INTERNATIONAL INDUCTIVE STUDY BIBLE

NEW AMERICAN STANDARD BIBLE

Portland, OR 97266

PRECEPT MINISTRIES

Chattanooga, TN 37422

INTERNATIONAL INDUCTIVE STUDY BIBLE

Dedicated to the Church of the living God . . .
to those whose passion is to be
"the pillar and support of the truth."
1 Timothy 3:15

Design by Bruce DeRoos
Maps and charts by Brian Davis
Illustrations by Stanley C. Stein

INTERNATIONAL INDUCTIVE STUDY BIBLE
© 1992 Precept Ministries
Published by Multnomah Press
10209 S.E. Division Street
Portland, Oregon 97266

Multnomah Press is a ministry of
Multnomah School of the Bible
8435 N.E. Glisan Street
Portland, Oregon 97220

Printed in the United States of America

Library of Congress Cataloging-in-Publication Data
Bible. English. New American Standard. 1992.
International Inductive Study Bible: New American Standard Bible
p. cm.
ISBN 0-88070-535-3 (genuine leather)
ISBN 0-88070-488-8 (premier limited edition)
ISBN 0-88070-531-0 (bonded leather)
ISBN 0-88070-532-9 (hardback)
I. Bible—Study and teaching. I. Title.
BS195.N35 1992
220.5'204–dc20 91-46964
CIP

1 2 3 4 5 6 7 8 9 / 97 96 95 94 93 92

FOREWORD

Scriptural Promise

"The grass withers, the flower fades, but the word of our God stands forever."

Isaiah 40:8

The New American Standard Bible has been produced with the conviction that the words of Scripture as originally penned in the Hebrew, Aramaic, and Greek were inspired by God. Since they are the eternal Word of God, the Holy Scriptures speak with fresh power to each generation, to give wisdom that leads to salvation, that men may serve Christ to the glory of God.

The Editorial Board had a twofold purpose in making this translation: to adhere as closely as possible to the original languages of the Holy Scriptures, and to make the translation in a fluent and readable style according to current English usage.

The Fourfold Aim of The Lockman Foundation

1. These publications shall be true to the original Hebrew, Aramaic, and Greek.
2. They shall be grammatically correct.
3. They shall be understandable to the masses.
4. They shall give the Lord Jesus Christ His proper place, the place which the Word gives Him; therefore, no work will ever be personalized.

Preface to the New American Standard Bible

In the history of English Bible translations, the King James Version is the most prestigious. This time-honored version of 1611, itself a revision of the Bishops' Bible of 1568, became the basis for the English Revised Version appearing in 1881 (New Testament) and 1885 (Old Testament). The American counterpart of this last work was published in 1901 as the American Standard Version. Recognizing the values of the American Standard Version, The Lockman Foundation felt an urgency to update it by incorporating recent discoveries of Hebrew and Greek textual sources and by rendering it into more current English. Therefore, in 1959 a new translation project was launched, based on the ASV. The result is the New American Standard Bible.

The American Standard Version (1901) has been highly regarded for its scholarship and accuracy. A product of both British and American scholarship, it has frequently been used as a standard for other translations. It is still recognized as a valuable tool for study of the Scriptures. The New American Standard Bible has sought to preserve these and other lasting values of the ASV.

Furthermore, in the preparation of this work numerous other translations have been consulted along with the linguistic tools and literature of biblical scholarship. Decisions about English renderings were made by consensus of a team composed of educators and pastors. Subsequently, review and evaluation by other Hebrew and Greek scholars outside the Editorial Board were sought and carefully considered.

The Editorial Board has continued to function since publication of the complete Bible in 1971. Minor revisions and refinements, recommended over the last several years, are presented in this edition.

Principles of Translation

Modern English Usage: The attempt has been made to render the grammar and terminology in contemporary English. When it was felt that the word-for-word literalness was unacceptable to the modern reader, a change was made in the direction of a more current English idiom. In the instances where this has been done, the more literal rendering has been indicated in the notes.

Alternative Readings: In addition to the more literal renderings, notations have been made to include alternate translations, readings of variant manuscripts and explanatory equivalents of the text. Only such notations have been used as have been felt justified in assisting the reader's comprehension of the terms used by the original author.

Hebrew Text: In the present translation the latest edition of Rudolph Kittel's *Biblia Hebraica* has been employed together with the most recent light from lexicography, cognate languages, and the Dead Sea Scrolls.

Hebrew Tenses: Consecution of tenses in Hebrew remains a puzzling factor in translation. The translators have been guided by the requirements of a literal translation, the sequence of tenses, and the immediate and broad contexts.

The Proper Name of God in the Old Testament: In the Scriptures, the name of God is most significant and understandably so. It is inconceivable to think of spiritual matters without a proper designation for the Supreme Deity. Thus the most common name for the Deity is God, a translation of the original *Elohim*. One of the titles for God is Lord, a translation of *Adonai*. There is yet another name which is particularly assigned to God as His special or proper name, that is, the four letters YHWH (Exodus 3:14 and Isaiah 42:8). This name has not been pronounced by the Jews because of reverence for the great sacredness of the divine name. Therefore, it has been consistently translated LORD. The only exception to this translation of YHWH is when it occurs in immediate proximity to the word Lord, that is, *Adonai*. In that case it is regularly translated GOD in order to avoid confusion. It is known that for many years YHWH has been transliterated as Yahweh, however no complete certainty attaches to this pronunciation.

Greek Text: Consideration was given to the latest available manuscripts with a view to determining the best Greek text. In most instances the 23rd edition of Eberhard Nestle's *Novum Testamentum Graece* was followed.

Greek Tenses: A careful distinction has been made in the treatment of the Greek aorist tense (usually translated as the English past, "He did") and the Greek imperfect tense (rendered either as English past progressive, "He was doing"; or, if inceptive, as "He *began* to do" or "He started to do"; or else if customary past, as "He used to do"). "Began" is italicized if it renders an imperfect tense, in order to distinguish it from the Greek verb for "begin."

On the other hand, not all aorists have been rendered as English pasts ("He did"), for some of them are clearly to be rendered as English perfects ("He has done"), or even as past perfects ("He had done"), judging from the context in which they occur. Such aorists have been rendered as perfects or past perfects in this translation.

As for the distinction between aorist and present imperatives, the translators have usually rendered these imperatives in the customary manner, rather than attempting any such fine distinction as "Begin to do!" (for the aorist imperative), or, "Continually do!" (for the present imperative).

As for sequence of tenses, the translators took care to follow English rules rather than Greek in translating Greek presents, imperfects and aorists. Thus, where English says, "We knew that he was doing," Greek puts it, "We knew that he does"; similarly, "We knew that he had done" is the Greek, "We knew that he did." Likewise, the English, "When he had come, they met him," is represented in Greek by: "When he came, they met him." in all cases a consistent transfer has been made from the Greek tense in the subordinate clause to the appropriate tense in English.

In the rendering of negative questions introduced by the particle *mē* (which always expects the answer "No") the wording has been altered from a mere, "Will he not do this?" to a more accurate, "He will not do this, will he?"

Editorial Board, The Lockman Foundation

Explanations of General Format

Notes and Cross References are placed in a column adjoining the text on the page and listed under verse numbers to which they refer. Superior numbers refer to literal renderings, alternate translations, or explanations. Superior letters refer to cross references. Cross references in italics are parallel passages.

Paragraphs are designated by a paragraph mark.

Quotation marks are used in the text in accordance with modern English usage.

"Thou," "Thee" and *"Thy"* are not used in this translation except in the language of prayer when addressing Deity.

Personal Pronouns are capitalized when pertaining to Deity.

Italics are used in the text to indicate words which are not found in the original Hebrew, Aramaic, or Greek but implied by it. Italics are used in the marginal notes to signify alternate readings for the text.

Small Caps in the New Testament are used in the text to indicate Old Testament quotations or obvious allusions to Old Testament texts. Variations of Old Testament wording are found in New Testament citations depending on whether the New Testament writer translated from a Hebrew text, used existing Greek or Aramaic translations, or paraphrased the material. It should be noted that modern rules for the indication of direct quotation were not used in biblical times thus allowing freedom for omissions or insertions without specific indication of these.

Asterisks are used to mark verbs that are historical presents in the Greek which have been translated with an English past tense in order to conform to modern usage. The translators recognized that in some contexts the present tense seems more unexpected and unjustified to the English reader than a past tense would have been. But Greek authors frequently used the present tense for the sake of heightened vividness, thereby transporting their readers in imagination to the actual scene at the time of occurrence. However, the translators felt that it would be wise to change these historical presents to English past tenses.

Abbreviations and Special Markings

Aram.	= Aramaic
DSS	= Dead Sea Scrolls
Gr.	= Greek translation of O.T. (Septuagint or LXX) or Greek text on N.T.
Heb.	= Hebrew text, usually Masoretic
Lat.	= Latin
M.T.	= Masoretic text
Syr.	= Syriac
Lit.	= A literal translation
Or	= An alternate translation justified by the Hebrew, Aramaic, or Greek
[ ]	= In text, brackets indicate words probably not in the original writings
[ ]	= In margin, brackets indicate references to a name, place or thing similar to, but not identical with that in the text
cf.	= compare
f., ff.	= following verse or verses
ms., mss.	= manuscript, manuscripts
v., vv.	= verse, verses

CONTENTS

THE BOOKS OF THE BIBLE

The Old Testament

The New Testament

Why Should I Use an International Inductive Study Bible?

If you long to understand and enjoy the Word of God for yourself . . . if you want to do more than just read through the Bible year after year, studying what others say . . . then you've picked up the right Bible.

Most Christians have been encouraged to study the Word of God, yet many have never been shown *how*. The International Inductive Study Bible guides you through a tried-and-true method that enables you to move through the Word of God, chapter by chapter, book by book, forming your own analysis of every book of the Bible.

Many people think only scholars or seminary students can have an in-depth grasp of the Word of God. How mistaken they are! The Bible was not written only for scholars; it is for everyone who desires to know God and His precepts for life.

There are three requirements for knowing and understanding the Word of God: the indwelling Spirit who leads and guides us into all truth, the commitment to study to show one's self approved unto God, and the willingness to obey His precepts.

While scholars have offered excellent supplements which have increased our understanding of difficult passages, such studies mean little if you and I do not know for ourselves what Scripture says, what it means, and how we are to apply it to our lives. That is the heart of inductive study—seeing truth for yourself through observation of the text, then discerning what it means by allowing scripture to interpret scripture, and finally applying that truth to your life. In inductive study, the Bible becomes its own commentary.

As the children of Israel found it necessary to gather manna daily (Deuteronomy 8:3), we too are to live daily by every word which comes out of the mouth of God.

The International Inductive Study Bible teaches you an inductive method which enables you to feed yourself solid food for the rest of your life. As you work your way through this Bible, you will find yourself more and more capable of discerning if what you hear or read from other sources is true to the whole counsel of God. You'll be amazed at all you remember about the content and purpose of each book of the Bible. You'll begin to see how the teachings of each book interrelates with the others.

There's no substitute for seeing, knowing, and understanding God's Word for *yourself*. No one can provide it for you except yourself. And no one can take that from you.

As you study the Bible inductively you will get to know God in a deep, exciting, and enlightening way—and "the people who know their God will be strong and do exploits" (Daniel 11:32b). Now your question may be:

When and how do I get started?

Start today. To know the Bible is the task of a lifetime.

• Prayerfully choose one of the Bible's sixty-six books and begin. If you don't have clear direction you might want to begin in Genesis, Luke, or Philippians.

• Take a minute and turn to the book you're going to study. You'll see several things.

The ***introduction*** presents an overview of the book's author and/or the current events at the time the book was written.

The *Things to Do* sections vary since each book is unique. Quickly read through this section for an overview of what you're going to do, but don't let the instructions overwhelm you. When you take them one by one and study one chapter at a time, they become very manageable. (Specific instructions on observing the text and marking key words follow.)

The *Things to Think About* section encourages you to get alone with God to consider how the truths of the book apply to you.

Old Testament historical or prophetical books have a *Historical Chart* just before the first chapter to help you see where the book fits historically and chronologically.

Each book of the Bible ends with an *At a Glance* chart, where you'll record the theme of each chapter. An explanation of how to do this is on page I-15.

Many of the books in the New Testament contain an *Observations Chart* on which to record information you are instructed to look for in the *Things to Do* section.

• When you have time, familiarize yourself with the information in the front of this Bible beginning on page I-55. This will be invaluable in your study.

How to Observe the Bible Chapter by Chapter

• *Begin with prayer.* It is the ministry and responsibility of the Holy Spirit to guide you into truth. Tell God you need His help.

• *Ask questions based on the five W's and an H: who, what, when, where, why, and how.* Train yourself to observe exactly what the text is saying by asking questions such as: Who is speaking? Who is being addressed? Who or what is this about? What are they to do, to say, to believe? What happened? When was it said or done? When will it happen and where? Why should they do that? What will be the result? How is it going to be done? How is it going to happen?

For example look at 1 Peter 5 on page I-17 and read only the text. If you were to do an inductive study of 1 Peter 5 you might begin by asking ***Who*** is speaking? First Peter 5 does not tell us; however, in 1 Peter 1:1, Peter has already identified himself. Next ask ***Who*** is Peter? According to 1 Peter 5:1 he is a fellow elder. Then ask, ***To whom*** is he speaking in chapter 5? The answer is again found in verse 1—to the elders. Now ask, ***What*** is he saying? Peter's telling them to shepherd the flock. Then ask ***Why***? ***How***? The answers are found in verses 1 through 4.

As you ask these questions and see what the text says, think about what you've observed and what it means. As you meditate on these truths, think about their place in your life, and how they apply to you so that your study doesn't become an intellectual pursuit of knowledge for its own sake.

• *Look for and mark the key words and phrases.* Key words and phrases unlock the meaning of the text and tend to be *repeated* in order to convey the author's point or purpose for writing. They may be repeated throughout a chapter, a segment of a book, or the book as a whole.

Many of the key words are listed under *Things to Do* or on the *At a Glance* chart which comes at the end of the book. If a key word has a synonym (a word that has the same meaning in that context) it's listed after the key word and is set off in parentheses ( ).

As you come to a key word, mark it in the text in a distinctive way with a symbol and/or color such as this:

God.

In the same way mark any synonyms. Also mark the key word's pronouns: I, you, he, it, we, our, and so on. Look at the sample chapter observations on page I-17 to see how key words were marked in 1 Peter 5.

• *In the margin of the chapter make a list* of what you learn from marking significant key words. For example, in the margin of 1 Peter 5 you could compile a list of all you learn about God from the text. (You don't need to make a list from every key word.)

• *Watch for lists in the text.* Many times you'll see various instructions, truths, qualities, and other elements listed in the text. When you see such lists, number them. Look at 1 Peter 5:2-3 for an example. See the list numbered in the text which tells the elders *how* to shepherd the flock. Look at the numbered list in 5:10 of *what* God will do to those who have suffered for awhile.

• *Mark any references to time and note the relationship of events in time.* The timing of something can be seen several ways: by an exact statement of time such as "on the tenth day of the eleventh month" or "at the feast of Tabernacles." These phrases can be marked in the margin with the symbol of a clock such as this .

Time is also indicated through words such as *until, then, when,* and *after.* These words show the relationship of one statement or event to another. Marking them will help you see the sequence of events.

• *Watch for and mark any things which are contrasted or compared.* Contrasts compare things that are different or opposite; comparisons point out similarities and likenesses. For example in 1 Peter 5:5, Peter contrasts how God treats the proud with how He treats the humble: "God opposes the proud . . . gives grace to the humble."

• *Watch for terms of conclusion.* The words *wherefore, therefore, for this reason* and *finally* show a sequence of thought. When you see a *therefore* or any term of conclusion, note what it's there for!

You will find a sample of how to mark John 1 on page 1884-85 in the appendix of the Bible. This will give you another example of what to look for when observing a chapter. Since this section is black and white, you will notice that symbols rather than colors are used to indicate the key words.

• *Record the theme of each chapter on the* AT A GLANCE *chart and in the text.* Determine the theme of the chapter by capturing the main idea or main event for that chapter in a summarizing statement. When you record the theme, be brief. Try to use words found in the text if possible. Possible themes or summaries of 1 Peter 5 could be "Exhortations to elders, younger men, and the suffering" or "God Gives Grace to the Humble."

Once you have recorded the theme of each chapter on the *AT A GLANCE* chart, you will be able to see if any chapters can be grouped under a common theme. If so, they form a *segment division.* When you get the broad view of a book through its segment divisions, it's easier to remember and understand its content and purpose. For example, Genesis 1 through 11 is historical and Genesis 12 through 50 is biographical. Paul's New Testament epistles usually have two major divisions: first doctrine, then application.

The chart below shows the features of the *AT A GLANCE* charts. On page 1886 you'll find a completed *AT A GLANCE* chart on the Gospel of John. You'll find it helpful to study how the "Segment Divisions" on this chart relate to "Chapter Themes."

The number and type of segment divisions will vary from book to book. Books may be divided into segment divisions according to dates, places, topics, doctrines, reigns of kings, and major characters or events.

1 PETER AT A GLANCE

Theme of 1 Peter:

Author:

Date:

Purpose:

Key Words:
suffering
(and all its synonyms)
grace
glory
salvation
Jesus Christ
God
Holy Spirit
called
chosen
holy

SEGMENT DIVISIONS	CHAPTER THEMES
	1
	2
	3
	4
	5

How can I remember what's in each book?
How can I make sure I interpret it correctly?

This is the purpose of the *AT A GLANCE* charts. Since accurate interpretation must always be based on thorough observation, before you interpret any verse or passage of Scripture you must:

- Consider the verses around it (the setting or context).
- View the setting within the framework or message of the entire book and in light of the author's purpose for writing the book.
- Finally, look for how that verse or passage relates to the entire Word of God. Scripture will never contradict scripture if you allow context to rule over all interpretation.

Can you see then how critical it is that you know what God's Word has to say—to know the "whole counsel of the Word of God" book by book?

When you finish observing a book of the Bible, recording its chapter themes, and seeing how it divides into segments, you will have its framework and therefore can examine every statement or truth in the book in the light of its proper context.

How will marking my Bible help me?

This interactive Bible is designed for you to feel free to mark the text and write notes in the margin. The more you interact with it, the more power it will have in your life.

The use of color and/or symbols to mark important words and themes will enhance your study of the Bible. As you return to these passages again and again, the visual impact of your notations will help you to identify quickly what's in the passage and to notice subjects which run throughout the Bible.

For this reason there are some key words you'll want to mark in the same distinctive way throughout the entire Bible. Write these on a card, color code them in the way you intend to mark them throughout your Bible, and keep it in your Bible. Use the card as a bookmark.

Some of the key words you'll want to mark throughout are on the next page in the color section. You may want to add other words to this list.

What should I use to mark my Bible?

Use a four-color, fine-ball-point pen and colored pencils. Keep a bottle of correction fluid to mark out anything you might want to change.

sin (wickedness, evil, iniquity)
covenant
death (die)
life (live)
repent
love
law

grace
believe (faith)
righteousness (righteous)
holy (holiness)
cry (cries, cried)
Babylon
nations
Day of the Lord (that day)

Satan (any reference to the devil, spirits, demons, mediums)
any reference to:
Jesus' first coming
Jesus' second coming

1 Peter 5

Chapter 5 ________________

5 [a]Therefore, I exhort the elders among you, as *your* [b]fellow elder
and witness of the sufferings of Christ, and a partaker also of
the glory that is to be revealed,
2 shepherd [a]the flock of God among you, exercising oversight [b]not
under compulsion, but voluntarily, according to *the will of* God; and
[c]not for sordid gain, but with eagerness;
3 nor yet as [a]lording it over [1]those allotted to your charge, but
[2]proving to be [b]examples to the flock.
4 And when the Chief [a]Shepherd appears, you will receive the
[b]unfading [1c]crown of glory.
5 [a]You younger men, likewise, [b]be subject to your elders; and all of
you, clothe yourselves with [c]humility toward one another, for [d]GOD
IS OPPOSED TO THE PROUD, BUT GIVES GRACE TO THE HUMBLE.
6 [a]Humble yourselves, therefore, under the mighty hand of God,
that He may exalt you at the proper time,
7 casting all your [a]anxiety upon Him, because He cares for you.
8 [a]Be of sober *spirit*, [b]be on the alert. Your adversary, [c]the devil,
prowls about like a roaring [d]lion, seeking someone to devour.
9 [1a]But resist him, [b]firm in *your* faith, knowing that [c]the same ex-
periences of suffering are being accomplished by your [2]brethren who
are in the world.
10 And after you have suffered [a]for a little while, the [b]God of all
grace, who [c]called you to His [d]eternal glory in Christ, will Himself
[e]perfect, [f]confirm, strengthen *and* establish you.
11 [a]To Him *be* dominion forever and ever. Amen.
12 Through [a]Silvanus, our faithful brother [1](for so I regard *him*), [b]I
have written to you briefly, exhorting and testifying that this is [c]the
true grace of God. [d]Stand firm in it!
13 [1]She who is in Babylon, chosen together with you, sends you
greetings, and *so does* my son, [a]Mark.
14 [a]Greet one another with a kiss of love.
[b]**P**eace be to you all who are in Christ.

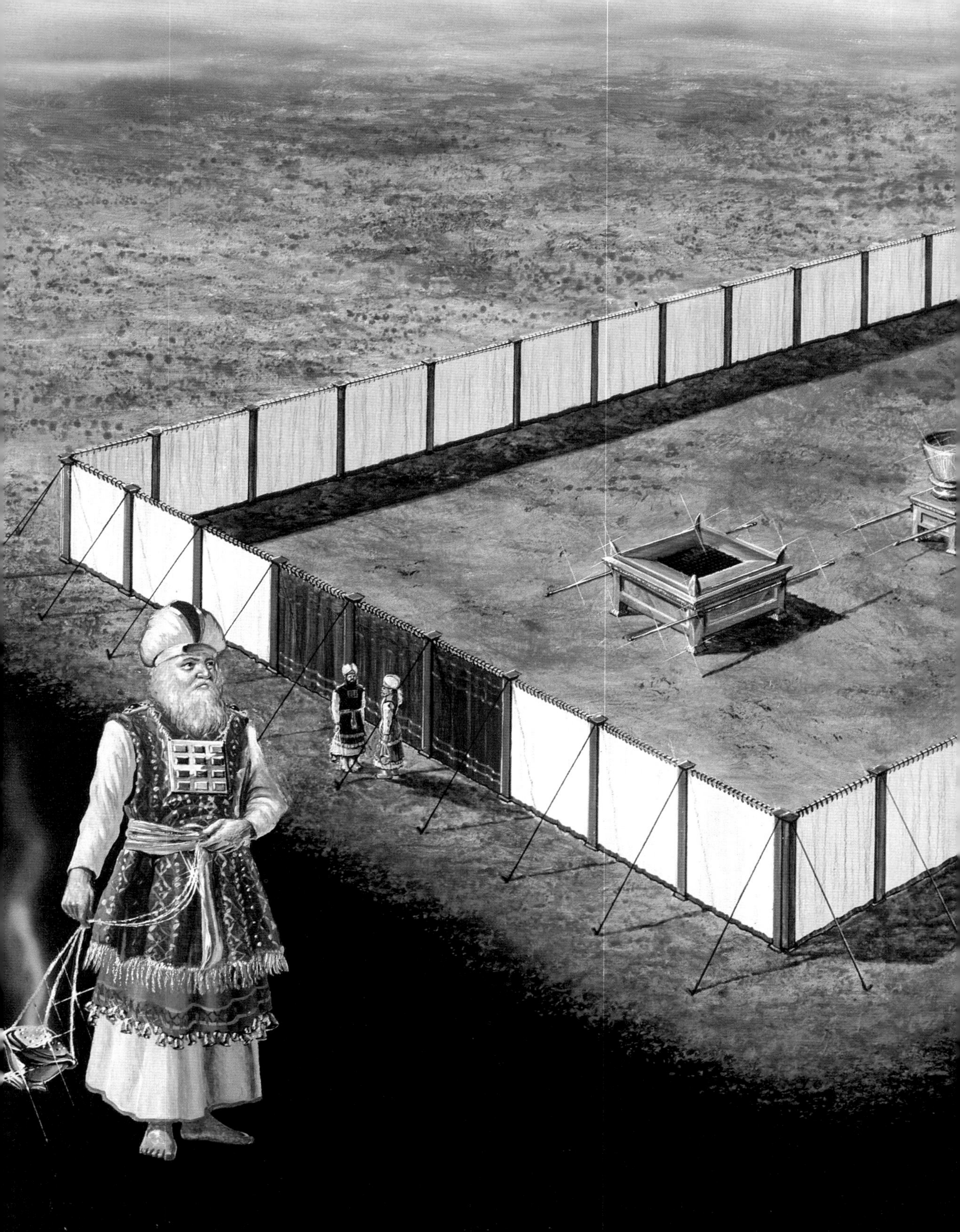

The Tabernacle
and the High Priest
in his priestly garments

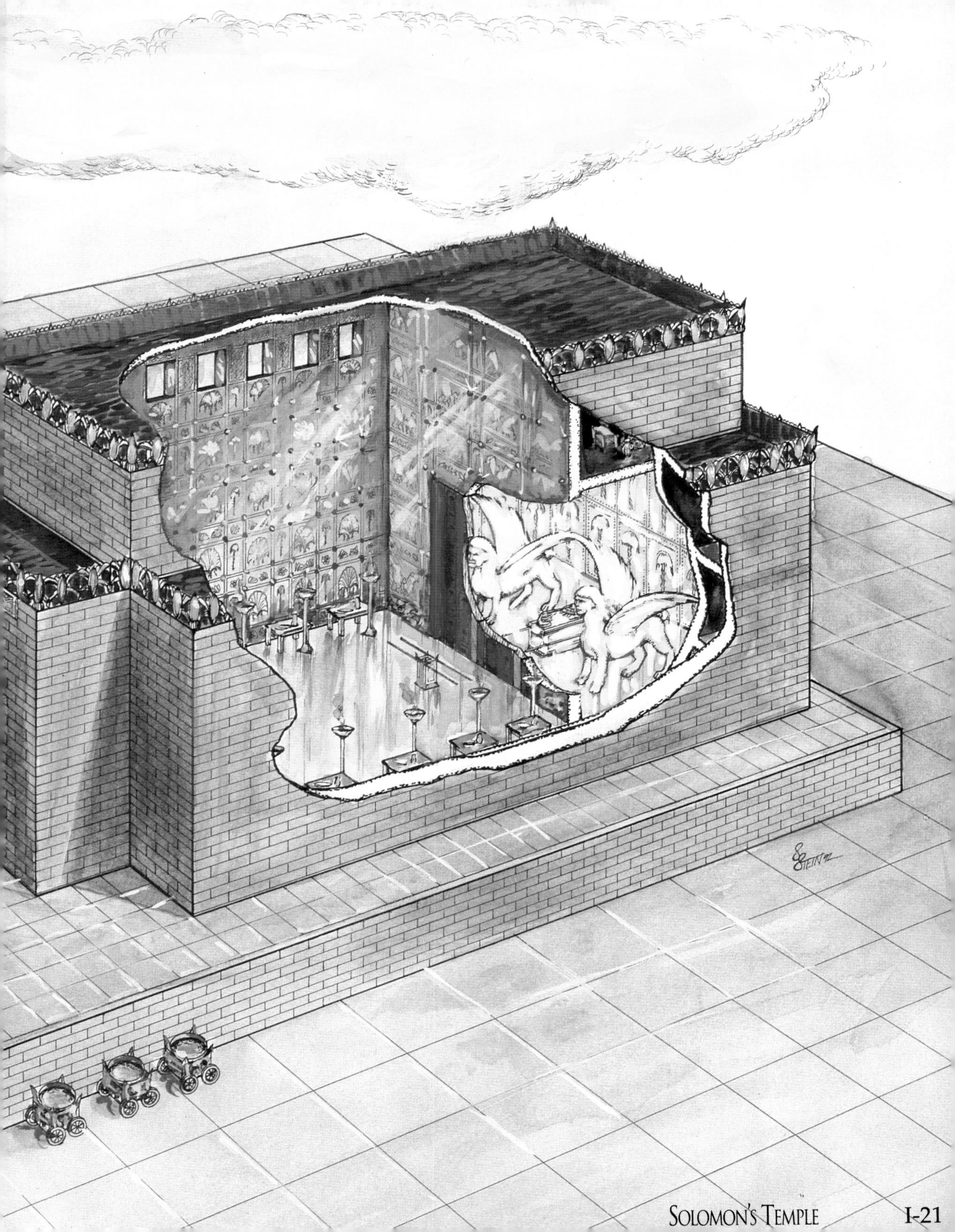

Herod's Temple at the Time of Jesus
During the Feast of Tabernacles
(For floor plan, see page I-50)

18
16
1
20
19
17
8
3
2
4
6
THE TEMPLE MOUNT
DURING THE SECOND TEMPLE PERIOD
1. Second Temple (Herod's)
2. Western Wall
3. Wilson's Arch*
4. Barclay's Gate*
5. Small Shops
6. Main N-S Street
7. Robinson's Arch*
8. Upper City
9. Royal Porch
10. Pilasters
11. Double Gate
12. Triple Gate
13. Plaza
14. Ritual Bathhouse
15. Council House
16. Herodian Tower
17. Largest Ashlars
18. Antonia Fortress
19. Warren's Gate*
20. Court of the Gentiles
21. Eastern Gate
*Named after nineteenth-century explorers
Note: See page I-50 for an inside floor plan of Herod's Temple

21
9
20
12
14
15
0
11
7
13

HISTORICAL CHART OF  ISRAEL'S HISTORY

FROM ADAM TO THE INTERTESTAMENT PERIOD

Panel 1

Scholars vary in the dating systems they use. The IISB follows John Witcomb's system throughout for the sake of consistency.

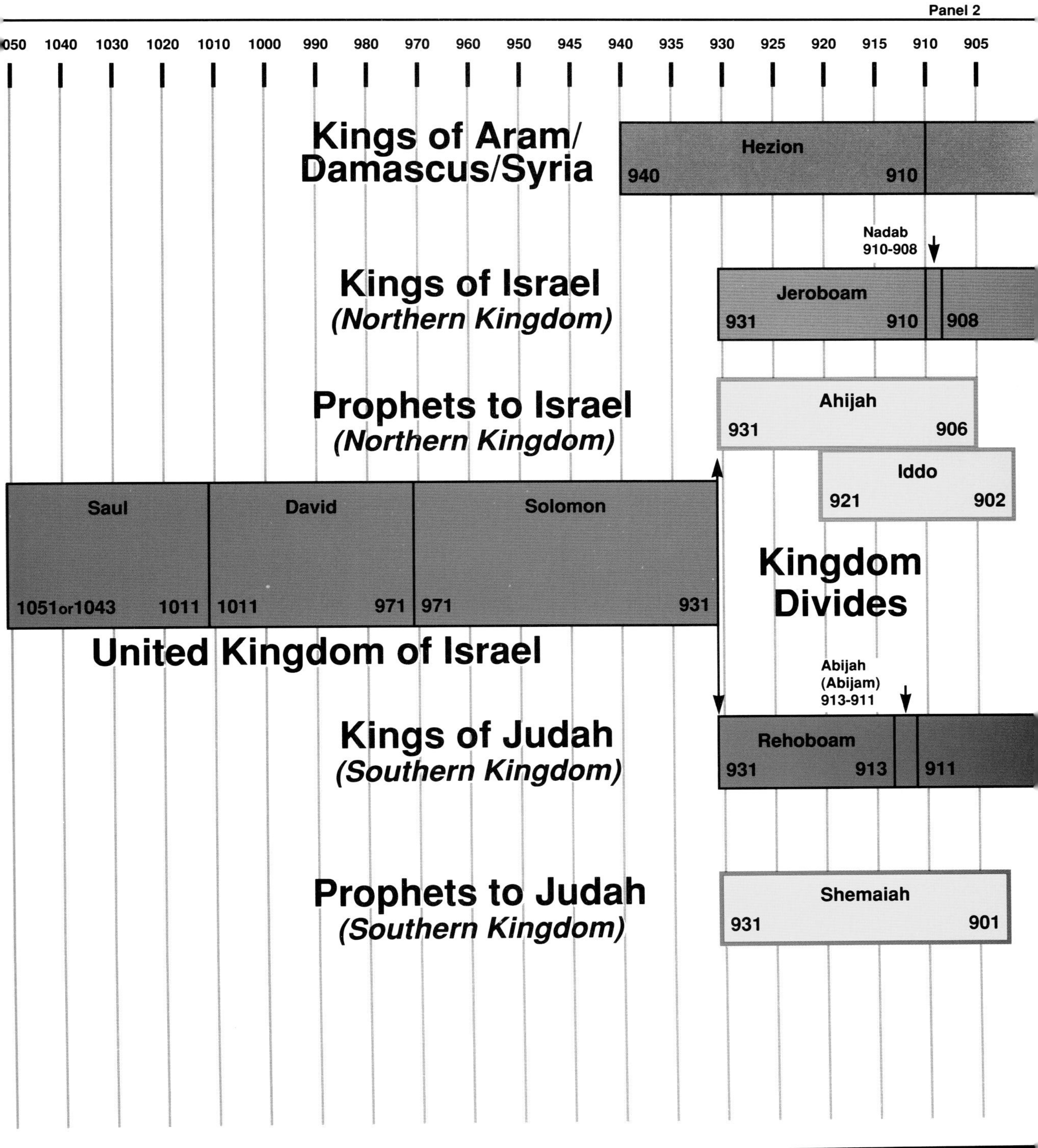

1050 | 1040 | 1030 | 1020 | 1010 | 1000 | 990 | 980 | 970 | 960 | 950 | 945 | 940 | 935 | 930 | 925 | 920 | 915 | 910 | 905

Kings of Aram/ Damascus/Syria

Hezion 940 – 910

Nadab 910-908

Kings of Israel
(Northern Kingdom)

Jeroboam 931 – 910

908

Prophets to Israel
(Northern Kingdom)

Ahijah 931 – 906

Iddo 921 – 902

Saul 1051 or 1043 – 1011

David 1011 – 971

Solomon 971 – 931

United Kingdom of Israel

Kingdom Divides

Abijah (Abijam) 913-911

Kings of Judah
(Southern Kingdom)

Rehoboam 931 – 913

911

Prophets to Judah
(Southern Kingdom)

Shemaiah 931 – 901

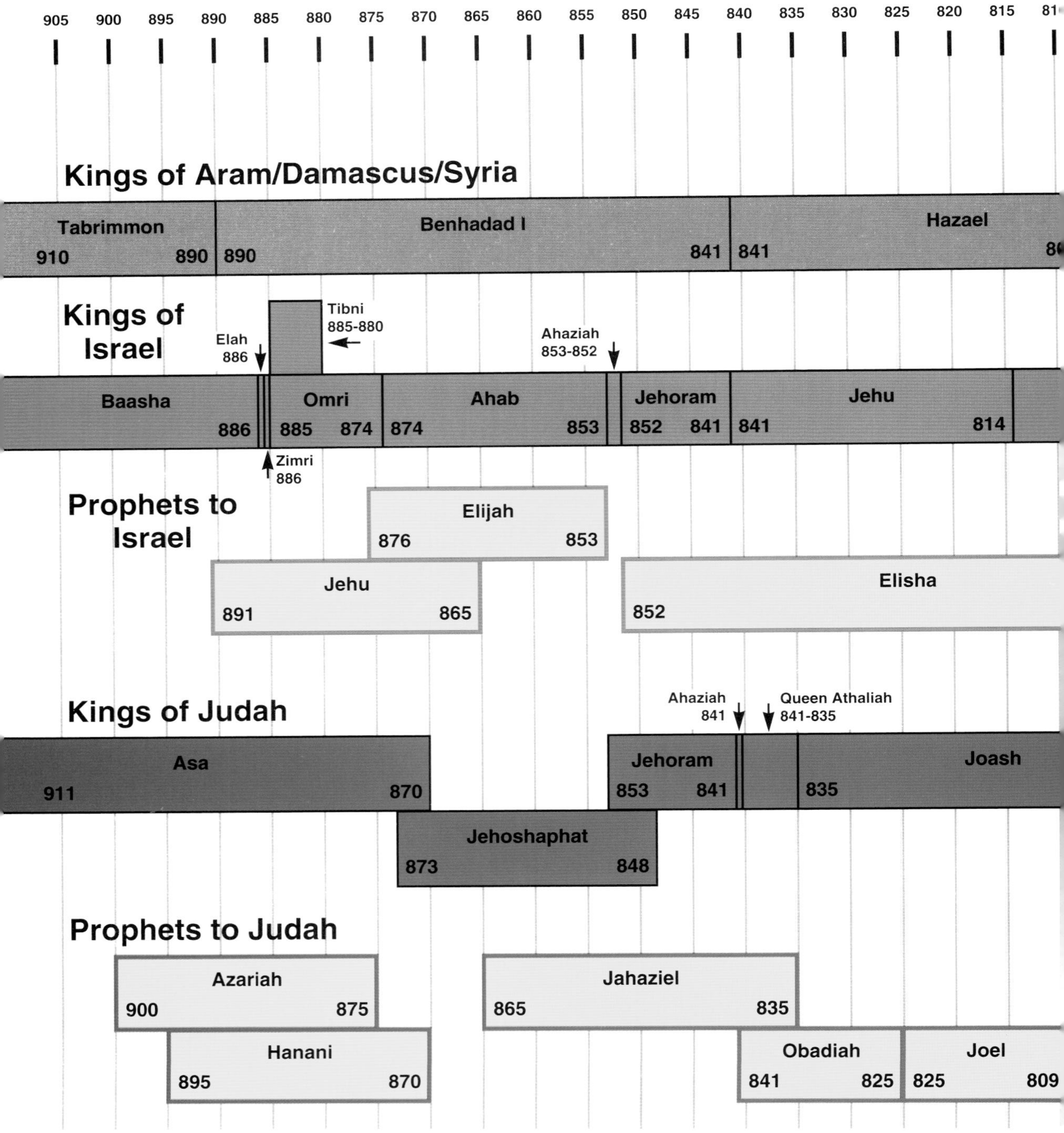

(continued)
Panel 3

905 900 895 890 885 880 875 870 865 860 855 850 845 840 835 830 825 820 815 81

Kings of Aram/Damascus/Syria

Tabrimmon 910 890
Benhadad I 890 841
Hazael 841 8

Kings of Israel

Elah 886
Tibni 885-880
Ahaziah 853-852
Baasha 886
Omri 885 874
Ahab 874 853
Jehoram 852 841
Jehu 841 814
Zimri 886

Prophets to Israel

Elijah 876 853
Jehu 891 865
Elisha 852

Kings of Judah

Ahaziah 841
Queen Athaliah 841-835
Asa 911 870
Jehoram 853 841
Joash 835
Jehoshaphat 873 848

Prophets to Judah

Azariah 900 875
Jahaziel 865 835
Hanani 895 870
Obadiah 841 825
Joel 825 809

Kings of Assyria

Timeline	810	805	800	795	790	785	780	775	770	765	760	755	750	745	740	735	730	725	720	715

Kings of Assyria:
- Shalmaneser IV 783–773
- Ashurdan III 773–755
- Ashur-nirari 755–745
- Tiglathpileser III 745–727
- Shalmaneser V 727-722

Syria:
- Benhadad II 801–?
- Rezin 750–732

Northern ten tribes taken captive by King Shalmaneser V of Assyria in 722 B.C.

Israel:
- Jehoahaz –798
- Jehoash 798–782
- Jeroboam II 793–753
- Zechariah 753-752
- Shallum (one month)
- Menahem 752–742
- Pekahiah 742-740
- Pekah 752–732
- Hoshea 732–722

Prophets:
- Elisha –796
- Jonah 784–772
- Amos 767–755
- Hosea 755–714

Judah:
- Joash –796
- Amaziah 796–767
- Uzziah or Azariah 790–740
- Jotham 750–731
- Ahaz 735–715

Prophets:
- Isaiah 740–681
- Micah 733–701

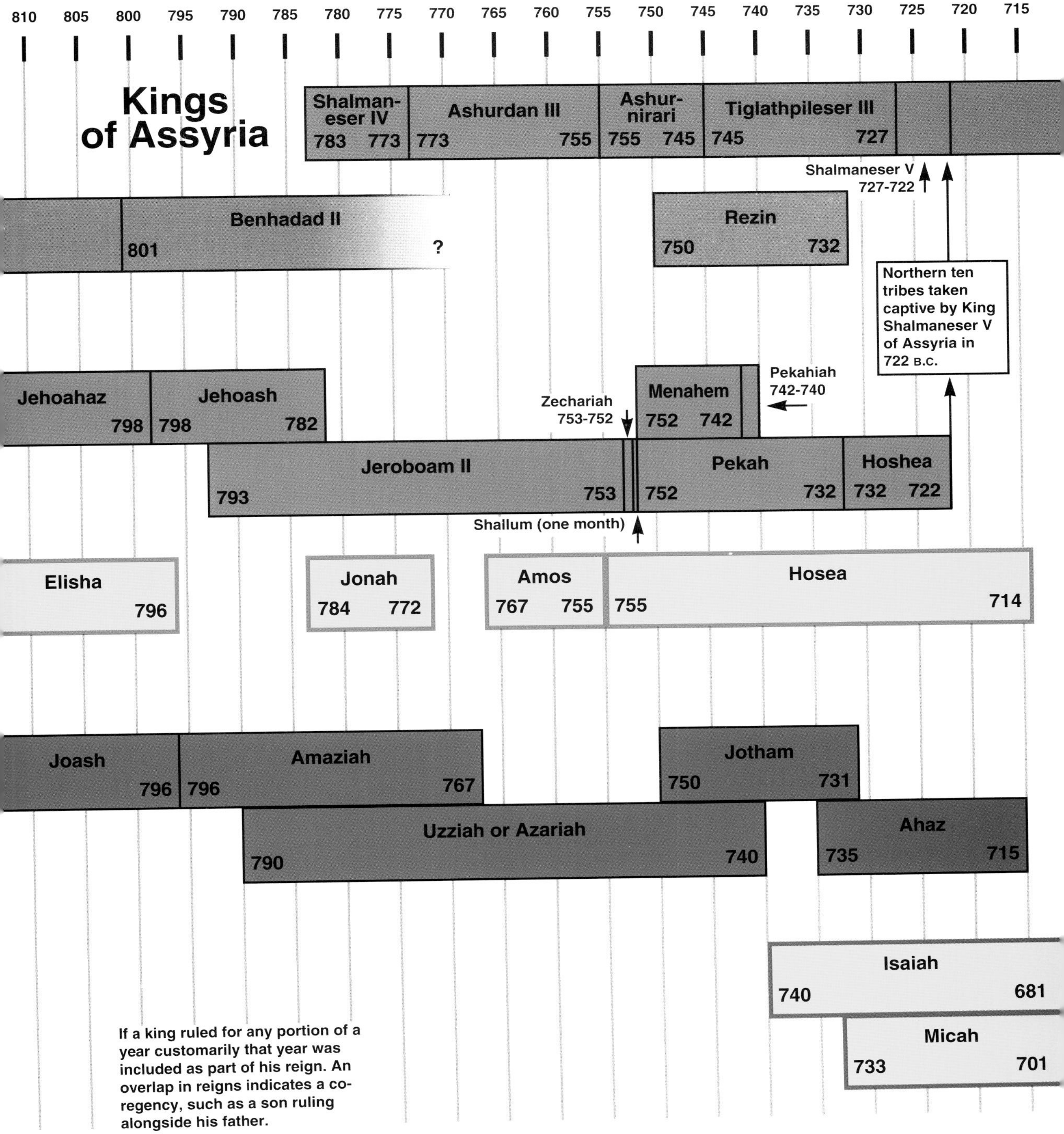

If a king ruled for any portion of a year customarily that year was included as part of his reign. An overlap in reigns indicates a co-regency, such as a son ruling alongside his father.

(continued)
Panel 5

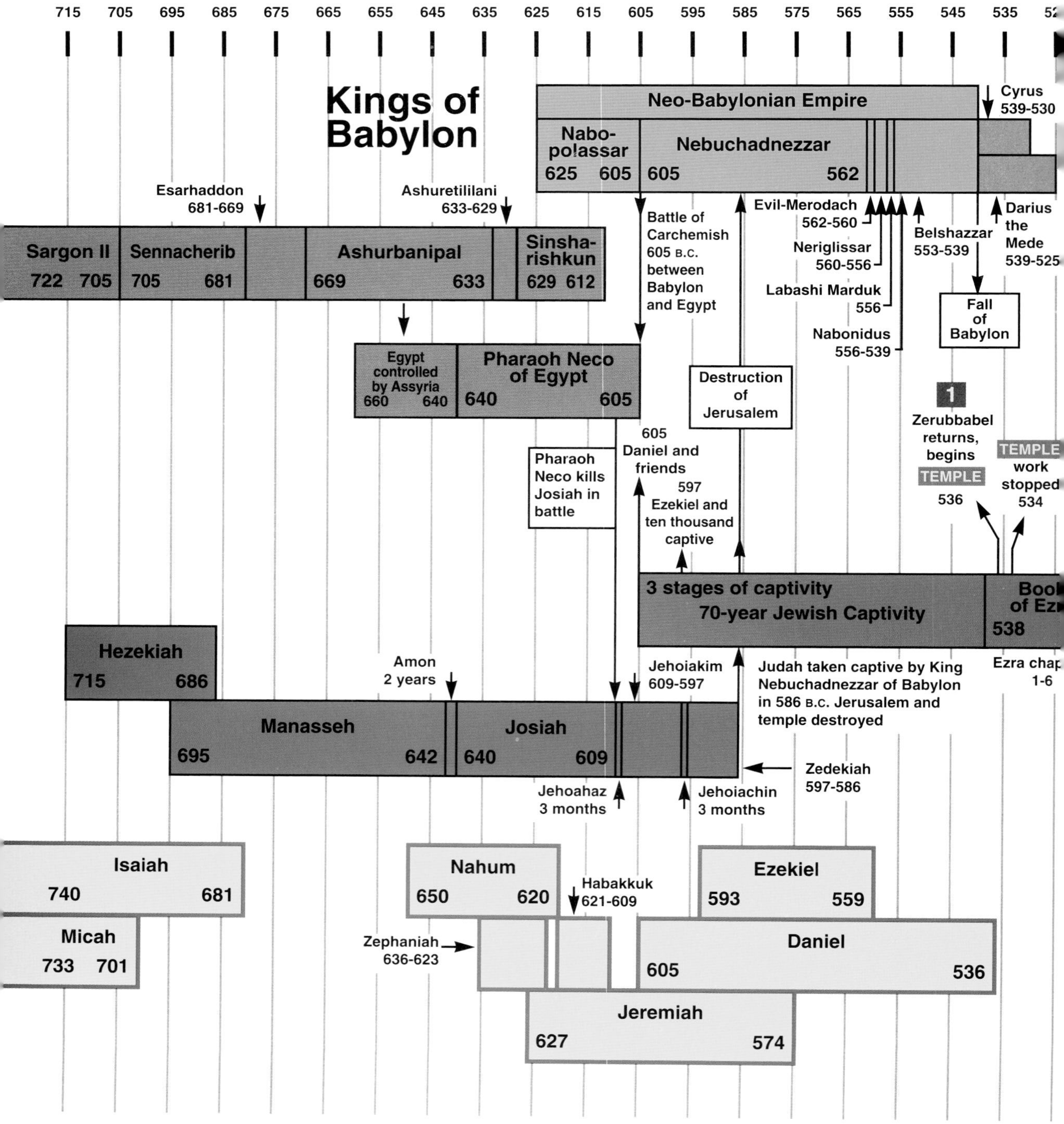

Kings of Babylon

715 705 695 685 675 665 655 645 635 625 615 605 595 585 575 565 555 545 535

Neo-Babylonian Empire
Nabo-polassar 625 605
Nebuchadnezzar 605 562
Cyrus 539-530
Esarhaddon 681-669
Ashuretililani 633-629
Sargon II 722 705
Sennacherib 705 681
Ashurbanipal 669 633
Sinsha-rishkun 629 612
Battle of Carchemish 605 B.C. between Babylon and Egypt
Evil-Merodach 562-560
Neriglissar 560-556
Labashi Marduk 556
Nabonidus 556-539
Belshazzar 553-539
Darius the Mede 539-525
Fall of Babylon
Egypt controlled by Assyria 660 640
Pharaoh Neco of Egypt 640 605
Destruction of Jerusalem
1
Zerubbabel returns, begins TEMPLE 536
TEMPLE work stopped 534
605 Daniel and friends
597 Ezekiel and ten thousand captive
Pharaoh Neco kills Josiah in battle
3 stages of captivity
70-year Jewish Captivity
Book of Ezra 538
Ezra chapters 1-6
Hezekiah 715 686
Amon 2 years
Jehoiakim 609-597
Judah taken captive by King Nebuchadnezzar of Babylon in 586 B.C. Jerusalem and temple destroyed
Manasseh 695 642
Josiah 640 609
Zedekiah 597-586
Jehoahaz 3 months
Jehoiachin 3 months
Isaiah 740 681
Nahum 650 620
Habakkuk 621-609
Ezekiel 593 559
Micah 733 701
Zephaniah 636-623
Daniel 605 536
Jeremiah 627 574

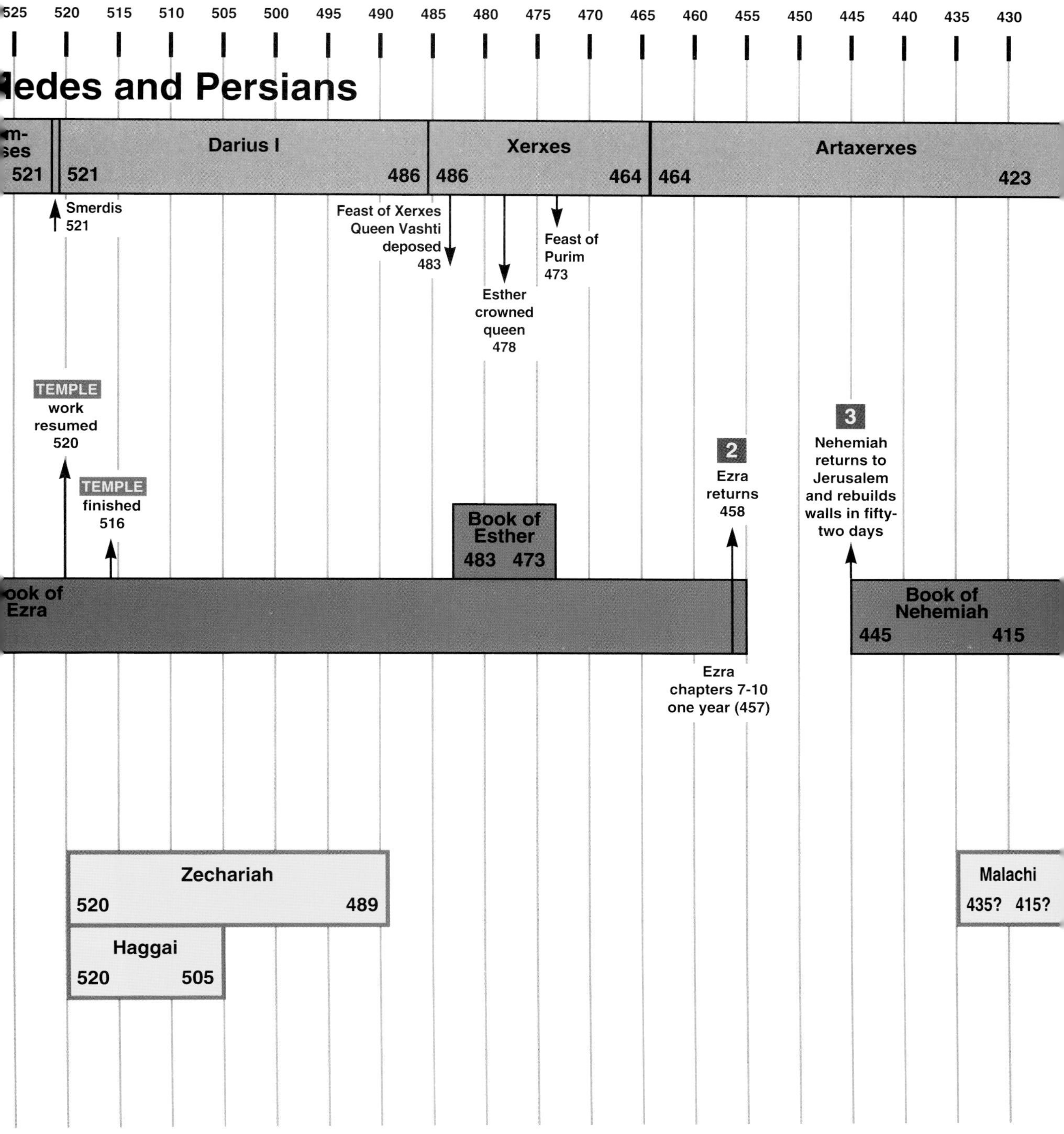

525 520 515 510 505 500 495 490 485 480 475 470 465 460 455 450 445 440 435 430

ledes and Persians

m-ses 521	Darius I 521 – 486	Xerxes 486 – 464	Artaxerxes 464 – 423

Smerdis 521

Feast of Xerxes Queen Vashti deposed 483

Esther crowned queen 478

Feast of Purim 473

TEMPLE work resumed 520

TEMPLE finished 516

Book of Esther 483 473

2 Ezra returns 458

3 Nehemiah returns to Jerusalem and rebuilds walls in fifty-two days

ook of Ezra

Ezra chapters 7-10 one year (457)

Book of Nehemiah 445 415

Zechariah 520 489

Haggai 520 505

Malachi 435? 415?

From the Intertestament Period to the 1990s

Panel 7

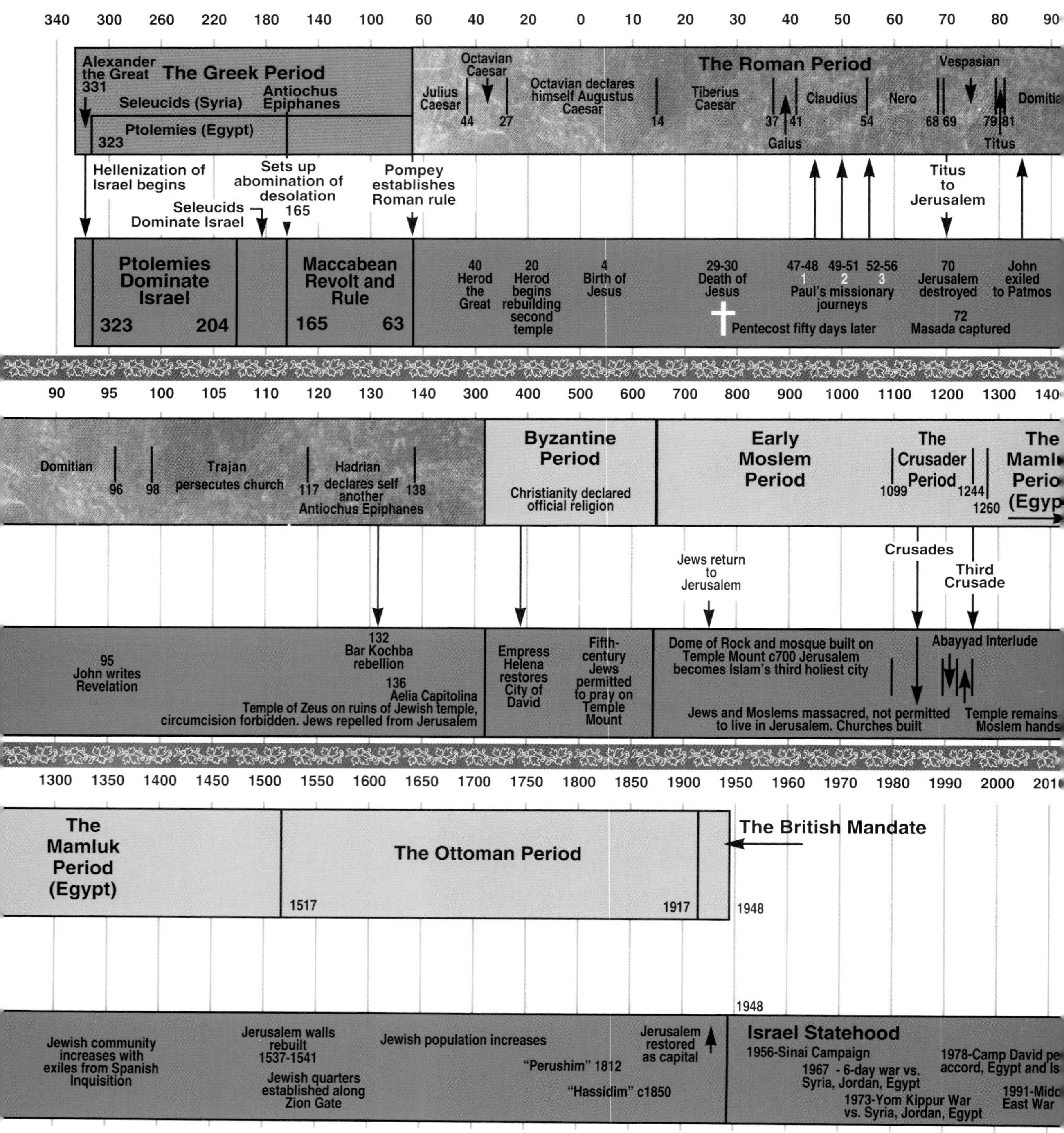

340 300 260 220 180 140 100 60 40 20 0 10 20 30 40 50 60 70 80 90

The Greek Period
Alexander the Great 331
Seleucids (Syria)
Antiochus Epiphanes
Ptolemies (Egypt) 323

The Roman Period
Julius Caesar 44
Octavian Caesar 27
Octavian declares himself Augustus Caesar 14
Tiberius Caesar 37
Gaius 41
Claudius 54
Nero 68 69
Vespasian 79 81
Titus
Domitia

Hellenization of Israel begins
Seleucids Dominate Israel
Sets up abomination of desolation 165
Pompey establishes Roman rule
Titus to Jerusalem

Ptolemies Dominate Israel 323 204
Maccabean Revolt and Rule 165 63
40 Herod the Great
20 Herod begins rebuilding second temple
4 Birth of Jesus
29-30 Death of Jesus
Pentecost fifty days later
47-48 49-51 52-56
1 2 3
Paul's missionary journeys
70 Jerusalem destroyed
72 Masada captured
John exiled to Patmos

90 95 100 105 110 120 130 140 300 400 500 600 700 800 900 1000 1100 1200 1300 140

Domitian 96 98
Trajan persecutes church 117
Hadrian declares self another Antiochus Epiphanes 138

Byzantine Period
Christianity declared official religion

Early Moslem Period

The Crusader Period 1099 1244 1260

The Maml Perio (Egyp

Jews return to Jerusalem
Crusades
Third Crusade

95 John writes Revelation
132 Bar Kochba rebellion
136 Aelia Capitolina Temple of Zeus on ruins of Jewish temple, circumcision forbidden. Jews repelled from Jerusalem
Empress Helena restores City of David
Fifth-century Jews permitted to pray on Temple Mount
Dome of Rock and mosque built on Temple Mount c700 Jerusalem becomes Islam's third holiest city
Jews and Moslems massacred, not permitted to live in Jerusalem. Churches built
Abayyad Interlude
Temple remains Moslem hands

1300 1350 1400 1450 1500 1550 1600 1650 1700 1750 1800 1850 1900 1950 1960 1970 1980 1990 2000 201

The Mamluk Period (Egypt)
The Ottoman Period 1517 1917
The British Mandate 1948

1948

Jewish community increases with exiles from Spanish Inquisition
Jerusalem walls rebuilt 1537-1541
Jewish quarters established along Zion Gate
Jewish population increases
"Perushim" 1812
"Hassidim" c1850
Jerusalem restored as capital

Israel Statehood
1956-Sinai Campaign
1967 - 6-day war vs. Syria, Jordan, Egypt
1973-Yom Kippur War vs. Syria, Jordan, Egypt
1978-Camp David pe accord, Egypt and Is
1991-Midc East War

Major Events in Israel's History

The Word of God takes on new life when a person understands the major events in Israel's history between the years of the Assyrian captivity and the birth of Christ. Old and New Testament prophecies regarding Israel and her relationship to various world powers are seen in a new dimension.

Once you're acquainted with the religious, cultural, and political setting of New Testament times, you'll better understand the Gospels and the book of Acts. You'll have a greater appreciation of the times in which our Lord lived and gave birth to His church.

From 722 B.C. until the Birth of Christ

After the death of Solomon, the kingdom of Israel divided. In 931 B.C. the tribes of Judah and Benjamin formed the southern kingdom of Judah with Jerusalem as their capital. The remaining ten tribes formed the northern kingdom of Israel and eventually made Samaria their capital. The northern kingdom immediately began to worship idols, so in 722 B.C. God allowed the Assyrians to take them captive.

Although the southern kingdom was warned by the prophets of God that they too would go into captivity if they did not repent of their disobedience and idolatry, Judah did not listen. In 605 B.C., just before Nebuchadnezzar became king of Babylon, he attacked Jerusalem and took the king and some of his nobles captive to Babylon. Among them was Daniel (Daniel 1:1-2). In 597 B.C. Nebuchadnezzar again attacked Judah, this time taking about ten thousand to Babylon, Ezekiel among them. Then in 586 B.C. Babylon, now the predominant world power, conquered Judah and destroyed not only the city of Jerusalem but the magnificent temple built by Solomon during his reign over Israel.

Separated from Jerusalem and their temple, the exiles established **synagogues** as a means of preserving their faith. The synagogues became centers of learning and worship and were formed wherever there were ten Jewish men. There the Jews recited the **Shema** (Deuteronomy 6:4), read from the law and the prophets, prayed, and delivered messages.

Men trained in writing who recorded events and decisions were called **scribes.** They assumed the responsibility of copying, preserving, and even

HEROD'S TEMPLE

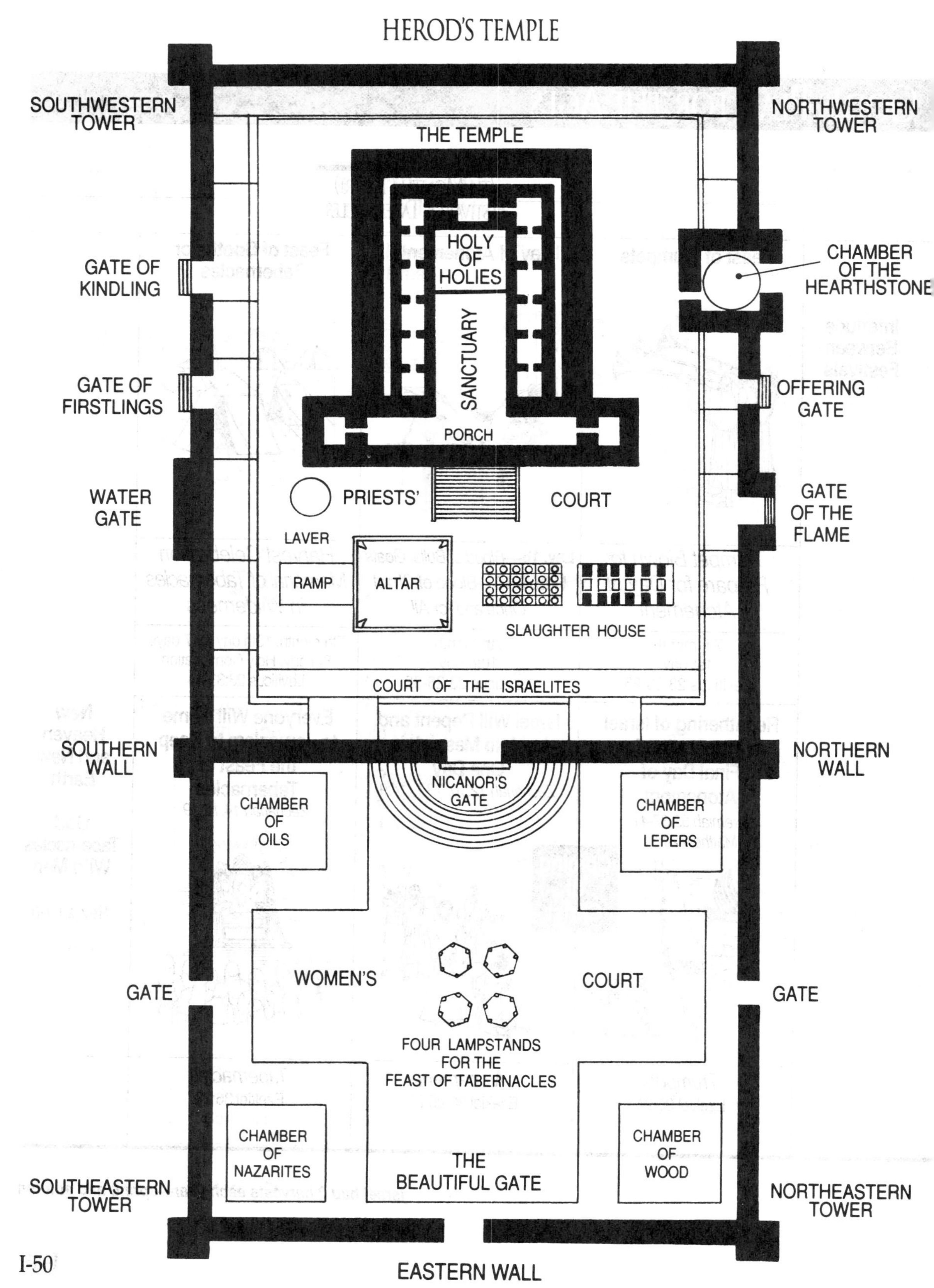

Understanding the Value of God's Word

What is the Bible?

The Bible is comprised of sixty-six separate writings or books. It was written over a period of approximately 1,400 to 1,800 years by more than forty authors from various walks of life. While many of the authors are identified, some remain unknown.

The Bible is divided into the Old Testament, comprised of thirty-nine books, and the New Testament, comprised of twenty-seven books. The Old Testament, the Bible of the nation of Israel, was divided into three segments: the Law or Torah, the Prophets or Nebi'im, and the Writings or Kethubim.

Although the Old Testament was written in Hebrew and Aramaic, it was translated into Koine (common) Greek around 250-150 B.C. This translation is referred to as the Septuagint or the LXX. Although nothing was altered in respect to the text, upon the completion of the Septuagint the order and breakdown of its various books was changed to the form now used in the Old Testament.

While the Old Testament was orginally written in two Semitic languages, Hebrew and Aramaic, the majority of it is in Hebrew. The New Testament was written in Koine Greek, the popular language used throughout the world in the time of the Lord Jesus Christ. However, some Aramaic phrases are found in the New Testament as Aramaic was the vernacular of the people of Israel. Jesus and His disciples also spoke Aramaic in addition to Koine Greek. Much of the Old Testament was translated into Aramaic and these works are referred to as the Targums.

How was the Bible written and translated ?

The Bible itself tells us how it was written: "All scripture is inspired by God" (2 Timothy 3:16). Men "moved by the Holy Spirit spoke from God"

(2 Peter 1:21). The Greek word for inspired, *theopneustos*, means "God-breathed." The Holy Spirit carried men along, moving and guiding them as they wrote in their own words what God wanted them to say. Thus we have *verbal* inspiration, because the words of the original text were inspired by God. And because all Scripture was given by inspiration we have *plenary inspiration*, which means total or complete inspiration. Every part of the Bible is inspired. The Bible does not merely contain the words of God, it is the Word of God. Thus the original writings, often called *autographs*, are infallible—without error. Those who hold to this belief say they believe in the verbal, plenary inspiration of the autographs.

Autographs

In the beginning writing was done on stone, clay tablets, leather (animal skins), and papyrus scrolls. The *autographs* were probably written on papyrus. Papyrus, made from the inner bark of a reed plant, was formed into a paper-like material which was glued together and rolled into a scroll. Normally the writing was done on only one side of the scroll so as it was read it was unrolled with one hand and rolled up with the other. The scrolls were kept in a cylindrical box called a *capsa*.

According to the Jewish Talmud, when the original autographs were copied they were to be copied only on the skins of what God deemed as clean animals such as sheep, calves, and goats. Parchment (dried animal skin) was costly but more durable and permanent than papyrus.

The Accuracy of the Copies

Eventually the scrolls were replaced by the *codex*. The codex (or *codices*) was made from folded sheets, *quires*, which were stitched together like a book. Copies of the original autographs of the Old Testament and copies of those copies were transcribed by hand under the strictest measures. The men who copied the manuscripts were called *scribes*. If one error was found the entire copy was destroyed. Thus the accuracy of the copies is phenomenal. This accuracy has been confirmed by the multiple number of copies, by the Septuagint, and by the Dead Sea Scrolls. Plus, there are more than five thousand ancient Greek copies of all or portions of the New Testament. Although there may be minor variances in the manuscripts, none deal with doctrinal issues.

The Canon

The same omnipotent Sovereign who inspired men to write the Word of God led other men to recognize that these were the books which would comprise the *canon* of Scripture. The canon is the list of books which are recognized to be inspired by God. This list comprises the Old and New Testaments. The Old Testament canon was already established in the days of Jesus Christ. Jesus, who is one with the Father, affirmed and never contradicted the Old Testament. Revelation, the last of the New Testament books to be written, was complete before the end of the first century A.D. By A.D. 367 Bishop Athanasius compiled the first known list of the current twenty-seven books of the New Testament.

Translations

The Hebrew/Aramaic and Greek copies of the autographs of the sixty-six books of the Bible are the basis of the translations made in the various languages of the world. A translator will study the original words of the copies of the autographs, determine what those words mean, and then select the best way to faithfully transmit the meaning of the original words in their context into the language of their translation. This is called a *primary translation*.

A *secondary translation* occurs when a translation is made from a primary translation of another language, say English, into a third language. Thus a secondary translation is not made from a copy of the autograph in its original language but from a second language translated from the original language (the primary translation).

How do we know the Bible is what it claims to be—the Word of God?

It's a matter of faith. You either believe what the Word of God says about itself or you don't. You either believe the testimony of Jesus Christ regarding the Word of God or you don't.

There are, however, several areas of objective evidence that test and support the veracity of the verbal, plenary inspiration of the autographs.

First, there is *bibliographic evidence* for its authenticity. No other ancient writings have as much manuscript evidence as does the Bible. Aside from 643 copies of Homer's works, which were written about 850 B.C., the other classical works written between 450 B.C. and 10 B.C. have anywhere from three to twenty copies each. And not only is there more than an ample *quantity* of copies, but the *quality* of the biblical manuscripts surpasses other manuscripts. This is largely due to the Jews' extreme caution in the translation and preservation of the manuscripts.

Time is also a factor. The Dead Sea Scrolls, which date from 200 B.C. to A.D. 68, greatly reduce the time span between the writing of the Old Testament books to our earliest existing copies of the Old Testament. The time span between the autographs of the New Testament and its existing copies is between one to two hundred years.

Second, there is *internal evidence* for the authenticity of the Bible. The Bible not only claims to be the Word of God, but also states that not the smallest letter or stroke will pass away from the law (the Old Testament) until it is all accomplished (Matthew 5:17-18). Many of the writers claimed to be eyewitnesses who wrote what they saw, heard, or experienced. Although over forty different authors wrote sixty-six separate books, you'll find that over a time span of almost two millennia there are no contradictions in what they wrote. Also, what was written in the Old Testament, sealed and canonized, is often seen fulfilled in the New Testament. Thus there is the internal evidence of fulfilled prophecy, some of which is being fulfilled even to this time.

Finally, there is an abundance of *external evidence* that supports the Bible's infallibility. When the Bible speaks on matters of history or science, it speaks accurately. There were times when it was supposed that science or history contradicted the Bible; however, later it was discovered that all the facts hadn't been uncovered.

More recent archeological evidence has affirmed the historicity of the Bible in a multitude of ways as it speaks regarding rulers, nations, languages, battles, customs, geographic locations, tragedies, and other events. Extrabiblical writings also affirm what the New Testament teaches about the historicity of Jesus Christ and other New Testament characters.

Yet despite all this evidence, men choose to believe only what they want to believe. Have you accepted the Bible as the inerrant Word of God, profitable for doctrine, reproof, correction, for training in righteousness that you may be adequate, equipped for every good work? (2 Timothy 3:16). As you study it, you'll discover that it's a supernatural book . . . the very words of life.

Inductive Bible Study Helps

The material in this portion of your International Inductive Study Bible *will provide you with additional tools to assist you in your inductive study of God's Word.*

You'll find it beneficial to take some time to familiarize yourself with the basic content of each part of this section so you'll know what's at your fingertips when you need it.

The Ark of the Covenant

The one piece of furniture that is the most holy to the Jews is the ark of the covenant. The following information will help you understand why it is so important to them and why orthodox Jews are still looking for it.

The ark, a box 4 feet long by 2 1/2 feet wide and 2 1/2 feet high, was constructed of acacia wood and overlaid with gold inside and out. Because it symbolized God's presence, no one was allowed to touch it. Four gold rings were attached to the feet of the ark. Poles, made of acacia wood and overlaid with gold, were slipped through these rings so that the ark could be carried from place to place (Exodus 25:10-22). Only the Kohathites (a division of the Levites) were allowed to move the ark.

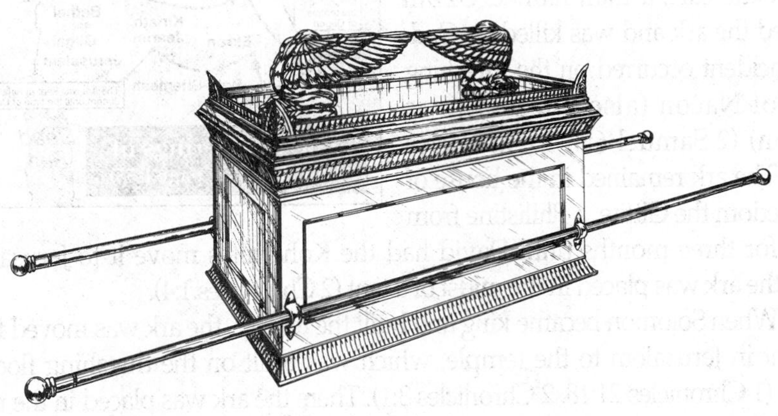

When the ark was in the tabernacle the cloud of God's presence hovered over the mercy seat (Leviticus 16:2, 1 Samuel 4:4). The mercy seat, made of pure gold with a gold cherub attached at each end, covered the ark of the covenant. On the day of atonement the high priest sprinkled the blood of sacrifice on the mercy seat as a covering for the sins of the people. (The Hebrew word for mercy is *kapporeth*, a covering.)

Inside the ark was the testimony, the stone tablets bearing the ten commandments (Exodus 40:20, Deuteronomy 10:2). For a period of time the ark also contained Aaron's rod which budded (Numbers 17:10) and a gold jar of manna (Hebrews 9:4).

The tabernacle, where the ark resided in the most holy place, and the furniture were made according to the pattern of God's throne in heaven. God gave Moses this pattern when He instructed him to build the tabernacle (Hebrews 8:1-5).

The ark journeyed before the children of Israel as they moved from Sinai to Canaan. It went before them as they crossed the Jordan and conquered Jericho. It rested at Gilgal, Shechem, Bethel, and Shiloh. Then the Philistines at Ebenezer captured it and kept it for seven months. They took it to Aphek, Ashdod, Gath, and Ekron. From Ekron it went to Beth-shemesh. It was at Beth-shemesh that 50,070 people were killed because they looked into the ark. From there the ark was taken to Kiriath-jearim (Gibeath) and the house of Abinadab, where it remained for twenty years.

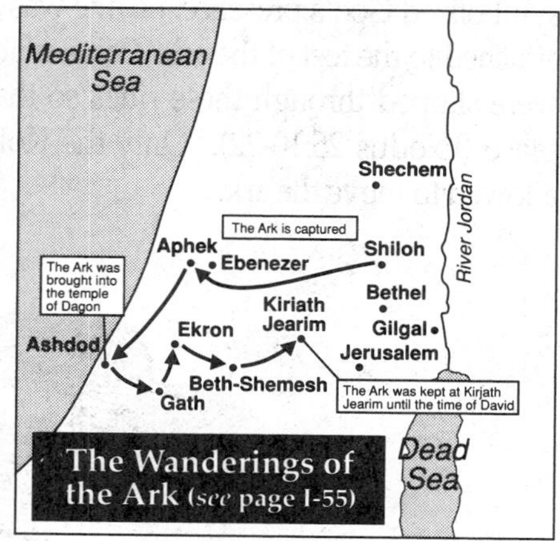

The Wanderings of the Ark (*see page I-55*)

When David became king he wanted to move the ark to Jerusalem. The Israelites broke God's command by moving it on a cart rather than carrying it by the poles. When the ark started to fall off the cart, a man named Uzzah touched the ark and was killed by God. This incident occurred on the threshing floor of Nacon (also referred to as Chidon) (2 Samuel 6:6, 1 Chronicles 13:9). The ark remained in the house of Obed-edom the Gittite, a Philistine from Gath, for three months until David had the Kohathites move it to Jerusalem. There the ark was placed in the midst of a tent (2 Chronicles 1:4).

When Solomon became king and built the temple, the ark was moved from the tent in Jerusalem to the temple, which was built on the threshing floor of Ornan (1 Chronicles 21:18, 2 Chronicles 3:1). There the ark was placed in the most holy place (1 Kings 8:6, 2 Chronicles 5:2-14).

There is no record of the whereabouts or fate of the ark since the destruction of the temple by the Babylonians in 586 B.C.

The last mention of the ark is in Revelation 11:19: "And the temple of God which is in heaven was opened; and the ark of His covenant appeared in His temple, and there were flashes of lightning and sounds and peals of thunder and an earthquake and a great hailstorm."

Understanding Gnosticism

Much like the church today, many members of the early church were significantly influenced by the prevailing philosophy of the day. While some of the New Testament was being written, the church in Asia was being threatened by gnosticism, a philosophy which became the major opponent of the gospel in the early apostolic church.

A familiarity with the teachings of gnosticism will give you a greater understanding of and appreciation for some of the warnings and teachings given in the epistles.

Many members of the early church were seeking enlightenment, and were easily deceived by Gnostic teachers and led astray from the simplicity and purity of devotion to Christ. Some had apparently left the church to form their own community purporting a different gospel than what the apostles had preached. This movement away from the church caused those who remained to question what was true, and thus confusion crept in.

The term *gnosticism* comes from the Greek word *gnosis*, meaning "to know." Gnosticism is a philosophy which centers on a search for higher knowledge. The Gnostics taught that this knowledge was not intellectual knowledge but a knowledge which the ordinary Christian was incapable of attaining. Once a believer came into possession of this extraordinary knowledge, according to Gnostic thought, he had "salvation."

Although Gnostic philosophy took many strange and divergent turns, two axioms were basic to its teaching:

- *The first major Gnostic doctrine was the supremacy of knowledge.*

  Certain *pneumatiko* or "enlightened ones" claimed to have special knowledge of the truth.

  Ordinary Christians did not or could not possess this secret of higher knowledge.

- *The second major doctrine of gnosticism was the separation of spirit and matter.*

  All matter was considered to be evil and the source of evil.

  The spirit was considered to be good and impervious to defilement by anything the body (matter) did.

Purporting a so-called higher knowledge beyond that revealed by God in Christ Jesus and through the prophets, gnosticism had it origins in the philosophies of the Greeks and the Romans, in the creeds of Plato and Philo, and in the religions of the East, especially those of Persia and India. While Christianity kept its Judaic roots, it was free from these heresies. However, when Christianity spread to Gentile territory, an attempt was made on the part of Eastern philosophical religion to form an alliance with it.

Many Gnostics allegorized the Old Testament and did not interpret its teachings literally. They strayed from the veracity of the Word which would have exposed their erroneous teaching regarding creation, sin, and the restoration of all things. They failed to see how a supreme God, pure in spirit and essentially good, could create a universe of matter which they considered evil.

When the Gnostics embraced Christianity, they split into two factions on the subject of Christ's deity.

- The Docetic Gnostics denied the humanity of Jesus. The word *docetic* comes from the Greek word *dokeo*, "to seem." According to the Docetists, it was impossible for God, who was spirit and good, to become flesh, which was matter and evil, in the person of Jesus Christ. They believed that Jesus was a phantom; He didn't possess a real flesh-and-blood body. He only seemed to have a body.
- The Cerinthian Gnostics (followers of Cerinthus) separated the man Jesus from the *aeon*, the power of Christ. They believed that when the dove came on Jesus at His baptism, the power of Christ came and rested on the man Jesus. This power then departed before His death on the cross. So it was simply the "man" Jesus who died, not Jesus Christ, God in the flesh.

These Gnostic heresies denied that God became man and walked this earth in the person of Jesus Christ to bring redemption and salvation to mankind. Having eliminated Jesus Christ as the only way to God, the Gnostics believed they could make their own way to God through their inquiry and knowledge. Faith and one's deeds were viewed as having no significance in salvation or the ensuing walk.

Understanding the basis of gnosticism and the forms of thought that it took in the early days of the Christian church will enable you to better understand the doctrinal heresy some of the New Testament writers addressed.

Guidelines for Interpreting Predictive Prophecy

From Genesis to Revelation the Bible is filled with prophecy. If you want to handle the prophecies in the Word of God accurately, the following guidelines will give you some important parameters.

The Greek word for prophecy, *propheteia*, comes from two Greek words, *pro*, meaning "forth," and *phemi*, meaning "to speak." It means to speak forth the mind and counsel of God. According to this definition, all Scripture is, in a sense, prophecy.

Predictive prophecy points to a future fulfillment and is of divine origin. In *Understanding and Applying the Bible*, Dr. Robertson McQuilkin says: "There are two purposes for predictive prophecy. The chief purpose is to affect the conduct of those who hear the prophecy. Another purpose is met only when the prophecy is fulfilled. That purpose is to build forth, to establish confidence in the God who miraculously foretold events (John 13:19, 14:29, 16:4)."

Some scholars divide predictive prophecy into two categories: *forthtelling* and *foretelling*. Forthtelling prophecies contain a message about the present or immediate time. (Often this is a call to godly living in the light of prophecy yet to be fulfilled.) Foretelling prophecies contain a message about what God will do *in the future*.

When a prophet spoke for God, the prophecy could refer to the following:

- a present or near fulfillment
- a future fulfillment
- a two-fold fulfillment: a near fulfillment and then a later, future fulfillment

As you read the prophecies of the Bible, keep in mind the following guidelines and discern if the prophecy refers to:

- the prophet's own time and/or a future time
- the captivity and/or restoration of Israel or Judah
- the first coming of Christ and any events connected with it
- the second coming of Christ
- the last days or end times

The Prophetic Points of History

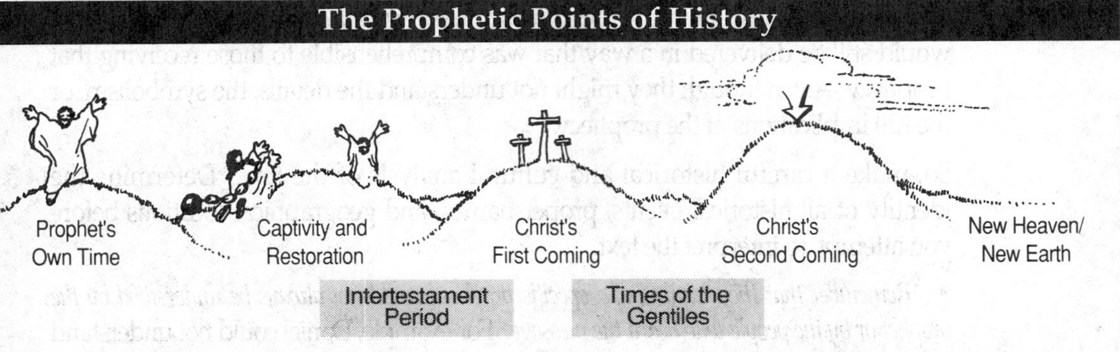

- *As you study prophecy, it is important to remember that the prophets did not always indicate intervals of time between events, nor did they write their prophecies in chronological order.* For example an Old Testament prophecy could include the first and second comings of Christ without any indication of the time span between the two comings. One such prophecy is found in Isaiah 65:17-25. In this prophecy, Isaiah first talks about the new heavens and the new earth (in which we know there is no death), and then in verses 18-25 he refers to a time when a youth dies at one hundred and the wolf and lamb lay down together. Chronologically, verse 17 will be fulfilled *after* verses 18-25 become a reality.

- *Always approach a prophecy as literal (in its simple, ordinary meaning) unless one of the following occurs:*

  The grammatical context shows it is figurative language by the use of similes, metaphors, parables, allegories, symbols, or types.

  A literal interpretation violates common sense, is contrary to what the author is saying, or is contrary to what the rest of Scripture teaches.

- *When a prophetic passage cannot be taken literally, look for what the author is trying to convey through his figurative or symbolic language.* To discern what the author is saying, look for answers in the following places:

  within the context of the book in which the passage appears

  in any other writings of that author

  in any other prophetic writings to which the author had access (for example, other prophetic books or passages in the Word of God)

- *Remember that often when a prophet refers to future events, he does not use the future tense.*

- *When you interpret Scripture, consider the historical context of that writing, remembering that God was delivering His prophecy to a particular people at a particular time.* Granted, it might have been a prophecy with a future fulfillment, but it would still be delivered in a way that was comprehensible to those receiving that prophecy—even though they might not understand the details, the symbolism, or the full implications of the prophecy.

So, make a careful historical and cultural analysis of the text. Determine the identity of all historical events, proper names, and geographical locations before you attempt to interpret the text.

- *Remember that the meaning of a specific prophecy could not always be understood by the prophet or by the people who heard the message.* For example, Daniel could not understand what he had written, as it was to remain sealed until the end time (Daniel 12:8-9).

However, many prophecies will come to light through the following:

a fulfillment as recorded in history

a fulfillment as recorded in the New Testament

an explanation given by an Old Testament or a New Testament writing (for example, Acts 4:24-28)

• *Remember that many New Testament prophecies include Old Testament quotations and allusions.* Scholars estimate that between 350 to over 400 Old Testament quotations or allusions appear in Revelation alone. Revelation is replete with the language of Isaiah, Jeremiah, Ezekiel, Daniel, and the minor prophets. It is obvious the author of Revelation was steeped in the Old Testament, for he talks in Old Testament phraseology. So to correctly interpret New Testament prophecy, check Old Testament cross-references.

• *When you study prophecy, watch for phrases which indicate periods of time.* For example, look for *in the last days, day of the Lord, day of wrath,* and *end of the age.* When you come across phrases such as these, carefully observe the things which occur during that particular time period. Then ask the following questions:

- Have these events ever occurred in history?
- Do these events coincide with any other particular period of time?
- Do these events parallel any events mentioned in another place in the Word of God?

Figures of Speech

Although the Bible is to be interpreted literally, it is important to remember that like other writings it contains figures of speech which must be interpreted for what they are and in the light of their intended purpose. As you seek to handle the Word of God accurately, you'll find it helpful to understand the definitions of the different types of figures of speech.

A *figure of speech* is a word, a phrase, or an expression used in an imaginative rather than a literal sense.

Discerning the use of figures of speech is important in biblical intrepretation. For example, there has been much controversy in the church over Jesus' statement regarding the bread at the Last Supper: "And when He had taken some bread and given thanks, He broke it, and gave it to them, saying, `This is My body which is given for you'" (Luke 22:19). Some believe that the bread actually becomes His body (the doctrine of transubstantiation); others believe Jesus was simply using a metaphor and that the bread is representative of His body.

Three principles for dealing with figurative language are:

- Identify the fact that the author is using figurative language.

- Identify the type of figurative language in use: simile, metaphor, hyperbole, and so on.
- Follow the guidelines for interpreting what the author meant by his use of that particular figure of speech.

You will be aided in your study of Scripture if you are able to identify when the author is using a figure of speech. The following are brief definitions of the types of figurative language used in the Bible.

- A *metaphor* is an implied comparison between two things which are different. In a metaphor the words of comparison—*like, as, as . . . so is*, and *such as*—are *not* used. An example is John 6:48, where Jesus says, "I am the bread of life."

- A *simile* is an expressed comparison of two different things or ideas that uses the words *like, as, as . . . so is,* and/or *such as.* An example is Revelation 1:14b, "His eyes were like a flame of fire."

- *Hyperbole* is a deliberate exaggeration for effect or emphasis. Hyperboles are found in all languages, and they are frequently used among Semitic peoples. For example, "My soul is crushed with longing" (Psalm 119:20).

- *Metonymy* is used when the name of one object or concept is used for that of another to which it is related. This is a figure of association. An example of a metonymy is found in the statement, "All the country of Judea was going out to Him." The metonymy is Judea, which refers to the people rather than the region itself. Note also the hyperbole, all the country.

- *Synecdoche* is another figure of association where the whole can refer to the part or the part to the whole. This is often found in the use of the term *the law,* which can refer to the Pentateuch (the first five books of the Old Testament), the Ten Commandments, or the whole Old Testament.

A synecdoche can also be a singular for a plural or a plural for a singular. An example is in Jeremiah 25:29. God says He is going to summon "a sword against all the inhabitants of the earth." The singular sword represents many swords.

- In *personification* an object is given characteristics or attributes that belong to people; for example, when the trees clap their hands and the mountains sing for joy (Isaiah 55:12).

- *Irony* is a statement which says the opposite of what is meant. Irony is used for emphasis or effect. When it is not easy to discern if a statement is ironic, then examine it first as a true statement. As such, does it make sense in its context? Second, examine it as figurative irony. If this makes sense and fits with the context, then accept it as irony. Otherwise, treat it as a truth.

Here are two examples of irony:

1. In 1 Kings 22:1-23, a true prophet tells the king what he wants to hear but it is a lie. It's obvious he's using irony because the king tells him to stop prophesying falsely and tell the truth.
2. In 1 Corinthians 4:8, Paul says to the Corinthians, "You are already filled, you have already become rich, you have become kings without us; and I would indeed that you had become kings so that we also might reign with you." When you read this, it is obvious the Corinthians are not kings, nor does Paul desire to reign with them.

Parables

A parable is a story which, although not usually factual, remains true to life and teaches a moral lesson or truth. Every detail of a parable will reinforce the main theme, but you shouldn't attempt to ascribe a spiritual meaning and application to each point.

Jesus frequently used parables in His teaching; He used them for two reasons: to reveal truth to believers and to hide truth from those who had rejected it and/or hardened their hearts against it.

To correctly interpret a parable:

• *Ascertain the occasion of the parable.* Since parables clarify or emphasize a truth, discover why the parable was told. What prompted it?

• *Look for the intended meaning of the parable.* The meaning will sometimes be stated. If not, it can usually be determined by the application of the parable to the hearer.

• *Don't impose any meaning beyond what is clearly stated or applied to the hearers by the speaker of the parable.*

• *Identify the central or focal idea of the parable.* Every parable has one central theme or emphasis. No detail of the story is to be given any meaning that is independent of the main teaching of the parable.

Since a parable has one central point of emphasis, identify relevant details. To attach meaning that is not in the context of the occasion or relevant to its central emphasis is to go away from the meaning of the parable. A detail is relevant only if it reinforces the central theme of the parable.

How many sermons have you heard on the parable of the prodigal son? Many teachers violate the occasion and meaning of this parable, attaching all sorts of meanings to the details of this story. Jesus told this parable because He wanted the Pharisees to see what their hearts were like as they grumbled, "This man receives sinners and eats with them" (Luke 15:2). In order to make His point Jesus told three consecutive parables about three things which were lost: a sheep, a coin, and a son. In each of the parables Jesus uses the following words: *lost, found, sin,* and *joy (rejoice).* When He gets to the story of the prodigal son, He shows them the kindness of the father's heart versus the hardness of the elder brother's, and in doing so, shows them their hearts are like the elder brother's, not the Father's.

• *Interpret parables in the context of the culture of Bible times rather than the culture of today.* For example, in the parable of the wise and foolish virgins, the central emphasis of the parable is, "Be on the alert then, for you do not know the day nor the hour" (Matthew 25:13). Understanding Eastern wedding traditions would give insight into the parable and explain why some were ready and others were not.

• *Do not establish doctrine when parables are the primary or only source for that teaching.* Parables should simply amplify or affirm doctrine, not establish it.

Allegory

An allegory is a description of one thing using the image of another—a story with an underlying meaning different from the surface facts of the story itself. Some refer to an allegory as an extended metaphor, which is an implied comparison between two different things. An allegory is a realistic or non-realistic story created to teach one or more truths which may or may not be related.

The following comparison of parables and allegories will help you distinguish one from the other.

Parable	**Allegory**
1. Has one central point	1. Can have more than one central point
2. Teaches one truth	2. Can teach a number of truths
3. Every relevant detail reinforces the central theme or point of emphasis	3. The details of an allegory may be many and varied, relating to more than one theme
4. Can have irrelevant details; all features of the parable do not have to be identified	4. Can have irrelevant details; all the features of an allegory do not have to be identified
5. Usually the story is separate from its interpretation and application	5. Intertwines the story and the meaning
6. Application usually follows the parable	6. Application is found within the allegory

When interpreting an allegory, follow these guidelines:

- List the features of the allegory.
- Note any interpretation given within the text of the allegory.
- Study the allegory's features according to sound principles of biblical exegesis. Do not contradict the clear teaching of the Word of God by interpreting an unexplained detail in an allegory in a way contrary to other truths.
- Do not try to identify all the features of an allegory.

Types

A type is a prophetic symbol designated by God.

The word *type* comes from the Greek word *tupos*. A *tupos* was a mark formed by a blow or an impression, creating a figure or an image on the object that was struck. Therefore, a type prefigures something or someone to come. That which it prefigures is called an *antitype*.

A type prefigures only one antitype, although it may parallel many points in the antitype. An illustration of this is the tabernacle, a type of man's redemption. According to Hebrews 10:20, the veil that separated the holy place from the Holy of Holies prefigured the flesh of Jesus Christ.

When determining types, although it may not be formally stated, there should be some evidence of divine affirmation of the corresponding type and antitype. If the Word does not designate something as a type, then the Bible expositor should simply show the parallels without calling it a type. In Romans 5:14 we read, "Nevertheless death reigned from Adam until Moses, even over those who had not sinned in the likeness of the offense of Adam, who is a type of Him who was to come." The word translated *type* is the Greek word *tupos*. Adam was a type or figure of Christ, who was to come. In 1 Corinthians 15:45, Christ is referred to as "the last Adam."

Symbols

A symbol is a picture or an object that stands for or represents another thing. For example, the seven candlesticks mentioned in Revelation 1:20 represent the seven churches described in Revelation 2 and 3.

When noting symbols it is important to remember the following:

- *The item used as a symbol can symbolize different things.* For example, water is used to symbolize the Word of God (Ephesians 5:26), and the Holy Spirit (John 7:37-39).
- *Although a symbol can represent many things when it does symbolize something in a given passage, a single parallel is intended.* For instance in John 7:37-39, water symbolized the Holy Spirit, not the Word.

- *Interpret symbols in the light of a biblical setting and culture rather than the culture of the current interpreter.*
- *Symbols are timeless and can symbolize something past, present, or future.*

Tense, Voice, and Mood of Greek Verbs

There are many excellent study tools which can help you examine the text in a more in-depth way through Greek word studies. If you would like to pursue Greek word studies further, a highly recommended book is The Complete Word Study New Testament *by Spiros Zodhiates, Th.D.*

The following explanation of the tense, voice, and mood of Greek verbs will help those who do not know Greek but want a better understanding of the implications of the kind of action indicated by the verbs.

Because verbs express action, they are often the most significant element in the expression of thought. Therefore, understanding the Greek verb is a key to correct interpretation and application of Scripture. (Context is the most important key to correct interpretation and application, since the Greek words get their meaning from the context.) The major features of Greek verbs are tense, voice, and mood.

Part of the beauty of the Greek language is that the construction of the verb clearly shows who does the action, whether the statement is a command or a suggestion, and whether the passage is speaking of reality or possibility.

By thinking through a simple, concise explanation of tense, voice, and mood, new vistas of insight will be opened to you. Keep in mind that the following is a simplified and nonexhaustive summarization of a complex subject. The purpose of this information is to give you an overview of terms that are frequently used in the more technical commentaries.

Tense
(Shows the Kind of Action)

Greek verb tenses differ from English verb tenses in that the kind of action portrayed is the most significant element, and time is a relatively minor consideration.

- **Action as continuous**

  Present tense—continuous action. It is primarily progressive or linear in that it shows action that is continuing.

  Examples:
  Jeff *is studying* the Bible.
  John 15:4b— "As the branch *cannot bear* fruit of itself, unless it *abides* in the vine, so neither can you, unless you *abide* in Me."

John 15:6—"If anyone *does not abide* in Me."

Imperfect tense—continuous action, usually in the past.

Examples:
Jeff *was studying* the Bible.
John 15:19a—"If you were of the world, the world *would love* its own." (Literally, "would have been loving" its own.)

- **Action as completed**

Perfect tense—punctiliar action in the past with the results continuing into the present.

Examples:
Jeff is being transformed by *having studied* the Bible.
John 15:3—"You are already clean because of the word which I *have spoken* to you."
John 15:10b—"Just as I *have kept* My Father's commandments, and abide in His love."

Pluperfect tense—punctiliar action in the past with the results continuing in the past.

Examples:
Jeff was transformed because he *had studied* the Bible.
John 9:22—"For the Jews *had* already *agreed*."

- **Action as occurring**

Aorist tense—punctiliar action. The aorist tense states an action as completed without regard to its duration; that is, it denotes the fact of an action without any reference to the length of that action. Compared to the present tense, the aorist tense expresses the action like a snapshot while the present tense action is like a moving picture, continuing on.

Examples:
Jeff *studied* the Bible.
John 15:4a—"*Abide* in Me, and I in you."

Future tense—indefinite action to occur in the future. Indicates continuing or punctiliar action in the future. This is the only tense that reflects the time of the action.

Examples:
Jeff *will be studying* his Bible.
John 15:7—"It *shall be done* for you."
John 15:8—"*So* prove to *be* My disciples."

Voice

(Shows How the Subject Is Related to the Action)

- **Active voice—indicates that the subject produces the action.**

  Examples:
  Jeff *hit* the ball.
  John 15:2b—"And every branch that bears fruit, He *prunes* it."

- **Passive voice—indicates that the subject was acted upon.**

  Examples:
  Jeff *was hit* by the ball.
  John 15:6—"And they *are burned*."

- **Middle voice—indicates that the subject initiates the action and also participates in the results of the action.** (This voice is unique to Greek construction.)

  Examples:
  Jeff *hit* himself with the ball.
  John 15:26—"That is the Spirit of truth, who *proceeds* from the Father, He will bear witness of Me."

One note of interest when looking up a verb in a Greek study tool: the middle and passive voices will have identical forms, but the context will show you if the subject is receiving the action (passive voice) or if the subject initiated the action and participated in it (middle voice).

Also, some verbs are *deponent verbs*. This means that their form in a Greek study tool may be listed as a passive or middle voice verb but their function or action is active. Usually your Greek study helps will list these as deponent verbs.

Mood

(Shows How the Action Is Related to Reality from the Speaker's Point of View)

- **Indicative mood—the declarative mood or mood of certainty.** It is a statement of fact which assumes reality from the speaker's point of view. This mood simply states a thing as being a fact.

  Examples:
  Bible study *has changed* Jeff's life.
  John 15:6—"He *is thrown* away as a branch, and *dries* up; and they *gather* them, and *cast* them into the fire, and they *are burned*."

- **Imperative mood—usually a command or entreaty.** It is the mood of volition or will. The imperative mood in the Greek makes a demand on the will of the reader to obey the command; it is used to indicate prohibition and authority.

Examples:
Jeff, *study* your homework.
John 15:4—"*Abide* in Me."
John 15:7—"*Ask* whatever you wish."
John 15:9—"*Abide* in My love."
John 15:20—"*Remember* the word that I said to you."

Something else which may help your study of God's Word is the understanding of the combination of the present tense and the imperative mood that is stating a negative command (a prohibition). The *present imperative prohibition* demands cessation of some act already in progress.

Example:
John 20:17—"Jesus said to her, '*Stop clinging* to Me.' " In other words, Mary was already clinging to Jesus, and Jesus was telling her to stop clinging and to go on refusing to cling to Him.

- **Subjunctive mood—the mood of probability.** It implies some doubt regarding the reality of the action from the speaker's point of view. It expresses an uncertainty or an action which may or should happen. This is the mood used for conditional clauses, strong suggestions, or "polite" commands.

Examples:
Jeff *may have done* his homework. Jeff, if you do not do your homework, you cannot participate in the class discussion.
John 15:2—"That it *may bear* more fruit."
John 15:4b—"As the branch cannot bear fruit of itself, unless it *abides* in the vine, so neither can you, unless you *abide* in Me."
John 15:6—"If anyone *does not abide* in Me."
John 15:7—"If you *abide* in Me, and My words *abide* in you."

Something else which may help you in your study of God's Word is an understanding of the combination of the aorist tense and the subjunctive mood that is stating a negative command (a prohibition). The *aorist subjunctive prohibition* is a warning or an exhortation against doing a thing not yet begun.

Example:
John 13:8a — "Peter said to Him, '*Never shall* You *wash* my feet!' " In other words, Peter was telling Jesus that He was not to wash his feet and Jesus was not even to start washing his feet.

- **Optative mood — the mood of possibility.** This mood presents no definite anticipation of realization but merely presents the action as conceivable from the speaker's point of view. (Used less frequently than the other moods.)

Examples:
I *wish* my neighbor, Jeff, would take the Precept Bible Studies.
2 Thessalonians 3:5 — "And may the Lord *direct* your hearts."

Tense, Mood, and Voice of Greek Verbs

Tense

The emphasis is on the *kind* of action, not the time of action.

Tense	Kind of Action	Example
Present	Continuous action	Jeff is studying the Bible.
Imperfect	Continuous action in the past	Jeff was studying the Bible.
Perfect	Punctiliar action in the past with the results continuing into the present	Jeff is being transformed by having studied the Bible.
Pluperfect	Punctiliar action in the past with the results continuing in the past	Jeff was transformed because he had studied the Bible.
Aorist	Punctiliar action (The time can be past, present, or future but is generally past.)	Jeff studied the Bible.
Future	Generally continuous action in the future, on occasion, it can be punctiliar. This is the only tense that reflects the time of action.	Jeff will be studying his Bible.

Mood

The mood expresses the relationship of the action to reality from the speaker's point of view.

Mood	Relation to Reality	Usage or Meaning	Example
Indicative	Mood of certainty (reality)	Used to declare a statement of fact as something which is true. Expresses that which is actual, factual, or real from the speaker's point of view.	Bible study has changed Jeff's life.
Imperative	Mood of volition or will (potential reality)	Usually used to express a command or entreaty. Denotes intention, authority, permission, or prohibition.	Jeff, study your homework.
Subjunctive	Mood of probability (probable reality)	Used to express an action which may or should happen but which is not necessarily true at the present, from the speaker's point of view. Expresses conditional or uncertain actions.	Jeff may have done his homework.
Optative	Mood of possibility (possible reality)	Merely presents an action as conceivable from the speaker's point of view, with no definite anticipation of realization.	I wish my neighbor, Jeff, would take the Precept Bible Studies.

Voice

The voice expresses the relationship of the subject to the action.

Voice	How the Subject Is Related to the Action	Example
Active	Indicates the subject produces the action	Jeff hit the ball
Passive	Indicates the subject is acted upon	Jeff was hit by the ball.
Middle	Indicates the subject initiates the action and participates in the results of the action	Jeff hit himself with the ball.

Prohibitions

This is when the speaker states a negative command.

Prohibition	Definition	Example
Present Imperative (used with a negative)	This prohibition demands cessation of some act already in progress.	John 20:17
Aorist Subjunctive (used with a negative)	This prohibition is a warning or exhortation against doing a thing not yet begun.	John 13:8

THE OLD TESTAMENT

NEW AMERICAN STANDARD BIBLE

ENESIS

hen there was nothing, there was God. Then God spoke.

NGS TO DO

eral Instructions

enesis falls into two segments. The first, chapters 1 through 11, covers four major events. The nd segment, chapters 12 through 50, covers the lives of four major characters. The instructions on to study this book will be divided according to these two segments.

As you read chapter by chapter train yourself to ask the five W's and an H about the text: Who? What? When? Where? Why? and How? Ask questions such as: Who is speaking? What is happening? When is it happening? Where will it happen? Why was this said or done and what were the consequences? How did it happen? How was it to be done? etc.

. Mark in a distinctive way any repeated words or phrases which are key to understanding the content of the chapter. There are several key words you should look for throughout the book of Genesis. These are listed on the GENESIS AT A GLANCE chart on pages 79 and 80. Write these on an index card and use it as a bookmark while you study Genesis. (Instructions on how to mark key words and observe the text are in the introduction of this Bible. If you haven't read them, do so before you proceed any further.)

. The timing of events can be very important. When you see a time phrase, in the margin draw a clock such as this in a color of your choice so you'll be able to see it immediately.

. In the margin, summarize the main things which occur in the chapter. List them in the order in which they occur. You may want to number them. For example, in Genesis 1 you could summarize what happens on each of the six days of creation.

. As you study you'll gain insights into God's character and ways. As you read each chapter, in the margin note what you learn about God. You may want to put a distinguishing mark such as this in the margin and then color it yellow so you easily can recognize it. Then list your insights under this symbol for God.

. Look for the theme (subject) of each chapter. Record it on GENESIS AT A GLANCE. Also record the theme on the line next to the chapter number in the text.

. Genesis often is referred to as the book of beginnings; it's the seedbed of truth. This is because the Word of God is a progressive revelation. *Progressive revelation* means that truth is unveiled over a period of time throughout various books of the Bible. God doesn't say everything He has to say about a particular subject at one time or in one place. Rather He'll introduce a truth and then progressively reveal more and more about it.

Since Genesis is the book of beginnings, when you come to the first of anything, record it in the chapter margin in a special way or color so you can spot it easily. For example, next to Genesis 1:26-27, you could write: "First man and woman."

apters 1-11

1. Genesis 1-2
   a. In the margin note what is created on each day.
   b. Notice when a day begins and ends.
   c. Chapter 2 gives a more detailed explanation of the creation of man: male and female. Note the order of events and the man's relationship and responsibilities to God and to the woman.

2. Genesis 3-5
   a. In the margin of chapter 3 list all you learn about the serpent and his tactics: how he te Eve, what he says. Then note what happens to Satan because he deceives Eve.
   b. Note Eve's progression into sin. List what happens before and after she sins.
   c. Watch what happens to Adam and Eve's relationship with God. Note the consequen Adam's disobedience.
   d. In chapters 3 through 5 note the consequences of sin's entrance into the world. Record insights in the chapter margins.
3. Genesis 6-9
   a. As you study these chapters observe the reasons for the flood, how and when it came, was affected and how.
   b. Watch the timing of events. Record these in the margin, e.g.: "Rains forty days and nig Mark time phrases with the clock symbol.
   c. Mark the word *covenant* and list all you learn from the text about covenant.
4. Genesis 10-11
   a. Observe who was separated and why, how they were separated, when and where thi curred and what happened as a result.
   b. Babylon plays an intermittently prominent role throughout the Bible, and of course, its are in Genesis. Therefore whenever you come to any mention of Babel or Babylon you nee record what you learn on WHAT THE BIBLE TEACHES ABOUT BABYLON, a chart in appendix of this Bible on pages 1876 and 1877. When you record your observation Babylon note the book, chapter, and verse for future reference.
5. When you finish reading Genesis 11, look at GENESIS AT A GLANCE. Under "Chapter Ther you'll find a place for segment divisions. Fill in the four main events covered in Gene through 11. The chapter divisions are noted on the chart.

Chapters 12-50

1. Genesis 12 through 50 covers the biographical segment of Genesis which focuses on the live four main characters: Abraham, Isaac, Jacob (also called Israel), and Joseph. So when you read
   a. Follow the "General Instructions" for studying each chapter (see page 1).
   b. Watch for and mark every reference to time in the life of each of the major characters in th chapters, including their wives and children. God often will tell how old the person was w certain events occurred in his or her life.
   c. The word *covenant* is more prominent in this last segment. Mark each occurrence of the w and then in the margin list everything you learn about covenant from observing the text.
   d. In the chapter margins note any insights or lessons you learned from the way these pec lived. Note how and why God deals with these men, their families, and their associates what happens as a result.
2. Watch when the focus of a chapter moves from Abraham to Isaac, then to Jacob, and ther Joseph. Then on GENESIS AT A GLANCE, on the line where you recorded the four major eve of Genesis 1 through 11, record the chapter segments that cover the lives of Abraham, Isa Jacob, and Joseph. Look at the chapter themes to see where the focus moves from one of th men to the other.
3. When you finish reading Genesis 50, record on GENESIS AT A GLANCE the theme of Genesis the segment divisions, record the "firsts" that you marked throughout Genesis. (There is a bla line for any other segment divisions you might want to note.)

THINGS TO THINK ABOUT

1. What have you learned from the lives of those mentioned in Genesis—from Adam and E through Joseph? Remember the things which were written in the Old Testament were written

our instruction, that through perseverance and the encouragement of Scripture we might have hope (Romans 15:4). What are the blessings of obedience and the consequences of disobedience?

What have you learned about God—His character, His attributes, and the ways He moves in the lives of men and nations? Since God never changes, can you trust Him? Can you rely on what the Word of God reveals about Him even though you may not understand His ways?

Jesus took the book of Genesis at face value. As you study the Gospels you'll see Jesus referred to the creation of Adam and Eve, to the flood, to the destruction of Sodom and Gomorrah. He even referred to Satan as a murderer from the beginning. Jesus never contradicted the teachings of Genesis; He only affirmed them. Are you going to take God's Word at face value and believe as Jesus did, or are you going to listen to the philosophies of men? Are you going to follow men with finite minds who critique God and His Word, or are you going to accept the Bible as the Word of God and then think and live accordingly?

Chapter 1

1 [a]In the beginning [b]God [c]created the heavens and the earth.
2 And the earth was [1a]formless and void, and [b]darkness was
over the [2]surface of the deep; and [c]the Spirit of God [d]was [3]moving
over the [2]surface of the waters.
3 Then [a]God said, "Let there be light"; and there was light.
4 And God saw that the light was [a]good; and God [b]separated the
light from the darkness.
5 And [a]God called the light day, and the darkness He called night.
And [b]there was evening and there was morning, one day.
6 Then God said, "Let there be [1]an [a]expanse in the midst of the
waters, and let it separate the waters from the waters."
7 And God made the [1]expanse, and separated [a]the waters which
were below the [1]expanse from the waters [b]which were above the
[1]expanse; and it was so.
8 And God called the [1]expanse heaven. And there was evening
and there was morning, a second day.
9 Then God said, "[a]Let the waters below the heavens be gathered
into one place, and let [b]the dry land appear"; and it was so.
10 And God called the dry land earth, and the [a]gathering of the
waters He called seas; and God saw that it was good.
11 Then God said, "Let the earth sprout [1a]vegetation, [2]plants yield-
ing seed, *and* fruit trees bearing fruit after [3]their kind, [4]with seed in
them, on the earth"; and it was so.
12 And the earth brought forth [1]vegetation, [2]plants yielding seed
after [3]their kind, and trees bearing fruit, [4]with seed in them, after
[3]their kind; and God saw that it was good.
13 And there was evening and there was morning, a third day.
14 Then God said, "Let there be [1a]lights in the [2b]expanse of the
heavens to separate the day from the night, and let them be for
[c]signs, and for [d]seasons, and for days and years;
15 and let them be for [1]lights in the [2]expanse of the heavens to give
light on the earth"; and it was so.
16 And God made the two [1]great lights, the [a]greater [2]light [3]to
govern the day, and the lesser [2]light [3]to govern the night; *He made*
[b]the stars also.
17 [a]And God placed them in the [1]expanse of the heavens to give
light on the earth,

[a]Ps. 102:25; Is. ...ohn 1:1, 2; Heb. ...Ps. 89:11; 90:2; ...:24; Rom. 1:20; ...3 [c]Job 38:4; Is. ...45:18; Rev. 4:11

...Or, *a waste and* ...*ss* [2]Lit., *face of* ..., *hovering* [a]Jer. ... [b]Job 38:9 [c]Ps. ...30; Is. 40:13, 14 ...t. 32:11; Is. 31:5

...3:6, 9; 2 Cor. 4:6

...s. 145:9, 10 [b]Is. 45:7

...74:16 [b]Ps. 65:8

...*a firmament* [a]Is. ...Jer. 10:12; 2 Pet. 3:5

...*firmament* [a]Job ...:8-11 [b]Ps. 148:4

...8 [1]Or, *firmament*

[a]Ps. 104:6-9; Jer. ...2; 2 Pet. 3:5 [b]Ps. 24:1, 2; 95:5

... [a]Ps. 33:7; 95:5; 146:6

...1 [1]Or, *grass* [2]Or, ...*s* [3]Lit., *its* [4]Lit., *in* ...*h is its seed* [a]Ps. ...-13; 104:14; Heb. 6:7

...2 [1]Or, *grass* [2]Or, ...*s* [3]Lit., *its* [4]Lit., *in which is its seed*

...4 [1]Or, *luminaries, light-bearers* [2]Or, ...*ament* [a]Ps. 74:16; ...7 [b]Ps. 19:1; 150:1 ...10:2 [d]Ps. 104:19

...5 [1]Or, *luminaries, light-bearers* [2]Or, *firmament*

...16 [1]Or, *luminaries, light-bearers* [2]Or, ...*minary, light-bearer for the dominion of* ...136:8, 9 [b]Job 38:7; Ps. 8:3; Is. 40:26

...Or, *firmament* [a]Jer. 33:20, 25

INSIGHT

The first five books of the Bible—Genesis, Exodus, Leviticus, Numbers, and Deuteronomy—are referred to as the Torah or the Pentateuch. **Torah**, a term used by the Jews, refers to the law or the teaching. **Pentateuch,** a word coined about A.D. 200, means "the five scrolls" or the "five-volume book."

18 and [1]to [a]govern the day and the night, and to separate the light
from the darkness; and God saw that it was good.
19 And there was evening and there was morning, a fourth day.
20 Then God said, "Let the waters [1]teem with swarms of living
creatures, and let birds fly above the earth [2]in the open [3]expanse of
the heavens."
21 And God created [a]the great sea monsters, and every living crea-
ture that moves, with which the waters swarmed after their kind,
and every winged bird after its kind; and God saw that it was good.
22 And God blessed them, saying, "Be fruitful and multiply, and fill
the waters in the seas, and let birds multiply on the earth."
23 And there was evening and there was morning, a fifth day.
24 [a]Then God said, "Let the earth bring forth living creatures after
[1]their kind: cattle and creeping things and beasts of the earth after
[1]their kind"; and it was so.
25 And God made the [a]beasts of the earth after [1]their kind, and the
cattle after [1]their kind, and everything that creeps on the ground
after its kind; and God saw that it was good.
26 Then God said, "Let [a]Us make [b]man in Our image, according to
Our likeness; and let them [c]rule over the fish of the sea and over the
birds of the [1]sky and over the cattle and over all the earth, and over
every creeping thing that creeps on the earth."
27 And God created man [a]in His own image, in the image of God
He created him; [b]male and female He created them.
28 And God blessed them; and God said to them, "[a]Be fruitful and
multiply, and fill the earth, and subdue it; and rule over the fish of
the sea and over the birds of the [1]sky, and over every living thing
that [2]moves on the earth."
29 Then God said, "Behold, [a]I have given you every plant yielding
seed that is on the [1]surface of all the earth, and every tree [2]which has
fruit yielding seed; it shall be food for you;
30 and [a]to every beast of the earth and to every bird of the [1]sky and
to every thing that [2]moves on the earth [3]which has life, *I have given*
every green plant for food"; and it was so.
31 And God saw all that He had made, and behold, it was very
[a]good. And there was evening and there was morning, the sixth day.

Chapter 2

2 Thus the heavens and the earth were completed, and all [a]their
hosts.
2 And by [a]the seventh day God completed His work which He
had done; and [b]He rested on the seventh day from all His work
which He had done.
3 Then God blessed the seventh day and sanctified it, because in it
He rested from all His work which God had created [1]and made.
4 [1a]This is the account of the heavens and the earth when they
were created, in [b]the day that the LORD God made earth and heaven.
5 [a]Now no shrub of the field was yet in the earth, and no plant of
the field had yet sprouted, [b]for the LORD God had not sent rain upon
the earth; and there was no man to [1]cultivate the ground.
6 But a [1]mist used to rise from the earth and water the whole
[2]surface of the ground.
7 Then the LORD God formed man of [a]dust from the ground, and

18 [1]Lit., *for the dominion of* [a]J

20 [1]Or, *swarm* *the face of* [3]Or *firmament*

21 [a]Ps. 104:25

24 [1]Lit., *its* [a]G 6:20; 7:14; 8:19

25 [1]Lit., *its* [a]Ge 22; Jer. 27:5

26 [1]Lit., *heaver* 3:22; 11:7 [b]Gen 9:6; 1 Cor. 11:7; 4:24; James 3:9 8:6-8

27 [a]Gen. 5:1f.; 11:7; Eph. 4:24; 3:10 [b]Matt. 19:4 10:6

28 [1]Lit., *heaven.* *creeps* [a]Gen. 9: Lev. 26:9; Ps. 12

29 [1]Lit., *face of* *which is the fruit tree yielding see* 104:14; 136:25

30 [1]Lit., *heavens* *creeps* [3]Lit., *in w* *a living soul* [a]Ps. 145:15, 16; 147:9

31 [a]Ps. 104:24, 119:68; 1 Tim. 4:4

2:1 [a]Deut. 4:19;

2 [a]Ex. 20:8-11; 31 [b]Heb. 4:4, 10

3 [1]Lit., *to make*

4 [1]Lit., *These are* *generations* [a]Job 38:4-11 [b]Gen. 1:3

5 [1]Lit., *work, serve* [a]Gen. 1:11 [b]Ps. 65 10; Jer. 10:12, 13

6 [1]Or, *flow* [2]Lit., *fa*

7 [a]Gen. 3:19

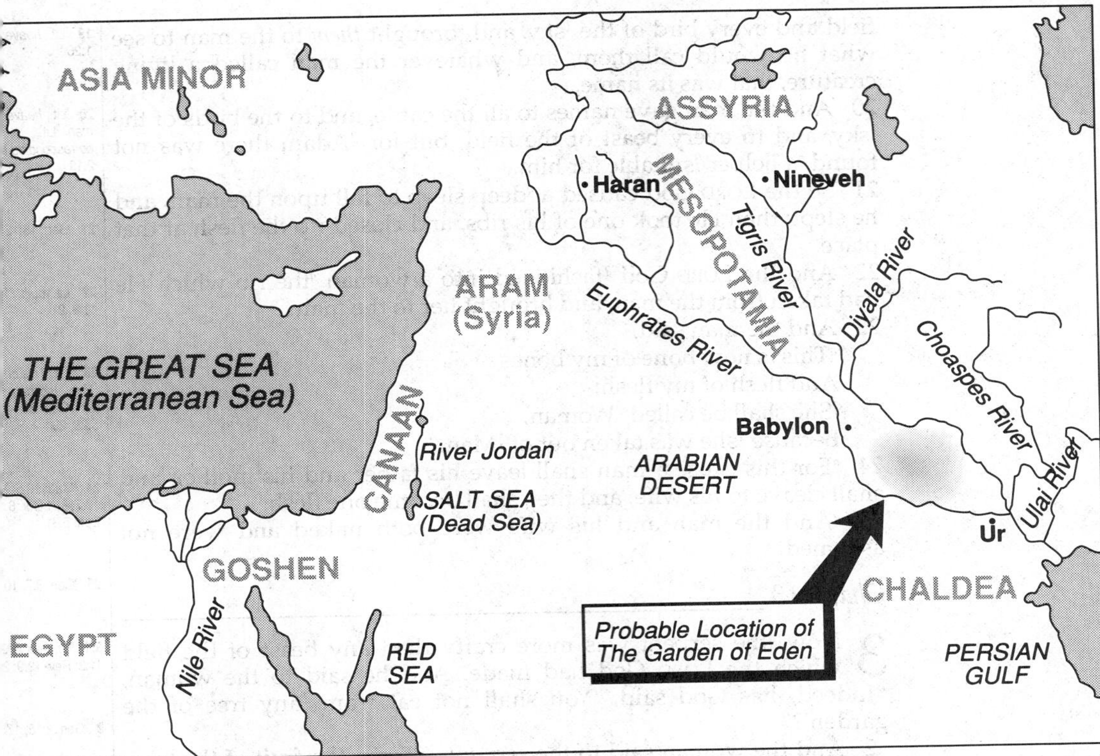

breathed into his nostrils the breath of life; and [b]man became a living
[1]being.
8 And the LORD God planted a [a]garden toward the east, in Eden;
and there He placed the man whom He had formed.
9 And out of the ground the LORD God caused to grow [a]every tree
that is pleasing to the sight and good for food; [b]the tree of life also in
the midst of the garden, and the tree of the knowledge of good and
evil.
10 Now a [a]river [1]flowed out of Eden to water the garden; and from
there it divided and became four [2]rivers.
11 The name of the first is Pishon; it [1]flows around the whole land
of [a]Havilah, where there is gold.
12 And the gold of that land is good; the bdellium and the onyx
stone are there.
13 And the name of the second river is Gihon; it [1]flows around the
whole land of Cush.
14 And the name of the third river is [1a]Tigris; it [2]flows east of As-
syria. And the fourth river is the [3b]Euphrates.
15 Then the LORD God took the man and put him into the garden of
Eden to cultivate it and keep it.
16 And the LORD God [a]commanded the man, saying, "From any
tree of the garden you may eat freely;
17 but from the tree of the knowledge of good and evil you shall
not [1]eat, for in the day that you eat from it [a]you shall surely die."
18 Then the LORD God said, "It is not good for the man to be alone;
[a]I will make him a helper [1]suitable for him."
19 And [a]out of the ground the LORD God formed every beast of the

[1]Lit., *soul* [b]1 Cor. 15:45
en. 13:10; Is. 51:3; Ezek. 28:13
Ezek. 47:12 [b]Gen. ; Rev. 2:7; 22:2, 14
[1]Lit., *was going out* ., *heads* [a]Ps. 46:4
11 [1]Lit., *surrounds* [a]Gen. 25:18
13 [1]Lit., *is the one surrounding*
14 [1]Heb., *Hiddekel* .it., *is the one going* Heb., *Perath* [a]Dan. 10:4 [b]Gen. 15:18
16 [a]Gen. 3:2, 3
17 [1]Lit., *eat from it* Deut. 30:15, 19, 20; om. 6:23; 1 Tim. 5:6; James 1:15
[1]Lit., *corresponding to* [a]1 Cor. 11:9
19 [a]Gen. 1:24

field and every bird of the [1]sky, and [b]brought *them* to the man to see what he would call them; and whatever the man called a living creature, that was its name.

20 And the man gave names to all the cattle, and to the birds of the [1]sky, and to every beast of the field, but for [2]Adam there was not found [a]a helper [3]suitable for him.

21 So the LORD God caused a [a]deep sleep to fall upon the man, and he slept; then He took one of his ribs, and closed up the flesh at that place.

22 And the LORD God [1]fashioned into a woman [a]the rib which He had taken from the man, and brought her to the man.

23 And the man said,

"[a]This is now bone of my bones,
And flesh of my flesh;
[1]She shall be called [2]Woman,
Because [1]she was taken out of [3]Man."

24 [a]For this cause a man shall leave his father and his mother, and shall cleave to his wife; and they shall become one flesh.

25 [a]And the man and his wife were both naked and were not ashamed.

Chapter 3

3 Now [a]the serpent was more crafty than any beast of the field which the LORD God had made. And he said to the woman, "Indeed, has God said, 'You shall not eat from [1]any tree of the garden'?"

2 And the woman said to the serpent, "[a]From the fruit of the trees of the garden we may eat;

3 but from the fruit of the tree which is in the middle of the garden, God has said, 'You shall not eat from it or touch it, lest you die.' "

4 [a]And the serpent said to the woman, "You surely shall not die!

5 "For God knows that in the day you eat from it your eyes will be opened, and [a]you will be like God, knowing good and evil."

6 [a]When the woman saw that the tree was good for food, and that it was a delight to the eyes, and that the tree was desirable to make *one* wise, she took from its fruit and ate; and she gave also to her husband with her, and he ate.

7 Then the eyes of both of them were opened, and they [a]knew that they were naked; and they sewed fig leaves together and made themselves [1]loin coverings.

8 And they heard the sound of [a]the LORD God walking in the garden in the [1]cool of the day, [b]and the man and his wife hid themselves from the presence of the LORD God among the trees of the garden.

9 Then the LORD God called to the man, and said to him, "[a]Where are you?"

10 And he said, "[a]I heard the sound of Thee in the garden, and I was afraid because I was naked; so I hid myself."

11 And He said, "Who told you that you were naked? Have you eaten from the tree of which I commanded you not to eat?"

12 [a]And the man said, "The woman whom Thou gavest *to be* with me, she gave me from the tree, and I ate."

13 Then the LORD God said to the woman, "What is this you have done?" And the woman said, "[a]The serpent deceived me, and I ate."

19 [1]Lit., *heave*
1:26

20 [1]Lit., *heaver*
man [3]Lit.,
corresponding t
2:18

21 [a]Gen. 15:12

22 [1]Lit., *built* [a]1
11:8, 9

23 [1]Lit., *This on*
[2]Heb., *Ishshah*
Ish [a]Gen. 29:14;
5:28, 29

24 [a]Matt. 19:5; M
10:7, 8; 1 Cor. 6:
Eph. 5:31

25 [a]Gen. 3:7, 10

3:1 [1]Or, *every* [a]2
11:3; Rev. 12:9; 2

2 [a]Gen. 2:16, 17

4 [a]John 8:44; 2 C
11:3

5 [a]Is. 14:14; Ezek
12-17

6 [a]Rom. 5:12-19;
2:14; James 1:14,
1 John 2:16

7 [1]Or, *girdles* [a]Is.
Lam. 1:8

8 [1]Lit., *wind, breez*
[a]Gen. 18:33; Lev. 2
Deut. 23:14 [b]Job 3
Ps. 139:1-12; Hos.
Amos 9:3; Rev. 6:1

9 [a]Gen. 4:9; 18:9

10 [a]Ex. 20:18, 19;
5:25

12 [a]Job 31:33; Prov
28:13

13 [a]2 Cor. 11:3; 1 T
2:14

ut. 28:15-20 [b]Is. 65:25; Mic. 7:17

14 And the LORD God said to the serpent,
"[a]Because you have done this,
Cursed are you more than all cattle,
And more than every beast of the field;
On your belly shall you go,
And [b]dust shall you eat
All the days of your life;

[1]Or, *crush* [a]Rev. .17 [b]Rom. 16:20

15 And I will put [a]enmity
Between you and the woman,
And between your seed and her seed;
[b]He shall [1]bruise you on the head,
And you shall bruise him on the heel."

6 [1]Lit., *and your ancy, conception* ohn 16:21; 1 Tim. 15 [b]1 Cor. 14:34

16 To the woman He said,
"I will greatly multiply
Your pain [1]in childbirth,
In pain you shall [a]bring forth children;
Yet your desire shall be for your husband,
And [b]he shall rule over you."

Or, *sorrow* [a]Gen. 9; Rom. 8:20-22; 8 [b]Job 5:7; 14:1; Eccl. 2:23

17 Then to Adam He said, "Because you have listened to the voice of your wife, and have eaten from the tree about which I commanded you, saying, 'You shall not eat from it';
[a]Cursed is the ground because of you;
[b]In [1]toil you shall eat of it
All the days of your life.

18 [1]Lit., *plant*

18 "Both thorns and thistles it shall grow for you;
And you shall eat the [1]plants of the field;

[a]Ps. 90:3; 104:29; cl. 12:7 [b]Gen. 2:7

19 By the sweat of your face
You shall eat bread,
Till you [a]return to the ground,
Because [b]from it you were taken;
For you are dust,
And to dust you shall return."

[1]I.e., living; or, life . 11:3; 1 Tim. 2:13

20 Now the man called his wife's name [1a]Eve, because she was the mother of all *the* living.

[a]Gen. 1:26 [b]Gen. 2:9; Rev. 22:14

21 And the LORD God made garments of skin for Adam and his wife, and clothed them.

Ezek. 31:11 [b]Gen. [c]Ex. 25:18-22; Ps. 4:4; Ezek. 10:1-20; Heb. 1:7 [d]Gen. 2:9

22 Then the LORD God said, "Behold, the man has become like one of [a]Us, knowing good and evil; and now, lest he stretch out his hand, and take also from [b]the tree of life, and eat, and live forever"—

23 therefore the LORD God sent him out from the garden of Eden, to cultivate the ground from which he was taken.

1 [1]Lit., *knew* [2]I.e., tten one [3]Or, *man, the LORD*

24 So [a]He drove the man out; and at the [b]east of the garden of Eden He stationed the [c]cherubim, and the flaming sword which turned every direction, to guard the way to [d]the tree of life.

Chapter 4

2 [a]Luke 11:50, 51 [b]Gen. 46:32; 47:3

4 Now the man [1]had relations with his wife Eve, and she conceived and gave birth to [2]Cain, and she said, "I have gotten a [3]manchild with *the help of* the LORD."

3 [1]Lit., *at the end of days*

2 And again, she gave birth to his brother Abel. And [a]Abel was [b]a keeper of flocks, but Cain was a tiller of the ground.

3 So it came about [1]in the course of time that Cain brought an offering to the LORD of the fruit of the ground.

4 [a]Heb. 11:4

4 And [a]Abel, on his part also brought of the firstlings of his flock

and of their fat portions. And [b]the LORD had regard for Abel and for
his offering;
5 but [a]for Cain and for his offering He had no regard. So [b]Cain
became very angry and his countenance fell.
6 Then the LORD said to Cain, "[a]Why are you angry? And why has
your countenance fallen?
7 "[a]If you do well, [1]will not *your countenance* be lifted up? [b]And if
you do not do well, sin is crouching at the door; and its desire is for
you, [c]but you must master it."
8 And Cain [1]told Abel his brother. And it came about when they
were in the field, that Cain rose up against Abel his brother and
[a]killed him.
9 Then the LORD said to Cain, "[a]Where is Abel your brother?" And
he said, "I do not know. Am I my brother's keeper?"
10 And He said, "What have you done? [a]The voice of your
brother's blood is crying to Me from the ground.
11 "And now [a]you are cursed from the ground, which has opened its
mouth to receive your brother's blood from your hand.
12 "[a]When you cultivate the ground, it shall no longer yield its
strength to you; [b]you shall be a vagrant and a wanderer on the
earth."
13 And Cain said to the LORD, "My punishment is too great to bear!
14 "Behold, Thou hast [a]driven me this day from the face of the
ground; and from Thy face I shall be hidden, and [b]I shall be a
vagrant and a wanderer on the earth, and it will come about that
[c]whoever finds me will kill me."
15 So the LORD said to him, "Therefore whoever kills Cain, ven-
geance will be taken on him [a]sevenfold." And the LORD [1b]appointed a
sign for Cain, lest anyone finding him should slay him.
16 Then Cain went out from the presence [a]of the LORD, and [1]settled
in the land of [2]Nod, east of Eden.
17 And Cain [1]had relations with his wife and she conceived, and
gave birth to Enoch; and he built a city, and called the name of the
city Enoch, after the name of his son.
18 Now to Enoch was born Irad; and Irad [1]became the father of
Mehujael; and Mehujael [1]became the father of Methushael; and
Methushael [1]became the father of Lamech.
19 And Lamech took to himself [a]two wives: the name of the one
was Adah, and the name of the other, Zillah.
20 And Adah gave birth to Jabal; he was the father of those who
dwell in tents and *have* livestock.
21 And his brother's name was Jubal; he was the father of all those
who play the lyre and pipe.
22 As for Zillah, she also gave birth to Tubal-cain, the forger of all
implements of bronze and iron; and the sister of Tubal-cain was
Naamah.
23 And Lamech said to his wives,
"Adah and Zillah,
Listen to my voice,
You wives of Lamech,
Give heed to my speech,
[a]For I [1]have killed a man for wounding me;
And a boy for striking me;

4 [b]1 Sam. 15:22
5 [a]1 Sam. 16:7 Jude 11
6 [a]Jon. 4:4
7 [1]Or, *surely you accepted* [a]Jer. 3 Mic. 7:18 [b]Num. [c]Job 11:14, 15; R 6:12, 16
8 [1]Lit., *said to* [a]M 23:35; Luke 11:51 1 John 3:12-15; J
9 [a]Gen. 3:9
10 [a]Num. 35:33; 21:1-9; Heb. 12:24 6:9, 10
11 [a]Gen. 3:14; De 28:15-20; Gal. 3:1
12 [a]Deut. 28:15-2 Joel 1:10-20 [b]Lev. 26:17, 36
14 [a]Gen. 3:24; Jer 52:3 [b]Deut. 28:64- [c]Num. 35:19
15 [1]Or, *set a mark* [a]Gen. 4:24 [b]Ezek.
16 [1]Lit., *dwelt* [2]I.e. wandering [a]2 Kin. 24:20; Jer. 23:39; 5
17 [1]Lit., *knew*
18 [1]Lit., *begot*
19 [a]Gen. 2:24
23 [1]Or, *kill* [a]Ex. 20: Lev. 19:18; Deut. 32 Ps. 94:1

24 If Cain is avenged [a]sevenfold,
Then Lamech seventy-sevenfold."
25 And [a]Adam [1]had relations with his wife again; and she gave
birth to a son, and named him [2]Seth, for, *she said,* "God [3]has ap-
pointed me another [4]offspring in place of Abel; [b]for Cain killed him."
26 And to Seth, to him also [a]a son was born; and he called his name
Enosh. Then *men* began [b]to call [1]upon the name of the LORD.

Chapter 5

5 This is the book of the generations of Adam. In the day when
God created man, He made him [a]in the likeness of God.
2 He created them [a]male and female, and He [b]blessed them and
named them [1]Man in the day when they were created.
3 When Adam had lived one hundred and thirty years, he [1]became
the father of *a son* in his own likeness, according to his image, and
named him Seth.
4 Then the days of Adam after he became the father of Seth were
eight hundred years, and he had *other* sons and daughters.
5 So all the days that Adam lived were nine hundred and thirty
years, and he died.
6 And Seth lived one hundred and five years, and became the
father of Enosh.
7 Then Seth lived eight hundred and seven years after he became
the father of Enosh, and he had *other* sons and daughters.
8 So all the days of Seth were nine hundred and twelve years, and
he died.
9 And Enosh lived ninety years, and became the father of Kenan.
10 Then Enosh lived eight hundred and fifteen years after he be-
came the father of Kenan, and he had *other* sons and daughters.
11 So all the days of Enosh were nine hundred and five years, and
he died.
12 And Kenan lived seventy years, and became the father of Maha-
lalel.
13 Then Kenan lived eight hundred and forty years after he became
the father of Mahalalel, and he had *other* sons and daughters.
14 So all the days of Kenan were nine hundred and ten years, and
he died.
15 And Mahalalel lived sixty-five years, and became the father of
Jared.
16 Then Mahalalel lived eight hundred and thirty years after he
became the father of Jared, and he had *other* sons and daughters.
17 So all the days of Mahalalel were eight hundred and ninety-five
years, and he died.
18 And Jared lived one hundred and sixty-two years, and became
the father of Enoch.
19 Then Jared lived eight hundred years after he became the father
of Enoch, and he had *other* sons and daughters.
20 So all the days of Jared were nine hundred and sixty-two years,
and he died.
21 And Enoch lived sixty-five years, and became the father of
Methuselah.
22 Then Enoch [a]walked with God three hundred years after he be-
came the father of Methuselah, and he had *other* sons and daughters.
23 So all the days of Enoch were three hundred and sixty-five years.

24 [a]Gen. 4:15

5 [1]Lit., *knew* [2]Heb., *Sheth* [3]Heb., *shath* [4]Lit., *seed* [a]Gen. 5:3 [b]Gen. 4:8

6 [1]Or, *by* [a]Luke 3:38 [b]n. 12:8; 26:25; 1 Kin. 3:24; Ps. 116:17; Joel :32; Zeph. 3:9; 1 Cor. 1:2

5:1 [a]Gen. 1:26, 27; Eph. 4:24; Col. 3:10

2 [1]Lit., *Adam* [a]Matt. 9:4; Mark 10:6 [b]Gen. 1:28

3 [1]Lit., *begot,* and so throughout the ch.

22 [a]Gen. 6:9; 17:1; 24:40; 48:15; Mic. 6:8; Mal. 2:6; 1 Thess. 2:12

The Overlapping of the Patriarchs' Lives

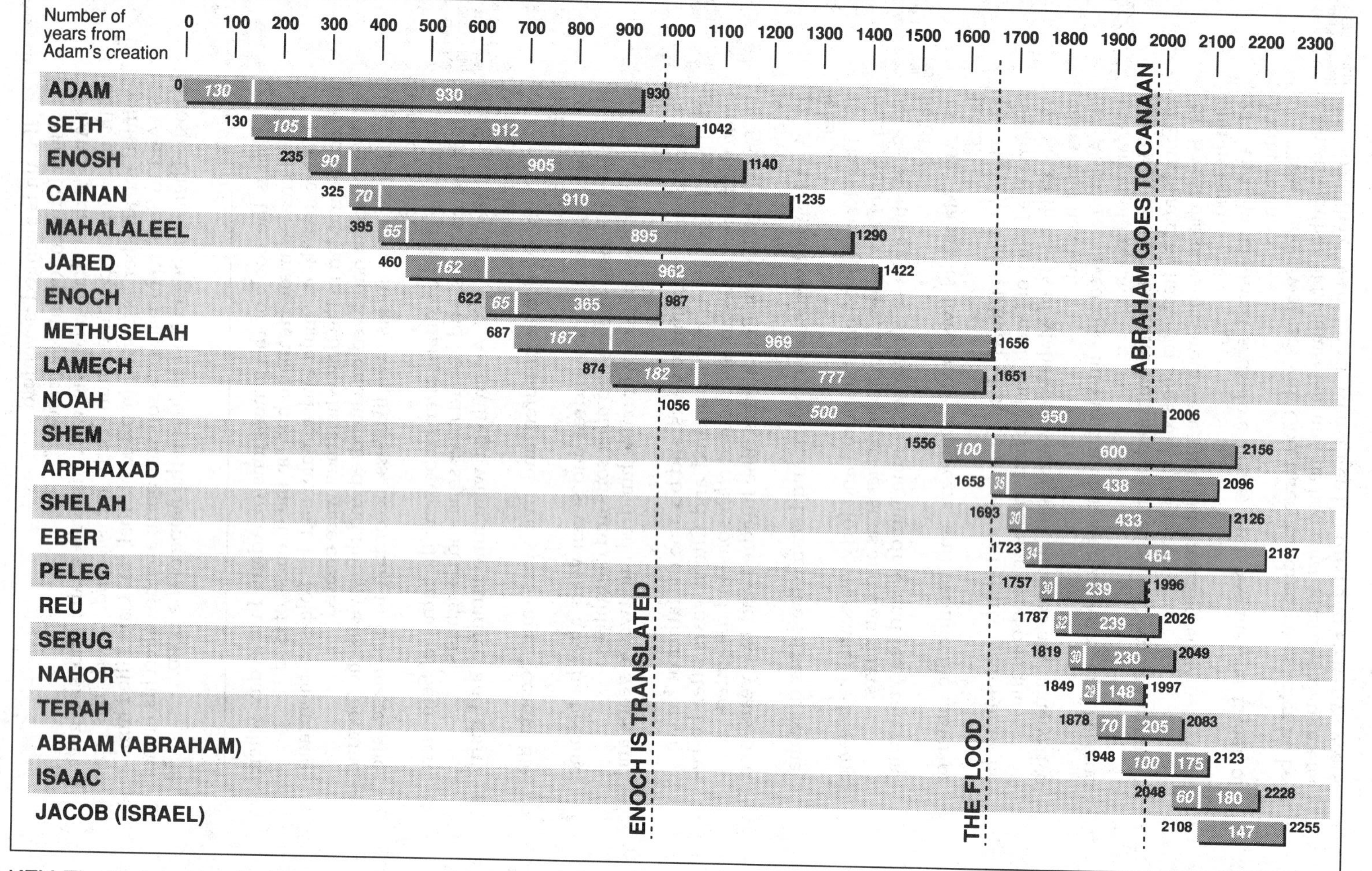

KEY: The first number inside the block is the man's age when his son (whose name is in the next line below) was born. The second number in the block is the number of years the man lived. The numbers preceding and following each block are the number of years from Adam's creation. Remember the years on this chart begin with Adam's creation and are *not* calendar years.

24 And [a]Enoch walked with God; and he was not, for God [b]took
him.
25 And Methuselah lived one hundred and eighty-seven years, and
became the father of Lamech.
26 Then Methuselah lived seven hundred and eighty-two years
after he became the father of Lamech, and he had *other* sons and
daughters.
27 So all the days of Methuselah were nine hundred and sixty-nine
years, and he died.
28 And Lamech lived one hundred and eighty-two years, and be-
came the father of a son.
29 Now he called his name Noah, saying, "This one shall [1]give us
rest from our work and from the toil of our hands *arising* from [a]the
ground which the LORD has cursed."
30 Then Lamech lived five hundred and ninety-five years after he
became the father of Noah, and he had *other* sons and daughters.
31 So all the days of Lamech were seven hundred and seventy-
seven years, and he died.
32 And Noah was [a]five hundred years old, and Noah became the
father of Shem, Ham, and Japheth.

Chapter 6

6 Now it came about, when men began to multiply on the face of
the land, and daughters were born to them,
2 that the sons of God saw that the daughters of men were [1]beauti-
ful; and they took wives for themselves, whomever they chose.
3 Then the LORD said, "[a]My Spirit shall not [1]strive with man
forever, [2b]because he also is flesh; [3]nevertheless his days shall be one
hundred and twenty years."
4 The [a]Nephilim were on the earth in those days, and also after-
ward, when the sons of God came in to the daughters of men, and
they bore *children* to them. Those were the mighty men who *were* of
old, men of renown.
5 Then the LORD saw that the wickedness of man was great on the
earth, and that [a]every intent of the thoughts of his heart was only
evil continually.
6 And [a]the LORD was sorry that He had made man on the earth,
and He was [b]grieved [1]in His heart.
7 And the LORD said, "[a]I will blot out man whom I have created
from the face of the land, from man to animals to creeping things
and to birds of the [1]sky; for [b]I am sorry that I have made them."
8 But [a]Noah [b]found favor in the eyes of the LORD.
9 These are *the records of* the generations of Noah. Noah was a
[a]righteous man, [1b]blameless in his [2]time; Noah [c]walked with God.
10 And Noah [1]became the father of three sons: Shem, Ham, and
Japheth.
11 Now the earth was [a]corrupt in the sight of God, and the earth
was [b]filled with violence.
12 And God looked on the earth, and behold, it was corrupt; for [a]all
flesh had corrupted their way upon the earth.
13 Then God said to Noah, "[a]The end of all flesh has come before
Me; for the earth is filled with violence because of them; and behold,
I am about to destroy them with the earth.

4 [a]2 Kin. 2:11; Jude 14 [b]2 Kin. 2:10; Ps. 15; 73:24; Heb. 11:5
9 [1]Lit., *comfort us in* [a]Gen. 3:17-19; 4:11
32 [a]Gen. 7:6
6:2 [1]Lit., *good*
3 [1]Or, *rule in;* some ncient versions read *abide in* [2]Or, *in his ing astray he is flesh* [3]Or, *therefore* [a]Gal. 5:16, 17; 1 Pet. 3:20 [b]Ps. 78:39
4 [a]Num. 13:33
5 [a]Gen. 8:21; Ps. 1-3; Prov. 6:18; Matt. 15:19; Rom. 1:28-32
6 [1]Lit., *to* [a]Gen. 6:7; r. 18:7-10 [b]Is. 63:10; Eph. 4:30
[1]Lit., *heavens* [a]Deut. 63; 29:20 [b]Gen. 6:6; Amos 7:3, 6
8 [a]Matt. 24:37; Luke 17:26; 1 Pet. 3:20 en. 19:19; Ex. 33:17; Luke 1:30
9 [1]Lit., *complete, perfect;* or, *having integrity* [2]Lit., *nerations* [a]Ps. 37:39; Pet. 2:5 [b]Gen. 17:1; Deut. 18:13; Job 1:1 [c]Gen. 5:24
10 [1]Lit., *begot*
1 [a]Deut. 31:29; Judg. 2:19 [b]Ezek. 8:17
12 [a]Ps. 14:1-3
13 [a]Is. 34:1-4; Ezek. 2, 3; Amos 8:2; 1 Pet. 4:7

14 "Make for yourself an ark of gopher wood; you shall make the
ark with rooms, and shall [1]cover it inside and out with pitch.
15 "And this is how you shall make it: the length of the ark three
hundred [1]cubits, its breadth fifty [1]cubits, and its height thirty [1]cubits.
16 "You shall make a [1]window for the ark, and finish it to a cubit
from [2]the top; and set the door of the ark in the side of it; you shall
make it with lower, second, and third decks.
17 "And behold, [a]I, even I am bringing the flood of water upon the
earth, to destroy all flesh in which is the breath of life, from under
heaven; everything that is on the earth shall perish.
18 "But I will establish [a]My covenant with you; and [b]you shall enter
the ark—you and your sons and your wife, and your sons' wives
with you.
19 "[a]And of every living thing of all flesh, you shall bring two of
every *kind* into the ark, to keep *them* alive with you; they shall be
male and female.
20 "[a]Of the birds after their kind, and of the animals after their kind,
of every creeping thing of the ground after its kind, two of every *kind*
shall come to you to keep *them* alive.
21 "And as for you, take for yourself some of all [a]food which is
edible, and gather *it* to yourself; and it shall be for food for you and
for them."
22 [a]Thus Noah did; according to all that God had commanded him,
so he did.

Chapter 7

7 Then the LORD said to Noah, "Enter the ark, you and all your
household; for you *alone* I have seen *to be* [a]righteous before Me in
this [1]time.
2 "You shall take [1]with you of every [a]clean animal [2]by sevens, a
male and his female; and of the animals that are not clean two, a
male and his female;
3 also of the birds of the [1]sky, [2]by sevens, male and female, to keep
[3]offspring alive on the face of all the earth.
4 "For after [a]seven more days, I will send rain on the earth [b]forty
days and forty nights; and I will blot out from the face of the land
[c]every living thing that I have made."
5 [a]And Noah did according to all that the LORD had commanded
him.
6 Now Noah was [a]six hundred years old when the flood of water
[1]came upon the earth.
7 Then [a]Noah and his sons and his wife and his sons' wives with
him entered the ark because of the water of the flood.
8 [a]Of clean animals and animals that are not clean and birds and
everything that creeps on the ground,
9 there went into the ark to Noah [1]by twos, male and female, as
God had commanded Noah.
10 And it came about after [a]the seven days, that the water of the
flood [1]came upon the earth.
11 In the [a]six hundredth year of Noah's life, in the second month,
on the seventeenth day of the month, on the same day all [b]the foun-
tains of the great deep burst open, and the [1]floodgates of the sky
were opened.
12 And [a]the rain [1]fell upon the earth for forty days and forty nights.

14 [1]Or, *pitch*
15 [1]I.e., One cubit equals approx. 18 i
16 [1]Or, *roof* [2]Lit., a
17 [a]2 Pet. 2:5
18 [a]Gen. 9:9-16; 1 [b]Gen. 7:7
19 [a]Gen. 7:2, 14,
20 [a]Gen. 7:3
21 [a]Gen. 1:29, 30
22 [a]Gen. 7:5; Heb.
7:1 [1]Lit., *generatio* [a]Gen. 6:9
2 [1]Lit., *to* [2]Lit., *sev seven* [a]Lev. 11:1-3 Deut. 14:3-20
3 [1]Lit., *heavens* [2]L *seven seven* [3]Lit.,
4 [a]Gen. 7:10 [b]Ger 7:12, 17 [c]Gen. 6:7,
5 [a]Gen. 6:22
6 [1]Lit., *was* [a]Gen.
7 [a]Gen. 6:18; 7:13; Matt. 24:38f.; Luke
8 [a]Gen. 6:19, 20; 7
9 [1]Lit., *two two*
10 [1]Lit., *were* [a]Ger
11 [1]Or, *windows of heavens* [a]Gen. 7:6 [b]Gen. 8:2
12 [1]Lit., *was* [a]Gen. 7:4, 17

13 On the very same day [a]Noah and Shem and Ham and Japheth,
the sons of Noah, and Noah's wife and the three wives of his sons
with them, entered the ark,
14 they and every beast after its kind, and all the cattle after [1]their
kind, and every creeping thing that creeps on the earth after its kind,
and every bird after its kind, [2]all sorts of birds.
15 So they went into the ark to Noah, [a]by twos of all flesh in which
was the breath of life.
16 And those that entered, male and female of all flesh, entered as
God had commanded him; and the LORD closed *it* behind him.
17 Then the flood [1]came upon the earth for [a]forty days; and the
water increased and lifted up the ark, so that it rose above the earth.
18 And the water prevailed and increased greatly upon the earth;
and the ark [1]floated on the [2]surface of the water.
19 And the water prevailed more and more upon the earth, so that
all the high mountains [1]everywhere under the heavens were
covered.
20 The water prevailed fifteen [1]cubits higher, [a]and the mountains
were covered.
21 [a]And all flesh that [1]moved on the earth perished, birds and cattle
and beasts and every swarming thing that swarms upon the earth,
and all mankind;
22 of all that was on the dry land, all [a]in whose nostrils was the
breath of the spirit of life, died.
23 Thus He blotted out [1]every living thing that was upon the face of
the land, from man to animals to creeping things and to birds of the
[2]sky, and they were blotted out from the earth; and only [a]Noah was
left, together with those that were with him in the ark.
24 [a]And the water prevailed upon the earth one hundred and fifty
days.

Chapter 8

8 But [a]God remembered Noah and all the beasts and all the cattle
that were with him in the ark; and [b]God caused a wind to pass
over the earth, and the water subsided.
2 Also [a]the fountains of the deep and the [1]floodgates of the sky
were closed, and [b]the rain from the sky was restrained;
3 and the water receded steadily from the earth, and at the end [a]of
one hundred and fifty days the water decreased.
4 And in the seventh month, on the seventeenth day of the month,
[a]the ark rested upon the mountains of Ararat.
5 And the water decreased steadily until the tenth month; in the
tenth month, on the first day of the month, the tops of the mountains
became visible.
6 Then it came about at the end of forty days, that Noah opened
the [a]window of the ark which he had made;
7 and he sent out a raven, and it [1]flew here and there until the
water was dried up [2]from the earth.
8 Then he sent out a dove from him, to see if the water was abated
from the face of the land;
9 but the dove found no resting place for the sole of her foot, so
she returned to him into the ark; for the water was on the [1]surface of
all the earth. Then he put out his hand and took her, and brought her
into the ark to himself.

13 [a]Gen. 6:18; 7:7
[1]Lit., *its* [2]Lit., *every bird, every wing*
15 [a]Gen. 6:19; 7:9
[1]Lit., *was* [a]Gen. 7:4
[1]Lit., *went* [2]Lit., *face*
19 [1]Lit., *which were* *nder all the heavens*
20 [1]I.e., One cubit equals approx. 18 in. [a]Gen. 8:4
21 [1]Or, *crept* [a]Gen. 6:7, 13, 17; 7:4
22 [a]Gen. 2:7
3 [1]Lit., *all existence* [2]Lit., *heavens* [a]Matt. :38, 39; Luke 17:26, 27; Heb. 11:7; 1 Pet. 3:20; 2 Pet. 2:5
24 [a]Gen. 8:3
8:1 [a]Gen. 19:29; Ex. :24; 1 Sam. 1:19; Ps. 105:42 [b]Ex. 14:21; 5:10; Job 12:15; Ps. 29:10; Is. 44:27; Nah. 1:4
[1]Or, *windows of the heavens* [a]Gen. 7:11 [b]Gen. 7:4, 12
3 [a]Gen. 7:24
4 [a]Gen. 7:20
6 [a]Gen. 6:16
[1]Lit., *went out, going* *d returning* [2]Lit., *from upon*
9 [1]Lit., *face*

10 So he waited yet another seven days; and again he sent out the
dove from the ark.
11 And the dove came to him toward [1]evening; and behold, in her
[2]beak was a freshly picked olive leaf. So Noah knew that the water
was abated from the earth.
12 Then he waited yet another seven days, and sent out [a]the dove;
but she did not return to him again.
13 Now it came about in the [a]six hundred and first year, in the first
month, on the first of the month, the water was dried up [1]from the
earth. Then Noah removed the covering of the ark, and looked, and
behold, the [2]surface of the ground was dried up.
14 And in the second month, on the twenty-seventh day of the
month, the earth was dry.
15 Then God spoke to Noah, saying,
16 "Go out of the ark, you and your wife and your sons and your
sons' wives with you.
17 "Bring out with you every living thing of all flesh that is with
you, birds and animals and every creeping thing that creeps on the
earth, that they may [1a]breed abundantly on the earth, and be fruitful
and multiply on the earth."
18 So Noah went out, and his sons and his wife and his sons' wives
with him.
19 Every beast, every creeping thing, and every bird, everything
that moves on the earth, went out [1]by their families from the ark.
20 Then Noah built [a]an altar to the LORD, and took of every [b]clean
animal and of every clean bird and offered [c]burnt offerings on the
altar.
21 And the LORD [a]smelled the soothing aroma; and the LORD said [1]to
Himself, "I will never again [b]curse the ground on account of man, for
[c]the [2]intent of man's heart is evil from his youth; [d]and I will never
again [3]destroy every living thing, as I have done.
22 "While the earth remains,
Seedtime and harvest,
And cold and heat,
And [a]summer and winter,
And [b]day and night
Shall not cease."

Chapter 9

9 And God blessed Noah and his sons and said to them, "[a]Be
fruitful and multiply, and fill the earth.
2 "And the fear of you and the terror of you shall be on every beast
of the earth and on every bird of the [1]sky; with everything that
creeps on the ground, and all the fish of the sea, into your hand they
are given.
3 "Every moving thing that is alive shall be food for you; I give all
to you, [a]as *I gave* the green plant.
4 "Only you shall not eat flesh with its life, *that is,* [a]its blood.
5 "And surely I will require [1a]your lifeblood; [2b]from every beast I
will require it. And [2]from *every* man, [2]from every man's brother I will
require the life of man.
6 "[a]Whoever sheds man's blood,
By man his blood shall be shed,
For [b]in the image of God

11 [1]Lit., *the time o* *evening* [2]Lit., *mou*

12 [a]Jer. 48:28

13 [1]Lit., *from upor* [2]Lit., *face* [a]Gen. 7:

17 [1]Or, *swarm* [a]G 1:22, 28

19 [1]Or, *according their kind*

20 [a]Gen. 12:7, 8; 22:9 [b]Gen. 7:2; Le 11:1-47 [c]Gen. 22: 10:25

21 [1]Lit., *to His hea* [2]Or, *inclination* [3]Lit *smite* [a]Ex. 29:18, [b]Gen. 3:17; 6:7, 13 Is. 54:9 [c]Gen. 6:5; 51:5; Jer. 17:9; Ro 1:21; 3:23; Eph. 2:1 [d]Gen. 9:11, 15

22 [a]Ps. 74:17 [b]Je 33:20, 25

9:1 [a]Gen. 1:28; 9:7

2 [1]Lit., *heavens*

3 [a]Gen. 1:29

4 [a]Lev. 7:26f.; 17:1 19:26; Deut. 12:16, 15:23; 1 Sam. 14:3 Acts 15:20, 29

5 [1]Lit., *your blood* *your lives* [2]Lit., *fror* *hand of* [a]Ex. 20:13; 21:12 [b]Ex. 21:28, 2

6 [a]Ex. 21:12-14; Le 24:17; Num. 35:33; Matt. 26:52 [b]Gen. 1:26, 27

He made man.
7 "And as for you, [a]be fruitful and multiply;
[1]Populate the earth abundantly and multiply in it."
8 Then God spoke to Noah and to his sons with him, saying,
9 "Now behold, [a]I Myself do establish My covenant with you, and
with your [1]descendants after you;
10 and with every living creature that is with you, the birds, the
cattle, and every beast of the earth with you; of all that comes out of
the ark, even every beast of the earth.
11 "And I establish My covenant with you; and all flesh shall [a]never
again be cut off by the water of the flood, [b]neither shall there again
be a flood to destroy the earth."
12 And God said, "This is [a]the sign of the covenant which I am
making between Me and you and every living creature that is with
you, for [1]all successive generations;
13 I set My [a]bow in the cloud, and it shall be for a sign of a covenant
between Me and the earth.
14 "And it shall come about, when I bring a cloud over the earth,
that the bow shall be seen in the cloud,
15 and [a]I will remember My covenant, which is between Me and
you and every living creature of all flesh; and [b]never again shall the
water become a flood to destroy all flesh.
16 "When the bow is in the cloud, then I will look upon it, to remem-
ber the [a]everlasting covenant between God and every living creature
of all flesh that is on the earth."
17 And God said to Noah, "This is the sign of the covenant which I
have established between Me and all flesh that is on the earth."
18 Now the sons of Noah who came out of the ark were Shem and
Ham and Japheth; and [a]Ham was the father of Canaan.
19 These three *were* the sons of Noah; and [a]from these the whole
earth was [1]populated.
20 Then Noah began [1]farming and planted a vineyard.
21 And he drank of the wine and [a]became drunk, and uncovered
himself inside his tent.
22 And Ham, the father of Canaan, [a]saw the nakedness of his father,
and told his two brothers outside.
23 But Shem and Japheth took a garment and laid it upon both their
shoulders and walked backward and covered the nakedness of their
father; and their faces were [1]turned away, so that they did not see
their father's nakedness.
24 When Noah awoke from his wine, he knew what his youngest
son had done to him.
25 So he said,
"[a]Cursed be Canaan;
[1b]A servant of servants
He shall be to his brothers."
26 He also said,
"[a]Blessed be the LORD,
The God of Shem;
And let Canaan be [1]his servant.
27 "[a]May God enlarge Japheth,
And let him dwell in the tents of Shem;
And let Canaan be [1]his servant."
28 And Noah lived three hundred and fifty years after the flood.

7 [1]Lit., *Swarm in the earth* [a]Gen. 9:1
[1]Lit., *seed* [a]Gen. 6:18
[a]Gen. 8:21 [b]Is. 54:9
12 [1]Or, *everlasting* *nerations* [a]Gen. 9:13, 17; 17:11
13 [a]Ezek. 1:28
15 [a]Lev. 26:42, 45; Deut. 7:9; Ezek. 16:60 [b]Gen. 9:11
16 [a]Gen. 17:13, 19; 2 Sam. 23:5
6 [a]Gen. 9:25-27; 10:6
19 [1]Lit., *scattered* [a]Gen. 9:1, 7; 10:32; 1 Chr. 1:4
0 [1]Lit., to be *a farmer*
21 [a]Prov. 20:1
22 [a]Hab. 2:15
23 [1]Lit., *backward*
25 [1]I.e., The lowest of servants [a]Deut. 27:16 [b]Josh. 9:23
26 [1]Or, *their* [a]Gen. 14:20; 24:27
27 [1]Or, *their* [a]Gen. 10:2-5; Is. 66:19

29 So all the days of Noah were nine hundred and fifty years, and he died.

Chapter 10

10 Now these are *the records of* the generations of Shem, Ham, and Japheth, the sons of Noah; and sons were born to them after the flood.

2 [a]The sons of Japheth *were* [b]Gomer and Magog and [c]Madai and [d]Javan and Tubal and [e]Meshech and Tiras.

3 And the sons of Gomer *were* [a]Ashkenaz and [1]Riphath and [b]Togarmah.

4 And the sons of Javan *were* Elishah and [a]Tarshish, Kittim and [1]Dodanim.

5 From these the coastlands of the nations [1]were separated into their lands, every one according to his language, according to their families, into their nations.

6 [a]And the sons of Ham *were* Cush and Mizraim and Put and Canaan.

7 And the sons of Cush *were* [a]Seba and Havilah and Sabtah and [b]Raamah and Sabteca; and the sons of Raamah *were* [b]Sheba and [c]Dedan.

8 Now Cush [1]became the father of Nimrod; he [2]became a mighty one on the earth.

9 He was a mighty hunter before the LORD; therefore it is said, "Like Nimrod a mighty hunter before the LORD."

10 And the beginning of his kingdom was [1a]Babel and Erech and Accad and Calneh, in the land of [b]Shinar.

11 From that land he went forth [a]into Assyria, and built Nineveh and Rehoboth-Ir and Calah,

12 and Resen between Nineveh and Calah; that is the great city.

13 And Mizraim [1]became the father of [a]Ludim and Anamim and Lehabim and Naphtuhim

14 and [a]Pathrusim and Casluhim (from which came the Philistines) and Caphtorim.

15 And Canaan [1]became the father of [a]Sidon, his first-born, and [b]Heth

16 and [a]the Jebusite and the Amorite and the Girgashite

17 and the Hivite and the Arkite and the Sinite

18 and the Arvadite and the Zemarite and the Hamathite; and afterward the families of the Canaanite were spread abroad.

19 And [a]the territory of the Canaanite [1]extended from Sidon as you go toward Gerar, as far as Gaza; as you go toward [b]Sodom and Gomorrah and Admah and Zeboiim, as far as Lasha.

20 These are the sons of Ham, according to their families, according to their languages, by their lands, by their nations.

21 And also to Shem, the father of all the children of Eber, *and* the [1]older brother of Japheth, children were born.

22 [a]The sons of Shem *were* [b]Elam and Asshur and [c]Arpachshad and [d]Lud and Aram.

23 And the sons of Aram *were* [a]Uz and Hul and Gether and Mash.

24 And Arpachshad [1]became the father of [a]Shelah; and Shelah [1]became the father of Eber.

25 And [a]two sons were born to Eber; the name of the one *was*

10:2 [a]1 Chr. 1:5-7 [b]Ezek. 38:2, 6 [c]2 Kin 17:6 [d]Is. 66:19 [e]Eze 38:2

3 [1]I.e., In 1 Chr. 1:6, *Diphath* [a]Jer. 51:27 [b]Ezek. 27:14

4 [1]I.e., In 1 Chr. 1:7, *Rodanim* [a]Ezek. 27:12, 25

5 [1]Or, *separated themselves*

6 [a]1 Chr. 1:8-10

7 [a]Is. 43:3 [b]Ezek. 27:22 [c]Ezek. 27:15,

8 [1]Lit., *begot* [2]Lit., *began to be*

10 [1]Or, *Babylon* [a]Ge 11:9 [b]Gen. 11:2; 14:1

11 [a]Mic. 5:6

13 [1]Lit., *begot* [a]Jer. 46:9

14 [a]1 Chr. 1:12

15 [1]Lit., *begot* [a]1 Ch 1:13; Jer. 47:4 [b]Gen 23:3

16 [a]Gen. 15:19-21

19 [1]Lit., *was* [a]Num. 34:2-12 [b]Gen. 14:2,

21 [1]Or, *the brother o Japheth the elder*

22 [a]1 Chr. 1:17 [b]Ge 14:1, 9 [c]Gen. 11:10 66:19

23 [a]Job 1:1; Jer. 25:

24 [1]Lit., *begot* [a]Gen. 11:12; Luke 3:35

25 [a]1 Chr. 1:19

[1]Peleg, for in his days the earth was divided; and his brother's name
was Joktan.
26 And Joktan [1]became the father of Almodad and Sheleph and
Hazarmaveth and Jerah
27 and Hadoram and Uzal and Diklah
28 and [1]Obal and Abimael and Sheba
29 and Ophir and Havilah and Jobab; all these were the sons of
Joktan.
30 Now their [1]settlement [2]extended from Mesha as you go toward
Sephar, the hill country of the east.
31 These are the sons of Shem, according to their families, accord-
ing to their languages, by their lands, according to their nations.
32 These are the families of the sons of Noah, according to their
genealogies, by their nations; and [a]out of these the nations were
separated on the earth after the flood.

Chapter 11

11 Now the whole earth [1]used the same language and [2]the same
words.
2 And it came about as they journeyed east, that they found a
plain in the land [a]of Shinar and [1]settled there.
3 And they said to one another, "Come, let us make bricks and
burn *them* thoroughly." And they used brick for stone, and they used
[a]tar for mortar.
4 And they said, "Come, let us build for ourselves a city, and a
tower whose top [a]*will reach* into heaven, and let us make for
ourselves [b]a name; lest we [c]be scattered abroad over the face of the
whole earth."
5 [a]And the LORD came down to see the city and the tower which
the sons of men had built.
6 And the LORD said, "Behold, they are one people, and they all
have [1a]the same language. And this is what they began to do, and
now nothing which they purpose to do will be [2]impossible for them.
7 "Come, [a]let Us go down and there [b]confuse their [1]language, that
they may not understand one another's [1]speech."
8 So the LORD [a]scattered them abroad from there over the face of
the whole earth; and they stopped building the city.
9 Therefore its name was called [1a]Babel, because there the LORD
confused the [2]language of the whole earth; and from there the LORD
scattered them abroad over the face of the whole earth.
10 [a]These are *the records of* the generations of Shem. Shem was one
hundred years old, and [1]became the father of Arpachshad two years
after the flood;
11 and Shem lived five hundred years after he became the father of
Arpachshad, and he had *other* sons and daughters.
12 And Arpachshad lived thirty-five years, and became the father
of Shelah;
13 and Arpachshad lived four hundred and three years after he
became the father of Shelah, and he had *other* sons and daughters.
14 And Shelah lived thirty years, and became the father of Eber;
15 and Shelah lived four hundred and three years after he became
the father of Eber, and he had *other* sons and daughters.
16 And Eber lived thirty-four years, and became the father of Peleg;

25 [1]I.e., division
26 [1]Lit., *begot*
[1]I.e., In 1 Chr. 1:22, *Ebal*
[1]Lit., *dwelling* [2]Lit., *was*
32 [a]Gen. 9:19
:1 [1]Lit., *was one lip* [2]Or, *few* or *one* set of *words*
2 [1]Lit., *dwelt* [a]Gen. 0:10; 14:1; Dan. 1:2
3 [a]Gen. 14:10
[a]Deut. 1:28; 9:1; Ps. 107:26 [b]Gen. 6:4; m. 8:13 [c]Deut. 4:27
[a]Gen. 18:21; Ex. 3:8; 19:11, 18, 20
6 [1]Lit., *one lip* [2]Lit., *withheld from* [a]Gen. 11:1
[1]Lit., *lip* [a]Gen. 1:26 Gen. 42:23; Ex. 4:11; eut. 28:49; Is. 33:19; Jer. 5:15
[a]Gen. 11:4; Ps. 92:9; Luke 1:51
9 [1]Or, *Babylon;* cf. Heb., *balal,* confuse [2]Lit., *lip* [a]Gen. 10:10
0 [1]Lit., *begot,* and so throughout the ch. [a]Gen. 10:22-25

17 and Eber lived four hundred and thirty years after he became
the father of Peleg, and he had *other* sons and daughters.
18 And Peleg lived thirty years, and became the father of Reu;
19 and Peleg lived two hundred and nine years after he became the
father of Reu, and he had *other* sons and daughters.
20 And Reu lived thirty-two years, and became the father of Serug;
21 and Reu lived two hundred and seven years after he became the
father of Serug, and he had *other* sons and daughters.
22 And Serug lived thirty years, and became the father of Nahor;
23 and Serug lived two hundred years after he became the father of
Nahor, and he had *other* sons and daughters.
24 And Nahor lived twenty-nine years, and became the father of
[a]Terah;
25 and Nahor lived one hundred and nineteen years after he became the father of Terah, and he had *other* sons and daughters.
26 And Terah lived seventy years, and became [a]the father of Abram,
Nahor and Haran.
27 Now these are *the records of* the generations of Terah. Terah became the father of Abram, Nahor and Haran; and [a]Haran became the
father of [b]Lot.
28 And Haran died [1]in the presence of his father Terah in the land
of his birth, in [a]Ur of the Chaldeans.
29 And Abram and [a]Nahor took wives for themselves. The name of
Abram's wife was [b]Sarai; and the name of Nahor's wife was [c]Milcah,
the daughter of Haran, the father of Milcah [1]and Iscah.
30 And [a]Sarai was barren; she had no
child.
31 And Terah took Abram his son, and Lot
the son of Haran, his grandson, and Sarai
his daughter-in-law, his son Abram's wife;
and they went out [1]together from [a]Ur of the
Chaldeans in order to enter the land of
Canaan; and they went as far as Haran, and
[2]settled there.
32 And the days of Terah were two
hundred and five years; and Terah died in
Haran.

Journeys of Abraham

Chapter 12

12 Now [a]the LORD said to Abram,
"[1]Go forth from your country,
And from your relatives
And from your father's house,
To the land which I will show you;
2 And [a]I will make you a great nation,
And [b]I will bless you,
And make your name great;
And so [1c]you shall be a blessing;
3 And [a]I will bless those who bless you,
And the one who [1]curses you I will [2]curse.
[b]And in you all the families of the earth shall be blessed."
4 So Abram went forth as the LORD had spoken to him; and [a]Lot
went with him. Now Abram was seventy-five years old when he
departed from Haran.

24 [a]Josh. 24:2

26 [a]Josh. 24:2

27 [a]Gen. 11:31; [b]Gen. 13:10; 14:1 19:1, 29

28 [1]Or, *during the lifetime of* [a]Gen.

29 [1]Lit., *and the f* *of* [a]Gen. 24:10 [b] 17:15; 20:12 [c]Gen 22:20, 23; 24:15

30 [a]Gen. 16:1

31 [1]Lit., *with them dwelt* [a]Gen. 15:7; 9:7; Acts 7:4

12:1 [1]Lit., *Go for yourself* [a]Gen. 15: Acts 7:3; Heb. 11:8

2 [1]Lit., *be a blessi* [a]Gen. 17:4-6; 18:18 46:3; Deut. 26:5 [b]G 22:17 [c]Zech. 8:13

3 [1]Or, *reviles* [2]Or, *under a curse* [a]Gen 24:35; 27:29; Num. 24:9 [b]Gen. 22:18; 28:14; Acts 3:25; Ga 3:8

4 [a]Gen. 11:27, 31

5 And Abram took Sarai his wife and Lot his nephew, and all their
[a]possessions which they had accumulated, and [b]the [1]persons which
they had acquired in Haran, and they [2]set out for the land of Canaan;
[c]thus they came to the land of Canaan.
6 And Abram passed through the land as far as the site of
[a]Shechem, to the [1]oak of Moreh. Now the Canaanite *was* then in the
land.
7 And the LORD [a]appeared to Abram and said, "[b]To your [1]descend-
ants I will give this land." So he built [c]an altar there to the LORD who
had appeared to him.
8 Then he proceeded from there to the mountain on the east of
Bethel, and pitched his tent, with [a]Bethel on the west and Ai on the
east; and there he built an altar to the LORD and [b]called upon the
name of the LORD.
9 And Abram journeyed on, continuing toward [a]the [1]Negev.
10 Now there was [a]a famine in the land; so Abram went down to
Egypt to sojourn there, for the famine was [b]severe in the land.
11 And it came about when he [1]came near to Egypt, that he said to
Sarai his wife, "See now, I know that you are a [2a]beautiful woman;
12 [a]and it will come about when the Egyptians see you, that they
will say, 'This is his wife'; and they will kill me, but they will let you
live.
13 "Please say that you are [a]my sister so that it may go well with me
because of you, and that [1b]I may live on account of you."
14 And it came about when Abram came into Egypt, the Egyptians
[1]saw that the woman was very beautiful.
15 And Pharaoh's officials saw her and praised her to Pharaoh; and
[a]the woman was taken into Pharaoh's house.
16 Therefore [a]he treated Abram well for her sake; and [1b]gave him
sheep and oxen and donkeys and male and female servants and
female donkeys and camels.
17 But the LORD [a]struck Pharaoh and his house with great plagues
because of Sarai, Abram's wife.
18 Then Pharaoh called Abram and said, "[a]What is this you have
done to me? Why did you not tell me that she was your wife?
19 "Why did you say, 'She is my sister,' so that I took her for my
wife? Now then, [1]here is your wife, take her and go."
20 And Pharaoh commanded *his* men concerning him; and they
[1]escorted him away, with his wife and all that belonged to him.

Chapter 13

13 So Abram went up from Egypt to [a]the [1]Negev, he and his wife
and all that belonged to him; and Lot with him.
2 Now Abram was [a]very rich in livestock, in silver and in gold.
3 And he went [1]on his journeys from the [2]Negev as far as Bethel,
to the place where his tent had been at the beginning, [a]between
Bethel and Ai,
4 to the place of the [a]altar, which he had made there formerly; and
there Abram called on the name of the LORD.
5 Now [a]Lot, who went with Abram, also had flocks and herds and
tents.
6 And [a]the land could not [1]sustain them [2]while dwelling together;
[b]for their possessions were so great that they were not able to remain
together.

[1]Lit., *souls* [2]Lit., *went forth to go to* [a]Gen. ...6 [b]Gen. 14:14; Lev. ...1 [c]Gen. 11:31; Heb. 11:8

[1]Or, *terebinth* [a]Gen. 35:4; Deut. 11:30

7 [1]Lit., *seed* [a]Gen. ...; 18:1 [b]Gen. 13:15; ...5:18; Deut. 34:4; Ps. ...:9-12; Acts 7:5; Gal. 3:16 [c]Gen. 13:4, 18; 22:9

[a]Josh. 8:9, 12 [b]Gen. 4:26; 21:33

[1]I.e., South country [a]Gen. 13:1, 3; 20:1; 24:62

...0 [a]Gen. 26:1 [b]Gen. 43:1

...1 [1]Lit., *drew near to enter* [2]Lit., *woman of beautiful appearance* [a]Gen. 26:7; 29:17

12 [a]Gen. 20:11

[1]Lit., *my soul* [a]Gen. ...0:2, 5, 12; 26:7 [b]Jer. 38:17, 20

14 [1]Lit., *saw the woman that she was*

15 [a]Gen. 20:2

... [1]Lit., *he had* [a]Gen. 20:14 [b]Gen. 13:2

[a]Gen. 20:18; 1 Chr. 16:21; Ps. 105:14

...Gen. 20:9, 10; 26:10

19 [1]Or, *behold*

20 [1]Lit., *sent*

13:1 [1]I.e., South country [a]Gen. 12:9

2 [a]Gen. 24:35

3 [1]Lit., *by his stages* [2]I.e., South country [a]Gen. 12:8

4 [a]Gen. 12:7, 8

5 [a]Gen. 12:5

6 [1]Lit., *bear* [2]Lit., *to ...ell* [a]Gen. 36:7 [b]Gen. 12:5, 16; 13:2

7 [a]And there was strife between the herdsmen of Abram's live-
stock and the herdsmen of Lot's livestock. Now [b]the Canaanite and
the Perizzite were dwelling then in the land.
8 [a]Then Abram said to Lot, "Please let there be no strife between
you and me, nor between my herdsmen and your herdsmen, for we
are brothers.
9 "Is not the whole land before you? Please separate from me: if *to*
the left, then I will go to the right; or if *to* the right, then I will go to
the left."
10 And Lot lifted up his eyes and saw all the [1a]valley of the Jordan,
that it was well watered everywhere—*this was* before the LORD [b]de-
stroyed Sodom and Gomorrah—like [c]the garden of the LORD, [d]like
the land of Egypt as you go to [e]Zoar.
11 So Lot chose for himself all the [1]valley of the Jordan; and Lot
journeyed eastward. Thus they separated from each other.
12 Abram [1]settled in the land of Canaan, while Lot [1]settled in [a]the
cities of the [2]valley, and moved his tents as far as Sodom.
13 Now [a]the men of Sodom were wicked [1]exceedingly and [b]sinners
against the LORD.
14 And the LORD said to Abram, after Lot had separated from him,
"[a]Now lift up your eyes and look from the place where you are,
[b]northward and southward and eastward and westward;
15 [a]for all the land which you see, [b]I will give it to you and to your
[1]descendants forever.
16 "And I will make your [1]descendants [a]as the dust of the earth; so
that if anyone can number the dust of the earth, then your [1]descend-
ants can also be numbered.
17 "Arise, [a]walk about the land through its length and breadth; for [b]I
will give it to you."
18 Then Abram moved his tent and came and dwelt by the [1a]oaks of
Mamre, which are in Hebron, and there he built [b]an altar to the LORD.

Chapter 14 ____________________

14 And it came about in the days of Amraphel king of [a]Shinar,
Arioch king of Ellasar, Chedorlaomer king of [b]Elam, and Tidal
king of [1]Goiim,
2 *that* they made war with Bera king of Sodom, and with Birsha
king of Gomorrah, Shinab king of [a]Admah, and Shemeber king of
[b]Zeboiim, and the king of Bela (that is, [c]Zoar).
3 All these [1]came as allies to [a]the valley of Siddim (that is, [b]the Salt
Sea).
4 Twelve years they had served Chedorlaomer, but the thirteenth
year they rebelled.
5 And in the fourteenth year Chedorlaomer and the kings that
were with him, came and [1]defeated the [a]Rephaim in [b]Ashteroth-
karnaim and the Zuzim in Ham and the Emim in [2c]Shaveh-
kiriathaim,
6 and the [a]Horites in their Mount Seir, as far as [b]El-paran, which is
by the wilderness.
7 Then they turned back and came to En-mishpat (that is, [a]Ka-
desh), and [1]conquered all the country of the Amalekites, and also the
Amorites, who lived in [b]Hazazon-tamar.
8 And the king of Sodom and the king of Gomorrah and the king
of Admah and the king of Zeboiim and the king of Bela (that is,

7 [a]Gen. 26:20 [b]G
12:6; 15:20, 21

8 [a]Prov. 15:18; 20

10 [1]Lit., *circle* [a]G
19:17-29; Deut. 34
[b]Gen. 19:24 [c]Gen
10 [d]Gen. 47:6 [e]G
14:2, 8; 19:22; Deu
34:3

11 [1]Lit., *circle*

12 [1]Lit., *dwelt* [2]Lit
circle [a]Gen. 14:2;
19:24, 25, 29

13 [1]Lit., *wicked an*
sinners exceedingl
[a]Gen. 18:20; Ezek.
16:49 [b]Gen. 39:9;
32:23; 2 Pet. 2:7, 8

14 [a]Deut. 3:27; 34
Is. 49:18 [b]Gen. 28

15 [1]Lit., *seed* [a]Ge
12:7 [b]Gen. 13:17;
17:8; 2 Chr. 20:7; A
7:5

16 [1]Lit., *seed* [a]Ge
16:10; 28:14; Num.
23:10

17 [a]Num. 13:17-24
[b]Gen. 13:15

18 [1]Or, *terebinths*
[a]Gen. 14:13 [b]Gen.
8:20; 12:7, 8

14:1 [1]Or, *nations* [a]
10:10; 11:2 [b]Gen.
10:22; Is. 11:11; Dar

2 [a]Gen. 10:19 [b]Deu
29:23 [c]Gen. 13:10;
19:22

3 [1]Lit., *joined togeth*
[a]Gen. 14:8, 10 [b]Nur
34:12; Deut. 3:17; Jo
3:16

5 [1]Lit., *smote* [2]Or, *t*
plain of Kiriathaim
[a]Deut. 3:11, 13 [b]Deu
1:4; Josh. 9:10 [c]Num
32:37

6 [a]Gen. 36:20; Deut
2:12, 22 [b]Gen. 21:21
Num. 10:12

7 [1]Lit., *smote* [a]Num.
13:26 [b]2 Chr. 20:2

Zoar) came out; and they arrayed for battle against them in [a]the
valley of Siddim,
9 against Chedorlaomer king of Elam and Tidal king of [1]Goiim
and Amraphel king of Shinar and Arioch king of Ellasar—four kings
against five.
10 Now the valley of Siddim was full of tar pits; and [a]the kings of
Sodom and Gomorrah fled, and they fell [1]into them. But those who
survived fled to the [b]hill country.
11 Then they took all the goods of Sodom and Gomorrah and all
their food supply, and departed.
12 And they also took Lot, [a]Abram's nephew, and his possessions
and departed, [b]for he was living in Sodom.
13 Then [1]a fugitive came and told Abram the [a]Hebrew. Now he was
[2]living by the [3b]oaks of Mamre the Amorite, brother of Eshcol and
brother of Aner, and these were [4c]allies with Abram.
14 And when Abram heard that [a]his [1]relative had been taken cap-
tive, he [2]led out his trained men, [b]born in his house, three hundred
and eighteen, and went in pursuit as far as [c]Dan.
15 And [a]he divided [1]his forces against them by night, he and his
servants, and [2]defeated them, and pursued them as far as Hobah,
which is [3]north of [b]Damascus.
16 And he [a]brought back all the goods, and also brought back [b]his
[1]relative Lot with his possessions, and also the women, and the
people.
17 Then after his return from the [1]defeat of Chedorlaomer and the
kings who were with him, [a]the king of Sodom went out to meet him
at the valley of Shaveh (that is, [b]the King's Valley).
18 And [a]Melchizedek king of Salem brought out [b]bread and wine;
now he was a [c]priest of [1]God Most High.
19 And he blessed him and said,
"Blessed be Abram of [1]God Most High,
[2a]Possessor of heaven and earth;
20 And blessed be [1]God Most High,
Who has delivered your enemies into your hand."
[a]And he gave him a tenth of all.
21 And the king of Sodom said to Abram, "Give the [1]people to me
and take the goods for yourself."
22 And Abram said to the king of Sodom, "I have [1]sworn to the
LORD [2a]God Most High, [3b]possessor of heaven and earth,
23 that [a]I will not take a thread or a sandal thong or anything that is
yours, lest you should say, 'I have made Abram rich.'
24 "[1]I will take nothing except what the young men have eaten, and
the share of the men who went with me, [a]Aner, Eshcol, and Mamre;
let them take their share."

Chapter 15

15 After these things [a]the word of the LORD came to Abram in a
vision, saying,
"[b]Do not fear, Abram,
I am [c]a shield to you;
[1]Your [d]reward shall be very great."
2 And Abram said, "O Lord [1]GOD, what wilt Thou give me, since I
[2]am childless, and the [3]heir of my house is Eliezer of Damascus?"

8 [a]Gen. 14:3
9 [1]Or, *nations*
[1]Lit., *there* [a]Gen. 4:17, 21, 22 [b]Gen. 19:17
[a]Gen. 11:27 [b]Gen. 13:12
13 [1]Lit., *the* [2]Lit., *...ing* [3]Or, *terebinths* *...possessors of the ...enant* [a]Gen. 40:15; 3:18 [b]Gen. 13:18; ...24 [c]Gen. 21:27, 32
[1]Lit., *brother* [2]Or, *...stered* [a]Gen. 14:12 ... 12:5; 15:3; 17:27; ...cl. 2:7 [c]Deut. 34:1; 18:29; 1 Kin. 15:20
[1]Lit., *himself* [2]Lit., *...ote* [3]Lit., *on the left* ...g. 7:16 [b]Gen. 15:2
16 [1]Lit., *brother* 1 Sam. 30:8, 18, 19 [b]Gen. 14:12, 14
[1]Lit., *smiting* [a]Gen. ...4:10 [b]2 Sam. 18:18
18 [1]Heb., *El Elyon* [a]Heb. 7:1-10 [b]Ps. ...15 [c]Ps. 110:4; Heb. 5:6, 10
[1]Heb., *El Elyon* [2]Or, *...Creator* [a]Gen. 14:22
20 [1]Heb., *El Elyon* [a]Heb. 7:4
21 [1]Lit., *soul*
22 [1]Lit., *lifted up my ...hand* [2]Heb., *El Elyon* [3]Or, *Creator* [a]Gen. 14:19 [b]Ps. 24:1
23 [a]2 Kin. 5:16
24 [1]Lit., *Not to me except* [a]Gen. 14:13
15:1 [1]Or, *Your very great reward* [a]Gen. 15:4; 46:2; 1 Sam. 15:10 [b]Gen. 21:17; ...:24; Is. 41:10 [c]Deut. ...:29 [d]Num. 18:20; Ps. 58:11
2 [1]Heb., *YHWH, ...sually rendered LORD* [2]Lit., *go* [3]Lit., *son of acquisition*

3 And Abram said, "[1]Since Thou hast given no [2]offspring to me,
[3]one [a]born in my house is my heir."
4 Then behold, the word of the LORD came to him, saying, "This
man will not be your heir; [a]but one who shall come forth from your
own [1]body, he shall be your heir."
5 And He took him outside and said, "Now look toward the heav-
ens, and [a]count the stars, if you are able to count them." And He said
to him, "[b]So shall your [1]descendants be."
6 [a]Then he believed in the LORD; and He reckoned it to him as
righteousness.
7 And He said to him, "I am the LORD who brought you out of [a]Ur
of the Chaldeans, to [b]give you this land to [1]possess it."
8 And he said, "O Lord [1]GOD, [a]how may I know that I shall [2]pos-
sess it?"
9 So He said to him, "[1]Bring Me a three year old heifer, and a three
year old female goat, and a three year old ram, and a turtledove, and
a young pigeon."
10 Then he [1]brought all these to Him and [a]cut them [2]in two, and
laid each half opposite the other; but he [b]did not cut the birds.
11 And the birds of prey came down upon the carcasses, and
Abram drove them away.
12 Now when the sun was going down, [a]a deep sleep fell upon
Abram; and behold, [1]terror *and* great darkness fell upon him.
13 And *God* said to Abram, "Know for certain that [a]your [1]descend-
ants will be strangers in a land that is not theirs, [2]where [b]they will be
enslaved and oppressed [c]four hundred years.
14 "But I will also judge the nation whom they will serve; and after-
ward they will come out [a]with [1]many possessions.
15 "And as for you, [a]you shall go to your fathers in peace; you shall
be buried at a good old age.
16 "Then in [a]the fourth generation they shall return here, for [b]the
iniquity of the Amorite is not yet complete."
17 And it came about when the sun had set, that it was very dark,
and behold, *there appeared* a smoking oven and a flaming torch which
[a]passed between these pieces.
18 On that day the LORD made a covenant with Abram, saying,
"[a]To your [1]descendants I have given this land,
From [b]the river of Egypt as far as the great river, the river
Euphrates:
19 [a]the Kenite and the Kenizzite and the Kadmonite
20 and the Hittite and the Perizzite and the Rephaim
21 and the Amorite and the Canaanite and the Girgashite and the
Jebusite."

Chapter 16

16 Now [a]Sarai, Abram's wife had borne him no *children*, and she
had [b]an Egyptian maid whose name was Hagar.
2 So Sarai said to Abram, "Now behold, the LORD has prevented
me from bearing *children*. [a]Please go in to my maid; perhaps I shall
[1]obtain children through her." And Abram listened to the voice of
Sarai.
3 And after Abram had [1]lived [a]ten years in the land of Canaan,
Abram's wife Sarai took Hagar the Egyptian, her maid, and gave her
to her husband Abram as his wife.

INSIGHT

Berith, the Hebrew word for covenant, is a solemn binding agreement made by passing through pieces of flesh. The Greek word for covenant, **diatheke**, means a testament or an agreement. The Bible is divided into the Old and New Testaments—or covenants. Everything God does is based on covenant.

3 [1]Lit., *Behold* [2]Li *seed* [3]Lit., *and be a son of* [a]Gen. 14

4 [1]Lit., *inward par* [a]Gal. 4:28

5 [1]Lit., *seed* [a]Gen 22:17; 26:4; Deut. [b]Ex. 32:13; Rom. 4 Heb. 11:12

6 [a]Rom. 4:3, 20-2 Gal. 3:6; James 2:

7 [1]Or, *inherit* [a]Gen 11:31 [b]Gen. 13:15

8 [1]Heb., *YHWH*, usually rendered *L* [2]Or, *inherit* [a]Judg. 6:36-40; Luke 1:18

9 [1]Lit., *Take*

10 [1]Lit., *took* [2]Lit., *the midst* [a]Gen. 15 [b]Lev. 1:17

12 [1]Or, *a terror of g darkness* [a]Gen. 2:2 28:11; Job 33:15

13 [1]Lit., *seed* [2]Lit., *shall serve them; a they shall afflict the* [a]Acts 7:6, 17 [b]Ex. Deut. 5:15 [c]Ex. 12: Gal. 3:17

14 [1]Lit., *great* [a]Ex. 12:32-38

15 [a]Gen. 25:8; 47:3

16 [a]Gen. 15:13 [b]Le 18:24-28

17 [a]Jer. 34:18, 19

18 [1]Lit., *seed* [a]Gen 17:8; Josh. 21:43; A 7:5 [b]Ex. 23:31; Num 34:1-15; Deut. 1:7, 8

19 [a]Ex. 3:17; 23:28; Josh. 24:11; Neh. 9:

16:1 [a]Gen. 11:30 [b]Gen. 12:16

2 [1]Lit., *be built from* [a]Gen. 30:3, 4, 9, 10

3 [1]Lit., *dwelt* [a]Gen.

4 And he went in to Hagar, and she conceived; and when she saw
that she had conceived, her mistress was despised in her sight.
5 And Sarai said to Abram, "[a]May the wrong done me be upon
you. I gave my maid into your [1]arms; but when she saw that she had
conceived, I was despised in her [2]sight. [b]May the LORD judge be-
tween [3]you and me."
6 But Abram said to Sarai, "Behold, your maid is in your [1]power;
do to her what is good in your [2]sight." So Sarai treated her harshly,
and [a]she fled from her presence.
7 Now [a]the angel of the LORD found her by a spring of water in the
wilderness, by the spring on the way to [b]Shur.
8 And he said, "Hagar, Sarai's maid, [a]where have you come from
and where are you going?" And she said, "I am fleeing from the
presence of my mistress Sarai."
9 Then the angel of the LORD said to her, "Return to your mistress,
and submit yourself [1]to her authority."
10 Moreover, the [a]angel of the LORD said to her, "[b]I will greatly
multiply your [1]descendants so that [2]they shall be too many to
count."
11 The angel of the LORD said to her further,
"Behold, you are with child,
And you shall bear a son;
And you shall call his name [1]Ishmael,
Because [a]the LORD [2]has given heed to your affliction.
12 "And he will be a [a]wild donkey of a man,
His hand *will be* against everyone,
And everyone's hand *will be* against him;
And he will [1]live [2b]to the east of all his brothers."
13 Then she called the name of the LORD who spoke to her, "[1]Thou
art [2]a God who sees"; for she said, "[a]Have I even [3]remained alive
here after seeing Him?"
14 Therefore the well was called [1]Beer-lahai-roi; behold, it is be-
tween [a]Kadesh and Bered.
15 So Hagar bore Abram a son; and Abram called the name of his
son, whom Hagar bore, Ishmael.
16 And Abram was [a]eighty-six years old when Hagar bore Ishmael
to [1]him.

Chapter 17

17 Now when Abram was ninety-nine years old, [a]the LORD ap-
peared to Abram and said to him,
"I am [1]God [b]Almighty;
Walk before Me, and be [2c]blameless.
2 "And I will [1]establish My [a]covenant between Me and you,
And I will [b]multiply you exceedingly."
3 And Abram [a]fell on his face, and God talked with him, saying,
4 "As for Me, behold, My covenant is with you,
And you shall be the father of a [a]multitude of nations.
5 "No longer shall your name be called [1]Abram,
But [a]your name shall be [2]Abraham;
For [b]I will make you the father of a multitude of nations.
6 "And I will make you exceedingly fruitful, and I will make na-
tions of you, and [a]kings shall come forth from you.
7 "And I will establish My covenant between Me and you and your

t., *bosom* [2]Lit., it., *me and you* er. 51:35 [b]Gen. 31:53; Ex. 5:21

hand [2]Lit., *eyes* [a]Gen. 16:9

Gen. 21:17, 18; 15; 31:11 [b]Gen. 20:1; 25:18

Gen. 3:9; 1 Kin. 19:9, 13

under her hands

[1]Lit., *seed* [2]Or, it ot be counted for multitude [a]Gen. -18 [b]Gen. 17:20

[1]I.e., God hears , has heard [a]Ex. 2:23, 24; 3:7, 9

[1]Lit., *dwell* [2]Lit., the face of; or, in nce of [a]Job 24:5; 9:5-8 [b]Gen. 25:18

r, *Thou, God, dost* ee me [2]Heb., *Elroi* seen here after the ho saw me [a]Gen. 2:30; Ps. 139:1-12

I.e., the well of the one who sees me [a]Gen. 14:7

[1]Lit., *Abram* [a]Gen. 12:4; 16:3

[1]Heb., *El Shaddai* , complete, perfect; or, having integrity n. 12:7; 18:1 [b]Gen. 3; 35:11 [c]Gen. 6:9; Deut. 18:13

2 [1]Lit., *give* [a]Gen. 3 [b]Gen. 13:16; 15:5

3 [a]Gen. 17:17; 18:2

[a]Gen. 35:11; 48:19

[1]I.e., exalted father [2]I.e., father of a multitude [a]Neh. 9:7 [b]Rom. 4:17

[a]Gen. 17:16; 35:11

[1]descendants after you throughout their generations for an [a]everlasting covenant, [b]to be God to you and [c]to your [1]descendants after you.

8 "And [a]I will give to you and to your [1]descendants after you, the land of your sojournings, all the land of Canaan, for an everlasting possession; and [b]I will be their God."

9 God said further to Abraham, "Now as for you, [a]you shall keep My covenant, you and your [1]descendants after you throughout their generations.

10 "[a]This is My covenant, which you shall keep, between Me and you and your [1]descendants after you: every male among you shall be circumcised.

11 "And [a]you shall be circumcised in the flesh of your foreskin; and it shall be the sign of the covenant between Me and you.

12 "And every male among you who is [a]eight days old shall be circumcised throughout your generations, a *servant* who is born in the house or who is bought with money from any foreigner, who is not of your [1]descendants.

13 "A *servant* who is born in your house or [a]who is bought with your money shall surely be circumcised; thus shall My covenant be in your flesh for an everlasting covenant.

14 "But an uncircumcised male who is not circumcised in the flesh of his foreskin, that person shall be [a]cut off from his people; he has broken My covenant."

15 Then God said to Abraham, "As for Sarai your wife, you shall not call her name Sarai, but [1]Sarah *shall be* her name.

16 "And I will bless her, and indeed I will give you [a]a son by her. Then I will bless her, and she shall be *a mother of* nations; [b]kings of peoples shall [1]come from her."

17 Then Abraham [a]fell on his face and laughed, and said in his heart, "Will a child be born to a man one hundred years old? And [b]will Sarah, who is ninety years old, bear *a child?*"

18 And Abraham said to God, "Oh that Ishmael might live before Thee!"

19 But God said, "No, but Sarah your wife shall bear you [a]a son, and you shall call his name [1]Isaac; and [b]I will establish My covenant with him for an everlasting covenant for his [2]descendants after him.

20 "And as for Ishmael, I have heard you; behold, I will bless him, and [a]will make him fruitful, and will multiply him exceedingly. [b]He shall [1]become the father of twelve princes, and I will make him a [c]great nation.

21 "But My covenant I will establish with [a]Isaac, whom [b]Sarah will bear to you at this season next year."

22 And when He finished talking with him, [a]God went up from Abraham.

23 Then Abraham took Ishmael his son, and all *the servants* who were [a]born in his house and all who were bought with his money, every male among the men of Abraham's household, and circumcised the flesh of their foreskin in the very same day, [b]as God had said to him.

24 Now Abraham was ninety-nine years old when [a]he was circumcised in the flesh of his foreskin.

25 And [a]Ishmael his son was thirteen years old when he was circumcised in the flesh of his foreskin.

7 [1]Lit., *seed* [a]... 17:13, 19; Ps. ... Luke 1:55 [b]Ge... Lev. 11:45; 26:... Heb. 11:16 [c]G... 28:13; Gal. 3:1...

8 [1]Lit., *seed* [a]... 12:7; 13:15, 17 ... 7:5 [b]Ex. 6:7; 2... 26:12; Deut. 29... 21:7

9 [1]Lit., *seed* [a]E...

10 [1]Lit., *seed* [a]... 7:22; Acts 7:8; R...

11 [a]Ex. 12:48; D... 10:16; Acts 7:8; ... 4:11

12 [1]Lit., *seed* [a]...

13 [a]Ex. 12:44

14 [a]Ex. 4:24-26

15 [1]I.e., princess

16 [1]Lit., *be* [a]Gen... 18:10 [b]Gen. 17:6...

17 [a]Gen. 17:3; 18... 21:6 [b]Gen. 21:7

19 [1]I.e., he laughs... *seed* [a]Gen. 17:16... 18:10; 21:2 [b]Gen. ... 26:2-5

20 [1]Lit., *beget twe...* *princes* [a]Gen. 16:... [b]Gen. 25:12-16 [c]G... 21:18

21 [a]Gen. 17:19; 18... 14 [b]Gen. 21:2

22 [a]Gen. 18:33; 35...

23 [a]Gen. 14:14 [b]G... 17:9-11

24 [a]Rom. 4:11

25 [a]Gen. 16:16

26 In the very same day Abraham was circumcised, and Ishmael his
son.
27 And all the men of his household, who were [a]born in the house
or bought with money from a foreigner, were circumcised with him.

Chapter 18

18 Now [a]the LORD appeared to him by the [1b]oaks of Mamre,
while he was sitting at the tent door in the heat of the day.
2 And when he lifted up his eyes and looked, behold, three [a]men
were standing opposite him; and when he saw *them,* he ran from the
tent door to meet them, and bowed himself to the earth,
3 and said, "[1]My lord, if now I have found favor in [2]your sight,
please do not [3]pass [2]your servant by.
4 "Please let a little water be brought and [a]wash your feet, and [1]rest
yourselves under the tree;
5 and I will [1a]bring a piece of bread, that you may [2]refresh your-
selves; after that you may go on, since you have [3]visited your ser-
vant." And they said, "So do, as you have said."
6 So Abraham hurried into the tent to Sarah, and said, "[1]Quickly,
prepare three [2]measures of fine flour, knead *it,* and make bread
cakes."
7 Abraham also ran to the herd, and took a tender and [1]choice calf,
and gave *it* to the servant; and he hurried to prepare it.
8 And he took curds and milk and the calf which he had prepared,
and placed *it* before them; and he was standing by them under the
tree [1]as they ate.
9 Then they said to him, "Where is Sarah your wife?" And he said,
"Behold, in the tent."
10 And he said, "[a]I will surely return to you [1]at this time next year;
and behold, Sarah your wife shall have a son." And Sarah was lis-
tening at the tent door, which was behind him.
11 Now [a]Abraham and Sarah were old, advanced in age; Sarah was
[b]past [1]childbearing.
12 And Sarah laughed [1]to herself, saying, "[a]After I have become
old, shall I have pleasure, my [b]lord being old also?"
13 And the LORD said to Abraham, "Why did Sarah laugh, saying,
'Shall I indeed [1]bear *a child,* when I am *so* old?'
14 "[a]Is anything too [1]difficult for the LORD? At the [b]appointed time I
will return to you, [2]at this time next year, and Sarah shall have a
son."
15 Sarah denied *it* however, saying, "I did not laugh"; for she was
afraid. And He said, "No, but you did laugh."
16 Then [a]the men rose up from there, and looked down toward
Sodom; and Abraham was walking with them to send them off.
17 And [a]the LORD said, "Shall I hide from Abraham [b]what I am
about to do,
18 since Abraham will surely become a great and [1]mighty nation,
and in him [a]all the nations of the earth will be blessed?
19 "For I have [1a]chosen him, in order that he may [b]command his
children and his household after him to [c]keep the way of the LORD by
doing righteousness and justice; in order that the LORD may bring
upon Abraham [d]what He has spoken about him."
20 And the LORD said, "[a]The outcry of Sodom and Gomorrah is
indeed great, and their sin is exceedingly grave.

[a]Gen. 14:14

[1]Or, *terebinths* :7; 17:1 [b]Gen. 13:18; 14:13

Gen. 18:16, 22; sh. 5:13; Judg. 6-11; Heb. 13:2

) *Lord* [2]Or, *Thy pass away from your servant*

, *support* [a]Gen. :2; 24:32; 43:24

[1]Lit., *take* [2]Lit., *your heart* [3]Lit., *to* [a]Judg. 6:18, 19; 13:15, 16

it., *Hasten three es* [2]Heb., *seah;* one seah equals prox. eleven qts.

7 [1]Lit., *good*

8 [1]Lit., *and*

it., *when the time rives* [a]Gen. 21:2; Rom. 9:9

it., *the manner of nen* [a]Gen. 17:17; 4:19 [b]Heb. 11:11

[1]Lit., *within* [a]Gen. 17:17; Luke 1:18 [b]1 Pet. 3:6

[1]Lit., *surely bear*

Or, *wonderful* [2]Lit., *n the time revives* r. 32:17, 27; Zech. Matt. 19:26; Luke Rom. 4:21 [b]Gen. 17:21; 18:10

Gen. 18:2, 22; 19:1

Gen. 18:22, 26, 33; s 3:7 [b]Gen. 18:21; 19:24

Or, *populous* [a]Gen. 3; 22:18; Acts 3:25; Gal. 3:8

[1]Lit., *known* [a]Neh. 7; Amos 3:2 [b]Deut. [c]Gen. 17:9 [d]Gen. 12:2, 3

[a]Gen. 19:13; Ezek. 16:49, 50

21 "I will [a]go down now, and see if they have done entirely accord-
ing to its outcry, which has come to Me; and if not, I will know."
22 Then [a]the men turned away from there and went toward Sodom,
while Abraham was still standing before [b]the LORD.
23 And Abraham came near and said, "[a]Wilt Thou indeed sweep
away the righteous with the wicked?
24 "Suppose there are fifty righteous within the city; wilt Thou in-
deed sweep *it* away and not [1]spare the place for the sake of the fifty
righteous who are in it?
25 "Far be it from Thee to do [1]such a thing, to slay the righteous with
the wicked, so that the righteous and the wicked are *treated* alike. Far
be it from Thee! Shall not [a]the Judge of all the earth [2]deal justly?"
26 So the LORD said, "[a]If I find in Sodom fifty righteous within the
city, then I will [1]spare the whole place on their account."
27 And Abraham answered and said, "Now behold, I have [1]ven-
tured to speak to the Lord, although I am *but* [a]dust and ashes.
28 "Suppose the fifty righteous are lacking five, wilt Thou destroy
the whole city because of five?" And He said, "I will not destroy *it* if
I find forty-five there."
29 And he spoke to Him yet again and said, "Suppose forty are
found there?" And He said, "I will not do *it* on account of the forty."
30 Then he said, "Oh may the Lord not be angry, and I shall speak;
suppose thirty are found there?" And He said, "I will not do *it* if I
find thirty there."
31 And he said, "Now behold, I have [1]ventured to speak to the
Lord; suppose twenty are found there?" And He said, "I will not
destroy *it* on account of the twenty."
32 Then he said, "[a]Oh may the Lord not be angry, and I shall speak
only this once; suppose ten are found there?" And He said, "I will
not destroy *it* on account of the ten."
33 And as soon as He had finished speaking to Abraham [a]the LORD
departed; and Abraham returned to his place.

Chapter 19

19 Now the [a]two angels came to Sodom in the evening as Lot
was sitting in the gate of Sodom. When [b]Lot saw *them*, he rose
to meet them and [1]bowed down *with his* face to the ground.
2 And he said, "Now behold, my lords, please turn aside into your
servant's house, and spend the night, and wash your feet; then you
may rise early and go on your way." They said however, "No, but
we shall spend the night in the square."
3 Yet he urged them strongly, so they turned aside to him and
entered his house; [a]and he prepared a feast for them, and baked
unleavened bread, and they ate.
4 Before they lay down, [a]the men of the city, the men of Sodom,
surrounded the house, both young and old, all the people [1]from
every quarter;
5 and they called to Lot and said to him, "[a]Where are the men who
came to you tonight? Bring them out to us that we may [1]have rela-
tions with them."
6 But Lot went out to them at the doorway, and shut the door
behind him,
7 and said, "Please, my brothers, do not act wickedly.
8 "Now behold, [a]I have two daughters who have not [1]had relations

21 [a]Gen. 11:5; Ps. 14:2
22 [a]Gen. 18:16 [b]Gen. 18:1, 17
23 [a]Ex. 23:7; N... 16:22; 2 Sam. 2... Ps. 11:4-7
24 [1]Or, *forgive*
25 [1]Lit., *after th... manner* [2]Lit., *do* [a]Deut. 1:16, 17; ... Job 8:3, 20; Ps. 94:2; Is. 3:10, 11 ... 3:5, 6
26 [1]Or, *forgive* ...
27 [1]Lit., *underta...* [a]Gen. 3:19; Job 3... 42:6
31 [1]Lit., *underta...*
32 [a]Judg. 6:39
33 [a]Gen. 17:22; 3...
19:1 [1]Lit., *bowed himself* [a]Gen. 18:2... [b]Gen. 18:2-5
3 [a]Gen. 18:6-8
4 [1]Or, *without exception;* lit., *from every end* [a]Gen. 1... 18:20
5 [1]I.e., have intercourse [a]Lev. 1... Judg. 19:22
8 [1]I.e., had intercou... [a]Judg. 19:24

with man; please let me bring them out to you, and do to them
[2]whatever you like; only do nothing to these men, inasmuch as they
have come under the [3]shelter of my roof."
9 But they said, "Stand aside." Furthermore, they said, "This one
came in [1]as an alien, and already [a]he is acting like a judge; now we
will treat you worse than them." So they pressed hard against [2]Lot
and came near to break the door.
10 But [a]the men reached out their [1]hands and brought Lot into the
house [2]with them, and shut the door.
11 And [a]they [1]struck the men who were at the doorway of the
house with blindness, both small and great, so that they wearied
themselves trying to find the doorway.
12 Then the men said to Lot, "Whom else have you here? A son-in-
law, and your sons, and your daughters, and whomever you have in
the city, bring *them* out of the place;
13 for we are about to destroy this place, because [a]their outcry has
become so great before the LORD that [b]the LORD has sent us to destroy
it."
14 And Lot went out and spoke to his sons-in-law, who [1]were to
marry his daughters, and said, "Up, [a]get out of this place, for the
LORD will destroy the city." [b]But he appeared to his sons-in-law [2]to be
jesting.
15 And when morning dawned, the angels urged Lot, saying, "Up,
take your wife and your two daughters, who are here, lest you be
swept away in the [1]punishment of the city."
16 But he hesitated. So the men [a]seized his hand and the hand of his
wife and the [1]hands of his two daughters, for [b]the compassion of the
LORD *was* upon him; and they brought him out, and put him outside
the city.
17 And it came about when they had brought them outside, that
[1]one said, "[a]Escape for your life! [b]Do not look behind you, and do not
stay [2]anywhere in the [c]valley; escape to [d]the [3]mountains, lest you be
swept away."
18 But Lot said to them, "Oh no, my lords!
19 "Now behold, your servant has found favor in your sight, and
you have magnified your lovingkindness, which you have shown
me by saving my life; but I cannot escape to the [1]mountains, lest the
disaster overtake me and I die;
20 now behold, this town is near *enough* to flee to, and it is small.
Please, let me escape there (is it not small?) [1]that my life may be
saved."
21 And he said to him, "Behold, I grant you this [1]request also, not
to overthrow the town of which you have spoken.
22 "Hurry, escape there, for I cannot do anything until you arrive
there." Therefore the name of the town was called [1a]Zoar.
23 The sun had risen over the earth when Lot came to Zoar.
24 Then the LORD [a]rained on Sodom and Gomorrah brimstone and
fire from the LORD out of heaven,
25 and [a]He overthrew those cities, and all the [1]valley, and all the
inhabitants of the cities, and what grew on the ground.
26 But his wife, from behind him, [a]looked *back;* and she became a
pillar of salt.
27 Now Abraham arose early in the morning *and went* to [a]the place
where he had stood before the LORD;

..., *as is good in* t [3]Lit., *shadow*

o *sojourn* [2]Lit., an, *against Lot* [a]Ex. 2:14

..., *hand* [2]Lit., *to* [a]Gen. 19:1

..., *smote* [a]Deut. 29; 2 Kin. 6:18; Acts 13:11

en. 18:20 [b]Lev. -33; Deut. 4:26; 45; 1 Chr. 21:15

had married; lit., *taking* [2]Lit., *like who was jesting* . 16:21, 45; Rev. 8:4 [b]Jer. 43:1, 2

15 [1]Or, *iniquity*

Lit., *hand* [a]Deut. ; 6:21; 7:8; 2 Pet. :7 [b]Ex. 34:7; Ps. 32:10; 33:18, 19

.it., *he* [2]Lit., *in all the circle* [3]Lit., ountain [a]Jer. 48:6 Gen. 19:26 [c]Gen. 3:10 [d]Gen. 14:10

9 [1]Lit., *mountain*

[1]Lit., *and my soul will live*

21 [1]Lit., *thing*

[1]I.e., small [a]Gen. 13:10; 14:2

[a]Deut. 29:23; Ps. :6; Is. 13:19; Ezek. 49, 50; Luke 17:29; Jude 7

[1]Lit., *circle* [a]Deut. :23; Ps. 107:34; Is. 19; Lam. 4:6; 2 Pet. 2:6

[a]Gen. 19:17; Luke 17:32

27 [a]Gen. 18:22

28 and he looked down toward Sodom and Gomorrah, and toward all the land of the [1]valley, and he saw, and behold, [a]the smoke of the land ascended like the smoke of a [2]furnace.

29 Thus it came about, when God destroyed the cities of the [1]valley, that [a]God remembered Abraham, and [b]sent Lot out of the midst of the overthrow, when He overthrew the cities in which Lot lived.

30 And Lot went up from Zoar, and [1a]stayed in the [2]mountains, and his two daughters with him; for he was afraid to [3]stay in Zoar; and he [1]stayed in a cave, he and his two daughters.

31 Then the first-born said to the younger, "Our father is old, and there is not a man [1]on earth to [a]come in to us after the manner of the earth.

32 "Come, [a]let us make our father drink wine, and let us lie with him, that we may preserve [1]our family through our father."

33 So they made their father drink wine that night, and the first-born went in and lay with her father; and he did not know when she lay down or when she arose.

34 And it came about on the morrow, that the first-born said to the younger, "Behold, I lay last night with my father; let us make him drink wine tonight also; then you go in and lie with him, that we may preserve [1]our family through our father."

35 So they made their father drink wine that night also, and the younger arose and lay with him; and he did not know when she lay down or when she arose.

36 Thus both the daughters of Lot were with child by their father.

37 And the first-born bore a son, and called his name [a]Moab; he is the father of the Moabites to this day.

38 And as for the younger, she also bore a son, and called his name Ben-ammi; he is the father of the [1]sons of [a]Ammon to this day.

Chapter 20

20 Now Abraham journeyed from [a]there toward the land of [b]the [1]Negev, and [2]settled between Kadesh and Shur; then he sojourned in [c]Gerar.

2 And Abraham said of Sarah his wife, "[a]She is my sister." So [b]Abimelech king of Gerar sent and took Sarah.

3 [a]But God came to Abimelech in a dream of the night, and said to him, "Behold, [b]you are a dead man because of the woman whom you have taken, for she is [1]married."

4 Now Abimelech had not come near her; and he said, "Lord, [a]wilt Thou slay a nation, even *though* [1]blameless?

5 "Did he not himself say to me, 'She is my sister'? And she [a]herself said, 'He is my brother.' In [b]the integrity of my heart and the innocence of my [1]hands I have done this."

6 Then God said to him in the dream, "Yes, I know that in the integrity of your heart you have done this, and I also [1a]kept you from sinning against Me; therefore I did not let you touch her.

7 "Now therefore, restore the man's wife, for [a]he is a prophet, and he will pray for you, and you will live. But if you do not restore *her*, know that you shall surely die, you and all who are yours."

8 So Abimelech arose early in the morning and called all his servants and told all these things in their hearing; and the men were greatly frightened.

9 [a]Then Abimelech called Abraham and said to him, "What have

28 [1]Lit., *circle* [a]Rev. 9:2; 18:9

29 [1]Lit., *circle* 7:8; 9:5, 27 [b]2 F

30 [1]Lit., *dwelt* *mountain* [3]Lit., [a]Gen. 19:17, 19

31 [1]Or, *in the la* [a]Gen. 16:2, 4; 38 Deut. 25:5

32 [1]Lit., *seed fro father* [a]Luke 21:

34 [1]Lit., *seed fro father*

37 [a]Deut. 2:9

38 [1]Heb., *Bene-Ammon* [a]D 2:19

20:1 [1]I.e., South country [2]Lit., *dwe* [a]Gen. 18:1 [b]Gen. [c]Gen. 26:1, 6

2 [a]Gen. 12:11-13; 20:12; 26:7 [b]Gen.

3 [1]Lit., *married to husband* [a]Gen. 12 18 [b]Gen. 20:7

4 [1]Lit., *righteous* 18:23-25

5 [1]Lit., *palms* [a]Ge 20:13 [b]1 Kin. 9:4; F 7:8; 26:6

6 [1]Lit., *restrained* [a]1 Sam. 25:26, 34

7 [a]1 Sam. 7:5; 2 Ki 5:11; Job 42:8

9 [a]Gen. 12:18

you done to us? And [1]how have I sinned against you, that you have
brought on me and on my kingdom [b]a great sin? You have done to
me [2]things that ought not to be done."
10 And Abimelech said to Abraham, "What have you [1]encountered,
that you have done this thing?"
11 And Abraham said, "Because I thought, surely there is no [a]fear of
God in this place; and [b]they will kill me because of my wife.
12 "Besides, she actually is my sister, the daughter of my father, but
not the daughter of my mother, and she became my wife;
13 and it came about, when [a]God caused me to wander from my
father's house, that I said to her, 'This is [1]the kindness which you
will show to me: [2]everywhere we go, [b]say of me, "He is my
brother." ' "
14 [a]Abimelech then took sheep and oxen and male and female ser-
vants, and gave them to Abraham, and restored his wife Sarah to
him.
15 And Abimelech said, "[a]Behold, my land is before you; [1]settle
wherever [2]you please."
16 And to Sarah he said, "Behold, I have given your [a]brother a
thousand pieces of silver; behold, it is [1]your vindication before all
who are with you, and before all men you are cleared."
17 And [a]Abraham prayed to God; and God healed Abimelech and
his wife and his maids, so that they bore *children*.
18 [a]For the LORD had closed fast all the wombs of the household of
Abimelech because of Sarah, Abraham's wife.

Chapter 21

21 [a]Then the LORD took note of Sarah as He had said, and the
LORD did for Sarah as He had [1]promised.
2 [a]So Sarah conceived and bore a son to Abraham in his old age, at
[b]the appointed time of which God had spoken to him.
3 And Abraham called the name of his son who was born to him,
whom Sarah bore to him, [a]Isaac.
4 Then Abraham circumcised his son Isaac when he was [a]eight
days old, as God had commanded him.
5 Now Abraham was [a]one hundred years old when his son Isaac
was born to him.
6 And Sarah said, "God has made [a]laughter for me; everyone who
hears will laugh [1]with me."
7 And she said, "[a]Who would have said to Abraham that Sarah
would nurse children? Yet I have borne him a son in his old age."
8 And the child grew and was weaned, and Abraham made a
great feast on the day that Isaac was weaned.
9 Now Sarah saw [a]the son of Hagar the Egyptian, whom she had
borne to Abraham, [1b]mocking.
10 Therefore she said to Abraham, "[a]Drive out this maid and her
son, for the son of this maid shall not be an heir with my son [1]Isaac."
11 [a]And the matter [1]distressed Abraham greatly because of his son.
12 But God said to Abraham, "[1]Do not be distressed because of the
lad and your maid; whatever Sarah tells you, listen to her, for
[a]through Isaac [2]your descendants shall be named.
13 "And of [a]the son of the maid I will make a nation also, because he
is your [1]descendant."
14 So Abraham rose early in the morning, and took bread and a

[1]Lit., *what* [2]Lit., *deeds* [b]Gen. 39:9

10 [1]Lit., *seen*

Neh. 5:15; Prov. Gen. 12:12; 26:7

Lit., *your* [2]Lit., *at every place where* Gen. 12:1-9 [b]Gen. 12:13; 20:5

14 [a]Gen. 12:16

, *dwell* [2]Lit., *it is good in your sight* 13:9; 34:10; 47:6

6 [1]Lit., *for you a covering of the eyes* [a]Gen. 20:5

Num. 12:13; 21:7; James 5:16

18 [a]Gen. 12:17

21:1 [1]Lit., *spoken* 17:16, 21; 18:10, 14; Gal. 4:23

Acts 7:8; Gal. 4:22; Heb. 11:11 [b]Gen. 17:21; 18:10, 14

3 [a]Gen. 17:19, 21

Gen. 17:12; Acts 7:8

5 [a]Gen. 17:17

, *for* [a]Gen. 18:13; Ps. 126:2; Is. 54:1

7 [a]Gen. 18:11, 13

[1]Or, *playing* [a]Gen. 16:1, 4, 15 [b]Gal. 4:29

10 [1]Lit., *with Isaac* [a]Gal. 4:30

11 [1]Lit., *was very grievous in Abraham's sight* [a]Gen. 17:18

[1]Lit., *Do not let it be grievous in your sight* Lit., *your seed will be called* [a]Rom. 9:7; Heb. 11:18

13 [1]Lit., *seed* [a]Gen. 16:10; 21:18; 25:12-18

[1]skin of water, and gave *them* to Hagar, putting *them* on her shoulder,
and *gave her* the boy, and sent her away. And she departed, and
wandered about in the wilderness of Beersheba.
15 And the water in the skin was used up, and she [1]left the boy
under one of the bushes.
16 Then she went and sat down opposite him, about a bowshot
away, for she said, "Do not let me [1]see the boy die." And she sat
opposite him, and [a]lifted up her voice and wept.
17 And God [a]heard the lad crying; and the angel of God called to
Hagar from heaven, and said to her, "What is the matter with you,
Hagar? [b]Do not fear, for God has heard the voice of the lad where
he is.
18 "Arise, lift up the lad, and hold him by [1]the hand; [a]for I will make
a great nation of him."
19 Then God [a]opened her eyes and she saw [b]a well of water; and
she went and filled the [1]skin with water, and gave the lad a drink.
20 And [a]God was with the lad, and he grew; and he [1]lived in the
wilderness, and became an archer.
21 And [a]he [1]lived in the wilderness of Paran; and his mother took a
wife for him from the land of Egypt.
22 Now it came about at that time, that [a]Abimelech and Phicol, the
commander of his army, spoke to Abraham, saying, "[b]God is with
you in all that you do;
23 now therefore, [a]swear to me here by God that you will not deal
falsely with me, or with my offspring, or with my posterity; but
according to the kindness that I have shown to you, you shall show
to me, and to the land in which you have sojourned."
24 And Abraham said, "I swear it."
25 But Abraham [1]complained to Abimelech because of the well of
water which the servants of Abimelech [a]had seized.
26 And Abimelech said, "I do not know who has done this thing;
neither did you tell me, nor did I hear of it [1]until today."
27 And Abraham took sheep and oxen, and gave them to
Abimelech; and [a]the two of them made a covenant.
28 Then Abraham set seven ewe lambs of the flock by themselves.
29 And Abimelech said to Abraham, "What do these seven ewe
lambs mean, which you have set by themselves?"
30 And he said, "You shall take these seven ewe lambs from my
hand in order that it may be a [a]witness to me, that I dug this well."
31 Therefore he called that place [a]Beersheba; because there the two
of them took an oath.
32 So they made a covenant at Beersheba; and Abimelech and
Phicol, the commander of his army, arose and returned to the land of
the Philistines.
33 And *Abraham* planted a tamarisk tree at Beersheba, and there [a]he
called on the name of the LORD, the [b]Everlasting God.
34 And Abraham sojourned [a]in the land of the Philistines for many
days.

Chapter 22

22 Now it came about after these things, that [a]God tested Abra-
ham, and said to him, "[b]Abraham!" And he said, "Here I am."
2 And He said, "Take now [a]your son, your only son, whom you

14 [1]I.e., a skin a bottle

15 [1]Lit., *cast*

16 [1]Lit., *look up death of the chil* 6:26; Amos 8:10

17 [a]Ex. 3:7; Deu Ps. 6:8 [b]Gen. 26

18 [1]Lit., *your* [a]G 16:10; 21:13; 25:

19 [1]V. 14, note 1 [a]Num. 22:31; 2 K 6:17 [b]Gen. 16:7,

20 [1]Lit., *dwelt* [a]G 28:15; 39:2, 3, 21

21 [1]Lit., *dwelt* [a]G 25:18

22 [a]Gen. 20:2, 14 26:26 [b]Gen. 26:2 8:10

23 [a]Josh. 2:12; 1 24:21

25 [1]Lit., *reproved* [a]Gen. 26:15, 18, 2

26 [1]Lit., *except*

27 [a]Gen. 26:31

30 [a]Gen. 31:48

31 [a]Gen. 21:14; 26

33 [a]Gen. 12:8 [b]Ex. 15:18; Deut. 32:40; 90:2; 93:2; Is. 40:28 Jer. 10:10; Hab. 1:1 Heb. 13:8

34 [a]Gen. 22:19

22:1 [a]Deut. 8:2, 16; Heb. 11:17; James 1:12-14 [b]Gen. 22:1

2 [a]Gen. 22:12, 16; J 3:16; 1 John 4:9

love, Isaac, and go to the land of [b]Moriah; and offer him there as a
[c]burnt offering on one of the mountains of which I will tell you."
3 So Abraham rose early in the morning and saddled his donkey,
and took two of his young men with him and Isaac his son; and he
split wood for the burnt offering, and arose and went to the place of
which God had told him.
4 On the third day Abraham raised his eyes and saw the place
from a distance.
5 And Abraham said to his young men, "Stay here with the
donkey, and I and the lad will go yonder; and we will worship and
return to you."
6 And Abraham took the wood of the burnt offering and [a]laid it on
Isaac his son, and he took in his hand the fire and the knife. So the
two of them walked on together.
7 And Isaac spoke to Abraham his father and said, "My father!"
And he said, "Here I am, my son." And he said, "Behold, the fire and
the wood, but where is the [a]lamb for the burnt offering?"
8 And Abraham said, "God will [1]provide for Himself the lamb for
the burnt offering, my son." So the two of them walked on together.
9 Then they came to [a]the place of which God had told him; and
Abraham built [b]the altar there, and arranged the wood, and bound
his son Isaac, and [c]laid him on the altar on top of the wood.
10 And Abraham stretched out his hand, and took the knife to slay
his son.
11 But [a]the angel of the LORD called to him from heaven, and said,
"Abraham, Abraham!" And he said, "Here I am."
12 And he said, "Do not stretch out your hand against the lad, and
do nothing to him; for now [a]I know that you [1]fear God, since you
have not withheld [b]your son, your only son, from Me."
13 Then Abraham raised his eyes and looked, and behold, behind
him a ram caught in the thicket by his horns; and Abraham went and
took the ram, and offered him up for a burnt offering in the place of
his son.
14 And Abraham called the name of that place [1]The LORD Will Pro-
vide, as it is said to this day, "In the mount of the LORD [a]it will [2]be
provided."
15 Then the angel of the LORD called to Abraham a second time
from heaven,
16 and said, "[a]By Myself I have sworn, declares the LORD, because
you have done this thing, and have not withheld your son, your
only son,
17 indeed I will greatly bless you, and I will greatly [a]multiply your
[1]seed as the stars of the heavens, and as [b]the sand which is on the
seashore; and [c]your [1]seed shall possess the gate of [2]their enemies.
18 "And [a]in your [1]seed all the nations of the earth shall [2]be blessed,
because you have [b]obeyed My voice."
19 [a]So Abraham returned to his young men, and they arose and
went together to Beersheba; and Abraham lived at Beersheba.
20 Now it came about after these things, that it was told Abraham,
saying, "Behold, [a]Milcah [1]also has borne children to your brother
Nahor:
21 Uz his first-born and Buz his brother and Kemuel the father of
Aram
22 and Chesed and Hazo and Pildash and Jidlaph and Bethuel."

Chr. 3:1 [c]Gen. 8:20
6 [a]John 19:17
[a]Ex. 29:38-42; John 1:29, 36; Rev. 13:8
8 [1]Lit., *see*
[a]Gen. 22:2 [b]Gen. 2:7, 8; 13:18 [c]Heb. :17-19; James 2:21
11 [a]Gen. 16:7-11; 21:17, 18
[1]Or, *reverence;* lit., *are a fearer of God* mes 2:21, 22 [b]Gen. 22:2, 16
[1]Heb., *YHWH-jireh* *be seen* [a]Gen. 22:8
16 [a]Ps. 105:9; Luke 1:73; Heb. 6:13, 14
7 [1]Or, *descendants* Lit., *his* [a]Gen. 15:5; 6:4; Jer. 33:22; Heb. 11:12 [b]Gen. 32:12 [c]Gen. 24:60
8 [1]Or, *descendants* Dr, *bless themselves* en. 12:3; 18:18; Acts ; Gal. 3:8, 16 [b]Gen. 18:19; 22:3, 10; 26:5
19 [a]Gen. 22:5
[1]Lit., *she also* [a]Gen. 11:29

INSIGHT

The words **love, obedience**, and **worship** are first used in Genesis 22. Note their context.

23 And Bethuel [1]became the father of [a]Rebekah: these eight Milcah
bore to Nahor, Abraham's brother.
24 And his concubine, whose name was Reumah, [1]also bore Tebah
and Gaham and Tahash and Maacah.

Chapter 23

23 Now [1]Sarah lived one hundred and twenty-seven years; *these*
were the years of the life of Sarah.
2 And Sarah died in [a]Kiriath-arba (that is, Hebron) in the land of
Canaan; and Abraham [1]went in to mourn for Sarah and to weep for
her.
3 Then Abraham rose from before his dead, and spoke to the [a]sons
of Heth, saying,
4 "I am [a]a stranger and a sojourner among you; [b]give me [1]a [c]burial
site among you, that I may bury my dead out of my sight."
5 And the sons of Heth answered Abraham, saying to him,
6 "Hear us, my lord, you are a [1a]mighty prince among us; bury your
dead in the choicest of our graves; none of us will refuse you his
grave for burying your dead."
7 So Abraham rose and bowed to the people of the land, the sons
of Heth.
8 And he spoke with them, saying, "If it is your [1]wish *for me* to
bury my dead out of my sight, hear me, and approach [a]Ephron the
son of Zohar for me,
9 that he may give me the cave of Machpelah which he owns,
which is at the end of his field; for the full price let him give it to me
in [1]your presence for [2]a burial site."
10 Now Ephron was sitting among the sons of Heth; and Ephron
the Hittite answered Abraham in the hearing of the sons of Heth;
even [a]of all who went in at the gate of his city, saying,
11 "No, my lord, hear me; [a]I give you the field, and I give you the
cave that is in it. In the presence of the sons of my people I give it to
you; bury your dead."
12 And Abraham bowed before the people of the land.
13 And he spoke to Ephron in the hearing of the people of the land,
saying, "If you will only please listen to me; I will give the price of
the field, accept *it* from me, that I may bury my dead there."
14 Then Ephron answered Abraham, saying to him,
15 "My lord, listen to me; a piece of land worth four hundred [a]shek-
els of silver, what is that between me and you? So bury your dead."
16 And Abraham listened to Ephron; and Abraham [a]weighed out
for Ephron the silver which he had named in the [1]hearing of the sons
of Heth, four hundred shekels of silver, [2]commercial standard.
17 So [a]Ephron's field, which was in Machpelah, which faced
Mamre, the field and cave which was in it, and all the trees which
were in the field, that were [1]within all the confines of its border,
[2]were deeded over
18 to Abraham for a possession [a]in the presence of the sons of Heth,
before all who went in at the gate of his city.
19 And after this, Abraham buried Sarah his wife in the cave of the
field at Machpelah facing Mamre (that is, Hebron) in the land of
Canaan.
20 So the field, and the cave that is in it, [1]were [a]deeded over to
Abraham for [2]a burial site by the sons of Heth.

23 [1]Lit., *begot* [a]Ge
24:15

24 [1]Lit., *she also*

23:1 [1]Lit., *the life o*
Sarah was

2 [1]Or, *proceeded*
[a]Josh. 14:15; 15:13
21:11

3 [a]Gen. 10:15; 15:2

4 [1]Lit., *possession*
grave [a]Gen. 17:8;
25:23; 1 Chr. 29:15
39:12; 105:12; 119:
Heb. 11:9, 13 [b]Acts
7:16 [c]Gen. 49:30

6 [1]Lit., *prince of G*
[a]Gen. 14:14; 20:7

8 [1]Lit., *soul* [a]Gen.

9 [1]Lit., *the midst of*
[2]Lit., *possession of*
burial place

10 [a]Gen. 23:18; 34
24; Ruth 4:1, 11

11 [a]2 Sam. 24:21-2

15 [a]Ex. 30:13; Eze
45:12

16 [1]Lit., *ears* [2]Lit.,
current according t
merchant [a]2 Sam.
14:26; Jer. 32:9, 10
Zech. 11:12

17 [1]Lit., *in all its bo*
around [2]Or, *were*
ratified [a]Gen. 25:9;
49:29, 30; 50:13

18 [a]Gen. 23:10

20 [1]Or, *were ratifie*
[2]Lit., *possession of*
burial place [a]Jer.
32:10-14

Chapter 24

24 Now [a]Abraham was old, advanced in age; and the LORD had
[b]blessed Abraham in every way.
2 And Abraham said to his servant, the oldest of his household,
who had [a]charge of all that he owned, "[b]Please place your hand
under my thigh,
3 and I will make you swear by the LORD, [a]the God of heaven and
the God of earth, that you [b]shall not take a wife for my son from the
daughters of [c]the Canaanites, among whom I live,
4 but you shall go to [a]my country and to my relatives, and take a
wife for my son Isaac."
5 And the servant said to him, "Suppose the woman will not be
willing to follow me to this land; should I take your son back to the
land from where you came?"
6 Then Abraham said to him, "[a]Beware lest you take my son back
there!
7 "[a]The LORD, the God of heaven, who took me from my father's
house and from the land of my birth, and who spoke to me, and who
swore to me, saying, '[b]To your [1]descendants I will give this land,' He
will send [c]His angel before you, and you will take a wife for my son
from there.
8 "But if the woman is not willing to follow you, then you will [a]be
free from this my oath; [b]only do not take my son back there."
9 So the servant [a]placed his hand under the thigh of Abraham his
master, and swore to him concerning this matter.
10 Then the servant took ten camels from the camels of his master,
and set out with a variety of [a]good things of his master's in his hand;
and he arose, and went to [1]Mesopotamia, to [b]the city of Nahor.
11 And he made the camels kneel down outside the city by [a]the
well of water at evening time, [b]the time when women go out to draw
water.
12 And he said, "[a]O LORD, the God of my master Abraham, please
[1b]grant me success today, and show lovingkindness to my master
Abraham.
13 "Behold, [a]I am standing by the [1]spring, and the daughters of the
men of the city are coming out to draw water;
14 now may it be that the girl to whom I say, 'Please let down your
jar so that I may drink,' and [1]who answers, 'Drink, and I will water
your camels also';—*may* she *be the one* whom Thou hast appointed
for Thy servant Isaac; and by this I shall know that Thou hast shown
lovingkindness to my master."
15 And it came about [a]before he had finished speaking, that behold,
[b]Rebekah who was born to Bethuel the son of [c]Milcah, the wife of
Abraham's brother Nahor, came out with her jar on her shoulder.
16 And the girl was [a]very beautiful, a virgin, and no man had [1]had
relations with her; and she went down to the spring and filled her
jar, and came up.
17 Then the servant ran to meet her, and said, "[a]Please let me drink
a little water from your jar."
18 And [a]she said, "Drink, my lord"; and she quickly lowered her jar
to her hand, and gave him a drink.
19 Now when she had finished giving him a drink, [a]she said, "I will
draw also for your camels until they have finished drinking."

1 [a]Gen. 18:11 ...2; 13:2; 24:35; Gal. 3:9
...39:4-6 [b]Gen. 24:9; 47:29
...Gen. 14:19, 22 ...eut. 7:3; 2 Cor. 6:14-17 [c]Gen. ...-19; 26:34, 35; 28:1, 8
...Gen. 12:1; Heb. 11:15
6 [a]Gen. 24:8
...Lit., *seed* [a]Gen. ...en. 12:7; 13:15; ...Ex. 32:13 [c]Gen. ...1:17; 22:11; Ex. 23:20, 23
...2:17-20 [b]Gen. 24:6
9 [a]Gen. 24:2
10 [1]Heb., ...*naharaim, Aram* ...*two rivers* [a]Gen. 24:22, 53 [b]Gen. 11:31, 32
...[a]Gen. 24:42 [b]Ex. ...2:16; 1 Sam. 9:11
...t., *cause to occur* [a]Gen. 24:27, 42, 26:24; Ex. 3:6, 15 [b]Gen. 27:20
...3 [1]Lit., *fountain of water* [a]Gen. 24:43
... [1]Lit., *she will say*
...[a]Gen. 24:45 [b]Gen. ...20, 23 [c]Gen. 11:29
...[1]Lit., *known* [a]Gen. 12:11; 26:7; 29:17
17 [a]John 4:7
18 [a]Gen. 24:14, 46
19 [a]Gen. 24:14

20 So she quickly emptied her jar into the trough, and ran back to the well to draw, and she drew for all his camels.

21 [a]Meanwhile, the man was gazing at her [1]in silence, to know whether the LORD had made his journey successful or not.

22 Then it came about, when the camels had finished drinking, that the man took a [a]gold ring weighing a half-shekel and two bracelets for her [1]wrists weighing ten shekels in gold,

23 and said, "Whose daughter are you? Please tell me, is there room for us to lodge in your father's house?"

24 And she said to him, "[a]I am the daughter of Bethuel, the son of Milcah, whom she bore to Nahor."

25 Again she said to him, "We have plenty of both straw and feed, and room to lodge in."

26 Then the man [a]bowed low and worshiped the LORD.

27 And he said, "[a]Blessed be the LORD, the God of my master Abraham, who has not forsaken [b]His lovingkindness and His truth toward my master; as for me, [c]the LORD has guided me in the way to the house of my master's brothers."

28 Then [a]the girl ran and told her mother's household about these things.

29 Now Rebekah had a brother whose name was [a]Laban; and Laban ran outside to the man at the spring.

30 And it came about that when he saw the ring, and the bracelets on his sister's [1]wrists, and when he heard the words of Rebekah his sister, saying, "[2]This is what the man said to me," he went to the man; and behold, he was standing by the camels at the spring.

31 And he said, "[a]Come in, [b]blessed of the LORD! Why do you stand outside since [c]I have prepared the house, and a place for the camels?"

32 So the man entered the house. Then [1a]Laban unloaded the camels, and he gave straw and feed to the camels, and water to wash his feet and the feet of the men who were with him.

33 But when *food* was set before him to eat, he said, "I will not eat until I have told my business." And he said, "Speak on."

34 So he said, "I am [a]Abraham's servant.

35 "And the LORD has greatly [a]blessed my master, so that he has become [1]rich; and He has given him [b]flocks and herds, and silver and gold, and servants and maids, and camels and donkeys.

36 "Now [a]Sarah my master's wife bore a son to my master [1]in her old age; and [b]he has given him all that he has.

37 "[a]And my master made me swear, saying, 'You shall not take a wife for my son from the daughters of the Canaanites, in whose land I [1]live;

38 but you shall go to my father's house, and to my relatives, and take a wife for my son.'

39 "[a]And I said to my master, 'Suppose the woman does not follow me.'

40 "And he said to me, '[a]The LORD, before whom I have [b]walked, will send [c]His angel with you to make your journey successful, and you will take a wife for my son from my relatives, and from my father's house;

41 [a]then you will be free from my oath, when you come to my relatives; and if they do not give her to you, you will be free from my oath.'

21 [1]Lit., *keepi* [a]Gen. 24:12-14

22 [1]Lit., *hands* 24:47; Ex. 32:2

24 [a]Gen. 24:1

26 [a]Gen. 24:48 4:31

27 [a]Gen. 24:12 Ex. 18:10; Ruth 1 Sam. 25:32; 2 18:28; Luke 1:6 32:10; Ps. 98:3 24:21, 48

28 [a]Gen. 29:12

29 [a]Gen. 29:5,

30 [1]Lit., *hands* *Thus the man*

31 [a]Gen. 29:13 26:29; Ruth 3:10 115:15 [c]Gen. 18 19:2, 3

32 [1]Lit., *he* [a]Gen 43:24; Judg. 19:2

34 [a]Gen. 24:2

35 [1]Lit., *great* [a]G 24:1 [b]Gen. 13:2

36 [1]Lit., *after she old* [a]Gen. 21:1-7 25:5

37 [1]Lit., *dwell* [a]G 24:2-4

39 [a]Gen. 24:5

40 [a]Gen. 24:7 [b]Ge 5:22, 24; 17:1 [c]Ex 23:20

41 [a]Gen. 24:8

42 "So [a]I came today to the spring, and said, 'O LORD, the God of my
master Abraham, if now Thou wilt make my journey on which I go
[b]successful;
43 behold, [a]I am standing by the [1]spring, and may it be that the
maiden who comes out to draw, and to whom I say, "[b]Please let me
drink a little water from your jar";
44 and she will say to me, "You drink, and I will draw for your
camels also"; let her be the woman whom the LORD has appointed
for my master's son.'
45 "Before I had finished [a]speaking in my heart, behold, [b]Rebekah
came out with her jar on her shoulder, and went down to the spring
and drew; and [c]I said to her, 'Please let me drink.'
46 "And she quickly lowered her jar from her *shoulder,* and said,
'[a]Drink, and I will water your camels also'; so I drank, and she
watered the camels also.
47 "[a]Then I asked her, and said, 'Whose daughter are you?' And she
said, 'The daughter of Bethuel, Nahor's son, whom Milcah bore to
him'; and I put the [b]ring on her nose, and the bracelets on her
[1]wrists.
48 "And I [a]bowed low and worshiped the LORD, and blessed the
LORD, the God of my master Abraham, [b]who had guided me in the
right way to take the daughter of my master's [1]kinsman for his son.
49 "So now if you are going to [1a]deal kindly and truly with my
master, tell me; and if not, let me know, that I may turn to the right
hand or the left."
50 Then Laban and Bethuel answered and said, "[a]The matter comes
from the LORD; [b]*so* we cannot speak to you bad or good.
51 "Behold, Rebekah is before you, take *her* and go, and let her be the
wife of your master's son, as the LORD has spoken."
52 And it came about when Abraham's servant heard their words,
that he [a]bowed himself to the ground [1]before the LORD.
53 And the servant brought out [a]articles of silver and articles of
gold, and garments, and gave them to Rebekah; he also gave pre-
cious things to her brother and to her mother.
54 Then he and the men who were with him ate and drank and
spent the night. When they arose in the morning, he said, "[a]Send me
away to my master."
55 But her brother and her mother said, "[a]Let the girl stay with us *a*
few days, say ten; afterward she may go."
56 And he said to them, "Do not delay me, since [a]the LORD has
prospered my way. Send me away that I may go to my master."
57 And they said, "We will call the girl and [1]consult her wishes."
58 Then they called Rebekah and said to her, "Will you go with this
man?" And she said, "I will go."
59 Thus they sent away their sister Rebekah and [a]her nurse with
Abraham's servant and his men.
60 And they blessed Rebekah and said to her,
"May you, our sister,
[a]Become thousands of ten thousands,
And may [b]your [1]descendants possess
The gate of those who hate them."
61 Then Rebekah arose with her maids, and they mounted the
camels and followed the man. So the servant took Rebekah and
departed.

[a]Gen. 24:11, 12 [b]Neh. 1:11
[1]Lit., *fountain of* ...*er* [a]Gen. 24:13 [b]Gen. 24:14
...am. 1:13 [b]Gen. ...15 [c]Gen. 24:17
[a]Gen. 24:18, 19
...it., *hands* [a]Gen. ...24:23, 24 [b]Ezek. 16:11, 12
...t., *brother* [a]Gen. ...52 [b]Gen. 24:27; ...; 48:14; Is. 48:17
49 [1]Lit., *show* ...*vingkindness and* ...Gen. 47:29; Josh. 2:14
[a]Ps. 118:23; Mark ... [b]Gen. 31:24, 29
52 [1]Lit., *to* [a]Gen. 24:26, 48
...Gen. 24:10, 22; Ex. 3:22; 11:2; 12:35
...4 [a]Gen. 24:56, 59; 30:25
55 [a]Judg. 19:4
56 [a]Gen. 24:40
[1]Lit., *ask her mouth*
59 [a]Gen. 35:8
...0 [1]Lit., *seed* [a]Gen. 17:16 [b]Gen. 22:17

62 Now Isaac had come from going to [a]Beer-lahai-roi; for he [1]was
living in [b]the [2]Negev.
63 And Isaac went out [a]to [1]meditate in the field toward evening;
and [b]he lifted up his eyes and looked, and behold, camels were
coming.
64 And Rebekah lifted up her eyes, and when she saw Isaac she
dismounted from the camel.
65 And she said to the servant, "Who is that man walking in the
field to meet us?" And the servant said, "He is my master." Then she
took her [1]veil and covered herself.
66 And the servant told Isaac all the things that he had done.
67 Then Isaac brought her into his mother Sarah's tent, and [a]he took
Rebekah, and she became his wife; and [b]he loved her; thus Isaac was
comforted after [c]his mother's death.

Chapter 25

25 Now Abraham took another wife, [1]whose name was Keturah.
2 And [a]she bore to him Zimran and Jokshan and Medan and
Midian and Ishbak and Shuah.
3 And Jokshan [1]became the father of Sheba and Dedan. And the
sons of Dedan were Asshurim and Letushim and Leummim.
4 And the sons of Midian *were* Ephah and Epher and Hanoch and
Abida and Eldaah. All these *were* the sons of Keturah.
5 [a]Now Abraham gave all that he had to Isaac;
6 but to the sons of [1]his concubines, Abraham gave gifts while he
was still living, and [a]sent them away from his son Isaac eastward, to
the land of the east.
7 And these are [1]all the years of Abraham's life that he lived, [a]one
hundred and seventy-five years.
8 And Abraham breathed his last and died [a]in a [1]ripe old age, an
old man and satisfied *with life;* and he was [b]gathered to his people.
9 Then his sons Isaac and Ishmael buried him in [a]the cave of
Machpelah, in the field of Ephron the son of Zohar the Hittite, facing
Mamre,
10 [a]the field which Abraham purchased from the sons of Heth;
there Abraham was buried with Sarah his wife.
11 And it came about after the death of Abraham, that [a]God blessed
his son Isaac; and Isaac [1]lived by [b]Beer-lahai-roi.
12 Now these are *the records of* the generations of [a]Ishmael,
Abraham's son, whom Hagar the Egyptian, Sarah's maid, bore to
Abraham;
13 and these are the names of [a]the sons of Ishmael, by their names,
[1]in the order of their birth: Nebaioth, the first-born of Ishmael, and
Kedar and Adbeel and Mibsam
14 and Mishma and Dumah and Massa,
15 Hadad and Tema, Jetur, Naphish and Kedemah.
16 These are the sons of Ishmael and these are their names, by their
villages, and by their camps; [a]twelve princes according to their
[1]tribes.
17 And these are the years of the life of Ishmael, [a]one hundred and
thirty-seven years; and he breathed his last and died, and was [b]gath-
ered to his people.
18 And they [1]settled from [a]Havilah to [b]Shur which is [2]east of Egypt

62 [1]Lit., *was d* [2]I.e., South cou [a]Gen. 16:14; 25 [b]Gen. 20:1

63 [1]Or, *stroll; m* uncertain [a]Josh Ps. 1:2; 77:12; 1 27, 48; 143:5; 1 [b]Gen. 18:2

65 [1]Or, *shawl*

67 [a]Gen. 25:20 29:18 [c]Gen. 23

25:1 [1]Lit., *and h*

2 [a]1 Chr. 1:32, 3

3 [1]Lit., *begot*

5 [a]Gen. 24:35, 3

6 [1]Lit., *concubin which belonged t Abraham* [a]Gen. 2

7 [1]Lit., *the days o* [a]Gen. 12:4

8 [1]Lit., *good* [a]Ge 15:15; 47:8, 9 [b]G 25:17; 35:29; 49:2

9 [a]Gen. 23:17, 18 49:29, 30; 50:13

10 [a]Gen. 23:3-16

11 [1]Lit., *dwelt* [a]G 12:2, 3; 22:17; 26: [b]Gen. 16:14; 24:62

12 [a]Gen. 16:15

13 [1]Lit., *in regard t their generations* [a]1 Chr. 1:29-31

16 [1]Or, *peoples* [a]G 17:20

17 [a]Gen. 16:16 [b]G 25:8; 49:33

18 [1]Lit., *dwelt* [2]Lit., *before* [a]1 Sam. 15:7 [b]Gen. 20:1

[3]as one goes toward Assyria; [c]he [4]settled in defiance of all his [5]rela-
tives.
19 Now these are *the records of* [a]the generations of Isaac, Abraham's
son: Abraham [1]became the father of Isaac;
20 and Isaac was forty years old when he took [a]Rebekah, the
[b]daughter of Bethuel the [1]Aramean of Paddan-aram, the [c]sister of
Laban the [1]Aramean, to be his wife.
21 And Isaac prayed to the LORD on behalf of his wife, because she
was barren; and [a]the LORD [1]answered him and Rebekah his wife
[b]conceived.
22 But the children struggled together within her; and she said, "If
it is so, why then am I *this way?*" So she went to [a]inquire of the LORD.
23 And the LORD said to her,
"[a]Two nations are in your womb;
[b]And two peoples shall be separated from your body;
And one people shall be stronger than the other;
And [c]the older shall serve the younger."
24 When her days to be delivered were fulfilled, behold, there were
twins in her womb.
25 Now the first came forth red, [a]all over like a hairy garment; and
they named him Esau.
26 And afterward his brother came forth with [a]his hand holding on
to Esau's heel, so [b]his name was called [1]Jacob; and Isaac was [c]sixty
years old when she gave birth to them.
27 When the boys grew up, Esau became a skillful hunter, a man of
the field; but Jacob was a [1]peaceful man, [2a]living in tents.
28 Now Isaac loved Esau, because [1]he had [a]a taste for game; [b]but
Rebekah loved Jacob.
29 And when Jacob had cooked [a]stew, Esau came in from the field
and he was [1]famished;
30 and Esau said to Jacob, "Please let me have a swallow of [1]that
red stuff there, for I am [2]famished." Therefore his name was called
[3]Edom.
31 But Jacob said, "[1]First sell me your [a]birthright."
32 And Esau said, "Behold, I am about to die; so of what *use* then is
the birthright to me?"
33 And Jacob said, "[1]First swear to me"; so he swore to him, and
[a]sold his birthright to Jacob.
34 Then Jacob gave Esau bread and lentil stew; and he ate and
drank, and rose and went on his way. Thus Esau despised his
birthright.

Chapter 26

26 Now there was [a]a famine in the land, besides the previous
famine that had occurred in the days of Abraham. So Isaac
went to Gerar, to [b]Abimelech king of the Philistines.
2 And the LORD [a]appeared to him and said, "Do not go down to
Egypt; [1b]stay in the land of which I shall tell you.
3 "Sojourn in this land and [a]I will be with you and [b]bless you, for [c]to
you and to your [1]descendants I will give all these lands, and I will
establish [d]the oath which I swore to your father Abraham.
4 "And [a]I will multiply your [1]descendants as the stars of heaven,
and will give your [1]descendants all these lands; and [b]by your [1]de-
scendants all the nations of the earth [2]shall be blessed;

you go [4]Lit., against [5]Lit., [c]Gen. 16:12
begot [a]Matt. 1:2
Syrian [a]Gen. 29, 67 [b]Gen. [c]Gen. 24:29
was entreated [a]1 Sam. 1:17; r. 5:20; 2 Chr. Ezra 8:23; Ps. 3 [b]Rom. 9:10
am. 9:9; 10:22
en. 17:4-6, 16; :14; Deut. 2:4, . 27:29 [c]Gen. l. 1:2, 3; Rom. 9:12
5 [a]Gen. 27:11
one who takes by the heel or nts [a]Hos. 12:3 6 [c]Gen. 25:20
complete [2]Lit., ling [a]Heb. 11:9
t., *game was in* th [a]Gen. 27:19 [b]Gen. 27:6-10
., *weary* [a]2 Kin. 4:38
Lit., *the red, this* Lit., *weary* [3]I.e., red
t., *Today* [a]Deut. 17; 1 Chr. 5:1, 2
it., *Today* [a]Heb. 12:16
6:1 [a]Gen. 12:10 [b]Gen. 20:1, 2
[1]Lit., *dwell* [a]Gen. 17:1; 18:1 [b]Gen. 12:1
[1]Lit., *seed* [a]Gen. 6:24; 28:15; 31:3 12:2 [c]Gen. 12:7; :15; 15:18 [d]Gen. :16-18; Ps. 105:9
, *seed* [2]Or, *bless* elves [a]Gen. 15:5; ; Ex. 32:13 [b]Gen. 22:18; Gal. 3:8

5 because Abraham [1a]obeyed Me and kept My charge, My com-
mandments, My statutes and My laws."
6 So Isaac [1]lived in Gerar.
7 When the men of the place asked about his wife, he said, "[a]She is
my sister," for he was [b]afraid to say, "my wife," *thinking*, "[1]the men
of the place might kill me on account of Rebekah, for she is [c]beauti-
ful."
8 And it came about, when he had been there a long time, that
Abimelech king of the Philistines looked out through a window, and
saw, and behold, Isaac was caressing his wife Rebekah.
9 Then Abimelech called Isaac and said, "Behold, certainly she is
your wife! How then did you say, 'She is my sister'?" And Isaac said
to him, "Because I said, 'Lest I die on account of her.' "
10 And [a]Abimelech said, "What is this you have done to us? One of
the people might easily have lain with your wife, and you would
have brought guilt upon us."
11 So Abimelech charged all the people, saying, "He who [a]touches
this man or his wife shall surely be put to death."
12 Now Isaac sowed in that land, and [1]reaped in the same year a
hundredfold. And [a]the LORD blessed him,
13 and the man [a]became rich, and continued to grow [1]richer until
he became very [1]wealthy;
14 for [a]he had possessions of flocks [1]and herds and a great
household, so that the Philistines envied him.
15 Now [a]all the wells which his father's servants had dug in the
days of Abraham his father, the Philistines stopped up [1]by filling
them with earth.
16 Then Abimelech said to Isaac, "Go away from us, for you are
[1a]too powerful for us."
17 And Isaac departed from there and camped in the valley of
Gerar, and [1]settled there.
18 Then Isaac dug again the wells of water which [1]had been dug in
the days of his father Abraham, for the Philistines had stopped them
up after the death of Abraham; and he [2]gave them the same names
which his father had [3]given them.
19 But when Isaac's servants dug in the valley and found there a
well of [1]flowing water,
20 the herdsmen of Gerar [a]quarreled with the herdsmen of Isaac,
saying, "The water is ours!" So he named the well [1]Esek, because
they contended with him.
21 Then they dug another well, and they quarreled over it too, so he
named it [1]Sitnah.
22 And he moved away from there and dug another well, and they
did not quarrel over it; so he named it [1]Rehoboth, for he said, "[2a]At
last the LORD has made [3]room for us, and we shall be [b]fruitful in the
land."
23 Then he went up from there to [a]Beersheba.
24 And the LORD [a]appeared to him the same night and said,
"[b]I am the God of your father Abraham;
[c]Do not fear, for I am with you.
I [d]will bless you, and multiply your [1]descendants,
For the sake of My servant Abraham."
25 So he built an [a]altar there, and called upon the name of the LORD,
and pitched his tent there; and there Isaac's servants dug a well.

5 [1]Lit., *hear* *voice* [a]Gen.
6 [1]Lit., *dwelt*
7 [1]Lit., *lest*. [a]Gen. 12:13; [b]Prov. 29:25 12:11; 24:16;
10 [a]Gen. 20:
11 [a]Ps. 105:1
12 [1]Lit., *found* 24:1; 26:3; Jo Prov. 10:22
13 [1]Lit., *great* 10:22
14 [1]Lit., *and* *possessions o* [a]Gen. 24:35; 2
15 [1]Lit., *and fi* [a]Gen. 21:25, 3
16 [1]Lit., *much* *than we* [a]Ex. 1
17 [1]Lit., *dwelt*
18 [1]Lit., *they h* [2]Lit., *called thei* *as the names* [3] *called*
19 [1]Lit., *living*
20 [1]I.e., *conten* [a]Gen. 21:25
21 [1]I.e., enmity
22 [1]I.e., broad p [2]Lit., *Truly now* *broad* [a]Ps. 4:1; 3 [b]Gen. 17:6; Ex
23 [a]Gen. 22:19
24 [1]Lit., *seed* [a]G 26:2 [b]Gen. 17:7, 24:12; Ex. 3:6; Ac 7:32 [c]Gen. 15:1 22:17; 26:3, 4
25 [a]Gen. 12:7, 8; 18; Ps. 116:17

6 [1]Lit., *and his* …nfidential friend [a]Gen. 21:22

26 Then [a]Abimelech came to him from Gerar [1]with his adviser
Ahuzzath, and Phicol the commander of his army.

27 [a]Judg. 11:7

27 And Isaac said to them, "[a]Why have you come to me, since you
hate me, and have sent me away from you?"

…Lit., *us and you* [a]Gen. 21:22, 23

28 And they said, "We see plainly [a]that the LORD has been with you;
so we said, 'Let there now be an oath between us, *even* between [1]you
and us, and let us make a covenant with you,

…, *and just as we* …:31; Ps. 115:15

29 that you will do us no harm, just as we have not touched you
[1]and have done to you nothing but good, and have sent you away in
peace. You are now the [a]blessed of the LORD.' "

30 [a]Gen. 19:3

30 Then [a]he made them a feast, and they ate and drank.
31 And in the morning they arose early and [1a]exchanged oaths; then
Isaac sent them away and they departed from him in peace.

…it., *swore one to* …her [a]Gen. 21:31

32 Now it came about on the same day, that Isaac's servants came
in and told him about the well which they had dug, and said to him,
"We have found water."

33 [a]Gen. 21:31

33 So he called it Shibah; therefore the name of the city is [a]Beer-
sheba to this day.

[1]Lit., *took as wife* [a]Gen. 28:8; 36:2

34 And when Esau was forty years old [a]he [1]married Judith the
daughter of Beeri the Hittite, and Basemath the daughter of Elon the
Hittite;

35 [1]Lit., *were a* …erness of spirit to [a]Gen. 27:46

35 and [a]they [1]brought grief to Isaac and Rebekah.

Chapter 27

7:1 [a]Gen. 48:10; …Sam. 3:2 [b]Gen. 25:25, 33, 34

27 Now it came about, when Isaac was old, and [a]his eyes were
too dim to see, that he called his [b]older son Esau and said to
him, "My son." And he said to him, "Here I am."

…, *he* [a]Gen. 47:29

2 [a]And [1]Isaac said, "Behold now, I am old *and* I do not know the
day of my death.

3 [a]Gen. 25:28

3 "Now then, please take your gear, your quiver and your bow, and
go out to the field and [a]hunt game for me;
4 and prepare a savory dish for me such as I love, and bring it to
me that I may eat, so that [a]my soul may bless you before I die."

…en. 27:19, 25, 31; …5, 16; Deut. 33:1; Heb. 11:20

5 And Rebekah was listening while Isaac spoke to his son Esau. So
when Esau went to the field to hunt for game to bring *home,*

6 [a]Gen. 25:28

6 [a]Rebekah said to her son Jacob, "Behold, I heard your father
speak to your brother Esau, saying,
7 'Bring me *some* game and prepare a savory dish for me, that I
may eat, and bless you in the presence of the LORD before my death.'

…Lit., *my voice* [2]Lit., *according to what* [a]Gen. 27:13, 43

8 "Now therefore, my son, [a]listen to [1]me [2]as I command you.

…Lit., *take* [2]Lit., *kids of goats*

9 "Go now to the flock and [1]bring me two choice [2]kids from there,
that I may prepare them *as* a savory dish for your father, such as he
loves.
10 "Then you shall bring *it* to your father, that he may eat, so that he
may bless you before his death."

[1]Lit., *said to* [a]Gen. 25:25

11 And Jacob [1]answered his mother Rebekah, "Behold, Esau my
brother is a [a]hairy man and I am a smooth man.

[1]Lit., *mocker* [a]Gen. 27:21, 22

12 "[a]Perhaps my father will feel me, then I shall be as a [1]deceiver in
his sight; and I shall bring upon myself a curse and not a blessing."

13 [a]Gen. 27:8

13 But his mother said to him, "Your curse be on me, my son; only
[a]obey my voice, and go, get *them* for me."
14 So he went and got *them,* and brought *them* to his mother; and
his mother made savory food such as his father loved.

…5 [1]Lit., *desirable;* or, *choice* [a]Gen. 27:27

15 Then Rebekah took the [1]best [a]garments of Esau her elder son,

which were with her in the house, and put them on Jacob her
younger son.
16 And she put the skins of the [1]kids on his hands and on the
smooth part of his neck.
17 She also gave the savory food and the bread, which she had
made, [1]to her son Jacob.
18 Then he came to his father and said, "My father." And he said,
"Here I am. Who are you, my son?"
19 And Jacob said to his father, "I am Esau your first-born; I have
done as you told me. [a]Get up, please, sit and eat of my game, that
[1b]you may bless me."
20 And Isaac said to his son, "How is it that you have *it* so quickly,
my son?" And he said, "[a]Because the LORD your God caused *it* to
happen to me."
21 Then Isaac said to Jacob, "Please come close, that [a]I may feel you,
my son, whether you are really my son Esau or not."
22 So Jacob came close to Isaac his father, and he felt him and said,
"The voice is the voice of Jacob, but the hands are the hands of
Esau."
23 And he did not recognize him, because his hands were [a]hairy
like his brother Esau's hands; so he blessed him.
24 And he said, "Are you really my son Esau?" And he said, "I
am."
25 So he said, "Bring *it* to me, and I will eat of my son's game, that
[1a]I may bless you." And he brought *it* to him, and he ate; he also
brought him wine and he drank.
26 Then his father Isaac said to him, "Please come close and kiss
me, my son."
27 So he came close and kissed him; and when he smelled the smell
of his garments, he [a]blessed him and said,
"See, [b]the smell of my son
Is like the smell of a field [c]which the LORD has blessed;
28 Now may [a]God give you of the dew of heaven,
And of the [b]fatness of the earth,
And an abundance of grain and new wine;
29 [a]May peoples serve you,
And nations bow down to you;
[b]Be master of your brothers,
[c]And may your mother's sons bow down to you.
[d]Cursed be those who curse you,
And blessed be those who bless you."
30 Now it came about, as soon as Isaac had finished blessing Jacob,
and Jacob had hardly gone out from the presence of Isaac his father,
that Esau his brother came in from his hunting.
31 Then he also made savory food, and brought it to his father; and
he said to his father, "[a]Let my father arise, and eat of his son's game,
that [1b]you may bless me."
32 And Isaac his father said to him, "[a]Who are you?" And he said,
"I am your son, [b]your first-born, Esau."
33 Then Isaac [1]trembled violently, and said, "[a]Who was he then that
hunted game and brought *it* to me, so that I ate of all *of it* before you
came, and blessed him? [b]Yes, and he shall be blessed."
34 When Esau heard the words of his father, [a]he cried out with an

16 [1]Lit., *kids of the goats*
17 [1]Lit., *into t*
19 [1]Lit., *your s* [a]Gen. 27:31 [b]
20 [a]Gen. 24:1
21 [a]Gen. 27:12
23 [a]Gen. 27:16
25 [1]Lit., *my sou* 27:4
27 [a]Heb. 11:20 4:11 [c]Ps. 65:10
28 [a]Gen. 27:39; 33:13, 28; Prov. Zech. 8:12 [b]Nur
29 [a]Gen. 25:23; 45:14; 49:7, 23; 14 [b]Gen. 9:26, 2 27:37 [c]Gen. 37:7 [d]Gen. 12:3; Num
31 [1]Lit., *your sou* [a]Gen. 27:19 [b]Ge
32 [a]Gen. 27:18 25:33, 34
33 [1]Lit., *trembled very great tremblin* [a]Gen. 27:35 [b]Gen 25:23; 28:3, 4; Nur 23:20
34 [a]Heb. 12:17

exceedingly great and bitter cry, and said to his father, "Bless me,
even me also, O my father!"
35 And he said, "[a]Your brother came deceitfully, and has taken
away your blessing."
36 Then he said, "[1]Is he not rightly named [a]Jacob, for he has sup-
planted me these two times? He took away my birthright, and be-
hold, now he has taken away my blessing." And he said, "Have you
not reserved a blessing for me?"
37 But Isaac answered and said to Esau, "Behold, I have made him
[a]your master, and all his [1]relatives I have given to him [2]as servants;
and with grain and new wine I have sustained him. Now as for you
then, what can I do, my son?"
38 And Esau said to his father, "Do you have only one blessing, my
father? Bless me, *even* me also, O my father." So Esau lifted his voice
and [a]wept.
39 Then [a]Isaac his father answered and said to him,
"Behold, [1b]away from the [2]fertility of the earth shall be your
dwelling,
And [1]away from the dew of heaven from above.
40 "And by your sword you shall live,
And your brother [a]you shall serve;
But it shall come about [b]when you become restless,
That you shall [1]break his yoke from your neck."
41 So Esau [a]bore a grudge against Jacob because of the blessing
with which his father had blessed him; and Esau said [1]to himself,
"[b]The days of mourning for my father are near; then I will kill my
brother Jacob."
42 Now when the words of her elder son Esau were reported to
Rebekah, she sent and called her younger son Jacob, and said to him,
"Behold your brother Esau is consoling himself concerning you, *by
planning* to kill you.
43 "Now therefore, my son, [a]obey my voice, and arise, [1]flee to
[b]Haran, to my brother [c]Laban!
44 "And stay with him [a]a few days, until your brother's fury [1]sub-
sides,
45 until your brother's anger [1]against you subsides, and he forgets
[a]what you did to him. Then I shall send and get you from there. Why
should I be bereaved of you both in one day?"
46 And Rebekah said to Isaac, "I am tired of [1]living because of [a]the
daughters of Heth; [b]if Jacob takes a wife from the daughters of Heth,
like these, from the daughters of the land, what good will my life be
to me?"

Chapter 28

28 So Isaac called Jacob and [a]blessed him and charged him, and
said to him, "[b]You shall not take a wife from the daughters of
Canaan.
2 "Arise, go to Paddan-aram, to the house of [a]Bethuel your
mother's father; and from there take to yourself a wife from the
daughters of Laban your mother's brother.
3 "And may [1a]God Almighty [b]bless you and [c]make you fruitful and
[d]multiply you, that you may become a [e]company of peoples.
4 "May He also give you the [a]blessing of Abraham, to you and to

35 [a]Gen. 27:19
36 [1]Or, *Was he then named Jacob that he* [a]Gen. 25:26, 32-34
[1]Lit., *brothers* [2]Lit., *for* [a]Gen. 27:28, 29
38 [a]Heb. 12:17
[1]Or, *of* [2]Lit., *fatness* [a]Heb. 11:20 [b]Gen. 27:28; Deut. 33:13, 28
[1]Lit., *tear off* [a]Gen. 25:23; 27:29 [b]2 Kin. 8:20-22
41 [1]Lit., *in his heart* Gen. 32:3-11; 37:4, 8 [b]Gen. 50:2-4, 10
43 [1]Lit., *flee for yourself* [a]Gen. 27:8, 13 [b]n. 11:31 [c]Gen. 24:29
44 [1]Lit., *turns away* [a]Gen. 31:41
45 [1]Lit., *turns away from you* [a]Gen. 27:12, 19, 35
46 [1]Lit., *my life* [a]Gen. 26:34, 35; 28:8 [b]Gen. 24:3
28:1 [a]Gen. 27:33 [b]Gen. 24:3, 4
2 [a]Gen. 25:20
3 [1]Heb., *El Shaddai* Gen. 17:1; 35:11; 48:3 n. 22:17 [c]Gen. 17:6, [d]Gen. 17:2; 26:4, 24 [e]Gen. 35:11; 48:4
4 [a]Gen. 12:2; 22:17

your [1]descendants with you; that you may [b]possess the land of your
[c]sojournings, which God gave to Abraham."
5 Then [a]Isaac sent Jacob away, and he went to Paddan-aram to
Laban, son of Bethuel the Aramean, the brother of Rebekah, the
mother of Jacob and Esau.
6 Now Esau saw that Isaac had blessed Jacob and sent him away
to Paddan-aram, to take to himself a wife from there, *and that* when
he blessed him he charged him, saying, "[a]You shall not take a wife
from the daughters of Canaan,"
7 and that Jacob had obeyed his father and his mother and had
gone to Paddan-aram.
8 So Esau saw that [a]the daughters of Canaan displeased [1]his father
Isaac;
9 and Esau went to Ishmael, and [1]married, [a]besides the wives that
he had, Mahalath the daughter of Ishmael, Abraham's son, the sister
of Nebaioth.
10 Then Jacob departed from [a]Beersheba and went toward [b]Haran.
11 And he [1]came to [2]a [a]certain place and spent the night there,
because the sun had set; and he took one of the stones of the place
and put it [3]under his head, and lay down in that place.
12 And [a]he had a dream, and behold, a ladder was set on the earth
with its top reaching to heaven; and behold, [b]the angels of God were
ascending and descending on it.
13 And behold, [a]the LORD stood [1]above it and said, "I am the LORD,
[b]the God of your father Abraham and the God of Isaac; the land on
which you lie, I will give it [c]to you and to [d]your [2]descendants.
14 "Your [1]descendants shall also be like [a]the dust of the earth, and
you shall [2]spread out [b]to the west and to the east and to the north
and to the south; and [c]in you and in your [1]descendants shall all the
families of the earth be blessed.
15 "And behold, [a]I am with you, and [b]will keep you wherever you
go, and [c]will bring you back to this land; for [d]I will not leave you
until I have done what I have [1]promised you."
16 Then Jacob [a]awoke from his sleep and said, "[b]Surely the LORD is
in this place, and I did not know it."
17 And he was afraid and said, "[a]How awesome is this place! This
is none other than the house of God, and this is the gate of heaven."
18 So Jacob rose early in the morning, and took [a]the stone that he
had put [1]under his head and set it up as a pillar, and poured oil on
its top.
19 And he called the name of that place [1a]Bethel; however, [2]pre-
viously the name of the city had been [b]Luz.
20 Then Jacob [a]made a vow, saying, "[b]If God will be with me and
will keep me on this journey that I [1]take, and will give me [2c]food to
eat and garments to wear,
21 and [a]I return to my father's house in [1]safety, [b]then the LORD will
be my God.
22 "And this stone, which I have set up as a pillar, [a]will be God's
house; and [b]of all that Thou dost give me I will surely give a tenth to
Thee."

Chapter 29 ____

29 Then Jacob [1]went on his journey, and came to the land of [a]the
sons of the east.

4 [1]Lit., *seed* 15:7, 8; 17:8 29:15; Ps. 39:
5 [a]Gen. 27:43
6 [a]Gen. 28:1
8 [1]Lit., *in the e his* [a]Gen. 24:3 35; 27:46
9 [1]Lit., *took fo* [a]Gen. 26:34; 3
10 [a]Gen. 26:2 12:4, 5; 27:43
11 [1]Lit., *lighted the place* [3]Lit., *head-place* [a]G
12 [a]Gen. 41:1; 12:6 [b]John 1:5
13 [1]Or, *beside* [2]Lit., *seed* [a]Ger Amos 7:7 [b]Gen 24 [c]Gen. 13:15 26:3 [d]Gen. 12:7
14 [1]Lit., *seed* [2] *break through* 13:16; 22:17 [b]G 13:14, 15 [c]Gen. 18:18; 22:18; 26
15 [1]Lit., *spoken* [a]Gen. 26:3, 24; [b]Num. 6:24; Ps. 7, 8 [c]Gen. 48:2 30:3 [d]Num. 23:1 Deut. 7:9; 31:6, 8
16 [a]1 Kin. 3:15; 31:26 [b]Ex. 3:4-6 5:13-15; Ps. 139
17 [a]Ps. 68:35
18 [1]Lit., *at his head-place* [a]Gen 28:11; 35:14
19 [1]I.e., the hous God [2]Lit., *at the f* [a]Judg. 1:23 [b]Gen 48:3
20 [1]Lit., *go* [2]Lit., [a]Gen. 31:13; Judg 11:30; 2 Sam. 15:8 [b]Gen. 28:15 [c]1 Tir
21 [1]Lit., *peace* [a]J 11:31 [b]Deut. 26:17
22 [a]Gen. 35:7 [b]Le 27:30; Deut. 14:22
29:1 [1]Lit., *lifted up feet* [a]Judg. 6:3, 33

2 And he looked, and [1]saw [a]a well in the field, and behold, three
flocks of sheep were lying there beside it, for from that well they
watered the flocks. Now the stone on the mouth of the well was
large.
3 When all the flocks were gathered there, they would then roll the
stone from the mouth of the well, and water the sheep, and put the
stone back in its place on the mouth of the well.
4 And Jacob said to them, "My brothers, where are you from?"
And they said, "We are from [a]Haran."
5 And he said to them, "Do you know Laban the [a]son of Nahor?"
And they said, "We know *him.*"
6 And he said to them, "Is it well with him?" And they said, "It is
well, and behold, [a]Rachel his daughter is coming with the sheep."
7 And he said, "Behold, it is still high day; it is not time for the
livestock to be gathered. Water the sheep, and go, pasture them."
8 But they said, "We cannot, until all the flocks are gathered, and
they roll the stone from the mouth of the well; then we water the
sheep."
9 While he was still speaking with them, Rachel came with her
father's sheep, for she was a shepherdess.
10 And it came about, when Jacob saw Rachel the daughter of
Laban his mother's brother, and the sheep of Laban his mother's
brother, that Jacob went up, and rolled the stone from the mouth of
the well, and watered the flock of Laban his mother's brother.
11 Then Jacob [a]kissed Rachel, and lifted his voice and wept.
12 And Jacob told Rachel that he was a [1a]relative of her father and
that he was Rebekah's son, and [b]she ran and told her father.
13 So it came about, when [a]Laban heard the news of Jacob his
sister's son, that he ran to meet him, and [b]embraced him and kissed
him, and brought him to his house. Then he related to Laban all
these things.
14 And Laban said to him, "Surely you are [a]my bone and my flesh."
And he stayed with him a month.
15 Then Laban said to Jacob, "Because you are my [1]relative, should
you therefore serve me for nothing? Tell me, what shall [a]your wages
be?"
16 Now Laban had two daughters; the name of the older was Leah,
and the name of the younger was Rachel.
17 And Leah's eyes were weak, but Rachel was [a]beautiful of form
and [1]face.
18 Now Jacob [a]loved Rachel, so he said, "[b]I will serve you seven
years for your younger daughter Rachel."
19 And Laban said, "It is better that I give her to you than that I
should give her to another man; stay with me."
20 So Jacob served seven years for Rachel and they seemed to him
but a few days [a]because of his love for her.
21 Then Jacob said to Laban, "Give *me* my wife, for my [1]time is
completed, that I may [a]go in to her."
22 And Laban gathered all the men of the place, and made a feast.
23 Now it came about in the evening that he took his daughter
Leah, and brought her to him; and *Jacob* went in to her.
24 Laban also gave his maid Zilpah to his daughter Leah as a maid.
25 So it came about in the morning that, behold, it was Leah! And

behold [a]Gen. 1; Ex. 2:15, 16
4 [a]Gen. 28:10
[a]Gen. 24:24, 29
6 [a]Ex. 2:16
11 [a]Gen. 33:4
...t., *brother* [a]Gen. 8:5 [b]Gen. 24:28
[a]Gen. 24:29-31 [b]Gen. 33:4
[a]Gen. 2:23; Judg. 9:2; 2 Sam. 5:1; 19:12, 13
...it., *brother* [a]Gen. 31:41
7 [1]Lit., *beautiful of appearance* [a]Gen. 12:11, 14; 26:7
[a]Gen. 24:67 [b]Hos. 12:12
20 [a]Song 8:7
21 [1]Lit., *days are* [a]Judg. 15:1

he said to Laban, "[a]What is this you have done to me? Was it not for
Rachel that I served with you? Why then have you [b]deceived me?"
26 But Laban said, "It is not [1]the practice in our place, to [2]marry off
the younger before the first-born.
27 "Complete the week of this one, and we will give you the other
also for the service which [a]you shall serve with me for another seven
years."
28 And Jacob did so and completed her week, and he gave him his
daughter Rachel as his wife.
29 Laban also gave his maid Bilhah to his daughter Rachel as her
maid.
30 So *Jacob* went in to Rachel also, and indeed [a]he loved Rachel
more than Leah, and he served with [1]Laban for [b]another seven years.
31 Now the LORD saw that Leah was [1]unloved, and He opened her
womb, but Rachel was barren.
32 And Leah conceived and bore a son and named him [1]Reuben, for
she said, "Because the LORD has [2a]seen my affliction; surely now my
husband will love me."
33 Then she conceived again and bore a son and said, "[a]Because the
LORD has [1]heard that I am [2]unloved, He has therefore given me this
son also." So she named him Simeon.
34 And she conceived again and bore a son and said, "Now this
time my husband will become [1]attached to me, because I have borne
him three sons." Therefore he was named [a]Levi.
35 And she conceived again and bore a son and said, "This time I
will [1]praise the LORD." Therefore she named him [2a]Judah. Then she
stopped bearing.

Chapter 30

30 Now when Rachel saw that [a]she bore Jacob no children, [1]she
became jealous of her sister; and she said to Jacob, "[b]Give me
children, or else I die."
2 Then Jacob's anger burned against Rachel, and he said, "Am I in
the place of God, who has [a]withheld from you the fruit of the
womb?"
3 And she said, "[a]Here is my maid Bilhah, go in to her, that she
may [b]bear on my knees, that [1c]through her I too may have children."
4 So [a]she gave him her maid Bilhah as a wife, and Jacob went in to
her.
5 And Bilhah conceived and bore Jacob a son.
6 Then Rachel said, "God has [1a]vindicated me, and has indeed
heard my voice and has given me a son." Therefore she named him
[2]Dan.
7 And Rachel's maid Bilhah conceived again and bore Jacob a
second son.
8 So Rachel said, "With [1]mighty wrestlings I have [2]wrestled
with my sister, *and* I have indeed prevailed." And she named him
Naphtali.
9 When Leah saw that she had stopped bearing, she took her maid
Zilpah and gave her to Jacob as a wife.
10 And Leah's maid Zilpah bore Jacob a son.
11 Then Leah said, "[1]How fortunate!" So she named him [2]Gad.
12 And Leah's maid Zilpah bore Jacob a second son.

25 [a]Gen. 12:1 26:10 [b]1 Sam

26 [1]Lit., *done* [2]Lit., *give*

27 [a]Gen. 31:4

30 [1]Lit., *him* [a] 29:17, 18 [b]Ge

31 [1]Lit., *hated*

32 [1]I.e., see, a [2]Lit., *looked up* 16:11; 31:42; E 4:31; Deut. 26: 25:18

33 [1]Heb., *sham* related to Sime *hated* [a]Deut. 21

34 [1]Heb., *lavah* to Levi [a]Gen. 4

35 [1]Heb., *Jada* related to Judah *Jehudah* [a]Gen. Matt. 1:2

30:1 [1]Lit., *Rach* [a]Gen. 29:31 [b]1 S 1:5, 6

2 [a]Gen. 20:18; 2

3 [1]Lit., *from her* *may be built* [a]Ge 16:2 [b]Gen. 50:23 3:12

4 [a]Gen. 16:3, 4

6 [1]Lit., *judged* [2]I. judged [a]Ps. 35:24 43:1; Lam. 3:59

8 [1]Lit., *wrestlings* *God* [2]Heb., *nipht* related to Naphtali

11 [1]Lit., *With fortu* Some versions rea *Fortune has come* Fortune

13 Then Leah said, "[1]Happy am I! For women [a]will call me happy."
So she named him [2]Asher.
14 Now in the days of wheat harvest Reuben went and found [a]man-
drakes in the field, and brought them to his mother Leah. Then
Rachel said to Leah, "Please give me some of your son's
mandrakes."
15 But she said to her, "Is it a small matter for you to take my
husband? And would you take my son's mandrakes also?" So
Rachel said, "Therefore he may lie with you tonight in return for
your son's mandrakes."
16 When Jacob came in from the field in the evening, then Leah
went out to meet him and said, "You must come in to me, for I have
surely hired you with my son's mandrakes." So he lay with her that
night.
17 And God gave heed to Leah, and she conceived and bore Jacob a
fifth son.
18 Then Leah said, "God has given me my [1]wages, because I gave
my maid to my husband." So she named him Issachar.
19 And Leah conceived again and bore a sixth son to Jacob.
20 Then Leah said, "God has endowed me with a good gift; now
my husband [1]will dwell with me, because I have borne him six
sons." So she named him Zebulun.
21 And afterward she bore a daughter and named her Dinah.
22 Then [a]God remembered Rachel, and God gave heed to her and
[b]opened her womb.
23 So she conceived and bore a son and said, "God has [a]taken away
my reproach."
24 And she named him Joseph, saying, "[a]May the LORD [1]give me
another son."
25 Now it came about when Rachel had borne Joseph, that Jacob
said to Laban, "[a]Send me away, that I may go to my own place and
to my own country.
26 "Give *me* my wives and my children [a]for whom I have served
you, and let me depart; for you yourself know my service which I
have [1]rendered you."
27 But Laban said to him, "If now [1]it pleases you, *stay with me;* I
have divined [a]that the LORD has blessed me on your account."
28 And he [1]continued, "[a]Name me your wages, and I will give it."
29 But he said to him, "[a]You yourself know how I have served you
and how your cattle have [1]fared with me.
30 "For you had little before [1]I came, and it has [2]increased to a
multitude; and the LORD has blessed you [3]wherever I turned. But
now, when shall I provide for my own household also?"
31 So he said, "What shall I give you?" And Jacob said, "You shall
not give me anything. If you will do this *one* thing for me, I will
again pasture *and* keep your flock:
32 let me pass through your entire flock today, removing from there
every [a]speckled and spotted sheep, and every black [1]one among the
lambs, and the spotted and speckled among the goats; and *such* shall
be my wages.
33 "So my [1]honesty will answer for me later, when you come con-
cerning my [2]wages. Every one that is not speckled and spotted
among the goats and black among the lambs, *if found* with me, will
be considered stolen."

[1]Lit., *With my* ...ss! [2]I.e., happy [a]Luke 1:48
14 [a]Song 7:13
[1]Heb., *sachar,* ...ated to Issachar
..., *zabal,* related ... Zebulun. Some ...nslate *will honor*
[a]1 Sam. 1:19, 20 [b]Gen. 29:31
...s. 4:1; Luke 1:25
[1]Lit., *add to me;* ..., *Joseph* [a]Gen. 35:17
[a]Gen. 24:54, 56
...Lit., *served* [a]Gen. ...9:18, 20, 27; Hos. 12:12
[1]Lit., *I have found favor in your eyes* 26:24; 39:3, 5; Is. 61:9
[1]Lit., *said* [a]Gen. 29:15; 31:7, 41
[1]Lit., *been* [a]Gen. 31:6
30 [1]Lit., *me* [2]Lit., ...*en forth* [3]Lit., *at my foot*
[1]Lit., *sheep* [a]Gen. 31:8
[1]Lit., *righteousness* ...it., *wages which are before you*

34 And Laban said, "[1]Good, let it be according to your word."
35 So he removed on that day the striped and spotted male goats
and all the speckled and spotted female goats, every one with white
in it, and all the black ones among the sheep, and gave them into the
[1]care of his sons.
36 And he put *a distance of* three days' journey between himself and
Jacob, and Jacob fed the rest of Laban's flocks.
37 Then Jacob [1]took fresh rods of poplar and almond and plane
trees, and peeled white stripes in them, exposing the white which
was [2]in the rods.
38 And he set the rods which he had peeled in front of the flocks in
the gutters, *even* in the watering troughs, where the flocks came to
drink; and they [1]mated when they came to drink.
39 So the flocks [1]mated by the rods, and the flocks brought forth
striped, speckled, and spotted.
40 And Jacob separated the lambs, and [1]made the flocks face
toward the striped and all the black in the flock of Laban; and he put
his own herds apart, and did not put them with Laban's flock.
41 Moreover, it came about whenever the [1]stronger of the flock
[2]were mating, that Jacob would place the rods in the sight of the
flock in the gutters, so that they might [3]mate by the rods;
42 but when the flock was feeble, he did not put *them* in; so the
feebler were Laban's and the [1]stronger Jacob's.
43 So [a]the man [1]became exceedingly prosperous, and had large
flocks and female and male servants and camels and donkeys.

Chapter 31

31 Now [1]Jacob heard the words of Laban's sons, saying, "Jacob
has taken away all that was our father's, and from what
belonged to our father he has made all this [2]wealth."
2 And Jacob saw the [1]attitude of Laban, and behold, it was not
friendly toward him as formerly.
3 Then the LORD said to Jacob, "[a]Return to the land of your fathers
and to your relatives, and [b]I will be with you."
4 So Jacob sent and called Rachel and Leah to his flock in the field,
5 and said to them, "[a]I see your father's [1]attitude, that it is not
friendly toward me as formerly, but [b]the God of my father has been
with me.
6 "And [a]you know that I have served your father with all my
strength.
7 "Yet your father has [a]cheated me and [b]changed my wages ten
times; however, [c]God did not allow him to hurt me.
8 "If [a]he spoke thus, 'The speckled shall be your wages,' then all the
flock brought forth speckled; and if he spoke thus, 'The striped shall
be your wages,' then all the flock brought forth striped.
9 "Thus God has [a]taken away your father's livestock and given
them to me.
10 "And it came about at the time when the flock were [1]mating that I
lifted up my eyes and saw in a dream, and behold, the male goats
which were [2]mating *were* striped, speckled, and mottled.
11 "Then [a]the angel of God said to me in the dream, 'Jacob,' and I
said, 'Here I am.'
12 "And he said, 'Lift up, now, your eyes and see *that* all the male

34 [1]Lit., *Beho* *that it might be*
35 [1]Lit., *hand*
37 [1]Lit., *took t* [2]Lit., *on*
38 [1]Or, *conce*
39 [1]Or, *concei*
40 [1]Lit., *set the*
41 [1]Lit., *bound* i.e., firm and co [2]Or, *conceived* *conceive*
42 [1]Lit., *bound* i.e., firm and co
43 [1]Lit., *broke f* [a]Gen. 12:16; 13. 24:35; 26:13, 14
31:1 [1]Lit., *he* [2]L
2 [1]Lit., *face*
3 [a]Gen. 32:9 [b]G 28:15
5 [1]Lit., *face* [a]Ge [b]Gen. 21:22; 28: 31:29, 42, 53; Is. Heb. 13:5
6 [a]Gen. 30:29
7 [a]Gen. 29:25 [b]G 31:41 [c]Gen. 15:1,
8 [a]Gen. 30:32
9 [a]Gen. 31:1, 16
10 [1]Or, *conceiving* [2]Lit., *leaping upon* *flock*
11 [a]Gen. 16:7-11; 22:11, 15; 31:13; 4

goats which are [1]mating are striped, speckled, and mottled; for [a]I
have seen all that Laban has been doing to you.
13 'I am [a]the God *of* Bethel, where you [b]anointed a pillar, where you
made a vow to Me; now arise, [1]leave this land, and [c]return to the
land of your birth.' "
14 And Rachel and Leah answered and said to him, "Do we still
have any portion or inheritance in our father's house?
15 "Are we not reckoned by him as foreigners? For [a]he has sold us,
and has also [1]entirely consumed [2]our purchase price.
16 "Surely all the wealth which God has taken away from our father
belongs to us and our children; now then, do whatever God has said
to you."
17 Then Jacob arose and put his children and his wives upon
camels;
18 and he drove away all his livestock and all his property which
he had gathered, his acquired livestock which he had gathered in
Paddan-aram, [a]to go to the land of Canaan to his father Isaac.
19 When Laban had gone to shear his flock, then Rachel stole the
[1a]household idols that were her father's.
20 And Jacob [1]deceived Laban the Aramean, by not telling him that
he was fleeing.
21 So he fled with all that he had; and he arose and crossed the
Euphrates River, and set his face toward the hill country of [a]Gilead.
22 When it was told Laban on the third day that Jacob had fled,
23 then he took his [1]kinsmen with him, and pursued him *a distance*
of seven days' journey; and he overtook him in the hill country of
Gilead.
24 And [a]God came to Laban the Aramean in a [b]dream of the night,
and said to him, "[1c]Be careful that you do not speak to Jacob either
good or bad."
25 And Laban caught up with Jacob. Now Jacob had pitched his
tent in the hill country, and Laban with his [1]kinsmen camped in the
hill country of Gilead.
26 Then Laban said to Jacob, "What have you done [1]by deceiving
me and carrying away my daughters like captives of the sword?
27 "Why did you flee secretly and [1]deceive me, and did not tell me,
so that I might have sent you away with joy and with songs, with
[a]timbrel and with [b]lyre;
28 and did not allow me [a]to kiss my sons and my daughters? Now
you have done foolishly.
29 "It is in [1]my power to do you harm, but [a]the God of your father
spoke to me last night, saying, '[2b]Be careful not to speak either good
or bad to Jacob.'
30 "And now you have indeed gone away because you longed great-
ly for your father's house; *but* why did you steal [a]my gods?"
31 Then Jacob answered and said to Laban, "Because I was afraid,
for I said, 'Lest you would take your daughters from me by force.'
32 "[a]The one with whom you find your gods shall not live; in the
presence of our [1]kinsmen [2]point out what is yours [3]among my
belongings and take *it* for yourself." For Jacob did not know that
Rachel had stolen them.
33 So Laban went into Jacob's tent, and into Leah's tent, and into
the tent of the two maids, but he did not find *them*. Then he went out
of Leah's tent and entered Rachel's tent.

..., *leaping upon* ... *flock* [a]Ex. 3:7

...it., *go out from* ...3:13, 19 [b]Gen. ...0 [c]Gen. 28:15; 32:9

...e., *enjoyed the* ...efit of [2]Lit., *our* ...*y* [a]Gen. 29:20, 23, 27

18 [a]Gen. 35:27

[1]Heb., *teraphim* 31:30, 34; 35:2; ...lg. 17:5; 1 Sam. 19:13; Hos. 3:4

...0 [1]Lit., *stole the heart of*

21 [a]Gen. 37:25

...3 [1]Lit., *brothers*

...it., *Take heed to* ...*rself* [a]Gen. 20:3; ...9 [b]Gen. 20:3, 6; ...:11 [c]Gen. 24:50; 31:7, 29

25 [1]Lit., *brothers*

...it., *and you have stolen my heart*

...it., *steal me* [a]Ex. 15:20 [b]Gen. 4:21

28 [a]Gen. 31:55

[1]Lit., *the power of* ...*y hand* [2]Lit., *Take* ...*to yourself* [a]Gen. ..., 24, 42, 53 [b]Gen. 31:24

[a]Gen. 31:19; Josh. 24:2; Judg. 18:24

[1]Lit., *brothers* [2]Lit., ...*ecognize* [3]Lit., *with me* [a]Gen. 44:9

who followed the droves, saying, "After this manner you shall speak
to Esau when you find him;
20 and you shall say, 'Behold, your servant Jacob also is behind
us.'" For he said, "I will appease him with the present that goes
before me. Then afterward I will see his face; perhaps he will accept
me."
21 So the present passed on before him, while he himself spent that
night in the camp.
22 Now he arose that same night and took his two wives and his
two maids and his eleven children, and crossed the ford of the
[a]Jabbok.
23 And he took them and sent them across the stream. And he sent
across whatever he had.
24 Then Jacob was left alone, and a man [a]wrestled with him until
daybreak.
25 And when he saw that he had not prevailed against him, he
touched the socket of his thigh; so the socket of Jacob's thigh was
dislocated while he wrestled with him.
26 Then he said, "Let me go, for the dawn is breaking." But he said,
"[a]I will not let you go unless you bless me."
27 So he said to him, "What is your name?" And he said, "Jacob."
28 And [a]he said, "Your name shall no longer be Jacob, but [1]Israel;
for you have striven with God and with men and have prevailed."
29 Then [a]Jacob asked him and said, "Please tell me your name." But
he said, "Why is it that you ask my name?" And he blessed him
there.
30 So Jacob named the place [1]Peniel, for *he said,* "[a]I have seen God
face to face, yet my [2]life has been preserved."
31 Now the sun rose upon him just as he crossed over [a]Penuel, and
he was limping on his thigh.
32 Therefore, to this day the sons of Israel do not eat the sinew of
the hip which is on the socket of the thigh, because he touched the
socket of Jacob's thigh in the sinew of the hip.

Chapter 33

33 Then Jacob lifted his eyes and looked, and behold, [a]Esau was
coming, and four hundred men with him. So he divided the
children [1]among Leah and Rachel and the two maids.
2 And he put the maids and their children [1]in front, and Leah and
her children [2]next, and Rachel and Joseph [2]last.
3 But he himself passed on ahead of them and [a]bowed down to the
ground seven times, until he came near to his brother.
4 Then Esau ran to meet him and embraced him, and [a]fell on his
neck and kissed him, and they wept.
5 And he lifted his eyes and saw the women and the children, and
said, "[1]Who are these with you?" So he said, "[a]The children whom
God has graciously given your servant."
6 Then the maids came near [1]with their children, and they bowed
down.
7 And Leah likewise came near with her children, and they bowed
down; and afterward Joseph came near with Rachel, and they
bowed down.
8 And he said, "What do you mean by [a]all this company which I
have met?" And he said, "[b]To find favor in the sight of my lord."

22 [a]Deut. 3:16 12:2
24 [a]Hos. 12:3,
26 [a]Hos. 12:4
28 [1]I.e., he who with God; or, God strives [a]Gen. 35 1 Kin. 18:31
29 [a]Judg. 13:17,
30 [1]I.e., the face God [2]Lit., *soul* [a] 16:13; Ex. 24:10, 33:20; Num. 12:8 6:22; 13:22
31 [a]Judg. 8:8
33:1 [1]Or, *to* [a]Gen
2 [1]Lit., *first* [2]Lit.,
3 [a]Gen. 42:6; 43:2
4 [a]Gen. 45:14, 15
5 [1]Or, *What relatio these to you?* [a]Gen 48:9; Ps. 127:3; Is.
6 [1]Lit., *they and*
8 [a]Gen. 32:13-16 [b]Gen. 32:5

9 But Esau said, "[a]I have plenty, my brother; let what you have be
your own."
10 And Jacob said, "No, please, if now I have found favor in your
sight, then take my present from my hand, [1]for I see your face as one
sees the face of God, and you have received me favorably.
11 "Please take my [1a]gift which has been brought to you, [b]because
God has dealt graciously with me, and because I have [2]plenty." Thus
he urged him and he took *it*.
12 Then [1]Esau said, "Let us take our journey and go, and I will go
before you."
13 But he said to him, "My lord knows that the children are frail
and that the flocks and herds which are nursing are [1]a care to me.
And if they are driven hard one day, all the flocks will die.
14 "Please let my lord pass on before his servant; and I will proceed
at my leisure, according to the pace of the cattle that are before me
and according to the pace of the children, until I come to my lord at
[a]Seir."
15 And Esau said, "Please let me leave with you some of the people
who are with me." But he said, "[1]What need is there? [a]Let me find
favor in the sight of my lord."
16 So Esau returned that day on his way to Seir.
17 And Jacob journeyed to [1a]Succoth; and built for himself a house,
and made booths for his livestock, therefore the place is named Suc-
coth.
18 Now Jacob came safely to the city of [a]Shechem, which is in the
land of Canaan, when he came from [b]Paddan-aram, and camped
before the city.
19 And [a]he bought the piece of land where he had pitched his tent
from the hand of the sons of Hamor, Shechem's father, for one
hundred [1]pieces of money.
20 Then he erected there an altar, and called it [1]El-Elohe-Israel.

Chapter 34

34 Now [a]Dinah the daughter of Leah, whom she had borne to
Jacob, went out to [1]visit the daughters of the land.
2 And when Shechem the son of Hamor [a]the Hivite, the prince of
the land, saw her, he took her and lay with her [1]by force.
3 And [1]he was deeply attracted to Dinah the daughter of Jacob,
and he loved the girl and [2]spoke tenderly to her.
4 So Shechem [a]spoke to his father Hamor, saying, "Get me this
young girl for a wife."
5 Now Jacob heard that he had defiled Dinah his daughter; but his
sons were with his livestock in the field, so Jacob kept silent until
they came in.
6 Then Hamor the father of Shechem went out to Jacob to speak
with him.
7 Now the sons of Jacob came in from the field when they heard *it;*
and the men were grieved, and they were very angry because he had
done a [1a]disgraceful thing in Israel [2]by lying with Jacob's daughter,
for such a thing ought not to be done.
8 But Hamor spoke with them, saying, "The soul of my son Shech-
em longs for your daughter; please give her to him [1]in marriage.
9 "And intermarry with us; give your daughters to us, and take our
daughters for yourselves.

9 [a]Gen. 27:39, 40
[1]Lit., *for therefore I* ... *seen your face like seeing God's face*
[1]Lit., *blessing* [2]Lit., *all* [a]1 Sam. 25:27 [b]Gen. 30:43
12 [1]Lit., *he*
13 [1]Lit., *upon me*
14 [a]Gen. 32:3
15 [1]Lit., *Why this?* [a]Ruth 2:13
[1]I.e., booths [a]Josh. ...7; Judg. 8:5, 14; Ps. 60:6
...8 [a]Gen. 12:6; Josh. ...4:1; Judg. 9:1 [b]Gen. 25:20; 28:2
19 [1]Heb., *qesitah* ...osh. 24:32; John 4:5
... [1]I.e., God, the God of Israel
...4:1 [1]Lit., *see* [a]Gen. 30:21
2 [1]Lit., *and humbled her* [a]Gen. 34:30
...3 [1]Lit., *his soul clung* ...it., *spoke to the heart of the girl*
4 [a]Judg. 14:2
[1]Lit., *senseless* [2]Lit., ...*lie* [a]Deut. 22:20-30; ...g. 20:6; 2 Sam. 13:12
8 [1]Lit., *for a wife*

10 "Thus you shall [1]live with us, and [a]the land shall be *open* before
you; [1]live and [b]trade in it, and [c]acquire property in it."
11 Shechem also said to her father and to her brothers, "If I find
favor in your sight, then I will give whatever you say to me.
12 "Ask me ever so much bridal payment and gift, and I will give
according as you say to me; but give me the girl [1]in marriage."
13 But Jacob's sons answered Shechem and his father Hamor, with
deceit, and spoke to them, because he had defiled Dinah their sister.
14 And they said to them, "We cannot do this thing, to give our
sister to [a]one who is uncircumcised, for that would be a disgrace
to us.
15 "Only on this *condition* will we consent to you: if you will become
like us, in that every male of you be circumcised,
16 then we will give our daughters to you, and we will take your
daughters for ourselves, and we will [1]live with you and become one
people.
17 "But if you will not listen to us to be circumcised, then we will
take our daughter and go."
18 Now their words seemed [1]reasonable to Hamor and Shechem,
Hamor's son.
19 And the young man did not delay to do the thing, because he
was delighted with Jacob's daughter. Now he was more respected
than all the household of his father.
20 So Hamor and his son Shechem came to the [a]gate of their city,
and spoke to the men of their city, saying,
21 "These men are [1]friendly with us; therefore let them [2]live in the
land and trade in it, for behold, the land is [3]large enough for them.
Let us take their daughters [4]in marriage, and give our daughters to
them.
22 "Only on this *condition* will the men consent to us to [1]live with us,
to become one people: that every male among us be circumcised as
they are circumcised.
23 "Will not their livestock and their property and all their animals
be ours? Only let us consent to them, and they will [1]live with us."
24 And [a]all who went out of the gate of his city listened to Hamor
and to his son Shechem, and every male was circumcised, all who
went out of the gate of his city.
25 Now it came about on the third day, when they were in pain,
that two of Jacob's sons, [a]Simeon and Levi, Dinah's brothers, each
took his sword and came upon the city unawares, and killed every
male.
26 And they killed Hamor and his son Shechem with the edge of
the sword, and took Dinah from Shechem's house, and went forth.
27 Jacob's sons came upon the slain and looted the city, because
they had defiled their sister.
28 They took their flocks and their herds and their donkeys, and
that which was in the city and that which was in the field;
29 and they captured and looted all their wealth and all their little
ones and their wives, even all that *was* in the houses.
30 Then Jacob said to Simeon and Levi, "You have [a]brought trouble
on me, by [b]making me odious among the inhabitants of the land,
among [c]the Canaanites and the Perizzites; and [1d]my men being few
in number, they will gather together against me and [2]attack me and I
shall be destroyed, I and my household."

10 [1]Lit., *dwell* [a]Gen 13:9; 20:15 [b]Gen. 42:34 [c]Gen. 47:27

12 [1]Lit., *for a wife*

14 [a]Gen. 17:14

16 [1]Lit., *dwell*

18 [1]Lit., *good*

20 [a]Ruth 4:1; 2 Sam 15:2

21 [1]Lit., *peaceful* [2]Lit., *dwell* [3]Lit., *wide of hands before them* [4]Lit., *to us for wives*

22 [1]Lit., *dwell*

23 [1]Lit., *dwell*

24 [a]Gen. 23:10

25 [a]Gen. 49:5-7

30 [1]Lit., *I, few in number* [2]Lit., *smite* [a]Josh. 7:25 [b]Ex. 5:2[illegible] 1 Sam. 13:4; 2 Sam. 10:6 [c]Gen. 13:7; 34[illegible] [d]Gen. 46:26, 27; De[illegible] 4:27; 1 Chr. 16:19; P[illegible] 105:12

31 But they said, "Should he [1]treat our sister as a harlot?"

Chapter 35

35 Then God said to Jacob, "Arise, go up to [a]Bethel, and [1]live
there; and make an altar there to [b]God, who appeared to you
[c]when you fled [2]from your brother Esau."
2 So Jacob said to his [a]household and to all who were with him,
"Put away [b]the foreign gods which are among you, and [c]purify your-
selves, and change your garments;
3 and let us arise and go up to Bethel; and I will make [a]an altar
there to God, [b]who answered me in the day of my distress, and [c]has
been with me [1]wherever I have gone."
4 So they gave to Jacob all the foreign gods which [1]they had, and
the rings which were in their ears; and Jacob hid them under the
[2]oak which was near Shechem.
5 As they journeyed, there was [1a]a great terror upon the cities
which were around them, and they did not pursue the sons of Jacob.
6 So Jacob came to [a]Luz (that is, Bethel), which is in the land of
Canaan, he and all the people who were with him.
7 And [a]he built an altar there, and called the place [1]El-bethel, be-
cause there God had revealed Himself to him, when he fled [2]from his
brother.
8 Now [a]Deborah, Rebekah's nurse, died, and she was buried
below Bethel under the oak; it was named [1]Allon-bacuth.
9 Then God appeared to Jacob again when he came from Paddan-
aram, and He [a]blessed him.
10 And [a]God said to him,
"Your name is Jacob;
[1]You shall no longer be called Jacob,
But Israel shall be your name."
Thus He called [2]him Israel.
11 God also said to him,
"I am [1a]God Almighty;
[b]Be fruitful and multiply;
A nation and a [c]company of nations shall [2]come from you,
And [d]kings shall [2]come forth from [3]you.
12 "And [a]the land which I gave to Abraham and Isaac,
I will give it to you,
And I will give the land to your [1]descendants after you."
13 Then [a]God went up from him in the place where He had spoken
with him.
14 And Jacob set up [a]a pillar in the place where He had spoken with
him, a pillar of stone, and he poured out a [1]libation on it; he also
poured oil on it.
15 So Jacob named the place where God had spoken with him,
[1a]Bethel.
16 Then they journeyed from Bethel; and when there was still some
distance to go to [a]Ephrath, Rachel began to give birth and she [1]suf-
fered severe labor.
17 And it came about when she was in severe labor that the mid-
wife said to her, "Do not fear, for now [a]you have *another* son."
18 And it came about as her soul was departing (for she died), that
she named him [1]Ben-oni; but his father called him [2]Benjamin.

31 [1]Or, *make*
[illegible]Lit., *dwell* [2]Lit., [illegible]*e face of* [a]Gen. [illegible]9 [b]Gen. 28:13 [c]Gen. 27:43
[illegible]en. 18:19; Josh. [illegible]Gen. 31:19, 30, [c]Ex. 19:10, 14
[1]Lit., *in the way* [a]Gen. 28:20-22 [illegible]:6 [c]Gen. 28:15; 31:3, 42
[illegible]it., *were in their* [illegible]*d* [2]Or, *terebinth*
[illegible], *a terror of God* [illegible]16; 23:27; Deut. 2:25
[illegible]Gen. 28:19; 48:3
[1]I.e., the God of [illegible]el [2]Lit., *from the* [illegible]*ce of* [a]Gen. 35:3
[illegible], oak of weeping [a]Gen. 24:59
9 [a]Gen. 32:29
[1]Lit., *Your name* [illegible], *his name* [a]Gen. 17:5; 32:28
[1]Heb., *El Shaddai* [illegible]*, come into being* [illegible]*, your loins* [a]Gen. 17:1; 28:3; Ex. 6:3 [illegible]9:1, 7 [c]Gen. 48:4 [illegible]n. 17:6, 16; 36:31
[1]Lit., *seed* [a]Gen. [illegible]2:7; 13:15; 26:3, 4; 28:13; Ex. 32:13
[a]Gen. 17:22; 18:33
[1]Or, *drink offering* [illegible]n. 28:18, 19; 31:45
[1]I.e., the house of God [a]Gen. 28:19
[illegible]Lit., *had difficulty in* [illegible]*r giving birth* [a]Gen. [illegible]19; 48:7; Ruth 4:11; Mic. 5:2
17 [a]Gen. 30:24
[1]I.e., the son of my [illegible]row [2]I.e., the son of the right hand

19 So [a]Rachel died and was buried on the way to [b]Ephrath (that is,
Bethlehem).
20 And Jacob set up a pillar over her grave; that is the [a]pillar of
Rachel's grave to this day.
21 Then Israel journeyed on and pitched his tent beyond the [1a]tower
of [2]Eder.
22 And it came about while Israel was dwelling in that land, that
[a]Reuben went and lay with Bilhah his father's concubine; and Israel
heard *of it*.
Now there were twelve sons of Jacob—
23 [a]the sons of Leah: Reuben, Jacob's first-born, then Simeon and
Levi and Judah and Issachar and Zebulun;
24 [a]the sons of Rachel: Joseph and Benjamin;
25 and [a]the sons of Bilhah, Rachel's maid: Dan and Naphtali;
26 and [a]the sons of Zilpah, Leah's maid: Gad and Asher. These are
the sons of Jacob who were born to him in Paddan-aram.
27 And Jacob came to his father Isaac at [a]Mamre of [b]Kiriath-arba
(that is, Hebron), where Abraham and Isaac had sojourned.
28 Now the days of Isaac were [a]one hundred and eighty years.
29 And Isaac breathed his last and died, and was [a]gathered to his
people, an [b]old man [1]of ripe age; and [c]his sons Esau and Jacob buried
him.

The Birth Order of Jacob's (Israel's) Sons

Mother	Son
Leah	Reuben (1) *(born 1921 B.C.)*
	Simeon (2)
	Levi (3)
	Judah (4)
Bilhah *(Rachel's maid)*	Dan (5)
	Naphtali (6)
Zilpah *(Leah's maid)*	Gad (7)
	Asher (8)
Leah	Issachar (9)
	Zebulun (10)
Rachel	Joseph (11) *(born 1914 B.C.)*
	Benjamin (12)

Chapter 36

36 Now these are *the records of* the generations of [a]Esau (that is,
Edom).
2 Esau [a]took his wives from the daughters of Canaan: Adah the
daughter of Elon the Hittite, and [b]Oholibamah the daughter of Anah
and the [c]granddaughter of Zibeon the Hivite;
3 also Basemath, Ishmael's daughter, the sister of Nebaioth.
4 And Adah bore [a]Eliphaz to Esau, and Basemath bore Reuel,
5 and Oholibamah bore Jeush and Jalam and Korah. These are the
sons of Esau who were born to him in the land of Canaan.
6 [a]Then Esau took his wives and his sons and his daughters and
all [1]his household, and his livestock and all his cattle and all his
goods which he had acquired in the land of Canaan, and went to
another land away from his brother Jacob.
7 [a]For their property had become too great for them to [1]live
together, and the [b]land where they [c]sojourned could not sustain them
because of their livestock.
8 So Esau lived in the hill country of [a]Seir; Esau is [b]Edom.
9 These then are *the records of* the generations of Esau the father of
[1]the Edomites in the hill country of Seir.
10 These are the names of Esau's sons: Eliphaz the son of Esau's
wife Adah, Reuel the son of Esau's wife Basemath.
11 And the sons of Eliphaz were Teman, Omar, [1]Zepho and Gatam
and Kenaz.
12 And Timna was a concubine of Esau's son Eliphaz and she bore
[a]Amalek to Eliphaz. These are the sons of Esau's wife Adah.
13 And these are the sons of Reuel: Nahath and Zerah, Shammah
and Mizzah. These were the sons of Esau's wife Basemath.
14 And these were the sons of Esau's wife Oholibamah, the daugh-
ter of Anah and the [1]granddaughter of Zibeon: [2]she bore to Esau,
Jeush and Jalam and Korah.

19 [a]Gen. 48:7 1:2; 4:11; Mic. 5
20 [a]1 Sam. 10.
21 [1]Heb., *Migo* [2]Or, *flock* [a]Mic.
22 [a]Gen. 49:4; 5:1
23 [a]Gen. 29:31 30:18-20; 46:8;
24 [a]Gen. 30:22 35:18
25 [a]Gen. 30:5-8
26 [a]Gen. 30:10-
27 [a]Gen. 13:18; 23:19 [b]Josh. 14:
28 [a]Gen. 25:26
29 [1]Lit., *and sati with days* [a]Gen. 49:33 [b]Gen. 15:1 [c]Gen. 25:9
36:1 [a]Gen. 25:30
2 [a]Gen. 28:9 [b]G 36:25 [c]Gen. 36:2
4 [a]1 Chr. 1:35
6 [1]Lit., *the souls o house* [a]Gen. 12:5
7 [1]Lit., *dwell* [a]Ge 13:6 [b]Gen. 17:8; 11:9 [c]1 Chr. 29:15 39:12
8 [a]Gen. 32:3 [b]Ge 36:1, 19
9 [1]Lit., *Edom*
11 [1]In 1 Chr. 1:36,
12 [a]Ex. 17:8-16; N 24:20; Deut. 25:17- 1 Sam. 15:2, 3
14 [1]Gr., *son* [2]Lit., *she*

15 These are the chiefs of the sons of Esau. The sons of Eliphaz, the
first-born of Esau, are chief Teman, chief Omar, chief Zepho, chief
Kenaz,
16 chief Korah, chief Gatam, chief Amalek. These are the chiefs [1]de-
scended from Eliphaz in the land of Edom; these are the sons of
Adah.
17 And these are the sons of Reuel, Esau's son: chief Nahath, chief
Zerah, chief Shammah, chief Mizzah. These are the chiefs [1]descend-
ed from Reuel in the land of Edom; these are the sons of Esau's wife
Basemath.
18 And these are the sons of Esau's wife Oholibamah: chief Jeush,
chief Jalam, chief Korah. These are the chiefs [1]descended from Esau's
wife Oholibamah, the daughter of Anah.
19 These are the sons of Esau (that is, Edom), and these are their
chiefs.
20 These are the sons of Seir [a]the Horite, the inhabitants of the land:
Lotan and Shobal and Zibeon and Anah,
21 and Dishon and Ezer and Dishan. These are the chiefs [1]descend-
ed from the Horites, the sons of Seir in the land of Edom.
22 And the sons of Lotan were Hori and [1]Hemam; and Lotan's
sister was Timna.
23 And these are the sons of Shobal: [1]Alvan and Manahath and
Ebal, [2]Shepho and Onam.
24 And these are the sons of Zibeon: Aiah and Anah—he is the
Anah who found the hot springs in the wilderness when he was
pasturing the donkeys of his father Zibeon.
25 And these are the children of Anah: Dishon, and Oholibamah,
the daughter of Anah.
26 And these are the sons of [1a]Dishon: [2]Hemdan and Eshban and
Ithran and Cheran.
27 These are the sons of Ezer: Bilhan and Zaavan and [1]Akan.
28 These are the sons of Dishan: Uz and Aran.
29 These are the chiefs [1]descended from the Horites: chief Lotan,
chief Shobal, chief Zibeon, chief Anah,
30 chief Dishon, chief Ezer, chief Dishan. These are the chiefs [1]de-
scended from the Horites, according to their *various* chiefs in the
land of Seir.
31 Now these are the kings who reigned in the land of Edom before
any [a]king reigned over the sons of Israel.
32 [1a]Bela the son of Beor reigned in Edom, and the name of his city
was Dinhabah.
33 Then Bela died, and Jobab the son of Zerah of Bozrah became
king in his place.
34 Then Jobab died, and Husham of the land of the Temanites be-
came king in his place.
35 Then Husham died, and Hadad the son of Bedad, who [1]defeated
Midian in the field of Moab, became king in his place; and the name
of his city was Avith.
36 Then Hadad died, and Samlah of Masrekah became king in his
place.
37 Then Samlah died, and Shaul of Rehoboth on the *Euphrates* River
became king in his place.

Lit., *of Eliphaz*
[1]Lit., *of Reuel*
of Oholibamah, Esau's wife
ien. 14:6; Deut. ; 1 Chr. 1:38-42
t., *of the Horites*
[1]In 1 Chr. 1:39, *Homam*
[1]In 1 Chr. 1:40, [2]In 1 Chr. 1:40, *Shephi*
Heb., *Dishan* [2]In hr. 1:41, *Hamran* [a]1 Chr. 1:41
7 [1]In 1 Chr. 1:42, *Jaakan*
[1]Lit., *of the Horites*
[1]Lit., *of the Horites*
31 [a]Gen. 17:6, 16; 35:11; 1 Chr. 1:43
32 [1]Lit., *And Bela* [a]1 Chr. 1:43
35 [1]Or, *smote*

38 Then Shaul died, and Baal-hanan the son of Achbor became king in his place.
39 Then Baal-hanan the son of Achbor died, and [1]Hadar became king in his place; and the name of his city was [2]Pau; and his wife's name was Mehetabel, the daughter of Matred, daughter of Mezahab.
40 Now these are the names of the chiefs [1]descended from Esau, according to their families *and* their localities, by their names: chief Timna, chief [2]Alvah, chief Jetheth,
41 chief Oholibamah, chief Elah, chief Pinon,
42 chief Kenaz, chief Teman, chief Mibzar,
43 chief Magdiel, chief Iram. These are the chiefs of Edom (that is, Esau, the father of [1]the Edomites), according to their habitations in the land of their possession.

Chapter 37

37 Now Jacob lived in [a]the land [1]where his father had sojourned, in the land of Canaan.
2 These are *the records of* the generations of Jacob.
Joseph, when [a]seventeen years of age, was pasturing the flock with his brothers while he was *still* a youth, along with [b]the sons of Bilhah and the sons of Zilpah, his father's wives. And Joseph brought back a [c]bad report about them to their father.
3 Now Israel loved Joseph more than all his sons, because he was [a]the son of his old age; and he made him a [1b]varicolored tunic.
4 And his brothers saw that their father loved him more than all his brothers; and *so* they [a]hated him and could not speak to him [1]on friendly terms.
5 Then Joseph [1a]had a dream, and when he told it to his brothers, they hated him even more.
6 And he said to them, "Please listen to this dream which I have [1]had;
7 for behold, we were binding sheaves in the field, and lo, my sheaf rose up and also stood erect; and behold, your sheaves gathered around and [a]bowed down to my sheaf."
8 Then his brothers said to him, "[a]Are you actually going to reign over us? Or are you really going to rule over us?" So they hated him even more for his dreams and for his words.
9 Now he [1]had still another dream, and related it to his brothers, and said, "Lo, I have [1]had still another dream; and behold, the sun and the moon and eleven stars were bowing down to me."
10 And he related *it* to his father and to his brothers; and his father rebuked him and said to him, "What is this dream that you have [1]had? Shall I and your mother and [a]your brothers actually come to bow ourselves down before you to the ground?"
11 And [a]his brothers were jealous of him, but his father [b]kept the saying *in mind*.
12 Then his brothers went to pasture their father's flock in Shechem.
13 And Israel said to Joseph, "Are not your brothers pasturing *the flock* in [a]Shechem? Come, and I will send you to them." And he said to him, "[1]I will go."
14 Then he said to him, "Go now and see about the welfare of your brothers and the welfare of the flock; and bring word back to me." So he sent him from the valley of [a]Hebron, and he came to Shechem.

39 [1]In 1 Chr. 1 *Hadad* [2]In 1 C *Pai*

40 [1]Lit., *of Esa* 1 Chr. 1:51, *Ali*

43 [1]Heb., *Edo*

37:1 [1]Lit., *of hi sojournings* [a]G 28:4

2 [a]Gen. 41:46 35:25, 26 [c]1 Sa 2:22-24

3 [1]Or, *full-lengt* [a]Gen. 44:20 [b]G 37:23, 32

4 [1]Lit., *in peace* 27:41; 1 Sam. 1

5 [1]Lit., *dreamed* 28:12; 31:10, 11,

6 [1]Lit., *dreamed*

7 [a]Gen. 42:6, 9; 44:14

8 [a]Gen. 49:26; D 33:16

9 [1]Lit., *dreamed*

10 [1]Lit., *dreamed* [a]Gen. 27:29

11 [a]Acts 7:9 [b]Dan 7:28; Luke 2:19, 51

13 [1]Lit., *Behold me* [a]Gen. 33:18-20

14 [a]Gen. 13:18; 23 19; 35:27; Josh. 14 15; Judg. 1:10

15 And a man found him, and behold, he was wandering in the
field; and the man asked him, [1]"What are you looking for?"
16 And he said, "I am looking for my brothers; please tell me where
they are pasturing *the flock*."
17 Then the man said, "They have moved from here; for I heard
them say, 'Let us go to [a]Dothan.'" So Joseph went after his brothers
and found them at Dothan.
18 [1]When they saw him from a distance and before he came close to
them, they [a]plotted against him to put him to death.
19 And they said to one another, "[1]Here comes this dreamer!
20 "Now then, come and let us kill him and throw him into one of
the pits; and [a]we will say, 'A wild beast devoured him.' Then let us
see what will become of his dreams!"
21 But [a]Reuben heard *this* and rescued him out of their hands and
said, "Let us not [1]take his life."
22 Reuben further said to them, "Shed no blood. Throw him into
this pit that is in the wilderness, but do not lay hands on him"—that
he might rescue him out of their hands, to restore him to his father.
23 So it came about, when Joseph [1]reached his brothers, that they
stripped Joseph of his [2]tunic, the varicolored tunic that was on him;
24 and they took him and threw him into the pit. Now the pit was
empty, without any water in it.
25 Then they sat down to eat [1]a meal. And as they raised their eyes
and looked, behold, a caravan of [a]Ishmaelites was coming from
Gilead, with their camels bearing [2b]aromatic gum and [3c]balm and
[4]myrrh, [5]on their way to bring *them* down to Egypt.
26 And Judah said to his brothers, "What profit is it for us to kill
our brother and [a]cover up his blood?
27 "[a]Come and let us sell him to the Ishmaelites and not lay our
hands on him; for he is our brother, our *own* flesh." And his brothers
listened *to him*.
28 Then some [a]Midianite traders passed by, so they pulled *him* up
and lifted Joseph out of the pit, and [b]sold [1]him to the Ishmaelites for
twenty *shekels* of silver. Thus [c]they brought Joseph into Egypt.
29 Now Reuben returned to the pit, and behold, Joseph was not in
the pit; so he [a]tore his garments.
30 And he returned to his brothers and said, "[a]The boy is not *there*;
as for me, where am I to go?"
31 So [a]they took Joseph's tunic, and slaughtered a male goat, and
dipped the tunic in the blood;
32 and they sent the varicolored tunic and brought it to their father
and said, "We found this; please [1]examine *it* to *see* whether it is your
son's tunic or not."
33 Then he [1]examined it and said, "It is my son's tunic. [a]A wild
beast has devoured him; [b]Joseph has surely been torn to pieces!"
34 So Jacob [a]tore his clothes, and put sackcloth on his loins, and
mourned for his son many days.
35 Then all his sons and all his daughters arose to comfort him, but
he refused to be comforted. And he said, "Surely I will [a]go down to
Sheol in mourning for my son." So his father wept for him.
36 Meanwhile, the [1]Midianites [a]sold him in Egypt to Potiphar, Pha-
raoh's officer, the captain of the bodyguard.

5 [1]Lit., *saying, 'What . . .?'*
17 [a]2 Kin. 6:13
...and [a]Ps. 31:13; ..., 32; Mark 14:1; ...:53; Acts 23:12
...Lit., *Behold, this ... dreams comes*
[a]Gen. 37:32, 33
...t., *smite his soul* [a]Gen. 42:22
...it., *came to* [2]Or, *full-length robe*
[1]Lit., *bread* [2]Or, ...*anum spice* [3]Or, ...*stic* [4]Or, *resinous* ...Lit., *going* [a]Gen. ..., 12; 37:28; 39:1 43:11 [c]Jer. 8:22; 46:11
26 [a]Gen. 37:20
27 [a]Gen. 42:21
...it., *Joseph* [a]Gen. Judg. 6:1-3; 8:22, [b]Gen. 45:4, 5; Ps. ...17; Acts 7:9 [c]Gen. 39:1
...Gen. 37:34; 44:13
...0 [a]Gen. 42:13, 36
31 [a]Gen. 37:3, 23
32 [1]Or, *recognize*
33 [1]Or, *recognized* [a]Gen. 37:20 [b]Gen. 44:28
34 [a]Gen. 37:29
... [a]Gen. 25:8; 35:29; 42:38; 44:29, 31
36 [1]Lit., *Medanites* [a]Gen. 39:1

Chapter 38

38 And it came about at that time, that Judah [1]departed from his
brothers, and [2]visited a certain [a]Adullamite, whose name was
Hirah.
2 And Judah saw there a daughter of a certain Canaanite whose
name was [a]Shua; and he took her and went in to her.
3 So she conceived and bore a son and he named him [a]Er.
4 Then she conceived again and bore a son and named him [a]Onan.
5 And she bore still another son and named him [a]Shelah; and it
was at Chezib [1]that she bore him.
6 Now Judah took a wife for Er his first-born, and her name *was*
Tamar.
7 But [a]Er, Judah's first-born, was evil in the sight of the LORD, so
the LORD took his life.
8 Then Judah said to Onan, "[a]Go in to your brother's wife, and
perform your duty as a brother-in-law to her, and raise up [1]offspring
for your brother."
9 And Onan knew that the [1a]offspring would not be his; so it came
about that when he went in to his brother's wife, he [2]wasted his seed
on the ground, in order not to give [1]offspring to his brother.
10 But what he did was displeasing in the sight of the LORD; so He
[a]took his life also.
11 Then Judah said to his daughter-in-law Tamar, "[a]Remain a
widow in your father's house until my son Shelah grows up"; for he
[1]thought, "[2]*I am afraid* that he too may die like his brothers." So
Tamar went and lived in her father's house.
12 Now [1]after a considerable time Shua's daughter, the wife of
Judah, died; and when [2]the time of mourning was ended, Judah
went up to his sheepshearers at [a]Timnah, he and his friend Hirah the
Adullamite.
13 And it was told to Tamar, "[1]Behold, your father-in-law is going
up to [a]Timnah to shear his sheep."
14 So she [1]removed her widow's garments and [a]covered *herself* with
a [2]veil, and wrapped herself, and sat in the gateway of [3]Enaim,
which is on the road to Timnah; for she saw that Shelah had grown
up, and [b]she had not been given to him as a wife.
15 When Judah saw her, he thought she *was* a harlot, for she had
covered her face.
16 So he turned aside to her by the road, and said, "[1]Here now, let
me come in to you"; for he did not know that she was his daughter-
in-law. And she said, "What will you give me, that you may come in
to me?"
17 He said, therefore, "I will send you a [1]kid from the flock." She
said, moreover, "Will you give a pledge until you send *it?*"
18 And he said, "What pledge shall I give you?" And she said,
"[a]Your seal and your cord, and your staff that is in your hand." So he
gave *them* to her, and went in to her, and she conceived by him.
19 Then she arose and departed, and [1]removed her [2]veil and put on
her widow's garments.
20 When Judah sent the [1]kid by his friend the Adullamite, to receive
the pledge from the woman's hand, he did not find her.
21 And he asked the men of her place, saying, "Where is the temple
prostitute who was by the road at Enaim?" But they said, "There has
been no temple prostitute here."

38:1 [1]Lit., *wen* [2]Lit., *turned asi* [a]Josh. 15:35; 1 22:1

2 [a]1 Chr. 2:3

3 [a]Gen. 46:12; 26:19

4 [a]Gen. 46:12

5 [1]Lit., *when* [a]N 26:20

7 [a]Gen. 46:12; N 26:19; 1 Chr. 2:3

8 [1]Lit., *seed* [a]De 25:5, 6; Matt. 22:

9 [1]Lit., *seed* [2]Lit *spilled on the gro* [a]Deut. 25:6

10 [a]Gen. 46:12; N 26:19

11 [1]Lit., *said* [2]Lit *he also die* [a]Ruth 1:12, 13

12 [1]Lit., *the days became many and Judah was comfo he* [a]Josh. 15:10, 5

13 [1]Lit., *saying, B* [a]Josh. 15:10, 57; J 14:1

14 [1]Lit., *removed herself* [2]Or, *shawl* Josh. 15:34, *Enam* [a]Gen. 24:65 [b]Gen. 38:11, 26

16 [1]Or, *Come, now*

17 [1]Lit., *kid of goat*

18 [a]Gen. 38:25; 41

19 [1]Lit., *removed fr herself* [2]Or, *shawl*

20 [1]Lit., *kid of goats the hand of*

22 So he returned to Judah, and said, "I did not find her; and fur-
thermore, the men of the place said, 'There has been no temple pros-
titute here.'"
23 Then Judah said, "Let her [1]keep them, lest we become a
laughingstock. [2]After all, I sent this kid, but you did not find her."
24 Now it was about three months later that Judah was informed,
"[1]Your daughter-in-law Tamar has played the harlot, and behold,
she is also with child by harlotry." Then Judah said, "Bring her out
and [a]let her be burned!"
25 It was while she was being brought out that she sent to her
father-in-law, saying, "I am with child by the man to whom these
things belong." And she said, "[a]Please examine and see, whose sig-
net ring and cords and staff are these?"
26 And Judah recognized *them*, and said, "[a]She is more righteous
than I, inasmuch as [b]I did not give her to my son Shelah." And he
did not [1]have relations with her again.
27 And it came about at the time she was giving birth, that behold,
there were [a]twins in her womb.
28 Moreover, it took place while she was giving birth, one put out a
hand, and the midwife took and tied a scarlet *thread* on his hand,
saying, "This one came out first."
29 But it came about as he drew back his hand, that behold, his
brother came out. Then she said, "What a breach you have made for
yourself!" So he was named [1a]Perez.
30 And afterward his brother came out who had the scarlet *thread*
on his hand; and he was named [1a]Zerah.

Chapter 39

39 Now Joseph had been taken down to Egypt; and Potiphar, an
Egyptian officer of Pharaoh, the captain of the bodyguard,
bought him [1]from the [a]Ishmaelites, who had taken him down there.
2 And [a]the LORD was with Joseph, so he became a [1]successful man.
And he was in the house of his master, the Egyptian.
3 Now his master [a]saw that the LORD was with him and *how* the
LORD [b]caused all that he did to prosper in his hand.
4 So Joseph [a]found favor in his sight, and [1]became his personal
servant; and he made him overseer over his house, and [b]all that he
owned he put in his [2]charge.
5 And it came about that from the time he made him overseer in
his house, and over all that he owned, the LORD [a]blessed the
Egyptian's house on account of Joseph; thus [b]the LORD's blessing was
upon all that he owned, in the house and in the field.
6 So he left everything he owned in Joseph's [1]charge; and with
him *there* he did not [2]concern himself with anything except the [3]food
which he [4]ate. Now Joseph was [a]handsome in form and appearance.
7 And it came about after these events [a]that his master's wife
[1]looked with desire at Joseph, and she said, "[b]Lie with me."
8 But [a]he refused and said to his master's wife, "Behold, with me
here, my master [1]does not concern himself with anything in the
house, and he has put all that he owns in my [2]charge.
9 "[1a]There is no one greater in this house than I, and he has with-
held nothing from me except you, because you are his wife. How
then could I do this great evil, and [b]sin against God?"

ake for herself [2]Lit., Behold
., saying, Your [a]Lev. 21:9
5 [a]Gen. 37:32
., know her yet [a]1 Sam. 24:17 [b]Gen. 38:14
[a]Gen. 25:24-26
[1]I.e., a breach 6:12; Ruth 4:12
e., a dawning or ess [a]1 Chr. 2:4
1 [1]Lit., from the of [a]Gen. 37:25, , 36; Ps. 105:17
[1]Or, prosperous 9:3, 21, 23; Acts 7:9
en. 21:22; 26:28 [b]Ps. 1:3
[1]Or, ministered to [2]Lit., hand [a]Gen. 9:19 [b]Gen. 24:2; 39:8, 22
en. 30:27 [b]Deut. 28:3, 4, 11
6 [1]Lit., hand [2]Lit., [3]Lit., bread [4]Or, used to eat [a]Gen. :17; 1 Sam. 16:12
[1]Lit., lifted up her s at [a]Prov. 7:15-20 [b]2 Sam. 13:11
Lit., does not know what is in the house [2]Lit., hand [a]Prov. 6:23, 24
r, He is not greater [a]Gen. 41:40 [b]Gen. 20:6; 42:18; 2 Sam. 12:13; Ps. 51:4

10 And it came about as she spoke to Joseph day after day, that he
did not listen to her to lie beside her, *or* be with her.
11 Now it happened [1]one day that he went into the house to do his
work, and none of the men of the household was there inside.
12 And she caught him by his garment, saying, "Lie with me!" And
he left his garment in her hand and fled, and went outside.
13 [1]When she saw that he had left his garment in her hand, and had
fled outside,
14 she called to the men of her household, and said to them, "See,
he has brought in a [1]Hebrew to us to make sport of us; he came in to
me to lie with me, and I [2]screamed.
15 "And it came about when he heard that I raised my voice and
[1]screamed, that he left his garment beside me and fled, and went
outside."
16 So she [1]left his garment beside her until his master came home.
17 Then she [a]spoke to him [1]with these words, "[2]The Hebrew slave,
whom you brought to us, came in to me to make sport of me;
18 and it happened as I raised my voice and [1]screamed, that he left
his garment beside me and fled outside."
19 Now it came about when his master heard the words of his wife,
which she spoke to him, saying, "[1]This is what your slave did to
me," that [a]his anger burned.
20 So Joseph's master took him and [a]put him into the jail, the place
where the king's prisoners were confined; and he was there in the
jail.
21 But [a]the LORD was with Joseph and extended kindness to him,
and [b]gave him favor in the sight of the chief jailer.
22 And the chief jailer [a]committed to Joseph's [1]charge all the
prisoners who were in the jail; so that whatever was done there, he
was [2]responsible *for it*.
23 [a]The chief jailer did not supervise anything under [1]Joseph's
charge because [b]the LORD was with him; and whatever he did, [c]the
LORD made to prosper.

Chapter 40

40 Then it came about after these things [a]the cupbearer and the
baker for the king of Egypt offended their lord, the king of
Egypt.
2 And Pharaoh was [a]furious with his two officials, the chief cup-
bearer and the chief baker.
3 So he put them in confinement in the house of the [a]captain of the
bodyguard, in the jail, the *same* place where Joseph was imprisoned.
4 And the captain of the bodyguard put Joseph in charge of them,
and he [1]took care of them; and they were in confinement for [2]some
time.
5 Then the cupbearer and the baker for the king of Egypt, who
were confined in jail, both had a dream the same night, each man
with his *own* dream *and* each dream with its *own* interpretation.
6 [1]When Joseph came to them in the morning and observed them,
[2]behold, they were dejected.
7 And he asked Pharaoh's officials who were with him in confine-
ment in his master's house, "[1a]Why are your faces so sad today?"
8 Then they said to him, "[a]We have [1]had a dream and there is no

11 [1]Lit., *abou*
13 [1]Lit., *And i… about when*
14 [1]Lit., *Hebre* [2]Lit., *called wit… voice.*
15 [1]Lit., *called*
16 [1]Lit., *let . . .*
17 [1]Lit., *accor* [2]Lit., *saying, "*… 23:1; Prov. 26:2
18 [1]Lit., *called*
19 [1]Lit., *Accor… these things yo* [a]Prov. 6:34
20 [a]Gen. 40:3; … 105:18
21 [a]Gen. 39:2; … 105:19; Acts 7:9 … 3:21; 11:3; 12:36
22 [1]Lit., *hand* [2]L… *doer* [a]Gen. 39:4
23 [1]Lit., *his hand* … 39:3, 8 [b]Gen. 39 … [c]Gen. 39:3
40:1 [a]Gen. 40:11 … Neh. 1:11
2 [a]Prov. 16:14
3 [a]Gen. 39:1, 20
4 [1]Lit., *ministered* [2]Lit., *days*
6 [1]Or, *And* [2]Lit., *a… behold*
7 [1]Lit., *saying, Wh…* [a]Neh. 2:2
8 [1]Lit., *dreamed* [a]… 41:15

1. 41:16; Dan. 2:27, 28

one to interpret it." Then Joseph said to them, "[b]Do not interpretations belong to God? Tell *it* to me, please."

9 So the chief cupbearer told his dream to Joseph, and said to him, "In my dream, [1]behold, *there was* a vine in front of me;

it., and behold

10 and on the vine *were* three branches. And as it was budding, its blossoms came out, *and* its clusters produced ripe grapes.

11 "Now Pharaoh's cup was in my hand; so I took the grapes and squeezed them into Pharaoh's cup, and I put the cup into Pharaoh's [1]hand."

11 [1]Lit., *palm*

12 Then Joseph said to him, "This is the [a]interpretation of it: the three branches are three days;

. 2:36; 4:18, 19

13 within three more days Pharaoh will [1]lift up your head and restore you to your [2]office; and you will put Pharaoh's cup into his hand according to your former custom when you were his cupbearer.

ossibly, *forgive you* [2]Lit., *place*

14 "Only [1]keep me in mind when it goes well with you, and please [a]do me a kindness [2]by mentioning me to Pharaoh, and get me out of this house.

, *remember me urself* [2]Lit., *and on* [a]Josh. 2:12; 20:14; 1 Kin. 2:7

15 "For [a]I was in fact kidnapped from the land of the Hebrews, and even here I have done nothing that they should have put me into the [1]dungeon."

5 [1]Or, *pit* [a]Gen. 37:26-28

16 When the chief baker saw that he had interpreted favorably, he said to Joseph, "I also *saw* in my dream, and behold, *there were* three baskets of white bread on my head;

17 and in the top basket *there were* some of all [1]sorts of baked food for Pharaoh, and the birds were eating them out of the basket on my head."

17 [1]Lit., *food for* *araoh made by a baker*

18 Then Joseph answered and said, "This is its interpretation: the three baskets are three days;

19 within three more days Pharaoh will lift up your head from you and will hang you on a tree; and the birds will eat your flesh off you."

Matt. 14:6 [b]2 Kin. 25:27; Jer. 52:31

20 Thus it came about on the third day, *which was* [a]Pharaoh's birthday, that he made a feast for all his servants; [b]and he lifted up the head of the chief cupbearer and the head of the chief baker among his servants.

Lit., *wine-pouring* *palm* [a]Gen. 40:13

21 And he restored the chief cupbearer to his [1]office, and [a]he put the cup into Pharaoh's [2]hand;

Gen. 40:19; Esth. 7:10

22 but [a]he hanged the chief baker, just as Joseph had interpreted to them.

23 Yet the chief cupbearer did not remember Joseph, but [a]forgot him.

23 [a]Job 19:14; Ps. 31:12; Eccl. 9:15

Chapter 41 ___

41 Now it happened at the end of two full years that Pharaoh had a dream, and behold, he was standing by the Nile.

:2 [1]Lit., *fat of flesh* Job 8:11; Is. 19:6, 7

2 And lo, from the Nile there came up seven cows, sleek and [1]fat; and they grazed in the [a]marsh grass.

3 Then behold, seven other cows came up after them from the Nile, ugly and [1]gaunt, and they stood by the *other* cows on the bank of the Nile.

3 [1]Lit., *lean of flesh*

4 And the ugly and [1]gaunt cows ate up the seven sleek and fat cows. Then Pharaoh awoke.

4 [1]Lit., *lean of flesh*

5 And he fell asleep and dreamed a second time; and behold,
seven ears of grain came up on a single stalk, plump and good.
6 Then behold, seven ears, thin and scorched by the east wind,
sprouted up after them.
7 And the thin ears swallowed up the seven plump and full ears.
Then Pharaoh awoke, and behold, *it was* a dream.
8 Now it came about in the morning that [a]his spirit was troubled,
so he sent and called for all the [1b]magicians of Egypt, and all its [c]wise
men. And Pharaoh told them his [2]dreams, but [d]there was no one
who could interpret them to Pharaoh.
9 Then the chief cupbearer spoke to Pharaoh, saying, "I would
make mention today of [a]my *own* [1]offenses.
10 "Pharaoh was [a]furious with his servants, and [b]he put me in
confinement in the house of the captain of the bodyguard, *both* me
and the chief baker.
11 "And [a]we had a dream [1]on the same night, [2]he and I; each of us
dreamed according to the interpretation of his *own* dream.
12 "Now a Hebrew youth *was* with us there, a [a]servant of the captain
of the bodyguard, and we related *them* to him, and [b]he interpreted
our dreams for us. To each one he interpreted according to his *own*
dream.
13 "And it came about that just [a]as he interpreted for us, so it hap-
pened; he restored me in my [1]office, but he hanged him."
14 Then Pharaoh sent and [a]called for Joseph, and they [b]hurriedly
brought him out of the dungeon; and when he had shaved himself
and changed his clothes, he came to Pharaoh.
15 And Pharaoh said to Joseph, "I have had a dream, [a]but no one
can interpret it; and [b]I have heard [1]it said about you, that [2]when you
hear a dream you can interpret it."
16 Joseph then answered Pharaoh, saying, "[1a]It is not in me; [b]God
will [2]give Pharaoh a favorable answer."
17 So Pharaoh spoke to Joseph, "In my dream, behold, I was stand-
ing on the bank of the Nile;
18 and behold, seven cows, [1]fat and sleek came up out of the Nile;
and they grazed in the marsh grass.
19 "And lo, seven other cows came up after them, poor and very
ugly and [1]gaunt, such as I had never seen for [2]ugliness in all the land
of Egypt;
20 and the lean and [1]ugly cows ate up the first seven fat cows.
21 "Yet when they had [1]devoured them, it could not be [2]detected that
they had [1]devoured them; [3]for they were just as ugly as [4]before. Then
I awoke.
22 "I saw also in my dream, and behold, seven ears, full and good,
came up on a single stalk;
23 and lo, seven ears, withered, thin, *and* scorched by the east wind,
sprouted up after them;
24 and the thin ears swallowed the seven good ears. Then [a]I told it
to the [1]magicians, but there was no one who could explain it to me."
25 Now Joseph said to Pharaoh, "Pharaoh's [1]dreams are one *and the*
same; [a]God has told to Pharaoh what He is about to do.
26 "The seven good cows are seven years; and the seven good ears
are seven years; the [1]dreams are one *and the same.*
27 "And the seven lean and ugly cows that came up after them are

8 [1]Or, *soothsa* *priests* [2]Lit., *d* [a]Dan. 2:1, 3 [b]... 22; Dan. 1:20; [c]Matt. 2:1 [d]Da 4:7

9 [1]Or, *sins* [a]G 40:14, 23

10 [a]Gen. 40:2, 39:20

11 [1]Lit., *one ni* *I and he* [a]Gen.

12 [a]Gen. 37:36 40:12

13 [1]Lit., *place* 40:21, 22

14 [a]Ps. 105:20 2:25

15 [1]Lit., *about y* *saying* [2]Lit., *you* *dream to interpr* [a]Gen. 41:8 [b]Dar

16 [1]Lit., *Apart fr* [2]Lit., *answer the* *of Pharaoh* [a]Dar Zech. 4:6; Acts 3 2 Cor. 3:5 [b]Gen. 41:25, 28, 32; De 29:29; Dan. 2:22,

18 [1]Lit., *fat of fle*

19 [1]Lit., *lean of f* [2]Lit., *badness*

20 [1]Lit., *bad*

21 [1]Lit., *entered t* *inward parts* [2]Or, *known* [3]Lit., *and* *in the beginning*

24 [1]Or, *soothsaye* *priests* [a]Is. 8:19; D 4:7

25 [1]Lit., *dream is* 41:28, 32; Dan. 2:2 29, 45

26 [1]Lit., *dream is*

seven years, and the seven thin ears scorched by the east wind [a]shall
be seven years of famine.
28 "[1]It is as I have spoken to Pharaoh: [a]God has shown to Pharaoh
what He is about to do.
29 "Behold, [a]seven years of great abundance are coming in all the
land of Egypt;
30 and after them [a]seven years of famine will [1]come, and all the
abundance will be forgotten in the land of Egypt; and the famine
will [2]ravage the land.
31 "So the abundance will be unknown in the land because of that
subsequent famine; for it *will be* very severe.
32 "Now as for the repeating of the dream to Pharaoh twice, *it means*
that [a]the matter is determined by God, and God will quickly bring it
about.
33 "And now let Pharaoh look for a man [a]discerning and wise, and
set him over the land of Egypt.
34 "Let Pharaoh take action to appoint overseers [1]in charge of the
land, and let him exact a fifth *of the produce* of the land of Egypt in
the seven years of abundance.
35 "Then let them [a]gather all the food of these good years that are
coming, and store up the grain for food in the cities under Pharaoh's
authority, and let them guard *it*.
36 "And let the food become as a reserve for the land for the seven
years of famine which will occur in the land of Egypt, so that the
land may not perish during the famine."
37 Now the [1]proposal seemed good [2]to Pharaoh and [2]to all his ser-
vants.
38 Then Pharaoh said to his servants, "Can we find a man like this,
[a]in whom is a divine spirit?"
39 So Pharaoh said to Joseph, "Since God has informed you of all
this, there is no one so [a]discerning and wise as you are.
40 "[a]You shall be over my house, and according to your [1]command
all my people shall [2]do homage; only in the throne I will be greater
than you."
41 And Pharaoh said to Joseph, "See I have set you [a]over all the
land of Egypt."
42 Then Pharaoh [a]took off his signet ring from his hand, and put it
on Joseph's hand, and clothed him in garments of fine linen, and
[b]put the gold necklace around his neck.
43 And he had him ride in [1]his second chariot; and they proclaimed
before him, "[2]Bow the knee!" And he set him over all the land of
Egypt.
44 Moreover, Pharaoh said to Joseph, "*Though* I am Pharaoh, yet
[a]without [1]your permission no one shall raise his hand or foot in all
the land of Egypt."
45 Then Pharaoh named Joseph [1]Zaphenath-paneah; and he gave
him Asenath, the daughter of Potiphera priest of [2a]On, as his wife.
And Joseph went forth over the land of Egypt.
46 Now Joseph was [a]thirty years old when he [1]stood before Pha-
raoh, king of Egypt. And Joseph went out from the presence of Pha-
raoh, and went through all the land of Egypt.
47 And during the seven years of plenty the land brought forth
[1]abundantly.
48 So he gathered all the food of *these* seven years which occurred

27 [a]2 Kin. 8:1
it., *That is the which I spoke* ien. 41:25, 32
9 [a]Gen. 41:47
.it., *arise* [2]Lit., [a]Gen. 41:54, 13; Ps. 105:16
Gen. 41:25, 28
3 [a]Gen. 41:39
34 [1]Lit., *over*
35 [a]Gen. 41:48
t., *word* [2]Lit., *in the sight of*
32:8; Dan. 4:8, 9, 18; 5:11, 14
39 [a]Gen. 41:33
Lit., *mouth* [2]Lit., Ps. 105:21; Acts 7:10
[a]Gen. 42:6; Ps. 1; Dan. 6:3; Acts 7:10
[a]Esth. 3:10; 8:2 [b]Dan. 5:7, 16, 29
t., *the second . . . ch was his* [2]Heb., *reck: Attention or Make way*
[1]Lit., *you no one* [a]Ps. 105:22
Probably Egyptian "God speaks; he es" [2]Or, *Heliopolis* 43:13; Ezek. 30:17
6 [1]Or, *entered the vice of* [a]Gen. 37:2
7 [1]Lit., *by handfuls*

in the land of Egypt, and placed the food in the cities; he placed in
every city the food from its own surrounding fields.
49 Thus Joseph stored up grain [1]in great abundance like the sand of
the sea, until he stopped [2]measuring *it*, for it was [3]beyond measure.
50 Now before the year of famine came, [a]two sons were born to
Joseph, whom Asenath, the daughter of Potiphera priest of [1]On, bore
to him.
51 And Joseph named the first-born [1]Manasseh, "For," *he said*, "God
has made me forget all my trouble and all my father's household."
52 And he named the second [1]Ephraim, "For," *he said*, "[a]God has
made me fruitful in the land of my affliction."
53 When the seven years of plenty which had been in the land of
Egypt came to an end,
54 and [a]the seven years of famine began to come, just as Joseph had
said, then there was famine in all the lands; but in all the land of
Egypt there was bread.
55 So when all the land of Egypt was famished, the people cried out
to Pharaoh for bread; and Pharaoh said to all the Egyptians, "Go to
Joseph; [a]whatever he says to you, you shall do."
56 When the famine was *spread* over all the face of the earth, then
Joseph opened all [1]the storehouses, and sold to the Egyptians; and
the famine was severe in the land of Egypt.
57 And *the people of* all the earth came to Egypt to buy grain from
Joseph, because [a]the famine was severe in all the earth.

Chapter 42

42 Now [a]Jacob saw that there was grain in Egypt, and Jacob said
to his sons, "Why are you staring at one another?"
2 And he said, "Behold, [a]I have heard that there is grain in Egypt;
go down there and buy *some* for us [1]from that place, [b]so that we may
live and not die."
3 Then ten brothers of Joseph went down to buy grain from Egypt.
4 But Jacob did not send Joseph's brother [a]Benjamin with his
brothers, for he said, "[1b]I am afraid that harm may befall him."
5 So the sons of Israel came to buy grain among those who were
coming, [a]for the famine was in the land of Canaan *also*.
6 Now [a]Joseph was the ruler over the land; he was the one who
sold to all the people of the land. And Joseph's brothers came and
[b]bowed down to him with *their* faces to the ground.
7 When Joseph saw his brothers he recognized them, but he dis-
guised himself to them and [a]spoke to them harshly. And he said to
them, "Where have you come from?" And they said, "From the land
of Canaan, to buy food."
8 But Joseph had recognized his brothers, although [a]they did not
recognize him.
9 And Joseph [a]remembered the dreams which he [1]had about them,
and said to them, "You are spies; you have come to look at the
[2]undefended parts of our land."
10 Then they said to him, "No, [a]my lord, but your servants have
come to buy food.
11 "We are all sons of one man; we are [a]honest men, your servants
are not spies."
12 Yet he said to them, "No, but you have come to look at the
[1]undefended parts of our land!"

49 [1]Lit., *very m* [2]Lit., *numbering without numbe*
50 [1]Or, *Heliop* [a]Gen. 48:5
51 [1]I.e., makin
52 [1]I.e., fruitful [a]Gen. 17:6; 28:3
54 [a]Gen. 41:30 105:16; Acts 7:1
55 [a]John 2:5
56 [1]Lit., *that wh in them*
57 [a]Gen. 12:10
42:1 [a]Acts 7:12
2 [1]Lit., *from there* 7:12 [b]Gen. 43:8; 33:18, 19
4 [1]Lit., *Lest harm* [a]Gen. 35:24 [b]Gen 42:38
5 [a]Gen. 12:10; 26 41:57; Acts 7:11
6 [a]Gen. 41:41, 55 [b]Gen. 37:7-10; 41 60:14
7 [a]Gen. 42:30
8 [a]Gen. 37:2; 41:4
9 [1]Lit., *had dream* [2]Lit., *nakedness of land* [a]Gen. 37:6-9
10 [a]Gen. 37:8
11 [a]Gen. 42:16, 19, 31, 34
12 [1]Lit., *nakedness the land*

13 But they said, "Your servants are twelve brothers *in all*, the sons
of one man in the land of Canaan; and behold, the youngest is with
[a]our father today, and [b]one is no more."
14 And Joseph said to them, "It is as I said [1]to you, you are spies;
15 by this you will be tested: [a]by the life of Pharaoh, you shall not
go from this place unless your youngest brother comes here!
16 "Send one of you that he may get your brother, while you remain
confined, that your words may be tested, whether there is [a]truth in
you. But if not, by the life of Pharaoh, surely you are spies."
17 So he put them all together in [a]prison for three days.
18 Now Joseph said to them on the third day, "Do this and live, for
[a]I fear God:
19 if you are honest men, let one of your brothers be confined in
[1]your prison; but as for *the rest of* you, go, carry grain for the famine
of your households,
20 and [a]bring your youngest brother to me, so your words may be
verified, and you will not die." And they did so.
21 Then they said to one another, "[a]Truly we are guilty concerning
our brother, because we saw the distress of his soul when he pleaded
with us, yet we would not listen; therefore this distress has come
upon us."
22 And Reuben answered them, saying, "[a]Did I not tell [1]you, 'Do
not sin against the boy'; and you would not listen? [2b]Now comes the
reckoning for his blood."
23 They did not know, however, that Joseph understood, for there
was an interpreter between them.
24 And he turned away from them and [a]wept. But when he
returned to them and spoke to them, he [b]took Simeon from them and
bound him before their eyes.
25 [a]Then Joseph gave orders to fill their bags with grain and to
restore every man's money in his sack, and to give them provisions
for the journey. And thus it was done for them.
26 So they loaded their donkeys with their grain, and departed
from there.
27 And as one *of them* opened his sack to give his donkey fodder at
the lodging place, he saw his [a]money; and behold, it was in the
mouth of his sack.
28 Then he said to his brothers, "My money has been returned, and
behold, it is even in my sack." And their hearts [1]sank, and they
turned [2]trembling to one another, saying, "[a]What is this that God has
done to us?"
29 When they came to their father Jacob in the land of Canaan, they
told him all that had happened to them, saying,
30 "The man, the lord of the land, [a]spoke harshly with us, and took
us for spies of the country.
31 "But we said to him, 'We are [a]honest men; we are not spies.
32 'We are twelve brothers, sons of our father; one is no more, and
the youngest is with our father today in the land of Canaan.'
33 "And the man, the lord of the land, said to us, "[a]By this I shall
know that you are honest men: leave one of your brothers with me
and take *grain for* the famine of your households, and go.
34 'But bring your youngest brother to me that I may know that you
are not spies, but [1]honest men. I will give your brother to you, and
you may [a]trade in the land.' "

n. 43:7 [b]Gen. ; 42:32; 44:20
to you, saying
[a]1 Sam. 17:55
6 [a]Gen. 42:11
[a]Gen. 40:4, 7
Gen. 39:9; Lev. 5:43; Neh. 5:15
it., *the house of your prison*
en. 42:34; 43:5; 44:23
[a]Gen. 37:26-28; 45:3; Hos. 5:15
[1]Lit., *you saying* . *And behold, his also is required* 37:21, 22 [b]Gen. :5, 6; 1 Kin. 2:32; . 24:22; Ps. 9:12
en. 43:30; 45:14, [b]Gen. 43:14, 23
[a]Gen. 44:1; Rom. 20, 21; 1 Pet. 3:9
[a]Gen. 43:21, 22
Lit., *went out* [2]Lit., *mbled* [a]Gen. 43:23
30 [a]Gen. 42:7
31 [a]Gen. 42:11
33 [a]Gen. 42:19, 20
Lit., *you are honest* [a]Gen. 34:10

35 Now it came about as they were emptying their sacks, that be-
hold, [a]every man's bundle of money *was* in his sack; and when they
and their father saw their bundles of money, they were dismayed.
36 And their father Jacob said to them, "You have [a]bereaved me of
my children: Joseph is no more, and Simeon is no more, and you
would take Benjamin; all these things are against me."
37 Then Reuben spoke to his father, saying, "You may put my two
sons to death if I do not bring him *back* to you; put him in my [1]care,
and I will return him to you."
38 But [1]Jacob said, "My son shall not go down with you; for his
[a]brother is dead, and he alone is left. [b]If harm should befall him on
the journey [2]you are taking, then you will [c]bring my gray hair down
to Sheol in sorrow."

35 [a]Gen. 43:1…
36 [a]Gen. 43:1…
37 [1]Lit., *hand*
38 [1]Lit., *he* [2]Li… *which you are g…* [a]Gen. 37:33, 34… 44:27, 28 [b]Gen… [c]Gen. 37:35; 44…

Chapter 43

43 [a]Now the famine was severe in the land.
2 So it came about when they had finished eating the grain
which they had brought from Egypt, that their father said to them,
"Go back, buy us a little food."
3 Judah spoke to him, however, saying, "[a]The man solemnly
warned [1]us, 'You shall not see my face unless your brother is with
you.'
4 "If you send our brother with us, we will go down and buy you
food.
5 "But if you do not send *him,* we will not go down; for the man
said to us, 'You shall not see my face unless your brother is with
you.' "
6 Then Israel said, "Why did you treat me so badly [1]by telling the
man whether you still had *another* brother?"
7 But they said, "The man questioned particularly about us and
our relatives, saying, '[a]Is your father still alive? Have you *another*
brother?' So we [1]answered his questions. Could we possibly know
that he would say, 'Bring your brother down'?"
8 And Judah said to his father Israel, "Send the lad with me, and
we will arise and go, [a]that we may live and not die, we as well as
you and our little ones.
9 "[a]I myself will be surety for him; [1]you may hold me responsible
for him. If I do not bring him *back* to you and set him before you,
then [2]let me bear the blame before you forever.
10 "For if we had not delayed, surely by now we could have
returned twice."
11 Then their father Israel said to them, "If *it must be* so, then do
this: take some of the best products of the land in your [1]bags, and
carry down to the man [a]as a present, a little [2b]balm and a little honey,
[3]aromatic gum and [4]myrrh, pistachio nuts and almonds.
12 "And take double *the* money in your hand, and take back in your
hand [a]the money that was returned in the mouth of your sacks;
perhaps it was a mistake.
13 "Take your brother also, and arise, return to the man;
14 and may [1a]God Almighty [b]grant you compassion in the sight of
the man, that he may release to you [c]your other brother and Ben-
jamin. And as for me, [d]if I am bereaved of my children, I am
bereaved."
15 So the men took [a]this present, and they took double *the* money in

43:1 [a]Gen. 12:… 41:56, 57
3 [1]Lit., *us, sayi…* [a]Gen. 43:5; 44:2…
6 [1]Lit., *to tell*
7 [1]Lit., *told him according to thes… words* [a]Gen. 42:… 43:27
8 [a]Gen. 42:2
9 [1]Lit., *from my h… you may require h…* [2]Lit., *I shall have s… before you all the…* [a]Gen. 42:37; 44:3… Philem. 18, 19
11 [1]Or, *vessels* [2]… *mastic* [3]Or, *ladan… spice* [4]Or, *resinou… bark* [a]Gen. 32:20; 43:25, 26 [b]Gen. 3… Jer. 8:22; Ezek. 27…
12 [a]Gen. 42:25, 3… 43:21, 22
14 [1]Heb., *El Shad…* [a]Gen. 17:1; 28:3; 3… [b]Ps. 106:46 [c]Gen. 42:24 [d]Gen. 42:36
15 [a]Gen. 43:11

their hand, and Benjamin; then they arose and went down to Egypt
and stood before Joseph.
16 When Joseph saw Benjamin with them, he said to his [a]house
steward, "Bring the men into the house, and slay *an animal* and make
ready; for the men are to dine with me at noon."
17 So the man did as Joseph said, and [1]brought the men to Joseph's
house.
18 Now the men were afraid, because they were brought to
Joseph's house; and they said, "*It is* because of the money that was
returned in our sacks the first time that we are being brought in, that
he may [1]seek occasion against us and fall upon us, and take us for
slaves with our donkeys."
19 So they came near to Joseph's house steward, and spoke to him
at the entrance of the house,
20 and said, "Oh, my lord, we indeed came down the first time to
buy food,
21 and it came about when we came to the lodging place, that we
opened our sacks, and behold, [a]each man's money was in the mouth
of his sack, our money in [1]full. So [b]we have brought it back in our
hand.
22 "We have also brought down other money in our hand to buy
food; we do not know who put our money in our sacks."
23 And he said, "[1]Be at ease, do not be afraid. [a]Your God and the
God of your father has given you treasure in your sacks; [2]I had your
money." Then [b]he brought Simeon out to them.
24 Then the man brought the men into Joseph's house and [a]gave
them water, and they [b]washed their feet; and he gave their donkeys
fodder.
25 So they prepared [a]the present [1]for Joseph's coming at noon; for
they had heard that they were to eat [2]a meal there.
26 When Joseph came home, they brought into the house to him the
present which was in their hand and [a]bowed to the ground before
him.
27 Then he asked them about their welfare, and said, "[a]Is your old
father well, of whom you spoke? Is he still alive?"
28 And they said, "Your servant our father is well; he is still alive."
[a]And they bowed down [1]in homage.
29 As he lifted his eyes and saw his brother Benjamin, his mother's
son, he said, "Is this [a]your youngest brother, of whom you spoke to
me?" And he said, "[b]May God be gracious to you, my son."
30 And Joseph hurried *out* for [1a]he was deeply stirred over his
brother, and he sought *a place* to weep; and he entered his chamber
and [b]wept there.
31 Then he washed his face, and came out; and he [a]controlled him-
self and said, "[1]Serve the meal."
32 So they served him by himself, and them by themselves, and the
Egyptians, who ate with him, by themselves; because the Egyptians
could not eat bread with the Hebrews, for that is [1a]loathsome to the
Egyptians.
33 Now they [1]were seated before him, [a]the first-born according to
his birthright and the youngest according to his youth, and the men
looked at one another in astonishment.
34 And he took portions to them from [1]his own table; [a]but

16 [a]Gen. 44:1
[1]Lit., *the man brought*
Lit., *roll himself upon us*
[1]Lit., *its weight* 2:27, 35 [b]Gen. 43:12, 15
.it., *Peace be to* .it., *your money* *ne to me* [a]Gen. 28 [b]Gen. 42:24
Gen. 18:4; 19:2; Luke 7:44; John 3:5; 1 Tim. 5:10
[1]Lit., *until* [2]Lit., [a]Gen. 43:11, 15
5 [a]Gen. 37:7, 10
[a]Gen. 43:7; 45:3
t., *and prostrated* *hemselves* [a]Gen. 37:7, 10
ien. 42:13 [b]Num. 6:25; Ps. 67:1
., *his compassion* *warm* [a]1 Kin. 3:26 1. 42:24; 45:2, 14, 15; 46:29
[1]Lit., *Set on bread.* [a]Gen. 45:1
32 [1]Lit., *an* *abomination* [a]Gen. 46:34; Ex. 8:26
.it., *sat* [a]Gen. 42:7
Lit., *his face* [a]Gen. 35:24; 45:22

Benjamin's portion was five times as much as any of theirs. So they
feasted and drank freely with him.

Chapter 44

44 [a]Then he commanded his house steward, saying, "Fill the
men's sacks with food, as much as they can carry, and put
each man's money in the mouth of his sack.
2 "And put my cup, the silver cup, in the mouth of the sack of the
youngest, and his money for the grain." And he did [1]as Joseph had
told *him*.
3 [1]As soon as it was light, the men were sent away, they with their
donkeys.
4 They had *just* gone out of [a]the city, *and* were not far off, when
Joseph said to his house steward, "Up, follow the men; and when
you overtake them, say to them, 'Why have you repaid evil for
good?
5 'Is not this the one from which my lord drinks, and which he
indeed uses for [a]divination? You have done wrong in doing this.' "
6 So he overtook them and spoke these words to them.
7 And they said to him, "Why does my lord speak such words as
these? Far be it from your servants to do such a thing.
8 "Behold, [a]the money which we found in the mouth of our sacks
we have brought back to you from the land of Canaan. How then
could we steal silver or gold from your lord's house?
9 "[a]With whomever of your servants it is found, let him die, and we
also will be my lord's [b]slaves."
10 So he said, "Now let it also be according to your words; he with
whom it is found shall be my slave, and *the rest of* you shall be
innocent."
11 Then they hurried, each man lowered his sack to the ground,
and each man opened his sack.
12 And he searched, beginning with the oldest and ending with the
youngest, and [a]the cup was found in Benjamin's sack.
13 Then they [a]tore their clothes, and when each man loaded his
donkey, they returned to [b]the city.
14 When Judah and his brothers came to Joseph's house, he was
still there, and [a]they fell to the ground before him.
15 And Joseph said to them, "What is this deed that you have
done? Do you not know that such a man as I can indeed practice
[a]divination?"
16 So Judah said, "What can we say to my lord? What can we
speak? And how can we justify ourselves? God has found out the
iniquity of your servants; behold, we are my lord's [a]slaves, both we
and the one in whose [1]possession the cup has been found."
17 But he said, "Far be it from me to do this. The man in whose
[1]possession the cup has been found, he shall be my slave; but as for
you, go up in peace to your father."
18 Then Judah approached him, and said, "Oh my lord, may your
servant please speak a word in my lord's ears, and [1a]do not be angry
with your servant; for [b]you are equal to Pharaoh.
19 "[a]My lord asked his servants, saying, 'Have you a father or a
brother?'
20 "And we said to my lord, 'We have an old father and [a]a little child

44:1 [a]Gen. 42:25
2 [1]Or, *according to word*
3 [1]Lit., *The morning was light*
4 [a]Gen. 44:13
5 [a]Gen. 30:27; 44:1[illegible] Lev. 19:26; Deut. 18:10-14
8 [a]Gen. 43:21
9 [a]Gen. 31:32 [b]Gen[illegible] 44:16
12 [a]Gen. 44:2
13 [a]Gen. 37:29, 34; Num. 14:6; 2 Sam. 1[illegible] [b]Gen. 44:4
14 [a]Gen. 37:7, 10
15 [a]Gen. 44:5
16 [1]Lit., *hand* [a]Gen. 44:9
17 [1]Lit., *hand*
18 [1]Lit., *let not your anger burn against* [a]Gen. 18:30, 32; Ex. 32:22 [b]Gen. 37:7, 8[illegible] 41:40-44
19 [a]Gen. 43:7
20 [a]Gen. 37:3; 43:8[illegible] 44:30

of *his* old age. Now [b]his brother is dead, so he alone is left of his
mother, and his father loves him.'
21 "Then you said to your servants, '[a]Bring him down to me, that I
may set my eyes on him.'
22 "But we said to my lord, 'The lad cannot leave his father, for if he
should leave his father, [1]his father would die.'
23 "You said to your servants, however, '[a]Unless your youngest
brother comes down with you, you shall not see my face again.'
24 "Thus it came about when we went up to your servant my father,
we told him the words of my lord.
25 "And [a]our father said, 'Go back, buy us a little food.'
26 "But we said, 'We cannot go down. If our youngest brother is
with us, then we will go down; for we cannot see the man's face
unless our youngest brother is with us.'
27 "And your servant my father said to us, 'You know that [a]my wife
bore me two sons;
28 and the one went out from me, and [a]I said, "Surely he is torn in
pieces," and I have not seen him since.
29 'And if you take this one also from [1]me, and harm befalls him,
you will [a]bring my gray hair down to Sheol in [2]sorrow.'
30 "Now, therefore, when I come to your servant my father, and the
lad is not with us, since [1a]his life is bound up in the lad's life,
31 it will come about when he sees that the lad is not *with us*, that
he will die. Thus your servants will [a]bring the gray hair of your
servant our father down to Sheol in sorrow.
32 "For your servant [a]became surety for the lad to my father, saying,
'If I do not bring him *back* to you, then [1]let me bear the blame before
my father forever.'
33 "Now, therefore, please let your servant remain instead of the lad
a slave to my lord, and let the lad go up with his brothers.
34 "For how shall I go up to my father if the lad is not with me, lest I
see the evil that would [1]overtake my father?"

Chapter 45

45 Then Joseph could not control himself before all those who
stood by him, and he cried, "Have everyone go out from me."
So there [1]was no man with him [a]when Joseph made himself known
to his brothers.
2 And [a]he [1]wept so loudly that the Egyptians heard *it*, and the
household of Pharaoh heard *of it*.
3 Then Joseph said to his brothers, "[a]I am Joseph! [b]Is my father still
alive?" But his brothers could not answer him, for [c]they were dis-
mayed at his presence.
4 Then Joseph said to his brothers, "Please come [1]closer to me."
And they came [1]closer. And he said, "I am your brother Joseph,
whom you [a]sold into Egypt.
5 "And now do not be grieved or angry [1]with yourselves, because
[a]you sold me here; for [b]God sent me before you to preserve life.
6 "For the famine *has been* in the land [a]these two years, and there are
still five years in which there will be neither plowing nor harvesting.
7 "And [a]God sent me before you to preserve for you a remnant in
the earth, and to keep you alive by a great [1]deliverance.
8 "Now, therefore, it was not you who sent me here, but God; and

[b]Gen. 37:33; 42:13, 38
[a]Gen. 42:15, 20
[1]Lit., *he would*
[a]Gen. 43:3, 5
25 [a]Gen. 43:2
27 [a]Gen. 46:19
[a]Gen. 37:31-35
[1]Lit., *my face* [2]Lit., ... [a]Gen. 42:38; 44:31
[1]Lit., *his soul is ... and with his soul* [a]1 Sam. 18:1
31 [a]Gen. 44:29
[1]Lit., *and I shall ... sinned for all the ... before my father* [a]Gen. 43:9
34 [1]Lit., *find*
[1]Lit., *stood* [a]Acts 7:13
[1]Lit., *gave forth his ... in weeping* [a]Gen. 45:14, 15; 46:29
[a]Acts 7:13 [b]Gen. ... [c]Gen. 37:20-28; 42:21, 22
[1]Lit., *near* [a]Gen. 37:28
[1]Lit., *in your eyes* [a]Gen. 37:28 [b]Gen. 45:7, 8; 50:20; Ps. 105:17
[a]Gen. 37:2; 41:46, 53
7 [1]Lit., *escaped company* [a]Gen. 45:5

He has made me a [a]father to Pharaoh and lord of all his household
and ruler over all the land of Egypt.
9 "Hurry and go up to my father, and [a]say to him, 'Thus says your
son Joseph, "God has made me lord of all Egypt; come down to me,
do not delay.
10 "And you shall [1]live in the land of [a]Goshen, and you shall be near
me, you and your children and your children's children and your
flocks and your herds and all that you have.
11 "There I will also [a]provide for you, for there are still five years of
famine *to come*, lest you and your household and all that you have be
impoverished."'
12 "And behold, your eyes see, and the eyes of my brother Benjamin
see, that it is my mouth which is speaking to you.
13 "Now you must tell my father of all my splendor in Egypt, and all
that you have seen; and you must hurry and [a]bring my father down
here."
14 Then he fell on his brother Benjamin's neck and [a]wept; and Ben-
jamin wept on his neck.
15 And he kissed all his brothers and wept on them, and afterward
his brothers talked with him.
16 Now when [a]the [1]news was heard in Pharaoh's house [2]that
Joseph's brothers had come, it [3]pleased Pharaoh and his servants.
17 Then Pharaoh said to Joseph, "Say to your brothers, 'Do this:
load your beasts and [1]go to the land of Canaan,
18 and take your father and your households and come to me, and
[a]I will give you the [1]best of the land of Egypt and you shall eat the
fat of the land.'
19 "Now you are ordered, 'Do this: [1]take [a]wagons from the land of
Egypt for your little ones and for your wives, and bring your father
and come.
20 'And do not [1]concern yourselves with your goods, for the [2]best of
all the land of Egypt is yours.' "
21 Then the sons of Israel did so; and Joseph gave them [a]wagons
according to the [1]command of Pharaoh, and gave them provisions
for the journey.
22 To [1]each of them he gave [a]changes of garments, but to Benjamin
he gave three hundred *pieces of* silver and [b]five changes of garments.
23 And to his father he sent [1]as follows: ten donkeys loaded with
the [2]best things of Egypt, and ten female donkeys loaded with grain
and bread and sustenance for his father [3]on the journey.
24 So he sent his brothers away, and [1]as they departed, he said to
them, "Do not [2]quarrel on the journey."
25 Then they went up from Egypt, and came to the land of Canaan
to their father Jacob.
26 And they told him, saying, "Joseph is still alive, and indeed he is
ruler over all the land of Egypt." But [1]he was stunned, for [a]he did not
believe them.
27 When they told him all the words of Joseph that he had spoken
to them, and when he saw the [a]wagons that Joseph had sent to carry
him, the spirit of their father Jacob revived.
28 Then Israel said, "It is enough; my son Joseph is still alive. I will
go and see him before I die."

8 [a]Judg. 17:10
9 [a]Acts 7:14
10 [1]Lit., *dwell* [a]
46:28, 34; 47:1
11 [a]Gen. 47:12
13 [a]Acts 7:14
14 [a]Gen. 45:2
16 [1]Lit., *voice* [a]
saying, ""Joseph
brothers have co
[3]Lit., *was good in*
eyes of [a]Acts 7:1
17 [1]Lit., *come, g*
18 [1]Lit., *good* [a]G
27:28
19 [1]Lit., *take for*
yourselves [a]Gen.
45:21, 27; 46:5; N
7:3-8
20 [1]Lit., *let your e*
look with regret up
your vessels [2]Lit.,
21 [1]Lit., *mouth* [a]G
45:19
22 [1]Lit., *all of them*
gave each man [a]2
5:5 [b]Gen. 43:34
23 [1]Lit., *like this* [2]L
good [3]Lit., *for*
24 [1]Lit., *they depar*
and he said [2]Lit., *be*
agitated
26 [1]Lit., *his heart gr*
numb [a]Gen. 37:31-
27 [a]Gen. 45:19

Chapter 46

46 So Israel set out with all that he had, and came to [a]Beersheba,
and offered sacrifices to the [b]God of his father Isaac.
2 And [a]God spoke to Israel [1]in visions of the night and said,
"[b]Jacob, Jacob." And he said, "Here I am."
3 And He said, "[a]I am God, the God of your father; do not be
afraid to go down to Egypt, for I will [b]make you a great nation there.
4 "[a]I will go down with you to Egypt, and [b]I will also surely bring
you up again; and [c]Joseph will [1]close your eyes."
5 Then Jacob arose from Beersheba; and the sons of Israel carried
their father Jacob and their little ones and their wives, in the [a]wagons
which Pharaoh had sent to carry him.
6 And they took their livestock and their property, which they had
acquired in the land of Canaan, and [a]came to Egypt, Jacob and all his
[1]descendants with him:
7 his sons and his grandsons with him, his daughters and his
granddaughters, and all his [1]descendants he brought with him to
Egypt.
8 Now these are the [a]names of the sons of Israel, Jacob and his
sons, who went to Egypt: Reuben, Jacob's first-born.
9 And the sons of Reuben: Hanoch and Pallu and Hezron and
Carmi.
10 And the [a]sons of Simeon: [1]Jemuel and Jamin and Ohad and
[2]Jachin and [3]Zohar and Shaul the son of a Canaanite woman.
11 And the sons of Levi: [1]Gershon, Kohath, and Merari.
12 And the sons of Judah: Er and Onan and Shelah and Perez and
Zerah (but Er and Onan died in the land of Canaan). And the [a]sons
of Perez were Hezron and Hamul.
13 And the sons of Issachar: Tola and [1]Puvvah and [2]Iob and Shim-
ron.
14 And the sons of Zebulun: Sered and Elon and Jahleel.
15 These are the sons of Leah, whom she bore to Jacob in Paddan-
aram, with his daughter Dinah; [1]all his sons and his daughters *num-
bered* thirty-three.
16 And the [a]sons of Gad: [1]Ziphion and Haggi, Shuni and [2]Ezbon,
Eri and [3]Arodi and Areli.
17 And the [a]sons of Asher: Imnah and Ishvah and Ishvi and Beriah
and their sister Serah. And the [b]sons of Beriah: Heber and Malchiel.
18 These are the sons of Zilpah, whom Laban gave to his daughter
Leah; and she bore to Jacob these sixteen persons.
19 The sons of Jacob's wife Rachel: Joseph and Benjamin.
20 [a]Now to Joseph in the land of Egypt were born Manasseh and
Ephraim, whom Asenath, the daughter of Potiphera, priest of On,
bore to him.
21 And the [a]sons of Benjamin: Bela and Becher and Ashbel, Gera
and Naaman, [1]Ehi and Rosh, [2]Muppim and [3]Huppim and Ard.
22 These are the sons of Rachel, who were born to Jacob; *there were*
fourteen persons in all.
23 And the sons of Dan: [1]Hushim.
24 And the sons of Naphtali: [1]Jahzeel and Guni and Jezer and
[2]Shillem.
25 These are the [a]sons of Bilhah, whom [b]Laban gave to his daughter
Rachel, and she bore these to Jacob; *there were* seven persons in all.
26 [a]All the persons belonging to Jacob, who came to Egypt, [1]his

[a]Gen. 21:31; [b]Gen. 26:24; 28:13; 31:42
n the visions ; Num. 12:6; 4, 15 [b]Gen. 22:11; 31:11
. 17:1; 28:13 12:2; Ex. 1:9; Deut. 26:5
t his hand on 28:15; 48:21 50:24; Ex. 3:8 [c]Gen. 50:1
[a]Gen. 45:21
, *seed* [a]Deut. osh. 24:4; Ps. Is. 52:4; Acts 7:15
7 [1]Lit., *seed*
x. 1:1-4; Num. 5; 1 Chr. 2:1ff.
um. 26:12 and 4, *Nemuel* [2]In 4:24, *Jarib* [3]In :13 and 1 Chr. *erah* [a]Ex. 6:15
[1]In 1 Chr. 6:16, *Gershom*
12 [a]1 Chr. 2:5
[1]In Num. 26:23, *h;* in 1 Chr. 7:1, [2]In Num. 26:24 hr. 7:1, *Jashub*
, *all the souls of*
[1]In Num. 26:15, *ephon* [2]In Num. , *Ozni* [3]In Num. 17, *Arod* [a]Num. 26:15-18
hr. 7:30 [b]1 Chr. 7:31
[a]Gen. 41:50-52
[1]In Num. 26:38, [2]In Num. 26:39, *upham;* in 1 Chr. 12, *Shuppim* [3]In . 26:39, *Hupham* [a]1 Chr. 7:6
[1]In Num. 26:42, *Shuham*
4 [1]In 1 Chr. 7:13, *el* [2]In 1 Chr. 7:13, *Shallum*
en. 30:5, 7 [b]Gen. 29:29
.it., *who came out his loins* [a]Ex. 1:5

direct descendants, not including the wives of Jacob's sons, *were* sixty-six persons in all,

27 and the sons of Joseph, who were born to him in Egypt were [1]two; [a]all the persons of the house of Jacob, who came to Egypt, *were* seventy.

28 Now he sent Judah before him to Joseph, to point out *the way* before him to [a]Goshen; and they came into the land of Goshen.

29 And Joseph [1]prepared his chariot and went up to Goshen to meet his father Israel; as soon as he appeared [2]before him, he fell on his neck and [a]wept on his neck a long time.

30 Then Israel said to Joseph, "Now let me die, since I have seen your face, that you are still alive."

31 And Joseph said to his brothers and to his father's household, "[a]I will go up and tell Pharaoh, and will say to him, 'My brothers and my father's household, who *were* in the land of Canaan, have come to me;

32 and the men are shepherds, for they have been [1]keepers of livestock; and they have brought their flocks and their herds and all that they have.'

33 "And it shall come about when Pharaoh calls you and says, '[a]What is your occupation?'

34 that you shall say, 'Your servants have been [1a]keepers of livestock from our youth even until now, both we and our fathers,' that you may [2]live in the land of [b]Goshen; for every shepherd is [3c]loathsome to the Egyptians."

Chapter 47

47 Then [a]Joseph went in and told Pharaoh, and said, "My father and my brothers and their flocks and their herds and all that they have, have come out of the land of Canaan; and behold, they are in the land of [b]Goshen."

2 And he took five men from among his brothers, and [a]presented them to Pharaoh.

3 Then Pharaoh said to his brothers, "[a]What is your occupation?" So they said to Pharaoh, "Your servants are [b]shepherds, both we and our fathers."

4 And they said to Pharaoh, "[a]We have come to sojourn in the land, for there is no pasture for your servants' flocks, for [b]the famine is severe in the land of Canaan. Now, therefore, please let your servants [1c]live in the land of Goshen."

5 Then Pharaoh said to [1]Joseph, "Your father and your brothers have come to you.

6 "The land of Egypt is [1]at your disposal; [2]settle your father and your brothers in [a]the best of the land, let them [3]live in the land of Goshen; and if you know any [b]capable men among them, then [4]put them in charge of my livestock."

7 Then Joseph brought his father Jacob and [1]presented him to Pharaoh; and Jacob [a]blessed Pharaoh.

8 And Pharaoh said to Jacob, "How many [1]years have you lived?"

9 So Jacob said to Pharaoh, "The [1a]years of my sojourning are one hundred and [2]thirty; few and [3]unpleasant have been the [1]years of my life, nor have they [4]attained [b]the [1]years [5]that my fathers lived during the days of their sojourning."

10 And Jacob [a]blessed Pharaoh, and went out from [1]his presence.

27 [1]Lit., *two s* 1:5; Deut. 10:2 7:14

28 [a]Gen. 45:1

29 [1]Lit., *tied, harnessed* [2]Li [a]Gen. 45:14, 1

31 [a]Gen. 47:1

32 [1]Lit., *men*

33 [a]Gen. 47:2,

34 [1]Lit., *men* [2] *dwell* [3]Lit., *an abomination* [a]C 13:7, 8; 26:20; [b]Gen. 45:10, 18 11 [c]Gen. 43:32

47:1 [a]Gen. 46: [b]Gen. 45:10; 46

2 [a]Acts 7:13

3 [a]Gen. 46:33 46:34

4 [1]Lit., *dwell* [a]G 15:13; Deut. 26: 105:23 [b]Gen. 43 7:11 [c]Gen. 46:3

5 [1]Lit., *Joseph,*

6 [1]Lit., *before yo cause them to dw* [3]Lit., *dwell* [4]Lit., *them rulers* [a]Ger 45:10, 18; 47:11 18:21, 25; 1 Kin. Prov. 22:29

7 [1]Lit., *set him be* [a]Gen. 47:10; 2 Sa 14:22; 1 Kin. 8:66

8 [1]Lit., *are the da the years of your*

9 [1]Lit., *days of the years* [2]Lit., *thirty* [3]Lit., *evil* [4]Lit., *rea* [5]Lit., *of the life of r fathers* [a]Heb. 11:9 [b]Gen. 25:7; 35:28

10 [1]Lit., *Pharaoh'* [a]Gen. 47:7

11 So Joseph [1]settled his father and his brothers, and gave them a possession in the land of Egypt, in [a]the best of the land, in the land of [b]Rameses, as Pharaoh had ordered.

12 And Joseph [a]provided his father and his brothers and all his father's household with [1]food, according to their little ones.

13 Now there was no [1]food in all the land, because the famine was very severe, so that [a]the land of Egypt and the land of Canaan languished because of the famine.

14 And [a]Joseph gathered all the money that was found in the land of Egypt and in the land of Canaan for the grain which they bought, and Joseph brought the money into Pharaoh's house.

15 And when the money was all spent in the land of Egypt and in the land of Canaan, all the Egyptians came to Joseph [1]and said, "Give us [2]food, for [a]why should we die in your presence? For *our* money [3]is gone."

16 Then Joseph said, "Give up your livestock, and I will give you *food* for your livestock, since *your* money [1]is gone."

17 So they brought their livestock to Joseph, and Joseph gave them [1]food in exchange for the horses and the [2]flocks and the herds and the donkeys; and he [3]fed them with [1]food in exchange for all their livestock [4]that year.

18 And when that year was ended, they came to him the [1]next year and said to him, "We will not hide from my lord that our money is all spent, and the [2]cattle are my lord's. There is nothing left [3]for my lord except our bodies and our lands.

19 "Why should we die before your eyes, both we and our land? Buy us and our land for [1]food, and we and our land will be slaves to Pharaoh. So give us seed, that we may live and not die, and that the land may not be desolate."

20 So Joseph bought all the land of Egypt for Pharaoh, for [1]every Egyptian sold his field, because the famine was severe upon them. Thus the land became Pharaoh's.

21 And as for the people, he removed them to the cities from one end of Egypt's border to the other.

22 Only the land of the priests he did not buy, for the priests had an allotment from Pharaoh, and they [1]lived off the allotment which Pharaoh gave them. Therefore, they did not sell their land.

23 Then Joseph said to the people, "Behold, I have today bought you and your land for Pharaoh; now, *here* is seed for you, and you may sow the land.

24 "And [1]at the harvest you shall give a [a]fifth to Pharaoh, and [2]four-fifths shall be your own for seed of the field and for your food and for those of your households and as food for your little ones."

25 So they said, "You have saved our lives! Let us find favor in the sight of my lord, and we will be Pharaoh's slaves."

26 And Joseph made it a statute concerning the land of Egypt *valid* to this day, that Pharaoh should have the fifth; [a]only the land of the priests [1]did not become Pharaoh's.

27 Now Israel [1]lived in the land of Egypt, in [2]Goshen, and they [a]acquired property in it and [b]were fruitful and became very numerous.

28 And Jacob lived in the land of Egypt [a]seventeen years; so the [1]length of Jacob's life was one hundred and forty-seven years.

29 When [1a]the time for Israel to die drew near, he called his son

, caused to ...en. 47:6, 27 1:11; 12:37
...read [a]Gen. 45:11
...read [a]Gen. ...30; Acts 7:11
[a]Gen. 41:56
saying [2]Or, [3]Lit., ceases [a]Gen. 47:19
[1]Lit., ceases
..., bread [2]Lit., ...k of the flocks ...estock of the ..., led them as ...d [4]Lit., in that year
second [2]Lit., ...k of the cattle ...e presence of
19 [1]Or, bread
..., Egypt, every man
[1]Lit., ate their allotment
...., it shall come ... that you shall ...ur parts [a]Gen. 41:34
[1]Lit., alone did [a]Gen. 47:22
...., dwelt [2]Lit., in land of Goshen ...:11 [b]Gen. 17:6; ...; 35:11; Ex. 1:7; 26:5; Acts 7:17
..., days of Jacob, ...e years of his life [a]Gen. 47:9
[1]Lit., the days of ...to die drew near 31:14; 1 Kin. 2:1

Joseph and said to him, "Please, if I have found favor in your sight,
[b]place now your hand under my thigh and [c]deal with me in kindness
and [2]faithfulness. Please do not bury me in Egypt,
30 but when I [a]lie down with my fathers, you shall carry me out of
Egypt and bury me in [b]their burial place." And he said, "I will do as
you have said."
31 And he said, "[a]Swear to me." So he swore to him. Then [b]Israel
bowed *in worship* at the head of the bed.

Chapter 48

48 Now it came about after these things that [1]Joseph was told,
"Behold, your father is sick." So he took his two sons [a]Ma-
nasseh and Ephraim with him.
2 When [1]it was told to Jacob, "Behold, your son Joseph has come
to you," Israel [2]collected his strength and sat [3]up in the bed.
3 Then Jacob said to Joseph, "[1a]God Almighty appeared to me at
[b]Luz in the land of Canaan and blessed me,
4 and He said to me, 'Behold, I will make you fruitful and
numerous, and I will make you a company of peoples, and will give
this land to your [1]descendants after you for [a]an everlasting posses-
sion.'
5 "And now your two sons, who were born to you in the land of
Egypt before I came to you in Egypt, are mine; [a]Ephraim and Manas-
seh shall be mine, as [b]Reuben and Simeon are.
6 "But your offspring that [1]have been born after them shall be
yours; they shall be called by the [2]names of their brothers in their
inheritance.
7 "Now as for me, when I came from [a]Paddan, [b]Rachel died, [1]to my
sorrow, in the land of Canaan on the journey, when there was still
some distance to go to Ephrath; and I buried her there on the way to
Ephrath (that is, Bethlehem)."
8 When Israel [a]saw Joseph's sons, he said, "Who are these?"
9 And Joseph said to his father, "[a]They are my sons, whom God
has given me here." So he said, "Bring them to me, please, that [b]I
may bless them."
10 Now [a]the eyes of Israel were *so* dim from age *that* he could not
see. Then [1]Joseph brought them close to him, and he [b]kissed them
and embraced them.
11 And Israel said to Joseph, "I never [1]expected to see your face,
and behold, God has let me see your [2]children as well."
12 Then Joseph [1]took them from his knees, and [a]bowed with his
face to the ground.
13 And Joseph took them both, Ephraim with his right hand
toward Israel's left, and Manasseh with his left hand toward Israel's
right, and brought them close to him.
14 But Israel stretched out his right hand and laid it on the head of
Ephraim, who was the younger, and his left hand on Manasseh's
head, [1]crossing his hands, [2]although [a]Manasseh was the first-born.
15 And he blessed Joseph, and said,

"[a]The God before whom my fathers Abraham and Isaac walked,
[b]The God who has been my shepherd [1]all my life to this day,
16 [a]The angel who has redeemed me from all evil,
[b]Bless the lads;
And may my name [1]live on in them,

29 [2]Lit., *truth* 24:2 [c]Gen. 2

30 [a]Gen. 15:1 31:16 [b]Gen. 2 25:9, 10; 35:2 49:29-32; 50:5 7:15, 16

31 [a]Gen. 21:2 24:3; 31:53; 50 [b]1 Kin. 1:47

48:1 [1]Lit., *one Joseph* [a]Gen. 52; Josh. 14:4

2 [1]Lit., *one to and said* [2]Lit., *strengthened* [3]Lit., *upon the*

3 [1]Heb., *El Sh* [a]Gen. 28:13f.; [b]Gen. 28:19; 3

4 [1]Lit., *seed* [a]

5 [a]Gen. 41:50- 46:20; 48:1; Jos [b]1 Chr. 5:1, 2

6 [1]Lit., *you hav begotten* [2]Lit.,

7 [1]Lit., *upon me* 33:18 [b]Gen. 35

8 [a]Gen. 48:10

9 [a]Gen. 33:5 [b]G 27:4

10 [1]Lit., *he* [a]Ge [b]Gen. 27:27

11 [1]Lit., *meditate judged* [2]Lit., *see*

12 [1]Lit., *made th come out* [a]Gen.

14 [1]Or, *consciou directing* [2]Lit., *wh* [a]Gen. 41:51, 52

15 [1]Lit., *from the continuance of m* [a]Gen. 17:1 [b]Gen.

16 [1]Lit., *be called* [a]Gen. 22:11, 15-1 28:13-15; 31:11 11:21

And the [2]names of my fathers Abraham and Isaac;
And [c]may they grow into a multitude in the midst of the earth."
17 When Joseph saw that his father [a]laid his right hand on
Ephraim's head, it displeased him; and he grasped his father's hand
to remove it from Ephraim's head to Manasseh's head.
18 And Joseph said to his father, "Not so, my father, for this one is
the first-born. Place your right hand on his head."
19 But his father refused and said, "I know, my son, I know; he also
shall become a people and he also shall be great. However, his
younger brother shall be greater than he, and [a]his [1]descendants shall
become a [2]multitude of nations."
20 And [a]he blessed them that day, saying,
"By you Israel shall pronounce blessing, saying,
'May God make you like Ephraim and Manasseh!' "
Thus he put Ephraim before Manasseh.
21 Then Israel said to Joseph, "Behold, I am about to die, but [a]God
will be with you, and [b]bring you back to the land of your fathers.
22 "And I give you one [1]portion more than your brothers, [a]which I
took from the hand of the Amorite with my sword and my bow."

Chapter 49

49 Then Jacob summoned his sons and said, "Assemble yourselves that I may tell you what shall befall you [a]in the [1]days to come.

2 "Gather together and hear, O sons of Jacob;
And [a]listen to Israel your father.

3 "Reuben, you are my first-born;
My might and [a]the beginning of my strength,
[1]Preeminent in dignity and [1]preeminent in power.
4 "[1]Uncontrolled as water, you shall not have preeminence,
[a]Because you went up to your father's bed;
Then you defiled *it*—he went up to my couch.

5 "[a]Simeon and Levi are brothers;
Their swords are implements of violence.
6 "[a]Let my soul not enter into their council;
Let not my glory be united with their assembly;
Because in their anger they slew [1]men,
And in their self-will they lamed [2]oxen.
7 "Cursed be their anger, for it is fierce;
And their wrath, for it is cruel.
[a]I will [1]disperse them in Jacob,
And scatter them in Israel.

8 "Judah, your brothers shall praise you;
Your hand shall be on the neck of your enemies;
[a]Your father's sons shall bow down to you.
9 "Judah is a [a]lion's whelp;
From the prey, my son, you have gone up.
[b]He [1]couches, he lies down as a lion,
And as a [2]lion, who [3]dares rouse him up?
10 "[a]The scepter shall not depart from Judah,
Nor the ruler's staff from between his feet,

name [c]Gen. 28:14; 46:3
[a]Gen. 48:14
.., *seed* [2]Lit., [a]Gen. 28:14; 46:3
[a]Heb. 11:21
ı. 26:3 [b]Gen. ;; 46:4; 50:24
[1]Or, *ridge*; lit., *ıoulder*; Heb., [a]Josh. 24:32; John 4:5
Lit., *end of the* ; [a]Num. 24:14
2 [a]Ps. 34:11
, *preeminence* :17; Ps. 78:51; 105:36
Boiling over; lit., *essness* [a]Gen. :2; Deut. 27:20; 1 Chr. 5:1
[a]Gen. 34:25-30
a man [2]Lit., *an ox* [a]Ps. 64:2
t., *divide* [a]Josh. 19:1, 9; 21:1-42
en. 27:29; 1 Chr. 5:2
bows down [2]Or, *oness* [3]Lit., *shall* . 19:5-7; Mic. 5:8 [b]Num. 24:9
[a]Num. 24:17; Ps. 60:7; 108:8

[1]Until Shiloh comes,
And [b]to him *shall be* the obedience of the peoples.
11 "[1a]He ties *his* foal to the vine,
And his donkey's colt to the choice vine;
[b]He washes his garments in wine,
And his robes in the blood of grapes.
12 "His eyes are [1]dull from wine,
And his teeth [2]white from milk.

13 "[a]Zebulun shall dwell at the seashore;
And he *shall be* [1]a haven for ships,
And his flank *shall be* toward Sidon.

14 "Issachar is [1]a strong donkey,
[a]Lying down between the [2]sheepfolds.
15 "When he saw that a resting place was good
And that the land was pleasant,
He bowed his shoulder to bear *burdens*,
And became a slave at forced labor.

16 "[a]Dan shall [b]judge his people,
As one of the tribes of Israel.
17 "Dan shall be a serpent in the way,
A horned snake in the path,
That bites the horse's heels,
So that his rider falls backward.
18 "[a]For Thy salvation I wait, O LORD.

19 "[a]As for Gad, [1]raiders shall raid him,
But he shall raid *at* their [2]heels.

20 "[1a]As for [b]Asher, his [2]food shall be [3]rich,
And he shall yield royal dainties.

21 "[a]Naphtali is a doe let loose,
He gives beautiful words.

22 "[a]Joseph is a fruitful [1]bough,
A fruitful [1]bough by a spring;
Its [2]branches run over a wall.
23 "The archers bitterly attacked him,
And shot *at him* and harassed him;
24 But his [a]bow remained [1]firm,
And [2b]his arms were agile,
From the hands of the [c]Mighty One of Jacob
(From there is [d]the Shepherd, [e]the Stone of Israel),
25 From [a]the God of your father who helps you,
And [1b]by the [2]Almighty who blesses you
With [c]blessings of heaven above,
Blessings of the deep that lies beneath,
Blessings of the breasts and of the womb.
26 "The blessings of your father
Have surpassed the blessings of my ancestors
Up to the [1]utmost bound of [a]the everlasting hills;

10 [1]Or, *Until* ... *to Shiloh;* or, ... *comes to wh*... *belongs* [b]Ps. 72:8-11; Is. 4...

11 [1]Lit., *Bind*... [a]Deut. 8:7, 8; ... 18:32 [b]Is. 63:...

12 [1]Or, *darke*... [2]Or, *whiter tha*...

13 [1]Lit., *for a* ... *ships* [a]Deut. 3...

14 [1]Lit., *a don*... *bone* [2]Or, *sad*... [a]Judg. 5:16; Ps...

16 [a]Deut. 33:2... 18:26, 27 [b]Ger...

18 [a]Ex. 15:2; ... 40:1-3; 119:166... 25:9; Mic. 7:7

19 [1]Lit., *a raidi*... [2]Lit., *heel* [a]Deu...

20 [1]Lit., *From* ... *bread* [3]Lit., *fat* ... 33:24, 25 [b]Gen....

21 [a]Deut. 33:23

22 [1]Lit., *son* [2]Li... *daughters* [a]Deu... 33:13-17

24 [1]I.e., in an unyielding positi... *the arms of his h*... [a]Job 29:20 [b]Ps. ... 73:23; Is. 41:10 ... 132:2, 5; Is. 1:24; ... [d]Ps. 23:1; 80:1 ... 118:22; Is. 28:16; ... 2:6-8

25 [1]Or, *with* [2]He... *Shaddai* [a]Gen. 2... 32:9 [b]Gen. 28:3; ... [c]Gen. 27:28

26 [1]Lit., *limit;* or, ... [a]Deut. 33:15, 16

May they be on the head of Joseph,
And on the crown of the head of the one distinguished among
his brothers.

27 "Benjamin is a [1]ravenous wolf;
In the morning he devours the prey,
And in the evening he divides the spoil."

28 All these are the twelve tribes of Israel, and this is what their
father said to them [1]when he blessed them. He blessed them, every
one [2]with the blessing appropriate to him.
29 Then he charged them and said to them, "I am about to be [a]gath-
ered to my people; [b]bury me with my fathers in the cave that is in
[c]the field of Ephron the Hittite,
30 in the [a]cave that is in the field of Machpelah, which is before
Mamre, in the land of Canaan, which Abraham bought along with
the field from Ephron the Hittite for a [1]burial site.
31 "There they buried [a]Abraham and his wife [b]Sarah, there they bur-
ied [c]Isaac and his wife Rebekah, and there I buried Leah—
32 the field and the cave that is in it, purchased from the sons of
Heth."
33 When Jacob finished charging his sons, he drew his feet into the
bed and [a]breathed his last, and was [b]gathered to his people.

Chapter 50

50 Then Joseph fell on his father's face, and wept over him and
kissed him.
2 And Joseph commanded his servants the physicians to embalm
his father. So the physicians [a]embalmed Israel.
3 Now forty days were [1]required for [2]it, for [3]such is the period
required for embalming. And the Egyptians [a]wept for him seventy
days.
4 And when the days of [1]mourning for him were past, Joseph
spoke to the household of Pharaoh, saying, "If now I have found
favor in your sight, please speak [2]to Pharaoh, saying,
5 '[a]My father made me swear, saying, "Behold, I am about to die;
in my grave [b]which I dug for myself in the land of Canaan, there you
shall bury me." Now therefore, please let me go up and bury my
father; then I will return.' "
6 And Pharaoh said, "Go up and bury your father, as he made you
swear."
7 So Joseph went up to bury his father, and with him went up all
the servants of Pharaoh, the elders of his household and all the
elders of the land of Egypt,
8 and all the household of Joseph and his brothers and his father's
household; they left only their little ones and their flocks and their
herds in the land of Goshen.
9 There also went up with him both chariots and horsemen; and it
was a very great company.
10 When they came to the [1]threshing floor of Atad, which is beyond
the Jordan, they [a]lamented there with a very great and [2]sorrowful
lamentation; and he [3]observed seven days mourning for his father.
11 Now when the inhabitants of the land, the Canaanites, saw the
mourning at [1]the threshing floor of Atad, they said, "This is a

...olf that tears
...it., and [2]Lit., his blessing
... 25:8 [b]Gen. ...en. 23:16-20; 50:13
...possession of ...place [a]Gen. 23:3-20
...n. 25:9 [b]Gen. ... [c]Gen. 35:29
...en. 25:8; Acts ...5 [b]Gen. 49:29
... [a]Gen. 50:26; ...r. 16:14; Matt. ...ark 16:1; John 19:39, 40
...t., fulfilled [2]Or, ..., so are fulfilled ...s of embalming ...n. 50:10; Num. ...:29; Deut. 34:8
[a]Gen. 47:29-31 ...16:14; Is. 22:16; Matt. 27:60
...weeping [2]Lit., In the ears of
10 [1]Heb., Goren Atad [2]Lit., heavy ...made a mourning ...n days [a]Acts 8:2
11 [1]Heb., Goren ha-Atad

[2]grievous [3]mourning for the Egyptians." Therefore it was named
[4]Abel-mizraim, which is beyond the Jordan.
12 And thus his sons did for him as he had charged them;
13 for his sons carried him to the land of Canaan, and buried him in
[a]the cave of the field of Machpelah before Mamre, which Abraham
had bought along with the field for a [1]burial site from Ephron the
Hittite.
14 And after he had buried his father, Joseph returned to Egypt, he
and his brothers, and all who had gone up with him to bury his
father.
15 When Joseph's brothers saw that their father was dead, they
said, "[a]What if Joseph should bear a grudge against us and pay us
back in full for all the wrong which we did to him!"
16 So they [1]sent *a message* to Joseph, saying, "Your father charged
before he died, saying,
17 'Thus you shall say to Joseph, "Please forgive, I beg you, the
transgression of your brothers and their sin, for they did you
wrong." ' And now, please forgive the transgression of the servants
of the God of your father." And Joseph wept when they spoke to
him.
18 Then his brothers also came and [a]fell down before him and said,
"Behold, we are your servants."
19 But Joseph said to them, "Do not be afraid, for am I in God's
place?
20 "And as for you, [a]you meant evil against me, *but* God meant it for
good in order to bring about [1]this present result, to preserve many
people alive.
21 "So therefore, do not be afraid; [a]I will provide for you and your
little ones." So he comforted them and spoke [1]kindly to them.
22 Now Joseph stayed in Egypt, he and his father's household, and
Joseph lived one hundred and ten years.
23 And Joseph saw the third generation of Ephraim's sons; also the
sons of Machir, the son of Manasseh, were [a]born on Joseph's knees.
24 And Joseph said to his brothers, "[a]I am about to die, but God will
surely [1]take care of you, and bring you up from this land to the land
which He [2]promised on oath to [b]Abraham, to [c]Isaac and to [d]Jacob."
25 Then Joseph made the sons of Israel swear, saying, "God will
surely [1]take care of you, and [a]you shall carry my bones up from
here."
26 So Joseph died at the age of one hundred and ten years; and [1]he
was [a]embalmed and placed in a coffin in Egypt.

11 [2]Lit., *heav* *ebel* [4]I.e., the (or mourning)

13 [1]Lit., *posse* *a burial place* 23:16-20; Acts

15 [a]Gen. 37:2 42:21, 22

16 [1]Lit., *comm*

18 [a]Gen. 37:8-

20 [1]Lit., *as it is* [a]Gen. 37:26, 27

21 [1]Lit., *to their* [a]Gen. 45:11; 47:

23 [a]Gen. 30:3

24 [1]Or, *visit* [2]Lit *swore* [a]Gen. 48: 3:16, 17; Heb. 11 [b]Gen. 13:15, 17; 18 [c]Gen. 26:3 [d] 28:13; 35:12

25 [1]Or, *visit* [a]Ge 47:29, 30; Ex. 13: Josh. 24:32; Heb

26 [1]Lit., *they em* *him* [a]Gen. 50:2

...ne of Genesis:

SEGMENT DIVISIONS

THE FIRSTS		4 MAIN EVENTS/4 CHARACTERS	TIME SPANS	CHAPTER THEMES
MAN	BEGINNINGS OF MAN		APPROXIMATELY 2080 YEARS	1
MARRIAGE				2
				3
				4
				5
				6
				7
				8
				9
				10
				11
	BEGINNINGS OF ISRAEL (CONTINUED NEXT PAGE)		APPROXIMATELY 300 YEARS (CONTINUED NEXT PAGE)	12
				13
				14
				15
				16
				17
				18
				19
				20
				21
				22
				23
				24
				25

Author:
Moses
(Luke 24:27)

Date:

Purpose:

Key Words:
God said
(or commanded)

generations of

covenant

altar

circumcised

Abram
(or Abraham)

GENESIS AT A GLANCE

SEGMENT DIVISIONS

	THE FIRSTS		4 MAIN EVENTS/4 CHARACTERS	TIME SPAN	CHAPTER THEMES
		BEGINNINGS OF ISRAEL (CONTINUED FROM PREVIOUS PAGE)		APPROXIMATELY 300 YEARS (CONTINUED FROM PREVIOUS PAGE)	26
					27
					28
					29
					30
					31
					32
					33
					34
					35
					36
					37
					38
					39
					40
					41
					42
					43
					44
					45
					46
					47
					48
					49
					50

ODUS

en Jacob and his family, a relatively small group, went into Egypt, they were welcomed and ed because they were relatives of Joseph. Four hundred and thirty years later the children of were Egypt's slaves, a people so numerous it frightened the Egyptians.

ey were God's covenant people, different from all the nations, a people of His own choosing. And se God is a covenant-keeping God He could not leave Jacob's people in Egypt—they had to be med by the blood of a lamb, a Passover lamb.

GS TO DO

ral Instructions

As Genesis comes to a close, the children of Israel are living in Egypt rather than in Canaan, the land of promise. The book that began with the creation of man in Eden ends with the children of Israel looking into a coffin in Egypt—but not without a promise that someday they'd leave Egypt. Read Genesis 50:22-26 and Exodus 1:1-7 and notice how the book of Exodus relates chronologically to the book of Genesis.

Exodus can be divided into three segments according to the location of the children of Israel. In Exodus 1 through 12 they're in Egypt. In Exodus 13 through 18 they journey to Sinai and then in Exodus 19 through 40 they camp at Sinai. Record this information on the EXODUS AT A GLANCE chart (pages 145 and 146) on the first line for segment divisions. This division will be the basis of some of your instructions.

Read through Exodus one chapter at a time. As you read do the following:

a. Remember you are reading a historical account. As you read, ask the five W's and an H: Who? What? When? Where? Why? and How? Ask questions such as: Who are the main characters in this chapter? What is happening? When and where is it happening? What were the consequences of their actions? How and why did this occur?

b. Mark key repeated words. Although a list of the key words for Exodus is recorded on EXODUS AT A GLANCE, remember there will be other words which are predominant in specific chapters. Don't miss these. You'll find it helpful to write the key words on an index card and use it as a bookmark while you study Exodus.

c. If you glean insights from the repeated use of a key word, list them in the margin of the chapter.

d. Mark all references to time in a distinctive way so you immediately can notice them. You might want to use a symbol such as this ⏰ .

e. List in the margin the main points or events covered in a particular chapter or group of chapters. This will give you a concise analysis of the chapter's content.

For example, Exodus 2 gives an account of Moses from his birth to the birth of his first son. In the margin you could list the major events in this chapter: Moses' birth, Moses' adoption by Pharaoh's daughter, Moses kills Egyptian, Moses flees to Midian, etc.

. When you finish reading a chapter record the main theme or subject of the chapter on EXODUS AT A GLANCE under "Chapter Themes." Also record it in the text next to the chapter number.

pters 1-12

. As you study these chapters, add *Pharaoh* and *staff* to your list of key words. Mark these words and their synonyms in a distinctive way. Then in the margin list everything you observe from marking them.

2. You can gain insights into God's character, power, and dealings with mankind from these ters. As you read each chapter, in the margin note what you learn about God. You may w put a distinguishing mark such as this △ in the margin and then color it yellow so yc recognize it easily. Then list your insights under the symbol for God.
3. There are lessons to be learned from Moses' life in these chapters. Although you probabl want to note these lessons in the margins, you'll also find it profitable to record what you le LESSONS FROM THE LIFE OF MOSES, a chart in the appendix of your Bible on page When you record an insight, make sure you note the book, chapter, and verse from which it
4. As you read chapters 7 through 12, in the margin of the chapter list the plagues as they app the text, numbering each one in the order in which they come.
5. When you come to Exodus 12, in the margin list everything you learn about the Passover. A five W's and an H: Who? What? When? Where? Why? and How?

Chapters 13-18

1. As you read:
   a. Watch for the key words, including those you marked in the first segment. Add *tes* *grumble,* along with their synonyms. In the margin note what the tests were and wh people grumbled. Also continue your list of insights on Pharaoh and on Moses' staff.
   b. Mark references to time with the clock symbol and note where events occur. Locate places on the map in the text on page 83.
2. Add to your list of insights on Moses and also note in the margin new insights on God. what He is called in 15:26 and 17:15 and the circumstances in which these names are reveale
3. In chapter 16 note in the margin all you learn from the text about manna and why it was g When you finish you might compare this with Deuteronomy 8:1-3.
4. In chapter 17 note the conditions under which Moses strikes the rock. Compare this 1 Corinthians 10:1-4 and John 7:37-39. Also note what happens after the rock is smitten an battle is fought in the valley.

Chapters 19-40

1. In chapters 19 through 24 God gives Moses the law. As you read these important chapters the five W's and an H.
   a. Chapter 20 presents the Ten Commandments. Number these within the text or list them i margin.
   b. Chapter 24 is very important as it deals with the inauguration of the law, the old covena the margin note the circumstances and procedure connected with its inauguration and the people respond.
2. In chapters 25 through 31 God gives the pattern for the tabernacle and all that is necessary fo priests.
   a. Note in the margin the main points of these chapters.
   b. Watch for other key words which are predominant in specific chapters. Mark them.
   c. In chapter 31 notice what is said about the Sabbath. List in the margin everything you l about it from the text.
3. Chapters 32 through 34 are significant in light of what happens.
   a. Note how Moses deals with this situation. Record your insights in the margin and on the c LESSONS FROM THE LIFE OF MOSES in the appendix on page 1875.
   b. Read 2 Corinthians 3:12-18 for additional insights regarding the veil over Moses' face.
4. Chapters 35 through 40 are an account of the construction of the tabernacle and the making o priest's garments. As you read, highlight or mark in a distinguishable way the specific inst tions which are given in regard to each piece of furniture.

'inally, after you have recorded all the chapter themes on EXODUS AT A GLANCE, see if any of he chapters can be grouped according to main events. Record these segment divisions on the ppropriate line under the chapter themes. Then decide on and record the theme of Exodus on he chart.

GS TO THINK ABOUT

Daniel 11:32b says, "The people who know their God will display strength and take action." What have you learned about God, His character, and His ways? What have you seen of His power and sovereignty? When we speak of God as being sovereign, we mean He rules over all. How do you see God's sovereignty and power manifested in Exodus? Meditate on what you have learned and then make it a matter of prayer and application.

Since the Bible is a progressive revelation of truth, keep in mind what you have observed about redemption and the Passover. These are Old Testament pictures of the salvation to be offered through the Lord Jesus Christ; therefore, they are pictures of truths to be applied to your life (1 Corinthians 5:6-8). Are you a slave to sin? Jesus Christ has provided for your redemption from sin through His blood. Have you been redeemed?

What have you learned from Moses' life? How did he deal with difficult situations and people? What was his overriding passion? What did you learn about Moses' relationship with God that you can apply to your own life today?

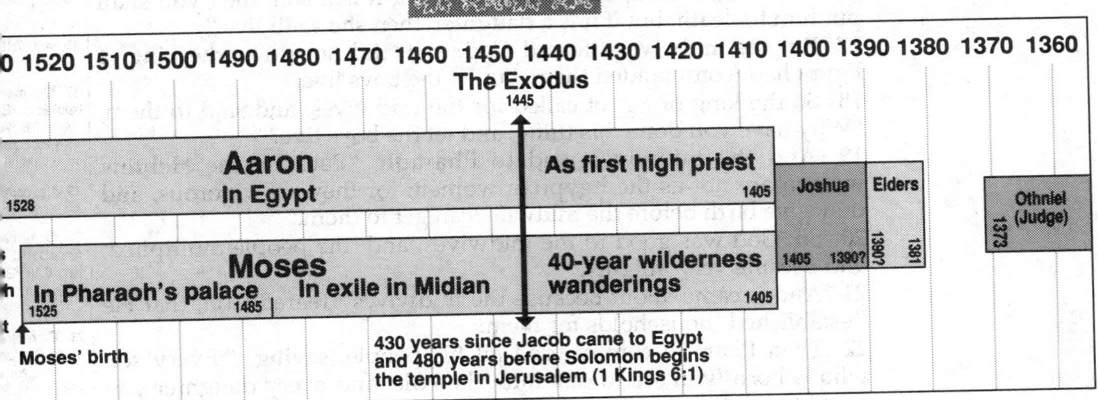

Chapter 1 ______

1 Now these are the [a]names of the sons of
Israel who came to Egypt with Jacob;
they came each one [1]with his household:
2 Reuben, Simeon, Levi and Judah;
3 Issachar, Zebulun and Benjamin;
4 Dan and Naphtali, Gad and Asher.
5 And all the [1]persons who came from
the loins of Jacob were [a]seventy [2]in number,
but Joseph was *already* in Egypt.
6 And [a]Joseph died, and all his brothers
and all that generation.
7 But the sons of Israel [a]were fruitful and
[1]increased greatly, and multiplied, and became exceedingly [2]mighty, so that the land
was filled with them.

THE GREAT SEA (Mediterranean Sea)
CANAAN
Mt. Nebo
Jericho
SALT SEA
MOAB
GOSHEN
Rameses
Succoth?
RED SEA Area
Etham?
Wilderness of Zin
Negev
EDOM
Kadesh-Barnea
Mt. Hor
EGYPT
Marah
Elim
Ezion-Geber
Wilderness of Sin
Rephidim
Mt. Sinai (Horeb)
RED SEA
?–Approximate location

The Exodus from Egypt to Canaan
(see page 1897)

[1]Lit., *and* [a]Gen. 46:8-27

[1]souls [2]Lit., *as to* [a]Gen. 46:26, 27; Deut. 10:22

6 [a]Gen. 50:26

[1]Lit., *swarmed* [2]Or, *numerous* [a]Gen. 12:2; 35:11; 46:3; 47:27; 48:4; Deut. 26:5; Ps. 105:24; Acts 7:17

8 Now a new [a]king arose over Egypt, who did not know Joseph.
9 And [a]he said to his people, "Behold, the people of the sons of
Israel are [1]more and mightier than we.
10 "Come, let us [a]deal wisely with them, lest they multiply and [1]in
the event of war, they also join themselves to those who hate us, and
fight against us, and [2]depart from the land."
11 So they appointed [a]taskmasters over them to afflict them with
[1b]hard labor. And they built for Pharaoh [c]storage cities, Pithom and
[d]Raamses.
12 But the more they afflicted them, [a]the more they multiplied and
the more they [1]spread out, so that they were in dread of the sons of
Israel.
13 And the Egyptians compelled the sons of Israel [a]to labor
rigorously;
14 and they made [a]their lives bitter with hard labor in mortar and
bricks and at all *kinds* of labor in the field, all their labors which they
rigorously [1]imposed on them.
15 Then the king of Egypt spoke to the Hebrew midwives, one of
whom [1]was named Shiphrah, and the other [1]was named Puah;
16 and he said, "When you are helping the Hebrew women to give
birth and see *them* upon the birthstool, [a]if it is a son, then you shall
put him to death; but if it is a daughter, then she shall live."
17 But the midwives [1a]feared God, and [b]did not do as the king of
Egypt had [2]commanded them, but let the boys live.
18 So the king of Egypt called for the midwives, and said to them,
"Why have you done this thing, and let the boys live?"
19 And the midwives said to Pharaoh, "Because the Hebrew
women are not as the Egyptian women; for they are vigorous, and
they give birth before the midwife [1]can get to them."
20 So [a]God was good to the midwives, and [b]the people multiplied,
and became very [1]mighty.
21 And it came about because the midwives [1a]feared God, that He
[2b]established [3]households for them.
22 Then Pharaoh commanded all his people, saying, "[a]Every son
who is born [1]you are to cast into [b]the Nile, and every daughter you
are to keep alive."

Chapter 2

2 Now a man from [a]the house of Levi went and [1]married a daugh-
ter of Levi.
2 And the woman conceived and bore a son; and when she saw
[1]that he was [2a]beautiful, she hid him for three months.
3 But when she could hide him no longer, she got him a [1a]wicker
[2]basket and covered it over with tar and pitch. Then she put the
child into it, and set *it* among the [b]reeds by the bank of the Nile.
4 And [a]his sister stood at a distance to [1]find out what would [2]hap-
pen to him.
5 Then the daughter of Pharaoh came down [a]to bathe at the Nile,
with her maidens walking alongside the Nile; and she saw the [1]bas-
ket among the reeds and sent her maid, and she brought it *to her.*
6 When she opened *it,* she [1]saw the child, and behold, *the* [2]boy was
crying. And she had pity on him and said, "This is one of the
Hebrews' children."
7 Then his sister said to Pharaoh's daughter, "Shall I go and call

8 [a]Acts 7:1

9 [1]Or, *too m mighty for u* 105:24, 25

10 [1]Lit., *it c when war b* [2]Lit., *go up f* 7:19

11 [1]Lit., *ther* [a]Gen. 15:13; 5:6 [b]Ex. 1:1 5:4-9; 6:6f. 2 Chr. 8:4 [d]

12 [1]Lit., *brok* [a]Ex. 1:7

13 [a]Gen. 15: 4:20

14 [1]Lit., *work them* [a]Ex. 2: Num. 20:15;

15 [1]Lit., *the n*

16 [a]Acts 7:19

17 [1]Or, *rever spoken to* [a]E Prov. 16:6 [b]A 4:18-20; 5:29

19 [1]Lit., *come*

20 [1]Or, *nume* [a]Prov. 11:18; E Heb. 6:10 [b]Ex 3:10

21 [1]Or, *revere made* [3]Or, *fam* 1:17 [b]1 Sam. 2 Sam. 7:11, 2 2:24; 11:38

22 [1]Some vers insert *to the He* [a]Acts 7:19 [b]Ge

2:1 [1]Lit., *took* 6:16, 18, 20

2 [1]Lit., *him tha good* [a]Acts 7:2 11:23

3 [1]I.e., papyrus [2]Or, *chest* [a]Is. 19:6

4 [1]Lit., *know* [2]L *done* [a]Ex. 15:2 26:59

5 [1]Or, *chest* [a]E 8:20

6 [1]Heb., *saw it, child* [2]Or, *lad*

[1]a nurse for you from the Hebrew women, that she may nurse the
child for you?"
8 And Pharaoh's daughter said to her, "Go *ahead.*" So the girl went
and called the child's mother.
9 Then Pharaoh's daughter said to her, "Take this child away and
nurse him for me and I shall give *you* your wages." So the woman
took the child and nursed him.
10 And the child grew, and she brought him to Pharaoh's daughter,
and [a]he became her son. And she named him [1]Moses, and said,
"Because I [2]drew him out of the water."
11 Now it came about in those days, [a]when Moses had grown up,
that he went out to his brethren and looked on their [1b]hard labors;
and [c]he saw an Egyptian beating a Hebrew, one of his brethren.
12 So he [1]looked this way and that, and when he saw there was no
one *around,* he [a]struck down the Egyptian and hid him in the sand.
13 And he went out [a]the next day, and behold, two Hebrews were
[1]fighting with each other; and he said to the [2]offender, "Why are you
striking your companion?"
14 But he said, "[a]Who made you a [1]prince or a judge over us? Are
you [2]intending to kill me, as you killed the Egyptian?" Then Moses
was afraid, and said, "Surely the matter has become known."
15 When Pharaoh heard of this matter, he tried to kill Moses. But
[a]Moses fled from the presence of Pharaoh and [1]settled in the land of
Midian; and he sat down [b]by a well.
16 Now [a]the priest of Midian had seven daughters; and [b]they came
to draw water, and filled the troughs to water their father's flock.
17 Then the shepherds came and drove them away, but [a]Moses
stood up and helped them, and watered their flock.
18 When they came to [a]Reuel their father, he said, "Why have you
come *back* so soon today?"
19 So they said, "An Egyptian delivered us from the hand of the
shepherds; and what is more, he even drew the water for us and
watered the flock."
20 And he said to his daughters, "Where is he then? Why is it that
you have left the man behind? Invite him [1]to have something to eat."
21 [a]And Moses was willing to dwell with the man, and he gave his
daughter [b]Zipporah to Moses.
22 Then she gave birth to [a]a son, and he named him [1]Gershom, for
he said, "I have been [b]a [2]sojourner in a foreign land."
23 Now it came about in *the course of* those many days that the king
of Egypt died. And the sons of Israel [a]sighed because of the bondage,
and they cried out; and [b]their cry for help because of *their* bondage
rose up to God.
24 So [a]God heard their groaning; and God remembered [b]His cove-
nant with Abraham, Isaac, and Jacob.
25 And [a]God saw the sons of Israel, and God [1]took notice *of them.*

Chapter 3

3 Now Moses was pasturing the flock of [a]Jethro his father-in-law,
the priest of Midian; and he led the flock to the [1]west side of the
wilderness, and came to [b]Horeb, the [c]mountain of God.
2 And [a]the angel of the LORD appeared to him in a blazing fire
from the midst of [1]a [b]bush; and he looked, and behold, the bush was
burning with fire, yet the bush was not consumed.

woman giving suck
Mosheh, from *ashah* [2]Heb., *ah* [a]Acts 7:21
ourdens [a]Acts Heb. 11:24-26 ; 5:4, 5; 6:6, 7 [c]Acts 7:24
, *turned* [a]Acts 7:24, 25
quarreling [2]Or, *uilty one* [a]Acts 7:26-28
man, a prince saying in your Gen. 19:9; Acts 7:27, 28
it., *dwelt* [a]Acts b. 11:27 [b]Gen. 24:11; 29:2
[a]Ex. 3:1; 18:12 . 24:11, 13, 19; 10; 1 Sam. 9:11
[a]Gen. 29:3, 10
3:1; Num. 10:29
that he may eat bread
[a]Acts 7:29 [b]Ex. 4:25; 18:2
eb., *ger sham, a ger there* [2]Heb., Ex. 4:20; 18:3, 4 23:4; Lev. 25:23; Acts 7:29; Heb. 11:13, 14
. 6:5, 9 [b]Ex. 3:7, 26:7; James 5:4
Ex. 6:5; Acts 7:34 5:13f.; 22:16-18; -5; 28:13-15; Ps. 105:8, 42
[1]Lit., *knew* them 7; 4:31; Acts 7:34
Or, *rear part* [a]Ex. 4:18; 18:12; Num. [b]Ex. 3:12; 17:6; ; 1 Kin. 19:8 [c]Ex. 4:27; 18:5; 24:13
2 [1]Lit., *the* [a]Gen. -11; 21:17; 22:11, 3:4-11, 16; Judg. 3:13-21; Acts 7:30 Deut. 33:16; Mark ; Luke 20:37; Acts 7:30

3 So Moses said, "[1a]I must turn aside now, and see this [2]marvelous
sight, why the bush is not burned up."
4 When the LORD saw that he turned aside to look, [a]God called to
him from the midst of the bush, and said, "Moses, Moses!" And he
said, "Here I am."
5 Then He said, "Do not come near here; [a]remove your sandals
from your feet, for the place on which you are standing is holy
ground."
6 He said also, "[a]I am the God of your father, the God of Abraham,
the God of Isaac, and the God of Jacob." [b]Then Moses hid his face,
for he was [c]afraid to look at God.
7 And the LORD said, "I have surely [a]seen the affliction of My
people who are in Egypt, and have given heed to their cry because of
their taskmasters, for I am aware of their sufferings.
8 "So I have come down [a]to deliver them from the [1]power of the
Egyptians, and to bring them up from that land to a [b]good and
spacious land, to a land flowing with milk and honey, to the place of
[c]the Canaanite and the Hittite and the Amorite and the Perizzite and
the Hivite and the Jebusite.
9 "And now, behold, [a]the cry of the sons of Israel has come to Me;
furthermore, I have seen the oppression with which the Egyptians
are oppressing them.
10 "Therefore, come now, and I will send you to Pharaoh, [a]so that
you may bring My people, the sons of Israel, out of Egypt."
11 But Moses said to God, "[a]Who am I, that I should go to Pharaoh,
and that I should bring the sons of Israel out of Egypt?"
12 And He said, "Certainly [a]I will be with you, and this shall be the
sign to you that it is I who have sent you: [b]when you have brought
the people out of Egypt, [c]you shall [1]worship God at this mountain."
13 Then Moses said to God, "Behold, I am going to the sons of
Israel, and I shall say to them, 'The God of your fathers has sent me
to you.' Now they may say to me, 'What is His name?' What shall I
say to them?"
14 And God said to Moses, "[1a]I AM WHO [1]I AM"; and He said,
"Thus you shall say to the sons of Israel, '[1]I AM has sent me to
you.'"
15 And God, furthermore, said to Moses, "Thus you shall say to the
sons of Israel, '[a]The LORD, the God of your fathers, the God of
Abraham, the God of Isaac, and the God of Jacob, has sent me to
you.' This is My name forever, and this is My [b]memorial-name [1]to all
generations.
16 "Go and [a]gather the elders of Israel together, and say to them,
'[b]The LORD, the God of your fathers, the God of Abraham, Isaac and
Jacob, has appeared to me, saying, "[1c]I am indeed concerned about
you and what has been done to you in Egypt.
17 "So [a]I said, I will bring you up out of the affliction of Egypt to the
land of [b]the Canaanite and the Hittite and the Amorite and the Periz-
zite and the Hivite and the Jebusite, to a land [c]flowing with milk and
honey."'
18 "And [a]they will [1]pay heed to what you say; and [b]you with the
elders of Israel will come to the king of Egypt, and you will say to
him, 'The LORD, the God of the Hebrews, has met with us. So now,
please, let us go a [c]three days' journey into the wilderness, that we
may sacrifice to the LORD our God.'

3 [1]Lit., *Let me* [2]Lit., *great* [a]A

4 [a]Ex. 4:5

5 [a]Josh. 5:15

6 [a]Gen. 28:13 3:16; 4:5; Matt Mark 12:26; L [b]Acts 7:32 [c]Ju 13:22; Rev. 1:

7 [a]Ex. 2:25; N Ps. 106:44; Is. Acts 7:34

8 [1]Lit., *hand* [a] 15:13-16; 46:4 25; Ex. 6:6-8; [b]Ex. 3:17; 13:5 13:27; Deut. 1: Jer. 11:5; Ezek. [c]Gen. 15:19-21 24:11

9 [a]Ex. 2:23

10 [a]Gen. 15:13 12:40, 41; Mic. 7:6, 7

11 [a]Ex. 4:10; 6 1 Sam. 18:18

12 [1]Or, *serve* [a] 31:3; Ex. 4:12, 33:14-16; Deut. Josh. 1:5; Is. 43 19:1 [c]Ex. 19:2, 7:7

14 [1]Related to t name of God, *Y* rendered *LORD*, derived from the *HAYAH, to be* [a] John 8:24, 28, 5 13:8; Rev. 1:8; 4

15 [1]Lit., *to gene generation* [a]Ex. [b]Ps. 30:4; 97:12; 102:12; 135:13; 12:5

16 [1]Lit., *Visiting visited* [a]Ex. 4:29 28:13; 48:15; Ex. 4:5 [c]Ex. 4:31; Ps 33:18f.

17 [a]Gen. 15:13-2 46:4; 50:24, 25 [b] 24:11 [c]Ex. 3:8

18 [1]Lit., *hear you voice* [a]Ex. 4:31 5:1 [c]Ex. 5:3; 8:27

19 "But I know that the king of Egypt [a]will not permit you to go,
[b]except [1]under compulsion.
20 "So I will stretch out [a]My hand, and strike Egypt with all My
[b]miracles which I shall do in the midst of it; and [c]after that he will let
you go.
21 "And I will grant this people [a]favor in the sight of the Egyptians;
and it shall be that when you go, you will not go empty-handed.
22 "But every woman [a]shall ask of her neighbor and the woman who
lives in her house, articles of silver and articles of gold, and clothing;
and you will put them on your sons and daughters. Thus you will
[b]plunder the Egyptians."

Chapter 4

4 Then Moses answered and said, "What if they will not believe
me, or [a]listen [1]to what I say? For they may say, '[b]The LORD has
not appeared to you.' "
2 And the LORD said to him, "What is that in your hand?" And he
said, "[a]A staff."
3 Then He said, "Throw it on the ground." So he threw it on the
ground, and [a]it became a serpent; and Moses fled from it.
4 But the LORD said to Moses, "Stretch out your hand and grasp *it*
by its tail"—so he stretched out his hand and caught it, and it be-
came a staff in his [1]hand—
5 "that [a]they may believe that [b]the LORD, the God of their fathers,
the God of Abraham, the God of Isaac, and the God of Jacob, has
appeared to you."
6 And the LORD furthermore said to him, "Now put your hand
into your bosom." So he put his hand into his bosom, and when he
took it out, behold, his hand was [a]leprous like snow.
7 Then He said, "Put your hand into your bosom again." So he put
his hand into his bosom again; and when he took it out of his bosom,
behold, [a]it was restored like *the rest of* his flesh.
8 "And it shall come about that if they will not believe you or [1]heed
the [2]witness of the first sign, they may believe the [2]witness of the last
sign.
9 "But it shall be that if they will not believe even these two signs or
heed what you say, then you shall take some water from the Nile
and pour it on the dry ground; and the water which you take from
the Nile [a]will become blood on the dry ground."
10 Then Moses said to the LORD, "Please, Lord, [a]I have never been
[1]eloquent, neither [2]recently nor in time past, nor since Thou hast
spoken to Thy servant; for I am [3]slow of speech and [3]slow of
tongue."
11 And the LORD said to him, "Who has made man's mouth? Or
[a]who makes *him* dumb or deaf, or seeing or blind? Is it not I, the
LORD?
12 "Now then go, and [a]I, even I, will be with your mouth, and [b]teach
you what you are to say."
13 But he said, "Please, Lord, now [1]send *the message* by whomever
Thou wilt."
14 Then the anger of the LORD burned against Moses, and He said,
"Is there not your brother Aaron the Levite? I know that [1]he speaks
fluently. And moreover, behold, [a]he is coming out to meet you; when
he sees you, he will be glad in his heart.

, *by a strong* 5:2 [b]Ex. 6:1
x. 6:1; 7:4, 5; 3, 9, 14 [b]Ex. ; Deut. 6:22; ; Ps. 105:27; r. 32:20; Acts 1:1; 12:31-33
. 11:3; 12:36; Kin. 8:50; Ps. 106:46; Prov. 16:7
en. 15:14; Ex. [b]Ezek. 39:10
t., *to my voice* .18; 6:30 [b]Ex. 3:15, 16
[a]Ex. 4:17, 20
3 [a]Ex. 7:10-12
4 [1]Lit., *palm*
31; 19:9 [b]Gen. 15; Ex. 3:6, 15
n. 12:10; 2 Kin. 5:27
Num. 12:13-15; 39; 2 Kin. 5:14; Luke 17:12-14
., *listen to* [2]Lit., *voice*
9 [a]Ex. 7:19, 20
) [1]Lit., *a man of* [2]Lit., *yesterday* *eavy* [a]Ex. 3:11; :1; 6:12; Jer. 1:6
Ps. 94:9; 146:8; 5; Luke 1:20, 64
. 4:15, 16; Deut. Is. 50:4; Jer. 1:9 10:19, 20; Mark ; Luke 12:11, 12; 21:14, 15
[1]Lit., *send by the hand which Thou sendest*
[1]Lit., *speaking he speaks* [a]Ex. 4:27

15 "And you are to speak to him and [a]put the words in his mouth;
and I, even I, will be with your mouth and his mouth, and I will
teach you what you are to do.
16 "Moreover, [a]he shall speak for you to the people; and it shall come
about that he shall be as a mouth for you, and you shall be as God to
him.
17 "And you shall take in your hand [a]this staff, [b]with which you
shall perform the signs."
18 Then Moses departed and returned to [1]Jethro [a]his father-in-law,
and said to him, "Please, let me go, that I may return to my brethren
who are in Egypt, and see if they are still alive." And Jethro said to
Moses, "Go in peace."
19 Now the LORD said to Moses in Midian, "Go [1]back to Egypt, for
[a]all the men who were seeking your life are dead."
20 So Moses took his wife and his [a]sons and mounted them on a
donkey, and he returned to the land of Egypt. Moses also took the
[b]staff of God in his hand.
21 And the LORD said to Moses, "When you go [1]back to Egypt see
that you perform before Pharaoh all [a]the wonders which I have put
in your [2]power; but [b]I will harden his heart so that he will not let the
people go.
22 "Then you shall say to Pharaoh, 'Thus says the LORD, "[a]Israel is
My son, My first-born.
23 "So I said to you, '[a]Let My son go, that he may serve Me'; but you
have refused to let him go. Behold, [b]I will kill your son, your first-
born." ' "
24 Now it came about at the lodging place on the way that the LORD
met him and [a]sought to put him to death.
25 Then Zipporah took [a]a flint and cut off her son's foreskin and
[1]threw *it* at Moses' feet, and she said, "You are indeed a bridegroom
of blood to me."
26 So He let him alone. At that time she said, "*You are* a bridegroom
of blood"—[1]because of the circumcision.
27 [a]Now the LORD said to Aaron, "Go to meet Moses in the wilder-
ness." So he went and met him at the [b]mountain of God, and he
kissed him.
28 And [a]Moses told Aaron all the words of the LORD with which He
had sent him, and [b]all the signs that He had commanded him *to do*.
29 Then Moses and Aaron went and [a]assembled all the elders of the
sons of Israel;
30 and [a]Aaron spoke all the words which the LORD had spoken to
Moses. He then performed the [b]signs in the sight of the people.
31 So [a]the people believed; and when they heard that the LORD
[1b]was concerned about the sons of Israel and that He had seen their
affliction, then [c]they bowed low and worshiped.

Chapter 5

5 And afterward Moses and Aaron came and said to Pharaoh,
"[a]Thus says the LORD, the God of Israel, '[b]Let My people go that
they may celebrate a feast to Me in the wilderness.' "
2 But Pharaoh said, "[a]Who is the LORD that I should obey His voice
to let Israel go? I do not know the LORD, and besides, [b]I will not let
Israel go."
3 Then they said, "[a]The God of the Hebrews has met with us.

15 [a]Ex. 4:12 Num. 23:5, 1 18:18; Is. 51 Jer. 1:9
16 [a]Ex. 7:1,
17 [a]Ex. 4:2, [b]Ex. 7:9-20;
18 [1]Heb., *Je* 2:21; 3:1
19 [1]Lit., *retur* 2:15, 23
20 [a]Ex. 18:3, 7:29 [b]Ex. 4:1 Num. 20:8, 9,
21 [1]Lit., *to ret hand* [a]Ex. 3:2 10 [b]Ex. 7:3, 1 35; 10:1, 20, 2 Deut. 2:30; Jo 1 Sam. 6:6; Is. John 12:40; R
22 [a]Is. 63:16; 31:9; Hos. 11:1
23 [a]Ex. 5:1; 6: [b]Ex. 11:5; 12:2 105:36; 135:8;
24 [a]Num. 22:2
25 [1]Lit., *made his feet* [a]Gen. Josh. 5:2, 3
26 [1]Lit., *with re*
27 [a]Ex. 4:14 [b]E 18:5; 24:13
28 [a]Ex. 4:15f.
29 [a]Ex. 3:16
30 [a]Ex. 4:15, 16 4:1-9
31 [1]Lit., *had vis* 3:18; 4:8f.; 19:9 50:24; Ex. 3:16 24:26; Ex. 12:27 29:20
5:1 [a]Ex. 3:18 [b]E 6:11; 7:16
2 [a]2 Kin. 18:35; 32:14; Job 21:15 3:19
3 [a]Ex. 3:18

Please, let us go a three days' journey into the wilderness that we may sacrifice to the LORD our God, lest He fall upon us with pestilence or with the sword."

4 But the king of Egypt said to them, "Moses and Aaron, why do you [1]draw the people away from their [2]work? Get *back* to your [3a]labors!"

5 Again Pharaoh said, "Look, [a]the people of the land are now many, and you would have them cease from their labors!"

6 So the same day Pharaoh commanded [a]the taskmasters over the people and their [b]foremen, saying,

7 "You are no longer to give the people straw to make brick as previously; let them go and gather straw for themselves.

8 "But the quota of bricks which they were making previously, you shall impose on them; you are not to reduce any of it. Because they are [a]lazy, therefore they cry out, '[1]Let us go and sacrifice to our God.'

9 "Let the labor be heavier on the men, and let them work at it that they may pay no attention to false words."

10 So [a]the taskmasters of the people and their foremen went out and spoke to the people, saying, "Thus says Pharaoh, 'I am not going to give you *any* straw.

11 'You go *and* get straw for yourselves wherever you can find *it;* but none of your labor will be reduced.' "

12 So the people scattered through all the land of Egypt to gather stubble for straw.

13 And the taskmasters pressed them, saying, "Complete your [1]work quota, [2]*your* daily amount, just as when [3]you had straw."

14 Moreover, [a]the foremen of the sons of Israel, whom Pharaoh's taskmasters had set over them, [b]were beaten [1]and were asked, "Why have you not completed your required amount either yesterday or today in making brick as previously?"

15 Then the foremen of the sons of Israel came and cried out to Pharaoh, saying, "Why do you deal this way with your servants?

16 "There is no straw given to your servants, yet they keep saying to us, 'Make bricks!' And behold, your servants are being beaten; but it is the fault of your *own* people."

17 But he said, "You are [a]lazy, *very* lazy; therefore you say, 'Let us go *and* sacrifice to the LORD.'

18 "So go now *and* work; for you shall be given no straw, yet you must deliver the quota of bricks."

19 And the foremen of the sons of Israel saw that they were in trouble [1]because they were told, "You must not reduce [2]*your* daily amount of bricks."

20 When they left Pharaoh's presence, they met Moses and Aaron as they were [1]waiting for them.

21 And [a]they said to them, "[b]May the LORD look upon you and judge *you,* for you have [c]made [1]us odious in Pharaoh's sight and in the sight of his servants, to put a sword in their hand to kill us."

22 Then Moses returned to the LORD and said, "[a]O Lord, why hast Thou brought harm to this people? Why didst Thou ever send me?

23 "Ever since I came to Pharaoh to speak in Thy name, he has done harm to this people; [a]and Thou hast not delivered Thy people at all."

loose [2]Lit., Lit., *burdens* ; 2:11; 6:5-7

5 [a]Ex. 1:7, 9

11; 3:7; 5:10, Ex. 5:10, 14, 15, 19

ing, 'Let [a]Ex. 5:17

1:11; 3:7; 5:6

orks [2]Lit., *the of a day in its* Lit., *there was*

., *saying* [a]Ex. 5:6 [b]Is. 10:24

17 [a]Ex. 5:8

., *saying* [2]Lit., *your bricks the a day in its day*

Lit., *standing to meet*

Lit., *our savor to* x. 14:11; 15:24; Gen. 16:5; 31:53 . 34:30; 1 Sam. ; 27:12; 2 Sam. 0:6; 1 Chr. 19:6

Num. 11:11; Jer. 4:10

23 [a]Ex. 3:8

Pharaoh is a title that was given to the kings of Egypt. An ancient Pharaoh had absolute power making him the high priest of all religions in Egypt.

Chapter 6

6 Then the LORD said to Moses, "Now you shall see what I will do
to Pharaoh; for [1a]under compulsion he shall let them go, and
[1]under compulsion he shall drive them out of his land."
2 God spoke further to Moses and said to him, "I am [a]the LORD;
3 and I appeared to Abraham, Isaac, and Jacob, as [1a]God Almighty,
but *by* [b]My name, [2]LORD, I did not make Myself known to them.
4 "And I also established [a]My covenant with them, to give them the
land of Canaan, the [1]land in which they sojourned.
5 "And furthermore I have [a]heard the groaning of the sons of Israel,
because the Egyptians are holding them in bondage; and I have
remembered My covenant.
6 "Say, therefore, to the sons of Israel, '[a]I am the LORD, and [b]I will
bring you out from under the burdens of the Egyptians, and I will
deliver you from their bondage. I will also [c]redeem you with [d]an
outstretched arm and with great judgments.
7 'Then I will take you [1a]for My people, and [b]I will be [2]your God;
and [c]you shall know that I am the LORD your God, who brought you
out from under the burdens of the Egyptians.
8 'And I will bring you to the land which [a]I [1]swore to give to
Abraham, Isaac, and Jacob, and [b]I will give it to you *for* a possession;
[c]I am the LORD.'"
9 So Moses spoke thus to the sons of Israel, but they did not listen
to Moses on [a]account of *their* [1]despondency and cruel bondage.
10 Now the LORD spoke to Moses, saying,
11 "[a]Go, [1]tell Pharaoh king of Egypt [2]to let the sons of Israel go out of
his land."
12 But Moses spoke before the LORD, saying, "Behold, the sons of
Israel have not listened to me; [a]how then will Pharaoh listen to me,
for I am [1b]unskilled in speech?"
13 Then the LORD spoke to Moses and to Aaron, and gave them a
charge to the sons of Israel and to Pharaoh king of Egypt, to bring
the sons of Israel out of the land of Egypt.
14 These are the heads of their fathers' households. [a]The sons of
Reuben, Israel's first-born: Hanoch and Pallu, Hezron and Carmi;
these are the families of Reuben.
15 And the [a]sons of Simeon: Jemuel and Jamin and Ohad and
Jachin and Zohar and Shaul the son of a Canaanite woman; these are
the families of Simeon.
16 And these are the names of [a]the sons of Levi according to their
generations: Gershon and Kohath and Merari; and the [1]length of
Levi's life was one hundred and thirty-seven years.
17 [a]The sons of Gershon: [1]Libni and Shimei, according to their
families.
18 And [a]the sons of Kohath: Amram and Izhar and Hebron and
Uzziel; and the [1]length of Kohath's life was one hundred and thirty-
three years.
19 And [a]the sons of Merari: Mahli and Mushi. These are the families
of the Levites according to their generations.
20 And [a]Amram [1]married his father's sister Jochebed, and she bore
him Aaron and Moses; and the [2]length of Amram's life was one
hundred and thirty-seven years.
21 And [a]the sons of Izhar: Korah and Nepheg and Zichri.
22 [a]And the sons of Uzziel: Mishael and [1]Elzaphan and Sithri.

6:1 [1]Lit., *by hand* [a]Ex. 3 5; 11:1; 12:3 13:3
2 [a]Ex. 3:14
3 [1]Heb., *El* [2]Heb., *YHW* rendered *LO* 17:1; 35:11; 68:4; 83:18; Jer. 16:21; E 37:6, 13
4 [1]Lit., *land sojournings* [a]Gen. 12:7; 7; 26:3, 4; 28
5 [a]Ex. 2:24
6 [a]Ex. 13:3; Deut. 6:12 [b] 7:4; 12:51; 1 Deut. 26:8; P [c]Ex. 15:13; D 1 Chr. 17:21; [d]Deut. 4:34; 5 Ps. 136:11f.
7 [1]Lit., *to Me people* [2]Lit., *God* [a]Ex. 19: 4:20; 7:6; 2 S [b]Gen. 17:7f.; 29:45f.; Lev. 26:12, 13, 45; 29:13 [c]Ex. 16 41:20; 49:23,
8 [1]Lit., *lifted u hand* [a]Gen. 1 Num. 14:30; N Ezek. 20:5, 6 24:13; Ps. 136 [c]Ex. 6:6
9 [1]Lit., *shortn spirit* [a]Ex. 2:2
11 [1]Lit., *speak that he let* [a]Ex
12 [1]Lit., *uncir of lips* [a]Ex. 4:1 6:30 [b]Jer. 1:6
14 [a]Gen. 46:9 26:5-11; 1 Chr.
15 [a]Gen. 46:10 4:24
16 [1]Lit., *years* 46:11; Num. 3:1 26:57f.; 1 Chr. 6
17 [1]In 1 Chr. 2 *Ladan* [a]Num. 3 1 Chr. 6:17-19
18 [1]Lit., *years* 3:19; 1 Chr. 6:2
19 [a]Num. 3:20; 6:19; 23:21
20 [1]Lit., *took to wife* [2]Lit., *years* 2:1, 2; Num. 26:
21 [a]Num. 16:1; 6:37, 38
22 [1]In Num. 3:3 *Elizaphan* [a]Lev. Num. 3:30

23 And Aaron [1]married Elisheba, the daughter of [a]Amminadab, the
sister of [b]Nahshon, and she bore him [c]Nadab and Abihu, Eleazar and
Ithamar.
24 And the [a]sons of Korah: Assir and Elkanah and [1]Abiasaph; these
are the families of the Korahites.
25 And Aaron's son [a]Eleazar [1]married one of the daughters of
Putiel, and she bore him [b]Phinehas. These are the heads of the
fathers' *households* of the Levites according to their families.
26 It was *the same* Aaron and Moses to whom the LORD said, "[a]Bring
out the sons of Israel from the land of Egypt according to their
[b]hosts."
27 They were the ones [a]who spoke to Pharaoh king of Egypt [1]about
bringing out the sons of Israel from Egypt; it was *the same* Moses and
Aaron.
28 Now it came about on the day when the LORD spoke to Moses in
the land of Egypt,
29 that the LORD spoke to Moses, saying, "[a]I am the LORD; [b]speak to
Pharaoh king of Egypt all that I speak to you."
30 But Moses said before the LORD, "Behold, I am [1a]unskilled in
speech; how then will Pharaoh listen to me?"

ook to him to uth 4:19, 20; [b]Num. 1:7; . 10:1; Num.); 1 Chr. 6:3; 24:1
Chr. 6:23 and saph [a]Num. ; 1 Chr. 6:22, 23, 37
ook to him to [a]Josh. 24:33 5:7-13; Josh. 3; Ps. 106:30
10; 6:13 [b]Ex. 7:4; 12:17, 51
., to bring out [a]Ex. 5:1
6:2, 6, 8 [b]Ex. 6:11; 7:2
uncircumcised Ex. 4:10; 6:12; Jer. 1:6

Chapter 7

7 Then the LORD said to Moses, "[a]See, I make you *as* God to Pha-
raoh, and your brother Aaron shall be your prophet.
2 "You shall speak all that I command you, and your brother
[a]Aaron shall speak to Pharaoh that he let the sons of Israel go out of
his land.
3 "But [a]I will harden Pharaoh's heart that I may [b]multiply My signs
and My wonders in the land of Egypt.
4 "When [a]Pharaoh will not listen to you, then I will lay My hand on
Egypt, and [b]bring out My hosts, My people the sons of Israel, from
the land of Egypt by [c]great judgments.
5 "And [a]the Egyptians shall know that I am the LORD, when I

7:1 [a]Ex. 4:16
2 [a]Ex. 4:15
:21 [b]Ex. 11:9; Acts 7:36
3:19, 20; 7:13, 8:15, 19; 9:12; Ex. 12:51; 13:3, 9 [c]Ex. 6:6
7:17; 8:19, 22; :7; 14:4, 18, 25

Some of the Gods of Egypt

god:	Ruled over:	How symbolized:
r	Earth-god • Helper of the dead	Two lion heads
n	Sun-god	
	Protection at birth • Dispenser of virility	Group of demons
et	Primordial goddess	Frog
	Goddess of life and healing	Human
epri	Primordial god • Rising sun	Scarabaeus (beetle)
um	Giver of the Nile • Creator of mankind	Human with ram's head
	"Eye of the sun"	Vulture or human
	Sky goddess • Mother of heavenly bodies	
iris	Dead pharaohs, Ruler of dead, life, vegetation	
	God of sun, earth and sky • National god	Human with falcon head
ket	Guardian of life • Protector of dead	Scorpion
h	God of chaos, desert and storm, crops	
this	God of Nile floodwaters	
ermuthis	Goddess of fertility and harvest; fate	Serpent

[b]stretch out My hand on Egypt and bring out the sons of Israel from
their midst."
6 So Moses and Aaron did *it;* [a]as the LORD commanded them, thus
they did.
7 And Moses was [a]eighty years old and Aaron [1]eighty-three, when
they spoke to Pharaoh.
8 Now the LORD spoke to Moses and Aaron, saying,
9 "When Pharaoh speaks to you, saying, '[1a]Work a miracle,' then
you shall say to Aaron, '[b]Take your staff and throw *it* down before
Pharaoh, *that* it may become a serpent.' "
10 So Moses and Aaron came to Pharaoh, and thus they did just as
the LORD had commanded; and Aaron threw his staff down before
Pharaoh and [1]his servants, and it [a]became a serpent.
11 Then Pharaoh also [a]called for *the* wise men and *the* sorcerers, and
they also, the [1b]magicians of Egypt, did [2]the same with [c]their secret
arts.
12 For each one threw down his staff and they turned into serpents.
But Aaron's staff swallowed up their staffs.
13 Yet [a]Pharaoh's heart was [1]hardened, and he did not listen to
them, as the LORD had said.
14 Then the LORD said to Moses, "Pharaoh's heart is [1]stubborn; he
refuses to let the people go.
15 "Go to Pharaoh in the morning [1]as [a]he is going out to the water,
and station yourself to meet him on the bank of the Nile; and you
shall take in your hand [b]the staff that was turned into a serpent.
16 "[a]And you will say to him, 'The LORD, the God of the Hebrews,
sent me to you, saying, "[b]Let My people go, that they may serve Me
in the wilderness. But behold, you have not listened until now."
17 'Thus says the LORD, "[a]By this you shall know that I am the LORD:
behold, I will strike [1]the water that is in the Nile with the staff that is
in my hand, and [b]it shall be turned to blood.
18 "And [a]the fish that are in the Nile will die, and the Nile will
[1]become foul; and the Egyptians will [2b]find difficulty in drinking
water from the Nile." ' "
19 Then the LORD said to Moses, "Say to Aaron, 'Take your staff and
[a]stretch out your hand over the waters of Egypt, over their rivers,
over their [1]streams, and over their pools, and over all their reservoirs
of water, that they may become blood; and there shall be blood
throughout all the land of Egypt, both in *vessels of* wood and in
vessels of stone.' "
20 So Moses and Aaron did even as the LORD had commanded. And
he lifted up [1a]the staff and struck the water that *was* in the Nile, in
the sight of Pharaoh and in the sight of his servants, and [b]all the
water that *was* in the Nile was turned to blood.
21 And the fish that *were* in the Nile died, and the Nile [1]became
foul, so that the Egyptians could not drink water from the Nile. And
the blood was through all the land of Egypt.
22 [a]But the [1]magicians of Egypt did [2]the same with their secret arts;
and Pharaoh's heart was [3]hardened, and he did not listen to them, as
the LORD had said.
23 Then Pharaoh turned and went into his house [1]with no concern
even for this.
24 So all the Egyptians dug around the Nile for water to drink, for
they could not drink of the water of the Nile.

5 [b]Ex. 3:20

6 [a]Gen. 6:2[illegible] 7:2

7 [1]Lit., *83 ye*[illegible] [a]Deut. 29:5; [illegible] Acts 7:23, 30

9 [1]Lit., *Show for yourselve*[illegible] John 2:18; 6:[illegible] 4:2, 17

10 [1]Lit., *befo*[illegible] 4:3; 7:9

11 [1]Or, *sooth*[illegible] *priests* [2]Lit., [illegible] 2:2; 4:6; 5:7 [illegible] Ex. 7:22; Dan [illegible] 2 Tim. 3:8 [c]E[illegible] 8:7, 18; 2 Tim [illegible] 13:13, 14

13 [1]Lit., *stron*[illegible] 4:21; 7:3, 22; [illegible] 32; 9:7, 12, 34 [illegible] 20, 27

14 [1]Or, *hard;* [illegible]

15 [1]Lit., *behol*[illegible] 2:5; 8:20 [b]Ex. 7:10

16 [a]Ex. 3:13, [illegible] 5:1 [b]Ex. 4:23; [illegible]

17 [1]Lit., *upon* [illegible] *waters* [a]Ex. 5:[illegible] 10:2; Ps. 9:16; [illegible] 25:17 [b]Ex. 4:9, [illegible] Rev. 11:6; 16:4, [illegible]

18 [1]I.e., have a[illegible] smell [2]Or, *be w*[illegible] [a]Ex. 7:21 [b]Ex. [illegible]

19 [1]Or, *canals* [illegible] 6, 16; 9:22; 10:[illegible] 14:21, 26

20 [1]Lit., *with the*[illegible] [a]Ex. 17:5 [b]Ps. 7[illegible] 105:29

21 [1]I.e., had a b[illegible]

22 [1]Or, *soothsa*[illegible] *priests* [2]Lit., *thus*[illegible] *strong* [a]Ex. 7:11 [illegible]

23 [1]Lit., *and he* [illegible] *set his heart eve*[illegible]

25 And seven days [1]passed after the LORD had struck the Nile.

Chapter 8

8 [1]Then the LORD said to Moses, "Go to Pharaoh and say to him,
'Thus says the LORD, "[a]Let My people go, that they may
serve Me.
2 "But if you refuse to let *them* go, behold, I will smite your whole
territory with frogs.
3 "And the Nile will [a]swarm with frogs, which will come up and go
into your house and into your bedroom and on your bed, and into
the houses of your servants and on your people, and into your ovens
and into your kneading bowls.
4 "So the frogs will come up on you and your people and all your
servants." ' "
5 [1]Then the LORD said to Moses, "Say to Aaron, '[a]Stretch out your
hand with your staff over the rivers, over the [2]streams and over the
pools, and make frogs come up on the land of Egypt.' "
6 So Aaron stretched out his hand over the waters of Egypt, and
the [1a]frogs came up and covered the land of Egypt.
7 [a]And the [1]magicians did [2]the same with their secret arts, [3]making
frogs come up on the land of Egypt.
8 Then Pharaoh [a]called for Moses and Aaron and said, "[b]Entreat
the LORD that He remove the frogs from me and from my people;
and [c]I will let the people go, that they may sacrifice to the LORD."
9 And Moses said to Pharaoh, "[1]The honor is yours to tell me:
when shall I entreat for you and your servants and your people, that
the frogs be [2]destroyed from you and your houses, *that* they may be
left only in the Nile?"
10 Then he said, "Tomorrow." So he said, "*May it be* according to
your word, that you may know that there is [a]no one like the LORD
our God.
11 "And the [a]frogs will depart from you and your houses and your
servants and your people; they will be left only in the Nile."
12 Then Moses and Aaron went out from Pharaoh, and [a]Moses
cried to the LORD concerning the frogs which He had [1]inflicted upon
Pharaoh.
13 And the LORD did according to the word of Moses, and the frogs
died out of the houses, the courts, and the fields.
14 So they piled them in heaps, and the land [1]became foul.
15 But when Pharaoh saw that there was relief, he [1]hardened his
heart and [a]did not listen to them, as the LORD had said.
16 Then the LORD said to Moses, "Say to Aaron, 'Stretch out your
staff and strike the dust of the earth, that it may become [1]gnats
through all the land of Egypt.' "
17 And they did so; and Aaron stretched out his hand with his staff,
and struck the dust of the earth, and there were [1]gnats on man and
beast. All the dust of the earth became [1a]gnats through all the land of
Egypt.
18 And the [1]magicians tried with their secret arts to bring forth
[2]gnats, but [a]they could not; so there were [2]gnats on man and beast.
19 Then the [1]magicians said to Pharaoh, "[a]This is the finger of
God." But Pharaoh's heart was [2]hardened, and he did not listen to
them, as the LORD had said.
20 Now the LORD said to Moses, "[a]Rise early in the morning and

were fulfilled
. 7:26 in Heb. 3; 4:23; 5:1, 3
3 [a]Ps. 105:30
1 in Heb. [2]Or, nals [a]Ex. 7:19
og [a]Ps. 78:45; 105:30
Or, soothsayer Lit., *thus* [3]Lit., [a]Ex. 7:11, 22
Ex. 8:25; 9:27; Ex. 8:28; 9:28; m. 21:7; 1 Kin. x. 8:15, 29, 32
Glory over me [2]Lit., *cut off*
Ex. 9:14; Deut. ; 33:26; 2 Sam. Chr. 17:20; Ps. :8; Is. 46:9; Jer. 10:6, 7
11 [a]Ex. 8:13
Lit., *placed* [a]Ex. :30; 9:33; 10:18
had a bad smell
Lit., *made heavy* [a]Ex. 7:4
16 [1]Or, *lice*
lice [a]Ps. 105:31
[1]Or, *soothsayer* sts [2]Or, *lice* [a]Ex. 7:11, 12; 8:7; 9:11
[1]Or, *soothsayer* iests [2]Lit., *strong* 7:5; 10:7; Ps. 8:3; Luke 11:20
20 [a]Ex. 7:15; 9:13

present yourself before Pharaoh, [1]as [b]he comes out to the water, and
say to him, 'Thus says the LORD, "[c]Let My people go, that they may
serve Me.
21 "For if you will not let My people go, behold, I will send swarms
of insects on you and on your servants and on your people and into
your houses; and the houses of the Egyptians shall be full of swarms
of insects, and also the ground on which they *dwell*.
22 "[a]But on that day I will set apart the land of Goshen, where My
people are [1]living, so that no swarms of insects will be there, in order
that you may know that [2b]I, the LORD, am in the midst of the land.
23 "And I will [1]put a division between My people and your people.
Tomorrow this sign shall occur."'"
24 Then the LORD did so. And there came [1]great swarms of insects
into the house of Pharaoh and the houses of his servants and the
land was [a]laid waste because of the swarms of insects in all the land
of Egypt.
25 And Pharaoh [a]called for Moses and Aaron and said, "[b]Go,
sacrifice to your God within the land."
26 But Moses said, "It is not right to do so, for we shall sacrifice to
the LORD our God [1]what is [a]an abomination to the Egyptians. If we
sacrifice [1]what is an abomination to the Egyptians before their eyes,
will they not then stone us?
27 "We must go a [a]three days' journey into the wilderness and
sacrifice to the LORD our God as He [1]commands us."
28 And Pharaoh said, "[a]I will let you go, that you may sacrifice to
the LORD your God in the wilderness; only you shall not go very far
away. [b]Make supplication for me."
29 Then Moses said, "Behold, I am going out from you, and I shall
make supplication to the LORD that the swarms of insects may depart
from Pharaoh, from his servants, and from his people tomorrow;
only do not let Pharaoh [a]deal deceitfully again in not letting the
people go to sacrifice to the LORD."
30 So [a]Moses went out from Pharaoh and made supplication to the
LORD.
31 And the LORD did [1]as Moses asked, and removed the swarms of
insects from Pharaoh, from his servants and from his people; not one
remained.
32 But Pharaoh [1]hardened his heart this time also, and [a]he did not
let the people go.

Chapter 9

9 Then the LORD said to Moses, "Go to Pharaoh and speak to him,
'Thus says the LORD, the God of the Hebrews, "[a]Let My people
go, that they may serve Me.
2 "For [a]if you refuse to let *them* go, and [1]continue to hold them,
3 behold, [a]the hand of the LORD [1]will come *with* a very severe
pestilence on your livestock which are in the field, on the horses, on
the donkeys, on the camels, on the herds, and on the flocks.
4 "[a]But the LORD will make a distinction between the livestock of
Israel and the livestock of Egypt, so that [b]nothing will die of all that
belongs to the sons of Israel."'"
5 And the LORD set a definite time, saying, "Tomorrow the LORD
will do this thing in the land."

20 [1]Lit., *beh* 2:5; 7:15 [c]Ex 4:23; 5:1, 3;
22 [1]Lit., *star* *am the LORD* *midst of the* 9:4, 6, 24; 10 [b]Ex. 9:29; 19
23 [1]Lit., *set a*
24 [1]Lit., *heav* 78:45; 105:31
25 [a]Ex. 8:8; 9 10:16 [b]Ex. 9:2 24; 12:31
26 [1]Lit., *the abomination o* [a]Gen. 43:32; 4 Deut. 7:25f.
27 [1]Lit., *says* 3:18; 5:3
28 [a]Ex. 8:8, 15 [b]Ex. 8:8; 9:28; 13:6
29 [a]Ex. 8:8, 15
30 [a]Ex. 8:12
31 [1]Lit., *accord* *the word of Mos*
32 [1]Lit., *made h* [a]Ex. 4:21; 8:8, 1
9:1 [a]Ex. 4:23; 8.
2 [1]Lit., *still hold*
3 [1]Lit., *will be* [a]E 1 Sam. 5:6; Ps. 3 Acts 13:11
4 [a]Ex. 8:22 [b]Ex.

6 So the LORD did this thing on the morrow, and [a]all the livestock
of Egypt died; [b]but of the livestock of the sons of Israel, not one died.
7 And Pharaoh sent, and behold, there was not even one of the
livestock of Israel dead. But [a]the heart of Pharaoh was [1]hardened,
and he did not let the people go.
8 Then the LORD said to Moses and Aaron, "Take for yourselves
handfuls of soot from a kiln, and let Moses throw it toward the sky
in the sight of Pharaoh.
9 "And it will become fine dust over all the land of Egypt, and will
become [a]boils breaking out with sores on man and beast through all
the land of Egypt."
10 So they took soot from a kiln, and stood before Pharaoh; and
Moses threw it toward the sky, and it became boils breaking out with
sores on man and beast.
11 [a]And the [1]magicians could not stand before Moses because of the
boils, for the boils were on the magicians [2]as well as on all the Egyp-
tians.
12 And [a]the LORD [1]hardened Pharaoh's heart, and he did not listen
to them, just as the LORD had spoken to Moses.
13 Then the LORD said to Moses, "[a]Rise up early in the morning and
stand before Pharaoh and say to him, 'Thus says the LORD, the God
of the Hebrews, "[b]Let My people go, that they may serve Me.
14 "For this time I will send all My plagues [1]on you and your ser-
vants and your people, so that [a]you may know that there is no one
like Me in all the earth.
15 "For *if by* now I had put forth My hand and struck you and your
people with pestilence, you would then have been cut off from the
earth.
16 "But, indeed, [a]for this cause I have allowed you to [1]remain, in
order to show you My power, and in order to proclaim My name
through all the earth.
17 "Still you exalt yourself against My people [1]by not letting
them go.
18 "Behold, about this time tomorrow, [a]I will [1]send a very heavy hail,
such as has not been *seen* in Egypt from the day it was founded
[2]until now.
19 "Now therefore send, bring [a]your livestock and whatever you
have in the field to safety. [b]Every man and beast that is found in the
field and is not brought home, when the hail comes down on them,
will die."' "
20 [a]The one among the servants of Pharaoh who [1]feared the word of
the LORD made his servants and his livestock flee into the houses;
21 but he who [1]paid no regard to the word of the LORD [2]left his
servants and his livestock in the field.
22 Now the LORD said to Moses, "Stretch out your hand toward the
sky, that [1a]hail may fall on all the land of Egypt, on man and on beast
and on every plant of the field, throughout the land of Egypt."
23 And Moses stretched out his staff toward the sky, and the LORD
[1]sent [2]thunder and [a]hail, and fire ran down to the earth. And the
LORD rained hail on the land of Egypt.
24 So there was hail, and fire [1]flashing continually in the midst of
the hail, very severe, such as had not been in all the land of Egypt
since it became a nation.
25 And [a]the hail struck all that was in the field through all the land

9, 20, 25; Ps. 3:48 [b]Ex. 9:4
., *heavy* [a]Ex. 7:14; 8:32
t. 28:27; Rev. 16:2
)r, *soothsayer* Lit., *and on all* [a]Ex. 8:18
, *made strong* 4:21; 10:1, 20; h. 11:20; John 12:40
3:20 [b]Ex. 4:23
., *to your heart* 10; Deut. 3:24; m. 7:22; 1 Chr. 0; Ps. 86:8; Is. :9; Jer. 10:6, 7
., *stand* [a]Prov. 6:4; Rom. 9:17
so as not to let
., *cause to rain* *until now* [a]Ex. 9:23, 24
. 9:6 [b]Ex. 9:25
revered [a]Prov. 13:13
., *did not set his to* [2]Lit., *then left*
it., *there may be hail* [a]Rev. 16:21
[1]Lit., *gave* [2]Lit., ds [a]Gen. 19:24; 10:11; Ps. 18:13; 05:32; Is. 30:30; . 38:22; Rev. 8:7
it., *taking hold of itself*
. 9:19; Ps. 78:47, 48; 105:32, 33

of Egypt, both man and beast; the hail also struck every plant of the
field and shattered every tree of the field.
26 [a]Only in the land of Goshen, where the sons of Israel *were*, there
was no hail.
27 Then Pharaoh [1a]sent for Moses and Aaron, and said to them, "[b]I
have sinned this time; the LORD is the righteous one, and I and my
people are the wicked ones.
28 "[a]Make supplication to the LORD, for there has been enough of
God's [1]thunder and hail; and [b]I will let you go, and you shall stay no
longer."
29 And Moses said to him, "As soon as I go out of the city, I will
[a]spread out my [1]hands to the LORD; the [2]thunder will cease, and there
will be hail no longer, that you may know that [b]the earth is the
LORD's.
30 "[a]But as for you and your servants, I know that [b]you do not yet
[1]fear [2]the LORD God."
31 (Now the flax and the [a]barley were [1]ruined, for the barley was in
the ear and the flax was in bud.
32 But the wheat and the spelt were not [1]ruined, for they *ripen* late.)
33 [a]So Moses went out of the city from Pharaoh, and spread out his
[1]hands to the LORD; and the [2]thunder and the hail ceased, and rain
[3]no longer poured on the earth.
34 But when Pharaoh saw that the rain and the hail and the
[1]thunder had ceased, he sinned again and [2]hardened his heart, he
and his servants.
35 And Pharaoh's heart was [1]hardened, and he did not let the sons
of Israel go, just as the [a]LORD had spoken through Moses.

Chapter 10

10 Then the LORD said to Moses, "Go to Pharaoh, for [a]I have
[1]hardened his heart and the heart of his servants, that I may
[2]perform these signs of Mine [3]among them,
2 and [a]that you may tell in the [1]hearing of your son, and of your
grandson, how I made a mockery of the Egyptians, and how I [2]per-
formed My signs among them; [b]that you may know that I am the
LORD."
3 And Moses and Aaron went to Pharaoh and said to him, "Thus
says the LORD, the God of the Hebrews, 'How long will you refuse
to [a]humble yourself before Me? [b]Let My people go, that they may
serve Me.
4 'For if you refuse to let My people go, behold, tomorrow I will
bring locusts into your territory.
5 'And they shall cover the surface of the land, so that no one shall
be able to see the land. [a]They shall also eat the rest of what has
escaped—what is left to you from the hail—and they shall eat every
tree which sprouts for you out of the field.
6 'Then [a]your houses shall be filled, and the houses of all your
servants and the houses of all the Egyptians, *something* which neither
your fathers nor your grandfathers have seen, from the day that they
[1]came upon the earth until this day.'" And he turned and went out
from Pharaoh.
7 And [a]Pharaoh's servants said to him, "How long will this man
be [b]a snare to us? Let the men go, that they may serve the LORD their
God. Do you not [1]realize that Egypt is destroyed?"

26 [a]Ex. 8:2
11:7

27 [1]Lit., *ser*
called [a]Ex.
10:16, 17; 2
Ps. 129:4; 1
1:18

28 [1]Lit., *sou*
8:8, 28; 10:1
8:25; 10:8, 2

29 [1]Lit., *palr*
sounds [a]1 K
Ps. 143:6; Is.
8:22; 19:5; 2
24:1; 1 Cor.

30 [1]Or, *reve*
before the L
8:29 [b]Is. 26:

31 [1]Lit., *smit*
1:22; 2:23

32 [1]Lit., *smit*

33 [1]Lit., *palm*
sounds [3]Lit.,
poured [a]Ex.

34 [1]Lit., *soun*
made heavy

35 [1]Lit., *stron*
4:21

10:1 [1]Lit., *ma*
[2]Lit., *put* [3]Lit.,
midst [a]Ex. 4:2
Josh. 11:20; Jo
Rom. 9:18

2 [1]Lit., *ears*
[a]Ex. 12:26, 27;
15; Deut. 4:9;
78:5; Joel 1:3
7:5, 17

3 [a]1 Kin. 21:29
34:27; James 4
1 Pet. 5:6 [b]Ex.

5 [a]Joel 1:4; 2:2

6 [1]Lit., *were* [a]E
8:3, 21

7 [1]Lit., *know* [a]E
8:19; 12:33 [b]Ex
Josh. 23:13; 1 S
18:21; Eccl. 7:2

8 So Moses and Aaron [a]were brought back to Pharaoh, and he said
to them, "[b]Go, serve the LORD your God! [1]Who are the ones that are
going?"
9 And Moses said, "[a]We shall go with our young and our old; with
our sons and our daughters, [b]with our flocks and our herds we will
go, for we [1]must hold a feast to the LORD."
10 Then he said to them, "Thus may the LORD be with you, [1]if ever I
let you and your little ones go! Take heed, for evil is [2]in your mind.
11 "Not so! Go now, the men *among you*, and serve the LORD, for [1]that
is what you desire." So [a]they were driven out from Pharaoh's pres-
ence.
12 Then the LORD said to Moses, "[a]Stretch out your hand over the
land of Egypt for the locusts, that they may come up on the land of
Egypt, and [b]eat every plant of the land, *even* all that the hail has left."
13 So Moses stretched out his staff over the land of Egypt, and the
LORD directed an east wind on the land all that day and all that
night; and when it was morning, the east wind [1]brought the [a]locusts.
14 And [a]the locusts came up over all the land of Egypt and settled
in all the territory of Egypt; *they were* very [1]numerous. There had
never been so *many* [2]locusts, nor would there be so *many* [3]again.
15 For they covered the surface of the whole land, so that the land
was darkened; and they [a]ate every plant of the land and all the fruit
of the trees that the hail had left. Thus nothing green was left on tree
or plant of the field through all the land of Egypt.
16 Then Pharaoh hurriedly [a]called for Moses and Aaron, and he
said, "[b]I have sinned against the LORD your God and against you.
17 "Now therefore, please forgive my sin only this once, and [a]make
supplication to the LORD your God, that He would only remove this
death from me."
18 And [a]he went out from Pharaoh and made supplication to the
LORD.
19 So the LORD shifted *the wind* to a very strong west wind which
took up the locusts and drove them into the [1]Red Sea; not one locust
was left in all the territory of Egypt.
20 But [a]the LORD [1]hardened Pharaoh's heart, and he did not let the
sons of Israel go.
21 Then the LORD said to Moses, "[a]Stretch out your hand toward the
sky, that there may be darkness over the land of Egypt, even a dark-
ness [b]which may be felt."
22 So Moses stretched out his hand toward the sky, and there was
[a]thick darkness in all the land of Egypt for three days.
23 They did not see one another, nor did anyone rise from his place
for three days, [a]but all the sons of Israel had light in their dwellings.
24 Then Pharaoh [a]called to Moses, and said, "Go, serve the LORD;
only let your flocks and your herds be detained. Even [b]your little
ones may go with you."
25 But Moses said, "You must also [1]let us have sacrifices and burnt
offerings, that we may [2]sacrifice *them* to the LORD our God.
26 "[a]Therefore, our livestock, too, will go with us; not a hoof will be
left behind, for we shall take some of them to serve the LORD our
God. And until we arrive there, we ourselves do not know with
what we shall serve the LORD."
27 But [a]the LORD [1]hardened Pharaoh's heart, and he was not willing
to let them go.

Who and who ...8:8 [b]Ex. 8:25
...have a feast ...2:37, 38 [b]Ex. 10:26
..., when I [2]Lit., *...fore your face*
..., you desire it [a]Ex. 10:28
[a]Ex. 7:19 [b]Ex. 10:5, 15
..., carried [a]Ps. 78:46; 105:34
...t., heavy [2]Lit., *...ke them before* [3]Lit., *after them* ...:38; Ps. 78:46; ...34; Joel 1:4, 7; ...:1-11; Rev. 9:3
[a]Ex. 10:5; Ps. 105:34f.
...8:8 [b]Ex. 9:27
...x. 8:8, 28; 9:28; 1 Kin. 13:6
18 [a]Ex. 8:30
..., Sea of Reeds
...it., made strong [a]Ex. 4:21; 11:10
[a]Ex. 9:22 [b]Deut. 28:29
...Ps. 105:28; Rev. 16:10
23 [a]Ex. 8:22
[a]Ex. 8:8, 25 [b]Ex. 10:10
[1]Lit., *give into our hand* [2]Lit., *make*
26 [a]Ex. 10:9
[1]Lit., *made strong* ...21; 10:20; 14:4, 8

28 Then Pharaoh said to him, "[a]Get away from me! [1]Beware, do not
see my face again, for in the day you see my face you shall die!"
29 And Moses said, "You are right; [a]I shall never see your face
again!"

Chapter 11

11 Now the LORD said to Moses, "One more plague I will bring
on Pharaoh and on Egypt; [a]after that he will let you go from
here. When he lets you go, he will surely drive you out from here
completely.
2 "Speak now in the [1]hearing of the people that [a]each man ask from
his neighbor and each woman from her neighbor for articles of silver
and articles of gold."
3 [a]And the LORD gave the people favor in the sight of the Egyp-
tians. [b]Furthermore, the man Moses *himself* was [1]greatly esteemed in
the land of Egypt, *both* in the sight of Pharaoh's servants and in the
sight of the people.
4 And Moses said, "Thus says the LORD, 'About [a]midnight I am
going out into the midst of Egypt,
5 and [a]all the first-born in the land of Egypt shall die, from the
first-born of the Pharaoh who sits on his throne, even to the first-
born of the slave girl who is behind the millstones; all the first-born
of the cattle as well.
6 'Moreover, there shall be [a]a great cry in all the land of Egypt,
such as there has not been *before* and such as shall never be again.
7 '[a]But against any of the sons of Israel a dog shall not *even* [1]bark,
whether against man or beast, that you may [2]understand how the
LORD makes a distinction between Egypt and Israel.'
8 "And [a]all these your servants will come down to me and bow
themselves [1]before me, saying, 'Go out, you and all the people who
[2]follow you,' and after that I will go out." [b]And he went out from
Pharaoh in hot anger.
9 Then the LORD said to Moses, "[a]Pharaoh will not listen to you, so
[b]that My wonders will be multiplied in the land of Egypt."
10 And [a]Moses and Aaron performed all these wonders before Pha-
raoh; yet [b]the LORD [1]hardened Pharaoh's heart, and he did not let the
sons of Israel go out of his land.

Chapter 12

12 Now the LORD said to Moses and Aaron in the land of [1]Egypt,
2 "[a]This month shall be the beginning of months for you; it is
to be the first month of the year to you.
3 "Speak to all the congregation of Israel, saying, 'On the tenth of
this month they are each one to take a [1]lamb for themselves, accord-
ing to their fathers' households, a [1]lamb for [2]each household.
4 'Now if the household is too small for a [1]lamb, then he and his
neighbor nearest to his house are to take one according to the [2]num-
ber of persons *in them;* according to [3]what each man should eat, you
are to [4]divide the lamb.
5 'Your [1]lamb shall be [a]an unblemished male a year old; you may
take it from the sheep or from the goats.
6 'And [1]you shall keep it until the [a]fourteenth day of the same
month, then the whole assembly of the congregation of Israel is to
kill it [2b]at twilight.

28 [1]Lit., *Ta*
yourself [a]E

29 [a]Ex. 11:

11:1 [a]Ex. 1

2 [1]Lit., *ears*
12:35, 36

3 [1]Lit., *very*
3:21; 12:36;
[b]Deut. 34:10

4 [a]Ex. 12:29

5 [a]Ex. 12:12
78:51; 105:3
136:10

6 [a]Ex. 12:30

7 [1]Lit., *sharp*
tongue [2]Lit.,
8:22; Josh. 1

8 [1]Lit., *to* [2]Li
your feet [a]Ex
[b]Heb. 11:27

9 [a]Ex. 7:4 [b]E

10 [1]Lit., *made*
[a]Ex. 4:21 [b]Ex
10:20, 27; Jos
Is. 63:17; John

12:1 [1]Lit., *Eg*

2 [a]Ex. 13:4; 2
34:18; Deut. 1

3 [1]Or, *kid* [2]Lit.

4 [1]Or, *kid* [2]Or,
[3]Lit., *each man*
[4]Lit., *compute*

5 [1]Or, *kid* [a]Lev
22:18-21; 23:12
9:14; 1 Pet. 1:1

6 [1]Lit., *it shall b*
for a guarding
between the two
evenings [a]Ex.
17; Lev. 23:5; N
9:1-3, 11; 28:16
16:12; Deut. 16:

7 '[a]Moreover, they shall take some of the blood and put it on the
two doorposts and on the lintel [1]of the houses in which they eat it.
8 'And they shall eat the flesh [a]that *same* night, [b]roasted with fire,
and they shall eat it with [c]unleavened bread [1d]and bitter herbs.
9 'Do not eat any of it raw or boiled at all with water, but rather
[a]roasted with fire, *both* its head and its legs along with [b]its entrails.
10 '[a]And you shall not leave any of it over until morning, but
whatever is left of it until morning, you shall burn with fire.
11 'Now you shall eat it in this manner: *with* your loins girded, your
sandals on your feet, and your staff in your hand; and you shall eat
it in haste—it is [a]the LORD's Passover.
12 'For [a]I will go through the land of Egypt on that night, and will
strike down all the first-born in the land of Egypt, both man and
beast; and [b]against all the gods of Egypt I will execute judgments—[c]I
am the LORD.
13 'And [a]the blood shall be a sign for you on the houses where you
[1]live; and when I see the blood I will pass over you, and no plague
will befall you [2]to destroy *you* when I strike the land of Egypt.
14 'Now [a]this day will be [b]a memorial to you, and you shall
celebrate it *as* a feast to the LORD; throughout your generations you
are to celebrate it *as* [1c]a permanent ordinance.
15 '[a]Seven days you shall eat unleavened bread, but on the first day
you shall [1]remove leaven from your houses; for whoever eats any-
thing leavened from the first day until the seventh day, [b]that [2]person
shall be cut off from Israel.
16 'And [a]on the first day you shall have a holy assembly, and *another*
holy assembly on the seventh day; no work at all shall be done on
them, except what must be eaten [1]by every person, that alone may be
[2]prepared by you.
17 'You shall also observe [a]the *Feast of* Unleavened Bread, for on this
[b]very day I brought your hosts out of the land of Egypt; therefore
you shall observe this day throughout your generations as [c]a [1]per-
manent ordinance.
18 '[a]In the first *month,* on the fourteenth day of the month at eve-
ning, you shall eat unleavened bread, until the twenty-first day of
the month at evening.
19 '[a]Seven days there shall be no leaven found in your houses; for
whoever eats what is leavened, that [1b]person shall be cut off from the
congregation of Israel, whether *he is* an alien or a native of the land.
20 'You shall not eat anything leavened; in all your dwellings you
shall eat unleavened bread.' "
21 Then [a]Moses called for all the elders of Israel, and said to them,
"[1]Go and [b]take for yourselves [2]lambs according to your families, and
slay [c]the Passover *lamb.*
22 "[a]And you shall take a bunch of hyssop and dip it in the blood
which is in the basin, and [1]apply some of the blood that is in the
basin to the lintel and the two doorposts; and none of you shall go
outside the door of his house until morning.
23 "For [a]the LORD will pass through to smite the Egyptians; and
when He sees the blood on the lintel and on the two doorposts, the
LORD will pass over the door and will [b]not allow the [c]destroyer to
come in to your houses to smite *you.*
24 "And [a]you shall observe this event as an ordinance for you and
your children forever.

ı [a]Ex. 12:22

n addition to
5; Num. 9:12
[c]Deut. 16:3,
[d]Num. 9:11

[b]Ex. 29:13,
17, 22

16:19; 23:18;
34:25

x. 12:13, 21,
27, 43

1:4, 5 [b]Num.
82:1 [c]Ex. 6:2

, *are* [2]Lit., *for*
ı [a]Heb. 11:28

ı *eternal* [a]Ex.
23:4, 5; 2 Kin.
Ex. 13:9 [c]Ex.
:17, 24; 13:10

[1]Lit., *cause to*
Lit., *soul* [a]Ex.
23:15; 34:18;
5; Num. 28:17;
16:3, 8 [b]Gen.
x. 12:19; Num.
9:13

., *pertaining to*
[a]Lev. 23:7, 8;
Num. 28:18, 25

eternal [a]Deut.
Ex. 12:41 [c]Ex.
12:14; 13:3, 10

[a]Ex. 12:2; Lev.
Num. 28:16-25

[1]Lit., *soul* [a]Ex.
5; 23:15; 34:18
[b]Num. 9:13

Draw out [2]Lit.,
Num. 9:4; Heb.
[b]Ex. 12:3 [c]Ex.
12:11

, *cause to touch*
[a]Ex. 12:7

11:4; 12:12, 13
7:3; 9:4 [c]1 Cor.
0:10; Heb. 11:28

[a]Ex. 12:14, 17;
13:5, 10

25 "And it will come about when you enter the land which the LORD
will give you, as He has [1]promised, that you shall observe this [2]rite.
26 "[a]And it will come about when your children will say to you,
'[1]What does this rite mean to you?'
27 that you shall say, 'It is a Passover sacrifice to [a]the LORD [1]who
passed over the houses of the sons of Israel in Egypt when He smote
the Egyptians, but [2]spared our homes.' " [b]And the people bowed low
and worshiped.
28 Then the sons of Israel went and did *so;* just as the LORD had
commanded Moses and Aaron, so they did.
29 Now it came about at [a]midnight that [b]the LORD struck all [c]the
first-born in the land of Egypt, from the first-born of Pharaoh who
sat on his throne to the first-born of the captive who was in the
dungeon, and all the first-born of [d]cattle.
30 And Pharaoh arose in the night, he and all his servants and all
the Egyptians; and there was [a]a great cry in Egypt, for there was no
home where there was not someone dead.
31 Then [a]he called for Moses and Aaron at night and said, "Rise up,
[b]get out from among my people, both you and the sons of Israel; and
go, [1]worship the LORD, as you have said.
32 "Take [a]both your flocks and your herds, as you have said, and go,
and bless me also."
33 And [a]the Egyptians urged the people, to send them out of the
land in haste, for they said, "We shall all be dead."
34 So the people took [a]their dough before it was leavened, *with* their
kneading bowls bound up in the clothes on their shoulders.
35 [a]Now the sons of Israel had done according to the word of
Moses, for they had requested from the Egyptians articles of silver
and articles of gold, and clothing;
36 and the LORD had given the people favor in the sight of the
Egyptians, so that they let them have their request. Thus they [a]plun-
dered the Egyptians.
37 Now the [a]sons of Israel journeyed from [b]Rameses to Succoth,
about [c]six hundred thousand men on foot, aside from children.
38 And a [a]mixed multitude also went up with them, [1]along with
flocks and herds, a [b]very large number of livestock.
39 And they baked the dough which they had brought out of Egypt
into cakes of unleavened bread. For it had not become leavened,
since they were [a]driven out of Egypt and could not delay, nor had
they [1]prepared any provisions for themselves.
40 Now the time [1]that the sons of Israel lived in Egypt was [a]four
hundred and thirty years.
41 And it came about at the end of four hundred and thirty years,
[1]to [a]the very day, that [b]all the hosts of the LORD went out from the
land of Egypt.
42 [a]It is a night [1]to be observed for the LORD for having brought
them out from the land of Egypt; this night is for the LORD, [1]to be
observed [2]by all the sons of Israel throughout their generations.
43 And the LORD said to Moses and Aaron, "This is the ordinance of
[a]the Passover: no [1b]foreigner is to eat of it;
44 but every man's [a]slave purchased with money, after you have
circumcised him, then he may eat of it.
45 "[a]A sojourner or a hired servant shall not eat of it.

25 [1]Lit., *sp*
service
26 [1]Lit., *Wh*
service to y
10:2; 13:8,
32:7; Josh.
27 [1]Lit., *bec*
[2]Lit., *deliver*
12:11 [b]Ex. 4
29 [a]Ex. 11:4
8:17; 33:4; P
136:10 [c]Ex.
78:51; 105:3
30 [a]Ex. 11:6
31 [1]Or, *serv*
[b]Ex. 8:25
32 [a]Ex. 10:9
33 [a]Ex. 10:7
12:39; Ps. 10
34 [a]Ex. 12:3
35 [a]Ex. 3:21,
3; Ps. 105:37
36 [a]Ex. 3:22
37 [a]Num. 33
47:11 [c]Ex. 38
1:46; 2:32; 11
38 [1]Lit., *and*
11:4 [b]Ex. 17:3
20:19; 32:1; D
39 [1]Lit., *made*
11:1; 12:31-33
40 [1]Or, *of the*
Israel who dw
15:13, 16; Acts
3:17
41 [1]Lit., *that it*
happened on t
day [a]Ex. 12:17
3:8, 10; 6:6
42 [1]Or, *of vigil*
the sons [a]Ex.
34:18; Deut. 16
43 [1]Lit., *son of*
stranger [a]Ex.
Num. 9:14 [b]Ex
44 [a]Gen. 17:12
Lev. 22:11
45 [a]Lev. 22:10

46 "It is to be eaten in a single house; you are not to bring forth any
of the flesh outside of the house, [a]nor are you to break any bone of it.
47 "[a]All the congregation of Israel are to [1]celebrate this.
48 "But [a]if a [1]stranger sojourns with you, and [2]celebrates the Pass-
over to the LORD, let all his males be circumcised, and then let him
come near to [3]celebrate it; and he shall be like a native of the land.
But no uncircumcised person may eat of it.
49 "[1a]The same law shall [2]apply to the native as to the [3]stranger who
sojourns among you."
50 Then all the sons of Israel did *so;* they did just as the LORD had
commanded Moses and Aaron.
51 And it came about on that same day that [a]the LORD brought the
sons of Israel out of the land of Egypt [1b]by their hosts.

Chapter 13

13 Then the LORD spoke to Moses, saying,
2 "[a]Sanctify to Me every first-born, the first [1]offspring of every
womb among the sons of Israel, both of man and beast; it belongs to
Me."
3 And Moses said to the people, "[a]Remember this day in which
you went out from Egypt, from the house of [1]slavery; for [b]by [2]a
powerful hand the LORD brought you out from this place. [c]And noth-
ing leavened shall be eaten.
4 "On this day in the [a]month of Abib, you are about to go forth.
5 "And it shall be when the LORD [a]brings you to the land of the
Canaanite, the Hittite, the Amorite, the Hivite and the Jebusite,
which [b]He swore to your fathers to give you, a land flowing with
milk and honey, [c]that you shall [1]observe this rite in this month.
6 "For [a]seven days you shall eat unleavened bread, and on the
seventh day there shall be a feast to the LORD.
7 "Unleavened bread shall be eaten throughout the seven days; and
[a]nothing leavened shall be seen [1]among you, nor shall any leaven be
seen [1]among you in all your borders.
8 "[a]And you shall tell your son on that day, saying, 'It is because of
what the LORD did for me when I came out of Egypt.'
9 "And [a]it shall [1]serve as a sign to you on your hand, and as a
reminder [2]on your forehead, that the law of the LORD may be in your
mouth; for with [b]a powerful hand the LORD brought you out of
Egypt.
10 "Therefore, you shall [a]keep this ordinance at its appointed time
from [1]year to year.
11 "Now it shall come about when [a]the LORD brings you to the land
of the Canaanite, as [b]He swore to you and to your fathers, and gives
it to you,
12 that [a]you shall [1]devote to the LORD the first [2]offspring of every
womb, and [3]the first offspring of every beast that you own; the
males belong to the LORD.
13 "But [a]every first [1]offspring of a donkey you shall redeem with a
lamb, but if you do not redeem *it,* then you shall break its neck; and
[b]every first-born of man among your sons you shall redeem.
14 "[a]And it shall be when your son asks you in time to come, saying,
'What is this?' then you shall say to him, '[b]With a [1]powerful hand the
LORD brought us out of Egypt, from the house of [2]slavery.
15 'And it came about, when Pharaoh was stubborn about letting us

m. 9:12; Ps. hn 19:33, 36
lo [a]Ex. 12:6; um. 9:13, 14
journer [2]Lit., it., *do* [a]Num. 9:14
One law [2]Lit., *journer* [a]Lev. ; Num. 15:15, 16, 29
, *according to* :41 [b]Ex. 6:26
opening [a]Ex. 13, 15; 22:29; 6; Num. 3:13; ; 18:15; Deut. 19; Luke 2:23
., *slaves* [2]Lit., *1 of hand* [a]Ex. eut. 16:3 [b]Ex. 6:1 [c]Ex. 12:19
x. 12:2; 23:15; 18; Deut. 16:1
[1]Lit., *serve this e* [a]Ex. 3:8, 17; 24:11 [b]Ex. 6:8 [c]Ex. 12:25
[a]Ex. 12:15-20
., *to* [a]Ex. 12:19
x. 10:2; 12:26f.; 13:14; Ps. 44:1
Lit., *be for* [2]Lit., *your eyes* [a]Ex. 14; 13:16; Num. Deut. 6:8; 11:18 [b]Ex. 13:3
it., *days to days* 12:24, 25; 13:5
[a]Ex. 13:5 [b]Gen. 17:8; 28:15; Ps. 105:42-45
t., *cause to pass* t., *opening* [3]Lit., *sue the offspring ast* [a]Ex. 13:1, 2; 2:29; 34:19; Lev. :26; Num. 18:15; 44:30; Luke 2:23
.it., *opening* [a]Ex. 4:20; Num. 18:15 [b]Num. 3:46
[1]Lit., *strength of* [2]Lit., *slaves* [a]Ex. ; 12:26, 27; 13:8; t. 6:20; Josh. 4:6, 21 [b]Ex. 13:3, 9

go, that the [a]LORD killed every first-born in the land of Egypt, both
the first-born of man and the first-born of beast. Therefore, I sacrifice
to the LORD the males, the first [1]offspring of every womb, but every
first-born of my sons I redeem.'
16 "So [a]it shall [1]serve as a sign on your hand, and as [2]phylacteries
[3]on your forehead, for with a [4]powerful hand the LORD brought us
out of Egypt."
17 Now it came about when Pharaoh had let the people go, that
God did not lead them by the way of the land of the Philistines, even
though it was near; for God said, "[a]Lest the people change their
minds when they see war, and they return to Egypt."
18 Hence God led the people around by the way of the wilderness
to the [1]Red Sea; and the sons of Israel went up [a]in martial array from
the land of Egypt.
19 And Moses took [a]the bones of Joseph with him, for he had made
the sons of Israel solemnly swear, saying, "God shall surely [1]take
care of you; and you shall carry my bones from here with you."
20 Then they set out from [a]Succoth and camped in Etham on the
edge of the wilderness.
21 And [a]the LORD was going before them in a pillar of cloud by day
to lead them on the way, and in a pillar of fire by night to give them
light, that they might [1]travel by day and by night.
22 [1]He [a]did not take away the pillar of cloud by day, nor the pillar
of fire by night, from before the people.

Chapter 14

14 Now the LORD spoke to Moses, saying,
2 "Tell the sons of Israel to turn back and camp before [a]Pi-
hahiroth, between [b]Migdol and the sea; you shall camp in front of
Baal-zephon, opposite it, by the sea.
3 "For Pharaoh will say of the sons of Israel, 'They are wandering
aimlessly in the land; the wilderness has shut them in.'
4 "Thus [a]I will [1]harden Pharaoh's heart, and [b]he will chase after
them; and I will be honored through Pharaoh and all his army, and
[c]the Egyptians will know that I am the LORD." And they did so.
5 When the king of Egypt was told that the people had fled, [1]Pha-
raoh and his servants had a change of heart toward the people, and
they said, "What is this we have done, that we have let Israel go
from serving us?"
6 So he made his chariot ready and took his people with him;
7 and he took six hundred select chariots, and all the *other* chariots
of Egypt with officers over all of them.
8 And [a]the LORD [1]hardened the heart of Pharaoh, king of Egypt,
and he chased after the sons of Israel as the sons of Israel were going
out [2b]boldly.
9 Then [a]the Egyptians chased after them *with* all the horses *and*
chariots of Pharaoh, his horsemen and his army, and they overtook
them camping by the sea, [b]beside Pi-hahiroth, in front of Baal-
zephon.
10 And as Pharaoh drew near, the sons of Israel [1]looked, and be-
hold, the Egyptians were marching after them, and they became
very frightened; [a]so the sons of Israel cried out to the LORD.
11 Then [a]they said to Moses, "Is it because there were no graves in

15 [1]Lit., *op*... 12:29

16 [1]Lit., *be* *frontlet-ban*... *between yo*... [4]Lit., *strengt*... [a]Ex. 13:9; D...

17 [a]Ex. 14:1... 14:1-4; Deut...

18 [1]Lit., *Sea*... [a]Josh. 1:14;...

19 [1]Lit., *visi*... 50:24, 25; Jo... Acts 7:15, 16...

20 [a]Ex. 12:3... 33:6

21 [1]Lit., *go*... 24; 33:9, 10;... 14:14; Deut.... 9:12; Ps. 78:1... 105:39; Is. 4:5... 10:1

22 [1]Or, *The p*... *cloud by day*... *pillar of fire by*... *not depart* [a]N...

14:2 [a]Num. 3... 44:1

4 [1]Lit., *make s*... [a]Ex. 4:21; 7:3;... [b]Ex. 14:23 [c]Ex... 14:25

5 [1]Lit., *the hea*... *Pharaoh . . . w*... *changed*

8 [1]Lit., *made s*... [2]Lit., *with a hig*... [a]Ex. 14:4 [b]Num... Acts 13:17

9 [a]Ex. 15:9; Jo... [b]Ex. 14:2

10 [1]Lit., *lifted u*... *eyes* [a]Josh. 24... 9:9; Ps. 34:17;...

11 [a]Ex. 5:21; 15... 16:2; Ps. 106:7,...

Egypt that you have taken us away to die in the wilderness? Why
have you dealt with us in this way, [1]bringing us out of Egypt?
12 "[a]Is this not the word that we spoke to you in Egypt, saying,
'[1]Leave us alone that we may serve the Egyptians'? For it would
have been better for us to serve the Egyptians than to die in the
wilderness."
13 But Moses said to the people, "[a]Do not fear! [1]Stand by and see
[b]the salvation of the LORD which He will accomplish for you today;
for the Egyptians whom you have seen today, you will never see
them again forever.
14 "[a]The LORD will fight for you while [b]you keep silent."
15 Then the LORD said to Moses, "Why are you crying out to Me?
Tell the sons of Israel to go forward.
16 "And as for you, lift up [a]your staff and stretch out your hand over
the sea and divide it, and the sons of Israel shall [1]go through the
midst of the sea on dry land.
17 "And as for Me, behold, [a]I will [1]harden the hearts of the Egyptians
so that they will go in after them; and I will be honored through
Pharaoh and all his army, through his chariots and his horsemen.
18 "[a]Then the Egyptians will know that I am the LORD, when I am
honored through Pharaoh, through his chariots and his horsemen."
19 And [a]the angel of God, who had been going before the camp of
Israel, moved and went behind them; and the pillar of cloud moved
from before them and stood behind them.
20 So it came between the camp of Egypt and the camp of Israel;
and there was the cloud [1]along with the darkness, yet it gave light at
night. Thus the one did not come near the other all night.
21 [a]Then Moses stretched out his hand over the sea; and the LORD
[1]swept the sea *back* by a strong east wind all night, and turned the
sea into [b]dry land, so [c]the waters were divided.
22 [a]And the sons of Israel [1]went through the midst of the sea on the
dry land, and [b]the waters *were like* a wall to them on their right hand
and on their left.
23 Then [a]the Egyptians took up the pursuit, and all Pharaoh's hor-
ses, his chariots and his horsemen went in after them into the midst
of the sea.
24 And it came about at the morning watch, that [a]the LORD looked
down on the [1]army of the Egyptians [2]through the pillar of fire and
cloud and brought the [1]army of the Egyptians into confusion.
25 And He [1]caused their chariot wheels to swerve, and He made
them drive with difficulty; so the Egyptians said, "Let [2]us flee from
Israel, [a]for the LORD is fighting for them against the Egyptians."
26 Then the LORD said to Moses, "[a]Stretch out your hand over the
sea so that the waters may come back over the Egyptians, over their
chariots and their horsemen."
27 So Moses stretched out his hand over the sea, and [a]the sea
returned to its normal state at daybreak, while the Egyptians were
fleeing [1]right into it; then the LORD [2b]overthrew the Egyptians in the
midst of the sea.
28 And the waters returned and covered the chariots and the horse-
men, [1]even Pharaoh's entire army that had gone into the sea after
them; [a]not even one of them remained.
29 But the sons of Israel walked on [a]dry land through the midst of

so as to bring
Cease from us [a]Ex. 6:9
[1]Or, *Take your* ...en. 15:1; 46:3; ...); 2 Chr. 20:15, ...s. 41:10, 13, 14 ...Ex. 14:30; 15:2
...Ex. 14:25; 15:3; ...:30; 3:22; Josh. ...Chr. 20:29; Neh. 4:20 [b]Is. 30:15
..., *enter the* [a]Ex. ...20; 7:19; 14:21, ...17:5, 6, 9; Num. ...9, 11; Is. 10:26
...Lit., *make strong* [a]Ex. 14:4, 8
18 [a]Ex. 14:25
...[a]Ex. 13:21, 22
20 [1]Lit., *and the darkness*
...Lit., *caused to go* ...7:19; 14:16 [b]Ps. ...06:9; 136:13, 14 ...15:8; Josh. 3:16; ...3; Neh. 9:11; Ps. ...; 78:13; 114:3, 5; Is. 63:12, 13
[1]Lit., *entered the* ...5:19; Josh. 3:17; ...22; Neh. 9:11; Ps. ...78:13; Heb. 11:29 [b]Ex. 14:29; 15:8
23 [a]Ex. 14:4, 17
[1]Lit., *camp* [2]Or, *in* [a]Ex. 13:21
...Or, *removed* [2]Lit., ...[a]Ex. 14:4, 14, 18
26 [a]Ex. 14:16
...Lit., *to meet it* [2]Lit., ...*ook off* [a]Josh. 4:18 ...15:1, 7; Deut. 11:4; ...eh. 9:11; Ps. 78:53; Heb. 11:29
... [1]Lit., *in respect to* [a]Ps. 78:53; 106:11
...Ex. 14:22; Ps. 66:6; Is. 11:15

the sea, and the waters *were like* a wall to them on their right hand
and on their left.
30 [a]Thus the LORD saved Israel that day from the hand of the Egyp-
tians, and Israel [b]saw the Egyptians dead on the seashore.
31 And when Israel saw the great [1]power which the LORD had [2]used
against the Egyptians, the people [3]feared the LORD, and [a]they
believed in the LORD and in His servant Moses.

Chapter 15

15 [a]Then Moses and the sons of Israel sang this song to the LORD,
[1]and said,
"[2b]I will sing to the LORD, for He [3]is highly exalted;
[c]The horse and its rider He has hurled into the sea.
2 "[1a]The LORD is my strength and song,
And He has become my salvation;
[b]This is my God, and I will praise Him;
[c]My father's God, and I will [d]extol Him.
3 "[a]The LORD is a warrior;
[1b]The LORD is His name.
4 "[a]Pharaoh's chariots and his army He has cast into the sea;
And the choicest of his officers are [1]drowned in the [2]Red Sea.
5 "The deeps cover them;
[a]They went down into the depths like a stone.
6 "[a]Thy right hand, O LORD, is majestic in power,
[b]Thy right hand, O LORD, shatters the enemy.
7 "And in the greatness of Thine [1]excellence Thou [a]dost overthrow
those who rise up against Thee;
[b]Thou dost send forth Thy burning anger, *and* it [c]consumes them
as chaff.
8 "[a]And at the blast of Thy nostrils the waters were piled up,
[b]The flowing waters stood up like a heap;
The deeps were congealed in the heart of the sea.
9 "[a]The enemy said, 'I will pursue, I will overtake, I will [b]divide the
spoil;
My [1]desire shall be [2]gratified against them;
I will draw out my sword, my hand shall [3]destroy them.'
10 "[a]Thou didst blow with Thy wind, the sea covered them;
[b]They sank like lead in the [1]mighty waters.
11 "[a]Who is like Thee among the gods, O LORD?
Who is like Thee, [b]majestic in holiness,
[c]Awesome in praises, [d]working wonders?
12 "[a]Thou didst stretch out Thy right hand,
The earth swallowed them.
13 "In Thy lovingkindness Thou hast [a]led the people whom Thou
hast [b]redeemed;
In Thy strength Thou hast guided *them* [c]to Thy holy habitation.
14 "[a]The peoples have heard, they tremble;
Anguish has gripped the inhabitants of Philistia.
15 "Then the [a]chiefs of Edom were dismayed;
[b]The leaders of Moab, trembling grips them;
[c]All the inhabitants of Canaan have melted away.
16 "[a]Terror and dread fall upon them;
[b]By the greatness of Thine arm they are motionless as stone;
Until Thy people pass over, O LORD,

30 [a]Ex. 14:1 106:8, 10; Is. [b]Ps. 58:10; 5

31 [1]Lit., *hand* *done* [3]Or, *re* 4:31; 19:9; Ps John 2:11; 11

15:1 [1]Lit., *an* *saying* [2]Or, *L* *sing* [3]Or, *triur* *gloriously* [a]Ps Rev. 15:3 [b]Is. 42:10-12 [c]Jer

2 [1]Heb., YAH 2; Is. 12:2; Ha [b]Ps. 48:14 [c]Ex 16 [d]2 Sam. 22 99:5; Is. 25:1

3 [1]Heb., *YHW* usually render [a]Ex. 14:14; Re [b]Ex. 3:15; 6:2, Ps. 24:8; 83:18

4 [1]Lit., *sunk* [2] *of Reeds* [a]Ex. 17, 28

5 [a]Ex. 15:10; N

6 [a]Ex. 3:20; 6: 118:15, 16

7 [1]Or, *exaltatio* 14:27 [b]Ps. 78:4 [c]Deut. 4:24; Is. Heb. 12:29

8 [a]Ex. 14:22, 2 4:9 [b]Ps. 78:13

9 [1]Lit., *soul* [2]Lit *filled with them* *dispossess, brin* *ruin* [a]Ex. 14:5, 8 [b]Judg. 5:30; Is. 5 Luke 11:22

10 [1]Or, *majestic* 14:27, 28 [b]Ex. 1

11 [a]Ex. 8:10; 9:1 Deut. 3:24; 2 Sar 1 Kin. 8:23; Ps. 7 86:8; Mic. 7:18 [b] Rev. 4:8 [c]Ps. 22: [d]Ps. 72:18; 136:4

12 [a]Ex. 15:6

13 [a]Neh. 9:12; Ps 77:20 [b]Ex. 15:16; 77:15 [c]Ex. 15:17; 78:54

14 [a]Deut. 2:25; H

15 [a]Gen. 36:15, 4 [b]Num. 22:3, 4 [c]Jo 2:9, 11, 24; 5:1

16 [a]Ex. 23:27; De 2:25; Josh. 2:9 [b]E 15:5, 6

Until the people pass over whom Thou [c]hast purchased.
17 "[a]Thou wilt bring them and [b]plant them in [c]the mountain of
Thine inheritance,
[d]The place, O LORD, which Thou hast made for Thy dwelling,
[e]The sanctuary, O Lord, which Thy hands have established.
18 "[a]The LORD shall reign forever and ever."
19 [a]For the horses of Pharaoh with his chariots and his horsemen
went into the sea, and the LORD brought back the waters of the sea
on them; but the sons of Israel walked on [b]dry land through the
midst of the sea.
20 And [a]Miriam the prophetess, Aaron's sister, took the [b]timbrel in
her hand, and all the women went out after her with timbrels and
with [1c]dancing.
21 And Miriam answered them,
"[a]Sing to the LORD, for He [1]is highly exalted;
The horse and his rider He has hurled into the sea."
22 [a]Then Moses [1]led Israel from the [2]Red Sea, and they went out
into [b]the wilderness of [c]Shur; and they went three days in the wilder-
ness and found no water.
23 And when they came to [a]Marah, they could not drink the waters
[1]of Marah, for they were [2]bitter; therefore it was named [3]Marah.
24 So the people [a]grumbled at Moses, saying, "What shall we
drink?"
25 Then he [a]cried out to the LORD, and the LORD showed him [b]a tree;
and he threw *it* into the waters, and the waters became sweet. There
He [c]made for them a statute and regulation, and there He [d]tested
them.
26 And He said, "[a]If you will give earnest heed to the voice of the
LORD your God, and do what is right in His sight, and give ear [b]to
His commandments, and keep all His statutes, [c]I will put none of the
diseases on you which I have put on the Egyptians; for I, [d]the LORD,
am your healer."
27 Then they came to [a]Elim where there *were* twelve springs of
water and seventy date palms, and they camped there beside the
waters.

Chapter 16

16 Then they set out from Elim, and all the congregation of the
sons of Israel came to the wilderness of [a]Sin, which is between
Elim and Sinai, on [b]the fifteenth day of the second month after their
departure from the land of Egypt.
2 And the whole congregation of the sons of Israel [a]grumbled
against Moses and Aaron in the wilderness.
3 And the sons of Israel said to them, "[a]Would that we had died by
the LORD's hand in the land of Egypt, [b]when we sat by the pots of
[1]meat, when we ate bread to the full; for you have brought us out
into this wilderness to kill this whole assembly with hunger."
4 Then the LORD said to Moses, "Behold, [a]I will rain bread from
heaven for you; and the people shall go out and gather a day's
portion every day, that I may [b]test them, whether or not they will
walk in My [1]instruction.
5 "And it will come about [a]on the sixth day, when they prepare
what they bring in, it will be twice as much as they gather daily."
6 So Moses and Aaron said to all the sons of Israel, "At evening

3; Ps. 74:2;
31:11; Titus
4; 2 Pet. 2:1
23:20; 32:34
0:8, 15 [c]Ps.
:54, 68 [d]Ps.
; 132:13, 14
[e]Ps. 78:69
0:16; 29:10;
Is. 57:15
:23, 28 [b]Ex.
14:22, 29
dances [a]Ex.
26:59; 1 Chr.
c. 6:4 [b]Judg.
1 Sam. 18:6;
6; Ps. 68:25;
9:3; Jer. 31:4
11:34; 21:21;
:6; Ps. 30:11;
150:4
has triumphed
usly [a]Ex. 15:1
caused Israel
y [2]Lit., *Sea of*
ds [a]Ps. 77:20;
3 [b]Num. 33:8
7; 20:1; 25:18
t., *from* [2]Heb.,
[3]I.e., bitterness
3:8; Ruth 1:20
4:11; 16:2; Ps.
106:13
. 14:10 [b]Ezek.
8 [c]Josh. 24:25
; Deut. 8:2, 16;
2:22; 3:1, 4; Ps.
66:10
. 19:5, 6; Deut.
2 [b]Ex. 20:2-17
7:15; 28:58, 60
25; Deut. 32:39;
4; 103:3; 147:3
27 [a]Num. 33:9
Num. 33:10, 11;
30:15 [b]Ex. 12:6,
51; 19:1
4:11; 15:24; Ps.
:25; 1 Cor. 10:10
flesh [a]Ex. 17:3;
um. 14:2, 3; 20:3;
:9 [b]Num. 11:4, 5
, *law* [a]Neh. 9:15;
78:23-25; 105:40;
6:31; 1 Cor. 10:3
:25; Deut. 8:2, 16
5 [a]Ex. 16:22

[1a]you will know that the LORD has brought you out of the land of
Egypt;
7 and in the morning [1]you will see [a]the glory of the LORD, for [b]He
hears your grumblings against the LORD; and [c]what are we, that you
grumble against us?"
8 And Moses said, "*This will happen* when the LORD gives you
[1]meat to eat in the evening, and bread to the full in the morning; for
the LORD hears your grumblings which you grumble against Him.
And what are we? Your grumblings are [a]not against us but against
the LORD."
9 Then Moses said to Aaron, "Say to all the congregation of the
sons of Israel, '[a]Come near before the LORD, for He has heard your
grumblings.' "
10 And it came about as Aaron spoke to the whole congregation of
the sons of Israel, that they [1]looked toward the wilderness, and be-
hold, [a]the glory of the LORD appeared in the cloud.
11 And the LORD spoke to Moses, saying,
12 "[a]I have heard the grumblings of the sons of Israel; speak to them,
saying, '[1]At twilight you shall eat [2]meat, and in the morning you
shall be filled with bread; and [b]you shall know that I am the LORD
your God.' "
13 So it came about at evening that [a]the quails came up and covered
the camp, and in the morning [b]there was a layer of dew around the
camp.
14 [a]When the layer of dew [1]evaporated, behold, on the [2]surface of
the wilderness [b]there was a fine flake-like thing, fine as the frost on
the ground.
15 When the sons of Israel saw *it*, they said to one another, "[1]What
is it?" For they did not know what it was. And Moses said to them,
"[a]It is the bread which the LORD has given you to eat.
16 "This is [1]what the LORD has commanded, 'Gather of it every man
[2]as much as he should eat; you shall take [3a]an omer apiece according
to the number of persons each of you has in his tent.' "
17 And the sons of Israel did so, and *some* gathered much and *some*
little.
18 When they measured it with an omer, [a]he who had gathered
much had no excess, and he who had gathered little had no lack;
every man gathered [1]as much as he should eat.
19 And Moses said to them, "[a]Let no man leave any of it until
morning."
20 But they did not listen to Moses, and some left part of it until
morning, and it bred worms and became foul; and Moses was angry
with them.
21 And they gathered it morning by morning, every man [1]as much
as he should eat; but when the sun grew hot, it would melt.
22 [a]Now it came about on the sixth day they gathered twice as
much bread, two omers for each one. When all the [b]leaders of the
congregation came and told Moses,
23 then he said to them, "This is what the LORD [1]meant: [a]Tomorrow
is a sabbath observance, a holy sabbath to the LORD. Bake what you
will bake and boil what you will boil, and [b]all that is left over [2]put
aside to be kept until morning."
24 So they [1]put it aside until morning, as Moses had ordered, and [a]it
did not become foul, nor was there any worm in it.

6 [1]Lit., an
7 [1]Lit., an 16:10, 12; John 11:4, 14:27; 17:5
8 [1]Or, *fles* 8:7; Luke 1 13:2; 1 The
9 [a]Num. 16
10 [1]Lit., *tur* 13:21; 16:7; 16:19; 1 Kin
12 [1]Lit., *Be two evening* [a]Ex. 16:8; N [b]Ex. 6:7; 16: 20:28; Joel 3
13 [a]Num. 11 78:27-29; 10 [b]Num. 11:9
14 [1]Lit., *had* [2]Lit., *face of* 11:7-9 [b]Ex. 1 9:15; Ps. 78:2
15 [1]Heb., *Ma* 31 [a]Ex. 16:4; Ps. 78:24; Joh 1 Cor. 10:3
16 [1]Lit., *the th* [2]Lit., *according eating* [3]Lit., *a a head* [a]Ex. 1
18 [1]Lit., *accor his eating* [a]2 C
19 [a]Ex. 12:10; 23:18
21 [1]Lit., *accord his eating*
22 [a]Ex. 16:5 [b]E
23 [1]Lit., *spoke up for you* [a]Gen Ex. 20:8-11; 23:1 31:15; 35:2; Lev. Neh. 9:13, 14 [b]E
24 [1]Lit., *laid it up* 16:20

25 And Moses said, "Eat it today, for today is a sabbath to the LORD;
today you will not find it in the field.
26 "[a]Six days you shall gather it, but on the seventh day, *the* sabbath,
there will be [1]none."
27 And it came about on the seventh day that some of the people
went out to gather, but they found none.
28 Then the LORD said to Moses, "[a]How long do you refuse to keep
My commandments and My [1]instructions?
29 "See, [1]the LORD has given you the sabbath; therefore He gives you
bread for two days on the sixth day. Remain every man in his place;
let no man go out of his place on the seventh day."
30 So the people rested on the seventh day.
31 And the house of [a]Israel named it [1]manna, and it was like [b]cori-
ander seed, white; and its taste was like wafers with honey.
32 Then Moses said, "This is [1]what the LORD has commanded, 'Let
an omerful of it be kept throughout your generations, that they may
see the bread that I fed you in the wilderness, when I brought you
out of the land of Egypt.' "
33 And Moses said to Aaron, "[a]Take a jar and put an omerful of
manna in it, and place it before the LORD, to be kept throughout your
generations."
34 As the LORD commanded Moses, so Aaron placed it before [a]the
Testimony, to be kept.
35 [a]And the sons of Israel ate the manna forty years, until they
came to an inhabited land; they ate the manna until they came to the
border of the land of Canaan.
36 (Now [a]an omer is a tenth of an [1]ephah.)

Chapter 17

17 Then all the congregation of the sons of Israel journeyed by
[1]stages from the wilderness of [a]Sin, according to the [2]com-
mand of the LORD, and camped at [b]Rephidim, and there was no
water for the people to drink.
2 Therefore the people [a]quarreled with Moses and said, "Give us
water that we may drink." And Moses said to them, "[b]Why do you
quarrel with me? [c]Why do you test the LORD?"
3 But the people thirsted there for water; and [1]they [a]grumbled
against Moses and said, "Why, now, have you brought us up from
Egypt, to kill [2]us and [3]our children and [3b]our livestock with thirst?"
4 So Moses cried out to the LORD, saying, "What shall I do to this
people? A [a]little more and they will stone me."
5 Then the LORD said to Moses, "Pass before the people and take
with you some of [a]the elders of Israel; and take in your hand your
staff with which [b]you struck the Nile, and go.
6 "Behold, I will stand before you there on the rock at [a]Horeb; and
[b]you shall strike the rock, and water will come out of it, that the
people may drink." And Moses did so in the sight of the elders of
Israel.
7 And he named the place [1a]Massah and [2b]Meribah because of the
quarrel of the sons of Israel, and because they [c]tested the LORD,
saying, "Is the LORD among us, or not?"
8 Then [a]Amalek came and fought against Israel at [b]Rephidim.
9 So Moses said to [a]Joshua, "Choose men for us, and go out, fight

against Amalek. Tomorrow I will station myself on the top of the hill
with [b]the staff of God in my hand."
10 And Joshua did as Moses [1]told him, [2]and fought against Amalek;
and Moses, Aaron, and [a]Hur went up to the top of the hill.
11 So it came about when Moses held his hand up, that Israel pre-
vailed, and when he let his hand [1]down, Amalek prevailed.
12 But Moses' hands were heavy. Then they took a stone and put it
under him, and he sat on it; and Aaron and Hur [a]supported his
hands, one on one side and one on the other. Thus his hands were
steady until the sun set.
13 So Joshua [1]overwhelmed Amalek and his people with the edge
of the sword.
14 Then the LORD said to Moses, "[a]Write this in [1]a book as a
memorial, and [2]recite it to Joshua, [3]that [b]I will utterly blot out the
memory of Amalek from under heaven."
15 And Moses built an [a]altar, and named it [b]The LORD is My Banner;
16 and he said, "[1a]The LORD has sworn; the LORD will have war
against Amalek from generation to generation."

Chapter 18

18 Now [a]Jethro, the priest of Midian, Moses' father-in-law, heard
of all that God had done for Moses and for Israel His people,
how the LORD had brought Israel out of Egypt.
2 And Jethro, Moses' father-in-law, took Moses' wife [a]Zipporah,
after he had sent her away,
3 and her [a]two sons, of whom [1]one was named Gershom, for he
said, "I have been [b]a [2]sojourner in a foreign land."
4 And [1]the other was named [2a]Eliezer, for *he said,* "[b]The God of my
father was my help, and delivered me from the sword of Pharaoh."
5 Then Jethro, Moses' father-in-law, came with his sons and his
wife to Moses [1]in the wilderness where he was camped, at [a]the
mount of God.
6 And he [1]sent word to Moses, "I, your father-in-law Jethro, am
coming to you with your wife and her two sons with her."
7 Then Moses went out to meet his father-in-law, and [a]he bowed
down and [b]kissed him; and they [c]asked each other of their welfare,
and went into the tent.
8 And Moses told his father-in-law all that the LORD had done to
Pharaoh and to the Egyptians [a]for Israel's sake, all the [b]hardship that
had befallen them on the journey, and *how* [c]the LORD had delivered
them.
9 And Jethro rejoiced over all [a]the goodness which the LORD had
done to Israel, [1]in delivering [2]them from the hand of the Egyptians.
10 So Jethro said, "[a]Blessed be the LORD who delivered you from the
hand of the Egyptians and from the hand of Pharaoh, *and* who de-
livered the people from under the hand of the Egyptians.
11 "Now I know that [a]the LORD is greater than all the gods; [1]indeed,
[b]it was proven when they dealt proudly against [2]the people."
12 [a]Then Jethro, Moses' father-in-law, took a burnt offering and
sacrifices for God, and Aaron came with all the elders of Israel to eat
[1]a meal with Moses' father-in-law before God.
13 And it came about the next day that Moses sat to judge the
people, and the people stood about Moses from the morning until
the evening.

9 [b]Ex. 4:20
10 [1]Lit., *sai*
fight [a]Ex. 24
11 [1]Lit., *rest*
12 [a]Is. 35:3
13 [1]Lit., *wea*
14 [1]Lit., *the*
place it in the
[3]Or, *for* [a]Ex.
34:27; Num.
[b]Deut. 25:19;
15:3
15 [a]Ex. 24:4
22:14; Judg. 6
16 [1]Or, *Beca*
hand is agains
throne of the
Because a ha
the throne of
22:16
18:1 [a]Ex. 2:16
2 [a]Ex. 2:21; 4
3 [1]Lit., *the nar*
one was [2]Heb.
[a]Ex. 2:22; 4:20;
7:29 [b]Ex. 2:22
4 [1]Lit., *the nam*
other was [2]Heb
El-ezer; i.e., my
help [a]1 Chr. 23
[b]Gen. 49:25
5 [1]Lit., *unto* [a]E
12; 4:27; 24:13
6 [1]Lit., *said*
7 [a]Gen. 43:26, 2
[b]Gen. 29:13; Ex.
[c]Gen. 43:27; 2 S
8 [a]Ex. 4:23; 7:4,
[b]Num. 20:14; Ne
[c]Ex. 15:6, 16
9 [1]Lit., *in that He*
delivered [2]Lit., *h*
63:7-14
10 [a]Gen. 14:20;
18:28; 1 Kin. 8:56
68:19, 20
11 [1]Lit., *indeed, i*
thing in which they
them [a]Ex. 12:12;
2 Chr. 2:5; Ps. 95:
97:9; 135:5 [b]Luke
12 [1]Lit., *bread* [a]G
31:54; Ex. 24:5

14 Now when Moses' father-in-law saw all that he was doing for the people, he said, "What is this thing that you are doing for the people? Why do you alone sit *as judge* and all the people stand about you from morning until evening?"

15 And Moses said to his father-in-law, "Because the people come to me [a]to inquire of God.

16 "When they have a [1a]dispute, it comes to me, and I judge between a man and his neighbor, and make known the statutes of God and His laws."

17 And Moses' father-in-law said to him, "The thing that you are doing is not good.

18 "[a]You will surely wear out, both yourself and [1]these people who are with you, for the [2]task is too heavy for you; [b]you cannot do it alone.

19 "Now listen to [1]me: I shall give you counsel, and God be with you. [2]You be the people's representative before God, and you [a]bring the [3]disputes to God,

20 [a]then teach them the statutes and the laws, and make known to them [b]the way in which they are to walk, and the work they are to do.

21 "Furthermore, you shall [1]select out of all the people [a]able men [b]who fear God, men of truth, those who [c]hate dishonest gain; and you shall place *these* over them, *as* leaders of thousands, [2]of hundreds, [2]of fifties and [2]of tens.

22 "And let them judge the people at all times; and let it be [a]that every major [1]dispute they will bring to you, but every minor [1]dispute they themselves will judge. So it will be easier for you, and [b]they will bear *the burden* with you.

23 "If you do this thing and God *so* commands you, then you will be able to [1]endure, and all [2]these people also will go to [3]their place in peace."

24 So Moses listened [1]to his father-in-law, and did all that he had said.

25 And Moses chose [a]able men out of all Israel, and made them heads over the people, leaders of thousands, [1]of hundreds, [1]of fifties and [1]of tens.

26 And they judged the people at all times; [a]the difficult [1]dispute they would bring to Moses, but every minor [1]dispute they themselves would judge.

27 Then Moses [1a]bade his father-in-law farewell, and he went his way into his own land.

Chapter 19

19 [a]In the third month after the sons of Israel had gone out of the land of Egypt, [1]on that very day they came into the wilderness of [b]Sinai.

2 When they set out from [a]Rephidim, they came to the wilderness of Sinai, and camped in the wilderness; and there Israel camped in front of [b]the mountain.

3 And Moses went up to God, and [a]the LORD called to him from the mountain, saying, "Thus you shall say to the house of Jacob and tell the sons of Israel:

4 '[a]You yourselves have seen what I did to the Egyptians, and *how* I bore you on [b]eagles' wings, and brought you to Myself.

. 9:6, 8; 27:5; Deut. 17:8-13
., matter [a]Ex. 24:14
[1]Lit., *this* [2]Lit., ...um. 11:14, 17; ...12 [b]Deut. 1:9
my voice [2]Lit., *...r the people in ...nt of God* [3]Lit., *...rs* [a]Num. 27:5
...ut. 1:18; 4:1, 5; 5:1 [b]Ps. 143:8
[1]Lit., *see* [2]Lit., *...s of* [a]Ex. 18:25; 1:13, 15; 2 Chr. ...-10; Ps. 15:1-5; 3 [b]Gen. 42:18; ...am. 23:3 [c]Deut. 16:19
..., *matter* [a]Deut. ...18 [b]Num. 11:17
[1]Lit., *stand* [2]Lit., *this* [3]Lit., *his*
...t., *to the voice of*
..., *leaders of* [a]Ex. 18:21; Deut. 1:15
[1]Lit., *matter* [a]Ex. 18:22
[1]Lit., *sent off his ...ther-in-law* [a]Num. 10:29, 30
1 [1]Lit., *on this day* [a]Ex. 12:6, 51; 16:1 ...1:6; 4:10, 15; 5:2
2 [a]Ex. 17:1; Num. [b]Ex. 3:1, 12; 18:5
3 [a]Ex. 3:4
[a]Deut. 29:2 [b]Deut. 32:11; Rev. 12:14

5 'Now then, [a]if you will indeed obey My voice and [b]keep My
covenant, then you shall be [c]My [1]own possession among all the peo-
ples, for [d]all the earth is Mine;
6 and you shall be to Me [a]a kingdom of priests and [b]a holy nation.'
These are the words that you shall speak to the sons of Israel."
7 [a]So Moses came and called the elders of the people, and set
before them all these words which the LORD had commanded him.
8 [a]And all the people answered together and said, "All that the
LORD has spoken we will do!" And Moses brought back the words of
the people to the LORD.
9 And the LORD said to Moses, "Behold, I shall come to you in [a]a
thick cloud, in order that the [b]people may hear when I speak with
you, and may also believe in you forever." Then Moses told the
words of the people to the LORD.
10 The LORD also said to Moses, "Go to the people and [a]consecrate
them today and tomorrow, and let them [b]wash their garments;
11 and let them be ready for the third day, for on [a]the third day the
LORD will come down on Mount Sinai in the sight of all the people.
12 "And you shall set bounds for the people all around, saying, '[1]Be-
ware that you do not go up on the mountain or touch the border of
it; [a]whoever touches the mountain shall surely be put to death.
13 'No hand shall touch him, but [a]he shall surely be stoned or [1]shot
through; whether beast or man, he shall not live.' When the ram's
horn sounds a long blast, they shall come up to [b]the mountain."
14 So Moses went down from the mountain to the people and con-
secrated the people, and they washed their garments.
15 And he said to the people, "Be ready for the third day; do not go
near a woman."
16 [a]So it came about on the third day, when it was morning, that
there were [1]thunder and lightning flashes and a thick cloud upon the
mountain and a very loud trumpet sound, so that all the people who
were in the camp trembled.
17 And Moses brought the people out of the camp to meet God,
and they stood at the [1]foot of the mountain.
18 [a]Now Mount Sinai *was* all in smoke because the LORD descended
upon it [b]in fire; and its smoke ascended like [c]the smoke of a furnace,
and [d]the whole mountain [1]quaked violently.
19 When the sound of the trumpet grew louder and louder, Moses
spoke and [a]God answered him with [1]thunder.
20 [a]And the LORD came down on Mount Sinai, to the top of the
mountain; and the LORD called Moses to the top of the mountain,
and Moses went up.
21 Then the LORD spoke to Moses, "Go down, [1]warn the people, lest
[a]they break through to the LORD to gaze, and many of them [2]perish.
22 "And also let the [a]priests who come near to the LORD consecrate
themselves, lest the LORD break out against them."
23 And Moses said to the LORD, "The people cannot come up to
Mount Sinai, for Thou didst [1]warn us, saying, '[a]Set bounds about the
mountain and consecrate it.' "
24 Then the LORD said to him, "[1]Go down and come up *again*, [a]you
and Aaron with you; but do not let the [b]priests and the people break
through to come up to the LORD, lest He break forth upon them."
25 So Moses went down to the people and told them.

5 [1]Or, *specia* [a]Ex. 15:26; D [b]Ps. 78:10 [c]D 7:6; 14:2; 26:1 135:4; Titus 2: 2:9 [d]Ex. 9:29; 10:14; Job 41 50:12; 1 Cor.
6 [a]1 Pet. 2:5, 1:6; 5:10 [b]Deu 14:21; 26:19; I
7 [a]Ex. 4:29, 30
8 [a]Ex. 4:31; 24 Deut. 5:27; 26:
9 [a]Ex. 19:16; 2 Deut. 4:11; Ps. [b]Deut. 4:12, 36
10 [a]Lev. 11:44, [b]Gen. 35:2; Lev Num. 8:7, 21; 1 Rev. 22:14
11 [a]Ex. 19:16
12 [1]Lit., *Take he yourselves* [a]Heb
13 [1]I.e., with arr [a]Heb. 12:20 [b]Ex
16 [1]Lit., *sounds* 12:18, 19, 21
17 [1]Lit., *lower pa*
18 [1]Or, *trembled* 4:11; Ps. 104:32; [b]Ex. 3:2; 24:17; D 5:4; 2 Chr. 7:1-3; 12:18 [c]Gen. 15:1 19:28 [d]Judg. 5:5; 68:7, 8; Jer. 4:24
19 [1]Or, *a voice; li sound* [a]Ps. 81:7
20 [a]Neh. 9:13
21 [1]Lit., *testify to fall* [a]Ex. 3:5; 1 San 6:19
22 [a]Ex. 19:24; 24:5 Lev. 10:3; 21:6-8
23 [1]Lit., *testify to* [a] 19:12
24 [1]Lit., *Go, desce* [a]Ex. 24:1, 9, 12 [b]Ex 19:22

Chapter 20

20 Then God spoke all these words, saying,
2 "[a]I am the LORD your God, [b]who brought you out of the land
of Egypt, out of the house of [1]slavery.
3 "[a]You shall have no other [b]gods [1]before Me.
4 "[a]You shall not make for yourself [1]an idol, or any likeness of what
is in heaven above or on the earth beneath or in the water under the
earth.
5 "[a]You shall not worship them or serve them; for I, the LORD your
God, am a [b]jealous God, [c]visiting the iniquity of the fathers on the
children, on the third and the fourth generations of those who
hate Me,
6 but showing lovingkindness to [a]thousands, to those who love
Me and keep My commandments.
7 "[a]You shall not take the name of the LORD your God in vain, for
the LORD will not [1]leave him unpunished who takes His name in
vain.
8 "Remember [a]the sabbath day, to keep it holy.
9 "[a]Six days you shall labor and do all your work,
10 but the seventh day is a sabbath of the LORD your God; *in it* [a]you
shall not do any work, you or your son or your daughter, your male
or your female servant or your cattle or your sojourner who [1]stays
with you.
11 "[a]For in six days the LORD made the heavens and the earth, the sea
and all that is in them, and rested on the seventh day; therefore the
LORD blessed the sabbath day and made it holy.
12 "[a]Honor your father and your mother, that your [b]days may be
prolonged in the land which the LORD your God gives you.
13 "[a]You shall not murder.
14 "[a]You shall not commit adultery.
15 "[a]You shall not steal.
16 "[a]You shall not bear false witness against your [b]neighbor.
17 "[a]You shall not covet your neighbor's house; [b]you shall not covet
your neighbor's wife or his male servant or his female servant or his
ox or his donkey or anything that belongs to your neighbor."
18 [a]And all the people perceived the [1]thunder and the lightning
flashes and the sound of the trumpet and the mountain smoking;
and when the people saw *it,* they trembled and stood at a distance.
19 [a]Then they said to Moses, "Speak [1]to us yourself and we will
listen; but let not God speak [1]to us, lest we die."
20 And Moses said to the people, "[a]Do not be afraid; for God has
come in order [b]to test you, and in order that [c]the fear of Him may
[1]remain with you, so that you may not sin."
21 So the people stood at a distance, while Moses approached [a]the
thick cloud where God *was.*
22 Then the LORD said to Moses, "Thus you shall say to the sons of
Israel, 'You yourselves have seen that [a]I have spoken [1]to you from
heaven.
23 '[a]You shall not make *other gods* besides Me; [b]gods of silver or gods
of gold, you shall not make for yourselves.
24 'You shall make [a]an altar of earth for Me, and you shall sacrifice
on it your [b]burnt offerings and your [c]peace offerings, [d]your sheep
and your oxen; in every place [e]where I cause My name to be remem-
bered, I will come to you and bless you.

...it., *slaves* [a]Lev. ...1; Deut. 5:6; Ps. [b]Ex. 13:3; 15:13, 16; Deut. 7:8
[1]Or, *besides Me* ...eut. 6:14; 2 Kin. ...Jer. 25:6; 35:15 [b]Ex. 15:11; 20:23
...*a graven image* ...19:4; 26:1; Deut. 4:15-19; 27:15
[a]Ex. 23:24; Josh. ...2 Kin. 17:35 [b]Ex. ...Deut. 4:24; Josh. ...9; Nah. 1:2 [c]Ex. ...Num. 14:18, 33; ...ut. 5:9, 10; 1 Kin. 21:29; Jer. 32:18
6 [a]Deut. 7:9
7 [1]Or, *hold him ...less* [a]Lev. 19:12; Deut. 6:13; 10:20
...23:12; 31:13-16; ...26:2; Deut. 5:12
...x. 34:21; 35:2, 3; ...23:3; Deut. 5:13; Luke 13:14
...0 [1]Lit., *is in your ...s* [a]Neh. 13:16-19
[a]Gen. 2:2, 3; Ex. 31:17
[a]Lev. 19:3; Deut. ...Matt. 15:4; 19:19; ...7:10; 10:19; Luke ...; Eph. 6:2 [b]Deut. ...5, 33; 6:2; 11:8, 9; Jer. 35:7
13 [a]Gen. 9:6; Ex. ...Lev. 24:17; Matt. ...9:18; Mark 10:19; ...18:20; Rom. 13:9; James 2:11
[a]Lev. 20:10; Deut. ...Matt. 5:27; 19:18; Rom. 13:9
...5 [a]Ex. 21:16; Lev. ...1, 13; Matt. 19:18; Rom. 13:9
[a]Ex. 23:1, 7; Deut. ...Matt. 19:18 [b]Lev. 19:18
[a]Deut. 5:21; Rom. ...; 13:9; Eph. 5:3, 5 ...v. 6:29; Matt. 5:28
[1]Lit., *sounds* [a]Ex. 19:16, 18; Heb. 12:18, 19
... [1]Lit., *with* [a]Deut. ..., 23-27; Gal. 3:19; Heb. 12:19
...it., *be before* [a]Ex. ...4:13; Is. 41:10, 13 ...15:25; Deut. 13:3 ...t. 4:10; 6:24; Prov. ...3:7; 16:6; Is. 8:13
... [a]Ex. 19:16; Deut. 5:22
...2 [1]Lit., *with* [a]Deut. ...5:24, 26; Neh. 9:13
...Ex. 20:3 [b]Ex. 32:1, 2, 4; Deut. 29:17
[a]Ex. 20:25; 27:1-8 ...10:25; 18:12 [c]Ex. ...:5; Lev. 1:2 [d]Deut. ...12:5; 16:6, 11; 26:2; ...hr. 6:6 [e]Deut. 12:5; 26:2

25 'And if you make an altar of stone for Me, [a]you shall not build it
of cut stones, for if you wield your tool on it, you will profane it.
26 'And you shall not go up by steps to My altar, that [a]your naked-
ness may not be exposed on it.'

Chapter 21

21 "Now these are the [a]ordinances which you are to set before
them.
2 "If you buy [a]a Hebrew slave, he shall serve for six years; but on
the seventh he shall go out as a free man without payment.
3 "If he comes [1]alone, he shall go out [1]alone; if he is the husband of
a wife, then his wife shall go out with him.
4 "If his master gives him a wife, and she bears him sons or daugh-
ters, the wife and her children shall belong to her master, and he
shall go out [1]alone.
5 "But [a]if the slave plainly says, 'I love my master, my wife and my
children; I will not go out as a free man,'
6 then his master shall bring him to [1]God, then he shall bring him
to the door or the doorpost. And his master shall pierce his ear with
an awl; and he shall serve him permanently.
7 "[a]And if a man sells his daughter as a female slave, she is not to
[1]go free [b]as the male slaves [1]do.
8 "If she is [1]displeasing in the eyes of her master [2]who designated
her for himself, then he shall let her be redeemed. He does not have
authority to sell her to a foreign people because of his [3]unfairness to
her.
9 "And if he designates her for his son, he shall deal with her ac-
cording to the custom of daughters.
10 "If he takes to himself another woman, he may not reduce her
[1]food, her clothing, or [a]her conjugal rights.
11 "And if he will not do these three *things* for her, then she shall go
out for nothing, without *payment of* money.
12 "[a]He who strikes a man so that he dies shall surely be put to
death.
13 "[a]But [1]if he did not lie in wait *for him,* but [b]God let *him* fall into his
hand, then I will appoint you a place to which he may flee.
14 "[a]If, however, a man acts presumptuously toward his neighbor, so
as to kill him craftily, you are to take him *even* from My altar, that he
may die.
15 "And he who strikes his father or his mother shall surely be put
to death.
16 "[a]And he who [1]kidnaps a man, whether he sells him or he is
found in his [2]possession, shall surely be put to death.
17 "[a]And he who curses his father or his mother shall surely be put
to death.
18 "And if men have a quarrel and one strikes the other with a stone
or with *his* fist, and he does not die but [1]remains in bed;
19 if he gets up and walks around outside on his staff, then he who
struck him shall go unpunished; he shall only pay for his [1]loss of
time, and [2]shall take care of him until he is completely healed.
20 "And if a man strikes his male or female slave with a rod and he
dies [1]at his hand, he shall [2]be punished.
21 "If, however, he [1]survives a day or two, no vengeance shall be
taken; [a]for he is his [2]property.

25 [a]Deut. 27:5, 6
8:31

26 [a]Ex. 28:42, 4

21:1 [a]Ex. 24:3, 4
4:14; 6:1

2 [a]Lev. 25:39-43
15:12-18; Jer. 34

3 [1]Lit., *by himsel*

4 [1]Lit., *by himsel*

5 [a]Deut. 15:16, 1

6 [1]Or, *the judges
acted in God's na*

7 [1]Lit., *go out* [a]N
5:5 [b]Ex. 21:2, 3

8 [1]Lit., *bad* [2]Ano
reading is *so that
not designate her
dealing treachero*

10 [1]Lit., *flesh* [a]1
7:3, 5

12 [a]Gen. 9:6; Lev
24:17; Num. 35:3
Matt. 26:52

13 [1]Lit., *he who* [a]
35:10-34; Deut. 19
Josh. 20:1-9 [b]1 S
24:4, 10, 18

14 [a]Deut. 19:11, 1
1 Kin. 2:28-34

16 [1]Lit., *steals* [2]L
hand [a]Deut. 24:7

17 [a]Lev. 20:9; Pro
20:20; Matt. 15:4;
7:10

18 [1]Lit., *lies*

19 [1]Lit., *his sitting
healing, he shall c
to be healed*

20 [1]Lit., *under* [2]Li
suffer vengeance

21 [1]Lit., *stands* [2]L
money [a]Lev. 25:44

22 "And *if* men struggle with each other and strike a woman with
child so that [1]she has a miscarriage, yet there is no *further* injury, he
shall surely be fined as the woman's husband [2]may demand of him;
and he shall [a]pay [3]as the judges *decide*.
23 "But if there is *any further* injury, [a]then you shall appoint *as a*
penalty life for life,
24 [a]eye for eye, tooth for tooth, hand for hand, foot for foot,
25 burn for burn, wound for wound, [1]bruise for bruise.
26 "And if a man strikes the eye of his male or female slave, and
destroys it, he shall let him go free on account of his eye.
27 "And if he [1]knocks out a tooth of his male or female slave, he
shall let him go free on account of his tooth.
28 "And if an ox gores a man or a woman [1]to death, [a]the ox shall
surely be stoned and its flesh shall not be eaten; but the owner of the
ox shall go unpunished.
29 "If, however, an ox was previously in the habit of goring, and its
owner has been warned, yet he does not confine it, and it kills a man
or a woman, the ox shall be stoned and its owner also shall be put to
death.
30 "If a ransom is [1]demanded of him, then he shall give for the
redemption of his life whatever is [1]demanded of him.
31 "Whether it gores a son or [1]a daughter, it shall be done to him
according to [2]the same rule.
32 "If the ox gores a male or female slave, [1]the owner shall give his *or*
her master [a]thirty shekels of silver, and the ox shall be stoned.
33 "And if a man opens a pit, or [1]digs a pit and does not cover it
over, and an ox or a donkey falls into it,
34 the owner of the pit shall make restitution; he shall [1]give money
to its owner, and the dead *animal* shall become his.
35 "And if one man's ox hurts another's so that it dies, then they
shall sell the live ox and divide its price equally; and also they shall
divide the dead *ox*.
36 "Or *if* it is known that the ox was previously in the habit of
goring, yet its owner has not confined it, he shall surely pay ox for
ox, and the dead *animal* shall become his.

Chapter 22

22 "[1]If a man steals an ox or a sheep, and slaughters it or sells it,
he shall pay five oxen for the ox and [a]four sheep for the
sheep.
2 "[1]If the [a]thief is [2]caught while breaking in, and is struck so that he
dies, there will be no bloodguiltiness on his account.
3 "*But* if the sun has risen on him, there will be bloodguiltiness on
his account. He shall surely make restitution; if he owns nothing,
then he shall be [a]sold for his theft.
4 "If what he stole is actually found alive in his [1]possession,
whether an ox or a donkey or a sheep, [a]he shall pay double.
5 "If a man lets a field or vineyard be grazed *bare* and lets his
animal loose so that it grazes in another man's field, he shall make
restitution from the best of his own field and the best of his own
vineyard.
6 "If a fire breaks out and spreads to thorn bushes, so that stacked
grain or the standing grain or the field *itself* is consumed, he who
started the fire shall surely make restitution.

an untimely urs; lit., her ne out [2]Lit., im [3]Lit., by [a]Ex. 21:30; t. 22:18, 19

24:19; Deut. 19:21

24:20; Deut. 1; Matt. 5:38

25 [1]Lit., welt

causes to fall

o that he dies 9:5; Ex. 21:32

it., laid on him

[1]Lit., gores a ghter [2]Lit., this judgment

[1]Lit., he [a]Zech. 2; Matt. 26:15; 27:3, 9

it., if a man digs

[1]Lit., give back

:1 [1]Ch. 21:37 in o. [a]2 Sam. 12:6; Luke 19:8

[1]Ch. 22:1 in Heb. ound [a]Matt. 6:19; 24:43; 1 Pet. 4:15

3 [a]Matt. 18:25

t., hand [a]Ex. 22:7

7 "[a]If a man gives his neighbor money or goods to keep *for him,* and
it is stolen from the man's house, if the thief is [1]caught, he shall pay
double.
8 "If the thief is not [1]caught, then the owner of the house shall
[2]appear before [3a]the judges, *to* determine whether he [4]laid his hands
on his neighbor's property.
9 "For every [1]breach of trust, *whether it is* for ox, for donkey, for
sheep, for clothing, *or* for any lost thing about which one says, 'This
is it,' the [2]case of both parties shall come before [3a]the judges; he
whom [3]the judges condemn shall pay double to his neighbor.
10 "If a man gives his neighbor a donkey, an ox, a sheep, or any
animal to keep *for him,* and it dies or is hurt or is driven away while
no one is looking,
11 an [a]oath before the LORD shall be made by the two of them, [1]that
he has not [2]laid hands on his neighbor's property; and its owner
shall accept *it,* and he shall not make restitution.
12 "But if it is actually stolen from him, he shall make restitution to
its owner.
13 "If it is all torn to pieces, let him bring it as evidence; he shall not
make restitution for what has been torn to pieces.
14 "And if a man [1]borrows *anything* from his neighbor, and it is
injured or dies while its owner is not with it, he shall make full
restitution.
15 "If its owner is with it, he shall not make restitution; if it is hired,
it came for its hire.
16 "[a]And if a man seduces a virgin who is not engaged, and lies with
her, he must pay a dowry for her *to be* his wife.
17 "If her father absolutely refuses to give her to him, he shall [1]pay
money equal to the [a]dowry for virgins.
18 "You shall not allow a [a]sorceress to live.
19 "[a]Whoever lies with an animal shall surely be put to death.
20 "[a]He who sacrifices to [1]any god, other than to the LORD alone,
shall be [2]utterly destroyed.
21 "And [a]you shall not wrong a stranger or oppress him, for you
were strangers in the land of Egypt.
22 "[a]You shall not afflict any widow or orphan.
23 "If you afflict him at all, *and* [a]if he does cry out to Me, [b]I will
surely hear his cry;
24 and My anger will be kindled, and I will kill you with the sword;
[a]and your wives shall become widows and your children fatherless.
25 "[a]If you lend money to My people, to the poor [1]among you, you
are not to [2]act as a creditor to him; you shall not [3]charge him
[b]interest.
26 "If you ever take your neighbor's cloak [a]as a pledge, you are to
return it to him before the sun sets,
27 for that is his only covering; it is his cloak for his [1]body. What
else shall he sleep in? And it shall come about that [a]when he cries out
to Me, I will hear *him,* for [b]I am gracious.
28 "You shall not [1a]curse God, [b]nor curse a ruler of your people.
29 "[a]You shall not delay *the offering from* [1]your harvest and your vin-
tage. [b]The first-born of your sons you shall give to Me.
30 "[a]You shall do the same with your oxen *and* with your sheep. It
shall be with its mother seven days; [b]on the eighth day you shall
give it to Me.

7 [1]Lit., *found* [a]L
6:1-7

8 [1]Lit., *found* [2]Li
approach to [3]Or,
[4]Lit., *stretched hi*
[a]Ex. 22:9; Deut. 1
19:17

9 [1]Or, *matter of*
transgression [2]L
matter [3]Or, *God*
22:8, 28; Deut. 2

11 [1]Lit., *whether*
stretched his han
[a]Heb. 6:16

14 [1]Lit., *asks*

16 [a]Deut. 22:28,

17 [1]Lit., *weigh o*
silver [a]Gen. 34:1
1 Sam. 18:25

18 [a]Lev. 19:31; 2
27; Deut. 18:10, 1
1 Sam. 28:3; Jer.
27:9, 10

19 [a]Lev. 18:23; 2
16; Deut. 27:21

20 [1]Lit., *the gods*
put under the ban
32:8; 34:15; Lev.
Num. 25:2; Deut.
3, 5; 1 Kin. 18:40;
10:25

21 [a]Ex. 23:9; Lev
19:33, 34; 25:35;
1:16; 10:19; 27:19
Zech. 7:10

22 [a]Deut. 24:17,
Prov. 23:10, 11; J
7:6, 7

23 [a]Deut. 15:9; J
35:9; Luke 18:7 [b]
10:18; Job 34:28;
10:14, 17, 18; 18
68:5; James 5:4

24 [a]Ps. 109:2, 9

25 [1]Lit., *with* [2]Lit.
[3]Lit., *lay upon* [a]Le
25:35-37; Deut. 1
[b]Deut. 23:19, 20;
5:7; Ps. 15:5; Eze

26 [a]Deut. 24:6, 1
Job 24:3; Prov. 20
Amos 2:8

27 [1]Lit., *skin* [a]Ex.
22:23 [b]Ex. 34:6

28 [1]Or, *revile* [a]Le
24:15, 16 [b]Eccl. 1
Acts 23:5

29 [1]Lit., *your fulne*
and your tears [a]E
23:16, 19; Deut.
26:2-11; Prov. 3:9
13:2, 12

30 [a]Deut. 15:19;
22:27 [b]Gen. 17:12
12:3

31 "[a]And you shall be holy men to Me, therefore [b]you shall not eat
any flesh torn to pieces in the field; you shall throw it to the dogs.

Chapter 23

23 "[a]You shall not bear a false report; do not join your hand with
a wicked man to be a [b]malicious witness.
2 "You shall not follow [1]a multitude in doing evil, nor shall you
[2]testify in a dispute so as to turn aside after [1]a multitude in order to
[a]pervert *justice;*
3 [a]nor shall you [1]be partial to a poor man in his dispute.
4 "[a]If you meet your enemy's ox or his donkey wandering away,
you shall surely return it to him.
5 "[a]If you see the donkey of one who hates you lying *helpless* under
its load, you shall refrain from leaving it to him, you shall surely
release *it* with him.
6 "[a]You shall not pervert the justice *due* to your needy *brother* in his
dispute.
7 "[a]Keep far from a false charge, and [b]do not kill the innocent or the
righteous, for [c]I will not acquit the guilty.
8 "[a]And you shall not take a bribe, for a bribe blinds the clear-
sighted and [1]subverts the cause of the just.
9 "[a]And you shall not oppress a [1]stranger, since you yourselves
know the [2]feelings of a [1]stranger, for you *also* were [1]strangers in the
land of Egypt.
10 "[a]And you shall sow your land for six years and gather in its
yield,
11 but *on* the seventh year you shall let it [1]rest and lie fallow, so that
the needy of your people may eat; and whatever they leave the beast
of the field may eat. You are to do the same with your vineyard *and*
your olive grove.
12 "[a]Six days you are to do your work, but on the seventh day you
shall cease *from labor* in order that your ox and your donkey may
rest, and the son of your female slave, as well as [1]your stranger, may
refresh themselves.
13 "Now [a]concerning everything which I have said to you, be on
your guard; and [b]do not mention the name of other gods, nor let
them be heard [1]from your mouth.
14 "[a]Three times a year you shall celebrate a feast to Me.
15 "You shall observe [a]the Feast of Unleavened Bread; for seven days
you are to eat unleavened bread, as I commanded you, at the ap-
pointed time in the [b]month Abib, for in it you came out of Egypt.
And [1c]none shall appear before Me empty-handed.
16 "Also *you shall observe* [a]the Feast of the Harvest *of* the first fruits of
your labors *from* what you sow in the field; also the Feast of the
Ingathering at the end of the year [b]when you gather in *the fruit of*
your labors from the field.
17 "[a]Three times a year all your males shall appear before the Lord
[1]GOD.
18 "[a]You shall not offer the blood of My sacrifice with leavened
bread; [b]nor is the fat of My [1]feast to remain overnight until morning.
19 "You shall bring [a]the choice first fruits of your soil into the house
of the LORD your God. [b]You are not to boil a kid in the milk of its
mother.
20 "Behold, I am going to send [a]an angel before you to guard you

19:6; Lev. [b]Lev. 7:24; Ezek. 4:14
20:16; Lev. ...t. 5:20; Ps. ...Prov. 10:18 ...:16-21; Ps. 19:5; Acts 6:11
...y men [2]Or, ...Deut. 16:19; 24:17
...r [a]Ex. 23:6; Deut. 1:17; 16:19
...Deut. 22:1-4
[a]Deut. 22:4
23:2, 3; Lev. 19:15
...x. 20:16; Ps. ...h. 4:25 [b]Ex. ...t. 27:25 [c]Ex. ...t. 25:1; Rom. 1:18
...r, *distorts the* [a]Deut. 10:17; ... 15:27; 17:8, ...3; Is. 5:22, 23
..., *sojourner(s)* ...l [a]Ex. 22:21; 19:33f.; Deut. 24:17f.; 27:19
[a]Lev. 25:1-7
11 [1]Lit., *drop*
the sojourner ...0:8-11; 31:15; ...; 35:2, 3; Lev. ...3; Deut. 5:13f.
on [a]Deut. 4:9, ...n. 4:16 [b]Josh. ...6:4; Hos. 2:17
14 [a]Ex. 23:17; ...24; Deut. 16:16
...it., *they . . . not* 12:14-20; Lev. Num. 28:16-25 12:2; 13:4 [c]Ex. 22:29; 34:20
[a]Ex. 34:22; Lev. 10; Num. 28:26 [b]Lev. 23:39
[1]Heb., *YHWH,* rendered *LORD* 14; 34:23; Deut. 16:16
...Or, *festival* [a]Ex. ...5; Lev. 2:11 [b]Ex. Lev. 7:15; Deut. 16:4
...Ex. 22:29; 34:26; ...t. 26:2, 10; Neh. Prov. 3:9 [b]Deut. 14:21
[a]Ex. 3:2; 14:19; ...3:23; 32:34; 33:2

along the way, and [b]to bring you into the place which I have
prepared.
21 "Be on your guard before him and obey his voice; [a]do not be
rebellious toward him, for he will not pardon your transgression,
since [b]My name is in him.
22 "But if you will truly obey his voice and do all that I say, then
[a]I will be an enemy to your enemies and an adversary to your
adversaries.
23 "[a]For My angel will go before you and bring you in to *the land of*
the Amorites, the Hittites, the Perizzites, the Canaanites, the Hivites
and the Jebusites; and I will completely destroy them.
24 "[a]You shall not worship their gods, nor serve them, nor do ac-
cording to their deeds; [b]but you shall utterly overthrow them, and
break their [c]*sacred* pillars in pieces.
25 "[a]But you shall serve the LORD your God, [1]and He will bless your
bread and your water; and [b]I will remove sickness from your midst.
26 "There shall be no one miscarrying or [a]barren in your land; [b]I will
fulfill the number of your days.
27 "I will [a]send My terror ahead of you, and [b]throw into confusion
all the people among whom you come, and I will [c]make all your
enemies turn *their* backs to you.
28 "And I will send [a]hornets ahead of you, that they may [b]drive out
the Hivites, the Canaanites, and the Hittites before you.
29 "[a]I will not drive them out before you in a single year, that the
land may not become desolate, and the beasts of the field become too
numerous for you.
30 "I will drive them out before you [a]little by little, until you become
fruitful and take possession of the land.
31 "[a]And I will fix your boundary from the [1]Red Sea to the sea of the
Philistines, and from the wilderness to the River *Euphrates;* [b]for I will
deliver the inhabitants of the land into your hand, and you will
[c]drive them out before you.
32 "[a]You shall [1]make no covenant with them [b]or with their gods.
33 "[a]They shall not live in your land, lest they make you sin against
Me; for *if* you serve their gods, [b]it will surely be a snare to you."

Chapter 24

24 Then He said to Moses, "[a]Come up to the LORD, you and
Aaron, [b]Nadab and Abihu and [c]seventy of the elders of Israel,
and you shall worship at a distance.
2 "Moses alone, however, shall come near to the LORD, but they
shall not come near, nor shall the people come up with him."
3 Then Moses came and recounted to the people all the words of
the LORD and all the [1]ordinances; and all the people answered with
one voice, and said, "[a]All the words which the LORD has spoken we
will do!"
4 And [a]Moses wrote down all the words of the LORD. Then he
arose early in the morning, and built an [b]altar [1]at the foot of the
mountain with twelve pillars for the twelve tribes of Israel.
5 And he sent young men of the sons of Israel, [a]and they offered
burnt offerings and sacrificed young bulls as peace offerings to the
LORD.
6 And [a]Moses took half of the blood and put *it* in basins, and the
other half of the blood he sprinkled on the altar.

20 [b]Ex. 15:
21 [a]Deut. 9 78:40, 56 [b] 6:3; 34:5-7
22 [a]Gen. 12 24:9; Deut. 3
23 [a]Ex. 23:2 24:8, 11
24 [a]Ex. 20:5 Deut. 12:30f. 33:52; Deut. 2 Kin. 18:4 [c] Lev. 26:1; 2 K
25 [1]Or, *that bless* [a]Lev. 2 Deut. 6:13; 1 28:1-14; Josh 1 Sam. 12:20 4:10 [b]Ex. 15: 7:15
26 [a]Deut. 7:1 4:40; Job 5:26
27 [a]Gen. 35:5 15:16; Deut. 2 2:9 [b]Deut. 7:2 18:40; 21:12
28 [a]Deut. 7:20 24:12 [b]Ex. 33.
29 [a]Deut. 7:22
30 [a]Deut. 7:22
31 [1]Lit., *Sea of* [a]Gen. 15:18; De 8; 11:24 [b]Deut. Josh. 21:44 [c]J 24:12, 18
32 [1]Lit., *cut* [a]Ex Deut. 7:2 [b]Ex. 2
33 [a]Deut. 7:1-5 [b]Ex. 34:12; Deut Josh. 23:13; Jud Ps. 106:36
24:1 [a]Ex. 19:24 6:23; 28:1; Lev. 1 [c]Num. 11:16
3 [1]Or, *judgments* 19:8; 24:7; Deut.
4 [1]Lit., *under* [a]E 17:14; 34:27; Deu 31:9 [b]Ex. 17:15
5 [a]Ex. 18:12
6 [a]Heb. 9:18

7 Then he took [a]the book of the covenant and read *it* in the hearing
of the people; and they said, "[b]All that the LORD has spoken we will
do, and we will be obedient!"
8 So [a]Moses took the blood and sprinkled *it* on the people, and
said, "Behold [b]the blood of the covenant, which the LORD has [1]made
with you [2]in accordance with all these words."
9 Then Moses went up [1]with Aaron, [a]Nadab and Abihu, and
seventy of the elders of Israel,
10 and [a]they saw the God of Israel; and under His feet [1b]there ap-
peared to be a pavement of sapphire, [2]as clear as the sky itself.
11 Yet He did not stretch out His hand against the nobles of the
sons of Israel; and [a]they beheld God, and they ate and drank.
12 Now the LORD said to Moses, "Come up to Me on the mountain
and [1]remain there, and [a]I will give you the stone tablets [2]with the law
and the commandment which I have written for their instruction."
13 So Moses arose [1]with [a]Joshua his [2]servant, and Moses went up to
[b]the mountain of God.
14 But to the elders he said, "[a]Wait here for us until we return to
you. And behold, [b]Aaron and Hur are with you; whoever [1]has a legal
matter, let him approach them."
15 Then Moses went up to the mountain, and [a]the cloud covered
the mountain.
16 And [a]the glory of the LORD [1]rested on Mount Sinai, and the cloud
covered it for six days; and on the seventh day He [b]called to Moses
from the midst of the cloud.
17 [a]And to the eyes of the sons of Israel the appearance of the glory
of the LORD was like a [b]consuming fire on the mountain top.
18 And Moses entered the midst of the cloud [1]as he went up to the
mountain; and Moses was on the mountain [a]forty days and forty
nights.

Chapter 25

25 Then the LORD spoke to Moses, saying,
2 "[a]Tell the sons of Israel to [1]raise a [2]contribution for Me;
[b]from every man whose heart moves him you shall [1]raise My [2]con-
tribution.
3 "And this is the [1]contribution which you are to [2]raise from them:
gold, silver and bronze,
4 [1a]blue, purple and scarlet *material*, fine linen, goat *hair*,
5 rams' skins dyed red, porpoise skins, acacia wood,
6 [a]oil for lighting, [b]spices for the anointing oil and for the fragrant
incense,
7 onyx stones and setting stones, for the [a]ephod and for the
[1b]breastpiece.
8 "And let them [a]construct a sanctuary for Me, [b]that I may dwell
among them.
9 "[a]According to all that I am going to show you, *as* the pattern of
the tabernacle and the pattern of all its furniture, just so you shall
construct *it*.
10 "[a]And they shall construct an ark of acacia wood two and a half
[1]cubits [2]long, and one and a half cubits [3]wide, and one and a half
cubits [4]high.
11 "And you shall [a]overlay it with pure gold, inside and out you
shall overlay it, and you shall make a gold molding [1]around it.

4; Heb. 9:19 [b]Ex. 24:3
it [2]Lit., *on all* 9, 20 [b]Zech. 26:28; Mark ; Luke 22:20; ; Heb. 13:20
and [a]Ex. 24:1
10 [1]Lit., *like a* [2]Lit., *and as* 1; Num. 12:8; hn 1:18; 6:46 26; 10:1; Rev. 4:3
16:13; 32:30; Ex. 24:10
, *be* [2]Lit., *and* ; 32:15; Deut. 5:22
[1]Lit., *and* [2]Or, [a]Ex. 17:9-14; 33:11 [b]Ex. 3:1
, *is a master of* *ers* [a]Gen. 22:5 [b]Ex. 17:10, 12
15 [a]Ex. 19:9
Lit., *dwelt* [a]Ex. um. 14:10 [b]Ps. 99:7
3:2; Ezek. 1:28 4:24; 9:3; Heb. 12:29
[1]Lit., *and* [a]Ex. Deut. 9:9; 10:10
[1]Lit., *take* [2]Or, *ve offering* [a]Ex. 4-9 [b]Ex. 35:21; 29:3, 5, 9; Ezra or. 8:11, 12; 9:7
r, heave offering [2]Lit., *take*
violet [a]Ex. 28:5, 6, 8
[a]Ex. 27:20 [b]Ex. 30:23f.
pouch [a]Ex. 28:4, [b]Ex. 28:4, 15-30
[a]Ex. 36:1-5 [b]Ex. 45, 46; Num. 5:3; 2:11; 1 Kin. 6:13; r. 6:16; Rev. 21:3
[a]Ex. 25:40; 26:30; 7:44; Heb. 8:2, 5
0 [1]I.e., One cubit ials approx. 18 in. *its length* [3]Lit., *its dth* [4]Lit., *its height* 37:1-9; Deut. 10:3; Heb. 9:4
1 [1]Lit., *on it round about* [a]Heb. 9:4

Each piece of furniture in the tabernacle was a picture of the work of the Lord Jesus Christ. Think about how each portrays this.

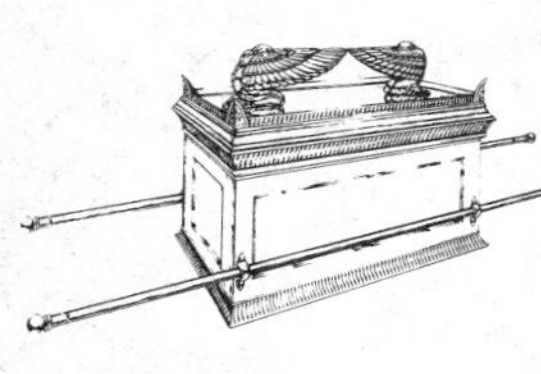
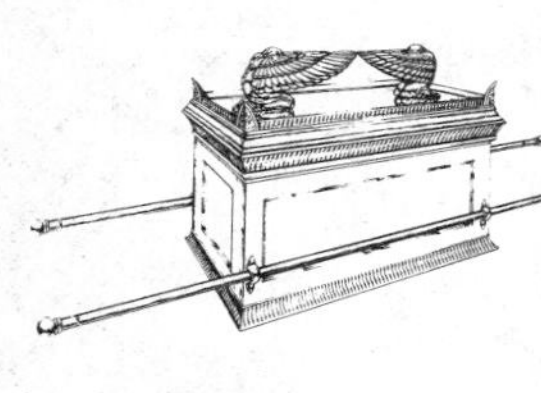

12 "And you shall cast four gold rings for it, and [1]fasten them on its
four feet, and two rings shall be on one side of it and two rings on
the other side of it.
13 "And you shall make poles of acacia wood and overlay them with
gold.
14 "And you shall put the poles into the rings on the sides of the ark,
to carry the ark with them.
15 "The [a]poles shall [1]remain in the rings of the ark; they shall not be
removed from it.
16 "And you shall [a]put into the ark the testimony which I shall give
you.
17 "And you shall [a]make a [1]mercy seat of pure gold, two and a half
[2]cubits [3]long and one and a half cubits [4]wide.
18 "And you shall make two cherubim of gold, make them of ham-
mered work [1]at the two ends of the mercy seat.
19 "And make one cherub [1]at one end and one cherub [1]at the other
end; you shall make the cherubim *of one piece* with the mercy seat at
its two ends.
20 "And [a]the cherubim shall have *their* wings spread upward, cover-
ing the mercy seat with their wings and [1]facing one another; the
faces of the cherubim are to be *turned* toward the mercy seat.
21 "And [a]you shall put the mercy seat [1]on top of the ark, and [b]in the
ark you shall put the testimony which I shall give to you.
22 "And [a]there I will meet with you; and from above the mercy seat,
from [b]between the two cherubim which are upon the ark of the
testimony, I will speak to you about all that I will give you in com-
mandment for the sons of Israel.

23 "[a]And you shall make a table of acacia wood, two cubits [1]long
and one cubit [2]wide and one and a half cubits [3]high.
24 "And you shall overlay it with pure gold and make a gold [a]border
around it.
25 "And you shall make for it a rim of a handbreadth around *it;* and
you shall make a gold border for the rim around it.
26 "And you shall make four gold rings for it and put rings on the
four corners which are on its four feet.
27 "The rings shall be close to the rim as holders for the poles to
carry the table.
28 "And you shall make the poles of acacia wood and overlay them
with gold, so that with them the table may be carried.
29 "And you shall make its [1a]dishes and its pans and its jars and its
[2]bowls, with which to pour libations; you shall make them of pure
gold.
30 "And you shall set [a]the bread of the [1]Presence on the table before
Me [2]at all times.

31 "[a]Then you shall make a lampstand of pure gold. The lampstand
and its base and its shaft are to be made of hammered work; its cups,
its [1]bulbs and its flowers shall be *of one piece* with it.
32 "And [a]six branches shall go out from its sides; three branches of
the lampstand from its one side, and three branches of the
lampstand from its [1]other side.
33 "[a]Three cups *shall be* shaped like almond *blossoms* in the one
branch, a [1]bulb and a flower, and three cups shaped like almond
blossoms in the [2]other branch, a [1]bulb and a flower—so for six
branches going out from the lampstand;

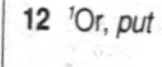

12 [1]Or, *put*

15 [1]Lit., *be*

16 [a]Ex. 40:2 10:2; 31:26; Heb. 9:4

17 [1]Lit., *prop* and so throug [2]I.e., One cub approx. 18 in. *length* [4]Lit., *it* [a]Ex. 37:6

18 [1]Lit., *from*

19 [1]Lit., *from*

20 [1]Lit., *their f* [a]1 Kin. 8:7; 1 C Heb. 9:5

21 [1]Lit., *above* [a]Ex. 26:34; 40:2 25:16

22 [a]Ex. 29:42, 36; Lev. 16:2; N 17:4 [b]Num. 7:8 1 Sam. 4:4; 2 S 2 Kin. 19:15; Ps Is. 37:16

23 [1]Lit., *its leng its width* [3]Lit., *its* [a]Ex. 37:10-16

24 [a]Ex. 25:11

29 [1]Or, *platters libation bowls* [a]E 37:16; Num. 4:7

30 [1]Lit., *Face* [2]C *continually* [a]Ex. 3 40:23; Lev. 24:5-9

31 [1]Or, *calyx* [a]Ex 37:17-24; 1 Kin. 7: Zech. 4:2

32 [1]Lit., *second* [a] 37:18

33 [1]Or, *calyx* [2]Lit., *branch* [a]Ex. 37:19

34 and [a]in the lampstand four cups shaped like almond *blossoms,* its
[1]bulbs and its flowers.
35 "[a]And a [1]bulb shall be under the *first* pair of branches *coming* out
of it, and a [1]bulb under the *second* pair of branches *coming* out of it,
and a [1]bulb under the *third* pair of branches *coming* out of it, for the
six branches coming out of the lampstand.
36 "[a]Their [1]bulbs and their branches *shall be of one piece* with it; all of
it shall be one piece of hammered work of pure gold.
37 "Then you shall make its lamps seven *in number;* and [a]they shall
[1]mount its lamps so as to shed light on the space in front of it.
38 "And its snuffers and [1]their trays *shall be* of pure gold.
39 "It shall be made from a talent of pure gold, with all these uten-
sils.
40 "And [a]see that you make *them* [b]after the pattern for them, which
was shown to you on the mountain.

Chapter 26

26 "[a]Moreover you shall make the tabernacle with ten curtains of
fine twisted linen and [1]blue and purple and scarlet *material;*
you shall make them with cherubim, the work of a skillful workman.
2 "The length of each curtain shall be twenty-eight [1]cubits, and the
width of each curtain four [1]cubits; all the curtains shall have [2]the
same measurements.
3 "Five curtains shall be [1]joined to one another; and *the other* five
curtains *shall be* [1]joined to one another.
4 "And you shall make loops of [1]blue on the edge of the [2]outermost
curtain in the *first* set, and likewise you shall make *them* on the edge
of the curtain that is outermost in the second [3]set.
5 "You shall make fifty loops in the one curtain, and you shall make
fifty loops on the [1]edge of the curtain that is in the second [2]set; the
loops shall be opposite each other.
6 "And you shall make fifty clasps of gold, and [1]join the curtains to
one another with the clasps, that the [2]tabernacle may be a unit.
7 "Then [a]you shall make curtains of goats' *hair* for a tent over the
tabernacle; you shall make eleven curtains in all.
8 "The length of each curtain *shall be* thirty [1]cubits, and the width of
each curtain four cubits; the eleven curtains shall have [2]the same
measurements.
9 "And you shall [1]join five curtains by themselves, and the *other* six
curtains by themselves, and you shall double over the sixth curtain
[2]at the front of the tent.
10 "And you shall make fifty loops on the edge of the [1]curtain that is
outermost in the *first* [2]set, and fifty loops on the edge of the curtain
that is outermost in the second [2]set.
11 "And you shall make fifty clasps of [1]bronze, and you shall put the
clasps into the loops and [2]join the tent together, that it may be [3]a
unit.
12 "And the [1]overlapping part that is left over in the curtains of the
tent, the half curtain that is left over, shall lap over the back of the
tabernacle.
13 "And the cubit on one side and the cubit on the other, of what is
left over in the length of the curtains of the tent, shall lap over the
sides of the tabernacle on one side and on the other, to cover it.

alyxes [a]Ex. 37:20
[a]Ex. 37:21
calyxes [a]Ex. 37:22
se up [a]Num. 8:2
s snuff dishes
3:5 [b]Ex. 25:9; Num. 8:4; Acts 7:44
Or, violet [a]Ex. 36:8-19
I.e., One cubit approx. 18 in. , one measure
3 [1]Or, coupled
violet [2]Lit., one from the end in e coupling [3]Lit., coupling
[1]Lit., end [2]Lit., coupling
[1]Or, couple [2]Or, ng place, and so roughout the ch.
7 [a]Ex. 36:14
8 [1]I.e., One cubit als approx. 18 in. Lit., one measure
[1]Or, couple [2]Lit., ard the front of the face of the tent
[1]Lit., one curtain [2]Lit., coupling
[1]Or, copper [2]Or, couple [3]Lit., one
12 [1]Lit., excess

14 "And [a]you shall make a covering for the tent of rams' skins [1]dyed
red, and a covering of porpoise skins above.
15 "Then you shall make [a]the boards for the tabernacle of acacia
wood, standing upright.
16 "Ten cubits *shall be* the length of [1]each board, and one and a half
cubits the width of each board.
17 "There *shall be* two tenons for each board, [1]fitted to one another;
thus you shall do for all the boards of the tabernacle.
18 "And you shall make the boards for the tabernacle: twenty boards
[1]for the south side.
19 "And you shall make forty [1a]sockets of silver under the twenty
boards, two [1]sockets under one board for its two tenons and two
[1]sockets under another board for its two tenons;
20 and for the second side of the tabernacle, on the north side,
twenty boards,
21 and their forty [1]sockets of silver; two [1]sockets under one board
and two [1]sockets under another board.
22 "And for the [1]rear of the tabernacle, to the west, you shall make
six boards.
23 "And you shall make two boards for the corners of the tabernacle
at the [1]rear.
24 "And they shall be double beneath, and together they shall be
complete [1]to its top [2]to the first ring; thus it shall be with both of
them: they shall form the two corners.
25 "And there shall be eight boards with their [1]sockets of silver,
sixteen [1]sockets; two [1]sockets under one board and two [1]sockets
under another board.
26 "Then you shall make [a]bars of acacia wood, five for the boards of
one side of the tabernacle,
27 and five bars for the boards of the [1]other side of the tabernacle,
and five bars for the boards of the side of the tabernacle for the [2]rear
side to the west.
28 "And the middle bar in the [1]center of the boards shall pass
through from end to end.
29 "And you shall overlay the boards with gold and make their rings
of gold *as* holders for the bars; and you shall overlay the bars with
gold.
30 "Then you shall erect the tabernacle [a]according to its plan which
you have been shown in the mountain.
31 "And you shall make [a]a veil of [1]blue and purple and scarlet
material and fine twisted linen; it shall be made with cherubim, the
work of a skillful workman.
32 "And you shall [1]hang it on four pillars of acacia overlaid with
gold, their hooks *also being of* gold, on four [2]sockets of silver.
33 "And you shall [1]hang up the veil under the clasps, and shall bring
in [a]the ark of the testimony there within the veil; and the veil shall
[2]serve for you as a partition [b]between the holy place and the holy of
holies.
34 "And [a]you shall put the mercy seat on the ark of the testimony in
the holy of holies.
35 "And [a]you shall set the table outside the veil, and the [b]lampstand
opposite the table on the side of the tabernacle toward the south; and
you shall put the table on the north side.
36 "And [a]you shall make a screen for the doorway of the tent of [1]blue

14 [1]Or, tan. 36:19
15 [a]Ex. 36:
16 [1]Lit., the
17 [1]Lit., bou
18 [1]Lit., tow. of the Negev south
19 [1]Or, base 38:27
21 [1]Or, bases
22 [1]Lit., extre
23 [1]Lit., extre
24 [1]Or, at its h with reference
25 [1]Or, bases
26 [a]Ex. 36:31
27 [1]Lit., secon extreme parts
28 [1]Lit., midst
30 [a]Ex. 25:9, 40 7:44; Heb. 8:5
31 [1]Or, violet [a]E 36:35, 36; 2 Chr. Matt. 27:51; Heb
32 [1]Lit., put [2]Or,
33 [1]Lit., put [2]Lit., separate for you between [a]Ex. 25 40:21 [b]Heb. 9:2f.
34 [a]Ex. 25:21; 40 Lev. 16:2
35 [a]Ex. 40:22 [b]Ex 40:24
36 [1]Or, violet [a]Ex.

and purple and scarlet *material* and fine twisted linen, the work of a
[2]weaver.
37 "And [a]you shall make five pillars of acacia for the screen, and
overlay them with gold, their hooks *also being of* gold; and you shall
cast five [1]sockets of [2]bronze for them.

Chapter 27

27 "And you shall make [a]the altar of acacia wood, five [1]cubits
long and five cubits wide; the altar shall be square, and its
height shall be three cubits.
2 "And you shall make [a]its horns on its four corners; its horns shall
be of one piece with it, and you shall overlay it with [1]bronze.
3 "And you shall make its pails for removing its ashes, and its
shovels and its basins and its forks and its firepans; you shall make
all its utensils of bronze.
4 "And you shall make for it a grating of network of bronze, and on
the net you shall make four bronze rings [1]at its four corners.
5 "And you shall put it beneath, under the ledge of the altar, that
the net may reach halfway up the altar.
6 "And you shall make poles for the altar, poles of acacia wood, and
overlay them with bronze.
7 "And its poles shall be inserted into the rings, so that the poles
shall be on the two sides of the altar [a]when it is carried.
8 "You shall make it hollow with planks; [a]as it was shown to you in
the mountain, so they shall make *it*.
9 "And you shall make [a]the court of the [1]tabernacle. [2]On the south
side *there shall be* hangings for the court of fine twisted linen one
hundred cubits long for one side;
10 and its pillars *shall be* twenty, with their twenty [1]sockets of
bronze; the hooks of the pillars and their [2]bands *shall be* of silver.
11 "And likewise for the north side in length *there shall be* hangings
one hundred *cubits* long, and its twenty pillars with their twenty
[1]sockets of bronze; the hooks of the pillars and their bands *shall be* of
silver.
12 "And *for* the width of the court on the west side *shall be* hangings
of fifty cubits *with* their ten pillars and their ten [1]sockets.
13 "And the width of the court on the [1]east side *shall be* fifty cubits.
14 "The hangings for the *one* [1]side *of the gate shall be* fifteen cubits
with their three pillars and their three [2]sockets.
15 "And for the [1]other [2]side *shall be* hangings of fifteen cubits *with*
their three pillars and their three [3]sockets.
16 "And for the gate of the court there *shall be* a screen of twenty
cubits, of [1]blue and purple and scarlet *material* and fine twisted linen,
the work of a [2]weaver, *with* their four pillars and their four [3]sockets.
17 "All the pillars around the court shall be furnished with silver
bands *with* their hooks of silver and their [1]sockets of bronze.
18 "The length of the court *shall be* one hundred cubits, and the
width fifty throughout, and the height five cubits of fine twisted
linen, and their [1]sockets of bronze.
19 "All the utensils of the tabernacle *used* in all its service, and all its
pegs, and all the pegs of the court, *shall be* of bronze.
20 "And you shall charge the sons of Israel, that they bring you
[a]clear oil of beaten olives for the [1]light, to make a lamp [2]burn
continually.

gator; i.e., r in colors
ases [2]Or, [a]Ex. 36:38
, One cubit prox. 18 in. [a]Ex. 38:1-7
per, and so throughout [a]Ps. 118:27
4 [1]Lit., on
[a]Num. 4:15
25:40; 26:30; :44; Heb. 8:5
welling place he side of the he south [a]Ex. 38:9-20
Or, bases [2]Or, fillets, rings
11 [1]Or, bases
12 [1]Or, bases
[1]Lit., east side eastward
., shoulder [2]Or, bases
t., second [2]Lit., ulder [3]Or, bases
[1]Or, violet [2]Lit., variegator; i.e., a er in colors [3]Or, bases
17 [1]Or, bases
18 [1]Or, bases
Or, luminary [2]Lit., end [a]Ex. 35:8, 28; Lev. 24:1-4

21 "In the [a]tent of meeting, outside [b]the veil which is before the testi-
mony, [c]Aaron and his sons shall keep it in order from evening to
morning before the LORD; *it shall be* a perpetual [d]statute throughout
their generations [1]for the sons of Israel.

Chapter 28 ______________________________

28 "Then [a]bring near to yourself Aaron your brother, and his
sons with him, from among the sons of Israel, to minister as
priest to Me—Aaron, [b]Nadab and Abihu, Eleazar and Ithamar,
Aaron's sons.
2 "And you shall make [a]holy garments for Aaron your brother, for
glory and for beauty.
3 "And you shall speak to all the [1a]skillful persons [b]whom I have
endowed with [2]the spirit of wisdom, that they make Aaron's gar-
ments to consecrate him, that he may minister as priest to Me.
4 "And these are the garments which they shall make: a
[1a]breastpiece and an ephod and a robe and a tunic of checkered
work, a turban and a sash, and they shall make holy garments for
Aaron your brother and his sons, that he may minister as priest
to Me.
5 "And they shall take [a]the gold and the [1]blue and the purple and
the scarlet *material* and the fine linen.
6 "They shall also make [a]the ephod of gold, of [1]blue and purple *and*
scarlet *material* and fine twisted linen, the work of the skillful
workman.
7 "It shall have two shoulder pieces joined to its two ends, that it
may be joined.
8 "And the skillfully woven band, which is on it, shall be like its
workmanship, [1]of the same material: of gold, of [2]blue and purple
and scarlet *material* and fine twisted linen.
9 "And you shall take two onyx stones and engrave on them the
names of the sons of Israel,
10 six of their names on the one stone, and the names of the remain-
ing six on the [1]other stone, according to their birth.
11 "[1]As a jeweler engraves a signet, you shall engrave the two stones
according to the names of the sons of Israel; you shall [2]set them in
filigree *settings* of gold.
12 "And you shall put the two stones on the shoulder pieces of the
ephod, *as* stones of memorial for the sons of Israel, and Aaron shall
[a]bear their names before the LORD on his two shoulders [b]for a
memorial.
13 "[a]And you shall make filigree *settings* of gold,
14 and two chains of pure gold; you shall make them of twisted
cordage work, and you shall put the corded chains on the filigree
settings.
15 "And [a]you shall make a [1]breastpiece of judgment, the work of a
skillful workman; like the work of the ephod you shall make it: of
gold, of [2]blue and purple and scarlet *material* and fine twisted linen
you shall make it.
16 "It shall be square *and* folded double, a span [1]in length and a span
[1]in width.
17 "And you shall [1]mount on it four rows of stones; the first row
shall be a row of ruby, topaz and emerald;
18 and the second row a turquoise, a sapphire and a diamond;

INSIGHT

The **ephod** was used to seek guidance from God. Described in Exodus 28, it is a linen garment worn by the priest and also by David when he was king (2 Samuel 6:14). The ephod was fastened on each shoulder by onyx clasps which had the name of six tribes engraved on one clasp, and six tribes engraved on the other. The **breastplate,** which was fastened to the ephod, had a linen pouch which held the **Urim** and **Thummim,** which may have been used as sacred lots to reveal God's will (1 Samuel 28:6).

21 [1]Lit., *fr*
25:22; 29:4
[b]Ex. 26:31,
30:8; 1 Sar
13:11 [d]Ex.
Lev. 3:17; 1
18:23; 19:2
30:25

28:1 [a]Num
99:6; Heb. 5
24:1, 9

2 [a]Ex. 29:5
39:1-31; Lev

3 [1]Lit., *wise*
[2]I.e., artistic
31:6; 35:25,
[b]Ex. 31:3; Is.
1 Cor. 12:7-1

4 [1]Or, *pouch*
28:15-43

5 [1]Or, *violet*

6 [1]Or, *violet*
39:2-7; Lev. 8

8 [1]Lit., *from it*

10 [1]Lit., *seco*

11 [1]Lit., *A wor*
lapidary, engra
seal [2]Lit., *mak*
be surrounded

12 [a]Ex. 28:29;
[b]Ex. 39:7; Lev.
Num. 31:54; Jos
1 Cor. 11:24f.

13 [a]Ex. 39:16-1

15 [1]Or, *pouch* [2]
violet [a]Ex. 39:8-

16 [1]Lit., *its*

17 [1]Lit., *fill in a s*
of stones, four ro
stones

19 and the third row a jacinth, an agate and an amethyst;
20 and the fourth row a beryl and an onyx and a jasper; they shall
be [1]set in gold filigree.
21 "And the stones shall be according to the names of the sons of
Israel: twelve, according to their names; they shall be *like* the engrav-
ings of a seal, each [a]according to his name for the twelve tribes.
22 "And you shall make on the [1]breastpiece chains of twisted cord-
age work in pure gold.
23 "And you shall make on the breastpiece two rings of gold, and
shall put the two rings on the two ends of the breastpiece.
24 "And you shall put the two cords of gold on the two rings at the
ends of the breastpiece.
25 "And you shall put the *other* two ends of the two cords on the two
filigree *settings,* and put them on the shoulder pieces of the ephod, at
the front of it.
26 "And you shall make two rings of gold and shall place them on
the two ends of the breastpiece, on the edge of it, which is toward
the inner side of the ephod.
27 "And you shall make two rings of gold and put them on the
bottom of the two shoulder pieces of the ephod, on the front of it
close to the place where it is joined, above the skillfully woven band
of the ephod.
28 "And they shall bind the breastpiece by its rings to the rings of
the ephod with a [1]blue cord, that it may be on the skillfully woven
band of the ephod, and that the breastpiece may not come loose
from the ephod.

29 "And Aaron shall carry the names of the sons of Israel in the
breastpiece of judgment over his heart when he enters the holy
place, for a memorial before the LORD continually.
30 "And [a]you shall put in the breastpiece of judgment the [1b]Urim and
the Thummim, and they shall be over Aaron's heart when he goes in
before the LORD; and Aaron shall carry the judgment of the sons of
Israel over his heart before the LORD continually.
31 "[a]And you shall make the robe of the ephod all of [1]blue.
32 "And there shall be an opening [1]at its top in the middle of it;
around its opening there shall be a binding of woven work, as *it were*
the opening of a coat of mail, that it may not be torn.
33 "And you shall make on its hem pomegranates of blue and
purple and scarlet *material,* all around on its hem, and bells of gold
between them all around:
34 a golden bell and a pomegranate, a golden bell and a pome-
granate, all around on the hem of the robe.
35 "And it shall be on Aaron [1]when he ministers; and [2]its tinkling
may be heard when he enters and [3]leaves the holy place before the
LORD, that he may not die.
36 "You shall also make [a]a plate of pure gold and shall engrave on it,
like the engravings of a seal, '[b]Holy to the LORD.'

37 "And you shall [1]fasten it on a [2]blue cord, and it shall be on the
turban; it shall be at the front of the turban.
38 "And it shall be on Aaron's forehead, and Aaron shall [1a]take away
the iniquity of the holy things which the sons of Israel consecrate,
with regard to all their holy gifts; and it shall always be on his
forehead, that [b]they may be accepted before the LORD.
39 "And you shall weave [a]the tunic of checkered work of fine linen,

woven with
eir settings

7:4-8; 21:12

uch, and so
nrough v. 30

8 [1]Or, violet

.e., lights and
ons [a]Lev. 8:8
27:21; Deut.
ra 2:63; Neh.
7:65

Or, violet [a]Ex.
39:22-26

Or, for his head

, for ministering
its sound [3]Lit.,
comes out from

. 39:30, 31; Lev.
9 [b]Zech. 14:20

[1]Lit., place [2]Or,
violet

[1]Or, bear [a]Lev.
):17; 22:16; Num.
[b]Lev. 1:4; 22:27;
23:11; Is. 56:7

39 [a]Ex. 39:27-29

and shall make a turban of fine linen, and you shall make a sash, the
work of a [1]weaver.
40 "And for Aaron's sons you shall make [a]tunics; you shall also
make sashes for them, and you shall make [1b]caps for them, for glory
and for beauty.
41 "And you shall put them on Aaron your brother and on his sons
with him; and you shall [a]anoint them and [1]ordain them and con-
secrate them, that they may serve Me as priests.
42 "And you shall make for them [a]linen breeches to cover *their* bare
flesh; they shall [1]reach from the loins even to the thighs.
43 "And they shall be on Aaron and on his sons when they enter the
tent of meeting, or [a]when they approach the altar to minister in the
holy place, so that they do not incur [1]guilt and die. [b]It *shall be* a
statute forever to him and to his [2]descendants after him.

Chapter 29

29 "[a]Now this is [1]what you shall do to them to consecrate them
to minister as priests to Me: take one young bull and two
rams without blemish,
2 and [a]unleavened bread and unleavened cakes mixed with oil,
and unleavened wafers [1]spread with oil; you shall make them of fine
wheat flour.
3 "And you shall put them in one basket, and present them in the
basket along with the bull and the two rams.
4 "Then [a]you shall bring Aaron and his sons to the doorway of the
tent of meeting, and wash them with water.
5 "And you shall take the garments, and put on Aaron the [a]tunic
and [b]the robe of the ephod and [c]the ephod and [d]the [1]breastpiece, and
gird him with the skillfully [e]woven band of the ephod;
6 and you shall set the [a]turban on his head, and put [b]the holy
crown on the turban.
7 "Then you shall take [a]the anointing oil, and pour it on his head
and anoint him.
8 "And you shall bring his sons and put [a]tunics on them.
9 "And you shall gird them with [a]sashes, Aaron and his sons, and
bind [1]caps on them, and they shall have [b]the priesthood by a per-
petual statute. So you shall [2c]ordain Aaron and his sons.
10 "Then you shall bring the bull before the tent of meeting, and
Aaron and his sons shall [a]lay their hands on the head of the bull.
11 "And you shall slaughter the bull before the LORD at the doorway
of the tent of meeting.
12 "And you shall [a]take some of the blood of the bull and put *it* on
[b]the horns of the altar with your finger; and you shall pour out all
the blood at the base of the altar.
13 "And you shall [a]take all the fat that covers the entrails and the
[1]lobe of the liver, and the two kidneys and the fat that is on them,
and offer them up in smoke on the altar.
14 "But [a]the flesh of the bull and its hide and its refuse, you shall
burn with fire outside the camp; it is a sin offering.
15 "[a]You shall also take the one ram, and Aaron and his sons shall
lay their hands on the head of the ram;
16 and you shall slaughter the ram and shall take its blood and
sprinkle it around on the altar.

39 [1]Lit., *va*
a weaver in

40 [1]Lit., *hea*
28:4; 39:27,
29:9; 39:28;
Ezek. 44:18

41 [1]Lit., *fill t*
[a]Ex. 29:7, 9;
40:15; Lev. 8

42 [1]Lit., *be*
Lev. 6:10; 16
44:18

43 [1]Or, *iniqu*
seed [a]Ex. 2C
27:21

29:1 [1]Lit., *the*
which [a]Lev. 8

2 [1]Or, *anointe*
2:4; 6:19-23

4 [a]Ex. 40:12;

5 [1]Or, *pouch*
[a]Ex. 28:39; Lev
[b]Ex. 28:31 [c]Ex
[d]Ex. 28:15 [e]Ex

6 [a]Ex. 28:4, 39
28:36, 37; Lev.

7 [a]Ex. 30:25; L
21:10; Num. 35
133:2

8 [a]Ex. 28:39, 4
8:13

9 [1]Lit., *headgea*
fill the hand of [a]
28:40 [b]Ex. 40:1
3:10; 18:7; 25:13
18:5 [c]Ex. 28:41;
8:1-36

10 [a]Lev. 1:4; 8:1

12 [a]Lev. 8:15 [b]E
27:2; 30:2

13 [1]Or, *appenda*
[a]Lev. 3:3, 4

14 [a]Lev. 4:11, 12,
Heb. 13:11

15 [a]Lev. 8:18

17 "Then you shall cut the ram into its pieces, and wash its entrails
and its legs, and put *them* [1]with its pieces and [2]its head.
18 "And you shall offer up in smoke the whole ram on the altar; it is
a burnt offering to the LORD: [a]it is a soothing aroma, an offering by
fire to the LORD.
19 "Then [a]you shall take the [1]other ram, and Aaron and his sons
shall lay their hands on the head of the ram.
20 "And you shall slaughter the ram, and take some of its blood and
put *it* on the lobe of Aaron's right ear and on the lobes of his sons'
right ears and on the thumbs of their right hands and on the big toes
of their right feet, and sprinkle the *rest of the* blood around on the
altar.
21 "Then you shall take some of the blood that is on the altar and
some of the [a]anointing oil, and sprinkle *it* on Aaron and on his
garments, and on his sons and on his sons' garments with him; so he
and his garments shall be consecrated, as well as his sons and his
sons' garments with him.
22 "You shall also take the fat from the ram and the fat tail, and the
fat that covers the entrails and the [1]lobe of the liver, and the two
kidneys and the fat that is on them and the right thigh (for it is a ram
of [2]ordination),
23 and one cake of bread and [a]one cake of bread *mixed with* oil and
one wafer from the basket of unleavened bread which is *set* before
the LORD;
24 and you shall put [1]all these [2]in the [3]hands of Aaron and [2]in the
[3]hands of his sons, and shall wave them as a wave offering before
the LORD.
25 "And [a]you shall take them from their hands, and offer them up in
smoke on the altar on the burnt offering for a soothing aroma before
the LORD; it is an offering by fire to the LORD.
26 "Then you shall take [a]the breast of Aaron's ram of [1]ordination,
and wave it as a wave offering before the LORD; and it shall be your
portion.
27 "And you shall consecrate the breast of the wave offering and the
thigh of the heave offering which was waved and which was [1]of-
fered from the ram of [2]ordination, from the one which was for Aaron
and from the one which was for his sons.
28 "And it shall be for Aaron and his sons as *their* portion forever
from the sons of Israel, for it is a heave offering; and it shall be a
heave offering from the sons of Israel from the sacrifices of their
peace offerings, *even* their heave offering to the LORD.
29 "And [a]the holy garments of Aaron shall be for his sons after him,
[1]that in them they may be anointed and ordained.
30 "For seven days the one of his sons who is priest in his stead shall
put them on when he enters the tent of meeting to minister in the
holy place.
31 "And you shall take the ram of [1]ordination and [a]boil its flesh in a
holy place.
32 "And Aaron and his sons shall eat the flesh of the ram, and the
bread that is in the basket, at the doorway of the tent of meeting.
33 "Thus [a]they shall eat [1]those things by which atonement was made
[2]at their ordination *and* consecration; but a [3b]layman shall not eat
them, because they are holy.
34 "And [a]if any of the flesh of [1]ordination or any of the bread

[2]Lit., *on its*
en. 8:21; Ex. 29:25
econd [a]Lev. 8:22f.
0:25, 31; Lev. 8:30
ppendage on [2]Lit., *filling*
23 [a]Lev. 8:26
he whole [2]Lit., on [3]Lit., *palms*
25 [a]Lev. 8:28
Lit., *filling* [a]Lev. 7:31, 34; 8:29
[1]Lit., *heaved*; or, d up [2]Lit., *filling*
, *for anointing in* n *and filling their* d *in them* [a]Num. 20:26, 28
[1]Lit., *filling* [a]Lev. 8:31
Lit., *them* [2]Lit., *to* ir *hand to sanctify* em [3]Lit., *stranger* [a]Lev. 10:14 [b]Lev. 22:10, 13
4 [1]Lit., *filling* [a]Ex. 2:10; 23:18; 34:25; Lev. 8:32

remains until morning, then you shall burn the remainder with fire;
it shall not be eaten, because it is holy.
35 "And thus you shall do to Aaron and to his sons, according to all
that I have commanded you; you shall [1]ordain them through [a]seven
days.
36 "And [a]each day you shall offer a bull as a sin offering for atone-
ment, and you shall [1]purify the altar when you make atonement [2]for
it; and [b]you shall anoint it to consecrate it.
37 "For seven days you shall make atonement [1]for the altar and
consecrate it; then [a]the altar shall be most holy, *and* whatever touches
the altar shall be holy.
38 "Now [a]this is what you shall offer on the altar: two one year old
lambs each day, continuously.
39 "The [a]one lamb you shall offer in the morning, and the [1]other
lamb you shall offer at [2]twilight;
40 and there *shall be* one-tenth *of an ephah* of fine flour mixed with
one-fourth of a hin of beaten oil, and one-fourth of a hin of wine for
a libation with one lamb.
41 "And the [1]other lamb you shall offer at [2]twilight, and shall offer
with it [3]the same grain offering as the morning and [4]the same liba-
tion, for a soothing aroma, an offering by fire to the LORD.
42 "It shall be a continual burnt offering throughout your genera-
tions at the doorway of the tent of meeting before the LORD, [a]where I
will meet with you, to speak to you there.
43 "And I will meet there with the sons of Israel, and it shall be
consecrated by My glory.
44 "And I will consecrate the tent of meeting and the altar; I will also
consecrate Aaron and his sons to minister as priests to Me.
45 "And [a]I will dwell among the sons of Israel and will be their God.
46 "And they shall know that [a]I am the LORD their God who brought
them out of the land of Egypt, that I might dwell among them; I am
the LORD their God.

Chapter 30

30 "Moreover, you shall make [a]an altar as a place for burning
incense; you shall make it of acacia wood.
2 "Its length *shall be* a [1]cubit, and its width a cubit, it shall be square,
and its height *shall be* two cubits; its horns *shall be* [2]of one piece
with it.
3 "And you shall overlay it with pure gold, its top and its [1]sides all
around, and its horns; and you shall make a gold molding all around
for it.
4 "And you shall make two gold rings for it under its molding; you
shall make *them* on its two side walls—on [1]opposite sides—and [2]they
shall be holders for poles with which to carry it.
5 "And you shall make the poles of acacia wood and overlay them
with gold.
6 "And you shall put [1]this altar in front of the veil that is [2]near the
ark of the testimony, in front of the [3a]mercy seat that is over *the ark of*
the testimony, where I will meet with you.
7 "And Aaron shall burn fragrant incense on it; he shall burn it
every morning when he trims the lamps.
8 "And when Aaron [1]trims the lamps at [2]twilight, he shall burn

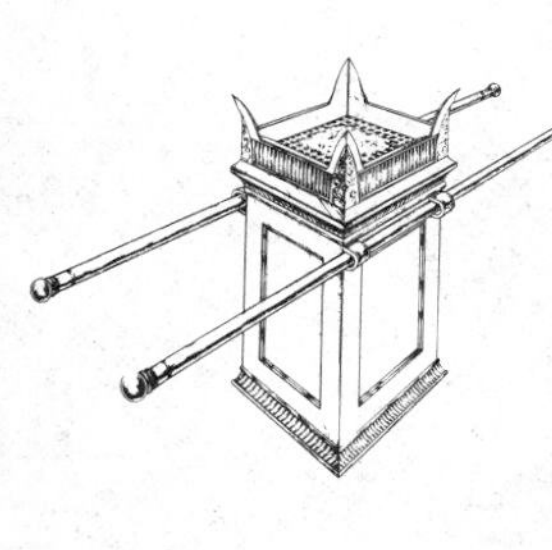

35 [1]Lit., *fill* [a]Lev. 8:33

36 [1]Or, *offe* *offering on t* [2]Lit., *upon* [a] [b]Ex. 40:10

37 [1]Lit., *upo* 30:28f.

38 [a]Num. 28 29:6-38

39 [1]Lit., *seco* *between the* *evenings* [a]Ez 46:13-15

41 [1]Lit., *seco* *between the t* *evenings* [3]Lit. *according to t* *offering of the* [4]Lit., *according*

42 [a]Ex. 25:22; 17:4

45 [a]Ex. 25:8; L 26:12; Num. 5: 12:11; Zech. 2: 2 Cor. 6:16; Re

46 [a]Ex. 20:2

30:1 [a]Ex. 37:25

2 [1]I.e., One cub equals approx. [2]Lit., *from itself*

3 [1]Lit., *walls*

4 [1]Lit., *its two* [2]L

6 [1]Lit., *it* [2]Lit., *up* *over* [3]Lit., *propiti* [a]Ex. 25:21f.

8 [1]Lit., *causes to ascend* [2]Lit., *betw* *the two evenings*

incense. *There shall be* perpetual incense before the LORD throughout
your generations.
9 "You shall not offer any strange incense on [1]this altar, or burnt
offering or meal offering; and you shall not pour out a libation on it.
10 "And Aaron shall [a]make atonement on its horns once a year; he
shall make atonement on it with the blood of the sin offering of
atonement once a year throughout your generations. It is most holy
to the LORD."
11 The LORD also spoke to Moses, saying,
12 "When you take [a]a [1]census of the sons of Israel [2]to number them,
then each one of them shall give [b]a ransom for [3]himself to the LORD,
when you [4]number them, that there may be no plague among them
when you [4]number them.
13 "This is what everyone who [1]is numbered shall give: half a shekel
according to the shekel of the sanctuary ([a]the shekel is twenty
gerahs), half a shekel as a [2]contribution to the LORD.
14 "Everyone who [1]is numbered, from twenty years old and over,
shall give the [2]contribution to the LORD.
15 "The rich shall not pay more, and the poor shall not pay less than
the half shekel, when you give the [1]contribution to the LORD to make
atonement for [2]yourselves.
16 "And you shall take the atonement money from the sons of Israel,
and shall give it for the service of the tent of meeting, that it may be
a memorial for the sons of Israel before the LORD, to make atonement
for [1]yourselves."
17 And the LORD spoke to Moses, saying,
18 "You shall also make [a]a laver of [1]bronze, with its base of bronze,
for washing; and you shall [b]put it between the tent of meeting and
the altar, and you shall put water in it.
19 "And Aaron and his sons shall [a]wash their hands and their feet
from it;
20 when they enter the tent of meeting, they shall wash with water,
that they may not die; or when they approach the altar to minister,
by offering up in smoke a fire *sacrifice* to the LORD.
21 "So they shall wash their hands and their feet, that they may not
die; and [a]it shall be a perpetual statute for them, for [1]Aaron and his
[2]descendants throughout their generations."
22 Moreover, the LORD spoke to Moses, saying,
23 "Take also for yourself the finest of spices: of flowing myrrh five
hundred *shekels,* and of fragrant cinnamon half as much, two
hundred and fifty, and of fragrant cane two hundred and fifty,
24 and of cassia five hundred, according to the shekel of the sanctu-
ary, and of olive oil a hin.
25 "And you shall make [1]of these a holy anointing oil, a perfume
mixture, the work of a perfumer; it shall be [a]a holy anointing oil.
26 "And with it [a]you shall anoint the tent of meeting and the ark of
the testimony,
27 and the table and all its utensils, and the lampstand and its
utensils, and the altar of incense,
28 and the altar of burnt offering and all its utensils, and the laver
and its stand.
29 "You shall also consecrate them, that they may be most holy;
whatever touches them shall be holy.

9 [1]Lit., *it*
10 [a]Lev. 16:18
Lit., *sum* [2]Lit., *for* …ir *being mustered* [3]Lit., *his soul* [4]Lit., …er [a]Ex. 38:25, 26; …1:2; 26:2 [b]Num. 31:50
…it., *passes over to those who are* …tered [2]Lit., *heave* …ering [a]Lev. 27:25; 3:47; Ezek. 45:12
…V. 13, note 1 [2]Lit., …ave offering of the LORD
…it., *heave offering* …e LORD [2]Lit., *your souls*
…6 [1]Lit., *your souls*
… [1]Or, *copper* [a]Ex. 38:8 [b]Ex. 40:30
…x. 40:31f.; Is. 52:11
…it., *him* [2]Lit., *seed* [a]Ex. 28:43
[1]Lit., *it* [a]Ex. 37:29; 40:9; Lev. 8:10
…Ex. 40:9; Lev. 8:10; Num. 7:1

30 "[a]And you shall anoint Aaron and his sons, and consecrate them,
that they may minister as priests to Me.
31 "And you shall speak to the sons of Israel, saying, 'This shall be a
holy anointing oil to Me throughout your generations.
32 'It shall not be poured on [1]anyone's body, nor shall you make *any*
like it, in [2]the same proportions; [a]it is holy, *and* it shall be holy to you.
33 '[a]Whoever shall mix *any* like it, or whoever puts any of it on a
[1]layman, [2b]shall be cut off from his people.' "
34 Then the LORD said to Moses, "Take for yourself spices, stacte
and onycha and galbanum, spices with pure frankincense; there
shall be an equal part of each.
35 "And with it you shall make incense, a perfume, the work of a
perfumer, salted, pure, *and* holy.
36 "And you shall beat some of it very fine, and put part of it before
the testimony in the tent of meeting, [a]where I shall meet with you; it
shall be most holy to you.
37 "And the incense which you shall make, [a]you shall not make in
[1]the same proportions for yourselves; it shall be holy to you for the
LORD.
38 "[a]Whoever shall make *any* like it, to [1]use as perfume, [2]shall be cut
off from his people."

Chapter 31

31 [a]Now the LORD spoke to Moses, saying,
2 "See, I have called by name Bezalel, the [a]son of Uri, the son
of Hur, of the tribe of Judah.
3 "And I have [a]filled him with the Spirit of God in wisdom, in
understanding, in knowledge, and in all *kinds of* [1]craftsmanship,
4 to [1]make artistic designs for work in gold, in silver, and in
[2]bronze,
5 and in the cutting of stones [1]for settings, and in the carving of
wood, that he may work in all *kinds of* [2]craftsmanship.
6 "And behold, I Myself have [1]appointed with him [a]Oholiab, the
son of Ahisamach, of the tribe of Dan; and in the hearts of all who
are [2]skillful I have put [3]skill, that they may make all that I have
commanded you:
7 [a]the tent of meeting, and [b]the ark of testimony, and [c]the [1]mercy
seat upon it, and all the furniture of the tent,
8 [a]the table also and its [1]utensils, and the [b]pure *gold* lampstand
with all its [1]utensils, and [c]the altar of incense,
9 [a]the altar of burnt offering also with all its [1]utensils, and [b]the
laver and its stand,
10 the [1a]woven garments as well, and the holy garments for Aaron
the priest, and the garments of his sons, *with which* to [2]carry on their
priesthood;
11 [a]the anointing oil also, and the [b]fragrant incense for the holy
place, they are to make *them* according to all that I have commanded
you."
12 And the LORD spoke to Moses, saying,
13 "But as for you, speak to the sons of Israel, saying, '[a]You shall
surely observe My sabbaths; for *this* is [b]a sign between Me and you
throughout your generations, that you may know that I am the LORD
who sanctifies you.
14 'Therefore you are to observe the sabbath, for it is holy to you.

30 [a]Ex. 29:7
32 [1]Lit., *the man* [2]Lit., *its* [a]Ex. 30:25, 3
33 [1]Lit., *stra* *even he shal* 30:38 [b]Gen. 12:15; Lev. 7
36 [a]Ex. 29:42
37 [1]Lit., *its pr* [a]Ex. 30:32
38 [1]Lit., *smell* *even he shall*
31:1 [a]Ex. 35:3
2 [a]1 Chr. 2:20
3 [1]Or, *workma* [a]Ex. 35:31; 1 Ki 1 Cor. 12:4-8
4 [1]Lit., *devise c* [2]Or, *copper*
5 [1]Lit., *to fill in (* *setting)* [2]Or, *workmanship*
6 [1]Lit., *given* [2]Li *of heart* [3]Lit., *wis* [a]Ex. 35:34
7 [1]Lit., *propitiato* 36:8-38 [b]Ex. 37:1 [c]Ex. 37:6-9
8 [1]Or, *vessels* [a]E 37:10-16 [b]Ex. 37 Lev. 24:4 [c]Ex. 37
9 [1]Or, *vessels* [a]E 38:1-7 [b]Ex. 38:8
10 [1]Or, *service garments* [2]Lit., *mi* *as priests* [a]Ex. 39
11 [a]Ex. 30:23-32 30:34-38
13 [a]Ex. 20:8 [b]Ex. 31:17; Ezek. 20:12,

[a]Everyone who profanes it shall surely be put to death; for whoever
does any work on it, that person shall be cut off from among his
people.
15 '[a]For six days work may be done, but on the seventh day there is
a [b]sabbath of complete rest, holy to the LORD; [c]whoever does any
work on the sabbath day shall surely be put to death.
16 'So the sons of Israel shall observe the sabbath, to [1]celebrate the
sabbath throughout their generations as a perpetual covenant.'
17 "[a]It is a sign between Me and the sons of Israel forever; [b]for in six
days the LORD made heaven and earth, but on the seventh day He
ceased *from labor*, and was refreshed."
18 And when He had finished speaking with him upon Mount
Sinai, He gave Moses [a]the two tablets of the testimony, tablets of
stone, [b]written by the finger of God.

Chapter 32

32 Now when the people saw that Moses [a]delayed to come
down from the mountain, the people assembled about Aaron,
and said to him, "Come, [b]make us [1]a god who will go before us; as
for [c]this Moses, the man who brought us up from the land of Egypt,
we do not know what has become of him."
2 And Aaron said to them, "[a]Tear off the gold rings which are in
the ears of your wives, your sons, and your daughters, and bring
them to me."
3 Then all the people tore off the gold rings which were in their
ears, and brought *them* to Aaron.
4 And he took *this* from their hand, and fashioned it with a grav-
ing tool, and made it into a [a]molten calf; and they said, "[1]This is your
god, O Israel, who brought you up from the land of Egypt."
5 Now when Aaron saw *this*, he built an altar before it; and Aaron
made a proclamation and said, "Tomorrow *shall be* a feast to the
LORD."
6 So the next day they rose early and [a]offered burnt offerings, and
brought peace offerings; and [b]the people sat down to eat and to
drink, and rose up [c]to play.
7 Then the LORD spoke to Moses, "Go [1]down at once, for your
people, whom [a]you brought up from the land of Egypt, have [b]cor-
rupted *themselves*.
8 "They have quickly turned aside from the way which I com-
manded them. [a]They have made for themselves a molten calf, and
have worshiped it, and [b]have sacrificed to it, and said, '[1c]This is your
god, O Israel, who brought you up from the land of Egypt!' "
9 [a]And the LORD said to Moses, "I have seen this people, and be-
hold, they are [1b]an obstinate people.
10 "Now then [a]let Me alone, that My anger may burn against them,
and that I may destroy them; and [b]I will make of you a great nation."
11 Then [a]Moses entreated the LORD his God, and said, "O LORD,
why doth Thine anger burn against Thy people whom Thou hast
brought out from the land of Egypt with great power and with a
mighty hand?
12 "Why should [a]the Egyptians speak, saying, 'With evil *intent* He
brought them out to kill them in the mountains and to destroy them
from the face of the earth'? Turn from Thy burning anger and change
Thy mind about *doing* harm to Thy people.

31:15; 35:2; 32, 35; John 7:23
9-11; 23:12; 2; Lev. 23:3; 12-14 [b]Gen. 16:23; 20:8; 3 [c]Ex. 31:14
16 [1]Lit., *do*
31:13; Ezek. en. 1:31; 2:2, 3; Ex. 20:11
24:12; 34:29; 3; 5:22; 9:10f. 16; 34:1, 28; Deut. 9:10
Or, *gods* [a]Ex. Deut. 9:11, 12 40 [c]Ex. 14:11
2 [a]Ex. 35:22
These are your eut. 9:16; Neh. s. 106:19; Acts 7:41
ts 7:41 [b]1 Cor. [c]Ex. 32:17-19; Num. 25:2
., *go down* [a]Ex. , 11; Deut. 9:12 [b]Gen. 6:11f.
These are your [a]Ex. 20:3, 4, 23 20; 34:15; Deut. 17 [c]1 Kin. 12:28
Or, *a stiff-necked* n. 14:11-20 [b]Ex. 5; 34:9; Is. 48:4; Acts 7:51
Deut. 9:14 [b]Num. 14:12
1 [a]Deut. 9:18, 26
[a]Num. 14:13-19; ut. 9:28; Josh. 7:9

13 "Remember Abraham, Isaac, and Israel, Thy servants to whom
Thou didst [a]swear by Thyself, and didst say to them, 'I will [b]multiply
your [1]descendants as the stars of the heavens, and [c]all this land of
which I have spoken I will give to your [1]descendants, and they shall
inherit *it* forever.' "
14 [a]So the LORD changed His mind about the harm which He said
He would do to His people.
15 [a]Then Moses turned and went down from the mountain with the
two tablets of the testimony in his hand, [b]tablets which were written
on both [1]sides; they were written on one *side* and the other.
16 And the tablets were God's work, and the writing was God's
writing engraved on the tablets.
17 Now when Joshua heard the sound of the people [1]as they
shouted, he said to Moses, "There is a sound of war in the camp."
18 But he said,

"It is not the sound of the cry of triumph,
Nor is it the sound of the cry of defeat;
But the sound of singing I hear."

19 And it came about, as soon as [1]Moses came near the camp, that
[a]he saw the calf and *the* dancing; and Moses' anger burned, and [b]he
threw the tablets from his hands and shattered them [2]at the foot of
the mountain.
20 [a]And he took the calf which they had made and burned *it* with
fire, and ground it to powder, and scattered it over the surface of the
water, and made the sons of Israel drink *it*.
21 Then Moses said to Aaron, "What did this people do to you, that
you have brought *such* great sin upon them?"
22 And Aaron said, "Do not let the anger of my lord burn; you
know the people yourself, [a]that they are [1]prone to evil.
23 "For [a]they said to me, 'Make [1]a god for us who will go before us;
for this Moses, the man who brought us up from the land of Egypt,
we do not know what has become of him.'
24 "And I said to them, 'Whoever has any gold, let them tear it off.'
So they gave *it* to me, and [a]I threw it into the fire, and out came this
calf."
25 Now when Moses saw that the people were [1]out of control—for
Aaron had [a]let them [2]get out of control to be a derision among [3]their
enemies—
26 then Moses stood in the gate of the camp, and said, "Whoever is
for the LORD, *come* to me!" And all the sons of Levi gathered together
to him.
27 And he said to them, "Thus says the LORD, the God of Israel,
'Every man *of you* put his sword upon his thigh, and go back and
forth from gate to gate in the camp, and kill every man his brother,
and every man his friend, and every man his [1]neighbor.' "
28 So [a]the sons of Levi did [1]as Moses instructed, and about three
thousand men of the people fell that day.
29 Then Moses said, "[1]Dedicate yourselves today to the LORD—for
every man has been against his son and against his brother—in
order that He may bestow a blessing upon you today."
30 And it came about on the next day that Moses said to the people,
"[a]You yourselves have [1]committed a great sin; and now I am going
up to the LORD, perhaps I can [b]make atonement for your sin."
31 Then Moses returned to the LORD, and said, "Alas, this people

13 [1]Lit., *se* 22:16-18; H [b]Gen. 15:5; 12:7; 13:15 35:12; Ex.

14 [a]Ps. 106

15 [1]Lit., *the* [a]Deut. 9:15

17 [1]Lit., *in its*

19 [1]Lit., *he* [2] *beneath* [a]Ex. Deut. 9:16 [b]D

20 [a]Deut. 9:2

22 [1]Lit., *in evi* 9:24

23 [1]Or, *gods* 32:1-4

24 [a]Ex. 32:4

25 [1]Lit., *let loos* *go loose* [3]Lit., *th* *who rise agains* [a]1 Kin. 12:28-30

27 [1]Or, *kin*

28 [1]Lit., *accordir* *Moses' word* [a]Nu 25:7-13; Deut. 33

29 [1]Lit., *Fill your*

30 [1]Lit., *sinned* [a]1 Sam. 12:20, 23 [b]Num. 25:13

has [1]committed a great sin, and they have made [2]a [a]god of gold for
themselves.
32 "But now, if Thou wilt, forgive their sin—and if not, please blot
me out from Thy [a]book which Thou hast written!"
33 And the LORD said to Moses, "Whoever has sinned against Me, [a]I
will blot him out of My book.
34 "But go now, lead the people [a]where I told you. Behold, [b]My angel
shall go before you; nevertheless [c]in the day when I [1]punish, [d]I will
[2]punish them for their sin."
35 [a]Then the LORD smote the people, because of [b]what they did with
the calf which Aaron had made.

Chapter 33

33 Then the LORD spoke to Moses, "Depart, go up from here, you
and the people whom you have brought up from the land of
Egypt, to the land of which [a]I swore to Abraham, [b]Isaac, and [c]Jacob,
saying, '[d]To your [1]descendants I will give it.'
2 "And I will send [a]an angel before you and [b]I will drive out the
Canaanite, the Amorite, the Hittite, the Perizzite, the Hivite and the
Jebusite.
3 "*Go up* to a land [a]flowing with milk and honey; for I will not go
up in your midst, because you are [1b]an obstinate people, lest [c]I
destroy you on the way."
4 When the people heard this [1]sad word, [a]they went into mourn-
ing, and none of them put on his ornaments.
5 For the LORD had said to Moses, "Say to the sons of Israel, 'You
are [1a]an obstinate people; should I go up in your midst for one mo-
ment, I would destroy you. Now therefore, put off your ornaments
from you, that I may know what I will do with you.' "
6 So the sons of Israel stripped themselves of their ornaments from
Mount Horeb *onward*.
7 Now Moses used to take [a]the tent and pitch it outside the camp,
a good distance from the camp, and he called it the tent of meeting.
And it came about, that [b]everyone who sought the LORD would go
out to the tent of meeting which was outside the camp.
8 And it came about, whenever Moses went out to the tent, that all
the people would arise and stand, each at the entrance of his tent,
and gaze after Moses until he entered the tent.
9 And it came about, whenever Moses entered the tent, [a]the pillar
of cloud would descend and stand at the entrance of the tent; [b]and
[1]the LORD would speak with Moses.
10 When all the people saw the pillar of cloud standing at the
entrance of the tent, all the people would arise and worship, each at
the entrance of his tent.
11 Thus [a]the LORD used to speak to Moses face to face, just as a man
speaks to his friend. When [1]Moses returned to the camp, [b]his servant
Joshua, the son of Nun, a young man, would not depart from the
tent.
12 Then Moses said to the LORD, "See, Thou dost say to me, '[a]Bring
up this people!' But Thou Thyself hast not let me know [b]whom Thou
wilt send with me. [c]Moreover, Thou hast said, 'I have known you by
name, and you have also found favor in My sight.'
13 "Now therefore, I pray Thee, if I have found favor in Thy sight,

sinned [2]Or, [a]Ex. 20:23
:28; Is. 4:3; ; Mal. 3:16, 3; Rev. 3:5; 21:27
17:14; Deut. 9:5; Rev. 3:5
sit [1]Lit., visit n upon them 7 [b]Ex. 23:20 35; Rom. 2:5, 6 [d]Ps. 99:8
x. 32:28 [b]Ex. 32:4, 24
.it., seed [a]Ex. [b]Gen. 26:1-3 0 [d]Gen. 12:7
Ex. 32:34 [b]Ex. 31; Josh. 24:11
, a stiff-necked , 17 [b]Ex. 32:9; 3:5 [c]Ex. 32:10
Lit., evil [a]Num. 14:1, 39
t., a stiff-necked [a]Ex. 33:3
18:7, 12-16 [b]Ex. 29:42f.
t., He [a]Ex. 13:21 [b]Ps. 99:7
., he [a]Num. 12:8; 34:10 [b]Ex. 24:13
2 [a]Ex. 3:10; 32:34 x. 33:2 [c]Ex. 33:17

[a]let me know Thy ways, that I may know Thee, so that I may find
favor in Thy sight. [b]Consider too, that this nation is Thy people."
14 And He said, "[a]My presence shall go *with you*, and [b]I will give
you rest."
15 Then he said to Him, "[a]If Thy presence does not go *with us*, do
not lead us up from here.
16 "For how then can it be known that I have found favor in Thy
sight, I and Thy people? Is it not by Thy going with us, so that [a]we, I
and Thy people, may be distinguished from all the *other* people who
are upon the face of the [1]earth?"
17 And the LORD said to Moses, "I will also do this thing of which
you have spoken; [a]for you have found favor in My sight, and I have
known you by name."
18 [a]Then [1]Moses said, "I pray Thee, show me Thy glory!"
19 And He said, "[a]I Myself will make all My goodness pass before
you, and will proclaim the name of the LORD before you; and [b]I will
be gracious to whom I will be gracious, and will show compassion
on whom I will show compassion."
20 But He said, "You cannot see My face, [a]for no man can see Me
and live!"
21 Then the LORD said, "Behold, there is a place [1]by Me, and [a]you
shall stand *there* on the rock;
22 and it will come about, while My glory is passing by, that I will
put you in the cleft of the rock and [a]cover you with My hand until I
have passed by.
23 "Then I will take My hand away and you shall see My back, but
[a]My face shall not be seen."

Chapter 34

34 Now the LORD said to Moses, "Cut out for yourself [a]two stone
tablets like the former ones, and [b]I will write on the tablets the
words that were on the former tablets which you shattered.
2 "So be ready by morning, and come up in the morning to [a]Mount
Sinai, and [1]present yourself there to Me on the top of the mountain.
3 "And [a]no man is to come up with you, nor let any man be seen
[1]anywhere on the mountain; even the flocks and the herds may not
graze in front of that mountain."
4 So he cut out [a]two stone tablets like the former ones, and Moses
rose up early in the morning and went up to Mount Sinai, as the
LORD had commanded him, and he took two stone tablets in his
hand.
5 And [a]the LORD descended in the cloud and stood there with him
as [1]he called upon the name of the LORD.
6 Then the LORD passed by in front of him and proclaimed, "The
LORD, the LORD God, [a]compassionate and gracious, slow to anger,
and abounding in lovingkindness and [1]truth;
7 who [a]keeps lovingkindness for thousands, who forgives iniquity,
transgression and sin; yet He [b]will by no means leave *the guilty* un-
punished, [c]visiting the iniquity of fathers on the children and on the
grandchildren to the third and fourth generations."
8 And Moses made haste [1a]to bow low toward the earth and wor-
ship.
9 And he said, "[a]If now I have found favor in Thy sight, O Lord, I
pray, let the Lord go along in our midst, even though [1b]the people are

13 [a]Ps. 25 51:13; 86: [b]Ex. 3:7, 1 14; Deut. 9

14 [a]Deut. [b]Deut. 12: Josh. 21:44

15 [a]Ps. 80

16 [1]Lit., *gr* 20:24, 26

17 [a]Ex. 33:

18 [1]Lit., *he* 33:20-23

19 [a]Ex. 34:6 9:15

20 [a]Is. 6:5;

21 [1]Lit., *with* 46; 27:5; 61:

22 [a]Ps. 91:1, 49:2; 51:16

23 [a]Ex. 33:20 1:18

34:1 [a]Ex. 24: 32:16, 19 [b]De

2 [1]Or, *place y before* [a]Ex. 19 18, 20

3 [1]Lit., *on all* 19:12, 13

4 [a]Ex. 34:1

5 [1]Or, *he calle the name of the* [a]Ex. 19:9; 33:9

6 [1]Or, *faithfulne* [a]Num. 14:18; D 4:31; Neh. 9:17 86:15; 103:8; 10 145:8; Joel 2:13 2:4

7 [a]Ex. 20:5, 6; D 5:10; 7:9; Ps. 10 130:3, 4; 1 John [b]Ex. 23:7; Deut. Job 10:14; Nah. [c]Deut. 5:9

8 [1]Lit., *and bowe worshiped* [a]Ex. 4

9 [1]Lit., *it is a peo stiff-necked* [a]Ex. [b]Ex. 32:9

so obstinate; and do Thou [c]pardon our iniquity and our sin, and
[d]take us as Thine own [2]possession."
10 Then [1]God said, "Behold, [a]I am going to make a covenant. Before
all your people [b]I will perform miracles which have not been
[2]produced in all the earth, nor among any of the nations; and all the
people [3]among whom you live will see the working of the LORD, for
it is a fearful thing that I am going to perform with you.
11 "[1]Be sure to observe what I am commanding you this day: behold,
[a]I am going to drive out the Amorite before you, and the Canaanite,
the Hittite, the Perizzite, the Hivite and the Jebusite.
12 "[a]Watch yourself that you make no covenant with the inhabitants
of the land into which you are going, lest it become a snare in your
midst.
13 "[a]But *rather,* you are to tear down their altars and smash their
sacred pillars and cut down their [1b]Asherim
14 —for [a]you shall not worship any other god, for the LORD, whose
name is Jealous, is a jealous God—
15 lest you make a covenant with the inhabitants of the land and
they play the harlot with their gods, and [a]sacrifice to their gods, and
someone [b]invite you [1]to eat of his sacrifice;
16 and [a]you take some of his daughters for your sons, and his
daughters play the harlot with their gods, and cause your sons *also*
to play the harlot with their gods.
17 "[a]You shall make for yourself no molten gods.
18 "You shall observe [a]the Feast of Unleavened Bread. For [b]seven
days you are to eat unleavened bread, [1]as I commanded you, at the
appointed time in the [c]month of Abib, for in the month of Abib you
came out of Egypt.
19 "[a]The first offspring from every womb belongs to Me, and all
your male livestock, the first offspring from [1]cattle and sheep.
20 "[a]And you shall redeem with a lamb the [1]first offspring from a
donkey; and if you do not redeem *it,* then you shall break its neck.
You shall redeem [b]all the first-born of your sons. And [2c]none shall
appear before Me empty-handed.
21 "You shall work [a]six days, but on the seventh day you shall rest;
even during plowing time and harvest you shall rest.
22 "And you shall celebrate [a]the Feast of Weeks, *that is,* the first fruits
of the wheat harvest, and the Feast of Ingathering at the turn of the
year.
23 "[a]Three times a year all your males are to appear before the Lord
[1]GOD, the God of Israel.
24 "For I will [1a]drive out nations before you and enlarge your bor-
ders, and no man shall covet your land when you go up three times
a year to appear before the LORD your God.
25 "[a]You shall not [1]offer the blood of My sacrifice with leavened
bread, [b]nor is the sacrifice of the Feast of the Passover to [2]be left over
until morning.
26 "You shall bring [a]the very first of the first fruits of your soil into
the house of the LORD your God. You shall not boil a kid in its
mother's milk."
27 Then the LORD said to Moses, "[a]Write [1]down these words, for in
accordance with these words I have made [b]a covenant with you and
with Israel."
28 So he was there with the LORD [a]forty days and forty nights; he

eritance [c]Ex. ...ut. 4:20; 9:26, ...2:9; Ps. 33:12

[1]Lit., *He* [2]Lit., ... [3]Lit., *in whose ... you are* [a]Ex. ...28; Deut. 5:2 ...32; Ps. 72:18; 136:4

..., *Observe for ...self* [a]Ex. 33:2

[a]Ex. 23:32, 33

[1]I.e., wooden ...ols of a female ...x. 23:24; Deut. ... [b]Deut. 16:21; ...6:25, 26; 2 Kin. ...4; 2 Chr. 34:3f.

... 20:3, 5; Deut. 4:24

...it., *and you eat* ...20; 32:8 [b]Num. ...Deut. 32:37, 38

...Deut. 7:3; Josh. ...3; 1 Kin. 11:1-4

...x. 20:4, 23; Lev. 19:4; Deut. 5:8

[1]Or, *which* [a]Ex. ...Lev. 23:6; Num. ... [b]Ex. 12:15, 16 [c]Ex. 12:2; 13:4

...*oxen* [a]Ex. 13:2; 22:29f.

..., *first opening of* ...*ey shall not* [a]Ex. ... [b]Ex. 13:15; Num. ...Ex. 22:29; 23:15; Deut. 16:16

...Ex. 20:9f.; 23:12; ...5; 35:2; Lev. 23:3; Deut. 5:13f.

[a]Ex. 23:16; Num. 28:26

23 [1]Heb., *YHWH,* ...lly rendered *LORD* [a]Ex. 23:14-17

...4 [1]Or, *dispossess* ...Ex. 33:2; Ps. 78:55

...it., *slaughter* [2]Lit., ...*main overnight* [a]Ex. 23:18 [b]Ex. 12:10

...6 [a]Ex. 23:19; Deut. 26:2

27 [1]Lit., *for yourself* ...x. 17:14; 24:4 [b]Ex. 34:10

28 [a]Ex. 24:18

did not eat bread or drink water. And [b]he wrote on the tablets the
words of the covenant, [c]the Ten [1]Commandments.
29 And it came about when Moses was coming down from Mount
Sinai (and the [a]two tablets of the testimony *were* in Moses' hand as
he was coming down from the mountain), that Moses did not know
that [b]the skin of his face shone because of his speaking with Him.
30 So when Aaron and all the sons of Israel saw Moses, behold, the
skin of his face shone, and [a]they were afraid to come near him.
31 Then Moses called to them, and Aaron and all the rulers in the
congregation returned to him; and Moses spoke to them.
32 And afterward all the sons of Israel came near, and he com-
manded them *to do* everything that the LORD had spoken [1]to him on
Mount Sinai.
33 When Moses had finished speaking with them, [a]he put a veil
over his face.
34 But whenever Moses went in before the LORD to speak with Him,
[a]he would take off the veil until he came out; and whenever he came
out and spoke to the sons of Israel what he had been commanded,
35 [a]the sons of Israel would see the face of Moses, that the skin of
Moses' face shone. So Moses would replace the veil over his face
until he went in to speak with Him.

Chapter 35

35 Then Moses assembled all the congregation of the sons of
Israel, and said to them, "[a]These are the things that the LORD
has commanded *you* to [1]do.
2 "[a]For six days work may be done, but on the seventh day you
shall have a holy *day,* [b]a sabbath of complete rest to the LORD;
[c]whoever does any work on it shall be put to death.
3 "[a]You shall not kindle a fire in any of your dwellings on the sab-
bath day."
4 And Moses spoke to all the congregation of the sons of Israel,
saying, "This is the thing which the LORD has commanded, saying,
5 '[a]Take from among you a [1]contribution to the LORD; whoever is of
a willing heart, let him bring it as the LORD's [1]contribution: gold,
silver, and [2]bronze,
6 and [1]blue, purple and scarlet *material,* fine linen, goats' *hair,*
7 and rams' skins [1]dyed red, and porpoise skins, and acacia wood,
8 and oil for lighting, and spices for the anointing oil, and for the
fragrant incense,
9 and onyx stones and setting stones, for the ephod and for the
[1]breastpiece.
10 'And [a]let every skillful man among you come, and make all that
the LORD has commanded:
11 the [1a]tabernacle, its tent and its covering, its hooks and its
boards, its bars, its pillars, and its [2]sockets;
12 the [a]ark and its poles, the [1]mercy seat, and the curtain of the
screen;
13 the [a]table and its poles, and all its [1]utensils, and the bread of the
[2]Presence;
14 the [a]lampstand also for the light and its utensils and its lamps
and the oil for the light;
15 and the [a]altar of incense and its poles, and the [b]anointing oil and

28 [1]Lit., *Wor*
31:18; 34:1
10:4
29 [a]Ex. 32:1
17:2; 2 Cor. 3
30 [a]2 Cor. 3:7
32 [1]Lit., *with*
33 [a]2 Cor. 3:1
34 [a]2 Cor. 3:1
35 [a]2 Cor. 3:13
35:1 [1]Lit., *do th*
[a]Ex. 34:32
2 [a]Ex. 20:9, 10;
31:15; 34:21; Le
Deut. 5:13f. [b]Ex
[c]Num. 15:32-36
3 [a]Ex. 12:16; 16
5 [1]Or, *heave off*
[2]Or, *copper* [a]Ex.
6 [1]Or, *violet*
7 [1]Or, *tanned*
9 [1]Or, *pouch*
10 [a]Ex. 31:6
11 [1]Lit., *dwelling p*
[2]Or, *bases* [a]Ex. 26
12 [1]Lit., *propitiator*
[a]Ex. 25:10-22
13 [1]Or, *vessels* [2]L
Face [a]Ex. 25:23-30
14 [a]Ex. 25:31ff.
15 [a]Ex. 30:1-6 [b]Ex.
30:25

the [c]fragrant incense, and the screen for the doorway at the [1]entrance
of the tabernacle;
16 [a]the altar of burnt offering with its [1]bronze grating, its poles, and
all its [2]utensils, the [3]basin and its stand;
17 [a]the hangings of the court, its pillars and its [1]sockets, and the
screen for the gate of the court;
18 the pegs of the tabernacle and the pegs of the court and their
cords;
19 the [1a]woven garments, for ministering in the holy place, the holy
garments for Aaron the priest, and the garments of his sons, to
minister as priests.' "
20 Then all the congregation of the sons of Israel departed from
Moses' presence.
21 And [a]everyone whose heart [1]stirred him and everyone whose
spirit [2]moved him came *and* brought the LORD's [3]contribution for the
work of the tent of meeting and for all its service and for the holy
garments.
22 Then all [1]whose hearts moved them, both men and women,
came *and* brought brooches and [2]earrings and signet rings and
bracelets, all articles of gold; so *did* every man who [3]presented an
offering of gold to the LORD.
23 And every man, [1]who had in his possession [2]blue and purple
and scarlet *material* and fine linen and goats' *hair* and rams' skins
[3]dyed red and porpoise skins, brought them.
24 Everyone who could make a [1]contribution of silver and [2]bronze
brought the LORD's [1]contribution; and every man, [3]who had in his
possession acacia wood for any work of the service, brought it.
25 And all the [1]skilled women spun with their hands, and brought
what they had spun, *in* [2]blue and purple *and* scarlet *material* and *in*
fine linen.
26 And all the women whose heart [1]stirred with a skill spun the
goats' *hair*.
27 And the rulers brought the onyx stones and the stones for setting
for the ephod and for the [1]breastpiece;
28 and [a]the spice and the oil for the light and for the anointing oil
and for the fragrant incense.
29 The [1]Israelites, all the men and women, whose heart [2]moved
them to bring *material* for all the work, which the LORD had com-
manded through Moses to be done, brought a [a]freewill offering to
the LORD.
30 [a]Then Moses said to the sons of Israel, "See, the LORD has called
by name Bezalel the son of Uri, the son of Hur, of the tribe of Judah.
31 "And He has filled him with the Spirit of God, in wisdom, in
understanding and in knowledge and in all [1]craftsmanship;
32 [1]to make designs for working in gold and in silver and in
[2]bronze,
33 and in the cutting of stones for settings, and in the carving of
wood, so as to perform in every inventive work.
34 "He also has put in his heart to teach, both he and [a]Oholiab, the
son of Ahisamach, of the tribe of Dan.
35 "[a]He has filled them with [1]skill to perform every work of an en-
graver and of a designer and of an embroiderer, in [2]blue and in
purple *and* in scarlet *material,* and in fine linen, and of a weaver, as
performers of every work and makers of designs.

doorway [c]Ex. 30:34-38
, copper [2]Or, Or, laver [a]Ex. 27:1-8
r, bases [a]Ex. 27:9-18
[1]Or, service ts [a]Ex. 31:10; 39:1
, lifted up [2]Or, m willing [3]Or, offering [a]Ex. :5, 22, 26, 29; 36:2
[1]Or, who were -hearted [2]Or, s [3]Lit., waved wave offering
with whom was [2]Or, violet [3]Or, tanned
heave offering pper [3]Lit., with hom was found
women wise of eart [2]Or, violet
., lifted them up in wisdom
27 [1]Or, pouch
28 [a]Ex. 30:23ff.
., sons of Israel ade them willing 5:21; 1 Chr. 29:9
30 [a]Ex. 31:1-6
31 [1]Or, work
., devise devices [2]Or, copper
34 [a]Ex. 31:6
[1]Lit., wisdom of [2]Or, violet [a]Ex. 3, 6; 35:31; 1 Kin. 7:14

Chapter 36

36 "Now Bezalel and Oholiab, and every [1]skillful person in whom the LORD has put [2]skill and understanding to know how to perform all the work [3]in the construction of the sanctuary, shall perform in accordance with all that the LORD has commanded."

2 Then Moses called Bezalel and Oholiab and every [1]skillful person in [2]whom the LORD had put [3]skill, [a]everyone whose heart stirred him, to come to the work to perform it.

3 And they received from Moses all the [1]contributions which the sons of Israel had brought [2]to perform the work [3]in the construction of the sanctuary. And they still *continued* bringing to him freewill offerings every morning.

4 And all the [1]skillful men who were performing all the work of the sanctuary came, each from [2]the work which [3]he was performing,

5 and they said to [1]Moses, "[a]The people are bringing much more than enough for the [2]construction work which the LORD commanded *us* to [3]perform."

6 So Moses issued a command, and a [1]proclamation was circulated throughout the camp, saying, "Let neither man nor woman any longer perform work for the [2]contributions of the sanctuary." Thus the people were restrained from bringing *any more.*

7 [a]For the [1]material they had was sufficient and more than enough for all the work, to perform it.

8 [a]And all the [1]skillful men among those who were performing the work made the [2]tabernacle with ten curtains; of fine twisted linen and [3]blue and purple and scarlet *material,* with cherubim, the work of a skillful workman, [4]Bezalel made them.

9 The length of each curtain was twenty-eight [1]cubits, and the width of each curtain four [1]cubits; all the curtains had [2]the same measurements.

10 And he [1]joined five curtains to one another, and *the other* five curtains he [1]joined to one another.

11 And he made loops of [1]blue on the edge of the [2]outermost curtain in the first [3]set; he did likewise on the edge of the curtain that was [2]outermost in the second [3]set.

12 He made [a]fifty loops in the one curtain and he made fifty loops on the [1]edge of the curtain that was in the second [2]set; the loops were opposite each other.

13 And he made [a]fifty clasps of gold, and [1]joined the curtains to one another with the clasps, so the tabernacle was [2]a unit.

14 Then [a]he made curtains of goats' *hair* for a tent over the tabernacle; he made eleven curtains [1]in all.

15 The length of each curtain was thirty cubits, and four cubits the width of each curtain; the eleven curtains had [1]the same measurements.

16 And he [1]joined five curtains by themselves, and *the other* six curtains by themselves.

17 Moreover, he made fifty loops on the edge of the curtain that was outermost in the *first* [1]set, and he made fifty loops on the edge of the curtain *that was outermost in* the second [1]set.

18 And he made fifty clasps of [1]bronze to [2]join the tent together, that it might be [3]a unit.

19 And he made a covering for the tent of rams' skins [1]dyed red, and a covering of porpoise skins above.

36:1 [1]Lit., *m* *heart* [2]Lit., *w* *connected w* *service of;* lit *service of*

2 [1]Lit., *man* *heart* [2]Lit., *w* [3]Lit., *wisdom* 35:21, 26

3 [1]Lit., *lifted* [2]Lit., *to perfor* *work* [3]Lit., *of* *service of*

4 [1]Lit., *wise* [3]Lit., *they wer*

5 [1]Lit., *Moses* [2]Lit., *service f* *work* [3]Lit., *pe* [a]2 Chr. 24:14;

6 [1]Lit., *voice* *heave offering*

7 [1]Lit., *work* 8:64

8 [1]Lit., *wise of* [2]Lit., *dwelling p* *violet* [4]Lit., *he* 26:1-14

9 [1]I.e., One cu equals approx. [2]Lit., *one meas*

10 [1]Or, *couple*

11 [1]Or, *violet* *curtain from the* *the coupling* [3]L *coupling*

12 [1]Lit., *end* [2]L *coupling* [a]Ex. 2

13 [1]Or, *coupled* *one* [a]Ex. 26:6

14 [1]Lit., *in numb* 26:7-14

15 [1]Lit., *one me*

16 [1]Or, *coupled*

17 [1]Lit., *coupling*

18 [1]Or, *copper* *couple* [3]Lit., *one*

19 [1]Or, *tanned*

20 [a]Then he made the boards for the tabernacle of acacia wood,
standing upright.
21 Ten cubits was the length of [1]each board, and one and a half
cubits the width of each board.
22 There were two tenons for each board, [1]fitted to one another;
thus he did for all the boards of the tabernacle.
23 And he made the boards for the tabernacle: twenty boards [1]for
the south side;
24 and he made forty [1]sockets of silver under the twenty boards;
two [1]sockets under one board for its two tenons and two [1]sockets
under another board for its two tenons.
25 Then for the second side of the tabernacle, on the north side, he
made twenty boards,
26 and their forty [1]sockets of silver; two [1]sockets under one board
and two [1]sockets under another board.
27 And for the [1]rear of the tabernacle, to the west, he made six
boards.
28 And he made two boards for the corners of the [1]tabernacle at the
[2]rear.
29 And they were double beneath, and together they were complete
to its [1]top [2]to the first ring; thus he did with both of them for the two
corners.
30 And there were eight boards with their [1]sockets of silver, sixteen
[1]sockets, [2]two under every board.
31 Then he made [a]bars of acacia wood, five for the boards of one
side of the tabernacle,
32 and five bars for the boards of the [1]other side of the tabernacle,
and five bars for the boards of the tabernacle for the [2]rear *side* to the
west.
33 And he made the middle bar to pass through in the [1]center of the
boards from end to end.
34 And he overlaid the boards with gold and made their rings of
gold *as* holders for the bars, and overlaid the bars with gold.
35 [a]Moreover, he made the veil of [1]blue and purple and scarlet *mate-*
rial, and fine twisted linen; he made it with cherubim, the work of a
skillful workman.
36 And he made four pillars of acacia for it, and overlaid them with
gold, with their hooks of gold; and he cast four [1]sockets of silver for
them.
37 And he made a [a]screen for the doorway of the tent, of [1]blue and
purple and scarlet *material,* and fine twisted linen, the work of a
[2]weaver;
38 and *he made* its [a]five pillars with their hooks, and he overlaid
their tops and their [1]bands with gold; but their five [2]sockets were of
[3]bronze.

Chapter 37

37 [a]Now Bezalel made the ark of acacia wood; its length was two
and a half [1]cubits, and its width one and a half cubits, and its
height one and a half cubits;
2 and he overlaid it with pure gold inside and out, and made a
gold molding for it all around.
3 And he cast four rings of gold for it on its four feet; even two
rings on one side of it, and two rings on the [1]other side of it.

[a]Ex. 26:15-29
21 [1]Lit., *the*
2 [1]Lit., *bound*
to the side of
v, to the south
24 [1]Or, *bases*
26 [1]Or, *bases*
extreme parts
dwelling place
extreme parts
head [2]Or, *with reference to*
bases [2]Lit., *two sockets*
[a]Ex. 26:26-29
Or, *second* [2]Lit., *extreme parts*
33 [1]Lit., *midst*
[1]Or, *violet* [a]Ex. 26:31-37
36 [1]Or, *bases*
[1]Or, *violet* [2]Lit., *variegator;* i.e., a
er in colors [a]Ex. 26:36
[1]Or, *fillets, rings*
ases [3]Or, *copper*
[a]Ex. 26:37
1 [1]I.e., One cubit
als approx. 18 in.
[a]Ex. 25:10-20
3 [1]Lit., *second*

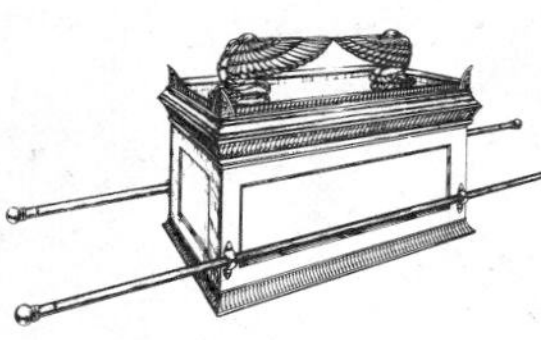

4 And he made poles of acacia wood and overlaid them with gold.
5 And he put the poles into the rings on the sides of the ark, to
carry [1]it.
6 And he made a [1]mercy seat of pure gold, two and a half cubits
[2]long, and one and a half cubits [3]wide.
7 And he made two cherubim of gold; he made them of ham-
mered work, [1]at the two ends of the mercy seat;
8 one cherub [1]at the one end, and one cherub [1]at the other end; he
made the cherubim *of one piece* with the mercy seat [1]at the two ends.
9 And the cherubim had *their* wings spread upward, covering the
[1]mercy seat with their wings, with their faces toward each other; the
faces of the cherubim were toward the mercy seat.
10 [a]Then he made the table of acacia wood, two [1]cubits [2]long and a
cubit [3]wide and one and a half cubits [4]high.

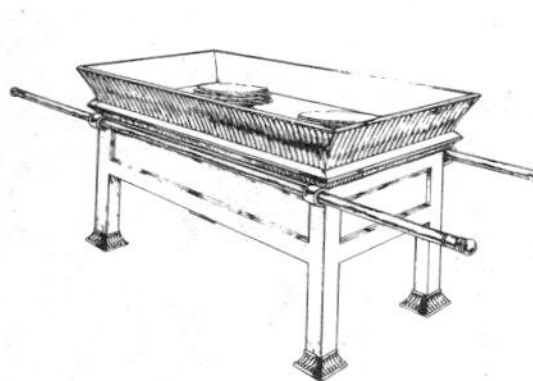

11 And he overlaid it with pure gold, and made a gold molding for
it all around.
12 And he made a rim for it of a handbreadth all around, and made
a gold molding for its rim all around.
13 And he cast four gold rings for it and put the rings on the four
corners that were on its four feet.
14 Close by the rim were the rings, the holders for the poles to carry
the table.
15 And he made the poles of acacia wood and overlaid them with
gold, to carry the table.
16 And he made the utensils which were on the table, its [1]dishes
and its pans and its [2]bowls and its jars, with which to pour out
libations, of pure gold.
17 [a]Then he made the lampstand of pure gold. He made the lamp-
stand of hammered work, its base and its shaft; its cups, its [1]bulbs
and its flowers were *of one piece* with it.

18 And there were six branches going out of its sides; three
branches of the lampstand from the one side of it, and three
branches of the lampstand from the [1]other side of it;
19 three cups shaped like almond *blossoms*, a [1]bulb and a flower in
one branch, and three cups shaped like almond *blossoms*, a [1]bulb and
a flower in the other branch—so for the six branches going out of the
lampstand.
20 And in the lampstand *there were* four cups shaped like almond
blossoms, its [1]bulbs and its flowers;
21 and a [1]bulb was under the *first* pair of branches *coming* out of it,
and a [1]bulb under the *second* pair of branches *coming* out of it, and a
[1]bulb under the *third* pair of branches *coming* out of it, for the six
branches coming out of the lampstand.
22 Their [1]bulbs and their branches were *of one piece* with it; the
whole of it *was* a single hammered work of pure gold.
23 And he made its seven lamps with its snuffers and its [1]trays of
pure gold.
24 He made it and all its utensils from a talent of pure gold.

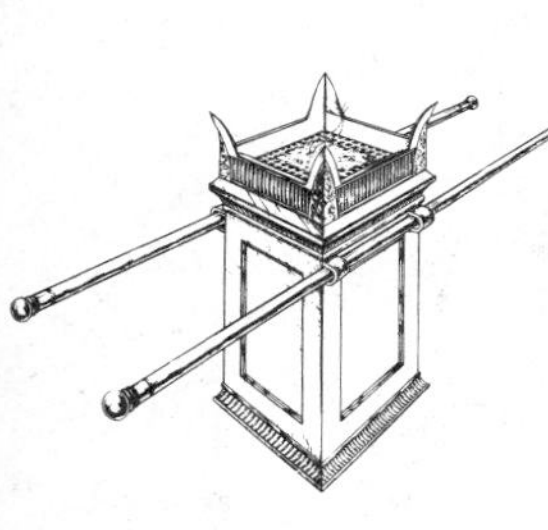

25 [a]Then he made the altar of incense of acacia wood: a cubit [1]long
and a cubit [2]wide, square, and two cubits [3]high; its horns were *of one
piece* with it.
26 And he overlaid it with pure gold, its top and its [1]sides all
around, and its horns; and he made a gold molding for it all around.
27 And he made two golden rings for it under its molding, on its

5 [1]Lit., *the ar*
6 [1]Lit., *propit* *its length* [3]Lit
7 [1]Lit., *from*
8 [1]Lit., *from*
9 [1]Lit., *propitia*
10 [1]I.e., One c equals approx. [2]Lit., *its length* *width* [4]Lit., *its* [a]Ex. 25:23-29
16 [1]Or, *platters* *libation bowls*
17 [1]Or, *calyxes* 25:31-39
18 [1]Lit., *second*
19 [1]Or, *calyx*
20 [1]Or, *calyxes*
21 [1]Or, *calyx*
22 [1]Or, *calyxes*
23 [1]Lit., *snuff dis*
25 [1]Lit., *its length* *its width* [3]Lit., *its* [a]Ex. 30:1-5
26 [1]Lit., *walls*

two sides—on opposite sides—as holders for poles with which to
carry it.
28 And he made the poles of acacia wood and overlaid them with
gold.
29 [a]And he made the holy anointing oil and the pure, fragrant
incense of spices, the work of a perfumer.

Chapter 38

38 [a]Then he made the altar of burnt offering of acacia wood, five
[1]cubits [2]long, and five cubits [3]wide, square, and three cubits
[4]high.
2 And he made its horns on its four corners, its horns [1]being *of one
piece* with it, and he overlaid it with [2]bronze.
3 And he made all the utensils of the altar, the pails and the
shovels and the basins, the flesh hooks and the firepans; he made all
its utensils of bronze.
4 And he made for the altar a grating of bronze network beneath,
under its ledge, reaching halfway up.
5 And he cast four rings on the four ends of the bronze grating *as*
holders for the poles.
6 And he made the poles of acacia wood and overlaid them with
bronze.
7 And he inserted the poles into the rings on the sides of the altar,
with which to carry it. He made it hollow with planks.
8 [a]Moreover, he made the laver of bronze with its base of bronze,
[1]from the mirrors of the serving women who served at the doorway
of the tent of meeting.
9 [a]Then he made the court: [1]for the south side the hangings of the
court were of fine twisted linen, one hundred cubits;
10 their twenty pillars, and their twenty [1]sockets, *made* of bronze;
the hooks of the pillars and their [2]bands *were* of silver.
11 And for the north side *there were* one hundred cubits; their twen-
ty pillars and their twenty [1]sockets *were* of bronze, the hooks of the
pillars and their [2]bands *were* of silver.
12 And for the west side *there were* hangings of fifty cubits *with* their
ten pillars and their ten [1]sockets; the hooks of the pillars and their
[2]bands *were* of silver.
13 And for the [1]east side fifty cubits.
14 The hangings for the *one* [1]side *of the gate were* fifteen cubits, *with*
their three pillars and their three [2]sockets,
15 and so for the [1]other [2]side. [3]On both sides of the gate of the court
were hangings of fifteen cubits, *with* their three pillars and their three
[4]sockets.
16 All the hangings of the court all around *were* of fine twisted
linen.
17 And the [1]sockets for the pillars *were* of [2]bronze, the hooks of the
pillars and their [3]bands, of silver; and the overlaying of their tops, of
silver, and all the pillars of the court were furnished with silver
[3]bands.
18 And the screen of the gate of the court was the work of the
[1]weaver, of [2]blue and purple and scarlet *material*, and fine twisted
linen. And the length was twenty cubits and the [3]height was five
cubits, corresponding to the hangings of the court.
19 And their four pillars and their four [1]sockets *were* of bronze; their

…. 30:23-25, 34, 35
…1 [1]I.e., One cubit …uals approx. 18 in. *its length* [3]Lit., *its* …*dth* [4]Lit., *its height* [a]Ex. 27:1-8
2 [1]Lit., *were* [2]Or, *copper*, and so for *bronze* throughout the ch.
…t., *with* [a]Ex. 30:18
…, *to the side of the …legev, to the south* [a]Ex. 27:9-19
…0 [1]Or, *bases* [2]Or, *fillets, rings*
…1 [1]Or, *bases* [2]Or, *fillets, rings*
…2 [1]Or, *bases* [2]Or, *fillets, rings*
…3 [1]Lit., *east side, eastward*
…Lit., *shoulder* [2]Or, *bases*
[1]Lit., *second* [2]Lit., …*ulder* [3]Lit., *On this …e and on that side* [4]Or, *bases*
…7 [1]Or, *bases* [2]Or, …r [3]Or, *fillets, rings*
…it., *variegator;* i.e., …aver in colors [2]Or, …olet [3]Lit., *height in width*
19 [1]Or, *bases*

hooks *were* of silver, and the overlaying of their tops and their [2]bands
were of silver.
20 And all the pegs of the [1]tabernacle and of the court all around
were of bronze.
21 [1]This is the number of *the things for* the [2]tabernacle, the [2]taber-
nacle of the testimony, as they were [3]numbered according to the
[4]command of Moses, for the service of the Levites, by the hand of
Ithamar, the son of Aaron the priest.
22 Now [a]Bezalel, the son of Uri the son of Hur, of the tribe of Judah,
made all that the LORD had commanded Moses.
23 And with him was [a]Oholiab, the son of Ahisamach, of the tribe
of Dan, an engraver and a skillful workman and a [1]weaver in [2]blue
and in purple and in scarlet *material,* and fine linen.
24 All the gold that was used for the work, in all the work of the
sanctuary, even the gold of the wave offering, was 29 talents and 730
shekels, according to [a]the shekel of the sanctuary.
25 [a]And the silver of those of the congregation who were [1]num-
bered was 100 talents and 1,775 shekels, according to the shekel of
the sanctuary;
26 [a]a beka a head (*that is,* half a shekel according to the shekel of the
sanctuary), for each one who passed over to those who were [1]num-
bered, from twenty years old and upward, for [b]603,550 men.
27 And the hundred talents of silver were for casting the [1]sockets of
the sanctuary and the [1]sockets of the veil; one hundred [1]sockets for
the hundred talents, a talent for a [1]socket.
28 And of the 1,775 *shekels,* he made hooks for the pillars and over-
laid their tops and made [1]bands for them.
29 And the bronze of the wave offering was 70 talents, and 2,400
shekels.
30 And with it he made the [1]sockets to the doorway of the tent of
meeting, and the bronze altar and its bronze grating, and all the
utensils of the altar,
31 and the [1]sockets of the court all around and the [1]sockets of the

19 [2]Or, *fillets, rin*

20 [1]Lit., *dwelling*

21 [1]Lit., *These a appointed things tabernacle* [2]Lit., *dwelling place* [3]L *appointed* [4]Lit., *n*

22 [a]Ex. 31:2

23 [1]Lit., *variegat a weaver in colors violet* [a]Ex. 31:6

24 [a]Ex. 30:13; Le 27:25; Num. 3:47;

25 [1]Lit., *mustere* 30:11-16

26 [1]Lit., *mustere* 30:13, 15 [b]Ex. 12 Num. 1:46; 26:51

27 [1]Or, *bases*

28 [1]Or, *fillets, rin*

30 [1]Or, *bases*

31 [1]Or, *bases*

The Tabernacle

gate of the court, and all the pegs of the [2]tabernacle and all the pegs
of the court all around.

Chapter 39

39 Moreover, from the [1a]blue and purple and scarlet *material,*
they made finely [b]woven garments for ministering in the holy
place, [2]as well as the holy garments which were for Aaron, just as the
LORD had commanded Moses.
2 [a]And he made the ephod of gold, *and* of [1]blue and purple and
scarlet *material,* and fine twisted linen.
3 Then they hammered out gold sheets and cut *them* into threads
[1]to be woven in *with* the [2]blue and the purple and the scarlet *material,*
and the fine linen, the work of a skillful workman.
4 They made attaching shoulder pieces for [1]the ephod; it was at-
tached at its two *upper* ends.
5 And the skillfully woven band which was on it was like its
workmanship, [1]of the same material: of gold *and* of [2]blue and purple
and scarlet *material,* and fine twisted linen, just as the LORD had
commanded Moses.
6 And [a]they made the onyx stones, set in gold filigree *settings;* they
were engraved *like* the engravings of a signet, according to the
names of the sons of Israel.
7 And [a]he placed them on the shoulder pieces of the ephod, *as*
memorial stones for the sons of Israel, just as the LORD had com-
manded Moses.
8 [a]And he made the breastpiece, the work of a skillful workman,
like the workmanship of the ephod: of gold *and* of [1]blue and purple
and scarlet *material* and fine twisted linen.
9 It was square; they made the breastpiece folded double, a span
[1]long and a span [2]wide when folded double.
10 And they [1]mounted four rows of stones on it. The first row *was* a
row of ruby, topaz, and emerald;
11 and the second row, a turquoise, a sapphire and a diamond;
12 and the third row, a jacinth, an agate, and an amethyst;
13 and the fourth row, a beryl, an onyx, and a jasper. They were set
in gold filigree *settings* when they were [1]mounted.
14 And the stones were corresponding to the names of the sons of
Israel; they were twelve, corresponding to their names, *engraved with*
the engravings of a signet, each with its name for the twelve tribes.
15 And they made on the breastpiece chains like cords, of twisted
cordage work in pure gold.
16 And they made two gold filigree *settings* and two gold rings, and
put the two rings on the two ends of the breastpiece.
17 Then they put the two gold cords in the two rings at the ends of
the breastpiece.
18 And they put the *other* two ends of the two cords on the two
filigree *settings,* and put them on the shoulder pieces of the ephod at
the front of it.
19 And they made two gold rings and placed *them* on the two ends
of the breastpiece, on its inner edge which was next to the ephod.
20 Furthermore, they made two gold rings and placed them on the
bottom of the two shoulder pieces of the ephod, on the front of it,
close to the place where it joined, above the woven band of the
ephod.

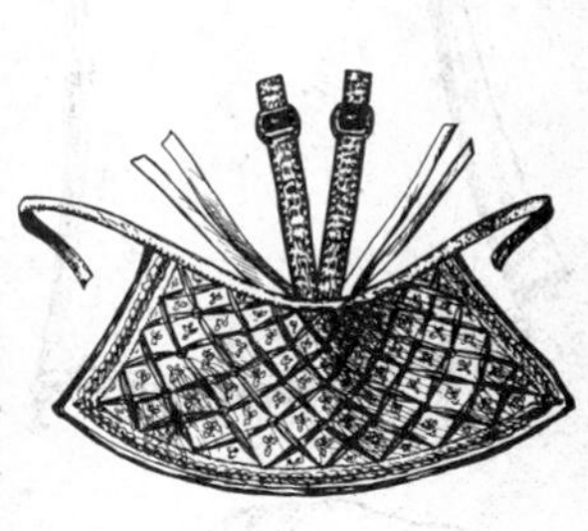

...velling place

..., violet [2]Lit., ...y made [a]Ex. 31:10; 35:19

...r, violet [a]Ex. 28:6-12

... to work [2]Or, violet

4 [1]Lit., *it*

...m it [2]Or, violet

6 [a]Ex. 28:9-11

7 [a]Ex. 28:12

[1]Or, violet [a]Ex. 28:15-28

... its length [2]Lit., its width

10 [1]Lit., *filled*

13 [1]Lit., *filled*

21 And they bound the breastpiece by its rings to the rings of the
ephod with a [1]blue cord, that it might be on the woven band of the
ephod, and that the breastpiece might not come loose from the
ephod, just as the LORD had commanded Moses.
22 [a]Then he made the robe of the ephod of woven work, all of [1]blue;
23 [a]and the opening of the robe was *at the top* in the center, as the
opening of a coat of mail, with a binding all around its opening, that
it might not be torn.
24 And they made pomegranates of [1]blue and purple and scarlet
material and twisted *linen* on the hem of the robe.
25 They also made bells of pure gold, and put the bells between the
pomegranates all around on the hem of the [1]robe,
26 [1]alternating a bell and a pomegranate all around on the hem of
the robe, for the service, just as the LORD had commanded Moses.
27 [a]And they made the tunics of finely woven linen for Aaron and
his sons,
28 and the turban of fine linen, and the decorated [1]caps of fine
linen, and the linen breeches of fine twisted linen,
29 and the sash of fine twisted linen, and [1]blue and purple and
scarlet *material*, the work of the [2]weaver, just as the LORD had com-
manded Moses.
30 [a]And they made the plate of the holy crown of pure gold, and
[1]inscribed it like the engravings of a signet, "Holy to the LORD."
31 And they [1]fastened a [2]blue cord to it, to [1]fasten it on the turban
above, just as the LORD had commanded Moses.
32 Thus all the work of the [1]tabernacle of the tent of meeting was
completed; and the sons of Israel did according to all that the LORD
had commanded Moses; so they did.
33 And they brought the tabernacle to Moses, the tent and all its
[1]furnishings: its clasps, its boards, its bars, and its pillars and its
[2]sockets;
34 and the covering of rams' skins [1]dyed red, and the covering of
porpoise skins, and the screening veil;
35 the ark of the testimony and its poles and the [1]mercy seat;
36 the table, all its utensils, and the bread of the [1]Presence;
37 the pure *gold* lampstand, [1]with its arrangement of lamps and all
its utensils, and the oil for the light;
38 and the gold altar, and the anointing oil and the fragrant incense,
and the veil for the doorway of the tent;
39 the [1]bronze altar and its [1]bronze grating, its poles and all its
utensils, the laver and its stand;
40 the hangings for the court, its pillars and its [1]sockets, and the
screen for the gate of the court, its cords and its pegs and all the
[2]equipment for the service of the tabernacle, for the tent of meeting;
41 the woven garments for ministering in the holy place and the
holy garments for Aaron the priest and the garments of his sons, to
minister as priests.
42 So the sons of Israel did all the work according to all that the
LORD had commanded Moses.
43 And Moses [1]examined all the work and behold, they had done it;
just as the LORD had commanded, this they had done. So Moses
[a]blessed them.

21 [1]Or, *viol*
22 [1]Or, *viol* 28:31, 34
23 [a]Ex. 28:3
24 [1]Or, *viole*
25 [1]Lit., *robe the pomegra*
26 [1]Lit., *a be pomegranate*
27 [a]Ex. 28:39
28 [1]Lit., *head*
29 [1]Or, *violet variegator;* i.e. weaver in colo
30 [1]Lit., *wrote writing* [a]Ex. 28
31 [1]Lit., *put* [2]
32 [1]Lit., *dwelli*
33 [1]Or, *utensil bases*
34 [1]Or, *tanned*
35 [1]Lit., *propiti*
36 [1]Lit., *Face*
37 [1]Lit., *its lamp lamps set in ord*
39 [1]Or, *copper*
40 [1]Or, *bases* [2] *utensils*
43 [1]Lit., *saw* [a]Le 9:22, 23; Num. 6

Inside of the Tabernacle

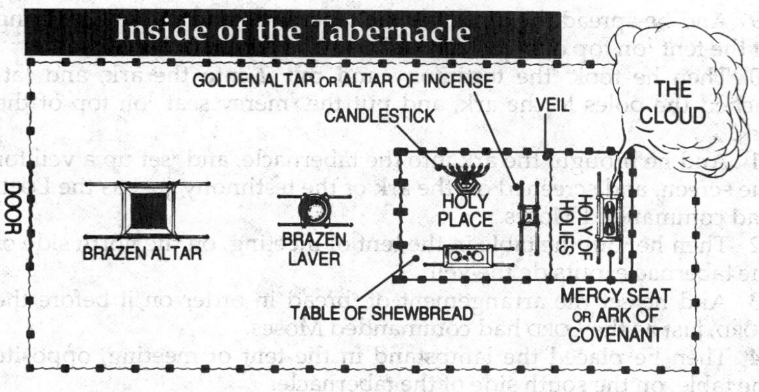

Chapter 40

40:2 [1]Lit., *dwelling* [a]Ex. 19:1; 40:17; Num. 1:1

40 Then the LORD spoke to Moses, saying,
2 "[a]On the first day of the first month you shall set up the
[1]tabernacle of the tent of meeting.

[a]Ex. 26:33; 40:21; Num. 4:5

3 "And [a]you shall place the ark of the testimony there, and you
shall screen the ark with the veil.

4 [1]Lit., *arrange its* [...]*ngement* [2]Or, *light* [...]26:35; 40:22 [b]Ex. 25:30; 40:23 [c]Ex. 40:24f.

4 "And you shall [a]bring in the table and [1b]arrange what belongs on
it; and you shall [c]bring in the lampstand and [2]mount its lamps.
5 "Moreover, you shall [a]set the gold altar of incense before the ark
of the testimony, and set up the veil for the doorway to the taber-
nacle.

5 [a]Ex. 40:26

6 "And you shall set the altar of burnt offering in front of the door-
way of the tabernacle of the tent of meeting.

7 [1]Lit., *there* [a]Ex. 30:18; 40:30

7 "And you shall [a]set the laver between the tent of meeting and the
altar, and put water [1]in it.
8 "And you shall set up the court all around and [1]hang up the veil
for the gateway of the court.

[...]Lit., *put the screen*

9 "Then you shall take the anointing oil and [a]anoint the tabernacle
and all that is in it, and shall consecrate it and all its [1]furnishings;
and it shall be holy.

[1]Or, *utensils* [a]Ex. 30:26; Lev. 8:10

10 "And you shall anoint the altar of burnt offering and all its uten-
sils, and consecrate the altar; and [a]the altar shall be most holy.
11 "And you shall anoint the laver and its stand, and consecrate it.

10 [a]Ex. 29:37

12 "Then you shall [a]bring Aaron and his sons to the doorway of the
tent of meeting and wash them with water.

12 [a]Lev. 8:1-6

13 "And [a]you shall put the holy garments on Aaron and anoint him
and consecrate him, that he may minister as a priest to Me.
14 "And you shall bring his sons and put tunics on them;

[...]x. 28:41; Lev. 8:13

15 and you shall anoint them even as you have anointed their
father, that they may minister as priests to Me; and their anointing
shall [1]qualify them for a [a]perpetual priesthood throughout their
generations."

[...] [1]Lit., *be for them* [...]29:9; Num. 25:13

16 Thus Moses did; according to all that the LORD had commanded
him, so he did.

17 [1]Lit., *in* [2]Lit., [...]*ng place* [a]Ex. 40:2

17 Now it came about [a]in the first month [1]of the second year, on the
first day of the month, that the [2]tabernacle was erected.
18 And Moses erected the tabernacle and [1]laid its [2]sockets, and set
up its boards, and [1]inserted its bars and erected its pillars.

[...]it., *put* [2]Or, *bases*

19 And he spread the tent over the tabernacle and put the covering
of the tent [1]on top of it, just as the LORD had commanded Moses.
20 Then he took [a]the testimony and put *it* into the ark, and [1]at-
tached the poles to the ark, and put the [2]mercy seat [3]on top of the
ark.
21 And he brought the ark into the tabernacle, and [a]set up a veil for
the screen, and screened off the ark of the testimony, just as the LORD
had commanded Moses.
22 Then he [a]put the table in the tent of meeting, on the north side of
the tabernacle, outside the veil.
23 And he set the arrangement of [a]bread in order on it before the
LORD, just as the LORD had commanded Moses.
24 Then he placed the lampstand in the tent of meeting, opposite
the table, on the south side of the tabernacle.
25 And he [a]lighted the lamps before the LORD, just as the LORD had
commanded Moses.
26 Then he [a]placed the gold altar in the tent of meeting in front of
the veil;
27 and he [a]burned fragrant incense on it, just as the LORD had com-
manded Moses.
28 Then he set up the [1]veil for the doorway of the tabernacle.
29 And he [a]set the altar of burnt offering *before* the doorway of the
tabernacle of the tent of meeting, and [b]offered on it the burnt offering
and the meal offering, just as the LORD had commanded Moses.
30 And he placed the laver between the tent of meeting and the
altar, and put water in it for washing.
31 [a]And from it Moses and Aaron and his sons washed their hands
and their feet.
32 When they entered the tent of meeting, and when they ap-
proached the altar, they washed, just as the LORD had commanded
Moses.
33 And he [a]erected the court all around the [1]tabernacle and the
altar, and [2]hung up the veil for the gateway of the court. Thus Moses
finished the work.
34 [a]Then the cloud covered the tent of meeting, and the [b]glory of the
LORD filled the tabernacle.
35 And Moses [a]was not able to enter the tent of meeting because the
cloud had settled on it, and the glory of the LORD filled the taber-
nacle.
36 And throughout all their journeys [a]whenever the cloud was
taken up from over the tabernacle, the sons of Israel would set out;
37 but [a]if the cloud was not taken up, then they did not set out until
the day when it was taken up.
38 For throughout all their journeys, [a]the cloud of the LORD was on
the tabernacle by day, and there was fire in it by night, in the sight of
all the house of Israel.

19 [1]Lit., *over it ab*
20 [1]Lit., *set* [2]Lit., *propitiatory* [3]Lit., *c the ark above* [a]Ex 25:16; Deut. 10:5; 8:9; 2 Chr. 5:10; H
21 [a]Ex. 26:33
22 [a]Ex. 26:35
23 [a]Ex. 25:30; Lev 24:5, 6
25 [a]Ex. 25:37; 40
26 [a]Ex. 30:6; 40:5
27 [a]Ex. 30:7
28 [1]Or, *screen*
29 [a]Ex. 40:6 [b]Ex. 29:38-42
31 [a]Ex. 30:19, 20
33 [1]Or, *dwelling p* [2]Lit., *put the scree* [a]Ex. 27:9-18; 40:8
34 [a]Num. 9:15-23 [b]1 Kin. 8:11; Ezek. 43:4f.; Rev. 15:8
35 [a]1 Kin. 8:11; 2 5:13, 14
36 [a]Num. 9:17; N 9:19
37 [a]Num. 9:19-22
38 [a]Ex. 13:21; Nu 9:12, 15; Ps. 78:14 4:5

EXODUS AT A GLANCE

ne of Exodus:

GMENT DIVISIONS

			CHAPTER THEMES
			1
			2
			3
			4
			5
			6
			7
			8
			9
			10
			11
			12
			13
			14
			15
			16
			17
			18
			19
			20

Author:

Date:

Purpose:

Key Words:

slave(s) (bondage)

deliver (delivered)

holy

the Lord commanded (I commanded)

covenant

cloud

tested

law

tabernacle (tent, tent of meeting)

SEGMENT DIVISIONS

			CHAPTER THEMES
			21
			22
			23
			24
			25
			26
			27
			28
			29
			30
			31
			32
			33
			34
			35
			36
			37
			38
			39
			40

EVITICUS

Genesis we see the ruin of man as he listens to the serpent rather than to God. The human race is emned to sin's awful wage—death. Yet, in the mercy and grace of God comes the promise of nption through the seed of the woman, through the seed of Abraham, as God calls out a people imself. God makes a covenant with Abraham which He confirms to Isaac and then to Jacob, later named Israel.

owever, as the book of Genesis comes to a close, the children of Israel are living in Egypt rather in Canaan, the land of promise. The book that began with the creation of man in Eden ends with hildren of Israel looking into a coffin in Egypt, yet not without a promise that someday they'd Egypt.

xodus plays out the drama of redemption as the nation of Israel is redeemed from slavery through lood of the Passover lamb. After the descendants of Abraham were enslaved and oppressed for hundred years, just as God promised, they left Egypt with great possessions as God went before in His cloud of glory.

nd what follows the redemption of ruined man? That is what the book of Leviticus is all about. y it well, for in picture form Leviticus shows us what God expects from those who have been emed.

NGS TO DO

eral Instructions

As you read Leviticus watch for the verses which attribute the authorship of this book to Moses. When you come across those references, record them under "Author" on the LEVITICUS AT A GLANCE chart on page 195.

Read Exodus 40:17, 32-38, and Leviticus 1:1-2 and note the uninterrupted transition from one book to the other. Then compare Numbers 1:1 with these verses. As you do this you'll see the book of Leviticus covers a period of one month.

. As you read through Leviticus one chapter at a time, do the following:

a. Ask the five W's and an H: Who? What? When? Where? Why? and How? For example: Who is to do what? When are they to do it? How are they to do it? Why? What if they didn't know why? Questions which interrogate the text help you see what is being said.

b. Mark the key repeated words listed on LEVITICUS AT A GLANCE. You'll find it helpful to list these key words on an index card that you can use as a bookmark while you study Leviticus. Also watch for any other key words which might be used in that particular chapter. If you gain insights from marking these words, list what you learn in the margin.

c. Record the main theme or subject of the chapter on the line next to the chapter number in the text. Then record it on LEVITICUS AT A GLANCE.

d. You may want to summarize the main points or the order of events covered in the chapter. Record them in the margin.

e. Record any new insights about the character and ways of God. You could identify your insights on God with this symbol △ and then color it yellow which would make it easy to recognize.

apters 1-7

1. After you read chapters 1 through 7, which give instructions regarding the various sacrifices or offerings, mark the text as instructed under "General Instructions" and then record what you

learn about each of the offerings on the chart THE OFFERINGS AND THEIR PURPOSE. chart is at the end of Leviticus, on page 194.

2. Watch what God says about unintentional sin, guilt, and restitution. Note what is to be when a leader sins and when the congregation sins. Write it in the margin or mark it in the te

Chapters 8-10

This segment covers the consecration of Aaron and his sons. There is an event in chapter 10 v occurs in conjunction with this. As you read these chapters, list in the margin of each chapter wha to be done and why. In chapter 10 note what happened, why it happened, and who was involved.

Chapters 11-15

This segment deals with laws of cleanliness.

1. In addition to the other key words, also mark *clean* and *unclean*.
2. In the margin record what the law covers. For example: food, women, infections, etc.

Chapters 16-17

These chapters cover the day of atonement and regulations regarding the blood.

1. In the margin of chapter 16 carefully outline what is to be done on the day of atonement. As do, you might want to consult the chart INSIDE OF THE TABERNACLE on page 173.
2. Note the regulations in chapter 17 regarding sacrifices and the blood.

Chapters 18-27

This segment lays out statutes on issues regarding moral laws, the priests, the celebration of an feasts, the land, etc.

1. As you read each chapter, in the margin list the main topics or situations.
2. If moral laws are given, note the consequences of breaking the laws and the reason for consequences.
3. In chapter 23 note the feasts, when they are to be celebrated, and how. When you finish stud the chapter, consult the chart THE FEASTS OF ISRAEL on pages I-48 and I-49.
4. Give special attention to any mention of the land—its Sabbath rest, principles of redemption, Mark the words *redeem, redemption,* and any other synonyms. Record your insights in the marg
5. When you finish reading through Leviticus, complete LEVITICUS AT A GLANCE.
   a. See if any of the chapters can be grouped categorically. If so, record this under "Segn Divisions" on the chart. Record any other possible segment divisions. For instance, you co do a segment division, "Laws Regarding."
   b. Record the theme of Leviticus.

THINGS TO THINK ABOUT

1. What have you learned about God and His attitude toward sin? What happens when sin g unpunished?
2. What have you learned about the occult and about the types of sexual sin? How severely w these sins to be dealt with? What does this tell you about how God feels regarding these sins their consequences? What do you think would happen in your country if these sins were d with according to God's law? Read 1 Timothy 1:8-11.
3. Jesus told the Jews that the Scriptures—the Old Testament—testified of Him. Think about h Jesus Christ and His work are foreshadowed in Leviticus.
4. What have you learned about holiness from Leviticus? If you want to be holy, how will you l your life? Are there any changes you need to make? Are you willing? If not, you need to ask, w not?

Chapter 1

1 Then [a]the LORD called to Moses and spoke to him from the tent
of meeting, saying,
2 "Speak to the sons of Israel and say to them, 'When any man of
you brings an [1a]offering to the LORD, you shall bring your [1]offering of
animals from [b]the herd or the flock.
3 'If his offering is a [a]burnt offering from the herd, he shall offer it,
a male [b]without defect; he shall offer it [c]at the doorway of the tent of
meeting, that he may be accepted before the LORD.
4 '[a]And he shall lay his hand on the head of the burnt offering, that
it may be accepted for him to make [b]atonement on his behalf.
5 'And [a]he shall slay the [1]young bull before the LORD; and Aaron's
sons, the priests, shall offer up [b]the blood and [c]sprinkle the blood
around on the altar that is at the doorway of the tent of meeting.
6 '[a]He shall then skin the burnt offering and cut it into its pieces.
7 '[a]And the sons of Aaron the priest shall put fire on the altar and
arrange wood on the fire.
8 'Then Aaron's sons, the priests, shall arrange the pieces, the
head, and the [a]suet over the wood which is on the fire that is on the
altar.
9 'Its [a]entrails, however, and its legs he shall wash with water. And
[b]the priest shall offer up in smoke all of it on the altar for a burnt
offering, an offering by fire of [c]a soothing aroma to the LORD.
10 'But if his offering is from the flock, of the sheep or of the goats,
for a burnt offering, he shall offer it a [a]male without defect.
11 'And [a]he shall slay it on the side of the altar northward before the
LORD, and Aaron's sons, the priests, shall sprinkle its blood around
on the altar.
12 'He shall then cut it into its pieces with its head and its [a]suet, and
the priest shall arrange them on the wood which is on the fire that is
on the altar.
13 'The entrails, however, and the legs he shall wash with water.
And [a]the priest shall offer all of it, and offer it up in smoke on the
altar; it is a burnt offering, an offering by fire of a soothing aroma to
the LORD.
14 'But if his offering to the LORD is a burnt offering of birds, then he
shall bring his offering from the [a]turtledoves or from young pigeons.
15 'And the priest shall bring it to the altar and wring off its head,
and offer it up in smoke on the altar; and its blood is to be drained
out [a]on the side of the altar.
16 'He shall also take away its crop with its feathers, and cast it
beside the altar eastward, to the place of the [1a]ashes.
17 'Then he shall tear it by its wings, *but* [a]shall not sever *it*. And the
priest shall offer it up in smoke on the altar on the wood which is on
the fire; [b]it is a burnt offering, an offering by fire of a soothing aroma
to the LORD.

Chapter 2

2 'Now when anyone presents a [a]grain offering as an offering to
the LORD, his offering shall be of fine flour, and he shall pour oil
on it and put frankincense on it.
2 'He shall then bring it to Aaron's sons, the priests; and shall take
from it [a]his handful of its fine flour and of its oil with all of its

. 19:3; 25:22; Num. 7:89
orban [a]Mark [b]Lev. 22:18f.
. 6:8-13 [b]Ex. .ev. 22:20-24; 21; 17:1 [c]Lev. ut. 12:5, 6, 11
29:10, 15, 19; 8 [b]Ex. 29:33; 26, 31; 2 Chr. 29:23, 24
ne of the herd; the herd [a]Ex. , 16, 20 [b]Lev. v. 1:11; 3:2, 8, . 12:24; 1 Pet. 1:2
6 [a]Lev. 7:8
7 [a]Lev. 6:8-13
12; 3:3, 4; 8:20
x. 12:9 [b]Num. 28:11-14 [c]Gen. 29:18, 25; Lev. um. 15:3; Eph. 5:2
. 12:5; Lev. 1:3; :22; 1 Pet. 1:19
. 24:6; Lev. 1:5; 8:19; 9:12
12 [a]Lev. 3:3, 4
3 [a]Num. 15:4-7; 28:11-14
n. 15:9; Lev. 5:7, 12:8; Luke 2:24
15 [a]Lev. 5:9
, fat ashes [a]Lev. 6:10
[a]Gen. 15:10; Lev. 5:8 [b]Lev. 9:13
ev. 6:14-18; Num. 15:4
2 [a]Lev. 5:12; 6:15

frankincense. And the priest shall offer *it* up in smoke *as* its
[b]memorial portion on the altar, an offering by fire of a soothing
aroma to the LORD.
3 'And [a]the remainder of the grain offering belongs to [b]Aaron and
his sons: a thing most holy, of the offerings to the LORD by fire.
4 'Now when you bring an offering of a grain offering baked in an
oven, *it shall be* [a]unleavened cakes of fine flour mixed with oil, or
unleavened wafers [1]spread with oil.
5 'And if your offering is a grain offering *made* [a]on the griddle, *it*
shall be of fine flour, unleavened, mixed with oil;
6 you shall break it into bits, and pour oil on it; it is a grain
offering.
7 'Now if your offering is a grain offering *made* [a]in a [1]pan, it shall
be made of fine flour with oil.
8 'When you bring in the grain offering which is made of these
things to the LORD, it shall be presented to the priest and he shall
bring it to the altar.
9 'The priest then shall take up from the grain offering [a]its
memorial portion, and shall offer *it* up in smoke on the altar *as* an
offering by fire of a soothing aroma to the LORD.
10 'And [a]the remainder of the grain offering belongs to Aaron and
his sons: a thing most holy, of the offerings to the LORD by fire.
11 '[a]No grain offering, which you bring to the LORD, shall be made
with leaven, for you shall not offer [1]up in smoke any leaven or any
honey as an [b]offering by fire to the LORD.
12 '[a]As an offering of first fruits, you shall bring them to the LORD,
but they shall not ascend for a soothing aroma on the altar.
13 'Every grain offering of yours, moreover, you shall season with
salt, so that [a]the salt of the covenant of your God shall not be lacking
from your grain offering; with all your offerings you shall offer salt.
14 'Also if you bring a grain offering of early ripened things to the
LORD, you shall bring [a]fresh heads of grain roasted in the fire, grits of
new growth, for the grain offering of your early ripened things.
15 'You shall then put oil on it and lay incense on it; it is a grain
offering.
16 'And the priest shall offer up in smoke [a]its memorial portion,
part of its grits and its oil with all its incense as an offering by fire to
the LORD.

Chapter 3

3 'Now if his offering is a [a]sacrifice of peace offerings, if he is
going to offer out of the herd, whether male or female, he shall
offer it [b]without defect before the LORD.
2 '[a]And he shall lay his hand on the head of his offering and [b]slay it
at the doorway of the tent of meeting, and Aaron's sons, the priests,
shall sprinkle the blood around on the altar.
3 'And from the sacrifice of the peace offerings, he shall present an
offering by fire to the LORD, the fat that covers the entrails and all the
fat that is on the entrails,
4 and the two kidneys with the fat that is on them, which is on the
loins, and the [1]lobe of the liver, which he shall remove with the
kidneys.
5 'Then [a]Aaron's sons shall offer *it* up in smoke on the altar [b]on the

2 [b]Lev. 2:9, 24:7; Acts 1(

3 [a]Lev. 2:10 10:12, 13

4 [1]Lit., *anoin* 29:2

5 [a]Lev. 6:21;

7 [1]Lit., *lidded pan* [a]Lev. 7:9

9 [a]Lev. 2:2, 1

10 [a]Lev. 2:3;

11 [1]Lit., *up fro* 23:18; 34:25; L 17 [b]Ex. 29:25;

12 [a]Ex. 34:22; 7:13; 23:10, 17

13 [a]Num. 18:1 13:5; Ezek. 43:

14 [a]Lev. 23:14

16 [a]Lev. 2:2

3:1 [a]Lev. 7:11-3 [b]Lev. 1:3; 22:20-

2 [a]Lev. 1:4 [b]Ex. 16, 20

4 [1]Or, *appendag*

5 [a]Lev. 7:28-34 29:38-42; Num. 2

burnt offering, which is on the wood that is on the fire; [c]it is an
offering by fire of a soothing aroma to the LORD.
6 'But if his offering for a sacrifice of peace offerings to the LORD is
from the flock, he shall offer it, male or female, [a]without defect.
7 'If he is going to offer [a]a lamb for his offering, then he shall offer
it [b]before the LORD,
8 and [a]he shall lay his hand on the head of his offering, and [b]slay it
before the tent of meeting; and Aaron's sons shall [c]sprinkle its blood
around on the altar.
9 'And from the [a]sacrifice of peace offerings he shall bring as an
offering by fire to the LORD, its fat, [1]the entire fat tail which he shall
remove close to the backbone, and the fat that covers the entrails and
all the fat that is on the entrails,
10 and the two kidneys with the fat that is on them, which is on the
loins, and the [1]lobe of the liver, which he shall remove [a]with the
kidneys.
11 'Then the priest shall offer *it* up in smoke [a]on the altar, *as* [b]food,
an offering by fire to the LORD.
12 'Moreover, if his offering is [a]a goat, then he shall offer it before
the LORD,
13 and he shall lay his hand on its head and slay it before the tent of
meeting; and the sons of Aaron shall sprinkle its blood around on
the altar.
14 'And from it he shall present his offering as an offering by fire to
the LORD, the fat that covers the entrails and all the fat that is on the
entrails,
15 and the two kidneys with the fat that is on them, which is on the
loins, and the [1]lobe of the liver, which he shall remove [a]with the
kidneys.
16 'And the priest shall offer them up in smoke on the altar *as* food,
an offering by fire for a soothing aroma; [a]all fat is the LORD's.
17 'It is a [a]perpetual statute throughout your generations in all your
dwellings: you shall not eat any fat [b]or any blood.' "

Chapter 4

4 Then the LORD spoke to Moses, saying,
2 "Speak to the sons of Israel, saying, 'If a person sins [a]uninten-
tionally in any of the [1]things which the LORD has [b]commanded not to
be done, and commits any of them,
3 [a]if the anointed priest sins so as to bring guilt on the people, then
let him offer to the LORD a [1]bull without defect as a sin offering for
the sin he has [2]committed.
4 'And he shall bring the bull to the doorway of the tent of meeting
before the LORD, and [a]he shall lay his hand on the head of the bull,
and slay the bull before the LORD.
5 'Then the [a]anointed priest is to take some of the blood of the bull
and bring it to the tent of meeting,
6 and the priest shall dip his finger in the blood, and sprinkle
some of the blood seven times before the LORD, in front of [a]the veil of
the sanctuary.
7 'The priest shall also put some of the blood on the horns of [a]the
altar of fragrant incense which is before the LORD in the tent of meet-
ing; and all the blood of the bull he shall pour out at the base of the
altar of burnt offering which is at the doorway of the tent of meeting.

um. 15:8-10; 28:12-14
:1; 22:20-24
:4, 5; 28:4-8 ; 1 Kin. 8:62
1:4 [b]Lev. 3:2 [c]Lev. 1:5
t., *the fat tail,* v. 17:5; Num. 1 Sam. 10:8; . 6:17; 1 Kin. 63, 64; 1 Chr. 16:1
appendage on [a]Lev. 3:4, 15
:5 [b]Lev. 3:16; 21:6, 8, 17, 22
[a]Num. 15:6-11
appendage on [a]Lev. 3:4; 7:4
[a]Lev. 7:23-25
6:18, 22; 7:34, 10:9, 15; 16:29; 23:14, 21; 24:3 7:26; 17:10-16
., *commands of* D *which are not* *one* [a]Lev. 4:22, 18; 22:14 [b]Lev. 4:13
, *bull of the herd* *ned* [a]Lev. 4:14, 23, 28
. 1:4; 4:15; Num. 8:12
5 [a]Lev. 4:3, 17
6 [a]Ex. 40:21, 26
. 4:18, 25, 30, 34; 8:15; 9:9; 16:18

8 '[a]And he shall remove from it all the fat of the bull of the sin offering: the fat that covers the entrails, and all the fat which is on the entrails,

9 and the two kidneys with the fat that is on them, which is on the loins, and the [1]lobe of the liver, which he shall remove [a]with the kidneys

10 (just as it is removed from the ox of the sacrifice of peace offerings), and the priest is to offer them up in smoke on the altar of burnt offering.

11 'But [a]the hide of the bull and all its flesh with its head and its legs and its entrails and its refuse,

12 [1]that is, all *the rest of* the bull, he is to bring out to [a]a clean place outside the camp where the [2]ashes are poured out, and burn it on wood with fire; where the [2]ashes are poured out it shall be burned.

13 '[a]Now if the whole congregation of Israel commits error, and the matter [1]escapes the notice of the assembly, and they commit any of the [2]things which the LORD has commanded not to be done, and they become guilty;

14 [a]when the sin [1]which they have [2]committed becomes known, then the assembly shall offer [b]a [3]bull of the herd for a sin offering, and bring it before the tent of meeting.

15 'Then [a]the elders of the congregation shall lay their hands on the head of the bull before the LORD, and the bull shall be slain [b]before the LORD.

16 'Then the anointed priest is to bring some of the blood of the bull to the tent of meeting;

17 and [a]the priest shall dip his finger in the blood, and sprinkle *it* seven times before the LORD, in front of the veil.

18 'And he shall put some of the blood on the horns of [a]the altar which is before the LORD [1]in the tent of meeting; and all the blood he shall pour out at the base of the altar of burnt offering which is at the doorway of the tent of meeting.

19 '[a]And he shall remove all its fat from it and offer it up in smoke on the altar.

20 'He shall also do with the bull just as he did with [a]the bull of the sin offering; thus he shall do with it. So [b]the priest shall make atonement for them, and they shall be forgiven.

21 'Then he is to bring out the bull to *a place* outside the camp, and burn it as he burned the first bull; it is [a]the sin offering for the assembly.

22 'When [a]a leader [b]sins and unintentionally does any one of all the [1]things which the LORD God has commanded not to be done, and he becomes guilty,

23 [1a]if his sin [2]which he has committed is made known to him, he shall bring for his offering a [3b]goat, [c]a male without defect.

24 'And he shall lay his hand on the head of the male goat, and slay it in the place where [1]they slay the burnt offering before the LORD; it is a sin offering.

25 'Then the priest is to take some of the blood of the sin offering with his finger, and put it on [a]the horns of the altar of burnt offering; and *the rest of* its blood he shall pour out at the base of the altar of burnt offering.

26 '[a]And all its fat he shall offer up in smoke on the altar as *in the case of* the fat of the sacrifice of peace offerings. Thus [b]the priest shall

8 [a]Lev. 3:3, 4

9 [1]Or, *appendage* [a]Lev. 3:4

11 [a]Lev. 9:11; Nur

12 [1]Lit., *and* [2]Or, *ashes are* [a]Lev. 4 6:10, 11; 16:27

13 [1]Lit., *is hidden the eyes of* [2]Lit., *commands of the which are not to b done* [a]Num. 15:24

14 [1]Lit., *concerni which* [2]Lit., *sinne son of the herd* [a]L 4:3 [b]Lev. 4:3, 23,

15 [a]Lev. 8:14, 18, Num. 8:10, 12 [b]Le

17 [a]Lev. 4:6

18 [1]Lit., *which is* [a]Lev. 4:7, 25, 30,

19 [a]Lev. 4:8

20 [a]Lev. 4:8, 21 15:25, 28

21 [a]Lev. 4:13f.; 16:15-17; Num. 15

22 [1]Lit., *comman the* LORD *which a to be done* [a]Num. 31:13; 32:2 [b]Lev.

23 [1]Lit., *or* [2]Lit., *which he has sinn* [3]Lit., *buck of the g* [a]Lev. 4:3 [b]Lev. 4: 28 [c]Lev. 4:28

24 [1]Lit., *one slays*

25 [a]Lev. 4:7, 18,

26 [a]Lev. 4:19 [b]Le 4:20, 31; 5:10, 13, 18; 6:7

make atonement for him in regard to his sin, and he shall be
forgiven.
27 'Now if [1]anyone of [2]the common people sins [a]unintentionally in
doing any of the [3]things which the LORD has commanded not to be
done, and becomes guilty,
28 [1a]if his sin, which he has [2]committed is made known to him, then
he shall bring for his offering a [3b]goat, a [c]female without defect, for
his sin which he has [2]committed.
29 'And [a]he shall lay his hand on the head of the sin offering, and
[b]slay the sin offering at the place of the burnt offering.
30 'And the priest shall take some of its blood with his finger and
put it on the horns of [a]the altar of burnt offering; and [b]all *the rest of* its
blood he shall pour out at the base of the altar.
31 '[a]Then he shall remove all its fat, just as the fat was removed
from the sacrifice of peace offerings; and the priest shall offer it up in
smoke on the altar for [b]a soothing aroma to the LORD. Thus the priest
shall make atonement for him, [1]and he shall be forgiven.
32 'But if he brings [a]a lamb as his offering for a sin offering, he shall
bring it, a female without defect.
33 'And [a]he shall lay his hand on the head of the sin offering, and
slay it for a sin offering [b]in the place where [1]they slay the burnt
offering.
34 'And the priest is to take some of the blood of the sin offering
with his finger and put it on the horns of [a]the altar of burnt offering;
and [b]all *the rest of* its blood he shall pour out at the base of the altar.
35 'Then he shall remove [a]all its fat, just as the fat of the lamb is
removed from the sacrifice of the peace offerings, and the priest shall
offer them up in smoke on the altar, on the offerings by fire to the
LORD. Thus [b]the priest shall make atonement for him in regard to his
sin which he has [1]committed, and he shall be forgiven.

Chapter 5

5 'Now if a person sins, after he hears a [1]public [a]adjuration *to
testify*, when he is a witness, whether he has seen or *otherwise*
known, if he does not tell *it*, then he will bear his [2]guilt.
2 'Or if a person touches [a]any unclean thing, whether a carcass of
an unclean beast, or the carcass of unclean cattle, or a carcass of
unclean swarming things, though it is hidden from him, and he is
unclean, then he will be guilty.
3 'Or if he touches human uncleanness, of whatever *sort* his un-
cleanness *may* be with which he becomes unclean, and it is hidden
from him, and then he comes to know *it*, he will be guilty.
4 'Or if a person [a]swears thoughtlessly with his lips to do evil or to
do good, in whatever matter a man may speak thoughtlessly with an
oath, and it is hidden from him, and then he comes to know *it*, he
will be guilty in one of these.
5 'So it shall be when he becomes guilty in one of these, that he
shall [a]confess that in which he has sinned.
6 'He shall also bring his guilt offering to the LORD for his sin
which he has [1]committed, [a]a female from the flock, a lamb or a [2]goat
as a sin offering. So the priest shall make atonement on his behalf for
his sin.
7 'But if [1]he cannot afford a lamb, then he shall bring to the LORD
his guilt offering for that in which he has sinned, two turtledoves or

one soul [2]Lit., ple of the land nmands of the hich are not to one [a]Lev. 4:2; Num. 15:27

or [2]Lit., sinned ale goat [a]Lev. ev. 4:3, 14, 23, 32 [c]Lev. 4:23

ev. 1:4; 4:4, 24 [b]Lev. 1:5, 11

4:7, 18, 25, 34 [b]Lev. 4:7

so that he may [a]Lev. 4:8 [b]Gen. Ex. 29:18; Lev. 9, 13; 2:2, 9, 12

32 [a]Lev. 4:28

[1]Lit., *one slays* :4, 5 [b]Lev. 4:29

. 4:7, 18, 25, 30 [b]Lev. 4:7

.it., *sinned* [a]Lev. :6, 31 [b]Lev. 4:20

[1]Lit., *voice of an* Or, *iniquity* [a]Prov. 29:24; Jer. 23:10

. 11:8, 11, 24-40; . 19:11-16; Deut. 14:8

[a]Num. 30:6, 8; Ps. 106:33

Lev. 16:21; 26:40; . 5:7; Prov. 28:13

[1]Lit., *sinned* [2]Lit., *female goat* [a]Lev. 4:28, 32

Lit., *his hand does t reach enough for*

two young pigeons, [a]one for a sin offering and the other for a burnt offering.

8 'And he shall bring them to the priest, who shall offer first that which is for the sin offering and shall nip its head at the front of its neck, but he [a]shall not sever *it*.

9 'He shall also sprinkle some of the blood of the sin offering [a]on the side of the altar, while the rest of the blood shall be drained out [b]at the base of the altar: it is a sin offering.

10 'The second he shall then prepare as a burnt offering [a]according to the ordinance. [b]So the priest shall make atonement on his behalf for his sin which he has [1]committed, and it shall be forgiven him.

11 'But [a]if his [1]means are insufficient for two turtledoves or two young pigeons, then for his offering for that which he has sinned, he shall bring the tenth of an [2]ephah of fine flour for a sin offering; [b]he shall not put oil on it or place incense on it, for it is a sin offering.

12 'And he shall bring it to the priest, and the priest shall take his handful of it as its memorial portion and offer *it* up in smoke on the altar, [1]with the offerings of the LORD by fire: it is a sin offering.

13 'So the priest shall make atonement for him concerning his sin which he has [1]committed from [a]one of these, and it shall be forgiven him; then [b]*the rest* shall become the priest's, like the grain offering.' "

14 Then the LORD spoke to Moses, saying,

15 "[a]If a person acts unfaithfully and sins [b]unintentionally against the LORD's holy things, then he shall bring his [c]guilt offering to the LORD: [d]a ram without defect from the flock, according to your valuation in silver by shekels, in *terms of* the [e]shekel of the sanctuary, for a guilt offering.

16 "[a]And he shall make restitution for that which he has sinned against the holy thing, and shall add to it a fifth part of it, and give it to the priest. [b]The priest shall then make atonement for him with the ram of the guilt offering, and it shall be forgiven him.

17 "Now if a person sins and does any of the things [1]which the LORD has commanded not to be done, [a]though he was unaware, still he is guilty, and shall bear his punishment.

18 "He is then to bring to the priest [a]a ram without defect from the flock, according to your valuation, for a guilt offering. So the priest shall make atonement for him concerning his error in which he sinned [b]unintentionally and did not know *it*, and it shall be forgiven him.

19 "It is a guilt offering; he was certainly guilty before the LORD."

Chapter 6

6 [1]Then the LORD spoke to Moses, saying,

2 "[a]When a person sins and acts unfaithfully against the LORD, and deceives his companion in regard to a deposit or a security entrusted *to him*, or through robbery, or *if* he has extorted from his companion,

3 or [a]has found what was lost and lied about it and sworn falsely, so that he sins in regard to any one of the things a man may do;

4 then it shall be, when he sins and becomes guilty, that he shall [a]restore what he took by robbery, or what he got by extortion, or the deposit which was [1]entrusted to him, or the lost thing which he found,

5 or anything about which he swore falsely; [a]he shall make

7 [a]Lev. 12:6, 8; 14:30, 31

8 [a]Lev. 1:17

9 [a]Lev. 1:15 [b]Lev. 4:7, 18

10 [1]Lit., *sinned* [a]Le 1:14-17 [b]Lev. 4:20, 5:13, 16

11 [1]Lit., *hand does reach* [2]I.e., Approx bu. [a]Lev. 14:21-32; 27:8 [b]Lev. 2:1, 2

12 [1]Lit., *upon*

13 [1]Lit., *sinned* [a]L 5:4, 5 [b]Lev. 2:3

15 [a]Num. 5:5-8 [b]L 4:2; 22:14 [c]Lev. 7: [d]Lev. 6:6 [e]Ex. 30:1

16 [a]Lev. 6:5; 22:14 Num. 5:7, 8 [b]Lev. 7

17 [1]Lit., *the comm of the LORD which* [a]Lev. 4:2; 5:19

18 [a]Lev. 5:15 [b]Lev

6:1 [1]Ch. 5:20 in He

2 [a]Ex. 22:7-15

3 [a]Ex. 23:4; Deut. 22:1-4

4 [1]Or, *deposited w* [a]Lev. 24:18, 21

5 [a]Lev. 5:16

restitution for it [1]in full, and add to it one-fifth more. [b]He shall give it
to the one to whom it belongs on the day *he presents* his guilt
offering.
6 "Then he shall bring to the priest his guilt offering to the LORD, [a]a
ram without defect from the flock, according to your valuation, for a
guilt offering,
7 and [a]the priest shall make atonement for him before the LORD;
and he shall be forgiven for any one of the things which he may
have done to incur guilt."
8 [1]Then the LORD spoke to Moses, saying,
9 "Command Aaron and his sons, saying, 'This is [a]the law for the
burnt offering: the burnt offering itself *shall remain* on the hearth on
the altar all night until the morning, and [b]the fire on the altar is to be
kept burning on it.
10 'And the priest is to put on [a]his linen robe, and he shall put on
undergarments next to his flesh; and he shall take up the [1]ashes *to*
which the fire [2]reduces the burnt offering on the altar, and place
them beside the altar.
11 'Then he shall take off his garments and put on other garments,
and carry the [1]ashes outside the camp to a clean place.
12 'And the fire on the altar shall be kept burning on it. It shall not
go out, but the priest shall burn wood on it every morning; and he
shall lay out the burnt offering on it, and offer up in smoke the fat
portions of the peace offerings [a]on it.
13 'Fire shall be kept burning continually on the altar; it is not to go
out.
14 'Now this is the law of the grain offering: the sons of Aaron shall
present it before the LORD in front of the altar.
15 '[a]Then one *of them* shall lift up from it a handful of the fine flour
of the grain offering, [1]with its oil and all the incense that is on the
grain offering, and he shall offer *it* up in smoke on the altar, a sooth-
ing aroma, as its memorial offering to the LORD.
16 '[a]And what is left of it Aaron and his sons are to eat. It shall be
eaten as unleavened cakes in a holy place; they are to eat it in the
court of the tent of meeting.
17 '[a]It shall not be baked with leaven. I have given it as their share
from My offerings by fire; [b]it is most holy, like the sin offering and
[c]the guilt offering.
18 '[a]Every male among the sons of Aaron may eat it; it is a
permanent ordinance throughout your generations, from the
offerings by fire to the LORD. [b]Whoever touches them shall become
consecrated.' "
19 Then the LORD spoke to Moses, saying,
20 "This is the offering which Aaron and his sons are to present to
the LORD on the day when he is anointed; the tenth of an [a]ephah of
fine flour as [b]a [1]regular grain offering, half of it in the morning and
half of it in the evening.
21 "It shall be prepared with oil on a [a]griddle. When it is *well* stirred,
you shall bring it. You shall present the grain offering in baked
pieces as a soothing aroma to the LORD.
22 "And the anointed priest who will be in his place [1]among his sons
shall [2]offer it. By a permanent ordinance it shall be entirely offered
up in smoke to the LORD.

Lit., *in its sum* [b]Num. 5:8
6 [a]Lev. 5:15
7 [a]Lev. 7:2-5
Ch. 6:1 in Heb.
29:38-42; Num. [b]Lev. 6:12, 13
fat ashes [2]Lit., ...*es* [a]Ex. 28:39, 42; 39:27, 28
[1]Or, *fat ashes*
12 [a]Lev. 3:5
Lit., *and some of* [a]Lev. 2:2, 9
...v. 2:3; 10:12-14; Ezek. 44:29
[a]Lev. 2:11 [b]Ex. ...Lev. 6:25, 26, 29, Num. 18:9 [c]Lev. 7:7; 10:16-18
8 [a]Lev. 6:29; 7:6; 18:10; 1 Cor. 9:13 [b]Lev. 6:27
[1]Lit., *grain offering* ...*tinually* [a]Lev. 5:11 [b]Num. 4:16
21 [a]Lev. 2:5
[1]Lit., *from among* [2]Lit., *do*

23 "So every grain offering of the priest shall be burned entirely. It
shall not be eaten."
24 Then the LORD spoke to Moses, saying,
25 "Speak to Aaron and to his sons, saying, 'This is the law of the sin
offering: [a]in the place where the burnt offering is slain the sin offer-
ing shall be slain before the LORD; it is most holy.
26 '[a]The priest who offers it for sin shall eat it. It shall be eaten in a
holy place, in the court of the tent of meeting.
27 '[a]Anyone who touches its flesh shall become consecrated; and
when any of its blood [1]splashes on a garment, in a holy place you
shall wash what was splashed on.
28 'Also [a]the earthenware vessel in which it was boiled shall be
broken; and if it was boiled in a bronze vessel, then it shall be
scoured and rinsed in water.
29 '[a]Every male among the priests may eat of it; [b]it is most holy.
30 'But no sin offering [a]of which any of the blood is brought into the
tent of meeting to make atonement [b]in the holy place shall be eaten;
[c]it shall be burned with fire.

Chapter 7

7 'Now this is the law of the [a]guilt offering; it is most holy.
2 'In [a]the place where they slay the burnt offering they are to
slay the guilt offering, and he shall sprinkle its blood around on the
altar.
3 'Then he shall offer from it all its fat: the [a]fat tail and the fat that
covers the entrails,
4 and the two kidneys with the fat that is on them, which is on the
loins, and the lobe on the liver he shall remove [a]with the kidneys.
5 'And the priest shall offer them up in smoke on the altar as an
offering by fire to the LORD; it is a guilt offering.
6 '[a]Every male among the priests may eat of it. It shall be eaten in a
holy place; it is most holy.
7 'The guilt offering is like the [a]sin offering, there is one law for
them; the [b]priest who makes atonement with it [1]shall have it.
8 'Also the priest who presents any man's burnt offering, [1]that
priest shall have for himself the skin of the burnt offering which he
has presented.
9 'Likewise, every grain offering that is baked in the oven, and
everything prepared in a [1]pan or on a [a]griddle, [2]shall belong to the
priest who presents it.
10 'And every grain offering mixed with oil, or dry, shall [1]belong to
all the sons of Aaron, [2]to all alike.
11 'Now this is the law of the [a]sacrifice of peace offerings which
shall be presented to the LORD.
12 'If he offers it by way of [a]thanksgiving, then along with the
sacrifice of thanksgiving he shall offer [b]unleavened cakes mixed with
oil, and unleavened wafers [1]spread with oil, and cakes *of well* stirred
fine flour mixed with oil.
13 'With the sacrifice of his peace offerings for thanksgiving, he
shall present his offering with cakes of [a]leavened bread.
14 'And of [1]this he shall present one of every offering as a [2]contribu-
tion to the LORD; [a]it shall [3]belong to the priest who sprinkles the
blood of the peace offerings.
15 '[a]Now *as for* the flesh of the sacrifice of his thanksgiving peace

25 [a]Lev. 1:11
26 [a]Lev. 6:29
27 [1]Lit., *one* [a]Lev. 7:19
28 [a]Lev. 11:3
29 [a]Lev. 6:18 6:17, 25
30 [a]Lev. 4:1-2 4:7, 18 [c]Lev. 4 12, 21
7:1 [a]Lev. 5:14
2 [a]Lev. 1:11
3 [a]Lev. 3:9
4 [a]Lev. 3:4
6 [a]Lev. 6:18, 2 18:9
7 [1]Lit., *it shall b him* [a]Lev. 6:25, [b]1 Cor. 9:13; 10
8 [1]Lit., *for the p shall be for him*
9 [1]Lit., *lidded c pan* [2]Lit., *for the it shall be for hi* 2:5
10 [1]Lit., *be* [2]Lit. *as his brother*
11 [a]Lev. 3:1
12 [1]Or, *anointed* 7:15 [b]Lev. 2:4; N 6:15
13 [a]Lev. 2:12; 23 18; Amos 4:5
14 [1]Lit., *it* [2]Or, *he offering* [3]Lit., *be f* [a]Num. 18:8, 11, 19
15 [a]Lev. 22:29, 30

offerings, it shall be eaten on the day of his offering; he shall not
leave any of it over until morning.
16 'But if the sacrifice of his offering is a [a]votive or a freewill offer-
ing, it shall be eaten on the day that he offers his sacrifice; and on the
[1]next day what is left of it may be eaten;
17 [a]but what is left over from the flesh of the sacrifice on the third
day shall be burned with fire.
18 'So if any of the flesh of the sacrifice of his peace offerings should
ever be eaten on the third day, he who offers it shall not be accepted,
and it shall not be reckoned to his *benefit*. It shall be an [a]offensive
thing, and the person who eats of it shall bear his *own* iniquity.
19 'Also the flesh that touches anything unclean shall not be eaten;
it shall be burned with fire. [1]As for *other* flesh, anyone who is clean
may eat *such* flesh.
20 '[a]But the person who eats the flesh of the sacrifice of peace offer-
ings which belong to the LORD, [1]in his uncleanness, that person [b]shall
be cut off from his people.
21 '[a]And when anyone touches anything unclean, whether human
uncleanness, or an unclean animal, or any unclean [1]detestable thing,
and eats of the flesh of the sacrifice of peace offerings which belong
to the LORD, that person shall be cut off from his people.'"
22 Then the LORD spoke to Moses, saying,
23 "Speak to the sons of Israel, saying, 'You shall not eat [a]any fat *from*
an ox, a sheep, or a goat.
24 'Also the fat of *an animal* which dies, and the fat of an animal
[a]torn *by beasts*, may be put to any other use, but you must certainly
not eat it.
25 'For whoever eats the fat of the animal from which [1]an offering
by fire is offered to the LORD, even the person who eats shall be cut
off from his people.
26 '[a]And you are not to eat any blood, either of bird or animal, in
any of your dwellings.
27 'Any person who eats any blood, even that person shall be cut off
from his people.'"
28 Then the LORD spoke to Moses, saying,
29 "Speak to the sons of Israel, saying, 'He who offers [a]the sacrifice
of his peace offerings to the LORD shall bring his offering to the LORD
from the sacrifice of his peace offerings.
30 'His own hands are to bring offerings by fire to the LORD. He
shall bring the fat with the breast, that the [a]breast may be [1]presented
as a wave offering before the LORD.
31 'And the priest shall offer up the fat in smoke on the altar; but
[a]the breast shall belong to Aaron and his sons.
32 'And you shall give [a]the right thigh to the priest as a [1]contribu-
tion from the sacrifices of your peace offerings.
33 'The one among the sons of Aaron who offers the blood of the
peace offerings and the fat, the right thigh shall be his as *his* portion.
34 'For I have taken [a]the breast of the wave offering and the thigh of
the [1]contribution from the sons of Israel from the sacrifices of their
peace offerings, and have given them to Aaron the priest and to his
sons as *their* due forever from the sons of Israel.
35 'This is [1]that which is consecrated to Aaron and [1]that [a]which is
consecrated to his sons from the offerings by fire to the LORD, in that
day when he presented them to serve as priests to the LORD.

morrow and [a]Lev. 19:5-8
7 [a]Ex. 12:10
7; Prov. 15:8
And the flesh
[1]Lit., and his ess is on him 22:3-7; Num. 13 [b]Lev. 7:25
me mss. read ng thing [a]Lev. 5:2, 3
23 [a]Lev. 3:17
Ex. 22:31; Lev. 17:15; 22:8
it., he offers an offering by fire
[a]Gen. 9:4; Lev. 6; 19:26; Deut. ; 1 Sam. 14:33; Acts 15:20
29 [a]Lev. 3:1
Lit., waved [a]Ex. 6, 27; Lev. 8:29; Num. 6:20
um. 18:11; Deut. 18:3
r, heave offering 29:27; Lev. 7:34; 9:21; Num. 6:20
Or, heave offering 29:27; Lev. 10:14, 15; Num. 18:18
[1]Lit., the anointed ion of [a]Num. 18:8

36 '[1]These the LORD had commanded to be given them from the sons of Israel in the day that He [a]anointed them. It is *their* due forever throughout their generations.' "

37 This is the law of the burnt offering, the grain offering and the sin offering and the guilt offering and [a]the ordination offering and the sacrifice of peace offerings,

38 [a]which the LORD commanded Moses at Mount Sinai in the day that He commanded the sons of Israel to [1]present their offerings to the LORD in the wilderness of Sinai.

Chapter 8

8 Then the LORD spoke to Moses, saying,

2 "[a]Take Aaron and his sons with him, and the [b]garments and [c]the anointing oil and the bull of the sin offering, and the two rams and the basket of unleavened bread;

3 and assemble all the congregation at the doorway of the tent of meeting."

4 So Moses did just as the LORD commanded him. When the congregation was assembled at the doorway of the tent of meeting,

5 Moses said to the congregation, "This is the thing which the LORD has commanded to do."

6 Then [a]Moses had Aaron and his sons come near, and [b]washed them with water.

7 And he [a]put the tunic on him and girded him with the sash, and clothed him with the robe, and put the ephod on him; and he girded him with the artistic band of the ephod, [1]with which he tied *it* to him.

8 He then placed the [1]breastpiece on him, and in the [1]breastpiece he put [2a]the Urim and the Thummim.

9 He also placed the turban on his head, and on the turban, at its front, he placed [a]the golden plate, the holy crown, just as the LORD had commanded Moses.

10 Moses then took [a]the anointing oil and anointed the [1]tabernacle and all that was in it, and consecrated them.

11 And he sprinkled some of it on the altar seven times and anointed the altar and all its utensils, and the basin and its stand, to [a]consecrate them.

12 Then he poured some of the [a]anointing oil on Aaron's head and anointed him, to consecrate him.

13 [a]Next Moses had Aaron's sons come near and clothed them with tunics, and girded them with sashes, and bound [1]caps on them, just as the LORD had commanded Moses.

14 Then he brought [a]the bull of the sin offering, and Aaron and his sons laid their hands on the head of the bull of the sin offering.

15 Next [1]Moses slaughtered *it* and took the blood and with his finger [a]put *some of it* around on the horns of the altar, and purified the altar. Then he poured out *the rest of* the blood at the base of the altar and consecrated it, to make atonement for it.

16 He also [a]took all the fat that was on the entrails and the [1]lobe of the liver, and the two kidneys and their fat; and Moses offered it up in smoke on the altar.

17 [a]But the bull and its hide and its flesh and its refuse, he burned in the fire outside the camp, just as the LORD had commanded Moses.

36 [1]Lit., *whic* 40:13-15; Lev

37 [a]Ex. 29:22 8:22, 23

38 [1]Or, *offer* 26:46; 27:34;

8:2 [a]Ex. 28:1 6:10 [c]Ex. 30:2

6 [a]Ex. 29:4-6 30:19, 20; Ps. 1 Cor. 6:11; Ep

7 [1]Lit., *and wit* 28:4

8 [1]Lit., *pouch* lights and perfe [a]Ex. 28:30; Nu Deut. 33:8; 1 Sa Ezra 2:63; Neh.

9 [a]Ex. 28:36

10 [1]Or, *dwelling* [a]Ex. 30:26-29; L

11 [a]Ex. 29:36, 3

12 [a]Ex. 29:7; 30 Lev. 21:10, 12; P

13 [1]Lit., *headgea* 29:8, 9

14 [a]Ex. 29:10; Le Ps. 66:15; Ezek.

15 [1]Lit., *he slaug it and Moses took* 29:12; Lev. 4:7; E 43:20

16 [1]Or, *appendag* [a]Ex. 29:13

17 [a]Ex. 29:14; Lev 4:11, 12

18 Then he presented [a]the ram of the burnt offering, and Aaron and
his sons laid their hands on the head of the ram.
19 And [1]Moses slaughtered *it* and sprinkled the blood around on
the altar.
20 When he had cut the ram into its pieces, Moses [a]offered up the
head and the pieces and the suet in smoke.
21 After he had washed the entrails and the legs with water, Moses
[a]offered up the whole ram in smoke on the altar. It was a burnt
offering for a soothing aroma; it was an offering by fire to the LORD,
just as the LORD had commanded Moses.
22 Then he presented the second ram, [a]the ram of [1]ordination; and
Aaron and his sons laid their hands on the head of the ram.
23 And [1]Moses slaughtered *it* and took some of its blood and [a]put it
on the lobe of Aaron's right ear, and on the thumb of his right hand,
and on the big toe of his right foot.
24 He also had Aaron's sons come near; and Moses put some of the
blood on the lobe of their right ear, and on the thumb of their right
hand, and on the big toe of their right foot. Moses then [a]sprinkled *the
rest of* the blood around on the altar.
25 And he took the fat, and the fat tail, and all the fat that was on
the entrails, and the [1]lobe of the liver and the two kidneys and their
fat and the right thigh.
26 And [a]from the basket of unleavened bread that was before the
LORD, he took one unleavened cake and one cake of bread *mixed with*
oil and one wafer, and placed *them* on the portions of fat and on the
right thigh.
27 He then [a]put all *these* on the hands of Aaron and on the hands of
his sons, and presented them as a wave offering before the LORD.
28 Then Moses [a]took them from their hands and offered them up in
smoke on the altar with the burnt offering. They were an ordination
offering for [b]a soothing aroma; it was an offering by fire to the LORD.
29 Moses also took [a]the breast and presented it for a wave offering
before the LORD; it was [b]Moses' portion of the ram of ordination, just
as the LORD had commanded Moses.
30 So Moses [a]took some of the anointing oil and some of the blood
which was on the altar, and sprinkled it on Aaron, on his garments,
on his sons, and on the garments of his sons with him; and he
consecrated Aaron, his garments, and his sons, and the garments of
his sons with him.
31 Then Moses said to Aaron and to his sons, "[a]Boil the flesh at the
doorway of the tent of meeting, and eat it there together with the
bread which is in the basket of the ordination offering, just as I
commanded, [b]saying, 'Aaron and his sons shall eat it.'
32 "And [a]the remainder of the flesh and of the bread you shall burn
in the fire.
33 "[a]And you shall not go outside the doorway of the tent of meeting
for seven days, until the day that the period of your ordination is
fulfilled; for he will [1]ordain you through seven days.
34 "The LORD has commanded to do as has been done this day, to
make atonement on your behalf.
35 "At the doorway of the tent of meeting, moreover, you shall
remain day and night for seven days, and [a]keep the charge of the
LORD, that you may not die, for so I have been commanded."

x. 29:15; Lev. 8:2
., *he slaughtered* / *Moses sprinkled*
20 [a]Lev. 1:8
21 [a]Ex. 29:18
.it., *filling,* and so hout the ch. [a]Ex. 29:31; Lev. 8:2
., *he slaughtered* / *Moses took* [a]Ex. 29:20, 21
24 [a]Heb. 9:18-22
Or, *appendage on*
26 [a]Ex. 29:23
27 [a]Ex. 29:24
[a]Ex. 29:25 [b]Gen. 8:21
ev. 7:31-34 [b]Ex. 29:26; Ps. 99:6
30 [a]Ex. 29:21
[a]Ex. 29:31 [b]Ex. 29:32
32 [a]Ex. 29:34
it., *fill your hands* [a]Ex. 29:35
[a]Num. 3:7; 9:19; .11:1; 1 Kin. 2:3; Ezek. 48:11

36 Thus Aaron and his sons did all the things which the LORD had
commanded through Moses.

Chapter 9

9 Now it came about [a]on the eighth day that Moses called Aaron
and his sons and the elders of Israel;
2 and he said to Aaron, "[a]Take for yourself a calf, a bull, for a sin
offering and a ram for a burnt offering, *both* without defect, and offer
them before the LORD.
3 "Then to the sons of Israel you shall speak, saying, 'Take a male
goat for a sin offering, and a calf and a lamb, both one year old,
without defect, for a burnt offering,
4 and an ox and a ram for peace offerings, to sacrifice before the
LORD, and a grain offering mixed with oil; for today [a]the LORD shall
appear to you.' "
5 So they took what Moses had commanded to the front of the tent
of meeting, and the whole congregation came near and stood before
the LORD.
6 And Moses said, "This is the thing which the LORD has com-
manded you to do, that [a]the glory of the LORD may appear to you."
7 Moses then said to Aaron, "Come near to the altar and [1a]offer
your sin offering and your burnt offering, that you may make atone-
ment for yourself and for the people; then make the offering [2]for the
people, that you may make atonement for them, just as the LORD has
commanded."
8 [a]So Aaron came near to the altar and slaughtered the calf of the
sin offering which was for himself.
9 [a]And Aaron's sons presented the blood to him; and he dipped
his finger in the blood, and [b]put *some* on the horns of the altar, and
poured out *the rest of* the blood at the base of the altar.
10 The fat and the kidneys and the [1]lobe of the liver of the sin
offering, he then offered up in smoke on the altar just as the LORD
had commanded Moses.
11 [a]The flesh and the skin, however, he burned with fire outside the
camp.
12 Then he slaughtered the burnt offering; and Aaron's sons
handed the blood to him and he sprinkled it around on the altar.
13 And they handed the burnt offering to him in [1]pieces with the
head, and he offered *them* up in smoke on the altar.
14 He also washed the entrails and the legs, and offered *them* up in
smoke with the burnt offering on the altar.
15 Then he presented the people's offering, and took the [a]goat of
the sin offering which was for the people, and slaughtered it and
offered it for sin, like the first.
16 He also presented the burnt offering, and [1]offered it according to
[a]the ordinance.
17 Next he presented [a]the grain offering, and filled his [1]hand with
some of it and offered *it* up in smoke on the altar, [b]besides the burnt
offering of the morning.
18 Then [a]he slaughtered the ox and the ram, the sacrifice of peace
offerings which was for the people; and Aaron's sons handed the
blood to him and he sprinkled it around on the altar.
19 As for the portions of fat from the ox and from the ram, the fat
tail, and the *fat* [a]covering, and the kidneys and the [1]lobe of the liver,

9:1 [a]Ezek. 43:27
2 [a]Ezek. 29:1; L
4 [a]Ex. 29:43
6 [a]Ex. 24:16; Le
7 [1]Lit., *make* [2]L [a]Heb. 5:3; 7:27
8 [a]Lev. 4:1-12
9 [a]Lev. 9:12, 18 4:7
10 [1]Or, *appenda*
11 [a]Lev. 4:11, 12
13 [1]Lit., *its piece*
15 [a]Lev. 4:27-31
16 [1]Lit., *made* [a] 1:1-13
17 [1]Lit., *palm* [a] 2:1-3 [b]Lev. 3:5
18 [a]Lev. 3:1-11
19 [1]Or, *appenda* [a]Lev. 3:9

20 they now placed the portions of fat on the breasts; and he offered
[1]them up in smoke on the altar.
21 But [a]the breasts and the right thigh Aaron [1]presented as a wave
offering before the LORD, just as Moses had commanded.
22 Then Aaron lifted up his hands toward the people and [a]blessed
them, and he stepped down after making the sin offering and the
burnt offering and the peace offerings.
23 And Moses and Aaron went into the tent of meeting. When they
came out and blessed the people, [a]the glory of the LORD appeared to
all the people.
24 [a]Then fire came out from before the LORD and consumed the
burnt offering and the portions of fat on the altar; and when all the
people saw *it*, they shouted and fell on their faces.

Chapter 10

10 Now [a]Nadab and Abihu, the sons of Aaron, took their respective [b]firepans, and after putting fire in them, placed incense
on it and offered strange fire before the LORD, which He had not
commanded them.
2 [a]And fire came out from the presence of the LORD and consumed
them, and they died before the LORD.
3 Then Moses said to Aaron, "It is what the LORD spoke, saying,
'By those who [a]come near Me I [1b]will be treated as holy,
And before all the people I will [c]be honored.' "
So Aaron, therefore, kept silent.
4 Moses called also to [a]Mishael and Elzaphan, the sons of Aaron's
uncle Uzziel, and said to them, "Come forward, carry your [1]relatives
away from the front of the sanctuary to the outside of the camp."
5 So they came forward and carried them still in their [a]tunics to the
outside of the camp, as Moses had said.
6 Then Moses said to Aaron and to his sons Eleazar and Ithamar,
"[a]Do not [1]uncover your heads nor tear your clothes, so that you may
not die, and that He may not [b]become wrathful against all the congregation. But your [2]kinsmen, the whole house of Israel, shall bewail
the burning which the LORD has [3]brought about.
7 "You shall not even go out from the doorway of the tent of meeting, lest you die; for [a]the LORD's anointing oil is upon you." So they
did according to the word of Moses.
8 The LORD then spoke to Aaron, saying,
9 "[a]Do not drink wine or strong drink, neither you nor your sons
with you, when you come into the tent of meeting, so that you may
not die—it is a perpetual statute throughout your generations—
10 and [a]so as to make a distinction between the holy and the
profane, and between the unclean and the clean,
11 and [a]so as to teach the sons of Israel all the statutes which the
LORD has spoken to them through Moses."
12 Then Moses spoke to Aaron, and to his surviving sons, [a]Eleazar
and Ithamar, "[b]Take the grain offering that is left over from the
LORD's offerings by fire and eat it unleavened beside the altar, for it is
most holy.
13 "You shall eat it, moreover, in a holy place, because it is your due
and your sons' due out of the LORD's offerings by fire; for thus I have
been commanded.
14 "[a]The breast of the wave offering, however, and the thigh of the

...e portions of fat
..., waved [a]Ex. ... Lev. 7:30-34
...um. 6:22-26; ...5; Luke 24:50
...ev. 9:6; Num. 16:19
...in. 18:38, 39; 2 Chr. 7:1
...24:1, 9; Num. ...1 [b]Lev. 16:12
...m. 3:4; 16:35; 26:61
...ll show Myself ...Ex. 19:22; Lev. ...x. 30:30; Ezek. ...x. 14:4, 17; Is. ...3; Ezek. 28:22
..., brothers [a]Ex. 6:22
...29:5; Lev. 8:13
...it., unbind [2]Lit., ...rs [3]Lit., burned ...v. 21:1-5, 10-12 ...1:53; 16:22, 46; ...osh. 7:1; 22:18, ...20; 2 Sam. 24:1
...8:41; Lev. 21:12
...v. 20:1; 31:5; Is. ...zek. 44:21; Hos. ...Luke 1:15; Eph. ...1 Tim. 3:3; Titus 1:7
...ev. 11:47; 20:25; Ezek. 22:26
[a]Deut. 17:10, 11; 33:10
...x. 6:23; Num. 3:2 [b]Lev. 6:14-18
...ev. 7:30-34; Num. 18:11

offering you may eat in a clean place, you and your sons and your
daughters with you; for they have been given as your due and your
sons' due out of the sacrifices of the peace offerings of the sons of
Israel.
15 "[a]The thigh offered by lifting up and the breast offered by waving,
they shall bring along with the offerings by fire of the portions of fat,
to present as a wave offering before the LORD; so it shall be a thing
perpetually due you and your sons with you, just as the LORD has
commanded."
16 But Moses searched carefully for the [a]goat of the sin offering, and
behold, it had been burned up! So he was angry with Aaron's sur-
viving sons Eleazar and Ithamar, saying,
17 "Why [a]did you not eat the sin offering at the holy place? For it is
most holy, and [1]He gave it to you to bear away [b]the guilt of the
congregation, to make atonement for them before the LORD.
18 "Behold, [a]since its blood had not been brought inside, into the
sanctuary, you should certainly have [b]eaten it in the sanctuary, just
as I commanded."
19 But Aaron spoke to Moses, "Behold, this very day they
[a]presented their sin offering and their burnt offering before the LORD.
When things like these happened to me, if I had eaten a sin offering
today, would it have been good in the sight of the LORD?"
20 And when Moses heard *that*, it seemed good in his sight.

Chapter 11

11 The LORD spoke again to Moses and to Aaron, saying to them,
2 "Speak to the sons of Israel, saying, '[a]These are the creatures
which you may eat from all the animals that are on the earth.
3 'Whatever divides a hoof, thus making split hoofs, *and* chews the
cud, among the animals, that you may eat.
4 'Nevertheless, [a]you are not to eat of these, among those which
chew the cud, or among those which divide the hoof: the camel, for
though it chews cud, it does not divide the hoof, it is unclean to you.
5 'Likewise, the rock badger, for though it chews cud, it does not
divide the hoof, it is unclean to you;
6 the [1]rabbit also, for though it chews cud, it does not divide the
hoof, it is unclean to you;
7 and the pig, for though it divides the hoof, thus making a split
hoof, it does not chew cud, it is unclean to you.
8 'You shall not eat of their flesh nor touch their carcasses; they are
unclean to you.
9 '[a]These you may eat, whatever is in the water: all that have fins
and scales, those in the water, in the seas or in the rivers, you may
eat.
10 '[a]But whatever is in the seas and in the rivers, that do not have
fins and scales among all the teeming life of the water, and among all
the living creatures that are in the water, they are detestable things to
you,
11 and they shall be [1]abhorrent to you; you may not eat of their
flesh, and their carcasses you shall detest.
12 'Whatever in the water does not have fins and scales is [1]abhor-
rent to you.
13 'These, moreover, [a]you shall detest among the birds; they are

15 [a]Lev. 7:3
16 [a]Lev. 9:3
17 [1]Or, *was* 6:24-30 [b]Ex. Lev. 22:16; N
18 [a]Lev. 6:30
19 [a]Lev. 9:8,
11:2 [a]Deut. 14
4 [a]Acts 10:14
6 [1]Or, *hare*
9 [a]Deut. 14:9
10 [a]Deut. 14:10
11 [1]Lit., *detesta things*
12 [1]Lit., *detestal things*
13 [a]Deut. 14:12-

[1]abhorrent, not to be eaten: the [2]eagle and the vulture and the
[3]buzzard,
14 and the kite and the falcon in its kind,
15 every raven in its kind,
16 and the ostrich and the owl and the sea gull and the hawk in its
kind,
17 and the little owl and the cormorant and the [1]great owl,
18 and the white owl and the [1]pelican and the carrion vulture,
19 and the stork, the heron in its kinds, and the hoopoe, and the bat.
20 'All the [1]winged insects that walk on *all* fours are detestable to
you.
21 'Yet these you may eat among all the [1]winged insects which walk
on *all* fours: those which have above their feet jointed legs with
which to jump on the earth.
22 'These of them you may eat: the locust in its kinds, and the
devastating locust in its kinds, and the cricket in its kinds, and the
grasshopper in its kinds.
23 'But all other [1]winged insects which are four-footed are detest-
able to you.
24 'By these, moreover, you will be made unclean: whoever touches
their carcasses becomes unclean until evening,
25 and [a]whoever picks up any of their carcasses shall wash his
clothes and be unclean until evening.
26 'Concerning all the animals which divide the hoof, but do not
make a split *hoof*, or which do not chew cud, they are unclean to you:
whoever touches them becomes unclean.
27 'Also whatever walks on its paws, among all the creatures that
walk on *all* fours, are unclean to you; whoever touches their carcas-
ses becomes unclean until evening,
28 and the one who picks up their carcasses shall wash his clothes
and be unclean until evening; they are unclean to you.
29 'Now these are to you the unclean among the swarming things
which swarm on the earth: the mole, and the mouse, and the [1]great
lizard in its kinds,
30 and the gecko, and the [1]crocodile, and the lizard, and the [2]sand
reptile, and the chameleon.
31 'These are to you the unclean among all the swarming things;
whoever touches them when they are dead becomes unclean until
evening.
32 'Also anything on which one of them may fall when they are
dead, becomes unclean, including any wooden article, or clothing, or
a skin, or a sack—any article [1]of which use is made—[a]it shall be put
in the water and be unclean until evening, then it becomes clean.
33 'As for any [a]earthenware vessel into which one of them may fall,
whatever is in it becomes unclean and you shall break [1]the vessel.
34 'Any of the [1]food which may be eaten, on which water comes,
shall become unclean; and any [1]liquid which may be drunk in every
vessel shall become unclean.
35 'Everything, moreover, on which part of their carcass may fall
becomes unclean; an oven or a [1]stove shall be smashed; they are
unclean and shall continue as unclean to you.
36 'Nevertheless a spring or a cistern [1]collecting water shall be
clean, though the one who touches their carcass shall be unclean.

, a detestable
r, vulture [3]Or, black vulture
cifically, great horned owl
owl or jackdaw
[1]Lit., swarming ngs with wings
[1]V. 20, note 1
[1]V. 20, note 1
25 [a]Lev. 11:40
[1]Or, thorn-tailed lizard
lizard [2]Species as yet undefined
[1]Lit., with which rk is done [a]Lev. 15:12
it., it [a]Lev. 6:28; 15:12
., if touched by a ass; cf. vv. 29-32
5 [1]Lit., hearth for porting (two) pots
, of a gathering of

37 'And if a part of their carcass falls on any seed for sowing which
is to be sown, it is clean.
38 'Though if water is put on the seed, and a part of their carcass
falls on it, it is unclean to you.
39 'Also if one of the animals dies which you have for food, the one
who touches its carcass becomes unclean until evening.
40 '[a]He too, who eats some of its carcass shall wash his clothes and
be unclean until evening; and the one who picks up its carcass shall
wash his clothes and be unclean until evening.
41 '[a]Now every swarming thing that swarms on the earth is detest-
able, not to be eaten.
42 'Whatever crawls on its belly, and whatever walks on *all* fours,
whatever has many feet, in respect to every swarming thing that
swarms on the earth, you shall not eat them, for they are detestable.
43 '[a]Do not render [1]yourselves detestable through any of the swarm-
ing things that swarm; and you shall not make yourselves unclean
with them so that you become unclean.
44 'For [a]I am the LORD your God. Consecrate yourselves therefore,
and [b]be holy; for I am holy. And you shall not make yourselves
unclean with any of the swarming things that swarm on the earth.
45 '[a]For I am the LORD, who brought you up from the land of Egypt,
to be your God; thus [b]you shall be holy for I am holy.' "
46 This is the law regarding the animal, and the bird, and every
living thing that moves in the waters, and everything that swarms
on the earth,
47 [a]to make a distinction between the unclean and the clean, and
between the edible creature and the creature which is not to be eaten.

Chapter 12

12 Then the LORD spoke to Moses, saying,
2 "Speak to the sons of Israel, saying, 'When a woman [1]gives
birth and bears a male *child*, then she shall be unclean for seven
days, [a]as in the days of [2]her menstruation she shall be unclean.
3 'And on [a]the eighth day the flesh of his foreskin shall be circum-
cised.
4 'Then she shall remain in the blood of *her* purification for thirty-
three days; she shall not touch any consecrated thing, nor enter the
sanctuary, until the days of her purification are completed.
5 'But if she bears a female *child*, then she shall be unclean for two
weeks, as in her [1]menstruation; and she shall remain in the blood of
her purification for sixty-six days.
6 'And [a]when the days of her purification are completed, for a son
or for a daughter, she shall bring to the priest at the doorway of the
tent of meeting, a one year old lamb for a burnt offering, and a
young pigeon or a turtledove [b]for a sin offering.
7 'Then he shall offer it before the LORD and make atonement for
her; and she shall be cleansed from the [1]flow of her blood. This is the
law for her who bears *a child, whether* a male or a female.
8 'But if [1]she cannot afford a lamb, then she shall take [a]two turtle-
doves or two young pigeons, [b]the one for a burnt offering and the
other for a sin offering; and the [c]priest shall make atonement for her,
and she shall be clean.' "

40 [a]Lev. 17:1[illegible] Deut. 14:21; [illegible]

41 [a]Lev. 11:2[illegible]

43 [1]Lit., *your* [a]Lev. 20:25

44 [a]Ex. 6:7; 1[illegible] 23:25; Is. 43:3 [b]Lev. 19:2; 1 P[illegible]

45 [a]Ex. 6:7; 2[illegible] 22:33; 25:38; 2[illegible] [b]Lev. 19:2; 1 P[illegible]

47 [a]Lev. 10:10[illegible] 22:26; 44:23

12:2 [1]Lit., *prod[illegible] seed* [2]Lit., *the [illegible] of her sickness* 15:19; 18:19

3 [a]Gen. 17:12; [illegible] 1:59; 2:21

5 [1]Lit., *impurity*

6 [a]Luke 2:22 [b]L[illegible]

7 [1]Lit., *fountain*

8 [1]Lit., *her hand [illegible] not find a sufficien[illegible] a lamb* [a]Luke 2:2[illegible] [b]Lev. 5:7 [c]Lev. 4:[illegible]

[1]Lit., *flesh* [2]Lit., *a* …rk, *stroke*, and so …hroughout the ch. [a]Deut. 24:8

Chapter 13

13 Then the LORD spoke to Moses and to Aaron, saying,
2 "When a man has on the skin of his [1]body a swelling or a
scab or a bright spot, and it becomes [2]an infection of leprosy on the
skin of his [1]body, [a]then he shall be brought to Aaron the priest, or to
one of his sons the priests.

3 [1]Lit., *flesh*

3 "And the priest shall look at the mark on the skin of the [1]body,
and if the hair in the infection has turned white and the infection
appears to be deeper than the skin of his [1]body, it is an infection of
leprosy; when the priest has looked at him, he shall pronounce him
unclean.

…it., *flesh* [2]Lit., *the* …arance of it is not …per [3]Lit., *shut up*

4 "But if the bright spot is white on the skin of his [1]body, and [2]it
does not appear to be deeper than the skin, and the hair on it has not
turned white, then the priest shall [3]isolate *him who has* the infection
for seven days.

…, *has stood* [2]Lit., *shut up*

5 "And the priest shall look at him on the seventh day, and if in his
eyes the infection [1]has not changed, *and* the infection has not spread
on the skin, then the priest shall [2]isolate him for seven more days.
6 "And the priest shall look at him again on the seventh day; and if
the infection has faded, and the mark has not spread on the skin,
then the priest shall pronounce him clean; it is *only* a scab. And he
shall [a]wash his clothes and be clean.

[a]Lev. 11:25; 14:8

7 "But if the scab spreads farther on the skin, after he has shown
himself to the priest for his cleansing, he shall appear again to the
priest.
8 "And the priest shall look, and if the scab has spread on the skin,
then the priest shall pronounce him unclean; it is leprosy.

…um. 12:10; 2 Kin. …; 2 Chr. 26:19, 20

9 "When the infection of leprosy is on a man, then he shall be
brought to the priest.
10 "The priest shall then look, and if there is a [a]white swelling in the
skin, and it has turned the hair white, and there is quick raw flesh in
the swelling,
11 it is [1]a chronic leprosy on the skin of his [2]body, and the priest
shall pronounce him unclean; he shall not [3]isolate him, for he is
unclean.

[1]Lit., *an old* [2]Lit., …esh [3]Lit., *shut up*

12 "And if the leprosy breaks out farther on the skin, and the leprosy
covers all the skin of *him who has* the infection from his head even to
his feet, [1]as far as the priest can see,
13 then the priest shall look, and behold, *if* the leprosy has covered
all his [1]body, he shall pronounce clean *him who has* the infection; it
has all turned white *and* he is clean.
14 "But whenever raw flesh appears on him, he shall be unclean.
15 "And the priest shall look at the raw flesh, and he shall
pronounce him unclean; the raw flesh is unclean, it is leprosy.

…it., *with regard to* …*whole sight of the priest's eyes*

13 [1]Lit., *flesh*

16 "Or if the raw flesh turns again and is changed to white, then he
shall [a]come to the priest,
17 and the priest shall look at him, and behold, *if* the infection has
turned to white, then the priest shall pronounce clean *him who has*
the infection; he is clean.

6 [a]Luke 5:12-14

18 "And when the [1]body has a boil on its skin, and it is healed,
19 and in the place of the boil there is a white swelling or a reddish-
white, bright spot, then it shall be shown to the priest;
20 and the priest shall look, and behold, *if* [1]it appears to be lower
than the skin, and the hair on it has turned white, then the priest

18 [1]Lit., *flesh*

…, *the appearance of it is lower*

shall pronounce him unclean; it is the infection of leprosy, it has 21 [1]Lit., *shut up*
broken out in the boil.
21 "But if the priest looks at it, and behold, there are no white hairs
in it and it is not lower than the skin and is faded, then the priest
shall [1]isolate him for seven days;
22 and if it spreads farther on the skin, then the priest shall
pronounce him unclean; it is an infection.
23 "But if the bright spot remains in its place, and does not spread, it 24 [1]Lit., *flesh*
is *only* the scar of the boil; and the priest shall pronounce him clean.
24 "Or if the [1]body sustains in its skin a burn by fire, and the raw
flesh of the burn becomes a bright spot, reddish-white, or white,
25 then the priest shall look at it. And if the hair in the bright spot
has [a]turned white, and it appears to be deeper than the skin, it is
leprosy; it has broken out in the burn. Therefore, the priest shall
pronounce him unclean; it is an infection of leprosy. 25 [a]Ex. 4:6; Nu
26 "But if the priest looks at it, and indeed, there is no white hair in 12:10; 2 Kin. 5:2
the bright spot, and it is no [1]deeper than the skin, but is dim, then
the priest shall [2]isolate him for seven days;
27 and the priest shall look at him on the seventh day. If it spreads
farther in the skin, then the priest shall pronounce him unclean; it is
an infection of leprosy.
28 "But if the bright spot remains in its place, and has not spread in
the skin, but is dim, it is the swelling from the burn; and the priest 26 [1]Lit., *lower* [2]
shall pronounce him clean, for it is *only* the scar of the burn. *shut up*
29 "Now if a man or woman has an infection on the head or on the
beard,
30 then the priest shall look at the infection, and if it appears to be
deeper than the skin, and there is thin yellowish hair in it, then the
priest shall pronounce him unclean; it is a scale, it is leprosy of the
head or of the beard.
31 "But if the priest looks at the infection of the scale, and indeed, it 31 [1]Lit., *shut up*
appears to be no deeper than the skin, and there is no black hair in it,
then the priest shall [1]isolate *the person* with the scaly infection for
seven days.
32 "And on the seventh day the priest shall look at the infection, and
if the scale has not spread, and no yellowish hair has [1]grown in it,
and the appearance of the scale is no deeper than the skin,
33 then he shall shave himself, but he shall not shave the scale; and 32 [1]Lit., *been*
the priest shall [1]isolate *the person* with the scale seven more days.
34 "Then on the seventh day the priest shall look at the scale, and if
the scale has not spread in the skin, and it appears to be no deeper
than the skin, the priest shall pronounce him clean; and he shall
wash his clothes and be clean.
35 "But if the scale spreads farther in the skin after his cleansing,
36 then the priest shall look at him, and if the scale has spread in
the skin, the priest need not seek for the yellowish hair; he is un- 33 [1]Lit., *shut up*
clean.
37 "If in his sight the scale has remained, however, and black hair
has grown in it, the scale has healed, he is clean; and the priest shall
pronounce him clean.
38 "And when a man or a woman has bright spots on the skin of the
[1]body, *even* white bright spots,
39 then the priest shall look, and if the bright spots on the skin of 38 [1]Lit., *flesh*

their [1]bodies are a faint white, it is [2]eczema that has broken out on
the skin; he is clean.
40 "Now if a [1]man loses the hair of his head, he is [a]bald; he is clean.
41 "And if his head becomes bald at the [1]front and sides, he is bald
on the forehead; he is clean.
42 "But if on the bald head or the bald forehead, there occurs a
reddish-white infection, it is leprosy breaking out on his bald head
or on his bald forehead.
43 "Then [a]the priest shall look at him; and if the swelling of the
infection is reddish-white on his bald head or on his bald forehead,
like the appearance of leprosy in the skin of the [1]body,
44 he is a leprous man, he is unclean. The priest shall surely pro-
nounce him unclean; his infection is on his head.
45 "As for the leper who has the infection, his clothes shall be torn,
and [a]the hair of his head shall be [1]uncovered, and he shall [b]cover his
mustache and cry, '[c]Unclean! Unclean!'
46 "He shall remain unclean all the days during which he has the
infection; he is unclean. He shall live alone; his dwelling shall be
[a]outside the camp.
47 "When a garment has a [1]mark of leprosy in it, whether it is a wool
garment or a linen garment,
48 whether in [1]warp or woof, of linen or of wool, whether in leather
or in any article made of leather,
49 if the mark is greenish or reddish in the garment or in the
leather, or in the [1]warp or in the woof, or in any article of leather, it is
a leprous mark and shall be shown to the priest.
50 "Then [a]the priest shall look at the mark, and shall [1]quarantine the
article with the mark for seven days.
51 "He shall then look at the mark on the seventh day; if the mark
has spread in the garment, whether in the warp or in the woof, or in
the leather, whatever the purpose for which the leather is used, the
mark is a [1]leprous malignancy, it is unclean.
52 "So he shall burn the garment, whether the warp or the woof, in
wool or in linen, or any article of leather in which the mark occurs,
for it is a [1]leprous malignancy; it shall be burned in the fire.
53 "But if the priest shall look, and indeed, the mark has not spread
in the garment, either in the warp or in the woof, or in any article of
leather,
54 then the priest shall order them to wash the thing in which the
mark occurs, and he shall [1]quarantine it for seven more days.
55 "After the article with the mark has been washed, the priest shall
again look, and if the mark has not changed its appearance, even
though the mark has not spread, it is unclean; you shall burn it in the
fire, whether an eating away has produced bareness on the top or on
the front of it.
56 "Then if the priest shall look, and if the mark has faded after it
has been washed, then he shall tear it out of the garment or out of
the leather, whether from the warp or from the woof;
57 and if it appears again in the garment, whether in the warp or in
the woof, or in any article of leather, it is an outbreak; the article with
the mark shall be burned in the fire.
58 "And the garment, whether the warp or the woof, or any article of
leather from which the mark has departed when you washed it, it
shall then be washed a second time and shall be clean."

h [2]Lit., tetter

, man's head bald [a]2 Kin. 2; Amos 8:10

border of his face

t., flesh [a]Lev. ; Ezek. 22:26

Or, disheveled . 10:6 [b]Ezek. 7, 22; Mic. 3:7 [c]Lam. 4:15

n. 5:1-4; 12:14

, infection, and oughout the ch.

[1]Or, weaving or texture

[1]Or, weaving or texture

, shut up [a]Ezek. 44:23

[1]Lit., malignant leprosy

2 [1]Lit., malignant leprosy

54 [1]Lit., shut up

59 This is the law for the mark of leprosy in a garment of wool or
linen, whether in the warp or in the woof, or in any article of leather,
for pronouncing it clean or unclean.

Chapter 14

14 Then the LORD spoke to Moses, saying,
2 "This shall be the law of the leper in the day of his cleans-
ing. [a]Now he shall be brought to the priest,
3 and the priest shall go [a]out to the outside of the camp. Thus the
priest shall look, and if the [1]infection of leprosy has been healed in
the leper,
4 then the priest shall give orders to take two live clean birds and
[a]cedar wood and a [1]scarlet string and hyssop for the one who is to be
cleansed.
5 "The priest shall also give orders to slay the one bird in an earth-
enware vessel over [1]running water.
6 "*As for* the live bird, he shall take it, together with [a]the cedar
wood and the [1]scarlet string and the [b]hyssop, and shall dip them and
the live bird in the blood of the bird that was slain over the [2]running
water.
7 "[a]He shall then sprinkle seven times the one who is to be cleansed
from the leprosy, and shall pronounce him clean, and shall let the
live bird go free over the open field.
8 "[a]The one to be cleansed shall then wash his clothes and shave off
all his hair, and bathe in water and [b]be clean. Now afterward, he
may enter the camp, but he [c]shall stay outside his tent for seven
days.
9 "And it will be on the seventh day that he shall shave off all his
hair: he shall shave his head and his beard and his eyebrows, even
all his hair. He shall then wash his clothes and bathe his [1]body in
water and [a]be clean.
10 "Now on the eighth day he is to take two male lambs without
defect, and a yearling ewe lamb without defect, and three-tenths *of
an* [1]*ephah* of fine flour mixed with oil for a grain offering, and one
[2a]log of oil;
11 and the priest who pronounces him clean shall present the man
to be cleansed and the [1]aforesaid before the LORD at the doorway of
the tent of meeting.
12 "Then the priest shall take the one male lamb and bring it for a
[a]guilt offering, with the [1b]log of oil, and present them as a [c]wave
offering before the LORD.
13 "Next he shall slaughter the male lamb in [a]the place where they
slaughter the sin offering and the burnt offering, at the place of the
sanctuary—for the guilt offering, [b]like the sin offering, belongs to the
priest; it is most holy.
14 "The priest shall then take some of the blood of the [a]guilt offering,
and the priest shall put *it* on [b]the lobe of the right ear of the one to be
cleansed, and on the thumb of his right hand, and on the big toe of
his right foot.
15 "The priest shall also take some of the [1a]log of oil, and pour *it* into
his left palm;
16 the priest shall then dip his right-hand finger into the oil that is
in his left palm, and with his finger sprinkle some of the oil seven
times before the LORD.

14:2 [a]Matt. 1:44; Luke 5

3 [1]Lit., *mark* and so throu ch. [a]Lev. 13

4 [1]Lit., *scarle and* [a]Lev. 14 52; Num. 19:

5 [1]Lit., *living*

6 [1]Lit., *scarle and* [2]Lit., *livin* 14:4 [b]Ps. 51:

7 [a]Ezek. 36:2

8 [a]Lev. 11:25; Num. 8:7 [b]Lev 20 [c]Num. 5:2, 15; 2 Chr. 26:2

9 [1]Lit., *flesh* [a]L 14:8, 20

10 [1]I.e., Approx bu. [2]I.e., Appro pt. [a]Lev. 14:12, 21, 24

11 [1]Lit., *them*

12 [1]I.e., Approx pt. [a]Lev. 5:6, 18 14:19 [b]Lev. 14: 29:22-24, 26

13 [a]Ex. 29:11; Le 1:11; 4:24 [b]Lev. 6:24-30; 7:7

14 [a]Lev. 14:19 [b] 29:20; Lev. 8:23,

15 [1]I.e., Approx. pt. [a]Lev. 14:10

17 "And of the remaining oil which is in his palm, the priest shall
put some on the right ear lobe of the one to be cleansed, and on the
thumb of his right hand, and on the big toe of his right foot, on the
blood of the guilt offering;
18 while the rest of the oil that is in the priest's palm, he shall put
on the head of the one to be cleansed. So the priest shall make
[a]atonement on his behalf before the LORD.
19 "The priest shall next offer the [a]sin offering and make atonement
for the one to be cleansed from his uncleanness. Then afterward, he
shall slaughter the burnt offering.
20 "And the priest shall offer up the burnt offering and the grain
offering on the altar. Thus the priest shall make atonement for him,
and [a]he shall be clean.
21 "[a]But if he is poor, and his [1]means are insufficient, then he is to
take one male lamb for a [b]guilt offering as a wave offering to make
atonement for him, and one-tenth *of an* [2]*ephah* of fine flour mixed
with oil for a grain offering, and a [3c]log of oil,
22 and two turtledoves or two young pigeons which [1]are within his
means, [a]the one shall be a [b]sin offering and the other a burnt offering.
23 "[a]Then the eighth day he shall bring them for his cleansing to the
priest, at the doorway of the tent of meeting, before the LORD.
24 "And the priest shall take the lamb of the guilt offering, and [a]the
[1]log of oil, and the priest shall offer them for a wave offering before
the LORD.
25 "Next he shall slaughter the lamb of the guilt offering; and the
priest is to take some of the blood of the guilt offering and put *it* on
[a]the lobe of the right ear of the one to be cleansed and on the thumb
of his right hand, and on the big toe of his right foot.
26 "The priest shall also pour some of the oil into his left palm;
27 and with his right-hand finger the priest shall sprinkle some of
the oil that is in his left palm seven times before the LORD.
28 "The priest shall then put some of the oil that is in his palm on the
lobe of the right ear of the one to be cleansed, and on the thumb of
his right hand, and on the big toe of his right foot, on the place of the
blood of the guilt offering.
29 "Moreover, the rest of the oil that is in the priest's palm he shall
put on the head of the one to be cleansed, to make atonement on his
behalf before the LORD.
30 "He shall then offer one of the turtledoves or young pigeons,
[1]which are within his means.
31 "*He shall offer* what [1]he can afford, [a]the one for a sin offering, and
the other for a burnt offering, together with the grain offering. So the
priest shall make atonement before the LORD on behalf of the one to
be cleansed.
32 "This is the law *for him* in whom there is an infection of leprosy,
whose [1]means are limited for his cleansing."
33 The LORD further spoke to Moses and to Aaron, saying,
34 "[a]When you enter the land of Canaan, which I give you for a
possession, and I put a mark of leprosy on a house in the land of
your possession,
35 then the one who owns the house shall come and tell the priest,
saying, '*Something* like [a]a mark *of leprosy* has become visible to me in
the house.'
36 "The priest shall then order that they empty the house before the

v. 4:26; Num. 28; Heb. 2:17
9 [a]Lev. 14:12
[a]Lev. 14:8, 9
it., *hand is not* [2]I.e., Approx. [3]I.e., Approx. .ev. 5:11; 12:8; ev. 14:22 [c]Lev. 14:10
[1]Lit., *his hand* [a]Lev. 5:7 [b]Lev. 14:21, 24, 25
[a]Lev. 14:10, 11
.e., Approx. one pt. [a]Lev. 14:10
25 [a]Lev. 14:14
[1]Lit., *from those* ich *his hand can reach*
Lit., *his hand can reach* [a]Lev. 5:7
it., *hand does not reach*
[a]Gen. 17:8; Num. 2; Deut. 7:1; 32:49
35 [a]Ps. 91:10

priest goes in to look at the mark, so that everything in the house
need not become unclean; and afterward the priest shall go in to
look at the house.
37 "So he shall look at the mark, and if the mark on the walls of the
house has greenish or reddish depressions, and appears deeper than
the [1]surface;
38 then the priest shall come out of the house, to the [1]doorway, and
[2]quarantine the house for seven days.
39 "And the priest shall return on the seventh day and [1]make an
inspection. If the mark has indeed spread in the walls of the house,
40 then the priest shall order them to tear out the stones with the
mark in them and throw them away [1]at an unclean place outside the
city.
41 "And he shall have the house scraped all around [1]inside, and they
shall dump the plaster that they scrape off at an unclean place out-
side the city.
42 "Then they shall take other stones and replace *those* stones; and he
shall take other plaster and replaster the house.
43 "If, however, the mark breaks out again in the house, after he has
torn out the stones and scraped the house, and after it has been
replastered,
44 then the priest shall come in and [1]make an inspection. If he sees
that the mark has indeed spread in the house, it is [a]a malignant mark
in the house; it is unclean.
45 "He shall therefore tear down the house, its stones, and its tim-
bers, and all the plaster of the house, and he shall take *them* outside
the city to an [a]unclean place.
46 "Moreover, whoever goes into the house during the time that he
has [1]quarantined it, becomes [a]unclean until evening.
47 "Likewise, whoever lies down in the house shall wash his clothes,
and whoever eats in the house shall wash his clothes.
48 "If, on the other hand, the priest comes in and [1]makes an inspec-
tion, and the mark has not indeed spread in the house after the
house has been replastered, then the priest shall pronounce the
house clean because the mark has [2]not reappeared.
49 "To cleanse the house then, he shall take [a]two birds and cedar
wood and a [1]scarlet string and hyssop,
50 and he shall slaughter the one bird in an earthenware vessel over
[1]running water.
51 "Then he shall take the cedar wood and the [a]hyssop and the [1]scar-
let string, with the live bird, and dip them in the blood of the slain
bird, as well as in the [2]running water, and sprinkle the house seven
times.
52 "He shall thus cleanse the house with the blood of the bird and
with the [1]running water, along with the live bird and with the cedar
wood and with the hyssop and with the [2]scarlet string.
53 "However, he shall let the live bird go free outside the city into
the open field. So he shall make atonement for the house, and it shall
be clean."
54 This is the law for any mark of leprosy—even for a [a]scale,
55 and for the [a]leprous garment or house,
56 and [a]for a swelling, and for a scab, and for a bright spot—
57 to teach [1]when they are unclean, and [2]when they are clean. This
is the law of leprosy.

37 [1]Lit., *wall*
38 [1]Lit., *doo* *house* [2]Lit., *s*
39 [1]Lit., *look*
40 [1]Lit., *to*
41 [1]Lit., *from* *around*
44 [1]Lit., *look* 13:51
45 [a]Lev. 14:41
46 [1]Lit., *shut u* 19:7, 10, 21, 22
48 [1]Lit., *looks* *healed*
49 [1]Lit., *scarlet* [a]Lev. 14:4
50 [1]Lit., *living*
51 [1]Lit., *scarlet* [2]Lit., *living* [a]1 Kir Ps. 51:7
52 [1]Lit., *living* [2]L *scarlet color*
54 [a]Lev. 13:30
55 [a]Lev. 13:47-52
56 [a]Lev. 13:2
57 [1]Lit., *in the day* *uncleanness* [2]Lit., *the day of cleanne*

Chapter 15

15 The LORD also spoke to Moses and to Aaron, saying,
2 "Speak to the sons of Israel, and say to them, '[a]When any
man has a discharge from his [1]body, [2]his discharge is unclean.
3 'This, moreover, shall be his uncleanness in his discharge: it is his
uncleanness whether his body allows its discharge to flow, or
whether his body obstructs its discharge.
4 'Every bed on which the person with the discharge lies becomes
unclean, and everything on which he sits becomes unclean.
5 'Anyone, moreover, who touches his bed shall wash his clothes
and bathe in water and be unclean until evening;
6 and whoever sits on the thing on which the man with the dis-
charge has been sitting, shall wash his clothes and bathe in water
and be unclean until evening.
7 'Also whoever touches the [1]person with the discharge shall wash
his clothes and bathe in water and be unclean until evening.
8 'Or if the man with the discharge spits on one who is clean, he
too shall wash his clothes and bathe in water and be unclean until
evening.
9 'And every saddle on which the person with the discharge rides
becomes unclean.
10 'Whoever then touches any of the things which were under him
shall be unclean until evening, and he who carries them shall wash
his clothes and bathe in water and be unclean until evening.
11 'Likewise, whomever the one with the discharge touches without
having rinsed his hands in water shall wash his clothes and bathe in
water and be unclean until evening.
12 'However, an [a]earthenware vessel which the person with the dis-
charge touches shall be broken, and every wooden vessel shall be
rinsed in water.
13 'Now when the man with the discharge becomes cleansed from
his discharge, then he [a]shall count off for himself seven days for his
cleansing; he shall then wash his clothes and bathe his body in [1]run-
ning water and shall become clean.
14 'Then on the eighth day he shall take for himself [a]two turtledoves
or two young pigeons, and come before the LORD to the doorway of
the tent of meeting, and give them to the priest;
15 and the priest shall offer them, [a]one for a sin offering, and the
other for a burnt offering. So [b]the priest shall make atonement on his
behalf before the LORD because of his discharge.
16 '[a]Now if a [1]man has a seminal emission, he shall bathe all his
body in water and be unclean until evening.
17 'As for any garment or any leather on which there is seminal
emission, it shall be washed with water and be unclean until eve-
ning.
18 'If a man lies with a woman *so that* there is a seminal emission,
they shall both bathe in water and be [a]unclean until evening.
19 '[a]When a woman has a discharge, *if* her discharge in her body is
blood, she shall continue in her menstrual impurity for seven days;
and whoever touches her shall be unclean until evening.
20 'Everything also on which she lies during her menstrual im-
purity shall be unclean, and everything on which she sits shall be
unclean.

[1]Lit., *flesh*, and so ...ghout the ch. [2]Or, ...*is discharge, he is* ...*nclean* [a]Lev. 22:4; ...n. 5:2; 2 Sam. 3:29

7 [1]Lit., *flesh*

...2 [a]Lev. 6:28; 11:33

...3 [1]Lit., *living* [a]Lev. 8:33; 14:8

14 [a]Lev. 14:22, 23

...5 [a]Lev. 5:7; 14:31 [b]Lev. 14:19, 31

...Lit., *man's . . . goes* ...*om him* [a]Lev. 22:4; Deut. 23:10, 11

18 [a]1 Sam. 21:4

19 [a]Lev. 12:2

21 'And anyone who touches her bed shall wash his clothes and
bathe in water and be unclean until evening.
22 'And whoever touches any thing on which she sits shall wash his
clothes and bathe in water and be unclean until evening.
23 'Whether it be on the bed or on the thing on which she is sitting,
when he touches it, he shall be unclean until evening.
24 '[a]And if a man actually lies with her, so that her menstrual im-
purity is on him, he shall be unclean seven days, and every bed on
which he lies shall be unclean.
25 "[a]Now if a woman has a discharge of her blood many days, not at
the period of her menstrual impurity, or if she has a discharge
beyond [1]that period, all the days of her impure discharge she shall
continue as though [2]in her menstrual impurity; she is unclean.
26 'Any bed on which she lies all the days of her discharge shall be
to her like [1]her bed at menstruation; and every thing on which she
sits shall be unclean, like [2]her uncleanness at that time.
27 'Likewise, whoever touches them shall be unclean and shall
wash his clothes and bathe in water and be unclean until evening.
28 'When she becomes clean from her discharge, she shall count off
for herself seven days; and afterward she shall be clean.
29 'Then on the eighth day she shall take for herself two turtledoves
or two young pigeons, and bring them in to the priest, to the door-
way of the tent of meeting.
30 'And the priest shall offer the [a]one for a sin offering and the other
for a burnt offering. So the priest shall make atonement on her behalf
before the LORD because of her impure discharge.'
31 "Thus you shall keep the sons of Israel separated from their un-
cleanness, lest they die in their uncleanness by their [a]defiling My
[1]tabernacle that is among them."
32 This is the law for the one with a discharge, and for the man
[1]who has a seminal emission so that he is unclean by it,
33 and for the woman who is ill because of menstrual impurity, and
for the one who has a discharge, whether a male or a female, or a
man who lies with an unclean woman.

Chapter 16

16 Now the LORD spoke to Moses after [a]the death of the two sons
of Aaron, when they had approached the presence of the
LORD and died.
2 And the LORD said to Moses, "Tell your brother Aaron that he
shall not enter [a]at any time into the holy place inside the veil, before
the [1]mercy seat which is on the ark, lest he die; for [b]I will appear in
the cloud over the [1]mercy seat.
3 "Aaron shall enter the holy place with this: with a [1]bull for a [a]sin
offering and a ram for a burnt offering.
4 "He shall put on the [a]holy linen tunic, and the linen undergar-
ments shall be next to his [1]body, and he shall be girded with the
linen sash, and attired with the linen turban (these are holy gar-
ments). Then he shall [b]bathe his [1]body in water and put them on.
5 "And he shall take from the congregation of the sons of Israel
[a]two male goats for a sin offering and one ram for a burnt offering.
6 "Then [a]Aaron shall offer the bull for the sin offering which is for
himself, that he may make atonement for himself and for his
household.

24 [a]Lev. 18:

25 [1]Lit., *her* *impurity* [2]Lit. *days of* [a]Mat Mark 5:25; Lu

26 [1]Lit., *the b* *menstrual im* *the uncleanne* *menstrual imp*

30 [a]Lev. 5:7

31 [1]Or, *dwellir* [a]Lev. 20:3; Nur 20; Ezek. 5:11;

32 [1]Lit., *whose* *emission goes* *him*

16:1 [a]Lev. 10:1

2 [1]Lit., *propitiato* 30:10; Heb. 6:19 25 [b]Ex. 25:21, 2 40:34; 1 Kin. 8:1

3 [1]Or, *bull of the* [a]Lev. 4:1-12; 16:6 9:7

4 [1]Lit., *flesh* [a]Ex. 28:39, 42 [b]Ex. 30 Lev. 16:24; Heb. 1

5 [a]Lev. 4:13-21; 2 29:21; Ezek. 45:22

6 [a]Heb. 5:3

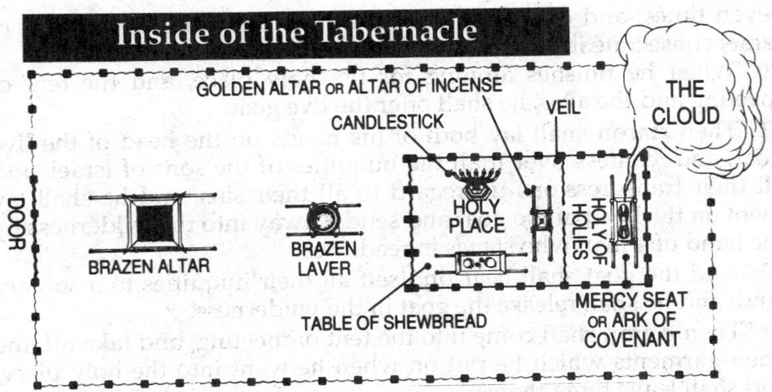

7 "And he shall take the two goats and present them before the
LORD at the doorway of the tent of meeting.
8 "And Aaron shall cast lots for the two goats, one lot for the LORD
and the other lot for the [1]scapegoat.
9 "Then Aaron shall offer the goat on which the lot for the LORD fell,
and make it a sin offering.
10 "But the goat on which the lot for the [1]scapegoat fell, shall be
presented alive before the LORD, to make [a]atonement upon it, to send
it into the wilderness as the [1]scapegoat.
11 "Then Aaron shall offer the bull of the sin offering [a]which is for
himself, and make atonement for himself and [b]for his household,
and he shall slaughter the bull of the sin offering which is for
himself.
12 "And he shall take a [a]firepan full of coals of fire from upon the
altar before the LORD, and [1]two handfuls of finely ground [b]sweet
incense, and bring *it* inside the veil.
13 "And he shall put the incense on the fire before the LORD, that the
cloud of incense may cover the [1a]mercy seat that is on *the ark of* the
testimony, [b]lest he die.
14 "Moreover, [a]he shall take some of the blood of the bull and
sprinkle *it* [b]with his finger on the [1]mercy seat on the east *side*; also in
front of the [1]mercy seat he shall sprinkle some of the blood with his
finger seven times.
15 "Then he shall slaughter the goat of the sin offering [a]which is for
the people, and bring its blood inside the veil, and do with its blood
as he did with the blood of the bull, and sprinkle it on the [1]mercy
seat and in front of the [1]mercy seat.
16 "And [a]he shall make atonement for the holy place, because of the
impurities of the sons of Israel, and because of their transgressions,
in regard to all their sins; and thus he shall do for the tent of meeting
which abides with them in the midst of their impurities.
17 "When he goes in to make atonement in the holy place, no one
shall be in the tent of meeting until he comes out, that he may make
atonement for himself and for his household and for all the assembly
of Israel.
18 "Then he shall go out to the altar that is before the LORD and make
atonement for it, and shall take some of the blood of the bull and of
the blood of the goat, and [a]put it on the horns of the altar on all sides.
19 "And [a]with his finger he shall sprinkle some of the blood on it

...at of removal, ...name: *Azazel*
... [1]Lit., *goat of* ...*oval, or else a* ...e: *Azazel* [a]Is. ...0; Rom. 3:25; 1 John 2:2
Heb. 7:27; 9:7 [b]Lev. 16:33
...*he filling of the* ...*w of his hands* ...:1; Num. 16:18 [b]Ex. 30:34-38
Lit., *propitiatory* ...:21 [b]Ex. 28:43; ...; Num. 4:15, 20
Lit., *propitiatory* ...25 [b]Lev. 4:6, 17
[1]Lit., *propitiatory* ...eb. 7:27; 9:7, 12
... [a]Ex. 29:36, 37; 30:10; Heb. 2:17
[a]Lev. 4:25; Ezek. 43:20, 22
...Lev. 16:14; Ezek. 43:20

seven times, and cleanse it, and from the impurities of the sons of Israel consecrate it.

20 "When he finishes atoning for the holy place, and the tent of meeting and the altar, he shall offer the live goat.

21 "Then Aaron shall lay both of his hands on the head of the live goat, and [a]confess over it all the iniquities of the sons of Israel, and all their transgressions [1]in regard to all their sins; and he shall lay them on the head of the goat and send *it* away into the wilderness by the hand of a man who *stands* in readiness.

22 "And the goat shall bear on itself all their iniquities to a solitary land; and he shall release the goat in the wilderness.

23 "Then Aaron shall come into the tent of meeting, and take off [a]the linen garments which he put on when he went into the holy place, and shall leave them there.

24 "And [a]he shall bathe his [1]body with water in a holy place and put on [b]his clothes, and come forth and offer his burnt offering and the burnt offering of the people, and make atonement for himself and for the people.

25 "Then he shall offer up in smoke the fat of the sin offering on the altar.

26 "And the one who released the goat as the [1]scapegoat [a]shall wash his clothes and bathe his [2]body with water; then afterward he shall come into the camp.

27 "But the bull of the sin offering and the goat of the sin offering, [a]whose blood was brought in to make atonement in the holy place, shall be taken outside the camp, and they shall burn their hides, their flesh, and their refuse in the fire.

28 "Then the [a]one who burns them shall wash his clothes and bathe his body with water, then afterward he shall come into the camp.

29 "And *this* shall be a permanent statute for you: [a]in the seventh month, on the tenth day of the month, you shall humble your souls, and not [b]do any work, whether the native, or the alien who sojourns among you;

30 for it is on this day that [1]atonement shall be made for you to [a]cleanse you; you shall be clean from all your sins before the LORD.

31 "It is to be a sabbath of solemn rest for you, that you may [a]humble your souls; it is a permanent statute.

32 "So the priest who is anointed and [1]ordained to serve as priest in his father's place shall make atonement: he shall thus put on [a]the linen garments, the holy garments,

33 and make atonement for the holy sanctuary; and he shall make atonement for the tent of meeting and for the altar. He shall also make atonement for [a]the priests and for all the people of the assembly.

34 "Now you shall have this as a [a]permanent statute, to [b]make atonement for the sons of Israel for all their sins once every year." And just as the LORD had commanded Moses, *so* he did.

Chapter 17

17 Then the LORD spoke to Moses, saying,
2 "Speak to Aaron and to his sons, and to all the sons of Israel, and say to them, 'This is what the LORD has commanded, saying,

21 [1]Lit., *in a* [a]Lev. 5:5

23 [a]Lev. 16: 42:14; 44:19

24 [1]Lit., *flesh* 16:4 [b]Ex. 28:

26 [1]Lit., *goat removal*, or el name: *Azazel* *flesh* [a]Lev. 11

27 [a]Lev. 6:30; 13:11

28 [a]Num. 19:8

29 [a]Lev. 23:27, 29:7 [b]Ex. 31:14

30 [1]Lit., *he sha atonement* [a]Ps. Jer. 33:8; Eph. 5

31 [a]Lev. 23:32; 8:21; Is. 58:3, 5; 10:12

32 [1]Lit., *whose h filled* [a]Lev. 16:4

33 [a]Lev. 16:11

34 [a]Lev. 23:31 [b] 9:7

3 "Any man from the house of Israel who slaughters an ox, or a
lamb, or a goat in the camp, or who slaughters it outside the camp,
4 and [a]has not brought it to the doorway of the tent of meeting to
present *it* as an offering to the LORD before the [1]tabernacle of the
LORD, bloodguiltiness is to be reckoned to that man. He has shed
blood and that man shall be cut off from among his people.
5 "[1]The reason is so that the sons of Israel may bring their sacrifices
which they were sacrificing in the open field, that they may bring
them in to the LORD, at the doorway of the tent of meeting to the
priest, and sacrifice them as sacrifices of peace offerings to the LORD.
6 "And the priest shall sprinkle the blood on the altar of the LORD at
the doorway of the tent of meeting, and [a]offer up the fat in smoke as
a soothing aroma to the LORD.
7 "And [a]they shall no longer sacrifice their sacrifices to the [1]goat
demons with which they play the harlot. This shall be a permanent
statute to them throughout their generations."'
8 "Then you shall say to them, 'Any man from the house of Israel,
or from the aliens who sojourn among them, who offers a burnt
offering or sacrifice,
9 and [a]does not bring it to the doorway of the tent of meeting to
[1]offer it to the LORD, that man also shall be cut off from his people.
10 '[a]And any man from the house of Israel, or from the aliens who
sojourn among them, who eats any blood, [b]I will set My face against
that person who eats blood, and will cut him off from among his
people.
11 'For [a]the [1]life of the flesh is in the blood, and I have given it to
you on the altar to make atonement for your souls; for [b]it is the blood
by reason of the [1]life that makes atonement.'
12 "Therefore I said to the sons of Israel, 'No person among you may
eat blood, nor may any alien who sojourns among you eat blood.'
13 "So when any man from the sons of Israel, or from the aliens who
sojourn among them, [1]in hunting catches a beast or a bird which
may be eaten, [a]he shall pour out its blood and cover it with earth.
14 "[a]For *as for the* [1]life of all flesh, its blood is *identified* with its [1]life.
Therefore I said to the sons of Israel, 'You are not to eat the blood of
any flesh, for the [1]life of all flesh is its blood; whoever eats it shall be
cut off.'
15 "[a]And when any person eats *an animal* which dies, or is torn *by
beasts*, whether he is a native or an alien, he shall wash his clothes
and bathe in water, and remain unclean until evening; then he will
become clean.
16 "But if he does not wash *them* or bathe his body, then [a]he shall
bear his [1]guilt."

Chapter 18

18 Then the LORD spoke to Moses, saying,
2 "Speak to the sons of Israel and say to them, '[a]I am the LORD
your God.
3 'You shall not do [1]what is [a]done in the land of Egypt where you
lived, nor are you to do [1]what is [b]done in the land of Canaan where I
am bringing you; you shall not walk in their statutes.
4 'You are to perform My judgments and keep My statutes, [1]to live
in accord with them; [a]I am the LORD your God.

[1]Lit., dwelling [a]Deut. 12:5-21
[1]In order that
[a]Num. 18:17
[1]goat-idols [a]Ex. ...; 32:8; 34:15; ... 32:17; 2 Chr. ...; Ps. 106:37f.; 1 Cor. 10:20
[1]do [a]Ex. 20:24; Lev. 17:4
... 9:4; Lev. 3:17; ... 7; Deut. 12:16, ...; 1 Sam. 14:33 ... 3, 6; Jer. 44:11
[1]soul [a]Gen. 9:4; ...:14 [b]Heb. 9:22
[1]who in hunting [a]Deut. 12:16
[1]soul [a]Gen. 9:4; Lev. 17:11
[a]Ex. 22:31; Lev. 22:8; Deut. 14:21
[1]Or, iniquity [a]Num. 19:20
18:2 [a]Ex. 6:7; Lev. 11:44; Ezek. 20:5
[1]Lit., according to the ... of [a]Ezek. 20:7, 8 ... Lev. 18:24-30; 20:23
[1]Lit., to walk in them [a]Lev. 18:2

5 'So you shall keep My statutes and My judgments, [a]by which a
man may live if he does them; I am the LORD.
6 'None of you shall approach any blood relative [1]of his to uncover
nakedness; I am the LORD.
7 '[a]You shall not uncover the nakedness of your father, that is, the
nakedness of your mother. She is your mother; you are not to un-
cover her nakedness.
8 '[a]You shall not uncover the nakedness of your father's wife; it is
your father's nakedness.
9 '[a]The nakedness of your sister, *either* your father's daughter or
your mother's daughter, whether born at home or born outside, their
nakedness you shall not uncover.
10 'The nakedness of your son's daughter or your daughter's
daughter, their nakedness you shall not uncover; for [1]their naked-
ness is yours.
11 'The nakedness of your father's wife's daughter, [1]born to your
father, she is your sister, you shall not uncover her nakedness.
12 '[a]You shall not uncover the nakedness of your father's sister; she
is your father's blood relative.
13 'You shall not uncover the nakedness of your mother's sister, for
she is your mother's blood relative.
14 '[a]You shall not uncover the nakedness of your father's brother;
you shall not approach his wife, she is your aunt.
15 '[a]You shall not uncover the nakedness of your daughter-in-law;
she is your son's wife, you shall not uncover her nakedness.
16 '[a]You shall not uncover the nakedness of your brother's wife; it is
your brother's nakedness.
17 '[a]You shall not uncover the nakedness of a woman and of her
daughter, nor shall you take her son's daughter or her daughter's
daughter, to uncover her nakedness; they are blood relatives. It is
[1]lewdness.
18 'And you shall not [1]marry a woman in addition to [2]her sister [3]as
a rival while she is alive, to uncover her nakedness.
19 '[a]Also you shall not approach a woman to uncover her naked-
ness during her [b]menstrual impurity.
20 '[a]And you shall not have intercourse with your neighbor's wife,
to be defiled with her.
21 'Neither shall you give any of your offspring [a]to [1]offer them to
Molech, nor shall you [b]profane the name of your God; I am the LORD.
22 '[a]You shall not lie with a male as [1]one lies with a female; it is an
abomination.
23 '[a]Also you shall not have intercourse with any animal to be
defiled with it, nor shall any woman stand before an animal to [1]mate
with it; it is a perversion.
24 'Do not defile yourselves by any of these things; for by all these
[a]the nations which I am casting out before you have become defiled.
25 'For the land has become defiled, [a]therefore I have visited its
[1]punishment upon it, so the land [b]has spewed out its inhabitants.
26 'But as for you, you are to keep My statutes and My judgments,
and shall not do any of these abominations, *neither* the native, nor
the alien who sojourns among you
27 (for the men of the land who have been before you have done all
these abominations, and the land has become defiled);

5 [a]Neh. 9:29
18:9; 20:11; L
Rom. 10:5; G
6 [1]Lit., *of his*
7 [a]Lev. 20:11
27:20; Ezek.
8 [a]Lev. 20:11
22:30; 27:20;
9 [a]Lev. 18:11;
Deut. 27:22
10 [1]Lit., *they*
nakedness
11 [1]Lit., *begot*
12 [a]Lev. 20:19
14 [a]Lev. 20:20
15 [a]Lev. 20:12
16 [a]Lev. 20:21
17 [1]Or, *wicked*
[a]Lev. 20:14
18 [1]Lit., *take a*
[2]Or, *another* [3]L
19 [a]Lev. 15:24;
[b]Lev. 12:2
20 [a]Lev. 20:10;
6:29; Matt. 5:27,
1 Cor. 6:9; Heb.
21 [1]Lit., *cause t*
over [a]Lev. 20:2-
12:31 [b]Lev. 19:1
21:6; Ezek. 36:2
1:12
22 [1]Lit., *those w*
[a]Lev. 20:13; Deu
mg.; Rom. 1:27
23 [1]Or, *lie* [a]Ex. 2
Lev. 20:15, 16; De
27:21
24 [a]Lev. 18:3; De
18:12
25 [1]Lit., *iniquity* [a]
20:23; Deut. 9:5; 1
[b]Lev. 18:28; 20:22

28 so that the land may not spew you out, should you defile it, as it
has spewed out the nation which has been before you.
29 'For whoever does any of these abominations, [1]those persons
who do *so* shall be cut off from among their people.
30 'Thus you are to keep [a]My charge, that you do not practice any of
the abominable customs which have been practiced before you, so as
not to defile yourselves with them; [b]I am the LORD your God.' "

Chapter 19

19 Then the LORD spoke to Moses, saying,
2 "Speak to all the congregation of the sons of Israel and say
to them, '[a]You shall be holy, for I the LORD your God am holy.
3 'Every one of you [a]shall reverence his mother and his father, and
you shall keep [b]My sabbaths; [c]I am the LORD your God.
4 'Do not turn to [a]idols or make for yourselves molten [b]gods; I am
the LORD your God.
5 'Now when you offer a sacrifice of peace offerings to the LORD,
you shall offer it so that you may be accepted.
6 'It shall be eaten the same day you offer *it*, and the next day; but
what remains until the third day shall be burned with fire.
7 'So if it is eaten at all on the third day, it is an offense; it will not
be accepted.
8 'And everyone who eats it will bear his iniquity, for he has
profaned the holy thing of the LORD; and that person shall be cut off
from his people.
9 '[a]Now when you reap the harvest of your land, you shall not
reap to the very corners of your field, neither shall you gather the
gleanings of your harvest.
10 'Nor shall you glean your vineyard, nor shall you gather the
fallen fruit of your vineyard; you shall leave them for the needy and
for the stranger. I am the LORD your God.
11 '[a]You shall not steal, nor deal falsely, [b]nor lie to one another.
12 '[a]And you shall not swear falsely by My name, so as to [b]profane
the name of your God; I am the LORD.
13 '[a]You shall not oppress your neighbor, nor rob *him*. [b]The wages of
a hired man are not to remain with you all night until morning.
14 'You shall not curse a deaf man, nor [a]place a stumbling block
before the blind, but you shall revere your God; I am the LORD.
15 '[a]You shall do no injustice in judgment; you shall not be partial to
the poor nor defer to the great, but you are to judge your neighbor
fairly.
16 'You shall not go about as [a]a slanderer among your people, and
you are not to [1]act against the [2b]life of your neighbor; I am the LORD.
17 'You [a]shall not hate your [1]fellow countryman in your heart; you
[b]may surely reprove your neighbor, but shall not incur sin because of
him.
18 '[a]You shall not take vengeance, [b]nor bear any grudge against the
sons of your people, but [c]you shall love your neighbor as yourself; I
am the LORD.
19 'You are to keep My statutes. You shall not breed together two
kinds of your cattle; [a]you shall not sow your field with two kinds of
seed, nor wear a garment upon you of two kinds of material mixed
together.
20 '[a]Now if a man lies carnally with a woman who is a slave

[1]Or, *and the*
v. 22:9; Deut. :1 [b]Lev. 18:2
Ex. 19:6; Lev. 20:7, 26; Eph. :4; 1 Pet. 1:16
20:12; 31:13; 5:16 [b]Ex. 20:8 [c]Lev. 11:44
26:1; Ps. 96:5; -7 [b]Ex. 20:23; 34:17
v. 23:22; Deut. 24:20-22
20:15, 16 [b]Jer. :3-5; Eph. 4:25
[a]Ex. 20:7; Deut. Matt. 5:33 [b]Lev. 18:21
22:7-15, 21-27 4:15; James 5:4
14 [a]Deut. 27:18
Ex. 23:3, 6; Deut. :17; 10:17; 16:19
[1]Lit., *stand* [2]Lit., *od* [a]Ps. 15:3; Jer. 3; 9:4; Ezek. 22:9 23:7; Deut. 27:25
17 [1]Lit., *brother* John 2:9, 11; 3:15 18:15; Luke 17:3
Deut. 32:35; Rom. ; Heb. 10:30 [b]Ps. 03:9 [c]Matt. 19:19; 12:31; Luke 10:27; m. 13:9; Gal. 5:14; James 2:8
19 [a]Deut. 22:9, 11
20 [a]Deut. 22:23-27

acquired for *another* man, but who has in no way been redeemed,
nor given her freedom, there shall be punishment; they shall not,
however, be put to death, because she was not free.
21 'And he shall bring his guilt offering to the LORD to the doorway
of the tent of meeting, [a]a ram for a guilt offering.
22 'The priest shall also make atonement for him with the ram of
the guilt offering before the LORD for his sin which he has com-
mitted, and the sin which he has committed shall be forgiven him.
23 'And when you enter the land and plant all kinds of trees for
food, then you shall count their fruit as [1]forbidden. Three years it
shall be [1]forbidden to you; *it* shall not be eaten.
24 'But in the fourth year all its fruit shall be holy, an offering of
praise to the LORD.
25 'And in the fifth year you are to eat of its fruit, that its yield may
increase for you; I am the LORD your God.
26 'You shall not eat *anything* [a]with the blood, nor practice [b]divina-
tion or soothsaying.
27 '[a]You shall not round off the side-growth of your heads, nor
harm the edges of your beard.
28 'You shall not make any cuts in your [1]body for the [2]dead, nor
make any tattoo marks on yourselves: I am the LORD.
29 '[a]Do not [1]profane your daughter by making her a harlot, so that
the land may not fall to harlotry, and the land become full of
lewdness.
30 'You shall [a]keep My sabbaths and [b]revere My sanctuary; I am the
LORD.
31 'Do not turn to [1a]mediums or spiritists; do not seek them out to
be defiled by them. I am the LORD your God.
32 '[a]You shall rise up before the grayheaded, and honor the [1]aged,
and you shall revere your God; I am the LORD.
33 '[a]When a stranger resides with you in your land, you shall not do
him wrong.
34 'The stranger who resides with you shall be to you as the native
among you, and [a]you shall love him as yourself; for you were aliens
in the land of Egypt: I am the LORD your God.
35 '[a]You shall do no wrong in judgment, in measurement of weight,
or capacity.
36 'You shall have [a]just balances, just weights, a just [1]ephah, and a
just [2]hin: I am the LORD your God, who brought you out from the
land of Egypt.
37 'You shall thus observe all My statutes, and all My ordinances,
and do them: I am the LORD.' "

Chapter 20

20 Then the LORD spoke to Moses, saying,
2 "You shall also say to the sons of Israel, 'Any man from the
sons of Israel or from the aliens sojourning in Israel, [a]who gives any
of his [1]offspring to Molech, shall surely be put to death; [b]the people
of the land shall stone him with stones.
3 'I will also set My face against that man and will cut him off from
among his people, because he has given some of his [1]offspring to
Molech, [a]so as to defile My sanctuary and [b]to profane My holy name.
4 'If the people of the land, however, [1]should ever disregard that

21 [a]Lev. 6:1
23 [1]Lit., *uncl*
26 [a]Gen. 9:4 7:26f.; 17:10; 12:16, 23 [b]D 2 Kin. 17:17
27 [a]Lev. 21:5 14:1
28 [1]Lit., *flesh*
29 [1]Or, *degra* 21:9; Deut. 22 23:17, 18
30 [a]Lev. 19:3
31 [1]Or, *ghosts* *spirits* [a]Lev. 20 Deut. 18:11; 1 S 28:3; Is. 8:19
32 [1]Lit., *face o* *aged* [a]Prov. 23 Lam. 5:12; 1 Tir
33 [a]Ex. 22:21; 24:17, 18
34 [a]Lev. 19:18
35 [a]Deut. 25:13 Ezek. 45:10
36 [1]I.e., Approx. bu. [2]I.e., Approx. gal. [a]Deut. 25:13 Prov. 20:10
20:2 [1]Lit., *seed* 18:21 [b]Lev. 20:27 24:14-23; Num. 1 36; Deut. 21:21
3 [1]Lit., *seed* [a]Lev 15:31 [b]Lev. 18:21
4 [1]Lit., *hiding they* *their eyes from*

man when he gives any of his [2]offspring to Molech, so as not to put
him to death,
5 then I Myself will set My face against that man and against his
family; and I will cut off from among their people both him and all
those who play the harlot after him, by playing the harlot after
Molech.
6 'As for the person who turns to [1a]mediums and to spiritists, to
play the harlot after them, I will also set My face against that person
and will cut him off from among his people.
7 'You shall consecrate yourselves therefore and [a]be holy, for I am
the LORD your God.
8 'And [a]you shall keep My statutes and practice them; I am the
LORD who sanctifies you.
9 '[a]If *there is* anyone who curses his father or his mother, he shall
surely be put to death; he has cursed his father or his mother, his
bloodguiltiness is upon him.
10 '[a]If *there is* a man who commits adultery with another man's
wife, one who commits adultery with his friend's wife, the adulterer
and the adulteress shall surely be put to death.
11 '[a]If *there is* a man who lies with his father's wife, he has un-
covered his father's nakedness; both of them shall surely be put to
death, their bloodguiltiness is upon them.
12 '[a]If *there is* a man who lies with his daughter-in-law, both of them
shall surely be put to death; they have committed [1]incest, their
bloodguiltiness is upon them.
13 '[a]If *there is* a man who lies with a male as those who lie with a
woman, both of them have committed a detestable act; they shall
surely be put to death. Their bloodguiltiness is upon them.
14 '[a]If *there is* a man who [1]marries a woman and her mother, it is
immorality; both he and they shall be burned with fire, that there
may be no immorality in your midst.
15 '[a]If *there is* a man who lies with an animal, he shall surely be put
to death; you shall also kill the animal.
16 'If *there is* a woman who approaches any animal to [1]mate with it,
you shall kill the woman and the animal; they shall surely be put to
death. Their bloodguiltiness is upon them.
17 '[a]If *there is* a man who takes his sister, his father's daughter or his
mother's daughter, so that he sees her nakedness and she sees his
nakedness, it is a disgrace; and they shall be cut off in the sight of the
sons of their people. He has uncovered his sister's nakedness; he
bears his guilt.
18 '[a]If *there is* a man who lies with a [1]menstruous woman and un-
covers her nakedness, he has laid bare her flow, and she has [2]ex-
posed the flow of her blood; thus both of them shall be cut off from
among their people.
19 '[a]You shall also not uncover the nakedness of your mother's
sister or of your father's sister, for such a one has made naked his
[1]blood relative; they shall bear their guilt.
20 '[a]If *there is* a man who lies with his uncle's wife he has uncovered
his uncle's nakedness; they shall bear their sin. They shall die
childless.
21 '[a]If *there is* a man who takes his brother's wife, it is [1]abhorrent; he
has uncovered his brother's nakedness. They shall be childless.
22 'You are therefore to keep all My statutes and all My ordinances

4 [2]Lit., *seed*
6 [1]Or, *ghosts and spirits* [a]Lev. 19:31
ph. 1:4; 1 Pet. 1:16
8 [a]Ex. 31:13
9 [a]Ex. 21:17; Deut. 27:16
10 [a]Ex. 20:14; Lev. 18:20; Deut. 5:18
[a]Lev. 18:7, 8; Deut. 27:20
[1]Lit., *confusion;* i.e., a violation of divine order [a]Lev. 18:15
13 [a]Lev. 18:22
4 [1]Lit., *takes* [a]Lev. 18:17; Deut. 27:23
[a]Lev. 18:23; Deut. 27:21
16 [1]Lit., *lie*
7 [a]Lev. 18:9; Deut. 27:22
18 [1]Lit., *sick* [2]Or, *overed* [a]Lev. 15:24; 18:19
19 [1]Lit., *flesh* [a]Lev. 18:12, 13
20 [a]Lev. 18:14
21 [1]Or, *an impure deed* [a]Lev. 18:16

and do them, so that the land to which I am bringing you to [1]live will not [a]spew you out.

23 'Moreover, you shall not [1]follow [a]the customs of the nation which I shall drive out before you, for they did all these things, and [b]therefore I have abhorred them.

24 'Hence I have said to you, "[a]You are to possess their land, and I Myself will give it to you to possess it, a land flowing with milk and honey." I am the LORD your God, who has [b]separated you from the peoples.

25 '[a]You are therefore to make a distinction between the clean animal and the unclean, and between the unclean bird and the clean; and you shall not make [1]yourselves detestable by animal or by bird or by anything [2]that creeps on the ground, which I have separated for you as unclean.

26 'Thus you are to be holy to Me, for I the LORD am holy; and I [a]have set you apart from the peoples to be Mine.

27 'Now a man or a woman [a]who is a medium or a [1]spiritist shall surely be put to death. They shall be stoned with stones, their bloodguiltiness is upon them.' "

Chapter 21

21 Then the LORD said to Moses, "Speak to the priests, the sons of Aaron, and say to them, '[a]No one shall defile himself for a *dead* person among his people,

2 [a]except for his relatives who are nearest to him, his mother and his father and his son and his daughter and his brother,

3 also for his virgin sister, who is near to him [1]because she has had no husband; for her he may defile himself.

4 'He shall not defile himself as a [1]relative by marriage among his people, and so profane himself.

5 '[a]They shall not make any baldness on their heads, [b]nor shave off the edges of their beards, [c]nor make any cuts in their flesh.

6 'They shall be holy to their God and [a]not profane the name of their God, for they present the offerings by fire [1]to the LORD, [b]the bread of their God; so they shall be holy.

7 '[a]They shall not take a woman who is profaned by harlotry, nor shall they take a woman divorced from her husband; for he is holy to his God.

8 'You shall consecrate him, therefore, for he offers [a]the bread of your God; he shall be holy to you; for I the LORD, who sanctifies you, am holy.

9 '[a]Also the daughter of any priest, if she profanes herself by harlotry, she profanes her father; she shall be burned with fire.

10 'And the priest who is the highest among his brothers, on whose head the anointing oil has been poured, and [1]who has been consecrated to wear the garments, [a]shall not [2]uncover his head, nor tear his clothes;

11 [a]nor shall he approach any dead person, nor defile himself *even* for his father or his mother;

12 [a]nor shall he go out of the sanctuary, nor profane the sanctuary of his God; for [b]the consecration of the anointing oil of his God is on him: I am the LORD.

13 'And he shall take a wife in her virginity.

14 '[a]A widow, or a divorced woman, or one who is profaned by

22 [1]Lit., *dwel*
18:28

23 [1]Lit., *walk statutes* [a]Lev.
[b]Lev. 18:25

24 [a]Ex. 13:5;
[b]Ex. 33:16; Le

25 [1]Lit., *your*
[2]Lit., *with whic ground creeps*
10:10; 11:1-47
14:3-21

26 [a]Lev. 20:24

27 [1]Lit., *spiritis them* [a]Lev. 19:

21:1 [a]Lev. 19:2
44:25

2 [a]Lev. 21:11

3 [1]Or, *whom no has had*

4 [1]Lit., *husban*

5 [a]Deut. 14:1; E
44:20 [b]Lev. 19:2
[c]Deut. 14:1

6 [1]Lit., *of* [a]Lev.
[b]Lev. 3:11

7 [a]Lev. 21:13, 14

8 [a]Lev. 21:6

9 [a]Gen. 38:24; Le
19:29

10 [1]Lit., *whose h has been filled* [2]L *unbind* [a]Lev. 10:6

11 [a]Lev. 19:28; N
19:14

12 [a]Lev. 10:7 [b]Ex
29:6, 7

14 [a]Lev. 21:7; Eze
44:22

harlotry, these he may not take; but rather he is to [1]marry a virgin of
his own people;
15 that he may not profane his [1]offspring among his people: for I
am the LORD who sanctifies him.' "
16 Then the LORD spoke to Moses, saying,
17 "Speak to Aaron, saying, 'No man of your [1]offspring throughout
their generations who has a defect shall approach to offer the [a]bread
of his God.
18 '[a]For no one who has a defect shall approach: a blind man, or a
lame man, or he who has a [1a]disfigured *face,* or any deformed *limb,*
19 or a man who has a broken foot or broken hand,
20 or a hunchback or a dwarf, or *one who has* a [1]defect in his eye or
eczema or scabs or [a]crushed testicles.
21 'No man among the [1]descendants of Aaron the priest, who has a
defect, is to come near to offer the LORD's offerings by fire; *since* he
has a defect, he shall not come near to offer [a]the bread of his God.
22 'He may eat [a]the bread of his God, *both* of the most holy and of
the holy,
23 only he shall not go in to the veil or come near the altar because
he has a defect, that he may not profane My sanctuaries. For I am the
LORD who sanctifies them.' "
24 So Moses spoke to Aaron and to his sons and to all the sons of
Israel.

Chapter 22

22 Then the LORD spoke to Moses, saying,
2 "Tell Aaron and his sons to be careful with the holy *gifts* of
the sons of Israel, which they dedicate to Me, so as not to profane
My holy name; I am the LORD.
3 "Say to them, '[a]If any man among all your [1]descendants
throughout your generations approaches the holy *gifts* which the
sons of Israel dedicate to the LORD, while he has an uncleanness, that
person shall be cut off from before Me. I am the LORD.
4 '[a]No man, of the [1]descendants of Aaron, who is a leper or who
has a discharge, may eat of the holy *gifts* until he is clean. [b]And if one
touches anything made unclean by a corpse or if [c]a man has a semi-
nal emission,
5 or [a]if a man touches any teeming things, by which he is made
unclean, or any man by whom he is made unclean, whatever his
uncleanness;
6 a [1]person who touches any such shall be unclean until evening,
and shall not eat of the holy *gifts,* unless he has bathed his [2]body in
water.
7 'But when the sun sets, he shall be clean, and afterward he shall
eat of the holy *gifts,* for [a]it is his [1]food.
8 'He shall not eat [a]*an animal* which dies or is torn *by beasts,* becom-
ing unclean by it; I am the LORD.
9 'They shall therefore keep [a]My charge, so that [b]they may not bear
sin because of it, and die thereby because they profane it; I am the
LORD who sanctifies them.
10 '[a]No [1]layman, however, is to eat the holy *gift;* a sojourner with the
priest or a hired man shall not eat of the holy *gift.*
11 '[a]But if a priest buys a [1]slave as *his* property with his money, [2]that

[1]Lit., *take as wife*
15 [1]Lit., *seed*
...t., *seed* [a]Lev. 21:6
18 [1]Lit., *slit* [a]Lev. 22:19-25
20 [1]Lit., *obscurity* ...ut. 23:1; Is. 56:3-5
...t., *seed* [a]Lev. 21:6
22 [a]1 Cor. 9:13
3 [1]Lit., *seed* [a]Lev. ...20, 21; Num. 19:13
4 [1]Lit., *seed* [a]Lev. ...32 [b]Lev. 11:24-28, ...40 [c]Lev. 15:16, 17
5 [a]Lev. 11:23-28
...it., *soul* [2]Lit., *flesh*
[1]Lit., *bread* [a]Num. 18:11
...ev. 7:24; 11:39, 40; 17:15
9 [a]Lev. 18:30 [b]Ex. ...; Lev. 22:16; Num. 18:22
[1]Lit., *stranger* [a]Ex. ...; Lev. 22:13; Num. 3:10
[1]Lit., *soul* [2]Lit., *he* ...y [a]Gen. 17:13; Ex. 12:44

one may eat of it, and those who are born in his house may eat of his
[3]food.
12 'And if a priest's daughter is married to a [1]layman, she shall not
eat of the [2]offering of the *gifts*.
13 'But if a priest's daughter becomes a widow or divorced, and has
no child and returns to her father's house as in her youth, she shall
eat of her father's [1]food; [a]but no [2]layman shall eat of it.
14 '[a]But if a man eats a holy *gift* unintentionally, then he shall add to
it a fifth of it and shall give the holy *gift* to the priest.
15 'And [a]they shall not profane the holy *gifts* of the sons of Israel
which they offer to the LORD,
16 and *so* cause them [a]to bear [1]punishment for guilt by eating their
holy *gifts*; for I am the LORD who sanctifies them.' "
17 Then the LORD spoke to Moses, saying,
18 "Speak to Aaron and to his sons and to all the sons of Israel, and
say to them, '[a]Any man of the house of Israel or of the aliens in Israel
who presents his offering, whether it is any of their [1]votive or any of
their freewill offerings, which they present to the LORD for a burnt
offering—
19 [a]for you to be accepted—*it must be* a male without defect from
the cattle, the sheep, or the goats.
20 '[a]Whatever has a defect, you shall not offer, for it will not be
accepted for you.
21 'And when a man offers a sacrifice of peace offerings to the LORD
[a]to [1]fulfill a special vow, or for a freewill offering, of the herd or of
the flock, it must be perfect to be accepted; there shall be no defect
in it.
22 'Those *that are* blind or fractured or maimed or having a running
sore or eczema or scabs, you shall not offer to the LORD, nor make of
them an offering by fire on the altar to the LORD.
23 'In respect to an ox or a lamb which has an [1]overgrown or
stunted *member*, you may present it for a freewill offering, but for a
vow it shall not be accepted.
24 'Also [a]anything *with its testicles* bruised or crushed or torn or cut,
you shall not offer to the LORD, or [1]sacrifice in your land,
25 nor shall you accept any such from the hand of a foreigner for
offering [a]as the [1]food of your God; for their corruption is in them,
they have a defect, they shall not be accepted for you.' "
26 Then the LORD spoke to Moses, saying,
27 "When an ox or a sheep or a goat is born, it shall [1]remain [a]seven
days [2]with its mother, and from the eighth day on it shall be ac-
cepted as a sacrifice of an offering by fire to the LORD.
28 "[a]But, *whether* it is an ox or a sheep, you shall not kill *both* it and
its young in one day.
29 "And when you sacrifice [a]a sacrifice of thanksgiving to the LORD,
you shall sacrifice it so that you may be accepted.
30 "It shall be eaten on the same day, you shall leave none of it until
morning: I am the LORD.
31 "[a]So you shall keep My commandments, and do them: I am the
LORD.
32 "And you shall not profane My holy name, but I will be sanctified
among the sons of Israel: I am the LORD who sanctifies you,
33 [a]who brought you out from the land of Egypt, to be your God: I
am the LORD."

11 [3]Lit., brea
12 [1]Lit., stra heave offerin
13 [1]Lit., brea stranger [a]Lev
14 [a]Lev. 5:15
15 [a]Num. 18:
16 [1]Or, iniquit requiring a gui [a]Lev. 10:17; 22
18 [1]Lit., vows 15:14
19 [a]Lev. 21:18 Deut. 15:21
20 [a]Deut. 15:2 Mal. 1:8, 14; He 1 Pet. 1:19
21 [1]Or, make a votive offering 15:3, 8
23 [1]Or, a deforr
24 [1]Lit., do [a]Lev
25 [1]Lit., bread [a] 21:22
27 [1]Lit., be [2]Lit., [a]Ex. 22:30
28 [a]Deut. 22:6, 7
29 [a]Lev. 7:12
31 [a]Lev. 19:37; N 15:40; Deut. 4:40
33 [a]Lev. 11:45

The Jewish Calendar

Babylonian names (B) for the months are still used today for the Jewish calendar. Canaanite names (C) were used prior to the Babylonian captivity. Four are mentioned in the Old Testament.
Adar-Sheni is an intercalary month used every two to three years or seven times in nineteen years.

1st month	2nd month	3rd month	4th month
Nisan (B) Abib (C) March-April	Iyyar (B) Ziv (C) April-May	Sivan (B) May-June	Tammuz (B) June-July
7th month	*8th month*	*9th month*	*10th month*
5th month	**6th month**	**7th month**	**8th month**
Ab (B) July-August	Elul (B) August-September	Tishri (B) Ethanim (C) September-October	Marcheshvan (B) Bul (C) October-November
11th month	*12th month*	*1st month*	*2nd month*
9th month	**10th month**	**11th month**	**12th month**
Kislev (B) November-December	Tebeth (B) December-January	Shebat (B) January-February	Adar (B) February-March
3rd month	*4th month*	*5th month*	*6th month*

Sacred calendar appears in black • Civil calendar appears in grey

Chapter 23

23 The LORD spoke again to Moses, saying,
2 "Speak to the sons of Israel, and say to them, '[a]The LORD's
appointed times which you shall [b]proclaim as holy convocations—
My appointed times are these:
3 '[a]For six days work may be done; but on the seventh day there is
a sabbath of complete rest, a holy convocation. You shall not do any
work; it is a sabbath to the LORD in all your dwellings.
4 'These are the [a]appointed times of the LORD, holy convocations
which you shall proclaim at the times appointed for them.
5 '[a]In the first month, on the fourteenth day of the month [1]at
twilight is the LORD's Passover.
6 'Then on the fifteenth day of the same month there is the [a]Feast of
Unleavened Bread to the LORD; for seven days you shall eat un-
leavened bread.
7 'On the first day you shall have a holy convocation; you shall
[a]not do any laborious work.
8 'But for seven days you shall present an offering by fire to the
LORD. On the seventh day is a holy convocation; you shall not do any
laborious work.' "
9 Then the LORD spoke to Moses, saying,
10 "Speak to the sons of Israel, and say to them, 'When you enter the
land which I am going to give to you and [a]reap its harvest, then you
shall bring in the sheaf of the first fruits of your harvest to the priest.
11 'And he shall wave the sheaf before the LORD for you to be ac-
cepted; on the day after the sabbath the priest shall wave it.
12 'Now on the day when you wave the sheaf, you shall offer a
male lamb one year old without defect for a burnt offering to the
LORD.
13 'Its [a]grain offering shall then be two-tenths *of an ephah* of fine
flour mixed with oil, an offering by fire to the LORD *for* a soothing
aroma, with its libation, a fourth of a [1]hin of wine.
14 'Until this same day, until you have brought in the offering of

v. 23:4, 37, 44; 39 [b]Lev. 23:21
20:9, 10; 23:12; 7; 35:2, 3; Lev. ; Deut. 5:13, 14
23:14; Lev. 23:2
between the two ings [a]Ex. 12:18, ; Num. 28:16-25; 16:1; Josh. 5:10
12:14-20; 23:15; :18; Deut. 16:3-8
[a]Lev. 23:8, 21, 25, 35, 36
[a]Ex. 23:19; 34:26
[1]I.e., Approx. one gal. [a]Lev. 6:20

your God, [a]you shall eat neither bread nor roasted grain nor new
growth. It is to be a perpetual statute throughout your generations in
all your dwelling places.
15 '[a]You shall also count for yourselves from the day after the sab-
bath, from the day when you brought in the sheaf of the wave offer-
ing; there shall be seven complete sabbaths.
16 'You shall count fifty days to the day after the seventh sabbath;
then you shall present a [a]new grain offering to the LORD.
17 'You shall bring in from your dwelling places two *loaves* of bread
for a wave offering, made of two-tenths *of an* [1]*ephah;* they shall be of
a fine flour, baked [a]with leaven as first fruits to the LORD.
18 'Along with the bread, you shall present seven one year old male
lambs without defect, and a bull of the herd, and two rams; they are
to be a burnt offering to the LORD, with their grain offering and their
libations, an offering by fire of a soothing aroma to the LORD.
19 'You shall also offer [a]one male goat for a sin offering and two
male lambs one year old for a sacrifice of peace offerings.
20 'The priest shall then wave them with the bread of the first fruits
for a wave offering with two lambs before the LORD; they are to be
holy to the LORD for the priest.
21 'On this same day you shall [a]make a proclamation as well; you
are to have a holy convocation. You shall do no laborious [b]work. It is
to be a perpetual statute in all your dwelling places throughout your
generations.
22 '[a]When you reap the harvest of your land, moreover, you shall
not reap to the very corners of your field, nor gather the gleaning of
your harvest; you are to leave them for the needy and the alien. I am
the LORD your God.' "
23 Again the LORD spoke to Moses, saying,
24 "Speak to the sons of Israel, saying, '[a]In the seventh month on the
first of the month, you shall have a [1]rest, a [b]reminder by blowing *of*
trumpets, a holy convocation.
25 'You shall [a]not do any laborious work, but you shall present an
offering by fire to the LORD.' "
26 And the LORD spoke to Moses, saying,
27 "On exactly [a]the tenth day of this seventh month is [b]the day of
atonement; it shall be a holy convocation for you, and you shall
humble your souls and present an offering by fire to the LORD.
28 "Neither shall you do any work on this same day, for it is a [a]day
of atonement, [b]to make atonement on your behalf before the LORD
your God.
29 "If there is any [1]person who will not humble himself on this same
day, [a]he shall be cut off from his people.
30 "As for any person who does any work on this same day, that
person I will destroy from among his people.
31 "You shall do no work at all. It is to be a perpetual statute
throughout your generations in all your dwelling places.
32 "It is to be a sabbath of complete rest to you, and you shall
humble your souls; on the ninth of the month at evening, from eve-
ning until evening you shall keep your sabbath."
33 Again the LORD spoke to Moses, saying,
34 "Speak to the sons of Israel, saying, 'On [a]the fifteenth of this
seventh month is the [b]Feast of Booths for seven days to the LORD.

14 [a]Ex. 34:2
15:20, 21
15 [a]Num. 28
Deut. 16:9-1
16 [a]Num. 28
17 [1]I.e., App
bu. [a]Lev. 2:1
19 [a]Lev. 4:23
28:30
21 [a]Lev. 23:2,
23:7
22 [a]Lev. 19:9,
24:19; Ruth 2:1
24 [1]Lit., *sabba*
[a]Num. 29:1 [b]N
10:9, 10
25 [a]Lev. 23:21
27 [a]Lev. 16:29;
Num. 29:7 [b]Ex.
Lev. 16:30; 23:2
29:7-11
28 [a]Lev. 23:27
16:34
29 [1]Lit., *soul* [a]G
17:14; Lev. 13:46
5:2
34 [a]Num. 29:12
23:42, 43; Deut. 1
16; Ezra 3:4; Neh
Zech. 14:16; John

35 'On the first day is a holy convocation; you shall do [a]no laborious
work of any kind.
36 '[a]For seven days you shall present an offering by fire to the LORD.
On [b]the eighth day you shall have a holy convocation and present an
offering by fire to the LORD; it is an assembly. You shall do no
laborious work.
37 'These are [a]the appointed times of the LORD which you shall
proclaim as holy convocations, to present offerings by fire to the
LORD—burnt offerings and grain offerings, sacrifices and libations,
[b]*each* day's matter on its own day—
38 besides *those of* the sabbaths of the LORD, and besides your gifts,
and besides all your [1]votive and freewill offerings, which you give to
the LORD.
39 'On exactly the fifteenth day of the seventh month, [a]when you
have gathered in the crops of the land, you shall celebrate the feast of
the LORD for seven days, with a [1]rest on the first day and a [1]rest on
the eighth day.
40 'Now on the first day you shall take for yourselves the [1]foliage of
beautiful trees, palm branches and boughs of leafy trees and willows
of the brook; and you shall rejoice before the LORD your God for
seven days.
41 'You shall thus celebrate it *as* a feast to the LORD for seven days in
the year. It *shall be* a perpetual statute throughout your generations;
you shall celebrate it in the seventh month.
42 'You shall [1]live [a]in booths for seven days; all the native-born in
Israel shall [1]live in booths,
43 so that [a]your generations may know that I had the sons of Israel
live in booths when I brought them out from the land of Egypt. I am
the LORD your God.' "
44 So Moses declared to the sons of Israel [a]the appointed times of
the LORD.

Chapter 24

24
Then the LORD spoke to Moses, saying,
2 "Command the sons of Israel that they bring to you
[a]clear oil from beaten olives for the [1]light, to make a lamp [2]burn
continually.
3 "Outside the veil of testimony in the tent of meeting, Aaron shall
keep it in order from evening to morning before the LORD continual-
ly; *it shall be* a perpetual statute throughout your generations.
4 "He shall keep the lamps in order on the [a]pure *gold* lampstand
before the LORD continually.
5 "[a]Then you shall take fine flour and bake twelve cakes with it;
two-tenths *of an ephah* shall be *in* each cake.
6 "And you shall set them *in* two rows, six *to* a row, on the [a]pure
gold table before the LORD.
7 "And you shall put pure frankincense on each row, that it may be
[a]a memorial portion for the bread, *even* an offering by fire to the
LORD.
8 "[a]Every sabbath day he shall set it in order before the LORD [b]con-
tinually; it is an everlasting covenant [1]for the sons of Israel.
9 "[a]And it shall be for Aaron and his sons, and they shall eat it in a
holy place; for it is most holy to him from the LORD's offerings by
fire, *his* portion forever."

5 [a]Lev. 23:25
Num. 29:12-34 Num. 29:35-38
ev. 23:2 [b]Num. 28:1-29:38
[1]Lit., *vows, and besides all your*
t., *sabbath rest* [a]Ex. 23:16
., *products, fruit*
Lit., *dwell* [a]Lev. 23:34
Deut. 31:13; Ps. 78:5f.
44 [a]Lev. 23:37
Or, *luminary* [2]Lit., nd [a]Ex. 27:20, 21
[a]Ex. 25:31; 31:8; 37:17
[a]Ex. 25:30; 39:36; 40:23
25:24; 1 Kin. 7:48
7 [a]Lev. 2:2, 9, 16
8 [1]Lit., *from* [a]Matt. 5 [b]Ex. 25:30; Num. 4:7; 2 Chr. 2:4
9 [a]Matt. 12:4; Mark 2:26; Luke 6:4

10 Now the son of an Israelite woman, whose father was an Egyp-
tian, went out among the sons of Israel; and the Israelite woman's
son and a man of Israel struggled with each other in the camp.
11 And the son of the Israelite woman blasphemed the [a]Name and
cursed. So they brought him to Moses. (Now his mother's name was
Shelomith, the daughter of Dibri, of the tribe of Dan.)
12 And they put him in [1]custody [2]so that [a]the command of the LORD
might be made clear to them.
13 Then the LORD spoke to Moses, saying,
14 "Bring the one who has cursed outside the camp, and let all who
heard him [a]lay their hands on his head; then [b]let all the congregation
stone him.
15 "And you shall speak to the sons of Israel, saying, '[a]If anyone
curses his God, then he shall bear his sin.
16 'Moreover, the one who [a]blasphemes the name of the LORD shall
surely be put to death; all the congregation shall certainly stone him.
The alien as well as the native, when he blasphemes the Name, shall
be put to death.
17 '[a]And if a man [1]takes the life of any human being, he shall surely
be put to death.
18 'And [a]the one who [1]takes the life of an animal shall make it good,
life for life.
19 'And if a man [1]injures his neighbor, just as he has done, so it shall
be done to him:
20 [a]fracture for fracture, [b]eye for eye, tooth for tooth; just as he has
[1]injured a man, so it shall be [2]inflicted on him.
21 'Thus the one who [1]kills an animal shall make it good, but [a]the
one who [1]kills a man shall be put to death.
22 'There shall be [a]one [1]standard for you; it shall be for the stranger
as well as the native, for I am the LORD your God.' "
23 Then Moses spoke to the sons of Israel, and they brought the one
who had cursed outside the camp and stoned him with stones. Thus
the sons of Israel did, just as the LORD had commanded Moses.

Chapter 25

25 The LORD then spoke to Moses [1]at Mount Sinai, saying,
2 "Speak to the sons of Israel, and say to them, 'When you
come into the land which I shall give you, then the land shall have a
sabbath to the LORD.
3 '[a]Six years you shall sow your field, and six years you shall
prune your vineyard and gather in its crop,
4 but during [a]the seventh year the land shall have a sabbath rest, a
sabbath to the LORD; you shall not sow your field nor prune your
vineyard.
5 'Your harvest's [1]aftergrowth you shall not reap, and your grapes
of untrimmed vines you shall not gather; the land shall have a sab-
batical year.
6 '[a]And all of you shall have the sabbath *products* of the land for
food; yourself, and your male and female slaves, and your hired
man and your foreign resident, those who live as aliens with you.
7 'Even your cattle and the animals that are in your land shall have
all its crops to eat.
8 'You are also to count off seven sabbaths of years for yourself,

11 [a]Ex. 3:15; 2 2:5, 9; Is. 8:21

12 [1]Or, *prison* *declare distinct them according mouth of the LO* 18:15; Num. 15

14 [a]Deut. 13:9; [b]Lev. 20:2, 27; D 21:21

15 [a]Ex. 22:28

16 [a]1 Kin. 21:10 12:31; Mark 3:28

17 [1]Lit., *smites* 9:6; Ex. 21:12; N 35:30, 31; Deut.

18 [1]Lit., *smites* 24:21

19 [1]Lit., *gives a b*

20 [1]Lit., *given a blemish* [2]Lit., *give* [a]Ex. 21:23; Deut. [b]Matt. 5:38

21 [1]Lit., *smites* [a] 24:17

22 [1]Lit., *judgment* 12:49; Num. 9:14; 15:15, 16, 29

25:1 [1]Or, *on*

3 [a]Ex. 23:10, 11

4 [a]Lev. 25:20

5 [1]Lit., *growth from spilled kernels*

6 [a]Lev. 25:20, 21

seven times seven years, so that you have the time of the seven
sabbaths of years, *namely*, forty-nine years.
9 'You shall then sound a ram's horn abroad on [a]the tenth day of
the seventh month; on the day of atonement you shall sound a horn
all through your land.
10 'You shall thus consecrate the fiftieth year and [a]proclaim [1]a
release through the land to all its inhabitants. It shall be a jubilee for
you, [2]and [b]each of you shall return to his own property, [2]and each of
you shall return to his family.
11 'You shall have the fiftieth year as a jubilee; you shall not sow,
nor reap its aftergrowth, nor gather in *from* its untrimmed vines.
12 'For it is a jubilee; it shall be holy to you. You shall eat its crops
out of the field.
13 '[a]On this year of jubilee each of you shall return to his own
property.
14 'If you make a sale, moreover, to your friend, or buy from your
friend's hand, [a]you shall not wrong one another.
15 'Corresponding to the number of years after the jubilee, you shall
buy from your [1]friend; he is to sell to you according to the number of
years of crops.
16 '[a]In proportion to the [1]extent of the years you shall increase its
price, and in proportion to the fewness of the years, you shall
diminish its price; for *it is* a number of crops he is selling to you.
17 'So [a]you shall not wrong one another, but you shall [1]fear your
God; for I am the LORD your God.
18 'You shall thus observe My statutes, and keep My judgments, so
as to carry them out, that [a]you may live securely on the land.
19 'Then the land will yield its produce, so that you can eat your fill
and live securely on it.
20 'But if you say, "[a]What are we going to eat on the seventh year [1]if
we do not sow or gather in our crops?"
21 then [a]I will so order My blessing for you in the sixth year that it
will bring forth the crop for three years.
22 'When you are sowing the eighth year, you can still eat [a]old
things from the crop, eating *the old* until the ninth year when its crop
comes in.
23 'The land, moreover, shall not be sold permanently, for [a]the land
is Mine; for [b]you are *but* aliens and sojourners with Me.
24 'Thus for every [1]piece of your property, you are to provide for
the redemption of the land.
25 '[a]If a [1]fellow countryman of yours becomes so poor he has to sell
part of his property, then his nearest kinsman is to come and buy
back what his [1]relative has sold.
26 'Or in case a man has no kinsman, but so [1]recovers his means as
to find sufficient for its redemption,
27 [a]then he shall calculate the years since its sale and refund the
balance to the man to whom he sold it, and so return to his property.
28 'But if [1]he has not found sufficient means to get it back for him-
self, then what he has sold shall remain in the hands of its purchaser
until the year of jubilee; but at the jubilee it shall [2]revert, that [a]he may
return to his property.
29 'Likewise, if a man sells a dwelling house in a walled city, then
his redemption right remains valid until a full year from its sale; his
right of redemption lasts a full year.

9 [a]Lev. 23:27
r, *liberty* [2]Or, . 34:8, 15, 17 25:13, 28, 54
. 25:10; 27:24
4 [a]Lev. 25:17
friend's hands
nultitude [a]Lev. 25:27, 51, 52
everence [a]Lev. 4; Prov. 14:31; :22; Jer. 7:5, 6; 1 Thess. 4:6
.ev. 26:5; Deut. 12:10; Jer. 23:6
r, *behold* [a]Lev. 25:4
21 [a]Deut. 28:8
22 [a]Lev. 26:10
[a]Ex. 19:5 [b]Gen. 1 Chr. 29:15; Ps. :12; Heb. 11:13; 1 Pet. 2:11
24 [1]Lit., *land*
it., *brother* [a]Ruth 2:20; 4:4, 6
26 [1]Lit., *his hand reaches*
27 [a]Lev. 25:16
[1]Lit., *his hand has found sufficient to* [2]Lit., *go out* [a]Lev. 25:10, 13

30 'But if it is not bought back for him within the space of a full
year, then the house that is in the walled city passes permanently to
its purchaser throughout his generations; it does not [1]revert in the
jubilee.
31 'The houses of the villages, however, which have no surrounding
wall shall be considered [1]as open fields; they have redemption rights
and [2]revert in the jubilee.
32 'As for [a]cities of the Levites, the Levites have a permanent right
of redemption for the houses of the cities which are their possession.
33 'What, therefore, [1]belongs to the Levites may be redeemed and a
house sale [2]in the city of this possession [3]reverts in the jubilee, for the
houses of the cities of the Levites are their possession among the
sons of Israel.
34 '[a]But pasture fields of their cities shall not be sold, for that is their
perpetual possession.
35 '[a]Now in case a [1]countryman of yours becomes poor and his
[2]means with regard to you falter, then you are to sustain him, like a
stranger or a sojourner, that he may live with you.
36 '[a]Do not take [1]usurious interest from him, but revere your God,
that your [2]countryman may live with you.
37 'You shall not give him your silver at interest, nor your food for
gain.
38 '[a]I am the LORD your God, who brought you out of the land of
Egypt to give you the land of Canaan *and* [b]to be your God.
39 '[a]And if a [1]countryman of yours becomes so poor with regard to
you that he sells himself to you, you shall not subject him to a slave's
service.
40 'He shall be with you as a hired man, as [a]if he were a sojourner;
he shall serve with you until the year of jubilee.
41 'He shall then go out from you, he and his sons with him, and
shall go back to his family, that he may return to the property of his
forefathers.
42 'For they are My servants whom I brought out from the land of
Egypt; they are not to be sold *in* a slave sale.
43 '[a]You shall not rule over him with severity, but are to revere your
God.
44 'As for your male and female slaves whom you may have—you
may acquire male and female slaves from the pagan nations that are
around you.
45 'Then, too, *it is* out of the sons of the sojourners who live as aliens
among you that you may gain acquisition, and out of their families
who are with you, whom they will have [1]produced in your land;
they also may become your possession.
46 'You may even bequeath them to your sons after you, to receive
as a possession; you can use them as permanent slaves. [a]But in
respect to your [1]countrymen, the sons of Israel, you shall not rule
with severity over one another.
47 'Now if the [1]means of a stranger or of a sojourner with you
becomes sufficient, and a [2]countryman of yours becomes so poor
with regard to him as to sell himself to a stranger who is sojourning
with you, or to the descendants of a stranger's family,
48 then he shall have redemption right after he has been sold. One
of his brothers may redeem him,
49 or his uncle, or his uncle's son, may redeem him, or one of his

30 [1]Lit., *go o*
31 [1]Lit., *acco* [2]Lit., *go out*
32 [a]Num. 35: 21:2
33 [1]Lit., *is fro* *and* [3]Lit., *goes*
34 [a]Num. 35:2
35 [1]Lit., *brothe* *hand* [a]Deut. 15 24:14, 15
36 [1]Lit., *interes* *usury* [2]Lit., *brot* 22:25; Deut. 23
38 [a]Lev. 11:45 17:7
39 [1]Lit., *brother* 21:2-6; Deut. 15. 1 Kin. 9:22
40 [a]Ex. 21:2
43 [a]Ex. 1:13, 14; 25:46, 53; Ezek. 3 Col. 4:1
45 [1]Lit., *begotten*
46 [1]Lit., *brothers* 25:43
47 [1]Lit., *hand . . . reaches* [2]Lit., *brot*

blood relatives from his family may redeem him; or [1a]if he prospers,
he may redeem himself.
50 'He then with his purchaser shall calculate from the year when
he sold himself to him up to the year of jubilee; and the price of his
sale shall correspond to the number of years. *It is* like the days of a
hired man *that* he shall be with him.
51 'If there are still many years, [a]he shall refund part of his purchase
price in proportion to them for his own redemption;
52 and if few years remain until the year of jubilee, he shall so
calculate with him. In proportion to his years he is to refund *the
amount for* his redemption.
53 'Like a man hired year by year he shall be with him; [a]he shall not
rule over him with severity in your sight.
54 'Even if he is not redeemed by [1]these *means*, [a]he shall still go out
in the year of jubilee, he and his sons with him.
55 'For the sons of Israel are My servants; they are My servants
whom I brought out from the land of Egypt. I am the LORD your
God.

Chapter 26

26 'You shall not make for yourselves [1a]idols, nor shall you set
up for yourselves [b]an image or [c]a *sacred* pillar, nor shall you
place a [d]figured stone in your land to bow down [2]to it; for I am the
LORD your God.
2 '[a]You shall keep My sabbaths and reverence My sanctuary; I am
the LORD.
3 '[a]If you walk in My statutes and keep My commandments so as
to carry them out,
4 then [a]I shall give you rains in their season, so that the land will
yield its produce and the trees of the field will bear their fruit.
5 '[a]Indeed, your threshing will last for you until grape gathering,
and grape gathering will last until sowing time. You will thus eat
your [1]food to the full and [b]live securely in your land.
6 '[a]I shall also grant peace in the land, so that [b]you may lie down
with no one making *you* tremble. [c]I shall also eliminate harmful
beasts from the land, and [d]no sword will pass through your land.
7 'But you will chase your enemies, and they will fall before you
by the sword;
8 [a]five of you will chase a hundred, and a hundred of you will
chase ten thousand, and your enemies will fall before you by the
sword.
9 'So I will turn toward you and [a]make you fruitful and multiply
you, and I will [b]confirm My covenant with you.
10 '[a]And you will eat the old supply and clear out the old because of
the new.
11 '[a]Moreover, I will make My [1]dwelling among you, and My soul
will not [2]reject you.
12 '[a]I will also walk among you and be your God, and you shall be
My people.
13 '[a]I am the LORD your God, who brought you out of the land of
Egypt so that *you* should not be their slaves, and [b]I broke the bars of
your yoke and made you walk erect.
14 '[a]But if you do not obey Me and do not carry out all these com-
mandments,

15 if, instead, you [a]reject My statutes, and if your soul abhors My ordinances so as not to carry out all My commandments, *and* so [b]break My covenant,

16 I, in turn, will do this to you: I will appoint over you a [a]sudden terror, consumption and fever that shall waste away the eyes and cause the [b]soul to pine away; also, [c]you shall sow your seed uselessly, for your enemies shall eat it up.

17 'And I will set My face against you so that you shall be struck down before your enemies; and [a]those who hate you shall rule over you, and [b]you shall flee when no one is pursuing you.

18 'If also after these things, you do not obey Me, then I will punish you [a]seven times more for your sins.

19 'And I will also [a]break down your pride of power; I will also make your sky like iron and your earth like bronze.

20 'And [a]your strength shall be spent uselessly, for your land shall not yield its produce and the trees of the land shall not yield their fruit.

21 'If then, you [1a]act with hostility against Me and are unwilling to obey Me, I will increase the plague on you [b]seven times according to your sins.

22 'And [a]I will let loose among you the beasts of the field, which shall bereave you of your children and destroy your cattle and reduce your number so that [b]your roads lie deserted.

23 '[a]And if by these things you are not turned to Me, but act with hostility against Me,

24 then I will [a]act with hostility against you; and I, even I, will strike you [b]seven times for your sins.

25 'I will also bring upon you a sword which will execute [a]vengeance for the covenant; and when you gather together into your cities, I will send [b]pestilence among you, so that you shall be delivered into enemy hands.

26 '[a]When I break your staff of bread, ten women will bake your bread in one oven, and they will bring back your bread [1]in rationed amounts, so that you will [b]eat and not be satisfied.

27 'Yet if in spite of this, you do not obey Me, but act with hostility against Me,

28 then [a]I will act with wrathful hostility against you; and I, even I, will punish you seven times for your sins.

29 'Further, [a]you shall eat the flesh of your sons and the flesh of your daughters you shall eat.

30 'I then [a]will destroy your high places, and cut down your [b]incense altars, and heap your [1]remains on the [1]remains of your idols; for My soul shall abhor you.

31 'I will [1]lay [a]waste your cities as well, and will make your [b]sanctuaries desolate; and I will not [c]smell your soothing aromas.

32 'And I will make [a]the land desolate [b]so that your enemies who settle in it shall be appalled over it.

33 'You, however, I [a]will scatter among the nations and will draw out a sword after you, as your land becomes desolate and your cities become waste.

34 '[a]Then the land will [1]enjoy its sabbaths all the days of the desolation, while you are in your enemies' land; then the land will rest and [1]enjoy its sabbaths.

15 [a]Lev. 26:1[…] 17:15 [b]Lev. 2[…]

16 [a]Deut. 28:[…] 78:33 [b]1 Sam[…] Ezek. 24:23; 3[…] [c]Judg. 6:3-6; J[…]

17 [a]Ps. 106:4[…] 26:36, 37; Ps. […] Prov. 28:1

18 [a]Lev. 26:21

19 [a]Is. 28:1-3; […] 24:21

20 [a]Ps. 127:1; […] 17:10, 11; 49:4[…] 12:13

21 [1]Lit., *walk,* […] throughout the […] 26:23, 27, 40 [b][…] 26:18

22 [a]2 Kin. 17:2[…] 5:6

23 [a]Lev. 26:21; […]

24 [a]Lev. 26:28, […] [b]Lev. 26:21

25 [a]Jer. 50:28; […] [b]Num. 14:12

26 [1]Lit., *by weig[…]* 3:1; Ezek. 4:16, […] 5:16 [b]Mic. 6:14

28 [a]Lev. 26:24, […] 59:18

29 [a]2 Kin. 6:29

30 [1]Lit., *corpses* [a]2 Kin. 23:20; Eze[…] 6; Amos 7:9 [b]2 C[…] 34:4, 7; Is. 27:9

31 [1]Lit., *give des[…] to* [a]Neh. 2:3; Jer. […] 6, 22 [b]Is. 63:18; […] 2:7 [c]Amos 5:21

32 [a]Jer. 9:11; 12:[…] 25:11; 33:10 [b]Jer. […] 18:16; 19:8

33 [a]Deut. 4:27; 2[…] Ps. 44:11; 106:27; […] 31:10; Ezek. 12:1[…] 20:23; Zech. 7:14

34 [1]Lit., *satisfy* [a]L[…] 26:43; 2 Chr. 36:2[…]

35 'All the days of *its* desolation it will observe the rest which it did
not observe on your sabbaths, while you were living on it.
36 'As for those of you who may be left, I will also bring [a]weakness
into their hearts in the lands of their enemies. And the sound of a
driven leaf will chase them and even when no one is pursuing, they
will flee [1]as though from the sword, and they will fall.
37 '[a]They will therefore stumble over each other as if *running* from
the sword, although no one is pursuing; and you will have *no
strength* [1]to stand up before your enemies.
38 'But [a]you will perish among the nations, and your enemies' land
will consume you.
39 '[a]So those of you who may be left will rot away because of their
iniquity in the lands of your enemies; and also because of the
iniquities of their forefathers they will rot away with them.
40 '[a]If they confess their iniquity and the iniquity of their
forefathers, in their unfaithfulness which they committed against
Me, and also in their acting with hostility against Me—
41 I also was acting with hostility against them, to bring them into
the land of their enemies—[a]or if their uncircumcised heart becomes
humbled so that [b]they then make amends for their iniquity,
42 then I will remember [a]My covenant with Jacob, and I will
remember also [b]My covenant with Isaac, and [c]My covenant with
Abraham as well, and I will remember the land.
43 '[a]For the land shall be abandoned by them, and shall make up for
its sabbaths while it is made desolate without them. They,
meanwhile, shall be making amends for their iniquity, [1]because they
rejected My ordinances and their [b]soul abhorred My statutes.
44 'Yet in spite of this, when they are in the land of their enemies, I
will not reject them, nor will I so [a]abhor them as [b]to destroy them,
[c]breaking My covenant with them; for I am the LORD their God.
45 'But I will remember for them the [a]covenant with their ancestors,
whom I brought out of the land of Egypt in the sight of the nations,
that [b]I might be their God. I am the LORD.' "
46 [a]These are the statutes and ordinances and laws which the LORD
established between Himself and the sons of Israel [1]through Moses
at Mount Sinai.

Chapter 27

27 Again, the LORD spoke to Moses, saying,
2 "Speak to the sons of Israel, and say to them, '[a]When a man
makes a difficult vow, he *shall be valued* according to your valuation
of persons belonging to the LORD.
3 'If your valuation is of the male from twenty years even to sixty
years old, then your valuation shall be fifty shekels of silver, after
[a]the shekel of the sanctuary.
4 'Or if it is a female, then your valuation shall be thirty shekels.
5 'And if it be from five years even to twenty years old then your
valuation for the male shall be twenty shekels, and for the female ten
shekels.
6 'But if *they are* from a month even up to five years old, then your
valuation shall be [a]five shekels of silver for the male, and for the
female your valuation shall be three shekels of silver.
7 'And if *they are* from sixty years old and upward, if it is a male,

flight of the
30:17; Lam.
; Ezek. 21:7

ou will stand
21; Nah. 3:3

[a]Deut. 4:26

. 4:17; 33:10

12-15; 14:20;
Hos. 5:15

4:4; 9:25, 26;
', 9; Acts 7:51
[b]Ezek. 20:43

ien. 28:13-15;
[b]Gen. 26:2-5
Gen. 22:15-18

, because and
e cause [a]Lev.
34 [b]Lev. 26:11

v. 26:11 [b]Deut.
Jer. 30:11 [c]Jer.
33:20-26

Ex. 6:6-8 [b]Gen.
17:7

, by the hand of
38; 27:34; Deut.
4:5; 29:1

[a]Num. 6:2; Deut.
23:21-23

[a]Ex. 30:13; Lev.
Num. 3:47; 18:16

6 [a]Num. 18:16

then your valuation shall be fifteen shekels, and for the female ten
shekels.
8 'But if he is poorer than your valuation, then he shall be placed
before the priest, and the priest shall value him; [a]according to [1]the
means of the one who vowed, the priest shall value him.
9 'Now if it is an animal of the kind which [1]men can present as an
offering to the LORD, any such that one gives to the LORD shall be
holy.
10 '[a]He shall not replace it or exchange it, a good for a bad, or a bad
for a good; or if he does exchange animal for animal, then both it and
its substitute shall become holy.
11 'If, however, it is any unclean animal of the kind which [1]men do
not present as an offering to the LORD, then he shall place the animal
before the priest.
12 'And the priest shall value it [1]as either good or bad; as you, the
priest, value it, so it shall be.
13 'But if he should ever *wish to* redeem it, then he shall add one-
fifth of it to your valuation.
14 'Now if a man consecrates his house as holy to the LORD, then the
priest shall value it [1]as either good or bad; as the priest values it, so it
shall stand.
15 'Yet if the one who consecrates it should *wish to* redeem his
house, then he shall add one-fifth of your valuation price to it, so
that it may be his.
16 'Again, if a man consecrates to the LORD part of the fields of his
own property, then your valuation shall be [1]proportionate to the
seed needed for it: a homer of barley seed at fifty shekels of silver.
17 'If he consecrates his field as of the year of jubilee, according to
your valuation it shall stand.
18 'If he consecrates his field after the jubilee, however, then the
priest shall calculate the price for [1]him [2]proportionate to the years
that are left until the year of jubilee; and it shall be deducted from
your valuation.
19 'And if the one who consecrates it should ever wish to redeem
the field, then he shall add one-fifth of your valuation price to it, so
that it may pass to him.
20 'Yet if he will not redeem the field, [1]but has sold the field to
another man, it may no longer be redeemed;
21 and when it [1]reverts in the jubilee, the field shall be holy to the
LORD, like a field [2]set apart; [a]it shall be for the priest as his [3]property.
22 'Or if he consecrates to the LORD a field which he has bought,
which is not a part of the field of his own [1]property,
23 then the priest shall calculate for [1]him the amount of your valua-
tion up to the year of jubilee; and he shall on that day give your
valuation as holy to the LORD.
24 'In the year of jubilee the field shall return to the one from whom
he bought it, to whom the possession of the land belongs.
25 'Every valuation of yours, moreover, shall be after [a]the shekel of
the sanctuary. The shekel shall be twenty gerahs.
26 '[a]However, a first-born among animals, which as a first-born
belongs to the LORD, no man may consecrate it; whether ox or sheep,
it is the LORD's.
27 'But if *it is* among the unclean animals, then he shall [1]redeem it

8 [1]Lit., *wha reaches* [a]L 14:21-24
9 [1]Lit., *they*
10 [a]Lev. 27
11 [1]Lit., *they*
12 [1]Lit., *betw*
14 [1]Lit., *betw*
16 [1]Lit., *acco seed*
18 [1]Or, *it* [2]Lit *according to th*
20 [1]Or, *if he*
21 [1]Lit., *goes devoted, banne possession* [a]N 18:14; Ezek. 44
22 [1]Lit., *posses*
23 [1]Or, *it*
25 [a]Ex. 30:13; L 27:3; Num. 3:47;
26 [a]Ex. 13:2
27 [1]Or, *ransom*

according to your valuation, and add to it one-fifth of it; and if it is
not redeemed, then it shall be sold according to your valuation.
28 'Nevertheless, [a]anything which a man [1]sets apart to the LORD out
of all that he has, of man or animal or of the fields of his own
property, shall not be sold or redeemed. Anything [2]devoted to
destruction is most holy to the LORD.
29 'No [1]one who may have been [2]set apart among men shall be
ransomed; he shall surely be put to death.
30 'Thus [a]all the tithe of the land, of the seed of the land or of the
fruit of the tree, is the LORD'S; it is holy to the LORD.
31 'If, therefore, a man wishes to redeem part of his tithe, he shall
add to it one-fifth of it.
32 'And for every tenth part of herd or flock, whatever [a]passes
under the rod, the tenth one shall be holy to the LORD.
33 '[a]He is not to be concerned whether *it is* good or bad, nor shall he
exchange it; or if he does exchange it, then both it and its substitute
shall become holy. It shall not be redeemed.' "
34 [a]These are the commandments which the LORD commanded
Moses for the sons of Israel at Mount Sinai.

28 [1]Lit., *anything* ...*evoted; or, banned* ...*uts under the ban* [a]Num. 18:14; Josh. 6:17-19

[1]Lit., *one devoted;* ...*r, banned* [2]Or, *put under the ban*

[a]Gen. 28:22; 2 Chr. 31:5; Neh. 13:12

[a]Jer. 33:13; Ezek. 20:37

33 [a]Lev. 27:10

[a]Lev. 26:46; Deut. 4:5

THE OFFERINGS AND THEIR PURPOSE

The Offering	Chapter/ Verse	Voluntary/ Involuntary	Reason/Purpose

LEVITICUS AT A GLANCE

ne of Leviticus:

GMENT DIVISIONS

LAWS REGARDING	MAIN DIVISION	CHAPTER THEMES
	WORSHIPING A HOLY GOD	1
		2
		3
		4
		5
		6
		7
		8
		9
		10
		11
		12
		13
		14
		15
		16
		17
	LIVING A HOLY LIFE	18
		19
		20
		21
		22
		23
		24
		25
		26
		27

Author:

Date:

Purpose:

Key Words:

- the Lord spoke to Moses saying
- tabernacle (tent of meeting)
- law
- sacrifice (offering)
- sin (iniquity)
- blood
- atonement
- holy
- covenant

NUMBERS

Then the Israelites cried out to God. And God heard and raised up Moses to deliver the childı Israel out of the land of Egypt, the house of bondage. The children of Israel had lived in Egypt fc years. Now after camping at Sinai, they were to go to Canaan, the land promised to Abraham, I and Jacob. At last they would see the land with their own eyes. And God would go with them pillar of cloud by day and a pillar of fire by night.

Soon the journey would begin, but first there must be a numbering of all the sons of Israel twenty years of age on up.

THINGS TO DO

General Instructions

The book of Numbers can be divided into three segments according to the journeys and enca ments of the children of Israel. In Numbers 1 through 10:10 they are encamped at Sinai. In Num 10:11 the cloud lifts and their journeying begins and does not end for about thirty-nine years. Th Numbers 22 Israel camps on the plains of Moab, opposite Jericho, as they prepare to enter the la promise.

Chapters 1-10:10

1. The first five books of the Bible, Genesis through Deuteronomy, are closely related. They fo each other chronologically. To put Numbers into context:
   a. Read Exodus 40:1-2, 17, 33-38 which gives an account of the building of the tabernac Mount Sinai.
   b. Read Leviticus 1:1 and then 27:34. All the book of Leviticus takes place at Mount Sinai.
   c. Then compare where Leviticus ends and Numbers begins. Read Numbers 1:1-2.
   d. Look at Exodus 40:17 again and Numbers 1:1 and you'll see one month elapsed between close of Exodus and the beginning of Numbers. Leviticus covers a period of only one mont
2. Read through this first segment chapter by chapter. As you do, do not become discouraged quit—Numbers gets more interesting and practical after this segment. As you read:
   a. Mark the following key words in a distinctive way: *number* or *census* (and their synonyms) *Lord spoke to, of the sons of* (then underline whose sons they were), *service, cloud, wilderness, (tabernacle)*, and *war*. Write them on an index card and use it as a bookmark as you st Numbers.
   b. Note every reference to time with a symbol such as this .
   c. In the margin of each chapter make lists of key truths you want to be able to find with e For instance next to 9:15 you might write: "Instructions re: Cloud" or simply "The Cloud."
   d. Note the theme of each chapter and record it on the NUMBERS AT A GLANCE chart on p 262 and on the line next to the chapter number in the text.

Chapters 10:11-21:35

1. This segment covers about thirty-nine years. As you study you'll discover why it takes so lon cover such a relatively short distance. As you read each chapter:
   a. Since much of what you will read in this segment is historical, you can learn a lot simply asking the five W's and an H. Ask: Who are the main characters in this chapter? Wha happening? Why is it happening? When and where is it happening? Why are they told to something? What were the consequences of their actions? How and why did this occur?

1) You might want to note in the margin when and where events occur.

2) Follow the movements of the Israelites on the map at Numbers 11 on page 217.

b. Mark key repeated words. Use the list you used in the first segment, although *war* won't be repeated until the final segment of Numbers. Watch for key words which are not on the list but will be significant in a particular chapter.

c. As you read, write on a piece of paper what you learn about the land the Israelites are to possess and what you learn about Korah and Balaam. (Balaam appears in Numbers 22.) These two men will be mentioned again, even in the New Testament, so it will be helpful to summarize all you learn about them. Record your insights on the chart INSIGHTS FROM NUMBERS at the end of Numbers on page 261.

d. There are lessons to be learned from Moses' life about leadership and about our relationship to God. Although you probably will want to note these lessons in the chapter margins, you'll also find it profitable to summarize what you learn on LESSONS FROM THE LIFE OF MOSES, a chart in the appendix of your Bible on page 1875. When you record your insights, make sure you note the book, chapter, and verse from which you took your insight.

As you did before, record each chapter theme on NUMBERS AT A GLANCE and in the text.

ters 22-36

This final segment of Numbers is a mixture of historical events, instructions, and numberings. As you read each chapter, remember to ask the five W's and an H and record any pertinent insights in the margin.

To your list of key words add the following: *Balaam, Moab* (Moab is first mentioned in Numbers 21, so go back and mark Moab in that chapter also), *Midian (Midianites), covenant, burnt offering,* and *sin offering.*

Balaam plays a major role in this last segment. Note all you learn about him on INSIGHTS FROM NUMBERS on page 261.

Record the main points or events of these chapters in the margin. As you near the end of Numbers you'll read more about Balaam, so note in the margin where these final verses on Balaam can be found.

Record what you learn about Moses. Give special attention to Numbers 27:12-23 in the light of Numbers 20. Next to Numbers 20:1-13 you might want to write Numbers 27:12-23 as a cross reference.

Record your chapter themes as you did before.

a. Record the predominant theme or event in each of the three segments of Numbers on NUMBERS AT A GLANCE.

b. See if any of the chapters can be grouped according to the types of commands, ordinances, and/or events. In other words, do several chapters cover similar topics or events? For example, chapters 1 and 2 cover the census. Note these on the second line under "Segment Divisions" and complete the chart.

NGS TO THINK ABOUT

Review all you learned from Moses' life and then pray about how it applies to your own life.

. Remember God is the same yesterday, today, and forever. His character did not change between the Old Testament and the New Testament. Think about what you have learned about God from the book of Numbers. Are you living accordingly?

. Are you jealous that the children of Israel had a cloud to guide them? Have you realized that God's presence in the form of the indwelling Spirit is there to guide you? Do you seek and ask for His Spirit to lead and guide you just as surely as He led the children of Israel? What can you learn from the children of Israel so you won't make the same mistakes?

Chapter 1

1 Then the LORD spoke to Moses in the wilderness of Sinai, in the
tent of meeting, on [a]the first of the second month, in the second
year after they had come out of the land of Egypt, saying,
2 "[a]Take a [1]census of all the congregation of the sons of Israel, by
their families, by their fathers' households, according to the number
of names, every male, head by head
3 from [a]twenty years old and upward, whoever *is able to* go out to
war in Israel, you and Aaron shall [1]number them by their armies.
4 "With you, moreover, there shall be a man of each tribe, [a]each one
head of his father's household.
5 "These then are the names of the men who shall stand with you:
[a]of Reuben, Elizur the son of Shedeur;
6 of Simeon, Shelumiel the son of Zurishaddai;
7 of Judah, [a]Nahshon the son of Amminadab;
8 of Issachar, Nethanel the son of Zuar;
9 of Zebulun, Eliab the son of Helon;
10 of the sons of Joseph: of Ephraim, Elishama the son of Ammi-
hud; of Manasseh, Gamaliel the son of Pedahzur;
11 of Benjamin, Abidan the son of Gideoni;
12 of Dan, Ahiezer the son of Ammishaddai;
13 of Asher, Pagiel the son of Ochran;
14 of Gad, Eliasaph the son of [a]Deuel;
15 of Naphtali, Ahira the son of Enan.
16 "These are they who were [a]called of the congregation, the leaders
of their fathers' tribes; they were the [b]heads of [1]divisions of Israel."
17 So Moses and Aaron took these men who had been designated
by name,
18 and they assembled all the congregation together on the [a]first of
the second month. Then they registered by [b]ancestry in their
families, by their fathers' households, according to the number of
names, from twenty years old and upward, head by head,
19 just as [a]the LORD had commanded Moses. So he numbered them
in the wilderness of Sinai.
20 [a]Now the sons of Reuben, Israel's first-born, their genealogical
registration by their families, by their fathers' households, according
to the number of names, head by head, every male from twenty
years old and upward, whoever *was able to* go out to war,
21 their numbered men, of the tribe of Reuben, *were* 46,500.
22 [a]Of the sons of Simeon, their genealogical registration by their
families, by their fathers' households, their numbered men, accord-
ing to the number of names, head by head, every male from twenty
years old and upward, [b]whoever *was able to* go out to war,
23 their numbered men, of the tribe of Simeon, *were* 59,300.
24 [a]Of the sons of Gad, their genealogical registration by their fami-
lies, by their fathers' households, according to the number of names,
from twenty years old and upward, whoever *was able to* go out to
war,
25 their numbered men, of the tribe of Gad, *were* 45,650.
26 [a]Of the sons of Judah, their genealogical registration by their
families, by their fathers' households, according to the number of
names, from twenty years old and upward, whoever *was able to* go
out to war,
27 their numbered men, of the tribe of Judah, *were* 74,600.

1:1 [a]Ex. 40:2

2 [1]Lit., *sum* [a]...
38:25, 26; Nu...

3 [1]Lit., *muste*...
throughout the...
30:14; 38:26

4 [a]Ex. 18:21, ...
1:16; Deut. 1:1...

5 [a]Gen. 29:32...
Deut. 33:6; Re...

7 [a]Ruth 4:20; 1...
2:10; Luke 3:32

14 [a]Num. 2:14

16 [1]Lit., *thousa*...
clans [a]Ex. 18:2...
7:2; 16:2; 26:9 ...
18:25

18 [a]Num. 1:1 [b]...
2:59; Heb. 7:3

19 [a]2 Sam. 24:1

20 [a]Num. 26:5-7

22 [a]Num. 26:12-1...
[b]Ps. 144:1

24 [a]Gen. 30:11; N...
26:15-18; Josh. 4:...
Jer. 49:1

28 [a]Of the sons of Issachar, their genealogical registration by their families, by their fathers' households, according to the number of names, from twenty years old and upward, whoever *was able to* go out to war,
29 their numbered men, of the tribe of Issachar, *were* 54,400.
30 [a]Of the sons of Zebulun, their genealogical registration by their families, by their fathers' households, according to the number of names, from twenty years old and upward, whoever *was able to* go out to war,
31 their numbered men, of the tribe of Zebulun, *were* 57,400.
32 [a]Of the sons of Joseph, *namely*, of the sons of Ephraim, their genealogical registration by their families, by their fathers' households, according to the number of names, from twenty years old and upward, whoever *was able to* go out to war,
33 their numbered men, of the tribe of Ephraim, *were* 40,500.
34 [a]Of the sons of Manasseh, their genealogical registration by their families, by their fathers' households, according to the number of names, from twenty years old and upward, whoever *was able to* go out to war,
35 their numbered men, of the tribe of Manasseh, *were* 32,200.
36 [a]Of the sons of Benjamin, their genealogical registration by their families, by their fathers' households, according to the number of names, from twenty years old and upward, whoever *was able to* go out to war,
37 their numbered men, of the tribe of Benjamin, *were* 35,400.
38 [a]Of the sons of Dan, their genealogical registration by their families, by their fathers' households, according to the number of names, from twenty years old and upward, whoever *was able to* go out to war,
39 their numbered men, of the tribe of Dan, *were* 62,700.
40 [a]Of the sons of Asher, their genealogical registration by their families, by their fathers' households, according to the number of names, from twenty years old and upward, whoever *was able to* go out to war,
41 their numbered men, of the tribe of Asher, *were* 41,500.
42 [a]Of the sons of Naphtali, their genealogical registration by their families, by their fathers' households, according to the number of names, from twenty years old and upward, whoever *was able to* go out to war,
43 their numbered men, of the tribe of Naphtali, *were* 53,400.
44 These are the ones who were numbered, whom Moses and Aaron numbered, with the leaders of Israel, twelve men, each of whom was of his father's household.
45 So all the numbered men of the sons of Israel by their fathers' households, from twenty years old and upward, whoever *was able to* go out to war in Israel,
46 even all the numbered men were [a]603,550.
47 [a]The Levites, however, were not numbered among them by their fathers' tribe.
48 For the LORD had spoken to Moses, saying,
49 "Only the tribe of Levi [a]you shall not number, nor shall you take their [1]census among the sons of Israel.
50 "But you shall [a]appoint the Levites over the [1]tabernacle of the testimony, and over all its furnishings and over all that belongs to it.

29:35; Num. 2 Sam. 24:9; :68; Matt. 1:2
um. 26:23-25
um. 26:26, 27
um. 26:35-37; 33:13-17; Jer. ':15; Obad. 19
Num. 26:28-34
n. 49:27; Num. ; 2 Chr. 17:17; Rev. 7:8
en. 30:6; 46:23; 2:25; 26:42, 43
[a]Num. 26:44-47
[a]Num. 26:48-50
x. 12:37; 38:26; um. 2:32; 26:51
n. 2:33; 3:14-39; 4:49; 26:57-64
[1]Lit., *sum* [a]Num. 26:62
., *dwelling place*, so throughout the [a]Ex. 38:21; Num. :6-8, 25-37; 4:15, 25-27, 31, 32

They shall carry the tabernacle and all its furnishings, and they shall
take care of it; they shall also camp around the [1]tabernacle.
51 "[a]So when the tabernacle is to set out, the Levites shall take it
down; and when the tabernacle encamps, the Levites shall set it up.
But [b]the [1]layman who comes near shall be put to death.
52 "[a]And the sons of Israel shall camp, each man by his own camp,
and each man by his own standard, according to their armies.
53 "[a]But the Levites shall camp around the tabernacle of the testi-
mony, that there may be [b]no wrath on the congregation of the sons of
Israel. [c]So the Levites shall keep charge of the tabernacle of the
testimony."
54 Thus the sons of Israel did; according to all which the LORD had
commanded Moses, so they did.

Chapter 2

2 Now the LORD spoke to Moses and to Aaron, saying,
2 "[a]The sons of Israel shall camp, each by his own standard, with
the [1]banners of their fathers' households; they shall camp around the
tent of meeting [2]at a distance.
3 "Now those who camp on the east side toward the sunrise *shall be*
of the standard of the camp of Judah, by their armies, and the leader
of the sons of Judah: [a]Nahshon the son of Amminadab,
4 and his army, even their [1]numbered men, 74,600.
5 "And those who camp next to him *shall be* the tribe of Issachar,
and the leader of the sons of Issachar: [a]Nethanel the son of Zuar,
6 and his army, even their numbered men, 54,400.
7 "Then *comes* the tribe of Zebulun, and the leader of the sons of
Zebulun: [a]Eliab the son of Helon,
8 and his army, even his numbered men, 57,400.
9 "The total of the numbered men of the camp of Judah: 186,400, by
their armies. [a]They shall set out first.
10 "On the south side *shall be* the standard of the camp of Reuben by
their armies, and the leader of the sons of Reuben: [a]Elizur the son of
Shedeur,
11 and his army, even their numbered men, 46,500.
12 "And those who camp next to him *shall be* the tribe of Simeon,
and the leader of the sons of Simeon: [a]Shelumiel the son of
Zurishaddai,
13 and his army, even their numbered men, 59,300.
14 "Then *comes* the tribe of Gad, and the leader of the sons of Gad:
[a]Eliasaph the son of [1]Deuel,
15 and his army, even their numbered men, 45,650.
16 "The total of the numbered men of the camp of Reuben: 151,450
by their armies. And [a]they shall set out second.
17 "[a]Then the tent of meeting shall set out *with* the camp of the
Levites in the midst of the camps; just as they camp, so they shall set
out, every man in his place, by their standards.
18 "On the west side *shall be* the standard of the camp of [a]Ephraim
by their armies, and the leader of the sons of Ephraim *shall be*
[b]Elishama the son of Ammihud,
19 and his army, even their numbered men, 40,500.
20 "And next to him *shall be* the tribe of Manasseh, and the leader of
the sons of Manasseh: [a]Gamaliel the son of Pedahzur,
21 and his army, even their numbered men, 32,200.

50 [1]Lit., *d*... and so thr... the ch.
51 [1]Lit., *st*... [a]Num. 4:1-... 3:10, 38; 4:...
52 [a]Num. 2...
53 [a]Num. 3... 38 [b]Lev. 10... 16:46; 18:5... 18:2-4; 1 Ch...
2:2 [1]Lit., *sig*... *facing it* [a]Nu... 24:2
3 [a]Num. 1:7... Ruth 4:20; 1... Luke 3:32, 3...
4 [1]Lit., *must*... so throughou...
5 [a]Num. 1:8...
7 [a]Num. 1:9
9 [a]Num. 10:1...
10 [a]Num. 1:5...
12 [a]Num. 1:6
14 [1]Many mss... *Reuel* [a]Num. ...
16 [a]Num. 10:1...
17 [a]Num. 1:53
18 [a]Gen. 48:14... 31:9, 18-20 [b]N...
20 [a]Num. 1:10

22 "Then *comes* the tribe of [a]Ben-
jamin, and the leader of the sons of
Benjamin: [b]Abidan the son of
Gideoni,
23 and his army, even their num-
bered men, 35,400.
24 "The total of the numbered men
of the camp of Ephraim: 108,100,
by their armies. And [a]they shall set
out third.
25 "On the north side *shall be* the
standard of the camp of Dan by
their armies, and the leader of the
sons of Dan: [a]Ahiezer the son of
Ammishaddai,
26 and his army, even their num-
bered men, 62,700.
27 "And those who camp next to
him *shall be* the tribe of Asher, and
the leader of the sons of Asher:
[a]Pagiel the son of Ochran,
28 and his army, even their numbered men, 41,500.
29 "Then *comes* the tribe of [a]Naphtali, and the leader of the sons of
Naphtali: [b]Ahira the son of Enan,
30 and his army, even their numbered men, 53,400.
31 "The total of the numbered men of the camp of Dan, *was* 157,600.
[a]They shall set out last by their standards."
32 These are the numbered men of the sons of Israel by their
fathers' households; the total of the numbered men of the camps by
their armies, [a]603,550.
33 [a]The Levites, however, were not numbered among the sons of
Israel, just as the LORD had commanded Moses.
34 Thus the sons of Israel did; according to all that the LORD com-
manded Moses, so they camped by their standards, and so they set
out, every one by his family, according to his father's household.

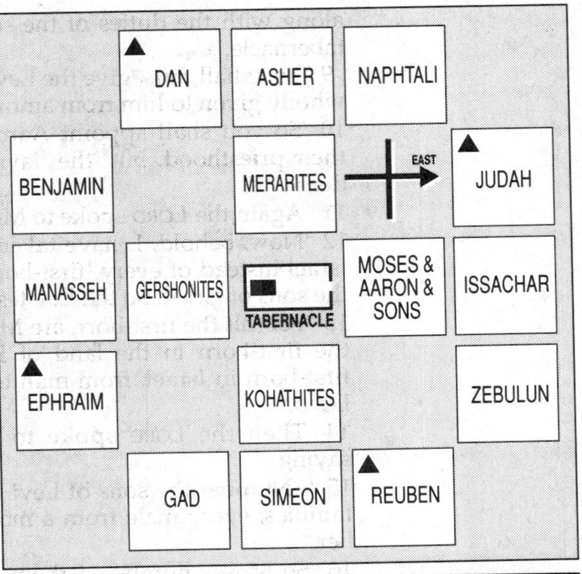
DAN
ASHER
NAPHTALI
BENJAMIN
MERARITES
EAST
JUDAH
MANASSEH
GERSHONITES
TABERNACLE
MOSES & AARON & SONS
ISSACHAR
EPHRAIM
KOHATHITES
ZEBULUN
GAD
SIMEON
REUBEN

Camp Arrangement of Israel's Tribes
Key: ▲ Denotes the leaders of each group

Chapter 3

3 [a]Now these are *the records of* the generations of Aaron and Moses
at the time when the LORD spoke with Moses on Mount Sinai.
2 [a]These then are the names of the sons of Aaron: Nadab the first-
born, and Abihu, Eleazar and Ithamar.
3 These are the names of the sons of Aaron, the [a]anointed priests,
whom he [1]ordained to serve as priests.
4 [a]But Nadab and Abihu died before the LORD when they offered
strange fire before the LORD in the wilderness of Sinai; and they had
no children. So Eleazar and Ithamar served as priests [1]in the lifetime
of their father Aaron.
5 Then the LORD spoke to Moses, saying,
6 "[a]Bring the tribe of Levi near and set them before Aaron the priest,
that they may serve him.
7 "And they shall perform the duties for [1]him and for the whole
congregation before the tent of meeting, to do the [a]service of the
tabernacle.
8 "They shall also keep all the furnishings of the tent of meeting,

8:27 [b]Num. 1:11
[a]Num. 10:22
5 [a]Num. 1:12
7 [a]Num. 1:13
. 30:8 [b]Num. 1:15
[a]Num. 10:25
x. 38:26; Num. 1:46
3 [a]Num. 1:47; 26:57-62
1 [a]Ex. 6:20-27
23; Num. 26:60
filled their hand [a]Ex. 28:41
, before the face
ev. 10:1, 2; Num. 26:61
. 8:6-22; 18:1-7; Deut. 10:8
[1]Lit., him and the uties of the whole gregation [a]Num. 1:50

along with the duties of the sons of Israel, to do the service of the
tabernacle.
9 "You shall thus [a]give the Levites to Aaron and to his sons; they are
wholly given to him from among the sons of Israel.
10 "So you shall appoint Aaron and his sons that [a]they may keep
their priesthood, but [b]the [1]layman who comes near shall be put to
death."
11 Again the LORD spoke to Moses, saying,
12 "Now, behold, I [a]have taken the Levites from among the sons of
Israel instead of every [b]first-born, the first issue of the womb among
the sons of Israel. So the Levites shall be Mine.
13 "For [a]all the first-born are Mine; on the day that I struck down all
the first-born in the land of Egypt, I sanctified to Myself all the
first-born in Israel, from man to beast. They shall be Mine; I am the
LORD."
14 Then the LORD spoke to Moses [a]in the wilderness of Sinai,
saying,
15 "[1a]Number the sons of Levi by their fathers' households, by their
families; every male from a month old and upward you shall num-
ber."
16 So Moses numbered them according to the [1]word of the LORD,
just as he had been commanded.
17 [a]These then are the sons of Levi by their names: Gershon and
Kohath and Merari.
18 And these are the names of the [a]sons of Gershon by their
families: Libni and Shimei;
19 and the sons of Kohath by their families: Amram and Izhar,
Hebron and Uzziel;
20 and the sons of Merari by their families: Mahli and Mushi. These
are the families of the Levites according to their fathers' households.
21 Of Gershon *was* the family of the Libnites and the family of the
Shimeites; these *were* the families of the Gershonites.
22 Their numbered men, in the numbering of every male from a
month old and upward, *even* their numbered men *were* 7,500.
23 The families of the Gershonites were to camp behind the [1]taber-
nacle westward,
24 and the leader of the fathers' households of the Gershonites *was*
Eliasaph the son of Lael.
25 Now [a]the duties of the sons of Gershon in the tent of meeting
involved the tabernacle and [b]the tent, its covering, and [c]the screen for
the doorway of the tent of meeting,
26 and [a]the hangings of the court, and [b]the screen for the doorway
of the court, which is around the tabernacle and the altar, and its
cords, according to all the service [1]concerning them.
27 And of Kohath *was* the family of the Amramites and the family
of the Izharites and the family of the Hebronites and the family of
the Uzzielites; these were the families of the Kohathites.
28 In the numbering of every male from a month old and upward,
there were 8,600, performing the duties of the sanctuary.
29 The families of the sons of Kohath were to camp on the south-
ward side of the tabernacle,
30 and the leader of the fathers' households of the Kohathite
families was [1]Elizaphan the son of Uzziel.
31 Now [a]their duties *involved* [b]the ark, [c]the table, [d]the lampstand,

9 [a]Num. 18
10 [1]Lit., *stra* 29:9 [b]Num.
12 [a]Num. 3 [b]Ex. 13:2
13 [a]Ex. 13:2 27:26; Neh. 1
14 [a]Ex. 19:1
15 [1]Lit., *mus* throughout th [a]Num. 1:47
16 [1]Lit., *mou*
17 [a]Ex. 6:16-2
18 [a]Ex. 6:17
23 [1]Lit., *dwelli* and so through the ch.
25 [a]Num. 4:24 26:1, 7, 14 [c]Ex
26 [1]Lit., *of it* [a]E 12, 14, 15 [b]Ex.
30 [1]In Ex. 6:22, *Elzaphan*
31 [a]Num. 4:15 25:10-22 [c]Ex. 2 [d]Ex. 25:31-40

[e]the altars, and the utensils of the sanctuary with which they minis-
ter, and the screen, and all the service [1]concerning them;
32 and Eleazar the son of Aaron the priest *was* the chief of the
leaders of Levi, *and had* the oversight of those who perform the
duties of the sanctuary.
33 Of Merari *was* the family of the Mahlites and the family of the
Mushites; these *were* the families of Merari.
34 Their numbered men in the numbering of every male from a
month old and upward, *were* 6,200.
35 And the leader of the fathers' households of the families of
Merari *was* Zuriel the son of Abihail. They *were* to [a]camp on the
northward side of the tabernacle.
36 Now the appointed duties of the sons of Merari *involved* the
frames of the tabernacle, its bars, its pillars, its sockets, all its equip-
ment, and the service concerning them,
37 and the pillars around the court with their sockets and their pegs
and their cords.
38 Now those who were to [a]camp before the tabernacle eastward,
before the tent of meeting toward the sunrise, are Moses and Aaron
and his sons, performing the duties of the sanctuary for the obliga-
tion of the sons of Israel; but [b]the [1]layman coming near was to be put
to death.
39 All the numbered men of the Levites, whom Moses and Aaron
numbered at the [1]command of the LORD by their families, every male
from a month old and upward, *were* [a]22,000.
40 Then the LORD said to Moses, "[a]Number every first-born male of
the sons of Israel from a month old and upward, and [1]make a list of
their names.
41 "And you [a]shall take the Levites for Me, I am the LORD, instead of
all the first-born among the sons of Israel, and the cattle of the
Levites instead of all the first-born among the cattle of the sons of
Israel."
42 So Moses numbered all the first-born among the sons of Israel,
just as the LORD had commanded him;
43 and all the first-born males by the number of names from a
month old and upward, for their numbered men were [a]22,273.
44 Then the LORD spoke to Moses, saying,
45 "[a]Take the Levites instead of all the first-born among the sons of
Israel and the cattle of the Levites. And the Levites shall be Mine; I
am the LORD.
46 "[a]And for the ransom of the 273 of the first-born of the sons of
Israel who are in excess beyond the Levites,
47 you shall take [a]five shekels apiece, per head; you shall take *them*
in [b]terms of the shekel of the sanctuary ([c]the shekel is twenty
[1]gerahs),
48 and give the money, the ransom of those who are in excess
among them, to Aaron and to his sons."
49 So Moses took the ransom money from those who were in ex-
cess, beyond those ransomed by the Levites;
50 from the first-born of the sons of Israel he took the money in
terms of the shekel of the sanctuary, 1,365.
51 Then Moses gave the ransom money to Aaron and to his sons, at
the [1]command of the LORD, just as the LORD had commanded Moses.

it [e]Ex. 27:1, 2; 30:1-5
n. 1:53; 2:25
[1]Lit., *stranger* 3; 2:3 [b]Num. 1:51
word [a]Num. 3; 4:48; 26:62
[1]Lit., *take the* *er* [a]Num. 3:15
Num. 3:12, 45
43 [a]Num. 3:39
45 [a]Num. 3:12
3:13, 15; Num. 18:15, 16
A gerah equals one-fortieth oz. 7:6; Num. 18:16 :13 [c]Lev. 27:25; Ezek. 45:12
51 [1]Lit., *mouth*

Chapter 4

4 Then the LORD spoke to Moses and to Aaron, saying,
2 "Take [1]a census of the [2]descendants of Kohath from among the
sons of Levi, by their families, by their fathers' households,
3 from [a]thirty years and upward, even to fifty years old, all who
enter the service to do the work in the tent of meeting.
4 "This is the work of the [1]descendants of Kohath in the tent of
meeting, *concerning* the most holy things.
5 "When the camp sets out, Aaron and his sons shall go in and they
shall take down [a]the veil of the screen and cover the [b]ark of the
testimony with it;
6 and they shall lay a [a]covering of porpoise skin on it, and shall
spread over *it* a cloth of pure [1]blue, and shall insert its poles.
7 "Over the table of the bread of the Presence they shall also spread
a cloth of [1]blue and put on it the dishes and the pans and the sacrifi-
cial bowls and the jars for the libation, and [a]the continual bread shall
be on it.
8 "And they shall spread over them a cloth of scarlet *material*, and
cover the same with a covering of porpoise skin, and they shall
insert its poles.
9 "Then they shall take a [1]blue cloth and cover the [a]lampstand for
the light, [b]along with its lamps and its snuffers, and its [2]trays and all
its oil vessels, by which they serve it;
10 and they shall put it and all its utensils in a covering of porpoise
skin, and shall put it on the carrying bars.
11 "And over the golden altar they shall spread a [1]blue cloth and
cover it with a covering of porpoise skin, and shall insert its poles;
12 and they shall take all the utensils of service, with which they
serve in the sanctuary, and put them in a [1]blue cloth and cover them
with a covering of porpoise skin, and put them on the carrying bars.
13 "Then they shall take away the [1]ashes from the [a]altar, and spread
a purple cloth over it.
14 "They shall also put on it all its utensils by which they serve in
connection with it: the firepans, the forks and shovels and the basins,
all the utensils of the altar; and they shall spread a cover of porpoise
skin over it and insert its poles.
15 "And when Aaron and his sons have finished covering the holy
objects and all the furnishings of the sanctuary, when the camp is to
set out, after that the sons of Kohath shall come to carry *them*, so that
they may not touch the holy *objects* [a]and die. These are the [1]things in
the tent of meeting which the sons of Kohath are to carry.
16 "And the responsibility of Eleazar the son of Aaron the priest is
[a]the oil for the light and the [b]fragrant incense and [c]the continual
grain offering and [d]the anointing oil—the responsibility of all the
[1]tabernacle and of all that is in it, with the sanctuary and its furnish-
ings."
17 Then the LORD spoke to Moses and to Aaron, saying,
18 "Do not let the tribe of the families of the Kohathites be cut off
from among the Levites.
19 "But do this to them that they may live and [a]not die when they
approach the most holy *objects:* Aaron and his sons shall go in and
assign each of them to his work and to his load;
20 but [a]they shall not go in to see the holy *objects* even for a mo-
ment, lest they die."

4:2 [1]Lit., *th*
sons

3 [a]Num. 4:
8:24; 1 Chr.
27; Ezra 3:8

4 [1]Lit., *sons*

5 [a]Ex. 40:5;
2 Chr. 3:14;
Heb. 9:3 [b]E

6 [1]Or, *violet*

7 [1]Or, *violet*
Lev. 24:5-9

9 [1]Or, *violet*
dishes [a]Ex. 2
25:37, 38

11 [1]Or, *violet*

12 [1]Or, *violet*

13 [1]Or, *fat ash*
soaked with fa
27:1-8

15 [1]Lit., *burde*
the sons [a]Num
4:19, 20; 2 Sam

16 [1]Lit., *dwellin*
and so through
ch. [a]Lev. 24:1-
30:34-38 [c]Lev.
[d]Ex. 30:22-33

19 [a]Num. 4:15

20 [a]Ex. 19:21; 1
6:19

21 Then the LORD spoke to Moses, saying,
22 "Take [1]a census of the sons of Gershon [2]also, by their fathers'
households, by their families;
23 from [a]thirty years and upward to fifty years old, you shall [1]num-
ber them; all who enter to perform the service to do the work in the
tent of meeting.
24 "This is the service of the families of the Gershonites, in serving
and in carrying:
25 they shall carry [a]the curtains of the tabernacle and the tent of
meeting *with* its covering and [b]the covering of porpoise skin that is
on top of it, and the screen for the doorway of the tent of meeting,
26 and [a]the hangings of the court, and the screen for the doorway of
the gate of the court which is around the tabernacle and the altar,
and their cords and all the equipment for their service; and all that is
to be done, [1]they shall perform.
27 "All the service of the sons of the Gershonites, in all their loads
and in all their work, shall be *performed* at the [1]command of Aaron
and his sons; and you shall assign to them as a duty all their loads.
28 "This is the service of the families of the sons of the Gershonites
in the tent of meeting, and their duties *shall be* [1]under the direction of
Ithamar the son of Aaron the priest.
29 "*As for* the sons of Merari, you shall number them by their
families, by their fathers' households;
30 from [a]thirty years and upward even to fifty years old, you shall
number them, everyone who enters the service to do the work of the
tent of meeting.
31 "Now this is the duty of their loads, for all their service in the tent
of meeting: the boards of the tabernacle and its bars and its pillars
and its [1]sockets,
32 and the pillars around the court and their [1]sockets and their pegs
and their cords, with all their equipment and with all their service;
and you shall assign *each man* by name the items [2]he is to carry.
33 "This is the service of the families of the sons of Merari, according
to all their service in the tent of meeting, [1]under the direction of
Ithamar the son of Aaron the priest."
34 So Moses and Aaron and the leaders of the congregation num-
bered the sons of the Kohathites by their families, and by their
fathers' households,
35 from [a]thirty years and upward even to fifty years old, everyone
who entered the service for work in the tent of meeting.
36 And their numbered men by their families were 2,750.
37 These are the numbered men of the Kohathite families, everyone
who was serving in the tent of meeting, whom Moses and Aaron
numbered according to the [1]commandment of the LORD [2]through
Moses.
38 And the numbered men of the sons of Gershon by their families,
and by their fathers' households,
39 from thirty years and upward even to fifty years old, everyone
who entered the service for work in the tent of meeting.
40 And their numbered men by their families, by their fathers'
households, were 2,630.
41 These are the numbered men of the families of the sons of Ger-
shon, everyone who was serving in the tent of meeting, whom

[1]Lit., *the sum* [2]Lit., *also them*

...it., *muster*, and so throughout the ch. ...n. 4:3; 1 Chr. 23:3, 24, 27

...5 [a]Ex. 40:19 [b]Ex. 26:14; Num. 4:6

[1]Lit., *so they shall serve* [a]Ex. 38:9

27 [1]Lit., *mouth*

...8 [1]Lit., *in the hand*

[a]Num. 4:3; 8:24-26

31 [1]Or, *bases*

[1]Or, *bases* [2]Lit., *of duty of their loads.*

...3 [1]Lit., *in the hand*

35 [a]1 Chr. 23:24

...it., *mouth* [2]Lit., *by the hand of*

Moses and Aaron numbered according to the [1]commandment of the
LORD.
42 And the numbered men of the families of the sons of Merari by
their families, by their fathers' households,
43 from [a]thirty years and upward even to fifty years old, everyone
who entered the service for work in the tent of meeting.
44 And their numbered men by their families were 3,200.
45 These are the numbered men of the families of the sons of
Merari, whom Moses and Aaron numbered according to the [1]com-
mandment of the LORD [2]through Moses.
46 All the numbered men of the Levites, whom Moses and Aaron
and the leaders of Israel numbered, by their families and by their
fathers' households,
47 from thirty years and upward even to fifty years old, everyone
who could enter to do the work of service and the work of carrying
in the tent of meeting.
48 And their numbered men were [a]8,580.
49 According to the [1]commandment of the LORD [2]through Moses,
they [a]were numbered, everyone by his serving or carrying; thus
these were his numbered men, just as the LORD had commanded
Moses.

Chapter 5

5 Then the LORD spoke to Moses, saying,
2 "Command the sons of Israel that they [a]send away from the
camp every leper and everyone having a [b]discharge and everyone
who is [c]unclean because of a *dead* person.
3 "You shall send away both male and female; you shall send them
outside the camp so that they will not defile their camp where I
dwell [a]in their midst."
4 And the sons of Israel did so and sent them outside the camp;
just as the LORD had spoken to Moses, thus the sons of Israel did.
5 Then the LORD spoke to Moses, saying,
6 "Speak to the sons of Israel, '[a]When a man or woman commits
any of the sins of mankind, acting unfaithfully against the LORD, and
that person is guilty,
7 then [1]he shall [a]confess [2]his sins which [3]he has committed, and he
[b]shall make restitution in full for his wrong, and add to it one-fifth of
it, and give *it* to him whom he has wronged.
8 'But if the man has no [1]relative to whom restitution may be made
for the wrong, the restitution which is made for the wrong *must go* to
the LORD for the priest, besides the ram of atonement, by which
atonement is made for him.
9 '[a]Also every [1]contribution pertaining to all the holy *gifts* of the
sons of Israel, which they offer to the priest, shall be his.
10 'So every man's holy *gifts* shall be his; whatever any man gives to
the priest, it [a]becomes his.' "
11 Then the LORD spoke to Moses, saying,
12 "Speak to the sons of Israel, and say to them, 'If any man's wife
[a]goes astray and is unfaithful to him,
13 and a man has [a]intercourse with her and it is hidden from the
eyes of her husband and she is [1]undetected, although she has defiled
herself, and there is no witness against her and she has not been
caught in the act,

41 [1]Lit., *mou*
43 [a]Num. 8:2
45 [1]Lit., *mout* *the hand of*
48 [a]Num. 3:39
49 [1]Lit., *mouth* *the hand of* [a]N
5:2 [a]Lev. 13:8, Num. 12:10, 14 [b]Lev. 15:2 [c]Lev Num. 9:6-10; 1
3 [a]Lev. 26:12; 35:34
6 [a]Lev. 5:14-6:7
7 [1]Lit., *they* [2]Li [3]Lit., *they have* 5:5; 26:40, 41; J 7:19 [b]Lev. 6:4, 5
8 [1]Lit., *redeeme*
9 [1]Lit., *heave off* [a]Lev. 7:32, 34; 10
10 [a]Lev. 10:13
12 [a]Num. 5:19-2
13 [1]Lit., *conceale* [a]Lev. 18:20; 20:10

14 [1]if a spirit of [a]jealousy comes over him and he is jealous of his wife when she has defiled herself, or if a spirit of jealousy comes over him and he is jealous of his wife when she has not defiled herself,

15 the man shall then bring his wife to the priest, and shall bring *as* [1]an offering for her one-tenth of an [2]ephah of barley meal; he shall not pour oil on it, nor put frankincense on it, for it is a grain offering of jealousy, a grain offering of memorial, [a]a reminder of iniquity.

16 'Then the priest shall bring her near and have her stand before the LORD,

17 and the priest shall take holy water in an earthenware vessel; and [1]he shall take some of the dust that is on the floor of the tabernacle and put *it* into the water.

18 'The priest shall then have the woman stand before the LORD and let *the hair of* the woman's head go loose, and place the grain offering of memorial [1]in her hands, which is the grain offering of jealousy, and in the hand of the priest is to be the water of bitterness that brings a curse.

19 'And the priest shall have her take an oath and shall say to the woman, "If no man has lain with you and if you have not [a]gone astray into uncleanness, *being* under *the authority of* your husband, be [1]immune to this water of bitterness that brings a curse;

20 if you, however, have [a]gone astray, *being* under *the authority of* your husband, and if you have defiled yourself and a man other than your husband has had intercourse with you"

21 (then the priest shall have the woman [a]swear with the oath of the curse, and the priest shall say to the woman), "the LORD make you a curse and an oath among your people by the LORD's making your thigh [1]waste away and your abdomen swell;

22 and this water that brings a curse shall go into your [1]stomach, and make your abdomen swell and your thigh [2]waste away." And the woman [a]shall say, "Amen. Amen."

23 'The priest shall then write these curses on a scroll, and he shall [1]wash them off into the water of bitterness.

24 'Then he shall make the woman drink the water of bitterness that brings a curse, so that the water which brings a curse will go into her [1]and *cause* bitterness.

25 'And the priest shall take the grain offering of jealousy from the woman's hand, and he shall wave the grain offering before the LORD and bring it to the altar;

26 and [a]the priest shall take a handful of the grain offering as its memorial offering and offer *it* up in smoke on the altar, and afterward he shall make the woman drink the water.

27 'When he has made her drink the water, then it shall come about, if she has defiled herself and has been unfaithful to her husband, that the water which brings a curse shall go into her [1]and *cause* bitterness, and her abdomen will swell and her thigh will [2]waste away, and the woman will become [a]a curse among her people.

28 'But if the woman has not defiled herself and is clean, she will then be free and conceive [1]children.

29 'This is the law of jealousy: when a wife, *being* under *the authority of* her husband, [a]goes astray and defiles herself,

30 or when a spirit of jealousy comes over a man and he is jealous

[1]Lit., *and* [a]Prov. 6:34; Song 8:6
15 [1]Lit., *her* [2]I.e., ...x. one bu. [a]1 Kin. ...7:18; Ezek. 29:16
...7 [1]Lit., *the priest*
[1]Lit., *on her palms*
19 [1]Lit., *free from* [a]Num. 5:12
20 [a]Num. 5:12
... [1]Lit., *fall* [a]Josh. ...26; 1 Sam. 14:24; Neh. 10:29
[1]Or, *inward parts* ... *fall* [a]Deut. 27:15
23 [1]Lit., *wipe*
24 [1]Lit., *to*
26 [a]Lev. 2:2, 9
[1]Lit., *to* [2]Lit., *fall* ...:18; 42:18; 44:12
28 [1]Lit., *seed*
29 [a]Num. 5:12

of his wife, he shall then make the woman stand before the LORD,
and the priest shall apply all this law to her.
31 'Moreover, the man shall be free from [1]guilt, but that woman
shall [a]bear her [1]guilt.' "

Chapter 6

6 Again the LORD spoke to Moses, saying,
2 "Speak to the sons of Israel, and say to them, 'When a man or
woman makes a [1]special vow, the vow of [a]a [2]Nazirite, to [3]dedicate
himself to the LORD,
3 he shall [a]abstain from wine and strong drink; he shall drink no
vinegar, whether made from wine or strong drink, neither shall he
drink any grape juice, nor eat fresh or dried grapes.
4 'All the days of his [1]separation he shall not eat anything that is
produced by the grape vine, from *the* seeds even to *the* skin.
5 'All the days of his vow of separation [a]no razor shall pass over
his head. He shall be holy until the days are fulfilled for which he
separated himself to the LORD; he shall let the locks of hair on his
head grow long.
6 '[a]All the days of his separation to the LORD he shall not go near to
a dead person.
7 'He [a]shall not make himself unclean for his father or for his
mother, for his brother or for his sister, when they die, because his
separation to God is on his head.
8 'All the days of his separation he is holy to the LORD.
9 'But if a man dies very suddenly beside him and he defiles his
dedicated head *of hair,* then [a]he shall shave his head on the day when
he becomes clean; [b]he shall shave it on the seventh day.
10 'Then on the eighth day he shall bring [a]two turtledoves or two
young pigeons to the priest, to the doorway of the tent of meeting.
11 'And the priest shall offer [a]one for a sin offering and *the* other for
a burnt offering, and make atonement for him [1]concerning his sin
because of the *dead* person. And that same day he shall consecrate
his head,
12 and shall dedicate to the LORD his days [1]as a [2]Nazirite, and shall
bring a male lamb a year old for a guilt offering; but the former days
shall be void because his separation was defiled.
13 'Now this is the law of the Nazirite [a]when the days of his separa-
tion are fulfilled, he shall bring [1]the offering to the doorway of the
tent of meeting.
14 'And he shall present his offering to the LORD: one male lamb a
year old without defect for a burnt offering and one [a]ewe-lamb a
year old without defect for a sin offering and one ram without defect
for a peace offering,
15 and a basket of [a]unleavened cakes of fine flour mixed with oil
and unleavened wafers spread with oil, along with [b]their grain offer-
ing and their libations.
16 'Then the priest shall present *them* before the LORD and shall offer
his sin offering and his burnt offering.
17 'He shall also offer the ram for a sacrifice of peace offerings to the
LORD, together with the basket of unleavened cakes; the priest shall
likewise offer its grain offering and its libation.
18 '[a]The Nazirite shall then shave his dedicated head *of hair* at the
doorway of the tent of meeting, and take the dedicated hair of his

31 [1]Or, *iniqu* 20:17

6:2 [1]Or, *diffic* one separate *as a Nazirite* 13:5; 16:17; A 2:11, 12

3 [a]Luke 1:15

4 [1]Or, *living a Nazirite,* and s v. 21

5 [a]1 Sam. 1:1

6 [a]Lev. 21:1-3 19:11-22

7 [a]Num. 9:6

9 [a]Lev. 14:8, 9 6:18

10 [a]Lev. 5:7; 1

11 [1]Lit., *becaus which he sinne* 5:7

12 [1]Or, *of dedic* [2]I.e., one separa

13 [1]Lit., *it* [a]Acts

14 [a]Lev. 14:10; 15:27

15 [a]Ex. 29:2; Le [b]Num. 15:1-7

18 [a]Num. 6:9; Ac 21:23, 24

head and put *it* on the fire which is under the sacrifice of peace
offerings.
19 '[a]And the priest shall take the ram's shoulder *when it has been*
boiled, and one unleavened cake out of the basket, and one un-
leavened wafer, and shall put *them* on the [1]hands of the Nazirite after
he has shaved his [2]dedicated *hair.*
20 'Then the priest shall wave them for a wave offering before the
LORD. It is holy for the priest, together with the breast offered by
waving and the thigh offered by lifting up; and [a]afterward the
Nazirite may drink wine.'
21 "This is the law of the Nazirite who vows his offering to the LORD
according to his separation, in addition to what *else* [1]he can afford;
according to his vow which he takes, so he shall do according to the
law of his separation."
22 Then the LORD spoke to Moses, saying,
23 "Speak to Aaron and to his sons, saying, 'Thus [a]you shall bless the
sons of Israel. You shall say to them:
24 The LORD [a]bless you, and [b]keep you;
25 The LORD [a]make His face shine on you,
And [b]be gracious to you;
26 The LORD [a]lift up His countenance on you,
And [b]give you peace.'
27 "So they shall [1a]invoke My name on the sons of Israel, and I then
will bless them."

Chapter 7

7 Now it came about on [a]the day that Moses had finished setting
up the tabernacle, he [b]anointed it and consecrated it with all its
furnishings and the altar and all its utensils; he anointed them and
consecrated them also.
2 Then [a]the leaders of Israel, the heads of their fathers' households,
[b]made an offering (they were the leaders of the tribes; they were the
ones who [1]were over the [2]numbered men).
3 When they brought their offering before the LORD, six [a]covered
carts and twelve oxen, a cart for *every* two of the leaders and an ox
for each one, then they presented them before the tabernacle.
4 Then the LORD spoke to Moses, saying,
5 "Accept *these things* from them, that they may be [1]used in the
service of the tent of meeting, and you shall give them to the Levites,
to each man according to his service."
6 So Moses took the carts and the oxen, and gave them to the
Levites.
7 Two carts and four oxen he gave to the sons of Gershon, accord-
ing to [a]their service,
8 and four carts and eight oxen he gave to the sons of Merari,
according to [a]their service, under the [1]direction of Ithamar the son of
Aaron the priest.
9 But he did not give *any* to the sons of Kohath because theirs *was*
[a]the service of the holy *objects, which* they carried on the shoulder.
10 And the leaders offered the dedication *offering* [1]for the altar
[2]when [a]it was anointed, so the leaders offered their offering before
the altar.
11 Then the LORD said to Moses, "Let them present their offering,
one leader each day, for the dedication of the altar."

...palms [2]Or, ...ev. 7:28-34
... [a]Eccl. 9:7
...is hand can reach
...1 Chr. 23:13
... 28:3-6; Ps. ...am. 2:9; Ps. 17:8
...3, 7, 19 [b]Ps. 86:16
...:6; 44:3 [b]Ps. 29:11; 37:37
...put [a]2 Sam. ...3; 2 Chr. 7:14
...x. 40:17 [b]Ex. ...1; Num. 7:10, 84, 88
...t., *stood* [2]Lit., ...*stered* [a]Num. ...6 [b]2 Chr. 35:8
3 [a]Is. 66:20
...Lit., *for serving*
[a]Num. 4:24-26
...t., *hand* [a]Num. 4:31, 32
9 [a]Num. 4:5-15
...t., *of* [2]Lit., *in the that* [a]Num. 7:1; 2 Chr. 7:9

12 Now the one who presented his offering on the first day *was*
Nahshon the son of Amminadab, of the tribe of Judah;
13 and his offering *was* one silver [1a]dish whose weight *was* one
hundred and thirty *shekels,* one silver bowl of seventy shekels, [b]ac-
cording to [2]the shekel of the sanctuary, both of them full of fine flour
mixed with oil for a grain offering;
14 one gold pan of ten *shekels,* full of incense;
15 one [1]bull, one ram, one male lamb one year old, for a burnt
offering;
16 [a]one male goat for a sin offering;
17 and for the sacrifice of peace offerings, two oxen, five rams, five
male goats, five male lambs one year old. This *was* the offering of
[a]Nahshon the son of Amminadab.
18 On the second day Nethanel the son of Zuar, leader of Issachar,
presented *an offering;*
19 he presented as his offering one silver dish whose weight *was*
one hundred and thirty *shekels,* one silver bowl of seventy shekels,
according to the shekel of the sanctuary, both of them full of fine
flour mixed with oil for a grain offering;
20 one gold pan of ten *shekels,* full of incense;
21 one bull, one ram, one male lamb one year old, for a burnt
offering;
22 one male goat for a sin offering;
23 and for the sacrifice of [a]peace offerings, two oxen, five rams, five
male goats, five male lambs one year old. This *was* the offering of
Nethanel the son of Zuar.
24 On the third day *it was* Eliab the son of Helon, leader of the sons
of Zebulun;
25 his offering *was* one silver dish whose weight *was* one hundred
and thirty *shekels,* one silver bowl of seventy shekels, according to
the shekel of the sanctuary, both of them full of fine flour mixed with
oil for a grain offering;
26 one gold pan of ten *shekels,* full of incense;
27 one young bull, one ram, one [a]male lamb one year old, for a
burnt offering;
28 one male goat for a sin offering;
29 and for the sacrifice of peace offerings, two oxen, five rams, five
male goats, five male lambs one year old. This *was* the offering of
Eliab the son of Helon.
30 On the fourth day *it was* Elizur the son of Shedeur, leader of the
sons of Reuben;
31 his offering *was* one silver dish whose weight *was* one hundred
and thirty *shekels,* one silver bowl of seventy shekels, according to
the shekel of the sanctuary, both of them full of fine flour mixed with
oil for a grain offering;
32 one gold pan of ten *shekels,* full of incense;
33 one bull, one ram, one [a]male lamb one year old, for a burnt
offering;
34 one male goat for a sin offering;
35 and for the sacrifice of peace offerings, two oxen, five rams, five
male goats, five male lambs one year old. This *was* the offering of
Elizur the son of Shedeur.
36 On the fifth day *it was* Shelumiel the son of Zurishaddai, leader
of the children of Simeon;

13 [1]Or, *plat*
through v. 85
[2]Approx. one
and so throu
[a]Ex. 25:29;
[b]Num. 3:47

15 [1]Or, *bull*
and so throug

16 [a]Lev. 4:23

17 [a]Luke 3:32

23 [a]Lev. 7:11-1

27 [a]Is. 53:7; Jo
1 Pet. 1:19

33 [a]Heb. 9:28

37 his offering *was* one silver dish whose weight *was* one hundred
and thirty *shekels,* one silver bowl of seventy shekels, according to
the shekel of the sanctuary, both of them full of fine flour mixed with
oil for a grain offering;
38 one gold pan of ten *shekels,* full of incense;
39 one bull, one ram, one male lamb one year old, for a burnt
offering;
40 one male goat for a sin offering;
41 and for the sacrifice of peace offerings, two oxen, five rams, five
male goats, five male lambs one year old. This *was* the offering of
Shelumiel the son of Zurishaddai.
42 On the sixth day *it was* [a]Eliasaph the son of Deuel, leader of the
sons of Gad;
43 his offering *was* one silver dish whose weight *was* one hundred
and thirty *shekels,* one silver bowl of seventy shekels, according to
the shekel of the sanctuary, both of them full of [a]fine flour mixed
with oil for a grain offering;
44 one gold pan of ten *shekels,* full of incense;
45 [a]one bull, one ram, one male lamb one year old, for a burnt
offering;
46 one male goat for a sin offering;
47 and for the sacrifice of peace offerings, two oxen, five rams, five
male goats, five male lambs one year old. This *was* the offering of
Eliasaph the son of Deuel.
48 On the seventh day *it was* [a]Elishama the son of Ammihud, leader
of the sons of Ephraim;
49 his offering *was* one silver dish whose weight *was* one hundred
and thirty *shekels,* one silver bowl of seventy shekels, according to
the shekel of the sanctuary, both of them full of fine flour mixed with
oil for a grain offering;
50 one gold pan of ten *shekels,* full of [a]incense;
51 [a]one bull, one ram, one male lamb one year old, for a burnt
offering;
52 one male goat for a sin offering;
53 and for the sacrifice of peace offerings, two oxen, five rams, five
male goats, five male lambs one year old. This *was* the offering of
Elishama the son of Ammihud.
54 On the eighth day *it was* [a]Gamaliel the son of Pedahzur, leader of
the sons of Manasseh;
55 his offering *was* one silver dish whose weight *was* one hundred
and thirty *shekels,* one silver bowl of seventy shekels, according to
the shekel of the sanctuary, both of them full of fine flour mixed with
oil for a grain offering;
56 one gold pan of ten *shekels,* full of [a]incense;
57 one bull, one ram, one [a]male lamb one year old, for a burnt
offering;
58 one male goat for a sin offering;
59 and for the [a]sacrifice of peace offerings, two oxen, five rams, five
male goats, five male lambs one year old. This *was* the offering of
Gamaliel the son of Pedahzur.
60 On the ninth day *it was* [a]Abidan the son of Gideoni, leader of the
sons of Benjamin;
61 his offering *was* one silver dish whose weight *was* one hundred
and thirty *shekels,* one silver bowl of seventy shekels, according to

um. 1:14; 10:20
[a]Lev. 2:5; 14:10
50:8-14; Is. 1:11
lum. 1:10; 2:18; 1 Chr. 7:26
ut. 33:10; Ezek. 8:11; Luke 1:10
51 [a]Mic. 6:6-8
54 [a]Num. 2:20
56 [a]Ex. 30:7
12:5; Acts 8:32; Rev. 5:6
59 [a]Lev. 3:1-17
[a]Num. 1:11; 2:22

the shekel of the sanctuary, both of them full of fine flour mixed with
oil for a grain offering;
62 one gold pan of ten *shekels,* full of [a]incense;
63 one bull, one ram, one male lamb one year old, for a burnt
offering;
64 one male goat for a [a]sin offering;
65 and for the sacrifice of [a]peace offerings, two oxen, five rams, five
male goats, five male lambs one year old. This *was* the offering of
Abidan the son of Gideoni.
66 On the tenth day *it was* [a]Ahiezer the son of Ammishaddai, leader
of the sons of Dan;
67 his offering *was* one silver dish whose weight *was* one hundred
and thirty *shekels,* one silver bowl of seventy shekels, according to
the [a]shekel of the sanctuary, both of them full of fine flour mixed
with oil for a grain offering;
68 one gold pan of ten *shekels,* full of [a]incense;
69 one bull, one ram, one male lamb one year old, for a burnt
offering;
70 one male goat for a sin offering;
71 and for the sacrifice of peace offerings, two oxen, five rams, five
male goats, five male lambs one year old. This *was* the offering of
Ahiezer the son of Ammishaddai.
72 On the eleventh day *it was* [a]Pagiel the son of Ochran, leader of
the sons of Asher;
73 his offering *was* one silver dish whose weight *was* one hundred
and thirty *shekels,* one silver bowl of seventy shekels, according to
the shekel of the sanctuary, both of them full of fine flour mixed with
oil for a grain offering;
74 one gold pan of ten *shekels,* full of [a]incense;
75 one bull, one ram, one male lamb one year old, for a burnt
offering;
76 one male goat for a sin offering;
77 and for the sacrifice of peace offerings, two oxen, five rams, five
male goats, five male lambs one year old. This *was* the offering of
Pagiel the son of Ochran.
78 On the twelfth day *it was* [a]Ahira the son of Enan, leader of the
sons of Naphtali;
79 his offering *was* one [a]silver dish whose weight *was* one hundred
and thirty *shekels,* one silver bowl of seventy shekels, according to
the shekel of the sanctuary, both of them full of fine flour mixed with
oil for a grain offering;
80 one gold pan of ten *shekels,* full of incense;
81 one bull, one ram, one male lamb one year old, for a burnt
offering;
82 one male goat for a sin offering;
83 and for the sacrifice of peace offerings, two oxen, five rams, five
male goats, five male lambs one year old. This *was* the offering of
Ahira the son of Enan.
84 This *was* [a]the dedication *offering* [1]for the altar from the leaders of
Israel [2]when [b]it was anointed: twelve silver dishes, twelve silver
bowls, twelve gold pans,
85 each silver dish *weighing* one hundred and thirty *shekels* and each
bowl seventy; all the silver of the utensils *was* 2,400 *shekels,* according
to the shekel of the sanctuary;

62 [a]Rev. 5:8;
64 [a]2 Cor. 5:2
65 [a]Col. 1:20
66 [a]Num. 1:1
67 [a]Ex. 30:13
27:25
68 [a]Ps. 141:2
72 [a]Num. 1:1
74 [a]Mal. 1:11
78 [a]Num. 1:1
79 [a]Ezra 1:9,
5:2
84 [1]Lit., *of* [2]
day that [a]Nu
[b]Num. 7:1

86 the twelve gold pans, full of incense, *weighing* ten *shekels* apiece,
according to the [a]shekel of the sanctuary, all the gold of the pans 120
shekels;
87 all the oxen for the burnt offering twelve bulls, *all* the rams
twelve, the male lambs one year old with their grain offering twelve,
and the male goats for a sin offering twelve;
88 and all the oxen for the sacrifice of peace offerings 24 bulls, *all*
the rams 60, the male goats 60, the male lambs one year old 60. [a]This
was the dedication *offering* for the altar after it was anointed.
89 Now when [a]Moses went into the tent of meeting to speak with
Him, he heard the voice speaking to him from above [b]the [1]mercy seat
that was on the ark of the testimony, from [c]between the two
cherubim, so He spoke to him.

Chapter 8

8 Then the LORD spoke to Moses, saying,
2 "Speak to Aaron and say to him, 'When you [1]mount the lamps,
the seven lamps will [a]give light in the front of the lampstand.' "
3 Aaron therefore did so; he [1]mounted its lamps at the front of the
lampstand, just as the LORD had commanded Moses.
4 [a]Now this was the workmanship of the lampstand, hammered
work of gold; from its base to its flowers, it was hammered work;
[b]according to the pattern which the LORD had showed Moses, so he
made the lampstand.
5 Again the LORD spoke to Moses, saying,
6 "Take the Levites from among the sons of Israel and [a]cleanse
them.
7 "And thus you shall do to them, for their [1]cleansing: *sprinkle*
[2]purifying [a]water on them, and let them [3b]use a razor over their
whole [4]body, and [c]wash their clothes, and they shall be clean.
8 "Then let them take a [1]bull with [a]its grain offering, fine flour
mixed with oil; and a second [1]bull you shall take for a sin offering.
9 "So [a]you shall present the Levites before the tent of meeting. [b]You
shall also assemble the whole congregation of the sons of Israel,
10 and present the Levites before the LORD; and the sons of Israel
[a]shall lay their hands on the Levites.
11 "Aaron then shall [1]present the Levites before the LORD as a [a]wave
offering from the sons of Israel, that they may [2]qualify to perform the
service of the LORD.
12 "Now [a]the Levites shall lay their hands on the heads of the bulls;
then offer the one for a sin offering and the other for a burnt offering
to the LORD, to make atonement for the Levites.
13 "And you shall have the Levites stand before Aaron and before
his sons so as to present them as a wave offering to the LORD.
14 "Thus you shall separate the Levites from among the sons of
Israel, and [a]the Levites shall be Mine.
15 "Then after that the Levites may go in to serve the tent of meet-
ing. But you shall cleanse them and [a]present them as a wave offer-
ing;
16 for they are [a]wholly given to Me from among the sons of Israel. I
have taken them for Myself [b]instead of every first issue of the womb,
the first-born of all the sons of Israel.
17 "For [a]every first-born among the sons of Israel is Mine, among the

6 [a]Ex. 30:13
Num. 7:1, 10
., *propitiatory*):34, 35 [b]Ex. 22 [c]Ps. 80:1; 99:1
raise up [a]Ex. '; Lev. 24:2, 4
Lit., *raised up*
25:31-40 [b]Ex. 31-40; 26:30; 37:17-24
6 [a]Is. 52:11
[1]Lit., *this their* [2]Lit., *water of* *cause to pass* *h* [a]Num. 19:9,) [b]Lev. 14:8, 9 [c]Num. 8:21
bull of the herd ; Num. 15:8-10
[a]Ex. 29:4; 40:12 [b]Lev. 8:3
10 [a]Lev. 1:4
t., *wave*, and so out the ch. [2]Lit., *e* [a]Lev. 7:30, 34
12 [a]Ex. 29:10
[a]Num. 3:12; 16:9
15 [a]Ex. 29:24
6 [a]Num. 3:9 [b]Ex. :2; Num. 3:12, 45
[a]Ex. 13:2, 12, 13, 15; Luke 2:23

men and among the animals; on the day that I struck down all the
first-born in the land of Egypt I sanctified them for Myself.
18 "But I have taken the Levites instead of every first-born among
the sons of Israel.
19 "And [a]I have given the Levites as [1]a gift to Aaron and to his sons
from among the sons of Israel, to perform the service of the sons of
Israel at the tent of meeting, and to make atonement on behalf of the
sons of Israel, that there may be no [b]plague among the sons of Israel
by [2]their coming near to the sanctuary."
20 Thus did Moses and Aaron and all the congregation of the sons
of Israel to the Levites; according to all that the LORD had com-
manded Moses concerning the Levites, so the sons of Israel did to
them.
21 [a]The Levites, too, purified themselves from sin and washed their
clothes; and Aaron presented them as a wave offering before the
LORD. Aaron also made atonement for them to cleanse them.
22 Then after that the Levites went in to perform their service in the
tent of meeting before Aaron and before his sons; just as the LORD
had commanded Moses concerning the Levites, so they did to them.
23 Now the LORD spoke to Moses, saying,
24 "This is what *applies* to the Levites: from [a]twenty-five years old
and upward [1]they shall enter to perform service in the work of the
tent of meeting.
25 "But at the age of fifty years they shall [1]retire from service in the
work and not work any more.
26 "They may, however, [1]assist their brothers in the tent of meeting,
[a]to keep an obligation; but they *themselves* shall do no work. Thus
you shall deal with the Levites concerning their obligations."

Chapter 9

9 Thus the LORD spoke to Moses in the wilderness of Sinai, in [a]the
first month of the second year after they had come out of the
land of Egypt, saying,
2 "Now, let the sons of Israel observe the Passover at [a]its appointed
time.
3 "On the fourteenth day of this month, [1]at twilight, you shall ob-
serve it at its appointed time; you shall observe it according to all its
statutes and according to all its ordinances."
4 So Moses [1]told the sons of Israel to observe the Passover.
5 And [a]they observed the Passover in the first *month*, on the four-
teenth day of the month, at twilight, in the wilderness of Sinai; [b]ac-
cording to all that the LORD had commanded Moses, so the sons of
Israel did.
6 But there were *some* men who were [a]unclean because of *the* [1]dead
person, so that they could not observe Passover on that day; so [b]they
came before Moses and Aaron on that day.
7 And those men said to him, "*Though* we are unclean because of
the [1]dead person, why are we restrained from presenting the offering
of the LORD at its appointed time among the sons of Israel?"
8 Moses therefore said to them, "[1a]Wait, and I will listen to what
the LORD will command concerning you."
9 Then the LORD spoke to Moses, saying,
10 "Speak to the sons of Israel, saying, 'If any one of you or of your

19 [1]Lit., *give* [2]Lit., *the son* [a]Num. 3:9 [b] 16:46

21 [a]Num. 8:7

24 [1]Lit., *he* [a] 1 Chr. 23:3, 2

25 [1]Lit., *retur*

26 [1]Lit., *serve* 1:53

9:1 [a]Ex. 40:2, 1:1

2 [a]Ex. 12:6; Le Deut. 16:1, 2

3 [1]Lit., *betwee evenings*, and s throughout the

4 [1]Lit., *spoke to*

5 [a]Josh. 5:10 [b] 12:1-13

6 [1]Lit., *soul of m* [a]Num. 5:2; 19:11 [b]Ex. 18:15; Num

7 [1]Lit., *soul of m*

8 [1]Lit., *Stand* [a]E 18:15; Ps. 85:8

generations becomes unclean because of a *dead* [1]person, or is on a
distant journey, he may, however, observe the Passover to the LORD.
11 'In the second month on the [a]fourteenth day at twilight, they
shall observe it; they [b]shall eat it with unleavened bread and bitter
herbs.
12 'They [a]shall leave none of it until morning, [b]nor break a bone of
it; according to all the statute of the Passover they shall observe it.
13 '[a]But the man who is clean and is not on a journey, and yet
[1]neglects to observe the Passover, that [2]person shall then be cut off
from his people, for he did not present the offering of the LORD at its
appointed time. That man [b]shall bear his sin.
14 '[a]And if an alien sojourns among you and [1]observes the Passover
to the LORD, according to the statute of the Passover and according to
its ordinance, so he shall do; you shall have [b]one statute, both for the
alien and for the native of the land.' "
15 Now on [a]the day that the tabernacle was erected [b]the cloud
covered the tabernacle, the [c]tent of the testimony, and [d]in the evening
it was like the appearance of fire over the tabernacle, until morning.
16 So it was continuously; [a]the cloud would cover it *by day,* and the
appearance of fire by night.
17 [a]And whenever the cloud was lifted from over the tent, after-
ward the sons of Israel would then set out; and in the place where
the cloud settled down, there the sons of Israel would camp.
18 At the [1]command of the LORD the sons of Israel would set out,
and at the [1]command of the LORD they would camp; [a]as long as the
cloud settled over the tabernacle, they remained camped.
19 Even when the cloud lingered over the tabernacle for many
days, [1]the sons of Israel would keep the LORD's charge and not set
out.
20 If [1]sometimes the cloud remained a few days over the tabernacle,
[a]according to the [2]command of the LORD they remained camped.
Then according to the [2]command of the LORD they set out.
21 If [1]sometimes the cloud [2]remained from evening until morning,
when the cloud was lifted in the morning, they would move out; or
if it remained in the daytime and at night, whenever the cloud was
lifted, they would set out.
22 Whether it was two days or a month or a year that the cloud
lingered over the tabernacle, staying above it, the sons of Israel re-
mained camped and did not set out; but [a]when it was lifted, they did
set out.
23 [a]At the [1]command of the LORD they camped, and at the [1]com-
mand of the LORD they set out; they kept the LORD's charge, accord-
ing to the [1]command of the LORD through Moses.

Chapter 10

10 The LORD spoke further to Moses, saying,
2 "Make yourself two trumpets of silver, of hammered work
you shall make them; and you shall use them for [a]summoning the
congregation and for having the camps set out.
3 "And [a]when both are blown, all the congregation shall gather
themselves to you at the doorway of the tent of meeting.
4 "Yet if *only* one is blown, then the [a]leaders, the heads of the
[1]divisions of Israel, shall assemble before you.

10 [1]Lit., *soul*
[a]2 Chr. 30:2, 15 [b]Ex. 12:8
[a]Ex. 12:10 [b]Ex. 12:46; John 19:36
[1]Or, *ceases* [2]Lit., [a]Gen. 17:14; Ex. 5, 47 [b]Num. 5:31
Or, *would observe* 12:48 [b]Ex. 12:49; 4:22; Num. 15:15, 16, 29
Ex. 40:2, 17 [b]Ex. [c]Num. 17:7 [d]Ex. 13:21, 22
40:34; Neh. 9:12
x. 40:36-38; Num. 10:11, 12
it., *mouth* [a]1 Cor. 10:1
19 [1]Lit., *and the*
0 [1]Lit., *it was that* nouth [a]Ps. 48:14; Prov. 3:5, 6
1 [1]Lit., *it was that* [2]Lit., *was*
22 [a]Ex. 40:36, 37
[1]Lit., *mouth* [a]Ps. 4; 107:7; Is. 63:14
10:2 [a]Is. 1:13
Jer. 4:5; Joel 2:15
it., *thousands;* or, [a]Ex. 18:21; Num. 1:16; 7:2

5 "But when you blow an alarm, the camps that are pitched [a]on the
east side shall set out.
6 "And when you blow an alarm the second time, the camps that
are pitched on [a]the south side shall set out; an alarm is to be blown
for them to set out.
7 "When convening the assembly, however, you shall blow without
[a]sounding an alarm.
8 "[a]The priestly sons of Aaron, moreover, shall blow the trumpets;
and [1]this shall be for you a perpetual statute throughout your
generations.
9 "And when you go to war in your land against the adversary
who [a]attacks you, then you shall sound an alarm with the trumpets,
that you may be [b]remembered before the LORD your God, and be
saved from your enemies.
10 "Also in the day of your gladness and in your appointed [1]feasts,
and on the first *days* of your months, [a]you shall blow the trumpets
over your burnt offerings, and over the sacrifices of your peace offer-
ings; and they shall be as a reminder of you before your God. I am
the LORD your God."
11 Now it came about in [a]the second year, in the second month, on
the twentieth of the month, that the cloud was lifted from over the
[1]tabernacle of the testimony;
12 and the sons of Israel set out on [a]their journeys from the wilder-
ness of Sinai. Then the cloud settled down in the [b]wilderness of
Paran.
13 [a]So they moved out for the first time according to the [1]command-
ment of the LORD through Moses.
14 And the standard of the camp of the sons of Judah, according to
their armies, [a]set out first, with Nahshon the son of Amminadab,
over its army,
15 and Nethanel the son of Zuar, over the tribal army of the sons of
Issachar;
16 and Eliab the son of Helon over the tribal army of the sons of
Zebulun.
17 [a]Then the tabernacle was taken down; and the sons of Gershon
and the sons of Merari, who were carrying the tabernacle, set out.
18 Next [a]the standard of the camp of Reuben, according to their
armies, set out with Elizur the son of Shedeur, over its army,
19 and Shelumiel the son of Zurishaddai over the tribal army of the
sons of Simeon,
20 and Eliasaph the son of Deuel was over the tribal army of the
sons of Gad.
21 [a]Then the Kohathites set out, carrying the holy *objects;* and [b]the
tabernacle was set up before their arrival.
22 [a]Next the standard of the camp of the sons of Ephraim, accord-
ing to their armies, was set out, with Elishama the son of Ammihud
over its army,
23 and Gamaliel the son of Pedahzur over the tribal army of the
sons of Manasseh;
24 and Abidan the son of Gideoni over the tribal army of the sons
of Benjamin.
25 [a]Then the standard of the camp of the sons of Dan, according to
their armies, *which formed* the [b]rear guard for all the camps, set out,
with Ahiezer the son of Ammishaddai over its army,

5 [a]Num. 10:14
6 [a]Num. 10:18
7 [a]Joel 2:1
8 [1]Lit., *it* [a]Num. Josh. 6:4; 2 Chr.
9 [a]Judg. 2:18; 1 10:18; Ps. 106:42 [b]Gen. 8:1; Ps. 10
10 [1]Or, *times* [a]P 81:3-5
11 [1]Lit., *dwelling* and so throughou ch. [a]Ex. 40:17
12 [a]Ex. 40:36 [b]C 21:21; Num. 12:1
13 [1]Lit., *mouth* [a] 1:6
14 [a]Num. 2:3-9
17 [a]Num. 4:21-3
18 [a]Num. 2:10-1
21 [a]Num. 4:4-20 [b]Num. 10:17
22 [a]Num. 2:18-2
25 [a]Num. 2:25-3 [b]Josh. 6:9, 13

26 and Pagiel the son of Ochran over the tribal army of the sons of
Asher;
27 and Ahira the son of Enan over the tribal army of the sons of
Naphtali.
28 [1]This was the order of march of the sons of Israel by their armies
as they set out.
29 Then Moses said to [a]Hobab the son of [b]Reuel the Midianite,
Moses' father-in-law, "We are setting out to the place of which the
LORD said, '[c]I will give it to you'; [d]come with us and we will do you
good, for the LORD [e]has [1]promised good concerning Israel."
30 But he said to him, "[a]I will not come, but rather will go to my
own land and relatives."
31 Then he said, "Please do not leave us, inasmuch as you know
where we should camp in the wilderness, and you [a]will be as eyes
for us.
32 "So it will be, if you go with us, it will come about that [1a]whatever
good the LORD [2]does for us, [b]we will [3]do for you."
33 [a]Thus they set out from the mount of the LORD three days' jour-
ney, with [b]the ark of the covenant of the LORD journeying in front of
them for the [1]three days, to seek out [c]a resting place for them.
34 [a]And the cloud of the LORD was over them by day, when they set
out from the camp.
35 Then it came about when the ark set out that Moses said,
"[a]Rise up, O LORD!
And let Thine enemies be scattered,
And let those [b]who hate Thee flee [1]before Thee."
36 And when it came to rest, he said,
"[a]Return Thou, O LORD,
To the myriad [b]thousands of Israel."

Chapter 11

11 Now the people became like [a]those who complain of adver-
sity [b]in the hearing of the LORD; and when the LORD heard *it*,
His anger was kindled, and the fire of the LORD burned among them
and consumed *some* of the outskirts of the camp.
2 [a]The people therefore cried out to Moses, and Moses prayed to
the LORD, and the fire [1]died out.
3 So the name of that place was called
[1a]Taberah, because the fire of the LORD
burned among them.
4 And the [a]rabble who were among them
[1]had greedy desires; and also the sons of
Israel wept again and said, "[b]Who will give
us [2]meat to eat?
5 "[a]We remember the fish which we used
to eat free in Egypt, the cucumbers and the
melons and the leeks and the onions and
the garlic,
6 but now [a]our [1]appetite is gone. There is
nothing at all [2]to look at except this
manna."
7 [a]Now the manna was like coriander
seed, and its appearance like that of
[b]bdellium.

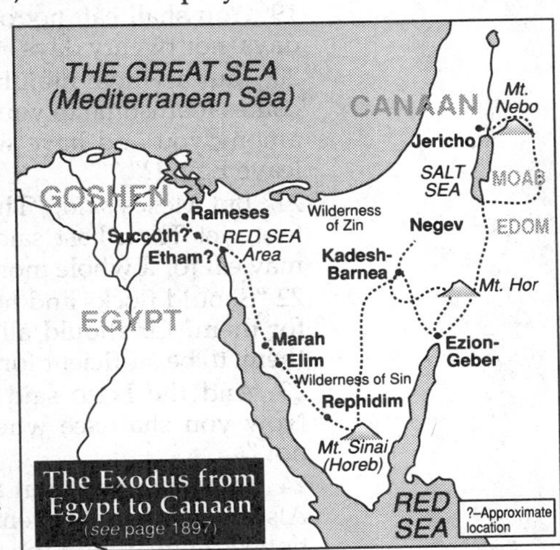

The Exodus from Egypt to Canaan
(see page 1897)

8 The people would go about and gather *it* and grind *it* [1]between
two millstones or beat *it* in the mortar, and boil *it* in the pot and
make cakes with it; and its taste was as the taste of [2]cakes baked with
oil.
9 [a]And when the dew fell on the camp at night, the manna would
fall [1]with it.
10 Now Moses heard the people weeping throughout their families,
each man at the doorway of his tent; and the anger of the LORD was
kindled greatly, and [1]Moses was displeased.
11 [a]So Moses said to the LORD, "Why hast Thou [1]been so hard on
Thy servant? And why have I not found favor in Thy sight, that
Thou hast laid the burden of all this people on me?
12 "Was it I who conceived all this people? Was it I who brought
them forth, that Thou shouldest say to me, 'Carry them in your
bosom as a [1a]nurse carries a nursing infant, to the land which [b]Thou
didst swear to their fathers'?
13 "Where am I to get meat to give to [a]all this people? For they weep
before me, saying, 'Give us meat that we may eat!'
14 "[a]I alone am not able to carry all this people, because it is too
[1]burdensome for me.
15 "[a]So if Thou art going to deal thus with me, please kill me at once,
if I have found favor in Thy sight, and do not let me see my
wretchedness."
16 The LORD therefore said to Moses, "Gather for Me [a]seventy men
from the elders of Israel, [b]whom you know to be the elders of the
people and their officers and bring them to the tent of meeting, and
let them take their stand there with you.
17 "[a]Then I will come down and speak with you there, and I will
take of [b]the Spirit who is upon you, and will put *Him* upon them;
and they shall bear the burden of the people with you, so that you
shall not bear *it* all alone.
18 "And say to the people, '[a]Consecrate yourselves for tomorrow,
and you shall eat meat; for you have wept [b]in the ears of the LORD,
saying, "Oh that someone would give us meat to eat! For we were
well-off in Egypt." Therefore the LORD will give you meat and you
shall eat.
19 'You shall eat, not one day, nor two days, nor five days, nor ten
days, nor twenty days,
20 [1]but a whole month, until it comes out of your nostrils and be-
comes loathsome to you; because [a]you have rejected the LORD who is
among you and have wept before Him, saying, "Why did we ever
leave Egypt?"' "
21 But Moses said, "The people, among whom I am, are 600,000 on
foot; yet Thou hast said, 'I will give them meat in order that they
may eat for a whole month.'
22 "Should flocks and herds be slaughtered for them, to be sufficient
for them? Or should all the fish of the sea be gathered together for
them, to be sufficient for them?"
23 And the LORD said to Moses, "Is [a]the LORD's [1]power limited?
Now you shall see whether [b]My word will [2]come true for you or
not."
24 So Moses went out and [a]told the people the words of the LORD.
Also, he gathered seventy men of the elders of the people, and sta-
tioned them around the tent.

8 [1]Lit., *with* ... *of oil*
9 [1]Lit., *on* ... 16:13, 14
10 [1]Lit., it w... *Moses' sigh*...
11 [1]Lit., *dea*... [a]Ex. 5:22; D...
12 [1]Or, *foste*... [a]2 Kin. 10:1, ... [b]Gen. 24:7; ... 33:1
13 [a]Num. 1... John 6:5-9
14 [1]Lit., *hea*... 18:18; Deut.
15 [a]Ex. 32:3...
16 [a]Ex. 24:1, ... 18:25
17 [a]Num. 11:... [b]1 Sam. 10:6;
18 [a]Ex. 19:10 [b]Num. 11:1
20 [1]Lit., *until* ... 24:27; 1 Sam.
23 [1]Lit., *hand* ... [2]Lit., *befall you* ... 50:2; 59:1 [b]Ez... 12:25; 24:14
24 [a]Num. 11:1...

25 [a]Then the LORD came down in the cloud and spoke to him; and
He took of the Spirit who was upon him and placed *Him* upon the
seventy elders. And it came about that when the Spirit rested upon
them, they prophesied. But they did not do *it* again.
26 But two men had remained in the camp; the name of one was
Eldad and the name of the [1]other Medad. And [a]the Spirit rested upon
them (now they were among those who had been registered, but had
not gone out to the tent), and they prophesied in the camp.
27 So a young man ran and told Moses and said, "Eldad and
Medad are prophesying in the camp."
28 Then [a]Joshua the son of Nun, the attendant of Moses from his
youth, answered and said, "[b]Moses, my lord, restrain them."
29 But Moses said to him, "Are you jealous for my sake? [a]Would
that all the LORD's people were prophets, that the LORD would put
His Spirit upon them!"
30 Then Moses [1]returned to the camp, *both* he and the elders of
Israel.
31 [a]Now there went forth a wind from the LORD, and it brought
quail from the sea, and let *them* fall beside the camp, about a day's
journey on this side and a day's journey on the other side, all around
the camp, and [1]about two [2]cubits *deep* on the surface of the ground.
32 And the people [1]spent all day and all night and all the next day,
and gathered the quail (he who gathered least gathered ten
[2a]homers) and they spread *them* out for themselves all around the
camp.
33 [a]While the meat was still between their teeth, before it was
chewed, the anger of the LORD was kindled against the people, and
the LORD struck the people with a very severe plague.
34 So the name of that place was called [1a]Kibroth-hattaavah, be-
cause there they buried the people who had been greedy.
35 From Kibroth-hattaavah [a]the people set out for Hazeroth, and
they [1]remained at Hazeroth.

Chapter 12

12 Then Miriam and Aaron spoke against Moses because of the
Cushite woman whom he had married (for he had married a
[a]Cushite woman);
2 [a]and they said, "Has the LORD indeed spoken only through
Moses? Has He not spoken through us as well?" And the LORD
heard it.
3 (Now the man Moses was [a]very humble, more than any man
who was on the face of the earth.)
4 And suddenly the LORD said to Moses and Aaron and to Miriam,
"You three come out to the tent of meeting." So the three of them
came out.
5 [a]Then the LORD came down in a pillar of cloud and stood at the
doorway of the tent, and He called [1]Aaron and Miriam. When they
had both come forward,
6 He said,
"Hear now My words:
If there is a prophet among you,
I, the LORD, shall make Myself known to him in a [a]vision.
I shall speak with him in a [b]dream.
7 "Not so, with [a]My servant Moses,

11:17; 12:5
cond [a]Num.
Sam. 10:6;
1; Neh. 9:30
33:11; Josh.
Mark 9:38-40
[a]1 Cor. 14:5
Lit., *removed himself*
om *about two*
ve [2]I.e., One
ls approx. 18
Ex. 16:13; Ps.
26-28; 105:40
ose [2]I.e., One
quals approx.
[a]Ezek. 45:11
[a]Ps. 78:29-31;
106:15
, the graves of
ss [a]Deut. 9:22
t., *were* [a]Num.
33:17
12:1 [a]Ex. 2:21
2 [a]Num. 16:3
3 [a]Matt. 11:29
[1]Or, "Aaron and
[a]Ex. 19:9; 34:5
en. 46:2; 1 Sam.
en. 31:11; 1 Kin.
3:5, 15
7 [a]Josh. 1:1

[b]He is faithful in all My household;
8 [a]With him I speak mouth to mouth,
Even openly, and not in dark sayings,
And he beholds [b]the form of the LORD.
Why then were you not afraid
To speak against My servant, against Moses?"
9 So the anger of the LORD burned against them and [a]He departed.
10 But when the cloud had withdrawn from over the tent, behold,
[a]Miriam *was* leprous, as [b]*white as* snow. As Aaron turned toward
Miriam, behold, she *was* leprous.
11 Then Aaron said to Moses, "Oh, my lord, I beg you, [a]do not
account *this* sin to us, in which we have acted foolishly and in which
we have sinned.
12 "Oh, do not let her be like one dead, whose flesh is half eaten
away when he comes from his mother's womb!"
13 And Moses cried out to the LORD, saying, "O God, [a]heal her, I
pray!"
14 But the LORD said to Moses, "If her father had but [a]spit in her
face, would she not bear her shame for seven days? Let her be shut
up for seven days [b]outside the camp, and afterward she may be
received again."
15 So [a]Miriam was shut up outside the camp for seven days, and
the people did not move on until Miriam was received again.
16 Afterward, however, the people moved out from Hazeroth and
camped in the wilderness of Paran.

Chapter 13

13 Then [a]the LORD spoke to Moses saying,
2 "[a]Send out for yourself men so that they may spy out the
land of Canaan, which I am going to give to the sons of Israel; you
shall send a man from each of their fathers' tribes, every one a leader
among them."
3 So Moses sent them from the wilderness of Paran at the [1]com-
mand of the LORD, all of them men who were heads of the sons of
Israel.
4 These then *were* their names: from the tribe of Reuben, Shammua
the son of Zaccur;
5 from the tribe of Simeon, Shaphat the son of Hori;
6 from the tribe of Judah, [a]Caleb the son of Jephunneh;
7 from the tribe of Issachar, Igal the son of Joseph;
8 from the tribe of Ephraim, [a]Hoshea the son of Nun;
9 from the tribe of Benjamin, Palti the son of Raphu;
10 from the tribe of Zebulun, Gaddiel the son of Sodi;
11 from the tribe of Joseph, from the tribe of Manasseh, Gaddi the
son of Susi;
12 from the tribe of Dan, Ammiel the son of Gemalli;
13 from the tribe of Asher, Sethur the son of Michael;
14 from the tribe of Naphtali, Nahbi the son of Vophsi;
15 from the tribe of Gad, Geuel the son of Machi.
16 These are the names of the men whom Moses sent to spy out the
land; but Moses called [a]Hoshea the son of Nun, Joshua.
17 When Moses sent them to spy out the land of Canaan, he said to
them, "Go up [1]there into [a]the [2]Negev; then go up into the hill
country.

7 [b]Heb. 3:2
8 [a]Deut. 34 12:13 [b]Ex. 11; Deut. 5:
9 [a]Gen. 17:
10 [a]Deut. 2 4:6; 2 Kin. 5
11 [a]2 Sam.
13 [a]Ps. 30:2 30:26; Jer. 17
14 [a]Deut. 25 17:6; 30:10; [b]Num. 5:1-4
15 [a]Deut. 24
13:1 [a]Deut. 1
2 [a]Deut. 1:22
3 [1]Lit., *mouth*
6 [a]Num. 14:6, 14:6
8 [a]Num. 13:16 32:44
16 [a]Num. 13:8 32:44
17 [1]Lit., *here* [2] South country, a throughout the [a]Gen. 12:9; 13:1

19 [1]Lit., *in*
it., *Use your* [a]Deut. 1:24, eut. 31:6, 23
the entrance [a]Num. 20:1; [b]Josh. 13:5
ost mss. read e came [2]Lit., [a]Num. 13:17 15:14 [c]Num. Ps. 78:12, 43
Or, *wadi* [2]I.e., [a]Gen. 14:13; 4; 32:9; Deut. 1:24
4 [1]I.e., cluster
o [a]Num. 20:1, 14; 32:8
x. 3:8, 17; 13:5 [b]Deut. 1:25
[1]Lit., *born ones* eut. 1:28; 9:1, 2 [b]Num. 13:33
n. 13:17; 14:25, sh. 10:6 [c]Num. 14:43, 45
30 [1]Lit., *toward*
Deut. 1:28; 9:1-3
, *settlers* [a]Num. 3, 37; Ps. 106:24 6:13, 14 [c]Amos 2:9
[a]Gen. 6:4 [b]Deut. , 9:2; Josh. 11:21
1 [1]Lit., *lifted and* *their voice* [2]Lit., *in* *that*
Num. 11:1 [b]Num. 5:13; 20:3, 4; 21:5
3 [a]Ex. 5:21; 16:3

18 "And see what the land is like, and whether the people who live
in it are strong *or* weak, whether they are few or many.
19 "And how is the land in which they live, is it good or bad? And
how are the cities in which they live, are *they* [1]like *open* camps or
with fortifications?
20 "And [a]how is the land, is it fat or lean? Are there trees in it or not?
[1]Make an [b]effort then to get some of the fruit of the land." Now the
time was the time of the first ripe grapes.
21 So they went up and spied out the land from [a]the wilderness of
Zin as far as Rehob, [1b]at Lebo-hamath.
22 When they had gone up into [a]the Negev, [1]they came to Hebron
where [b]Ahiman, Sheshai and Talmai, the [2]descendants of [c]Anak
were. (Now Hebron was built seven years before [d]Zoan in Egypt.)
23 Then they came to the [1]valley of [2a]Eshcol and from there cut
down a branch with a single cluster of grapes; and they carried it on
a pole between two *men,* with some of the pomegranates and the
figs.
24 That place was called the valley of [1]Eshcol, because of the cluster
which the sons of Israel cut down from there.
25 When they returned from spying out the land, at the end of forty
days,
26 they proceeded to come to Moses and Aaron and to all the
congregation of the sons of Israel [1]in the wilderness of Paran, at
[a]Kadesh; and they brought back word to them and to all the con-
gregation and showed them the fruit of the land.
27 Thus they told him, and said, "We went in to the land where you
sent us; and [a]it certainly does flow with milk and honey, and [b]this is
its fruit.
28 "Nevertheless, [a]the people who live in the land are strong, and the
cities are fortified *and* very large; and moreover, we saw [b]the [1]de-
scendants of Anak there.
29 "Amalek is living in the land of [a]the Negev and the Hittites and
the Jebusites and [b]the Amorites are living in the hill country, and [c]the
Canaanites are living by the sea and by the side of the Jordan."
30 Then Caleb quieted the people [1]before Moses, and said, "We
should by all means go up and take possession of it, for we shall
surely overcome it."
31 But the men who had gone up with him said, "[a]We are not able
to go up against the people, for they are too strong for us."
32 So they gave out to the sons of Israel [a]a bad report of the land
which they had spied out, saying, "The land through which we have
gone, in spying it out, is [b]a land that devours its [1]inhabitants; and [c]all
the people whom we saw in it are men of *great* size.
33 "There also we saw the [a]Nephilim (the sons of Anak are part of
the Nephilim); and [b]we became like grasshoppers in our own sight,
and so we were in their sight."

Chapter 14

14 Then all the congregation [1]lifted up their voices and cried,
and the people wept [2]that night.
2 And all the sons of Israel [a]grumbled against Moses and Aaron;
and the whole congregation said to them, "[b]Would that we had died
in the land of Egypt! Or would that we had died in this wilderness!
3 "And why is the LORD bringing us into this land, [a]to fall by the

sword? [b]Our wives and our little ones will become plunder; would it
not be better for us to return to Egypt?"
4 So they said to one another, "[a]Let us appoint a leader and return
to Egypt."
5 [a]Then Moses and Aaron fell on their faces in the presence of all
the assembly of the congregation of the sons of Israel.
6 And Joshua the son of Nun and Caleb the son of Jephunneh, of
those who had spied out the land, tore their clothes;
7 and they spoke to all the congregation of the sons of Israel,
saying, "[a]The land which we passed through to spy out is an exceed-
ingly good land.
8 "[a]If the LORD is pleased with us, then He will bring us into this
land, and give it to us—[b]a land which flows with milk and honey.
9 "Only [a]do not rebel against the LORD; and do not [b]fear the people
of the land, for they shall be our [1]prey. Their [2]protection has been
removed from them, and the LORD is with us; do not fear them."
10 [a]But all the congregation said to stone them with stones. Then
[b]the glory of the LORD appeared in the tent of meeting to all the sons
of Israel.
11 [a]And the LORD said to Moses, "How long will this people spurn
Me? And how long will [b]they not believe in Me, despite all the signs
which I have performed in their midst?
12 "I will smite them with [1a]pestilence and dispossess them, and I
[b]will make you into a nation greater and mightier than they."
13 [a]But Moses said to the LORD, "Then the Egyptians will hear of it,
for by Thy strength Thou didst bring up this people from their
midst,
14 and they will tell *it* to the inhabitants of this land. They have
heard that Thou, O LORD, art in the midst of this people, for [a]Thou, O
LORD, art seen eye to eye, while Thy cloud stands over them; and
Thou dost go before them in a pillar of cloud by day and in a pillar
of fire by night.
15 "Now if Thou dost slay this people as one man, [a]then the nations
who have heard of Thy fame will [1]say,
16 'Because the LORD [a]could not bring this people into the land
which He promised them by oath, therefore He slaughtered them in
the wilderness.'
17 "But now, I pray, let the power of the Lord be great, just as Thou
hast [1]declared,
18 '[a]The LORD is slow to anger and abundant in lovingkindness,
forgiving iniquity and transgression; but [b]He will by no means clear
the guilty, [c]visiting the iniquity of the fathers on the children [1]to the
third and the fourth *generations.*'
19 "[a]Pardon, I pray, the iniquity of this people according to the great-
ness of Thy lovingkindness, just as Thou also hast forgiven this
people, from Egypt even until now."
20 So the LORD said, "[a]I have pardoned *them* according to your
word;
21 but indeed, [a]as I live, [1b]all the earth will be filled with the glory of
the LORD.
22 "Surely [a]all the men who have seen My glory and My signs,
which I performed in Egypt and in the wilderness, yet [b]have put Me
to the test these ten times and have not listened to My voice,

3 [b]Num. 14
1:39

4 [a]Neh. 9:1

5 [a]Num. 16

7 [a]Num. 13
1:25

8 [a]Deut. 10:
3:8; Num. 13

9 [1]Lit., *food*
shadow [a]De
9:23, 24 [b]De

10 [a]Ex. 17:4
16:10; Lev. 9

11 [a]Ex. 32:9
106:24

12 [1]Lit., *the p*
[a]Lev. 26:25; D
28:21 [b]Ex. 32

13 [a]Ex. 32:11
106:23

14 [a]Ex. 13:21

15 [1]Lit., *speak*
[a]Ex. 32:12

16 [a]Josh. 7:7

17 [1]Lit., *spoke*

18 [1]Lit., *on* [a]E
34:6, 7; Deut. 5
Ps. 103:8; 145
4:2 [b]Ex. 20:5;
7:10 [c]Ex. 34:7

19 [a]Ex. 32:32;

20 [a]Mic. 7:18-2

21 [1]Lit., *and all*
14:28; Deut. 32
49:18 [b]Is. 6:3;

22 [a]1 Cor. 10:5
5:21; 14:11; 15:2
17:2, 3; 32:1; Nu
11:1, 4; 12:1; 14

23 [a]shall by no means see the land which I swore to their fathers,
nor shall any of those who spurned Me see it.
24 "But My servant Caleb, [a]because he has had a different spirit and
has followed Me fully, [1b]I will bring into the land [2]which he entered,
and his [3]descendants shall take possession of it.
25 "[a]Now the Amalekites and the Canaanites live in the valleys; turn
tomorrow and set out to the wilderness by the way of the [1]Red Sea."
26 And the LORD spoke to Moses and Aaron, saying,
27 "How long *shall I bear* with this evil congregation who are [a]grum-
bling against Me? I have heard the complaints of the sons of Israel,
which they are [1]making against Me.
28 "Say to them, '[a]As I live,' says the LORD, 'just as [b]you have spoken
in My hearing, so I will surely do to you;
29 [a]your corpses shall fall in this wilderness, even all [b]your [1]num-
bered men, according to your complete number from twenty years
old and upward, who have grumbled against Me.
30 'Surely you shall not come into the land in which I [1]swore to
settle you, [a]except Caleb the son of Jephunneh and Joshua the son of
Nun.
31 '[a]Your children, however, whom you said would become a
prey—I will bring them in, and they shall know the land which you
have rejected.
32 '[a]But as for you, your corpses shall fall in this wilderness.
33 'And your sons shall be shepherds for [a]forty years in the wilder-
ness, and they shall [1]suffer *for* your [2]unfaithfulness, until your
corpses [3]lie in the wilderness.
34 'According to the [a]number of days which you spied out the land,
forty days, for every day you shall bear your [1]guilt a year, *even* forty
years, and you shall know My opposition.
35 '[a]I, the LORD, have spoken, surely this I will do to all this evil
congregation who are gathered together against Me. In this wilder-
ness they shall be destroyed, and there they shall die.' "
36 [a]As for the men whom Moses sent to spy out the land and who
returned and made all the congregation grumble against him by
bringing out a bad report concerning the land,
37 even [a]those men who brought out the very bad report of the land
died by a [b]plague before the LORD.
38 But Joshua the son of Nun and Caleb the son of Jephunneh
remained alive out of those men who went to spy out the land.
39 And when Moses spoke [a]these words to all the sons of Israel,
[b]the people mourned greatly.
40 In the morning, however, they rose up early and went up to the
[1]ridge of the hill country, saying, "[a]Here we are; [2]we have indeed
sinned, but we will go up to the place which the LORD has
promised."
41 But Moses said, "[a]Why then are you transgressing the [1]com-
mandment of the LORD, when it will not succeed?
42 "[a]Do not go up, lest you be struck down before your enemies, for
the LORD is not among you.
43 "For the Amalekites and the Canaanites will be there in front of
you, and you will fall by the sword, inasmuch as you have turned
back from following the LORD. And the LORD will not be with you."
44 But they went up heedlessly to the [1]ridge of the hill country;
neither [a]the ark of the covenant of the LORD nor Moses left the camp.

26:65; 32:11; Heb. 3:18
it., *him I* [2]Lit., *ere* [3]Lit., *seed* 14:6-9 [b]Num. ; 32:12; Deut. Josh. 14:6-15
Sea of Reeds [a]Num. 13:29
., *complaining* [a]Num. 11:1
. 14:21 [b]Num. Deut. 2:14, 15; Heb. 3:17
[1]Lit., *mustered* b. 3:17 [b]Num. 1:45, 46
[1]Lit., *raised My* *d* [a]Num. 14:24
31 [a]Num. 14:3
Num. 26:64, 65; :13; 1 Cor. 10:5
[1]Lit., *bear* [2]Lit., *ations* [3]Lit., *are* [a]Deut. 2:7; 8:2, 4; 29:5
4 [1]Or, *iniquities* [a]Num. 13:25
35 [a]Num. 23:19
Num. 13:4-16, 32
Cor. 10:10; Heb. 18 [b]Num. 16:49
[a]Num. 14:28-35 [b]Ex. 33:4
40 [1]Or, *top of the* *ntain* [2]Or, *and we* *'l go up . . . for we* *ve sinned* [a]Deut. 1:41-44
it., *mouth* [a]2 Chr. 24:20
42 [a]Deut. 1:42
44 [1]Or, *top of the* *untain* [a]Num. 31:6

45 Then the Amalekites and the Canaanites who lived in that hill
country came down, and struck them and beat them down as far as
[a]Hormah.

Chapter 15

15 Now the LORD spoke to Moses, saying,
2 "[a]Speak to the sons of Israel, and say to them, 'When you
enter the land [1]where you are to live, which I am giving you,
3 then make [a]an offering by fire to the LORD, a burnt offering or a
sacrifice to [1b]fulfill a special vow, or as a freewill offering or in your
[c]appointed times, to make a [d]soothing aroma to the LORD, from the
herd or from the flock.
4 '[a]And the one who presents his offering shall present to the LORD
a grain offering of one-tenth *of an ephah* of fine flour mixed with
one-fourth of a [1]hin of oil,
5 and you shall prepare wine for the libation, one-fourth of a hin,
with the burnt offering or for the sacrifice, for [a]each lamb.
6 'Or for a ram you shall prepare as a grain offering two-tenths *of
an ephah* of fine flour mixed with one-third of a hin of oil;
7 and for the libation you shall offer one-third of a hin of wine as a
soothing aroma to the LORD.
8 'And when you prepare [a]a bull as a burnt offering or a sacrifice,
to [1]fulfill a special vow, or for peace offerings to the LORD,
9 then you shall offer with the bull a grain offering of three-tenths
of an ephah of fine flour mixed with one-half a hin of oil;
10 and you shall offer as the libation one-half a hin of wine as an
offering by fire, as a soothing aroma to the LORD.
11 'Thus it shall be done for each ox, or for each ram, or for each of
the male lambs, or of the goats.
12 'According to the number that you prepare, so you shall do for
everyone according to their number.
13 'All who are native shall do these things in this manner, in
presenting an offering by fire, as a soothing aroma to the LORD.
14 'And if an alien sojourns with you, or one who may be among
you throughout your generations, and he *wishes to* make an offering
by fire, as a soothing aroma to the LORD, just as you do, so he
shall do.
15 '*As for* the assembly, there shall be [a]one statute for you and for
the alien who sojourns *with you*, a perpetual statute throughout your
generations; as you are, so shall the alien be before the LORD.
16 'There is to be [a]one law and one ordinance for you and for the
alien who sojourns with you.'"
17 Then the LORD spoke to Moses, saying,
18 "Speak to the sons of Israel, and say to them, 'When you enter the
land where I bring you,
19 then it shall be, that when you eat of the [1a]food of the land, you
shall lift up [2]an offering to the LORD.
20 '[a]Of the first of your [1]dough you shall lift up a cake as an [2]offer-
ing; as [b]the [2]offering of the threshing floor, so you shall lift it up.
21 'From the first of your [1]dough you shall give to the LORD an
[2]offering throughout your generations.
22 'But when you [a]unwittingly fail and do not observe all these
commandments, which the LORD has spoken to Moses,
23 *even* all that the LORD has commanded you [1]through Moses, from

45 [a]Num. 21
15:2 [1]Lit., *of dwellings* [a]Le
3 [1]Or, *make a votive offering* 1:2, 3 [b]Lev. 2 23:1-44 [c]Gen 2 Cor. 2:15, 1 4:18
4 [1]I.e., Approx gal., and so th v. 10 [a]Num. 2
5 [a]Lev. 1:10; 3 15:11
8 [1]Or, *make a votive offering* 1:3; 3:1
15 [a]Num. 9:14;
16 [a]Lev. 24:22
19 [1]Lit., *bread* *heave offering* 5:11, 12
20 [1]Or, *coarse* [2]Or, *heave offeri* 34:26; Lev. 23:1 [b]Deut. 14:22, 23
21 [1]Or, *coarse* [2]Or, *offering lifted*
22 [a]Lev. 4:2
23 [1]Lit., *by the ha*

the day when the LORD gave commandment and onward throughout
your generations,
24 then it shall be, if it is done [a]unintentionally, [1]without the knowl-
edge of the congregation, that all the congregation shall offer one
bull for a burnt offering, as a soothing aroma to the LORD, [b]with its
grain offering, and its libation, according to the ordinance, and one
male goat for a sin offering.
25 'Then [a]the priest shall make atonement for all the congregation of
the sons of Israel, and they shall be forgiven; for it was an error, and
they have brought their offering, an offering by fire to the LORD, and
their sin offering before the LORD, for their error.
26 'So all the congregation of the sons of Israel will be forgiven,
with the alien who sojourns among them, for *it happened* to all the
people through [a]error.
27 'Also if one person sins [a]unintentionally, then he shall offer a one
year old female goat for a sin offering.
28 'And [a]the priest shall make atonement before the LORD for the
person who goes astray when he sins unintentionally, making atone-
ment for him [1]that he may be forgiven.
29 'You shall have one law for him who does *anything* unintention-
ally, for him who is native among the sons of Israel and for the alien
who sojourns among them.
30 'But the person who does *anything* [a]defiantly, whether he is na-
tive or an alien, that one is blaspheming the LORD; and that person
shall be cut off from among his people.
31 'Because he has [a]despised the word of the LORD and has broken
His commandment, that person shall be completely cut off; [b]his
[1]guilt *shall be* on him.' "
32 Now while the sons of Israel were in the wilderness, they found
a man [a]gathering wood on the sabbath day.
33 And those who found him gathering wood brought him to
Moses and Aaron, and to all the congregation;
34 and they put him in [1]custody [a]because it had not been [2]declared
what should be done to him.
35 Then the LORD said to Moses, "The man shall surely be put to
death; [a]all the congregation shall stone him with stones outside the
camp."
36 So all the congregation brought him outside the camp, and
stoned him [1]to death with stones, just as the LORD had commanded
Moses.
37 The LORD also spoke to Moses, saying,
38 "Speak to the sons of Israel, and tell them that they shall make for
themselves [a]tassels on the corners of their garments throughout their
generations, and that they shall put on the tassel of each corner a
cord of blue.
39 "And it shall be a tassel for you [1]to look at and [a]remember all the
commandments of the LORD, so as to do them and not [2]follow after
your own heart and your own eyes, after which you played the
harlot,
40 in order that you may remember to do all My commandments,
and [a]be holy to your God.
41 "I am the LORD your God who brought you out from the land of
Egypt to be your God; I am the LORD your God."

om the eyes congregation 22, 27; 5:15, um. 15:8-10
0; Heb. 2:17
[a]Num. 15:24
:27-31; Luke 12:48
, and he shall [a]Lev. 4:35
um. 14:40-44; 43; 17:12, 13
quity [a]2 Sam. 9; Prov. 13:13 [b]Ezek. 18:20
[a]Ex. 31:14, 15; 35:2, 3
Or, prison [2]Lit., clared distinctly [a]Num. 9:8
[a]Lev. 20:2, 27; 23; Deut. 21:21
with stones and he died
eut. 22:12; Matt. 23:5
t., and you shall k at it [2]Lit., seek 4:23; 6:12; 8:11, 14, 19
[a]Lev. 11:44, 45

Chapter 16

16 Now [a]Korah the son of Izhar, the son of Kohath, the son of
Levi, with [b]Dathan and Abiram, the sons of Eliab, and On the
son of Peleth, sons of Reuben, took *action,*
2 and they rose up before Moses, [1]together with some of the sons
of Israel, two hundred and fifty leaders of the congregation, [2a]chosen
in the assembly, men of renown.
3 And they assembled together [a]against Moses and Aaron, and
said to them, "[1b]You have gone far enough, for all the congregation
are holy, every one of them, and [c]the LORD is in their midst; so why
do you exalt yourselves above the assembly of the LORD?"
4 When Moses heard *this,* [a]he fell on his face;
5 and he spoke to Korah and all his company, saying, "Tomorrow
morning the LORD will show who is His, and [a]who is holy, and will
bring *him* near to Himself; even [b]the one whom He will choose, He
will bring near to Himself.
6 "Do this: take censers for yourselves, Korah and all [1]your
company,
7 and put fire in them, and lay incense upon them in the presence
of the LORD tomorrow; and the man whom the LORD chooses *shall be*
the one who is holy. [1a]You have gone far enough, you sons of Levi!"
8 Then Moses said to Korah, "Hear now, you sons of Levi,
9 [a]is it [1]not enough for you that the God of Israel has separated
you from the *rest of* the congregation of Israel, [b]to bring you near to
Himself, to do the service of the tabernacle of the LORD, and to stand
before the congregation to minister to them;
10 and that He has brought you near, *Korah,* and all your brothers,
sons of Levi, with you? And are you [a]seeking for the priesthood
also?
11 "Therefore you and all your company are gathered together
[a]against the LORD; but as for Aaron, [1]who is he that [b]you grumble
against him?"
12 Then Moses sent [1]a summons to Dathan and Abiram, the sons of
Eliab; but they said, "We will not come up.
13 "Is it [1]not enough that you have brought us up out of a [a]land
flowing with milk and honey [b]to have us die in the wilderness, but
you would also lord it over us?
14 "Indeed, you have not brought us [a]into a land flowing with milk
and honey, nor have you given us an inheritance of [b]fields and vine-
yards. Would you [1c]put out the eyes of [2]these men? We will not come
up!"
15 Then Moses became very angry and said to the LORD, "[a]Do not
regard their offering! [b]I have not taken a single donkey from them,
nor have I done harm to any of them."
16 And Moses said to Korah, "You and all your company be
present before the LORD tomorrow, both you and they along with
Aaron.
17 "And each of you take his firepan and put incense on [1]it, and each
of you bring his censer before the LORD, two hundred and fifty
firepans; also you and Aaron *shall* each *bring* his firepan."
18 So they each took his *own* censer and put fire on [1]it, and laid
incense on [1]it; and they stood at the doorway of the tent of meeting,
with Moses and Aaron.
19 Thus Korah assembled all the congregation against them at the

16:1 [a]Ex. 6 11 [b]Num. 2 11:6
2 [1]Lit., *and* [2]Lit., *called* [a]Num. 1:16;
3 [1]Lit., *It is you* [a]Num. 106:16 [b]Nu [c]Num. 5:3
4 [a]Num. 14.
5 [a]Lev. 10:3 [b]Num. 17:5,
6 [1]Lit., *his*
7 [1]Lit., *It is m you* [a]Num. 1
9 [1]Or, *too litt* [a]Is. 7:13 [b]Nu Deut. 10:8
10 [a]Num. 3:1
11 [1]Lit., *what* [b]1 Cor. 10:10
12 [1]Lit., *to cal*
13 [1]Lit., *a little* [a]Ex. 16:3; Num [b]Num. 14:2, 3
14 [1]Lit., *bore o those* [a]Num. 1 14:8 [b]Ex. 22:5 11; Num. 20:5 16:21; 1 Sam.
15 [a]Gen. 4:4, 5 [b]1 Sam. 12:3
17 [1]Lit., *them*
18 [1]Lit., *them*

doorway of the tent of meeting. And [a]the glory of the LORD appeared
to all the congregation.
20 Then the LORD spoke to Moses and Aaron, saying,
21 "[a]Separate yourselves from among this congregation, [b]that I may
consume them instantly."
22 But they fell on their faces, and said, "O God, [a]Thou God of the
spirits of all flesh, [b]when one man sins, wilt Thou be angry with the
entire congregation?"
23 Then the LORD spoke to Moses, saying,
24 "Speak to the congregation, saying, '[a]Get back from around the
dwellings of Korah, Dathan and Abiram.' "
25 Then Moses arose and went to Dathan and Abiram, with the
elders of Israel following him,
26 and he spoke to the congregation, saying, "[a]Depart now from the
tents of these wicked men, and touch nothing that belongs to them,
[b]lest you be swept away in all their sin."
27 So they got back from around the dwellings of Korah, Dathan
and Abiram; and Dathan and Abiram came out *and* stood at the
doorway of their tents, along with their wives and [a]their sons and
their little ones.
28 And Moses said, "By this you shall know that [a]the LORD has sent
me to do all these deeds; for this is not [1]my doing.
29 "If these men die [1]the death of all men, or [2]if they suffer the [a]fate
of all men, *then* the LORD has not sent me.
30 "But [a]if the LORD [1]brings about an entirely new thing and the
ground opens its mouth and swallows them up with all that is
theirs, and they [b]descend alive into [2]Sheol, then you will understand
that these men have spurned the LORD."
31 Then it came about as he finished speaking all these words, that
the ground that was under them split open;
32 and [a]the earth opened its mouth and swallowed them up, and
their households, and [b]all the men who belonged to Korah, with *their*
possessions.
33 So they and all that belonged to them went down alive to [1]Sheol;
and the earth closed over them, and they perished from the midst of
the assembly.
34 And all Israel who *were* around them fled at their [1]outcry, for
they said, "[2]The earth may swallow us up!"
35 [a]Fire also came forth from the LORD and consumed the [b]two hun-
dred and fifty men who were offering the incense.
36 [1]Then the LORD spoke to Moses, saying,
37 "Say to Eleazar, the son of Aaron the priest, that he shall take up
the censers out of the midst of the [1]blaze, for they are holy; and you
scatter the [2]burning coals abroad.
38 "As for the censers of these [1]men who have sinned at the cost of
their lives, let them be made into hammered sheets for a plating of
the altar, since they did present them before the LORD and they are
holy; and [a]they shall be for a sign to the sons of Israel."
39 So Eleazar the priest took the bronze censers which the men who
were burned had offered; and they hammered them out as a plating
for the altar,
40 as a [1]reminder to the sons of Israel that [a]no [2]layman who is not of
the [3]descendants of Aaron should come near [b]to burn incense before

...:10; 16:42; 20:6
16:45 [b]Ex. 32:10, 12
...7:16 [b]Gen. 32; Lev. 4:3
[a]Num. 16:45
...52:11 [b]Gen. 19:15, 17
[a]Num. 26:11
...om my heart ...-15; 4:12, 15
...ike the death ...isitation of all visited upon ...n [a]Eccl. 3:19
...reates a new ...tion [2]I.e., the ...d [a]Job 31:2, 3 [b]Ps. 55:15
... 26:10; Deut. ...06:17 [b]Num. 26:11
...e nether world
...oice [2]Lit., Lest the earth
... 11:1-3; 26:10 [b]Num. 16:2
...n. 17:1 in Heb.
... [1]Or, place of ...ng [2]Lit., the fire
...sinners against ...es [a]Ezek. 14:8; 2 Pet. 2:6
...memorial [2]Lit., ...nger [3]Lit., seed ...51 [b]Ex. 30:7-10

the LORD; that he might not become like Korah and his company—
just as the LORD had spoken to him [4]through Moses.
41 But on the next day all the congregation of the sons of Israel
[a]grumbled against Moses and Aaron, saying, "You are the ones who
have caused the death of the LORD's people."
42 It came about, however, when the congregation had assembled
against Moses and Aaron, that they turned toward the tent of meet-
ing, and behold, the cloud covered it and [a]the glory of the LORD
appeared.
43 Then Moses and Aaron came to the front of the tent of meeting,
44 and the LORD spoke to Moses, saying,
45 "[1a]Get away from among this congregation, that I may consume
them instantly." Then they fell on their faces.
46 And Moses said to Aaron, "Take your censer and put in it fire
from the altar, and lay incense *on it;* then bring it quickly to the
congregation and [a]make atonement for them, for [b]wrath has gone
forth from the LORD, the plague has begun!"
47 Then Aaron took *it* as Moses had spoken, and ran into the midst
of the assembly, for behold, the plague had begun among the people.
[a]So he put *on* the incense and made atonement for the people.
48 And he took his stand between the dead and the living, so that
the plague was checked.
49 [a]But those who died by the plague were 14,700, besides those
who [b]died on account of Korah.
50 Then Aaron returned to Moses at the doorway of the tent of
meeting, for the plague had been checked.

Chapter 17

17 [1]Then the LORD spoke to Moses, saying,
2 "Speak to the sons of Israel, and get from them a rod for
each father's household: twelve rods, from all their leaders accord-
ing to their fathers' households. You shall write each name on his
rod,
3 and write Aaron's name on the rod of Levi; for there is one rod
for the head *of each* of their fathers' households.
4 "You shall then deposit them in the tent of meeting in front of [a]the
testimony, where I meet with you.
5 "And it will come about that the rod of [a]the man whom I choose
will sprout. Thus I shall lessen from upon Myself the grumblings of
the sons of Israel, who are grumbling against you."
6 Moses therefore spoke to the sons of Israel, and all their leaders
gave him a rod apiece, for each leader according to their fathers'
households, twelve rods, with the rod of Aaron among their rods.
7 So Moses deposited the rods before the LORD in [a]the tent of the
testimony.
8 Now it came about on the next day that Moses went into the tent
of the testimony; and behold, [a]the rod of Aaron for the house of Levi
had sprouted and put forth buds and produced blossoms, and it
bore ripe almonds.
9 Moses then brought out all the rods from the presence of the
LORD to all the sons of Israel; and they looked, and each man took his
rod.
10 But the LORD said to Moses, "Put back the rod of Aaron [a]before
the testimony [1]to be kept as a sign against the [2b]rebels, that you may

40 [4]Lit., *by*
41 [a]Num. 1
42 [a]Num. 1
45 [1]Or, *Aris* 16:21, 24
46 [a]Num. 25 7 [b]Num. 18: 9:22
47 [a]Num. 25
49 [a]Num. 25 16:32, 35
17:1 [1]Ch. 17:
4 [a]Ex. 25:16, Num. 17:7
5 [a]Num. 16:5
7 [a]Num. 1:50,
8 [a]Ezek. 17:24
10 [1]Lit., *for pres* [2]Lit., *sons of reb* [a]Num. 17:4 [b]De 9:7, 24

put an end to their grumblings against Me, so that they should not die."

11 Thus Moses did; just as the LORD had commanded him, so he did.

12 Then the sons of Israel spoke to Moses, saying, "[a]Behold, we perish, we are dying, we are all dying!

13 "[a]Everyone who comes near, who comes near to the tabernacle of the LORD, must die. Are we to perish completely?"

Chapter 18

18 So the LORD said to Aaron, "You and your sons and your father's household with you shall [a]bear the guilt [1]in connection with the sanctuary; and you and your sons with you shall bear the guilt [2]in connection with your priesthood.

2 "But bring with you also your brothers, the tribe of Levi, the tribe of your father, that they may be [a]joined with you and serve you, while you and your sons with you are before the tent of the testimony.

3 "And they shall thus attend to your obligation and the obligation of all the tent, but [a]they shall not come near to the furnishings of the sanctuary and [b]the altar, lest both they and you die.

4 "And they shall be joined with you and attend to the obligations of the tent of meeting, for all the service of the tent; but an [1]outsider may not come near you.

5 "So you shall attend to the [a]obligations of the sanctuary and the obligations of the altar, [b]that there may no longer be wrath on the sons of Israel.

6 "And behold, I Myself [a]have taken your [1]fellow Levites from among the sons of Israel; they are [b]a gift to you, [2]dedicated to the LORD, to perform the service for the tent of meeting.

7 "But you and your sons with you shall [a]attend to your priesthood for everything concerning the altar and inside the veil, and you are to perform service. I am giving you the priesthood as [b]a [1]bestowed service, but [c]the [2]outsider who comes near shall be put to death."

8 Then the LORD spoke to Aaron, "Now behold, I Myself have given you charge of My [1a]offerings, even all the holy gifts of the sons of Israel, I have given them to you as a portion, and to your sons as a perpetual allotment.

9 "This shall be yours from the most holy *gifts, reserved* from the fire; every offering of theirs, even [a]every grain offering and every [b]sin offering and every guilt offering, which they shall render to Me, shall be most holy for you and for your sons.

10 "As the most holy *gifts* you shall eat it; every male shall eat it. It shall be holy to you.

11 "This also is yours, [a]the offering of their gift, even all the wave offerings of the sons of Israel; I have [b]given them to you and to your sons and daughters with you, as a perpetual allotment. Everyone of your household who is clean may eat it.

12 "[a]All the [1]best of the fresh oil and all the [1]best of the fresh wine and of the grain, the first fruits of those which they give to the LORD, I give them to you.

13 "[a]The first ripe fruits of all that is in their land, which they bring to the LORD, shall be yours; everyone of your household who is clean may eat it.

12 [a]Is. 6:5
[a]Num. 1:51
[1]Lit., *of the* [2]Lit., *of your* [a]Ex. 28:38; 10:17; 22:16
[a]Num. 3:5-10
Num. 4:15-20 m. 1:51; 18:7
it., *a stranger*
:21; Lev. 24:3 [b]Num. 16:46
., *brethren the n* [a]Num. 3:12, 45 [b]Num. 3:9
, *service of gift nger* [a]Ex. 29:9 n. 18:20; Deut. att. 10:8; 1 Pet. , 3 [c]Num. 1:51
eave offerings, throughout the [a]Lev. 6:16, 18; 7:28-34
ev. 2:1-16 [b]Lev. 6:30
um. 18:1; Deut. 3 [b]Lev. 22:1-16
fat [a]Deut. 18:4; s. 81:16; 147:14
Ex. 22:29; 23:19; 34:26

14 "[a]Every devoted thing in Israel shall be yours.

15 "[1a]Every first issue of the womb of all flesh, whether man or animal, which they offer to the LORD, shall be yours; nevertheless the first-born of man you shall surely redeem, and the first-born of unclean animals you shall redeem.

16 "And as to their redemption price, from a month old you shall redeem them, by your valuation, five [1]shekels in silver, according to the [1]shekel of the sanctuary, which is twenty gerahs.

17 "But [a]the first-born of an ox or the first-born of a sheep or the first-born of a goat, you shall not redeem; they are holy. [b]You shall sprinkle their blood on the altar and shall offer up their fat in smoke *as* an offering by fire, for a soothing aroma to the LORD.

18 "And their [1]meat shall be yours; it shall be yours like the [a]breast of a wave offering and like the right thigh.

19 "[a]All the offerings of the holy *gifts,* which the sons of Israel offer to the LORD, I have given to you and your sons and your daughters with you, as a perpetual allotment. It is [b]an everlasting covenant of salt before the LORD to you and your [1]descendants with you."

20 Then the LORD said to Aaron, "[a]You shall have no inheritance in their land, nor own any portion among them; [b]I am your portion and your inheritance among the sons of Israel.

21 "And to the sons of Levi, behold, I have given all the [a]tithe in Israel for an inheritance, in return for their service which they perform, the service of the tent of meeting.

22 "And [a]the sons of Israel shall not come near the tent of meeting again, lest they bear sin and die.

23 "Only the Levites shall perform the service of the tent of meeting, and they shall [a]bear their iniquity; it shall be a perpetual statute throughout your generations, and among the sons of Israel [b]they shall have no inheritance.

24 "For the tithe of the sons of Israel, which they offer as an offering to the LORD, I have given to the Levites for an inheritance; therefore I have said concerning them, '[a]They shall have no inheritance among the sons of Israel.' "

25 Then the LORD spoke to Moses, saying,

26 "Moreover, you shall speak to the Levites and say to them, 'When you take from the sons of Israel [a]the tithe which I have given you from them for your inheritance, then you shall present an offering from it to the LORD, a [b]tithe of the tithe.

27 'And your offering shall be reckoned to you as the grain from the threshing floor or the full produce from the wine vat.

28 'So you shall also present an offering to the LORD from your tithes, which you receive from the sons of Israel; and from it you shall give the LORD's offering to Aaron the priest.

29 'Out of all your gifts you shall present every offering due to the LORD, from all the [1]best of them, [2]the sacred part from them.'

30 "And you shall say to them, 'When you have [1]offered from it the best of it, then *the rest* shall be reckoned to the Levites as the product of the threshing floor, and as the product of the wine vat.

31 'And you may eat it anywhere, you and your households, for it is your compensation in return for your service in the tent of meeting.

32 'And you shall bear no sin by reason of it, when you have [1]offered the [2]best of it. But you shall not [a]profane the sacred gifts of the sons of Israel, lest you die.' "

14 [a]Lev. 27:

15 [1]Lit., *Eve opens* [a]Ex. 1 Num. 3:46

16 [1]I.e., A sh equals appro: one-half oz.

17 [a]Deut. 15: 3:2

18 [1]Lit., *flesh*

19 [1]Lit., *seed* 18:11 [b]2 Chr.

20 [a]Deut. 10:9 14:27, 29 [b]De Josh. 13:33; E

21 [a]Lev. 27:30 Deut. 14:22-29

22 [a]Num. 1:51

23 [a]Num. 18:1 18:20

24 [a]Deut. 10:9

26 [a]Num. 18:21 10:38

29 [1]Lit., *fat* [2]Lit.

30 [1]Lit., *lifted*

32 [1]Lit., *lifted* [2]L [a]Lev. 22:15, 16

Chapter 19

19 Then the LORD spoke to Moses and Aaron, saying,
2 "This is the statute of the law which the LORD has com-
manded, saying, 'Speak to the sons of Israel that they bring you an
[a]unblemished red heifer in which is no defect, *and* [b]on which a yoke
has never [1]been placed.
3 'And you shall give it to [a]Eleazar the priest, and it shall [b]be
brought outside the camp and be slaughtered in his presence.
4 'Next Eleazar the priest shall take some of its blood with his
finger, and [a]sprinkle some of its blood toward the front of the tent of
meeting seven times.
5 'Then the heifer shall be burned in his sight; [a]its hide and its flesh
and its blood, with its refuse, shall be burned.
6 'And the priest shall take [a]cedar wood and hyssop and scarlet
material, and cast it into the midst of the [1]burning heifer.
7 'The priest [a]shall then wash his clothes and bathe his [1]body in
water, and afterward come into the camp, but the priest shall be
unclean until evening.
8 'The one who burns it shall also wash his clothes in water and
bathe his [1]body in water, and shall be unclean until evening.
9 'Now a man who is clean shall gather up the ashes of the heifer
and deposit them outside the camp in a clean place, and [1]the con-
gregation of the sons of Israel shall keep it as [a]water to remove
impurity; it is [2]purification from sin.
10 'And the one who gathers the ashes of the heifer [a]shall wash his
clothes and be unclean until evening; and it shall be a perpetual
statute to the sons of Israel and to the alien who sojourns among
them.
11 '[a]The one who touches the corpse of any [1]person shall be unclean
for seven days.
12 'That one shall [a]purify himself from uncleanness with [1]the water
on the third day and on the seventh day, *and then* he shall be clean;
but if he does not purify himself on the third day and on the seventh
day, he shall not be clean.
13 '[a]Anyone who touches a corpse, the [1]body of a man who has
died, and does not purify himself, [b]defiles the [2]tabernacle of the
LORD; and that person shall be cut off from Israel. Because the water
for impurity was not [3c]sprinkled on him, he shall be unclean; his
uncleanness is still on him.
14 'This is the law when a man dies in a tent: everyone who comes
into the tent and everyone who is in the tent shall be unclean for
seven days.
15 'And every open vessel, which has no covering [1]tied down on it,
shall be unclean.
16 '[a]Also, anyone who in the open field touches one who has been
slain with a sword or who has died *naturally,* or a human bone or a
grave, shall be unclean for seven days.
17 'Then for the unclean *person* they shall take some of the [1]ashes of
the [2]burnt [3a]purification from sin and [4]flowing water shall be [5]added
to them in a vessel.
18 'And a clean person shall take hyssop and dip *it* in the water, and
sprinkle *it* on the tent and on all the furnishings and on the persons
who were there, and on the one who touched the bone or the one
slain or the one dying *naturally* or the grave.

[1]Lit., *come up* :20-25 [b]Deut. 21:3
3:4 [b]Lev. 4:11, 21; Num. 19:9
4:6, 17; 16:14
Ex. 29:14; Lev. 4:11, 12
, *burning of the* *eifer* [a]Lev. 14:4
[1]Lit., *flesh* [a]Lev. 16:26, 28; 22:6
8 [1]Lit., *flesh*
it shall be to the *gation . . . Israel,* *uarding as water* *purity* [2]Or, *a sin* *ering* [a]Num. 8:7; 31:23
10 [a]Num. 19:7
[1]Lit., *soul of man* :1, 11; Num. 5:2; 6; Acts 21:26, 27
., *it* [a]Num. 19:19; 31:19
3 [1]Lit., *soul* [2]Lit., *welling place* [3]Or, *hrown* [a]Lev. 7:21; 2:3-7 [b]Lev. 15:31; 20:3; Num. 19:20 [c]Num. 19:19
15 [1]Lit., *cord*
16 [a]Num. 31:19
17 [1]Lit., *dust* [2]Lit., *ning of the* [3]Or, *sin offering* [4]Lit., *living* .it., *put* [a]Num. 19:9

19 'Then the clean *person* [a]shall sprinkle on the unclean on the third
day and on the seventh day; and on the seventh day he shall purify
him from uncleanness, and he shall wash his clothes and bathe *him-*
self in water and shall be clean by evening.
20 'But the man who is unclean and does not purify himself from
uncleanness, that person shall be cut off from the midst of the as-
sembly, because he has [a]defiled the sanctuary of the LORD; the water
for impurity has not been sprinkled on him, he is unclean.
21 'So it shall be a perpetual statute for them. And he [a]who
sprinkles the water for impurity shall wash his clothes, and he who
touches the water for impurity shall be unclean until evening.
22 '[a]Furthermore, anything that the unclean *person* touches shall be
unclean; and the person who touches *it* shall be unclean until
evening.' "

Chapter 20

20 Then the sons of Israel, the whole congregation, came to the
[a]wilderness of Zin in the first month; and the people stayed at
Kadesh. Now Miriam died there and was buried there.
2 [a]And there was no water for the congregation; [b]and they as-
sembled themselves against Moses and Aaron.
3 [a]The people thus contended with Moses and spoke, saying, "[b]If
only we had perished [c]when our brothers perished before the LORD!
4 "[a]Why then have you brought the LORD's assembly into this
wilderness, for us and our beasts to die [1]here?
5 "And why have you made us come up from Egypt, to bring us in
to this wretched place? [a]It is not a place of [1]grain or figs or vines or
pomegranates, nor is there water to drink."
6 Then Moses and Aaron came in from the presence of the assemb-
ly to the doorway of the tent of meeting, and [a]fell on their faces.
Then the glory of the LORD appeared to them;
7 and the LORD spoke to Moses, saying,
8 "Take [a]the rod; and you and your brother Aaron assemble the
congregation and speak to the rock before their eyes, that it may
yield its water. You shall thus bring forth water for them out of the
rock and let the congregation and their beasts drink."
9 So Moses took the rod [a]from before the LORD, just as He had
commanded him;
10 and Moses and Aaron gathered the assembly before the rock.
And he said to them, "[a]Listen now, you rebels; shall we bring forth
water for you out of this rock?"
11 Then Moses lifted up his hand and struck the rock twice with his
rod; and [a]water came forth abundantly, and the congregation and
their beasts drank.
12 But the LORD said to Moses and Aaron, "[a]Because you have not
believed Me, to treat Me as holy in the sight of the sons of Israel,
therefore you shall not bring this assembly into the land which I
have given them."
13 Those *were* the waters of [1a]Meribah, [2]because the sons of Israel
contended with the LORD, and He proved Himself holy among them.
14 From Kadesh Moses then sent messengers to [a]the king of Edom:
"Thus your brother Israel has said, 'You [b]know all the hardship that
has befallen us;

19 [a]Ezek. 36
10:22
20 [a]Num. 19
21 [a]Num. 19:
22 [a]Lev. 5:2,
22:5, 6
20:1 [a]Num. 1
27:14; 33:36
2 [a]Ex. 17:1 [b]N
16:19, 42
3 [a]Ex. 17:2 [b]N
14:2, 3 [c]Num.
4 [1]Lit., *there* [a]
5 [1]Lit., *seed* [a]N
16:14
6 [a]Num. 14:5
8 [a]Ex. 4:17, 20;
9 [a]Num. 17:10
10 [a]Ps. 106:33
11 [a]Ps. 78:16; Is
1 Cor. 10:4
12 [a]Num. 20:24;
Deut. 1:37; 3:26,
13 [1]I.e., contentio
where [a]Ex. 17:7;
95:8
14 [a]Gen. 36:31-3
Deut. 2:4 [b]Josh. 2
10; 9:9, 10, 24

15 that our fathers went down to Egypt, and we stayed in Egypt a
long time, and the Egyptians treated us and our fathers badly.
16 'But [a]when we cried out to the LORD, He heard our voice and sent
[b]an angel and brought us out from Egypt; now behold, we are at
Kadesh, a town on the edge of your territory.
17 'Please [a]let us pass through your land. We shall not pass through
field or through vineyard; we shall not even drink water from a well.
We shall go along the king's highway, not turning to the right or left,
until we pass through your territory.' "
18 [a]Edom, however, said to him, "You shall not pass through [1]us,
lest I come out with the sword against you."
19 Again, the sons of Israel said to him, "We shall go up by the
highway, and if I and [a]my livestock do drink any of your water, [b]then
I will [1]pay its price. Let me only pass through on my feet, [2]nothing
else."
20 But he said, "[a]You shall not pass through." And Edom came out
against him with a heavy [1]force, and with a strong hand.
21 [a]Thus Edom refused to allow Israel to pass through his territory;
[b]so Israel turned away from him.
22 Now when they set out from [a]Kadesh, the sons of Israel, the
whole congregation, came to Mount Hor.
23 Then the LORD spoke to Moses and Aaron at [a]Mount Hor by the
border of the land of Edom, saying,
24 "Aaron shall be [a]gathered to his people; for he shall not enter the
land which I have given to the sons of Israel, because [b]you rebelled
against My [1]command at the waters of Meribah.
25 "Take Aaron and his son [a]Eleazar, and bring them up to Mount
Hor;
26 and strip Aaron of his garments and put them on his son Eleazar.
So Aaron will be [a]gathered *to his people,* and will die there."
27 So Moses did just as the LORD had commanded, and they went
up to Mount Hor in the sight of all the congregation.
28 And after Moses had stripped Aaron of his garments and [a]put
them on his son Eleazar, [b]Aaron died there on the mountain top.
Then Moses and Eleazar came down from the mountain.
29 And when all the congregation saw that Aaron had died, all the
house of Israel wept for Aaron thirty [a]days.

Chapter 21

21 When the Canaanite, the king of [a]Arad, who lived in the
[1]Negev, heard that Israel was coming by the way of [2]Atharim,
then he fought against Israel, and took some of them captive.
2 So [a]Israel made a vow to the LORD, and said, "If Thou wilt indeed
deliver this people into my hand, then I will [1]utterly destroy their
cities."
3 And the LORD heard the voice of Israel, and delivered up the
Canaanites; then they [1]utterly destroyed them and their cities. Thus
the name of the place was called [2a]Hormah.
4 Then they set out from Mount Hor by the way of the [1]Red Sea, to
[a]go around the land of Edom; and the [2]people became impatient
because of the journey.
5 And the people spoke against God and Moses, "[a]Why have you
brought us up out of Egypt to die in the wilderness? For there is no
[1]food and no water, and [2b]we loathe this miserable food."

:23; 3:7 [b]Ex. 14:19
[a]Num. 21:22
it., *me* [a]Num. 24:18
, *give* [2]Or, *no* ng [a]Ex. 12:38 [b]Deut. 2:6, 28
people [a]Judg. 11:17
. 11:17 [b]Deut. 2:8
Num. 20:1, 14
3 [a]Num. 33:37
, *mouth* [a]Gen. Num. 20:5, 10
25 [a]Num. 3:4
6 [a]Num. 20:24
. 29:29 [b]Num. eut. 10:6; 32:50
n. 1:5; 50:3, 10; Deut. 34:8
1:1 [1]I.e., South y [2]Or, *the spies* m. 33:40; Josh. 2:14; Judg. 1:16
[1]Lit., *devote to* estruction [a]Gen. :20; Judg. 11:30
[1]Lit., *devoted to* struction [2]I.e., a evoted thing; or, struction [a]Num. 14:45
it., *Sea of Reeds* oul of the people *short* [a]Deut. 2:8
, *bread* [2]Lit., *our* ul *loathes* [a]Num. :2, 3 [b]Num. 11:6

6 [a]And the LORD sent fiery serpents among the people and [b]they bit the people, so that [c]many people of Israel died.

7 [a]So the people came to Moses and said, "We have sinned, because we have spoken against the LORD and you; [b]intercede with the LORD, that He may remove the serpents from us." And Moses interceded for the people.

8 Then the LORD said to Moses, "[1]Make a [a]fiery *serpent*, and set it on a standard; and it shall come about, that everyone who is bitten, when he looks at it, he shall live."

9 And Moses made a [a]bronze serpent and set it on the standard; and it came about, that if a serpent bit any man, when he looked to the bronze serpent, he lived.

10 [a]Now the sons of Israel moved out and camped in Oboth.

11 And they journeyed from Oboth, and camped at Iyeabarim, in the wilderness which is opposite Moab, to the [1]east.

12 [a]From there they set out and camped in [1]Wadi Zered.

13 From there they journeyed and camped on the other side of the Arnon, which is in the wilderness that comes out of the border of the Amorites, [a]for the Arnon is the border of Moab, between Moab and the Amorites.

14 Therefore it is said in the Book of the Wars of the LORD,
"Waheb in Suphah,
And the wadis of the Arnon,
15 And the slope of the wadis
That extends to the site of [a]Ar,
And leans to the border of Moab."

16 [a]And from there *they continued* to [1]Beer, that is the well where the LORD said to Moses, "Assemble the people, that I may give them water."

17 [a]Then Israel sang this song:
"Spring up, O well! Sing to it!
18 "The well, which the leaders sank,
Which the nobles of the people dug,
With the scepter *and* with their staffs."
And from the wilderness *they continued* to Mattanah,

19 and from Mattanah to Nahaliel, and from Nahaliel to Bamoth,

20 and from Bamoth to the valley that is in the land of Moab, at the top of Pisgah which overlooks the [1]wasteland.

21 [a]Then Israel sent messengers to Sihon, king of the Amorites, saying,

22 "[a]Let me pass through your land. We will not turn off into field or vineyard; we will not drink water from wells. We will go by the king's highway until we have passed through your border."

23 [a]But Sihon would not permit Israel to pass through his border. So Sihon gathered all his people and went out against Israel in the wilderness, and came to [b]Jahaz and fought against Israel.

24 Then [a]Israel [1]struck him with the edge of the sword, and took possession of his land from the Arnon to the Jabbok, as far as the sons of Ammon; for the [b]border of the sons of Ammon *was* [2]Jazer.

25 And Israel took all these cities and [a]Israel lived in all the cities of the Amorites, in Heshbon, and in all her [1]villages.

26 For Heshbon was the city of Sihon, king of the Amorites, who had fought against the former king of Moab and had taken all his land out of his hand, as far as the Arnon.

6 [a]Deut. 8: 8:17 [c]1 Cor

7 [a]Num. 11 78:34; Is. 26 5:15 [b]Ex. 8: 12:19; Acts

8 [1]Lit., *Make yourself* [a]Is. 30:6; John 3

9 [a]2 Kin. 18: 3:14, 15

10 [a]Num. 33

11 [1]Lit., *sunr*

12 [1]I.e., a dry except during season [a]Num

13 [a]Num. 22: 11:18

15 [a]Num. 21: 2:9, 18, 29

16 [1]I.e., a well 33:46-49

17 [a]Ex. 15:1; P

20 [1]Or, *Jeshim*

21 [a]Deut. 2:26 Judg. 11:19

22 [a]Num. 20:1

23 [a]Num. 20:2 2:32

24 [1]Lit., *smote,* Gr. and Lat. [2]M. *strong* [a]Amos 2 [b]Deut. 2:37

25 [1]Lit., *daughte* [a]Amos 2:10

3 [1]Lit., *lords of the* [2]Or, *Bamoth* [a]Jer. 3:45 [b]Num. 21:15 m. 22:41; Is. 15:2; 16:12

27 Therefore those who use proverbs say,
"Come to Heshbon! Let it be built!
So let the city of Sihon be established.
28 "[a]For a fire went forth from Heshbon,
A flame from the town of Sihon;
It devoured [b]Ar of Moab,
The [1c]dominant [2]heights of the Arnon.

[a]Jer. 48:46 [b]Judg. 1:24; 1 Kin. 11:33; in. 23:13 [c]Is. 15:5 [d]Is. 16:2

29 "[a]Woe to you, O Moab!
You are ruined, O people of [b]Chemosh!
[c]He has given his sons as fugitives,
[d]And his daughters into captivity,
To an Amorite king, Sihon.

um. 32:3, 34; Jer. 48:18, 22

30 "But we have cast them down,
Heshbon is ruined as far as [a]Dibon,
Then we have laid waste even to Nophah,
Which *reaches* to Medeba."

[a]Num. 32:1, 3, 35; Jer. 48:32

31 Thus Israel lived in the land of the Amorites.
32 And Moses sent to spy out [a]Jazer, and they captured its villages
and dispossessed the Amorites who *were* there.

Lit., *he and* [a]Deut. :1-7 [b]Josh. 13:12

33 [a]Then they turned and went up by the way of Bashan, and Og
the king of Bashan went out [1]with all his people, for battle at [b]Edrei.
34 But the LORD said to Moses, "[a]Do not fear him, for I have given
him into your hand, and all his people and his land; and you shall
do to him as you did to Sihon, king of the Amorites, who lived at
Heshbon."

34 [a]Deut. 3:2

Lit., *smote* [a]Deut. 3:3, 4

35 So [a]they [1]killed him and his sons and all his people, until there
was no remnant left him; and they possessed his land.

Chapter 22

[a]Num. 33:48, 49

22 [a]Then the sons of Israel journeyed, and camped in the plains
of Moab beyond the Jordan *opposite* Jericho.
2 Now [a]Balak the son of Zippor saw all that Israel had done to the
Amorites.

2 [a]Judg. 11:25

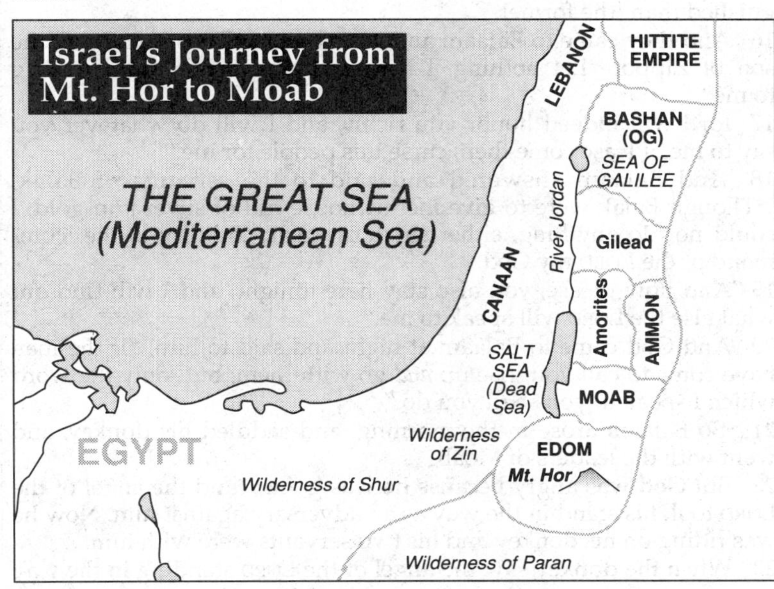

Midian was the son of Abraham by his concubine Keturah (Genesis 25:2). Midian's descendants, the Midianites, took Joseph to Egypt (Genesis 37:28, 36). After killing the Egyptian, Moses fled to Midian and there married the daughter of a priest.

3 [a]So Moab was in great fear because of the people, for they were
numerous; and Moab was in dread of the sons of Israel.
4 And Moab said to the elders of [a]Midian, "Now this [1]horde will
lick up all that is around us, as the ox licks up the grass of the field."
And Balak the son of Zippor was king of Moab at that time.
5 So he sent messengers to [a]Balaam the son of Beor, at [b]Pethor,
which is near the [1]River, *in* the land of the sons of his people, to call
him, saying, "Behold, a people came out of Egypt; behold, they
cover the surface of the land, and they are living opposite me.
6 "[a]Now, therefore, please come, [b]curse this people for me since
they are too [1]mighty for me; perhaps I may be able to [2]defeat them
and drive them out of the land. For I know that he whom you bless
is blessed, and he whom you curse is cursed."
7 So the elders of Moab and the elders of Midian departed with
the *fees for* [a]divination in their hand; and they came to Balaam and
[1]repeated Balak's words to him.
8 And he said to them, "Spend the night here, and I will bring
word back to you as the LORD may speak to me." And the leaders of
Moab stayed with Balaam.
9 Then [a]God came to Balaam and said, "Who are these men with
you?"
10 And Balaam said to God, "Balak the son of Zippor, king of
Moab, has sent *word* to me,
11 'Behold, there is a people who came out of Egypt and they cover
the surface of the land; now come, curse them for me; perhaps I may
be able to fight against them, and drive them out.'"
12 And God said to Balaam, "Do not go with them; [a]you shall not
curse the people; for they [b]are blessed."
13 So Balaam arose in the morning and said to Balak's leaders, "Go
back to your land, for the LORD has refused to let me go with you."
14 And the leaders of Moab arose and went to Balak, and said,
"Balaam refused to come with us."
15 Then Balak again sent leaders, more numerous and more distin-
guished than [1]the former.
16 And they came to Balaam and said to him, "Thus says Balak the
son of Zippor, 'Let nothing, I beg you, hinder you from coming
to me;
17 for I will indeed honor you richly, and I will do whatever you
say to me. [a]Please come then, curse this people for me.'"
18 And Balaam answered and said to the servants of Balak,
"[a]Though Balak were to give me his house full of silver and gold, I
could not do anything, either small or great, contrary to the [1]com-
mand of the LORD my God.
19 "And now please, you also stay here tonight, and I will find out
what else the LORD will speak to me."
20 And God came to Balaam at night and said to him, "If the men
have come to call you, rise up *and* go with them; but [a]only the word
which I speak to you shall you do."
21 [a]So Balaam arose in the morning, and saddled his donkey, and
went with the leaders of Moab.
22 But God was angry because he was going, [a]and the angel of the
LORD took his stand in the way as an adversary against him. Now he
was riding on his donkey and his two servants were with him.
23 When the donkey saw the angel of the LORD standing in the way

3 [a]Ex. 15:15
4 [1]Lit., *assembly* [a]Num. 25:15-18; 3
5 [1]I.e., Euphrates [a]Josh. 24:9; 2 Pet 2:15f.; Jude 11 [b]D 23:4
6 [1]Or, *numerous* [2]*smite* [a]Num. 22:1 23:7, 8 [b]Num. 22 24:9
7 [1]Lit., *spoke* [a]N 23:23; 24:1; Josh
9 [a]Gen. 20:3
12 [a]Num. 23:8; 2 [b]Gen. 12:2; 22:17
15 [1]Lit., *these*
17 [a]Num. 22:6
18 [1]Lit., *mouth* [a] 22:38; 24:13; 1 Ki 22:14; 2 Chr. 18:1
20 [a]Num. 22:35; 12, 16, 26; 24:13
21 [a]2 Pet. 2:15
22 [a]Ex. 23:20

[a]James 1:19

with his drawn sword in his hand, the donkey turned off from the
way and went into the field; but Balaam struck the donkey to turn
her back into the way.
24 Then the angel of the LORD stood in a narrow path of the
vineyards, *with* a wall on this side and a wall on that side.

[a]2 Pet. 2:16

25 When the donkey saw the angel of the LORD, she pressed herself
to the wall and pressed Balaam's foot against the wall, so he struck
her again.
26 And the angel of the LORD went further, and stood in a narrow
place where there was no way to turn to the right hand or the left.

. 12:10; Matt. 15:19

27 When the donkey saw the angel of the LORD, she lay down
under Balaam; so [a]Balaam was angry and struck the donkey with his
stick.
28 And [a]the LORD opened the mouth of the donkey, and she said to
Balaam, "What have I done to you, that you have struck me these
three times?"

and prostrated self to his face [a]Josh. 5:13-15

29 Then Balaam said to the donkey, "Because you have made a
mockery of me! If there had been a sword in my hand, [a]I would have
killed you by now."
30 And the donkey said to Balaam, "Am I not your donkey on
which you have ridden all your life to this day? Have I ever been
accustomed to do so to you?" And he said, "No."

[1]Lit., *reckless* [a]2 Pet. 2:15

31 Then the LORD opened the eyes of Balaam, and he saw [a]the angel
of the LORD standing in the way with his drawn sword in his hand;
and he bowed [1]all the way to the ground.
32 And the angel of the LORD said to him, "Why have you struck
your donkey these three times? Behold, I have come out as an adver-
sary, because your way was [1a]contrary to me.

4 [a]Num. 14:40

33 "But the donkey saw me and turned aside from me these three
times. If she had not turned aside from me, I would surely have
killed you just now, and let her live."
34 And Balaam said to the angel of the LORD, "[a]I have sinned, for I
did not know that you were standing in the way against me. Now
then, if it is displeasing to you, I will turn back."

speak to [a]Num. 22:20

35 But the angel of the LORD said to Balaam, "Go with the men, but
[a]you shall speak only the word which I shall [1]tell you." So Balaam
went along with the leaders of Balak.

[1]Lit., *which is at*

36 When Balak heard that Balaam was coming, he went out to meet
him at the city of Moab, which is on the Arnon border, [1]at the ex-
treme end of the border.
37 Then Balak said to Balaam, "Did I not urgently send to you to
call you? Why did you not come to me? Am I really unable to honor
you?"

38 [a]Num. 22:18

38 So Balaam said to Balak, "Behold, I have come now to you! [a]Am
I able to speak anything at all? The word that God puts in my
mouth, that I shall speak."
39 And Balaam went with Balak, and they came to Kiriath-huzoth.
40 And Balak sacrificed oxen and sheep, and sent *some* to Balaam
and the leaders who were with him.

[1]Or, *Bamoth-baal* [2]it., *the end of the* *mp* [a]Num. 21:28 [b]Num. 23:13

41 Then it came about in the morning that Balak took Balaam, and
brought him up to [1a]the high places of Baal; and he saw from there [2]a
[b]portion of the people.

Chapter 23

23 Then Balaam said to Balak, "Build seven altars for me here, and prepare seven bulls and seven rams for me here."

2 And Balak did just as Balaam had spoken, and Balak and Balaam offered up a bull and a ram on each altar.

3 Then Balaam said to Balak, "Stand beside your burnt offering, and I will go; perhaps the LORD will come to meet me, and whatever He shows me I will tell you." So he went to a bare hill.

4 Now God met Balaam, and he said to Him, "I have set up the seven altars, and I have offered up a bull and a ram on each altar."

5 Then the LORD [a]put a word in Balaam's mouth and said, "Return to Balak, and you shall speak thus."

6 So he returned to him, and behold, he was standing beside his burnt offering, he and all the leaders of Moab.

7 And he took up his [1]discourse and said,
"From [a]Aram Balak has brought me,
Moab's king from the mountains of the East,
'[b]Come curse Jacob for me,
And come, denounce Israel!'
8 "[a]How shall I curse, whom God has not cursed?
And how can I denounce, whom the LORD has not denounced?
9 "As I see him from the top of the rocks,
And I look at him from the hills;
[a]Behold, a people *who* dwells apart,
And shall not be reckoned among the nations.
10 "[a]Who can count the dust of Jacob,
Or number the fourth part of Israel?
[b]Let [1]me die the death of the upright,
[c]And let my end be like his!"

11 Then Balak said to Balaam, "What have you done to me? [a]I took you to curse my enemies, but behold, you have actually blessed them!"

12 And he answered and said, "Must I not be careful to speak [a]what the LORD puts in my mouth?"

13 Then Balak said to him, "Please come with me to another place from where you may see them, although you will only see the extreme end of them, and will not see all of them; and curse them for me from there."

14 So he took him to the field of Zophim, to the top of Pisgah, and built seven altars and offered a bull and a ram on *each* altar.

15 And he said to Balak, "Stand here beside your burnt offering, while I myself meet *the LORD* yonder."

16 Then the LORD met Balaam and [a]put a word in his mouth and said, "Return to Balak, and thus you shall speak."

17 And he came to him, and behold, he was standing beside his burnt offering, and the leaders of Moab with him. And Balak said to him, "What has the LORD spoken?"

18 Then he took up his [1]discourse and said,
"Arise, O Balak, and hear;
Give ear to me, O son of Zippor!
19 "[a]God is not a man, that He should lie,
Nor a son of man, that He should repent;
[b]Has He said, and will He not do it?
Or has He spoken, and will He not make it good?

23:5 [a]Num. Deut. 18:18;
7 [1]Lit., *parab* 22:5; Deut. 23 22:6
8 [a]Num. 22:1
9 [a]Deut. 32:8;
10 [1]Lit., *my so* 13:16; 28:14 [b] [c]Ps. 37:37
11 [a]Neh. 13:2
12 [a]Num. 22:20
16 [a]Num. 22:20
18 [1]Lit., *parable*
19 [a]1 Sam. 15:29 40:8; 55:11

20 "Behold, I have received *a command* to bless;
[a]When He has blessed, then [b]I cannot revoke it.
21 "[a]He has not observed [1]misfortune in Jacob;
[b]Nor has He seen trouble in Israel;
[c]The LORD his God is with him,
[d]And the shout of a king is among them.
22 "[a]God brings them out of Egypt,
He is for them like the [b]horns of the wild ox.
23 "[a]For there is no omen against Jacob,
Nor is there any divination against Israel;
At the proper time it shall be said to Jacob
And to Israel, what God has done.
24 "[a]Behold, a people rises like a lioness,
And as a lion it lifts itself;
It shall not lie down until it devours the prey,
And drinks the blood of the slain."
25 Then Balak said to Balaam, "Do not curse them at all nor bless
them at all!"
26 But Balaam answered and said to Balak, "Did I not tell you,
'[1a]Whatever the LORD speaks, that I must do'?"
27 Then Balak said to Balaam, "Please come, I will take you to
another place; perhaps it will be [1]agreeable with God that you curse
them for me from there."
28 So Balak took Balaam to the top of Peor which overlooks the
[1]wasteland.
29 And Balaam said to Balak, "Build seven altars for me here and
prepare seven bulls and seven rams for me here."
30 And Balak did just as Balaam had said, and offered up a bull and
a ram on *each* altar.

Chapter 24

24 When Balaam saw that it [1]pleased the LORD to bless Israel, he
did not go as at other times to [2]seek [a]omens but he set his face
toward the [b]wilderness.
2 And Balaam lifted up his eyes and saw Israel [1]camping tribe by
tribe; and [a]the Spirit of God came upon him.
3 And he took up his [1]discourse and said,
"[a]The oracle of Balaam the son of Beor,
And the oracle of the man whose eye is opened;
4 The oracle of him who [a]hears the [1]words of God,
Who sees the [b]vision of [2]the Almighty,
Falling down, yet having his eyes uncovered,
5 How fair are your tents, O Jacob,
Your dwellings, O Israel!
6 "Like [1]valleys that stretch out,
Like gardens beside the river,
Like [a]aloes planted by the LORD,
Like [b]cedars beside the waters.
7 "Water shall flow from his buckets,
And his seed *shall be* by many waters,
And his king shall be higher than [a]Agag,
[b]And his kingdom shall be exalted.
8 "[a]God brings him out of Egypt,
He is for him like the horns of the wild ox.

12:2; 22:17;
2 [b]Is. 43:13
iquity [a]Num.
34; Ps. 32:2,
24; 32:5; Jer.
. 3:12; Deut.
eut. 33:5; Ps.
89:15-18
. 24:8 [b]Deut.
33:17
m. 22:7; 24:1;
Josh. 13:22
en. 49:9; Nah.
2:11, 12
[1]Lit., *saying,*
[a]Num. 22:18
Lit., *right in the sight of God*
[1]Or, *Jeshimon*
it., *was good in*
ne eyes of [2]Lit.,
ter [a]Num. 22:7;
3 [b]Num. 23:28
dwelling [a]Num.
; 1 Sam. 19:20;
Rev. 1:10
parable, and so
roughout the ch.
[a]Num. 24:15, 16
, *sayings* [2]Heb.,
dai [a]Num. 22:20
15:1; Num. 12:6
Or possibly, *palm*
Ps. 45:8 [b]Ps. 1:3
m. 24:20; 1 Sam.
8 [b]Ps. 145:11-13
8 [a]Num. 23:22

[b]He shall devour the nations *who are* his adversaries,
And shall crush their bones in pieces,
And shatter *them* with his [c]arrows.
9 "[a]He [1]couches, he lies down as a lion,
And as a [2]lion, who [3]dares rouse him?
[b]Blessed is everyone who blesses you,
And cursed is everyone who curses you."
10 Then Balak's anger burned against Balaam, and he struck his
[1]hands together; and Balak said to Balaam, "I called you to curse my
enemies, but behold, you have persisted in blessing them these three
times!
11 "Therefore, [1]flee to your place now. I said I would honor you
greatly, but behold, the LORD has held you back from honor."
12 And Balaam said to Balak, "[a]Did I not tell your messengers
whom you had sent to me, saying,
13 'Though Balak were to give me his house full of silver and gold, I
could not do anything contrary to the [1]command of the LORD, either
good or bad, [a]of my own [2]accord. [b]What the LORD speaks, that I will
speak'?
14 "And now behold, [a]I am going to my people; come, *and* I will
advise you what this people will do to your people in the [1]days to
come."
15 And he took up his discourse and said,
"[a]The oracle of Balaam the son of Beor,
And the oracle of the man whose eye is opened,
16 The oracle of him who hears the [1]words of God,
And knows the knowledge of the [2]Most High,
Who sees the vision of [3]the Almighty,
Falling down, yet having his eyes uncovered.
17 "I see him, but not now;
I behold him, but not near;
A star shall come forth from Jacob,
[a]And a scepter shall rise from Israel,
[b]And shall crush through the [1]forehead of Moab,
And [2]tear down all the sons of [3]Sheth.
18 "[a]And Edom shall be a possession,
[b]Seir, its enemies, also shall be a possession,
While Israel performs valiantly.
19 "One from Jacob shall have dominion,
And shall destroy the remnant from the city."
20 And he looked at Amalek and took up his discourse and said,
"Amalek was the first of the nations,
[a]But his end *shall be* [1]destruction."
21 And he looked at the [a]Kenite, and took up his discourse and
said,
"Your dwelling place is enduring,
And your nest is set in the cliff.
22 "Nevertheless Kain shall be consumed;
How long shall [a]Asshur [1]keep you captive?"
23 And he took up his discourse and said,
"Alas, who can live except God has ordained it?
24 "But ships *shall come* from the coast of [a]Kittim,
And they shall afflict Asshur and shall afflict [b]Eber;
[c]So they also *shall come* to destruction."

8 [b]Num. 23:24; P
[c]Ps. 45:5

9 [1]Lit., *bows dow* *lioness* [3]Lit., *shal* [a]Gen. 49:9; Num. [b]Gen. 12:3; 27:29

10 [1]Lit., *palms*

11 [1]Lit., *flee for y*

12 [a]Num. 22:18

13 [1]Lit., *mouth* [2]L *heart* [a]Num. 16:2 [b]Num. 22:20

14 [1]Lit., *end of the days* [a]Num. 31:8, Josh. 13:22

15 [a]Num. 24:3, 4

16 [1]Lit., *sayings* *Elyon* [3]Heb., *Sha*

17 [1]Lit., *corners* [2]Another reading *crown of the head* [3]I.e., tumult [a]Gen 49:10 [b]Num. 21:2 15:1-16:14

18 [a]Gen. 27:29; 9:11, 12 [b]Gen. 32

20 [1]Lit., *to destro* [a]Num. 24:24

21 [a]Gen. 15:19

22 [1]Lit., *take* [a]Ge 10:21, 22

24 [a]Gen. 10:4; E 27:6 [b]Gen. 10:21 [c]Num. 24:20

25 Then Balaam arose and departed and returned to [a]his place, and Balak also went his way.

Chapter 25

25 While Israel remained at [a]Shittim, the people began [b]to play the harlot with the daughters of Moab.

2 For [a]they invited the people to the sacrifices of their gods, and the people ate and bowed down to their gods.

3 So [a]Israel joined themselves to [1]Baal of Peor, and the LORD was angry against Israel.

4 And the LORD said to Moses, "Take all the leaders of the people and execute them [1]in broad daylight before the LORD, [a]so that the fierce anger of the LORD may turn away from Israel."

5 So Moses said to the judges of Israel, "Each of you [a]slay his men who have joined themselves to [1]Baal of Peor."

6 Then behold, one of the sons of Israel came and brought to his [1]relatives a [a]Midianite woman, in the sight of Moses and in the sight of all the congregation of the sons of Israel, [b]while they were weeping at the doorway of the tent of meeting.

7 [a]When Phinehas the son of Eleazar, the son of Aaron the priest, saw it, he arose from the midst of the congregation, and took a spear in his hand;

8 and he went after the man of Israel into the [1]tent, and pierced both of them through, the man of Israel and the woman, through the [2]body. [a]So the plague on the sons of Israel was checked.

9 [a]And those who died by the plague were 24,000.

10 Then the LORD spoke to Moses, saying,

11 "[a]Phinehas the son of Eleazar, the son of Aaron the priest, has turned away My wrath from the sons of Israel, in that he was jealous with My jealousy among them, so that I did not destroy the sons of Israel [b]in My jealousy.

12 "Therefore say, '[a]Behold, I give him My [b]covenant of peace;

13 and it shall be for him and his [1]descendants after him, a covenant of a [a]perpetual priesthood, because he was jealous for his God, and [b]made atonement for the sons of Israel.' "

14 Now the name of the [1]slain man of Israel who was [1]slain with the Midianite woman, was Zimri the son of Salu, a leader of a father's household among the Simeonites.

15 And the name of the Midianite woman who was [1]slain was [a]Cozbi the daughter of [b]Zur, [2]who was head of the people of a father's household in Midian.

16 Then the LORD spoke to Moses, saying,

17 "[a]Be hostile to the Midianites and strike them;

18 for they have been hostile to you with their tricks, with which they have deceived you in the affair of Peor, and in the affair of Cozbi, the daughter of the leader of Midian, their sister who was slain on the day of the plague because of Peor."

Chapter 26

26 [1]Then it came about after the [a]plague, [2]that the LORD spoke to Moses and to Eleazar the son of Aaron the priest, saying,

2 "[a]Take a [1]census of all the congregation of the sons of Israel from twenty years old and upward, by their fathers' households, whoever is able to go out to war in Israel."

25 [a]Num. 24:14
:1 [a]Num. 33:49; :1 [b]Num. 31:16; 10:8; Rev. 2:14
Ex. 34:15; Deut. 32:38
Baal-peor [a]Ps. 8, 29; Hos. 9:10
it., *in front of the un* [a]Deut. 13:17
Baal-peor [a]Ex. 32:27
brothers [a]Num. 22:4 [b]Joel 2:17
7 [a]Ps. 106:30
nner rooms [2]Or, [a]Num. 16:46-48
9 [a]Num. 14:37; 16:48-50; 31:16
[a]Ps. 106:30 [b]Ex. 20:5
. 106:30, 31 [b]Is. 10; Ezek. 34:25; 37:26
[1]Lit., *seed* [a]Ex. 9:9 [b]Num. 16:46
14 [1]Lit., *smitten*
.it., *smitten* [2]Lit., m. 25:18 [b]Num. 31:8
Num. 25:1; 22:4; 31:1-3
:1 [1]Ch. 25:19 in [2]Ch. 26:1 in Heb. [a]Num. 25:9
2 [1]Lit., *sum* [a]Ex. 11-16; 38:25, 26; Num. 1:2

3 So Moses and Eleazar the priest spoke with them [a]in the plains
of Moab by the Jordan at Jericho, saying,
4 "*Take a census of the people* from twenty years old and upward, as
the LORD has commanded Moses."
Now the sons of Israel who came out of the land of Egypt *were:*
5 Reuben, Israel's first-born, the sons of Reuben: *of* Hanoch, the
family of the Hanochites; of Pallu, the family of the Palluites;
6 of Hezron, the family of the Hezronites; of Carmi, the family of
the Carmites.
7 These are the families of the Reubenites, and those who were
numbered of them were [a]43,730.
8 And the son of Pallu: Eliab.
9 And the sons of Eliab: Nemuel and Dathan and Abiram. These
are the Dathan and Abiram who were [a]called by the congregation,
who contended against Moses and against Aaron in the company of
Korah, when they contended against the LORD,
10 and [a]the earth opened its mouth and swallowed them up along
with Korah, when that company died, [b]when the fire devoured 250
men, so that they became a [1]warning.
11 [a]The sons of Korah, however, did not die.
12 The sons of Simeon according to their families: of [1]Nemuel, the
family of the Nemuelites; of Jamin, the family of the Jaminites; of
[2]Jachin, the family of the Jachinites;
13 of [1]Zerah, the family of the Zerahites; of Shaul, the family of the
Shaulites.
14 These are the families of the Simeonites, [a]22,200.
15 The sons of Gad according to their families: of [1]Zephon, the
family of the Zephonites; of Haggi, the family of the Haggites; of
Shuni, the family of the Shunites;
16 of [1]Ozni, the family of the Oznites; of Eri, the family of the Erites;
17 of [1]Arod, the family of the Arodites; of Areli, the family of the
Arelites.
18 These are the families of the sons of Gad according to those who
were numbered of them, [a]40,500.
19 The [a]sons of Judah *were* Er and Onan, but Er and Onan died in
the land of Canaan.
20 And the [a]sons of Judah according to their families were: of
Shelah, the family of the Shelanites; of Perez, the family of the
Perezites; of Zerah, the family of the Zerahites.
21 And the sons of Perez were: of Hezron, the family of the Hez-
ronites; of Hamul, the family of the Hamulites.
22 These are the families of Judah according to those who were
numbered of them, [a]76,500.
23 The [a]sons of Issachar according to their families: *of* Tola, the
family of the Tolaites; of [1]Puvah, the family of the Punites;
24 of [1]Jashub, the family of the Jashubites; of Shimron, the family of
the Shimronites.
25 These are the families of Issachar according to those who were
numbered of them, [a]64,300.
26 The [a]sons of Zebulun according to their families: of Sered, the
family of the Seredites; of Elon, the family of the Elonites; of Jahleel,
the family of the Jahleelites.
27 These are the families of the Zebulunites according to those who
were numbered of them, [a]60,500.

3 [a]Num. 22:1 35:1
7 [a]Num. 1:21
9 [a]Num. 1:16
10 [1]Lit., *sign* 16:32 [b]Num.
11 [a]Num. 16: Deut. 24:16
12 [1]In Gen. 4 Ex. 6:15, *Jem* 1 Chr. 4:24, *Ja*
13 [1]In Gen. 4 *Zohar*
14 [a]Num. 1:2
15 [1]In Gen. 46 *Ziphion*
16 [1]In Gen. 46 *Ezbon*
17 [1]In Gen. 46
18 [a]Num. 1:25
19 [a]Gen. 38:2;
20 [a]Gen. 49:8; 2:3; Rev. 7:5
22 [a]Num. 1:27
23 [1]In Gen. 46 *Puvvah;* in 1 Ch *Puah* [a]Gen. 46 1 Chr. 7:1
24 [1]In Gen. 46:
25 [a]Num. 1:29
26 [a]Gen. 46:14
27 [a]Num. 1:31

28 The [a]sons of Joseph according to their families: Manasseh and Ephraim.
29 The sons of Manasseh: of Machir, the family of the Machirites; and [a]Machir [1]became the father of Gilead: of Gilead, the family of the Gileadites.
30 These are the sons of Gilead: *of* [1]Iezer, the family of the [a]Iezerites; of Helek, the family of the Helekites;
31 and *of* Asriel, the family of the Asrielites; and *of* Shechem, the family of the Shechemites;
32 and *of* Shemida, the family of the Shemidaites; and *of* Hepher, the family of the Hepherites.
33 Now Zelophehad the son of Hepher had no sons, but only daughters; and [a]the names of the daughters of Zelophehad were Mahlah, Noah, Hoglah, Milcah and Tirzah.
34 These are the families of Manasseh; and those who were numbered of them were [a]52,700.
35 These are the sons of Ephraim according to their families: of Shuthelah, the family of the Shuthelahites; of [1]Becher, the family of the Becherites; of Tahan, the family of the Tahanites.
36 And these are the sons of Shuthelah: of Eran, the family of the Eranites.
37 These are the families of the sons of Ephraim according to those who were numbered of them, [a]32,500. These are the sons of Joseph according to their families.
38 The sons of Benjamin according to their families: of Bela, the family of the Belaites; of Ashbel, the family of the Ashbelites; of [1]Ahiram, the family of the Ahiramites;
39 of [1]Shephupham, the family of the Shuphamites; of [2]Hupham, the family of the Huphamites.
40 And the sons of Bela were [1]Ard and Naaman: *of Ard*, the family of the Ardites; of Naaman, the family of the Naamites.
41 These are the sons of Benjamin according to their families; and those who were numbered of them were [a]45,600.
42 These are the sons of Dan according to their families: of [1]Shuham, the family of the Shuhamites. These are the families of Dan according to their families.
43 All the families of the Shuhamites, according to those who were numbered of them, were [a]64,400.
44 The [a]sons of Asher according to their families: of Imnah, the family of the Imnites; of Ishvi, the family of the Ishvites; of Beriah, the family of the Beriites.
45 Of the sons of Beriah: of Heber, the family of the Heberites; of Malchiel, the family of the Malchielites.
46 And the name of the daughter of Asher *was* Serah.
47 These are the families of the sons of Asher according to those who were numbered of them, [a]53,400.
48 The [a]sons of Naphtali according to their families: of Jahzeel, the family of the Jahzeelites; of Guni, the family of the Gunites;
49 of Jezer, the family of the Jezerites; of [a]Shillem, the family of the Shillemites.
50 These are the families of Naphtali according to their families; and those who were numbered of them were [a]45,400.
51 These are those who were numbered of the sons of Israel, [a]601,730.

52 Then the LORD spoke to Moses, saying,

53 "[1]Among these the land shall be divided for an inheritance according to the number of names.

54 "[a]To the larger *group* you shall increase their inheritance, and to the smaller *group* you shall diminish their inheritance; each shall be given their inheritance according to those who were numbered of them.

55 "But the land shall be [a]divided by lot. They shall [1]receive their inheritance according to the names of the tribes of their fathers.

56 "According to the selection by lot, their inheritance shall be divided between the larger and the smaller *groups*."

57 And [a]these are those who were numbered of the Levites according to their families: of Gershon, the family of the Gershonites; of Kohath, the family of the Kohathites; of Merari, the family of the Merarites.

58 These are the families of Levi: the family of the Libnites, the family of the Hebronites, the family of the Mahlites, the family of the Mushites, the family of the Korahites. [a]And Kohath [1]became the father of Amram.

59 And the name of Amram's wife [a]was Jochebed, the daughter of Levi, who was born to Levi in Egypt; and she bore to Amram: Aaron and Moses and their sister Miriam.

60 [a]And to Aaron were born Nadab and Abihu, Eleazar and Ithamar.

61 [a]But Nadab and Abihu died when they offered strange fire before the LORD.

62 And those who were numbered of them were [a]23,000, every male from a month old and upward, for [b]they were not numbered among the sons of Israel [c]since no inheritance was given to them among the sons of Israel.

63 These are those who were numbered by Moses and Eleazar the priest, who numbered the sons of Israel in the plains of Moab by the Jordan at Jericho.

64 [a]But among these there was not a man of those who were numbered by Moses and Aaron the priest, who numbered the sons of Israel in the wilderness of Sinai.

65 For the LORD had said [1]of them, "[a]They shall surely die in the wilderness." And not a man was left of them, [b]except Caleb the son of Jephunneh, and Joshua the son of Nun.

Chapter 27

27 Then [a]the daughters of Zelophehad, the son of Hepher, the son of Gilead, the son of Machir, the son of Manasseh, of the families of Manasseh the son of Joseph, came near; and these are [b]the names of his daughters: Mahlah, Noah and Hoglah and Milcah and Tirzah.

2 And they stood before Moses and before Eleazar the priest and before the leaders and all the congregation, at the doorway of the tent of meeting, saying,

3 "Our father [a]died in the wilderness, yet he was not among the company of those who gathered themselves together against the LORD in the company of Korah; but he died in his own sin, and [b]he had no sons.

4 "Why should the name of our father be withdrawn from among

53 [1]Lit., *To*
54 [a]Num. 33
55 [1]Lit., *inhe according to* 33:54; 34:13
57 [a]Gen. 46:1 6:16; 1 Chr. 6
58 [1]Lit., *bego*
59 [a]Ex. 2:1, 2;
60 [a]Num. 3:2
61 [a]Lev. 10:1, 3:4
62 [a]Num. 3:39 1:47 [c]Num. 18:
64 [a]Num. 14:29 Deut. 2:14-16; H
65 [1]Or, *to* [a]Num 14:26-35; Ps. 90 1 Cor. 10:5 [b]De Josh. 14:6-10
27:1 [a]Num. 26:3 36:1 [b]Num. 26:3
3 [a]Num. 26:64, 6 [b]Num. 26:33

his family because he had no son? Give us a possession among our
father's brothers."
5 [a]And Moses brought their case before the LORD.
6 Then the LORD spoke to Moses, saying,
7 "[a]The daughters of Zelophehad are right in *their* statements. You
shall surely give them a hereditary possession among their father's
brothers, and you shall transfer the inheritance of their father to
them.
8 "Further, you shall speak to the sons of Israel, saying, 'If a man
dies and has no son, then you shall transfer his inheritance to his
daughter.
9 'And if he has no daughter, then you shall give his inheritance to
his brothers.
10 'And if he has no brothers, then you shall give his inheritance to
his father's brothers.
11 'And if his father has no brothers, then you shall give his inheri-
tance to his nearest relative in his own family, and he shall possess it;
and it shall be a [a]statutory ordinance to the sons of Israel, just as the
LORD commanded Moses.' "
12 [a]Then the LORD said to Moses, "Go up to this [b]mountain of
Abarim, and see the land which I have given to the sons of Israel.
13 "And when you have seen it, you too [a]shall be gathered to your
people, [b]as Aaron your brother [1]was;
14 for in the wilderness of Zin, during the strife of the congregation,
[a]you rebelled against My [1]command [2]to treat Me as holy before their
eyes at the water." (These are the waters of Meribah of Kadesh in the
wilderness of Zin.)
15 Then Moses spoke to the LORD, saying,
16 "[a]May the LORD, the God of the spirits of all flesh, appoint a man
over the congregation,
17 who [a]will go out [1]and come in before them, and who will lead
them out and [2]bring them in, that the congregation of the LORD may
not be [b]like sheep which have no shepherd."
18 So the LORD said to Moses, "[1]Take Joshua the son of Nun, a man
[a]in whom is the Spirit, and [b]lay your hand on him;
19 and have him stand before Eleazar the priest and before all the
congregation; and [a]commission him in their sight.
20 "And you shall put some of your [1]authority on him, in order that
all the congregation of the sons of Israel may obey *him*.
21 "Moreover, he shall stand before Eleazar the priest, who shall
inquire for him [a]by the judgment of the Urim before the LORD. At his
[1]command they shall go out and at his [1]command they shall come in,
both he and the sons of Israel with him, even all the congregation."
22 And Moses did just as the LORD commanded him; and he took
Joshua and set him before Eleazar the priest, and before all the
congregation.
23 Then he laid his hands on him and [a]commissioned him, just as
the LORD had spoken [1]through Moses.

Chapter 28

28 Then the LORD spoke to Moses, saying,
2 "Command the sons of Israel and say to them, 'You shall [1]be
careful to present My offering, My [a]food for My offerings by fire, of a
soothing aroma to Me, at their appointed time.'

. 9:8; 27:21
36:2; Josh. 17:4
[a]Num. 35:29
eut. 3:23-27; -8-52 [b]Num. 33:47, 48
vas gathered . 31:2 [b]Num. 8; Deut. 10:6
outh [2]Lit., *for anctity* [a]Num. ut. 32:51; Ps. 106:32
[a]Num. 16:22
., *before them will* [2]Lit., *who g* [a]Deut. 31:2; r. 1:10 [b]1 Kin. ek. 34:5; Matt. :36; Mark 6:34
[1]Lit., *Take for yourself* [a]Num. -29; Deut. 34:9 [b]Num. 27:23
t. 3:28; 31:3, 7, 8, 23
0 [1]Lit., *majesty*
Lit., *mouth* [a]Ex. 30; 1 Sam. 28:6
., *by the hand of* [a]Deut. 31:23
Lit., *watch* [a]Lev. 3:11

3 "[a]And you shall say to them, 'This is the offering by fire which
you shall offer to the LORD; two male lambs one year old without
defect *as* a continual burnt offering every day.
4 'You shall offer the one lamb in the morning, and the other lamb
you shall offer [1]at twilight;
5 also [a]a tenth of an ephah of fine flour for a [b]grain offering, mixed
with a fourth of a hin of beaten oil.
6 'It is a continual burnt offering which was ordained in Mount
Sinai as a soothing aroma, an offering by fire to the LORD.
7 'Then the libation with it *shall be* a fourth of a hin for each lamb,
[a]in the holy place you shall pour out a libation of strong drink to the
LORD.
8 'And the other lamb you shall offer [1]at twilight; as the grain
offering of the morning and as its libation, you shall offer it, an
offering by fire, a soothing aroma to the LORD.
9 'Then on the sabbath day two male lambs one year old without
defect, and two-tenths *of an* [1]*ephah* of fine flour mixed with oil as a
grain offering, and its libation:
10 '*This is* the burnt offering of every sabbath in addition to the
[a]continual burnt offering and its libation.
11 'Then [a]at the beginning of each of your months you shall present
a burnt offering to the LORD; two [1]bulls and one ram, seven male
lambs one year old without defect,
12 [a]and three-tenths *of an* [1]*ephah* of fine flour for a grain offering,
mixed with oil, for each bull; and two-tenths of fine flour for a grain
offering, mixed with oil, for the one ram;
13 and a tenth *of an* [1]*ephah* of fine flour mixed with oil for a grain
offering for each lamb, for a burnt offering of a soothing aroma, an
offering by fire to the LORD.
14 'And their libations shall be half a hin of wine for a bull and a
third of a hin for the ram and a fourth of a hin for a lamb; this is the
burnt offering of each month throughout the months of the year.
15 'And one male goat for a sin offering to the LORD; it shall be
offered with its libation in addition to the [a]continual burnt offering.
16 '[a]Then on the fourteenth day of the first month shall be the
LORD's Passover.
17 'And [a]on the fifteenth day of this month *shall be* a [b]feast, un-
leavened bread *shall be* eaten for seven days.
18 'On the [a]first day *shall be* a holy convocation; you shall do no
laborious work.
19 'And you shall present an offering by fire, a burnt offering to the
LORD: two [1]bulls and one ram and seven male lambs one year old,
[a]having them without defect.
20 'And for their grain offering, you shall offer fine flour mixed
with oil: three-tenths *of an* [1]*ephah* for a bull and two-tenths for the
ram.
21 'A tenth *of an* [1]*ephah* you shall offer for [2]each of the seven lambs,
22 and one male goat for a [a]sin offering, to make atonement for you.
23 'You shall present these besides [a]the burnt offering of the morn-
ing, which is for a continual burnt offering.
24 'After this manner you shall present daily, for seven days, [a]the
food of the offering by fire, of a soothing aroma to the LORD; it shall
be presented with its libation in addition to the [b]continual burnt
offering.

3 [a]Ex. 29:38
4 [1]Lit., betw... evenings
5 [a]Ex. 16:36 15:4 [b]Lev. 2
7 [a]Ex. 29:42
8 [1]Lit., betw... evenings
9 [1]I.e., Appro...
10 [a]Num. 28...
11 [1]Lit., bulls... herd [a]Num. ... Ezek. 46:6, 7
12 [1]I.e., Appr... bu. [a]Num. 15...
13 [1]I.e., Appr...
15 [a]Num. 28:...
16 [a]Ex. 12:1-... 23:5-8; Deut. ...
17 [a]Lev. 23:6 23:15; 34:18; D... 16:3-8
18 [a]Lev. 23:7
19 [1]Or, bulls o... herd [a]Deut. 15...
20 [1]I.e., Approx...
21 [1]I.e., Approx... bu. [2]Lit., each l...
22 [a]Lev. 16:18; 8:3; Gal. 4:4f.
23 [a]Num. 28:3
24 [a]Lev. 3:11 [b]... 28:3

25 'And on the seventh day you shall have a holy convocation; [a]you
shall do no laborious work.
26 'Also on [a]the day of the first fruits, when you present a new grain
offering to the LORD in your *Feast of* Weeks, you shall have a holy
convocation; [b]you shall do no laborious work.
27 'And you shall offer a burnt offering for a soothing aroma to the
LORD, two young bulls, one ram, seven male lambs one year old,
28 and their grain offering, fine flour mixed with oil, three-tenths *of*
an [1]*ephah* for each bull, two-tenths for the one ram,
29 a tenth for [1]each of the seven lambs,
30 one male goat to make atonement for you.
31 '[a]Besides the continual burnt offering and its grain offering, you
shall present *them* with their libations. They shall be [1]without defect.

Chapter 29

29 '[a]Now in the seventh month, on the first day of the month,
you shall also have a holy convocation; [b]you shall do no
laborious work. It will be to you a day for blowing trumpets.
2 'And you shall offer a burnt offering as a soothing aroma to the
LORD: one [1]bull, one ram, *and* seven male lambs one year old without
defect;
3 also their grain offering, fine flour mixed with oil, three-tenths *of*
an [1]*ephah* for the bull, two-tenths for the ram,
4 and one-tenth for [1]each of the seven lambs.
5 'And *offer* one male goat for a sin offering, to make atonement for
you,
6 [a]besides the burnt offering of the new moon, and its grain offer-
ing, and the [b]continual burnt offering and its grain offering, and
their libations, according to their ordinance, for a soothing aroma, an
offering by fire to the LORD.
7 'Then on [a]the tenth day of this seventh month you shall have a
holy convocation, and you shall humble yourselves; you shall not do
any work.
8 'And you shall present a burnt offering to the LORD *as* a soothing
aroma: one bull, one ram, seven male lambs one year old, [a]having
them without defect;
9 and their grain offering, fine flour mixed with oil, three-tenths *of*
an [1]*ephah* for the bull, two-tenths for the one ram,
10 a tenth for each of the seven lambs;
11 one male goat for a sin offering, besides [a]the sin offering of
atonement and [b]the continual burnt offering and its grain offering,
and their libations.
12 'Then on [a]the fifteenth day of the seventh month you shall have a
holy convocation; you [b]shall do no laborious work, and you shall
observe a feast to the LORD for seven days.
13 'And you shall present a burnt offering, an offering by fire as a
soothing aroma to the LORD: thirteen bulls, two rams, fourteen male
lambs one year old, which are without defect,
14 and their grain offering, fine flour mixed with oil, three-tenths *of*
an [1]*ephah* for [2]each of the thirteen bulls, two-tenths for [3]each of the
two rams,
15 and a tenth for each of the fourteen lambs;
16 and one male goat for a sin offering, [a]besides the continual burnt
offering, its grain offering and its libation.

Num. 28:18
3:16; 34:22; 5-21; Deut. Num. 28:18
rox. one bu.
, *each lamb*
ithout defect [a]Num. 28:3
23:16; 34:22; 23-25 [b]Num. 28:26
ull of a herd, o throughout the ch.
prox. one bu.
ach lamb, and ghout the ch.
28:27 [b]Num. 28:3
Lev. 16:29-34; 23:26-32
v. 22:20; Deut. 15:21; 17:1
pprox. one bu.
16:3, 5 [b]Num. 28:3
[a]Lev. 23:33-35; 6:13-15 [b]Num. 29:1
.e., Approx. one , *each bull* [3]Lit., *each ram*
16 [a]Num. 28:3

17 'Then on [a]the second day: twelve bulls, two rams, fourteen male lambs one year old without defect;

18 and their grain offering and their libations for the bulls, for the rams and for the lambs, by their number [a]according to the ordinance;

19 and one male goat for a sin offering, [a]besides the continual burnt offering and its grain offering, and their libations.

20 'Then on the third day: eleven bulls, two rams, fourteen male lambs one year old without defect;

21 and their grain offering and their libations for the bulls, for the rams and for the lambs, by their number according to the ordinance;

22 and one male goat for a sin offering, besides the continual burnt offering and its grain offering and its libation.

23 'Then on the fourth day: ten bulls, two rams, fourteen male lambs one year old without defect;

24 their grain offering and their libations for the bulls, for the rams and for the lambs, by their number according to the ordinance;

25 and one male goat for a sin offering, besides the continual burnt offering, its grain offering and its libation.

26 'Then on the fifth day: nine bulls, two rams, fourteen male lambs one year old [a]without defect;

27 and their grain offering and their libations for the bulls, for the rams and for the lambs, by their number according to the ordinance;

28 and one male goat for a sin offering, besides the continual burnt offering and its grain offering and its libation.

29 'Then on the sixth day: eight bulls, two rams, fourteen male lambs one year old without defect;

30 and their grain offering and their libations for the bulls, for the rams and for the lambs, by their number according to the ordinance;

31 and one male goat for a sin offering, besides the continual burnt offering, its grain offering and its libations.

32 'Then on the seventh day: seven bulls, two rams, fourteen male lambs one year old without defect;

33 and their grain offering and their libations for the bulls, for the rams and for the lambs, by their number according to the ordinance;

34 and one male goat for a sin offering, besides the continual burnt offering, its grain offering and its libation.

35 '[a]On the eighth day you shall have a solemn assembly; you shall do no laborious work.

36 'But you shall present a burnt offering, an offering by fire, as a soothing aroma to the LORD: one bull, one ram, seven male lambs one year old without defect;

37 their grain offering and their libations for the bull, for the ram and for the lambs, by their number according to the ordinance;

38 and one male goat for a sin offering, besides the continual burnt offering and its grain offering and its libation.

39 'You shall present these to the LORD at your [a]appointed times, besides your [1]votive offerings and your freewill offerings, for your burnt offerings and for your grain offerings and for your libations and for your peace offerings.' "

40 [1]And Moses spoke to the sons of Israel in accordance with all that the LORD had commanded Moses.

17 [a]Lev. 23

18 [a]Lev. 2:1

19 [a]Num. 28

26 [a]Heb. 7:2

35 [a]Lev. 23:36

39 [1]Lit., *vows* 23:2

40 [1]Ch. 30:1 in

1:4, 16; 7:2

Chapter 30

30 Then Moses spoke to [a]the heads of the tribes of the sons of
Israel, saying, "This is the word which the LORD has com-
manded.
2 "[a]If a man makes a vow to the LORD, or takes an oath to bind
himself with a binding obligation, he shall not violate his word; he
shall do according to all that proceeds out of his mouth.
3 "Also if a woman makes a vow to the LORD, and binds herself by
an obligation in her father's house in her youth,

:21-23; Matt. 5:33

4 and her father hears her vow and her obligation by which she
has bound herself, and her father [1]says nothing to her, then all her
vows shall stand, and every obligation by which she has bound
herself shall stand.
5 "But if her father should forbid her on the day he hears *of it,* none
of her vows or her obligations by which she has bound herself shall
stand; and the LORD will forgive her because her father had forbid-
den her.
6 "However, if she should [1]marry while [2]under her vows or the
rash statement of her lips by which she has bound herself,

's silent to her, so throughout the ch.

7 and her husband hears of it and says nothing to her on the day
he hears *it,* then her vows shall stand and her obligations by which
she has bound herself shall stand.
8 "But if on the day her husband hears *of it,* he forbids her, then he
shall annul her vow which [1]she is under and the rash statement of
her lips by which she has bound herself; and the LORD will forgive
her.
9 "But the vow of a widow or of a divorced woman, everything by
which she has bound herself, shall stand against her.
10 "However, if she vowed in her husband's house, or bound herself
by an obligation with an oath,

e to a husband 'ows are on her

11 and her husband heard *it,* but said nothing to her *and* did not
forbid her, then all her vows shall stand, and every obligation by
which she bound herself shall stand.
12 "But if her husband indeed annuls them on the day he hears *them,*
then whatever proceeds out of her lips concerning her vows or con-
cerning the obligation of herself, shall not stand; her husband has
annulled them, and the LORD will forgive her.
13 "Every vow and every binding oath to humble herself, her hus-
band may confirm it or her husband may annul it.
14 "But if her husband indeed says nothing to her from day to day,
then he confirms all her vows or all her obligations which are on her;
he has confirmed them, because he said nothing to her on the day he
heard them.

8 [1]Lit., *is on her*

15 "But if he indeed annuls them after he has heard them, then he
shall bear her guilt."
16 These are the statutes which the LORD commanded Moses, *as*
between a man and his wife, *and as* between a father and his daugh-
ter, *while she is* in her youth in her father's house.

Chapter 31

31 Then the LORD spoke to Moses, saying,
2 "[a]Take full vengeance for the sons of Israel on the
Midianites; afterward you will be [b]gathered to your people."

[a]Num. 25:1, 16, [b]Num. 20:24, 26; 27:13

3 And Moses spoke to the people, saying, "Arm men from among
you for the war, that they may [1]go against Midian, to execute [a]the
LORD's vengeance on Midian.
4 "A thousand from each tribe of all the tribes of Israel you shall
send to the war."
5 So there were [1]furnished from the thousands of Israel, a
thousand from each tribe, twelve thousand armed for war.
6 And Moses sent them, a thousand from each tribe, to the war,
and Phinehas the son of Eleazar the priest, to the war with them,
[a]and the holy vessels and [b]the trumpets for the alarm in his hand.
7 So they made war against Midian, just as the LORD had com-
manded Moses, and [a]they killed every male.
8 And they killed the kings of Midian along with the *rest of* their
slain: [a]Evi and Rekem and [b]Zur and Hur and Reba, the five kings of
Midian; they also killed [c]Balaam the son of Beor with the sword.
9 And the sons of Israel captured the women of Midian and their
little ones; and all their cattle and all their flocks and all their goods,
they plundered.
10 Then they burned all their cities where they lived and all their
camps with fire.
11 And [a]they took all the spoil and all the prey, both of man and of
beast.
12 And they brought the captives and the prey and the spoil to
Moses, and to Eleazar the priest and to the congregation of the sons
of Israel, to the camp at the plains of Moab, which are by the Jordan
opposite Jericho.
13 And Moses and Eleazar the priest and all the leaders of the
congregation went out to meet them outside the camp.
14 And Moses was angry with the officers of the army, the captains
of thousands and the captains of hundreds, who had come from
service in the war.
15 And Moses said to them, "Have you [1]spared [a]all the women?
16 "[a]Behold, these [1]caused the sons of Israel, through the [2]counsel of
[b]Balaam, to [3]trespass against the LORD in the matter of Peor, so the
plague was among the congregation of the LORD.
17 "[a]Now therefore, kill every male among the little ones, and kill
every woman who has known man [1]intimately.
18 "But all the [1]girls who have not known man [2]intimately, [3]spare for
yourselves.
19 "[a]And you, camp outside the camp seven days; whoever has
killed any person, and whoever has touched any slain, purify your-
selves, you and your captives, on the third day and on the seventh
day.
20 "And you shall purify for yourselves every garment and every
article of [1]leather and all the work of goats' *hair,* and all articles of
wood."
21 Then Eleazar the priest said to the men of war who had gone to
battle, "This is the statute of the law which the LORD has com-
manded Moses:
22 only the gold and the silver, the bronze, the iron, the tin and the
lead,
23 everything that can stand the fire, you shall pass through the
fire, and it shall be clean, but it shall be purified with [a]water for

3 [1]Lit., *be*
5 [1]Lit., *deli*
6 [a]Num. 14 10:8, 9
7 [a]Deut. 20: 21:11; 1 Kin.
8 [a]Josh. 13: 25:15 [c]Num. Josh. 13:22
11 [a]Deut. 20:
15 [1]Lit., *let* . . [a]Deut. 20:14
16 [1]Lit., *were word* [3]Possib *from the Lord* 25:1-9 [b]Num.
17 [1]Lit., *by lyir man* [a]Deut. 7: 20:16-18
18 [1]Lit., *female children* [2]Lit., *b with a man* [3]Lit *alive*
19 [a]Num. 19:11
20 [1]Or, *skin*
23 [a]Num. 19:9,

[1]Lit., *of captives*

impurity. But whatever cannot stand the fire you shall pass through
the water.
24 "And you shall wash your clothes on the seventh day and be
clean, and afterward you may enter the camp."
25 Then the LORD spoke to Moses, saying,
26 "You and Eleazar the priest and the heads of the fathers'

27 [a]Josh. 22:8

households of the congregation, take a count of the booty [1]that was
captured, both of man and of animal;
27 and [a]divide the booty between the warriors who went out to
battle and all the congregation.
28 "[a]And levy a tax for the LORD from the men of war who went out
to battle, one [1]in five hundred of the persons and of the cattle and of

8 [1]Lit., *soul from*
[a]Num. 18:21-30

the donkeys and of the sheep;
29 take it from their half and give it to Eleazar the priest, as an
[1]offering to the LORD.
30 "And from the sons of Israel's half, you shall take one drawn out
of every fifty of the persons, of the cattle, of the donkeys and of the
sheep, from all the animals, and give them to the Levites who [a]keep
charge of the tabernacle of the LORD."

., *heave offering,*
nd so throughout
the ch.

31 And Moses and Eleazar the priest did just as the LORD had com-
manded Moses.
32 Now the booty that remained from the spoil which the [1]men of
war had plundered was 675,000 sheep,
33 and 72,000 cattle,
34 and 61,000 donkeys,
35 and of human beings, of the women who had not known man
[1]intimately, all the persons were 32,000.

m. 3:7, 8, 25, 26,
1, 36, 37; 18:3, 4

36 And the half, the portion of those who went out to war, was *as*
follows: the number of sheep was 337,500,
37 and the LORD's levy of the sheep was 675,
38 and the cattle were 36,000, from which the LORD's levy was 72.
39 And the donkeys were 30,500, from which the LORD's levy
was 61.

32 [1]Lit., *people*

40 And the human beings were 16,000, from whom the LORD's levy
was 32 persons.
41 And Moses gave the levy *which was* the LORD's offering to
Eleazar the priest, just [a]as the LORD had commanded Moses.
42 As for the sons of Israel's half, which Moses [1]separated from the
men who had gone to war—

t., *by lying with a*
man

43 now the congregation's half was 337,500 sheep,
44 and 36,000 cattle,
45 and 30,500 donkeys,
46 and the human beings were 16,000—
47 and from the sons of Israel's half, Moses took one drawn out of
every fifty, both of man and of animals, and gave them to the
Levites, who kept charge of the tabernacle of the LORD, just as the

m. 5:9, 10; 18:19

LORD had commanded Moses.
48 Then the officers who were over the thousands of the army, the
captains of thousands and the captains of hundreds, approached
Moses;
49 and they said to Moses, "Your servants have taken a census of
men of war who are in our charge, and no man of us is missing.

42 [1]Or, *divided*

50 "So we have brought as an offering to the LORD what each man

found, articles of gold, armlets and bracelets, signet rings, earrings
and necklaces, [a]to make atonement for ourselves before the LORD."
51 And Moses and Eleazar the priest took the gold from them, all
kinds of wrought articles.
52 And all the gold of the offering which they offered up to the
LORD, from the captains of thousands and the captains of hundreds,
was 16,750 shekels.
53 [a]The men of war had taken booty, every man for himself.
54 So Moses and Eleazar the priest took the gold from the captains
of thousands and of hundreds, and brought it to the tent of meeting
as [a]a memorial for the sons of Israel before the LORD.

Chapter 32

32 Now the sons of Reuben and the sons of Gad had an [a]exceed-
ingly large number of livestock. So when they saw the land of
[b]Jazer and the land of Gilead, that [1]it was indeed a place suitable for
livestock,
2 the sons of Gad and the sons of Reuben came and spoke to
Moses and to Eleazar the priest and to the leaders of the congrega-
tion, saying,
3 "[a]Ataroth, Dibon, Jazer, Nimrah, Heshbon, Elealeh, Sebam, Nebo
and Beon,
4 the land [a]which the LORD [1]conquered before the congregation of
Israel, is a land for livestock; and your servants have livestock."
5 And they said, "If we have found favor in your sight, let this
land be given to your servants as a possession; do not take us across
the Jordan."
6 But Moses said to the sons of Gad and to the sons of Reuben,
"Shall your brothers go to war while you yourselves sit here?
7 "[a]Now why are you [1]discouraging the sons of Israel from crossing
over into the land which the LORD has given them?
8 "[1]This is what your fathers did when I sent them from [a]Kadesh-
barnea to see the land.
9 "For when they went up to [a]the [1]valley of Eshcol and saw the
land, they [2]discouraged the sons of Israel so that they did not go into
the land which the LORD had given them.
10 "So [a]the LORD's anger burned in that day, and He swore, saying,
11 '[a]None of the men who came up from Egypt, from twenty years
old and upward, shall see the land which I swore to Abraham, to
Isaac and to Jacob; for they did not follow Me fully,
12 except Caleb the son of Jephunneh the Kenizzite and Joshua the
son of Nun, [a]for they have followed the LORD fully.'
13 "[a]So the LORD's anger burned against Israel, and He made them
wander in the wilderness forty years, until the entire generation of
those who had done evil in the sight of the LORD was destroyed.
14 "Now behold, you have risen up in your fathers' place, a brood of
sinful men, to add still more to the burning [a]anger of the LORD
against Israel.
15 "For if you [a]turn away from following Him, He will once more
abandon them in the wilderness; and you will destroy all these
people."
16 Then they came near to him and said, "We will build here sheep-
folds for our livestock and cities for our little ones;
17 [a]but we ourselves will be armed ready *to go* before the sons of

50 [a]Ex. 30
53 [a]Num. 3
20:14
54 [a]Ex. 30:
32:1 [1]Lit., *b*
place, a pla
12:38 [b]Num
3 [a]Num. 32
4 [1]Lit., *smo*
21:34
7 [1]Lit., *restra*
hearts of [a]N
13:27-14:4
8 [1]Lit., *Thus*
fathers [a]Num
Deut. 1:19-25
9 [1]Or, *wadi* [2]
restrained the
[a]Num. 13:24;
10 [a]Num. 14:
1:34
11 [a]Num. 14:2
12 [a]Deut. 1:36
14:8f.
13 [a]Num. 14:3
14 [a]Deut. 1:34
15 [a]Deut. 30:17
2 Chr. 7:19, 20
17 [a]Josh. 4:12,

Israel, until we have brought them to their place, while our little
ones live in the fortified cities because of the inhabitants of the land.
18 "[a]We will not return to our homes until every one of the sons of
Israel has possessed his inheritance.
19 "For we will not have an inheritance with them on the other side
of the Jordan and beyond, because our inheritance has fallen to us
[a]on this side of the Jordan toward the east."
20 [a]So Moses said to them, "If you will do [1]this, if you will arm
yourselves before the LORD for the war,
21 and all of you armed men cross over the Jordan before the LORD
until He has driven His enemies out from before Him,
22 [a]and the land is subdued before the LORD, then afterward you
shall return and be free of obligation toward the LORD and toward
Israel, and this land shall be yours for a possession before the LORD.
23 "But if you will not do so, behold, you have sinned against the
LORD, and be sure [a]your sin will find you out.
24 "Build yourselves cities for your little ones, and sheepfolds for
your sheep; and [a]do [1]what you have promised."
25 And the sons of Gad and the sons of Reuben spoke to Moses,
saying, "Your servants will do just as my lord commands.
26 "[a]Our little ones, our wives, our livestock and all our cattle shall
[1]remain there in the cities of Gilead;
27 while your servants, everyone who is armed for war, will [a]cross
over in the presence of the LORD to battle, just as my lord says."
28 So Moses gave command concerning them to Eleazar the priest,
and to Joshua the son of Nun, and to the heads of the fathers'
households of the tribes of the sons of Israel.
29 And Moses said to them, "If the sons of Gad and the sons of
Reuben, everyone who is armed for battle, will cross with you over
the Jordan in the presence of the LORD, and the land will be subdued
before you, then you shall give them the land of Gilead for a
possession;
30 but if they will not cross over with you armed, they shall have
possessions among you in the land of Canaan."
31 And the sons of Gad and the sons of Reuben answered, saying,
"As the LORD has said to your servants, so we will do.
32 "We ourselves will cross over armed in the presence of the LORD
into the land of Canaan, and the possession of our inheritance *shall
remain* with us across the Jordan."
33 [a]So Moses gave to them, to the sons of Gad and to the sons of
Reuben and to the half-tribe of Joseph's son Manasseh, the kingdom
of Sihon, king of the Amorites and the kingdom of Og, the king of
Bashan, the land with its cities with *their* [1]territories, the cities of the
surrounding land.
34 And the sons of Gad built Dibon and Ataroth and [a]Aroer,
35 and Atroth-shophan and Jazer and Jogbehah,
36 and [a]Beth-nimrah and Beth-haran as fortified cities, and sheep-
folds for sheep.
37 And the sons of Reuben built Heshbon and Elealeh and
Kiriathaim,
38 and [a]Nebo and Baal-meon—*their* names being changed—and
Sibmah, and they gave *other* names to the cities which they built.
39 And the sons of [a]Machir the son of Manasseh went to Gilead and
took it, and dispossessed the Amorites who were in it.

18 [a]Josh. 22:1-4
[a]Josh. 12:1; 13:8
20 [1]Lit., *this thing* [a]Deut. 3:18
22 [a]Deut. 3:20
Gen. 4:7; 44:16; Is. 59:12
Lit., *that which has* out of your mouth [a]Num. 30:2
Lit., *be* [a]Josh. 1:14
27 [a]Josh. 4:12
Lit., *borders* [a]Deut. 8-17; Josh. 12:1-6
34 [a]Deut. 2:36
36 [a]Num. 32:3
38 [a]Is. 46:1
39 [a]Gen. 50:23

40 So Moses gave [a]Gilead to Machir the son of Manasseh, and he
lived in it.
41 And Jair the son of Manasseh went and took its [1]towns, and
called them [2a]Havvoth-jair.
42 And Nobah went and took Kenath and its villages, and called it
Nobah after [a]his own name.

Chapter 33

33 These are the journeys of the sons of Israel, by which they
came out from the land of Egypt by their armies, under [a]the
[1]leadership of Moses and Aaron.
2 And Moses recorded their starting places according to their jour-
neys by the [1]command of the LORD, and these are their journeys
according to their starting places.
3 [a]And they journeyed from Rameses in the first month, on the
fifteenth day of the first month; on the [1]next day after the Passover
the sons of Israel [b]started out [2]boldly in the sight of all the Egyptians,
4 while the Egyptians were burying all their first-born whom the
LORD had struck down among them. The LORD had also executed
judgments [a]on their gods.
5 Then [a]the sons of Israel journeyed from Rameses, and camped in
Succoth.
6 [a]And they journeyed from Succoth, and camped in Etham, which
is on the edge of the wilderness.
7 [a]And they journeyed from Etham, and turned back to Pi-
hahiroth, which faces Baal-zephon; and they camped before Migdol.
8 [a]And they journeyed [1]from before Hahiroth, and passed through
the midst of the sea into the wilderness; and [b]they went three days'
journey in the wilderness of Etham, and camped at Marah.
9 [a]And they journeyed from Marah, and came to Elim; and in Elim
there were twelve springs of water and seventy palm trees; and they
camped there.
10 And they journeyed from Elim, and camped by the [1]Red Sea.
11 And they journeyed from the [1]Red Sea, and camped in [a]the
wilderness of Sin.
12 And they journeyed from the wilderness of Sin, and camped at
Dophkah.
13 And they journeyed from Dophkah, and camped at Alush.
14 And they journeyed from Alush, and camped [a]at Rephidim; now
it was there that the people had no water to drink.
15 And they journeyed from Rephidim, and camped in [a]the wilder-
ness of Sinai.
16 And they journeyed from the wilderness of Sinai, and camped at
[a]Kibroth-hattaavah.
17 And they journeyed from Kibroth-hattaavah, and camped at
[a]Hazeroth.
18 And they journeyed from Hazeroth, and camped at Rithmah.
19 And they journeyed from Rithmah, and camped at Rimmon-
perez.
20 And they journeyed from Rimmon-perez, and camped at
[a]Libnah.
21 And they journeyed from Libnah, and camped at Rissah.
22 And they journeyed from Rissah, and camped in Kehelathah.

40 [a]Deut. 3:12, 1
Josh. 17:1

41 [1]Lit., *tent villag*
[2]I.e., the towns of
[a]Deut. 3:14; Judg.

42 [a]2 Sam. 18:18
49:11

33:1 [1]Lit., *hand* [a]
77:20; 105:26; Mi

2 [1]Lit., *mouth*

3 [1]Lit., *morrow* [2]
with a high hand
12:37 [b]Ex. 14:8

4 [a]Ex. 12:12

5 [a]Ex. 12:37

6 [a]Ex. 13:20

7 [a]Ex. 14:1, 2

8 [1]Many mss. re
from Pi-hahiroth
14:22 [b]Ex. 15:22

9 [a]Ex. 15:27

10 [1]Lit., *Sea of R*

11 [1]Lit., *Sea of R*
[a]Ex. 16:1

14 [a]Ex. 17:1

15 [a]Ex. 19:1

16 [a]Num. 11:34

17 [a]Num. 11:35

20 [a]Deut. 1:1

23 And they journeyed from Kehelathah, and camped at Mount Shepher.
24 And they journeyed from Mount Shepher, and camped at Haradah.
25 And they journeyed from Haradah, and camped at Makheloth.
26 And they journeyed from Makheloth, and camped at Tahath.
27 And they journeyed from Tahath, and camped at Terah.
28 And they journeyed from Terah, and camped at Mithkah.
29 And they journeyed from Mithkah, and camped at Hashmonah.
30 And they journeyed from Hashmonah, and camped at [a]Moseroth.
31 And they journeyed from Moseroth, and camped at Bene-jaakan.
32 And they journeyed from [a]Bene-jaakan, and camped at Hor-haggidgad.
33 And they journeyed from Hor-haggidgad, and camped at [a]Jotbathah.
34 And they journeyed from Jotbathah, and camped at Abronah.
35 And they journeyed from Abronah, and camped at [a]Ezion-geber.
36 And they journeyed from Ezion-geber, and camped in the wilderness of [a]Zin, that is, Kadesh.
37 And they journeyed from Kadesh, and camped at [a]Mount Hor, [b]at the edge of the land of Edom.
38 [a]Then Aaron the priest went up to Mount Hor at the [1]command of the LORD, and died there, in the fortieth year after the sons of Israel had come from the land of Egypt on the first *day* in the fifth month.
39 And Aaron was one hundred twenty-three years old when he died on Mount Hor.
40 Now the Canaanite, the king of [a]Arad [1]who lived in the [2]Negev in the land of Canaan, heard of the coming of the sons of Israel.
41 Then they journeyed from Mount Hor, and camped at Zalmonah.
42 And they journeyed from Zalmonah, and camped at Punon.
43 And they journeyed from Punon, and camped at [a]Oboth.
44 And they journeyed from Oboth, and camped at Iye-abarim, at the border of Moab.
45 And they journeyed from Iyim, and camped at Dibon-gad.
46 And they journeyed from Dibon-gad, and camped at Almon-diblathaim.
47 And they journeyed from Almon-diblathaim, and camped in the mountains of [a]Abarim, before Nebo.
48 And they journeyed from the mountains of Abarim, and [a]camped in the plains of Moab by the Jordan *opposite* Jericho.
49 And they camped by the Jordan, from Beth-jeshimoth as far as [a]Abel-shittim in the plains of Moab.
50 Then the LORD spoke to Moses in the plains of Moab by the Jordan *opposite* Jericho, saying,
51 "Speak to the sons of Israel and say to them, '[a]When you cross over the Jordan into the land of Canaan,
52 then you shall drive out all the inhabitants of the land from before you, and [a]destroy all their figured stones, and destroy all their molten images and demolish all their high places;
53 [a]and you shall take possession of the land and live in it, for I have given the land to you to possess it.

30 [a]Deut. 10:6
...Gen. 36:27; Deut. 10:6; 1 Chr. 1:42
33 [a]Deut. 10:7
35 [a]Deut. 2:8
36 [a]Num. 20:1
...um. 20:22 [b]Num. 20:16
...it., *mouth* [a]Num. 20:28; Deut. 10:6
[1]Lit., *and he* [2]I.e., ...th country [a]Num. 21:1
[a]Num. 21:10, 11
47 [a]Num. 27:12
48 [a]Num. 22:1
49 [a]Num. 25:1
51 [a]Josh. 3:17
... [a]Ex. 23:24; Lev. ...; Deut. 7:5; 12:3, ...30; Ps. 106:34-36
...eut. 11:31; 17:14; Josh. 21:43

54 '[a]And you shall inherit the land by lot according to your families;
to the larger you shall give more inheritance, and to the smaller you
shall give less inheritance. Wherever the lot falls to anyone, that shall
be his. You shall inherit according to the tribes of your fathers.
55 'But if you do not drive out the inhabitants of the land from
before you, then it shall come about that those whom you let remain
of them *will become* [a]as pricks in your eyes and as thorns in your
sides, and they shall trouble you in the land in which you live.
56 'And it shall come about that as I plan to do to them, so I will do
to you.' "

Chapter 34

34 Then the LORD spoke to Moses, saying,
2 "Command the sons of Israel and say to them, 'When you
enter [a]the land of Canaan, this is the land that shall fall to you as an
inheritance, *even the* land of Canaan according to its borders.
3 '[a]Your southern [1]sector shall [2]extend from the wilderness of Zin
along the side of Edom, and your southern border shall [2]extend from
the end of the Salt Sea [b]eastward.
4 'Then your border shall turn *direction* from the south to the ascent
of Akrabbim, and [1]continue to Zin, and its [2]termination shall be to
the south of [a]Kadesh-barnea; and it shall [3]reach Hazaraddar, and
[1]continue to Azmon.

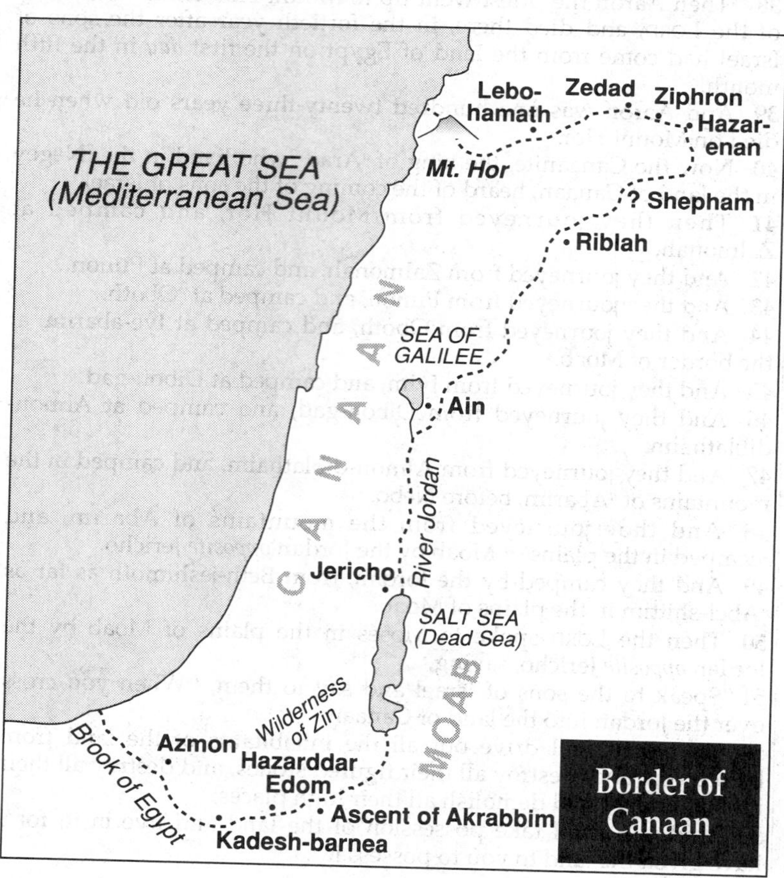

54 [a]Num. 2…

55 [a]Josh. 23…

34:2 [a]Gen. 1… 78:54, 55; 10…

3 [1]Lit., *side* [2]… [a]Josh. 15:1-3 … 15:5

4 [1]Lit., *pass a…* *goings out,* an… throughout the… *go forth to* [a]Nu…

5 'And the border shall turn *direction* from Azmon to the brook of
Egypt, and its termination shall be at [a]the sea.
6 'As for the western border, you shall have the Great Sea, that is,
its [1]coastline; this shall be your west border.
7 '[a]And this shall be your north border: you shall draw your *border*
line from the Great Sea to Mount Hor.
8 'You shall draw a line from Mount Hor to [a]the [1]Lebo-hamath, and
the termination of the border shall be at Zedad;
9 and the border shall proceed to Ziphron, and its termination
shall be at Hazar-enan. This shall be your north border.
10 'For your eastern border you shall also draw a line from Hazar-
enan to Shepham,
11 and the border shall go down from Shepham to [a]Riblah on the
east side of Ain; and the border shall go down and reach to the
[1]slope on the east side of the Sea of [b]Chinnereth.
12 'And the border shall go down to the Jordan and its termination
shall be at the Salt Sea. This shall be your land according to its
borders all around.' "
13 So Moses commanded the sons of Israel, saying, "[a]This is the
land that you are to apportion by lot among you as a possession,
which the LORD has commanded to give to the nine and a half tribes.
14 "[a]For the tribe of the sons of Reuben have received *theirs* accord-
ing to their fathers' households, and the tribe of the sons of Gad
according to their fathers' households, and the half-tribe of Manas-
seh have received their possession.
15 "The two and a half tribes have received their possession across
the Jordan opposite Jericho, eastward toward the sunrising."
16 Then the LORD spoke to Moses, saying,
17 "[a]These are the names of the men who shall apportion the land to
you for inheritance: Eleazar the priest and Joshua the son of Nun.
18 "And you shall take one leader of every tribe to apportion the
land for inheritance.
19 "And these are the names of the men: of the tribe of [a]Judah, [b]Caleb
the son of Jephunneh.
20 "And of the tribe of the sons of [a]Simeon, Samuel the son of Am-
mihud.
21 "Of the tribe of [a]Benjamin, Elidad the son of Chislon.
22 "And of the tribe of the sons of Dan a leader, Bukki the son of
Jogli.
23 "Of the sons of Joseph: of the tribe of the sons of Manasseh a
leader, Hanniel the son of Ephod.
24 "And of the tribe of the sons of Ephraim a leader, Kemuel the son
of Shiphtan.
25 "And of the tribe of the sons of Zebulun a leader, Elizaphan the
son of Parnach.
26 "And of the tribe of the sons of Issachar a leader, Paltiel the son of
Azzan.
27 "And of the tribe of the sons of Asher a leader, Ahihud the son of
Shelomi.
28 "And of the tribe of the sons of Naphtali a leader, Pedahel the son
of Ammihud."
29 These are those whom the LORD commanded to apportion the
inheritance to the sons of Israel in the land of Canaan.

[a]Josh. 15:4
[1]Lit., *border*
...zek. 47:15-17
...r, *entrance of* ...h [a]Josh. 13:5
[1]Lit., *shoulder* ...23:33 [b]Deut. ...7; Josh. 13:27
...n. 15:18; Num. ...6; Deut. 11:24; Josh. 14:1-5
...4 [a]Num. 32:33
... [a]Josh. 14:1, 2
...en. 29:35; Deut. ...Ps. 60:7 [b]Num. ...30; 26:65; Deut. 1:36
...Gen. 29:33; 49:5; Ezek. 48:24
...Gen. 49:27; Deut. 33:12; Ps. 68:27

Chapter 35

35 [a]Now the LORD spoke to Moses in the plains of Moab by the
Jordan opposite Jericho, saying,
2 "Command the sons of Israel that they give to the Levites from
the inheritance of their possession, cities to live in; and you shall
give to the Levites pasture lands around the cities.
3 "And the cities shall be theirs to live in; and their pasture lands
shall be for their cattle and for their herds and for all their beasts.
4 "And the pasture lands of the cities which you shall give to the
Levites *shall extend* from the wall of the city [1]outward a thousand
cubits around.
5 "You shall also measure outside the city on the east side two
thousand cubits, and on the south side two thousand cubits, and on
the west side two thousand cubits, and on the north side two
thousand cubits, with the city in the center. This shall become theirs
as pasture lands for the cities.
6 "And the cities which you shall give to the Levites *shall be* the [a]six
cities of refuge, which you shall give for the manslayer to flee to; and
in addition to them you shall give forty-two cities.
7 "All the cities which you shall give to the Levites *shall be* [a]forty-
eight cities, [1]together with their pasture lands.
8 "[a]As for the cities which you shall give from the possession of the
sons of Israel, you shall take more from the larger and you shall take
less from the smaller; each shall give some of his cities to the Levites
in proportion to his possession which he inherits."
9 Then the LORD spoke to Moses, saying,
10 "[a]Speak to the sons of Israel and say to them, 'When you cross the
Jordan into the land of Canaan,
11 [a]then you shall select for yourselves cities to be your [b]cities of
refuge, that the manslayer who has [1]killed any person [c]unintention-
ally may flee there.
12 'And [a]the cities shall be to you as a refuge from the avenger, so
that the manslayer may not die until he stands before the congrega-
tion for [1]trial.
13 'And the cities which you are to give shall be your six cities of
refuge.
14 'You [a]shall give three cities across the Jordan and three cities [1]in
the land of Canaan; they are to be cities of refuge.
15 'These six cities shall be for refuge for the sons of Israel, and for
the alien and for the sojourner among them; that anyone who [1]kills a
person [a]unintentionally may flee there.
16 '[a]But if he struck him down with an iron object, so that he died,
he is a murderer; the murderer shall surely be put to death.
17 'And if he struck him down with a stone in the hand, by which
he may die, and *as a result* he died, he is a murderer; the murderer
[a]shall surely be put to death.
18 'Or if he struck him with a wooden object in the hand, by which
he may die, and *as a result* he died, he is a murderer; the murderer
shall surely be put to death.
19 'The blood avenger himself shall put the murderer to death; he
shall put him to death when he meets him.
20 'And [a]if he pushed him of hatred, or threw something at him
[b]lying in wait and *as a result* he died,
21 or if he struck him down with his hand in enmity, and *as a result*

35:1 [a]Lev. 2
4 [1]Lit., *and*
6 [a]Josh. 20:
7 [1]Lit., *them*
21:41
8 [a]Lev. 25:32
26:54; 33:54;
21:1-42
10 [a]Josh. 20:
11 [1]Lit., *smote*
19:1-13 [b]Josh
[c]Ex. 21:13; Lev
22f.; Num. 35:
12 [1]Lit., *judgm*
[a]Deut. 19:4-6;
20:2, 3
14 [1]Lit., *you sh*
in [a]Deut. 4:41
15 [1]Lit., *smites*
35:11
16 [a]Ex. 21:12,
24:17
17 [a]Num. 35:31
20 [a]Gen. 4:8; 2 S
3:27; 20:10 [b]Ex.
Deut. 19:11

he died, the one who struck him shall surely be put to death, he is a murderer; the blood avenger shall put the murderer to death when he meets him.

22 '[a]But if he pushed him suddenly without enmity, or threw something at him without lying in wait,

23 or with any [1]deadly object of stone, and without seeing it dropped on him so that he died, while he was not his enemy nor seeking his injury,

24 then [a]the congregation shall judge between the slayer and the blood avenger according to these ordinances.

25 'And the congregation shall deliver the manslayer from the hand of the blood avenger, and the congregation shall restore him to his city of refuge to which he fled; and he shall live in it until the death of the high priest who was anointed with the holy oil.

26 'But if the manslayer shall at any time go beyond the border of his city of refuge to which he may flee,

27 and the blood avenger finds him outside the border of his city of refuge, and the blood avenger kills the manslayer, he shall not be guilty of blood

28 because he should have remained in his city of refuge until the death of the high priest. But after the death of the high priest the manslayer shall return to the land of his possession.

29 'And these things shall be for a [a]statutory ordinance to you throughout your generations in all your dwellings.

30 '[a]If anyone kills a person, the murderer shall be put to death at the [1]evidence of witnesses, but [b]no person shall be put to death on the testimony of one witness.

31 'Moreover, you shall not take ransom for the life of a murderer who is guilty of death, but he shall surely be put to death.

32 'And you shall not take ransom for him who has fled to his city of refuge, that he may return to live in the land [1]before the death of the priest.

33 '[a]So you shall not pollute the land in which you are; for blood pollutes the land and no expiation can be made for the land for the blood that is shed on it, except [b]by the blood of him who shed it.

34 'And you shall not [a]defile the land in which you live, in the midst of which [b]I dwell; for I the LORD am dwelling in the midst of the sons of Israel.' "

Chapter 36

36 [a]And the heads of the fathers' *households* of the family of the sons of Gilead, the son of Machir, the son of Manasseh, of the families of the sons of Joseph, came near and spoke before Moses and before the leaders, the heads of the fathers' *households* of the sons of Israel,

2 and they said, "The LORD commanded my lord to give the land by lot to the sons of Israel as an inheritance, and my lord [a]was commanded by the LORD to give the inheritance of Zelophehad our brother to his daughters.

3 "But if they [1]marry one of the sons of the *other* tribes of the sons of Israel, their inheritance will be withdrawn from the inheritance of our fathers and will be added to the inheritance of the tribe to which they belong; thus it will be withdrawn from our allotted inheritance.

4 "And when the [a]jubilee of the sons of Israel [1]comes, then their

[a]Num. 35:11
by which he may die
[a]Josh. 20:6
[a]Num. 27:11
mouth [a]Num. [b]Deut. 17:6; . 18:16; John 7:51; 8:17, 18
32 [1]*Or, until*
ut. 21:7, 8; Ps. :38 [b]Gen. 9:6
[a]Lev. 18:24, 25 [b]Num. 5:3
:1 [a]Num. 27:1
2 [a]Num. 27:5-7
., *become wives to*, in this ch.
t., *shall be* [a]Lev. 25:10

inheritance will be added to the inheritance of the tribe to which
they belong; so their inheritance will be withdrawn from the inheri-
tance of the tribe of our fathers."
5 Then Moses commanded the sons of Israel according to the
[1]word of the LORD, saying, "The tribe of the sons of Joseph are right
in *their* statements.
6 "[a]This is [1]what the LORD has commanded concerning the daugh-
ters of Zelophehad, saying, 'Let them marry [2]whom they wish; only
they must marry within the family of the tribe of their father.'
7 "Thus [a]no inheritance of the sons of Israel shall [1]be transferred
from tribe to tribe, for the sons of Israel shall each [2]hold to the
inheritance of the tribe of his fathers.
8 "[a]And every daughter who comes into possession of an inheri-
tance of any tribe of the sons of Israel, shall be wife to one of the
family of the tribe of her father, so that the sons of Israel each may
possess the inheritance of his fathers.
9 "Thus no inheritance shall [1]be transferred from one tribe to
another tribe, for the tribes of the sons of Israel shall each [2]hold to his
own inheritance."
10 Just as the LORD had commanded Moses, so the daughters of
Zelophehad did:
11 [a]Mahlah, Tirzah, Hoglah, Milcah and Noah, the daughters of
Zelophehad married their uncles' sons.
12 They married *those* from the families of the sons of Manasseh the
son of Joseph, and their inheritance [1]remained with the tribe of the
family of their father.
13 [a]These are the commandments and the ordinances which the
LORD commanded to the sons of Israel through Moses in the plains
of Moab by the Jordan *opposite* Jericho.

5 [1]Lit., *mouth*

6 [1]Lit., *the thing* [2]Lit., *to the good* *their eyes* [a]Num

7 [1]Lit., *turn abo* *cleave* [a]1 Kin. 2

8 [a]1 Chr. 23:22

9 [1]Lit., *turn abou* *cleave*

11 [a]Num. 26:33

12 [1]Lit., *was*

13 [a]Lev. 26:46; Num. 22:1

Insights from Numbers

The Land	Balaam	Korah

Theme of Numbers:

Author:

Date:

Purpose:

Key Words:

SEGMENT DIVISIONS

	JOURNEYS/ ENCAMP- MENTS	CHAPTER THEMES
		1
		2
		3
		4
		5
		6
		7
		8
		9
		10
		11
		12
		13
		14
		15
		16
		17
		18
		19
		20
		21
		22
		23
		24
		25
		26
		27
		28
		29
		30
		31
		32
		33
		34
		35
		36

EUTERONOMY

uteronomy is the crown jewel of the Pentateuch. It lays before us, clearly, what God expects from who have been redeemed: a life of uncompromising obedience.

d raised up Moses to deliver His people from the land of Egypt, the land of bondage. That Moses one. Now he stood at Pisgah before the land of promise. He was 120 years old.

hen Moses struck the rock a second time, he failed to treat God as holy. Because of this he could nter the land of promise. But the people he had led so faithfully for the last forty years would go in possess it.

oses had to do one more thing before God took him home: tell God's children how to live in the which the God of their fathers was giving them.

IGS TO DO

ral Instructions

For the book's historical context, read Numbers 21:21-22:1; 36:13 and Deuteronomy 1:1-5.

a. Record the author, date, and geographical setting on the DEUTERONOMY AT A GLANCE chart on page 319.

b. When you study Deuteronomy watch for any verses which confirm Moses' authorship. Although the last chapter tells of Moses' death, this doesn't negate the fact that Moses wrote the rest of the book. The last chapter would be an appropriate postscript after his death.

Read Romans 15:4 and 1 Corinthians 10:1-14 and keep these verses in mind as you study.

a. As you study each chapter, note in the margin insights you glean in respect to the character of God and the ways He deals with His children and with unbelievers.

b. Also note in the margin any specific instructions or admonitions that are to be followed in respect to God, for example, "Fear Him."

c. It would also be good to record any "Lessons for Life" you learn from the text. Mark or color them in a distinctive way so they can be recognized immediately. Then under the heading "LFL" list the lesson(s) you saw in that particular chapter.

There are insightful lessons to be learned from Moses' life about leadership and about our relationship to God. As you study Deuteronomy note these lessons in the chapter margins. Also record all that you learn about Moses on the chart LESSONS FROM THE LIFE OF MOSES in the appendix of your Bible on page 1875. When you record your insights, make sure you note the book, chapter, and verse from which they came.

pters 1-3

Ioses rehearses what happened from the time they left Horeb (Mount Sinai) until they camped in valley opposite Beth-peor at the foot of Mount Nebo (Pisgah).

. As you read these three chapters:

a. Ask the five W's and an H: Who? What? When? Where? Why? and How? Watch what happens in each chapter, where it happened and to whom, why it happened, and what the consequences or results were. Also note how things were accomplished.

b. Mark every use of *then* so you can see the sequence of events.

c. Look at the map in chapter 1 on page 266 to see where the events took place.

. In a distinctive way mark these key words and their synonyms: *fear, heart, command (commanded),* and *listen*. Write these on an index card to use as a bookmark while studying Deuteronomy.

3. Choose the theme of each chapter and record it in the text on the line next to the chapter n
and on DEUTERONOMY AT A GLANCE.

Chapters 4-11

Moses instructs the children of Israel regarding what they are to do when they enter the land.

1. Read this segment chapter by chapter, keeping in mind the five W's and an H. Words su *when, then, watch, hear, listen, beware,* and *you shall therefore* will come to your attention. Whe see *when*, look and see if *then* eventually follows it. If so, connect them with a line as illustrat
2. Add the following key words to your list and mark them when you come to them in th *observe (keep, do), love, remember,* and *commandment (statutes).*
3. Record the main points of each chapter in the margin or underline and note them in the tex a number 1, 2, 3, etc.
4. Record the chapter themes as you did previously.

Chapters 12-26

Moses gives the people the statutes and the judgments they are to observe.

1. Add the following phrase to your list of key words and make sure you mark every occurre it in these chapters: *you shall purge* [remove] *the evil.* Also add the words *life, death, curse blessing.*
2. As you read these chapters note in the margin of the text what the people are to do and why.
3. Go back and read number 2 under "General Instructions." Don't forget this important proce
4. Record the theme of the chapters on DEUTERONOMY AT A GLANCE and in the text.

Chapters 27-30

Moses tells the people about the necessity of obedience and that if they obey they will be ble but if they disobey they will be cursed.

1. Add to your list of key words the following items along with their synonyms and pron *curse(s), blessing, the Lord will, nation (nations, enemies, people), captivity,* and *covenant.* List i margin what you observe from marking these words.
2. As you read these chapters keep asking the five W's and an H. Note who and/or what w affected by their obedience or disobedience. Also note everything that will happen if they ob disobey.
3. Don't forget to note what you learn about God from these chapters and to record the then each chapter.

Chapters 31-34

This segment contains Moses' parting words, song, and blessing and the account of his death.

1. Mark the key repeated words listed on your index card.
2. As Moses sings his song in chapter 32 he recounts Israel's relationship to God and God's dea with them. *Jeshurun* in 32:15 is a reference to Israel.
   a. Pay attention to what you learn about Israel. Observe what led to Israel's downfall and the consequences were.
   b. Remember that although Moses begged God to change His mind and allow him to ente promised land, God said no. Keep this in mind as you read these chapters and see M heart and hear his words in respect to God. Take note of all you learn about God from t significant chapters. Make a list in the margin of what you learn about "the Rock."
3. Observe what Moses says will happen after his death and note this in the margin.
4. When you study chapter 33, mark the name of each of the tribes of Israel and carefully obs how they are described and what is said about each one of them. Underline every occurren *they shall.*

Don't forget to record what you learn about Moses from this final chapter on the chart LESSONS FROM THE LIFE OF MOSES in the appendix of your Bible on page 1875.

NGS TO THINK ABOUT

Since we are under the new covenant of grace, what is our relationship to the commands of God? Do you think grace allows us to continue in sin and disobedience without any consequences or chastening from the Father?

What kind of allegiance does God call for from Israel? Do you think He expects anything less from the church, the body of the Lord Jesus Christ?

What have you learned regarding the long-suffering of God and His gracious ways with His covenant people?

How does a child of God demonstrate his love for the Lord?

erhaps Red Sea 4:46 [b]Deut. 2:8

3:1; 17:6 [b]Gen. ...um. 13:26; 32:8; Deut. 9:23

...m. 33:38 [b]Deut. 4:1, 2

...smitten [2]So with ...ent versions; M.T. omits *and* [a]Num. ...6; Deut. 2:26-35; 13:10; Neh. 9:22 ... 21:33-35; Josh. 3:12 [c]Josh. 12:4

[1]Lit., *dwelt* [a]Num. 10:11-13

...e., South country ...Gen. 15:18; Deut. ...1:24; Josh. 10:40 [b]Gen. 12:9

[1]Lit., *seed* [a]Gen. ...7; 26:3; 28:13; Ex. 33:1; Num. 14:23; ...:11; Heb. 6:13, 14

...x. 18:18, 24; Num. 11:14

[a]Gen. 15:5; 22:17; ... 32:13; Deut. 7:7; 10:22; 26:5; 28:62

11 [1]Lit., *spoken to* [a]Deut. 1:8, 10

13 [1]Lit., *Give for* ...rselves [a]Ex. 18:21

Chapter 1

1 These are the words which Moses spoke to all Israel [a]across the
Jordan in the wilderness, in the [b]Arabah opposite [1]Suph, be-
tween Paran and Tophel and Laban and Hazeroth and Dizahab.
2 It is eleven days' *journey* from [a]Horeb by the way of Mount [b]Seir
to [c]Kadesh-barnea.
3 And it came about in the [a]fortieth year, on the first day of the
eleventh month, that Moses spoke to the children of Israel, [b]accord-
ing to all that the LORD had commanded him *to give* to them,
4 after he had [1a]defeated Sihon the king of the Amorites, who lived
in Heshbon, and [b]Og the king of Bashan, who lived in [c]Ashtaroth
[2]and Edrei.
5 Across the Jordan in the land of Moab, Moses undertook to ex-
pound this law, saying,
6 "The LORD our God [a]spoke to us at Horeb, saying, 'You have
[1]stayed long enough at this mountain.
7 'Turn and set your journey, and go to [a]the hill country of the
Amorites, and to all their neighbors in the Arabah, in the hill country
and in the lowland and in [b]the [1]Negev and by the seacoast, the land
of the Canaanites, and Lebanon, as far as the great river, the river
Euphrates.
8 'See, I have placed the land before you; go in and possess the
land which the LORD [a]swore to give to your fathers, to Abraham, to
Isaac, and to Jacob, to them and their [1]descendants after them.'
9 "And I spoke to you at that time, saying, '[a]I am not able to bear *the
burden* of you alone.
10 'The LORD your God has [a]multiplied you, and behold, you are
this day as the stars of heaven for multitude.
11 'May the LORD, the God of your fathers, increase you a thousand-
fold more than you are, and bless you, [a]just as He has [1]promised
you!
12 'How can I alone bear the load and burden of you and your
strife?
13 '[1a]Choose wise and discerning and experienced men from your
tribes, and I will appoint them as your heads.'
14 "And you answered me and said, 'The thing which you have said
to do is good.'
15 "So I took the heads of your tribes, wise and experienced men,

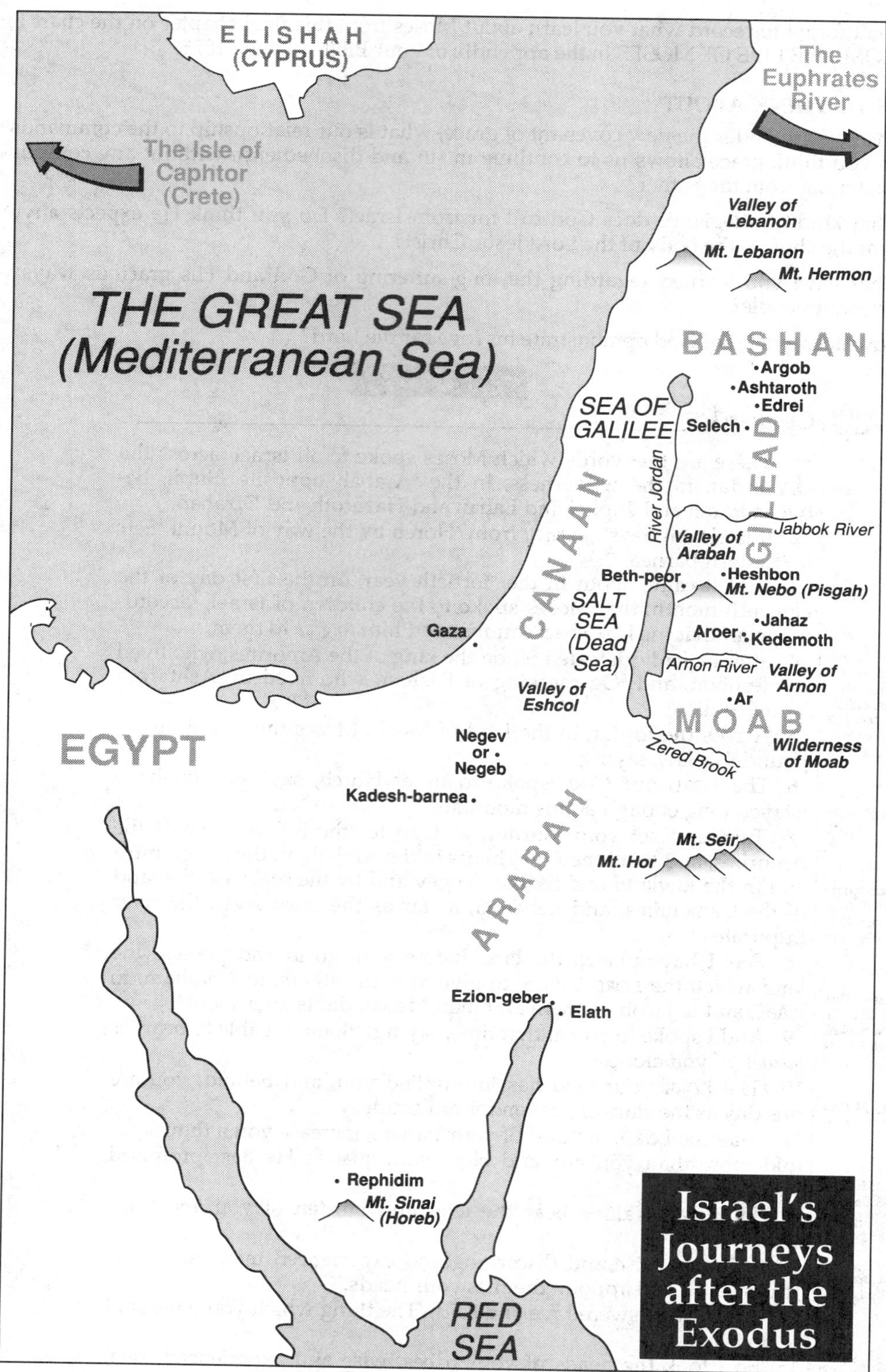
ELISHAH
(CYPRUS)
The Euphrates River
The Isle of Caphtor (Crete)
Valley of Lebanon
Mt. Lebanon
Mt. Hermon
THE GREAT SEA
(Mediterranean Sea)
BASHAN
•Argob
•Ashtaroth
•Edrei
SEA OF GALILEE
Selech •
GILEAD
River Jordan
CANAAN
Jabbok River
Valley of Arabah
Beth-peor
•Heshbon
Mt. Nebo (Pisgah)
SALT SEA (Dead Sea)
•Jahaz
Aroer •Kedemoth
Gaza
Arnon River
Valley of Arnon
Valley of Eshcol
•Ar
MOAB
EGYPT
Negev or Negeb
Zered Brook
Wilderness of Moab
Kadesh-barnea
ARABAH
Mt. Seir
Mt. Hor
Ezion-geber
• Elath
• Rephidim
Mt. Sinai (Horeb)
RED SEA
Israel's Journeys after the Exodus

and [1]appointed them heads over you, leaders of thousands, and [2]of
hundreds, [2]of fifties and [2]of tens, and officers for your tribes.
16 "Then I charged your judges at that time, saying, 'Hear *the cases*
between your [1]fellow countrymen, and [a]judge righteously between a
man and his [2]fellow countryman, or the alien who is with him.
17 '[a]You shall not show partiality in judgment; you shall hear the
small and the great alike. You shall [b]not fear [1]man, for the judgment
is God's. And [c]the case that is too hard for you, you shall bring to
me, and I will hear it.'
18 "[a]And I commanded you at that time all the things that you
should do.
19 "Then we set out from [a]Horeb, and went through all that [b]great
and terrible wilderness which you saw, on the way to the [c]hill
country of the Amorites, just as the LORD our God had commanded
us; and we came to [a]Kadesh-barnea.
20 "And I said to you, 'You have come to the hill country of the
Amorites which the LORD our God is about to give us.
21 'See, the LORD your God has placed the land before you; go up,
take possession, as the LORD, the God of your fathers, has spoken to
you. [a]Do not fear or be dismayed.'
22 "[a]Then all of you approached me and said, 'Let us send men
before us, that they may search out the land for us, and bring back to
us word of the way by which we should go up, and the cities which
we shall enter.'
23 "And the thing pleased me and I took twelve of your men, one
man for each tribe.
24 "And [a]they turned and went up into the hill country, and came to
the valley of Eshcol, and spied it out.
25 "Then they took *some* of the fruit of the land in their hands and
brought it down to us; and they brought us back a report and said,
'It is a good land which the LORD our God is about to give us.'
26 "[a]Yet you were not willing to go up, but [b]rebelled against the
[1]command of the LORD your God;
27 and [a]you grumbled in your tents and said, 'Because the LORD
hates us, He has brought us out of the land of Egypt to deliver us
into the hand of the Amorites to destroy us.
28 'Where can we go up? Our brethren have made our hearts melt,
saying, "The people are bigger and taller than we; the cities are large
and fortified to heaven. And besides, we saw [a]the sons of the
Anakim there." '
29 "Then I said to you, 'Do not be shocked, nor fear them.
30 'The LORD your God who goes before you will [a]Himself fight on
your behalf, [1]just as He did for you in Egypt before your eyes,
31 and in the wilderness where you saw how [a]the LORD your God
carried you, just as a man carries his son, in all the way which you
have walked, until you came to this place.'
32 "But [1a]for all this, you did not trust the LORD your God,
33 [a]who goes before you on *your* way, [b]to seek out a place for you to
encamp, in fire by night and cloud by day, to show you the way in
which you should go.
34 "Then the LORD heard the sound of your words, and He was
angry and [a]took an oath, saying,
35 '[a]Not one of these men, this evil generation, shall see the good
land which I swore to give your fathers,

Lit., *gave* [2]Lit., *leaders of*
, *brothers* [2]Lit., r [a]Deut. 16:18; John 7:24
Lit., *because of* n [a]Deut. 10:17; 9; 24:17; 2 Chr. Prov. 24:23-26; :34; James 2:1, rov. 29:25 [c]Ex. 18:22, 26
18 [a]Ex. 18:20
eut. 1:2 [b]Deut. 8:15; 32:10; Jer. 2:6 [c]Deut. 1:7
21 [a]Josh. 1:6, 9
2 [a]Num. 13:1-3
[a]Num. 13:21-25
t., *mouth* [a]Num. :1-4 [b]Deut. 9:23
[a]Deut. 9:28; Ps. 106:25
[a]Num. 13:28, 33; Deut. 9:2
., *according to all* [a]Ex. 14:14; Deut. ; 20:4; Neh. 4:20
eut. 32:10-12; Is. ; 63:9; Hos. 11:3; Acts 13:18
Lit., *in this matter* [a]Num. 14:11; Ps. 4; Heb. 3:19; 4:2; Jude 5
[a]Ex. 13:21; Num. 23; Neh. 9:12; Ps. 3:14 [b]Num. 10:33
[a]Num. 14:28-30; Heb. 3:18
Ps. 95:11; 106:26; zek. 20:15; 1 Cor. 0:5; Heb. 3:14-19

36 except Caleb the son of Jephunneh; he shall see it, and [a]to him
and to his sons I will give the land on which he has set foot, because
he has followed the LORD fully.'
37 "[a]The LORD was angry with me also on your account, saying,
'[b]Not even you shall enter there.
38 'Joshua the son of Nun, who stands before you, [a]he shall enter
there; encourage him, for [b]he shall cause Israel to inherit it.
39 'Moreover, [a]your little ones who you said would become a prey,
and your sons, who this day have [b]no knowledge of good or evil,
shall enter there, and I will give it to them, and they shall possess it.
40 'But as for you, [a]turn around and set out for the wilderness by
the way to the [1]Red Sea.'
41 "[a]Then you answered and said to me, 'We have sinned against the
LORD; we will indeed go up and fight, just as the LORD our God
commanded us.' And every man of you girded on his weapons of
war, and regarded it as easy to go up into the hill country.
42 "[a]And the LORD said to me, 'Say to them, "Do not go up, nor fight,
for I am not among you; lest you be [1]defeated before your
enemies." '
43 "So I spoke to you, but you would not listen. Instead [a]you
rebelled against the [1]command of the LORD, and acted
presumptuously and went up into the hill country.
44 "[a]And the Amorites who [1]lived in that hill country came out
against you, and chased you [b]as bees do, and crushed you from Seir
to Hormah.
45 "Then you returned and wept before the LORD; but the [a]LORD did
not listen to your voice, nor give ear to you.
46 "So you remained in [a]Kadesh many days, [1]the days that you spent
there.

Chapter 2

2 "[a]Then we turned and set out for the wilderness by the way to
the [1]Red Sea, as the LORD spoke to me, and circled [b]Mount Seir
for many days.
2 "And the LORD spoke to me, saying,
3 'You have circled this mountain long enough. *Now* turn north,
4 [a]and command the people, saying, "You will pass through the
[b]territory of your brothers the sons of Esau who live in Seir; and
[c]they will be afraid of you. So be very careful;
5 do not [1]provoke them, for I will not give you any of their land,
even *as little as* a [2]footstep [a]because I have given Mount Seir to Esau
as a possession.
6 "You shall buy food from them with money so that you may eat,
and you shall also purchase water from them with money so that
you may drink.
7 "For the LORD your God has blessed you in all [1]that you have
done; He has known your [2]wanderings through this [a]great wilder-
ness. These [b]forty years the LORD your God has been with you; you
have not lacked a thing." '
8 "So we passed beyond our brothers the sons of Esau, who live in
Seir, away from the [a]Arabah road, away from Elath and [b]from Ezion-
geber. And we turned and passed through by the way of the wilder-
ness of Moab.
9 "Then the LORD said to me, 'Do not harass Moab, nor provoke

36 [a]Num. 14:2 14:9

37 [a]Num. 20:1 3:26; 4:21 [b]Nu 27:13, 18

38 [a]Num. 14:3 34:17; Deut. 3: Josh. 11:23

39 [a]Num. 14:3 7:15, 16

40 [1]Lit., *Sea o* [a]Num. 14:25

41 [a]Num. 14:40

42 [1]Lit., *smitten* 14:41-43

43 [1]Lit., *mouth* 14:40

44 [1]Lit., *dwelt* [a] 14:45 [b]Ps. 118:

45 [a]Job 27:8, 9; 66:18; John 9:31

46 [1]Lit., *as the d* [a]Num. 20:1, 22; 2:7, 14; Judg. 11

2:1 [1]Lit., *Sea of* [a]Num. 21:4 [b]Deu

4 [a]Num. 20:14-2 [b]Gen. 36:8 [c]Ex. 15:15, 16

5 [1]Or, *engage in with* [2]Lit., *treading sole of a foot* [a]Ge 36:8; Josh. 24:4

7 [1]Lit., *the work o hand* [2]Lit., *goings* [a]Deut. 1:19 [b]Num 14:33, 34; 32:13; 2:14

8 [a]Deut. 1:1 [b]Nu 33:35; 1 Kin. 9:26

them to war, for I will not give you any of [1]their land as a possession,
because I have given [a]Ar to [b]the sons of Lot as a possession.
10 (The [a]Emim lived there formerly, a people as great, numerous,
and tall as the Anakim.
11 Like the Anakim, they are also regarded as [a]Rephaim, but the
Moabites call them Emim.
12 [a]The Horites formerly lived in Seir, but the sons of Esau dispos-
sessed them and destroyed them from before them and settled in
their place, [b]just as Israel did to the land of [1]their possession which
the LORD gave to them.)
13 'Now arise and cross over the [1]brook Zered yourselves.' So we
crossed over the [1]brook Zered.
14 "Now the [1]time that it took for us to come from Kadesh-barnea,
until we crossed over the [2]brook Zered, was [a]thirty-eight years; until
[b]all the generation of the men of war perished from within the camp,
as [c]the LORD had sworn to them.
15 "[a]Moreover the hand of the LORD was against them, to destroy
them from within the camp, until they all perished.
16 "So it came about when [a]all the men of war had finally perished
from among the people,
17 that the LORD spoke to me, saying,
18 'You shall cross over [a]Ar, the border of Moab, today.
19 'And when you come opposite the [a]sons of Ammon, do not
harass them nor provoke them, for I will not give you any of the
land of the sons of Ammon as a possession, because I have given it
to [b]the sons of Lot as a possession.'
20 (It is also regarded as the land of the [a]Rephaim, *for* Rephaim
formerly lived in it, but the Ammonites call them Zamzummin,
21 a people as great, numerous, and tall as the Anakim, but the
LORD destroyed them before them. And they dispossessed them and
settled in their place,
22 just as He did for the sons of Esau, who [a]live in Seir, when He
destroyed [b]the Horites from before them; and they dispossessed
them, and settled in their place even to this day.
23 And the [a]Avvim, who lived in villages as far as Gaza, the
[1b]Caphtorim who came from [2c]Caphtor, destroyed them and lived in
their place.)
24 'Arise, set out, and pass through the [1a]valley of Arnon. Look! I
have given Sihon the Amorite, king of Heshbon, and his land into
your hand; begin to take possession and contend with him in battle.
25 'This day I will begin to put [a]the dread and fear of you [1]upon the
peoples [2]everywhere under the heavens, who, when they hear the
report of you, [b]shall tremble and be in anguish because of you.'
26 "[a]So I sent messengers from the wilderness of Kedemoth to Sihon
king of Heshbon with words of peace, saying,
27 'Let me pass through your land, I will [1]travel only on the high-
way; I will not turn aside to the right or to the left.
28 'You will sell me food for money so that I may eat, and give me
water for money so that I may drink, [a]only let me pass through on
[1]foot,
29 just as the sons of Esau who live in Seir and the Moabites who
live in [a]Ar did for me, until I cross over the Jordan into the land
which the LORD our God is giving to us.'
30 "But [a]Sihon king of Heshbon was not willing for us to pass

Lit., *his* [a]Num. 28; Deut. 2:18, Gen. 19:36, 37

10 [a]Gen. 14:5

en. 14:5; Deut. 2:20

[1]Lit., *his* [a]Gen. :20; Deut. 2:22 Num. 21:25, 35

13 [1]Or, *wadi*

., *days in which went* [2]Or, *wadi* eut. 2:7 [b]Num. ; 26:64, 65; Ps. :26; 1 Cor. 10:5 [c]Deut. 1:34, 35

15 [a]Jude 5

16 [a]Deut. 2:14

18 [a]Deut. 2:9

en. 19:38 [b]Deut. 2:9

20 [a]Deut. 2:11

Gen. 36:8; Deut. 2:5 [b]Deut. 2:12

[1]I.e., Philistines rete [a]Josh. 13:3 en. 10:14; 1 Chr. [c]Jer. 47:4; Amos 9:7

[1]Or, *wadi* [a]Num. , 14; Judg. 11:18

., *in front of* [2]Lit., *er all the heavens* 3:27; Deut. 11:25; :9 [b]Ex. 15:14-16

[a]Num. 21:21-32; Deut. 1:4; Judg. 11:19-21

Lit., *go by the way*

it., *my feet* [a]Num. 20:19

29 [a]Deut. 2:9

30 [a]Num. 21:23

[1]through his land; for the [b]LORD your God hardened his spirit and
made his heart obstinate, in order to deliver him into your hand, as
he is today.
31 "And the LORD said to me, 'See, I have begun to deliver Sihon and
his land [1]over to you. Begin to [2]occupy, that you may possess his
land.'
32 "Then Sihon [1]with all his people came out to meet us in battle at
Jahaz.
33 "And [a]the LORD our God delivered him [1]over to us; and we [2b]de-
feated him with his sons and all his people.
34 "So we captured all his cities at that time, and [1a]utterly destroyed
[2]the men, women and children of every city. We left no survivor.
35 "We took [a]only the animals as our booty and the spoil of the cities
which we had captured.
36 "From [a]Aroer which is on the edge of the [1]valley of Arnon and
from the city which is in the [1]valley, even to Gilead, there was no city
that was too high for us; the LORD our God delivered all [2]over to us.
37 "[a]Only you did not go near to the land of the sons of Ammon, all
along the [1]river [b]Jabbok and the cities of the hill country, and
wherever the LORD our God had commanded us.

Chapter 3

3 "[a]Then we turned and went up the road to Bashan, and Og, king
of Bashan, [1]with all his people came out to meet us in battle at
Edrei.
2 "But the LORD said to me, 'Do not fear him, for I have delivered
him and all his people and his land into your hand; and you shall do
to him just as you did to Sihon king of the Amorites, who lived at
Heshbon.'
3 "So the LORD our God delivered Og also, king of Bashan, with all
his people into our hand, and we smote [1]them until no survivor was
[2]left.
4 "And we captured all his cities at that time; there was not a city
which we did not take from them: sixty cities, all the region of
[a]Argob, the kingdom of Og in Bashan.
5 "All these were cities fortified with high walls, gates and bars,
besides a great many [1]unwalled towns.
6 "And we [1]utterly destroyed them, as we did to [a]Sihon king of
Heshbon, [2b]utterly destroying [3]the men, women and children of
every city.
7 "[a]But all the animals and the spoil of the cities we took as our
booty.
8 "[a]Thus we took the land at that time from the hand of the two
kings of the Amorites who were beyond the Jordan, from the [1]valley
of Arnon to Mount Hermon
9 (Sidonians [a]call Hermon [b]Sirion, and the Amorites call it [c]Senir):
10 all the cities of the tableland and all Gilead and [a]all Bashan, as far
as Salecah and Edrei, cities of the kingdom of Og in Bashan.
11 (For only Og king of Bashan was left of the remnant of the
[a]Rephaim. Behold, his [1]bedstead was an iron [1]bedstead; it is in
[b]Rabbah of the sons of Ammon. Its length was nine cubits and its
width four cubits [2]by ordinary cubit.)
12 "So we took possession of this land at that time. From [a]Aroer,

30 [1]Lit., *by hi*
4:21; Josh. 11

31 [1]Lit., *befor*
[2]Lit., *possess*

32 [1]Lit., *he an*

33 [1]Lit., *before*
smote [a]Ex. 23
7:2 [b]Deut. 29:

34 [1]Or, *put un*
ban [2]Lit., *ever*
man . . . [a]Deut

35 [a]Deut. 3:7

36 [1]Or, *wadi* [2]
before us [a]Deu
4:48; Josh. 12:2

37 [1]Or, *wadi* [a]
2:19 [b]Gen. 32:2
21:24; Deut. 3:1

3:1 [1]Lit., *he an*
21:33-35

3 [1]Lit., *him* [2]Lit.
him

4 [a]Deut. 3:13, 1
4:13

5 [1]Or, *rural*

6 [1]Or, *put them*
the ban [2]Or, *putt*
under the ban [3]L
every city of men
[a]Deut. 1:4 [b]Deut.

7 [a]Deut. 2:35

8 [1]Or, *wadi* [a]Nur
32:33; Josh. 12:1
13:8-12

9 [a]Deut. 4:48; Jos
11:17; Ps. 42:6; 1
[b]Ps. 29:6 [c]1 Chr.

10 [a]Josh. 13:11

11 [1]Or, *couch* [2]Li
a man's forearm
14:5; Deut. 2:11, 2
[b]2 Sam. 11:1; 12:2
49:2

12 [a]Deut. 2:36

which is by the [1]valley of Arnon, and half the hill country of [b]Gilead
and its cities, I gave to the Reubenites and to the Gadites.
13 "And the rest of Gilead, and all Bashan, the kingdom of Og, I
gave to the half-tribe of Manasseh, all the region of Argob (concern-
ing all Bashan, it is called the land of Rephaim.
14 [a]Jair the son of Manasseh took all the region of Argob as far as
the border of the Geshurites and the Maacathites, and called [1]it, *that
is*, Bashan, after his own name, [2]Havvoth-jair, *as it is* to this day.)
15 "[a]And to Machir I gave Gilead.
16 "And to the Reubenites and to the Gadites, I gave from Gilead
even as far as the [1]valley of Arnon, the middle of the [1]valley [2]as a
border and as far as the [1]river [a]Jabbok, the border of the sons of
Ammon;
17 the Arabah also, with the Jordan [1]as *a* border, from [2a]Chinnereth
[b]even as far as the sea of the Arabah, [c]the Salt Sea, [3]at the foot of the
slopes of Pisgah on the east.
18 "Then I commanded you at that time, saying, '[a]The LORD your
God has given you this land to possess it; [b]all you valiant men shall
cross over armed before your brothers, the sons of Israel.
19 '[a]But your wives and your little ones and your livestock (I know
that you have [b]much livestock), shall remain in your cities which I
have given you,
20 [a]until the LORD gives rest to your fellow countrymen as to you,
and they also possess the land which the LORD your God will give
them beyond the Jordan. [b]Then you may return every man to his
possession, which I have given you.'
21 "And I commanded Joshua at that time, saying, 'Your eyes have
seen all that the LORD your God has done to these two kings; so the
LORD shall do to all the kingdoms into which you are about to cross.
22 'Do not fear them, for the LORD your God [a]is the one fighting for
you.'
23 "I also pleaded with the LORD at that time, saying,
24 'O Lord [1]GOD, Thou hast begun to show Thy servant [a]Thy great-
ness and Thy strong hand; for what [b]god is there in heaven or on
earth who can do such works and mighty acts as Thine?
25 'Let me, I pray, cross over and see the [a]fair land that is beyond
the Jordan, [1]that good hill country and Lebanon.'
26 "But [a]the LORD was angry with me on your account, and would
not listen to me; and the LORD said to me, '[1]Enough! Speak to Me no
more of this matter.
27 'Go up to the top of [a]Pisgah and lift up your eyes to the west and
north and south and east, and see *it* with your eyes, [b]for you shall
not cross over this Jordan.
28 '[a]But charge Joshua and encourage him and strengthen him; [b]for
he shall go across [1]at the head of this people, and he shall give them
as an inheritance the land which you will see.'
29 "So we remained in the valley opposite [a]Beth-peor.

Chapter 4

4 "And now, O Israel, listen to the statutes and the judgments
which [a]I am teaching you to perform, in order that [b]you may live
and go in and take possession of the land which the LORD, the God
of your fathers, is giving you.
2 "[a]You shall not add to the word which [b]I am commanding you,

', *wadi* [b]Num. Josh. 13:8-13
hem [2]I.e., the of Jair [a]Num. 41; 1 Chr. 2:22
Num. 32:39, 40
wadi [2]Lit., *and* :24; Deut. 2:37
, *and* [2]I.e., the of Galilee [3]Lit., [a]Num. 34:11; . 13:27 [b]Josh. en. 14:3; Josh. 3:16
sh. 1:13 [b]Num. ; Josh. 4:12, 13
Josh. 1:14 [b]Ex. 12:38
sh. 1:15 [b]Josh. 22:4
Ex. 14:14; Deut. 20:4; Neh. 4:20
[1]Heb., *YHWH*, rendered *LORD* . 11:2 [b]Ex. 8:10; 2 Sam. 7:22; Ps. 71:19; 86:8
this [a]Deut. 4:22
[1]Lit., *Enough for you* [a]Deut. 1:37
um. 23:14; 27:12 [b]Deut. 1:37
3 [1]Lit., *before this* ople [a]Num. 27:18; eut. 31:3, 7, 8, 23 [b]Deut. 1:38
Num. 25:1-3; Deut. 4:46; 34:6
1 [a]Deut. 1:3 [b]Lev. :5; Deut. 5:33; 8:1; 0; 30:16, 19; Ezek. 20:11; Rom. 10:5
[a]Deut. 12:32; Prov. Rev. 22:18 [b]Deut. 4:5, 14, 40

nor take away from it, that you may keep the commandments of the
LORD your God which I command you.
3 "[a]Your eyes have seen what the LORD has done in the case of
Baal-peor, for all the men who followed Baal-peor, the LORD your
God has destroyed [1]them from among you.
4 "But you who held fast to the LORD your God are alive today,
every one of you.
5 "See, I have taught you statutes and judgments [a]just as the LORD
my God commanded me, that you should do thus in the land where
you are entering to possess it.
6 "So keep and do *them*, [a]for that is your wisdom and your under-
standing in the sight of the peoples who will hear all these statutes
and say, 'Surely this great nation is a wise and understanding
people.'
7 "For [a]what great nation is there that has a god [b]so near to it as is
the LORD our God [c]whenever we call on Him?
8 "Or what great nation is there that has [a]statutes and judgments as
righteous as this whole law which I am setting before you today?
9 "Only [a]give heed to yourself and keep your soul diligently, lest
you forget the things which your eyes have seen, and lest they
depart from your heart [b]all the days of your life; but [c]make them
known to your sons and your grandsons.
10 "*Remember* the day you stood before the LORD your God at Horeb,
when the LORD said to me, 'Assemble the people to Me, that I may
let them hear My words [a]so they may learn to [1]fear Me all the days
they live on the earth, and that they may [b]teach their children.'
11 "And you came near and stood at the foot of the mountain, [a]and
the mountain burned with fire to the *very* heart of the heavens: dark-
ness, cloud and thick gloom.
12 "Then the LORD spoke to you from the midst of the fire; you heard
the sound of words, but you saw no form—only a voice.
13 "So He declared to you His covenant which He commanded you
to perform, *that is*, [a]the Ten [1]Commandments; and [b]He wrote them on
two tablets of stone.
14 "And the LORD commanded me at that time to teach you statutes
and judgments, that you might perform them in the land where you
are going over to possess it.
15 "So [a]watch yourselves carefully, since you did not see any [b]form
on the day the LORD spoke to you at Horeb from the midst of the fire,
16 lest you [a]act corruptly and [b]make a graven image for yourselves
in the form of any figure, the likeness of male or female,
17 the likeness of any animal that is on the earth, the likeness of
[a]any winged bird that flies in the sky,
18 the likeness of anything that creeps on the ground, the likeness
of any fish that is in the water below the earth.
19 "And *beware*, lest you lift up your eyes to heaven and see the sun
and the moon and the stars, [a]all the host of heaven, [b]and be drawn
away and worship them and serve them, those which the LORD your
God has allotted to all the peoples under the whole heaven.
20 "But the LORD has taken you and brought you out of [a]the iron
furnace, from Egypt, to [b]be a people for His own possession, as
today.
21 "[a]Now the LORD was angry with me on your account, and swore

3 [1]Lit., *him* [a]... 25:1-9
5 [a]Lev. 26:46;
6 [a]Deut. 30:19 32:46, 47; Job Ps. 19:7; 111:1 1:7; 2 Tim. 3:15
7 [a]Deut. 4:32- 2 Sam. 7:23 [b]... 18; 145:18; 148 55:6 [c]Ps. 34:18
8 [a]Ps. 89:14; 9 119:144, 160, 1
9 [a]Deut. 4:23; 8:11, 14, 19; Pr 23:19 [b]Deut. 6 16:3 [c]Gen. 18: 4:10; 6:7, 20-25 32:46; Ps. 78:5, 22:6; Eph. 6:4
10 [1]Or, *reveren* [a]Deut. 14:23; 17 31:12, 13 [b]Deut
11 [a]Ex. 19:18; 12:18, 19
13 [1]Lit., *Words* 34:28; Deut. 10: 31:18; 34:1, 28
15 [a]Josh. 23:11 40:18
16 [a]Deut. 4:25; 9 31:29 [b]Ex. 20:4; 26:1; Deut. 5:8, 9 27:15; Rom. 1:23
17 [a]Rom. 1:23
19 [a]Gen. 2:1; De 17:3; 2 Kin. 17:16 [b]Deut. 13:5, 10; J 31:26-28
20 [a]1 Kin. 8:51; J 11:4 [b]Ex. 19:5; De 7:6; 14:2; 26:18; T 2:14; 1 Pet. 2:9
21 [a]Num. 20:12; 1:37

that I should not cross the Jordan, and that I should not enter the good land which the LORD your God is giving you as an inheritance.
22 "For [a]I shall die in this land, I shall not cross the Jordan, but you shall cross and take possession of this [b]good land.
23 "So watch yourselves, [a]lest you forget the covenant of the LORD your God, which He made with you, and [b]make for yourselves a graven image in the form of anything *against* which the LORD your God has commanded you.
24 "For the LORD your God is a [a]consuming fire, a [b]jealous God.
25 "When you [1]become the father of children and children's children and have remained long in the land, and [a]act corruptly, and [b]make an [2]idol in the form of anything, and [c]do that which is evil in the sight of the LORD your God *so as* to provoke Him to anger,
26 I [a]call heaven and earth to witness against you today, that you shall [b]surely perish quickly from the land where you are going over the Jordan to possess it. You shall not [1]live long on it, but shall be utterly destroyed.
27 "And the LORD will [a]scatter you among the peoples, and you shall be left few in number among the nations, where the LORD shall drive you.
28 "And [a]there you will serve gods, the work of man's hands, [b]wood and stone, [c]which neither see nor hear nor eat nor smell.
29 "[a]But from there you will seek the LORD your God, and you will find *Him* if you search for Him [b]with all your heart and all your soul.
30 "When you [a]are in distress and all these things have come upon you, [b]in the latter days, [c]you will return to the LORD your God and listen to His voice.
31 "For the LORD your God is a [a]compassionate God; [b]He will not fail you nor [c]destroy you nor [d]forget the covenant with your fathers which He swore to them.
32 "Indeed, [a]ask now concerning the former days which were before you, since the [b]day that God created [1]man on the earth, and *inquire* [c]from one end of the heavens to the other. [d]Has *anything* been done like this great thing, or has *anything* been heard like it?
33 "[a]Has *any* people heard the voice of God speaking from the midst of the fire, as you have heard *it*, and survived?
34 "[a]Or has a god tried to go to take for himself a nation from within *another* nation [b]by trials, by signs and wonders and by war and [c]by a mighty hand and by an outstretched arm and by great terrors, [1]as the LORD your God did for you in Egypt before your eyes?
35 "To you it was shown that you might know that the LORD, He is God; [a]there is no other besides Him.
36 "[a]Out of the heavens He let you hear His voice [b]to discipline you; and on earth He let you see His great fire, and you heard His words from the midst of the fire.
37 "[1a]Because He loved your fathers, therefore He chose [2]their descendants after them. And He [3b]personally brought you from Egypt by His great power,
38 driving out from before you nations greater and mightier than you, to bring you in *and* [a]to give you their land for an inheritance, as it is today.
39 "Know therefore today, and take it to your heart, that [a]the LORD, He is God in heaven above and on the earth below; there is no other.
40 "[a]So you shall keep His statutes and His commandments which I

um. 27:13, 14 [b]Deut. 3:25
eut. 4:9 [b]Deut. 4:16
x. 24:17; Deut. . 30:27; 33:14; :29 [b]Deut. 5:9; 6:15
t., *beget* [2]Or, *a* *image* [a]Deut. 16 [b]Deut. 4:23 [c]2 Kin. 17:17
t., *prolong your* s [a]Deut. 30:19; 2:1; Is. 1:2; Mic. ut. 7:4; 8:19, 20
ev. 26:33; Deut. 29:28; Neh. 1:8
Deut. 28:36, 64; 13 [b]Deut. 29:17 :4-8; 135:15-18; Is. 44:12-20
Deut. 30:1-3, 10; 5:4; Is. 55:6; Jer. Deut. 6:5; 10:12
[a]Ps. 18:6; 59:16; 3 [b]Deut. 31:29; 23:20; Hos. 3:5; . 1:2 [c]Jer. 4:1, 2
[a]Ex. 34:6; 2 Chr. 9; Neh. 9:31; Ps. 11:4; 116:5; Jon. 2 [b]Deut. 31:6, 8; :5; 1 Chr. 28:20; 13:5 [c]Jer. 30:11 [d]Lev. 26:45
Or, *Adam* [a]Deut. 7; Job 8:8 [b]Gen. , Is. 45:12 [c]Deut. 28:64; Matt. 24:31 4:7; 2 Sam. 7:23
[a]Ex. 20:22; Deut. 5:24, 26
t., *according to all* [a]Ex. 14:30; Deut. 33:29 [b]Deut. 7:19 ut. 5:15; 6:21; Ps. 136:12
5 [a]Ex. 8:10; 9:14; t. 4:39; 32:12, 39; 1 Sam. 2:2; Is. 43:10-12; 44:6-8; 45:5-7; Mark 12:32
x. 19:9, 19; 20:18, ; Deut. 4:33; Neh. Heb. 12:25 [b]Deut. 8:5
[1]Lit., *And instead,* use [2]Lit., *his seed* *with His presence* Deut. 7:7, 8; 10:15; [b]Ex. 33:14; Is. 63:9
38 [a]Num. 32:4; 34:14, 15
[a]Deut. 4:35; Josh. 2:11
[a]Lev. 22:31; Deut. 4:2; Ps. 105:45

am [1]giving you today, that [b]it may go well with you and with your
children after you, and [c]that you may [2]live long on the land which
the LORD your God is giving you for all time."
41 [a]Then Moses set apart three cities across the Jordan to the [1]east,
42 that a manslayer might flee there, who unintentionally slew his
neighbor without having enmity toward him in time past; and by
fleeing to one of these cities he might live:
43 [a]Bezer in the wilderness on the plateau for the Reubenites, and
Ramoth in Gilead for the Gadites, and Golan in Bashan for the
Manassites.
44 Now this is the law which Moses set before the sons of Israel;
45 these are the testimonies and the statutes and the ordinances
which Moses spoke to the sons of Israel, when they came out from
Egypt,
46 across the Jordan, in the valley [a]opposite Beth-peor, in the land of
[b]Sihon king of the Amorites who lived at Heshbon, whom Moses
and the sons of Israel [1]defeated when they came out from Egypt.
47 And they took possession of his land and the land of [a]Og king of
Bashan, the two kings of the Amorites, *who were* across the Jordan to
the [1]east,
48 from [a]Aroer, which is on the edge of the [1]valley of Arnon, even
as far as [b]Mount Sion (that is, Hermon),
49 with all the Arabah across the Jordan to the east, even as far as
the sea of the Arabah, [1]at the foot of the slopes of Pisgah.

Chapter 5

5 Then Moses summoned all Israel, and said to them, "Hear, O
Israel, the statutes and the ordinances which I am speaking
today in your [1]hearing, that you may learn them and observe [2]them
carefully.
2 "The LORD our God made [a]a covenant with us at Horeb.
3 "[a]The LORD did not make this covenant with our fathers, but with
us, *with* all those of [1]us alive here today.
4 "The LORD spoke to you [a]face to face at the mountain [b]from the
midst of the fire,
5 *while* [a]I was standing between the LORD and you at that time, to
declare to you the word of the LORD; [b]for you were afraid because of
the fire and did not go up the mountain. [1]He said,
6 '[a]I am the LORD your God, who brought you out of the land of
Egypt, out of the house of [1]slavery.
7 '[a]You shall have no other gods [1]before Me.
8 '[a]You shall not make for yourself [1]an idol, *or* any likeness *of* what
is in heaven above [2]or on the earth beneath [2]or in the water under
the earth.
9 'You shall not worship them or serve them; for I, the LORD your
God, am a jealous God, [a]visiting the iniquity of the fathers on the
children, and on the third and the fourth *generations* of those who
hate Me,
10 but [a]showing lovingkindness to thousands, to those who love
Me and keep My commandments.
11 '[a]You shall not take the name of the LORD your God in vain, for
the LORD will not [1]leave him unpunished who takes His name in
vain.

40 [1]Lit., *comm* [2]Lit., *prolong yo* [b]Deut. 4:1; 5:16 6:3, 18; 12:25, 2 [c]Ex. 23:26; Deu

41 [1]Lit., *sunrise* 35:6; Deut. 19:2 Josh. 20:7-9

43 [a]Josh. 20:8

46 [1]Lit., *smote* 3:29 [b]Num. 21:2

47 [1]Lit., *sunrise* 1:4; 3:3, 4

48 [1]Or, *wadi* [a]D 2:36; 3:12 [b]Deu Ps. 133:3

49 [1]Lit., *under*

5:1 [1]Lit., *ears* [2]L *do them*

2 [a]Ex. 19:5; Mal.

3 [1]Lit., *us oursel* [a]Jer. 31:32; Heb.

4 [a]Num. 14:14; D 34:10 [b]Deut. 4:33

5 [1]Lit., *saying* [a]G 3:19 [b]Ex. 19:16, 2 20:18; Heb. 12:18

6 [1]Lit., *slaves* [a]Ex 20:2-17; Lev. 26:1 Deut. 6:4; Ps. 81:1

7 [1]Or, *besides* [a]E 20:3

8 [1]Or, *a graven im* [2]Lit., *or what is* [a]Ex 20:4-6; Lev. 26:1; 4:15-18; 27:15; Ps.

9 [a]Ex. 34:7; Num. 14:18; Deut. 7:10

10 [a]Num. 14:18; D 7:9; Jer. 32:18

11 [1]Or, *hold him guiltless* [a]Ex. 20:7; 19:12; Deut. 6:13; 10:20; Matt. 5:33

12 ‘[a]Observe the sabbath day to keep it holy, as the LORD your God
commanded you.
13 ‘Six days you shall labor and do all your work,
14 but [a]the seventh day is a sabbath of the LORD your God; *in it* you
shall not do any work, you or your son or your daughter or your
male servant or your female servant or your ox or your donkey or
any of your cattle or your sojourner who [1]stays with you, so that
your male servant and your female servant may rest as well as you.
15 ‘[a]And you shall remember that you were a slave in the land of
Egypt, and the LORD your God brought you out of there by a mighty
hand and by an outstretched arm; therefore the LORD your God com-
manded you to observe the sabbath day.
16 ‘[a]Honor your father and your mother, as the LORD your God has
commanded you, [b]that your days may be prolonged, and that it may
go well with you on the land which the LORD your God gives you.
17 ‘[a]You shall not murder.
18 ‘[a]You shall not commit adultery.
19 ‘[a]You shall not steal.
20 ‘[a]You shall not bear false witness against your neighbor.
21 ‘[a]You shall not covet your neighbor's wife, and you shall not
desire your neighbor's house, his field or his male servant or his
female servant, his ox or his donkey or anything that belongs to your
neighbor.’
22 “These words the LORD spoke to all your assembly at the moun-
tain from the midst of the fire, *of* the cloud and *of* the thick gloom,
with a great voice, and He added no more. And [a]He wrote them on
two tablets of stone and gave them to me.
23 “And it came about, when you heard the voice from the midst of
the darkness, while the mountain was burning with fire, that you
came near to me, all the heads of your tribes and your elders.
24 “And you said, ‘Behold, the LORD our God has shown us His
glory and His greatness, and we have heard His voice from the
midst of the fire; we have seen today that God speaks with man, yet
he lives.
25 ‘[a]Now then why should we die? For this great fire will consume
us; if we hear the voice of the LORD our God any longer, then we
shall die.
26 ‘For [a]who is there of all flesh, who has heard the voice of the
living God speaking from the midst of the fire, as we *have*, and lived?
27 ‘[1]Go near and hear all that the LORD our God says; then speak to
us all that the LORD our God will speak to you, and we will hear and
do *it*.’
28 “And the LORD heard the voice of your words when you spoke to
me, [a]and the LORD said to me, ‘I have heard the voice of the words of
this people which they have spoken to you. They have done well in
all that they have spoken.
29 ‘[a]Oh that they had such a heart in them, that they would fear Me,
and [b]keep all My commandments always, that [c]it may be well with
them and with their sons forever!
30 ‘Go, say to them, “Return to your tents.”
31 ‘[a]But as for you, stand here by Me, that I may speak to you all the
commandments and the statutes and the judgments which you shall
teach them, that they may observe *them* in the land which I give
them to possess.’

12 [a]Ex. 16:23-30; [20]:8-11; 31:13f.; Mark 2:27f.
14 [1]Lit., *is in your* [gat]*es* [a]Gen. 2:2; Heb. 4:4
15 [a]Ex. 20:11
16 [a]Ex. 20:12; Lev. [19:3]; Deut. 27:16; Matt. [15:]4; 19:19; Mark 7:10; [10:1]9; Luke 18:20; Eph. [6:2f.]3; Col. 3:20 [b]Deut. 4:40
17 [a]Gen. 9:6; Ex. [20:1]3; Lev. 24:17; Matt. 5:21f.; 19:18; Mark 10:19; Rom. 13:9; James 2:11
18 [a]Ex. 20:14; Lev. 20:10; Matt. 5:27f.; [19:1]8; Mark 10:19; Luke 18:20; Rom. 13:9; James 2:11
19 [a]Ex. 20:15; Lev. 19:11
[2]0 [a]Ex. 20:16; 23:1; Matt. 19:18
[21] [a]Ex. 20:17; Rom. 7:7; 13:9
[22] [a]Ex. 24:12; 31:18; Deut. 4:13
[25 a E]x. 20:18, 19; Deut. 18:16
26 [a]Deut. 4:33
[2]7 [1]Lit., *Go yourself*
28 [a]Deut. 18:17
29 [a]Ps. 81:13; Is. 48:18 [b]Deut. 11:1 [c]Deut. 5:16, 33
31 [a]Ex. 24:12

32 "So you shall observe to do just as the LORD your God has com-
manded you; [a]you shall not turn aside to the right or to the left.
33 "[a]You shall walk in all the way which the LORD your God has
commanded you, [b]that you may live, and that it may be well with
you, and that you may prolong *your* days in the land which you
shall possess.

Chapter 6

6 "Now this is the commandment, the statutes and the judgments
which the LORD your God has commanded *me* to teach you, that
you might do *them* in the land where you are going over to pos-
sess it,
2 so that you and your son and your grandson might [a]fear the
LORD your God, to keep all His statutes and His commandments,
which I command you, [b]all the days of your life, and that your days
may be prolonged.
3 "O Israel, you should listen and [1]be careful to do *it*, that [a]it may be
well with you and that you may multiply greatly, just as the LORD,
the God of your fathers, has promised you, *in* [b]a land flowing with
milk and honey.
4 "[a]Hear, O Israel! The LORD is our God, the [b]LORD is one!
5 "And [a]you shall love the LORD your God [b]with all your heart and
with all your soul and with all your might.
6 "And [a]these words, which I am commanding you today, shall be
on your heart;
7 and [a]you shall teach them diligently to your sons and shall talk
of them when you sit in your house and when you walk by the way
and when you lie down and when you rise up.
8 "[a]And you shall bind them as a sign on your hand and they shall
be as [1]frontals [2]on your forehead.
9 "[a]And you shall write them on the doorposts of your house and
on your gates.
10 "Then it shall come about when the LORD your God brings you
into the land which He swore to your fathers, Abraham, Isaac and
Jacob, to give you, [a]great and splendid cities which you did not
build,
11 and houses full of all good things which you did not fill, and
hewn cisterns which you did not dig, vineyards and olive trees
which you did not plant, and [a]you shall eat and be satisfied,
12 then watch yourself, lest [a]you forget the LORD who brought you
from the land of Egypt, out of the house of [1]slavery.
13 "[a]You shall [1]fear *only* the LORD your God; and you shall [2]worship
Him, and [b]swear by His name.
14 "[a]You shall not follow other gods, any of the gods of the peoples
who surround you,
15 for the LORD your God in the midst of you is a [a]jealous God;
otherwise the anger of the LORD your God will be kindled against
you, and He will [1]wipe you off the face of the earth.
16 "[a]You shall not put the LORD your God to the test, [b]as you tested
Him at Massah.
17 "[a]You should diligently keep the commandments of the LORD
your God, and His testimonies and His statutes which He has com-
manded you.
18 "And you shall do what is right and good in the sight of the LORD,

32 [a]Deut. 17:20; 28 Josh. 1:7; 23:6; Pro 4:27

33 [a]Deut. 10:12; Je 7:23; Luke 1:6 [b]De 4:1, 40; 12:25, 28; Eph. 6:3

6:2 [a]Ex. 20:20; De 10:12; Ps. 111:10; 128:1; Eccl. 12:13 [b]Deut. 4:9

3 [1]Lit., *keep* [a]Deu 5:33 [b]Ex. 3:8, 17

4 [a]Matt. 22:37; Ma 12:29, 30; Luke 10: [b]Deut. 4:35, 39; Jo 10:30; 1 Cor. 8:4; E 4:6

5 [a]Matt. 22:37; Ma 12:30; Luke 10:27 [b]Deut. 4:29; 10:12

6 [a]Deut. 11:18

7 [a]Deut. 4:9; 11:19 Eph. 6:4

8 [1]Or, *frontlet ban* [2]Lit., *between your eyes* [a]Ex. 12:14; 1 16; Deut. 11:18; Pr 3:3; 6:21; 7:3

9 [a]Deut. 11:20

10 [a]Deut. 9:1; 19: Josh. 24:13; Ps. 1

11 [a]Deut. 8:10; 11 14:29

12 [1]Lit., *slaves* [a]D 4:9

13 [1]Or, *reverence* *serve* [a]Deut. 13:4 4:10; Luke 4:8 [b]D 5:11; 10:20; Ps. 63 Matt. 5:33

14 [a]Jer. 25:6

15 [1]Lit., *destroy* [a] 4:24; 5:9

16 [a]Matt. 4:7; Luk 4:12 [b]Ex. 17:7

17 [a]Deut. 11:22; F 119:4

that [a]it may be well with you and that you may go in and possess the
good land which the LORD swore to *give* your fathers,
19 by driving out all your enemies from before you, as the LORD has
spoken.
20 "[a]When your son asks you in time to come, saying, 'What *do* the
testimonies and the statutes and the judgments *mean* which the LORD
our God commanded you?'
21 then you shall say to your son, 'We were slaves to Pharaoh in
Egypt; and the LORD brought us from Egypt with a mighty hand.
22 'Moreover, the LORD showed great and distressing signs and
wonders before our eyes against Egypt, Pharaoh and all his
household;
23 and He brought us out from there in order to bring us in, to give
us the land which He had sworn to our fathers.'
24 "So the LORD commanded us to observe all these statutes, [a]to fear
the LORD our God for our good always and [b]for our survival, as *it is*
today.
25 "And [a]it will be righteousness for us if we [1]are careful to observe
all this commandment before the LORD our God, just as He com-
manded us.

Chapter 7

7 "[a]When the LORD your God shall bring you into the land where
you are entering to possess it, and shall clear away many nations
before you, the Hittites and the Girgashites and the Amorites and the
Canaanites and the Perizzites and the Hivites and the Jebusites,
[b]seven nations greater and stronger than you,
2 and when the LORD your God shall deliver them before you, and
you shall [1]defeat them, [a]then you shall [2]utterly destroy them. [b]You
shall make no covenant with them [c]and show no favor to them.
3 "Furthermore, [a]you shall not intermarry with them; you shall not
give your [1]daughters to [2]their sons, nor shall you take [3]their daugh-
ters for your [4]sons.
4 "For [1]they will turn your [2]sons away from [3]following Me to serve
other gods; then the anger of the LORD will be kindled against you,
and [a]He will quickly destroy you.
5 "But thus you shall do to them: [a]you shall tear down their altars,
and smash their *sacred* pillars, and hew down their [1]Asherim, and
burn their graven images with fire.
6 "For you are [a]a holy people to the LORD your God; the LORD your
God has chosen you to be [b]a people for His [1]own possession out of
all the peoples who are on the face of the [2]earth.
7 "[a]The LORD did not set His love on you nor choose you because
you were more in number than any of the peoples, for you were the
fewest of all peoples,
8 but because the LORD loved you and kept the [a]oath which He
swore to your forefathers, [b]the LORD brought you out by a mighty
hand, and redeemed you from the house of [1]slavery, from the hand
of Pharaoh king of Egypt.
9 "Know therefore that the LORD your God, [a]He is God, [b]the faithful
God, [c]who keeps [1]His covenant and [1]His lovingkindness to a thou-
sandth generation with those who [d]love Him and keep His com-
mandments;
10 but [a]repays those who hate Him to [1]their faces, to destroy [2]them;

18 [a]Deut. 4:40
20 [a]Ex. 13:8, 14
[a]Deut. 10:12; Jer. 39 [b]Ps. 41:2; Luke 10:28
[1]Lit., *keep* [a]Deut. 24:13; Rom. 10:3
:1 [a]Deut. 20:16-18 [b]Acts 13:19
2 [1]Lit., *smite* [2]Lit., *surely devote to the* [a]Num. 31:17; Josh. [b]Ex. 23:32 [c]Deut. 7:16; 13:8
[1]Lit., *daughter* [2]Lit., *his son* [3]Lit., *his hter* [4]Lit., *son* [a]Ex. 5, 16; Josh. 23:12; Ezra 9:2
[1]Lit., *he* [2]Lit., *son* ., *after* [a]Deut. 4:26
5 [1]I.e., wooden ymbols of a female [a]Ex. 23:24; 34:13; Deut. 12:3
Or, *special treasure* , *ground* [a]Ex. 19:6; 14:2, 21; Ps. 50:5; :3 [b]Ex. 19:5; Deut. 20; 14:2; 26:18; Ps. 4; Titus 2:14; 1 Pet. 2:9
7 [a]Deut. 4:37
8 [1]Lit., *slaves* [a]Ex. 32:13 [b]Ex. 13:3
t., *the* [a]Deut. 4:35, Is. 49:7; 1 Cor. 1:9; Thess. 5:24; 2 Tim. 13 [c]Ex. 20:6; Dan. 9:4 [d]Deut. 5:10
[1]Lit., *his face* [2]Lit., [a]Is. 59:18; Nah. 1:2

He will not delay [3]with him who hates Him, He will repay him to
his face.
11 "Therefore, you shall keep the commandment and the statutes
and the judgments which I am commanding you today, to do them.
12 "[a]Then it shall come about, because you listen to these judgments
and keep and do them, that the LORD your God will keep with you
[1]His covenant and [1]His lovingkindness which He swore to your
forefathers.
13 "And He will [a]love you and bless you and [b]multiply you; He will
also bless the fruit of your womb and the fruit of your ground, your
grain and your new wine and your oil, the increase of your herd and
the young of your flock, [1]in the land which He swore to your fore-
fathers to give you.
14 "You shall be blessed above all peoples; there shall be no male or
female [a]barren among you or among your cattle.
15 "And [a]the LORD will remove from you all sickness; and He will
not put on you any of the harmful diseases of Egypt which you have
known, but He will lay them on all who hate you.
16 "And you shall consume all the peoples whom the LORD your
God will deliver to you; [a]your eye shall not pity them, neither shall
you serve their gods, for that *would be* [b]a snare to you.
17 "If you should say in your heart, 'These nations are greater than I;
how can I [a]dispossess them?'
18 you shall not be afraid of them; you shall well [a]remember what
the LORD your God did to Pharaoh and to all Egypt:
19 [a]the great trials which your eyes saw and the signs and the won-
ders and the mighty hand and the outstretched arm by which the
LORD your God brought you out. So shall the LORD your God do to
all the peoples of whom you are afraid.
20 "Moreover, the LORD your God will send [a]the hornet against them,
until those who are left and hide themselves from you perish.
21 "You shall not dread [1]them, for [a]the LORD your God is in your
midst, [b]a great and awesome God.
22 "[a]And the LORD your God will clear away these nations before
you little by little; you will not be able to put an end to them quickly,
lest the [1]wild beasts grow too numerous for you.
23 "[a]But the LORD your God shall deliver them before you, and will
[1]throw them into great confusion until they are destroyed.
24 "[a]And He will deliver their kings into your hand so that you shall
make their name perish from under heaven; [b]no man will be able to
stand before you until you have destroyed them.
25 "The graven images of their gods you are to [a]burn with fire; you
shall [b]not covet the silver or the gold that is on them, nor take it for
yourselves, lest you be [c]snared by it, for it is an [d]abomination to the
LORD your God.
26 "And you shall not bring an abomination into your house, and
like it come under the [a]ban; you shall utterly detest it and you shall
utterly abhor it, for it is something banned.

Chapter 8

8 "All the commandments that I am commanding you today you
shall be careful to do, that you [a]may live and multiply, and go in
and possess the land which the LORD swore *to give* to your
forefathers.

10 [3]Lit., *to*
12 [1]Lit., *the* [a]L
26:3-13; Deut.
13 [1]Lit., *on the*
[a]Ps. 146:8; Pro
John 14:21 [b]Le
Deut. 13:17; 30
14 [a]Ex. 23:26
15 [a]Ex. 15:26
16 [a]Deut. 7:2 [b]
23:33; Judg. 8:2
106:36
17 [a]Num. 33:53
18 [a]Ps. 105:5
19 [a]Deut. 4:34
20 [a]Ex. 23:28; Jo
24:12
21 [1]Lit., *from bef*
them [a]Ex. 29:45;
3:10 [b]Deut. 10:17
1:5; 9:32
22 [1]Lit., *beasts o*
field [a]Ex. 23:29, 3
23 [1]Lit., *confuse t*
with [a]Ex. 23:27; J
10:10
24 [a]Josh. 6:2;
10:23-25 [b]Deut. 1
Josh. 1:5; 10:8; 23
25 [a]Ex. 32:20; De
12:3; 1 Chr. 14:12
20:17 [c]Deut. 7:16;
Judg. 8:27 [d]Deut.
26 [a]Lev. 27:28f.
8:1 [a]Deut. 4:1

2 "[a]And you shall remember all the way which the LORD your God
has [b]led you in the wilderness these forty years, that He might
humble you, [c]testing you, to know what was in your heart, whether
you would keep His commandments or not.
3 "And He humbled you and let you be hungry, and fed you with
manna which you did not know, nor did your fathers know, that He
might make you [1]understand that [a]man does not live by bread alone,
but man lives by everything that proceeds out of the mouth of the
LORD.
4 "[a]Your clothing did not wear out on you, nor did your foot swell
these forty years.
5 "[a]Thus you are to know in your heart that the LORD your God was
disciplining you just as a man disciplines his son.
6 "Therefore, you shall keep the commandments of the LORD your
God, to walk in His ways and to [1]fear Him.
7 "For [a]the LORD your God is bringing you into a good land, a land
of brooks of water, of fountains and springs, flowing forth in valleys
and hills;
8 a land of wheat and barley, of vines and fig trees and pome-
granates, a land of olive oil and honey;
9 a land where you shall eat food without scarcity, in which you
shall not lack anything; a land whose stones are iron, and out of
whose hills you can dig copper.
10 "When [a]you have eaten and are satisfied, you shall bless the LORD
your God for the good land which He has given you.
11 "[1]Beware lest you [a]forget the LORD your God by not keeping His
commandments and His ordinances and His statutes which I am
commanding you today;
12 lest, [a]when you have eaten and are satisfied, and have built good
houses and lived *in them,*
13 and when your herds and your flocks multiply, and your silver
and gold multiply, and all that you have multiplies,
14 then your heart becomes [1]proud, and you [a]forget the LORD your
God who brought you out from the land of Egypt, out of the house
of [2]slavery.
15 "He led you through [a]the great and terrible wilderness, *with its*
[b]fiery serpents and scorpions and thirsty ground where there was no
water; He [c]brought water for you out of the rock of flint.
16 "In the wilderness He fed you manna [a]which your fathers did not
know, that He might humble you and that He might [b]test you, to do
good for you [1]in the end.
17 "Otherwise, [a]you may say in your heart, 'My power and the
strength of my hand made me this wealth.'
18 "But you shall remember the LORD your God, for [a]it is He who is
giving you power to make wealth, that He may confirm His cove-
nant which He swore to your fathers, as *it is* this day.
19 "And it shall come about if you ever forget the LORD your God,
and go after other gods and serve them and worship them, [a]I testify
against you today that you shall surely perish.
20 "Like the nations that the LORD makes to perish before you, so
[a]you shall perish; because you would not listen to the voice of the
LORD your God.

2 [a]Deut. 8:16 [b]Ps. ...16; Amos 2:10 [c]Ex. 15:25; 20:20; 2 Chr. 32:31

...t., *know* [a]Matt. 4:4; Luke 4:4

...eut. 29:5; Neh. 9:21

[a]Deut. 4:36; 2 Sam. ...4; Prov. 3:12; Heb. 12:6; Rev. 3:19

6 [1]Or, *reverence*

[a]Deut. 11:9-12; Jer. 2:7

10 [a]Deut. 6:11

[1]Lit., *Take heed to yourself* [a]Deut. 4:9

...2 [a]Prov. 30:9; Hos. 13:6

[1]Lit., *lifted up* [2]Lit., ...*es* [a]Deut. 8:11; Ps. 106:21

...Deut. 1:19; Jer. 2:6 ...um. 21:6 [c]Ex. 17:6; Num. 20:11; Deut. ...3; Ps. 78:15; 114:8

...6 [1]Lit., *at your end* ...x. 16:15 [b]Deut. 8:2

17 [a]Deut. 9:4

[a]Prov. 10:22; Hos. 2:8

[a]Deut. 4:26; 30:18

20 [a]Ezek. 5:5-17

Chapter 9

9 "Hear, O Israel! You are crossing over the Jordan today to go in
to dispossess [a]nations greater and mightier than you, great cities
[1b]fortified to heaven,
2 a people great and tall, the sons of the Anakim, whom you know
and of whom you have heard *it said,* '[a]Who can stand before the sons
of Anak?'
3 "Know therefore today that [a]it is the LORD your God who is cross-
ing over before you as [b]a consuming fire. He will destroy them and
He will subdue them before you, so that [c]you may drive them out
and destroy them quickly, just as the LORD has spoken to you.
4 "[a]Do not say in your heart when the LORD your God has driven
them out before [1]you, 'Because of my righteousness the LORD has
brought me in to possess this land,' but *it is* [b]because of the wicked-
ness of these nations *that* the LORD is dispossessing them before you.
5 "It is [a]not for your righteousness or for the uprightness of your
heart that you are going to possess their land, but *it is* because of the
wickedness of these nations *that* the LORD your God is driving them
out before you, in order to confirm [b]the [1]oath which the LORD swore
to your fathers, to Abraham, Isaac and Jacob.
6 "Know, then, *it is* not because of your righteousness *that* the LORD
your God is giving you this good land to possess, for you are [a]a
[1]stubborn people.
7 "Remember, do not forget how you provoked the LORD your God
to wrath in the wilderness; [a]from the day that you left the land of
Egypt until you arrived at this place, you have been rebellious
against the LORD.
8 "Even [a]at Horeb you provoked the LORD to wrath, and the LORD
was so angry with you that He would have destroyed you.
9 "When I went up to the mountain to receive the tablets of stone,
the tablets of the covenant which the LORD had made with you, then
I remained on the mountain forty days and nights; [a]I neither ate
bread nor drank water.
10 "And the LORD gave me the two tablets of stone [a]written by the
finger of God; and on them *were* all the words which the LORD had
spoken with you at the mountain from the midst of the fire on the
day of the assembly.
11 "And it came about [a]at the end of forty days and nights that the
LORD gave me the two tablets of stone, the tablets of the covenant.
12 "[a]Then the LORD said to me, 'Arise, go down from here quickly,
for your people whom you brought out of Egypt have acted corrupt-
ly. They have [b]quickly turned aside from the way which I com-
manded them; they have made a molten image for themselves.'
13 "The [a]LORD spoke further to me, saying, 'I have seen this people,
and indeed, it is a [1b]stubborn people.
14 '[a]Let Me alone, that I may destroy them and [b]blot out their name
from under heaven; and I will make of you a nation mightier and
greater than they.'
15 "[a]So I turned and came down from the mountain while the moun-
tain was burning with fire, and the two tablets of the covenant were
in my two hands.
16 "And I saw that you had indeed sinned against the LORD your
God. You had made for yourselves a molten calf; you had turned
aside quickly from the way which the LORD had commanded you.

9:1 [1]Lit., *and f* [a]Deut. 4:38; 7:1 [b]Deut. 1:28
2 [a]Num. 13:22 Josh. 11:21, 22
3 [a]Deut. 31:3; 3:11 [b]Deut. 4:2 12:29 [c]Ex. 23:3 7:24
4 [1]Lit., *you say* [a]Deut. 8:17; 9:7 31:27 [b]Lev. 18: Deut. 12:31; 18
5 [1]Lit., *word* [a]T [b]Gen. 12:7; 13:1 17:8; 26:4; 28:13
6 [1]Or, *stiff-neck* [a]Deut. 9:13; 10:1
7 [a]Ex. 14:10f.; N 14:22
8 [a]Ex. 32:7-10; P 106:19
9 [a]Ex. 24:18; 34: Deut. 8:3; 9:18
10 [a]Deut. 4:13
11 [a]Deut. 9:9
12 [a]Ex. 32:7, 8 [b]J 2:17
13 [1]Or, *stiff-necke* [a]Ex. 32:9 [b]Deut. 1 31:27; 2 Kin. 17:14
14 [a]Ex. 32:10 [b]Ps 109:13
15 [a]Ex. 32:15-19

17 "And I took hold of the two tablets and threw them from my
hands, and smashed them before your eyes.
18 "[a]And I fell down before the LORD, [b]as at the first, forty days and
nights; [c]I neither ate bread nor drank water, [d]because of all your sin
which you had committed in doing what was evil in the sight of the
LORD to provoke Him to anger.
19 "For [a]I was afraid of the anger and hot displeasure with which the
LORD was wrathful against you in order to destroy you, [b]but the
LORD listened to me that time also.
20 "And the LORD was angry enough with Aaron to destroy him; so I
also prayed for Aaron at the same time.
21 "[a]And I took your [1]sinful *thing*, the calf which you had made, and
burned it with fire and crushed it, grinding it very small until it was
as fine as dust; and I threw its dust into the brook that came down
from the mountain.
22 "Again at [a]Taberah and at [b]Massah and at [c]Kibroth-hattaavah you
provoked the LORD to wrath.
23 "And when the LORD sent you from [a]Kadesh-barnea, saying, '[b]Go
up and possess the land which I have given you,' then you rebelled
against the [1]command of the LORD your God; [c]you neither believed
Him nor listened to His voice.
24 "[a]You have been rebellious against the LORD from the day I knew
you.
25 "[a]So I fell down before the LORD the forty days and nights, which I
[1]did because the LORD had said He would destroy you.
26 "[a]And I prayed to the LORD, and said, 'O Lord GOD, do not
destroy Thy people, even Thine inheritance, whom Thou hast
redeemed through Thy greatness, whom Thou hast brought out of
Egypt with a mighty hand.
27 'Remember Thy servants, Abraham, Isaac, and Jacob; do not look
at the stubbornness of this people or at their wickedness or their sin.
28 'Otherwise the land from which Thou didst bring us may say,
"[a]Because the LORD was not able to bring them into the land which
He had [1]promised them and because He hated them He has brought
them out to slay them in the wilderness."
29 'Yet they are Thy people, even [a]Thine inheritance, whom Thou
hast brought out by Thy [b]great power and Thine outstretched arm.'

Chapter 10

10 "At that time the LORD said to me, '[a]Cut out for yourself two
tablets of stone like the former ones, and come up to Me on
the mountain, and [b]make an ark of wood for yourself.
2 'And [a]I will write on the tablets the words that were on the
former tablets which you shattered, and [b]you shall put them in the
ark.'
3 "So [a]I made an ark of acacia wood and [b]cut out two tablets of
stone like the former ones, and went up on the mountain with the
two tablets in my hand.
4 "And He wrote on the tablets, like the former writing, [a]the Ten
[1]Commandments [b]which the LORD had spoken to you on the moun-
tain from the midst of the fire [c]on the day of the assembly; and the
LORD gave them to me.
5 "Then I turned and [a]came down from the mountain, and [b]put the

[a]Ex. 34:28 [b]Deut. 0 [c]Deut. 9:9 [d]Ex. 34:9
[a]Ex. 32:10f.; Heb. [b]Ex. 34:10; Deut. 10:10
.it., *sin* [a]Ex. 32:20
[a]Num. 11:3 [b]Ex. 17:7 [c]Num. 11:34
Lit., *mouth* [a]Deut. [b]Deut. 1:21 [c]Deut. 1:26; Ps. 106:24
[a]Deut. 9:7; 31:27
25 [1]Lit., *fell down* [a]Deut. 9:18
26 [a]Ex. 32:11-13; Sam. 7:9; Jer. 15:1
it., *spoken to* [a]Ex. 32:12; Num. 14:16
[a]Deut. 4:20; 1 Kin. 51; Neh. 1:10; Ps. 06:40 [b]Deut. 4:34
:1 [a]Ex. 34:1 [b]Ex. 25:10
[a]Deut. 4:13 [b]Ex. 25:16
[a]Ex. 25:5; 37:1-9 [b]Ex. 34:4
[1]Lit., *Words* [a]Ex. 8; Deut. 4:13 [b]Ex. [c]Deut. 9:10; 18:16
. 34:29 [b]Ex. 40:20

tablets in the ark which I had made; [c]and there they are, as the LORD commanded me."

6 (Now the sons of Israel set out from [1]Beeroth [a]Bene-jaakan to Moserah. [b]There Aaron died and there he was buried and Eleazar his son ministered as priest in his place.

7 [a]From there they set out to Gudgodah; and from Gudgodah to Jotbathah, a land of brooks of water.

8 [a]At that time the LORD set apart the tribe of Levi to carry the ark of the covenant of the LORD, to stand before the LORD [b]to serve Him and to bless in His name until this day.

9 [a]Therefore, Levi does not have a portion or inheritance with his brothers; the LORD is his inheritance, just as the LORD your God spoke to him.)

10 "[a]I, moreover, stayed on the mountain forty days and forty nights like the first time, and the LORD listened to me that time also; the LORD was not willing to destroy you.

11 "Then the LORD said to me, 'Arise, proceed on your journey ahead of the people, that they may go in and possess the land which I swore to their fathers to give them.'

12 "[a]And now, Israel, what does the LORD your God require from you, but to [1]fear the LORD your God, to walk in all His ways and [b]love Him, and to serve the LORD your God with [c]all your heart and with all your soul,

13 *and* to keep the LORD's commandments and His statutes which I am commanding you today for your good?

14 "Behold, [a]to the LORD your God belong heaven and the [1]highest heavens, [b]the earth and all that is in it.

15 "[a]Yet on your fathers did the LORD set His affection to love them, and He chose their [1]descendants after them, *even* you above all peoples, as *it is* this day.

16 "[a]Circumcise then [1]your heart, and [b]stiffen your neck no more.

17 "[a]For the LORD your God is the God of gods and the [b]Lord of lords, the great, the mighty, and the awesome God [c]who does not show partiality, nor [d]take a bribe.

18 "He executes justice for [a]the orphan and the widow, and shows His love for the alien by giving him food and clothing.

19 "[a]So show your love for the alien, for you were aliens in the land of Egypt.

20 "You shall fear the LORD your God; you shall serve Him and [a]cling to Him, and [b]you shall swear by His name.

21 "He is [a]your praise and He is your God, who has done these great and awesome things for you which your eyes have seen.

22 "[a]Your fathers went down to Egypt seventy persons *in all*, [b]and now the LORD your God has made you as numerous as the stars of heaven.

Chapter 11

11 "You shall therefore [a]love the LORD your God, and always [b]keep His charge, His statutes, His ordinances, and His commandments.

2 "And know this day [a]that I *am* not *speaking* with your sons who have not known and who have not seen the [1]discipline of the LORD your God—His greatness, His mighty hand, and His outstretched arm,

5 [c]1 Kin. 8:9
6 [1]Or, *the wel*
sons of Jaaka
33:30, 31 [b]Nu
20:25-28; 33:3
7 [a]Num. 33:3
8 [a]Num. 3:6;
Deut. 31:9 [b]D
17:12; 18:5; 21
9 [a]Num. 18:20
Deut. 18:1, 2; E
44:28
10 [a]Ex. 34:28;
9:18
12 [1]Or, *revere*
[a]Mic. 6:8 [b]Deu
Matt. 22:37; 1 T
[c]Deut. 4:29
14 [1]Lit., *heave*
heavens [a]1 Kin
Neh. 9:6; Ps. 68
115:16 [b]Ps. 24.
15 [1]Lit., *seed* [a]
4:37
16 [1]Lit., *the fore*
your heart [a]Lev
Jer. 4:4 [b]Deut.
17 [a]Josh. 22:22
136:2; Dan. 2:47
6:15; Rev. 19:16
17:14 [c]Deut. 1:1
10:34; Rom. 2:11
2:6; Eph. 6:9 [d]D
16:19
18 [a]Ex. 22:22-24
68:5; 146:9
19 [a]Lev. 19:34; E
47:22, 23
20 [a]Deut. 11:22;
[b]Deut. 5:11; 6:13;
63:11
21 [a]Ps. 109:1; 14
Jer. 17:14
22 [a]Gen. 46:27
15:5; 22:17; Deut.
11:1 [a]Deut. 6:5; 1
[b]Lev. 18:30; 22:9
2 [1]Or, *instruction*
[a]Deut. 4:34

3 and [a]His signs and His works which He did in the midst of
Egypt to Pharaoh the king of Egypt and to all his land;
4 and what He did to Egypt's army, to its horses and its chariots,
[a]when He made the water of the [1]Red Sea to [2]engulf them while they
were pursuing you, and the LORD [3]completely destroyed them;
5 and what He did to you in the wilderness until you came to this
place;
6 and [a]what He did to Dathan and Abiram, the sons of Eliab, the
son of Reuben, when the earth opened its mouth and swallowed
them, their households, their tents, and [b]every living thing that [1]fol-
lowed them, among all Israel—
7 but your own eyes have seen all the great work of the LORD
which He did.
8 "You shall therefore keep every commandment which I am com-
manding you today, [a]so that you may be strong and go in and pos-
sess the land into which you are about to cross to possess it;
9 [a]so that you may prolong *your* days on the land which the LORD
swore to your fathers to give to them and to their [1]descendants, [b]a
land flowing with milk and honey.
10 "For the land, into which you are entering to possess it, is not like
the land of Egypt from which you came, where you used to sow
your seed and water it with your [1]foot like a vegetable garden.
11 "But [a]the land into which you are about to cross to possess it, a
land of hills and valleys, drinks water from the rain of heaven,
12 a land for which the LORD your God cares; [a]the eyes of the LORD
your God are always on it, from the [1]beginning even to the end of
the year.
13 "And it shall come about, [a]if you listen obediently to my com-
mandments which I am commanding you today, [b]to love the LORD
your God and to serve Him [c]with all your heart and all your soul,
14 that [1a]He will give the rain for your land in its season, the [2b]early
and [3]late rain, that you may gather in your grain and your new wine
and your oil.
15 "And [1a]He will give grass in your fields for your cattle, and [b]you
shall eat and be satisfied.
16 "[1a]Beware, lest your hearts be deceived and you turn away and
serve other gods and worship them.
17 "Or [a]the anger of the LORD will be kindled against you, and He
will [b]shut up the heavens [c]so that there will be no rain and the
ground will not yield its fruit; and [d]you will perish quickly from the
good land which the LORD is giving you.
18 "[a]You shall therefore [1]impress these words of mine on your heart
and on your soul; and you shall bind them as a sign on your hand,
and they shall be as [2]frontals [3]on your forehead.
19 "[a]And you shall teach them to your sons, talking of them when
you sit in your house and when you walk along the road and when
you lie down and when you rise up.
20 "[a]And you shall write them on the doorposts of your house and
on your gates,
21 so that [a]your days and the days of your sons may be multiplied
on the land which the LORD swore to your fathers to give them, as
[1b]long as the heavens *remain* above the earth.
22 "For if you are [a]careful to keep all this commandment which I am

3 [a]Ex. 7:8-21
, *Sea of Reeds* , *flow over their* [3]Lit., *to this day* :28; Deut. 1:40; 2:1
was at their feet m. 16:1-35; Ps. 06:16-18 [b]Num. 26:10, 11
eut. 31:6, 7, 23; Josh. 1:6, 7
.it., *seed* [a]Deut. 6, 33; 6:2; Prov. 10:27 [b]Ex. 3:8
[1]I.e., probably a treadmill
11 [a]Deut. 8:7
[1]Lit., *beginning of* *year* [a]1 Kin. 9:3
[a]Lev. 26:3; Deut. Deut. 11:1 [c]Deut. 4:29
[1]So some ancient ions; M.T. reads *I* I.e., autumn [3]I.e., [a]Lev. 26:4; Deut. 28:12 [b]Joel 2:23; James 5:7
[1]So some ancient sions; M.T. reads *I* 04:14 [b]Deut. 6:11
16 [1]Lit., *Watch selves* [a]Job 31:27
[a]Deut. 6:15; 9:19 . 8:35; 2 Chr. 6:26; 7:13 [c]Deut. 28:24 [d]Deut. 4:26
18 [1]Lit., *put* [2]Lit., *frontlet bands* [3]Lit., *een your eyes* [a]Ex. 13:9, 16; Deut. 6:8
[a]Deut. 4:9, 10; 6:7; Prov. 22:6
20 [a]Deut. 6:9
[1]Lit., *the days of the heavens* [a]Prov. 3:2; 4:10; 9:11 [b]Ps. 72:5
22 [a]Deut. 6:17

commanding you, to do it, [b]to love the LORD your God, to walk in all
His ways and [c]hold fast to Him;
23 then the LORD will [a]drive out all these nations from before you,
and you will [b]dispossess nations greater and mightier than you.
24 "[a]Every place on which the sole of your foot shall tread shall be
yours; [b]your border shall be from the wilderness to Lebanon, *and*
from the river, the river Euphrates, as far as [1]the western sea.
25 "[a]There shall no man be able to stand before you; the LORD your
God shall lay the dread of you and the fear of you on all the land on
which you set foot, as He has spoken to you.
26 "[a]See, I am setting before you today a blessing and a curse:
27 the [a]blessing, if you listen to the commandments of the LORD
your God, which I am commanding you today;
28 and the [a]curse, if you do not listen to the commandments of the
LORD your God, but turn aside from the way which I am command-
ing you today, [1]by following other gods which you have not known.
29 "And it shall come about, when the LORD your God brings you
into the land where you are entering to possess it, [a]that you shall
place the blessing on Mount Gerizim and the curse on Mount Ebal.
30 "Are they not across the Jordan, west of the way toward the sun-
set, in the land of the Canaanites who live in the Arabah, opposite
[a]Gilgal, beside [b]the [1]oaks of Moreh?
31 "For you are about to cross the Jordan to go in to possess the land
which the LORD your God is giving you, and [a]you shall possess it
and live in it,
32 and you shall be careful to do all the statutes and the judgments
which I am setting before you today.

Chapter 12

12 "These are the statutes and the judgments which you shall
carefully observe in the land which the LORD, the God of your
fathers, has given you to possess [1a]as long as you live on the [2]earth.
2 "You shall utterly destroy all the places where the nations whom
you shall dispossess serve their gods, on the [a]high mountains and on
the hills and under every green tree.
3 "And [a]you shall tear down their altars and smash their *sacred*
pillars and burn their [1]Asherim with fire, and you shall cut down the
engraved images of their gods, and you shall [b]obliterate their name
from that place.
4 "You shall not act like this toward the LORD your God.
5 "[a]But you shall seek *the LORD* at the place which the LORD your
God shall choose from all your tribes, to establish His name there for
His dwelling, and there you shall come.
6 "And there you shall bring your burnt offerings, your sacrifices,
[a]your tithes, the [1]contribution of your hand, your votive offerings,
your freewill offerings, and the first-born of your herd and of your
flock.
7 "There also you and your households shall eat before the LORD
your God, and [a]rejoice in all [1]your undertakings in which the LORD
your God has blessed you.
8 "You shall not do at all what we are doing here today, every man
doing whatever is right in his own eyes;
9 for you have not as yet come to [a]the resting place and the [b]in-
heritance which the LORD your God is giving you.

22 [b]Deut. 11:1 10:20
23 [a]Deut. 4:38 9:1
24 [1]I.e., the Mediterranean 1:3; 14:9 [b]Gen Ex. 23:31; Deut
25 [a]Ex. 23:27; 7:24
26 [a]Deut. 30:1,
27 [a]Deut. 28:1-
28 [1]Lit., *to follow* [a]Deut. 28:15-68
29 [a]Deut. 27:12 8:33
30 [1]Lit., *terebint* [a]Josh. 4:19 [b]Ge
31 [a]Deut. 17:14; 21:43
12:1 [1]Lit., *all the* [2]Lit., *ground* [a]De 10; 1 Kin. 8:40
2 [a]2 Kin. 16:4; 17
3 [1]I.e., wooden symbols of a fema deity [a]Num. 33:52 Deut. 7:5; Judg. 2 [b]Ex. 23:13; Ps. 16 Zech. 13:2
5 [a]Ex. 20:24; Deu 12:11, 13; 2 Chr. 7 Ps. 78:68
6 [1]Or, *heave offer* [a]Deut. 14:22
7 [1]Lit., *the putting of your hand* [a]Lev. 23:40; Deut. 12:12, 14:26; 28:47; Eccl. 13; 5:18-20
9 [a]Deut. 3:20; 25:1 Ps. 95:11 [b]Deut. 4:

10 "When you cross the Jordan and live in the land which the LORD
your God is giving you to inherit, and [a]He gives you rest from all
your enemies around *you* so that you live in security,
11 [a]then it shall come about that the place in which the LORD your
God shall choose for His name to dwell, there you shall bring all that
I command you: your burnt offerings and your sacrifices, your tithes
and the [1]contribution of your hand, and all your choice votive offer-
ings which you will vow to the LORD.
12 "And you shall [a]rejoice before the LORD your God, you and your
sons and daughters, your male and female servants, and the [b]Levite
who is within your gates, since [c]he has no portion or inheritance
with you.
13 "[a]Be careful that you do not offer your burnt offerings in every
cultic place you see,
14 but in the place which the LORD chooses in one of your tribes,
there you shall offer your burnt offerings, and there you shall do all
that I command you.
15 "[a]However, you may slaughter and eat meat within any of your
gates, [1]whatever you desire, according to the blessing of the LORD
your God which He has given you; the unclean and the clean may
eat of it, as of [b]the gazelle and the deer.
16 "[a]Only you shall not eat the blood; [b]you are to pour it out on the
ground like water.
17 "[a]You are not allowed to eat within your gates the tithe of your
grain, or new wine, or oil, or the first-born of your herd or flock, or
any of your votive offerings which you vow, or your freewill offer-
ings, or the [1]contribution of your hand.
18 "But [a]you shall eat them before the LORD your God in [b]the place
which the LORD your God will choose, you and your son and daugh-
ter, and your male and female servants, and the [c]Levite who is
within your gates; and you shall [d]rejoice before the LORD your God in
all [1]your undertakings.
19 "[a]Be careful that you do not forsake the Levite [1]as long as you live
in your land.
20 "When the LORD your God extends your border [a]as He has
promised you, and you say, 'I will eat meat,' because [1]you desire to
eat meat, *then* you may eat meat, [2]whatever you desire.
21 "If the place which the LORD your God chooses to put His name is
too far from you, then you may slaughter of your herd and flock
which the LORD has given you, as I have commanded you; and you
may eat within your gates [1]whatever you desire.
22 "Just as a gazelle or a deer is eaten, so you shall eat it; the unclean
and the clean alike may eat of it.
23 "Only be sure [a]not to eat the blood, for the blood is the [1]life, and
you shall not eat the [1]life with the flesh.
24 "You shall not eat it; you shall pour it out on the ground like
water.
25 "You shall not eat it, in order that [a]it may be well with you and
your sons after you, for [b]you will be doing what is right in the sight
of the LORD.
26 "[a]Only your holy things which you may have and your votive
offerings, you shall take and go to the place which the LORD chooses.
27 "And [a]you shall offer your burnt offerings, the flesh and the
blood, on the altar of the LORD your God; and the blood of your

10 [a]Josh. 11:23
Or, heave offering
12:5; 15:20; 16:2; 17:8; 18:6
Deut. 12:7 [b]Deut.
:18, 19; 26:11-13
Deut. 10:9; 14:29
3 [a]Deut. 12:5, 11
t., in every desire
your soul [a]Deut.
23 [b]Deut. 12:22; 14:5; 15:22
en. 9:4; Lev. 7:26;
17:10-12; 1 Sam.
3f.; Acts 15:20, 29
[b]Deut. 15:23
it., heave offering
[a]Deut. 12:26
., the putting forth
your hand [a]Deut.
4:23 [b]Deut. 12:5
eut. 12:12 [d]Deut.
12:7; Eccl. 3:12f.;
5:18-20
[1]Lit., all your days
your land [a]Deut.
14:27
20 [1]Lit., your soul
res [2]Lit., in every
desire of your soul
Gen. 15:18; Deut.
11:24; 19:8
t., in every desire
of your soul
., soul [a]Gen. 9:4;
v. 17:10-14; Deut.
12:16
eut. 4:40; Is. 3:10
5:26; 1 Kin. 11:38
Num. 5:9f.; 18:19;
Deut. 12:17
27 [a]Lev. 1:9, 13

sacrifices shall be poured out on the altar of the LORD your God, and [b]you shall eat the flesh.
28 "Be careful to listen to all these words which I command you, in order that [a]it may be well with you and your sons after you forever, for you will be doing what is good and right in the sight of the LORD your God.
29 "When [a]the LORD your God cuts off before you the nations which you are going in to dispossess, and you dispossess them and dwell in their land,
30 beware that you are not ensnared [1]to follow them, after they are destroyed before you, and that you do not inquire after their gods, saying, 'How do these nations serve their gods, that I also may do likewise?'
31 "[a]You shall not behave thus toward the LORD your God, for every abominable act which the LORD hates they have done for their gods; for [b]they even burn their sons and daughters in the fire to their gods.
32 "[1a]Whatever I command you, you shall be careful to do; [b]you shall not add to nor take away from it.

Chapter 13

13 "[1a]If a prophet or a dreamer of dreams arises among you and gives you a sign or a wonder,
2 and the sign or the wonder comes true, concerning which he spoke to you, saying, '[a]Let us go after other gods (whom you have not known) and let us serve them,'
3 you shall not listen to the words of that prophet or that dreamer of dreams; for the LORD your God is [a]testing you to find out if [b]you love the LORD your God with all your heart and with all your soul.
4 "[a]You shall follow the LORD your God and fear Him; and you shall keep His commandments, listen to His voice, serve Him, and [b]cling to Him.
5 "But that prophet or that dreamer of dreams shall be [a]put to death, because he has [1]counseled [2]rebellion against the LORD your God who brought you from the land of Egypt and redeemed you from the house of [3]slavery, [b]to seduce you from the way in which the LORD your God commanded you to walk. [c]So you shall purge the evil from among you.
6 "[a]If your brother, your mother's son, or your son or daughter, or the wife [1]you cherish, or your friend who is as your own soul, entice you secretly, saying, '[b]Let us go and serve other gods' (whom neither you nor your fathers have known,
7 of the gods of the peoples who are around you, near you or far from you, from one end of the earth to the other end),
8 [a]you shall not yield to him or listen to him; [b]and your eye shall not pity him, nor shall you spare or conceal him.
9 "[a]But you shall surely kill him; [b]your hand shall be first against him to put him to death, and afterwards the hand of all the people.
10 "So you shall stone him [1]to death because he has sought [a]to seduce you from the LORD your God who brought you out from the land of Egypt, out of the house of [2]slavery.
11 "Then [a]all Israel will hear and be afraid, and will never again do such a wicked thing among you.
12 "If you hear in one of your cities, which the LORD your God is giving you to live in, *anyone* saying *that*

27 [b]Lev. 3:1-
28 [a]Deut. 4:4 8:12
29 [a]Josh. 23
30 [1]Lit., *after*
31 [a]Deut. 9:5 18:21; Deut. 106:37; Jer. 3
32 [1]Lit., *Eve* [a]Deut. 4:2; Jo [b]Prov. 30:6; F
13:1 [1]Ch. 13 [a]Matt. 24:24; 13:22; 2 Thes
2 [a]Deut. 13:6
3 [a]Ex. 20:20 16; 1 Cor. 11 6:5
4 [a]2 Kin. 23: 34:31; 2 John 10:20
5 [1]Lit., *spoke turning aside slaves* [a]Deut 17:5; 1 Kin. 1 [b]Deut. 4:19; [c]1 Cor. 5:13
6 [1]Lit., *of yo* [a]Deut. 17:2-7 [b]Deut. 13:2
8 [a]Prov. 1:10
9 [a]Deut. 13:5 24:14; Deut.
10 [1]Lit., *with that he dies slaves* [a]Deu
11 [a]Deut. 19

13 some worthless men have gone out from among you and have
seduced the inhabitants of their city, saying, "[a]Let us go and serve
other gods' (whom you have not known),
14 then you shall investigate and search out and inquire thorough-
ly. And if it is true *and* the matter established that this abomination
has been done among you,
15 [a]you shall surely strike the inhabitants of that city with the edge
of the sword, [1]utterly destroying it and all that is in it and its cattle
with the edge of the sword.
16 "[a]Then you shall gather all its booty into the middle of its open
square and burn the city and all its booty with fire as a whole burnt
offering to the LORD your God; and it shall be a [1b]ruin forever. It shall
never be rebuilt.
17 "And nothing from that which is put under the ban shall cling to
your hand, in order that the LORD may turn from [a]His burning anger
and [b]show mercy to you, and have compassion on you and [c]make
you increase, just [d]as He has sworn to your fathers,
18 [1]if you will listen to the voice of the LORD your God, [2]keeping all
His commandments which I am commanding you today, [3]and doing
what is right in the sight of the LORD your God.

Chapter 14

14 "You are [a]the sons of the LORD your God; [b]you shall not cut
yourselves nor [1]shave your forehead for the sake of the dead.
2 "For you are [a]a holy people to the LORD your God; and the LORD
has chosen you to be a [b]people for His [1]own possession out of all the
peoples who are on the face of the earth.
3 "[a]You shall not eat any detestable thing.
4 "[a]These are the animals which you may eat: the ox, the sheep, the
goat,
5 [1]the deer, the gazelle, the roebuck, the wild goat, the ibex, the
antelope and the mountain sheep.
6 "And any animal that divides the hoof and has the hoof split in
[1]two *and* [2]chews the cud, among the animals, that you may eat.
7 "Nevertheless, you are not to eat of these among those which
[1]chew the cud, or among those that divide the hoof in [2]two: the
camel and the [3]rabbit and the rock-badger, for though they [1]chew the
cud, they do not divide the hoof; they are unclean for you.
8 "And the pig, because it divides the hoof but *does* not *chew* the
cud, it is unclean for you. You shall not eat any of their flesh nor
touch their carcasses.
9 "These you may eat of all that are in water: anything that has fins
and scales you may eat,
10 but anything that does not have fins and scales you shall not eat;
it is unclean for you.
11 "You may eat any clean bird.
12 "But [a]these are the ones which you shall not eat: the [1]eagle and
the vulture and the [2]buzzard,
13 and the red kite, the falcon, and the kite in their kinds,
14 and every raven in its kind,
15 and the ostrich, the owl, the sea gull, and the hawk in their
kinds,
16 the little owl, the [1]great owl, the white owl,
17 the pelican, the carrion vulture, the cormorant,

[a]Deut. 13:2
...utting it under ...n [a]Deut. 13:5
...mound [a]Deut. ...osh. 8:28; Is. ...25:2; Jer. 49:2
...: 32:12; Num. ...t. 30:3 [c]Deut. ...n. 22:17; 26:4, 24; 28:14
...Or, for [2]Lit., to ...eep [3]Lit., to do
[1]Lit., make a ...s between your ...Rom. 8:16; 9:8, ...al. 3:26; 1 John ...ev. 19:28; 21:5; Jer. 16:6; 41:5
...special treasure ...0:26; Deut. 7:6; 12:1 [b]Ex. 19:5; ...20; 26:18; Titus 2:14; 1 Pet. 2:9
3 [a]Ezek. 4:14
...ev. 11:2-45; Acts 10:14
...act identification ...these animals is uncertain
..., two hoofs [2]Lit., brings up
...brings up [2]Lit., a ...eaving [3]Or, hare
[1]Or, vulture [2]Or, ...ulture [a]Lev. 11:13
...great horned owl

18 the stork, and the heron in their kinds, and the hoopoe and the
bat.
19 "And all the [1]teeming life with wings are unclean to you; they
shall not be eaten.
20 "You may eat any clean bird.
21 "[a]You shall not eat anything which dies *of itself*. You may give it to
the alien who is in your [1]town, so that he may eat it, or you may sell
it to a foreigner, for you are [b]a holy people to the LORD your God.
[c]You shall not boil a kid in its mother's milk.
22 "You [a]shall surely tithe all the produce from [1]what you sow,
which comes out of the field every year.
23 "And you shall eat in the presence of the LORD your God, [a]at the
place where He chooses to establish His name, the tithe of your
grain, your new wine, your oil, and the first-born of your herd and
your flock, in order that you may [b]learn to fear the LORD your God
always.
24 "And if the [1]distance is so great for you that you are not able to
[2]bring *the tithe,* since the place where the LORD your God chooses [a]to
set His name is too far away from you when the LORD your God
blesses you,
25 then you shall [1]exchange *it* for money, and bind the money in
your hand and go to the place which the LORD your God chooses.
26 "And you may spend the money for whatever your [1]heart desires,
for oxen, or sheep, or wine, or strong drink, or whatever your [1]heart
[2]desires; and [a]there you shall eat in the presence of the LORD your
God and rejoice, you and your household.
27 "Also you shall not neglect [a]the Levite who is in your [1]town, [b]for
he has no portion or inheritance among you.
28 "[a]At the end of every third year you shall bring out all the tithe of
your produce in that year, and shall deposit *it* in your [1]town.
29 "And the Levite, [a]because he has no portion or inheritance among
you, and [b]the alien, the [1]orphan and the widow who are in your
[2]town, shall come and [c]eat and be satisfied, in order that [d]the LORD
your God may bless you in all the work of your hand which you do.

Chapter 15

15 "[a]At the end of *every* seven years you shall [1]grant a remission
of debts.
2 "And this is the manner of remission: every creditor shall release
what he has loaned to his neighbor; he shall not exact it of his neigh-
bor and his brother, because the LORD's remission has been
proclaimed.
3 "[a]From a foreigner you may exact *it,* but your hand shall release
whatever of yours is with your brother.
4 "However, there shall be no poor among you, since [a]the LORD will
surely bless you in the land which the LORD your God is giving you
as an inheritance to possess,
5 if only you listen obediently to the voice of the LORD your God,
to observe carefully all this commandment which I am commanding
you today.
6 "[a]For the LORD your God shall bless you as He has promised you,
and you will lend to many nations, but you will not borrow; and you
will rule over many nations, but they will not rule over you.
7 "If there is [a]a poor man with you, one of your brothers, in any of

19 [1]I.e., flyin
21 [1]Lit., *gate* 17:15; 22:8; E 44:31 [b]Deut. 23:19; 34:26
22 [1]Lit., *your* [a]Lev. 27:30; D 17; Neh. 10:3
23 [a]Deut. 12:5 4:10; Ps. 2:11; 147:11; Is. 8:1 32:38-40
24 [1]Lit., *way* it [a]Deut. 12:5,
25 [1]Lit., *give ir*
26 [1]Lit., *soul* [2] *of you* [a]Deut. 1
27 [1]Lit., *gates* 12:12 [b]Num. 1 Deut. 10:9; 18:1
28 [1]Lit., *gates* 26:12
29 [1]Or, *fatherle gates* [a]Deut. 10 [b]Deut. 16:11, 14 24:19-21; 26:12; 94:6; Is. 1:17 [c]D 6:11 [d]Deut. 15:1 3:10
15:1 [1]Lit., *make release* [a]Deut. 3
3 [a]Deut. 23:20
4 [a]Deut. 28:8
6 [a]Deut. 28:12, 1
7 [a]Lev. 25:35; De 15:11

your [1]towns in your land which the LORD your God is giving you,
[b]you shall not harden your heart, nor close your hand from your
poor brother;
8 but [a]you shall freely open your hand to him, and shall generous-
ly lend him sufficient for his need *in* whatever he lacks.
9 "Beware, lest there is a base [1]thought in your heart, saying, '[a]The
seventh year, the year of remission, is near,' and [b]your eye is hostile
toward your poor brother, and you give him nothing; then he [c]may
cry to the LORD against you, and it will be a sin in you.
10 "You shall generously give to him, and your heart shall not be
grieved when you give to him, because [a]for this thing the LORD your
God will bless you in all your work and in all [1]your undertakings.
11 "[a]For the poor will never cease *to be* [1]in the land; therefore I com-
mand you, saying, 'You shall freely open your hand to your brother,
to your needy and poor in your land.'
12 "[a]If your [1]kinsman, a Hebrew man or woman, is sold to you, then
he shall serve you six years, but in the seventh year you shall set him
[2]free.
13 "And when you set him [1]free, you shall not send him away
empty-handed.
14 "You shall furnish him liberally from your flock and from your
threshing floor and from your wine vat; you shall give to him as the
LORD your God has blessed you.
15 "And you shall remember that you were a slave in the land of
Egypt, and the LORD your God redeemed you; therefore I command
you [1]this today.
16 "And it shall come about [a]if he says to you, 'I will not go out from
you,' because he loves you and your household, since he fares well
with you;
17 then you shall take an awl and pierce it through his ear into the
door, and he shall be your servant forever. And also you shall do
likewise to your maidservant.
18 "It shall not seem hard to you when you set him [1]free, for he has
given you six years *with* [2]double the service of a hired man; so the
LORD your God will bless you in whatever you do.
19 "[a]You shall consecrate to the LORD your God all the first-born
males that are born of your herd and of your flock; you shall not
work with the first-born of your herd, nor shear the first-born of
your flock.
20 "[a]You and your household shall eat it every year before the LORD
your God in the place which the LORD chooses.
21 "[a]But if it has any [1]defect, *such as* lameness or blindness, *or* any
serious [1]defect, you shall not sacrifice it to the LORD your God.
22 "You shall eat it within your gates; [a]the unclean and the clean
alike *may eat it*, as [a]a gazelle or a deer.
23 "Only [a]you shall not eat its blood; you are to pour it out on the
ground like water.

Chapter 16

16 "Observe [a]the month of Abib and [1b]celebrate the Passover to
the LORD your God, for in the month of Abib the LORD your
God brought you out of Egypt by night.
2 "And you shall sacrifice the Passover to the LORD your God from

ates [b]1 John 3:17
tt. 5:42; Luke 34; Gal. 2:10
, *word* [a]Deut. tt. 20:15 [c]Ex. ut. 24:15; Job . 12:5; James 5:4
e putting forth r hand [a]Deut. 's. 41:1; Prov. 22:9
in the midst of 11; Mark 14:7; John 12:8
, *brother* [2]Lit., *from you* [a]Ex. Lev. 25:39-43; Jer. 34:14
., *free from you*
[1]Lit., *this thing*
16 [a]Ex. 21:5, 6
., *free from you uble the amount*
9 [a]Ex. 13:2, 12
. 7:15-18; Deut. 12:5; 14:23
t., *blemish* [a]Lev. 9-25; Deut. 17:1
eut. 12:15, 16, 22
en. 9:4; Lev. 7:26; :10; 19:26; Deut. 12:16, 23
Lit., *perform* [a]Ex. 2:2 [b]Num. 28:16

the flock and the herd, in the place where the LORD chooses to establish His name.

3 "[a]You shall not eat leavened bread with it; seven days you shall eat with it unleavened bread, the bread of affliction (for you came out of the land of Egypt in haste), in order that you may remember [b]all the days of your life the day when you came out of the land of Egypt.

4 "For seven days no leaven shall be seen with you in all your territory, and [a]none of the flesh which you sacrifice on the evening of the first day shall remain overnight until morning.

5 "You are not allowed to sacrifice the Passover in any of your [1]towns which the LORD your God is giving you;

6 but [a]at the place where the LORD your God chooses to establish His name, you shall sacrifice the Passover in the evening at sunset, at the time that you came out of Egypt.

7 "And you shall [a]cook and eat *it* in the place which the LORD your God chooses. And in the morning you are to return to your tents.

8 "Six days you shall eat unleavened bread, and [a]on the seventh day there shall be [b]a solemn assembly to the LORD your God; you shall do no work *on it*.

9 "[a]You shall count seven weeks for yourself; you shall begin to count seven weeks from the time you begin to put the sickle to the standing grain.

10 "Then you shall [1]celebrate the Feast of Weeks to the LORD your God with a tribute of a freewill offering of your hand, which you shall give just as the LORD your God blesses you;

11 and you shall [a]rejoice before the LORD your God, you and your son and your daughter and your male and female servants and [b]the Levite who is in your [1]town, and [c]the stranger and the [2]orphan and the widow who are in your midst, in the place where the LORD your God chooses to establish His name.

12 "And [a]you shall remember that you were a slave in Egypt, and you shall be careful to observe these statutes.

13 "[a]You shall [1]celebrate the Feast of Booths seven days after you have gathered in from your threshing floor and your wine vat;

14 and you shall [a]rejoice in your feast, you and your son and your daughter and your male and female servants and the Levite and the stranger and the [1]orphan and the widow who are in your [2]towns.

15 "Seven days you shall celebrate a feast to the LORD your God in the place which the LORD chooses, because the LORD your God will bless you in all your produce and in all the work of your hands, so that you shall be altogether joyful.

16 "[a]Three times in a year all your males shall appear before the LORD your God in the place which He chooses, at the Feast of Unleavened Bread and at the Feast of Weeks and at the Feast of Booths, and [b]they shall not appear before the LORD empty-handed.

17 "Every man [1]shall give as he is able, according to the blessing of the LORD your God which He has given you.

18 "You shall appoint for yourself judges and officers in all your [1]towns which the LORD your God is giving you, according to your tribes, and they shall judge the people with righteous judgment.

19 "[a]You shall not distort justice; [b]you shall not [1]be partial, and [c]you shall not take a bribe, for a bribe blinds the eyes of the wise and perverts the words of the righteous.

3 [a]Ex. 12:8, 13:3; 34:18

4 [a]Ex. 12:8,

5 [1]Lit., *gates*

6 [a]Deut. 12:5

7 [a]Ex. 12:8; 2

8 [a]Num. 28:2 12:16; 13:6; L 23:8, 36

9 [a]Ex. 23:16; Lev. 23:15; Nu

10 [1]Lit., *perfo*

11 [1]Lit., *gates fatherless* [a]De [b]Deut. 12:12 [c] 14:29

12 [a]Deut. 15:1

13 [1]Lit., *perforr* 23:34-43

14 [1]Or, *fatherle gates* [a]Deut. 16

16 [a]Ex. 23:14-1 34:23, 24 [b]Ex. 3

17 [1]Lit., *accordi the gift of his ha*

18 [1]Lit., *gates*

19 [1]Lit., *regard persons* [a]Ex. 23 19:15; Deut. 1:17 10:17 [b]Prov. 24:2 23:8; Prov. 17:23 7:7

20 "Justice, *and only* justice, you shall pursue, that [a]you may live and
possess the land which the LORD your God is giving you.
21 "[a]You shall not plant for yourself an [1]Asherah of any kind of tree
beside the altar of the LORD your God, which you shall make for
yourself.
22 "[a]Neither shall you set up for yourself a *sacred* pillar which the
LORD your God hates.

Chapter 17

17 "[a]You shall not sacrifice to the LORD your God an ox or a
sheep which has a blemish or any [1]defect, for that is a detest-
able thing to the LORD your God.
2 "[a]If there is found in your midst, in any of your [1]towns, which the
LORD your God is giving you, a man or a woman who does what is
evil in the sight of the LORD your God, by transgressing His cove-
nant,
3 and has gone and [a]served other gods and worshiped them, [b]or
the sun or the moon or any of the heavenly host, [c]which I have not
commanded,
4 and if it is told you and you have heard of it, then you shall
inquire thoroughly. And behold, if it is true and the thing certain that
this detestable thing has been done in Israel,
5 then you shall bring out that man or that woman who has done
this evil deed, to your gates, *that is,* the man or the woman, and [a]you
shall stone them to [1]death.
6 "[a]On the [1]evidence of two witnesses or three witnesses, he who is
to die shall be put to death; he shall not be put to death on the
[1]evidence of one witness.
7 "[a]The hand of the witnesses shall be first against him to put him
to death, and afterward the hand of all the people. [b]So you shall
purge the evil from your midst.
8 "[a]If any case is too difficult for you to decide, between [1]one kind
of homicide or another, between [2]one kind of lawsuit or another, and
between [3]one kind of assault or another, being cases of dispute in
your [4]courts, then you shall arise and go up to [b]the place which the
LORD your God chooses.
9 "So you shall come to [a]the Levitical priest or the judge who is *in
office* in those days, and you shall inquire *of them,* and they will
declare to you the verdict in the case.
10 "And you shall do according to the [1]terms of the verdict which
they declare to you from that place which the LORD chooses; and you
shall be careful to observe according to all that they teach you.
11 "[a]According to the [1]terms of the law which they teach you, and
according to the verdict which they tell you, you shall do; you shall
not turn aside from the word which they declare to you, to the right
or the left.
12 "And the man who acts [a]presumptuously by not listening to the
priest who stands there to serve the LORD your God, nor to the judge,
that man shall die; thus you shall purge the evil from Israel.
13 "Then all the people will hear and be afraid, and will not act
[a]presumptuously again.
14 "When you enter the land which the LORD your God gives you,
and you [a]possess it and live in it, and you say, '[b]I will set a king over
me like all the nations who are around me,'

20 [a]Deut. 4:1
[1]I.e., wooden ...ol of a female ...ut. 7:5; 2 Kin. ...3; 2 Chr. 33:3
22 [a]Lev. 26:1
[1]Lit., *evil thing* [a]Deut. 15:21
..., *gates* [a]Deut. 13:6-11
...Ex. 22:20 [b]Job ...-28 [c]Jer. 7:22
...Lit., *death with ...es* [a]Lev. 24:14; Josh. 7:25
..., *mouth* [a]Num. ...30; Deut. 19:15; ...:16; John 8:17; ...:1; 1 Tim. 5:19; Heb. 10:28
...ev. 24:14; Deut. ...:9 [b]1 Cor. 5:13
..., *blood to blood* ...Lit., *judgment to ...nt* [3]Lit., *stroke to ...roke* [4]Lit., *gates* ...Chr. 19:10; Hag. ... [b]Deut. 12:5; Ps. 122:5
9 [a]Deut. 19:17
10 [1]Lit., *mouth*
...it., *mouth* [a]Deut. 25:1
...Num. 15:30; Deut. 17:13; 18:20; Hos. 4:4
13 [a]Deut. 17:12
...Deut. 11:31; Josh. ...3 [b]1 Sam. 8:5, 19, 20; 10:19

15 you shall surely set a king over you whom the LORD your God
chooses, *one* [a]from among your [1]countrymen you shall set as king
over yourselves; you may not put a foreigner over yourselves who is
not your [1]countryman.
16 "[a]Moreover, he shall not multiply horses for himself, nor shall he
[b]cause the people to return to Egypt to multiply horses, since [c]the
LORD has said to you, 'You shall never again return that way.'
17 "[a]Neither shall he multiply wives for himself, [1]lest his heart turn
away; nor shall he greatly increase silver and gold for himself.
18 "Now it shall come about when he sits on the throne of his king-
dom, he shall write for himself a copy of this law on a scroll [1a]in the
presence of the Levitical priests.
19 "And it shall be with him, and he shall read it [a]all the days of his
life, that he may learn to fear the LORD his God, [1]by carefully observ-
ing all the words of this law and these statutes,
20 that his heart may not be lifted up above his [1]countrymen [a]and
that he may not turn aside from the commandment, to the right or
the left; in order that he and his sons may continue long in his
kingdom in the midst of Israel.

Chapter 18

18 "[a]The Levitical priests, the whole tribe of Levi, shall have no
portion or inheritance with Israel; they shall eat the LORD's
offerings by fire and His [1]portion.
2 "[a]And they shall have no inheritance among their [1]countrymen;
the LORD is their inheritance, as He [2]promised them.
3 "[a]Now this shall be the priests' due from the people, from those
who offer a sacrifice, either an ox or a sheep, of which they shall give
to the priest the shoulder and the two cheeks and the stomach.
4 "You shall give him the [a]first fruits of your grain, your new wine,
and your oil, and the first shearing of your sheep.
5 "[a]For the LORD your God has chosen him and his sons from all
your tribes, to [b]stand [1]and serve in the name of the LORD forever.
6 "Now if a Levite comes from any of your [1]towns throughout Isra-
el where he [a]resides, and comes [2]whenever he desires to the place
which the LORD chooses,
7 then he shall serve in the name of the LORD his God, like all his
fellow Levites who stand there before the LORD.
8 "[a]They shall eat [1]equal portions, except *what they receive* from the
sale of their fathers' *estates.*
9 "When you enter the land which the LORD your God gives you,
you shall not learn to [1a]imitate the detestable things of those nations.
10 "There shall not be found among you anyone [a]who makes his son
or his daughter pass through the fire, one who uses divination, one
[b]who practices witchcraft, or one who interprets omens, or a sorcerer,
11 or one who casts a spell, [a]or a medium, or a spiritist, or one who
calls up the dead.
12 "For whoever does these things is detestable to the LORD; and
[a]because of these detestable things the LORD your God will drive
them out before you.
13 "[a]You shall be [1]blameless before the LORD your God.
14 "For those nations, which you shall dispossess, listen to those
who [a]practice witchcraft and to diviners, but as for you, the LORD
your God has not allowed you *to do* so.

15 [1]Lit., *broth*
30:21

16 [a]1 Kin. 4:2
10:26-29; Ps.
31:1; Ezek. 17
13:17, 18; Hos

17 [1]Lit., *nor* [a]
5:13; 12:11; 1
11:3, 4

18 [1]Lit., *from t*
[a]Deut. 31:24-2

19 [1]Lit., *to kee*
them [a]Deut. 4:
Josh. 1:8

20 [1]Lit., *brothe*
[a]Deut. 5:32; 1

18:1 [1]Or, *inher*
[a]Deut. 10:9; 1 C

2 [1]Lit., *brothers*
spoke to [a]Num

3 [a]Lev. 7:32-34
18:11, 12

4 [a]Num. 18:12

5 [1]Lit., *to* [a]Ex. 2
[b]Deut. 10:8

6 [1]Lit., *gates* [2]L
all the desire of
[a]Num. 35:2, 3

8 [1]Lit., *portion li*
portion [a]Lev. 27:
Num. 18:21-24;
31:4; Neh. 12:44

9 [1]Lit., *do accor*
[a]Deut. 9:5

10 [a]Deut. 12:31
22:18; Lev. 19:26
20:6; Jer. 27:9, 10
3:5

11 [a]Lev. 19:31

12 [a]Lev. 18:24

13 [1]Lit., *complete*
perfect; or, *having*
integrity [a]Gen. 6:
17:1; Matt. 5:48

14 [a]2 Kin. 21:6

15 "[a]The LORD your God will raise up for you a prophet like me from
among you, from your [1]countrymen, you shall listen to him.
16 "This is [a]according to all that you asked of the LORD your God in
Horeb on the day of the assembly, saying, 'Let me not hear again the
voice of the LORD my God, let me not see this great fire anymore, lest
I die.'
17 "[a]And the LORD said to me, 'They have [1]spoken well.
18 'I will raise up a prophet from among their [1]countrymen like
you, and [a]I will put My words in his mouth, and [b]he shall speak to
them all that I command him.
19 '[a]And it shall come about that whoever will not listen to My
words which he shall speak in My name, I Myself will require *it* of
him.
20 'But the prophet who shall speak a word [a]presumptuously in My
name which I have not commanded him to speak, or [b]which he shall
speak in the name of other gods, [1]that prophet shall die.'
21 "And [1]you may say in your heart, 'How shall we know the word
which the LORD has not spoken?'
22 "[a]When a prophet speaks in the name of the LORD, if the thing
does not come about or come true, that is the thing which the LORD
has not spoken. The prophet has spoken it [b]presumptuously; you
shall not be afraid of him.

Chapter 19

19 "[a]When the LORD your God cuts off the nations, whose land
the LORD your God gives you, and you dispossess them and
settle in their cities and in their houses,
2 [a]you shall set aside three cities for yourself in the midst of your
land, which the LORD your God gives you to [1]possess.
3 "You shall prepare the [1]roads for yourself, and divide into three
parts the territory of your land, which the LORD your God will give
you as a possession, [2]so that any manslayer may flee there.
4 "[a]Now this is the case of the manslayer who may flee there and
live: when he [1]kills his friend [2]unintentionally, [3]not hating him
previously—
5 as when *a man* goes into the forest with his friend to cut wood,
and his hand [1]swings the axe to cut down the tree, and the iron *head*
slips off the [2]handle and [3]strikes his friend so that he dies—he may
flee to one of these cities and live;
6 lest the avenger of blood pursue the manslayer [1]in the heat of his
anger, and overtake him, because the way is long, and [2]take his life,
though he was not deserving of death, since he had not hated him
previously.
7 "Therefore, I command you, saying, 'You shall set aside three
cities for yourself.'
8 "And if the LORD your God [a]enlarges your territory, just as He has
sworn to your fathers, and gives you all the land which He
[1]promised to give your fathers—
9 if you [1]carefully observe all this commandment, which I com-
mand you today, [a]to love the LORD your God, and to walk in His
ways always—[b]then you shall add three more cities for yourself,
besides these three.

thers [a]Matt. uke 2:25-34;); John 1:21, ts 3:22; 7:37
18, 19; Deut. 5:23-27
ne well what have spoken [a]Deut. 5:28
brothers [a]Is. n 17:8 [b]John 28; 12:49, 50
cts 3:23; Heb. 12:25
nd that [a]Deut. [b]Deut. 13:1, 4; Zech. 13:3
Lit., *if you say*
er. 28:9 [b]Deut. 18:20
[a]Deut. 6:10, 11
Lit., *possess it* :41; Josh. 20:2
oad [2]Lit., *and it all be for every er to flee there*
it., *smites* [2]Lit., *nowledge* [3]Lit., *was not hating eviously* [a]Num. 35:9-34
it., *is thrust with wood* [3]Lit., *finds*
while his heart is Lit., *smite him in the soul*
Lit., *spoke* [a]Gen. 15:18
keep . . . to do it 6:5 [b]Josh. 20:7

10 "So innocent blood will not be shed in the midst of your land
which the LORD your God gives you as an inheritance, and
[a]bloodguiltiness be on you.
11 "But [a]if there is a man who hates his neighbor and lies in wait for
him and rises up against him and strikes [1]him so that he dies, and he
flees to one of these cities,
12 then the elders of his city shall send and take him from there and
deliver him into the hand of the avenger of blood, that he may die.
13 "[1a]You shall not pity him, but [b]you shall purge the blood of the
innocent from Israel, that it may go well with you.
14 "[a]You shall not move your neighbor's boundary mark, which the
ancestors have set, in your inheritance which you shall inherit in the
land that the LORD your God gives you to [1]possess.
15 "[a]A single witness shall not rise up against a man on account of
any iniquity or any sin [1]which he has committed; on the [2]evidence of
two or three witnesses a matter shall be confirmed.
16 "[a]If a malicious witness rises up against a man to [1]accuse him of
[2]wrongdoing,
17 then both the men who have the dispute shall stand [a]before the
LORD, before the priests and the judges who will be *in office* in those
days.
18 "And the judges [a]shall investigate thoroughly; and if the witness
is a false witness *and* he has [1]accused his brother falsely,
19 then [a]you shall do to him just as he had intended to do to his
brother. Thus you shall purge the evil from among you.
20 "And [a]the rest will hear and be afraid, and will never again do
such an evil thing among you.
21 "Thus [1a]you shall not show pity: [b]life for life, [c]eye for eye, tooth for
tooth, hand for hand, foot for foot.

Chapter 20

20 "When you go out to battle against your enemies and see
[a]horses and chariots *and* people more numerous than you, [b]do
not be afraid of them; for the LORD your God, who brought you up
from the land of Egypt, is with you.
2 "Now it shall come about that when you are approaching the
battle, the priest shall come near and speak to the people.
3 "And he shall say to them, 'Hear, O Israel, you are approaching
the battle against your enemies today. Do not be fainthearted. [a]Do
not be afraid, or panic, or tremble before them,
4 for the LORD your God [a]is the one who goes with you, to fight for
you against your enemies, to save you.'
5 "The officers also shall speak to the people, saying, 'Who is the
man that has built a new house and has not [a]dedicated it? Let him
depart and return to his house, lest he die in the battle and another
man dedicate it.
6 'And who is the man that has planted a vineyard and has not
[1]begun to use its fruit? Let him depart and return to his house, lest
he die in the battle and another man [1]begin to use its fruit.
7 '[a]And who is the man that is engaged to a woman and has not
[1]married her? Let him depart and return to his house, lest he die in
the battle and another man [2]marry her.'

10 [a]Num. 3
21:1-9

11 [1]Lit., *hir*
[a]Ex. 21:12;
1 John 3:15

13 [1]Lit., *Yo*
[a]Deut. 7:2

14 [1]Lit., *pos*
[a]Deut. 27:17
Prov. 22:28;

15 [1]Lit., *in a*
which he sin
mouth of two
or by the mo
three [a]Num.
Deut. 17:6;
John 8:17; 2
1 Tim. 5:19;

16 [1]Lit., *test*
[2]Lit., *turning*
23:1; Ps. 27:

17 [a]Deut. 17

18 [1]Lit., *testi*
against [a]Deu

19 [a]Prov. 19:

20 [a]Deut. 17:

21 [1]Lit., *your*
[a]Deut. 19:13
21:23; Lev. 24
5:38

20:1 [a]Deut. 3:
31:6, 8; Ps. 20
31:1 [b]2 Chr. 3
23:4; Is. 41:10

3 [a]Deut. 20:1;
23:10

4 [a]Deut. 1:30;
Josh. 23:10

5 [a]Neh. 12:27

6 [1]Lit., *treat(ed*
common

7 [1]Lit., *taken* [2]
[a]Deut. 24:5

8 "Then the officers shall speak further to the people, and they shall
say, '[a]Who is the man that is afraid and fainthearted? Let him depart
and return to his house, so that [1]he might not make his brothers'
hearts melt like his heart.'
9 "And it shall come about that when the officers have finished
speaking to the people, they shall appoint commanders of armies at
the head of the people.
10 "When you approach a city to fight against it, you shall [1]offer it
terms of peace.
11 "And it shall come about, if it [1]agrees to make peace with you and
opens to you, then it shall be that all the people who are found in it
shall become your [a]forced labor and shall serve you.
12 "However, if it does not make peace with you, but makes war
against you, then you shall besiege it.
13 "When the LORD your God gives it into your hand, [a]you shall
strike all the [1]men in it with the edge of the sword.
14 "Only the women and the children and [a]the animals and all that is
in the city, all its spoil, you shall take as booty for yourself; and you
shall [1]use the spoil of your enemies which the LORD your God has
given you.
15 "Thus you shall do to all the cities that are very far from you,
which are not of the cities of these nations [1]nearby.
16 "[a]Only in the cities of these peoples that the LORD your God is
giving you as an inheritance, you shall not leave alive anything that
breathes.
17 "But you shall [1]utterly destroy them, the Hittite and the Amorite,
the Canaanite and the Perizzite, the Hivite and the Jebusite, as the
LORD your God has commanded you,
18 in order that they may not teach you to do [a]according to all their
detestable things which they have done for their gods, so that you
would [b]sin against the LORD your God.
19 "When you besiege a city a long time, to make war against it in
order to capture it, you shall not destroy its trees by swinging an axe
against them; for you may eat from them, and you shall not cut them
down. [1]For is the tree of the field a man, that it should [2]be besieged
by you?
20 "Only the trees which you know [1]are not fruit trees you shall
destroy and cut down, that you may construct siegeworks against
the city that is making war with you until it falls.

Chapter 21

21 "If a slain person is found lying in the open country in the
land which the LORD your God gives you to [1]possess, *and* it is
not known who has struck him,
2 then your elders and your judges shall go out and measure *the
distance* to the cities which are around the slain one.
3 "And it shall be that the city which is nearest to the slain man,
that is, the elders of that city, shall take a heifer of the herd, which
has not been worked and which has not pulled in a yoke;
4 and the elders of that city shall bring the heifer down to a valley
with running water, which has not been plowed or sown, and shall
break the heifer's neck there in the valley.
5 "Then [a]the priests, the sons of Levi, shall come near, for the LORD
your God has chosen them to serve Him and to bless in the name of

Gr. and other rsions [a]Judg. 7:3
it., *call to it for peace*
[1]Lit., *answers* e [a]1 Kin. 9:21
males [a]Num. 31:7
eat [a]Josh. 8:2
15 [1]Lit., *here*
23:31-33; Num. , 3; Deut. 7:1-5; Josh. 11:14
put them under the ban
34:12-16; Deut. ; 12:30, 31 [b]Ex. ; 2 Kin. 21:3-15; Ps. 106:34-41
19 [1]Read as interrogative with nt versions [2]Lit., *before you in the siege*
[1]Lit., *they are not trees for food*
1 [1]Lit., *possess it*
ut. 17:9-11; 19:17; 1 Chr. 23:13

the LORD; and every dispute and every [1]assault [2]shall be settled by
them.
6 "And all the elders of that city [1]which is nearest to the slain man
shall [a]wash their hands over the heifer whose neck was broken in the
valley;
7 and they shall answer and say, 'Our hands have not shed this
blood, nor did our eyes see *it*.
8 '[1]Forgive Thy people Israel whom Thou hast redeemed, O LORD,
and do not place the guilt of [a]innocent blood in the midst of Thy
people Israel.' And the bloodguiltiness shall be [2]forgiven them.
9 "[a]So you shall remove the guilt of innocent blood from your
midst, when you do what is right in the eyes of the LORD.
10 "When you go out to battle against your enemies, and [a]the LORD
your God delivers them into your hands, and you take them away
captive,
11 and see among the captives a beautiful woman, and have a
desire for her and would take her as a wife for yourself,
12 then you shall bring her home to your house, and she shall
[a]shave her head and [1]trim her nails.
13 "She shall also [1]remove the clothes of her captivity and shall
remain in your house, and [a]mourn her father and mother a full
month; and after that you may go in to her and be her husband and
she shall be your wife.
14 "And it shall be, if you are not pleased with her, then you shall let
her go [1]wherever she wishes; but you shall certainly not sell her for
money, you shall not [2]mistreat her, because you have [a]humbled her.
15 "If a man has two wives, the one loved and [a]the other [1]unloved,
and *both* the loved and the [1]unloved have borne him sons, if the
first-born son belongs to the [1]unloved,
16 then it shall be in the day he [1]wills what he has to his sons, he
cannot make the son of the loved the first-born before the son of the
[2]unloved, who is the first-born.
17 "But he shall acknowledge the first-born, the son of the [1]unloved,
by giving him a double portion of all that [2]he has, for he is the
[a]beginning of his strength; [b]to him belongs the right of the first-born.
18 "If any man has a stubborn and rebellious son who will [a]not obey
his father or his mother, and when they chastise him, he will not
even listen to them,
19 then his father and mother shall seize him, and bring him out to
the elders of his city [1]at the gateway of his home town.
20 "And they shall say to the elders of his city, 'This son of ours is
stubborn and rebellious, he will not obey us, he is a glutton and a
drunkard.'
21 "[a]Then all the men of his city shall stone him to death; so [b]you
shall remove the evil from your midst, and [c]all Israel shall hear *of it*
and fear.
22 "And if a man has committed a sin [a]worthy of death, and he is
put to death, and you hang him on a tree,
23 [a]his corpse shall not hang all night on the tree, but you shall
surely bury him on the same day (for [b]he who is hanged is [1]accursed
of God), so that you [c]do not defile your land which the LORD your
God gives you as an inheritance.

5 [1]Lit., *strok* *shall be acc* *their mouth*

6 [1]Lit., *who* 27:24

8 [1]Lit., *Cove* *atone for* [2]Li *over, atoned* 35:33, 34; Jo

9 [a]Deut. 19:1

10 [a]Josh. 21.

12 [1]Lit., *do* [a] 9; Num. 6:9

13 [1]Lit., *remo* *her* [a]Ps. 45:1

14 [1]Lit., *accor* *her soul* [2]Or, [a]Gen. 34:2

15 [1]Lit., *hated* 29:33

16 [1]Lit., *make* *inherit* [2]Lit., *ha*

17 [1]Lit., *hated* *found with him* 49:3 [b]Gen. 25:

18 [a]Ex. 20:12; 19:3; Prov. 1:8; 6:1-3

19 [1]Lit., *and to* *of his place*

21 [a]Lev. 20:2, 2 24:14-23; Num. 36 [b]Deut. 19:19 13:11

22 [a]Deut. 22:26 26:66; Mark 14:6 23:29

23 [1]Lit., *the curs* *God* [a]Josh. 8:29 27; John 19:31 [b] 3:13 [c]Lev. 18:25 35:34

Chapter 22

22 "[a]You shall not see your [1]countryman's ox or his sheep stray-
ing away, and [2]pay no attention to them; you shall certainly
bring them back to your countryman.
2 "And if your countryman is not near you, or if you do not know
him, then you shall bring it home to your house, and it shall remain
with you until your countryman looks for it; then you shall restore it
to him.
3 "And thus you shall do with his donkey, and you shall do the
same with his garment, and you shall do likewise with anything lost
by your countryman, which he has lost and you have found. You are
not allowed to [1]neglect *them*.
4 "You shall not see your countryman's donkey or his ox fallen
down on the way, and [1]pay no attention to them; you shall certainly
help him to raise *them* up.
5 "A woman shall not wear man's clothing, nor shall a man put on
a woman's clothing; for whoever does these things is an abomina-
tion to the LORD your God.
6 "If you happen to come upon a bird's nest along the way, in any
tree or on the ground, with young ones or eggs, and the mother
sitting on the young or on the eggs, [a]you shall not take the mother
with the young;
7 you shall certainly let the mother go, but the young you may
take for yourself, [a]in order that it may be well with you, and that you
may prolong your days.
8 "When you build a new house, you shall make a parapet for your
roof, that you may not bring bloodguilt on your house if anyone falls
from it.
9 "[a]You shall not sow your vineyard with two kinds of seed, lest [1]all
the produce of the seed which you have sown, and the increase of
the vineyard become defiled.
10 "[a]You shall not plow with an ox and a donkey together.
11 "[a]You shall not wear a material mixed of wool and linen together.
12 "[a]You shall make yourself tassels on the four corners of your gar-
ment with which you cover yourself.
13 "[a]If any man takes a wife and goes in to her and *then* [1]turns
against her,
14 and charges her with shameful deeds and [1]publicly defames her,
and says, 'I took this woman, *but* when I came near her, I did not
find her a virgin,'
15 then the girl's father and her mother shall take and bring out the
evidence of the girl's virginity to the elders of the city at the gate.
16 "And the girl's father shall say to the elders, 'I gave my daughter
to this man for a wife, but he [1]turned against her;
17 and behold, he has charged her with shameful deeds, saying, "I
did not find your daughter a virgin." But [1]this is the *evidence* of my
daughter's virginity.' And they shall spread the garment before the
elders of the city.
18 "So [a]the elders of that city shall take the man and chastise him,
19 and they shall fine him a hundred *shekels* of silver and give it to
the girl's father, because he [1]publicly defamed a virgin of Israel. And
she shall remain his wife; he cannot [2]divorce her all his days.
20 "But if this [1a]charge is true, that the girl was not found a virgin,
21 then they shall bring out the girl to the doorway of her father's

1 [1]Lit., *brother*, and so through v. 4 [2]Lit., *yourself from them* [a]Ex. 23:4, 5; Prov. 27:10; Zech. 7:9
3 [1]Lit., *hide yourself*
4 [1]Lit., *hide yourself from them*
6 [a]Lev. 22:28
7 [a]Deut. 4:40
9 [1]Lit., *the fulness* [a]Lev. 19:19
10 [a]2 Cor. 6:14-16
11 [a]Lev. 19:19
12 [a]Num. 15:37-41; Matt. 23:5
13 [1]Lit., *hates her* [a]...29:21; Deut. 24:1; Judg. 15:1
14 [1]Lit., *causes an evil name to go out against her*
16 [1]Lit., *hated her*
17 [1]Lit., *these are*
18 [a]Ex. 18:21; Deut. 1:9-18
19 [1]Lit., *caused an evil name to go out against a virgin* [2]Lit., *send her away*
20 [1]Lit., *matter* [a]Deut. 17:4

house, and the men of her city shall stone her [1]to death because she has [a]committed an act of folly in Israel, by playing the harlot in her father's house; thus [b]you shall purge the evil from among you.

22 "[a]If a man is found lying with a married woman, then both of them shall die, the man who lay with the woman, and the woman; thus you shall purge the evil from Israel.

23 "[a]If there is a girl who is a virgin engaged to a man, and *another* man finds her in the city and lies with her,

24 then you shall bring them both out to the gate of that city and you shall stone them [1]to death; the girl, because she did not cry out in the city, and the man, because he has violated his neighbor's wife. Thus you shall purge the evil from among you.

25 "But if in the field the man finds the girl who is engaged, and the man forces her and lies with her, then only the man who lies with her shall die.

26 "But you shall do nothing to the girl; there is no sin in the girl worthy of death, for just as a man rises against his neighbor and murders him, so is this case.

27 "When he found her in the field, the engaged girl cried out, but there was no one to save her.

28 "[a]If a man finds a girl who is a virgin, who is not engaged, and seizes her and lies with her and they are discovered,

29 then the man who lay with her shall give to the girl's father fifty *shekels* of silver, and she shall become his wife because he has violated her; he cannot divorce her all his days.

30 "[1a]A man shall not take his father's wife so that he shall not uncover his father's skirt.

Chapter 23

23 "[a]No one who is [1]emasculated, or has his male organ cut off, shall enter the assembly of the LORD.

2 "No one of illegitimate birth shall enter the assembly of the LORD; none of his *descendants,* even to the tenth generation, shall enter the assembly of the LORD.

3 "[a]No Ammonite or Moabite shall enter the assembly of the LORD; none of their *descendants,* even to the tenth generation, shall ever enter the assembly of the LORD,

4 [a]because they did not meet you with [1]food and water on the way when you came out of Egypt, and because they hired against you [b]Balaam the son of Beor from Pethor of [2]Mesopotamia, to curse you.

5 "Nevertheless, the LORD your God was not willing to listen to Balaam, but the LORD your God [a]turned the curse into a blessing for you because the LORD your God [b]loves you.

6 "[a]You shall never seek their peace or their prosperity all your days.

7 "You shall not detest an Edomite, for [a]he is your brother; you shall not detest an Egyptian, [b]because you were an alien in his land.

8 "The sons of the third generation who are born to them may enter the assembly of the LORD.

9 "When you go out as [1]an army against your enemies, then you shall keep yourself from every evil thing.

10 "[a]If there is among you any man who is unclean because of a nocturnal emission, then he must go outside the camp; he may not [1]reenter the camp.

21 [1]Lit., *with stor* *that she dies* [a]Ge 34:7; Lev. 19:29; Deut. 23:17, 18; J 20:5-10; 2 Sam. 1 13 [b]Deut. 13:5; 1 19:19

22 [a]Lev. 20:10; E 16:38; Matt. 5:27, John 8:5; 1 Cor. 6 Heb. 13:4

23 [a]Lev. 19:20-2 1:18, 19

24 [1]Lit., *with stor* *that they die*

28 [a]Ex. 22:16

30 [1]Ch. 23:1 in H [a]Lev. 18:8; 20:11; 27:20; 1 Cor. 5:1

23:1 [1]Lit., *wounc* *crushing* of testicl [a]Lev. 21:20; 22:2

3 [a]Neh. 13:1, 2

4 [1]Lit., *bread* [2]H *Aram-naharaim* 13:2 [b]Num. 22:5, Josh. 24:9; 2 Pet. Jude 11

5 [a]Prov. 26:2 [b]D 4:37

6 [a]Ezra 9:12

7 [a]Gen. 25:24-26 Obad. 10, 12 [b]E 22:21; 23:9; Lev. Deut. 10:19

9 [1]Or, *a camp*

10 [1]Lit., *come to* *midst of* [a]Lev. 15

[1]Lit., come to the midst of
[1]Lit., peg [2]Lit., and
14 [1]Lit., give [2]Lit., edness of anything t., and [a]Lev. 26:12 [b]Ex. 3:5
15 [1]Lit., delivered self [a]1 Sam. 30:15
6 [1]Lit., gates [a]Ex. 22:21; Prov. 22:22
[a]Lev. 19:29; Deut. 22:21 [b]Gen. 19:5; 2 Kin. 23:7
e., male prostitute, omite [a]Lev. 18:22; 20:13
[1]Lit., brothers [a]Ex. :25; Lev. 25:35-37; eh. 5:2-7; Ps. 15:5
[1]Lit., brother [2]Lit., utting forth of your d [3]Lit., possess it eut. 28:12 [b]Deut. 15:10
21 [1]Lit., for [a]Num. , 2; Job 22:27; Ps. Eccl. 5:4, 5; Matt. 5:33
[1]Lit., spoken with your mouth
[1]Lit., according to satisfaction of your soul [2]Or, vessel
[a]Matt. 12:1; Mark 2:23; Luke 6:1
4:1 [1]Lit., if [a]Num. 5:12, 28; Deut. 13-21 [b]Matt. 5:31; :7-9; Mark 10:4, 5
3 [1]Lit., hates her
4 [a]Jer. 3:1

11 "But it shall be when evening approaches, he shall bathe himself
with water, and at sundown he may [1]reenter the camp.
12 "You shall also have a place outside the camp and go out there,
13 and you shall have a [1]spade among your tools, and it shall be
when you sit down outside, you shall dig with it and shall turn [2]to
cover up your excrement.
14 "Since [a]the LORD your God walks in the midst of your camp to
deliver you and to [1]defeat your enemies before you, therefore your
camp must be [b]holy; and He must not see [2]anything indecent among
you [3]lest He turn away from you.
15 "[a]You shall not hand over to his master a slave who has [1]escaped
from his master to you.
16 "He shall live with you in your midst, in the place which he shall
choose in one of your [1]towns where it pleases him; [a]you shall not
mistreat him.
17 "[a]None of the daughters of Israel shall be a cult prostitute, [b]nor
shall any of the sons of Israel be a cult prostitute.
18 "You shall not bring the hire of a harlot or the wages of a [1a]dog
into the house of the LORD your God for any votive offering, for both
of these are an abomination to the LORD your God.
19 "[a]You shall not charge interest to your [1]countrymen: interest on
money, food, *or* anything that may be loaned at interest.
20 "[a]You may charge interest to a foreigner, but to your [1]countryman
you shall not charge interest, so that [b]the LORD your God may bless
you in all [2]that you undertake in the land which you are about to
enter to [3]possess.
21 "[a]When you make a vow to the LORD your God, you shall not
delay to pay it, for it would be sin in you, [1]and the LORD your God
will surely require it of you.
22 "However, if you refrain from vowing, it would not be sin in you.
23 "You shall be careful to perform what goes out from your lips,
just as you have voluntarily vowed to the LORD your God, what you
have [1]promised.
24 "When you enter your neighbor's vineyard, then you may eat
grapes [1]until you are fully satisfied, but you shall not put any in
your [2]basket.
25 "[a]When you enter your neighbor's standing grain, then you may
pluck the heads with your hand, but you shall not wield a sickle in
your neighbor's standing grain.

Chapter 24

24 "When a man takes a wife and marries her, and it happens
[1]that she finds no favor in his eyes because he has found some
[a]indecency in her, and [b]he writes her a certificate of divorce and puts
it in her hand and sends her out from his house,
2 and she leaves his house and goes and becomes another man's
wife,
3 and if the latter husband [1]turns against her and writes her a
certificate of divorce and puts *it* in her hand and sends her out of his
house, or if the latter husband dies who took her to be his wife,
4 *then* her [a]former husband who sent her away is not allowed to
take her again to be his wife, since she has been defiled; for that is an
abomination before the LORD, and you shall not bring sin on the land
which the LORD your God gives you as an inheritance.

5 "[a]When a man takes a new wife, he shall not go out with the
army, nor be charged with any duty; he shall be free at home one
year and shall [b]give happiness to his wife whom he has taken.
6 "No one shall take a handmill or an upper millstone in pledge, for
he would be taking a life in pledge.
7 "[a]If a man is [1]caught kidnapping any of his [2]countrymen of the
sons of Israel, and he deals with him violently, or sells him, then that
thief shall die; so you shall purge the evil from among you.
8 "[a]Be careful against [1]an infection of leprosy, that you diligently
observe and do according to all that the Levitical priests shall teach
you; as I have commanded them, so you shall be careful to do.
9 "Remember what the LORD your God did [a]to Miriam on the way
as you came out of Egypt.
10 "[a]When you make your neighbor a loan of any sort, you shall not
enter his house to take his pledge.
11 "You shall remain outside, and the man to whom you make the
loan shall bring the pledge out to you.
12 "And if he is a poor man, you shall not sleep with his pledge.
13 "[a]When the sun goes down you shall surely return the pledge to
him, that he may sleep in his cloak and bless you; and [b]it will be
righteousness for you before the LORD your God.
14 "[a]You shall not oppress a hired servant *who is* poor and needy,
whether *he is* one of your [1]countrymen or one of your aliens who is
in your land in your [2]towns.
15 "[a]You shall give him his wages on his day [1]before the sun sets, for
he is poor and sets his [2]heart on it; so that [b]he may not cry against
you to the LORD and it become sin in you.
16 "[a]Fathers shall not be put to death [1]for *their* sons, nor shall sons be
put to death [1]for *their* fathers; everyone shall be put to death for his
own sin.
17 "[a]You shall not pervert the justice [1]due an alien *or* [2]an orphan, nor
[b]take a widow's garment in pledge.
18 "But you shall remember that you were a slave in Egypt, and that
the LORD your God redeemed you from there; therefore I am com-
manding you to do this thing.
19 "[a]When you reap your harvest in your field and have forgotten a
sheaf in the field, you shall not go back to get it; it shall be [b]for the
alien, for the [1]orphan, and for the widow, in order that the LORD your
God [c]may bless you in all the work of your hands.
20 "[a]When you beat your olive tree, you shall not go over the boughs
[1]again; it shall be [b]for the alien, for the [2]orphan, and for the widow.
21 "When you gather the grapes of your vineyard, you shall not [1]go
over it again; it shall be for the alien, for the [2]orphan, and for the
widow.
22 "And you shall remember that you were a slave in the land of
Egypt; therefore I am commanding you to do this thing.

Chapter 25

25 "[a]If there is a dispute between men and they go to [1]court, and
[2]the judges decide their case, [b]and they justify the righteous
and condemn the wicked,
2 then it shall be if the wicked man [1a]deserves to be beaten, the
judge shall then make him lie down and be beaten in his presence
with the number of stripes according to his [2]guilt.

5 [a]Deut. 20:7 [b]P
5:18

7 [1]Lit., *found ste*
[2]Lit., *brothers* [a]E

8 [1]Lit., *a mark o*
stroke [a]Lev. 13:

9 [a]Num. 12:10

10 [a]Ex. 22:26, 2

13 [a]Ex. 22:26 [b]
6:25; Ps. 106:31
4:27

14 [1]Lit., *brother*
gates [a]Lev. 19:1
25:35-43; Deut.
Prov. 14:31; Am
1 Tim. 5:18

15 [1]Lit., *that the*
shall not go dow
[2]Lit., *soul* [a]Lev.
Jer. 22:13; Jame
[b]Ex. 22:23; Deu
Job 35:9; James

16 [1]Or, *with* [a]2
14:6; 2 Chr. 25:
31:29, 30; Ezek

17 [1]Lit., *of* [2]Or,
fatherless [a]Ex.
Lev. 19:33; Deu
10:17; 16:19; 27
[b]Ex. 22:22

19 [1]Or, *fatherle*
19:9, 10; 23:22
14:29 [c]Prov. 19

20 [1]Lit., *after yo*
[2]Or, *fatherless*
19:10 [b]Deut. 24

21 [1]Lit., *glean i*
yourself [2]Or, *fa*

25:1 [1]Lit., *the j*
[2]Lit., *they judge*
[a]Deut. 17:8-13;
[b]Deut. 1:16, 17

2 [1]Lit., *is a son*
beating [2]Or,
wickedness [a]P
19:29; Luke 12:

3 "[a]He may beat him forty times *but* no more, lest he beat him with
many more stripes than these, and your brother be [b]degraded in
your eyes.
4 "[a]You shall not muzzle the ox while he is threshing.
5 "When brothers live together and one of them dies and has no
son, the wife of the deceased shall not be *married* outside *the family* to
a strange man. [a]Her husband's brother shall go in to her and take her
to himself as wife and perform the duty of a husband's brother to
her.
6 "And it shall be that the first-born whom she bears shall [1]assume
the name of his dead brother, that [a]his name may not be blotted out
from Israel.
7 "[a]But if the man does not desire to take his brother's wife, then his
brother's wife shall go up to the gate to the elders and say, 'My
husband's brother refuses to establish a name for his brother in
Israel; he is not willing to perform the duty of a husband's brother to
me.'
8 "Then the elders of his city shall summon him and speak to him.
And *if* he persists and says, 'I do not desire to take her,'
9 [a]then his brother's wife shall come to him in the sight of the
elders, and pull his sandal off his foot and [b]spit in his face; and she
shall [1]declare, 'Thus it is done to the man who does not build up his
brother's house.'
10 "And in Israel his name shall be called, 'The house of him whose
sandal is removed.'
11 "If *two* men, a man and his [1]countryman, are struggling together,
and the wife of one comes near to deliver her husband from the
hand of the one who is striking him, and puts out her hand and
seizes his genitals,
12 then you shall cut off her [1]hand; [2a]you shall not show pity.
13 "[a]You shall not have in your bag [1]differing weights, a large and a
small.
14 "You shall not have in your house [1]differing measures, a large
and a small.
15 "You shall have a full and just weight; you shall have a full and
just [1]measure, [a]that your days may be prolonged in the [2]land which
the LORD your God gives you.
16 "For [a]everyone who does these things, everyone who acts unjust-
ly is an abomination to the LORD your God.
17 "[a]Remember what Amalek did to you along the way when you
came out from Egypt,
18 how he met you along the way and attacked among you all the
stragglers at your rear when you were faint and weary; and he [a]did
not [1]fear God.
19 "Therefore it shall come about when the LORD your God has given
you [a]rest from all your surrounding enemies, in the land which the
LORD your God gives you as an inheritance to [1]possess, you shall
blot out the memory of Amalek from under heaven; you must not
forget.

Chapter 26

26 "Then it shall be, when you enter the land which the LORD
your God gives you as an inheritance, and you possess it and
live in it,

3 [a]2 Cor. 11:24 [b]Job 18:3
4 [a]Prov. 12:10; 1 Cor. 9:9; 1 Tim. 5:18
5 [a]Matt. 22:24; Mark 12:19; Luke 20:28
6 [1]Lit., *stand on* [a]Ruth 4:5, 10
7 [a]Ruth 4:5, 6
9 [1]Lit., *answer and say* [a]Ruth 4:7, 8 [b]Num. 12:14
11 [1]Lit., *brother*
12 [1]Lit., *palm* [2]Lit., *your eye* [a]Deut. 7:2; 19:13
13 [1]Lit., *a stone and a stone* [a]Lev. 19:35-37; Prov. 11:1; 20:23; Ezek. 45:10; Mic. 6:11
14 [1]Lit., *an ephah and an ephah*
15 [1]Lit., *ephah* [2]Lit., *ground* [a]Ex. 20:12
16 [a]Prov. 11:1
17 [a]Ex. 17:8-16
18 [1]Or, *reverence* [a]Ps. 36:1; Rom. 3:18
19 [1]Lit., *possess it* [a]Deut. 12:9

2 that you shall take some of [a]the first of all the produce of the
ground which you shall bring in from your land that the LORD your
God gives you, and you shall put *it* in a basket and [b]go to the place
where the LORD your God chooses to establish His name.
3 "And you shall go to the priest who is in office at that time, and
say to him, 'I declare this day to the LORD [1]my God that I have
entered the land which the LORD swore to our fathers to give us.'
4 "Then the priest shall take the basket from your hand and set it
down before the altar of the LORD your God.
5 "And you shall answer and say before the LORD your God, '[a]My
father was a [1]wandering Aramean, and he went down to Egypt and
[2]sojourned there, [b]few in number; but there he became a [c]great,
mighty and populous nation.
6 'And the [a]Egyptians treated us harshly and afflicted us, and im-
posed hard labor on us.
7 'Then [a]we cried to the LORD, the God of our fathers, and the LORD
heard our voice and saw our affliction and our toil and our oppres-
sion;
8 [a]and the LORD brought us out of Egypt with a mighty hand and
an outstretched arm and with great terror and with signs and
wonders;
9 and He has brought us to this place, and has given us this land,
[a]a land flowing with milk and honey.
10 'And now behold, I have brought the first of the produce of the
ground [a]which Thou, O LORD hast given me.' And you shall set it
down before the LORD your God, and worship before the LORD your
God;
11 and you and [a]the Levite and the alien who is among you shall
[b]rejoice in all the good which the LORD your God has given you and
your household.
12 "[a]When you have finished [1]paying all the tithe of your increase in
the third year, the year of tithing, then you shall give it to the Levite,
to the stranger, to the [2]orphan and to the widow, that they may eat in
your [3]towns, and be satisfied.
13 "And you shall say before the LORD your God, 'I have removed
the sacred *portion* from *my* house, and also have given it to the Levite
and the alien, the [1]orphan and the widow, according to all Thy com-
mandments which Thou hast commanded me; [a]I have not trans-
gressed or forgotten any of Thy commandments.
14 'I have not eaten of it [1]while mourning, nor have I removed any
of it while I was unclean, nor offered any of it to the dead. I have
listened to the voice of the LORD my God; I have done according to
all that Thou hast commanded me.
15 '[a]Look down from Thy holy habitation, from heaven, and bless
Thy people Israel, and the ground which Thou hast given us, [b]a land
flowing with milk and honey, as Thou didst swear to our fathers.'
16 "This day the LORD your God commands you to do these statutes
and ordinances. You shall therefore be careful to do them [a]with all
your heart and with all your soul.
17 "[a]You have today declared the LORD to be your God, and [1]that you
would walk in His ways and keep His statutes, His commandments
and His ordinances, and listen to His voice.
18 "And the LORD has today declared you to be [a]His people, a

26:2 [a]Ex. 22:29; 23: 19; Num. 18:13; Pro 3:9 [b]Deut. 12:5

3 [1]So with Gr.; Heb. *your*

5 [1]Or, *perishing* [2]O *lived as an alien* [a]G 43:1-14 [b]Gen. 46:27 [c]Deut. 1:10; 10:22

6 [a]Ex. 1:8-11

7 [a]Ex. 2:23-25; 3:9

8 [a]Deut. 4:34; 34:11

9 [a]Ex. 3:8, 17

10 [a]Deut. 8:18; Pro 10:22

11 [a]Deut. 12:12 [b]D 12:7; 16:11; Eccl. 3: 13; 5:18-20

12 [1]Lit., *tithing* [2]Or, *fatherless* [3]Lit., *gate* [a]Lev. 27:30; Num. 18:24; Deut. 14:28, Heb. 7:5, 9, 10

13 [1]Or, *fatherless* [a] 119:141, 153, 176

14 [1]Lit., *while in my*

15 [a]Ps. 80:14; Is. 63:15; Zech. 2:13 [b]Deut. 26:9

16 [a]Deut. 4:29

17 [1]Lit., *to walk in* [a] 48:14

18 [a]Ex. 6:7; 19:5; D 4:20; 7:6; 14:2; 28:9 29:13; Titus 2:14; 1 2:9

18 [1]Lit., *to keep all*

treasured possession, as He promised you, and [1]that you should
keep all His commandments;

19 [1]Lit., *to set you* ...eut. 4:7, 8; 28:1, 13 ... 19:6; Deut. 7:6; Is. ... Jer. 2:3; 1 Pet. 2:9

19 and [1]that He shall [a]set you high above all nations which He has
made, for praise, fame, and honor; and that you shall be [b]a con-
secrated people to the LORD your God, as He has spoken."

Chapter 27

7:2 [a]Josh. 8:30-32

27 Then Moses and the elders of Israel charged the people,
saying, "Keep all the commandments which I command you
today.

...t., *spoke to* [a]Deut. 26:9

2 "[a]So it shall be on the day when you shall cross the Jordan to the
land which the LORD your God gives you, that you shall set up for
yourself large stones, and coat them with lime

[1]Lit., *which* [a]Deut. 11:29; Josh. 8:30

3 and write on them all the words of this law, when you cross
over, in order that you may enter the land which the LORD your God
gives you, [a]a land flowing with milk and honey, as the LORD, the God
of your fathers, [1]promised you.

5 [1]Lit., *lift up* [a]Ex. 20:25; Josh. 8:31

4 "So it shall be when you cross the Jordan, you shall set up [a]on
Mount Ebal, these stones, [1]as I am commanding you today, and you
shall coat them with lime.

6 [1]Lit., *whole*

5 "Moreover, you shall build there an altar to the LORD your God,
an altar of stones; you [a]shall not [1]wield an iron *tool* on them.

7 [a]Deut. 26:11

6 "You shall build the altar of the LORD your God of [1]uncut stones;
and you shall offer on it burnt offerings to the LORD your God;
7 and you shall sacrifice peace offerings and eat there, and you
shall [a]rejoice before the LORD your God.

[1]I.e., stones coated with lime, cf. v. 4

8 "And you shall write on the [1]stones all the words of this law very
distinctly."

...0 [1]Lit., *listen to the voice of*

9 Then Moses and the Levitical priests spoke to all Israel, saying,
"Be silent and listen, O Israel! This day you have become a people
for the LORD your God.
10 "You shall therefore [1]obey the LORD your God, and do His com-
mandments and His statutes which I command you today."

...Deut. 11:29 [b]Josh. 8:33-35

11 Moses also charged the people on that day, saying,
12 "When you cross the Jordan, these shall stand on [a]Mount Gerizim
to bless the people: [b]Simeon, Levi, Judah, Issachar, Joseph, and Ben-
jamin.

...Or, *a graven image* ...Ex. 20:4, 23; 34:17; ...v. 19:4; 26:1; Deut. 16, 23; 5:8; Is. 44:9 [b]1 Cor. 14:16

13 "And for the curse, these shall stand on Mount Ebal: Reuben,
Gad, Asher, Zebulun, Dan, and Naphtali.
14 "The Levites shall then answer and say to all the men of Israel
with a loud voice,

[a]Ex. 20:12; 21:17; ...v. 19:3; 20:9; Deut. 5:16; Ezek. 22:7

15 'Cursed is the man who makes [1a]an idol or a molten image, an
abomination to the LORD, the work of the hands of the craftsman,
and sets *it* up in secret.' And [b]all the people shall answer and say,
'Amen.'

[a]Deut. 19:14; Prov. 22:28

16 '[a]Cursed is he who dishonors his father or mother.' And all the
people shall say, 'Amen.'
17 '[a]Cursed is he who moves his neighbor's boundary mark.' And
all the people shall say, 'Amen.'

18 [a]Lev. 19:14

18 '[a]Cursed is he who misleads a blind *person* on the road.' And all
the people shall say, 'Amen.'

[1]Or, *fatherless* [a]Ex. ...1; 23:9; Lev. 19:33; Deut. 10:18; 24:17

19 '[a]Cursed is he who distorts the justice due an alien, [1]orphan, and
widow.' And all the people shall say, 'Amen.'

20 '[a]Cursed is he who lies with his father's wife, because he has
uncovered his father's skirt.' And all the people shall say, 'Amen.'
21 '[a]Cursed is he who lies with any animal.' And all the people shall
say, 'Amen.'
22 '[a]Cursed is he who lies with his sister, the daughter of his father
or of his mother.' And all the people shall say, 'Amen.'
23 '[a]Cursed is he who lies with his mother-in-law.' And all the
people shall say, 'Amen.'
24 '[a]Cursed is he who strikes his neighbor in secret.' And all the
people shall say, 'Amen.'
25 '[a]Cursed is he who accepts a bribe to strike down an innocent
person.' And all the people shall say, 'Amen.'
26 '[a]Cursed is he who does not confirm the words of this law by
doing them.' And all the people shall say, 'Amen.'

Chapter 28

28 "[a]Now it shall be, if you will diligently [1]obey the LORD your
God, being careful to do all His commandments which I com-
mand you today, the LORD your God [b]will set you high above all the
nations of the earth.
2 "And all these blessings shall come upon you and [a]overtake you,
if you will [1]obey the LORD your God.
3 "Blessed *shall* you *be* in the city, and blessed *shall* you *be* [a]in the
[1]country.
4 "Blessed *shall be* the [1]offspring of your [2]body and the [1]produce of
your ground and the [1]offspring of your beasts, the increase of your
herd and the young of your flock.
5 "Blessed *shall be* your basket and your kneading bowl.
6 "Blessed *shall* you *be* [a]when you come in, and blessed *shall* you *be*
when you go out.
7 "The LORD will cause your enemies who rise up against you to be
[1]defeated before you; they shall come out against you one way and
shall flee before you seven ways.
8 "The LORD will command the blessing upon you in your barns
and in [a]all that you put your hand to, and He will bless you in the
land which the LORD your God gives you.
9 "[a]The LORD will establish you as a holy people to Himself, as He
swore to you, if you will keep the commandments of the LORD your
God, and walk in His ways.
10 "So all the peoples of the earth shall see that [1a]you are called by
the name of the LORD; and they shall be afraid of you.
11 "[a]And the LORD will make you abound in prosperity, in the [1]off-
spring of your [2]body and in the [1]offspring of your beast and in the
[1]produce of your ground, in the land which the LORD swore to your
fathers to give you.
12 "The LORD will open for you His good storehouse, the heavens, to
give rain to your land in its season and to bless all the work of your
hand; and [a]you shall lend to many nations, but you shall not borrow.
13 "[a]And the LORD shall make you the head and not the tail, and you
only shall be above, and you shall not be underneath, if you will
listen to the commandments of the LORD your God, which I charge
you today, to [1]observe *them* carefully,
14 and [a]do not turn aside from any of the words which I command

20 [a]Lev. 18:8 Deut. 22:30; 1
21 [a]Ex. 22:19 18:23; 20:15
22 [a]Lev. 18:9
23 [a]Lev. 20:1
24 [a]Ex. 21:12 24:17; Num. 3
25 [a]Ex. 23:7; 10:17; Ps. 15:5 22:12
26 [a]Ps. 119:2 11:3; Gal. 3:10
28:1 [1]Lit., *liste voice of* [a]Ex. 1 23:22-27; Lev. Deut. 7:12-26; [b]Deut. 28:13; 2 1 Chr. 14:2
2 [1]Lit., *listen to voice of* [a]Zech.
3 [1]Or, *field* [a]Ge
4 [1]Lit., *fruit* [2]Lit
6 [a]Ps. 121:8
7 [1]Lit., *smitten*
8 [a]Deut. 15:10
9 [a]Ex. 19:5
10 [1]Lit., *the nam LORD is called up you* [a]2 Chr. 7:14
11 [1]Lit., *fruit* [2]Or, *womb* [a]Deut. 28: Prov. 10:22
12 [a]Deut. 23:20
13 [1]Lit., *keep and* [a]Deut. 28:1, 44
14 [a]Deut. 5:32; Jo 1:7

you today, to the right or to the left, to go after other gods to serve
them.
15 "[a]But it shall come about, if you will not [1]obey the LORD your God,
to observe to do all His commandments and His statutes with which
I charge you today, that all these curses shall come upon you and
overtake you.
16 "[a]Cursed *shall* you *be* in the city, and cursed *shall* you *be* in the
[1]country.
17 "[a]Cursed *shall be* your basket and your kneading bowl.
18 "[a]Cursed *shall be* the [1]offspring of your [2]body and the [1]produce of
your ground, the increase of your herd and the young of your flock.
19 "[a]Cursed *shall* you *be* when you come in, and cursed *shall* you *be*
when you go out.
20 "[a]The LORD will send upon you curses, confusion, and [b]rebuke, in
all [1]you undertake to do, until you are destroyed and until [c]you
perish quickly, on account of the evil of your deeds, because you
have forsaken Me.
21 "[a]The LORD will make the pestilence cling to you until He has
consumed you from the land, where you are entering to possess it.
22 "[a]The LORD will smite you with consumption and with fever and
with inflammation and with fiery heat and with [1]the sword and
[b]with blight and with mildew, and they shall pursue you until [c]you
perish.
23 "And [1]the heaven which is over your head shall be bronze, and
the earth which is under you, iron.
24 "[a]The LORD will make the rain of your land powder and dust;
from heaven it shall come down on you until you are destroyed.
25 "[a]The LORD will cause you to be [1]defeated before your enemies;
you shall go out one way against them, but you shall flee seven
ways before them, and you shall [b]be *an example of* terror to all the
kingdoms of the earth.
26 "[a]And your carcasses shall be food to all birds of the sky and to
the beasts of the earth, and there shall be no one to frighten *them*
away.
27 "[a]The LORD will smite you with the boils of Egypt and with
[b]tumors and with the scab and with the itch, from which you cannot
be healed.
28 "The LORD will smite you with madness and with blindness and
with bewilderment of heart;
29 and you shall [1a]grope at noon, as the blind man gropes in dark-
ness, and you shall not prosper in your ways; but you shall only be
oppressed and robbed continually, with none to save you.
30 "[a]You shall betroth a wife, but another man shall violate her; [b]you
shall build a house, but you shall not live in it; you shall plant a
vineyard, but you shall not [1]use its fruit.
31 "Your ox shall be slaughtered before your eyes, but you shall not
eat of it; your donkey shall be torn away from you, and shall not be
restored to you; your sheep shall be given to your enemies, and you
shall have none to save you.
32 "[a]Your sons and your daughters shall be given to another people,
while your eyes shall look on and yearn for them continually; but
there shall be nothing [1]you can do.
33 "[a]A people whom you do not know shall eat up the produce of

..., *listen to the* ...ev. 26:14-43; ...15; Dan. 9:11
...d [a]Deut. 28:3
...7 [a]Deut. 28:5
[1]Lit., *fruit* [2]Or, ...*nb* [a]Deut. 28:4
19 [a]Deut. 28:6
...*he putting forth* ...*and which you* ...Deut. 28:8; Mal. [b]Ps. 80:16; Is. ...15 [c]Deut. 4:26
...ev. 26:25; Num. ...er. 24:10; Amos 4:10
...*other reading is* ...*ght* [a]Lev. 26:16 ...4:9 [c]Deut. 4:26
23 [1]Lit., *your*
...eut. 11:17; 28:12
..., *smitten* [a]Deut. ...Is. 30:17 [b]2 Chr. ...3; Jer. 15:4; 24:9; Ezek. 23:46
...[a]Jer. 7:33; 16:4; 19:7; 34:20
...x. 9:9; Deut. 7:15; ...0, 61 [b]1 Sam. 5:6
...9 [1]Lit., *be groping* [a]Ex. 10:21
[1]Lit., *begin it* [a]Job ...); Jer. 8:10 [b]Amos 5:11
...Lit., *in the power of* ...*hand* [a]Deut. 28:41
33 [a]Jer. 5:15, 17

your ground and all your labors, and you shall never be anything
but oppressed and crushed continually.
34 "And you shall be driven mad by the sight of [1]what you see.
35 "[a]The LORD will strike you on the knees and legs with sore boils,
from which you cannot be healed, from the sole of your foot to the
crown of your head.
36 "[a]The LORD will bring you and your king, whom you shall set
over you, to a nation which neither you nor your fathers have
known, and there you shall serve other gods, [b]wood and stone.
37 "And [a]you shall become a horror, a proverb, and a taunt among
all the people where the LORD will drive you.
38 "[a]You shall bring out much seed to the field but you shall gather
in little, for [b]the locust shall consume it.
39 "[a]You shall plant and cultivate vineyards, but you shall neither
drink of the wine nor gather *the grapes,* for the worm shall devour
them.
40 "[a]You shall have olive trees throughout your territory but you
shall not anoint yourself with the oil, for your olives shall drop off.
41 "[a]You shall [1]have sons and daughters but they shall not be yours,
for they shall go into captivity.
42 "[a]The cricket shall possess all your trees and the produce of your
ground.
43 "[a]The alien who is among you shall rise above you higher and
higher, but you shall go down lower and lower.
44 "[a]He shall lend to you, but you shall not lend to him; [b]he shall be
the head, and you shall be the tail.
45 "So all these curses shall come on you and pursue you and over-
take you [a]until you are destroyed, because you would not [1]obey the
LORD your God by keeping His commandments and His statutes
which He commanded you.
46 "And they shall become [a]a sign and a wonder on you and your
[1]descendants forever.
47 "[a]Because you did not serve the LORD your God with joy and a
glad heart, for the abundance of all things;
48 therefore you shall serve your enemies whom the LORD shall
send against you, [a]in hunger, in thirst, in nakedness, and in the lack
of all things; and He [b]will put an iron yoke on your neck until He has
destroyed you.
49 "[a]The LORD will bring a nation against you from afar, from the
end of the earth, [b]as the eagle swoops down, a nation whose lan-
guage you shall not understand,
50 a nation of fierce countenance who shall [a]have no respect for the
old, nor show favor to the young.
51 "Moreover, it shall eat the [1]offspring of your herd and the
produce of your ground until you are destroyed, who also leaves
you no grain, new wine, or oil, nor the increase of your herd or the
young of your flock until they have caused you to perish.
52 "[a]And it shall besiege you in all your [1]towns until your high and
fortified walls in which you trusted come down throughout your
land, and it shall besiege you in all your [1]towns throughout your
land which the LORD your God has given you.
53 "[a]Then you shall eat the [1]offspring of your own body, the flesh of
your sons and of your daughters whom the LORD your God has

34 [1]Lit., *your which you*
35 [a]Deut. 28.
36 [a]2 Kin. 17 24:12, 14; 25: 2 Chr. 36:1-21 39:1-9 [b]Deut. 16:13
37 [a]1 Kin. 9:7 19:8; 24:9; 25
38 [a]Is. 5:10; M Hag. 1:6 [b]Ex. 1:4
39 [a]Is. 5:10; 1
40 [a]Jer. 11:16
41 [1]Lit., *beget* 28:32
42 [a]Deut. 28:3
43 [a]Deut. 28:1
44 [a]Deut. 28:12 28:13
45 [1]Lit., *listen to voice of* [a]Deut.
46 [1]Lit., *seed* [a] 26:10; Is. 8:18; E 5:15; 14:8
47 [a]Deut. 12:7; 9:35-37
48 [a]Lam. 4:4-6 28:13, 14
49 [a]Is. 5:26-30; 7:18-20; Jer. 5:15 23 [b]Jer. 48:40; 4 Lam. 4:19; Hos. 8
50 [a]Is. 47:6
51 [1]Lit., *fruit*
52 [1]Lit., *gates* [a]J 10:17, 18; Zeph. 1
53 [1]Lit., *fruit* [a]Lev 26:29; 2 Kin. 6:28, Jer. 19:9; Lam. 2:2 4:10

given you, during the siege and the distress by which your enemy shall [2]oppress you.

54 "The man who is [1]refined and very delicate among you [2]shall be hostile toward his brother and toward the wife [3]he cherishes and toward the rest of his children who remain,

55 so that he will not give *even* one of them any of the flesh of his children which he shall eat, since he has nothing *else* left, during the siege and the distress by which your enemy shall [1]oppress you in all your [2]towns.

56 "[a]The [1]refined and delicate woman among you, who would not venture to set the sole of her foot on the ground for delicateness and [2]refinement, [3]shall be hostile toward the husband [4]she cherishes and toward her son and daughter,

57 and toward her afterbirth which issues from between her [1]legs and toward her children whom she bears; for [a]she shall eat them secretly for lack of anything *else,* during the siege and the distress by which your enemy shall [2]oppress you in your [3]towns.

58 "If you are not careful to observe all the words of this law which are written in this book, to [1a]fear this honored and awesome [b]name, [2]the LORD your God,

59 then the LORD will bring extraordinary plagues on you and [1]your descendants, even [2]severe and lasting plagues, and miserable and chronic sicknesses.

60 "[a]And He will bring back on you all the diseases of Egypt of which you were afraid, and they shall cling to you.

61 "Also every sickness and every plague which, not written in the book of this law, the LORD will bring on you [a]until you are destroyed.

62 "Then you shall be left few in number, [a]whereas you were as the stars of heaven for multitude, because you did not [1]obey the LORD your God.

63 "And it shall come about that as the LORD [a]delighted over you to prosper you, and multiply you, so the LORD will [b]delight over you to make you perish and destroy you; and you shall be [c]torn from the land where you are entering to possess it.

64 "Moreover, the LORD will [a]scatter you among all peoples, from one end of the earth to the other end of the earth; and there you shall [b]serve other gods, wood and stone, which you or your fathers have not known.

65 "And [a]among those nations you shall find no rest, and there shall be no resting place for the sole of your foot; but there [b]the LORD will give you a trembling heart, failing of eyes, and despair of soul.

66 "So your life shall [1]hang in doubt before you; and you shall be in dread night and day, and shall have no assurance of your life.

67 "[a]In the morning you shall say, 'Would that it were evening!' And at evening you shall say, 'Would that it were morning!' because of the dread of your heart which you dread, and for the sight of your eyes which you shall see.

68 "And the LORD will bring you back to Egypt in ships, by the way about which I spoke to you, 'You will never see it again!' And there you shall offer yourselves for sale to your enemies as male and female slaves, but there will be no buyer."

53 [2]Or, *distress*

t., *tender* [2]Lit., *his* *hall be evil toward* [3]Lit., *of his bosom*

[1]Or, *distress* [2]Lit., *gates*

[1]Lit., *tender* [2]Lit., *nderness* [3]Lit., *her* *hall be evil toward* [4]Lit., *of her bosom* [a]Lam. 4:10

57 [1]Lit., *feet* [2]Or, *istress* [3]Lit., *gates* Kin. 6:28, 29; Lam. 4:10

58 [1]Or, *reverence* Heb., *YHWH* [a]Ps. Mal. 1:14 [b]Is. 42:8

it., *plague on your seed* [2]Lit., *great*

60 [a]Deut. 28:27

61 [a]Deut. 4:25, 26

[1]Lit., *listen to the* *ce of* [a]Deut. 1:10; Neh. 9:23

[a]Jer. 32:41 [b]Prov. [c]Jer. 12:14; 45:4

[a]Lev. 26:33; Deut. 7; Neh. 1:8 [b]Deut. 4:28; 29:26; 32:17

[a]Lam. 1:3 [b]Lev. 26:36

t., *be hung for you in front*

67 [a]Job 7:4

Chapter 29

29 [1a]These are the words of the covenant which the LORD com-
manded Moses to make with the sons of Israel in the land of
Moab, besides the [b]covenant which He had made with them at
Horeb.
2 [1]And Moses summoned all Israel and said to them, "You have
seen all that the LORD did before your eyes in the land of Egypt to
Pharaoh and all his servants and all his land;
3 [a]the great trials which your eyes have seen, those great signs and
wonders.
4 "Yet to this day [a]the LORD has not given you a heart to know, nor
eyes to see, nor ears to hear.
5 "And I have led you forty years in the wilderness; [a]your clothes
have not worn out on you, and your sandal has not worn out on
your foot.
6 "[a]You have not eaten bread, nor have you drunk wine or strong
drink, in order that you might know that I am the LORD your God.
7 "[a]When you [1]reached this place, Sihon the king of Heshbon and
Og the king of Bashan came out to meet us for battle, but we
[2]defeated them;
8 and we took their land and [a]gave it as an inheritance to the
Reubenites, the Gadites, and the half-tribe of the Manassites.
9 "[a]So keep the words of this covenant to do them, [b]that you may
prosper in all that you do.
10 "You stand today, all of you, before the LORD your God: your
chiefs, your tribes, your elders and your officers, *even* all the men of
Israel,
11 your little ones, your wives, and the alien who is within your
camps, from [a]the one who chops your wood to the one who draws
your water,
12 that you may enter into the covenant with the LORD your God,
and into His oath which the LORD your God is making with you
today,
13 in order that He may establish you today as His people and that
[a]He may be your God, just as He spoke to you and as He swore to
your fathers, to Abraham, Isaac, and Jacob.
14 "Now not with you alone am I [a]making this covenant and this
oath,
15 [a]but both with those who stand here with us today in the pres-
ence of the LORD our God and with those who are not with us here
today
16 (for you know how we lived in the land of Egypt, and how we
came through the midst of the nations through which you passed.
17 "Moreover, you have seen their abominations and their idols *of*
[a]wood, stone, silver, and gold, which *they had* with them);
18 [a]lest there shall be among you a man or woman, or family or
tribe, whose heart turns away today from the LORD our God, to go
and serve the gods of those nations; lest there shall be among you [b]a
root bearing poisonous fruit and wormwood.
19 "And it shall be when he hears the words of this curse, that he
will [1]boast, saying, 'I have peace though I walk in the stubbornness
of my heart in order [2]to destroy the watered *land* with the dry.'
20 "The LORD shall never be willing to forgive him, but rather the
anger of the LORD and [a]His jealousy will [1b]burn against that man, and

29:1 [1]Ch. 28 Heb. [a]Lev. 2 27:34 [b]Deut.
2 [1]Ch. 29:1 i
3 [a]Deut. 4:34
4 [a]Is. 6:9, 10; 12:2; Matt. 13 28:26, 27; Ro
5 [a]Deut. 8:4
6 [a]Deut. 8:3
7 [1]Lit., *came t* *smote* [a]Num. 33, 35; Deut. 2
8 [a]Num. 32:32 Deut. 3:12, 13
9 [a]Deut. 4:6; 1 [b]Josh. 1:7
11 [a]Josh. 9:21
13 [a]Gen. 17:7;
14 [a]Jer. 31:31; 8:7, 8
15 [a]Acts 2:39
17 [a]Ex. 20:23; 4:28; 28:36
18 [a]Deut. 13:6 32:32; Heb. 12:1
19 [1]Lit., *bless hi* *his heart* [2]I.e., to destroy everythin
20 [1]Lit., *smoke* 79:5; Ezek. 23:25 74:1; 80:4

every curse which is written in this book will [2]rest on him, and the
LORD will [c]blot out his name from under heaven.
21 "Then the LORD will single him out for [1]adversity from all the
tribes of Israel, according to all the curses of the covenant [a]which are
written in this book of the law.
22 "Now the generation to come, your sons who rise up after you
and [a]the foreigner who comes from a distant land, when they see the
plagues of the land and the diseases with which the LORD has [1]af-
flicted it, will say,
23 'All its land is [a]brimstone and salt, [b]a burning waste, [1]unsown
and unproductive, and no grass grows in it, like the overthrow of
[c]Sodom and Gomorrah, Admah and Zeboiim, which the LORD over-
threw in His anger and in His wrath.'
24 "And all the nations shall say, '[a]Why has the LORD done thus to
this land? Why this great [1]outburst of anger?'
25 "Then *men* shall say, '[a]Because they forsook the covenant of the
LORD, the God of their fathers, which He made with them when He
brought them out of the land of Egypt.
26 'And they went and served other gods and worshiped them,
gods whom they have not known and whom He had not [1]allotted to
them.
27 'Therefore, the anger of the LORD burned against that land, [a]to
bring upon it every curse which is written in this book;
28 and [a]the LORD uprooted them from their land in anger and in
fury and in great wrath, and cast them into another land, as *it is* this
day.'
29 "[a]The secret things belong to the LORD our God, but [b]the things
revealed belong to us and to our sons forever, that we may observe
all the words of this law.

Chapter 30

30 "So it shall be when all of these things have come upon you,
[a]the blessing and the curse which I have set before you, and
you [1]call *them* to mind [b]in all nations where the LORD your God has
banished you,
2 and you [a]return to the LORD your God and [1]obey Him [b]with all
your heart and soul according to all that I command you today, you
and your sons,
3 then the LORD your God will [a]restore [1]you from captivity, and
have compassion on you, and [b]will gather you again from all the
peoples where the LORD your God has [c]scattered you.
4 "If your outcasts are at the ends of the [1]earth, [a]from there the LORD
your God will gather you, and from there He will [2]bring you back.
5 "And [a]the LORD your God will bring you into the land which your
fathers possessed, and you shall possess it; and He will prosper you
and [b]multiply you more than your fathers.
6 "Moreover [a]the LORD your God will circumcise your heart and the
heart of your [1]descendants, [b]to love the LORD your God with all your
heart and with all your soul, in order that you may live.
7 "[a]And the LORD your God will [1]inflict all these curses on your
enemies and on those who hate you, who persecuted you.
8 "And you shall again [1]obey the LORD, and observe all His com-
mandments which I command you today.
9 "[a]Then the LORD your God will [1]prosper you abundantly in all the

.., *lie down* [c]Ex. ...eut. 9:14; 2 Kin. 14:27
[1]Lit., *evil* [a]Deut. 30:10
...Lit., *made it sick* ...:8; 49:17; 50:13
...it., *it is not sown* ...oes not cause to [a]Gen. 19:24; Is. Jer. 17:6; Zeph. 9 [b]Is. 1:7; 64:11 [c]Jude 7
Lit., *heat* [a]1 Kin. 9:8; Jer. 22:8
[a]2 Kin. 17:9-23; 2 Chr. 36:13-21
6 [1]Lit., *portioned*
27 [a]Dan. 9:11
[a]2 Chr. 7:20; Ps. Prov. 2:22; Ezek. 19:12, 13
[a]Acts 1:7 [b]John Acts 17:11; 2 Tim. 3:16
[1]Lit., *cause them* ...eturn to your heart ...t. 11:26; 30:15, 19 ...v. 26:40-45; Deut. 29:28; 1 Kin. 8:47
[1]Lit., *listen to His* ...e [a]Deut. 4:29, 30; ...h. 1:9 [b]Deut. 4:29
[1]Lit., *your captivity* ... 28:15; 48:21; Ps. 126:1, 4; Jer. 29:14 ... 147:2; Jer. 32:37; 34:13 [c]Deut. 4:27
[1]Lit., *sky* [2]Lit., *take* [a]Neh. 1:9; Is. 43:6; 48:20; 62:11
5 [a]Jer. 29:14; 30:3 [b]Deut. 7:13; 13:17
6 [1]Lit., *seed* [a]Deut. 10:16 [b]Deut. 6:5
Lit., *put* [a]Deut. 7:15
8 [1]Lit., *listen to the voice of*
[1]Lit., *make you have* ...xcess for good [a]Jer. 31:27, 28

work of your hand, in the [2]offspring of your [3]body and in the [2]off-
spring of your cattle and in the [2]produce of your ground, for [b]the
LORD will again rejoice over you for good, just as He rejoiced over
your fathers;
10 [1]if you [2]obey the LORD your God to keep His commandments
and His statutes which [a]are written in this book of the law, [1]if you
turn to the LORD your God [b]with all your heart and soul.
11 "For this commandment which I command you today is not too
difficult for you, nor is it [1]out of reach.
12 "It is not in heaven, [1]that you should say, '[a]Who will go up to
heaven for us to get it for us and make us hear it, that we may
observe it?'
13 "Nor is it beyond the sea, [1]that you should say, 'Who will cross
the sea for us to get it for us and make us hear it, that we may
observe it?'
14 "But the word is very near you, in your mouth and in your heart,
that you may observe it.
15 "See, [a]I have set before you today life and [1]prosperity, and death
and [2]adversity;
16 in that I command you today [a]to love the LORD your God, to
walk in His ways and to keep His commandments and His statutes
and His judgments, that you [b]may live and multiply, and that the
LORD your God may bless you in the land where you are entering to
possess it.
17 "But if your heart turns away and you will not obey, but are
drawn away and worship other gods and serve them,
18 I declare to you today that [a]you shall surely perish. You shall not
prolong *your* days in the land where you are crossing the Jordan to
enter [1]and possess it.
19 "[a]I call heaven and earth to witness against you today, that I have
set before you life and death, [b]the blessing and the curse. So choose
life in order that you may live, you and your [1]descendants,
20 [a]by loving the LORD your God, by obeying His voice, and [b]by
holding fast to Him; [c]for [1]this is your life and the length of your
days, [2]that you may live in [d]the land which the LORD swore to your
fathers, to Abraham, Isaac, and Jacob, to give them."

Chapter 31

31 So Moses went and spoke these words to all Israel.
2 And he said to them, "I am [a]a hundred and twenty years
old today; [b]I am no longer able to come and go, and the LORD has
said to me, '[c]You shall not cross this Jordan.'
3 "[a]It is the LORD your God who will cross ahead of you; He will
destroy these nations before you, and you shall dispossess them.
[b]Joshua is the one who will cross ahead of you, just as the LORD has
spoken.
4 "And the LORD will do to them just as He did to Sihon and Og, the
kings of the Amorites, and to their land, when He destroyed them.
5 "And [a]the LORD will deliver them up before you, and you shall do
to them according to all the commandments which I have com-
manded you.
6 "[a]Be strong and courageous, [b]do not be afraid or tremble at them,
for [c]the LORD your God is the one who goes with you. [d]He will not
fail you or forsake you."

9 [2]Lit., *fruit* [3]Lit., *wo* [b]Jer. 32:41

10 [1]Or, *for you will* [2]Lit., *listen to the voi* *of* [a]Deut. 29:21 [b]De 4:29

11 [1]Lit., *far off*

12 [1]Lit., *to say* [a]Ro 10:6-8

13 [1]Lit., *to say*

15 [1]Lit., *good* [2]Lit., [a]Deut. 11:26

16 [a]Deut. 6:5 [b]Deu 4:1; 30:19

18 [1]Lit., *to* [a]Deut. 4 8:19

19 [1]Lit., *seed* [a]Deu 4:26 [b]Deut. 30:1

20 [1]Lit., *that* [2]Lit., *to dwell* [a]Deut. 6:5 [b]D 10:20 [c]Deut. 4:1; 32 Acts 17:25, 28 [d]Ger 12:7; 17:1-8

31:2 [a]Deut. 34:7 [b]N 27:17; 1 Kin. 3:7 [c]D 1:37; 3:27

3 [a]Deut. 9:3 [b]Num. 27:18

5 [a]Deut. 7:2

6 [a]Josh. 10:25; 1 C 22:13 [b]Deut. 1:29; 7 20:1 [c]Deut. 20:4 [d]J 1:5; Heb. 13:5

eut. 1:38; 3:28

7 Then Moses called to Joshua and said to him in the sight of all Israel, "[a]Be strong and courageous, for you shall go with this people into the land which the LORD has sworn to their fathers to give them, and you shall give it to them as an inheritance.

x. 13:21; 33:14 31:6; Josh. 1:5; Heb. 13:5

8 "And [a]the LORD is the one who goes ahead of you; He will be with you. [b]He will not fail you or forsake you. Do not fear, or be dismayed."

Num. 4:5, 6, 15; 10:8; 31:25, 26; Josh. 3:3

9 So Moses wrote this law and gave it to the priests, the sons of Levi [a]who carried the ark of the covenant of the LORD, and to all the elders of Israel.

ut. 15:1, 2 [b]Lev. :34; Deut. 16:13

10 Then Moses commanded them, saying, "At the end of *every* seven years, at the time of [a]the year of remission of debts, at the [b]Feast of Booths,

ut. 16:16 [b]Deut. osh. 8:34; 2 Kin. 23:2

11 when all Israel comes [a]to appear before the LORD your God at [b]the place which He will choose, [c]you shall read this law in front of all Israel in their hearing.

your alien [2]Lit., *ates* [a]Deut. 4:10

12 "Assemble the people, the men and the women and children and [1]the alien who is in your [2]town, in order that they may hear and [a]learn and fear the LORD your God, and be careful to observe all the words of this law.

[1]Lit., *where* [2]Lit., *possess it*

13 "And their children, who have not known, will hear and learn to fear the LORD your God, as long as you live on the land [1]which you are about to cross the Jordan to [2]possess."

[1]Lit., *your days to are* [a]Num. 27:12, Deut. 4:22; 32:50 [b]Ex. 33:9-11

14 Then the LORD said to Moses, "Behold, [1a]the time for you to die is near; call Joshua, and present yourselves at the tent of meeting, that I may commission him." [b]So Moses and Joshua went and presented themselves at the tent of meeting.

15 [a]Ex. 33:9

15 [a]And the LORD appeared in the tent in a pillar of cloud, and the pillar of cloud stood at the doorway of the tent.

[a]Gen. 15:15 [b]Ex. 15; Deut. 4:25-28; Judg. 2:11, 12, 17 [c]Judg. 10:6; 1 Kin. 8; 19:10; Jer. 2:13

16 And the LORD said to Moses, "Behold, [a]you are about to lie down with your fathers; and [b]this people will arise and play the harlot with the strange gods of the land, into the midst of which they are going, and [c]will forsake Me and break My covenant which I have made with them.

[a]Judg. 2:14; 6:13 r. 15:2; 24:20 [c]Ps. 29; Is. 8:17 [d]Num. 14:42

17 "[a]Then My anger will be kindled against them in that day, and [b]I will forsake them and [c]hide My face from them, and they shall be consumed, and many evils and troubles shall come upon them; so that they will say in that day, '[d]Is it not because our God is not among us that these evils have come upon us?'

18 "But I will surely hide My face in that day because of all the evil which they will do, for they will turn to other gods.

Lit., *in their mouths* [a]Deut. 31:22

19 "Now therefore, [a]write this song for yourselves, and teach it to the sons of Israel; put it [1]on their lips, in order that this song may be a witness for Me against the sons of Israel.

20 [1]Lit., *fat* [a]Deut. 12; 8:10, 19; 11:16, 17 [b]Deut. 32:15-17

20 "[a]For when I bring them into the land flowing with milk and honey, which I swore to their fathers, and they have eaten and are satisfied and [b]become [1]prosperous, then they will turn to other gods and serve them, and spurn Me and break My covenant.

21 [1]Lit., *mouth of its seed* [2]Lit., *making* v. 26:41; Deut. 4:30 [b]1 Chr. 28:9; John 2:24, 25

21 "Then it shall come about, [a]when many evils and troubles have come upon them, that this song will testify before them as a witness (for it shall not be forgotten from the [1]lips of their descendants); for [b]I know their intent which they are [2]developing today, before I have brought them into the land which I swore."

22 [a]So Moses wrote this song the same day, and taught it to the sons
of Israel.
23 [a]Then He commissioned Joshua the son of Nun, and said, "[b]Be
strong and courageous, for you shall bring the sons of Israel into the
land which I swore to them, and [c]I will be with you."
24 And it came about, when Moses finished writing the words of
this law in a book until they were complete,
25 that Moses commanded the Levites [a]who carried the ark of the
covenant of the LORD, saying,
26 "Take this book of the law and place it beside the ark of the
covenant of the LORD your God, that it may [1]remain there as a wit-
ness against you.
27 "For I know [a]your rebellion and [b]your [1]stubbornness; behold,
while I am still alive with you today, you have been rebellious
against the LORD; how much more, then, after my death?
28 "Assemble to me all the elders of your tribes and your officers,
that I may speak these words in their hearing and [a]call the heavens
and the earth to witness against them.
29 "For I know that after my death you will [a]act corruptly and turn
from the way which I have commanded you; and evil will befall you
in the latter days, for you will do that which is evil in the sight of the
LORD, provoking Him to anger with the work of your hands."
30 Then Moses spoke in the hearing of all the assembly of Israel the
words of this song, until they were complete:

Chapter 32

32 "[a]Give ear, O heavens, and let me speak;
And let the earth hear the words of my mouth.
2 "[a]Let my teaching drop as the rain,
My speech distill as the dew,
[b]As the droplets on the fresh grass
And as the showers on the herb.
3 "[a]For I proclaim the name of the LORD;
[b]Ascribe greatness to our God!
4 "[a]The Rock! His work is perfect,
[b]For all His ways are [1]just;
[c]A God of faithfulness and without injustice,
Righteous and upright is He.
5 "[1][a]They have acted corruptly toward Him,
They are not His children, because of their defect;
[b]*But are* a perverse and crooked generation.
6 "Do you thus [a]repay the LORD,
[b]O foolish and unwise people?
[c]Is not He your Father who has bought you?
[d]He has made you and established you.
7 "Remember the days of old,
Consider the years of all generations.
[a]Ask your father, and he will inform you,
Your elders, and they will tell you.
8 "[a]When the Most High gave the nations their inheritance,
When He separated the sons of [1]man,
He set the boundaries of the peoples
[b]According to the number of the sons of Israel.
9 "[a]For the LORD's portion is His people;

22 [a]Deut. 31:19
23 [a]Num. 27:23; De 31:7 [b]Josh. 1:6 [c]Ex. 3:12
25 [a]Deut. 31:9
26 [1]Lit., *be*
27 [1]Lit., *stiff neck* [a]Deut. 9:7, 24 [b]Ex. 32:9; Deut. 9:6, 13
28 [a]Deut. 4:26; 30:1 32:1
29 [a]Judg. 2:19
32:1 [a]Deut. 4:26; Ps 50:4; Is. 1:2; Jer. 6:1
2 [a]Is. 55:10, 11 [b]Ps. 72:6
3 [a]Ex. 33:19; 34:5, 6 [b]Deut. 3:24; 5:24
4 [1]Or, *judgment* [a]De 32:15, 18, 30; 2 Sam 22:31 [b]Gen. 18:25; Dan. 4:37 [c]Deut. 7:9
5 [1]Lit., *It has* [a]Deut. 4:25; 31:29 [b]Matt. 1
6 [a]Ps. 116:12 [b]Deut 32:28 [c]Deut. 1:31; P 74:2; Is. 63:16 [d]Deu 32:15
7 [a]Ex. 12:26; Ps. 78
8 [1]Or, *Adam* [a]Acts 17:26 [b]Num. 23:9; Deut. 33:28
9 [a]1 Sam. 10:1; 1 Ki 8:51, 53; Jer. 10:16

ıt. 1:19 [b]Ps.
2; Zech. 2:8

Jacob is the allotment of His inheritance.
10 "[a]He found him in a desert land,
And in the howling waste of a wilderness;
He encircled him, He cared for him,
He guarded him as [b]the pupil of His eye.

. 19:4; Deut.
Ps. 18:10-18

11 "[a]Like an eagle that stirs up its nest,
That hovers over its young,
[b]He spread His wings and caught them,
He carried them on His pinions.

eut. 4:35, 39
.39; Is. 43:12

12 "[a]The LORD alone guided him,
[b]And there was no foreign god with him.

58:14 [b]Deut.
16 [c]Job 29:6

13 "[a]He made him ride on the high places of the earth,
And he ate the produce of the field;
[b]And He made him suck honey from the rock,
And [c]oil from the flinty rock,

31:16; 147:14
[b]Gen. 49:11

14 Curds of cows, and milk of the flock,
With fat of lambs,
And rams, the breed of Bashan, and goats,
[a]With the finest of the wheat—
And of the [b]blood of grapes you drank wine.

Israel [a]Deut.
0 [b]Judg. 10:6
5 [d]Deut. 32:4;
Ps. 89:26

15 "[a]But [1]Jeshurun grew fat and kicked—
You are grown fat, thick, and sleek—
[b]Then he forsook God [c]who made him,
And scorned [d]the Rock of his salvation.

Ps. 78:58 [b]Ps.
106:29

16 "[a]They made Him jealous with strange *gods;*
[b]With abominations they provoked Him to anger.

ev. 17:7; 1 Cor.
) [b]Deut. 28:64
[c]Judg. 5:8

17 "[a]They sacrificed to demons who were not God,
[b]To gods whom they have not known,
[c]New *gods* who came lately,
Whom your fathers did not dread.

eut. 32:4 [b]Ps.
106:21

18 "You neglected [a]the Rock who begot you,
[b]And forgot the God who gave you birth.

Lev. 26:30; Ps.
[b]Jer. 44:21-23

19 "[a]And the LORD saw *this,* and spurned *them*
[b]Because of the provocation of His sons and daughters.

ıt. 31:29 [b]Deut.
2:5 [c]Deut. 9:23

20 "Then He said, 'I will hide My face from them,
[a]I will see what their end *shall be;*
[b]For they are a perverse generation,
[c]Sons in whom is no faithfulness.

vanities [a]Deut.
16; 1 Cor. 10:22
eut. 32:17; 1 Kin.
26 [c]Rom. 10:19

21 '[a]They have made Me jealous with *what* is not God;
They have provoked Me to anger with their [1b]idols.
[c]So I will make them jealous with *those who* are not a people;
I will provoke them to anger with a foolish nation,

[1]I.e., the nether
[a]Num. 16:33-35;
8:7, 8; Lam. 4:11
[b]Lev. 26:20

22 [a]For a fire is kindled in My anger,
And burns to the lowest part of [1]Sheol,
[b]And consumes the earth with its yield,
And sets on fire the foundations of the mountains.

Deut. 29:21 [b]Ps.
18:14; 45:5

23 '[a]I will heap misfortunes on them;
[b]I will use My arrows on them.

[1]Lit., *burning heat*
ıt. 28:22, 48 [b]Ps.
91:6 [c]Lev. 26:22

24 '[a]*They shall be* wasted by famine, and consumed by [1]plague
[b]And bitter destruction;
[c]And the teeth of beasts I will send upon them,

[d]With the venom of crawling things of the dust.
25 '[a]Outside the sword shall bereave,
And inside terror—
[b]Both young man and virgin,
The nursling with the man of gray hair.
26 'I would have said, "[a]I will cut them to pieces,
[b]I will remove the memory of them from men,"
27 Had I not feared the provocation by the enemy,
Lest their adversaries should misjudge,
Lest they should say, "[a]Our hand is [1]triumphant,
And the LORD has not done all this." '

28 "[a]For they are a nation [1]lacking in counsel,
And there is no understanding in them.
29 "[a]Would that they were wise, that they understood this,
[b]That they would discern their [1]future!
30 "[a]How could one chase a thousand,
And two put ten thousand to flight,
Unless their [b]Rock had sold them,
And the LORD had given them up?
31 "Indeed their rock is not like our Rock,
[a]Even our enemies [1]themselves judge this.
32 "For their vine is from the vine of Sodom,
And from the fields of Gomorrah;
Their grapes are grapes of [a]poison,
Their clusters, bitter.
33 "Their wine is the venom of [1]serpents,
And the [2]deadly poison of cobras.

34 '[a]Is it not laid up in store with Me,
Sealed up in My treasuries?
35 '[a]Vengeance is Mine, and retribution,
[b]In due time their foot will slip;
[c]For the day of their calamity is near,
And the impending things are hastening upon them.'
36 "[a]For the LORD will vindicate His people,
[b]And will have compassion on His servants;
When He sees that *their* [1]strength is gone,
And there is none *remaining,* bond or free.
37 "And He will say, '[a]Where are their gods,
The rock in which they sought refuge?
38 '[a]Who ate the fat of their sacrifices,
And drank the wine of their libation?
[b]Let them rise up and help you,
Let them be your hiding place!
39 '[a]See now that I, I am He,
[b]And there is no god besides Me;
[c]It is I who put to death and give life.
[d]I have wounded, and it is I who heal;
[e]And there is no one who can deliver from My hand.
40 'Indeed, [a]I lift up My hand to heaven,
And say, as I live forever,
41 [a]If I sharpen My [1]flashing sword,
And My hand takes hold on justice,

24 [d]Amos 5:
25 [a]Lam. 1:2 7:15 [b]2 Chr. Lam. 2:21
26 [a]Deut. 4:2 [b]Deut. 9:14
27 [1]Lit., *high* 15:30
28 [1]Lit., *peris* [a]Deut. 32:6
29 [1]Or, *latter* [a]Deut. 5:29 [b]
30 [a]Lev. 26:7, 32:4; Ps. 44:12
31 [1]Lit., *are ju* [a]Ex. 14:25
32 [a]Deut. 29:1
33 [1]Lit., *drago* *cruel*
34 [a]Job 14:17; 44:21
35 [a]Ps. 94:1; R 12:19; Heb. 10: 23:12 [c]Ezek. 7:
36 [1]Lit., *hand* [a] 135:14; Heb. 10 [b]Lev. 26:43-45; 30:1-3
37 [a]Judg. 10:14 2:28
38 [a]Num. 25:1, 11:12
39 [a]Is. 41:4; 43:1 [b]Deut. 32:12; Is. [c]1 Sam. 2:6; Ps. [d]Ps. 51:8 [e]Ps. 50
40 [a]Ezek. 20:5, 21:4, 5
41 [1]Or, *lightning* 34:6-8

[b]I will render vengeance on My adversaries,
And I will repay those who hate Me.
42 '[a]I will make My arrows drunk with blood,
[b]And My sword shall devour flesh,
With the blood of the slain and the captives,
From the long-haired [1]leaders of the enemy.'
43 "[a]Rejoice, O nations, *with* His people;
[b]For He will avenge the blood of His servants,
[c]And will render vengeance on His adversaries,
[d]And will atone for His land *and* His people."

44 Then Moses came and spoke all the words of this song in the
hearing of the people, he, with [1a]Joshua the son of Nun.
45 When Moses had finished speaking all these words to all Israel,
46 he said to them, "[a]Take to your heart all the words with which I
am warning you today, which you shall command [b]your sons to
observe [1]carefully, *even* all the words of this law.
47 "For it is not an idle word for you; indeed [a]it is your life. And [b]by
this word you shall prolong your days in the land, [1]which you are
about to cross the Jordan to [2]possess."
48 And [a]the LORD spoke to Moses that very same day, saying,
49 "[a]Go up to this mountain of the Abarim, Mount Nebo, which is in
the land of Moab [1]opposite Jericho, and look at the land of Canaan,
which I am giving to the sons of Israel for a possession.
50 "Then die on the mountain where you ascend, and be [a]gathered
to your people, as Aaron your brother died on Mount Hor and was
gathered to his people,
51 [a]because you broke faith with Me in the midst of the sons of
Israel at the waters of Meribah-kadesh, in the [b]wilderness of Zin,
because you did not treat Me as holy in the midst of the sons of
Israel.
52 "[a]For you shall see the land at a distance, but [b]you shall not go
there, into the land which I am giving the sons of Israel."

Chapter 33

33 Now this is the blessing with which Moses [a]the man of God
blessed the sons of Israel before his death.
2 And he said,
"[a]The LORD came from Sinai,
[b]And [1]dawned on them from Seir;
[c]He shone forth from Mount Paran,
And He came from [d]the [2]midst of ten thousand holy ones;
[e]At His right hand there was [3]flashing lightning for them.
3 "[a]Indeed, He loves [1]the people;
[b]All [2]Thy holy ones are in Thy hand,
[c]And they [3]followed in Thy steps;
Everyone receives of Thy words.
4 "[a]Moses charged us with a law,
[b]A possession for the assembly of Jacob.
5 "[a]And He was king in Jeshurun,
When the heads of the people were gathered,
The tribes of Israel together.
6 "[a]May Reuben live and not die,
Nor his men be few."

[b]Jer. 50:28-32
, *head* [a]Deut. 3 [b]Jer. 12:12; 46:10, 14
15:10 [b]2 Kin. 6:10; 19:2 [c]Is. 25 [d]Ps. 65:3; 79:9; 85:1
Hoshea [a]Num. 13:8, 16
., *to do* [a]Ezek. 4:5 [b]Deut. 4:9
it., *where* [2]Lit., *s it* [a]Deut. 8:3; ut. 4:40; 33:25
8 [a]Num. 27:12
9 [1]Lit., *which is opposite* [a]Num. 2-14; Deut. 3:27
50 [a]Gen. 25:8
n. 20:12 [b]Num. 27:14
ut. 34:1-3 [b]Deut. 1:37; 3:27
33:1 [a]Josh. 14:6
Lit., *rose to* [2]Lit., *of holiness* [3]Or, *law* [a]Ex. 19:18, 68:8, 17 [b]Judg. Num. 10:12; Hab. [d]Dan. 7:10; Acts 53 [e]Ex. 23:20-22
Lit., *peoples* [2]Lit., r, *lie down at Thy* [a]Deut. 4:37; Mal. 2 [b]Deut. 7:6; 14:2 6:1-9; Luke 10:39
ut. 4:2; John 7:19 [b]Ps. 119:111
5 [a]Num. 23:21
6 [a]Gen. 49:3, 4

7 [a]And this regarding Judah; so he said,
"Hear, O LORD, the voice of Judah,
And bring him to his people.
With his hands he contended for [1]them;
And mayest Thou be a help against his adversaries."

8 And of Levi he said,
"*Let* Thy [a]Thummim and Thy Urim *belong* to [1]Thy [b]godly man,
[c]Whom Thou didst prove at Massah,
With whom Thou didst contend at the waters of Meribah;
9 [a]Who said of his father and his mother,
'I did not consider them';
And he did not acknowledge his brothers,
Nor did he regard his own sons,
For [b]they observed Thy word,
And kept Thy covenant.
10 "[a]They shall teach Thine ordinances to Jacob,
And Thy law to Israel.
[b]They shall put incense [1]before Thee,
And [c]whole burnt offerings on Thine altar.
11 "O LORD, bless his substance,
And accept the work of his hands;
Shatter the loins of those who rise up against him,
And those who hate him, so that they may not rise *again*."

12 Of Benjamin he said,
"[a]May the beloved of the LORD dwell in security by Him,
[b]Who shields him all the day,
[c]And he dwells between His shoulders."

13 And of Joseph he said,
"[a]Blessed of the LORD *be* his land,
With the choice things of heaven, with the dew,
And from the deep lying beneath,
14 And with the choice yield of the sun,
And with the choice produce of the months.
15 "And with the [1]best things of [a]the ancient mountains,
And with the choice things of the everlasting hills,
16 And with the choice things of the earth and its fulness,
And the favor [a]of Him who dwelt in the bush.
Let it come to the head of Joseph,
And to the crown of the head of the one distinguished among his brothers.
17 "As the first-born of his ox, majesty is his,
And his horns are the horns of [a]the wild ox;
With them he shall [b]push the peoples,
All [1]at once, *to* the ends of the earth.
And those are the ten thousands of Ephraim,
And those are the thousands of Manasseh."

18 [a]And of Zebulun he said,
"Rejoice, Zebulun, in your going forth,
And, Issachar, in your tents.
19 "[a]They shall call peoples *to* the mountain;

7 [1]Lit., *him* [a]G
49:8-12

8 [1]Lit., *him* [a]E
Lev. 8:8 [b]Ps. 1
[c]Ex. 17:7; Num
24; Deut. 6:16

9 [a]Ex. 32:27-29
2:5

10 [1]Lit., *in Thy*
[a]Lev. 10:11; Deu
31:9-13 [b]Lev. 1
[c]Ps. 51:19

12 [a]Deut. 4:37f.
[b]Deut. 32:11 [c]Ex

13 [a]Gen. 27:27,
49:22-26

15 [1]Or, *chief* [a]H

16 [a]Ex. 2:2-6; 3:2

17 [1]Or, *together*
23:22 [b]1 Kin. 22:1
44:5

18 [a]Gen. 49:13-15

19 [a]Ex. 15:17; Ps.
Is. 2:3

There they shall offer [b]righteous sacrifices;
For they shall [1]draw out [c]the abundance of the seas,
And the hidden treasures of the sand."

20 [a]And of Gad he said,
"Blessed is the one who enlarges Gad;
He lies down [b]as a [1]lion,
And tears the arm, also the crown of the head.
21 "[a]Then he [1]provided the first *part* for himself,
[b]For there the ruler's portion was [2]reserved;
[c]And he came *with* the leaders of the people;
[d]He executed the justice of the LORD,
And His ordinances with Israel."

22 [a]And of Dan he said,
"Dan is [b]a lion's whelp,
That leaps forth from Bashan."

23 And of Naphtali he said,
"[a]O Naphtali, satisfied with favor,
And full of the blessing of the LORD,
Take possession of the sea and the south."

24 [a]And of Asher he said,
"More blessed than sons is Asher;
May he be favored by his brothers,
[b]And may he dip his foot in oil.
25 "[a]Your locks shall be iron and bronze,
[b]And according to your days, so shall your leisurely walk be.

26 "[a]There is none like the God of [1]Jeshurun,
[b]Who rides the heavens [2]to your help,
And through the skies in His majesty.
27 "[a]The eternal God is a [1]dwelling place,
[b]And underneath are the everlasting arms;
[c]And He drove out the enemy from before you,
[d]And said, 'Destroy!'
28 "[a]So Israel dwells in security,
[b]The fountain of Jacob secluded,
[c]In a land of grain and new wine;
[d]His heavens also drop down dew.
29 "[a]Blessed are you, O Israel;
[b]Who is like you, a people saved by the LORD,
[c]Who is the shield of your help,
[d]And the sword of your majesty!
[e]So your enemies shall cringe before you,
[f]And you shall tread upon their high places."

Chapter 34

34 [a]Now Moses went up from the plains of Moab to Mount
Nebo, to the top of Pisgah, which is opposite Jericho. And the
LORD [b]showed him all the land, Gilead as far as Dan,
2 and all Naphtali and the land of Ephraim and Manasseh, and all
the land of Judah as far as the [1a]western sea,

uck [b]Ps. 4:5; :19 [c]Is. 60:5

ioness [a]Gen. 9 [b]Gen. 49:9

Lit., *saw* [2]Or, *red up* [a]Num. [b]Num. 34:14 1. 4:12 [d]Josh. 22:1-3

49:16 [b]Ezek. 19:2, 3

3 [a]Gen. 49:21

en. 49:20 [b]Job 29:6

147:13 [b]Deut. 4:40; 32:47

., Israel [2]Lit., *in* :11; Deut. 4:35; . 86:8; Jer. 10:6 0:14; Ps. 68:33, 104:3; Hab. 3:8

[1]Or, *refuge* [a]Ps. , 2 [b]Gen. 49:24 :11; Josh. 24:18 [d]Deut. 7:2

Deut. 33:12; Jer. Num. 23:9; Deut. [c]Gen. 27:28, 37 [d]Deut. 33:13

[a]Ps. 1:1; 32:1, 2 eut. 4:32; 2 Sam. 3 [c]Gen. 15:1; Ps. 20; 115:9-11 [d]Ps. [e]Ps. 66:3 [f]Num. 33:52

34:1 [a]Deut. 32:49 [b]Deut. 32:52

.e., Mediterranean Sea [a]Deut. 11:24

3 and the [1]Negev and the plain in the valley of Jericho, [a]the city of
palm trees, as far as Zoar.
4 Then the LORD said to him, "This is the land which [a]I swore to
Abraham, Isaac, and Jacob, saying, 'I will give it to your [1]descend-
ants'; I have let you see *it* with your eyes, but you shall not go over
there."
5 So Moses [a]the servant of the LORD [b]died there in the land of
Moab, according to the [1]word of the LORD.
6 And He buried him in the valley in the land of Moab, [a]opposite
Beth-peor; but [b]no man knows his burial place to this day.
7 Although Moses was [a]one hundred and twenty years old when
he died, [b]his eye was not dim, nor his vigor abated.
8 So the sons of Israel wept for Moses in the plains of Moab thirty
days; then the days of weeping *and* mourning for Moses came to an
end.
9 Now Joshua the son of Nun was [a]filled with the spirit of wis-
dom, for Moses had laid his hands on him; and the sons of Israel
listened to him and did as the LORD had commanded Moses.
10 Since then [a]no prophet has risen in Israel like Moses, whom [b]the
LORD knew face to face,
11 for all the signs and wonders which the LORD sent him to per-
form in the land of Egypt against Pharaoh, all his servants, and all
his land,
12 and for all the mighty [1]power and for all the great terror which
Moses performed in the sight of all Israel.

3 [1]I.e., South cou [a]Judg. 1:16; 3:13; 28:15

4 [1]Lit., *seed* [a]Ger 12:7; 26:3; 28:13

5 [1]Lit., *mouth* [a]Nu 12:7; Josh. 1:1, 2 [b]Deut. 32:50

6 [a]Deut. 3:29; 4:46 [b]Jude 9

7 [a]Deut. 31:2 [b]Ge 27:1; 48:10

9 [a]Num. 27:18, 23; 11:2

10 [a]Deut. 18:15, 18 [b]Ex. 33:11; Num. 12 Deut. 5:4

12 [1]Lit., *hand*

DEUTERONOMY AT A GLANCE

me of Deuteronomy:

MENT DIVISIONS

		CHAPTER THEMES
		1
		2
		3
		4
		5
		6
		7
		8
		9
		10
		11
		12
		13
		14
		15
		16
		17
		18
		19
		20
		21
		22
		23
		24
		25
		26
		27
		28
		29
		30
		31
		32
		33
		34

Author:

Date:

Geographical Location:

Purpose:

Key Words:

JOSHUA

For years Joshua faithfully had served Moses—and God. How well Joshua understood the mea of his name, "The Lord is salvation." All his contemporaries, except Caleb, had died in the wilder because they had not believed God. But God had spared Joshua and Caleb because they had follo Him fully.

Now Moses was dead and God had appointed Joshua to lead the children of Israel into the lar promise. Their salvation from their enemies would not come from the east nor from the west but the One who made the heaven and the earth!

God's words rang in Joshua's heart: "Be strong and courageous."

THINGS TO DO

General Instructions

1. If you aren't familiar with who Joshua is, before you begin studying the book, read Number 14, 27:18-23, and Deuteronomy 34:9.
2. As you study Joshua one chapter at a time, it will help you keep everything in context if yo remember that Joshua falls into four segments. In chapters 1 through 5 the children of Is prepare to enter the land. Chapters 6 through 12 describe the conquest of the land. Chapter through 21 tell of the allocation of the land. In chapters 22 through 24 Joshua calls Israel to se the Lord who gave them the land.
3. As you read each chapter, ask the five W's and an H: Who? What? When? Where? Why? How? For example, in a historical book such as Joshua ask: What is this chapter about? Who the main characters? What is taking place? Where is it happening and when? Who is involv Why is this occurring, being said, or to be done? What are the consequences? How is it goin happen? How should it be done? Record the main points or events of the chapter in the margi
4. Notice the various cities and places mentioned throughout this book. Look them up on the n at the beginning of Joshua (*see* page 323) so you can keep the book in its geographical context.
5. Mark every reference to time with a symbol such as this ⏰ . This will help you see when eve occurred and the chronological relationship of one event to another.
6. After you finish studying each chapter, write the theme or event covered in that chapter on line next to the chapter number. Then record it on the JOSHUA AT A GLANCE chart on page 3

Chapters 1-5

1. As you read these chapters, mark the following key words and their synonyms: *Joshua, la strong, courageous, firm, command (commanded, as the Lord commanded, in accordance with the co mand of the Lord), possess, covenant, ark of the Lord (ark of the covenant),* and *Israel*. Write these on index card that you can use as a bookmark while studying this segment.
2. Watch how the events or the instructions prepare the Israelites to enter the land. Also note procedure for entering the land and the requirements placed on them as they arrive in the lar You might list these in the margin under the heading "Possessing the Land."
3. If while reading chapter 5 you need a review of circumcision, read Genesis 17 and Exod 4:24-26.
4. Don't forget to record the theme of each chapter in the text and on JOSHUA AT A GLANCE.

Chapters 6-12

1. As you study this section keep in mind the general instructions above.

Although you'll mark many of the same key words, make a new bookmark of the following key words: *God, Lord, Joshua, covenant, strong, courageous, land, fear, command (commanded), fight (fought), capture (captured), ark of the Lord,* and *Israel.*

Carefully observe what God tells the people to do when they conquer a city. Read Genesis 15:7-21 and note that God told Abraham He would bring his descendants into Canaan when "the iniquity of the Amorites was complete." Also recall the covenant God made with Abraham on that day. You might write "Genesis 15:7-21" in the margin of this section as a cross-reference.

As you read, watch what happens when the people fail to consult God or to obey His commands in respect to the inhabitants of the land. Note this in the margin.

When you come to chapter 8, note where Mt. Ebal and Gerizim are located and what takes place there. Refer back to Deuteronomy 11:29 and Deuteronomy 27:11-14. Use the map on page 323 to locate these places. Also mark all clues to time with a drawing of a clock in the margin or above the verse where it occurs.

Record the theme of each chapter.

ters 13-21

Once again make a new bookmark of the following key words, although some words will remain the same: *Israel, land, Joshua, Caleb, strong, fear, command (commanded, commandments), fought, captured, inheritance, possession, possessed* (also mark *possession* in chapter 12), and *promised.*

Continue to consult the map on page 323 so you are aware of the geographical location of the places mentioned in this segment. Also mark the name of each tribe as it is allotted its portion of the land.

As you read, watch for any mention of Caleb. Remember what you read about Joshua and Caleb in Numbers 13-14. There are lessons to be learned from their example.

Pay careful attention to chapter 20 and what you learn about the cities of refuge.

Also note the inheritance given to the Levites in Joshua 21.

Don't forget to record the chapter themes.

pters 22-24

Make this final bookmark of key words and mark them in the text: *land, possess (possession), covenant, strong, firm, fear, command (commandment, commanded), serve (served), inheritance, Israel, Joshua, promised, fought,* and *inheritance.*

In the margin also list God's instructions and what the people are to do in order to keep them. Also note in the margin the consequences of disobedience.

. As you read Joshua 23, mark the word *cling.* Then read Jeremiah 13:1-11.

. Complete JOSHUA AT A GLANCE. Fill in the four main segment divisions and any others you see.

. Compare what Joshua tells the children of Israel in chapter 23 with God's word to Joshua in chapter 1. You might write "Joshua 1:7-9" in the margin of Joshua 23.

NGS TO THINK ABOUT

. Do you consult the Lord and His Word and then walk in obedience to what He says?

. Joshua was admonished to be strong and courageous. What do you think this means? Read Revelation 21:8 and note what is said about the cowardly.

. Have you decided whom you are going to follow? Have you counted the cost? What would cause you to compromise? Could you get away with compromise? What would it cost you? Will it be worth it?

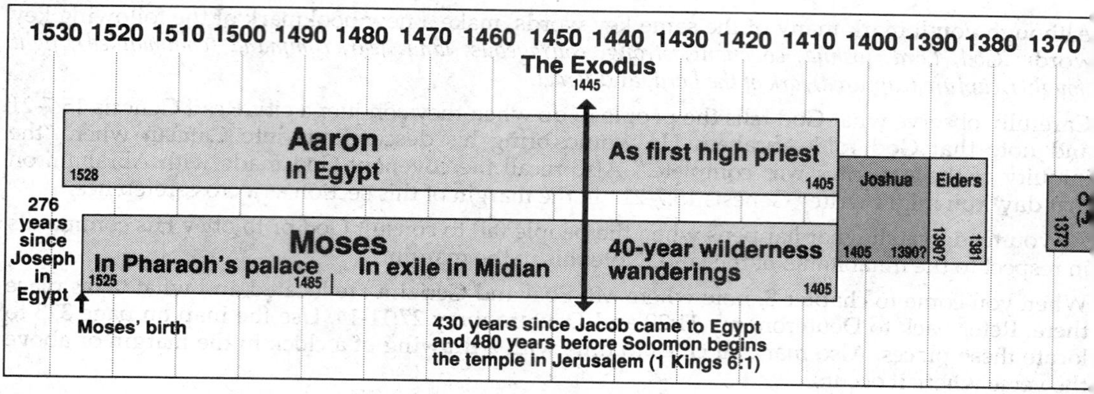

Chapter 1

1 Now it came about after the death of Moses the servant of the
LORD that the LORD spoke to Joshua the son of Nun, Moses'
[1]servant, saying,
2 "Moses [a]My servant is dead; now therefore arise, [b]cross this Jor-
dan, you and all this people, to the land which I am giving to them,
to the sons of Israel.
3 "[a]Every place on which the sole of your foot treads, I have given it
to you, just as I spoke to Moses.
4 "[a]From the wilderness and this Lebanon, even as far as the great
river, the river Euphrates, all the land of the Hittites, and as far as the
Great Sea toward the setting of the sun, will be your territory.
5 "[a]No man will *be able to* stand before you all the days of your life.
Just as I have been with Moses, I will be with you; [b]I will not fail you
or forsake you.
6 "[a]Be strong and courageous, for you shall give this people posses-
sion of the land which I swore to their fathers to give them.
7 "Only be strong and very courageous; [1a]be careful to do according
to all the law which Moses My servant commanded you; do not turn
from it to the right or to the left, so that you may [2]have success
wherever you go.
8 "[a]This book of the law shall not depart from your mouth, but you
shall meditate on it day and night, so that you may [1]be careful to do
according to all that is written in it; [b]for then you will make your
way prosperous, and then you will [2]have success.
9 "Have I not commanded you? [a]Be strong and courageous! [b]Do not
tremble or be dismayed, for the LORD your God is with you
wherever you go."
10 Then Joshua commanded the officers of the people, saying,
11 "Pass through the midst of the camp and command the people,
saying, 'Prepare provisions for yourselves, for within [a]three days
you are to cross this Jordan, to go in to possess the land which the
LORD your God is giving you, to possess it.'"
12 [a]And to the Reubenites and to the Gadites and to the half-tribe of
Manasseh, Joshua [1]said,
13 "Remember the word which Moses the servant of the LORD com-
manded you, saying, '[a]The LORD your God gives you rest, and will
give you this land.'
14 "Your wives, your little ones, and your cattle shall remain in the

1:1 [1]Or, minist

2 [a]Num. 12:7; D 34:5 [b]Josh. 1:1

3 [a]Deut. 11:24

4 [a]Gen. 15:18; 34:3

5 [a]Deut. 7:24 [b] 31:6, 7; Heb. 13

6 [a]Deut. 31:6, 7,

7 [1]Lit., *observe wisely* [a]Deut. 5:3

8 [1]Lit., *observe wisely* [a]Deut. 31 Josh. 8:34 [b]Deu Ps. 1:1-3

9 [a]Josh. 1:7 [b]De

11 [a]Josh. 3:2

12 [1]Lit., *said, say* [a]Num. 32:20-22

13 [a]Deut. 3:18-20

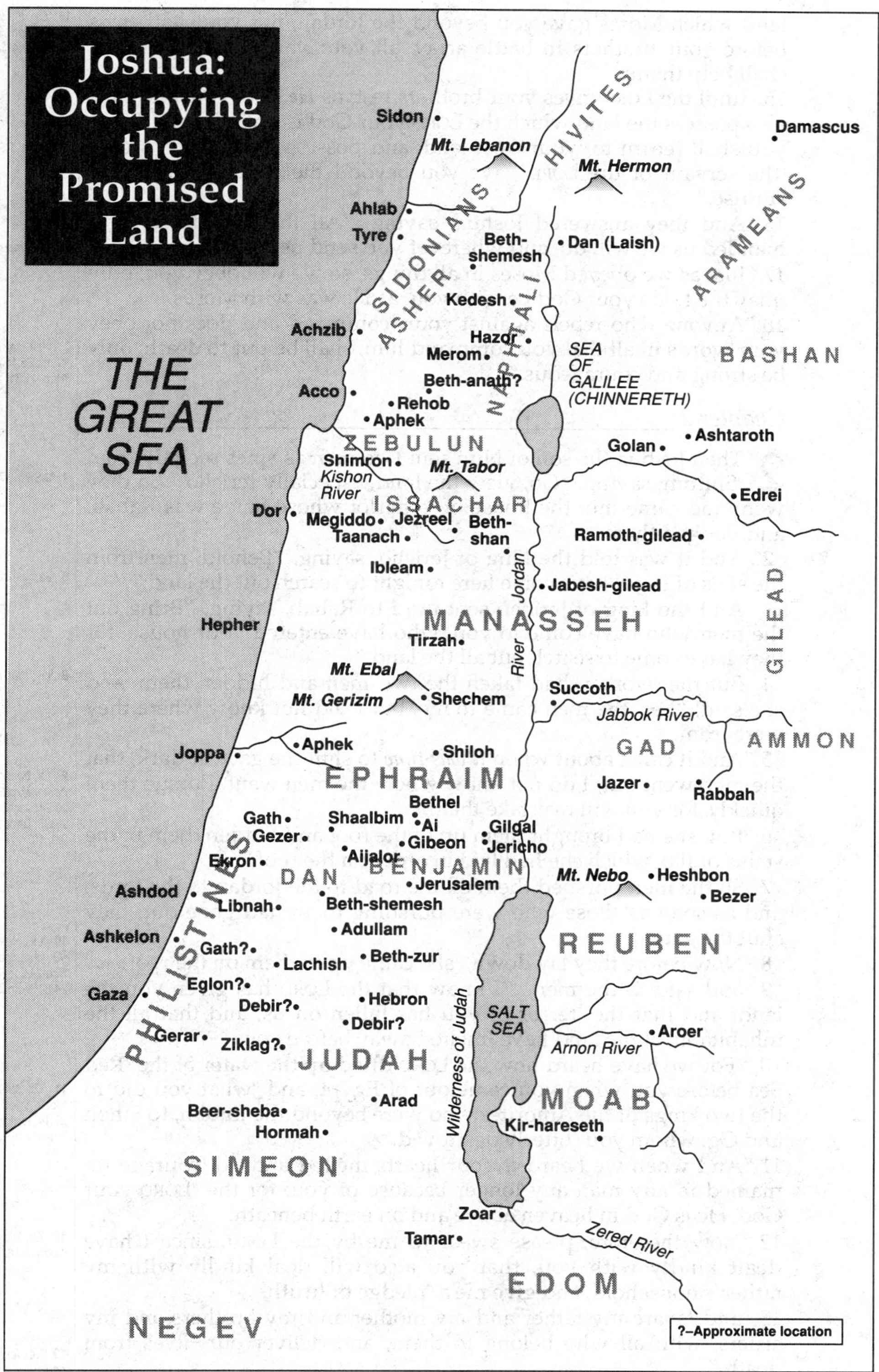
Joshua: Occupying the Promised Land
THE GREAT SEA
Sidon
Damascus
Mt. Lebanon
HIVITES
Mt. Hermon
SIDONIANS
ARAMEANS
Ahlab
Tyre
Beth-shemesh
Dan (Laish)
ASHER
NAPHTALI
Kedesh
Achzib
Hazor
Merom
SEA OF GALILEE (CHINNERETH)
BASHAN
Acco
Beth-anath?
Rehob
Aphek
ZEBULUN
Golan
Ashtaroth
Shimron
Mt. Tabor
Kishon River
ISSACHAR
Edrei
Dor
Megiddo
Jezreel
Beth-shan
Taanach
Ramoth-gilead
Ibleam
River Jordan
Jabesh-gilead
MANASSEH
GILEAD
Hepher
Tirzah
Mt. Ebal
Mt. Gerizim
Shechem
Succoth
Jabbok River
Joppa
Aphek
Shiloh
GAD
AMMON
EPHRAIM
Jazer
Rabbah
Gath
Shaalbim
Bethel
Ai
Gilgal
Gezer
Gibeon
Jericho
Aijalon
Ekron
DAN
BENJAMIN
Mt. Nebo
Heshbon
Ashdod
Jerusalem
Libnah
Beth-shemesh
Bezer
Adullam
Ashkelon
REUBEN
Gath?
Beth-zur
Lachish
PHILISTINES
Eglon?
Gaza
Hebron
Debir?
Debir?
SALT SEA
Wilderness of Judah
Aroer
Gerar
Ziklag?
Arnon River
JUDAH
MOAB
Arad
Beer-sheba
Kir-hareseth
Hormah
SIMEON
Zoar
Tamar
Zered River
EDOM
NEGEV
?–Approximate location

land which Moses gave you beyond the Jordan, but you shall cross before your brothers in battle array, all your valiant warriors, and shall help them,

15 until the LORD gives your brothers rest, as *He gives* you, and they also possess the land which the LORD your God is giving them. [a]Then you shall return to [1]your own land, and possess [2]that which Moses [b]the servant of the LORD gave you beyond the Jordan toward the sunrise."

16 And they answered Joshua, saying, "All that you have commanded us we will do, and wherever you send us we will go.

17 "Just as we obeyed Moses in all things, so we will obey you; only [a]may the LORD your God be with you, as He was with Moses.

18 "Anyone who rebels against your [1]command and does not obey your words in all that you command him, shall be put to death; only be strong and courageous."

Chapter 2

2 Then Joshua the son of Nun sent two men as spies secretly from [a]Shittim, saying, "Go, view the land, especially Jericho." So they went and came into the house of [b]a harlot whose name was Rahab, and [1]lodged there.

2 And it was told the king of Jericho, saying, "Behold, men from the sons of Israel have come here tonight to search out the land."

3 And the king of Jericho sent *word* to Rahab, saying, "Bring out the men who have come to you, who have entered your house, for they have come to search out all the land."

4 But the [a]woman had taken the two men and hidden them, and she said, "Yes, the men came to me, but I did not know where they were from.

5 "And it came about when *it was time* to shut the gate, at dark, that the men went out; I do not know where the men went. Pursue them quickly, for you will overtake them."

6 But [a]she had brought them up to the roof and hidden them in the stalks of flax which she had laid in order on the roof.

7 So the men pursued them on the road to the Jordan to the fords; and as soon as those who were pursuing them had gone out, they shut the gate.

8 Now before they lay down, [1]she came up to them on the roof,

9 and said to the men, "[a]I know that the LORD has given you the land, and that the [b]terror of you has fallen on us, and that all the inhabitants of the land have [1]melted away before you.

10 "[a]For we have heard how the LORD dried up the water of the [1]Red Sea before you when you came out of Egypt, and [b]what you did to the two kings of the Amorites who were beyond the Jordan, to Sihon and Og, whom you [2]utterly destroyed.

11 "And when we heard *it,* [a]our hearts melted and no [1]courage remained in any man any longer because of you; for the [b]LORD your God, He is God in heaven above and on earth beneath.

12 "Now therefore, please swear to me by the LORD, since I have dealt kindly with you, that you also will deal kindly with my father's household, and give me a [a]pledge of [1]truth,

13 and [1]spare my father and my mother and my brothers and my sisters, with all who belong to them, and deliver our [2]lives from death."

15 [1]Lit., *the land of* [2]Lit., *it* [a]Josh. 22:4 [b]Josh. 1

17 [a]Josh. 1:5, 9

18 [1]Lit., *mouth*

2:1 [1]Lit., *lay down* [a]Num. 25:1; Josh. 3: [b]Heb. 11:31; James

4 [a]2 Sam. 17:19

6 [a]James 2:25

8 [1]Lit., *then she*

9 [1]Or, *become demoralized* [a]Num. 20:24; Josh. 9:24 [b] 23:27; Deut. 2:25; J 9:9, 10

10 [1]Lit., *Sea of Ree* [2]Or, *put under the b* [a]Ex. 14:21; Num. 23 24:8 [b]Num. 21:21-3

11 [1]Lit., *spirit arose* [a]Josh. 5:1; 7:5; Ps. 22:14; Is. 13:7; 19:1 [b]Deut. 4:39

12 [1]Or, *faithfulness* [a]Josh. 2:18, 19

13 [1]Lit., *let live* [2]Lit *souls*

14 So the men said to her, "Our [1]life [2]for yours if you do not tell this
business of ours; and it shall come about when the LORD gives us the
land that we will [a]deal kindly and [3]faithfully with you."
15 Then she let them down by a rope through the window, for her
house was on the city wall, so that she was living on the wall.
16 And she said to them, "[a]Go to the hill country, lest the pursuers
happen upon you, and hide yourselves there for three days, until the
pursuers return. Then afterward you may go on your way."
17 And the men said to her, "[a]We *shall be* free from this oath [1]to you
which you have made us swear,
18 [1]unless, when we come into the land, you tie this cord of scarlet
thread in the window through which you let us down, and [a]gather to
yourself into the house your father and your mother and your
brothers and all your father's household.
19 "And it shall come about that anyone who goes out of the doors
of your house into the street, his blood *shall be* on his own head, and
we *shall be* free; but anyone who is with you in the house, [a]his blood
shall be on our head, if a hand is *laid* on him.
20 "But if you tell this business of ours, then we shall be free from
the oath which you have made us swear."
21 And she said, "According to your words, so be it." So she sent
them away, and they departed; and she tied the scarlet cord in the
window.
22 And they departed and came to the hill country, and remained
there for three days until the pursuers returned. Now the pursuers
had sought *them* [1]all along the road, but had not found *them*.
23 Then the two men returned and came down from the hill
country and crossed over and came to Joshua the son of Nun, and
they related to him all that had happened to them.
24 And they said to Joshua, "Surely the LORD has given all the land
into our hands, and [a]all the inhabitants of the land, moreover, have
[1]melted away before us."

Chapter 3 ______

3 Then Joshua rose early in the morning; and he and all the sons of
Israel set out from [a]Shittim and came to the Jordan, and they
lodged there before they crossed.
2 And it came about [a]at the end of three days that the officers went
through the midst of the camp;
3 and they commanded the people, saying, "When you see the
[a]ark of the covenant of the LORD your God with the Levitical priests
carrying it, then you shall set out from your place and go after it.
4 "However, there shall be between you and it a distance of about
2,000 [1]cubits by measure. Do not come near it, that you may know
the way by which you shall go, for you have not passed this way
before."
5 Then Joshua said to the people, "[a]Consecrate yourselves, for to-
morrow the LORD will do wonders among you."
6 And Joshua spoke to the priests, saying, "Take up the ark of the
covenant and cross over ahead of the people." So they took up the
ark of the covenant and went ahead of the people.
7 Now the LORD said to Joshua, "This day I will begin to [a]exalt you
in the sight of all Israel, that they may know that just as I have been
with Moses, I will be with you.

14 [1]Lit., *soul* [2]Lit., *instead of you to die* [3]Or, *truly* [a]Gen. 24:49

16 [a]James 2:25

17 [1]Lit., *of yours* [a]Gen. 24:8

18 [1]Lit., *behold* [a]Josh. 2:12

19 [a]Matt. 27:25

22 [1]Lit., *through all the road*

24 [1]Or, *become demoralized* [a]Josh. 2:9

3:1 [a]Josh. 2:1

2 [a]Josh. 1:11

3 [a]Deut. 31:9

4 [1]I.e., One cubit equals approx. 18 in.

5 [a]Ex. 19:10, 11; Josh. 7:13

7 [a]Josh. 4:14

8 "You shall, moreover, command the priests who are carrying the ark of the covenant, saying, 'When you come to the edge of the waters of the Jordan, you shall stand *still* in the Jordan.' "

9 Then Joshua said to the sons of Israel, "Come here, and hear the words of the LORD your God."

10 And Joshua said, "By this you shall know that [a]the living God is among you, and that He will assuredly [b]dispossess from before you the Canaanite, the Hittite, the Hivite, the Perizzite, the Girgashite, the Amorite, and the Jebusite.

11 "Behold, the ark of the covenant of [a]the Lord of all the earth is crossing over ahead of you into the Jordan.

12 "Now then, [a]take for yourselves twelve men from the tribes of Israel, one man for each tribe.

13 "And it shall come about when the soles of the feet of the priests who carry the ark of the LORD, the Lord of all the earth, shall rest in the waters of the Jordan, the waters of the Jordan shall be cut off, *and* the waters which are [1]flowing down from above [2]shall [a]stand in one heap."

14 So it came about when the people set out from their tents to cross the Jordan with the priests carrying [a]the ark of the covenant before the people,

15 and when those who carried the ark came into the Jordan, and the feet of the priests carrying the ark were dipped in the edge of the water (for the [a]Jordan overflows all its banks all the days of harvest),

16 [a]that the waters which were [1]flowing down from above stood *and* rose up in [b]one heap, a great distance away at Adam, the city that is beside Zarethan; and those which were [1]flowing down toward the sea of the [c]Arabah, the Salt Sea, were completely cut off. So the people crossed opposite Jericho.

17 And the priests who carried the ark of the covenant of the LORD stood firm [a]on dry ground in the middle of the Jordan while all Israel crossed on dry ground, until all the nation had finished crossing the Jordan.

Chapter 4

4 Now it came about when all the nation had finished crossing the [a]Jordan, that the LORD spoke to Joshua, saying,

2 "[a]Take for yourselves twelve men from the people, one man from each tribe,

3 and command them, saying, 'Take up for yourselves twelve stones from here out of the middle of the Jordan, from the place where the priests' feet are standing firm, and carry them over with you, and lay them down in [a]the lodging place where you will lodge tonight.' "

4 So Joshua called the twelve men whom he had appointed from the sons of Israel, one man from each tribe;

5 and Joshua said to them, "[1]Cross again to the ark of the LORD your God into the middle of the Jordan, and each of you take up a stone on his shoulder, according to the number of the tribes of the sons of Israel.

6 "[1]Let this be a sign among you, so that [a]when your children ask [2]later, saying, 'What do these stones mean to you?'

7 then you shall say to them, 'Because the [a]waters of the Jordan were cut off before the ark of the covenant of the LORD; when it

10 [a]Deut. 5:26; 1 Thess. 1:9 [b]Deut. 7:1
11 [a]Job 41:11; Zech. 6:5
12 [a]Josh. 4:2
13 [1]Lit., *going* *they shall* [a]Ex.
14 [a]Ps. 132:8; 7:44f.
15 [a]1 Chr. 12:1… 12:5; 49:19
16 [1]Lit., *going* 66:6; 74:15; 114 [b]Josh. 3:13 [c]De
17 [a]Ex. 14:21, 2
4:1 [a]Deut. 27:2; 3:17
2 [a]Josh. 3:12
3 [a]Josh. 4:20
5 [1]Lit., *Cross bef* *ark*
6 [1]Lit., *That this n* *be* [2]Lit., *tomorrow* 12:26; 13:14; Josh
7 [a]Josh. 3:13

crossed the Jordan, the waters of the Jordan were cut off.' So these
stones shall become a [b]memorial to the sons of Israel forever."
8 And thus the sons of Israel did, as Joshua commanded, and took
up twelve stones from the middle of the Jordan, just as the LORD
spoke to Joshua, according to the number of the tribes of the sons of
Israel; and they carried them over with them to [a]the lodging place,
and put them down there.
9 Then Joshua set up twelve [a]stones in the middle of the Jordan at
the place where the feet of the priests who carried the ark of the
covenant were standing, and they are there to this day.
10 For the priests who carried the ark were standing in the middle
of the Jordan until everything was completed that the LORD had
commanded Joshua to speak to the people, according to all that
Moses had commanded Joshua. And the people hurried and crossed;
11 and it came about when all the people had finished crossing, that
the ark of the LORD and the priests crossed before the people.
12 [a]And the sons of Reuben and the sons of Gad and the half-tribe
of Manasseh crossed over in battle array before the sons of Israel,
just as Moses had spoken to them;
13 about 40,000, equipped for war, crossed for battle before the
LORD to the desert plains of Jericho.
14 [a]On that day the LORD exalted Joshua in the sight of all Israel; so
that they [1]revered him, just as they had [1]revered Moses all the days
of his life.
15 Now the LORD said to [1]Joshua,
16 "Command the priests who carry [a]the ark of the testimony that
they come up from the Jordan."
17 So Joshua commanded the priests, saying, "Come up from the
Jordan."
18 And it came about when the priests who carried the ark of the
covenant of the LORD had come up from the middle of the Jordan,
and the soles of the priests' feet were [1]lifted up to the dry ground,
that the waters of the Jordan returned to their place, and went over
all its banks as before.
19 Now the people came up from the Jordan on the [a]tenth of the
first month and camped at Gilgal on the eastern edge of Jericho.
20 [a]And [1]those twelve stones which they had taken from the Jordan,
Joshua set up [b]at Gilgal.
21 And he said to the sons of [1]Israel, "When your children ask their
fathers in time to come, saying, 'What are these stones?'
22 then you shall inform your children, saying, 'Israel crossed this
Jordan on [a]dry ground.'
23 "For the LORD your God dried up the waters of the Jordan before
you until you had crossed, just as the LORD your God had done to
the [1]Red Sea, [a]which He dried up before us until we had crossed;
24 that [a]all the peoples of the earth may know that the [b]hand of the
LORD is mighty, so that you may [1c]fear the LORD your God [2]forever."

Chapter 5

5 Now it came about when all the kings of the Amorites who *were*
beyond the Jordan to the west, and all the kings of the
[a]Canaanites who *were* by the sea, [b]heard how the LORD had dried up
the waters of the Jordan before the sons of Israel until [1]they had

. 12:14; Num. 16:40
8 [a]Josh. 4:20
ı. 28:18; Josh. ·.; 1 Sam. 7:12
2 [a]Num. 32:17
feared [a]Josh. 3:7
Joshua, saying
16 [a]Ex. 25:16
[1]Lit., *drawn out*
19 [a]Deut. 1:3
t., *these* [a]Josh. :8 [b]Josh. 4:3, 8
., *Israel, saying,*
22 [a]Josh. 3:17
t., *Sea of Reeds* [a]Ex. 14:21
reverence [2]Lit., *the days* [a]1 Kin. 2 Kin. 19:19; Ps. Ex. 15:16; 1 Chr. ; Ps. 89:13 [c]Ex. ; Ps. 76:7f.; Jer. 10:7
[1]Other mss. read ım. 13:29 [b]Josh. 2:10, 11

crossed, that their hearts melted, and there was no spirit in them any
longer, because of the sons of Israel.
2 At that time the LORD said to Joshua, "Make for yourself [a]flint
knives and circumcise again the sons of Israel the second time."
3 So Joshua made himself flint knives and circumcised the sons of
Israel at [1]Gibeath-haaraloth.
4 And this is the reason why Joshua circumcised them: [a]all the
people who came out of Egypt who were males, all the men of war,
died in the wilderness along the way, after they came out of Egypt.
5 For all the people who came out were circumcised, but all the
people who were born in the wilderness along the way as they came
out of Egypt had not been circumcised.
6 For the sons of Israel walked [a]forty years in the wilderness, until
all the nation, *that is,* the men of war who came out of Egypt,
[1]perished because they did not listen to the voice of the LORD, [b]to
whom the LORD had sworn that He would not let them see the land
which the LORD had sworn to their fathers to give us, a land flowing
with milk and honey.
7 And their children whom He raised up in their place, Joshua
[1]circumcised; for they were uncircumcised, because they had not
circumcised them along the way.
8 Now it came about when they had finished circumcising all the
nation, that they remained in their places in the camp until they
were [1]healed.
9 Then the LORD said to Joshua, "Today I have rolled away [a]the
reproach of Egypt from you." So the name of that place is called
[1]Gilgal to this day.
10 While the sons of Israel camped at Gilgal, [a]they observed the
Passover on the evening of the [b]fourteenth day of the month on the
desert plains of Jericho.
11 And on the [1]day after the Passover, on [2]that very day, they ate
some of the produce of the land, unleavened cakes and parched
grain.
12 And [a]the manna ceased on the [1]day after they had eaten some of
the produce of the land, so that the sons of Israel no longer had
manna, but they ate some of the yield of the land of Canaan during
that year.
13 Now it came about when Joshua was by Jericho, that he lifted up
his eyes and looked, and behold, [a]a man was standing opposite him
with his sword drawn in his hand, and Joshua went to him and said
to him, "Are you for us or for our adversaries?"
14 And he said, "No, rather I indeed come now *as* captain of the
host of the LORD." And Joshua [a]fell on his face to the earth, and
bowed down, and said to him, "What has my lord to say to his
servant?"
15 And the captain of the LORD's host said to Joshua, "[a]Remove
your sandals from your feet, for the place where you are standing is
holy." And Joshua did so.

Chapter 6 ____________________________________

6 Now Jericho was tightly shut because of the sons of Israel; no
one went out and no one came in.
2 And the LORD said to Joshua, "See, I have given Jericho into your
hand, with [a]its king *and* the valiant warriors.

2 [a]Ex. 4:25
3 [1]I.e., the hill foreskins
4 [a]Deut. 2:14
6 [1]Lit., *were fin* [a]Deut. 2:7, 14 14:29-35; 26:63
7 [1]Lit., *circumc them*
8 [1]Lit., *revived*
9 [1]I.e., rolling [a] 2:8
10 [a]Ex. 12:18 [b] 4:19
11 [1]Lit., *morrow this*
12 [1]Lit., *morrow* 16:35
13 [a]Gen. 18:1, 2 30; Num. 22:31
14 [a]Gen. 17:3
15 [a]Ex. 3:5
6:2 [a]Deut. 7:24

3 "And you shall march around the city, all the men of war circling
the city once. You shall do so for six days.
4 "Also seven priests shall carry seven [a]trumpets of rams' horns
before the ark; then on the seventh day you shall march around the
city seven times, and the priests shall blow the trumpets.
5 "And it shall be that when they make a long blast with the ram's
horn, and when you hear the sound of the trumpet, all the people
shall shout with a great shout; and the wall of the city will fall down
[1]flat, and the people will go up every man [2]straight ahead."
6 So Joshua the son of Nun called the priests and said to them,
"Take up the ark of the covenant, and let seven priests carry seven
trumpets of rams' horns before the ark of the LORD."
7 Then [1]he said to the people, "Go forward, and march around the
city, and let the armed men go on before the ark of the LORD."
8 And it was *so,* that when Joshua had spoken to the people, the
seven priests carrying the seven trumpets of rams' horns before the
LORD went forward and blew the trumpets; and the ark of the cove-
nant of the LORD followed them.
9 And the armed men went before the priests who blew the trum-
pets, and [a]the rear guard came after the ark, while they continued to
blow the trumpets.
10 But Joshua commanded the people, saying, "You shall not shout
nor let your voice be heard, nor let a word proceed out of your
mouth, until the day I tell you, 'Shout!' Then you shall shout!"
11 So he had the ark of the LORD [1]taken around the city, circling *it*
once; then they came into the camp and spent the night in the camp.
12 Now Joshua rose early in the morning, and the priests took up
the ark of the LORD.
13 And [a]the seven priests carrying the seven trumpets of rams'
horns before the ark of the LORD went on continually, and blew the
trumpets; and the armed men went before them, and [b]the rear guard
came after the ark of the LORD, while they continued to blow the
trumpets.
14 Thus the second day they marched around the city once and
returned to the camp; they did so for six days.
15 Then it came about on the seventh day that they rose early at the
dawning of the day and marched around the city in the same man-
ner seven times; only on that day they marched around the city
seven times.
16 And it came about at the seventh time, when the priests blew the
trumpets, Joshua said to the people, "[a]Shout! For the LORD has given
you the city.
17 "And the city shall be [a]under the ban, it and all that is in it
belongs to the LORD; only Rahab the harlot [1]and all who are with her
in the house shall live, because she hid the messengers whom we
sent.
18 "But as for you, only keep yourselves from the things under the
ban, lest you [1]covet *them* and [a]take some of the things under the ban,
so you would make the camp of Israel accursed and bring trouble
on it.
19 "[a]But all the silver and gold and articles of bronze and iron are
holy to the LORD; they shall go into the treasury of the LORD."
20 So the people shouted, and [1]*priests* blew the trumpets; and it
came about, when the people heard the sound of the trumpet, that

4 [a]Lev. 25:9
, *in its place* [2]Lit., *before himself*
7 [1]Or, *they*
sh. 6:13; Is. 52:12
Lit., *to go around*
h. 6:4 [b]Josh. 6:9
6 [a]2 Chr. 13:14f.
[1]Lit., *she and all*
7:28; Deut. 20:17
., *devote* [a]Josh. 7:1
[a]Num. 31:11, 12, 21-23
20 [1]Or, *they*

the people shouted with a great shout and the [a]wall fell down [2]flat,
so that the people went up into the city, every man straight [3]ahead,
and they took the city.
21 [a]And they [1]utterly destroyed everything in the city, both man
and woman, young and old, and ox and sheep and donkey, with the
edge of the sword.
22 And Joshua said to the two men who had spied out the land,
"[a]Go into the harlot's house and bring the woman and all she has
out of there, as you have sworn to her."
23 So the young men who were spies went in and [a]brought out
Rahab and her father and her mother and her brothers and all she
had; they also brought out all her relatives, and placed them outside
the camp of Israel.
24 [a]And they burned the city with fire, and all that was in it. Only
the silver and gold and articles of bronze and iron, they put into the
treasury of the [1]house of the LORD.
25 However, [a]Rahab the harlot and her father's household and all
she had, Joshua [1]spared; and she has lived in the midst of Israel to
this day, for [b]she hid the messengers whom Joshua sent to spy out
Jericho.
26 Then Joshua made them take an oath at that time, saying,
"[a]Cursed before the LORD is the man who rises up and builds this
city Jericho; with *the loss of* his first-born he shall lay its foundation,
and with *the loss of* his youngest son he shall set up its gates."
27 So [a]the LORD was with Joshua, and his [b]fame was in all the land.

Chapter 7

7 [a]But the sons of Israel acted unfaithfully in regard to the things
under the ban, for Achan, the son of Carmi, the son of Zabdi, the
son of Zerah, from the tribe of Judah, took some of the things under
the ban, therefore the anger of the LORD burned against the sons of
Israel.
2 Now Joshua sent men from Jericho to Ai, which is near [a]Beth-
aven, east of Bethel, and said to them, "[1]Go up and spy out the
land." So the men went up and spied out Ai.
3 And they returned to Joshua and said to him, "Do not let all the
people go up; *only* about two or three thousand men need go up [1]to
Ai; do not make all the people toil up there, for they are few."
4 So about three thousand men from the people went up there, but
[a]they fled [1]from the men of Ai.
5 And the men of Ai struck down about thirty-six of their men,
and pursued them [1]from the gate as far as Shebarim, and struck
them down on the descent, so the [a]hearts of the people melted and
became as water.
6 Then Joshua [a]tore his clothes and fell to the earth on his face
before the ark of the LORD until the evening, *both* he and the elders of
Israel; and [b]they put dust on their heads.
7 And Joshua said, "Alas, O Lord [1]GOD, why didst Thou ever
bring this people over the Jordan, *only* to deliver us into the hand of
the Amorites, to destroy us? If only we had been willing [2]to dwell
beyond the Jordan!
8 "O Lord, what can I say since Israel has turned *their* [1]back before
their enemies?
9 "[a]For the Canaanites and all the inhabitants of the land will hear

20 [2]Lit., *in its* [3]Lit., *before h* [a]Heb. 11:30
21 [1]Or, *put u* *ban* [a]Deut. 2
22 [a]Josh. 2:1
23 [a]Heb. 11:
24 [1]I.e., tabe [a]Deut. 20:16-
25 [1]Lit., *let li* 11:31 [b]Josh.
26 [a]1 Kin. 16
27 [a]Gen. 39 1:19 [b]Josh.
7:1 [a]Josh. 6
2 [1]Lit., *sayir* [a]Josh. 18:12 13:5; 14:23
3 [1]Lit., *and s*
4 [1]Lit., *befo* 26:17; Deut.
5 [1]Or, *befor* 26:36; Josh. 21:7; Nah. 2
6 [a]Job 2:12 Lam. 2:10; F
7 [1]Heb., *YH* usually rend [2]Lit., *and ha*
8 [1]Lit., *neck*
9 [a]Ex. 32:1

of it, and they will surround us and cut off our name from the earth.
And what wilt Thou do for Thy great name?"
10 So the LORD said to Joshua, "Rise up! Why is it that you have
fallen on your face?
11 "Israel has sinned, and [a]they have also transgressed My covenant
which I commanded them. And they have even taken some of the
things under the ban and have both stolen and deceived. Moreover,
they have also put *them* among their own things.
12 "Therefore the [a]sons of Israel cannot stand before their enemies;
they turn *their* [1]backs before their enemies, for they have become
accursed. I will not be with you anymore unless you destroy the
things under the ban from your midst.
13 "Rise up! [a]Consecrate the people and say, 'Consecrate yourselves
for tomorrow, for thus the LORD, the God of Israel, has said, "[b]There
are things under the ban in your midst, O Israel. You cannot stand
before your enemies until you have removed the things under the
ban from your midst."
14 'In the morning then you shall come near by your tribes. And it
shall be that the tribe which [a]the LORD takes *by lot* shall come near by
families, and the family which the LORD takes shall come near by
households, and the household which the LORD takes shall come
near man by man.
15 'And [a]it shall be that the one who is taken with the things under
the ban shall be burned with fire, he and all that belongs to him,
because he has transgressed the covenant of the LORD, and because
he [b]has committed a disgraceful thing in Israel.' "
16 So Joshua arose early in the morning and brought Israel near by
[1]tribes, and the tribe of Judah was taken.
17 And he brought the family of Judah near, and he took the family
of the Zerahites; and he brought the family of the Zerahites near
man by man, and Zabdi was taken.
18 And he brought his household near man by man; and [a]Achan,
son of Carmi, son of Zabdi, son of Zerah, from the tribe of Judah,
was taken.
19 Then Joshua said to Achan, "My son, I implore you, [a]give glory
to the LORD, the God of Israel, and give praise to Him; and tell me
now what you have done. Do not hide it from me."
20 So Achan answered Joshua and said, "Truly, I have sinned
against the LORD, the God of Israel, and [1]this is what I did:
21 when I saw among the spoil a beautiful mantle from Shinar and
two hundred shekels of silver and a bar of gold fifty shekels in
weight, then I [a]coveted them and took them; and behold, they are
concealed in the earth inside my tent with the silver underneath it."
22 So Joshua sent messengers, and they ran to the tent; and behold,
it was concealed in his tent with the silver underneath it.
23 And they took them from inside the tent and brought them to
Joshua and to all the sons of Israel, and they poured them out before
the LORD.
24 Then Joshua and all Israel with him, took Achan the son of
Zerah, the silver, the mantle, the bar of gold, his sons, his daughters,
his [1]oxen, his donkeys, his sheep, his tent and all that belonged to
him; and they brought them up to [a]the valley of [2]Achor.
25 And Joshua said, "Why have you [a]troubled us? The LORD will

osh. 6:18, 19
necks [a]Num. ...5; Judg. 2:14
...sh. 3:5 [b]Josh. 6:18
[a]Prov. 16:33
1 Sam. 14:38f. ...4:7; Judg. 20:6
[1]Lit., *its tribes*
...um. 32:23; Acts 5:1-10
...Sam. 6:5; 2 Chr. ...Jer. 13:16; John 9:24
..., *thus and thus I did*
[a]Eph. 5:5; 1 Tim. 6:10
[1]Or, *cattle* [2]I.e., ...ouble [a]Josh. 15:7
25 [a]Josh. 6:18

trouble you this day." And all Israel stoned [1]them with stones; and
they burned them with fire [2]after they had stoned them with stones.
26 And they raised over him a great heap of stones that stands to
this day, and the LORD turned from the fierceness of His anger.
Therefore the name of that place has been called [a]the valley of
[1]Achor to this day.

Chapter 8 ____________________

8 Now the LORD said to Joshua, "[a]Do not fear or be dismayed. Take
all the people of war with you and arise, go up to Ai; see, [b]I have
given into your hand the king of Ai, his people, his city, and his land.
2 "And you shall do to Ai and its king just as you did to Jericho and
its king; you shall [a]take only its spoil and its cattle as plunder for
yourselves. [1]Set an ambush for the city behind it."
3 So Joshua rose with all the people of war to go up to Ai; and
Joshua chose 30,000 men, valiant warriors, and sent them out at
night.
4 And he commanded them, saying, "See, you are [a]going to am-
bush the city from behind [1]it. Do not go very far from the city, but all
of you be ready.
5 "Then I and all the people who are with me will approach the city.
And it will come about when they come out to meet us as at the first,
that [a]we will flee before them.
6 "And they will come out after us until we have drawn them away
from the city, for they will say, '*They* are fleeing before us as at the
first.' So we will flee before them.

25 [1]Lit., *they stor*

26 [1]I.e., 65:10; Ho

8:1 [a]Josh [b]Josh. 6:2

2 [1]Lit., *Se* [a]Deut. 20:

4 [1]Lit., *the* 20:29

5 [a]Judg. 2

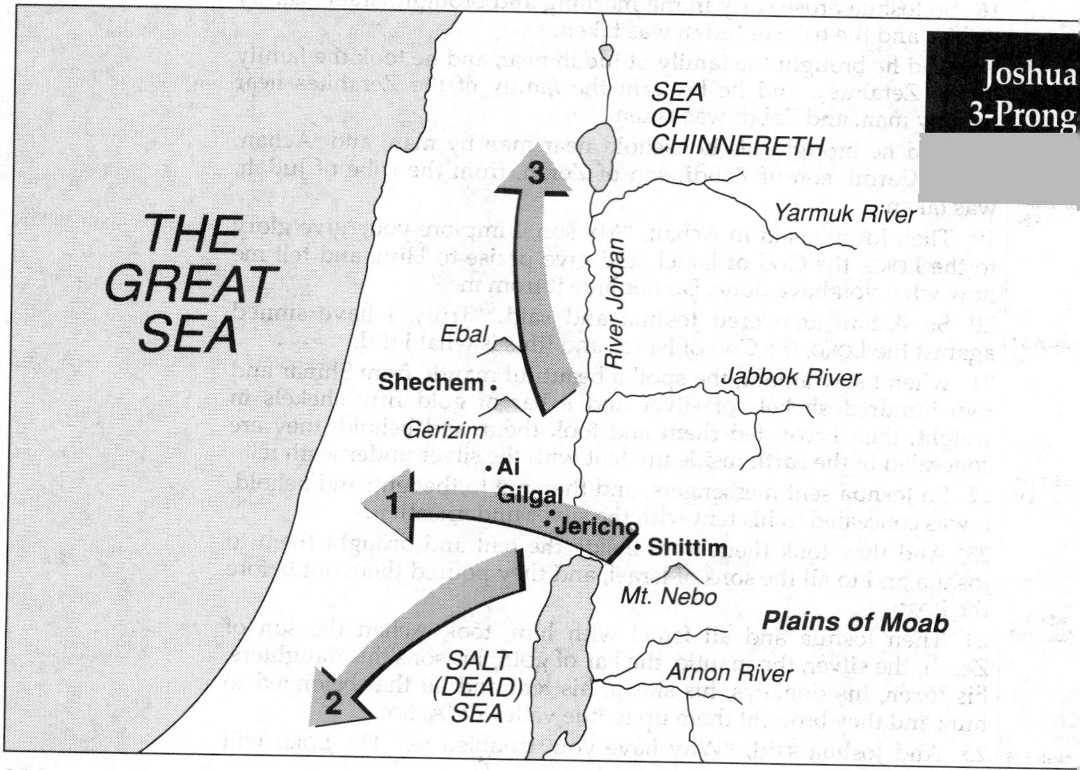

Joshua
3-Prong

THE GREAT SEA
SEA OF CHINNERETH
Yarmuk River
River Jordan
Ebal
Shechem
Jabbok River
Gerizim
Ai
Gilgal
Jericho
Shittim
Mt. Nebo
Plains of Moab
SALT (DEAD) SEA
Arnon River
1
2
3

7 "And you shall rise from *your* ambush and take possession of the
city, for the LORD your God will deliver it into your hand.
8 "Then it will be when you have seized the city, that you shall set
the city on fire. You shall do *it* [a]according to the word of the LORD.
See, I have commanded you."
9 So Joshua sent them away, and they went to the place of ambush
and remained between Bethel and Ai, on the west side of Ai; but
Joshua spent that night among the people.
10 Now Joshua [a]rose early in the morning and mustered the people,
and he went up with the elders of Israel before the people to Ai.
11 Then all the people of war who *were* with him went up and drew
near and arrived in front of the city, and camped on the north side of
Ai. Now *there was* a valley between him and Ai.
12 And he took about 5,000 men and set them in ambush between
[a]Bethel and Ai, on the west side of the [1]city.
13 So they stationed the people, all the army that was on the north
side of the city, and its rear guard on the west side of the city, and
Joshua spent that night in the midst of the valley.
14 And it came about when the king of Ai saw *it*, that the men of
the city hurried and rose up early and went out to meet Israel in
battle, he and all his people at the appointed place before the desert
plain. But he did not know that *there was* an ambush against him
behind the city.
15 And Joshua and all Israel pretended to be beaten before them,
and fled [a]by the way of the wilderness.
16 And all the people who were in the city were called together to
pursue them, and they pursued Joshua, and [a]were drawn away from
the city.
17 So not a man was left in Ai or Bethel who had not gone out after
Israel, and they left the city [1]unguarded and pursued Israel.
18 Then the LORD said to Joshua, "[a]Stretch out the javelin that is in
your hand toward Ai, for I will give it into your hand." So Joshua
stretched out the javelin that was in his hand toward the city.
19 And the *men in* ambush rose quickly from their place, and when
he had stretched out his hand, they ran and entered the city and
captured it; and they quickly set the city on fire.
20 When the men of Ai turned [1]back and looked, behold, the smoke
of the city ascended to the sky, and they had no place to flee this way
or that, for the people who had been fleeing to the wilderness turned
against the pursuers.
21 When Joshua and all Israel saw that the *men in* ambush had
captured the city and that the smoke of the city ascended, they
turned back and [1]slew the men of Ai.
22 And [1]the others came out from the city to encounter them, so
that they were *trapped* in the midst of Israel, [2]some on this side and
some on that side; and they [3]slew them until [a]no one was left [4]of
those who survived or escaped.
23 But they took alive the king of Ai and brought him to Joshua.
24 Now it came about when Israel had finished killing all the in-
habitants of Ai in the field in the wilderness where they pursued
them, and all of them were fallen by the edge of the sword until they
were destroyed, then all Israel returned to Ai and struck it with the
edge of the sword.

20:16-18; Josh. 8:2
[a]Gen. 22:3
[a]Gen. 12:8; Judg. 1:22
15:61; 16:1; 18:12
[a]Judg. 20:31
7 [1]Lit., *open*
:16; 17:9-13; Josh. 8:26
, *behind them*
1 [1]Lit., *smote*
it., *these came*
hese . . . those
note [4]Lit., *for it*
[a]Josh. 8:8

25 [a]And all who fell that day, both men and women, were 12,000—
all the [1]people of Ai.
26 For Joshua [a]did not withdraw his hand with which he stretched
out the javelin until he had [1]utterly destroyed all the inhabitants
of Ai.
27 [a]Israel took only the cattle and the spoil of that city as plunder
for themselves, according to the word of the LORD which He had
commanded Joshua.
28 So Joshua burned Ai and made it [a]a heap forever, a desolation
until this day.
29 [a]And he hanged the king of Ai on a tree until evening; and at
sunset Joshua gave command and they took his body down from the
tree, and threw it at the entrance of the city gate, and raised over it a
great heap of stones *that stands* to this day.
30 Then Joshua built an altar to the LORD, the God of Israel, in
[a]Mount Ebal,
31 just as Moses the servant of the LORD had commanded the sons
of Israel, as it is written in the book of the law of Moses, [a]an altar of
uncut stones, on which no man had wielded an iron *tool;* and they
offered burnt offerings on it to the LORD, and sacrificed peace offer-
ings.
32 And he [a]wrote there on the stones a copy of the law of Moses,
which [1]he had written, in the presence of the sons of Israel.
33 [a]And all Israel with their elders and officers and their judges
were standing on both sides of the ark before the Levitical priests
who carried the ark of the covenant of the LORD, the stranger as well
as the native. Half of them *stood* in front of [b]Mount Gerizim and half
of them in front of Mount Ebal, just as Moses the servant of the LORD
had given command at first to bless the people of Israel.
34 Then afterward he read all the words of the law, the blessing and
the curse, according to all that is written in [a]the book of the law.
35 There was not a word of all that Moses had commanded which
Joshua did not read before all the assembly of Israel [a]with the
women and the little ones and the strangers who were [1]living among
them.

Chapter 9

9 Now it came about when [a]all the kings who were beyond the
Jordan, in the hill country and in the lowland and on all the
[b]coast of the Great Sea toward Lebanon, [c]the Hittite and the Amorite,
the Canaanite, the Perizzite, the Hivite and the Jebusite, heard of it,
2 that they gathered themselves together with [1a]one accord to fight
with Joshua and with Israel.
3 When the inhabitants of [a]Gibeon heard what Joshua had done to
Jericho and to Ai,
4 they also acted craftily and [1]set out as envoys, and took worn-
out sacks on their donkeys, and wineskins, worn-out and torn and
[2]mended,
5 and worn-out and patched sandals on their feet, and worn-out
clothes on themselves; and all the bread of their provision was dry
and had become crumbled.
6 And they went to Joshua to the [a]camp at Gilgal, and said to him
and to the men of Israel, "We have come from a far country; now
therefore, make a covenant with us."

25 [1]Lit., *m* 20:16-18
26 [1]Or, *put ban* [a]Ex. 1
27 [a]Josh. 8
28 [a]Deut. 1
29 [a]Deut. 2
30 [a]Deut. 2
31 [a]Ex. 20:2
32 [1]I.e., Mos 27:2, 3, 8
33 [a]Deut. 27 [b]Deut. 11:29
34 [a]Josh. 1:8
35 [1]Lit., *walk* 12:38; Deut. 3 Zech. 8:23
9:1 [a]Num. 13 3:10 [b]Num. 34 3:17; 23:23
2 [1]Lit., *one m* 83:3, 5
3 [a]Josh. 9:17, 21:17
4 [1]Lit., *went ar traveled as en* [2]Lit., *tied up*
6 [a]Josh. 5:10

7 And the men of Israel said to the [a]Hivites, "Perhaps you are
living [1]within our land; [b]how then shall we make a covenant with
you?"
8 But they said to Joshua, "[a]We are your servants." Then Joshua
said to them, "Who are you, and where do you come from?"
9 And they said to him, "Your servants have come from [a]a very far
country because of the [1]fame of the LORD your God; for [b]we have
heard the report of Him and all that He did in Egypt,
10 and all that He did to the two kings of the Amorites who were
beyond the Jordan, to Sihon king of Heshbon and to Og king of
Bashan who was at Ashtaroth.
11 "So our elders and all the inhabitants of our country spoke to us,
saying, 'Take provisions in your hand for the journey, and go to meet
them and say to them, "[a]We are your servants; now then, make a
covenant with us."'
12 "This our bread *was* warm *when* we took it for our provisions out
of our houses on the day that we left to come to you; but now
behold, it is dry and has become crumbled.
13 "And these wineskins which we filled were new, and behold,
they are torn; and these our clothes and our sandals are worn out
because of the very long journey."
14 So the men *of Israel* took some of their provisions, and [a]did not
ask for the [1]counsel of the LORD.
15 [a]And Joshua made peace with them and made a covenant with
them, to let them live; and the leaders of the congregation swore *an
oath* to them.
16 And it came about at the end of three days after they had made a
covenant with them, that they heard that they were neighbors and
that they were living [1]within their land.
17 Then the sons of Israel set out and came to their cities on the
third day. Now their cities *were* [a]Gibeon and Chephirah and Beeroth
and Kiriath-jearim.
18 And the sons of Israel did not strike them because the leaders of
the congregation had sworn to them by the LORD the God of Israel.
And the whole congregation grumbled against the leaders.
19 But all the leaders said to the whole congregation, "We have
sworn to them by the LORD, the God of Israel, and now we cannot
touch them.
20 "This we will do to them, even let them live, lest wrath be upon
us for the oath which we swore to them."
21 And the leaders said to them, "Let them live." So they became
[a]hewers of wood and drawers of water for the whole congregation,
just as the leaders had spoken to them.
22 Then Joshua called for them and spoke to them, saying, "Why
have you deceived us, saying, 'We are very far from you,' [a]when you
are living [1]within our land?
23 "Now therefore, you are [a]cursed, and [1]you shall never cease being
slaves, both hewers of wood and drawers of water for the house of
my God."
24 So they answered Joshua and said, "[a]Because it was certainly
told your servants that the LORD your God had commanded His
servant Moses to give you all the land, and to destroy all the in-
habitants of the land before you; therefore we feared greatly for our
lives because of you, and have done this thing.

t., *among us*
; 11:19 [b]Ex.
32; Deut. 7:2
20:11; 2 Kin.
10:5
name [a]Josh.
osh. 2:9; 9:24
11 [a]Josh. 9:8
mouth [a]Num.
27:21
15 [a]Ex. 23:32
t., *among them*
7 [a]Josh. 18:25
1 [a]Deut. 29:11
[1]Lit., *among us*
[a]Josh. 9:16
., *a servant shall*
cut off from you
[a]Gen. 9:25
24 [a]Josh. 9:9

25 "And now behold, [a]we are in your hands; do as it seems good and
right in your sight to do to us."
26 Thus he did to them, and delivered them from the hands of the
sons of Israel, and they did not kill them.
27 But Joshua made them that day hewers of wood and drawers of
water for the congregation and for the altar of the LORD, to this day,
[a]in the place which He would choose.

Chapter 10

10 Now it came about when Adoni-zedek king of Jerusalem
heard that Joshua had captured Ai, and had [1]utterly
destroyed it (just [a]as he had done to Jericho and its king, so he had
done to Ai and its king), and that the inhabitants of Gibeon had
[b]made peace with Israel and were [2]within their land,
2 that [1]he [a]feared greatly, because Gibeon *was* a great city, like one
of the royal cities, and because it was greater than Ai, and all its men
were mighty.
3 Therefore Adoni-zedek king of Jerusalem sent *word* [a]to Hoham
king of Hebron and to Piram king of Jarmuth and to Japhia king of
Lachish and to Debir king of Eglon, saying,
4 "Come up to me and help me, and let us [1]attack Gibeon, for it has
[a]made peace with Joshua and with the sons of Israel."
5 So the five kings of [a]the Amorites, the king of Jerusalem, the king
of Hebron, the king of Jarmuth, the king of Lachish, *and* the king of
Eglon, gathered together and went up, they with all their armies,
and camped by Gibeon and fought against it.
6 Then the men of Gibeon sent *word* to Joshua to the camp at
Gilgal, saying, "Do not [1]abandon your servants; come up to us
quickly and save us and help us, for all the kings of the Amorites
that live in the hill country have assembled against us."
7 So Joshua went up from Gilgal, he and [a]all the people of war
with him and all the valiant warriors.
8 And the LORD said to Joshua, "[a]Do not fear them, for I have given
them into your hands; not [1]one of them shall stand before you."
9 So Joshua came upon them suddenly [1]by marching all night
from Gilgal.
10 [a]And the LORD confounded them before Israel, and He [1]slew
them with a great slaughter at Gibeon, and pursued them by the
way of the ascent of Beth-horon, and struck them as far as Azekah
and Makkedah.
11 And it came about as they fled from before Israel, *while* they
were at the descent of Beth-horon, that [a]the LORD threw large stones
from heaven on them as far as Azekah, and they died; *there were*
more who died [1]from the hailstones than those whom the sons of
Israel killed with the sword.
12 Then Joshua spoke to the LORD in the day when the LORD
delivered up the Amorites before the sons of Israel, and he said in
the sight of Israel,

"O [a]sun, stand still at Gibeon,
And O moon in the valley of Aijalon."

13 [a]So the sun stood still, and the moon stopped,
Until the nation avenged themselves of their enemies.

Is it not written in [b]the book of Jashar? And [c]the sun stopped in the

25 [a]Gen. 16:6
27 [a]Deut. 12:5
10:1 [1]Or, *put u*... *ban* [2]Lit., *amor*... [a]Josh. 8:21f. [b]J...
2 [1]Lit., *they* [a]E... 15:14-16
3 [a]Josh. 10:23
4 [1]Lit., *smite* [a]J... 9:15
5 [a]Num. 13:29
6 [1]Lit., *slacken y*... *hands from*
7 [a]Josh. 8:1
8 [1]Lit., *a man* [a]J... 1:5, 9
9 [1]Lit., *he went u*...
10 [1]Lit., *struck* [a]... 7:23
11 [1]Lit., *with* [a]Ps 18:12f.; Is. 28:2
12 [a]Hab. 3:11
13 [a]Hab. 3:11 [b]2... 1:18 [c]Is. 38:8

middle of the sky, and did not hasten to go *down* for about a whole
day.
14 And there was no day like that before it or after it, when the
LORD listened to the voice of a man; for [a]the LORD fought for Israel.
15 Then Joshua and all Israel with him returned to the camp to
Gilgal.
16 Now these [a]five kings had fled and hidden themselves in the
cave at Makkedah.
17 And it was told Joshua, saying, "The five kings have been found
hidden in the cave at Makkedah."
18 And Joshua said, "Roll large stones against the mouth of the
cave, and assign men by it to guard them,
19 but do not stay *there* yourselves; pursue your enemies and [1]at-
tack them in the rear. Do not allow them to enter their cities, for the
LORD your God has delivered them into your hand."
20 And it came about when Joshua and the sons of Israel had
finished [1]slaying them with a very great slaughter, [a]until they were
destroyed, and the survivors *who* remained of them [2]had entered the
fortified cities,
21 that all the people returned to the camp to Joshua at Makkedah
in peace. No one [1]uttered a word against any of the sons of Israel.
22 Then Joshua said, "Open the mouth of the cave and bring these
five kings out to me from the cave."
23 And they did so, and [a]brought these five kings out to him from
the cave: the king of Jerusalem, the king of Hebron, the king of
Jarmuth, the king of Lachish, *and* the king of Eglon.
24 And it came about when they brought these kings out to Joshua,
that Joshua called for all the men of Israel, and said to the chiefs of
the men of war who had gone with him, "Come near, [a]put your feet
on the necks of these kings." So they came near and put their feet on
their necks.
25 Joshua then said to them, "[a]Do not fear or be dismayed! Be
strong and courageous, for thus the LORD will do to all your enemies
with whom you fight."
26 So afterward Joshua struck them and put them to death, and he
[a]hanged them on five trees; and they hung on the trees until evening.
27 And it came about at [1]sunset that Joshua commanded, and [a]they
took them down from the trees and threw them into the cave where
they had hidden themselves, and put large stones over the mouth of
the cave, to this very day.
28 Now Joshua captured Makkedah on that day, and struck it and
its king with the edge of the sword; [a]he [1]utterly destroyed [2]it and
every [3]person who was in it. He left no survivor. Thus he did to the
king of Makkedah [b]just as he had done to the king of Jericho.
29 Then Joshua and all Israel with him passed on from Makkedah
to [a]Libnah, and fought against Libnah.
30 And the LORD gave it also with its king into the hands of Israel,
and he struck it and every person who *was* in it with the edge of the
sword. He left no survivor in it. Thus he did to its king just as he had
done to the king of Jericho.
31 And Joshua and all Israel with him passed on from Libnah to
Lachish, and they camped by it and fought against it.
32 And the LORD gave Lachish into the hands of Israel; and he
captured it on the second day, and struck it and every person who

[a]Ex. 14:14; Deut. 1:30; Josh. 10:42
16 [a]Josh. 10:5
Lit., *smite their tail*
[1]Lit., *striking* [2]Lit., *had* [a]Deut. 20:16
Lit., *sharpened his tongue*
23 [a]Deut. 7:24
24 [a]Mal. 4:3
25 [a]Josh. 10:8
26 [a]Josh. 8:29
Lit., *the time of the* ... *of the sun* [a]Deut. 21:22, 23
Or, *put under the* ... [2]Some mss. read ... [3]Lit., *soul*, and so throughout the ch. ...0:16 [b]Josh. 6:21
...sh. 15:42; 21:13

was in it with the edge of the sword, according to all that he had
done to Libnah.
33 Then Horam king of [a]Gezer came up to help Lachish, and Joshua
[1]defeated him and his people until he had left him no survivor.
34 And Joshua and all Israel with him passed on from Lachish to
Eglon, and they camped by it and fought against it.
35 And they captured it on that day and struck it with the edge of
the sword; and he [1]utterly destroyed that day every person who *was*
in it, according to all that he had done to Lachish.
36 Then Joshua and all Israel with him went up from Eglon to
[a]Hebron, and they fought against it.
37 And they captured it and struck it and its king and all its cities
and all the persons who *were* in it with the edge of the sword. He left
no survivor, according to all that he had done to Eglon. And he
[1]utterly destroyed it and every person who *was* in it.
38 Then Joshua and all Israel with him returned to [a]Debir, and they
fought against it.
39 And he captured it and its king and all its cities, and they struck
them with the edge of the sword, and [1]utterly destroyed every per-
son *who was* in it. He left no survivor. Just as he had done to Hebron,
so he did to Debir and its king, as he had also done to Libnah and its
king.
40 Thus Joshua struck all the land, [a]the hill country and the [1]Negev
and the lowland and the slopes and [b]all their kings. He left no sur-
vivor, but [c]he [2]utterly destroyed all who breathed, just as the LORD,
the God of Israel, had commanded.
41 And Joshua struck them from Kadesh-barnea even as far as
Gaza, and all the country of [a]Goshen even as far as Gibeon.
42 And Joshua captured all these kings and their lands at one time,
because [a]the LORD, the God of Israel, fought for Israel.
43 So Joshua and all Israel with him returned to the camp at Gilgal.

Chapter 11

11 Then it came about, when Jabin king of [a]Hazor heard *of it,*
that he sent to Jobab king of Madon and to the king of Shim-
ron and to the king of Achshaph,
2 and to the kings who were of the north in the hill country, and in
the [a]Arabah—south of [1]Chinneroth and in the lowland and on the
[2]heights of Dor on the west—
3 to the Canaanite on the east and on the west, and the Amorite
and the Hittite and the Perizzite and the Jebusite in the hill country,
and [a]the Hivite [1]at the foot of [b]Hermon in the land of [c]Mizpeh.
4 And they came out, they and all their armies with them, [a]*as*
many people *as* the sand that is on the seashore, with very many
horses and chariots.
5 So all of these kings having agreed to meet, came and encamped
together at the waters of Merom, to fight against Israel.
6 Then the LORD said to Joshua, "[a]Do not be afraid because of
them, for tomorrow at this time I will deliver all of them slain before
Israel; you shall [b]hamstring their horses and burn their chariots with
fire."
7 So Joshua and all the people of war with him came upon them
suddenly by the waters of Merom, and attacked them.
8 And the LORD delivered them into the hand of Israel, so that they

33 [1]Lit., *smote* [a]... 16:3, 10; Judg ... 1 Kin. 9:16f.
35 [1]Or, *put un*... *ban*
36 [a]Num. 13:2... 1:10, 20; 2 Sam... 5, 13; 2 Chr. 11...
37 [1]Or, *put it u*... *ban*
38 [a]Josh. 15:1... 1:11; 1 Chr. 6:5...
39 [1]Or, *put it u*... *ban*
40 [1]I.e., South [2]Or, *put it under*... [a]Deut. 1:7 [b]Deu... [c]Deut. 20:16
41 [a]Josh. 11:16
42 [a]Josh. 10:14
11:1 [a]Josh. 11:1...
2 [1]I.e., Sea of G... [2]Or, *Naphoth-do*... [a]Josh. 12:3; 13:2...
3 [1]Lit., *under* [a]D... 7:1; Judg. 3:3, 5; 9:20 [b]Josh. 11:1... 11 [c]Josh. 15:38; ...
4 [a]Judg. 7:12
6 [a]Josh. 10:8 [b]2... 8:4

[1]Lit., *smote* [a]Josh. 13:6 [b]Josh. 11:3

[1]defeated them, and pursued them as far as Great Sidon and
[a]Misrephoth-maim and the valley of [b]Mizpeh to the east; and they
struck them until no survivor was left to them.
9 And Joshua did to them as the LORD had told him; he
[a]hamstrung their horses, and burned their chariots with fire.
10 Then Joshua turned back at that time, and captured [a]Hazor and
struck its king with the sword; for Hazor formerly was the head of
all these kingdoms.
11 [a]And they struck every person who was in it with the edge of the
sword, [1]utterly destroying *them;* there was no one left who breathed.
And he burned Hazor with fire.
12 And Joshua captured all the cities of these kings, and all their
kings, and he struck them with the edge of the sword, *and* utterly
destroyed them; just [a]as Moses the servant of the LORD had commanded.
13 However, Israel did not burn any cities that stood on their
mounds, except Hazor alone, *which* Joshua burned.
14 [a]And all the spoil of these cities and the cattle, the sons of Israel
took as their plunder; but they struck every man with the edge of the
sword, until they had destroyed them. They left no one who
breathed.
15 Just as the LORD had commanded Moses his servant, so Moses
commanded Joshua, and so Joshua did; he left nothing undone of all
that the LORD had commanded Moses.
16 Thus Joshua took all that land: [a]the hill country and all the
[1]Negev, all that land of Goshen, the lowland, [b]the Arabah, the hill
country of Israel and its lowland
17 from [a]Mount Halak, that rises toward Seir, even as far as Baal-gad in the valley of Lebanon [1]at the foot of Mount Hermon. And he
captured [b]all their kings and struck them down and put them to
death.
18 Joshua waged war a long time with all these kings.
19 There was not a city which made peace with the sons of Israel
except [a]the Hivites living in Gibeon; they took them all in battle.
20 [a]For it was of the LORD to [1]harden their hearts, to meet Israel in
battle in order that he might [b]utterly destroy them, that they might
[2]receive no mercy, but that he might destroy them, just as the LORD
had commanded Moses.
21 Then Joshua came at that time and cut off [a]the Anakim from the
hill country, from Hebron, from Debir, from Anab and from all the
hill country of Judah and from all the hill country of Israel. Joshua
utterly destroyed them with their cities.
22 There were no Anakim left in the land of the sons of Israel; only
in Gaza, in [a]Gath, and in [b]Ashdod some remained.
23 So Joshua took the whole land, according to all that the LORD
had spoken to Moses, and [a]Joshua gave it for an inheritance to Israel
according to their divisions by their tribes. [b]Thus the land had rest
from war.

9 [a]Josh. 11:6
10 [a]Josh. 11:1
[1]Or, *putting them* *...er the ban,* and so throughout the ch. [a]Deut. 20:16
...2 [a]Num. 33:50-52; Deut. 7:2; 20:16f.
...4 [a]Num. 31:11, 12
[1]I.e., South country ... 10:40, 41 [b]Josh. 11:2
[1]Lit., *under* [a]Josh. 12:7 [b]Deut. 7:24
19 [a]Josh. 9:3, 7
[1]Lit., *make strong* ..., *have* [a]Ex. 14:17 [b]Deut. 7:16
...Num. 13:33; Deut. 9:2
...Sam. 17:4; 1 Kin. ... 1 Chr. 8:13 [b]Josh. ...6f.; 1 Sam. 5:1; Is. 20:1
...Deut. 1:38 [b]Deut. ...0; 25:19; Heb. 4:8

Chapter 12

12 Now these are the [a]kings of the land whom the sons of Israel
[1]defeated, and whose land they possessed beyond the Jordan
toward the sunrise, from the valley of the Arnon as far as Mount
Hermon, and all the Arabah to the east:

...Lit., *smote* [a]Num. ...2:33; Deut. 3:8-17

2 Sihon king of the Amorites, who lived in Heshbon, *and* ruled
[a]from Aroer, which is on the edge of the valley of the Arnon, both the
middle of the valley and half of Gilead, even as far as the brook
Jabbok, the border of the sons of Ammon;
3 and the [a]Arabah as far as the Sea of [1]Chinneroth toward the east,
and as far as the sea of the Arabah, *even* the Salt Sea, eastward
[2]toward [b]Beth-jeshimoth, and on the south, [3]at the foot of the slopes
of Pisgah;
4 and the territory of Og king of Bashan, one of [a]the remnant of
Rephaim, who lived at [b]Ashtaroth and at Edrei,
5 and ruled over Mount Hermon and [a]Salecah and all Bashan, as
far as [b]the border of the Geshurites and the Maacathites, and half of
Gilead, *as far as* the border of Sihon king of Heshbon.
6 Moses the servant of the LORD and the sons of Israel [1]defeated
them; and [a]Moses the servant of the LORD gave it to the Reubenites
and the Gadites, and the half-tribe of Manasseh as a possession.
7 Now these are the kings of the land whom Joshua and the sons
of Israel [1]defeated beyond the Jordan toward the west, from Baal-
gad in the valley of Lebanon even as far as [a]Mount Halak, which
rises toward Seir; and Joshua gave it to the tribes of Israel as a
possession according to their divisions,
8 in [a]the hill country, in the lowland, in the Arabah, on the slopes,
and in the wilderness, and in the [1]Negev; the Hittite, the Amorite
and the Canaanite, the Perizzite, the Hivite and the Jebusite:
9 the [a]king of Jericho, one; the [b]king of Ai, which is beside Bethel,
one;
10 the [a]king of Jerusalem, one; the king of Hebron, one;
11 the king of Jarmuth, one; the king of Lachish, one;
12 the king of Eglon, one; the king of Gezer, one;
13 the king of Debir, one; the king of Geder, one;
14 the king of Hormah, one; the king of [a]Arad, one;
15 the king of Libnah, one; the king of Adullam, one;
16 the king of Makkedah, one; the king of Bethel, one;
17 the king of Tappuah, one; the [a]king of Hepher, one;
18 the king of [a]Aphek, one; the king of Lasharon, one;
19 the king of Madon, one; the king of Hazor, one;
20 the king of Shimron-meron, one; the king of Achshaph, one;
21 the king of Taanach, one; the king of Megiddo, one;
22 the king of [a]Kedesh, one; the king of Jokneam in Carmel, one;
23 the king of Dor in the [1]heights of Dor, one; the king of [a]Goiim in
Gilgal, one;
24 the king of Tirzah, one: [a]in all, thirty-one kings.

Chapter 13

13 Now [a]Joshua was old *and* advanced in years when the LORD
said to him, "You are old *and* advanced in years, and very
much of the land remains to be possessed.
2 "This is the land that remains: all the regions *of* the Philistines and
all *those of* the [a]Geshurites;
3 from the Shihor which is [1]east of Egypt, even as far as the border
of Ekron to the north (it is counted as Canaanite); the [a]five lords of
the Philistines: the Gazite, the Ashdodite, the Ashkelonite, the Git-
tite, the Ekronite; and the Avvite
4 [1]to the south, all the land of the Canaanite, and Mearah that

2 [a]Deut. 2:36

3 [1]I.e., Galilee *way of* [3]Lit., ur [a]Josh. 11:2 [b]Jo

4 [a]Deut. 3:11

5 [a]Deut. 3:10; 13:11; 1 Chr. 5: [b]Deut. 3:14; 1 S

6 [1]Lit., *smote* 32:33; Deut. 3:1

7 [1]Lit., *smote* 11:17

8 [1]I.e., South co [a]Josh. 11:16

9 [a]Josh. 6:2 [b]Jo

10 [a]Josh. 10:23

14 [a]Num. 21:1

17 [a]1 Kin. 4:10

18 [a]Josh. 13:4; 2 13:17

22 [a]Josh. 19:37; 21:32

23 [1]Or, *Naphath-* [a]Gen. 14:1

24 [a]Deut. 7:24

13:1 [a]Josh. 14:10

2 [a]Josh. 13:11; 1 27:8

3 [1]Lit., *on the face* [a]1 Sam. 6:4, 16

4 [1]Or, *from the Te*

belongs to the Sidonians, as far as [a]Aphek, to the border of the
[b]Amorite;
5 and the land of the [a]Gebalite, and all of Lebanon, toward the
[1]east, [b]from Baal-gad below Mount Hermon as far as [2]Lebo-hamath.
6 "All the inhabitants of the hill country from Lebanon as far as
[a]Misrephoth-maim, all the Sidonians, I will [1]drive them out from
before the sons of Israel; [b]only allot it to Israel for an inheritance as I
have commanded you.
7 "Now therefore, apportion this land for an inheritance to the nine
tribes, and the half-tribe of Manasseh."
8 With [1]the other half-tribe, the Reubenites and the Gadites
received their inheritance which Moses gave them [a]beyond the Jor-
dan to the east, just as Moses the servant of the LORD gave to them;
9 from Aroer, which is on the edge of the valley of the Arnon, with
the city which is in the middle of the valley, and all the plain of
Medeba, as far as Dibon;
10 and all the cities of Sihon king of the Amorites, who reigned in
Heshbon, as far as the border of the sons of Ammon;
11 and [a]Gilead, and the [1]territory of the Geshurites and Maacathites,
and all Mount Hermon, and all Bashan as far as Salecah;
12 all the kingdom of [a]Og in Bashan, who reigned in Ashtaroth and
in Edrei (he alone was left of the remnant of the Rephaim); for Moses
[b]struck them and dispossessed them.
13 But the sons of Israel did not dispossess the Geshurites or the
Maacathites; for Geshur and Maacath live among Israel until this
day.
14 [a]Only to the tribe of Levi he did not give an inheritance; the
offerings by fire to the LORD, the God of Israel, are [1]their inheritance,
as He spoke to him.
15 So Moses gave *an inheritance* to the tribe of the sons of Reuben
according to their families.
16 And their [1]territory was [a]from Aroer, which is on the edge of the
valley of the Arnon, with the city which is in the middle of the valley
and all the plain by Medeba;
17 Heshbon, and all its cities which are on the plain: Dibon and
Bamoth-baal and Beth-baal-meon,
18 and [a]Jahaz and Kedemoth and Mephaath,
19 and [a]Kiriathaim and Sibmah and Zereth-shahar on the hill of the
valley,
20 and Beth-peor and the slopes of Pisgah and Beth-jeshimoth,
21 even all the cities of the plain and all the kingdom of Sihon king
of the Amorites who reigned in Heshbon, whom Moses struck with
the chiefs of Midian, [a]Evi and Rekem and Zur and Hur and Reba, the
princes of Sihon, who lived in the land.
22 The sons of Israel also killed [a]Balaam the son of Beor, the diviner,
with the sword among *the rest of* their slain.
23 And the border of the sons of Reuben was the [1]Jordan. This was
the inheritance of the sons of Reuben according to their families, the
cities and their villages.
24 Moses also gave *an inheritance* to the tribe of Gad, to the sons of
Gad, according to their families.
25 And their territory was [a]Jazer, and all the cities of Gilead, and
half the land of the sons of Ammon, as far as Aroer which is before
Rabbah;

sh. 12:18; 19:30; Sam. 4:1; 1 Kin. 30 [b]Ezek. 16:3; Amos 2:10
sunrise [2]Or, the ance of Hamath :18 [b]Josh. 12:7
[1]Or, dispossess :8 [b]Num. 33:54
it., *it, the* [a]Josh. 12:1-6
r, *border* [a]Gen. 25; Num. 32:29; sh. 13:25; 17:5f.
eut. 3:11 [b]Num. 21:24
[1]Lit., *his* [a]Deut. 18:1, 2
r, *border* [a]Josh. 13:9
m. 21:23; Judg. 20; Is. 15:4; Jer. 48:34
Num. 32:37; Jer. , 23; Ezek. 25:9
21 [a]Num. 31:8
22 [a]Num. 31:8
[1]Lit., *Jordan and border*
m. 21:32; Josh. 39; 2 Sam. 24:5; 6:81; 26:31; Is. 6:8f.; Jer. 48:32

26 and from Heshbon as far as Ramath-mizpeh and Betonim, and from Mahanaim as far as the border of [1]Debir;

27 and in the valley, Beth-haram and Beth-nimrah and Succoth and Zaphon, the rest of the kingdom of Sihon king of Heshbon, with the Jordan [1]as a border, as far as the *lower* end of the Sea of [2a]Chinnereth beyond the Jordan to the east.

28 This is the inheritance of the sons of Gad according to their families, the cities and their villages.

29 Moses also gave *an inheritance* to the half-tribe of Manasseh; and it was for the half-tribe of the sons of Manasseh according to their families.

30 And their territory was from Mahanaim, all Bashan, all the kingdom of Og king of Bashan, and all [a]the [1]towns of Jair, which are in Bashan, sixty cities;

31 also half of Gilead, with [a]Ashtaroth and Edrei, the cities of the kingdom of Og in Bashan, *were* for the sons of Machir the son of Manasseh, for half of the sons of Machir according to their families.

32 These are *the territories* which Moses apportioned for an inheritance in the plains of Moab, beyond the Jordan at Jericho to the east.

33 But [a]to the tribe of Levi, Moses did not give an inheritance; the LORD, the God of Israel, is their inheritance, as He had [1]promised to them.

Chapter 14

14 Now these are *the territories* which the sons of Israel inherited in the land of Canaan, which [a]Eleazar the priest, and Joshua the son of Nun, and the heads of the [1]households of the tribes of the sons of Israel apportioned to them for an inheritance,

2 by the [a]lot of their inheritance, as the LORD commanded [1]through Moses, for the nine tribes and the half-tribe.

3 For [a]Moses had given the inheritance of the two tribes and the half-tribe beyond the Jordan; but [b]he did not give an inheritance to the Levites among them.

4 For the sons of Joseph were two tribes, [a]Manasseh and Ephraim, and they did not give a portion to the Levites in the land, except cities to live in, with their pasture lands for their livestock and for their property.

5 Thus the sons of Israel did just [a]as the LORD had commanded Moses, and they divided the land.

6 Then the sons of Judah drew near to Joshua in Gilgal, and [a]Caleb the son of Jephunneh the Kenizzite said to him, "You know the word which the LORD spoke to Moses the man of God concerning [1]you and me in Kadesh-barnea.

7 "I was forty years old when [a]Moses the servant of the LORD sent me from Kadesh-barnea to spy out the land, and I brought word back to him as *it was* in my heart.

8 "Nevertheless my brethren who went up with me made the heart of the people [1]melt with fear; but [a]I followed the LORD my God fully.

9 "So Moses swore on that day, saying, 'Surely [a]the land on which your foot has trodden shall be an inheritance to you and to your children forever, because you have followed the LORD my God fully.'

10 "And now behold, the LORD has let me live, just as He spoke, these forty-five years, from the time that the LORD spoke this word to

26 [1]Or, *Lide*

27 [1]Lit., *and* [2]I.e., Galilee [a]34:11; Deut.

30 [1]Lit., *tent* [a]Num. 32:41

31 [a]Josh. 9: 13:12; Judg. 1 Sam. 7:3f.; 1 Chr. 6:71

33 [1]Lit., *spok* [a]Deut. 18:1f.; 13:14

14:1 [1]Lit., *fat* [a]Num. 34:16-

2 [1]Lit., *by the* [a]Num. 26:55; 34:13

3 [a]Num. 32:3 13:14

4 [a]Gen. 41:51 48:1, 5; Num. 2 Chr. 30:1

5 [a]Num. 35:1f. 21:2

6 [1]Lit., *me and concerning you* 13:6, 30; 14:6,

7 [a]Num. 13:1-3

8 [1]Lit., *become demoralized* [a]N 14:24; Deut. 1:3

9 [a]Deut. 1:36

Moses, when Israel walked in the wilderness; and now behold, I am
eighty-five years old today.
11 "[a]I am still as strong today as I was in the day Moses sent me; as
my strength was then, so my strength is now, for war and for [b]going
out and coming in.
12 "Now then, give me this hill country about which the LORD spoke
on that day, for you heard on that day that [a]Anakim *were* there, with
great fortified cities; perhaps the LORD will be with me, and I shall
[1]drive them out as the LORD has spoken."
13 So Joshua [a]blessed him, and [b]gave Hebron to Caleb the son of
Jephunneh for an inheritance.
14 Therefore, Hebron became the inheritance of Caleb the son of
Jephunneh the Kenizzite until this day, because he followed the
LORD God of Israel fully.
15 Now the name of Hebron was formerly [1]Kiriath-arba; *for Arba*
was the greatest man among the Anakim. [a]Then the land had rest
from war.

Chapter 15

15 Now [a]the lot for the tribe of the sons of Judah according to
their families [1]reached the [b]border of Edom, southward to the
[c]wilderness of Zin at the extreme south.
2 And their south border was from the lower end of the Salt Sea,
from the bay that turns to the south.
3 Then it proceeded southward to the ascent of Akrabbim and
continued to Zin, then went up by the south of Kadesh-barnea and
continued to Hezron, and went up to Addar and turned about to
Karka.
4 And it [a]continued to Azmon and proceeded to the [1b]brook of
Egypt; and the [2]border ended at the sea. This shall be your south
border.
5 And the [a]east border *was* the Salt Sea, as far as the [1]mouth of the
Jordan. And the [b]border of the north side was from the bay of the sea
at the [1]mouth of the Jordan.
6 Then the border went up to Beth-hoglah, and continued on the
north of Beth-arabah, and the border went up to the stone of Bohan
the son of Reuben.
7 And the border went up to Debir from [a]the valley of Achor, and
turned northward toward Gilgal which is opposite the ascent of
Adummim, which is on the south of the valley; and the border con-
tinued to the waters of En-shemesh, and [1]it ended at En-rogel.
8 Then the border went up the valley of Ben-hinnom to the slope
of the [a]Jebusite on the south (that is, Jerusalem); and the border went
up to the top of the mountain which is before the valley of Hinnom
to the west, which is at the end of the valley of Rephaim toward the
north.
9 And from the top of the mountain the border curved to the
spring of the waters of Nephtoah and proceeded to the cities of
Mount Ephron, then the border curved to [a]Baalah (that is, [b]Kiriath-
jearim).
10 And the border turned about from Baalah westward to Mount
Seir, and continued to the slope of Mount Jearim on the north (that
is, Chesalon), and went down to Beth-shemesh and continued
through [a]Timnah.

34:7 [b]Deut. 31:2
; *dispossess* [a]Num. 13:33
22:6 [b]Judg. 1 Chr. 6:55f.
e city of Arba [a]Josh. 11:23
[1]Lit., *was to* 4:3, 4 [b]Num. [c]Deut. 32:51
Or, *wadi* [2]Lit., *t of the border* n. 34:5 [b]Gen. 18; 1 Kin. 8:65
d [a]Num. 34:3, Josh. 18:15-19
e goings out of ere [a]Josh. 7:24
8 [a]Josh. 15:63
Chr. 13:6 [b]Judg. 18:12
en. 38:13; Judg. 14:1

11 And the border proceeded to the side of Ekron northward. Then
the border curved to Shikkeron and continued to Mount Baalah and
proceeded to Jabneel, and the [1]border ended at the sea.
12 And the west border *was* [a]at the Great Sea, even *its* [1]coastline.
This is the border around the sons of Judah according to their
families.
13 Now [a]he gave to Caleb the son of Jephunneh a portion [b]among
the sons of Judah, according to the [1]command of the LORD to Joshua,
namely, [2]Kiriath-arba, *Arba being* the father of Anak (that is, Hebron).
14 And [a]Caleb [1]drove out from there the three [b]sons of Anak:
Sheshai and Ahiman and Talmai, the children of Anak.
15 Then [a]he went up from there against the inhabitants of Debir;
now the name of Debir formerly was Kiriath-sepher.
16 And Caleb said, "The one who [1]attacks Kiriath-sepher and cap-
tures it, [2]I will give him Achsah my daughter as a wife."
17 And [a]Othniel the son of Kenaz, the brother of Caleb, captured it;
so he gave him Achsah his daughter as a wife.
18 [a]And it came about that when she came *to him,* she persuaded
him to ask her father for a field. So she alighted from the donkey,
and Caleb said to her, "What do you want?"
19 Then she said, "Give me a blessing; since you have given me the
land of the [1]Negev, give me also springs of water." So he gave her
the upper springs and the lower springs.
20 This is the inheritance of the tribe of the sons of Judah according
to their families.
21 Now the cities at the extremity of the tribe of the sons of Judah
toward the border of Edom in the south were Kabzeel and [a]Eder and
Jagur,
22 and Kinah and Dimonah and Adadah,
23 and Kedesh and Hazor and Ithnan,
24 Ziph and Telem and Bealoth,
25 and Hazor-hadattah and Kerioth-hezron (that is, Hazor),
26 Amam and Shema and Moladah,
27 and Hazar-gaddah and Heshmon and Beth-pelet,
28 and Hazar-shual and [a]Beersheba and Biziothiah,
29 Baalah and Iim and Ezem,
30 and Eltolad and Chesil and Hormah,
31 and [a]Ziklag and Madmannah and Sansannah,
32 and Lebaoth and Shilhim and Ain and Rimmon; in all, twenty-
nine cities with their villages.
33 In the lowland: [a]Eshtaol and Zorah and Ashnah,
34 and Zanoah and En-gannim, Tappuah and Enam,
35 Jarmuth and [a]Adullam, Socoh and Azekah,
36 and Shaaraim and Adithaim and Gederah and Gederothaim;
fourteen cities with their villages.
37 Zenan and Hadashah and Migdal-gad,
38 and Dilean and Mizpeh and Joktheel,
39 [a]Lachish and Bozkath and Eglon,
40 and Cabbon and Lahmas and Chitlish,
41 and Gederoth, Beth-dagon and Naamah and Makkedah; sixteen
cities with their villages.
42 Libnah and Ether and Ashan,
43 and Iphtah and Ashnah and Nezib,

11 [1]Lit., *go*
were

12 [1]Lit., *bo*
34:6

13 [1]Lit., *mo*
the city of A
14:13-15 [b]N

14 [1]Or, *disp*
[a]Josh. 11:21
13:33; Deut.

15 [a]Josh. 1(

16 [1]Lit., *smi*
and I

17 [a]Judg. 1:

18 [a]Judg. 1:1

19 [1]I.e., Sout

21 [a]Gen. 35:

28 [a]Gen. 21:3

31 [a]1 Sam. 2

33 [a]Judg. 13:2

35 [a]1 Sam. 22

39 [a]Josh. 10:3
14:19

44 and Keilah and Achzib and Mareshah; nine cities with their
villages.
45 Ekron, with its towns and its villages;
46 from Ekron even to the sea, all that were by the [1]side of Ashdod,
with their villages.
47 Ashdod, its towns and its villages; Gaza, its towns and its vil-
lages; as far as [a]the [1]brook of Egypt and the Great Sea, even *its*
[2]coastline.
48 And in the hill country: Shamir and Jattir and Socoh,
49 and Dannah and Kiriath-sannah (that is, Debir),
50 and Anab and Eshtemoh and Anim,
51 and Goshen and Holon and Giloh; eleven cities with their
villages.
52 Arab and Dumah and Eshan,
53 and Janum and Beth-tappuah and Aphekah,
54 and Humtah and Kiriath-arba (that is, Hebron), and Zior; nine
cities with their villages.
55 Maon, Carmel and Ziph and Juttah,
56 and Jezreel and Jokdeam and Zanoah,
57 Kain, Gibeah and Timnah; ten cities with their villages.
58 Halhul, Beth-zur and Gedor,
59 and Maarath and Beth-anoth and Eltekon; six cities with their
villages.
60 Kiriath-baal (that is, Kiriath-jearim), and Rabbah; two cities with
their villages.
61 In the wilderness: Beth-arabah, Middin and Secacah,
62 and Nibshan and the City of Salt and Engedi; six cities with their
villages.
63 Now as for the [a]Jebusites, the inhabitants of Jerusalem, the sons
of Judah could not [1]drive them out; so the Jebusites live with the
sons of Judah at Jerusalem until this day.

Chapter 16

16 Then the lot for the sons of Joseph went from the Jordan at
Jericho to the waters of Jericho on the east into [a]the wilder-
ness, going up from Jericho through the hill country to Bethel.
2 And it went from Bethel to Luz, and [a]continued to the border of
the Archites at Ataroth.
3 And it went down westward to the territory of the Japhletites, as
far as the territory of lower [a]Beth-horon even to [b]Gezer, and [1]it ended
at the sea.
4 And the [a]sons of Joseph, Manasseh and Ephraim, received their
inheritance.
5 Now *this* was the territory of the sons of Ephraim according to
their families: the border of their inheritance eastward was [a]Ataroth-
addar, as far as upper Beth-horon.
6 Then the border went westward at [a]Michmethath on the north,
and the border turned about eastward to Taanath-shiloh, and con-
tinued *beyond* it to the east of Janoah.
7 And it went down from Janoah to Ataroth and to [a]Naarah, then
reached Jericho and came out at the Jordan.
8 From [a]Tappuah the border continued westward to the [1]brook of
Kanah, and [2]it ended at the sea. This is the inheritance of the tribe of
the sons of Ephraim according to their families,

46 [1]Lit., *hand*
[1]Or, *wadi* [2]Lit., ...*der* [a]Josh. 15:4
[1]Or, *dispossess* ...*em* [a]Judg. 1:21; ...5:6; 1 Chr. 11:4
...osh. 8:15; 18:12
2 [a]Josh. 18:13
the goings out of ...*ere* [a]Josh. 18:13; ...:17 [b]Josh. 10:33
4 [a]Josh. 17:14
5 [a]Josh. 18:13
6 [a]Josh. 17:7
7 [a]1 Chr. 7:28
[1]Or, *wadi* [2]Lit., *the* ...*oings out of it were* [a]Josh. 17:8

9 *together* with the cities which were set apart for the sons of
Ephraim in the midst of the inheritance of the sons of Manasseh, all
the cities with their villages.
10 [a]But they did not [1]drive out the Canaanites who lived in Gezer,
so [b]the Canaanites live in the midst of Ephraim to this day, and they
became forced laborers.

Chapter 17

17 Now *this* was the lot for the tribe of [a]Manasseh, for he was the
first-born of Joseph. To Machir the first-born of Manasseh, the
father of Gilead, [1]was allotted Gilead and Bashan, because he was a
man of war.
2 So *the lot* was *made* for the rest of the sons of Manasseh according
to their families: for the sons of Abiezer and for the sons of Helek
and for the sons of Asriel and for the sons of Shechem and for the
sons of Hepher and for the sons of Shemida; these *were* the male
descendants of Manasseh the son of Joseph according to their families.
3 However, [a]Zelophehad, the son of Hepher, the son of Gilead, the
son of Machir, the son of Manasseh, had no sons, only daughters;
and these are the names of his daughters: Mahlah and Noah,
Hoglah, Milcah and Tirzah.
4 And they came near before Eleazar the priest and before Joshua
the son of Nun and before the leaders, saying, "The LORD com-
manded Moses to give us an inheritance among our brothers." So
[a]according to the [1]command of the LORD he gave them an inheritance
among their father's brothers.
5 Thus there fell ten portions to Manasseh, besides the land of
Gilead and Bashan, which is beyond the Jordan,
6 because the daughters of Manasseh received an inheritance
among his sons. And the [a]land of Gilead belonged to the rest of the
sons of Manasseh.
7 And the border of Manasseh [1]ran from Asher to Michmethath
which was east of Shechem; then the border went [2]southward to the
inhabitants of En-tappuah.
8 The land of Tappuah belonged to Manasseh, but [a]Tappuah on
the border of Manasseh *belonged* to the sons of Ephraim.
9 And the [a]border went down to the [1]brook of Kanah, southward
of the [1]brook (these cities *belonged* to Ephraim among the cities of
Manasseh), and the border of Manasseh *was* on the north side of the
[1]brook, and [2]it ended at the sea.
10 The south side *belonged* to Ephraim and the north side to Manas-
seh, and the sea was [1]their border; and they reached to Asher on the
north and to Issachar on the east.
11 And in Issachar and in Asher, [a]Manasseh had Beth-shean and its
towns and Ibleam and its towns, and the inhabitants of Dor and its
towns, and the inhabitants of En-dor and its towns, and the in-
habitants of Taanach and its towns, and the inhabitants of Megiddo
and its towns, the third is [b]Napheth.
12 [a]But the sons of Manasseh could not take possession of these
cities, because the Canaanites persisted in living in that land.
13 And it came about when the sons of Israel became strong, [a]they
put the Canaanites to forced labor, but they did not [1]drive them out
completely.
14 Then the [a]sons of Joseph spoke to Joshua, saying, "Why have

10 [1]Or, *dispos* [a]Judg. 1:29; 1 [b]Josh. 17:12, 1

17:1 [1]Lit., *and was to him* [a]G 41:51; 46:20; 4

3 [a]Num. 26:33

4 [1]Lit., *mouth* 27:5-7

6 [a]Josh. 13:30,

7 [1]Lit., *was* [2]Li *right hand*

8 [a]Josh. 16:8

9 [1]Or, *wadi* [2]Lit *goings out of it* [a]Josh. 16:8f.

10 [1]Lit., *its*

11 [a]1 Chr. 7:29 11:2; 12:23

12 [a]Judg. 1:27

13 [1]Or, *disposse* [a]Josh. 16:10

14 [a]Num. 13:7

) for yourself you given me only one lot and one portion for an inheritance, since I
.it., cut down am a numerous people whom the LORD has thus far blessed?"
15 And Joshua said to them, "If you are a numerous people, go [1]up
to the forest and [2]clear a place for yourself there in the land of the
Perizzites and of the Rephaim, since the hill country of Ephraim is
17:18; Judg. too narrow for you."
1:19; 4:3, 13 16 And the sons of Joseph said, "The hill country is not enough for
us, and all the Canaanites who live in the valley land have [a]chariots
of iron, both those who are in Beth-shean and its towns, and those
who are in the valley of Jezreel."
t., cut it down 17 And Joshua spoke to the house of Joseph, to Ephraim and
ings out [3]Or, Manasseh, saying, "You are a numerous people and have great
[a]Josh. 17:16 power; you shall not have one lot *only*,
18 but the hill country shall be yours. For though it is a forest, you
shall [1]clear it, and to its [2]farthest borders it shall be yours; for you
shall [3]drive out the Canaanites, even though they have [a]chariots of
dg. 21:19; Jer. iron *and* though they are strong."
7:12; 26:6, 9

Chapter 18

18 Then the whole congregation of the sons of Israel assembled
themselves at [a]Shiloh, and set up the tent of meeting there;
3 [a]Judg. 18:9 and the land was subdued before them.
2 And there remained among the sons of Israel seven tribes who
had not divided their inheritance.
3 So Joshua said to the sons of Israel, "[a]How long will you put off
he [2]Lit., come entering to take possession of the land which the LORD, the God of
your fathers, has given you?
4 "Provide for yourselves three men from [1]each tribe that I may
send them, and that they may arise and walk through the land and
write a description of it according to their inheritance; then they
5 [a]Josh. 15:1 shall [2]return to me.
5 "And they shall divide it into seven portions; [a]Judah shall stay in
its territory on the south, and the house of Joseph shall stay in their
territory on the north.
6 [a]Josh. 14:2 6 "And you shall describe the land in seven divisions, and bring *the
description* here to me. [a]And I will cast lots for you here before the
LORD our God.
7 "For [a]the Levites have no portion among you, because the priest-
hood of the LORD is [1]their inheritance. Gad and Reuben and the
his [a]Num. 18:7, half-tribe of Manasseh also have received their inheritance eastward
20; Josh. 13:33 beyond the Jordan, which Moses the servant of the LORD gave them."
8 Then the men arose and went, and Joshua commanded those
who went to describe the land, saying, "Go and walk through the
land and describe it, and return to me; then I will cast lots for you
8 [a]Josh. 18:1 here before the LORD in [a]Shiloh."
9 So the men went and passed through the land, and described it
by cities in seven divisions in a book; and they came to Joshua to the
camp at Shiloh.
[a]Num. 34:16-29; 10 And [a]Joshua cast lots for them in Shiloh before the LORD, and
Josh. 19:51 there Joshua divided the land to the sons of Israel according to their
divisions.
11 Now the lot of the tribe of the sons of Benjamin came up accord-
ing to their families, and the territory of their lot [1]lay between the
11 [1]Lit., went out sons of Judah and the sons of Joseph.

12 And [a]their border on the north side was from the Jordan, then
the border went up to the side of Jericho on the north, and went up
through the hill country westward; and [1]it ended at the wilderness
of Beth-aven.
13 And from there the border continued to [a]Luz, to the side of Luz
(that is, Bethel) southward; and the border went down to Ataroth-
addar, near the hill which *lies* on the south of [b]lower Beth-horon.
14 And the border extended *from there,* and turned round on the
west side southward, from the hill which *lies* before Beth-horon
southward; and [1]it ended at Kiriath-baal (that is, Kiriath-jearim), a
city of the sons of Judah. This *was* the west side.
15 Then the [a]south side *was* from the edge of Kiriath-jearim, and the
border went westward and went to the fountain of the waters of
Nephtoah.
16 And the border went down to the edge of the hill which is in the
[a]valley of Ben-hinnom, which is in the valley of Rephaim northward;
and it went down to the valley of Hinnom, to the slope of the
Jebusite southward, and went down to En-rogel.
17 And it extended northward and went to En-shemesh and went
to Geliloth, which is opposite the ascent of Adummim, and it went
down to the [a]stone of Bohan the son of Reuben.
18 And it continued to the side in front of the Arabah northward,
and went down to the Arabah.
19 And the border continued to the side of Beth-hoglah northward;
and the [1]border ended at the north bay of the Salt Sea, at the south
end of the Jordan. This *was* the south border.
20 Moreover, the Jordan was its border on the east side. This *was*
the inheritance of the sons of Benjamin, according to their families
and according to its borders all around.
21 Now the cities of the tribe of the sons of Benjamin according to
their families were Jericho and Beth-hoglah and Emek-keziz,
22 and Beth-arabah and Zemaraim and Bethel,
23 and Avvim and Parah and Ophrah,
24 and Chephar-ammoni and Ophni and [a]Geba; twelve cities with
their villages.
25 Gibeon and Ramah and Beeroth,
26 and Mizpeh and Chephirah and Mozah,
27 and Rekem and Irpeel and Taralah,
28 and [a]Zelah, Haeleph and the Jebusite (that is, Jerusalem), Gibeah,
Kiriath; fourteen cities with their villages. This is the inheritance of
the [b]sons of Benjamin according to their families.

Chapter 19

19 Then the second lot [1]fell to Simeon, to the tribe of the sons of
Simeon according to their families, and their inheritance was
in the midst of the inheritance of the sons of Judah.
2 So they had as their inheritance Beersheba or [1]Sheba and
Moladah,
3 and Hazar-shual and Balah and Ezem,
4 and Eltolad and Bethul and Hormah,
5 and Ziklag and Beth-marcaboth and Hazar-susah,
6 and Beth-lebaoth and Sharuhen, thirteen cities with their
villages;

12 [1]Lit., *the g... of it were* [a]Jo...
13 [a]Gen. 28:... 1:23 [b]Josh. 1...
14 [1]Lit., *the g... of it were*
15 [a]Josh. 15:...
16 [a]2 Kin. 23:...
17 [a]Josh. 15:6...
19 [1]Lit., *goings... the border were*
24 [a]Ezra 2:26;...
28 [a]2 Sam. 21:... [b]Num. 26:38
19:1 [1]Lit., *came...*
2 [1]In Josh. 15:2... *Shema*

7 Ain, Rimmon and Ether and Ashan, four cities with their villages;

8 and all the villages which *were* around these cities as far as Baalath-beer, Ramah of the [1]Negev. This *was* the inheritance of the tribe of the sons of Simeon according to their families.

9 The inheritance of the sons of Simeon *was taken* from the portion of the sons of Judah, for the share of the sons of Judah was too large for them; so the sons of Simeon received *an* inheritance in the midst of [1]Judah's inheritance.

10 Now the third lot came up for the sons of Zebulun according to their families. And the territory of their inheritance was as far as Sarid.

11 Then their border went up to the west and to Maralah, it then [1]touched Dabbesheth, and reached to the [2]brook that is before Jokneam.

12 Then it turned from Sarid to the east toward the sunrise as far as the border of Chisloth-tabor, and it proceeded to Daberath and [1]up to Japhia.

13 And from there it continued eastward toward the sunrise to Gath-hepher, to Eth-kazin, and it proceeded to Rimmon [1]which stretches to Neah.

14 And the border circled around it on the north to Hannathon, and [1]it ended at the valley of Iphtahel.

15 *Included* also *were* Kattah and Nahalal and Shimron and Idalah and Bethlehem; twelve cities with their villages.

16 This *was* the inheritance of the sons of Zebulun according to their families, these cities with their villages.

17 The fourth lot [1]fell to Issachar, to the sons of Issachar according to their families.

18 And their territory was to Jezreel and *included* Chesulloth and [a]Shunem,

19 and Hapharaim and Shion and Anaharath,

20 and Rabbith and Kishion and Ebez,

21 and Remeth and En-gannim and En-haddah and Beth-pazzez.

22 And the border reached to [a]Tabor and Shahazumah and Beth-shemesh, and [1]their border ended at the Jordan; sixteen cities with their villages.

23 This *was* the inheritance of the tribe of the sons of Issachar according to their families, the cities with their villages.

24 Now the fifth lot [1]fell to the tribe of the sons of Asher according to their families.

25 And their territory was Helkath and Hali and Beten and Achshaph,

26 and Allammelech and Amad and Mishal; and it reached to Carmel on the west and to Shihor-libnath.

27 And it turned toward the [1]east to Beth-dagon, and reached to Zebulun, and to the valley of Iphtahel northward to Beth-emek and Neiel; then it proceeded on [2]north to [a]Cabul,

28 and Ebron and Rehob and Hammon and Kanah, as far as Great [a]Sidon.

29 And the border turned to Ramah, and to the fortified city of Tyre; then the border turned to Hosah, and [1]it ended at the sea by the region of [a]Achzib.

.e., South country

9 [1]Lit., their

r, reached to [2]Or, wadi

12 [1]Lit., went up

Or, and is marked off

.it., the goings out of it were

17 [1]Lit., came out

Sam. 28:4; 2 Kin. 4:8

.it., the goings out their border were

dg. 4:6; Ps. 89:12

24 [1]Lit., came out

Lit., sunrise [2]Lit., from the left hand [a]1 Kin. 9:13

Gen. 10:19; Judg. 1:31; Acts 27:3

it., the goings out were [a]Judg. 1:31

30 *Included* also *were* Ummah, and Aphek and Rehob; twenty-two
cities with their villages.
31 This *was* the inheritance of the tribe of the sons of Asher accord-
ing to their families, these cities with their villages.
32 The sixth lot [1]fell to the sons of Naphtali; to the sons of Naphtali
according to their families.
33 And their border was from Heleph, from the oak in Zaanannim
and Adami-nekeb and Jabneel, as far as Lakkum; and [1]it ended at the
Jordan.
34 Then the border turned westward to Aznoth-tabor, and
proceeded from there to Hukkok; and it reached to Zebulun on the
south and [1]touched Asher on the west, and to Judah at the Jordan
toward the [2]east.
35 And the fortified cities *were* Ziddim, Zer and [a]Hammath, Rak-
kath and [b]Chinnereth,
36 and Adamah and Ramah and Hazor,
37 and Kedesh and Edrei and En-hazor,
38 and Yiron and Migdal-el, Horem and Beth-anath and Beth-
shemesh; nineteen cities with their villages.
39 This *was* the inheritance of the tribe of the sons of Naphtali ac-
cording to their families, the cities with their villages.
40 The seventh lot [1]fell to the tribe of the sons of Dan according to
their families.
41 And the territory of their inheritance was Zorah and Eshtaol and
Ir-shemesh,
42 and Shaalabbin and Aijalon and Ithlah,
43 and Elon and Timnah and Ekron,
44 and Eltekeh and Gibbethon and Baalath,
45 and Jehud and Bene-berak and Gath-rimmon,
46 and Me-jarkon and Rakkon, with the territory over against
[1]Joppa.
47 And the territory of the [a]sons of Dan proceeded [1]beyond them;
for the sons of Dan went up and fought with Leshem and captured
it. Then they struck it with the edge of the sword and possessed it
and [2]settled in it; and they called [3b]Leshem Dan after the name of
Dan their father.
48 This *was* the inheritance of the tribe of the sons of Dan according
to their families, these cities with their villages.
49 When they finished apportioning the land for inheritance by its
borders, the sons of Israel gave an inheritance in their midst to
Joshua the son of Nun.
50 In accordance with the [1]command of the LORD they gave him the
city for which he asked, [a]Timnath-serah in the hill country of
Ephraim. So he built the city and [2]settled in it.
51 [a]These are the inheritances which Eleazar the priest and Joshua
the son of Nun and the heads of the [1]households of the tribes of the
sons of Israel distributed by lot in Shiloh before the LORD, at the
doorway of the tent of meeting. So they finished dividing the land.

Chapter 20

20 Then the LORD spoke to Joshua, saying,
2 "Speak to the sons of Israel, saying, '[1]Designate [a]the cities of
refuge, of which I spoke to you [2]through Moses,
3 that the manslayer who [1]kills any person unintentionally,

32 [1]Lit., *came ou*
33 [1]Lit., *the going of it were*
34 [1]Or, *reached* [2]Lit., *sunrise*
35 [a]Gen. 10:18; 8:65 [b]Deut. 3:17
40 [1]Lit., *came ou*
46 [1]Heb., *Japho*
47 [1]Lit., *from* [2]Li *dwelt* [3]I.e., Laish [a]Judg. 18:1 [b]Jud 18:29
50 [1]Lit., *mouth* *dwelt* [a]Num. 13: 24:30
51 [1]Lit., *fathers* 18:10
20:2 [1]Lit., *Set fo yourselves* [2]Lit., *hand of* [a]Num. 3 Deut. 4:41-43; 1
3 [1]Lit., *smites*

without premeditation, may flee there, and they shall become your
refuge from the avenger of blood.
4 'And he shall flee to one of these cities, and shall stand at the
entrance of the [a]gate of the city and state his case in the hearing of
the elders of that city; and they shall [1]take him into the city to them
and give him a place, so that he may dwell among them.
5 'Now [a]if the avenger of blood pursues him, then they shall not
deliver the manslayer into his hand, because he struck his neighbor
without premeditation and did not hate him beforehand.
6 'And he shall dwell in that city [a]until he stands before the con-
gregation for judgment, until the death of the one who is high priest
in those days. Then the manslayer shall [1]return to his own city and
to his own house, to the city from which he fled.' "
7 So they [1]set apart [a]Kedesh in [2]Galilee in the hill country of Naph-
tali and Shechem in the hill country of Ephraim, and Kiriath-arba
(that is, Hebron) in [b]the hill country of Judah.
8 And beyond the Jordan east of Jericho, they [1]designated Bezer in
the wilderness on the plain from the tribe of Reuben, and Ramoth in
Gilead from the tribe of Gad, and Golan in Bashan from the tribe of
Manasseh.
9 [a]These were the appointed cities for all the sons of Israel and for
the stranger who sojourns among them, that whoever [1]kills any per-
son unintentionally may flee there, and not die by the hand of the
avenger of blood until he stands before the congregation.

Chapter 21

21 Then the heads of [1]households of [a]the Levites approached
Eleazar the priest and Joshua the son of Nun and the heads of
[1]households of the tribes of the sons of Israel.
2 And they spoke to them at Shiloh in the land of Canaan, saying,
"[a]The LORD commanded [1]through Moses to give us cities to live in,
with their pasture lands for our cattle."
3 So the sons of Israel gave the Levites from their inheritance these
cities with their pasture lands, according to the [1]command of the
LORD.
4 Then the lot came out for the families of the Kohathites. And the
sons of Aaron the priest, who were of the Levites, [1]received thirteen
cities by lot from the tribe of Judah and from the tribe of the
Simeonites and from the tribe of Benjamin.
5 And the rest of the sons of Kohath [1]received ten cities by lot from
the families of the tribe of Ephraim and from the tribe of Dan and
from the half-tribe of Manasseh.
6 And the sons of Gershon [1]received thirteen cities by lot from the
families of the tribe of Issachar and from the tribe of Asher and from
the tribe of Naphtali and from the half-tribe of Manasseh in Bashan.
7 The sons of Merari according to their families [1]received twelve
cities from the tribe of Reuben and from the tribe of Gad and from
the tribe of Zebulun.
8 Now the [a]sons of Israel gave by lot to the Levites these cities
with their pasture lands, as the LORD had commanded [1]through
Moses.
9 And they gave these cities which are *here* mentioned by name
from the tribe of the sons of Judah and from the tribe of the sons of
Simeon;

ather [a]Ruth
4; Jer. 38:7
Num. 35:12
, *return and*
[a]Num. 35:12
t., *sanctified*
Galil [a]Josh.
; 1 Chr. 6:76
1; Luke 1:39
8 [1]Lit., *set*
mites [a]Num.
35:13ff.
[1]Lit., *fathers*
[a]Num. 35:1-8
by the hand of
[a]Num. 35:2
3 [1]Lit., *mouth*
4 [1]Lit., *had*
5 [1]Lit., *had*
6 [1]Lit., *had*
7 [1]Lit., *had*
, *by the hand of*
[a]Gen. 49:5ff.

10 and they were for the sons of Aaron, one of the families of the Kohathites, of the sons of Levi, for the lot was theirs first.

11 Thus [a]they gave them Kiriath-arba, *Arba being* the [b]father of Anak (that is, Hebron), in the hill country of Judah, with its surrounding pasture lands.

12 But the fields of the city and its villages, they gave to Caleb the son of Jephunneh as his possession.

13 So [a]to the sons of Aaron the priest they gave [b]Hebron, the city of refuge for the manslayer, with its pasture lands, and [c]Libnah with its pasture lands,

14 and [a]Jattir with its pasture lands and [b]Eshtemoa with its pasture lands,

15 and [1]Holon with its pasture lands and [a]Debir with its pasture lands,

16 and [1]Ain with its pasture lands and [a]Juttah with its pasture lands *and* [b]Beth-shemesh with its pasture lands; nine cities from these two tribes.

17 And from the tribe of Benjamin, [a]Gibeon with its pasture lands, [b]Geba with its pasture lands,

18 Anathoth with its pasture lands and [1]Almon with its pasture lands; four cities.

19 All the cities of the sons of Aaron, the priests, were thirteen cities with their pasture lands.

20 Then the cities from the tribe of Ephraim were allotted to the [a]families of the sons of Kohath, the Levites, *even to* the rest of the sons of Kohath.

21 And they gave them [a]Shechem, the city of refuge for the manslayer, with its pasture lands, in the hill country of Ephraim, and Gezer with its pasture lands,

22 and Kibzaim with its pasture lands and Beth-horon with its pasture lands; four cities.

23 And from the tribe of Dan, Elteke with its pasture lands, Gibbethon with its pasture lands,

24 Aijalon with its pasture lands, Gath-rimmon with its pasture lands; four cities.

25 And from the half-tribe of Manasseh, *they allotted* Taanach with its pasture lands and Gath-rimmon with its pasture lands; two cities.

26 All the cities with their pasture lands for the families of the rest of the sons of Kohath were ten.

27 And [a]to the sons of Gershon, one of the families of the Levites, from the half-tribe of Manasseh, *they gave* Golan in Bashan, the city of refuge for the manslayer, with its pasture lands, and Be-eshterah with its pasture lands; two cities.

28 And from the tribe of Issachar, *they gave* Kishion with its pasture lands, Daberath with its pasture lands,

29 Jarmuth with its pasture lands, En-gannim with its pasture lands; four cities.

30 And from the tribe of Asher, *they gave* Mishal with its pasture lands, Abdon with its pasture lands,

31 Helkath with its pasture lands and Rehob with its pasture lands; four cities.

32 And from the tribe of Naphtali, *they gave* [a]Kedesh in Galilee, the city of refuge for the manslayer, with its pasture lands and

11 [a]1 Chr. 6:5 14:15; 15:13

13 [a]1 Chr. 6:5 15:54 [c]Josh. 1

14 [a]Josh. 15:4 15:50

15 [1]In 1 Chr. 6: *Hilen* [a]Josh. 15

16 [1]In 1 Chr. 6: *Ashan* [a]Josh. 1 [b]Josh. 15:10

17 [a]Josh. 18:2 18:24

18 [1]In 1 Chr. 6 *Allemeth*

20 [a]1 Chr. 6:66

21 [a]Josh. 20:7

27 [a]1 Chr. 6:7

32 [a]Josh. 20:7

Hammoth-dor with its pasture lands and Kartan with its pasture
lands; three cities.
33 All the cities of the Gershonites according to their families were
thirteen cities with their pasture lands.
34 And to the families of [a]the sons of Merari, the rest of the Levites,
they gave from the tribe of Zebulun, Jokneam with its pasture lands
and Kartah with its pasture lands.
35 Dimnah with its pasture lands, Nahalal with its pasture lands;
four cities.
36 And from the tribe of Reuben, *they gave* [a]Bezer with its pasture
lands and Jahaz with its pasture lands,
37 Kedemoth with its pasture lands and Mephaath with its pasture
lands; four cities.
38 And from the tribe of Gad, *they gave* [a]Ramoth in Gilead, the city
of refuge for the manslayer, with its pasture lands and [b]Mahanaim
with its pasture lands,
39 Heshbon with its pasture lands, Jazer with its pasture lands; four
cities in all.
40 All *these were* the cities of the sons of Merari according to their
families, the rest of the families of the Levites; and their lot was
twelve cities.
41 [a]All the cities of the Levites in the midst of the possession of the
sons of Israel were forty-eight cities with their pasture lands.
42 These cities each had its surrounding pasture lands; thus *it was*
with all these cities.
43 [a]So the LORD gave Israel all the land which He had sworn to give
to their fathers, and [b]they possessed it and lived in it.
44 And the LORD [a]gave them rest on every side, according to all that
He had sworn to their fathers, and [b]no one of all their enemies stood
before them; [c]the LORD gave all their enemies into their hand.
45 [a]Not [1]one of the good promises which the LORD had [2]made to the
house of Israel failed; all came to pass.

Chapter 22

22 [a]Then Joshua summoned the Reubenites and the Gadites and
the half-tribe of Manasseh,
2 and said to them, "You have kept all that Moses the servant of
the LORD commanded you, [a]and have listened to my voice in all that
I commanded you.
3 "You have not forsaken your brothers these many days to this
day, but have kept the charge of the commandment of the LORD your
God.
4 "And now [a]the LORD your God has given rest to your brothers, as
He spoke to them; therefore turn now and go to your tents, to the
land of your possession, which Moses the servant of the LORD gave
you beyond the Jordan.
5 "Only be very careful to observe the commandment and the law
which Moses the servant of the LORD commanded you, to [a]love the
LORD your God and walk in all His ways and keep His command-
ments and hold fast to Him and serve Him [b]with all your heart and
with all your soul."
6 So Joshua [a]blessed them and sent them away, and they went to
their tents.
7 Now [a]to the one half-tribe of Manasseh Moses had given *a*

[a]1 Chr. 6:77
...t. 4:43; Josh. 20:8
...t. 4:43; 1 Kin. ...3 [b]Gen. 32:2; 2 Sam. 2:8
41 [a]Num. 35:7
...t. 34:4 [b]Num. ...3; Deut. 11:31; 17:14
...osh. 1:13; 23:1 ...:24 [c]Ex. 23:31
...it., *a word from* ...*good word* [2]Lit., ...*n* [a]Josh. 23:14; 1 Kin. 8:56
[a]Num. 32:20-22
[a]Josh. 1:12-18
...um. 32:18; Deut. 3:20
...eut. 5:10 [b]Deut. 4:29
[a]Gen. 47:7; Josh. ...:13; 2 Sam. 6:18; Luke 24:50
7 [a]Num. 32:33

possession in Bashan, but [b]to the other half Joshua gave *a possession* among their brothers westward beyond the Jordan. So when Joshua sent them away to their tents, he blessed them,

8 and said to [1]them, "Return to your tents with great riches and with very much livestock, with silver, gold, bronze, iron, and with very many clothes; [a]divide the spoil of your enemies with your brothers."

9 And the sons of Reuben and the sons of Gad and the half-tribe of Manasseh returned *home* and departed from the sons of Israel at Shiloh which is in the land of Canaan, to go to the [a]land of Gilead, to the land of their possession which they had possessed, according to the [1]command of the LORD [2]through Moses.

10 And when they came to the region of the Jordan which is in the land of Canaan, the sons of Reuben and the sons of Gad and the half-tribe of Manasseh built an altar there by the Jordan, a large altar in appearance.

11 And the sons of Israel heard *it* [1]said, "Behold, the sons of Reuben and the sons of Gad and the half-tribe of Manasseh have [a]built an altar at the [2]frontier of the land of Canaan, in the region of the Jordan, on the side *belonging to* the sons of Israel."

12 And when the sons of Israel heard *of it,* the whole congregation of the sons of Israel gathered themselves at [a]Shiloh, to go up against them in war.

13 Then the sons of Israel sent to the sons of Reuben and to the sons of Gad and to the half-tribe of Manasseh, into the land of Gilead, [a]Phinehas the son of Eleazar the priest,

14 and with him ten chiefs, one chief for each father's household from each of the tribes of Israel; and [a]each one of them *was* the head of his father's household among the [1]thousands of Israel.

15 And they came to the sons of Reuben and to the sons of Gad and to the half-tribe of Manasseh, to the land of Gilead, and they spoke with them saying,

16 "Thus says the whole congregation of the LORD, 'What is this unfaithful act which you have committed against the God of Israel, turning away from following the LORD this day, by [a]building yourselves an altar, to rebel against the LORD this day?

17 'Is not [a]the iniquity of Peor [1]enough for us, from which we have not cleansed ourselves to this day, although a plague came on the congregation of the LORD,

18 that you must turn away this day from following the LORD? And it will come about if you rebel against the LORD today, that [a]He will be angry with the whole congregation of Israel tomorrow.

19 'If, however, the land of your possession is unclean, then [1]cross into the land of the possession of the LORD, where the LORD's tabernacle [2]stands, and take possession among us. Only do not rebel against the LORD, or rebel against us by [a]building an altar for yourselves, besides the altar of the LORD our God.

20 'Did not [a]Achan the son of Zerah act unfaithfully in the things under the ban, and wrath fall on all the congregation of Israel? And that man did not perish alone in his iniquity.' "

21 Then the sons of Reuben and the sons of Gad and the half-tribe of Manasseh answered, and spoke to the heads of the [1]families of Israel.

22 "The [a]Mighty One, God, the LORD, the Mighty One, God, the

7 [b]Josh. 17:1
8 [1]Lit., *them, "Return* [a]Nun
1 Sam. 30:16
9 [1]Lit., *mouth*
the hand of [a]
26, 29
11 [1]Lit., *sayin*
front [a]Deut. 1
22:19
12 [a]Josh. 18:1
13 [a]Num. 25:7
14 [1]Or, *familie*
1:4
16 [a]Josh. 22:11
17 [1]Lit., *little fo*
[a]Num. 25:1-9
18 [a]Num. 16:22
19 [1]Lit., *cross fo*
yourselves [2]Lit.,
[a]Josh. 22:11
20 [a]Josh. 7:1-26
21 [1]Lit., *thousan*
22 [a]Deut. 10:17

LORD! [b]He knows, and may Israel itself know. If *it was* in rebellion, or
if in an unfaithful act against the LORD do not Thou save us this day!
23 "If we have built us an altar to turn away from following the
LORD, or if to [a]offer a burnt offering or grain offering on it, or if to
offer sacrifices of peace offerings on it, may the LORD Himself re-
quire it.
24 "But truly we have done this out of concern, [1]for a reason, saying,
'In time to come your sons may say to our [2]sons, "What have you to
do with the LORD, the God of Israel?
25 "For the LORD has made the Jordan a border between us and you,
you sons of Reuben and sons of Gad; you have no portion in the
LORD." So your sons may make our sons stop fearing the LORD.'
26 "Therefore we said, 'Let us [1]build an altar, not for burnt offering
or for sacrifice;
27 rather it shall be [a]a witness between us and you and between our
generations after us, that we are to [b]perform the service of the LORD
before Him with our burnt offerings, and with our sacrifices and
with our peace offerings, that your sons may not say to our sons in
time to come, "You have no portion in the LORD." '
28 "Therefore we said, 'It shall also come about if they say *this* to us
or to our generations in time to come, then we shall say, "See the
copy of the altar of the LORD which our fathers made, not for burnt
offering or for sacrifice; rather it is a witness between us and you." '
29 "Far be it from us that we should rebel against the LORD and turn
away from following the LORD this day, by [a]building an altar for
burnt offering, for grain offering or for sacrifice, besides the altar of
the LORD our God which is before His [1]tabernacle."
30 So when Phinehas the priest and the leaders of the congregation,
even the heads of the [1]families of Israel who *were* with him, heard
the words which the sons of Reuben and the sons of Gad and the
sons of Manasseh spoke, it pleased them.
31 And Phinehas the son of Eleazar the priest said to the sons of
Reuben and to the sons of Gad and to the sons of Manasseh, "Today
we know that the [a]LORD is in our midst, because you have not com-
mitted this unfaithful act against the LORD; now you have delivered
the sons of Israel from the hand of the LORD."
32 Then Phinehas the son of Eleazar the priest and the leaders re-
turned from the sons of Reuben and from the sons of Gad, from the
land of Gilead, to the land of Canaan, to the sons of Israel, and
brought back word to them.
33 And the word pleased the sons of Israel, and the sons of Israel
[a]blessed God; and they did not speak of going up against them in
war, to destroy the land in which the sons of Reuben and the sons of
Gad were living.
34 And the sons of Reuben and the sons of Gad [a]called the altar
Witness; "For," *they said,* "it is a witness between us that the LORD is
God."

Chapter 23

23 Now it came about after many days, when the LORD had
given [a]rest to Israel from all their enemies [1]on every side, and
Joshua was old, advanced in years,
2 that [a]Joshua called for all Israel, for their elders and their heads

in. 8:39; Job :7; Ps. 44:21
[a]Deut. 12:11
it., *from* [2]Lit., *sons, saying*
epare to build *for ourselves*
. 31:48; Josh. eut. 12:6, 11, 26f.
dwelling place [a]Deut. 12:13f.
Lit., *thousands*
[a]Ex. 25:8; Lev. 1f.; 2 Chr. 15:2
hr. 29:20; Dan. 2:19; Luke 2:28
[a]Gen. 31:47-49
[1]Lit., *from round* *ut* [a]Josh. 21:44
2 [a]Josh. 24:1

and their judges and their officers, and said to them, "I am old,
advanced in years.
3 "And you have seen all that the LORD your God has done to all
these nations because of you, for [a]the LORD your God is He who has
been fighting for you.
4 "See, [a]I have apportioned to you these nations which remain as an
inheritance for your tribes, with all the nations which I have cut off,
from the Jordan even to the Great Sea toward the setting of the sun.
5 "And the LORD your God, He shall thrust them out from before
you and [1a]drive them from before you; and [b]you shall possess their
land, just as the LORD your God [2]promised you.
6 "[a]Be very firm, then, to keep and do all that is written in the book
of the law of Moses, so that you may not turn aside from it to the
right hand or to the left,
7 in order that you may not [1]associate with these nations, these
which remain among you, or [a]mention the name of their gods, or
[b]make *anyone* swear *by them,* or [c]serve them, or bow down to them.
8 "But you are to cling to the LORD your God, as you have done to
this day.
9 "[a]For the LORD has [1]driven out great and strong nations from
before you; and as for you, [b]no man has stood before you to this day.
10 "[a]One of your men puts to flight a thousand, for the LORD your
God is [b]He who fights for you, just as He [1]promised you.
11 "So take diligent heed to yourselves to love the LORD your God.
12 "For if you ever go back and [a]cling to the rest of these nations,
these which remain among you, and [b]intermarry with them, so that
you [1]associate with them and they with you,
13 know with certainty that the LORD your God will not continue to
[1]drive these nations out from before you; but they shall be a [a]snare
and a trap to you, and a whip on your sides and thorns in your eyes,
until you perish from off this good land which the LORD your God
has given you.
14 "Now behold, today [a]I am going the way of all the earth, and you
know in all your hearts and in all your souls that [b]not one word of
all the good words which the LORD your God spoke concerning you
has failed; all have [1]been fulfilled for you, not [2]one of them has
failed.
15 "And it shall come about that just as all the good words which the
LORD your God spoke to you have come upon you, so [a]the LORD will
bring upon you all the threats, until He has destroyed you from off
this good land which the LORD your God has given you.
16 "[a]When you transgress the covenant of the LORD your God, which
He commanded you, and go and serve other gods, and bow down to
them, then the anger of the LORD will burn against you, and you
shall perish quickly from off the good land which He has given
you."

Chapter 24

24 Then [a]Joshua gathered all the tribes of Israel to Shechem, and
called for the elders of Israel and for their heads and their
judges and their officers; and they presented themselves before God.
2 And Joshua said to all the people, "Thus says the LORD, the God
of Israel, 'From ancient times your fathers lived beyond the [1]River,

3 [a]Deut. 1:3
4 [a]Ex. 23:30
5 [1]Or, *dispo*
spoke to [a]E
[b]Num. 33:53
6 [a]Deut. 5:3
7 [1]Lit., *go ar*
23:13; Ps. 16
6:13; 10:20 [c]
9 [1]Or, *dispos*
[a]Ex. 23:23, 30
7:24
10 [1]Lit., *spok*
26:8; Deut. 28
[b]Deut. 3:22; J
12 [1]Lit., *go ar*
34:15, 16; Ps.
35 [b]Deut. 7:3,
9:2; Neh. 13:2
13 [1]Or, *dispos*
[a]Ex. 23:33; 34
7:16
14 [1]Lit., *come*
word [a]1 Kin. 2
21:45
15 [a]Lev. 26:14
Deut. 28:15
16 [a]Deut. 4:25,
24:1 [a]Josh. 23
2 [1]I.e., Euphrat

namely, [a]Terah, the father of Abraham and the father of Nahor, and
they served other gods.
3 'Then [a]I took your father Abraham from beyond the [1]River, and
led him through all the land of Canaan, and [b]multiplied his [2]de-
scendants and gave him [c]Isaac.
4 'And to Isaac I gave [a]Jacob and Esau, and [b]to Esau I gave Mount
Seir, to possess it; but [c]Jacob and his sons went down to Egypt.
5 'Then [a]I sent Moses and Aaron, and I plagued Egypt [1]by what I
did in its midst; and afterward I brought you out.
6 'And I brought your fathers out of Egypt, and [a]you came to the
sea; and Egypt pursued your fathers with chariots and horsemen to
the [1]Red Sea.
7 'But when they cried out to the LORD, He put darkness between
you and the Egyptians, and brought the sea upon them and covered
them; and your own eyes saw what I did in Egypt. And [a]you lived in
the wilderness for a long time.
8 'Then [a]I brought you into the land of the Amorites who lived
beyond the Jordan, and they fought with you; and I gave them into
your hand, and you took possession of their land when I destroyed
them before you.
9 'Then [a]Balak the son of Zippor, king of Moab, arose and fought
against Israel, and he sent and summoned Balaam the son of Beor to
curse you.
10 'But I [a]was not willing to listen to Balaam. So he had to bless you,
and I delivered you from his hand.
11 'And [a]you crossed the Jordan and came to Jericho; and the
citizens of Jericho fought against you, *and* [b]the Amorite and the
Perizzite and the Canaanite and the Hittite and the Girgashite, the
Hivite and the Jebusite. Thus [c]I gave them into your hand.
12 'Then I [a]sent the hornet before you and it [1]drove out the two
kings of the Amorites from before you, *but* [b]not by your sword or
your bow.
13 'And [a]I gave you a land on which you had not labored, and cities
which you had not built, and you have lived in them; you are eating
of vineyards and olive groves which you did not plant.'
14 "Now, therefore, [1a]fear the LORD and serve Him in sincerity and
[2]truth; and put away the gods which your fathers served beyond the
[3]River and in Egypt, and serve the LORD.
15 "And if it is disagreeable in your sight to serve the LORD, choose
for yourselves today whom you will serve: whether the gods which
your fathers served which were beyond the River, or [a]the gods of the
Amorites in whose land you are living; but as for me and my house,
we will serve the LORD."
16 And the people answered and said, "Far be it from us that we
should forsake the LORD to serve other gods;
17 for the LORD our God is He who brought us and our fathers up
out of the land of Egypt, from the house of [1]bondage, and who did
these great signs in our sight and preserved us through all the way
in which we went and among all the peoples through whose midst
we passed.
18 "And the LORD drove out from before us all the peoples, even the
Amorites who lived in the land. We also will serve the LORD, for He
is our God."
19 Then Joshua said to the people, "You will not be able to serve the

Gen. 11:27-32
uphrates [2]Lit.,
en. 12:1; 24:7
:5 [c]Gen. 21:3
Gen. 25:25, 26
36:8; Deut. 2:5
[c]Gen. 46:6, 7
., *according to*
[a]Ex. 4:14-17
, *Sea of Reeds*
[a]Ex. 14:2-31
Deut. 1:46; 2:14
[a]Num. 21:21-32
9 [a]Num. 22:2-6
10 [a]Deut. 23:5
sh. 3:14-17 [b]Ex.
23, 28; Deut. 7:1
[c]Ex. 23:31
, *drove them out*
23:28; Deut. 7:20
[b]Ps. 44:3
3 [a]Deut. 6:10, 11
r, *reverence* [2]Or,
faithfulness [3]I.e.,
Euphrates [a]Deut.
2; 18:13; 1 Sam.
12:24
15 [a]Judg. 6:10
17 [1]Lit., *bondmen*

LORD, [a]for He is a holy God. He is [b]a jealous God; [c]He will not forgive
your transgression or your sins.
20 "[a]If you forsake the LORD and serve foreign gods, then He will
turn and do you harm and consume you after He has done good to
you."
21 And the people said to Joshua, "No, but we will serve the LORD."
22 And Joshua said to the people, "You are witnesses against your-
selves that [a]you have chosen for yourselves the LORD, to serve Him."
And they said, "We are witnesses."
23 "Now therefore, put away the foreign gods which are in your
midst, and [a]incline your hearts to the LORD, the God of Israel."
24 [a]And the people said to Joshua, "We will serve the LORD our God
and we will [1]obey His voice."
25 [a]So Joshua made a covenant with the people that day, and made
for them a statute and an ordinance in Shechem.
26 And Joshua [a]wrote these words in the book of the law of God;
and he took a large stone and set it up there under the oak that was
by the sanctuary of the LORD.
27 And Joshua said to all the people, "Behold, [a]this stone shall be
for a witness against us, for it has heard all the words of the LORD
which He spoke [1]to us; thus it shall be for a witness against you, lest
you deny your God."
28 Then Joshua dismissed the people, each to his inheritance.
29 And it came about after these things that Joshua the son of Nun,
the servant of the LORD, died, being one hundred and ten years old.
30 And they buried him in the territory of his inheritance in
[a]Timnath-serah, which is in the hill country of Ephraim, on the north
of Mount Gaash.
31 And [a]Israel served the LORD all the days of Joshua and all the
days of the elders who [1]survived Joshua, and had known all the
deeds of the LORD which He had done for Israel.
32 Now [a]they buried the bones of Joseph, which the sons of Israel
brought up from Egypt, at Shechem, in the piece of ground [b]which
Jacob had bought from the sons of Hamor the father of Shechem for
one hundred [1]pieces of money; and they became the inheritance of
Joseph's sons.
33 And Eleazar the son of Aaron died; and they buried him [1]at
Gibeah of [a]Phinehas his son, which was given him in the hill country
of Ephraim.

19 [a]Lev. 19:2; 20 [b]Ex. 20:5; 34:14 23:21

20 [a]Deut. 4:25, 2

22 [a]Ps. 119:173

23 [a]1 Kin. 8:57, 5 119:36; 141:4

24 [1]Lit., *listen to* 19:8; 24:3, 7; Deu

25 [a]Ex. 24:8

26 [a]Deut. 31:24

27 [1]Lit., *with* [a]Jos 22:27, 34

30 [a]Josh. 19:50

31 [1]Lit., *prolonge after* [a]Judg. 2:6f.

32 [1]Heb., *qesitah* [a]Gen. 50:24, 25; E 13:19 [b]Gen. 33:1 John 4:5; Acts 7:1

33 [1]Or, *on the hil* [a]Josh. 22:13

JOSHUA AT A GLANCE

ne of Joshua:

NT DIVISIONS

		CHAPTER THEMES
		1
		2
		3
		4
		5
		6
		7
		8
		9
		10
		11
		12
		13
		14
		15
		16
		17
		18
		19
		20
		21
		22
		23
		24

Author:

Date:

Purpose:

Key Words:

JUDGES

During Joshua's leadership Israel finally entered the land promised to Abraham. There were in the land, but none who were greater than God. The Captain of the Host was able to sub Israel's enemies—in one battle the sun even stood still and the moon stopped until the nation of avenged themselves of their enemies.

Then there arose a generation which did not know war; nor did they know the Lord or the w had done for Israel. Israel went from victory to defeat and plunged into 325 to 400 years of dar These were the days of the judges, days from which we can learn valuable lessons.

THINGS TO DO

Chapters 1-2

1. Because the book of Judges is not chronological, it's helpful to understand the setting of the Read chapters 1 through 2. Then go to the end of Judges and read Judges 17:6, 18:1, 19: 21:25 and look for the key repeated phrase. Mark this phrase in a distinctive way and recor the JUDGES AT A GLANCE chart (page 399) under "Key Words."
2. Now read chapters 1 through 2 again and do the following:
   a. Mark in a distinctive way the key repeated phrases that are listed on JUDGES AT A GLA Put these on an index card that you can use as a bookmark while you study Judges.
   b. Chapter 1 also contains an important key phrase which is not on this list because it is no after chapter 2. Look for that phrase and mark its repeated use in a distinctive way. Ther up Exodus 23:20-33, Deuteronomy 7:1-11,16, and Joshua 23:5-13. Record these references margin of chapter 1 for cross-references.
   c. As you read each chapter question the text with the five W's and an H: Who? What? W Where? Why? and How? You won't always find the answer to every question. As you make sure you note who does what and why. Watch for where events take place and Always ask how something was accomplished, happened, or is to be done.
   d. Write in the chapter margin the names of key persons or groups of people (such as "the of Israel" and "judges"). Then list everything you learn about them from that chapter. D with the references to the Lord also.
3. When you finish your observations of chapter 2, review all you have learned, especially verses 11 through 23. Notice the cycle of events. Make sure you record this in the margin; the pattern for chapters 3 through 16.
4. Discern the theme of these chapters and record them on JUDGES AT A GLANCE and in th on the line next to the chapter number.

Chapters 3-16

1. Study chapters 3 through 16 the same way you did chapters 1 through 2: mark key words, as five W's and an H, list your insights in the margin, and record the theme of each chapter i appropriate places.
2. As you read Judges 3 through 16, note the names of the judges and record them in the ch margin where they appear. List everything you learn about them from the text. Then record information on the chart THE JUDGES OF ISRAEL on page 398. To understand when t judges ruled and what their relationship was to each other, carefully study the historical ch the beginning of Judges on page 361.
3. At the beginning of Judges on page 362 is a map showing the locations mentioned in Judges

you study each judge, note where the judge is from and write his or her name on the map next to the proper location.

ers 17-21

There is no indication that chapters 17 through 21 chronologically follow chapters 3 through 16. Rather, they give an overview of the moral setting of the time. Examine each chapter carefully as you have done the other chapters of Judges and note your insights. Watch the progression of events.

As you read these chapters, keep in mind the key phrase you marked when you began your study. Note how the result of this phrase is manifested in the way the people live.

Record the chapter themes as you have done previously on JUDGES AT A GLANCE. Also record the main theme of each segment division and any other segment division you may see. Finally record the main theme of Judges.

IGS TO THINK ABOUT

What have you learned from Judges about carefully listening to and obeying the commands of the Lord? What have you seen about the consequences of doing what is right in your own eyes? What parallels do you see between the sins committed in Judges 17 through 21 and today? What does it tell you?

Why wasn't the cycle of sin broken in the days of the judges? Are you caught in a cycle of sin in your own life? What will it take to break it?

What have you learned by studying the lives of the judges? Carefully review your chart on the judges (page 398) and meditate on the lessons you can apply to your own life.

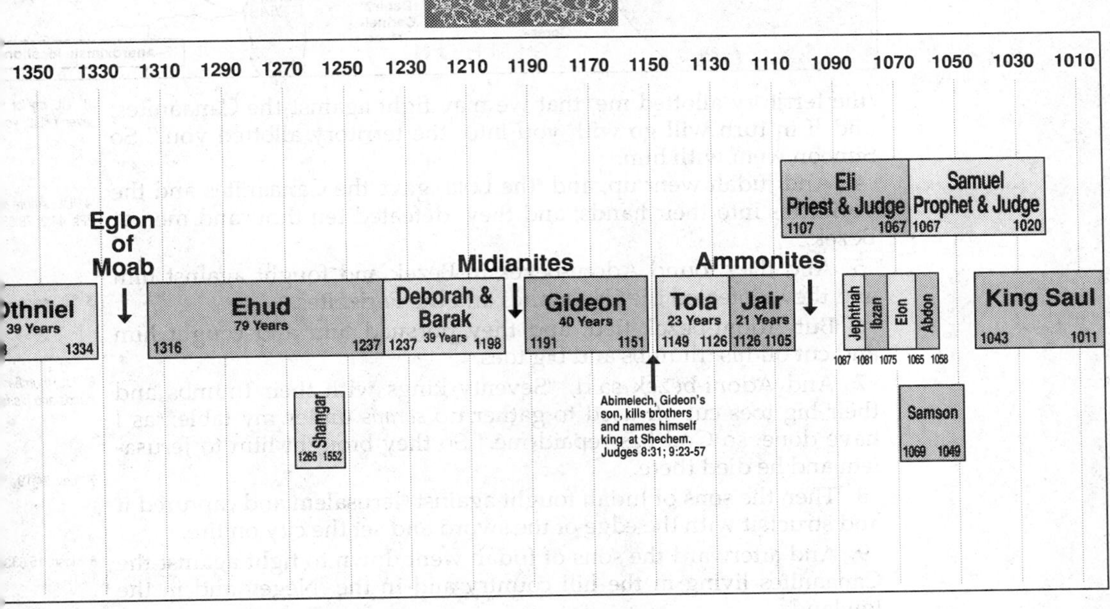

1:1 [a]Num. 27:21 [b]Jdg. 1:27; 2:21-23; 3:1-6

Chapter 1

1 Now it came about after the death of Joshua that the sons of
Israel [a]inquired of the LORD, saying, "Who shall go up first for us
[b]against the Canaanites, to fight against them?"
2 And the LORD said, "[a]Judah shall go up; behold, I have given the
land into his hand."
3 Then Judah said to Simeon his brother, "Come up with me into

2 [a]Gen. 49:8

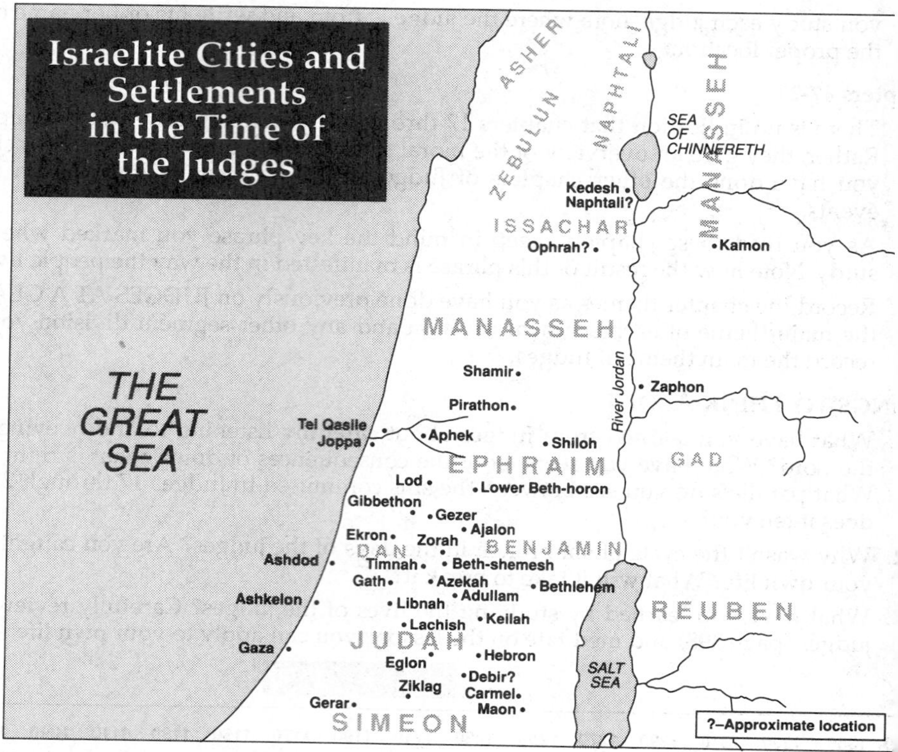

[1]the territory allotted me, that we may fight against the Canaanites;
and [2]I in turn will go with you into [3]the territory allotted you." So
Simeon went with him.
4 And Judah went up, and [a]the LORD gave the Canaanites and the
Perizzites into their hands; and they [1]defeated ten thousand men at
Bezek.
5 And they found Adoni-bezek in Bezek and fought against him
and they [1]defeated the Canaanites and the Perizzites.
6 But Adoni-bezek fled; and they pursued him and caught him
and cut off his [1]thumbs and big toes.
7 And Adoni-bezek said, "Seventy kings with their thumbs and
their big toes cut off used to gather up *scraps* under my table; [a]as I
have done, so God has repaid me." So they brought him to Jerusa-
lem and he died there.
8 Then the sons of Judah fought against [a]Jerusalem and captured it
and struck it with the edge of the sword and set the city on fire.
9 And afterward the sons of Judah went down to fight against the
Canaanites living in the hill country and in the [1]Negev and in the
lowland.
10 [a]So Judah went against the Canaanites who lived in Hebron
(now the name of Hebron formerly *was* Kiriath-arba); and they
struck Sheshai and Ahiman and Talmai.
11 Then [a]from there he went against the inhabitants of Debir (now
the name of Debir formerly *was* Kiriath-sepher).
12 And Caleb said, "The one who attacks Kiriath-sepher and cap-
tures it, I will even give him my daughter Achsah for a wife."

3 [1]Lit., *my lot* [2]Li *even I* [3]Lit., *your*
4 [1]Lit., *smote the* [a]Ps. 44:2; 78:55
5 [1]Lit., *smote*
6 [1]Lit., *thumbs of hands and his fee*
7 [a]Lev. 24:19
8 [a]Josh. 15:63; J 1:21
9 [1]I.e., South cou
10 [a]Josh. 15:13-
11 [a]Josh. 15:15

13 And [a]Othniel the son of Kenaz, Caleb's younger brother, cap-
tured it; so he gave him his daughter Achsah for a wife.
14 Then [a]it came about when she came *to him,* that she persuaded
him to ask her father for a field. Then she alighted from [1]her donkey,
and Caleb said to her, "What [2]do you want?"
15 And she said to him, "Give me a blessing, since you have given
me the land of the [1]Negev, give me also springs of water." So Caleb
gave her the upper springs and the lower springs.
16 And the [1]descendants of [a]the Kenite, Moses' father-in-law, went
up from the [b]city of palms with the sons of Judah, to the wilderness
of Judah which is in the south of [c]Arad; and they went and lived
with the people.
17 Then Judah went with Simeon his brother, and they struck the
Canaanites living in Zephath, and utterly destroyed it. So the name
of the city was called [a]Hormah.
18 And Judah took [a]Gaza with its territory and Ashkelon with its
territory and Ekron with its territory.
19 Now the LORD was with Judah, and they took possession of the
hill country; but they could not [1]drive out the inhabitants of the
valley because they had [a]iron chariots.
20 Then they gave Hebron to Caleb, [a]as Moses had [1]promised; and
he drove out from there [b]the three sons of Anak.
21 [a]But the sons of Benjamin did not drive out the [b]Jebusites who
lived in Jerusalem; so the Jebusites have lived with the sons of Ben-
jamin in Jerusalem to this day.
22 Likewise the house of Joseph went up against Bethel, and the
LORD was with them.
23 And the house of Joseph spied out Bethel ([a]now the name of the
city was formerly Luz).
24 And the spies saw a man coming out of the city, and they said to
him, "Please show us the entrance to the city and [a]we will treat you
kindly."
25 So he showed them the entrance to the city, and they struck the
city with the edge of the sword, [a]but they let the man and all his
family go free.
26 And the man went into the land of the Hittites and built a city
and named it Luz [1]which is its name to this day.
27 [a]But Manasseh did not take possession of Beth-shean and its
villages, or Taanach and its villages, or the inhabitants of Dor and its
villages, or the inhabitants of Ibleam and its villages, or the in-
habitants of Megiddo and its villages; so [b]the Canaanites persisted in
living in that land.
28 And it came about when Israel became strong, that they put the
Canaanites to forced labor, but they did not drive them out com-
pletely.
29 [a]Neither did Ephraim drive out the Canaanites who were living
in Gezer; so the Canaanites lived in Gezer among them.
30 Zebulun did not drive out the inhabitants of Kitron, or the in-
habitants of Nahalol; so the Canaanites lived among them and be-
came subject to forced labor.
31 Asher did not drive out the inhabitants of Acco, or the in-
habitants of Sidon, or of Ahlab, or of Achzib, or of Helbah, or of
Aphik, or of Rehob.

13 [a]Judg. 3:9
, *the* [2]Lit., *for*
[a]Josh. 15:18
South country
., *sons* [a]Num.
32; Judg. 4:11
:3; Judg. 3:13
[c]Num. 21:1
17 [a]Num. 21:3
8 [a]Josh. 11:22
Or, *dispossess*
h. 17:16; Judg.
4:3, 13
spoken [a]Josh.
9 [b]Josh. 15:14;
Judg. 1:10
sh. 15:63; Judg.
1:8 [b]1 Chr. 11:4
23 [a]Gen. 28:19
24 [a]Josh. 2:12
25 [a]Josh. 6:25
26 [1]Lit., *it*
sh. 17:12 [b]Judg.
1:1
29 [a]Josh. 16:10

32 So the Asherites lived among the Canaanites, the inhabitants of
the land; for they did not drive them out.
33 Naphtali did not drive out the inhabitants of Beth-shemesh, or
the inhabitants of Beth-anath, but lived among the Canaanites, the
inhabitants of the land; and the inhabitants of Beth-shemesh and
Beth-anath became forced labor for them.
34 Then the Amorites [1]forced the sons of Dan into the hill country,
for they did not allow them to come down to the valley;
35 yet the Amorites persisted in [1]living in Mount Heres, in Aijalon
and in Shaalbim; but when the [2]power of the house of Joseph [3]grew
strong, they became forced labor.
36 And the border of the Amorites ran from the [a]ascent of Akrab-
bim, from Sela and upward.

Chapter 2

2 Now [a]the angel of the LORD came up from Gilgal to [b]Bochim.
And he said, "[c]I brought you up out of Egypt and led you into
the land which I have sworn to your fathers; and I said, '[d]I will never
break My covenant with you,
2 and as for you, [a]you shall make no covenant with the inhabitants
of this land; [b]you shall tear down their altars.' But you have not
[1]obeyed Me; what is this you have done?
3 "Therefore I also said, '[a]I will not drive them out before you; but
they shall [1]become [b]*as thorns* in your sides, and their gods shall be a
snare to you.' "
4 And it came about when the angel of the LORD spoke these
words to all the sons of Israel, that the people lifted up their voices
and wept.
5 So they named that place [1]Bochim; and there they sacrificed to
the LORD.
6 [a]When Joshua had dismissed the people, the sons of Israel went
each to his inheritance to possess the land.
7 And the people served the LORD all the days of Joshua, and all
the days of the elders who [1]survived Joshua, who had seen all the
great work of the LORD which He had done for Israel.
8 Then Joshua the son of Nun, the servant of the LORD, died at the
age of one hundred and ten.
9 And they buried him in the territory of [a]his inheritance in
Timnath-heres, in the hill country of Ephraim, north of Mount
Gaash.
10 And all that generation also were gathered to their fathers; and
there arose another generation after them who [a]did not know the
LORD, nor yet the work which He had done for Israel.
11 Then the sons of Israel did [a]evil in the sight of the LORD, and
[1]served the [b]Baals,
12 and [a]they forsook the LORD, the God of their fathers, who had
brought them out of the land of Egypt, and followed other gods
from *among* the gods of the peoples who were around them, and
bowed themselves down to them; thus they provoked the LORD to
anger.
13 So they forsook the LORD and [a]served Baal and the Ashtaroth.
14 [a]And the anger of the LORD burned against Israel, and He gave
them into the hands of plunderers who plundered them; and [b]He

INSIGHT

Baal, which meant "lord, owner, possessor, or husband," was the Canaanite god of fertility. **Baal** was part of several compound names for locations where Canaanite deities were worshiped, such as Baal-peor.

Ashtaroth, the plural form of Ashtoreth, is the Canaanite goddess of fertility, love, and war. According to Greek mythology she is the wife of Baal.

34 [1]Lit., *press*
35 [1]Lit., *dwell* ... *hand* [3]Lit., *wa*
36 [a]Josh. 15:3
2:1 [a]Judg. 6:1 ... 13:2-21 [b]Judg ... 20:2 [c]Gen. 17 ... 26:42, 44; Deu
2 [1]Lit., *listened* ... *voice* [a]Ex. 23:3 ... 7:2-5 [b]Ex. 34:1
3 [1]Some ancie ... read *be advers.* ... *and* [a]Josh. 23:1 ... [b]Num. 33:55
5 [1]I.e., *weepers*
6 [a]Josh. 24:28-
7 [1]Lit., *prolonge* ... *after*
9 [a]Josh. 19:49f.
10 [a]Ex. 5:2; 1 Sa
11 [1]Or, *worshipe* ... [a]Judg. 3:7, 12; 4: ... [b]Judg. 6:25; 8:33
12 [a]Deut. 31:16
13 [a]Judg. 10:6
14 [a]Deut. 31:17; ... 106:40-42 [b]Deut ... 32:30

sold them into the hands of their enemies around *them*, so that they
could no longer stand before their enemies.
15 Wherever they went, the hand of the LORD was against them for
evil, as the LORD had spoken and [a]as the LORD had sworn to them, so
that they were severely distressed.
16 [a]Then the LORD raised up judges [1]who delivered them from the
hands of those who plundered them.
17 And yet they did not listen to their judges, for they played the
harlot after other gods and bowed themselves down to them. They
turned aside quickly from the way [a]in which their fathers had
walked in obeying the commandments of the LORD; they did not do
as *their fathers*.
18 And when the LORD raised up judges for them, [a]the LORD was
with the judge and delivered them from the hand of their enemies all
the days of the judge; for the LORD was [b]moved to pity by their
groaning because of those who oppressed and afflicted them.
19 But it came about when the judge died, that they would turn
back and act more corruptly than their fathers, in following other
gods to serve them and bow down to them; they did not abandon
their practices or their stubborn ways.
20 [a]So the anger of the LORD burned against Israel, and He said,
"Because this nation has transgressed My covenant which I com-
manded their fathers, and has not listened to My voice,
21 [a]I also will no longer drive out before them any of the nations
which Joshua left when he died,
22 in order to [a]test Israel by them, whether they will keep the way
of the LORD to walk in it as their fathers [1]did, or not."
23 So the LORD allowed those nations to remain, not driving them
out quickly; and He did not give them into the hand of Joshua.

Chapter 3

3 [a]Now these are the nations which the LORD left, to test Israel by
them (*that is,* all who had not [1]experienced any of the wars of
Canaan;
2 only in order that the generations of the sons of Israel might [1]be
taught war, [2]those who had not [3]experienced it formerly).
3 *These nations are:* the five lords of the Philistines and all the
Canaanites and the Sidonians and [a]the Hivites who lived in Mount
Lebanon, from Mount Baal-hermon as far as [1]Lebo-hamath.
4 And they were for [1a]testing Israel, to find out if they would [2]obey
the commandments of the LORD, which He had commanded their
fathers [3]through Moses.
5 And [a]the sons of Israel lived among the Canaanites, the Hittites,
the Amorites, the Perizzites, the Hivites, and the Jebusites;
6 and [a]they took their daughters for themselves as wives, and gave
their own daughters to their sons, and served their gods.
7 And the sons of Israel did [a]what was evil in the sight of the LORD,
and [b]forgot the LORD their God, and [c]served the Baals and the
[1]Asheroth.
8 Then the anger of the LORD was kindled against Israel, so that He
sold them into the hands of Cushan-rishathaim king of
[1]Mesopotamia; and the sons of Israel served Cushan-rishathaim
eight years.
9 And when the sons of Israel cried to the LORD, the LORD raised

up a deliverer for the sons of Israel to deliver them, [a]Othniel the son of Kenaz, Caleb's younger brother.

10 And [a]the Spirit of the LORD came upon him, and he judged Israel. When he went out to war, the LORD gave Cushan-rishathaim king of [1]Mesopotamia into his hand, so that [2]he prevailed over Cushan-rishathaim.

11 Then the land had rest forty years. And Othniel the son of Kenaz died.

12 Now the sons of Israel again [a]did evil in the sight of the LORD. So [b]the LORD strengthened Eglon the king of Moab against Israel, because they had done evil in the sight of the LORD.

13 And he gathered to himself the sons of Ammon and Amalek; and he went and [1]defeated Israel, and they possessed [a]the city of the palm trees.

14 And the sons of Israel served Eglon the king of Moab eighteen years.

15 But when the sons of Israel [a]cried to the LORD, the LORD raised up a deliverer for them, Ehud the son of Gera, the Benjamite, a left-handed man. And the sons of Israel sent tribute by [1]him to Eglon the king of Moab.

16 And Ehud made himself a sword which had two edges, a cubit in length; and he bound it on his right thigh under his cloak.

17 And he presented the tribute to Eglon king of Moab. Now Eglon was a very fat man.

18 And it came about when he had finished presenting the tribute, that he sent away the people who had carried the tribute.

19 But he himself turned back from the idols which were at Gilgal, and said, "I have a secret message for you, O king." And he said, "Keep silence." And all who attended him left him.

20 And Ehud came to him while he was sitting alone in his cool roof chamber. And Ehud said, "I have a message from God for you." And he arose from his seat.

21 And Ehud stretched out his left hand, took the sword from his right thigh and thrust it into his belly.

22 The handle also went in after the blade, and the fat closed over the blade, for he did not draw the sword out of his belly; and the refuse came out.

23 Then Ehud went out into the vestibule and shut the doors of the roof chamber behind him, and locked *them*.

24 When he had gone out, his servants came and looked, and behold, the doors of the roof chamber were locked; and they said, "[a]He is only [1]relieving himself in the cool room."

25 And they waited until they [1]became anxious; but behold, he did not open the doors of the roof chamber. Therefore they took the key and opened them, and behold, their master had fallen to the [2]floor dead.

26 Now Ehud escaped while they were delaying, and he passed by the idols and escaped to Seirah.

27 And it came about when he had arrived, that [a]he blew the trumpet in the hill country of Ephraim; and the sons of Israel went down with him from the hill country, and he *was* in front of them.

28 And he said to them, "Pursue *them*, for the LORD has given your enemies the Moabites into your hands." So they went down after

9 [a]Judg. 1:13

10 [1]Heb., *Ara... his hand was s...* [a]Num. 11:25-2...

12 [a]Judg. 2:11 2:14

13 [1]Lit., *smote* 34:3; Judg. 1:1...

15 [1]Lit., *his har...* 78:34

24 [1]Lit., *coverin... feet* [a]1 Sam. 24...

25 [1]Lit., *were as* [2]Lit., *earth*

27 [a]Judg. 6:34; ... 13:3

him and seized [a]the fords of the Jordan opposite Moab, and did not
allow anyone to cross.
29 And they struck down at that time about ten thousand Moabites,
all robust and valiant men; and no one escaped.
30 So Moab was subdued that day under the hand of Israel. And
the land was undisturbed for eighty years.
31 And after him came [a]Shamgar the son of Anath, who struck
down six hundred Philistines with an oxgoad; and he also saved
Israel.

Chapter 4

4 Then [a]the sons of Israel again did evil in the sight of the LORD,
after Ehud died.
2 And the LORD sold them into the hand of [a]Jabin king of Canaan,
who reigned in Hazor; and the commander of his army was Sisera,
who lived in [b]Harosheth-hagoyim.
3 And the sons of Israel cried to the LORD; for he had nine hundred
[a]iron chariots, and he oppressed the sons of Israel severely for twen-
ty years.
4 Now Deborah, a [1]prophetess, the wife of Lappidoth, was judg-
ing Israel at that time.
5 And she used to [1]sit under the [a]palm tree of Deborah between
Ramah and Bethel in the hill country of Ephraim; and the sons of
Israel came up to her for judgment.
6 Now she sent and summoned [a]Barak the son of Abinoam from
Kedesh-naphtali, and said to him, "[1]Behold, the LORD, the God of
Israel, has commanded, 'Go and march to Mount Tabor, and take
with you ten thousand men from the sons of Naphtali and from the
sons of Zebulun.
7 'And I will draw out to you Sisera, the commander of Jabin's
army, with his chariots and his [1]many *troops* to the river Kishon; and
[a]I will give him into your hand.' "
8 Then Barak said to her, "If you will go with me, then I will go;
but if you will not go with me, I will not go."
9 And she said, "I will surely go with you; nevertheless, the honor
shall not be yours on the journey that you are about to take, [a]for the
LORD will sell Sisera into the hands of a woman." Then Deborah
arose and went with Barak to Kedesh.
10 And Barak called [a]Zebulun and Naphtali together to Kedesh,
and ten thousand men went up [1b]with him; Deborah also went up
with him.
11 Now Heber [a]the Kenite had separated himself from the Kenites,
from the sons of Hobab the father-in-law of Moses, and had pitched
his tent as far away as the [1]oak in [b]Zaanannim, which is near
Kedesh.
12 Then they told Sisera that Barak the son of Abinoam had gone
up to Mount Tabor.
13 And Sisera called together all his chariots, [a]nine hundred iron
chariots, and all the people who *were* with him, from [b]Harosheth-
hagoyim to the river Kishon.
14 And Deborah said to Barak, "Arise! For this is the day in which
the LORD has given Sisera into your hands; [1]behold, [a]the LORD has
gone out before you." So Barak went down from Mount Tabor with
ten thousand men following him.

[a]Judg. 7:24; 12:5
31 [a]Judg. 5:6
4:1 [a]Judg. 2:19
2 [a]Josh. 11:1, 10 [b]Judg. 4:13, 16
3 [a]Judg. 1:19
4 [1]Lit., *woman prophetess*
...r, *live* [a]Gen. 35:8
...6 [1]Or, *Has not . . . commanded . . . ?* [a]Heb. 11:32
...it., *multitude* [a]Ps. 83:9
9 [a]Judg. 4:21
...0 [1]Lit., *at his feet* ...Judg. 5:18 [b]Judg. 4:14; 5:15
..., *terebinth* [a]Judg. ...1:16 [b]Josh. 19:33
...[a]Judg. 4:3 [b]Judg. 4:2
...4 [1]Or, *has not the ...gone . . . ?* [a]Deut. 2 Sam. 5:24; Ps. 68:7

15 [a]And the LORD [1]routed Sisera and all *his* chariots and all *his* army,
with the edge of the sword before Barak; and Sisera alighted from *his*
chariot and fled away on foot.
16 But Barak pursued the chariots and the army as far as
Harosheth-hagoyim, and all the army of Sisera fell by the edge of the
sword; [a]not even one was left.
17 Now Sisera fled away on foot to the tent of Jael the wife of Heber
the Kenite, for *there was* peace between Jabin the king of Hazor and
the house of Heber the Kenite.
18 And Jael went out to meet Sisera, and said to him, "Turn aside,
my master, turn aside to me! Do not be afraid." And he turned aside
to her into the tent, and she covered him with a [1]rug.
19 [a]And he said to her, "Please give me a little water to drink, for I
am thirsty." So she opened a [1]bottle of milk and gave him a drink;
then she covered him.
20 And he said to her, "Stand in the doorway of the tent, and it
shall be if anyone comes and inquires of you, and says, 'Is there
anyone here?' that you shall say, 'No.' "
21 But Jael, Heber's wife, [a]took a tent peg and [1]seized a hammer in
her hand, and went secretly to him and drove the peg into his
temple, and it went through into the ground; for he was sound
asleep and exhausted. So he died.
22 And behold, as Barak pursued Sisera, Jael came out to meet him
and said to him, "Come, and I will show you the man whom you are
seeking." And he entered [1]with her, and behold Sisera was lying
dead with the tent peg in his temple.
23 So [a]God subdued on that day Jabin the king of Canaan before the
sons of Israel.
24 And the hand of the sons of Israel pressed heavier and heavier
upon Jabin the king of Canaan, until they had [1]destroyed Jabin the
king of Canaan.

Chapter 5

5 [a]Then Deborah and Barak the son of Abinoam sang on that day,
saying,

2 "[a]That [1]the leaders led in Israel,
That [b]the people volunteered,
Bless the LORD!
3 "Hear, O kings; give ear, O rulers!
[a]I—to the LORD, I will sing,
I will sing praise to the LORD, the God of Israel.
4 "[a]LORD, when Thou didst go out from Seir,
When Thou didst march from the field of Edom,
[b]The earth quaked, the heavens also dripped,
Even the clouds dripped water.
5 "[a]The mountains [1]quaked at the presence of the LORD,
[b]This Sinai, at the presence of the LORD, the God of Israel.

6 "In the days of [a]Shamgar the son of Anath,
In the days of [b]Jael, the highways [1]were deserted,
And travelers [2]went by [3]roundabout ways.
7 "The peasantry ceased, they ceased in Israel,
Until I, Deborah, arose,
Until I arose, a mother in Israel.

15 [1]Lit., *confused* [a]Deut. 7:23; Josh. 1

16 [a]Ex. 14:28; Ps.

18 [1]Or, *blanket*

19 [1]I.e., skin conta [a]Judg. 5:24-27

21 [1]Lit., *placed* [a]J 5:26

22 [1]Lit., *to*

23 [a]Neh. 9:24; Ps

24 [1]Lit., *cut off*

5:1 [a]Ex. 15:1

2 [1]Or, *locks hung in* [a]Judg. 5:9 [b]Ps

3 [a]Ps. 27:6

4 [a]Deut. 33:2; Ps [b]Ps. 68:8, 9

5 [1]Lit., *flowed* [a]E 19:18 [b]Ps. 68:8

6 [1]Lit., *had cease* [2]Lit., *walked* [3]Lit. *twisted* [a]Judg. 3: [b]Judg. 4:17

8 "[a]New gods were chosen;
Then war *was* in the gates.
Not a shield or a spear was seen
Among forty thousand in Israel.
9 "My heart *goes out* to [a]the commanders of Israel,
The volunteers among the people;
Bless the LORD!
10 "[a]You who ride on [1]white donkeys,
You who sit on *rich* carpets,
And you who travel on the road—[2]sing!
11 "At the sound of those who divide *flocks* among [a]the watering places,
There they shall recount [b]the righteous deeds of the LORD,
The righteous deeds for His [1]peasantry in Israel.
Then the people of the LORD went down [c]to the gates.

12 "[a]Awake, awake, Deborah;
Awake, awake, [1]sing a song!
Arise, Barak, and [b]take away your captives, O son of Abinoam.
13 "Then survivors came down to the nobles;
The people of the LORD came down to me as warriors.
14 "From Ephraim those whose root is [a]in Amalek *came down*,
Following you, Benjamin, with your peoples;
From Machir commanders came down,
And from Zebulun those who wield the staff of [1]office.
15 "And the [1]princes of Issachar *were* with Deborah;
As *was* Issachar, so *was* Barak;
Into the valley they rushed [a]at his [2]heels;
Among the divisions of Reuben
There were great resolves of heart.
16 "Why did you sit among [a]the [1]sheepfolds,
To hear the piping for the flocks?
Among the divisions of Reuben
There were great searchings of heart.
17 "[a]Gilead [1]remained across the Jordan;
And why did Dan stay in ships?
Asher sat at the seashore,
And [1]remained by its landings.
18 "[a]Zebulun *was* a people who despised their lives *even* to death,
And Naphtali also, on the high places of the field.

19 "[a]The kings came *and* fought;
Then fought the kings of Canaan
[b]At Taanach near the waters of Megiddo;
[c]They took no plunder in silver.
20 "[a]The stars fought from heaven,
From their courses they fought against Sisera.
21 "The torrent of Kishon swept them away,
The ancient torrent, the torrent Kishon.
[a]O my soul, march on with strength.
22 "[a]Then the horses' hoofs beat
From the dashing, the dashing of his [1]valiant steeds.
23 'Curse Meroz,' said the angel of the LORD,
'Utterly curse its inhabitants;

8 [a]Deut. 32:17
9 [a]Judg. 5:2
10 [1]Or, *tawny* [2]Or, *...are it* [a]Judg. 10:4; 12:14
[1]Or, *rural dwellers* ...Gen. 24:11; 29:2, 3 ...Sam. 12:7; Mic. 6:5 [c]Judg. 5:8
Or, *utter* [a]Ps. 57:8 ...Ps. 68:18; Eph. 4:8
14 [1]Lit., *the scribe* [a]Judg. 12:15
15 [1]So with ancient versions; Heb., *My princes* [2]Lit., *feet* [a]Judg. 4:10
16 [1]Or, *saddlebags* ...Num. 32:1, 2, 24, 36
[1]Or, *dwelt* [a]Josh. 22:9
18 [a]Judg. 4:6, 10
...Josh. 11:1-5; Judg. 4:13 [b]Judg. 1:27 [c]Judg. 5:30
20 [a]Josh. 10:12-14
...Ex. 15:2; Ps. 44:5
[1]Lit., *mighty ones* [a]Job 39:19-25

[a]Because they did not come to the help of the LORD,
To the help of the LORD against the warriors.'

24 "[a]Most blessed of women is Jael,
The wife of Heber the Kenite;
Most blessed is she of women in the tent.
25 "He asked for water *and* she gave him milk;
In a magnificent bowl she brought him curds.
26 "She reached out her hand for the tent peg,
And her right hand for the workmen's hammer.
Then she struck Sisera, she smashed his head;
And she shattered and pierced his temple.
27 "Between her feet he bowed, he fell, he lay;
Between her feet he bowed, he fell;
Where he bowed, there he fell [1]dead.

28 "Out of the window she looked and lamented,
The mother of Sisera through the [1]lattice,
'Why does his chariot delay in coming?
Why do the [2]hoofbeats of his chariots tarry?'
29 "Her wise princesses would answer her,
Indeed she repeats her words to herself,
30 '[a]Are they not finding, are they not dividing the spoil?
A maiden, two maidens for every warrior;
To Sisera a spoil of dyed work,
A spoil of dyed work embroidered,
Dyed work of double embroidery on the [1]neck of the spoiler?'
31 "[a]Thus let all Thine enemies perish, O LORD;
[b]But let those who love Him be like the rising of the sun in its might."
And the land was undisturbed for forty years.

Chapter 6

6 Then the sons of Israel [a]did what was evil in the sight of the
LORD; and the LORD gave them into the hands of [b]Midian seven
years.
2 And the [1]power of Midian prevailed against Israel. Because of
Midian the sons of Israel made for themselves [a]the dens which were
in the mountains and the caves and the strongholds.
3 For it was when Israel had sown, that the Midianites would
come up with the Amalekites and the sons of the east and [1]go
against them.
4 So they would camp against them and [a]destroy the produce of
the earth [1]as far as Gaza, and [b]leave no sustenance in Israel as well as
no sheep, ox, or donkey.
5 For they would come up with their livestock and their tents, they
would come in [a]like locusts for number, both they and their camels
were innumerable; and they came into the land to devastate it.
6 So Israel was brought [a]very low because of Midian, and the sons
of Israel cried to the LORD.
7 Now it came about when the sons of Israel cried to the LORD on
account of Midian,
8 that the LORD sent a prophet to the sons of Israel, and [a]he said to

23 [a]Judg. 5:1
24 [a]Judg. 4:1
27 [1]Lit., *devas*
28 [1]Or, *windo steps*
30 [1]Lit., *necks spoil* [a]Ex. 15:9
31 [a]Ps. 68:2; 9 19:4-6; 89:36, 3
6:1 [a]Judg. 2:11 22:4; 25:15-18;
2 [1]Lit., *hand* [a]1 13:6; Heb. 11:38
3 [1]Lit., *go up*
4 [1]Lit., *until you coming to* [a]Lev. [b]Deut. 28:31
5 [a]Judg. 7:12; 8
6 [a]Deut. 28:43
8 [a]Judg. 2:1, 2

them, "Thus says the LORD, the God of Israel, 'It was I who brought
you up from Egypt, and brought you out from the house of [1]slavery.
9 'And I delivered you from the hands of the Egyptians and from
the hands of all your oppressors, and dispossessed them before you
and gave you their land,
10 and I said to you, "I am the LORD your God; you [a]shall not fear
the gods of the Amorites in whose land you live. But you have not
[1]obeyed Me."'"
11 Then [a]the angel of the LORD came and sat under the [1]oak that
was in Ophrah, which belonged to Joash the [b]Abiezrite as his son
[c]Gideon was beating out wheat in the wine press in order to save *it*
from the Midianites.
12 And the angel of the LORD appeared to him and said to him,
"The LORD is with you, O valiant warrior."
13 Then Gideon said to him, "O my lord, if the LORD is with us,
why then has all this happened to us? And where are all His
miracles which our fathers told us about, saying, 'Did not the LORD
bring us up from Egypt?' But [a]now the LORD has abandoned us and
given us into the hand of Midian."
14 And the LORD [1]looked at him and said, "[a]Go in this your strength
and deliver Israel from the hand of Midian. Have I not sent you?"
15 [a]And he said to Him, "O Lord, [1]how shall I deliver Israel? Be-
hold, my family is the least in [b]Manasseh, and I am the youngest in
my father's house."
16 [a]But the LORD said to him, "Surely I will be with you, and you
shall [1]defeat Midian as one man."
17 So [1]Gideon said to Him, "If now I have found favor in Thy sight,
then show me [a]a sign that it is Thou who speakest with me.
18 "Please do not depart from here, until I come *back* to Thee, and
bring out my offering and lay it before Thee." And He said, "I will
remain until you return."
19 Then Gideon went in and [a]prepared a kid and unleavened bread
from an [1]ephah of flour; he put the meat in a basket [2]and the broth in
a pot, and brought *them* out to him under the [3]oak, and presented
them.
20 And the angel of God said to him, "Take the meat and the un-
leavened bread and lay them on this rock, and pour out the broth."
And he did so.
21 Then the angel of the LORD put out the end of the staff that was
in his hand and touched the meat and the unleavened bread; and
[a]fire sprang up from the rock and consumed the meat and the un-
leavened bread. Then the angel of the LORD [1]vanished from his sight.
22 [a]When Gideon saw that he was the angel of the LORD, [1]he said,
"Alas, O Lord [2]GOD! For now I have seen the angel of the LORD face
to face."
23 And the LORD said to him, "Peace to you, do not fear; you shall
not die."
24 Then Gideon built an altar there to the LORD and named it [1]The
LORD is Peace. To this day it is still [a]in Ophrah of the Abiezrites.
25 Now the same night it came about that the LORD said to him,
"Take your father's bull [1]and a second bull seven years old, and pull
down the altar of Baal which belongs to your father, and cut down
the [2a]Asherah that is beside it;
26 and build an altar to the LORD your God on the top of this

[1]Lit., *slaves*

...istened to My ...n. 17:35; Jer. 10:2

...ebinth [a]Judg. ...; 13:3 [b]Josh. ...g. 6:15 [c]Heb. 11:32

... 6:1; Ps. 44:9

...turned toward ...Heb. 11:32-34

...with what [a]Ex. ...11 [b]Judg. 6:11

...Lit., *smite* [a]Ex. 3:12; Josh. 1:5

[1]Lit., *he* [a]Judg. 6:37; Is. 38:7, 8

...e., Approx. one [2]Lit., *and he put* ...terebinth [a]Gen. 18:6-8

...departed [a]Lev. 9:24

..., Gideon [2]Heb., *YHWH*, usually ...red LORD [a]Gen. ...Ex. 33:20; Judg. 13:21, 22

... [1]Heb., *Yahweh-* ...alom [a]Judg. 8:32

...5 [1]Or, *even* [2]I.e., ...oden symbol of a deity, also vv. 26, 28, 30 [a]Ex. 34:13

stronghold in an orderly manner, and take a second bull and offer a burnt offering with the wood of the Asherah which you shall cut down."

27 Then Gideon took ten men of his servants and did as the LORD had spoken to him; and it came about, because he was too afraid of his father's household and the men of the city to do it by day, that he did it by night.

28 When the men of the city arose early in the morning, behold, the altar of Baal was torn down, and the Asherah which was beside it was cut down, and the second bull was offered on the altar which had been built.

29 And they said to one another, "Who did this thing?" And when they searched about and inquired, they said, "Gideon the son of Joash did this thing."

30 Then the men of the city said to Joash, "Bring out your son, that he may die, for he has torn down the altar of Baal, and indeed, he has cut down the Asherah which was beside it."

31 But Joash said to all who stood against him, "Will you contend for Baal, or will you deliver him? Whoever will [1]plead for him shall be put to death by morning. If he is a god, let him contend for himself, because someone has torn down his altar."

32 Therefore on that day he named him [a]Jerubbaal, that is to say, "Let Baal contend against him," because he had torn down his altar.

33 Then all the Midianites and the Amalekites and the sons of the east assembled themselves; and they crossed over and camped in [a]the valley of Jezreel.

34 So [a]the Spirit of the LORD [1]came upon Gideon; and he [b]blew a trumpet, and the Abiezrites were called together to follow him.

35 And he sent messengers throughout Manasseh, and they also were called together to follow him; and he sent messengers to Asher, [a]Zebulun, and Naphtali, and [b]they came up to meet them.

36 Then Gideon said to God, "[a]If Thou wilt deliver Israel [1]through me, as Thou hast spoken,

37 behold, I will put a fleece of wool on the threshing floor. If there is dew on the fleece only, and it is dry on all the ground, then I will know that Thou wilt deliver Israel [1]through me, as Thou hast spoken."

38 And it was so. When he arose early the next morning and squeezed the fleece, he drained the dew from the fleece, a bowl full of water.

39 Then Gideon said to God, "[a]Do not let Thine anger burn against me that I may speak once more; please let me make a test once more with the fleece, let it now be dry only on the fleece, and let there be dew on all the ground."

40 And God did so that night; for it was dry only on the fleece, and dew was on all the ground.

Chapter 7

7 Then [a]Jerubbaal (that is, Gideon) and all the people who were with him, rose early and camped beside [1]the spring of Harod; and the camp of Midian was on the north side of [2]them by the hill of [b]Moreh in the valley.

2 And the LORD said to Gideon, "The people who are with you are

31 [1]Or, *contend*

32 [a]Judg. 7:1

33 [a]Josh. 17:16

34 [1]Lit., *clothed* [a]Judg. 3:10 [b]Judg. 3:27

35 [a]Judg. 4:6, 10; [b]Judg. 7:3

36 [1]Lit., *by my ha* [a]Judg. 6:14, 16, 1

37 [1]Lit., *by my ha*

39 [a]Gen. 18:32

7:1 [1]Or, *En-Haro* *him* [a]Judg. 6:32 12:6; Deut. 11:30

too many for Me to give Midian into their hands, [a]lest Israel [1]become boastful, saying, 'My own [2]power has delivered me.'

3 "Now therefore [1]come, proclaim in the hearing of the people, saying, '[a]Whoever is afraid and trembling, let him return and depart from Mount Gilead.'" So 22,000 people returned, but 10,000 remained.

4 [a]Then the LORD said to Gideon, "The people are still too many; bring them down to the water and I will test them for you there. Therefore it shall be that he of whom I say to you, 'This one shall go with you,' he shall go with you; but everyone of whom I say to you, 'This one shall not go with you,' he shall not go."

5 So he brought the people down to the water. And the LORD said to Gideon, "You shall separate everyone who laps the water with his tongue, as a dog laps, as well as everyone who kneels to drink."

6 Now the number of those who lapped, putting their hand to their mouth, was 300 men; but all the rest of the people kneeled to drink water.

7 And the LORD said to Gideon, "I will deliver you [a]with the 300 men who lapped and will give the Midianites into your hands; so let all the *other* people go, each man to his [1]home."

8 So [1]the 300 men took the people's provisions and their trumpets into their hands. And [2]Gideon sent all the *other* men of Israel, each to his tent, but retained the 300 men; and the camp of Midian was below him in the valley.

9 Now the same night it came about that the LORD said to him, "Arise, go down against the camp, [a]for I have given it into your hands.

10 "But if you are afraid to go down, go with Purah your servant down to the camp,

11 and you will hear what they say; and [a]afterward your hands will be strengthened that you may go down against the camp." So he went with Purah his servant down to the [1]outposts of the army that was in the camp.

12 Now the Midianites and the Amalekites and all the sons of the east were lying in the valley [a]as numerous as locusts; and their camels were without number, [b]as numerous as the sand on the seashore.

13 When Gideon came, behold, a man was relating a dream to his friend. And he said, "Behold, I [1]had a dream; [2]a loaf of barley bread was tumbling into the camp of Midian, and it came to the tent and struck it so that it fell, and turned it [3]upside down so that the tent lay flat."

14 And his friend answered and said, "This is nothing less than the sword of Gideon the son of Joash, a man of Israel; God has given Midian and all the camp [a]into his hand."

15 And it came about when Gideon heard the account of the dream and its interpretation, that he bowed in worship. He returned to the camp of Israel and said, "Arise, for the LORD has given the camp of Midian into your hands."

16 And he divided the 300 men into three [1]companies, and he put trumpets and empty pitchers into the hands of all of them, with torches inside the pitchers.

17 And he said to them, "Look at me, and do likewise. And behold, when I come to the outskirts of the camp, [1]do as I do.

, glorify itself ...e [2]Lit., *hand* ...eut. 8:17, 18

...*lease* [a]Deut. 20:8

[a]1 Sam. 14:6

...*place* [a]1 Sam. 14:6

, they [2]Lit., *he*

...2:24; 10:8; 11:6

extremity of the ...ay [a]Judg. 7:15; ... Sam. 14:9, 10

[a]Judg. 6:5; 8:10 [b]Josh. 11:4

., dreamed [2]Lit., ...*hold, a loaf* [3]Lit., *upwards*

14 [a]Josh. 2:9

16 [1]Lit., *heads*

[1]Lit., *it shall come* ...*it that just as I do, so you shall do.*

18 "When I and all who are with me blow the trumpet, then you also
blow the trumpets all around the camp, and say, 'For the LORD and
for Gideon.' "
19 So Gideon and the hundred men who were with him came to the
outskirts of the camp at the beginning of the middle watch, when
they had just posted the watch; and they blew the trumpets and
smashed the pitchers that were in their hands.
20 When the three [1]companies blew the trumpets and broke the
pitchers, they held the torches in their left hands and the trumpets in
their right hands for blowing, and cried, "A sword for the LORD and
for Gideon!"
21 And each stood in his place around the camp; and [a]all the [1]army
ran, crying out as they fled.
22 And when they blew 300 trumpets, the [a]LORD set the sword of
one against another even throughout the whole [1]army; and the
[1]army fled as far as Beth-shittah toward Zererah, as far as the edge of
[b]Abel-meholah, by Tabbath.
23 And the men of Israel were summoned from [a]Naphtali and
Asher and all Manasseh, and they pursued Midian.
24 And Gideon sent messengers throughout all the hill country of
Ephraim, saying, "Come down [1]against Midian and [a]take the waters
before them, as far as Beth-barah and the Jordan." So all the men of
Ephraim were summoned, and they took the waters as far as Beth-
barah and the Jordan.
25 And they captured the two leaders of Midian, [a]Oreb and Zeeb,
and they killed Oreb at the rock of Oreb, and they killed Zeeb at the
wine press of Zeeb, while they pursued Midian; and they brought
the heads of Oreb and Zeeb to Gideon [b]from across the Jordan.

Chapter 8

8 Then the men of Ephraim said to him, "[a]What is this thing you
have done to us, not calling us when you went to fight against
Midian?" And they contended with him vigorously.
2 But he said to them, "What have I done now in comparison with
you? Is not the gleaning *of the grapes* of Ephraim better than the
vintage of Abiezer?
3 "God has given the leaders of Midian, Oreb and Zeeb into your
hands; and what was I able to do in comparison with you?" Then
their [1]anger toward him subsided when he said [2]that.
4 Then Gideon and the 300 men who were with him came [a]to the
Jordan *and* crossed over, weary yet pursuing.
5 And he said to the men of [a]Succoth, "Please give loaves of bread
to the people who are following me, for they are weary, and I am
pursuing Zebah and Zalmunna, the kings of Midian."
6 And the leaders of Succoth said, "[1a]Are the hands of Zebah and
Zalmunna already in your hands, that we should give bread to your
army?"
7 And Gideon said, "[1]All right, [a]when the LORD has given Zebah
and Zalmunna into my hand, then I will [2]thrash your [3]bodies with
the thorns of the wilderness and with briers."
8 And he went up from there to [1a]Penuel, and spoke similarly to
them; and the men of Penuel answered him just as the men of Suc-
coth had answered.

20 [1]Lit., *heads*
21 [1]Or, *camp* 7:7
22 [1]Or, *camp* 14:20 [b]1 Kin. 4 19:16
23 [a]Judg. 6:35
24 [1]Lit., *to mee* 3:28
25 [a]Ps. 83:11; I [b]Judg. 8:4
8:1 [a]Judg. 12:1
3 [1]Lit., *spirit* [2]Lit *thing*
4 [a]Judg. 7:25
5 [a]Gen. 33:17
6 [1]Lit., *Is the palr* [a]Judg. 8:15
7 [1]Lit., *For thus* [2] *trample* [3]Lit., *fles* [a]Judg. 7:15
8 [1]In Gen. 32:30, *Peniel* [a]Gen. 32:3

9 So he spoke also to the men of Penuel, saying, "When I return
safely, [a]I will tear down this tower."
10 Now Zebah and Zalmunna were in Karkor, and their [1]armies
with them, about 15,000 men, all who were left of the entire [2]army of
the sons of the east; [a]for the fallen were 120,000 [3]swordsmen.
11 And Gideon went up by the way of those who lived in tents on
the east of Nobah and Jogbehah, and [1]attacked the camp, when the
camp was [2]unsuspecting.
12 When Zebah and Zalmunna fled, he pursued them and captured
the two kings of Midian, Zebah and Zalmunna, and routed the
whole [1]army.
13 Then Gideon the son of Joash returned from the battle [1]by the
ascent of Heres.
14 And he captured a youth [1]from Succoth and questioned him.
Then *the youth* wrote down for him the princes of Succoth and its
elders, seventy-seven men.
15 And he came to the men of Succoth and said, "Behold Zebah and
Zalmunna, concerning whom you taunted me, saying, '[1a]Are the
hands of Zebah and Zalmunna already in your hand, that we should
give bread to your men who are weary?' "
16 And he took the elders of the city, and thorns of the wilderness
and briers, and he [1]disciplined the men of Succoth with them.
17 [a]And he tore down the tower of Penuel and killed the men of the
city.
18 Then he said to Zebah and Zalmunna, "What kind of men *were*
they whom you killed at Tabor?" And they said, "They were like
you, each one [1]resembling the son of a king."
19 And he said, "They *were* my brothers, the sons of my mother. *As*
the LORD lives, if only you had let them live, I would not kill you."
20 So he said to Jether his first-born, "Rise, kill them." But the youth
did not draw his sword, for he was afraid, because he was still a
youth.
21 Then Zebah and Zalmunna said, "Rise up yourself, and fall on
us; for as the man, so is his strength." [a]So Gideon arose and killed
Zebah and Zalmunna, and [b]took the crescent ornaments which were
on their camels' necks.
22 Then the men of Israel said to Gideon, "Rule over us, both you
and your son, also your son's son, for you have delivered us from
the hand of Midian."
23 But Gideon said to them, "I will not rule over you, nor shall my
son rule over you; [a]the LORD shall rule over you."
24 Yet Gideon said to them, "I would [1]request of you, that each of
you give me [2]an earring from his spoil." (For they had gold earrings,
because they were [a]Ishmaelites.)
25 And they said, "We will surely give *them*." So they spread out a
garment, and every one of them threw an earring there from his
spoil.
26 And the weight of the gold earrings that he requested was 1,700
shekels of gold, besides the crescent ornaments and the pendants and
the purple robes which *were* on the kings of Midian, and besides the
neck bands that *were* on their camels' necks.
27 And Gideon made it into [a]an ephod, and placed it in his city,
Ophrah, and all Israel played the harlot with it there, so that it be-
came a snare to Gideon and his household.

[a]Judg. 8:17

r, camps [2]Or, Lit., *men who* rd [a]Judg. 6:5; 7:12; Is. 9:4

t., *smote* [2]Or, *secure*

12 [1]Or, *camp*

13 [1]Or, *from*

., *of the men of*

Lit., *Is the palm* [a]Judg. 8:6

made the men . . . to know

17 [a]Judg. 8:9

., *like the form of the sons*

Ps. 83:11 [b]Judg. 8:26

Sam. 8:7; 10:19; 12:12; Ps. 10:16

24 [1]Lit., *request a* *quest* [2]Or, *a nose* *g* [a]Gen. 25:13-16

Ex. 28:6-35; Judg. 17:5; 18:14-20

28 So Midian was subdued before the sons of Israel, and they did
not lift up their heads anymore. And the land was undisturbed for
forty years in the days of Gideon.
29 Then [a]Jerubbaal the son of Joash went and lived in his own
house.
30 Now Gideon had [a]seventy sons who [1]were his direct descend-
ants, for he had many wives.
31 And his concubine who was in Shechem also bore him a son,
and he [1]named him Abimelech.
32 And Gideon the son of Joash died at a ripe old age and was
buried in the tomb of his father Joash, in Ophrah of the Abiezrites.
33 Then it came about, as soon as Gideon was dead, [a]that the sons
of Israel again played the harlot with the Baals, and made [b]Baal-
berith their god.
34 Thus the sons of Israel [a]did not remember the LORD their God,
who had delivered them from the hands of all their enemies on
every side;
35 [a]nor did they show kindness to the household of Jerubbaal (*that
is,* Gideon), in accord with all the good that he had done to Israel.

Chapter 9

9 And [a]Abimelech the son of Jerubbaal went to Shechem to his
mother's [1]relatives, and spoke to them and to the whole clan of
the household of his mother's father, saying,
2 "Speak, now, in the hearing of all the leaders of Shechem, 'Which
is better for you, that [a]seventy men, all the sons of Jerubbaal, rule
over you, or that one man rule over you?' Also, remember that I am
[b]your bone and your flesh."
3 And his mother's [1]relatives spoke all these words on his behalf
in the hearing of all the leaders of Shechem; and [2]they were inclined
to follow Abimelech, for they said, "He is [a]our [3]relative."
4 And they gave him seventy *pieces* of silver from the house of
[a]Baal-berith with which Abimelech hired worthless and reckless fel-
lows, and they followed him.
5 Then he went to his father's house at Ophrah, and [a]killed his
brothers the sons of Jerubbaal, [b]seventy men, on one stone. But
Jotham the youngest son of Jerubbaal was left, for he hid himself.
6 And all the men of Shechem and all [1]Beth-millo assembled to-
gether, and they went and made Abimelech king, by the [2]oak of the
pillar which was in Shechem.
7 Now when they told Jotham, he went and stood on the top of
[a]Mount Gerizim, and lifted his voice and called out. Thus he said to
them, "Listen to me, O men of Shechem, that God may listen to you.
8 "Once the trees went forth to anoint a king over them, and they
said to the olive tree, 'Reign over us!'
9 "But the olive tree said to them, 'Shall I leave my fatness with
[1]which God and men are honored, and go to wave over the trees?'
10 "Then the trees said to the fig tree, 'You come, reign over us!'
11 "But the fig tree said to them, 'Shall I leave my sweetness and my
good [1]fruit, and go to wave over the trees?'
12 "Then the trees said to the vine, 'You come, reign over us!'
13 "But the vine said to them, 'Shall I leave my new wine, which
cheers God and men, and go to wave over the trees?'

29 [a]Judg. 7:1
30 [1]Lit., *cam* *loins* [a]Judg. 9
31 [1]Lit., *appo* *name*
33 [a]Judg. 2:1 [b]Judg. 9:4, 27,
34 [a]Deut. 4:9;
35 [a]Judg. 9:16
9:1 [1]Lit., *broth* [a]Judg. 8:31, 35
2 [a]Judg. 8:30; [b]Gen. 29:14
3 [1]Lit., *brothers* *their hearts inc* *after* [3]Lit., *broth* [a]Gen. 29:15
4 [a]Judg. 8:33
5 [a]2 Kin. 11:1, 2 8:30; 9:2, 18
6 [1]Or, *the house* *Millo* [2]Or, *terebir*
7 [a]Deut. 11:29, 3
9 [1]Lit., *which by*
11 [1]Or, *produce*

14 "Finally all the trees said to the bramble, 'You come, reign over
us!'
15 "And the bramble said to the trees, 'If in [1]truth you are anointing
me as king over you, come and take refuge in my shade; but if not,
may fire come out from the bramble and consume the cedars of
Lebanon.'
16 "Now therefore, if you have dealt in [1]truth and integrity in
making Abimelech king, and if you have dealt well with [a]Jerubbaal
and his house, and [2]have dealt with him [3]as he deserved—
17 for my father fought for you and [1]risked his life and delivered
you from the hand of Midian;
18 but you have risen against my father's house today and have
killed [a]his sons, seventy men, on one stone, and have made
Abimelech, [b]the son of his maidservant, king over the men of
Shechem, because he is your [1]relative—
19 if then you have dealt in [1]truth and integrity with Jerubbaal and
his house this day, rejoice in Abimelech, and let him also rejoice in
you.
20 "But if not, let fire come out from Abimelech and consume the
men of Shechem and [1]Beth-millo; and let fire come out from the men
of Shechem and from [1]Beth-millo, and consume Abimelech."
21 Then Jotham escaped and fled, and went to Beer and remained
there because of Abimelech his brother.
22 Now Abimelech ruled over Israel three years.
23 [a]Then God sent an evil spirit between Abimelech and the men of
Shechem; and the men of Shechem [b]dealt treacherously with
Abimelech,
24 [a]in order that the violence [1]done to the seventy sons of Jerubbaal
might come, and [b]their blood might be laid on Abimelech their
brother, who killed them, and on the men of Shechem, who
strengthened his hands to kill his brothers.
25 And the men of Shechem set [1]men in ambush against him on the
tops of the mountains, and they robbed all who might pass by them
along the road; and it was told to Abimelech.
26 Now Gaal the son of Ebed came with his [1]relatives, and crossed
over into Shechem; and the men of Shechem put their trust in him.
27 And they went out into the field and gathered *the grapes of* their
vineyards and trod *them,* and held a [1]festival; and they went into the
house of [a]their god, and ate and drank and cursed Abimelech.
28 Then Gaal the son of Ebed said, "Who is Abimelech, and who is
Shechem, that we should serve him? Is he not the son of Jerubbaal,
and *is* Zebul *not* his [1]lieutenant? Serve the men of [a]Hamor the father
of Shechem; but why should we serve him?
29 "[1a]Would, therefore, that this people were under my authority!
Then I would remove Abimelech." And he said to Abimelech, "In-
crease your army, and come out."
30 And when Zebul the ruler of the city heard the words of Gaal
the son of Ebed, his anger burned.
31 And he sent messengers to Abimelech [1]deceitfully, saying, "Be-
hold, Gaal the son of Ebed and his [2]relatives have come to Shechem;
and behold, they are [3]stirring up the city against you.
32 "Now therefore, arise by night, you and the people who are with
you, and lie in wait in the field.
33 "And it shall come about in the morning, as soon as the sun is up,

[1]Or, sincerity
...cerity [2]Lit., if ...u have [3]Lit., ...o the dealing ... [a]Judg. 8:35
...ast his soul in front
...rother [a]Judg. ...5 [b]Judg. 8:31
[1]Or, sincerity
..., the house of Millo
...Sam. 16:14; Is. ...2, 14 [b]Is. 33:1
... of the seventy ...t. 27:25; Judg. ...7 [b]Num. 35:33
...liers-in-wait for
...6 [1]Lit., brothers
...7 [1]Lit., rejoicing ...Judg. 8:33; 9:46
...8 [1]Lit., overseer [a]Gen. 34:2
...Lit., And who will ...is people into my ...nd [a]2 Sam. 15:4
..., in Tormah [2]Lit., ...'s [3]Lit., besieging

that you shall rise early and rush upon the city; and behold, when he
and the people who are with him come out against you, you shall
[a]do to them [1]whatever you can."
34 So Abimelech and all the people who *were* with him arose by
night and lay in wait against Shechem in four [1]companies.
35 Now Gaal the son of Ebed went out and stood in the entrance of
the city gate; and Abimelech and the people who *were* with him
arose from the ambush.
36 And when Gaal saw the people, he said to Zebul, "[1]Look, people
are coming down from the tops of the mountains." But Zebul said to
him, "You are seeing the shadow of the mountains as *if they were*
men."
37 And Gaal spoke again and said, "Behold, people are coming
down from [a]the [1]highest part of the land, and one [2]company comes
by the way of [3]the diviners' [4]oak."
38 Then Zebul said to him, "Where is your [1]boasting now with
which you said, 'Who is Abimelech that we should serve him?' Is
this not the people whom you despised? Go out now and fight with
them!"
39 So Gaal went out before the leaders of Shechem and fought with
Abimelech.
40 And Abimelech chased him, and he fled before him; and many
fell wounded up to the entrance of the gate.
41 Then Abimelech remained at Arumah, but Zebul drove out Gaal
and his [1]relatives so that they could not remain in Shechem.
42 Now it came about the next day, that the people went out to the
field, and it was told to Abimelech.
43 So he took [1]his people and divided them into three [2]companies,
and lay in wait in the field; when he looked and [3]saw the people
coming out from the city, he arose against them and [4]slew them.
44 Then Abimelech and the [1]company who was with him dashed
forward and stood in the entrance of the city gate; the other two
[2]companies then dashed against all who *were* in the field and [3]slew
them.
45 And Abimelech fought against the city all that day, and he cap-
tured the city and killed the people who *were* in it; then he [a]razed the
city and sowed it with salt.
46 When all the leaders of the tower of Shechem heard of *it*, they
entered the inner chamber of the [1]temple of [a]El-berith.
47 And it was told Abimelech that all the leaders of the tower of
Shechem were gathered together.
48 So Abimelech went up to Mount [a]Zalmon, he and all the people
who *were* with him; and Abimelech took [1]an axe in his hand and cut
down a branch from the trees, and lifted it and laid *it* on his
shoulder. Then he said to the people who *were* with him, "What you
have seen me do, hurry *and* do [2]likewise."
49 And all the people also cut down each one his branch and fol-
lowed Abimelech, and put *them* on the inner chamber and set the
inner chamber on fire over those *inside*, so that all the men of the
tower of Shechem also died, about a thousand men and women.
50 Then Abimelech went to Thebez, and he camped against Thebez
and captured it.
51 But there was a strong tower in the center of the city, and all the

33 [1]Lit., *as y... can find* [a]1 S...

34 [1]Lit., *hea...*

36 [1]Lit., *Beh...*

37 [1]Or, *cente... head* [3]Heb., *Elommeonen... terebinth* [a]Ez...

38 [1]Lit., *mout...*

41 [1]Lit., *brothe...*

43 [1]Lit., *the* [2]L... *heads* [3]Lit., *be...* [4]Lit., *smote*

44 [1]Singular w... Heb. plural, *hea... heads* [3]Lit., *sm...*

45 [a]2 Kin. 3:25

46 [1]Lit., *house* ... 8:33

48 [1]Lit., *the axes... like me* [a]Ps. 68:1...

2 Sam. 11:21
men and women with all the leaders of the city fled there and shut
themselves in; and they went up on the roof of the tower.
52 So Abimelech came to the tower and fought against it, and ap-
proached the entrance of the tower to burn it with fire.
, *his* [a]1 Sam. 31:4
53 But [a]a certain woman threw an upper millstone on Abimelech's
head, crushing his skull.
54 Then [a]he called quickly to the young man, his armor bearer, and
said to him, "Draw your sword and kill me, lest it be said of me, 'A
55 [1]Lit., *place*
woman slew him.' " So [1]the young man pierced him through, and he
died.
55 And when the men of Israel saw that Abimelech was dead, each
departed to his [1]home.
56 Thus [a]God repaid the wickedness of Abimelech, which he had
en. 9:5, 6; Ps. 94:23
done to his father, in killing his seventy brothers.
57 Also God returned all the wickedness of the men of Shechem on
their heads, and the curse of Jotham the son of Jerubbaal came [1]upon
them.

57 [1]Lit., *to*

Chapter 10

10 Now after Abimelech died, Tola the son of Puah, the son of
Dodo, a man of Issachar, [a]arose to save Israel; and he lived in
:1 [a]Judg. 2:16
Shamir in the hill country of Ephraim.
2 And he judged Israel twenty-three years. Then he died and was
buried in Shamir.
3 And after him, Jair the Gileadite arose, and judged Israel twenty-
it., *which are in* ie towns of Jair [a]Num. 32:41
two years.
4 And he had thirty sons who rode on thirty donkeys, and they
had thirty cities [1]in the land of Gilead [a]that are called [2]Havvoth-jair
to this day.
5 And Jair died and was buried in Kamon.
dg. 2:13 [b]Judg. Deut. 31:16, 17; 32:15
6 Then the sons of Israel again did evil in the sight of the LORD,
[a]served the Baals and the Ashtaroth, the gods of Aram, the gods of
Sidon, the gods of Moab, [b]the gods of the sons of Ammon, and the
gods of the Philistines; thus [c]they forsook the LORD and did not serve
Him.
7 [a]1 Sam. 12:9
7 And the anger of the LORD burned against Israel, and He [a]sold
them into the hands of the Philistines, and into the hands of the sons
of Ammon.
8 And they [1]afflicted and crushed the sons of Israel [2]that year; for
, *shattered* [2]Lit., [3]Lit., *which is in*
eighteen years they *afflicted* all the sons of Israel who were beyond
the Jordan [3]in Gilead in the land of the Amorites.
9 And the sons of Ammon crossed the Jordan to fight also against
Judah, Benjamin, and the house of Ephraim, so that Israel was great-
ly distressed.
0 [a]1 Sam. 12:10
10 Then the [a]sons of Israel cried out to the LORD, saying, "We have
sinned against Thee, for indeed, we have forsaken our God and
served the Baals."
11 And the LORD said to the sons of Israel, *"Did I* not *deliver you*
udg. 2:12 [b]Num. 1-25 [c]Judg. 3:13
[a]from the Egyptians, [b]the Amorites, [c]the sons of Ammon, and the
Philistines?
12 "Also when the Sidonians, the Amalekites and the Maonites [a]op-
pressed you, you cried out to Me, and I delivered you from their
12 [a]Ps. 106:42
hands.

13 "Yet [a]you have forsaken Me and served other gods; therefore I
will deliver you no more.
14 "[a]Go and cry out to the gods which you have chosen; let them
deliver you in the time of your distress."
15 And the sons of Israel said to the LORD, "We have sinned, [a]do to
us whatever seems good to Thee; only please deliver us this day."
16 [a]So they put away the foreign gods from among them, and
served the LORD; and [1b]He could bear the misery of Israel no longer.
17 Then the sons of Ammon were summoned, and they camped in
Gilead. And the sons of Israel gathered together, and camped in
[a]Mizpah.
18 And the people, the leaders of Gilead, said to one another, "Who
is the man who will begin to fight against the sons of Ammon? He
shall become head over all the inhabitants of Gilead."

Chapter 11

11 Now [a]Jephthah the Gileadite was a [1]valiant warrior, but he
was the son of a harlot. And Gilead [2]was the father of Jeph-
thah.
2 And Gilead's wife bore him sons; and when his wife's sons grew
up, they drove Jephthah out and said to him, "You shall not have an
inheritance in our father's house, for you are the son of another
woman."
3 So Jephthah fled from his brothers and lived in the land of [a]Tob;
and worthless fellows gathered themselves [1]about Jephthah, and
they went out with him.
4 And it came about after a while that [a]the sons of Ammon fought
against Israel.
5 And it happened when the sons of Ammon fought against Israel
that the elders of Gilead went to get Jephthah from the land of Tob;
6 and they said to Jephthah, "Come and be our chief that we may
fight against the sons of Ammon."
7 Then Jephthah said to the elders of Gilead, "[a]Did you not hate
me and drive me from my father's house? So why have you come to
me now when you are in trouble?"
8 And the elders of Gilead said to Jephthah, "For this reason we
have now returned to you, that you may go with us and fight with
the sons of Ammon and [a]become head over all the inhabitants of
Gilead."
9 So Jephthah said to the elders of Gilead, "If you take me back to
fight against the sons of Ammon and the LORD gives them up [1]to me,
will I become your head?"
10 And the elders of Gilead said to Jephthah, "[a]The LORD is [1]witness
between us; surely we will do [2]as you have said."
11 Then Jephthah went with the elders of Gilead, and the people
made him head and chief over them; and Jephthah spoke all his
words before the LORD at [a]Mizpah.
12 Now Jephthah sent messengers to the king of the sons of
Ammon, saying, "What is between you and me, that you have come
to me to fight against my land?"
13 And the king of the sons of Ammon said to the messengers of
Jephthah, "Because Israel [a]took away my land when they came up
from Egypt, from the Arnon as far as the [b]Jabbok and the Jordan;
therefore, return them peaceably now."

13 [a]Jer. 2:13
14 [a]Deut. 32:
15 [a]1 Sam. 3:
16 [1]Lit., *His sc short with the* [a]Josh. 24:23 [b] 32:36
17 [a]Judg. 11:2
11:1 [1]Or, *migh valor* [2]Lit., *beg* 11:32
3 [1]Lit., *to* [a]2 Sa 10:6, 8
4 [a]Judg. 10:9, 1
7 [a]Gen. 26:27
8 [a]Judg. 10:18
9 [1]Lit., *before*
10 [1]Lit., *hearer* *according to your* [a]Gen. 31:50; Jer. 42:5; Mic. 1:2
11 [a]Judg. 10:17; 20:1; 1 Sam. 10:1
13 [a]Num. 21:24 32:22

14 But Jephthah sent messengers again to the king of the sons of
Ammon,
15 and they said to him, "Thus says Jephthah, 'Israel did not take
away the land of Moab, nor the land of the sons of Ammon.
16 'For when they came up from Egypt, and Israel [a]went through
the wilderness to the [1]Red Sea and [b]came to Kadesh,
17 then Israel [a]sent messengers to the king of Edom, saying, "Please
let us pass through your land," but the king of Edom would not
listen. [b]And they also sent to the king of Moab, but he would not
consent. So Israel remained at Kadesh.
18 'Then they went through the wilderness and [a]around the land of
Edom and the land of Moab, and came to the east side of the land of
Moab, and they camped beyond the Arnon; but they [b]did not enter
the territory of Moab, for the Arnon *was* the border of Moab.
19 'And Israel sent [a]messengers to Sihon king of the Amorites, the
king of Heshbon, and Israel said to him, "Please let us pass through
your land to our place."
20 'But Sihon did not trust Israel to pass through his territory; so
Sihon gathered all his people and camped in Jahaz, and fought with
Israel.
21 'And the LORD, the God of Israel, gave Sihon and all his people
into the hand of Israel, and they [1a]defeated them; so Israel possessed
all the land of the Amorites, the inhabitants of that country.
22 '[a]So they possessed all the territory of the Amorites, from the
Arnon as far as the Jabbok, and from the wilderness as far as the
Jordan.
23 'Since now the LORD, the God of Israel, drove out the Amorites
from before His people Israel, are you then to possess it?
24 'Do you not possess what [a]Chemosh your god gives you to pos-
sess? So whatever the LORD our God has driven out before us, we
will possess it.
25 'And now are you any better than [a]Balak the son of Zippor, king
of Moab? Did he ever strive with Israel, or did he ever fight against
them?
26 '[a]While Israel lived in Heshbon and its villages, and in Aroer and
its villages, and in all the cities that are on the banks of the Arnon,
three hundred years, why did you not recover them within that
time?
27 'I therefore have not sinned against you, but you are doing me
wrong by making war against me; [a]may the LORD, the Judge, judge
today between the sons of Israel and the sons of Ammon.' "
28 But the king of the sons of Ammon [1]disregarded the message
which Jephthah sent him.
29 Now [a]the Spirit of the LORD came upon Jephthah, so that he
passed through Gilead and Manasseh; then he passed through Miz-
pah of Gilead, and from Mizpah of Gilead he went on to the sons of
Ammon.
30 And Jephthah made a vow to the LORD and said, "If Thou wilt
indeed give the sons of Ammon into my hand,
31 then it shall be that whatever comes out of the doors of my
house to meet me when I return in peace from the sons of Ammon, it
shall be the LORD's, and I will offer it up as a burnt offering."
32 So Jephthah crossed over to the sons of Ammon to fight against
them; and the LORD gave them into his hand.

Sea of Reeds 14:25; Deut. ...m. 20:1, 4-21
...um. 20:14-21 [b]Josh. 24:9
...m. 21:4; Deut. ...ut. 2:9, 18, 19
...um. 21:21-32; Deut. 2:26-36
..., *smote* [a]Num. ...; Deut. 2:32-34
[a]Deut. 2:36, 37
...m. 21:29; 1 Kin. 11:7
...um. 22:2; Josh. 24:9; Mic. 6:5
[a]Num. 21:25, 26; Deut. 2:36
...Gen. 16:5; 18:25; 1 Sam. 24:12, 15
...t., *did not listen to the words*
29 [a]Judg. 3:10

33 And he struck them with a very great slaughter from Aroer [1]to the entrance of [a]Minnith, twenty cities, and as far as Abel-keramim. So the sons of Ammon were subdued before the sons of Israel.

34 When Jephthah came to his house at [a]Mizpah, behold, his daughter was coming out to meet him [b]with tambourines and with dancing. Now she was his one *and* only child; besides her he had neither son nor daughter.

35 And it came about when he saw her, that he tore his clothes and said, "Alas, my daughter! You have brought me very low, and you are among those who trouble me; for I have [1]given my word to the LORD, and [a]I cannot take *it* back."

36 So she said to him, "My father, you have [1]given your word to the LORD; [a]do to me [2]as you have said, since the LORD has avenged you of your enemies, the sons of Ammon."

37 And she said to her father, "Let this thing be done for me; let me alone two months, that I may [1]go to the mountains and weep because of [a]my virginity, I and my companions."

38 Then he said, "Go." So he sent her away for two months; and she left with her companions, and wept on the mountains because of her virginity.

39 And it came about at the end of two months that she returned to her father, who did to her according to the vow which he had made; and she [1]had no relations with a man. Thus it became a custom in Israel,

40 that the daughters of Israel went yearly to [1]commemorate the daughter of Jephthah the Gileadite four days in the year.

Chapter 12

12 Then the men of Ephraim were summoned, and they crossed [1]to Zaphon and [a]said to Jephthah, "Why did you cross over to fight against the sons of Ammon without calling us to go with you? We will burn your house down on you."

2 And Jephthah said to them, "I and my people were at great strife with the sons of Ammon; when I called you, you did not deliver me from their hand.

3 "And when I saw that you would not deliver *me,* I [1a]took my life in my hands and crossed over against the sons of Ammon, and the LORD gave them into my hand. Why then have you come up to me this day, to fight against me?"

4 Then Jephthah gathered all the men of Gilead and fought Ephraim; and the men of Gilead [1]defeated Ephraim, because they said, "You are fugitives of Ephraim, O Gileadites, in the midst of Ephraim *and* in the midst of Manasseh."

5 And the Gileadites [a]captured the fords of the Jordan opposite Ephraim. And it happened when *any of* the fugitives of Ephraim said, "Let me cross over," the men of Gilead would say to him, "Are you an Ephraimite?" If he said, "No,"

6 then they would say to him, "Say now, 'Shibboleth.'" But he said, "Sibboleth," for he could not [1]pronounce it correctly. Then they seized him and slew him at the fords of the Jordan. Thus there fell at that time 42,000 of Ephraim.

7 And Jephthah judged Israel six years. Then Jephthah the Gileadite died and was buried in *one of* the cities of Gilead.

8 Now Ibzan of Bethlehem judged Israel after him.

33 [1]Lit., *even are coming to* 27:17

34 [a]Judg. 10:1 [b]Ex. 15:20; 1 S Jer. 31:4

35 [1]Lit., *opene mouth* [a]Num. 3 Eccl. 5:4, 5

36 [1]Lit., *opene mouth* [2]Lit., *ac to what has pro from your mout* 30:2

37 [1]Lit., *go and down on* [a]Gen. Luke 1:25

39 [1]Lit., *knew n*

40 [1]Lit., *recount* ancient versions

12:1 [1]Or, *northw* [a]Judg. 8:1

3 [1]Lit., *put my so my palm* [a]1 Sam 28:21; Job 13:14

4 [1]Lit., *smote*

5 [a]Judg. 3:28

6 [1]Lit., *speak so*

9 And he had thirty sons, and thirty daughters *whom* he [1]gave in
marriage outside *the family,* and he brought in thirty daughters from
outside for his sons. And he judged Israel seven years.
10 Then Ibzan died and was buried in Bethlehem.
11 Now Elon the Zebulunite judged Israel after him; and he judged
Israel ten years.
12 Then Elon the Zebulunite died and was buried at Aijalon in the
land of Zebulun.
13 Now Abdon the son of Hillel the Pirathonite judged Israel after
him.
14 And he had forty sons and thirty grandsons who rode on seven-
ty donkeys; and he judged Israel eight years.
15 Then Abdon the son of Hillel the Pirathonite died and was bur-
ied at Pirathon in the land of Ephraim, in the hill country of the
Amalekites.

Chapter 13

13 Now the sons of Israel [a]again did evil in the sight of the LORD,
so that the LORD gave them into the hands of the Philistines
forty years.
2 And there was a certain man of [a]Zorah, of the family of the
Danites, whose name was Manoah; and his wife was barren and had
borne no *children.*
3 [a]Then the angel of the LORD appeared to the woman, and said to
her, "Behold now, you are barren and have borne no *children,* but
you shall conceive and give birth to a son.
4 "Now therefore, be careful [a]not to drink wine or strong drink, nor
eat any unclean thing.
5 "[a]For behold, you shall conceive and give birth to a son, and no
razor shall come upon his head, for the boy shall be a [b]Nazirite to
God from the womb; and he shall begin to deliver Israel from the
hands of the Philistines."
6 Then the woman came and told her husband, saying, "[a]A man of
God came to me and his appearance was like the appearance of the
angel of God, very awesome. And I did not ask him where he *came*
from, nor did he tell me his name.
7 "But he said to me, 'Behold, you shall conceive and give birth to a
son, and now you shall not drink wine or strong drink nor eat any
unclean thing, for the boy shall be a Nazirite to God from the womb
to the day of his death.' "
8 Then Manoah entreated the LORD and said, "O Lord, please let
[a]the man of God whom Thou hast sent come to us again that he may
teach us what to do for the boy who is to be born."
9 And God listened to the voice of Manoah; and [a]the angel of God
came again to the woman as she was sitting in the field, but Manoah
her husband was not with her.
10 So the woman ran quickly and told her [1]husband, "Behold, [a]the
man who [2]came the *other* day has appeared to me."
11 Then Manoah arose and followed his wife, and when he came to
the man he said to him, "Are you [a]the man who spoke to the
woman?" And he said, "I am."
12 And Manoah said, "Now when your words come *to pass,* what
shall be the boy's mode of life and his vocation?"

sent outside
[a]Judg. 2:11
[a]Josh. 19:41
:11, 14; 13:6, Luke 1:11-13
n. 6:2, 3; Luke 1:15
ke 1:15 [b]Num. 6:2-5
udg. 6:11; 13:8, 10, 11
[a]Judg. 13:3, 7
9 [a]Judg. 13:8
t., *husband, and him* [2]Lit., *came me* [a]Judg. 13:9
11 [a]Judg. 13:8

13 So [a]the angel of the LORD said to Manoah, "[b]Let the woman pay attention [1]to all that I said.
14 "She should not eat anything that comes from the [a]vine nor drink wine or strong drink, nor eat any unclean thing; let her observe all that I commanded."
15 Then Manoah said to [a]the angel of the LORD, "Please let us detain you so that we may prepare a kid for you."
16 And the angel of the LORD said to Manoah, "Though you detain me, [a]I will not eat your [1]food, but if you prepare a burnt offering, *then* offer it to the LORD." For Manoah did not know that he was the angel of the LORD.
17 And Manoah said to the angel of the LORD, "[a]What is your name, so that when your words come *to pass*, we may honor you?"
18 But the angel of the LORD said to him, "Why do you ask my name, seeing it is [1a]wonderful?"
19 So [a]Manoah took the kid with the grain offering and offered it on the rock to the LORD, and He performed wonders while Manoah and his wife looked on.
20 For it came about when the flame went up from the altar toward heaven, that the angel of the LORD ascended in the flame of the altar. When Manoah and his wife saw *this*, they [a]fell on their faces to the ground.
21 Now the angel of the LORD appeared no more to Manoah or his wife. [a]Then Manoah knew that he was the angel of the LORD.
22 So Manoah said to his wife, "[a]We shall surely die, for we have seen God."
23 But his wife said to him, "If the LORD had desired to kill us, He would not have accepted a burnt offering and a grain offering from our hands, nor would He have [a]shown us all these things, nor would He have let us hear *things* like this at this time."
24 Then the woman gave birth to a son and named him Samson; and the [a]child grew up and the LORD blessed him.
25 And [a]the Spirit of the LORD began to stir him in [1b]Mahaneh-dan, between Zorah and Eshtaol.

Chapter 14

14 Then Samson went down to Timnah and saw a woman in Timnah, *one* of the daughters of the Philistines.
2 So he came [1]back and told his father and [2]mother, "I saw a woman in Timnah, *one* of the daughters of the Philistines; now therefore, get her for me as a wife."
3 Then his father and his mother said to him, "Is there no woman among the daughters of your [1a]relatives, or among all [2]our people, that you go to [b]take a wife from the uncircumcised Philistines?" But Samson said to his father, "Get her for me, for she [3]looks good to me."
4 However, his father and mother did not know that [a]it was of the LORD, for He was seeking an occasion against the Philistines. Now at that time the Philistines were ruling over Israel.
5 Then Samson went down to Timnah with his father and mother, and came as far as the vineyards of Timnah; and behold, a young lion *came* roaring toward him.
6 And [a]the Spirit of the LORD [1]came upon him mightily, so that [b]he

13 [1]Lit., *from* 13:11 [b]Judg.
14 [a]Num. 6:4
15 [a]Judg. 13
16 [1]Lit., *brea* 6:20
17 [a]Gen. 32:
18 [1]I.e., incomprehens 9:6
19 [a]Judg. 6:2
20 [a]Lev. 9:24; 21:16; Ezek. 1. 17:6
21 [a]Judg. 13:1
22 [a]Gen. 32:3 5:26; Judg. 6:2
23 [a]Ps. 25:14
24 [a]1 Sam. 3:1 1:80
25 [1]I.e., the ca Dan [a]Judg. 3:1 18:11, 12
14:2 [1]Lit., *up* [2] *mother, saying,*
3 [1]Lit., *brothers my* [3]Lit., *is right eyes* [a]Gen. 24:3 [b]Ex. 34:16; Deut.
4 [a]Josh. 11:20
6 [1]Lit., *rushed u* [a]Judg. 3:10 [b]1 S 17:34-36

, was right in msons's eyes

tore him as one tears a kid though he had nothing in his hand; but
he did not tell his father or mother what he had done.
7 So he went down and talked to the woman; and she [1]looked
good to Samson.
8 When he returned later to take her, he turned aside to look at the
carcass of the lion; and behold, a swarm of bees and honey were in
the body of the lion.
9 So he scraped [1]the honey into his [2]hands and went on, eating as
he went. When he came to his father and mother, he gave *some* to
them and they ate *it;* but he did not tell them that he had scraped the
honey out of the body of the lion.
10 Then his father went down to the woman; and Samson made a
feast there, for the young men customarily did this.
11 And it came about when they saw him that they brought thirty
companions to be with him.
12 Then Samson said to them, "Let me now [a]propound a riddle to
you; if you will indeed tell it to me within the seven days of the feast,
and find it out, then I will give you thirty linen wraps and thirty
[b]changes of clothes.
13 "But if you are unable to tell me, then you shall give me thirty
linen wraps and thirty changes of clothes." And they said to him,
"Propound your riddle, that we may hear it."
14 So he said to them,

"Out of the eater came something to eat,
And out of the strong came something sweet."

But they could not tell the riddle in three days.
15 Then it came about on the [1]fourth day that they said to Samson's
wife, "[a]Entice your husband, that he may tell us the riddle, [b]lest we
burn you and your father's house with fire. Have you invited us to
impoverish us? Is this not *so?"*
16 And Samson's wife wept before him and said, "[a]You only hate
me, and you do not love me; you have propounded a riddle to the
sons of my people, and have not told *it* to me." And he said to her,
"Behold, I have not told *it* to my father or mother; so should I tell
you?"
17 However she wept before him seven days while their feast
lasted. And it came about on the seventh day that he told her be-
cause she pressed him so hard. She then told the riddle to the sons of
her people.
18 So the men of the city said to him on the seventh day before the
sun went down,

"What is sweeter than honey?
And what is stronger than a lion?"

And he said to them,

"If you had not plowed with my heifer,
You would not have found out my riddle."

19 Then [a]the Spirit of the LORD [1]came upon him mightily, and he
went down to Ashkelon and killed thirty of them and took their
spoil, and gave the changes *of clothes* to those who told the riddle.
And his anger burned, and he went up to his father's house.
20 But Samson's wife was [a]*given* to his companion who had been
his [1]friend.

it [2]Lit., *palms*

k. 17:2 [b]Gen. 22; 2 Kin. 5:22

[1]So with some versions; Heb., *th* [a]Judg. 16:5 [b]Judg. 15:6

6 [a]Judg. 16:15

.it., *rushed upon* udg. 3:10; 13:25

20 [1]Or, *best man* [a]Judg. 15:2

Chapter 15

15 But after a while, in the time of wheat harvest, it came about
that Samson visited his wife [a]with a young goat, and said, "I
will go in to my wife in *her* room." But her father did not let him
enter.
2 And her father said, "I really thought that you hated her intense-
ly; so I [a]gave her to your companion. Is not her younger sister [1]more
beautiful than she? Please let her be yours [2]instead."
3 Samson then said to them, "This time I shall be blameless in
regard to the Philistines when I do them harm."
4 And Samson went and caught three hundred foxes, and took
torches, and turned *the foxes* tail to tail, and put one torch in the
middle between two tails.
5 When he had set fire to the torches, he released [1]the foxes into
the standing grain of the Philistines, thus burning up both the
shocks and the standing grain, along with the vineyards *and* groves.
6 Then the Philistines said, "Who did this?" And they said, "Sam-
son, the son-in-law of the Timnite, because [1]he took his wife and
gave her to his companion." So the Philistines came up and [a]burned
her and her father with fire.
7 And Samson said to them, "Since you act like this, I will surely
take revenge on you, but after that I will quit."
8 And he struck them [1]ruthlessly with a great slaughter; and he
went down and lived in the cleft of the rock of Etam.
9 Then the Philistines went up and camped in Judah, and spread
out in Lehi.
10 And the men of Judah said, "Why have you come up against
us?" And they said, "We have come up to bind Samson in order to
do to him as he did to us."
11 Then 3,000 men of Judah went down to the cleft of the rock of
Etam and said to Samson, "Do you not know [a]that the Philistines are
rulers over us? What then is this that you have done to us?" And he
said to them, "As they did to me, so I have done to them."
12 And they said to him, "We have come down to bind you so that
we may give you into the hands of the Philistines." And Samson
said to them, "Swear to me that you will not [1]kill me."
13 So they said to [1]him, "No, but we will bind you fast and give
you into their hands; yet surely we will not kill you." Then they
bound him with two new ropes and brought him up from the rock.
14 When he came to Lehi, the Philistines shouted as they met him.
And [a]the Spirit of the LORD [1]came upon him mightily so that the
ropes that were on his arms were as flax that is burned with fire, and
his bonds [2]dropped from his hands.
15 And he found a fresh jawbone of a donkey, so he [1]reached out
and took it and [2]killed [a]a thousand men with it.
16 Then Samson said,

"With the jawbone of a donkey,
[1]Heaps upon heaps,
With the jawbone of a donkey
I have [2]killed a thousand men."

17 And it came about when he had finished speaking, that he threw
the jawbone from his hand; and he named that place [1]Ramath-lehi.
18 Then he became very thirsty, and he [a]called to the LORD and said,
"Thou hast given this great deliverance by the hand of Thy servant,

15:1 [a]Gen. 3
2 [1]Lit., *better* *instead of her* 14:20
5 [1]Lit., *them*
6 [1]I.e., the Tim [a]Judg. 14:15
8 [1]Lit., *leg on*
11 [a]Lev. 26:25 28:43f.; Judg. 1 14:4; Ps. 106:4
12 [1]Lit., *fall up* *yourselves*
13 [1]Lit., *him, sa*
14 [1]Lit., *rushed* [2]Lit., *were melte* [a]Judg. 14:19; 1 S 11:6
15 [1]Lit., *stretche* *his hand* [2]Lit., *s* [a]Lev. 26:8; Josh.
16 [1]Lit., *Heap, tw* *heaps;* Heb. is sa root as donkey [2] *smitten*
17 [1]I.e., the high of the jawbone
18 [a]Judg. 16:28

and now [1]shall I die of thirst [2]and fall into the hands of the uncir-
cumcised?"
19 But God split the hollow place that is in Lehi so that water came
out of it. When he drank, [a]his [1]strength returned and he revived.
Therefore, he named it [2]En-hakkore, which is in Lehi to this day.
20 So [a]he judged Israel twenty years in [b]the days of the Philistines.

Chapter 16

16 Now Samson went to [a]Gaza and saw a harlot there, and went
in to her.
2 *When it was told* to the Gazites, saying, "Samson has come here,"
they [a]surrounded *the place* and lay in wait for him all night at the
gate of the city. And they kept silent all night, saying, "*Let us wait*
until the morning light, then we will kill him."
3 Now Samson lay until midnight, and at midnight he arose and
took hold of the doors of the city gate and the two posts and pulled
them up along with the bars; then he put them on his shoulders and
carried them up to the top of the mountain which is opposite
Hebron.
4 After this it came about that he loved a woman in the valley of
Sorek, whose name was Delilah.
5 And the [a]lords of the Philistines came up to her, and said to her,
"[b]Entice him, and see where his great strength *lies* and [1]how we may
overpower him that we may bind him to afflict him. Then we will
each give you eleven hundred *pieces* of silver."
6 So Delilah said to Samson, "Please tell me where your great
strength is and [1]how you may be bound to afflict you."
7 And Samson said to her, "If they bind me with seven fresh cords
that have not been dried, then I shall become weak and be like any
other man."
8 Then the lords of the Philistines brought up to her seven fresh
cords that had not been dried, and she bound him with them.
9 Now she had *men* lying in wait in an inner room. And she said to
him, "The Philistines are upon you, Samson!" But he snapped the
cords as a string of tow snaps when it [1]touches fire. So his strength
was not discovered.
10 Then Delilah said to Samson, "Behold, you have deceived me
and told me lies; now please tell me, [1]how you may be bound."
11 And he said to her, "If they bind me tightly with new ropes
[1]which have not been used, then I shall become weak and be like any
other man."
12 So Delilah took new ropes and bound him with them and said to
him, "The Philistines are upon you, Samson!" For the *men* were lying
in wait in the inner room. But he snapped [1]the ropes from his arms
like a thread.
13 Then Delilah said to Samson, "Up to now you have deceived me
and told me lies; tell me [1]how you may be bound." And he said to
her, "If you weave the seven locks of my [2]hair with the web [3][and
fasten it with a pin, then I shall become weak and be like any other
man."
14 So while he slept, Delilah took the seven locks of his [1]hair and
wove them into the web]. And she fastened *it* with the pin, and said
to him, "The Philistines are upon you, Samson!" But he awoke from
his sleep and pulled out the pin of the loom and the web.

18 [1]Or, *I shall . . .* [u]ncircumcised [2]Or, *or*

[1]Lit., *spirit* [2]I.e., the spring of him who called [a]Is. 40:29

[a]Judg. 16:31; Heb. 11:32 [b]Judg. 13:1

16:1 [a]Josh. 15:47

[a]1 Sam. 23:26; Ps. 118:10-12

[1]L]it., *by what* [a]Josh. 13:3 [b]Judg. 14:15

6 [1]Lit., *by what*

9 [1]Lit., *smells*

10 [1]Lit., *by what*

[1]Lit., *with which* [w]as *not been done*

12 [1]Lit., *them*

[1]Lit., *by what* [2]Lit., ... [3]The passage in [brack]ets is found in Gr. ... in any Heb. mss.

14 [1]Lit., *head*

15 Then she said to him, "[a]How can you say, 'I love you,' when
your heart is not with me? You have deceived me these three times
and have not told me where your great strength is."
16 And it came about when she pressed him daily with her words
and urged him, that his soul was [1]annoyed to death.
17 So he told her all *that was* in his heart and said to her, "A razor
has never come on my head, for I have been a [a]Nazirite to God from
my mother's womb. If I am shaved, then my strength will leave me
and I shall become weak and be like any *other* man."
18 When Delilah saw that he had told her all *that was* in his heart,
she sent and called the lords of the Philistines, saying, "Come up
once more, for he has told me all *that is* in his heart." Then the lords
of the Philistines came up to her, and brought the money in their
hands.
19 And she made him sleep on her knees, and called for a man and
had him shave off the seven locks of his [1]hair. Then she began to
afflict him, and his strength left him.
20 And she said, "The Philistines are upon you, Samson!" And he
awoke from his sleep and said, "I will go out as at other times and
shake myself free." But he did not know that [a]the LORD had departed
from him.
21 Then the Philistines seized him and gouged out his eyes; and
they brought him down to Gaza and bound him with bronze chains,
and he was a grinder in the prison.
22 However, the hair of his head began to grow again after it was
shaved off.
23 Now the lords of the Philistines assembled to offer a great
sacrifice to [a]Dagon their god, and to rejoice, for they said,
"Our god has given Samson our enemy into our hands."
24 When the people saw him, [a]they praised their god, for they said,
"Our god has given our enemy into our hands,
Even the destroyer of our country,
Who has slain many of us."
25 It so happened when [1]they were in high spirits, that they said,
"Call for Samson, that he may amuse us." So they called for Samson
from the prison, and he [2]entertained them. And they made him
stand between the pillars.
26 Then Samson said to the boy who was holding his hand, "Let
me feel the pillars on which the house rests, that I may lean against
them."
27 Now the house was full of men and women, and all the lords of
the Philistines were there. And about 3,000 men and women were on
the roof looking on while Samson was amusing *them*.
28 [a]Then Samson called to the LORD and said, "O Lord [1]GOD, please
remember me and please strengthen me just this time, O God, that I
may at once [b]be avenged of the Philistines for my two eyes."
29 And Samson grasped the two middle pillars on which the house
rested, and braced himself against them, the one with his right hand
and the other with his left.
30 And Samson said, "Let me die with the Philistines!" And he bent
with [1]all his might so that the house fell on the lords and all the
people who were in it. So the dead whom he killed at his death were
more than those whom he killed in his life.
31 Then his brothers and all his father's household came down,

15 [a]Judg. 14:16

16 [1]Lit., *impatient* *point of*

17 [a]Num. 6:2, 5; J 13:5

19 [1]Lit., *head*

20 [a]Num. 14:42, Josh. 7:12; 1 Sam

23 [a]1 Sam. 5:2

24 [a]1 Sam. 31:9; 10:9; Ps. 97:7

25 [1]Lit., *their hea* *pleasant* [2]Lit., *ma* *sport before them*

28 [1]Heb., *YWH* usually rendered [a]Judg. 15:18 [b]Je

30 [1]Lit., *strength*

took him, brought him up, and buried him between Zorah and Esh-
taol in the tomb of Manoah his father. [a]Thus he had judged Israel
twenty years.

Chapter 17

17 Now there was a man of the hill country of Ephraim whose
name was Micah.
2 And he said to his mother, "The eleven hundred *pieces* of silver
which were taken from you, about which you uttered a curse [1]in my
hearing, behold, the silver is with me; I took it." And his mother
said, "Blessed be my son by the LORD."
3 He then returned the eleven hundred *pieces* of silver to his
mother, and his mother said, "I wholly dedicate the silver from my
hand to the LORD for my son [a]to make a graven image and a molten
image; now therefore, I will return [1]them to you."
4 So when he returned the silver to his mother, his mother took
two hundred *pieces* of silver and gave them to the silversmith who
made [1]them into a graven image and a molten image, and [2]they were
in the house of Micah.
5 And the man Micah had a [1a]shrine and he made an [b]ephod and
[2c]household idols and [3]consecrated one of his sons, [d]that he might
become his priest.
6 In those days [a]there was no king in Israel; [b]every man did what
was right in his own eyes.
7 Now there was a young man from [a]Bethlehem in Judah, of the
family of Judah, who was a Levite; and he was [1]staying there.
8 Then the man departed from the city, from Bethlehem in Judah,
to [1]stay wherever he might find *a place;* and as he made his journey,
he came to the [a]hill country of Ephraim to the house of Micah.
9 And Micah said to him, "Where do you come from?" And he
said to him, "I am a Levite from Bethlehem in Judah, and I am going
to [1]stay wherever I may find *a place.*"
10 Micah then said to him, "Dwell with me and be [a]a father and a
priest to me, and I will give you ten *pieces* of silver a year, a suit of
clothes, and your maintenance." So the Levite went *in.*
11 And the Levite agreed to live with the man; and the young man
became to him like one of his sons.
12 So Micah [1]consecrated the Levite, and the young man [a]became
his priest and [2]lived in the house of Micah.
13 Then Micah said, "Now I know that the LORD will prosper me,
seeing I have a Levite as priest."

Chapter 18

18 [a]In those days there was no king of Israel; and [b]in those days
the tribe of the Danites was seeking an inheritance for them-
selves to live in, for until that day [1]an inheritance had not [2]been
allotted to them as a possession among the tribes of Israel.
2 So the sons of Dan sent from their family five men out of their
whole number, [1]valiant men from [a]Zorah and Eshtaol, to spy out the
land and to search it; and they said to them, "Go, search the land."
And they came to [b]the hill country of Ephraim, to the house of
Micah, and lodged there.
3 When they were near the house of Micah, they recognized the
voice of the young man, the Levite; and they turned aside there, and

[a]Judg. 15:20

[1]Lit., *and also*
…e it in my ears

[a]Ex. 20:4, 23; 34:17

…it [2]Lit., *it was*

…house of gods
…eraphim [3]Lit.,
…and of [a]Judg.
…4 [b]Judg. 8:27;
…4 [c]Gen. 31:19
[d]Num. 3:10

…dg. 18:1; 19:1
…8; Judg. 21:25

[1]Or, *sojourning*
…:1; Ruth 1:1, 2;
…. 5:2; Matt. 2:1

sojourn [a]Josh. 24:33

9 [1]Or, *sojourn*

10 [a]Judg. 18:19

…, *filled the hand*
[2]Lit., *was* [a]Num.
16:10; 18:1-7

…Lit., *it* [2]Lit., *fallen*
…7:6; 19:1 [b]Josh.
19:40-48

…Lit., *men, sons of*
…alor [a]Judg. 13:25
[b]Judg. 17:1

said to him, "Who brought you here? And what are you doing in
this *place?* And what do you have here?"
4 And he said to them, "Thus and so has Micah done to me, and
he has hired me, and [a]I have become his priest."
5 And they said to him, "Inquire of God, please, that we may
know whether our way on which we are going will be prosperous."
6 And the priest said to them, "Go in peace; your way in which
you are going [1]has the LORD's approval."
7 Then the five men departed and came to [a]Laish and saw the
people who were in it living in security, after the manner of the
Sidonians, quiet and secure; for there was no [1]ruler humiliating *them*
for anything in the land, and they were far from the Sidonians and
had no dealings with anyone.
8 When they came back to their brothers at Zorah and Eshtaol,
their brothers said to them, "What *do* you *report?*"
9 And they said, "Arise, and let us go up against them; for we
have seen the land, and behold, it is very good. And will you [1]sit
still? Do not delay to go, to enter, to possess the land.
10 "When you enter, you shall come to a secure people with a spa-
cious land; for God has given it into your hand, [a]a place where there
is no lack of anything that is on the earth."
11 Then from the family of the Danites, from Zorah and from Esh-
taol, six hundred men armed with weapons of war set out.
12 And they went up and camped at Kiriath-jearim in Judah. There-
fore they called that place [1a]Mahaneh-dan to this day; behold, it is
[2]west of Kiriath-jearim.
13 And they passed from there to the hill country of Ephraim and
came to the house of Micah.
14 Then the five men who went to spy out the country of Laish
answered and said to their kinsmen, "Do you know that there are in
these houses [a]an ephod and [1]household idols and a graven image
and a molten image? Now therefore, consider what you should do."
15 And they turned aside there and came to the house of the young
man, the Levite, to the house of Micah, and asked him of his welfare.
16 And the six hundred men armed with their weapons of war,
who were of the sons of Dan, stood by the entrance of the gate.
17 Now the five men who went to spy out the land went up *and*
entered there, *and* took [a]the graven image and the ephod and [1]house-
hold idols and the molten image, while the priest stood by the
entrance of the gate with the six hundred men armed with weapons
of war.
18 And when these went into Micah's house and took the graven
image, the ephod and [1]household idols and the molten image, the
priest said to them, "What are you doing?"
19 And they said to him, "Be silent, [a]put your hand over your
mouth and come with us, and be to us [b]a father and a priest. Is it
better for you to be a priest to the house of one man, or to be priest to
a tribe and a family in Israel?"
20 And the priest's heart was glad, and he took the ephod and
[1]household idols and the graven image, and went among the people.
21 Then they turned and departed, and put the little ones and the
livestock and the valuables in front of them.
22 When they had gone some distance from the house of Micah, the

4 [a]Judg. 17:

6 [1]Lit., *is bef* *LORD*

7 [1]Lit., *posse* *restraint* [a]Jos Judg. 18:29

9 [1]Lit., *be*

10 [a]Deut. 8:9

12 [1]I.e., the ca Dan [2]Lit., *behi* [a]Judg. 13:25

14 [1]Heb., *terap* [a]Judg. 17:5

17 [1]Heb., *terap* [a]Gen. 31:19, 30 41:29; Mic. 5:13

18 [1]Heb., *teraph*

19 [a]Job 21:5; 29 40:4 [b]Judg. 17:1

20 [1]Heb., *teraph*

men who *were* in the houses near Micah's house assembled and
overtook the sons of Dan.
23 And they cried to the sons of Dan, who turned [1]around and said
to Micah, "What is *the matter* with you, that you have assembled
together?"
24 And he said, "You have taken away my gods which I made, and
the priest, and have gone away, and what do I have besides? So how
can you say to me, 'What is *the matter* with you?' "
25 And the sons of Dan said to him, "Do not let your voice be heard
among us, lest [1]fierce men fall upon you and you [2]lose your life, with
the lives of your household."
26 So the sons of Dan went on their way; and when Micah saw that
they were too strong for him, he turned and went back to his house.
27 Then they took what Micah had made and the priest who had
belonged to him, and came to [a]Laish, to a people quiet and secure,
and struck them with the edge of the sword; and they burned the
city with fire.
28 And there was no one to deliver *them*, because it was far from
Sidon and they had no dealings with anyone, and it was in the
valley which is near [a]Beth-rehob. And they rebuilt the city and lived
in it.
29 And [a]they called the name of the city Dan, after the name of Dan
their father who was born in Israel; however, the name of the city
formerly was Laish.
30 And the sons of Dan set up for themselves [a]the graven image;
and Jonathan, the son of [b]Gershom, the son of [1]Manasseh, [a]he and his
sons were priests to the tribe of the Danites until the day of the
captivity of the land.
31 So they set up for themselves Micah's graven image which he
had made, all the time that the [a]house of God was at Shiloh.

Chapter 19

19 Now it came about in those days, when [a]there was no king in
Israel, that there was a certain Levite [1]staying in the remote
part of the hill country of Ephraim, who took a concubine for him-
self from Bethlehem in Judah.
2 But his concubine played the harlot against him, and she went
away from him to her father's house in Bethlehem in Judah, and was
there for a period of four months.
3 Then her husband arose and went after her to [a]speak [1]tenderly to
her in order to bring her back, [2]taking with him his servant and a
pair of donkeys. So she brought him into her father's house, and
when the girl's father saw him, he was glad to meet him.
4 And his father-in-law, the girl's father, detained him; and he
remained with him three days. So they ate and drank and lodged
there.
5 Now it came about on the fourth day that they got up early in
the morning, and he [1]prepared to go; and the girl's father said to his
son-in-law, "[a]Sustain [2]yourself with a piece of bread, and afterward
you may go."
6 So both of them sat down and ate and drank together; and the
girl's father said to the man, "Please be willing to spend the night,
and [a]let your heart be merry."

[1]Lit., *their faces*
...it., *bitter of soul* [2]Lit., *gather*
...sh. 19:47; Judg. 18:7
28 [a]2 Sam. 10:6
29 [a]Josh. 19:47
... [1]Some ancient ...ions read *Moses* ...Judg. 17:3, 5 [b]Ex. 2:22; 18:3
31 [a]Josh. 18:1
1 [1]Or, *sojourning* [a]Judg. 18:1
[1]Lit., *to her heart* ..., *and* [a]Gen. 34:3; 50:21
..., *arose* [2]Lit., *your* [a]Gen. 18:5; Judg. 19:8
[a]Judg. 16:25; 19:9, 22; Ruth 3:7; 1 Kin. 21:7; Esth. 1:10

7 Then the man arose to go, but his father-in-law urged him so
that he spent the night there again.
8 And on the fifth day he arose to go early in the morning, and the
girl's father said, "Please sustain [1]yourself, and wait until [2]after-
noon"; so both of them ate.
9 When the man arose to go along with his concubine and servant,
his father-in-law, the girl's father, said to him, "Behold now, the day
has drawn [1]to a close; please spend the night. Lo, the day is [2]coming
to an end; spend the night here that your heart may be merry. Then
tomorrow you may arise early for your journey so that you may go
[3]home."
10 But the man was not willing to spend the night, so he arose and
departed and came to *a place* opposite [a]Jebus (that is, Jerusalem). And
there were with him a pair of saddled donkeys; his concubine also
was with him.
11 When they *were* near Jebus, the day was almost gone; and [a]the
servant said to his master, "Please come, and let us turn aside into
this city of the Jebusites and spend the night in it."
12 However, his master said to him, "We will not turn aside into the
city of foreigners who are not of the sons of Israel; but we will go on
as far as Gibeah."
13 And he said to his servant, "Come and let us approach one of
these places; and we will spend the night in Gibeah or Ramah."
14 So they passed along and went their way, and the sun set on
them near Gibeah which belongs to Benjamin.
15 And they turned aside there in order to enter *and* lodge in
Gibeah. When [1]they entered, [1]they sat down in the open square of
the city, for no one took them into *his* house to spend the night.
16 Then behold, an old man was coming out of the field from his
work at evening. Now the man was from [a]the hill country of
Ephraim, and he was [1]staying in Gibeah, but the men of the place
[b]were Benjamites.
17 And he lifted up his eyes and saw the traveler in the open square
of the city; and the old man said, "Where are you going, and where
do you come from?"
18 And he said to him, "We are passing from Bethlehem in Judah to
the remote part of the hill country of Ephraim, *for* I am from there,
and I went to Bethlehem in Judah. But I am *now* going to [1]my house,
and no man will take me into his house.
19 "Yet there is both straw and fodder for our donkeys, and also
bread and wine for me, [1]your maidservant, and [a]the young man who
is with your servants; there is no lack of anything."
20 And the old man said, "[a]Peace to you. Only let me *take care of* all
your needs; however, do not spend the night in the open square."
21 [a]So he took him into his house and gave the donkeys fodder, and
they washed their feet and ate and drank.
22 While they were [1]making merry, behold, [a]the men of the city,
certain [2b]worthless fellows, surrounded the house, pounding the
door; and they spoke to the owner of the house, the old man, saying,
"Bring out the man who came into your house that we may have
[3]relations with him."
23 Then the man, the owner of the house, went out to them and
said to them, "No, my fellows, please do not act so wickedly; since
this man has come into my house, [a]do not commit this act of folly.

8 [1]Lit., *your hea* *the day declines*

9 [1]Lit., *toward e* [2]Lit., *declining* [3] *your tent*

10 [a]1 Chr. 11:4,

11 [a]Judg. 19:19

15 [1]So with Gr.;

16 [1]Or, *sojourni* [a]Judg. 19:1 [b]Jud 19:14

18 [1]Heb., *the ho* *the LORD*, cf. v. 2

19 [1]I.e., my conc [a]Judg. 19:11

20 [a]Gen. 43:23; 6:23

21 [a]Gen. 24:32, 3

22 [1]Lit., *making th hearts merry* [2]Lit., *of Belial* [3]Lit., *intercourse* [a]Gen. 5; Ezek. 16:46-48 [b]Deut. 13:13; 1 Sa 2:12; 1 Kin. 21:10; 2 Cor. 6:15

23 [a]Gen. 34:7; De 22:21; Judg. 20:6; 2 Sam. 13:12

Lit., *the good in* ...ves [a]Gen. 19:8

24 "[a]Here is my virgin daughter and his concubine. Please let me bring them out that you may ravish them and do to them [1]whatever you wish. But do not commit such an act of folly against this man."

25 But the men would not listen to him, so the man seized his concubine and brought *her* out to them. And they raped her and abused her all night until morning, then let her go at the approach of dawn.

, *At the turning of the morning*

26 [1]As the day began to dawn, the woman came and fell down at the doorway of the man's house where her master was, until *full* daylight.

t., *place* [a]Judg. 20:5

27 When her master arose in the morning and opened the doors of the house and went out to go on his way, then behold, his concubine was lying at the doorway of the house, with her hands on the threshold.

28 And he said to her, "Get up and let us go," [a]but there was no answer. Then he placed her on the donkey; and the man arose and went to his [1]home.

29 [a]1 Sam. 11:7

29 When he entered his house, he took a knife and laid hold of his concubine and [a]cut her in twelve pieces, limb by limb, and sent her throughout the territory of Israel.

udg. 20:7; Prov. 13:10

30 And it came about that all who saw *it* said, "Nothing like this has *ever* happened or been seen from the day when the sons of Israel came up from the land of Egypt to this day. Consider it, [a]take counsel and speak up!"

Chapter 20

0:1 [a]1 Sam. 7:5

20 Then all the sons of Israel from Dan to Beersheba, including the land of Gilead, came out, and the congregation assembled as one man to the LORD at [a]Mizpah.

Lit., *cornerstones* ...men [a]Judg. 8:10

2 And the [1]chiefs of all the people, *even* of all the tribes of Israel, took their stand in the assembly of the people of God, 400,000 foot [2]soldiers [a]who drew the sword.

3 (Now the sons of Benjamin heard that the sons of Israel had gone up to Mizpah.) And the sons of Israel said, "Tell *us*, how did this wickedness take place?"

dg. 19:22 [b]Judg. 19:25f.

4 So the Levite, the husband of the woman who was murdered, answered and said, "I came with my concubine to spend the night at Gibeah which belongs to Benjamin.

5 "But the [a]men of Gibeah rose up against me and surrounded the house at night because of me. They intended to kill me; instead, they [b]ravished my concubine so that she died.

udg. 19:29 [b]Gen. 34:7; Josh. 7:15

6 "And I [a]took hold of my concubine and cut her in pieces and sent her throughout the land of Israel's inheritance; for [b]they have committed a lewd and disgraceful act in Israel.

7 [a]Judg. 19:30

7 "Behold, all you sons of Israel, [a]give your advice and counsel here."

8 Then all the people arose as one man, saying, "Not one of us will go to his tent, nor will any of us return to his house.

9 "But now this is the thing which we will do to Gibeah; *we will go up* against it by lot.

[1]Lit., *take* [2]Heb., *Geba*

10 "And we will take 10 men out of 100 throughout the tribes of Israel, and 100 out of 1,000, and 1,000 out of 10,000 to [1]supply food for the people, that when they come to [2]Gibeah of Benjamin, they

may [3]punish *them* for all the disgraceful acts that they have committed in Israel."
11 Thus all the men of Israel were gathered against the city, united as one man.
12 Then the tribes of Israel sent men through the entire [1]tribe of Benjamin, saying, "What is this wickedness that has taken place among you?
13 "Now then, deliver up the men, the [1a]worthless fellows in Gibeah, that we may put them to death and [b]remove *this* wickedness from Israel." But the sons of Benjamin would not listen to the voice of their brothers, the sons of Israel.
14 And the sons of Benjamin gathered from the cities to Gibeah, to go out to battle against the sons of Israel.
15 And from the cities on that day the [a]sons of Benjamin were [1]numbered, 26,000 men who draw the sword, besides the inhabitants of Gibeah who were [1]numbered, 700 choice men.
16 Out of all these people 700 [a]choice men were left-handed; each one could sling a stone at a hair and not miss.
17 Then the men of Israel besides Benjamin were [1]numbered, 400,000 men who draw the sword; all these were men of war.
18 Now the sons of Israel arose, went up to Bethel, and [a]inquired of God, and said, "Who shall go up first for us to battle against the sons of Benjamin?" Then the LORD said, "Judah *shall go up* first."
19 So the sons of Israel arose in the morning and camped against Gibeah.
20 And the men of Israel went out to battle against Benjamin, and the men of Israel arrayed for battle against them at Gibeah.
21 Then the sons of Benjamin came out of Gibeah and [1a]felled to the ground on that day 22,000 men of Israel.
22 But the people, the men of Israel, encouraged themselves and arrayed for battle again in the place where they had arrayed themselves the first day.
23 [a]And the sons of Israel went up and wept before the LORD until evening, and [b]inquired of the LORD, saying, "Shall we again draw near for battle against the sons of my brother Benjamin?" And the LORD said, "Go up against him."
24 Then the sons of Israel [1]came against the sons of Benjamin the second day.
25 And Benjamin went out [1]against them from Gibeah the second day and [2]felled to the ground again 18,000 men of the sons of Israel; all these drew the sword.
26 Then [a]all the sons of Israel and all the people went up and came to Bethel and wept; thus they remained there before the LORD and fasted that day until evening. And they offered burnt offerings and peace offerings before the LORD.
27 And the sons of Israel [a]inquired of the LORD (for the ark of the covenant of God *was* there in those days,
28 and Phinehas the son of Eleazar, Aaron's son, stood before it to *minister* in those days), saying, "Shall I yet again go out to battle against the sons of my brother Benjamin, or shall I cease?" And the LORD said, "Go up, [a]for tomorrow I will deliver them into your hand."
29 [a]So Israel set men in ambush around Gibeah.
30 And the sons of Israel went up against the sons of Benjamin on

10 [3]Lit., *do*
12 [1]Lit., *tribes*
13 [1]Lit., *sons of B*
[a]2 Cor. 6:15 [b]Deut 13:5; 17:12; 1 Cor.
15 [1]Or, *mustered* [a]Num. 1:36, 37; 2:2 26:41
16 [a]Judg. 3:15; 1 C 12:2
17 [1]Or, *mustered*
18 [a]Num. 27:21; J 20:23, 27
21 [1]Lit., *destroyed* [a]Judg. 20:25
23 [a]Josh. 7:6, 7 [b] 20:18
24 [1]Lit., *approach*
25 [1]Lit., *to meet* [2] *destroyed*
26 [a]Judg. 20:23; 2
27 [a]Judg. 20:18
28 [a]Judg. 7:9
29 [a]Josh. 8:4

the third day and arrayed themselves against Gibeah, as at other
times.
31 [a]And the sons of Benjamin went out [1]against the people and
were drawn away from the city, and they began to strike [2]and kill
some of the people, as at other times, on the highways, one of which
goes up to Bethel and the other to Gibeah, *and* in the field, about
thirty men of Israel.
32 And the sons of Benjamin said, "They are struck down before us,
as at the first." But the sons of Israel said, "Let us flee that we may
draw them away from the city to the highways."
33 Then all the men of Israel arose from their place and arrayed
themselves at Baal-tamar; [a]and the men of Israel in ambush broke
out of their place, even out of Maareh-geba.
34 When ten thousand choice men from all Israel came against
Gibeah, the battle became [1]fierce; [a]but [2]Benjamin did not know that
[3]disaster was [4]close to them.
35 And the LORD struck Benjamin before Israel, so that the sons of
Israel destroyed 25,100 men of Benjamin that day, all [1]who draw the
sword.
36 So the sons of Benjamin saw that they were [1]defeated. [a]When the
men of Israel gave [2]ground to Benjamin because they relied on the
men in ambush whom they had set against Gibeah,
37 [a]the men in ambush hurried and rushed against Gibeah; the men
in ambush also deployed and struck all the city with the edge of the
sword.
38 Now the appointed sign between the men of Israel and the men
in ambush was [a]that they should make a great cloud of smoke rise
from the city.
39 Then the men of Israel turned in the battle, and Benjamin began
to strike [1]and kill about thirty men of Israel, [a]for they said, "Surely
they are [2]defeated before us, as in the first battle."
40 But when the cloud began to rise from the city in a column of
smoke, Benjamin looked [a]behind them; and behold, the whole city
was going up *in smoke* to heaven.
41 Then the men of Israel turned, and the men of Benjamin were
terrified; for they saw that [1a]disaster was [2]close to them.
42 Therefore, they turned their backs before the men of Israel
[a]toward the direction of the wilderness, but the battle overtook them
while those who came out of the cities destroyed them in the midst
of them.
43 [a]They surrounded Benjamin, pursued them without rest *and* trod
them down opposite Gibeah toward the [1]east.
44 Thus 18,000 men of Benjamin fell; all these were valiant warriors.
45 [1]The rest turned and fled toward the wilderness to the rock of
[a]Rimmon, but they [2]caught 5,000 of them on the highways and over-
took them [3]at Gidom and [4]killed 2,000 of them.
46 So all of Benjamin who fell that day were 25,000 men who draw
the sword; all these were valiant warriors.
47 But 600 men turned and fled toward the wilderness to the rock
of Rimmon, and they remained at the rock of Rimmon four months.
48 The men of Israel then turned back against the sons of Benjamin
and struck them with the edge of the sword, both the entire city with
the cattle and all that they found; they also set on fire all the cities
which they found.

to meet [2]Lit., ...s [a]Josh. 8:16
...3 [a]Josh. 8:19
...t., *heavy* [2]Lit., [3]Lit., *evil* [4]Lit., ...g [a]Josh. 8:14; Job 21:13
35 [1]Lit., *these*
..., *smitten* [2]Lit., ...ce [a]Josh. 8:15
37 [a]Josh. 8:19
38 [a]Josh. 8:20
[1]Lit., *slain ones* ... *smitten* [a]Judg. 20:32
40 [a]Josh. 8:20
...1 [1]Lit., *evil* [2]Lit., ...hing [a]Prov. 5:22; 11:5, 6; 29:6
... [a]Josh. 8:15, 24
...it., *sunrise* [a]Hos. 9:9; 10:9
...So with Gr.; Heb., ...hey [2]Lit., *gleaned* ...it., *as far as* [4]Lit., ...note [a]Judg. 21:13

Chapter 21

21 Now the men of Israel [a]had sworn in Mizpah, saying, "None
of us shall give his daughter to Benjamin [1]in marriage."
2 [a]So the people came to Bethel and sat there before God until
evening, and lifted up their voices and wept [1]bitterly.
3 And they said, "Why, O LORD, God of Israel, has this come about
in Israel, so that one tribe should be *missing* today in Israel?"
4 And it came about the next day that the people arose early and
built [a]an altar there, and offered burnt offerings and peace offerings.
5 Then the sons of Israel said, "Who is there among all the tribes of
Israel who did not come up in the assembly to the LORD?" For [1]they
had taken a great oath concerning him [a]who did not come up to the
LORD at Mizpah, saying, "He shall surely be put to death."
6 And the sons of Israel were sorry for their brother Benjamin and
said, "One tribe is cut off from Israel today.
7 "What shall we do for wives for those who are left, since we have
[a]sworn by the LORD not to give them any of our daughters in
marriage?"
8 And they said, "What one is there of the tribes of Israel who did
not come up to the LORD at Mizpah?" And behold, no one had come
to the camp from Jabesh-gilead to the assembly.
9 For when the people were [1]numbered, behold, not one of the
inhabitants of Jabesh-gilead was there.
10 And the congregation sent 12,000 of the valiant warriors there,
and commanded them, saying, "Go and [a]strike the inhabitants of
Jabesh-gilead with the edge of the sword, with the women and the
little ones.
11 "And this is the thing that you shall do: you [a]shall utterly destroy
every man and every woman who has [1]lain with a man."
12 And they found among the inhabitants of Jabesh-gilead 400
young virgins who had not known a man by lying with [1]him; and
they brought them to the camp at Shiloh, which is in the land of
Canaan.
13 Then the whole congregation sent *word* and spoke to the sons of
Benjamin who were [a]at the rock of Rimmon, and [b]proclaimed peace
to them.
14 And Benjamin returned at that time, and they gave them the
women whom they had kept alive from the women of Jabesh-gilead;
yet they [1]were not enough for them.
15 And the people were sorry for Benjamin because the LORD had
made a breach in the tribes of Israel.
16 Then the elders of the congregation said, "What shall we do for
wives for those who are left, since the women are destroyed out of
Benjamin?"
17 And they said, "*There must be* an inheritance for the survivors of
Benjamin, that a tribe may not be blotted out from Israel.
18 "But we cannot give them wives of our daughters." For the sons
of Israel [a]had sworn, saying, "Cursed is he who gives a wife to
Benjamin."
19 So they said, "Behold, there is a feast of the LORD from year to
year in [a]Shiloh, which is on the north side of Bethel, on the east side
of the highway that goes up from Bethel to Shechem, and on the
south side of Lebonah."

21:1 [1]Lit., *for* [a]Judg. 21:7, 1
2 [1]Lit., *with gr* *weeping* [a]Jud
4 [a]Deut. 12:5; 24:25
5 [1]Lit., *there w* *great oath* [a]Ju
7 [a]Judg. 21:1
9 [1]Or, *mustere*
10 [a]Num. 31:17 5:23; 1 Sam. 11
11 [1]Lit., *known with* [a]Num. 31:1
12 [1]Lit., *a male*
13 [a]Judg. 20:47 20:10
14 [1]Lit., *did not f*
18 [a]Judg. 21:1
19 [a]Josh. 18:1; J 18:31; 1 Sam. 1:3

...it., *dance* [a]Ex. ...0; Judg. 11:34

20 And they commanded the sons of Benjamin, saying, "Go and lie
in wait in the vineyards,
21 and watch; and behold, if the daughters of Shiloh come out to
[1a]take part in the dances, then you shall come out of the vineyards
and each of you shall catch his wife from the daughters of Shiloh,
and go to the land of Benjamin.

[1]Lit., *his* [2]Lit., [a]Judg. 21:1, 18

22 "And it shall come about, when their fathers or their brothers
come to complain to us, that we shall say to them, 'Give them to us
voluntarily, because we did not take for each man *of Benjamin* [1]a wife
in battle, [2a]nor did you give *them* to them, *else* you would now be
guilty.' "
23 And the sons of Benjamin did so, and took wives according to
their number from those who danced, whom they carried away. And

3 [a]Judg. 20:48

they went and returned to their inheritance, and [a]rebuilt the cities
and lived in them.
24 And the sons of Israel departed from there at that time, every
man to his tribe and family, and each one of them went out from
there to his inheritance.

...dg. 17:6; 18:1; 19:1

25 [a]In those days there was no king in Israel; everyone did what
was right in his own eyes.

Judges of Israel

Judge	Chapter/ Verse	Years/ Judged	Major Facts/Accomplishments	Lessons for My Life

Judges at a Glance

e of Judges:

r Divisions

	Chapter Themes
	1
	2
	3
	4
	5
	6
	7
	8
	9
	10
	11
	12
	13
	14
	15
	16
	17
	18
	19
	20
	21

Author:

Date:

Purpose:

Key Words:

sons of Israel did evil

sold (served)

sons of Israel cried

the Lord raised up a deliverer (or judges)

judge(s)

RUTH

The book of Ruth is set chronologically in the midst of the dark years of the judges. It c encouragement and hope to those who decide to follow God. This story of love and dedic revolves around three people who determine in their hearts to walk in integrity, clinging to their and His precepts—three people who know who their King is and who do what is right in His eyes.

THINGS TO DO

1. As you read Ruth one chapter at a time:
   a. First read each chapter simply to catch the flavor of the lives of these people.
   b. Then read each chapter again, observing the events of that chapter. Examine what you re light of the five W's and an H, asking questions such as: Who are these people? What learn about them? What is happening to them? When is it happening and where? Why do do what they do? How will they accomplish their tasks? What will be the end result? Re pertinent insights in the margin.
   c. Watch for and mark the key repeated words listed on the RUTH AT A GLANCE chart on 406. After you finish marking key words in a chapter, observe what you learn about eac there's something significant you want to remember, write it in the margin.
2. Determine the theme of each chapter and record it on RUTH AT A GLANCE and on the line to the chapter number in the text.
3. When you finish reading Ruth and marking every reference to *redeem*, *kinsman*, and *close relati*
   a. List everything you learn about the process of redeeming a close relative. Pay attention tc process in chapter 4.
   b. Look up the laws regarding redemption in Leviticus 25:23-28 and Deuteronomy 25:5-10. may want to record these cross-references in the margin next to your insights on redemptic
4. Complete RUTH AT A GLANCE.

THINGS TO THINK ABOUT

1. What have you learned about loyalty from the story of Ruth? What does it mean to be loy God, to His people, to His precepts, and to trust God to do what He says He will do?
2. As you think of Boaz redeeming Ruth, remember you have a kinsman redeemer, the Lord J Christ. Think of how the Lord has acted on your behalf as your kinsman redeemer by becon human so He could break death's hold by paying for your sin (Hebrews 2:14-15). Remember were not redeemed from your empty way of life with silver or gold, but with the precious b of the Lamb of God, a lamb without spot or blemish (1 Peter 1:18-19).
3. The final verses of Ruth show us that Ruth was included in the genealogy of David, and there in the human lineage of our Lord Jesus Christ. Not only did a sovereign God include the ha Rahab, in the genealogy of His Son, He also chose a Gentile, Ruth. Both of these women chos believe God when those around them didn't! What about you?
4. In the book of Judges Israel forsook the true God and turned to idols while in Ruth the opposi seen. One Gentile woman turns from idols to serve the only true God. In which category do find yourself?

Chapter 1

1 Now it came about in the days [a]when the judges [1]governed, that
there was [b]a famine in the land. And a certain man [c]of Bethlehem
in Judah went to sojourn in the land of Moab [2]with his wife and his
two sons.
2 And the name of the man *was* Elimelech, and the name of his
wife, Naomi; and the names of his two sons *were* Mahlon and
Chilion, Ephrathites of Bethlehem in Judah. Now they [a]entered the
land of Moab and remained there.
3 Then Elimelech, Naomi's husband, died; and she was left with
her two sons.
4 And they took for themselves Moabite women *as* wives; the
name of the one was Orpah and the name of the other Ruth. And
they lived there about ten years.
5 Then [1]both Mahlon and Chilion also died; and the woman was
bereft of her two children and her husband.
6 Then she arose with her daughters-in-law that she might return
from the land of Moab, for she had heard in the land of Moab that
the LORD had [a]visited His people in [b]giving them food.
7 So she departed from the place where she was, and her two
daughters-in-law with her; and they went on the way to return to
the land of Judah.
8 And Naomi said to her two daughters-in-law, "Go, return each
of you to her mother's house. [a]May the LORD deal kindly with you as
you have dealt with the dead and with me.
9 "May the LORD grant that you may find rest, each in the house of
her husband." Then she kissed them, and they lifted up their voices
and wept.
10 And they said to her, "*No,* but we will surely return with you to
your people."
11 But Naomi said, "Return, my daughters. Why should you go
with me? Have I yet sons in my womb, that [a]they may be your
husbands?
12 "Return, my daughters! Go, for I am too old to have a husband. If
I said I have hope, if I should even have a husband tonight and also
bear sons,
13 would you therefore wait until they were grown?
Would you therefore refrain from marrying? No, my
daughters; for it is [1]harder for me than for you, for [a]the
hand of the LORD has gone forth against me."
14 And they lifted up their voices and wept again; and
Orpah kissed her mother-in-law, but Ruth clung to her.
15 Then she said, "Behold, your sister-in-law has gone
back to her people and her [a]gods; return after your sister-
in-law."
16 But Ruth said, "Do not urge me to leave you *or* turn
back from following you; for where you go, I will go, and
where you lodge, I will lodge. Your people *shall be* my
people, and your God, my God.
17 "Where you die, I will die, and there I will be buried.
Thus may [a]the LORD do to me, and worse, if *anything but*
death parts you and me."
18 When [a]she saw that she was determined to go with
her, she [1]said no more to her.

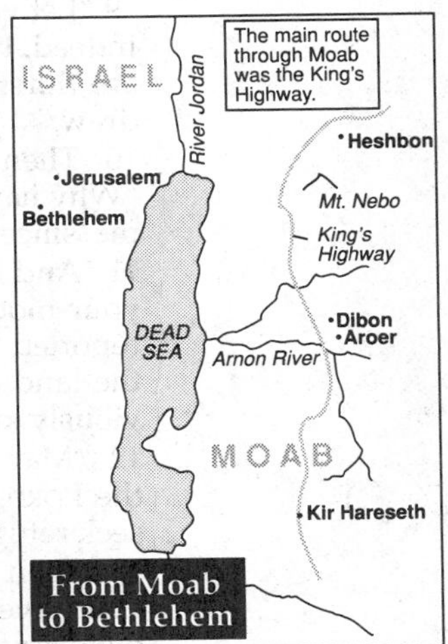

From Moab to Bethlehem

r, *judged* [2]Lit., [a]Judg. 2:16-18 ...0; 26:1; 2 Kin. ... 17:8; Mic. 5:2

2 [a]Judg. 3:30

...t., *both of them*

...4:31; Jer. 29:10; ...:7 [b]Ps. 132:15; Matt. 6:11

8 [a]2 Tim. 1:16

...en. 38:11; Deut. 25:5

[1]Lit., *more bitter* ...2:15; Job 19:21; Ps. 32:4

...osh. 24:15; Judg. 11:24

...Sam. 3:17; 2 Kin. 6:31

18 [1]Lit., *ceased to speak* [a]Acts 21:14

19 So they both went until they came to Bethlehem. And it came
about when they had come to Bethlehem, that [a]all the city was
stirred because of them, and [1]the women said, "Is this Naomi?"
20 And she said to them, "Do not call me [1]Naomi; call me [2]Mara,
for [3a]the Almighty has dealt very bitterly with me.
21 "I went out full, but [a]the LORD has brought me back empty. Why
do you call me Naomi, since the LORD has witnessed against me and
[1]the Almighty has afflicted me?"
22 So Naomi returned, and with her Ruth the Moabitess, her
daughter-in-law, who returned from the land of Moab. And they
came to Bethlehem at [a]the beginning of barley harvest.

Chapter 2

2 Now Naomi had [1]a kinsman of her husband, a [2]man of great
wealth, of the family of [a]Elimelech, whose name was Boaz.
2 And Ruth the Moabitess said to Naomi, "Please let me go to the
field and [a]glean among the ears of grain after one in whose sight I
may find favor." And she said to her, "Go, my daughter."
3 So she departed and went and gleaned in the field after the
reapers; and [1]she happened to come to the portion of the field
belonging to Boaz, who was of the family of Elimelech.
4 Now behold, Boaz came from Bethlehem and said to the reapers,
"[a]May the LORD be with you." And they said to him, "May the LORD
bless you."
5 Then Boaz said to his servant who was [1]in charge of the reapers,
"Whose young woman is this?"
6 And the servant [1]in charge of the reapers answered and said,
"She is the young Moabite woman who returned with Naomi from
the land of Moab.
7 "And she said, 'Please let me glean and gather after the reapers
among the sheaves.' Thus she came and has remained from the
morning until now; she has been sitting in the house for a little
while."
8 Then Boaz said to Ruth, "[1]Listen carefully, my daughter. Do not
go to glean in another field; furthermore, do not go on from this one,
but stay here with my maids.
9 "Let your eyes be on the field which they reap, and go after them.
Indeed, I have commanded the servants not to touch you. When you
are thirsty, go to the [1]water jars and drink from what the servants
draw."
10 Then she [a]fell on her face, bowing to the ground and said to him,
"Why have I found favor in your sight that you should take notice of
me, since I am a foreigner?"
11 And Boaz answered and said to her, "All that you have done for
your mother-in-law after the death of your husband has been fully
reported to me, and how you left your father and your mother and
the land of your birth, and came to a people that you did not pre-
viously know.
12 "[a]May the LORD reward your work, and your wages be full from
the LORD, the God of Israel, [b]under whose wings you have come to
seek refuge."
13 Then she said, "I have found favor in your sight, my lord, for
you have comforted me and indeed have spoken [1]kindly to your
maidservant, though I am not like one of your maidservants."

19 [1]Lit., *they* 21:10

20 [1]I.e., pleas bitter [3]Heb., S [a]Ex. 6:3; Job 6

21 [1]Heb., *Sha* [a]Job 1:21

22 [a]Ex. 9:31; L 23:10, 11

2:1 [1]Or, *an acquaintance mighty, valiant* [a]Ruth 1:2

2 [a]Lev. 19:9, 1 Deut. 24:19; Ru

3 [1]Lit., *her cha chanced upon*

4 [a]Judg. 6:12; 129:8; Luke 1:2 2 Thess. 3:16

5 [1]Lit., *appointe*

6 [1]Lit., *who was appointed over*

8 [1]Lit., *Have yo heard*

9 [1]Lit., *vessels*

10 [a]1 Sam. 25:2

12 [a]1 Sam. 24:1 [b]Ruth 1:16; Ps. 1 36:7; 57:1; 61:4; 91:4

13 [1]Lit., *to the he your*

Lit., *Draw near*
ld out to [a]Ruth 2:18
., *her* [2]Lit., *her*
ety [a]Ruth 2:14
19 [a]Ps. 41:1
[1]Lit., *near to us*
[2]Lit., *redeemers*
[a]2 Sam. 2:5
[1]Lit., *Also that*
23 [a]Deut. 16:9
3:1 [1]Lit., *rest*
Or, *acquaintance*
[a]Deut. 25:5-10
4 [1]Lit., *know*
.ph. 6:1; Col. 3:20
7 [a]Judg. 19:6, 9;
Sam. 13:28; 1 Kin. 21:7; Esth. 1:10
.it., *twisted himself*

14 And at mealtime Boaz said to her, "[1]Come here, that you may eat
of the bread and dip your piece of bread in the vinegar." So she sat
beside the reapers; and he [2]served her roasted grain, and she ate and
was satisfied [a]and had some left.
15 When she rose to glean, Boaz commanded his servants, saying,
"Let her glean even among the sheaves, and do not insult her.
16 "And also you shall purposely pull out for her *some grain* from the
bundles and leave *it* that she may glean, and do not rebuke her."
17 So she gleaned in the field until evening. Then she beat out what
she had gleaned, and it was about an ephah of barley.
18 And she took *it* up and went into the city, and her mother-in-law
saw what she had gleaned. She also took *it* out and [a]gave [1]Naomi
what she had left after [2]she was satisfied.
19 Her mother-in-law then said to her, "Where did you glean today
and where did you work? May he who [a]took notice of you be
blessed." So she told her mother-in-law with whom she had worked
and said, "The name of the man with whom I worked today is
Boaz."
20 And Naomi said to her daughter-in-law, "[a]May he be blessed of
the LORD who has not withdrawn his kindness to the living and to
the dead." Again Naomi said to her, "The man is [1]our relative, he is
one of our [2]closest relatives."
21 Then Ruth the Moabitess said, "[1]Furthermore, he said to me,
'You should stay close to my servants until they have finished all my
harvest.' "
22 And Naomi said to Ruth her daughter-in-law, "It is good, my
daughter, that you go out with his maids, lest *others* fall upon you in
another field."
23 So she stayed close by the maids of Boaz in order to glean until
[a]the end of the barley harvest and the wheat harvest. And she lived
with her mother-in-law.

Chapter 3

3 Then Naomi her mother-in-law said to her, "My daughter, shall I
not seek [1]security for you, that it may be well with you?
2 "And now is not Boaz [a]our [1]kinsman, with whose maids you
were? Behold, he winnows barley at the threshing floor tonight.
3 "Wash yourself therefore, and anoint yourself and put on your
best clothes, and go down to the threshing floor; *but* do not make
yourself known to the man until he has finished eating and
drinking.
4 "And it shall be when he lies down, that you shall [1]notice the
place where he lies, and you shall go and uncover his feet and lie
down; then he will tell you what you shall do."
5 And she said to her, "[a]All that you say I will do."
6 So she went down to the threshing floor and did according to all
that her mother-in-law had commanded her.
7 When Boaz had eaten and drunk and [a]his heart was merry, he
went to lie down at the end of the heap of grain; and she came
secretly, and uncovered his feet and lay down.
8 And it happened in the middle of the night that the man was
startled and [1]bent forward; and behold, a woman was lying at his
feet.
9 And he said, "Who are you?" And she answered, "I am Ruth

your maid. So spread your covering over your maid, for you are a
[1]close relative."
10 Then he said, "[a]May you be blessed of the LORD, my daughter.
You have shown your last kindness to be better than the first by not
going after young men, whether poor or rich.
11 "And now, my daughter, do not fear. I will do for you whatever
you [1]ask, for all my people in the [2]city know that you are [a]a woman
of excellence.
12 "And now it is true I am a [1]close relative; however, there is a
[1]relative closer than I.
13 "Remain this night, and when morning comes, [a]if he will [1]redeem
you, good; let him redeem you. But if he does not wish to [1]redeem
you, then I will redeem you, [b]as the LORD lives. Lie down until morn-
ing."
14 So she lay at his feet until morning and rose before one could
recognize another; and he said, "[a]Let it not be known that the
woman came to the threshing floor."
15 Again he said, "Give me the cloak that is on you and hold it." So
she held it, and he measured six *measures* of barley and laid *it* on her.
Then [1]she went into the city.
16 And when she came to her mother-in-law, she said, "[1]How did it
go, my daughter?" And she told her all that the man had done for
her.
17 And she said, "These six *measures* of barley he gave to me, for he
said, 'Do not go to your mother-in-law empty-handed.' "
18 Then she said, "Wait, my daughter, until you know how the
matter [1]turns out; for the man will not rest until he has [2]settled it
today."

Chapter 4

4 Now Boaz went up to the gate and sat down there, and behold,
[a]the [1]close relative of whom Boaz spoke was passing by, so he
said, "Turn aside, [2]friend, sit down here." And he turned aside and
sat down.
2 And he took ten men of the [a]elders of the city and said, "Sit
down here." So they sat down.
3 Then he said to the [1]closest relative, "Naomi, who has come back
from the land of Moab, has to sell the piece of land [a]which belonged
to our brother Elimelech.
4 "So I thought to [1]inform you, saying, '[a]Buy *it* before those who are
sitting *here,* and before the elders of my people. If you will redeem *it,*
redeem *it;* but if [2]not, tell me that I may know; for [b]there is no one
but you to redeem *it,* and I am after you.' " And he said, "I will
redeem *it.*"
5 Then Boaz said, "On the day you buy the field from the hand of
Naomi, you must also acquire Ruth the Moabitess, the widow of the
deceased, in order [a]to raise up the name of the deceased on his
inheritance."
6 And [a]the [1]closest relative said, "I cannot redeem *it* for myself, lest
I [2]jeopardize my own inheritance. Redeem *it* for yourself; you *may
have* my right of redemption, for I cannot redeem *it.*"
7 Now this was [a]*the custom* in former times in Israel concerning the
redemption and the exchange *of land* to confirm any matter: a man

9 [1]Or, *redeem*
10 [a]Ruth 2:20
11 [1]Lit., *say* [2]L
[a]Prov. 12:4; 31
12 [1]Or, *redeem*
13 [1]Or, *act as c*
relative to [a]Deu
Matt. 22:24 [b]Ju
Jer. 4:2; 12:16
14 [a]Rom. 14:16
8:21
15 [1]So with mar
M.T., *he*
16 [1]Lit., *Who ar*
18 [1]Lit., *falls* [2]L
finished the matt
4:1 [1]Or, *redeem*
a certain one [a]R
2 [a]1 Kin. 21:8; P
31:23
3 [1]Lit., *redeemer*
25:25
4 [1]Lit., *uncover y*
ear [2]Lit., *no one*
redeem [a]Jer. 32:
[b]Lev. 25:25
5 [a]Gen. 38:8; De
25:5f.; Matt. 22:24
6 [1]Lit., *redeemer*
ruin [a]Lev. 25:25
7 [a]Deut. 25:8-10

8 [1]Lit., *redeemer*

[1]Lit., *gate* [a]Deut. 25:6

11 [1]Lit., *gate* [2]Or, ower [3]Lit., *call the* in [a]Gen. 29:25-30

[1]Lit., *seed* [a]Gen. 9; 46:12; Ruth 4:18

13 [1]Lit., *gave her conception* [a]Gen. 29:31; 33:5

Or, *closest relative be called in* [a]Luke 1:58

5 [1]Lit., *who* [a]Ruth 1:16, 17; 2:11, 12

6 [1]I.e., as her own

Lit., *begot*, and so rough v. 22 [a]Matt. 1:3-6

removed his sandal and gave it to another; and this was the *manner*
of attestation in Israel.
8 So the [1]closest relative said to Boaz, "Buy *it* for yourself." And he
removed his sandal.
9 Then Boaz said to the elders and all the people, "You are wit-
nesses today that I have bought from the hand of Naomi all that
belonged to Elimelech and all that belonged to Chilion and Mahlon.
10 "Moreover, I have acquired Ruth the Moabitess, the widow of
Mahlon, to be my wife in order to raise up the name of the deceased
on his inheritance, so [a]that the name of the deceased may not be cut
off from his brothers or from the [1]court of his *birth* place; you are
witnesses today."
11 And all the people who were in the [1]court, and the elders, said,
"*We are* witnesses. May the LORD make the woman who is coming
into your home [a]like Rachel and Leah, both of whom built the house
of Israel; and may you achieve [2]wealth in Ephrathah and [3]become
famous in Bethlehem.
12 "Moreover, may your house be like the house of [a]Perez whom
Tamar bore to Judah, through the [1]offspring which the LORD shall
give you by this young woman."
13 So Boaz took Ruth, and she became his wife, and he went in to
her. And [a]the LORD [1]enabled her to conceive, and she gave birth to a
son.
14 Then the [a]women said to Naomi, "Blessed is the LORD who has
not left you without a [1]redeemer today, and may his name [2]become
famous in Israel.
15 "May he also be to you a restorer of life and a sustainer of your
old age; for your daughter-in-law, who loves you [1a]and is better to
you than seven sons, has given birth to him."
16 Then Naomi took the child [1]and laid him in her lap, and became
his nurse.
17 And the neighbor women gave him a name, saying, "A son has
been born to Naomi!" So they named him Obed. He is the father of
Jesse, the father of David.
18 Now these are the generations of Perez: [a]to Perez [1]was born
Hezron,
19 and to Hezron was born Ram, and to Ram, Amminadab,
20 and to Amminadab was born Nahshon, and to Nahshon,
Salmon,
21 and to Salmon was born Boaz, and to Boaz, Obed,
22 and to Obed was born Jesse, and to Jesse, David.

The Genealogy of Boaz

Abram+Sarai
(Abraham + Sarah)
↓
Isaac + Rebekah
↓
Jacob + Leah
↓
Judah + Tamar
↓
Perez
↓
Hezron
↓
Jerahmeel
↓
Ram
↓
Amminadab
↓
Nahshon
↓
Salmon + **Rahab** (the harlot)
↓
Boaz + Ruth (the Gentile)
↓
Obed
↓
Jesse
↓
David
"from whom came Mary the mother of Jesus"

See **The Genealogy of Jesus Christ** on page 1874.

RUTH AT A GLANCE

Theme of Ruth:

Author:

Date:

Purpose:

Key Words:

- redeem (redemption)
- relative (closest relative, kinsman)
- Naomi
- Ruth
- Boaz

SEGMENT DIVISIONS		CHAPTER THEMES
		1
		2
		3
		4

SAMUEL

e days of the judges were dark until God raised up Samuel as a prophet, priest, and judge. el would do what was right in God's eyes. But the people weren't satisfied. They cried, "Now nt a king for us to judge us like all the nations." With that plea they rejected the Lord as their What would it be like to live under a monarchy rather than a theocracy? The children of Israel soon to find out as the times of the kings began.

e books of 1 and 2 Samuel, 1 and 2 Kings, and 1 and 2 Chronicles record the days of the kings of The kingdom, at first united, was divided because of the disobedience of the kings. Children of who have been made "to be a kingdom, priests" and who "will reign upon the earth" (Revelation 10) can learn many valuable lessons from these books. The lessons begin in 1 Samuel as God s Saul and chooses as king a man after His own heart. And what will such a man be like? Will he perfect life? Is this what will make him a man after God's own heart—or are there other reasons?

IGS TO DO

ral Instructions

you study this book never forget that these are people, frail but not without access to God, nor to recepts and statutes of life. Observe the text prayerfully and carefully and as you study, note in argin God's lessons for life. You might want to give them the heading "LFL" (Lessons for Life) olor it in a distinctive way so you can recognize it immediately.

ters 1-7: Samuel, the Last Judge

As you observe these first seven chapters, mark the following words in a distinctive way and then note in the margin what you learn from observing each word in its context:

a. Mark: *ark (of the Lord, of God, of the covenant), ephod, judge (judged), king, Ichabod*, and *Ebenezer*. The last three words are only used one time in these chapters but are significant. *Ephod* is used only twice in this segment but will have greater significance in the last segment of 1 Samuel. List these key words on an index card you can use as a bookmark for this segment.

b. Mark all geographical references on the map on page 457. This will help you gain perspective of events and familiarity with biblical locations.

Since 1 Samuel is a historical account, note the focus of each chapter. Who and/or what event does the chapter center on?

a. In the margin list your insights about the main characters in each chapter. You might note who they are. For example, Elkanah's two wives:
   1) Hannah (childless)
   2) Peninnah (had sons/daughters)

b. Especially observe the lives of Hannah, Samuel, and Eli and list what you learn.

c. In the margin list any progression of events which occur. For example in chapter 1 Hannah:
   1) Weeps because barren
   2) Asks for son/makes vow to God
   3) Is confronted by Eli
   4) Conceives
   5) Keeps vow to God

d. Note in the margin your insights about God and His ways. For instance, in chapter 1 God closes the womb and opens the womb.

. Record the theme of each chapter on the 1 SAMUEL AT A GLANCE chart on page 456 and in the text next to the chapter number.

Chapters 8-15: From Samuel to Saul, from Judge to King

1. As you observe this segment of 1 Samuel:
   a. Mark the following key words: *judge (judges), king* (don't include foreign kings), *sin sinned), evil, Spirit of God (of the Lord), ark of God,* and *ephod*. Put them on an index card to a bookmark.
   b. In the margin list what you learn about Samuel, Saul, King Agag, and the Amalekites.
   c. Note all you learn about God and His ways.
   d. Mark any reference to time, i.e. when Saul begins his reign, etc. Mark these with a time such as .
   e. There are no references to the ark in 1 Samuel after this segment. Review what you le about the ark in this book and note in the margin where it is last mentioned and its loc (Read "The Ark of the Covenant" in the introduction of this Bible on page I-55.)
2. Carefully observe all you learn from marking the word *king*. Watch for the following and r your insights in the margin:
   a. Why the people wanted a king, how they perceived the kingship, and what kind of king wanted.
   b. How God responded to the people's request, what God desired in a kingship, and how success or failure of a king was determined.
3. Examine each chapter as you did in the previous segment, watching for and recording the event of each chapter and any pertinent subpoints. Don't forget to record the chapter then 1 SAMUEL AT A GLANCE and in the text.

Chapters 16-31: The Preparation of Another King

1. In this segment:
   a. Make a new bookmark and mark the following key words: *king* (not foreign kings), *evil spirit, sin (sinned), judge, covenant, inquire (inquired),* and *ephod*. Don't forget to record what are learning from marking *king* and *ephod*.
   b. Mark all references to time and to geographical locations as before.
2. Observe and record in the margin of each chapter what you learn about Samuel, Saul, and Da Give special attention to all that happens to David and how he responds to God and to Watch for and note in the margin the "LFL" (Lessons for Life).
3. In the margin write "Covenant" and list what you've observed from the text. Ask the five and an H: Who makes the covenant? How is it made? What is done? What is promised? Wha the conditions? When is it made? Where is it made? Why? Remember you are in covenant God if you are a child of God (Matthew 26:26-29); watch for any principles which might app you. (See the "Insight" on covenant at Genesis 15.)
4. As you read each chapter watch for insights on God, note the events of each chapter and subpoints of the chapter, and record the chapter themes.
5. Complete 1 SAMUEL AT A GLANCE. Watch for any additional segment divisions in 1 San Look at the chapter themes and see if there is any other way 1 Samuel might be segmented: any chapters be grouped in respect to David's relationship to Saul, to Jonathan, to the Philisti or others? Or is there any geographical segmentation, such as where Samuel, Saul, and Da spend their time?
6. Record the theme of 1 Samuel on 1 SAMUEL AT A GLANCE.

THINGS TO THINK ABOUT

1. What lessons did you learn from Eli's dealing with his sons? Do you see your accountab before God to discipline your children?
2. What do you learn from Samuel, Saul, and David's lives regarding seeking God, listening to H and obeying Him? Are there consequences when you don't?

Did you notice that much time has elapsed since the time David was anointed to be king? Still, as 1 Samuel comes to a close, David is not king over Israel. Think about all that transpired since Samuel anointed David. What can you learn from this about God's promises, His purpose, and His timing? Are you waiting patiently on God for the fulfillment of His promise to you?

Review the "Lessons for Life" you observed and the insights you recorded about God in the margins of 1 Samuel. Make these a matter of prayer.

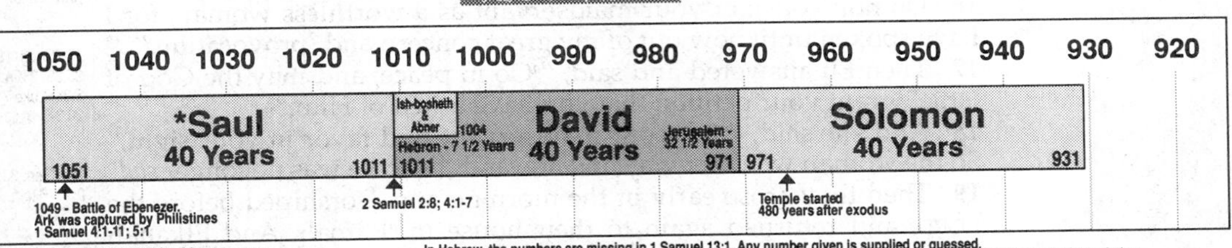

13:1 says that Saul was king for thirty-two years.
ays that Saul was king for forty years.
umbers from 1-19 are singular and numbers 20 and above are plural.
the number is plural, so we know it is 20+ years.

In Hebrew, the numbers are missing in 1 Samuel 13:1. Any number given is supplied or guessed.
The first word of 1 Samuel 13:2 is a connector word. It can be used in ten different ways. "And" would be a good translation.
In any case, that connector word tells us Saul was in his thirty-second year when what follows happened.

Chapter 1

1 Now there was a certain man from [a]Ramathaim-zophim from
the [b]hill country of Ephraim, and his name was [c]Elkanah the son
of Jeroham, the son of Elihu, the son of Tohu, the son of Zuph, an
Ephraimite.
2 And he had [a]two wives: the name of one was [b]Hannah and the
name of the other Peninnah; and Peninnah had children, but Han-
nah had no children.
3 Now this man would go up from his city [a]yearly [b]to worship and
to sacrifice to the LORD of hosts in [c]Shiloh. And the two sons of Eli,
Hophni and Phinehas were priests to the LORD there.
4 And when the day came that Elkanah sacrificed, he [a]would give
portions to Peninnah his wife and to all her sons and her daughters;
5 but to Hannah he would give a double portion, for he loved
Hannah, [a]but the LORD had closed her womb.
6 Her rival, however, [a]would provoke her bitterly to irritate her,
because the LORD had closed her womb.
7 And it happened year after year, as often as she went up to the
house of the LORD, she would provoke her, so she wept and would
not eat.
8 Then Elkanah her husband said to her, "Hannah, why do you
weep and why do you not eat and why is your heart sad? [a]Am I not
better to you than ten sons?"
9 Then Hannah rose after eating and drinking in Shiloh. Now Eli
the priest was sitting on the seat by the doorpost of [a]the temple of
the LORD.
10 And she, [1]greatly distressed, prayed to the LORD and wept bit-
terly.
11 And she [a]made a vow and said, "O LORD of hosts, if Thou wilt
indeed [b]look on the affliction of Thy maidservant and remember me,
and not forget Thy maidservant, but wilt give Thy maidservant a
[1]son, then I will give him to the LORD all the days of his life, and [c]a
razor shall never come on his head."
12 Now it came about, as she [1]continued praying before the LORD,
that Eli was watching her mouth.

[a]1 Sam. 1:19 7:17, 18; 24:33 6:22-28, 33-38
[a]Deut. 21:15-17 [b]Luke 2:36
. 34:23; 1 Sam. Luke 2:41 [b]Ex. 4; Deut. 12:5-7; :16 [c]Josh. 18:1
[a]Deut. 12:17, 18
[a]Gen. 16:1; 30:1
6 [a]Job 24:21
8 [a]Ruth 4:15
9 [a]1 Sam. 3:3
[1]Lit., *bitter of soul*
[1]Lit., *seed of men* m. 30:6-11 [b]Gen. [c]Num. 6:5; Judg. 13:5
12 [1]Lit., *multiplied*

INSIGHT

A **Nazarite** (which means "consecration, devotion, and separation") was someone who was bound by a vow of consecration to God's service for either a specific period of time or for life. A Nazarite's devotion to God was evidenced outwardly by not cutting the hair, abstaining from wine and alcoholic drinks, and avoiding contact with the dead. Violation of these brought defilement and need of purification.

13 As for Hannah, [a]she was speaking in her heart, only her lips
were moving, but her voice was not heard. So Eli thought she was
drunk.
14 Then Eli said to her, "[a]How long will you make yourself drunk?
Put away your wine from you."
15 But Hannah answered and said, "No, my lord, I am a woman
[1]oppressed in spirit; I have drunk neither wine nor strong drink, but
I [a]have poured out my soul before the LORD.
16 "Do not [1]consider your maidservant as a worthless woman; for I
have spoken until now out of my great concern and [2]provocation."
17 Then Eli answered and said, "[a]Go in peace; and may the God of
Israel [b]grant your petition that you have asked of Him."
18 And she said, "[a]Let your maidservant find favor in your sight."
So the woman went her way and ate, and [b]her face was no longer *sad*.
19 Then they arose early in the morning and worshiped before the
LORD, and returned again to their house in [a]Ramah. And Elkanah
[1]had relations with Hannah his wife, and [b]the LORD remembered her.
20 And it came about [1]in due time, after Hannah had conceived,
that she gave birth to a son; and she named him Samuel, *saying*,
"[a]Because I have asked him of the LORD."
21 Then the man Elkanah [a]went up with all his household to offer
to the LORD the yearly sacrifice and *pay* his vow.
22 But Hannah did not go up, for she said to her husband, "*I will
not go up* until the child is weaned; then I will [a]bring him, that he
may appear before the LORD and [b]stay there forever."
23 And [a]Elkanah her husband said to her, "Do what seems best [1]to
you. Remain until you have weaned him; only [b]may the LORD con-
firm His word." So the woman remained and nursed her son until
she weaned him.
24 Now when she had weaned him, [a]she took him up with her,
with a three-year-old bull and one ephah of flour and a jug of wine,
and brought him to [b]the house of the LORD in Shiloh, although the
child was young.
25 Then [a]they slaughtered the bull, and [b]brought the boy to Eli.
26 And she said, "Oh, my lord! [a]As your soul lives, my lord, I am
the woman who stood here beside you, praying to the LORD.
27 "[a]For this boy I prayed, and the LORD has given me my petition
which I asked of Him.
28 "[a]So I have also [1]dedicated him to the LORD; as long as he lives he
is [1]dedicated to the LORD." And [b]he worshiped the LORD there.

Chapter 2

2 Then Hannah [a]prayed and said,
"My heart exults in the LORD;
[b]My [1]horn is exalted in the LORD,
My mouth [2]speaks boldly against my enemies,
Because [c]I rejoice in Thy salvation.
2 "[a]There is no one holy like the LORD,
Indeed, [b]there is no one besides Thee,
[c]Nor is there any rock like our God.
3 "[1]Boast no more so very proudly,
[a]Do not let arrogance come out of your mouth;
[b]For the LORD is a God of knowledge,
[c]And with Him actions are weighed.

13 [a]Gen. 24:4

14 [a]Acts 2:4,

15 [1]Lit., *sever* 30:16; Ps. 42:4 Lam. 2:19

16 [1]Lit., *give provocation*

17 [a]Judg. 18:6 25:35; 2 Kin. 5: 5:34; Luke 7:50 20:3-5

18 [a]Gen. 33:15 2:13 [b]Rom. 15

19 [1]Lit., *knew* 1:1; 2:11 [b]Gen. 30:22

20 [1]Lit., *at the the days* [a]Gen. 52; Ex. 2:10, 22 1:21

21 [a]Deut. 12:11 1:3

22 [a]Luke 2:22 1:11, 28

23 [1]Lit., *in your* [a]Num. 30:7, 10, [b]1 Sam. 1:17

24 [a]Num. 15:9, Deut. 12:5, 6 [b]Jo 18:1; 1 Sam. 4:3,

25 [a]Lev. 1:5 [b]Lu

26 [a]2 Kin. 2:2, 4,

27 [a]1 Sam. 1:11- 6:9; 66:19, 20

28 [1]Lit., *lent* [a]1 S 1:11, 22 [b]Gen. 24

2:1 [1]I.e., strength *is enlarged* [a]1 Sa 2:1-10; Luke 1:46 [b]Deut. 33:17; Job Ps. 75:10; 89:17, 92:10; 112:9 [c]Ps. 13:5; 35:9; Is. 12:2

2 [a]Ex. 15:11; Lev. Ps. 86:8 [b]2 Sam. [c]Deut. 32:30, 31

3 [1]Lit., *Talk much* [a]Prov. 8:13 [b]1 Sar 16:7; 1 Kin. 8:39 [c] 16:2; 24:12

5; 46:9 [b]Ps.
Heb. 11:32-34
15; Ps. 113:9
[b]Jer. 15:9
nether world
39; 2 Kin. 5:7;
18 [b]Is. 26:19
8:17, 18 [b]Job
. 75:7; James
4:10
42:10-12; Ps.
13:7 [b]2 Sam.
. 2:48; James
[c]Job 36:7; Ps.
ob 38:4-6; Ps.
75:3; 104:5
:11, 12; 121:3;
:26; 1 Pet. 1:5
Matt. 8:12 [c]Ps.
33:16, 17
, strength [a]Ex.
s. 2:9 [b]1 Sam.
am. 22:14; Ps.
14 [c]Ps. 96:13;
Matt. 25:31, 32
1, 7 [e]Ps. 89:24
[a]1 Sam. 1:1, 19
1:28; 2:18; 3:1
., sons of Belial
8; 9:3, 6; 2 Cor.
6:15
3 [a]Lev. 7:29-34
[a]Lev. 3:3-5, 16
[1]Lit., offer up in
oke [2]Lit., like the
y [3]Lit., your soul
17 [a]Mal. 2:7-9
[1]Lit., girded with
[a]1 Sam. 2:11; 3:1
Sam. 2:28; 22:18;
Sam. 6:14; 1 Chr.
15:27
x. 28:31 [b]1 Sam.
1:3, 21
it., seed [2]Lit., the
e asked for which
as lent [3]Lit., place
uke 2:34 [b]1 Sam.
1:11, 27, 28
Gen. 21:1 [b]Judg.
3:24; 1 Sam. 2:26;
1; Luke 1:80; 2:40

4 "[a]The bows of the mighty are shattered,
[b]But the feeble gird on strength.
5 "Those who were full hire themselves out for bread,
But those who were hungry cease *to hunger.*
[a]Even the barren gives birth to seven,
But [b]she who has many children languishes.
6 "[a]The LORD kills and makes alive;
[b]He brings down to [1]Sheol and raises up.
7 "[a]The LORD makes poor and rich;
[b]He brings low, He also exalts.
8 "[a]He raises the poor from the dust,
[b]He lifts the needy from the ash heap
[c]To make them sit with nobles,
And inherit a seat of honor;
[d]For the pillars of the earth are the LORD's,
And He set the world on them.
9 "[a]He keeps the feet of His godly ones,
[b]But the wicked ones are silenced in darkness;
[c]For not by might shall a man prevail.
10 "[a]Those who contend with the LORD will be shattered;
[b]Against them He will thunder in the heavens,
[c]The LORD will judge the ends of the earth;
[d]And He will give strength to His king,
[e]And will exalt the [1]horn of His anointed."

11 Then Elkanah went to his home at [a]Ramah. [b]But the boy minis-
tered to the LORD before Eli the priest.
12 Now the sons of Eli were [1a]worthless men; they did not know the
LORD
13 [a]and the custom of the priests with the people. When any man
was offering a sacrifice, the priest's servant would come while the
meat was boiling, with a three-pronged fork in his hand.
14 Then he would thrust it into the pan, or kettle, or caldron, or pot;
all that the fork brought up the priest would take for himself. Thus
they did in Shiloh to all the Israelites who came there.
15 Also, before [a]they burned the fat, the priest's servant would
come and say to the man who was sacrificing, "Give the priest meat
for roasting, as he will not take boiled meat from you, only raw."
16 And if the man said to him, "They must surely [1]burn the fat
[2]first, and then take as much as [3]you desire," then he would say,
"No, but you shall give *it to me* now; and if not, I will take it by
force."
17 Thus the sin of the young men was very great before the LORD,
for the men [a]despised the offering of the LORD.
18 Now [a]Samuel was ministering before the LORD, *as* a boy [1b]wear-
ing a linen ephod.
19 And his mother would make him a little [a]robe and bring it to
him from year to year when she would come up with her husband
to offer [b]the yearly sacrifice.
20 Then Eli would [a]bless Elkanah and his wife and say, "May the
LORD give you [1]children from this woman in place of [2]the one she
[b]dedicated to the LORD." And they went to their own [3]home.
21 And [a]the LORD visited Hannah; and she conceived and gave
birth to three sons and two daughters. And [b]the boy Samuel grew
before the LORD.

The **ephod** was used to seek guidance from God. Described in Exodus 28, it is a linen garment worn by the priest and also by David when he was king (2 Samuel 6:14). The ephod was fastened on each shoulder by onyx clasps which had the name of six tribes engraved on one clasp, and six tribes engraved on the other. The **breastplate,** which was fastened to the ephod, had a linen pouch which held the **Urim** and **Thummim,** which may have been used as sacred lots to reveal God's will (1 Samuel 28:6).

22 Now Eli was very old; and he heard [a]all that his sons were doing
to all Israel, and how they lay with [b]the women who served at the
doorway of the tent of meeting.
23 And he said to them, "Why do you do such things, the evil
things that I hear from all these people?
24 "No, my sons; for the report is not good [a]which I hear [1]the LORD's
people circulating.
25 "If one man sins against another, [a]God will mediate for him; but
[b]if a man sins against the LORD, who can intercede for him?" But they
would not listen to the voice of their father, for the [c]LORD desired to
put them to death.
26 Now the boy [a]Samuel [1]was growing in stature and in favor both
with the LORD and with men.
27 Then [a]a man of God came to Eli and said to him, "Thus says the
LORD, '[b]Did I *not* indeed reveal Myself to the house of your father
when they were in Egypt *in bondage* to Pharaoh's house?
28 'And [a]did I *not* choose them from all the tribes of Israel to be My
priests, to go up to My altar, to burn incense, to carry an ephod
before Me; and did I *not* [b]give to the house of your father all the fire
offerings of the sons of Israel?
29 'Why do you [a]kick at My sacrifice and at My offering [b]which I
have commanded *in My* [c]dwelling, and [d]honor your sons above Me,
by making yourselves fat with the [1]choicest of every offering of My
people Israel?'
30 "Therefore the LORD God of Israel declares, '[a]I did indeed say that
your house and the house of your father should walk before Me
forever'; but now the LORD declares, 'Far be it from Me—for [b]those
who honor Me I will honor, and those [c]who despise Me will be
lightly esteemed.
31 'Behold, [a]the days are coming when I will break your [1]strength
and the [1]strength of your father's house so that there will not be an
old man in your house.
32 'And you will see [a]the distress of *My* dwelling, in *spite of* all that
[1]I do good for Israel; and an [b]old man will not be in your house
forever.
33 'Yet I will not cut off every man of yours from My altar [1]that your
eyes may fail *from weeping* and your soul grieve, and all the increase
of your house will die [2]in the prime of life.
34 'And this will be [a]the sign to you which shall come concerning
your two sons, Hophni and Phinehas: [b]on the same day both of them
shall die.
35 'But [a]I will raise up for Myself a faithful priest who will do ac-
cording to what is in My heart and in My soul; and [b]I will build him
an enduring house, and he will walk before [c]My anointed always.
36 'And it shall come about that everyone who is left in your house
shall come and bow down to him for a [1]piece of silver or a loaf of
bread, and say, "Please [2]assign me to one of the priest's offices so
that I may eat a piece of bread." ' "

Chapter 3

3 Now [a]the boy Samuel was ministering to the LORD before Eli.
And [b]word from the LORD was rare in those days, [1]visions were
infrequent.
2 And it happened at that time as Eli was lying down in his place

22 [a]1 Sam. 2: [b]Ex. 38:8
24 [1]Or, *makin LORD's people transgress* [a]1
25 [a]Deut. 1:17 15:30; 1 Sam. Heb. 10:26, 27 11:20
26 [1]Lit., *was g both great and* [a]1 Sam. 2:21; L
27 [a]Deut. 33:1 13:6 [b]Ex. 4:14- 12:1, 43
28 [a]Ex. 28:1-4; Lev. 8:7, 8 [b]Lev 7:35, 36
29 [1]Or, *first* [a]1 2:13-17 [b]Deut. [c]Ps. 26:8 [d]Matt
30 [a]Ex. 29:9; N 25:13 [b]Ps. 50:2 2:9
31 [1]Or, *arm* [a]1 4:11-18; 22:17-2
32 [1]Lit., *He doe* [a]1 Kin. 2:26, 27 8:4
33 [1]Lit., *to waste your eyes and to your soul* [2]Lit., *a*
34 [a]1 Sam. 10:7 1 Kin. 13:3 [b]1 Sa 4:11, 17
35 [a]1 Sam. 3:1; 9:12, 13 [b]1 Sam. 25:28; 2 Sam. 7:1 1 Kin. 11:38 [c]1 S 10:9, 10; 12:3; 16
36 [1]Or, *payment attach*
3:1 [1]Lit., *no visio spread abroad* [a]1 2:11, 18 [b]Ps. 74:9 Ezek. 7:26; Amos 8:11, 12

(now [a]his eyesight had begun to grow dim *and* he could not see
well),
3 and [a]the lamp of God had not yet gone out, and Samuel was
lying down in the temple of the LORD where the ark of God *was*,
4 that the LORD called Samuel; and he said, "[a]Here I am."
5 Then he ran to Eli and said, "Here I am, for you called me." But
he said, "I did not call, lie down again." So he went and lay down.
6 And the LORD called yet again, "Samuel!" So Samuel arose and
went to Eli, and said, "Here I am, for you called me." But he
[1]answered, "I did not call, my son, lie down again."
7 [a]Now Samuel did not yet know the LORD, nor had the word of
the LORD yet been revealed to him.
8 So the LORD called Samuel again for the third time. And he arose
and went to Eli, and said, "Here I am, for you called me." Then Eli
discerned that the LORD was calling the boy.
9 And Eli said to Samuel, "Go lie down, and it shall be if He calls
you, that you shall say, 'Speak, LORD, for Thy servant is listening.' "
So Samuel went and lay down in his place.
10 Then the LORD came and stood and called as at other times,
"Samuel! Samuel!" And Samuel said, "Speak, for Thy servant is lis-
tening."
11 And the LORD said to Samuel, "Behold, [a]I am about to do a thing
in Israel at which both ears of everyone who hears it will tingle.
12 "In that day [a]I will carry out against Eli all that I have spoken
concerning his house, from beginning to end.
13 "For [a]I have told him that I am about to judge his house forever
for [b]the iniquity which he knew, because [c]his sons brought a curse on
themselves and [d]he did not rebuke them.
14 "And therefore I have sworn to the house of Eli that [a]the iniquity
of Eli's house shall not be atoned for by sacrifice or offering forever."
15 So Samuel lay down until morning. Then he [a]opened the doors
of the house of the LORD. But Samuel was afraid to tell [b]the vision to
Eli.
16 Then Eli called Samuel and said, "Samuel, my son." And he said,
"Here I am."
17 And he said, "What is the word that He spoke to you? Please do
not hide it from me. [a]May God do so to you, and more also, if you
hide anything from me of all the words that He spoke to you."
18 So Samuel told him everything and hid nothing from him. And
he said, "[a]It is the LORD; let Him do what seems good to Him."
19 Thus [a]Samuel grew and [b]the LORD was with him and [c]let none of
his words [1]fail.
20 And all Israel [a]from Dan even to Beersheba knew that Samuel
was confirmed as a prophet of the LORD.
21 And [a]the LORD appeared again at Shiloh, [b]because the LORD re-
vealed Himself to Samuel at Shiloh by the word of the LORD.

Chapter 4

4 Thus the word of Samuel came to all Israel. Now Israel went out
to meet the Philistines in battle and camped beside [a]Ebenezer
while the Philistines camped in [b]Aphek.
2 And the Philistines drew up in battle array to meet Israel. When
the battle spread, Israel was [1]defeated before the Philistines who
killed about four thousand men on the battlefield.

ɜen. 27:1; 48:10; 1 Sam. 4:15
x. 25:31-37; Lev. 24:2, 3
4 [a]Is. 6:8
6 [1]Lit., *said*
[a]Acts 19:2; 1 Cor. 13:11
[a]2 Kin. 21:12; Jer. 19:3
[a]1 Sam. 2:27-36
[a]1 Sam. 2:29-31 am. 2:22 [c]1 Sam. 12, 17, 22 [d]Deut. 17:12; 21:18
/. 15:31; Is. 22:14
15 [a]1 Chr. 15:23 [b]1 Sam. 3:10
17 [a]2 Sam. 3:35
[a]Ex. 34:5-7; Lev. Job 2:10; Is. 39:8
19 [1]Lit., *fall to the* und [a]1 Sam. 2:21 ɜen. 21:22; 28:15; 39:2 [c]1 Sam. 9:6
20 [a]Judg. 20:1
ɜen. 12:7 [b]1 Sam. 3:10
4:1 [a]1 Sam. 7:12 ısh. 12:18; 1 Sam. 29:1
2 [1]Lit., *smitten*

3 When the people came into the camp, the elders of Israel said,
"[a]Why has the LORD defeated us today before the Philistines? [b]Let us
take to ourselves from Shiloh the ark of the covenant of the LORD,
that [1]it may come among us and deliver us from the power of our
enemies."
4 So the people sent to Shiloh, and from there they carried the ark
of the covenant of the LORD of hosts [a]who sits *above* the cherubim;
and the two sons of Eli, Hophni and Phinehas, *were* there with the
ark of the covenant of God.
5 And it happened as the ark of the covenant of the LORD came
into the camp, that [a]all Israel shouted with a great shout, so that the
earth resounded.
6 And when the Philistines heard the noise of the shout, they said,
"What *does* the noise of this great shout in the camp of the Hebrews
mean?" Then they understood that the ark of the LORD had come into
the camp.
7 And the Philistines were afraid, for they said, "God has come
into the camp." And they said, "[a]Woe to us! For nothing like this has
happened before.
8 "Woe to us! Who shall deliver us from the hand of these mighty
gods? These are the gods who smote the Egyptians with all *kinds of*
plagues in the wilderness.
9 "[a]Take courage and be men, O Philistines, lest you become slaves
to the Hebrews, [b]as they have been slaves to you; therefore, be men
and fight."
10 So the Philistines fought and [a]Israel was [1]defeated, and [b]every
man fled to his tent, and the slaughter was very great; for there fell
of Israel thirty thousand foot soldiers.
11 And the ark of God was taken; and [a]the two sons of Eli, Hophni
and Phinehas, died.
12 Now a man of Benjamin ran from the battle line and came to
Shiloh the same day with [a]his clothes torn and [1]dust on his head.
13 When he came, behold, [a]Eli was sitting on *his* seat [1]by the road
eagerly watching, because his heart was trembling for the ark of
God. So the man came to tell *it* in the city, and all the city cried out.
14 When Eli heard the noise of the outcry, he said, "What *does* the
noise of this commotion *mean?*" Then the man came hurriedly and
told Eli.
15 Now Eli was ninety-eight years old, and [a]his eyes were set so
that he could not see.
16 And the man said to Eli, "I am the one who came from the battle
line. Indeed, I escaped from the battle line today." And he said,
"[a]How did things go, my son?"
17 Then the one who brought the news answered and said, "Israel
has fled before the Philistines and there has also been a great
slaughter among the people, and your two sons also, Hophni and
Phinehas, are dead, and the ark of God has been taken."
18 And it came about when he mentioned the ark of God that [1a]Eli
fell off the seat backward beside the gate, and his neck was broken
and he died, for [2]he was old and heavy. Thus he judged Israel forty
years.
19 Now his daughter-in-law, Phinehas' wife, was pregnant and
about to give birth; and when she heard the news that the ark of God

3 [1]Or, *he* [a]Jo
[b]Num. 10:35;

4 [a]Ex. 25:22;
6:2; Ps. 80:1

5 [a]Josh. 6:5,

7 [a]Ex. 15:14

9 [a]1 Cor. 16:13
13:1; 1 Sam. 1

10 [1]Lit., *smitte*
28:15, 25; 1 Sa
[b]2 Sam. 18:17;
2 Kin. 14:12; 2
25:22

11 [a]1 Sam. 2:34
78:56-64

12 [1]Lit., *ground*
7:6; 2 Sam. 1:2;
Neh. 9:1; Job 2:

13 [1]Gr. version
beside the gate
watching the roa
[a]1 Sam. 1:9; 4:18

15 [a]1 Sam. 3:2;
14:4

16 [a]2 Sam. 1:4

18 [1]Lit., *he* [2]Lit.,
man [a]1 Sam. 4:1

Gen. 35:16-19

was taken and that her father-in-law and her husband had died, she
kneeled down and gave birth, for her pains came upon her.
20 And about the time of her death the women who stood by her
said to her, "[a]Do not be afraid, for you have given birth to a son." But
she did not answer or pay attention.
21 And she called the boy [1]Ichabod, saying, "[a]The glory has
departed from Israel," because [b]the ark of God was taken and be-
cause of her father-in-law and her husband.
22 And she said, "The glory has departed from Israel, for the ark of
God was taken."

No glory [a]Ps. 2:11 [b]1 Sam. 4:11

Sam. 4:1; 7:12 [b]Josh. 13:3

Chapter 5

5 Now the Philistines took the ark of God and [a]brought it from
Ebenezer to [b]Ashdod.
2 Then the Philistines took the ark of God and brought it to [a]the
house of Dagon, and set it by Dagon.
3 When the Ashdodites arose early the next morning, behold,
[a]Dagon had fallen on his face to the ground before the ark of the
LORD. So they took Dagon and [b]set him in his place again.
4 But when they arose early the next morning, behold, [a]Dagon had
fallen on his face to the ground before the ark of the LORD. And the
head of Dagon and both the palms of his hands *were* cut off on the
threshold; [1]only the trunk of Dagon was left to him.
5 Therefore neither the priests of Dagon nor all who enter Dagon's
house [a]tread on the threshold of Dagon in Ashdod to this day.
6 Now [a]the hand of the LORD was heavy on the Ashdodites, and
[b]He ravaged them and smote them with [c]tumors, both Ashdod and
its territories.
7 When the men of Ashdod saw that it was so, they said, "The ark
of the God of Israel must not remain with us, for His hand is severe
on us and on Dagon our god."
8 So they sent and [a]gathered all the lords of the Philistines to them
and said, "What shall we do with the ark of the God of Israel?" And
they said, "Let the ark of the God of Israel be brought around to
Gath." And they brought the ark of the God of Israel *around*.
9 And it came about that after they had brought it around, [a]the
hand of the LORD was against the city with very great confusion; and
He smote the men of the city, both young and
old, so that [b]tumors broke out on them.
10 So they sent the ark of God to Ekron. And it
happened as the ark of God came to Ekron that
the Ekronites cried out, saying, "They have
brought the ark of the God of Israel around to
[1]us, to kill [1]us and [2]our people."
11 They [a]sent therefore and gathered all the
lords of the Philistines and said, "Send away the
ark of the God of Israel, and let it return to its
own place, that it may not kill [1]us and [2]our
people." For there was a deadly confusion
throughout the city; [b]the hand of God was very
heavy there.
12 And the men who did not die were smitten
with tumors and [a]the cry of the city went up to
heaven.

udg. 16:23-30; 1 Chr. 10:8-10

:1; 46:1, 2 [b]Is. 46:7

So with ancient ons; Heb., *only* 1 [a]Ezek. 6:4, 6; Mic. 1:7

5 [a]Zeph. 1:9

9:3; 1 Sam. 5:7, s. 32:4; 145:20; 47:6; Acts 13:11 Sam. 6:5 [c]Deut. 28:27; Ps. 78:66

m. 5:11; 29:6-11

eut. 2:15; 1 Sam. 5:11; 7:13; 12:15 [b]1 Sam. 5:6

[1]Lit., *me* [2]Lit., *my*

[1]Lit., *me* [2]Lit., *my* Sam. 5:8 [b]1 Sam. 5:6, 9

Ex. 12:30; Is. 15:3

INSIGHT

Dagon, the chief deity of the Philistines, dates back to Mesopotamia and the third millennium B.C. According to ancient literature Dagon was the father of Baal. (See Judges 16:23, 1 Chronicles 10:10).

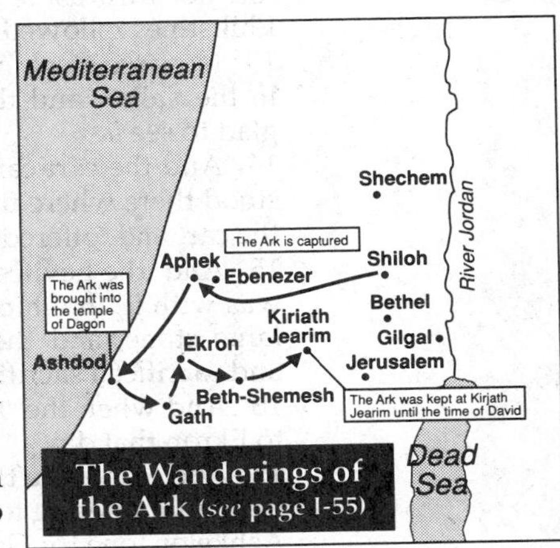

The Wanderings of the Ark (*see page I-55*)

Chapter 6

6 Now the ark of the LORD had been in the [1]country of the Philis-
tines seven months.
2 And [a]the Philistines called for the priests and the diviners,
saying, "What shall we do with the ark of the LORD? Tell us [1]how we
shall send it to its place."
3 And they said, "If you send away the ark of the God of Israel,
[a]do not send it empty; but you shall surely [b]return to Him a guilt
offering. Then you shall be healed and it shall be known to you why
His hand is not removed from you."
4 Then they said, "What shall be the guilt offering which we shall
return to Him?" And they said, "Five golden [a]tumors and five gold-
en mice [b]*according to* the number of the lords of the Philistines, for
one plague was on all of [1]you and on your lords.
5 "So you shall make likenesses of your tumors and likenesses of
your mice that ravage the land, and [a]you shall give glory to the God
of Israel; perhaps [b]He will ease His hand from you, [c]your gods, and
your land.
6 "Why then do you harden your hearts [a]as the Egyptians and Pha-
raoh hardened their hearts? When He had severely dealt with them,
[b]did they not allow [1]the people to go, and they departed?
7 "Now therefore take and [a]prepare a new cart and two milch cows
on which there [b]has never been a yoke; and hitch the cows to the cart
and take their calves home, away from them.
8 "And take the ark of the LORD and place it on the cart; and put
[a]the articles of gold which you return to Him as [b]a guilt offering in a
box by its side. Then send it away that it may go.
9 "And watch, if it goes up by the way of its own territory to [a]Beth-
shemesh, then He has done us this great evil. But if not, then [b]we
shall know that it was not His hand that struck us; it happened to us
by chance."
10 Then the men did so, and took two milch cows and hitched them
to the cart, and shut up their calves at home.
11 And they put the ark of the LORD on the cart, and the box with
the golden mice and the likenesses of their tumors.
12 And the cows took the straight way in the [1]direction of [a]Beth-
shemesh; they went along [b]the highway, lowing as they went, and
did not turn aside to the right or to the left. And the lords of the
Philistines followed them to the border of Beth-shemesh.
13 Now *the people of* Beth-shemesh were reaping their wheat harvest
in the valley, and they raised their eyes and saw the ark and were
glad to see *it*.
14 And the cart came into the field of Joshua the Beth-shemite and
stood there where there *was* a large stone; and they split the wood of
the cart and [a]offered the cows as a burnt offering to the LORD.
15 And [a]the Levites took down the ark of the LORD and the box that
was with it, in which were the articles of gold, and put them on the
large stone; and the men of Beth-shemesh offered burnt offerings
and sacrificed sacrifices that day to the LORD.
16 And when the [a]five lords of the Philistines saw it, they returned
to Ekron that day.
17 And [a]these are the golden tumors which the Philistines returned
for a guilt offering to the LORD: one for Ashdod, one for Gaza, one for
Ashkelon, one for Gath, one for Ekron;

6:1 [1]Lit., *field*
2 [1]Or, *with wh*... 41:8; Ex. 7:11; ...
3 [a]Ex. 23:15; ... 16:16 [b]Lev. 5:...
4 [1]Lit., *them* [a]... 5:6, 9, 12; 6:17 ... 13:3; Judg. 3:3 ... 6:17, 18
5 [a]Josh. 7:19; ... 16:28, 29; Is. 4... 13:16; John 9:2... 14:7 [b]1 Sam. 5... [c]1 Sam. 5:3, 4, ...
6 [1]Lit., *them* [a]E... 8:15, 32; 9:34; ... [b]Ex. 12:31
7 [a]2 Sam. 6:3 ... 19:2; Deut. 21:3
8 [a]1 Sam. 6:4, 5 [b]1 Sam. 6:3
9 [a]Josh. 15:10; ... [b]1 Sam. 6:3
12 [1]Lit., *way* [a]1 ... 6:9 [b]Num. 20:19
14 [a]2 Sam. 24:22; 1 Kin. 19:21
15 [a]Josh. 3:3
16 [a]Josh. 13:3; J... 3:3
17 [a]1 Sam. 6:4

18 and the golden mice, *according* to the number of all the cities of
the Philistines belonging to the five lords, [a]both of fortified cities and
of country villages. [b]The large [1]stone on which they set the ark of the
LORD *is a witness* to this day in the field of Joshua the Beth-shemite.
19 And [a]He struck down some of the men of Beth-shemesh because
they had looked into the ark of the LORD. He struck down of all the
people, 50,070 men, and the people mourned because the LORD had
struck the people with a great slaughter.
20 And the men of Beth-shemesh said, "[a]Who is able to stand before
the LORD, this holy God? And to whom shall He go up from us?"
21 So they sent messengers to the inhabitants of [a]Kiriath-jearim,
saying, "The Philistines have brought back the ark of the LORD; come
down and take it up to you."

Chapter 7

7 And the men of Kiriath-jearim came and took the ark of the
LORD and [a]brought it into the house of Abinadab on the hill, and
consecrated Eleazar his son to keep the ark of the LORD.
2 And it came about from the day that the ark remained at Kiriath-
jearim that the time was long, for it was twenty years; and all the
house of Israel lamented after the LORD.
3 Then Samuel spoke to all the house of Israel, saying, "[a]If you
return to the LORD with all your heart, [b]remove the foreign gods and
the [c]Ashtaroth from among you and [d]direct your hearts to the LORD
and [e]serve Him alone; and He will deliver you from the hand of the
Philistines."
4 So the sons of Israel removed the Baals and the Ashtaroth and
served the LORD alone.
5 Then Samuel said, "Gather all Israel to [a]Mizpah, and [b]I will pray
to the LORD for you."
6 And they gathered to Mizpah, and drew water and [a]poured it
out before the LORD, and [b]fasted on that day, and said there, "[c]We
have sinned against the LORD." And Samuel judged the sons of Israel
at Mizpah.
7 Now when the Philistines heard that the sons of Israel had
gathered to Mizpah, the lords of the Philistines went up against
Israel. And when the sons of Israel heard it, [a]they were afraid of the
Philistines.
8 Then the sons of Israel said to Samuel, "[a]Do not cease to cry to
the LORD our God for us, that He may save us from the hand of the
Philistines."
9 And Samuel took [a]a suckling lamb and offered it for a whole
burnt offering to the LORD; and Samuel cried to the LORD for Israel
and [b]the LORD answered him.
10 Now Samuel was offering up the burnt offering, and the Philis-
tines drew near to battle against Israel. But [a]the LORD thundered with
a great [1]thunder on that day against the Philistines and [b]confused
them, so that they were [2]routed before Israel.
11 And the men of Israel went out of Mizpah and pursued the
Philistines, and struck them down as far as below Beth-car.
12 Then Samuel [a]took a stone and set it between Mizpah and Shen,
and named it [1]Ebenezer, saying, "Thus far the LORD has helped us."
13 [a]So the Philistines were subdued and [b]they did not come

So some mss. and ersions; Heb., *Abel* [a]Deut. 3:5 [b]1 Sam. 6:14, 15

[a]Ex. 19:21; Num. 15, 20; 2 Sam. 6:7

20 [a]Lev. 11:44, 45; Sam. 6:9; Mal. 3:2; Rev. 6:17

[a]Josh. 9:17; 15:9, 60; 1 Chr. 13:5, 6

7:1 [a]2 Sam. 6:3, 4

Kin. 8:48; Is. 55:7; . 6:1; Joel 2:12-14 35:2; Josh. 24:14, udg. 10:16 [c]Judg. 2:13; 1 Sam. 31:10 . 13:4; 2 Chr. 19:3 6:13; 10:20; 13:4; 24:14; Matt. 4:10; Luke 4:8

[a]Judg. 10:17; 20:1 Sam. 8:6; 12:17-19

[a]1 Sam. 1:15; Ps. ; Lam. 2:19 [b]Lev. ; Neh. 9:1 [c]Judg. 0; 1 Kin. 8:47; Ps. 106:6

Sam. 13:6; 17:11

Sam. 12:19-24; Is. 37:4

[a]Lev. 22:27 [b]Ps. 99:6; Jer. 15:1

[1]Lit., *voice* [2]Lit., *ten* [a]1 Sam. 2:10; am. 22:14, 15; Ps. 3, 4 [b]Josh. 10:10; Ps. 18:14

[1]I.e., The stone of Gen. 35:14; Josh. 4:9; 24:26

3 [a]Judg. 13:1-15 [b]1 Sam. 13:5

anymore within the border of Israel. And the hand of the LORD was
against the Philistines all the days of Samuel.
14 And the cities which the Philistines had taken from Israel were
restored to Israel, from Ekron even to Gath; and Israel delivered their
territory from the hand of the Philistines. So there was peace be-
tween Israel and [a]the Amorites.
15 Now Samuel [a]judged Israel all the days of his life.
16 And he used to go annually on circuit to [a]Bethel and [b]Gilgal and
[c]Mizpah, and he judged Israel in all these places.
17 Then his return *was* to [a]Ramah, for his house *was* there, and there
he judged Israel; and he [b]built there an altar to the LORD.

Chapter 8

8 And it came about when Samuel was old that [a]he appointed his
sons judges over Israel.
2 Now the name of his first-born was Joel, and the name of his
second, Abijah; *they* were judging in [a]Beersheba.
3 His sons, however, did not walk in his ways, but turned aside
after dishonest gain and [a]took bribes and perverted justice.
4 Then all the elders of Israel gathered together and came to
Samuel at [a]Ramah;
5 and they said to him, "Behold, you have grown old, and your
sons do not walk in your ways. Now [a]appoint a king for us to judge
us like all the nations."
6 But the thing was [1a]displeasing in the sight of Samuel when they
said, "Give us a king to judge us." And [b]Samuel prayed to the LORD.
7 And the LORD said to Samuel, "Listen to the voice of the people
in regard to all that they say to you, for [a]they have not rejected you,
but they have rejected Me from being king over them.
8 "Like all the deeds which they have done since the day that I
brought them up from Egypt even to this day—in that they have
forsaken Me and served other gods—so they are doing to you also.
9 "Now then, listen to their voice; [a]however, you shall solemnly
[1]warn them and tell them of [b]the [2]procedure of the king who will
reign over them."
10 So Samuel spoke all the words of the LORD to [a]the people who
had asked of him a king.
11 And he said, "[a]This will be the [1]procedure of the king who will
reign over you: [b]he will take your sons and place *them* for himself in
his chariots and among his horsemen and [c]they will run before his
chariots.
12 "And [a]he will appoint for himself commanders of thousands and
of fifties, and *some* to [1]do his plowing and to reap his harvest and to
make his weapons of war and equipment for his chariots.
13 "He will also take your daughters for perfumers and cooks and
bakers.
14 "And [a]he will take the best of your fields and your vineyards and
your olive groves, and give *them* to his servants.
15 "And he will take a tenth of your seed and of your vineyards, and
give to his officers and to his servants.
16 "He will also take your male servants and your female servants
and your best young men and your donkeys, and [1]use *them* for his
work.

14 [a]Num. 13:29; Jo 10:5-10
15 [a]1 Sam. 7:6
16 [a]Gen. 28:19; 35 [b]Josh. 5:9, 10 [c]1 S 7:5
17 [a]1 Sam. 1:1, 19 2:11 [b]Judg. 21:4
8:1 [a]Deut. 16:18,
2 [a]Gen. 22:19; 1 K 19:3; Amos 5:5
3 [a]Ex. 23:6, 8; De 16:19
4 [a]1 Sam. 7:17
5 [a]Deut. 17:14, 15
6 [1]Or, *evil* [a]1 Sam 12:17 [b]1 Sam. 15:
7 [a]Ex. 16:8; 1 Sar 10:19
9 [1]Lit., *testify to* [2]*custom* [a]Ezek. 3:1 [b]1 Sam. 8:11-18;
10 [a]1 Sam. 8:4
11 [1]Lit., *custom* 17:14-20; 1 Sam. [b]1 Sam. 14:52 [c]2 15:1
12 [1]Lit., *plow his plowing* [a]Num. 3 1 Sam. 22:7
14 [a]1 Kin. 21:7; E 46:18
16 [1]Lit., *make*

17 "He will take a tenth of your flocks, and you yourselves will
become his servants.
18 "Then [a]you will cry out in that day because of your king whom
you have chosen for yourselves, but [b]the LORD will not answer you
in that day."
19 Nevertheless, the people [a]refused to listen to the voice of Samuel,
and they said, "No, but there shall be a king over us,
20 [a]that we also may be like all the nations, that our king may judge
us and go out before us and fight our battles."
21 Now after Samuel had heard all the words of the people, [a]he
repeated them in the LORD's hearing.
22 And the LORD said to Samuel, "[a]Listen to their voice, and [1]ap-
point them a king." So Samuel said to the men of Israel, "Go every
man to his city."

Chapter 9

9 Now there was a man of Benjamin whose name was [a]Kish the
son of Abiel, the son of Zeror, the son of Becorath, the son of
Aphiah, the son of a Benjamite, a mighty man of [1]valor.
2 And he had a son whose name was Saul, a [a]choice and hand-
some *man,* and there was not a more handsome person than he
among the sons of Israel; [b]from his shoulders and up he was taller
than any of the people.
3 Now the donkeys of Kish, Saul's father, were lost. So Kish said to
his son Saul, "Take now with you one of the servants, and arise, go
search for the donkeys."
4 And he passed through [a]the hill country of Ephraim and passed
through the land of [b]Shalishah, but they did not find *them.* Then they
passed through the land of [c]Shaalim, but *they were* not *there.* Then he
passed through the land of the Benjamites, but they did not find
them.
5 When they came to the land of [a]Zuph, Saul said to his servant
who was with him, "Come, and let us return, [b]lest my father cease *to
be concerned* about the donkeys and become anxious for us."
6 And he said to him, "Behold now, there is [a]a man of God in this
city, and the man is held in honor; [b]all that he says surely comes true.
Now let us go there, [c]perhaps he can tell us about our journey on
which we have set out."
7 Then Saul said to his servant, "But behold, if we go, what shall
we bring the man? For the bread is gone from our sack and there is
[a]no present to bring to the man of God. What do we have?"
8 And the servant answered Saul again and said, "Behold, I have
in my hand a fourth of a shekel of silver; I will give *it* to the man of
God and he will [a]tell us our way."
9 (Formerly in Israel, when a man went to inquire of God, he used
to say, "Come, and let us go to the seer"; for *he who is called* a prophet
now was formerly called [a]a seer.)
10 Then Saul said to his servant, "Well said; come, let us go." So
they went to the city where the man of God was.
11 As they went up the slope to the city, [a]they found young women
going out to draw water, and said to them, "Is the seer here?"
12 And they answered them and said, "He is; [1]see, *he is* ahead of
you. Hurry now, for he has come into the city today, for [a]the people
have a sacrifice on [b]the high place today.

18 [a]Is. 8:21 [b]Prov. ..5-28; Is. 1:15; Mic. 3:4
[a]Is. 66:4; Jer. 44:16
20 [a]1 Sam. 8:5
21 [a]Judg. 11:11
..it., *cause a king to ..n for them* [a]1 Sam. 8:7
9:1 [1]Or, *wealth* or *influence* [a]1 Sam. 14:51; 1 Chr. 8:33; 9:36-39
2 [a]1 Sam. 10:24 [b]1 Sam. 10:23
..osh. 24:33 [b]2 Kin. 4:42 [c]Josh. 19:42
..Sam. 1:1 [b]1 Sam. 10:2
[a]Deut. 33:1; 1 Kin. ..2 Kin. 5:8 [b]1 Sam. 3:19 [c]Gen. 24:42
[a]1 Kin. 14:3; 2 Kin. ..8:8, 9; Ezek. 13:19
8 [a]1 Sam. 9:6
..Sam. 24:11; 2 Kin. 17:13; 1 Chr. 9:22; ..; 29:29; Is. 30:10; Amos 7:12
[a]Gen. 24:11, 15; 29:8, 9; Ex. 2:16
[1]Or, *behold* [a]Gen. ..4; Num. 28:11-15; ..3:2 [b]1 Sam. 7:17; 10:5

13 "As soon as you enter the city you will find him before he goes up
to the high place to eat, for the people will not eat until he comes,
because [a]he must bless the sacrifice; afterward those who are invited
will eat. Now therefore, go up for you will find him at once."
14 So they went up to the city. As they came into the city, behold,
Samuel was coming out toward them to go up to the high place.
15 Now a day before Saul's coming, [a]the LORD had [1]revealed *this* to
Samuel saying,
16 "About this time tomorrow I will send you a man from the land
of Benjamin, and [a]you shall anoint him to be prince over My people
Israel; and he shall deliver My people from the hand of the Philis-
tines. For [b]I have regarded My people, because their cry has come to
Me."
17 When Samuel saw Saul, the LORD [1]said to him, "[a]Behold, the
man of whom I spoke to you! This one shall rule over My people."
18 Then Saul approached Samuel in the gate, and said, "Please tell
me where the seer's house is."
19 And Samuel answered Saul and said, "I am the seer. Go up
before me to the high place, for you shall eat with me today; and in
the morning I will let you go, and will tell you all that is on your
mind.
20 "And [a]as for your donkeys which were lost three days ago, do not
set your mind on them, for they have been found. And [b]for whom is
all that is desirable in Israel? Is it not for you and for all your father's
household?"
21 And Saul answered and said, "[a]Am I not a Benjamite, of [b]the
smallest of the tribes of Israel, and my family the least of all the
families of the [1]tribe of Benjamin? Why then do you speak to me in
this way?"
22 Then Samuel took Saul and his servant and brought them into
the hall, and gave them a place at the head of those who were in-
vited, who were about thirty men.
23 And Samuel said to the cook, "[1]Bring the portion that I gave you,
concerning which I said to you, 'Set it [2]aside.'"
24 Then the cook [a]took up the leg with what was on it and set *it*
before Saul. And *Samuel* said, "Here is what has been reserved! Set *it*
before you *and* eat, because it has been kept for you until the ap-
pointed time, [1]since I said I have invited the people." So Saul ate
with Samuel that day.
25 When they came down from the high place into the city, *Samuel*
spoke with Saul [a]on the roof.[1]
26 And they arose early; and it came about at daybreak that Samuel
called to Saul on the roof, saying, "Get up, that I may send you
away." So Saul arose, and both he and Samuel went out into the
street.
27 As they were going down to the edge of the city, Samuel said to
Saul, "Say to the servant that he might go ahead of us and pass on,
but you remain standing now, that I may proclaim the word of God
to you."

Chapter 10 ______________________

10 Then [a]Samuel took the flask of oil, poured it on his head,
[b]kissed him and said, "Has not [c]the LORD anointed you a ruler
over [d]His inheritance?

13 [a]Luke 9:16; Joh 6:11

15 [1]Lit., *uncovere ear* [a]1 Sam. 15:1; 13:21

16 [a]1 Sam. 10:1 [b] 3:7, 9

17 [1]Lit., *answere* [a]1 Sam. 16:12

20 [a]1 Sam. 9:3 [b]1 Sam. 8:5; 12:13

21 [1]So some anc versions; Heb., *tri* [a]1 Sam. 15:17 [b]Ju 20:46-48

23 [1]Lit., *Give* [2]Lit *you*

24 [1]Lit., *saying* [a] 29:22, 27; Lev. 7:3 Num. 18:18

25 [1]Gr. adds *and spread a bed for S on the roof and he slept.* [a]Deut. 22:8 5:19; Acts 10:9

10:1 [a]Ex. 30:23-3 1 Sam. 16:13; 2 K 9:3, 6 [b]Ps. 2:12 [c]1 Sam. 16:13; 26 2 Sam. 1:14 [d]De 32:9; Ps. 78:71

2 "When you go from me today, then you will find two men close
to [a]Rachel's tomb in the territory of Benjamin at Zelzah; and they
will say to you, '[b]The donkeys which you went to look for have been
found. Now behold, your father has [1]ceased to be concerned about
the donkeys and is anxious for you, saying, "What shall I do about
my son?"'
3 "Then you will go on further from there, and you will come as far
as the [1a]oak of Tabor, and there three men going up [b]to God at Bethel
will meet you, one carrying three kids, another carrying three loaves
of bread, and another carrying a jug of wine;
4 and they will greet you and give you two *loaves* of bread, which
you will accept from their hand.
5 "Afterward you will come to [1a]the hill of God where the Philistine
garrison is; and it shall be as soon as you have come there to the city,
that you will meet [b]a group of prophets coming down from the high
place with harp, tambourine, flute, and a lyre before them, and [c]they
will be prophesying.
6 "Then [a]the Spirit of the LORD will come upon you mightily, and
[b]you shall prophesy with them and be changed into another man.
7 "And it shall be when these signs come to you, [a]do for yourself
what [1]the occasion requires; for [b]God is with you.
8 "And [a]you shall go down before me to Gilgal; and behold, I will
come down to you to offer burnt offerings and [b]sacrifice peace offer-
ings. [c]You shall wait seven days until I come to you and show you
what you should do."
9 Then it happened when he turned his back to leave Samuel, God
[a]changed [1]his heart; and all those signs came about on that day.
10 [a]When they came to [1]the hill there, behold, a group of prophets
met him; and the Spirit of God came upon him mightily, so that he
prophesied among them.
11 And it came about, when all who knew him previously saw that
he prophesied now with the prophets, that the people said to one
another, "What has happened to the son of Kish? [a]Is Saul also among
the prophets?"
12 And a man there answered and said, "Now, who is their father?"
Therefore it became a proverb: "[a]Is Saul also among the prophets?"
13 When he had finished prophesying, he came to the high place.
14 Now [a]Saul's uncle said to him and his servant, "Where did you
go?" And he said, "[b]To look for the donkeys. When we saw that they
could not be found, we went to Samuel."
15 And Saul's uncle said, "Please tell me what Samuel said to you."
16 So Saul said to his uncle, "[a]He told us plainly that the donkeys
had been found." But he did not tell him about the matter of the
kingdom which Samuel had mentioned.
17 Thereafter Samuel called the [a]people together to the LORD at Miz-
pah;
18 and he said to the sons of Israel, "[a]Thus says the LORD, the God
of Israel, 'I brought Israel up from Egypt, and I delivered you from
the hand of the Egyptians, and from the [1]power of all the kingdoms
that were oppressing you.'
19 "But you [a]today rejected your God, who delivers you from all
your calamities and your distresses; yet you have [1]said, 'No, but set
a king over us!' Now therefore, [b]present yourselves before the LORD
by your tribes and by your clans."

…it., *abandoned the matter of* [a]Gen. …6-20; 48:7 [b]1 Sam. 9:3-5
…Or, *terebinth* [a]Gen. … [b]Gen. 28:19; 35:1, 3, 7
5 [1]Or, *Gibeath-haelohim* [a]1 Sam. 13:2, 3 … Sam. 19:20; 2 Kin. …5, 15 [c]2 Kin. 3:15; …Chr. 25:1-6; 1 Cor. 14:1
…6 [a]Num. 11:25, 29; …udg. 14:6 [b]1 Sam. 10:10; 19:23, 24
…it., *your hand finds* …l. 9:10 [b]Josh. 1:5; …dg. 6:12; Heb. 13:5
…1 Sam. 11:14; 13:8 …am. 11:15 [c]1 Sam. 13:8
…it., *for him another heart* [a]1 Sam. 10:6
10 [1]Or, *Gibeath* …am. 10:5, 6; 19:20
11 [a]1 Sam. 19:24; …mos 7:14, 15; Matt. …3:54-57; John 7:15
[a]1 Sam. 19:23, 24
14 [a]1 Sam. 14:50 [b]1 Sam. 9:3-6
16 [a]1 Sam. 9:20
…Judg. 20:1; 1 Sam. 7:5
[1]Lit., *hand* [a]Judg. 6:8, 9
…9 [1]So with several …and versions; M.T., …*aid to Him* [a]1 Sam. …6, 7; 12:12 [b]Josh. …:14-18; 24:1; Prov. 16:33

20 Thus Samuel brought all the tribes of Israel near, and the tribe of
Benjamin was taken by lot.
21 Then he brought the tribe of Benjamin near by its families, and
the Matrite family was taken. And Saul the son of Kish was taken;
but when they looked for him, he could not be found.
22 Therefore [a]they inquired further of the LORD, "Has the man come
here yet?" So the LORD said, "Behold, he is hiding himself by the
baggage."
23 So they ran and took him from there, and when he stood among
the people, [a]he was taller than any of the people from his shoulders
upward.
24 And Samuel said to all the people, "Do you see him [a]whom the
LORD has chosen? Surely there is no one like him among all the
people." So all the people shouted and said, "[1b]*Long* live the king!"
25 Then Samuel told the people [a]the ordinances of the kingdom,
and wrote *them* in the book and [b]placed *it* before the LORD. And
Samuel sent all the people away, each one to his house.
26 And Saul also went [a]to his house at Gibeah; and the valiant *men*
whose hearts God had touched went with him.
27 But certain [1a]worthless men said, "How can this one deliver us?"
And they despised him and [b]did not bring him any present. But he
kept silent.

Chapter 11

11 Now [a]Nahash the Ammonite came up and [1]besieged [b]Jabesh-
gilead; and all the men of Jabesh said to Nahash, "Make [c]a
covenant with us and we will serve you."
2 But Nahash the Ammonite said to them, "I will make *it* with you
on this condition, [a]that I will gouge out the right eye of every one of
you, thus I will make it [b]a reproach on all Israel."
3 And [a]the elders of Jabesh said to him, "Let us alone for seven
days, that we may send messengers throughout the territory of Isra-
el. Then, if there is no one to deliver us, we will come out to you."
4 Then the messengers came [a]to Gibeah of Saul and spoke these
words in the hearing of the people, and all the people [b]lifted up their
voices and wept.
5 Now behold, Saul was coming from the field [a]behind the oxen;
and [1]he said, "What is *the matter* with the people that they weep?" So
they related to him the words of the men of Jabesh.
6 Then [a]the Spirit of God came upon Saul mightily when he heard
these words, and [1]he became very angry.
7 And he took a yoke of oxen and [a]cut them in pieces, and sent
them throughout the territory of Israel by the hand of messengers,
saying, "[b]Whoever does not come out after Saul and after Samuel, so
shall it be done to his oxen." Then the dread of the LORD fell on the
people, and they came out [c]as one man.
8 And he [1]numbered them in [a]Bezek; and the [b]sons of Israel were
300,000, and the men of Judah 30,000.
9 And they said to the messengers who had come, "Thus you shall
say to the men of Jabesh-gilead, 'Tomorrow, by the time the sun is
hot, you shall have deliverance.' " So the messengers went and told
the men of Jabesh; and they were glad.
10 Then the men of Jabesh said, "[a]Tomorrow we will come out to
you, and you may do to us whatever seems good [1]to you."

22 [a]1 Sam. 23:2, 4

23 [a]1 Sam. 9:2

24 [1]Lit., *May the k*[…] *live* [a]Deut. 17:15; 2 Sam. 21:6 [b]1 Kin. 1:25, 34, 39

25 [a]Deut. 17:14-2[…] 1 Sam. 8:11-18 [b]D[…] 31:26

26 [a]1 Sam. 11:4; […]

27 [1]Lit., *sons of B*[…] cf. 2 Cor. 6:15 [a]De[…] 13:13; 1 Sam. 25:[…] [b]1 Kin. 10:25; 2 Ch[…]

11:1 [1]Lit., *camped against* [a]1 Sam. 1[…] [b]Judg. 21:8; 1 Sam 31:11 [c]Gen. 26:28 1 Kin. 20:34; Job 4[…] Ezek. 17:13

2 [a]Num. 16:14 [b]1 17:26; Ps. 44:13

3 [a]1 Sam. 8:4

4 [a]1 Sam. 10:26; [b]Gen. 27:38; Judg. 20:23, 26; 21:2; 1 30:4

5 [1]Lit., *Saul* [a]1 Ki[…] 19:19

6 [1]Lit., *his anger* […] *exceedingly* [a]Jud[…] 3:10; 6:34; 11:29; 14:6; 1 Sam. 10:1[…] 16:13

7 [a]Judg. 19:29 [b]J[…] 21:5, 8 [c]Judg. 20

8 [1]Lit., *mustered* [a]Judg. 1:5 [b]Judg.

10 [1]Lit., *in your s*[…] [a]1 Sam. 11:3

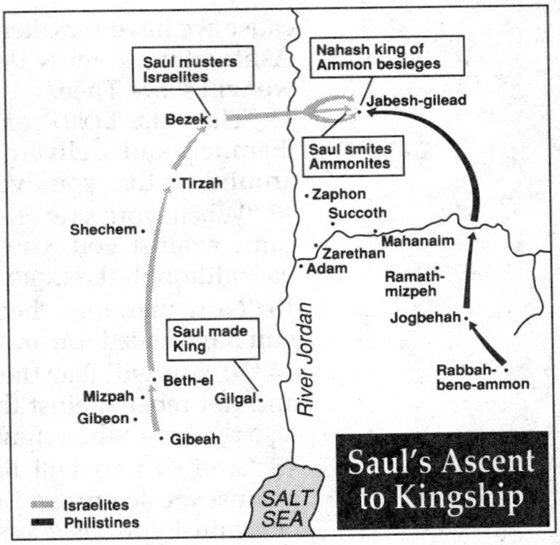

Saul's Ascent to Kingship

[a]Judg. 7:16, 20
, Give [a]1 Sam. ...7 [b]Luke 19:27
[a]1 Sam. 10:27; ...am. 19:22 [b]Ex. ...30; 1 Sam. 19:5
...Sam. 7:16; 10:8 [b]1 Sam. 10:25
[a]1 Sam. 10:17 [b]1 Sam. 10:8
...2:1 [1]Lit., *made* ...Sam. 8:7, 9, 22 ...10:24; 11:14, 15
2 [a]1 Sam. 8:20 ...8:1, 5 [c]1 Sam. ...5 [d]1 Sam. 3:10, 19, 20
...Sam. 10:1; 24:6; ...1:14 [b]Ex. 20:17; ...6:15; Acts 20:33 ...23:8; Deut. 16:19
[a]Acts 23:9; 24:20 [b]Ex. 22:4
made [a]Ex. 6:26; Mic. 6:4
...Ezek. 20:35; Mic. 6:1-5
8 [1]Lit., *and they* ...*ght* [a]Gen. 46:5, 6 ...2:23-25 [c]Ex. 3:10; ...16 [d]1 Sam. 10:18
...Deut. 32:18; Judg. [b]Judg. 4:2 [c]Judg. 10:7; 13:1 [d]Judg. 3:12-30
10 [a]Judg. 10:10

11 And it happened the next morning that Saul put the people [a]in three companies; and they came into the midst of the camp at the morning watch, and struck down the Ammonites until the heat of the day. And it came about that those who survived were scattered, so that no two of them were left together.

12 Then the people said to Samuel, "[a]Who is he that said, 'Shall Saul reign over us?' [1b]Bring the men, that we may put them to death."

13 But Saul said, "[a]Not a man shall be put to death this day, for today [b]the LORD has accomplished deliverance in Israel."

14 Then Samuel said to the people, "Come and let us go to [a]Gilgal and [b]renew the kingdom there."

15 So all the people went to Gilgal, and there they made Saul king [a]before the LORD in Gilgal. There they also [b]offered sacrifices of peace offerings before the LORD; and there Saul and all the men of Israel rejoiced greatly.

Chapter 12

12 Then Samuel said to all Israel, "Behold, [a]I have listened to your voice in all that you said to me, and I [b]have [1]appointed a king over you.

2 "And now, [a]here is the king walking before you, but [b]I am old and gray, and behold [c]my sons are with you. And [d]I have walked before you from my youth even to this day.

3 "Here I am; bear witness against me before the LORD and [a]His anointed. [b]Whose ox have I taken, or whose donkey have I taken, or whom have I defrauded? Whom have I oppressed, or [c]from whose hand have I taken a bribe to blind my eyes with it? I will restore *it* to you."

4 And they said, "You have not defrauded us, or oppressed us, or taken anything from any man's hand."

5 And he said to them, "The LORD is witness against you, and His anointed is witness this day that [a]you have found nothing [b]in my hand." And they said, "*He is* witness."

6 Then Samuel said to the people, "It is the LORD who [1a]appointed Moses and Aaron and who brought your fathers up from the land of Egypt.

7 "So now, take your stand, [a]that I may plead with you before the LORD concerning all the righteous acts of the LORD which He did for you and your fathers.

8 "[a]When Jacob went into Egypt and [b]your fathers cried out to the LORD, then [c]the LORD sent Moses and Aaron [1d]who brought your fathers out of Egypt and settled them in this place.

9 "But [a]they forgot the LORD their God, so [b]He sold them into the hand of Sisera, captain of the army of Hazor, and [c]into the hand of the Philistines and [d]into the hand of the king of Moab, and they fought against them.

10 "And [a]they cried out to the LORD and said, 'We have sinned be-

cause we have forsaken the LORD and have served [b]the Baals and the
Ashtaroth; but [c]now deliver us from the hands of our enemies, and
we will serve Thee.'
11 "Then the LORD sent [a]Jerubbaal and [1b]Bedan and [c]Jephthah and
[d]Samuel, and delivered you from the hands of your enemies all
around, so that you lived in security.
12 "When you saw [a]that Nahash the king of the sons of Ammon
came against you, you said to me, '[b]No, but a king shall reign over
us,' [c]although the LORD your God *was* your king.
13 "Now therefore, [a]here is the king whom you have chosen, [b]whom
you have asked for, and behold, the LORD has set a king over you.
14 "[a]If you will fear the LORD and serve Him, and listen to His voice
and not rebel against the [1]command of the LORD, then both you and
also the king who reigns over you will follow the LORD your God.
15 "And [a]if you will not listen to the voice of the LORD, but rebel
against the [1]command of the LORD, then [b]the hand of the LORD will
be against you, [c]*as it was* against your fathers.
16 "Even now, [a]take your stand and see this great thing which the
LORD will do before your eyes.
17 "[a]Is it not the wheat harvest today? [b]I will call to the LORD, that He
may send [1]thunder and rain. Then you will know and see that [c]your
wickedness is great which you have done in the sight of the LORD by
asking for yourselves a king."
18 So Samuel called to the LORD, and the LORD sent [1]thunder and
rain that day; and [a]all the people greatly feared the LORD and
Samuel.
19 Then all the people said to Samuel, "[a]Pray for your servants to
the LORD your God, so that we may not die, for we have added to all
our sins [b]*this* evil by asking for ourselves a king."
20 And Samuel said to the people, "Do not fear. You have com-
mitted all this evil, yet [a]do not turn aside from following the LORD,
but serve the LORD with all your heart.
21 "And you must not turn aside, for *then you would go* after [a]futile
things which can not profit or deliver, because they are futile.
22 "For [a]the LORD will not abandon His people [b]on account of His
great name, because the LORD [c]has been pleased to make you a
people for Himself.
23 "Moreover, as for me, [a]far be it from me that I should sin against
the LORD by ceasing to pray for you; but [b]I will instruct you in the
good and right way.
24 "[a]Only [1]fear the LORD and serve Him in truth with all your heart;
for consider [b]what great things He has done for you.
25 "[a]But if you still do wickedly, [b]both you and your king [c]shall be
swept away."

Chapter 13 ____________________

13 Saul was *forty* years old when he began to reign, and he
reigned *thirty*-two years over Israel.
2 Now Saul chose for himself 3,000 men of Israel, of which 2,000
were with Saul in [a]Michmash and in the hill country of Bethel, while
1,000 were with Jonathan at [b]Gibeah of Benjamin. But he sent away
the rest of the people, each to his tent.
3 And Jonathan smote [a]the garrison of the Philistines that was in

10 [b]Judg. 2:1 [c]Judg. 10:15,
11 [1]Gr. and S *Barak* [a]Judg. 7:1 [b]Judg. 4:6 [c]Judg. 11:29 3:20
12 [a]1 Sam. 11 [b]1 Sam. 8:6, 1 8:23; 1 Sam. 8
13 [a]1 Sam. 10 [b]1 Sam. 8:5; 1 Hos. 13:11
14 [1]Lit., *mouth* 24:14
15 [1]Lit., *mouth* 26:14, 15; Josh Is. 1:20 [b]1 Sam [c]1 Sam. 12:9
16 [a]Ex. 14:13,
17 [1]Lit., *sound* 26:1 [b]1 Sam. 7 James 5:16ff. 8:7
18 [1]Lit., *sound* 14:31
19 [a]Ex. 9:28; 1 12:23; Jer. 15:1 5:16 [b]1 Sam. 1
20 [a]Deut. 11:16
21 [a]Deut. 11:16 41:29; Hab. 2:18
22 [a]Deut. 31:6; 6:13 [b]Ex. 32:12 14:13; Josh. 7:9 106:8; Jer. 14:21 7:6-11; 1 Pet. 2:
23 [a]Rom. 1:9; 1 9:16; Col. 1:9; 1 3:10; 2 Tim. 1:3 8:36; Ps. 34:11; 4:11
24 [1]Or, *reverence* [a]Eccl. 12:13 [b]De 10:21; Is. 5:12
25 [a]Is. 1:20; 3:11 [b]Josh. 24:20 [c]1 S 31:1-5; Hos. 10:3
13:2 [a]1 Sam. 13. 14:31 [b]1 Sam. 10
3 [a]1 Sam. 10:5

[b]Geba, and the Philistines heard of *it*. Then Saul [c]blew the
trumpet throughout the land, saying, "Let the Hebrews
hear."
4 And all Israel heard [1]the news that Saul had smitten
the garrison of the Philistines, and also that Israel [a]had
become odious to the Philistines. The people were then
summoned [2]to Saul at Gilgal.
5 Now the Philistines assembled to fight with Israel,
30,000 chariots and 6,000 horsemen, and [a]people like the
sand which is on the seashore in abundance; and they
came up and camped in Michmash, east of [b]Beth-aven.
6 When the men of Israel saw that they were in a strait
(for the people were hard-pressed), then [a]the people hid
themselves in caves, in thickets, in cliffs, in cellars, and in
pits.
7 Also *some of* the Hebrews crossed the Jordan into the
land of [a]Gad and Gilead. But as for Saul, he *was* still in
Gilgal, and all the people followed him trembling.

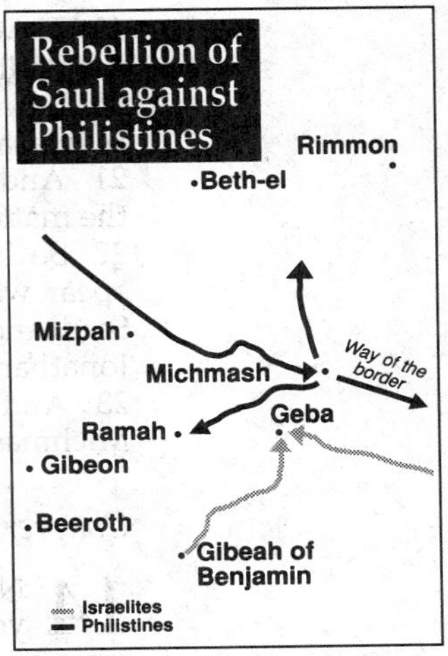
Rebellion of Saul against Philistines
Rimmon
Beth-el
Mizpah
Michmash
Way of the border
Geba
Ramah
Gibeon
Beeroth
Gibeah of Benjamin
Israelites
Philistines

8 Now [a]he waited seven days, according to the appointed time set
by Samuel, but Samuel did not come to Gilgal; and the people were
scattering from him.
9 So Saul said, "Bring to me the burnt offering and the peace offer-
ings." And [a]he offered the burnt offering.
10 And it came about as soon as he finished offering the burnt
offering, that behold, Samuel came; and [a]Saul went out to meet him
and to [1]greet him.
11 But Samuel said, "What have you done?" And Saul said, "Be-
cause I saw that the people were scattering from me, and that you
did not come within the appointed days, and that [a]the Philistines
were assembling at Michmash,
12 therefore I said, 'Now the Philistines will come down against me
at Gilgal, and I have not asked the favor of the LORD.' So I forced
myself and offered the burnt offering."
13 And Samuel said to Saul, "[a]You have acted foolishly; [b]you have
not kept the commandment of the LORD your God, which He com-
manded you, for now the LORD would have established your king-
dom [1]over Israel [c]forever.
14 "But [a]now your kingdom shall not endure. [b]The LORD has sought
out for Himself a man after His own heart, and the LORD has ap-
pointed him as ruler over His people, because you have not kept
what the LORD commanded you."
15 Then Samuel arose and went up from Gilgal to [a]Gibeah of Ben-
jamin. And Saul [1]numbered the people who were present with him,
[b]about six hundred men.
16 Now Saul and his son Jonathan and the people who were
present with them were staying in [a]Geba of Benjamin while the Phi-
listines camped at Michmash.
17 And [a]the [1]raiders came from the camp of the Philistines in three
[2]companies: one [3]company turned [4]toward [b]Ophrah, to the land of
Shual,
18 and another [1]company turned [2]toward [a]Beth-horon, and another
[1]company turned [2]toward the border which overlooks the valley of
[b]Zeboim toward the wilderness.

m. 13:16; 14:5 Judg. 3:27; 6:34
t., *saying* [2]Lit., Gen. 34:30; Ex. .1; 2 Sam. 10:6
sh. 11:4 [b]Josh. ; 1 Sam. 14:23
6 [a]Judg. 6:2
7 [a]Num. 32:33
8 [a]1 Sam. 10:8
[a]Deut. 12:5-14; 24:25; 1 Kin. 3:4
., *bless* [a]1 Sam. 15:13
[a]1 Sam. 13:2, 5, 16, 23
, *to* [a]2 Chr. 16:9 am. 15:11, 22, 28 [c]1 Sam. 1:22
Sam. 15:28 [b]Acts 7:46; 13:22
5 [1]Lit., *mustered* am. 13:2 [b]1 Sam. 13:2, 6, 7; 14:2
6 [a]1 Sam. 13:2, 3
7 [1]Lit., *destroyers* heads [3]Lit., *head* [4]Lit., *toward the* ection of [a]1 Sam. 4:15 [b]Josh. 18:23
Lit., *head* [2]Lit., *the* on of [a]Josh. 16:3; 3, 14 [b]Neh. 11:34

19 Now [a]no blacksmith could be found in all the land of Israel, for
the Philistines said, "Lest the Hebrews make [1b]swords or spears."
20 So all Israel went down to the Philistines, each to sharpen his
plowshare, his mattock, his axe, and his hoe.
21 And the charge was [1]two-thirds of a shekel for the plowshares,
the mattocks, the forks, and the axes, and to fix the hoes.
22 So it came about on the day of battle that [a]neither sword nor
spear was found in the hands of any of the people who *were* with
Saul and Jonathan, but they were found with Saul and his son
Jonathan.
23 And [a]the garrison of the Philistines went out to [b]the pass of
Michmash.

Chapter 14

14 Now the day came that Jonathan, the son of Saul, said to the
young man who was carrying his armor, "Come and let us
cross over to the Philistines' garrison that is on yonder side." But he
did not tell his father.
2 And Saul was staying in the outskirts of [a]Gibeah under the
pomegranate tree which is in [b]Migron. And the people who *were*
with him *were* [c]about six hundred men,
3 and Ahijah, the [a]son of Ahitub, [b]Ichabod's brother, the son of
Phinehas, the son of Eli, the priest of the LORD at [c]Shiloh, [d]was [1]wear-
ing an ephod. And the people did not know that Jonathan had gone.
4 And [a]between the passes by which Jonathan sought to cross over
to the Philistines' garrison, there was a sharp crag on the one side,
and a sharp crag on the other side, and the name of the one was
Bozez, and the name of the other Seneh.

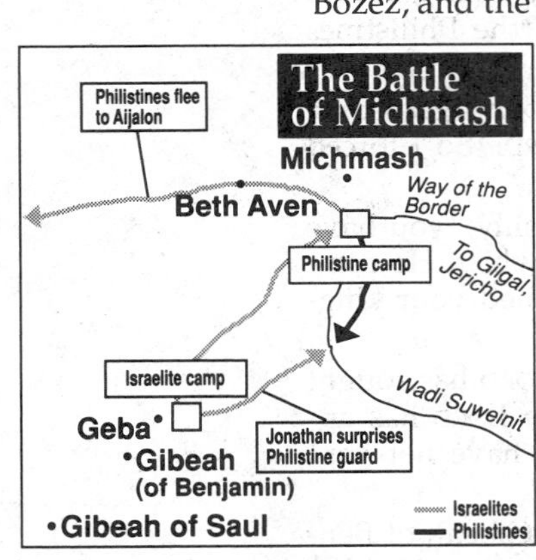

5 The one crag rose on the north opposite Mich-
mash, and the other on the south opposite Geba.
6 Then Jonathan said to the young man who was
carrying his armor, "Come and let us cross over to
the garrison of [a]these uncircumcised; perhaps the
LORD will work for us, for [b]the LORD is not restrained
to save by many or by few."
7 And his armor bearer said to him, "Do all that is
in your heart; turn yourself, *and* here I am with you
according to your [1]desire."
8 Then Jonathan said, "[a]Behold, we will cross over
to the men and reveal ourselves to them.
9 "If they [1]say to us, 'Wait until we come to you';
then we will stand in our place and not go up to
them.
10 "But if they [1]say, 'Come up to us,' then we will go up, for the
LORD has given them into our hands; and [a]this shall be the sign to
us."
11 And when both of them revealed themselves to the garrison of
the Philistines, the Philistines said, "Behold, [a]Hebrews are coming
out of the holes where they have hidden themselves."
12 So the men of the garrison [1]hailed Jonathan and his armor bearer
and said, "Come up to us and [a]we will tell you something." And
Jonathan said to his armor bearer, "Come up after me, for [b]the LORD
has given them into the hands of Israel."
13 Then Jonathan climbed up on his hands and feet, with his armor

19 [1]Lit., *sword or s* [a]Judg. 5:8; 2 Kin. 2 Jer. 24:1; 29:2 [b]Ju 5:8
21 [1]Heb., *pim*
22 [a]Judg. 5:8
23 [a]1 Sam. 14:1; 2 Sam. 23:14 [b]1 S 14:4, 5; Is. 10:28
14:2 [a]1 Sam. 13:1 [b]Is. 10:28 [c]1 Sam.
3 [1]Lit., *carrying* [a]1 Sam. 22:9-12, 2 [b]1 Sam. 4:21 [c]1 S 1:3 [d]1 Sam. 2:28
4 [a]1 Sam. 13:23
6 [a]1 Sam. 17:26, Jer. 9:25, 26 [b]Jud 7; 1 Sam. 17:46, 4 115:3; 135:6; Zech Matt. 19:26
7 [1]Lit., *heart*
8 [a]Judg. 7:9-14
9 [1]Lit., *say thus*
10 [1]Lit., *say thus* 24:14; Judg. 6:36
11 [a]1 Sam. 13:6;
12 [1]Lit., *answere* [a]1 Sam. 17:43, 44 [b]2 Sam. 5:24

bearer behind him; and they fell before Jonathan, and his armor
bearer put some to death after him.
14 And that first slaughter which Jonathan and his armor bearer
made was about twenty men within about half a furrow in an acre of
land.
15 And there was a trembling in the camp, in the field, and among
all the people. Even the garrison and [a]the raiders trembled, and [b]the
earth quaked so [c]that it became a [1]great trembling.
16 Now Saul's watchmen in Gibeah of Benjamin looked, and be-
hold, the multitude melted away; and they went here and *there*.
17 And Saul said to the people who *were* with him, "[1]Number now
and see who has gone from us." And when they had [1]numbered,
behold, Jonathan and his armor bearer were not *there*.
18 Then Saul said to Ahijah, "[a]Bring the ark of God here." For the
ark of God was at that time with the sons of Israel.
19 And it happened [a]while Saul talked to the priest, that the com-
motion in the camp of the Philistines continued and increased; so
Saul said to the priest, "Withdraw your hand."
20 Then Saul and all the people who *were* with him rallied and
came to the battle; and behold, [a]every man's sword was against his
fellow, *and there was* very great confusion.
21 Now the Hebrews *who* were with the Philistines previously, who
went up with them all around in the camp, even [a]they also *turned* to
be with the Israelites who *were* with Saul and Jonathan.
22 When all the [a]men of Israel who had hidden themselves in the
hill country of Ephraim heard that the Philistines had fled, even they
also pursued them closely in the battle.
23 So [a]the LORD delivered Israel that day, and the battle [1]spread
beyond [b]Beth-aven.
24 Now the men of Israel were hard-pressed on that day, for Saul
had [a]put the people under oath, saying, "Cursed be the man who
eats food [1]before evening, and until I have avenged myself on my
enemies." So none of the people tasted food.
25 And all *the people of* the land entered the forest, and there was
honey on the ground.
26 When the people entered the forest, behold, [a]*there was* a flow of
honey; but no man put his hand to his mouth, for the people feared
the oath.
27 But Jonathan had not heard when his father put the people
under oath; therefore, [a]he put out the end of the staff that *was* in his
hand and dipped it in the honeycomb, and put his hand to his
mouth, and [b]his eyes brightened.
28 Then one of the people answered and said, "Your father strictly
put the people under oath, saying, 'Cursed be the man who eats
food today.' " And the people were weary.
29 Then Jonathan said, "[a]My father has troubled the land. See now,
how my eyes have brightened because I tasted a little of this honey.
30 "How much more, if only the people had eaten freely today of the
spoil of their enemies which they found! For now the slaughter
among the Philistines has not been great."
31 And they struck among the Philistines that day from [a]Michmash
to [b]Aijalon. And the people were very weary.
32 And [a]the people [1]rushed greedily upon the spoil, and took sheep

15 [1]Lit., *trembling of* ...d [a]1 Sam. 13:17, 18 [b]1 Sam. 7:10 [c]Gen. 35:5; 2 Kin. 7:6
17 [1]Lit., *muster(ed)*
[a]1 Sam. 23:9; 30:7
19 [a]Num. 27:21
[a]Judg. 7:22; 2 Chr. 20:23
21 [a]1 Sam. 29:4
22 [a]1 Sam. 13:6
...3 [1]Lit., *passed over* [a]Ex. 14:30; 1 Sam. ...0:19; 14:23; 1 Chr. ...4; 2 Chr. 32:22; Ps. 44:7 [b]1 Sam. 13:5
...4 [1]Lit., *until* [a]Josh. 6:26
26 [a]Matt. 3:4
27 [a]1 Sam. 14:43 [b]1 Sam. 30:12
[a]Josh. 7:25; 1 Kin. 18:18
...Sam. 14:5 [b]Josh. 10:12
...Lit., *did with regard* ...*the spoil* [a]1 Sam. 15:19

and oxen and calves, and slew *them* on the ground; and the people
ate *them* [b]with the blood.
33 Then they told Saul, saying, "Behold, the people are [a]sinning
against the LORD by eating with the blood." And he said, "You have
acted treacherously; roll a great stone to me today."
34 And Saul said, "Disperse yourselves among the people and say
to them, 'Each one of you bring me his ox or his sheep, and slaughter
it here and eat; and do not sin against the LORD by eating with the
blood.' " So all the people that night brought each one his ox [1]with
him, and slaughtered *it* there.
35 And [a]Saul built an altar to the LORD; it was the first altar that he
built to the LORD.
36 Then Saul said, "Let us go down after the Philistines by night
and take spoil among them until the morning light, and let us not
leave a man of them." And they said, "Do whatever seems good [1]to
you." So [a]the priest said, "Let us draw near to God here."
37 And Saul [a]inquired of God, "Shall I go down after the Philis-
tines? Wilt Thou give them into the hand of Israel?" But [b]He did not
answer him on that day.
38 And Saul said, "[a]Draw near here, all you [1]chiefs of the people,
and investigate and see how this sin has happened today.
39 "For [a]as the LORD lives, who delivers Israel, though it is in
Jonathan my son, he shall surely die." But not one of all the people
answered him.
40 Then he said to all Israel, "You shall be on one side and I and
Jonathan my son will be on the other side." And the people said to
Saul, "Do what seems good [1]to you."
41 Therefore, Saul said to the LORD, the God of Israel, "[a]Give a
perfect *lot*." And Jonathan and Saul were taken, but the people
escaped.
42 And Saul said, "Cast *lots* between me and Jonathan my son."
And Jonathan was taken.
43 Then Saul said to Jonathan, "[a]Tell me what you have done." So
Jonathan told him and said, "[b]I indeed tasted a little honey with the
end of the staff that was in my hand. Here I am, I must die!"
44 And Saul said, "[a]May God do [1]this *to me* and more also, for [b]you
shall surely die, Jonathan."
45 But the people said to Saul, "Must Jonathan die, who has
[1]brought about this great deliverance in Israel? Far from it! As the
LORD lives, [a]there shall not one hair of his head fall to the ground, for
[b]he has worked with God this day." So the people [2]rescued Jonathan
and he did not die.
46 Then Saul went up from [1]pursuing the Philistines, and the Phi-
listines went to their own place.
47 Now when Saul had taken the kingdom over Israel, he fought
against all his enemies on every side, against Moab, [a]the sons of
Ammon, Edom, [b]the kings of Zobah, and [c]the Philistines; and
wherever he turned, he [1]inflicted punishment.
48 And he acted valiantly and [1a]defeated the Amalekites, and
delivered Israel from the hands of [2]those who plundered them.
49 Now [a]the sons of Saul were Jonathan and Ishvi and Malchi-shua;
and the names of his two daughters *were these:* the name of the
first-born [b]Merab and the name of the younger [c]Michal.
50 And the name of Saul's wife was Ahinoam the daughter of

32 [b]Gen. 9:4; Lev. 17:10-14; 19:26; D 12:16, 23; Acts 15:
33 [a]Lev. 7:26, 27; 19:26; Deut. 12:16, 23-25; 15:23
34 [1]Lit., *in his han*
35 [a]1 Sam. 7:12, 2 Sam. 24:25; Jam
36 [1]Lit., *in your ey* [a]1 Sam. 14:3, 18,
37 [a]1 Sam. 10:22 [b]1 Sam. 28:6
38 [1]Lit., *corners* [a] 7:11, 12; 1 Sam. 10:19, 20
39 [a]1 Sam. 14:24, 2 Sam. 12:5
40 [1]Lit., *in your e*
41 [a]Acts 1:24
43 [a]Josh. 7:19 [b]1 14:27
44 [1]Lit., *thus* [a]Ru 1:17; 1 Sam. 25:2 [b]1 Sam. 14:39
45 [1]Lit., *worked* [2] *ransomed* [a]2 Sam 14:11; 1 Kin. 1:52; 21:18; Acts 27:34 [b]2 Cor. 6:1
46 [1]Lit., *after*
47 [1]Or, *condemn* [a]1 Sam. 11:1-13 [b]2 Sam. 8:3-10 [c]1 14:52
48 [1]Lit., *smote* [2]L *plunderers* [a]1 Sa 15:3, 7
49 [a]1 Sam. 31:2; 8:33; 10:2 [b]1 Sa 18:17-19 [c]1 Sam. 18:20, 27; 19:12; 2 Sam. 6:20-23

1 Samuel 14:49-51: Saul's Family Tree

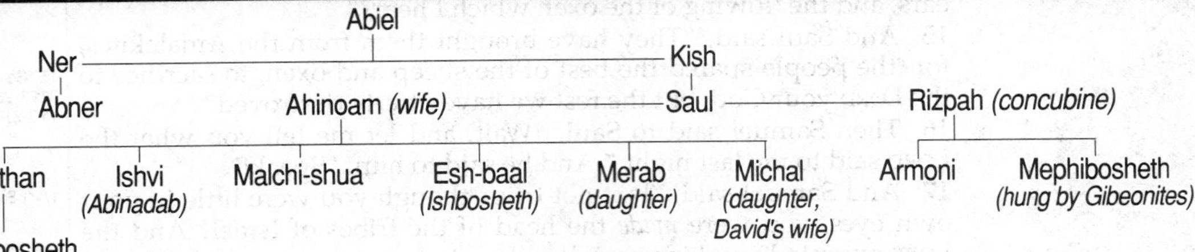

Ahimaaz. And [a]the name of the captain of his army was Abner the
son of Ner, Saul's uncle.
51 [a]And Kish *was* the father of Saul, and Ner the father of Abner *was*
the son of Abiel.
52 Now the war against the Philistines was severe all the days of
Saul; and when Saul saw any mighty man or any valiant man, he
[1a]attached him to [2]his staff.

Chapter 15

15 Then Samuel said to Saul, "[a]The LORD sent me to anoint you
as king over His people, over Israel; now therefore, listen to
the [1]words of the LORD.
2 "Thus says the LORD of hosts, 'I will [1]punish Amalek [a]*for* what he
did to Israel, how he set himself against him on the way while he
was coming up from Egypt.
3 'Now go and strike Amalek and [a]utterly destroy all that he has,
and do not spare him; but [b]put to death both man and woman, child
and infant, ox and sheep, camel and donkey.' "
4 Then Saul summoned the people and [1]numbered them in
[a]Telaim, 200,000 foot soldiers and 10,000 men of Judah.
5 And Saul came to the city of Amalek, and set an ambush in the
valley.
6 And Saul said to [a]the Kenites, "Go, depart, go down from among
the Amalekites, lest I destroy you with them; for [b]you showed kind-
ness to all the sons of Israel when they came up from Egypt." So the
Kenites departed from among the Amalekites.
7 So [a]Saul [1]defeated the Amalekites, from [b]Havilah as you go to
[c]Shur, which is [2]east of Egypt.
8 And he captured [a]Agag the king of the Amalekites alive, and
[b]utterly destroyed all the people with the edge of the sword.
9 But Saul and the people [a]spared Agag and the best of the sheep,
the oxen, the fatlings, the lambs, and all that was good, and were not
willing to destroy them utterly; but everything despised and worth-
less, that they utterly destroyed.
10 Then the word of the LORD came to Samuel, saying,
11 "[a]I regret that I have made Saul king, for [b]he has turned back from
[1]following Me, and has not carried out My commands." And Samuel
was distressed and [c]cried out to the LORD all night.
12 And Samuel rose early in the morning to meet Saul; and it was
told Samuel, saying, "Saul came to [a]Carmel, and behold, he set up a
monument for himself, then turned and proceeded on [1]down to
[b]Gilgal."
13 And Samuel came to Saul, and Saul said to him, "[a]Blessed are
you of the LORD! I have carried out the command of the LORD."

50 [a]2 Sam. 2:8
[a]1 Sam. 9:1, 21
, *gathered* [2]Lit., *elf* [a]1 Sam. 8:11
.it., *sound of the 's* [a]1 Sam. 9:16; 10:1
2 [1]Or, *visit* [a]Ex. 16; Num. 24:20; Deut. 25:17-19
um. 24:20; Deut. 8; Josh. 6:17-21 [b]1 Sam. 22:19
mustered [a]Josh. 15:24
um. 24:21; Judg. ; 4:11 [b]Ex. 18:9,); Num. 10:29-32
[1]Lit., *smote* [2]Lit., *re* [a]1 Sam. 14:48 5:18 [c]Gen. 16:7; 5:22; 1 Sam. 27:8
um. 24:7; 1 Sam. 15:20; Esth. 3:1 am. 27:8, 9; 30:1; 2 Sam. 8:12
Sam. 15:3, 15, 19
[1]Lit., *after* [a]Gen. 6:6, 7; Ex. 32:14; am. 15:35; 2 Sam. :16 [b]Josh. 22:16; Sam. 13:13; 1 Kin. , 7 [c]Ex. 32:11-13; Luke 6:12
12 [1]Lit., *and went own* [a]Josh. 15:55; Sam. 25:2 [b]1 Sam. 13:12, 15
[a]Gen. 14:19; Judg. Ruth 3:10; 2 Sam. 2:5

14 But Samuel said, "[a]What then is this [1]bleating of the sheep in my
ears, and the [1]lowing of the oxen which I hear?"
15 And Saul said, "They have brought them from the Amalekites,
for [a]the people spared the best of the sheep and oxen, to sacrifice to
the LORD your God; but the rest we have utterly destroyed."
16 Then Samuel said to Saul, "Wait, and let me tell you what the
LORD said to me last night." And he said to him, "Speak!"
17 And Samuel said, "Is it not true, [a]though you were little in your
own eyes, you were *made* the head of the tribes of Israel? And the
LORD anointed you king over Israel,
18 and the LORD sent you on a [1]mission, and said, '[a]Go and utterly
destroy the sinners, the Amalekites, and fight against them until
they are exterminated.'
19 "Why then did you not obey the voice of the LORD, [a]but rushed
upon the spoil and did what was evil in the sight of the LORD?"
20 Then Saul said to Samuel, "[a]I did obey the voice of the LORD, and
went on the [1]mission on which the LORD sent me, and have brought
back Agag the king of Amalek, and have utterly destroyed the
Amalekites.
21 "But [a]the people took *some* of the spoil, sheep and oxen, the
choicest of the things devoted to destruction, to sacrifice to the LORD
your God at Gilgal."
22 And Samuel said,
"[a]Has the LORD as much delight in burnt offerings and sacrifices
As in obeying the voice of the LORD?
Behold, [b]to obey is better than sacrifice,
And to heed than the fat of rams.
23 "For rebellion is as the sin of [a]divination,
And insubordination is as [b]iniquity and idolatry.
Because you have rejected the word of the LORD,
[c]He has also rejected you from *being* king."
24 Then Saul said to Samuel, "[a]I have sinned; [b]I have indeed trans-
gressed the [1]command of the LORD and your words, because I feared
the people and listened to their voice.
25 "Now therefore, [a]please pardon my sin and return with me, that I
may worship the LORD."
26 But Samuel said to Saul, "I will not return with you; for [a]you
have rejected the word of the LORD, and the LORD has rejected you
from being king over Israel."
27 And as Samuel turned to go, [a]*Saul* seized the edge of his robe,
and it tore.
28 So Samuel said to him, "[a]The LORD has torn the kingdom of
Israel from you today, and has given it to your neighbor who is
better than you.
29 "And also the [1a]Glory of Israel [b]will not lie or change His mind;
for He is not a man that He should change His mind."
30 Then he said, "I have sinned; [a]*but* please honor me now before
the elders of my people and before Israel, and go back with me, [b]that
I may worship the LORD your God."
31 So Samuel went back following Saul, and Saul worshiped the
LORD.
32 Then Samuel said, "Bring me Agag, the king of the Amalekites."
And Agag came to him [1]cheerfully. And Agag said, "Surely the bit-
terness of death is past."

14 [1]Lit., *sour* 32:21-24
15 [a]Gen. 3:1 32:22, 23; 1 S 15:9, 21
17 [a]1 Sam. 9.
18 [1]Lit., *way* 15:3
19 [a]1 Sam. 14
20 [1]Lit., *way* 15:13
21 [a]Ex. 32:22, 1 Sam. 15:15
22 [a]Ps. 40:6-8 17; Is. 1:11-15; 6:6-8; Heb. 10: 7:22, 23; Hos. 12:7; Mark 12:3
23 [a]Deut. 18:1 31:19, 34 [c]1 Sa
24 [1]Lit., *mouth* 22:34; 2 Sam. 1 Ps. 51:4 [b]Prov. Is. 51:12, 13
25 [a]Ex. 10:17
26 [a]1 Sam. 13:
27 [a]1 Kin. 11:30
28 [a]1 Sam. 28:1 1 Kin. 11:31
29 [1]Or, *Eminenc* [a]1 Chr. 29:11 [b]N 23:19; Ezek. 24: Titus 1:2
30 [a]John 5:44; 1 [b]Is. 29:13
32 [1]Or, *in bonds*

33 But Samuel said, "[a]As your sword has made women childless, so shall your mother be childless among women." And Samuel hewed Agag to pieces before the LORD at Gilgal.
34 Then Samuel went to [a]Ramah, but Saul went up to his house at [b]Gibeah of Saul.
35 And [a]Samuel did not see Saul again until the day of his death; for Samuel [b]grieved over Saul. And the LORD regretted that He had made Saul king over Israel.

Chapter 16

16 Now the LORD said to Samuel, "[a]How long will you grieve over Saul, since [b]I have rejected him from being king over Israel? [c]Fill your horn with oil, and go; I will send you to [d]Jesse the Bethlehemite, for I have [e]selected a king for Myself among his sons."
2 But Samuel said, "How can I go? When Saul hears *of it*, he will kill me." And the LORD said, "[a]Take a heifer with you, and say, 'I have come to sacrifice to the LORD.'
3 "And you shall invite Jesse to the sacrifice, and [a]I will show you what you shall do; and [b]you shall anoint for Me the one whom I [1]designate to you."
4 So Samuel did what the LORD said, and came to [a]Bethlehem. And the elders of the city came trembling to meet him and said, "[b]Do you come in peace?"
5 And he said, "In peace; I have come to sacrifice to the LORD. [a]Consecrate yourselves and come with me to the sacrifice." He also consecrated Jesse and his sons, and invited them to the sacrifice.
6 Then it came about when they entered, that he looked at [a]Eliab and thought, "Surely the LORD's anointed is before Him."
7 But the LORD said to Samuel, "Do not look at his appearance or at the height of his stature, because I have rejected him; for [1]God *sees* not as man sees, for man looks at the outward appearance, [a]but the LORD looks at the heart."
8 Then Jesse called [a]Abinadab, and made him pass before Samuel. And he said, "Neither has the LORD chosen this one."
9 Next Jesse made [1a]Shammah pass by. And he said, "Neither has the LORD chosen this one."
10 Thus Jesse made seven of his sons pass before Samuel. But Samuel said to Jesse, "The LORD has not chosen these."
11 And Samuel said to Jesse, "Are these all the children?" And he said, "[a]There remains yet the youngest, and behold, he is tending the sheep." Then Samuel said to Jesse, "Send and [1]bring him; for we will not sit down until he comes here."
12 So he sent and brought him in. Now he was ruddy, with [a]beautiful eyes and a handsome appearance. And the LORD said, "[b]Arise, anoint him; for this is he."
13 Then Samuel took the horn of oil and [a]anointed him in the midst of his brothers; and [b]the Spirit of the LORD came mightily upon David from that day forward. And Samuel arose and went to Ramah.
14 [a]Now the Spirit of the LORD departed from Saul, and [b]an evil spirit from the LORD terrorized him.
15 Saul's servants then said to him, "Behold now, an evil spirit from God is terrorizing you.
16 "Let our lord now command your servants who are before you.

9:6; Judg. 1:7; Matt. 7:2
[a]1 Sam. 7:17 [b]1 Sam. 11:4
[a]1 Sam. 19:24 [b]1 Sam. 16:1
[a]1 Sam. 15:35 ...am. 13:13, 14; [c]1 Sam. 9:16; Kin. 9:1 [d]Ruth [e]Ps. 78:70, 71; Acts 13:22
[a]1 Sam. 20:29
...say to you [a]Ex. Acts 9:6 [b]Deut. ...5; 1 Sam. 9:16
. 48:7; Luke 2:4 :13; 2 Kin. 9:22; Chr. 12:17, 18
35:2; Ex. 19:10
[a]1 Sam. 17:13
...ith Gr.; Heb., He ...ot see *what man* ...es [a]1 Sam. 2:3; :39; 1 Chr. 28:9; Luke 16:15
8 [a]1 Sam. 17:13
[1]In 2 Sam. 13:3, ...h; in 1 Chr. 2:13, ...a [a]1 Sam. 17:13
...it., *take* [a]1 Sam. ...:12; 2 Sam. 13:3
...en. 39:6; Ex. 2:2; .20 [b]1 Sam. 9:17
...Sam. 10:1 [b]Num. ...:18; 1 Sam. 10:6, 9, 10
14 [a]Judg. 16:20; Sam. 11:6; 18:12; ...8:15 [b]Judg. 9:23; 1 Sam. 16:15, 16; 18:10; 19:9; 1 Kin. 22:19-22

Let them seek a man who is a skillful player on the harp; and it shall
come about when the evil spirit from God is on you, that [a]he shall
play *the harp* with his hand, and you will be well."
17 So Saul said to his servants, "Provide for me now a man who can
play well, and bring *him* to me."
18 Then one of the young men answered and said, "Behold, I have
seen a son of Jesse the Bethlehemite who is a skillful musician, [a]a
mighty man of valor, a warrior, one prudent in speech, and a hand-
some man; and [b]the LORD is with him."
19 So Saul sent messengers to Jesse, and said, "Send me your son
David who is with the flock."
20 And Jesse [a]took a donkey *loaded with* bread and a jug of wine and
a young goat, and sent *them* to Saul by David his son.
21 Then David came to Saul and [1a]attended him, and [2]Saul loved
him greatly; and he became his armor bearer.
22 And Saul sent to Jesse, saying, "Let David now stand before me;
for he has found favor in my sight."
23 So it came about whenever [a]the *evil* spirit from God came to
Saul, David would take the harp and play *it* with his hand; and Saul
would be refreshed and be well, and the evil spirit would depart
from him.

Chapter 17

17 Now [a]the Philistines gathered their armies for battle; and they
were gathered at Socoh which belongs to Judah, and they
camped between [b]Socoh and [c]Azekah, in [d]Ephes-dammim.
2 And Saul and the men of Israel were gathered, and camped in
[a]the valley of Elah, and drew up in battle array to encounter the
Philistines.
3 And the Philistines stood on the mountain on one side while
Israel stood on the mountain on the other side, with the valley be-
tween them.
4 Then a champion came out from the armies of the Philistines
named [a]Goliath, from [b]Gath, whose height was six [1]cubits and a
span.
5 And *he had* a bronze helmet on his head, and he was clothed
with scale-armor [1]which weighed five thousand shekels of bronze.
6 *He* also *had* bronze [1]greaves on his legs and a [a]bronze javelin
slung between his shoulders.
7 And [a]the shaft of his spear was like a weaver's beam, and the
head of his spear *weighed* six hundred shekels of iron; [b]his shield-car-
rier also walked before him.
8 And he stood and shouted to the ranks of Israel, and said to
them, "Why do you come out to draw up in battle array? Am I not
the Philistine and you [a]servants of Saul? Choose a man for your-
selves and let him come down to me.
9 "[a]If he is able to fight with me and [1]kill me, then we will become
your servants; but if I prevail against him and [1]kill him, then you
shall become our servants and serve us."
10 Again the Philistine said, "[a]I defy the ranks of Israel this day;
give me a man that we may fight together."
11 When Saul and all Israel heard these words of the Philistine, they
were dismayed and greatly afraid.
12 Now David was [a]the son of [1]the [b]Ephrathite of Bethlehem in

16 [a]1 Sam. 18:10; 2 Kin. 3:15
18 [a]1 Sam. 17:32- [b]1 Sam. 3:19
20 [a]1 Sam. 10:4, 2 Prov. 18:16
21 [1]Lit., *stood befo him* [2]Lit., *he* [a]Gen 41:46; Prov. 22:29
23 [a]1 Sam. 16:14-
17:1 [a]1 Sam. 13:5 [b]Josh. 15:35; 2 Chr 28:18 [c]Josh. 10:10 [d]1 Chr. 11:13
2 [a]1 Sam. 21:9
4 [1]I.e., One cubit equals approx. 18 [a]2 Sam. 21:19 [b]Jo 11:22
5 [1]Lit., *and the we of the armor* was
6 [1]Or, *shin guards* [a]1 Sam. 17:45
7 [a]2 Sam. 21:19; 11:23 [b]1 Sam. 17:
8 [a]1 Sam. 8:17
9 [1]Lit., *smite* [a]2 S 2:12-16
10 [a]1 Sam. 17:26 45; 2 Sam. 21:21
12 [1]Lit., *this* [a]Rut 4:22; 1 Sam. 16:1 [b]Gen. 35:19

Judah, whose name was Jesse, and [c]he had eight sons. And [2]Jesse was old in the days of Saul, advanced *in years* among men.

13 And the three older sons of Jesse had [1]gone after Saul to the battle. And [a]the names of his three sons who went to the battle were Eliab the first-born, and the second to him Abinadab, and the third Shammah.

14 And [a]David was the youngest. Now the three oldest followed Saul,

15 [a]but David went back and forth from Saul [b]to tend his father's flock at Bethlehem.

16 And the Philistine came [1]forward morning and evening for forty days, and took his stand.

17 Then Jesse said to David his son, "[a]Take now for your brothers an ephah of this roasted grain and these ten loaves, and run to the camp to your brothers.

18 "[a]Bring also these ten cuts of cheese to the commander of *their* thousand, [b]and look into the welfare of your brothers, and bring back [1]news of them.

19 "For Saul and they and all the men of Israel are in the valley of Elah, fighting with the Philistines."

20 So David arose early in the morning and left the flock with a keeper and took *the supplies* and went as Jesse had commanded him. And he came to the [a]circle of the camp while the army was going out in battle array shouting the war cry.

21 And Israel and the Philistines drew up in battle array, army against army.

22 Then David left his [a]baggage in the [1]care of the baggage keeper, and ran to the battle line and entered in order to greet his brothers.

23 As he was talking with them, behold, the champion, the Philistine from Gath named Goliath, was coming up from the army of the Philistines, and he spoke [a]these same words; and David heard *them*.

24 When all the men of Israel saw the man, they fled from him and were greatly afraid.

25 And the men of Israel said, "Have you seen this man who is coming up? Surely he is coming up to defy Israel. And it will be that the king will enrich the man who kills him with great riches and [a]will give him his daughter and make his father's house [1]free in Israel."

26 Then David spoke to the men who were standing by him, saying, "What will be done for the man who kills this Philistine, and takes away [a]the reproach from Israel? For who is this [b]uncircumcised Philistine, that he should [c]taunt the armies of [d]the living God?"

27 And the people [1]answered him in accord with this word, saying, "[a]Thus it will be done for the man who kills him."

28 Now Eliab his oldest brother heard when he spoke to the men; and [a]Eliab's anger burned against David and he said, "Why have you come down? And with whom have you left those few sheep in the wilderness? I know your insolence and the wickedness of your heart; for you have come down in order to see the battle."

29 But David said, "What have I done now? Was it not just a [1]question?"

30 Then he turned [1]away from him to another and [a]said the same thing; and the people answered the same thing as [2]before.

12 [2]Lit., *the man* [c]1 Sam. 16:10, 11; 1 Chr. 2:13-15
13 [1]Lit., *gone; they* [a]1 Sam. 16:6, 8, 9
14 [a]1 Sam. 16:11
[a]1 Sam. 16:21-23 [b]1 Sam. 16:11, 19
16 [1]Lit., *near*
17 [a]1 Sam. 25:18
8 [1]Lit., *their pledge* Sam. 16:20 [b]Gen. 37:13, 14
20 [a]1 Sam. 26:5, 7
[1]Lit., *hand* [a]Judg. 18:21; Is. 10:28
3 [a]1 Sam. 17:8-10
I.e., free from taxes and public service [a]Josh. 15:16
26 [a]1 Sam. 11:2 1 Sam. 14:6; 17:36; r. 9:25, 26 [c]1 Sam. 17:10 [d]Deut. 5:26; Kin. 19:4; Jer. 10:10
27 [1]Lit., *said to* [a]1 Sam. 17:25
8 [a]Gen. 37:4, 8-36; 18:19; Matt. 10:36
29 [1]Lit., *word*
0 [1]Lit., *from beside im* [2]Lit., *the former* [a]1 Sam. 17:26, 27

31 When the words which David spoke were heard, they told *them* [1]to Saul, and he sent for him.
32 And David said to Saul, "[a]Let no man's heart fail on account of him; [b]your servant will go and fight with this Philistine."
33 Then Saul said to David, "[a]You are not able to go against this Philistine to fight with him; for you are *but* a youth while he has been a warrior from his youth."
34 But David said to Saul, "Your servant was tending his father's sheep. When a lion or a bear came and took a lamb from the flock,
35 I went out after him and [1]attacked him, and [a]rescued *it* from his mouth; and when he rose up against me, I seized *him* by his beard and [1]struck him and killed him.
36 "Your servant has [1]killed both the lion and the bear; and this uncircumcised Philistine will be like one of them, since he has taunted the armies of the living God."
37 And David said, "[a]The LORD who delivered me from the paw of the lion and from the paw of the bear, He will deliver me from the hand of this Philistine." And Saul said to David, "[b]Go, and may the LORD be with you."
38 Then Saul clothed David with his garments and put a bronze helmet on his head, and he clothed him with armor.
39 And David girded his sword over his armor and tried to walk, for he had not tested *them*. So David said to Saul, "I cannot go with these, for I have not tested *them*." And David took them [1]off.
40 And he took his stick in his hand and chose for himself five smooth stones from the brook, and put them in the shepherd's bag which he had, even in *his* pouch, and [a]his sling was in his hand; and he approached the Philistine.
41 Then the Philistine came on and approached David, with the shield-bearer in front of him.
42 When the Philistine looked and saw David, [a]he disdained him; for he was *but* a youth, and [b]ruddy, with a handsome appearance.
43 And the Philistine said to David, "[a]Am I a dog, that you come to me with sticks?" And [b]the Philistine cursed David by his gods.
44 The Philistine also said to David, "Come to me, and I will give your flesh [a]to the birds of the sky and the beasts of the field."
45 Then David said to the Philistine, "You come to me with a sword, a spear, and a javelin, [a]but I come to you in the name of the LORD of hosts, the God of the armies of Israel, whom you have taunted.
46 "This day the LORD will deliver you up into my hands, and I will strike you down and remove your head from you. And I will give the [a]dead bodies of the army of the Philistines this day to the birds of the sky and the wild beasts of the earth, [b]that all the earth may know that there is a God in Israel,
47 and that all this assembly may know that [a]the LORD does not deliver by sword or by spear; [b]for the battle is the LORD's and He will give you into our hands."
48 Then it happened when the Philistine rose and came and drew near to meet David, that [a]David ran quickly toward the battle line to meet the Philistine.
49 And David put his hand into his bag and took from it a stone and slung *it*, and struck the Philistine on his forehead. And the stone sank into his forehead, so that he fell on his face to the ground.

31 [1]Lit., *befor*
32 [a]Deut. 20:1 [b]1 Sam. 16:18
33 [a]Num. 13:3
35 [1]Lit., *smote* 3:12
36 [1]Lit., *smitten*
37 [a]2 Cor. 1:10 4:17, 18 [b]1 Sar 1 Chr. 22:11, 16
39 [1]Lit., *off from*
40 [a]Judg. 20:16
42 [a]Ps. 123:4; F 16:18 [b]1 Sam. 1
43 [a]1 Sam. 24:1 2 Sam. 3:8; 2 Kin [b]1 Kin. 20:10
44 [a]1 Sam. 17:4
45 [a]2 Sam. 22:3 2 Chr. 32:8; Ps. 1 Heb. 11:32-34
46 [a]Deut. 28:26 4:24; 1 Kin. 8:43; 2 Kin. 19:19; Is. 3
47 [a]1 Sam. 14:6; 14:11; 20:15; Ps. 4 Hos. 1:7; Zech. 4: [b]2 Chr. 20:15
48 [a]Ps. 27:3

50 Thus David prevailed over the Philistine with a sling and a
stone, and he struck the Philistine and killed him; but there was no
sword in David's hand.
51 Then David ran and stood over the Philistine and [a]took his
sword and drew it out of its sheath and killed him, and cut off his
head with it. [b]When the Philistines saw that their champion was
dead, they fled.
52 And the men of Israel and Judah arose and shouted and pursued
the Philistines [1]as far as the valley, and to the gates of [a]Ekron. And
the slain Philistines [2]lay along the way to [b]Shaaraim, even to Gath
and Ekron.
53 And the sons of Israel returned from chasing the Philistines and
plundered their camps.
54 Then David took the Philistine's head and brought it to Jerusa-
lem, but he put his weapons in his tent.
55 Now when Saul saw David going out against the Philistine, he
said to Abner the commander of the army, "Abner, whose son is [a]this
young man?" And Abner said, "By your life, O king, I do not know."
56 And the king said, "You inquire whose son the youth is."
57 So when David returned from killing the Philistine, Abner took
him and [a]brought him before Saul with the Philistine's head in his
hand.
58 And Saul said to him, "Whose son are you, young man?" And
David answered, "[a]*I am* the son of your servant Jesse the Beth-
lehemite."

Chapter 18

18 Now it came about when he had finished speaking to Saul,
that [a]the soul of Jonathan was knit to the soul of David, and
[b]Jonathan loved him as himself.
2 And Saul took him that day and [a]did not let him return to his
father's house.
3 Then [a]Jonathan made a covenant with David because he loved
him as himself.
4 And [a]Jonathan stripped himself of the robe that was on him and
gave it to David, with his armor, including his sword and his bow
and his belt.
5 So David went out wherever Saul sent him, *and* [1]prospered; and
Saul set him over the men of war. And it was pleasing in the sight of
all the people and also in the sight of Saul's servants.
6 And it happened as they were coming, when David returned
from killing the Philistine, that [a]the women came out of all the cities
of Israel, singing and dancing, to meet King Saul, with tambourines,
with joy and with [1]musical instruments.
7 And the women [a]sang as they [1]played, and said,
"[b]Saul has slain his thousands,
[c]And David his ten thousands."
8 Then Saul became very angry, for this saying [1]displeased him;
and he said, "They have ascribed to David ten thousands, but to me
they have ascribed thousands. Now [a]what more can he have but the
kingdom?"
9 And Saul looked at David with suspicion from that day on.
10 Now it came about on the next day that [a]an evil spirit from God
came mightily upon Saul, and [b]he raved in the midst of the house,

51 [a]1 Sam. 21:9; 2 Sam. 23:21 [b]Heb. 11:34
52 [1]Lit., *until your coming to* [2]Lit., *fell* [a]Josh. 15:11 [b]Josh. 15:36
55 [a]1 Sam. 16:12, 21, 22
57 [a]1 Sam. 17:54
58 [a]1 Sam. 17:12
18:1 [a]Gen. 44:30 [b]Deut. 13:6; 1 Sam. 20:17; 2 Sam. 1:26
2 [a]1 Sam. 17:15
3 [a]1 Sam. 20:8-17
Gen. 41:42; 1 Sam. 17:38; Esth. 6:8
5 [1]Or, *acted wisely*
[1]I.e., triangles; or, three-stringed ments [a]Ex. 15:20, 1; Judg. 11:34; Ps. 68:25; 149:3
[1]Or, *danced* [a]Ex. 5:21; 1 Sam. 21:11; 29:5 [b]1 Sam. 21:11 [c]2 Sam. 18:3
[1]Lit., *was evil in his yes* [a]1 Sam. 15:28
10 [a]1 Sam. 16:14 [b]1 Sam. 19:23, 24

while David was playing *the harp* with his hand, [1c]as usual; and [2d]a
spear *was* in Saul's hand.
11 And [a]Saul hurled the spear for he thought, "I will [1]pin David to
the wall." But David [2]escaped from his presence twice.
12 Now [a]Saul was afraid of David, [b]for the LORD was with him but
[c]had departed from Saul.
13 Therefore Saul removed him from [1]his presence, and appointed
him as his commander of a thousand; and [a]he went out and came in
before the people.
14 And David was [1]prospering in all his ways for [a]the LORD *was*
with him.
15 When Saul saw that he was [1]prospering greatly, he dreaded him.
16 But [a]all Israel and Judah loved David, and he went out and came
in before them.
17 Then Saul said to David, "[a]Here is my older daughter Merab; I
will give her to you as a wife, only be a valiant man for me and fight
[b]the LORD's battles." For Saul thought, "My hand shall not be against
him, but [c]let the hand of the Philistines be against him."
18 But David said to Saul, "[a]Who am I, and what is my life *or* my
father's family in Israel, that I should be the king's son-in-law?"
19 So it came about at the time when Merab, Saul's daughter,
should have been given to David, that she was given to [a]Adriel [b]the
Meholathite for a wife.
20 Now [a]Michal, Saul's daughter, loved David. When they told
Saul, the thing was agreeable [1]to him.
21 And Saul thought, "I will give her to him that she may become a
snare to him, and [a]that the hand of the Philistines may be against
him." Therefore Saul said to David, "[b]For a second time you may be
my son-in-law today."
22 Then Saul commanded his servants, "Speak to David secretly,
saying, 'Behold, the king delights in you, and all his servants love
you; now therefore, become the king's son-in-law.' "
23 So Saul's servants spoke these words [1]to David. But David said,
"Is it trivial in your sight to become the king's son-in-law, [a]since I am
a poor man and lightly esteemed?"
24 And the servants of Saul reported to him [1]according to these
words *which* David spoke.
25 Saul then said, "Thus you shall say to David, 'The king does not
desire any [a]dowry except a hundred foreskins of the Philistines, [b]to
take vengeance on the king's enemies.' " Now [c]Saul planned to make
David fall by the hand of the Philistines.
26 When his servants told David these words, [1]it pleased David to
become the king's son-in-law. [2a]Before the days had expired
27 David rose up and went, [a]he and his men, and struck down two
hundred men among the Philistines. Then [b]David brought their
foreskins, and they gave them in full number to the king, that he
might become the king's son-in-law. So Saul gave him Michal his
daughter for a wife.
28 When Saul saw and knew that the LORD was with David, and
that Michal, Saul's daughter, loved him,
29 then Saul was even more afraid of David. Thus Saul was David's
enemy continually.
30 Then the commanders of the Philistines [a]went out *to battle*, and it
happened as often as they went out, that David [b]behaved himself

10 [1]Lit., *day b* [2]Lit., *the* [c]1 Sa [d]1 Sam. 19:9

11 [1]Lit., *strike and the wall* [2]L *turned about* [a] 19:10; 20:33

12 [a]1 Sam. 18: [b]1 Sam. 16:13, [c]1 Sam. 16:14;

13 [1]Lit., *with hi* [a]Num. 27:17; 1 18:16; 2 Sam. 5

14 [1]Or, *acting* [a]Gen. 39:2, 3, 2 6:27; 1 Sam. 16

15 [1]Or, *acting wisely*

16 [a]1 Sam. 18:

17 [a]1 Sam. 17: [b]Num. 21:14; 1 17:36, 47; 25:28 [c]1 Sam. 18:21, 2

18 [a]1 Sam. 9:21 2 Sam. 7:18

19 [a]2 Sam. 21:8 7:22; 1 Kin. 19:1

20 [1]Lit., *in his s* [a]1 Sam. 18:28

21 [a]1 Sam. 18:1 [b]1 Sam. 18:26

23 [1]Lit., *in the ea* [a]Gen. 29:20; 34:1

24 [1]Lit., *by sayin according*

25 [a]Gen. 34:12; 22:17 [b]1 Sam. 14 [c]1 Sam. 18:17

26 [1]Lit., *it was agreeable in the s of* [2]Lit., *And the d had not expired* [a]1 Sam. 18:21

27 [a]1 Sam. 18:17 [b]2 Sam. 3:14

30 [a]2 Sam. 11:1 [b]1 Sam. 18:5

more wisely than all the servants of Saul. So his name was highly
esteemed.

Chapter 19

19 Now Saul told Jonathan his son and all his servants [a]to put
David to death. But [b]Jonathan, Saul's son, greatly delighted in
David.
2 So Jonathan told David saying, "Saul my father is seeking to put
you to death. Now therefore, please be on guard in the morning, and
stay in a secret place and hide yourself.
3 "And I will go out and stand beside my father in the field where
you are, and I will speak with my father about you; [a]if I [1]find out
anything, then I shall tell you."
4 Then Jonathan [a]spoke well of David to Saul his father, and said
to him, "[b]Do not let the king sin against his servant David, since he
has not sinned against you, and since his deeds *have been* very
[1]beneficial to you.
5 "For [a]he took his life in his hand and struck the Philistine, and
[b]the LORD brought about a great deliverance for all Israel; you saw *it*
and rejoiced. [c]Why then will you sin against innocent blood, by put-
ting David to death without a cause?"
6 And Saul listened to the voice of Jonathan, and Saul vowed, "As
the LORD lives, he shall not be put to death."
7 Then Jonathan called David, and Jonathan told him all these
words. And Jonathan brought David to Saul, and he was in his
presence as [a]formerly.
8 When there was war again, David went out and fought with the
Philistines, and [1]defeated them with great slaughter, so that they fled
before him.
9 Now there was [a]an evil spirit from the LORD on Saul as he was
sitting in his house [b]with his spear in his hand, [c]and David was
playing *the harp* with *his* hand.
10 [a]And Saul tried to [1]pin David to the wall with the spear, but he
slipped away out of Saul's presence, so that he [2]stuck the spear into
the wall. And David fled and escaped that night.
11 Then [a]Saul sent messengers to David's house to watch him, in
order to put him to death in the morning. But Michal, David's wife,
told him, saying, "If you do not save your life tonight, tomorrow
you will be put to death."
12 [a]So Michal let David down through a window, and he went out
and fled and escaped.
13 And Michal took [a]the [1]household idol and laid *it* on the bed, and
put a quilt of goats' *hair* at its head, and covered *it* with clothes.
14 When Saul sent messengers to take David, she said, "[a]He is
sick."
15 Then Saul sent messengers to see David, saying, "Bring him up
to me on [1]his bed, that I may put him to death."
16 When the messengers entered, behold, the [1]household idol *was*
on the bed with the quilt of goats' *hair* at its head.
17 So Saul said to Michal, "Why have you deceived me like this and
let my enemy go, so that he has escaped?" And Michal said to Saul,
"He said to me, 'Let me go! [a]Why should I put you to death?' "
18 Now David fled and escaped and came [a]to Samuel at Ramah,

Sam. 18:8, 9
Sam. 18:1-3
see [a]1 Sam. 20:9, 13
good [a]1 Sam. ; Prov. 31:8, 9 . 42:22; Prov. 13; Jer. 18:20
. 9:17; 1 Sam. 50; 28:21; Ps. [b]1 Sam. 11:13; . 11:14 [c]Deut. 1 Sam. 20:32; :21; Matt. 27:4
m. 16:21; 18:2, 10, 13
8 [1]Lit., *smote*
. 16:14; 18:10, [b]1 Sam. 18:10 [c]1 Sam. 16:16
.it., *strike David* *d the wall* [2]Lit., [a]1 Sam. 18:11; 0:33; Prov. 1:16
[a]Judg. 16:2; Ps. 59:title
Josh. 2:15; Acts :25; 2 Cor. 11:33
[1]Heb., *teraphim* ien. 31:19; Judg. 18:14, 17
14 [a]Josh. 2:5
15 [1]Lit., *the*
[1]Heb., *teraphim*
17 [a]2 Sam. 2:22
18 [a]1 Sam. 7:17

and told him all that Saul had done to him. And he and Samuel went
and stayed in [b]Naioth.
19 And it was told Saul, saying, "Behold, David is at Naioth in
Ramah."
20 Then [a]Saul sent messengers to take David, but when they saw
[b]the company of the prophets prophesying, with Samuel standing
and presiding over them, the Spirit of God came upon the mes-
sengers of Saul; and [c]they also prophesied.
21 And when it was told Saul, he sent other messengers, and they
also prophesied. So Saul sent messengers again the third time, and
they also prophesied.
22 Then he himself went to Ramah, and came as far as the large
well that is in Secu; and he asked and said, "Where are Samuel and
David?" And *someone* said, "Behold, they are at Naioth in Ramah."
23 And he [1]proceeded there to Naioth in Ramah; and [a]the Spirit of
God came upon him also, so that he went along prophesying con-
tinually until he came to Naioth in Ramah.
24 And he also stripped off his clothes, and he too prophesied
before Samuel and [1]lay down [2a]naked all that day and all that night.
Therefore they say, "[b]Is Saul also among the prophets?"

Chapter 20

20 Then David fled from Naioth in Ramah, and came and [a]said
[1]to Jonathan, "What have I done? What is my iniquity? And
what is my sin before your father, that he is seeking my life?"
2 And he said to him, "Far from it, you shall not die. Behold, my
father does nothing either great or small [1]without disclosing it to me.
So why should my father hide this thing from me? It is not so!"
3 Yet David [a]vowed again, [1]saying, "Your father knows well that I
have found favor in your sight, and he has said, 'Do not let Jonathan
know this, lest he be grieved.' But truly [b]as the LORD lives and as
your soul lives, there is [2]hardly a step between me and death."
4 Then Jonathan said to David, "Whatever [1]you say, I will do for
you."
5 So David said to Jonathan, "Behold, tomorrow is [a]the new moon,
and I ought [b]to sit down to eat with the king. But let me go, [c]that I
may hide myself in the field until the third evening.
6 "If your father misses me at all, then say, 'David earnestly asked
leave of me to run to [a]Bethlehem his city, because it is [b]the yearly
sacrifice there for the whole family.'
7 "If he [1]says, 'It is good,' your servant *shall be* safe; but if he is very
angry, [a]know that he has decided on evil.
8 "Therefore deal kindly with your servant, for [a]you have brought
your servant into a covenant of the LORD with you. But [b]if there is
iniquity in me, put me to death yourself; for why then should you
bring me to your father?"
9 And Jonathan said, "Far be it from you! For if I should indeed
learn that evil has been decided by my father to come upon you,
then would I not tell you about it?"
10 Then David said to Jonathan, "Who will tell me [1]if your father
answers you harshly?"
11 And Jonathan said to David, "Come, and let us go out into the
field." So both of them went out to the field.
12 Then Jonathan said to David, "The LORD, the God of Israel, *be*

18 [b]1 Sam. 1…

20 [a]1 Sam. 1… John 7:32 [b]1… 10:5, 6, 10 [c]N… 11:25; Joel 2:2…

23 [1]Lit., *went* 10:10

24 [1]Lit., *fell* [2]I… without outwar… garments [a]2 S… Is. 20:2; Mic. 1… [b]1 Sam. 10:10-…

20:1 [1]Lit., *befo…* [a]1 Sam. 24:9

2 [1]Lit., *and he uncover my ea…*

3 [1]Lit., *and sai… about* [a]Deut. 6:… [b]1 Sam. 25:26; …

4 [1]Lit., *your sou…*

5 [a]Num. 10:10; 28:11-15; Amos … [b]1 Sam. 20:24, 2… [c]1 Sam. 19:2

6 [a]1 Sam. 17:58… 12:5; 1 Sam. 9:1…

7 [1]Lit., *says thus* [a]1 Sam. 25:17

8 [a]1 Sam. 18:3; 2… [b]2 Sam. 14:32

10 [1]Lit., *or what*

witness! When I have sounded out my father about this time tomorrow, *or* the third day, behold, if there is good *feeling* toward David, shall I not then send to you and [1]make it known to you?
13 "If it please my father *to do* you harm, [a]may the LORD do so to Jonathan and more also, if I do not [1]make it known to you and send you away, that you may go in safety. And [b]may the LORD be with you as He has been with my father.
14 "And if I am still alive, will you not show me the lovingkindness of the LORD, that I may not die?
15 "And [a]you shall not cut off your lovingkindness from my house forever, not even when the LORD cuts off every one of the enemies of David from the face of the earth."
16 So Jonathan made a *covenant* with the house of David, *saying,* "[a]May the LORD require *it* at the hands of David's enemies."
17 And Jonathan made David vow again because of his love for him, because [a]he loved him as he loved his own life.
18 Then Jonathan said to him, "[a]Tomorrow is the new moon, and you will be missed because your seat will be empty.
19 "When you have stayed for three days, you shall go down quickly and come to the place where you hid yourself on that eventful day, and you shall remain by the stone Ezel.
20 "And I will shoot three arrows to the side, as though I shot at a target.
21 "And behold, I will send the lad, *saying,* 'Go, find the arrows.' If I specifically say to the lad, 'Behold, the arrows are on this side of you, get them,' then come; for there is safety for you and [1]no harm, as the LORD lives.
22 "But if I [1]say to the youth, '[a]Behold, the arrows are beyond you,' go, for the LORD has sent you away.
23 "[a]As for the [1]agreement of which you and I have spoken, behold, [b]the LORD is between you and me forever."
24 So David hid in the field; and when the new moon came, the king sat down to eat food.
25 And the king sat on his seat as usual, the seat by the wall; then Jonathan rose up and Abner sat down by Saul's side, but [a]David's place was empty.
26 Nevertheless Saul did not speak anything that day, for he thought, "It is an accident, [a]he is not clean, surely *he is* not clean."
27 And it came about the next day, the second *day* of the new moon, that David's place was empty; so Saul said to Jonathan his son, "Why has the son of Jesse not come to the meal, either yesterday or today?"
28 Jonathan then answered Saul, "[a]David earnestly asked leave of me *to go* to Bethlehem,
29 for he said, 'Please [1]let me go, since our family has a sacrifice in the city, and my brother has commanded me to attend. And now, if I have found favor in your sight, please let me get away that I may see my brothers.' For this reason he has not come to the king's table."
30 Then Saul's anger burned against Jonathan and he said to him, "You son of a perverse, rebellious woman! Do I not know that you are choosing the son of Jesse to your own shame and to the shame of your mother's nakedness?
31 "For [1]as long as the son of Jesse lives on the earth, neither you nor

[1]Lit., *uncover your ear*

[1]Lit., *uncover your* [a]Ruth 1:17; 1 Sam. [b]Josh. 1:5; 1 Sam. 7:37; 18:12; 1 Chr. 22:11, 16

15 [a]2 Sam. 9:1, 3

16 [a]Deut. 23:21; 1 Sam. 25:22

17 [a]1 Sam. 18:1

[a]1 Sam. 20:5, 25

t., *there is nothing*

22 [1]Lit., *say thus* [a]1 Sam. 20:37

.it., *word* [a]1 Sam. , 15 [b]Gen. 31:49, 53; 1 Sam. 20:42

25 [a]1 Sam. 20:18

ev. 7:20, 21; 15:5; 1 Sam. 16:5

28 [a]1 Sam. 20:6

.it., *send me away*

[1]Lit., *all the days which*

your kingdom will be established. Therefore now, send and bring
him to me, for [a]he [2]must surely die."
32 But Jonathan answered Saul his father and said to him, "[a]Why
should he be put to death? What has he done?"
33 Then [a]Saul hurled his spear at him to strike him down; [b]so
Jonathan knew that his father had decided to put David to death.
34 Then Jonathan arose from the table in fierce anger, and did not
eat food on the second day of the new moon, for he was grieved
over David because his father had dishonored him.
35 Now it came about in the morning that Jonathan went out into
the field for the appointment with David, and a little lad *was* with
him.
36 And he said to his lad, "[a]Run, find now the arrows which I am
about to shoot." As the lad was running, he shot [1]an arrow past him.
37 When the lad reached the place of the arrow which Jonathan had
shot, Jonathan called after the lad, and said, "[a]Is not the arrow
beyond you?"
38 And Jonathan called after the lad, "Hurry, be quick, do not stay!"
And Jonathan's lad picked up the arrow and came to his master.
39 But the lad was not aware of anything; only Jonathan and David
knew about the matter.
40 Then Jonathan gave his weapons to his lad and said to him, "Go,
bring *them* to the city."
41 When the lad was gone, David rose from the south side and fell
on his face to the ground, and [a]bowed three times. And they kissed
each other and wept together, but [b]David more.
42 And Jonathan said to David, "[a]Go in safety, inasmuch as we
have sworn to each other in the name of the LORD, saying, '[b]The LORD
will be between me and you, and between my [1]descendants and
your [1]descendants forever.' " [2]Then he rose and departed, while
Jonathan went into the city.

Chapter 21

21 Then David came to [a]Nob to Ahimelech the priest; and Ahi-
melech [b]came trembling to meet David, and said to him,
"Why are you alone and no one with you?"
2 And David said to Ahimelech the priest, "The king has commis-
sioned me with a matter, and has said to me, '[a]Let no one know
anything about the matter on which I am sending you and with
which I have commissioned you; and I have directed the young men
to a certain place.'
3 "Now therefore, what [1]do you have on hand? Give [2]me five
loaves of bread, or whatever can be found."
4 And the priest answered David and said, "There is no ordinary
bread [1]on hand, but there is [a]consecrated bread; if only the young
men have [b]kept themselves from women."
5 And David answered the priest and said to him, "[a]Surely women
have been kept from us as previously when I set out and the [b]vessels
of the young men were holy, though it was an ordinary journey; how
much more then today will [1]their vessels *be holy*?"
6 So [a]the priest gave him consecrated *bread*; for there was no bread
there but the [b]bread of the Presence which was removed from before
the LORD, in order to put hot bread *in its place* when it was taken
away.

31 [2]Lit., *is a son o* *death* [a]2 Sam. 12

32 [a]Gen. 31:36; 1 19:5; Prov. 31:9; M 27:23

33 [a]1 Sam. 18:11; 19:10 [b]1 Sam. 20

36 [1]Lit., *the* [a]1 Sa 20:20, 21

37 [a]1 Sam. 20:22

41 [a]Gen. 42:6 [b]1 18:3

42 [1]Lit., *seed* [2]C in Heb. [a]1 Sam. [b]1 Sam. 20:15, 16

21:1 [a]1 Sam. 22 Neh. 11:32; Is. 10 [b]1 Sam. 16:4

2 [a]Ps. 141:3

3 [1]Lit., *is under* *hand?* [2]Lit., *in m*

4 [1]Lit., *under my* [a]Ex. 25:30; Lev. Matt. 12:4 [b]Ex. 1

5 [1]Lit., *it be holy* *vessel* [a]Ex. 19:1 [b]1 Thess. 4:4

6 [a]Matt. 12:3, 4; 6:3, 4 [b]Lev. 24:5

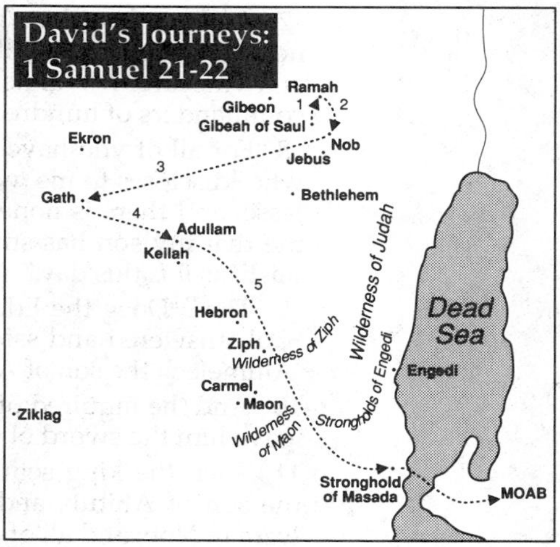

David's Journeys: 1 Samuel 21-22

1 Sam. 14:47; 22:9; Ps. 52: title [b]1 Chr. 27:29, 31

7 Now one of the servants of Saul was there that day, detained before the LORD; and his name was [a]Doeg the Edomite, the [b]chief of Saul's shepherds.

8 [1]Lit., *under your* ...nd [2]Lit., *in my hand*

8 And David said to Ahimelech, "Now is there not a spear or a sword [1]on hand? For I brought neither my sword nor my weapons [2]with me, because the king's matter was urgent."

...Lit., *smote* [a]1 Sam. ...1, 54 [b]1 Sam. 17:2

9 Then the priest said, "[a]The sword of Goliath the Philistine, whom you [1]killed [b]in the valley of Elah, behold, it is wrapped in a cloth behind the ephod; if you would take it for yourself, take *it*. For there is no other except it here." And David said, "There is none like it; give it to me."

10 [a]Ps. 34:title

10 Then David arose and fled that day from Saul, and went to [a]Achish king of Gath.

...Ps. 56:title [b]1 Sam. 18:7; 29:5

11 But the [a]servants of Achish said to him, "Is this not David the king of the land? [b]Did they not sing of this one as they danced, saying,

'Saul has slain his thousands,
And David his ten thousands'?"

...[1]Lit., *in his* [a]Luke 2:19

12 And David [a]took these words [1]to heart, and greatly feared Achish king of Gath.

13 So he [a]disguised his sanity before them, and acted insanely in their hands, and scribbled on the doors of the gate, and let his saliva run down into his beard.

14 Then Achish said to his servants, "Behold, you see the man behaving as a madman. Why do you bring him to me?

13 [a]Ps. 34:title

15 "Do I lack madmen, that you have brought this one to act the madman in my presence? Shall this one come into my house?"

Chapter 22

22:1 [a]Ps. 57:title ...Josh. 12:15; 15:35; 2 Sam. 23:13; Ps. 142:title

22 So David departed from there and [a]escaped to [b]the cave of Adullam; and when his brothers and all his father's household heard *of it*, they went down there to him.

2 And everyone who was in distress, and everyone who [1]was in debt, and everyone who was [2]discontented, gathered to him; and he became captain over them. Now there were [a]about four hundred men with him.

[1]Lit., *had a creditor* [2]Lit., *bitter of soul* ...Sam. 23:13; 25:13

3 And David went from there to Mizpah of Moab; and he said to the king of Moab, "Please let my father and my mother come *and stay* with you until I know what God will do for me."

4 Then he left them with the king of Moab; and they stayed with him all the time that David was in the stronghold.

...Sam. 24:11; 1 Chr. 29:29; 2 Chr. 29:25

5 And [a]the prophet Gad said to David, "Do not stay in the stronghold; depart, and go into the land of Judah." So David departed and went into the forest of Hereth.

6 Then Saul heard that David and the men who were with him had been discovered. Now [a]Saul was sitting in Gibeah, under the tamarisk tree on the height with his spear in his hand, and all his servants were standing around him.

[a]Judg. 4:5; 1 Sam. 14:2

7 And Saul said to his servants who stood around him, "Hear
now, O Benjamites! Will the son of Jesse also give to all of you fields
and vineyards? [a]Will he make you all commanders of thousands and
commanders of hundreds?
8 "For all of you have conspired against me so that there is no one
who [1]discloses to me [a]when my son makes *a covenant* with the son of
Jesse, and there is none of you [b]who is sorry for me or [1]discloses to
me that my son has stirred up my servant against me to lie in am-
bush, as *it is* this day."
9 Then [a]Doeg the Edomite, who was [1]standing by the servants of
Saul, answered and said, "[b]I saw the son of Jesse coming to Nob, to
[c]Ahimelech the son of Ahitub.
10 "And [a]he inquired of the LORD for him, [b]gave him provisions, and
[c]gave him the sword of Goliath the Philistine."
11 Then the king sent someone to summon Ahimelech the priest,
the son of Ahitub, and all his father's household, the priests who
were in Nob; and all of them came to the king.
12 And Saul said, "Listen now, son of Ahitub." And he [1]answered,
"Here I am, my lord."
13 Saul then said to him, "Why have you and the son of Jesse
conspired against me, in that you have given him bread and a sword
and have inquired of God for him, that he should rise up against me
[a]by lying in ambush as *it is* this day?"
14 [a]Then Ahimelech answered the king and said, "And who among
all your servants is as faithful as David, even the king's son-in-law,
who [1]is captain over your guard, and is honored in your house?
15 "Did I *just* begin [a]to inquire of God for him today? Far be it from
me! [b]Do not let the king impute anything to his servant *or* to any of
the household of my father, for your servant knows nothing [1]at all of
this whole affair."
16 But the king said, "You shall surely die, Ahimelech, you and all
your father's household!"
17 And [a]the king said to the [1]guards who were attending him,
"Turn around and put the priests of the LORD to death, because their
hand also is with David and because they knew that he was fleeing
and did not [2]reveal it to me." But the [b]servants of the king were not
willing to put forth their hands to [3]attack the priests of the LORD.
18 Then the king said to Doeg, "You turn around and [1]attack the
priests." And Doeg the Edomite turned around and [2]attacked the
priests, and [a]he killed that day eighty-five men [b]who wore the linen
ephod.
19 And [a]he struck Nob the city of the priests with the edge of the
sword, both men and women, children and infants; also oxen, don-
keys, and sheep, *he struck* with the edge of the sword.
20 But [a]one son of Ahimelech the son of Ahitub, named Abiathar,
[b]escaped and fled after David.
21 And Abiathar told David that Saul had killed the priests of the
LORD.
22 Then David said to Abiathar, "I knew on that day, when [a]Doeg
the Edomite was there, that he would surely tell Saul. I have brought
about *the death* of every person in your father's household.
23 "Stay with me, do not be afraid, for [a]he who seeks my life seeks
your life; for you are [1]safe with me."

7 [a]1 Sam. 8:1... 12:16-18
8 [1]Lit., *uncove... ear* [a]1 Sam. 1... 20:16 [b]1 Sam. ...
9 [1]Or, *set over* 52:title [b]1 Sam... [c]1 Sam. 14:3; 2...
10 [a]Num. 27:2... 1 Sam. 10:22 [b]... 21:6 [c]1 Sam. 2...
12 [1]Lit., *said*
13 [a]1 Sam. 22:...
14 [1]So with Gr.; *turns aside to* [a]... 19:4, 5; 20:32
15 [1]Lit., *small o...* [a]2 Sam. 5:19, 23 [b]2 Sam. 19:18, 1...
17 [1]Lit., *runners* ... *uncover my ear* ... *fall upon* [a]2 Kin. ... [b]Ex. 1:17
18 [1]Lit., *smite* [a]... *smote* [a]1 Sam. 2... [b]1 Sam. 2:18
19 [a]1 Sam. 15:3
20 [a]1 Sam. 23:6, 30:7; 1 Kin. 2:26, ... [b]1 Sam. 23:6
22 [a]1 Sam. 21:7
23 [1]Lit., *a charge* [a]1 Kin. 2:26

Chapter 23

23 Then they told David, saying, "Behold, the Philistines are
fighting against [a]Keilah, and are plundering the threshing
floors."
2 So David [a]inquired of the LORD, saying, "Shall I go and [1]attack
these Philistines?" And the LORD said to David, "Go and [1]attack the
Philistines, and deliver Keilah."
3 But David's men said to him, "Behold, we are afraid here in
Judah. How much more then if we go to Keilah against the ranks of
the Philistines?"
4 Then David inquired of the LORD once more. And the LORD
answered him and said, "Arise, go down to Keilah, for [a]I will give
the Philistines into your hand."
5 So David and his men went to Keilah and fought with the Philis-
tines; and he led away their livestock and struck them with a great
slaughter. Thus David delivered the inhabitants of Keilah.
6 Now it came about, when Abiathar the son of Ahimelech [a]fled to
David at Keilah, *that* he came down *with* an ephod in his hand.
7 When it was told Saul that David had come to Keilah, Saul said,
"God has [1]delivered him into my hand, for he shut himself in by
entering a city with double gates and bars."
8 So Saul summoned all the people for war, to go down to Keilah
to besiege David and his men.
9 Now David knew that Saul was plotting evil against him; so he
said to [a]Abiathar the priest, "[b]Bring the ephod here."
10 Then David said, "O LORD God of Israel, Thy servant has heard
for certain that Saul is seeking to come to Keilah to destroy the city
on my account.
11 "Will the men of Keilah surrender me into his hand? Will Saul
come down just as Thy servant has heard? O LORD God of Israel, I
pray, tell Thy servant." And the LORD said, "He will come down."
12 Then David said, "Will the men of Keilah surrender me and my
men into the hand of Saul?" And the LORD said, "[a]They will sur-
render you."
13 Then David and his men, [a]about six hundred, arose and
departed from Keilah, and they went [b]wherever they could go.
When it was told Saul that David had escaped from Keilah, he [1]gave
up the pursuit.
14 And David stayed in the wilderness in the strongholds, and re-
mained in the hill country in the wilderness of [a]Ziph. And Saul
sought him every day, but [b]God did not deliver him into his hand.
15 Now David [1]became aware that Saul had come out to seek his
life while David was in the wilderness of Ziph at Horesh.
16 And Jonathan, Saul's son, arose and went to David at Horesh,
and [1a]encouraged him in God.
17 Thus he said to him, "[a]Do not be afraid, because the hand of Saul
my father shall not find you, and you will be king over Israel and I
will be next to you; and [b]Saul my father knows that also."
18 So [a]the two of them made a covenant before the LORD; and David
stayed at Horesh while Jonathan went to his house.
19 Then [a]Ziphites came up to Saul at Gibeah, saying, "Is David not
hiding with us in the strongholds at Horesh, on [b]the hill of Hachilah,
which is on the [1]south of [2]Jeshimon?
20 "Now then, O king, come down according to all the desire of your

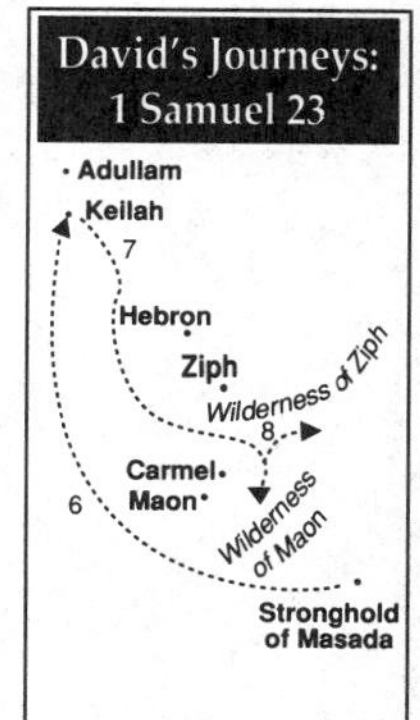

[a]Josh. 15:44; Neh. 3:17, 18
[1]Lit., *smite* [a]1 Sam. 23:4, 6, 9-12; 2 Sam. 5:19, 23
[a]Josh. 8:7; Judg. 7:7
6 [a]1 Sam. 22:20
7 [1]Lit., *alienated*
9 [a]1 Sam. 22:20 [b]1 Sam. 23:6; 30:7
12 [a]Judg. 15:10-13; 1 Sam. 23:20
[1]Lit., *ceased going out* [a]1 Sam. 22:2; 25:13 [b]2 Sam. 15:20
[a]Josh. 15:55; 2 Chr. 11:8 [b]Ps. 32:7
15 [1]Lit., *saw*
[1]Lit., *strengthened hand* [a]1 Sam. 30:6; Neh. 2:18
[a]Ps. 27:1, 3; 118:6; Is. 54:17; Heb. 13:6 Sam. 20:31; 24:20
18 [a]1 Sam. 18:3; 20:12-17, 42; 2 Sam. 9:1; 21:7
[1]Lit., *right side* [2]Or, *the desert* [a]1 Sam. 26:1; Ps. 54:title [b]1 Sam. 26:3

soul to [1]do so; and [a]our part *shall be* to surrender him into the king's
hand."
21 And Saul said, "May you be blessed of the LORD; [a]for you have
had compassion on me.
22 "Go now, make more sure, and investigate and see his place
where his [1]haunt is, *and* who has seen him there; for I am told that he
is very cunning.
23 "So look, and learn about all the hiding places where he hides
himself, and return to me with certainty, and I will go with you; and
it shall come about if he is in the land that I will search him out
among all the thousands of Judah."
24 Then they arose and went to Ziph before Saul. Now David and
his men were in the wilderness of [a]Maon, in the Arabah to the [1]south
of [2]Jeshimon.
25 When Saul and his men went to seek *him*, they told David, and
he came down to the rock and stayed in the wilderness of Maon.
And when Saul heard *it*, he pursued David in the wilderness of
Maon.
26 And Saul went on one side of the mountain, and David and his
men on the other side of the mountain; and David was hurrying to
get away from Saul, for Saul and his men [a]were surrounding David
and his men to seize them.
27 But a messenger came to Saul, saying, "Hurry and come, for the
Philistines have made a raid on the land."
28 So Saul returned from pursuing David, and went to meet the
Philistines; therefore they called that place [1]the Rock of Escape.
29 [1]And David went up from there and stayed in the strongholds of
[a]Engedi.

David's Journeys: 1 Samuel 24

Engedi
9
Strongholds of Engedi
Dead Sea
Stronghold of Masada

Chapter 24 ______________________________

24 Now it came about [a]when Saul returned from pursuing the
Philistines, [b]he was told, saying, "Behold, David is in the
wilderness of Engedi."
2 Then [a]Saul took three thousand chosen men from all Israel, and
went to seek David and his men in front of the Rocks of the Wild
Goats.
3 And he came to the sheepfolds on the way, where there *was* a
cave; and Saul [a]went in to [1]relieve himself. Now [b]David and his men
were sitting in the inner recesses of the cave.
4 And the men of David said to him, "Behold, [a]*this is* the day of
which the LORD said to you, 'Behold; [b]I am about to give your enemy
into your hand, and you shall do to him as it seems good [1]to you.' "
Then David arose and cut off the edge of Saul's robe secretly.
5 And it came about afterward that [a]David's [1]conscience bothered
him because he had cut off the edge of Saul's *robe*.
6 So he said to his men, "[a]Far be it from me because of the LORD
that I should do this thing to my lord, the LORD's anointed, to stretch
out my hand against him, since he is the LORD's anointed."
7 And David [1]persuaded his men with *these* words and did not
allow them to rise up against Saul. And Saul arose, [2]left the cave, and
went on *his* way.
8 Now afterward David arose and went out of the cave and called
after Saul, saying, "My lord the king!" And when Saul looked

20 [1]Lit., *come* [a]1 Sam. 23:12
21 [a]1 Sam. 22:
22 [1]Lit., *foot*
24 [1]Lit., *right si* *the desert* [a]Jos 1 Sam. 25:2
26 [a]Ps. 17:9
28 [1]Heb., *Sela-hammahlek*
29 [1]Ch. 24:1 in [a]Josh. 15:62; 2 C
24:1 [a]1 Sam. 23 [b]1 Sam. 23:19
2 [a]1 Sam. 26:2
3 [1]Lit., *cover his* [a]Judg. 3:24 [b]Ps. 57:title; 142:title
4 [1]Lit., *in your sig* [a]1 Sam. 23:17; 25:28-30 [b]1 Sam. 26:8, 11
5 [1]Lit., *heart struc* [a]2 Sam. 24:10
6 [a]1 Sam. 26:11
7 [1]Lit., *tore apart from*

behind him, [a]David bowed with his face to the ground and
prostrated himself.
9 And David said to Saul, "Why do you listen to the words of
men, saying, 'Behold, David seeks [1]to harm you'?
10 "[a]Behold, this day your eyes have seen that the LORD had given
you today into my hand in the cave, and [b]some said to kill you, but
my eye had pity on you; and I said, 'I will not stretch out my hand
against my lord, for he is the LORD's anointed.'
11 "Now, [a]my father, see! Indeed, see the edge of your robe in my
hand! For in that I cut off the edge of your robe and did not kill you,
know and perceive that there is no evil or [1]rebellion in my hands,
and I have not sinned against you, though you [b]are lying in wait for
my life to take it.
12 "[a]May the LORD judge between [1]you and me, and may the LORD
avenge me on you; but my hand shall not be against you.
13 "As the proverb of the ancients says, '[a]Out of the wicked comes
forth wickedness'; but my hand shall not be against you.
14 "After whom has the king of Israel come out? Whom are you
pursuing? [a]A dead dog, [b]a single flea?
15 "[a]The LORD therefore be judge and decide between [1]you and me;
and may He see and [b]plead my cause, and [2]deliver me from your
hand."
16 Now it came about when David had finished speaking these
words to Saul, that Saul said, "[a]Is this your voice, my son David?"
Then Saul lifted up his voice and wept.
17 [a]And he said to David, "You are more righteous than I; for [b]you
have dealt well with me, while I have dealt wickedly with you.
18 "And you have declared today that you have done good to me,
that [a]the LORD delivered me into your hand and *yet* you did not
kill me.
19 "For if a man [a]finds his enemy, will he let him go away [1]safely?
May the LORD therefore reward you with good in return for what
you have done to me this day.
20 "And now, behold, [a]I know that you shall surely be king, and that
[b]the kingdom of Israel shall be established in your hand.
21 "So now [a]swear to me by the LORD that you will not cut off my
[1]descendants after me, and that you will not destroy my name from
my father's household."
22 And David swore to Saul. And Saul went to his home, but David
and his men went up to [a]the stronghold.

Chapter 25

25 [a]Then Samuel died; and all Israel gathered together and
[b]mourned for him, and [c]buried him at his house in Ramah.
And David arose and went down to the [d]wilderness of Paran.
2 Now *there was* a man in [a]Maon whose business was in [b]Carmel;
and the man was very [1]rich, and he had three thousand sheep and a
thousand goats. And it came about while [c]he was shearing his sheep
in Carmel
3 (now the man's name was Nabal, and his [a]wife's name was
Abigail. And the woman was [1]intelligent and beautiful in ap-
pearance, but the man was harsh and evil in *his* dealings, and he was
[b]a Calebite),

[a]1 Sam. 25:23, 24; 1 Kin. 1:31
9 [1]Lit., *your hurt*
[a]Ps. 7:3, 4 [b]1 Sam. 24:4
[1]Lit., *transgression* 2 Kin. 5:13 [b]1 Sam. 23:14, 23; 26:20
2 [1]Lit., *me and you* . 16:5; 31:53; Judg. 7; 1 Sam. 26:10, 23
13 [a]Matt. 7:16-20
14 [a]2 Sam. 9:8 [b]1 Sam. 26:20
5 [1]Lit., *me and you vindicate* [a]1 Sam. 12 [b]Ps. 35:1; 43:1; 119:154; Mic. 7:9
16 [a]1 Sam. 26:17
17 [a]1 Sam. 26:21 [b]Matt. 5:44
18 [a]1 Sam. 26:23
19 [1]Lit., *on a good* *oad* [a]1 Sam. 23:17
20 [a]1 Sam. 23:17 [b]1 Sam. 13:14
[1]Lit., *seed* [a]Gen. ; 1 Sam. 20:14-17; 2 Sam. 21:6-8
22 [a]1 Sam. 23:29
25:1 [a]1 Sam. 28:3 Num. 20:29; Deut. 34:8 [c]2 Kin. 21:18; 2 Chr. 33:20 [d]Gen. , Num. 10:12; 13:3
Lit., *great* [a]1 Sam. 3:24 [b]Josh. 15:55 Gen. 38:13; 2 Sam. 13:23
3 [1]Lit., *of good* *lerstanding* [a]Prov. 1:10 [b]Josh. 15:13; 1 Sam. 30:14

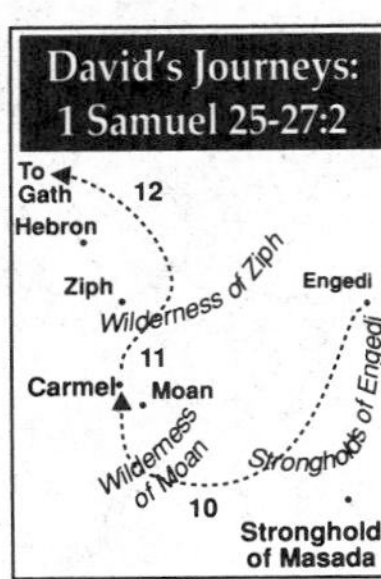

4 that David heard in the wilderness that Nabal was shearing his
sheep.
5 So David sent ten young men, and David said to the young men,
"Go up to Carmel, [1]visit Nabal and greet him in my name;
6 and thus you shall say, '[1]Have a long life, [a]peace be to you, and
peace be to your house, and peace be to all that you have.
7 'And now I have heard [a]that you have shearers; now your shep-
herds have been with us and we have not insulted them, [b]nor have
they missed anything all the days they were in Carmel.
8 'Ask your young men and they will tell you. Therefore let *my*
young men find favor in your eyes, for we have come on [a]a [1]festive
day. Please give whatever you find at hand to your servants and to
your son David.' "
9 When David's young men came, they spoke to Nabal according
to all these words in David's name; then they waited.
10 But Nabal answered David's servants, and said, "[a]Who is David?
And who is the son of Jesse? There are many servants today who are
each breaking away from his master.
11 "Shall I then [a]take my bread and my water and my meat that I
have slaughtered for my shearers, and give it to men [1]whose origin I
do not know?"
12 So David's young men retraced their way and went back; and
they came and told him according to all these words.
13 And David said to his men, "Each *of you* gird on his sword." So
each man girded on his sword. And David also girded on his sword,
and about [a]four hundred men went up behind David while two
hundred [b]stayed with the baggage.
14 But one of the young men told Abigail, Nabal's wife, saying,
"Behold, David sent messengers from the wilderness to [1a]greet our
master, and he scorned them.
15 "Yet the men were very good to us, and we were not [a]insulted,
nor did we miss anything [1]as long as we went about with them,
while we were in the fields.
16 "[a]They were a wall to us both by night and by day, all the time we
were with them tending the sheep.
17 "Now therefore, know and [1]consider what you should do, for evil
is plotted against our master and against all his household; and he is
such a [2]worthless man that no one can speak to him."
18 Then Abigail hurried and [a]took two hundred *loaves* of bread and
two jugs of wine and five sheep already prepared and five measures
of roasted grain and a hundred clusters of raisins and two hundred
cakes of figs, and loaded *them* on donkeys.
19 And she said to her young men, "[a]Go on before me; behold, I am
coming after you." But she did not tell her husband Nabal.
20 And it came about as she was riding on her donkey and coming
down by the hidden part of the mountain, that behold, David and
his men were coming down toward her; so she met them.
21 Now David had said, "Surely in vain I have guarded all that this
man has in the wilderness, so that nothing was missed of all that
belonged to him; and he has [a]returned me evil for good.
22 "[a]May God do so to the enemies of David, and more also, [b]if by
morning I leave *as much as* one [1]male of any who belong to him."
23 When Abigail saw David, she hurried and dismounted from her

5 [1]Lit., *go into*
6 [1]Lit., *To life* [a]1 12:18; Ps. 122:7; 10:5
7 [a]2 Sam. 13:23 [b]1 Sam. 25:15, 2
8 [1]Lit., *good* [a]Ne 8:10-12; Esth. 9:
10 [a]Judg. 9:28
11 [1]Lit., *from wh they are* [a]Judg.
13 [a]1 Sam. 23:1 [b]1 Sam. 30:24
14 [1]Lit., *bless* [a] 13:10; 15:13
15 [1]Lit., *all the* [a]1 Sam. 25:7, 21
16 [a]Ex. 14:22;
17 [1]Lit., *see* [2]L *of Belial*
18 [a]2 Sam. 16: 12:40
19 [a]Gen. 32:16
21 [a]Ps. 109:5; 17:13
22 [1]Lit., *who u against the wal* [a]1 Sam. 3:17; 2 [b]1 Kin. 14:10

donkey, and fell on her face before David, [a]and bowed herself to the
ground.
24 And she fell at his feet and said, "On me [1]alone, my lord, be the
blame. And please let your maidservant speak [2]to you, and listen to
the words of your maidservant.
25 "Please do not let my lord [1]pay attention to this [2]worthless man,
Nabal, for as his name is, so is he. [3]Nabal is his name and folly is
with him; but I your maidservant did not see the young men of my
lord whom you sent.
26 "Now therefore, my lord, as the LORD lives, and as your soul lives,
since the LORD has restrained you from [1]shedding blood, and [a]from
[2]avenging yourself by your own hand, now then [b]let your enemies,
and those who seek evil against my lord, be as Nabal.
27 "And now let [a]this [1]gift which your maidservant has brought to
my lord be given to the young men who [2]accompany my lord.
28 "Please forgive [a]the transgression of your maidservant; for [b]the
LORD will certainly make for my lord an enduring house, because
my lord is [c]fighting the battles of the LORD, and [d]evil shall not be
found in you all your days.
29 "And should anyone rise up to pursue you and to seek your [1]life,
then the [1]life of my lord shall be bound in the bundle of the living
with the LORD your God; but the [1]lives of your enemies [a]He will sling
out [2]as from the hollow of a sling.
30 "And it shall come about when the LORD shall do for my lord
according to all the good that He has spoken concerning you, and
[a]shall appoint you ruler over Israel,
31 that this will not [1]cause grief or a troubled heart to my lord, both
by having shed blood without cause and by my lord having
[2]avenged himself. [a]When the LORD shall deal well with my lord, then
remember your maidservant."
32 Then David said to Abigail, "[a]Blessed be the LORD God of Israel,
who sent you this day to meet me,
33 and blessed be your discernment, and blessed be you, [a]who have
kept me this day from [1]bloodshed, and from [2]avenging myself by my
own hand.
34 "Nevertheless, as the LORD God of Israel lives, [a]who has
restrained me from harming you, unless you had come quickly to
meet me, surely there would not have been left to Nabal until the
morning light *as much as* one [1]male."
35 So David received from her hand what she had brought him,
and he said to her, "[a]Go up to your house in peace. See, I have
listened to [1]you and [2b]granted your request."
36 Then Abigail came to Nabal, and behold, he was holding [a]a feast
in his house, like the feast of a king. And Nabal's heart was merry
within him, [b]for he was very drunk; so [c]she did not tell him anything
[1]at all until the morning light.
37 But it came about in the morning, when the wine had gone out
of Nabal, that his wife told him these things, and his heart died
within him so that he became *as* a stone.
38 And about ten days later, it happened that [a]the LORD struck
Nabal, and he died.
39 When David heard that Nabal was dead, he said, "Blessed be the
LORD, who has [a]pleaded the cause of my reproach from the hand of
Nabal, and [b]has kept back His servant from evil. The LORD has also

23 [a]1 Sam. 20:41
[1]Lit., *even me* [2]Lit., *in your ears*
[1]Lit., *set his heart to* [2]*man of Belial* [3]I.e., Fool
[1]Lit., *coming in with blood* [2]Lit., *saving* [a]Heb. 10:30 [b]2 Sam. 18:32
[1]Lit., *blessing* [2]Lit., *walk at the feet of* [a]Gen. 33:11; 1 Sam. 30:26
28 [a]1 Sam. 25:24 [b]2 Sam. 22:14; 2 Sam. 7:11, 16 [c]1 Sam. 18:17 [d]1 Sam. 24:11; Ps. 7:3
[1]Lit., *soul* [2]Lit., *in the midst* [a]Jer. 10:18
30 [a]1 Sam. 13:14
31 [1]Lit., *become a staggering to you or a stumbling of the heart* [2]Lit., *saved* [a]Gen. 40:14; 1 Sam. 25:30
[a]Ex. 18:10; 1 Kin. 1:48; Ps. 41:13; 72:18; 106:48; Luke 1:68
[1]Lit., *coming in with blood* [2]Lit., *saving* [a]1 Sam. 25:26
[1]Lit., *who urinates against the wall* [a]1 Sam. 25:26
35 [1]Lit., *your voice* [2]*lifted up your face* [a]1 Sam. 20:42; 2 Kin. 5:19 [b]Gen. 19:21
[1]Lit., *small or large* [a]2 Sam. 13:28 [b]Prov. 20:1; Is. 5:11; Hos. 4:11 [c]1 Sam. 25:19
38 [a]1 Sam. 26:10; Rom. 6:7; Ps. 104:29
[a]1 Sam. 24:15; Prov. 22:23 [b]1 Sam. 25:26, 34

returned the evildoing of Nabal on his own head." Then David sent
[1c]a proposal to Abigail, to take her as his wife.
40 When the servants of David came to Abigail at Carmel, they
spoke to her, saying, "David has sent us to you, to take you as his
wife."
41 And she arose [a]and bowed with her face to the ground and said,
"Behold, your maidservant is a maid [b]to wash the feet of my lord's
servants."
42 Then [a]Abigail quickly arose, and rode on a donkey, with her five
maidens who [1]attended her; and she followed the messengers of
David, and became his wife.
43 David had also taken Ahinoam of [a]Jezreel, and [b]they both be-
came his wives.
44 Now Saul had given [a]Michal his daughter, David's wife, to Palti
the son of Laish, who was from [b]Gallim.

Chapter 26

26 Then the Ziphites came to Saul at Gibeah, saying, "[a]Is not
David hiding on the hill of Hachilah, *which is* before
[1]Jeshimon?"
2 So Saul arose and went down to the wilderness of Ziph, having
with him [a]three thousand chosen men of Israel, to search for David
in the wilderness of Ziph.
3 And Saul camped in the hill of Hachilah, which is before [1]Jeshi-
mon, [a]beside the road, and David was staying in the wilderness.
When [b]he saw that Saul came after him into the wilderness,
4 David sent out spies, and he knew that Saul was definitely com-
ing.
5 David then arose and came to the place where Saul had camped.
And David saw the place where Saul lay, and [a]Abner the son of Ner,
the commander of his army; and Saul was lying in the circle of the
camp, and the people were camped around him.
6 Then David answered and said to Ahimelech [a]the Hittite and to
[b]Abishai the son of Zeruiah, Joab's brother, saying, "Who [c]will go
down with me to Saul in the camp?" And Abishai said, "I will go
down with you."
7 So David and Abishai came to the people by night, and behold,
Saul lay sleeping inside the circle of the camp, with his spear stuck
in the ground at his head; and Abner and the people were lying
around him.
8 Then Abishai said to David, "Today God has delivered your
enemy into your hand; now therefore, please let me strike him with
the spear [1]to the ground with one stroke, and I will not [2]strike him
the second time."
9 But David said to Abishai, "Do not destroy him, for [a]who can
stretch out his hand against the LORD's anointed and be without
guilt?"
10 David also said, "As the LORD lives, [a]surely the LORD will strike
him, or [b]his day will come that he dies, or [c]he will go down into
battle and perish.
11 "[a]The LORD forbid that I should stretch out my hand against the
LORD's anointed; but now please take the spear that is at his head
and the jug of water, and let us go."
12 So David took the spear and the jug of water from *beside* Saul's

39 [1]Lit., *and s*... [c]Song 8:8

41 [a]1 Sam. 25... [b]Mark 1:7

42 [1]Lit., *walke*... *feet* [a]Gen. 24:6...

43 [a]Josh. 15:5... [b]1 Sam. 27:3; 3...

44 [a]1 Sam. 18... 2 Sam. 3:14 [b]Is...

26:1 [1]Or, *the d*... [a]1 Sam. 23:19; ... 54:title

2 [a]1 Sam. 13:2; ...

3 [1]Or, *the deser*... [a]1 Sam. 24:3 [b]1... 23:15

5 [a]1 Sam. 14:50... 17:55

6 [a]Gen. 23:3; 26... Josh. 3:10; 1 Kin... 2 Kin. 7:6 [b]1 Chr... [c]Judg. 7:10, 11

8 [1]Lit., *even into*... *repeat with respe*... *him*

9 [a]1 Sam. 24:6, 7... 2 Sam. 1:14, 16

10 [a]Deut. 32:35; 1 Sam. 25:26, 38; 12:19; Heb. 10:30 [b]Gen. 47:29; Deut 31:14; Ps. 37:13 [c]1 Sam. 31:6

11 [a]1 Sam. 24:6, ... Rom. 12:17, 19; 1... 3:9

head, and they went away, but no one saw or knew *it*, nor did any
awake, for they were all asleep, because [a]a sound sleep from the
LORD had fallen on them.
13 Then David crossed over to the other side, and stood on top of
the mountain at a distance *with* a large area between them.
14 And David called to the people and to Abner the son of Ner,
saying, "Will you not answer, Abner?" Then Abner answered and
said, "Who are you who calls to the king?"
15 So David said to Abner, "Are you not a man? And who is like
you in Israel? Why then have you not guarded your lord the king?
For one of the people came to destroy the king your lord.
16 "This thing that you have done is not good. As the LORD lives, *all*
of you [1a]must surely die, because you did not guard your lord, the
LORD's anointed. And now, see where the king's spear is, and the jug
of water that was at his head."
17 Then Saul recognized David's voice and said, "[a]Is this your
voice, my son David?" And David said, "It is my voice, my lord the
king."
18 He also said, "[a]Why then is my lord pursuing his servant? For
what have I done? Or what evil is in my hand?
19 "Now therefore, please let my lord the king listen to the words of
his servant. If [a]the LORD has stirred you up against me, [b]let Him
[1]accept an offering; but [c]if it is [2]men, cursed are they before the LORD,
for [d]they have driven me out today that I should have no attachment
with the inheritance of the LORD, saying, 'Go, serve other gods.'
20 "Now then, do not let my blood fall to the ground away from the
presence of the LORD; for the king of Israel has come out to search for
[a]a single flea, just as one hunts a partridge in the mountains."
21 Then Saul said, "[a]I have sinned. Return, my son David, for I will
not harm you again because my life was precious in your sight this
day. Behold, I have played the fool and have committed a serious
error."
22 And David answered and said, "Behold the spear of the king!
Now let one of the young men come over and take it.
23 "And [a]the LORD will repay each man *for* his righteousness and his
faithfulness; for the LORD delivered you into *my* hand today, but [b]I
refused to stretch out my hand against the LORD's anointed.
24 "Now behold, as your life was [a]highly valued in my sight this
day, so may my life be highly valued in the sight of the LORD, and
may He [b]deliver me from all distress."
25 Then Saul said to David, "[a]Blessed are you, my son David; you
will both accomplish much and surely prevail." So [b]David went on
his way, and Saul returned to his place.

Chapter 27

27 Then David said [1]to himself, "Now I will perish one day by
the hand of Saul. [a]There is nothing better for me than [2]to
escape into the land of the Philistines. Saul then will despair of
searching for me anymore in all the territory of Israel, and I will
escape from his hand."
2 So David arose and crossed over, he and [a]the six hundred men
who were with him, to [b]Achish the son of Maoch, king of Gath.
3 And David lived with Achish at Gath, he and his men, [a]each

n. 2:21; 15:12; Is. 29:10
are surely sons [a]1 Sam. 20:31
[a]1 Sam. 24:16
am. 24:9, 11-14
Lit., *smell* [2]Lit., of men [a]2 Sam. :11 [b]Gen. 8:21 am. 24:9 [d]Josh. 22:25-27
[a]1 Sam. 24:14
Ex. 9:27; 1 Sam. 15:24, 30; 24:17
Sam. 24:19; Ps. 7:8; 18:20; 62:12 [b]1 Sam. 24:12
Sam. 18:30 [b]Ps. 54:7
5 [a]1 Sam. 24:19 [b]1 Sam. 24:22
[1]Lit., *in his heart* hat I should surely oe [a]1 Sam. 26:19
2 [a]1 Sam. 25:13 Sam. 21:10; 1 Kin. 2:39
Sam. 30:3; 2 Sam. 2:3

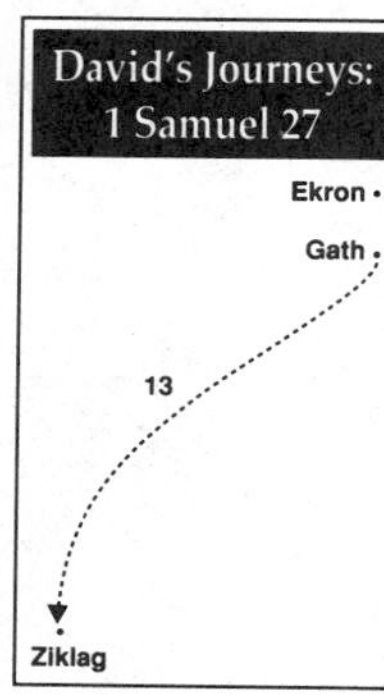

David's Journeys: 1 Samuel 27

with his household, *even* David with [b]his two wives, Ahinoam the
Jezreelitess, and Abigail the Carmelitess, Nabal's [1]widow.
4 Now it was told Saul that David had fled to Gath, so he no
longer searched for him.
5 Then David said to Achish, "If now I have found favor in your
sight, let them give me a place in one of the cities in the country, that
I may live there; for why should your servant live in the royal city
with you?"
6 So Achish gave him Ziklag that day; therefore [a]Ziklag has
belonged to the kings of Judah to this day.
7 And the number of days that David lived in the country of the
Philistines was [a]a year and four months.
8 Now David and his men went up and raided [a]the Geshurites and
the Girzites and [b]the Amalekites; for they were the inhabitants of the
land from ancient times, as you come to [c]Shur even as far as the land
of Egypt.
9 And David [1]attacked the land and did not leave a man or a
woman alive, and he [a]took away the sheep, the cattle, the donkeys,
the camels, and the clothing. Then he returned and came to Achish.
10 Now Achish said, "Where have you [a]made a raid today?" And
David said, "Against the [1]Negev of Judah and against the [1]Negev of
[b]the Jerahmeelites and against the [1]Negev of [c]the Kenites."
11 And David did not leave a man or a woman alive, to bring to
Gath, saying, "Lest they should tell about us, saying, 'So has David
done and so *has been* his practice all the time he has lived in the
country of the Philistines.' "
12 So Achish believed David, saying, "He has surely made himself
odious among his people Israel; therefore he will become my servant
forever."

Chapter 28

28 Now it came about in those days that [a]the Philistines gathered
their armed camps for war, to fight against Israel. And Achish
said to David, "Know assuredly that you will go out with me in the
camp, you and your men."
2 And David said to Achish, "Very well, you shall know what
your servant can do." So Achish said to David, "Very well, I will
make you [1]my bodyguard [a]for life."
3 Now [a]Samuel was dead, and all Israel had lamented him and
buried him [b]in Ramah his own city. And Saul had removed from the
land those who [c]were mediums and spiritists.
4 So the Philistines gathered together and came and camped [a]in
Shunem; and Saul gathered all Israel together and they camped in
[b]Gilboa.
5 When Saul saw the camp of the Philistines, he was afraid and his
heart trembled greatly.
6 [a]When Saul inquired of the LORD, [b]the LORD did not answer him,
either by [c]dreams or by [d]Urim or by prophets.
7 Then Saul said to his servants, "Seek for me a woman who is a
medium, that I may go to her and inquire of her." And his servants
said to him, "Behold, [a]there is a woman who is a medium at [b]En-
dor."
8 Then Saul [a]disguised himself by putting on other clothes, and
went, he and two men with him, and they came to the woman by

3 [1]Lit., *wife* [b]1 25:42, 43
6 [a]Josh. 15:31 Neh. 11:28
7 [a]1 Sam. 29:3
8 [a]Josh. 13:2, 1 17:8; 1 Sam. 15 [c]Ex. 15:22
9 [1]Lit., *smote* [a] 15:3; Job 1:3
10 [1]I.e., South c [a]1 Sam. 23:27 [b] 30:29; 1 Chr. 2:9 [c]Judg. 1:16; 4:11
28:1 [a]1 Sam. 29
2 [1]Lit., *keeper o head* [a]1 Sam. 1:
3 [a]1 Sam. 25:1 [b]1 Sam. 7:17 [c]Le 19:31; 20:27; Deu 18:10; 1 Sam. 15
4 [a]Josh. 19:18; 1 28:4; 1 Kin. 1:3; 2 4:8 [b]1 Sam. 31:1
6 [a]1 Chr. 10:13, 1 [b]1 Sam. 14:37; Pr 1:24-31 [c]Num. 12 Joel 2:28 [d]Ex. 28 Num. 27:21
7 [a]Acts 16:16 [b]Jo 17:11; Ps. 83:10
8 [a]2 Chr. 18:29; 3

night; and he said, "[b]Conjure up for me, please, and [c]bring up for me
whom I shall [1]name to you."
9 But the woman said to him, "Behold, you know [a]what Saul has
done, how he has cut off those who are mediums and spiritists from
the land. Why are you then laying a snare for my life to bring about
my death?"
10 And Saul vowed to her by the LORD, saying, "As the LORD lives,
there shall no punishment come upon you for this thing."
11 Then the woman said, "Whom shall I bring up for you?" And he
said, "Bring up Samuel for me."
12 When the woman saw Samuel, she cried out with a loud voice;
and the woman spoke to Saul, saying, "Why have you deceived me?
For you are Saul."
13 And the king said to her, "Do not be afraid; but what do you
see?" And the woman said to Saul, "I see a [1]divine being coming up
out of the earth."
14 And he said to her, "What is his form?" And she said, "An old
man is coming up, and [a]he is wrapped with a robe." And Saul knew
that it was Samuel, and [b]he bowed with his face to the ground and
did homage.
15 Then Samuel said to Saul, "Why have you disturbed me by
bringing me up?" And Saul answered, "I am greatly distressed; for
the Philistines are waging war against me, and [a]God has departed
from me and [b]answers me no more, either through prophets or by
dreams; therefore I have called you, that you may make known to
me what I should do."
16 And Samuel said, "Why then do you ask me, since the LORD has
departed from you and has become your adversary?
17 "And the LORD has done [1]accordingly [a]as He spoke through me;
for the LORD has torn the kingdom out of your hand and given it to
your neighbor, to David.
18 "As [a]you did not [1]obey the LORD and did not execute His fierce
wrath on Amalek, so the LORD has done this thing to you this day.
19 "Moreover the LORD will also give over Israel along with you into
the hands of the Philistines, therefore tomorrow [a]you and your sons
will be with me. Indeed the LORD will give over the army of Israel
into the hands of the Philistines!"
20 Then Saul immediately fell full length upon the ground and was
very afraid because of the words of Samuel; also there was no
strength in him, for he had eaten no [1]food all day and all night.
21 And the woman came to Saul and saw that he was terrified, and
said to him, "Behold, your maidservant has [1]obeyed you, and [a]I have
[2]taken my life in my hand, and have listened to your words which
you spoke to me.
22 "So now also, please listen to the voice of your maidservant, and
let me set a piece of bread before you that *you may* eat and have
strength when you go on *your* way."
23 But he refused and said, "[a]I will not eat." [b]However, his servants
together with the woman urged him, and he listened to [1]them. So he
arose from the ground and sat on [c]the bed.
24 And the woman had a [a]fattened calf in the house, and she quick-
ly slaughtered it; and she [b]took flour, kneaded it, and baked un-
leavened bread from it.

8 [1]Lit., *say* [b]1 Chr. ...0:13; Is. 8:19 [c]Deut. 18:10, 11
9 [a]1 Sam. 28:3
13 [1]Or, *god*
14 [a]1 Sam. 15:27 [b]1 Sam. 24:8
15 [a]1 Sam. 16:14; ...18:12 [b]1 Sam. 28:6
17 [1]Lit., *for himself* [a]1 Sam. 15:28
...8 [1]Lit., *listen to the ...e of* [a]1 Sam. 15:20, 26; 1 Kin. 20:42
...[a]1 Sam. 31:2; Job 3:17-19
20 [1]Lit., *bread*
...Lit., *listened to your ...ce* [2]Lit., *put* [a]Judg. ...3; 1 Sam. 19:5; Job 13:14
...3 [1]Lit., *their voices* [a]1 Kin. 21:4 [b]2 Kin. ...3 [c]Esth. 1:6; Ezek. 23:41
...4 [a]Gen. 18:7; Luke ...27, 30 [b]Gen. 18:6

25 And she brought *it* before Saul and his servants, and they ate.
Then they arose and went away that night.

Chapter 29

29 Now [a]the Philistines gathered together all their armies to
[b]Aphek, while the Israelites were camping by the spring
which is in [c]Jezreel.
2 And the lords of the Philistines were proceeding on by hundreds
and by thousands, and [a]David and his men were proceeding on in
the rear with Achish.
3 Then the commanders of the Philistines said, "What *are* these
Hebrews *doing here*?" And Achish said to the commanders of the
Philistines, "Is this not David, the servant of Saul the king of Israel,
[a]who has been with me these days, or *rather* these years, and [b]I have
found no fault in him from the day he [1]deserted *to me* to this day?"
4 But the commanders of the Philistines were angry with him, and
the commanders of the Philistines said to him, "Make the man go
back, that he may return [a]to his place where you have assigned him,
and do not let him go down to battle with us, [b]lest in the battle he
become an adversary to us. For with what could this *man* make
himself acceptable to his lord? *Would it* not *be* with the heads of
[1]these men?
5 "Is this not David, [a]of whom they sing in the dances, saying,
'Saul has slain his thousands,
And David his ten thousands'?"

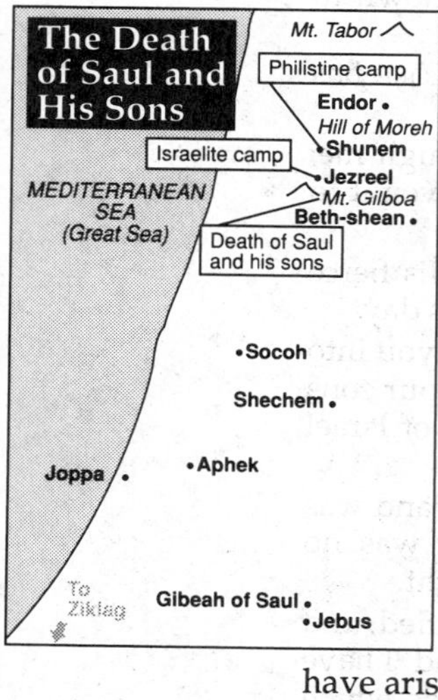

The Death of Saul and His Sons

6 Then Achish called David and said to him, "*As* the
LORD lives, you *have been* upright, and [a]your going out and
your coming in with me in the army are pleasing in my
sight; [b]for I have not found evil in you from the day of
your coming to me to this day. Nevertheless, you are not
pleasing in the sight of the lords.
7 "Now therefore return, and go in peace, that you may
not displease the lords of the Philistines."
8 And David said to Achish, "[a]But what have I done?
And what have you found in your servant from the day
when I came before you to this day, that I may not go and
fight against the enemies of my lord the king?"
9 But Achish answered and said to David, "I know that
you are pleasing in my sight, [a]like an angel of God; never-
theless [b]the commanders of the Philistines have said, 'He
must not go up with us to the battle.'
10 "Now then arise early in the morning [a]with the servants
of your lord who have come with you, and as soon as you
have arisen early in the morning and have light, depart."
11 So David arose early, he and his men, to depart in the morning,
to return to the land of the Philistines. And the Philistines went up to
Jezreel.

Chapter 30

30 Then it happened when David and his men came to [a]Ziklag
on the third day, that [b]the Amalekites had made a raid on the
[1]Negev and on [c]Ziklag, and had [2]overthrown Ziklag and burned it
with fire;
2 and they took captive the women *and all* who were in it, both

29:1 [a]1 Sam. 2 [b]Josh. 12:18; 1 1 Sam. 4:1; 1 K 20:30 [c]1 Kin. 2 2 Kin. 9:30

2 [a]1 Sam. 28:1,

3 [1]Lit., *fell* [a]1 S 27:7 [b]1 Sam. 27 1 Chr. 12:19, 20 6:5

4 [1]Lit., *those* [a]1 27:6 [b]1 Sam. 14

5 [a]1 Sam. 18:7;

6 [a]2 Sam. 3:25; 19:27; Is. 37:28 [b]1 Sam. 27:8-12;

8 [a]1 Sam. 27:10-

9 [a]2 Sam. 14:17, 19:27 [b]1 Sam. 29

10 [a]1 Chr. 12:19,

30:1 [1]I.e., South country [2]Lit., *smo* [a]1 Sam. 29:4, 11 [b]1 Sam. 15:7; 27:8 [c]1 Sam. 27:6, 8

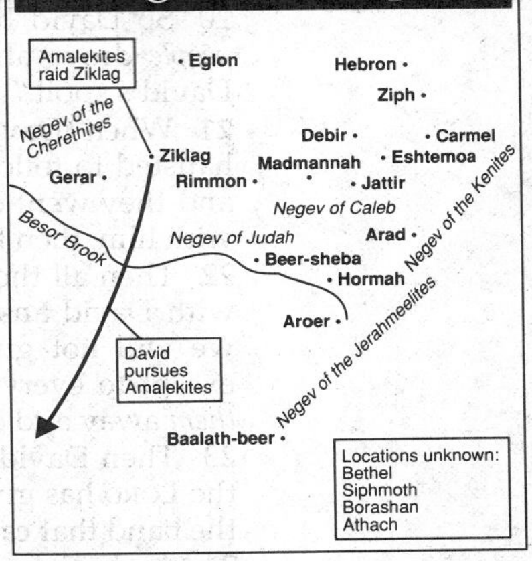
Amalekites raid Ziklag
Eglon
Hebron
Ziph
Negev of the Cherethites
Debir
Carmel
Ziklag
Madmannah
Eshtemoa
Gerar
Rimmon
Jattir
Negev of the Kenites
Negev of Caleb
Besor Brook
Negev of Judah
Arad
Beer-sheba
Hormah
Aroer
Negev of the Jerahmeelites
David pursues Amalekites
Baalath-beer
Locations unknown:
Bethel
Siphmoth
Borashan
Athach
Ziklag and the Spoils

[1]Lit., *they did not kill* [a]1 Sam. 27:11

small and great, [1a]without killing anyone, and carried *them* off and went their way.

4 [a]Num. 14:1

3 And when David and his men came to the city,
behold, it was burned with fire, and their wives and
their sons and their daughters had been taken captive.
4 Then David and the people who were with him
[a]lifted their voices and wept until there was no
strength in them to weep.

[1]Lit., *wife* [a]1 Sam. ...5:42, 43; 2 Sam. 2:2

5 Now [a]David's two wives had been taken captive, Ahinoam the Jezreelitess and Abigail the
[1]widow of Nabal the Carmelite.

6 [1]Lit., *bitter in soul* [a]Ex. 17:4; John 8:59 ...am. 23:16; Ps. 18:2; ...7:14; 31:24; 71:4, 5; Rom. 4:20

6 Moreover David was greatly distressed because
[a]the people spoke of stoning him, for all the people
were [1]embittered, each one because of his sons and
his daughters. But [b]David strengthened himself in
the LORD his God.

7 [a]1 Sam. 23:6, 9 [b]1 Sam. 22:20-23

7 Then [a]David said to [b]Abiathar the priest, the son
of Ahimelech, "Please bring me the ephod." So Abiathar brought the
ephod to David.

...[a]1 Sam. 23:2, 4; Ps. ...5; 91:15 [b]Ex. 15:9 [c]1 Sam. 30:18

8 And [a]David inquired of the LORD, saying, "[b]Shall I pursue this
band? Shall I overtake them?" And He said to him, "Pursue, for you
shall surely overtake them, [c]and you shall surely rescue *all*."
9 So David went, [a]he and the six hundred men who were with
him, and came to the brook Besor, *where* those left behind remained.

9 [a]1 Sam. 27:2

10 But David pursued, he and four hundred men, for [a]two hundred
who were too exhausted to cross the brook Besor, remained *behind*.

...0 [a]1 Sam. 30:9, 21

11 Now they found an Egyptian in the field and brought him to
David, and gave him bread and he ate, and they provided him water
to drink.

12 [1]Lit., *returned to him* [a]Judg. 15:19

12 And they gave him a piece of fig cake and two clusters of raisins,
and he ate; [a]then his spirit [1]revived. For he had not eaten bread or
drunk water for three days and three nights.
13 And David said to him, "To whom do you belong? And where
are you from?" And he said, "I am a young man of Egypt, a servant
of an Amalekite; and my master left me behind when I fell sick three
days ago.

[1]I.e., South country [a]1 Sam. 30:1, 16; 2 Sam. 8:18; 1 Kin. ...8, 44; Ezek. 25:16; ... 2:5 [b]Josh. 14:13; ...:13; 21:12 [c]1 Sam. 30:1

14 "We made a raid on [a]the [1]Negev of the Cherethites, and on that
which belongs to Judah, and on [b]the [1]Negev of Caleb, and [c]we
burned Ziklag with fire."
15 Then David said to him, "Will you bring me down to this band?"
And he said, "Swear to me by God that you will not kill me or
deliver me into the hands of my master, and I will bring you down
to this band."

16 [1]Lit., *left* [2]Lit., ...*ping a pilgrim-feast* ...Luke 12:19; 17:27f. [b]1 Sam. 30:14

16 And when he had brought him down, behold, they were [1]spread
over all the land, [a]eating and drinking and [2]dancing because of [b]all
the great spoil that they had taken from the land of the Philistines
and from the land of Judah.

...7 [1]Lit., *smote* [2]Lit., ...*ven until* [3]Lit., *their* ...Sam. 11:11 [b]Judg. 7:12; 1 Sam. 15:3

17 And David [1]slaughtered them [a]from the twilight [2]until the evening of [3]the next day; and not a man of them escaped, except four
hundred young men who rode on [b]camels and fled.

...Lit., *David rescued* [a]Gen. 14:16

18 So David [a]recovered all that the Amalekites had taken, and [1]rescued his two wives.
19 But nothing of theirs was missing, whether small or great, sons

or daughters, spoil or anything that they had taken for themselves;
[a]David brought *it* all back.
20 So David had [1]captured all the sheep and the cattle *which the*
people drove ahead of [2]the *other* livestock, and they said, "[a]This is
David's spoil."
21 When [a]David came to the two hundred men who were too ex-
hausted to follow David, who had also been left at the brook Besor,
and they went out to meet David and to meet the people who were
with him, then David approached the people and greeted them.
22 Then all the wicked and worthless men among those who went
with David answered and said, "Because they did not go with [1]us,
we will not give them any of the spoil that we have recovered,
except to every man his wife and his children, that they may lead
them away and depart."
23 Then David said, "You must not do so, my brothers, with what
the LORD has given us, who has kept us and delivered into our hand
the band that came against us.
24 "And who will listen to you in this matter? For [a]as his share is
who goes down to the battle, so shall his share be who stays by the
baggage; they shall share alike."
25 And so it has been from that day forward, that he made it a
statute and an ordinance for Israel to this day.
26 Now when David came to Ziklag, he sent *some* of the spoil to the
elders of Judah, to his friends, saying, "Behold, [a]a [1]gift for you from
the spoil of [b]the enemies of the LORD:
27 to those who were in [a]Bethel, and to those who were in [b]Ramoth
of the [1]Negev, and to those who were in [c]Jattir,
28 and to those who were in [a]Aroer, and to those who were in
Siphmoth, and to those who were in [b]Eshtemoa,
29 and to those who were in Racal, and to those who were in the
cities of [a]the Jerahmeelites, and to those who were in the cities of [b]the
Kenites,
30 and to those who were in [a]Hormah, and to those who were in
[b]Bor-ashan, and to those who were in Athach,
31 and to those who were in [a]Hebron, and to all the places where
David himself and his men were accustomed to [b]go."

Chapter 31

31 [a]Now the Philistines were fighting against Israel, and the men
of Israel fled from before the Philistines and fell slain [b]on
Mount Gilboa.
2 And the Philistines overtook Saul and his sons; and the Philis-
tines [1]killed [a]Jonathan and Abinadab and Malchi-shua the sons of
Saul.
3 And [a]the battle went heavily against Saul, and the archers [1]hit
him; and he was badly wounded by the archers.
4 [a]Then Saul said to his armor bearer, "Draw your sword and
pierce me through with it, lest [b]these uncircumcised come and pierce
me through and make sport of me." But his armor bearer would not,
for he was greatly afraid. [c]So Saul took his sword and fell on it.
5 And when his armor bearer saw that Saul was dead, he also fell
on his sword and died with him.
6 Thus Saul died with his three sons, his armor bearer, and all his
men on that day together.

19 [a]1 Sam. 30:

20 [1]Lit., *taken* *those livestock* 30:26-31

21 [a]1 Sam. 30:

22 [1]Lit., *me*

24 [a]Num. 31:27 22:8

26 [1]Lit., *blessing* [a]1 Sam. 25:27 [b] 18:17; 25:28

27 [1]I.e., South c [a]Gen. 12:8; Josh 8:9; 16:1 [b]Josh. [c]Josh. 15:48; 21

28 [a]Josh. 13:16; 11:44 [b]Josh. 15:

29 [a]1 Sam. 27:1 [b]Judg. 1:16; 1 Sa

30 [a]Num. 14:45; Josh. 12:14; 15:3 19:4; Judg. 1:17 15:42; 19:7

31 [a]Num. 13:22; 14:13-15; 21:11-1 2 Sam. 2:1 [b]1 Sa 23:22

31:1 [a]1 Chr. 10:1 [b]1 Sam. 28:4

2 [1]Lit., *smote* [a]1 8:33f.

3 [1]Lit., *found* [a]2 S 1:6

4 [a]Judg. 9:54; 1 C 10:4 [b]Judg. 14:3; 1 Sam. 14:6; 17:26 [c]2 Sam. 1:6, 10

7 And when the men of Israel who were on the other side of the
valley, with those who were beyond the Jordan, saw that the men of
Israel had fled and that Saul and his sons were dead, they aban-
doned the cities and fled; then the Philistines came and lived in
them.
8 And it came about on the [1]next day when the Philistines came to
strip the slain, that they found Saul and his three sons fallen on
Mount Gilboa.
9 And they cut off his head, and stripped off his weapons, and
sent *them* [1]throughout the land of the Philistines, [a]to carry the good
news [b]to the house of their idols and to the people.
10 And they put his weapons in the [1]temple of [a]Ashtaroth, and
[b]they fastened his body to the wall of [c]Beth-shan.
11 Now when [a]the inhabitants of Jabesh-gilead heard [1]what the Phi-
listines had done to Saul,
12 [a]all the valiant men rose and walked all night, and took the body
of Saul and the bodies of his sons from the wall of Beth-shan, and
they came to Jabesh, and [b]burned them there.
13 And they took their bones and [a]buried them under [b]the tamarisk
tree at Jabesh, and [c]fasted seven days.

8 [1]Lit., *morrow*

Lit., *into . . . around* 2 Sam. 1:20 [b]Judg. 16:23, 24

[1]Lit., *house* [a]Judg. 2:13; 1 Sam. 7:3 Sam. 31:12; 2 Sam. 21:12 [c]Josh. 17:11

11 [1]Lit., *about him* at [a]1 Sam. 11:1-13

12 [a]2 Sam. 2:4-7 [b]2 Chr. 16:14

[a]2 Sam. 21:12-14 Sam. 22:6 [c]2 Sam. 1:12

1 Samuel at a Glance

Theme of 1 Samuel:

Author:

Date:

Purpose:

Key Words:

Segment Divisions

		Main Divisions		Chapter Themes
		Samuel, the Last Judge	1	
			2	
			3	
			4	
			5	
			6	
			7	
		From Samuel to Saul From Judges to Kings	8	
			9	
			10	
			11	
			12	
			13	
			14	
			15	
		The Preparation of Another King	16	
			17	
			18	
			19	
			20	
			21	
			22	
			23	
			24	
			25	
			26	
			27	
			28	
			29	
			30	
			31	

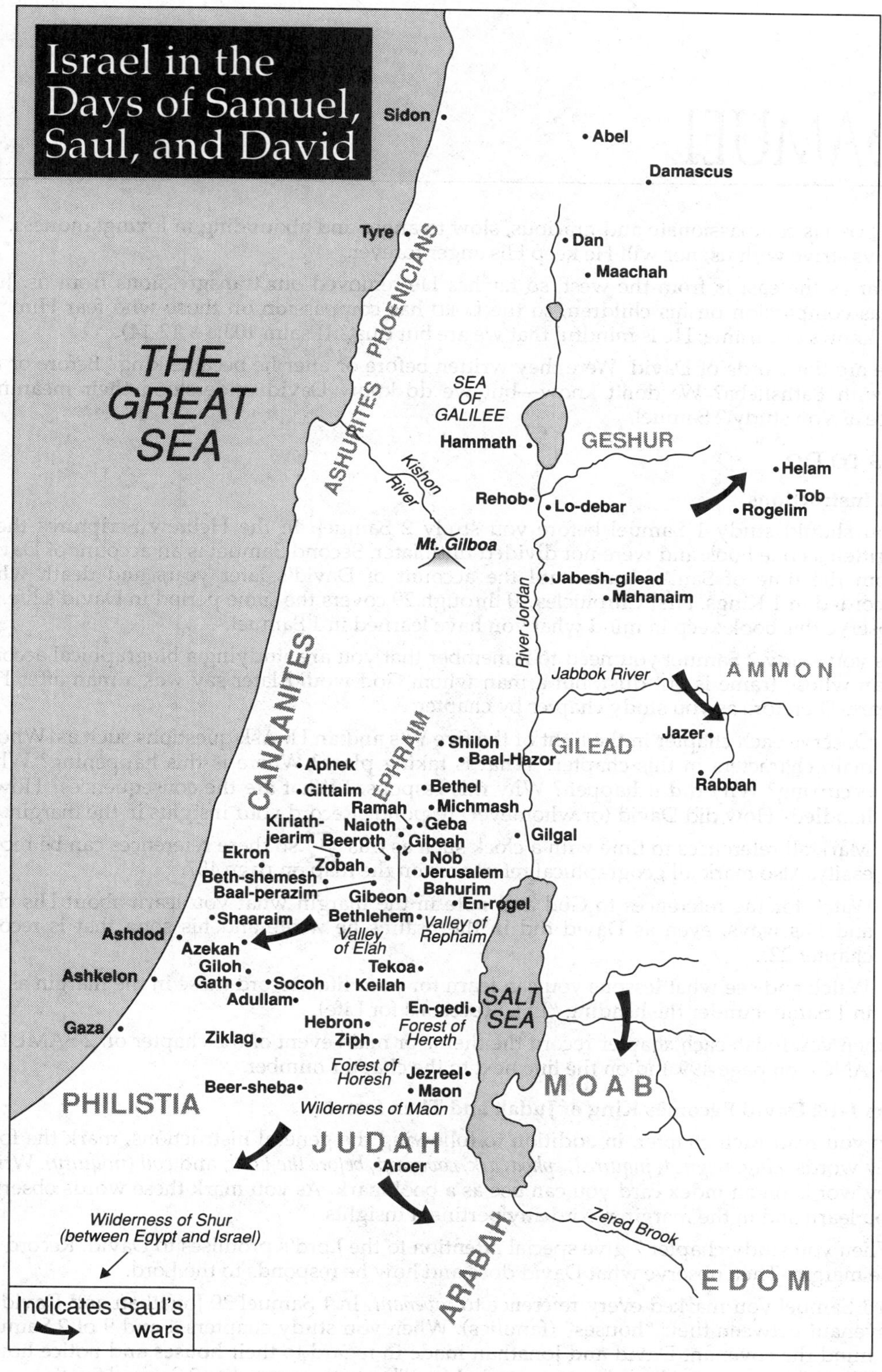

Israel in the Days of Samuel, Saul, and David
Sidon
Abel
Damascus
Tyre
Dan
Maachah
PHOENICIANS
THE GREAT SEA
ASHURITES
SEA OF GALILEE
Hammath
GESHUR
Kishon River
Helam
Tob
Rogelim
Rehob
Lo-debar
Mt. Gilboa
Jabesh-gilead
Mahanaim
River Jordan
CANAANITES
Jabbok River
AMMON
Jazer
EPHRAIM
Shiloh
Baal-Hazor
GILEAD
Aphek
Rabbah
Gittaim
Bethel
Ramah
Michmash
Kiriath-jearim
Naioth
Geba
Beeroth
Gibeah
Gilgal
Ekron
Zobah
Nob
Jerusalem
Beth-shemesh
Baal-perazim
Gibeon
Bahurim
En-rogel
Shaaraim
Bethlehem
Valley of Rephaim
Ashdod
Azekah
Valley of Elah
Giloh
Tekoa
Ashkelon
Gath
Socoh
Keilah
Adullam
SALT SEA
En-gedi
Hebron
Forest of Hereth
Gaza
Ziklag
Ziph
Forest of Horesh
Jezreel
Beer-sheba
Maon
MOAB
PHILISTIA
Wilderness of Maon
JUDAH
Aroer
Wilderness of Shur (between Egypt and Israel)
Zered Brook
ARABAH
EDOM
Indicates Saul's wars

2 SAMUEL

"The LORD is compassionate and gracious, slow to anger and abounding in lovingkindness. He w not always strive with us; nor will He keep His anger forever.

"As far as the east is from the west, so far has He removed our transgressions from us. Just a father has compassion on his children, so the LORD has compassion on those who fear Him. For Himself knows our frame; He is mindful that we are but dust" (Psalm 103:8-9,12-14).

These are the words of David. Were they written before or after he became king? Before or after sinned with Bathsheba? We don't know—but we do know David understood their meaning. T you'll see as you study 2 Samuel.

THINGS TO DO

General Instructions

1. You should study 1 Samuel before you study 2 Samuel. In the Hebrew Scriptures they w written as one book and were not divided until later. Second Samuel is an account of David's from the time of Saul's death until the account of David's later years and death which recorded in 1 Kings. First Chronicles 10 through 29 covers the same period in David's life. As observe this book keep in mind what you have learned in 1 Samuel.
2. As you study 2 Samuel you need to remember that you are studying a biographical account man whose frame is but dust, but a man whom God would later say was a man after His o heart. Therefore as you study chapter by chapter:
   a. Observe each chapter in the light of the five W's and an H. Ask questions such as: Who are main characters in this chapter? What is taking place? Where is this happening? When occurring? Why did it happen? Why this response? What are the consequences? How wa handled? How did David (or whomever) respond? Record your insights in the margin.
   b. Mark all references to time with a clock such as this so these references can be recogni easily. Also mark all geographical references on the map on page 457.
   c. Watch for the references to God and note in the margin what you learn about His chara and His ways, even as David did in the psalms he wrote and his song that is recorde chapter 22.
   d. Watch and see what lessons you can learn for your life. Record these in the margin as you in 1 Samuel under the heading "LFL" (Lessons for Life).
3. When you finish each chapter record the theme or main event of the chapter on 2 SAMUEL A GLANCE on page 499 and on the line next to the chapter number.

Chapters 1-10: David Becomes King of Judah and Then Israel

1. As you read each chapter, in addition to following the general instructions, mark the follow key words: *king, reigned, inquired, ephod, ark, covenant, before the Lord,* and *evil (iniquity).* Write th key words on an index card you can use as a bookmark. As you mark these words observe w you learn and in the margin record any pertinent insights.
2. When you study chapter 7 give special attention to the Lord's promises to David. Record thes the margin. Then observe what David does and how he responds to the Lord.
3. In 1 Samuel you marked every reference to *covenant*. In 1 Samuel 20 Jonathan and David ma covenant between their "houses" (families). When you study chapters 4 and 9 of 2 Samuel k in mind the covenant David and Jonathan made in regard to their houses and notice how Da fulfills this covenant. Also when you study Mephibosheth, remember 2 Samuel 5:6-8.

ters 11-12: David's Sins

Mark the following key words: *inquired, ark,* and *evil (sinned, sin).* Make a new bookmark for this segment.

Carefully watch the progression of events in these two chapters. Note in the margin the progression of sin and the things which could have served as admonitions against sin had David heeded them. Also list the consequences of David's sin and how the consequences parallel his sin.

Remember to follow the "General Instructions." Don't forget the "Lessons for Life" (LFL) in these two chapters.

Study Psalm 51. Note when the psalm was written.

ters 13-24: Consequences of David's Sins

Mark the following key words: *inquired, ark, covenant, before the Lord, evil (iniquity, sinned),* and *Spirit.* Make a new bookmark for this segment.

Follow the "General Instructions." Pay attention to who's who in these chapters—there are many key characters. Record their names in the margin along with a brief description of who they are. Observe the consequences of their actions.

Note who David's children are and how he deals with them. Watch Absalom carefully and keep a running record in the margin of what you learn about him. Record your "LFL" in the margin.

As you study these final chapters give special attention to David's relationship to the Lord and what David has to say about God even after God told him He would chasten him. Spend time meditating on chapter 22 and 23:1-7. When you come to *covenant,* review what you learned in chapter 7 and add any new insights.

IGS TO THINK ABOUT

What have you learned about sin and its consequences? Did you think that if God forgave you, you'd never reap sin's harvest? What do you think now?

In light of all you have learned, why do you think God referred to David as a man after His own heart (1 Samuel 13:14; Acts 13:22)? Give this some serious thought. Then think about what such a statement about David, after his death, would mean to you. If you wanted to be a man, a woman, a teen, a child after God's own heart, what do you think it would require on your part?

Review the "Lessons for Life" you marked in the margin. What did you see that you can make a matter of prayer? Did you learn anything about inquiring or sitting before the Lord? Did you learn anything from marking "before the Lord"?

:1 [a]1 Sam. 31:6
am. 30:1, 17, 26

Chapter 1

1 Now it came about after [a]the death of Saul, when David had returned from [b]the slaughter of the Amalekites, that David remained two days in Ziklag.

2 And it happened on the third day, that behold, [a]a man came out of the camp from Saul, [b]with his clothes torn and [1]dust on his head. And it came about when he came to David that [c]he fell to the ground and prostrated himself.

ground [a]2 Sam.
10 [b]1 Sam. 4:12
[c]1 Sam. 25:23

3 Then David said to him, "From where do you come?" And he said to him, "I have escaped from the camp of Israel."

4 And David said to him, "[a]How did things go? Please tell me." And he said, "The people have fled from the battle, and also many of the people have fallen and are dead; and Saul and Jonathan his son are dead also."

5 So David said to the young man who told him, "How do you know that Saul and his son Jonathan are dead?"

4 [a]1 Sam. 4:16

6 And the young man who told him said, "By chance I happened
to be on [a]Mount Gilboa, and behold, [b]Saul was leaning on his spear.
And behold, the chariots and the horsemen pursued him closely.
7 "And when he looked behind him, he saw me and called to me.
And I said, 'Here I am.'
8 "And he said to me, 'Who are you?' And I [1]answered him, '[a]I am
an Amalekite.'
9 "Then he said to me, 'Please stand beside me and kill me; for
agony has seized me because my [1]life still lingers in me.'
10 "So I stood beside him [a]and killed him, because I knew that he
could not live after he had fallen. And [b]I took the crown which *was*
on his head and the bracelet which *was* on his arm, and I have
brought them here to my lord."
11 Then [a]David took hold of his clothes and tore them, and *so* also
did all the men who *were* with him.
12 And they mourned and wept and [a]fasted until evening for Saul
and his son Jonathan and for the people of the LORD and the house of
Israel, because they had fallen by the sword.
13 And David said to the young man who told him, "Where are
you from?" And he [1]answered, "[a]I am the son of an alien, an
Amalekite."
14 Then David said to him, "How is it you were not afraid [a]to
stretch out your hand to destroy the LORD's anointed?"
15 And David called one of the young men and said, "Go, [1]cut him
down." [a]So he struck him and he died.
16 And David said to him, "[a]Your blood is on your head, for [b]your
mouth has testified against you, saying, 'I have killed the LORD's
anointed.' "
17 Then David [a]chanted with this lament over Saul and Jonathan
his son,
18 and he told *them* to teach the sons of Judah *the song of* the bow;
behold, it is written in [a]the book of Jashar.
19 "[1]Your beauty, O Israel, is slain on your high places!
[a]How have the mighty fallen!
20 "[a]Tell *it* not in Gath,
Proclaim it not in the streets of Ashkelon;
Lest [b]the daughters of the Philistines rejoice,
Lest the daughters of [c]the uncircumcised exult.
21 "[a]O mountains of Gilboa,
[b]Let not dew or rain be on you, nor fields of offerings;
For there the shield of the mighty was defiled,
The shield of Saul, not [c]anointed with oil.
22 "[a]From the blood of the slain, from the fat of the mighty,
[b]The bow of Jonathan did not turn back,
And the sword of Saul did not return empty.
23 "Saul and Jonathan, beloved and pleasant in their life,
And in their death they were not parted;
[a]They were swifter than eagles,
[b]They were stronger than lions.
24 "O daughters of Israel, weep over Saul,
Who clothed you luxuriously in scarlet,
Who put ornaments of gold on your apparel.
25 "[a]How have the mighty fallen in the midst of the battle!
Jonathan is slain on your high places.

The **book of Jashar** was a collection of poetical writings of important events in Israel's history which was gathered in the time of David or Solomon. It is often compared to "The Book of the Wars of the Lord." Bible authors are believed to have quoted from this book.

6 [a]1 Sam. 28 1 Chr. 10:4-1 31:2-4
8 [1]Lit., *said t* 15:3; 30:1, 13
9 [1]Lit., *whole in me*
10 [a]Judg. 9:5 11:12
11 [a]Gen. 37:2 Josh. 7:6; 2 C Ezra 9:3
12 [a]2 Sam. 3:
13 [1]Lit., *said* 1:8
14 [a]1 Sam. 24 11, 16
15 [1]Lit., *fall up* [a]2 Sam. 4:10,
16 [a]1 Sam. 26 2 Sam. 3:28, 29 2:32 [b]2 Sam. 1 Luke 19:22
17 [a]2 Chr. 35:2
18 [a]Josh. 10:13
19 [1]Lit., *The* [a]2 1:25, 27
20 [a]1 Sam. 31:8 Mic. 1:10 [b]Ex. 21; 1 Sam. 18:6 [c]1 Sam. 14:6
21 [a]1 Sam. 31:1 31:15 [c]Is. 21:5
22 [a]Deut. 32:42, 34:6 [b]1 Sam. 18
23 [a]Jer. 4:13 [b]J 14:18
25 [a]2 Sam. 1:19,

26 "I am distressed for you, my brother Jonathan;
You have been very pleasant to me.
[a]Your love to me was more wonderful
Than the love of women.
27 "[a]How have the mighty fallen,
And [b]the weapons of war perished!"

Chapter 2

2 Then it came about afterwards that [a]David inquired of the LORD,
saying, "Shall I go up to one of the cities of Judah?" And the
LORD said to him, "Go up." So David said, "Where shall I go up?"
And He said, "[b]To Hebron."
2 So David went up there, and [a]his two wives also, Ahinoam the
Jezreelitess and Abigail the [1]widow of Nabal the Carmelite.
3 And [a]David brought up his men who *were* with him, each with
his household; and they lived in the cities of Hebron.
4 Then the men of Judah came and there [a]anointed David king
over the house of Judah.
And they told David, saying, "It was [b]the men of Jabesh-gilead
who buried Saul."
5 And David sent messengers to the men of Jabesh-gilead, and
said to them, "[a]May you be blessed of the LORD because you have
[1]shown this kindness to Saul your lord, and have buried him.
6 "And now [a]may the LORD [1]show lovingkindness and truth to you;
and I also will [1]show this goodness to you, because you have done
this thing.
7 "Now therefore, let your hands be strong, and be [1]valiant; for Saul
your lord is dead, and also the house of Judah has anointed me king
over them."
8 But [a]Abner the son of Ner, commander of Saul's army, had taken
[1]Ish-bosheth the son of Saul, and brought him over to [b]Mahanaim.
9 And he made him king over [a]Gilead, over the [b]Ashurites, over
[c]Jezreel, over Ephraim, and over Benjamin, even over all Israel.
10 Ish-bosheth, Saul's son, was forty years old when he became
king over Israel, and he was king for two years. The house of Judah,
however, followed David.
11 And [a]the [1]time that David was king in Hebron over the house of
Judah was seven years and six months.
12 Now Abner the son of Ner, went out from Mahanaim to [a]Gibeon
with the servants of Ish-bosheth the son of Saul.
13 And [a]Joab the son of Zeruiah and the servants of David went out
and met [1]them by the pool of Gibeon; and they sat down, [2]one on the
one side of the pool and [2]the other on the other side of the pool.
14 Then Abner said to Joab, "Now let the young men arise and
[1a]hold a contest before us." And Joab said, "Let them arise."
15 So they arose and went over by count, twelve for Benjamin and
Ish-bosheth the son of Saul, and twelve of the servants of David.
16 And each one of them seized his [1]opponent by the head, and
thrust his sword in his [2]opponent's side; so they fell down together.
Therefore that place was called [3]Helkath-hazzurim, which is in
Gibeon.
17 And that day the battle was very severe, and [a]Abner and the
men of Israel were beaten before the servants of David.
18 Now [a]the three sons of Zeruiah were there, Joab and Abishai and

Sam. 18:1-4
Sam. 1:19, 25 [b]Is. 13:5
Sam. 23:2, 4, [b]Josh. 14:13; 1 Sam. 30:31
wife [a]1 Sam. 25:42, 43
n. 30:9; 1 Chr. 12:1
[a]1 Sam. 16:13; 5:3, 5 [b]1 Sam. 31:11-13
done [a]1 Sam. 21; Ps. 115:15
, do [a]Ex. 34:6; 2 Tim. 1:16
., sons of valor
man of shame; . 8:33, *Eshbaal* n. 14:50 [b]Gen. 2; 2 Sam. 17:24
sh. 22:9 [b]Judg. 2 [c]1 Sam. 29:1
[1]Lit., *number of* ays [a]2 Sam. 5:5
sh. 10:12; 18:25
t., *them together* ., *these* [a]2 Sam. 1 Chr. 2:16; 11:6
[1]Lit., *make sport* [a]2 Sam. 2:16, 17
[1]Lit., *fellow* [2]Lit., [3]I.e., the field of sword-edges
17 [a]2 Sam. 3:1
18 [a]1 Chr. 2:16

Asahel; and Asahel *was* [b]*as* [1]swift-footed as one of the gazelles which
is in the field.
19 And Asahel pursued Abner and did not [1]turn to the right or to
the left from following Abner.
20 Then Abner looked behind him and said, "Is that you, Asahel?"
And he answered, "It is I."
21 So Abner said to him, "[1]Turn to your right or to your left, and
take hold of one of the young men for yourself, and take for yourself
his spoil." But Asahel was not willing to turn aside from following
him.
22 And Abner repeated again to Asahel, "Turn [1]aside from follow-
ing me. Why should I strike you to the ground? [a]How then could I
lift up my face to your brother Joab?"
23 However, he refused to turn aside; therefore Abner struck him in
the belly with the butt end of the spear, so that the spear came out at
his back. And he fell there and died on the spot. And it came about
that all who came to the place where [a]Asahel had fallen and died,
stood still.
24 But Joab and Abishai pursued Abner, and when the sun was
going down, they came to the hill of Ammah, which is in front of
Giah by the way of the wilderness of Gibeon.
25 And the sons of Benjamin gathered together behind Abner and
became one band, and they stood on the top of a certain hill.
26 Then Abner called to Joab and said, "Shall the sword devour
forever? Do you not know that it will be bitter in the end? How long
will you [1]refrain from telling the people to turn back from following
their brothers?"
27 And Joab said, "As God lives, if you had not spoken, surely then
the people would have gone away in the morning, each from follow-
ing his brother."
28 So Joab blew the trumpet; and all the people halted and pursued
Israel no longer, [a]nor did they continue to fight anymore.
29 Abner and his men then went through the Arabah all that night;
so they crossed the Jordan, walked all morning, and came to [a]Maha-
naim.
30 Then Joab returned from following Abner; when he had
gathered all the people together, [1]nineteen of David's servants be-
sides Asahel were missing.
31 But the servants of David had struck down many of Benjamin
and Abner's men, *so that* three hundred and sixty men died.
32 And they took up Asahel and buried him [a]in his father's tomb
which was in Bethlehem. Then Joab and his men went all night until
the day [1]dawned at Hebron.

Chapter 3

3 Now [a]there was a long war between the house of Saul and the
house of David; and David grew steadily stronger, but the house
of Saul grew weaker continually.
2 [a]Sons were born to David at Hebron: his first-born was Amnon,
by [b]Ahinoam the Jezreelitess;
3 and his second, Chileab, by Abigail the [1]widow of Nabal the
Carmelite; and the third, Absalom the son of [a]Maacah, the daughter
of Talmai, king of [b]Geshur;

18 [1]Lit., *light in* [b]1 Chr. 12:8; Ha
19 [1]Lit., *turn to go*
21 [1]Lit., *Turn for y*
22 [1]Lit., *aside for yourself* [a]2 Sam.
23 [a]2 Sam. 20:12
26 [1]Lit., *not tell th people*
28 [a]2 Sam. 3:1
29 [a]2 Sam. 2:8
30 [1]Lit., *nineteen*
32 [1]Lit., *lighted o them* [a]Gen. 47:29 Judg. 8:32
3:1 [a]1 Kin. 14:30 46:9
2 [a]1 Chr. 3:1-3 [b] 25:42, 43
3 [1]Lit., *wife* [a]1 S 27:8; 1 Chr. 3:2 14:32; 15:8

4 and the fourth, [a]Adonijah the son of Haggith; and the fifth,
Shephatiah the son of Abital;
5 and the sixth, Ithream, by David's wife Eglah. These were born
to David at Hebron.
6 And it came about while there was war between the house of
Saul and the house of David that [a]Abner was making himself strong
in the house of Saul.
7 Now Saul had a concubine whose name was [a]Rizpah, the daugh-
ter of Aiah; and [1]Ish-bosheth said to Abner, "Why have you gone in
to my father's concubine?"
8 Then Abner was very angry over the words of Ish-bosheth and
said, "[a]Am I a dog's head that belongs to Judah? Today I show
kindness to the house of Saul your father, to his brothers and to his
friends, and have not delivered you into the hands of David; and yet
today you charge me with a guilt concerning the woman.
9 "[a]May God do so to Abner, and more also, if [b]as the LORD has
sworn to David, I do not accomplish this for him,
10 [a]to transfer the kingdom from the house of Saul, and to establish
the throne of David over Israel and over Judah, [b]from Dan even to
Beersheba."
11 And he could no longer answer Abner a word, because he was
afraid of him.
12 Then Abner sent messengers to David in his place, saying,
"Whose is the land? Make your covenant with me, and behold, my
hand shall be with you to bring all Israel over to you."
13 And he said, "Good! I will make a covenant with you, but I
demand one thing of you, [1]namely, [a]you shall not see my face unless
you [b]first bring Michal, Saul's daughter, when you come to see [2]me."
14 So David sent messengers to Ish-bosheth, Saul's son, saying,
"Give me my wife Michal, to whom I was betrothed [a]for a hundred
foreskins of the Philistines."
15 And Ish-bosheth sent and took her from *her* husband, from [1]Pal-
tiel the son of Laish.
16 But her husband went with her, weeping as he went, and fol-
lowed her as far as [a]Bahurim. Then Abner said to him, "Go, return."
So he returned.
17 Now Abner had [1]consultation with [a]the elders of Israel, saying,
"In times past you were seeking for David to be king over you.
18 "Now then, do *it*! For the LORD has spoken of David, saying, '[a]By
the hand of My servant David [1]I will save My people Israel from the
hand of the Philistines and from the hand of all their enemies.'"
19 And Abner also spoke in the hearing of Benjamin; and in addi-
tion Abner went to speak in the hearing of David in Hebron all that
seemed good to Israel and to [a]the whole house of Benjamin.
20 Then Abner and twenty men with him came to David at Hebron.
And David made a feast for Abner and the men who were with him.
21 And Abner said to David, "Let me arise and go, and [a]gather all
Israel to my lord the king that they may make a covenant with you,
and that [b]you may be king over all that your soul desires." So David
sent Abner away, and he went in peace.
22 And behold, [a]the servants of David and Joab came from a raid
and brought much spoil with them; but Abner was not with David
in Hebron, for he had sent him away, and he had gone in peace.
23 When Joab and all the army that was with him arrived, they told

4 [a]1 Kin. 1:5
[a]2 Sam. 2:8, 9
...some ancient versions; M.T., ...2 Sam. 21:8-11
[a]1 Sam. 24:14; 2 Sam. 9:8
...19:2 [b]1 Sam. 15:28
[a]1 Sam. 15:28 [b]1 Sam. 3:20
...Lit., *saying* [2]Lit., *face* [a]Gen. 43:3 ...m. 18:20; 19:11
...Sam. 18:25, 27
...in 1 Sam. 25:44, *Palti*
...Sam. 16:5; 19:16
17 [1]Lit., *a word* [a]1 Sam. 8:4
...So many ancient ...nd versions; M.T., ...Sam. 9:16; 15:28
...Sam. 10:20, 21; 1 Chr. 12:29
[a]2 Sam. 3:10, 12 [b]1 Kin. 11:37
22 [a]1 Sam. 27:8

Joab, saying, "Abner the son of Ner came to the king, and he has
sent him away, and he has gone in peace."
24 Then Joab came to the king and said, "What have you done?
Behold, Abner came to you; why then have you sent him away and
he is already gone?
25 "You know Abner the son of Ner, that he came to deceive you and
to learn of [a]your going out and coming in, and to find out all that
you are doing."
26 When Joab came out from David, he sent messengers after
Abner, and they brought him back from the well of Sirah; but David
did not know *it*.
27 So when Abner returned to Hebron, Joab took him aside into the
middle of the gate to speak with him privately, and there [a]he struck
him in the belly so that he died on account of the blood of Asahel his
brother.
28 And afterward when David heard it, he said, "I and my king-
dom are innocent before the LORD forever of the blood of Abner the
son of Ner.
29 "[a]May it [1]fall on the head of Joab and on all his father's house;
and may there not fail from the house of Joab [b]one who has a dis-
charge, or who is a leper, or who takes hold of a distaff, or who falls
by the sword, or who lacks bread."
30 So Joab and Abishai his brother killed Abner [a]because he had put
their brother Asahel to death in the battle at Gibeon.
31 Then David said to Joab and to all the people who were with
him, "[a]Tear your clothes and gird on sackcloth and lament before
Abner." And King David walked behind the bier.
32 Thus they buried Abner in Hebron; and the king lifted up his
voice and wept at [a]the grave of Abner, and all the people wept.
33 And [a]the king chanted a *lament* for Abner and said,
"Should Abner die as a fool dies?
34 "Your hands were not bound, nor your feet put in fetters;
As one falls before the [1]wicked, you have fallen."
And all the people wept again over him.
35 Then all the people came [a]to [1]persuade David to eat bread while
it was still day; but David vowed, saying, "[b]May God do so to me,
and more also, if I taste bread or anything else [c]before the sun goes
down."
36 Now all the people took note *of it,* and it [1]pleased them, just as
everything the king did [2]pleased all the people.
37 So all the people and all Israel understood that day that it had
not been *the will* of the king to put Abner the son of Ner to death.
38 Then the king said to his servants, "Do you not know that a
prince and a great man has fallen this day in Israel?
39 "And I am [a]weak today, though anointed king; and these men [b]the
sons of Zeruiah are too difficult for me. [c]May the LORD repay the
evildoer according to his evil."

Chapter 4

4 Now when [1]Ish-bosheth, Saul's son, heard that [a]Abner had died
in Hebron, [2b]he lost courage, and all Israel was disturbed.
2 And Saul's son *had* two men who were commanders of bands:
the name of the one was Baanah and the name of the other Rechab,

25 [a]Deut. 28:6; 29:6; Is. 37:28

27 [a]2 Sam. 2:2[…] 10; 1 Kin. 2:5

29 [1]Lit., *whirl* […] 21:6-9; 1 Kin. 2[…] [b]Lev. 13:46

30 [a]2 Sam. 2:2[…]

31 [a]Gen. 37:34 […] 11:35

32 [a]Job 31:28, […] Prov. 24:17

33 [a]2 Sam. 1:17 […] 35:25

34 [1]Lit., *sons of wickedness*

35 [1]Lit., *cause* […] 12:17 [b]1 Sam. 3[…] [c]2 Sam. 1:12

36 [1]Lit., *was goo[d…] their eyes* [2]Lit., *[…] good in the eyes*

39 [a]1 Chr. 29:1; […] 13:7 [b]2 Sam. 19:[…] [c]1 Kin. 2:32-34

4:1 [1]So some an[…] mss.; M.T., *he* [2]L[…] *hands dropped* [a]… 3:27 [b]Ezra 4:4

sons of Rimmon the Beerothite, of the sons of Benjamin (for [a]Beeroth
is also considered [b]*part* of Benjamin,
3 and the Beerothites fled to [a]Gittaim, and have been aliens there
until this day).
4 Now [a]Jonathan, Saul's son, had a son crippled in his feet. He was
five years old when the [b]report of Saul and Jonathan came from
Jezreel, and his nurse took him up and fled. And it happened that in
her hurry to flee, he fell and became lame. And his name was
[1c]Mephibosheth.
5 So the sons of Rimmon the Beerothite, Rechab and Baanah, de-
parted and came to the house of [a]Ish-bosheth in the heat of the day
while he was taking his midday rest.
6 [1]And they came to the middle of the house as [2]if to get wheat,
and [a]they struck him in the belly; and Rechab and Baanah his
brother escaped.
7 Now when they came into the house, as he was lying on his bed
in his bedroom, they struck him and killed him and beheaded him.
And they took his head and [1a]traveled by way of the Arabah all
night.
8 Then they brought the head of Ish-bosheth to David at Hebron,
and said to the king, "Behold, the head of Ish-bosheth, [a]the son of
Saul, your enemy, who sought your life; thus the LORD has given my
lord the king vengeance this day on Saul and his [1]descendants."
9 And David answered Rechab and Baanah his brother, sons of
Rimmon the Beerothite, and said to them, "As the LORD lives, [a]who
has redeemed my life from all distress,
10 [a]when one told me, saying, 'Behold, Saul is dead,' and [1]thought
he was bringing good news, I seized him and killed him in Ziklag,
which was the reward I gave him for *his* news.
11 "How much more, when wicked men have killed a righteous man
in his own house on his bed, shall I not now [a]require his blood from
your hand, and [1]destroy you from the earth?"
12 Then [a]David commanded the young men, and they killed them
and cut off their hands and feet, and hung them up beside the pool
in Hebron. But they took the head of Ish-bosheth [b]and buried it in
the grave of Abner in Hebron.

Chapter 5

5 [a]Then all the tribes of Israel came to David at Hebron and [1]said,
"Behold, we are [b]your bone and your flesh.
2 "Previously, when Saul was king over us, [a]you were the one who
led Israel out and in. And the LORD said to you, '[b]You will shepherd
My people Israel, and you will be [c]a ruler over Israel.' "
3 So all the elders of Israel came to the king at Hebron, and King
David [a]made a covenant with them before the LORD at Hebron; then
[b]they anointed David king over Israel.
4 David was [a]thirty years old when he became king, *and* [b]he
reigned forty years.
5 At Hebron [a]he reigned over Judah seven years and six months,
and in Jerusalem he reigned thirty-three years over all Israel and
Judah.
6 [a]Now the king and his men went to [b]Jerusalem against the Jebu-
sites, the inhabitants of the land, and they said to [1]David, "You shall

9:17 [b]Josh. 18:25
[a]Neh. 11:33
..., Merib-baal ...3, 6 [b]1 Sam. ...hr. 8:34; 9:40
[a]2 Sam. 2:8
...nd here [2]Lit., ...heat [a]2 Sam. 2:23
...went [a]2 Sam. 2:29
...seed [a]1 Sam. 24:4; 25:29
... 48:16; 1 Kin. 1:29; Ps. 31:7
..., he was as a ...f good news in ... eyes [a]2 Sam. 1:2, 4, 15
...it., burn [a]Gen. 9:5; Ps. 9:12
...2 [a]2 Sam. 1:15 [b]2 Sam. 3:32
...it., said, saying ...11:1-3 [b]2 Sam. 19:13
...am. 18:5, 13, 16 ... 49:24; 2 Sam. ... [c]1 Sam. 25:30
3 [a]2 Sam. 3:21 ... 16:13; 2 Sam. 2:4
...en. 41:46; Num. ...uke 3:23 [b]1 Kin. ...11; 1 Chr. 26:31
...Sam. 2:11; 1 Chr. 3:4; 29:27
...it., David, saying ...hr. 11:4-9 [b]Josh. 8:28; Judg. 1:21

not come in here, but the blind and lame shall turn you away";
[2]thinking, "David cannot enter here."
7 Nevertheless, David captured the stronghold of Zion, that is [a]the
city of David.
8 And David said on that day, "Whoever would strike the
Jebusites, let him reach the lame and the blind, who are hated by
David's soul, through the water tunnel." Therefore they say, "The
blind or the lame shall not come into the house."
9 So David lived in the stronghold, and called it [a]the city of David.
And David built all around from the [1b]Millo and inward.
10 And [a]David became greater and greater, for the LORD God of
hosts was with him.
11 [a]Then Hiram king of Tyre sent messengers to David with cedar
trees and carpenters and stonemasons; and [b]they built a house for
David.
12 And David realized that the LORD had established him as king
over Israel, and that He had exalted his kingdom for the sake of His
people Israel.
13 Meanwhile [a]David took more concubines and wives from Jeru-
salem, after he came from Hebron; and more sons and daughters
were born to David.
14 Now [a]these are the names of those who were born to him in
Jerusalem: Shammua, Shobab, Nathan, Solomon,
15 Ibhar, Elishua, Nepheg, Japhia,
16 Elishama, Eliada and Eliphelet.
17 When the Philistines heard that they had anointed David king
over Israel, [a]all the Philistines went up to seek out David; and when
David heard *of it,* he went down to the [b]stronghold.
18 Now the Philistines came and spread themselves out in [a]the val-
ley of Rephaim.
19 Then [a]David inquired of the LORD, saying, "Shall I go up against
the Philistines? Wilt Thou give them into my hand?" And [b]the LORD
said to David, "Go up, for I will certainly give the Philistines into
your hand."
20 So David came to [a]Baal-perazim, and [1]defeated them there; and
he said, "The LORD has broken through my enemies before me like
the breakthrough of waters." Therefore he named that place [2]Baal-
perazim.
21 And they abandoned their idols there, so [a]David and his men
carried them away.
22 Now [a]the Philistines came up once again and spread themselves
out in the valley of Rephaim.
23 And when [a]David inquired of the LORD, He said, "You shall not
go *directly* up; circle around behind them and come at them in front
of the [1]balsam trees.
24 "And it shall be, when [a]you hear the sound of marching in the
tops of the [1]balsam trees, then you shall act promptly, for then [b]the
LORD will have gone out before you to strike the army of the Philis-
tines."
25 Then David did so, just as the LORD had commanded him, and
struck down the Philistines from [1a]Geba [2]as far as [b]Gezer.

6 [2]Lit., *sayin*

7 [a]2 Sam. 6:1 1 Kin. 2:10; 9

9 [1]I.e., citade 5:7 [b]1 Kin. 9:

10 [a]2 Sam. 3:

11 [a]1 Kin. 5:1 1 Chr. 14:1 [b]P

13 [a]Deut. 17: 3:9

14 [a]1 Chr. 3:5

17 [a]1 Sam. 29 [b]2 Sam. 23:14; 11:16

18 [a]Gen. 14:5; 15:8; 17:15; 18

19 [a]1 Sam. 23 [b]2 Sam. 2:1

20 [1]Lit., *David* [2]I.e., the master breakthrough [a] 14:11; Is. 28:21

21 [a]1 Chr. 14:1

22 [a]2 Sam. 5:18

23 [1]Or, *baka-sh* [a]2 Sam. 5:19

24 [1]Or, *baka-sh* [a]2 Kin. 7:6 [b]Jud

25 [1]In 1 Chr. 14: *Gibeon* [2]Lit., *unt are coming to* [a]Is 28:21 [b]Josh. 12: 21:21

Chapter 6

6 [a]Now David again gathered all the chosen men of Israel, thirty
thousand.
2 And David arose and went with all the people who were with
him to [1a]Baale-judah, to bring up from there the ark of God which is
called by the [b]Name, the very name of the LORD of hosts who [c]is
[2]enthroned *above* the cherubim.
3 And they [1]placed the ark of God on [a]a new cart that they might
bring it from the house of Abinadab which was on the hill; and
Uzzah and Ahio, the sons of Abinadab, were leading the new cart.
4 So [a]they brought it with the ark of God from the house of
Abinadab, which was on the hill; and Ahio was walking ahead of
the ark.
5 Meanwhile, David and all the house of Israel [a]were celebrating
before the LORD [b]with all kinds of *instruments made of* [1]fir wood, and
with lyres, harps, tambourines, castanets and cymbals.
6 But when they came to the [a]threshing floor of Nacon, Uzzah
[b]reached out toward the ark of God and took hold of it, for the oxen
nearly upset *it*.
7 And the anger of the LORD burned against Uzzah, and [a]God
struck him down there for [1]his irreverence; and he died there by the
ark of God.
8 And David became angry because [1]of the LORD's outburst
against Uzzah, and that place is called [2]Perez-uzzah to this day.
9 So [a]David was afraid of the LORD that day; and he said, "How
can the ark of the LORD come to me?"
10 And David was unwilling to move the ark of the LORD into the
city of David with him; but David took it aside to the house of
[a]Obed-edom the Gittite.
11 Thus the ark of the LORD remained in the house of Obed-edom
the Gittite three months, and the LORD [a]blessed Obed-edom and all
his household.
12 Now it was told King David, saying, "The LORD has blessed the
house of Obed-edom and all that belongs to him, on account of the
ark of God." [a]And David went and brought up the ark of God from
the house of Obed-edom into [b]the city of David with gladness.
13 And so it was, that when the [a]bearers of the ark of the LORD had
gone six paces, he sacrificed an [b]ox and a fatling.
14 And [a]David was dancing before the LORD with all *his* might, and
David was [1b]wearing a linen ephod.
15 So David and all the house of Israel were bringing up the ark of
the LORD with shouting and the sound of the trumpet.
16 Then it happened *as* the ark of the LORD came into the city of
David that [a]Michal the daughter of Saul looked out of the window
and saw King David leaping and dancing before the LORD; and she
despised him in her heart.
17 So they brought in the ark of the LORD and set it [a]in its place
inside the tent which David had pitched for it; and [b]David offered
burnt offerings and peace offerings before the LORD.
18 And when David had finished offering the burnt offering and
the peace offering, [a]he blessed the people in the name of the LORD of
hosts.
19 Further, he distributed to all the people, to all the multitude of
Israel, both to men and women, a cake of bread and one of dates and

:1 [a]1 Chr. 13:5-14

[1]I.e., Kiriath-jearim
sitting [a]Josh. 15:9,
; 1 Sam. 7:1 [b]Lev.
24:16 [c]Ex. 25:22

Lit., *caused to ride*
. 7:4-9; 1 Sam. 6:7

[a]1 Sam. 7:1; 1 Chr.
13:7

, cypress [a]1 Sam.
3:6, 7 [b]1 Chr. 13:8

1 Chr. 13:9 [b]Num.
4:15, 19, 20

the [a]1 Sam. 6:19

t., *the* LORD *broke*
gh a breakthrough
the breakthrough
of Uzzah

119:120; Luke 5:8

10 [a]1 Chr. 26:4-8

[a]Gen. 30:27; 39:5

[a]1 Chr. 15:25-16:3
[b]1 Kin. 8:1

[a]Num. 4:15; Josh.
:3; 1 Chr. 15:2, 15
[b]1 Kin. 8:5

[1]Lit., *girded with*
. 15:20, 21; Judg.
[b]Ex. 19:6; 1 Sam.
2:18, 28

16 [a]2 Sam. 3:14

Chr. 15:1; 2 Chr.
4 [b]1 Kin. 8:62-65

3 [a]1 Kin. 8:14, 15

one of raisins to each one. Then all the people departed each to his
house.
20 But when David returned to bless his household, Michal the
daughter of Saul came out to meet David and said, "How the king of
Israel distinguished himself today! [a]He uncovered himself today in
the eyes of his servants' maids as one of the [b]foolish ones shameless-
ly uncovers himself!"
21 So David said to Michal, "[a]*It was* before the LORD, who chose me
above your father and above all his house, to appoint me ruler over
the people of the LORD, over Israel; therefore I will celebrate before
the LORD.
22 "And I will be more lightly esteemed than this and will be
humble in my own eyes, but with the maids of whom you have
spoken, with them I will be distinguished."
23 And Michal the daughter of Saul had no child to the day of her
death.

Chapter 7

7 [a]Now it came about when the king lived in his house, and the
LORD had given him rest on every side from all his enemies,
2 that the king said to [a]Nathan the prophet, "See now, I dwell in [b]a
house of cedar, but the ark of God [c]dwells within tent curtains."
3 And Nathan said to the king, "[a]Go, do all that is in your mind,
for the LORD is with you."
4 But it came about in the same night that the word of the LORD
came to Nathan, saying,
5 "Go and say to My servant David, 'Thus says the LORD, "[a]Are you
the one who should build Me a house to dwell in?
6 "For [a]I have not dwelt in a house since the day I brought up the
sons of Israel from Egypt, even to this day; but I have been moving
about [b]in a tent, even in a [1]tabernacle.
7 "[a]Wherever I have gone with all the sons of Israel, did I speak a
word with one of the tribes of Israel, [b]which I commanded to
shepherd My people Israel, saying, 'Why have you not built Me a
house of cedar?' " '
8 "Now therefore, thus you shall say to My servant David, 'Thus
says the LORD of hosts, "[a]I took you from the pasture, from following
the sheep, [b]that you should be ruler over My people Israel.
9 "And [a]I have been with you wherever you have gone and [b]have
cut off all your enemies from before you; and I will make you a great
name, like the names of the great men who are on the earth.
10 "I will also appoint a place for My people Israel and [a]will plant
them, that they may live in their own place and not be disturbed
again, [b]nor will the [1]wicked afflict them any more as formerly,
11 even [a]from the day that I commanded judges to be over My
people Israel; and [b]I will give you rest from all your enemies. The
LORD also declares to you that [c]the LORD will make a house for you.
12 "[a]When your days are complete and you [b]lie down with your
fathers, [c]I will raise up your [1]descendant after you, who will come
forth from [2]you, and I will establish his kingdom.
13 "[a]He shall build a house for My name, and [b]I will establish the
throne of his kingdom forever.
14 "[a]I will be a father to him and he will be a son to Me; [b]when he

20 [a]2 Sam. 6:14, 1 Eccl. 7:17 [b]Judg. 9
21 [a]1 Sam. 13:14;
7:1 [a]1 Chr. 17:1-27
2 [a]2 Sam. 7:17; 12 1 Kin. 1:22; 1 Chr. 29:29; 2 Chr. 9:29 [b]2 Sam. 5:11 [c]Ex.
3 [a]1 Kin. 8:17, 18; 1 Chr. 22:7
5 [a]1 Kin. 5:3, 4; 8:
6 [1]Lit., *dwelling pla* [a]Josh. 18:1; 1 Kin. [b]Ex. 40:18, 34
7 [a]Lev. 26:11, 12 [b]2 Sam. 5:2
8 [a]1 Sam. 16:11, Ps. 78:70, 71 [b]2 S 6:21
9 [a]1 Sam. 5:10 [b]P 18:37-42
10 [1]Lit., *sons of wickedness* [a]Ex. Is. 5:2, 7 [b]Ps. 89: 23; Is. 60:18
11 [a]Judg. 2:14-16 1 Sam. 12:9-11 [b]2 7:1 [c]1 Sam. 25:28 2 Sam. 7:27
12 [1]Lit., *seed* [2]Li *bowels* [a]1 Kin. 2: [b]Deut. 31:16; Acts 13:36 [c]1 Kin. 8:2 132:11
13 [a]1 Kin. 6:12; 8 [b]Is. 9:7; 49:8
14 [a]Ps. 89:26, 27 2 Cor. 6:18; Heb. [b]1 Kin. 11:34; Ps. 89:30-33

commits iniquity, I will correct him with the rod of men and the
strokes of the sons of men,
15 but My lovingkindness shall not depart from him, [a]as I took *it*
away from Saul, whom I removed from before you.
16 "And [a]your house and your kingdom shall endure before [1]Me
forever; your throne shall be established forever." ' "
17 In accordance with all these words and all this vision, so Nathan
spoke to David.
18 Then David the king went in and sat before the LORD, and he
said, "[a]Who am I, O Lord [1]GOD, and what is my house, that Thou
hast brought me this far?
19 "And yet this was insignificant in Thine eyes, O Lord GOD, [a]for
Thou hast spoken also of the house of Thy servant concerning the
distant future. And [b]this is the [1]custom of man, O Lord GOD.
20 "And again what more can David say to Thee? For [a]Thou
knowest Thy servant, O Lord GOD!
21 "[a]For the sake of Thy word, and according to Thine own heart,
Thou hast done all this greatness to let Thy servant know.
22 "For this reason [a]Thou art great, O Lord GOD; for [b]there is none
like Thee, and there is no God besides Thee, [c]according to all that we
have heard with our ears.
23 "And [a]what one nation on the earth is like Thy people Israel,
whom God went to redeem for Himself as a people and to make a
name for Himself, and [b]to do a great thing for Thee and awesome
things for Thy land, before [c]Thy people whom [d]Thou hast redeemed
for Thyself from Egypt, *from* nations and their gods?
24 "For [a]Thou hast established for Thyself Thy people Israel as Thine
own people forever, and [b]Thou, O LORD, hast become their God.
25 "Now therefore, O LORD God, the word that Thou hast spoken
concerning Thy servant and his house, confirm *it* forever, and do as
Thou hast spoken,
26 [a]that Thy name may be magnified forever, by saying, 'The LORD
of hosts is God over Israel'; and may the house of Thy servant David
be established before Thee.
27 "For Thou, O LORD of hosts, the God of Israel, hast [1]made a
revelation to Thy servant, saying, '[a]I will build you a house'; there-
fore Thy servant has found [2]courage to pray this prayer to Thee.
28 "And now, O Lord GOD, Thou art God, and [a]Thy words are truth,
and Thou hast [1]promised this good thing to Thy servant.
29 "Now therefore, may it please Thee to bless the house of Thy
servant, that it may continue forever before Thee. For Thou, O Lord
GOD, hast spoken; and [a]with Thy blessing may the house of Thy
servant be blessed forever."

Chapter 8

8 [a]Now after this it came about that David [1]defeated the Philistines
and subdued them; and David took [2]control of the chief city
from the hand of the Philistines.
2 And [a]he [1]defeated [b]Moab, and measured them with the line,
making them lie down on the ground; and he measured two lines to
put to death and one full line to keep alive. And [c]the Moabites be-
came servants to David, [d]bringing tribute.
3 Then David [1]defeated [a]Hadadezer, the son of Rehob king of
Zobah, as [b]he went to restore his [2]rule at the [3]River.

Sam. 15:23; 16:14

6 [1]So with Gr. and some ancient mss.; *you* [a]2 Sam. 7:13; Ps. 89:36, 37

18 [1]Heb., *YHWH*, ...lly rendered *LORD*, ...d so throughout the [a]Ex. 3:11; 1 Sam. 18:18

[1]Or, *law* [a]2 Sam. ...11-16; 1 Chr. 17:17 [b]Is. 55:8, 9

[a]1 Sam. 16:7; John 21:17

[a]1 Chr. 17:19; Eph. 4:32

..2 [a]Deut. 3:24; Ps. 86:10 [b]Ex. 15:11; ...am. 2:2 [c]Ex. 10:2; Ps. 44:1

23 [a]Deut. 4:32-38 ...Deut. 10:21 [c]Deut. 15:15 [d]Deut. 9:26

[a]Deut. 32:6 [b]Gen. 17:7, 8; Ex. 6:7

...s. 72:18, 19; Matt. 6:9

...Lit., *uncovered the* ...*r of* [2]Lit., *his heart* [a]2 Sam. 7:13

[1]Or, *spoken* [a]Ex. 34:6; John 17:17

29 [a]Num. 6:24-26

[1]Lit., *smote* [2]Lit., ...*ridle of the mother city* [a]1 Chr. 18

...Lit., *smote* [a]Num. ...7 [b]1 Sam. 22:3, 4 ...m. 8:6; 1 Kin. 4:21 [d]2 Kin. 3:4; 17:3

[1]Lit., *smote* [2]Lit., ...*d* [3]I.e., Euphrates ...am. 14:47; 2 Sam. ...10:16, 19 [b]2 Sam. 10:15-19

4 And David captured from him 1,700 horsemen and 20,000 foot soldiers; and David [a]hamstrung the chariot horses, but reserved *enough* of them for 100 chariots.

5 And when [a]the Arameans of Damascus came to help Hadadezer, king of Zobah, David [1]killed 22,000 Arameans.

6 Then David put garrisons among the Arameans of Damascus, and [a]the Arameans became servants to David, bringing tribute. And [b]the LORD helped David wherever he went.

7 And David took the shields of gold which were [1]carried by the servants of Hadadezer, and brought them to Jerusalem.

8 And from [1]Betah and from [a]Berothai, cities of Hadadezer, King David took a very large amount of bronze.

9 Now when Toi king of [a]Hamath heard that David had [1]defeated all the army of Hadadezer,

10 Toi sent [1]Joram his son to King David to [2]greet him and bless him, because he had fought against Hadadezer and [3]defeated him; for Hadadezer [4]had been at war with Toi. And [5]*Joram* brought with him articles of silver, of gold and of bronze.

11 King David also [a]dedicated these to the LORD, with the silver and gold that he had dedicated from all the nations which he had subdued:

12 from [1]Aram and [a]Moab and [b]the sons of Ammon and [c]the Philistines and [d]Amalek, and from the spoil of Hadadezer, son of Rehob, king of Zobah.

13 So [a]David made a name *for himself* when he returned from [1]killing 18,000 [2]Arameans in [b]the Valley of Salt.

14 And he put garrisons in Edom. In all Edom he put garrisons, and [a]all the Edomites became servants to David. And [b]the LORD helped David wherever he went.

15 So David reigned over all Israel; and David [1]administered justice and righteousness for all his people.

16 And [a]Joab the son of Zeruiah *was* over the army, and [b]Jehoshaphat the son of Ahilud *was* [c]recorder.

17 And [a]Zadok the son of Ahitub and Ahimelech the son of Abiathar *were* [b]priests, and Seraiah *was* [c]secretary.

18 And [a]Benaiah the son of Jehoiada [1]was over the [b]Cherethites and the Pelethites; and David's sons were [2c]chief ministers.

Chapter 9

9 Then David said, "Is there yet [1]anyone left of the house of Saul, [a]that I may show him kindness for Jonathan's sake?"

2 Now there was a servant of the house of Saul whose name was Ziba, and they called him to David; and the king said to him, "Are you [a]Ziba?" And he said, "*I am* your servant."

3 And the king said, "Is there not yet anyone of the house of Saul to whom I may show the [a]kindness of God?" And Ziba said to the king, "[b]There is still a son of Jonathan who is crippled in both feet."

4 So the king said to him, "Where is he?" And Ziba said to the king, "Behold, he is [a]in the house of Machir the son of Ammiel in Lo-debar."

5 Then King David sent and brought him from the house of Machir the son of Ammiel, from Lo-debar.

6 And [a]Mephibosheth, the son of Jonathan the son of Saul, came to

4 [a]Josh. 11:6, 9

5 [1]Lit., *smote* [a]1 K 11:23-25

6 [a]2 Sam. 8:2 [b]2 S 3:18

7 [1]Lit., *on*

8 [1]In 1 Chr. 18:8, *Tibhath* [a]Ezek. 47:

9 [1]Lit., *smitten* [a]1 8:65; 2 Chr. 8:4

10 [1]In 1 Chr. 18:10 *Hadoram* [2]Lit., *ask of his welfare* [3]Lit., *smitten* [4]Lit., *was a man of wars* [5]Lit., *were in his hand*

11 [a]1 Kin. 7:51

12 [1]Some mss. re *Edom* [a]2 Sam. 8:2 [b]2 Sam. 10:14 [c]2 S 5:17-25 [d]1 Sam. 2 30:17-20

13 [1]Lit., *smiting* [2]S mss. read *Edom* [a]2 Sam. 7:9 [b]2 Kin

14 [a]Gen. 27:37-40 Num. 24:17, 18 [b]2 Sam. 8:6

15 [1]Lit., *was doing*

16 [a]1 Chr. 11:6 [b]1 4:3 [c]2 Kin. 18:18,

17 [a]1 Chr. 6:4-8 [b] 16:39, 40 [c]2 Kin.

18 [1]Lit., *and the Cherethites* [2]Lit., *priests* [a]1 Kin. 4:4 [b]1 Sam. 30:14; 2 S 15:18; 20:7, 23; 1 1:38, 44 [c]1 Chr. 1

9:1 [1]Lit., *he who* [a]1 Sam. 20:14-17,

2 [a]2 Sam. 16:1-4; 19:17, 29

3 [a]1 Sam. 20:14 [b]2 Sam. 4:4

4 [a]2 Sam. 17:27-

6 [a]2 Sam. 16:4; 19:24-30

David's Family Tree

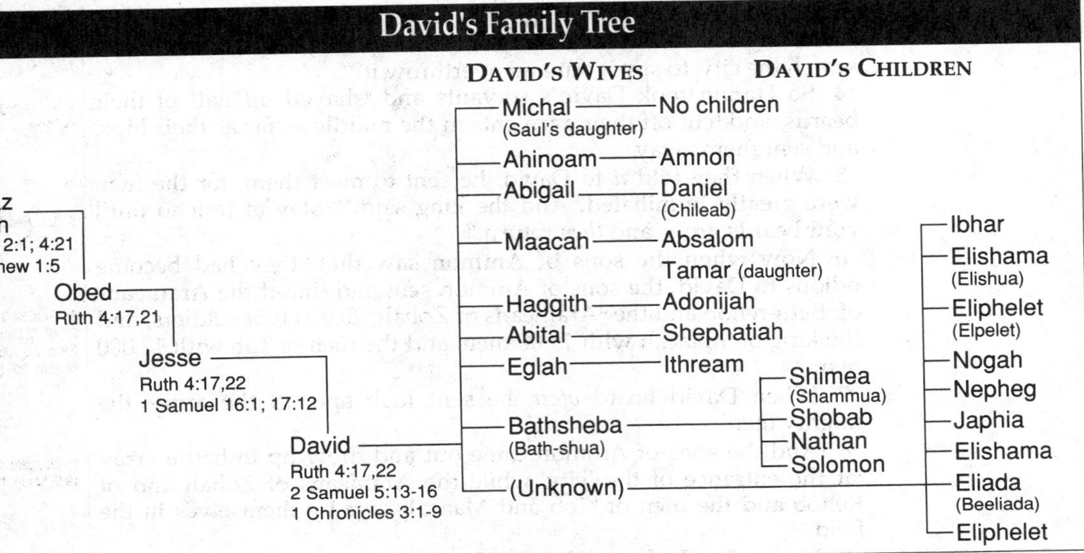

b1 Sam. 25:23

David and [b]fell on his face and prostrated himself. And David said,
"Mephibosheth." And he said, "Here is your servant!"

ield [2]Lit., father bread [a]2 Sam. 3 [b]2 Sam. 12:8 m. 19:28; 1 Kin. 2:7; 2 Kin. 25:29

7 And David said to him, "Do not fear, for [a]I will surely show
kindness to you for the sake of your father Jonathan, and [b]will re-
store to you all the [1]land of your [2]grandfather Saul; and [c]you shall
[3]eat at my table regularly."
8 Again he prostrated himself and said, "What is your servant,
that you should regard [a]a dead dog like me?"

am. 16:9; 24:14

9 Then the king called Saul's servant Ziba, and said to him, "[a]All
that belonged to Saul and to all his house I have given to your
master's [1]grandson.

.it., son [a]2 Sam. 16:4; 19:29

10 "And you and your sons and your servants shall cultivate the
land for him, and you shall bring in *the produce* so that your master's
grandson may have food; nevertheless [a]Mephibosheth your master's
grandson [b]shall [1]eat at my table regularly." Now Ziba had fifteen
sons and twenty servants.

[1]Lit., eat bread Sam. 9:7, 11, 13 19:28; 1 Kin. 2:7

11 Then Ziba said to the king, "According [a]to all that my lord the
king commands his servant so your servant will do." So
Mephibosheth ate at [1]David's table as one of the king's sons.

[1]Lit., my [a]2 Sam. 16:1-4; 19:24-30

12 And Mephibosheth had a young son whose name was Mica.
And all who lived in the house of Ziba were servants to
Mephibosheth.

[a]2 Sam. 9:7, 11 [b]2 Sam. 9:3

13 So Mephibosheth lived in Jerusalem, for [a]he ate at the king's
table regularly. Now [b]he was lame in both feet.

Chapter 10

1 [a]1 Chr. 19:1-19 [b]1 Sam. 11:1

10 [a]Now it happened afterwards that [b]the king of the Ammonites
died, and Hanun his son became king in his place.

.it., by the hand of [a]1 Sam. 11:1

2 Then David said, "I will show kindness to Hanun the son of
[a]Nahash, just as his father showed kindness to me." So David sent
[1]some of his servants to console him concerning his father. But when
David's servants came to the land of the Ammonites,

.it., In your eyes is David honoring

3 the princes of the Ammonites said to Hanun their lord, "[1]Do you

think that David is honoring your father because he has sent con-
solers to you? [a]Has David not sent his servants to you in order to
search the city, to spy it out and overthrow it?"
4 So Hanun took David's servants and [a]shaved off half of their
beards, and [b]cut off their garments in the middle as far as their hips,
and sent them away.
5 When they told *it* to David, he sent to meet them, for the men
were greatly humiliated. And the king said, "[1]Stay at Jericho until
your beards grow, and *then* return."
6 Now when the sons of Ammon saw that [a]they had become
odious to David, the sons of Ammon sent and [b]hired the Arameans
of [c]Beth-rehob and the [d]Arameans of Zobah, 20,000 foot soldiers, and
the king of [e]Maacah with 1,000 men, and the men of Tob with 12,000
men.
7 When David heard *of it,* he sent Joab and all the army, the
mighty men.
8 And the sons of Ammon came out and drew up in battle array
[a]at the entrance of the [1]city, while the Arameans of Zobah and of
Rehob and the men of [b]Tob and Maacah *were* by themselves in the
field.
9 Now when Joab saw that [1]the battle was set against him in front
and in the rear, he selected from all the choice men of Israel, and
arrayed *them* against the Arameans.
10 But the remainder of the people he placed in the hand of Abishai
his brother, and he arrayed *them* against the sons of Ammon.
11 And he said, "If the Arameans are too strong for me, then you
shall help me, but if the sons of Ammon are too strong for you, then
I will come to help you.
12 "[a]Be strong, and let us show ourselves courageous for the sake of
our people and for the cities of our God; and [b]may the LORD do what
is good in His sight."
13 So Joab and the people who were with him drew near to the
battle against the Arameans, and [a]they fled before him.
14 When the sons of Ammon saw that the Arameans fled, they *also*
fled before Abishai and entered the city. [a]Then Joab returned from
fighting against the sons of Ammon and came to Jerusalem.
15 When the Arameans saw that they had been [1]defeated by Israel,
they gathered themselves together.
16 [a]And Hadadezer sent and brought out the Arameans who were
beyond the [1]River, and they came to Helam; and [b]Shobach the com-
mander of the army of Hadadezer [2]led them.
17 Now when it was told David, he gathered all Israel together and
crossed the Jordan, and came to Helam. And the Arameans arrayed
themselves to meet David and fought against him.
18 But the Arameans fled before Israel, and David killed [a]700
charioteers of the Arameans and 40,000 horsemen and struck down
Shobach the commander of their army, and he died there.
19 When all the kings, servants of Hadadezer, saw that they were
[1]defeated by Israel, [a]they made peace with Israel and served them.
So the Arameans feared to help the sons of Ammon anymore.

Chapter 11

11 [a]Then it happened [1b]in the spring, at the time when kings go
out *to battle,* that David sent Joab and his servants with him

3 [a]Gen. 42:9;
4 [a]Is. 15:2; Je [b]Is. 20:4
5 [1]Lit., *Return*
6 [a]Gen. 34:30, 27:12 [b]2 Sam. 2 Kin. 7:6 [c]Jud [d]2 Sam. 8:3 [e]D
8 [1]Lit., *gate* [a]1 19:9 [b]Judg. 11.
9 [1]Lit., *the face battle were aga*
12 [a]Deut. 31:6; 1:6; 1 Cor. 16:13 [b]1 Sam. 3:18
13 [a]1 Kin. 20:13
14 [a]2 Sam. 11:1
15 [1]Lit., *smitten*
16 [1]I.e., Euphrat [2]Lit., *before* [a]2 S 8:3-8 [b]1 Chr. 19:
18 [a]1 Chr. 19:18
19 [1]Lit., *smitten b* [a]2 Sam. 8:6
11:1 [1]Lit., *at the of the year* [a]1 Ch [b]2 Sam. 10:14; 1 I 20:22, 26

and all Israel, and they destroyed the sons of Ammon and [c]besieged
Rabbah. But David stayed at Jerusalem.
2 Now when evening came David arose from his bed and walked
around on [a]the roof of the king's house, and from the roof he saw a
woman bathing; and the woman was very beautiful in appearance.
3 So David sent and inquired about the woman. And one said, "Is
this not [a]Bathsheba, the daughter of Eliam, the wife of [b]Uriah the
Hittite?"
4 And David sent messengers and took her, and when she came to
him, [a]he lay with her; [b]and when she had purified herself from her
uncleanness, she returned to her house.
5 And the woman conceived; and she sent and told David, and
said, "[a]I am pregnant."
6 Then David sent to Joab, *saying,* "Send me Uriah the Hittite." So
Joab sent Uriah to David.
7 When Uriah came to him, [a]David asked concerning the welfare
of Joab and [1]the people and the state of the war.
8 Then David said to Uriah, "Go down to your house, and [a]wash
your feet." And Uriah went out of the king's house, and a present
from the king [1]was sent out after him.
9 But Uriah slept [a]at the door of the king's house with all the
servants of his lord, and did not go down to his house.
10 Now when they told David, saying, "Uriah did not go down to
his house," David said to Uriah, "Have you not come from a jour-
ney? Why did you not go down to your house?"
11 And Uriah said to David, "[a]The ark and Israel and Judah are
staying in [1]temporary shelters, and my lord Joab and [b]the servants of
my lord are camping in the open field. Shall I then go to my house to
eat and to drink and to lie with my wife? By your life and the life of
your soul, I will not do this thing."
12 Then David said to Uriah, "[a]Stay here today also, and tomorrow
I will let you go." So Uriah remained in Jerusalem that day and the
[1]next.
13 Now David called him, and he ate and drank before him, and he
[a]made him drunk; and in the evening he went out to lie on his bed
[b]with his lord's servants, but he did not go down to his house.
14 Now it came about in the morning that David [a]wrote a letter to
Joab, and sent *it* by the hand of Uriah.
15 And [a]he had written in the letter, saying, "[1]Place Uriah in the
front line of the [2]fiercest battle and withdraw from him, [b]so that he
may be struck down and die."
16 So it was as Joab kept watch on the city, that he put Uriah at the
place where he knew there *were* valiant men.
17 And the men of the city went out and fought against Joab, and
some of the people among David's servants fell; and [a]Uriah the Hit-
tite also died.
18 Then Joab sent and reported to David all the events of the war.
19 And he charged the messenger, saying, "When you have
finished telling all the events of the war to the king,
20 and if it happens that the king's wrath rises and he says to you,
'Why did you go so near to the city to fight? Did you not know that
they would shoot from the wall?
21 'Who [a]struck down Abimelech the son of Jerubbesheth? Did not
a woman throw an upper millstone on him from the wall so that he

am. 12:26-29; 3; Amos 1:14
22:8; 1 Sam. tt. 24:17; Acts 10:9
r. 3:5 [b]2 Sam. 23:39
51:title; James [b]Lev. 12:2-5; 5:18-28; 18:19
v. 20:10; Deut. 22:22
elfare of [a]Gen. ; 1 Sam. 17:22
went out [a]Gen. 3:24; Luke 7:44
1 Kin. 14:27, 28
booths [a]2 Sam. 6 [b]2 Sam. 20:6
t., *morrow* [a]Job 20:12-14
13 [a]Prov. 20:1; 35 [b]2 Sam. 11:9
[a]1 Kin. 21:8-10
[1]Lit., *Give* [2]Lit., [a]Eccl. 8:11; Jer. 7:9 [b]2 Sam. 12:9
7 [a]2 Sam. 11:21
1 [a]Judg. 9:50-54

died at Thebez? Why did you go so near the wall?'—then you shall
say, 'Your servant Uriah the Hittite is dead also.' "
22 So the messenger departed and came and reported to David all
that Joab had sent him *to tell.*
23 And the messenger said to David, "The men prevailed against
us and came out against us in the field, but we [1]pressed them as far
as the entrance of the gate.
24 "Moreover, the archers shot at your servants from the wall; so
some of the king's servants are dead, and your servant Uriah the
Hittite is also dead."
25 Then David said to the messenger, "Thus you shall say to Joab,
'Do not let this thing [1]displease you, for the sword devours one as
well as another; make your battle against the city stronger and over-
throw it'; and *so* encourage him."
26 Now when the wife of Uriah heard that Uriah her husband was
dead, [a]she mourned for her husband.
27 When the *time of* mourning was over, David sent and [1]brought
her to his house and [a]she became his wife; then she bore him a son.
But [b]the thing that David had done was evil in the sight of the LORD.

Chapter 12

12 Then the LORD sent [a]Nathan to David. And [b]he came to him,
and [1]said,
"There were two men in one city, the one rich and the other poor.
2 "The rich man had a great many flocks and herds.
3 "But the poor man had nothing except [a]one little ewe lamb
Which he bought and nourished;
And it grew up together with him and his children.
It would eat of his [1]bread and drink of his cup and lie in his
bosom,
And was like a daughter to him.
4 "Now a traveler came to the rich man,
And he [1]was unwilling to take from his own flock or his own
herd,
To prepare for the wayfarer who had come to him;
Rather he took the poor man's ewe lamb and prepared it for the
man who had come to him."
5 Then David's anger burned greatly against the man, and he said
to Nathan, "As the LORD lives, surely the man who has done this
[1a]deserves to die.
6 "And he must make restitution for the lamb [a]fourfold, because he
did this thing and had no compassion."
7 Nathan then said to David, "[a]You are the man! Thus says the
LORD God of Israel, '[b]It is I who anointed you king over Israel and it
is I who delivered you from the hand of Saul.
8 'I also gave you [a]your master's house and your master's wives
into your [1]care, and I gave you the house of Israel and Judah; and if
that had been too little, I would have added to you many more things
like these!
9 'Why [a]have you despised the word of the LORD by doing evil in
His sight? [b]You have struck down Uriah the Hittite with the sword,
[c]have taken his wife to be your wife, and have killed him with the
sword of the sons of Ammon.
10 'Now therefore, [a]the sword shall never depart from your house,

23 [1]Lit., *were*

25 [1]Lit., *be ev*
sight

26 [a]Gen. 50:1
34:8; 1 Sam. 3

27 [1]Lit., *gathe*
[a]2 Sam. 12:9
51:4, 5

12:1 [1]Lit., *said*
[a]2 Sam. 7:2, 4,
51:title

3 [1]Lit., *morsel*
11:3

4 [1]Lit., *spared*

5 [1]Lit., *is a son*
death [a]1 Sam. 2

6 [a]Ex. 22:1; Luk

7 [a]1 Kin. 20:42
16:13

8 [1]Lit., *bosom* [a]
9:7

9 [a]1 Sam. 15:23
[b]2 Sam. 11:14-17
[c]2 Sam. 11:27

10 [a]2 Sam. 13:28
18:14; 1 Kin. 2:25

because you have despised Me and have taken the wife of Uriah the
Hittite to be your wife.'
11 "Thus says the LORD, 'Behold, I will raise up evil against you from
your own household; [a]I will even take your wives before your eyes,
and give *them* to your companion, and he shall lie with your wives
in [1]broad daylight.
12 'Indeed [a]you did it secretly, but [b]I will do this thing before all
Israel, and [1]under the sun.' "
13 Then David said to Nathan, "[a]I have sinned against the LORD."
And Nathan said to David, "The LORD also has [1b]taken away your
sin; you shall not die.
14 "However, because by this deed you have [a]given occasion to the
enemies of the LORD to blaspheme, the child also that is born to you
shall surely die."
15 So Nathan went to his house.
Then the LORD struck the child that Uriah's [1]widow bore to
David, so that he was *very* sick.
16 David therefore inquired of God for the child; and David [a]fasted
and went and [b]lay all night on the ground.
17 And [a]the elders of his household stood beside him in order to
raise him up from the ground, but he was unwilling and would not
eat food with them.
18 Then it happened on the seventh day that the child died. And
the servants of David were afraid to tell him that the child was dead,
for they said, "Behold, while the child was *still* alive, we spoke to
him and he did not listen to our voice. How then can we tell him that
the child is dead, since he might do *himself* harm!"
19 But when David saw that his servants were whispering together,
David perceived that the child was dead; so David said to his ser-
vants, "Is the child dead?" And they said, "He is dead."
20 So David arose from the ground, [a]washed, anointed *himself*, and
changed his clothes; and he came into the house of the LORD and
[b]worshiped. Then he came to his own house, and when he re-
quested, they set food before him and he ate.
21 Then his servants said to him, "What is this thing that you have
done? [1]While the child was alive, you fasted and wept; but when the
child died, you arose and ate food."
22 And he said, "While the child was *still* alive, [a]I fasted and wept;
for I said, '[b]Who knows, the LORD may be gracious to me, that the
child may live.'
23 "But now he has died; why should I fast? Can I bring him back
again? [a]I shall go to him, but [b]he will not return to me."
24 Then David comforted his wife Bathsheba, and went in to her
and lay with her; and she gave birth to a son, and [1a]he named him
Solomon. Now the LORD loved him
25 and sent *word* through Nathan the prophet, and he named him
[1]Jedidiah for the LORD's sake.
26 [a]Now Joab fought against [b]Rabbah of the sons of Ammon, and
captured the royal city.
27 And Joab sent messengers to David and said, "I have fought
against Rabbah, I have even captured the city of waters.
28 "Now therefore, gather the rest of the people together and camp
against the city and capture it, lest I capture the city myself and it be
named after me."

...e sight of this [a]Deut. 28:30; ...m. 16:21, 22
...fore [a]2 Sam. ...2 Sam. 16:22
..., caused your to pass away ...m. 15:24, 30; ....24:10; Luke ... [b]Lev. 20:10; ...v. 28:13; Mic. 7:18
...:5; Rom. 2:24
15 [1]Lit., *wife*
...1:4 [b]2 Sam. 13:31
17 [a]Gen. 24:2
...Ruth 3:3; Matt. ...95:6-8; 103:1, ...8-17; Prov. 3:7
..., *On account of*
...8:1-3 [b]Jon. 3:9
...ien. 37:35 [b]Job 7:8-10
...Some mss. read ...Chr. 22:9; Matt. 1:6
...., beloved of the LORD
...6 [a]1 Chr. 20:1-3 [b]Deut. 3:11

A **brickkiln** was an oven, furnace, or heated enclosure which was used for drying or firing bricks.

29 So David gathered all the people and went to Rabbah, fought against it, and captured it.

30 Then [a]he took the crown of [1]their king from his head; and its weight *was* a talent of gold, and *in it* [2]*was* a precious stone; and it was *placed* on David's head. And he brought out the spoil of the city in great amounts.

31 He also brought out the people who were in it, and [a]set *them* under saws, sharp iron instruments, and iron axes, and made them pass through the brickkiln. And thus he did to all the cities of the sons of Ammon. Then David and all the people returned *to* Jerusalem.

Chapter 13

13 Now it was after this that [a]Absalom the son of David had a beautiful sister whose name was [b]Tamar, and [c]Amnon the son of David loved her.

2 And Amnon was so frustrated because of his sister Tamar that he made himself ill, for she was a virgin, and it seemed [1]hard to Amnon to do anything to her.

3 But Amnon had a friend whose name was Jonadab, the son of [1a]Shimeah, David's brother; and Jonadab was a very shrewd man.

4 And he said to him, "O son of the king, why are you so depressed morning after morning? Will you not tell me?" Then Amnon said to him, "I am in love with Tamar, the sister of my brother Absalom."

5 Jonadab then said to him, "Lie down on your bed and pretend to be ill; when your father comes to see you, say to him, 'Please let my sister Tamar come and give me *some* food to eat, and let her prepare the food in my sight, that I may see *it* and eat from her hand.' "

6 So Amnon lay down and pretended to be ill; when the king came to see him, Amnon said to the king, "Please let my sister Tamar come and [a]make me a couple of cakes in my sight, that I may eat from her hand."

7 Then David sent to the house for Tamar, saying, "Go now to your brother Amnon's house, and prepare food for him."

8 So Tamar went to her brother Amnon's house, and he was lying down. And she took dough, kneaded *it*, made cakes in his sight, and baked the cakes.

9 And she took the pan and [1]dished *them* out before him, but he refused to eat. And Amnon said, "[a]Have everyone go out from me." So everyone went out from him.

10 Then Amnon said to Tamar, "Bring the food into the [1]bedroom, that I may eat from your hand." So Tamar took the cakes which she had made and brought them into the bedroom to her brother Amnon.

11 When she brought *them* to him to eat, he [a]took hold of her and said to her, "Come, lie with me, my sister."

12 But she answered him, "No, my brother, do not violate me, for [a]such a thing is not done in Israel; do not do this [b]disgraceful thing!

13 "As for me, where could I [1]get rid of my reproach? And as for you, you will be like one of the [2]fools in Israel. Now therefore, please speak to the king, for [a]he will not withhold me from you."

14 However, he would not listen to [1]her; since he was stronger than she, he [a]violated her and lay with her.

30 [1]Or, *Malca* Zeph. 1:5 [2]O *precious ston* 20:2

31 [a]1 Chr. 20 11:37

13:1 [a]2 Sam. 1 Chr. 3:2 [b]1 [c]2 Sam. 3:2

2 [1]Lit., *hard in eyes*

3 [1]In 1 Sam. 1 *Shammah;* in 1 2:13, *Shimea* 16:9

6 [a]Gen. 18:6

9 [1]Lit., *poured* 45:1

10 [1]Or, *inner ro*

11 [a]Gen. 39:12

12 [a]Lev. 20:17 19:23; 20:6

13 [1]Lit., *cause t* [2]Or, *disgraceful* [a]Gen. 20:12

14 [1]Lit., *her voic* 18:9; Deut. 22:25 27:22; 2 Sam. 12

15 Then Amnon hated her with a very great hatred; for the hatred
with which he hated her was greater than the love with which he
had loved her. And Amnon said to her, "Get up, go away!"
16 But she said to him, "No, because this wrong in sending me
away is greater than the other that you have done to me!" Yet he
would not listen to her.
17 Then he called his young man who attended him and said,
"Now throw this woman out of my *presence,* and lock the door be-
hind her."
18 Now she had on [a]a [1]long-sleeved garment; for in this manner the
virgin daughters of the king dressed themselves in robes. Then his
attendant took her out and locked the door behind her.
19 And [a]Tamar put [1]ashes on her head, and [b]tore her [2]long-sleeved
garment which *was* on her; and [c]she put her hand on her head and
went away, crying aloud as she went.
20 Then Absalom her brother said to her, "Has Amnon your brother
been with you? But now keep silent, my sister, he is your brother; do
not take this matter to heart." So Tamar remained and was desolate
in her brother Absalom's house.
21 Now when King David heard of all these matters, he was very
angry.
22 But Absalom did not speak to Amnon [a]either good or bad; for
[b]Absalom hated Amnon because he had violated his sister Tamar.
23 Now it came about after two full years that Absalom [a]had sheep-
shearers in Baal-hazor, which is near Ephraim, and Absalom invited
all the king's sons.
24 And Absalom came to the king and said, "Behold now, your
servant has sheepshearers; please let the king and his servants go
with your servant."
25 But the king said to Absalom, "No, my son, we should not all go,
lest we be burdensome to you." Although he [1]urged him, he would
not go, but blessed him.
26 Then [a]Absalom said, "If not, please let my brother Amnon go
with us." And the king said to him, "Why should he go with you?"
27 But when Absalom [1]urged him, he let Amnon and all the king's
sons go with him.
28 And Absalom commanded his servants, saying, "See now, [a]when
Amnon's heart is merry with wine, and when I say to you, 'Strike
Amnon,' then put him to death. Do not fear; have not I myself com-
manded you? Be courageous and be [1]valiant."
29 And the servants of Absalom did to Amnon just as Absalom had
commanded. Then all the king's sons arose and each mounted [a]his
mule and fled.
30 Now it was while they were on the way that the report came to
David, saying, "Absalom has struck down all the king's sons, and
not one of them is left."
31 Then the king arose, [a]tore his clothes and [b]lay on the ground; and
all his servants were standing by with clothes torn.
32 And [a]Jonadab, the son of Shimeah, David's brother, [1]responded,
"Do not let my lord [2]suppose they have put to death all the young
men, the king's sons, for Amnon alone is dead; because by the [3]in-
tent of Absalom this has been determined since the day that he vio-
lated his sister Tamar.
33 "Now therefore, do not let my lord the king [a]take the report to

a varicolored
Gen. 37:3, 23
Or, dust [2]Lit.,
icolored tunic
:12; Esth. 4:1
37:29; 2 Sam.
11 [c]Jer. 2:37
. 31:24 [b]Lev.
John 2:9, 11;
3:10, 12, 15
[a]1 Sam. 25:7
broke through
[a]2 Sam. 3:27;
11:13-15
, broke through
t., sons of valor
dg. 19:6, 9, 22;
Sam. 25:36-38
am. 18:9; 1 Kin.
1:33, 38
31 [a]2 Sam. 1:11
[b]2 Sam. 12:16
t., answered and
d [2]Lit., say [3]Lit.,
[a]2 Sam. 13:3-5
3 [a]2 Sam. 19:19

[1]heart, namely, 'all the king's sons are dead,' for only Amnon is
dead."
34 Now [a]Absalom had fled. And [b]the young man who was the
watchman raised his eyes and looked, and behold, many people
were coming from the road behind him by the side of the mountain.
35 And Jonadab said to the king, "Behold, the king's sons have
come; according to your servant's word, so it happened."
36 And it came about as soon as he had finished speaking, that
behold, the king's sons came and lifted their voices and wept; and
also the king and all his servants wept [1]very bitterly.
37 Now [a]Absalom fled and went to [b]Talmai the son of Ammihud,
the king of [c]Geshur. And *David* mourned for his son every day.
38 [a]So Absalom had fled and gone to Geshur, and was there three
years.
39 And *the heart of* King David longed to go out to Absalom; for [a]he
was comforted concerning Amnon, since he was dead.

Chapter 14

14 Now Joab the son of Zeruiah perceived that [a]the king's heart
was inclined toward Absalom.
2 So Joab sent to [a]Tekoa and [1]brought a wise woman from there
and said to her, "Please pretend to be a mourner, and put on mourn-
ing garments now, and do not [b]anoint yourself with oil, but be like a
woman who has been mourning for the dead many days;
3 then go to the king and speak to him in this manner." So Joab
put [a]the words in her mouth.
4 Now when the woman of Tekoa [1]spoke to the king, she fell on
her face to the ground and [a]prostrated herself and said, "[b]Help, O
king."
5 And the king said to her, "What is your trouble?" And she
[1]answered, "Truly I am a widow, for my husband is dead.
6 "And your maidservant had two sons, but the two of them strug-
gled together in the field, and there was no [1]one to separate them, so
one struck the other and killed him.
7 "Now behold, [a]the whole family has risen against your maidser-
vant, and they say, 'Hand over the one who struck his brother, that
we may put him to death for the life of his brother whom he killed,
[b]and destroy the heir also.' Thus they will extinguish my coal which
is left, so as to [1]leave my husband neither name nor remnant on the
face of the earth."
8 Then the king said to the woman, "Go to your house, and I will
give orders concerning you."
9 And the woman of Tekoa said to the king, "O my lord, the king,
[a]the iniquity is on me and my father's house, but [b]the king and his
throne are guiltless."
10 So the king said, "Whoever speaks to you, bring him to me, and
he will not touch you anymore."
11 Then she said, "Please let the king remember the LORD your God,
[a]*so that* the avenger of blood may not continue to destroy, lest they
destroy my son." And he said, "[b]As the LORD lives, not one hair of
your son shall fall to the ground."
12 Then the woman said, "Please let your maidservant speak a
word to my lord the king." And he said, "Speak."
13 And the woman said, "[a]Why then have you planned such a

33 [1]Lit., *his h*
34 [a]2 Sam. 1
[b]2 Sam. 18:24
36 [1]Lit., *with a great weeping*
37 [a]2 Sam. 13
[b]2 Sam. 3:3 [c]2
14:23, 32
38 [a]2 Sam. 13
39 [a]2 Sam. 12
14:1 [a]2 Sam.
2 [1]Lit., *took* [a]2
23:26; 2 Chr. 11
Amos 1:1 [b]2 S
3 [a]2 Sam. 14:1
4 [1]Many mss. a
ancient versions
came [a]1 Sam. 2
[b]2 Kin. 6:26-28
5 [1]Lit., *said*
6 [1]Lit., *deliverer between*
7 [1]Lit., *set* [a]Nu
35:19; Deut. 19:1
[b]Matt. 21:38
9 [a]Gen. 43:9; 1 S
25:24 [b]1 Kin. 2:3
11 [a]Num. 35:19,
Deut. 19:4-10 [b]1
14:45; 1 Kin. 1:52
10:30
13 [a]2 Sam. 12:7;
20:40-42

thing against the people of God? For in speaking this word the king
is as one who is guilty, *in that* the king does not bring back [b]his
banished one.
14 "For [a]we shall surely die and are [b]like water spilled on the ground
which cannot be gathered up again. Yet God does not take away life,
but plans [1]ways so that [c]the banished one may not be cast out from
him.
15 "Now [1]the reason I have come to speak this word to my lord the
king is because the people have made me afraid; so your maidser-
vant said, 'Let me now speak to the king, perhaps the king will
perform the [2]request of his maidservant.
16 'For the king will hear [1]and deliver his maidservant from the
[2]hand of the man who would destroy [3]both me and my son from [a]the
inheritance of God.'
17 "Then your maidservant said, 'Please let the word of my lord the
king be [1]comforting, for as [a]the angel of God, so is my lord the king
to discern good and evil. And may the LORD your God be with
you.' "
18 Then the king answered and said to the woman, "Please do not
hide anything from me that I am about to ask you." And the woman
said, "Let my lord the king please speak."
19 So the king said, "Is the hand of Joab with you in all this?" And
the woman answered and said, "As your soul lives, my lord the
king, no one can turn to the right or to the left from anything that my
lord the king has spoken. Indeed, it was [a]your servant Joab who
commanded me, and it was he who put all these words in the mouth
of your maidservant;
20 in order to change the appearance of things your servant Joab
has done this thing. But my lord is wise, [a]like the wisdom of the
angel of God, to know all that is in the earth."
21 Then the king said to Joab, "Behold now, [a]I will surely do this
thing; go therefore, bring back the young man Absalom."
22 And Joab fell on his face to the ground, prostrated himself and
blessed the king; then Joab said, "Today your servant knows that I
have found favor in your sight, O my lord, the king, in that the king
has performed the [1]request of his servant."
23 So Joab arose and went to [a]Geshur, and brought Absalom to
Jerusalem.
24 However the king said, "Let him turn to [a]his own house, and let
him not see my face." So Absalom turned to his own house and did
not see the king's face.
25 Now in all Israel was no one as handsome as Absalom, so highly
praised; [a]from the sole of his foot to the crown of his head there was
no defect in him.
26 And when he [a]cut the hair of his head (and it was at the end of
every year that he cut *it*, for it was heavy on him so he cut it), he
weighed the hair of his head at 200 shekels by the king's weight.
27 And [a]to Absalom there were born three sons, and one daughter
whose name was [b]Tamar; she was a woman of beautiful appearance.
28 Now Absalom lived two full years in Jerusalem, [a]and did not see
the king's face.
29 Then Absalom sent for Joab, to send him to the king, but he
would not come to him. So he sent again a second time, but he
would not come.

[b]2 Sam. 13:37, 38
[1]Lit., *devices* [a]Job 3; 34:15; Heb. 9:27 58:7 [c]Num. 35:15, 25, 28
Lit., *that* [2]Lit., *word*
[1]Lit., *to* [2]Lit., *palm* Lit., *together* [a]Deut. 32:9; 1 Sam. 26:19
17 [1]Lit., *for rest* Sam. 29:9; 2 Sam. 14:20; 19:27
19 [a]2 Sam. 14:3
Sam. 14:17; 19:27
21 [a]2 Sam. 14:11
22 [1]Lit., *word*
Deut. 3:14; 2 Sam. 13:37, 38
24 [a]2 Sam. 13:20
[a]Deut. 28:35; Job 2:7; Is. 1:6
26 [a]Ezek. 44:20
27 [a]2 Sam. 18:18 [b]2 Sam. 13:1
28 [a]2 Sam. 14:24

30 Therefore he said to his servants, "See, [a]Joab's [1]field is next to
mine, and he has barley there; go and set it on fire." So Absalom's
servants set the [1]field on fire.
31 Then Joab arose, came to Absalom at his house and said to him,
"Why have your servants set my [1]field on fire?"
32 And Absalom [1]answered Joab, "Behold, I sent for you, saying,
'Come here, that I may send you to the king, to say, "Why have I
come from Geshur? It would be better for me still to be there." ' Now
therefore, let me see the king's face; [a]and if there is iniquity in me, let
him put me to death."
33 So when Joab came to the king and told him, he called for Ab-
salom. Thus he came to the king and prostrated himself on his face
to the ground before the king, and [a]the king kissed Absalom.

Chapter 15

15 Now it came about after this that [a]Absalom provided for him-
self a chariot and horses, and fifty men as runners before him.
2 And Absalom used to rise early and [a]stand beside the way to the
gate; and it happened that when any man had a suit to come to the
king for judgment, Absalom would call to him and say, "From what
city are you?" And he would say, "Your servant is from one of the
tribes of Israel."
3 Then Absalom would say to him, "See, [a]your [1]claims are good
and right, but no man listens to you on the part of the king."
4 Moreover, Absalom would say, "[a]Oh that one would appoint me
judge in the land, then every man who has any suit or cause could
come to me, and I would give him justice."
5 And it happened that when a man came near to prostrate him-
self before him, he would put out his hand and take hold of him and
[a]kiss him.
6 And in this manner Absalom dealt with all Israel who came to
the king for judgment; [a]so Absalom stole away the hearts of the men
of Israel.
7 Now it came about at the end of [1]forty years that Absalom said
to the king, "Please let me go and pay my vow which I have vowed
to the LORD, in [a]Hebron.
8 "For your servant [a]vowed a vow while I was living at Geshur in
Aram, saying, '[b]If the LORD shall indeed bring me back to Jerusalem,
then I will serve the LORD.' "
9 And the king said to him, "Go in peace." So he arose and went to
Hebron.
10 But Absalom sent spies throughout all the tribes of Israel, saying,
"As soon as you hear the sound of the trumpet, then you shall say,
'[a]Absalom is king in Hebron.' "
11 Then two hundred men went with Absalom from Jerusalem,
[a]who were invited and [b]went [1]innocently, and they did not know
anything.
12 And Absalom sent for [a]Ahithophel the Gilonite, David's coun-
selor, from his city [b]Giloh, while he was offering the sacrifices. And
the conspiracy was strong, for [c]the people increased continually with
Absalom.
13 Then a messenger came to David, saying, "[a]The hearts of the
men of Israel are [1]with Absalom."
14 And David said to all his servants who were with him at

30 [1]Lit., por
15:3-5
31 [1]Lit., por
32 [1]Lit., said [a]1 Sam. 20:8
28:13
33 [a]Gen. 33:
15:20
15:1 [a]1 Kin.
2 [a]Ruth 4:1;
19:8
3 [1]Lit., *words*
12:2
4 [a]Judg. 9:29
5 [a]2 Sam. 14:
6 [a]Rom. 16:18
7 [1]Some ancie
versions rende
[a]2 Sam. 3:2, 3
8 [a]2 Sam. 13:3
[b]Gen. 28:20, 21
10 [a]1 Kin. 1:34
9:13
11 [1]Lit., *in their integrity* [a]1 Sam
[b]1 Sam. 22:15
12 [a]2 Sam. 15:3
[b]Josh. 15:51 [c]P
13 [1]Lit., *after* [a]J
9:3; 2 Sam. 15:6

Jerusalem, "[a]Arise and let us flee, for *otherwise* none of us shall es-
cape from Absalom. Go in haste, lest he overtake us quickly and
bring down calamity on us and strike the city with the edge of the
sword."
15 Then the king's servants said to the king, "Behold, your servants
are ready to do whatever my lord the king chooses."
16 So the king went out and all his household [1]with him. But [a]the
king left ten concubines to keep the house.
17 And the king went out and all the people [1]with him, and they
stopped at the last house.
18 Now all his servants passed on beside him, [a]all the Cherethites,
all the Pelethites, and all the Gittites, [b]six hundred men who had
come [1]with him from Gath, passed on before the king.
19 Then the king said to [a]Ittai the Gittite, "Why will you also go
with us? Return and remain with the king, for you are a foreigner
and also an exile; *return* to your own place.
20 "You came *only* yesterday, and shall I today make you wander
with us, while [a]I go where I will? Return and take back your
brothers; [b]mercy and [1]truth be with you."
21 But Ittai answered the king and said, "As the LORD lives, and as
my lord the king lives, surely [a]wherever my lord the king may be,
whether for death or for life, there also your servant will be."
22 Therefore David said to Ittai, "Go and pass over." So Ittai the
Gittite passed over with all his men and all the little ones who *were*
with him.
23 While all the country was weeping with a loud voice, all the
people passed over. The king also passed over [a]the brook Kidron,
and all the people passed over toward [b]the way of the wilderness.
24 Now behold, [a]Zadok also *came,* and all the Levites with him
[b]carrying the ark of the covenant of God. And they set down the ark
of God, and [c]Abiathar came up until all the people had finished
passing from the city.
25 And the king said to Zadok, "Return the ark of God to the city. If
I find favor in the sight of the LORD, then [a]He will bring me back
again, and show me both it and [b]His habitation.
26 "But if He should say thus, '[a]I have no delight in you,' behold,
here I am, [b]let Him do to me as seems good [1]to Him."
27 The king said also to Zadok the priest, "Are you *not* [a]a seer?
Return to the city in peace and your [b]two sons with you, your son
Ahimaaz and Jonathan the son of Abiathar.
28 "See, I am going to wait [a]at the fords of the wilderness until word
comes from you to inform me."
29 Therefore Zadok and Abiathar returned the ark of God to Jeru-
salem and remained there.
30 And David went up the ascent of the *Mount of* Olives, and wept
as he went, and [a]his head was covered and he walked [b]barefoot.
Then all the people who were with him each covered his head and
went up weeping as they went.
31 Now someone told David, saying, "[a]Ahithophel is among the
conspirators with Absalom." And David said, "O LORD, I pray,
[b]make the counsel of Ahithophel foolishness."
32 It happened as David was coming to the summit, where God
was worshiped, that behold, Hushai the [a]Archite met him with his
[1]coat torn, and [2]dust on his head.

...m. 12:11; Ps. 3:title
...Lit., *at his feet* ...am. 16:21, 22
...Lit., *at his feet*
Lit., *at his feet* ...8:18 [b]1 Sam. 25:13; 30:1, 9
[a]2 Sam. 18:2
...Or, *faithfulness* ...23:13 [b]2 Sam. 2:6
...1:16, 17; Prov. 17:17
...n. 15:13; 2 Chr. [b]2 Sam. 15:28; 16:2
...am. 8:17; 20:25 ...:15; 1 Sam. 4:4, ... [c]1 Sam. 22:20
[a]Ps. 43:3 [b]Ex. 5:13; Jer. 25:30
[1]Lit., *in His sight* ...m. 11:27; 1 Chr. ...:7 [b]1 Sam. 3:18
...7 [a]1 Sam. 9:6-9 [b]2 Sam. 17:17
...sh. 5:10; 2 Sam. 17:16
Esth. 6:12; Ezek. ...7, 23 [b]Is. 20:2-4
...31 [a]2 Sam. 15:12 ... 16:23; 17:14, 23
...2 [1]Or, *tunic* [2]Lit., ...round [a]Josh. 16:2

33 And David said to him, "If you pass over with me, then you will
be [a]a burden to me.
34 "But if you return to the city, and [a]say to Absalom, 'I will be your
servant, O king; as I have been your father's servant in time past, so
I will now be your servant,' then you can thwart the counsel of
Ahithophel for me.
35 "And are not Zadok and Abiathar the priests with you there? So it
shall be that [a]whatever you hear from the king's house, you shall
report to Zadok and Abiathar the priests.
36 "Behold [a]their two sons are with them there, Ahimaaz, Zadok's
son and Jonathan, Abiathar's son; and [b]by them you shall send me
everything that you hear."
37 So Hushai, [a]David's friend, came into the city, and [b]Absalom
came into Jerusalem.

Chapter 16

16 Now when David had passed [a]a little beyond the summit,
behold, [b]Ziba the servant of Mephibosheth met him [c]with a
couple of saddled donkeys, and on them *were* two hundred loaves of
bread, a hundred clusters of raisins, a hundred summer fruits, and a
jug of wine.
2 And the king said to Ziba, "Why do you have these?" And Ziba
said, "[a]The donkeys are for the king's household to ride, and the
bread and summer fruit for the young men to eat, and the wine, [b]for
whoever is faint in the wilderness to drink."
3 Then the king said, "And where is [a]your master's son?" And
[b]Ziba said to the king, "Behold, he is staying in Jerusalem, for he
said, 'Today the house of Israel will restore the kingdom of my father
to me.'"
4 So the king said to Ziba, "Behold, all that belongs to
Mephibosheth is yours." And Ziba said, "I prostrate myself; let me
find favor in your sight, O my lord, the king!"
5 When King David came to [a]Bahurim, behold, there came out
from there a man of the family of the house of Saul [b]whose name
was Shimei, the son of Gera; he came out [c]cursing continually as he
came.
6 And he threw stones at David and at all the servants of King
David; and all the people and all the mighty men were at his right
hand and at his left.
7 And thus Shimei said when he cursed, "Get out, get out, [a]you
man of bloodshed, and worthless fellow!
8 "[a]The LORD has returned upon you all [b]the bloodshed of the house
of Saul, in whose place you have reigned; and the LORD has given
the kingdom into the hand of your son Absalom. And behold, you
are *taken* in your own evil, for you are a man of bloodshed!"
9 Then [a]Abishai the son of Zeruiah said to the king, "Why should
[b]this dead dog [c]curse my lord the king? Let me go over now, and [1]cut
off his head."
10 But the king said, "[a]What have I to do with you, O sons of
Zeruiah? [b]If he curses, and if the LORD has told him, 'Curse David,'
[c]then who shall say, 'Why have you done so?'"
11 Then David said to Abishai and to all his servants, "Behold, [a]my
son who came out from [1]me seeks my life; how much more now this

33 [a]2 Sam. 1
34 [a]2 Sam. 1
35 [a]2 Sam. 1
36 [a]2 Sam. 1 [b]2 Sam. 17:17
37 [a]2 Sam. 16 1 Chr. 27:33 [b] 16:15
16:1 [a]2 Sam. [b]2 Sam. 9:2-13 25:18
2 [a]Judg. 10:4 17:29
3 [a]2 Sam. 9:9, [b]2 Sam. 19:26,
5 [a]2 Sam. 3:16 [b]2 Sam. 19:16-2 2:8, 9, 44 [c]Ex. 1 Sam. 17:43
7 [a]2 Sam. 12:9
8 [a]2 Sam. 21:1- [b]2 Sam. 1:16; 3: 4:11, 12
9 [1]Lit., *take off* 26:8; 2 Sam. 19: Luke 9:54 [b]2 Sa [c]Ex. 22:28
10 [a]2 Sam. 3:39 [b]John 18:11 [c]Ro
11 [1]Lit., *my bod* [a]2 Sam. 12:11

Benjamite? Let him alone and let him curse, [b]for the LORD has told
him.
12 "Perhaps the LORD will look on my affliction and [1a]return good to
me instead of his cursing this day."
13 So David and his men went on the way; and Shimei went along
on the hillside parallel with him and as he went he cursed, and cast
stones and threw dust at him.
14 And the king and all the people who were with him arrived
weary and he refreshed himself there.
15 [a]Then Absalom and all the people, the men of Israel, entered
Jerusalem, and Ahithophel with him.
16 Now it came about when [a]Hushai the Archite, David's friend,
came to Absalom, that [b]Hushai said to Absalom, "[c]*Long* live the king!
Long live the king!"
17 And Absalom said to Hushai, "Is this your [1]loyalty to your
friend? [a]Why did you not go with your friend?"
18 Then Hushai said to Absalom, "No! For whom the LORD, this
people, and all the men of Israel have chosen, his will I be, and with
him I will remain.
19 "And besides, [a]whom should I serve? *Should I* not *serve* in the
presence of his son? As I have served in your father's presence, so I
will be in your presence."
20 Then Absalom said to Ahithophel, "Give your advice. What
shall we do?"
21 And Ahithophel said to Absalom, "[a]Go in to your father's con-
cubines, whom he has left to keep the house; then all Israel will hear
that you have made yourself odious to your father. The hands of all
who are with you will also be strengthened."
22 So they pitched a tent for Absalom on the roof, [a]and Absalom
went in to his father's concubines [b]in the sight of all Israel.
23 And [a]the advice of Ahithophel, which he [1]gave in those days,
was as if one inquired of the word of God; [b]so was all the advice of
Ahithophel *regarded* by both David and Absalom.

Chapter 17

17 Furthermore, Ahithophel said to Absalom, "Please let me
choose 12,000 men that I may arise and pursue David tonight.
2 "And [a]I will come upon him while he is weary and [1]exhausted
and will terrify him so that all the people who are with him will flee.
Then [b]I will strike down the king alone,
3 and I will bring back all the people to you. [1]The return of
everyone depends on the man you seek; *then* all the people shall be
at [a]peace."
4 So the [1]plan pleased Absalom and all the elders of Israel.
5 Then Absalom said, "Now call [a]Hushai the Archite also, and let
us hear what [1]he has to say."
6 When Hushai had come to Absalom, Absalom said to [1]him,
"Ahithophel has spoken [2]thus. Shall we [3]carry out his plan? If not,
you speak."
7 So Hushai said to Absalom, "[a]This time the advice that
Ahithophel has [1]given is not good."
8 Moreover, Hushai said, "You know your father and his men, that
they are mighty men and they are [1]fierce, [a]like a bear robbed of her

[b]Gen. 45:5; 1 Sam. 26:19
[1]Lit., *the LORD will return* [a]Deut. 23:5; Rom. 8:28
[a]2 Sam. 15:12, 37
16 [a]2 Sam. 15:37 …am. 15:34 [c]1 Sam. 10:24; 2 Kin. 11:12
17 [1]Or, *kindness* [a]2 Sam. 19:25
19 [a]2 Sam. 15:34
…Sam. 15:16; 20:3
…Sam. 15:16; 20:3 [b]2 Sam. 12:11, 12
23 [1]Lit., *advised* [a]2 Sam. 17:14, 23 [b]2 Sam. 15:12
17:2 [1]Lit., *slack of …ds* [a]2 Sam. 16:14 [b]1 Kin. 22:31
…*Like the return of … whole is the man …m you seek* [a]Jer. 6:14
4 [1]Lit., *word was …sing in the sight of*
5 [1]Lit., *is in his mouth—even he* [a]2 Sam. 15:32-34
[1]Lit., *him, saying … according to this* [3]Lit., *do his word*
7 [1]Lit., *advised* [a]2 Sam. 16:21
[1]Lit., *bitter of soul* [a]Hos. 13:8

cubs in the field. And your father is an [2]expert in warfare, and will
not spend the night with the people.
9 "Behold, he has now hidden himself in one of the [1]caves or in
another place; and it will be [2]when he falls on them at the first attack,
that whoever hears *it* will say, 'There has been a slaughter among the
people who follow Absalom.'
10 "And even the one who is valiant, whose heart is like the heart of
a lion, [a]will completely [1]lose heart; for all Israel knows that your
father is a mighty man and those who are with him are valiant men.
11 "But I counsel that all Israel be surely gathered to you, [a]from Dan
even to Beersheba, [b]as the sand that is by the sea in abundance, and
that [1]you personally go into battle.
12 "So we shall come to him in one of the places where he can be
found, and we will [1]fall on him [a]as the dew falls on the ground; and
of him and of all the men who are with him, not even one will be
left.
13 "And if he withdraws into a city, then all Israel shall bring ropes
to that city, and we will [a]drag it into the [1]valley until not even a small
stone is found there."
14 Then Absalom and all the men of Israel said, "The counsel of
Hushai the Archite is better than the counsel of Ahithophel." For [a]the
LORD had ordained to thwart the good counsel of Ahithophel, in
order that the LORD might bring calamity on Absalom.
15 Then [a]Hushai said to Zadok and to Abiathar the priests, "[1]This is
what Ahithophel counseled Absalom and the elders of Israel, and
[1]this is what I have counseled.
16 "Now therefore, send quickly and tell David, saying, '[a]Do not
spend the night at the fords of the wilderness, but by all means cross
over, lest the king and all the people who are with him be
[1]destroyed.' "
17 [a]Now Jonathan and Ahimaaz were staying at [b]En-rogel, and a
maidservant would go and tell them, and they would go and tell
King David, for they could not be seen entering the city.
18 But a lad did see them, and told Absalom; so the two of them
departed quickly and came to the house of a man [a]in Bahurim, who
had a well in his courtyard, and they went down [1]into it.
19 And [a]the woman [1]took a covering and spread it over the well's
mouth and scattered grain on it, so that nothing was known.
20 Then Absalom's servants came to the woman at the house and
said, "Where are Ahimaaz and Jonathan?" And [a]the woman said
to them, "They have crossed the brook of water." And when they
searched and could not find *them*, they returned to Jerusalem.
21 And it came about after they had departed that they came up out
of the well and went and told King David; and they said to David,
"[a]Arise and cross over the water quickly for thus Ahithophel has
counseled against you."
22 Then David and all the people who *were* with him arose and
crossed the Jordan; and by [1]dawn not even one remained who had
not crossed the Jordan.
23 Now when Ahithophel saw that his counsel was not [1]followed,
he [2]saddled *his* donkey and arose and went to his home, to [a]his city,
and [3b]set his house in order, and [c]strangled himself; thus he died and
was buried in the grave of his father.

8 [2]Lit., *man of wa*

9 [1]Lit., *pits* [2]Lit., *according to a fall among them*

10 [1]Lit., *melt* [a]Jo 2:9-11

11 [1]Lit., *your face* [a]1 Sam. 3:20 [b]Ge 22:17; 1 Sam. 13:

12 [1]Lit., *settle do* [a]Ps. 110:3; Mic. 5

13 [1]Or, *wadi* [a]Mi

14 [a]2 Sam. 15:3 Ps. 9:15, 16

15 [1]Lit., *Thus an* [a]2 Sam. 15:35, 36

16 [1]Lit., *swallow* [a]2 Sam. 15:28

17 [a]2 Sam. 15:2 [b]Josh. 15:7; 18:1

18 [1]Lit., *there* [a]2 3:16; 16:5

19 [1]Lit., *took an spread the cover* [a]Josh. 2:4-6

20 [a]Lev. 19:11; 2:3-5; 1 Sam. 19

21 [a]2 Sam. 17:1

22 [1]Lit., *the ligh morning*

23 [1]Lit., *done* [2] *bound* [3]Lit., *gav charge to* [a]2 Sa 15:12 [b]2 Kin. 20 [c]Matt. 27:5

24 Then David came to [a]Mahanaim. And Absalom crossed the Jor-
dan, he and all the men of Israel with him.
25 And Absalom set [a]Amasa over the army in place of Joab. Now
Amasa was the son of a man whose name was [1]Ithra the Israelite,
who went in to Abigail the daughter of [b]Nahash, sister of Zeruiah,
Joab's mother.
26 And Israel and Absalom camped in the land of Gilead.
27 Now when David had come to Mahanaim, Shobi [a]the son of
Nahash from [b]Rabbah of the sons of Ammon, [c]Machir the son of
Ammiel from Lo-debar, and [d]Barzillai the Gileadite from Rogelim,
28 brought [a]beds, basins, pottery, wheat, barley, flour, parched
grain, beans, lentils, parched *seeds,*
29 honey, curds, sheep, and cheese of the herd, for David and for
the people who *were* with him, [a]to eat; for they said, "The people are
hungry and weary and thirsty in the wilderness."

Chapter 18

18 Then David [1]numbered the people who were with him and
[a]set over them commanders of thousands and commanders of
hundreds.
2 And David sent the people out, [a]one third under the [1]command
of Joab, one third under the [1]command of Abishai the son of
Zeruiah, Joab's brother, and one third under the [1]command of [b]Ittai
the Gittite. And the king said to the people, "I myself will surely go
out with you also."
3 But the people said, "[a]You should not go out; for if we indeed
flee, they will not care about us, even if half of us die, they will not
care about us. But [1]you are worth ten thousand of us; therefore now
it is better that you *be ready* to help us from the city."
4 Then the king said to them, "Whatever seems best to you I will
do." So [a]the king stood beside the gate, and all the people went out
by hundreds and thousands.
5 And the king charged Joab and Abishai and Ittai, saying, "*Deal*
gently for my sake with the young man Absalom." And [a]all the
people heard when the king charged all the commanders concerning
Absalom.
6 Then the people went out into the field against Israel, and the
battle took place in [a]the forest of Ephraim.
7 And the people of Israel were [1]defeated there before the servants
of David, and the slaughter there that day was great, 20,000 men.
8 For the battle there was spread over the whole countryside, and
the forest devoured more people that day than the sword devoured.
9 Now Absalom happened to meet the servants of David. For Ab-
salom was riding on *his* mule, and the mule went under the thick
branches of a great oak. And [a]his head caught fast in the oak, so he
was [1]left hanging between heaven and earth, while the mule that
was under him kept going.
10 When a certain man saw *it,* he told Joab and said, "Behold, I saw
Absalom hanging in an oak."
11 Then Joab said to the man who had told him, "Now behold, you
saw *him!* Why then did you not strike him there to the ground? And
I would have given you ten *pieces* of silver and a belt."
12 And the man said to Joab, "Even if I should receive a thousand
pieces of silver in my hand, I would not put out my hand against the

Gen. 32:2, 10; 2 Sam. 2:8
n 1 Chr. 2:17, *the Ishmaelite* 9:13; 20:9-12; :5, 32 [b]1 Chr. 2:16
[a]1 Sam. 11:1;):1, 2 [b]2 Sam. 9 [c]2 Sam. 9:4 9:31-39; 1 Kin. 2:7
v. 11:25; Matt. 5:7
Sam. 16:2, 14; :26; Eccl. 11:1; Rom. 12:13
[1]Lit., *mustered* 5; Num. 31:14; 1 Sam. 22:7
t., *hand* [a]Judg. 6; 1 Sam. 11:11 Sam. 15:19-22
[1]So with some versions; M.T., *ow there are ten thousand like us* [a]2 Sam. 21:17
[a]2 Sam. 18:24
5 [a]2 Sam. 18:12
[a]Josh. 17:15, 18; 2 Sam. 17:26
7 [1]Lit., *smitten*
, *placed* [a]2 Sam. 14:26

king's son; for [a]in our hearing the king charged you and Abishai and
Ittai, saying, '[1]Protect for me the young man Absalom!'
13 "Otherwise, if I had dealt treacherously against his life (and [a]there
is nothing hidden from the king), then you yourself would have
stood aloof."
14 Then Joab said, "I will not [1]waste time here with you." [a]So he
took three spears in his hand and thrust them through the heart of
Absalom while he was yet alive in the [2]midst of the oak.
15 And ten young men who carried Joab's armor gathered around
and struck Absalom and killed him.
16 Then [a]Joab blew the trumpet, and the people returned from pur-
suing Israel, for Joab restrained the people.
17 And they took Absalom and cast him into [1]a deep pit in the
forest and [a]erected over him a very great heap of stones. And [b]all
Israel fled, each to his tent.
18 Now Absalom in his lifetime had taken and [a]set up for himself a
pillar which is in [b]the King's Valley, for he said, "[c]I have no son [1]to
preserve my name." So he named the pillar after his own name, and
it is called Absalom's monument to this day.
19 Then [a]Ahimaaz the son of Zadok said, "Please let me run and
bring the king news [b]that the LORD has [1]freed him from the hand of
his enemies."
20 But Joab said to him, "You are not the man to carry news this
day, but you shall carry news another day; however, you shall carry
no news today because the king's son is dead."
21 Then Joab said to the Cushite, "Go, tell the king what you have
seen." So the Cushite bowed to Joab and ran.
22 Now Ahimaaz the son of Zadok said once more to Joab, "But
whatever happens, please let me also run after the Cushite." And
Joab said, "Why would you run, my son, since [a]you will have no
reward for going?"
23 "But whatever happens," *he said*, "I will run." So he said to him,
"Run." Then Ahimaaz ran by way of the plain and passed up the
Cushite.
24 Now [a]David was sitting between the two gates; and [b]the
watchman went up to the roof of the gate by the wall, and raised his
eyes and looked, and behold, a man running by himself.
25 And the watchman called and told the king. And the king said,
"If he is by himself there is good news in his mouth." And he came
nearer and nearer.
26 Then the watchman saw another man running; and the
watchman called to the gatekeeper and said, "Behold, *another* man
running by himself." And the king said, "This one also is bringing
good news."
27 And the watchman said, "I [1]think the running of the first one [a]is
like the running of Ahimaaz the son of Zadok." And the king said,
"[b]This is a good man and comes with good news."
28 And Ahimaaz called and said to the king, "[1]All is well." And [a]he
prostrated himself before the king with his face to the ground. And
he said, "[b]Blessed is the LORD your God, who has delivered up the
men who lifted their hands against my lord the king."
29 And the king said, "[a]Is it well with the young man Absalom?"
And Ahimaaz answered, "When Joab sent the king's servant, and
your servant, I saw a great tumult, but [b]I did not know what *it was*."

12 [1]So with and the anci versions; M. *care whoeve of* [a]2 Sam. 1

13 [a]2 Sam.

14 [1]Lit., *tarr heart* [a]2 San

16 [a]2 Sam. 2

17 [1]Lit., *the g* [a]Deut. 21:20, 7:26; 8:29 [b]2 19:8; 20:1, 22

18 [1]Lit., *for th remembering* 15:12 [b]Gen. [c]2 Sam. 14:27

19 [1]Lit., *vindic* [a]2 Sam. 15:36 18:31

22 [a]2 Sam. 18

24 [a]2 Sam. 19 [b]2 Sam. 13:34; 9:17

27 [1]Lit., *see* [a]2 9:20 [b]1 Kin. 1:4

28 [1]Lit., *Peace.* [a]1 Sam. 25:23; 14:4 [b]1 Sam. 17

29 [a]2 Sam. 20:9 4:26 [b]2 Sam. 18

30 Then the king said, "Turn aside and stand here." So he turned
aside and stood still.
31 And behold, the Cushite arrived, and the Cushite said, "Let my
lord the king receive good news, for [a]the LORD has [1]freed you this
day from the hand of all those who rose up against you."
32 Then the king said to the Cushite, "[a]Is it well with the young
man Absalom?" And the Cushite answered, "[b]Let the enemies of my
lord the king, and all who rise up against you for evil, be as that
young man!"
33 [1]And the king was deeply moved and went up to the chamber
over the gate and wept. And thus he said as he walked, "[a]O my son
Absalom, my son, my son Absalom! [b]Would I had died instead of
you, O Absalom, my son, my son!"

Chapter 19

19 Then it was told Joab, "Behold, [a]the king is weeping and
mourns for Absalom."
2 And the [1]victory that day was turned to mourning for all the
people, for the people heard *it* said that day, "The king is grieved for
his son."
3 So the people went by stealth into the city that day, as people
who are humiliated steal away when they flee in battle.
4 And the king [a]covered his face and [1]cried out with a loud voice,
"[b]O my son Absalom, O Absalom, my son, my son!"
5 Then Joab came into the house to the king and said, "Today you
have covered with shame the faces of all your servants, who today
have saved your life and the lives of your sons and daughters, the
lives of your wives, and the lives of your concubines,
6 by loving those who hate you, and by hating those who love
you. For you have shown today that [1]princes and servants are noth-
ing to you; for I know this day that if Absalom were alive and all of
us were dead today, then [2]you would be pleased.
7 "Now therefore arise, go out and speak [1]kindly to your servants,
for I swear by the LORD, if you do not go out, surely [a]not a man will
pass the night with you, and this will be worse for you than all the
evil that has come upon you from your youth until now."
8 So the king arose and sat in the gate. When they told all the
people, saying, "Behold, the king is [a]sitting in the gate," then all the
people came before the king.
Now [b]Israel had fled, each to his tent.
9 And all the people were quarreling throughout all the tribes of
Israel, saying, "[a]The king delivered us from the [1]hand of our enemies
and [b]saved us from the [1]hand of the Philistines, but now [c]he has fled
out of the land from Absalom.
10 "However, Absalom, whom we anointed over us, has died in
battle. Now then, why are you silent about bringing the king back?"
11 Then King David sent to [a]Zadok and Abiathar the priests,
saying, "Speak to the elders of Judah, saying, 'Why are you the last
to bring the king back to his house, since the word of all Israel has
come to the king, *even* to his house?
12 'You are my brothers; [a]you are my bone and my flesh. Why then
should you be the last to bring back the king?'
13 "And say to [a]Amasa, 'Are you not my bone and my flesh? [b]May

it., *vindicated* 5:31; 2 Sam. 18:19
[a]2 Sam. 18:29 [b]1 Sam. 25:26
ı. 19:1 in Heb. am. 19:4 [b]Ex. 2:32; Rom. 9:3
Sam. 18:5, 14
[1]Lit., *salvation*
, *the king cried* 15:30 [b]2 Sam. 18:33
r, *commanders* *vould be right in your eyes*
Lit., *to the heart* [a]Prov. 14:28
am. 15:2; 18:24 [b]2 Sam. 18:17
t., *palm* [a]2 Sam. 4 [b]2 Sam. 5:20; 1 [c]2 Sam. 15:14
1 [a]2 Sam. 15:29
12 [a]2 Sam. 5:1
3 [a]2 Sam. 17:25 [b]1 Kin. 19:2

God do so to me, and more also, if you will not be [c]commander of
the army before me continually [d]in place of Joab.' "
14 Thus he turned the hearts of all the men of Judah [a]as one man, so
that they sent *word* to the king, *saying,* "Return, you and all your
servants."
15 The king then returned and came as far as the Jordan. And Judah
came to [a]Gilgal in order to go to meet the king, to bring the king
across the Jordan.
16 Then [a]Shimei the son of Gera, the Benjamite who was from
Bahurim, hurried and came down with the men of Judah to meet
King David.
17 And there were a thousand men of Benjamin with him, with
[a]Ziba the servant of the house of Saul, and his fifteen sons and his
twenty servants with him; and they rushed to the Jordan before the
king.
18 Then they kept crossing the ford to bring over the king's house-
hold, and to do what was good in his sight. And Shimei the son of
Gera fell down before the king as he was about to cross the Jordan.
19 So he said to the king, "[a]Let not my lord consider me guilty, nor
remember what your servant did wrong on the day when my lord
the king came out from Jerusalem, so that the king should [1]take *it* to
heart.
20 "For your servant knows that I have sinned; therefore behold, I
have come today, [a]the first of all the house of Joseph to go down to
meet my lord the king."
21 But Abishai the son of Zeruiah answered and said, "[a]Should not
Shimei be put to death for this, [b]because he cursed the LORD's
anointed?"
22 David then said, "[a]What have I to do with you, O sons of
Zeruiah, that you should this day be an adversary to me? [b]Should
any man be put to death in Israel today? For do I not know that I am
king over Israel today?"
23 And the king said to Shimei, "[a]You shall not die." Thus the king
swore to him.
24 Then [a]Mephibosheth the [1]son of Saul came down to meet the
king; and [b]he had neither [2]cared for his feet, nor [2]trimmed his mus-
tache, nor [c]washed his clothes, from the day the king departed until
the day he came *home* in peace.
25 And it was when he came from Jerusalem to meet the king, that
the king said to him, "[a]Why did you not go with me, Mephibo-
sheth?"
26 So he answered, "O my lord, the king, my servant deceived me;
for your servant said, 'I will saddle a donkey for myself that I may
ride on it and go with the king,' [a]because your servant is lame.
27 "Moreover, [a]he has slandered your servant to my lord the king;
but my lord the king is [b]like the angel of God, therefore do what is
good in your sight.
28 "For [a]all my father's household was nothing but dead men before
my lord the king; [b]yet you set your servant among those who ate at
your own table. What right do I have yet that I should [1]complain
anymore to the king?"
29 So the king said to him, "Why do you still speak of your affairs?
I have [1]decided, 'You and Ziba shall divide the land.' "

13 [c]2 Sam. 8 [d]2 Sam. 3:27
14 [a]Judg. 20
15 [a]Josh. 5:9 11:14, 15
16 [a]2 Sam. 1 1 Kin. 2:8
17 [a]2 Sam. 1 19:26, 27
19 [1]Lit., *set* [a] 22:15; 2 Sam.
20 [a]2 Sam. 16
21 [a]2 Sam. 16 [b]Ex. 22:28
22 [a]2 Sam. 3:3 10 [b]1 Sam. 11
23 [a]1 Kin. 2:8
24 [1]I.e., grands *done* [a]2 Sam. 9 [b]2 Sam. 12:20 19:10
25 [a]2 Sam. 16:1
26 [a]2 Sam. 9:3
27 [a]2 Sam. 16:3 [b]2 Sam. 14:17, 2
28 [1]Lit., *cry out* [a]2 Sam. 21:6-9 9:7, 10, 13
29 [1]Lit., *said*

, send [a]2 Sam.
7-29; 1 Kin. 2:7

30 And Mephibosheth said to the king, "Let him even take it all,
since my lord the king has come safely to his own house."
31 Now [a]Barzillai the Gileadite had come down from Rogelim; and
he went on to the Jordan with the king to [1]escort him over the Jor-
dan.

r, provided food
Sam. 17:27-29

32 Now Barzillai was very old, being eighty years old; and he had
[1a]sustained the king while he stayed at Mahanaim, for he was a very
great man.

provide food for

33 And the king said to Barzillai, "You cross over with me and I
will [1]sustain you in Jerusalem with me."
34 But Barzillai said to the king, "[a]How long [1]have I yet to live, that
I should go up with the king to Jerusalem?

, are the days of
years of my life
[a]Gen. 47:8

35 "I am [1]now [a]eighty years old. Can I distinguish between good and
bad? Or can your servant taste what I eat or what I drink? Or can I
hear anymore [b]the voice of singing men and women? [c]Why then
should your servant be an added burden to my lord the king?

[1]Lit., *today* [a]Ps.
0 [b]Eccl. 2:8; Is.
2 [c]2 Sam. 15:33

36 "Your servant would merely cross over the Jordan with the king.
Why should the king compensate me *with* this reward?
37 "Please let your servant return, that I may die in my own city near
the grave of my father and my mother. However, here is your ser-
vant [a]Chimham, let him cross over with my lord the king, and do for
him what is good in your sight."

[a]2 Sam. 19:40;
1. 2:7; Jer. 41:17

38 And the king answered, "Chimham shall cross over with me,
and I will do for him what is good in your sight; and whatever you
[1]require of me, I will do for you."

38 [1]Lit., *choose*

39 All the people crossed over the Jordan and the king crossed too.
The king then [a]kissed Barzillai and blessed him, and he returned to
his place.

Gen. 31:55; Ruth
14; 2 Sam. 14:33

40 Now the king went on to Gilgal, and Chimham went on with
him; and all the people of Judah and also [a]half the people of Israel
[1]accompanied the king.

Lit., *crossed over*
[a]2 Sam. 19:9, 10

41 And behold, all the men of Israel came to the king and said to
the king, "[a]Why had our brothers [b]the men of Judah stolen you away,
and brought the king and his household and all David's men with
him over the Jordan?"

[a]Judg. 8:1; 12:1
[b]2 Sam. 19:11, 12

42 Then all the men of Judah answered the men of Israel, "Because
[a]the king is a close relative to [1]us. Why then [2]are you angry about
this matter? Have we eaten at all at the king's *expense*, or has [3]any-
thing been taken for us?"

[1]Lit., *me* [2]Lit., *is it*
to you [3]Or, *a gift*
[a]2 Sam. 19:12

43 But the men of Israel answered the men of Judah and said, "[1a]We
have ten parts in the king, therefore [1]we also have more *claim* on
David than you. Why then did you treat us with contempt? Was it
not [1]our advice first to bring back [1]our king?" Yet the words of the
men of Judah were harsher than the words of the men of Israel.

[1]Singular in Heb.
2 Sam. 5:1; 1 Kin.
11:30, 31

Chapter 20

20 Now [a]a worthless fellow happened to be there whose name
was Sheba, the son of [b]Bichri, a Benjamite; and he blew the
trumpet and said,

"[c]We have no portion in David,
Nor do we have inheritance in [d]the son of Jesse;
[e]Every man to his tents, O Israel!"

20:1 [a]2 Sam. 16:7
en. 46:21 [c]2 Sam.
19:43; 1 Kin. 12:16
m. 22:7-9 [e]1 Sam.
3:2; 2 Sam. 18:17;
2 Chr. 10:16

2 So all the men of Israel [1]withdrew from following David, *and*

2 [1]Lit., *went up*

followed Sheba the son of Bichri; but the men of Judah [2]remained
steadfast to their king, from the Jordan even to Jerusalem.
3 Then David came to his house at Jerusalem, and [a]the king took
the ten women, the concubines whom he had left to keep the house,
and placed them under guard and provided them with sustenance,
but did not go in to them. So they were shut up until the day of their
death, living as widows.
4 Then the king said to [a]Amasa, "Call out the men of Judah for me
within three days, and be present here yourself."
5 So Amasa went to call out *the men of* Judah, but he [a]delayed
longer than the set time which he had appointed him.
6 And David said to [a]Abishai, "Now Sheba the son of Bichri will
do us more harm than Absalom; [b]take your lord's servants and pursue him, lest he find for himself fortified cities and escape from our
sight."
7 So Joab's men went out after him, [a]along with the Cherethites
and the Pelethites and all the mighty men; and they went out from
Jerusalem to pursue Sheba the son of Bichri.
8 When they were at the large stone which is in [a]Gibeon, Amasa
came [1]to meet them. Now Joab was [2]dressed in his military attire,
and over it was a belt with a sword in its sheath fastened at his
waist; and as he went forward, it fell out.
9 And Joab said to Amasa, "Is it well with you, my brother?" And
[a]Joab took Amasa by the beard with his right hand to kiss him.
10 But Amasa was not on guard against the sword which was in
Joab's hand so [a]he struck him in the belly with it and poured out his
inward parts on the ground, and did not *strike* him again; and he
died. Then Joab and Abishai his brother pursued Sheba the son of
Bichri.
11 Now there stood by him one of Joab's young men, and said,
"Whoever favors Joab and whoever is for David, [a]*let him* follow
Joab."
12 But Amasa lay wallowing in *his* blood in the middle of the highway. And when the man saw that all the people stood still, he [1]removed Amasa from the highway into the field and threw a garment
over him when he saw that everyone who came by him stood still.
13 As soon as he was removed from the highway, all the men
passed on after Joab to pursue Sheba the son of Bichri.
14 Now he went through all the tribes of Israel to Abel even to
Beth-maacah and all the Berites; and they were gathered together
and also went after him.
15 And they came and besieged him in [a]Abel Beth-maacah, and
[b]they [1]cast up a mound against the city, and it stood by the rampart;
and all the people who were with Joab were wreaking destruction in
order to topple the wall.
16 Then [a]a wise woman called from the city, "Hear, hear! Please tell
Joab, 'Come here that I may speak with you.' "
17 So he approached her, and the woman said, "Are you Joab?"
And he answered, "I am." Then she said to him, "Listen to the
words of your maidservant." And he answered, "I am listening."
18 Then she spoke, saying, "Formerly they used to say, 'They will
surely ask *advice* at Abel,' and thus they ended *the dispute*.
19 "I am of those who are peaceable *and* faithful in Israel. [a]You are

2 [2]Lit., *clung*
3 [a]2 Sam. 15: 16:21, 22
4 [a]2 Sam. 17:
5 [a]1 Sam. 13:8
6 [a]2 Sam. 21:1 [b]2 Sam. 11:11; 1:33
7 [a]2 Sam. 8:18 1:38
8 [1]Lit., *before* [2]*girded with milit garment as clot* [a]2 Sam. 2:13; 3
9 [a]Matt. 26:49
10 [a]2 Sam. 2:23 1 Kin. 2:5
11 [a]2 Sam. 20:1
12 [1]Lit., *caused*
15 [1]Lit., *poured* [a]1 Kin. 15:20; 2 K 15:29 [b]2 Kin. 19: Ezek. 4:2
16 [a]2 Sam. 14:2
19 [a]Deut. 20:10

seeking to destroy a city, even a mother in Israel. Why would you
swallow up [b]the inheritance of the LORD?"
20 And Joab answered and said, "Far be it, far be it from me that I
should swallow up or destroy!
21 "Such is not the case. But a man from [a]the hill country of
Ephraim, [b]Sheba the son of Bichri by name, has lifted up his hand
against King David. Only hand him over, and I will depart from the
city." And the woman said to Joab, "Behold, his head will be thrown
to you over the wall."
22 Then the woman [a]wisely came to all the people. And they cut off
the head of Sheba the son of Bichri and threw it to Joab. So [b]he blew
the trumpet, and they were dispersed from the city, each to his tent.
Joab also returned to the king at Jerusalem.
23 [a]Now Joab was over the whole army of Israel, and Benaiah the
son of Jehoiada was over the Cherethites and the Pelethites;
24 and Adoram was over the forced labor, and [a]Jehoshaphat the son
of Ahilud was the recorder;
25 and Sheva was scribe, and Zadok and [a]Abiathar were priests;
26 and Ira the Jairite was also a priest to David.

Chapter 21

21 Now there was [a]a famine in the days of David for three years,
year after year; and [b]David sought the presence of the LORD.
And the LORD said, "It is for Saul and his bloody house, because he
put the Gibeonites to death."
2 So the king called the Gibeonites and spoke to them (now the
Gibeonites were not of the sons of Israel but of the remnant of the
Amorites, and [a]the sons of Israel [1]made a covenant with them, but
Saul had sought to [2]kill them in his zeal for the sons of Israel and
Judah).
3 Thus David said to the Gibeonites, "What should I do for you?
And how can I make atonement that you may bless [a]the inheritance
of the LORD?"
4 Then the Gibeonites said to him, "[a]We have no *concern* of silver
or gold with Saul or his house, nor is it for us to put any man to
death in Israel." And he said, "I will do for you whatever you say."
5 So they said to the king, "[a]The man who consumed us, and who
planned [1]to exterminate us from remaining within any border of
Israel,
6 let seven men from his sons be given to us, and we will [1]hang
them [a]before the LORD in Gibeah of Saul, [b]the chosen of the LORD."
And the king said, "I will give *them*."
7 But the king spared [a]Mephibosheth, the son of Jonathan the son
of Saul, [b]because of the oath of the LORD which was between them,
between David and Saul's son Jonathan.
8 So the king took the two sons of [a]Rizpah the daughter of Aiah,
Armoni and Mephibosheth whom she had born to Saul, and the five
sons of [1b]Merab the daughter of Saul, whom she had born to Adriel
the son of Barzillai the [c]Meholathite.
9 Then he gave them into the hands of the Gibeonites, and they
[1]hanged them in the mountain before the LORD, so that the seven of
them fell together; and they were put to death in the first days of
harvest at [a]the beginning of barley harvest.
10 [a]And Rizpah the daughter of Aiah took sackcloth and spread it

19 [b]1 Sam. 26:19; 2 Sam. 14:16; 21:3
21 [a]Josh. 24:33 [b]2 Sam. 20:2
2 Sam. 20:16; Eccl. 3-16 [b]2 Sam. 20:1
3 [a]2 Sam. 8:16-18; 1 Kin. 4:3-6
24 [a]1 Kin. 4:3
25 [a]1 Kin. 4:4
[a]Gen. 12:10; 26:1; 42:5 [b]Num. 27:21
[1]Lit., *had sworn to* .., *smite* [a]Josh. 9:3, 15-20
3 [a]1 Sam. 26:19; 2 Sam. 20:19
4 [a]Num. 35:31, 32
Lit., *against us that we should be* *erminated* [a]2 Sam. 21:1
[1]Lit., *expose them* lum. 25:4 [b]1 Sam. 10:24
[a]2 Sam. 4:4; 9:10 m. 18:3; 20:12-17; 3:18; 2 Sam. 9:1-7
[1]So Gr. and Heb. mss. [a]2 Sam. 3:7 Sam. 18:19 [c]1 Kin. 19:16
Lit., *exposed them* [a]Ex. 9:31, 32
10 [a]Deut. 21:23

for herself on the rock, from the beginning of harvest until [1]it rained
on them from the sky; and [b]she [2]allowed neither the birds of the sky
to rest on them by day nor the beasts of the field by night.
11 When it was told David what Rizpah the daughter of Aiah, the
concubine of Saul, had done,
12 then David went and took [a]the bones of Saul and the bones of
Jonathan his son from the men of Jabesh-gilead, who had stolen
them from the open square of [b]Beth-shan, [c]where the Philistines had
hanged them on the day [d]the Philistines struck down Saul in Gilboa.
13 And he brought up the bones of Saul and the bones of Jonathan
his son from there, and they gathered the bones of those who had
been [1]hanged.
14 And they buried the bones of Saul and Jonathan his son in the
country of Benjamin in [a]Zela, in the grave of Kish his father; thus
they did all that the king commanded, and after that [b]God was
moved by entreaty for the land.
15 Now when [a]the Philistines were at war again with Israel, David
went down and his servants with him; and as they fought against
the Philistines, David became weary.
16 Then Ishbi-benob, who was [a]among the descendants of the
[1]giant, the weight of whose spear was three hundred *shekels* of
bronze in weight, [2]was girded with a new *sword,* and he [3]intended to
kill David.
17 But [a]Abishai the son of Zeruiah helped him, and struck the Phi-
listine and killed him. Then the men of David swore to him, saying,
"[b]You shall not go out again with us to battle, that you may not
extinguish [c]the lamp of Israel."
18 [a]Now it came about after this that there was war again with the
Philistines at Gob; then [b]Sibbecai the Hushathite struck down Saph,
who was among the descendants of the [1]giant.
19 And there was war with the Philistines again at Gob, and El-
hanan the son of Jaare-oregim the Bethlehemite [1]killed [2]Goliath the
Gittite, [a]the shaft of whose spear was like a weaver's beam.
20 And there was war at Gath again, where there was a man of
great stature who had six fingers on each hand and six toes on each
foot, twenty-four in number; and he also had been born [a]to the
[1]giant.
21 And when he defied Israel, Jonathan the son of Shimei, David's
brother, struck him down.
22 [a]These four were born to the [1]giant in Gath, and they fell by the
hand of David and by the hand of his servants.

Chapter 22

22 [a]And David spoke [b]the words of this song to the LORD in the
day that the LORD delivered him from the [1]hand of all his
enemies and from the [1]hand of Saul.
2 And he said,
"[a]The LORD is my [1]rock and my fortress and my deliverer;
3 [1a]My God, my rock, in whom I take refuge;
My [b]shield and [c]the horn of my salvation, my stronghold and
[d]my refuge;
My savior, Thou dost save me from violence.
4 "I call upon the LORD, [a]who is worthy to be praised;
And I am saved from my enemies.

10 [1]Lit., *wate... poured* [2]Lit., ... [b]1 Sam. 17:44
12 [a]1 Sam. 3... [b]Josh. 17:11 ... 31:10 [d]1 Sam...
13 [1]Lit., *expo...*
14 [a]Josh. 18:... 7:26; 2 Sam. 2...
15 [a]2 Sam. 5:...
16 [1]Heb., *Rap... and he was* [3]L... [a]Num. 13:22, 2... 15:14; 2 Sam. ...
17 [a]2 Sam. 20... [b]2 Sam. 18:3 ... 22:29 1 Kin. 11...
18 [1]Heb., *Rap...* [a]1 Chr. 20:4-8 ... 11:29; 27:11
19 [1]Lit., *smote* ... 1 Chr. 20:5, *La... brother of Golia...* [a]1 Sam. 17:7
20 [1]Heb., *Raph...* [a]2 Sam. 21:16, ...
22 [1]Heb., *Raph...* [a]1 Chr. 20:8
22:1 [1]Lit., *palm* ... 18:2-50 [b]Ex. 15... Deut. 31:30
2 [1]Lit., *crag* [a]1 ... 23:25; 24:2; Ps. 71:3
3 [1]Lit., *God of m...* [a]Deut. 32:4, 37; ... 2:2 [b]Gen. 15:1; ... 33:29 [c]Luke 1:6... 9:9
4 [a]Ps. 48:1; 96:4...

5 "For [a]the waves of death encompassed me;
[b]The torrents of [1]destruction [2]overwhelmed me;
6 [a]The cords of [1]Sheol surrounded me;
The snares of death confronted me.
7 "[a]In my distress I called upon the LORD,
Yes, I [1]cried to my God;
And from His temple He heard my voice,
And my cry for help *came* into His ears.
8 "Then [a]the earth shook and quaked,
[b]The foundations of heaven were trembling
And were shaken, because He was angry.
9 "Smoke went up [1]out of His nostrils,
[a]And fire from His mouth devoured;
[b]Coals were kindled by it.
10 "He bowed the heavens also, and came down
With [a]thick darkness under His feet.
11 "[a]And He rode on a cherub and flew;
And He [1]appeared on [b]the wings of the wind.
12 "[a]And He made darkness [1]canopies around Him,
A mass of waters, thick clouds of the sky.
13 "From the brightness before Him
[a]Coals of fire were kindled.
14 "[a]The LORD thundered from heaven,
And the Most High uttered His voice.
15 "[a]And He sent out arrows, and scattered them,
Lightning, and [1]routed them.
16 "Then the channels of the sea appeared,
The foundations of the world were [1]laid bare,
By the rebuke of the LORD,
[a]At the blast of the breath of His nostrils.
17 "[a]He sent from on high, He took me;
[b]He drew me out of many waters.
18 "He delivered me from my strong enemy,
From those who hated me, for they were too strong for me.
19 "They confronted me in the day of my calamity,
[a]But the LORD was my support.
20 "[a]He also brought me forth into a broad place;
He rescued me, [b]because He delighted in me.
21 "[a]The LORD has rewarded me according to my righteousness;
[b]According to the cleanness of my hands He has recompensed
me.
22 "[a]For I have kept the ways of the LORD,
And have not acted wickedly against my God.
23 "[a]For all His ordinances *were* before me;
And *as for* His statutes, I did not depart from [1]them.
24 "[a]I was also [1]blameless toward Him,
And I kept myself from my iniquity.
25 "[a]Therefore the LORD has recompensed me according to my
righteousness,
According to my cleanness before His eyes.
26 "[a]With the [1]kind Thou dost show Thyself [1]kind,
With the [2]blameless Thou dost show Thyself [2]blameless;
27 [a]With the pure Thou dost show Thyself pure,
[b]And with the perverted Thou dost show Thyself [1]astute.

eb., *Belial* [2]Or, [a]Ps. 93:4; Jon. [b]Ps. 69:14, 15
ne nether world [a]Ps. 116:3
[1]Or, *called* [a]Ps. 116:4; 120:1
g. 5:4; Ps. 97:4 [b]Job 26:11
His wrath [a]Ps. 7:3; Heb. 12:29 [b]2 Sam. 22:13
Ex. 19:16; 1 Kin. . 97:2; Nah. 1:3
Many mss. read 2 Sam. 6:2 [b]Ps. 104:3
, *pavilions* [a]Job 36:29
13 [a]2 Sam. 22:9
37:2-5; Ps. 29:3
5 [1]Lit., *confused* eut. 32:23; Josh. :10; 1 Sam. 7:10
uncovered [a]Ex. 15:8; Nah. 1:4
144:7 [b]Ex. 2:10
19 [a]Ps. 23:4
[a]Ps. 31:8; 118:5 [b]2 Sam. 15:26
[a]1 Sam. 26:23; n. 8:32 [b]Ps. 24:4
[a]Gen. 18:19; Ps. 128:1; Prov. 8:32
., *it* [a]Deut. 6:6-9; Ps. 119:30, 102
Lit., *complete;* or, *ng integrity* [a]Gen. 7:1; Eph. 1:4; Col. 1:21, 22
25 [a]2 Sam. 22:21
26 [1]Or, *loyal* [2]Lit., *mplete;* or, *having ntegrity* [a]Matt. 5:7
Lit., *twisted* [a]Matt. ; 1 John 3:3 [b]Lev. 23, 24; Rom. 1:28

28 "[a]And Thou dost save an afflicted people;
[b]But Thine eyes are on the haughty *whom* Thou dost abase.
29 "[a]For Thou art my lamp, O LORD;
And the LORD illumines my darkness.
30 "[a]For by Thee I can [1]run upon a troop;
By my God I can leap over a wall.
31 "[a]As for God, His way is [1]blameless;
[b]The word of the LORD is tested;
[c]He is a shield to all who take refuge in Him.
32 "[a]For who is God, besides the LORD?
[b]And who is a rock, besides our God?
33 "[a]God is my strong fortress;
And He [1]sets the [2]blameless in [3]His way.
34 "[a]He makes [1]my feet like hinds' *feet*,
[b]And sets me on my high places.
35 "[a]He trains my hands for battle,
[b]So that my arms can bend a bow of bronze.
36 "Thou hast also given me [a]the shield of Thy salvation,
And Thy [1]help makes me great.
37 "[a]Thou dost enlarge my steps under me,
And my [1]feet have not slipped.
38 "I pursued my enemies and [a]destroyed them,
And I did not turn back until they were consumed.
39 "And I have devoured them and shattered them, so that they did not rise;
And [a]they fell under my feet.
40 "For Thou hast girded me with strength for battle;
Thou hast [1]subdued under me [a]those who rose up against me.
41 "Thou hast also [a]made my enemies turn *their* backs to me,
And I [1]destroyed those who hated me.
42 "[a]They looked, but there was none to save;
[b]*Even* to the LORD, but He did not answer them.
43 "[a]Then I pulverized them as the dust of the earth,
[b]I crushed *and* stamped them as the mire of the streets.
44 "[a]Thou hast also delivered me from the contentions of my people;
[b]Thou hast kept me as head of the nations;
[c]A people whom I have not known serve me.
45 "[a]Foreigners pretend obedience to me;
As soon as they hear, they obey me.
46 "Foreigners [1]lose heart,
[a]And [2]come trembling out of their [3]fortresses.
47 "The LORD lives, and blessed be my rock;
And exalted be [1a]God, the rock of my salvation,
48 [a]The God who executes vengeance for me,
[b]And brings down peoples under me,
49 Who also brings me out from my enemies;
Thou dost even lift me above [a]those who rise up against me;
[b]Thou dost rescue me from the violent man.
50 "[a]Therefore I will give thanks to Thee, O LORD, among the nations,
And I will sing praises to Thy name.
51 "[a]*He* is a tower of [1]deliverance to His king,
And [b]shows lovingkindness to His anointed,
[c]To David and his [2]descendants forever."

28 [a]Ex. 3:7, 8 72:12, 13 [b]Is. 17; 5:15

29 [a]2 Sam. 21 1 Kin. 11:36; P

30 [1]Or, *crush* [a]2 Sam. 5:6-8

31 [1]Lit., *comp having integrity* 32:4; Matt. 5:4 12:6; 119:140; 30:5 [c]2 Sam. 2 84:9

32 [a]1 Sam. 2:2 [b]2 Sam. 22:2

33 [1]Or, *sets fr complete;* or, *h. integrity* [3]Anoth reading is *my* 22:2; Ps. 31:3,

34 [1]Another re *His* [a]2 Sam. 2: 3:19 [b]Deut. 32

35 [a]Ps. 144:1 20:24

36 [1]Lit., *answe* [a]Eph. 6:16, 17

37 [1]Lit., *ankles* [a]2 Sam. 22:20; 4:12

38 [a]Ex. 15:9

39 [a]Mal. 4:3

40 [1]Lit., *caused down* [a]Ps. 44:5

41 [1]Or, *silence* 23:27; Josh. 10:

42 [a]Is. 17:7, 8 [b] 28:6; Is. 1:15

43 [a]2 Kin. 13:7 10:6; Mic. 7:10

44 [a]2 Sam. 3:1; 14 [b]2 Sam. 8:1- 55:5

45 [a]Ps. 66:3; 81

46 [1]Lit., *languish gird themselves fastnesses* [a]1 Sa 14:11; Mic. 7:17

47 [1]Lit., *the God rock* [a]2 Sam. 22: 89:26

48 [a]1 Sam. 24:12 25:39; 2 Sam. 4:8 94:1 [b]Ps. 144:2

49 [a]Ps. 44:5 [b]Ps 140:1, 4, 11

50 [a]Rom. 15:9

51 [1]I.e., victories; *salvation* [2]Lit., *se* [a]Ps. 144:10 [b]Ps. [c]2 Sam. 7:12-16

Chapter 23

23 Now these are the last words of David.
David the son of Jesse declares,
[a]And the man who was raised on high declares,
[b]The anointed of the God of Jacob,
And the sweet psalmist of Israel,
2 "[a]The Spirit of the LORD spoke by me,
And His word was on my tongue.
3 "The God of Israel said,
[a]The Rock of Israel spoke to me,
'[b]He who rules over men righteously,
[c]Who rules in the fear of God,
4 [a]Is as the light of the morning *when* the sun rises,
A morning without clouds,
When the tender grass *springs* out of the earth,
Through sunshine after rain.'
5 "Truly is not my house so with God?
For [a]He has made an everlasting covenant with me,
Ordered in all things, and secured;
For all my salvation and all *my* desire,
Will He not indeed make *it* grow?
6 "[a]But the worthless, every one of them will be thrust away like
thorns,
Because they cannot be taken in hand;
7 But the man who touches them
Must be [1]armed with iron and the shaft of a spear,
And [a]they will be completely burned with fire in *their* [2]place."
8 [a]These are the names of the mighty men whom David had:
Josheb-basshebeth a Tahchemonite, chief of the [1]captains, he was
called Adino the Eznite, because of eight hundred slain *by him* at one
time;
9 and after him was Eleazar the son of [a]Dodo the [b]Ahohite, one of
the three mighty men with David when they [1]defied the Philistines
who were gathered there to battle and the men of Israel had [2]with-
drawn.
10 [a]He arose and struck the Philistines until his hand was weary
and [1]clung to the sword, and [b]the LORD brought about a great [2]vic-
tory that day; and the people returned after him only to strip *the*
slain.
11 Now after him was Shammah the son of Agee a [a]Hararite. And
the Philistines were gathered [1]into a troop, where there was a plot of
ground full of lentils, and the people fled from the Philistines.
12 But he took his stand in the midst of the plot, defended it and
struck the Philistines; and [a]the LORD brought about a great [1]victory.
13 Then three of the thirty chief men went down and came to David
in the harvest time to the [a]cave of Adullam, while the troop of the
Philistines was camping in [b]the valley of Rephaim.
14 And David was then [a]in the stronghold, while the garrison of the
Philistines was then in Bethlehem.
15 [a]And David had a craving and said, "Oh that someone would
give me water to drink from the well of Bethlehem which is by the
gate!"
16 [a]So the three mighty men broke through the camp of the Philis-
tines, and drew water from the well of Bethlehem which was by the

am. 7:8, 9; Ps. 0, 71 [b]1 Sam. 13; Ps. 89:20
. 22:43; 2 Pet. 1:21
am. 22:2, 3, 32 :1-3; Is. 11:1-5 [c]2 Chr. 19:7, 9
5:31; Ps. 72:6
n. 7:12-16; Ps. 89:29; Is. 55:3
6 [a]Matt. 13:41
[1]Lit., *filled* [2]Lit., *ng* [a]Matt. 3:10; 13:30; Heb. 6:8
)r, *three* [a]1 Chr. 11:11-47
Lit., *reproached* *gone up* [a]1 Chr. 27:4 [b]1 Chr. 8:4
, *his hand clung* *salvation* [a]1 Chr. [b]1 Sam. 11:13; 19:5
Possibly, at Lehi [a]2 Sam. 23:33
2 [1]Lit., *salvation* [a]2 Sam. 23:10
13 [a]1 Sam. 22:1 [b]2 Sam. 5:18
[a]1 Sam. 22:4, 5
15 [a]1 Chr. 11:17
16 [a]1 Chr. 11:18

gate, and took *it* and brought *it* to David. Nevertheless he would not
drink it, but [b]poured it out to the LORD;
17 and he said, "Be it far from me, O LORD, that I should do this.
[a]*Shall I drink* the blood of the men who went in *jeopardy* of their
lives?" Therefore he would not drink it. These things the three
mighty men did.
18 And [a]Abishai, the brother of Joab, the son of Zeruiah, was [b]chief
of the [1]thirty. And he swung his spear against three hundred [2]and
killed *them,* and had a name as well as the three.
19 He was most honored of the thirty, therefore he became their
commander; however, he did not attain to the three.
20 Then [a]Benaiah the son of Jehoiada, the son of a valiant man of
[b]Kabzeel, who had done mighty deeds, [1]killed the [2]two *sons of* Ariel
of Moab. He also went down and killed a lion in the middle of a pit
on a snowy day.
21 And he [1]killed an Egyptian, [2]an impressive man. Now the Egyp-
tian *had* a spear in his hand, but he went down to him with a club
and snatched the spear from the Egyptian's hand, and killed him
with his own spear.
22 These *things* [a]Benaiah the son of Jehoiada did, and had a name as
well as the three mighty men.
23 He was honored among the thirty, but he did not attain to the
three. And David appointed him over his guard.
24 [a]Asahel the brother of Joab was among the thirty; Elhanan the
son of Dodo of Bethlehem,
25 [a]Shammah the [b]Harodite, Elika the Harodite,
26 Helez the Paltite, Ira the son of Ikkesh the [a]Tekoite,
27 Abiezer the [a]Anathothite, Mebunnai the Hushathite,
28 Zalmon the Ahohite, Maharai the [a]Netophathite,
29 [a]Heleb the son of Baanah the Netophathite, Ittai the son of Ribai
of [b]Gibeah of the sons of Benjamin,
30 Benaiah a [a]Pirathonite, Hiddai of the brooks of [b]Gaash,
31 Abi-albon the Arbathite, Azmaveth the [a]Barhumite,
32 Eliahba the [a]Shaalbonite, the sons of Jashen, Jonathan,
33 [a]Shammah the Hararite, Ahiam the son of Sharar the Ararite,
34 Eliphelet the son of Ahasbai, the son of [a]the Maacathite, [b]Eliam
the son of [c]Ahithophel the Gilonite,
35 [a]Hezro the [b]Carmelite, Paarai the Arbite,
36 Igal the son of Nathan of [a]Zobah, Bani the Gadite,
37 Zelek the Ammonite, Naharai the [a]Beerothite, armor bearers of
Joab the son of Zeruiah,
38 Ira the [a]Ithrite, Gareb the Ithrite,
39 [a]Uriah the Hittite; thirty-seven in all.

Chapter 24

24 [a]Now [b]again the anger of the LORD burned against Israel, and
it incited David against them to say, "[c]Go, number Israel and
Judah."
2 And the king said to Joab the commander of the army who was
with him, "Go about now through all the tribes of Israel, [a]from Dan
to Beersheba, and [1]register the people, that I may know the number
of the people."
3 But Joab said to the king, "[a]Now may the LORD your God add to
the people a hundred times as many as they are, while the eyes of

16 [b]Gen. 35:1
17 [a]Lev. 17:1
18 [1]So two H… and Syriac; M… [2]Lit., *slain one* … 10:10, 14; 18:… 11:20, 21
20 [1]Lit., *smot…* *lion-like heroe…* 8:18; 20:23 [b]J…
21 [1]Lit., *smote* … *man of appear…*
22 [a]2 Sam. 23…
24 [a]2 Sam. 2:… 27:7
25 [a]1 Chr. 11:… 7:1
26 [a]2 Sam. 14…
27 [a]Josh. 21:1…
28 [a]2 Kin. 25:2…
29 [a]1 Chr. 11:3… 18:28
30 [a]Judg. 12:1… [b]Josh. 24:30
31 [a]2 Sam. 3:1…
32 [a]Josh. 19:4…
33 [a]2 Sam. 23:…
34 [a]2 Sam. 10:… 20:14 [b]2 Sam. … [c]2 Sam. 15:12
35 [a]1 Chr. 11:3… 15:55
36 [a]2 Sam. 8:3
37 [a]2 Sam. 4:2
38 [a]1 Chr. 2:53
39 [a]2 Sam. 11:3
24:1 [a]1 Chr. 21:… [b]2 Sam. 21:1, 2 … 27:23, 24
2 [1]Lit., *muster* [a]… 20:1; 2 Sam. 3:1…
3 [a]Deut. 1:11

my lord the king *still* see; but why does my lord the king delight in
this thing?"
4 Nevertheless, the king's word prevailed against Joab and against
the commanders of the army. So Joab and the commanders of the
army went out from the presence of the king, to [1]register the people
of Israel.
5 And they crossed the Jordan and camped in [a]Aroer, on the right
side of the city that is in the middle of the valley of Gad, and toward
[b]Jazer.
6 Then they came to Gilead and to [1]the land of Tahtim-hodshi, and
they came to Dan-jaan and around to [a]Sidon,
7 and came to the [a]fortress of Tyre and to all the cities of the
[b]Hivites and of the Canaanites, and they went out to the south of
Judah, *to* [c]Beersheba.
8 So when they had gone about through the whole land, they
came to Jerusalem at the end of nine months and twenty days.
9 And Joab gave [a]the number of the [1]registration of the people to
the king; and there were in Israel [b]eight hundred thousand valiant
men who drew the sword, and the men of Judah were five hundred
thousand men.
10 Now [a]David's heart [1]troubled him after he had numbered the
people. So David said to the LORD, "[b]I have sinned greatly in what I
have done. But now, O LORD, please [2]take away the iniquity of Thy
servant, for [c]I have acted very foolishly."
11 When David arose in the morning, the word of the LORD came to
[a]the prophet Gad, David's [b]seer, saying,
12 "Go and speak to David, 'Thus the LORD says, "I am offering you
three things; choose for yourself one of them, which I may do to
you." ' "
13 So Gad came to David and told him, and said to him, "Shall
[a]seven years of famine come to you in your land? Or will you flee
three months before your foes while they pursue you? Or shall there
be three days' pestilence in your land? Now consider and see what
answer I shall return to Him who sent me."
14 Then David said to Gad, "I am in great distress. Let us now fall
into the hand of the LORD [a]for His mercies are great, but do not let
me fall into the hand of man."
15 So [a]the LORD [1]sent a pestilence upon Israel from the morning
until the appointed time; and seventy thousand men of the people
[b]from Dan to Beersheba died.
16 [a]When the angel stretched out his hand toward Jerusalem to
destroy it, [b]the LORD relented from the calamity, and said to the angel
who destroyed the people, "It is enough! Now relax your hand!"
And the angel of the LORD was by the threshing floor of Araunah the
Jebusite.
17 Then David spoke to the LORD when he saw the angel who was
striking down the people, and said, "Behold, [a]it is I who have
sinned, and it is I who have done wrong; but [b]these sheep, what
have they done? Please let Thy hand be against me and against my
father's house."
18 So Gad came to David that day and said to him, "[a]Go up, erect
an altar to the LORD on the threshing floor of [1]Araunah the Jebusite."
19 And David went up according to the word of Gad, just as the
LORD had commanded.

4 [1]Lit., *muster*

[a]Deut. 2:36; Josh. , 16 [b]Num. 21:32; 32:35

[1]Or, *Kadesh in the f the Hittite* [a]Josh. 19:28; Judg. 1:31

osh. 19:29 [b]Josh. 3; Judg. 3:3 [c]Gen. 21:22-33

.it., *muster* [a]Num. .4-46 [b]1 Chr. 21:5

[1]Lit., *smote* [2]Lit., *use to pass away* am. 24:5 [b]2 Sam. 3 [c]1 Sam. 13:13; 2 Chr. 16:9

Sam. 22:5; 1 Chr. 9:29 [b]1 Sam. 9:9

Chr. 21:12; Ezek. 14:21

Ps. 51:1; 130:4, 7

Lit., *gave* [a]1 Chr. 4; 27:24 [b]2 Sam. 24:2

[a]Ex. 12:23; 2 Kin. ; Acts 12:23 [b]Ex. 14; 1 Sam. 15:11

7 [a]2 Sam. 24:10 am. 7:8; Ps. 74:1

18 [1]In 2 Chr. 3:1, *an* [a]1 Chr. 21:18

20 And Araunah looked down and saw the king and his servants
crossing over toward him; and Araunah went out and bowed his
face to the ground before the king.
21 Then Araunah said, "Why has my lord the king come to his
servant?" And David said, "To buy the threshing floor from you, in
order to build an altar to the LORD, [a]that the plague may be held back
from the people."
22 And Araunah said to David, "Let my lord the king take and
offer up what is good in his sight. Look, [a]the oxen for the burnt
offering, the threshing sledges and the yokes of the oxen for the
wood.
23 "Everything, O king, Araunah gives to the king." And Araunah
said to the king, "May the LORD your God [a]accept you."
24 However, the king said to Araunah, "No, but I will surely buy *it*
from you for a price, for [a]I will not offer burnt offerings to the LORD
my God [1]which cost me nothing." So [b]David bought the threshing
floor and the oxen for fifty shekels of silver.
25 And David built there an altar to the LORD, and offered burnt
offerings and peace offerings. [a]Thus the LORD was moved by
entreaty for the land, and the plague was held back from Israel.

21 [a]Num. 16.

22 [a]1 Sam. 6
19:21

23 [a]Ezek. 20:

24 [1]Lit., *gratu*
[a]Mal. 1:13, 14
21:24, 25

25 [a]2 Sam. 21

2 Samuel at a Glance

e of 2 Samuel:

Divisions

	Chapter Themes
	1
	2
	3
	4
	5
	6
	7
	8
	9
	10
	11
	12
	13
	14
	15
	16
	17
	18
	19
	20
	21
	22
	23
	24

Author:

Date:

Purpose:

Key Words:

1 KINGS

David—the warrior, the great king, the man loved but chastened by God—was old and very col the end of his life many were vying for his throne. First Kings, which records the final events of Da life, begins a new era for Israel, one that begins with untold glory and ends with . . . you read the st

The account of the kings who followed David is full of wonderful but sobering lessons. It' history of Israel and their God who made them a people of His own possession.

We don't know who wrote 1 Kings. We only know that this is His Word preserved "for our ins tion, that through perseverance and the encouragement of the Scriptures we might have h (Romans 15:4).

THINGS TO DO

General Instructions

Chapter 12 of 1 Kings records a dramatic, pivotal point in the history of Israel. Therefore as we s 1 Kings, we will divide it into two segments with two sets of instructions.

Chapters 1-11

Read through this first segment of 1 Kings one chapter at a time.

1. Remember, you're studying the lives of real people. Observe the opportunities God gives th His instructions to them, and how they respond. Watch when they succeed, when they fail, why—and learn! Pray and ask God to speak to your heart. In the margin of each chapte applicable, make a list of these two things: "Lessons for Life" (LFL) and "Insights on God."
2. Mark in a distinctive way the following words and phrases: *word* or any reference to the *Wo the Lord, heart, pray (cry, cried), covenant, wisdom (wise), command (commandments), pro (promised), high places, house* (when it refers to God's house, their place of worship), and *(sinned)*. The first occurrence of the word *sin* is in chapter 8.
   a. List the key words on an index card and use it as a bookmark while you study this segme 1 Kings.
   b. When you read "and the Lord said," highlight or underline what the Lord said. Then un line anything you want to remember.
3. The main characters of these first chapters are David and Solomon. List in the margins what learn about them.
   a. When you come to Solomon's reign, read Deuteronomy 7:2-6 and 17:14-20 to underst Solomon's actions as he took over the kingdom. Remember sin was to be judged and n derers were to be put to death; otherwise the land would be polluted.
   b. Second Chronicles 1 through 9 is an excellent cross reference on 1 Kings 1 through 11.
4. Mark every reference to time. Draw a time clock such as this ⏰ .
5. After you finish reading a chapter, record the theme or subject of that chapter next to the cha number in the text and on the appropriate place on 1 KINGS AT A GLANCE on page 549.
6. When you finish chapter 11 see if any of the first eleven chapters can be grouped unde common theme or as part of an event: e.g. the building of the temple. These are called segm divisions and can be recorded in the designated place on 1 KINGS AT A GLANCE.

Chapters 12-22

1. Read chapter 12 and then turn to the end of 2 Kings. Look at the chart ISRAEL'S DIVISION A CAPTIVITY on page 551. Note the division of the kingdom which occurred in 931 B.C. Write

date at the beginning of chapter 12. From this point on whenever "Israel" is used you will need to distinguish whether it is a reference to the ten tribes of the northern kingdom (which it usually will be) or to the nation of Israel as a whole.

Add *according to* to your key word list. When you come to this phrase, note what was "according to" what. You'll gain some good insights.

Watch for insights the Lord gives you into Himself, His ways, and into life in general through the example of the kings and God's people. Record these in the margin under "Insights on God" or "Lessons for Life" just as you did in the first section of 1 Kings.

When you read of a king or another key figure consult Part 1 of THE HISTORICAL CHART OF THE KINGS AND PROPHETS OF ISRAEL AND JUDAH which is located on pages 596 through 598 between 2 Kings and 1 Chronicles.

Each time you finish reading about a king, record your insights on the chart, THE KINGS OF ISRAEL AND JUDAH on pages 599 and 600 between 2 Kings and 1 Chronicles. Also fill in the information on Solomon.

a. Make sure you note on the chart whether each king ruled over the northern (Israel) or southern (Judah) kingdom. Also note on the chart under whose reign the kingdom was divided.

b. Mark every reference to time. You might find it helpful to record in the margin the dates the king reigned. These are on the chart THE KINGS OF ISRAEL AND JUDAH.

In chapter 17 when you come to Elijah, in the margin compile a list of everything you learn about this prophet. Also, compare 17:1 with Deuteronomy 28:1-2,12,15,23-24 and James 5:17-18. What could be the scriptural basis for Elijah's prayer and word to Ahab? Think about it.

Record the chapter themes and any segment divisions you see on 1 KINGS AT A GLANCE. Also fill in any other pertinent information. You might try coming up with a title which best describes what happens during this period in Israel's history.

Second Kings is a continuation of 1 Kings. You'll want to study it next.

NGS TO THINK ABOUT

Have you seen God's graciousness, His longsuffering? God doesn't retaliate, rather He brings us to repentance and obedience. What does this provoke in your heart? And how should you live if He's in control of your life?

Have you seen how a person can start so well in their walk with the Lord and then turn away? What do you think causes this? What can you do to prevent this in your own life? Go back and review what you've listed in the margin regarding the kings and their relationship with the Lord. What lessons have you learned that you can apply to your life?

Did you notice the sovereignty of God—how He turns hearts, directs spirits, raises up and puts down kings and others in order to accomplish His purpose and will? Are you living in the light of this truth about God?

Have you been thinking that you had to be absolutely perfect before God could use you? Did you see how Elijah was a man "of like passions" just like you and yet God used him? What have you learned in 1 Kings? When David's life was over, didn't God call David a man after His own heart? Frailties and all, David was a man of God because he believed God.

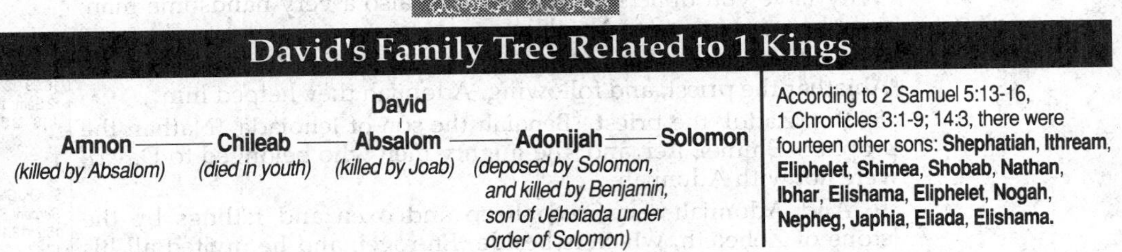

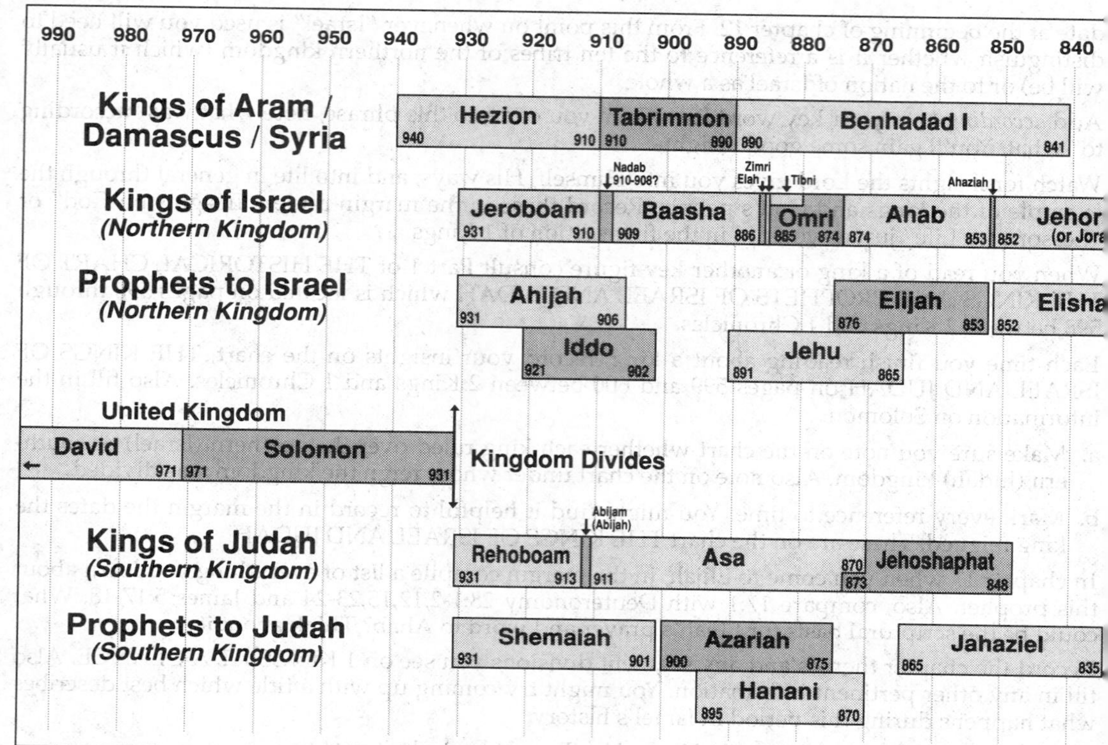

Chapter 1

1 Now King David was old, advanced in age; and they covered
him with clothes, but he could not keep warm.
2 So his servants said to him, "Let them seek a young virgin for
my lord the king, and let her [1]attend the king and become his nurse;
and let her lie in your bosom, that my lord the king may keep
warm."
3 So they searched for a beautiful girl throughout all the territory
of Israel, and found Abishag the [a]Shunammite, and brought her to
the king.
4 And the girl was very beautiful; and she became the king's nurse
and served him, but the king did not [1]cohabit with her.
5 Now [a]Adonijah the son of Haggith exalted himself, saying, "I
will be king." So [b]he prepared for himself chariots and horsemen
with fifty men to run before him.
6 And his father had never [1]crossed him at any time by asking,
"Why have you done so?" And he was also a very handsome man;
and [2a]he was born after Absalom.
7 And [1]he had conferred with [a]Joab the son of Zeruiah and with
[b]Abiathar the priest; and following [c]Adonijah they helped him.
8 But [a]Zadok the priest, [b]Benaiah the son of Jehoiada, [c]Nathan the
prophet, [d]Shimei, Rei, and [e]the mighty men who belonged to David,
were not with Adonijah.
9 And Adonijah sacrificed sheep and oxen and fatlings by the
[1]stone of Zoheleth, which is beside [a]En-rogel; and he invited all his

1:2 [1]Lit., *stand*

3 [a]Josh. 19:18; 28:4

4 [1]Lit., *know he*

5 [a]2 Sam. 3:4 15:1

6 [1]Lit., *pained h* *she gave him bi* [a]2 Sam. 3:3, 4

7 [1]Lit., *his words* [a]1 Chr. 11:6 [b]1 S 22:20, 23; 2 Sam 20:25 [c]1 Kin. 2:2

8 [a]2 Sam. 20:25 16:39 [b]2 Sam. 8 [c]2 Sam. 12:1 [d]1 4:18 [e]2 Sam. 23

9 [1]Or, *Gliding or* *Serpent Stone* [a]J 15:7; 18:16; 2 Sa 17:17

brothers, the king's sons, and all the men of Judah, the king's ser-
vants.
10 But he did not invite Nathan the prophet, Benaiah, the mighty
men, and [a]Solomon his brother.
11 Then Nathan spoke to [a]Bathsheba the mother of Solomon,
saying, "Have you not heard that Adonijah the son of Haggith has
become king, and David our lord does not know *it*?
12 "So now come, please let me [a]give you counsel and save your life
and the life of your son Solomon.
13 "Go [1]at once to King David and say to him, 'Have you not, my
lord, O king, sworn to your maidservant, saying, "[a]Surely Solomon
your son shall be king after me, and he shall sit on my throne"? Why
then has Adonijah become king?'
14 "Behold, while you are still there speaking with the king, I will
come in after you and confirm your words."
15 So Bathsheba went in to the king in the bedroom. Now [a]the king
was very old, and Abishag the Shunammite was ministering to the
king.
16 Then Bathsheba bowed and prostrated herself [1]before the king.
And the king said, "What [2]do you wish?"
17 And she said to him, "My lord, you swore to your maidservant
by the LORD your God, *saying,* '[a]Surely your son Solomon shall be
king after me and he shall sit on my throne.'
18 "And now, behold, Adonijah is king; and now, my lord the king,
you do not know *it*.
19 "And [a]he has sacrificed oxen and fatlings and sheep in abun-
dance, and has invited all the sons of the king and Abiathar the
priest and Joab the commander of the army; but he has not invited
Solomon your servant.
20 "And as for you now, my lord the king, the eyes of all Israel are
on you, to tell them who shall sit on the throne of my lord the king
after him.
21 "Otherwise it will come about, [a]as soon as my lord the king sleeps
with his fathers, that I and my son Solomon will be considered [1]of-
fenders."
22 And behold, while she was still speaking with the king, Nathan
the prophet came in.
23 And they told the king, saying, "Here is Nathan the prophet."
And when he came in before the king, he prostrated himself [1]before
the king with his face to the ground.
24 Then Nathan said, "My lord the king, have you said, 'Adonijah
shall be king after me, and he shall sit on my throne'?
25 "[a]For he has gone down today and has sacrificed oxen and fat-
lings and sheep in abundance, and has invited all the king's sons
and the commanders of the army and Abiathar the priest, and be-
hold, they are eating and drinking before him; and they say, '[b]*Long*
live King Adonijah!'
26 "[a]But me, *even* me your servant, and Zadok the priest and Benaiah
the son of Jehoiada and your servant Solomon, he has not invited.
27 "Has this thing been done by my lord the king, and you have not
shown to your [1]servants who should sit on the throne of my lord the
king after him?"
28 Then King David answered and said, "Call Bathsheba to me."
And she came into the king's presence and stood before the king.

10 [a]2 Sam. 12:24
11 [a]2 Sam. 12:24
12 [a]Prov. 15:22
13 [1]Lit., *and enter* ...1 Kin. 1:30; 1 Chr. 22:9-13
15 [a]1 Kin. 1:1
...it., *to* [2]Lit., *to you*
17 [a]1 Kin. 1:13
19 [a]1 Kin. 1:9
...it., *sinners* [a]Deut. ...:16; 2 Sam. 7:12; 1 Kin. 2:10
23 [1]Lit., *to*
...Kin. 1:9 [b]1 Sam. 10:24
26 [a]1 Kin. 1:8, 10
[1]Some mss. read *servant*

29 And the king vowed and said, "[a]As the LORD lives, who has
redeemed my life from all distress,
30 surely as [a]I vowed to you by the LORD the God of Israel, saying,
'Your son Solomon shall be king after me, and he shall sit on my
throne in my place'; I will indeed do so this day."
31 Then Bathsheba bowed with her face to the ground, and
prostrated herself [1]before the king and said, "[a]May my lord King
David live forever."
32 Then King David said, "Call to me [a]Zadok the priest, Nathan the
prophet, and Benaiah the son of Jehoiada." And they came into the
king's presence.
33 And the king said to them, "Take with you [a]the servants of your
lord, and have my son Solomon ride on my own mule, and bring
him down to [b]Gihon.
34 "And let Zadok the priest and Nathan the prophet [a]anoint him
there as king over Israel, and [b]blow the trumpet and say, '[c]*Long* live
King Solomon!'
35 "Then you shall come up after him, and he shall come and sit on
my throne and be king in my place; for I have appointed him to be
ruler over Israel and Judah."
36 And Benaiah the son of Jehoiada answered the king and said,
"Amen! Thus may the LORD, the God of my lord the king, say.
37 "[a]As the LORD has been with my lord the king, so may He be with
Solomon, and [b]make his throne greater than the throne of my lord
King David!"
38 So [a]Zadok the priest, Nathan the prophet, Benaiah the son of
Jehoiada, [b]the Cherethites, and the Pelethites went down and had
Solomon ride on King David's mule, and brought him to [c]Gihon.
39 Zadok the priest then [a]took the horn of oil from the tent and
[b]anointed Solomon. Then they [c]blew the trumpet, and all the people
said, "[d]*Long* live King Solomon!"
40 And all the people went up after him, and the people [1]were
playing on flutes and rejoicing with great joy, so that the earth
[2]shook at their noise.
41 Now Adonijah and all the guests who were with him heard *it*, as
they finished eating. When Joab heard the sound of the trumpet, he
said, "Why [1]is the city making such an uproar?"
42 While he was still speaking, behold, [a]Jonathan the son of
Abiathar the priest came. Then Adonijah said, "Come in, for [b]you are
a valiant man and bring good news."
43 But Jonathan answered and said to Adonijah, "No! Our lord
King David has made Solomon king.
44 "The king has also sent with him Zadok the priest, Nathan the
prophet, Benaiah the son of Jehoiada, the Cherethites, and the Pele-
thites; and they have made him ride on the king's mule.
45 "And Zadok the priest and Nathan the prophet have anointed
him king in Gihon, and they have come up from there rejoicing, [a]so
that the city is in an uproar. This is the noise which you have heard.
46 "Besides, [a]Solomon has even taken his seat on the throne of the
kingdom.
47 "And moreover, the king's servants came to bless our lord King
David, saying, 'May [a]your God make the name of Solomon better
than your name and his throne greater than your throne!' And [b]the
king bowed himself on the bed.

29 [a]2 Sam. 4:9
30 [a]1 Kin. 1:13, 1
31 [1]Lit., *to* [a]Dan. 3:9
32 [a]1 Kin. 1:8
33 [a]2 Sam. 20:6, [b]2 Chr. 32:30; 33:
34 [a]1 Sam. 10:1; 12; 2 Sam. 5:3; 1 19:16; 2 Kin. 9:3 [b]2 Sam. 15:10 [c]1 1:25
37 [a]Josh. 1:5, 17 1 Sam. 20:13 [b]1 1:47
38 [a]1 Kin. 1:8 [b]2 8:18 [c]1 Kin. 1:33
39 [a]Ex. 30:23-32 89:20 [b]1 Chr. 29 [c]1 Kin. 1:34 [d]1 S 10:24
40 [1]Lit., *fluting* [2]*was split*
41 [1]Lit., *is the so the city an uproa*
42 [a]2 Sam. 15:2 17:17 [b]2 Sam. 1
45 [a]1 Kin. 1:40
46 [a]1 Chr. 29:23
47 [a]1 Kin. 1:37 47:31

48 "The king has also said thus, 'Blessed be the LORD, the God of
Israel, who [a]has granted one to sit on my throne today while my
own eyes see *it*.' "
49 Then all the guests of Adonijah were terrified; and they arose
and each went on his way.
50 And Adonijah was afraid of Solomon, and he arose, went and
[a]took hold of the horns of the altar.
51 Now it was told Solomon, saying, "Behold, Adonijah is afraid of
King Solomon, for behold, he has taken hold of the horns of the altar,
saying, 'Let King Solomon swear to me today that he will not put his
servant to death with the sword.' "
52 And Solomon said, "If he will be a worthy man, [a]not one of his
hairs will fall to the ground; but if wickedness is found in him, he
will die."
53 So King Solomon sent, and they brought him down from the
altar. And he came and prostrated himself [1]before King Solomon,
and Solomon said to him, "Go to your house."

Chapter 2

2 As David's [1a]time to die drew near, he charged Solomon his son,
saying,
2 "[a]I am going the way of all the earth. [b]Be strong, therefore, and
[1]show yourself a man.
3 "And keep the charge of the LORD your God, to walk in His ways,
to keep His statutes, His commandments, His ordinances, and His
testimonies, [a]according to what is written in the law of Moses, that
[b]you may succeed in all that you do and wherever you turn,
4 so that [a]the LORD may carry out His promise which He spoke
concerning me, saying, [b]'If your sons are careful of their way, [c]to
walk before Me in [1]truth with all their heart and with all their soul,
[2d]you shall not lack a man on the throne of Israel.'
5 "Now you also know what Joab the [a]son of Zeruiah did to me,
what he did to the two commanders of the armies of Israel, to [b]Abner
the son of Ner, and to [c]Amasa the son of Jether, whom he killed; he
also [1]shed the blood of war in peace. And he put the blood of war on
his belt [2]about his waist, and on his sandals [3]on his feet.
6 "[a]So act according to your wisdom, and do not let his gray hair go
down to [1]Sheol in peace.
7 "But [a]show kindness to the sons of Barzillai the Gileadite, and [b]let
them be among those who eat at your table; [c]for they [1]assisted me
when I fled from Absalom your brother.
8 "And behold, [a]there is with you Shimei the son of Gera the Ben-
jamite, of Bahurim; now it was he who cursed me with a [1]violent
curse on the day I went to Mahanaim. But when [b]he came down to
me at the Jordan, I swore to him by the LORD, saying, 'I will not put
you to death with the sword.'
9 "Now therefore, do not let him go unpunished, [a]for you are a wise
man; and you will know what you ought to do to him, and you will
bring his gray hair down to [1]Sheol with blood."
10 Then [a]David slept with his fathers and was buried in [b]the city of
David.
11 And [a]the days that David reigned over Israel *were* forty years:
[b]seven years he reigned in Hebron, and thirty-three years he reigned
in Jerusalem.

2 Sam. 7:12; 1 Kin. 3:6
0 [a]Ex. 27:2; 30:10; 1 Kin. 2:28
52 [a]1 Sam. 14:45; ı. 14:11; Acts 27:34
53 [1]Lit., *to*
[1]Lit., *days* [a]Gen. 47:29; Deut. 31:14
.it., *become a man* Josh. 23:14 [b]Deut. :7, 23; Josh. 1:6, 7
3 [a]Deut. 17:18-20 [b]1 Chr. 22:12, 13
·, *faithfulness* [2]Lit., *re shall not be cast to you a man from before Me* [a]2 Sam. 7:25 [b]Ps. 132:12 Kin. 20:3 [d]2 Sam. 13; 1 Kin. 8:25; 9:5
it., *made* [2]Lit., *that as about* [3]Lit., *that e on* [a]2 Sam. 2:13, 2 Sam. 3:27; 1 Kin. :32 [c]2 Sam. 20:10
., the nether world [a]1 Kin. 2:9
[1]Lit., *came near to* [a]2 Sam. 19:31-38 n. 9:7, 10 [c]2 Sam. 17:27-29
8 [1]Or, *grievous* m. 16:5-8 [b]2 Sam. 19:18-23
., the nether world [a]1 Kin. 2:6
[a]Acts 2:29; 13:36 am. 5:7; 1 Kin. 3:1
11 [a]2 Sam. 5:4, 5; Chr. 3:4; 29:26, 27 [b]2 Sam. 5:5

12 And [a]Solomon sat on the throne of David his father, and his kingdom was firmly established.

13 Now Adonijah the son of Haggith came to Bathsheba the mother of Solomon. And she said, "[a]Do you come peacefully?" And he said, "Peacefully."

14 Then he said, "I have something *to say* to you." And she said, "Speak."

15 So he said, "You know that [a]the kingdom was mine and [b]that all Israel [1]expected me to be king; [c]however, the kingdom has turned about and become my brother's, [d]for it was his from the LORD.

16 "And now I am making one request of you; do not [1]refuse me." And she said to him, "Speak."

17 Then he said, "Please speak to Solomon the king, for he will not [1]refuse you, that he may give me [a]Abishag the Shunammite as a wife."

18 And Bathsheba said, "Very well; I will speak to the king for you."

19 So Bathsheba went to King Solomon to speak to him for Adonijah. And the king arose to meet her, bowed before her, and sat on his throne; then he [a]had a throne set for the king's mother, and [b]she sat on his right.

20 Then she said, "I am making one small request of you; [a]do not [1]refuse me." And the king said to her, "Ask, my mother, for I will not [2]refuse you."

21 So she said, "[a]Let Abishag the Shunammite be given to Adonijah your brother as a wife."

22 And King Solomon answered and said to his mother, "And why are you asking Abishag the Shunammite for Adonijah? [a]Ask for him also the kingdom—[b]for he is my older brother—even for him, for [c]Abiathar the priest, and for Joab the son of Zeruiah!"

23 Then King Solomon swore by the LORD, saying, "May God do so to me and more also, if Adonijah has [a]not spoken this word against his own [1]life.

24 "Now therefore, as the LORD lives, who has established me and set me on the throne of David my father, and [a]who has made me a house as He promised, surely Adonijah will be put to death today."

25 So King Solomon [a]sent Benaiah the son of Jehoiada; and he fell upon him so that he died.

26 Then to Abiathar the priest the king said, "[a]Go to Anathoth to your own field, [b]for you [1]deserve to die; but I will not put you to death at this time, because [c]you carried the ark of the Lord [2]GOD before my father David, and because [d]you were afflicted in everything with which my father was afflicted."

27 So Solomon dismissed Abiathar from being priest to the LORD, in order to fulfill [a]the word of the LORD, which He had spoken concerning the house of Eli in Shiloh.

28 Now the news came to Joab, [a]for Joab had followed Adonijah, [b]although he had not followed Absalom. And Joab fled to the tent of the LORD and [c]took hold of the horns of the altar.

29 And it was told King Solomon that Joab had fled to the tent of the LORD, and behold, he is beside the altar. Then Solomon [a]sent Benaiah the son of Jehoiada, saying, "[b]Go, fall upon him."

30 So Benaiah came to the tent of the LORD, and said to him, "Thus the king has said, 'Come out.' " But he said, "No, for I will die here."

12 [a]1 Chr. 29... 1:1

13 [a]1 Sam. 16...

15 [1]Lit., *set th... on me* [a]2 Sam... 1 Kin. 2:22 [b]1... 1:5-25 [c]1 Kin. [d]1 Chr. 22:9, 10...

16 [1]Lit., *turn a... face*

17 [1]Lit., *turn a... face* [a]1 Kin. 1:3...

19 [a]1 Kin. 15:1... 45:9

20 [1]Lit., *turn a... face* [2]Lit., *turn a... your face* [a]1 Kin...

21 [a]1 Kin. 1:3, 4...

22 [a]2 Sam. 12:8... 1:6; 2:15; 1 Chr. [c]1 Kin. 1:7

23 [1]Lit., *soul* [a]R...

24 [a]2 Sam. 7:11, 1 Chr. 22:10

25 [a]2 Sam. 8:18

26 [1]Lit., *are a ma... death* [2]Heb., *YH...* usually rendered ... [a]Josh. 21:18; Jer. [b]1 Sam. 26:16 [c]1... 23:6; 2 Sam. 15:2... [d]1 Sam. 22:20-23... 23:8, 9

27 [a]1 Sam. 2:27-3...

28 [a]1 Kin. 1:7 [b]2... 17:25; 18:2 [c]1 Kin...

29 [a]1 Kin. 2:25 [b]E... 21:14

And Benaiah brought the king word again, saying, "Thus spoke Joab, and thus he answered me."

31 And the king said to him, "[a]Do as he has spoken and fall upon him and bury him, [b]that you may remove from me and from my father's house the blood which Joab shed without cause.

32 "And [a]the LORD will return his blood on his own head, [b]because he fell upon two men more righteous and better than he and killed them with the sword, while my father David did not know *it:* [c]Abner the son of Ner, commander of the army of Israel, and [d]Amasa the son of Jether, commander of the army of Judah.

33 "[a]So shall their blood return on the head of Joab and on the head of his [1]descendants forever; but to David and his [1]descendants and his house and his throne, may there be peace from the LORD forever."

34 Then [a]Benaiah the son of Jehoiada went up and fell upon him and put him to death, and he was buried at his own house [b]in the wilderness.

35 And [a]the king appointed Benaiah the son of Jehoiada over the army in his place, and the king appointed [b]Zadok the priest [c]in the place of Abiathar.

36 Now the king sent and called for [a]Shimei and said to him, "Build for yourself a house in Jerusalem and live there, and do not go out from there to any place.

37 "For it will happen on the day you go out and [a]cross over the [1]brook Kidron, you will know for certain that you shall surely die; [b]your blood shall be on your own head."

38 Shimei then said to the king, "The word is good. As my lord the king has said, so your servant will do." So Shimei lived in Jerusalem many days.

39 But it came about at the end of three years, that two of the servants of Shimei ran away [a]to Achish son of Maacah, king of Gath. And they told Shimei, saying, "Behold, your servants are in Gath."

40 Then Shimei arose and saddled his donkey, and went to Gath to Achish to look for his servants. And Shimei went and brought his servants from Gath.

41 And it was told Solomon that Shimei had gone from Jerusalem to Gath, and had returned.

42 So the king sent and called for Shimei and said to him, "Did I not make you swear by the LORD and solemnly warn you, saying, 'You will know for certain that on the day you depart and go anywhere, you shall surely die'? And you said to me, 'The word which I have heard is good.'

43 "Why then have you not kept the oath of the LORD, and the command which I [1]have laid on you?"

44 The king also said to Shimei, "[a]You know all the evil which [1]you acknowledge in your heart, which you did to my father David; therefore [b]the LORD shall return your evil on your own head.

45 "But King Solomon shall be blessed, and [a]the throne of David shall be established before the LORD forever."

46 [a]So the king commanded Benaiah the son of Jehoiada, and he went out and fell upon him so that he died. [b]Thus the kingdom was established in the hands of Solomon.

[a]Ex. 21:14 [b]Num. 35:33; Deut. 19:13; 21:8, 9

[a]Gen. 9:6; Judg. 9:24, 57; Ps. 7:16 [b]2 Chr. 21:13, 14 ...am. 3:27 [d]2 Sam. 20:9, 10

...it., *seed* [a]2 Sam. 3:29

...Kin. 2:25 [b]Josh. 15:61; Matt. 3:1

...1 Kin. 4:4 [b]1 Chr. 6:53; 24:3; 29:22 [c]1 Kin. 2:27

...Sam. 16:5; 1 Kin. 2:8

...Or, *wadi* [a]2 Sam. ...2 Kin. 23:6; John 18:1 [b]Josh. 2:19; ...Sam. 1:16; Ezek. 18:13

39 [a]1 Sam. 27:2

...Lit., *commanded*

... [1]Lit., *your heart* ...wledges [a]2 Sam. ...3 [b]1 Sam. 25:39; ... 11:1, 12-16; Ps. 7:16

...Sam. 7:13; Prov. 25:5

... [a]1 Kin. 2:25, 34 ... 2:12; 2 Chr. 1:1

Chapter 3

3 Then [a]Solomon [1]formed a marriage alliance with Pharaoh king of Egypt, and took Pharaoh's daughter [b]and brought her to the city of David, [c]until he had finished building his own house and the house of the LORD and [d]the wall around Jerusalem.

2 [a]The people were still sacrificing on the high places, because there was no house built for the name of the LORD until those days.

3 Now [a]Solomon loved the LORD, [b]walking in the statutes of his father David, except he sacrificed and burned incense on the high places.

4 [a]And the king went to [b]Gibeon to sacrifice there, [c]for that was the great high place; Solomon offered a thousand burnt offerings on that altar.

5 [a]In Gibeon the LORD appeared to Solomon [b]in a dream at night; and God said, "[c]Ask what *you wish* me to give you."

6 Then Solomon said, "[a]Thou hast shown great lovingkindness to Thy servant David my father, [b]according as he walked before Thee in [1]truth and righteousness and uprightness of heart toward Thee; and [c]Thou hast [2]reserved for him this great lovingkindness, that Thou hast given him a son to sit on his throne, as *it is* this day.

7 "And now, O LORD my God, [a]Thou hast made Thy servant king in place of my father David, yet [b]I am but a little child; [c]I do not know how to go out or come in.

8 "And [a]Thy servant is in the midst of Thy people which Thou hast chosen, [b]a great people who cannot be numbered or counted for multitude.

9 "So [a]give Thy servant [1]an understanding heart to judge Thy people [b]to discern between good and evil. For who is able to judge this [2]great people of Thine?"

10 And [1]it was pleasing in the sight of the Lord that Solomon had asked this thing.

11 And God said to him, "Because you have asked this thing and have [a]not asked for yourself [1]long life, nor have asked riches for yourself, nor have you asked for the life of your enemies, but have asked for yourself [2]discernment to understand justice,

12 behold, [a]I have done according to your words. Behold, [b]I have given you a wise and discerning heart, so that there has been no one like you before you, nor shall one like you arise after you.

13 "[a]And I have also given you what you have not asked, both [b]riches and honor, so that there will not be any among the kings like you all your days.

14 "And [a]if you walk in My ways, keeping My statutes and commandments, as your father David walked, then I will [b]prolong your days."

15 Then [a]Solomon awoke, and behold, it was a dream. And he came to Jerusalem and stood before the ark of the covenant of the Lord, and offered burnt offerings and made peace offerings, and [b]made a feast for all his servants.

16 Then two women who were harlots came to the king and stood before him.

17 And the one woman said, "Oh, my lord, [1]this woman and I live in the same house; and I gave birth to a child while she *was* in the house.

18 "And it happened on the third day after I gave birth, that this

3:1 [1]Lit., *made hi[s] a son-in-law of Ph* [a]1 Kin. 7:8; 9:16, 2 2 Chr. 8:11 [b]1 Kin [c]1 Kin. 7:1; 9:10 [c] 9:15

2 [a]Lev. 17:3-5; D 12:2, 13, 14; 1 Kin

3 [a]Deut. 6:5; 10: 11:13; 30:16; Ps. 145:20; 1 Cor. 8:3 [b]1 Kin. 2:3; 9:4; 11 6, 38

4 [a]2 Chr. 1:3 [b]Jo 18:21-25 [c]1 Chr. 21:29

5 [a]1 Kin. 9:2; 11: [b]Num. 12:6; Matt. 2:13 [c]John 15:7

6 [1]Or, *faithfulnes* *kept* [a]2 Sam. 7:8 2 Chr. 1:8 [b]1 Kin. [c]1 Kin. 1:48

7 [a]1 Chr. 22:9-13 [b]1 Chr. 29:1; Jer. [c]Num. 27:17

8 [a]Ex. 19:6; Deu [b]Gen. 15:5; 22:17

9 [1]Lit., *a hearing heavy* [a]2 Chr. 1: 72:1, 2; Prov. 2:3 James 1:5 [b]2 Sa 14:17; Heb. 5:14

10 [1]Lit., *the thing*

11 [1]Lit., *many da* [2]Lit., *hearing* [a]Ja

12 [a]1 John 5:14, [b]1 Kin. 4:29-31; 5 10:23, 24; Eccl. 1

13 [a]1 Kin. 4:21-2 10:23, 27; Matt. 6 Eph. 3:20 [b]Prov.

14 [a]1 Kin. 3:6 [b]P 91:16; Prov. 3:2

15 [a]Gen. 41:7 [b] 8:65

17 [1]Lit., *I and th[is] woman*

woman also gave birth to a child, and we were together. There was
no stranger with us in the house, only the two of us in the house.
19 "And this woman's son died in the night, because she lay on it.
20 "So she arose in the middle of the night and took my son from
beside me while your maidservant slept, and laid him in her bosom,
and laid her dead son in my bosom.
21 "And when I rose in the morning to nurse my son, behold, he was
dead; but when I looked at him carefully in the morning, behold, he
was not my son, whom I had borne."
22 Then the other woman said, "No! For the living one is my son,
and the dead one is your son." But [1]the first woman said, "No! For
the dead one is your son, and the living one is my son." Thus they
spoke before the king.
23 Then the king said, "[1]The one says, 'This is my son who is living,
and your son is the dead one'; and [1]the other says, 'No! For your son
is the dead one, and my son is the living one.' "
24 And the king said, "Get me a sword." So they brought a sword
before the king.
25 And the king said, "Divide the living child in two, and give half
to the one and half to the other."
26 Then the woman whose child *was* the living one spoke to the
king, for [1a]she was deeply stirred over her son and said, "Oh, my
lord, give her the living child, and by no means kill him." But the
other said, "He shall be neither mine nor yours; divide *him!*"
27 Then the king answered and said, "Give [1]the first woman the
living child, and by no means kill him. She is his mother."
28 When all Israel heard of the judgment which the king had
[1]handed down, they feared the king; for [a]they saw that the wisdom
of God was in him to [2]administer justice.

Chapter 4

4 Now King Solomon was king over all Israel.
2 And these were his officials: Azariah the son of Zadok *was* [a]the
priest;
3 Elihoreph and Ahijah, the sons of Shisha *were* secretaries; [a]Jeho-
shaphat the son of Ahilud *was* the recorder;
4 and [a]Benaiah the son of Jehoiada *was* over the army; and Zadok
and [b]Abiathar *were* priests;
5 and Azariah the son of Nathan *was* over [a]the deputies; and
Zabud the son of Nathan, a priest, *was* the king's friend;
6 and Ahishar was over the household; and Adoniram the son of
Abda *was* over the men subject to forced labor.
7 And Solomon had twelve deputies over all Israel, who [1]provided
for the king and his household; each man had to [2]provide for a
month in the year.
8 And these are their names: Ben-hur, in the [a]hill country of
Ephraim;
9 Ben-deker in Makaz and [a]Shaalbim and [b]Beth-shemesh and
Elonbeth-hanan;
10 Ben-hesed, in Arubboth ([a]Socoh *was* his and all the land of
[b]Hepher);
11 Ben-abinadab, *in* all [1]the [a]height of Dor (Taphath the daughter of
Solomon was his wife);
12 Baana the son of Ahilud, *in* [a]Taanach and Megiddo, and all

[1]Lit., *this one was saying*
23 [1]Lit., *this one*
26 [1]Lit., *her [c]ompassion grew warm* [a]...n. 43:30; Is. 49:15; ...r. 31:20; Hos. 11:8
[1]Lit., *her the living child*
[1]Lit., *judged* [2]Lit., [a]1 Kin. 3:9, 11, 12; ...n. 1:17; Col. 2:2, 3
4:2 [a]1 Chr. 6:10
3 [a]2 Sam. 8:16
...1 Kin. 2:35 [b]1 Kin. 2:27
5 [a]1 Kin. 4:7
...t., *nourished* [2]Lit., *nourish*
8 [a]Josh. 24:33
...[a]Judg. 1:35 [b]Josh. 21:16
...osh. 15:35 [b]Josh. 12:17
[1]Or, *Naphoth-dor* [a]Josh. 11:1, 2
12 [a]Judg. 5:19

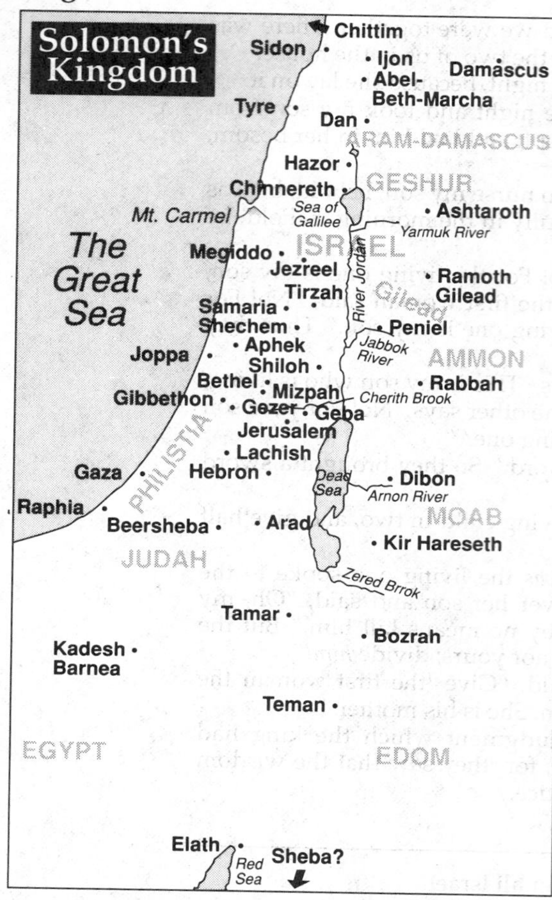

[b]Beth-shean which is beside [c]Zare-
than below Jezreel, from Beth-
shean to [d]Abel-meholah as far as
the other side of [e]Jokmeam;
13 Ben-geber, in [a]Ramoth-gilead
([b]the towns of Jair, the son of Ma-
nasseh, which are in Gilead were
his: [c]the region of Argob, which is
in Bashan, sixty great cities with
walls and bronze bars *were* his);
14 Ahinadab the son of Iddo, *in*
[a]Mahanaim;
15 [a]Ahimaaz, in Naphtali (he also
married Basemath the daughter of
Solomon);
16 Baana the son of [a]Hushai, in
Asher and [1]Bealoth;
17 Jehoshaphat the son of Paruah,
in Issachar;
18 [a]Shimei the son of Ela, in Ben-
jamin;
19 Geber the son of Uri, in the
land of Gilead, [a]the country of
Sihon king of the Amorites and of
Og king of Bashan; and *he was* the
only deputy who *was* in the land.
20 [a]Judah and Israel *were* as nu-
merous as the sand that is on the
[1]seashore in abundance; *they* were
eating and drinking and rejoicing.
21 [1a]Now Solomon ruled over all
the kingdoms [b]from the [2]River *to*
the land of the Philistines and to
the border of Egypt; [c]*they* brought
tribute and served Solomon all the days of his life.
22 And Solomon's [1]provision for one day was thirty [2]kors of fine
flour and sixty [2]kors of meal,
23 ten fat oxen, twenty [1]pasture-fed oxen, a hundred sheep besides
deer, gazelles, roebucks, and fattened fowl.
24 For he had dominion over everything [1]west of the [2]River, from
Tiphsah even to [a]Gaza, [b]over all the kings [1]west of the [2]River; and [c]he
had peace on all sides around about him.
25 [a]So Judah and Israel lived in safety, every man under his vine
and his fig tree, [b]from Dan even to Beersheba, all the days of Solo-
mon.
26 [a]And Solomon had [1]40,000 stalls of horses for his chariots, and
12,000 horsemen.
27 And those deputies [1]provided for King Solomon and all who
came to King Solomon's table, each in his month; they left nothing
lacking.
28 They also brought barley and straw for the horses and [a]swift
steeds to the place where it should be, each according to his charge.
29 Now [a]God gave Solomon wisdom and very great discernment
and breadth of [1]mind, [b]like the sand that is on the seashore.

12 [b]Josh. 17:
3:16 [d]1 Kin. 1
[e]1 Chr. 6:68

13 [a]1 Kin. 22:
[b]Num. 32:41

14 [a]Josh. 13:2

15 [a]2 Sam. 15

16 [1]Or, *in Alot*
[a]2 Sam. 15:32

18 [a]1 Kin. 1:8

19 [a]Deut. 3:8-1

20 [1]Lit., *sea* [a]
22:17; 32:12; 1

21 [1]Ch. 5:1 in
[2]I.e., Euphrates
9:26 [b]Gen. 15:
1:4 [c]2 Sam. 8:2

22 [1]Lit., *bread*
kor equals appr
bu.

23 [1]Lit., *oxen o*
pasture

24 [1]Lit., *beyond*
Euphrates [a]Jud
[b]Ps. 72:11 [c]1 Ch

25 [a]Jer. 23:6; M
Zech. 3:10 [b]1 S

26 [1]One ms. rea
4000, cf. 2 Chr. 9
[a]1 Kin. 10:26; 2 C

27 [1]Or, *nourishe*

28 [a]Esth. 8:10,
1:13

29 [1]Lit., *heart* [a]1
3:12 [b]1 Kin. 4:20

30 And Solomon's wisdom surpassed the wisdom of all [a]the sons of
the east and [b]all the wisdom of Egypt.
31 For [a]he was wiser than all men, than [b]Ethan the Ezrahite,
Heman, [c]Calcol and [1]Darda, the sons of Mahol; and his [2]fame was
known in all the surrounding nations.
32 [a]He also spoke 3,000 proverbs, and his songs were 1,005.
33 And he spoke of trees, from the cedar that is in Lebanon even to
the hyssop that grows on the wall; he spoke also of animals and
birds and creeping things and fish.
34 And [1]men [a]came from all peoples to hear the wisdom of Solo-
mon, from all the kings of the earth who had heard of his wisdom.

Chapter 5

5 [1a]Now Hiram king of Tyre sent his servants to Solomon, when he
heard that they had anointed him king in place of his father, for
[b]Hiram had [2]always been a friend of David.
2 Then [a]Solomon sent *word* to Hiram, saying,
3 "You know that [a]David my father was unable to build a house for
the name of the LORD his God because of the wars which surrounded
him, until the LORD put them under the soles of his feet.
4 "But now [a]the LORD my God has given me rest on every side;
there is neither adversary nor [1]misfortune.
5 "And behold, [a]I [1]intend to build a house for the name of the LORD
my God, as the LORD spoke to David my father, saying, 'Your son,
whom I will set on your throne in your place, he will build the house
for My name.'
6 "Now therefore, command that they cut for me [a]cedars from
Lebanon, and my servants will be with your servants; and I will give
you wages for your servants according to all that you say, for you
know that there is no one among us who knows how to cut timber
like the Sidonians."
7 And it came about when Hiram heard the words of Solomon,
that he rejoiced greatly and said, "Blessed be the LORD today, who
has given to David a wise son over this great people."
8 So Hiram sent *word* to Solomon, saying, "I have heard *the mes-
sage* which you have sent me; I will do [1]what you desire concerning
the cedar and cypress timber.
9 "My servants will bring *them* down from Lebanon to the sea; and
I will make them into rafts *to go* by sea [a]to the place where you
[1]direct me, and I will have them broken up there, and you shall carry
them away. Then [b]you shall accomplish my desire by giving food to
my household."
10 So [1]Hiram [2]gave Solomon [3]as much as he desired of the cedar
and cypress timber.
11 [a]Solomon then gave Hiram 20,000 [1]kors of wheat as food for his
household, and twenty [1]kors of beaten oil; thus Solomon would give
Hiram year by year.
12 And [a]the LORD gave wisdom to Solomon, just as He [1]promised
him; and there was peace between Hiram and Solomon, and the two
of them made a covenant.
13 Now [a]King Solomon [1]levied forced laborers from all Israel; and
the forced laborers [2]numbered 30,000 men.
14 And he sent them to Lebanon, 10,000 a month in relays; they

...n. 29:1; Judg. ...s. 19:11; Acts 7:22
...Chr. 2:6, *Dara* ...e [a]1 Kin. 3:12 ...Chr. 15:19; Ps. ...tle [c]1 Chr. 2:6
...Prov. 1:1; 10:1; ...ccl. 12:9; Song 1:1
...it., *they* [a]1 Kin. ...0:1; 2 Chr. 9:23
...h. 5:15 in Heb. ...*the day* [a]2 Chr. ...am. 5:11; 1 Chr. 14:1
2 [a]2 Chr. 2:3
...Sam. 7:5; 1 Chr. 28:2, 3
evil occurrence ...4:24; 1 Chr. 22:9
...Lit., *say* [a]2 Sam. ...13; 1 Chr. 17:12; ...; 28:6; 2 Chr. 2:4
6 [a]2 Chr. 2:8
all your pleasure
Lit., *send* [a]2 Chr. [b]Ezra 3:7; Ezek. 27:17
Heb., *Hirom* [2]Lit., *giving* [3]Lit., *all his desire*
[1]I.e., 1 kor equals ...ox. 10 bu. [a]2 Chr. 2:10
12 [1]Lit., *spoke to* [a]1 Kin. 3:12
...Lit., *raised up* [2]Lit., ...as [a]1 Kin. 4:6; 9:15

were in Lebanon a month *and* two months at home. And [a]Adoniram
was over the forced laborers.
15 Now [a]Solomon had 70,000 [1]transporters, and 80,000 hewers *of*
stone in the mountains,
16 [a]besides Solomon's 3,300 chief deputies who *were* over the
[1]project *and* who ruled over the people who were doing the work.
17 Then [a]the king commanded, and they quarried great stones,
costly stones, to lay the foundation of the house with cut stones.
18 So Solomon's builders and [1]Hiram's builders and [a]the Gebalites
[2]cut them, and prepared the timbers and the stones to build the
house.

The Jewish Calendar

Babylonian names (B) for the months are still used today for the Jewish calendar. Canaanite names (C) were used prior to the Babylonian captivity. Four are mentioned in the Old Testament.
Adar-Sheni is an intercalary month used every two to three years or seven times in nineteen years.

1st month	2nd month	3rd month	4th month
Nisan (B) Abib (C) March-April	Iyyar (B) Ziv (C) April-May	Sivan (B) May-June	Tammuz (B) June-July
7th month	*8th month*	*9th month*	*10th month*
5th month	**6th month**	**7th month**	**8th month**
Ab (B) July-August	Elul (B) August-September	Tishri (B) Ethanim (C) September-October	Marcheshvan (B) Bul (C) October-November
11th month	*12th month*	*1st month*	*2nd month*
9th month	**10th month**	**11th month**	**12th month**
Kislev (B) November-December	Tebeth (B) December-January	Shebat (B) January-February	Adar (B) February-March
3rd month	*4th month*	*5th month*	*6th month*

Sacred calendar appears in black • Civil calendar appears in grey

Chapter 6

6 [a]Now it came about in the four hundred and eightieth year after
the sons of Israel came out of the land of Egypt, in the fourth
year of Solomon's reign over Israel, in the month of Ziv which is the
second month, that he [1]began to build the house of the LORD.
2 As for the house which King Solomon built for the LORD, its
length *was* sixty [1]cubits and its width twenty *cubits* and its height
thirty cubits.
3 And the porch in front of the nave of the house *was* twenty
cubits [1]in length, [2]corresponding to the width of the house, *and* its
[3]depth along the front of the house *was* ten cubits.
4 Also for the house [a]he made windows with *artistic* frames.
5 And [a]against the wall of the house he built stories encompassing
the walls of the house around both the nave and the [b]inner sanctu-
ary; thus he made [c]side chambers all around.
6 The lowest story *was* five cubits wide, and the middle *was* six
cubits wide, and the third *was* seven cubits wide; for on the outside
he [1]made offsets *in the wall* of the house all around in order that *the*
beams should not [2]be inserted in the walls of the house.
7 And [a]the house, while it was being built, was built of stone [1]pre-
pared at the quarry, and there was neither hammer nor axe nor any
iron tool heard in the house while it was being built.

14 [a]1 Kin. 4:6

15 [1]Or, *burde* [a]1 Kin. 9:20-22 2:17, 18

16 [1]Lit., *work* 9:23

17 [a]1 Kin. 6:7; 22:2

18 [1]Heb., *Hiror* *chiseled* [a]Josh. Ezek. 27:9

6:1 [1]Lit., *built* [a] 3:1, 2

2 [1]I.e., One cub equals approx. 1

3 [1]Lit., *in its leng* [2]Lit., *on the face* *width*

4 [a]Ezek. 40:16; 4

5 [a]Ezek. 41:6 [b]1 6:16, 19, 20 [c]Eze

6 [1]Lit., *gave* [2]Lit., *hold*

7 [1]Lit., *finished* [a]E 20:25; Deut. 27:5,

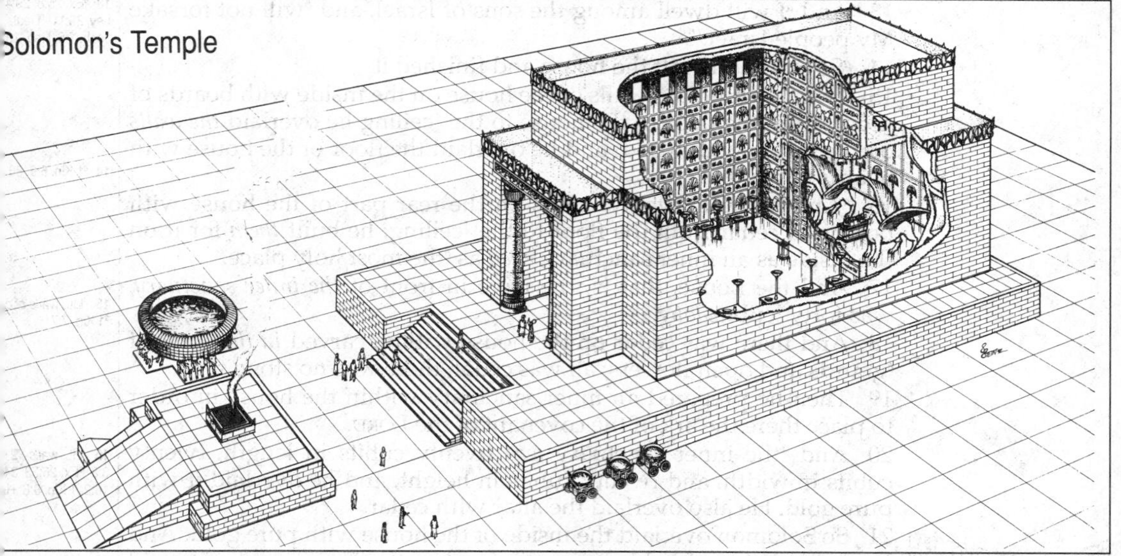

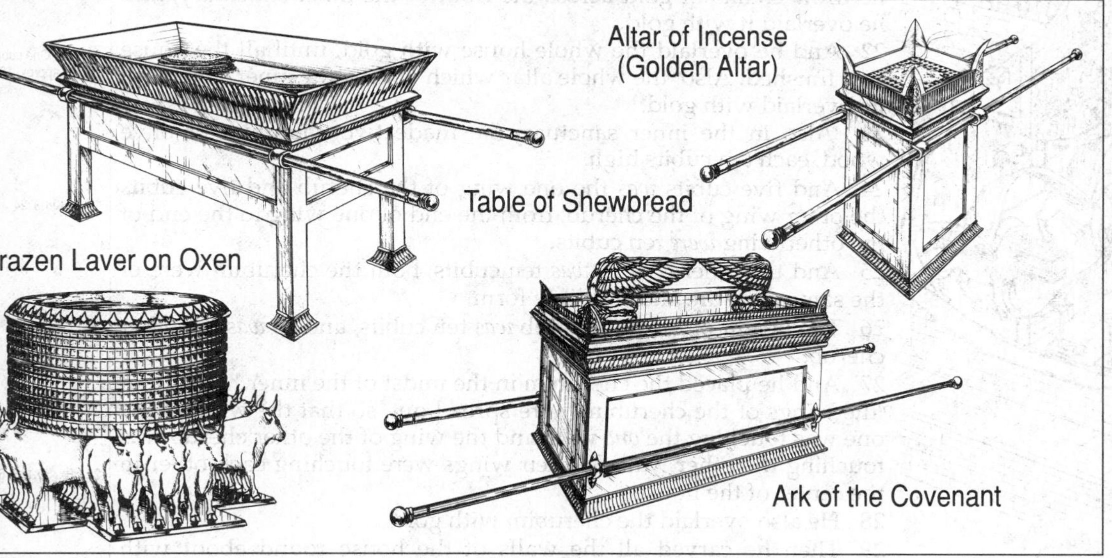

8 The doorway for the [1]lowest side chamber *was* on the right side
of the house; and they would go up by winding stairs to the middle
story, and from the middle to the third.

9 So [a]he built the house and finished it; and he covered the house
with beams and [1]planks of cedar.

10 He also built the stories against the whole house, each five [1]cu-
bits high; and they [2]were fastened to the house with timbers of cedar.

11 Now the word of the LORD came to Solomon saying,

12 "*Concerning* this house which you are building, [a]if you will walk
in My statutes and execute My ordinances and keep all My com-
mandments by walking in them, then I will carry out My word with
you which I spoke to David your father.

8 [1]So with Gr. and ...ions; M.T., *middle*

9 [1]Lit., *rows* [a]1 Kin. 6:14, 38

10 [1]I.e., One cubit ...als approx. 18 in. [2]Lit., *took hold*

12 [a]2 Sam. 7:5-16; 1 Kin. 9:4

13 "And [a]I will dwell among the sons of Israel, and [b]will not forsake
My people Israel."
14 [a]So Solomon built the house and finished it.
15 Then he [a]built the walls of the house on the inside with boards of
cedar; from the floor of the house to the [1]ceiling he overlaid *the walls*
on the inside with wood, and he overlaid the floor of the house with
boards of cypress.
16 [a]And he built twenty cubits on the rear part of the house with
boards of cedar from the floor to the [1]ceiling; he built *them* for it on
the inside as an inner sanctuary, *even* as [b]the most holy place.
17 And the house, that is, the nave in front of *the inner sanctuary,*
was forty [1]cubits *long.*
18 And there was cedar on the house within, carved *in the shape* of
[a]gourds and open flowers; all was cedar, there was no stone seen.
19 Then he prepared an inner sanctuary within the house in order
to place there the ark of the covenant of the LORD.
20 And [1]the inner sanctuary *was* twenty cubits in length, twenty
cubits in width, and twenty cubits in height, and he overlaid it with
pure gold. He also overlaid the altar with cedar.

21 So Solomon overlaid the inside of the house with pure gold. And
he drew chains of gold across the front of the inner sanctuary; and
he overlaid it with gold.
22 And he overlaid the whole house with gold, until all the house
was finished. Also [a]the whole altar which was by the inner sanctuary
he overlaid with gold.
23 [a]Also in the inner sanctuary he made two cherubim of olive
wood, each ten cubits high.
24 And five cubits *was* the one wing of the cherub and five cubits
the other wing of the cherub; from the end of one wing to the end of
the other wing *were* ten cubits.
25 And the other cherub *was* ten cubits; both the cherubim were of
the same measure and the same form.
26 The height of the one cherub *was* ten cubits, and so *was* the other
cherub.
27 And he placed the cherubim in the midst of the inner house, and
[a]the wings of the cherubim were spread out, so that the wing of the
one was touching the *one* wall, and the wing of the other cherub was
touching the other wall. So their wings were touching each other in
the center of the house.
28 He also overlaid the cherubim with gold.
29 Then he carved all the walls of the house round about with
carved engravings of cherubim, palm trees, and open flowers, inner
and outer *sanctuaries.*
30 And he overlaid the floor of the house with gold, inner and
outer *sanctuaries.*
31 And for the entrance of the inner sanctuary he made doors of
olive wood, the lintel *and* five-sided doorposts.
32 So *he made* two doors of olive wood, and he carved on them
carvings of cherubim, palm trees, and open flowers, and overlaid
them with gold; and he spread the gold on the cherubim and on the
palm trees.
33 So also he made for the entrance of the nave four-sided door-
posts of olive wood
34 and [a]two doors of cypress wood; the two leaves of the one door

13 [a]Ex. 25:8; Lev. 26:11 [b]D Josh. 1:5; He
14 [a]1 Kin. 6:9
15 [1]Lit., *walls* [a]1 Kin. 7:7
16 [1]Lit., *walls* 3:8 [b]Ex. 26:33, 16:2; 1 Kin. 8:6
17 [1]I.e., One cu equals approx.
18 [a]1 Kin. 7:24
20 [1]Lit., *before*
22 [a]Ex. 30:1, 3,
23 [a]Ex. 37:7-9; 2 3:10-12
27 [a]Ex. 25:20; 37 1 Kin. 8:7
34 [a]Ezek. 41:23-2

turned on pivots, and the two [1]leaves of the other door turned on pivots.
35 And he carved *on it* cherubim, palm trees, and open flowers; and he overlaid *them* with gold evenly applied on the engraved work.
36 And [a]he built the inner court with three rows of cut stone and a row of cedar beams.
37 [a]In the fourth year the foundation of the house of the LORD was laid, in the month of Ziv.
38 And in the eleventh year, in the month of Bul, which is the eighth month, the house was finished throughout all its parts and according to all its plans. So he was seven years in building it.

Chapter 7

7 Now [a]Solomon was building his own house thirteen years, and he finished all his house.
2 And [a]he built the house of the forest of Lebanon; its length was
100 [1]cubits and its width 50 cubits and its height 30 cubits, on four rows of cedar pillars with cedar beams on the pillars.
3 And it was paneled with cedar above the side chambers which were on the 45 pillars, 15 in each row.
4 And *there were artistic window* frames in three rows, and window was opposite window in three ranks.
5 And all the doorways and doorposts *had* squared *artistic* frames, and window was opposite window in three ranks.
6 Then he made [a]the hall of pillars; its length was 50 cubits and its width 30 cubits, and a porch *was* in front of them and pillars and a [b]threshold in front of them.
7 And he made the hall of the [a]throne where he was to judge, the hall of judgment, and [b]it was paneled with cedar from floor to floor.
8 And his house where he was to live, the other court inward from the hall, was of the same workmanship. [a]He also made a house like this hall for Pharaoh's daughter, [b]whom Solomon had married.
9 All these were of costly stones, of stone cut according to measure, sawed with saws, inside and outside; even from the foundation to the coping, and so on the outside to the great court.
10 And the foundation was of costly stones, *even* large stones, stones of ten cubits and stones of eight cubits.
11 And above were costly stones, stone cut according to measure, and cedar.
12 So [a]the great court all around *had* three rows of cut stone and a row of cedar beams even as the inner court of the house of the LORD, and [b]the porch of the house.
13 Now [a]King Solomon sent and brought Hiram from Tyre.
14 [a]He was a widow's son from the tribe of Naphtali, and his father was a man of Tyre, a worker in bronze; and [b]he was filled with wisdom and understanding and skill for doing any work in bronze. So he came to King Solomon and [c]performed all his work.
15 And he fashioned [a]the two pillars of bronze; [b]eighteen cubits was the height of one pillar, and a line of twelve cubits [1]measured the circumference of both.
16 He also made two capitals of molten bronze to set on the tops of the pillars; the height of the one capital was five [1]cubits and the height of the other capital was five cubits.
17 *There were* nets of network and twisted threads of chainwork for

ith Gr.; M.T., *curtains*

Kin. 7:12; Jer. 36:10

37 [a]1 Kin. 6:1

Kin. 3:1; 9:10; 2 Chr. 8:1

[1]I.e., One cubit approx. 18 in. :17, 21; 2 Chr. 9:16

n. 7:12 [b]Ezek. 41:25, 26

Ps. 122:5; Prov. [b]1 Kin. 6:15, 16

Kin. 9:24; 2 Chr. 8:11 [b]1 Kin. 3:1

Kin. 6:36 [b]1 Kin. 7:6

hr. 2:13, 14; 4:11

[a]2 Chr. 2:14 [b]Ex. :3; 31:3-5; 35:31; 1 [c]2 Chr. 4:11-16

[1]Lit., *went around ther pillar* [a]2 Kin. 2 Chr. 3:15; 4:12; 52:21 [b]1 Kin. 7:41

6 [1]I.e., One cubit uals approx. 18 in.

the capitals which were on the top of the pillars; seven for the one
capital and seven for the other capital.
18 So he made the pillars, and two rows around on the one network
to cover the capitals which were on the top of the pomegranates; and
so he did for the other capital.
19 And the capitals which *were* on the top of the pillars in the porch
were of lily design, four cubits.
20 And *there were* capitals on the two pillars, even above *and* close
to the [1]rounded projection which was beside the network; and [a]the
pomegranates *numbered* two hundred in rows around [2]both capitals.
21 [a]Thus he set up the pillars at the [b]porch of the nave; and he set
up the right pillar and named it [1]Jachin, and he set up the left pillar
and named it [2]Boaz.
22 And on the top of the pillars was lily design. So the work of the
pillars was finished.
23 [a]Now he made the sea of [b]cast *metal* ten cubits from brim to brim,
circular in form, and its height was five cubits, and [1]thirty cubits in
circumference.
24 And under its brim [a]gourds went around encircling it ten to a
cubit, [b]completely surrounding the sea; the gourds were in two rows,
cast [1]with the rest.

25 [a]It stood on twelve oxen, three facing north, three facing west,
three facing south, and three facing east; and the sea *was set* on top of
them, and all their rear parts *turned* inward.
26 And it was a handbreadth thick, and its brim was made like the
brim of a cup, *as* a lily blossom; it could hold two thousand baths.
27 Then [a]he made the ten stands of bronze; the length of each stand
was four cubits and its width four cubits and its height three cubits.
28 And this was the design of the stands: they had borders, even
borders between the [1]frames,
29 and on the borders which were between the [1]frames *were* lions,
oxen and cherubim; and on the [1]frames there *was* a pedestal above,
and beneath the lions and oxen *were* wreaths of hanging work.
30 Now each stand had four bronze wheels with bronze axles, and
its four feet had supports; beneath the basin *were* cast supports with
wreaths at each side.
31 And its opening inside the crown at the top *was* a cubit, and its
opening *was* round like the design of a pedestal, a cubit and a half;
and also on its opening *there were* engravings, and their borders were
square, not round.
32 And the four wheels *were* underneath the borders, and the axles
of the wheels *were* on the stand. And the height of a wheel *was* a
cubit and a half.

33 And the workmanship of the wheels *was* like the workmanship
of a chariot wheel. Their axles, their rims, their spokes, and their
hubs *were* all cast.
34 Now *there were* four supports at the four corners of each stand;
its supports *were* part of the stand itself.
35 And on the top of the stand *there was* a circular form half a [1]cubit
high, and on the top of the stand its [2]stays and its borders *were* part
of it.
36 And he engraved on the plates of its stays and on its borders,
cherubim, lions and palm trees, according to the clear space on each,
with wreaths *all* around.

20 [1]Lit., *belly* ... *the other capi*... 7:42; 2 Chr. 3... Jer. 52:23

21 [1]I.e., he sh... establish [2]I.e. ... strength [a]2 Ch... [b]1 Kin. 6:3

23 [1]Lit., *a line* ... *cubits went ar*... [a]2 Chr. 4:2 [b]2 ... 16:17; 25:13

24 [1]Lit., *in its c*... [a]1 Kin. 6:18 [b]2 ...

25 [a]2 Chr. 4:4, ... 52:20

27 [a]1 Kin. 7:38; ... 25:13; 2 Chr. 4:1...

28 [1]Or, *crossbar*...

29 [1]Or, *crossbars*

35 [1]I.e., One cubit ... equals approx. 18 ... [2]Lit., *hands*

37 [a]He made the ten stands like this: all of them had one casting,
one measure and one form.
38 [a]And he made ten basins of bronze, one basin held forty baths;
each basin *was* four cubits, *and* on each of the ten stands *was* one
basin.
39 Then he set the stands, five on the right side of the house and
five on the left side of the house; and he set the sea *of cast metal* on
the right side of the house eastward toward the south.
40 Now Hiram made the basins and the shovels and the bowls. So
Hiram finished doing all the work which he performed for King
Solomon *in* the house of the LORD:
41 the two pillars and the *two* bowls of the capitals which *were* on
the top of the [a]two pillars, and the two networks to cover the two
bowls of the capitals which *were* on the top of the pillars;
42 and the [a]four hundred pomegranates for the two networks, two
rows of pomegranates for each network to cover the two bowls of
the capitals which *were* on the tops of the pillars;
43 and the ten stands with the ten basins on the stands;
44 and [a]the one sea and the twelve oxen under the sea;
45 and [a]the pails and the shovels and the bowls; even all these
utensils which Hiram made for King Solomon *in* the house of the
LORD *were* of polished bronze.
46 [a]In the plain of the Jordan the king cast them, in the clay ground
between [b]Succoth and [c]Zarethan.
47 And Solomon left all the utensils *unweighed,* because *they were*
too many; [a]the weight of the bronze could not be ascertained.
48 And Solomon made all the furniture which *was in* the house of
the LORD: [a]the golden altar and the golden table on which *was* the
[b]bread of the Presence;
49 and the lampstands, five on the right side and five on the left, in
front of the inner sanctuary, of pure gold; and [a]the flowers and the
lamps and the tongs, of gold;
50 and the cups and the snuffers and the bowls and the spoons and
the [a]firepans, of pure gold; and the hinges both for the doors of the
inner house, the most holy place, *and* for the doors of the house, *that
is,* of the nave, of gold.
51 [a]Thus all the work that King Solomon performed *in* the house of
the LORD was finished. And [b]Solomon brought in the things dedi-
cated by his father David, the silver and the gold and the utensils,
and he put them in the treasuries of the house of the LORD.

Chapter 8

8 [a]Then Solomon assembled the elders of Israel and all [b]the heads
of the tribes, the leaders of the fathers' *households* of the sons of
Israel, to King Solomon in Jerusalem, [c]to bring up the ark of the
covenant of the LORD from [d]the city of David, which is Zion.
2 And all the men of Israel assembled themselves to King Solomon
at [a]the feast, in the month Ethanim, which is the seventh month.
3 Then all the elders of Israel came, and [a]the priests took up the
ark.
4 And they brought up the ark of the LORD and [a]the tent of meet-
ing and all the holy utensils, which were in the tent, and the priests
and the Levites brought them up.
5 And King Solomon and all the congregation of Israel, who were

[a]2 Chr. 4:14
18; 2 Chr. 4:6
Kin. 7:17, 18
2 [a]1 Kin. 7:20
1 Kin. 7:23, 25
:3; 2 Chr. 4:16
hr. 4:17 [b]Gen.
7; Josh. 13:27
[c]Josh. 3:16
[a]1 Chr. 22:3, 14
48 [a]Ex. 30:1-3;
0-29; 2 Chr. 4:8
[b]Ex. 25:30
9 [a]Ex. 25:31-38
[a]Ex. 27:3; 2 Kin.
25:15
Chr. 5:1 [b]2 Sam.
11; 1 Chr. 18:11;
2 Chr. 5:1
1 [a]2 Chr. 5:2-10
1:4; 7:2 [c]2 Sam.
6:12-17; 1 Chr.
5-29 [d]2 Sam. 5:7
Lev. 23:34; 1 Kin.
:65; 2 Chr. 7:8-10
[a]Num. 7:9; Deut.
31:9; Josh. 3:3, 6
Kin. 3:4; 2 Chr. 1:3

See the illustration of Solomon's temple on page I-20.

assembled to him, [a]were with him before the ark, sacrificing [1]so
many sheep and oxen they could not be counted or numbered.
6 Then [a]the priests brought the ark of the covenant of the LORD [b]to
its place, into the inner sanctuary of the house, to the most holy
place, [c]under the wings of the cherubim.
7 For the cherubim spread *their* wings over the place of the ark,
and the cherubim made a covering over the ark and its poles from
above.
8 But [a]the poles were so long that the ends of the poles could be
seen from the holy place before the inner sanctuary, but they could
not be seen outside; they are there to this day.
9 [a]There was nothing in the ark except the two tablets of stone
which Moses put there at Horeb, where [b]the LORD made a covenant
with the sons of Israel, when they came out of the land of Egypt.
10 And it came about when the priests came from the holy place,
that [a]the cloud filled the house of the LORD,
11 so that the priests could not stand to minister because of the
cloud, for the glory of the LORD filled the house of the LORD.
12 [a]Then Solomon said,
"The LORD has said that [b]He would dwell in the thick cloud.
13 "[a]I have surely built Thee a lofty house,
[b]A place for Thy dwelling forever."
14 Then the king [1]faced about and [a]blessed all the assembly of Isra-
el, while all the assembly of Israel was standing.
15 And he said, "[a]Blessed be the LORD, the God of Israel, [b]who
spoke with His mouth to my father David and has fulfilled *it* with
His hand, saying,
16 '[a]Since the day that I brought My people Israel from Egypt, I did
not choose a city out of all the tribes of Israel *in which* to build a
house that [b]My name might be there, but [c]I chose David to be over
My people Israel.'
17 "[a]Now it was [1]in the heart of my father David to build a house for
the name of the LORD, the God of Israel.
18 "But the LORD said to my father David, 'Because it was [1]in your
heart to build a house for My name, you did well that it was [1]in your
heart.
19 '[a]Nevertheless you shall not build the house, but your son who
[1]shall be born to you, he shall build the house for My name.'
20 "Now the LORD has fulfilled His word which He spoke; for [a]I have
risen in place of my father David and sit on the throne of Israel, as
the LORD [1]promised, and have built the house for the name of the
LORD, the God of Israel.
21 "And there I have set a place for the ark, [a]in which is the covenant
of the LORD, which He made with our fathers when He brought them
from the land of Egypt."
22 Then [a]Solomon stood before the altar of the LORD in the presence
of all the assembly of Israel and [b]spread out his hands toward
heaven.
23 And he said, "O LORD, the God of Israel, [a]there is no God like
Thee in heaven above or on earth beneath, [b]who art keeping cove-
nant and *showing* lovingkindness to Thy servants who walk before
Thee with all their heart,
24 who hast kept with Thy servant, my father David, that which

5 [1]Lit., *sheep . . . numbered multitude* [a]2 S 2 Chr. 1:6
6 [a]1 Kin. 8:3 6:19 [c]1 Kin. 6
8 [a]Ex. 25:13-
9 [a]Ex. 25:16, 10:2-5; Heb. 9 24:7, 8; 40:20; 4:13
10 [a]Ex. 40:34, 2 Chr. 7:1, 2
12 [a]2 Chr. 6:1 16:2; Ps. 18:11
13 [a]2 Sam. 7:1 15:17; Ps. 132:
14 [1]Lit., *turned about* [a]2 Sam. 1 Kin. 8:55
15 [a]1 Chr. 29:1 Neh. 9:5; Luke [b]2 Sam. 7:12, 1 22:10
16 [a]2 Sam. 7:4, 1 Chr. 17:3-10; 6:5 [b]Deut. 12:5, [c]1 Sam. 16:1; 2
17 [1]Lit., *with* [a]2 7:2, 3; 1 Chr. 17.
18 [1]Lit., *with*
19 [1]Lit., *is to co from your loins* 7:5, 12, 13; 1 Kin 1 Chr. 17:11, 12;
20 [1]Lit., *spoke* [a] 28:5, 6
21 [a]Deut. 31:26; 8:9
22 [a]1 Kin. 8:54; 2 6:12 [b]Ex. 9:33; E
23 [a]1 Sam. 2:2; 2 7:22 [b]Deut. 7:9; N 1:5; 9:32; Dan. 9:4

Thou hast [1]promised him; indeed, Thou hast spoken with Thy
mouth and hast fulfilled it with Thy hand as it is this day.
25 "Now therefore, O LORD, the God of Israel, keep with Thy servant
David my father that which Thou hast [1]promised him, saying, '[2a]You
shall not lack a man to sit on the throne of Israel, if only your sons
take heed to their way to walk before Me as you have walked.'
26 "Now therefore, O God of Israel, let Thy word, I pray Thee, be
confirmed [a]which Thou hast spoken to Thy servant, my father
David.
27 "But will God indeed dwell on the earth? Behold, [a]heaven and the
[1]highest heaven cannot contain Thee, how much less this house
which I have built!
28 "Yet have regard to the [a]prayer of Thy servant and to his supplica-
tion, O LORD my God, to listen to the cry and to the prayer which
Thy servant prays before Thee today;
29 [a]that Thine eyes may be open toward this house night and day,
toward [b]the place of which Thou hast said, 'My name shall be there,'
to listen to the prayer which Thy servant shall pray toward this
place.
30 "And [a]listen to the supplication of Thy servant and of Thy people
Israel, [b]when they pray toward this place; hear Thou in heaven Thy
dwelling place; hear and [c]forgive.
31 "[a]If a man sins against his neighbor and is made to take an oath,
and he comes *and* takes an oath before Thine altar in this house,
32 then hear Thou in heaven and act and judge Thy servants, [a]con-
demning the wicked by bringing his way on his own head and
justifying the righteous by giving him according to his right-
eousness.
33 "[a]When Thy people Israel are [1]defeated before an enemy, because
they have sinned against Thee, [b]if they turn to Thee again and con-
fess Thy name and pray and make supplication to Thee in this
house,
34 then hear Thou in heaven, and forgive the sin of Thy people
Israel, and bring them back to the land which Thou didst give to
their fathers.
35 "[a]When the heavens are shut up and there is no rain, because they
have sinned against Thee, and they pray toward this place and con-
fess Thy name and turn from their sin when Thou dost afflict them,
36 then hear Thou in heaven and forgive the sin of Thy servants
and of Thy people Israel, [a]indeed, teach them the good way in which
they should walk. And [b]send rain on Thy land, which Thou hast
given Thy people for an inheritance.
37 "[a]If there is famine in the land, if there is pestilence, if there is
blight *or* mildew, locust *or* grasshopper, if their enemy besieges them
in the land of their [1]cities, whatever plague, whatever sickness
there is,
38 whatever prayer or supplication is made by any man *or* by all
Thy people Israel, [1]each knowing the [2]affliction of his own heart, and
spreading his [3]hands toward this house;
39 then hear Thou in heaven Thy dwelling place, and forgive and
act and render to each according to all his ways, [a]whose heart Thou
knowest, for [b]Thou alone dost know the hearts of all the sons of men,
40 that they may [1]fear Thee all the days that they live [2]in the land
which Thou hast given to our fathers.

[1]Lit., *spoken to*
poken to [2]Lit., *shall not be cut* *ou a man from Me.* [a]1 Kin. 2:4
[a]2 Sam. 7:25
[1]Lit., *heaven of* *ns* [a]2 Chr. 2:6; :7-16; Is. 66:1; 3:24; Acts 7:49
28 [a]Phil. 4:6
Chr. 7:15; Neh. 6 [b]Deut. 12:11
Neh. 1:6 [b]Dan. Ex. 34:6, 7; Ps. an. 9:9; 1 John 1:9
31 [a]Ex. 22:8-11
32 [a]Deut. 25:1
., *smitten* [a]Lev. 25; Deut. 28:25, [b]Lev. 26:40-42
ev. 26:19; Deut. :16, 17; 2 Sam. 24:10-13
Sam. 12:23; Ps. ; 25:4, 5; 27:11; 11; 119:133; Jer. :16 [b]1 Kin. 18:1, 41-45; Jer. 14:22
[1]Lit., *gates* [a]Lev. 16, 25, 26; Deut. 28:21-23, 38-42
, *who shall know* Lit., *plague* [3]Lit., *palms*
[a]1 Sam. 2:3; 16:7 r. 28:9; Ps. 11:4; 7:10; John 2:24, 25; Acts 1:24
r, *revere* [2]Lit., *on* *e face of the land*

41 "Also concerning the foreigner who is not of Thy people Israel,
when he comes from a far country for Thy name's sake
42 (for they will hear of Thy great name [a]and Thy mighty hand, and
of Thine outstretched arm); when he comes and prays toward this
house,
43 hear Thou in heaven Thy dwelling place, and do according to all
for which the foreigner calls to Thee, in order [a]that all the peoples of
the earth may know Thy name, to [1]fear Thee, as *do* Thy people Israel,
and that they may know that [2]this house which I have built is called
by Thy name.
44 "When Thy people go out to battle against [1]their enemy, by what-
ever way Thou shalt send them, and [a]they pray to the LORD [2]toward
the city which Thou hast chosen and the house which I have built for
Thy name,
45 then hear in heaven their prayer and their supplication, and
maintain their [1]cause.
46 "When they sin against Thee (for [a]there is no man who does not
sin) and Thou art angry with them and dost deliver them to an
enemy, so that [1]they take them away captive [b]to the land of the
enemy, far off or near;
47 [a]if they [1]take thought in the land where they have been taken
captive, and repent and make supplication to Thee in the land of
those who have taken them captive, saying, '[b]We have sinned and
have committed iniquity, we have acted wickedly';
48 [a]if they return to Thee with all their heart and with all their soul
in the land of their enemies who have taken them captive, and [b]pray
to Thee toward their land which Thou hast given to their fathers, the
city which Thou hast chosen, and the house which I have built for
Thy name;
49 then hear their prayer and their supplication in heaven Thy
dwelling place, and maintain their [1]cause,
50 and forgive Thy people who have sinned against Thee and all
their transgressions which they have transgressed against Thee, and
[a]make them *objects of* compassion before those who have taken them
captive, that they may have compassion on them
51 ([a]for they are Thy people and Thine inheritance which Thou hast
brought forth from Egypt, [b]from the midst of the iron furnace),
52 [a]that Thine eyes may be open to the supplication of Thy servant
and to the supplication of Thy people Israel, to listen to them when-
ever they call to Thee.
53 "For Thou hast separated them from all the peoples of the earth
as Thine inheritance, [a]as Thou didst speak through Moses Thy ser-
vant, when Thou didst bring our fathers forth from Egypt, O Lord
[1]GOD."
54 [a]And it came about that when Solomon had finished praying this
entire prayer and supplication to the LORD, [b]he arose from before the
altar of the LORD, from kneeling on his knees with his [1]hands spread
toward heaven.
55 And he stood and [a]blessed all the assembly of Israel with a loud
voice, saying,
56 "Blessed be the LORD, who has given rest to His people Israel,
[a]according to all that He [1]promised; [b]not one word has [2]failed of all
His good [3]promise, which He [1]promised through Moses His servant.

42 [a]Ex. 13:3; D
43 [1]Or, *revere* *Thy name is ca* *this house whic* *built* [a]Josh. 4:2 1 Sam. 17:46; I
44 [1]Lit., *his* [2]Li *way of* [a]2 Chr.
45 [1]Lit., *right or*
46 [1]Lit., *their ca* *take them capti* 130:3, 4; 143:2; 20:9; Eccl. 7:20 3:23; 1 John 1:8 [b]Lev. 26:34-39; 17:6, 18; 25:21
47 [1]Lit., *return* *heart* [a]Lev. 26:4 Neh. 9:2 [b]Ezra Neh. 1:6; Ps. 10 Dan. 9:5
48 [a]Deut. 4:29; 7:3, 4; Neh. 1:9 6:10; Jon. 2:4
49 [1]Lit., *judgme*
50 [a]2 Chr. 30:9; 106:46; Acts 7:1
51 [a]Ex. 32:11, 1 9:26-29 [b]Deut. 4 Jer. 11:4
52 [a]1 Kin. 8:29
53 [1]Heb., *YHWH* usually rendered [a]Ex. 19:5, 6; Deu 9:26-29
54 [1]Lit., *palms* [a] 7:1 [b]2 Chr. 6:13
55 [a]Num. 6:23-2 2 Sam. 6:18; 1 Ki
56 [1]Lit., *spoke* [2]L *fallen* [3]Lit., *word* 12:10 [b]Josh. 21:4 23:14, 15

57 "May the LORD our God be with us, as He was with our fathers;
[a]may He not leave us or forsake us,
58 that [a]He may incline our hearts to Himself, to walk in all His
ways and to keep His commandments and His statutes and His
ordinances, which He commanded our fathers.
59 "And may these words of mine, with which I have made suppli-
cation before the LORD, be near to the LORD our God day and night,
that He may maintain the [1]cause of His servant and the [1]cause of His
people Israel, [2]as each day requires,
60 so [a]that all the peoples of the earth may know that [b]the LORD is
God; there is no one else.
61 "[a]Let your heart therefore be [1]wholly devoted to the LORD our
God, to walk in His statutes and to keep His commandments, as at
this day."
62 [a]Now the king and all Israel with him [b]offered sacrifice before
the LORD.
63 And Solomon offered for the sacrifice of peace offerings, which
he offered to the LORD, 22,000 oxen and 120,000 sheep. [a]So the king
and all the sons of Israel dedicated the house of the LORD.
64 On the same day the king consecrated the middle of the court
that *was* before the house of the LORD, because there he [1]offered the
burnt offering and the grain offering and the fat of the peace offer-
ings; for [a]the bronze altar that *was* before the LORD *was* too small to
hold the burnt offering and the grain offering and the fat of the
peace offerings.
65 So [a]Solomon observed the feast at that time, and all Israel with
him, a great assembly [b]from the entrance of Hamath [c]to the brook of
Egypt, before the LORD our God, for seven days and seven *more* days,
even fourteen days.
66 On the eighth day he sent the people away and they blessed the
king. Then they went to their tents joyful and glad of heart for all the
goodness that the LORD had [1]shown to David His servant and to
Israel His people.

Chapter 9

9 [a]Now it came about when Solomon had finished building the
house of the LORD, and [b]the king's house, and [c]all [1]that Solomon
desired to do,
2 that [a]the LORD appeared to Solomon a second time, as He had
appeared to him at Gibeon.
3 And the LORD said to him, "[a]I have heard your prayer and your
supplication, which you have made before Me; I have consecrated
this house which you have built [b]by putting My name there forever,
and [c]My eyes and My heart will be there perpetually.
4 "And as for you, [a]if you will walk before Me as your father David
walked, in integrity of heart and uprightness, doing according to all
that I have commanded you *and* will keep My statutes and My or-
dinances,
5 then [a]I will establish the throne of your kingdom over Israel
forever, just as I [1]promised to your father David, saying, '[2]You shall
not lack a man on the throne of Israel.'
6 "[a]But if you or your sons shall indeed turn away from following
Me, and shall not keep My commandments and My statutes which I

Deut. 31:6, 17; 1 Sam. 12:22; :31; Heb. 13:5
s. 119:36; Jer. 31:33
udgment [2]Lit., *of a day in its day*
. 4:24; 1 Sam. in. 8:43; 2 Kin. 9 [b]Deut. 4:35; Kin. 18:39; Jer. 10:10-12
complete with t. 18:13; 1 Kin. 1:4; 2 Kin. 20:3
[a]2 Chr. 7:4-10 . 6:17-19; Ezra 6:16, 17
a 6:15-18; Neh. 12:27
, made [a]2 Chr. 4:1
[a]Lev. 23:34-42; 3:2 [b]Num. 34:8; 13:5; Judg. 3:3; in. 14:25 [c]Gen. Ex. 23:31; Num. 34:5; Josh. 13:3
66 [1]Lit., *done*
[1]Lit., *Solomon's re which he was ed to do* [a]2 Chr. 11 [b]1 Kin. 7:1, 2 [c]2 Chr. 8:6
[a]1 Kin. 3:5; 11:9; 2 Chr. 1:7
[a]2 Kin. 20:5; Ps. 7; 34:17 [b]1 Kin. 29 [c]Deut. 11:12; 2 Chr. 6:40
Kin. 3:6, 14; 11:4, ; 2 Kin. 20:3; Ps. 128:1
[1]Lit., *spoke* [2]Lit., *e shall not be cut off to you a man* . 7:12, 16; 1 Kin. :12; 1 Chr. 22:10
[a]2 Sam. 7:14-16; 28:9; Ps. 89:30ff.

have set before you and shall go and serve other gods and worship
them,
7 [a]then I will cut off Israel from the land which I have given them,
and [b]the house which I have consecrated for My name, I will [1]cast
out of My sight. So [c]Israel will become a proverb and a byword
among all peoples.
8 "And this house will become [1a]a heap of ruins; everyone who
passes by will be astonished and hiss and say, '[b]Why has the LORD
done thus to this land and to this house?'
9 "And they will say, '[a]Because they forsook the LORD their God,
who brought their fathers out of the land of Egypt, and adopted
other gods and worshiped them and served them, therefore the LORD
has brought all this adversity on them.' "
10 [a]And it came about [b]at the end of twenty years in which Solomon
had built the two houses, the house of the LORD and the king's house
11 (Hiram king of Tyre had supplied Solomon with cedar and
cypress timber and gold according to all his desire), then King
Solomon gave Hiram twenty cities in the land of Galilee.
12 So Hiram came out from Tyre to see the cities which Solomon
had given him, and they [1]did not please him.
13 And he said, "What are these cities which you have given me,
my brother?" So [1]they were called the land of [2a]Cabul to this day.
14 [a]And Hiram sent to the king 120 talents of gold.
15 Now this is the account of the forced labor which King Solomon
[a]levied to build the house of the LORD, his own house, the [1b]Millo, the
wall of Jerusalem, [c]Hazor, [d]Megiddo, and [e]Gezer.
16 *For* Pharaoh king of Egypt had gone up and captured Gezer, and
burned it with fire, and killed the [a]Canaanites who lived in the city,
and had [b]given it *as* a dowry to his daughter, Solomon's wife.
17 So Solomon rebuilt Gezer and the lower [a]Beth-horon
18 and [a]Baalath and Tamar in the wilderness, in the land *of Judah,*
19 and all the storage cities which Solomon had, even [a]the cities for
[1]his chariots and the cities for [1b]his horsemen, and [2c]all that it pleased
Solomon to build in Jerusalem, in Lebanon, and in all the land
[3]under his rule.
20 *As for* all the people who were left of the Amorites, the Hittites,
the Perizzites, the Hivites and the Jebusites, who were not of the
sons of Israel,
21 [a]their descendants who were left after them in the land [b]whom
the sons of Israel were unable to destroy utterly, [c]from them Solomon
levied [d]forced laborers, even to this day.
22 But Solomon [a]did not make slaves of the sons of Israel; for they
were men of war, his servants, his princes, his captains, his chariot
commanders, and his horsemen.
23 These *were* the [1a]chief officers who were over Solomon's work,
five hundred and fifty, [b]who ruled over the people doing the work.
24 As soon as [a]Pharaoh's daughter came up from the city of David
to her house which *Solomon* had built for her, [b]then he built the Millo.
25 Now [a]three times in a year Solomon offered burnt offerings and
peace offerings on the altar which he built to the LORD, burning
incense with them *on the altar* which *was* before the LORD. So he
finished the house.
26 King Solomon also built a [a]fleet of ships in [b]Ezion-geber, which is
near Eloth on the shore of the [1]Red Sea, in the land of Edom.

7 [1]Lit., *send* [a]L... 18:24-29; Deut. ... 2 Kin. 17:23 [b]J... 7:4-14 [c]Deut. 2... Ps. 44:14; Jer. 2...

8 [1]Heb., *high* ... 25:9; 2 Chr. 36:... [b]Deut. 29:24-26... 7:21; Jer. 22:8,...

9 [a]Deut. 29:25-... 2:10-13

10 [a]2 Chr. 8:1 ... 6:37, 38; 7:1; 9:...

12 [1]Lit., *were n... in his sight*

13 [1]Lit., *he calle...* [2]I.e., as good as nothing [a]Josh. 1...

14 [a]1 Kin. 9:11

15 [1]I.e., citadel ... 5:13 [b]2 Sam. 5:... 9:24 [c]Josh. 11:1... [d]Josh. 17:11 [e]Ju...

16 [a]Josh. 16:10 ... 3:1; 7:8

17 [a]Josh. 10:10;... 21:22; 2 Chr. 8:5

18 [a]Josh. 19:44

19 [1]Lit., *the* [2]Lit... *desire of Solomo... which he desired... build in Jerusaler... of* [a]1 Kin. 10:26;... 1:14 [b]1 Kin. 4:26 [c]1 Kin. 9:1

21 [a]Judg. 1:21-2... [b]Josh. 15:63; 17:... [c]Judg. 1:28, 35 ... 9:25, 26; Ezra 2:5...

22 [a]Lev. 25:39

23 [1]Or, *officers o... deputies* [a]2 Chr. ... [b]1 Kin. 5:16

24 [a]1 Kin. 3:1; 7:... [b]2 Sam. 5:9; 1 Kin... 11:27; 2 Chr. 32:5

25 [a]Ex. 23:14-17;... 16:16

26 [1]Lit., *Sea of R...* [a]1 Kin. 22:48 [b]Nu... 33:35; Deut. 2:8; ... 22:48

27 [a]And Hiram sent his servants with the fleet, sailors who knew
the sea, along with the servants of Solomon.
28 And they went to [a]Ophir, and took four hundred and twenty
talents of gold from there, and brought *it* to King Solomon.

Chapter 10

10 [a]Now when the [a]queen of [b]Sheba heard about the fame of
Solomon concerning the name of the LORD, she came [c]to test
him with difficult questions.
2 So she came to Jerusalem with a very large retinue, with camels
[a]carrying spices and very much gold and precious stones. When she
came to Solomon, she spoke with him about all that was in her heart.
3 And Solomon [1]answered all her questions; nothing was hidden
from the king which he did not [2]explain to her.
4 When the queen of Sheba perceived all the wisdom of Solomon,
the house that he had built,
5 the food of his table, the seating of his servants, the attendance of
his waiters and their attire, his cupbearers, and [1]his stairway by
which he went up to the house of the LORD, there was no more spirit
in her.
6 Then she said to the king, "It was a true report which I heard in
my own land about your words and your wisdom.
7 "Nevertheless I did not believe the [1]reports, until I came and my
eyes had seen it. And behold, the half was not told me. You exceed *in*
wisdom and prosperity the report which I heard.
8 "How [a]blessed are your men, how blessed are these your servants
who stand before you continually *and* hear your wisdom.
9 "[a]Blessed be the LORD your God who delighted in you to set you
on the throne of Israel; [b]because the LORD loved Israel forever, there-
fore He made you king, [c]to do justice and righteousness."
10 And [a]she gave the king a hundred and twenty talents of gold,
and a very great *amount* of spices and precious stones. Never again
did such abundance of spices come in as that which the queen of
Sheba gave King Solomon.
11 [a]And also the ships of Hiram, which brought gold from Ophir,
brought in from Ophir a very great *number of* almug trees and pre-
cious stones.
12 And [a]the king made of the almug trees supports for the house of
the LORD and for the king's house, also lyres and harps for the
singers; such almug trees have not come in *again,* nor have they been
seen to this day.
13 And King Solomon gave to the queen of Sheba all her desire
which she requested, besides what he gave her according to [1]his
royal bounty. Then she turned and went to her own land [2]together
with her servants.
14 [a]Now the weight of gold which came in to Solomon in one year
was 666 talents of gold,
15 besides *that* from the traders and the [1]wares of the merchants
and all the kings of the [a]Arabs and the governors of the country.
16 And [a]King Solomon made 200 large shields of beaten gold,
[1]using 600 *shekels of* gold on each large shield.
17 And *he made* [a]300 shields of beaten gold, [1]using three minas of
gold on each shield, and [b]the king put them in the house of the forest
of Lebanon.

[a]1 Kin. 5:6, 9; 10:11
[a]1 Chr. 29:4; 2 Chr. 8:18
1 [a]2 Chr. 9:1; Matt. 12:42; Luke 11:31 [b]Gen. 10:7, 28; Ps. 72:10, 15 [c]Judg. 14:12-14; Ps. 49:4
2 [a]1 Kin. 10:10
[1]Lit., *told her all her words* [2]Lit., *tell her*
…r, *his burnt offering which he offered*
7 [1]Lit., *words*
8 [a]Prov. 8:34
[a]1 Kin. 5:7 [b]1 Chr. 17:22; 2 Chr. 2:11 …am. 8:15; 23:3; Ps. 72:2
10 [a]1 Kin. 10:2
…Kin. 9:27, 28; Job 22:24
12 [a]2 Chr. 9:11
…3 [1]Lit., *the hand of Solomon* [2]Lit., *she and*
14 [a]2 Chr. 9:13-28
[1]Or, *traffic* [a]2 Chr. 9:14
…Lit., *he brought up* …n. 14:26-28; 2 Chr. 12:9, 10
…Lit., *he brought up* …14:26 [b]1 Kin. 7:2

18 Moreover, the king made a great throne of [a]ivory and overlaid it
with refined gold.
19 There *were* six steps to the throne and a round top to the throne
at its rear, and [1]arms [2]on each side of the seat, and two lions standing
beside the [1]arms.
20 And twelve lions were standing there on the six steps on the one
side and on the other; nothing like *it* was made for any other king-
dom.
21 And all King Solomon's drinking vessels *were* of gold, and all the
vessels of the house of the forest of Lebanon *were* of pure gold. None
was of silver; it was not considered [1]valuable in the days of
Solomon.
22 For [a]the king had at sea the ships of Tarshish with the ships of
Hiram; once every three years the ships of Tarshish came bringing
gold and silver, ivory and apes and peacocks.
23 [a]So King Solomon became greater than all the kings of the earth
in riches and in wisdom.
24 And all the earth was seeking the presence of Solomon, [a]to hear
his wisdom which God had put in his heart.
25 And [a]they brought every man his gift, articles of silver and gold,
garments, weapons, spices, horses, and mules, so much year by year.
26 [a]Now Solomon gathered chariots and horsemen; and he had
1,400 chariots and 12,000 horsemen, and he [1]stationed them in the
[b]chariot cities and with the king in Jerusalem.
27 [a]And the king made silver *as common* as stones in Jerusalem, and
he made cedars as plentiful as sycamore trees that are in the
[1]lowland.
28 [a]Also Solomon's import of horses was from Egypt and Kue, and
the king's merchants procured *them* from Kue for a price.
29 And a chariot [1]was imported from Egypt for 600 *shekels* of silver,
and a horse for 150; and [2]by the same means they exported them [a]to
all the kings of the Hittites and to the kings of the Arameans.

Chapter 11

11 Now [a]King Solomon loved many foreign women along with
the daughter of Pharaoh: Moabite, Ammonite, Edomite,
Sidonian, and Hittite women,
2 from the nations concerning which the LORD had said to the sons
of Israel, "[a]You shall not [1]associate with them, neither shall they
[1]associate with you, *for* they will surely turn your heart away after
their gods." Solomon held fast to these in love.
3 [a]And he had seven hundred wives, princesses, and three
hundred concubines, and his wives turned his heart away.
4 For it came about when Solomon was old, his wives turned his
heart away after other gods; and [a]his heart was not [1]wholly devoted
to the LORD his God, as the heart of David his father *had been*.
5 For Solomon went after [a]Ashtoreth the goddess of the Sidonians
and after [1b]Milcom the detestable idol of the Ammonites.
6 And Solomon did what was evil in the sight of the LORD, and did
not follow the LORD fully, as David his father *had done*.
7 Then Solomon built a high place for [a]Chemosh the detestable
idol of Moab, on the mountain which is [1]east of Jerusalem, and for
[b]Molech the detestable idol of the sons of Ammon.

18 [a]1 Kin. 10:22; 2 C 9:17; Ps. 45:8

19 [1]Lit., *hands* [2]Lit., *this side and on this the place of the seat*

21 [1]Lit., *anything*

22 [a]1 Kin. 9:26-28; 22:48; 2 Chr. 20:36

23 [a]1 Kin. 3:12, 13;

24 [a]1 Kin. 3:9, 12, 2

25 [a]Ps. 68:29

26 [1]So with ancient versions; Heb., *led* [a]1 Kin. 4:26; 2 Chr. 1:14-17; 9:25 [b]1 Kir 9:19

27 [1]Heb., *Shephela* [a]Deut. 17:17; 2 Chr.

28 [a]Deut. 17:16; 2 1:16; 9:28

29 [1]Lit., *came up a went out from* [2]Lit., *like manner by their hand* [a]2 Kin. 7:6, 7

11:1 [a]Deut. 17:17; 13:23-27

2 [1]Lit., *go among* 23:31-33; 34:12-16 Deut. 7:3

3 [a]2 Sam. 5:13-16

4 [1]Lit., *complete w* [a]1 Kin. 9:4

5 [1]In Jer. 49:1, 3, *Malcam* [a]Judg. 2:1 10:6; 1 Sam. 7:3, 4 [b]1 Kin. 11:7

7 [1]Lit., *before* [a]Nu 21:29; Judg. 11:24 2 Kin. 23:13 [b]Lev. 20:2-5; 2 Kin. 23:1 Acts 7:43

8 Thus also he did for all his foreign wives, who burned incense
and sacrificed to their gods.
9 Now [a]the LORD was angry with Solomon [b]because his heart was
turned away from the LORD, the God of Israel, [c]who had appeared to
him twice,
10 and [a]had commanded him concerning this thing, that he should
not go after other gods; but he did not observe what the LORD had
commanded.
11 So the LORD said to Solomon, "Because [1]you have done this, and
you have not kept My covenant and My statutes, which I have com-
manded you, [a]I will surely tear the kingdom from you, and will give
it to your servant.
12 "Nevertheless I will not do it in your days for the sake of your
father David, *but* I will tear it out of the hand of your son.
13 "However, [a]I will not tear away all the kingdom, *but* [b]I will give
one tribe to your son for the sake of My servant David and [c]for the
sake of Jerusalem which I have chosen."
14 Then the LORD raised up an adversary to Solomon, Hadad the
Edomite; he was of the [1]royal line in Edom.
15 For it came about, [a]when David was in Edom, and Joab the
commander of the army had gone up to bury the slain, and had
[b]struck down every male in Edom
16 (for Joab and all Israel stayed there six months, until he had cut
off every male in Edom),
17 that Hadad fled [1]to Egypt, he and certain Edomites of his
father's servants with him, while Hadad *was* a young boy.
18 And they arose from Midian and came to [a]Paran; and they took
men with them from Paran and came to Egypt, to Pharaoh king of
Egypt, who gave him a house and assigned him food and gave him
land.
19 Now Hadad found great favor [1]before Pharaoh, so that he gave
him in marriage the sister of his own wife, the sister of Tahpenes the
queen.
20 And the sister of Tahpenes bore his son Genubath, whom Tah-
penes weaned in Pharaoh's house; and Genubath was in Pharaoh's
house among the sons of Pharaoh.
21 But [a]when Hadad heard in Egypt that David slept with his
fathers, and that Joab the commander of the army was dead, Hadad
said to Pharaoh, "Send me away, that I may go to my own country."
22 Then Pharaoh said to him, "But what have you lacked with me,
that behold, you are seeking to go to your own country?" And he
answered, "Nothing; nevertheless you must surely [1]let me go."
23 [a]God also raised up *another* adversary to him, Rezon the son of
Eliada, who had fled from his lord [b]Hadadezer king of Zobah.
24 And he gathered men to himself and became leader of a
marauding band, [a]after David slew them of *Zobah;* and they went to
Damascus and stayed [1]there, and reigned in Damascus.
25 So he was an adversary to Israel all the days of Solomon, along
with the evil that Hadad *did;* and he abhorred Israel and reigned
over Aram.
26 Then [a]Jeroboam the son of Nebat, an Ephraimite of Zeredah,
Solomon's servant, whose mother's name was Zeruah, a widow,
[b]also [1]rebelled against the king.
27 Now this was the reason why he [1]rebelled against the king:

s. 90:7 [b]1 Kin. [c]1 Kin. 3:5; 9:2
in. 6:12; 9:6, 7
this is with you
m. 2:30; 1 Kin. 12:15, 16, 20; Kin. 17:15, 21
m. 7:15; 1 Chr. . 89:33 [b]1 Kin. ; 12:20 [c]1 Kin. 8:29
.it., *king's seed*
m. 8:14; 1 Chr. 3 [b]Deut. 20:13
[1]Lit., *to go into*
m. 10:12; Deut. 1:1
., *in the sight of*
21 [a]1 Kin. 2:10
, *send me away*
23 [a]1 Kin. 11:14 Sam. 8:3; 10:16
.it., *in it* [a]2 Sam. 10:8, 18
[1]Lit., *lifted up a* [a]1 Kin. 11:11, 28; ., 20; 2 Chr. 13:6 [b]2 Sam. 20:21
, *lifted up a hand*

INSIGHT

Religious Influences of Solomon's Wives

1. **The Gods of Egypt** (see page 91).
2. **Ashtoreth**—*Sidonian* (Canaanite) goddess of fertility, love, and war. Later she became the spouse of Baal (2 Kings 23:13).
3. **Milcom**—*Ammonite* god that means king. At the request of his pagan wives, Solomon built sanctuaries to Milcom on the Mount of Olives (2 Kings 23:13).
4. **Chemosh**—*god of Moab*—divine name meaning to "subdue." Solomon erected a sanctuary for Chemosh on a mountain east of Jerusalem (2 Kings 23:13; Jeremiah 48:7, 13, 46).
5. **Molech**—a pagan deity from Ammon to whom human sacrifices, usually children, were made. This practice was condemned by God (Leviticus 18:21; 20: 3-5; 2 Kings 23:10; Jeremiah 32:35). Compare with 2 Kings 17:31 and Jeremiah 7:31; 19:5.

For more information, look up these names in a Bible dictionary.

[a]Solomon built the [2]Millo, *and* closed up the breach of the city of his father David.

28 Now the man Jeroboam was a valiant warrior, and when [a]Solomon saw that the young man was [1]industrious, he appointed him over all the [2]forced labor of the house of Joseph.

29 And it came about at that time, when Jeroboam went out of Jerusalem, that [a]the prophet Ahijah the Shilonite found him on the road. Now [1]Ahijah had clothed himself with a new cloak; and both of them were alone in the field.

30 Then [a]Ahijah took hold of the new cloak which was on him, and tore it into twelve pieces.

31 And he said to Jeroboam, "Take for yourself ten pieces; for thus says the LORD, the God of Israel, 'Behold, [a]I will tear the kingdom out of the hand of Solomon and give you ten tribes

32 ([a]but he will have one tribe, for the sake of My servant David and for the sake of Jerusalem, [b]the city which I have chosen from all the tribes of Israel),

33 because they have forsaken Me, and [a]have worshiped Ashtoreth the goddess of the Sidonians, [b]Chemosh the god of Moab, and Milcom the god of the sons of Ammon; and they have not walked in My ways, doing what is right in My sight and *observing* My statutes and My ordinances, as his father David *did.*

34 'Nevertheless I will not take the whole kingdom out of his hand, but I will make him [1]ruler all the days of his life, for the sake of My servant David whom I chose, who observed My commandments and My statutes;

35 but [a]I will take the kingdom from his son's hand and give it to you, *even* ten tribes.

36 'But [a]to his son I will give one tribe, [b]that My servant David may have a lamp always before Me in Jerusalem, [a]the city where I have chosen for Myself to put My name.

37 'And I will take you, and you shall reign over whatever [1]you desire, and you shall be king over Israel.

38 'Then it will be, that if you listen to all that I command you and walk in My ways, and do what is right in My sight by observing My statutes and My commandments, as My servant David did, then [a]I will be with you and [b]build you an enduring house as I built for David, and I will give Israel to you.

39 'Thus I will afflict the [1]descendants of David for this, but not always.' "

40 Solomon sought therefore to put Jeroboam to death; but Jeroboam arose and fled to Egypt to [a]Shishak king of Egypt, and he was in Egypt until the death of Solomon.

41 [a]Now the rest of the acts of Solomon and whatever he did, and his wisdom, are they not written in the book of the acts of Solomon?

42 Thus [a]the time that Solomon reigned in Jerusalem over all Israel was forty years.

43 And Solomon [a]slept with his fathers and was buried in the city of his father David, and his son [b]Rehoboam reigned in his place.

Chapter 12

12 [a]Then Rehoboam went to Shechem, for all Israel had come to [b]Shechem to make him king.

2 Now it came about [a]when Jeroboam the son of Nebat heard *of it,*

27 [2]I.e., citad 9:15, 24
28 [1]Lit., *a doe* [2]Lit., *burden* [a] 22:29
29 [1]Lit., *he* [a]1 12:15; 14:2; 2
30 [a]1 Sam. 15
31 [a]1 Kin. 11:1
32 [a]1 Kin. 11:1 [b]1 Kin. 11:13; 1
33 [a]1 Sam. 7:3 11:5-8 [b]Num. 2 Jer. 48:7, 13
34 [1]Or, *prince*
35 [a]1 Kin. 11:12 12:16, 17
36 [a]1 Kin. 11:13 15:4; 2 Kin. 8:19 132:17
37 [1]Lit., *your so* *desires*
38 [a]Deut. 31:8; 1:5 [b]2 Sam. 7:1
39 [1]Lit., *seed*
40 [a]1 Kin. 14:25 12:2-9
41 [a]2 Chr. 9:29
42 [a]2 Chr. 9:30
43 [a]1 Kin. 2:10; 2 9:31 [b]1 Kin. 14:2 Matt. 1:7
12:1 [a]2 Chr. 10:1 [b]Judg. 9:6
2 [a]1 Kin. 11:26, 4

that [1]he was living in Egypt (for he was yet in Egypt, where he had
fled from the presence of King Solomon).
3 Then they sent and called him, and Jeroboam and all the assemb-
ly of Israel came and spoke to Rehoboam, saying,
4 "[a]Your father made our yoke hard; now therefore lighten the hard
service of your father and his heavy yoke which he put on us, and
we will serve you."
5 Then he said to them, "[a]Depart [1]for three days, then return to
me." So the people departed.
6 And King Rehoboam [a]consulted with the elders who had [1]served
his father Solomon while he was still alive, saying, "How do you
counsel *me* to answer this people?"
7 Then they spoke to him, saying, "[a]If you will be a servant to this
people today, will serve them, [1]grant them their petition, and speak
good words to them, then they will be your servants forever."
8 But he forsook the counsel of the elders which they had given
him, and consulted with the young men who grew up with him [1]and
served him.
9 So he said to them, "What counsel do you give that we may
answer this people who have spoken to me, saying, 'Lighten the
yoke which your father put on us'?"
10 And the young men who grew up with him spoke to him,
saying, "Thus you shall say to this people who spoke to you, saying,
'Your father made our yoke heavy, now you make it lighter for us!'
But you shall speak to them, 'My little finger is thicker than my
father's loins!
11 'Whereas my father loaded you with a heavy yoke, I will add to
your yoke; my father disciplined you with whips, but I will dis-
cipline you with scorpions.' "
12 Then Jeroboam and all the people came to Rehoboam on the
third day as the king had [1]directed, saying, "[a]Return to me on the
third day."
13 And the king answered the people harshly, for he forsook the
advice of the elders which they had [1]given him,
14 and he spoke to them according to the advice of the young men,
saying, "[a]My father made your yoke heavy, but I will add to your
yoke; my father disciplined you with whips, but I will discipline you
with scorpions."
15 So the king did not listen to the people; [a]for it was a turn *of events*
from the LORD, [b]that He might establish His word, which the LORD
spoke through Ahijah the Shilonite to Jeroboam the son of Nebat.
16 When all Israel *saw* that the king did not listen to them, the
people answered the king, saying,

> "What portion do we have in David?
> *We have* no inheritance in the son of Jesse;
> [a]To your tents, O Israel!
> Now look after your own house, David!"

So Israel departed to their tents.
17 But [a]as for the sons of Israel who lived in the cities of Judah,
Rehoboam reigned over them.
18 Then King Rehoboam sent [a]Adoram, who was over the forced
labor, and all Israel stoned him [1]to death. And King Rehoboam made
haste to mount his chariot to flee to Jerusalem.

2 [1]Lit., *Jeroboam*
4 [a]1 Sam. 8:11-18; Kin. 4:7, 21-25; 9:15
Lit., *yet three* [a]1 Kin. 12:12
6 [1]Lit., *stood before* in. 4:1-6; Job 12:12; 32:7
7 [1]Lit., *answer them* Chr. 10:7; Prov. 15:1
it., *who stood before*
[1]Lit., *spoken* [a]1 Kin. 12:5
13 [1]Lit., *advised*
[a]Ex. 1:13, 14; 5:5-9, 16-18
[a]Deut. 2:30; Judg. 14:4; 1 Kin. 12:24; 2 Chr. 10:15 [b]1 Kin. 11:11, 31
16 [a]2 Sam. 20:1
7 [a]1 Kin. 11:13, 36
it., *with stones that* ied [a]2 Sam. 20:24; 1 Kin. 4:6; 5:14

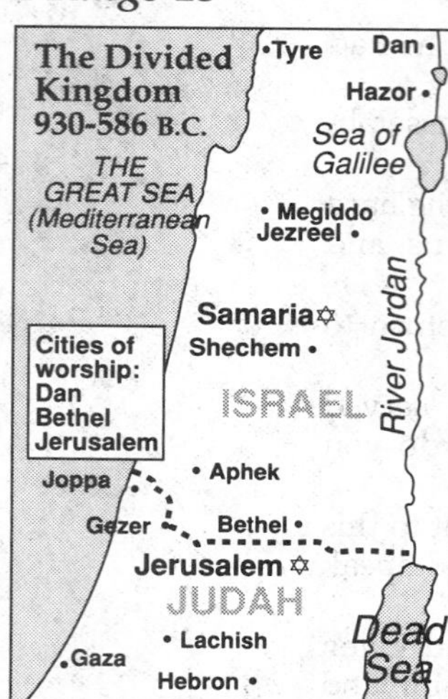

19 [a]So Israel has been in rebellion against the house of
David to this day.
20 And it came about when all Israel heard that Jeroboam
had returned, that they sent and called him to the assem-
bly and made him king over all Israel. [a]None but the tribe
of Judah followed the house of David.
21 [a]Now when Rehoboam had come to Jerusalem, he as-
sembled all the house of Judah and the tribe of Benjamin,
180,000 chosen men who were warriors, to fight against
the house of Israel to restore the kingdom to Rehoboam
the son of Solomon.
22 But the word of God came to [a]Shemaiah the man of
God, saying,
23 "Speak to Rehoboam the son of Solomon, king of
Judah, and to all the house of Judah and Benjamin and to
the [a]rest of the people, saying,
24 'Thus says the LORD, "You must not go up and fight
against your [1]relatives the sons of Israel; return every man
to his house, [a]for this thing has come from Me."'" So they listened
to the word of the LORD, and returned and went *their way* according
to the word of the LORD.
25 Then [a]Jeroboam built Shechem in the hill country of Ephraim,
and lived [1]there. And he went out from there and built [b]Penuel.
26 And Jeroboam said in his heart, "Now the kingdom will return
to the house of David.
27 "[a]If this people go up to offer sacrifices in the house of the LORD at
Jerusalem, then the heart of this people will return to their lord, *even*
to Rehoboam king of Judah; and they will kill me and return to
Rehoboam king of Judah."
28 So the king [1]consulted, and [a]made two golden [b]calves, and he
said to them, "It is too much for you to go up to Jerusalem; [c]behold
your gods, O Israel, that brought you up from the land of Egypt."
29 And he set [a]one in [b]Bethel, and the other he put in [c]Dan.
30 Now [a]this thing became a sin, for the people went *to worship*
before the one as far as Dan.
31 And [a]he made houses on high places, and [b]made priests from
among [1]all the people who were not of the sons of Levi.
32 And Jeroboam [1]instituted a feast in the eighth month on the
fifteenth day of the month, [a]like the feast which is in Judah, and he
[2]went up to the altar; thus he did in Bethel, sacrificing to the calves
which he had made. And he stationed in Bethel [b]the priests of the
high places which he had made.
33 Then he [1]went up to the altar which he had made in Bethel on
the fifteenth day in the eighth month, even in the month which he
had [2a]devised [3]in his own heart; and he [2]instituted a feast for the sons
of Israel, and [1]went up to the altar [b]to burn [4]incense.

Chapter 13 ______________________________

13 Now behold, there came [a]a man of God from Judah to Bethel
by the word of the LORD, while Jeroboam was standing by the
altar [b]to burn incense.
2 And [a]he cried against the altar by the word of the LORD, and said,
"O altar, altar, thus says the LORD, 'Behold, a son shall be born to the
house of David, [b]Josiah by name; and on you he shall sacrifice the

19 [a]2 Kin. 17:2
20 [a]1 Kin. 11:1
21 [a]2 Chr. 11:1
22 [a]2 Chr. 11:2
23 [a]1 Kin. 12:1
24 [1]Lit., *brothe* [a]1 Kin. 12:15
25 [1]Lit., *in it* [a]G 12:6; Judg. 9:45 [b]Gen. 32:30, 31 8:8, 17
27 [a]Deut. 12:5-
28 [1]Lit., *took co* [a]2 Kin. 10:29; 1 Hos. 8:4-7 [b]Hos [c]Ex. 32:4, 8
29 [a]Hos. 10:5 28:19 [c]Judg. 18
30 [a]1 Kin. 13:34 17:21
31 [1]Or, *extremit* [a]1 Kin. 13:32 [b]1 13:33; 2 Kin. 17: 2 Chr. 11:15; 13:
32 [1]Lit., *made* [2] *offered upon* [a]Le 23:33, 34; Num. 1 Kin. 8:2, 5 [b]Am 7:10-13
33 [1]Or, *offered u* [2]Lit., *made* [3]Lit., [4]Or, *sacrifices* [a]N 15:39 [b]1 Kin. 13
13:1 [a]1 Kin. 12:2 2 Kin. 23:17 [b]1 K 12:33
2 [a]1 Kin. 13:32 [b] 23:15, 16

priests of the high places who burn incense on you, and human
bones shall be burned on you.' "
3 Then he gave a [1]sign the same day, saying, "[a]This is the [1]sign
which the LORD has spoken, 'Behold, the altar shall be split apart and
the [2]ashes which are on it shall be poured out.' "
4 Now it came about when the king heard the saying of the man of
God, which he cried against the altar in Bethel, that Jeroboam
stretched out his hand from the altar, saying, "Seize him." But his
hand which he stretched out against him dried up, so that he could
not draw it back to himself.
5 The altar also was split apart and the [1]ashes were poured out
from the altar, according to the [2]sign which the man of God had
given by the word of the LORD.
6 And the king answered and said to the man of God, "Please
[1a]entreat the LORD your God, and pray for me, that my hand may be
restored to me." So [b]the man of God [2]entreated the LORD, and the
king's hand was restored to him, and it became as it was before.
7 Then the king said to the man of God, "Come home with me and
refresh yourself, and [a]I will give you a reward."
8 But the man of God said to the king, "[a]If you were to give me
half your house I would not go with you, nor would I eat bread or
drink water in this place.
9 "For so [1]it was commanded me by the word of the LORD, saying,
'You shall eat no bread, nor drink water, nor return by the way
which you came.' "
10 So he went another way, and did not return by the way which he
came to Bethel.
11 Now [a]an old prophet was living in Bethel; and his [1]sons came
and told him all the deeds which the man of God had done that day
in Bethel; the words which he had spoken to the king, these also they
related to their father.
12 And their father said to them, "[1]Which way did he go?" Now his
sons [2]had seen the way which the man of God who came from Judah
had gone.
13 Then he said to his sons, "Saddle the donkey for me." So they
saddled the donkey for him and he rode away on it.
14 So he went after the man of God and found him sitting under
[1]an oak; and he said to him, "Are you the man of God who came
from Judah?" And he said, "I am."
15 Then he said to him, "Come home with me and eat bread."
16 And he said, "[a]I cannot return with you, nor go with you, nor
will I eat bread or drink water with you in this place.
17 "For a command *came* to me [a]by the word of the LORD, 'You shall
eat no bread, nor drink water there; do not return by going the way
which you came.' "
18 And he said to him, "[a]I also am a prophet like you, and [b]an angel
spoke to me by the word of the LORD, saying, 'Bring him back with
you to your house, that he may eat bread and drink water.' " *But* [c]he
lied to him.
19 So he went back with him, and ate bread in his house and drank
water.
20 Now it came about, as they were sitting down at the table, that
the word of the LORD came to the prophet who had brought him
back;

3 [1]Lit., *wonder* [2]Lit., *…shes of fat* [a]Ex. 4:1-5; Judg. 6:17; Is. 38:7; John 2:18; 1 Cor. 1:22

5 [1]Lit., *ashes of fat* [2]Lit., *wonder*

[1]Lit., *soften the face of* [2]Lit., *softened the face of* [a]Ex. 8:8, 28; …:28; 10:17; Acts 8:24; James 5:16 [b]Luke 6:27, 28

[a]1 Sam. 9:7, 8; 2 Kin. 5:15

[a]Num. 22:18; 24:13; 1 Kin. 13:16, 17

[1]Lit., *he commanded me*

11 [1]Lit., *son* [a]1 Kin. 13:25; 2 Kin. 23:18

…2 [1]Lit., *Where is the …ay he went* [2]Some …ncient versions read *showed him*

14 [1]Or, *a terebinth*

16 [a]1 Kin. 13:8, 9

17 [a]1 Kin. 20:35

[a]Matt. 7:15; 1 John …:1 [b]Gal. 1:8 [c]Prov. 12:19, 22; 19:5; Jer. …, 32; Ezek. 13:8, 9; 1 Tim. 4:1, 2

21 and he cried to the man of God who came from Judah, saying, "Thus says the LORD, 'Because you have [1]disobeyed the [2]command of the LORD, and have not observed the commandment which the LORD your God commanded you,

22 but have returned and eaten bread and drunk water in the place of which He said to you, "Eat no bread and drink no water"; your body shall not come to the grave of your fathers.'"

23 And it came about after he had eaten bread and after he had drunk, that he saddled the donkey for him, for the prophet whom he had brought back.

24 Now when he had gone, [a]a lion met him on the way and killed him, and his body was thrown on the road, with the donkey standing beside it; the lion also was standing beside the body.

25 And behold, men passed by and saw the body thrown on the road, and the lion standing beside the body; so they came and told *it* in the city where [a]the old prophet lived.

26 Now when the prophet who brought him back from the way heard *it*, he said, "It is the man of God, who [1]disobeyed the [2]command of the LORD; therefore the LORD has given him to the lion, which has torn him and killed him, according to the word of the LORD which He spoke to him."

27 Then he spoke to his sons, saying, "Saddle the donkey for me." And they saddled *it*.

28 And he went and found his body thrown on the road with the donkey and the lion standing beside the body; the lion had not eaten the body nor torn the donkey.

29 So the prophet took up the body of the man of God and laid it on the donkey, and brought it back and he came to the city of the old prophet to mourn and to bury him.

30 And he laid his body in his own grave, and they mourned over him, *saying*, "[a]Alas, my brother!"

31 And it came about after he had buried him, that he spoke to his sons, saying, "When I die, bury me in the grave in which the man of God is buried; [a]lay my bones beside his bones.

32 "[a]For the thing shall surely come to pass which he cried by the word of the LORD against the altar in Bethel and [b]against all the houses of the high places which are in the cities of [c]Samaria."

33 After this event Jeroboam did not return from his evil way, but [a]again he made priests of the high places from among [1]all the people; [b]any who would, he ordained, to be priests of the high places.

34 [a]And [1]this event became sin to the house of Jeroboam, [b]even to blot *it* out and destroy *it* from off the face of the earth.

Chapter 14

14 At that time Abijah the son of Jeroboam became sick.

2 And Jeroboam said to his wife, "Arise now, and [a]disguise yourself so that they may not know that you are the wife of Jeroboam, and go to [b]Shiloh; behold, Ahijah the prophet is there, who [c]spoke concerning me *that I would be* king over this people.

3 "[a]And take ten loaves with you, *some* cakes and a jar of honey, and go to him. He will tell you what will happen to the boy."

4 And Jeroboam's wife did so, and arose and went to [a]Shiloh, and came to the house of [b]Ahijah. Now Ahijah could not see, [c]for his eyes were [1]dim because of his age.

21 [1]Lit., *rebelle*... against [2]Lit., *m*...

24 [a]1 Kin. 20:36

25 [a]1 Kin. 13:11

26 [1]Lit., *rebelled* against [2]Lit., *mo*...

30 [a]Jer. 22:18

31 [a]Ruth 1:17; 2... 23:17, 18

32 [a]1 Kin. 13:2 ... 26:30; 1 Kin. 12:3... [c]1 Kin. 16:24; Joh... Acts 8:14

33 [1]Or, *extremiti*... [a]1 Kin. 12:31, 32 ... 17:5

34 [1]Lit., *by this th... became* [a]1 Kin. 1... 2 Kin. 17:21 [b]1 K... 14:10; 15:29, 30

14:2 [a]1 Sam. 28:8... 2 Sam. 14:2; 2 Ch... 18:29 [b]Josh. 18:1 [c]1 Kin. 11:29-31

3 [a]1 Sam. 9:7, 8; ... 13:7; 2 Kin. 4:42

4 [1]Lit., *set* [a]1 Kin. ... [b]1 Kin. 11:29 [c]1 Sa... 3:2; 4:15

5 Now the LORD had said to Ahijah, "Behold, the wife of Jeroboam
is coming to [1]inquire of you concerning her son, for he is sick. You
shall say thus and thus to her, for it will be when she arrives that
[a]she will pretend to be another woman."
6 And it came about when Ahijah heard the sound of her feet
coming in the doorway, that he said, "Come in, wife of Jeroboam,
why do you pretend to be another woman? For I am sent to you *with*
a harsh *message.*
7 "Go, say to Jeroboam, 'Thus says the LORD God of Israel,
"[a]Because I exalted you from among the people and made you
leader over My people Israel,
8 and [a]tore the kingdom away from the house of David and gave it
to you—[b]yet you have not been like My servant David, who kept My
commandments and who followed Me with all his heart, [c]to do only
that which was right in My sight;
9 you also have done more evil than all who were before you, and
[a]have gone and made for yourself other gods and [b]molten images to
provoke Me to anger, and have [c]cast Me behind your back—
10 therefore behold, I am bringing calamity on the house of
Jeroboam, and [a]will cut off from Jeroboam [1]every male person, [b]both
bond and free in Israel, and I [c]will make a clean sweep of the house
of Jeroboam, as one sweeps away dung until it is all gone.
11 "[a]Anyone belonging to Jeroboam who dies in the city the dogs
will eat. And he who dies in the field the birds of the heavens will
eat; for the LORD has spoken *it.*"'
12 "Now you arise, go to your house. [a]When your feet enter the city
the child will die.
13 "And all Israel shall mourn for him and bury him, for [1]he alone of
Jeroboam's *family* shall come to the grave, because in him [a]something
good was found toward the LORD God of Israel in the house of
Jeroboam.
14 "Moreover, [a]the LORD will raise up for Himself a king over Israel
who shall cut off the house of Jeroboam this day [1]and from now on.
15 "For the LORD will strike Israel, as a reed is shaken in the water;
and [a]He will uproot Israel from [b]this good land which He gave to
their fathers, and [c]will scatter them beyond the *Euphrates* River,
[d]because they have made their [1]Asherim, provoking the LORD to
anger.
16 "And He will give up Israel [a]on account of the sins of Jeroboam,
which he [1]committed and with which he made Israel to sin."
17 Then Jeroboam's wife arose and departed and came to [a]Tirzah.
[b]As she was entering the threshold of the house, the child died.
18 [a]And all Israel buried him and mourned for him, according to
the word of the LORD which He spoke through His servant Ahijah
the prophet.
19 Now the rest of the acts of Jeroboam, [a]how he made war and
how he reigned, behold, they are written in the Book of the
Chronicles of the Kings of Israel.
20 And the time that Jeroboam reigned *was* twenty-two years; and
he slept with his fathers, and Nadab his son reigned in his place.
21 [a]Now Rehoboam the son of Solomon reigned in Judah.
Rehoboam was forty-one years old when he became king, and he
reigned seventeen years in Jerusalem, [b]the city which the LORD had

5 [1]Lit., *seek a word from* [a]2 Sam. 14:2

[a]2 Sam. 12:7; 1 Kin. 11:28-31; 16:2

1 Kin. 11:31 [b]1 Kin. :33, 38 [c]1 Kin. 15:5

[a]1 Kin. 12:28; 2 Chr. 5 [b]Ex. 34:17 [c]Neh. :26; Ps. 50:17; Ezek. 23:35

10 [1]Lit., *him who urinates against the wall* [a]1 Kin. 21:21; . 9:8 [b]Deut. 32:36; 2 Kin. 14:26 [c]1 Kin. 15:29

[a]1 Kin. 16:4; 21:24

12 [a]1 Kin. 14:17

it., *the one* [a]2 Chr. 19:3

Lit., *and what even* ? [a]1 Kin. 15:27-29

15 [1]I.e., wooden ymbols of a female leity [a]Deut. 29:28; Kin. 17:6; Ps. 52:5 . 23:15, 16 [c]2 Kin. 29 [d]Ex. 34:13, 14; Deut. 12:3, 4

Lit., *sinned* [a]1 Kin. ; 13:34; 15:30, 34; 16:2

[a]1 Kin. 15:21, 33; :6-9, 15, 23; Song 6:4 [b]1 Kin. 14:12

18 [a]1 Kin. 14:13

Kin. 14:30; 2 Chr. 13:2-20

21 [a]2 Chr. 12:13 [b]1 Kin. 11:32, 36

chosen from all the tribes of Israel to put His name there. And his
mother's name was Naamah the Ammonitess.
22 [a]And Judah did evil in the sight of the LORD, and they [b]provoked
Him to jealousy more than all that their fathers had done, with [1]the
sins which they [2]committed.
23 For they also built for themselves [a]high places and *sacred* [b]pillars
and [1c]Asherim on every high hill and [d]beneath every luxuriant tree.
24 And there were also [a]male cult prostitutes in the land. They did
according to all the abominations of the nations which the LORD
dispossessed before the sons of Israel.
25 [a]Now it came about in the fifth year of King Rehoboam, that
Shishak the king of Egypt came up against Jerusalem.
26 And he took away the treasures of the house of the LORD and the
treasures of the king's house, and [a]he took everything, [1b]even taking
all the shields of gold which Solomon had made.
27 So King Rehoboam made shields of bronze in their place, and
[a]committed them to the [1]care of the commanders of the [2]guard who
guarded the doorway of the king's house.
28 Then it happened as often as the king entered the house of the
LORD, that the [1]guards would carry them and would bring them back
into the [1]guards' room.
29 [a]Now the rest of the acts of Rehoboam and all that he did, are
they not written in the Book of the Chronicles of the Kings of Judah?
30 [a]And there was war between Rehoboam and Jeroboam con-
tinually.
31 And Rehoboam slept with his fathers, and was buried with his
fathers in the city of David; and [a]his mother's name was Naamah the
Ammonitess. And Abijam his son became king in his place.

Chapter 15

15 [a]Now in the eighteenth year of King Jeroboam, the son of
Nebat, Abijam became king over Judah.
2 He reigned three years in Jerusalem; and his mother's name was
[1a]Maacah the daughter of [2b]Abishalom.
3 And he walked in all the sins of his father which he had com-
mitted before him; and [a]his heart was not [1]wholly devoted to the
LORD his God, like the heart of his father David.
4 But for David's sake the LORD his God gave him a [a]lamp in
Jerusalem, to raise up his son after him and to establish Jerusalem;
5 [a]because David did what was right in the sight of the LORD, and
had not turned aside from anything that He commanded him all the
days of his life, [b]except in the case of Uriah the Hittite.
6 [a]And there was war between Rehoboam and Jeroboam all the
days of his life.
7 Now [a]the rest of the acts of Abijam and all that he did, are they
not written in the Book of the Chronicles of the Kings of Judah?
[b]And there was war between Abijam and Jeroboam.
8 [a]And Abijam slept with his fathers and they buried him in the
city of David; and Asa his son became king in his place.
9 So in the twentieth year of Jeroboam the king of Israel, Asa
began to reign as king of Judah.
10 And he reigned forty-one years in Jerusalem; and [a]his mother's
name was Maacah the daughter of Abishalom.

22 [1]Lit., *their sinned* [a]2 Chr. [b]Deut. 32:21; P 1 Cor. 10:22

23 [1]I.e., woode symbols of a fe deity [a]Deut. 12 16:24 [b]Deut. 1 [c]1 Kin. 14:15 [d] 17:10; Is. 57:5;

24 [a]Gen. 19:5; 23:17; 1 Kin. 15 22:46; 2 Kin. 23

25 [a]1 Kin. 11:4 12:2, 9

26 [1]Lit., *and he away* [a]1 Kin. 1 2 Chr. 12:9 [b]1 10:17; 2 Chr. 9

27 [1]Lit., *hand runner* [a]1 Sam. 22:17

28 [1]Lit., *runner*

29 [a]2 Chr. 12:1

30 [a]1 Kin. 12:2

31 [a]1 Kin. 14:21

15:1 [a]2 Chr. 13

2 [1]In 2 Chr. 13: *Micaiah, the dau Uriel* [2]In 2 Chr. *Absalom* [a]2 Chr [b]2 Chr. 11:21

3 [1]Lit., *complete* [a]1 Kin. 11:4; Ps.

4 [a]2 Sam. 21:17 11:36; 2 Chr. 21

5 [a]1 Kin. 9:4; 14 Luke 1:6 [b]2 Sam 15-17; 12:9, 10

6 [a]1 Kin. 14:30; 12:15-13:20

7 [a]2 Chr. 13:2, 2 [b]2 Chr. 13:3-20

8 [a]2 Chr. 14:1

10 [a]1 Kin. 15:2

11 And [a]Asa did what was right in the sight of the LORD, like David
his father.
12 [a]He also put away the male cult prostitutes from the land, and
[b]removed all the idols which his fathers had made.
13 [a]And [1]he also removed Maacah his mother from *being* queen
mother, because she had made a horrid image [2]as an Asherah; and
Asa cut down her horrid image and [b]burned *it* at the brook Kidron.
14 [a]But the high places were not taken away; nevertheless [b]the heart
of Asa was [1]wholly devoted to the LORD all his days.
15 And [a]he brought into the house of the LORD the dedicated things
of his father and his own dedicated things: silver and gold and utensils.
16 [a]Now there was war between Asa and Baasha king of Israel all
their days.
17 [a]And Baasha king of Israel went up against Judah and [1b]fortified
Ramah [c]in order to prevent *anyone* from going out or coming in to
Asa king of Judah.
18 Then [a]Asa took all the silver and the gold which were left in the
treasuries of the house of the LORD and the treasuries of the king's
house, and delivered them into the hand of his servants. And [b]King
Asa sent them to Ben-hadad the son of Tabrimmon, the son of
Hezion, king of Aram, who lived in [c]Damascus, saying,
19 "*Let there be* a [a]treaty between [1]you and me, *as* between my father
and your father. Behold, I have sent you a present of silver and gold;
go, break your treaty with Baasha king of Israel so that he will withdraw from me."
20 So Ben-hadad listened to King Asa and sent the commanders of
his armies against the cities of Israel, and [1]conquered [a]Ijon, [b]Dan,
[c]Abel-beth-maacah and all [d]Chinneroth, besides all the land of Naphtali.
21 And it came about when Baasha heard *of it* that [a]he ceased [1]fortifying Ramah, and remained in [b]Tirzah.
22 Then King Asa made a proclamation to all Judah—none was
exempt—and they carried away the stones of Ramah and its timber
with which Baasha had built. And King Asa built with them [a]Geba of
Benjamin and Mizpah.
23 [a]Now the rest of all the acts of Asa and all his might and all that
he did and the cities which he built, are they not written in the Book
of the Chronicles of the Kings of Judah? But in the time of his old age
he was diseased in his feet.
24 And Asa slept with his fathers and was buried with his fathers
in the city of David his father; and [a]Jehoshaphat his son reigned in
his place.
25 Now [a]Nadab the son of Jeroboam became king over Israel in the
second year of Asa king of Judah, and he reigned over Israel two
years.
26 And he did evil in the sight of the LORD, and [a]walked in the way
of his father and [b]in his sin which he made Israel sin.
27 Then [a]Baasha the son of Ahijah of the house of Issachar conspired against him, and Baasha struck him down at [b]Gibbethon,
which belonged to the Philistines, while Nadab and all Israel were
laying siege to Gibbethon.
28 So Baasha killed him in the third year of Asa king of Judah, and
reigned in his place.

11 [a]2 Chr. 14:2
[a]Deut. 23:17; 1 Kin. 14:24; 22:46 [b]1 Kin. 11:7, 8; 14:23; 2 Chr. 14:2-5
13 [1]Lit., *also Maacah his mother and he removed her* [2]Or, *for Asherah* [a]2 Chr. 15:16-18 [b]Ex. 32:20
[1]Lit., *complete with* [a]1 Kin. 22:43; 2 Kin. ...:3 [b]1 Kin. 8:61; 15:3
15 [a]1 Kin. 7:51
16 [a]1 Kin. 15:32
17 [1]Lit., *built* [a]2 Chr. 16:1-6 [b]Josh. 18:25; ...in. 15:21, 22 [c]1 Kin. 12:26-29
[a]1 Kin. 14:26; 15:15 ...Kin. 12:17, 18; 2 Chr. ... [c]Gen. 14:15; 1 Kin. 11:23, 24
19 [1]Lit., *me and you* [a]2 Chr. 16:7
[1]Lit., *smote* [a]2 Kin. 15:29 [b]Judg. 18:29; ...Kin. 12:29 [c]2 Sam. 20:15; 2 Kin. 15:29 [d]Josh. 11:2; 12:3
...Lit., *building* [a]1 Kin. 15:17 [b]1 Kin. 14:17; 16:15-18
[a]Josh. 18:24; 21:17
23 [a]2 Chr. 16:11-14
24 [a]1 Kin. 22:41-44; ...Chr. 17:1; Matt. 1:8
25 [a]1 Kin. 14:20
26 [a]1 Kin. 12:28-33; ...3, 34 [b]1 Kin. 14:16; 15:30, 34
...1 Kin. 14:14 [b]Josh. 19:44; 21:23; 1 Kin. 16:15

29 And it came about, as soon as he was king, he struck down all the household of Jeroboam. He did not leave to Jeroboam [1]any persons alive, until he had destroyed them, [a]according to the word of the LORD, which He spoke by His servant Ahijah the Shilonite,

30 *and* because of the sins of Jeroboam which he sinned, and [a]which he made Israel sin, because of his provocation with which he provoked the LORD God of Israel to anger.

31 [a]Now the rest of the acts of Nadab and all that he did, are they not written in the Book of the Chronicles of the Kings of Israel?

32 [a]And there was war between Asa and Baasha king of Israel all their days.

33 In the third year of Asa king of Judah, Baasha the son of Ahijah became king over all Israel at Tirzah, *and reigned* twenty-four years.

34 And he did evil in the sight of the LORD, and [a]walked in the way of Jeroboam and in his sin which he made Israel sin.

Chapter 16

16 Now the word of the LORD came to [a]Jehu the son of [b]Hanani against Baasha, saying,

2 "Inasmuch as I [a]exalted you from the dust and made you leader over My people Israel, and [b]you have walked in the way of Jeroboam and have made My people Israel sin, provoking Me to anger with their sins,

3 behold, [a]I will consume [b]Baasha and his house, and [c]I will make your house like the house of Jeroboam the son of Nebat.

4 "[a]Anyone of Baasha who dies in the city the dogs shall eat, and anyone of his who dies in the field the birds of the heavens will eat."

5 [a]Now the rest of the acts of Baasha and what he did and his might, are they not written in the Book of the Chronicles of the Kings of Israel?

6 And Baasha slept with his fathers and was buried in [a]Tirzah, and Elah his son became king in his place.

7 Moreover, the word of the LORD through [a]the prophet Jehu the son of Hanani also came against Baasha and his household, both because of all the evil which he did in the sight of the LORD, provoking Him to anger with [b]the work of his hands, in being like the house of Jeroboam, and because [c]he struck [1]it.

8 In the twenty-sixth year of Asa king of Judah, Elah the son of Baasha became king over Israel at Tirzah, *and reigned* two years.

9 And his servant [a]Zimri, commander of half his chariots, conspired against him. Now he *was* at Tirzah drinking himself drunk in the house of Arza, [b]who *was* over the household at Tirzah.

10 Then Zimri went in and struck him and put him to death, in the twenty-seventh year of Asa king of Judah, and became king in his place.

11 And it came about, when he became king, as soon as he sat on his throne, that [a]he [1]killed all the household of Baasha; he did not leave [2]a single male, neither of his [3]relatives nor of his friends.

12 Thus Zimri destroyed all the household of Baasha, [a]according to the word of the LORD, which He spoke against Baasha through [b]Jehu the prophet,

13 for all the sins of Baasha and the sins of Elah his son, which they sinned and which they made Israel sin, [a]provoking the LORD God of Israel to anger with their [1]idols.

29 [1]Lit., *any bre* [a]1 Kin. 14:9-16
30 [a]1 Kin. 15:26
31 [a]1 Kin. 14:19
32 [a]1 Kin. 15:16
34 [a]1 Kin. 15:26
16:1 [a]1 Kin. 16:7 19:2; 20:34 [b]2 C 16:7-10
2 [a]1 Sam. 2:8; 1 14:7 [b]1 Kin. 15:3
3 [a]1 Kin. 14:10; 2 [b]1 Kin. 16:11 [c]1 K 15:29
4 [a]1 Kin. 14:11; 2
5 [a]1 Kin. 14:19; 1
6 [a]1 Kin. 14:17; 1
7 [1]Or, *him* [a]1 Kin [b]Ps. 115:4; Is. 2:8 [c]1 Kin. 14:14; 15:2
9 [a]2 Kin. 9:30-33 24:2; 39:4; 1 Kin. 1
11 [1]Lit., *smote* [2]L *him who urinates against the wall* [3] *redeemers* [a]1 Kin 15:29; 16:3
12 [a]1 Kin. 16:3 [b]2 19:2; 20:34
13 [1]Lit., *vanities* [a] 32:21; 1 Kin. 15:30

14 [a]1 Kin. 16:5

14 [a]Now the rest of the acts of Elah and all that he did, are they not written in the Book of the Chronicles of the Kings of Israel?

15 [a]1 Kin. 15:27

15 In the twenty-seventh year of Asa king of Judah, Zimri reigned seven days at Tirzah. Now the people were camped against [a]Gibbethon, which belonged to the Philistines.

16 [1]Lit., *saying*

16 And the people who were camped heard [1]it said, "Zimri has conspired and has also struck down the king." Therefore all Israel made Omri, the commander of the army, king over Israel that day in the camp.

18 [a]1 Sam. 31:4, 5; 2 Sam. 17:23

17 Then Omri and all Israel with him went up from Gibbethon, and they besieged Tirzah.

18 And it came about, when Zimri saw that the city was taken, that he went into the citadel of the king's house and burned the king's house over him with fire, and [a]died,

[a]1 Kin. 12:28; 14:16; 15:26

19 because of his sins which he sinned, doing evil in the sight of the LORD, [a]walking in the way of Jeroboam, and in his sin which he did, making Israel sin.

20 [1]Lit., *conspired* [a]1 Kin. 16:5, 14, 27

20 [a]Now the rest of the acts of Zimri and his conspiracy which he [1]carried out, are they not written in the Book of the Chronicles of the Kings of Israel?

21 Then the people of Israel were divided into two parts: half of the people followed Tibni the son of Ginath, to make him king; the *other* half followed Omri.

23 [a]1 Kin. 15:21

22 But the people who followed Omri prevailed over the people who followed Tibni the son of Ginath. And Tibni died and Omri became king.

4 [1]Heb., *Shomeron* [a]1 Kin. 16:28, 29, 32

23 In the thirty-first year of Asa king of Judah, Omri became king over Israel, *and reigned* twelve years; he reigned six years at [a]Tirzah.

24 And he bought the hill [1]Samaria from Shemer for two talents of silver; and he built on the hill, and named the city which he built [1a]Samaria, after the name of Shemer, the owner of the hill.

[a]Mic. 6:16 [b]1 Kin. 14:9; 16:30-33

25 And [a]Omri did evil in the sight of the LORD, and [b]acted more wickedly than all who *were* before him.

Lit., *vanities* [a]1 Kin. 16:19

26 For he [a]walked in all the way of Jeroboam the son of Nebat and in his sins which he made Israel sin, provoking the LORD God of Israel with their [1]idols.

27 [1]Lit., *did*

27 Now the rest of the acts of Omri which he did and his might which he [1]showed, are they not written in the Book of the Chronicles of the Kings of Israel?

[a]1 Kin. 14:9; 16:25

28 So Omri slept with his fathers, and was buried in Samaria; and Ahab his son became king in his place.

29 Now Ahab the son of Omri became king over Israel in the thirty-eighth year of Asa king of Judah, and Ahab the son of Omri reigned over Israel in Samaria twenty-two years.

[a]Deut. 7:1-5 [b]Judg. 18:7; 1 Kin. 11:1-5; 2 Kin. 10:18; 17:16

30 And Ahab the son of Omri did evil in the sight of the LORD [a]more than all who were before him.

2 Kin. 10:21, 26, 27

31 And it came about, as though it had been a trivial thing for him to walk in the sins of Jeroboam the son of Nebat, that [a]he married Jezebel the daughter of Ethbaal king of the [b]Sidonians, and went to serve Baal and worshiped him.

33 [1]I.e., wooden symbol of a female deity [a]2 Kin. 13:6 Kin. 14:9; 16:29, 30; 21:25

32 So he erected an altar for Baal in [a]the house of Baal, which he built in Samaria.

33 And Ahab also made [a]the [1]Asherah. Thus [b]Ahab did more to

provoke the LORD God of Israel than all the kings of Israel who were
before him.
34 [a]In his days Hiel the Bethelite built Jericho; he laid its founda-
tions with the *loss of* Abiram his first-born, and set up its gates with
the *loss of* his youngest son Segub, according to the word of the LORD,
which He spoke by Joshua the son of Nun.

Chapter 17

17 Now Elijah the Tishbite, who was of [1a]the settlers of Gilead,
said to Ahab, "[b]As the LORD, the God of Israel lives, before
whom I stand, surely [c]there shall be neither dew nor rain these years,
except by my word."
2 And the word of the LORD came to him, saying,
3 "Go away from here and turn eastward, and hide yourself by the
brook Cherith, which is [1]east of the Jordan.
4 "And it shall be that you shall drink of the brook, and [a]I have
commanded the ravens to provide for you there."
5 So he went and did according to the word of the LORD, for he
went and lived by the brook Cherith, which is [1]east of the Jordan.
6 And the ravens brought him bread and meat in the morning and
bread and meat in the evening, and he would drink from the brook.
7 And it happened after a while, that the brook dried up, because
there was no rain in the land.
8 Then the word of the LORD came to him, saying,
9 "Arise, go to [a]Zarephath, which belongs to Sidon, and stay there;
behold, [b]I have commanded a widow there to provide for you."
10 So he arose and went to Zarephath, and when he came to the
gate of the city, behold, a widow was there gathering sticks; and [a]he
called to her and said, "Please get me a little water in a [1]jar, that I
may drink."
11 And as she was going to get *it*, he called to her and said, "Please
bring me a piece of bread in your hand."
12 But she said, "[a]As the LORD your God lives, [b]I have no [1]bread,
only a handful of flour in the [2]bowl and a little oil in the jar; and
behold, I am gathering [3]a few sticks that I may go in and prepare for
me and my son, that we may eat it and [c]die."
13 Then Elijah said to her, "Do not fear; go, do as you have said, but
make me a little bread cake from [1]it first, and bring *it* out to me, and
afterward you may make *one* for yourself and for your son.
14 "For thus says the LORD God of Israel, 'The [1]bowl of flour shall
not be exhausted, nor shall the jar of oil [2]be empty, until the day that
the LORD sends rain on the face of the earth.' "
15 So she went and did according to the word of Elijah, and she and
he and her household ate for *many* days.
16 The [1]bowl of flour was not exhausted nor did the jar of oil [2]be-
come empty, according to the word of the LORD which He spoke
through Elijah.
17 Now it came about after these things, that the son of the woman,
the mistress of the house, became sick; and his sickness was so
severe, that there was no breath left in him.
18 So she said to Elijah, "[a]What do I have to do with you, O [b]man of
God? [1]You have come to me to bring my iniquity to remembrance,
and to put my son to death!"
19 And he said to her, "Give me your son." Then he took him from

34 [a]Josh. 6:26

17:1 [1]Or, *Tishbe i Gilead* [a]Judg. 12: [b]1 Kin. 18:10; 22:1 2 Kin. 3:14; 5:20 [c] 18:1; Luke 4:25; J 5:17

3 [1]Lit., *before*

4 [a]1 Kin. 17:9

5 [1]Lit., *before*

9 [a]Obad. 20; Luk [b]1 Kin. 17:4

10 [1]Or, *vessel* [a] 24:17; John 4:7

12 [1]Lit., *cake* [2]L *pitcher* [3]Lit., *two* 17:1 [b]2 Kin. 4:2- [c]Gen. 21:15, 16

13 [1]Lit., *there*

14 [1]Lit., *pitcher* *lack*

16 [1]Lit., *pitcher* *lack*

18 [1]Or, *Have y . . . death?* [a]2 S 16:10; 2 Kin. 3:1 4:34; John 2:4 12:22

her bosom and carried him up to the upper room where he was
living, and laid him on his own bed.
20 And he called to the LORD and said, "O LORD my God, hast Thou
also brought calamity to the widow with whom I am [1]staying, by
causing her son to die?"
21 [a]Then he stretched himself upon the child three times, and called
to the LORD, and said, "O LORD my God, I pray Thee, let this child's
life return [1]to him."
22 And the LORD heard the voice of Elijah, [a]and the life of the child
returned [1]to him and he revived.
23 And Elijah took the child, and brought him down from the
upper room into the house and gave him to his mother; and Elijah
said, "See, your son is alive."
24 Then the woman said to Elijah, "[a]Now I know that you are a
man of God, and that the word of the LORD in your mouth is truth."

Chapter 18

18 Now it came about [a]*after* many days, that the word of the
LORD came to Elijah in the third year, saying, "Go, show your-
self to Ahab, and [b]I will send rain on the face of the earth."
2 So Elijah went to show himself to Ahab. Now the famine *was*
severe in Samaria.
3 And Ahab called Obadiah [a]who *was* over the household. (Now
Obadiah [1b]feared the LORD greatly;
4 for it came about, [a]when Jezebel [1]destroyed the prophets of the
LORD, that Obadiah took a hundred prophets and hid them by fifties
in a cave, and [b]provided them with bread and water.)
5 Then Ahab said to Obadiah, "Go through the land to all the
springs of water and to all the valleys; perhaps we will find grass
and keep the horses and mules alive, and not [1]have to kill some of
the cattle."
6 So they divided the land between them to [1]survey it; Ahab went
one way by himself and Obadiah went another way by himself.
7 Now as Obadiah was on the way, behold, Elijah [1]met him, [a]and
he recognized him and fell on his face and said, "Is this you, Elijah
my master?"
8 And he said to him, "It is I. Go, say to your master, 'Behold,
Elijah *is here.*' "
9 And he said, "What [1]sin have I committed, that you are giving
your servant into the hand of Ahab, to put me to death?
10 "[a]As the LORD your God lives, there is no nation or kingdom
where my master has not sent to search for you; and when they said,
'He is not *here,*' he made the kingdom or nation swear that they
could not find you.
11 "And now you are saying, 'Go, say to your master, "Behold, Elijah
is here." '
12 "And it will come about when I leave you [a]that the Spirit of the
LORD will carry you where I do not know; so when I come and tell
Ahab and he cannot find you, he will kill me, although *I* your ser-
vant have [1]feared the LORD from my youth.
13 "[a]Has it not been told to my master what I did when Jezebel killed
the prophets of the LORD, that I hid [1]a hundred prophets of the LORD
by fifties in a cave, and provided them with bread and water?

t., *sojourning*
[1]Lit., *upon his* *d part* [a]2 Kin. 5; Acts 20:10
[1]Lit., *upon his* *rt* [a]Luke 7:14; Heb. 11:35
ohn 2:11; 3:2; 16:30
in. 17:1; Luke 5; James 5:17 [b]Deut. 28:12
evered [a]1 Kin. [b]Neh. 7:2; Job 28:28
cut off [a]1 Kin. Matt. 10:40-42
5 [1]Lit., *cut off*
., *pass through*
to meet [a]2 Kin. 1:6-8
., *have I sinned*
10 [a]1 Kin. 17:1
revered [a]2 Kin. ; Ezek. 3:12, 14; Acts 8:39
, *a hundred men* *prophets* [a]1 Kin. 18:4

14 "And now you are saying, 'Go, say to your master, "Behold,
Elijah *is here*" '; he will then kill me."
15 And Elijah said, "[a]As the LORD of hosts lives, before whom I
stand, I will surely show myself to him today."
16 So Obadiah went to meet Ahab, and told him; and Ahab went to
meet Elijah.
17 And it came about, when Ahab saw Elijah that [a]Ahab said to
him, "Is this you, you troubler of Israel?"
18 And he said, "I have not troubled Israel, but you and your
father's house *have*, because [a]you have forsaken the commandments
of the LORD, and [b]you have followed the Baals.
19 "Now then send *and* gather to me all Israel at [a]Mount Carmel,
[b]*together* with 450 prophets of Baal and 400 prophets of [c]the Asherah,
who eat at Jezebel's table."
20 So Ahab sent *a message* among all the sons of Israel, and brought
the prophets together at Mount Carmel.
21 And Elijah came near to all the people and said, "[a]How long *will*
you [1]hesitate between two opinions? [b]If the LORD is God, follow Him;
but if Baal, follow him." But the people did not answer him a word.
22 Then Elijah said to the people, "I [a]alone am left a prophet of the
LORD, but Baal's prophets are [b]450 men.
23 "Now let them give us two oxen; and let them choose one ox for
themselves and cut it up, and place it on the wood, but put no fire
under it; and I will prepare the other ox, and lay it on the wood, and I
will not put a fire *under it*.
24 "Then you call on the name of your god, and I will call on the
name of the LORD, and [a]the God who answers by fire, He is God."
And all the people answered and said, "[1]That is a good idea."
25 So Elijah said to the prophets of Baal, "Choose one ox for your-
selves and prepare it first for you are many, and call on the name of
your god, but put no fire *under it*."
26 Then they took the ox which [1]was given them and they prepared
it and called on the name of Baal from morning until noon saying,
"O Baal, answer us." But there was [a]no voice and no one answered.
And they [2]leaped about the altar which [3]they made.
27 And it came about at noon, that Elijah mocked them and said,
"Call out with a loud voice, for he is a god; either he is occupied or
gone aside, or is on a journey, or perhaps he is asleep and needs to
be awakened."
28 So they cried with a loud voice and [a]cut themselves according to
their custom with swords and lances until the blood gushed out on
them.
29 And it came about when midday was past, that they [1]raved
[a]until the time of the offering of the *evening* sacrifice; but there was
no voice, no one answered, and no [2]one paid attention.
30 Then Elijah said to all the people, "Come near to me." So all the
people came near to him. And [a]he repaired the altar of the LORD
which had been torn down.
31 And Elijah took twelve stones according to the number of the
tribes of the sons of Jacob, to whom the word of the LORD had come,
saying, "[a]Israel shall be your name."
32 So with the stones he built an altar in [a]the name of the LORD, and
he made a trench around the altar, large enough to hold two
[1]measures of seed.

15 [a]1 Kin.
17 [a]Josh.
21:20
18 [a]1 Kin.
15:2 [b]1 Kin
21:25, 26
19 [a]Josh. 1
2:25 [b]1 Kin
[c]1 Kin. 16:3
21 [1]Lit., *lim*
divided opir
17:41; Matt.
24:15
22 [a]1 Kin. 1
[b]1 Kin. 18:1
24 [1]Lit., *The*
good [a]1 Kin
26 [1]Lit., *he*
limped; i.e.,
ceremonial c
some mss. a
ancient vers
he [a]Ps. 115.
10:5
28 [a]Lev. 19:
14:1
29 [1]Lit., *prop*
[2]Lit., *attentive*
29:39, 41
30 [a]1 Kin. 19
2 Chr. 33:16
31 [a]Gen. 32:
2 Kin. 17:34
32 [1]Heb., *sea*
one seah equ
approx. 11 qts
3:17

33 [a]Then he arranged the wood and cut the ox in pieces and laid *it*
on the wood. And he said, "Fill four pitchers with water and pour *it*
on the burnt offering and on the wood."
34 And he said, "Do it a second time," and they did it a second
time. And he said, "Do it a third time," and they did it a third time.
35 And the water flowed around the altar, and he also filled the
trench with water.
36 Then it came about [a]at the time of the offering of the *evening*
sacrifice, that Elijah the prophet came near and said, "[b]O LORD, the
God of Abraham, Isaac and Israel, today let it be known that [c]Thou
art God in Israel, and that I am Thy servant, and [d]that I have done all
these things at Thy word.
37 "Answer me, O LORD, answer me, that this people may know that
Thou, O LORD, art God, and *that* Thou hast turned their heart back
again."
38 Then the [a]fire of the LORD fell, and consumed the burnt offering
and the wood and the stones and the dust, and licked up the water
that was in the trench.
39 And when all the people saw it, they fell on their faces; and they
said, "[a]The LORD, He is God; the LORD, He is God."
40 Then Elijah said to them, "Seize the prophets of Baal; do not let
one of them escape." So they seized them; and Elijah brought them
down to [a]the brook Kishon, [b]and slew them there.
41 Now Elijah said to Ahab, "Go up, eat and drink; for there is the
sound of the roar of a *heavy* shower."
42 So Ahab went up to eat and drink. But Elijah went up to the top
of [a]Carmel; and he [b]crouched down on the earth, and put his face
between his knees.
43 And he said to his servant, "Go up now, look toward the sea." So
he went up and looked and said, "There is nothing." And he said,
"Go back" seven times.
44 And it came about at the seventh *time,* that he said, "Behold, [a]a
cloud as small as a man's hand is coming up from the sea." And he
said, "Go up, say to Ahab, '[1]Prepare *your chariot* and go down, so
that the *heavy* shower does not stop you.' "
45 So it came about in a little while, that the sky grew black with
clouds and wind, and there was a heavy shower. And Ahab rode
and went to [a]Jezreel.
46 Then [a]the hand of the LORD was on Elijah, and [b]he girded up his
loins and [1]outran Ahab [2]to Jezreel.

Chapter 19

19 Now Ahab told Jezebel all that Elijah had done, and [1a]how he
had killed all the prophets with the sword.
2 Then Jezebel sent a messenger to Elijah, saying, "[a]So may the
gods do to me and even more, if I do not make your [1]life as the [1]life
of one of them by tomorrow about this time."
3 And he [1]was afraid and arose and ran for his [2]life and came to
[a]Beersheba, which belongs to Judah, and left his servant there.
4 But he himself went a day's journey into the wilderness, and
came and sat down under a [1]juniper tree; and [a]he requested for
himself that he might die, and said, "It is enough; now, O LORD, take
my [2]life, for I am not better than my fathers."

33 [a]Gen. 22:9; Lev. 1:7, 8
[a]1 Kin. 18:29 [b]Gen. ...3; Ex. 3:6; 4:5; Matt. 22:32 [c]1 Kin. 8:43 [d]Num. 16:28-32
...8 [a]Gen. 15:17; Lev. 9:24; 10:1, 2; Judg. ...; 2 Kin. 1:12; 1 Chr. ...1:26; 2 Chr. 7:1; Job 1:16
...39 [a]1 Kin. 18:21, 24
40 [a]Judg. 4:7; 5:21 [b]Deut. 13:5; 18:20; 2 Kin. 10:24, 25
...2 [a]1 Kin. 18:19, 20 [b]James 5:18
... [1]Lit., *Tie, harness* [a]Luke 12:54
[a]Josh. 17:16; Judg. 6:33
46 [1]Lit., *ran before* [2]Lit., *until you are* ...*ing to* [a]2 Kin. 3:15; Is. 8:11; Ezek. 3:14 ...Kin. 4:29; Jer. 1:17; 1 Pet. 1:13
19:1 [1]Lit., *all* about *how* [a]1 Kin. 18:40
...t., *soul* [a]Ruth 1:17; ... 20:10; 2 Kin. 6:31
[1]Reading of many ...nss.; Heb. text may ...ead *saw* [2]Lit., *soul* [a]Gen. 21:31
...r, *broom-tree* [2]Lit., ... [a]Num. 11:15; Jer. ...0:14-18; Jon. 4:3, 8

5 And he lay down and slept under a [1]juniper tree; and behold,
there was [a]an angel touching him, and he said to him, "Arise, eat."
6 Then he looked and behold, there was at his head a bread cake
baked on hot stones, and a jar of water. So he ate and drank and lay
down again.
7 And the angel of the LORD came again a second time and
touched him and said, "Arise, eat, because the journey is too great
for you."
8 So he arose and ate and drank, and went in the strength of that
food [a]forty days and forty nights to [b]Horeb, the mountain of God.
9 Then he came there to a cave, and lodged there; and behold, [a]the
word of the LORD *came* to him, and He said to him, "What are you
doing here, Elijah?"
10 And he said, "[a]I have been very zealous for the LORD, the God of
hosts; for the sons of Israel have forsaken Thy covenant, [b]torn down
Thine altars and killed Thy prophets with the sword. And [c]I alone
am left; and they seek my life, to take it away."
11 So He said, "[a]Go forth, and stand on the mountain before the
LORD." And behold, the LORD was passing by! And [b]a great and
strong wind was rending the mountains and breaking in pieces the
rocks before the LORD; *but* the LORD
was not in the wind. And after the
wind an earthquake, *but* the LORD
was not in the earthquake.
12 And after the earthquake a
fire, *but* the LORD *was* not in the
fire; and after the fire [a]a sound of a
gentle blowing.
13 And it came about when Elijah
heard *it*, that [a]he wrapped his face
in his mantle, and went out and
stood in the entrance of the cave.
And behold, [b]a voice *came* to him
and said, "What are you doing
here, Elijah?"
14 Then he said, "[a]I have been
very zealous for the LORD, the God
of hosts; for the sons of Israel have
forsaken Thy covenant, torn down
Thine altars and killed Thy
prophets with the sword. And I
alone am left; and they seek my
life, to take it away."
15 And the LORD said to him,
"Go, return on your way to the
wilderness of Damascus, and
when you have arrived, [a]you shall
anoint Hazael king over Aram;
16 and [a]Jehu the son of Nimshi
you shall anoint king over Israel;
and [b]Elisha the son of Shaphat of
Abel-meholah you shall anoint as
prophet in your place.
17 "And it shall come about, the

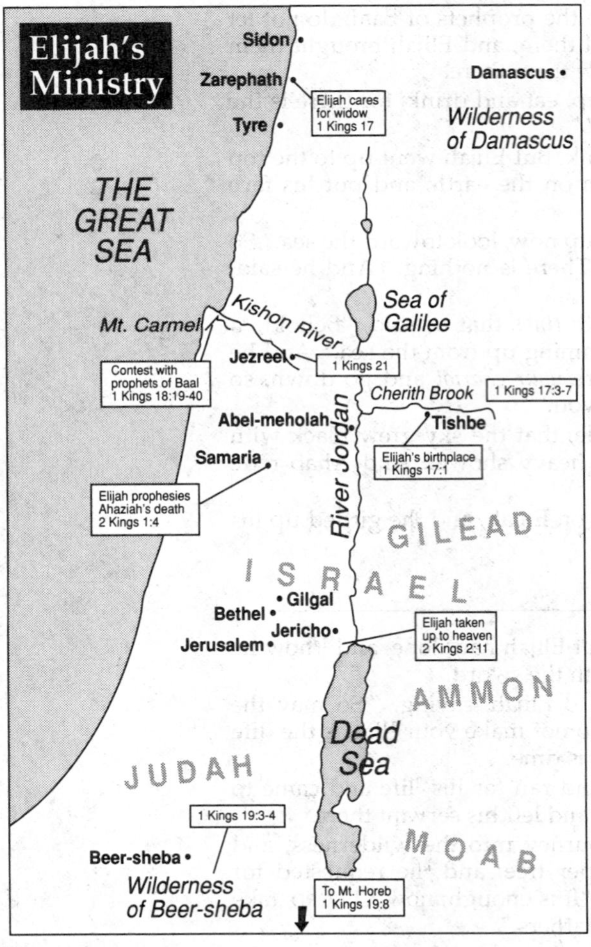

5 [1]Or, *broom-tree* [a]Gen. 28:12
8 [a]Ex. 24:18; 34:2 Deut. 9:9-11, 18; 4:2 [b]Ex. 3:1; 4:27
9 [a]Ex. 33:21, 22
10 [a]Ex. 20:5; 34 [b]Rom. 11:3, 4 [c]1 18:22
11 [a]Ex. 19:20; 24 18 [b]Ezek. 1:4
12 [a]Job 4:16; Ze
13 [a]Ex. 3:6 [b]1 K
14 [a]1 Kin. 19:10
15 [a]2 Kin. 8:8-1
16 [a]2 Kin. 9:1-1 [b]1 Kin. 19:19-21 2:9, 15

[a]one who escapes from the sword of Hazael, Jehu [b]shall put to death,
and the one who escapes from the sword of Jehu, Elisha shall put to
death.
18 "[a]Yet I will leave 7,000 in Israel, all the knees that have not bowed
to Baal and every mouth that has not [b]kissed him."
19 So he departed from there and found Elisha the son of Shaphat,
while he was plowing with twelve pairs *of oxen* before him, and he
with the twelfth. And Elijah passed over to him and threw [a]his
mantle on him.
20 And he left the oxen and ran after Elijah and said, "Please [a]let me
kiss my father and my mother, then I will follow you." And he said
to him, "Go back again, for what have I done to you?"
21 So he returned from following him, and took the pair of oxen
and sacrificed them and [a]boiled their flesh with the implements of
the oxen, and gave *it* to the people and they ate. Then he arose and
followed Elijah and ministered to him.

Chapter 20

20 Now [a]Ben-hadad king of Aram gathered all his army, [b]and
there *were* thirty-two kings with him, and horses and chariots.
And he went up and [c]besieged Samaria, and fought against it.
2 Then he sent messengers to the city to Ahab king of Israel, and
said to him, "Thus says Ben-hadad,
3 'Your silver and your gold are mine; your most beautiful wives
and children are also mine.' "
4 And the king of Israel answered and said, "It is according to
your word, my lord, O king; I am yours, and all that I have."
5 Then the messengers returned and said, "Thus says [1]Ben-hadad,
'Surely, I sent to you saying, "You shall give me your silver and your
gold and your wives and your children,"
6 but about this time tomorrow I will send my servants to you,
and they will search your house and the houses of your servants;
and it shall come about, [1]whatever is desirable in your eyes, they
will [2]take in their hand and carry away.' "
7 Then the king of Israel called all the elders of the land and said,
"Please observe and [a]see how this man is looking for trouble; for he
sent to me for my wives and my children and my silver and my
gold, and I did not refuse him."
8 And all the elders and all the people said to him, "Do not listen
or consent."
9 So he said to the messengers of Ben-hadad, "Tell my lord the
king, 'All that you sent for to your servant at the first I will do, but
this thing I cannot do.' " And the messengers departed and brought
him word again.
10 And Ben-hadad sent to him and said, "May [a]the gods do so to
me and more also, if the dust of Samaria shall suffice for handfuls for
all the people who [1]follow me."
11 Then the king of Israel answered and said, "Tell *him*, '[a]Let not
him who girds on *his armor* boast like him who takes *it* off.' "
12 And it came about when *Ben-hadad* heard this message, as [a]he
was drinking [1]with the kings in the [2]temporary shelters, that he said
to his servants, "Station *yourselves*." So they stationed *themselves*
against the city.
13 Now behold, a prophet approached Ahab king of Israel and said,

[a]2 Kin. 8:12; 13:3, [b]2 Kin. 9:14-10:25

[a]Rom. 11:4 [b]Hos. 13:2

19 [a]1 Sam. 28:14; 2 Kin. 2:8, 13, 14

att. 8:21, 22; Luke :61, 62; Acts 20:37

21 [a]2 Sam. 24:22

[a]1 Kin. 15:18, 20; 2 Kin. 6:24 [b]1 Kin. 2:31 [c]1 Kin. 16:24; 2 Kin. 6:24

5 [1]Lit., *Ben-hadad, saying*

it., *all the desire of your eyes* [2]Lit., *put*

7 [a]2 Kin. 5:7

[1]Lit., *are at my feet* n. 19:2; 2 Kin. 6:31

11 [a]Prov. 27:1

[1]Lit., *he and* [2]Or, *ooths* [a]1 Kin. 16:9; Prov. 31:4, 5

"Thus says the LORD, 'Have you seen all this great multitude? Be-
hold, [a]I will deliver them into your hand today, and [b]you shall know
that I am the LORD.' "
14 And Ahab said, "By whom?" So he said, "Thus says the LORD,
'By the young men of the rulers of the provinces.' " Then he said,
"Who shall [1]begin the battle?" And he [2]answered, "You."
15 Then he mustered the young men of the rulers of the provinces,
and there were 232; and after them he mustered all the people, *even*
all the sons of Israel, 7,000.
16 And they went out at noon, while [a]Ben-hadad was drinking him-
self drunk in the [1]temporary shelters [2]with the thirty-two kings who
helped him.
17 And the young men of the rulers of the provinces went out first;
and Ben-hadad sent out and they told him, saying, "Men have come
out from Samaria."
18 [a]Then he said, "If they have come out for peace, take them alive;
or if they have come out for war, take them alive."
19 So these went out from the city, the young men of the rulers of
the provinces, and the army which followed them.
20 And they [1]killed each his man; and the Arameans fled, and Israel
pursued them, and Ben-hadad king of Aram escaped on a horse
with horsemen.
21 And the king of Israel went out and [1]struck the horses and
chariots, and [1]killed the Arameans with a great slaughter.
22 Then [a]the prophet came near to the king of Israel, and said to
him, "Go, strengthen yourself and observe and see what you have to
do; for [b]at the turn of the year the king of Aram will come up against
you."
23 Now the servants of the king of Aram said to him, "[a]Their gods
are gods of the mountains, therefore they were stronger than we; but
rather let us fight against them in the plain, *and* surely we shall be
stronger than they.
24 "And do this thing: remove the kings, each from his place, and
put captains in their place,
25 and [1]muster an army like the army that you have lost, horse for
horse, and chariot for chariot. Then we will fight against them in the
plain, and surely we shall be stronger than they." And he listened to
their voice and did so.
26 So it came about [a]at the turn of the year, that Ben-hadad
mustered the Arameans and went up to [b]Aphek to fight against
Israel.
27 And the sons of Israel were mustered and were provisioned and
went to meet them; and the sons of Israel camped before them like
two little flocks of goats, [a]but the Arameans filled the country.
28 Then [a]a man of God came near and spoke to the king of Israel
and said, "Thus says the LORD, 'Because the Arameans have said,
"[b]The LORD is a god of *the* mountains, but He is not a god of *the*
valleys"; therefore [c]I will give all this great multitude into your
hand, and you shall know that I am the LORD.' "
29 So they camped one over against the other seven days. And it
came about that on the seventh day, the battle was joined, and the
sons of Israel [1]killed *of* the Arameans 100,000 foot soldiers in one day.
30 But the rest fled to [a]Aphek into the city, and the wall fell on

13 [a]1 Kin. 20:... 18:36
14 [1]Lit., *bind*
16 [1]Or, *booths* [2]*and the 32 king...* 16:9; 20:12; Pr...
18 [a]2 Kin. 14:8
20 [1]Lit., *smote*
21 [1]Lit., *smote*
22 [a]1 Kin. 20:1... [b]2 Sam. 11:1; 1... 20:26
23 [a]1 Kin. 14:23... 16:19-21; Rom...
25 [1]Lit., *number*
26 [a]1 Kin. 20:22... 13:17
27 [a]Judg. 6:3-5; 13:5-8
28 [a]1 Kin. 17:18... 20:23 [c]1 Kin. 20...
29 [1]Lit., *smote*
30 [a]1 Kin. 20:26

27,000 men who were left. And Ben-hadad fled and came into the
city [b]into an inner chamber.
31 And [a]his servants said to him, "Behold now, we have heard that
the kings of the house of Israel are merciful kings, please let us [b]put
sackcloth on our loins and ropes on our heads, and go out to the
king of Israel; perhaps he will save your [1]life."
32 So [a]they girded sackcloth on their loins and *put* ropes on their
heads, and came to the king of Israel and said, "[b]Your servant Ben-
hadad says, 'Please let me live.' " And he said, "Is he still alive? He is
my brother."
33 Now the men [1]took this as an omen, and quickly [2]catching his
word said, "Your brother Ben-hadad." Then he said, "Go, bring
him." Then Ben-hadad came out to him, and he [3]took him up into
the chariot.
34 And *Ben-hadad* said to him, "[a]The cities which my father took
from your father I will restore, and you shall make streets for your-
self in Damascus, as my father made in Samaria." *Ahab said,* "And I
will let you go with this covenant." So he made a covenant with him
and let him go.
35 Now a certain man of [a]the sons of the prophets said to [1]another
[b]by the word of the LORD, "Please strike me." But the man refused to
strike him.
36 Then he said to him, "Because you have not listened to the voice
of the LORD, behold, as soon as you have departed from me, [a]a lion
will [1]kill you." And as soon as he had departed from him a lion
found him, and [2]killed him.
37 Then he found another man and said, "Please [1]strike me." And
the man [2]struck him, [3]wounding him.
38 So the prophet departed and waited for the king by the way, and
[a]disguised himself with a bandage over his eyes.
39 And as the king passed by, he cried to the king and said, "Your
servant went out into the midst of the battle; and behold, a man
turned aside and brought a man to me and said, 'Guard this man; if
for any reason he is missing, [a]then your life shall be for his life, or
else you shall pay a talent of silver.'
40 "And while your servant was busy here and there, he was gone."
And the king of Israel said to him, "So shall your judgment be; you
yourself have decided *it*."
41 Then he hastily took the bandage away from his eyes, and the
king of Israel recognized him that he was of the prophets.
42 And he said to him, "Thus says the LORD, 'Because you have let
go out of *your* hand the man whom I had devoted to destruction,
therefore [a]your [1]life shall go for his [1]life, and your people for his
people.' "
43 So [a]the king of Israel went to his house sullen and vexed, and
came to Samaria.

Chapter 21

21 Now it came about after these things, that Naboth the Jez-
reelite had a vineyard which *was* in [a]Jezreel beside the palace
of Ahab king of Samaria.
2 And Ahab spoke to Naboth, saying, "[a]Give me your vineyard,
that I may have it for a vegetable garden because it is close beside

. 22:25; 2 Chr. 18:24
t., *soul* [a]1 Kin. ; [b]Gen. 37:34; 2 Sam. 3:31
. 20:31 [b]1 Kin. 20:3-6
., *divined* [2]Lit., *from him* [3]Lit., *him to come up*
[a]1 Kin. 15:20
it., *his neighbor* n. 2:3-7 [b]1 Kin. 13:17, 18
Lit., *smite* [2]Lit., *e* [a]1 Kin. 13:24
Lit., *smite* [2]Lit., Lit., *striking and wounding*
38 [a]1 Kin. 14:2
39 [a]2 Kin. 10:24
Lit., *soul* [a]1 Kin. 20:39
43 [a]1 Kin. 21:4
udg. 6:33; 1 Kin. 18:45, 46
2 [a]1 Sam. 8:14

my house, and I will give you a better vineyard than it in its place; if
[1]you like, I will give you the price of [2]it in money."
3 But Naboth said to Ahab, "The LORD forbid me [a]that I should
give you the inheritance of my fathers."
4 [a]So Ahab came into his house sullen and vexed because of the
word which Naboth the Jezreelite had spoken to him; for he said, "I
will not give you the inheritance of my fathers." And he lay down
on his bed and turned away his face and ate no [1]food.
5 But Jezebel his wife came to him and said to him, "How is it that
your spirit is so sullen that you are not eating [1]food?"
6 So he said to her, "Because I spoke to Naboth the Jezreelite, and
said to him, 'Give me your vineyard for money; or else, if it pleases
you, I will give you a vineyard in its place.' But he said, 'I will not
give you my vineyard.' "
7 And Jezebel his wife said to him, "[a]Do you now [1]reign over
Israel? Arise, eat bread, and let your heart be joyful; I will give you
the vineyard of Naboth the Jezreelite."
8 [a]So she wrote letters in Ahab's name and sealed them with his
seal, and sent letters to [b]the elders and to the nobles who were living
with Naboth in his city.
9 Now she wrote in the letters, saying, "Proclaim a fast, and seat
Naboth at the head of the people;
10 and seat two [a]worthless men before him, and let them testify
against him, saying, '[b]You cursed God and the king.' Then take him
out and [c]stone him [1]to death."
11 So the men of his city, the elders and the nobles who lived in his
city, did as Jezebel had sent *word* to them, just as it was written in the
letters which she had sent them.
12 They [a]proclaimed a fast and seated Naboth at the head of the
people.
13 Then the two worthless men came in and sat before him; and the
worthless men testified against him, even against Naboth, before the
people, saying, "Naboth cursed God and the king." [a]So they took
him outside the city and stoned him [1]to death with stones.
14 Then they sent *word* to Jezebel, saying, "Naboth has been stoned,
and is dead."
15 And it came about when Jezebel heard that Naboth had been
stoned and was dead, that Jezebel said to Ahab, "Arise, take posses-
sion of the vineyard of Naboth, the Jezreelite, which he refused to
give you for money; for Naboth is not alive, but dead."
16 And it came about when Ahab heard that Naboth was dead, that
Ahab arose to go down to the vineyard of Naboth the Jezreelite, to
take possession of it.
17 Then the word of the LORD came to Elijah the Tishbite, saying,
18 "Arise, go down to meet Ahab king of Israel, [a]who is in Samaria;
behold, he is in the vineyard of Naboth where he has gone down to
take possession of it.
19 "And you shall speak to him, saying, 'Thus says the LORD, "[a]Have
you murdered, and also taken possession?" ' And you shall speak to
him, saying, 'Thus says the LORD, "[b]In the place where the dogs
licked up the blood of Naboth the dogs shall lick up your blood,
even yours." ' "
20 And Ahab said to Elijah, "[a]Have you found me, O my enemy?"

2 [1]Lit., *it is go*[…] *eyes* [2]Lit., *th*[…]

3 [a]Lev. 25:23; […] 36:7; Ezek. 4[…]

4 [1]Lit., *bread* […] 20:43

5 [1]Lit., *bread*

7 [1]Lit., *exercis*[…] *kingship* [a]1 Sa[…]

8 [a]Esth. 3:12; [b]1 Kin. 20:7

10 [1]Lit., *so tha*[…] [a]1 Sam. 2:12; […] 20:1 [b]Ex. 22:2[…] 24:15, 16; Acts […] [c]Lev. 24:14

12 [a]Is. 58:4

13 [1]Lit., *with st*[…] *that he died* [a]2[…] 9:26; 2 Chr. 24:[…] 7:58, 59; Heb. 1[…]

18 [a]1 Kin. 16:29

19 [a]2 Sam. 12:9[…] 22:38; 2 Kin. 9:2[…]

20 [a]1 Kin. 18:17

And he [1]answered, "I have found *you,* [b]because you have sold your-
self to do evil in the sight of the LORD.
21 "Behold, I will bring evil upon you, and [a]will utterly sweep you
away, and will cut off from Ahab every male, both bond and free in
Israel;
22 and [a]I will make your house [b]like the house of Jeroboam the son
of Nebat, and like the house of Baasha the son of Ahijah, because of
the provocation with which you have provoked *Me* to anger, and
because you [c]have made Israel sin.
23 "And of Jezebel also has the LORD spoken, saying, '[a]The dogs shall
eat Jezebel in the [1]district of Jezreel.'
24 "[a]The one belonging to Ahab, who dies in the city, the dogs shall
eat, and the one who dies in the field the birds of heaven shall eat."
25 [a]Surely there was no one like Ahab who sold himself to do evil
in the sight of the LORD, [1]because Jezebel his wife incited him.
26 And [a]he acted very abominably in following idols, [b]according to
all that the Amorites had done, whom the LORD cast out before the
sons of Israel.
27 And it came about when Ahab heard these words, that [a]he tore
his clothes and put [1]on sackcloth and fasted, and he lay in sackcloth
and went about [2]despondently.
28 Then the word of the LORD came to Elijah the Tishbite, saying,
29 "Do you see how Ahab has humbled himself before Me? Because
he has humbled himself before Me, I will not bring the evil in his
days, *but* I will bring the evil upon his house [a]in his son's days."

Chapter 22

22 And [1]three years passed without war between Aram and
Israel.
2 [a]And it came about in the third year, that [b]Jehoshaphat the king
of Judah came down to the king of Israel.
3 Now the king of Israel said to his servants, "Do you know that
[a]Ramoth-gilead belongs to us, and we [1]are still doing nothing to take
it out of the hand of the king of Aram?"
4 And he said to Jehoshaphat, "Will you go with me to battle at
Ramoth-gilead?" And Jehoshaphat said to the king of Israel, "[a]I am
as you are, my people as your people, my horses as your horses."
5 Moreover, Jehoshaphat said to the king of Israel, "Please inquire
[1]first for the word of the LORD."
6 Then [a]the king of Israel gathered the prophets together, about
four hundred men, and said to them, "Shall I go against Ramoth-
gilead to battle or shall I refrain?" And they said, "Go up, for the
Lord will give *it* into the hand of the king."
7 But [a]Jehoshaphat said, "Is there not yet a prophet of the LORD
here, that we may inquire of him?"
8 And the king of Israel said to Jehoshaphat, "There is yet one man
by whom we may inquire of the LORD, but I hate him, because he
does not prophesy good concerning me, but evil. *He is* Micaiah son
of Imlah." But Jehoshaphat said, "Let not the king say so."
9 Then the king of Israel called an officer and said, "[1]Bring quickly
Micaiah son of Imlah."
10 Now the king of Israel and Jehoshaphat king of Judah were
sitting each on his throne, arrayed in *their* robes, at the threshing

20 [1]Lit., *said* [b]1 Kin. 21:25; 2 Kin. 17:17; Rom. 7:14
[a]1 Kin. 14:10; 2 Kin. 9:8
1 Kin. 15:29 [b]1 Kin. :3, 11 [c]1 Kin. 12:30; 13:34; 14:16
[1]Lit., *portion;* some mss. read *rampart* [a]2 Kin. 9:10, 30-37
[a]1 Kin. 14:11; 16:4
[1]Or, *whom Jezebel wife incited* [a]1 Kin. 16:30-33; 21:20
[a]1 Kin. 15:12; 2 Kin. 2 [b]Gen. 15:16; Lev. 25-30; 2 Kin. 21:11
[1]Lit., *sackcloth on his flesh* [2]Or, *softly* Gen. 37:34; 2 Sam. 3:31; 2 Kin. 6:30
29 [a]2 Kin. 9:25-37
1 [1]Lit., *they sat for three years*
2 Chr. 18:2 [b]1 Kin. 15:24
it., *are silent so as* [a]Deut. 4:43; Josh. 21:38; 1 Kin. 4:13
4 [a]2 Kin. 3:7
5 [1]Lit., *as the day*
6 [a]1 Kin. 18:19
7 [a]2 Kin. 3:11
t., *Hasten Micaiah*

floor at the entrance of the gate of Samaria; and [a]all the prophets
were prophesying before them.
11 Then Zedekiah the son of Chenaanah made [a]horns of iron for
himself and said, "Thus says the LORD, '[b]With these you shall gore
the Arameans until they are consumed.' "
12 And all the prophets were prophesying thus, saying, "Go up to
Ramoth-gilead and prosper, for the LORD will give *it* into the hand of
the king."
13 Then the messenger who went to summon Micaiah spoke to him
saying, "Behold now, the words of the prophets are uniformly favor-
able to the king. Please let your word be like the word of one of
them, and speak favorably."
14 But Micaiah said, "[a]As the LORD lives, what [b]the LORD says to me,
that I will speak."
15 When he came to the king, the king said to him, "Micaiah, shall
we go to Ramoth-gilead to battle, or shall we refrain?" And he [1]an-
swered him, "[a]Go up and succeed, and the LORD will give *it* into the
hand of the king."
16 Then the king said to him, "How many times must I adjure you
to speak to me nothing but the truth in the name of the LORD?"
17 So he said,

"I saw all Israel
Scattered on the mountains,
[a]Like sheep which have no shepherd.
And the LORD said, 'These have no master.
Let each of them return to his house in peace.' "

18 Then the king of Israel said to Jehoshaphat, "[a]Did I not tell you
that he would not prophesy good concerning me, but evil?"
19 And [1]Micaiah said, "Therefore, hear the word of the LORD. [a]I saw
the LORD sitting on His throne, and [b]all the host of heaven standing
by Him on His right and on His left.
20 "And the LORD said, 'Who will entice Ahab to go up and fall at
Ramoth-gilead?' And one said this while another said that.
21 "Then a spirit came forward and stood before the LORD and said,
'I will entice him.'
22 "And the LORD said to him, 'How?' And he said, 'I will go out and
[a]be a deceiving spirit in the mouth of all his prophets.' Then He said,
'You are to entice *him* and also prevail. Go and do so.'
23 "Now therefore, behold, [a]the LORD has put a deceiving spirit in
the mouth of all these your prophets; and the LORD has proclaimed
disaster against you."
24 Then [a]Zedekiah the son of Chenaanah came near and struck
Micaiah on the cheek and said, "[b]How did the Spirit of the LORD pass
from me to speak to you?"
25 And Micaiah said, "Behold, you shall see on that day when you
[a]enter an inner room to hide yourself."
26 Then the king of Israel said, "Take Micaiah and return him to
Amon the governor of the city and to Joash the king's son;
27 and say, 'Thus says the king, "[a]Put this man in prison, and feed
him [1]sparingly with bread and water until I return safely." ' "
28 And Micaiah said, "[a]If you indeed return safely the LORD has not
spoken by me." And he said, "[b]Listen, all you people."
29 So [a]the king of Israel and Jehoshaphat king of Judah went up
against Ramoth-gilead.

10 [a]1 Kin. 22:6
11 [a]Zech. 1:18 [b]Deut. 33:17
14 [a]1 Kin. 18:1 [b]Num. 22:18; 2
15 [1]Lit., *said to* 22:12
17 [a]Num. 27:1 22:34-36; 2 Chr Matt. 9:36; Mar
18 [a]1 Kin. 22:8
19 [1]Lit., *he* [a]Is. Ezek. 1:26-28; 10 [b]Job 1:6; 2:1 103:20, 21; Dan Matt. 18:10; Heb
22 [a]Judg. 9:23; 16:14; 18:10; 19 Ezek. 14:9; 2 Th 2:11
23 [a]Ezek. 14:9
24 [a]1 Kin. 22:11 5:39; Acts 23:2, 3 [b]2 Chr. 18:23
25 [a]1 Kin. 20:30
27 [1]Lit., *with bre affliction and wat affliction* [a]2 Chr. 18:25-27
28 [a]Deut. 18:22 1:2
29 [a]1 Kin. 22:3, 4

30 And the king of Israel said to Jehoshaphat, "[a]I will disguise
myself and go into the battle, but you put on your robes." So the
king of Israel disguised himself and went into the battle.
31 Now [a]the king of Aram had commanded the thirty-two captains
of his chariots, saying, "Do not fight with small or great, but with the
king of Israel alone."
32 So it came about, when the captains of the chariots saw Jehosha-
phat, that they said, "Surely it is the king of Israel," and they turned
aside to fight against him, and Jehoshaphat cried out.
33 Then it happened, when the captains of the chariots saw that it
was not the king of Israel, that they turned back from pursuing him.
34 Now a certain man drew his bow at random and struck the king
of Israel [1]in a joint of the armor. So he said to the driver of his
chariot, "Turn [2]around, and take me out of the [3]fight; [a]for I am
severely wounded."
35 And the battle [1]raged that day, and the king was propped up in
his chariot in front of the Arameans, and died at evening, and the
blood from the wound ran into the bottom of the chariot.
36 [a]Then a cry passed throughout the army close to sunset, saying,
"Every man to his city and every man to his [1]country."
37 So the king died and was brought to Samaria, and they buried
the king in Samaria.
38 And they washed the chariot by the pool of Samaria, and the
dogs licked up his blood (now the harlots bathed themselves *there*),
[a]according to the word of the LORD which He spoke.
39 Now the rest of the acts of Ahab and all that he did and [a]the
ivory house which he built and all the cities which he built, are they
not written in the Book of the Chronicles of the Kings of Israel?
40 So Ahab slept with his fathers, and Ahaziah his son became king
in his place.
41 [a]Now Jehoshaphat the son of Asa became king over Judah in the
fourth year of Ahab king of Israel.
42 Jehoshaphat was thirty-five years old when he became king, and
he reigned twenty-five years in Jerusalem. And his mother's name
was Azubah the daughter of Shilhi.
43 [a]And he walked in all the way of Asa his father; he did not turn
aside from it, doing right in the sight of the LORD. [b]However, the high
places were not taken away; the people still sacrificed and burnt
incense on the high places.
44 [a]Jehoshaphat also made peace with the king of Israel.
45 Now the rest of the acts of Jehoshaphat, and his might which he
showed and how he warred, are they not written [a]in the Book of the
Chronicles of the Kings of Judah?
46 And the remnant of [a]the sodomites who remained in the days of
his father Asa, he [1]expelled from the land.
47 Now [a]there was no king in Edom; a deputy was king.
48 Jehoshaphat made [a]ships of Tarshish to go to [b]Ophir for gold, but
[c]they did not go for the ships were broken at [d]Ezion-geber.
49 Then Ahaziah the son of Ahab said to Jehoshaphat, "Let my
servants go with your servants in the ships." But Jehoshaphat was
not willing.
50 [a]And Jehoshaphat slept with his fathers and was buried with his
fathers in the city of his father David, and Jehoram his son became
king in his place.

30 [a]2 Chr. 35:22
1 Kin. 20:1, 16, 24; 2 Chr. 18:30
[1]Lit., *between the* *cale-armor and the* *astplate* [2]Lit., *your hand* [3]Lit., *camp* [a]2 Chr. 35:23
35 [1]Lit., *went up*
[1]Lit., *land* [a]2 Kin. 14:12
38 [a]1 Kin. 21:19
39 [a]Amos 3:15
41 [a]2 Chr. 20:31
2 Chr. 17:3 [b]1 Kin. 15:14; 2 Kin. 12:3
[a]1 Kin. 22:2; 2 Kin. 16, 18; 2 Chr. 19:2
45 [a]2 Chr. 20:34
6 [1]Lit., *consumed* 19:5; Deut. 23:17; Kin. 14:24; 15:12; Jude 7
Sam. 8:14; 2 Kin. 3:9
Kin. 10:22; 2 Chr. 20:36 [b]1 Kin. 9:28 Chr. 20:37 [d]1 Kin. 9:26
50 [a]2 Chr. 21:1

51 Ahaziah the son of Ahab [a]became king over Israel in Samaria in
the seventeenth year of Jehoshaphat king of Judah, and he reigned
two years over Israel.
52 And he did evil in the sight of the LORD and [a]walked in the way
of his father and in the way of his mother and in the way of
Jeroboam the son of Nebat, who caused Israel to sin.
53 [a]So he served Baal and worshiped him and provoked the LORD
God of Israel to anger according to all that his father had done.

51 [a]1 Kin. 22:40

52 [a]1 Kin. 15:26; 2

53 [a]Judg. 2:11; 1
16:30-32

1 Kings at a Glance

e of 1 Kings:

Divisions

	Chapter Themes
	1
	2
	3
	4
	5
	6
	7
	8
	9
	10
	11
	12
	13
	14
	15
	16
	17
	18
	19
	20
	21
	22

Author:

Date:

Purpose:

Key Words:

2 KINGS

"Where is the God of Elijah?"

As you study 2 Kings, the continuation of 1 Kings, you'll see God at work setting up and rem kings and kingdoms. You'll be introduced to His spokesmen, the prophets, who spoke His Worc Israel and then Judah were led into captivity.

THINGS TO DO

1. As you read through 2 Kings one chapter at a time:
   a. Mark the following key repeated words: *according to the Word of the Lord, heart, sin, high* and *covenant*. Always watch for and mark words which are distinctive to a particular ch such as *customs* in chapter 17. Write these key words on an index card you can use bookmark while studying 2 Kings.
   b. Look for what you learn about God: His requirements, His ways, His judgments, an character. Record your insights in the margin of the text.
   c. Watch for any reforms instituted by a king. In the margin note these reforms and the re As you finish reading about the reign of a king, record what you learn on the chart KINGS OF ISRAEL AND JUDAH on pages 599 and 600.
   d. Record the theme or main event of each chapter on 2 KINGS AT A GLANCE on page 59 in the text next to the chapter number.
2. Second Kings has some key or pivotal events:
   a. In 1:1 through 8:15 the prophetic ministries of Elijah and then Elisha are prominent. List margin the miracles accomplished through these men. Several miraculous things occur 8:15— watch for them.
   b. Second Kings gives the account of the Assyrian invasion and subsequent captivity c northern kingdom of Israel. Give special attention to the details of this invasion and w came about. Note these in the margin of the text under the heading "The Assyrian Captivi
   c. After the Assyrian captivity all that is left is the southern kingdom of Judah. Watch how J conducts herself after seeing God's judgment on the northern kingdom. All this came to just as God's prophets said it would.
   d. Watch for the account of the Babylonian captivity of the southern kingdom of Judah an ensuing events. Record this in the margin as you did the Assyrian captivity.
3. Between 2 Kings and 1 Chronicles are charts which identify the major characters and ever 2 Kings.
   a. The first chart, ISRAEL'S DIVISION AND CAPTIVITY on page 551, gives a broad overvie the division of the kingdom through the three sieges of Jerusalem by the Babylonians.
   b. The second is a three-part chart: THE HISTORICAL CHART OF THE KINGS PROPHETS OF ISRAEL AND JUDAH on pages 596 through 598. This chart shows relationship of the kings and prophets to one another and to other foreign kings and kingdoms. You might color these charts so that the kings of the northern and southern k doms and the prophets can be distinguished readily from one another.
   c. When you read of key figures or events in 2 Kings consult these charts.
4. Complete the chart 2 KINGS AT A GLANCE on page 595. Considering the key events or sonages featured in 2 Kings, see which chapters of 2 Kings can be grouped together und common theme or topic. Record the theme of each segment under "Segment Divisions." Also

might want to note on the chart the chapters which tell when the Assyrian and Babylonian invasions occur.

HINGS TO THINK ABOUT

1. As you consider the lives of Elijah and Elisha, what do you learn about faith and trusting God?
2. As you think about the captivity of Israel and Judah, and the reasons for their captivity, what do you learn about the necessity of living a righteous life? What practical applications can you make to your own life? Remember, walking your own way may be pleasurable for awhile, but a just God must hold you accountable, and He must judge sin.
3. As you studied 1 and 2 Kings you saw that what God says will happen eventually comes to pass. Since His Word stands and none can alter it, can you see how critical it is that you believe God and hold to His Word no matter what others say or do?

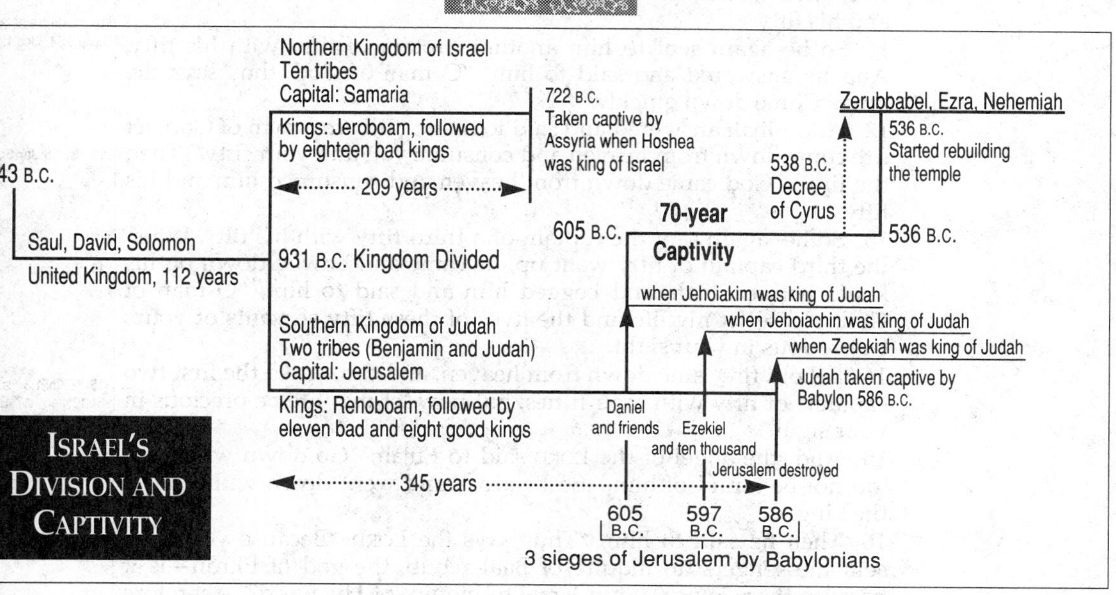

Chapter 1

a2 Sam. 8:2; 2 Kin. 3:5

1 Now [a]Moab rebelled against Israel after the death of Ahab.
2 And Ahaziah fell through the lattice in his upper chamber
which *was* in Samaria, and became ill. So he sent messengers and
said to them, "Go, [a]inquire of Baal-zebub, the god of Ekron, [b]whether
I shall recover from this sickness."

a2 Kin. 1:3, 6, 16; Matt. 10:25; Mark 3:22 b2 Kin. 8:7-10

3 But the angel of the LORD said to [a]Elijah the Tishbite, "Arise, go
up to meet the messengers of the king of Samaria and say to them,
'Is it because there is no God in Israel *that* you are going to inquire of
[b]Baal-zebub, the god of Ekron?'

a1 Kin. 17:1; 21:17 b2 Kin. 1:2

4 "Now therefore thus says the LORD, '[1a]You shall not come down
from the bed where you have gone up, but you shall surely die.'"
Then Elijah departed.

1Lit., *The bed where you went up, you shall not come down from it* a2 Kin. 1:6, 16

5 When the messengers returned to him he said to them, "[1]Why
have you returned?"
6 And they said to him, "A man came up to meet us and said to
us, 'Go, return to the king who sent you and say to him, "Thus says
the LORD, 'Is it because there is no God in Israel *that* you are sending

1Lit., *What is this that you have returned?*

[a]to inquire of Baal-zebub, the god of Ekron? Therefore [1]you shall not
come down from the bed where you have gone up, but shall surely
die.' " ' "
7 And he said to them, "What kind of man was he who came up to
meet you and spoke these words to you?"
8 And they [1]answered him, "[a]*He was* a hairy man with a leather
girdle [2]bound about his loins." And he said, "It is Elijah the Tish-
bite."
9 Then *the king* [a]sent to him a captain of fifty with his fifty. And he
went up to him, and behold, he was sitting on the top of the hill.
And he said to him, "O man of God, the king says, 'Come down.' "
10 And Elijah answered and said to the captain of fifty, "If I am a
man of God, [a]let fire come down from heaven and consume you and
your fifty." [b]Then fire came down from heaven and consumed him
and his fifty.
11 So he again sent to him another captain of fifty with his fifty.
And he answered and said to him, "O man of God, thus says the
king, 'Come down quickly.' "
12 And Elijah answered and said to them, "If I am a man of God, let
fire come down from heaven and consume you and your fifty." Then
the fire of God came down from heaven and consumed him and his
fifty.
13 So he [a]again sent the captain of a third fifty with his fifty. When
the third captain of fifty went up, he came and bowed down on his
knees before Elijah, and begged him and said to him, "O man of
God, please let my life and the lives of these fifty servants of yours
be precious in your sight.
14 "Behold fire came down from heaven, and consumed the first two
captains of fifty with their fifties; but now let my [1]life be precious in
your sight."
15 And [a]the angel of the LORD said to Elijah, "Go down with him;
[b]do not be afraid of him." So he arose and went down with him to
the king.
16 Then he said to him, "Thus says the LORD, 'Because you have
sent messengers [a]to inquire of Baal-zebub, the god of Ekron—is it
because there is no God in Israel to inquire of His word?—therefore
[1]you shall not come down from the bed where you have gone up,
but shall surely die.' "
17 So Ahaziah died according to the word of the LORD which Elijah
had spoken. And because he had no son, Jehoram became king in his
place [a]in the second year of Jehoram the son of Jehoshaphat, king of
Judah.
18 Now the rest of the acts of Ahaziah which he did, are they not
written in the Book of the Chronicles of the Kings of Israel?

Chapter 2

2 And it came about when the LORD was about to [a]take up Elijah
by a [1]whirlwind to heaven, that Elijah went with [b]Elisha from
[c]Gilgal.
2 And Elijah said to Elisha, "[a]Stay here please, for the LORD has
sent me as far as [b]Bethel." But Elisha said, "[c]As the LORD lives and as
you yourself live, I will not leave you." So they went down to Bethel.
3 Then [a]the sons of the prophets who *were at* Bethel came out to
Elisha and said to him, "Do you know that the LORD will take away

6 [1]V. 4, note 1 1:2

8 [1]Lit., *said* [2]([a]Zech. 13:4; M Mark 1:6

9 [a]2 Kin. 6:13,

10 [a]1 Kin. 18:3 Luke 9:54 [b]Job

13 [a]Is. 1:5; Jer.

14 [1]Lit., *soul*

15 [a]2 Kin. 1:3 [b] 51:12; Jer. 1:17; 2:6

16 [1]V. 4, note 1 1:3

17 [a]2 Kin. 3:1; 8

2:1 [1]Or, *windstor* [a]Gen. 5:24; Heb. [b]1 Kin. 19:16-21 4:19

2 [a]Ruth 1:15 [b]1 K 12:28, 29 [c]1 Sam 2 Kin. 2:4, 6

3 [a]2 Kin. 4:1, 38;

your master from over [1]you today?" And he said, "Yes, I know; be still."

4 And Elijah said to him, "Elisha, please [a]stay here, for the LORD has sent me to [b]Jericho." But he said, "[a]As the LORD lives, and as you yourself live, I will not leave you." So they came to Jericho.

5 And [a]the sons of the prophets who *were* at Jericho approached Elisha and said to him, "[a]Do you know that the LORD will take away your master from over [1]you today?" And he [2]answered, "Yes, I know; be still."

6 Then Elijah said to him, "Please [a]stay here, for the LORD has sent me to [b]the Jordan." And he said, "As the LORD lives, and as you yourself live, I will not leave you." So the two of them went on.

7 Now [a]fifty men of the sons of the prophets went and stood opposite *them* at a distance, while the two of them stood by the Jordan.

8 And Elijah [a]took his mantle and folded it together and [b]struck the waters, and they were divided here and there, so that the two of them crossed over on dry ground.

9 Now it came about when they had crossed over, that Elijah said to Elisha, "Ask what I shall do for you before I am taken from you." And Elisha said, "Please, let a [a]double portion of your spirit be upon me."

10 And he said, "You have asked a hard thing. *Nevertheless,* if you [a]see me when I am taken from you, it shall be so for you; but if not, it shall not be *so.*"

11 Then it came about as they were going along and talking, that behold, *there appeared* [a]a chariot of fire and horses of fire which separated the two of them. And Elijah went up by a [1]whirlwind to heaven.

12 And Elisha saw *it* and cried out, "[a]My father, my father, the [1]chariots of Israel and its horsemen!" And he saw him no more. Then [b]he took hold of his own clothes and tore them in two pieces.

13 He also took up the mantle of Elijah that fell from him, and returned and stood by the bank of the Jordan.

14 And he took the mantle of Elijah that fell from him, and struck the waters and said, "Where is the LORD, the God of Elijah?" And when he also had [a]struck the waters, they were divided here and there; and Elisha crossed over.

15 Now when [a]the sons of the prophets who *were* at Jericho opposite *him* saw him, they said, "The spirit of Elijah rests on

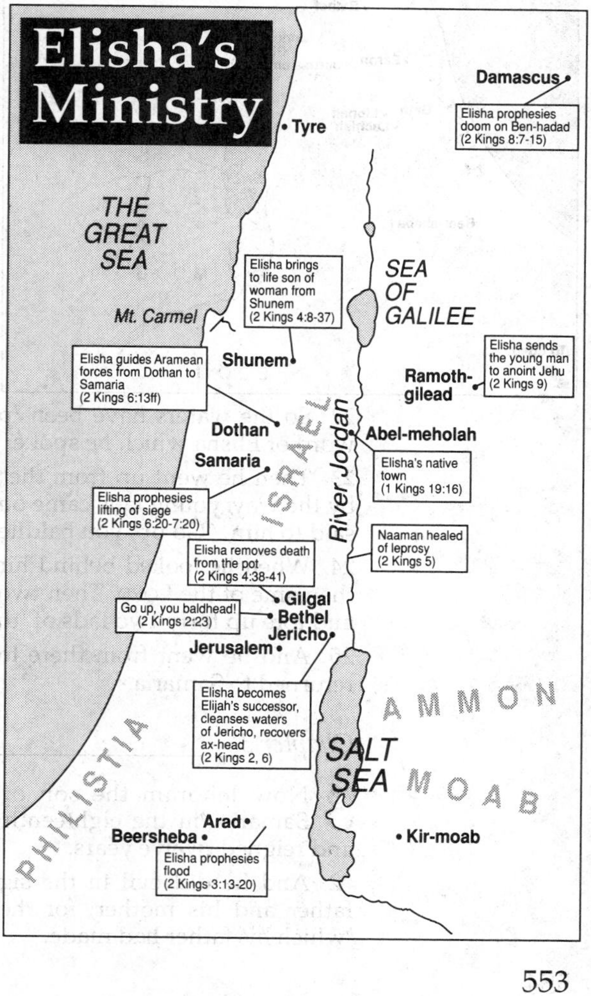
Elisha's Ministry
Damascus
Elisha prophesies doom on Ben-hadad (2 Kings 8:7-15)
Tyre
THE GREAT SEA
Elisha brings to life son of woman from Shunem (2 Kings 4:8-37)
SEA OF GALILEE
Mt. Carmel
Elisha guides Aramean forces from Dothan to Samaria (2 Kings 6:13ff)
Shunem
Elisha sends the young man to anoint Jehu (2 Kings 9)
Ramoth-gilead
ISRAEL
River Jordan
Dothan
Abel-meholah
Samaria
Elisha's native town (1 Kings 19:16)
Elisha prophesies lifting of siege (2 Kings 6:20-7:20)
Naaman healed of leprosy (2 Kings 5)
Elisha removes death from the pot (2 Kings 4:38-41)
Gilgal
Go up, you baldhead! (2 Kings 2:23)
Bethel
Jericho
Jerusalem
Elisha becomes Elijah's successor, cleanses waters of Jericho, recovers ax-head (2 Kings 2, 6)
AMMON
PHILISTIA
SALT SEA
MOAB
Arad
Beersheba
Kir-moab
Elisha prophesies flood (2 Kings 3:13-20)

3 [1]Lit., *your head*
[a]2 Kin. 2:2 [b]Josh. 6:26
it., *your head* [2]Lit., *said* [a]2 Kin. 2:3
[a]2 Kin. 2:2 [b]Josh. 3:8, 15-17
7 [a]2 Kin. 2:15, 16
Kin. 19:13, 19 [b]Ex. 21, 22; 2 Kin. 2:14
[a]Num. 11:17-25; Deut. 21:17
10 [a]Acts 1:10
1 [1]Or, *windstorm* [a]2 Kin. 6:17
it., *chariot* [a]2 Kin. [b]Gen. 37:34; Job 1:20
14 [a]2 Kin. 2:8
15 [a]2 Kin. 2:7

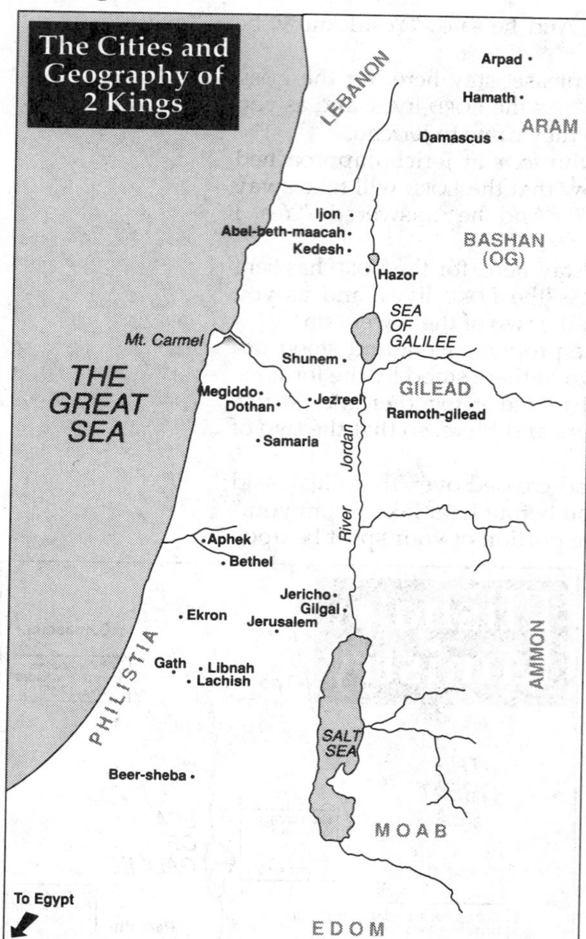

Elisha." And they came to meet
him and bowed themselves to the
ground before him.
16 And they said to him, "Behold
now, there are with your servants
fifty strong men, please let them go
and search for your master; [1]per-
haps [a]the Spirit of the LORD has
taken him up and cast him on
some mountain or into some val-
ley." And he said, "You shall not
send."
17 But when [a]they urged him
until he was ashamed, he said,
"Send." They sent therefore fifty
men; and they searched three days,
but did not find him.
18 And they returned to him
while he was staying at Jericho;
and he said to them, "Did I not say
to you, 'Do not go'?"
19 Then the men of the city said to
Elisha, "Behold now, the situation
of this city is pleasant, as my lord
sees; but the water is bad, and the
land [1]is unfruitful."
20 And he said, "Bring me a new
jar, and put salt [1]in it." So they
brought *it* to him.
21 And he went out to the spring
of water, and [a]threw salt [1]in it and
said, "Thus says the LORD, 'I have
[2]purified these waters; there shall
not be from there death or [3]unfruit-
fulness any longer.' "
22 So the waters have been [1]purified to this day, according to the
word of Elisha which he spoke.
23 Then he went up from there to Bethel; and as he was going up
by the way, young lads came out from the city and [a]mocked him and
said to him, "Go up, you baldhead; go up, you baldhead!"
24 When he looked behind him and saw them, he [a]cursed them in
the name of the LORD. Then two female bears came out of the woods
and tore up forty-two lads of [1]their number.
25 And he went from there to [a]Mount Carmel, and from there he
returned to Samaria.

Chapter 3

3 Now Jehoram the son of Ahab became king over Israel at
Samaria [a]in the eighteenth year of Jehoshaphat king of Judah,
and reigned twelve years.
2 And he did evil in the sight of the LORD, though not like his
father and his mother; for [a]he put away the *sacred* pillar of Baal
[b]which his father had made.

16 [1]Lit., *lest* 18:12; Acts 8

17 [a]2 Kin. 8:

19 [1]Lit., *caus* *barrenness*

20 [1]Lit., *there*

21 [1]Lit., *there healed* [3]Lit., *barrenness* [a]E 26; 2 Kin. 4:41

22 [1]Lit., *healed*

23 [a]2 Chr. 36:1 31:17, 18

24 [1]Lit., *them* [a] 13:25-27

25 [a]1 Kin. 18:19 2 Kin. 4:25

3:1 [a]2 Kin. 1:17

2 [a]Ex. 23:24; 2 K 10:18, 26-28 [b]1 K 16:31, 32

3 Nevertheless, [a]he clung to the sins of Jeroboam the son of Nebat,
[b]which he made Israel sin; he did not depart from them.
4 Now Mesha king of Moab was a sheep breeder, and [a]used to pay
the king of Israel 100,000 lambs and the wool of 100,000 rams.
5 But it came about, [a]when Ahab died, the king of Moab rebelled
against the king of Israel.
6 And King Jehoram went out of Samaria [1]at that time and
mustered all Israel.
7 Then he went and sent *word* to Jehoshaphat the king of Judah,
saying, "The king of Moab has rebelled against me. Will you go with
me to fight against Moab?" And he said, "I will go up; [a]I am as you
are, my people as your people, my horses as your horses."
8 And he said, "Which way shall we go up?" And he [1]answered,
"The way of the wilderness of Edom."
9 So [a]the king of Israel went with [b]the king of Judah and [c]the king
of Edom; and they made a circuit of seven days' journey, and there
was no water for the army or for the cattle that followed them.
10 Then the king of Israel said, "Alas! For the LORD has called these
three kings to give them into the hand of Moab."
11 But Jehoshaphat said, "[a]Is there not a prophet of the LORD here,
that we may inquire of the LORD by him?" And one of the king of
Israel's servants answered and said, "[b]Elisha the son of Shaphat is
here, [c]who used to pour water on the hands of Elijah."
12 And Jehoshaphat said, "The word of the LORD is with him." So
the king of Israel and Jehoshaphat and the king of Edom went down
to him.
13 Now Elisha said to the king of Israel, "What do I have to do with
you? [a]Go to the prophets of your father and to the prophets of your
mother." And the king of Israel said to him, "No, for the LORD has
called these three kings *together* to give them into the hand of Moab."
14 And Elisha said, "[a]As the LORD of hosts lives, before whom I
stand, were it not that I regard the presence of Jehoshaphat the king
of Judah, I would not look at you nor see you.
15 "But now [a]bring me a minstrel." And it came about, when the
minstrel played, that [b]the hand of the LORD came upon him.
16 And he said, "Thus says the LORD, 'Make this valley full of
trenches.'
17 "For thus says the LORD, 'You shall not see wind nor shall you see
rain; yet that valley [a]shall be filled with water, so that you shall
drink, both you and your cattle and your beasts.
18 'And this is but a [a]slight thing in the sight of the LORD; He shall
also give the Moabites into your hand.
19 '[a]Then you shall strike every fortified city and every choice city,
and fell every good tree and stop all springs of water, and mar every
good piece of land with stones.' "
20 And it happened in the morning [a]about the time of offering the
sacrifice, that behold, water came by the way of Edom, and the
country was filled with water.
21 Now all the Moabites heard that the kings had come up to fight
against them. And all who were able to [1]put on armor and older
were summoned, and stood on the border.
22 And they rose early in the morning, and the sun shone on the
water, and the Moabites saw the water opposite *them* as red as blood.
23 Then they said, "This is blood; the kings have surely fought

3 [a]1 Kin. 12:28-32 [b]1 Kin. 14:9, 16
4 [a]2 Sam. 8:2; Is. 16:1, 2
5 [a]2 Kin. 1:1
6 [1]Lit., *in that day*
7 [a]1 Kin. 22:4
8 [1]Lit., *said*
[a]2 Kin. 3:1 [b]2 Kin. 3:7 [c]1 Kin. 22:47
[a]1 Kin. 22:7 [b]2 Kin. [c]1 Kin. 19:21; John 13:4, 5, 13, 14
13 [a]1 Kin. 18:19; 22:6-11, 22-25
[a]1 Kin. 17:1; 2 Kin. 5:16
15 [a]1 Sam. 16:23; 1 Chr. 25:1 [b]1 Kin. 18:46; Ezek. 1:3
17 [a]Ps. 107:35
18 [a]Jer. 32:17, 27; k 10:27; Luke 1:37
19 [a]2 Kin. 3:25
20 [a]Ex. 29:39, 40
21 [1]Lit., *gird* nselves *with a belt*

together, and they have slain one another. Now therefore, Moab, to the spoil!"

24 But when they came to the camp of Israel, the Israelites arose and struck the Moabites, so that they fled before them; and they went forward [1]into the land, [2]slaughtering the Moabites.

25 [a]Thus they destroyed the cities; and each one threw a stone on every piece of good land and filled it. So they stopped all the springs of water and felled all the good trees, until in [b]Kir-hareseth *only* they left its stones; however, the slingers went about *it* and struck it.

26 When the king of Moab saw that the battle was too fierce for him, he took with him 700 men who drew swords, to break through to the king of Edom; but they could not.

27 Then he took his oldest son who was to reign in his place, and [a]offered him as a burnt offering on the wall. And there came great wrath against Israel, and they departed from him and returned to their own land.

Chapter 4

4 Now a certain woman of the wives of [a]the sons of the prophets cried out to [1]Elisha, "Your servant my husband is dead, and you know that your servant feared the LORD; and [b]the creditor has come to take my two children to be his slaves."

2 And Elisha said to her, "What shall I do for you? Tell me, what do you have in the house?" And she said, "Your maidservant has nothing in the house except [a]a jar of oil."

3 Then he said, "Go, borrow vessels at large for yourself from all your neighbors, *even* empty vessels; do not get a few.

4 "And you shall go in and shut the door behind you and your sons, and pour out into all these vessels; and you shall set aside what is full."

5 So she went from him and shut the door behind her and her sons; they were bringing *the vessels* to her and she poured.

6 And it came about when [a]the vessels were full, that she said to her son, "Bring me another vessel." And he said to her, "There is not one vessel more." And the oil stopped.

7 Then she came and told [a]the man of God. And he said, "Go, sell the oil and pay your debt, and you *and* your sons can live on the rest."

8 Now there came a day when Elisha passed over to [a]Shunem, where there was a [1]prominent woman, and she persuaded him to eat [2]food. And so it was, as often as he passed by, he turned in there to eat [2]food.

9 And she said to her husband, "Behold now, I perceive that this is a holy [a]man of God passing by us continually.

10 "Please, let us [a]make a little walled upper chamber and let us set a bed for him there, and a table and a chair and a lampstand; and it shall be, when he comes to us, *that* he can turn in there."

11 [1]One day he came there and turned in to the upper chamber and [2]rested.

12 Then he said to [a]Gehazi his servant, "Call this Shunammite." And when he had called her, she stood before him.

13 And he said to him, "Say now to her, 'Behold, you have been [1]careful for us with all this [2]care; what can I do for you? Would you

24 [1]Lit., *into it* *smiting*

25 [a]2 Kin. 3:19 16:7; Jer. 48:31

27 [a]Amos 2:1;

4:1 [1]Lit., *Elisha* [a]2 Kin. 2:3 [b]Lev 25:39-41, 48; 1 22:2; Neh. 5:2-5

2 [a]1 Kin. 17:12

6 [a]Matt. 14:20

7 [a]1 Kin. 12:22

8 [1]Lit., *great* [2]Li *bread* [a]Josh. 19

9 [a]2 Kin. 4:7

10 [a]Matt. 10:41, 25:40; Rom. 12:1

11 [1]Lit., *Now a d came that* [2]Lit., *la*

12 [a]2 Kin. 4:29-3 5:20-27; 8:4, 5

13 [1]Lit., *fearful* [2]L *fear*

be spoken for to the king or to the captain of the army?' " And she
[3]answered, "I live among my own people."
14 So he said, "What then is to be done for her?" And Gehazi [1]an-
swered, "Truly she has no son and her husband is old."
15 And he said, "Call her." When he had called her, she stood in the
doorway.
16 Then he said, "[a]At this season [1]next year you shall embrace a
son." And she said, "No, my lord, O man of God, [b]do not lie to your
maidservant."
17 And the woman conceived and bore a son at that season [1]the
next year, as Elisha had said to her.
18 When the child was grown, the day came that he went out to his
father to the reapers.
19 And he said to his father, "My head, my head." And he said to
his servant, "Carry him to his mother."
20 When he had taken him and brought him to his mother, he sat
on her [1]lap until noon, and *then* died.
21 And she went up and [a]laid him on the bed of [b]the man of God,
and shut *the door* behind him, and went out.
22 Then she called to her husband and said, "Please send me one of
the servants and one of the donkeys, that I may run to the man of
God and return."
23 And he said, "Why will you go to him today? It is neither [a]new
moon nor sabbath." And she said, "*It will be* well."
24 Then she saddled a donkey and said to her servant, "Drive and
go forward; do not slow down [1]the pace for me unless I tell you."
25 So she went and came to the man of God to [a]Mount Carmel. And
it came about when the man of God saw her at a distance, that he
said to Gehazi his servant, "Behold, [1]yonder is the Shunammite.
26 "Please run now to meet her and say to her, 'Is it well with you? Is
it well with your husband? Is it well with the child?' " And she
[1]answered, "It is well."
27 When she came to the man of God [a]to the hill, she caught hold of
his feet. And Gehazi came near to push her away; but the man of
God said, "Let her alone, for her soul is [1]troubled within her; and the
LORD has hidden it from me and has not told me."
28 Then she said, "Did I ask for a son from my lord? Did I not say,
'[a]Do not deceive me'?"
29 Then he said to Gehazi, "[a]Gird up your loins and [b]take my staff
in your hand, and go your way; if you meet any man, do not [c]salute
him, and if anyone salutes you, do not answer him; and [d]lay my staff
on the lad's face."
30 And the mother of the lad said, "[a]As the LORD lives and as you
yourself live, I will not leave you." And he arose and followed her.
31 Then Gehazi passed on before them and laid the staff on the
lad's face, but there was neither sound nor [1]response. So he returned
to meet him and told [2]him, "The lad [a]has not awakened."
32 When Elisha came into the house, behold the lad was dead and
laid on his bed.
33 So he entered and [a]shut the door behind them both, and prayed
to the LORD.
34 And [a]he went up and lay on the child, and put his mouth on his
mouth and his eyes on his eyes and his hands on his hands, and he
stretched himself on him; and the flesh of the child became warm.

13 [3]Lit., *said*
14 [1]Lit., *said*
[1]Lit., *when the time* [re]*vives* [a]Gen. 18:14 [b]2 Kin. 4:28
[1]Lit., *when the time revived*
20 [1]Lit., *knees*
[a]2 Kin. 4:32 [b]2 Kin. 4:7
[a]Num. 10:10; 28:11; 1 Chr. 23:31
24 [1]Lit., *riding*
25 [1]Lit., *this* [Sh]*unammite* [a]2 Kin. 2:25
26 [1]Lit., *said*
[1]Lit., *bitter* [a]2 Kin. 4:25
28 [a]2 Kin. 4:16
[a]1 Kin. 18:46; 2 Kin. [b]Ex. 4:17; 2 Kin. [c]Luke 10:4 [d]Ex. 7:19, 20; 14:16
30 [a]2 Kin. 2:2, 4
[1]Lit., *attentiveness* [2]*him, saying* [a]John 11:11
[a]2 Kin. 4:4; Matt. 6:6; Luke 8:51
[a]1 Kin. 17:21-23

35 Then he returned and walked in the house once back and forth,
and went up and [a]stretched himself on him; and the lad sneezed
seven times and the lad opened his eyes.
36 And he called Gehazi and said, "Call this Shunammite." So he
called her. And when she came in to him, he said, "Take up your
son."
37 Then she went in and fell at his feet and bowed herself to the
ground, and [a]she took up her son and went out.
38 When Elisha returned to [a]Gilgal, *there was* [b]a famine in the land.
[1]As [c]the sons of the prophets [d]were sitting before him, he said to his
servant, "[e]Put on the large pot and boil stew for the sons of the
prophets."
39 Then one went out into the field to gather herbs, and found a
wild vine and gathered from it his lap full of wild gourds, and came
and sliced them into the pot of stew, for they did not know *what they
were.*
40 So they poured *it* out for the men to eat. And it came about as
they were eating of the stew, that they cried out and said, "O man of
God, there is [a]death in the pot." And they were unable to eat.
41 But he said, "Now bring meal." [a]And he threw it into the pot,
and he said, "Pour *it* out for the people that they may eat." Then
there was no harm in the pot.
42 Now a man came from Baal-shalishah, and brought the man of
God bread of the first fruits, twenty loaves of barley and fresh ears of
grain in his sack. And he said, "[a]Give *them* to the people that they
may eat."
43 And his attendant said, "What, [a]shall I set this before a hundred
men?" But he said, "Give *them* to the people that they may eat, for
thus says the LORD, 'They shall eat and have *some* left over.' "
44 So he set *it* before them, and they ate and [a]had *some* left over,
according to the word of the LORD.

INSIGHT

The land of Baal-Salishah, meaning "the third," was evidently the tribal territory of Ephraim (1 Samuel 9:4). Modern-day Kefr Thilth may be on the site of the ancient city. However, the exact location of Baal-Shalishah has recently been questioned.

Chapter 5

5 Now [a]Naaman, captain of the army of the king of Aram, was a
great man [1]with his master, and highly respected, because by
him the LORD had given victory to Aram. The man was also a valiant
warrior, *but he was* a leper.
2 Now the Arameans had gone out [a]in bands, and had taken cap-
tive a little girl from the land of Israel; and she [1]waited on Naaman's
wife.
3 And she said to her mistress, "I wish that my master were [1]with
the prophet who is in Samaria! Then he would cure him of his
leprosy."
4 And [1]Naaman went in and told his master, saying, "Thus and
thus spoke the girl who is from the land of Israel."
5 Then the king of Aram said, "Go [1]now, and I will send a letter to
the king of Israel." And he departed and [a]took with him ten talents
of silver and six thousand *shekels* of gold and ten [b]changes of clothes.
6 And he brought the letter to the king of Israel, saying, "And now
as this letter comes to you, behold, I have sent Naaman my servant
to you, that you may cure him of his leprosy."
7 And it came about when the king of Israel read the letter, that [a]he
tore his clothes and said, "[b]Am I God, to kill and to make alive, that

35 [a]1 Kin. 17
37 [a]Heb. 11:3
38 [1]Lit., *And* 2:1 [b]2 Kin. 8: 2:3 [d]Luke 10: 22:3 [e]Ezek. 24:3
40 [a]Ex. 10:17
41 [a]Ex. 15:25; 2:21
42 [a]Matt. 14:1 15:32-38
43 [a]Luke 9:13;
44 [a]Matt. 14:20 John 6:13
5:1 [1]Lit., *before* 4:27
2 [1]Lit., *was bef* [a]2 Kin. 6:23; 13:
3 [1]Lit., *before*
4 [1]Lit., *he*
5 [1]Lit., *enter* [a]1 9:7; 2 Kin. 4:42 14:12; 2 Kin. 5:22
7 [a]Gen. 37:29 30:2; 1 Sam. 2:6

this man is sending *word* to me to cure a man of his leprosy? But
[c]consider now, and see how he is seeking [1]a quarrel against me."
8 And it happened when Elisha [a]the man of God heard that the
king of Israel had torn his clothes, that he sent *word* to the king,
saying, "Why have you torn your clothes? Now let him come to me,
and he shall know that there is a prophet in Israel."
9 So Naaman came with his horses and his chariots, and stood at
the doorway of the house of Elisha.
10 And Elisha sent a messenger to him, saying, "[a]Go and wash in
the Jordan seven times, and your flesh shall be restored to you and
you shall be clean."
11 But Naaman was furious and went away and said, "Behold, I
[1]thought, 'He will surely come out to me, and stand and call on the
name of the LORD his God, and wave his hand over the place, and
cure the leper.'
12 "Are not [1]Abanah and Pharpar, the rivers of Damascus, better
than all the waters of Israel? Could I not wash in them and be
clean?" So he turned and [a]went away in a rage.
13 [a]Then his servants came near and spoke to him and said, "[b]My
father, had the prophet told you *to do some* great thing, would you
not have done *it*? How much more *then*, when he says to you, 'Wash,
and be clean'?"
14 So he went down and dipped *himself* seven times in the Jordan,
according to the word of the man of God; and [a]his flesh was restored
like the flesh of a little child, and [b]he was clean.
15 When he returned to the man of God [1]with all his company, and
came and stood before him, he said, "Behold now, [a]I know that there
is no God in all the earth, but in Israel; so please [b]take a [2]present
from your servant now."
16 But he said, "[a]As the LORD lives, before whom I stand, [b]I will take
nothing." And he urged him to take *it*, but he refused.
17 And Naaman said, "If not, please let your servant at least be
given two mules' load of [a]earth; for your servant will no more offer
burnt offering nor will he sacrifice to other gods, but to the LORD.
18 "In this matter may the LORD pardon your servant: when my
master goes into the house of Rimmon to worship there, and [a]he
leans on my hand and I bow myself in the house of Rimmon, when I
bow myself in the house of Rimmon, the LORD pardon your servant
in this matter."
19 And he said to him, "[a]Go in peace." So he departed from him
some distance.
20 But [a]Gehazi, the servant of Elisha the man of God, [1]thought,
"Behold, my master has spared this Naaman the Aramean, [2]by not
receiving from his hands what he brought. [b]As the LORD lives, I will
run after him and take something from him."
21 So Gehazi pursued Naaman. When Naaman saw one running
after him, he came down from the chariot to meet him and said, "Is
all well?"
22 And he said, "[a]All is well. My master has sent me, saying, 'Be-
hold, just now two young men of the sons of the prophets have come
to me from [b]the hill country of Ephraim. Please give them a talent of
silver and [c]two changes of clothes.' "
23 And Naaman said, "[a]Be pleased to take two talents." And he
urged him, and bound two talents of silver in two bags with two

7 [1]Lit., *an occasion* ...Kin. 20:7; Luke 11:54
8 [a]1 Kin. 12:22
10 [a]John 9:7
11 [1]Lit., *said*
[1]Another reading is ...*nanah* [a]Prov. 14:17; 16:32; 19:11
13 [a]1 Sam. 28:23 ...2 Kin. 2:12; 6:21; 8:9
14 [a]2 Kin. 5:10; Job ...25 [b]Luke 4:27; 5:13
...5 [1]Lit., *he and* [2]Lit., ...*lessing* [a]Josh. 2:11; ...m. 17:46, 47; 2 Kin. 5:8 [b]1 Sam. 25:27
[a]2 Kin. 3:14 [b]Gen. ...23; 2 Kin. 5:20, 26
17 [a]Ex. 20:24
18 [a]2 Kin. 7:2, 17
[a]Ex. 4:18; 1 Sam. 1:17; Mark 5:34
...Lit., *said* [2]Lit., *from* ...4:12, 31, 36 [b]Ex. 20:7; 2 Kin. 6:31
[a]2 Kin. 4:26 [b]Josh. 24:33 [c]2 Kin. 5:5
23 [a]2 Kin. 6:3

INSIGHT

The **Arameans,** the descendants of Noah through Shem, lived in a confederation of towns and settlements in what is now Syria. Some settled as far as Babylon. Jacob's father, Abraham, was Aramean (Deuteronomy 26:5).

changes of clothes, and gave them to two of his servants; and they
carried *them* before him.
24 When he came to the [1]hill, he took them from their hand and
[a]deposited them in the house, and he sent the men away, and they
departed.
25 But he went in and stood before his master. And Elisha said to
him, "Where have you been, Gehazi?" And he said, "[a]Your servant
went nowhere."
26 Then he said to him, "Did not my heart go *with you,* when the
man turned from his chariot to meet you? [a]Is it a time to receive
money and to receive clothes and olive groves and vineyards and
sheep and oxen and male and female servants?
27 "Therefore, the leprosy of Naaman shall cleave to you and to your
[1]descendants forever." So he went out from his presence [a]a leper *as
white* as snow.

Chapter 6

6 Now [a]the sons of the prophets said to Elisha, "Behold now, the
place before you where we are living is too limited for us.
2 "Please let us go to the Jordan, and each of us take from there a
beam, and let us make a place there for ourselves where we may
live." So he said, "Go."
3 Then one said, "Please be willing to go with your servants." And
he [1]answered, "I shall go."
4 So he went with them; and when they came to the Jordan, they
cut down trees.
5 But as one was felling a beam, [1]the axe head fell into the water;
and he cried out and said, "Alas, my master! For it was borrowed."
6 Then the man of God said, "Where did it fall?" And when he
showed him the place, [a]he cut off a stick, and threw *it* in there, and
made the iron float.
7 And he said, "Take it up for yourself." So he put out his hand
and took it.
8 Now the king of Aram was warring against Israel; and he [1]coun-
seled with his servants saying, "In such and such a place shall be my
camp."
9 And [a]the man of God sent *word* to the king of Israel saying,
"Beware that you do not pass this place, for the Arameans are com-
ing down there."
10 And the king of Israel sent to the place about which the man of
God had told him; thus he warned him, so that he guarded himself
there, [1]more than once or twice.
11 Now the heart of the king of Aram was enraged over this thing;
and he called his servants and said to them, "Will you tell me which
of us is for the king of Israel?"
12 And one of his servants said, "No, my lord, O king; but Elisha,
the prophet who is in Israel, tells the king of Israel the words that
you speak in your bedroom."
13 So he said, "Go and see where he is, that I may send and take
him." And it was told him, saying, "Behold, he is in [a]Dothan."
14 And he sent horses and chariots and a great army there, and
they came by night and surrounded the city.
15 Now when the attendant of the man of God had risen early and
gone out, behold, an army with horses and chariots was circling the

24 [1]Lit., *Ophe*... 7:1, 11, 12, 21; 21:16
25 [a]2 Kin. 5:22
26 [a]2 Kin. 5:16
27 [1]Lit., *seed* [a]Num. 12:10
6:1 [a]2 Kin. 2:3
3 [1]Lit., *said*
5 [1]Lit., *as for the fell*
6 [a]Ex. 15:25; 2 K... 2:21; 4:41
8 [1]Lit., *took coun*...
9 [a]2 Kin. 4:1, 7; 6...
10 [1]Lit., *not once twice*
13 [a]Gen. 37:17

city. And his servant said to him, "Alas, my master! [1]What shall we
do?"
16 So he [1]answered, "[a]Do not fear, for [b]those who are with us are
more than those who are with them."
17 Then Elisha prayed and said, "[a]O LORD, I pray, open his eyes that
he may see." And the LORD opened the servant's eyes, and he saw;
and behold, the mountain was full of [b]horses and chariots of fire all
around Elisha.
18 And when they came down to him, Elisha prayed to the LORD
and said, "Strike this [1]people with blindness, I pray." So He [a]struck
them with blindness according to the word of Elisha.
19 Then Elisha said to them, "This is not the way, nor is this the
city; follow me and I will bring you to the man whom you seek."
And he brought them to Samaria.
20 And it came about when they had come into Samaria, that Elisha
said, "O [a]LORD, open the eyes of these *men*, that they may see." So the
LORD opened their eyes, and they saw; and behold, they were in the
midst of Samaria.
21 Then the king of Israel when he saw them, said to Elisha, "[a]My
father, shall I [1]kill them? Shall I [1]kill them?"
22 And he [1]answered, "You shall not [2]kill *them*. Would you [2a]kill
those you have taken captive with your sword and with your bow?
[b]Set bread and water before them, that they may eat and drink and
go to their master."
23 So he prepared a great feast for them; and when they had eaten
and drunk he sent them away, and they went to their master. And
[a]the marauding bands of Arameans did not come again into the land
of Israel.
24 Now it came about after this, that [a]Ben-hadad king of Aram
gathered all his army and went up and besieged Samaria.
25 And there was a great [a]famine in Samaria; and behold, they
besieged it, until a donkey's head was sold for eighty *shekels* of sil-
ver, and a fourth of a [1]kab of dove's dung for five *shekels* of silver.
26 And as the king of Israel was passing by on the wall a woman
cried out to him, saying, "Help, my lord, O king!"
27 And he said, "[1]If the LORD does not help you, from where shall I
help you? From the threshing floor, or from the wine press?"
28 And the king said to her, "[a]What [1]is the matter with you?" And
she [2]answered, "This woman said to me, 'Give your son that we may
eat him today, and we will eat my son tomorrow.'
29 "[a]So we boiled my son and ate him; and I said to her on the next
day, 'Give your son, that we may eat him'; but she has hidden her
son."
30 And it came about when the king heard the words of the
woman, that [a]he tore his clothes—now he was passing by on the
wall—and the people looked, and behold, he had sackcloth [1]beneath
on his [2]body.
31 Then he said, "May [a]God do so to me and more also, if the head
of Elisha the son of Shaphat [1]remains on him today."
32 Now Elisha was sitting in his house, and [a]the elders were sitting
with him. And *the king* sent a man from his presence; but before the
messenger came to him, he said to the elders, "Do you [b]see how this
son of a murderer has sent to take away my head? Look, when the

15 [1]Lit., *How*
[1]Lit., *said* [a]Ex. [b]2 Chr. 32:7, 8; Rom. 8:31
Kin. 6:20 [b]2 Kin. Ps. 68:17; Zech. 6:1-7
it., *nation* [a]Gen. 19:11
20 [a]2 Kin. 6:17
Lit., *smite* [a]2 Kin. 2:12; 5:13; 8:9
2 [1]Lit., *said* [2]Lit., [a]Deut. 20:11-16; r. 28:8-15 [b]Rom. 12:20
[a]2 Kin. 5:2; 24:2
24 [a]1 Kin. 20:1
e., one kab equals pprox. 2 qts. [a]Lev. 26:26
7 [1]Lit., *No, let the LORD help you*
[1]Lit., *to you* [2]Lit., *said* [a]Judg. 18:23
29 [a]Lev. 26:27-29; Deut. 28:52, 53, 57; Lam. 4:10
0 [1]Lit., *within* [2]Lit., *flesh* [a]1 Kin. 21:27
[1]Lit., *stands* [a]Ruth 1:17; 1 Kin. 19:2
32 [a]Ezek. 8:1; 14:1; 0:1 [b]1 Kin. 18:4, 13, 14; 21:10, 13

messenger comes, shut the door and [1]hold the door shut against
him. Is not the sound of his master's feet behind him?"
33 And while he was still talking with them, behold, the messenger
came down to him, and he said, "[a]Behold, this evil is from the LORD;
why should I wait for the LORD any longer?"

Chapter 7

7 Then Elisha said, "Listen to the word of the LORD; thus says the
LORD, '[a]Tomorrow about this time a [1]measure of fine flour shall
be *sold* for a shekel, and two measures of barley for a shekel, in the
gate of Samaria.' "
2 And [a]the royal officer on whose hand the king was leaning an-
swered the man of God and said, "Behold, [b]if the LORD should make
windows in heaven, could this thing be?" Then he said, "Behold you
shall see it with your own eyes, but you shall not eat [1]of it."
3 Now there were four [a]leprous men at the entrance of the gate;
and they said to one another, "Why do we sit here until we die?
4 "If we say, 'We will enter the city,' then the famine is in the city
and we shall die there; and if we sit here, we die also. Now therefore
come, and let us [1]go over to [a]the camp of the Arameans. If they spare
us, we shall live; and if they kill us, we shall but die."
5 And they arose at twilight to go to the camp of the Arameans;
when they came to the outskirts of the camp of the Arameans, be-
hold, there was no one there.
6 For [a]the Lord had caused the army of the Arameans to hear a
sound of chariots and a sound of horses, *even* the sound of a great
army, so that they said to one another, "Behold, the king of Israel has
hired against us [b]the kings of the Hittites and [c]the kings of the Egyp-
tians, to come upon us."
7 Therefore they [a]arose and fled in the twilight, and left their tents
and their horses and their donkeys, even the camp just as it was, and
fled for their life.
8 When these lepers came to the outskirts of the camp, they
entered one tent and ate and drank, and [a]carried from there silver
and gold and clothes, and went and hid *them*; and they returned and
entered another tent and carried from there *also*, and went and hid
them.
9 Then they said to one another, "We are not doing right. This day
is a day of good news, but we are keeping silent; if we wait until
morning light, punishment will [1]overtake us. Now therefore come,
let us go and tell the king's household."
10 So they came and called to the gatekeepers of the city, and they
told them, saying, "We came to the camp of the Arameans, and
behold, there was no one there, nor the voice of man, only the horses
tied and the donkeys tied, and the tents just as they were."
11 And the gatekeepers called, and told *it* within the king's house-
hold.
12 Then the king arose in the night and said to his servants, "I will
now tell you what the Arameans have done to us. They know that
[a]we are hungry; therefore they have gone from the camp [b]to hide
themselves in the field, saying, 'When they come out of the city, we
shall capture them alive and get into the city.' "
13 And one of his servants answered and said, "Please, let some
men take five of the horses which remain, which are left [1]in the city.

32 [1]Lit., *press* *the door*

33 [a]Is. 8:21

7:1 [1]Heb., *seah* 7:18

2 [1]Lit., *from ther* [a]2 Kin. 5:18; 7:17 [b]Gen. 7:11; Mal.

3 [a]Lev. 13:45, 46 5:2-4; 12:10-14

4 [1]Lit., *fall* [a]2 Kin

6 [a]2 Sam. 5:24 [b] 10:29 [c]2 Chr. 12: Is. 31:1; 36:9

7 [a]Ps. 48:4-6; Pro

8 [a]Josh. 7:21

9 [1]Lit., *find*

12 [a]2 Kin. 6:25-29 [b]Josh. 8:4-12

13 [1]Lit., *in it*

Behold, they *will be in any case* like all the multitude of Israel who are
left in it; behold, they *will be in any case* like all the multitude of Israel
who have already perished, so let us send and see."
14 They took therefore two chariots with horses, and the king sent
after the army of the Arameans, saying, "Go and see."
15 And they went after them to the Jordan, and behold, all the way
was full of clothes and equipment, which the Arameans had thrown
away in their haste. Then the messengers returned and told the king.
16 So the people went out and plundered the camp of the
Arameans. Then a [1]measure of fine flour *was sold* for a shekel and
two [1]measures of barley for a shekel, [a]according to the word of the
LORD.
17 Now the king appointed [a]the royal officer on whose hand he
leaned [1]to have charge of the gate; but the people trampled on him at
the gate, and he died just as the man of God had said, [b]who spoke
when the king came down to him.
18 And it came about just as the man of God had spoken to the
king, saying, "[a]Two [1]measures of barley for a shekel and a [1]measure
of fine flour for a shekel, shall be *sold* tomorrow about this time at
the gate of Samaria."
19 Then the royal officer answered the man of God and said, "Now
behold, [a]if the LORD should make windows in heaven, could such a
thing be?" And he said, "Behold, you shall see it with your own
eyes, but you shall not eat [1]of it."
20 And so it happened to him, for the people trampled on him at
the gate, and he died.

Chapter 8

8 Now [a]Elisha spoke to the woman whose son he had restored to
life, saying, "Arise and go [1]with your household, and sojourn
wherever you can sojourn; for the [b]LORD has called for a famine, and
[c]it shall even come on the land for seven years."
2 So the woman arose and did according to the word of the man of
God, and she went with her household and sojourned in the land of
the Philistines seven years.
3 And it came about at the end of seven years, that the woman
returned from the land of the Philistines; and she went out to [1]appeal
to the king for her house and for her field.
4 Now the king was talking with [a]Gehazi, the servant of the man
of God, saying, "Please relate to me all the great things that Elisha
has done."
5 And it came about, as he was relating to the king [a]how he had
restored to life the one who was dead, that behold, the woman
whose son he had restored to life, [1]appealed to the king for her
house and for her field. And Gehazi said, "My lord, O king, this is
the woman and this is her son, whom Elisha restored to life."
6 When the king asked the woman, she related *it* to him. So the
king appointed for her a certain officer, saying, "Restore all that was
hers and all the produce of the field from the day that she left the
land even until now."
7 Then Elisha came to [a]Damascus. Now [b]Ben-hadad king of Aram
was sick, and it was told him, saying, "[c]The man of God has come
here."
8 And the king said to [a]Hazael, "[b]Take a gift in your hand and go

eb., *seah;* i.e., e seah equals 11 qts. [a]2 Kin. 7:1
, *over the gate* :2 [b]2 Kin. 6:32
Heb., *seah;* i.e., ne seah equals 11 qts. [a]2 Kin. 7:1
[1]Lit., *from there* [a]2 Kin. 7:2
it., *you and your* :18, 31-35; [b]Ps. 05:16; Hag. 1:11 [c]Gen. 41:27, 54
3 [1]Lit., *cry out*
Kin. 4:12; 5:20-27
cried out [a]2 Kin. 4:35
Kin. 11:24 [b]2 Kin. 6:24 [c]2 Kin. 5:20
[a]1 Kin. 19:15, 17 [b]1 Kin. 14:3

to meet the man of God, and [c]inquire of the LORD by him, saying,
'Will I recover from this sickness?' "
9 So Hazael went to meet him and took a gift in his hand, even
every kind of good thing of Damascus, forty camels' loads; and he
came and stood before him and said, "[a]Your son Ben-hadad king of
Aram has sent me to you, saying, 'Will I recover from this sick-
ness?' "
10 Then Elisha said to him, "[a]Go, say to him, 'You shall surely
recover,' but the [b]LORD has shown me that he will certainly die."
11 And he [1]fixed his gaze steadily *on him* [a]until he was ashamed,
and [b]the man of God wept.
12 And Hazael said, "Why does my lord weep?" Then he
[1]answered, "Because [a]I know the evil that you will do to the sons of
Israel: their strongholds you will set on fire, and their young men
you will kill with the sword, and their little ones you [b]will dash in
pieces, and their women with child you will rip up."
13 Then Hazael said, "But what is your servant, [a]*who is but* a dog,
that he should do this great thing?" And Elisha [1]answered, "[b]The
LORD has shown me that you will be king over Aram."
14 So he departed from Elisha and returned to his master, who said
to him, "What did Elisha say to you?" And he [1]answered, "He told
me that [a]you would surely recover."
15 And it came about on the morrow, that he took the cover and
dipped it in water and spread it on his face, [a]so that he died. And
Hazael became king in his place.
16 Now in the fifth year of [a]Joram the son of Ahab king of Israel,
Jehoshaphat being then the king of Judah, Jehoram the son of Jeho-
shaphat king of Judah became king.
17 He was [a]thirty-two years old when he became king, and he
reigned eight years in Jerusalem.
18 And he walked in the way of the kings of Israel, just as the house
of Ahab had done, for [a]the daughter of Ahab became his wife; and he
did evil in the sight of the LORD.
19 However, the LORD was not willing to destroy Judah, for the sake
of David His servant, [a]since He had [1]promised him to give a [2]lamp to
him through his sons always.
20 In his days [a]Edom revolted from under the hand of Judah, and
made a king over themselves.
21 Then Joram crossed over to Zair, and all his chariots with him.
And it came about that he arose by night and struck the Edomites
who had surrounded him and the captains of the chariots; [a]but *his*
[1]army fled to their tents.
22 [a]So Edom revolted [1]against Judah to this day. Then [b]Libnah re-
volted at the same time.
23 And the rest of the acts of Joram and all that he did, are they not
written in the Book of the Chronicles of the Kings of Judah?
24 So Joram slept with his fathers, and [a]was buried with his fathers
in the city of David; and [b]Ahaziah his son became king in his place.
25 [a]In the twelfth year of Joram the son of Ahab king of Israel,
Ahaziah the son of Jehoram king of Judah began to reign.
26 [a]Ahaziah *was* twenty-two years old when he became king, and
he reigned one year in Jerusalem. And his mother's name *was* Atha-
liah the granddaughter of Omri king of Israel.
27 And [a]he walked in the way of the house of Ahab, and did evil in

8 [c]2 Kin. 1:2
9 [a]2 Kin. 5:13
10 [a]2 Kin. 8:14 8:15
11 [1]Lit., *made stand fast and* [a]2 Kin. 2:17 [b]L
12 [1]Lit., *said* [a] 10:32, 33; 12:1 7 [b]2 Kin. 15:16 3:10
13 [1]Lit., *said* [a] 17:43; 2 Sam. 9 [b]1 Kin. 19:15
14 [1]Lit., *said* [a]2 8:10
15 [a]2 Kin. 8:10
16 [a]2 Kin. 1:17;
17 [a]2 Chr. 21:5-
18 [a]2 Kin. 8:27
19 [1]Lit., *said* [2]I.e. descendant on the throne [a]2 Sam. 1 Kin. 11:36
20 [a]1 Kin. 22:47; 3:9, 26, 27; 8:22
21 [1]Lit., *the peop* [a]2 Sam. 18:17; 19
22 [1]Lit., *from und hand of* [a]Gen. 27 [b]Josh. 21:13; 2 Ki
24 [a]2 Chr. 21:20 [b]2 Chr. 21:1, 7
25 [a]2 Chr. 22:1-6
26 [a]2 Chr. 22:2
27 [a]2 Chr. 22:3

INSIGHT

Zair's exact location is in question. The name means "small." Some believe it was south of the Dead Sea near Edom, while others equate it with Zoar (Genesis 13:10) or Zior (Joshua 15:54).

the sight of the LORD, like the house of Ahab *had done*, because he
was a son-in-law of the house of Ahab.
28 Then he went with Joram the son of Ahab to war against [a]Hazael
king of Aram at [b]Ramoth-gilead, and the Arameans [1]wounded
Joram.
29 So [a]King Joram returned to be healed in Jezreel of the wounds
which the Arameans had [1]inflicted on him at [b]Ramah, when he
fought against Hazael king of Aram. Then [c]Ahaziah the son of
Jehoram king of Judah went down to see Joram the son of Ahab in
Jezreel because he was sick.

Chapter 9

9 Now Elisha the prophet called one of [a]the sons of the prophets,
and said to him, "[b]Gird up your loins, and [c]take this flask of oil
in your hand, and go to [d]Ramoth-gilead.
2 "When you arrive there, [1]search out [a]Jehu the son of Jehoshaphat
the son of Nimshi, and go in and [2b]bid him arise from among his
brothers, and bring him to an inner room.
3 "Then take the flask of oil and pour it on his head and say, 'Thus
says the LORD, "[a]I have anointed you king over Israel."' Then open
the door and flee and do not wait."
4 So [a]the young man, the servant of the prophet, went to Ramoth-
gilead.
5 When he came, behold, the captains of the army were sitting,
and he said, "I have a word for you, O captain." And Jehu said,
"[1]For which *one* of us?" And he said, "For you, O captain."
6 And he arose and went into the house, and he poured the oil on
his head and said to him, "Thus says the LORD, the God of Israel, '[a]I
have anointed you king over the people of the LORD, *even* over Israel.
7 'And you shall strike the house of Ahab your master, [a]that I may
avenge [b]the blood of My servants the prophets, and the blood of all
the servants of the LORD, [c]at the hand of Jezebel.
8 'For the whole house of Ahab shall perish, and [a]I will cut off from
Ahab [b]every male person [c]both bond and free in Israel.
9 'And [a]I will make the house of Ahab like the house of Jeroboam
the son of Nebat, and [b]like the house of Baasha the son of Ahijah.
10 'And [a]the dogs shall eat Jezebel in the territory of Jezreel, and
none shall bury *her*.'" Then he opened the door and fled.
11 Now Jehu came out to the servants of his master, and one said to
him, "[a]Is all well? Why did this [b]mad fellow come to you?" And he
said to them, "You know *very well* the man and his talk."
12 And they said, "It is a lie, tell us now." And he said, "Thus and
thus he said to me, 'Thus says the LORD, "I have anointed you king
over Israel."'"
13 Then [a]they hurried and each man took his garment and placed it
under him on the bare steps, and [b]blew the trumpet, saying, "Jehu is
king!"
14 So Jehu the son of Jehoshaphat the son of Nimshi conspired
against Joram. [a]Now Joram [1]with all Israel was [2]defending Ramoth-
gilead against Hazael king of Aram,
15 but [a]King [1]Joram had returned to Jezreel to be healed of the
wounds which the Arameans had [2]inflicted on him when he fought
with Hazael king of Aram. So Jehu said, "If this is your mind, *then*
let no one escape *or* [3]leave the city to go tell *it* in Jezreel."

…8 [1]Lit., *smote* [a]2 Kin. 8:15 [b]1 Kin. 22:3, 29

…9 [1]Lit., *struck* [a]2 Kin. …5 [b]2 Kin. 8:28; 2 Chr. 22:5, 6 [c]2 Kin. 9:16

1 [a]2 Kin. 2:3 [b]2 Kin. 4:29 [c]1 Sam. 10:1; …1; 1 Kin. 1:39 [d]2 Kin. 8:28, 29

[1]Lit., *and look there* …or [2]Lit., *cause him to* …Kin. 19:16, 17; 2 Kin. …4, 20 [b]2 Kin. 9:5, 11

3 [a]2 Chr. 22:7

4 [a]2 Kin. 9:1

[1]Lit., *To whom of us all?*

…[a]1 Sam. 2:7, 8; 1 Kin. …16; 2 Kin. 9:3; 2 Chr. 22:7

7 [a]Deut. 32:35, 43 …Kin. 18:4; 21:15, 21, 25 [c]2 Kin. 9:32-37

[a]1 Kin. 21:21; 2 Kin. …0:17 [b]1 Sam. 25:22 [c]Deut. 32:36; 2 Kin. 14:26

9 [a]1 Kin. 14:10, 11; …5:29 [b]1 Kin. 16:3-5, 11, 12

[a]1 Kin. 21:23; 2 Kin. 9:35, 36

[a]2 Kin. 9:17, 19, 22 …Jer. 29:26; Hos. 9:7; Mark 3:21

[a]Matt. 21:7, 8; Mark …7, 8 [b]2 Sam. 15:10; 1 Kin. 1:34, 39

…4 [1]Lit., *he and* [2]Lit., …*eeping* [a]1 Kin. 22:3; 2 Kin. 8:28

15 [1]Heb., *Jehoram* …, *struck* [3]Lit., *go out from* [a]2 Kin. 8:29

16 Then Jehu rode in a chariot and went to Jezreel, for Joram was
lying there. [a]And Ahaziah king of Judah had come down to see
Joram.
17 Now the watchman was standing on the tower in Jezreel and he
saw the [1]company of Jehu as he came, and said, "I see a [1]company."
And Joram said, "Take a horseman and send him to meet them and
let him say, 'Is it peace?' "
18 So a horseman went to meet him and said, "Thus says the king,
'Is it peace?' " And Jehu said, "[a]What have you to do with peace?
Turn behind me." And the watchman [1]reported, "The messenger
came to them, but he did not return."
19 Then he sent out a second horseman, who came to them and
said, "Thus says the king, 'Is it peace?' " And Jehu [1]answered, "What
have you to do with peace? Turn behind me."
20 And the watchman [1]reported, "He came even to them, and he
did not return; and [a]the driving is like the driving of [b]Jehu the son of
Nimshi, for he drives furiously."
21 Then [1]Joram said, "[2]Get ready." And they made his chariot
ready. [a]And [1]Joram king of Israel and Ahaziah king of Judah went
out, each in his chariot, and they went out to meet Jehu and found
him in the [3b]property of Naboth the Jezreelite.
22 And it came about, when [1]Joram saw Jehu, that he said, "Is it
peace, Jehu?" And he [2]answered, "What peace, [a]so long as the har-
lotries of your mother Jezebel and her witchcrafts are so many?"
23 So [1]Joram [2]reined about and fled and said to Ahaziah, "[a]*There is*
treachery, O Ahaziah!"
24 And [a]Jehu [1]drew his bow with his full strength and [2]shot [3]Joram
between his arms; and the arrow went [4]through his heart, and he
sank in his chariot.
25 Then *Jehu* said to Bidkar his officer, "Take *him* up and [a]cast him
into the [1]property of the field of Naboth the Jezreelite, for I remem-
ber when [2]you and I were riding together after Ahab his father, that
the [b]LORD laid this [c]oracle against him:
26 'Surely [a]I have seen yesterday the blood of Naboth and the blood
of his sons,' says the LORD, 'and [b]I will repay you in this [1]property,'
says the LORD. Now then, take and cast him into the [1]property, ac-
cording to the word of the LORD."
27 [a]When Ahaziah the king of Judah saw *this,* he fled by the way of
the garden house. And Jehu pursued him and said, "[1]Shoot him too,
in the chariot." *So they shot him* at the ascent of Gur, which is at
[b]Ibleam. But he fled to Megiddo and died there.
28 [a]Then his servants carried him in a chariot to Jerusalem, and
buried him in his grave with his fathers in the city of David.
29 Now in [a]the eleventh year of Joram, the son of Ahab, Ahaziah
became king over Judah.
30 When Jehu came to Jezreel, Jezebel heard *of it,* and [a]she painted
her eyes and adorned her head, and looked out the window.
31 And as Jehu entered the gate, she said, "[a]Is it [1]well, Zimri, [2]your
master's murderer?"
32 Then he lifted up his face to the window and said, "Who is on
my side? Who?" And two or three officials looked down at him.
33 And he said, "Throw her down." So they threw her down, and
some of her blood was sprinkled on the wall and on the horses, and
he trampled her under foot.

16 [a]2 Kin. 8:29

17 [1]Lit., *multitude*

18 [1]Lit., *told, saying* [a]2 Kin. 9:19, 22

19 [1]Lit., *said*

20 [1]Lit., *told, saying* [a]2 Sam. 18:27 [b]1 Ki
19:17

21 [1]Heb., *Jehoram* [2]Lit., *Yoke the chario* [3]Lit., *portion* [a]2 Chr. 22:7 [b]1 Kin. 21:1-7, 15-19; 2 Kin. 9:26

22 [1]Heb., *Jehoram* [2]Lit., *said* [a]1 Kin. 16:30-33; 18:19; 2 C
21:13

23 [1]Heb., *Jehoram* [2]Lit., *turned his hanc* [a]2 Kin. 11:14

24 [1]Lit., *filled his ha with the bow* [2]Lit., *smote* [3]Heb., *Jehor* [4]Lit., *out at* [a]1 Kin. 2

25 [1]Lit., *portion* [2]Li *and you* [a]1 Kin. 21: [b]1 Kin. 21:19, 24-29
13:1

26 [1]Lit., *portion* [a]1
21:13, 19 [b]2 Kin. 9:21, 25

27 [1]Lit., *smite* [a]2 C
22:7, 9 [b]Josh. 17:1
Judg. 1:27

28 [a]2 Kin. 23:30

29 [a]2 Kin. 8:25

30 [a]Jer. 4:30; Ezek
23:40

31 [1]Lit., *peace* [2]Li *his* [a]1 Kin. 16:9-20; 2 Kin. 9:18-22

21:25 [b]1 Kin. 16:31
portion [a]1 Kin. 21:23
., portion [a]Jer. 8:1-3
1 Kin. 16:24-29
t., and with you the [a]2 Kin. 5:6
it., most upright
[a]2 Kin. 9:24, 27
h. 9:8, 11; 1 Kin. 32; 2 Kin. 18:14
. 9:5; 2 Kin. 11:1
just [2]Lit., smote . 9:14-24 [b]2 Kin. 10:6
it., by the hand of in. 9:7-10 [b]1 Kin. 21:19-29
[1]Lit., smote [a]Hos. 1:4
12 [1]I.e., house of binding
3 [1]Lit., found [2]Lit., rs [3]Lit., said [4]Lit., bout the welfare of in. 8:24, 29; 2 Chr. 21:17; 22:8

34 When he came in, he ate and drank; and he said, "See now to
[a]this cursed woman and bury her, for [b]she is a king's daughter."
35 And they went to bury her, but they found no more of her than
the skull and the feet and the palms of her hands.
36 Therefore they returned and told him. And he said, "This is the
word of the LORD, which He spoke by His servant Elijah the Tishbite,
saying, '[a]In the [1]property of Jezreel the dogs shall eat the flesh of
Jezebel;
37 and [a]the corpse of Jezebel shall be as dung on the face of the field
in the [1]property of Jezreel, so they cannot say, "This is Jezebel." ' "

Chapter 10

10 Now Ahab had seventy sons in [a]Samaria. And Jehu wrote
letters and sent *them* to Samaria, to the rulers of Jezreel, the
elders, and to the guardians of *the children of* Ahab, saying,
2 "And now, [a]when this letter comes to you, since your master's
sons are with you, [1]as well as the chariots and horses and a fortified
city and the weapons,
3 select the best and [1]fittest of your master's sons, and set *him* on
his father's throne, and fight for your master's house."
4 But they feared greatly and said, "Behold, [a]the two kings did not
stand before him; how then can we stand?"
5 And the one who *was* over the household, and he who *was* over
the city, the elders, and the guardians of *the children*, sent *word* to
Jehu, saying, "[a]We are your servants, all that you say to us we will
do, we will not make any man king; do what is good in your sight."
6 Then he wrote a letter to them a second time saying, "If you are
on my side, and you will listen to my voice, take the heads of the
men, your master's sons, and come to me at Jezreel tomorrow about
this time." Now the king's sons, seventy persons, *were* with the great
men of the city, *who* were rearing them.
7 And it came about when the letter came to them, that they took
the king's sons, and [a]slaughtered *them*, seventy persons, and put
their heads in baskets, and sent *them* to him at Jezreel.
8 When the messenger came and told him, saying, "They have
brought the heads of the king's sons," he said, "Put them in two
heaps at the entrance of the gate until morning."
9 Now it came about in the morning, that he went out and stood,
and said to all the people, "You are [1]innocent; behold, [a]I conspired
against my master and killed him, but [b]who [2]killed all these?
10 "Know then that [a]there shall fall to the earth nothing of the word
of the LORD, which the LORD spoke concerning the house of Ahab, for
the LORD has done [b]what He spoke [1]through His servant Elijah."
11 So Jehu [1]killed all who remained of the house of Ahab in [a]Jezreel,
and all his great men and his acquaintances and his priests, until he
left him without a survivor.
12 Then he arose and departed, and went to Samaria. On the way
while he was at [1]Beth-eked of the shepherds,
13 [a]Jehu [1]met the [2]relatives of Ahaziah king of Judah and said,
"Who are you?" And they [3]answered, "We are the [2]relatives of
Ahaziah; and we have come down [4]to greet the sons of the king and
the sons of the queen mother."
14 And he said, "Take them alive." So they took them alive, and

INSIGHT

After killing all the members of King Ahab's house, Jehu met the relatives of King Ahaziah of Judah at Beth-eked and killed them (2 Kings 10:12-14). The name of the city means "shearing house," which indicates it must have been a meeting place for shepherds. Tradition says the location was at Beit Qad, but more recent studies question this location.

killed them at the pit of Beth-eked, forty-two men; and he left none of them.

15 Now when he had departed from there, he [1]met [a]Jehonadab the son of [b]Rechab *coming* to meet him; and he [2]greeted him and said to him, "Is your heart right, as my heart is with your heart?" And Jehonadab [3]answered, "It is." *Jehu said,* "If it is, [c]give *me* your hand." And he gave him his hand, and he took him up to him into the chariot.

16 And he said, "Come with me and [a]see my zeal for the LORD." So [1]he made him ride in his chariot.

17 And when he came to Samaria, [a]he [1]killed all who remained to Ahab in Samaria, until he had destroyed him, [b]according to the word of the LORD, which He spoke to Elijah.

18 Then Jehu gathered all the people and said to them, "[a]Ahab served Baal a little; Jehu will serve him much.

19 "And now, [a]summon all the prophets of Baal, all his worshipers and all his priests; let no one be missing, for I have a great sacrifice for Baal; whoever is missing shall not live." But Jehu did it in [1]cunning, in order that he might destroy the worshipers of Baal.

20 And Jehu said, "[a]Sanctify a solemn assembly for Baal." And [b]they proclaimed *it.*

21 Then Jehu sent [1]throughout Israel and all the worshipers of Baal came, so that there was not a man left who did not come. And when they went into [a]the house of Baal, the house of Baal was filled from one end to the other.

22 And he said to the one who *was* [1]in charge of the wardrobe, "Bring out garments for all the worshipers of Baal." So he brought out garments for them.

23 And Jehu went into the house of Baal with Jehonadab the son of Rechab; and he said to the worshipers of Baal, "Search and see that there may be here with you none of the servants of the LORD, but only the worshipers of Baal."

24 Then they went in to offer sacrifices and burnt offerings. Now Jehu had stationed for himself eighty men outside, and he had said, "[a]The one who permits any of the men whom I bring into your hands to escape, [1]shall give up his life in exchange."

25 Then it came about, as soon as he had finished offering the burnt offering, that Jehu said to the [1a]guard and to the royal officers, "[b]Go in, [2]kill them; let none come out." And they [3]killed them with the edge of the sword; and the [1]guard and the royal officers threw *them* out, and went to the [4]inner room of the house of Baal.

26 And they brought out the *sacred* [a]pillars of the house of Baal, and burned them.

27 They also broke down the *sacred* pillar of Baal and broke down the house of Baal, and [a]made it a latrine to this day.

28 Thus Jehu eradicated Baal out of Israel.

29 However, [a]*as for* the sins of Jeroboam the son of Nebat, which he made Israel sin, from these Jehu did not depart, *even* the [b]golden calves that *were* at Bethel and that *were* at Dan.

30 And the LORD said to Jehu, "Because you have done well in executing what is right in My eyes, *and* have done to the house of Ahab according to all that *was* in My heart, [a]your sons of the fourth generation shall sit on the throne of Israel."

31 But Jehu [1a]was not careful to walk in the law of the LORD, the

15 [1]Lit., *found* *blessed* [3]Lit., s 35:6-19 [b]1 Chr [c]Ezra 10:19; Ez

16 [1]Lit., *they* [a] 19:10

17 [1]Lit., *smote* 9:8 [b]2 Kin. 10:1

18 [a]1 Kin. 16:3

19 [1]Lit., *insidiou* [a]1 Kin. 18:19; 22

20 [a]Joel 1:14 [b] 32:4-6

21 [1]Lit., *in all* [a]1 16:32; 2 Kin. 11:

22 [1]Lit., *over the*

24 [1]Lit., *his soul* *soul* [a]1 Kin. 20:3

25 [1]Lit., *runners* *smite* [3]Lit., *smote* *city* [a]1 Sam. 22:1 [b]1 Kin. 18:40

26 [a]1 Kin. 14:23; 3:2

27 [a]Ezra 6:11; Da 3:29

29 [a]1 Kin. 12:28-3 13:33, 34 [b]1 Kin. 1

30 [a]2 Kin. 15:12

31 [1]Lit., *did not wa* [a]Prov. 4:23

God of Israel, with all his heart; [b]he did not depart from the sins of
Jeroboam, which he made Israel sin.
32 In those days the [a]LORD began to cut off *portions* [1]from Israel; and
[b]Hazael [2]defeated them throughout the territory of Israel:
33 from the Jordan eastward, all the land of Gilead, the Gadites and
the Reubenites and the Manassites, from [a]Aroer, which is by the
valley of the Arnon, even [b]Gilead and Bashan.
34 Now the rest of the acts of Jehu and all that he did and all his
might, are they not written in the Book of the Chronicles of the Kings
of Israel?
35 And Jehu slept with his fathers, and they buried him in Samaria.
And Jehoahaz his son became king in his place.
36 Now the [1]time which Jehu reigned over Israel in Samaria *was*
twenty-eight years.

Chapter 11

11 [a]When Athaliah the mother of Ahaziah saw that her son was
dead, she rose and destroyed all the royal [1]offspring.
2 But Jehosheba, the daughter of King Joram, sister of Ahaziah,
[a]took Joash the son of Ahaziah and stole him from among the king's
sons who were being put to death, and placed him and his nurse in
the bedroom. So they hid him from Athaliah, and he was not put to
death.
3 So he was hidden with her in the house of the LORD six years,
while Athaliah was reigning over the land.
4 [a]Now in the seventh year Jehoiada sent and brought the captains
of hundreds of [b]the Carites and of the [1]guard, and brought them to
him in the house of the LORD. Then he made a covenant with them
and put them under oath in the house of the LORD, and showed them
the king's son.
5 And he commanded them, saying, "This is the thing that you
shall do: [a]one third of you, who come in on the sabbath and keep
watch over the king's house
6 (one third also *shall be* at the gate Sur, and one third at the gate
behind the [1]guards), [2]shall keep watch over the house for defense.
7 "And two parts of you, *even* all who go out on the sabbath, shall
also keep watch over the house of the LORD for the king.
8 "Then you shall surround the king, each with his weapons in his
hand; and whoever comes within the ranks shall be put to death.
And [a]be with the king when he goes out and when he comes in."
9 So the captains of hundreds [a]did according to all that Jehoiada
the priest commanded. And each one of them took his men who
were to come in on the sabbath, with those who were to go out on
the sabbath, and came to Jehoiada the priest.
10 And [a]the priest gave to the captains of hundreds the spears and
shields that had been King David's, which *were* in the house of the
LORD.
11 And the [1]guards stood each with his weapons in his hand, from
the right [2]side of the house to the left [2]side of the house, by the altar
and by the house, around the king.
12 Then he brought the king's son out and [a]put the crown on him,
and *gave him* [b]the testimony; and they made him king and anointed
him, and they clapped their hands and said, "[c]*Long* live the king!"

31 [b]2 Kin. 10:29
[1]Lit., *in* [2]Lit., *smote*
[a]2 Kin. 13:25; 14:25
[b]1 Kin. 19:17; 2 Kin. 8:12; 13:22
[a]Deut. 2:36 [b]Amos 1:3-5
36 [1]Lit., *days*
[1]Lit., *seed* [a]2 Chr. 22:10-12
[a]2 Kin. 11:21; 12:1
it., *runners* [a]2 Chr. -21 [b]2 Sam. 20:23; 2 Kin. 11:19
5 [a]1 Chr. 9:25
[1]Lit., *runners* [2]Lit., *and shall*
8 [a]Num. 27:16, 17
9 [a]2 Chr. 23:8
[a]2 Sam. 8:7; 1 Chr. 18:7
[1]Lit., *runners* [2]Lit., *shoulder*
[a]2 Sam. 1:10 [b]Ex. :16; 31:18 [c]1 Sam. 10:24

13 [a]When Athaliah heard the noise of the guard *and of* the people,
she came to the people in the house of the LORD.
14 And she looked and behold, the king was standing [a]by the pillar,
according to the custom, with the captains and the [1]trumpeters be-
side the king; and [b]all the people of the land rejoiced and blew trum-
pets. Then Athaliah [c]tore her clothes and cried, "[d]Treason! Treason!"
15 And Jehoiada the priest commanded the captains of hundreds
who were appointed over the army, and said to them, "Bring her out
[1]between the ranks, and whoever follows her put to death with the
sword." For the priest said, "Let her not be put to death in the house
of the LORD."
16 So they [1]seized her, and when she arrived at the horses' entrance
of the king's house, she was [a]put to death there.
17 Then [a]Jehoiada made a covenant between the LORD and the king
and the people, that they should be the LORD's people, also [b]between
the king and the people.
18 And all the people of the land went to [a]the house of Baal, and
tore it down; [b]his altars and his images they broke in pieces
thoroughly, and [c]killed Mattan the priest of Baal before the altars.
And the priest appointed [1]officers over the house of the LORD.
19 And he took the captains of hundreds and the [a]Carites and the
[1]guards and all the people of the land; and they brought the king
down from the house of the LORD, and came by the way of [b]the gate
of the [1]guards to the king's house. And he sat on the throne of the
kings.
20 So [a]all the people of the land rejoiced and the city was quiet. For
they had put Athaliah to death with the sword at the king's house.
21 [1a]Jehoash was seven years old when he became king.

Chapter 12

12 In the seventh year of Jehu, [a]Jehoash became king, and he
reigned forty years in Jerusalem; and his mother's name was
Zibiah of Beersheba.
2 And Jehoash did right in the sight of the LORD all his days in
which Jehoiada the priest instructed him.
3 Only [a]the high places were not taken away; the people still sacri-
ficed and burned incense on the high places.
4 Then Jehoash said to the priests, "All the money of the sacred
things [a]which is brought into the house of the LORD, in current
money, *both* [b]the money of each man's assessment *and* all the money
[1]which any man's heart prompts him to bring into the house of the
LORD,
5 let the priests take it for themselves, each from his acquaintance;
and they shall repair the [1]damages of the house wherever any
damage may be found.
6 But it came about that in the twenty-third year of King Jehoash
[a]the priests had not repaired the damages of the house.
7 Then King Jehoash called for Jehoiada the priest, and for the
other priests and said to them, "Why do you not repair the damages
of the house? Now therefore take no *more* money from your acquain-
tances, but pay it for the damages of the house."
8 So the priests agreed that they should take no *more* money from
the people, nor repair the damages of the house.
9 But [a]Jehoiada the priest took a chest and bored a hole in its lid,

13 [a]2 Chr. 23:1

14 [1]Lit., *trump* [a]2 Kin. 23:3; 2 34:31 [b]1 Kin. 1 [c]Gen. 37:29; 44 [d]2 Kin. 9:23

15 [1]Lit., *from w*

16 [1]Lit., *placed to her* [a]Gen. 9: 24:17

17 [a]Josh. 24:25 15:12-14; 34:31 [b]1 Sam. 10:25; 2 5:3

18 [1]Lit., *offices* 10:26, 27 [b]Deut 3 [c]1 Kin. 18:40

19 [1]Lit., *runners* 11:4 [b]2 Kin. 11:6

20 [a]Prov. 11:10

21 [1]Ch. 12:1 in H [a]2 Chr. 24:1-14

12:1 [a]2 Chr. 24:1

3 [a]2 Kin. 14:4; 15

4 [1]Lit., *which it co into . . . to bring* [a] 22:4 [b]Ex. 30:13-1 35:5, 22, 29; 1 Ch 29:3-9

5 [1]Lit., *breaches,* so through v. 12

6 [a]2 Chr. 24:5

9 [a]Mark 12:41; Lu 21:1

and put it beside the altar, on the right side as one comes into the
house of the LORD; and the priests who guarded the threshold put in
it all the money which was brought into the house of the LORD.
10 And when they saw that there was much money in the chest,
[a]the king's scribe and the high priest came up and tied *it* in bags and
counted the money which was found in the house of the LORD.
11 And they gave the money which was weighed out into the
hands of those who did the work, who had the oversight of the
house of the LORD; and they [1]paid it out to the carpenters and the
builders, who worked on the house of the LORD;
12 and [a]to the masons and the stonecutters, and for buying timber
and hewn stone to repair the damages to the house of the LORD, and
for all that was [1]laid out for the house to repair it.
13 But [a]there were not made for the house of the LORD [b]silver cups,
snuffers, bowls, trumpets, any vessels of gold, or vessels of silver
from the money which was brought into the house of the LORD;
14 for they gave that to those who did the work, and with it they
repaired the house of the LORD.
15 Moreover, [a]they did not require an accounting from the men into
whose hand they gave the money to pay to those who did the work,
for they dealt faithfully.
16 The [a]money from the guilt offerings and [b]the money from the sin
offerings, was not brought into the house of the LORD; [c]it was for the
priests.
17 Then [a]Hazael king of Aram went up and fought against Gath
and captured it, and [b]Hazael set his face to go up to Jerusalem.
18 And [a]Jehoash king of Judah took all the sacred things that Jeho-
shaphat and Jehoram and Ahaziah, his fathers, kings of Judah, had
dedicated, and [b]his own sacred things and all the gold that was
found among the treasuries of the house of the LORD and of the
king's house, and sent *them* to Hazael king of Aram. Then he went
away from Jerusalem.
19 Now the rest of the acts of Joash and all that he did, are they not
written in the Book of the Chronicles of the Kings of Judah?
20 [a]And his servants arose and made a conspiracy, and [b]struck
down Joash at [c]the house of Millo *as he was* going down to Silla.
21 For Jozacar the son of Shimeath, and Jehozabad the son of
[a]Shomer, his servants, struck *him*, and he died; and they buried him
with his fathers in the city of David, and [b]Amaziah his son became
king in his place.

Chapter 13

13 In the twenty-third year of Joash the son of Ahaziah, king of
Judah, Jehoahaz the son of Jehu became king over Israel at
Samaria, *and he reigned* seventeen years.
2 And he did evil in the sight of the LORD, and followed the sins of
Jeroboam the son of Nebat, [a]with which he made Israel sin; he did
not turn from them.
3 [a]So the anger of the LORD was kindled against Israel, and He
gave them continually into the hand of [b]Hazael king of Aram, and
into the hand of [c]Ben-hadad the son of Hazael.
4 Then [a]Jehoahaz entreated the favor of the LORD, and the LORD
listened to him; for [b]He saw the oppression of Israel, how the king of
Aram oppressed them.

[a]2 Sam. 8:17; 2 Kin. 19:2; 22:3, 4, 12
11 [1]Lit., *brought*
12 [1]Lit., *went out* [a]2 Kin. 22:5, 6
13 [a]2 Chr. 24:14 [b]1 Kin. 7:48, 50
5 [a]2 Kin. 22:7; 1 Cor. 4:2; 2 Cor. 8:20
[a]Lev. 5:15-18 [b]Lev. 4:24, 29 [c]Lev. 7:7; Num. 18:19
[a]1 Kin. 19:17; 2 Kin. 2; 10:32, 33 [b]2 Chr. 24:23, 24
[a]1 Kin. 14:26; 15:18; Kin. 16:8; 18:15, 16 [b]2 Kin. 12:4
20 [a]2 Chr. 24:25-27 Kin. 14:5 [c]Judg. 9:6; am. 5:9; 1 Kin. 11:27
21 [a]2 Chr. 24:26 [b]2 Kin. 14:1
3:2 [a]1 Kin. 12:26-33
[a]Judg. 2:14 [b]2 Kin. 17 [c]2 Kin. 13:24, 25
[a]Num. 21:7-9 [b]Ex. 3:7, 9; 2 Kin. 14:26

INSIGHT

Silla's exact location is indefinite, but is believed to be near Jerusalem.

5 And the LORD gave Israel a [1a]deliverer, so that they [2]escaped from
under the hand of the Arameans; and the sons of Israel lived in their
tents as formerly.
6 Nevertheless they did not turn away from the sins of the house
of Jeroboam, [a]with which he made Israel sin, but walked in [1]them;
and [b]the Asherah also remained standing in Samaria.
7 For he left to Jehoahaz of the [1]army not more than fifty horsemen
and ten chariots and 10,000 footmen, for the king of Aram had de-
stroyed them and [a]made them like the dust at threshing.
8 Now the rest of the acts of Jehoahaz, and all that he did and his
might, are they not written in the Book of the Chronicles of the Kings
of Israel?
9 And Jehoahaz slept with his fathers, and they buried him in
Samaria; and Joash his son became king in his place.
10 In the thirty-seventh year of Joash king of Judah, Jehoash the son
of Jehoahaz, became king over Israel in Samaria, *and reigned* sixteen
years.
11 And he did evil in the sight of the LORD; he did not turn away
from all the sins of Jeroboam the son of Nebat, with which he made
Israel sin, but he walked in [1]them.
12 [a]Now the rest of the acts of Joash and all that he did and his
might with which he fought against Amaziah king of Judah, are they
not written in the Book of the Chronicles of the Kings of Israel?
13 So Joash slept with his fathers, and Jeroboam sat on his throne;
and Joash was buried in Samaria with the kings of Israel.
14 When Elisha [1]became sick with the illness of which he was to
die, Joash the king of Israel came down to him and wept over [2]him
and said, "[a]My father, my father, the chariots of Israel and its horse-
men!"
15 And Elisha said to him, "Take a bow and arrows." So he [1]took a
bow and arrows.
16 Then he said to the king of Israel, "Put your hand on the bow."
And he put his hand *on it,* then Elisha laid his hands on the king's
hands.
17 And he said, "Open the window toward the east," and he
opened *it*. Then Elisha said, "Shoot!" And he shot. And he said, "The
LORD's arrow of victory, even the arrow of victory over Aram; for
you shall [1]defeat the Arameans at [a]Aphek until you have [2]destroyed
them."
18 Then he said, "Take the arrows," and he took them. And he said
to the king of Israel, "Strike the ground," and he struck *it* three times
and [1]stopped.
19 So [a]the man of God was angry with him and said, "You should
have struck five or six times, then you would have struck Aram until
you would have [1]destroyed *it*. But now you shall strike Aram [b]*only*
three times."
20 And Elisha died, and they buried him. Now [a]the bands of the
Moabites would invade the land in the spring of the year.
21 And as they were burying a man, behold, they saw a marauding
band; and they cast the man into the grave of Elisha. And when the
man [1]touched the bones of Elisha he [a]revived and stood up on his
feet.
22 Now [a]Hazael king of Aram had oppressed Israel all the days of
Jehoahaz.

5 [1]Or, *savior* [2]... *out* [a]2 Kin. 13:2... 14:25, 27; Neh.
6 [1]Lit., *it* [a]2 Kin... [b]1 Kin. 16:33
7 [1]Lit., *people* ... 1:3
11 [1]Lit., *it*
12 [a]2 Kin. 13:14 14:8-15
14 [1]Lit., *was sick ... his sickness* [2]Lit. *face* [a]2 Kin. 2:12
15 [1]Lit., *took to h...*
17 [1]Lit., *smite* [2]L... *made an end of* [a]... 20:26
18 [1]Lit., *stood*
19 [1]Lit., *made an ... of* [a]2 Kin. 5:20 [b]2 ... 13:25
20 [a]2 Kin. 3:7; 24:...
21 [1]Lit., *went and touched* [a]Matt. 27:5...
22 [a]2 Kin. 8:12, 13

[a]2 Kin. 14:27 [b]1 Kin. 28 [c]Gen. 13:16, 17; 17:2-5

23 But the [a]LORD was gracious to them and [b]had compassion on
them and turned to them because of [c]His covenant with Abraham,
Isaac, and Jacob, and would not destroy them or cast them from His
presence until now.

[1]Lit., *smote* [a]2 Kin. 32, 33; 14:25 [b]2 Kin. 13:18, 19

24 When Hazael king of Aram died, Ben-hadad his son became
king in his place.
25 Then [a]Jehoash the son of Jehoahaz took again from the hand of
Ben-hadad the son of Hazael the cities which he had taken in war
from the hand of Jehoahaz his father. [b]Three times Joash [1]defeated
him and recovered the cities of Israel.

14:1 [a]2 Chr. 25:1 [b]2 Kin. 13:10

Chapter 14

[a]2 Kin. 12:3 [b]2 Kin. 16:4

14 [a]In the second year of Joash son of Joahaz king of Israel,
[b]Amaziah the son of Joash king of Judah became king.
2 He was twenty-five years old when he became king, and he
reigned twenty-nine years in Jerusalem. And his mother's name was
Jehoaddin of Jerusalem.

[1]Lit., *smote* [a]2 Kin. 12:20

3 And he did right in the sight of the LORD, yet not like David his
father; he did according to all that Joash his father had done.
4 Only [a]the high places were not taken away; [b]the people still
sacrificed and burned incense on the high places.

[1]Lit., *smiters* [a]Deut. 24:16 [b]Jer. 31:30; Ezek. 18:4, 20

5 Now it came about, as soon as the kingdom was firmly in his
hand, that he [1a]killed his servants who had slain the king his father.
6 But the sons of the [1]slayers he did not put to death, according to
what is written in the book of the law of Moses, as the LORD com-
manded, saying, "[a]The fathers shall not be put to death for the sons,
nor the sons be put to death for the fathers; but [b]each shall be put to
death for his own sin."

Lit., *smote* [a]2 Sam. 8:13; 1 Chr. 18:12; Chr. 25:11 [b]Is. 16:1 [c]Josh. 15:38

7 He [1]killed *of* Edom in [a]the Valley of Salt 10,000 and took [b]Sela by
war, and named it [c]Joktheel to this day.

8 [a]2 Chr. 25:17-24 [b]2 Sam. 2:14-17

8 [a]Then Amaziah sent messengers to Jehoash, the son of Jehoahaz
son of Jehu, king of Israel, saying, "[b]Come, let us face each other."
9 And Jehoash king of Israel sent to Amaziah king of Judah,
saying, "[a]The thorn bush which was in Lebanon sent to the cedar
which was in Lebanon, saying, 'Give your daughter to my son in
marriage.' But there passed by a wild beast that was in Lebanon, and
trampled the thorn bush.

9 [a]Judg. 9:8-15

[1]Lit., *smitten* [2]Lit., *lifted you up* [a]2 Kin. [b]Deut. 8:14; 2 Chr. 26:16

10 "[a]You have indeed [1]defeated Edom, and [b]your heart has
[2]become proud. Enjoy your glory and stay at home; for
why should you provoke trouble so that you, even you,
should fall, and Judah with you?"
11 But Amaziah would not listen. So Jehoash king of Isra-
el went up; and he and Amaziah king of Judah faced each
other at [a]Beth-shemesh, which belongs to Judah.

11 [a]Josh. 19:38

12 And Judah was defeated [1]by Israel, and [a]they fled each
to his tent.

Lit., *before* [a]2 Sam. 18:17

13 Then Jehoash king of Israel captured Amaziah king of
Judah, the son of Jehoash the son of Ahaziah, at Beth-
shemesh, and came to Jerusalem and tore down the wall of
Jerusalem from [a]the Gate of Ephraim to [b]the Corner Gate,
400 [1]cubits.

13 [1]I.e., One cubit equals approx. 18 in. [a]Neh. 8:16; 12:39 [b]2 Chr. 25:23

14 And [a]he took all the gold and silver and all the utensils
which were found in the house of the LORD, and in the
treasuries of the king's house, the hostages also, and
returned to Samaria.

1 Kin. 14:26; 2 Kin. 12:18

Jerusalem of Old Testament
Sheep Gate
Fish Gate
Northwestern Hill
Muster Gate
Temple
East Gate
Altar
Temple Hill
Horse Gate
Kidron Valley
Ophel
Ephraim Gate
Corner Gate
CENTRAL VALLEY
Gihon Spring
MAKTESH
Valley Gate
Southeastern Hill (Zion)
Siloam Channel
Hezekiah's Tunnel
Siloam Pool
Lower Pool
Water Gate (Fountain Gate)
Valley Gate
Dung Gate

15 [a]Now the rest of the acts of Jehoash which he did, and his might
and how he fought with Amaziah king of Judah, are they not written
in the Book of the Chronicles of the Kings of Israel?
16 So Jehoash slept with his fathers and was buried in Samaria with
the kings of Israel; and Jeroboam his son became king in his place.
17 [a]And Amaziah the son of Joash king of Judah lived fifteen years
after the death of Jehoash son of Jehoahaz king of Israel.
18 Now the rest of the acts of Amaziah, are they not written in the
Book of the Chronicles of the Kings of Judah?
19 And they conspired against him in Jerusalem, and he fled to
[a]Lachish; but they sent after him to Lachish and killed him there.
20 Then they brought him on horses and he was buried at Jerusa-
lem with his fathers in the city of David.
21 And all the people of Judah took [1]Azariah, who *was* sixteen
years old, and made him king in the place of his father Amaziah.
22 [a]He built Elath and restored it to Judah, after the king slept with
his fathers.
23 In the fifteenth year of Amaziah the son of Joash king of Judah,
Jeroboam the son of Joash king of Israel became king in Samaria, *and
reigned* forty-one years.
24 And he did evil in the sight of the LORD; he did not depart from
all the sins of Jeroboam the son of Nebat, which he made Israel sin.
25 [a]He restored the border of Israel from [b]the entrance of Hamath as
far as [c]the Sea of the Arabah, according to the word of the LORD, the
God of Israel, which He spoke [1]through His servant [d]Jonah the son
of Amittai, the prophet, who was of [e]Gath-hepher.
26 For the [a]LORD saw the affliction of Israel, *which was* very bitter;
for [b]there was neither bond nor free, nor was there any helper for
Israel.
27 And the [a]LORD did not say that He would blot out the name of
Israel from under heaven, but He saved them by the hand of
Jeroboam the son of Joash.
28 Now the rest of the acts of Jeroboam and all that he did and his
might, how he fought and how he recovered for Israel, [a]Damascus
and [b]Hamath, *which had belonged* to Judah, are they not written in the
Book of the Chronicles of the Kings of Israel?
29 And Jeroboam slept with his fathers, even with the kings of
Israel, and Zechariah his son became king in his place.

Chapter 15

15 [a]In the twenty-seventh year of Jeroboam king of Israel,
Azariah son of Amaziah king of Judah became king.
2 He was [a]sixteen years old when he became king, and he reigned
fifty-two years in Jerusalem; and his mother's name was [1]Jecoliah of
Jerusalem.
3 And he did right in the sight of the LORD, according to all that his
father Amaziah had done.
4 Only [a]the high places were not taken away; the people still sacri-
ficed and burned incense on the high places.
5 [a]And the LORD struck the king, so that he was a leper to the day
of his death. And he [b]lived in a separate house, [1]while Jotham the
king's son was over the household, judging the people of the land.
6 Now the rest of the acts of Azariah and all that he did, are they
not written in the Book of the Chronicles of the Kings of Judah?

15 [a]2 Kin. 13:12, 13
17 [a]2 Chr. 25:25-28
19 [a]Josh. 10:31; 2 K 18:14, 17
21 [1]In 2 Chr. 26:1, *Uzziah*
22 [a]1 Kin. 9:26; 2 K 16:6; 2 Chr. 8:17
25 [1]Lit., *by* [a]2 Kin. 10:32; 13:25 [b]1 Kin 8:65 [c]Deut. 3:17 [d] 1:1; Matt. 12:39, 40 [e]Josh. 19:13
26 [a]2 Kin. 13:4 [b]D 32:36
27 [a]2 Kin. 13:23
28 [a]1 Kin. 11:24 [b]2 8:3
15:1 [a]2 Kin. 14:17
2 [1]In 2 Chr. 26:3, *Jechiliah* [a]2 Chr. 2
4 [a]2 Kin. 12:3
5 [1]Lit., *and* [a]2 Chr 26:21-23 [b]Lev. 13 Num. 12:14

8 [a]2 Kin. 15:1 7 And Azariah slept with his fathers, and they buried him with his
fathers in the city of David, and Jotham his son became king in his
place.
8 [a]In the thirty-eighth year of Azariah king of Judah, Zechariah the
smote [a]Amos 7:9 son of Jeroboam became king over Israel in Samaria *for* six months.
9 And he did evil in the sight of the LORD, as his fathers had done;
he did not depart from the sins of Jeroboam the son of Nebat, which
he made Israel sin.
10 Then Shallum the son of Jabesh conspired against him and
[a]2 Kin. 10:30 [a]struck him before the people and [1]killed him, and reigned in his
place.
11 Now the rest of the acts of Zechariah, behold they are written in
the Book of the Chronicles of the Kings of Israel.
12 This is [a]the word of the LORD which He spoke to Jehu, saying,
[a]2 Kin. 15:1, 8 [b]1 Kin. 16:24 "Your sons to the fourth generation shall sit on the throne of Israel."
And so it was.
13 Shallum son of Jabesh became king in the [a]thirty-ninth year of
Uzziah king of Judah, and he reigned one month in [b]Samaria.
14 Then Menahem son of Gadi went up from [a]Tirzah and came to
4 [a]1 Kin. 14:17 Samaria, and struck Shallum son of Jabesh in Samaria, and killed
him and became king in his place.
15 Now the rest of the acts of Shallum and his conspiracy which he
made, behold they are written in the Book of the Chronicles of the
Kin. 8:12; Hos. 13:16 Kings of Israel.
16 Then Menahem struck Tiphsah and all who were in it and its
borders from Tirzah, because they did not open *to him,* therefore he
struck *it;* and he ripped up [a]all its women who were with child.
17 In the [a]thirty-ninth year of Azariah king of Judah, Menahem son
Kin. 15:1, 8, 13 of Gadi became king over Israel *and reigned* ten years in Samaria.
18 And he did evil in the sight of the LORD; he did not depart all his
days from the sins of Jeroboam the son of Nebat, which he made
Israel sin.
[a]1 Chr. 5:25, 26 **19** [a]Pul, king of Assyria, came against the land, and Menahem gave

Some of the Pagan Gods Worshiped by the Israelites

ne god:	Ruled over / description:	Reference:
drammelech	War, love	2 Kings 17:31
nammelech	Demanded child sacrifice	2 Kings 17:31
sherah	Wife of Baal	2 Kings 13:6
shima	God of Hittites	2 Kings 17:30
shtoreth (Astarte, Ishtar)	Sex, fertility, queen of heaven	2 Kings 23:13
aal	Rain, wind, clouds, fertility of land	2 Kings 3:2
aal-Zebub	God of Ekron	2 Kings 1:2
hemosh	Provider of land	2 Kings 23:13
olech (Milcom)	National god of Moabites, worship involved human sacrifice	2 Kings 23:10
ebo	Wisdom, literature, arts	1 Chronicles 5:8
ergal	Underworld, death	2 Kings 17:30
ibhaz	Worshiped by the Avvites *(a people transplanted to Samaria from Assyria)*	2 Kings 17:31
isroch	God worshiped in Nineveh	2 Kings 19:37
immon	Thunder, lightning, rain	2 Samuel 4:5
uccoth Benoth	Mistress of Marduk, God of war	2 Chronicles 4:17
artak	Fertility (worshiped by Avvites)	2 Kings 17:31

Pul a thousand talents of silver so that his hand might be with him to [b]strengthen the kingdom [1]under his rule.

20 Then Menahem exacted the money from Israel, even from all the mighty men of wealth, from each man fifty shekels of silver to pay the king of Assyria. So the king of Assyria returned and did not remain there in the land.

21 Now the rest of the acts of Menahem and all that he did, are they not written in the Book of the Chronicles of the Kings of Israel?

22 And Menahem slept with his fathers, and Pekahiah his son became king in his place.

23 In [a]the fiftieth year of Azariah king of Judah, Pekahiah son of Menahem became king over Israel in Samaria, *and reigned* two years.

24 And he did evil in the sight of the LORD; he did not depart from the sins of Jeroboam son of Nebat, which he made Israel sin.

25 Then Pekah son of Remaliah, his officer, conspired against him and struck him in Samaria, in [a]the castle of the king's house with Argob and Arieh; and with him were fifty men of the Gileadites, and he killed him and became king in his place.

26 Now the rest of the acts of Pekahiah and all that he did, behold they are written in the Book of the Chronicles of the Kings of Israel.

27 In [a]the fifty-second year of Azariah king of Judah, [b]Pekah son of Remaliah became king over Israel in Samaria, *and reigned* twenty years.

28 And he did evil in the sight of the LORD; he did not depart from the sins of Jeroboam son of Nebat, which he made Israel sin.

29 In the days of Pekah king of Israel, [1a]Tiglath-pileser king of Assyria came and [2]captured Ijon and Abel-beth-maacah and Janoah and Kedesh and Hazor and Gilead and Galilee, all the land of Naphtali; and [b]he carried them captive to Assyria.

30 And Hoshea the son of Elah made a conspiracy against Pekah the son of Remaliah, and struck him and put him to death and became king in his place, in the twentieth year of Jotham the son of Uzziah.

31 Now the rest of the acts of Pekah and all that he did, behold, they are written in the Book of the Chronicles of the Kings of Israel.

32 In the second year of Pekah the son of Remaliah king of Israel, Jotham the son of [1]Uzziah king of Judah became king.

33 [a]He was twenty-five years old when he became king, and he reigned sixteen years in Jerusalem; and his mother's name *was* Jerusha the daughter of Zadok.

34 And [a]he did what was right in the sight of the LORD; he did according to all that his father Uzziah had done.

35 Only [a]the high places were not taken away; the people still sacrificed and burned incense on the high places. [b]He built the upper gate of the house of the LORD.

36 Now the rest of the acts of Jotham and all that he did, are they not written in the Book of the Chronicles of the Kings of Judah?

37 In those days [a]the LORD began to send Rezin king of Aram and Pekah the son of Remaliah against Judah.

38 And Jotham slept with his fathers, and he was buried with his fathers in the city of David his father; and Ahaz his son became king in his place.

19 [1]Lit., *in his* [b]2 Kin. 14:5

23 [a]2 Kin. 15:1 13, 17

25 [a]1 Kin. 16:1

27 [a]2 Kin. 15:2 [b]2 Chr. 28:6; Is.

29 [1]In 1 Chr. 5: *Tilgath-pilneser took* [a]2 Kin. 15. [b]2 Kin. 17:6

32 [1]I.e., Azariah

33 [a]2 Chr. 27:1

34 [a]2 Kin. 15:3, 4 2 Chr. 26:4, 5

35 [a]2 Kin. 12:3 [b] 23:20; 27:3

37 [a]2 Kin. 16:5; Is

Chapter 16

16 In the seventeenth year of Pekah the son of Remaliah, [a]Ahaz
the son of Jotham, king of Judah, became king.
2 [a]Ahaz *was* twenty years old when he became king, and he
reigned sixteen years in Jerusalem; and he did not do what was right
in the sight of the LORD his God, as his father David *had done.*
3 But he walked in the way of the kings of Israel, [a]and even made
his son pass through the fire, [b]according to the abominations of the
nations whom the LORD had [1]driven out from before the sons of
Israel.
4 And he [a]sacrificed and burned incense on the high places and on
the hills and under every green tree.
5 Then [a]Rezin king of Aram and Pekah son of Remaliah, king of
Israel, came up to Jerusalem to *wage* war; and they besieged Ahaz,
[b]but could not [1]overcome him.
6 At that time Rezin king of Aram recovered [a]Elath for Aram, and
cleared the Judeans out of [1]Elath entirely; and the [2]Arameans came
to Elath, and have lived there to this day.
7 [a]So Ahaz sent messengers to [b]Tiglath-pileser king of Assyria,
saying, "I am your servant and your son; come up and deliver me
from the [1]hand of the king of Aram, and from the [1]hand of the king
of Israel, who are rising up against me."
8 And [a]Ahaz took the silver and gold that was found in the house
of the LORD and in the treasuries of the king's house, and sent a
present to the king of Assyria.
9 [a]So the king of Assyria listened to him; and the king of Assyria
went up against Damascus and [b]captured it, and carried *the people of*
it away into exile to [c]Kir, and put Rezin to death.
10 Now King Ahaz went to Damascus to meet [a]Tiglath-pileser king
of Assyria, and saw the altar which *was* at Damascus; and King Ahaz
sent to [b]Urijah the priest the [1]pattern of the altar and its model,
according to all its workmanship.
11 So Urijah the priest built an altar; according to all that King Ahaz
had sent from Damascus, thus Urijah the priest made *it,* [1]before the
coming of King Ahaz from Damascus.
12 And when the king came from Damascus, the king saw the altar;
then [a]the king approached the altar and [1]went up to it,
13 and [1]burned his burnt offering and his meal offering, and
poured his libation and sprinkled the blood of his peace offerings on
the altar.
14 And [a]the bronze altar, which *was* before the LORD, [1]he brought
from the front of the house, from between [b]*his* altar and the house of
the LORD, and he put it on the north side of *his* altar.
15 Then King Ahaz [1]commanded Urijah the priest, saying, "Upon
the great altar [2]burn [a]the morning burnt offering and the evening
meal offering and the king's burnt offering and his meal offering,
with the burnt offering of all the people of the land and their meal
offering and their libations; and sprinkle on it all the blood of the
burnt offering and all the blood of the sacrifice. But [b]the bronze altar
shall be for me to inquire *by.*"
16 So Urijah the priest did according to all that King Ahaz com-
manded.
17 Then King Ahaz [a]cut off the borders of the stands, and removed

1 [a]2 Chr. 28:1
[a]2 Chr. 28:1-4
, *dispossessed* ...v. 18:21; 2 Kin. ...7; 21:6 [b]Deut. ...2 Kin. 21:2, 11
...eut. 12:2; 2 Kin. 14:4
...it., *fight* [a]2 Kin. ...; Is. 7:1 [b]2 Chr. 28:5, 6
..., *Eloth* [2]So with ...ncient versions; ...domites [a]2 Kin. ...:22; 2 Chr. 26:2
...it., *palm* [a]2 Chr. ...6 [b]2 Kin. 15:29
...2 Kin. 12:17, 18; 18:15
...hr. 28:21 [b]Amos ... [c]Is. 22:6; Amos 9:7
10 [1]Lit., *likeness* ...in. 15:29 [b]Is. 8:2
11 [1]Lit., *until*
[1]Or, *offered on it* [a]2 Chr. 26:16, 19
...3 [1]Lit., *offered in smoke*
[1]Lit., *he also* [a]Ex. ...2; 40:6, 29; 2 Chr. 4:1 [b]2 Kin. 16:11
[1]Lit., *commanded* ...rijah [2]Lit., *offer in* ...oke [a]Ex. 29:39-41 [b]2 Kin. 16:14
...1 Kin. 7:27, 28, 38

the laver from them; he also [b]took down the sea from the bronze oxen which were under it, and put it on a pavement of stone.

18 And the covered way for the sabbath which they had built in the house, and the outer entry of the king, he removed from the house of the LORD because of the king of Assyria.

19 Now the rest of the acts of Ahaz which he did, are they not written [a]in the Book of the Chronicles of the Kings of Judah?

20 So [a]Ahaz slept with his fathers, and [b]was buried with his fathers in the city of David; and his son Hezekiah reigned in his place.

Chapter 17

17 In the twelfth year of Ahaz king of Judah, [a]Hoshea the son of Elah became king over Israel in Samaria, *and reigned* nine years.

2 And he did evil in the sight of the LORD, only not as the kings of Israel who were before him.

3 [a]Shalmaneser king of Assyria came up [b]against him, and Hoshea became his servant and paid him tribute.

4 But the king of Assyria found conspiracy in Hoshea, who had sent messengers to So king of Egypt and had offered no tribute to the king of Assyria, as *he had done* year by year; so the king of Assyria shut him up and bound him in prison.

Carchemish
Haran
Gozan
Nineveh
To Media
ASSYRIA
Habor River
Tigris River
Hamath
Tadmor
Euphrates River
Babylon
Samaria

Exiles of Israel to Assyria

(For a more detailed map, see page 594)

5 Then the king of Assyria invaded the whole land and went up to [a]Samaria and besieged it three years.

6 In the ninth year of Hoshea, [a]the king of Assyria captured Samaria and [b]carried Israel away into exile to Assyria, and [c]settled them in Halah and Habor, *on* the river of [d]Gozan, and [e]in the cities of the Medes.

7 Now [a]*this* came about, because the sons of Israel had sinned against the LORD their God, [b]who had brought them up from the land of Egypt from under the hand of Pharaoh, king of Egypt, [c]and they had [1]feared other gods

8 and [a]walked in the [1]customs of the nations whom the LORD had driven out before the sons of Israel, and *in the customs* [b]of the kings of Israel which they had [2]introduced.

9 And the sons of Israel [1]did things secretly which were not right, against the LORD their God. Moreover, they built for themselves high places in all their towns, from [a]watchtower to fortified city.

10 And [a]they set for themselves *sacred* pillars and [1b]Asherim on every high hill and under every green tree,

11 and there they burned incense on all the high places as the nations *did* which the LORD had carried away to exile before them; and they did evil things provoking the LORD.

12 And they served idols, [a]concerning which the LORD had said to them, "You shall not do this thing."

13 Yet the [a]LORD warned Israel and Judah, [b]through all His prophets *and* [c]every seer, saying, "[d]Turn from your evil ways and keep My commandments, My statutes according to all the law which I commanded your fathers, and which I sent to you through My servants the prophets."

17 [b]1 Kin. 7:
19 [a]2 Chr. 28
20 [a]Is. 14:28 28:27
17:1 [a]2 Kin. 1
3 [a]Hos. 10:14 18:9-12
5 [a]Hos. 13:16
6 [a]Hos. 13:16 28:64; 29:27, 2 18:11; 1 Chr. 5 37:12 [e]Is. 13:1
7 [1]Lit., *reverec* throughout the [a]Josh. 23:16 [b] 14:15-30 [c]Judg
8 [1]Lit., *statutes* *made* [a]Lev. 18: 18:9 [b]2 Kin. 16
9 [1]Or, *uttered w* *which* [a]2 Kin. 1
10 [1]I.e., *wooder* *symbols of a fem* *deity* [a]Ex. 34:12 [b]1 Kin. 14:23; Mi
12 [a]Ex. 20:4
13 [a]Neh. 9:29, 3 [b]2 Kin. 17:23 [c]1 9:9 [d]Jer. 7:3-7; 1 Ezek. 18:31

ke the neck of 2:9; 33:3; Acts 7:51

14 However, they did not listen, but [a]stiffened their neck [1]like their fathers, who did not believe in the LORD their God.

[a]Jer. 8:9 [b]Ex. 8; Deut. 29:25 2:21 [d]Jer. 2:5; :21-23 [e]Deut. 12:30, 31

15 And [a]they rejected His statutes and [b]His covenant which He made with their fathers, and His warnings with which He warned them. And [c]they followed vanity and [d]became vain, and *went* after the nations which surrounded them, concerning which the [e]LORD had commanded them not to do like them.

[1]I.e., a wooden bol of a female [a]1 Kin. 12:28 :15, 23 [c]Deut. n. 21:3 [d]1 Kin. 16:31

16 And they forsook all the commandments of the LORD their God and made for themselves molten images, *even* [a]two calves, and [b]made an [1]Asherah and [c]worshiped all the host of heaven and [d]served Baal.

17 Then [a]they made their sons and their daughters pass through the fire, and [b]practiced divination and enchantments, and [c]sold themselves to do evil in the sight of the LORD, provoking Him.

Kin. 16:3 [b]Lev. Deut. 18:10-12 [c]1 Kin. 21:20

18 So the LORD was very angry with Israel, and [a]removed them from His [1]sight; [b]none was left except the tribe of Judah.

19 Also [a]Judah did not keep the commandments of the LORD their God, but [b]walked in the [1]customs [2]which Israel had [3]introduced.

it., *face* [a]2 Kin. 5 [b]1 Kin. 11:13, 32, 36

20 And the LORD rejected all the [1]descendants of Israel and afflicted them and [a]gave them into the hand of plunderers, until He had cast them [2]out of His sight.

., *statutes* [2]Lit., srael which they ., *made* [a]1 Kin. 23 [b]2 Kin. 16:3

21 When [a]He had torn Israel from the house of David, [b]they made Jeroboam the son of Nebat king. Then [c]Jeroboam drove Israel away from following the LORD, and made them [1]commit a great sin.

22 And the sons of Israel walked in all the sins of Jeroboam which he did; they did not depart from them,

[1]Lit., *seed* [2]Lit., *His face* [a]2 Kin. 15:29

23 [a]until the LORD removed Israel from His sight, [b]as He spoke through all His servants the prophets. [c]So Israel was carried away into exile from their own land to Assyria until this day.

[1]Lit., *sin* [a]1 Kin. 31 [b]1 Kin. 12:20 [c]1 Kin. 12:28-33

24 [a]And the king of Assyria brought *men* from Babylon and from Cuthah and from [1b]Avva and from [c]Hamath and Sephar-vaim, and settled *them* in the cities of Samaria in place of the sons of Israel. So they possessed Samaria and lived in its cities.

Kin. 17:6 [b]2 Kin. 17:13

25 And it came about at the beginning of their living there, that they [a]did not fear the LORD; therefore the LORD sent lions among them which killed some of them.

[1]In 2 Kin. 18:34, ah [a]Ezra 4:2, 10 in. 18:34 [c]1 Kin. 8:65

26 So they spoke to the king of Assyria, saying, "The nations whom you have carried away into exile in the cities of Samaria do not know the custom of the god of the land; so he has sent lions among them, and behold, they kill them because they do not know the custom of the god of the land."

[a]2 Kin. 17:32-41

27 Then the king of Assyria commanded, saying, "Take there one of the priests whom you carried away into [1]exile, and let [2]him go and live there; and let him teach them the custom of the god of the land."

7 [1]Lit., *exile from there* [2]Lit., *them*

28 So one of the priests whom they had carried away into exile from Samaria came and lived at Bethel, and taught them how they should fear the LORD.

Kin. 12:31; 13:32

29 But every nation still made gods of its own and put them [a]in the houses of the high places which the people of Samaria had made, every nation in their cities in which they lived.

30 [a]2 Kin. 17:24

30 And [a]the men of Babylon made Succoth-benoth, the men of Cuth made Nergal, the men of Hamath made Ashima,

31 [a]2 Kin. 17:17

31 and the Avvites made Nibhaz and Tartak; and [a]the Sepharvites

Cuthah (or Cuth), located in Mesopotamia about eighteen miles northeast of Babylon, was the center of worship for Nergel, the god of death or the underworld. The Assyrians took the people of Cuthah captive and exiled them to Israel (2 Kings 17:24). There they made an idol to Nergel (2 Kings 17:30), and became yet another influence upon people's tendency to worship other gods alongside Yahweh of Israel.

burned their children in the fire to [b]Adrammelech and Anammelech
the gods of [c]Sepharvaim.
32 [a]They also feared the LORD and [1b]appointed from among them-
selves priests of the high places, who acted for them in the houses of
the high places.
33 They feared the LORD and served their own gods according to
the custom of the nations from among whom they had been carried
away into exile.
34 To this day they do according to the earlier customs: they do not
fear the LORD, nor do they [1]follow their statutes or their ordinances
or the law, or the commandments which the LORD commanded the
sons of Jacob, [a]whom He named Israel;
35 with whom the LORD made a covenant and commanded them,
saying, "[a]You shall not fear other gods, nor [b]bow down yourselves to
them nor [c]serve them nor sacrifice to them.
36 "But the LORD, [a]who brought you up from the land of Egypt with
great power and with [b]an outstretched arm, [c]Him you shall fear, and
to Him you shall bow yourselves down, and to Him you shall
sacrifice.
37 "And the statutes and the ordinances and the law and the com-
mandment, which He wrote for you, [a]you shall observe to do
forever; and you shall not fear other gods.
38 "And the covenant that I have made with you, [a]you shall not
forget, nor shall you fear other gods.
39 "But the LORD your God you shall fear; and He will deliver you
from the hand of all your enemies."
40 However, they did not listen, but they did according to their
earlier custom.
41 [a]So while these nations feared the LORD, they also served their
[1]idols; their children likewise and their grandchildren, as their
fathers did, so they do to this day.

Chapter 18

18 Now it came about [a]in the third year of Hoshea, the son of
Elah king of Israel, that [b]Hezekiah the son of Ahaz king of
Judah became king.
2 He was [a]twenty-five years old when he became king, and he
reigned twenty-nine years in Jerusalem; and his mother's name was
Abi the daughter of Zechariah.
3 [a]And he did right in the sight of the LORD, according to all that
his father David had done.
4 [a]He removed the high places and broke down the *sacred* pillars
and cut down the [1]Asherah. He also broke in pieces [b]the bronze
serpent that Moses had made, for until those days the sons of Israel
burned incense to it; and it was called [2]Nehushtan.
5 [a]He trusted in the LORD, the God of Israel; [b]so that after him there
was none like him among all the kings of Judah, nor *among those*
who were before him.
6 For he [a]clung to the LORD; he did not depart from following Him,
but kept His commandments, which the LORD had commanded
Moses.
7 [a]And the LORD was with him; wherever he went he prospered.
And [b]he rebelled against the king of Assyria and did not serve him.

31 [b]2 Kin. 19:3 17:24
32 [1]Lit., *made themselves fro among* [a]Zeph. [b]1 Kin. 12:31
34 [1]Lit., *do acc to* [a]Gen. 32:28
35 [a]Judg. 6:10 20:5 [c]Deut. 5:9
36 [a]Ex. 14:15-3 6:6; 9:15 [c]Lev. Deut. 6:13
37 [a]Deut. 5:32
38 [a]Deut. 4:23;
41 [1]Or, *graven* [a]Zeph. 1:5; Matt
18:1 [a]2 Kin. 16: [b]2 Chr. 28:27
2 [a]2 Chr. 29:1, 2
3 [a]2 Kin. 20:3; 2 31:20
4 [1]I.e., a wooden symbol of a fema deity [2]I.e., a piec bronze [a]2 Kin. 18 2 Chr. 31:1 [b]Nun 21:8, 9
5 [a]2 Kin. 19:10 [b] 23:25
6 [a]Deut. 10:20; J 23:8
7 [a]Gen. 39:2, 3; 1 18:14 [b]2 Kin. 16:

8 [a]He [1]defeated the Philistines as far as Gaza and its territory, from
[b]watchtower to fortified city.
9 Now it came about in the fourth year of King Hezekiah, which
was the seventh year of Hoshea son of Elah king of Israel, that [a]Shal-
maneser king of Assyria came up against Samaria and besieged it.
10 And at the end of three years they captured it; in the sixth year
of Hezekiah, which was [a]the ninth year of Hoshea king of Israel,
Samaria was captured.
11 Then the king of Assyria carried Israel away into exile to As-
syria, and put them in [a]Halah and on the Habor, the river of Gozan,
and in the cities of the Medes,
12 because they [a]did not obey the voice of the LORD their God, but
transgressed His covenant, even all that Moses the servant of the
LORD commanded; they would neither listen, nor do *it*.
13 [a]Now in the fourteenth year of King Hezekiah, Sennacherib king
of Assyria came up against all the fortified cities of Judah and seized
them.
14 Then Hezekiah king of Judah sent to the king of Assyria at
Lachish, saying, "[a]I have done wrong. [1]Withdraw from me; whatever
you [2]impose on me I will bear." So the king of Assyria [3]required of
Hezekiah king of Judah three hundred talents of silver and thirty
talents of gold.
15 And [a]Hezekiah gave *him* all the silver which was found in the
house of the LORD, and in the treasuries of the king's house.
16 At that time Hezekiah cut off *the gold from* the doors of the
temple of the LORD, and *from* the doorposts which Hezekiah king of
Judah had overlaid, and gave it to the king of Assyria.
17 Then the king of Assyria sent [a]Tartan and Rab-saris and Rab-
shakeh from Lachish to King Hezekiah with a large army to Jerusa-
lem. So they went up and came to Jerusalem. And when they went
up, they came and stood by the [b]conduit of the upper pool, which is
on the highway of the [1]fuller's field.
18 When they called to the king, [a]Eliakim the son of Hilkiah, who
was over the household, and [b]Shebnah the scribe and Joah the son of
Asaph the recorder, came out to them.
19 Then Rabshakeh said to them, "Say now to Hezekiah, 'Thus says
the great king, the king of Assyria, "[a]What is this confidence that you
[1]have?
20 "You say (but *they are* [1]only empty words), '*I have* counsel and
strength for the war.' Now on whom do you rely, [a]that you have
rebelled against me?
21 "Now behold, you [1a]rely on the staff of this crushed reed, *even* on
Egypt; on which if a man leans, it will go into his [2]hand and pierce it.
So is Pharaoh king of Egypt to all who rely on him.
22 "But if you say to me, 'We trust in the LORD our God,' is it not He
whose high places and [a]whose altars Hezekiah has taken away, and
has said to Judah and to Jerusalem, 'You shall worship before this
altar in Jerusalem'?
23 "Now therefore, [1]come, make a bargain with my master the king
of Assyria, and I will give you two thousand horses, if you are able
on your part to set riders on them.
24 "How then can you [1]repulse one [2]official of the least of my
master's servants, and [3]rely on Egypt for chariots and for horsemen?
25 "Have I now come up [1]without the LORD's approval against this

smote [a]2 Chr. 14:29 [b]2 Kin. 17:9
[a]2 Kin. 17:3-7
10 [a]2 Kin. 17:6
11 [a]1 Chr. 5:26
[a]1 Kin. 9:6; Dan. 9:6, 10
[a]2 Chr. 32:1; Is. 36:1-39:8
Lit., *Return* [2]Lit., *put on* [a]2 Kin. 18:7
[a]1 Kin. 15:18, 19; 2 Kin. 12:18; 16:8
[1]I.e., launderer's [b]2 Kin. 20:20; Is. 7:3
[a]2 Kin. 19:2; Is. 22:20 [b]Is. 22:15
[1]Lit., *trust* [a]2 Chr. 32:10
Lit., *a word of the lips* [a]2 Kin. 18:7
21 [1]Lit., *rely for* [2]Lit., *palm* [a]Is. 36:6, 7; Ezek. 29:6, 7
[a]2 Kin. 18:4; 2 Chr. 31:1
23 [1]Lit., *please exchange pledges*
[1]Lit., *turn away the face of* [2]Or, *governor* [3]Lit., *rely for yourself*
25 [1]Lit., *without the LORD*

place to destroy it? The LORD said to me, 'Go up against this land
and destroy it.' " ' "
26 Then Eliakim the son of Hilkiah, and Shebnah and Joah, said to
Rabshakeh, "Speak now to your servants in Aramaic, for we [1]under-
stand *it;* and do not speak with us in [2a]Judean, in the hearing of the
people who are on the wall."
27 But Rabshakeh said to them, "Has my master sent me only to
your master and to you to speak these words, *and* not to the men
who sit on the wall, *doomed* to eat their own dung and drink their
own urine with you?"
28 Then Rabshakeh stood and cried with a loud voice in Judean,
[1]saying, "Hear the word of the great king, the king of Assyria.
29 "Thus says the king, '[a]Do not let Hezekiah deceive you, for he will
not be able to deliver you from [1]my hand;
30 nor let Hezekiah make you trust in the LORD, saying, "The LORD
will surely deliver us, and this city shall not be given into the hand
of the king of Assyria."
31 'Do not listen to Hezekiah, for thus says the king of Assyria,
"[1]Make your peace with me and come out to me, and eat [a]each of his
vine and each of his fig tree and drink each of the waters of his own
cistern,
32 until I come and take you away [a]to a land like your own land, a
land of grain and new wine, a land of bread and vineyards, a land of
olive trees and honey, that you may live and not die." But do not
listen to Hezekiah, when he misleads you, saying, "The LORD will
deliver us."
33 '[a]Has any one of the gods of the nations delivered his land from
the hand of the king of Assyria?
34 '[a]Where are the gods of Hamath and [b]Arpad? Where are the gods
of Sepharvaim, Hena and [1c]Ivvah? Have they delivered Samaria
from my hand?
35 'Who among all the gods of the lands [1]have delivered their land
from my hand, [a]that the LORD should deliver Jerusalem from my
hand?' "
36 But the people were silent and answered him not a word, for the
king's commandment was, "Do not answer him."
37 Then [a]Eliakim the son of Hilkiah, who was over the household,
and Shebna the scribe and Joah the son of Asaph, the recorder, came
to Hezekiah [b]with their clothes torn and told him the words of Rab-
shakeh.

Chapter 19

19 [a]And when King Hezekiah heard *it,* he [b]tore his clothes, [c]cov-
ered himself with sackcloth and entered the house of the
LORD.
2 Then he sent Eliakim who was over the household with Shebna
the scribe and the elders of the priests, [a]covered with sackcloth, to
[b]Isaiah the prophet the son of Amoz.
3 And they said to him, "Thus says Hezekiah, 'This day is a day of
distress, rebuke, and rejection; for children have come to birth, and
there is no strength to *deliver.*
4 '[a]Perhaps the LORD your God will hear all the words of Rab-
shakeh, whom his master the king of Assyria has sent [b]to reproach

INSIGHT

Ivvah (also spelled Ava or Avva) refers to the people the Assyrians conquered and took to Israel to replace the people taken into exile (2 Kings 17:24). Since the gods of the Ivvahian people did not come to their rescue against the Assyrians, they were used by Sennacherib as an example to call Jerusalem to surrender in 701 B.C. (2 Kings 18:34). Ivvah is believed to have been in Syria. Sennacherib used the same ploy against the city of Hena, which could possibly have been Ana or Anat on the Euphrates River.

26 [1]Lit., *hear* Hebrew [a]Ezr. 2:4
28 [1]Lit., *and s* *saying,*
29 [1]Heb., *his* 32:15
31 [1]Lit., *Make a blessing* [a]1 4:20, 25
32 [a]Deut. 8:7-9
33 [a]2 Kin. 19: 10:10, 11
34 [1]In 2 Kin. 17 *Avva* [a]2 Kin. 19 10:9 [c]2 Kin. 17
35 [1]Lit., *who ha* 2:1-3; 59:7
37 [a]2 Kin. 18:26 6:30
19:1 [a]2 Chr. 32: Is. 37:1 [b]2 Kin. 1 [c]1 Kin. 21:27
2 [a]2 Sam. 3:31 2:1
4 [a]Josh. 14:12; 2 16:12 [b]2 Kin. 18: 1:9

the living God, and will rebuke the words which the LORD your God
has heard. Therefore, offer a prayer for [c]the remnant that is left.' "
5 So the servants of King Hezekiah came to Isaiah.
6 And Isaiah said to them, "Thus you shall say to your master,
'Thus says the LORD, "Do not be afraid because of the words that you
have heard, with which the [a]servants of the king of Assyria [b]have
blasphemed Me.
7 "Behold, I will put a spirit in him so that [a]he shall hear a rumor
and return to his own land. And [b]I will make him fall by the sword
in his own land." ' "
8 Then Rabshakeh returned and found the king of Assyria fighting
against [a]Libnah, for he had heard that [1]the king had left [b]Lachish.
9 When he heard *them* say concerning Tirhakah king of [1]Cush,
"Behold, he has come out to fight against you," he sent messengers
again to Hezekiah saying,
10 "Thus you shall say to Hezekiah king of [1]Judah, 'Do not [a]let your
God in whom you trust deceive you saying, "[b]Jerusalem shall not be
given into the hand of the king of Assyria."
11 'Behold, you have heard what the kings of Assyria have done to
all the lands, destroying them completely. So will you be [1]spared?
12 '[a]Did the gods of [1]those nations which my fathers destroyed
deliver them, *even* [b]Gozan and [c]Haran and Rezeph and [d]the sons of
Eden who *were* in Telassar?
13 '[a]Where is the king of Hamath, the king of Arpad, the king of the
city of Sepharvaim, and *of* Hena and Ivvah?' "
14 Then [a]Hezekiah took the [1]letter from the hand of the messengers
and read it, and he went up to the house of the LORD and [2]spread it
out before the LORD.
15 And Hezekiah prayed before the LORD and said, "O LORD, the
God of Israel, [a]who art [1]enthroned *above* the cherubim, [b]Thou art the
God, Thou alone, of all the kingdoms of the earth. Thou hast made
heaven and earth.
16 "[a]Incline Thine ear, O LORD, and hear; [b]open Thine eyes, O LORD,
and see; and listen to the words of Sennacherib, which he has sent [c]to
reproach the living God.
17 "Truly, O LORD, the kings of Assyria have devastated the nations
and their lands
18 and have cast their gods into the fire, [a]for they were not gods but
the work of men's hands, wood and stone. So they have destroyed
them.
19 "And now, O LORD our God, I pray, deliver us from his hand [a]that
all the kingdoms of the earth may know that Thou alone, O [b]LORD,
art God."
20 Then Isaiah the son of Amoz sent to Hezekiah saying, "Thus
says the LORD, the God of Israel, 'Because you have prayed to Me
about Sennacherib king of Assyria, [a]I have heard *you*.'
21 "This is the word that the LORD has spoken against him:
'She has despised you and mocked you,
[a]The virgin daughter of Zion;
She [b]has shaken *her* head behind you,
The daughter of Jerusalem!
22 'Whom have you [a]reproached and [b]blasphemed?
And against whom have you raised *your* voice,
And [1]haughtily lifted up your eyes?

. 18:17 [b]2 Kin. 8:22-25; 30:35
Kin. 7:6 [b]2 Kin. 19:37
e [a]Josh. 10:29 [b]2 Kin. 18:14
9 [1]Or, *Ethiopia*
Judah, saying, n. 18:5 [b]2 Kin. 18:30
[1]Lit., *delivered*
Lit., *the* [a]2 Kin. 33 [b]2 Kin. 17:6 1:31 [d]Is. 37:12
3 [a]2 Kin. 18:34
letters . . . read [2]Lit., *Hezekiah read* [a]Is. 37:14
Lit., *seated* [a]Ex. s. 37:14 [b]2 Kin. 5:15
s. 31:2; Is. 37:17 3:29; 2 Chr. 6:40 [c]2 Kin. 19:4
Is. 44:9-20; Acts 17:29
[a]1 Kin. 8:42, 43 [b]2 Kin. 19:15
20 [a]2 Kin. 20:5
[a]Jer. 14:17; Lam. Ps. 109:25; Matt. 27:39
., *on high* [a]2 Kin. [b]2 Kin. 19:6 [c]Is. 5:24; 30:11-15

Against the [c]Holy One of Israel!
23 '[a]Through your messengers you have reproached the Lord,
And you have said, "With my many chariots
I came up to the heights of the mountains,
To the remotest parts of Lebanon;
And I [1]cut down its tall cedars *and* its choice cypresses.
And I [1]entered its farthest lodging place, its [b]thickest forest.
24 "I dug *wells* and drank foreign waters,
And with the sole of my feet I [1a]dried up
All the rivers of [2]Egypt."

25 '[a]Have you not heard?
Long ago I did it;
From ancient times I planned it.
[b]Now I have brought it to pass,
That you should turn fortified cities into ruinous heaps.
26 'Therefore their inhabitants were short of strength,
They were dismayed and put to shame;
They were [a]as the vegetation of the field and as the green herb,
As grass on the housetops is scorched before it is grown up.
27 'But [a]I know your sitting down,
And your going out and your coming in,
And your raging against Me.
28 'Because of your raging against Me,
And because your [1]arrogance has come up to My ears,
Therefore I [a]will put My hook in your nose,
And My bridle in your lips,
And [b]I will turn you back by the way which you came.
29 'Then this shall be [a]the sign for you: [1]you shall eat this year what
grows of itself, in the second year what springs from the same, and
in the third year sow, reap, plant vineyards, and eat their fruit.
30 '[a]And the surviving remnant of the house of Judah shall again
take root downward and bear fruit upward.
31 'For out of Jerusalem shall go forth a remnant, and [a]out of Mount
Zion [1]survivors. [b]The zeal of [2]the LORD shall perform this.
32 'Therefore thus says the LORD concerning the king of Assyria,
"[a]He shall not come to this city or shoot an arrow there; neither shall
he come before it with a shield, nor throw up a mound against it.
33 "[a]By the way that he came, by the same he shall return, and he
shall not come to this city," ' declares the LORD.
34 '[a]For I will defend this city to save it for My own sake and [b]for
My servant David's sake.' "
35 [a]Then it happened that night that the angel of the LORD went out,
and struck 185,000 in the camp of the Assyrians; and when [1]men
rose early in the morning, behold, all of them were [2]dead.
36 So [a]Sennacherib king of Assyria departed and returned *home,*
and lived at [b]Nineveh.
37 And it came about as he was worshiping in the house of Nisroch
his god, that [1a]Adrammelech and Sharezer killed him with the
sword; and they escaped into [b]the land of Ararat. And [c]Esarhaddon
his son became king in his place.

23 [1]So with sc ancient version *will cut . . . will* [a]2 Kin. 18:17 26:10; Is. 10:18

24 [1]So with sc ancient version *will dry up* [2]Lit *besieged place*

25 [a]Is. 45:7 [b]Is

26 [a]Ps. 129:6

27 [a]Ps. 139:1

28 [1]Lit., *compl* [a]Ezek. 19:9; 29 [b]2 Kin. 19:33, 3

29 [1]Lit., *eating* 3:12; 2 Kin. 20:8

30 [a]2 Kin. 19:4; 32:22, 23

31 [1]Lit., *those w escape* [2]Some mss. read *the L hosts* [a]Is. 10:20

32 [a]Is. 8:7-10

33 [a]2 Kin. 19:28

34 [a]2 Kin. 20:6; 31:5 [b]1 Kin. 11:1

35 [1]Lit., *they* [2]L *bodies* [a]2 Sam. 2 Chr. 32:21

36 [a]2 Kin. 19:7, [b]Jon. 1:2

37 [1]Some ancie read *Adrammele Sharezer his son smote him* [a]2 Kin 19:17, 31 [b]Gen. Jer. 51:27 [c]Ezra

Chapter 20

20 [a]In those days Hezekiah became [1]mortally ill. And Isaiah the
prophet the son of Amoz came to him and said to him, "Thus
says the LORD, '[b]Set your house in order, for you shall die and not
live.' "
2 Then he turned his face to the wall, and prayed to the LORD,
saying,
3 "[a]Remember now, O LORD, I beseech Thee, [b]how I have walked
before Thee in truth and with a whole heart, and have done what is
good in Thy sight." And [c]Hezekiah wept [1]bitterly.
4 And it came about before Isaiah had gone out of the middle
court, that the word of the LORD came to him, saying,
5 "Return and say to [a]Hezekiah the leader of My people, 'Thus says
the LORD, the God of your father David, "[b]I have heard your prayer,
[c]I have seen your tears; behold, I will heal you. On the third day you
shall go up to the house of the LORD.
6 "And I will add fifteen years to your [1]life, and I will deliver you
and this city from the hand of the king of Assyria; and [a]I will defend
this city for My own sake and for My servant David's sake." ' "
7 Then Isaiah said, "Take a cake of figs." And they took and laid *it*
on the boil, and he recovered.
8 Now Hezekiah said to Isaiah, "What will be the sign that the
LORD will heal me, and that I shall go up to the house of the LORD the
third day?"
9 And Isaiah said, "[a]This shall be the sign to you from the LORD,
that the LORD will do the thing that He has spoken: shall the shadow
go forward ten steps or go back ten steps?"
10 So Hezekiah [1]answered, "It is easy for the shadow to decline ten
steps; no, but let the shadow turn backward ten steps."
11 And Isaiah the prophet cried to the LORD, and [a]He brought the
shadow on the [1]stairway back ten steps by which it had gone down
on the [1]stairway of Ahaz.
12 [a]At that time [1]Berodach-baladan a son of Baladan, king of Baby-
lon, sent letters and a present to Hezekiah, for he heard that Heze-
kiah had been sick.
13 And Hezekiah listened to them, and showed them [a]all his treas-
ure house, the silver and the gold and the spices and the precious oil
and the house of his armor and all that was found in his treasuries.
There was nothing in his house, nor in all his dominion, that Heze-
kiah did not show them.
14 Then Isaiah the prophet came to King Hezekiah and said to him,
"What did these men say, and from where have they come to you?"
And Hezekiah said, "They have come from a far country, from Baby-
lon."
15 And he said, "What have they seen in your house?" So Hezekiah
[1]answered, "They have seen all that is in my house; there is nothing
among my treasuries that I have not shown them."
16 Then Isaiah said to Hezekiah, "Hear the word of the LORD.
17 'Behold, the days are coming when [a]all that is in your house, and
all that your fathers have laid up in store to this day shall be carried
to Babylon; nothing shall be left,' says the LORD.
18 'And some [a]of your sons who shall issue from you, whom you
shall beget, shall be taken away; and they shall become [b]officials in
the palace of the king of Babylon.' "

20:1 [1]Lit., *sick to the* [p]*oint of death* [a]2 Chr. 32:24; Is. 38:1-22 [b]2 Sam. 17:23
[1]Lit., *great weeping* [N]eh. 5:19; 13:14, 22, 31 [b]2 Kin. 18:3-6 [c]2 Sam. 12:21, 22
[a]1 Sam. 9:16; 10:1 ...n. 19:20 [c]Ps. 39:12
6 [1]Lit., *days* [a]2 Kin. 19:34
9 [a]Is. 38:7
10 [1]Lit., *said*
[1]Lit., *steps* [a]Josh. 10:12-14; Is. 38:8
2 [1]Many mss. and ...cient versions read ...*rodach-baladan;* cf. 39:1 [a]2 Chr. 32:31; Is. 39:1-8
13 [a]2 Chr. 32:27
15 [1]Lit., *said*
17 [a]2 Kin. 24:13; ...3-15; 2 Chr. 36:10; Jer. 52:17-19
...2 Kin. 24:12; 2 Chr. 33:11 [b]Dan. 1:3-7

19 Then Hezekiah said to Isaiah, "The word of the LORD which you have spoken is [a]good." For he [1]thought, "Is it not so, if there shall be peace and truth in my days?"

20 [a]Now the rest of the acts of Hezekiah and all his might, and how he [b]made the pool and the conduit, and brought water into the city, are they not written in the Book of the Chronicles of the Kings of Judah?

21 [a]So Hezekiah slept with his fathers, and Manasseh his son became king in his place.

Chapter 21

21 [a]Manasseh was twelve years old when he became king, and he reigned fifty-five years in Jerusalem; and his mother's name was Hephzibah.

2 And [a]he did evil in the sight of the LORD, [b]according to the abominations of the nations whom the LORD dispossessed before the sons of Israel.

3 For [a]he rebuilt the high places which Hezekiah his father had destroyed; and [b]he erected altars for Baal and made an [1]Asherah, as Ahab king of Israel had done, and [c]worshiped all the host of heaven and served them.

4 And [a]he built altars in the house of the LORD, of which the LORD had said, "[b]In Jerusalem I will put My name."

5 For he built altars for [a]all the host of heaven in [b]the two courts of the house of the LORD.

6 And [a]he made his son pass through the fire, [b]practiced witchcraft and used divination, and dealt with mediums and spiritists. He did much evil in the sight of the LORD provoking *Him to anger.*

7 Then [a]he set the carved image of Asherah that he had made, in the house of which the LORD said to David and to his son Solomon, "[b]In this house and in Jerusalem, which I have chosen from all the tribes of Israel, I will put My name forever.

8 "And I [a]will not make the feet of Israel wander anymore from the land which I gave their fathers, if only they will observe to do according to all that I have commanded them, and according to all the law that My servant Moses commanded them."

9 But they did not listen, and Manasseh [a]seduced them to do evil more than the nations whom the LORD destroyed before the sons of Israel.

10 Now the LORD spoke through His servants the prophets, saying,

11 "[a]Because Manasseh king of Judah has done these abominations, [b]having done wickedly more than all the Amorites did who *were* before him, and [c]has also made Judah sin [d]with his idols;

12 therefore thus says the LORD, the God of Israel, 'Behold, I am bringing *such* calamity on Jerusalem and Judah, that whoever hears of it, [a]both his ears shall tingle.

13 '[a]And I will stretch over Jerusalem the line of Samaria and the plummet of the house of Ahab, and I will wipe Jerusalem as one wipes a dish, wiping it and turning it upside down.

14 'And I will abandon the remnant of My inheritance and deliver them into the hand of their enemies, and they shall become as plunder and spoil to all their enemies;

15 because they have done evil in My sight, and have been

19 [1]Lit., *said* ... 3:18

20 [a]2 Chr. 32:... 3:16

21 [a]2 Chr. 32:...

21:1 [a]2 Chr. 33...

2 [a]Jer. 15:4 [b]2...

3 [1]I.e., a wood... symbol of a fem... deity [a]2 Kin. 18... [b]1 Kin. 16:31-33... 17:2-5; 2 Kin. 17... 23:5

4 [a]2 Kin. 16:10-... [b]2 Sam. 7:13; 1...

5 [a]2 Kin. 23:4, 5... 7:12; 2 Kin. 23:1...

6 [a]Lev. 18:21; 2... 16:3; 17:17 [b]Lev... 31; Deut. 18:10-...

7 [a]Deut. 16:21; ... 23:6 [b]1 Kin. 8:29... 2 Chr. 7:12, 16

8 [a]2 Sam. 7:10; ... 18:11, 12

9 [a]Prov. 29:12

11 [a]2 Kin. 21:2; 2... [b]Gen. 15:16; 1 Kin... 21:26 [c]2 Kin. 21:1... [d]2 Kin. 21:21

12 [a]1 Sam. 3:11; ... 19:3

13 [a]Is. 34:11; Am... 7:7, 8

[a]2 Kin. 24:4 [b]2 Kin. 21:11 provoking Me to anger, since the day their fathers came from Egypt,
even to this day.' "
16 [a]Moreover, Manasseh shed very much innocent blood until he
had filled Jerusalem from one end to another; besides his sin [b]with
[1]Lit., *sinned* [a]2 Chr. 33:11-19 which he made Judah sin, in doing evil in the sight of the LORD.
17 [a]Now the rest of the acts of Manasseh and all that he did and his
sin which he [1]committed, are they not written in the Book of the
Chronicles of the Kings of Judah?
18 [a]2 Chr. 33:20 [b]2 Kin. 21:26 18 [a]And Manasseh slept with his fathers and was buried in the
garden of his own house, [b]in the garden of Uzza, and Amon his son
became king in his place.
19 [a]2 Chr. 33:21-23 **19** [a]Amon was twenty-two years old when he became king, and he
reigned two years in Jerusalem; and his mother's name *was* Meshul-
lemeth the daughter of Haruz of Jotbah.
2 Kin. 21:2-6, 11, 16 20 And he did evil in the sight of the LORD, [a]as Manasseh his father
had done.
21 For he walked in all the way that his father had walked, and
served the idols that his father had served and worshiped them.
2 Kin. 22:17; 1 Chr. 28:9 22 So [a]he forsook the LORD, the God of his fathers, and did not walk
in the way of the LORD.
23 And [a]the servants of Amon conspired against him and killed the
[a]2 Kin. 12:20; 14:19 king in his own house.
24 Then [a]the people of the land [1]killed all those who had conspired
against King Amon, and the people of the land made Josiah his son
king in his place.
[1]Lit., *smote* [a]2 Kin. 14:5 25 Now the rest of the acts of Amon which he did, are they not
written in the Book of the Chronicles of the Kings of Judah?
26 And he was buried in his grave [a]in the garden of Uzza, and
26 [a]2 Kin. 21:18 Josiah his son became king in his place.

Chapter 22

22:1 [a]2 Chr. 34:1 [b]Josh. 15:39 **22** [a]Josiah was eight years old when he became king, and he
reigned thirty-one years in Jerusalem; and his mother's name
was Jedidah the daughter of Adaiah of [b]Bozkath.
2 And he did right in the sight of the LORD and walked in all the
Deut. 5:32; Josh. 1:7 way of his father David, nor did he [a]turn aside to the right or to the
left.
3 Now [a]it came about in the eighteenth year of King Josiah that the
3 [a]2 Chr. 34:8 king sent Shaphan, the son of Azaliah the son of Meshullam the
scribe, to the house of the LORD saying,
4 "[a]Go up to Hilkiah the high priest that he may [1]count the money
4 [1]Or, *total* [a]2 Kin. 12:4, 9, 10 brought in to the house of the LORD which the doorkeepers have
gathered from the people.
5 "[a]And let them deliver it into the hand of the workmen who have
the oversight of the house of the LORD, and let them give it to the
[1]Lit., *breach* [a]2 Kin. 12:11-14 workmen who are in the house of the LORD to repair the [1]damages of
the house,
6 to the carpenters and the builders and the masons and for
buying timber and hewn stone to repair the house.
2 Kin. 12:15; 1 Cor. 4:2 7 "Only [a]no accounting shall be made with them for the money
delivered into their hands, for they deal faithfully."
8 Then Hilkiah the high priest said to Shaphan the scribe, "[a]I have
[a]Deut. 31:24-26; 2 Chr. 34:14, 15 found the book of the law in the house of the LORD." And Hilkiah
gave the book to Shaphan who read it.

9 And Shaphan the scribe came to the king and brought back
word to the king and said, "Your servants have emptied out the
money that was found in the house, and have delivered it into the
hand of the workmen who have the oversight of the house of the
LORD."
10 Moreover, Shaphan the scribe told the king saying, "Hilkiah the
priest has given me a book." And Shaphan read it in the presence of
the king.
11 And it came about when the king heard the words of the book of
the law, that [a]he tore his clothes.
12 Then the king commanded Hilkiah the priest, [a]Ahikam the son
of Shaphan, [1b]Achbor the son of Micaiah, Shaphan the scribe, and
Asaiah the king's servant saying,
13 "Go, inquire of the LORD for me and the people and all Judah
concerning the words of this book that has been found, for [a]great is
the wrath of the LORD that burns against us, because our fathers have
not listened to the words of this book, to do according to all that is
written concerning us."
14 So Hilkiah the priest, Ahikam, Achbor, Shaphan, and Asaiah
went to Huldah the prophetess, the wife of Shallum the son of
[1a]Tikvah, the son of Harhas, keeper of the wardrobe (now she lived
in Jerusalem in the [b]Second Quarter); and they spoke to her.
15 And she said to them, "Thus says the LORD God of Israel, 'Tell
the man who sent you to me,
16 thus says the LORD, "Behold, I [a]bring evil on this place and on its
inhabitants, *even* all the words of the book which the king of Judah
has read.
17 "[a]Because they have forsaken Me and have burned incense to
other gods that they might provoke Me to anger with all the work of
their hands, therefore My wrath burns against this place, and it shall
not be quenched." '
18 "But to [a]the king of Judah who sent you to inquire of the LORD
thus shall you say to him, 'Thus says the LORD God of Israel,
"*Regarding* the words which you have heard,
19 [a]because your heart was tender and [b]you humbled yourself
before the LORD when you heard what I spoke against this place and
against its inhabitants that they should become [c]a desolation and a
[d]curse, and you have [e]torn your clothes and wept before Me, I truly
have heard you," declares the LORD.
20 "Therefore, behold, I will gather you to your fathers, and [a]you
shall be gathered to your grave in peace, neither shall your eyes see
all the evil which I will bring on this place." ' " So they brought back
word to the king.

Chapter 23

23 [a]Then the king sent, and they gathered to him all the elders of
Judah and of Jerusalem.
2 And the king went up to the house of the LORD and all the men
of Judah and all the inhabitants of Jerusalem with him, and the
priests and the prophets and all the people, both small and great;
and [a]he read in their hearing all the words of the book of the cove-
nant, [b]which was found in the house of the LORD.
3 And [a]the king stood by the pillar and made a covenant before
the LORD, [b]to walk after the LORD, and to keep His commandments

11 [a]Gen. 37:34; Jos 7:6

12 [1]In 2 Chr. 34:20 *Abdon, son of Mica* [a]2 Kin. 25:22; Jer. 26:24 [b]2 Chr. 34:20

13 [a]Deut. 29:23-28 31:17, 18

14 [1]In 2 Chr. 34:22 *Tokhath, son of Ha* [a]2 Chr. 34:22 [b]Zep 1:10

16 [a]Deut. 29:27; D 9:11-14

17 [a]Deut. 29:25, 2 2 Kin. 21:22

18 [a]2 Chr. 34:26

19 [a]1 Sam. 24:5; 51:17 [b]Ex. 10:3; 1 21:29 [c]Lev. 26:31 26:6 [e]2 Kin. 22:11

20 [a]2 Kin. 23:30

23:1 [a]2 Chr. 34:2

2 [a]Deut. 31:10-13 [b]2 Kin. 22:8

3 [a]2 Kin. 11:14, 1 [b]Deut. 13:4

and His testimonies and His statutes with all *his* heart and all *his* soul, to carry out the words of this covenant that were written in this book. And all the people [1]entered into the covenant.

4 Then the king commanded Hilkiah the high priest and [a]the priests of the second order and the [1]doorkeepers, [b]to bring out of the temple of the LORD all the vessels that were made for Baal, for [2]Asherah, and for all the host of heaven; and [c]he burned them outside Jerusalem in the fields of the Kidron, and carried their ashes to Bethel.

5 And he did away with the idolatrous priests whom the kings of Judah had appointed to burn incense in the high places in the cities of Judah and in the surrounding area of Jerusalem, also those who burned incense to Baal, to the sun and to the moon and to the constellations and to all the [a]host of heaven.

6 And he brought out the Asherah from the house of the LORD outside Jerusalem to the brook Kidron, and burned it at the brook Kidron, and [a]ground *it* to dust, and [b]threw its dust on the graves of the [1]common people.

7 He also broke down the houses of the [a]*male* cult prostitutes which *were* in the house of the LORD, where [b]the women were weaving [1]hangings for the Asherah.

8 Then he brought all the priests from the cities of Judah, and defiled the high places where the priests had burned incense, from [a]Geba to Beersheba; and he broke down the high places of the gates which *were* at the entrance of the gate of Joshua the governor of the city, which *were* on one's left at the city gate.

9 Nevertheless [a]the priests of the high places did not go up to the altar of the LORD in Jerusalem, but they ate unleavened bread among their brothers.

10 [a]He also defiled [1]Topheth, which is in the valley of the son of Hinnom, [b]that no man might make his son or his daughter pass through the fire for [c]Molech.

11 And he did away with the horses which the kings of Judah had given to the [a]sun, at the entrance of the house of the LORD, by the chamber of Nathan-melech the official, which *was* in the precincts; and he burned the chariots of the sun with fire.

12 And [a]the altars which *were* on the roof, the upper chamber of Ahaz, which the kings of Judah had made, and [b]the altars which Manasseh had made in the two courts of the house of the LORD, the king broke down; and he [1]smashed them there, and [c]threw their dust into the brook Kidron.

13 And the high places which *were* before Jerusalem, which *were* on the right of [a]the mount of destruction which Solomon the king of Israel had built for [b]Ashtoreth the abomination of the Sidonians, and for [c]Chemosh the abomination of Moab, and for Milcom the abomination of the sons of Ammon, the king defiled.

14 And [a]he broke in pieces the *sacred* pillars and cut down the Asherim and [b]filled their places with human bones.

15 Furthermore, [a]the altar that *was* at Bethel *and* the [b]high place which Jeroboam the son of Nebat, who made Israel sin, had made, even that altar and the high place he broke down. Then he [1c]demolished its stones, ground them to dust, and burned the Asherah.

16 Now when Josiah turned, he saw the graves that *were* there on the mountain, and he sent and took the bones from the graves and

[1]Lit., *took a stand in*

[1]Lit., *keepers of the threshold* [2]I.e., a wooden symbol of a female deity, and so throughout the ch. [a]2 Kin. 25:18; Jer. 52:24 [b]2 Kin. 21:3?; ... 33:3 [c]2 Kin. 23:15

5 [a]2 Kin. 21:3

6 [1]Lit., *sons of the people* [a]2 Kin. 23:15 [b]2 Chr. 34:4

... *Or, tents*; lit., *houses* [a]1 Kin. 14:24; 15:12 ... Ex. 35:25, 26; Ezek. 16:16

[a]Josh. 21:17; 1 Kin. 15:22

9 [a]Ezek. 44:10-14

10 [1]I.e., place of ...ing [a]Is. 30:33; Jer. ...1, 32; 19:4-6 [b]Lev. 18:21 [c]1 Kin. 11:7

1 [a]Deut. 4:19; Job 31:26; Ezek. 8:16

[1]Or, *ran from there* ...r. 19:13; Zeph. 1:5 ...1. 21:5; 2 Chr. 33:5 [c]2 Kin. 23:4, 6

[a]1 Kin. 11:7 [b]1 Kin. 11:5 [c]Num. 21:29

14 [a]Deut. 7:5, 25 [b]2 Kin. 23:16

[1]So the Gr.; Heb., ...*ned the high place* 1 Kin. 13:1 [b]1 Kin. ...28-33 [c]2 Kin. 23:6

burned *them* on the altar and defiled it [a]according to the word of the LORD which the man of God proclaimed, who proclaimed these things.

17 Then he said, "What is this monument that I see?" And the men of the city told him, "[a]It is the grave of the man of God who came from Judah and proclaimed these things which you have done against the altar of Bethel."

18 And he said, "Let him alone; let no one disturb his bones." So they [1]left his bones undisturbed [a]with the bones of the prophet who came from Samaria.

19 And Josiah also removed all the houses of the high places which *were* [a]in the cities of Samaria, which the kings of Israel had made provoking [1]the LORD; and he did to them [2]just as he had done in Bethel.

20 And all the priests of the high places who *were* there [a]he slaughtered on the altars and burned human bones on them; then he returned to Jerusalem.

21 Then the king commanded all the people saying, "[a]Celebrate the Passover to the LORD your God [b]as it is written in this book of the covenant."

22 [a]Surely such a Passover had not been celebrated from the days of the judges who judged Israel, nor in all the days of the kings of Israel and of the kings of Judah.

23 But in the eighteenth year of King Josiah, this Passover was observed to the LORD in Jerusalem.

24 Moreover, Josiah [1]removed [a]the mediums and the spiritists and the [b]teraphim and [c]the idols and all the abominations that were seen in the land of Judah and in Jerusalem, [d]that he might [2]confirm the words of the law which were written [e]in the book that Hilkiah the priest found in the house of the LORD.

25 And before him there was no king [a]like him who turned to the LORD with all his heart and with all his soul and with all his might, according to all the law of Moses; nor did any like him arise after him.

26 However, the LORD did not turn from the fierceness of His great wrath with which His anger burned against Judah, [a]because of all the provocations with which Manasseh had provoked Him.

27 And the LORD said, "I will remove Judah also from My sight, [a]as I have removed Israel. And [b]I will cast off Jerusalem, this city which I have chosen, and the [1]temple of which I said, 'My name shall be there.' "

28 Now the rest of the acts of Josiah and all that he did, are they not written in the Book of the Chronicles of the Kings of Judah?

29 [a]In his days [b]Pharaoh Neco king of Egypt went up to the king of Assyria to the river Euphrates. And King Josiah went to meet him, and when *Pharaoh Neco* saw him he killed him at [c]Megiddo.

30 And [a]his servants drove [1]his body in a chariot from Megiddo, and brought him to Jerusalem and buried him in his own tomb. [b]Then the people of the land took Jehoahaz the son of Josiah and anointed him and made him king in place of his father.

31 [a]Jehoahaz was twenty-three years old when he became king, and he reigned three months in Jerusalem; and his mother's name was [b]Hamutal the daughter of Jeremiah of Libnah.

16 [a]1 Kin. 13:2

17 [a]1 Kin. 13:1, 30,

18 [1]Lit., *let his bone* *escape with* [a]1 Kin. 13:11, 31

19 [1]So with ancient versions [2]Lit., *according to all the* [a]2 Chr. 34:6, 7

20 [a]2 Kin. 10:25; 11

21 [a]2 Chr. 35:1-17 [b]Num. 9:2-4; Deut. 16:2-8

22 [a]2 Chr. 35:18, 1

24 [1]Lit., *consumed* *perform* [a]Lev. 19:3 2 Kin. 21:6 [b]Gen. 3 mg. [c]2 Kin. 21:11, [d]Deut. 18:10-22 [e]2 22:8

25 [a]2 Kin. 18:5

26 [a]2 Kin. 21:11-1 Jer. 15:4

27 [1]Lit., *house* [a]2 18:11 [b]2 Kin. 21:1

29 [a]2 Chr. 35:20-2 [b]Jer. 46:2 [c]Judg. 5

30 [1]Lit., *him, dead* [a]2 Kin. 9:28 [b]2 Ch 36:1-4

31 [a]1 Chr. 3:15; Je 22:11 [b]2 Kin. 24:1

32 And he did evil in the sight of the LORD, [a]according to all that his
fathers had done.
33 And [a]Pharaoh Neco imprisoned him at [b]Riblah in the land of
[c]Hamath, that he might not reign in Jerusalem; and he imposed on
the land a fine of one hundred talents of silver and a talent of gold.
34 And Pharaoh Neco made [a]Eliakim the son of Josiah king in the
place of Josiah his father, and [b]changed his name to Jehoiakim. But
he took Jehoahaz away and [1c]brought *him* to Egypt, and he died
there.
35 So Jehoiakim [a]gave the silver and gold to Pharaoh, but he taxed
the land in order to give the money at the [1]command of Pharaoh. He
exacted the silver and gold from the people of the land, each accord-
ing to his valuation, to give it to Pharaoh Neco.
36 [a]Jehoiakim was twenty-five years old when he became king, and
he reigned eleven years in Jerusalem; and his mother's name *was*
Zebidah the daughter of Pedaiah of Rumah.
37 And he did evil in the sight of the LORD, [a]according to all that his
fathers had done.

Chapter 24

24 [a]In his days Nebuchadnezzar king of Babylon came up, and
Jehoiakim became his servant *for* three years; then he turned
and rebelled against him.
2 And the LORD sent against him [a]bands
of Chaldeans, [b]bands of Arameans, [c]bands
of Moabites, and bands of Ammonites. So
He sent them against Judah to destroy it,
[d]according to the word of the LORD, which
He had spoken through His servants the
prophets.
3 [a]Surely at the [1]command of the LORD it
came upon Judah, to remove *them* from His
sight [b]because of the sins of Manasseh, ac-
cording to all that he had done,
4 and [a]also for the innocent blood which he shed, for he filled
Jerusalem with innocent blood; and the LORD would not forgive.
5 Now the rest of the acts of Jehoiakim and all that he did, are they
not written in the Book of the Chronicles of the Kings of Judah?
6 So [a]Jehoiakim slept with his fathers, and Jehoiachin his son be-
came king in his place.
7 And [a]the king of Egypt did not come out of his land again, [b]for
the king of Babylon had taken all that belonged to the king of Egypt
from [c]the brook of Egypt to the river Euphrates.
8 [a]Jehoiachin was [b]eighteen years old when he became king, and
he reigned three months in Jerusalem; and his mother's name *was*
Nehushta the daughter of Elnathan of Jerusalem.
9 And he did evil in the sight of the LORD, [a]according to all that his
father had done.
10 At that time the servants of Nebuchadnezzar king of Babylon
went up to Jerusalem, and the city came under siege.
11 And Nebuchadnezzar the king of Babylon came to the city, while
his servants were besieging it.
12 And [a]Jehoiachin the king of Judah went out to the king of Baby-
lon, he and his mother and his servants and his captains and his

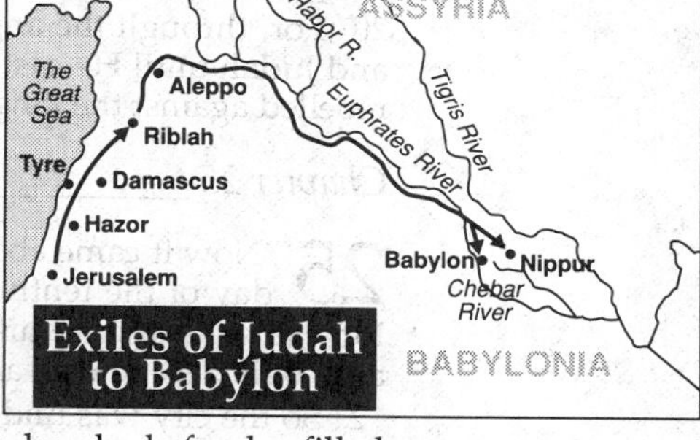

Exiles of Judah to Babylon

32 [a]2 Kin. 21:2-7
2 Kin. 23:29 [b]2 Kin. 25:6 [c]1 Kin. 8:65
[1]So with Gr.; Heb., came [a]1 Chr. 3:15 2 Kin. 24:17; 2 Chr. 36:4 [c]Jer. 22:11, 12; Ezek. 19:3, 4
[1]Lit., *mouth* [a]2 Kin. 23:33
6 [a]2 Chr. 36:5; Jer. 22:18, 19; 26:1
37 [a]2 Kin. 23:32
1 [a]2 Chr. 36:6; Jer. 25:1; Dan. 1:1, 2
Jer. 35:11f. [b]2 Kin. 6:23 [c]2 Kin. 13:20 [d]2 Kin. 23:27
[1]Lit., *mouth* [a]2 Kin. 8:25 [b]2 Kin. 23:26
4 [a]2 Kin. 21:16
6 [a]Jer. 22:18, 19
[a]Jer. 37:5-7 [b]Jer. 46:2 [c]Gen. 15:18
Chr. 3:16 [b]2 Chr. 36:9
9 [a]2 Kin. 21:2-7
er. 22:24-30; 24:1; 29:1, 2

officials. So [b]the king of Babylon took him captive in the eighth year
of his reign.
13 And [a]he carried out from there all the treasures of the house of
the LORD, and the treasures of the king's house, and [b]cut in pieces all
the vessels of gold [c]which Solomon king of Israel had made in the
temple of the LORD, just as the LORD had said.
14 Then [a]he led away into exile all Jerusalem and all the captains
and all the mighty men of valor, [b]ten thousand captives, and [c]all the
craftsmen and the smiths. None remained [d]except the poorest people
of the land.
15 So [a]he led Jehoiachin away into exile to Babylon; also the king's
mother and the king's wives and his officials and the leading men of
the land, he led away into exile from Jerusalem to Babylon.
16 And all the men of valor, [a]seven thousand, and the craftsmen
and the smiths, one thousand, all strong and fit for war, and these
the king of Babylon brought into exile to Babylon.
17 [a]Then the king of Babylon made [1]his uncle Mattaniah, king in his
place, and changed his name to Zedekiah.
18 [a]Zedekiah was twenty-one years old when he became king, and
he reigned eleven years in Jerusalem; and his mother's name *was*
[b]Hamutal the daughter of Jeremiah of Libnah.
19 And he did evil in the sight of the LORD, [a]according to all that
Jehoiakim had done.
20 For [a]through the anger of the LORD *this* came about in Jerusalem
and Judah until He cast them out from His presence. And [b]Zedekiah
rebelled against the king of Babylon.

Chapter 25

25 [a]Now it came about in the ninth year of his reign, on the tenth
day of the tenth month, that [b]Nebuchadnezzar king of Baby-
lon came, he and all his army, against Jerusalem, camped against it,
and [c]built a siege wall all around [1]it.
2 So the city was under siege until the eleventh year of King Zede-
kiah.
3 On the ninth day of the *fourth* month [a]the famine was so severe
in the city that there was no food for the people of the land.
4 [a]Then the city was broken into, and all the men of war *fled* by
night by way of the gate between the two walls beside [b]the king's
garden, though the Chaldeans were all around the city. And [1]they
went by way of the Arabah.
5 But the army of the Chaldeans pursued the king and overtook
him in the plains of Jericho and all his army was scattered from him.
6 Then [a]they captured the king and [b]brought him to the king of
Babylon at [c]Riblah, and [1]he passed sentence on him.
7 And [a]they slaughtered the sons of Zedekiah before his eyes, then
[b]put out the eyes of Zedekiah and bound him with bronze fetters
and brought him to Babylon.
8 [a]Now on the seventh day of the [b]fifth month, which was the
nineteenth year of King Nebuchadnezzar, king of Babylon, Nebu-
zaradan the captain of the guard, a servant of the king of Babylon,
came to Jerusalem.
9 And [a]he burned the house of the LORD, [b]the king's house, and all
the houses of Jerusalem; even every great house he burned with fire.

12 [b]2 Chr. 36:10
13 [a]2 Kin. 20:17; Is. 39:6 [b]2 Kin. 25:13-1 [c]1 Kin. 7:48-50
14 [a]Jer. 24:1 [b]2 Kir 24:16; Jer. 52:28 [c]J 24:1; 29:2 [d]2 Kin. 2
15 [a]2 Chr. 36:10; Je 22:24-28; Ezek. 17:
16 [a]2 Kin. 24:14
17 [1]I.e., Jehoiachin uncle [a]2 Chr. 36:1C Jer. 37:1
18 [a]Jer. 27:1; 28:1; 52:1 [b]2 Kin. 23:31
19 [a]2 Kin. 23:37
20 [a]Deut. 4:24; 29 2 Kin. 23:26 [b]2 Ch 36:13; Ezek. 17:15
25:1 [1]Lit., *against* [a]2 Chr. 36:17-20; J 39:1-7 [b]Jer. 21:2; 2; Ezek. 24:2 [c]Eze 21:22
3 [a]2 Kin. 6:24, 25; 4:9, 10
4 [1]So some ancie mss. and versions *he* [a]Ezek. 33:21 3:15
6 [1]Lit., *they spok judgment with hin* 34:21, 22 [b]Jer. 32 [c]2 Kin. 23:33
7 [a]Jer. 39:6, 7 [b]E 12:13
8 [a]Jer. 52:12 [b]Je 39:8-12
9 [a]1 Kin. 9:8; 2 C 36:19; Ps. 74:3-7 [b]Amos 2:5

10 So all the army of the Chaldeans who *were with* the captain of the
guard [a]broke down the walls around Jerusalem.
11 Then [a]the rest of the people who were left in the city and the
deserters who had deserted to the king of Babylon and the rest of the
multitude, Nebuzaradan the captain of the guard carried away into
exile.
12 But the captain of the guard left some of [a]the poorest of the land
to be vinedressers and plowmen.
13 [a]Now the bronze pillars which were in the house of the LORD,
and the stands and [b]the bronze sea which were in the house of the
LORD, the Chaldeans broke in pieces and carried the [1]bronze to Baby-
lon.
14 [a]And they took away the pots, the shovels, the snuffers, the
spoons, and all the bronze vessels which were used in *temple* service.
15 The captain of the guard also took away the firepans and the
basins, what was fine gold and what was fine silver.
16 The two pillars, the one sea, and the stands which Solomon had
made for the house of the LORD—[a]the bronze of all these vessels was
beyond weight.
17 [a]The height of the one pillar was eighteen [1]cubits, and a bronze
capital was on it; the height of the capital was three [1]cubits, with a
network and pomegranates on the capital all around, all of bronze.
And the second pillar was like these with network.
18 Then the captain of the guard took [a]Seraiah the chief priest and
[b]Zephaniah the second priest, with the three [1]officers of the temple.
19 And from the city he took one official who was overseer of the
men of war, and [a]five [1]of the king's advisers who were found in the
city; and the [2]scribe of the captain of the army, who mustered the
people of the land; and sixty men of the people of the land who were
found in the city.
20 And Nebuzaradan the captain of the guard took them and
brought them to the king of Babylon at [a]Riblah.
21 Then the king of Babylon struck them down and put them to
death at Riblah in the land of Hamath. [a]So Judah was led away into
exile from its land.
22 Now *as for* the people who were left in the land of Judah, whom
Nebuchadnezzar king of Babylon had left, he appointed [a]Gedaliah
the son of Ahikam, the son of Shaphan over them.
23 [a]When all the captains of the forces, they and *their* men, heard
that the king of Babylon had appointed Gedaliah *governor,* they came
to Gedaliah to [b]Mizpah, namely, Ishmael the son of Nethaniah, and
Johanan the son of Kareah, and Seraiah the son of Tanhumeth the
Netophathite, and Jaazaniah the son of the Maacathite, they and
their men.
24 And Gedaliah swore to them and their men and said to them,
"Do not be afraid of the servants of the Chaldeans; live in the land
and serve the king of Babylon, and it will be well with you."
25 [a]But it came about in the seventh month, that Ishmael the son of
Nethaniah, the son of Elishama, of the royal [1]family, came [2]with ten
men and struck Gedaliah down so that he died along with the Jews
and the Chaldeans who were with him at Mizpah.
26 [a]Then all the people, both small and great, and the captains of
the forces arose and went to Egypt; for they were afraid of the Chal-
deans.

[a]2 Kin. 14:13; Neh. 1:3
11 [a]2 Chr. 36:20
[a]2 Kin. 24:14; Jer. 40:7
...it., *bronze of them* ...Kin. 7:15-22; 2 Kin. ...17; 2 Chr. 3:15-17; ...8 [b]1 Kin. 7:23-26; 2 Chr. 4:2-4
...4 [a]Ex. 27:3; 1 Kin. ...47-50; 2 Chr. 4:16
16 [a]1 Kin. 7:47
...17 [1]I.e., One cubit ...uals approx. 18 in. [a]1 Kin. 7:15-22
...it., *keepers of the* [a]1 Chr. 6:14; Ezra ...er. 21:1; 29:25, 29
...Lit., *men of those ...ing the king's face ..., scribe, a captain* [a]Esth. 1:14
20 [a]2 Kin. 23:33
...eut. 28:64; 2 Kin. 23:27
...Jer. 39:14; 40:7-9
...er. 40:7-9 [b]Josh. 18:26
..., *seed* [2]Lit., *and ...en with him* [a]Jer. 41:1, 2
26 [a]Jer. 43:4-7

27 [a]Now it came about in the thirty-seventh year of [b]the exile of
Jehoiachin king of Judah, in the twelfth month, on the twenty-
seventh *day* of the month, that Evil-merodach king of Babylon, in the
year that he became king, [1c]released Jehoiachin king of Judah from
prison;
28 and he [a]spoke kindly to him and set his throne above the throne
of the kings who *were* with him in Babylon.
29 And [1]Jehoiachin changed his prison clothes, and [2a]had his meals
in [3]the king's presence regularly all the days of his life;
30 and for his [a]allowance, a regular allowance was given him by the
king, a portion for each day, all the days of his life.

27 [1]Lit., *lifted* ... *head of* [a]Jer. 5... [b]2 Kin. 24:12, 1... 40:13, 20

28 [a]Dan. 2:37;...

29 [1]Lit., *he* [2]Li... *bread* [3]Lit., *his* ... *presence* [a]2 S...

30 [a]Neh. 11:23...

The Assyrian Captivity of Israel

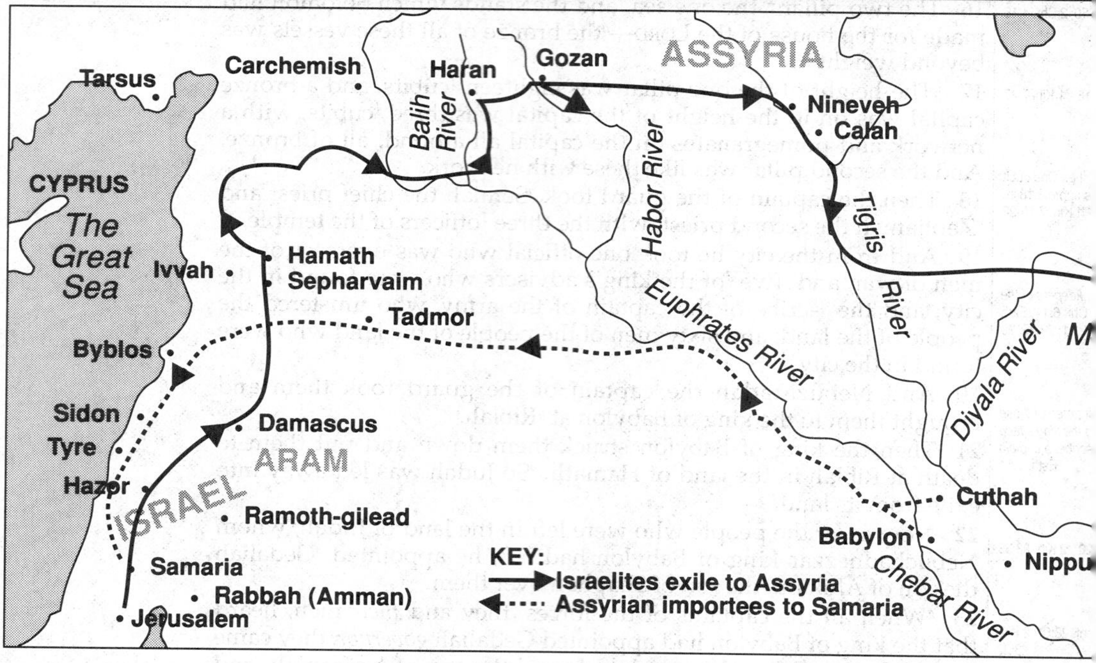

2 KINGS AT A GLANCE

e of 2 Kings:

r DIVISIONS

	CHAPTER THEMES
	1
	2
	3
	4
	5
	6
	7
	8
	9
	10
	11
	12
	13
	14
	15
	16
	17
	18
	19
	20
	21
	22
	23
	24
	25

Author:

Date:

Purpose:

Key Words:

The Historical Chart of the Kings and Prophets of Israel and Judah

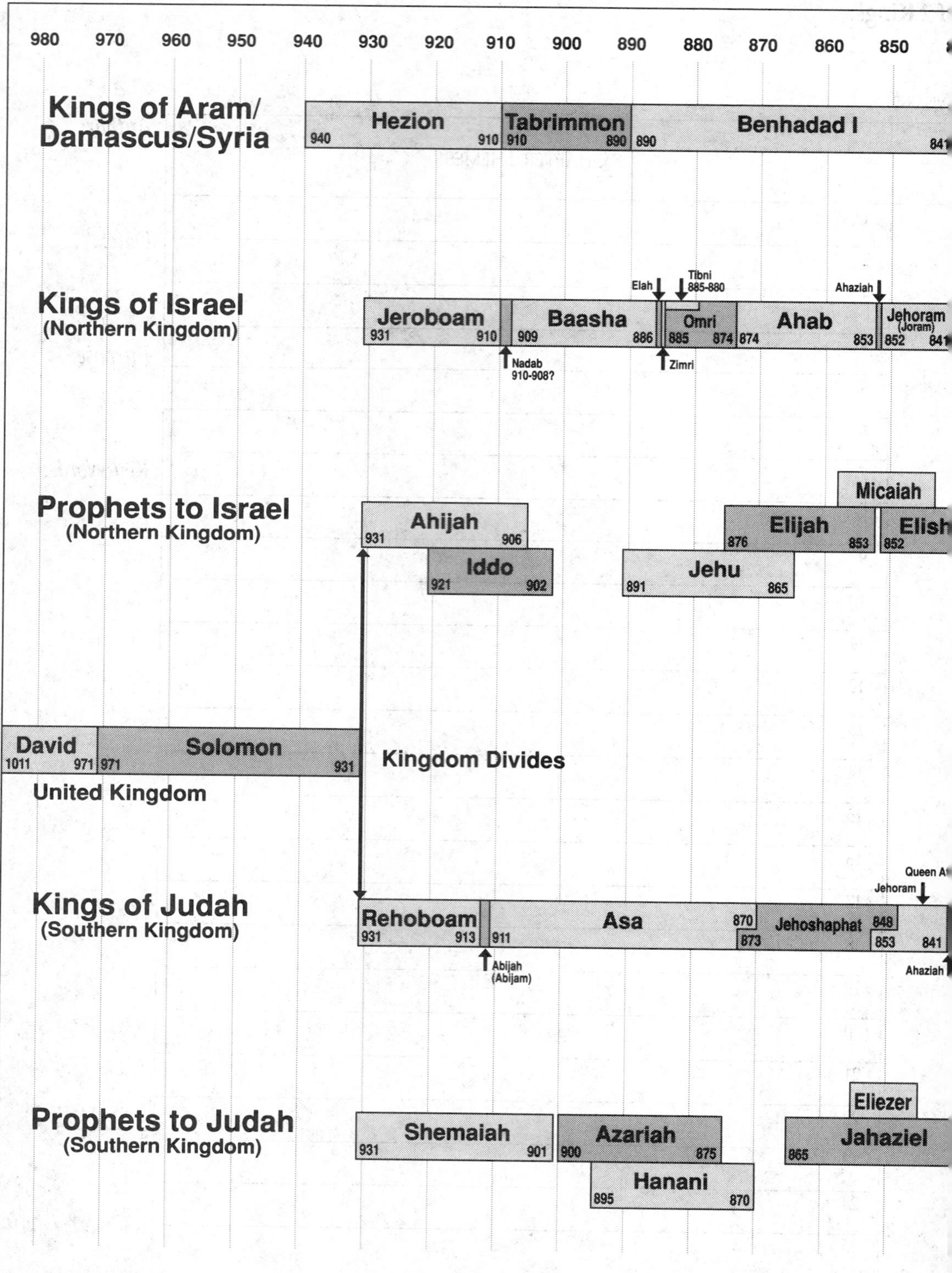

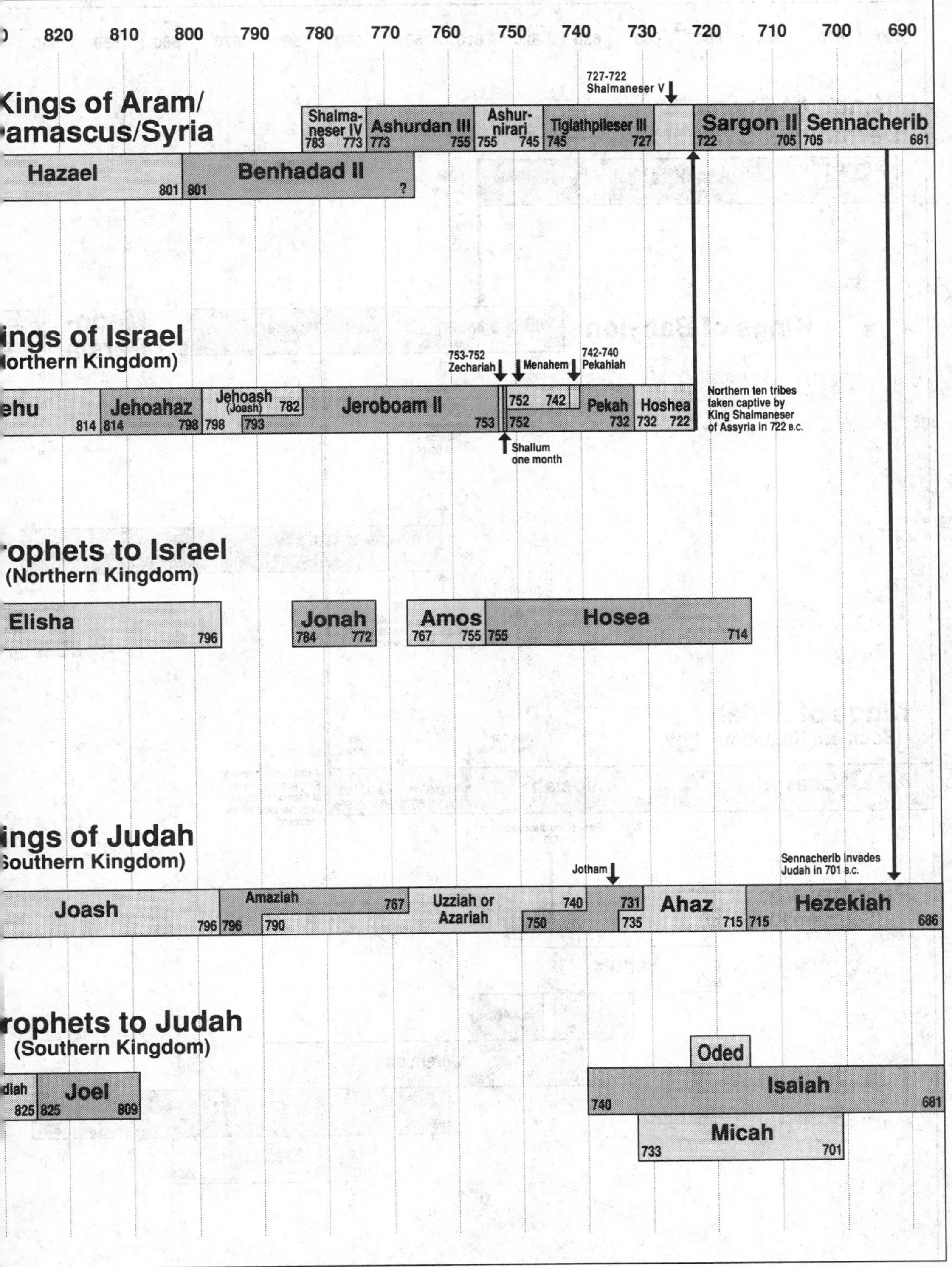

820
810
800
790
780
770
760
750
740
730
720
710
700
690
Kings of Aram/
amascus/Syria
727-722
Shalmaneser V
Shalma-
neser IV
783 773
Ashurdan III
773 755
Ashur-
nirari
755 745
Tiglathpileser III
745 727
Sargon II
722 705
Sennacherib
705 681
Hazael
801
Benhadad II
801 ?
ings of Israel
orthern Kingdom)
753-752
Zechariah
Menahem
742-740
Pekahiah
ehu
814
Jehoahaz
814 798
Jehoash
(Joash)
798 782
793
Jeroboam II
753
752 742
752
Pekah
732
Hoshea
732 722
Northern ten tribes
taken captive by
King Shalmaneser
of Assyria in 722 B.C.
Shallum
one month
rophets to Israel
(Northern Kingdom)
Elisha
796
Jonah
784 772
Amos
767 755
Hosea
755 714
ings of Judah
Southern Kingdom)
Jotham
Sennacherib invades
Judah in 701 B.C.
Joash
796
Amaziah
796 767
790
Uzziah or
Azariah
750 740
731
735
Ahaz
715
Hezekiah
715 686
rophets to Judah
(Southern Kingdom)
diah
825
Joel
825 809
Oded
Isaiah
740 681
Micah
733 701

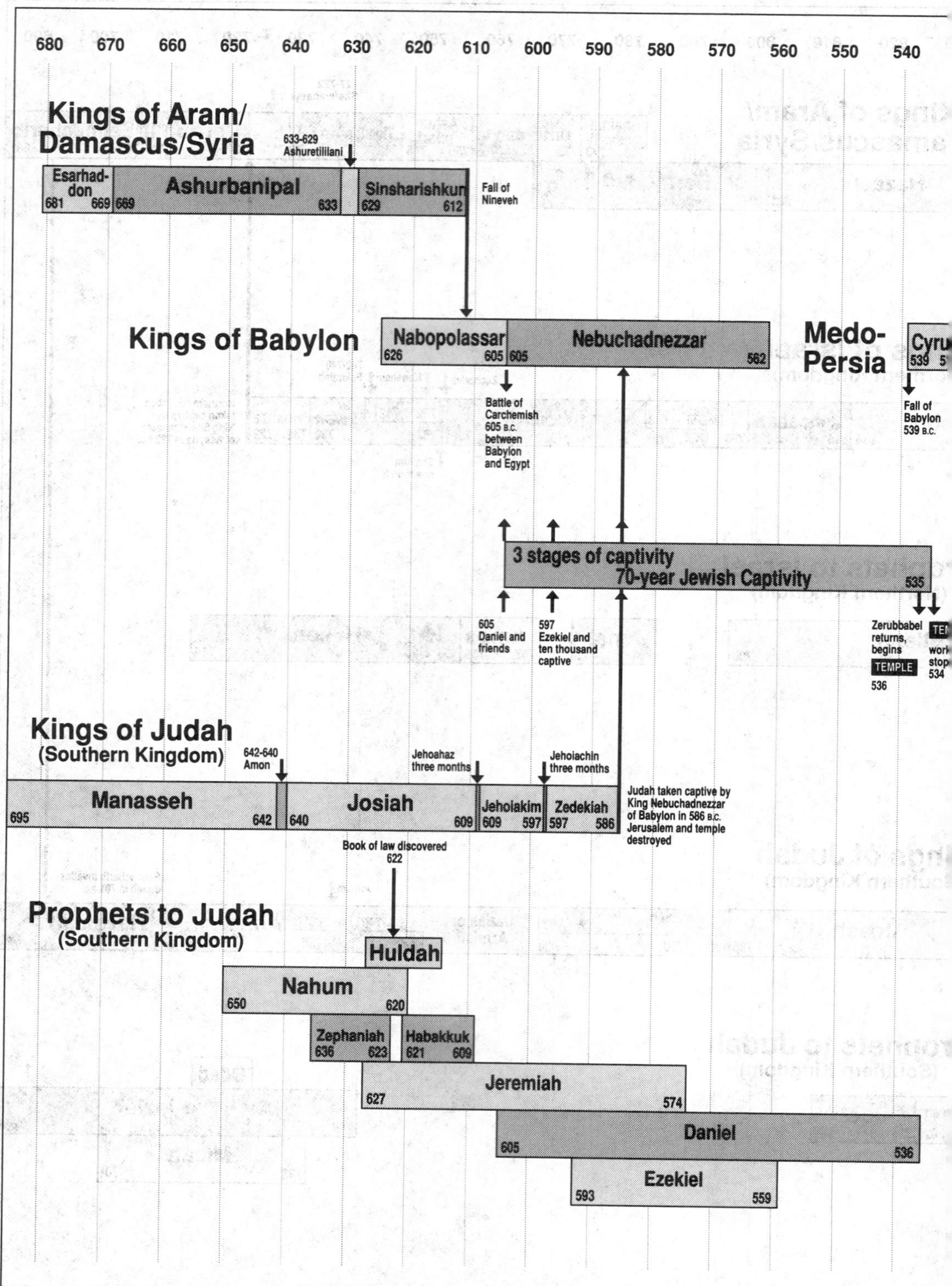
680 670 660 650 640 630 620 610 600 590 580 570 560 550 540
Kings of Aram/ Damascus/Syria
633-629 Ashuretililani
Esarhad-don 681 669
Ashurbanipal 669 633
Sinsharishkun 629 612
Fall of Nineveh
Kings of Babylon
Nabopolassar 626 605
Nebuchadnezzar 605 562
Medo-Persia
Cyru 539
Fall of Babylon 539 B.C.
Battle of Carchemish 605 B.C. between Babylon and Egypt
3 stages of captivity
70-year Jewish Captivity 535
605 Daniel and friends
597 Ezekiel and ten thousand captive
Zerubbabel returns, begins TEMPLE 536
TEM work stop 534
Kings of Judah (Southern Kingdom)
642-640 Amon
Jehoahaz three months
Jehoiachin three months
Manasseh 695 642
Josiah 640 609
Jehoiakim 609 597
Zedekiah 597 586
Judah taken captive by King Nebuchadnezzar of Babylon in 586 B.C. Jerusalem and temple destroyed
Book of law discovered 622
Prophets to Judah (Southern Kingdom)
Huldah
Nahum 650 620
Zephaniah 636 623
Habakkuk 621 609
Jeremiah 627 574
Daniel 605 536
Ezekiel 593 559

The Kings of Israel and Judah

	King	Kingdom Ruled Over and How Long	Insights on How King Lived and Died
	Solomon son of:		
	Rehoboam son of:		
	Jeroboam son of:		
	Abijam or **Abijah** son of:		
	Asa son of:		
	Nadab son of:		
	Baasha son of:		
	Elah son of:		
	Zimri son of:		
	Omri son of:		
	Jehoshaphat son of:		
	Ahab son of:		
	Ahaziah son of Ahab		
	Jehoram or **Joram** son of Ahab		
	Jehoram son of Jehoshaphat		
	Ahaziah son of Jehoram, grandson of Jehoshaphat		
5	**Queen Athaliah** mother of:		
4	**Jehu** son of:		
6	**Joash** son of:		
7	**Amaziah** son of:		

If a king ruled for any portion of a year, customarily that year was included as part of his reign.
An overlap in reigns indicates a co-regency, such as a son ruling alongside his father.

The Kings of Israel and Judah

Dates	King	Kingdom Ruled Over and How Long	Insights on How King Lived and D
814-798	**Jehoahaz** or **Joahaz** son of:		
798-782	**Jehoash** or **Joash** son of:		
790-740	**Azariah** or **Uzziah** son of:		
793-753	**Jeroboam II** son of:		
753-752	**Zechariah** son of:		
752	**Shallum** son of:		
752-742	**Menahem** son of:		
742-740	**Pekahiah** son of:		
752-732	**Pekah** son of:		
750-731	**Jotham** son of:		
735-715	**Ahaz** son of:		
732-722	**Hoshea** son of:		
715-686	**Hezekiah** son of:		
695-642	**Manasseh** son of:		
642-640	**Amon** son of:		
640-609	**Josiah** son of:		
609	**Jehoahaz** or **Shallum** son of:		
609-597	**Jehoiakim** or **Eliakim** son of:		
597 *three months*	**Jehoiachin** or (**Coniah** or **Jeconiah**) son of:		
597-586	**Zedekiah** or **Mattaniah** son of:		

If a king ruled for any portion of a year, customarily that year was included as part of his reign.
An overlap in reigns indicates a co-regency, such as a son ruling alongside his father.

CHRONICLES

ɔdah had watched Assyria capture Israel in 722 B.C. In 586 B.C. when the Babylonians besieged ılem for the third and final time, Judah lost her temple, the city of David, and the reign of the sons vid came to a halt. All seemed lost. Judah was held captive for seventy years. Then a Persian king, s, sent out a decree telling the exiles they could return and rebuild Jerusalem and their temple.

ıt if they did could they be assured that the God of Abraham, Isaac, and Jacob would be with ? Had He abandoned His people and His promise to Abraham because of their sin? Would the ern and southern kingdoms ever be united again? Would God still send Messiah? Would David a descendant who would sit on the throne of David forever?

ıd the temple? . . . Between the time of Solomon and the Babylonian captivity king after king had cted it or desecrated it with idols. If they were to restore it, would it do any good?

ıd what of the prophets? What was God's Word, the prophets' message, regarding Israel, Judah, heir future? Would the Word of God alter? Would the messages of the prophets be valid after l and Judah had sinned so grievously?

aving returned from captivity, God's people had to be reminded of "the events or annals of the . the years" and so Chronicles was written. We don't know who wrote it for certain; maybe it was However, whoever wrote it, we know it was part of God's plan, for God included it in the canon ripture.

NGS TO DO

eral Instructions

If possible, study 1 and 2 Samuel and then 1 and 2 Kings before you study 1 and 2 Chronicles. Chronicles is to these other historical books what John is to the synoptic Gospels (Matthew, Mark, and Luke). Both John and Chronicles are supplemental and yet bring unique insight and understanding. Study the chart which follows.

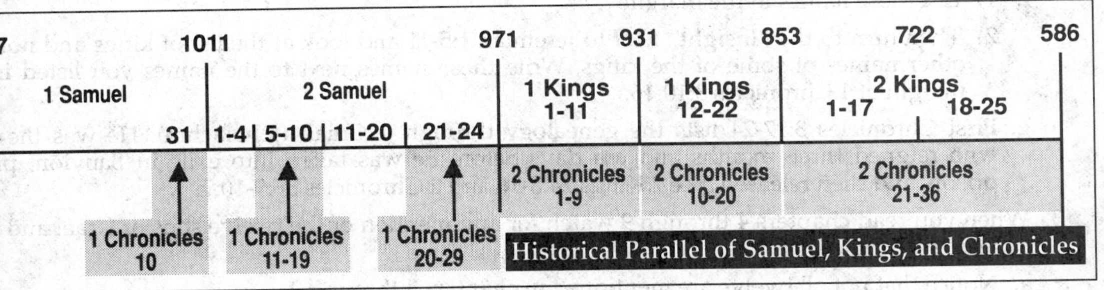

Historical Parallel of Samuel, Kings, and Chronicles

First and 2 Chronicles are not written chronologically. Keep this in mind as you study. When you wonder about the timing of something, look at the chart above.

. As you read 1 Chronicles watch for references to time, to any mention of dates or periods of time as well as who is reigning at the time. Mark these with a drawing of a clock such as this ⏰.

. When you finish observing each chapter, record its theme on the 1 CHRONICLES AT A GLANCE chart on page 647 and on the line next to the chapter number in the text.

pters 1-9: The Genealogies of the Nation of Israel

. This section may seem boring because it's primarily genealogies with a few historical sidelights.

However, remember this information has a purpose and that's why God included it in His Some genealogies, such as 4:1-23, are not included anywhere else.

a. Don't skip this section—you'll gain valuable insights which will help you in the study rest of the book.

b. To discover the scope of the genealogies, read the following verses and then write margin of 1:1 when the genealogies begin and end according to the historical event represent. Read 1:1 and 9:1-2. Keeping in mind what was said in the introducti 1 Chronicles, notice in 9:2 the words: "The first who lived in their possessions in their citi

2. In this segment the key words to mark or underline are the names of people who play vita in Israel's history.

a. Mark the following key words in a distinctive way: *Adam, Noah,* and Noah's three sons, *Ham,* and *Japheth.* Then mark the phrases: *the sons of Japheth, the sons of Ham,* and *the s Shem.*

b. Mark: *the sons of Abraham were Isaac and Ishmael, and Abraham became the father of Isaac,* a *sons of Isaac were Esau and Israel* (remember Israel was called Jacob until God changed his to Israel).

c. In chapter 2 mark *these are the sons of Israel.* Then count the sons. How many were there? became the heads of the tribes of Israel. Record their names on a card and look for any where they are repeated in this segment. Use this card as a bookmark.

1) Read Genesis 49:1-28 where Jacob (Israel) gives a prophetic blessing to each of these m

2) Look at the chart on page 605 which shows the birth order and mother of each of Is sons.

d. In 2:3-15 mark *the sons of Judah* and then look for *David.* In the margin list David's gene from Judah through David's immediate father, Jesse. Remember that the author of Chro gives the genealogy of Judah before the other sons of Israel. Why? What would be imp to the exiles who now repossessed their cities? Wouldn't it be God's promises to David? this in mind as you study the second-to-the-last segment of 1 Chronicles.

e. In 3:1 mark the names of the sons of David, then list their names in the margin.

f. First Chronicles 3:10-16 gives the line of kings which come from David through Solomon.

1) List these names in the margin.

2) Then turn to the "Insight" next to Jeremiah 1:5-11 and look at the list of kings and no other names of some of the kings. Write these names next to the names you listed i margin of 1 Chronicles 3:10-16.

g. First Chronicles 3:17-24 lists the genealogy through Jeconiah (Jehoiachin). He was the who reigned three months and ten days before he was taken into exile in Babylon, p prison, and then released. See 2 Kings 24:8-16 and 2 Chronicles 36:9-10.

3. When you read chapters 4 through 9 watch for any mention of the twelve sons of Israel and genealogy. As you do:

a. Notice that not all twelve are mentioned in chapters 4 through 9.

b. Joseph's sons Manasseh and Ephraim are mentioned in Scripture as part of the twelve trib Israel. The reason for this is given in 1 Chronicles 5:1-2. Take special note of this.

1) Write "Joseph's son" next to any mention of Manasseh and Ephraim.

2) Manasseh is named twice. The tribe split when Canaan was divided. Half the tri Manasseh took land east of the Jordan, the other half went west of the Jordan, thu reference to the "half tribe of Manasseh."

4. Read the section on the sons of Levi carefully and either underline what they were to do or n in the margin. Also observe and note what Aaron and his sons were to do. This will help you come to the final chapters of 1 Chronicles.

5. Don't forget to record the chapter themes in the text and on 1 CHRONICLES AT A GLANCE.

apters 10-19: God Turns the Kingdom to David

1. As you read this segment see how it fits with 1 and 2 Samuel. To do this consult the chart THE HISTORICAL PARALLEL OF SAMUEL, KINGS, AND CHRONICLES on page 601.
   a. Read 1 Chronicles 10, mark any reference to *kingdom*, and list the events of that chapter.
   b. Also note where it says whose son David was. Keep in mind what you just studied in the first segment.
   c. Note in the margin why Saul died, who died with him, and what happened to Saul's body.
2. Read this segment chapter by chapter and do the following:
   a. Mark the following key words: *city of David, ark,* and *covenant*. Observe what you learn from these words and record your insights in the margin.
   b. Ask the five W's and an H as you read each chapter. Who are the key characters? What happens? When? (Draw a clock next to any mention of time.) Where do events occur? Why do they occur? How do things happen? Record your insights in the margin.
   c. Don't forget to record chapter themes on 1 CHRONICLES AT A GLANCE and in the text next to the chapter number.
3. Watch for any prophecies (promises), speeches, songs, or psalms of praise. Who gives them? Why? What is said in each? Record your insights in the margin. Also ask: How can I apply these truths in my life?

apters 20-29: David Builds an Altar and Prepares for God's House

1. Note where this portion of 1 Chronicles comes in respect to 2 Samuel.
   a. When you read chapter 20, compare the wording of verse 1 with 2 Samuel 11:1. Then as you look at the content of 2 Samuel 11-12, note what the author of Chronicles leaves out.
   b. Compare 1 Chronicles 21 with 2 Samuel 24. Why was this event included in 1 Chronicles when David's other sin was omitted? See the "Insight" on page 635 next to 1 Chronicles 21:26-29. Remember, the temple is very important to the returning exiles.
2. As you read each chapter, mark the following key words and note in the margin what you learn from each: *house (home, temple, sanctuary), ark, heart, Levi (Levites),* and *Aaron*.
   a. The word *house* has been used numerous times in 1 Chronicles; however with one or two exceptions "house" referred to someone's family, such as the house of David. In this segment it is used primarily to refer to the house of the Lord. As you mark it note what you learn. Keep in mind this is the book for the exiles who had returned to rebuild the temple and thus the emphasis is on the house of God and its importance. When difficulties arose this historical account would affirm God's enduring purpose and promises.
   b. As you mark the references to the Levites and to Aaron and his sons, observe carefully the types of duties they were to perform and which Levite family was to perform each type of duty. Also go back and review what you marked in the first segment regarding Levi, Aaron, and Aaron's other sons.
3. Read each chapter as you did in the last segment, asking the five W's and an H. Note in the margin what you observe. Also as you did in the last segment watch for any speeches, prophecies, etc. and note the same things you looked for previously.
4. Complete 1 CHRONICLES AT A GLANCE. There are two lines for any additional segment divisions you might see and want to mark.

NGS TO THINK ABOUT

1. Second Timothy 2:13 says, "If we are faithless, He remains faithful; for He cannot deny Himself." What have you seen of the faithfulness of God in the book of Chronicles? What assurance does this give you for your life?

2. You marked the word *heart* in this last segment. Go back over these references in chapter 29 review what you observed about the heart. Also review what you observed as David blessed Lord. Think about your own heart. What is your heart like in respect to the Lord? How can turn what David did into a prayer to the Lord?

3. As you think about all you learned about the priests and their duties and you think of you and other Christians as a kingdom of priests unto God (Revelation 1 and 5), do you see application you can make to your responsibilities as a priest unto God?

Chapter 1 ______________________

1 [a]Adam, Seth, Enosh,
2 Kenan, Mahalalel, Jared,
3 Enoch, Methuselah, Lamech,
4 Noah, Shem, Ham and Japheth.
5 [a]The sons of Japheth *were* Gomer, Magog, Madai, Javan, Tubal,
Meshech, and Tiras.
6 And the sons of Gomer *were* Ashkenaz, [1]Diphath, and Togarmah.
7 And the sons of Javan *were* Elishah, Tarshish, Kittim, and [1]Roda-
nim.
8 The sons of Ham *were* Cush, Mizraim, Put, and Canaan.
9 And the sons of Cush *were* Seba, Havilah, Sabta, Raama, and
Sabteca; and the sons of Raamah *were* Sheba and Dedan.
10 And Cush [1]became the father of Nimrod; he began to be a
mighty one in the earth.
11 [a]And Mizraim became the father of the people of Lud, Anam,
Lehab, Naphtuh,
12 Pathrus, Casluh, from which the [1]Philistines came, and Caphtor.
13 And Canaan became the father of Sidon, his first-born, Heth,
14 and the Jebusites, the Amorites, the Girgashites,
15 the Hivites, the Arkites, the Sinites,
16 the Arvadites, the Zemarites, and the Hamathites.
17 [a]The sons of Shem *were* Elam, Asshur, Arpachshad, Lud, Aram,
Uz, Hul, Gether, and [1]Meshech.
18 And Arpachshad became the father of Shelah and Shelah be-
came the father of Eber.
19 And two sons were born to Eber, the name of the one was Peleg,
for in his days the earth was divided, and his brother's name was
Joktan.
20 And Joktan became the father of Almodad, Sheleph, Hazar-
maveth, Jerah,
21 Hadoram, Uzal, Diklah,
22 [1]Ebal, Abimael, Sheba,
23 Ophir, Havilah, and Jobab; all these *were* the sons of Joktan.
24 [a]Shem, Arpachshad, Shelah,
25 Eber, Peleg, Reu,
26 Serug, Nahor, Terah,
27 Abram, that is Abraham.
28 The sons of Abraham *were* Isaac and Ishmael.
29 [a]These are their genealogies: the first-born of Ishmael *was* Neba-
ioth, then Kedar, Adbeel, Mibsam,
30 Mishma, Dumah, Massa, Hadad, Tema,
31 Jetur, Naphish and Kedemah; these *were* the sons of Ishmael.
32 [a]And the sons of Keturah, Abraham's concubine, *whom* she bore,

1:1 [a]Gen. 4:25-5
5 [a]Gen. 10:2-4
6 [1]In Gen. 10:3,
7 [1]In Gen. 10:4, *Dodanim*
10 [1]Lit., *begot,* throughout the c
11 [a]Gen. 10:13
12 [1]Or, *people*
17 [1]In Gen. 10 *Mash* [a]Gen. 10
22 [1]In Gen. 10
24 [a]Gen. 11:10 Luke 3:34-36
29 [a]Gen. 25:1
32 [a]Gen. 25:1

[a]1 Chr. 1:28 [b]Gen. 25:25, 26; 32:28

were Zimran, Jokshan, Medan, Midian, Ishbak, and Shuah. And the
sons of Jokshan *were* Sheba and Dedan.
33 And the sons of Midian *were* Ephah, Epher, Hanoch, Abida, and
Eldaah. All these were the sons of Keturah.

35 [a]Gen. 36:4-10

34 And [a]Abraham became the father of Isaac. The sons of Isaac *were*
[b]Esau and Israel.

36 [1]In Gen. 36:11, *Zepho*

35 [a]The sons of Esau *were* Eliphaz, Reuel, Jeush, Jalam, and Korah.
36 The sons of Eliphaz *were* Teman, Omar, [1]Zephi, Gatam, Kenaz,
Timna, and Amalek.
37 The sons of Reuel *were* Nahath, Zerah, Shammah, and Mizzah.

38 [a]Gen. 36:20-28

38 [a]And the sons of Seir *were* Lotan, Shobal, Zibeon, Anah, Dishon,
Ezer, and Dishan.
39 And the sons of Lotan *were* Hori and [1]Homam; and Lotan's sister

39 [1]In Gen. 36:22, *Hemam*

was Timna.
40 The sons of Shobal *were* [1]Alian, Manahath, Ebal, [2]Shephi, and
Onam. And the sons of Zibeon *were* Aiah and Anah.

40 [1]In Gen. 36:23, *[Alv]an* [2]In Gen. 36:23, *Shepho*

41 The [1]son of Anah *was* Dishon. And the sons of Dishon *were*
[2]Hamran, Eshban, Ithran, and Cheran.
42 The sons of Ezer *were* Bilhan, Zaavan and [1]Jaakan. The sons of
Dishan *were* Uz and Aran.

[41] [1]Lit., *sons* [2]In Gen. 36:26, *Hemdan*

43 [a]Now these are the kings who reigned in the land of Edom
before any king of the sons of Israel reigned. Bela *was* the son of
Beor, and the name of his city was Dinhabah.
44 When Bela died, Jobab the son of Zerah of [a]Bozrah became king
in his place.

42 [1]Or, *Akan*, as in Gen. 36:27

45 When Jobab died, Husham of the land of [a]the Temanites became
king in his place.
46 When Husham died, Hadad the son of Bedad, who [1]defeated

43 [a]Gen. 36:31-43

Midian in the field of Moab, became king in his place; and the name
of his city *was* Avith.
47 When Hadad died, Samlah of Masrekah became king in his

44 [a]Is. 34:6

place.
48 When Samlah died, Shaul of Rehoboth by the River became king
in his place.

45 [a]Job 2:11

49 When Shaul died, Baal-hanan the son of Achbor became king in
his place.
50 When Baal-hanan died, [1]Hadad became king in his place; and

46 [1]Lit., *smote*

the name of his city was [2]Pai, and his wife's name was Mehetabel,
the daughter of Matred, the daughter of Mezahab.
51 Then Hadad died. Now the chiefs of Edom were: chief Timna,

50 [1]In Gen. 36:39, *[Had]ar* [2]In Gen. 36:39, *Pau*

chief [1]Aliah, chief Jetheth,
52 chief Oholibamah, chief Elah, chief Pinon,
53 chief Kenaz, chief Teman, chief Mibzar,
54 chief Magdiel, chief Iram. These *were* the chiefs of Edom.

[51 [1]In] Gen. 36:40, *Alvah*

Chapter 2

1 [a]Gen. 35:22-26; 46:8-25

2 [a]These are the sons of Israel: Reuben, Simeon, Levi, Judah, Is-
sachar, Zebulun,
2 Dan, Joseph, Benjamin, Naphtali, Gad, and Asher.
3 [a]The sons of Judah *were* Er, Onan, and Shelah; *these* three were

3 [a]Gen. 38:2-10

born to him by Bath-shua the Canaanitess. And Er, Judah's first-
born, was wicked in the sight of the LORD, so He put him to death.
4 And [a]Tamar his daughter-in-law bore him Perez and Zerah.

4 [a]Gen. 38:13-30

Judah had five sons in all.

Jacob's twelve sons, in order of birth, were: Reuben, Simeon, Levi, Judah (by Leah), Dan, Naphtali (by Bilhah, Rachel's maid), Gad, Asher (by Zilpah, Leah's maid), Issachar, Zebulun (by Leah), Joseph, and Benjamin (by Rachel).

5 The sons of Perez *were* Hezron and Hamul.
6 And the sons of Zerah *were* [1]Zimri, Ethan, Heman, Calcol, and
[2]Dara; five of them in all.
7 And the [1]son of Carmi *was* [2a]Achar, the troubler of Israel, who
violated the ban.
8 And the [1]son of Ethan *was* Azariah.
9 Now the sons of Hezron, who were born to him *were* Jerahmeel,
Ram, and Chelubai.
10 And Ram [1]became the father of Amminadab, and Amminadab
became the father of Nahshon, leader of the sons of Judah;
11 Nahshon became the father of Salma, Salma became the father of
Boaz,
12 Boaz became the father of Obed, and Obed became the father of
Jesse;
13 and Jesse became the father of Eliab his first-born, then
Abinadab the second, [1]Shimea the third,
14 Nethanel the fourth, Raddai the fifth,
15 Ozem the sixth, David the seventh;
16 and their sisters *were* Zeruiah and Abigail. And the three sons of
Zeruiah *were* [1]Abshai, Joab, and Asahel.
17 And Abigail bore Amasa, and the father of Amasa was [1]Jether
the Ishmaelite.
18 Now Caleb the son of Hezron had sons by Azubah *his* wife, and
by Jerioth; and these were her sons: Jesher, Shobab, and Ardon.
19 When Azubah died, Caleb married Ephrath, who bore him Hur.
20 And Hur became the father of Uri, and Uri became the father of
Bezalel.
21 Afterward Hezron went in to the daughter of Machir the father
of Gilead, whom he married when he was sixty years old; and she
bore him Segub.
22 And Segub became the father of Jair, who had twenty-three cities
in the land of Gilead.
23 But Geshur and Aram took [1]the towns of Jair from them, with
Kenath and its villages, *even* sixty cities. All these were the sons of
Machir, the father of Gilead.
24 And after the death of Hezron in Caleb-ephrathah, Abijah, Hez-
ron's wife, bore him Ashhur the father of Tekoa.
25 Now the sons of Jerahmeel the first-born of Hezron *were* Ram the
first-born, then Bunah, Oren, Ozem, *and* Ahijah.
26 And Jerahmeel had another wife, whose name was Atarah; she
was the mother of Onam.
27 And the sons of Ram, the first-born of Jerahmeel, were Maaz,
Jamin, and Eker.
28 And the sons of Onam were Shammai and Jada. And the sons of
Shammai *were* Nadab and Abishur.
29 And the name of Abishur's wife *was* Abihail, and she bore him
Ahban and Molid.
30 And the sons of Nadab *were* Seled and Appaim, and Seled died
without sons.
31 And the [1]son of Appaim *was* Ishi. And the [1]son of Ishi *was*
Sheshan. And the [1]son of Sheshan *was* Ahlai.
32 And the sons of Jada the brother of Shammai *were* Jether and
Jonathan, and Jether died without sons.

6 [1]In Josh. 7:1, *Zab* [2]In 1 Kin. 4:31, *Dar*

7 [1]Lit., *sons* [2]In Jo 7:18, *Achan* [a]Josh

8 [1]Lit., *sons*

10 [1]Lit., *begot*, and throughout the ch.

13 [1]In 1 Sam. 16: *Shammah;* in 2 Sa 13:3, *Shimeah*

16 [1]In 2 Sam. 2:1 *Abishai*

17 [1]In 2 Sam. 17 *Ithra the Israelite*

23 [1]Or, *Havvoth-*

31 [1]Lit., *sons*

33 And the sons of Jonathan *were* Peleth and Zaza. These were the sons of Jerahmeel.

34 Now Sheshan had no sons, only daughters. And Sheshan had an Egyptian servant whose name was Jarha.

35 And Sheshan gave his daughter to Jarha his servant in marriage, and she bore him Attai.

36 And Attai became the father of Nathan, and Nathan became the father of Zabad,

37 and Zabad became the father of Ephlal, and Ephlal became the father of Obed,

38 and Obed became the father of Jehu, and Jehu became the father of Azariah,

39 and Azariah became the father of Helez, and Helez became the father of Eleasah,

40 and Eleasah became the father of Sismai, and Sismai became the father of Shallum,

41 and Shallum became the father of Jekamiah, and Jekamiah became the father of Elishama.

42 Now the sons of Caleb, the brother of Jerahmeel, *were* Mesha his first-born, who was the father of Ziph; and [1]his son was Mareshah, the father of Hebron.

43 And the sons of Hebron *were* Korah and Tappuah and Rekem and Shema.

44 And Shema became the father of Raham, the father of Jorkeam; and Rekem became the father of Shammai.

45 And the son of Shammai was Maon, and Maon *was* the father of Bethzur.

46 And Ephah, Caleb's concubine, bore Haran, Moza, and Gazez; and Haran became the father of Gazez.

47 And the sons of Jahdai *were* Regem, Jotham, Geshan, Pelet, Ephah, and Shaaph.

48 Maacah, Caleb's concubine, bore Sheber and Tirhanah.

49 She also bore Shaaph the father of Madmannah, Sheva the father of Machbena and the father of Gibea; and the daughter of Caleb *was* Achsah.

50 These were the sons of Caleb.

The [1]sons of Hur, the first-born of Ephrathah, *were* Shobal the father of Kiriath-jearim,

51 Salma the father of Bethlehem *and* Hareph the father of Bethgader.

52 And Shobal the father of Kiriath-jearim had sons: Haroeh, half of the Manahathites,

53 and the families of Kiriath-jearim: the Ithrites, the Puthites, the Shumathites, and the Mishraites; from these came the Zorathites and the Eshtaolites.

54 The sons of Salma *were* Bethlehem and the Netophathites, Atroth-beth-joab and half of the Manahathites, the Zorites.

55 And the families of scribes who lived at Jabez *were* the Tirathites, the Shimeathites, *and* the Sucathites. Those are the Kenites who came from Hammath, the father of the house of Rechab.

42 [1]Lit., *the sons of*

50 [1]Lit., *son*

Chapter 3

3 [a]Now these were the sons of David who were born to him in
Hebron: the first-born *was* Amnon, by Ahinoam the Jezreelitess;
the second *was* Daniel, by Abigail the Carmelitess;
2 the third *was* Absalom the son of Maacah, the daughter of Talmai
king of Geshur; the fourth *was* Adonijah the son of Haggith;
3 the fifth *was* Shephatiah, by Abital; the sixth *was* Ithream, by his
wife Eglah.
4 Six were born to him in Hebron, and [a]there he reigned seven
years and six months. And in Jerusalem he reigned thirty-three
years.
5 [a]And these were born to him in Jerusalem: Shimea, Shobab, Na-
than, and [b]Solomon, four, by [c]Bath-shua the daughter of Ammiel;
6 and Ibhar, Elishama, Eliphelet,
7 Nogah, Nepheg, and Japhia,
8 Elishama, Eliada, and Eliphelet, nine.
9 All *these were* the sons of David, besides the sons of the con-
cubines; and [a]Tamar *was* their sister.
10 Now Solomon's son *was* Rehoboam, Abijah *was* his son, Asa his
son, Jehoshaphat his son,
11 Joram his son, Ahaziah his son, Joash his son,
12 Amaziah his son, Azariah his son, Jotham his son,
13 Ahaz his son, Hezekiah his son, Manasseh his son,
14 Amon his son, Josiah his son.
15 And the sons of Josiah *were* Johanan the first-born, and the
second *was* Jehoiakim, the third Zedekiah, the fourth Shallum.
16 And the sons of Jehoiakim *were* Jeconiah his son, Zedekiah his
son.
17 And the sons of Jeconiah, the prisoner, *were* Shealtiel his son,
18 and Malchiram, Pedaiah, Shenazzar, Jekamiah, Hoshama, and
Nedabiah.
19 And the sons of Pedaiah *were* Zerubbabel and Shimei. And the
[1]sons of Zerubbabel *were* Meshullam and Hananiah, and Shelomith
was their sister;
20 and Hashubah, Ohel, Berechiah, Hasadiah, and Jushab-hesed,
five.
21 And the [1]sons of Hananiah *were* Pelatiah and Jeshaiah, the sons
of Rephaiah, the sons of Arnan, the sons of Obadiah, the sons of
Shecaniah.
22 And the [1]son of Shecaniah *was* Shemaiah, and the sons of
Shemaiah *were* Hattush, Igal, Bariah, Neariah, and Shaphat, six.
23 And the [1]sons of Neariah *were* Elioenai, Hizkiah, and Azrikam,
three.
24 And the sons of Elioenai *were* Hodaviah, Eliashib, Pelaiah,
Akkub, Johanan, Delaiah, and Anani, seven.

Chapter 4

4 [a]The sons of Judah *were* Perez, Hezron, Carmi, Hur, and Shobal.
2 And Reaiah the son of Shobal [1]became the father of Jahath,
and Jahath became the father of Ahumai and Lahad. These *were* the
families of the Zorathites.
3 And these *were* the [1]sons of Etam: Jezreel, Ishma, and Idbash;
and the name of their sister *was* Hazzelelponi.

3:1 [a]2 Sam. 3:2-5
4 [a]2 Sam. 2:11; 5:4 1 Kin. 2:11; 1 Chr. 2
5 [a]2 Sam. 5:14-16; 1 Chr. 14:4-7 [b]2 Sa 12:24, 25 [c]2 Sam.
9 [a]2 Sam. 13:1
19 [1]Lit., *son*
21 [1]Lit., *son*
22 [1]Lit., *sons*
23 [1]Lit., *son*
4:1 [a]1 Chr. 2:3
2 [1]Lit., *begot*, an throughout the ch
3 [1]So with some ancient versions; *father*

[1]Another reading is *Zohar*

4 And Penuel *was* the father of Gedor, and Ezer the father of
Hushah. These *were* the sons of Hur, the first-born of Ephrathah, the
father of Bethlehem.
5 And Ashhur, the father of Tekoa, had two wives, Helah and
Naarah.
6 And Naarah bore him Ahuzzam, Hepher, Temeni, and Haahash-
tari. These were the sons of Naarah.
7 And the sons of Helah *were* Zereth, [1]Izhar and Ethnan.
8 And Koz became the father of Anub and Zobebah, and the
families of Aharhel the son of Harum.
9 And Jabez was more honorable than his brothers, and his
mother named him Jabez saying, "Because I bore *him* with pain."
10 Now Jabez called on the God of Israel, saying, "Oh that Thou
wouldst bless me indeed, and enlarge my border, and that Thy hand
might be with me, and that Thou wouldst keep *me* from harm, that *it*
may not pain me!" And God granted him what he requested.
11 And Chelub the brother of Shuhah became the father of Mehir,
who was the father of Eshton.
12 And Eshton became the father of Beth-rapha and Paseah, and
Tehinnah the father of [1]Ir-nahash. These are the men of Recah.
13 Now the sons of Kenaz *were* Othniel and Seraiah. And the [1]son of
Othniel *was* Hathath.
14 And Meonothai became the father of Ophrah, and Seraiah be-
came the father of Joab the father of [1]Ge-harashim, for they were
craftsmen.
15 And the sons of Caleb the son of Jephunneh *were* Iru, Elah and
Naam; and the [1]son of Elah *was* [2]Kenaz.
16 And the sons of Jehallelel *were* Ziph and Ziphah, Tiria and
Asarel.
17 And the [1]sons of Ezrah *were* Jether, Mered, Epher, and Jalon.
([2]And these are the sons of Bithia the daughter of Pharaoh, whom
Mered took) and she conceived *and bore* Miriam, Shammai, and Ish-
bah the father of Eshtemoa.
18 And his Jewish wife bore Jered the father of Gedor, and Heber
the father of Soco, and Jekuthiel the father of Zanoah.
19 And the sons of the wife of Hodiah, the sister of Naham, *were* the
[1]fathers of Keilah the Garmite and Eshtemoa the Maacathite.
20 And the sons of Shimon *were* Amnon and Rinnah, Benhanan and
Tilon. And the sons of Ishi *were* Zoheth and Ben-zoheth.
21 The sons of Shelah the son of Judah *were* Er the father of Lecah
and Laadah the father of Mareshah, and the families of the house of
the linen workers at Beth-ashbea;
22 and Jokim, the men of Cozeba, Joash, Saraph, who ruled in
Moab, and Jashubi-lehem. And the [1]records are ancient.
23 These were the potters and the inhabitants of Netaim and
Gederah; they lived there with the king for his work.
24 The sons of Simeon *were* [1]Nemuel and Jamin, [2]Jarib, [3]Zerah,
Shaul;
25 Shallum his son, Mibsam his son, Mishma his son.
26 And the sons of Mishma *were* Hammuel his son, Zaccur his son,
Shimei his son.
27 Now Shimei had sixteen sons and six daughters; but his brothers
did not have many sons, nor did all their family multiply like the
sons of Judah.

12 [1]Or, *the city of Nahash*

13 [1]Lit., *sons*

14 [1]Or, *valley of craftsmen*

…it., *sons* [2]Lit., *and Kenaz*

… [1]Lit., *son* [2]In the …he words in ( ) are at the end of v. 18

19 [1]Lit., *father*

22 [1]Lit., *words*

…n Gen. 46:10 and … 6:15, *Jemuel* [2]In … 26:12, *Jachin* [3]In …en. 46:10 and Ex. 6:15, *Zohar*

28 And they lived at Beersheba, Moladah, and Hazar-shual,
29 at Bilhah, Ezem, Tolad,
30 Bethuel, Hormah, Ziklag,
31 Beth-marcaboth, Hazar-susim, Beth-biri, and Shaaraim. These
were their cities until the reign of David.
32 And their villages *were* Etam, Ain, Rimmon, Tochen, and Ashan,
five cities;
33 and all their villages that *were* around the same cities as far as
[1]Baal. These *were* their settlements, and they have their genealogy.
34 And Meshobab and Jamlech and Joshah the son of Amaziah,
35 and Joel and Jehu the son of Joshibiah, the son of Seraiah, the son
of Asiel,
36 and Elioenai, Jaakobah, Jeshohaiah, Asaiah, Adiel, Jesimiel,
Benaiah,
37 Ziza the son of Shiphi, the son of Allon, the son of Jedaiah, the
son of Shimri, the son of Shemaiah;
38 these mentioned by name *were* leaders in their families; and their
fathers' houses increased greatly.
39 And they went to the entrance of Gedor, even to the east side of
the valley, to seek pasture for their flocks.
40 And they found rich and good pasture, and [a]the land was broad
and quiet and peaceful; for those who lived there formerly *were*
Hamites.
41 And [a]these, recorded by name, came in the days of Hezekiah
king of Judah, and [1]attacked their tents, and the Meunites who were
found there, and destroyed them utterly to this day, and lived in
their place; because there was pasture there for their flocks.
42 And from them, from the sons of Simeon, five hundred men
went to [a]Mount Seir, with Pelatiah, Neariah, Rephaiah, and Uzziel,
the sons of Ishi, as their leaders.
43 And [a]they [1]destroyed the remnant of the Amalekites who es-
caped, and have lived there to this day.

Chapter 5

5 Now the sons of Reuben the first-born of Israel (for [a]he was the
first-born, but because [b]he defiled his father's bed, [c]his birthright
was given to the sons of Joseph the son of Israel; so that he is not
enrolled in the genealogy according to the birthright.
2 [a]Though Judah prevailed over his brothers, and [b]from him *came*
the leader, yet the birthright belonged to Joseph),
3 [a]the sons of Reuben the first-born of Israel *were* Hanoch and
Pallu, Hezron and Carmi.
4 The sons of Joel *were* Shemaiah his son, Gog his son, [a]Shimei his
son,
5 Micah his son, Reaiah his son, Baal his son,
6 Beerah his son, whom [1]Tilgath-pilneser king of Assyria carried
away into exile; he was leader of the Reubenites.
7 And his [1]kinsmen by their families, [a]in the genealogy of their
generations, *were* Jeiel the chief, then Zechariah
8 and Bela the son of Azaz, the son of Shema, the son of Joel, who
lived in [a]Aroer, even to Nebo and Baal-meon.
9 And to the east he settled as far as the entrance of the wilderness
from the river Euphrates, [a]because their cattle had increased in the
land of Gilead.

33 [1]In Josh. 19
Baalath
40 [a]Judg. 18:7
41 [1]Lit., *smote*
4:33-38
42 [a]Gen. 36:8,
43 [1]Lit., *smote*
15:7, 8; 30:17
5:1 [a]Gen. 29:32
2:1 [b]Gen. 35:22
[c]Gen. 48:15-22
2 [a]Gen. 49:8-10
60:7; 108:8 [b]Mic
Matt. 2:6
3 [a]Gen. 46:9; Ex
Num. 26:5-9
4 [a]1 Chr. 5:8
6 [1]In 2 Kin. 15:29
Tiglath-pileser
7 [1]Lit., *brothers*
5:17
8 [a]Num. 32:34; J
12:2
9 [a]Josh. 22:8, 9

The Land Allotted to the Twelve Tribes

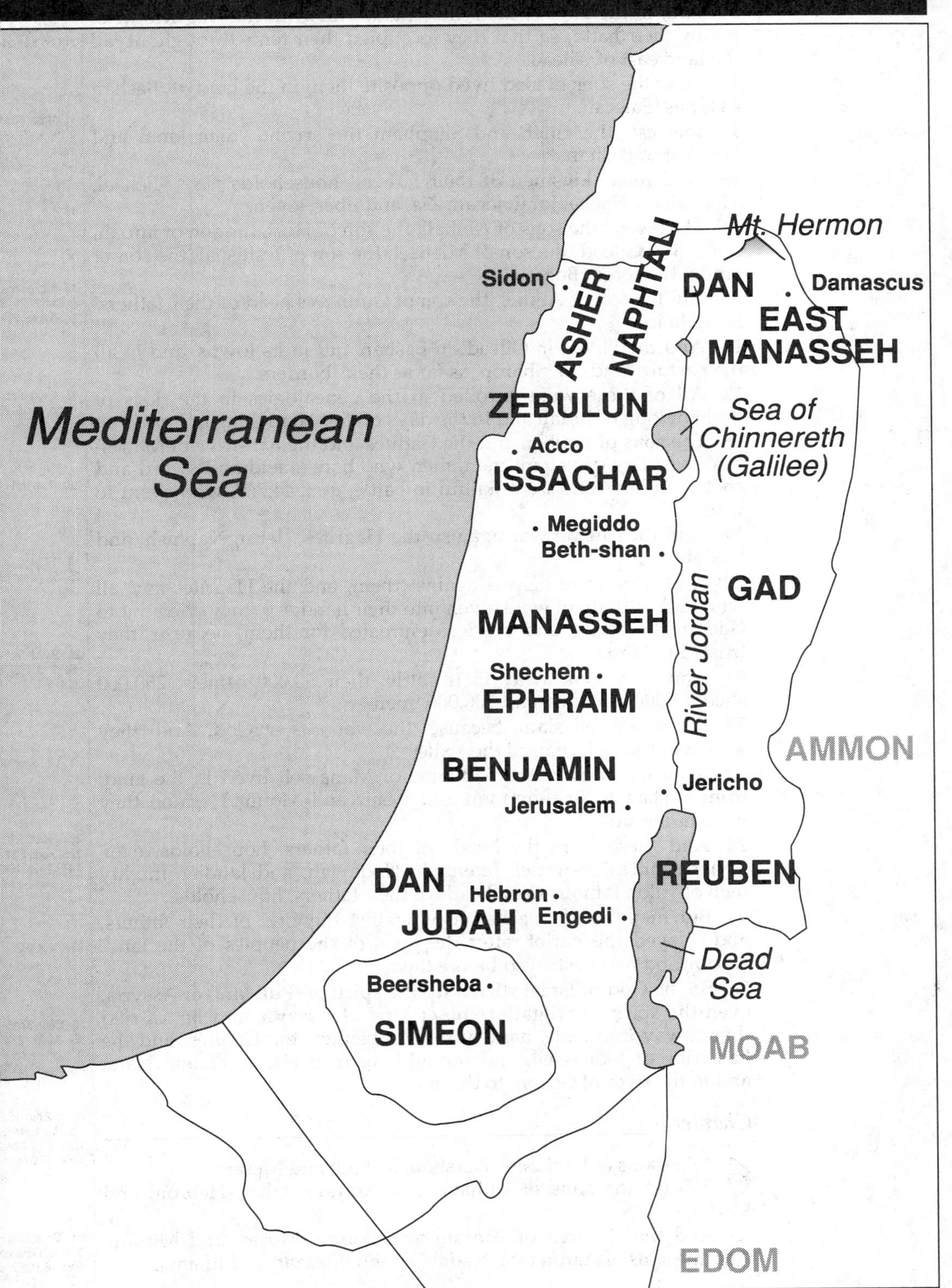

10 And in the days of Saul [a]they made war with the Hagrites, who
fell by their hand, so that they [1]occupied their tents throughout [2]all
the land east of Gilead.
11 Now the sons of Gad lived opposite them in the land of [a]Bashan
as far as [b]Salecah.
12 Joel *was* the chief, and Shapham the second, then Janai and
Shaphat in Bashan.
13 And their [1]kinsmen of their fathers' households *were* Michael,
Meshullam, Sheba, Jorai, Jacan, Zia, and Eber, seven.
14 These *were* the sons of Abihail, the son of Huri, the son of Jaroah,
the son of Gilead, the son of Michael, the son of Jeshishai, the son of
Jahdo, the son of Buz;
15 Ahi the son of Abdiel, the son of Guni, *was* head of their fathers'
households.
16 And they lived in Gilead, in Bashan and in its towns, and in all
the pasture lands of [a]Sharon, as far as their [1]borders.
17 All of these were enrolled in the genealogies in the days of
[a]Jotham king of Judah and in the days of [b]Jeroboam king of Israel.
18 The sons of Reuben and the Gadites and the half-tribe of Manas-
seh, *consisting* of valiant men, men who bore shield and sword and
shot with bow, and *were* skillful in battle, *were* 44,760, who [a]went to
war.
19 And they made war against [a]the Hagrites, [b]Jetur, Naphish, and
Nodab.
20 And they were helped against them, and the Hagrites and all
who *were* with them were given into their hand; for [a]they cried out to
God in the battle, and He was entreated for them, because [b]they
trusted in Him.
21 And they took away their cattle: their 50,000 camels, 250,000
sheep, 2,000 donkeys, and 100,000 [1]men.
22 For many fell slain, because [a]the war *was* of God. And [b]they
settled in their place until the [c]exile.
23 Now the sons of the half-tribe of Manasseh lived in the land;
from Bashan to Baal-hermon and [a]Senir and Mount Hermon they
were numerous.
24 And these were the heads of their fathers' households, even
Epher, Ishi, Eliel, Azriel, Jeremiah, Hodaviah, and Jahdiel, mighty
men of valor, famous men, heads of their fathers' households.
25 But they [a]acted treacherously against the God of their fathers,
and [b]played the harlot [c]after the gods of the peoples of the land,
whom God had destroyed before them.
26 So the God of Israel stirred up the spirit of [a]Pul, king of Assyria,
even the spirit of [1]Tilgath-pilneser king of Assyria, and he [b]carried
them away into exile, namely the Reubenites, the Gadites, and the
half-tribe of Manasseh, and brought them to Halah, Habor, Hara,
and to the river of Gozan, to this day.

Chapter 6

6 [1a]The sons of Levi *were* [2]Gershon, Kohath and Merari.
2 And the sons of Kohath *were* Amram, Izhar, Hebron, and
Uzziel.
3 And the children of Amram *were* Aaron, Moses, and Miriam.
And the sons of Aaron *were* Nadab, Abihu, Eleazar, and Ithamar.

10 [1]Lit., *dwelt* *all the face of th* [a]1 Chr. 5:18-21

11 [a]Josh. 13:11 3:10

13 [1]Lit., *brothe*

16 [1]Lit., *goings* [a]1 Chr. 27:29; S Is. 35:2; 65:10

17 [a]2 Kin. 15:5, [b]2 Kin. 14:16, 28

18 [a]Num. 1:3

19 [a]1 Chr. 5:10 25:15; 1 Chr. 1:3

20 [a]2 Chr. 14:11 [b]Ps. 9:10; 20:7, 8 22:4, 5

21 [1]Lit., *souls of*

22 [a]Josh. 23:10; 32:8; Rom. 8:31 4:41 [c]2 Kin. 15:2

23 [a]Deut. 3:9

25 [a]Deut. 32:15-1 [b]Ex. 34:15 [c]2 Kin

26 [1]In 2 Kin. 15:2 *Tiglath-pileser* [a]2 15:19, 29; 2 Chr. 2 [b]2 Kin. 17:6

6:1 [1]Ch. 5:27 in H [2]In v. 16, *Gershom* [a]Gen. 46:11; Ex. 6

[1]Lit., *begot*, and so throughout the ch.
8 [a]2 Sam. 8:17 [b]2 Sam. 15:27
10 [a]2 Chr. 26:17 Kin. 6:1; 2 Chr. 3:1
11 [a]Ezra 7:3
12 [1]In ch. 9:11, *Meshullam*
14 [a]Neh. 11:11
Lit., *by the hand of*
ch. 6:1 in Heb. [2]In 1, *Gershon* [a]Gen. 46:11; Ex. 6:16
Num. 3:33; 1 Chr. 23:21
1 Sam. 8:2; 1 Chr. 6:33
Chr. 15:16-22, 27; 4-6 [b]2 Sam. 6:17; 1 Kin. 8:4; 1 Chr. 15:25-16:1
[1]Lit., *stood over*
33 [1]Lit., *stood*

4 Eleazar [1]became the father of Phinehas, *and* Phinehas became the
father of Abishua,
5 and Abishua became the father of Bukki, and Bukki became the
father of Uzzi,
6 and Uzzi became the father of Zerahiah, and Zerahiah became
the father of Meraioth,
7 Meraioth became the father of Amariah, and Amariah became
the father of Ahitub,
8 and [a]Ahitub became the father of Zadok, and Zadok [b]became the
father of Ahimaaz,
9 and Ahimaaz became the father of Azariah, and Azariah became
the father of Johanan,
10 and Johanan became the father of Azariah ([a]it was he who
served as the priest in the house [b]which Solomon built in Jerusalem),
11 and [a]Azariah became the father of Amariah, and Amariah be-
came the father of Ahitub,
12 and Ahitub became the father of Zadok, and Zadok became the
father of [1]Shallum,
13 and Shallum became the father of Hilkiah, and Hilkiah became
the father of Azariah,
14 and Azariah became the father of [a]Seraiah, and Seraiah became
the father of Jehozadak;
15 and Jehozadak went *along* when the LORD carried Judah and
Jerusalem away into exile [1]by Nebuchadnezzar.
16 [1a]The sons of Levi *were* [2]Gershom, Kohath, and Merari.
17 And these are the names of the sons of Gershom: Libni and
Shimei.
18 And the sons of Kohath *were* Amram, Izhar, Hebron, and Uzziel.
19 The sons of [a]Merari *were* Mahli and Mushi. And these are the
families of the Levites according to their fathers' *households*.
20 Of Gershom: Libni his son, Jahath his son, Zimmah his son,
21 Joah his son, Iddo his son, Zerah his son, Jeatherai his son.
22 The sons of Kohath *were* Amminadab his son, Korah his son,
Assir his son,
23 Elkanah his son, Ebiasaph his son, and Assir his son,
24 Tahath his son, Uriel his son, Uzziah his son, and Shaul his son.
25 And the sons of Elkanah *were* Amasai and Ahimoth.
26 *As for* Elkanah, the sons of Elkanah *were* Zophai his son and
Nahath his son,
27 Eliab his son, Jeroham his son, Elkanah his son.
28 And the sons of Samuel *were* [a]Joel, the first-born and Abijah, the
second.
29 The sons of Merari *were* Mahli, Libni his son, Shimei his son,
Uzzah his son,
30 Shimea his son, Haggiah his son, Asaiah his son.
31 [a]Now these are those whom David appointed over the service of
song in the house of the LORD, [b]after the ark rested *there*.
32 And they ministered with song before the tabernacle of the tent
of meeting, until Solomon had built the house of the LORD in Jerusa-
lem; and they [1]served in their office according to their order.
33 And these are those who [1]served with their sons. From the sons
of the Kohathites *were* Heman the singer, the son of Joel, the son of
Samuel,

34 the son of Elkanah, the son of Jeroham, the son of Eliel, the son
of Toah,
35 the son of Zuph, the son of Elkanah, the son of Mahath, the son
of Amasai,
36 the son of Elkanah, the son of Joel, the son of Azariah, the son of
Zephaniah,
37 the son of Tahath, the son of Assir, the son of Ebiasaph, the son
of Korah,
38 the son of Izhar, the son of Kohath, the son of Levi, the son of
Israel.
39 And *Heman's* brother Asaph stood at his right hand, even Asaph
the son of Berechiah, the son of Shimea,
40 the son of Michael, the son of Baaseiah, the son of Malchijah,
41 the son of Ethni, the son of Zerah, the son of Adaiah,
42 the son of Ethan, the son of Zimmah, the son of Shimei,
43 the son of Jahath, the son of Gershom, the son of Levi.
44 And on the left hand *were* their [1]kinsmen the sons of Merari:
Ethan the son of Kishi, the son of Abdi, the son of Malluch,
45 the son of Hashabiah, the son of Amaziah, the son of Hilkiah,
46 the son of Amzi, the son of Bani, the son of Shemer,
47 the son of Mahli, the son of Mushi, the son of Merari, the son of
Levi.
48 And their [1]kinsmen the Levites were [2]appointed for all the ser-
vice of the tabernacle of the house of God.
49 But Aaron and his sons [1a]offered on the altar of burnt offering
and [b]on the altar of incense, for all the work of the most holy place,
and [c]to make atonement for Israel, according to all that Moses the
servant of God had commanded.
50 [a]And these are the sons of Aaron: Eleazar his son, Phinehas his
son, Abishua his son,
51 Bukki his son, Uzzi his son, Zerahiah his son,
52 Meraioth his son, Amariah his son, Ahitub his son,
53 Zadok his son, Ahimaaz his son.
54 Now these are their settlements according to their camps within
their borders. To the sons of Aaron of the families of the Kohathites
(for theirs was the [a]*first* lot),
55 to them they gave [a]Hebron in the land of Judah, and its pasture
lands around it;
56 [a]but the fields of the city and its villages, they gave to Caleb the
son of Jephunneh.
57 And [a]to the sons of Aaron they gave the *following* cities of refuge:
Hebron, Libnah also with its pasture lands, Jattir, Eshtemoa with its
pasture lands,
58 [1]Hilen with its pasture lands, Debir with its pasture lands,
59 [1]Ashan with its pasture lands, and Beth-shemesh with its pas-
ture lands;
60 and from the tribe of Benjamin: Geba with its pasture lands,
[1]Allemeth with its pasture lands, and Anathoth with its pasture
lands. All their cities throughout their families were thirteen cities.
61 [a]Then to the rest of the sons of Kohath *were given* by lot, from the
family of the tribe, from the half-tribe, the half of Manasseh, ten
cities.
62 And to the sons of Gershom, according to their families, *were*

44 [1]Lit., *broth*

48 [1]Lit., *brothe* [2]*given*

49 [1]Lit., *offere smoke* [a]Ex. 27 30:1-7 [c]Ex. 30

50 [a]1 Chr. 6:4- 7:5

54 [a]Josh. 21:4

55 [a]Josh. 14:13

56 [a]Josh. 15:13

57 [a]Josh. 21:13

58 [1]In Josh. 21: *Holon*

59 [1]In Josh. 21:

60 [1]In Josh. 21: *Almon*

61 [a]Josh. 21:5; 1 6:66-70

h. 21:7, 34-40

given from the tribe of Issachar and from the tribe of Asher, the tribe of Naphtali, and the tribe of Manasseh, thirteen cities in Bashan.
63 [a]To the sons of Merari *were given* by lot, according to their families, from the tribe of Reuben, the tribe of Gad, and the tribe of Zebulun, twelve cities.
64 [a]So the sons of Israel gave to the Levites the cities with their pasture lands.
65 And they gave by lot from the tribe of the sons of Judah, the tribe of the sons of Simeon, and the tribe of the sons of Benjamin, [a]these cities which are mentioned by name.

. 35:1-8; Josh. 21:3, 41, 42

66 [a]Now some of the families of the sons of Kohath had cities of their territory from the tribe of Ephraim.
67 And they gave to them the *following* cities of refuge: Shechem in the hill country of Ephraim with its pasture lands, Gezer also with its pasture lands,
68 Jokmeam with its pasture lands, Beth-horon with its pasture lands,
69 Aijalon with its pasture lands, and Gath-rimmon with its pasture lands;
70 and from the half-tribe of Manasseh: Aner with its pasture lands and Bileam with its pasture lands, for the rest of the family of the sons of Kohath.

[a]1 Chr. 6:57-60

71 To the sons of Gershom *were given,* from the family of the half-tribe of Manasseh: Golan in Bashan with its pasture lands and Ashtaroth with its pasture lands;
72 and from the tribe of Issachar: Kedesh with its pasture lands, Daberath with its pasture lands,
73 and Ramoth with its pasture lands, Anem with its pasture lands;
74 and from the tribe of Asher: Mashal with its pasture lands, Abdon with its pasture lands,
75 Hukok with its pasture lands, and Rehob with its pasture lands;

[a]Josh. 21:20-26

76 and from the tribe of Naphtali: Kedesh in Galilee with its pasture lands, Hammon with its pasture lands, and Kiriathaim with its pasture lands.
77 To the rest of *the Levites,* the sons of Merari, *were given,* from the tribe of Zebulun: Rimmono with its pasture lands, Tabor with its pasture lands;
78 and beyond the Jordan at Jericho, on the east side of the Jordan, *were given them,* from the tribe of Reuben: Bezer in the wilderness with its pasture lands, Jahzah with its pasture lands,
79 Kedemoth with its pasture lands, and Mephaath with its pasture lands;
80 and from the tribe of Gad: Ramoth in Gilead with its pasture lands, Mahanaim with its pasture lands,
81 Heshbon with its pasture lands, and Jazer with its pasture lands.

[1]In Gen. 46:13, *h*; in Num. 26:23, [2]In Gen. 46:13, *Iob*

Chapter 7

7 Now the sons of Issachar *were* four: Tola, [1]Puah, [2]Jashub, and Shimron.
2 And the sons of Tola *were* Uzzi, Rephaiah, Jeriel, Jahmai, Ibsam, and Samuel, heads of their fathers' households. *The sons* of Tola *were* mighty men of valor in their generations; [a]their number in the days of David was 22,600.

2 [a]2 Sam. 24:1-9

3 And the [1]son of Uzzi *was* Izrahiah. And the sons of Izrahiah *were*
Michael, Obadiah, Joel, Isshiah; all five of them *were* [a]chief men.
4 And with them by their generations according to their fathers'
households were 36,000 [1]troops of the army for war, for they had
many wives and sons.
5 And their [1]relatives among all the families of Issachar *were*
mighty men of valor, enrolled by genealogy, in all 87,000.
6 [a]*The sons of* Benjamin *were* three: Bela and Becher and Jediael.
7 And the sons of Bela were five: Ezbon, Uzzi, Uzziel, Jerimoth,
and Iri. They *were* heads of fathers' households, mighty men of valor,
and were 22,034 enrolled by genealogy.
8 And the sons of Becher *were* Zemirah, Joash, Eliezer, Elioenai,
Omri, Jeremoth, Abijah, Anathoth, and Alemeth. All these *were* the
sons of Becher.
9 And they were enrolled by genealogy, according to their generations, heads of their fathers' households, 20,200 mighty men of valor.
10 And the [1]son of Jediael *was* Bilhan. And the sons of Bilhan *were*
Jeush, Benjamin, Ehud, Chenaanah, Zethan, Tarshish, and
Ahishahar.
11 All these *were* sons of Jediael, according to the heads of their
fathers' households, 17,200 mighty men of valor, who were [1]ready to
go out with the army to war.
12 And [1]Shuppim and [2]Huppim *were* the sons of [3]Ir; Hushim *was*
the [4]son of [5]Aher.
13 The sons of Naphtali *were* [1]Jahziel, Guni, Jezer, and [2]Shallum, the
sons of Bilhah.
14 The sons of Manasseh *were* Asriel, whom his Aramean concubine
bore; she bore Machir the father of Gilead.
15 And Machir took a wife for Huppim and Shuppim, [1]whose sister's name was Maacah. And the name of the second was Zelophehad, and Zelophehad had daughters.
16 And Maacah the wife of Machir bore a son, and she named him
Peresh; and the name of his brother *was* Sheresh, and his sons *were*
Ulam and Rakem.
17 And the [1]son of Ulam *was* Bedan. These *were* the sons of Gilead
the son of Machir, the son of Manasseh.
18 And his sister Hammolecheth bore Ishhod and [1]Abiezer and
Mahlah.
19 And the sons of Shemida were Ahian and Shechem and Likhi
and Aniam.
20 And [a]the sons of Ephraim *were* Shuthelah and [1]Bered his son,
Tahath his son, Eleadah his son, Tahath his son,
21 Zabad his son, Shuthelah his son, and Ezer and Elead whom the
men of Gath who were born in the land killed, because they came
down to take their livestock.
22 And their father Ephraim [a]mourned many days, and his relatives
[b]came to comfort him.
23 Then he went in to his wife, and she conceived and bore a son,
and he named him [1]Beriah, because misfortune had come upon his
house.
24 And his daughter was Sheerah, [a]who built lower and upper
Beth-horon, also Uzzen-sheerah.
25 And Rephah was his son *along* with Resheph, Telah his son,
Tahan his son,

3 [1]Lit., *sons* [a]
5:24

4 [1]Or, *bands*

5 [1]Lit., *brothe*
throughout the

6 [a]1 Chr. 8:1-4

10 [1]Lit., *sons*

11 [1]Lit., *going*

12 [1]In Num. 26
Shephupham [2]
26:39, *Hupham*
Iri [4]Lit., *sons* [5]
26:38, *Ahiram*

13 [1]In Gen. 46:
Jahzeel [2]In Ger
and Num. 26:49

15 [1]Lit., *and his*

17 [1]Lit., *sons*

18 [1]In Num. 26:

20 [1]In Num. 26:
Becher [a]Num. 2

22 [a]Gen. 37:34
2:11; John 11:19

23 [1]I.e., on misfo

24 [a]Josh. 16:3, 5
2 Chr. 8:5

26 Ladan his son, Ammihud his son, Elishama his son,

27 [1]Non his son, and [a]Joshua his son.

28 And [a]their possessions and settlements *were* Bethel with its towns, and to the east [1]Naaran, and to the west Gezer with its towns, and Shechem with its towns as far as [2]Ayyah with its towns,

29 and along the borders of the sons of Manasseh, Beth-shean with its towns, Taanach with its towns, Megiddo with its towns, Dor with its towns. In these lived the [a]sons of Joseph the son of Israel.

30 [a]The sons of Asher *were* Imnah, Ishvah, Ishvi and Beriah, and Serah their sister.

31 And the sons of Beriah *were* Heber and Malchiel, who was the father of Birzaith.

32 And Heber [1]became the father of Japhlet, [2]Shomer and Hotham, and Shua their sister.

33 And the sons of Japhlet *were* Pasach, Bimhal, and Ashvath. These were the sons of Japhlet.

34 And the sons of [1]Shemer *were* Ahi and Rohgah, Jehubbah and Aram.

35 And the [1]sons of his brother Helem *were* Zophah, Imna, Shelesh, and Amal.

36 The sons of Zophah *were* Suah, Harnepher, Shual, Beri, and Imrah,

37 Bezer, Hod, Shamma, Shilshah, Ithran, and Beera.

38 And the sons of Jether *were* Jephunneh, Pispa, and Ara.

39 And the sons of Ulla *were* Arah, Hanniel, and Rizia.

40 All these *were* the sons of Asher, heads of the fathers' houses, choice and mighty men of valor, heads of the princes. And the number of them enrolled by genealogy for service in war was 26,000 men.

Chapter 8

8 And [a]Benjamin [1]became the father of Bela his first-born, Ashbel the second, [b]Aharah the third,

2 Nohah the fourth, and Rapha the fifth.

3 And Bela had sons: [1]Addar, Gera, Abihud,

4 Abishua, Naaman, Ahoah,

5 Gera, Shephuphan, and Huram.

6 And these are the sons of Ehud: these are the heads of fathers' *households* of the inhabitants of Geba, and they carried them into exile to Manahath,

7 namely, Naaman, Ahijah, and Gera—he carried them into exile; and he became the father of Uzza and Ahihud.

8 And Shaharaim became the father of children in the [1]country of Moab, after he had [2]sent away Hushim and Baara his wives.

9 And by Hodesh his wife he became the father of Jobab, Zibia, Mesha, Malcam,

10 Jeuz, Sachia, Mirmah. These were his sons, heads of fathers' *households*.

11 And by Hushim he became the father of Abitub and Elpaal.

12 And the sons of Elpaal *were* Eber, Misham, and Shemed, who built Ono and Lod, with its towns;

13 and Beriah and Shema, who were heads of fathers' *households* of the inhabitants of Aijalon, who put to flight the inhabitants of Gath;

14 and [1]Ahio, Shashak, and Jeremoth.

7 [1]In Ex. 33:11, *Nun* [a]Ex. 17:9-14; 24:13

28 [1]In Josh. 16:7, *Naarah* [2]Many mss. *Azzah* [a]Josh. 16:2

29 [a]Judg. 1:22-29

[a]Gen. 46:17; Num. 26:44-46

[1]Lit., *begot* [2]In v. 34, *Shemer*

[1]In v. 32, *Shomer*

35 [1]Lit., *son*

[1]Lit., *begot*, and so throughout the ch. [a]Gen. 46:21; 1 Chr. 7:6-12 [b]1 Chr. 7:12

[1]In Gen. 46:21 and Num. 26:40, *Ard*

[1]Lit., *field* [2]Lit., *sent them away*

[1]Or, *his brothers*

15 And Zebadiah, Arad, Eder,
16 Michael, Ishpah, and Joha *were* the sons of Beriah.
17 And Zebadiah, Meshullam, Hizki, Heber,
18 Ishmerai, Izliah, and Jobab *were* the sons of Elpaal.
19 And Jakim, Zichri, Zabdi,
20 Elienai, Zillethai, Eliel,
21 Adaiah, Beraiah, and Shimrath *were* the sons of [1]Shimei.
22 And Ishpan, Eber, Eliel,
23 Abdon, Zichri, Hanan,
24 Hananiah, Elam, Anthothijah,
25 Iphdeiah, and Penuel *were* the sons of Shashak.
26 And Shamsherai, Shehariah, Athaliah,
27 Jaareshiah, Elijah, and Zichri *were* the sons of Jeroham.
28 These were heads of the fathers' *households* according to their
generations, chief men, [1]who lived in Jerusalem.
29 [a]Now in Gibeon, *Jeiel,* the father of Gibeon lived, and his wife's
name was Maacah;
30 and his first-born son *was* Abdon, then Zur, Kish, Baal, Nadab,
31 Gedor, Ahio, and [1]Zecher.
32 And Mikloth became the father of [1]Shimeah. And they also lived
with their [2]relatives in Jerusalem opposite their *other* [2]relatives.
33 [a]And Ner became the father of Kish, and Kish became the father
of Saul, and Saul became the father of Jonathan, Malchi-shua,
[1]Abinadab, and [2]Eshbaal.
34 And the son of Jonathan *was* [1]Merib-baal, and Merib-baal be-
came the father of Micah.
35 And the sons of Micah *were* Pithon, Melech, [1]Tarea, and Ahaz.
36 And Ahaz became the father of [1]Jehoaddah, and Jehoaddah be-
came the father of Alemeth, Azmaveth, and Zimri; and Zimri be-
came the father of Moza.
37 And Moza became the father of Binea; [1]Raphah *was* his son,
Eleasah his son, Azel his son.
38 And Azel had six sons, and these *were* their names: Azrikam,
Bocheru, Ishmael, Sheariah, Obadiah and Hanan. All these *were* the
sons of Azel.
39 And the sons of Eshek his brother *were* Ulam his first-born, Jeush
the second, and Eliphelet the third.
40 And the sons of Ulam were mighty men of valor, archers, and
had many sons and grandsons, 150 *of them.* All these *were* of the sons
of Benjamin.

Chapter 9

9 So all Israel was enrolled by genealogies; and behold, they are
written in the Book of the Kings of Israel. And [a]Judah was car-
ried away into exile to Babylon for their unfaithfulness.
2 [a]Now the first who lived in their possessions in their cities *were*
Israel, the priests, the Levites and [b]the [1]temple servants.
3 And some of the sons of Judah, of the sons of Benjamin, and of
the sons of Ephraim and Manasseh lived in [a]Jerusalem:
4 Uthai the son of Ammihud, the son of Omri, the son of Imri, the
son of Bani, from the sons of Perez the [a]son of Judah.
5 And from the Shilonites *were* Asaiah the first-born and his sons.
6 And from the sons of Zerah *were* Jeuel and their [1]relatives, 690 *of*
them.

21 [1]In v. 13, *Shema*
28 [1]Lit., *these*
29 [a]1 Chr. 9:35-38
31 [1]In ch. 9:37, *Zechariah*
32 [1]In ch. 9:38, *Shimeam* [2]Lit., *bro*
33 [1]1 Sam. 14:49, [2]In 2 Sam. 2:8, *Ish-bosheth* [a]1 Chr 9:39-44
34 [1]In 2 Sam. 4:4, *Mephibosheth*
35 [1]In 9:41, *Tahrea*
36 [1]In 9:42, *Jarah*
37 [1]In 9:43, *Repha*
9:1 [a]1 Chr. 5:25, 2
2 [1]Heb., *Nethinim* [a]Ezra 2:70; Neh. 7 11:3-22 [b]Ezra 2:43 8:20
3 [a]Neh. 11:1
4 [a]Gen. 46:12; Nu 26:20
6 [1]Lit., *brothers,* a throughout the ch.

7 And from the sons of Benjamin *were* Sallu the son of Meshullam,
the son of Hodaviah, the son of Hassenuah,
8 and Ibneiah the son of Jeroham, and Elah the son of Uzzi, the
son of Michri, and Meshullam the son of Shephatiah, the son of
Reuel, the son of Ibnijah;
9 and their relatives according to their generations, [a]956. All these
were heads of fathers' *households* according to their fathers' houses.
10 [a]And from the priests *were* Jedaiah, Jehoiarib, Jachin,
11 and [1]Azariah the son of Hilkiah, the son of Meshullam, the son
of Zadok, the son of Meraioth, the son of Ahitub, [a]the chief officer of
the house of God;
12 and Adaiah the son of Jeroham, the son of Pashhur, the son of
Malchijah, and Maasai the son of Adiel, the son of Jahzerah, the son
of Meshullam, the son of Meshillemith, the son of Immer;
13 and their relatives, heads of their fathers' households, 1,760 very
able men for the work of the service of the house of God.
14 [a]And of the Levites *were* Shemaiah the son of Hasshub, the son of
Azrikam, the son of Hashabiah, of the sons of Merari;
15 and Bakbakkar, Heresh and Galal and Mattaniah the son of
Mica, the son of [1]Zichri, the son of Asaph,
16 and [1]Obadiah the son of [2]Shemaiah, the son of Galal, the son of
Jeduthun, and Berechiah the son of Asa, the son of Elkanah, who
lived in the villages of the Netophathites.
17 Now the gatekeepers *were* [1]Shallum and Akkub and Talmon and
Ahiman and their relatives (Shallum the chief
18 *being stationed* until now at [a]the king's gate to the east). These
were the gatekeepers for the camp of the sons of Levi.
19 And Shallum the son of Kore, the son of [1]Ebiasaph, the son of
Korah, and his relatives, of his father's house, the Korahites, *were*
over the work of the service, keepers of the thresholds of the tent;
and their fathers had been over the camp of the LORD, keepers of the
entrance.
20 And [a]Phinehas the son of Eleazar was ruler over them pre-
viously, *and* the LORD was with him.
21 [a]Zechariah the son of Meshelemiah was gatekeeper of the
entrance of the tent of meeting.
22 All these who were chosen to be gatekeepers in the thresholds
were 212. These were enrolled by genealogy in their villages, [a]whom
David and Samuel the seer appointed [b]in their office of trust.
23 So they and their sons [1]had charge of the gates of the house of
the LORD, *even* the house of the tent, as guards.
24 The gatekeepers were [1]on the four sides, to the east, west, north,
and south.
25 And their relatives in their villages [a]*were* to come in every seven
days from time to time *to be* with [1]them;
26 for the four chief gatekeepers who *were* Levites, were in an office
of trust, and were over the chambers and over the treasuries in the
house of God.
27 And they spent the night around the house of God, [a]because the
watch was [1]committed to them; and they *were* [2]in charge of opening
it morning by morning.
28 Now some of them [1]had charge of the utensils of service, for
[2]they counted them when they brought them in and when they took
them out.

9 [a]Neh. 11:8
10 [a]Neh. 11:10-14
11 [1]In Neh. 11:11, *Seraiah* [a]Jer. 20:1
14 [a]Neh. 11:15-19
…n Neh. 11:17, *Zabdi*
16 [1]In Neh. 11:17, …*bda* [2]In Neh. 11:17, *Shammua*
17 [1]In v. 21, …*helemiah;* in 26:14, *Shelemiah;* in Neh. 12:25, *Meshullam*
…Ezek. 44:1; 46:1, 2
19 [1]In Ex. 6:24, *Abiasaph*
20 [a]Num. 25:7-13
…1 [a]1 Chr. 26:2, 14
… Chr. 26:1 [b]2 Chr. 31:15, 18
…[1]Lit., *were over the gates*
…4 [1]Lit., *to the four winds*
[1]Lit., *these* [a]2 Kin. …1:5, 7; 2 Chr. 23:8
…Lit., *on them* [2]Lit., *over the opening* [a]1 Chr. 23:30-32
…Lit., *were over the* …Lit., *by count they* …*ght them in and by* …*hey took them out*

29 Some of them also were appointed over the furniture and over all the utensils of the sanctuary and [a]over the fine flour and the wine and the oil and the frankincense and the spices.

30 And some of [a]the sons of the priests prepared the mixing of the spices.

31 And Mattithiah, one of the Levites, who was the first-born of Shallum the Korahite, had [a]the [1]responsibility over the things which were baked in pans.

32 And some of their relatives of the sons of the Kohathites [a]*were* over the showbread to prepare it every sabbath.

33 Now these are [a]the singers, heads of fathers' *households* of the Levites, *who lived* in the chambers *of the temple* free *from other service;* for they were [1]engaged [b]in their work day and night.

34 These were heads of fathers' *households* of the Levites according to their generations, chief men, [1]who lived in Jerusalem.

35 [a]And in Gibeon Jeiel the father of Gibeon lived, and his wife's name was Maacah,

36 and his first-born son *was* Abdon, then Zur, Kish, Baal, Ner, Nadab,

37 Gedor, Ahio, Zechariah, and Mikloth.

38 And Mikloth became the father of Shimeam. And they also lived with their relatives in Jerusalem opposite their *other* relatives.

39 [a]And Ner became the father of Kish, and Kish became the father of Saul, and Saul became the father of Jonathan, Malchi-shua, Abinadab, and Eshbaal.

40 And the son of Jonathan *was* Merib-baal; and Merib-baal became the father of Micah.

41 And the sons of Micah *were* Pithon, Melech, Tahrea, [a]*and Ahaz.*

42 And Ahaz became the father of Jarah, and Jarah became the father of Alemeth, Azmaveth, and Zimri; and Zimri became the father of Moza,

43 and Moza became the father of Binea and Rephaiah his son, Eleasah his son, Azel his son.

44 And Azel had six sons whose names are these: Azrikam, Bocheru and Ishmael and Sheariah and Obadiah and Hanan. These were the sons of Azel.

Chapter 10

10 [a]Now the Philistines fought against Israel; and the men of Israel fled before the Philistines, and fell slain on Mount Gilboa.

2 And the Philistines closely pursued Saul and his sons, and the Philistines struck down Jonathan, [1a]Abinadab and Malchi-shua, the sons of Saul.

3 And the battle became heavy against Saul, and the archers [1]overtook him; and he was wounded by the archers.

4 Then Saul said to his armor bearer, "Draw your sword and thrust me through with it, lest these uncircumcised come and abuse me." But his armor bearer would not, for he was greatly afraid. [a]Therefore Saul took his sword and fell on it.

5 And when his armor bearer saw that Saul was dead, he likewise fell on his sword and died.

6 [a]Thus Saul died with his three sons, and all *those* of his house died together.

29 [a]1 Chr. 23:29
30 [a]Ex. 30:23-25
31 [1]Lit., *office of t* [a]1 Chr. 9:22
32 [a]Lev. 24:5-8
33 [1]Lit., *over ther the work* [a]1 Chr. 6:31-47; 25:1 [b]Ps
34 [1]Lit., *these*
35 [a]1 Chr. 8:29-3
39 [a]1 Chr. 8:33-3
41 [a]1 Chr. 8:35-3
10:1 [a]1 Sam. 31
2 [1]In 1 Sam. 14: *Ishvi* [a]1 Sam. 31
3 [1]Lit., *found hir*
4 [a]1 Sam. 31:4
6 [a]1 Sam. 31:6

7 When all the men of Israel who were in the valley saw that they
had fled, and that Saul and his sons were dead, they forsook their
cities and fled; and the Philistines came and lived in them.
8 And it came about the next day, when the Philistines came to
strip the slain, that they found Saul and his sons fallen on Mount
Gilboa.
9 [a]So they stripped him and took his head and his armor and sent
messengers around the land of the Philistines, to carry the good news
to their idols and to the people.
10 And they put his armor in the house of their gods and fastened
his head in the house of Dagon.
11 When all Jabesh-gilead heard all that the Philistines had done to
Saul,
12 [a]all the valiant men arose and took away the body of Saul and
the bodies of his sons, and brought them to Jabesh and buried their
bones under the oak in Jabesh, and fasted seven days.
13 [a]So Saul died for his trespass which he committed against the
LORD, because of the word of the LORD which he did not keep; and
also [b]because he asked counsel of a medium, making inquiry *of it,*
14 and did not inquire of the LORD. Therefore He killed him, and
[a]turned the kingdom to David the son of Jesse.

Chapter 11

11 [a]Then all Israel gathered to David at Hebron [1]and said, "Be-
hold, we are your bone and your flesh.
2 "In times past, even when Saul was king, you *were* the one who
led out and brought in Israel; and the LORD your God said to you,
'[a]You shall shepherd My people Israel, and you shall be prince over
My people Israel.' "
3 So all the elders of Israel came to the king at Hebron, and David
made a covenant with them in Hebron before the LORD; and [a]they
anointed David king over Israel, [b]according to the word of the LORD
through Samuel.
4 Then David and all Israel went to Jerusalem ([a]that is, Jebus); and
the Jebusites, the inhabitants of the land, *were* there.
5 And the inhabitants of Jebus said to David, "You shall not enter
here." Nevertheless David captured the stronghold of Zion (that is,
the city of David).
6 Now David had said, "Whoever strikes down a Jebusite first
shall be chief and commander." [a]And Joab the son of Zeruiah went
up first, so he became chief.
7 Then David dwelt in the stronghold; therefore it was called the
city of David.
8 And he [1]built the city all around, from the [2]Millo even to the
surrounding area; and Joab [3]repaired the rest of the city.
9 And [a]David became greater and greater, for the LORD of hosts
was with him.
10 [a]Now these are the heads of the mighty men whom David had,
who gave him strong support in his kingdom, together with all Isra-
el, to make him king, [b]according to the word of the LORD concerning
Israel.
11 And these *constitute* the list of the mighty men whom David had:
[a]Jashobeam, the son of a Hachmonite, [b]the chief of the thirty; he

9 [a]1 Sam. 31:9
12 [a]1 Sam. 31:12f.
13 [a]1 Sam. 13:13, 14; [b]Lev. 19:31; 20:6; 1 Sam. 28:7
14 [a]1 Sam. 15:28; 1 Chr. 12:23
11:1 [1]Lit., *saying* [a]2 Sam. 5:1, 3, 6-10
2 [a]2 Sam. 5:2; 7:7
3 [a]2 Sam. 2:4; 5:3, [b]1 Sam. 16:1, 3, 12, 13
4 [a]Josh. 15:8, 63; Judg. 1:21
6 [a]2 Sam. 8:16
8 [1]Or, *fortified* [2]I.e., citadel [3]Lit., *revived*
9 [a]2 Sam. 3:1
10 [a]2 Sam. 23:8-39 [b]1 Chr. 11:3
11 [a]2 Sam. 23:8 [b]1 Chr. 12:18

lifted up his spear against three hundred [1]whom he killed at one
time.
12 And after him was Eleazar the son of [a]Dodo, the Ahohite, who
was [1]one of the three mighty men.
13 He was with David at [1]Pasdammim [a]when the Philistines were
gathered together there to battle, and there was a plot of ground full
of barley; and the people fled before the Philistines.
14 And they took their stand in the midst of the plot, and defended
it, and struck down the Philistines; and the LORD saved them by a
great [1]victory.
15 Now three of the thirty chief men went down to the rock to
David, into the cave of Adullam, while [a]the army of the Philistines
was camping in the valley of Rephaim.
16 And David was then in the stronghold, while [a]the garrison of the
Philistines *was* then in Bethlehem.
17 And David had a craving and said, "Oh that someone would
give me water to drink from the well of Bethlehem, which is by the
gate!"
18 So the three broke through the camp of the Philistines, and drew
water from the well of Bethlehem which *was* by the gate, and took *it*
and brought *it* to David; nevertheless David would not drink it, but
poured it out to the LORD;
19 and he said, "Be it far from me before my God that I should do
this. Shall I drink the blood of these men *who went* [1]at the risk of their
lives? For at the risk of their lives they brought it." Therefore he
would not drink it. These things the three mighty men did.
20 As for [1]Abshai the brother of Joab, he was chief of the [2]thirty, and
he swung his spear against three hundred [3]and killed them; and he
had a name as well as the [2]thirty.
21 Of the three in the second *rank* he was the most honored, and
became their commander; however, he did not attain to the *first*
three.
22 [a]Benaiah the son of Jehoiada, the son of a valiant man of Kabzeel,
mighty in deeds, struck down the [1]two *sons of* Ariel of Moab. He also
went down and [2]killed a lion inside a pit on a snowy day.
23 And he [1]killed an Egyptian, a man of *great* stature five [2]cubits
tall. Now in the Egyptian's hand *was* [a]a spear like a weaver's beam,
but he went down to him with a club and snatched the spear from
the Egyptian's hand, and [1]killed him with his own spear.
24 These *things* Benaiah the son of Jehoiada did, and had a name as
well as the three mighty men.
25 Behold, he was honored among the thirty, but he did not attain
to the three; and David appointed him over his guard.
26 Now the mighty men of the armies *were* Asahel the brother of
Joab, Elhanan the son of Dodo of Bethlehem,
27 [1]Shammoth the Harorite, Helez the [2]Pelonite,
28 Ira the son of Ikkesh the Tekoite, Abiezer the Anathothite,
29 [1]Sibbecai the Hushathite, [2]Ilai the Ahohite,
30 Maharai the Netophathite, [1]Heled the son of Baanah the
Netophathite,
31 Ithai the son of Ribai of Gibeah of the sons of Benjamin, Benaiah
the Pirathonite,
32 [1]Hurai of the brooks of Gaash, [2]Abiel the Arbathite,
33 Azmaveth the Baharumite, Eliahba the Shaalbonite,

11 [1]Lit., *slain ones*

12 [1]Lit., *among* [a]1
27:4

13 [1]In 1 Sam. 17:1,
Ephesdammim [a]2
23:11, 12

14 [1]Or, *salvation*

15 [a]1 Chr. 14:9

16 [a]1 Sam. 10:5

19 [1]Lit., *with their*

20 [1]In 2 Sam. 23:
Abishai [2]So Syriac
M.T., *three* [3]Lit., *sl*
ones

22 [1]Or, *two lion-lik*
heroes of [2]Lit., *sm*
[a]2 Sam. 8:18

23 [1]Lit., *smote* [2]
One cubit equals
approx. 18 in. [a]1
17:7

27 [1]In 2 Sam. 23:
Shammah the Har
[2]In 2 Sam. 23:26,

29 [1]In 2 Sam. 23:
Mebunnai [2]In 2 S
23:28, *Zalmon*

30 [1]In 2 Sam. 23:
Heleb

32 [1]In 2 Sam. 23:
Hiddai [2]In 2 Sam
23:31, *Abi-albon*

34 the sons of [1]Hashem the Gizonite, Jonathan the son of Shagee the
Hararite,
35 Ahiam the son of [1]Sacar the Hararite, [2]Eliphal the son of Ur,
36 Hepher the Mecherathite, Ahijah the Pelonite,
37 Hezro the Carmelite, [1]Naarai the son of Ezbai,
38 Joel the brother of Nathan, Mibhar the son of Hagri,
39 Zelek the Ammonite, Naharai the Berothite, the armor bearer of
Joab the son of Zeruiah,
40 Ira the Ithrite, Gareb the Ithrite,
41 Uriah the Hittite, Zabad the son of Ahlai,
42 Adina the son of Shiza the Reubenite, a chief of the Reubenites,
and thirty with him,
43 Hanan the son of Maacah and Joshaphat the Mithnite,
44 Uzzia the Ashterathite, Shama and Jeiel the sons of Hotham the
Aroerite,
45 Jediael the son of Shimri and Joha his brother, the Tizite,
46 Eliel the Mahavite and Jeribai and Joshaviah, the sons of Elnaam,
and Ithmah the Moabite,
47 Eliel and Obed and Jaasiel the Mezobaite.

Chapter 12

12 [a]Now these are the ones who came to David at Ziklag, while
he was still restricted because of Saul the son of Kish; and
they were among the mighty men who helped *him* in war.
2 They were equipped with bows, [a]using both the right hand and
the left *to sling* stones and *to shoot* arrows from the bow; [b]*they were*
Saul's kinsmen from Benjamin.
3 The chief was Ahiezer, then Joash, the sons of Shemaah the
Gibeathite; and Jeziel and Pelet, the sons of Azmaveth, and Beracah
and Jehu the Anathothite,
4 and Ishmaiah the Gibeonite, a mighty man among the thirty, and
over the thirty. [1]Then Jeremiah, Jahaziel, Johanan, Jozabad the
Gederathite,
5 [1]Eluzai, Jerimoth, Bealiah, Shemariah, Shephatiah the Haruphite,
6 Elkanah, Isshiah, Azarel, Joezer, Jashobeam, the Korahites,
7 and Joelah and Zebadiah, the sons of Jeroham of Gedor.
8 And from the Gadites there [1]came over to David in the strong-
hold in the wilderness, mighty men of valor, men trained for war,
who could handle shield and spear, and whose faces were like the
faces of lions, and [a]*they were* as swift as the gazelles on the moun-
tains.
9 Ezer *was* the first, Obadiah the second, Eliab the third,
10 Mishmannah the fourth, Jeremiah the fifth,
11 Attai the sixth, Eliel the seventh,
12 Johanan the eighth, Elzabad the ninth,
13 Jeremiah the tenth, Machbannai the eleventh.
14 These of the sons of Gad were [1]captains of the army; [a]he who
was least was equal to a hundred and the greatest to a thousand.
15 [a]These are the ones who crossed the Jordan in the first month
when it was overflowing all its banks and they put to flight all those
in the valleys, both to the east and to the west.
16 Then some of the sons of Benjamin and Judah came to the
stronghold to David.
17 And David went out to meet them, and answered and said to

34 [1]In 2 Sam. 23:32, *Jashen*

35 [1]In 2 Sam. 23:33, *Sharar* [2]In 2 Sam. 23:34, *Eliphelet the son of Ahasbai*

37 [1]In 2 Sam. 23:35, *Paarai the Arbite*

12:1 [a]1 Sam. 27:2-6

2 [a]Judg. 3:15; 20:16 [b]1 Chr. 12:29

4 [1]In Heb. the beginning of v. 5, making 41 vv. in ch.

5 [1]V. 6 in Heb.

8 [1]Lit., *separated themselves* [a]2 Sam. 2:18

14 [1]Or, *chiefs* [a]Deut. 32:30

15 [a]Josh. 3:15; 4:18

them, "If you come peacefully to me to help me, my heart shall be
united with you; but if to betray me to my adversaries, since there is
no [1]wrong in my hands, may the God of our fathers look on *it* and
decide."
18 Then [a]the Spirit [1]came upon [b]Amasai, who was the chief of the
thirty, *and he said,*

"*We* are yours, O David,
And with you, O son of Jesse!
[c]Peace, peace to you,
And peace to him who helps you;
Indeed, your God helps you!"

Then David received them and made them [2]captains of the band.
19 [a]From Manasseh also some defected to David, when he was
about to go to battle with the Philistines against Saul. But they did
not help them, for the lords of the Philistines after consultation sent
him away, saying, "At *the cost of* our heads he may defect to his
master Saul."
20 As he went to Ziklag, there defected to him from Manasseh:
Adnah, Jozabad, Jediael, Michael, Jozabad, Elihu, and Zillethai, [1]cap-
tains of thousands who belonged to Manasseh.
21 And they helped David against [a]the band of raiders, for they
were all mighty men of valor, and were captains in the army.
22 For day by day *men* came to David to help him, until there was a
great army [a]like the army of God.
23 Now these are the numbers of the [1]divisions equipped for war,
[a]who came to David at Hebron, [b]to turn the kingdom of Saul to him,
[c]according to the [2]word of the LORD.
24 The sons of Judah who bore shield and spear *were* 6,800,
equipped for war.
25 Of the sons of Simeon, mighty men of valor for war, 7,100.
26 Of the sons of Levi 4,600.
27 Now Jehoiada was the leader of *the house of* Aaron, and with him
were 3,700,
28 also [a]Zadok, a young man mighty of valor, and of his father's
house twenty-two captains.
29 And of the sons of Benjamin, [a]Saul's kinsmen, 3,000; for until
now [b]the greatest part of them had kept their allegiance to the house
of Saul.
30 And of the sons of Ephraim 20,800, mighty men of valor, famous
men in their fathers' households.
31 And of the half-tribe of Manasseh 18,000, who were designated
by name to come and make David king.
32 And of the sons of Issachar, [a]men who understood the times,
with knowledge of what Israel should do, their chiefs were two
hundred; and all their kinsmen were at their command.
33 Of Zebulun, there were 50,000 who went out in the army, who
could draw up in battle formation with all kinds of weapons of war
and helped *David* [1]with [a]an undivided heart.
34 And of Naphtali *there were* 1,000 captains, and with them 37,000
with shield and spear.
35 And of the Danites who could draw up in battle formation, *there
were* 28,600.
36 And of Asher *there were* 40,000 who went out in the army to
draw up in battle formation.

17 [1]Lit., *violence*
18 [1]Lit., *clothed* [2]Or, *chiefs* [a]Judg. 3:1… 6:34 [b]1 Chr. 2:17 [c]1 Sam. 25:5, 6
19 [a]1 Sam. 29:2…
20 [1]Or, *chiefs*
21 [a]1 Sam. 30:1
22 [a]Gen. 32:2; Jo… 5:13-15
23 [1]Lit., *heads* [2]L… *mouth* [a]2 Sam. 2:… [b]1 Chr. 10:14 [c]1 C… 11:10
28 [a]2 Sam. 8:17; 1… 6:8, 53
29 [a]1 Chr. 12:2 [b]2 Sam. 2:8, 9
32 [a]Esth. 1:13
33 [1]Lit., *not of dou… heart* [a]Ps. 12:2

38 [a]2 Sam. 5:1-3; 1 Chr. 12:33
40 [a]1 Sam. 25:18
13:3 [a]1 Sam. 7:1, 2
[a]2 Sam. 6:1; 1 Kin. 8:65; 1 Chr. 15:3 [b]1 Sam. 6:21; 7:1
6 [a]2 Sam. 6:2-11 h. 15:9 [c]Ex. 25:22; 2 Kin. 19:15
[1]Lit., *caused to ride* [a]1 Sam. 7:1
8 [a]1 Chr. 15:16
9 [a]2 Sam. 6:6
) [a]1 Chr. 15:13, 15 [b]Lev. 10:2
[1]Lit., *the LORD had broken through a* kthrough [2]i.e., the akthrough of Uzza
13 [a]1 Chr. 15:25

37 And from the other side of the Jordan, of the Reubenites and the
Gadites and of the half-tribe of Manasseh, *there were* 120,000 with all
kinds of weapons of war for the battle.
38 All these, being men of war, who could draw up in battle forma-
tion, came to Hebron with [a]a perfect heart, to make David king over
all Israel; and all the rest also of Israel were of one mind to make
David king.
39 And they were there with David three days, eating and drinking;
for their kinsmen had prepared for them.
40 Moreover those who were near to them, *even* as far as Issachar
and Zebulun and Naphtali, [a]brought food on donkeys, camels,
mules, and on oxen, great quantities of flour cakes, fig cakes and
bunches of raisins, wine, oil, oxen and sheep. There was joy indeed
in Israel.

Chapter 13

13 Then David consulted with the captains of the thousands and
the hundreds, even with every leader.
2 And David said to all the assembly of Israel, "If it seems good to
you, and if it is from the LORD our God, let us send everywhere to
our kinsmen who remain in all the land of Israel, also to the priests
and Levites who are with them in their cities with pasture lands, that
they may meet with us;
3 and let us bring back the ark of our God to us, [a]for we did not
seek it in the days of Saul."
4 Then all the assembly said that they would do so, for the thing
was right in the eyes of all the people.
5 [a]So David assembled all Israel together, from the Shihor of Egypt
even to the entrance of Hamath, [b]to bring the ark of God from
Kiriath-jearim.
6 [a]And David and all Israel went up to [b]Baalah, *that is,* to Kiriath-
jearim, which belongs to Judah, to bring up from there the ark of
God, the LORD [c]who is enthroned *above* the cherubim, where His
name is called.
7 And they [1]carried the ark of God on a new cart from [a]the house
of Abinadab, and Uzza and Ahio drove the cart.
8 And David and all Israel were celebrating before God with all
their might, [a]even with songs and with lyres, harps, tambourines,
cymbals, and with trumpets.
9 When they came to [a]the threshing floor of
Chidon, Uzza put out his hand to hold the ark,
because the oxen nearly upset *it*.
10 And the anger of the LORD burned against
Uzza, so He struck him down [a]because he put
out his hand to the ark; [b]and he died there
before God.
11 Then David became angry because [1]of the
LORD's outburst against Uzza; and he called that
place [2]Perez-uzza to this day.
12 And David was afraid of God that day,
saying, "How can I bring the ark of God *home* to
me?"
13 So David did not take the ark with him to
the city of David, but took it aside [a]to the house
of Obed-edom the Gittite.

Mediterranean Sea
Shechem
River Jordan
The Ark is captured
Aphek
Ebenezer
Shiloh
The Ark was brought into the temple of Dagon
Bethel
Kiriath Jearim
Gilgal
Ekron
Ashdod
Jerusalem
Beth-Shemesh
Gath
The Ark was kept at Kirjath Jearim until the time of David
Dead Sea

The Wanderings of the Ark (*see* page I-55)

14 Thus the ark of God remained with the family of Obed-edom in
his house three months; and [a]the LORD blessed the family of Obed-
edom with all that he had.

Chapter 14

14 [a]Now Hiram king of Tyre sent messengers to David with
cedar trees, masons, and carpenters, to build a house for him.
2 And David realized that the LORD had established him as king
over Israel, *and* that his kingdom was highly exalted, for the sake of
His people Israel.
3 Then David took more wives at Jerusalem, and David [1]became
the father of more sons and daughters.
4 [a]And these are the names of the children [1]born *to him* in Jerusa-
lem: Shammua, Shobab, Nathan, Solomon,
5 Ibhar, Elishua, Elpelet,
6 Nogah, Nepheg, Japhia,
7 Elishama, Beeliada and Eliphelet.
8 When the Philistines heard that David had been anointed king
over all Israel, all the Philistines went up in search of David; and
David heard of it and went out against them.
9 Now the Philistines had come and [a]made a raid in the valley of
Rephaim.
10 And David inquired of God, saying, "Shall I go up against the
Philistines? And wilt Thou give them into my hand?" Then the LORD
said to him, "Go up, for I will give them into your hand."
11 So they came up to Baal-perazim, and David [1]defeated them
there; and David said, "God has broken through my enemies by my
hand, like the breakthrough of waters." Therefore they named that
place [2]Baal-perazim.
12 And they abandoned their gods there; so David gave the order
and they were burned with fire.
13 And the Philistines made [a]yet another raid in the valley.
14 And David inquired again of God, and God said to him, "You
shall not go up after them; circle around [1]behind them, and come at
them in front of the [2]balsam trees.
15 "And it shall be when you hear the sound of marching in the tops
of the balsam trees, then you shall go out to battle, for God will have
gone out before you to strike the army of the Philistines."
16 And David did just as God had commanded him, and they
struck down the army of the Philistines from [1]Gibeon even as far as
Gezer.
17 Then the fame of David went out into all the lands; and [a]the
LORD brought the fear of him on all the nations.

Chapter 15

15 Now *David* built houses for himself in the city of David; and
he prepared a place for the ark of God, and [a]pitched a tent
for it.
2 Then David said, "[a]No one is to carry the ark of God but the
Levites; for the LORD chose them to carry the ark of God, and to
minister to Him forever."
3 And [a]David assembled all Israel at Jerusalem, to bring up the ark
of the LORD [b]to its place, which he had prepared for it.

14 [a]1 Chr. 26:4
14:1 [a]2 Sam. 5
3 [1]Lit., *begot*
4 [1]Lit., *were to* 3:5-8
9 [a]1 Chr. 11:15;
11 [1]Lit., *smote* master of breakt
13 [a]1 Chr. 14:9
14 [1]Lit., *from up* *baka shrubs*
16 [1]In 2 Sam. 5: *Geba*
17 [a]Ex. 15:14-16 2:25
15:1 [a]1 Chr. 15:3 17:1-5
2 [a]Num. 4:15; De 10:8
3 [a]1 Kin. 8:1; 1 Ch 13:5 [b]Ex. 40:20f.; 2 Sam. 6:12, 17; 1 15:1, 12

4 And David gathered together the sons of Aaron, and [a]the Levites:
5 of the sons of Kohath, Uriel the chief, and 120 of his [1]relatives;
6 of the sons of Merari, Asaiah the chief, and 220 of his relatives;
7 of the sons of Gershom, Joel the chief, and 130 of his relatives;
8 of the sons of Elizaphan, Shemaiah the chief, and 200 of his relatives;
9 of the sons of Hebron, Eliel the chief, and 80 of his relatives;
10 of the sons of Uzziel, Amminadab the chief, and 112 of his relatives.
11 Then David called for [a]Zadok and [b]Abiathar the priests, and for the Levites, for Uriel, Asaiah, Joel, Shemaiah, Eliel, and Amminadab,
12 and said to them, "You are the heads of the fathers' *households* of the Levites; [a]consecrate yourselves both you and your relatives, that you may bring up the ark of the LORD God of Israel, [b]to *the place* that I have prepared for it.
13 "[a]Because you did not *carry it* at the first, the LORD our God made an outburst on us, for we did not seek Him according to the ordinance."
14 [a]So the priests and the Levites consecrated themselves to bring up the ark of the LORD God of Israel.
15 And the sons of [a]the Levites carried the ark of God on their shoulders, with the poles thereon as Moses had commanded according to the word of the LORD.
16 Then David spoke to the chiefs of the Levites [a]to appoint their relatives the singers, with instruments of music, harps, lyres, loud-sounding cymbals, to raise sounds of joy.
17 So [a]the Levites appointed Heman the son of Joel, and from his relatives, Asaph the son of Berechiah; and from the sons of Merari their relatives, Ethan the son of Kushaiah,
18 and with them their relatives of the second rank, Zechariah, [1]Ben, Jaaziel, Shemiramoth, Jehiel, Unni, Eliab, Benaiah, Maaseiah, Mattithiah, Eliphelehu, Mikneiah, Obed-edom, and Jeiel, the gatekeepers.
19 So the singers, Heman, Asaph, and Ethan *were appointed* to sound aloud cymbals of bronze;
20 and Zechariah, Aziel, Shemiramoth, Jehiel, Unni, Eliab, Maaseiah, and Benaiah, with [1]harps *tuned* to [a]alamoth;
21 and Mattithiah, Eliphelehu, Mikneiah, Obed-edom, Jeiel, and Azaziah, to lead with [1]lyres tuned to [a]the sheminith.
22 And Chenaniah, chief of the Levites, was *in charge of* the singing; he gave instruction in singing because he was skillful.
23 And Berechiah and Elkanah were gatekeepers for the ark.
24 And Shebaniah, Joshaphat, Nethanel, Amasai, Zechariah, Benaiah, and Eliezer, the priests, [a]blew the trumpets before the ark of God. Obed-edom and Jehiah also *were* gatekeepers for the ark.
25 [a]So *it was* David, with the elders of Israel and the captains over thousands, who went to bring up the ark of the covenant of the LORD from [b]the house of Obed-edom with joy.
26 And it came about because God was helping the Levites who were carrying the ark of the covenant of the LORD, that they sacrificed [a]seven bulls and seven rams.
27 Now David was clothed with a robe of fine linen with all the Levites who were carrying the ark, and the singers and Chenaniah

Chr. 6:16-30; 12:26
5 [1]Lit., *brothers;* i.e., w tribesmen, and so throughout the ch.
11 [a]1 Chr. 12:28 am. 22:20-23; 1 Kin. 2:26, 35
12 [a]Ex. 19:14, 15; 2 Chr. 35:6 [b]1 Chr. 15:1, 3
[a]2 Sam. 6:3; 1 Chr. 13:7
14 [a]1 Chr. 15:12
5 [a]Ex. 25:14; Num. 4:5f.
6 [a]1 Chr. 13:8; 25:1
17 [a]1 Chr. 25:1
[1]Omitted in Gr. and many mss.
20 [1]Or, *harps of aiden-like tone* [a]Ps. 46:title
[1]Or, *octave harps* [a]Ps. 6:title
[a]1 Chr. 15:28; 16:6
5 [a]2 Sam. 6:12, 15 [b]1 Chr. 13:13
[a]Num. 23:1-4, 29

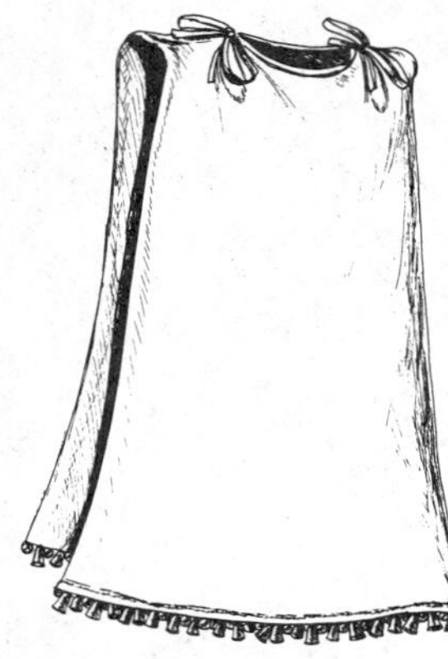

the leader of the singing *with* the singers. [a]David also wore an ephod
of linen.
28 Thus all Israel brought up the ark of the covenant of the LORD
with shouting, and with sound of the horn, with trumpets, with
loud-sounding cymbals, with harps and lyres.
29 And it happened when the ark of the covenant of the LORD came
to the city of David, that [a]Michal the daughter of Saul looked out of
the window, and saw King David leaping and making merry; and
she despised him in her heart.

Chapter 16

16 And they brought in the ark of God and [a]placed it inside the
tent which David had pitched for it, and they offered burnt
offerings and peace offerings before God.
2 When David had finished offering the burnt offering and the
peace offerings, he blessed the people in the name of the LORD.
3 And he distributed to everyone of Israel, both man and woman,
to everyone a loaf of bread and a portion *of meat* and a raisin cake.
4 And he appointed some of the Levites *as* ministers before the ark
of the LORD, even to celebrate and to thank and praise the LORD God
of Israel:
5 Asaph the chief, and second to him Zechariah, *then* [1]Jeiel,
Shemiramoth, Jehiel, Mattithiah, Eliab, Benaiah, Obed-edom, and
Jeiel, with musical instruments, harps, lyres; also Asaph *played* loud-
sounding cymbals,
6 and Benaiah and Jahaziel the priests *blew* trumpets continually
before the ark of the covenant of God.
7 Then on that day David [a]first assigned [1]Asaph and his [2]relatives
to give thanks to the LORD.

8 [a]Oh give thanks to the LORD, call upon His name;
[b]Make known His deeds among the peoples.
9 Sing to Him, sing praises to Him;
[1]Speak of all His [2]wonders.
10 [1]Glory in His holy name;
Let the heart of those who seek the LORD be glad.
11 [a]Seek the LORD and His strength;
Seek His face continually.
12 [a]Remember His wonderful deeds which He has done,
[b]His marvels and the judgments from His mouth,
13 O seed of Israel His servant,
Sons of Jacob, His chosen ones!
14 He is the LORD our God;
[a]His judgments are in all the earth.
15 Remember His covenant forever,
The word which He commanded to a thousand generations,
16 [a]*The covenant* which He made with Abraham,
And His oath to Isaac.
17 [a]He also confirmed it to Jacob for a statute,
To Israel as an everlasting covenant,
18 Saying, "[a]To you I will give the land of Canaan,
As the portion of your inheritance."
19 [a]When they were only a few in number,
Very few, and strangers in it,
20 And they wandered about from nation to nation,

27 [a]2 Sam. 6:14
29 [a]2 Sam. 3:13f.; 6
16:1 [a]1 Chr. 15:1
5 [1]In 1 Chr. 15:18, *Jaaziel*
7 [1]Lit., *by the hand Asaph* [2]Lit., *brother* [a]2 Sam. 22:1; 23:1
8 [a]1 Chr. 16:8-36; Ps 105:1-15 [b]1 Kin. 8:4 2 Kin. 19:19
9 [1]Or, *Meditate on* [2]I.e., wonderful acts
10 [1]Or, *Boast*
11 [a]Ps. 24:6
12 [a]Ps. 103:2 [b]Ps. 78:43-68
14 [a]Ps. 48:10
16 [a]Gen. 12:7; 17:2 22:16-18; 26:3
17 [a]Gen. 35:11, 12
18 [a]Gen. 13:15
19 [a]Gen. 34:30; De 7:7

And from *one* kingdom to another people,
21 He permitted no man to oppress them,
And [a]He reproved kings for their sakes, *saying*,
22 "Do not touch My anointed ones,
And [a]do My prophets no harm."
23 [a]Sing to the LORD, all the earth;
Proclaim good tidings of His salvation from day to day.
24 Tell of His glory among the nations,
His wonderful deeds among all the peoples.
25 For [a]great is the LORD, and greatly to be praised;
He also is [b]to be feared above all gods.
26 For all the gods of the peoples are [1a]idols,
[b]But the LORD made the heavens.
27 Splendor and majesty are before Him,
Strength and joy are in His place.
28 Ascribe to the LORD, O families of the peoples,
Ascribe to the LORD glory and strength.
29 Ascribe to the LORD the glory due His name;
Bring an [1]offering, and come before Him;
[a]Worship the LORD in [2]holy array.
30 Tremble before Him, all the earth;
Indeed, the world is firmly established, it will not be moved.
31 [a]Let the heavens be glad, and let the earth rejoice;
And let them say among the nations, "[b]The LORD reigns."
32 [a]Let the sea [1]roar, and [2]all it contains;
Let the field exult, and all that is in it.
33 Then the trees of the forest will sing for joy before the LORD;
For He is coming to judge the earth.
34 [a]O give thanks to the LORD, for *He is* good;
For His lovingkindness is everlasting.
35 [a]Then say, "Save us, O God of our salvation,
And gather us and deliver us from the nations,
To give thanks to Thy holy name,
And [1]glory in Thy praise."
36 [a]Blessed be the LORD, the God of Israel,
From everlasting even to everlasting.
Then all the people [b]said, "Amen," and praised the LORD.

37 So he left Asaph and his [1]relatives there [a]before the ark of the covenant of the LORD, to minister before the ark continually, [b]as every day's work required;

38 and [a]Obed-edom with [1]his 68 relatives; Obed-edom, also the son of Jeduthun, and [b]Hosah as gatekeepers.

39 And *he left* [a]Zadok the priest and his [1]relatives the priests [b]before the [2]tabernacle of the LORD in the high place which *was* at Gibeon,

40 to offer burnt offerings to the LORD on the altar of burnt offering continually morning and evening, [a]even according to all that is written in the law of the LORD, which He commanded Israel.

41 And with them *were* [a]Heman and Jeduthun, and [b]the rest who were chosen, who were designated by name, to [c]give thanks to the LORD, because His lovingkindness is everlasting.

42 And with them *were* Heman and Jeduthun *with* trumpets and cymbals for those who should sound aloud, and *with* instruments *for* [a]the songs of God, and the sons of Jeduthun for the gate.

[a]Gen. 12:17; 20:3; Ex. 7:15-18
22 [a]Gen. 20:7
23 [a]Ps. 96:1-13
[a]Ps. 144:3-6 [b]Ps. 89:7
6 [1]Or, *non-existent gs* [a]Lev. 19:4 [b]Ps. 102:25
[1]Or, *a grain offering* [2]Or, *the splendor of holiness* [a]Ps. 29:2
1 [a]Is. 44:23; 49:13 [b]Ps. 93:1; 96:10
r, *thunder* [2]Lit., *its fulness* [a]Ps. 98:7
[a]2 Chr. 5:13; 7:3; ra 3:11; Ps. 106:1; 136:1; Jer. 33:11
5 [1]Lit., *boast* [a]Ps. 106:47, 48
Kin. 8:15, 56; Ps. 2:18 [b]Deut. 27:15; Neh. 8:6
37 [1]Lit., *brothers* hr. 16:4, 5 [b]2 Chr. 8:14; Ezra 3:4
Lit., *their brothers, 68* [a]1 Chr. 13:14 [b]1 Chr. 26:10
Lit., *brothers* [2]Lit., *lling place* [a]1 Chr. 15:11 [b]1 Kin. 3:4
x. 29:38-42; Num. 28:3, 4
Chr. 6:33 [b]1 Chr. 5:1-6 [c]2 Chr. 5:13
1 Chr. 25:7; 2 Chr. 7:6; 29:27

43 [a]Then all the people departed each to his house, and David re-
turned to bless his household.

Chapter 17

17 [a]And it came about, when David dwelt in his house, that
David said to Nathan the prophet, "Behold, I am dwelling in
a house of cedar, but the ark of the covenant of the LORD is under
curtains."
2 Then Nathan said to David, "Do all that is in your heart, for God
is with you."
3 And it came about the same night, that the word of God came to
Nathan, saying,
4 "Go and tell David My servant, 'Thus says the LORD, [a]"You shall
not build a house for Me to dwell in;
5 for I have not dwelt in a house since the day that I brought up
Israel to this day, [a]but I have [1]gone from tent to tent and from *one*
dwelling place *to another.*
6 "In all places where I have walked with all Israel, have I spoken a
word [a]with any of the judges of Israel, whom I commanded to shep-
herd My people, saying, 'Why have you not built for Me a house of
cedar?' " '
7 "Now, therefore, thus shall you say to My servant David, 'Thus
says the LORD of hosts, "I took you from the pasture, from following
the sheep, that you should be leader over My people Israel.
8 "And I have been with you wherever you have gone, and have
cut off all your enemies from before you; and I will make you a
name like the name of the great ones who are in the earth.
9 "And I will appoint a place for My people Israel, and will plant
them, that they may dwell in their own place and be moved no
more; neither shall the [1]wicked waste them anymore as formerly,
10 even from the day that I commanded judges *to be* over My
people Israel. And I will subdue all your enemies. Moreover, I tell
you that the LORD will build a house for you.
11 "And it shall come about when your days are fulfilled that you
must go *to be* with your fathers, that I will set up *one of* your [1]de-
scendants after you, who shall be of your sons; and I will establish
his kingdom.
12 "He shall build for Me a house, and I will establish his throne
forever.
13 "[a]I will be his father, and he shall be My son; and I will not take
My lovingkindness away from him, [b]as I took it from him who was
before you.
14 "But I will settle him in My house and in My kingdom forever,
and his throne shall be established forever." ' "
15 According to all these words and according to all this vision, so
Nathan spoke to David.
16 Then David the king went in and sat before the LORD and said,
"[a]Who am I, O LORD God, and what is my house that Thou hast
brought me this far?
17 "And this was a small thing in Thine eyes, O God; but Thou hast
spoken of Thy servant's house for a great while to come, and hast
regarded me according to the standard of a man of high degree, O
LORD God.

43 [a]2 Sam. 6:19
17:1 [a]2 Sam. 7
4 [a]1 Chr. 28:2,
5 [1]Lit., *been* [a]
3; 2 Sam. 7:6
6 [a]2 Sam. 7:7
9 [1]Lit., *sons o*
wickedness
11 [1]Lit., *seed*
13 [a]2 Cor. 6:
1:5 [b]1 Chr. 10
16 [a]2 Sam. 7

18 "What more can David still *say* to Thee concerning the honor
bestowed on Thy servant? For Thou knowest Thy servant.
19 "O LORD, [a]for Thy servant's sake, and according to Thine own
heart, Thou hast wrought all this greatness, to make known all these
great things.
20 "O LORD, there is none like Thee, neither is there any God besides
Thee, according to all that we have heard with our ears.
21 "And what one nation in the earth is like Thy people Israel,
whom God went to redeem for Himself *as* a people, to make Thee a
name by great and terrible things, in driving out nations from before
Thy people, whom Thou didst redeem out of Egypt?
22 "[a]For Thy people Israel Thou didst make Thine own people
forever, and Thou, O LORD, didst become their God.
23 "And now, O LORD, let the word that Thou hast spoken concern-
ing Thy servant and concerning his house, be established forever,
and do as Thou hast spoken.
24 "And let Thy name be established and magnified forever, saying,
'The LORD of hosts is the God of Israel, *even* a God to Israel; and the
house of David Thy servant is established before Thee.'
25 "For Thou, O my God, hast revealed to Thy servant that Thou
wilt build for him a house; therefore Thy servant hath found *courage*
to pray before Thee.
26 "And now, O LORD, Thou art God, and hast [1]promised this good
thing to Thy servant.
27 "And now it hath pleased Thee to bless the house of Thy servant,
that it may [1]continue forever before Thee; for Thou, O LORD, hast
blessed, and it is blessed forever."

Chapter 18

18 Now after this [a]it came about that David [1]defeated the Philis-
tines and subdued them and took Gath and its towns from
the hand of the Philistines.
2 And he defeated Moab, and the Moabites became servants to
David, bringing tribute.
3 David also defeated Hadadezer king of Zobah *as far as* Hamath,
as he went to establish his [1]rule to the Euphrates River.
4 And David took from him 1,000 chariots and 7,000 horsemen
and 20,000 foot soldiers, and David hamstrung all the chariot horses,
but reserved *enough* of them for 100 chariots.
5 When the Arameans of [1]Damascus came to help Hadadezer king
[a]of Zobah, David [2]killed 22,000 men of the Arameans.
6 Then David put *garrisons* among the Arameans of [1]Damascus;
and the Arameans became servants to David, bringing tribute. And
the LORD helped David wherever he went.
7 And David took the shields of gold which were [1]carried by the
servants of Hadadezer, and brought them to Jerusalem.
8 Also from [1]Tibhath and from Cun, cities of Hadadezer, David
took a very large amount of bronze, with which [a]Solomon made the
bronze sea and the pillars and the bronze utensils.
9 Now when [1]Tou king of Hamath heard that David had [2]defeated
all the army of Hadadezer king of Zobah,
10 he sent [1]Hadoram his son to King David, to [2]greet him and to
bless him, because he had fought against Hadadezer and had

19 [a]2 Sam. 7:21; Is. 37:35
22 [a]Ex. 19:5, 6
26 [1]Lit., *said*
27 [1]Lit., *be*
1 [1]Lit., *smote*, and in vv. 1-3. [a]2 Sam. 8:1-18
3 [1]Lit., *hand*
5 [1]Heb., *Darmeseq* [2]Lit., *smote* [a]1 Chr. 19:6
6 [1]Heb., *Darmeseq*
7 [1]Lit., *on*
8 [1]In 2 Sam. 8:8, *Betah* [a]1 Kin. 7:40-47; 2 Chr. 4:11-18
9 [1]In 2 Sam. 8:9, *Toi* [2]Lit., *smitten*
10 [1]In 2 Sam. 8:10, *Joram* [2]Lit., *ask him of his welfare*

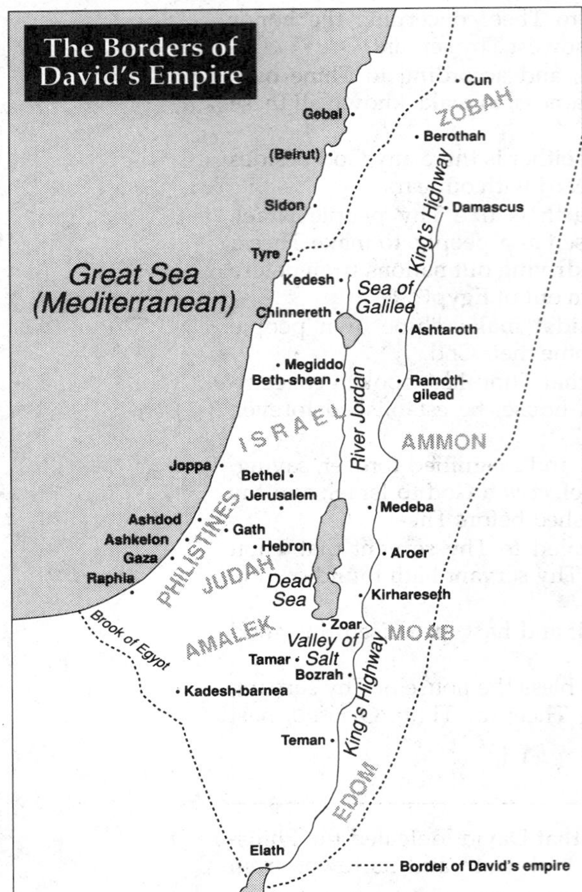

[3]defeated him; for Hadadezer had
been at war with Tou. And *Hado-
ram brought* all kinds of articles of
gold and silver and bronze.
11 King David also dedicated
these to the LORD with the silver
and the gold which he had carried
away from all the nations: from
Edom, Moab, the sons of Ammon,
the Philistines, and from Amalek.
12 Moreover Abishai the son of
Zeruiah [1]defeated 18,000 Edomites
in the Valley of Salt.
13 Then he put garrisons in
Edom, and all the Edomites be-
came servants to David. And the
LORD helped David wherever he
went.
14 So David reigned over all Isra-
el; and he [1]administered justice
and righteousness for all his
people.
15 And [a]Joab the son of Zeruiah
was over the army, and Jehosha-
phat the son of Ahilud *was* re-
corder;
16 and Zadok the son of Ahitub
and Abimelech the son of Abiathar
were priests, and Shavsha *was*
secretary;
17 and Benaiah the son of Jehoi-
ada *was* over the Cherethites and
the Pelethites, and the sons of
David *were* chiefs at the king's side.

10 [3]Lit., *smitte*
12 [1]Lit., *smot*
14 [1]Lit., *was*
15 [a]1 Chr. 11

Chapter 19

19 [a]Now it came about after this, that Nahash the king of the
sons of Ammon died, and his son became king in his place.
2 Then David said, "I will show kindness to Hanun the son of
Nahash, because his father showed kindness to me." So David sent
messengers to console him concerning his father. And David's ser-
vants came into the land of the sons of Ammon to Hanun, to console
him.
3 But the princes of the sons of Ammon said to Hanun, "[1]Do you
think that David is honoring your father, in that he has sent com-
forters to you? Have not his servants come to you to search and to
overthrow and to spy out the land?"
4 So Hanun took David's servants and shaved them, and cut off
their garments in the middle as far as their hips, and sent them away.
5 Then *certain persons* went and told David about the men. And he
sent to meet them, for the men were greatly humiliated. And the
king said, "[1]Stay at Jericho until your beards grow, and *then* return."
6 When the sons of Ammon saw that they had made themselves
odious to David, Hanun and the sons of Ammon sent 1,000 talents of

19:1 [a]2 Sam
3 [1]Lit., *In yo David honori father becau*
5 [1]Lit., *Retu*

6 [a]1 Chr. 18:5, 9

silver to hire for themselves chariots and horsemen from Mesopo-
tamia, from Aram-maacah, and [a]from Zobah.
7 So they hired for themselves 32,000 chariots, and the king of
Maacah and his people, who came and camped before [a]Medeba. And
the sons of Ammon gathered together from their cities and came to
battle.

[a]Num. 21:30; Josh. 13:9, 16

8 When David heard *of it*, he sent Joab and all the army, the
mighty men.
9 And the sons of Ammon came out and drew up in battle array at
the entrance of the city, and the kings who had come were by them-
selves in the field.
10 Now when Joab saw that the [1]battle was set against him in front

[1]Lit., *the face of the battle*

and in the rear, he selected from all the choice men of Israel and they
arrayed themselves against the Arameans.
11 But the remainder of the people he placed in the hand of [1]Abshai
his brother; and they arrayed themselves against the sons of
Ammon.
12 And he said, "If the Arameans are too strong for me, then you
shall help me; but if the sons of Ammon are too strong for you, then

1 [1]In 2 Sam. 10:10, *Abishai*

I will help you.
13 "Be strong, and let us show ourselves courageous for the sake of
our people and for the cities of our God; and may the LORD do what
is good in His sight."
14 So Joab and the people who were with him drew near to the
battle against the Arameans, and they fled before him.
15 When the sons of Ammon saw that the Arameans fled, they also

[1]Lit., *smitten before* e., Euphrates [3]Lit., *before*

fled before Abshai his brother, and entered the city. Then Joab came
to Jerusalem.
16 When the Arameans saw that they had been [1]defeated by Israel,
they sent messengers, and brought out the Arameans who were
beyond the [2]River, with Shophach the commander of the army of
Hadadezer [3]leading them.
17 When it was told David, he gathered all Israel together and

[1]Lit., *smitten before*

crossed the Jordan, and came upon them and drew up in formation
against them. And when David drew up in battle array against the
Arameans, they fought against him.
18 And the Arameans fled before Israel, and David killed of the
Arameans 7,000 charioteers and 40,000 foot soldiers, and put to
death Shophach the commander of the army.

1 [1]Lit., *at the return of the year* [a]2 Sam. 11:1 [b]2 Sam. 12:26

19 So when the servants of Hadadezer saw that they were [1]defeated
by Israel, they made peace with David and served him. Thus the
Arameans were not willing to help the sons of Ammon anymore.

Chapter 20

20 [a]Then it happened [1]in the spring, at the time when kings go
out *to battle*, that Joab led out the army and ravaged the land

2 [1]In Zeph. 1:5, *Malcam* [a]2 Sam. 12:30, 31

of the sons of Ammon, and came and besieged Rabbah. But David
stayed at Jerusalem. And [b]Joab struck Rabbah and overthrew it.
2 [a]And David took the crown of [1]their king from his head, and he
found it to weigh a talent of gold, and there was a precious stone in
it; and it was placed on David's head. And he brought out the spoil
of the city, a very great amount.
3 And he brought out the people who *were* in it, [a]and cut *them* with

3 [a]2 Sam. 12:31

saws and with sharp instruments and with axes. And thus David

did to all the cities of the sons of Ammon. Then David and all the
people returned *to* Jerusalem.
4 [a]Now it came about after this, that war [1]broke out at [2]Gezer with
the Philistines; then Sibbecai the Hushathite [3]killed Sippai, one of the
descendants of the [4]giants, and they were subdued.
5 And there was war with the Philistines again, and Elhanan the
son of [a]Jair [1]killed Lahmi the brother of Goliath the Gittite, the [b]shaft
of whose spear *was* like a weaver's beam.
6 And again there was war at Gath, where there was a man of
great stature who had twenty-four fingers and toes, six *fingers on each
hand* and six *toes on each foot;* and he also was descended from the
giants.
7 And when he taunted Israel, Jonathan the son of Shimea,
David's brother, [1]killed him.
8 These were descended from the giants in Gath, and they fell by
the hand of David and by the hand of his servants.

Chapter 21

21 [a]Then Satan stood up against Israel and moved David to
number Israel.
2 So David said to Joab and to the princes of the people, "[a]Go,
number Israel from Beersheba even to Dan, and bring me *word* that I
may know their number."
3 And Joab said, "[a]May the LORD add to His people a hundred
times as many as they are! But, my lord the king, are they not all my
lord's servants? Why does my lord seek this thing? Why should he
be a cause of guilt to Israel?"
4 Nevertheless, the king's word prevailed against Joab. Therefore,
Joab departed and went throughout all Israel, and came to Jerusa-
lem.
5 And Joab gave the number of the [1]census of *all* the people to
David. And [a]all Israel were 1,100,000 men who drew the sword; and
Judah *was* 470,000 men who drew the sword.
6 [a]But he did not [1]number Levi and Benjamin among them, for the
king's [2]command was abhorrent to Joab.
7 And [1]God was displeased with this thing, so He struck Israel.
8 And David said to God, "I have sinned greatly, in that I have
done this thing. [a]But now, please take away the iniquity of Thy ser-
vant, for I have done very foolishly."
9 And the LORD spoke to [a]Gad, David's [b]seer, saying,
10 "Go and speak to David, saying, 'Thus says the LORD, "I [1]offer
you three things; choose for yourself one of them, that I may do *it* to
you." ' "
11 So Gad came to David and said to him, "Thus says the LORD,
'Take for yourself
12 [a]either three years of famine, or three months to be swept away
before your foes, while the sword of your enemies overtakes *you*, or
else three days of the sword of the LORD, even pestilence in the land,
and the angel of the LORD destroying throughout all the territory of
Israel.' Now, therefore, consider what answer I shall return to Him
who sent me."
13 And David said to Gad, "I am in great distress; please let me fall
into the hand of the LORD, [a]for His mercies are very great. But do not
let me fall into the hand of man."

4 [1]Lit., *stood u* 2 Sam. 21:18, [3]Lit., *smote* [4]H *Raphah*, and s
8 [a]2 Sam. 21:1
5 [1]Lit., *smote* 21:19 [b]1 Sam. 1 Chr. 11:23
7 [1]Lit., *smote*
21:1 [a]2 Sam. 2
2 [a]1 Chr. 27:23,
3 [a]Deut. 1:11
5 [1]Lit., *muster* 24:9
6 [1]Lit., *muster* *word* [a]1 Chr. 27:
7 [1]Lit., *it was evi sight of God*
8 [a]2 Sam. 12:13
9 [a]2 Sam. 24:11; 29:29 [b]1 Sam. 9:9
10 [1]Lit., *stretch ou*
12 [a]2 Sam. 24:13
13 [a]Ps. 51:1; 130:

14 [a]So the LORD [1]sent a pestilence on Israel; 70,000 men of Israel fell.

15 And God sent an angel to Jerusalem to destroy it; but as he was about to destroy *it*, the LORD saw and [a]was sorry over the calamity, and said to the destroying angel, "It is enough; now relax your hand." And the angel of the LORD was standing by the threshing floor of [1]Ornan the Jebusite.

16 Then David lifted up his eyes and saw the angel of the LORD standing between earth and heaven, with his drawn sword in his hand stretched out over Jerusalem. Then David and the elders, [a]covered with sackcloth, fell on their faces.

17 And David said to God, "Is it not I who [1]commanded to count the people? Indeed, I am the one who has sinned and done very wickedly, [a]but these sheep, what have they done? O LORD my God, please let Thy hand be against me and my father's household, but not against Thy people that they should be plagued."

18 [a]Then the angel of the LORD [1]commanded Gad to say to David, that David should go up and build an altar to the LORD on the threshing floor of Ornan the Jebusite.

19 So David went up at the word of Gad, which he spoke in the name of the LORD.

20 Now Ornan turned back and saw the angel, and his four sons *who were* with him hid themselves. And Ornan was threshing wheat.

21 And as David came to Ornan, Ornan looked and saw David, and went out from the threshing floor, and prostrated himself [1]before David with his face to the ground.

22 Then David said to Ornan, "Give me the [1]site of *this* threshing floor, that I may build on it an altar to the LORD; for the full price you shall give it to me, that the plague may be restrained from the people."

23 And Ornan said to David, "Take *it* for yourself; and let my lord the king do what is good in his sight. See, I will give the oxen for burnt offerings and the threshing sledges for wood and the wheat for the grain offering; I will give *it* all."

24 But King David said to Ornan, "No, but I will surely buy *it* for the full price; for I will not take what is yours for the LORD, or offer a burnt offering [1]which costs me nothing."

25 So [a]David gave Ornan 600 shekels of gold by weight for the [1]site.

26 Then David built an altar to the LORD there, and offered burnt offerings and peace offerings. And he called to the LORD and [a]He answered him with fire from heaven on the altar of burnt offering.

27 And the LORD commanded the angel, and he put his sword back in its sheath.

28 At that time, when David saw that the LORD had answered him on the threshing floor of Ornan the Jebusite, he offered sacrifice there.

29 [a]For the tabernacle of the LORD, which Moses had made in the wilderness, and the altar of burnt offering *were* in the high place at Gibeon at that time.

30 But David could not go before it to inquire of God, for he was terrified by the sword of the angel of the LORD.

Chapter 22 ______________________________

22 Then David said, "[a]This is the house of the LORD God, and this is the altar of burnt offering for Israel."

[1]Lit., *gave* [a]1 Chr. 27:24

5 [1]In 2 Sam. 24:16, *...raunah* [a]Ex. 32:14; ...m. 15:11; Jon. 3:10

16 [a]1 Kin. 21:27

[1]Lit., *said* [a]2 Sam. 7:8; Ps. 74:1

[1]Lit., *said to* [a]2 Chr. 3:1

21 [1]Lit., *to*

22 [1]Lit., *place*

4 [1]Lit., *gratuitously*

[1]Lit., *place* [a]2 Sam. 24:24

6 [a]Lev. 9:24; Judg. 6:21

[a]1 Kin. 3:4; 1 Chr. 16:39

1 [a]1 Chr. 21:18-28; 2 Chr. 3:1

See 2 Chronicles 3:1 for what happened at this threshing floor.

There were basically three historical temples: **Solomon's** (pre-exilic), **Zerubbabel's**, called the second temple (post-exilic), and **Herod's** (New Testament). Since Herod's temple was an expansion/rebuilding of the second temple, it is often referred to as the second temple rather than "the third." All were located on a hill north of David's capital city which he took from the Jebusites (2 Samuel 5:6-7). David acquired the temple hill to build an altar and offer sacrifices (2 Samuel 24:18-25). Second Chronicles identifies this hill with Mount Moriah, where Abraham was willing to offer Isaac (2 Chronicles 3:1, Genesis 22:1-14).

2 So David [1]gave orders to gather [a]the foreigners who were in the
land of Israel, and [b]he set stonecutters to hew out stones to build the
house of God.
3 And David [a]prepared large quantities of iron [1]to make the nails
for the doors of the gates and for the clamps, and more [b]bronze than
could be weighed;
4 and timbers of cedar logs beyond number, for [a]the Sidonians and
Tyrians brought large quantities of cedar timber to David.
5 And David said, "My son [a]Solomon is young and inexperienced,
and the house that is to be built for the LORD shall be exceedingly
magnificent, famous and glorious throughout all lands. *Therefore*
now I will make preparation for it." So David made ample prepara-
tions before his death.
6 Then [a]he called for his son Solomon, and charged him to build a
house for the LORD God of Israel.
7 And David said to Solomon, "[a]My son, [1]I had intended to build a
house to the name of the LORD my God.
8 "But the word of the LORD came to me, saying, '[a]You have shed
much blood, and have [1]waged great wars; you shall not build a
house to My name, because you have shed *so* much blood on the
earth before Me.
9 'Behold, a son shall be born to you, who shall be a man of rest;
and [a]I will give him rest from all his enemies on every side; for [b]his
name shall be [1]Solomon, and I will give peace and quiet to Israel in
his days.
10 '[a]He shall build a house for My name, and he shall be My son,
and I will be his father; and I will establish the throne of his king-
dom over Israel forever.'
11 "Now, my son, [a]the LORD be with you that you may be successful,
and build the house of the LORD your God just as He has spoken
concerning you.
12 "[a]Only the LORD give you discretion and understanding, and give
you charge over Israel, so that you may [b]keep the law of the LORD
your God.
13 "[a]Then you shall prosper, if you are careful to observe the statutes
and the ordinances which the LORD commanded Moses concerning
Israel. [b]Be strong and courageous, do not fear nor be dismayed.
14 "Now behold, [1]with great pains I have prepared for the house of
the LORD [a]100,000 talents of gold and 1,000,000 talents of silver, and
[b]bronze and iron beyond weight, for [2]they are in great quantity; also
timber and stone I have prepared, and you may add to them.
15 "Moreover, there are many workmen with you, stonecutters and
masons of stone and carpenters, and all men who are skillful in
every kind of work.
16 "Of the gold, the silver and the bronze and the iron, there is no
limit. Arise and work, and may [a]the LORD be with you."
17 [a]David also commanded all the leaders of Israel to help his son
Solomon, *saying*,
18 "Is not the LORD your God with you? And [a]has He not given you
rest on every side? For He has given the inhabitants of the land into
my hand, and the land is subdued before the LORD and before His
people.
19 "Now [a]set your heart and your soul to seek the LORD your God;
arise, therefore, and build the sanctuary of the LORD God, [b]so that

2 [1]Lit., *said to* 9:20, 21; 2 Chr. [b]1 Kin. 5:17, 18
3 [1]Lit., *for* [a]1 C 7 [b]1 Chr. 22:14
4 [a]1 Kin. 5:6-1
5 [a]1 Kin. 3:7; 1
6 [a]1 Kin. 2:1
7 [1]Lit., *as for m* *in my heart* [a]2 7:2, 3; 1 Chr. 1
8 [1]Lit., *made* 28:3
9 [1]I.e., peacef 4:20, 25 [b]2 Sa 12:24, 25
10 [a]2 Sam. 7: 1 Chr. 17:12
11 [a]1 Chr. 22:
12 [a]1 Kin. 3:9 1:10 [b]1 Kin. 2
13 [a]1 Chr. 28 1:6-9
14 [1]Lit., *in my* [2]Lit., *it is* [a]1 C [b]1 Chr. 22:3
16 [a]1 Chr. 22
17 [a]1 Chr. 28
18 [a]1 Chr. 22
19 [a]1 Chr. 28 8:6, 21; 2 Chr

you may bring the ark of the covenant of the LORD, and the holy
vessels of God into the house that is to be built [c]for the name of the
LORD."

Chapter 23

23 [a]Now when David [1]reached old age, [b]he made his son
Solomon king over Israel.
2 And he gathered together all the leaders of Israel with the priests
and the Levites.
3 And [a]the Levites were numbered from thirty years old and up-
ward, and [b]their number by [1]census of men was 38,000.
4 Of these, 24,000 were [a]to oversee the work of the house of the
LORD; and 6,000 *were* [b]officers and judges,
5 and 4,000 *were* gatekeepers, and [a]4,000 *were* praising the LORD
with the instruments which [1]David made for giving praise.
6 And David divided them into divisions [a]according to the sons of
Levi: Gershon, Kohath, and Merari.
7 Of the Gershonites *were* [1]Ladan and Shimei.
8 The sons of Ladan *were* Jehiel the first and Zetham and Joel,
three.
9 The sons of Shimei *were* Shelomoth and Haziel and Haran, three.
These were the heads of the fathers' *households* of Ladan.
10 And the sons of Shimei *were* Jahath, [1]Zina, Jeush, and Beriah.
These four *were* the sons of Shimei.
11 And Jahath was the first, and Zizah the second; but Jeush and
Beriah did not have many sons, so they became a father's household,
one [1]class.
12 The sons of Kohath were four: Amram, Izhar, Hebron and Uz-
ziel.
13 [a]The sons of Amram were Aaron and Moses. And [b]Aaron was set
apart to sanctify him as most holy, he and his sons forever, [c]to burn
incense before the LORD, to minister to Him and to bless in His name
forever.
14 But *as for* [a]Moses the man of God, his sons were named among
the tribe of Levi.
15 The sons of Moses *were* Gershom and Eliezer.
16 The [1]son of Gershom *was* [2]Shebuel the chief.
17 And the [1]son of Eliezer was Rehabiah the chief; and Eliezer had
no other sons, but the sons of Rehabiah were very many.
18 The [1]son of Izhar was [2]Shelomith the chief.
19 The sons of Hebron *were* Jeriah the first, Amariah the second,
Jahaziel the third and Jekameam the fourth.
20 The sons of Uzziel *were* Micah the first and Isshiah the second.
21 The sons of Merari were Mahli and Mushi. The sons of Mahli
were Eleazar and Kish.
22 And Eleazar died and had no sons, but daughters only, so their
brothers, the sons of Kish, took them *as wives*.
23 The sons of Mushi *were* three: Mahli, Eder, and Jeremoth.
24 [a]These were the sons of Levi according to their fathers' house-
holds, *even* the heads of the fathers' *households* of those of them who
were [1]counted, in the number of names by their [2]census, doing the
work for the service of the house of the LORD, [b]from twenty years old
and upward.

19 [c]1 Chr. 22:7
:1 [1]Lit., *became old and sated with days* 1 Chr. 29:28 [b]1 Kin. 1:1-40; 2:12; 1 Chr. 28:5; 29:22
3 [1]Lit., *their heads* Num. 4:3-49 [b]Num. 4:48; 1 Chr. 23:24
[a]Ezra 3:8, 9 [b]1 Chr. 26:29
[1]Lit., *I made* [a]1 Chr. 15:16
6 [a]1 Chr. 6:1
[1]In Ex. 6:17, *Libni*
10 [1]In v. 11, *Zizah*
11 [1]Lit., *mustering*
[a]Ex. 6:20 [b]Ex. 28:1 [c]Ex. 30:6-10
14 [a]Deut. 33:1; Ps. 90:title
[1]Lit., *sons* [2]In ch. 24:20, *Shubael*
[1]Lit., *sons . . . were*
[1]Lit., *sons* [2]In ch. 24:22, *Shelomoth*
.it., *mustered* [2]Lit., *s* [a]Num. 10:17, 21 [b]1 Chr. 23:3

25 For David said, "The LORD God of Israel [a]has given rest to His
people, and He dwells in Jerusalem forever.
26 "And also, [a]the Levites will no longer need to carry the tabernacle
and all its utensils for its service."
27 For by the last words of David the sons of Levi *were* numbered,
from twenty years old and upward.
28 For their office is [1]to assist the sons of Aaron with the service of
the house of the LORD, in the courts and in the chambers and in the
purifying of all holy things, even the work of the service of the house
of God,
29 [a]and with the showbread, and [b]the fine flour for a grain offering,
and unleavened wafers, or [c]*what is baked in* the pan, or [d]what is
well-mixed, and [e]all measures of volume and size.
30 And they are to stand every morning to thank and to praise the
LORD, and likewise at evening,
31 and to offer all burnt offerings to the LORD, [a]on the sabbaths, the
new moons and [b]the fixed festivals in the number *set* by the ordinance
concerning them, continually before the LORD.
32 Thus [a]they are to keep charge of the tent of meeting, and charge
of the holy place, and [b]charge of the sons of Aaron their [1]relatives, for
the service of the house of the LORD.

Chapter 24

24 Now the divisions of the [1]descendants of Aaron *were these:*
[a]the sons of Aaron *were* Nadab, Abihu, Eleazar, and Ithamar.
2 [a]But Nadab and Abihu died before their father and had no [1]sons.
So Eleazar and Ithamar served as priests.
3 And David, with [a]Zadok of the sons of Eleazar and Ahimelech of
the sons of Ithamar, divided them according to their offices [1]for their
ministry.
4 Since more chief men were found from the [1]descendants of
Eleazar than the [1]descendants of Ithamar, they divided them thus:
there were sixteen heads of fathers' households of the [1]descendants of
Eleazar, and eight of the [1]descendants of Ithamar according to their
fathers' households.
5 [a]Thus they were divided by lot, the one as the other; for they
were officers of the sanctuary and officers of God, both from the
[1]descendants of Eleazar and the [1]descendants of Ithamar.
6 And Shemaiah, the son of Nethanel the scribe, from the Levites,
recorded them in the presence of the king, the princes, Zadok the
priest, [a]Ahimelech the son of Abiathar, and the heads of the fathers'
households of the priests and of the Levites; one father's household
taken for Eleazar and one taken for Ithamar.
7 Now the first lot came out for Jehoiarib, the second for Jedaiah,
8 the third for Harim, the fourth for Seorim,
9 the fifth for Malchijah, the sixth for Mijamin,
10 the seventh for Hakkoz, the eighth for [a]Abijah,
11 the ninth for Jeshua, the tenth for Shecaniah,
12 the eleventh for Eliashib, the twelfth for Jakim,
13 the thirteenth for Huppah, the fourteenth for Jeshebeab,
14 the fifteenth for Bilgah, the sixteenth for Immer,
15 the seventeenth for Hezir, the eighteenth for Happizzez,
16 the nineteenth for Pethahiah, the twentieth for Jehezkel,
17 the twenty-first for Jachin, the twenty-second for Gamul,

25 [a]1 Chr. 22:1

26 [a]Num. 4:5, 1 Deut. 10:8

28 [1]Lit., *at the h*

29 [a]Lev. 24:5-9 6:20 [c]1 Chr. 9:3 6:21 [e]Lev. 19:35

31 [a]Is. 1:13, 14 23:2-4

32 [1]Lit., *brothers* [a]Num. 1:53; 1 Ch [b]Num. 3:6-9, 38

24:1 [1]Lit., *sons* 6:23

2 [1]Or, *children* [a] 10:2

3 [1]Lit., *in their se* [a]1 Chr. 6:8

4 [1]Lit., *sons*

5 [1]Lit., *sons* [a]1 C 24:31

6 [a]1 Chr. 18:16

10 [a]Neh. 12:4; Lu

18 the twenty-third for Delaiah, the twenty-fourth for Maaziah.
19 [a]These were their offices for their ministry, when *they* came in to
the house of the LORD according to the ordinance *given* to them
through Aaron their father, just as the LORD God of Israel had com-
manded him.
20 Now for the rest of the sons of Levi: of the sons of Amram,
[1]Shubael; of the sons of Shubael, Jehdeiah.
21 Of Rehabiah: of the sons of Rehabiah, Isshiah the first.
22 Of the Izharites, [1]Shelomoth; of the sons of Shelomoth, Jahath.
23 And the sons [a]*of Hebron:* Jeriah *the first,* Amariah the second,
Jahaziel the third, Jekameam the fourth.
24 *Of* the sons of Uzziel, Micah; of the sons of Micah, Shamir.
25 The brother of Micah, Isshiah; of the sons of Isshiah, Zechariah.
26 The sons of Merari, Mahli and Mushi; the sons of Jaaziah, Beno.
27 The sons of Merari: by Jaaziah *were* Beno, Shoham, Zaccur, and
Ibri.
28 By Mahli: Eleazar, who had no sons.
29 By Kish: the sons of Kish, Jerahmeel.
30 And the sons of Mushi: Mahli, Eder, and Jerimoth. These *were*
the sons of the Levites according to their fathers' households.
31 [a]These also cast lots just as their [1]relatives the sons of Aaron in
the presence of David the king, [b]Zadok, Ahimelech, and the heads of
the fathers' *households* of the priests and of the Levites—the head of
fathers' *households* as well as those of his younger brother.

Chapter 25

25 Moreover, David and the commanders of the army set apart
for the service *some* of the sons of [a]Asaph and of Heman and
of Jeduthun, who *were* to [b]prophesy with lyres, [c]harps, and cymbals;
and the number of [1]those who performed their service was:
2 Of the sons of Asaph: Zaccur, Joseph, Nethaniah, and
[1]Asharelah; the sons of Asaph *were* under the [2]direction of Asaph,
who prophesied under the [2]direction of the king.
3 [a]Of Jeduthun, the sons of Jeduthun: Gedaliah, [1]Zeri, Jeshaiah,
[2]Shimei, Hashabiah, and Mattithiah, six, under the [3]direction of their
father Jeduthun with the harp, who prophesied in giving thanks and
praising the LORD.
4 Of Heman, the sons of Heman: Bukkiah, Mattaniah, [1]Uzziel,
[2]Shebuel and Jerimoth, Hananiah, Hanani, Eliathah, Giddalti and
Romamti-ezer, Joshbekashah, Mallothi, Hothir, Mahazioth.
5 All these *were* the sons of Heman [a]the king's seer to [1]exalt him
according to the words of God, for God gave fourteen sons and three
daughters to Heman.
6 All these were under the [1]direction of their father to sing in the
house of the LORD, [a]with cymbals, harps and lyres, for the service of
the house of God. [b]Asaph, Jeduthun and Heman *were* under the
[1]direction of the king.
7 And their number who were trained in singing to the LORD, with
their [1]relatives, all who were skillful, *was* [a]288.
8 And [a]they cast lots for their duties, all alike, the small as well as
the great, the teacher *as well* as the pupil.
9 Now the first lot came out for Asaph to Joseph, the second for
Gedaliah, he with his relatives and sons *were* twelve;
10 the third to Zaccur, his sons and his relatives, twelve;

19 [a]1 Chr. 9:25
[1]In 23:16, *Shebuel*
n 23:18, *Shelomith*
23 [a]1 Chr. 23:19
31 [1]Lit., *brothers* Chr. 24:5, 6 [b]1 Chr. 24:6
5:1 [1]Lit., *workmen according to their* rvice [a]1 Chr. 6:33, 2 Kin. 3:15 [c]1 Chr. 15:16
n v. 14, *Jesharelah* [2]Lit., *hand(s)*
v. 11, *Izri* [2]So with mss. and ancient ons, cf. v. 17 [3]Lit., [a]1 Chr. 16:41, 42
v. 18, *Azarel* [2]In v. 20, *Shubael*
Lit., *lift up the horn* Sam. 24:11; 1 Chr. 21:9
Lit., *hands* [a]1 Chr. 5:16 [b]1 Chr. 15:19
, *brothers,* and so throughout the ch. [a]1 Chr. 23:5
8 [a]1 Chr. 26:13

11 the fourth to [1]Izri, his sons and his relatives, twelve;
12 the fifth to Nethaniah, his sons and his relatives, twelve;
13 the sixth to Bukkiah, his sons and his relatives, twelve;
14 the seventh to [1]Jesharelah, his sons and his relatives, twelve;
15 the eighth to Jeshaiah, his sons and his relatives, twelve;
16 the ninth to Mattaniah, his sons and his relatives, twelve;
17 the tenth to Shimei, his sons and his relatives, twelve;
18 the eleventh to Azarel, his sons and his relatives, twelve;
19 the twelfth to Hashabiah, his sons and his relatives, twelve;
20 for the thirteenth, Shubael, his sons and his relatives, twelve;
21 for the fourteenth, Mattithiah, his sons and his relatives, twelve;
22 for the fifteenth to Jeremoth, his sons and his relatives, twelve;
23 for the sixteenth to Hananiah, his sons and his relatives, twelve;
24 for the seventeenth to Joshbekashah, his sons and his relatives,
twelve;
25 for the eighteenth to Hanani, his sons and his relatives, twelve;
26 for the nineteenth to Mallothi, his sons and his relatives, twelve;
27 for the twentieth to Eliathah, his sons and his relatives, twelve;
28 for the twenty-first to Hothir, his sons and his relatives, twelve;
29 for the twenty-second to Giddalti, his sons and his relatives,
twelve;
30 for the twenty-third to Mahazioth, his sons and his relatives,
twelve;
31 for the twenty-fourth to Romamti-ezer, his sons and his relatives,
twelve.

Chapter 26

26 For the divisions of the gatekeepers *there were* of the Kora-
hites, [1]Meshelemiah the son of Kore, of the sons of [2]Asaph.
2 And Meshelemiah had sons: Zechariah the first-born, Jediael the
second, Zebadiah the third, Jathniel the fourth,
3 Elam the fifth, Johanan the sixth, Eliehoenai the seventh.
4 And [a]Obed-edom had sons: Shemaiah the first-born, Jehozabad
the second, Joah the third, Sacar the fourth, Nethanel the fifth,
5 Ammiel the sixth, Issachar the seventh, *and* Peullethai the eighth;
God had indeed blessed him.
6 Also to his son Shemaiah sons were born who ruled over the
house of their father, for they were mighty men of valor.
7 The sons of Shemaiah *were* Othni, Rephael, Obed, and Elzabad,
whose brothers, Elihu and Semachiah, were valiant men.
8 All these *were* of the sons of Obed-edom; they and their sons and
their [1]relatives *were* able men with strength for the service, 62 from
Obed-edom.
9 And Meshelemiah had sons and relatives, 18 valiant men.
10 Also [a]Hosah, *one* of the sons of Merari had sons: Shimri the first
(although he was not the first-born, his father made him first),
11 Hilkiah the second, Tebaliah the third, Zechariah the fourth; all
the sons and relatives of Hosah *were* 13.
12 To these divisions of the gatekeepers, the chief men, *were given*
duties like their relatives to minister in the house of the LORD.
13 [a]And they cast lots, the small and the great alike, according to
their fathers' households, for every gate.
14 And the lot to the east fell to [1]Shelemiah. Then they cast lots *for*

11 [1]In v. 3, *Ze*

14 [1]In v. 2, *As*

26:1 [1]In v. 14 *Shelemiah* [2]In *Ebiasaph*

4 [a]2 Sam. 6:1 13:14

8 [1]Lit., *brothe* throughout th

10 [a]1 Chr. 16

13 [a]1 Chr. 24

14 [1]In 9:17,

his son Zechariah, a counselor with insight, and his lot came out to
the north.
15 For Obed-edom *it fell* to the south, and to his sons went the
storehouse.
16 For Shuppim and Hosah *it was* to the west, by the gate of Shal-
lecheth, on the ascending highway. Guard corresponded to guard.
17 On the east there were six Levites, on the north four daily, on the
south four daily, and at the storehouse two by two.
18 At the [1a]Parbar on the west *there were* four at the highway and
two at the Parbar.
19 These were the divisions of the gatekeepers of the sons of Korah
and of the sons of Merari.
20 [1]And the Levites, their relatives, [2]had [a]charge of the treasures of
the house of God, and of the treasures of the dedicated gifts.
21 The sons of Ladan, the sons of the Gershonites belonging to
Ladan, *namely,* the Jehielites, *were* the heads of the fathers' *households,*
belonging to Ladan the Gershonite.
22 The sons of Jehieli, Zetham and Joel his brother, [1]had charge of
the treasures of the house of the LORD.
23 As for the Amramites, the Izharites, the Hebronites, and the
Uzzielites,
24 Shebuel the son of Gershom, the son of Moses, was officer over
the treasures.
25 And his relatives by Eliezer *were* Rehabiah his son, Jeshaiah his
son, Joram his son, Zichri his son, and Shelomoth his son.
26 This Shelomoth and his relatives [1]had charge of all the treasures
of the dedicated gifts, [a]which King David and the heads of the
fathers' *households,* the commanders of thousands and hundreds, and
commanders of the army, had dedicated.
27 They dedicated [1]part of the spoil won in battles to repair the
house of the LORD.
28 And all that Samuel the seer had dedicated and Saul the son of
Kish, Abner the son of Ner and Joab the son of Zeruiah, everyone
who had dedicated *anything, all of this* was [1]in the care of [2]Shelomoth
and his relatives.
29 As for the Izharites, Chenaniah and his sons [a]were *assigned* to
outside duties for Israel, as [b]officers and judges.
30 As for the Hebronites, [a]Hashabiah and his relatives, 1,700
capable men, had charge of the affairs of Israel [1]west of the Jordan,
for all the work of the LORD and the service of the king.
31 As for the Hebronites, [a]Jerijah the chief [1](these Hebronites were
investigated according to their genealogies and fathers' *households,* in
the fortieth year of David's reign, and men of outstanding capability
were found among them at [b]Jazer of Gilead)
32 and his relatives, capable men, *were* 2,700 in number, heads of
fathers' *households.* And King David made them overseers of the
Reubenites, the Gadites and the half-tribe of the Manassites [a]con-
cerning [1]all the affairs of God and of the king.

Chapter 27

27 Now *this is* the enumeration of the sons of Israel, the heads of
fathers' *households,* the commanders of thousands and of hun-
dreds, and their officers who served the king in all the affairs of the

[1]Possibly *court or* ...*nade* [a]2 Kin. 23:11

...So Gr.; Heb., *As for* ...*Levites, Ahijah had* *were over* [a]1 Chr. ...:22, 24, 26; 28:12; Ezra 2:69

...22 [1]Lit., *were over*

...26 [1]Lit., *were over* [a]2 Sam. 8:11

...27 [1]Heb., *from the* ...*attles and from the* *spoil*

...28 [1]Lit., *under the* ... [2]Heb., *Shelomith*

...Neh. 11:16 [b]1 Chr. 23:4

...0 [1]Lit., *beyond the Jordan westward* [a]1 Chr. 27:17

...Heb., *according to the Hebronites . . .* ...*ather's households* ...Chr. 23:19 [b]1 Chr. 6:81

...it., *every matter of* ...*d and matter of the* ...*king.* [a]2 Chr. 19:11

divisions which came in and went out month by month throughout all the months of the year, each division *numbering* 24,000.
2 Jashobeam the son of Zabdiel [1][a]had charge of the first division for the first month; and in his division *were* 24,000.
3 *He was* from the sons of Perez, *and was* chief of all the commanders of the army for the first month.
4 Dodai the Ahohite and his division had charge of the division for the second month, Mikloth *being* the chief officer; and in his division *were* 24,000.
5 The third commander of the army for the third month *was* Benaiah, the son of Jehoiada the priest, *as* chief; and in his division *were* 24,000.
6 This Benaiah *was* the mighty man of the thirty, and had charge of thirty; and over his division was Ammizabad his son.
7 The fourth for the fourth month *was* Asahel the brother of Joab, and Zebadiah his son after him; and in his division *were* 24,000.
8 The fifth for the fifth month *was* the commander Shamhuth the Izrahite; and in his division *were* 24,000.
9 The sixth for the sixth month *was* Ira the son of Ikkesh the Tekoite; and in his division *were* 24,000.
10 The seventh for the seventh month *was* Helez the Pelonite of the sons of Ephraim; and in his division *were* 24,000.
11 The eighth for the eighth month *was* Sibbecai the Hushathite of the Zerahites; and in his division *were* 24,000.
12 The ninth for the ninth month *was* Abiezer the Anathothite of the Benjamites; and in his division *were* 24,000.
13 The tenth for the tenth month *was* Maharai the Netophathite of the Zerahites; and in his division *were* 24,000.
14 The eleventh for the eleventh month *was* Benaiah the Pirathonite of the sons of Ephraim; and in his division *were* 24,000.
15 The twelfth for the twelfth month *was* Heldai the Netophathite of Othniel; and in his division *were* 24,000.
16 Now in charge of the tribes of Israel: chief officer for the Reubenites was Eliezer the son of Zichri; for the Simeonites, Shephatiah the son of Maacah;
17 for Levi, Hashabiah the son of Kemuel; for Aaron, Zadok;
18 for Judah, Elihu, *one* of David's brothers; for Issachar, Omri the son of Michael;
19 for Zebulun, Ishmaiah the son of Obadiah; for Naphtali, Jeremoth the son of Azriel;
20 for the sons of Ephraim, Hoshea the son of Azaziah; for the half-tribe of Manasseh, Joel the son of Pedaiah;
21 for the half-tribe of Manasseh in Gilead, Iddo the son of Zechariah; for Benjamin, Jaasiel the son of Abner;
22 for Dan, Azarel the son of Jeroham. [a]These *were* the princes of the tribes of Israel.
23 But David did not [1]count those twenty years of age and under, [a]because the LORD had said He would multiply Israel [b]as the stars of heaven.
24 Joab the son of Zeruiah had begun to count *them*, but did not finish; and because of [a]this, wrath came upon Israel, and the number was not included in the account of the chronicles of King David.
25 Now Azmaveth the son of Adiel had charge of the king's storehouses. And Jonathan the son of Uzziah had charge of the

27:2 [1]Lit., *was* and so through ch. [a]2 Sam. 2 1 Chr. 11:11-3

22 [a]1 Chr. 28

23 [1]Lit., *take number from* 21:2-5 [b]Gen. 22:17; 26:4

24 [a]2 Sam. 1 Chr. 21:1-7

storehouses in the country, in the cities, in the villages, and in the
towers.
26 And Ezri the son of Chelub had charge of the [1]agricultural
workers who tilled the soil.
27 And Shimei the Ramathite had charge of the vineyards; and
Zabdi the Shiphmite had charge of the [1]produce of the vineyards
stored in the wine cellars.
28 And Baal-hanan the Gederite had charge of the olive and [a]syca-
more trees in the [1]Shephelah; and Joash had charge of the stores of
oil.
29 And Shitrai the Sharonite had charge of the cattle which were
grazing in [a]Sharon; and Shaphat the son of Adlai had charge of the
cattle in the valleys.
30 And Obil the Ishmaelite had charge of the camels; and Jehdeiah
the Meronothite had charge of the donkeys.
31 And Jaziz the [a]Hagrite had charge of the flocks. All these were
[1]overseers of the property which belonged to King David.
32 Also Jonathan, David's uncle, *was* a counselor, a man of under-
standing, and a scribe; and Jehiel the son of Hachmoni [1]tutored the
king's sons.
33 And [a]Ahithophel was counselor to the king; and [b]Hushai the
Archite was the king's friend.
34 And Jehoiada the son of [a]Benaiah, and [b]Abiathar [1]succeeded
Ahithophel; and Joab was the [c]commander of the king's army.

Chapter 28

28 Now [a]David assembled at Jerusalem all the officials of Israel,
the princes of the tribes, and the commanders of the divisions
that served the king, and the commanders of thousands, and the
commanders of hundreds, and the overseers of all the property and
livestock belonging to the king and his sons, with the officials and
[b]the mighty men, even all the valiant men.
2 Then King David rose to his feet and said, "Listen to me, my
brethren and my people; I [a]*had* [1]intended to build a [2]permanent
home for the ark of the covenant of the LORD and for [b]the footstool of
our God. So I had made preparations to build *it*.
3 "But God said to me, '[a]You shall not build a house for My name
because you are a man of war and have shed blood.'
4 "Yet, the LORD, the God of Israel, [a]chose me from all the house of
my father to be king over Israel [b]forever. For [c]He has chosen Judah to
be a leader; and [d]in the house of Judah, my father's house, and
among the sons of my father He took pleasure in me to make *me*
king over all Israel.
5 "And [a]of all my sons (for the LORD has given me many sons), [b]He
has chosen my son Solomon to sit on the throne of the kingdom of
the LORD over Israel.
6 "And He said to me, 'Your son [a]Solomon is the one who shall
build My house and My courts; for I have chosen him to be a son to
Me, and I will be a father to him.
7 'And I will establish his kingdom forever, [a]if he resolutely per-
forms My commandments and My ordinances, as [1]is done now.'
8 "So now, in the sight of all Israel, the assembly of the LORD, and
in the hearing of our God, observe and seek after all the

26 [1]Lit., *doers of the* ...rk *of the field for the tilling of*...
...[1]Lit., *what was in the vineyards of the storehouses of wine*
28 [1]Or, *lowlands* ...1. 10:27; 2 Chr. 1:15
29 [a]1 Chr. 5:16
...[1]Or, *rulers* [a]1 Chr. 5:10
32 [1]Lit., *was with*
33 [a]2 Sam. 15:12 [b]2 Sam. 15:32, 37
...[1]Lit., *after* [a]1 Chr. ... [b]1 Kin. 1:7 [c]1 Chr. 11:6
28:1 [a]1 Chr. 23:2; ...1 [b]1 Chr. 11:10-47
..., *in my heart* [2]Lit., ...*use of rest* [a]1 Chr. ...1, 2 [b]Ps. 132:7; Is. 66:1
3 [a]1 Chr. 22:8
4 [a]1 Sam. 16:6-13 ...r. 17:23, 27 [c]Gen. 49:8-10; 1 Chr. 5:2 [d]1 Sam. 16:1
...Chr. 3:1-9; 14:3-7 [b]1 Chr. 22:9, 10
... [a]2 Sam. 7:13, 14
7 [1]Lit., *at this day* [a]1 Chr. 22:13

commandments of the LORD your God in order that you may possess
the good land and bequeath *it* to your sons after you forever.
9 "As for you, my son Solomon, know the God of your father, and
[a]serve Him with [1]a whole heart and a willing [2]mind; [b]for the LORD
searches all hearts, and understands every intent of the thoughts. [c]If
you seek Him, He will let you find Him; but if you forsake Him, He
will reject you forever.
10 "Consider now, for the LORD has chosen you to build a house for
the sanctuary; [a]be courageous and act."
11 Then David gave to his son Solomon [a]the plan of [b]the porch *of the
temple,* its buildings, its storehouses, its upper rooms, its inner
rooms, and [c]the room for the mercy seat;
12 and the plan of all that he had in [1]mind, for the courts of the
house of the LORD, and for all the surrounding rooms, for [a]the store-
houses of the house of God, and for the storehouses of the dedicated
things;
13 also for [a]the divisions of the priests and [b]the Levites and for all
the work of the service of the house of the LORD and for all the
utensils of service in the house of the LORD;
14 for the golden *utensils,* the weight of gold for all utensils for
every kind of service; for the silver utensils, the weight *of silver* for all
utensils for every kind of service;
15 and the weight *of gold* for the [a]golden lampstands and their gold-
en lamps, with the weight of each lampstand and its lamps; and *the
weight of silver* for the silver lampstands, with the weight of each
lampstand and its lamps according to the use of each lampstand;
16 and the gold by weight for the tables of showbread, for each
table; and silver for the silver tables;
17 and the forks, the basins, and the pitchers of pure gold; and for
the golden bowls with the weight for each bowl; and for the silver
bowls with the weight for each bowl;
18 and for [a]the altar of incense refined gold by weight; and gold for
the model of the chariot, *even* [b]the cherubim, that spread out *their
wings,* and covered the ark of the covenant of the LORD.
19 "All *this," said David,* "the LORD made me understand in writing
by His hand upon me, [a]all the [1]details of this pattern."
20 Then David said to his son Solomon, "[a]Be strong and
courageous, and act; do not fear nor be dismayed, for the LORD God,
my God, is with you. [b]He will not fail you nor forsake you until all
the work for the service of the house of the LORD is finished.
21 "Now behold, [a]*there are* the divisions of the priests and the Levites
for all the service of the house of God, and [b]every willing man of any
skill will be with you in all the work for all kinds of service. The
officials also and all the people will be entirely at your command."

Chapter 29

29 Then King David said to the entire assembly, "My son
Solomon, whom alone God has chosen, [a]is still young and
inexperienced and the work is great; for [b]the [1]temple is not for man,
but for the LORD God.
2 "Now [a]with all my ability I have provided for the house of my
God the gold for the *things of* gold, and the silver for the *things of*
silver, and the bronze for the *things of* bronze, the iron for the *things
of* iron, and wood for the *things of* wood, onyx stones and inlaid

9 [1]Or, *the san*
soul [a]1 Kin. 8:
29:17-19 [b]1 S
[c]2 Chr. 15:2; J

10 [a]1 Chr. 22:

11 [a]Ex. 25:40
28:12, 19 [b]1 K
[c]Ex. 25:17-22

12 [1]Lit., *the s*
him [a]1 Chr. 2

13 [a]1 Chr. 24
23:6

15 [a]Ex. 25:3

18 [a]Ex. 30:1-
25:18-22

19 [1]Lit., *work*
28:11, 12

20 [a]1 Chr. 22
1:5; Heb. 13:5

21 [a]1 Chr. 28
35:25-35; 36:

29:1 [1]Lit., *pa*
[a]1 Chr. 22:5 [b]
29:19

2 [a]1 Chr. 22:

stones, stones of antimony, and stones of various colors, and all kinds
of precious stones, and alabaster in abundance.
3 "And moreover, in my delight in the house of my God, the trea-
sure I have of gold and silver, I give to the house of my God, over
and above all that I have already provided for the holy [1]temple,
4 *namely,* [a]3,000 talents of gold, of [b]the gold of Ophir, and 7,000
talents of refined silver, to overlay the walls of the [1]buildings;
5 of gold for the *things of* gold, and of silver for the *things of* silver,
that is, for all the work [1]done by the craftsmen. Who then is willing
[2]to consecrate himself this day to the LORD?"
6 Then [a]the rulers of the fathers' *households,* and the princes of the
tribes of Israel, and the commanders of thousands and of hundreds,
with [b]the overseers over the king's work, offered willingly;
7 and for the service for the house of God they gave 5,000 talents
and 10,000 [a]darics of gold, and 10,000 talents of silver, and 18,000
talents of brass, and 100,000 talents of iron.
8 And [1]whoever possessed *precious* stones gave them to the trea-
sury of the house of the LORD, [2]in care of [a]Jehiel the Gershonite.
9 Then the people rejoiced because they had offered so willingly,
for they made their offering to the LORD [a]with a whole heart, and
King David also rejoiced greatly.
10 So David blessed the LORD in the sight of all the assembly; and
David said, "Blessed art Thou, O LORD God of Israel our father,
forever and ever.
11 "[a]Thine, O LORD, is the greatness and the power and the glory and
the victory and the majesty, indeed everything that is in the heavens
and the earth; Thine is the dominion, O LORD, and Thou dost exalt
Thyself as head over all.
12 "[a]Both riches and honor *come* from Thee, and Thou dost rule over
all, and [b]in Thy hand is power and might; and it lies in Thy hand to
make great, and to strengthen everyone.
13 "Now therefore, our God, we thank Thee, and praise Thy glorious
name.
14 "But who am I and who are my people that we should [1]be able to
offer as generously as this? For all things come from Thee, and from
Thy hand we have given Thee.
15 "For [a]we are sojourners before Thee, and tenants, as all our fathers
were; [b]our days on the earth are like a shadow, and there is no hope.
16 "O LORD our God, all this abundance that we have provided to
build Thee a house for Thy holy name, it is from Thy hand, and all is
Thine.
17 "Since I know, O my God, that [a]Thou triest the heart and [b]de-
lightest in uprightness, I, in the integrity of my heart, have willingly
offered all these *things;* so now with joy I have seen Thy people, who
are present here, make *their* offerings willingly to Thee.
18 "O LORD, the God of Abraham, Isaac, and Israel, our fathers,
preserve this forever in the [1]intentions of the heart of Thy people,
and direct their heart to Thee;
19 "and [a]give to my son Solomon a perfect heart to keep Thy com-
mandments, Thy testimonies, and Thy statutes, and to do *them* all,
and [b]to build the [1]temple, for which I have made provision."
20 Then David said to all the assembly, "Now bless the LORD your
God." And [a]all the assembly blessed the LORD, the God of their

3 [1]Lit., *house*
ouses [a]1 Chr.
4 [b]1 Kin. 9:28
by the hand of
ftsmen [2]Lit., *to*
fill his hand
Chr. 27:1; 28:1
Chr. 27:25-31
2:69; Neh. 7:70
ose with whom
und [2]Lit., *under*
of [a]1 Chr. 23:8
8:61; 2 Cor. 9:7
Matt. 6:13; Rev.
5:13
hr. 1:12 [b]2 Chr.
20:6
., *retain strength*
[a]Lev. 25:23 [b]Job
14:2, 10-12
[a]1 Chr. 28:9 [b]Ps.
15:2
[1]Lit., *intent of the*
ughts of the heart
t., *palace* [a]1 Chr.
; Ps. 72:1 [b]1 Chr.
29:1, 2
20 [a]Josh. 22:33

fathers, and [b]bowed low and did homage to the LORD and to the
king.
21 And on the next day [a]they [1]made sacrifices to the LORD and
offered burnt offerings to the LORD, 1,000 bulls, 1,000 rams *and* 1,000
lambs, with their libations and sacrifices in abundance for all Israel.
22 So they ate and drank that day before the LORD with great glad-
ness.

And they made Solomon the son of David king [a]a second time,
and they [b]anointed *him* as ruler for the LORD and Zadok as priest.
23 Then [a]Solomon sat on the throne of the LORD as king instead of
David his father; and he prospered, and all Israel obeyed him.
24 And all the officials, the mighty men, and also all the sons of
King David [1]pledged allegiance to King Solomon.
25 And [a]the LORD highly exalted Solomon in the sight of all Israel,
and [b]bestowed on him royal majesty which had not been on any
king before him in Israel.
26 Now [a]David the son of Jesse reigned over all Israel.
27 [a]And the period which he reigned over Israel *was* forty years; he
reigned in Hebron seven years and [1]in Jerusalem thirty-three *years*.
28 Then he died in [a]a [1]ripe old age, [b]full of days, riches and honor;
and his son Solomon reigned in his place.
29 Now the acts of King David, from first to last, are written in the
chronicles of [a]Samuel the seer, in the chronicles of [b]Nathan the
prophet, and in the chronicles of [c]Gad the seer,
30 with all his reign, his power, and the circumstances which came
on him, on Israel, and on all the kingdoms of the lands.

20 [b]Ex. 4
21 [1]Lit., s
[a]1 Kin. 8:
22 [a]1 Ch
1:33-39
23 [a]1 Kin
24 [1]Lit., p
under Sol
25 [a]2 Chr
3:13; 2 Ch
26 [a]1 Chr
27 [1]Lit., h
[a]2 Sam. 5.
2:11; 1 Ch
28 [1]Lit., g
15:15; Acts
[b]1 Chr. 23
29 [a]1 Sam
[b]2 Sam. 7:
[c]1 Sam. 22

1 Chronicles at a Glance

e of 1 Chronicles:

MENT DIVISIONS

		CHAPTER THEMES
		1
		2
		3
		4
		5
		6
		7
		8
		9
		10
		11
		12
		13
		14
		15
		16
		17
		18
		19
		20
		21
		22
		23
		24
		25
		26
		27
		28
		29

Author:

Date:

Purpose:

Key Words:

2 CHRONICLES

When King David wanted to build a house for the Lord, the Lord promised David He would bu house for him. God said He would establish David's house forever and that David's son would b God's house. At this point in David's life the writers of the Septuagint divided Chronicles. Sec Chronicles tells of the house of David and of the house David's son built for the Lord.

THINGS TO DO

If you haven't already done so, study 1 Chronicles (at the very least read the introductio 1 Chronicles) before you begin your study of 2 Chronicles.

Second Chronicles is filled with truths and lessons for life which, if heeded, will help you in y pursuit of holiness. Second Chronicles focuses on the reigns of the kings of Judah and their relation to God and His house from the time of Solomon until the Babylonian exile. Read all the instruct before you begin. In each chapter:

1. Examine every chapter in the light of the five W's and an H. Record your insights in the margi
   a. Look for three *who's*: the king, the prophet, and the Lord. Of the three, the Lord and the are most prominent. Ask: Who are the associates of the king? Who influences, opposes assists him?
   b. Look for *what* each king does, *what* God does in respect to that king, and *what* role the pro plays, if at all. In 2 Chronicles the "house" of God takes center stage, therefore in each r observe what the king's relationship is to the Lord and to His house.
   c. Also keep track of *when* events occur. Don't forget to note references to time with a c drawing such as this ⏰.
   d. Because this is a historical book also watch *where* things occur.
   e. Observing *why* events occur will bring insight into the character and sovereignty of God in affairs of men and nations. Keep asking why. If the king does evil, ask why.
   f. Ask *how?* How did the king seek the Lord? How did the king do evil? How did God respon
2. Record your insights on the kings mentioned in 2 Chronicles. Put these on the chart THE KIN OF ISRAEL AND JUDAH located on pages 599 and 600 between 2 Kings and 1 Chronicles.
3. Make a list of the key repeated words printed on the 2 CHRONICLES AT A GLANCE char page 697. Use this list as a bookmark while you study 2 Chronicles.
   a. In the margin record all you learn from marking each of these key words. Note that a chapter 8, *ark*, one of the key words, is used once more in chapter 35.
   b. You'll also observe key words and phrases which will play a major role in only one or chapters. Don't miss these. They'll come to the surface as you prayerfully read and medi on a chapter.
4. As you study each chapter take notes in the margin of all you learn about God. You'll gain and maybe surprising insights. Also mark and record any lessons for life ("LFL").
5. Remember that 1 and 2 Chronicles were written as one book. Second Chronicles is a continuat of 1 Chronicles. Chronicles has a number of speeches, prophecies, and prayers, some of which not mentioned in Samuel or Kings. Watch for these and pay attention to what is said, by wh and why. Highlight or note your insights in the margin.
6. When you finish reading each chapter, record its theme on 2 CHRONICLES AT A GLANCE page 697 and on the line next to the chapter number. Also watch for the major historical eve which occur in 2 Chronicles. Highlight these on the chart.

Complete 2 CHRONICLES AT A GLANCE. As you review the chapter themes you've recorded, see how this book could be segmented and record this under segment divisions.

NGS TO THINK ABOUT

Many lessons about prayer and seeking God can be learned from this book. Review what you have seen from marking the key words. Think about what you learned regarding sin, prayer, confession, and repentance in 2 Chronicles 6.

Second Chronicles is filled with illustrations of how people dealt with difficulties and testings. How did you relate to these people? What did you learn from their lives—men such as Asa, Jehoshaphat, Hezekiah, Uzziah? As you studied these did God prick your heart? With what warnings or cautions?

What did you learn about the heart from this book? Do you serve the Lord wholeheartedly . . . or halfheartedly? And what did you learn about crying to the Lord? What happened to those who cried out to Him? Did they always deserve to be heard?

What did you learn about the sovereignty of God? How active or involved is God in the affairs of men? What were the different ways God afflicted those who disobeyed? Do you have a healthy fear of God?

Chapter 1

[a]1 Kin. 2:12, 46 [b]1 Chr. 29:25

1 Now [a]Solomon the son of David established himself securely
over his kingdom, and the LORD his God *was* with him and
[b]exalted him greatly.

2 [a]1 Chr. 28:1

2 And Solomon spoke to all Israel, [a]to the commanders of
thousands and of hundreds and to the judges and to every leader in
all Israel, the heads of the fathers' *households*.

Kin. 3:4 [b]Ex. 36:8

3 Then Solomon, and all the assembly with him, went to [a]the high
place which was at Gibeon; [b]for God's tent of meeting was there,
which Moses the servant of the LORD had made in the wilderness.

Lit., *where David* ad *prepared for it* 15:25-28 [b]2 Chr. 6:2

4 However, David had brought up [a]the ark of God from Kiriath-
jearim [1]to [b]the place he had prepared for it; for he had pitched a tent
for it in Jerusalem.

[1]Lit., *he put* [a]Ex. 31:9; 38:1-7

5 Now [a]the bronze altar, which Bezalel the son of Uri, the son of
Hur, had made, [1]was there before the tabernacle of the LORD, and
Solomon and the assembly sought it out.

6 [a]1 Kin. 3:4

6 And Solomon went up there before the LORD to the bronze altar
which *was* at the tent of meeting, and [a]offered a thousand burnt
offerings on it.

7 [a]1 Kin. 3:5-14

7 [a]In that night God appeared to Solomon and said to him, "Ask
what I shall give you."

8 [a]1 Chr. 28:5

8 And Solomon said to God, "Thou hast dealt with my father
David with great lovingkindness, and [a]hast made me king in his
place.

Lit., *word* [a]2 Sam. 2-16 [b]Gen. 13:16; 22:17; 28:14

9 "Now, O LORD God, [a]Thy [1]promise to my father David is fulfilled;
for Thou hast made me king over [b]a people as numerous as the dust
of the earth.

[a]1 Kin. 3:9 [b]Num. 27:17; 2 Sam. 5:2

10 "[a]Give me now wisdom and knowledge, [b]that I may go out and
come in before this people; for who can rule this great people of
Thine?"

t., *this was in your heart* [a]1 Kin. 3:11

11 [a]And God said to Solomon, "Because [1]you had this in mind, and
did not ask for riches, wealth, or honor, or the life of those who hate
you, nor have you even asked for long life, but you have asked for

Read ***The Ark of the Covenant*** on page I-55.

yourself wisdom and knowledge, that you may rule My people, over
whom I have made you king,
12 wisdom and knowledge have been granted to you. And [a]I will
give you riches and wealth and honor, [1]such as none of the kings
who were before you has possessed, nor those who will [2]come after
you."
13 [a]So Solomon went [1]from the high place which was at Gibeon,
from the tent of meeting, to Jerusalem, and he reigned over Israel.
14 [a]And Solomon amassed chariots and horsemen. [b]He had 1,400
chariots, and 12,000 horsemen, and he stationed them in [c]the chariot
cities and with the king at Jerusalem.
15 And [a]the king made [b]silver and gold as plentiful in Jerusalem as
stones, and he made cedars as plentiful as sycamores in the
[1]lowland.
16 And Solomon's [a]horses were imported from Egypt and from
Kue; the king's traders procured them from Kue for a price.
17 And they [1]imported chariots from Egypt for 600 *shekels* of silver
apiece, and horses for 150 apiece, and [2]by the same means they
[3]exported them to all the kings of the Hittites and the kings of Aram.

Chapter 2

2 [1a]Now Solomon [2]decided to build a house for the name of the
LORD, and a [3]royal palace for himself.
2 [1]So [a]Solomon [2]assigned 70,000 men to carry loads, and 80,000
men to quarry *stone* in the mountains, and 3,600 to supervise them.
3 [a]Then Solomon sent *word* to [1]Huram the king of Tyre, saying,
"[b]As you dealt with David my father, and sent him cedars to build
him a house to dwell in, so do for me.
4 "Behold, I am about to build a house for the name of the LORD my
God, dedicating it to Him, [a]to burn fragrant incense before Him, and
to set out [b]the showbread continually, and to offer [c]burnt offerings
morning and evening, [d]on sabbaths and on new moons and on the
appointed feasts of the LORD our God, this *being required* forever in
Israel.
5 "And the house which I am about to build *will be* great; for
[a]greater is our God than all the gods.
6 "But [a]who is able to build a house for Him, for the heavens and
the highest heavens cannot contain Him? So who am I,
that I should build a house for Him, except to [1]burn *in-*
cense before Him?
7 "And now [a]send me a skilled man to work in gold,
silver, brass and iron, and in purple, crimson and violet
fabrics, and who knows how to make engravings, to *work*
with the skilled men [1b]whom I have in Judah and Jerusa-
lem, whom David my father provided.
8 "[a]Send me also cedar, cypress and algum timber from
Lebanon, for I know that your servants know how to cut
timber of Lebanon; and indeed, [b]my servants *will work*
with your servants,
9 to prepare timber in abundance for me, for the house
which I am about to build *will be* great and wonderful.
10 "Now behold, [a]I will give to your servants, the woods-
men who cut the timber, 20,000 [1]kors of crushed wheat,
and 20,000 [1]kors of barley, and 20,000 baths of wine, and
20,000 baths of oil."

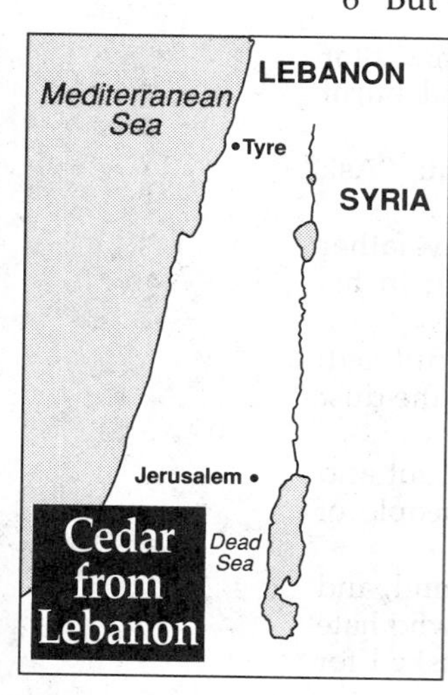

Cedar from Lebanon

12 [1]Lit., w... *so to the k... were befo... be* [a]1 Chr. 9:22

13 [1]Lit., *to*...

14 [a]1 Kin. ... [b]1 Kin. 4:2...

15 [1]Heb., ... [a]1 Kin. 10:... 17:17

16 [a]Deut. ...

17 [1]Lit., *br... brought ou... like manne... hand* [3]Lit., ...

2:1 [1]Ch. 1:... [2]Lit., *said* [3]... *for his roya...*

2 [1]Ch. 2:1 ... *numbered* ... 16; 2 Chr. 2...

3 [1]In 1 Kin. ... [a]1 Kin. 5:2-... 14:1

4 [a]Ex. 30:7 ... [c]Ex. 29:38-... 28:9, 10

5 [a]Ex. 15:11 ... 16:25

6 [1]Lit., *offer smoke* [a]1 K... 2 Chr. 6:18

7 [1]Lit., *who ... me* [a]Ex. 31:... 2:13, 14 [b]1 C...

8 [a]1 Kin. 5:6 ... 9:10, 11

10 [1]I.e., A ko... approx. 10 bu... 5:11

11 Then Huram, king of Tyre, [1]answered in a letter sent to Solomon:
"[a]Because the LORD loves His people, He has made you king over
them."
12 Then Huram [1]continued, "Blessed be [a]the LORD, the God of Isra-
el, who has made heaven and earth, who has given King David a
wise son, [2]endowed with discretion and understanding, [b]who will
build a house for the LORD and a [3]royal palace for himself.
13 "And now I am sending a skilled man, [1]endowed with under-
standing, Huram-abi,
14 [a]the son of a [1]Danite woman and [2]a Tyrian father, who knows
how to work in gold, silver, bronze, iron, stone and wood, *and* in
purple, violet, linen and crimson fabrics, and *who knows how* to make
all kinds of engravings and to [3]execute any design which may be
assigned to him, *to work* with your skilled men, and with [4]those of
my lord David your father.
15 "Now then, let my lord send to his servants wheat and barley, oil
and wine, of [a]which he has spoken.
16 "And [a]we will cut whatever timber you need from Lebanon, and
bring it to you on rafts by sea to Joppa, so that you may carry it up to
Jerusalem."
17 And Solomon numbered all the aliens who *were* in the land of
Israel, [a]following the [1]census which his father David had [2]taken; and
153,600 were found.
18 [a]And he appointed 70,000 of them to carry loads, and 80,000 to
quarry *stones* in the mountains, and 3,600 supervisors to make the
people work.

Chapter 3

3 [a]Then Solomon began to build the house of the LORD in Jerusa-
lem on Mount Moriah, where *the Lord* had appeared to his father
David, at the place that David had prepared, [b]on the threshing floor
of [1]Ornan the Jebusite.
2 And he began to build on the second *day* in the second month [1]of
the fourth year of his reign.
3 Now these are the [1]foundations which [a]Solomon laid for build-
ing the house of God. The length in [2]cubits, according to the old
standard *was* sixty cubits, and the width twenty cubits.
4 And the porch which was in front of the house [a]was as long as
the width of the house, twenty cubits, and the height 120; and inside
he overlaid it with pure gold.
5 And he overlaid [a]the [1]main room with cypress wood and over-
laid it with fine gold, and [2]ornamented it with palm trees and chains.
6 Further, he [1]adorned the house with precious stones; and the
gold was gold from [2]Parvaim.
7 [a]He also overlaid the house with gold—the beams, the
thresholds, and its walls, and its doors; and he [b]carved cherubim on
the walls.
8 Now he made [a]the [1]room of the holy of holies: its length, across
the width of the house, *was* twenty cubits, and its width *was* twenty
cubits; and he overlaid it with fine gold, *amounting* to 600 talents.
9 And the weight of the nails was fifty shekels of gold. He also
overlaid [a]the upper rooms with gold.
10 [a]Then he made two [1]sculptured cherubim in the room of the holy
of holies and overlaid them with gold.

[1]Lit., *said . . . and he*
t [a]1 Kin. 10:9; 2 Chr. 9:8

12 [1]Lit., *said* [2]Lit., *wing discretion* [3]Lit., *house for his royalty* [a]Ps. 33:6; 102:25 [b]2 Chr. 2:1

13 [1]Lit., *knowing understanding*

[1]Lit., *a woman of the ughters of Dan* [2]Lit., *ose father is a Tyrian an* [3]Lit., *devise any device* [4]Lit., *skilled men* [a]1 Kin. 7:14

15 [a]2 Chr. 2:10

16 [a]1 Kin. 5:8, 9

17 [1]Lit., *numbering , numbered of them* [a]1 Chr. 22:2

18 [a]2 Chr. 2:2

1 [1]In 2 Sam. 24:18, *Araunah* [a]1 Kin. 6:1 [b]1 Chr. 21:18

2 [1]Lit., *in*

3 [1]Lit., *founding of omon to build* [2]I.e., One cubit equals prox. 18 in. [a]1 Kin. 6:2

4 [a]1 Kin. 6:3

5 [1]Lit., *great house* [2]Lit., *put on it palm trees* [a]1 Kin. 6:17

Lit., *overlaid . . . for uty* [2]Or, *country of gold*

7 [a]1 Kin. 6:20-22 [b]1 Kin. 6:29-35

8 [1]Lit., *house* [a]Ex. 26:33; 1 Kin. 6:16

9 [a]1 Chr. 28:11

[1]Lit., *cherubim of ulptured work* [a]Ex. -20; 1 Kin. 6:23-28

11 And the wingspan of the cherubim *was* twenty cubits; the wing of one, of five cubits, touched the wall of the house, and *its* other wing, of five cubits, touched the wing of the other cherub.

12 And the wing of the other cherub, of five cubits, touched the wall of the house; and *its* other wing of five cubits, was attached to the wing of the [1]first cherub.

13 The wings of these cherubim extended twenty cubits, and they stood on their feet [1]facing the *main* room.

14 [a]And he made the veil of violet, purple, crimson and fine linen, and he worked cherubim on it.

15 [a]He also made two pillars for the front of the house, thirty-five cubits [1]high, and the capital on the top of each *was* five cubits.

16 And he made chains in the inner sanctuary, and placed *them* on the tops of the pillars; and he made one hundred pomegranates and placed *them* on the chains.

17 [a]And he erected the pillars in front of the temple, one on the right and the other on the left, and named the one on the right Jachin and the one on the left Boaz.

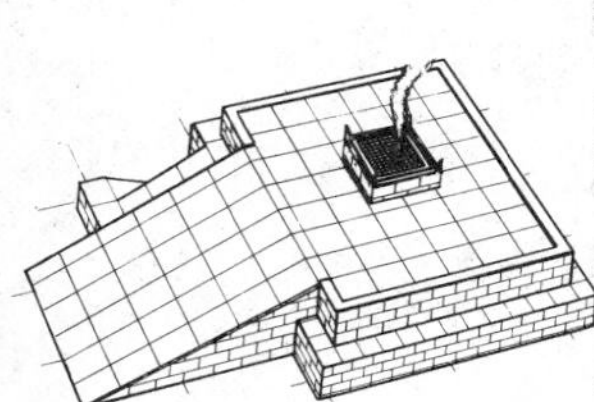
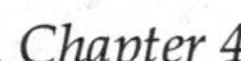

Chapter 4

4 Then [a]he made a bronze altar, twenty cubits in length and twenty cubits in width and ten cubits in height.

2 [a]Also he made the cast *metal* sea, ten cubits from brim to brim, circular in form, and its height *was* five cubits and [1]its circumference thirty cubits.

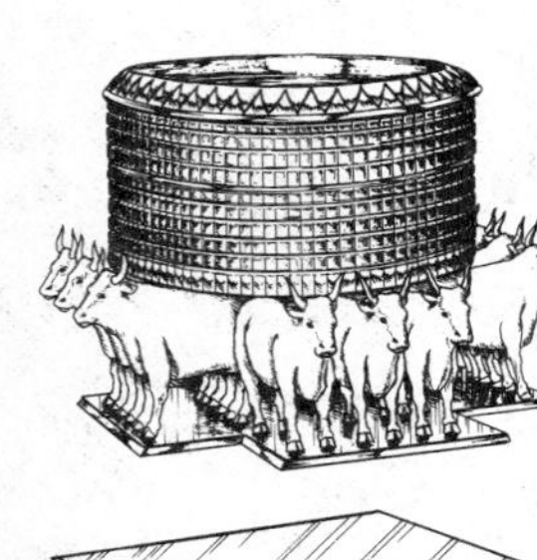

3 Now figures like oxen *were* under it *and* all around it, ten cubits, entirely encircling the sea. The oxen *were* in two rows, cast [1]in one piece.

4 It stood on twelve oxen, three facing the north, three facing west, three facing south, and three facing east; and the sea *was set* on top of them, and all their hindquarters turned inwards.

5 And it was a handbreadth thick, and its brim was made like the brim of a cup, *like* a lily blossom; it [a]could hold 3,000 baths.

6 [a]He also made ten basins in which to wash, and he set five on the right side and five on the left, [1]to rinse things for the burnt offering; but the sea *was* for the priests to wash in.

7 Then [a]he made the ten golden lampstands in the way prescribed for them, and he set them in the temple, five on the right side and five on the left.

8 He also made [a]ten tables and placed them in the temple, five on the right side and five on the left. And he made one hundred golden bowls.

9 Then he made [a]the court of the priests and [b]the great court and doors for the court, and overlaid their doors with bronze.

10 And [a]he set the sea on the right [1]side *of the house* toward the southeast.

11 [a]Huram also made the pails, the shovels, and the bowls. So Huram finished doing the work which he performed for King Solomon in the house of God:

12 the two pillars, the bowls and the two capitals on top of the pillars, and the two networks to cover the two bowls of the capitals which were on top of the pillars,

13 and [a]the four hundred pomegranates for the two networks, two

12 [1]Lit., *other*

13 [1]Lit., *and th faces to*

14 [a]Ex. 26:31

15 [1]Lit., *long* [a] 7:15-20

17 [a]1 Kin. 7:2

4:1 [a]Ex. 27:1, 16:14

2 [1]Lit., *a line c cubits encirclir about* [a]1 Kin.

3 [1]Lit., *in its c*

5 [a]1 Kin. 7:26

6 [1]Lit., *in whi* 30:17-21; 1 Ki

7 [a]Ex. 25:31- 7:49

8 [a]1 Kin. 7:48

9 [a]1 Kin. 6:36 21:5

10 [1]Lit., *shou* [a]1 Kin. 7:39

11 [a]1 Kin. 7:

13 [a]1 Kin. 7:

14 [a]1 Kin. 7:27-43
rows of pomegranates for each network to cover the two bowls of
the capitals which were on the pillars.
14 [a]He also made the stands and he made the basins on the stands,
15 *and* the one sea with the twelve oxen under it.
[a]1 Kin. 7:14; 2 Chr. 2:13
16 And the pails, the shovels, the forks, and all its utensils, [a]Huram-
abi made of polished bronze for King Solomon for the house of the
LORD.
18 [a]1 Kin. 7:47
17 On the plain of the Jordan the king cast them, in the clay ground
between Succoth and Zeredah.
18 [a]Thus Solomon made all these utensils in great quantities, for the
weight of the bronze could not be found out.
19 [a]2 Chr. 4:8
19 Solomon also made all the things that *were* in the house of God:
even the golden altar, [a]the tables with the bread of the Presence on
them,
20 the lampstands with their lamps of pure gold, [a]to burn in front of
20 [a]Ex. 25:31-37; 2 Chr. 5:7
the inner sanctuary in the way prescribed;
21 the flowers, the lamps, and the tongs of gold, of purest gold;
22 and the snuffers, the bowls, the spoons, and the firepans of pure
gold; and the entrance of the house, its inner doors for the holy of
5:1 [1]Lit., *dedicated* gs *of David*, [a]1 Kin. 7:51 [b]2 Sam. 8:11; 1 Chr. 18:11
holies, and the doors of the house, *that is*, of the nave, of gold.

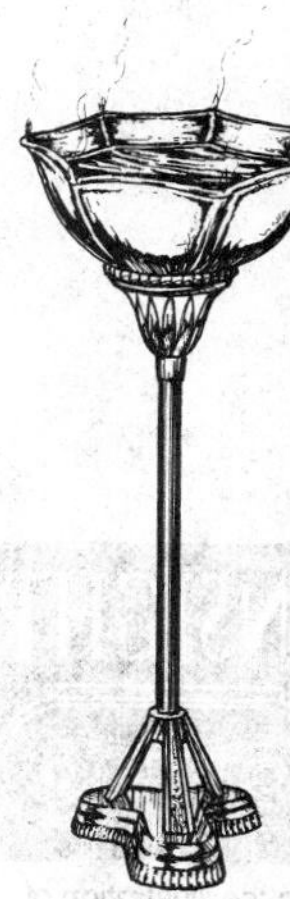

Chapter 5

5 [a]Thus all the work that Solomon performed for the house of the
LORD was finished. And Solomon brought in the [1b]things that
David his father had dedicated, even the silver and the gold and all
Kin. 8:1-9 [b]2 Sam. 6:12-15; 1 Chr. 5:25-28; 2 Chr. 1:4
the utensils, *and* put *them* in the treasuries of the house of God.
2 [a]Then Solomon assembled to Jerusalem the elders of Israel and
all the heads of the tribes, the leaders of the fathers' *households* of the
sons of Israel, [b]to bring up the ark of the covenant of the LORD out of
[a]1 Kin. 8:2 [b]2 Chr. 7:8-10
the city of David, which is Zion.
3 And [a]all the men of Israel assembled themselves to the king at
[b]the feast, that is *in* the seventh month.
4 Then all the elders of Israel came, and [a]the Levites took up the
ark.
osh. 3:6; 2 Chr. 5:7
5 And they brought up the ark and the tent of meeting and all the
holy utensils which *were* in the tent; the Levitical priests brought
them up.
6 [1]Lit., *sheep . . .* *bered for multitude*
6 And King Solomon and all the congregation of Israel who were
assembled with him before the ark were sacrificing [1]so many sheep
and oxen, that they could not be counted or numbered.
7 Then the priests brought the ark of the covenant of the LORD to
[1]Lit., *poles above*
its place, into the inner sanctuary of the house, to the holy of holies,
under the wings of the cherubim. 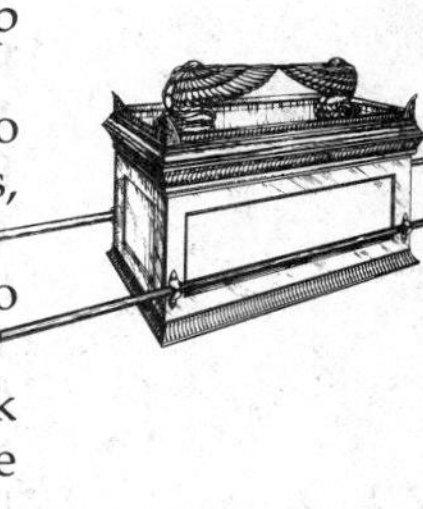
8 For the cherubim spread their wings over the place of the ark, so
that the cherubim made a covering over the ark and its [1]poles.
, *it is* [a]1 Kin. 8:8, 9
9 And the poles were so long that [a]the ends of the poles of the ark
could be seen in front of the inner sanctuary, but they could not be
seen outside; and [1]they are there to this day.
10 [a]There was nothing in the ark except the two tablets which
Deut. 10:2-5; Heb. 9:4
Moses put *there* at Horeb, where the LORD made a covenant with the
sons of Israel, when they came out of Egypt.
11 And when the priests came forth from the holy place (for all the
priests who were present had sanctified themselves, without regard
11 [a]1 Chr. 24:1-5
[a]to divisions),

12 and all the Levitical singers, [a]Asaph, Heman, Jeduthun, and their
sons and kinsmen, clothed in fine linen, [b]with cymbals, harps, and
lyres, standing east of the altar, and with them one hundred and
twenty priests [c]blowing trumpets
13 in unison when the trumpeters and the singers were to make
themselves heard with one voice to praise and to glorify the LORD,
and when they lifted up their voice [a]accompanied by trumpets and
cymbals and instruments of music, and when they praised the LORD
saying, "[b]He indeed is good for His lovingkindness is everlasting,"
then the house, the house of the LORD, was filled with a cloud,
14 so that the priests could not stand to minister because of the
cloud, for [a]the glory of the LORD filled the house of God.

Chapter 6

INSIGHT

See the illustration of Solomon's temple on page I-20.

6 [a]Then Solomon said,
"The LORD has said that He would dwell in the thick cloud.
2 "I have built Thee a lofty house,
And a place for Thy dwelling forever."
3 Then the king [1]faced about and blessed all the assembly of Israel,
while all the assembly of Israel was standing.
4 And he said, "Blessed be the LORD, the God of Israel, who spoke
with His mouth to my father David and has fulfilled *it* with His
hands, saying,
5 'Since the day that I brought My people from the land of Egypt, I
did not choose a city out of all the tribes of Israel *in which* to build a
house that My name might be there, nor did I choose any man for a
leader over My people Israel;
6 but [a]I have chosen Jerusalem that My name might be there, and I
[b]have chosen David to be over My people Israel.'
7 "[a]Now it was [1]in the heart of my father David to build a house for
the name of the LORD, the God of Israel.
8 "But the LORD said to my father David, 'Because it was [1]in your
heart to build a house for My name, you did well that it was [1]in your
heart.
9 'Nevertheless you shall not build the house, but your son who
[1]shall be born to you, he shall build the house for My name.'
10 "Now the LORD has fulfilled His word which He spoke; for I have
risen in the place of my father David and sit on the throne of Israel,
as the LORD [1]promised, and have built the house for the name of the
LORD, the God of Israel.
11 "And there I have set the ark, [a]in which is the covenant of the
LORD, which He made with the sons of Israel."
12 Then he stood before the altar of the LORD in the presence of all
the assembly of Israel and spread out his hands.
13 [a]Now Solomon had made a bronze platform, five cubits long,
five cubits wide, and three cubits high, and had set it in the midst of
the court; and he stood on it, [b]knelt on his knees in the presence of all
the assembly of Israel, and spread out his hands toward heaven.
14 And he said, "O LORD, the God of Israel, [a]there is no god like
Thee in heaven or on earth, [b]keeping covenant and *showing* loving-
kindness to Thy servants who walk before Thee with all their heart;
15 [a]who has kept with Thy servant David, my father, that which
Thou hast [1]promised him; indeed, Thou hast spoken with Thy
mouth, and hast fulfilled it with Thy hand, as it is this day.

12 [a]1 Chr. 25:1 [b]1 Chr. 13:8; 15 [c]2 Chr. 7:6
13 [a]1 Chr. 16:4 [b]1 Chr. 16:34; 2 7:3; Ezra 3:11; 100:5; Jer. 33:1
14 [a]Ex. 40:35; 8:11
6:1 [a]1 Kin. 8:12
3 [1]Lit., *turned h about*
6 [a]2 Chr. 12:13 28:4
7 [1]Lit., *with* [a]1 K 1 Chr. 28:2
8 [1]Lit., *with*
9 [1]Lit., *is to com from your loins*
10 [1]Lit., *spoke*
11 [a]2 Chr. 5:7, 10
13 [a]Neh. 8:4 [b]1 K 8:54
14 [a]Ex. 15:11; De 3:24 [b]Deut. 7:9
15 [1]Lit., *spoken t* [a]1 Chr. 22:9, 10

16 "Now therefore, O LORD, the God of Israel, keep with Thy servant
David, my father, that which Thou hast [1]promised him, saying,
'[2a]You shall not lack a man to sit on the throne of Israel, if only your
sons take heed to their way, to walk in My law as you have walked
before Me.'
17 "Now therefore, O LORD, the God of Israel, let Thy word be con-
firmed which Thou hast spoken to Thy servant David.
18 "But [a]will God indeed dwell with mankind on the earth? Behold,
[b]heaven and the [1]highest heaven cannot contain Thee; how much
less this house which I have built.
19 "Yet have regard to the prayer of Thy servant and to his supplica-
tion, O LORD my God, to listen to the cry and to the prayer which
Thy servant prays before Thee;
20 that Thine [a]eyes may be open toward this house day and night,
toward [b]the place of which Thou hast said that *Thou wouldst* put Thy
name there, to listen to the prayer which Thy servant shall pray
toward this place.
21 "And listen to the supplications of Thy servant and of Thy people
Israel, when they pray toward this place; hear Thou from Thy dwell-
ing place, from heaven; [a]hear Thou and forgive.
22 "If a man sins against his neighbor, and is made to take an oath,
and he comes *and* takes an oath before Thine altar in this house,
23 then hear Thou from heaven and act and judge Thy servants,
[1a]punishing the wicked by bringing his way on his own head and
justifying the righteous by giving him according to his right-
eousness.
24 "And if Thy people Israel [1]are defeated before an enemy, because
[a]they have sinned against Thee, and they return *to Thee* and confess
Thy name, and pray and make supplication before Thee in this
house,
25 then hear Thou from heaven and forgive the sin of Thy people
Israel, and bring them back to the land which Thou hast given to
them and to their fathers.
26 "When the [a]heavens are shut up and there is no rain because they
have sinned against Thee, and they pray toward this place and con-
fess Thy name, and turn from their sin when Thou dost afflict them;
27 then hear Thou in heaven and forgive the sin of Thy servants
and Thy people Israel, indeed, [a]teach them the good way in which
they should walk. And send rain on Thy land, which Thou hast
given to Thy people for an inheritance.
28 "If there is [a]famine in the land, if there is pestilence, if there is
blight or mildew, if there is locust or grasshopper, if their enemies
besiege them in the land of their [1]cities, whatever plague or what-
ever sickness *there is*,
29 whatever prayer or supplication is made by any man or by all
Thy people Israel, [1]each knowing his own affliction and his own
pain, and spreading his hands toward this house,
30 then hear Thou from heaven Thy dwelling place, and forgive,
and render to each according to all his ways, whose heart Thou
knowest [a]for Thou alone dost know the hearts of the sons of men,
31 that they may [1]fear Thee, to walk in Thy ways [2]as long as they
live in the land which Thou hast given to our fathers.
32 "Also concerning [a]the foreigner who is not from Thy people
Israel, when he comes from a far country for Thy great name's sake

...poken to [2]Lit., ...hall not be cut ...ou a man from ...e [a]1 Kin. 2:4; 2 Chr. 7:18

Lit., *heaven of* ... [a]Ps. 113:5, 6 ...r. 2:6; Is. 66:1; Acts 7:49

...s. 33:18; 34:15 [b]Deut. 12:11

... 43:25; 44:22; Mic. 7:18

, returning [a]Is. ...11; Rom. 2:8, 9

...t., *smitten* [a]Ps. 51:4

26 [a]1 Kin. 17:1

27 [a]Ps. 94:12

...t., *gates* [a]2 Chr. 20:9

...t., *whoever shall know*

...Sam. 16:7; 1 Chr. 28:9

, reverence [2]Lit., *...he days that they ...on the face of the land*

32 [a]Is. 56:3-8

and Thy mighty hand and Thine outstretched arm, when they come
and pray toward this house,
33 then hear Thou from heaven, from Thy dwelling place, and do
according to all for which the foreigner calls to Thee, in order that all
the peoples of the earth may know Thy name, and [1]fear Thee, as *do*
Thy people Israel, and that they may know that [2]this house which I
have built is [a]called by Thy name.
34 "When Thy people go out to battle against their enemies, by
whatever way Thou shalt send them, and they pray to Thee toward
this city which Thou hast chosen, and the house which I have built
for Thy name,
35 then hear Thou from heaven their prayer and their supplication,
and maintain their cause.
36 "When they sin against Thee ([a]for there is no man who does not
sin) and Thou art angry with them and dost deliver them to an
enemy, so that [1]they take them away captive to a land far off or near,
37 if they [1]take thought in the land where they are taken captive,
and repent and make supplication to Thee in the land of their cap-
tivity, saying, 'We have sinned, we have committed iniquity, and
have acted wickedly';
38 [a]if they return to Thee with all their heart and with all their soul
in the land of their captivity, where they have been taken captive,
and pray toward their land which Thou hast given to their fathers,
and the city which Thou hast chosen, and toward the house which I
have built for Thy name,
39 then hear from heaven, from Thy dwelling place, their prayer
and supplications, and maintain their cause, and forgive Thy people
who have sinned against Thee.
40 "Now, O my God, I pray Thee, [a]let Thine eyes be open, and [b]Thine
ears attentive to the prayer *offered* in this place.
41 "[a]Now therefore arise, O LORD God, to Thy resting place, Thou
and the ark of Thy might; let Thy priests, O LORD God, be clothed
with salvation, and let Thy godly ones rejoice in what is good.
42 "O LORD God, do not turn away the face of Thine anointed;
[a]remember *Thy* lovingkindness to Thy servant David."

Chapter 7

7 [a]Now when Solomon had finished praying, [b]fire came down
from heaven and consumed the burnt offering and the sacrifices;
and the glory of the LORD filled the house.
2 And [a]the priests could not enter into the house
of the LORD, because the glory of the LORD filled the
LORD'S house.
3 And all the sons of Israel, seeing the fire come
down and the glory of the LORD upon the house,
bowed down on the pavement with their faces to
the ground, and they worshiped and gave praise to
the LORD, *saying*, "[a]Truly He is good, truly His
lovingkindness is everlasting."
4 [a]Then the king and all the people offered
sacrifice before the LORD.
5 And King Solomon offered a sacrifice of 22,000
oxen, and 120,000 sheep. Thus the king and all the
people dedicated the house of God.
6 And the priests stood at their posts and [a]the

Solomon's Temple: Place of Sacrifice

33 [1]Or, *revere* ... *Thy name is c*... *this house* [a]2 ...
36 [1]Lit., *their* ... *take them cap*... 15:14-16; Jam... 1 John 1:8-10
37 [1]Lit., *return* ... *heart*
38 [a]Jer. 29:12, ...
40 [a]2 Chr. 7:15 ... 1:6, 11 [b]Ps. 17 ...
41 [a]Ps. 132:8, ...
42 [a]Ps. 89:24, ... 132:10-12; Is. 5...
7:1 [a]1 Kin. 8:54 ... 9:23f.; 1 Kin. 18 ...
2 [a]2 Chr. 5:14
3 [a]2 Chr. 5:13; 2...
4 [a]1 Kin. 8:62, 6...
6 [1]Lit., *David*

Levites, with the instruments of music to the LORD, which King
David had made for giving praise to the LORD—"for His loving-
kindness is everlasting"—whenever [1]he gave praise by their [2]means,
while [b]the priests on the other side blew trumpets; and all Israel was
standing.
7 [a]Then Solomon consecrated the middle of the court that *was*
before the house of the LORD, for there he offered the burnt offerings
and the fat of the peace offerings, because the bronze altar which
Solomon had made was not able to contain the burnt offering, the
grain offering, and the fat.
8 So [a]Solomon observed the feast at that time for seven days, and
all Israel with him, a very great assembly, *who came* from the
entrance of Hamath to the [b]brook of Egypt.
9 And on the eighth day they held [a]a solemn assembly, for the
dedication of the altar they observed seven days, and the feast seven
days.
10 Then on the twenty-third day of the seventh month he sent the
people to their tents, rejoicing and happy of heart because of the
goodness that the LORD had shown to David and to Solomon and to
His people Israel.
11 [a]Thus Solomon finished the house of the LORD and the king's
palace, and successfully completed all that [1]he had planned on doing
in the house of the LORD and in his palace.
12 Then the LORD appeared to Solomon at night and said to him, "I
have heard your prayer, and [a]have chosen this place for Myself as a
house of sacrifice.
13 "[a]If I shut up the heavens so that there is no rain, or if I command
the locust to devour the land, or if I send pestilence among My
people,
14 [a]and My people [1]who are called by My name humble themselves
and pray, and seek My face and turn from their wicked ways, then I
will hear from heaven, will forgive their sin, and will heal their land.
15 "[a]Now My eyes shall be open and My ears attentive to the [1]prayer
offered in this place.
16 "For [a]now I have chosen and consecrated this house that My
name may be there forever, and My eyes and My heart will be there
perpetually.
17 "And as for you, if you walk before Me as your father David
walked even to do according to all that I have commanded you and
will keep My statutes and My ordinances,
18 then I will establish your royal throne as I covenanted with your
father David, saying, '[1a]You shall not lack a man *to be* ruler in Israel.'
19 "[a]But if you turn away and forsake My statutes and My com-
mandments which I have set before you and shall go and serve other
gods and worship them,
20 [a]then I will uproot you from My land which I have given [1]you,
and this house which I have consecrated for My name I will cast out
of My sight, and I will make it [b]a proverb and a byword among all
peoples.
21 "As for this house, which was exalted, everyone who passes by it
will be astonished and say, '[a]Why has the LORD done thus to this
land and to this house?'
22 "And they will say, 'Because [a]they forsook the LORD, the God of
their fathers, who brought them from the land of Egypt, and they

[2]Lit., *hand* [a]1 Chr. :16-21 [b]2 Chr. 5:12
7 [a]1 Kin. 8:64-66
[a]1 Kin. 8:65 [b]Gen. 15:18
9 [a]Lev. 23:36
Lit., *came upon the* *rt of Solomon to do* [a]1 Kin. 9:1-9
12 [a]Deut. 12:5, 11
13 [a]2 Chr. 6:26-28
.it., *over whom My* *ne is called* [a]2 Chr. 37-39; James 4:10
[1]Lit., *prayer of this* *ce* [a]2 Chr. 6:20, 40
16 [a]2 Chr. 7:12
it., *There shall not* *ut off to you a man* n. 2:4; 2 Chr. 6:16
9 [a]Lev. 26:14, 33; Deut. 28:15
[1]Ancient versions d Heb. read *them* Deut. 29:28; 1 Kin. 4:15 [b]Deut. 28:37
[a]Deut. 29:24-27
22 [a]Judg. 2:13

adopted other gods and worshiped them and served them, therefore
He has brought all this adversity on them.' "

Chapter 8

8 [a]Now it came about at the end of the twenty years in which
Solomon had built the house of the LORD and his own house
2 that he built the cities which Huram had given to [1]him, and
settled the sons of Israel there.
3 Then Solomon went to Hamath-zobah and captured it.
4 And he built Tadmor in the wilderness and all the storage cities
which he had built in Hamath.
5 He also built upper [a]Beth-horon and lower Beth-horon, [b]fortified
cities *with* walls, gates, and bars;
6 and Baalath and all the storage cities that Solomon had, and all
the cities for [1]his chariots and cities for [1]his horsemen, and all that it
pleased Solomon to build in Jerusalem, in Lebanon, and in all the
land [2]under his rule.
7 [a]All of the people who were left of the Hittites, the Amorites, the
Perizzites, the Hivites, and the Jebusites, who were not of Israel,
8 namely, from their descendants who were left after them in the
land whom the sons of Israel had not destroyed, [a]them Solomon
raised as forced laborers to this day.
9 But Solomon did not make slaves for his work from the sons of
Israel; they were men of war, his chief captains, and commanders of
his chariots and his horsemen.
10 And these were the chief [1]officers of King Solomon, two hundred
and fifty who ruled over the people.
11 [a]Then Solomon brought Pharaoh's daughter up from the city of
David to the house which he had built for her; for he said, "My wife
shall not dwell in the house of David king of Israel, because [1]the
places are holy where the ark of the LORD has entered."
12 Then Solomon offered burnt offerings to the LORD on [a]the altar of
the LORD which he had built before the porch;
13 and [a]*did so* according to the daily rule, offering *them* up [b]accord-
ing to the commandment of Moses, for [c]the sabbaths, [d]the new
moons, and the [e]three annual feasts—the Feast of Unleavened Bread,
the Feast of Weeks, and the Feast of Booths.
14 Now according to the ordinance of his father David, he ap-
pointed [a]the divisions of the priests for their service, and [b]the Levites
for their duties of praise and ministering before the priests according
to the daily rule, and [c]the gatekeepers by their divisions at every
gate; for [d]David the man of God had so commanded.
15 And they did not depart from the commandment of the king to
the priests and Levites in any manner or concerning the storehouses.
16 Thus all the work of Solomon was carried out [1]from the day of
the foundation of the house of the LORD, and until it was finished. So
the house of the LORD was completed.
17 Then Solomon went to [a]Ezion-geber and to [b]Eloth on the
seashore in the land of Edom.
18 And Huram by his servants sent him ships and servants who
knew the sea; and they went with Solomon's servants to Ophir, and
[a]took from there four hundred and fifty talents of gold, and brought
them to King Solomon.

8:1 [a]1 Kin. 9:10
2 [1]Lit., *Solomo*
5 [a]1 Chr. 7:24 14:7
6 [1]Lit., *the* [2]Lit
7 [a]Gen. 15:18- 1 Kin. 9:20
8 [a]1 Kin. 4:6; 9
10 [1]Or, *deputi*
11 [1]Lit., *they a* [a]1 Kin. 3:1; 7:8
12 [a]2 Chr. 4:1
13 [a]Ex. 29:38 [b]Num. 28:3 [c]N 10 [d]Num. 28: 23:14-17; 34:2 Deut. 16:16
14 [a]1 Chr. 24 25:1 [c]1 Chr. 2 12:24, 36
16 [1]So ancie versions; M.T
17 [a]1 Kin. 9:2 14:22
18 [a]2 Chr. 9:

9:1 [a]1 Kin. 10:1-13; . 12:42; Luke 11:31

[1]Lit., told her all her words [2]Lit., tell

r, his burnt offering which he offered

7 [1]Or, happy

[a]1 Chr. 28:5; 29:23 ut. 7:8; 2 Chr. 2:11

Kin. 10:11; 2 Chr. 8:18

3 [a]1 Kin. 10:14-28

[a]Ps. 68:29; 72:10

.it., he brought up

.it., he brought up

t., hands [2]Lit., on side and on this at place of the seat

Chapter 9

9 [a]Now when the queen of Sheba heard of the fame of Solomon,
she came to Jerusalem to test Solomon with difficult questions.
She had a very large retinue, with camels carrying spices, and a large
amount of gold and precious stones; and when she came to Solo-
mon, she spoke with him about all that was on her heart.
2 And Solomon [1]answered all her questions; nothing was hidden
from Solomon which he did not [2]explain to her.
3 And when the queen of Sheba had seen the wisdom of Solomon,
the house which he had built,
4 the food at his table, the seating of his servants, the attendance of
his ministers and their attire, his cupbearers and their attire, and [1]his
stairway by which he went up to the house of the LORD, she was
breathless.
5 Then she said to the king, "It was a true report which I heard in
my own land about your words and your wisdom.
6 "Nevertheless I did not believe their reports until I came and my
eyes had seen it. And behold, the half of the greatness of your wis-
dom was not told me. You surpass the report that I heard.
7 "How [1]blessed are your men, how [1]blessed are these your ser-
vants who stand before you continually and hear your wisdom.
8 "Blessed be the LORD your God who delighted in you, [a]setting you
on His throne as king for the LORD your God; [b]because your God
loved Israel establishing them forever, therefore He made you king
over them, to do justice and righteousness."
9 Then she gave the king one hundred and twenty talents of gold,
and a very great *amount of* spices and precious stones; there had
never been spice like that which the queen of Sheba gave to King
Solomon.
10 And the servants of Huram and the servants of Solomon [a]who
brought gold from Ophir, also brought algum trees and precious
stones.
11 And from the algum the king made steps for the house of the
LORD and for the king's palace, and lyres and harps for the singers;
and none like that was seen before in the land of Judah.
12 And King Solomon gave to the queen of Sheba all her desire
which she requested besides *a return for* what she had brought to the
king. Then she turned and went to her own land with her servants.
13 [a]Now the weight of gold which came to Solomon in one year
was 666 talents of gold,
14 besides that which the traders and merchants brought; and all
[a]the kings of Arabia and the governors of the country brought gold
and silver to Solomon.
15 And King Solomon made 200 large shields of beaten gold,
[1]using 600 *shekels of* beaten gold on each large shield.
16 And *he made* 300 shields of beaten gold, [1]using three hundred
shekels of gold on each shield, and the king put them in the house of
the forest of Lebanon.
17 Moreover, the king made a great throne of ivory and overlaid it
with pure gold.
18 And *there were* six steps to the throne and a footstool in gold
attached to the throne, and [1]arms [2]on each side of the seat, and two
lions standing beside the [1]arms.
19 And twelve lions were standing there on the six steps on the one

side and on the other; nothing like *it* was made for any *other* king-
dom.
20 And all King Solomon's drinking vessels *were* of gold, and all the
vessels of the house of the forest of Lebanon *were* of pure gold; silver
was not considered [1]valuable in the days of Solomon.
21 [a]For the king had ships which went to Tarshish with the servants
of Huram; once every three years the ships of Tarshish came bring-
ing gold and silver, ivory and apes and peacocks.
22 [a]So King Solomon became greater than all the kings of the earth
in riches and wisdom.
23 And all the kings of the earth were seeking the presence of Solo-
mon, to hear his wisdom which God had put in his heart.
24 And [a]they brought every man his gift, articles of silver and gold,
garments, weapons, spices, horses, and mules, so much year by year.
25 Now Solomon had [a]4,000 stalls for horses and chariots and
12,000 horsemen, and he stationed them in the chariot cities and
with the king in Jerusalem.
26 [a]And he was the ruler over all the kings from the Euphrates
River even to the land of the Philistines, and as far as the border of
Egypt.
27 [a]And the king made silver *as common* as stones in Jerusalem, and
he made cedars as plentiful as sycamore trees that are in the
[1]lowland.
28 [a]And they were bringing horses for Solomon from Egypt and
from all countries.
29 [a]Now the rest of the acts of Solomon, from first to last, [b]are they
not written in the [1]records of Nathan the prophet, and in the prophe-
cy of Ahijah the Shilonite, and in the visions of [2]Iddo the seer con-
cerning Jeroboam the son of Nebat?
30 And [a]Solomon reigned forty years in Jerusalem over all Israel.
31 And Solomon slept with his fathers and was buried in [a]the city
of his father David; and his son Rehoboam reigned in his place.

Chapter 10

10 [a]Then Rehoboam went to Shechem, for all Israel had come to
Shechem to make him king.
2 And it came about when Jeroboam the son of Nebat heard *of it*
(for [a]he was in Egypt where he had fled from the presence of King
Solomon), that Jeroboam returned from Egypt.
3 So they sent and summoned him. When Jeroboam and all Israel
came, they spoke to Rehoboam, saying,
4 "Your father made our [a]yoke hard; now therefore lighten the hard
service of your father and his heavy yoke which he put on us, and
we will serve you."
5 And he said to them, "Return to me again in three days." So the
people departed.
6 Then King Rehoboam [a]consulted with the elders who had
[1]served his father Solomon while he was still alive, saying, "How do
you counsel *me* to answer this people?"
7 And they spoke to him, saying, "If you will be kind to this
people and please them and [a]speak good words to them, then they
will be your servants forever."
8 But he [a]forsook the counsel of the elders which they had given

20 [1]Lit., *anythi*
21 [a]2 Chr. 20:3
22 [a]1 Kin. 3:13 1:12
24 [a]Ps. 72:10
25 [a]Deut. 17:1 4:26; 10:26; 2
26 [a]Gen. 15:1 4:21, 24
27 [1]Heb., *she* [a]2 Chr. 1:15-17
28 [a]2 Chr. 1:1
29 [1]Lit., *words* *Jedo* [a]1 Kin. 1 [b]1 Chr. 29:29
30 [a]1 Kin. 11:
31 [a]1 Kin. 2:1
10:1 [a]1 Kin. 1
2 [a]1 Kin. 11:4
4 [a]1 Kin. 5:13
6 [1]Lit., *stood* [a]Job 8:8, 9; 3
7 [a]Prov. 15:1
8 [a]2 Sam. 17 13:20

him, and consulted with the young men who grew up with him [1]and
served him.
9 So he said to them, "What counsel do you give that we may
answer this people, who have spoken to me, saying, 'Lighten the
yoke which your father put on us'?"
10 And the young men who grew up with him spoke to him,
saying, "Thus you shall say to the people who spoke to you, saying,
'Your father made our yoke heavy, but you make it lighter for us.'
Thus you shall say to them, 'My little finger is thicker than my
father's loins!
11 'Whereas my father loaded you with a heavy yoke, I will add to
your yoke; my father disciplined you with whips, but I *will discipline*
you with scorpions.'"
12 So Jeroboam and all the people came to Rehoboam on the third
day as the king had [1]directed, saying, "Return to me on the third
day."
13 And the king answered them harshly, and King Rehoboam for-
sook the counsel of the elders.
14 And he spoke to them according to the advice of the young men,
saying, "[1]My father made your yoke heavy, but I will add to it; my
father disciplined you with whips, but I *will discipline you* with scor-
pions."
15 So the king did not listen to the people, [a]for it was a turn *of events*
from God [b]that the LORD might establish His word, which He spoke
through Ahijah the Shilonite to Jeroboam the son of Nebat.
16 And when all Israel *saw* that the king did not listen to them the
people answered the king, saying,

"[a]What portion do we have in David?
We have no inheritance in the son of Jesse.
Every man to your tents, O Israel;
Now look after your own house, David."

[b]So all Israel departed to their tents.
17 But as for the sons of Israel who lived in the cities of Judah,
Rehoboam reigned over them.
18 Then King Rehoboam sent Hadoram, who was [a]over the forced
labor, and the sons of Israel stoned him [1]to death. And King Reho-
boam made haste to mount his chariot to flee to Jerusalem.
19 So [a]Israel has been in rebellion against the house of David to this
day.

Chapter 11

11 [a]Now when Rehoboam had come to Jerusalem, he assembled
the house of Judah and Benjamin, 180,000 chosen men who
were warriors, to fight against Israel to restore the kingdom to Reho-
boam.
2 But the word of the LORD came to [a]Shemaiah the man of God,
saying,
3 "Speak to Rehoboam the son of Solomon, king of Judah, and to all
Israel in Judah and Benjamin, saying,
4 'Thus says the LORD, "You shall not go up or fight against [a]your
[1]relatives; return every man to his house, [b]for this thing is from
Me."'" So they listened to the words of the LORD and returned from
going against Jeroboam.

[1]Lit., *who stood before*

12 [1]Lit., *spoken*

4 [1]Many mss. read *I have made*

15 [a]2 Chr. 25:16-20 [b]1 Kin. 11:29-39

16 [a]2 Sam. 20:1 [b]2 Chr. 10:19

Lit., *with stones that ed* [a]1 Kin. 4:6; 5:14

19 [a]1 Kin. 12:19

1 [a]1 Kin. 12:21-24

[a]2 Chr. 12:5-7, 15

., *brothers* [a]2 Chr. 8-11 [b]2 Chr. 10:15

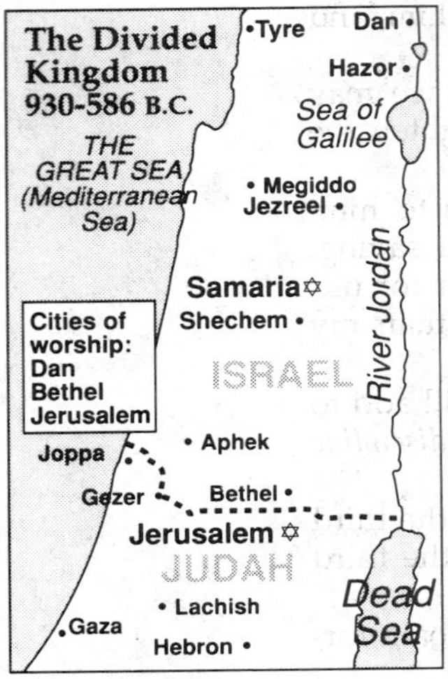

5 Rehoboam lived in Jerusalem and [a]built cities for
defense in Judah.
6 Thus he built Bethlehem, Etam, Tekoa,
7 Beth-zur, Soco, Adullam,
8 Gath, Mareshah, Ziph,
9 Adoraim, Lachish, Azekah,
10 Zorah, Aijalon, and Hebron, which are fortified cities
in Judah and in Benjamin.
11 He also strengthened the fortresses and put officers in
them and stores of food, oil and wine.
12 And *he put* shields and spears in every city and
strengthened them greatly. So he held Judah and Ben-
jamin.
13 Moreover, the priests and the Levites who were in all
Israel stood with him from all their districts.
14 For [a]the Levites left their pasture lands and their
property and came to Judah and Jerusalem, for [b]Jeroboam
and his sons had excluded them from serving as priests to
the LORD.
15 And [a]he set up priests of his own for the high places, for the
satyrs, and for the calves which he had made.
16 And [a]those from all the tribes of Israel who set their hearts on
seeking the LORD God of Israel, [1]followed them to Jerusalem to
sacrifice to the LORD God of their fathers.
17 [a]And they strengthened the kingdom of Judah and supported
Rehoboam the son of Solomon for three years, for they walked in the
way of David and Solomon for three years.
18 Then Rehoboam took as a wife Mahalath the daughter of
Jerimoth the son of David *and of* Abihail the daughter of [a]Eliab the
son of Jesse,
19 and she bore him sons: Jeush, Shemariah, and Zaham.
20 And after her he took [a]Maacah the daughter of [1]Absalom, and
she bore him Abijah, Attai, Ziza, and Shelomith.
21 And Rehoboam loved Maacah the daughter of Absalom more
than all his *other* wives and concubines. For [a]he had taken eighteen
wives and sixty concubines and fathered twenty-eight sons and sixty
daughters.
22 And [a]Rehoboam appointed Abijah the son of Maacah as head
and leader among his brothers, for he *intended* to make him king.
23 And he acted wisely and distributed [1]some of his sons through
all the territories of Judah and Benjamin to all the fortified cities, and
he gave them food in abundance. And he sought many wives *for
them*.

Chapter 12

12 It took place [a]when the kingdom of Rehoboam was estab-
lished and strong that [b]he and all Israel with him forsook the
law of the LORD.
2 [a]And it came about in King Rehoboam's fifth year, because they
had been unfaithful to the LORD, that [b]Shishak king of Egypt came
up against Jerusalem
3 with 1,200 chariots and 60,000 horsemen. And the people who
came with him from Egypt were without number: [a]the Lubim, the
Sukkiim, and the Ethiopians.

5 [a]2 Chr. 8:2-6;
14 [a]Num. 35:2-
[b]1 Kin. 12:28-33
13:9
15 [a]1 Kin. 12:31
16 [1]Lit., *came a*
[a]2 Chr. 15:9
17 [a]2 Chr. 12:1
18 [a]1 Sam. 16:
20 [1]In 1 Kin. 15
Abishalom [a]1 K
2 Chr. 13:2
21 [a]Deut. 17:1
22 [a]Deut. 21:1
23 [1]Lit., *from a*
12:1 [a]2 Chr. 1
12:13 [b]2 Chr.
2 [a]1 Kin. 14:2
11:40
3 [a]2 Chr. 16:8

4 And he captured [a]the fortified cities of Judah and came as far as
Jerusalem.
5 Then [a]Shemaiah the prophet came to Rehoboam and the princes
of Judah who had gathered at Jerusalem because of Shishak, and he
said to them, "Thus says the LORD, '[b]You have forsaken Me, so I also
have forsaken you [1]to Shishak.' "
6 So the princes of Israel and the king humbled themselves and
said, "The [a]LORD is righteous."
7 And when the LORD saw that they humbled themselves, the
word of the LORD came to Shemaiah, saying, "[a]They have humbled
themselves so I will not destroy them, but I will grant them some
measure of deliverance, and [b]My wrath shall not be poured out on
Jerusalem by means of Shishak.
8 "But they will become his slaves so [a]that they may learn *the dif-
ference between* My service and the service of the kingdoms of the
countries."
9 [a]So Shishak king of Egypt came up against Jerusalem, and took
the treasures of the house of the LORD and the treasures of the king's
palace. He took everything; [b]he even took the golden shields which
Solomon had made.
10 Then King Rehoboam made shields of bronze in their place, and
committed them to the [1]care of the commanders of the [2]guard who
guarded the door of the king's house.
11 And it happened as often as the king entered the house of the
LORD, the [1]guards came and carried them and *then* brought them
back into the [1]guards' room.
12 And [a]when he humbled himself, the anger of the LORD turned
away from him, so as not to destroy *him* completely; and also condi-
tions [b]were good in Judah.
13 [a]So King Rehoboam strengthened himself in Jerusalem, and
reigned. Now Rehoboam was forty-one years old when he began to
reign, and he reigned seventeen years in Jerusalem, the city which
the LORD had chosen from all the tribes of Israel, to put His name
there. And his mother's name was Naamah the Ammonitess.
14 And he did evil [a]because he did not set his heart to seek the
LORD.
15 [a]Now the acts of Rehoboam, from first to last, are they not writ-
ten in the [1]records of [b]Shemaiah the prophet and of [c]Iddo the seer,
according to genealogical enrollment? And *there were* wars between
Rehoboam and Jeroboam continually.
16 And Rehoboam slept with his fathers, and was buried in the city
of David; and his son [a]Abijah became king in his place.

Chapter 13

13 [a]In the eighteenth year of King Jeroboam, Abijah became king
over Judah.
2 He reigned three years in Jerusalem; and his mother's name was
Micaiah the daughter of Uriel of Gibeah. [a]And there was war be-
tween Abijah and Jeroboam.
3 And Abijah began the battle with an army of valiant warriors,
400,000 chosen men, while Jeroboam drew up in battle formation
against him with 800,000 chosen men *who were* valiant warriors.
4 Then Abijah stood on Mount [a]Zemaraim, which is in the hill
country of Ephraim, and said, "Listen to me, Jeroboam and all Israel:

4 [a]2 Chr. 11:5-12
[1]Lit., *in the hand of* [a]2 Chr. 11:2 [b]Deut. 28:15; 2 Chr. 15:2
[a]Ex. 9:27; Dan. 9:14
[a]1 Kin. 21:29 [b]2 Chr. 34:25-27; Ps. 78:38
8 [a]Deut. 28:47, 48
9 [a]1 Kin. 14:26-28 [b]1 Kin. 10:16, 17; 2 Chr. 9:15, 16
10 [1]Lit., *hands* [2]Lit., *runners*
11 [1]Lit., *runners*
12 [a]2 Chr. 12:6, 7 [b]2 Chr. 19:3
13 [a]1 Kin. 14:21
14 [a]2 Chr. 19:3
[1]Lit., *words* [a]1 Kin. 14:29 [b]2 Chr. 12:5 [c]2 Chr. 9:29
16 [a]2 Chr. 11:20
13:1 [a]1 Kin. 15:1, 2
2 [a]1 Kin. 15:7
4 [a]Josh. 18:22

5 "Do you not know that [a]the LORD God of Israel gave the rule over
Israel forever to David [1]and his sons by [b]a covenant of salt?
6 "Yet [a]Jeroboam the son of Nebat, the servant of Solomon the son
of David, rose up and rebelled against his [1]master,
7 and worthless men gathered about him, scoundrels, who proved
too strong for Rehoboam, the son of Solomon, when [1a]he was young
and timid and could not hold his own against them.
8 "So now you intend to resist the kingdom of the LORD [1]through
the sons of David, [2]being a great multitude and *having* with you [a]the
golden calves which Jeroboam made for gods for you.
9 "[a]Have you not driven out the priests of the LORD, the sons of
Aaron and the Levites, and made for yourselves priests like the
peoples of *other* lands? Whoever comes [b]to consecrate himself with a
young bull and seven rams, even he may become a priest of *what are*
[c]no gods.
10 "But as for us, the LORD is our God, and we have not forsaken
Him; and the sons of Aaron are ministering to the LORD as priests,
and the Levites [1]attend to their work.
11 "And every morning and evening [a]they [1]burn to the LORD burnt
offerings and fragrant incense, and [b]the showbread is *set* on the clean
table, and the golden lampstand with its lamps is *ready* to light every
evening; for we keep the charge of the LORD our God, but you have
forsaken Him.
12 "Now behold, God is with us at *our* head and [a]His priests with the
signal trumpets to sound the alarm against you. O sons of Israel, do
not fight against the LORD God of your fathers, for you will not
succeed."
13 But Jeroboam [a]had set an ambush to come from the rear, so that
Israel was in front of Judah, and the ambush was behind them.
14 When Judah turned around, behold, [1]they were attacked both
front and rear; so [a]they cried to the LORD, and the priests blew the
trumpets.
15 Then the men of Judah raised a war cry, and when the men of
Judah raised the war cry, then it was that God [1a]routed Jeroboam and
all Israel before Abijah and Judah.
16 And when the sons of Israel fled before Judah, [a]God gave them
into their hand.
17 And Abijah and his people defeated them with a great slaughter,
so that 500,000 chosen men of Israel fell slain.
18 Thus the sons of Israel were subdued at that time, and the sons
of Judah [1]conquered [a]because they trusted in the LORD, the God of
their fathers.
19 And Abijah pursued Jeroboam, and captured from him *several*
cities, Bethel with its villages, Jeshanah with its villages, and
[1]Ephron with its villages.
20 And Jeroboam did not again recover strength in the days of
Abijah; and the [a]LORD struck him and [b]he died.
21 But Abijah became powerful, and took fourteen wives to
himself; and became the father of twenty-two sons and sixteen
daughters.
22 Now the rest of the acts of Abijah, and his ways and his words
are written in [a]the [1]treatise of [b]the prophet Iddo.

5 [1]Lit., *to him a* *sons* [a]2 Sam. 7 [b]Lev. 2:13; Num

6 [1]Or, *lord* [a]1 K

7 [1]Lit., *Rehobo* [a]2 Chr. 12:13

8 [1]Lit., *in the h* [2]Lit., *and you a* [a]1 Kin. 12:28; 2 11:15

9 [a]2 Chr. 11:14 29:29-33 [c]Jer.

10 [1]Lit., *in the*

11 [1]Lit., *offer u* *smoke* [a]Ex. 29 2 Chr. 2:4 [b]Ex. 25:30-39; Lev.

12 [a]Num. 10:8

13 [a]Josh. 8:4-

14 [1]Lit., *the ba* *before and beh* [a]2 Chr. 14:11

15 [1]Lit., *smote* 14:12

16 [a]2 Chr. 16:

18 [1]Lit., *were* [a]2 Chr. 14:11

19 [1]Another re *Ephrain*

20 [a]1 Sam. 25 [b]1 Kin. 14:20

22 [1]Heb., *mid* [a]2 Chr. 24:27 9:29

14:1 [1]Ch. 13:23 in Heb. [a]1 Kin. 15:8

Chapter 14

[1]Ch. 14:1 in Heb.

14 [1a]So Abijah slept with his fathers, and they buried him in the city of David, and his son Asa became king in his place. The land was undisturbed for ten years during his days.

2 [1]And Asa did good and right in the sight of the LORD his God,

3 [1]I.e., wooden ...mbols of a female [a]Deut. 7:5 [b]1 Kin. ...:12-14 [c]Ex. 34:13

3 for he removed [a]the foreign altars and [b]high places, tore down the *sacred* pillars, cut down the [1c]Asherim,

4 and commanded Judah to seek the LORD God of their fathers and to observe the law and the commandment.

5 [a]2 Chr. 34:4, 7

5 He also removed the high places and the [a]incense altars from all the cities of Judah. And the kingdom was undisturbed under him.

...Lit., *there was not ...th him war* [a]2 Chr. ...1:5 [b]2 Chr. 15:15

6 And [a]he built fortified cities in Judah, since the land was undisturbed, and [1]there was no one at war with him during those years, [b]because the LORD had given him rest.

7 [1]Lit., *before us* [a]2 Chr. 8:5

7 For he said to Judah, "[a]Let us build these cities and surround *them* with walls and towers, gates and bars. The land is still [1]ours, because we have sought the LORD our God; we have sought Him, and He has given us rest on every side." So they built and prospered.

8 [a]2 Chr. 13:3

8 Now Asa had an army of [a]300,000 from Judah, bearing large shields and spears, and 280,000 from Benjamin, bearing shields and wielding bows; all of them were valiant warriors.

...Chr. 12:2, 3; 16:8 [b]2 Chr. 11:8

9 Now Zerah the Ethiopian [a]came out against them with an army of a million men and 300 chariots, and he came to [b]Mareshah.

...) [1]Lit., *before him*

10 So Asa went out [1]to meet him, and they drew up in battle formation in the valley of Zephathah at Mareshah.

11 [a]2 Chr. 13:14 [b]2 Chr. 13:18

11 Then Asa [a]called to the LORD his God, and said, "LORD, there is no one besides Thee to help *in the battle* between the powerful and those who have no strength; so help us, O LORD our God, [b]for we trust in Thee, and in Thy name have come against this multitude. O LORD, Thou art our God; let not man prevail against Thee."

...Lit., *struck* [a]2 Chr. 13:15

12 So [a]the LORD [1]routed the Ethiopians before Asa and before Judah, and the Ethiopians fled.

...r, *there was none alive* [a]Gen. 10:19

13 And Asa and the people who *were* with him pursued them as far as [a]Gerar; and so many Ethiopians fell that [1]they could not recover, for they were shattered before the LORD, and before His army. And they carried away very much plunder.

...it., *smote* [a]2 Chr. 17:10

14 And they [1]destroyed all the cities around Gerar, [a]for the dread of the LORD had fallen on them; and they despoiled all the cities, for there was much plunder in them.

15 [1]Lit., *tents of livestock*

15 They also struck down [1]those who owned livestock, and they carried away large numbers of sheep and camels. Then they returned to Jerusalem.

...:1 [a]2 Chr. 20:14; 24:20

Chapter 15

[1]Lit., *before Asa* ...hr. 20:17 [b]2 Chr. 15:4, 15

15 Now [a]the Spirit of God came on Azariah the son of Oded,

2 and he went out [1]to meet Asa and said to him, "Listen to me, Asa, and all Judah and Benjamin: [a]the LORD is with you when you are with Him. And [b]if you seek Him, He will let you find Him; but if you forsake Him, He will forsake you.

[a]1 Kin. 12:28-33 ...v. 10:8-11; 2 Chr. 17:9

3 "And [a]for many days Israel was without the true God and without [b]a teaching priest and without law.

4 "But [a]in their distress they turned to the LORD God of Israel, and
they sought Him, and He let them find Him.
5 "[a]And in those times there was no peace to him who went out or
to him who came in, for many disturbances [1]afflicted all the in-
habitants of the lands.
6 "And [a]nation was crushed by nation, and city by city, for God
troubled them with every kind of distress.
7 "But you, [a]be strong and do not [1]lose courage, for there is [b]reward
for your work."
8 Now when Asa heard these words and the [1]prophecy which
Azariah the son of Oded the prophet spoke, he took courage and
removed the abominable idols from all the land of Judah and Ben-
jamin and from [a]the cities which he had captured in the hill country
of Ephraim. [b]He then restored the altar of the LORD which was in
front of the porch of the LORD.
9 And he gathered all Judah and Benjamin and those from
Ephraim, Manasseh, and Simeon [a]who resided with them, for many
defected to him from Israel when they saw that the LORD his God
was with him.
10 So they assembled at Jerusalem in the third month of the fif-
teenth year of Asa's reign.
11 And [a]they sacrificed to the LORD that day 700 oxen and 7,000
sheep from the spoil they had brought.
12 And [a]they entered into the covenant to seek the LORD God of
their fathers with all their heart and soul;
13 and whoever would not seek the LORD God of Israel [a]should be
put to death, whether small or great, man or woman.
14 Moreover, they made an oath to the LORD with a loud voice, with
shouting, with trumpets, and with horns.
15 And all Judah rejoiced concerning the oath, for they had sworn
with their whole heart and had sought Him [1]earnestly, and He let
them find Him. So [a]the LORD gave them rest on every side.
16 [a]And he also removed Maacah, the mother of King Asa, from the
position of queen mother, because she had made a horrid image [1]as
[b]an Asherah, and [c]Asa cut down her horrid image, crushed *it* and
burned *it* at the brook Kidron.
17 But the high places were not removed from Israel; nevertheless
Asa's heart was blameless all his days.
18 And he brought into the house of God the dedicated things of
his father and his own dedicated things: silver and gold and utensils.
19 And there was no more war until the thirty-fifth year of Asa's
reign.

Chapter 16

16 In the thirty-sixth year of Asa's reign [a]Baasha king of Israel
came up against Judah and [1]fortified Ramah in order to
prevent *anyone* from going out or coming in to Asa king of Judah.
2 Then Asa brought out silver and gold from the treasuries of the
house of the LORD and the king's house, and sent them to Ben-hadad
king of Aram, who lived in Damascus, saying,
3 "*Let there be* a treaty between [1]you and me, *as* between my father
and your father. Behold, I have sent you silver and gold; go, break
your treaty with Baasha king of Israel so that he will withdraw from
me."

4 [a]Deut. 4:29
5 [1]Lit., *were o*
5:6
6 [a]Matt. 24:7
7 [1]Lit., *let you*
drop [a]Josh. 1
58:11
8 [1]With sever
versions; Heb
prophecy, Ode
prophet [a]2 Ch
[b]2 Chr. 4:1; 8:
9 [a]2 Chr. 11:1
11 [a]2 Chr. 14
12 [a]2 Chr. 23
13 [a]Ex. 22:20
13:6-9
15 [1]Lit., *with*
desire [a]2 Chr
16 [1]Or, *for A*
[a]1 Kin. 15:13-
34:13 [c]2 Chr.
16:1 [1]Lit., *bu*
15:17-22
3 [1]Lit., *me a*

4 So Ben-hadad listened to King Asa and sent the commanders of
his armies against the cities of Israel, and they [1]conquered Ijon, Dan,
Abel-maim, and all [a]the [2]store cities of Naphtali.
5 And it came about when Baasha heard *of it* that he ceased [1]for-
tifying Ramah and stopped his work.
6 Then King Asa brought all Judah, and they carried away the
stones of Ramah and its timber with which Baasha had been build-
ing, and with them he [1]fortified Geba and Mizpah.
7 At that time [a]Hanani the seer came to Asa king of Judah and said
to him, "[b]Because you have relied on the king of Aram and have not
relied on the LORD your God, therefore the army of the king of Aram
has escaped out of your hand.
8 "Were not [a]the Ethiopians and the Lubim [b]an immense army with
very many chariots and horsemen? Yet, [c]because you relied on the
LORD, He delivered them into your hand.
9 "For [a]the eyes of the LORD move to and fro throughout the earth
that He may strongly support those [b]whose heart is completely His.
You have acted foolishly in this. Indeed, from now on you will sure-
ly have wars."
10 Then Asa was angry with the seer and put him in [1]prison, for he
was enraged at him for this. And Asa oppressed some of the people
at the same time.
11 [a]And now, the acts of Asa from first to last, behold, they are
written in the Book of the Kings of Judah and Israel.
12 And in the thirty-ninth year of his reign Asa became diseased in
his feet. His disease was severe, yet even in his disease he [a]did not
seek the LORD, but the physicians.
13 So Asa slept with his fathers, [1]having died in the forty-first year
of his reign.
14 And they buried him in his own tomb which he had cut out for
himself in the city of David, and they laid him in the resting place
which he had filled [a]with spices of various kinds blended by the
perfumers' art; and [b]they made a very great fire for him.

Chapter 17

17 [a]Jehoshaphat his son then became king in his place, and made
his position over Israel firm.
2 He placed troops in all [a]the fortified cities of Judah, and set gar-
risons in the land of Judah, and in the cities of Ephraim [b]which Asa
his father had captured.
3 And the LORD was with Jehoshaphat because he [1]followed the
example of his father David's earlier days and did not seek the Baals,
4 but sought the God of his father, [1]followed His commandments,
[a]and did not act as Israel did.
5 So the LORD established the kingdom in his [1]control, and all
Judah brought tribute to Jehoshaphat, and [a]he had great riches and
honor.
6 And [1]he took great pride in the ways of the LORD and again
[a]removed the high places and the Asherim from Judah.
7 Then in the third year of his reign he sent his officials, Ben-hail,
Obadiah, Zechariah, Nethanel, and Micaiah, [a]to teach in the cities of
Judah;
8 and with them [a]the Levites, Shemaiah, Nethaniah, Zebadiah,

[1]Lit., *smote* [2]Lit., *...rage places of the cities* [a]Ex. 1:11
5 [1]Lit., *building*
6 [1]Lit., *built*
[a]1 Kin. 16:1; 2 Chr. ...9:2 [b]2 Chr. 14:11; 32:7, 8
...Chr. 14:9 [b]2 Chr. ... [c]2 Chr. 13:16, 18
[a]Prov. 15:3; Jer. 16:17; Zech. 4:10 [b]2 Chr. 15:17
[1]Lit., *the house of the stocks*
[a]1 Kin. 15:23, 24
12 [a]Jer. 17:5
13 [1]Lit., *and*
[a]Gen. 50:2; John ...40 [b]2 Chr. 21:19
...7:1 [a]1 Kin. 15:24
...Chr. 11:5 [b]2 Chr. 15:8
...Lit., *walked in the ways of his father*
4 [1]Lit., *walked in* [a]1 Kin. 12:28
...Lit., *hand* [a]2 Chr. 18:1
...Lit., *his heart was ...igh* [a]2 Chr. 15:17
[a]2 Chr. 15:3; 35:3
8 [a]2 Chr. 19:8

Asahel, Shemiramoth, Jehonathan, Adonijah, Tobijah, and Tobadoni- 9 [a]Deut. 6:4-9
jah, the Levites; and with them Elishama and Jehoram, the priests.
9 And they taught in Judah, *having* [a]the book of the law of the
LORD with them; and they went throughout all the cities of Judah
and taught among the people.
10 Now [a]the dread of the LORD was on all the kingdoms of the lands
which *were* around Judah, so that they did not make war against 10 [a]2 Chr. 14:
Jehoshaphat.
11 And some of the Philistines [a]brought gifts and silver as tribute to
Jehoshaphat; the Arabians also brought him flocks, 7,700 rams and
7,700 male goats.
12 So Jehoshaphat grew greater and greater, and he built fortresses
and store cities in Judah.
13 And he had large supplies in the cities of Judah, and warriors, 11 [a]2 Chr. 9:1
valiant men, in Jerusalem.
14 And this was their muster according to their fathers' households:
of Judah, commanders of thousands, Adnah *was* the commander,
and with him 300,000 valiant warriors;
15 and next to him *was* Johanan the commander, and with him
280,000;
16 and next to him Amasiah the son of Zichri, [a]who volunteered for 16 [a]Judg. 5:2
the LORD, and with him 200,000 valiant warriors; 29:9
17 and of Benjamin, Eliada a valiant warrior, and with him 200,000
armed with bow and shield;
18 and next to him Jehozabad, and with him 180,000 equipped for
war.
19 These are they who served the king, apart from [a]those whom the
king put in the fortified cities through all Judah. 19 [a]2 Chr. 17

Chapter 18

18 Now [a]Jehoshaphat had great riches and honor; and he allied
himself by marriage with Ahab.
2 [a]And some years later he went down to *visit* Ahab at Samaria.
And Ahab slaughtered many sheep and oxen for him and the people 18:1 [a]2 Chr. 1
who were with him, and induced him to go up against Ramoth-
gilead.
3 And Ahab king of Israel said to Jehoshaphat king of Judah, "Will
you go with me *against* Ramoth-gilead?" And he said to him, "I am
as you are, and my people as your people, and *we will be* with you in
the battle."
4 Moreover, Jehoshaphat said to the king of Israel, "Please inquire 2 [a]1 Kin. 22:2
[1]first for the word of the LORD."
5 Then the king of Israel assembled the prophets, four hundred
men, and said to them, "Shall we go against Ramoth-gilead to battle,
or shall I refrain?" And they said, "Go up, for God will give *it* into
the hand of the king."
6 But Jehoshaphat said, "Is there not yet a prophet of the LORD 4 [1]Lit., *as the*
here that we may inquire of him?"
7 And the king of Israel said to Jehoshaphat, "There is yet one man
by whom we may inquire of the LORD, but I hate him, for he never
prophesies good concerning me but always evil. He is Micaiah, son
of Imla." But Jehoshaphat said, "Let not the king say so."
8 Then the king of Israel called an officer and said, "[1]Bring quickly
Micaiah, Imla's son." 8 [1]Lit., *Haste*

9 Now the king of Israel and Jehoshaphat the king of Judah were
sitting each on his throne, arrayed in *their* robes, and *they* were sit-
ting [a]at the threshing floor at the entrance of the gate of Samaria; and
all the prophets were prophesying before them.
10 And Zedekiah the son of Chenaanah made horns of iron for
himself and said, "Thus says the LORD, 'With these you shall gore the
Arameans, until they are consumed.' "
11 And all the prophets were prophesying thus, saying, "Go up to
Ramoth-gilead and succeed, for the LORD will give *it* into the hand of
the king."
12 Then the messenger who went to summon Micaiah spoke to him
saying, "Behold, the words of the prophets are uniformly favorable
to the king. So please let your word be like one of them and speak
favorably."
13 But Micaiah said, "As the LORD lives, [a]what my God says, that I
will speak."
14 And when he came to the king, the king said to him, "Micaiah,
shall we go to Ramoth-gilead to battle, or shall I refrain?" He said,
"Go up and succeed, for they will be given into your hand."
15 Then the king said to him, "How many times must I adjure you
to speak to me nothing but the truth in the name of the LORD?"
16 So he said,

"I saw all Israel
Scattered on the mountains,
[a]Like sheep which have no shepherd;
And the LORD said,
'These have no master.
Let each of them return to his house in peace.' "

17 Then the king of Israel said to Jehoshaphat, "Did I not tell you
that he would not prophesy good concerning me, but evil?"
18 And Micaiah said, "Therefore, hear the word of the LORD. [a]I saw
the LORD sitting on His throne, and all the host of heaven standing
on His right and on His left.
19 "And the LORD said, 'Who will entice Ahab king of Israel to go up
and fall at Ramoth-gilead?' And one said this while another said
that.
20 "Then a [a]spirit came forward and stood before the LORD and said,
'I will entice him.' And the LORD said to him, 'How?'
21 "And he said, 'I will go and be [a]a deceiving spirit in the mouth of
all his prophets.' Then He said, 'You are to entice *him* and prevail
also. Go and do so.'
22 "Now therefore, behold, [a]the LORD has put a deceiving spirit in
the mouth of these your prophets; for the LORD has proclaimed di-
saster against you."
23 Then Zedekiah the son of Chenaanah came near and [a]struck
Micaiah on the cheek and said, "[1]How did the Spirit of the LORD pass
from me to speak to you?"
24 And Micaiah said, "Behold, you shall see on that day, when you
enter an inner room to hide yourself."
25 Then the king of Israel said, "[a]Take Micaiah and return him to
Amon [b]the governor of the city, and to Joash the king's son;
26 and say, 'Thus says the king, "[a]Put this *man* in prison, and feed
him [1]sparingly with bread and water until I return safely." ' "

9 [a]Ruth 4:1
22:18-20, 35
27:17; 1 Kin.
"; Ezek. 34:5;
tt. 9:36; Mark
6:34
s. 6:1-5; Dan.
7:9, 10
1:6; 2 Thess.
2:9
21 [a]John 8:44
.14; Ezek. 14:9
Lit., *Which way*
:2; Mark 14:65;
Acts 23:2
hr. 18:8 [b]2 Chr.
34:8
.it., *with bread of*
tion and water of
on [a]2 Chr. 16:10

27 And Micaiah said, "If you indeed return safely, the LORD has not spoken by me." And he said, "[a]Listen, all you people."

28 So the king of Israel and Jehoshaphat king of Judah went up against Ramoth-gilead.

29 And the king of Israel said to Jehoshaphat, "I will disguise myself and go into battle, but you put on your robes." So the king of Israel disguised himself, and they went into battle.

30 Now the king of Aram had commanded the captains of his chariots, saying, "Do not fight with small or great, but with the king of Israel alone."

31 So it came about when the captains of the chariots saw Jehoshaphat, that they said, "It is the king of Israel," and they turned aside to fight against him. But Jehoshaphat [a]cried out, and the LORD helped him, and God diverted them from him.

32 Then it happened when the captains of the chariots saw that it was not the king of Israel, that they turned back from pursuing him.

33 And a certain man drew his bow at random and struck the king of Israel [1]in a joint of the armor. So he said to the driver of the chariot, "Turn [2]around, and take me out of the [3]fight; for I am severely wounded."

34 And the battle raged that day, and the king of Israel propped himself up in his chariot in front of the Arameans until the evening; and at sunset he died.

Chapter 19

19 Then Jehoshaphat the king of Judah returned in safety to his house in Jerusalem.

2 And [a]Jehu the son of Hanani the seer went out to meet him and said to King Jehoshaphat, "[b]Should you help the wicked and love those who hate the LORD and [1c]so *bring* wrath on yourself from the LORD?

3 "But [1a]there is *some* good in you, for [b]you have removed the [2]Asheroth from the land and you [c]have set your heart to seek God."

4 So Jehoshaphat lived in Jerusalem and went out again among the people from Beersheba to the hill country of Ephraim and [a]brought them back to the LORD, the God of their fathers.

5 And he appointed [a]judges in the land in all the fortified cities of Judah, city by city.

6 And he said to the judges, "Consider what you are doing, for [a]you do not judge for man but for the LORD who is with you [1]when you render judgment.

7 "Now then let the fear of the LORD be upon you; [1]be very careful what you do, for [2]the LORD our God will [a]have no part in unrighteousness, [b]or partiality, or the taking of a bribe."

8 And in Jerusalem also Jehoshaphat appointed some [a]of the Levites and priests, and some of the heads of the fathers' *households* of Israel, for the judgment of the LORD and to judge [1]disputes among the inhabitants of Jerusalem.

9 Then he charged them saying, "Thus you shall do in the fear of the LORD, faithfully and wholeheartedly.

10 "[a]And whenever any dispute comes to you from your brethren who live in their cities, between blood and blood, between law and commandment, statutes and ordinances, you shall warn them that

27 [a]Mic. 1:2

31 [a]2 Chr. 1

33 [1]Lit., *betw* *scale-armor* *breastplate* [2] *hand* [3]Lit., *ca*

19:2 [1]Lit., *by* [a]1 Kin. 16:1; 2 20:34 [b]2 Chr. [c]2 Chr. 24:18

3 [1]Lit., *good t* *found* [2]I.e., w pillars [a]2 Chr. [b]2 Chr. 17:6 [c] 12:14

4 [a]2 Chr. 15:8

5 [a]Deut. 16:18

6 [1]Lit., *in the w* *judgment* [a]Lev. Deut. 1:17

7 [1]Lit., *be caref* *do* [2]Lit., *there is* *with the LORD o* [a]Gen. 18:25; De [b]Deut. 10:17, 18

8 [1]So the versio Heb. reads *disp* *And they returne* *Jerusalem*. Or, *A* *lived in Jerusale* [a]2 Chr. 17:8, 9

10 [a]Deut. 17:8

they may not be guilty before the LORD, and [b]wrath may *not* come on
you and your brethren. Thus you shall do and you will not be guilty.
11 "And behold, Amariah the chief priest will be over you in [1a]all
that pertains to the LORD; and Zebadiah the son of Ishmael, the ruler
of the house of Judah, in [1]all that pertains to the king. Also the
Levites shall be officers before you. [2b]Act resolutely, and the LORD be
with the upright."

Chapter 20

20 Now it came about after this that the sons of Moab and the
sons of Ammon, together with some of the [1a]Meunites, came
to make war against Jehoshaphat.
2 Then some came and reported to Jehoshaphat, saying, "A great
multitude is coming against you from beyond the sea, out of [1]Aram
and behold, they are in [a]Hazazon-tamar (that is Engedi)."
3 And Jehoshaphat was afraid and [1a]turned his attention to seek
the LORD; and [b]proclaimed a fast throughout all Judah.
4 So Judah gathered together to [a]seek help from the LORD; they
even came from all the cities of Judah to seek the LORD.
5 Then Jehoshaphat stood in the assembly of Judah and Jerusalem,
in the house of the LORD before the new court,
6 and he said, "O LORD, the God of our fathers, [a]art Thou not God
in the heavens? And [b]art Thou not ruler over all the kingdoms of the
nations? Power and might are in Thy hand so that no one can stand
against Thee.
7 "Didst Thou not, O our God, drive out the inhabitants of this land
before Thy people Israel, and [a]give it to the descendants of [b]Abraham
Thy friend forever?
8 "And they lived in it, and have built Thee a sanctuary there for
Thy name, saying,
9 '[a]Should evil come upon us, the sword, *or* judgment, or pes-
tilence, or famine, we will stand before this house and before Thee
(for [b]Thy name is in this house) and cry to Thee in our distress, and
Thou wilt hear and deliver *us*.'
10 "And now behold, [a]the sons of Ammon and Moab and [1]Mount
Seir, [b]whom Thou didst not let Israel invade when they came out of
the land of Egypt (they turned aside from them and did not destroy
them),
11 behold *how* they are rewarding us, by [a]coming to drive us out
from Thy possession which Thou hast given us as an inheritance.
12 "O our God, [a]wilt Thou not judge them? For we are powerless
before this great multitude who are coming against us; nor do we
know what to do, but [b]our eyes are on Thee."
13 And all Judah was standing before the LORD, with their infants,
their wives, and their children.
14 Then in the midst of the assembly [a]the Spirit of the LORD came
upon Jahaziel the son of Zechariah, the son of Benaiah, the son of
Jeiel, the son of Mattaniah, the Levite of the sons of Asaph;
15 and he said, "Listen, all Judah and the inhabitants of Jerusalem
and King Jehoshaphat: thus says the LORD to you, '[a]Do not fear or be
dismayed because of this great multitude, for [b]the battle is not yours
but God's.
16 'Tomorrow go down against them. Behold, they will come up by

0 [b]2 Chr. 19:2
every matter of
strong and do
r. 19:8 [b]1 Chr. 28:20
with Gr.; Heb.,
nonites [a]1 Chr.
:41; 2 Chr. 26:7
other reading is
om [a]Gen. 14:7
Lit., *set his face*
r. 19:3 [b]1 Sam. 7:6; Ezra 8:21
4 [a]Joel 1:14
eut. 4:39 [b]1 Chr. 29:11
1:8 [b]James 2:23
[a]2 Chr. 6:28-30 [b]2 Chr. 6:20
e., Edom [a]2 Chr. 20:1, 22 [b]Num. 20:17-21
11 [a]Ps. 83:12
[a]Judg. 11:27 [b]Ps. 25:15; 121:1, 2
2 Chr. 15:1; 24:20
[a]Ex. 14:13; Deut.
:1-4; 2 Chr. 32:7, 8
[b]1 Sam. 17:47

the ascent of Ziz, and you will find them at the end of the valley in
front of the wilderness of Jeruel.
17 'You *need* not fight in this *battle;* station yourselves, [a]stand and
see the salvation of the LORD on your behalf, O Judah and Jerusa-
lem.' Do not fear or be dismayed; tomorrow go out to face them, [b]for
the LORD is with you."
18 And Jehoshaphat [a]bowed his head with *his* face to the ground,
and all Judah and the inhabitants of Jerusalem fell down before the
LORD, worshiping the LORD.
19 And the Levites, from the sons of the Kohathites and of the sons
of the Korahites, stood up to praise the LORD God of Israel, with a
very loud voice.
20 And they rose early in the morning and went out to the wilder-
ness of Tekoa; and when they went out, Jehoshaphat stood and said,
"Listen to me, O Judah and inhabitants of Jerusalem, [a]put your trust
in the LORD your God, and you will be established. Put your trust in
His prophets and succeed."
21 And when he had consulted with the people, he appointed those
who sang to the LORD and those who [a]praised *Him* in holy attire, as
they went out before the army and said, "[b]Give thanks to the LORD,
for His lovingkindness is everlasting."
22 And when they began singing and praising, the LORD [a]set am-
bushes against the sons of [b]Ammon, Moab, and Mount Seir, who had
come against Judah; so they were [1]routed.
23 For the sons of Ammon and Moab rose up against the inhabit-
ants of Mount Seir destroying *them* completely, and when they had
finished with the inhabitants of Seir, [a]they helped to destroy one
another.
24 When Judah came to the lookout of the wilderness, they looked
toward the multitude; and behold, they *were* corpses lying on the
ground, and no one had escaped.
25 And when Jehoshaphat and his people came to take their spoil,
they found much among them, *including* goods, [1]garments, and
valuable things which they took for themselves, more than they
could carry. And they were three days taking the spoil because there
was so much.
26 Then on the fourth day they assembled in the valley of Beracah,
for there they blessed the LORD. Therefore they have named that
place "The Valley of [1]Beracah" until today.
27 And every man of Judah and Jerusalem returned with Jehosha-
phat at their head, returning to Jerusalem with joy, [a]for the LORD had
made them to rejoice over their enemies.
28 And they came to Jerusalem with harps, lyres, and trumpets to
the house of the LORD.
29 And [a]the dread of God was on all the kingdoms of the lands
when they heard that the LORD had fought against the enemies of
Israel.
30 So the kingdom of Jehoshaphat was at peace, [a]for his God gave
him rest on all sides.
31 [a]Now Jehoshaphat reigned over Judah. He *was* thirty-five years
old when he became king, and he reigned in Jerusalem twenty-five
years. And his mother's name *was* Azubah the daughter of Shilhi.
32 And he walked in the way of his father Asa and did not depart
from it, doing right in the sight of the LORD.

17 [a]Ex. 14:13 15:2
18 [a]Ex. 4:31
20 [a]Is. 7:9
21 [a]1 Chr. 16:2 29:2 [b]1 Chr. 16
22 [1]Lit., *struck* [a]2 Chr. 13:13 [b] 20:10
23 [a]Judg. 7:22; 14:20
25 [1]So several mss.; others rea *corpses*
26 [1]I.e., blessing
27 [a]Neh. 12:43
29 [a]2 Chr. 14:14;
30 [a]2 Chr. 14:6, 7
31 [a]1 Kin. 22:41-4

33 [a]The high places, however, were not removed; [b]the people had
not yet directed their hearts to the God of their fathers.
34 Now the rest of the acts of Jehoshaphat, first [1]to last, behold, they
are written in the annals of [a]Jehu the son of Hanani, which is
[2]recorded in the Book of the Kings of Israel.
35 [a]And after this Jehoshaphat king of Judah allied himself with
Ahaziah king of Israel. He acted wickedly [1]in so doing.
36 So he allied himself with him to make ships to go [a]to Tarshish,
and they made the ships in Ezion-geber.
37 Then Eliezer the son of Dodavahu of Mareshah prophesied
against Jehoshaphat saying, "Because you have allied yourself with
Ahaziah, the LORD has destroyed your works." So the ships were
broken and could not go to Tarshish.

Chapter 21

21 [a]Then Jehoshaphat slept with his fathers and was buried with
his fathers in the city of David, and Jehoram his son became
king in his place.
2 And he had brothers, the sons of Jehoshaphat: Azariah, Jehiel,
Zechariah, [1]Azaryahu, Michael, and Shephatiah. All these *were* the
sons of Jehoshaphat king [a]of Israel.
3 And their father gave them many gifts of silver, gold and pre-
cious things, [a]with fortified cities in Judah, but he gave the kingdom
to Jehoram because he was the first-born.
4 Now when Jehoram had [1]taken over the kingdom of his father
and made himself [2]secure, he [a]killed all his brothers with the sword,
and some of the rulers of Israel also.
5 [a]Jehoram *was* thirty-two years old when he became king, and he
reigned eight years in Jerusalem.
6 [a]And he walked in the way of the kings of Israel, just as the
house of Ahab did ([b]for Ahab's daughter was his wife), and he did
evil in the sight of the LORD.
7 Yet the LORD was not willing to destroy the house of David be-
cause of the covenant which He had made with David, [a]and since He
had promised to give a lamp to him and his sons forever.
8 In his days [a]Edom revolted [1]against the rule of Judah, and set up
a king over themselves.
9 Then Jehoram crossed over with his commanders and all his
chariots with him. And it came about that he arose by night and
struck down the Edomites who were surrounding him and the com-
manders of the chariots.
10 So Edom revolted [1]against Judah to this day. Then Libnah
revolted at the same time [2]against his rule, because he had forsaken
the LORD God of his fathers.
11 Moreover, [a]he made high places in the mountains of Judah, and
caused the inhabitants of Jerusalem [b]to play the harlot and led Judah
astray.
12 Then a letter came to him from Elijah the prophet saying, "Thus
says the LORD God of your father David, 'Because [a]you have not
walked in the ways of Jehoshaphat your father [b]and the ways of Asa
king of Judah,
13 but [a]have walked in the way of the kings of Israel, and have
caused Judah and the inhabitants of Jerusalem to play the harlot [b]as

r. 17:6 [b]2 Chr. 19:3
nd [2]Lit., *taken*
up [a]2 Chr. 19:2
., *to do* [a]1 Kin. 22:48, 49
36 [a]2 Chr. 9:21
1 [a]1 Kin. 22:50
Azariah [a]2 Chr. 12:6; 23:2
3 [a]2 Chr. 11:5
., *risen up* [2]Lit.,
Gen. 4:8; Judg. 9:5
[a]2 Kin. 8:17-22
[a]1 Kin. 12:28-30 [b]2 Chr. 18:1
2 Sam. 7:12-17; 1 Kin. 11:13, 36
., *from under the*
of [a]2 Chr. 20:22, 23; 21:10
t., *from under the*
and of [2]Lit., *from under his hand*
[a]1 Kin. 11:7 [b]Lev. 20:5
2 [a]2 Chr. 17:3, 4 [b]2 Chr. 14:2-5
Chr. 21:6 [b]1 Kin. 16:31-33

the house of Ahab played the harlot, and you [c]have also killed your
brothers, [1]your own family, who were better than you,
14 behold, the LORD is going to strike your people, your sons, your
wives, and all your possessions with a great [1]calamity;
15 and [a]you will suffer [1]severe sickness, a disease of your bowels,
until your bowels come out because of the sickness, day by day.' "
16 Then [a]the LORD stirred up against Jehoram the spirit of the Philis-
tines and [b]the Arabs who [1]bordered the Ethiopians;
17 and they came against Judah and invaded it, and carried away
all the possessions found in the king's house together with his sons
and his wives, so that no son was left to him except [1a]Jehoahaz, the
youngest of his sons.
18 So after all this the LORD smote him [a]in his bowels with an in-
curable sickness.
19 Now it came about in the course of time, at the end of two years,
that his bowels came out because of his sickness and he died in great
pain. And his people made no fire for him like [a]the fire for his
fathers.
20 He was thirty-two years old when he became king, and he
reigned in Jerusalem eight years; and he departed [1a]with no one's
regret, and they buried him in the city of David, [b]but not in the
tombs of the kings.

Chapter 22

22 [a]Then the inhabitants of Jerusalem made [1]Ahaziah, his
youngest son, king in his place, for the band of men who
came with [b]the Arabs to the camp had slain all the older *sons*. So
Ahaziah the son of Jehoram king of Judah began to reign.
2 Ahaziah *was* [1]twenty-two years old when he became king, and
he reigned one year in Jerusalem. And his mother's name was
Athaliah, the [2]granddaughter of Omri.
3 He also walked in the ways of the house of Ahab, for his mother
was his counselor to do wickedly.
4 And he did evil in the sight of the LORD like the house of Ahab,
for they were his counselors after the death of his father, to [a]his
destruction.
5 He also walked according to their counsel, and went with Jeho-
ram the son of Ahab king of Israel to wage war against Hazael king
of Aram at Ramoth-gilead. But the [1a]Arameans [2]wounded [3]Joram.
6 So he returned to be healed in Jezreel of the wounds [1]which they
had inflicted on him at Ramah, when he fought against Hazael king
of Aram. And [2]Ahaziah, the son of Jehoram king of Judah, went
down to see Jehoram the son of Ahab in Jezreel, because he was sick.
7 Now [a]the destruction of Ahaziah was from God, in that [1]he went
to Joram. For when he came, [b]he went out with Jehoram against Jehu
the son of Nimshi, [c]whom the LORD had anointed to cut off the house
of Ahab.
8 [a]And it came about when Jehu was executing judgment on the
house of Ahab, he found the princes of Judah and the sons of
Ahaziah's brothers, ministering to Ahaziah, and slew them.
9 [a]He also sought Ahaziah, and they caught him while he was
hiding in Samaria; they brought him to Jehu, put him to death, [b]and
buried him. For they said, "He is the son of Jehoshaphat, [c]who

13 [1]Lit., *your house* [c]2 Chr
14 [1]Lit., *blow*
15 [1]Lit., *in ma sicknesses* [a]2 21:18, 19
16 [1]Lit., *were hand of* [a]2 Ch [b]2 Chr. 17:11;
17 [1]In 2 Chr. *Ahaziah* [a]2 C
18 [a]2 Chr. 21:
19 [a]2 Chr. 16:1
20 [1]Lit., *withou* [a]Jer. 22:18, 28 24:25; 28:27
22:1 [1]In 2 Chr. *Jehoahaz* [a]2 K 8:24-29 [b]2 Chr.
2 [1]So some ve and 2 Kin. 8:26; *42 years* [2]Lit., *c*
4 [a]Prov. 13:20
5 [1]Heb., *archer smote* [3]I.e., Jeh [a]2 Kin. 8:28
6 [1]Lit., *with whic smitten* [2]So with 8:29; Heb., *Azar*
7 [1]Lit., *to go* [a]2 10:15 [b]2 Kin. 9:2 [c]2 Kin. 9:6, 7
8 [a]2 Kin. 10:11-1
9 [a]2 Kin. 9:27 [b]2 9:28 [c]2 Chr. 17:4

sought the LORD with all his heart." So there was no one of the house
of Ahaziah to retain the power of the kingdom.
10 [a]Now when Athaliah the mother of Ahaziah saw that her son
was dead, she rose and destroyed all the royal [1]offspring of the
house of Judah.
11 But Jehoshabeath the king's daughter took Joash the son of Aha-
ziah, and stole him from among the king's sons who were being put
to death, and placed him and his nurse in the bedroom. So Jehoshab-
eath, the daughter of King Jehoram, the wife of Jehoiada the priest
(for she was the sister of Ahaziah), hid him from Athaliah so that she
would not put him to death.
12 And he was hidden with them in the house of God six years
while Athaliah reigned over the land.

Chapter 23

23 [a]Now in the seventh year Jehoiada strengthened himself, and
took captains of hundreds: Azariah the son of Jeroham, Ish-
mael the son of Johanan, Azariah the son of Obed, Maaseiah the son
of Adaiah, and Elishaphat the son of Zichri, *and they entered* into a
covenant with him.
2 And they went throughout Judah and gathered the Levites from
all the cities of Judah, and the heads of the fathers' *households* of
[a]Israel, and they came to Jerusalem.
3 Then all the assembly made a covenant with the king in the
house of God. And [1]Jehoiada said to them, "Behold, the king's son
shall reign, [a]as the LORD has spoken concerning the sons of David.
4 "This is the thing which you shall do: one third of you, of the
priests and Levites [a]who come in on the sabbath, *shall be* gatekeepers,
5 and one third *shall be* at the king's house, and a third at the Gate
of the Foundation; and all the people *shall be* in the courts of the
house of the LORD.
6 "But let no one enter the house of the LORD except the priests and
[a]the ministering Levites; they may enter, for they are holy. And let all
the people keep the charge of the LORD.
7 "And the Levites will surround the king, each man with his
weapons in his hand; and whoever enters the house, let him be
killed. Thus be with the king when he comes in and when he goes
out."
8 So the Levites and all Judah did according to all that Jehoiada
the priest commanded. And each one of them took his men who
were to come in on the sabbath, with those who were to go out on
the sabbath, for Jehoiada the priest did not dismiss *any of* [a]the
divisions.
9 Then Jehoiada the priest gave to the captains of hundreds the
spears and the large and small shields which had been King David's,
which *were* in the house of God.
10 And he stationed all the people, each man with his weapon in
his hand, from the right [1]side of the house to the left [1]side of the
house, by the altar and by the house, around the king.
11 Then they brought out the king's son and put the crown on him,
and *gave him* [a]the testimony, and made him king. And Jehoiada and
his sons anointed him and said, "[b]*Long* live the king!"
12 When Athaliah heard the noise of the people running and prais-
ing the king, she came into the house of the LORD to the people.

) [1]Lit., *seed* [a]2 Kin. 11:1-3

3:1 [a]2 Kin. 11:4-20

Chr. 11:13-17; 21:2

3 [1]Lit., *he* [a]2 Sam. 7:12; 2 Chr. 21:7

4 [a]1 Chr. 9:25

6 [a]1 Chr. 23:28-32

8 [a]1 Chr. 24:1

10 [1]Lit., *shoulder*

11 [a]Ex. 25:16, 21 [b]1 Sam. 10:24

13 And she looked, and behold, the king was standing by his pillar at the entrance, and the captains and the [1]trumpeters *were* beside the king. And all the people of the land rejoiced and blew trumpets, the singers with *their* musical instruments [2]leading the praise. Then Athaliah tore her clothes and said, "Treason! Treason!"

14 And Jehoiada the priest brought out the captains of hundreds who were appointed over the army, and said to them, "Bring her out [1]between the ranks; and whoever follows her, put to death with the sword." For the priest said, "Let her not be put to death in the house of the LORD."

15 So they [1]seized her, and when she arrived at the entrance of [a]the Horse Gate of the king's house, they [b]put her to death there.

16 Then [a]Jehoiada made a covenant between himself and all the people and the king, that they should be the LORD's people.

17 And all the people went to the house of Baal, and tore it down, and they broke in pieces his altars and his images, and [a]killed Mattan the priest of Baal before the altars.

18 Moreover, Jehoiada placed the offices of the house of the LORD under the [1]authority of [a]the Levitical priests, [b]whom David had assigned over the house of the LORD, to offer the burnt offerings of the LORD, as it is written in the law of Moses—[c]with rejoicing and singing according to the [2]order of David.

19 And he stationed [a]the gatekeepers of the house of the LORD, so that no one should enter *who was* in any way unclean.

20 And [a]he took the captains of hundreds, the nobles, the rulers of the people, and all the people of the land, and brought the king down from the house of the LORD, and came through the upper gate to the king's house. And they placed the king upon the royal throne.

21 So [a]all of the people of the land rejoiced and the city was quiet. For they had put Athaliah to death with the sword.

Chapter 24

24 [a]Joash *was* seven years old when he became king, and he reigned forty years in Jerusalem; and his mother's name *was* Zibiah from Beersheba.

2 And [a]Joash did what was right in the sight of the LORD all the days of Jehoiada the priest.

3 And Jehoiada took two wives for him, and he became the father of sons and daughters.

4 Now it came about after this that Joash [1]decided [a]to restore the house of the LORD.

5 And he gathered the priests and Levites, and said to them, "Go out to the cities of Judah, and collect money from all [a]Israel to [1]repair the house of your God [2]annually, and you shall do the matter quickly." But the Levites did not act quickly.

6 So the king summoned Jehoiada the chief *priest* and said to him, "Why have you not required the Levites to bring in from Judah and from Jerusalem [a]the levy *fixed by* Moses the servant of the LORD on the congregation of Israel [b]for the tent of the testimony?"

7 For [a]the sons of the wicked Athaliah had broken into the house of God and even [1]used the holy things of the house of the LORD for the Baals.

8 So the king commanded, and [a]they made a chest and set it outside by the gate of the house of the LORD.

13 [1]Lit., *trumpets* *and leading for pra*

14 [1]Lit., *from withi*

15 [1]Lit., *placed ha* *to her* [a]Neh. 3:28; 31:40 [b]2 Chr. 22:1

16 [a]2 Kin. 11:17

17 [a]Deut. 13:6-9; 18:40

18 [1]Lit., *hand* [2]Lit. *hands of* [a]2 Chr. 5 [b]1 Chr. 23:6, 25-31 [c]1 Chr. 25:1

19 [a]1 Chr. 9:22

20 [a]2 Kin. 11:19

21 [a]2 Kin. 11:20

24:1 [a]2 Kin. 11:21 12:1-15

2 [a]2 Chr. 26:4, 5

4 [1]Lit., *was with a* [a]2 Chr. 24:7

5 [1]Lit., *to strength* [2]Lit., *from year to* [a]2 Chr. 21:2

6 [a]Ex. 30:12-16 1:50

7 [1]Lit., *made* [a]2 C 21:17

8 [a]2 Kin. 12:9

9 And [a]they made a proclamation in Judah and Jerusalem to bring
to the LORD [b]the levy *fixed by* Moses the servant of God on Israel in
the wilderness.
10 And all the officers and all the people rejoiced and brought in
their levies and [1]dropped *them* into the chest until they had finished.
11 And it came about whenever the chest was brought in to the
king's officer by the Levites, and when [a]they saw that there was
much money, then the king's scribe and the chief priest's officer
would come, empty the chest, take it, and return it to its place. Thus
they did daily and collected much money.
12 And the king and Jehoiada gave it to those who did the work of
the service of the house of the LORD; and they hired masons and
carpenters to restore the house of the LORD, and also workers in iron
and bronze to [1]repair the house of the LORD.
13 So the workmen labored, and the repair work progressed in their
hands, and they [1]restored the house of God [2]according to its speci-
fications, and strengthened it.
14 And when they had finished, they brought the rest of the money
before the king and Jehoiada; and it was made into utensils for the
house of the LORD, utensils for the service and the burnt offering,
and pans and utensils of gold and silver. And they offered burnt
offerings in the house of the LORD continually all the days of
Jehoiada.
15 Now when Jehoiada [1]reached a ripe old age he died; he was one
hundred and thirty years old at his death.
16 And they buried him [a]in the city of David among the kings,
because he had done well in [b]Israel and [1]to God and His house.
17 But after the death of Jehoiada the officials of Judah came and
bowed down to the king, and the king listened to them.
18 And they abandoned [a]the house of the LORD, the God of their
fathers, and [b]served the [1]Asherim and the idols; so [c]wrath came upon
Judah and Jerusalem for this their guilt.
19 Yet [a]He sent prophets to them to bring them back to the LORD;
though they testified against them, they would not listen.
20 [a]Then the Spirit of God [1]came on Zechariah the son of Jehoiada
the priest; and he stood above the people and said to them, "Thus
God has said, '[b]Why do you transgress the commandments of the
LORD and do not prosper? [c]Because you have forsaken the LORD, He
has also forsaken you.'"
21 So [a]they conspired against him and at the command of the king
they stoned him [1]to death in the court of the house of the LORD.
22 Thus Joash the king did not remember the kindness which his
father Jehoiada had shown him, but he murdered his son. And as he
died he said, "May [a]the LORD see and [1]avenge!"
23 Now it came about at the turn of the year that [a]the army of the
Arameans came up against him; and they came to Judah and Jeru-
salem, destroyed all the officials of the people from among the
people, and sent all their spoil to the king of Damascus.
24 Indeed the army of the Arameans came with a small number of
men; yet [a]the LORD delivered a very great army into their hands,
[b]because they had forsaken the LORD, the God of their fathers. Thus
they executed judgment on Joash.
25 [a]And when they had departed from him (for they left him very
sick), his own servants conspired against him because of the blood of

Chr. 36:22 [b]2 Chr. 24:6
10 [1]Lit., *threw*
11 [a]2 Kin. 12:10
[1]Lit., *to strengthen*
3 [1]Lit., *set up* [2]Lit., *upon its proportion*
5 [1]Lit., *became old satisfied with days*
[1]Lit., *with* [a]2 Chr. 21:20 [b]2 Chr. 21:2
18 [1]I.e., wooden symbols of a female [a]2 Chr. 24:4 [b]Ex. 2-14 [c]Josh. 22:20
19 [a]Jer. 7:25
[1]Lit., *clothed* [a]2 Chr. 0:14 [b]Num. 14:41 [c]2 Chr. 15:2
[1]Lit., *with stones* [a]Neh. 9:26; Matt. 23:34, 35
22 [1]Lit., *seek*, or *require* [a]Gen. 9:5
23 [a]2 Kin. 12:17
24 [a]2 Chr. 16:7, 8 [b]2 Chr. 24:20
[a]2 Kin. 12:20, 21

the [1]son of Jehoiada the priest, and murdered him on his bed. So he
died, and they buried him in the city of David, but they did not bury
him in the tombs of the kings.
26 Now these are those who conspired against him: Zabad the son
of Shimeath the Ammonitess, and Jehozabad the son of Shimrith the
Moabitess.
27 As to his sons and the many [1]oracles against him and [a]the
[2]rebuilding of the house of God, behold, they are written in the
[3b]treatise of the Book of the Kings. Then Amaziah his son became
king in his place.

Chapter 25

25 [a]Amaziah was twenty-five years old when he became king,
and he reigned twenty-nine years in Jerusalem. And his
mother's name was Jehoaddan of Jerusalem.
2 And he did right in the sight of the LORD, [a]yet not with a whole
heart.
3 Now [a]it came about as soon as the kingdom was [1]firmly in his
grasp, that he killed his servants who had slain his father the king.
4 However, he did not put their children to death, but *did* as it is
written in the law in the book of Moses, which the LORD com-
manded, saying, "[a]Fathers shall not be put to death for sons, nor
sons be put to death for fathers, but each shall be put to death for his
own sin."
5 Moreover, Amaziah assembled Judah and appointed them ac-
cording to *their* fathers' households under commanders of thousands
and commanders of hundreds throughout Judah and Benjamin; and
he [1]took a census of those [a]from twenty years old and upward, and
found them to be [b]300,000 choice men, *able* to go to war *and* handle
spear and shield.
6 He hired also 100,000 valiant warriors out of Israel for one
hundred talents of silver.
7 But [a]a man of God came to him saying, "O king, do not let the
army of Israel go with you, for the LORD is not with Israel *nor with*
any of the sons of Ephraim.
8 "But if you do go, do *it*, be strong for the battle; *yet* God will
[1]bring you down before the enemy, [a]for God has power to help and
to [1]bring down."
9 And Amaziah said to the man of God, "But what *shall we* do for
the hundred talents which I have given to the troops of Israel?" And
the man of God answered, "[a]The LORD has much more to give you
than this."
10 Then Amaziah [1]dismissed them, the troops which came to him
from Ephraim, to go home; so their anger burned against Judah and
they returned [2]home in fierce anger.
11 Now Amaziah strengthened himself, and led his people forth,
and went to [a]the Valley of Salt, and struck down 10,000 of the sons of
Seir.
12 The sons of Judah also captured 10,000 alive and brought them
to the top of the cliff, and threw them down from the top of the cliff
so that they were all dashed to pieces.
13 But the [1]troops whom Amaziah sent back from going with him
to battle, raided the cities of Judah, from Samaria to Beth-horon, and
struck down 3,000 of them, and plundered much spoil.

25 [1]So some anci versions; Heb., *sor*
27 [1]Or, *burdens u* [2]Lit., *founding* [3]He *midrash* [a]2 Chr. 24 [b]2 Chr. 13:22
25:1 [a]2 Kin. 14:1-
2 [a]2 Chr. 25:14
3 [1]Lit., *firm upon* [a]2 Kin. 14:5
4 [a]Deut. 24:16
5 [1]Lit., *mustered* 1:3 [b]2 Chr. 26:13
7 [a]2 Kin. 4:9
8 [1]Lit., *cause to stumble* [a]2 Chr. 1 20:6
9 [a]Deut. 8:18; Pr 10:22
10 [1]Lit., *separate* [2]Lit., *to their own*
11 [a]2 Kin. 14:7
13 [1]Lit., *sons of t troops*

14 [a]2 Chr. 28:23
14 Now it came about after Amaziah came from slaughtering the
Edomites that [a]he brought the gods of the sons of Seir, set them up as
his gods, bowed down before them, and burned incense to them.
15 Then the anger of the LORD burned against Amaziah, and He
5 [a]2 Chr. 25:11, 12
sent him a prophet who said to him, "Why have you sought the
gods of the people [a]who have not delivered their own people from
your hand?"
16 And it came about as he was talking with him that [1]the king said
to him, "Have we appointed you a royal counselor? Stop! Why
16 [1]Lit., *he*
should you be struck down?" Then the prophet stopped and said, "I
know that God has planned to destroy you, because you have done
this, and have not listened to my counsel."
17 [a]Then Amaziah king of Judah took counsel and sent to Joash the
son of Jehoahaz the son of Jehu, the king of Israel, saying, "Come, let
17 [a]2 Kin. 14:8-14
us face each other."
18 And Joash the king of Israel sent to Amaziah king of Judah,
saying, "[a]The thorn bush which was in Lebanon sent to the cedar
which was in Lebanon, saying, 'Give your daughter to my son in
18 [a]Judg. 9:8-15
marriage.' But there passed by a wild beast that was in Lebanon, and
trampled the thorn bush.
19 "You said, 'Behold, you have [1]defeated Edom.' And [a]your heart
has [2]become proud in boasting. Now stay at home; for why should
you provoke trouble that you, even you, should fall and Judah with
[1]Lit., *smitten* [2]Lit., *ted you up to boast* 2 Chr. 26:16; 32:25
you?"
20 But Amaziah would not listen, for it was from God, that He
might deliver them into the hand *of Joash* because they had sought
the gods of Edom.
21 So Joash king of Israel went up, and he and Amaziah king of
22 [1]Lit., *before*
Judah faced each other at Beth-shemesh, which belonged to Judah.
22 And Judah was defeated [1]by Israel, and they fled each to his tent.
23 Then Joash king of Israel captured Amaziah king of Judah, the
son of Joash the son of [a]Jehoahaz, at Beth-shemesh, and brought him
to Jerusalem, and tore down the wall of Jerusalem from the Gate of
23 [1]I.e., One cubit quals approx. 18 in. [a]2 Chr. 21:17; 22:1
Ephraim to the Corner Gate, 400 [1]cubits.
24 And *he took* all the gold and silver, and all the utensils which
were found in the house of God with [a]Obed-edom, and the treasures
of the king's house, the hostages also, and returned to Samaria.
25 [a]And Amaziah, the son of Joash king of Judah, lived fifteen years
after the death of Joash, son of Jehoahaz, king of Israel.
24 [a]1 Chr. 26:15
26 Now the rest of the acts of Amaziah, from first to last, behold,
are they not written in the Book of the Kings of Judah and Israel?
27 And from the time that Amaziah turned away from following
the LORD they conspired against him in Jerusalem, and he fled to
Lachish; but they sent after him to Lachish and killed him there.
5 [a]2 Kin. 14:17-22
28 Then they brought him on horses and buried him with his
fathers in the city of Judah.

Chapter 26

:1 [1]In 2 Kin. 14:21, *Azariah*
26 And all the people of Judah took [1]Uzziah, who *was* sixteen
years old, and made him king in the place of his father
Amaziah.
2 He built Eloth and restored it to Judah after the king slept with
his fathers.
3 [a]2 Kin. 15:2, 3
3 Uzziah was [a]sixteen years old when he became king, and he

reigned fifty-two years in Jerusalem; and his mother's name was [1]Jechiliah of Jerusalem.

4 And he did right in the sight of the LORD according to all that his father Amaziah had done.

5 And [a]he continued to seek God in the days of Zechariah, [b]who had understanding [1]through the vision of God; and [2c]as long as he sought the LORD, God prospered him.

6 Now he went out and [a]warred against the Philistines, and broke down the wall of Gath and the wall of Jabneh and the wall of Ashdod; and he built cities in *the area of* Ashdod and among the Philistines.

7 And [a]God helped him against the Philistines, and against the Arabians who lived in Gur-baal, and the Meunites.

8 The Ammonites also gave [a]tribute to Uzziah, and his [1]fame extended to the border of Egypt, for he became very strong.

9 Moreover, Uzziah built towers in Jerusalem at [a]the Corner Gate and at the [b]Valley Gate and at the corner buttress and fortified them.

10 And he built towers in the wilderness and [a]hewed many cisterns, for he had much livestock, both in the [1]lowland and in the plain. *He also had* plowmen and vinedressers in the hill country and the fertile fields, for he loved the soil.

11 Moreover, Uzziah had an army ready for battle, which [1]entered combat by divisions, according to the number of their muster, [2]prepared by Jeiel the scribe and Maaseiah the official, under the direction of Hananiah, one of the king's officers.

12 The total number of the heads of the [1]households, of valiant warriors, was 2,600.

13 And under their direction was an [1]elite army of [a]307,500, who could wage war with great power, to help the king against the enemy.

14 Moreover, Uzziah prepared [1]for all the army shields, spears, helmets, body armor, bows and sling stones.

15 And in Jerusalem he made engines *of war* invented by skillful men to be on the towers and on the corners, for the purpose of shooting arrows and great stones. Hence his [1]fame spread afar, for he was marvelously helped until he *was* strong.

16 But [a]when he became strong, his heart was so [1]proud that he acted corruptly, and he was unfaithful to the LORD his God, for [b]he entered the temple of the LORD to burn incense on the altar of incense.

17 Then [a]Azariah the priest entered after him and with him eighty priests of the LORD, valiant men.

18 And [a]they opposed Uzziah the king and said to him, "[b]It is not for you, Uzziah, to burn incense to the LORD, [c]but for the priests, the sons of Aaron who are consecrated to burn incense. Get out of the sanctuary, for you have been unfaithful, and will have no honor from the LORD God."

19 But Uzziah, with a censer in his hand for burning incense, was enraged; and while he was enraged with the priests, [a]the leprosy broke out on his forehead before the priests in the house of the LORD, beside the altar of incense.

20 And Azariah the chief priest and all the priests looked at him, and behold, he *was* leprous on his forehead; and they hurried him

3 [1]In 2 Kin. 15 *Jecoliah*

5 [1]Many mss. *the fear of God* *the days of his* [a]2 Chr. 24:2 [b]D [c]2 Chr. 15:2

6 [a]Is. 14:29

7 [a]2 Chr. 21:16

8 [1]Lit., *name w* *the entering of E* [a]2 Chr. 17:11

9 [a]2 Chr. 25:23 2:13, 15; 3:13

10 [1]Heb., *shep* [a]Gen. 26:18-21

11 [1]Lit., *goes ou* [2]Lit., *by the hand*

12 [1]Lit., *fathers*

13 [1]Lit., *powerfu* [a]2 Chr. 25:5

14 [1]Lit., *for them*

15 [1]Lit., *name*

16 [1]Lit., *lifted up* 32:15; 2 Chr. 25:1 [b]1 Kin. 13:1-4

17 [a]1 Chr. 6:10

18 [a]2 Chr. 19:2 [b]N 3:10; 16:39, 40 [c]E 30:7, 8

19 [a]2 Kin. 5:25-27

22 Now in the time of his distress this same King Ahaz [a]became yet
more unfaithful to the LORD.
23 [a]For he sacrificed to the gods of Damascus which had [1]defeated
him, and said, "[b]Because the gods of the kings of Aram helped them,
I will sacrifice to them that they may help me." But they became the
[2]downfall of him and all Israel.
24 Moreover, when Ahaz gathered together the utensils of the
house of God, he [a]cut the utensils of the house of God in pieces; and
he [b]closed the doors of the house of the LORD, and [c]made altars for
himself in every corner of Jerusalem.
25 And in every city of Judah he made high places to burn incense
to other gods, and provoked the LORD, the God of his fathers, to
anger.
26 [a]Now the rest of his acts and all his ways, from first to last,
behold, they are written in the Book of the Kings of Judah and Israel.
27 [a]So Ahaz slept with his fathers, and they buried him in the city,
in Jerusalem, for they did not bring him into the tombs of the kings
of [b]Israel; and Hezekiah his son reigned in his place.

Chapter 29

29 [a]Hezekiah became king *when he was* twenty-five years old;
and he reigned twenty-nine years in Jerusalem. And his
mother's name *was* Abijah, the daughter of Zechariah.
2 And [a]he did right in the sight of the LORD, according to all that
his father David had done.
3 In the first year of his reign, in the first month, he [a]opened the
doors of the house of the LORD and repaired them.
4 And he brought in the priests and the Levites, and gathered
them into the square on the east.
5 Then he said to them, "Listen to me, O Levites. [a]Consecrate your-
selves now, and consecrate the house of the LORD, the God of your
fathers, and carry the uncleanness out from the holy place.
6 "For our fathers have been unfaithful and have done evil in the
sight of the LORD our God, and have forsaken Him and [a]turned their
faces away from the dwelling place of the LORD, and have [1]turned
their backs.
7 "They have also [a]shut the doors of the porch and put out the
lamps, and have not burned incense or offered burnt offerings in the
holy place to the God of Israel.
8 "Therefore [a]the wrath of the LORD was against Judah and Jerusa-
lem, and He has made them an object of terror, of horror, and of
[b]hissing, as you see with your own eyes.
9 "For behold, [a]our fathers have fallen by the sword, and our sons
and our daughters and our wives are in captivity for this.
10 "Now it is in my heart [a]to make a covenant with the LORD God of
Israel, that His burning anger may turn away from us.
11 "My sons, do not be negligent now, for [a]the LORD has chosen you
to stand before Him, to minister to Him, and to be His ministers and
burn incense."
12 Then the Levites arose: [a]Mahath, the son of Amasai and Joel the
son of Azariah, from the sons of [b]the Kohathites; and from the sons
of Merari, Kish the son of Abdi and Azariah the son of Jehallelel; and
from the Gershonites, Joah the son of Zimmah and Eden the son of
Joah;

22 [a]Is. 1:5; Jer. 5:3; Rev. 16:11
[1]Lit., *smitten* [2]Lit., *stumbling* [a]2 Chr. 5:14 [b]Jer. 44:17, 18
24 [a]2 Kin. 16:17 [b]2 Chr. 29:7 [c]2 Chr. 30:14; 33:3-5
26 [a]2 Kin. 16:19, 20
[a]2 Kin. 16:20; 2 Chr. 5; Is. 14:28 [b]2 Chr. 21:2
29:1 [a]2 Kin. 18:1-3
2 [a]2 Chr. 28:1; 34:2
[a]2 Chr. 28:24; 29:7
Chr. 29:15, 34; 35:6
[1]Lit., *given* [a]Ezek. 8:16
7 [a]2 Chr. 28:24
[a]2 Chr. 24:20 [b]Jer. 25:9, 18
[a]2 Chr. 28:5-8, 17
10 [a]2 Chr. 23:16
11 [a]Num. 3:6; 8:6
Chr. 31:13 [b]Num. 3:19, 20

13 and from the sons of Elizaphan, Shimri and [1]Jeiel; and from the
sons of Asaph, Zechariah and Mattaniah;
14 and from the sons of Heman, [1]Jehiel and Shimei; and from the
sons of Jeduthun, Shemaiah and Uzziel.
15 And they assembled their brothers, [a]consecrated themselves, and
went in [b]to cleanse the house of the LORD, according to the com-
mandment of the king [c]by the words of the LORD.
16 So the priests went in to the inner part of the house of the LORD
to cleanse *it*, and every unclean thing which they found in the
temple of the LORD they brought out to the court of the house of the
LORD. Then the Levites received *it* to carry out to [a]the Kidron [1]valley.
17 Now they began [1]the consecration [a]on the first *day* of the first
month, and on the eighth day of the month they entered the porch of
the LORD. Then they consecrated the house of the LORD in eight days,
and finished on the sixteenth day of the first month.
18 Then they went in to King Hezekiah and said, "We have
cleansed the whole house of the LORD, the altar of burnt offering
with all of its utensils, and the table of showbread with all of its
utensils.
19 "Moreover, [a]all the utensils which King Ahaz had discarded
during his reign in his unfaithfulness, we have prepared and con-
secrated; and behold, they are before the altar of the LORD."
20 Then King Hezekiah arose early and assembled the princes of
the city and went up to the house of the LORD.
21 And they brought seven bulls, seven rams, seven lambs, and
seven male goats [a]for a sin offering for the kingdom, the sanctuary,
and Judah. And he ordered the priests, the sons of Aaron, to offer
them on the altar of the LORD.
22 So they slaughtered the bulls, and the priests took the blood and
sprinkled it on the altar. They also slaughtered the rams and
sprinkled the blood on the altar; they slaughtered the lambs also and
[a]sprinkled the blood on the altar.
23 Then they brought the male goats of the sin offering before the
king and the assembly, and [a]they laid their hands on them.
24 And the priests slaughtered them and purged the altar with their
blood [a]to atone for all Israel, for the king ordered the burnt offering
and the sin offering for all Israel.
25 [a]He then stationed the Levites in the house of the LORD with
cymbals, with harps, and with lyres, [b]according to the command of
David and of [c]Gad the king's seer, and of [d]Nathan the prophet; for
the command was from the LORD through His prophets.
26 And the Levites stood with [a]the *musical* instruments of David,
and [b]the priests with the trumpets.
27 Then Hezekiah gave the order to offer the burnt offering on the
altar. When the burnt offering began, [a]the song to the LORD also
began with the trumpets, [1]*accompanied* by the instruments of David,
king of Israel.
28 While the whole assembly worshiped, the singers also sang and
the trumpets sounded; all this *continued* until the burnt offering was
finished.
29 Now at the completion of the burnt offerings, [a]the king and all
who were present with him bowed down and worshiped.
30 Moreover, King Hezekiah and the officials ordered the Levites to

13 [1]Or, *Jeuel*

14 [1]Or, *Jehuel*, 15:18, 20

15 [a]2 Chr. 29:5 23:28 [c]2 Chr. 3

16 [1]Or, *wadi* [a]2 15:16

17 [1]Lit., *to cons* [a]2 Chr. 29:3

19 [a]2 Chr. 28:24

21 [a]Lev. 4:3-14

22 [a]Lev. 4:18

23 [a]Lev. 4:15

24 [a]Lev. 4:26

25 [a]1 Chr. 25:6 [b] 8:14 [c]2 Sam. 24:1 [d]2 Sam. 7:2

26 [a]1 Chr. 23:5 [b] 5:12

27 [1]Lit., *and acco to the authority of instruments* [a]2 Ch 23:18

29 [a]2 Chr. 20:18

sing praises to the LORD with the words of David and Asaph the seer. [a]So they sang praises with joy, and bowed down and worshiped.

31 Then Hezekiah answered and said, "[a]Now *that* you have [1]consecrated yourselves to the LORD, come near and bring sacrifices and thank offerings to the house of the LORD." And the assembly brought sacrifices and thank offerings, and [b]all those who were [2]willing *brought* burnt offerings.

32 And the number of the burnt offerings which the assembly brought was 70 bulls, 100 rams, and 200 lambs; all these were for a burnt offering to the LORD.

33 And the consecrated things were 600 bulls and 3,000 sheep.

34 But the priests were too few, so that they were unable to skin all the burnt offerings; [a]therefore their brothers the Levites helped them until the work was completed, and until the *other* priests had consecrated themselves. For [b]the Levites were more [1]conscientious to consecrate themselves than the priests.

35 And there *were* also [1a]many burnt offerings with [b]the fat of the peace offerings and with [c]the libations for the burnt offerings. Thus the service of the house of the LORD was established *again*.

36 Then Hezekiah and all the people rejoiced over what God had prepared for the people, because the thing came about suddenly.

Chapter 30

30 Now Hezekiah sent to all Israel and Judah and wrote letters also to Ephraim and Manasseh, that they should come to the house of the LORD at Jerusalem to [1]celebrate the Passover to the LORD God of Israel.

2 For the king and his princes and all the assembly in Jerusalem had decided [a]to celebrate the Passover in the second month,

3 since they could not celebrate it [a]at that time, because the priests had not consecrated themselves in sufficient numbers, nor had the people been gathered to Jerusalem.

4 Thus the thing was right in the sight of the king and [1]all the assembly.

5 So they established a decree to circulate a [1]proclamation throughout all Israel [a]from Beersheba even to Dan, that they should come to celebrate the Passover to the LORD God of Israel at Jerusalem. For they had not celebrated *it* in great numbers as it was [2]prescribed.

6 And [a]the [1]couriers went throughout all Israel and Judah with the letters from the hand of the king and his princes, even according to the command of the king, saying, "O sons of Israel, return to the LORD God of Abraham, Isaac, and Israel, that He may return to those of you who escaped *and* are left from [b]the [2]hand of the kings of Assyria.

7 "[a]And do not be like your fathers and your brothers, who were unfaithful to the LORD God of their fathers, so that [b]He made them a horror, as you see.

8 "Now do not [a]stiffen your neck like your fathers, but [1]yield to the LORD and enter His sanctuary which He has consecrated forever, and serve the LORD your God, [b]that His burning anger may turn away from you.

9 "For [a]if you return to the LORD, your brothers and your sons *will find* compassion before those who led them captive, and will return

100:1; 106:12

[1]Lit., *filled your* [2]Lit., *willing of* Chr. 13:9 [b]Ex. 35:5, 22

[1]Lit., *upright of* t [a]2 Chr. 35:11 [b]2 Chr. 30:3

[1]Lit., *the burnt offerings to an* ndance [a]2 Chr. ev. 3:16 [c]Num. 15:5-10

it., *do*, so in vv. 3, 5, 13, 21, 23

[a]Num. 9:10, 11; 2 Chr. 30:13, 15

2 Chr. 29:17, 34

in the sight of all

[1]Lit., *voice* [2]Lit., *tten* [a]Judg. 20:1

it., *runners* [2]Lit., [a]Esth. 8:14; Job er. 51:31 [b]2 Chr. 28:20

ek. 20:13 [b]2 Chr. 29:8

[1]Lit., *give a hand* 2:9 [b]2 Chr. 29:10

9 [a]Deut. 30:2

to this land. [b]For the LORD your God is gracious and compassionate,
and will not turn *His* face away from you if you return to Him."
10 So the [1]couriers passed from city to city through the country of
Ephraim and Manasseh, and as far as Zebulun, but [a]they laughed
them to scorn, and mocked them.
11 Nevertheless [a]some men of Asher, Manasseh, and Zebulun
humbled themselves and came to Jerusalem.
12 The [a]hand of God was also on Judah to give them one heart to do
what the king and the princes commanded by the word of the LORD.
13 Now many people were gathered at Jerusalem to celebrate the
Feast of Unleavened Bread [a]in the second month, a very large as-
sembly.
14 And they arose and removed the altars which *were* in Jerusalem;
they also [a]removed all the incense altars and [b]cast *them* into the
brook Kidron.
15 Then [a]they slaughtered the Passover *lambs* on the fourteenth of
the second month. And [b]the priests and Levites were ashamed of
themselves and consecrated themselves, and brought burnt offerings
to the house of the LORD.
16 And [a]they stood at their stations after their custom, according to
the law of Moses the man of God; the priests sprinkled the blood
which they received from the hand of the Levites.
17 For *there were* many in the assembly who had not consecrated
themselves; therefore, [a]the Levites *were* over the slaughter of the
Passover *lambs* for everyone who *was* unclean, in order to consecrate
them to the LORD.
18 For a multitude of the people, [a]*even* many from Ephraim and
Manasseh, Issachar and Zebulun, had not purified themselves, [b]yet
they ate the Passover [c]otherwise than [1]prescribed. For Hezekiah
prayed for them, saying, "May the good LORD pardon
19 [a]everyone who prepares his heart to seek God, the LORD God of
his fathers, though not according to the purification *rules* of the sanc-
tuary."
20 So the LORD heard Hezekiah and [a]healed the people.
21 And the sons of Israel present in Jerusalem [a]celebrated the Feast
of Unleavened Bread *for* seven days with great joy, and the Levites
and the priests praised the LORD day after day with loud instruments
to the LORD.
22 Then Hezekiah [a]spoke [1]encouragingly to all the Levites who
showed good insight *in the things* of the LORD. So they ate for the
appointed seven days, sacrificing peace offerings and [b]giving thanks
to the LORD God of their fathers.
23 Then the whole assembly [a]decided to celebrate *the feast* another
seven days, so they celebrated the seven days with joy.
24 For [a]Hezekiah king of Judah had contributed to the assembly
1,000 bulls and 7,000 sheep, and the princes had contributed to the
assembly 1,000 bulls and 10,000 sheep; and [b]a large number of
priests consecrated themselves.
25 And all the assembly of Judah rejoiced, with the priests and the
Levites, and [a]all the assembly that came from Israel, both the so-
journers who came from the land of Israel and those living in Judah.
26 So there was great joy in Jerusalem, because there was nothing
like this in Jerusalem [a]since the days of Solomon the son of David,
king of Israel.

9 [b]Ex. 34:6, 7
10 [1]Lit., *runn* [a]2 Chr. 36:16
11 [a]2 Chr. 30
12 [a]2 Cor. 3:5 2:13; Heb. 13:
13 [a]2 Chr. 30:
14 [a]2 Chr. 28: [b]2 Chr. 29:16
15 [a]2 Chr. 30: [b]2 Chr. 29:34
16 [a]2 Chr. 35:
17 [a]2 Chr. 29:3
18 [1]Lit., *written* 30:11, 25 [b]Num [c]Ex. 12:43-49
19 [a]2 Chr. 19:3
20 [a]James 5:16
21 [a]Ex. 12:15;
22 [1]Lit., *to the h* [a]2 Chr. 32:6 [b]Ez
23 [a]1 Kin. 8:65
24 [a]2 Chr. 35:7, [b]2 Chr. 29:34; 30
25 [a]2 Chr. 30:11,
26 [a]2 Chr. 7:8-10

27 Then [a]the Levitical priests arose and [b]blessed the people; and
their voice was heard and their prayer came to [c]His holy dwelling
place, to heaven.

Chapter 31

31 Now when all this was finished, all Israel who were present
went out to the cities of Judah, [a]broke the pillars in pieces, cut
down the [1]Asherim, and pulled down the high places and the altars
throughout all Judah and Benjamin, as well as in Ephraim and
Manasseh, [2]until they had destroyed them all. Then all the sons of
Israel returned to their cities, each to his possession.
2 And Hezekiah appointed [a]the divisions of the priests and the
Levites by their divisions, each according to his service, *both* the
priests and the Levites, [b]for burnt offerings and for peace offerings,
to minister and to give thanks and to praise in the gates of the camp
of the LORD.
3 *He* also *appointed* [a]the king's portion of his goods for the burnt
offerings, *namely,* for the morning and evening burnt offerings, and
the burnt offerings for the sabbaths and for the new moons and for
the fixed festivals, [b]as it is written in the law of the LORD.
4 Also he [1]commanded the people who lived in Jerusalem to give
[a]the portion due to the priests and the Levites, that they might
devote themselves to [b]the law of the LORD.
5 And as soon as the [1]order spread, the sons of Israel provided in
abundance the first fruits of grain, new wine, oil, honey, and of all
the produce of the field; and they brought in abundantly [a]the tithe of
all.
6 And the sons of Israel and Judah who lived in the cities of Judah,
also brought in the tithe of oxen and sheep, and [a]the tithe of [1]sacred
gifts which were consecrated to the LORD their God, and placed *them*
in heaps.
7 In the third month they began to [1]make the heaps, and finished
them by the seventh month.
8 And when Hezekiah and the rulers came and saw the heaps,
they blessed the LORD and [a]His people Israel.
9 Then Hezekiah questioned the priests and the Levites concern-
ing the heaps.
10 And Azariah the chief priest [a]of the house of Zadok said to [1]him,
"[b]Since the contributions began to be brought into the house of the
LORD, we have had enough to eat with plenty left over, for the LORD
has blessed His people, and this great quantity is left over."
11 Then Hezekiah commanded *them* to prepare [a]rooms in the house
of the LORD, and they prepared *them*.
12 And they faithfully brought in the contributions and the tithes
and the consecrated things; and Conaniah the Levite *was* the officer
in charge [a]of them and his brother Shimei *was* second.
13 And Jehiel, Azaziah, Nahath, Asahel, Jerimoth, Jozabad, Eliel,
Ismachiah, Mahath, and Benaiah *were* overseers [1]under the authority
of Conaniah and Shimei his brother by the appointment of King
Hezekiah, and [a]Azariah *was* the *chief* officer of the house of God.
14 And Kore the son of Imnah the Levite, the keeper of the eastern
gate, was over the freewill offerings of God, to apportion the con-
tributions for the LORD and the most holy things.
15 And [1]under his authority *were* [a]Eden, Miniamin, Jeshua,

: Chr. 23:18 [b]Num. 3 [c]Deut. 26:15; Ps. 68:5

31:1 [1]I.e., wooden ymbols of a female deity [2]Lit., *even to* letion [a]2 Kin. 18:4

Chr. 24:1 [b]1 Chr. 23:28-31

2 Chr. 35:7 [b]Num. 28:1-29:40

Lit., *said to* [a]Num. 18:8 [b]Mal. 2:7

[1]Lit., *word* [a]Neh. 13:12

[1]Lit., *consecrated* ings [a]Lev. 27:30; Deut. 14:28

7 [1]Lit., *found*

[a]Deut. 33:29; Ps. 33:12; 144:15

[1]Lit., *him, and he* aid [a]1 Chr. 6:8, 9 [b]Mal. 3:10

11 [a]1 Kin. 6:5, 8

12 [a]2 Chr. 35:9

it., *from the hand of* [a]2 Chr. 31:10

., *under his hand* [a]2 Chr. 29:12

Shemaiah, Amariah, and Shecaniah in [b]the cities of the priests, to
distribute faithfully *their portions* to their brothers by divisions,
whether great or small,
16 without regard to their genealogical enrollment, to the males
from [1a]thirty years old and upward—everyone who entered the
house of the LORD [b]for his daily obligations—for their work in their
duties according to their divisions;
17 as well as the priests who were enrolled genealogically accord-
ing to their fathers' households, and the Levites [a]from twenty years
old and upwards, by their duties *and* their divisions.
18 And the genealogical enrollment *included* [1]all their little children,
their wives, their sons, and their daughters, for the whole assembly,
for they consecrated themselves [2]faithfully in holiness.
19 Also for the sons of Aaron the priests *who were* in [a]the pasture
lands of their cities, or in each and every city, [b]*there were* men who
were designated by name to distribute portions to every male
among the priests and to everyone genealogically enrolled among
the Levites.
20 And thus Hezekiah did throughout all Judah; and [a]he did what
was good, right, and true before the LORD his God.
21 And every work which he began in the service of the house of
God in law and in commandment, seeking his God, he did with all
his heart and [a]prospered.

Chapter 32

32 After these [1]acts of faithfulness [a]Sennacherib king of Assyria
came and invaded Judah and besieged the fortified cities, and
[2]thought to break into them for himself.
2 Now when Hezekiah saw that Sennacherib had come, and that
[1]he intended to make war on Jerusalem,
3 he decided with his officers and his warriors to cut off the *supply
of* water from the springs which *were* outside the city, and they
helped him.
4 So many people assembled [a]and stopped up all the springs and
[b]the stream which flowed [1]through the region, saying, "Why should
the kings of Assyria come and find abundant water?"
5 And he took courage and [a]rebuilt all the wall that had been
broken down, and [1]erected towers on it, and *built* [b]another outside
wall, and strengthened the [c]Millo *in* the city of David, and made
weapons and shields in great number.
6 And he appointed military officers over the people, and
gathered them to him in the square at the city gate, and [a]spoke
[1]encouragingly to them, saying,
7 "[a]Be strong and courageous, do not fear or be dismayed because
of the king of Assyria, nor because of all the multitude which is with
him; [b]for the one with us is greater than the one with him.
8 "With him is *only* [a]an arm of flesh, but [b]with us is the LORD our
God to help us and to fight our battles." And the people relied on the
words of Hezekiah king of Judah.
9 After this [a]Sennacherib king of Assyria sent his servants to Jeru-
salem while he *was* [1]besieging Lachish with all his forces with him,
against Hezekiah king of Judah and against all Judah who *were* at
Jerusalem, saying,

15 [b]Josh. 21
16 [1]Heb., *thr* 23:3 [b]Ezra 3
17 [a]1 Chr. 23
18 [1]Lit., *with* *their faithfulne*
19 [a]Lev. 25:3 35:2-5 [b]2 Chr
20 [a]2 Kin. 20:
21 [a]Deut. 29:9 3:9, 10
32:1 [1]Lit., *thin* *this faithfulness* *said* [a]2 Kin. 18 37; Is. 36:1-37:
2 [1]Lit., *his face* *against*
4 [1]Lit., *in the m* *the land* [a]2 Kin. [b]2 Chr. 32:30
5 [1]Lit., *raised o* *towers* [a]2 Chr. [b]2 Kin. 25:4 [c]1
6 [1]Lit., *upon the* *hearts* [a]2 Chr. 3
7 [a]1 Chr. 22:13 6:16
8 [a]Jer. 17:5 [b]2 C 20:17
9 [1]Lit., *against* [a] 18:17

10 "Thus says Sennacherib king of Assyria, 'On what are you trust-
ing that you are remaining in Jerusalem under siege?
11 'Is not Hezekiah misleading you to give yourselves over to die by
hunger and by thirst, saying, "The LORD our God will deliver us
from the [1]hand of the king of Assyria"?
12 '[a]Has not the same Hezekiah taken away His high places and His
altars, and said to Judah and [1]Jerusalem, "You shall worship before
one altar, and on it you shall [2]burn incense"?
13 'Do you not know what I and my fathers have done to all the
peoples of the lands? [a]Were the gods of the nations of the lands able
at all to deliver their land from my hand?
14 '[a]Who *was there* among all the gods of those nations which my
fathers utterly destroyed who could deliver his people out of my
hand, that your God should be able to deliver you from my hand?
15 'Now therefore, do not let Hezekiah deceive you or mislead you
like this, and do not believe him, for [a]no god of any nation or king-
dom was able to deliver his people from my hand or from the hand
of my fathers. How much less shall your God deliver you from my
hand?' "
16 And his servants spoke further against the LORD God and
against His servant Hezekiah.
17 He also wrote letters to insult the LORD God of Israel, and to
speak against Him, saying, "[a]As the gods of the nations of the lands
[1]have not delivered their people from my hand, so the God of Heze-
kiah shall not deliver His people from my hand."
18 And [a]they called this out with a loud voice in the language of
Judah to the people of Jerusalem who were on the wall, to frighten
and terrify them, so that they might take the city.
19 And they spoke [1]of the God of Jerusalem as of [a]the gods of the
peoples of the earth, the work of men's hands.
20 But King Hezekiah and Isaiah the prophet, the son of Amoz,
prayed about this and cried out to heaven.
21 And the LORD sent an angel who destroyed every mighty war-
rior, commander and officer in the camp of the king of Assyria. So he
returned [1]in shame to his own land. And when he had entered the
temple of his god, some of his own children killed him there with
the sword.
22 So the LORD [a]saved Hezekiah and the inhabitants of Jerusalem
from the hand of Sennacherib the king of Assyria, and from the hand
of all *others,* and [1]guided them on every side.
23 And [a]many were bringing gifts to the LORD at Jerusalem and
choice presents to Hezekiah king of Judah, so that [b]he was exalted in
the sight of all nations thereafter.
24 [a]In those days Hezekiah became [1]mortally ill; and he prayed to
the LORD, and [2]the LORD spoke to him and gave him a sign.
25 But Hezekiah gave no return for the benefit [1]he received,
[a]because his heart was [2]proud; [b]therefore wrath came on him and on
Judah and Jerusalem.
26 However, [a]Hezekiah [1]humbled the pride of his heart, both he and
the inhabitants of Jerusalem, so that the wrath of the LORD did not
come on them in the days of Hezekiah.
27 Now Hezekiah had immense riches and honor; and he made for
himself treasuries for silver, gold, precious stones, spices, shields and
all kinds of valuable articles,

11 [1]Lit., *palm*
12 [1]Lit., *Jerusalem,* ...*ng,* [2]Lit., *offer up in smoke* [a]2 Chr. 31:1
13 [a]2 Kin. 18:33-35
14 [a]Is. 10:9-11
15 [a]Ex. 5:2; Is. ...6:18-20; Dan. 3:15
17 [1]Lit., *who have* [a]2 Chr. 32:14
18 [a]2 Kin. 18:28
...it., *to* [a]Ps. 115:4-8
[1]Lit., *in shame of face*
...Another reading is ...*them rest* [a]Is. 31:5
23 [a]2 Sam. 8:10 [b]2 Chr. 1:1
...t., *sick to the point of death* [2]Lit., *He* [a]2 Kin. 20:1-11; Is. 38:1-8
[1]Lit., *to him* [2]Lit., ...*igh* [a]2 Chr. 26:16; ...2:31 [b]2 Chr. 24:18
26 [1]Lit., *humbled himself in* [a]Jer. 26:18, 19

28 storehouses also for the produce of grain, wine and oil, pens for
all kinds of cattle and [1]sheepfolds for the flocks.
29 And he made cities for himself, and acquired flocks and herds in
abundance; for [a]God had given him very great [1]wealth.
30 It was Hezekiah who [a]stopped the upper outlet of the waters of
[b]Gihon and directed them to the west side of the city of David. And
Hezekiah prospered in all that he did.
31 And even *in the matter of* [a]the envoys of the rulers of Babylon,
who sent to him to inquire of [b]the wonder that had happened in the
land, God left him *alone only* [c]to test him, that He might know all that
was in his heart.
32 Now the rest of the acts of Hezekiah and his deeds of devotion,
behold, they are written in the vision of Isaiah the prophet, the son
of Amoz, in the Book of the Kings of Judah and Israel.
33 So Hezekiah slept with his fathers, and they buried him in the
[1]upper section of the tombs of the sons of David; and all Judah and
the inhabitants of Jerusalem [a]honored him at his death. And his son
Manasseh became king in his place.

Chapter 33

33 [a]Manasseh was twelve years old when he became king, and
he reigned fifty-five years in Jerusalem.
2 And [a]he did evil in the sight of the LORD according to the abomi-
nations of the nations whom the LORD dispossessed before the sons
of Israel.
3 For [a]he rebuilt the high places which Hezekiah his father had
broken down; [b]he also erected altars for the Baals and made
[1]Asherim, and worshiped all the host of heaven and served them.
4 And [a]he built altars in the house of the LORD of which the LORD
had said, "My name shall be [b]in Jerusalem forever."
5 For he built altars for all the host of heaven in [a]the two courts of
the house of the LORD.
6 And [a]he made his sons pass through the fire in the valley of
Ben-hinnom; and he practiced witchcraft, used divination, practiced
sorcery, and [b]dealt with mediums and spiritists. He did much evil in
the sight of the LORD, provoking Him *to anger.*
7 Then he put [a]the carved image of the idol which he had made in
the house of God, of which God had said to David and to Solomon
his son, "[b]In this house and in Jerusalem, which I have chosen from
all the tribes of Israel, I will put My name forever;
8 and I will not again remove the foot of Israel from the land
[a]which I have appointed for your fathers, if only they will observe to
do all that I have commanded them according to all the law, the
statutes, and the ordinances *given* through Moses."
9 Thus Manasseh misled Judah and the inhabitants of Jerusalem to
do more evil than the nations whom the LORD destroyed before the
sons of Israel.
10 And the LORD spoke to Manasseh and his people, but [a]they paid
no attention.
11 [a]Therefore the LORD brought the commanders of the army of the
king of Assyria against them, and they captured Manasseh with
[1]hooks, [b]bound him with bronze *chains,* and took him to Babylon.
12 And when [a]he was in distress, he entreated the LORD his God
and [b]humbled himself greatly before the God of his fathers.

28 [1]So ancient versions; Heb., *for the sheepfo*
29 [1]Lit., *posses property* [a]1 Ch
30 [a]2 Kin. 20:2 1:33
31 [a]2 Kin. 20:12 39:1 [b]2 Chr. 32 38:7, 8 [c]Deut. 8
33 [1]Or, *ascent* 112:6; Prov. 10:
33:1 [a]2 Kin. 21:
2 [a]2 Chr. 28:3; J
3 [1]I.e., wooden symbols of a fem deity [a]2 Chr. 31: [b]Deut. 16:21; 2 K 23:5, 6
4 [a]2 Chr. 28:24 [b]2 Sam. 7:13; 2 C
5 [a]2 Chr. 4:9
6 [a]2 Chr. 28:3 [b]L 19:31; 20:27
7 [a]2 Chr. 33:15 [b] 9:3-5; 2 Chr. 7:16;
8 [a]2 Sam. 7:10
10 [a]Neh. 9:29; Je
11 [1]I.e., thongs pu through the nose 28:36 [b]2 Chr. 36:6
12 [a]Ps. 118:5; 120 130:1, 2 [b]2 Chr. 3

13 When he prayed to Him, [a]He was moved by his entreaty and
heard his supplication, and brought him again to Jerusalem to his
kingdom. Then Manasseh [b]knew that the LORD *was* God.
14 Now after this he built the outer wall of the city of David on the
west side of [a]Gihon, in the valley, even to the entrance of the [b]Fish
Gate; and he encircled the [c]Ophel *with it* and made it very high. Then
he put army commanders in all the fortified cities of Judah.
15 He also [a]removed the foreign gods and the idol from the house
of the LORD, as well as all the altars which he had built on the
mountain of the house of the LORD and in Jerusalem, and he threw
them outside the city.
16 And he set up the altar of the LORD and sacrificed [a]peace offer-
ings and thank offerings on it; and he ordered Judah to serve the
LORD God of Israel.
17 Nevertheless [a]the people still sacrificed in the high places, *al-
though* only to the LORD their God.
18 Now the rest of the acts of Manasseh even [a]his prayer to his God,
and the words of [b]the seers who spoke to him in the name of the
LORD God of Israel, behold, they are among the records of the kings
of [c]Israel.
19 His prayer also and [a]*how God* was entreated by him, and all his
sin, his unfaithfulness, and [b]the sites on which he built high places
and erected the Asherim and the carved images, before he humbled
himself, behold, they are written in the records of the [1]Hozai.
20 So Manasseh slept with his fathers, and they buried him in his
own house. And Amon his son became king in his place.
21 [a]Amon *was* twenty-two years old when he became king, and he
reigned two years in Jerusalem.
22 And he did evil in the sight of the LORD as Manasseh his father
[a]had done, and Amon sacrificed to all [b]the carved images which his
father Manasseh had made, and he served them.
23 Moreover, he did not humble himself before the LORD [a]as his
father Manasseh had [1]done, but Amon multiplied guilt.
24 Finally [a]his servants conspired against him and put him to death
in his own house.
25 But the people of the land [1]killed all the conspirators against
King Amon, and the people of the land made Josiah his son king in
his place.

Chapter 34

34 [a]Josiah *was* eight years old when he became king, and he
reigned thirty-one years in Jerusalem.
2 And [a]he did right in the sight of the LORD, and walked in the
ways of his father David and did not turn aside to the right or to the
left.
3 For in the eighth year of his reign while he was still a youth, he
began to [a]seek the God of his father David; and in the twelfth year he
began [b]to purge Judah and Jerusalem of the high places, the
Asherim, the carved images, and the molten images.
4 And they tore down the altars of the Baals in his presence, and
[a]the incense altars that were high above them he chopped down; also
the Asherim, the carved images, and the molten images he broke in
pieces and [b]ground to powder and scattered *it* on the graves of those
who had sacrificed to them.

r. 5:20; Ezra
3 [b]Dan. 4:32

. 1:33 [b]Neh.
[c]2 Chr. 27:3

2 Chr. 33:3-7

[a]Lev. 7:11-18

[a]2 Chr. 32:12

Chr. 33:12, 13
33:10 [c]2 Chr.
21:2

r. reads *seers*
33:13 [b]2 Chr.
33:3

2 Kin. 21:19-24

[a]2 Chr. 33:2-7
[b]2 Chr. 34:3, 4

[1]Lit., *humbled himself* [a]2 Chr.
33:12, 19

4 [a]2 Chr. 25:27

25 [1]Lit., *smote*

[a]2 Kin. 22:1, 2;
Jer. 1:2; 3:6

2 [a]2 Chr. 29:2

2 Chr. 15:2; Prov.
Kin. 13:2; 2 Chr.
33:22

[a]2 Kin. 23:4, 5, 11
[b]Ex. 32:20

5 Then [a]he burned the bones of the priests on their altars, and
purged Judah and Jerusalem.
6 And [a]in the cities of Manasseh, Ephraim, Simeon, even as far as
Naphtali, in their surrounding ruins,
7 he also tore down the altars and [a]beat the Asherim and the
carved images into powder, and chopped down all the incense altars
throughout the land of Israel. Then he returned to Jerusalem.
8 [a]Now in the eighteenth year of his reign, when he had purged
the land and the house, he sent Shaphan the son of Azaliah, and
Maaseiah [b]an official of the city, and Joah the son of Joahaz the
recorder, to repair the house of the LORD his God.
9 And they came to [a]Hilkiah the high priest and delivered the
money that was brought into the house of God, which the Levites,
the [1]doorkeepers, had collected [2]from [b]Manasseh and Ephraim, and
from all the remnant of Israel, and from all Judah and Benjamin and
the inhabitants of Jerusalem.
10 Then they gave *it* into the hands of the workmen who had the
oversight of the house of the LORD, and the workmen who were
working in the house of the LORD [1]used it to restore and repair the
house.
11 They in turn gave *it* to the carpenters and to the builders to buy
quarried stone and timber for couplings and to make beams for the
houses [a]which the kings of Judah had let go to ruin.
12 And [a]the men did the work faithfully with foremen over them to
supervise: Jahath and Obadiah, the Levites of the sons of Merari,
Zechariah and Meshullam of the sons of the Kohathites, and [b]the
Levites, all who were skillful with musical instruments.
13 *They were* also over [a]the burden bearers, and supervised all the
workmen from job to job; and *some* of the Levites *were* scribes and
officials and gatekeepers.
14 When they were bringing out the money which had been
brought into the house of the LORD, [a]Hilkiah the priest found the
book of the law of the LORD *given* by Moses.
15 And Hilkiah responded and said to Shaphan the scribe, "I have
found the book of the law in the house of the LORD." And Hilkiah
gave the book to Shaphan.
16 Then Shaphan brought the book to the king and [1]reported fur-
ther word to the king, saying, "Everything that was [2]entrusted to
your servants they are doing.
17 "They have also emptied out the money which was found in the
house of the LORD, and have delivered it into the hands of the super-
visors and the workmen."
18 Moreover, Shaphan the scribe told the king saying, "Hilkiah the
priest gave me a book." And Shaphan read from it in the presence of
the king.
19 And it came about when the king heard [a]the words of the law
that [b]he tore his clothes.
20 Then the king commanded Hilkiah, Ahikam the son of Shaphan,
[1]Abdon the son of Micah, Shaphan the scribe, and Asaiah the king's
servant, saying,
21 "Go, inquire of the LORD for me and for those who are left in Israel
and in Judah, concerning the words of the book which has been
found; for [a]great is the wrath of the LORD which is poured out on us

5 [a]1 Kin. 13:2 23:20
6 [a]2 Kin. 23:1
7 [a]2 Chr. 31:1
8 [a]2 Kin. 22:3 [b]2 Chr. 18:25
9 [1]Lit., *guardia threshold* [2]Lit. *hand of* [a]2 Ch [b]2 Chr. 30:10,
10 [1]Lit., *gave*
11 [a]2 Chr. 33:4
12 [a]2 Kin. 12:1 [b]1 Chr. 25:1
13 [a]Neh. 4:10
14 [a]2 Chr. 34:9
16 [1]Lit., *returne given into the ha*
19 [a]Deut. 28:3-6 [b]Josh. 7:6
20 [1]In 2 Kin. 22: *Achbor, son of M*
21 [a]2 Chr. 29:8

2 [1]So with Gr. [2]In because our fathers have not observed the word of the LORD, to do
22:14 *Tikvah, son* according to all that is written in this book."
of Harhas **22** So Hilkiah and *those* whom the king [1]had told went to Huldah
the prophetess, the wife of Shallum the son of [2]Tokhath, the son of
Hasrah, the keeper of the wardrobe (now she lived in Jerusalem in
the Second Quarter); and they spoke to her regarding this.
4 [a]2 Chr. 36:14-20 23 And she said to them, "Thus says the LORD, the God of Israel,
[b]Deut. 28:15-68 'Tell the man who sent you to Me,
24 thus says the LORD, "Behold, [a]I am bringing evil on this place
and on its inhabitants, *even* all [b]the curses written in the book which
they have read in the presence of the king of Judah.
25 [a]2 Chr. 33:3 25 "[a]Because they have forsaken Me and have burned incense to
other gods, that they might provoke Me to anger with all the works
of their hands, therefore My wrath will be poured out on this place,
and it shall not be quenched." '
26 "But to the king of Judah who sent you to inquire of the LORD,
Kin. 22:19; 2 Chr. thus you will say to him, 'Thus says the LORD God of Israel *regarding*
12:7; 32:26 the words which you have heard,
27 "[a]Because your heart was tender and you humbled yourself
before God, when you heard His words against this place and
against its inhabitants, and *because* you humbled yourself before Me,
29 [a]2 Kin. 23:1-3 tore your clothes, and wept before Me, I truly have heard you,"
declares the LORD.
28 "Behold, I will gather you to your fathers and you shall be
gathered to your grave in peace, so your eyes shall not see all the
evil which I will bring on this place and on its inhabitants." ' " And
30 [a]Neh. 8:1-3 they brought back word to the king.
29 [a]Then the king sent and gathered all the elders of Judah and
Jerusalem.
30 And the king went up to the house of the LORD and [a]all the men
of Judah, the inhabitants of Jerusalem, the priests, the Levites, and all
2 Kin. 11:14; 23:3; the people, from the greatest to the least; and he read in their hearing
Chr. 30:16 [b]2 Chr. all the words of the book of the covenant which was found in the
23:16; 29:10 house of the LORD.
31 Then the king [a]stood in his place and [b]made a covenant before
the LORD to walk after the LORD, and to keep His commandments
and His testimonies and His statutes with all his heart and with all
[1]Lit., *days* [a]2 Chr. his soul, to perform the words of the covenant written in this book.
34:3-7 32 Moreover, he made all who were present in Jerusalem and Ben-
jamin to stand *with him.* So the inhabitants of Jerusalem did accord-
ing to the covenant of God, the God of their fathers.
33 And Josiah [a]removed all the abominations from all the lands
[a]2 Kin. 23:21 [b]Ex. belonging to the sons of Israel, and made all who were present in
12:6; Num. 9:3 Israel to serve the LORD their God. Throughout his [1]lifetime they did
not turn from following the LORD God of their fathers.

Chapter 35

2 [a]2 Chr. 29:11 **35** Then Josiah [a]celebrated the Passover to the LORD in Jerusalem,
and [b]they slaughtered the Passover *animals* on the fourteenth
day of the first month.
2 And he set the priests in their offices and [a]encouraged them in
the service of the house of the LORD.
Chr. 17:8, 9; Neh. 3 He also said to [a]the Levites who taught all Israel *and* who were
8:7 holy to the LORD, "Put the holy ark in the house which Solomon the

son of David king of Israel built; [b]it will be a burden on *your*
shoulders no longer. Now serve the LORD your God and His people
Israel.
4 "And [a]prepare *yourselves* by your fathers' households in your
divisions, according to the writing of David king of Israel and [b]ac-
cording to the writing of his son Solomon.
5 "Moreover, [a]stand in the holy place according to the sections of
the fathers' households of your brethren the [1]lay people, and accord-
ing to the Levites, by division of a father's household.
6 "Now [a]slaughter the Passover *animals*, [b]sanctify yourselves, and
prepare for your brethren to do according to the word of the LORD by
Moses."
7 And Josiah contributed to the lay people, to all who were pres-
ent, flocks of lambs and kids, all for the Passover offerings, number-
ing 30,000 plus 3,000 bulls; these were from the king's possessions.
8 His officers also contributed a freewill offering to the people, the
priests, and the Levites. Hilkiah and Zechariah and Jehiel, [a]the offi-
cials of the house of God, gave to the priests for the Passover offer-
ings 2,600 *from the flocks* and 300 bulls.
9 [a]Conaniah also, and Shemaiah and Nethanel, his brothers, and
Hashabiah and Jeiel and Jozabad, the officers of the Levites, con-
tributed to the Levites for the Passover offerings 5,000 *from the flocks*
and 500 bulls.
10 So the service was prepared, and [a]the priests stood at their sta-
tions and the Levites by their divisions according to the king's com-
mand.
11 And [1a]they slaughtered the Passover *animals*, and while [b]the
priests sprinkled [2]the blood *received* from their hand, [c]the Levites
skinned *them*.
12 Then they removed the burnt offerings that *they* might give them
to the sections of the fathers' households of the lay people to present
to the LORD, as it is written in the book of Moses. *They did* this also
with the bulls.
13 So [a]they roasted the Passover *animals* on the fire according to the
ordinance, and they boiled [b]the holy things in pots, in kettles, in
pans, and carried *them* speedily to all the lay people.
14 And afterwards they prepared for themselves and for the priests,
because the priests, the sons of Aaron, *were* offering the burnt offer-
ings and the fat until night; therefore the Levites prepared for them-
selves and for the priests, the sons of Aaron.
15 The singers, the sons of Asaph, *were* also at their stations [a]accord-
ing to the command of David, Asaph, Heman, and Jeduthun the
king's seer; and [b]the gatekeepers at each gate did not have to depart
from their service, because the Levites their brethren prepared for
them.
16 So all the service of the LORD was prepared on that day to
celebrate the Passover, and to offer burnt offerings on the altar of the
LORD according to the command of King Josiah.
17 Thus [a]the sons of Israel who were present celebrated the Pass-
over at that time, and the Feast of Unleavened Bread seven days.
18 And [a]there had not been celebrated a Passover like it in Israel
since the days of Samuel the prophet; nor had any of the kings of
Israel celebrated such a Passover as Josiah did with the priests, the

3 [b]1 Chr. 23:2

4 [a]1 Chr. 9:10 [b]2 Chr. 8:14

5 [1]Lit., *sons o*
people, and so
throughout the
[a]Ezra 6:18

6 [a]2 Chr. 35:1
29:5

8 [a]2 Chr. 31:13

9 [a]2 Chr. 31:12

10 [a]2 Chr. 35:5

11 [1]I.e., the Lev
[2]So with Gr. [a]2
35:1, 6 [b]2 Chr. 2
[c]2 Chr. 29:34

13 [a]Ex. 12:8, 9
6:28

15 [a]1 Chr. 25:1
26:12-19

17 [a]Ex. 12:1-20;
30:21

18 [a]2 Kin. 23:21;
30:5

Levites, all Judah and Israel who were present, and the inhabitants of Jerusalem.
19 In the eighteenth year of Josiah's reign this Passover was celebrated.
20 [a]After all this, when Josiah had set the [1]temple in order, Neco king of Egypt came up to make war at [b]Carchemish on the Euphrates, and Josiah went out to engage him.
21 But [1]Neco sent messengers to him, saying, "[a]What have we to do with each other, O King of Judah? *I am* not *coming* against you today but against the house with which I am at war, and God has ordered me to hurry. Stop for your own sake from *interfering with* God who is with me, that He may not destroy you."
22 However, Josiah would not turn [1]away from him, but [a]disguised himself in order to make war with him; nor did he listen to the words of Neco [b]from the mouth of God, but came to make war on the plain of [c]Megiddo.
23 And the archers shot King Josiah, and the king said to his servants, "Take me away, for I am badly wounded."
24 So his servants took him out of the chariot and carried him in the second chariot which he had, and brought him to Jerusalem [1]where he died and was buried in the tombs of his fathers. [a]And all Judah and Jerusalem mourned for Josiah.
25 Then [a]Jeremiah chanted a lament for Josiah. And all the male and female singers speak about Josiah in their lamentations to this day. And they made them an ordinance in Israel; behold, they are also written in the Lamentations.
26 Now the rest of the acts of Josiah and his deeds of devotion as written in the law of the LORD,
27 and his acts, first to last, behold, they are written in the Book of the Kings of Israel and Judah.

Chapter 36

36 [a]Then the people of the land took [1b]Joahaz the son of Josiah, and made him king in place of his father in Jerusalem.
2 Joahaz was twenty-three years old when he became king, and he reigned three months in Jerusalem.
3 Then the king of Egypt deposed him at Jerusalem, and imposed on the land a fine of one hundred talents of silver and one talent of gold.
4 And the king of Egypt made Eliakim his brother king over Judah and Jerusalem, and changed his name to Jehoiakim. But [a]Neco took Joahaz his brother and brought him to Egypt.
5 [a]Jehoiakim was twenty-five years old when he became king, and he reigned eleven years in Jerusalem; and he did evil in the sight of the LORD his God.
6 Nebuchadnezzar king of Babylon came up [a]against him and [b]bound him with bronze *chains* to take him to Babylon.
7 [a]Nebuchadnezzar also brought *some* of the articles of the house of the LORD to Babylon and put them in his temple at Babylon.
8 [a]Now the rest of the acts of Jehoiakim and [1]the abominations which he did, and what was found against him, behold, they are written in the Book of the Kings of Israel and Judah. And Jehoiachin his son became king in his place.
9 [a]Jehoiachin was eight years old when he became king, and he

Lit., *house* [a]2 Kin. , 30 [b]Is. 10:9; Jer. 46:2
1 [1]Lit., *he* [a]2 Chr. 25:19
22 [1]Lit., *his face* Chr. 18:29 [b]2 Chr. 35:21 [c]Judg. 5:19
[1]Lit., *and* [a]Zech. 12:11
[a]Jer. 22:10; Lam. 4:20
[1]I.e., short form of Jehoahaz [a]2 Kin. :30-34 [b]Jer. 22:11
4 [a]Jer. 22:10-12
Kin. 23:36, 37; Jer. :13-19; 26:1; 35:1
[a]2 Kin. 24:1; Jer. :1-9 [b]2 Chr. 33:11
7 [a]2 Kin. 24:13
t., *his* [a]2 Kin. 24:5
9 [a]2 Kin. 24:8-17

reigned three months and ten days in Jerusalem, and he did evil in
the sight of the LORD.
10 And [a]at the turn of the year King Nebuchadnezzar sent and
brought him to Babylon with the valuable articles of the house of the
LORD, and he made his kinsman [b]Zedekiah king over Judah and
Jerusalem.
11 [a]Zedekiah was twenty-one years old when he became king, and
he reigned eleven years in Jerusalem.
12 And he did evil in the sight of the LORD his God; [a]he did not
humble himself [b]before Jeremiah the prophet [1]who spoke for the
LORD.
13 And [a]he also rebelled against King Nebuchadnezzar who had
made him swear *allegiance* by God. But [b]he stiffened his neck and
hardened his heart against turning to the LORD God of Israel.
14 Furthermore, all the officials of the priests and the people were
very unfaithful *following* all the abominations of the nations; and
they defiled the house of the LORD which He had sanctified in Jeru-
salem.
15 And the LORD, the God of their fathers, [a]sent *word* to them again
and again by His messengers, because He had compassion on His
people and on His dwelling place;
16 but they *continually* [a]mocked the messengers of God, [b]despised
His words and scoffed at His prophets, [c]until the wrath of the LORD
arose against His people, until there was no remedy.
17 [a]Therefore He brought up against them the king of the Chalde-
ans who slew their young men with the sword in the house of their
sanctuary, and had no compassion on young man or virgin, old man
or infirm; He gave *them* all into his hand.
18 And [a]all the articles of the house of God, great and small, and the
treasures of the house of the LORD, and the treasures of the king and
of his officers, he brought *them* all to Babylon.
19 Then [a]they burned the house of God, and broke down the wall of
Jerusalem and burned all its fortified buildings with fire, and
destroyed all its valuable articles.
20 And those who had escaped from the sword he [a]carried away to
Babylon; and [b]they were servants to him and to his sons until the
rule of the kingdom of Persia,
21 [a]to fulfill the word of the LORD by the mouth of Jeremiah, until
[b]the land had enjoyed its sabbaths. [c]All the days of its desolation it
kept sabbath [1d]until seventy years were complete.
22 [a]Now in the first year of Cyrus king of Persia—in order to fulfill
the word of the LORD [b]by the mouth of Jeremiah—the LORD [c]stirred
up the spirit of Cyrus king of Persia, so that he sent a proclamation
throughout his kingdom, and also *put it* in writing, saying,
23 "Thus says Cyrus king of Persia, 'The LORD, the God of heaven,
has given me all the kingdoms of the earth, and He has appointed
me to build Him a house in Jerusalem, which is in Judah. Whoever
there is among you of all His people, may the LORD his God be with
him, and let him go up!' "

10 [a]2 Sam. 22:25; 24:1; 17:12 [b]Jer. 3
11 [a]2 Kin. 24 Jer. 27:1; 28:
12 [1]Lit., *from of the LORD* 33:23 [b]Jer. 2
13 [a]Jer. 52:3; 17:15 [b]2 Chr.
15 [a]Jer. 7:13;
16 [a]2 Chr. 30: 5:12, 13 [b]Prov [c]Ezra 5:12
17 [a]2 Kin. 25:1 21:1-10
18 [a]2 Chr. 36:7
19 [a]1 Kin. 9:8; 2 25:9; Jer. 52:13
20 [a]2 Kin. 25:11 27:7
21 [1]Lit., *to fulfill years* [a]Jer. 29:10 26:34 [c]Lev. 25:4 25:11
22 [a]Ezra 1:1-3 [b] 25:12; 29:10 [c]Is.

2 CHRONICLES AT A GLANCE

e of 2 Chronicles:

MENT DIVISIONS

		CHAPTER THEMES
		1
		2
		3
		4
		5
		6
		7
		8
		9
		10
		11
		12
		13
		14
		15
		16
		17
		18
		19
		20
		21
		22
		23
		24
		25
		26
		27
		28
		29
		30
		31
		32
		33
		34
		35
		36

Author:

Date:

Purpose:

Key Words:

house

ark

covenant

cry (cried)

seek (sought)

heart

pray (prayer, prayed)

prophet(s)

EZRA

Every seventh year the land was to lie fallow. This was God's ordinance to His people, part law by which they were to govern their lives.

However, for 490 years God's people had not paid attention to this statute, nor to others. The had missed seventy sabbaths. As prophesied by Jeremiah, God would exact seventy years for the Then the Spirit of God would move on behalf of His people. He would stir up the spirit of Cyrus of Persia, so that Cyrus would send out a written decree, proclaiming, "The LORD, the God of he has given me all the kingdoms of the earth, and He has appointed me to build Him a hou Jerusalem, which is in Judah. Whoever there is among you of all His people, may the LORD his G with him, and let him go up!" (2 Chronicles 36:23).

And so a remnant returned from the land of exile to the land promised to Abraham, Isaac, and as an everlasting possession. Ezra tells us what happened.

THINGS TO DO

To better understand Ezra, look at Isaiah's prophecy in 44:28-45:7. This was written about 175 before Cyrus was born.

Ezra falls into two main segments: chapters 1 through 6 and chapters 7 through 10. There is a of approximately fifty-eight to sixty years between these two segments.

Chapters 1-6

1. Read this segment chapter by chapter and do the following:
   a. In a distinctive way mark the key words listed on the EZRA AT A GLANCE chart on page
   b. Pay attention to any references to time. Mark these in a way that will enable you to spot immediately. You may want to put a clock such as this in the margin next to the refer to time.
   c. When you come to a reference of a particular king, consult the historical chart E NEHEMIAH, AND ESTHER at the end of Ezra on page 713. This will help you appreciat historical setting of the book of Ezra and see the relationship of Ezra to Esther and Neher who were contemporaries of Ezra.
   d. If specific people play a significant role, record their names and briefly describe what they
2. There are seven official documents or letters in the book of Ezra, all of which, except the were written in Aramaic, the international language of the times. The first document writte Cyrus, the Persian king, is in Hebrew. These documents or letters are found in Ezra 1:2-4; 4:1 4:17-22; 5:7-17; 6:2-5; and 6:6-12. The last one is in the second segment of the book, 7:12-26.

   As you come to each document or letter in the text, underline who presented it. Then ir margin list the major points of the document or letter. This information will help you keep t of the opposition the Jews faced and how God moved on their behalf.
3. After you finish reading each chapter, identify the main subject, theme, or event and record the line next to the chapter number and on EZRA AT A GLANCE.
4. The book of Ezra records when the temple construction began and when it was completed. V this information in the margin in bold print so you can find it easily.
5. For a better understanding of the Jewish feasts, consult the chart THE FEASTS OF ISRAEL ir front of your Bible on pages I-48 and I-49.

ters 7-10

This is the first time Ezra's name appears in this book. Note how he is described. Observe this man and the lessons you can learn from his life. List your insights in the margin.

Don't forget to mark the key words listed on EZRA AT A GLANCE. Also, note your insights on the last official document in 7:12-26.

Watch for and mark references to time and to kings. Note these as you did before.

Record the theme of each chapter as you did in the first segment of Ezra.

How does the second segment of Ezra, chapters 7 through 10, differ from the first?

a. Record the theme or subject of the first six chapters on EZRA AT A GLANCE under "Segment Divisions." Do the same for the last segment, chapters 7 through 10.

b. On the second line for segment divisions write in the name of the central character(s) of each segment.

c. Consult the historical chart EZRA, NEHEMIAH, AND ESTHER on page 713 and then record the number of years covered in the first and second segments of Ezra.

What is the theme or teaching of Ezra? Record this and any other requested information in the appropriate place on EZRA AT A GLANCE.

NGS TO THINK ABOUT

How did the people in Ezra's time deal with their sin? What showed you whether their sorrow led to repentance or simply regret? How do you deal with sin in your own life? How is it dealt with within your church congregation?

What did you learn about prayer and fasting? Are either of these integral parts of your walk with the Lord? Why?

As you review what you have learned in Ezra, what have you learned about your God, His promises, and His ways? What difference can this knowledge make in your life?

Chapter 1

2 Chr. 36:22; Jer. 9:10 [b]Ezra 5:13

1 [a]Now in the first year of Cyrus king of Persia, in order to fulfill
the word of the LORD by the mouth of Jeremiah, the LORD stirred
up the spirit of Cyrus king of Persia, so that he [b]sent a proclamation
throughout all his kingdom, and also *put it* in writing, saying,

:28; 45:1, 12, 13

2 "Thus says Cyrus king of Persia, 'The LORD, the God of heaven,
has given me all the kingdoms of the earth, and [a]He has appointed
me to build Him a house in Jerusalem, which is in Judah.

. 8:23; 18:39; Is. 37:16; Dan. 6:26

3 'Whoever there is among you of all His people, may his God be
with him! Let him go up to Jerusalem which is in Judah, and rebuild
the house of the LORD, the God of Israel; [a]He is the God who is in
Jerusalem.

[1]Or, *reside as an alien* [2]Lit., *his*

4 'And every survivor, at whatever place he may [1]live, let the men
of [2]that place support him with silver and gold, with goods and
cattle, together with a freewill offering for the house of God which is
in Jerusalem.' "

5 [a]Ezra 1:1, 2

5 Then the heads of fathers' *households* of Judah and Benjamin and
the priests and the Levites arose, [a]even everyone whose spirit God
had stirred to go up and rebuild the house of the LORD which is in
Jerusalem.

Lit., *strengthened hands* [a]Neh. 6:9; Is. 35:3

6 And all those about them [1a]encouraged them with articles of
silver, with gold, with goods, with cattle, and with valuables, aside
from all that was given as a freewill offering.

7 [a]Also King Cyrus brought out the articles of the house of the
LORD, [b]which Nebuchadnezzar had carried away from Jerusalem
and put in the house of his gods;
8 and Cyrus, king of Persia, had them brought out by the hand of
Mithredath the treasurer, and he counted them out to [a]Sheshbazzar,
the prince of Judah.
9 Now this *was* their number: 30 [a]gold dishes, 1,000 silver dishes,
29 [1]duplicates;
10 30 gold bowls, 410 silver bowls of a second *kind, and* 1,000 other
articles.
11 All the articles of gold and silver *numbered* 5,400. Sheshbazzar
brought them all up with the exiles who went up from Babylon to
Jerusalem.

Chapter 2

2 [a]Now these are the [1]people of the province who came up out of
the captivity of the exiles whom Nebuchadnezzar the king of
Babylon had carried away to Babylon, and returned to Jerusalem
and Judah, each to his city.
2 [1]These came with Zerubbabel, Jeshua, Nehemiah, [2]Seraiah, [3]Re-
elaiah, Mordecai, Bilshan, [4]Mispar, Bigvai, [5]Rehum, and Baanah.
The number of the men of the people of Israel:
3 the sons of Parosh, 2,172;
4 the sons of Shephatiah, 372;
5 the sons of [a]Arah, 775;
6 the sons of [a]Pahath-moab of the sons of Jeshua *and* Joab, 2,812;
7 the sons of Elam, 1,254;
8 the sons of Zattu, 945;
9 the sons of Zaccai, 760;
10 the sons of [1]Bani, 642;
11 the sons of Bebai, 623;
12 the sons of Azgad, 1,222;
13 the sons of [a]Adonikam, 666;
14 the sons of Bigvai, 2,056;
15 the sons of Adin, 454;
16 the sons of Ater of Hezekiah, 98;
17 the sons of Bezai, 323;
18 the sons of [1]Jorah, 112;
19 the sons of Hashum, 223;
20 the sons of [1]Gibbar, 95;
21 the [1]men of [a]Bethlehem, 123;
22 the men of Netophah, 56;
23 the men of Anathoth, 128;
24 the sons of [1]Azmaveth, 42;
25 the sons of [1]Kiriath-arim, Chephirah, and Beeroth, 743;
26 the sons of [a]Ramah and Geba, 621;
27 the men of Michmas, 122;
28 the men of Bethel and Ai, 223;
29 the sons of Nebo, 52;
30 the sons of Magbish, 156;
31 the sons of the other Elam, 1,254;
32 the sons of Harim, 320;
33 the sons of Lod, Hadid, and Ono, 725;
34 the [1]men of [a]Jericho, 345;

7 [a]Ezra 5:14; [b]2 Kin. 24:13;
8 [a]Ezra 5:14
9 [1]Heb. obscu possible mean *knives, censer* 8:27
2:1 [1]Lit., *sons* 24:14-16; 25:1 36:20; Neh. 7:6
2 [1]Lit., *who* [2]In Neh. 7:7, A [3]In Neh. 7:7, R [4]In Neh. 7:7, M [5]In Neh. 7:7, N
5 [a]Neh. 7:10
6 [a]Neh. 7:11
10 [1]In Neh. 7:1
13 [a]Ezra 8:13
18 [1]In Neh. 7:2
20 [1]In Neh. 7:25 *Gibeon*
21 [1]Lit., *sons* [a](35:19; Matt. 2:6
24 [1]In Neh. 7:28 *Beth-azmaveth*
25 [1]In Neh. 7:29 *Kiriath-jearim*
26 [a]Josh. 18:25
34 [1]Lit., *sons* [a]1 16:34; 2 Chr. 28:1

35 the sons of Senaah, 3,630.
36 [a]The priests: the sons of Jedaiah of the house of Jeshua, 973;
37 the sons of [a]Immer, 1,052;
38 [a]the sons of Pashhur, 1,247;
39 the sons of [a]Harim, 1,017.
40 The Levites: the sons of Jeshua and Kadmiel, of the sons of
[1]Hodaviah, 74.
41 The singers: the sons of Asaph, 128.
42 The sons of the gatekeepers: the sons of Shallum, the sons of
Ater, the sons of Talmon, the sons of Akkub, the sons of Hatita, the
sons of Shobai, in all 139.
43 The [a]temple servants: the sons of Ziha, the sons of Hasupha, the
sons of Tabbaoth,
44 the sons of Keros, the sons of [1]Siaha, the sons of Padon,
45 the sons of Lebanah, the sons of Hagabah, the sons of Akkub,
46 the sons of Hagab, the sons of Shalmai, the sons of Hanan,
47 the sons of Giddel, the sons of Gahar, the sons of Reaiah,
48 the sons of Rezin, the sons of Nekoda, the sons of Gazzam,
49 the sons of Uzza, the sons of Paseah, the sons of Besai,
50 the sons of Asnah, the sons of Meunim, the sons of [1]Nephisim,
51 the sons of Bakbuk, the sons of Hakupha, the sons of Harhur,
52 the sons of [1]Bazluth, the sons of Mehida, the sons of Harsha,
53 the sons of Barkos, the sons of Sisera, the sons of Temah,
54 the sons of Neziah, the sons of Hatipha.
55 The sons of [a]Solomon's servants: the sons of Sotai, the sons of
[1]Hassophereth, the sons of [2]Peruda,
56 the sons of Jaalah, the sons of Darkon, the sons of Giddel,
57 the sons of Shephatiah, the sons of Hattil, the sons of Pochereth-
hazzebaim, the sons of [1]Ami.
58 All the [a]temple servants, and the sons of [b]Solomon's servants,
were 392.
59 Now these are those who came up from Tel-melah, Tel-harsha,
Cherub, [1]Addan, *and* Immer, but they were not able to [2]give evidence
of their fathers' households, and their [3]descendants, whether they
were of Israel:
60 the sons of Delaiah, the sons of Tobiah, the sons of Nekoda, 652.
61 And of the sons of the priests: the sons of [1]Habaiah, the sons of
Hakkoz, the sons of [a]Barzillai, who took a wife from the daughters of
Barzillai the Gileadite, and he was called by their name.
62 These searched *among* their ancestral registration, but they could
not be located; [a]therefore they were considered unclean *and excluded*
from the priesthood.
63 And the [1]governor said to them [a]that they should not eat from
the most holy things until a priest stood up with [b]Urim and Thum-
mim.
64 The whole assembly [1]numbered 42,360,
65 besides their male and female servants, [1]who numbered 7,337;
and they had 200 [a]singing men and women.
66 Their horses were 736; their mules, 245;
67 their camels, 435; *their* donkeys, 6,720.
68 And some of the heads of fathers' *households,* when they arrived
at the house of the LORD which is in Jerusalem, offered willingly for
the house of God to [1]restore it on its foundation.
69 According to their ability they gave [a]to the treasury for the work

36 [a]1 Chr. 24:7-18
37 [a]1 Chr. 24:14
38 [a]1 Chr. 9:12
39 [a]1 Chr. 24:8
[1]In Ezra 3:9, *Judah;* [N]eh. 7:43, *Hodevah*
43 [a]1 Chr. 9:2
[1]In Neh. 7:47, *Sia*
50 [1]In Neh. 7:52, *Nephushesim*
Neh. 7:54, *Bazlith*
55 [1]In Neh. 7:57, *[S]ophereth* [2]In Neh. *[P]erida* [a]1 Kin. 9:21
[i]n Neh. 7:59, *Amon*
[a]1 Chr. 9:2 [b]1 Kin. 9:21
59 [1]In Neh. 7:61, *[Ad]don* [2]Lit., *tell* [3]Lit., *seed*
61 [1]In Neh. 7:63, *[Hobai]ah* [a]2 Sam. 17:27; 1 Kin. 2:7
[6]2 [a]Num. 16:39, 40
Heb., *Tirshatha,* a [Pers]ian title [a]Lev. 2:3, [b]Ex. 28:30; Num. 27:21
[1]Lit., *together was*
[6]5 [1]Lit., *they were* [a]2 Chr. 35:25
68 [1]Lit., *establish*
69 [a]Ezra 8:25-34

61,000 gold drachmas, and 5,000 silver minas, and 100 priestly [1]gar-
ments.
70 [a]Now the priests and the Levites, some of the people, the singers,
the gatekeepers, and the temple servants lived in their cities, and all
Israel in their cities.

Chapter 3

3 Now when the seventh month came, and [a]the sons of Israel *were*
in the cities, the people gathered together as one man to Jerusa-
lem.
2 Then [a]Jeshua the son of Jozadak and his brothers the priests, and
[b]Zerubbabel the son [c]of Shealtiel, and his brothers arose and [d]built
the altar of the God of Israel, to offer burnt offerings on it, [e]as it is
written in the law of Moses, the man of God.
3 So they set up the altar on its foundation, for [1a]they were terrified
because of the peoples of the lands; and they [b]offered burnt offerings
on it to the LORD, burnt offerings morning and evening.
4 And they celebrated the [a]Feast of [1]Booths, [b]as it is written, and
offered [2]the fixed number of burnt offerings daily, [c]according to the
ordinance, as each day required;
5 and afterward *there was* a [a]continual burnt offering, also [b]for the
new moons and [c]for all the fixed festivals of the LORD that were
consecrated, and from everyone who offered a freewill offering to
the LORD.
6 From the first day of the seventh month they began to offer
burnt offerings to the LORD, but the foundation of the temple of the
LORD had not been laid.
7 Then they gave money to the masons and carpenters, and [a]food,
drink, and oil to the Sidonians and to the Tyrians, [b]to bring cedar
wood from Lebanon to the sea at [c]Joppa, according to the permission
they had [1]from [d]Cyrus king of Persia.
8 Now in the second year of their coming to the house of God at
Jerusalem in the second month, [a]Zerubbabel the son of Shealtiel and
Jeshua the son of Jozadak and the rest of their brothers the priests
and the Levites, and all who came from the captivity to Jerusalem,
began *the work* and [b]appointed the Levites from twenty years and
older to oversee the work of the house of the LORD.
9 Then [a]Jeshua *with* his sons and brothers stood united *with* Kad-
miel and his sons, the sons of [1]Judah *and* the sons of Henadad *with*
their sons and brothers the Levites, to oversee the workmen in the
temple of God.
10 Now when the builders had [a]laid the foundation of the temple of
the LORD, [1]the priests stood in their apparel with trumpets, and the
Levites, the sons of Asaph, with cymbals, to praise the LORD [b]accord-
ing to the [2]directions of King David of Israel.
11 And [a]they sang, praising and giving thanks to the LORD, *saying*,
"[b]For He is good, for His lovingkindness is upon Israel forever." And
all the people shouted with a great shout when they praised the
LORD because the foundation of the house of the LORD was laid.
12 Yet many of the priests and Levites and heads of fathers'
households, [a]the old men who had seen the first [1]temple, wept with a
loud voice when the foundation of this house was laid before their
eyes, while many shouted aloud for joy;
13 so that the people could not distinguish the sound of the shout

69 [1]Or, *tunics*
70 [a]1 Chr. 9:2; Ne 11:3
3:1 [a]Neh. 7:73; 8:
2 [a]Neh. 12:1, 8 [b] 2:2; Hag. 1:1; 2:2 [c]1 Chr. 3:17 [d]Ex. [e]Deut. 12:5, 6
3 [1]Lit., *terror* was *them* [a]Ezra 4:4 [b] 28:2
4 [1]Or, *Tabernacle* [2]Lit., *by number* [a] 8:14; Zech. 14:16 23:16 [c]Num. 29:1
5 [a]Ex. 29:38; Nu 28:3 [b]Num. 28:11 [c]Num. 29:39
7 [1]Lit., *of* [a]2 Chr. Acts 12:20 [b]2 Ch [c]Acts 9:36 [d]Ezra
8 [a]Ezra 3:2; 4:3 23:4, 24
9 [1]In Ezra 2:40, *Hodaviah* [a]Ezra
10 [1]So with the some mss.; M.T., *set the priests* [2]L *hands* [a]Zech. 4: [b]1 Chr. 6:31; 25:1
11 [a]2 Chr. 7:3; N 12:24, 40 [b]1 Chr 2 Chr. 5:13; Ps. 106:1; 107:1; 118 131:1; Jer. 33:11
12 [1]Lit., *house* 2:3

of joy from the sound of the weeping of the people, for the people
shouted with a loud shout, and the sound was heard far away.

Chapter 4

4 Now when [a]the enemies of Judah and Benjamin heard that [b]the
people of the exile were building a temple to the LORD God of
Israel,
2 they approached Zerubbabel and the heads of fathers' *households,*
and said to them, "Let us build with you, for we, like you, seek your
God; [a]and we have been sacrificing to Him since the days of [b]Esar-
haddon king of Assyria, who brought us up here."
3 But Zerubbabel and Jeshua and the rest of the heads of fathers'
households of Israel said to them, "[a]You have nothing in common
with us in building a house to our God; but we ourselves will
together build to the LORD God of Israel, [b]as King Cyrus, the king of
Persia has commanded us."
4 Then [a]the people of the land [1]discouraged the people of Judah,
and frightened them from building,
5 and hired counselors against them to frustrate their counsel all
the days of Cyrus king of Persia, even until the reign of Darius king
of Persia.
6 Now in the reign of [1a]Ahasuerus, in the beginning of his reign,
they wrote an accusation against the inhabitants of Judah and Jeru-
salem.
7 And in the days of [1]Artaxerxes, Bishlam, Mithredath, Tabeel, and
the rest of his colleagues, wrote to Artaxerxes king of Persia; and the
[2]text of the letter was written in Aramaic and translated [a]*from*
Aramaic.
8 [1]Rehum the commander and Shimshai the scribe wrote a letter
against Jerusalem to King Artaxerxes, as follows—
9 then *wrote* Rehum the commander and Shimshai the scribe and
[a]the rest of their colleagues, the judges and [b]the lesser governors, the
officials, the secretaries, the men of Erech, the Babylonians, the men
of Susa, that is, the Elamites,
10 and the rest of the nations which the great and honorable [1]Os-
nappar deported and settled in the city of Samaria, and in the rest of
the region beyond the [2]River. [a]And now
11 this is the copy of the letter which they sent to him: "To King
Artaxerxes: Your servants, the men in the region beyond the River,
and now
12 let it be known to the king, that the Jews who came up from you
have come to us at Jerusalem; they are rebuilding [a]the rebellious and
evil city, and [b]are finishing the walls and repairing the foundations.
13 "Now let it be known to the king, that if that city is rebuilt and the
walls are finished, [a]they will not pay tribute, custom, or toll, and it
will damage the revenue of the kings.
14 "Now because we [1]are in the service of the palace, and it is not
fitting for us to see the king's dishonor, therefore we have sent and
informed the king,
15 so that a search may be made in the record books of your fathers.
And you will discover in the record books, and learn that that city is
a rebellious city and damaging to kings and provinces, and that they
have incited revolt within it in past days; therefore that city was laid
waste.

[a]Ezra 4:7-10 [b]Ezra 1:11
2 Kin. 17:32 [b]2 Kin. 19:37
3 [a]Neh. 2:20 [b]Ezra 1:1, 2
[1]Lit., *weakened the hands of* [a]Ezra 3:3
[1]Or, *Xerxes;* Heb., *hash-verosh* [a]Esth. 1:1; Dan. 9:1
eb., *Artah-shashta* [2]Lit., *writing* [a]2 Kin. 18:26; Dan. 2:4
[1]Ch. 4:8-6:18 is in Aram.
2 Kin. 17:24 [b]Ezra 5:6; 6:6
10 [1]I.e., probably Ashurbanipal [2]I.e., ates River, and so throughout the ch. Ezra 4:11, 17; 7:12
Chr. 36:13 [b]Ezra 5:3, 9
3 [a]Ezra 4:20; 7:24
4 [1]Lit., *eat the salt*

16 "We inform the king that, if that city is rebuilt and the walls
finished, as a result you will have no possession in *the province*
beyond the River."
17 *Then* the king sent an answer to Rehum the commander, to Shim-
shai the scribe, and to the rest of their colleagues who live in Samaria
and in the rest of *the provinces* beyond the River: "Peace. And now
18 the document which you sent to us has been [1a]translated and
read before me.
19 "And a decree has been [1]issued by me, and a search has been
made and it has been discovered that that city has risen up against
the kings in past days, that rebellion and revolt have been per-
petrated in it,
20 [a]that mighty kings have [1]ruled over Jerusalem, governing all *the
provinces* [b]beyond the River, and that [c]tribute, custom, and toll were
paid to them.
21 "So, now issue a decree to make these men stop *work,* that the city
may not be rebuilt until a decree is issued by me.
22 "And beware of being negligent in carrying out this *matter;* why
should damage increase to the detriment of the kings?"
23 Then as soon as the copy of King Artaxerxes' document was
read before Rehum and Shimshai the scribe and their colleagues,
they went in haste to Jerusalem to the Jews and stopped them by
force of arms.
24 Then work on the house of God in Jerusalem ceased, and it was
stopped until the second year of the reign of Darius king of Persia.

Chapter 5

5 When the prophets, [a]Haggai the prophet and [b]Zechariah the son
of Iddo, prophesied to the Jews who were in Judah and Jerusa-
lem, in the name of the God of Israel, who was over them,
2 then [a]Zerubbabel the son of Shealtiel and Jeshua the son of Joza-
dak arose and began to rebuild the house of God which is in Jerusa-
lem; and [b]the prophets of God were with them supporting them.
3 At that time [a]Tattenai, the governor of *the province* beyond the
[1]River, and Shethar-bozenai and their colleagues came to them and
spoke to them thus, "[b]Who issued you a decree to rebuild this
[2]temple and to finish this structure?"
4 [a]Then we told them accordingly what the names of the men were
who were reconstructing this building.
5 But [a]the eye of their God was on the elders of the Jews, and they
did not stop them until a report should come to Darius, and then a
written reply be returned concerning it.
6 *This is* the copy of the letter which [a]Tattenai, the governor of *the
province* beyond the River, and Shethar-bozenai and his colleagues
[b]the officials, who were beyond the River, sent to Darius the king.
7 They sent a report to him in which it was written thus: "To
Darius the king, all peace.
8 "Let it be known to the king, that we have gone to the province of
Judah, to the house of the great God, which is being built with huge
stones, and [1]beams are being laid in the walls; and this work is going
on with great care and is succeeding in their hands.
9 "Then we asked those elders and said to them thus, 'Who issued
you a decree to rebuild this temple and to finish this structure?'

18 [1]Lit., *plain... before* [a]Neh. ...

19 [1]Lit., *put fo...*

20 [1]Lit., *been* ... 4:21; 1 Chr. 18... 15:18; Josh. 1:... 4:13; 7:24

5:1 [a]Hag. 1:1 ... 1:1

2 [a]Ezra 3:2; Ha... Zech. 4:6-9 [b]Ez... Hag. 2:4; Zech. ...

3 [1]I.e., Euphrat... and so througho... ch. [2]Lit., *house,* in vv. 9, 11, 12 ... 6:6, 13 [b]Ezra 1:...

4 [a]Ezra 5:10

5 [a]Ezra 7:6, 28

6 [a]Ezra 5:3 [b]Ezr...

8 [1]Lit., *timber is*

10 "We also asked them their names so as to inform you, and that we
might write down the names of the men who were at their head.
11 "And thus they [1]answered us, saying, 'We are the servants of the
God of heaven and earth and are rebuilding the temple that was
built many years ago, [a]which a great king of Israel built and finished.
12 'But [a]because our fathers had provoked the God of heaven to
wrath, [b]He gave them into the hand of Nebuchadnezzar king of
Babylon, the Chaldean, *who* destroyed this temple and deported the
people to Babylon.
13 'However, [a]in the first year of Cyrus king of Babylon, King Cyrus
[b]issued a decree to rebuild this house of God.
14 'And also [a]the gold and silver utensils of the house of God which
Nebuchadnezzar had taken from the temple [1]in Jerusalem, and
brought them to the temple of Babylon, these King Cyrus took from
the temple of Babylon, and they were given to one [b]whose name was
Sheshbazzar, whom he had appointed governor.
15 'And he said to him, "Take these utensils, go *and* deposit them in
the temple [1]in Jerusalem, and let the house of God be rebuilt in its
place."
16 'Then that Sheshbazzar came *and* [a]laid the foundations of the
house of God [1]in Jerusalem; and from then until now it has been
under construction, and it is [b]not *yet* completed.'
17 "And now, if it pleases the king [a]let a search be conducted in the
king's treasure house, which is there in Babylon, if it be that a decree
was issued by King Cyrus to rebuild this house of God at Jerusalem;
and let the king send to us his decision concerning this *matter*."

Chapter 6

6 Then King Darius issued a decree, and [a]search was made in the
[1]archives, where the treasures were stored in Babylon.
2 And in [1]Ecbatana in the fortress, which is [a]in the province of
Media, a scroll was found and there was written in it as follows:
"Memorandum—
3 "[a]In the first year of King Cyrus, Cyrus the king issued a decree:
'*Concerning* the house of God at Jerusalem, let the temple, the place
where sacrifices are offered, be rebuilt and let its foundations be
[1]retained, its height being 60 cubits and its width 60 cubits;
4 [a]with three layers of huge stones, and [1]one layer of timbers. And
let the cost be paid from the [2]royal treasury.
5 'And also let [a]the gold and silver utensils of the temple of God,
which Nebuchadnezzar took from the temple in Jerusalem and
brought to Babylon, be returned and [1]brought to their places in the
temple in Jerusalem; and you shall put *them* in the house of God.'
6 "Now *therefore,* [a]Tattenai, governor of *the province* beyond the
[1]River, Shethar-bozenai, and [2]your colleagues, the officials of *the*
provinces beyond the [1]River, [3]keep away from there.
7 "Leave this work on the house of God alone; let the governor of
the Jews and the elders of the Jews rebuild this house of God on its
site.
8 "Moreover, [a]I issue a decree concerning what you are to do for
these elders of Judah in the rebuilding of this house of God: the full
cost is to be paid to these people from the royal treasury out of the
taxes of *the provinces* beyond the River, and that without delay.
9 "And whatever is needed, both young bulls, rams, and lambs for

[1]Lit., *returned us the word* [a]1 Kin. 6:1, 38

12 [a]2 Chr. 36:16, 17 [b]2 Kin. 25:8-11; Jer. 52:12-15

13 [a]Ezra 1:1 [b]Ezra 1:1-4

14 [1]Lit., *that was in* [a]Ezra 1:7; 6:5; Dan. 5:2 [b]Ezra 1:8; 5:16

15 [1]Lit., *that is in*

16 [1]Lit., *that is in* [a]Ezra 3:8, 10 [b]Ezra 6:15

17 [a]Ezra 6:1, 2

1 [1]Lit., *house of the books* [a]Ezra 5:17

2 [1]Aram., *Achmetha* [a]2 Kin. 17:6

3 [1]Or, *fixed, laid* [a]Ezra 1:1; 5:13

4 [1]So Gr.; Aram., *a layer of new timber* [2]Lit., *king's house* [a]1 Kin. 6:36

5 [1]Lit., *go* [a]Ezra 1:7; 5:14

6 [1]I.e., Euphrates River, and so throughout the ch. [2]Aram., *their* [3]Lit., *distant* [a]Ezra 5:3; 6:13

8 [a]Ezra 6:4; 7:14-22

a burnt offering to the God of heaven, and wheat, salt, wine, and
anointing oil, as the priests in Jerusalem request, *it* is to be given to
them daily without fail,
10 that they may offer [1]acceptable sacrifices to the God of heaven
and [a]pray for the life of the king and his sons.
11 "And I issued a decree that [a]any man who violates this edict, a
timber shall be drawn from his house and he shall be impaled on it
and [b]his house shall be made a refuse heap on account of this.
12 "And may the God who [a]has caused His name to dwell there
overthrow any king or people who [1]attempts to change *it*, so as to
destroy this house of God in Jerusalem. I, Darius, have issued *this*
decree, let *it* be carried out with all diligence!"
13 Then [a]Tattenai, the governor of *the province* beyond the River,
Shethar-bozenai, and their colleagues carried out *the decree* with all
diligence, just as King Darius had sent.
14 And [a]the elders of the Jews [1]were successful in building through
the prophesying of Haggai the prophet and Zechariah the son of
Iddo. And [2]they finished building according to the command of the
God of Israel and the decree [b]of Cyrus, [c]Darius, and [d]Artaxerxes king
of Persia.
15 And this temple was completed [1]on the third day of the [a]month
Adar; it was the sixth year of the reign of King Darius.
16 And the sons of Israel, the priests, the Levites, and the rest of the
[1]exiles, [a]celebrated the dedication of this house of God with joy.
17 And they offered for the dedication of this temple of God 100
bulls, 200 rams, 400 lambs, and as a sin offering for all Israel [a]12 male
goats, corresponding to the number of the tribes of Israel.
18 Then they appointed the priests to [a]their divisions and the
Levites in [b]their orders for the service of God [1]in Jerusalem, [c]as it is
written in the book of Moses.
19 And [a]the exiles observed the Passover on [b]the fourteenth of the
first month.
20 [a]For the priests and the Levites had purified themselves
together; all of them were pure. Then [b]they slaughtered the Passover
lamb for all the exiles, both for their brothers the priests and for
themselves.
21 And the sons of Israel who returned from exile and [a]all those
who had separated themselves from [b]the impurity of the nations of
the land to *join* them, to seek the LORD God of Israel, ate *the Passover.*
22 And [a]they observed the Feast of Unleavened Bread seven days
with joy, for the LORD had caused them to rejoice, and [b]had turned
the heart of [c]the king of Assyria toward them to [1]encourage them in
the work of the house of God, the God of Israel.

Chapter 7

7 [a]Now after these things, in the reign of [b]Artaxerxes king of Persia, *there went up* Ezra son of Seraiah, son of Azariah, son of
Hilkiah,
2 son of Shallum, son of Zadok, son of Ahitub,
3 son of Amariah, son of Azariah, son of Meraioth,
4 son of Zerahiah, son of Uzzi, son of Bukki,
5 son of Abishua, son of Phinehas, son of Eleazar, son of Aaron the
chief priest.
6 This Ezra went up from Babylon, and he was a [a]scribe skilled in

10 [1]Lit., *pleasing, sweet-smelling sacrifices* [a]Ezra Jer. 29:7; 1 Tim.
11 [a]Ezra 7:26 [b] 2:5; 3:29
12 [1]Lit., *sends h hand* [a]Deut. 12: 1 Kin. 9:3
13 [a]Ezra 6:6
14 [1]Lit., *were bu and succeeding built and finishe* 5:1, 2 [b]Ezra 1:1 [c]Ezra 4:24; 6:12 7:1
15 [1]Lit., *until* [a]E
16 [1]Lit., *sons o captivity* [a]1 Kin. 2 Chr. 7:5
17 [a]Ezra 8:35
18 [1]Lit., *which* [a]1 Chr. 24:1; 2 C 35:5 [b]1 Chr. 23 [c]Num. 3:6; 8:9
19 [a]Ezra 1:11
20 [a]2 Chr. 29:3 [b]2 Chr. 35:11
21 [a]Neh. 9:2; 1 [b]Ezra 9:11
22 [1]Lit., *streng hands* [a]Ex. 12: [b]Ezra 7:27; Pro [c]Ezra 1:1; 6:1
7:1 [a]1 Chr. 6:4 [b]Ezra 7:12, 21;
6 [a]Ezra 7:11, 1

the law of Moses, which the LORD God of Israel had given; and the
king granted him all [1]he requested [b]because the hand of the LORD his
God *was* upon him.
7 And [a]some of the sons of Israel and some of the priests, the
Levites, the singers, the gatekeepers, and the temple servants went
up to Jerusalem in the seventh year of King Artaxerxes.
8 And he came to Jerusalem in the fifth month, which was in the
seventh year of the king.
9 For on the first of the first month [1]he began to go up from Baby-
lon; and on the first of the fifth month he came to Jerusalem,
[a]because the good hand of his God *was* upon him.
10 For Ezra had set his heart to [1]study the law of the LORD, and to
practice *it*, and [a]to teach *His* statutes and ordinances in Israel.
11 Now this is the copy of the decree which King Artaxerxes gave
to Ezra the priest, the scribe, [1]learned in the words of the command-
ments of the LORD and His statutes to Israel:
12 "[1]Artaxerxes, [a]king of kings, to Ezra the priest, the scribe of the
law of the God of heaven, perfect *peace*. And now
13 [a]I have issued a decree that any of the people of Israel and their
priests and the Levites in my kingdom who are willing to go to
Jerusalem, may go with you.
14 "Forasmuch as you are sent [1]by the king and his [a]seven coun-
selors to inquire concerning Judah and Jerusalem according to the
law of your God which is in your hand,
15 and to bring the silver and gold, which the king and his coun-
selors have freely offered to the God of Israel, [a]whose dwelling is in
Jerusalem,
16 with [a]all the silver and gold which you shall find in the whole
province of Babylon, along [b]with the freewill offering of the people
and of the priests, who [c]offered willingly for the house of their God
which is in Jerusalem;
17 with this money, therefore, you shall diligently buy bulls, rams,
and lambs, [a]with their grain offerings and their libations and [b]offer
them on the altar of the house of your God which is in Jerusalem.
18 "And whatever seems good to you and to your brothers to do
with the rest of the silver and gold, you may do according to the will
of your God.
19 "Also the utensils which are given to you for the service of the
house of your God, deliver in full before the God of Jerusalem.
20 "And the rest of the needs for the house of your God, for which
you may have occasion to provide, [a]provide *for it* from the royal
treasury.
21 "And I, even I King Artaxerxes, issue a decree to all the treasurers
who are *in the provinces* beyond the [1]River, that whatever Ezra the
priest, [a]the scribe of the law of the God of heaven, may require of
you, it shall be done diligently,
22 *even* up to 100 talents of silver, 100 [1]kors of wheat, 100 baths of
wine, 100 baths of oil, and salt [2]as needed.
23 "Whatever is [1]commanded by the God of heaven, let it be done
with zeal for the house of the God of heaven, [a]lest there be wrath
against the kingdom of the king and his sons.
24 "We also inform you that [a]it is not allowed to [1]impose tax, tribute
or toll [b]*on* any of the priests, Levites, singers, doorkeepers, Nethinim,
or servants of this house of God.

6 [1]Lit., *his request* [b]Ezra 7:9, 28; 8:22
7 [a]Ezra 8:1-20
9 [1]Lit., *was the* [fou]*ndation* [a]Ezra 7:6; Neh. 2:8
[10] [1]Lit., *seek* [a]Deut. [33:1]0; Ezra 7:25; Neh. 8:1
[11] [1]Lit., *the scribe of*
[12] [1]Ch. 7:12-26 is in [A]ram. [a]Ezek. 26:7; Dan. 2:37
13 [a]Ezra 6:1
[14] [1]Lit., *from before* [a][E]zra 7:15, 28; 8:25
[15] [a]2 Chr. 6:2; Ezra 6:12; Ps. 135:21
[16] [a]Ezra 8:25 [b]Ezra [1]:4, 6 [c]1 Chr. 29:6
17 [a]Num. 15:4-13 [b]Deut. 12:5-11
20 [a]Ezra 6:4
[2]1 [1]I.e., Euphrates River, and so throughout the ch. [a]Ezra 7:6
[22] [1]I.e., One kor equals [ap]prox. ten bu. [2]Lit., [w]*ithout prescription*
23 [1]Lit., *from the* [dec]*ree of* [a]Ezra 6:10
[24] [1]Lit., *throw on them* [a]...:13, 20 [b]Ezra 7:7

25 "And you, Ezra, according to the wisdom of your God which is in
your hand, [a]appoint magistrates and judges that they may judge all
the people who are in *the province* beyond the River, *even* all those
who know the laws of your God; and you may [b]teach anyone who is
ignorant *of them*.
26 "And [a]whoever will not observe the law of your God and the law
of the king, let judgment be executed upon him strictly, whether for
death or for [1]banishment or for confiscation of goods or for im-
prisonment."
27 Blessed be the LORD, the God of our fathers, [a]who has put *such a*
thing as this in the king's heart, to adorn the house of the LORD which
is in Jerusalem,
28 and [a]has extended lovingkindness to me before the king and his
counselors and before all the king's mighty princes. Thus I was
strengthened according to [b]the hand of the LORD my God upon me,
and I gathered [1]leading men from Israel to go up with me.

Chapter 8

8 Now these are the heads of their fathers' *households* and the
genealogical enrollment of those who went up with me from
Babylon in the reign of King Artaxerxes:
2 of the sons of Phinehas, Gershom; of the sons of Ithamar, Daniel;
of the sons of David, [a]Hattush;
3 of the sons of Shecaniah *who was* of the sons of [a]Parosh,
Zechariah and with him 150 males *who were in* the genealogical list;
4 of the sons of Pahath-moab, Eliehoenai the son of Zerahiah and
200 males with him;
5 of the sons of Shecaniah, the son of Jahaziel and 300 males with
him;
6 and of the sons of [a]Adin, Ebed the son of Jonathan and 50 males
with him;
7 and of the sons of Elam, Jeshaiah the son of Athaliah and 70
males with him;
8 and of the sons of Shephatiah, Zebadiah the son of Michael and
80 males with him;
9 of the sons of Joab, Obadiah the son of Jehiel and 218 males with
him;
10 and of the sons of Shelomith, the son of Josiphiah and 160 males
with him;
11 and of the sons of Bebai, Zechariah the son of Bebai and 28 males
with him;
12 and of the sons of Azgad, Johanan the son of Hakkatan and 110
males with him;
13 and of the sons of Adonikam, the last ones, these being their
names, Eliphelet, Jeuel, and Shemaiah and 60 males with them;
14 and of the sons of Bigvai, Uthai and [1]Zabbud and 70 males with
[2]them.
15 Now I assembled them at [a]the river that runs to Ahava, where
we camped for three days; and when I observed the people and the
priests, I [b]did not find any Levites there.
16 So I sent for Eliezer, Ariel, Shemaiah, Elnathan, Jarib, Elnathan,
Nathan, Zechariah, and Meshullam, [1]leading men, and for Joiarib
and Elnathan, teachers.
17 And I sent them to Iddo the [1]leading man at the place Casiphia;

25 [a]Ex. 18:21; Deu 16:18 [b]Ezra 7:10; 2:7; Col. 1:28
26 [1]Lit., *rooting ou* [a]Ezra 6:11, 12
27 [a]Ezra 6:22
28 [1]Lit., *heads* [a]E 9:9 [b]Ezra 5:5
8:2 [a]1 Chr. 3:22
3 [a]Ezra 2:3
6 [a]Ezra 2:15; Neh 7:20; 10:16
14 [1]Or, *Zakkur* [2]
15 [a]Ezra 8:21, 31 [b]Ezra 7:7; 8:2
16 [1]Lit., *heads*
17 [1]Lit., *head*

and I [2]told them what to say to [3]Iddo *and* his brothers, [a]the temple
servants at the place Casiphia, *that is,* to bring ministers to us for the
house of our God.
18 And [a]according to the good hand of our God upon us they
brought us a [b]man of insight of the sons of Mahli, the son of Levi, the
son of Israel, namely Sherebiah, and his sons and brothers, 18 men;
19 and Hashabiah and [1]Jeshaiah of the sons of Merari, with his
brothers and their sons, 20 men;
20 and 220 of [a]the temple servants, whom David and the princes
had given for the service of the Levites, all of them designated by
name.
21 Then I proclaimed [a]a fast there at [b]the river of Ahava, that we
might [c]humble ourselves before our God to seek from Him a [1]safe
journey for us, our little ones, and all our possessions.
22 For I was ashamed to request from the king troops and horse-
men to [1]protect us from the enemy on the way, because we had said
to the king, "[a]The hand of our God is [2]favorably disposed to all those
who seek Him, but [b]His power and His anger are against all those
who [c]forsake Him."
23 So we fasted and sought our God concerning this *matter,* and He
[1a]listened to our entreaty.
24 Then I set apart twelve of the leading priests, [a]Sherebiah, Hasha-
biah, and with them ten of their brothers;
25 and I [a]weighed out to them [b]the silver, the gold, and the utensils,
the offering for the house of our God which the king and [c]his coun-
selors and his princes, and all Israel present *there,* had offered.
26 [a]Thus I weighed into their hands 650 talents of silver, and silver
utensils *worth* 100 talents, *and* 100 gold talents,
27 and 20 gold bowls, *worth* 1,000 darics; and two utensils of fine
shiny bronze, precious as gold.
28 Then I said to them, "[a]You are holy to the LORD, and the [b]utensils
are holy; and the silver and the gold are a freewill offering to the
LORD God of your fathers.
29 "Watch and keep *them* [a]until you weigh *them* before the leading
priests, the Levites, and the heads of the fathers' *households* of Israel
at Jerusalem, *in* the chambers of the house of the LORD."
30 So the priests and the Levites [a]accepted the weighed out silver
and gold and the utensils, to bring *them* to Jerusalem to the house of
our God.
31 Then we journeyed from [a]the river Ahava on [b]the twelfth of the
first month to go to Jerusalem; and [c]the hand of our God was over
us, and He delivered us from the hand of the enemy and the am-
bushes by the way.
32 [a]Thus we came to Jerusalem and remained there three days.
33 And on the fourth day the silver and the gold and the utensils
[a]were weighed out in the house of our God into the hand of [b]Mere-
moth the son of Uriah the priest, and with him *was* Eleazar the son of
Phinehas; and with them *were* the Levites, Jozabad the son of Jeshua
and Noadiah the son of Binnui.
34 Everything *was* numbered and weighed, and all the weight was
recorded at that time.
35 [a]The exiles who had come from the captivity offered burnt offer-
ings to the God of Israel: [b]12 bulls for all Israel, 96 rams, 77 lambs, 12
male goats for a sin offering, all as a burnt offering to the LORD.

...it., *put words in* ...*outh to say* [3]So ...; Heb., *Iddo his* ...*ther* [a]Ezra 2:43

...8 [a]Ezra 7:6, 28 [b]2 Chr. 30:22

...o Gr.; Heb., *with him Jeshaiah*

[a]Ezra 2:43; 7:7

Lit., *straight way* ... 7:6; 2 Chr. 20:3 ...a 8:15, 31 [c]Lev. 23:29; Is. 58:3, 5

... *help* [2]Lit., *upon* ... *for good* [a]Ezra ...28 [b]Josh. 22:16 [c]2 Chr. 15:2

...t., *was entreated* ... *us* [a]1 Chr. 5:20; 2 Chr. 33:13

...4 [a]Ezra 8:18, 19

[a]Ezra 8:33 [b]Ezra ...5, 16 [c]Ezra 7:14

26 [a]Ezra 1:9-11

...Lev. 21:6-8 [b]Lev. 22:2, 3

29 [a]Ezra 8:33, 34

30 [a]Ezra 1:9

31 [a]Ezra 8:15, 21 ...zra 7:9 [c]Ezra 8:22

32 [a]Neh. 2:11

[a]Ezra 8:30 [b]Neh. 3:4, 21

...zra 2:1 [b]Ezra 6:17

36 Then [a]they delivered the king's edicts to [b]the king's satraps, and
to the governors *in the provinces* beyond the [1]River, and they sup-
ported the people and the house of God.

Chapter 9

9 Now when these things had been completed, the princes ap-
proached me, saying, "The people of Israel and the priests and
the Levites have not [a]separated themselves from the peoples of the
lands, [b]according to their abominations, *those* of the Canaanites, the
Hittites, the Perizzites, the Jebusites, the Ammonites, the Moabites,
the Egyptians, and the Amorites.
2 "For [a]they have taken some of their daughters *as wives* for them-
selves and for their sons, so that [b]the holy [1]race has [c]intermingled
with the peoples of the lands; indeed, the hands of the princes and
the rulers have been foremost in this unfaithfulness."
3 And when I heard about this matter, I [a]tore my garment and my
robe, and pulled some of the hair from my head and my beard, and
[b]sat down appalled.
4 Then [a]everyone who trembled at the words of the God of Israel
on account of the unfaithfulness of the exiles gathered to me, and I
sat appalled until [b]the evening offering.
5 But at the evening offering I arose from my [1]humiliation, even
with my garment and my robe torn, and I fell on my knees and
[a]stretched out my [2]hands to the LORD my God;
6 and I said, "O my God, I am ashamed and embarrassed to lift up
my face to Thee, my God, for our iniquities have [1]risen above our
heads, and our [a]guilt has grown even to the heavens.
7 "[a]Since the days of our fathers to this day we *have been* in great
guilt, and on account of our iniquities we, our kings *and* our priests
have been given into the hand of the kings of the lands, to the sword,
to captivity, and to plunder and to [1b]open shame, as *it is* this day.
8 "But now for a brief moment grace has been *shown* from the LORD
our God, [a]to leave us an escaped remnant and to give us a [b]peg in
His holy place, that our God may [c]enlighten our eyes and grant us a
little reviving in our bondage.
9 "[a]For we are slaves; yet in our bondage, our God has not forsaken
us, but [b]has extended lovingkindness to us in the sight of the kings
of Persia, to give us reviving to raise up the house of our God, to
restore its ruins, and to give us a wall in Judah and Jerusalem.
10 "And now, our God, what shall we say after this? For we have
forsaken Thy commandments,
11 which Thou hast commanded by Thy servants the prophets,
saying, 'The land which you are entering to possess is an unclean
land with the uncleanness of the peoples of the lands, with their
abominations which have filled it from end to end *and* [a]with their
impurity.
12 'So now do not [a]give your daughters to their sons nor take their
daughters to your sons, and [b]never seek their peace or their
prosperity, that you may be strong and eat the good *things* of the
land and [c]leave *it* as an inheritance to your sons forever.'
13 "And after all that has come upon us for our evil deeds and [a]our
great guilt, since Thou our God hast requited *us* less than our
iniquities *deserve*, and hast given us [b]an escaped remnant as this,
14 [a]shall we again break Thy commandments and intermarry with

36 [1]I.e., Euphr River [a]Ezra 7:2 [b]Ezra 4:7; 5:6

9:1 [a]Ezra 6:21; 9:2 [b]Lev. 18:24

2 [1]Lit., *seed* [a] Ezra 10:2, 18 [b] 22:31; Deut. 14 6:14 [c]Neh. 13:3

3 [a]2 Kin. 18:37 1:4

4 [a]Ezra 10:3; Is [b]Ex. 29:39

5 [1]Or, *fasting* [2] *palms* [a]Ex. 9:29

6 [1]Lit., *multiplie the head* [a]2 Chr Ezra 9:13, 15; R

7 [1]Lit., *shame o* [a]2 Chr. 29:6; Ps. [b]Dan. 9:7

8 [a]Ezra 9:13-15 22:23 [c]Ps. 13:3

9 [a]Neh. 9:36 [b]E

11 [a]Ezra 6:21

12 [a]Ex. 34:15, 16 7:3; Ezra 9:2 [b]De 23:6 [c]Prov. 13:22

13 [a]Ezra 9:6, 7 [b] 9:8

14 [a]Ezra 9:2

the peoples [1]who commit these abominations? [b]Wouldst Thou not be
angry with us [2]to the point of destruction, until there is no remnant
nor any who escape?
15 "O LORD God of Israel, [a]Thou art righteous, for we have been left
an escaped remnant, as *it is* this day; behold, we are before Thee in
[b]our guilt, for [c]no one can stand before Thee because of this."

Chapter 10

10 Now [a]while Ezra was praying and making confession, weep-
ing and prostrating himself [b]before the house of God, a very
large assembly, men, women, and children, gathered to him from
Israel; for the people wept bitterly.
2 And Shecaniah the son of Jehiel, one of the sons of Elam,
answered and said to Ezra, "[a]We have been unfaithful to our God,
and have [1]married foreign women from the peoples of the land; yet
now there is hope for Israel in spite of this.
3 "So now [a]let us make a covenant with our God to put away all the
wives and [1b]their children, according to the counsel of [2]my lord and
of [c]those who tremble at the commandment of our God; and let it be
done [d]according to the law.
4 "Arise! For *this* matter is [1]your responsibility, but we will be with
you; [a]be courageous and act."
5 Then Ezra rose and [a]made the leading priests, the Levites, and all
Israel, take oath that they would do according to this [1]proposal; so
they took the oath.
6 Then Ezra [a]rose from before the house of God and went into the
chamber of Jehohanan the son of Eliashib. Although he went there,
[b]he did not eat bread, nor drink water, for he was mourning over the
unfaithfulness of the exiles.
7 And they made a proclamation throughout Judah and Jerusalem
to all the exiles, that they should assemble at Jerusalem,
8 and that whoever would not come within three days, according
to the counsel of the leaders and the elders, all his possessions
should be forfeited and he himself excluded from the assembly of
the exiles.
9 So all the men of Judah and Benjamin assembled at Jerusalem
within the three days. It was the ninth month on the twentieth of the
month, and all the people sat in the open square *before* the house of
God, [a]trembling because of this matter and the heavy rain.
10 Then Ezra the priest stood up and said to them, "You have been
unfaithful and have married foreign wives adding to the guilt of
Israel.
11 "Now, therefore, [a]make confession to the LORD God of your
fathers, and [b]do His will; and [c]separate yourselves from the peoples
of the land and from the foreign wives."
12 Then all the assembly answered and said with a loud voice,
"That's right! As you have said, so it is [1]our duty to do.
13 "But there are many people, it is the rainy season, and we are not
able to stand in the open. Nor *can* the task *be done* in one or two days,
for we have transgressed greatly in this matter.
14 "Let our leaders [1]represent the whole assembly and let all those in
our cities who have married foreign wives come at appointed times,
together with the elders and judges of each city, until the [a]fierce
anger of our God on account of this matter is turned away from us."

14 [1]Lit., *of these* [ab]ominations [2]Lit., *to* [de]stroy [b]Deut. 9:8, 14
[1]5 [a]Neh. 9:33; Dan. [b]Ezra 9:6 [c]Job 9:2; Ps. 130:3
10:1 [a]Dan. 9:4, 20 [b]2 Chr. 20:9
[2 1]Lit., *given dwelling* [aE]zra 9:2; Neh. 13:27
[3 1]Lit., *that which is* [bor]n *of them* [2]Or, *the* *Lord* [a]2 Chr. 34:31 [bEz]ra 10:44 [c]Ezra 9:4 [d]Deut. 7:2, 3
4 [1]Lit., *upon you* [a]1 Chr. 28:10
5 [1]Lit., *word, thing* [a]Neh. 5:12; 13:25
[6] [a]Ezra 10:1 [b]Deut. 9:18
[9 a1] Sam. 12:18; Ezra 9:4; 10:3
[11] [a]Lev. 26:40; Prov. 28:13 [b]Rom. 12:2 [c]Ezra 10:3
12 [1]Lit., *upon us*
14 [1]Lit., *stand for* [a2] Kin. 23:26; 2 Chr. [29:]1-13; 29:10; 30:8

15 Only Jonathan the son of Asahel and Jahzeiah the son of Tikvah
[1]opposed this, with Meshullam and Shabbethai the Levite support-
ing them.
16 But the exiles did so. And [1]Ezra the priest selected men *who were*
heads of fathers' *households* for *each of* their father's households, all of
them by name. So they [2]convened on the first day of the tenth month
to investigate the matter.
17 And they finished *investigating* all the men who had married
foreign wives by the first of the first month.
18 And among the sons of the priests who had married foreign
wives were found of the sons of [a]Jeshua the son of Jozadak, and his
brothers: Maaseiah, Eliezer, Jarib, and Gedaliah.
19 And they [1]pledged to put away their wives, and being guilty,
[a]*they offered* a ram of the flock for their offense.
20 And of the sons of Immer *there were* Hanani and Zebadiah;
21 and of the sons of Harim: Maaseiah, Elijah, Shemaiah, Jehiel, and
Uzziah;
22 and of the sons of Pashhur: Elioenai, Maaseiah, Ishmael,
Nethanel, Jozabad, and Elasah.
23 And of Levites *there were* Jozabad, Shimei, Kelaiah (that is,
Kelita), Pethahiah, Judah, and Eliezer.
24 And of the singers *there was* Eliashib; and of the gatekeepers:
Shallum, Telem, and Uri.
25 And of Israel, of the sons of [a]Parosh *there were* Ramiah, Izziah,
Malchijah, Mijamin, Eleazar, Malchijah, and Benaiah;
26 and of the sons of Elam: Mattaniah, Zechariah, Jehiel, Abdi, Jere-
moth, and Elijah;
27 and of the sons of [a]Zattu: Elioenai, Eliashib, Mattaniah, Jeremoth,
Zabad, and Aziza;
28 and of the sons of Bebai: Jehohanan, Hananiah, Zabbai, *and*
Athlai;
29 and of the sons of Bani: Meshullam, Malluch, and Adaiah,
Jashub, Sheal, *and* Jeremoth;
30 and of the sons of Pahath-moab: Adna, Chelal, Benaiah,
Maaseiah, Mattaniah, Bezalel, Binnui, and Manasseh;
31 and *of* the sons of Harim: Eliezer, Isshijah, [a]Malchijah, Shemaiah,
Shimeon,
32 Benjamin, Malluch, *and* Shemariah;
33 of the sons of Hashum: Mattenai, Mattattah, Zabad, Eliphelet,
Jeremai, Manasseh, *and* Shimei;
34 of the sons of Bani: Maadai, Amram, Uel,
35 Benaiah, Bedeiah, Cheluhi,
36 Vaniah, Meremoth, Eliashib,
37 Mattaniah, Mattenai, Jaasu,
38 Bani, Binnui, Shimei,
39 Shelemiah, Nathan, Adaiah,
40 Machnadebai, Shashai, Sharai,
41 Azarel, Shelemiah, Shemariah,
42 Shallum, Amariah, *and* Joseph.
43 Of the sons of [a]Nebo *there were* Jeiel, Mattithiah, Zabad, Zebina,
Jaddai, Joel, *and* Benaiah.
44 All these had married [a]foreign wives, and some of them had
wives *by whom* they had children.

15 [1]Lit., *stoo*

16 [1]Heb. rea *were set apa priest, men . .*

18 [a]Ezra 5:2; 12; 2:4; Zech.

19 [1]Lit., *gave hand* [a]Lev. 5:1

25 [a]Ezra 2:3; 7:8

27 [a]Ezra 2:8;

31 [a]Neh. 3:11

43 [a]Num. 32:3 2:29

44 [a]1 Kin. 11:1- 10:3

ne of Ezra:

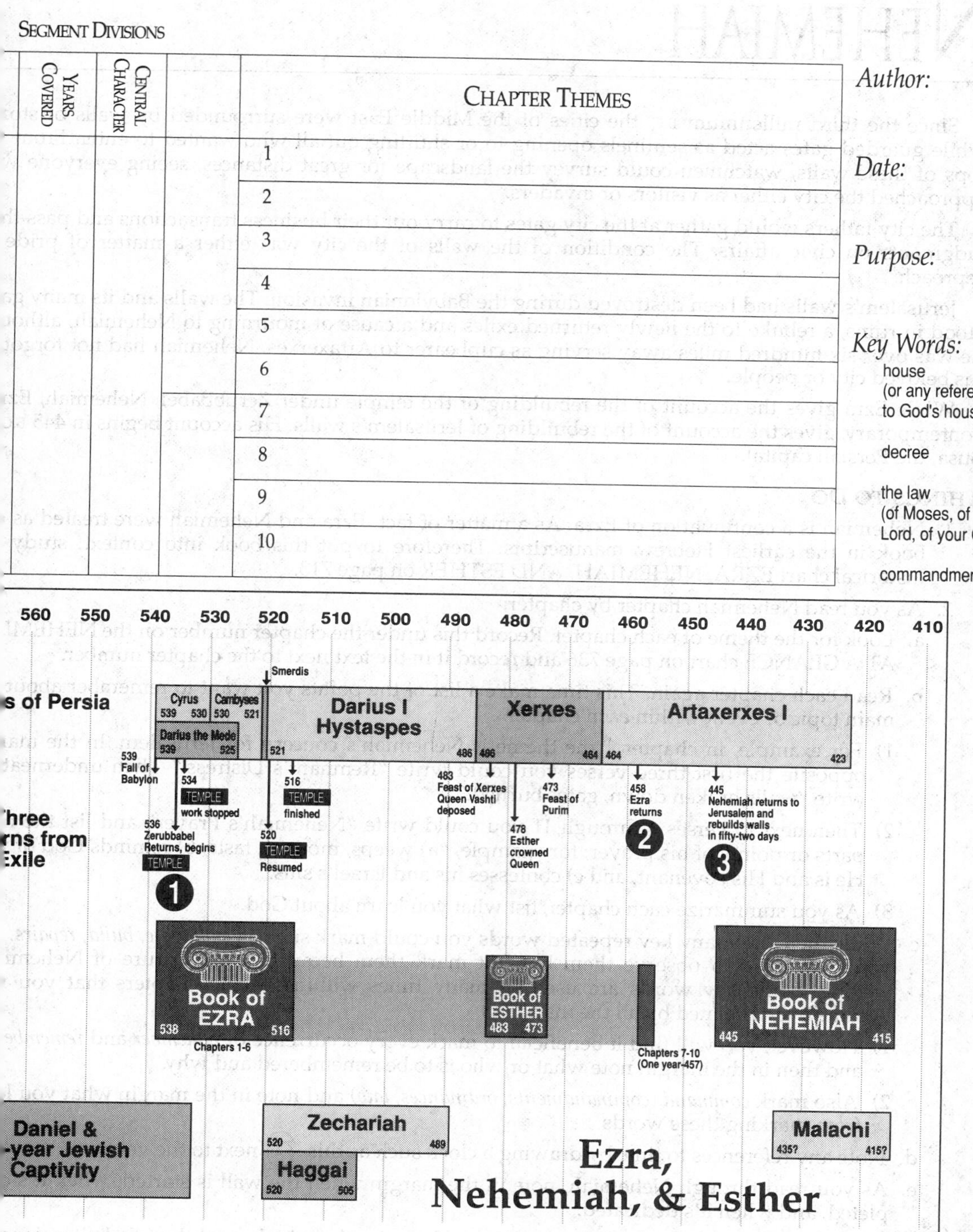

SEGMENT DIVISIONS
YEARS COVERED
CENTRAL CHARACTER
CHAPTER THEMES
1
2
3
4
5
6
7
8
9
10
Author:
Date:
Purpose:
Key Words:
house
(or any reference to God's house)
decree
the law
(of Moses, of the Lord, of your God)
commandments
560 550 540 530 520 510 500 490 480 470 460 450 440 430 420 410
s of Persia
Smerdis
Cyrus 539 530
Cambyses 530 521
Darius the Mede 539 525
Darius I Hystaspes 521 486
Xerxes 486 464
Artaxerxes I 464 423
539 Fall of Babylon
534 TEMPLE work stopped
516 TEMPLE finished
483 Feast of Xerxes Queen Vashti deposed
473 Feast of Purim
458 Ezra returns
445 Nehemiah returns to Jerusalem and rebuilds walls in fifty-two days
478 Esther crowned Queen
Three
rns from
Exile
536 Zerubbabel Returns, begins TEMPLE
520 TEMPLE Resumed
1
2
3
Book of EZRA 538 516
Chapters 1-6
Book of ESTHER 483 473
Chapters 7-10 (One year-457)
Book of NEHEMIAH 445 415
Daniel &
-year Jewish
Captivity
Zechariah 520 489
Haggai 520 505
Malachi 435? 415?
Ezra, Nehemiah, & Esther

NEHEMIAH

Since the third millennium B.C. the cities of the Middle East were surrounded by walls of s while guarded gates acted as sentinels opening to or shutting out all who wanted to enter. Fror tops of these walls, watchmen could survey the landscape for great distances, seeing everyone approached the city either as visitors or invaders.

The city fathers would gather at the city gates to carry out their business transactions and pass judgments on civic affairs. The condition of the walls of the city was either a matter of pric reproach.

Jerusalem's walls had been destroyed during the Babylonian invasion. The walls and its many stood in ruins, a rebuke to the newly returned exiles and a cause of mourning to Nehemiah, alth he was over six hundred miles away serving as cupbearer to Artaxerxes. Nehemiah had not forg his beloved city or people.

While Ezra gives the account of the rebuilding of the temple under Zerubbabel, Nehemiah, E contemporary, gives the account of the rebuilding of Jerusalem's walls. His account begins in 445 B Susa, the Persian capital.

THINGS TO DO

1. Nehemiah is a continuation of Ezra. As a matter of fact, Ezra and Nehemiah were treated as book in the earliest Hebrew manuscripts. Therefore to put this book into context, study historical chart EZRA, NEHEMIAH, AND ESTHER on page 713.
2. As you read Nehemiah chapter by chapter:
   a. Look for the theme of each chapter. Record this under the chapter number on the NEHEM AT A GLANCE chart on page 736 and record it in the text next to the chapter number.
   b. Read each chapter again. This time make a list of the points you want to remember abou main topic or event within each chapter.
      1) For example, in chapter 1 the theme is Nehemiah's concern for Jerusalem. In the ma opposite the first three verses you could write "Remnant's Distress." Then undernea write "walls broken down, gates burned."
      2) Then next to verses 4 through 11 you could write "Nehemiah's Prayer" and list the parts or points of his prayer; for example, "a) weeps, mourns, fasts, b) reminds God of He is and His covenant, and c) confesses his and Israel's sins."
      3) As you summarize each chapter, list what you learn about God.
   c. While there are many key repeated words you could mark such as *wall, gate, build, repairs,* you may want to observe them but not mark them because of the nature of Nehem writing. Some key words are used so many times within specific chapters that you become overwhelmed by all the markings.
      1) However, you will find it beneficial to mark every occurrence of *remember* and *remembe* and then in the margin note what or who is to be remembered and why.
      2) Also mark *command (commandments, ordinances, law)* and note in the margin what you l from marking these words.
   d. Note any references to time by drawing a clock such as this ⏰ next to the verse.
   e. As you read through Nehemiah, note in the margin when the wall is started, when it's c pleted, and when it's dedicated.
3. There are valuable lessons to be learned from observing how Nehemiah handled situations

you see how Nehemiah related to God in each situation, how he dealt with the people (including those who opposed him), and the example he set, you will see principles you can apply to your life. As you study, record your insights on the chart at the end of this book, LESSONS FROM THE LIFE OF NEHEMIAH on page 737.

When you finish recording the theme of every chapter on NEHEMIAH AT A GLANCE, look for the main division of the book, where one emphasis ends and another begins. On the line under the chapter themes, record this division and the theme or subject of the two segments of the book. Also fill in the rest of the chart.

IGS TO THINK ABOUT

Read Nehemiah chapter 9 again and think about the character of God and how He dealt with Israel. What can you learn about God and also about Israel's behavior that you can apply to your own life?

Have you thought about what could happen if the congregation of a church gathered together and publicly confessed their sins and then the sins of their nation?

What have you learned from Nehemiah's life? How are you going to apply it to your life in a practical way?

Chapter 1

[1]Or, *palace* or *del* [a]Neh. 10:1 . 7:1 [c]Neh. 2:1 ı. 1:2; Dan. 8:2

1 The words of [a]Nehemiah the son of Hacaliah.
Now it happened in [b]the month Chislev, [c]*in* the twentieth year, while I was in [d]Susa the [1]capitol,

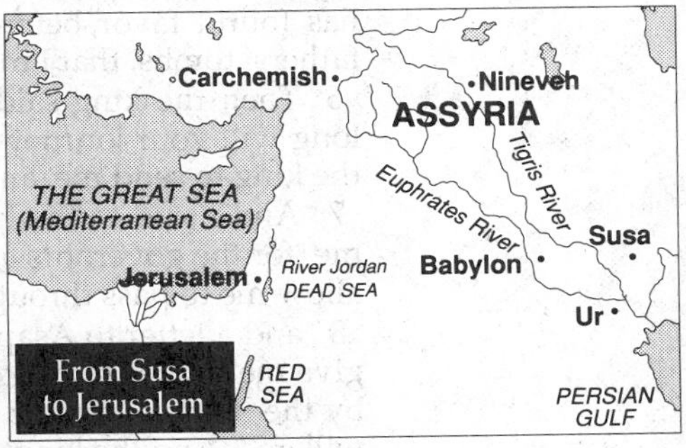

Carchemish
Nineveh
ASSYRIA
Tigris River
Euphrates River
THE GREAT SEA (Mediterranean Sea)
Susa
Babylon
Jerusalem
River Jordan
DEAD SEA
Ur
RED SEA
PERSIAN GULF

From Susa to Jerusalem

., *he and some* [a]Neh. 7:2

2 that [a]Hanani, one of my brothers, and [1]some men from Judah came; and I asked them concerning the Jews who had escaped *and* had survived the captivity, and about Jerusalem.

7:6 [b]Neh. 2:17 [c]Neh. 2:3

3 And they said to me, "The remnant there in the [a]province who survived the captivity are in great distress and [b]reproach, and [b]the wall of Jerusalem is broken down and [c]its gates are burned with fire."

9:3; 10:1 [b]Neh. 2:4

4 Now it came about when I heard these words, [a]I sat down and wept and mourned for days; and I was fasting and praying before [b]the God of heaven.

Neh. 4:14; 9:32; [b]Ex. 20:6; Ps. 89:2, 3

5 And I said, "I beseech Thee, O LORD God of heaven, [a]the great and awesome God, [b]who preserves the covenant and lovingkindness for those who love Him and keep His commandments,

Dan. 9:17 [b]Ezra an. 9:20 [c]2 Chr. 29:6

6 [a]let Thine ear now be attentive and Thine eyes open to hear the prayer of Thy servant which I am praying before Thee now, day and night, on behalf of the sons of Israel Thy servants, [b]confessing the sins of the sons of Israel which we have sinned against Thee; [c]I and my father's house have sinned.

Dan. 9:5 [b]Deut. 28:14

7 "[a]We have acted very corruptly against Thee and have not kept the commandments, nor the statutes, nor the ordinances [b]which Thou didst command Thy servant Moses.

8 [a]Lev. 26:33

8 "Remember the word which Thou didst command Thy servant Moses, saying, '[a]If you are unfaithful I will scatter you among the peoples;

9 [a]Deut. 30:2, 3

9 [a]but if you return to Me and keep My commandments and do them, though those of you who have been scattered were in the most

remote part of the heavens, I [b]will gather them from there and will
bring them [c]to the place where I have chosen to cause My name to
dwell.'
10 "And [a]they are Thy servants and Thy people whom Thou didst
redeem by Thy great power and by Thy strong hand.
11 "O Lord, I beseech Thee, [a]may Thine ear be attentive to the prayer
of Thy servant and the prayer of Thy servants who delight to [1]revere
Thy name, and make Thy servant successful today, and grant him
compassion before this man."
Now I was the [b]cupbearer to the king.

Chapter 2

2 And it came about in the month Nisan, [a]in the twentieth year of
King [b]Artaxerxes, that wine *was* before him, and [c]I took up the
wine and gave it to the king. Now I had not been sad in his presence.
2 So the king said to me, "Why is your face sad though you are not
sick? [a]This is nothing but sadness of heart." Then I was very much
afraid.
3 And I said to the king, "[a]Let the king live forever. Why should
my face not be sad [b]when the city, the place of my fathers' tombs, lies
desolate and its gates have been consumed by fire?"
4 Then the king said to me, "What would you request?" [a]So I
prayed to the God of heaven.
5 And I said to the king, "If it please the king, and if your servant
has found favor before you, send me to Judah, to the city of my
fathers' tombs, that I may rebuild it."
6 Then the king said to me, the queen sitting beside him, "How
long will your journey be, and when will you return?" So it pleased
the king to send me, and [a]I gave him a definite time.
7 And I said to the king, "If it please the king, let letters be given
me [a]for the governors *of the provinces* beyond the River, that they may
allow me to pass through until I come to Judah,
8 and a letter to Asaph the keeper of the king's [a]forest, that he may
give me timber to make beams for the gates of [b]the fortress which is
by the [1]temple, for the wall of the city, and for the house to which I
will go." And the king granted *them* to me because [c]the good hand of
my God *was* on me.
9 Then I came to [a]the governors *of the provinces* beyond the River
and gave them the king's letters. Now [b]the king had sent with me
officers of the army and horsemen.
10 And when [a]Sanballat the Horonite and Tobiah the Ammonite
[1]official heard *about it,* it was very displeasing to them that someone
had come to seek the welfare of the sons of Israel.
11 So I [a]came to Jerusalem and was there three days.
12 And I arose in the night, I and a few men with me. I did not tell
anyone what my God was putting into my [1]mind to do for Jerusalem
and there was no animal with me except the animal on which I was
riding.
13 So I went out at night by [a]the Valley Gate in the direction of the
Dragon's Well and *on* to the [1]Refuse Gate, inspecting the walls of
Jerusalem [b]which were broken down and its [c]gates which were con-
sumed by fire.
14 Then I passed on to [a]the Fountain Gate and [b]the King's Pool, but
there was no place for [1]my mount to pass.

9 [b]Deut. 30:4 12:5
10 [a]Ex. 32:11 9:29
11 [1]Or, *fear* [b]Gen. 40:21; N
2:1 [a]Neh. 1:1 7:1 [c]Neh. 1:11
2 [a]Prov. 15:13
3 [a]Dan. 2:4 [b]2 25:8-10; 2 Chr. Neh. 1:3; Jer.
4 [a]Neh. 1:4
6 [a]Neh. 13:6
7 [a]Ezra 7:21; 8
8 [1]Lit., *house* 2:5, 6 [b]Neh. 7: 7:6; Neh. 2:18
9 [a]Neh. 2:7 [b]E
10 [1]Lit., *servan* 2:19; 4:1
11 [a]Ezra 8:32
12 [1]Lit., *heart*
13 [1]Lit., *Gate of Ash-heaps* [a]Neh [b]Neh. 1:3 [c]Neh.
14 [1]Lit., *the anim under me* [a]Neh. [b]2 Kin. 20:20

15 [a]John 18:1 15 So I went up at night by the [a]ravine and inspected the wall. Then
I entered the Valley Gate again and returned.
16 And the officials did not know where I had gone or what I had
17 [a]Neh. 1:3 done; nor had I as yet told the Jews, the priests, the nobles, the
officials, or the rest who did the work.
17 Then I said to them, "You see the bad situation we are in, that
18 [a]2 Sam. 2:7 [a]Jerusalem is desolate and its gates burned by fire. Come, let us
rebuild the wall of Jerusalem that we may no longer be a reproach."
18 And I told them how the hand of my God had been favorable to
[1]Lit., *servant* [a]Neh. me, and also about the king's words which he had spoken to me.
6:6 [b]Neh. 4:1 Then they said, "Let us arise and build." [a]So they put their hands to
the good *work*.
19 But when Sanballat the Horonite, and Tobiah the Ammonite [1]of-
Ezra 4:3 [b]Neh. 2:4; ficial, and [a]Geshem the Arab heard *it*, [b]they mocked us and despised
Acts 8:21 us and said, "What is this thing you are doing? [a]Are you rebelling
against the king?"
20 So I answered them and said to them, "[a]The God of heaven will
[1]Lit., *it* [a]Neh. 3:20; 13:28 [b]Neh. 3:32; give us success; therefore we His servants will arise and build, [b]but
:39 [c]Neh. 6:1; 7:1 12:39 [e]Jer. 31:38 you have no portion, right, or memorial in Jerusalem."

Chapter 3

3 Then [a]Eliashib the high priest arose with his brothers the priests
it., *him* [a]Neh. 7:36 and built [b]the Sheep Gate; they consecrated it and [c]hung its
doors. They consecrated [1]the wall to [d]the Tower of the Hundred *and*
[e]the Tower of Hananel.
3 [a]Neh. 12:39 2 And next to him [a]the men of Jericho built, and next to
[1]them Zaccur the son of Imri built.
3 Now the sons of Hassenaah built [a]the Fish Gate; they
4 [1]Lit., *them* laid its beams and hung its doors with its bolts and bars.
4 And next to them Meremoth the son of Uriah the son
of Hakkoz made repairs. And next to him Meshullam the
, *them* [2]Lit., *bring* son of Berechiah the son of Meshezabel made repairs. And
their neck to next to [1]him Zadok the son of Baana also made repairs.
5 Moreover, next to [1]him the Tekoites made repairs, but
6 [a]Neh. 12:39 their nobles did not [2]support the work of their masters.
6 And Joiada the son of Paseah and Meshullam the son
of Besodeiah repaired [a]the Old Gate; they laid its beams
and hung its doors, with its bolts and its bars.
which was under 7 Next to them Melatiah the Gibeonite and Jadon the
jurisdiction of the Meronothite, the men of Gibeon and of Mizpah, [1]also
or of the province made repairs for the official seat of the [a]governor *of the*
nd the River, also *repairs* [a]Neh. 2:7 *province* beyond the River.
8 Next to him Uzziel the son of Harhaiah of the [a]goldsmiths made
h. 3:31, 32 [b]Neh. repairs. And next to him Hananiah, one of the perfumers, made
12:38 repairs, and they restored Jerusalem as far as [b]the Broad Wall.
9 And next to them Rephaiah the son of Hur, [a]the official of half
the district of Jerusalem, made repairs.
9 [a]Neh. 3:12, 17 10 Next to them Jedaiah the son of Harumaph made repairs op-
posite his house. And next to him Hattush the son of Hashabneiah
made repairs.
11 [a]Neh. 12:38 11 Malchijah the son of Harim and Hasshub the son of Pahath-
moab repaired another section and [a]the Tower of Furnaces.
12 And next to him Shallum the son of Hallohesh, [a]the official of
12 [a]Neh. 3:9 half the district of Jerusalem, made repairs, he and his daughters.

The Gates in Nehemiah's Time

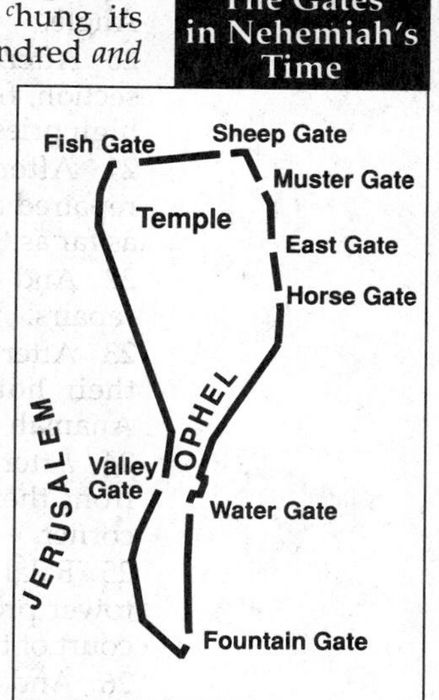

13 Hanun and the inhabitants of Zanoah repaired [a]the Valley Gate.
They built it and hung its doors with its bolts and its bars, and a
thousand cubits of the wall to the [1]Refuse Gate.
14 And Malchijah the son of Rechab, the official of the district of
[a]Beth-haccherem repaired the [1b]Refuse Gate. He built it and hung its
doors with its bolts and its bars.
15 Shallum the son of Col-hozeh, the official of the district of Miz-
pah, [a]repaired the Fountain Gate. He built it, covered it, and hung its
doors with its bolts and its bars, and the wall of the Pool of Shelah at
[b]the king's garden as far as [c]the steps that descend from the city of
David.
16 After him Nehemiah the son of Azbuk, [a]official of half the dis-
trict of Beth-zur, made repairs as far as *a point* opposite the tombs of
David, and as far as [b]the artificial pool and the house of the mighty
men.
17 After him the Levites carried out repairs *under* Rehum the son of
Bani. Next to him Hashabiah, the official of half the district of Keilah,
carried out repairs for his district.
18 After him their brothers carried out repairs *under* Bavvai the son
of Henadad, official of *the other* half of the district of Keilah.
19 And next to him Ezer the son of Jeshua, [a]the official of Mizpah,
repaired [1]another section, in front of the ascent of the armory [b]at the
Angle.
20 After him Baruch the son of Zabbai zealously repaired another
section, from the Angle to the doorway of the house of [a]Eliashib the
high priest.
21 After him Meremoth the son of Uriah the son of Hakkoz
repaired another section, from the doorway of Eliashib's house even
as far as the end of [1]his house.
22 And after him the priests, [a]the men of the [1]valley, carried out
repairs.
23 After [1]them Benjamin and Hasshub carried out repairs in front of
their house. After [1]them Azariah the son of Maaseiah, son of
Ananiah carried out repairs beside his house.
24 After him Binnui the son of Henadad repaired another section,
from the house of Azariah as far as [a]the Angle and as far as the
corner.
25 Palal the son of Uzai *made repairs* in front of the Angle and the
tower projecting from the upper house of the king, which is by [a]the
court of the guard. After him Pedaiah the son of Parosh *made repairs*.
26 And [a]the temple servants living in [b]Ophel *made repairs* as far as
the front of [c]the Water Gate toward the east and the projecting tower.
27 After him [a]the Tekoites repaired another section in front of the
great projecting tower and as far as the wall of Ophel.
28 Above [a]the Horse Gate the priests carried out repairs, each in
front of his house.
29 After [1]them Zadok the son of Immer carried out repairs in front
of his house. And after him Shemaiah the son of Shecaniah, the
keeper of the East Gate, carried out repairs.
30 After him Hananiah the son of Shelemiah, and Hanun the sixth
son of Zalaph, repaired another section. After him Meshullam the
son of Berechiah carried out repairs in front of his own [1]quarters.
31 After him Malchijah [1]one of [a]the goldsmiths, carried out repairs
as far as the house of the temple servants and of the merchants, in

13 [1]Lit., *Gate Ash-heaps* [a]N

14 [1]Lit., *Gate Ash-heaps* [a]J [b]Neh. 2:13

15 [a]Neh. 2:17 25:4 [c]Neh. 12

16 [a]Neh. 3:9, [b]2 Kin. 20:20; Is

19 [1]Lit., *a secc measure*, and s 20, 21, 24, 30 3:15 [b]2 Chr. 26

20 [a]Neh. 3:1

21 [1]Lit., *Eliash*

22 [1]Lit., *circle;* lower Jordan va [a]Neh. 12:28

23 [1]Lit., *him*

24 [a]Neh. 3:19

25 [a]Jer. 32:2

26 [a]Neh. 7:46 11:21 [c]Neh. 8:1

27 [a]Neh. 3:5

28 [a]2 Kin. 11:16 23:15; Jer. 31:40

29 [1]Lit., *him*

30 [1]Or, *cell*

31 [1]Lit., *son of* 3:8, 32

front of the [2]Inspection Gate and as far as the upper room of the
corner.
32 And between the upper room of the corner and [a]the Sheep Gate
the goldsmiths and the merchants carried out repairs.

Chapter 4

4 [1]Now it came about that when [a]Sanballat heard that we were
rebuilding the wall, he became furious and very angry and
mocked the Jews.
2 And he spoke in the presence of his brothers and [a]the [1]wealthy
men of Samaria and said, "What are these feeble Jews doing? Are
they going to restore *it* for themselves? Can they offer sacrifices? Can
they finish in a day? Can they revive the stones from the [2b]dusty
rubble even the burned ones?"
3 Now Tobiah the Ammonite *was* near him and he said, "Even
what they are building—[a]if a fox should [1]jump on *it,* he would break
their stone wall down!"
4 [a]Hear, O our God, how we are despised! [b]Return their reproach
on their own heads and give them up for plunder in a land of cap-
tivity.
5 Do not [1a]forgive their iniquity and let not their sin be blotted out
before Thee, for they have [2]demoralized the builders.
6 So we built the wall and the whole wall was joined together to
half its *height,* for the people had a [1]mind to work.
7 [1]Now it came about when Sanballat, Tobiah, the Arabs, the Am-
monites, and the Ashdodites heard that the [2]repair of the walls of
Jerusalem went on, *and* that the breaches began to be closed, they
were very angry.
8 And all of them [a]conspired together to come *and* fight against
Jerusalem and to cause a disturbance in it.
9 But we prayed to our God, and because of them we [a]set up a
guard against them day and night.
10 Thus [1]in Judah it was said,
"The strength of the burden bearers is failing,
Yet there is much [2]rubbish;
And we ourselves are unable
To rebuild the wall."
11 And our enemies said, "They will not know or see until we come
among them, kill them, and put a stop to the work."
12 And it came about when the Jews who lived near them came
and told us ten times, "[1]They will come up against us from every
place where you may turn,"
13 then I stationed *men* in the lowest parts of the space behind the
wall, the [1]exposed places, and I [a]stationed the people in families with
their swords, spears, and bows.
14 When I saw *their fear,* I rose and spoke to the nobles, the officials,
and the rest of the people: "[a]Do not be afraid of them; remember the
Lord who is great and awesome, and [b]fight for your brothers, your
sons, your daughters, your wives, and your houses."
15 And it happened when our enemies heard that it was known to
us, and that [a]God had frustrated their plan, then all of us returned to
the wall, each one to his work.
16 And it came about from that day on, that half of my servants
carried on the work while half of them held the spears, the shields,

31 [2]Or, *Mustering*
32 [a]Neh. 3:1; 12:39
:1 [1]Ch. 3:33 in Heb. [a]Neh. 2:10
)r, *army* [2]Lit., *heaps* *f dust* [a]Ezra 4:9, 10 [b]Neh. 4:10
3 [1]Lit., *go up* [a]Lam. 5:18
[a]Ps. 123:3, 4 [b]Ps. 79:12
5 [1]Lit., *cover* [2]Lit., *ended against* [a]Ps. 9:27, 28; Jer. 18:23
6 [1]Lit., *heart*
h. 4:1 in Heb. [2]Lit., *healing*
8 [a]Ps. 83:3
9 [a]Neh. 4:11
0 [1]Lit., *Judah said* [2]Lit., *dust*
So Gr.; Heb. omits *they . . . up*
[1]Lit., *bare* [a]Neh. 4:17, 18
[a]Num. 14:9; Deut. 30 [b]2 Sam. 10:12
5 [a]2 Sam. 17:14

the bows, and the breastplates; and the captains *were* behind the
whole house of Judah.
17 Those who were rebuilding the wall and those who carried bur-
dens took *their* load with one hand doing the work and the other
holding a weapon.
18 As for the builders, each *wore* his sword girded at his side as he
built, while [1]the trumpeter *stood* near me.
19 And I said to the nobles, the officials, and the rest of the people,
"The work is great and extensive, and we are separated on the wall
far from one another.
20 "At whatever place you hear the sound of the trumpet, [1]rally to
us there. [a]Our God will fight for us."
21 So we carried on the work with half of them holding spears from
[1]dawn until the stars [2]appeared.
22 At that time I also said to the people, "Let each man with his
servant spend the night within Jerusalem so that they may be a
guard for us by night and a laborer by day."
23 So neither I, my brothers, my servants, nor the men of the guard
who followed me, none of us removed our clothes, each *took* his
weapon *even to* the water.

Chapter 5

5 Now [a]there was a great outcry of the people and of their wives
against their [b]Jewish brothers.
2 For there were those who said, "We, our sons and our daughters,
are many; therefore let us [a]get grain that we may eat and live."
3 And there were others who said, "We are mortgaging our fields,
our vineyards, and our houses that we might get grain because of
the famine."
4 Also there were those who said, "We have borrowed money [a]for
the king's tax *on* our fields and our vineyards.
5 "And now [a]our flesh is like the flesh of our brothers, our children
like their children. Yet behold, [b]we are forcing our sons and our
daughters to be slaves, and some of our daughters are forced into
bondage *already,* and [1]we are helpless because our fields and vine-
yards belong to others."
6 Then I was very [a]angry when I had heard their outcry and these
words.
7 And I consulted with myself, and contended with the nobles and
the rulers and said to them, "[a]You are exacting usury, each from his
brother!" Therefore, I held a great assembly against them.
8 And I said to them, "We according to our ability [a]have
[1]redeemed our Jewish brothers who were sold to the nations; now
would you even sell your brothers that they may be sold to us?"
Then they were silent and could not find a word *to say.*
9 Again I said, "The thing which you are doing is not good;
should you not walk in the fear of our God because of [a]the reproach
of the nations, our enemies?
10 "And likewise I, my brothers and my servants, are lending them
money and grain. Please, let us leave off this usury.
11 "Please, give back to them this very day their fields, their vine-
yards, their olive groves, and their houses, also the hundredth *part* of
the money and of the grain, the new wine, and the oil that you are
exacting from them."

18 [1]Lit., *he who sounded the trum*
20 [1]Lit., *assemb yourselves* [a]Ex. Deut. 1:30
21 [1]Lit., *rising of dawn* [2]Lit., *came*
5:1 [a]Lev. 25:35 15:7
2 [a]Hag. 1:6
4 [a]Ezra 4:13; 7:
5 [1]Lit., *there is power in our ha* [a]Gen. 37:27 [b]L
6 [a]Ex. 11:8
7 [a]Ex. 22:25; L 25:36; Deut. 23
8 [1]Lit., *bought* 25:48
9 [a]Neh. 4:4

12 Then they said, "We [a]will give *it* back and [b]will require nothing
from them; we will do exactly as you say." So I called the priests and
[c]took an oath from them that they would do according to this
[1]promise.
13 I [a]also shook out the [1]front of my garment and said, "Thus may
God shake out every man from his house and from his possessions
who does not fulfill this [2]promise; even thus may he be shaken out
and emptied." And [b]all the assembly said, "Amen!" And they
praised the LORD. Then the people did according to this [2]promise.
14 Moreover, from the day that I was appointed to be their gover-
nor in the land of Judah, from [a]the twentieth year to the [b]thirty-
second year of King Artaxerxes, *for* twelve years, neither I nor my
[1]kinsmen have eaten the governor's food *allowance.*
15 But the former governors who were before me [1]laid burdens on
the people and took from them bread and wine besides forty shekels
of silver; even their servants domineered the people. But I did not do
so [a]because of the fear of God.
16 And I also [1]applied myself to the work on this wall; we did not
buy any land, and all my servants were gathered there for the work.
17 Moreover, [a]*there were* at my table one hundred and fifty Jews and
officials, besides those who came to us from the nations that were
around us.
18 Now [a]that which was prepared for each day was one ox *and* six
choice sheep, also birds were prepared for me; and once in ten days
all sorts of wine *were furnished* in abundance. Yet for all this [b]I did not
demand the governor's food *allowance,* because the servitude was
heavy on this people.
19 [a]Remember me, O my God, for good, *according to* all that I have
done for this people.

Chapter 6

6 Now it came about when it was reported to Sanballat, Tobiah, to
Geshem the Arab, and to the rest of our enemies that I had
rebuilt the wall, and *that* no breach remained in it, [a]although at that
time I had not set up the doors in the gates,
2 that Sanballat and Geshem sent *a message* to me, saying, "Come,
let us meet together at [1]Chephirim in the plain of [a]Ono." But they
were planning to [2]harm me.
3 So I sent messengers to them, saying, "I am doing a great work
and I cannot come down. Why should the work stop while I leave it
and come down to you?"
4 And they sent *messages* to me four times in this manner, and I
answered them in the same way.
5 Then Sanballat sent his servant to me in the same manner a fifth
time with an open letter in his hand.
6 In it was written, "It is reported among the nations, and [1]Gash-
mu says, that [a]you and the Jews are planning to rebel; therefore you
are rebuilding the wall. And you are to be their king, according to
these reports.
7 "And you have also appointed prophets to proclaim in Jerusalem
concerning [1]you, 'A king is in Judah!' And now it will be reported to
the king according to these reports. So come now, let us take counsel
together."
8 Then I sent *a message* to him saying, "Such things as you are

, *word* [a]2 Chr. 5 [b]Neh. 10:31 [c]Ezra 10:5

t., *bosom* [2]Lit., cts 18:6 [b]Neh. 8:6

brothers [a]Neh. 1:1 [b]Neh. 13:6

it., *made heavy* . 5:9; Job 31:23

6 [1]Or, *held fast*

7 [a]1 Kin. 18:19

[a]1 Kin. 4:22, 23 [b]2 Thess. 3:8

eh. 13:14, 22, 31

6:1 [a]Neh. 3:1, 3

nother reading is, *the villages* [2]Lit., *vil to me* [a]1 Chr. 8:12

6 [1]In v. 1 and ewhere, *Geshem* [a]Neh. 2:19

[1]Lit., *you, saying*

saying have not been done, but you are [a]inventing them [1]in your
own mind."
9 For all of them were *trying* to frighten us, [1]thinking, "[2]They will
become discouraged with the work and it will not be done." But
now, [a]*O God,* strengthen my hands.
10 And when I entered the house of Shemaiah the son of Delaiah,
son of Mehetabel, [a]who was [1]confined at home, he said, "Let us meet
together in the house of God, within the temple, and let us close the
doors of the temple, for they are coming to kill you, and they are
coming to kill you at night."
11 But I said, "[a]Should a man like me flee? And could one such as I
go into the temple [1]to save his life? I will not go in."
12 Then I perceived [1]that surely God had not sent him, but he ut-
tered *his* prophecy against me because Tobiah and Sanballat had
hired him.
13 He was hired for this reason, [a]that I might become frightened
and act accordingly and sin, so that they might have an evil report in
order that they could reproach me.
14 [a]Remember, O my God, Tobiah and Sanballat according to these
works of theirs, and also Noadiah [b]the prophetess and the rest of the
prophets who were *trying* to frighten me.
15 So [a]the wall was completed on the twenty-fifth of *the month* Elul,
in fifty-two days.
16 And it came about [a]when all our enemies heard *of it,* and all the
nations surrounding us saw *it,* they [1]lost their confidence; for [b]they
recognized that this work had been accomplished [2]with the help of
our God.
17 Also in those days many letters went from the nobles of Judah to
Tobiah, and Tobiah's *letters* came to them.
18 For many in Judah were bound by oath to him because he was
the son-in-law of Shecaniah the son of Arah, and his son Jehohanan
had married the daughter of Meshullam the son of Berechiah.
19 Moreover, they were speaking about his good deeds in my pres-
ence and reported my words to him. Then Tobiah sent letters to
frighten me.

Chapter 7

7 Now it came about when [a]the wall was rebuilt and I had set up
the doors, and the gatekeepers and the singers and the Levites
were appointed,
2 that I put [a]Hanani my brother, and [b]Hananiah the commander of
[c]the fortress, in charge of Jerusalem, for he was [d]a faithful man and
feared God more than many.
3 Then I said to them, "Do not let the gates of Jerusalem be opened
until the sun is hot, and while they are standing *guard,* let them shut
and bolt the doors. Also appoint guards from the inhabitants of
Jerusalem, each at his post, and each in front of his own house."
4 Now the city was large and spacious, but the people in it were
few and the houses were not built.
5 [a]Then my God put it into my heart to assemble the nobles, the
officials, and the people to be enrolled by genealogies. Then I found
the book of the genealogy of those who came up first [1]in which I
found the following record:
6 [a]These are the [1]people of the province who came up from the

8 [1]Lit., *from yo* [a]Job 13:4; Ps.
9 [1]Lit., *saying, Their hands w from* [a]Ps. 138
10 [1]Lit., *shut u* 36:5
11 [1]Lit., *and liv* 28:1
12 [1]Lit., *and be*
13 [a]Neh. 6:6
14 [a]Neh. 13:29 13:17
15 [a]Neh. 4:1, 2
16 [1]Lit., *fell exc in their own eye from our God* [a]N 2:10; 4:1, 7 [b]Ex
7:1 [a]Neh. 6:1, 1
2 [a]Neh. 1:2 [b]Ne 10:23 [c]Neh. 2:8 13:13
5 [1]Lit., *and I fou written in it* [a]Pro 3:6
6 [1]Lit., *sons* [a]Ez 2:1-70

captivity of the exiles whom Nebuchadnezzar the king of Babylon
had carried away, and who returned to Jerusalem and Judah, each to
his city,
7 who came with Zerubbabel, Jeshua, Nehemiah, [1]Azariah, [2]Ra-
amiah, Nahamani, Mordecai, Bilshan, [3]Mispereth, Bigvai, [4]Nehum,
Baanah.
The number of men of the people of Israel:
8 the sons of Parosh, 2,172;
9 the sons of Shephatiah, 372;
10 the sons of Arah, 652;
11 the sons of Pahath-moab of the sons of Jeshua and Joab, 2,818;
12 the sons of Elam, 1,254;
13 the sons of Zattu, 845;
14 the sons of Zaccai, 760;
15 the sons of [1]Binnui, 648;
16 the sons of Bebai, 628;
17 the sons of Azgad, 2,322;
18 the sons of Adonikam, 667;
19 the sons of Bigvai, 2,067;
20 the sons of Adin, 655;
21 the sons of Ater, of Hezekiah, 98;
22 the sons of Hashum, 328;
23 the sons of Bezai, 324;
24 the sons of [1]Hariph, 112;
25 the sons of [1]Gibeon, 95;
26 the men of Bethlehem and Netophah, 188;
27 the men of Anathoth, 128;
28 the men of [1]Beth-azmaveth, 42;
29 the men of [1]Kiriath-jearim, Chephirah, and Beeroth, 743;
30 the men of Ramah and Geba, 621;
31 the men of Michmas, 122;
32 the men of Bethel and Ai, 123;
33 the men of the other Nebo, 52;
34 the sons of the other Elam, 1,254;
35 the sons of Harim, 320;
36 the [1]men of Jericho, 345;
37 the sons of Lod, Hadid, and Ono, 721;
38 the sons of Senaah, 3,930.
39 The priests: the sons of Jedaiah of the house of Jeshua, 973;
40 the sons of Immer, 1,052;
41 the sons of Pashhur, 1,247;
42 the sons of Harim, 1,017.
43 The Levites: the sons of Jeshua, of Kadmiel, of the sons of [1]Hode-
vah, 74.
44 The singers: the sons of Asaph, 148.
45 The gatekeepers: the sons of Shallum, the sons of Ater, the sons
of Talmon, the sons of Akkub, the sons of Hatita, the sons of Sho-
bai, 138.
46 The temple servants: the sons of Ziha, the sons of Hasupha, the
sons of Tabbaoth,
47 the sons of Keros, the sons of [1]Sia, the sons of Padon,
48 the sons of Lebana, the sons of Hagaba, the sons of Shalmai,
49 the sons of Hanan, the sons of Giddel, the sons of Gahar,
50 the sons of Reaiah, the sons of Rezin, the sons of Nekoda,

In Ezra 2:2, *Seraiah* [2]In Ezra 2:2, *Reelaiah* [3]In Ezra 2:2, *Mispar* [4]In Ezra 2:2, *Rehum*

[1]In Ezra 2:10, *Bani*

[1]In Ezra 2:18, *Jorah*

[1]In Ezra 2:20, *Gibbar*

28 [1]In Ezra 2:24, *Azmaveth*

29 [1]In Ezra 2:25, *Kiriath-arim*

36 [1]Lit., *sons*

43 [1]In Ezra 2:40, *Hodaviah*

[1]In Ezra 2:44, *Siaha*

51 the sons of Gazzam, the sons of Uzza, the sons of Paseah,
52 the sons of Besai, the sons of Meunim, the sons of [1]Nephu-
shesim,
53 the sons of Bakbuk, the sons of Hakupha, the sons of Harhur,
54 the sons of [1]Bazlith, the sons of Mehida, the sons of Harsha,
55 the sons of Barkos, the sons of Sisera, the sons of Temah,
56 the sons of Neziah, the sons of Hatipha.
57 The sons of Solomon's servants: the sons of Sotai, the sons of
[1]Sophereth, the sons of [2]Perida,
58 the sons of Jaala, the sons of Darkon, the sons of Giddel,
59 the sons of Shephatiah, the sons of Hattil, the sons of Pochereth-
hazzebaim, the sons of [1]Amon.
60 All the temple servants and the sons of Solomon's servants
were 392.

61 And these *were* they who came up from Tel-melah, Tel-harsha,
Cherub, [1]Addon, and Immer; but they could not show their fathers'
houses or their [2]descendants, whether they were of Israel:
62 the sons of Delaiah, the sons of Tobiah, the sons of Nekoda, 642.
63 And of the priests: the sons of [1]Hobaiah, the sons of Hakkoz, the
sons of Barzillai, who took a wife of the daughters of Barzillai, the
Gileadite, and was named after them.
64 These searched *among* their ancestral registration, but it could
not be located; therefore they were considered unclean *and excluded*
from the priesthood.
65 And [a]the [1]governor said to them that they should not eat from
the most holy things until a priest arose with [b]Urim and Thummim.
66 The whole assembly together *was* 42,360,
67 besides their male and their female servants, [1]of whom *there*
were 7,337; and they had 245 male and female singers.
68 [1a]Their horses were 736; their mules, 245;
69 *their* camels, 435; *their* donkeys, 6,720.
70 And some from among the heads of fathers' *households* gave to
the work. The [1a]governor gave to the treasury 1,000 gold drach-
mas, 50 basins, 530 priests' garments.
71 And some of the heads of fathers' *households* gave into the
treasury of the work 20,000 gold drachmas, and 2,200 silver minas.
72 And that which the rest of the people gave was 20,000 gold
drachmas and 2,000 silver minas, and 67 priests' garments.
73 Now [a]the priests, the Levites, the gatekeepers, the singers, some
of the people, the temple servants, and all Israel, lived in their cities.
[b]**And** when the seventh month came, the sons of Israel *were* in
their cities.

Chapter 8

8 And all the people gathered as one man at the square which was
in front of [a]the Water Gate, and they [1]asked [b]Ezra the scribe to
bring [c]the book of the law of Moses which the LORD had [2]given to
Israel.
2 Then [a]Ezra the priest brought the law before the assembly of
men, women, and all who *could* listen with understanding, on [b]the
first day of the seventh month.
3 And he read from it before the square which was in front of [a]the
Water Gate from [1]early morning until midday, in the presence of

52 [1]In Ezra 2:5 *Nephisim*
54 [1]In Ezra 2:5 *Bazluth*
57 [1]In Ezra 2:5 *Hassophereth* 2:55, *Peruda*
59 [1]In Ezra 2:5
61 [1]In Ezra 2:59 *Addan* [2]Lit., *see*
63 [1]In Ezra 2:61 *Habaiah*
65 [1]Heb., *Tirsha* Persian title [a]Ne 10:1 [b]Ex. 28:30; 33:8
67 [1]Lit., *these*
68 [1]So with som ancient mss. and [a]Ezra 2:66
70 [1]Heb., *Tirsha* Persian title [a]Ne 8:9
73 [a]1 Chr. 9:2 [b]E
8:1 [1]Lit., *said to* *commanded* [a]Ne 3:26 [b]Ezra 7:6 [c]2 34:15
2 [a]Deut. 31:9-11; 8:9 [b]Lev. 23:24
3 [1]Lit., *the light* [a] 8:1

men and women, those who could understand; and all the people
were attentive to the book of the law.
4 And Ezra the scribe stood at a wooden podium which they had
made for the purpose. And beside him stood Mattithiah, Shema,
Anaiah, Uriah, Hilkiah, and Maaseiah on his right hand; and
Pedaiah, Mishael, Malchijah, Hashum, Hashbaddanah, Zechariah,
and Meshullam on his left hand.
5 And Ezra opened [a]the book in the sight of all the people for he
was standing above all the people; and when he opened it, all the
people [b]stood up.
6 Then Ezra blessed the LORD the great God. And all the people
answered, "[a]Amen, Amen!" while lifting up their hands; then [b]they
bowed low and worshiped the LORD with *their* faces to the ground.
7 Also Jeshua, Bani, Sherebiah, Jamin, Akkub, Shabbethai, Hodiah,
Maaseiah, Kelita, Azariah, Jozabad, Hanan, Pelaiah, and the Levites,
explained the law to the people while the people *remained* in their
place.
8 And they read from the book, from the law of God, [1]translating
to give the sense so that they understood the reading.
9 Then Nehemiah, who was the [1a]governor, and Ezra [b]the priest
and scribe, and the Levites who taught the people said to all the
people, "[c]This day is holy to the LORD your God; [d]do not mourn or
weep." For all the people were weeping when they heard the words
of the law.
10 Then he said to them, "Go, eat of the fat, drink of the sweet, and
[a]send portions to him who has nothing prepared; for this day is holy
to our Lord. Do not be grieved, for the joy of the LORD is your
strength."
11 So the Levites calmed all the people, saying, "Be still, for the day
is holy; do not be grieved."
12 And all the people went away to eat, to drink, [a]to send portions
and to [1]celebrate a great festival, [b]because they understood the
words which had been made known to them.
13 Then on the second day the heads of fathers' *households* of all the
people, the priests, and the Levites were gathered to Ezra the scribe
that they might gain insight into the words of the law.
14 And they found written in the law how the LORD had com-
manded through Moses that the sons of Israel [a]should live in booths
during the feast of the seventh month.
15 [1a]So they proclaimed and circulated a proclamation in all their
cities and [b]in Jerusalem, saying, "[c]Go out to the hills, and bring olive
branches, and [2]wild olive branches, myrtle branches, palm branches,
and branches of *other* leafy trees, to make booths, as it is written."
16 So the people went out and brought *them* and made booths for
themselves, each [a]on his roof, and in their courts, and in the courts of
the house of God, and in the square at [b]the Water Gate, and in the
square at [c]the Gate of Ephraim.
17 And the entire assembly of those who had returned from the
captivity made booths and lived in [1]them. The sons of Israel [a]had
indeed not done so from the days of Joshua the son of Nun to that
day. And [b]there was great rejoicing.
18 And [a]he read from the book of the law of God daily, from the
first day to the last day. And they [b]celebrated the feast seven days,

leh. 8:3 [b]Judg. ; 1 Kin. 8:12-14

5:13 [b]Ex. 4:31

[1]Or, *explaining*

eb., *Tirshatha*, a title [a]Neh. 7:65, eh. 12:26 [c]Neh. [d]Deut. 12:7, 12

[a]Deut. 26:11-13

it., *make a great cing* [a]Neh. 8:10 [b]Neh. 8:7, 8

ev. 23:34, 40, 42

it., *And that they ause to be heard* , *oil tree*, species nown [a]Lev. 23:4 6:16 [c]Lev. 23:40

Jer. 32:29 [b]Neh. Kin. 14:13; Neh. 12:39

[1]Lit., *the booths* 7:8; 8:13 [b]2 Chr. 30:21

Deut. 31:11 [b]Lev. 23:36

and on [c]the eighth day *there was* a solemn assembly according to the
ordinance.

Chapter 9

9 Now on the twenty-fourth day of [a]this month the sons of Israel
assembled [b]with fasting, in sackcloth, and with [c]dirt upon them.
2 And the [1a]descendants of Israel separated themselves from all
foreigners, and stood and [b]confessed their sins and the iniquities of
their fathers.
3 While [a]they stood in their place, they read from the book of the
law of the LORD their God for a fourth of the day; and for *another*
fourth they confessed and worshiped the LORD their God.
4 [a]Now on the Levites' platform stood Jeshua, Bani, Kadmiel,
Shebaniah, Bunni, Sherebiah, Bani, *and* Chenani, and they cried with
a loud voice to the LORD their God.
5 Then the Levites, Jeshua, Kadmiel, Bani, Hashabneiah, Shere-
biah, Hodiah, Shebaniah, *and* Pethahiah, said, "Arise, bless the LORD
your God forever and ever!

O may Thy glorious name be blessed
And exalted above all blessing and praise!
6 "[a]Thou alone art the LORD.
[b]Thou hast made the heavens,
The heaven of heavens with all their host,
The earth and all that is on it,
The seas and all that is in them.
[c]Thou dost give life to all of them
And the heavenly host bows down before Thee.
7 "Thou art the LORD God,
[a]Who chose Abram
And brought him out from [b]Ur of the Chaldees,
And [c]gave him the name Abraham.
8 "And Thou didst find [a]his heart faithful before Thee,
And didst make a covenant with him
To give *him* the land of the Canaanite,
Of the Hittite and the Amorite,
Of the Perizzite, the Jebusite, and the Girgashite—
To give *it* to his [1]descendants.
And Thou [b]hast fulfilled Thy promise,
For Thou art righteous.

9 "[a]Thou didst see the affliction of our fathers in Egypt,
And didst [b]hear their cry by the [1]Red Sea.
10 "Then Thou didst perform [a]signs and wonders against Pharaoh,
Against all his servants and all the people of his land;
For Thou didst know that [b]they acted arrogantly toward them,
And [c]didst make a name for Thyself as *it is* this day.
11 "And [a]Thou didst divide the sea before them,
So they passed through the midst of the sea on dry ground;
And [b]their pursuers Thou didst hurl into the depths,
Like a stone into [1]raging waters.
12 "And with a pillar of cloud [a]Thou didst lead them by day,
And with a pillar of fire by night
To light for them the way
In which they were to go.

18 [c]Num. 2

9:1 [a]Neh. 8
8:23 [c]1 Sam

2 [1]Lit., *seed*
10:11; Neh.
28:13; Jer. 3

3 [a]Neh. 8:4

4 [a]Neh. 8:7

6 [a]Deut. 6:4;
19:15 [b]Gen.
1:16f.

7 [a]Gen. 12:1
11:31 [c]Gen.

8 [1]Lit., *seed*
15:6, 18-21 [b]
21:43-45

9 [1]Lit., *Sea o*
[a]Ex. 3:7 [b]Ex.
14:10-14, 31

10 [a]Ex. 7:8-1
5:2 [c]Ex. 9:16

11 [1]Lit., *stron*
[a]Ex. 14:21 [b]E
5, 10

12 [a]Ex. 13:21

3 [a]Ex. 19:11, 18-20 x. 20:1 [c]Ps. 19:7-9

13 "Then [a]Thou didst come down on Mount Sinai,
And didst [b]speak with them from heaven;
Thou didst give to them [c]just ordinances and true laws,
Good statutes and commandments.

4 [a]Ex. 16:23; 20:8

14 "So Thou didst make known to them [a]Thy holy sabbath,
And didst lay down for them commandments, statutes, and law,
Through Thy servant Moses.

15 [1]Lit., *lift up Thy* d [a]Ex. 16:4, 14, 15 [b]Ex. 17:6; Num. -13 [c]Deut. 1:8, 21

15 "Thou didst [a]provide bread from heaven for them for their hunger,
Thou didst [b]bring forth water from a rock for them for their thirst,
And Thou didst [c]tell them to enter in order to possess
The land which Thou didst [1]swear to give them.

[1]Lit., *stiffened their neck;* so also v. 17 [a]Neh. 9:10 [b]Deut. 26-33; 31:27; Neh. 9:29

16 "But they, our fathers, [a]acted arrogantly;
They [1b]became stubborn and would not listen to Thy commandments.

[1]So Gr. and some . mss.; Heb. reads *their rebellion* [a]Ps. 3:11, 42-55 [b]Num. [c]Ex. 34:6, 7; Num. 14:18

17 "And they refused to listen,
And [a]did not remember Thy wondrous deeds which Thou hadst performed among them;
So they became stubborn and [b]appointed a leader to return to their slavery [1]in Egypt.
But Thou art a God [c]of forgiveness,
Gracious and compassionate,
Slow to anger, and abounding in lovingkindness;
And Thou didst not forsake them.

18 [1]Lit., *acts of contempt* [a]Ex 32:4-8, 31

18 "Even when they [a]made for themselves
A calf of molten metal
And said, 'This is your God
Who brought you up from Egypt,'
And committed great [1]blasphemies,

[a]Deut. 8:2-4; Neh. 27, 31 [b]Neh. 9:12

19 [a]Thou, in Thy great compassion,
Didst not forsake them in the wilderness;
[b]The pillar of cloud did not leave them by day,
To guide them on their way,
Nor the pillar of fire by night, to light for them the way in which they were to go.

Num. 11:17; Neh. 9:30; Is. 63:11-14

20 "And [a]Thou didst give Thy good Spirit to instruct them,
Thy manna Thou didst not withhold from their mouth,
And Thou didst give them water for their thirst.

21 [a]Deut. 2:7

21 "Indeed, [a]forty years Thou didst provide for them in the wilderness *and* they were not in want;
Their clothes did not wear out, nor did their feet swell.

[1]Lit., *side, corner* So the Gr. and the ; Heb. reads *and and of the king of Heshbon* [a]Num. 21:21-35

22 "Thou didst also give them kingdoms and peoples,
And Thou didst allot *them* to them as a [1]boundary.
[a]And they took possession of the land of Sihon [2]the king of Heshbon,
And the land of Og the king of Bashan.

Gen. 15:5; 22:17

23 "And Thou didst make their sons numerous as [a]the stars of heaven,
And Thou didst bring them into the land
Which Thou hadst told their fathers to enter and possess.

osh. 11:23; 21:43

24 "[a]So their sons entered and possessed the land.

And [b]Thou didst subdue before them the inhabitants of the land,
the Canaanites,
And Thou didst give them into their hand, with their kings, and
the peoples of the land,
To do with them [1]as they desired.
25 "And [a]they captured fortified cities and a [1b]fertile land.
They took possession of [c]houses full of every good thing,
Hewn cisterns, vineyards, olive groves,
Fruit trees in abundance.
So they ate, were filled, and [d]grew fat,
And [e]reveled in Thy great goodness.

26 "[a]But they became disobedient and rebelled against Thee,
And [b]cast Thy law behind their backs
And [c]killed Thy prophets who had [d]admonished them
So that they might return to Thee,
And [e]they committed great [1]blasphemies.
27 "Therefore Thou didst [a]deliver them into the hand of their
oppressors who oppressed them,
But when they cried to Thee [b]in the time of their distress,
Thou didst hear from heaven, and according to Thy great
compassion
Thou didst [c]give them deliverers who delivered them from the
hand of their oppressors.
28 "But [a]as soon as they had rest, they did evil again before Thee;
Therefore Thou didst abandon them to the hand of their
enemies, so that they ruled over them.
When they cried again to Thee, Thou didst hear from heaven,
And [b]many times Thou didst rescue them according to Thy
compassion,
29 And [a]admonished them in order to turn them back to Thy law.
Yet [b]they acted arrogantly and did not listen to Thy
commandments but sinned against Thine ordinances,
By [c]which if a man observes them he shall live.
And they [1d]turned a stubborn shoulder and stiffened their neck,
and would not listen.
30 "[a]However, Thou didst bear with them for many years,
And [b]admonished them by [c]Thy Spirit through Thy prophets,
Yet they would not give ear.
Therefore Thou didst give them into the hand of the peoples of
the lands.
31 "Nevertheless, in Thy great compassion Thou [a]didst not make an
end of them or forsake them,
For Thou art [b]a gracious and compassionate God.

32 "Now therefore, our God, [a]the great, the mighty, and the
awesome God, who dost keep covenant and
lovingkindness,
Do not let all the hardship seem insignificant before Thee,
Which has come upon us, our kings, our princes, our priests,
our prophets, our fathers, and on all Thy people,
[b]From the days of the kings of Assyria to this day.
33 "However, [a]Thou art just in all that has come upon us;
For Thou hast dealt faithfully, but we have acted wickedly.

24 [1]Lit., *accordin* *their desire* [b]Josh

25 [1]Lit., *fat* [a]Deu [b]Num. 13:27 [c]De 6:11 [d]Deut. 32:15 [e]1 Kin. 8:66

26 [1]Lit., *acts of contempt* [a]Judg. [b]1 Kin. 14:9 [c]2 C 36:16 [d]Neh. 9:30 9:18

27 [a]Judg. 2:14 4:29 [c]Judg. 2:16

28 [a]Judg. 3:11 106:43

29 [1]Lit., *gave* [a] 9:26, 30 [b]Neh. [c]Lev. 18:5 [d]Zec

30 [a]Ps. 95:10; 13:18 [b]2 Kin. 1 2 Chr. 36:15, 16 9:26, 29 [c]Neh.

31 [a]Jer. 4:27 [b]

32 [a]Neh. 1:5 [b] 15:19, 29; 2 Kin Ezra 4:2, 10

33 [a]Gen. 18:25 12:1

34 "For our kings, our leaders, our priests, and our fathers have not
kept Thy law
Or paid attention to Thy commandments and Thine
[1]admonitions with which Thou hast [2]admonished them.
35 "But [a]they, in their own kingdom,
[b]With Thy great goodness which Thou didst give them,
With the broad and rich land which Thou didst set before them,
Did not serve Thee or turn from their evil deeds.
36 "Behold, [a]we are slaves today,
And as to the land which Thou didst give to our fathers to eat of
its fruit and its bounty,
Behold, we are slaves on it.
37 "And [a]its abundant produce is for the kings
Whom Thou hast set over us because of our sins;
They also rule over our bodies
And over our cattle as they please,
So we are in great distress.
38 "[1]Now because of all this
[a]We are making an agreement in writing;
And on the [b]sealed document *are the names of* our leaders, our
Levites *and* our priests."

Chapter 10

10 [1]Now on the [a]sealed document *were the names of:* Nehemiah
the [2]governor, the son of Hacaliah, and Zedekiah,
2 Seraiah, Azariah, Jeremiah,
3 Pashhur, Amariah, Malchijah,
4 Hattush, Shebaniah, Malluch,
5 Harim, Meremoth, Obadiah,
6 Daniel, Ginnethon, Baruch,
7 Meshullam, Abijah, Mijamin,
8 Maaziah, Bilgai, Shemaiah. These *were* the priests.
9 And the Levites: Jeshua the son of Azaniah, Binnui of the sons of
Henadad, Kadmiel;
10 also their brothers Shebaniah, Hodiah, Kelita, Pelaiah, Hanan,
11 Mica, Rehob, Hashabiah,
12 Zaccur, Sherebiah, Shebaniah,
13 Hodiah, Bani, Beninu.
14 The leaders of the people: Parosh, Pahath-moab, Elam, Zattu,
Bani,
15 Bunni, Azgad, Bebai,
16 Adonijah, Bigvai, Adin,
17 Ater, Hezekiah, Azzur,
18 Hodiah, Hashum, Bezai,
19 Hariph, Anathoth, Nebai,
20 Magpiash, Meshullam, Hezir,
21 Meshezabel, Zadok, Jaddua,
22 Pelatiah, Hanan, Anaiah,
23 Hoshea, Hananiah, Hasshub,
24 Hallohesh, Pilha, Shobek,
25 Rehum, Hashabnah, Maaseiah,
26 Ahiah, Hanan, Anan,
27 Malluch, Harim, Baanah.
28 Now [a]the rest of the people, the priests, the Levites, the

[1]Lit., *testimonies* [2]Or, *witnessed*
Deut. 28:47 [b]Neh. 9:25
36 [a]Deut. 28:48
37 [a]Deut. 28:33
[1]Ch. 10:1 in Heb. 10:29 [b]Neh. 10:1
[1]Ch. 10:2 in Heb. Heb., *Tirshatha,* a in title [a]Neh. 9:38
28 [a]Ezra 2:36-58

gatekeepers, the singers, the temple servants, and [b]all those who had separated themselves from the peoples of the lands to the law of God, their wives, their sons and their daughters, all those who had knowledge and understanding,

29 are joining with their [1]kinsmen, their nobles, and are [2a]taking on themselves a curse and an oath to walk in God's law, which was given through Moses, God's servant, and to keep and to observe all the commandments of [3]GOD our Lord, and His ordinances and His statutes;

30 and [a]that we will not give our daughters to the peoples of the land or take their daughters for our sons.

31 As [a]for the peoples of the land who bring wares or any grain on the sabbath day to sell, we will not buy from them on the sabbath or a holy day; and we will forego *the crops* the [b]seventh year and the [c]exaction of every debt.

32 We also [1]placed ourselves under obligation to contribute yearly [a]one third of a shekel for the service of the house of our God:

33 for the [a]showbread, for the continual grain offering, for the continual burnt offering, the sabbaths, the new moon, for the appointed times, for the holy things and for the sin offerings to make atonement for Israel, and all the work of the house of our God.

34 Likewise [a]we cast lots [b]for the supply of wood *among* the priests, the Levites, and the people in order that they might bring it to the house of our God, according to our fathers' households, at fixed times annually, to burn on the altar of the LORD our God as it is written in the law;

35 and in order that they might bring the first fruits of our ground and [a]the first fruits of all the fruit of every tree to the house of the LORD annually,

36 and [a]bring to the house of our God the first-born of our sons and of our cattle, and the first-born of our herds and our flocks as it is written in the law, for the priests who are ministering in the house of our God.

37 [a]We will also bring the first of our [1]dough, our contributions, the fruit of every tree, the new wine and the oil [b]to the priests at the chambers of the house of our God, and the [c]tithe of our ground to the Levites, for the Levites are they who receive the tithes in all the rural towns.

38 And [a]the priest, the son of Aaron, shall be with the Levites when the Levites receive tithes, and the Levites shall bring up the tenth of the tithes to the house of our God, to the chambers of [b]the storehouse.

39 For the sons of Israel and the sons of Levi shall bring the [a]contribution of the grain, the new wine and the oil, to the chambers; there are the utensils of the sanctuary, the priests who are ministering, the gatekeepers, and the singers. Thus [b]we will not [1]neglect the house of our God.

Chapter 11

11 Now [a]the leaders of the people lived in Jerusalem, but the rest of the people [b]cast lots to bring one out of ten to live in Jerusalem, [c]the holy city, while nine-tenths *remained* in the *other* cities.

2 And the people blessed all the men who [a]volunteered to live in Jerusalem.

28 [b]Neh. 9:2

29 [1]Lit., *brothe* *entering into a* *YHWH,* usually rendered *LORD* 5:12

30 [a]Ex. 34:16;

31 [a]Neh. 13:15 23:10, 11; Lev. [c]Deut. 15:1, 2

32 [1]Lit., *impose* *commandments* [a]Ex. 30:11-16; 17:24

33 [a]Lev. 24:5, 6 2:4

34 [a]Neh. 11:1 13:31

35 [a]Ex. 23:19; 3 Deut. 26:2

36 [a]Ex. 13:2

37 [1]Or, *coarse m* [a]Lev. 23:17 [b]Neh 9 [c]Lev. 27:30; N 18:21

38 [a]Num. 18:26 13:12, 13

39 [1]Lit., *forsake* 12:6 [b]Neh. 13:10

11:1 [a]Neh. 7:4 10:34 [c]Neh. 11:18 48:2

2 [a]Judg. 5:9

[1]Lit., *Israel* [2]Heb., *Nethinim* [3]Lit., *sons*
Chr. 9:2-34 [b]Neh.
3; 11:20 [c]Ezra 2:43
[d]Neh. 7:57

9 [1]Lit., *over*

[1]Lit., *brothers*, and throughout the ch.
[2]Lit., *house*

[1]Or, *the great ones*

[1]Lit., *heads* [2]Lit.,
over [a]1 Chr. 26:29

17 [1]In 1 Chr. 9:15,
hri [2]Lit., *head* [3]In
Chr. 9:16, *Obadiah*
[4]In 1 Chr. 9:16,
Shemaiah

18 [a]Neh. 11:1

20 [a]Neh. 11:3

, *over* [a]Neh. 3:26

[1]Or, *work* [a]Neh.
11:9, 14

3 [a]Ezra 6:8; 7:20
[b]Neh. 12:47

[1]Lit., *hand* [a]Gen.
30 [b]1 Chr. 18:17

3 [a]Now these are the heads of the provinces who lived in Jerusa-
lem, but in the cities of Judah [b]each lived on his own property in
their cities—the [1]Israelites, the priests, the Levites, the [2c]temple ser-
vants and the [3d]descendants of Solomon's servants.
4 And some of the sons of Judah and some of the sons of Benjamin
lived in Jerusalem. From the sons of Judah: Athaiah the son of Uz-
ziah, the son of Zechariah, the son of Amariah, the son of Shepha-
tiah, the son of Mahalalel, of the sons of Perez;
5 and Maaseiah the son of Baruch, the son of Col-hozeh, the son of
Hazaiah, the son of Adaiah, the son of Joiarib, the son of Zechariah,
the son of the Shilonite.
6 All the sons of Perez who lived in Jerusalem were 468 able men.
7 Now these are the sons of Benjamin: Sallu the son of Meshullam,
the son of Joed, the son of Pedaiah, the son of Kolaiah, the son of
Maaseiah, the son of Ithiel, the son of Jeshaiah;
8 and after him Gabbai *and* Sallai, 928.
9 And Joel the son of Zichri was their overseer, and Judah the son
of Hassenuah was second [1]in command of the city.
10 From the priests: Jedaiah the son of Joiarib, Jachin,
11 Seraiah the son of Hilkiah, the son of Meshullam, the son of
Zadok, the son of Meraioth, the son of Ahitub, the leader of the
house of God,
12 and their [1]kinsmen who performed the work of the [2]temple, 822;
and Adaiah the son of Jeroham, the son of Pelaliah, the son of Amzi,
the son of Zechariah, the son of Pashhur, the son of Malchijah,
13 and his kinsmen, heads of fathers' *households*, 242; and Amashsai
the son of Azarel, the son of Ahzai, the son of Meshillemoth, the son
of Immer,
14 and their brothers, valiant warriors, 128. And their overseer was
Zabdiel, the son of [1]Haggedolim.
15 Now from the Levites: Shemaiah the son of Hasshub, the son of
Azrikam, the son of Hashabiah, the son of Bunni;
16 and Shabbethai and Jozabad, from the [1]leaders of the Levites,
who were [2]in charge of [a]the outside work of the house of God;
17 and Mattaniah the son of Mica, the son of [1]Zabdi, the son of
Asaph, who was the [2]leader in beginning the thanksgiving at prayer,
and Bakbukiah, the second among his brethren; and [3]Abda the son
of [4]Shammua, the son of Galal, the son of Jeduthun.
18 All the Levites in [a]the holy city *were* 284.
19 Also the gatekeepers, Akkub, Talmon, and their brethren, who
kept watch at the gates, *were* 172.
20 And the rest of Israel, of the priests, *and* of the Levites, *were* in all
the cities of Judah, each [a]on his own inheritance.
21 But [a]the temple servants were living in Ophel, and Ziha and
Gishpa were [1]in charge of the temple servants.
22 Now [a]the overseer of the Levites in Jerusalem was Uzzi the son
of Bani, the son of Hashabiah, the son of Mattaniah, the son of Mica,
from the sons of Asaph, who were the singers for the [1]service of the
house of God.
23 [a]For *there was* a commandment from the king concerning them
and a firm regulation for the song leaders [b]day by day.
24 And Pethahiah the son of Meshezabel, of the sons [a]of Zerah the
son of Judah, was the [b]king's [1]representative in all matters concern-
ing the people.

25 Now as for the villages with their fields, some of the sons of
Judah lived in [a]Kiriath-arba and its [1]towns, in [b]Dibon and its [1]towns,
and in Jekabzeel and its villages,
26 and in Jeshua, in Moladah and Beth-pelet,
27 and in Hazar-shual, in Beersheba and its towns,
28 and in Ziklag, in Meconah and in its towns,
29 and in En-rimmon, in Zorah and in Jarmuth,
30 Zanoah, Adullam, and their villages, Lachish and its fields, Aze-
kah and its towns. So they encamped from Beersheba as far as the
valley of Hinnom.
31 The sons of Benjamin also *lived* from Geba *onward,* at Michmash
and Aija, at Bethel and its towns,
32 at Anathoth, Nob, Ananiah,
33 Hazor, Ramah, Gittaim,
34 Hadid, Zeboim, Neballat,
35 Lod and Ono, the valley of craftsmen.
36 And from the Levites, *some* divisions in Judah belonged to Ben-
jamin.

Chapter 12

12 Now these are [a]the priests and the Levites who came up with
Zerubbabel the son of Shealtiel, and Jeshua: Seraiah, Jeremi-
ah, Ezra,
2 Amariah, Malluch, Hattush,
3 Shecaniah, Rehum, Meremoth,
4 Iddo, Ginnethoi, Abijah,
5 Mijamin, Maadiah, Bilgah,
6 Shemaiah and Joiarib, Jedaiah,
7 Sallu, Amok, Hilkiah, and Jedaiah. These were the heads of the
priests and their [1]kinsmen in the days of Jeshua.
8 And the Levites *were* Jeshua, Binnui, Kadmiel, Sherebiah, Judah,
and Mattaniah *who was* [1]in charge of the songs of thanksgiving, he
and his brothers.
9 Also Bakbukiah and Unni, their brothers, stood opposite them
[a]in *their* service divisions.
10 And Jeshua [1]became the father of Joiakim, and Joiakim [1]became
the father of Eliashib, and Eliashib [1]became the father of Joiada,
11 and Joiada became the father of Jonathan, and Jonathan became
the father of Jaddua.
12 Now in the days of Joiakim the priests, the heads of fathers'
households were: of Seraiah, Meraiah; of Jeremiah, Hananiah;
13 of Ezra, Meshullam; of Amariah, Jehohanan;
14 of [1]Malluchi, Jonathan; of Shebaniah, Joseph;
15 of Harim, Adna; of Meraioth, Helkai;
16 of Iddo, Zechariah; of Ginnethon, Meshullam;
17 of Abijah, Zichri; of Miniamin, of Moadiah, Piltai;
18 of Bilgah, Shammua; of Shemaiah, Jehonathan;
19 of Joiarib, Mattenai; of Jedaiah, Uzzi;
20 of Sallai, Kallai; of Amok, Eber;
21 of Hilkiah, Hashabiah; of Jedaiah, Nethanel.
22 As for the Levites, the heads of fathers' *households* were
registered in the days of Eliashib, Joiada, and Johanan, and Jaddua;
so *were* the priests in the reign of Darius the Persian.
23 The sons of Levi, the heads of fathers' *households,* were registered

25 [1]Lit., *daughters,* so throughout the ch [a]Josh. 14:15 [b]Josh. 13:9, 17

12:1 [a]Ezra 2:1; 7:7

7 [1]Lit., *brothers*

8 [1]Lit., *over*

9 [a]Neh. 12:24

10 [1]Lit., *begot,* ar in vv. 11, 12

14 [1]In Neh. 12:2 *Malluch*

in the Book of the Chronicles up to the days of Johanan the son of
Eliashib.
24 And the heads of the Levites *were* Hashabiah, Sherebiah, and
Jeshua the son of Kadmiel, with their brothers opposite them, [a]to
praise *and* give thanks, [1]as prescribed by David the man of God,
[b]division corresponding to division.
25 Mattaniah, and Bakbukiah, Obadiah, Meshullam, Talmon, *and*
Akkub were gatekeepers keeping watch at [a]the storehouses of the
gates.
26 These *served* in the days of Joiakim the son of Jeshua, the son of
Jozadak, and in the days of [a]Nehemiah the governor and of Ezra the
priest *and* scribe.
27 Now at the dedication of the wall of Jerusalem they sought out
the Levites from all their places, to bring them to Jerusalem so that
they might celebrate the dedication with gladness, with hymns of
thanksgiving and with songs [a]*to the accompaniment* of cymbals, harps,
and lyres.
28 So the sons of the singers were assembled from the district
around Jerusalem, and from [a]the villages of the Netophathites,
29 from Beth-gilgal, and from *their* fields in Geba and Azmaveth,
for the singers had built themselves villages around Jerusalem.
30 And the priests and the Levites [a]purified themselves; they also
purified the people, the gates, and the wall.
31 Then I had the leaders of Judah come up on top of the wall, and I
appointed two great [1]choirs, [2a]the first proceeding to the right on top
of the wall toward [b]the Refuse Gate.
32 Hoshaiah and half of the leaders of Judah followed them,
33 with Azariah, Ezra, Meshullam,
34 Judah, Benjamin, Shemaiah, Jeremiah,
35 and some of the sons of the priests with trumpets; *and* Zechariah
the son of Jonathan, the son of Shemaiah, the son of Mattaniah, the
son of Micaiah, the son of Zaccur, the son of Asaph,
36 and his [1]kinsmen, Shemaiah, Azarel, Milalai, Gilalai, Maai,
Nethanel, Judah *and* Hanani, [a]with the musical instruments of David
the man of God. And Ezra the scribe went before them.
37 And at [a]the Fountain Gate they went directly up [b]the steps of the
city of David by the stairway of the wall above the house of David to
[c]the Water Gate on the east.
38 [a]The second [1]choir proceeded to the [2]left, while I followed them
with half of the people on the wall, [b]above the Tower of Furnaces, to
[c]the Broad Wall,
39 and above [a]the Gate of Ephraim, by [b]the Old Gate, by the [c]Fish
Gate, [d]the Tower of Hananel, and the Tower of the Hundred, as far as
the Sheep Gate, and they stopped at [e]the Gate of the Guard.
40 Then the two choirs took their stand in the house of God. So did
I and half of the officials with me;
41 and the priests, Eliakim, Maaseiah, Miniamin, Micaiah, Elioenai,
Zechariah, and Hananiah, with the trumpets;
42 and Maaseiah, Shemaiah, Eleazar, Uzzi, Jehohanan, Malchijah,
Elam, and Ezer. And the singers [1]sang, with Jezrahiah *their* leader,
43 and on that day they offered great sacrifices and rejoiced because
[a]God had given them great joy, even the women and children
rejoiced, so that the joy of Jerusalem was heard from afar.
44 On that day [a]men were also appointed over the chambers for the

24 [1]Lit., *in the* ...*nandment of* [a]Neh. 11:17 [b]Neh. 12:9
25 [a]1 Chr. 26:15
26 [a]Neh. 8:9
... [a]1 Chr. 15:16, 28
28 [a]1 Chr. 9:16
...0 [a]Neh. 13:22, 30
... [1]Lit., *thanksgiving choirs* [2]Heb., *and* ...*ssions to the right* 12:38 [b]Neh. 2:13
...t., *brothers* [a]Neh. 12:24
... [a]Neh. 2:14 [b]Neh. 3:15 [c]Neh. 3:26
... [1]Lit., *thanksgiving* [2]Lit., *front* [a]Neh. ... [b]Neh. 3:11 [c]Neh. 3:8
... [a]Neh. 8:16 [b]Neh. ... [c]Neh. 3:3 [d]Neh. 3:1 [e]Neh. 3:25
... [1]Lit., *caused their* ...*oices to be heard*
43 [a]Ps. 9:2; 92:4
...h. 13:4, 5, 12, 13

stores, the contributions, the first fruits, and the tithes, to gather into
them from the fields of the cities the portions required by the law for
the priests and Levites; for Judah rejoiced over the priests and
Levites who [1]served.
45 For they performed the [1]worship of their God and the service of
purification, together with the singers and the gatekeepers [a]in ac-
cordance with the command of David *and* of his son Solomon.
46 For in the days of David and [a]Asaph, in ancient times, *there were*
[1b]leaders of the singers, songs of praise and hymns of thanksgiving
to God.
47 And so all Israel in the days of Zerubbabel and Nehemiah gave
the portions due the singers and the gatekeepers [a]as each day re-
quired, and [b]set apart the consecrated *portion* for the Levites, and the
Levites set apart the consecrated *portion* for the sons of Aaron.

Chapter 13

13 On that day [a]they read aloud from the book of Moses in the
hearing of the people; and there was found written in it that
[b]no Ammonite or Moabite should ever enter the assembly of God,
2 because they did not meet the sons of Israel with bread and
water, but [a]hired Balaam against them to curse them. However, [b]our
God turned the curse into a blessing.
3 So it came about, that when they heard the law, [a]they excluded
[b]all foreigners from Israel.
4 Now prior to this, Eliashib the priest, [a]who was appointed over
the chambers of the house of our God, being [1]related to [b]Tobiah,
5 had prepared a large [1]room for him, where formerly they put the
grain offerings, the frankincense, the utensils, and the tithes of grain,
wine and oil [a]prescribed for the Levites, the singers and the gate-
keepers, and the [2]contributions for the priests.
6 But during all this *time* I was not in Jerusalem, for in [a]the thirty-
second year of [b]Artaxerxes king of Babylon I had gone to the king.
After some time, however, I asked leave from the king,
7 and I came to Jerusalem and [1]learned about the evil that Eliashib
had done for Tobiah, [a]by preparing a [2]room for him in the courts of
the house of God.
8 And it was very displeasing to me, so I [a]threw all of Tobiah's
household goods out of the room.
9 Then I gave an order and [a]they cleansed the rooms; and I
returned there the utensils of the house of God with the grain offer-
ings and the frankincense.
10 I also [1]discovered that [a]the portions of the Levites had not been
given *them*, so that the Levites and the singers who performed the
service had [2]gone away, [b]each to his own field.
11 So I [1a]reprimanded the officials and said, "[b]Why is the house of
God forsaken?" Then I gathered them together and restored them to
their posts.
12 All Judah then brought [a]the tithe of the grain, wine, and oil into
the storehouses.
13 And in charge of the storehouses I appointed Shelemiah the
priest, Zadok the scribe, and Pedaiah of the Levites, and in addition
to them was Hanan the son of Zaccur, the son of Mattaniah; for [a]they
were considered reliable, and it was [1]their task to distribute to their
[2]kinsmen.

44 [1]Lit., *stood*

45 [1]Lit., *service* 25:1

46 [1]Lit., *heads* 29:30 [b]1 Chr. 9

47 [a]Neh. 11:23 18:21

13:1 [a]Neh. 9:3 23:3-5; Neh. 13

2 [a]Num. 22:3-1 23:5

3 [a]Neh. 9:2; 10 12:38

4 [1]Lit., *close to* 12:44 [b]Neh. 2:1 17, 18

5 [1]Or, *chamber* *heave offerings* 18:21

6 [a]Neh. 5:14 [b]E

7 [1]Or, *understoo* *chamber*, and so 8, 9 [a]Neh. 13:5

8 [a]John 2:13-16

9 [a]2 Chr. 29:5, 1

10 [1]Or, *knew* [2]Li [a]Deut. 12:19; Neh 10:37 [b]Neh. 12:2

11 [1]Or, *contende* [a]Neh. 13:17, 25 [b] 10:39

12 [a]Neh. 10:37; 1 Mal. 3:10

13 [1]Lit., *on them* [2]Lit., *brothers* [a]Ne

14 [a]Remember me for this, O my God, and do not blot out my loyal
deeds which I have performed for the house of my God and its
services.
15 In those days I saw in Judah some who were treading wine
presses [a]on the sabbath, and bringing in sacks of grain and loading
them on donkeys, as well as wine, grapes, figs, and all kinds of loads,
[b]and they brought *them* into Jerusalem on the sabbath day. So [c]I
admonished *them* on the day they sold food.
16 Also men of Tyre were living [1]there *who* imported fish and all
kinds of merchandise, and sold *them* to the sons of Judah on the
sabbath, even in Jerusalem.
17 Then [a]I [1]reprimanded the nobles of Judah and said to them,
"What is this evil thing you are doing, [2]by profaning the sabbath
day?
18 "[a]Did not your fathers do the same so that our God brought on us,
and on this city, all this trouble? Yet you are adding to the wrath on
Israel by profaning the sabbath."
19 [a]And it came about that just as it grew dark at the gates of
Jerusalem before the sabbath, I commanded that the doors should be
shut [1]and that they should not open them until after the sabbath.
Then I stationed some of my servants at the gates *that* no load
should enter on the sabbath day.
20 Once or twice the traders and merchants of every kind of mer-
chandise spent the night outside Jerusalem.
21 Then [a]I [1]warned them and said to them, "Why do you spend the
night in front of the wall? If you do so again, I will [2]use force against
you." From that time on they did not come on the sabbath.
22 And I commanded the Levites that [a]they should purify them-
selves and come as gatekeepers to sanctify the sabbath day. *For* this
also [b]remember me, O my God, and have compassion on me accord-
ing to the greatness of Thy lovingkindness.
23 In those days I also saw that the Jews had [1a]married women from
[b]Ashdod, [c]Ammon, *and* Moab.
24 As for their children, half spoke in the language of Ashdod, and
none of them was able to speak the language of Judah, but [1]the
language of his own people.
25 So [a]I contended with them and cursed them and [b]struck some of
them and pulled out their hair, and [c]made them swear by God, "You
shall not give your daughters to their sons, nor take of their daugh-
ters for your sons or for yourselves.
26 "[a]Did not Solomon king of Israel sin regarding these things? [b]Yet
among the many nations there was no king like him, and [c]he was
loved by his God, and God made him king over all Israel; neverthe-
less the foreign women caused even him to sin.
27 "[1]Do we then hear about you that you have committed all this
great evil [a]by acting unfaithfully against our God by [2]marrying
foreign women?"
28 Even one of the sons of Joiada, the son of Eliashib the high
priest, was a son-in-law of [a]Sanballat the Horonite, so I drove him
away from me.
29 [a]Remember them, O my God, [1]because they have defiled the
priesthood and the [b]covenant of the priesthood and the Levites.
30 [a]Thus I purified them from everything foreign and appointed
duties for the priests and the Levites, each in his task,

eh. 5:19; 13:22, 31
5 [a]Ex. 20:8; 34:21; Deut. 5:12-14; Jer. 2 [b]Neh. 10:31; Jer. [c]Neh. 9:29; 13:21
16 [1]Lit., *in it*
Or, *contended with* [2]Lit., *and* [a]Neh. 13:11, 25
8 [a]Ezra 9:13; Jer. 17:21
19 [1]Lit., *and* anded [a]Lev. 23:32
21 [1]Lit., *witnessed* ainst [2]Lit., *send a* and against [a]Neh. 13:15
1 Chr. 15:12; Neh. 0 [b]Neh. 13:14, 31
.it., *given dwelling* x. 34:11-16; Deut. -5; Ezra 9:2; Neh. [b]Neh. 4:7 [c]Ezra 9:1; Neh. 13:1
[1]Lit., *according to tongue of people and people*
5 [a]Neh. 13:11, 17 Deut. 25:2 [c]Neh. 10:29, 30
Kin. 11:1 [b]1 Kin. 3:13; 2 Chr. 1:12 2 Sam. 12:24, 25
[1]Or, *Is it reported giving dwelling to* 10:2; Neh. 13:23
eh. 2:10, 19; 4:1
, *for the defilings* Neh. 6:14 [b]Num. 25:13
30 [a]Neh. 10:30

31 and *I arranged* [a]for the supply of wood at appointed times and
for the first fruits. [b]Remember me, O my God, for good.

31 [a]Neh. 10:34 [b]Ne 13:14, 22

NEHEMIAH AT A GLANCE

Theme of Nehemiah:

Author:

Date:

Purpose:

Key Words:

SEGMENT DIVISIONS

		CHAPTER THEMES
		1
		2
		3
		4
		5
		6
		7
		8
		9
		10
		11
		12
		13

LESSONS FROM THE LIFE OF NEHEMIAH

The Situation	How Nehemiah Related to God	How Nehemiah Related to People	Nehemiah's Example

ESTHER

Throughout time people have attempted to destroy the nation of Israel, the "apple of God's ey Why? Because from the Jews came the covenants, the promises, the law, and the Messiah—salvation the world. The people of God are the enemy of Satan, the prince of this world.

While a remnant from Judah returned to the land promised to Abraham, Isaac, and Jacob, other Je remained in the cities of their captivity. Some were welcomed as valuable members of their cc munities, but others were despised and hated. Some were even targeted for extermination.

Esther tells the story. The book of Esther records a ten-year span during the fifty-eight to sixty y interlude in the book of Ezra. Esther tells us of the celebration of a feast which has endured over t thousand years all because of one woman who, for the sake of her people, was willing to say, " perish, I perish."

THINGS TO DO

Reading Esther is like reading a novel—a divinely inspired one. It reveals the sovereignty of G although God never is mentioned in this book. As you read:

1. Consult the historical chart EZRA, NEHEMIAH, AND ESTHER on page 713 in order to see setting of Esther.
2. As you read, observe the main events which occur in each chapter. Examine each chapter un the scrutiny of the five W's and an H: Who? What? When? Where? Why? and How? Ask: V was involved? What happened? When did it occur? Where did it take place and why? How di come about? etc.
   a. List in the margin the major points you want to remember about each event under the heac you give that event. For example Esther 1:3-4 could be titled, "King Ahasuerus's Banqu Then under the heading you could list these major points: 1) attended by his princes, at dants, etc., 2) given to display riches, 3) lasted 180 days.
   b. While the main event of each chapter will not always be a banquet, they play an impor role in Esther. So, mark in a distinctive way each use of the words *banquet* or *feast*. Ask the W's and an H about each banquet and list your insights in the margin.
   c. Make sure you underline or mark in a distinctive way the main characters in each chapter.
3. Mark every reference to time with the diagram of a clock such as this so it can be s immediately. This will help you see the timing of the events. Also consult the calendar on p 739 so you can keep track of the references to the various months.
4. Mark every occurrence of the words *Jew* or *Jews* (with their pronouns and synonyms, such as *people, my kindred,* or *people*). *Jews* was a term used to describe the people who came from Judal
5. Carefully observe the timing of events, such as when the king can't sleep and needs somethir read. Remember the truth in Daniel 4:34-35.
6. When you finish studying each chapter, record the theme of that chapter in the appropriate p on the ESTHER AT A GLANCE chart on page 750. Also record this in the text next to the cha number.
7. In a chapter margin, list all you learn about Esther and then list all you learn about Mordecai.
8. When you finish reading Esther, complete ESTHER AT A GLANCE. See if any of the chapters be grouped according to events. If so, record these segment divisions on the chart under chapter themes.

HINGS TO THINK ABOUT

1. What can you learn from the lives of each of the main characters of this historical event? Review what you've listed about Esther and Mordecai. Have you ever realized that you, too, have come to the kingdom for such a time as this? What are the good works God would have you do? Read John 15:16 and Ephesians 2:8-10.
2. Have you thought about why Mordecai was unwilling to bow before Haman? Have you "bowed" to someone or something and in doing so compromised your calling and position as a child of God? Read Galatians 1:10.
3. Esther and Mordecai relied heavily on fasting and prayer to turn the tide of events. What about you?

The Jewish Calendar

Babylonian names (B) for the months are still used today for the Jewish calendar. Canaanite names (C) were used prior to the Babylonian captivity. Four are mentioned in the Old Testament.
Adar-Sheni is an intercalary month used every two to three years or seven times in nineteen years.

1st month	2nd month	3rd month	4th month
Nisan (B) Abib (C) March-April	Iyyar (B) Ziv (C) April-May	Sivan (B) May-June	Tammuz (B) June-July
7th month	*8th month*	*9th month*	*10th month*
5th month	**6th month**	**7th month**	**8th month**
Ab (B) July-August	Elul (B) August-September	Tishri (B) Ethanim (C) September-October	Marcheshvan (B) Bul (C) October-November
11th month	*12th month*	*1st month*	*2nd month*
9th month	**10th month**	**11th month**	**12th month**
Kislev (B) November-December	Tebeth (B) December-January	Shebat (B) January-February	Adar (B) February-March
3rd month	*4th month*	*5th month*	*6th month*

Sacred calendar appears in black • Civil calendar appears in grey

Chapter 1

1 Now it took place in the days of [a]Ahasuerus, the Ahasuerus who
reigned [b]from India to [1]Ethiopia over [c]127 provinces,
2 in those days as King Ahasuerus [a]sat on his royal throne which
was in [b]Susa the capital,
3 in the third year of his reign, [a]he gave a banquet for all his
princes and attendants, the army *officers* of Persia and Media, the
nobles, and the princes of his provinces being in his presence.
4 [1]And he displayed the riches of his royal glory and the splendor
of his great majesty for many days, 180 days.
5 And when these days were completed, the king gave a banquet
lasting seven days for all the people who were present in Susa the
capital, from the greatest to the least, in the court of [a]the garden of
the king's palace.
6 *There were hangings of* fine white and violet linen held by cords of
fine purple linen on silver rings and marble columns, *and* [a]couches of
gold and silver on a mosaic pavement of porphyry, marble, mother-
of-pearl, and precious stones.
7 Drinks were served in golden vessels of various kinds, and the
royal wine was plentiful [a]according to the king's [1]bounty.
8 And the drinking was *done* according to the law, there was no

[1]Lit., *Cush* [a]Ezra ...an. 9:1 [b]Esth. 8:9 [c]Esth. 9:30
[a]1 Kin. 1:46 [b]Neh. 1:1; Dan. 8:2
3 [a]Esth. 2:18
4 [1]Lit., *When*
5 [a]Esth. 7:7, 8
...zek. 23:41; Amos 6:4
...*hand* [a]Esth. 2:18

compulsion, for so the king had given orders to each official of his
household that he should do according to the desires of each person.
9 Queen Vashti also gave a banquet for the women in the [1]palace
which belonged to King Ahasuerus.
10 On the seventh day, when the heart of the king was [a]merry with
wine, he commanded Mehuman, Biztha, Harbona, Bigtha, Abagtha,
Zethar, and Carkas, the seven eunuchs who served in the presence of
King Ahasuerus,
11 to bring Queen Vashti before the king with *her* royal [a]crown in
order to display her beauty to the people and the princes, for she
was beautiful.
12 But Queen Vashti refused to come at the king's command
delivered by the eunuchs. Then the king became very angry and his
wrath burned within him.
13 Then the king said to [a]the wise men [b]who understood the
times—for it was the custom of the king so *to speak* before all who
knew law and justice,
14 and were close to him: Carshena, Shethar, Admatha, Tarshish,
Meres, Marsena, and Memucan, the seven princes of Persia and
Media [a]who [1]had access to the king's presence and sat in the first
place in the kingdom—
15 "According to law, what is to be done with Queen Vashti, because
she did not [1]obey the command of King Ahasuerus *delivered* by the
eunuchs?"
16 And in the presence of the king and the princes, Memucan said,
"Queen Vashti has wronged not only the king but *also* all the princes,
and all the peoples who are in all the provinces of King Ahasuerus.
17 "For the queen's conduct will [1]become known to all the women
causing them [2]to look with contempt on their husbands by saying,
'King Ahasuerus commanded Queen Vashti to be brought in to his
presence, but she did not come.'
18 "And this day the ladies of Persia and Media who have heard of
the queen's conduct will speak in *the same way* to all the king's
princes, and there will be plenty of contempt and anger.
19 "If it pleases the king, let a royal [1]edict be issued by him and let it
be written in the laws of Persia and Media so [a]that it cannot [2]be
repealed, that Vashti should come no more into the presence of King
Ahasuerus, and let the king give her royal position to [3]another who
is more worthy than she.
20 "And when the king's edict which he shall make is heard
throughout all his kingdom, [1]great as it is, then [a]all women will give
honor to their husbands, great and small."
21 And *this* word pleased the king and the princes, and the king did
[1]as Memucan proposed.
22 So he sent letters to all the king's provinces, [a]to each province
according to its script and to every people according to their lan-
guage, that every man should [b]be the master in his own house and
the one who speaks in the language of his own people.

Chapter 2

2 After these things [a]when the anger of King Ahasuerus had sub-
sided, he remembered Vashti and what she had done and [b]what
had been decreed against her.

9 [1]Lit., *royal h*
10 [a]Judg. 16:2
11 [a]Esth. 2:17
13 [a]Jer. 10:7; [b]1 Chr. 12:32
14 [1]Lit., *saw th the king* [a]2 Kin Matt. 18:10
15 [1]Lit., *do*
17 [1]Lit., *go for to despise . . . i eyes*
19 [1]Lit., *word g from* [2]Lit., *pass* [3]Lit., *her neighb* [a]Esth. 8:8; Dan.
20 [1]Lit., *for grea* [a]Eph. 5:22; Col.
21 [1]Lit., *accord the word of*
22 [a]Esth. 3:12; 8 [b]Eph. 5:22-24
2:1 [a]Esth. 7:10 1:19, 20

2 Then the king's attendants, who served him, said, "[a]Let beautiful young virgins be sought for the king.

3 "And let the king appoint overseers in [a]all the provinces of his kingdom that they may gather every beautiful young virgin to Susa the capital, to the harem, into the custody of [b]Hegai, the king's eunuch, who was in charge of the women; and [c]let their cosmetics be given *them*.

4 "Then let the young lady who pleases the king be queen in place of Vashti." And the matter pleased the king, and he did accordingly.

5 *Now* there was a Jew in Susa the capital whose name was [a]Mordecai, the son of Jair, the son of Shimei, the son of Kish, a Benjamite,

6 [a]who had been taken into exile from Jerusalem with the captives who had been exiled with Jeconiah king of Judah, whom Nebuchadnezzar the king of Babylon had exiled.

7 And he was bringing up Hadassah, that is [a]Esther, his uncle's daughter, for she had neither father nor mother. Now the young lady was beautiful of form and [1]face, and when her father and her mother died, Mordecai took her as his own daughter.

8 So it came about when the command and decree of the king were heard and [a]many young ladies were gathered to Susa the capital into the custody of [b]Hegai, that Esther was taken to the king's [1]palace into the custody of Hegai, who was in charge of the women.

9 Now the young lady pleased him and found favor with him. So he quickly provided her with her [a]cosmetics and [1]food, gave her seven choice maids from the king's palace, and transferred her and her maids to the best place in the harem.

10 [a]Esther did not make known her people or her kindred, for Mordecai had instructed her that she should not make *them* known.

11 And every day Mordecai walked back and forth in front of the court of the harem to learn how Esther was and how she fared.

12 Now when the turn of each young lady came to go in to King Ahasuerus, after the end of her twelve months under the regulations for the women—for the days of their beautification were completed as follows: six months with oil of myrrh and six months with spices and the cosmetics for women—

13 the young lady would go in to the king in this way: anything that she [1]desired was given her to take with her from the harem to the king's palace.

14 In the evening she would go in and in the morning she would return to the second harem, to the [1]custody of Shaashgaz, the king's eunuch who was in charge of the concubines. She would not again go in to the king unless the king delighted in her and she was summoned by name.

15 Now when the turn of Esther, [a]the daughter of Abihail the uncle of Mordecai who had taken her as his daughter, came to go in to the king, she did not request anything except what [b]Hegai, the king's eunuch who was in charge of the women, [1]advised. And Esther found favor in the eyes of all who saw her.

16 So Esther was taken to King Ahasuerus to his royal palace in the tenth month which is the month Tebeth, in the seventh year of his reign.

17 And the king loved Esther more than all the women, and she found favor and kindness with him more than all the virgins, so that

2 [a]1 Kin. 1:2

Esth. 1:1, 2 [b]Esth. , 15 [c]Esth. 2:9, 12

5 [a]Esth. 3:2

[a]2 Kin. 24:14, 15; 2 Chr. 36:10

7 [1]Lit., *good of* *rance* [a]Esth. 2:15

Lit., *house* [a]Esth. 2:3 [b]Esth. 2:3, 15

., *portions* [a]Esth. 2:3, 12

10 [a]Esth. 2:20

13 [1]Lit., *said*

14 [1]Lit., *hand*

[1]Lit., *said* [a]Esth. 29 [b]Esth. 2:3, 8

[a]he set the royal crown on her head and made her queen instead of Vashti.

18 Then [a]the king gave a great banquet, Esther's banquet, for all his princes and his servants; he also made a holiday for the provinces and gave gifts [b]according to the king's bounty.

19 And [a]when the virgins were gathered together the second time, then Mordecai [b]was sitting at the king's gate.

20 [a]Esther had not yet made known her kindred or her people, even as Mordecai had commanded her, for Esther did [1]what Mordecai told her as she had done [b]when under his care.

21 In those days, while Mordecai was sitting at the king's gate, [a]Bigthan and Teresh, two of the king's officials from those who guarded the door, became angry and sought to [1]lay hands on King Ahasuerus.

22 But the [1]plot became known to Mordecai, and [a]he told Queen Esther, and Esther [2]informed the king in Mordecai's name.

23 Now when the plot was investigated and found *to be so,* they were both hanged on a [1]gallows; and it was written in [a]the Book of the Chronicles in the king's presence.

Chapter 3

Agagite, possibly a synonym for Amalekite, is a reference to a descendant of Agag. Haman, the arch villain in Esther, was an Agagite.

3 After these events King Ahasuerus [a]promoted Haman, the son of Hammedatha [b]the Agagite, and [a]advanced him and [1]established his authority over all the princes who *were* with him.

2 And all the king's servants who were at the king's gate bowed down [1]and paid homage to Haman; for so the king had commanded concerning him. But [a]Mordecai neither bowed down nor paid homage.

3 Then the king's servants who were at [a]the king's gate said to Mordecai, "[b]Why are you transgressing the king's command?"

4 Now it was when they had spoken daily to him and he would not listen to them, that they told Haman to see whether Mordecai's reason would stand; for he had told them that he was a Jew.

5 When Haman saw that [a]Mordecai neither bowed down nor paid homage to him, Haman was filled with rage.

6 But he [1]disdained to [2]lay hands on Mordecai alone, for they had told him *who* the people of Mordecai *were;* therefore Haman [a]sought to destroy all the Jews, the people of Mordecai, who *were* throughout the whole kingdom of Ahasuerus.

7 In the first month, which is the month Nisan, in the twelfth year of King Ahasuerus, [1]Pur, that is the lot, was [a]cast before Haman from day to day and from month *to month,* [2]until the twelfth month, that is [b]the month Adar.

8 Then Haman said to King Ahasuerus, "There is a certain people scattered and dispersed among the peoples in all the provinces of your kingdom; [a]their laws are different from *those* of all *other* people, and they do not observe the king's laws, so it is not in the king's interest to let them remain.

9 "If it is pleasing to the king, let it be [1]decreed that they be destroyed, and I will pay ten thousand talents of silver into the hands of those who carry on the *king's* business, to put into the king's treasuries."

10 Then [a]the king took his signet ring from his hand and gave it to

17 [a]Esth. 1:11

18 [a]Esth. 1:3 [b]Es

19 [a]Esth. 2:3, 4 [b] 2:21; 3:2

20 [1]Lit., *the word Mordecai* [a]Esth. 2 [b]Esth. 2:7

21 [1]Lit., *send a h against* [a]Esth. 6:2

22 [1]Lit., *matter, s* v. 23 [2]Lit., *told* [a]E 6:1, 2

23 [1]Lit., *tree* [a]Es

3:1 [1]Lit., *set his s* [a]Esth. 5:11 [b]Esth 8:3

2 [1]Lit., *and prost themselves befor* [a]Esth. 2:19; 5:9

3 [a]Esth. 2:19 [b]E

5 [a]Esth. 5:9

6 [1]Lit., *despised eyes* [2]Lit., *send against* [a]Ps. 83:4

7 [1]Lit., *he cast P before* [2]Gr., *and fell on the thirtee of* [a]Esth. 9:24-26 6:15

8 [a]Ezra 4:12-15; 16:20, 21

9 [1]Lit., *written*

10 [a]Gen. 41:42; 8:2

Haman, the son of Hammedatha [b]the Agagite, [c]the enemy of the
Jews.
11 And the king said to Haman, "The silver is [1]yours, and the
people *also,* to do with them as you please."
12 [a]Then the king's scribes were summoned on the thirteenth day of
the first month, and it was written just as Haman commanded to
[b]the king's satraps, to the governors who were over each province,
and to the princes of each people, each province according to its
script, each people according to its language, being written [c]in the
name of King Ahasuerus and sealed with the king's signet ring.
13 And letters were sent by [a]couriers to all the king's provinces [b]to
destroy, to kill, and to annihilate all the Jews, both young and old,
women and children, [c]in one day, the thirteenth *day* of the twelfth
month, which is the month Adar, and to [d]seize their possessions as
plunder.
14 [a]A copy of the edict to be [1]issued as law in every province was
published to all the peoples so that they should be ready for this day.
15 The couriers went out impelled by the king's command while
the decree was [1]issued in Susa the capital; and while the king and
Haman sat down to drink, [a]the city of Susa was in confusion.

Chapter 4

4 When Mordecai learned [a]all that had been done, [1]he tore his
clothes, put on sackcloth and ashes, and went out into the midst
of the city and wailed loudly and bitterly.
2 And he went as far as the king's gate, for no one was to enter the
king's gate clothed in sackcloth.
3 And in each and every province where the command and decree
of the king came, there was great mourning among the Jews, with
[a]fasting, weeping, and wailing; and many lay on sackcloth and
ashes.
4 Then Esther's maidens and her eunuchs came and told her, and
the queen writhed in great anguish. And she sent garments to clothe
Mordecai that he might remove his sackcloth from him, but he did
not accept *them.*
5 Then Esther summoned Hathach from the king's eunuchs,
whom [1]the king had appointed to attend her, and ordered him *to go*
to Mordecai to learn what this *was* and why it *was.*
6 So Hathach went out to Mordecai to the city square in front of
the king's gate.
7 And Mordecai told him all that had happened to him, and [a]the
exact amount of money that Haman had promised to pay to the
king's treasuries for the destruction of the Jews.
8 He also gave him [a]a copy of the text of the edict which had been
issued in Susa for their destruction, that he might show Esther and
inform her, and to order her to go in to the king to implore his favor
and to plead with him for her people.
9 And Hathach came back and related Mordecai's words to Esther.
10 Then Esther spoke to Hathach and ordered him *to reply* to Mor-
decai:
11 "All the king's servants and the people of the king's provinces
know that for any man or woman who [a]comes to the king to the
inner court who is not summoned, [b]he has but one law, that he be
put to death, unless the king holds out [c]to him the golden scepter so

[b]Esth. 3:1 [c]Esth. 7:6
11 [1]Lit., *given to you*
12 [a]Esth. 8:9 [b]Ezra 8:36 [c]1 Kin. 21:8; Esth. 8:8, 10
13 [a]2 Chr. 30:6; Esth. 8:10, 14 [b]Esth. 7:4 [c]Esth. 8:12 [d]Esth. 8:11; 9:10
14 [1]Lit., *given* [a]Esth. 8:13, 14
15 [1]Lit., *given* [a]Esth. 8:15
4:1 [1]Lit., *Mordecai* [a]2 Sam. 1:11; Esth. 3:8-10; Jon. 3:5,6
3 [a]Esth. 4:16
5 [1]Lit., *he*
7 [a]Esth. 3:9
8 [a]Esth. 3:14
11 [a]Esth. 5:1; 6:4 [b]Dan. 2:9 [c]Esth. 5:2; 8:4

that he may live. And I have not been summoned to come to the king for these thirty days."

12 And they related Esther's words to Mordecai.

13 Then Mordecai told *them* to reply to Esther, "Do not imagine that you in the king's palace can escape any more than all the Jews.

14 "For if you remain silent at this time, relief and [a]deliverance will arise for the Jews from another place and you and your father's house will perish. And who knows whether you have not attained royalty for such a time as this?"

15 Then Esther told *them* to reply to Mordecai,

16 "Go, assemble all the Jews who are found in Susa, and fast for me; [a]do not eat or drink for [b]three days, night or day. I and my maidens also will fast in the same way. And thus I will go in to the king, which is not according to the law; and if I perish, I perish."

17 So Mordecai went away and did just as Esther had commanded him.

Chapter 5

5 Now it came about [a]on the third day that Esther put on her royal robes and stood [b]in the inner court of the king's palace in front of the king's [1]rooms, and the king was sitting on his royal throne in the [2]throne room, opposite the entrance to the palace.

2 And it happened when the king saw Esther the queen standing in the court, [a]she obtained favor in his sight; and [b]the king extended to Esther the golden scepter which was in his hand. So Esther came near and touched the top of the scepter.

3 Then the king said to her, "What is *troubling* you, Queen Esther? And what is your request? [a]Even to half of the kingdom it will be given to you."

4 And Esther said, "If it please the king, may the king and Haman come this day to the banquet that I have prepared for him."

5 Then the king said, "[a]Bring Haman quickly that we may do [1]as Esther desires." So the king and Haman came to the banquet which Esther had prepared.

6 And, [1]as they drank their wine at the banquet, [a]the king said to Esther, "[b]What is your petition, for it shall be granted to you. And what is your request? Even to half of the kingdom it shall be done."

7 So Esther answered and said, "My petition and my request is:

8 [a]if I have found favor in the sight of the king, and if it please the king to grant my petition and do [1]what I request, may the king and Haman come to [b]the banquet which I shall prepare for them, and tomorrow I will do [2]as the king says."

9 Then Haman went out that day glad and pleased of heart; but when Haman saw Mordecai [a]in the king's gate, and [b]that he did not stand up or [1]tremble before him, Haman was filled with anger against Mordecai.

10 Haman controlled himself, however, went to his house, and [1]sent for his friends and his wife [a]Zeresh.

11 Then Haman recounted to them the glory of his riches, and the [1a]number of his sons, and every *instance* where the king had magnified him, and how he had [2b]promoted him above the princes and servants of the king.

12 Haman also said, "Even Esther the queen let no one but me

14 [a]Lev. 26:42 13:5

16 [a]Joel 1:14; [b]Esth. 5:1

5:1 [1]Lit., *house royal house* [a]E 4:16 [b]Esth. 4:1

2 [a]Esth. 2:9 [b]E 4:11; 8:4

3 [a]Esth. 7:2; Ma

5 [1]Lit., *the word Esther* [a]Esth. 6:

6 [1]Lit., *at the ba wine* [a]Esth. 7:2 5:3

8 [1]Lit., *my reque according to the the king* [a]Esth. 7 [b]Esth. 6:14

9 [1]Or, *move for* 2:19 [b]Esth. 3:5

10 [1]Lit., *sent and brought* [a]Esth. 6:

11 [1]Lit., *multitude lifted* [a]Esth. 9:7-1 [b]Esth. 3:1

come with the king to the banquet which she had prepared; and
[a]tomorrow also I am [1]invited by her with the king.
13 "Yet all of this [1]does not satisfy me every time I see Mordecai the
Jew sitting at [a]the king's gate."
14 Then Zeresh his wife and all his friends said to him, "[a]Have a
[1]gallows fifty cubits high made and in the morning ask the king to
have Mordecai hanged on it, then go joyfully with the king to the
banquet." And the [2]advice pleased Haman, so he had the gallows
made.

Chapter 6

6 During that night [1]the king [a]could not sleep so he gave an order
to bring [b]the book of records, the chronicles, and they were read
before the king.
2 And it was found written what [a]Mordecai had reported concern-
ing Bigthana and Teresh, two of the king's eunuchs who were door-
keepers, that they had sought to lay hands on King Ahasuerus.
3 And the king said, "What honor or dignity has been bestowed
on Mordecai for this?" Then the king's servants who attended him
said, "Nothing has been done for him."
4 So the king said, "Who is in the court?" Now Haman had just
[a]entered the outer court of the king's palace in order to speak to the
king about [b]hanging Mordecai on the gallows which he had
prepared for him.
5 And the king's servants said to him, "Behold, Haman is standing
in the court." And the king said, "Let him come in."
6 So Haman came in and the king said to him, "What is to be done
for the man [a]whom the king desires to honor?" And Haman said [1]to
himself, "Whom would the king desire to honor more than me?"
7 Then Haman said to the king, "For the man whom the king
desires to honor,
8 let them bring a royal robe which the king has worn, and [a]the
horse on which the king has ridden, and on whose head [b]a royal
crown has been placed;
9 and let the robe and the horse be handed over to one of the
king's most noble princes and let them array the man whom the
king desires to honor and lead him on horseback through the city
square, [a]and proclaim before him, 'Thus it shall be done to the man
whom the king desires to honor.'"
10 Then the king said to Haman, "Take quickly the robes and the
horse as you have said, and do so for Mordecai the Jew, who is
sitting at the king's gate; do not fall short in anything of all that you
have said."
11 So Haman took the robe and the horse, and arrayed Mordecai,
and led him *on horseback* through the city square, and proclaimed
before him, "Thus it shall be done to the man whom the king desires
to honor."
12 Then Mordecai returned to the king's gate. But Haman hurried
home, mourning, [a]with *his* head covered.
13 And Haman recounted [a]to Zeresh his wife and all his friends
everything that had happened to him. Then his wise men and
Zeresh his wife said to him, "If Mordecai, before whom you have
begun to fall, is [1]of Jewish origin, you will not overcome him, but
will surely fall before him."

[1]Lit., *summoned to her* [a]Esth. 5:8

[1]Lit., *is not suitable to me* [a]Esth. 5:9

14 [1]Lit., *tree* [2]Lit., ...g [a]Esth. 6:4; 7:9, 10

6:1 [1]Lit., *the king's* ...*eep fled* [a]Dan. 6:18 [b]Esth. 2:23; 10:2

2 [a]Esth. 2:21, 22

[a]Esth. 4:11 [b]Esth. 5:14

6 [1]Lit., *in his heart* [a]Esth. 6:7, 9, 11

[a]1 Kin. 1:33 [b]Esth. 1:11; 2:17

9 [a]Gen. 41:43

12 [a]2 Sam. 15:30

...Lit., *from the seed* ...*Jews* [a]Esth. 5:10

14 While they were still talking with him, the king's eunuchs ar-
rived and hastily [a]brought Haman to the banquet which Esther had
prepared.

Chapter 7

7 Now the king and Haman came to drink *wine* with Esther the
queen.
2 And the king said to Esther on the second day also [1]as they
drank their wine at the banquet, "[a]What is your petition, Queen
Esther? It shall be granted you. And what is your request? [b]Even to
half of the kingdom it shall be done."
3 Then Queen Esther answered and said, "[a]If I have found favor in
your sight, O king, and if it please the king, let my life be given me
as my petition, and my people as my request;
4 for [a]we have been sold, I and my people, to be destroyed, [b]to be
killed and to be annihilated. Now if we had only been sold as slaves,
men and women, I would have remained silent, for the [1]trouble
would not be commensurate with the [2]annoyance to the king."
5 Then King Ahasuerus [1]asked Queen Esther, "Who is he, and
where is he, [2]who would presume to do thus?"
6 And Esther said, "[a]A foe and an enemy, is this wicked Haman!"
Then Haman became terrified before the king and queen.
7 And the king arose [a]in his anger from [1]drinking wine *and went*
into [b]the palace garden; but Haman stayed to beg for his life from
Queen Esther, for he saw that harm had been determined against
him by the king.
8 Now when the king returned from the palace garden into the
[1]place where they were drinking wine, Haman was falling on [a]the
couch where Esther was. Then the king said, "Will he even assault
the queen with me in the house?" As the word went out of the king's
mouth, they covered Haman's face.
9 Then Harbonah, one of the eunuchs who *were* before the king
said, "Behold indeed, [a]the gallows standing at Haman's house fifty
cubits high, which Haman made for Mordecai [b]who spoke good on
behalf of the king!" And the king said, "Hang him on it."
10 [a]So they hanged Haman on the [1]gallows which he had prepared
for Mordecai, [b]and the king's anger subsided.

Chapter 8

8 On that day King Ahasuerus gave the house of Haman, [a]the
enemy of the Jews, to Queen Esther; and Mordecai came before
the king, for Esther had disclosed [b]what he was to her.
2 [a]And the king took off his signet ring which he had taken away
from Haman, and gave it to Mordecai. And Esther set Mordecai over
the house of Haman.
3 Then Esther spoke again to the king, fell at his feet, wept, and
implored him to avert the evil *scheme* of Haman the Agagite and his
plot which he had devised against the Jews.
4 [a]And the king extended the golden scepter to Esther. So Esther
arose and stood before the king.
5 Then she said, "[a]If it pleases the king and if I have found favor
before him and the matter *seems* proper to the king and I am pleasing
in his sight, let it be written to revoke the [b]letters devised by Haman,

14 [a]Esth. 5:8

7:2 [1]Lit., *at the ba*
of wine [a]Esth. 5:6
[b]Esth. 5:3

3 [a]Esth. 5:8; 8:5

4 [1]Or, *enemy co*
compensate for th
loss [2]Or, *damage*
[a]Esth. 3:9 [b]Esth.

5 [1]Lit., *said and*
[2]Lit., *whose hear*
been filled

6 [a]Esth. 3:10

7 [1]Lit., *the banq*
wine [a]Esth. 1:12
1:5

8 [1]Lit., *house of*
banquet of wine
1:6

9 [a]Esth. 5:14 [b]
2:22

10 [1]Lit., *tree* [a]P
94:23 [b]Esth. 7:

8:1 [a]Esth. 7:6
2:7, 15

2 [a]Esth. 3:10

4 [a]Esth. 4:11; 5

5 [a]Esth. 5:8; 7
3:13

the son of Hammedatha the Agagite, which he wrote to destroy the
Jews who are in all the king's provinces.
6 "For [a]how can I endure to see the calamity which shall befall my
people, and how can I endure to see the destruction of my kindred?"
7 So King Ahasuerus said to Queen Esther and to Mordecai the
Jew, "Behold, [a]I have given the house of Haman to Esther, and him
they have hanged on the gallows because he had stretched out his
hands against the Jews.
8 "Now you write to the Jews [1]as you see fit, in the king's name,
and [a]seal *it* with the king's signet ring; for a decree which is written
in the name of the king and sealed with the king's signet ring [b]may
not be revoked."
9 [a]So the king's scribes were called at that time in the third month
(that is, the month Sivan), on the twenty-third [1]day; and it was writ-
ten according to all that Mordecai commanded to the Jews, the sa-
traps, the governors, and the princes of the provinces which *extended*
[b]from India to [2]Ethiopia, 127 provinces, to [c]every province according
to its script, and to every people according to their language, as well
as to the Jews according to their script and their language.
10 And he wrote in the name of King Ahasuerus, and sealed it with
the king's signet ring, and sent letters by couriers on [a]horses, riding
on steeds sired by the royal stud.
11 [1]In them the king granted the Jews who were in each and every
city *the right* [a]to assemble and to defend their lives, [b]to destroy, to kill,
and to annihilate the entire army of any people or province which
might attack them, including children and women, and [c]to plunder
their spoil,
12 on [a]one day in all the provinces of King Ahasuerus, the thir-
teenth *day* of the twelfth month (that is, the month Adar).
13 [a]A copy of the edict to be [1]issued as law in each and every
province, was published to all the peoples, so that the Jews should
be ready for this day to avenge themselves on their enemies.
14 The couriers, hastened and impelled by the king's command,
went out, riding on the royal steeds; and the decree was given out in
Susa the capital.
15 Then Mordecai went out from the presence of the king [a]in royal
robes of [1]blue and white, with a large crown of gold and [b]a garment
of fine linen and purple; and [c]the city of Susa shouted and rejoiced.
16 For the Jews there was [a]light and gladness and joy and honor.
17 And in each and every province, and in each and every city,
wherever the king's commandment and his decree arrived, there
was gladness and joy for the Jews, a feast and a [1a]holiday. And
[b]many among the peoples of the land became Jews, for the dread of
the Jews had fallen on them.

Chapter 9

9 Now [a]in the twelfth month (that is, the month Adar), on [b]the
thirteenth [1]day [c]when the king's command and edict [2]were
about to be executed, on the day when the enemies of the Jews
hoped to gain the mastery over them, it was turned to the contrary
so that the Jews themselves gained the mastery over those who
hated them.
2 [a]The Jews assembled in their cities throughout all the provinces
of King Ahasuerus to lay hands on those who sought their harm;

[a]Esth. 7:4; 9:1
7 [a]Esth. 8:1
ccording to the
od in your eyes
2; 8:10 [b]Esth. 1:19
in it [2]Lit., *Cush*
3:12 [b]Esth. 1:1
Esth. 1:22; 3:12
10 [a]1 Kin. 4:28
, *Which* [a]Esth.
sth. 3:13 [c]Esth. 9:10
[a]Esth. 3:13; 9:1
t., *given* [a]Esth. 3:14
Or, *violet* [a]Esth.
11 [b]Gen. 41:42
[c]Esth. 3:15
Ps. 97:11; 112:4
[1]Lit., *good day*
9:19 [b]Esth. 9:27
t., *day in it* [2]Lit.,
near [a]Esth. 8:12
9:17 [c]Esth. 3:13
th. 8:11; 9:15-18

and no one could stand before them, [b]for the dread of them had
fallen on all the peoples.
3 Even all the princes of the provinces, [a]the satraps, the governors,
and those who were doing the king's business [1]assisted the Jews,
because the dread of Mordecai had fallen on them.
4 Indeed, Mordecai was great in the king's house, and his fame
spread throughout all the provinces; for the man Mordecai [a]became
greater and greater.
5 Thus [a]the Jews struck all their enemies with [1]the sword, killing
and destroying; and they did what they pleased to those who hated
them.
6 And in Susa the capital the Jews killed and destroyed five
hundred men,
7 and Parshandatha, Dalphon, Aspatha,
8 Poratha, Adalia, Aridatha,
9 Parmashta, Arisai, Aridai, and Vaizatha,
10 [a]the ten sons of Haman the son of Hammedatha, the Jews'
enemy; but [b]they did not lay their hands on the plunder.
11 On that day the number of those who were killed in Susa the
capital [1]was reported to the king.
12 And the king said to Queen Esther, "The Jews have killed and
destroyed five hundred men and the ten sons of Haman in Susa the
capital. What then have they done in the rest of the king's provinces!
[a]Now what is your petition? It shall even be granted you. And what
is your further request? It shall also be done."
13 Then said Esther, "If it pleases the king, [a]let tomorrow also be
granted to the Jews who are in Susa to do according to the edict of
today; and let Haman's ten sons be hanged on the gallows."
14 So the king commanded that it should be done so; and an edict
was issued in Susa, and Haman's ten sons were hanged.
15 And the Jews who were in Susa assembled also on the four-
teenth day of the month Adar and killed [a]three hundred men in
Susa, but [b]they did not lay their hands on the plunder.
16 Now [a]the rest of the Jews who *were* in the king's provinces [b]as-
sembled, to defend their lives and [1]rid themselves of their enemies,
and kill 75,000 of those who hated them; but they did not lay their
hands on the plunder.
17 *This was done* on [a]the thirteenth day of the month Adar, and [b]on
the fourteenth [1]day they rested and made it a day of feasting and
rejoicing.
18 But the Jews who were in Susa [a]assembled on the thirteenth and
[b]the fourteenth [1]of the same month, and they rested on the fifteenth
[1]day and made it a day of feasting and rejoicing.
19 Therefore the Jews of the rural areas, who live in [a]the rural
towns, make the fourteenth day of the month Adar *a* [1b]holiday for
rejoicing and feasting and [c]sending portions *of food* to one another.
20 Then Mordecai recorded these events, and he sent letters to all
the Jews who were in all the provinces of King Ahasuerus, both near
and far,
21 obliging them to celebrate the fourteenth day of the month Adar,
and the fifteenth day [1]of the same month, annually,
22 because on those days the Jews [1]rid themselves of their enemies,
and *it was a* month which was [a]turned for them from sorrow into
gladness and from mourning into a [2]holiday; that they should make

2 [b]Esth. 8:17
3 [1]Lit., *lifted u*
8:36
3
4 [a]2 Sam. 3:1;
11:9
5 [1]Lit., *the stro*
[a]Esth. 3:13
10 [a]Esth. 5:11
8:11
11 [1]Lit., *came*
12 [a]Esth. 5:6; 7
13 [a]Esth. 8:11;
15 [a]Esth. 9:12
9:10
16 [1]Lit., *have re*
[a]Esth. 9:2 [b]Lev.
Esth. 8:11
17 [1]Lit., *in it* [a]E
[b]Esth. 9:21
18 [1]Lit., *in it* [a]E
8:11; 9:2 [b]Esth.
19 [1]Lit., *rejoicin*
feasting and a g
and sending [a]De
Zech. 2:4 [b]Esth.
[c]Neh. 8:10
21 [1]Lit., *in it*
22 [1]Lit., *had res*
[2]Lit., *good day* [a]
30:11

22 [b]Neh. 8:12

them days of feasting and rejoicing and [b]sending portions *of food* to one another and gifts to the poor.

24 [a]Esth. 3:7

23 Thus the Jews undertook what they had started to do, and what Mordecai had written to them.

24 For Haman the son of Hammedatha, the Agagite, the adversary of all the Jews, had schemed against the Jews to destroy them, and [a]had cast Pur, that is the lot, to disturb them and destroy them.

[1]Lit., *before the king,* [2]Lit., *schemed* [3]Lit., *tree* [a]Esth. 7:4-10 ...sth. 3:6-15 [c]Ps. 7:16

25 But [a]when it came [1]to the king's attention, he commanded by letter [b]that his wicked scheme which he had [2]devised against the Jews, [c]should return on his own head, and that he and his sons should be hanged on the [3]gallows.

26 [1]Lit., *Therefore because of all the words* [a]Esth. 9:20

26 Therefore they called these days Purim after the name of Pur. [1]And [a]because of the instructions in this letter, both what they had seen in this regard and what had happened to them,

[1]Lit., *received* [2]Lit., ...*d* [3]Lit., *it should not ...s away* [4]Lit., *writing* [a]Esth. 8:17 [b]Esth. 9:20, 21

27 the Jews established and [1]made a custom for themselves, and for their [2]descendants, and for [a]all those who allied themselves with them, so that [3]they should not fail [b]to celebrate these two days according to their [4]regulation, and according to their appointed time annually.

28 [1]Lit., *pass away* ...Lit., *end* [3]Lit., *seed*

28 So these days were to be remembered and celebrated throughout every generation, every family, every province, and every city; and these days of Purim were not to [1]fail from among the Jews, or their memory [2]fade from their [3]descendants.

[a]Esth. 2:15 [b]Esth. 9:20, 21

29 Then Queen Esther, [a]daughter of Abihail, with Mordecai the Jew, wrote with full authority to confirm [b]this second letter about Purim.

30 [a]Esth. 1:1

30 And he sent letters to all the Jews, [a]to the 127 provinces of the kingdom of Ahasuerus, namely, words of peace and truth,

31 [1]Lit., *seed* [2]Lit., *words* [a]Esth. 4:3

31 to establish these days of Purim at their appointed times, just as Mordecai the Jew and Queen Esther had established for them, and just as they had established for themselves and for their [1]descendants with [2]instructions [a]for their times of fasting and their lamentations.

[1]Lit., *words* [a]Esth. 9:26

32 And the command of Esther established these [1]customs for [a]Purim, and it was written in the book.

Chapter 10

...1 [a]Is. 11:11; 24:15

10 Now King Ahasuerus laid a tribute on the land and on the [a]coastlands of the sea.

[1]Lit., *doings* [2]Lit., ...*e him great* [a]Esth. ...5; 9:4 [b]Esth. 2:23

2 And all the [1]accomplishments of his authority and strength, and the full account of the greatness of Mordecai, [a]to which the king [2]advanced him, are they not written in [b]the Book of the Chronicles of the Kings of Media and Persia?

3 [a]Gen. 41:43, 44 [b]Neh. 2:10

3 For Mordecai the Jew was [a]second *only* to King Ahasuerus and great among the Jews, and in favor with the multitude of his kinsmen, [b]one who sought the good of his people and one who spoke for the welfare of his whole nation.

Esther at a Glance

Theme of Esther:

Author:

Date:

Purpose:

Key Words:

Segment Divisions		Chapter Themes
		1
		2
		3
		4
		5
		6
		7
		8
		9
		10

OB

Job is a book of poetry, born out of pain. Job's pain was so crushing he wanted to die; he wished d never been born. His pain was compounded because his friends wrestled with the reason for his fering. Job's affliction brought God's character and ways into question. Ultimately it brought deeper imacy with God.

Job, the first and probably oldest of the poetical books of the Bible, is for those who need answers m God, for those who want to say with Job, "It is still my consolation, and I rejoice in unsparing n, that I have not denied the words of the Holy One" (6:10).

INGS TO DO

1. Chapters 1 and 2 provide the setting of Job's pain. Read through these two chapters. Mark every reference to Satan and to God. Then on the OBSERVATIONS CHART on page 798:
   a. List what you learn about Satan—his person and his relationship to God and to Job.
   b. List what you learn about God.
   c. List what you learn about Job: what God says about him; what Satan says; how he responds to God, to his pain, and to the counsel of his wife.
2. In order to understand Job and the ensuing discourses of his friends, read Job 1:8 and 2:3,11-13 again and then Job 42:7-9. Stop and do this before you proceed any further. Pay attention to what God says about Job and to what God says about what Job's three friends said.
3. In chapter 3 Job pours out his anguish, and then in chapters 4 through 42:6 there is a series of discourses given either by Job, his friends, or by God Himself. Read through this section chapter by chapter and do the following:
   a. At the top of every chapter, on the line next to the chapter number, note who is speaking, and to whom. Then record this under chapter themes on the JOB AT A GLANCE chart on page 799.
   b. Job 42:7 says that Job's friends did not speak what was right concerning God. Therefore if one of these three men speaks, in the margin note how his reasoning is wrong in respect to God and to Job's suffering. Watch carefully to see where or how (if it tells) Job's friend came up with his conclusion. Then watch how Job answers each of his friends. Record pertinent notes in the margin.
4. As you read Job 4 through 42 observe what the text says about:
   a. Man and God
   b. What God expects from man and what He does not expect
   c. Nature
   d. Sin and righteousness
   e. Physical life and death
   f. How to deal with those in pain

   Record your insights on the OBSERVATIONS CHART on page 798 as you read each chapter.
5. Mark key words or phrases which play a significant role in a particular chapter or which recur throughout the book. For instance, the word *wisdom*. Note in the margin the insights you glean from marking *wisdom* and other key words. Also highlight or underline verses which speak to your heart.
6. Don't fail to compare Job's end with his beginning and notice what came from Satan's challenge.

7. When you finish reading Job, and you have filled in JOB AT A GLANCE, note how the b
divides itself into a pattern of discourses. Record this under "Segment Divisions."

THINGS TO THINK ABOUT

1. Think about Job's end compared to his beginning and then ask yourself if Job's suffering
worth it. What about your suffering? What can it produce if you will respond in the proper w
What is the proper way? What did you learn from Job?
2. What have you learned about Satan and Satan's relationship to God from this book? How
those insights comfort you?
3. Read Job 31 again and if you didn't mark it the first time, mark in a distinctive way every *if*
every *if I have.* Think about how Job appealed to his own integrity in various matters of
Examine those areas carefully. How does your integrity measure up in those areas? What do
need to remember, do, hold onto, let go of, begin, or stop? Will you?

Chapter 1 ______

1 There was a man in the [a]land of Uz, whose name was [b]Job, and
that man was [c]blameless, upright, [d]fearing God, and [e]turning
away from evil.
2 [a]And seven sons and three daughters were born to him.
3 [a]His possessions also were 7,000 sheep, 3,000 camels, 500 yoke of
oxen, 500 female donkeys, and very many servants; and that man
was [b]the greatest of all the [1]men of the east.
4 And his sons used to go and hold a feast in the house of each one
on his day, and they would send and invite their three sisters to eat
and drink with them.
5 And it came about, when the days of feasting had completed
their cycle, that Job would send and consecrate them, rising up early
in the morning and offering [a]burnt offerings *according to* the number
of them all; for Job said, "[b]Perhaps my sons have sinned and [c]cursed
God in their hearts." Thus Job did continually.
6 [a]Now there was a day when the [b]sons of God came to present
themselves before the LORD, and [1]Satan also came among them.
7 And the LORD said to Satan, "From where do you come?" Then
Satan answered the LORD and said, "[a]From roaming about on the
earth and walking around on it."
8 And the LORD said to Satan, "Have you [1]considered [a]My servant
Job? For there is no one like him on the earth, [b]a blameless and
upright man, [2]fearing God and turning away from evil."
9 Then [a]Satan answered the [1]LORD, "Does Job fear God for noth-
ing?
10 "[a]Hast Thou not made a hedge about him and his house and all
that he has, on every side? [b]Thou hast blessed the work of his hands,
and his [c]possessions have increased in the land.
11 "[a]But put forth Thy hand now and [b]touch all that he has; he will
surely curse Thee to Thy face."
12 Then the LORD said to Satan, "Behold, all that he has is in your
[1]power, only do not put forth your hand on him." So Satan departed
from the presence of the LORD.
13 Now it happened on the day when his sons and his daughters
were eating and drinking wine in their oldest brother's house,
14 that a messenger came to Job and said, "The oxen were plowing
and the [1]donkeys feeding beside them,

1:1 [a]Jer. 25:20; L
4:21 [b]Ezek. 14:14
James 5:11 [c]Gen
17:1; Deut. 18:13
22:12; 42:18; Ex.
Prov. 8:13 [e]Job 2

2 [a]Job 42:13

3 [1]Lit., *sons* [a]Job
42:12 [b]Job 29:25

5 [a]Gen. 8:20; Job
[b]Job 8:4 [c]1 Kin.
21:10, 13

6 [1]I.e., the advers
and so throughou
1 and 2 [a]Job 2:1
38:7

7 [a]1 Pet. 5:8

8 [1]Lit., *set your*
[2]Or, *revering* [a]Nu
12:7; Josh. 1:2, 7
42:7, 8 [b]Job 1:1

9 [1]Lit., *LORD and*
[a]Rev. 12:9f.

10 [a]Job 29:2-6;
34:7 [b]Job 31:25
1:3; 31:25

11 [a]Job 2:5 [b]Jo

12 [1]Lit., *hand*

14 [1]Lit., *female*

15 and [1]the [a]Sabeans [2]attacked and took them. They also [3]slew the
servants with the edge of the sword, and [4]I alone have escaped to tell
you."
16 While he was still speaking, another also came and said, "[a]The
fire of God fell from heaven and burned up the sheep and the ser-
vants and consumed them, and I alone have escaped to tell you."
17 While he was still speaking, another also came and said, "The
[a]Chaldeans formed three bands and made a raid on the camels and
took them and [1]slew the servants with the edge of the sword; and I
alone have escaped to tell you."
18 While he was still speaking, another also came and said, "Your
sons and your daughters were eating and drinking wine in their
oldest brother's house,
19 and behold, a great wind came from across the wilderness and
struck the four corners of the house, and it fell on the young people
and they died; and I alone have escaped to tell you."
20 Then Job arose and [a]tore his robe and shaved his head, and he
fell to the ground and worshiped.
21 And he said,

"[a]Naked I came from my mother's womb,
And naked I shall return there.
The [b]LORD gave and the LORD has taken away.
Blessed be the name of the LORD."

22 [a]Through all this Job did not sin nor did he [1]blame God.

Chapter 2

2 [a]Again there was a day when the sons of God came to present
themselves before the LORD, and Satan also came among them to
present himself before the LORD.
2 And the LORD said to Satan, "Where have you come from?" Then
Satan answered the LORD and said, "From roaming about on the
earth, and walking around on it."
3 And the LORD said to Satan, "Have you [1]considered My servant
Job? For there is no one like him on the earth, a blameless and
upright man [2]fearing God and turning away from evil. And he still
[a]holds fast his integrity, although you incited Me against him, to
[3]ruin him without cause."
4 And Satan answered the LORD and said, "Skin for skin! Yes, all
that a man has he will give for his life.
5 "[a]However, put forth Thy hand, now, and [b]touch his bone and his
flesh; he will curse Thee to Thy face."
6 So the LORD said to Satan, "Behold, he is in your [1]power, only
spare his life."
7 Then Satan went out from the presence of the LORD, and smote
Job with [a]sore boils from the sole of his foot to the crown of his head.
8 And he took a potsherd to scrape himself while [a]he was sitting
among the ashes.
9 Then his wife said to him, "Do you still hold fast your integrity?
Curse God and die!"
10 But he said to her, "You speak as one of the foolish women
speaks. [a]Shall we indeed accept good from God and not accept ad-
versity?" [b]In all this Job did not sin with his lips.
11 Now when Job's three friends heard of all this adversity that had
come upon him, they came each one from his own place, Eliphaz the

5 [1]Lit., *Sheba* [2]Lit., *ell upon* [3]Lit., *smote* .it., *only I alone,* and ɔ also vv. 16, 17, 19 Gen. 10:7; Job 6:19

6 [a]Gen. 19:24; Lev. 10:2; Num. 11:1-3

[1]Lit., *smote* [a]Gen. 11:28, 31

0 [a]Gen. 37:29, 34; Josh. 7:6

Eccl. 5:15 [b]1 Sam. 2:7, 8; Job 2:10

22 [1]Lit., *ascribe seemliness to* [a]Job 2:10

2:1 [a]Job 1:6-8

.., *set your heart to* [2]Or, *revering* [3]Lit., *allow him up* [a]Job 27:5, 6

b 1:11 [b]Job 19:20

6 [1]Lit., *hand*

ut. 28:35; Job 7:5; :28; 30:17, 18, 30

ob 42:6; Jer. 6:26; k. 27:30; Jon. 3:6

0 [a]Job 1:21 [b]Job ; Ps. 39:1; James 1:12

[a]Temanite, Bildad the [b]Shuhite, and Zophar the Naamathite; and
they made an appointment together to come to [c]sympathize with
him and comfort him.
12 And when they lifted up their eyes at a distance, and did not
recognize him, they raised their voices and wept. And each of them
[a]tore his robe, and they [b]threw dust over their heads toward the sky.
13 [a]Then they sat down on the ground with him for seven days and
seven nights with no one speaking a word to him, for they saw that
his pain was very great.

Chapter 3

3 Afterward Job opened his mouth and cursed [1]the day of his *birth*.

2 And Job [1]said,

3 "[a]Let the day perish on which I was to be born,
And the night *which* said, 'A [1]boy is conceived.'
4 "May that day be darkness;
Let not God above care for it,
Nor light shine on it.
5 "Let [a]darkness and black gloom claim it;
Let a cloud settle on it;
Let the blackness of the day terrify it.
6 "*As for* that night, let darkness seize it;
Let it not rejoice among the days of the year;
Let it not come into the number of the months.
7 "Behold, let that night be barren;
Let no joyful shout enter it.
8 "Let those curse it who curse the day,
Who are [1]prepared to [a]rouse Leviathan.
9 "Let the stars of its twilight be darkened;
Let it wait for light but have none,
Neither let it see the [1]breaking dawn;
10 Because it did not shut the opening of my *mother's* womb,
Or hide trouble from my eyes.

11 "[a]Why did I not die [1]at birth,
Come forth from the womb and expire?
12 "Why did the knees receive me,
And why the breasts, that I should suck?
13 "For now I [a]would have lain down and been quiet;
I would have slept then, I would have been at rest,
14 With [a]kings and *with* [b]counselors of the earth,
Who rebuilt [c]ruins for themselves;
15 Or with [a]princes [b]who had gold,
Who were filling their houses *with* silver.
16 "Or like a miscarriage which is [1]discarded, I would not be,
As infants that never saw light.
17 "There the wicked cease from raging,
And there the [1]weary are at [a]rest.
18 "The prisoners are at ease together;
They do not hear the voice of the taskmaster.
19 "The small and the great are there,
And the slave is free from his master.

11 [a]Gen. 36:11; Job 6:19; Jer. 49:7 [b]Gen. 25:2 [c]Job 42:11; Ro[m.] 12:15

12 [a]Job 1:20 [b]Josh. 7:6; Neh. 9:1; Lam. 2:10; Ezek. 27:30

13 [a]Gen. 50:10; Ez[ek.] 3:15

3:1 [1]Lit., *his day*

2 [1]Lit., *answered a[nd] said*

3 [1]Lit., *man-child* [a][Jer.] 20:14-18

5 [a]Jer. 13:16

8 [1]Or, *skillful* [a]Job 41:1, 25

9 [1]Lit., *eyelids*

11 [1]Lit., *from the w[omb]* [a]Job 10:18, 19

13 [a]Job 3:13-19; 7:8-10, 21; 10:21, [22]; 14:10-15, 20-22; 1[6:22]; 17:13-16; 19:25-27; 21:13, 23-26; 24:19; 26:5, 6; 34:22

14 [a]Job 12:18 [b]Jo[b] 12:17 [c]Job 15:28; [Is.] 58:12

15 [a]Job 12:21 [b]Jo[b] 27:16, 17

16 [1]Lit., *hidden*

17 [1]Lit., *weary of strength* [a]Job 17:1[6]

20 "Why is [a]light given to him who suffers,
And life to the bitter of soul;
21 Who [1a]long for death, but there is none,
And dig for it more than for [b]hidden treasures;
22 Who rejoice greatly,
They exult when they find the grave?
23 "*Why is light given* to a man [a]whose way is hidden,
And whom [b]God has hedged in?
24 "For [a]my groaning comes at the sight of my food,
And [b]my cries pour out like water.
25 "For [1a]what I fear comes upon me,
And what I dread befalls me.
26 "I [a]am not at ease, nor am I quiet,
And I am not at rest, but turmoil comes."

Chapter 4

4 Then Eliphaz the Temanite [1]answered,
2 "If one ventures a word with you, will you become impatient?
But [a]who can refrain [1]from speaking?
3 "Behold [a]you have admonished many,
And you have strengthened weak hands.
4 "Your words have [1]helped the tottering to stand,
And you have strengthened [2]feeble knees.
5 "But now it has come to you, and you [a]are impatient;
It [b]touches you, and you are dismayed.
6 "Is not your [1a]fear *of God* [b]your confidence,
And the integrity of your ways your hope?

7 "Remember now, [a]who *ever* perished being innocent?
Or where were the upright destroyed?
8 "According to what I have seen, [a]those who plow iniquity
And those who sow trouble harvest it.
9 "By [a]the breath of God they perish,
And [b]by the [1]blast of His anger they come to an end.
10 "The [a]roaring of the lion and the voice of the *fierce* lion,
And the teeth of the young lions are broken.
11 "The [a]lion perishes for lack of prey,
And the [b]whelps of the lioness are scattered.

12 "Now a word [a]was brought to me stealthily,
And my ear received a [b]whisper of it.
13 "Amid disquieting [a]thoughts from the visions of the night,
When deep sleep falls on men,
14 Dread came upon me, and trembling,
And made [1]all my bones shake.
15 "Then a [1]spirit passed by my face;
The hair of my flesh bristled up.
16 "It stood still, but I could not discern its appearance;
A form *was* before my eyes;
There was silence, then I heard a voice:
17 'Can [a]mankind be just [1]before God?
Can a man be pure [1]before his [b]Maker?
18 '[a]He puts no trust even in His servants;
And against His angels He charges error.

20 [a]Jer. 20:18
[1]Lit., *wait* [a]Rev. 9:6 [b]Prov. 2:4
23 [a]Job 19:6, 8, 12 [b]Job 19:8; Ps. 88:8; Lam. 3:7
24 [a]Job 6:7; 33:20 [b]Job 30:16; Ps. 42:4
[1]Lit., *the fear I fear* ...nd [a]Job 9:28; 30:15
26 [a]Job 7:13, 14
[1]Lit., *answered and said*
[1]Lit., *in words* [a]Job 32:18-20
...b 4:3, 4; 29:15, 16, 21, 25
[1]Lit., *caused* [2]Lit., *bowing*
...b 6:14 [b]Job 19:21
...Or, *reverence* [a]Job 1:1 [b]Prov. 3:26
[a]Job 8:20; 36:6, 7; Ps. 37:25
...ob 15:31, 35; Prov. ...8; Hos. 10:13; Gal. 6:7
9 [1]Lit., *wind* [a]Job ...30; Is. 11:4; 30:33; 2 Thess. 2:8 [b]Job 40:11-13
...Job 5:15; Ps. 58:6
...1 [a]Job 29:17; Ps. ...0 [b]Job 5:4; 20:10; 27:14
12 [a]Job 4:12-17; ...15-18 [b]Job 26:14
13 [a]Job 33:15
...t., *the multitude of*
...Or, *breath passed over*
...it., *from* [a]Job 9:2; [b]Job 31:15; 32:22; 35:10; 36:3
18 [a]Job 15:15

19 'How much more those who dwell in [a]houses of clay,
Whose [b]foundation is in the dust,
Who are crushed before the moth!
20 '[a]Between morning and evening they are broken in pieces;
Unobserved, they [b]perish forever.
21 'Is not their [a]tent-cord plucked up within them?
They die, yet [b]without wisdom.'

Chapter 5

5 "Call now, is there anyone who will answer you?
And to which of the [a]holy ones will you turn?
2 "For [a]vexation slays the foolish man,
And anger kills the simple.
3 "I have seen the [a]foolish taking root,
And I [b]cursed his abode immediately.
4 "His [a]sons are far from safety,
They are even [1]oppressed in the gate,
Neither is there a deliverer.
5 "[1]His harvest the hungry devour,
And take it to a *place of* thorns;
And the [2a]schemer is eager for their wealth.
6 "For [a]affliction does not come from the dust,
Neither does trouble sprout from the ground,
7 For [a]man is born for trouble,
As sparks fly upward.

8 "But as for me, I would [a]seek God,
And I would place my cause before God;
9 Who [a]does great and unsearchable things,
[1]Wonders without number.
10 "He [a]gives rain on the earth,
And sends water on the fields,
11 So that [a]He sets on high those who are lowly,
And those who mourn are lifted to safety.
12 "He [a]frustrates the plotting of the shrewd,
So that their hands cannot attain success.
13 "He [a]captures the wise by their own shrewdness
And the advice of the cunning is quickly thwarted.
14 "By day they [a]meet with darkness,
And grope at noon as in the night.
15 "But He saves from [a]the sword of their mouth,
And [b]the poor from the hand of the mighty.
16 "So the helpless has hope,
And [a]unrighteousness must shut its mouth.

17 "Behold, how [a]happy is the man whom God reproves,
So do not despise the [b]discipline of [1]the Almighty.
18 "For [a]He inflicts pain, and [1]gives relief;
He wounds, and His hands *also* heal.
19 "[1]From six troubles [a]He will deliver you,
Even in seven [b]evil will not touch you.
20 "In [a]famine He will redeem you from death,
And [b]in war from the power of the sword.
21 "You will be [a]hidden from the scourge of the tongue,

19 [a]Job 10:9; 33:6 [b]Gen. 2:7; 3:19; Job 22:16

20 [a]Job 14:2 [b]Job 14:20; 20:7

21 [a]Job 8:22 [b]Job 18:21; 36:12

5:1 [a]Job 15:15

2 [a]Prov. 12:16; 27:3

3 [a]Jer. 12:2 [b]Job 24:18; 31:30

4 [1]Lit., *crushed* [a]Jo 4:11

5 [1]Lit., *Whose* [2]Anc versions read *thirsty* [a]Job 18:8-10; 22:10

6 [a]Job 15:35

7 [a]Job 14:1

8 [a]Job 13:2, 3; Ps. 50:15

9 [1]Or, *Miracles* [a]Jo 9:10; 37:14, 16; 42:

10 [a]Job 36:27-29; 37:6-11; 38:26

11 [a]Job 22:29; 36:7

12 [a]Ps. 33:10

13 [a]Job 37:24; 1 C 3:19

14 [a]Job 12:25; 15: 18:18; 20:26; 24:13

15 [a]Job 4:10, 11; F 35:10 [b]Job 29:17; 34:28; 36:6, 15; 38

16 [a]Ps. 107:42

17 [1]Heb., *Shadda* so throughout ch. 6 [a]Ps. 94:12 [b]Job 36 16; Prov. 3:11; Heb 12:5-11; James 1:1

18 [1]Lit., *binds* [a]De 32:39; 1 Sam. 2:6; 30:26; Hos. 6:1

19 [1]Lit., *In* [a]Ps. 34 [b]Ps. 91:10

20 [a]Ps. 33:19; 37: [b]Ps. 144:10

21 [a]Job 5:15; Ps.

[b]Neither will you be afraid of violence when it comes.
22 "You will [a]laugh at violence and famine,
[b]Neither will you be afraid of [1]wild beasts.
23 "For you will be in league with the stones of the field;
And [a]the beasts of the field will be at peace with you.
24 "And you will know that your [a]tent is secure,
For you will visit your abode and fear no loss.
25 "You will know also that your [1a]descendants will be many,
And [b]your offspring as the grass of the earth.
26 "You will [a]come to the grave in full vigor,
Like the stacking of grain in its season.
27 "Behold this, we have investigated it, thus it is;
Hear it, and know for yourself."

Chapter 6

6 Then Job [1]answered,
2 "[a]Oh that my vexation were actually weighed,
And laid in the balances together with my iniquity!
3 "For then it would be [a]heavier than the sand of the seas,
Therefore my words have been rash.
4 "For the [a]arrows of the Almighty are within me;
[1]Their [b]poison my spirit drinks;
The [c]terrors of God are arrayed against me.
5 "Does the [a]wild donkey bray over *his* grass,
Or does the ox low over his fodder?
6 "Can something tasteless be eaten without salt,
Or is there any taste in the [1]white of an egg?
7 "My soul [a]refuses to touch *them;*
They are like loathsome food to me.

8 "Oh that my request might come to pass,
And that God would grant my longing!
9 "Would that God were [a]willing to crush me;
That He would loose His hand and cut me off!
10 "But it is still my consolation,
And I rejoice in unsparing pain,
That I [a]have not [1]denied the words of the Holy One.
11 "What is my strength, that I should wait?
And what is my end, that I should [1a]endure?
12 "Is my strength the strength of stones,
Or is my flesh bronze?
13 "Is it that my [a]help is not within me,
And that [1b]deliverance is driven from me?

14 "For the [a]despairing man *there should be* kindness from his friend;
Lest he [b]forsake the [1]fear of the Almighty.
15 "My brothers have acted [a]deceitfully like a [1]wadi,
Like the torrents of [1]wadis which vanish,
16 Which are turbid because of ice,
And into which the snow [1]melts.
17 "When [a]they become waterless, they [1]are silent,
When it is hot, they vanish from their place.
18 "The [1]paths of their course wind along,
They go up into nothing and perish.

21 [b]Ps. 91:5, 6
22 [1]Lit., *beasts of the earth* [a]Job 8:21 [b]Ps. 91:13; Ezek. 34:25; Hos. 2:18
23 [a]Is. 11:6-9; 65:25
24 [a]Job 8:6
25 [1]Lit., *seed* [a]Ps. 2 [b]Is. 44:3, 4; 48:19
26 [a]Job 42:17
[1]Lit., *answered and said*
2 [a]Job 31:6
3 [a]Job 23:2
4 [1]Lit., *Whose* [a]Job 6:13; Ps. 38:2 [b]Job 6; 21:20 [c]Job 30:15
5 [a]Job 39:5-8
6 [1]Heb., *hallamuth,* meaning uncertain. rhaps the juice of a plant.
7 [a]Job 3:24; 33:20
[a]Num. 11:15; 1 Kin. 9:4; Job 7:16; 9:21; 10:1
[1]Lit., *hidden* [a]Job 22:22; 23:11, 12
11 [1]Lit., *prolong my soul* [a]Job 21:4
13 [1]So ancient versions [a]Job 26:2 [b]Job 26:3
r, *reverence* [a]Job 4:5 [b]Job 1:5; 15:4
[1]Or, *brooks* [a]Jer. 15:18
6 [1]Lit., *hides itself*
[1]Or, *cease* [a]Job 24:19
[1]Or, *caravans turn their course, they up into the waste and perish.*

19 "The caravans of [a]Tema looked,
The travelers of [b]Sheba hoped for them.
20 "They [a]were [1]disappointed for they had trusted,
They came there and were confounded.
21 "Indeed, you have now become such,
[a]You see a terror and are afraid.
22 "Have I said, 'Give me *something*,'
Or, 'Offer a bribe for me from your wealth,'
23 Or, 'Deliver me from the hand of the adversary,'
Or, 'Redeem me from the hand of the tyrants'?

24 "Teach me, and [a]I will be silent;
And show me how I have erred.
25 "How painful are honest words!
But what does your argument prove?
26 "Do you intend to reprove *my* words,
When the [a]words of one in despair belong to the wind?
27 "You would even [a]cast *lots* for [b]the orphans,
And [c]barter over your friend.
28 "And now please look at me,
And *see* if I [a]lie to your face.
29 "Desist now, let there be no injustice;
Even desist, [a]my righteousness is yet in it.
30 "Is there injustice on my tongue?
Cannot [a]my palate discern [1]calamities?

Chapter 7

7 "[1]Is not man [a]forced to labor on earth,
And *are not* his days like the days of [b]a hired man?
2 "As a slave who pants for the shade,
And as a hired man who eagerly waits for his wages,
3 So am I allotted months of vanity,
And [a]nights of trouble are appointed me.
4 "When I [a]lie down I say,
'When shall I arise?'
But the night continues,
And I am [1]continually tossing until dawn.
5 "My [a]flesh is clothed with worms and a crust of dirt;
My skin hardens and runs.
6 "My days are [a]swifter than a weaver's shuttle,
And come to an end [b]without hope.

7 "Remember that my life [a]is *but* breath,
My eye will [b]not again see good.
8 "The [a]eye of him who sees me will behold me no more;
Thine eyes *will be* on me, but [b]I will not be.
9 "When a [a]cloud vanishes, it is gone,
So [b]he who goes down to [c]Sheol does not come up.
10 "He will not return again to his house,
Nor will [a]his place know him anymore.

11 "Therefore, [a]I will not restrain my mouth;
I will speak in the anguish of my spirit,
I will complain in the bitterness of my soul.

19 [a]Gen. 25:15; Is. 21:14; Jer. 25:23 [b]Jo 1:15

20 [1]Lit., *ashamed* [a]J 14:3

21 [a]Ps. 38:11

24 [a]Ps. 39:1

26 [a]Job 8:2; 15:2; 1

27 [a]Joel 3:3; Nah. 3 [b]Job 22:9; 24:3, 9 [c]2 Pet. 2:3

28 [a]Job 27:4; 33:3;

29 [a]Job 13:18; 19:6 23:10; 27:5, 6; 34:5; 42:1-6

30 [1]Or, *words* [a]Job 12:11

7:1 [1]Lit., *Has not m compulsory labor* [a] 5:7; 10:17; 14:1, 14 [b]Job 14:6

3 [a]Job 16:7

4 [1]Lit., *sated with* [a]Deut. 28:67; Job 7:13, 14

5 [a]Job 2:7; 17:14

6 [a]Job 9:25 [b]Job 13:15; 14:19; 17:15 19:10

7 [a]Job 7:16; Ps. 78 James 4:14 [b]Job 9

8 [a]Job 8:18; 20:9 7:21

9 [a]Job 30:15 [b]Job 3:13-19 [c]2 Sam. 1 Job 11:8; 14:13; 17:13, 16

10 [a]Job 8:18; 20:9 27:21, 23

11 [a]Job 10:1; 21:4 23:2; Ps. 40:9

12 "Am I the sea, or [a]the sea monster,
That Thou dost set a guard over me?
13 "If I say, '[a]My bed will comfort me,
My couch will [1]ease my complaint,'
14 Then Thou dost frighten me with dreams
And terrify me by visions;
15 So that my soul would choose suffocation,
Death rather than my [1]pains.
16 "I [1a]waste away; I will not live forever.
Leave me alone, [b]for my days are *but* a breath.
17 "[a]What is man that Thou dost magnify him,
And that Thou [1]art concerned about him,
18 That [a]Thou dost examine him every morning,
And try him every moment?
19 "[1a]Wilt Thou never turn Thy gaze away from me,
Nor let me alone until I swallow my spittle?
20 "[a]Have I sinned? What have I done to Thee,
O [b]watcher of men?
Why hast Thou set me as Thy target,
So that I am a burden to myself?
21 "Why then [a]dost Thou not pardon my transgression
And take away my iniquity?
For now I will [b]lie down in the dust;
And Thou wilt seek me, [c]but I will not be."

Chapter 8

8 Then Bildad the Shuhite [1]answered,
2 "How long will you say these *things*,
And the [a]words of your mouth be a mighty wind?
3 "Does [a]God pervert justice
Or does [1]the Almighty pervert what is right?
4 "[a]If your sons sinned against Him,
Then He delivered them into the [1]power of their transgression.
5 "If you would [a]seek God
And implore the compassion of [1]the Almighty,
6 If you are pure and upright,
Surely now [a]He would rouse Himself for you
And restore your righteous [1b]estate.
7 "Though your beginning was insignificant,
Yet your [a]end will increase greatly.

8 "Please [a]inquire of past generations,
And consider the things searched out by their fathers.
9 "For we are *only* of yesterday and know nothing,
Because [a]our days on earth are as a shadow.
10 "Will they not teach you *and* tell you,
And bring forth words from their minds?

11 "Can the papyrus grow up without marsh?
Can the rushes grow without water?
12 "While it is still green *and* not cut down,
Yet it withers before any *other* [1]plant.
13 "So are the paths of [a]all who forget God,
And the [b]hope of the godless will perish,

[a]Ezek. 32:2, 3
bear [a]Job 7:4; Ps. 6:6
15 [1]Lit., *bones*
athe [a]Job 6:9; 10:1 [b]Job 7:7
t., *shouldst set on* [a]Job 22:2; 44:3; Heb. 2:6
18 [a]Job 14:3
., *How long wilt not* [a]Job 9:18; 10:20; 14:6
ob 35:3, 6 [b]Ps. 36:6
Job 9:28; 10:14 10:9 [c]Job 7:8
, *answered and said*
2 [a]Job 6:26
[1]Heb., *Shaddai* 3:25; Deut. 32:4; 19:7; Job 34:10, 23; 37:23; Rom. 3:5
, *hand* [a]Job 1:5, 18, 19
., *Shaddai* [a]Job 5:17-27
[1]Lit., *place* [a]Job 7; 34:28; Ps. 7:6 [b]Job 5:24
7 [a]Job 42:12
t. 4:32; 32:7; Job 15:18; 20:4
9 [a]Job 14:2
12 [1]Lit., *reed*
3 [a]Ps. 9:17 [b]Job 20; 13:16; 15:34; 20:5; 27:8

14 Whose confidence is fragile,
And whose trust a [a]spider's [1]web.
15 "He [1]trusts in his [a]house, but it does not stand;
He holds fast to it, but it does not endure.
16 "He [1a]thrives before the sun,
And his [b]shoots spread out over his garden.
17 "His roots wrap around a rock pile,
He [1]grasps a house of stones.
18 "If he is [1]removed from [a]his place,
Then it will deny him, *saying,* '[b]I never saw you.'
19 "Behold, [a]this is the joy of His way;
And out of the dust others will spring.
20 "Lo, [a]God will not reject *a man of* integrity,
Nor [b]will He [1]support the evildoers.
21 "He will yet fill [a]your mouth with laughter,
And your lips with shouting.
22 "Those who hate you will be [a]clothed with shame;
And the [b]tent of the wicked will be no more."

Chapter 9

9 Then Job [1]answered,
2 "In truth I know that this is so,
But how can a [a]man be in the right [1]before God?
3 "If one wished to [a]dispute with Him,
He could not answer Him once in a thousand *times.*
4 "[a]Wise in heart and [b]mighty in strength,
Who has [1c]defied Him [2]without harm?
5 "[a]*It is God* who removes the mountains, they know not *how,*
When He overturns them in His anger;
6 Who [a]shakes the earth out of its place,
And its [b]pillars tremble;
7 Who commands the [a]sun [1]not to shine,
And sets a seal upon the stars;
8 Who alone [a]stretches out the heavens,
And [1b]tramples down the waves of the sea;
9 Who makes the [a]Bear, Orion, and the Pleiades,
And the [b]chambers of the south;
10 Who [a]does great things, [1]unfathomable,
And wondrous works without number.
11 "Were He to pass by me, [a]I would not see Him;
Were He to move past *me,* I would not perceive Him.
12 "Were He to snatch away, who could [a]restrain Him?
Who could say to Him, '[b]What art Thou doing?'

13 "God will not turn back His anger;
Beneath Him crouch the helpers of [a]Rahab.
14 "How then can [a]I [1]answer Him,
And choose my words [2]before Him?
15 "For [a]though I were right, I could not [1]answer;
I would have to [b]implore the mercy of my judge.
16 "If I called and He answered me,
I could not believe that He was listening to my voice.
17 "For He [a]bruises me with a tempest,
And multiplies my wounds without cause.

14 [1]Lit., *hous*
59:5, 6
15 [1]Lit., *lean*
8:22; 27:18; P
16 [1]Lit., *is lus*
37:35; Jer. 11
80:11
17 [1]Heb., *se*
18 [1]Lit., *swal*
[a]Job 7:10 [b]Jo
19 [a]Job 20:5
20 [1]Lit., *stren*
hand of [a]Job
21:30
21 [a]Job 5:22;
126:1, 2
22 [a]Ps. 132:1
8:15; 15:34; 18
9:1 [1]Lit., *answ*
said
2 [1]Lit., *with* [a]J
25:4
3 [a]Job 10:2; 1
23:6; 40:2
4 [1]Lit., *stiffene*
neck against [2]
remained safe
11:6; 12:13; 28
38:36, 37 [b]Job
23:6 [c]2 Chr. 13
Prov. 29:1
5 [a]Job 9:5-10;
41:11
6 [a]Is. 2:19, 21;
Hag. 2:6 [b]Ps. 7
7 [1]Lit., *and it d*
shine [a]Is. 13:10
32:7, 8
8 [1]Lit., *treads u*
heights of [a]Ger
Job 37:18; Ps. 1
40:22 [b]Job 38:
77:19
9 [a]Job 38:31, 3
5:8 [b]Job 37:9
10 [1]Lit., *until the*
searching out [a]
11 [a]Job 23:8, 9;
12 [a]Job 10:7; 1
45:9
13 [a]Job 26:12; P
89:10; Is. 30:7; 5
14 [1]Or, *plead m*
[2]Lit., *with* [a]Job 9
15 [1]Or, *plead m*
[a]Job 9:20, 21; 10
[b]Job 8:5
17 [a]Job 16:12, 1

18 "He will [a]not allow me to get my breath,
But saturates me with [b]bitterness.
19 "If *it is a matter* of power, [a]behold, *He is* the strong one!
And if *it is a matter* of justice, who can summon [1]Him?
20 "[a]Though I am righteous, my mouth will [b]condemn me;
Though I am guiltless, He will declare me guilty.
21 "I am [a]guiltless;
I do not take notice of myself;
I [b]despise my life.
22 "It is *all* one; therefore I say,
'He [a]destroys the guiltless and the wicked.'
23 "If the scourge kills suddenly,
He [a]mocks the despair of the innocent.
24 "The earth [a]is given into the hand of the wicked;
He [b]covers the faces of its judges.
If *it is* not *He*, then who is it?

25 "Now [a]my days are swifter than a runner;
They flee away, [b]they see no good.
26 "They slip by like [a]reed boats,
Like an [b]eagle that swoops on [1]its prey.
27 "Though I say, 'I will forget [a]my complaint,
I will leave off my *sad* countenance and be cheerful,'
28 I am [a]afraid of all my pains,
I know that [b]Thou wilt not acquit me.
29 "I am accounted [a]wicked,
Why then should I toil in vain?
30 "If I should [a]wash myself with snow
And cleanse [b]my hands with lye,
31 Yet Thou wouldst plunge me into the pit,
And my own clothes would abhor me.
32 "For [a]*He is* not a man as I am that [b]I may answer Him,
That we may go to [1]court together.
33 "There is no [a]umpire between us,
Who may lay his hand upon us both.
34 "Let Him [a]remove His rod from me,
And let not dread of Him terrify me.
35 "*Then* I [a]would speak and not fear Him;
But I am not like that in myself.

Chapter 10

10 "[1][a]I loathe my own life;
I will give full vent to [b]my complaint;
I will speak in the bitterness of my soul.
2 "I will say to God, '[a]Do not condemn me;
Let me know why Thou dost contend with me.
3 'Is it [1]right for Thee indeed to [a]oppress,
To reject [b]the labor of Thy hands,
And [2]to look favorably on [c]the schemes of the wicked?
4 'Hast Thou eyes of flesh?
Or dost Thou [a]see as a man sees?
5 'Are Thy days as the days of a mortal,
Or [a]Thy years as man's years,
6 That [a]Thou shouldst seek for my guilt,

ob 7:19; 10:20 ob 13:26; 27:2
with Gr.; Heb., *me* [a]Job 9:4
[a]Job 9:15 [b]Job 9:29; 15:6
[a]Job 1:1; 12:4; 3:18 [b]Job 7:16
22 [a]Job 10:7, 8
23 [a]Job 24:12
[a]Job 10:3; 12:6; 5:11 [b]Job 12:17
ob 7:6 [b]Job 7:7
t., *food* [a]Is. 18:2 39:29; Hab. 1:8
27 [a]Job 7:11
[a]Job 3:25 [b]Job 7:21; 10:14
› 10:2; Ps. 37:33
. 2:22 [b]Job 31:7
2 [1]Lit., *judgment* :l. 6:10 [b]Job 9:3; Rom. 9:20
[a]1 Sam. 2:25; Job 9:19; Is. 1:18
34 [a]Job 13:21
35 [a]Job 13:22
0:1 [1]Lit., *My soul* *s* [a]Job 7:16 [b]Job 7:11
2 [a]Job 9:29
it., *good* [2]Lit., *you shine forth* [a]Job 22-24; 16:11; 19:6; [b]Job 10:8; 14:15; 38:8; Is. 64:8 [c]Job 21:16; 22:18
[a]1 Sam. 16:7; Job 28:24; 34:21
5 [a]Job 36:26
6 [a]Job 14:16

And search after my sin?
7 'According to Thy knowledge [a]I am indeed not guilty;
Yet there is [b]no deliverance from Thy hand.

8 '[a]Thy hands fashioned and made me [1]altogether,
[b]And wouldst Thou destroy me?
9 'Remember now, that Thou hast made me as [a]clay;
And wouldst Thou [b]turn me into dust again?
10 'Didst Thou not pour me out like milk,
And curdle me like cheese;
11 Clothe me with skin and flesh,
And knit me together with bones and sinews?
12 'Thou hast [a]granted me life and lovingkindness;
And Thy care has preserved my spirit.
13 'Yet [a]these things Thou hast concealed in Thy heart;
I know that this is within Thee:
14 If I sin, then Thou wouldst [a]take note of me,
And [b]wouldst not acquit me of my guilt.
15 'If [a]I am wicked, woe to me!
And [b]if I am righteous, I dare not lift up my head.
I am sated with disgrace and [1]conscious of my misery.
16 'And should *my head* be lifted up, [a]Thou wouldst hunt me like a lion;
And again Thou wouldst show Thy [b]power against me.
17 'Thou dost renew [a]Thy witnesses against me,
And increase Thine anger toward me,
[1b]Hardship after hardship is with me.

18 '[a]Why then hast Thou brought me out of the womb?
Would that I had died and no eye had seen me!
19 'I should have been as though I had not been,
Carried from womb to tomb.'
20 "Would He not let [a]my few days alone?
[1b]Withdraw from me that I may have a little cheer
21 Before I go—[a]and I shall not return—
[b]To the land of darkness and [c]deep shadow;
22 The land of utter gloom as darkness *itself*,
Of deep shadow without order,
And which shines as the darkness."

Chapter 11

11 Then Zophar the Naamathite [1]answered,
2 "Shall a multitude of words go unanswered,
And a [a]talkative man be acquitted?
3 "Shall your boasts silence men?
And shall you [a]scoff and none rebuke?
4 "For [a]you have said, 'My teaching is pure,
And [b]I am innocent in your eyes.'
5 "But would that God might speak,
And open His lips against you,
6 And show you the secrets of wisdom!
For sound wisdom [1a]has two sides.
Know then that God [2]forgets a part of [b]your iniquity.

7 [a]Job 9:21; [b]Job 9:12; 23:
8 [1]Lit., *togeth about* [a]Job 10 119:73 [b]Job 9
9 [a]Job 4:19; 3 7:21
12 [a]Job 33:4
13 [a]Job 23:13
14 [a]Job 7:20 [b] 7:21; 9:28
15 [1]Lit., *see* [a]J Is. 3:11 [b]Job 6:
16 [a]Is. 38:13; L 3:10; Hos. 13:7
17 [1]Lit., *Chang warfare are with* [a]Ruth 1:21; Job [b]Job 7:1
18 [a]Job 3:11-13
20 [1]Lit., *Put* [a]Jo [b]Job 7:16, 19
21 [a]2 Sam. 12:2 3:13-19; 16:22 [b] 88:12 [c]Job 10:2 34:22; 38:17; Ps
11:1 [1]Lit., *answe and said*
2 [a]Job 8:2; 15:2;
3 [a]Job 17:2; 21:3
4 [a]Job 6:10 [b]Job
6 [1]Lit., *is double causes to be forg for you* [a]Job 9:4 15:5; 22:5

7 "[a]Can you discover the depths of God?
Can you discover the limits of the Almighty?
8 "*They are* [a]high as [1]the heavens, what can you do?
Deeper than [2b]Sheol, what can you know?
9 "Its measure is longer than the earth,
And broader than the sea.
10 "If He passes by or shuts up,
Or calls an assembly, [a]who can restrain Him?
11 "For [a]He knows false men,
And He [b]sees iniquity [1]without investigating.
12 "And [1a]an idiot will become intelligent
When the [2]foal of a [b]wild donkey is born a man.

13 "[a]If you would [b]direct your heart right,
And [c]spread out your hand to Him;
14 If iniquity is in your hand, [a]put it far away,
And do not let wickedness dwell in your tents.
15 "Then, indeed, you could [a]lift up your face without *moral* defect,
And you would be steadfast and [b]not fear.
16 "For you would [a]forget *your* trouble,
As [b]waters that have passed by, you would remember *it*.
17 "And your [1]life would be [2a]brighter than noonday;
Darkness would be like the morning.
18 "Then you would trust, because there is hope;
And you would look around and rest securely.
19 "You would [a]lie down and none would disturb *you*,
And many would [b]entreat your [1]favor.
20 "But the [a]eyes of the wicked will fail,
And [1]there will [b]be no escape for them;
And their [c]hope is [2d]to breathe their last."

Chapter 12

12 Then Job [1]responded,
2 "Truly then [a]you are the people,
And with you wisdom will die!
3 "But [a]I have intelligence as well as you;
I am not inferior to you.
And [1]who does not know such things as these?
4 "I am a [a]joke to [1]my friends,
The one who called on God, and He answered him;
The just *and* [b]blameless *man* is a joke.
5 "[1]He who is at ease holds calamity in contempt,
As prepared for those whose feet slip.
6 "The [a]tents of the destroyers prosper,
And those who provoke God [b]are secure,
[1]Whom God brings [c]into their power.

7 "But now ask the beasts, and let them teach you;
And the birds of the heavens, and let them tell you.
8 "Or speak to the earth, and let it teach you;
And let the fish of the sea declare to you.
9 "Who among all these does not know
That [a]the hand of the LORD has done this,
10 [a]In whose hand is the life of every living thing,

:12, 13; 36:26; 23; Rom. 11:33
, *the heights of* [1]I.e., the nether ob 22:12; 35:5 ob 26:6; 38:17
10 [a]Job 9:12
even He does consider [a]Job 23 [b]Job 24:23; 28:24; 31:4
., *a hollow man* nkey [a]Ps. 39:5, :9; 144:4; Eccl. 1:10 [b]Job 39:5
3 [a]Job 5:17-27; 20 [b]1 Sam. 7:3; 8:8 [c]Job 22:27; Ps. 88:9; 143:6
14 [a]Job 22:23
Job 22:26 [b]Ps. 27:3; 46:2
5:16 [b]Job 22:11
., *duration of life* *above noonday* [a]Job 22:26
[1]Lit., *face* [a]Lev. s. 17:2; Mic. 4:4; . 3:13 [b]Is. 45:14
[1]Lit., *escape has* *rished from them* *e expiring of the* Deut. 28:65; Job Job 27:22; 34:22 ob 8:13 [d]Job 6:9
[1]Lit., *answered and said*
2 [a]Job 17:10
Lit., *with whom is re not like these?* [a]Job 13:2
it., *his* [a]Job 17:6; 9, 10; 34:7 [b]Job 6:29
Lit., *Contempt for* *nity is the thought* *im who is at ease*
Or, *He who brings* *nto his hand* [a]Job 9:24; 21:7-9 [b]Job 24:23 [c]Job 22:18
9 [a]Is. 41:20
10 [a]Acts 17:28

And [b]the breath of all mankind?
11 "Does not [a]the ear test words,
As the palate [1]tastes its food?
12 "Wisdom is with [a]aged men,
With [1]long life is understanding.

13 "With Him are [a]wisdom and [a]might;
To Him belong counsel and [b]understanding.
14 "Behold, He [a]tears down, and it cannot be rebuilt;
He [1b]imprisons a man, and [2]there can be no release.
15 "Behold, He [a]restrains the waters, and they dry up;
And He [b]sends them out, and they [1]inundate the earth.
16 "With Him are strength and sound wisdom,
The [a]misled and the misleader belong to Him.
17 "He makes [a]counselors walk [1]barefoot,
And makes fools of [b]judges.
18 "He [a]loosens the [1]bond of kings,
And binds their loins with a girdle.
19 "He makes priests walk [1]barefoot,
And overthrows [a]the secure ones.
20 "He deprives the trusted ones of speech,
And [a]takes away the discernment of the elders.
21 "He [a]pours contempt on nobles,
And [b]loosens the belt of the strong.
22 "He [a]reveals mysteries from the darkness,
And brings the deep darkness into light.
23 "He [a]makes the nations great, then destroys them;
He [1]enlarges the nations, then leads them away.
24 "He [a]deprives of intelligence the chiefs of the earth's people,
And makes them wander in a pathless waste.
25 "They [a]grope in darkness with no light,
And He makes them [b]stagger like a drunken man.

Chapter 13

13 "[a]Behold, my eye has seen all *this*,
My ear has heard and understood it.
2 "[a]What you know I also know.
I am not inferior to you.

3 "But [a]I would speak to [1]the Almighty,
And I desire to [b]argue with God.
4 "But you [a]smear with lies;
You are all [b]worthless physicians.
5 "O that you would [a]be completely silent,
And that it would become your wisdom!
6 "Please hear my argument,
And listen to the contentions of my lips.
7 "Will you [a]speak what is unjust for God,
And speak what is deceitful for Him?
8 "Will you [a]show partiality for Him?
Will you contend for God?
9 "Will it be well when He examines you?
Or [a]will you deceive Him as one deceives a man?
10 "He will surely reprove you,

10 [b]Job 27:3;

11 [1]Lit., *tastes itself* [a]Job 34:

12 [1]Lit., *lengt* [a]Job 15:10; 32

13 [a]Job 9:4 [b] 26:12; 32:8; 36

14 [1]Lit., *shuts* [2]Lit., *it is not o* [a]Job 19:10; Is. [b]Job 37:7

15 [1]Lit., *overt* [a]Deut. 11:17; 1 8:35; 17:1 [b]Ge

16 [a]Job 13:7,

17 [1]Or, *strippe* 3:14 [b]Job 9:24

18 [1]Or, *discipli* 116:16

19 [1]Or, *strippe* 24:22; 34:24-28

20 [a]Job 17:4;

21 [a]Job 34:19; 107:40 [b]Job 12

22 [a]Dan. 2:22; 4:5

23 [1]Or, *spreads* 9:3; 26:15

24 [a]Job 12:20

25 [a]Job 5:14 [b]

13:1 [a]Job 12:9

2 [a]Job 12:3

3 [1]Heb., *Shadd* 13:22; 23:4 [b]Job

4 [a]Ps. 119:69 [b] 23:32

5 [a]Job 13:13; 21 Prov. 17:28

7 [a]Job 27:4

8 [a]Lev. 19:15; P 24:23

9 [a]Job 12:16

If you secretly [a]show partiality.
11 "Will not [a]His [1]majesty terrify you,
And the dread of Him fall on you?
12 "Your memorable sayings are proverbs of ashes,
Your defenses are defenses of clay.

13 "[a]Be silent before me so that I may speak;
Then let come on me what may.
14 "Why should I take my flesh in my teeth,
And [a]put my life in my [1]hands?
15 "[a]Though He slay me,
I will hope in Him.
Nevertheless I [b]will argue my ways [1]before Him.
16 "This also will be my [a]salvation,
For [b]a godless man may not come before His presence.
17 "Listen carefully to my speech,
And let my declaration *fill* your ears.
18 "Behold now, I have [a]prepared my case;
I know that [b]I will be vindicated.
19 "[a]Who will contend with me?
For then I would be silent and [b]die.

20 "Only two things do not do to me,
Then I will not hide from Thy face:
21 [a]Remove Thy [1]hand from me,
And let not the dread of Thee terrify me.
22 "Then call, and [a]I will answer;
Or let me speak, then reply to me.
23 "[a]How many are my iniquities and sins?
Make known to me my [1]rebellion and my sin.
24 "Why dost Thou [a]hide Thy face,
And consider me [b]Thine enemy?
25 "Wilt Thou cause a [a]driven leaf to tremble?
Or wilt Thou pursue the dry [b]chaff?
26 "For Thou dost write [a]bitter things against me,
And dost [b]make me to inherit the iniquities of my youth.
27 "Thou [a]dost put my feet in the stocks,
And dost watch all my paths;
Thou dost [1]set a limit for the soles of my feet,
28 While [1]I am decaying like a [a]rotten thing,
Like a garment that is moth-eaten.

Chapter 14

14 "[a]Man, who is born of woman,
Is [1]short-lived and [b]full of turmoil.
2 "[a]Like a flower he comes forth and withers.
He also flees like [b]a shadow and does not remain.
3 "Thou also dost [a]open Thine eyes on him,
And [b]bring [1]him into judgment with Thyself.
4 "[a]Who can make the clean out of the unclean?
No one!
5 "Since his days are determined,
The [a]number of his months is with Thee,
And his limits Thou hast [1]set so that he cannot pass.

ob 13:8; 32:21; 34:19
exaltation [a]Job 31:23
13 [a]Job 13:5
[1]Lit., *palm* [a]Ps. 119:109
[1]Lit., *to His face* ɔ 7:6 [b]Job 27:5
b 23:7; Is. 12:1; [b]Job 34:21-23
[a]Job 23:4 [b]Job 9:21; 10:7; 12:4
50:8 [b]Job 7:21; 10:8
[1]Lit., *palm* [a]Job 9:34; Ps. 39:10
[a]Job 9:16; 14:15
Or, *transgression* [a]Job 7:21
[a]Ps. 13:1; 44:24; 14; Is. 8:17 [b]Job ; 33:10; Lam. 2:5
[a]Lev. 26:36 [b]Job 21:18
ob 9:18 [b]Ps. 25:7
t., *carve for* [a]Job 33:11
it., *he is* [a]Job 2:7
[1]Lit., *short of days* ob 5:7 [b]Eccl. 2:23
s. 90:5, 6; 103:15; :6, 7; James 1:10; Pet. 1:24 [b]Job 8:9
3 [1]So with some ent versions; M.T., s. 8:4; 144:3 [b]Ps. 143:2
ob 15:14; 25:4; Ps. 51:5
5 [1]Lit., *made* [a]Job 21:21

6 "[a]Turn Thy gaze from him that he may [1]rest,
Until he [2]fulfills his day like a hired man.

7 "For there is hope for a tree,
When it is cut down, that it will sprout again,
And its shoots will not [1]fail.
8 "Though its roots grow old in the ground,
And its stump dies in the dry soil,
9 At the scent of water it will flourish
And put forth sprigs like a plant.
10 "But [a]man dies and lies prostrate.
Man [b]expires, and where is he?
11 "*As* [a]water [1]evaporates from the sea,
And a river becomes parched and dried up,
12 So [a]man lies down and does not rise.
Until the heavens be no more,
[1]He will not awake nor be aroused out of [2]his sleep.

13 "Oh that Thou wouldst hide me in [1]Sheol,
That Thou wouldst conceal me [a]until Thy wrath returns *to Thee,*
That Thou wouldst set a limit for me and remember me!
14 "If a man dies, will he live *again?*
All the days of my struggle I will wait,
Until my change comes.
15 "Thou wilt call, and I will answer Thee;
Thou wilt long for [a]the work of Thy hands.
16 "For now Thou dost [a]number my steps,
Thou dost not [b]observe my sin.
17 "My transgression is [a]sealed up in a bag,
And Thou dost [1]wrap up my iniquity.

18 "But the falling mountain [1]crumbles away,
And the rock moves from its place;
19 Water wears away stones,
Its torrents wash away the dust of the earth;
So Thou dost [a]destroy man's hope.
20 "Thou dost forever overpower him and he [a]departs;
Thou dost change his appearance and send him away.
21 "His sons achieve honor, but [a]he does not know *it;*
Or they become insignificant, but he does not perceive it.
22 "But his [1]body pains him,
And he mourns only for himself."

Chapter 15

15 Then Eliphaz the Temanite [1]responded,
2 "Should a wise man answer with windy knowledge,
[a]And fill [1]himself with the east wind?
3 "Should he argue with useless talk,
Or with words which are not profitable?
4 "Indeed, you do away with [1]reverence,
And hinder meditation before God.
5 "For [a]your guilt teaches your mouth,
And you choose the language of [b]the crafty.
6 "Your [a]own mouth condemns you, and not I;

6 [1]Lit., *cease* ... *makes accepta*... 7:19; Ps. 39:13

7 [1]Or, *cease*

10 [a]Job 3:13; ... [b]Job 13:9

11 [1]Lit., *disapp*... 19:5

12 [1]Lit., *They* ... *their* [a]Job 3:13

13 [1]I.e., the net... world [a]Is. 26:20

15 [a]Job 10:3

16 [a]Job 31:4; 3... Ps. 139:1-3; Pro... [b]Job 10:6

17 [1]Lit., *plaster;* *together* [a]Deut. 32:32-34

18 [1]Lit., *withers*

19 [a]Job 7:6

20 [a]Job 4:20; 20...

21 [a]Eccl. 9:5

22 [1]Lit., *flesh*

15:1 [1]Lit., *answe*... *and said*

2 [1]Lit., *his belly* [a]... 6:26

4 [1]Lit., *fear*

5 [a]Job 22:5 [b]Job 5:12, 13

6 [a]Job 18:7

And your own lips testify against you.

7 "Were you the first man to be born,
Or [a]were you brought forth before the hills?
8 "Do you hear the [a]secret counsel of God,
And limit wisdom to yourself?
9 "[a]What do you know that we do not know?
What do you understand that [1]we do not?
10 "Both the [a]gray-haired and the aged are among us,
Older than your father.
11 "Are [a]the consolations of God too small for you,
Even the [b]word *spoken* gently with you?
12 "Why does your [a]heart carry you away?
And why do your eyes flash,
13 That you should turn your spirit against God,
And allow *such* words to go out of your mouth?
14 "What is man, that [a]he should be pure,
Or [b]he who is born of a woman, that he should be righteous?
15 "Behold, He puts no trust in His [a]holy ones,
And the [b]heavens are not pure in His sight;
16 How much less one who is [a]detestable and corrupt,
Man, who [b]drinks iniquity like water!

17 "I will tell you, listen to me;
And what I have seen I will also declare;
18 What wise men have told,
And have not concealed from [a]their fathers,
19 To whom alone the land was given,
And no alien passed among them.
20 "The wicked man writhes [a]in pain all *his* days,
And [1]numbered are the years [b]stored up for the ruthless.
21 "[1]Sounds of [a]terror are in his ears,
[b]While at peace the destroyer comes upon him.
22 "He does not believe that he will [a]return from darkness,
And he is destined for [b]the sword.
23 "He wanders about for food, saying, 'Where is it?'
He knows that a day of [a]darkness is [1]at hand.
24 "Distress and anguish terrify him,
They overpower him like a king ready for the attack,
25 Because he has stretched out his hand against God,
And conducts himself [a]arrogantly against [1]the Almighty.
26 "He rushes [1]headlong at Him
With [2]his massive shield.
27 "For he has [a]covered his face with his fat,
And made his thighs heavy with flesh.
28 "And he has [a]lived in desolate cities,
In houses no one would inhabit,
Which are destined to become [1]ruins.
29 "He [a]will not become rich, nor will his wealth endure;
And his grain will not bend down to the ground.
30 "He will [a]not [1]escape from darkness;
The [b]flame will wither his shoots,
And by [c]the breath of His mouth he will go away.
31 "Let him not [a]trust in emptiness, deceiving himself;

38:4, 21; Prov. 8:25
ob 29:4; Rom. 34; 1 Cor. 2:11
not within us? [a]Job 12:3; 13:2
12:12; 32:6, 7
5:17-19; 36:15, ob 6:10; 23:12
ob 11:13; 36:13
Job 14:4; Prov. Eccl. 7:20 [b]Job 25:4
5:1 [b]Job 25:5
4:1 [b]Job 34:7; Prov. 19:28
[a]Job 8:8; 20:4
, the number of are [a]Job 15:24 Job 24:1; 27:13
[1]Lit., *A sound of* s is [a]Job 15:24; 1; 20:25; 24:17; :20 [b]Job 20:21; 1 Thess. 5:3
[a]Job 15:30 [b]Job 9; 27:14; 33:18; 36:12
Lit., *ready at his* [a]Job 15:22, 30
[1]Heb., *Shaddai* [a]Job 36:9
[1]Lit., *with a stiff neck* [2]Lit., *the* k-bossed shields
[a]Ps. 73:7; 119:70
[1]Or, *heaps* [a]Job 3:14; Is. 5:8, 9
[a]Job 27:16, 17
, *turn aside* [a]Job 5:22 [b]Job 15:34; :26; 22:20; 31:12 [c]Job 4:9
ob 35:13; Is. 59:4

For emptiness will be his [1]reward.
32 "It will be accomplished [a]before his time,
And his palm [b]branch will not be green.
33 "He will drop off his unripe grape like the vine,
And will [a]cast off his flower like the olive tree.
34 "For the company of [a]the godless is barren,
And fire consumes [b]the tents of [1]the corrupt.
35 "They [a]conceive [1]mischief and bring forth iniquity,
And their [2]mind prepares deception."

Chapter 16

16 Then Job [1]answered,
2 "I have heard many such things;
[1a]Sorry comforters are you all.
3 "Is there *no* limit to [a]windy words?
Or what plagues you that you answer?
4 "I too could speak like you,
If [1]I were in your place.
I could compose words against you,
And [a]shake my head at you.
5 "I could strengthen you with my mouth,
And the solace of my lips could lessen *your pain.*

6 "If I speak, [a]my pain is not lessened,
And if I hold back, what has left me?
7 "But now He has [a]exhausted me;
Thou hast laid [b]waste all my company.
8 "And Thou hast shriveled me up,
[a]It has become a witness;
And my [b]leanness rises up against me,
It testifies to my face.
9 "His anger has [a]torn me and [1]hunted me down,
He has [b]gnashed at me with His teeth;
My [c]adversary [2]glares at me.
10 "They have [a]gaped at me with their mouth,
They have [1b]slapped me on the cheek with contempt;
They have [c]massed themselves against me.
11 "God hands me over to ruffians,
And tosses me into the hands of the wicked.
12 "I was at ease, but [a]He shattered me,
And He has grasped me by the neck and shaken me to pieces;
He has also set me up as His [b]target.
13 "His [a]arrows surround me.
Without mercy He splits my kidneys open;
He pours out [b]my gall on the ground.
14 "He [a]breaks through me with breach after breach;
He [b]runs at me like a warrior.
15 "I have sewed [a]sackcloth over my skin,
And [b]thrust my horn in the dust.
16 "My face is flushed from [a]weeping,
[b]And deep darkness is on my eyelids,
17 Although there is no [a]violence in my hands,
And [b]my prayer is pure.

31 [1]Lit., *exch*
32 [a]Job 22:16 7:17 [b]Job 18:
33 [a]Job 14:2
34 [1]Lit., *a brib* 8:13 [b]Job 8:22
35 [1]Or, *pain* [2] [a]Ps. 7:14; Is. 5
16:1 [1]Lit., *ans and said*
2 [1]Lit., *Comfo trouble* [a]Job 1
3 [a]Job 6:26
4 [1]Lit., *your so in place of my s* 22:7; 109:25; Z 2:15; Matt. 27:3
6 [a]Job 9:27, 28
7 [a]Job 7:3 [b]Jo 19:13-15
8 [a]Job 10:17 [b] 19:20; Ps. 109:
9 [1]Lit., *borne a against me* [2]Lit. *sharpens his ey* 19:11; Hos. 6:1 35:16; Lam. 2:1 7:54 [c]Job 13:24
10 [1]Lit., *struck* 22:13 [b]Is. 50:6; 3:30; Acts 23:2 30:12; Ps. 35:15
12 [a]Job 9:17 [b]J 7:20; Lam. 3:12
13 [a]Job 6:4; 19: 25:3 [b]Job 20:25
14 [a]Job 9:17 [b]J
15 [a]Gen. 37:34; 69:11 [b]Ps. 7:5
16 [a]Job 16:20 [b]J 24:17
17 [a]Is. 59:6; Jon. [b]Job 27:4

18 "O earth, do not cover my blood,
And let there be no *resting* place for my cry.
19 "Even now, behold, [a]my witness is in heaven,
And my [1]advocate is [b]on high.
20 "My friends are my scoffers;
[a]My eye [1]weeps to God.
21 "O that a man might plead with God
As a man with his neighbor!
22 "For when a few years are past,
I shall go the way [a]of no return.

Chapter 17

17 "My spirit is broken, my days are extinguished,
The [1a]grave is *ready* for me.
2 "[a]Surely mockers are with me,
And my eye [1]gazes on their provocation.

3 "Lay down, now, a pledge [a]for me with Thyself;
Who is there that will [1]be my guarantor?
4 "For Thou hast [1a]kept their heart from understanding;
Therefore Thou wilt not exalt *them.*
5 "He who [a]informs against friends for a share *of the spoil,*
The [b]eyes of his children also shall languish.

6 "But He has made me a [a]byword of the people,
And I am [1]one at whom men [b]spit.
7 "My eye has also grown [a]dim because of grief,
And all my [b]members are as a shadow.
8 "The upright shall be appalled at this,
And the [a]innocent shall stir up himself against the godless.
9 "Nevertheless [a]the righteous shall hold to his way,
And [b]he who has clean hands shall grow stronger and stronger.
10 "But come again all of [1]you now,
For I [a]do not find a wise man among you.
11 "My [a]days are past, my plans are torn apart,
Even the wishes of my heart.
12 "They make night into day, *saying,*
'The light is near,' in the presence of darkness.
13 "If I look for [a]Sheol as my home,
I [1]make my bed in the darkness;
14 If I call to the [a]pit, 'You are my father';
To the [b]worm, 'my mother and my sister';
15 Where now is [a]my hope?
And who regards my hope?
16 "[1]Will it go down with me to Sheol?
Shall we together [a]go down into the dust?"

Chapter 18

18 Then Bildad the Shuhite [1]responded,
2 "How long will you hunt for words?
Show understanding and then we can talk.
3 "Why are we [a]regarded as beasts,
As stupid in your eyes?
4 "O [1]you who tear yourself in your anger—

itness [a]Gen. ob 19:25-27; :9; Phil. 1:8; :5 [b]Job 31:2
os [a]Job 17:7
22 [a]Job 3:13
graves [a]Ps. 88:3, 4
lodges [a]Job 12:4; 17:6
ke hands with . 119:122; Is. 38:14
, hidden [a]Job 12:20
9:13, 16 [b]Job 11:20
spitting to the Job 17:2 [b]Job 30:10
:16 [b]Job 16:8
8 [a]Job 22:19
rov. 4:18 [b]Job 22:30; 31:7
some ancient versions; M.T., hem [a]Job 12:2
11 [a]Job 7:6
Lit., *spread out* [a]Job 3:13
Job 7:5; 13:28; Job 21:26; 25:6
15 [a]Job 7:6
So the Gr.; Heb. ly, *Let my limbs down to Sheol, ere is rest in the r all.* [a]Job 3:17; 21:33
[1]Lit., *answered and said*
3 [a]Ps. 73:22
Lit., *he . . . tears himself . . . his*

For your sake is the earth to be abandoned,
Or the rock to be moved from its place?

5 "Indeed, the [a]light of the wicked goes out,
And the [1]flame of his fire gives no light.
6 "The light in his tent is [a]darkened,
And his lamp goes out above him.
7 "His [1]vigorous stride is shortened,
And his [a]own scheme brings him down.
8 "For he is [a]thrown into the net by his own feet,
And he steps on the webbing.
9 "A snare seizes *him* by the heel,
And a trap snaps shut on him.
10 "A noose for him is hidden in the ground,
And a trap for him on the path.
11 "All around [a]terrors frighten him,
And [b]harry him at every step.
12 "His strength is [a]famished,
And calamity is ready at his side.
13 "[1]His skin is devoured by disease,
The first-born of death [a]devours his [2]limbs.
14 "He is [a]torn from [1]the security of his tent,
And [2]they march him before the king of [b]terrors.
15 "[1]There dwells in his tent nothing of his;
[a]Brimstone is scattered on his habitation.
16 "His [a]roots are dried below,
And his [b]branch is cut off above.
17 "[a]Memory of him perishes from the earth,
And he has no name abroad.
18 "[1]He is driven from light [a]into darkness,
And [b]chased from the inhabited world.
19 "He has no [a]offspring or posterity among his people,
Nor any survivor where he sojourned.
20 "Those [1]in the west are appalled at [a]his [2]fate,
And those [3]in the east are seized with horror.
21 "Surely such are the [a]dwellings of the wicked,
And this is the place of him who does not know God."

Chapter 19

19 Then Job [1]responded,
2 "How long will you torment [1]me,
And crush me with words?
3 "These ten times you have insulted me,
You are not ashamed to wrong me.
4 "Even if I have truly erred,
My error lodges with me.
5 "If indeed you [a]vaunt yourselves against me,
And prove my disgrace to me,
6 Know then that [a]God has wronged me,
And has closed [b]His net around me.

7 "Behold, [a]I cry, 'Violence!' but I get no answer;
I shout for help, but there is no justice.
8 "He has [a]walled up my way so that I cannot pass;

5 [1]Lit., *spark* 21:17; Prov. 24:20
6 [a]Job 12:25
7 [1]Lit., *steps strength* [a]Job
8 [a]Job 22:10 35:8; Is. 24:1
11 [a]Job 15:2 18:18; 20:8
12 [a]Is. 8:21
13 [1]Heb., *It e of his skin* [2]O [a]Zech. 14:12
14 [1]Lit., *his te trust* [2]Or, *you shall march* [a] 18:6 [b]Job 15:
15 [1]A sugges reading is *Fire his tent* [a]Ps. 1
16 [a]Is. 5:24; H Amos 2:9; Ma [b]Job 15:30, 32
17 [a]Job 24:20 34:16; Prov. 10
18 [1]Lit., *They . . . And chase* 5:14; Is. 8:22; 1 [b]Job 20:8; 27:2
19 [a]Job 27:14, 14:22
20 [1]Lit., *who c after* [2]Lit., *day who have gone* [a]Ps. 37:13; Jer. Obad. 12
21 [a]Job 21:28
19:1 [1]Lit., *answ and said*
2 [1]Lit., *my soul*
5 [a]Ps. 35:26; 38 55:12, 13
6 [a]Job 16:11; 27 18:8-10; Ps. 66: 1:13
7 [a]Job 9:24; 30: Hab. 1:2
8 [a]Job 3:23; Lar

And He has put [b]darkness on my paths.
9 "He has [a]stripped my honor from me,
And removed the [b]crown from my head.
10 "He [a]breaks me down on every side, and I am gone;
And He has uprooted my [b]hope [c]like a tree.
11 "He has also [a]kindled His anger against me,
And [b]considered me as His enemy.
12 "His [a]troops come together,
And [b]build up their [1]way against me,
And camp around my tent.

13 "He has [a]removed my brothers far from me,
And my [b]acquaintances are completely estranged from me.
14 "My relatives have failed,
And my [a]intimate friends have forgotten me.
15 "Those who live in my house and my maids consider me a stranger.
I am a foreigner in their sight.
16 "I call to my servant, but he does not answer,
I have to implore him with my mouth.
17 "My breath is [1]offensive to my wife,
And I am loathsome to my own brothers.
18 "Even young children despise me;
I rise up and they speak against me.
19 "All [1]my [a]associates abhor me,
And those I love have turned against me.
20 "My [a]bone clings to my skin and my flesh,
And I have escaped *only* by the skin of my teeth.
21 "Pity me, pity me, O you my friends,
For the [a]hand of God has struck me.
22 "Why do you [a]persecute me as God *does*,
And are not satisfied with my flesh?

23 "Oh that my words were written!
Oh that they were [a]inscribed in a book!
24 "That with an iron stylus and lead
They were engraved in the rock forever!
25 "And as for me, I know that [a]my [1]Redeemer lives,
And [2]at the last He will take His stand on the [3]earth.
26 "Even after my skin [1]is destroyed,
Yet from my flesh I shall [a]see God;
27 Whom I [1]myself shall behold,
And whom my eyes shall see and not another.
My [2]heart [a]faints [3]within me.
28 "If you say, 'How shall we [a]persecute him?'
And '[1]What pretext for a case against him can we find?'
29 "*Then* be afraid of [a]the sword for yourselves,
For wrath *brings* the punishment of the sword,
So that you may know [b]there is judgment."

Chapter 20

20 Then Zophar the Naamathite [1]answered,
2 "Therefore my disquieting thoughts make me [1]respond,
Even because of my [2]inward agitation.

8 [b]Job 30:26
12:17, 19; Ps.
Job 16:15; Ps.
39; Lam. 5:16
ob 12:14 [b]Job
:6 [c]Job 24:20
Job 16:9 [b]Job
13:24; 33:10
I.e., siegework
13 [b]Job 30:12
16:7; Ps. 69:8
0; Ps. 88:8, 18
14 [a]Job 19:19
7 [1]Lit., *strange*
, the men of my
ncil [a]Ps. 38:11;
55:12, 13
ob 16:8; 33:21;
102:5; Lam. 4:8
b 1:11; Ps. 38:2
[a]Job 13:24, 25;
19:6; Ps. 69:26
. 30:8; Jer. 36:2
[1]Or, *Vindicator,*
der; lit., *kinsman*
as the Last [3]Lit.,
[a]Job 16:19; Ps.
; Prov. 23:11; Is.
43:14; Jer. 50:34
[1]Lit., *which they*
ut off [a]Ps. 17:15;
:8; 1 Cor. 13:12;
1 John 3:2
[1]Or, *on my side*
neys [3]Lit., *in my*
loins [a]Ps. 73:26
Or, *the root of the*
er is found in him
[a]Job 19:22
[a]Job 15:22 [b]Job
Ps. 1:5; 9:7; Eccl.
12:14
1 [1]Lit., *answered*
and said
[1]Lit., *return* [2]Lit.,
haste within me

3 "I listened to [a]the reproof which insults me,
And the spirit of my understanding makes me answer.
4 "Do you know this from [a]of old,
From the establishment of man on earth,
5 That the [a]triumphing of the wicked is short,
And [b]the joy of the godless momentary?
6 "Though his loftiness [1a]reaches the heavens,
And his head touches the clouds,
7 He [a]perishes forever like his refuse;
Those who have seen him [b]will say, 'Where is he?'
8 "He flies away like a [a]dream, and they cannot find him;
Even like a vision of the night he is [b]chased away.
9 "The [a]eye which saw him sees him no more,
And [b]his place no longer beholds him.
10 "His [a]sons [1]favor the poor,
And his hands [b]give back his wealth.
11 "His [a]bones are full of his youthful vigor,
But it lies down with him [1]in the dust.

12 "Though [a]evil is sweet in his mouth,
And he hides it under his tongue,
13 *Though* he [1]desires it and will not let it go,
But holds it [a]in his [2]mouth,
14 *Yet* his food in his stomach is changed
To the [1]venom of cobras within him.
15 "He swallows riches,
But will [a]vomit them up;
God will expel them from his belly.
16 "He sucks [a]the poison of cobras;
The viper's tongue slays him.
17 "He does not look at [a]the streams,
The rivers flowing with honey and curds.
18 "He [a]returns what he has attained
And cannot swallow *it;*
As to the riches of his trading,
He cannot even enjoy *them.*
19 "For he has [a]oppressed *and* forsaken the poor;
He has seized a house which he has not built.

20 "Because he knew no quiet [1]within him
He does [a]not retain anything he desires.
21 "Nothing remains [1]for him to devour,
Therefore [a]his prosperity does not endure.
22 "In the fulness of his plenty he will be cramped;
The [a]hand of everyone who suffers will come *against* him.
23 "When he [a]fills his belly,
God will send His fierce anger on him
And will [b]rain *it* on him [1]while he is eating.
24 "He may [a]flee from the iron weapon,
But the bronze bow will pierce him.
25 "It is drawn forth and comes out of his back,
Even the glittering point from [a]his gall.
[b]Terrors come upon him,
26 Complete [a]darkness is held in reserve for his treasures,

3 [a]Job 19:3
4 [a]Job 8:8
5 [a]Job 8:12, 37:35, 36 [b]Jo
6 [1]Lit., *goes* 14:13, 14; Ob
7 [a]Job 4:20; [b]Job 7:10; 8:1
8 [a]Ps. 73:20; 18:18; 27:21-
9 [a]Job 7:8; 8: 7:10
10 [1]Or, *seek of* [a]Job 5:4; 2 20:18; 27:16,
11 [1]Lit., *on* [a]J 21:23, 24
12 [a]Job 15:16
13 [1]Lit., *has compassion or palate* [a]Num. 33; Job 20:23
14 [1]Lit., *gall*
15 [a]Job 20:10,
16 [a]Deut. 32:2
17 [a]Deut. 32:1 Job 29:6
18 [a]Job 20:10,
19 [a]Job 24:2-4
20 [1]Lit., *in his b* [a]Eccl. 5:13-15
21 [1]Or, *of what devours* [a]Job 1
22 [a]Job 5:5
23 [1]Or, *as his fo* [a]Job 20:13, 14 [b] 11:18-20, 33; Ps. 78:30, 31
24 [a]Is. 24:18; Am 5:19
25 [a]Job 16:13 [b] 18:11, 14
26 [a]Job 18:18

And unfanned [b]fire will devour him;
It will consume the survivor in his tent.
27 "The [a]heavens will reveal his iniquity,
And the earth will rise up against him.
28 "The [a]increase of his house will depart;
His possessions will flow away [b]in the day of His anger.
29 "This is the wicked man's [a]portion from God,
Even the heritage decreed to him by God."

Chapter 21

21 Then Job [1]answered,
2 "Listen carefully to my speech,
And let this be your *way of* consolation.
3 "Bear with me that I may speak;
Then after I have spoken, you may [a]mock.
4 "As for me, is [a]my complaint [1]to man?
And [b]why should [2]I not be impatient?
5 "Look at me, and be astonished,
And [a]put *your* hand over *your* mouth.
6 "Even when I remember, I am disturbed,
And [a]horror takes hold of my flesh.
7 "Why [a]do the wicked *still* live,
Continue on, also become very [b]powerful?
8 "Their [1a]descendants are established with them in their sight,
And their offspring before their eyes,
9 Their houses [a]are safe from fear,
Neither is the rod of God on them.
10 "His ox mates [1]without fail;
His cow calves and does not abort.
11 "They send forth their little ones like the flock,
And their children skip about.
12 "They [1]sing to the timbrel and harp
And rejoice at the sound of the flute.
13 "They [a]spend their days in prosperity,
And [1]suddenly they go down to [2]Sheol.
14 "And they say to God, '[a]Depart from us!
We do not even desire the knowledge of Thy ways.
15 '[1]Who is [2]the Almighty, that we should serve Him,
And [a]what would we gain if we entreat Him?'
16 "Behold, their prosperity is not in their hand;
The [a]counsel of the wicked is far from me.

17 "How often is [a]the lamp of the wicked put out,
Or *does* their [b]calamity fall on them?
Does [1]God apportion destruction in His anger?
18 "Are they as [a]straw before the wind,
And like [b]chaff which the storm carries away?
19 "*You say,* '[a]God stores away [1]a man's iniquity for his sons.'
Let [2]God repay him so that he may know *it*.
20 "Let his [a]own eyes see his decay,
And let him [b]drink of the wrath of [1]the Almighty.
21 "For what does he care for his household [1]after him,
When the number of his months is cut off?
22 "Can anyone [a]teach God knowledge,

5:30; Ps. 21:9
eut. 31:28; Is. 26:21
ut. 28:31 [b]Job 20:15; 21:30
27:13; 31:2, 3
[1]Lit., *answered and said*
[a]Job 11:3; 17:2
gainst [2]Lit., *my* [a]Job 7:11 [b]Job 6:11
udg. 18:19; Job 13:5; 29:9; 40:4
6 [a]Ps. 55:5
9:24; Ps. 73:3; 12:1; Hab. 1:13 [b]Job 12:19
eed [a]Ps. 17:14
9 [a]Job 12:6
t., *and does not fail*
Lit., *lifted up the voice*
3 [1]So with most rsions; M.T., *are* ttered by Sheol. the nether world Job 21:23; 36:11
14 [a]Job 22:17
it., *What* [2]Heb., ddai [a]Job 22:17; 34:9
16 [a]Job 22:18
., *He* [a]Job 18:5, 6 [b]Job 31:2, 3
[a]Job 13:25; Ps. Ps. 1:4; 35:5; Is. 17:13; Hos. 13:3
it., *his* [2]Lit., *Him* 20:5; Jer. 31:29; Ezek. 18:2
[1]Heb., *Shaddai* m. 14:28-32; Jer. ; Ezek. 18:4 [b]Ps.):3; Is. 51:17; Jer. 25:15; Rev. 14:10
[1]I.e., *after he dies*
Job 35:11; 36:22; 0:14; Rom. 11:34

In that He [b]judges those on high?
23 "One [a]dies in his full strength,
Being wholly at ease and [1]satisfied;
24 His [1]sides are filled out with fat,
And the [a]marrow of his bones is moist,
25 While another dies with a bitter soul,
Never even [1]tasting *anything* good.
26 "Together they [a]lie down in the dust,
And [b]worms cover them.

27 "Behold, I know your thoughts,
And the plans by which you would wrong me.
28 "For you say, 'Where is the house of [a]the nobleman,
And where is the [b]tent, the dwelling places of the wicked?'
29 "Have you not asked wayfaring men,
And do you not recognize their [1]witness?
30 "For the [a]wicked is reserved for the day of calamity;
They will be led forth at [b]the day of fury.
31 "Who will [1]confront him with his actions,
And who will repay him for what he has done?
32 "While he is carried to the grave,
Men will keep watch over *his* tomb.
33 "The [a]clods of the valley will [1]gently cover him;
Moreover, [b]all men will [2]follow after him,
While countless ones *go* before him.
34 "How then will you vainly [a]comfort me,
For your answers remain *full of* [1]falsehood?"

Chapter 22

22 Then Eliphaz the Temanite [1]responded,
2 "Can a vigorous [a]man be of use to God,
Or a wise man be useful to himself?
3 "Is there any pleasure to [1]the Almighty if you are righteous,
Or profit if you make your ways perfect?
4 "Is it because of your [1]reverence that He reproves you,
That He [a]enters into judgment against you?
5 "Is not [a]your wickedness great,
And your iniquities without end?
6 "For you have [a]taken pledges of your brothers without cause,
And [b]stripped [1]men naked.
7 "To the weary you have [a]given no water to drink,
And from the hungry you have [b]withheld bread.
8 "But the earth [a]belongs to the [b]mighty man,
And [c]the honorable man dwells in it.
9 "You have sent [a]widows away empty,
And the [1]strength of the [b]orphans has been crushed.
10 "Therefore [a]snares surround you,
And sudden [b]dread terrifies you,
11 Or [a]darkness, so that you cannot see,
And an [b]abundance of water covers you.

12 "Is not God [a]*in* the height of heaven?
Look also at the [1]distant stars, how high they are!
13 "And you say, '[a]What does God know?

22 [b]Job 4:18; Ps. 82:1
23 [1]Or, *quiet* 20:11; 21:13
24 [1]So with S uncertain. Son as, *his pails a milk* [a]Prov. 3:8
25 [1]Lit., *eating*
26 [a]Job 3:13; Eccl. 9:2 [b]Job 14:11
28 [a]Job 1:3; 3 [b]Job 8:22; 18:2
29 [1]Lit., *signs*
30 [a]Job 20:29; 16:4; 2 Pet. 2:9 21:17, 20; 40:1
31 [1]Lit., *declar to his face*
33 [1]Lit., *be sw him* [2]Lit., *draw* 3:22; 17:16 [b]Jo 24:24
34 [1]Or, *faithles* [a]Job 16:2
22:1 [1]Lit., *answ and said*
2 [a]Job 35:7; Lu
3 [1]Heb., *Shado*
4 [1]Or, *fear* [a]Jo 19:29
5 [a]Job 11:6; 15:
6 [1]Lit., *clothing naked* [a]Ex. 22:2 24:6, 17; Job 24 Ezek. 18:16 [b]Jo 31:19, 20
7 [a]Job 31:16, 17 31:31
8 [a]Job 9:24 [b]Jo 12:19 [c]Is. 3:3; 9
9 [1]Lit., *arms* [a]Jo 21; 29:13; 31:16, [b]Job 6:27
10 [a]Job 18:8 [b]Jo 15:21
11 [a]Job 5:14 [b]Jo 38:34; Ps. 69:2; 1 Lam. 3:54
12 [1]Lit., *head, to* [a]Job 11:7-9
13 [a]Ps. 10:11; 59 64:5; 94:7; Is. 29: Ezek. 8:12

Can He judge through the thick darkness?
14 "[a]Clouds are a hiding place for Him, so that He cannot see;
And He walks on the [1]vault of heaven.'
15 "Will you keep to the ancient path
Which [a]wicked men have trod,
16 Who were snatched away [a]before their time,
Whose [b]foundations were [1]washed away by a river?
17 "They [a]said to God, 'Depart from us!'
And 'What can [1]the Almighty do to them?'
18 "Yet He [a]filled their houses with good *things;*
But [b]the counsel of the wicked is far from me.
19 "The [a]righteous see and are glad,
And the innocent mock them,
20 *Saying,* 'Truly our adversaries are cut off,
And their [1]abundance [a]the fire has consumed.'

21 "[1a]Yield now and be at peace with Him;
Thereby good will come to you.
22 "Please receive [1a]instruction from His mouth,
And establish His words in your heart.
23 "If you [a]return to [1]the Almighty, you will be [2]restored;
If you [b]remove unrighteousness far from your tent,
24 And [a]place *your* [1]gold in the dust,
And *the gold of* Ophir among the stones of the brooks,
25 Then [1]the Almighty will be your [2]gold
And choice silver to you.
26 "For then you will [a]delight in [1]the Almighty,
And lift up your face to God.
27 "You will [a]pray to Him, and [b]He will hear you;
And you will pay your vows.
28 "You will also decree a thing, and it will be established for you;
And [a]light will shine on your ways.
29 "When [1]you are cast down, you will speak with [2]confidence
And the [3a]humble person He will save.
30 "He will deliver one who is not innocent,
And he will be [a]delivered through the cleanness of your hands."

Chapter 23

23 Then Job [1]replied,
2 "Even today my [a]complaint is rebellion;
[1]His hand is [b]heavy despite my groaning.
3 "Oh that I knew where I might find Him,
That I might come to His seat!
4 "I would [a]present *my* case before Him
And fill my mouth with arguments.
5 "I would learn the words *which* He would [1]answer,
And perceive what He would say to me.
6 "Would He contend with me by [a]the greatness of *His* power?
No, surely He would pay attention to me.
7 "There the upright would [a]reason with Him;
And I [1]would be [b]delivered forever from my Judge.

8 "Behold, I go forward but He is not *there,*
And backward, but I [a]cannot perceive Him;

ircle [a]Job 26:9
15 [a]Job 34:36
Lit., *poured out* 5:32; 21:13, 18 9; Ps. 90:5; Is. ; Matt. 7:26, 27
[1]Heb., *Shaddai* [a]Job 21:14, 15
[a]Job 12:6 [b]Job 21:16
Ps. 52:6; 58:10; 107:42
r, *excess* [a]Job 15:30
21 [1]Or, *Know tely* [a]Ps. 34:10
law [a]Job 6:10; 23:12; Prov. 2:6
[1]Heb., *Shaddai ilt up* [a]Job 8:5; Is. 19:22; 31:6; 1:3 [b]Job 11:14
[1]Lit., *ore* [a]Job 31:24, 25
[1]Heb., *Shaddai* [2]Lit., *ore*
[1]Heb., *Shaddai* 10; Ps. 37:4; Is. 58:14
ob 11:13; 33:26; 58:9 [b]Job 34:28
11:17; Ps. 112:4
t., *they cast you* [2]Lit., *pride* [3]Lit., *eyes* [a]Job 5:11; 5:7; Matt. 23:12; s 4:6; 1 Pet. 5:5
Job 42:7, 8; Ps. 18:20; 24:3, 4
[1]Lit., *answered and said*
ith Gr. and Syr.; ., *My* [a]Job 7:11 6:2, 3; Ps. 32:4
4 [a]Job 13:18
[1]Lit., *answer me*
6 [a]Job 9:4
r, *bring forth my ice forever* [a]Job Job 13:16; 23:10
[a]Job 9:11; 35:14

9 When He acts on the left, I cannot behold *Him;*
He turns on the right, I cannot see Him.
10 "But He knows the [1]way I take;
When He has [a]tried me, I shall come forth as gold.
11 "My foot has [a]held fast to His path;
I have kept His way and not turned aside.
12 "I have not departed from the command of His lips;
I have treasured the [a]words of His mouth [1]more than my
[2]necessary food.
13 "But He is unique and who can turn Him?
And *what* His soul desires, that He does.
14 "For He performs what is appointed for me,
And many such *decrees* are with Him.
15 "Therefore, I would be dismayed at His presence;
When I consider, I am terrified of Him.
16 "*It is* God *who* has made my [a]heart faint,
And the Almighty *who* has dismayed me,
17 But I [a]am not silenced by the darkness,
Nor [b]deep gloom *which* covers *me.*

Chapter 24

24 "[a]Why are [1]times not stored up by the Almighty,
And why do those who know Him not see [b]His days?
2 "[1]Some [a]remove the landmarks;
They seize and [2]devour flocks.
3 "They drive away the donkeys of the [a]orphans;
They take the [b]widow's ox for a pledge.
4 "They push [a]the needy aside from the road;
The [b]poor of the land are made to hide themselves altogether.
5 "Behold, as [a]wild donkeys in the wilderness
They [b]go forth seeking food in their activity,
As [1]bread for *their* children in the desert.
6 "They harvest their fodder in the field,
And they glean the vineyard of the wicked.
7 "[a]They spend the night naked, without clothing,
And have no covering against the cold.
8 "They are wet with the mountain rains,
And they hug the rock for want of a shelter.
9 "[1]Others snatch the [a]orphan from the breast,
And against the poor they take a pledge.
10 "They cause *the poor* to go about naked without clothing,
And they take away the sheaves from the hungry.
11 "Within the walls they produce oil;
They tread wine presses but thirst.
12 "From the city men groan,
And the souls of the wounded cry out;
Yet God [a]does not pay attention to folly.

13 "[1]Others have been with those who rebel against the light;
They do not want to know its ways,
Nor abide in its paths.
14 "The murderer [a]arises at dawn;
He [b]kills the poor and the needy,
And at night he is as a thief.

10 [1]Lit., *way w*
[a]Job 7:18; Ps. 66:10; Zech. 1
1 Pet. 1:7

11 [a]Job 31:7;
44:18

12 [1]Or, with sc
versions, *in my*
[2]Lit., *prescribed*
[a]Job 6:10; 22:2

16 [a]Deut. 20:3
27:2; Jer. 51:46

17 [a]Job 10:18,
19:8

24:1 [1]I.e., time
judgment [a]Acts
2:12; Jer. 46:10
15; Zeph. 1:7

2 [1]Lit., *They* [2]
pasture [a]Deut.
27:17; Prov. 23

3 [a]Job 6:27 [b]D
24:17; Job 22:9

4 [a]Job 24:14; 2
30:25; 31:19 [b]J
29:12; Ps. 41:1;
14:31; 28:28; Ar

5 [1]Lit., *his brea*
39:5-8 [b]Ps. 104

7 [a]Ex. 22:26; J

9 [1]Lit., *They* [a]J

12 [a]Job 9:23, 2

13 [1]Lit., *They*

14 [a]Mic. 2:1 [b]P

15 "And the eye of the [a]adulterer waits for the twilight,
Saying, 'No eye will see me.'
And he [1]disguises his face.
16 "In the dark they [a]dig into houses,
They [b]shut themselves up by day;
They do not know the light.
17 "For the morning is the same to him as thick darkness,
For he is familiar with the [a]terrors of thick darkness.

18 "They are [1a]insignificant on the surface of the water;
Their portion is [b]cursed on the earth.
They do not turn [2]toward the [c]vineyards.
19 "Drought and heat [1a]consume the snow waters,
So does [2b]Sheol *those who* have sinned.
20 "A [1a]mother will forget him;
The [b]worm feeds sweetly till he is remembered [c]no more.
And wickedness will be broken [d]like a tree.
21 "He wrongs the [1]barren woman,
And does no good for [a]the widow.
22 "But He drags off the valiant by [a]His power;
He rises, but [b]no one has assurance of life.
23 "He provides them [a]with security, and they are supported;
And His [b]eyes are on their ways.
24 "They are exalted a [a]little while, then they are gone;
Moreover, they are [b]brought low and like everything
gathered up;
Even like the heads of grain they are cut off.
25 "Now if it is not so, [a]who can prove me a liar,
And make my speech worthless?"

Chapter 25

25 Then Bildad the Shuhite [1]answered,
2 "[a]Dominion and awe [1]belong to Him
Who establishes peace in [b]His heights.
3 "Is there any number to [a]His troops?
And upon whom does His light not rise?
4 "How then can a man be [a]just with God?
Or how can he be [b]clean who is born of woman?
5 "If even [a]the moon has no brightness
And the [b]stars are not pure in His sight,
6 How much less [a]man, *that* [b]maggot,
And the son of man, *that* worm!"

Chapter 26

26 Then Job [1]responded,
2 "What a help you are to [1a]the weak!
How you have saved the arm [b]without strength!
3 "What counsel you have given to *one* without wisdom!
What helpful insight you have abundantly [1]provided!
4 "To whom have you uttered words?
And whose [1]spirit was expressed through you?

5 "The [1a]departed spirits tremble
Under the waters and their inhabitants.

...outs a covering ...face [a]Prov. 7:9
[a]Ex. 22:2; Matt. ...:19 [b]John 3:20
17 [a]Job 15:21
...Or, *light* or *swift* ...*he path of* [a]Job ...16; 27:20 [b]Job ...3 [c]Job 24:6, 11
...Lit., *seize* [2]I.e., ...orld [a]Job 6:16, ...17 [b]Job 21:13
[1]Lit., *womb* [a]Is. ...Job 21:26 [c]Job ...Ps. 34:16; Prov. ...Job 19:10; Dan. 4:14
...Lit., *barren who* ...*bear* [a]Job 22:9
...9:4 [b]Job 18:20
[a]Job 12:6 [b]Job 10:4; 11:11
[a]Ps. 37:10 [b]Job 14:21
[a]Job 6:28; 27:4
[1]Lit., *answered and said*
...it., *are with Him* ...ob 9:4; 36:5, 22; ...2:2 [b]Job 16:19; 31:2
3 [a]Job 16:13
...o 4:17; 9:2 [b]Job 14:4
[a]Job 31:26 [b]Job 15:15
...7:17 [b]Job 17:14
[1]Lit., *responded and said*
..., *no power* [a]Job 11, 12 [b]Ps. 71:9
...it., *made known*
...*breath has gone forth*
...r, *shades;* Heb., ...*n* [a]Job 3:13; Ps. 88:10

6 "Naked is [1a]Sheol before Him
And [2b]Abaddon has no covering.
7 "He [a]stretches out the north over empty space,
And hangs the earth on nothing.
8 "He [a]wraps up the waters in His clouds;
And the cloud does not burst under them.
9 "He [1a]obscures the face of the [2]full moon,
And spreads His cloud over it.
10 "He has inscribed a [a]circle on the surface of the waters,
At the [b]boundary of light and darkness.
11 "The pillars of heaven tremble,
And are amazed at His rebuke.
12 "He [a]quieted the sea with His power,
And by His [b]understanding He shattered [c]Rahab.
13 "By His breath the [a]heavens are [1]cleared;
His hand has pierced [b]the fleeing serpent.
14 "Behold, these are the fringes of His ways;
And how faint [a]a word we hear of Him!
But His mighty [b]thunder, who can understand?"

Chapter 27

27 Then Job [1]continued his [a]discourse and said,
2 "As God lives, [a]who has taken away my right,
And the Almighty, [b]who has embittered my soul,
3 For as long as [1]life is in me,
And the [2a]breath of God is in my nostrils,
4 My lips certainly will not speak unjustly,
Nor will [a]my tongue mutter deceit.
5 "Far be it from me that I should declare you right;
Till I die [a]I will not put away my integrity from me.
6 "I [a]hold fast my righteousness and will not let it go.
My heart does not reproach any of my days.

7 "May my enemy be as the wicked,
And [1]my opponent as the unjust.
8 "For what is [a]the hope of the godless [1]when he is cut off,
When God requires [b]his [2]life?
9 "Will God [a]hear his cry,
When [b]distress comes upon him?
10 "Will he take [a]delight in the Almighty,
Will he call on God at all times?
11 "I will instruct you in the [1]power of God;
What is with the Almighty I will not conceal.
12 "Behold, all of you have seen *it;*
Why then do you [1]act foolishly?

13 "This is [a]the portion of a wicked man from God,
And the inheritance *which* [b]tyrants receive from the Almighty.
14 "Though his sons are many, [1]they are destined [a]for the sword;
And his [b]descendants will not be satisfied with bread.
15 "His survivors will be buried because of the plague,
And [1]their [a]widows will not be able to weep.
16 "Though he piles up silver like dust,
And prepares garments as *plentiful as* the clay;

6 [1]I.e., the ne [2]I.e., place of destruction [a]J 26:6-14; 38:17 [b]Job 28:22; 31

7 [a]Job 9:8

8 [a]Job 37:11;

9 [1]Lit., *covers* *throne* [a]Job 2 97:2; 105:39

10 [a]Job 38:1- 8:29 [b]Job 38:

12 [a]Is. 51:15; 31:35 [b]Job 12 9:13

13 [1]Lit., *made* [a]Job 9:8 [b]Is. 2

14 [a]Job 4:12 36:29; 37:4, 5

27:1 [1]Or, *agai* [a]Job 13:12; 29

2 [a]Job 16:11; 9:18

3 [1]Lit., *breath* *spirit* [a]Job 32:8

4 [a]Job 6:28; 3

5 [a]Job 6:29

6 [a]Job 2:3; 13:

7 [1]Lit., *he who* *against me*

8 [1]Or, *though* [2]Lit., *soul* [a]Job 11:20 [b]Job 12:

9 [a]Job 35:12, 18:41; Prov. 1:2 1:15; Jer. 14:12 3:4 [b]Prov. 1:27

10 [a]Job 22:26, 37:4; Is. 58:14

11 [1]Lit., *hand*

12 [1]Or, *speak*

13 [a]Job 20:29 15:20

14 [1]Lit., *the swo* *them* [a]Job 15:2 18:19 [b]Job 20:1

15 [1]So ancient versions; Heb., 78:64

17 He may prepare *it,* [a]but the just will wear *it,*
And the innocent will divide the silver.
18 "He has built his [a]house like the [1]spider's web,
Or as a hut *which* the watchman has made.
19 "He lies down rich, but never [1]again;
He opens his eyes, and [a]it is no more.
20 "[a]Terrors overtake him like a flood;
A tempest steals him away [b]in the night.
21 "The east [a]wind carries him away, and he is gone,
For it whirls him [b]away from his place.
22 "For it will hurl at him [a]without sparing;
He will surely try to [b]flee from its [1]power.
23 "*Men* will clap their hands at him,
And will [a]hiss him from his place.

Chapter 28

28 "Surely there is a [1]mine for silver,
And a place [2]where they refine gold.
2 "Iron is taken from the dust,
And from rock copper is smelted.
3 "*Man* puts an end to darkness,
And [a]to the farthest limit he searches out
The rock in gloom and deep shadow.
4 "He [1]sinks a shaft far from [2]habitation,
Forgotten by the foot;
They hang and swing to and fro far from men.
5 "The earth, from it comes food,
And underneath it is turned up as fire.
6 "Its rocks are the [1]source of sapphires,
And its dust *contains* gold.
7 "The path no bird of prey knows,
Nor has the falcon's eye caught sight of it.
8 "The [1]proud beasts have not trodden it,
Nor has the *fierce* lion passed over it.
9 "He puts his hand on the flint;
He overturns the mountains at the [1]base.
10 "He hews out channels through the rocks;
And his eye sees anything precious.
11 "He dams up the streams from [1]flowing;
And what is hidden he brings out to the light.

12 "But [a]where can wisdom be found?
And where is the place of understanding?
13 "[a]Man does not know its value,
Nor is it found in the land of the living.
14 "The deep says, 'It is not in me';
And the sea says, 'It is not with me.'
15 "[a]Pure gold cannot be given in exchange for it,
Nor can silver be weighed as its price.
16 "It cannot be valued in the gold of Ophir,
In precious onyx, or sapphire.
17 "[a]Gold or glass cannot equal it,
Nor can it be exchanged for articles of fine gold.
18 "Coral and crystal are not to be mentioned;

17 [a]Job 20:18-21
18 [1]So ancient versions; Heb., *moth* [a]Job 8:15; 18:14
19 [1]So ancient versions; Heb., *will be gathered* [a]Job 7:8, 21; 20:7
20 [a]Job 15:21 [b]Job 20:8; 34:20
21 [a]Job 21:18 [b]Job 7:10
22 [1]Lit., *hand* [a]Jer. 13:14; Ezek. 5:11; 24:14 [b]Job 11:20
3 [a]Job 18:18; 20:8
1 [1]Or, *source* [2]Lit., *for gold they refine*
3 [a]Eccl. 1:13
4 [1]Lit., *breaks open* [2]Lit., *sojourning*
6 [1]Or, *place*
8 [1]Lit., *sons of pride*
9 [1]Lit., *roots*
11 [1]Lit., *weeping*
12 [a]Job 28:23, 28; Eccl. 7:24
13 [a]Matt. 13:44-46
15 [a]Prov. 3:13, 14; 8:10, 11; 16:16
17 [a]Prov. 8:10; 16:16

And the acquisition of [a]wisdom is above *that of* pearls.
19 "The topaz of Ethiopia cannot equal it,
Nor can it be valued in [a]pure gold.
20 "[a]Where then does wisdom come from?
And where is the place of understanding?
21 "Thus it is hidden from the eyes of all living,
And concealed from the birds of the sky.
22 "[1a]Abaddon and Death say,
'With our ears we have heard a report of it.'

23 "[a]God understands its way;
And He knows its place.
24 "For He [a]looks to the ends of the earth,
And sees everything under the heavens.
25 "When He imparted [a]weight to the wind,
And [b]meted out the waters by measure,
26 When He set a [a]limit for the rain,
And a course for the [b]thunderbolt,
27 Then He saw it and declared it;
He established it and also searched it out.
28 "And to man He said, 'Behold, the [a]fear of the Lord, that is wisdom;
And to depart from evil is understanding.' "

Chapter 29

29 And Job again took up his [a]discourse and said,
2 "Oh that I were as in months gone by,
As in the days when God [a]watched over me;
3 When [a]His lamp shone over my head,
And [b]by His light I walked through darkness;
4 As I was in [1]the prime of my days,
When the [2a]friendship of God *was* over my tent;
5 When [1]the Almighty was yet with me,
And my children were around me;
6 When my steps were bathed in [a]butter,
And the [b]rock poured out for me streams of oil!
7 "When I went out to [a]the gate of the city,
When I [1]took my seat in the square;
8 The young men saw me and hid themselves,
And the old men arose *and* stood.
9 "The princes [a]stopped talking,
And [b]put *their* hands on their mouths;
10 The voice of the nobles was [1a]hushed,
And their [b]tongue stuck to their palate.
11 "For when [a]the ear heard, it called me blessed;
And when the eye saw, it gave witness of me,
12 Because I delivered [a]the poor who cried for help,
And the [b]orphan who had no helper.
13 "The blessing of the one [a]ready to perish came upon me,
And I made the [b]widow's heart sing for joy.
14 "I [a]put on righteousness, and it clothed me;
My justice was like a robe and a turban.
15 "I was [a]eyes to the blind,
And feet to the lame.

18 [a]Prov. 8:11
19 [a]Prov. 8:19
20 [a]Job 28:23, 28
22 [1]I.e., Destruction [a]Job 26:6; Prov. 8:3
23 [a]Job 9:4; Prov. 8:22-36
24 [a]Ps. 11:4; 33:13 66:7; Prov. 15:3
25 [a]Ps. 135:7 [b]Job 12:15; 38:8-11
26 [a]Job 37:6, 11, 1 38:26-28 [b]Job 37:3 38:25
28 [a]Ps. 111:10; Pr 1:7; 9:10; Eccl. 12:
29:1 [a]Num. 23:7; Job 13:12; 27:1
2 [a]Jer. 31:28
3 [a]Job 18:6 [b]Job
4 [1]Lit., *the days of autumn* [2]Lit., *cour* [a]Job 15:8; Ps. 25:1 Prov. 3:32
5 [1]Heb., *Shaddai*
6 [a]Deut. 32:14; Jo 20:17 [b]Deut. 32:1 81:16
7 [1]Lit., *set up* [a]Jo 31:21
9 [a]Job 29:21 [b]Jo
10 [1]Lit., *hidden* [a] 29:22 [b]Ps. 137:6
11 [a]Job 4:3, 4
12 [a]Job 24:4, 9; 3 Ps. 72:12; Prov. 2 [b]Job 31:17, 21
13 [a]Job 31:19 [b]J 22:9
14 [a]Job 27:5, 6; 132:9; Is. 59:17; 6 Eph. 6:14
15 [a]Num. 10:31

16 "I was a father to [a]the needy,
And I investigated the case which I did not know.
17 "And I [a]broke the jaws of the wicked,
And snatched the prey from his teeth.
18 "Then I [1]thought, 'I shall die [2]in my nest,
And I shall multiply *my* days as the sand.
19 'My [a]root is spread out to the waters,
And [b]dew lies all night on my branch.
20 'My glory is *ever* new with me,
And my [a]bow is renewed in my hand.'

21 "To me [a]they listened and waited,
And kept silent for my counsel.
22 "After my words they did not [a]speak again,
And [b]my speech dropped on them.
23 "And they waited for me as for the rain,
And opened their mouth as for the spring rain.
24 "I smiled on them when they did not believe,
And the light of my face they did not cast down.
25 "I chose a way for them and sat as [a]chief,
And dwelt as a king among the troops,
As one who [b]comforted the mourners.

Chapter 30

30 "But now those younger than I [a]mock me,
Whose fathers I disdained to put with the dogs of my flock.
2 "Indeed, what *good was* the strength of their hands to me?
Vigor had perished from them.
3 "From want and famine they are gaunt
Who gnaw the dry ground by night in waste and desolation,
4 Who pluck [1]mallow by the bushes,
And whose food is the root of the broom shrub.
5 "They are driven from the community;
They shout against them as *against* a thief,
6 So that they dwell in dreadful [1]valleys,
In holes of the earth and of the rocks.
7 "Among the bushes they [1]cry out;
Under the nettles they are gathered together.
8 "[1]Fools, even [2]those without a name,
They were scourged from the land.

9 "And now I have become their [1a]taunt,
I have even become a [b]byword to them.
10 "They abhor me *and* stand aloof from me,
And they do not [1]refrain from [a]spitting at my face.
11 "Because [1]He has loosed [2]His [3]bowstring and [a]afflicted me,
They have cast off [b]the bridle before me.
12 "On the right hand their [1]brood arises;
They [a]thrust aside my feet [b]and build up against me their ways
of destruction.
13 "They [a]break up my path,
They profit [1]from my destruction,
No one restrains them.
14 "As *through* a wide breach they come,

ob 24:4; Prov. 29:7
17 [a]Ps. 3:7
[1]Lit., *said* [2]Lit., *with*
er. 17:8 [b]Hos. 14:5
0 [a]Gen. 49:24; Ps. 18:34
21 [a]Job 4:3; 29:9
[a]Job 29:10 [b]Deut. 32:2
25 [a]Job 1:3; 31:37 [b]Job 4:4; 16:5
30:1 [a]Job 12:4
e., plant of the salt marshes
6 [1]Or, *wadis*
7 [1]Or, *bray*
Lit., *Sons of fools* [2]Lit., *sons*
, *song* [a]Job 12:4 o 17:6; Ps. 69:11; Lam. 3:14, 63
[1]Lit., *withhold spit n my face* [a]Num. ; Deut. 25:9; Job :6; Is. 50:6; Matt. 26:67
[1]Or, *they* [2]Some ead *my* [3]Or, *cord* th 1:21; Ps. 88:7 [b]Ps. 32:9
ossibly, *sprout* or ng [a]Ps. 140:4, 5 [b]Job 19:12
Lit., *for* [a]Is. 3:12

[1]Amid the tempest they roll on.
15 "[a]Terrors are turned against me,
They pursue my [1]honor as the wind,
And my [2]prosperity has passed away [b]like a cloud.

16 "And now [a]my soul is poured out [1]within me;
Days of affliction have seized me.
17 "At night it pierces [a]my bones [1]within me,
And my gnawing *pains* take no rest.
18 "By a great force my garment is [a]distorted;
It binds me about as the collar of my coat.
19 "He has cast me into the [a]mire,
And I have become like dust and ashes.
20 "I [a]cry out to Thee for help, but Thou dost not answer me;
I stand up, and Thou dost turn Thy attention against me.
21 "Thou hast [1]become cruel to me;
With the might of Thy hand Thou dost [a]persecute me.
22 "Thou dost [a]lift me up to the wind *and* cause me to ride;
And Thou dost dissolve me in a storm.
23 "For I know that Thou [a]wilt bring me to death
And to the [b]house of meeting for all living.

24 "Yet does not one in a heap of ruins stretch out *his* hand,
Or in his disaster therefore [a]cry out for help?
25 "Have I not [a]wept for the [1]one whose life is hard?
Was not my soul grieved for [b]the needy?
26 "When I [a]expected good, then evil came;
When I waited for light, [b]then darkness came.
27 "[1]I am seething [a]within, and cannot relax;
Days of affliction confront me.
28 "I go about [1a]mourning without comfort;
I stand up in the assembly *and* [b]cry out for help.
29 "I have become a brother to [a]jackals,
And a companion of ostriches.
30 "My [a]skin turns black [1]on me,
And my [b]bones burn with [2]fever.
31 "Therefore my [a]harp [1]is turned to mourning,
And my flute to the sound of those who weep.

Chapter 31

31 "I Have made a covenant with my [a]eyes;
How then could I gaze at a virgin?
2 "And what is [a]the portion of God from above
Or the heritage of the Almighty from on high?
3 "Is it not [a]calamity to the unjust,
And disaster to [b]those who work iniquity?
4 "Does He not [a]see my ways,
And [b]number all my steps?

5 "If I have [a]walked with falsehood,
And my foot has hastened after deceit,
6 Let Him [a]weigh me with [1]accurate scales,
And let God know [b]my integrity.
7 "If my step has [a]turned from the way,

14 [1]Lit., *Unde*
15 [1]Or, *nobili* *welfare* [a]Job 31:23; Ps. 55 7:9; Hos. 13:3
16 [1]Lit., *upon* 1:15; Job 3:24 22:14; 42:4; Is
17 [1]Lit., *from* [a]Job 30:30
18 [a]Job 2:7
19 [a]Ps. 69:2,
20 [a]Job 19:7
21 [1]Lit., *turne* [a]Job 10:3; 16: 19:6, 22
22 [a]Job 9:17;
23 [a]Job 9:22; [b]Job 3:19; Ecc
24 [a]Job 19:7
25 [1]Lit., *hard* [a]Ps. 35:13, 14; 12:15 [b]Job 24
26 [a]Job 3:25, 8:15 [b]Job 19:8
27 [1]Lit., *My in* *parts are boilin* 2:11
28 [1]Or, *blacke* *not by the heat* *sun* [a]Job 30:31 38:6; 42:9; 43:2 19:7
29 [a]Ps. 44:19;
30 [1]Lit., *from u* [2]Lit., *heat* [a]Job 102:3
31 [1]Lit., *becom* 24:8
31:1 [a]Matt. 5:2
2 [a]Job 20:29
3 [a]Job 18:12; 2 [b]Job 34:22
4 [a]2 Chr. 16:9; 24:23; 28:24; 34 36:7; Prov. 5:21 [b]Job 14:16; 31:3
5 [a]Job 15:31; M
6 [1]Lit., *just* [a]Job [b]Job 23:10; 27:5
7 [a]Job 23:11

Or my heart [1]followed my eyes,
Or if any [b]spot has stuck to my hands,
8 Let me [a]sow and another eat,
And let my [1b]crops be uprooted.

9 "If my heart has been [a]enticed by a woman,
Or I have lurked at my neighbor's doorway,
10 May my wife [a]grind for another,
And let [b]others [1]kneel down over her.
11 "For that would be a [a]lustful crime;
Moreover, it would be [b]an iniquity *punishable by* judges.
12 "For it would be [a]fire that consumes to [1b]Abaddon,
And would [c]uproot all my [2]increase.

13 "If I have [a]despised the claim of my male or female slaves
When they filed a complaint against me,
14 What then could I do when God arises,
And when He calls me to account, what will I answer Him?
15 "Did not [a]He who made me in the womb make him,
And the same one fashion us in the womb?

16 "If I have kept [a]the poor from *their* desire,
Or have caused the eyes of [b]the widow to fail,
17 Or have [a]eaten my morsel alone,
And [b]the orphan has not [1]shared it
18 (But from my youth he grew up with me as with a father,
And from [1]infancy I guided her),
19 If I have seen anyone perish [a]for lack of clothing,
Or that [b]the needy had no covering,
20 If his loins have not [1]thanked me,
And if he has not been warmed with the fleece of my sheep,
21 If I have lifted up my hand against [a]the orphan,
Because I saw [1]I had support [b]in the gate,
22 Let my shoulder fall from the [1]socket,
And my [a]arm be broken off [2]at the elbow.
23 "For [a]calamity from God is a terror to me,
And because of [b]His [1]majesty I can do nothing.

24 "If I have put my confidence *in* [a]gold,
And called fine gold my trust,
25 If I have [a]gloated because my wealth was great,
And because my hand had secured *so* much;
26 If I have [a]looked at the [1]sun when it shone,
Or the moon going in splendor,
27 And my heart became secretly enticed,
And my hand [1]threw a kiss from my mouth,
28 That too would have been [a]an iniquity *calling for* [1]judgment,
For I would have [b]denied God above.

29 "Have I [a]rejoiced at the extinction of my enemy,
Or [1]exulted when evil befell him?
30 "[1]No, [a]I have not [2]allowed my mouth to sin
By asking for his life in [b]a curse.
31 "Have the men of my tent not said,

..., *walked after* [b]Job 9:30
...*offspring* [a]Lev. ...ob 20:18; Mic. ...15 [b]Job 31:12
...ob 24:15; 31:1
...0 [1]I.e., sexual ...tions [a]Is. 47:2 ...8:30; Jer. 8:10
...v. 20:10; Deut. ...24 [b]Job 31:28
[1]I.e., place of ...tion [2]Or, *yield* ...5:30 [b]Job 26:6 ...ob 20:28; 31:8
...eut. 24:14, 15
15 [a]Job 10:3
...ob 5:16; 20:19 ...2-24; Job 22:9
..., *eaten from it* ...2:7 [b]Job 29:12
..., *my mother's womb*
...ob 22:6; 29:13 [b]Job 24:4
... [1]Lit., *blessed*
..., *my help* [a]Job ...1:17 [b]Job 29:7
...t., *shoulder;* or, ... [2]Lit., *from the ... the upper arm* [a]Job 38:15
...*exaltation* [a]Job ...1:3 [b]Job 13:11
...ob 22:24; Mark 10:23-25
...Job 1:3, 10; Ps. 62:10
...it., *light* [a]Deut. ...7:3; Ezek. 8:16
[1]Lit., *kissed my mouth*
..., *judges* [a]Deut. ...:2-7; Job 31:11 ...24:27; Is. 59:13
...*lifted myself up* ...ov. 17:5; 24:17; Obad. 12
[1]Lit., *And* [2]Lit., *my palate* [a]Ps. 7:4 [b]Job 5:3

'Who can [1]find one who has not been [a]satisfied with his meat'?
32 "The alien has not lodged outside,
For I have opened my doors to the [1]traveler.
33 "Have I [a]covered my transgressions like [1]Adam,
By hiding my iniquity in my bosom,
34 Because I [a]feared the great multitude,
And the contempt of families terrified me,
And kept silent and did not go out of doors?
35 "Oh that I had one to hear me!
Behold, here is my [1]signature;
[a]Let the Almighty answer me!
And the indictment which my [b]adversary has written,
36 Surely I would carry it on my shoulder;
I would bind it to myself like a crown.
37 "I would declare to Him [a]the number of my steps;
Like [b]a prince I would approach Him.

38 "If my [a]land cries out against me,
And its furrows weep together;
39 If I have [a]eaten its [1]fruit without money,
Or have [b]caused [2]its owners to lose their lives,
40 Let [a]briars [1]grow instead of wheat,
And stinkweed instead of barley."
The words of Job are ended.

Chapter 32

32 Then these three men ceased answering Job, because he was
[a]righteous in his own eyes.
2 But the anger of Elihu the son of Barachel the [a]Buzite, of the
family of Ram burned; against Job his anger burned, [b]because he
justified himself [1c]before God.
3 And his anger burned against his three friends because they had
found no answer, and yet had condemned Job.
4 Now Elihu had waited [1]to speak to Job because they were years
older than he.
5 And when Elihu saw that there was no answer in the mouth of
the three men his anger burned.
6 So Elihu the son of Barachel the Buzite [1]spoke out and said,
"I am young in years and you are [a]old;
Therefore I was shy and afraid to tell you [2]what I think.
7 "I [1]thought [2a]age should speak,
And [3]increased years should teach wisdom.
8 "But it is a spirit in man,
And the [a]breath of the Almighty gives them [b]understanding.
9 "The [1]abundant *in years* may not be wise,
Nor may [a]elders understand justice.
10 "So I [1]say, 'Listen to me,
I too will tell [2]what I think.'

11 "Behold, I waited for your words,
I listened to your reasonings,
While you [1]pondered what to say.
12 "I even paid close attention to you,
[1]Indeed, there was no one who refuted Job,

31 [1]Lit., *give*

32 [1]M.T., *way*

33 [1]Or, *manki*
3:10; Prov. 28:

34 [a]Ex. 23:2

35 [1]Lit., *mark*
19:7; 30:20, 24
35:14 [b]Job 27

37 [a]Job 31:4
29:25

38 [a]Job 24:2

39 [1]Lit., *streng*
the soul of its o
expire [a]Job 24
10-12; James 5
[b]1 Kin. 21:19

40 [1]Lit., *come*
[a]Job 32:13; Is.

32:1 [a]Job 10:7
27:5, 6; 31:6

2 [1]Or, *more th*
22:21 [b]Job 27:
[c]Job 30:21

4 [1]Lit., *for Job*
words; or possi
they were spea
Job

6 [1]Lit., *answere*
my knowledge
15:10

7 [1]Lit., *said* [2]L
[3]Lit., *many* [a]Job

8 [a]Job 33:4 [b]J

9 [1]Or, *nobles*

10 [1]Or, *said* [2]L
knowledge

11 [1]Lit., *search*
words

12 [1]Lit., *Behold*

Not one of you who answered his words.
13 "[1]Do not say,
'[a]We have found wisdom;
God will [2]rout him, not man.'
14 "For he has not arranged *his* words against me;
Nor will I reply to him with your [1]arguments.

15 "They are dismayed, they answer no more;
Words have [1]failed them.
16 "And shall I wait, because they do not speak,
Because they [1]stop *and* answer no more?
17 "I too will answer my share,
I also will tell my opinion.
18 "For I am full of words;
The spirit within me constrains me.
19 "Behold, my belly is like unvented wine,
Like new wineskins it is about to burst.
20 "Let me speak that I may get relief;
Let me open my lips and answer.
21 "Let me now [a]be partial to no one;
Nor flatter *any* man.
22 "For I do not know how to flatter,
Else my Maker would soon take me away.

Chapter 33

33 "However now, Job, please [a]hear my speech,
And listen to all my words.
2 "Behold now, I open my mouth,
My tongue in my [1]mouth speaks.
3 "My words are *from* the uprightness of my heart;
And my lips speak [a]knowledge sincerely.
4 "The [a]Spirit of God has made me,
And the [b]breath of [1]the Almighty gives me life.
5 "[a]Refute me if you can;
Array yourselves before me, take your stand.
6 "Behold, I belong to God like you;
I too have been [1]formed out of the [a]clay.
7 "Behold, [a]no fear of me should terrify you,
Nor should my pressure weigh heavily on you.

8 "Surely you have spoken in my hearing,
And I have heard the sound of *your* words:
9 'I am [a]pure, [b]without transgression;
I am innocent and there [c]is no guilt in me.
10 'Behold, He [1]invents pretexts against me;
He [a]counts me as His enemy.
11 'He [a]puts my feet in the stocks;
He watches all my paths.'
12 "Behold, let me [1]tell you, [a]you are not right in this,
For God is greater than man.

13 "Why do you [a]complain against Him,
That He does not give an account of all His doings?
14 "Indeed [a]God speaks once,

., Lest you say ive away [a]Jer. 9:23
14 [1]Lit., *words*
., *moved away from*
16 [1]Lit., *stand*
Lev. 19:15; Job 13:8, 10; 34:19
33:1 [a]Job 13:6
2 [1]Lit., *palate*
5:28; 27:4; 36:4
[1]Heb., *Shaddai* . 2:7; Job 10:3; 32:8 [b]Job 27:3
5 [a]Job 33:32
cut out of [a]Job 4:19
7 [a]Job 13:21
[a]Job 9:21; 10:7; 6:17 [b]Job 7:21; 4:17 [c]Job 10:14
[1]Lit., *finds* [a]Job 13:24
11 [a]Job 13:27
., *answer* [a]Eccl. 7:20
ob 40:2; Is. 45:9
Job 33:29; 40:5; Ps. 62:11

Or twice, *yet* no one notices it.
15 "In a [a]dream, a vision of the night,
When sound sleep falls on men,
While they slumber in their beds,
16 Then [a]He opens the ears of men,
And seals their instruction,
17 That He may turn man aside *from his* conduct,
And [1]keep man from pride;
18 He [a]keeps back his soul from the pit,
And his life from [1]passing over [b]into Sheol.

19 "[1]Man is also chastened with [a]pain on his bed,
And with unceasing complaint in his bones;
20 So that his life [a]loathes bread,
And his soul favorite food.
21 "His [a]flesh wastes away from sight,
And his [b]bones which were not seen stick out.
22 "Then [a]his soul draws near to the pit,
And his life to those who bring death.

23 "If there is an angel *as* [a]mediator for him,
One out of a thousand,
To remind a man what is [1]right for him,
24 Then let him be gracious to him, and say,
'Deliver him from [a]going down to the pit,
I have found a [b]ransom';
25 Let his flesh become fresher than in youth,
Let him return to the days of his youthful vigor;
26 Then he will [a]pray to God, and He will accept him,
That [b]he may see His face with joy,
And He may restore His righteousness to man.
27 "He will sing to men and say,
'I [a]have sinned and perverted what is right,
And it is not [b]proper for me.
28 'He has redeemed my soul from going to the pit,
And my life shall [a]see the light.'

29 "Behold, God does [a]all these [1]oftentimes with men,
30 To [a]bring back his soul from the pit,
That he may be enlightened with the light of life.
31 "Pay attention, O Job, listen to me;
Keep silent and let me speak.
32 "*Then* if [1]you have anything to say, answer me;
Speak, for I desire to justify you.
33 "If not, [a]listen to me;
Keep silent, and I will teach you wisdom."

Chapter 34

34 Then Elihu continued and said,
2 "Hear my words, you wise men,
And listen to me, you who know.
3 "For [a]the ear tests words,
As the palate tastes food.
4 "Let us choose for ourselves what is right;

15 [a]Job 4:12- 33:15-18
16 [a]Job 36:1
17 [1]Lit., *hide*
18 [1]M.T., *peri the sword* [a]Jo 24, 28, 30 [b]Jo
19 [1]Lit., *He* [a]
20 [a]Job 3:24; 107:18
21 [a]Job 16:8 19:20; Ps. 22:
22 [a]Job 33:18
23 [1]Lit., *his uprightness* [a]
24 [a]Job 33:18 38:17 [b]Job 36 49:7
26 [a]Job 22:27; Ps. 50:14, 15 22:26
27 [a]2 Sam. 12 15:21 [b]Rom. 6
28 [a]Job 22:28
29 [1]Lit., *twice, times* [a]Eph. 1:1 2:13
30 [a]Job 33:18; 9:11
32 [1]Lit., *there a*
33 [a]Ps. 34:11
34:3 [a]Job 12:11

Let us know among ourselves what is good.
5 "For Job has said, '[a]I am righteous,
But [b]God has taken away my right;
6 [1]Should I lie concerning my right?
My [2a]wound is incurable, *though I am* without transgression.'
7 "What man is like Job,
Who [a]drinks up derision like water,
8 Who goes [a]in company with the workers of iniquity,
And walks with wicked men?
9 "For he has said, '[a]It profits a man nothing
When he [1]is pleased with God.'

10 "Therefore, listen to me, you men of understanding.
Far be it from God to [a]do wickedness,
And from the Almighty to do wrong.
11 "For He pays a man according to [a]his work,
And makes [1]him find it according to his way.
12 "Surely, [a]God will not act wickedly,
And the Almighty will not pervert justice.
13 "Who [a]gave Him authority over the earth?
And who [b]has laid *on Him* the whole world?
14 "If He should [1]determine to do so,
If He should [a]gather to Himself His spirit and His breath,
15 All [a]flesh would perish together,
And man would [b]return to dust.

16 "But if *you have* understanding, hear this;
Listen to the sound of my words.
17 "Shall [a]one who hates justice rule?
And [b]will you condemn a righteous mighty one,
18 Who says to a king, 'Worthless one,'
To nobles, 'Wicked ones';
19 Who shows no [a]partiality to princes,
Nor regards the rich above the poor,
For they all are the [b]work of His hands?
20 "In a moment they die, and [a]at midnight
People are shaken and pass away,
And [b]the mighty are taken away without a hand.

21 "For [a]His eyes are upon the ways of a man,
And He sees all his steps.
22 "There is [a]no darkness or deep shadow
Where the workers of iniquity may hide themselves.
23 "For He does not [a]*need to* consider a man further,
That he should go before God in judgment.
24 "He breaks in pieces [a]mighty men without inquiry,
And sets others in their place.
25 "Therefore He [a]knows their works,
And [b]He overthrows *them* in the night,
And they are crushed.
26 "He [a]strikes them like the wicked
[1]In a public place,
27 Because they [a]turned aside from following Him,
And [b]had no regard for any of His ways;

ob 13:18; 33:9 [b]Job 27:2
Although I am n accounted a rrow [a]Job 6:4
7 [a]Job 15:16
8 [a]Job 22:15
akes delight in ob 21:15; 35:3; Ps. 50:18
ı. 18:25; Deut. Job 8:3; 34:12; Rom. 9:14
t., a man [a]Job s. 62:12; Prov. r. 32:19; Ezek. 0; Matt. 16:27; :6; 2 Cor. 5:10; Rev. 22:12
12 [a]Job 34:10
38:4 [b]Job 38:5
set His mind on [a]Job 12:10; Ps. 4:29; Eccl. 12:7
Gen. 7:21; Job [b]Gen. 3:19; Job 10:9
Sam. 23:3; Job 4:30 [b]Job 40:8
ev. 19:15; Deut. Chr. 19:7; Acts Rom. 2:11; Gal. . 6:9; Col. 3:25; 1:17 [b]Job 10:3
[a]Ex. 12:29; Job :20 [b]Job 12:19
lob 24:23; 31:4; 5:21; 15:3; Jer. 16:17
[a]Ps. 139:11, 12; Amos 9:2, 3
23 [a]Job 11:11
24 [a]Job 12:19
[a]Job 34:11 [b]Job 34:20
., In the place of nes seeing [a]Ps. 9:5; 11:5
am. 15:11 [b]Job 21:14

28 So that they caused [a]the cry of the poor to come to Him,
And that He might [b]hear the cry of the afflicted—
29 When He keeps quiet, who then can condemn?
And when He hides His face, who then can behold Him,
That is, in regard to both nation and man?—
30 So that [a]godless men should not rule,
Nor be snares of the people.

31 "For has anyone said to God,
'I have borne *chastisement;*
I will not offend *anymore;*
32 Teach Thou me what I do not see;
If I have [a]done iniquity,
I will do it no more'?
33 "Shall He [a]recompense on your terms, because you have
rejected *it?*
For you must choose, and not I;
Therefore declare what you know.
34 "Men of understanding will say to me,
And a wise man who hears me,
35 'Job [a]speaks without knowledge,
And his words are without wisdom.
36 'Job ought to be tried [1]to the limit,
Because he answers [a]like wicked men.
37 'For he adds [a]rebellion to his sin;
He [b]claps his hands among us,
And multiplies his words against God.' "

Chapter 35

35 Then Elihu continued and said,
2 "Do you think this is according to [a]justice?
Do you say, 'My righteousness is more than God's'?
3 "For you say, '[a]What advantage will it be to [1]You?
[b]What profit shall I have, more than if I had sinned?'
4 "I will answer you,
And your friends with you.
5 "[a]Look at the heavens and see;
And behold [b]the clouds—they are higher than you.
6 "If you have sinned, [a]what do you accomplish against Him?
And if your transgressions are many, what do you do to Him?
7 "If you are righteous, [a]what do you give to Him?
Or what does He receive from your hand?
8 "Your wickedness is for a man like yourself,
And your righteousness is for a son of man.

9 "Because of the [a]multitude of oppressions they cry out;
They cry for help because of the arm [b]of the mighty.
10 "But [a]no one says, 'Where is God my Maker,
Who [b]gives songs in the night,
11 Who [a]teaches us more than the beasts of the earth,
And makes us wiser than the birds of the heavens?'
12 "There [a]they cry out, but He does not answer
Because of the pride of evil men.
13 "Surely [a]God will not listen to [1]an empty *cry,*

28 [a]Job 35:9; J
5:4 [b]Ex. 22:23;
22:27

30 [a]Job 5:15; 3
34:17; Prov. 29

32 [a]Job 33:27

33 [a]Job 41:11

35 [a]Job 35:16;

36 [1]Or, *to the e*
22:15

37 [a]Job 23:2 [b]
27:23

35:2 [a]Job 27:2

3 [1]Or, *you* [a]Job
[b]Job 9:30, 31

5 [a]Gen. 15:5; P
[b]Job 22:12

6 [a]Job 7:20; Pr
Jer. 7:19

7 [a]Job 22:2, 3;
9:12; Luke 17:10
11:35

9 [a]Ex. 2:23 [b]Jo

10 [a]Job 21:14;
36:13; Is. 51:13
8:21; Ps. 42:8; 7
149:5; Acts 16:2

11 [a]Job 36:22; P
94:12; Jer. 32:33

12 [a]Prov. 1:28

13 [1]Or, *falsehoo*
27:9; Prov. 15:29
1:15; Jer. 11:11;

Nor will the Almighty regard it.
14 "How much less when [a]you say you do not behold Him,
The [b]case is before Him, and you must wait for Him!
15 "And now, because He has not visited *in* His anger,
Nor has He acknowledged [1]transgression well,
16 So Job opens his mouth [1]emptily;
He multiplies words [a]without knowledge."

Chapter 36

36 Then Elihu continued and said,
2 "Wait for me a little, and I will show you
That there [1]is yet more to be said in God's behalf.
3 "I will fetch my knowledge from afar,
And I will ascribe [a]righteousness to my Maker.
4 "For truly [a]my words are not false;
One who is [b]perfect in knowledge is with you.
5 "Behold, God is mighty but does not [a]despise *any;*
He is [b]mighty in strength of understanding.
6 "He does not [a]keep the wicked alive,
But gives justice to [b]the afflicted.
7 "He does not [a]withdraw His eyes from the righteous;
But [b]with kings on the throne
He has seated them forever, and they are exalted.
8 "And if they are bound in fetters,
And are caught in the cords of [a]affliction,
9 Then He declares to them their work
And their transgressions, that they have [a]magnified themselves.
10 "And [a]He opens their ear to instruction,
And [b]commands that they return from evil.
11 "If they hear and serve *Him,*
They shall [a]end their days in prosperity,
And their years in [b]pleasures.
12 "But if they do not hear, they shall [1]perish [a]by the sword,
And they shall [b]die without knowledge.
13 "But the godless in heart lay up anger;
They do not cry for help when He binds them.
14 "[1]They die in youth,
And their life *perishes* among the [a]cult prostitutes.
15 "He delivers the afflicted in [1]their [a]affliction,
And [b]opens their ear [2]in *time of* oppression.
16 "Then indeed, He [a]enticed you from the mouth of distress,
Instead of it, a broad place with no constraint;
And that which was set on your table was full of [1]fatness.

17 "But you were full of [a]judgment on the wicked;
Judgment and justice take hold *of you.*
18 "*Beware* lest [a]wrath entice you to scoffing;
And do not let the greatness of the [b]ransom turn you aside.
19 "Will your [1]riches keep *you* from distress,
Or all the forces of *your* strength?
20 "Do not long for [a]the night,
When people [1]vanish in their place.
21 "Be careful, do [a]not turn to evil;
For you have preferred this to [b]affliction.

[a]Job 9:11; 23:8, 9 [b]Job 31:35
15 [1]Or, *arrogance*
6 [1]Lit., *vainly* [a]Job 34:35; 38:2
[1]Lit., *are yet words for God*
3 [a]Job 8:3; 37:23
b 33:3 [b]Job 37:16
[a]Ps. 22:24; 69:33; 02:17 [b]Job 12:13
[a]Job 8:22; 34:26 [b]Job 5:15
[a]Ps. 33:18; 34:15 ob 5:11; Ps. 113:8
8 [a]Job 36:15, 21
9 [a]Job 15:25
[a]Job 33:16; 36:15 [b]2 Kin. 17:13; Job 36:21; Jon. 3:8
[a]1 Tim. 4:8 [b]Ps. 16:11
[1]Lit., *pass away* 15:22 [b]Job 4:21
r, *Their soul dies* [a]Deut. 23:17
[1]Lit., *his* [2]Or, *in ity* [a]Job 36:8, 21 [b]Job 36:10
, *rich food* [a]Hos. 2:14
[a]Job 22:5, 10, 11
Jon. 4:4, 9 [b]Job 33:24
19 [1]Or, *cry*
[1]Lit., *go up* [a]Job 34:20, 25
[a]Job 36:10; Ps. 6:18 [b]Job 36:8, 15; Heb. 11:25

22 "Behold, God is exalted in His power;
Who is a [a]teacher like Him?
23 "Who has appointed Him His way,
And who has said, '[a]Thou hast done wrong'?
24 "Remember that you should [a]exalt His work,
Of which men have [b]sung.
25 "All men have seen it;
Man beholds from afar.
26 "Behold, God is [a]exalted, and [b]we do not know *Him;*
The [c]number of His years is unsearchable.
27 "For [a]He draws up the drops of water,
They distill rain from [1]the [2]mist,
28 Which the clouds pour down,
They drip upon man abundantly.
29 "Can anyone understand the [a]spreading of the clouds,
The [b]thundering of His [1]pavilion?
30 "Behold, He spreads His [1]lightning about Him,
And He covers the depths of the sea.
31 "For by these He [a]judges peoples;
He [b]gives food in abundance.
32 "He covers *His* hands with the [1]lightning,
And [a]commands it to strike the mark.
33 "Its [a]noise declares [1]His presence;
The cattle also, concerning what is coming up.

Chapter 37

37 "At this also my heart trembles,
And leaps from its place.
2 "Listen closely to the [a]thunder of His voice,
And the rumbling that goes out from His mouth.
3 "Under the whole heaven He lets it loose,
And His [1]lightning to the [a]ends of the earth.
4 "After it, a voice roars;
He thunders with His majestic voice;
And He does not restrain [1]the lightnings when His voice is heard.
5 "God [a]thunders with His voice wondrously,
Doing [b]great things which we cannot comprehend.
6 "For to [a]the snow He says, 'Fall on the earth,'
And to the [1b]downpour and the rain, 'Be strong.'
7 "He [a]seals the hand of every man,
That [b]all men may know His work.
8 "Then the beast goes into its [a]lair,
And remains in its [1]den.
9 "Out of the [1a]south comes the storm,
And out of the [2]north the cold.
10 "From the breath of God [a]ice is made,
And the expanse of the waters is frozen.
11 "Also with moisture He [a]loads the thick cloud;
He [b]disperses [c]the cloud of His [1]lightning.
12 "And it changes direction, turning around by His guidance,
That [1]it may do whatever He [a]commands [2]it
On the [b]face of the inhabited earth.

22 [a]Job 35:1
23 [a]Deut. 32
24 [a]Ps. 92:5; [b]Ex. 15:1; Juc 1 Chr. 16:9; P 138:5
26 [a]Job 11:7 [b]1 Cor. 13:12 Ps. 90:2; 102 Heb. 1:12
27 [1]Lit., *its* [2] [a]Job 5:10; 36: 37:6, 11; 38:2 147:8
29 [1]Lit., *booth* 37:11, 16 [b]Jol
30 [1]Lit., *light*
31 [a]Job 37:13 104:27; 136:2 14:17
32 [1]Lit., *light* 37:11, 12, 15
33 [1]Lit., *conce Him* [a]Job 37:2
37:2 [a]Job 36: 5; Ps. 29:3-9
3 [1]Lit., *light* [a] 37:11, 12; 38:1
4 [1]Lit., *them*
5 [a]Job 26:14 37:14, 16, 23
6 [1]Lit., *showe and shower of* [a]Job 38:22 [b]Jo
7 [a]Job 12:14
8 [1]Lit., *dens* [a] 38:40; Ps. 104
9 [1]Lit., *chamb scattering winc* 9:9
10 [a]Job 38:29; 147:17
11 [1]Lit., *light* [a] 36:27 [b]Job 36: 37:15
12 [1]Lit., *they* [2] *them* [a]Job 36:3 148:8 [b]Is. 14:2

13 "Whether for [1a]correction, or for [b]His world,
Or for [c]lovingkindness, He causes it to [2]happen.

14 "Listen to this, O Job,
Stand and consider the wonders of God.
15 "Do you know how God establishes them,
And makes the [1]lightning of His cloud to shine?
16 "Do you know about the layers of the thick clouds,
The [a]wonders of one [b]perfect in knowledge,
17 You whose garments are hot,
When the land is still because of the south wind?
18 "Can you, with Him, [a]spread out the skies,
Strong as a molten mirror?
19 "Teach us what we shall say to Him;
We [a]cannot arrange *our case* because of darkness.
20 "Shall it be told Him that I would speak?
[1]Or should a man say that he would be swallowed up?

21 "And now [1]men do not see the light which is bright in the skies;
But the wind has passed and cleared them.
22 "Out of the north comes golden *splendor;*
Around God is awesome majesty.
23 "The Almighty—[a]we cannot find Him;
He is [b]exalted in power;
And [c]He will not do violence [d]to justice and abundant
righteousness.
24 "Therefore men [a]fear Him;
He does not [b]regard any who are wise of heart."

Chapter 38

38 Then the LORD [a]answered Job out of the whirlwind and said,
2 "Who is this that [a]darkens counsel
By words without knowledge?
3 "Now [a]gird up your loins like a man,
And [b]I will ask you, and you instruct Me!
4 "Where were you [a]when I laid the foundation of the earth?
Tell *Me,* if you [1]have understanding,
5 Who set its [a]measurements, since you know?
Or who stretched the line on it?
6 "On what [a]were its bases sunk?
Or who laid its cornerstone,
7 When the morning stars sang together,
And all the [a]sons of God shouted for joy?

8 "Or *who* [a]enclosed the sea with doors,
When, bursting forth, it went out from the womb;
9 When I made a cloud its garment,
And thick darkness its swaddling band,
10 And I [1a]placed boundaries on it,
And I set a bolt and doors,
11 And I said, 'Thus far you shall come, but no farther;
And here shall your proud waves stop'?

12 "Have you [1]ever in your life commanded the morning,

[1]Lit., *the rod* [2]Lit., *und* [a]Ex. 9:18, 23; ...m. 12:18, 19 [b]Job 38:26, 27 [c]1 Kin. 18:41-46

15 [1]Lit., *light*

[a]Job 37:5, 14, 23 [b]Job 36:4

...ob 9:8; Ps. 104:2; 44:24; 45:12; Jer. 10:12; Zech. 12:1

...o 9:14; Rom. 8:26

...r, *If a man speak, surely he shall be swallowed up*

21 [1]Lit., *they*

...Job 11:7, 8; Rom. ... 1 Tim. 6:16 [b]Job ...5 [c]Is. 63:9; Lam. ... Ezek. 18:23, 32; 33:11 [d]Job 8:3

...Matt. 10:28 [b]Job ...att. 11:25; 1 Cor. 1:26

38:1 [a]Job 40:6

[a]Job 35:16; 42:3

...o 40:7 [b]Job 42:4

4 [1]Lit., *know ...erstanding* [a]Job ... Ps. 104:5; Prov. 8:29; 30:4

...v. 8:29; Is. 40:12

6 [a]Job 26:7

7 [a]Job 1:6

...8 [a]Gen. 1:9; Ps. ... Prov. 8:29; Jer. 5:22

[1]Lit., *broke My ...on it* [a]Gen. 1:9; ...3:7; 104:9; Prov. 8:29; Jer. 5:22

...*from your days*

And caused the dawn to know its place;
13 That it might take hold of [a]the ends of the earth,
And [b]the wicked be shaken out of it?
14 "It is changed like clay *under* the seal;
And they stand forth like a garment.
15 "And [a]from the wicked their light is withheld,
And the [b]uplifted arm is broken.

16 "Have you entered into [a]the springs of the sea?
Or have you walked [1]in the recesses of the deep?
17 "Have the gates of death been revealed to you?
Or have you seen the gates of [a]deep darkness?
18 "Have you understood the [1]expanse of [a]the earth?
Tell *Me,* if you know all this.

19 "Where is the way to the dwelling of light?
And darkness, where is its place,
20 That you may take it to [a]its territory,
And that you may discern the paths to its [1]home?
21 "You know, for [a]you were born then,
And the number of your days is great!
22 "Have you entered the storehouses [a]of the snow,
Or have you seen the storehouses of the [b]hail,
23 Which I have reserved for the time of distress,
For the day of war and battle?
24 "Where is the way that [a]the light is divided,
Or the east wind scattered on the earth?

25 "Who has cleft a channel for the flood,
Or a way for the thunderbolt;
26 To bring [a]rain on a land without [1]people,
On a desert without a man in it,
27 To [a]satisfy the waste and desolate land,
And to make the [1]seeds of grass to sprout?
28 "Has [a]the rain a father?
Or who has begotten the drops of dew?
29 "From whose womb has come the [a]ice?
And the frost of heaven, who has given it birth?
30 "Water [1]becomes hard like stone,
And the surface of the deep is imprisoned.

31 "Can you bind the chains of the [a]Pleiades,
Or loose the cords of Orion?
32 "Can you lead forth a [1]constellation in its season,
And guide the Bear with her [2]satellites?
33 "Do you know the [a]ordinances of the heavens,
Or fix their rule over the earth?

34 "Can you lift up your voice to the clouds,
So that an [a]abundance of water may cover you?
35 "Can you [a]send forth lightnings that they may go
And say to you, 'Here we are'?
36 "Who has [a]put wisdom in the innermost being,
Or has given [b]understanding to the [1]mind?

13 [a]Job 28:... [b]Job 34:25, ...
15 [a]Job 5:1... 15:30; Ps. 1...
16 [1]Or, *in se...* [a]Gen. 7:11; ... 8:24, 28
17 [a]Job 10:2... 34:22
18 [1]Or, *widt...* 28:24
20 [1]Lit., *hous...* 26:10
21 [a]Job 15:7
22 [a]Job 37:6... Josh. 10:11; ... Ezek. 13:11, ... 16:21
24 [a]Job 26:1...
26 [1]Lit., *man* 36:27
27 [1]Or, *growt...* 104:13, 14; 1...
28 [a]Job 36:2... 147:8; Jer. 14...
29 [a]Job 37:10... 147:17
30 [1]Lit., *hides*
31 [a]Job 9:9; A...
32 [1]Heb., *Maz...* [2]Lit., *sons*
33 [a]Ps. 148:6; ... 31:35, 36
34 [a]Job 22:11; ... 28; 38:37
35 [a]Job 36:32; ...
36 [1]Or, *cock* [a]... Ps. 51:6; Eccl. ... [b]Job 32:8

37 "Who can count the clouds by wisdom,
Or [a]tip the water jars of the heavens,
38 When the dust hardens into a mass,
And the clods stick together?

39 "Can you hunt the [a]prey for the lion,
Or satisfy the appetite of the young lions,
40 When they [a]crouch in *their* dens,
And lie in wait in *their* lair?
41 "Who prepares for [a]the raven its nourishment,
When its young cry to God,
And wander about without food?

Chapter 39

39 "Do you know the time the [1a]mountain goats give birth?
Do you observe the calving of the [b]deer?
2 "Can you count the months they fulfill,
Or do you know the time they give birth?
3 "They kneel down, they bring forth their young,
They get rid of their labor pains.
4 "Their offspring become strong, they grow up in the open field;
They leave and do not return to them.

5 "Who sent out the [a]wild donkey free?
And who loosed the bonds of the swift donkey,
6 To whom I gave [a]the wilderness for a home,
And the salt land for his dwelling place?
7 "He scorns the tumult of the city,
The shoutings of the driver he does not hear.
8 "He explores the mountains for his pasture,
And he searches after every green thing.
9 "Will the [a]wild ox consent to serve you?
Or will he spend the night at your manger?
10 "Can you bind the wild ox in a furrow with [1]ropes?
Or will he harrow the valleys after you?
11 "Will you trust him because his strength is great
And leave your labor to him?
12 "Will you have faith in him that he will return your [1]grain,
And gather *it from* your threshing floor?

13 "The ostriches' wings flap joyously
With the pinion and plumage of [1]love,
14 For she abandons her eggs to the earth,
And warms them in the dust,
15 And she forgets that a foot may crush [1]them,
Or that a wild beast may trample [1]them.
16 "She treats her young [a]cruelly, as if *they* were not hers;
Though her labor be in vain, *she* is [1]unconcerned;
17 Because God has made her forget wisdom,
And has not given her a share of understanding.
18 "When she lifts herself [1]on high,
She laughs at the horse and his rider.

19 "Do you give the horse *his* might?

37 [a]Job 38:34
39 [a]Ps. 104:21
40 [a]Job 37:8
[a]Ps. 147:9; Matt. 6:26; Luke 12:24
[1]Lit., *goats of the rock* [a]Deut. 14:5; 1 Sam. 24:2; Ps. 104:18 [b]Ps. 29:9
6:5; 11:12; 24:5; Ps. 104:11
b 24:5; Jer. 2:24; Hos. 8:9
um. 23:22; Deut. Ps. 22:21; 29:6; 92:10; Is. 34:7
0 [1]Lit., *his rope*
12 [1]Lit., *seed*
13 [1]Or, *a stork*
15 [1]Lit., *it*
Lit., *without fear* [a]Lam. 4:3
18 [1]Or, *to flee*

Do you clothe his neck with a mane?
20 "Do you make him [a]leap like the locust?
His majestic [b]snorting is terrible.
21 "[1]He paws in the valley, and rejoices in *his* strength;
He [a]goes out to meet the weapons.
22 "He laughs at fear and is not dismayed;
And he does not turn back from the sword.
23 "The quiver rattles against him,
The flashing spear and javelin.
24 "With shaking and rage he [1]races over the ground;
And he does not stand still at the voice of the trumpet.
25 "As often as the trumpet *sounds* he says, 'Aha!'
And he scents the battle from afar,
And thunder of the captains, and the war cry.

26 "Is it by your understanding that the hawk soars,
Stretching his wings toward the south?
27 "Is it at your [1]command that the eagle mounts up,
And makes [a]his nest on high?
28 "On the cliff he dwells and lodges,
Upon the rocky crag, an inaccessible place.
29 "From there he [a]spies out food;
His eyes see *it* from afar.
30 "His young ones also suck up blood;
And [a]where the slain are, there is he."

Chapter 40

40 Then the LORD said to Job,
2 "Will the faultfinder [a]contend with the Almighty?
Let him who [b]reproves God answer it."

3 Then Job answered the LORD and said,
4 "Behold, I am insignificant; what can I reply to Thee?
I [a]lay my hand on my mouth.
5 "Once I have spoken, and [a]I will not answer;
Even twice, and I will add no more."

6 Then the [a]LORD answered Job out of the storm, and said,
7 "Now [a]gird up your loins like a man;
I will [b]ask you, and you instruct Me.
8 "Will you really [a]annul My judgment?
Will you [b]condemn Me [c]that you may be justified?
9 "Or do you have an arm like God,
And can you [a]thunder with a voice like His?

10 "[a]Adorn yourself with eminence and dignity;
And clothe yourself with honor and majesty.
11 "Pour out [a]the overflowings of your anger;
And look on everyone who is [b]proud, and make him low.
12 "Look on everyone who is proud, *and* [a]humble him;
And [b]tread down the wicked [1]where they stand.
13 "[a]Hide them in the dust together;
Bind [1]them in the hidden *place*.
14 "Then I will also [1]confess to you,

20 [a]Joel 2:5
21 [1]Lit., *They* 8:6
24 [1]Or, *swall*
27 [1]Lit., *mout* 49:16; Obad.
29 [a]Job 9:26
30 [a]Matt. 24:2 17:37
40:2 [a]Job 9:3; 33:13; Is. 45:9 13:3; 23:4; 31:
4 [a]Job 21:5; 2
5 [a]Job 9:3, 15
6 [a]Job 38:1
7 [a]Job 38:3 [b]J 42:4
8 [a]Rom. 3:4 [b] 7; 16:11; 19:6; [c]Job 13:18; 27:
9 [a]Job 37:5; Ps
10 [a]Ps. 93:1; 1
11 [a]Is. 42:25; N 8 [b]Is. 2:12; Dar
12 [1]Lit., *under* [a]1 Sam. 2:7; Is. 13:11; Dan. 4:37 63:3
13 [1]Or, *their fac* 2:10-12
14 [1]Or, *praise y*

That your own right hand can save you.

15 “Behold now, [1]Behemoth, which [a]I made [2]as well as you;
He eats grass like an ox.
16 “Behold now, his strength in his loins,
And his power in the muscles of his belly.
17 “He bends his tail like a cedar;
The sinews of his thighs are knit together.
18 “His bones are tubes of bronze;
His [1]limbs are like bars of iron.

19 “He is the [a]first of the ways of God;
Let his [b]maker bring near his sword.
20 “Surely the mountains [a]bring him food,
And all the beasts of the field [b]play there.
21 “Under the lotus plants he lies down,
In the covert of the reeds and the marsh.
22 “The lotus plants cover him with [1]shade;
The willows of the brook surround him.
23 “If a river [1]rages, he is not alarmed;
He is confident, though the [a]Jordan rushes to his mouth.
24 “Can anyone capture him [1]when he is on watch,
With [2]barbs can anyone pierce *his* nose?

Chapter 41

41 “[1]Can you draw out [2a]Leviathan with a fishhook?
Or press down his tongue with a cord?
2 “Can you [a]put a [1]rope in his nose?
Or pierce his jaw with a [2]hook?
3 “Will he make many supplications to you?
Or will he speak to you soft words?
4 “Will he make a covenant with you?
Will you take him for a servant forever?
5 “Will you play with him as with a bird?
Or will you bind him for your maidens?
6 “Will the [1]traders bargain over him?
Will they divide him among the merchants?
7 “Can you fill his skin with harpoons,
Or his head with fishing spears?
8 “Lay your hand on him;
Remember the battle; [1]you will not do it again!
9 “[1]Behold, [2]your expectation is false;
Will [3]you be laid low even at the sight of him?
10 “No one is so fierce that he dares to [a]arouse him;
Who then is he that can stand before Me?
11 “Who has [1a]given to Me that I should repay *him?*
Whatever is [b]under the whole heaven is Mine.

12 “I will not keep silence concerning his limbs,
Or his mighty strength, or his [1]orderly frame.
13 “Who can [1]strip off his outer armor?
Who can come within his double [2]mail?
14 “Who can open the doors of his face?
Around his teeth there is terror.

15 [1]Or, the ...opopotamus [2]Lit., with [a]Job 40:19
18 [1]Lit., bones
[a]Job 41:33 [b]Job 40:15
[a]Ps. 104:14 [b]Ps. 104:26
2 [1]Lit., his shade
3 [1]Or, oppresses [a]Gen. 13:10
[1]Lit., in his eyes [2]Lit., snares
...:1 [1]Ch. 40:25 in ... [2]Or, the crocodile ...b 3:8; Ps. 74:14; 104:26; Is. 27:1
...t., rope of rushes ...m or ring [a]2 Kin. 19:28; Is. 37:29
6 [1]Lit., partners
[1]Lit., do not add
Ch. 41:1 in Heb. ...Lit., his [3]Lit., he
10 [a]Job 3:8
[1]Lit., anticipated ...11:35 [b]Ex. 19:5; ...:14; Job 9:5-10; ...6-14; 28:24; Ps. ...12; 1 Cor. 10:26
...12 [1]Or, graceful
...Lit., uncover the ...is garment [2]So ...Gr.; Heb., bridle

15 "*His* [1]strong scales are *his* pride,
Shut up *as with* a tight seal.
16 "One is so near to another,
That no air can come between them.
17 "They are joined one to another;
They clasp each other and cannot be separated.
18 "His sneezes flash forth light,
And his eyes are like the [a]eyelids of the morning.
19 "Out of his mouth go burning torches;
Sparks of fire leap forth.
20 "Out of his nostrils smoke goes forth,
As *from* a boiling pot and *burning* rushes.
21 "His breath kindles coals,
And a flame goes forth from his mouth.
22 "In his neck lodges strength,
And dismay leaps before him.
23 "The folds of his flesh are joined together,
Firm on him and immovable.
24 "His heart is as hard as a stone;
Even as hard as a lower millstone.
25 "When he raises himself up, the [1]mighty fear;
Because of the crashing they are bewildered.
26 "The sword that reaches him cannot avail;
Nor the spear, the dart, or the javelin.
27 "He regards iron as straw,
Bronze as rotten wood.
28 "The [1]arrow cannot make him flee;
Slingstones are turned into stubble for him.
29 "Clubs are regarded as stubble;
He laughs at the rattling of the javelin.
30 "His underparts are *like* sharp potsherds;
He [1]spreads out *like* a threshing sledge on the mire.
31 "He makes the depths boil like a pot;
He makes the sea like a jar of ointment.
32 "Behind him he makes a wake to shine;
One would think the deep to be gray-haired.
33 "[a]Nothing on [1]earth is like him,
One made without fear.
34 "[1]He looks on everything that is high;
He is king over all the [a]sons of pride."

Chapter 42

42 Then Job answered the LORD, and said,
2 "I know that [a]Thou canst do all things,
And that no purpose of Thine can be thwarted.
3 'Who is this that [a]hides counsel without knowledge?'
"Therefore I have declared that which I did not understand,
Things [b]too wonderful for me, which I did not know."
4 'Hear, now, and I will speak;
I will [a]ask Thee, and do Thou instruct me.'
5 "I have [a]heard of Thee by the hearing of the ear;
But now my [b]eye sees Thee;
6 Therefore I retract,
And I repent in dust and ashes."

15 [1]Lit., *rows*
18 [a]Job 3:9
25 [1]Or, *gods*
28 [1]Lit., *son o*
30 [1]Or, *moves*
33 [1]Lit., *dust*
34 [1]Ch. 41:26 [a]Job 28:8
42:2 [a]Gen. 18: 19:26
3 [a]Job 38:2 [b]P 131:1; 139:6
4 [a]Job 38:3; 40
5 [a]Job 26:14; R 10:17 [b]Is. 6:5; E 1:17, 18

7 And it came about after the LORD had spoken these words to Job,
that the LORD said to Eliphaz the Temanite, "My wrath is kindled
against you and against your two friends, because you have not
spoken of Me what is right [a]as My servant Job has.
8 "Now therefore, take for yourselves [a]seven bulls and seven rams,
and go to My servant Job, and offer up a [b]burnt offering for your-
selves, and My servant Job will [c]pray for you. [d]For I will [1]accept him
so that I may not do with you *according to your* folly, because you
have not spoken of Me what is right, as My servant Job has."
9 So Eliphaz the Temanite and Bildad the Shuhite *and* Zophar the
Naamathite went and did as the LORD told them; and the LORD [1]ac-
cepted Job.
10 And the LORD [a]restored the fortunes of Job when he prayed for
his friends, and the LORD increased all that Job had twofold.
11 Then all his [a]brothers, and all his sisters, and all who had known
him before, came to him, and they ate bread with him in his house;
and they [b]consoled him and comforted him for all the evil that the
LORD had brought on him. And each one gave him one [1]piece of
money, and each a ring of gold.
12 [a]And the LORD blessed the latter *days* of Job more than his begin-
ning, [b]and he had 14,000 sheep, and 6,000 camels, and 1,000 yoke of
oxen, and 1,000 female donkeys.
13 And [a]he had seven sons and three daughters.
14 And he named the first Jemimah, and the second Keziah, and
the third Keren-happuch.
15 And in all the land no women were found so fair as Job's daugh-
ters; and their father gave them inheritance among their brothers.
16 And after this Job lived 140 years, and saw his sons, and his
grandsons, four generations.
17 [a]And Job died, an old man and full of days.

ob 40:3-5; 42:1-6

it., *lift up his face*
m. 23:1 [b]Job 1:5
en. 20:17; James
John 5:16 [d]Job
22:30

[1]Lit., *lifted up the face of*

ut. 30:3; Job 1:2,
Ps. 14:7; 85:1-3;
126:1-6

b., *qesitah* [a]Job
19:13 [b]Job 2:11

[a]Job 1:10; 8:7;
es 5:11 [b]Job 1:3

13 [a]Job 1:2

en. 15:15; 25:8;
Job 5:26

Job Observations Chart

Insights Regarding Satan

Character

Tactics

Power

Insights Regarding God

His character

His ways

His power

over Satan

over nature

over man

Insights Regarding Job

Character

Relationship to God

Relationship to his friends

What God Says Regarding

Job

Job's friends

Insights Regarding God's Expectations of Man

Insights into Life and Death

Lessons I learned about dealing with those in pain

JOB AT A GLANCE

e of Job:

T DIVISIONS

		CHAPTER THEMES
		1
		2
		3
		4
		5
		6
		7
		8
		9
		10
		11
		12
		13
		14
		15
		16
		17
		18
		19
		20
		21
		22
		23
		24
		25
		26
		27
		28
		29
		30
		31
		32
		33
		34
		35
		36
		37
		38
		39
		40
		41
		42

Author:

Date:

Purpose:

Key Words:

Psalms

Man needs to communicate with God in prayer and in song. He needs to come before Hi honestly present that which is on his heart—whether it be distress or joy, confusion or confidence

Man needs to lift up his voice in worship, to speak to God and to one another in psalms and l and spiritual songs, singing and making melody with his heart to the Lord (*see* Ephesians 5:19).

Thus, the psalms—praises, prayers, and songs—are to be accompanied on stringed instrume David, writer of many psalms, appointed Levites over the service of song in the house of the They ministered with song before the tabernacle of the tent of meeting until Solomon had bu house of the Lord in Jerusalem (*see* 1 Chronicles 6:31).

Worship is befitting to God alone. Psalms is a book of prayer and praise, written by men, inspi God. "For from Him and through Him and to Him are all things. To Him be the glory forever. A (Romans 11:36).

Things to Do

1. As you study Psalms, remember psalms are poetry whether they are prayers or songs. H poetry does not contain rhyme and meter. Its distinctive feature is parallelism of some where one line relates to another in various ways. Usually the poetic lines are composed o or sometimes three, balanced segments where typically the second is shorter than the firs repeats, contrasts, or completes the first segment.

   The psalms vary in design. Nine are alphabetical with each stanza beginning with a letter the Hebrew alphabet. The alphabetical psalms are 9, 10, 25, 34, 37, 111, 112, 119, and 145.

2. The majority of the psalms have a superscription at the beginning, which designates o several things: the composer, the occasion of the psalm, who it is for, how it is to be accomp and what kind of psalm it is, i.e. a *maskil*, *shiggaion*, etc. If a psalm has a superscription, read consult the NASB cross references if it's referenced. This will help put the psalm into context

3. Watch for the theme of the psalm and how it is developed. Sometimes the theme will be sta the very beginning of the psalm, at other times the key thematic scheme will be found i center of the psalm. Each will have a theme and will be developed in accordance wit author's design for the psalm.

   a. Some of the psalms give insights into the history of Israel, such as Psalm 78. Study carefully. Note the events, God's intervention, and watchcare.

   b. If a psalm makes a reference to a person or circumstance which is discussed in one c historical books of the Bible, you might go back to that book and record the psalm that ap to that person or circumstance. For instance, in the margin of 2 Samuel 12, record Psalm 51

4. Key words bring out the theme of the psalm's song or prayer. Sometimes a key phrase will and close the psalm. Watch for and mark these phrases. Also watch for the following key w and mark them in a distinctive way: *righteous, wicked, sin (iniquity), prayer (pray), praise, sing refuge, hope, save (saves, saved, salvation),* and *cry (cried)*. Write these key words on an index and use it as a bookmark when you study and meditate on the psalms.

5. Don't miss the central focus of these psalms—God. There's so much to be learned about Him then worshiped and adored. Observe His names, His titles, His attributes, and how man respond to Him.

   a. Don't forget to look for Jesus, who is God, one with the Father, for He said, "All things w are written about Me in the Law of Moses and the Prophets and the Psalms must be fulfi (Luke 24:44).

b. The psalms are for the heart and soul, but they also address the mind. In the margin record your insights about God. As you do this, meditate on what you learn. Spend time in praise and prayer. Let the book of Psalms help you love the Lord your God with all your heart, mind, body, soul, and strength.

6. When you finish each psalm, record the theme of that psalm on the line in the text under the number of the psalm and on the PSALMS AT A GLANCE chart on pages 923 through 928.

7. Psalms has five segments which are marked on PSALMS AT A GLANCE.

   a. Give each segment a title or record its theme.

   b. Read Psalms 41:13; 72:18-19; 89:52; 106:48; and 150:6; and notice what is said and how each segment concludes.

   c. Complete PSALMS AT A GLANCE.

INGS TO THINK ABOUT

1. When you are distressed, confused, afraid, hurt, or when you need to talk with someone who will understand, turn to Psalms and with the psalmist, be still (cease striving) and know He is God.

2. Think about the practical value of Psalms and let it serve as your primary counselor when you need wisdom and understanding. Remember, blessed is the man who does not walk in the counsel of the wicked . . . but whose delight is in the law of the Lord, and who meditates in that law day and night (*see* Psalm 1).

3. Have you thought about ending each day as the book of Psalms ends—with a psalm of praise? "Let the godly ones exult in glory; let them sing for joy on their beds, let the high praises of God be in their mouth. . . . Let everything that has breath praise the Lord. Praise the Lord" (Psalm 149:5-6; 150:6). Try it and see what God does.

The following expressions occur often in the Psalms:

Selah May mean *Pause, Crescendo,* or *Musical Interlude*
Maskil Possibly, *Contemplative,* or *Didactic,* or *Skillful Psalm*
Mikhtam Possibly, *Epigrammatic Poem,* or *Atonement Psalm*
Sheol The nether world

BOOK 1

Psalm 1 ______________________

1 How blessed is the man who [a]does not walk in the [b]counsel of
the wicked,
Nor stand in the [1c]path of sinners,
Nor [d]sit in the seat of scoffers!
2 But his [a]delight is [b]in the law of the LORD,
And in His law he meditates [c]day and [d]night.
3 And he will be like [a]a tree *firmly* planted by [1]streams of water,
Which yields its fruit in its season,
And its [2]leaf does not wither;
And [3]in whatever he does, [b]he prospers.

4 The wicked are not so,
But they are like [a]chaff which the wind drives away.
5 Therefore [a]the wicked will not stand in the [b]judgment,
Nor sinners in [c]the assembly of the righteous.
6 For the LORD [1a]knows the way of the righteous,
But the way of [b]the wicked will perish.

1 [1]Or, *way* [a]Prov. 4:14 [b]Ps. 5:9, 10;):2-11; 36:1-4 [c]Ps. 17:4; 119:104 [d]Ps. 26:4, 5; Jer. 15:17

[a]Ps. 119:14, 16, 35 osh. 1:8 [c]Ps. 25:5 [d]Ps. 63:5, 6

3 [1]Or, *canals* [2]Or, *ge* [3]Or, *all that he oes prospers* [a]Ps. 2:12-14; Jer. 17:8; 19:10 [b]Gen. 39:2, 3, 23; Ps. 128:2

b 21:18; Ps. 35:5; Is. 17:13

s. 5:5 [b]Ps. 9:7, 8, 16 [c]Ps. 89:5, 7

r, *approves* or *has ard to* [a]Ps. 37:18; 1. 1:7; John 10:14; . 2:19 [b]Ps. 9:5, 6; 11:6

Psalm 2

2 Why are [a]the [1]nations in an uproar,
And the peoples [b]devising a vain thing?
2 The [a]kings of the earth take their stand,
And the rulers take counsel together
[b]Against the LORD and against His [1c]Anointed:
3 "Let us [a]tear their fetters apart,
And cast away their cords from us!"

4 He who [1]sits in the heavens [a]laughs,
The Lord [b]scoffs at them.
5 Then He will speak to them in His [a]anger
And [b]terrify them in His fury:
6 "But as for Me, I have [1]installed [a]My King
Upon Zion, [b]My holy mountain."

7 "I will surely tell of the [1]decree of the LORD:
He said to Me, 'Thou art [a]My Son,
Today I have begotten Thee.
8 'Ask of Me, and [a]I will surely give [b]the [1]nations as Thine inheritance,
And the *very* [c]ends of the earth as Thy possession.
9 'Thou shalt [1a]break them with a [2]rod of iron,
Thou shalt [b]shatter them like [3]earthenware.' "

10 Now therefore, O kings, [a]show discernment;
Take warning, O [1]judges of the earth.
11 [1]Worship the LORD with [2a]reverence,
And rejoice with [b]trembling.
12 [1]Do homage to [a]the Son, lest He become angry, and you perish *in* the way,
For [b]His wrath may [2]soon be kindled.
How blessed are all who [c]take refuge in Him!

Psalm 3

A Psalm of David, when [+]he fled from Absalom his son.

3 O LORD, how [a]my adversaries have increased!
Many are rising up against me.
2 Many are saying [1]of my soul,
"There is no [2a]deliverance for him in God." [3]Selah.

3 But Thou, O LORD, art [a]a shield about me,
My [b]glory, and the One who [c]lifts my head.
4 I was crying to the LORD with my voice,
And He [a]answered me from [b]His holy [1]mountain. Selah.
5 [1]I [a]lay down and slept;
I awoke, for the LORD sustains me.
6 I will [a]not be afraid of ten thousands of people
Who have [b]set themselves against me round about.

7 [a]Arise, O LORD; [b]save me, O my God!
For Thou [1]hast [c]smitten all my enemies on the [2]cheek;
Thou [3]hast [d]shattered the teeth of the wicked.

2:1 [1]Or, *Gentiles* [a]... 46:6; 83:2-5; Acts 4... 26 [b]Ps. 21:11

2 [1]Or, *Messiah* [a]P... 48:4-6 [b]Ps. 74:18, [c]John 1:41

3 [a]Jer. 5:5

4 [1]Or, *is enthroned* [a]Ps. 37:13 [b]Ps. 59...

5 [a]Ps. 21:8, 9; 76:... [b]Ps. 78:49, 50

6 [1]Or, *consecrated* [a]Ps. 45:6 [b]Ps. 48:1...

7 [1]Or, *decree: The LORD said to Me* [a]... 13:33; Heb. 1:5; 5:...

8 [1]Or, *Gentiles* [a]P... 21:1, 2 [b]Ps. 22:27 67:7

9 [1]Another readin... *rule* [2]Or, *scepter* o... *staff* [3]Lit., *potter's* [a]Ps. 89:23; 110:5, ... Rev. 2:26, 27; 12:5... 19:15 [b]Ps. 28:5; 5... 72:4

10 [1]Or, *leaders* [a]P... 8:15; 27:11

11 [1]Or, *Serve* [2]Or... [a]Ps. 5:7 [b]Ps. 119:... 120

12 [1]Lit., *Kiss;* som... ancient versions r... *Do homage purely*... *Lay hold of instruc*... [2]Or, *quickly, sudde*... *easily* [a]Ps. 2:7 [b]P... 6:16, 17 [c]Ps. 5:11

[+]2 Sam. 15:13-17, ...

3:1 [a]2 Sam. 15:12... 69:4

2 [1]Or, *to* [2]Or, *sal*... [3]*Selah* may mean *Pause, Crescend*... *Musical interlude* ... 22:7, 8; 71:11

3 [a]Ps. 5:12; 28:7 ... 62:7 [c]Ps. 9:13; 27...

4 [1]Or, *hill* [a]Ps. 4:... 34:4 [b]Ps. 2:6; 15:...

5 [1]Or, *As for me,* [a]Lev. 26:6; Ps. 4:8... 3:24

6 [a]Ps. 23:4; 27:3 118:10-13

7 [1]Or, *dost smite* ... *jaw* [3]Or, *dost sha*... [a]Ps. 7:6 [b]Ps. 6:4; ... [c]Job 16:10 [d]Ps. 5... 58:6

8 [1a]Salvation belongs to the LORD;
Thy [b]blessing [2]*be* upon Thy people! Selah.

Psalm 4

[+]For the choir director; on stringed instruments. A Psalm of David.

4 [a]Answer me when [b]I call, O God [1]of my righteousness!
Thou hast [2c]relieved me in my distress;
Be [d]gracious to me and [e]hear my prayer.

2 O sons of men, how long will [a]my [1]honor become [b]a reproach?
How long will you love [c]what is worthless and aim at [d]deception? [2]Selah.

3 But know that the LORD has [1a]set apart the [b]godly man for Himself;
The LORD [c]hears when I call to Him.

4 [1a]Tremble, [2b]and do not sin;
[3c]Meditate in your heart upon your bed, and be still. Selah.
5 Offer [1]the [a]sacrifices of righteousness,
And [b]trust in the LORD.

6 Many are saying, "[a]Who will show us *any* good?"
[b]Lift up the light of Thy countenance upon us, O LORD!
7 Thou hast put [a]gladness in my heart,
More than when their grain and new wine abound.
8 In peace I will [1]both [a]lie down and sleep,
For Thou alone, O LORD, dost make me to [b]dwell in safety.

Psalm 5

For the choir director; for [+]flute accompaniment. A Psalm of David.

5 [a]Give ear to my words, O LORD,
Consider my [1b]groaning.
2 Heed [a]the sound of my cry for help, [b]my King and my God,
For to Thee do I pray.
3 In the morning, O LORD, [1]Thou wilt hear my voice;
In the [a]morning I will order *my* [2]*prayer* to Thee and *eagerly* [b]watch.

4 For Thou art not a God [a]who takes pleasure in wickedness;
[b]No evil [1]dwells with Thee.
5 The [a]boastful shall not [b]stand before Thine eyes;
Thou [c]dost hate all who do iniquity.
6 Thou [a]dost destroy those who speak falsehood;
The LORD abhors [b]the man of bloodshed and deceit.
7 But as for me, [a]by Thine abundant lovingkindness I will enter Thy house,
[1]At Thy holy temple I will [b]bow in [c]reverence for Thee.

8 O LORD, [a]lead me [b]in Thy righteousness [c]because of [1]my foes;
Make Thy way [2]straight before me.
9 There is [a]nothing [1]reliable in [2]what they say;
Their [b]inward part is destruction *itself*;
Their [c]throat is an open grave;

erance [2]Or, 8:8; 35:3; Is. [b]Ps. 29:11
onging to the oir director's anthology
:1 [1]I.e., who nest my right ade room for :6 [b]Ps. 18:6 :18, 19 [d]Ps. . 17:6; 39:12
glory [2]Selah nean: *Pause,* do or Musical [a]Ps. 3:3 [b]Ps. , 19, 20 [c]Ps. 6 [d]Ps. 31:18
ner reading is nderfully with 4 [b]Ps. 31:23; 2 [c]Ps. 6:8, 9; 17:6
with anger or [2]Or, *but* [3]Lit., Ps. 99:1 [b]Ps. ph. 4:26 [c]Ps. 77:6
[1]Or, *righteous* [a]Deut. 33:19; [b]Ps. 37:3, 5; 62:8
7; 9:25 [b]Num. Ps. 80:3, 7, 19
11, 12; Is. 9:3; Acts 14:17
the same time 11:19; Ps. 3:5 v. 25:18; Deut. 12:10; Ps. 16:9
Heb., *Nehiloth*
[1]Or, *meditation* 2 [b]Ps. 104:34
40:6 [b]Ps. 84:3
, mayest Thou , *sacrifice* [a]Ps. :13 [b]Ps. 130:5
, sojourns [a]Ps. :16 [b]Ps. 92:15
73:3; 75:4 [b]Ps. [c]Ps. 11:5; 45:7
Ps. 52:4, 5 [b]Ps. 55:23
Or, *Toward* [a]Ps. [b]Ps. 138:2 [c]Ps. 115:11, 13
those who lie in wait for me [2]Or, [a]Ps. 31:3 [b]Ps. 31:1 [c]Ps. 27:11
Or, *true* [2]Lit., *his* [a]Ps. 52:3 [b]Ps. :14 [c]Rom. 3:13

They [3]flatter with their tongue.
10 Hold them guilty, O God;
[a]By their own devices let them fall!
In the multitude of their transgressions [b]thrust them out,
For they are [c]rebellious against Thee.

11 But let all who [a]take refuge in Thee [b]be glad,
Let them ever sing for joy;
And [1]mayest Thou [c]shelter them,
That those who [d]love Thy name may exult in Thee.
12 For it is Thou who dost [a]bless the righteous man, O LORD,
Thou dost [b]surround him with favor as with a shield.

Psalm 6

For the choir director; with stringed instruments,
[+]upon an eight-string lyre. A Psalm of David.

6 O LORD, [a]do not rebuke me in Thine anger,
Nor chasten me in Thy wrath.
2 Be gracious to me, O LORD, for I *am* [a]pining away;
[b]Heal me, O LORD, for [c]my bones are dismayed.
3 And my [a]soul is greatly dismayed;
But Thou, O LORD—[b]how long?

4 Return, O LORD, [a]rescue my [1]soul;
Save me because of Thy lovingkindness.
5 For [a]there is no [1]mention of Thee in death;
In [2]Sheol who will give Thee thanks?

6 I am [a]weary with my sighing;
Every night I make my bed swim,
I dissolve my couch with [b]my tears.
7 My [a]eye has wasted away with grief;
It has become old because of all my adversaries.

8 [a]Depart from me, all you who do iniquity,
For the LORD [b]has heard the voice of my weeping.
9 The LORD [a]has heard my supplication,
The LORD [b]receives my prayer.
10 All my enemies shall [a]be ashamed and greatly dismayed;
They shall [1]turn back, they shall [b]suddenly be ashamed.

Psalm 7

A [+]Shiggaion of David, which he sang to the LORD
•concerning Cush, a Benjamite.

7 O LORD my God, [a]in Thee I have taken refuge;
Save me from all those who pursue me, and [b]deliver me,
2 Lest he tear [1]my soul [a]like a lion,
[2]Dragging me away, while there is none to deliver.

3 O LORD my God, if I have done this,
If there is [a]injustice in my hands,
4 If I have [a]rewarded evil to [1]my friend,
Or have [b]plundered [2]him who without cause was my adversary,

9 [3]Or, *make tongue smoo*

10 [a]Ps. 9:16 36:12 [c]Ps. 1

11 [1]Or, *Thou shelter* [a]Ps. 2 33:1; 64:10 [c] [d]Ps. 69:36

12 [a]Ps. 29:11 32:7, 10

[+]Or, *according lower octave* (*Sheminith*)

6:1 [a]Ps. 38:1

2 [a]Ps. 102:4, 41:4; 147:3; H [c]Ps. 22:14; 31

3 [a]Ps. 88:3; Jo 12:27 [b]Ps. 90:

4 [1]Or, *life* [a]Ps

5 [1]Or, *rememb* [2]I.e., the nethe [a]Ps. 30:9; 88:1 115:17; Eccl. 9 38:18

6 [a]Ps. 69:3 [b]P

7 [a]Job 17:7; Ps 38:10

8 [a]Ps. 119:115; 7:23; Luke 13:2 3:4; 28:6

9 [a]Ps. 116:1 [b]P 66:19, 20

10 [1]Or, *again b ashamed sudde* 71:13, 24 [b]Ps. 7

[+]I.e., Dithyrambi rhythm; or, wild passionate song *concerning the*

7:1 [a]Ps. 31:1; 7 [b]Ps. 31:15

2 [1]Or, *me* [2]Or, *it in pieces, while* 57:4; Is. 38:13

3 [a]1 Sam. 24:11

4 [1]Lit., *him who peace with me* [2] *adversary withou cause* [a]Ps. 109: [b]1 Sam. 24:7; 26

5 Let the enemy pursue [1]my soul and overtake [2]*it*;
And let him trample my life down to the ground,
And lay my glory in the dust. [3]Selah.

6 [a]Arise, O LORD, in Thine anger;
[b]Lift up Thyself against [c]the rage of my adversaries,
And [d]arouse Thyself [1]for me; Thou hast appointed judgment.
7 And let the assembly of the [a]peoples encompass Thee;
And over [1]them return Thou on high.
8 The LORD [a]judges the peoples;
[1b]Vindicate me, O LORD, according to my righteousness and my integrity that is in me.
9 O let [a]the evil of the wicked come to an end, but [b]establish the righteous;
For the righteous God [c]tries the hearts and [1]minds.
10 My [a]shield is [1]with God,
Who [b]saves the upright in heart.
11 God is a [a]righteous judge,
And a God who has [b]indignation every day.

12 If [1]a man [a]does not repent, He will [b]sharpen His sword;
He has [c]bent His bow and [2]made it ready.
13 He has also prepared [1]for Himself deadly weapons;
He makes His [a]arrows fiery shafts.
14 Behold, he travails with wickedness,
And he [a]conceives mischief, and brings forth falsehood.
15 He has dug a pit and hollowed it out,
And has [a]fallen into the hole which he made.
16 His [a]mischief will return upon his own head,
And his [b]violence will descend upon [1]his own pate.

17 I will give thanks to the LORD [a]according to His righteousness,
And will [b]sing praise to the name of the LORD Most High.

Psalm 8

For the choir director; on the Gittith. A Psalm of David.

8 O LORD, our Lord,
How majestic is Thy name in all the earth,
Who hast [1a]displayed Thy splendor above the heavens!
2 [a]From the mouth of infants and nursing babes Thou hast established [1b]strength,
Because of Thine adversaries,
To make [c]the enemy and the revengeful cease.

3 When I [1a]consider [b]Thy heavens, the work of Thy fingers,
The [c]moon and the stars, which Thou hast [2]ordained;
4 [a]What is man, that Thou [1]dost take thought of him?
And the son of man, that Thou dost care for him?
5 Yet Thou hast made him a [a]little lower than [1]God,
And [b]dost crown him with [c]glory and majesty!
6 Thou dost make him to [a]rule over the works of Thy hands;
Thou hast [b]put all things under his feet,
7 All sheep and oxen,
And also the [1]beasts of the field,

me [2]Or, me may mean: *rescendo* or *cal interlude*
cient version *ny God* [a]Ps. s. 94:2 [c]Ps. 35:23; 44:23
it [a]Ps. 22:27
Judge [a]Ps. [b]Ps. 18:20; ; 35:24; 43:1
Lit., *kidneys*, or inner man ; 94:23 [b]Ps. [c]Ps. 11:4, 5; 20; Rev. 2:23
t., *upon* [a]Ps. Ps. 97:10, 11; 125:4
):6 [b]Ps. 90:9
he [2]Lit., *fixed* . 58:5 [b]Deut. :41 [c]Ps. 64:7
Or, *His deadly s* [a]Ps. 18:14; 45:5
5:35; Is. 59:4; James 1:15
4:8; Ps. 57:6
., the crown of n head [a]Esth. Ps. 140:9 [b]Ps. 140:11
71:15, 16 [b]Ps. 9:2; 66:1, 2, 4
set [a]Ps. 57:5, ; 113:4; 148:13
bulwark [a]Matt. Cor. 1:27 [b]Ps. :14 [c]Ps. 44:16
[1]Or, *see* [2]Or, *nted, fixed* [a]Ps. s. 89:11; 144:5 [c]Ps. 136:9
dost remember [a]Job 7:17; Ps. 44:3; Heb. 2:6-8
e angels; Heb., [a]Gen. 1:26; Ps. [b]Ps. 103:4 [c]Ps. 21:5
[a]Gen. 1:26, 28 Cor. 15:27; Eph. 1:22; Heb. 2:8
7 [1]Or, *animals*

8 The birds of the heavens, and the fish of the sea,
Whatever passes through the paths of the seas.

9 [a]O LORD, our Lord,
How majestic is Thy name in all the earth!

Psalm 9

For the choir director; on +Muth-labben. A Psalm of David.

9 I will give thanks to the LORD with all [a]my heart;
I will [b]tell of all Thy [1]wonders.
2 I will be glad and [a]exult in Thee;
I will [b]sing praise to Thy name, O [c]Most High.

3 When my enemies turn back,
They stumble and [a]perish before Thee.
4 For Thou hast [a]maintained [1]my just cause;
Thou dost sit on the throne [2b]judging righteously.
5 Thou hast [a]rebuked the nations; Thou hast destroyed the wicked;
Thou hast [b]blotted out their name forever and ever.
6 [1]The enemy has come to an end in perpetual ruins,
And Thou hast uprooted the cities;
The very [a]memory of them has perished.

7 But the [a]LORD [1]abides forever;
He has established His [b]throne for judgment,
8 And He will [a]judge the world in righteousness;
He will execute judgment for the peoples with equity.
9 [1]The LORD also will be a [a]stronghold for the oppressed,
A stronghold in times of trouble,
10 And [1]those who [a]know Thy name will put their trust in Thee;
For Thou, O LORD, hast not [b]forsaken those who seek Thee.

11 Sing praises to the LORD, who [a]dwells in Zion;
[b]Declare among the peoples His deeds.
12 For [a]He who [1]requires blood remembers them;
He does not forget [b]the cry of the afflicted.
13 Be gracious to me, O LORD;
Behold my affliction from those [a]who hate me,
Thou who [b]dost lift me up from the gates of death;
14 That I may tell of [a]all Thy praises,
That in the gates of the daughter of Zion
I may [b]rejoice in Thy [1]salvation.
15 The nations have sunk down [a]in the pit which they have made;
In the [b]net which they hid, their own foot has been caught.
16 The LORD has [a]made Himself known;
He has [b]executed judgment.
In the work of his own hands the wicked is snared.
[1]Higgaion [2]Selah.

17 The wicked will [1a]return to [2]Sheol,
Even all the nations who [b]forget God.
18 For the [a]needy will not always be forgotten,
Nor the [b]hope of the afflicted perish forever.
19 [a]Arise, O LORD, do not let man prevail;

9 [a]Ps. 8:1

+I.e., "Death

9:1 [1]Or, *mira* 86:12 [b]Ps. 2

2 [a]Ps. 5:11; [b]Ps. 66:2, 4 92:1

3 [a]Ps. 27:2

4 [1]Lit., *my rig cause* [2]Or, *a Judge* [a]Ps. 1 50:6

5 [a]Ps. 119:21 69:28; Prov. 1

6 [1]Or, *O ener desolations ar forever; And t Thou hast plu* [a]Ps. 34:16

7 [1]Or, *sits as* 10:16 [b]Ps. 89

8 [a]Ps. 96:13;

9 [1]Or, *Let the also be* [a]Ps. 3 16, 17

10 [1]Or, *let tho name put* [a]Ps. [b]Ps. 37:28; 94:

11 [a]Ps. 76:2 [b] 105:1; 107:22

12 [1]I.e., aveng bloodshed [a]Ge Ps. 72:14 [b]Ps.

13 [a]Ps. 38:19 30:3; 86:13

14 [1]Or, *deliver* [a]Ps. 106:2 [b]Ps 20:5; 35:9; 51:1

15 [a]Ps. 7:15, 1 57:6

16 [1]Perhaps, resounding mus meditation [2]Se mean: *Pause, Crescendo* or *M interlude* [a]Ex. 7 9:4

17 [1]Or, *turn* [2]I.e nether world [a]P 49:14 [b]Job 8:13 50:22

18 [a]Ps. 9:12; 12 62:5; 71:5; Prov.

19 [a]Num. 10:35

Let the nations be [b]judged before Thee.
20 Put them [a]in fear, O LORD;
Let the nations know that they are [b]but men. Selah.

Psalm 10

10 Why [a]dost Thou stand afar off, O LORD?
Why [b]dost Thou hide [1]*Thyself* in times of trouble?
2 In [a]pride the wicked [1]hotly pursue the afflicted;
[2]Let them be [b]caught in the plots which they have devised.

3 For the wicked [a]boasts of his [b]heart's desire,
And [1]the greedy man curses *and* [c]spurns the LORD.
4 The wicked, in the haughtiness of his countenance, [a]does not
seek *Him*.
All his [1]thoughts are, "[b]There is no God."

5 His ways [1a]prosper at all times;
Thy judgments are on high, [b]out of his sight;
As for all his adversaries, he snorts at them.
6 He says to himself, "[a]I shall not be moved;
[1]Throughout all generations [b]I shall not be in adversity."
7 His [a]mouth is full of curses and deceit and [b]oppression;
[c]Under his tongue is mischief and wickedness.
8 He sits in the [a]lurking places of the villages;
In the hiding places he [b]kills the innocent;
His eyes [1]stealthily watch for the [2c]unfortunate.
9 He lurks in a hiding place as [a]a lion in his [1]lair;
He [b]lurks to catch [c]the afflicted;
He catches the afflicted when he draws him into his [d]net.
10 He [1]crouches, he [2]bows down,
And the [3]unfortunate fall [4]by his mighty ones.
11 He [a]says to himself, "God has forgotten;
He has hidden His face; He will never see it."

12 Arise, O LORD; O God, [a]lift up Thy hand.
[b]Do not forget the afflicted.
13 Why has the wicked [a]spurned God?
He has said to himself, "Thou wilt not require *it*."
14 Thou hast seen *it*, for Thou hast beheld [a]mischief and vexation
to [1]take it into Thy hand.
The [2b]unfortunate commits *himself* to Thee;
Thou hast been the [c]helper of the orphan.
15 [a]Break the arm of the wicked and the evildoer,
[1b]Seek out his wickedness until Thou dost find none.

16 The LORD is [a]King forever and ever;
[b]Nations have perished from His land.
17 O LORD, Thou hast heard the [a]desire of the [1]humble;
Thou wilt [b]strengthen their heart, [c]Thou wilt incline Thine ear
18 To [1]vindicate the [a]orphan and the [b]oppressed,
That man who is of the earth may cause [c]terror no more.

19 [b]Ps. 9:5
[a]Ps. 14:5 [b]Ps. 62:9
:1 [1]Or, Thine eyes 2:1 [b]Ps. 13:1; 55:1
it., *burn* [2]Or, *They will be caught* [a]Ps. 8 [b]Ps. 7:16; 9:16
3 [1]Or, *blesses the* *dy man* [a]Ps. 49:6; 4:3, 4 [b]Ps. 112:10 [c]Ps. 10:13
, *plots* [a]Ps. 10:13; :2 [b]Ps. 14:1; 36:1
t., *are strong* [a]Ps. 52:7 [b]Ps. 28:5
.it., *To* [a]Ps. 49:11; l. 8:11 [b]Rev. 18:7
[a]Rom. 3:14 [b]Ps. 8 [c]Job 20:12; Ps. 140:3
.it., *lie in wait* [2]Or, *oor* [a]Ps. 11:2 [b]Ps. 94:6 [c]Ps. 72:12
[1]Or, *thicket* [a]Ps. 12 [b]Ps. 59:3; Mic. s. 10:2 [d]Ps. 140:5
)r, *is crushed* [2]Or, *bowed down* [3]Or, [4]Or, *into his claws*
11 [a]Ps. 10:4
[a]Ps. 17:7; Mic. 5:9 [b]Ps. 9:12
13 [a]Ps. 10:3
.it., *put, give* [2]Or, *or* [a]Ps. 10:7 [b]Ps. 22:11 [c]Ps. 68:5
[1]Or, *Mayest Thou* [a]Ps. 37:17 [b]Ps. 140:11
[a]Ps. 29:10 [b]Deut. 8:20
[1]Or, *afflicted* [a]Ps. 1 Chr. 29:18 [c]Ps. 34:15
[1]Lit., *judge* [a]Ps. 9 [b]Ps. 9:9; 74:21 [c]Is. 29:20

Psalm 11

For the choir director. *A Psalm* of David.

11 In the LORD I [a]take refuge;
How can you say to my soul, "Flee *as* a bird to your
[b]mountain;
2 For, behold, the wicked [a]bend the bow,
They [1b]make ready their arrow upon the string,
To [c]shoot in darkness at the upright in heart.
3 If the [a]foundations are destroyed,
What can the righteous do?"

4 The LORD is in His [a]holy temple; the [1]LORD's [b]throne is in heaven;
His [c]eyes behold, His eyelids test the sons of men.
5 The LORD [a]tests the righteous and [b]the wicked,
And the one who loves violence His soul hates.
6 Upon the wicked He will [a]rain [1]snares;
[b]Fire and brimstone and [c]burning wind will be the portion of
[d]their cup.
7 For the LORD is [a]righteous; [b]He loves [1]righteousness;
The upright will [c]behold His face.

Psalm 12

For the choir director; [+]upon an eight-stringed lyre. A Psalm of David.

12 Help, LORD, for [a]the godly man ceases to be,
For the faithful disappear from among the sons of men.
2 They [a]speak [1]falsehood to one another;
With [b]flattering [2]lips and with a double heart they speak.
3 May the LORD cut off all flattering lips,
The tongue that [a]speaks great things;
4 Who [a]have said, "With our tongue we will prevail;
Our lips are [1]our own; who is lord over us?"
5 "Because of the [a]devastation of the afflicted, because of the
groaning of the needy,
Now [b]I will arise," says the LORD; "I will [c]set him in the safety
for which he longs."

6 The [a]words of the LORD are pure words;
As silver [b]tried in a furnace on the earth, refined seven times.
7 Thou, O LORD, wilt keep them;
Thou wilt [a]preserve him from this generation forever.
8 The [a]wicked strut about on every side,
When [1b]vileness is exalted among the sons of men.

Psalm 13

For the choir director. A Psalm of David.

13 How long, O LORD? Wilt Thou [a]forget me forever?
How long [b]wilt Thou hide Thy face from me?
2 How long shall I [a]take counsel in my soul,
Having [b]sorrow in my heart all the day?
How long will my enemy be exalted over me?

3 [a]Consider *and* answer me, O LORD, my God;

11:1 [a]Ps. 2:12 [b]P
121:1

2 [1]Or, *fixed* [a]Ps.
37:14 [b]Ps. 64:3
64:4

3 [a]Ps. 82:5; 87:1;
119:152

4 [1]Lit., *LORD, His throne* [a]Ps. 18:6;
1:2; Hab. 2:20 [b]Ps
103:19; Is. 66:1; M
5:34; Rev. 4:2 [c]Ps
33:18; 34:15, 16

5 [a]Gen. 22:1; Ps.
34:19; James 1:12
5:5

6 [1]Or, *coals of fire*
18:13, 14 [b]Gen. 1
Ezek. 38:22 [c]Jer.
12 [d]Ps. 75:8

7 [1]Or, *righteous* c
[a]Ps. 7:9, 11 [b]Ps.
45:7 [c]Ps. 16:11;

[+]Or, *according to*
lower octave (Heb
Sheminith)

12:1 [a]Is. 57:1; Mi

2 [1]Or, *emptiness*
lip [a]Ps. 10:7; 41:6
28:3; 55:21; Jer. 9
Rom. 16:18

3 [a]Dan. 7:8; Rev.

4 [1]Lit., *with us* [a]P
73:8, 9

5 [a]Ps. 9:9; 10:18
33:10 [c]Ps. 34:6;

6 [a]2 Sam. 22:31;
18:30; 19:8, 10;
119:140 [b]Prov. 3

7 [a]Ps. 37:28; 97

8 [1]Or, *worthlessn*
[a]Ps. 55:10, 11 [b]Is

13:1 [a]Ps. 44:24
13:24; Ps. 89:46

2 [a]Ps. 42:4 [b]Ps.

3 [a]Ps. 5:1

[b]Enlighten my eyes, lest I [c]sleep the *sleep of* death,
4 Lest my enemy [a]say, "I have overcome him,"
Lest [b]my adversaries rejoice when I am shaken.

5 But I have [a]trusted in Thy lovingkindness;
My heart shall [b]rejoice in Thy salvation.
6 I will [a]sing to the LORD,
Because He has [b]dealt bountifully with me.

Psalm 14

For the choir director. *A Psalm* of David.

14 The fool has [a]said in his heart, "There is no God."
They are corrupt, they have committed abominable [1]deeds;
There is [b]no one who does good.
2 The LORD has [a]looked down from heaven upon the sons of men,
To see if there are any who [1b]understand,
Who [c]seek after God.
3 They have all [a]turned aside; together they have become corrupt;
There is [b]no one who does good, not even one.

4 Do all the workers of wickedness [a]not know,
Who [b]eat up my people *as* they eat bread,
And [c]do not call upon the Lord?
5 There they are in great dread,
For God is with the [a]righteous generation.
6 You would put to shame the counsel of the afflicted,
But the LORD is his [a]refuge.

7 Oh, that [a]the salvation of Israel [1]would come out of Zion!
When the LORD [2b]restores His captive people,
Jacob will rejoice, Israel will be glad.

Psalm 15

A Psalm of David.

15 O LORD, who may [1]abide [a]in Thy tent?
Who may dwell on Thy [b]holy hill?
2 He who [a]walks with integrity, and works righteousness,
And [b]speaks truth in his heart.
3 He [a]does not slander [1]with his tongue,
Nor [b]does evil to his neighbor,
Nor [c]takes up a reproach against his friend;
4 In [1]whose eyes a reprobate is despised,
But [2]who [a]honors those who fear the LORD;
He [b]swears to his own hurt, and does not change;
5 He [a]does not put out his money [1]at interest,
Nor [b]does he take a bribe against the innocent.
[c]He who does these things will never be shaken.

Psalm 16

A [+]Mikhtam of David.

16 [a]Preserve me, O God, for [b]I take refuge in Thee.
2 [1]I said to the LORD, "Thou art [2]my Lord;
I [a]have no good besides Thee."

n. 14:29; Ezra Job 33:30; Ps. 28 [c]Jer. 51:39
2:4 [b]Ps. 25:2; 38:16
52:8 [b]Ps. 9:14
s. 96:1, 2 [b]Ps. ; 119:17; 142:7
it., *doings* [a]Ps. :1 [b]Ps. 14:1-3; ; Rom. 3:10-12
act wisely [a]Ps. 4; 102:19 [b]Ps. 6 [c]1 Chr. 22:19
58:3 [b]Ps. 143:2
82:5 [b]Ps. 27:2; 5; Mic. 3:3 [c]Ps. 79:6; Is. 64:7
Ps. 73:15; 112:2
9:9; 40:17; 46:1; 142:5
., *would be* [2]Or, *s the fortunes of people* [a]Ps. 53:6 [b]Ps. 85:1, 2
Lit., *sojourn* [a]Ps. 5; 61:4 [b]Ps. 24:3
s. 24:4; Is. 33:15 . 8:16; Eph. 4:25
[1]Lit., *according to* 50:20 [b]Ps. 28:3 [c]Ex. 23:1
[1]Lit., *his* [2]Lit., *he* cts 28:10 [b]Judg. 11:35
5 [1]I.e., to a fellow aelite [a]Ex. 22:25; 5:36; Deut. 23:20; k. 18:8 [b]Ex. 23:8; 6:19 [c]2 Pet. 1:10
bly, *Epigrammatic* oem *or Atonement Psalm*
[a]Ps. 17:8 [b]Ps. 7:1
Or, *O my soul, you* [2]Or, *the Lord* [a]Ps. 73:25

3 As for the [1a]saints who are in the earth,
[2]They are the majestic ones [b]in whom is all my delight.
4 The [1a]sorrows of those who have [2]bartered for another *god* will be multiplied;
I shall not pour out their libations of [b]blood,
Nor shall I [c]take their names upon my lips.

5 The LORD is the [a]portion of my inheritance and my [b]cup;
Thou dost support my [c]lot.
6 The [a]lines have fallen to me in pleasant places;
Indeed, my heritage is [b]beautiful to me.

7 I will bless the LORD who has [a]counseled me;
Indeed, my [1b]mind instructs me in the night.
8 [a]I have [b]set the LORD continually before me;
Because He is [c]at my right hand, [d]I will not be shaken.
9 Therefore [a]my heart is glad, and [b]my glory rejoices;
My flesh also will [c]dwell securely.
10 For Thou [a]wilt not abandon my soul to [1]Sheol;
Neither wilt Thou [2b]allow Thy [3]Holy One to [4]undergo decay.
11 Thou wilt make known to me [a]the path of life;
In [b]Thy presence is fulness of joy;
In Thy right hand there are [c]pleasures forever.

Psalm 17

A Prayer of David.

17 Hear a [a]just cause, O LORD, [b]give heed to my cry;
[c]Give ear to my prayer, which is not from [d]deceitful lips.
2 Let [a]my [1]judgment come forth from Thy presence;
Let Thine eyes look with [b]equity.
3 Thou hast [a]tried my heart;
Thou hast visited *me* by night;
Thou hast [b]tested me and [c]dost find [1]nothing;
I have [d]purposed that my mouth will not transgress.
4 As for the deeds of men, [a]by the word of Thy lips
I have kept from the [b]paths of the violent.
5 My [a]steps have held fast to Thy [1]paths.
My [b]feet have not slipped.

6 I have [a]called upon Thee, for Thou wilt answer me, O God;
[b]Incline Thine ear to me, hear my speech.
7 [a]Wondrously show Thy lovingkindness,
O [b]Savior of those who take refuge [1]at Thy right hand
From those who rise up *against them*.
8 Keep me as [1]the [a]apple of the eye;
Hide me [b]in the shadow of Thy wings,
9 From the [a]wicked who despoil me,
My [b]deadly enemies, who surround me.
10 They have [a]closed their [1]unfeeling *heart*;
With their mouth they [b]speak proudly.
11 They have now [a]surrounded us in our steps;
They set their eyes [b]to cast *us* down to the ground.
12 He is [a]like a lion that is eager to tear,
And as a young lion [b]lurking in hiding places.

3 [1]Lit., *holy o…* the godly [2]Lit. *majestic ones … delight* [a]Ps. 1… 119:63

4 [1]I.e., sorrow… idolatry [2]Or, *h… to* [a]Ps. 32:10 … 106:37, 38 [c]E… Josh. 23:7

5 [a]Ps. 73:26; … 142:5; Lam. 3:… 23:5 [c]Ps. 125:…

6 [a]Ps. 78:55 [b]…

7 [1]Lit., *kidneys…* figurative for in… [a]Ps. 73:24 [b]Ps…

8 [a]Ps. 16:8-11; … 2:25-28 [b]Ps. 2… 123:1, 2 [c]Ps. 7… 110:5; 121:5 [d]…

9 [a]Ps. 4:7; 13:… 30:12; 57:8; 10… 4:8

10 [1]I.e., the ne… world [2]Lit., *give… godly one* [4]Or, *corruption* or *th…* [a]Ps. 49:15; 86:… 13:35

11 [a]Ps. 139:24, … 7:14 [b]Ps. 21:6; … [c]Job 36:11; Ps. … 46:4

17:1 [a]Ps. 9:4 [b]… 61:1; 142:6 [c]Ps… [d]Is. 29:13

2 [1]I.e., vindicati… 103:6 [b]Ps. 98:9

3 [1]Or, *no evil de… me; My mouth* [a]… 26:1, 2 [b]Job 23:… 66:10; Zech. 13:… 1 Pet. 1:7 [c]Jer. … [d]Ps. 39:1

4 [a]Ps. 119:9, 10… 10:5-11

5 [1]Lit., *tracks* [a]J… 23:11; Ps. 44:18; … 119:133 [b]Ps. 18:… 37:31

6 [a]Ps. 86:7; 116:… 88:2

7 [1]Or, *from those rise up . . . at Thy hand* [a]Ps. 31:21 … 20:6

8 [1]Lit., *the pupil, daughter of the e…* [a]Deut. 32:10; Zec… [b]Ruth 2:12; Ps. 3… 57:1; 61:4; 63:7; …

9 [a]Ps. 31:20 [b]Ps…

10 [1]Lit., *fat* [a]Job … Ps. 73:7 [b]1 Sam. … Ps. 31:18; 73:8

11 [a]Ps. 88:17 [b]P… 37:14

12 [a]Ps. 7:2 [b]Ps. …

13 [a]Arise, O LORD, confront him, [b]bring him low;
[c]Deliver my soul from the wicked with [d]Thy sword,
14 From men with [a]Thy hand, O LORD,
From men [1]of the world, [b]whose portion is in *this* life;
And whose belly Thou [c]dost fill with Thy treasure;
They are satisfied with children,
And leave their abundance to their babes.
15 As for me, I shall [a]behold Thy face in righteousness;
[b]I will be satisfied [1]with Thy [c]likeness when I awake.

Psalm 18

For the choir director. *A Psalm* of David the servant of the LORD, [+]who spoke to the LORD the words of this song in the day that the LORD delivered him from the hand of all his enemies and from the hand of Saul. And he said,

18 "I love Thee, O LORD, [a]my strength."
2 The LORD is [a]my [1]rock and [b]my fortress and my [c]deliverer,
My God, my rock, in whom I take refuge;
My [d]shield and the [e]horn of my salvation, my [f]stronghold.
3 I call upon the LORD, who is [a]worthy to be praised,
And I am [b]saved from my enemies.

4 The [a]cords of death encompassed me,
And the [b]torrents of [1]ungodliness [2]terrified me.
5 The [a]cords of [1]Sheol surrounded me;
The snares of death confronted me.
6 In my [a]distress I called upon the LORD,
And cried to my God for help;
He heard my voice [b]out of His temple,
And my [c]cry for help before Him came into His ears.

7 Then the [a]earth shook and quaked;
And the [b]foundations of the mountains were trembling
And were shaken, because He was angry.
8 Smoke went up [1]out of His nostrils,
And [a]fire from His mouth devoured;
Coals were kindled by it.
9 He [a]bowed the heavens also, and came down
With thick [b]darkness under His feet.
10 And He rode upon a [a]cherub and flew;
And He sped upon the [b]wings of the wind.
11 He made [a]darkness His hiding place, [b]His [1]canopy around Him,
Darkness of waters, thick clouds of the skies.
12 From the [a]brightness before Him passed His thick clouds,
Hailstones and [b]coals of fire.
13 The LORD also [a]thundered in the heavens,
And the Most High uttered His voice,
Hailstones and coals of fire.
14 And He [a]sent out His arrows, and scattered them,
And lightning flashes in abundance, and [1]routed them.
15 Then the [a]channels of water appeared,
And the foundations of the world were [1]laid bare
At Thy [b]rebuke, O LORD,
At the blast of the [c]breath of Thy nostrils.

7 [b]Ps. 55:23
20 [d]Ps. 7:12
whose portion
's of the world
[b]Ps. 73:3-7;
:25 [c]Ps. 49:6
with beholding
6:11; 140:13;
:2 [b]Ps. 4:6, 7
[c]Num. 12:8
Sam. 22:1-51
:1 [a]Ps. 59:17
r, crag [a]Deut.
Sam. 2:2; Ps.
46; 28:1; 31:3;
:3; 78:15 [b]Ps.
Ps. 19:14 [d]Ps.
0; 59:11; 84:9,
Prov. 30:5 [e]Ps.
5:10 [f]Ps. 59:9
Ps. 48:1; 96:4;
45:3 [b]Ps. 34:6
Or, *destruction;*
elial [2]Or, *were*
ing or *terrifying*
16:3 [b]Ps. 69:2;
124:3, 4
ne nether world
[a]Ps. 116:3
s. 50:15; 120:1
3:4 [c]Ps. 34:15
g. 5:4; Ps. 68:7,
13:13; Hag. 2:6
[b]Ps. 114:4, 6
His wrath [a]Ps.
50:3
144:5 [b]Ps. 97:2
80:1; 99:1 [b]Ps.
104:3
, pavilion [a]Deut.
4:11 [b]Ps. 97:2
[a]Ps. 104:2 [b]Ps.
140:10; Hab. 3:4
[a]Ps. 29:3; 104:7
t., confused [a]Ps.
144:6; Hab. 3:11
, uncovered [a]Ps.
:9 [b]Ps. 76:6 [c]Ps.
18:8

16 He [a]sent from on high, He took me;
He drew me out of [b]many waters.
17 He [a]delivered me from my strong enemy,
And from those who hated me, for they were [b]too mighty for me.
18 They confronted me in [a]the day of my calamity,
But [b]the LORD was my stay.
19 He brought me forth also into a [a]broad place;
He rescued me, because [b]He delighted in me.

20 The LORD has [a]rewarded me according to my righteousness;
According to the [b]cleanness of my hands He has
recompensed me.
21 For I have [a]kept the ways of the LORD,
And have [b]not wickedly departed from my God.
22 For all [a]His ordinances were before me,
And I did not put away His [b]statutes from me.
23 I was also [1a]blameless with Him,
And I [b]kept myself from my iniquity.
24 Therefore the LORD has [a]recompensed me according to my
righteousness,
According to the cleanness of my hands in His eyes.

25 With [a]the kind Thou dost show Thyself kind;
With the [1]blameless [b]Thou dost show Thyself blameless;
26 With the pure Thou dost show Thyself [a]pure;
And with the crooked [b]Thou dost show Thyself [1]astute.
27 For Thou dost [a]save an afflicted people;
But [b]haughty eyes Thou dost abase.
28 For Thou dost [a]light my lamp;
The LORD my God [b]illumines my darkness.
29 For by Thee I can [1a]run upon a troop;
And by my God I can [b]leap over a wall.

30 As for God, His way is [1a]blameless;
The [b]word of the LORD is tried;
He is a [c]shield to all who take refuge in Him.
31 For [a]who is God, but the LORD?
And who is a [b]rock, except our God,
32 The God who [a]girds me with strength,
And [1]makes my way [2b]blameless?
33 He [a]makes my feet like hinds' *feet*,
And [b]sets me upon my high places.
34 He [a]trains my hands for battle,
So that my arms can [b]bend a bow of bronze.
35 Thou hast also given me [a]the shield of Thy salvation,
And Thy [b]right hand upholds me;
And [c]Thy [1]gentleness makes me great.
36 Thou dost [a]enlarge my steps under me,
And my [1b]feet have not slipped.

37 I [a]pursued my enemies and overtook them,
And I did not turn back [b]until they were consumed.
38 I shattered them, so that they were [a]not able to rise;
They fell [b]under my feet.

16 [a]Ps. 144:

17 [a]Ps. 59:1
35:10; 142:6

18 [a]Ps. 59:1

19 [a]Ps. 4:1;
118:5 [b]Ps. 3

20 [a]1 Sam. 2
33:26; Ps. 7:
22:30; Ps. 24

21 [a]Ps. 37:3
Prov. 8:32 [b]2
34:33; Ps. 11

22 [a]Ps. 119:
119:83

23 [1]Lit., *com*
having integri
perfect [a]Ps. 1
19:12, 13; 25

24 [a]1 Sam. 2
18:20

25 [1]V. 23, no
[a]1 Kin. 8:32; F
Matt. 5:7 [b]Ps.

26 [1]Lit., *twist*
25:5; Hab. 1:1
26:23, 24, 27,
3:34

27 [a]Ps. 72:12
101:5; Prov. 6

28 [a]1 Kin. 15:
18:6; Ps. 132:
27:1

29 [1]Or, *crush*
[a]Ps. 118:10-12
18:33; 40:2

30 [1]V. 23, note
[a]Deut. 32:4; Ps
145:17; Rev. 1
12:6 [c]Ps. 17:7

31 [a]Deut. 32:3
1 Sam. 2:2; Ps
Is. 45:5 [b]Deut.
Ps. 18:2; 62:2

32 [1]Or, *has ma*
complete; or, *h*
integrity [a]Ps. 1
45:5 [b]Ps. 18:2

33 [a]Hab. 3:19
32:13

34 [a]Ps. 144:1
29:20

35 [1]Or, *condes*
[a]Ps. 33:20 [b]Ps.
119:117 [c]Ps. 1

36 [1]Lit., *ankles*
18:33 [b]Ps. 66:9
4:12

37 [a]Ps. 44:5 [b]P

38 [a]Ps. 36:12 [b]

39 For Thou hast [a]girded me with strength for battle;
Thou hast [1b]subdued under me those who rose up against me.
40 Thou hast also made my enemies [a]turn their backs to me,
And I [1b]destroyed those who hated me.
41 They cried for help, but there was [a]none to save,
Even to the LORD, but [b]He did not answer them.
42 Then I beat them fine as the [a]dust before the wind;
I emptied them out as the mire of the streets.

43 Thou hast delivered me from the [a]contentions of the people;
Thou hast placed me as [b]head of the nations;
A [c]people whom I have not known serve me.
44 As soon as they hear, they obey me;
Foreigners [1a]submit to me.
45 Foreigners [a]fade away,
And [b]come trembling out of their [1]fortresses.

46 The LORD [a]lives, and blessed be [b]my rock;
And exalted be [c]the God of my salvation,
47 The God who [a]executes vengeance for me,
And [b]subdues peoples under me.
48 He [a]delivers me from my enemies;
Surely Thou [b]dost lift me above those who rise up against me;
Thou dost rescue me from the [c]violent man.
49 Therefore I will [a]give thanks to Thee among the nations, O LORD,
And I will [b]sing praises to Thy name.
50 He gives great [1a]deliverance to His king,
And shows lovingkindness to [b]His anointed,
To David and [c]his [2]descendants forever.

Psalm 19

For the choir director. A Psalm of David.

19 The [a]heavens are telling of the glory of God;
And their [b]expanse is declaring the work of His hands.
2 Day to [a]day pours forth speech,
And [b]night to night reveals knowledge.
3 There is no speech, nor are there words;
Their voice is not heard.
4 Their [1a]line has gone out through all the earth,
And their utterances to the end of the world.
In them He has [b]placed a tent for the sun,
5 Which is as a bridegroom coming out of his chamber;
It rejoices as a strong man to run his course.
6 Its [a]rising is from [1]one end of the heavens,
And its circuit to the [2]other end of them;
And there is nothing hidden from its heat.

7 [a]The law of the LORD is [1b]perfect, [c]restoring the soul;
The testimony of the LORD is [d]sure, making [e]wise the simple.
8 The precepts of the LORD are [a]right, [b]rejoicing the heart;
The commandment of the LORD is [c]pure, [d]enlightening the eyes.
9 The fear of the LORD is clean, enduring forever;
The judgments of the LORD are [a]true; they are [b]righteous
altogether.

caused to bow [a]Ps. 18:32 [b]Ps. 18:47
silenced [a]Ps. ...:12 [b]Ps. 94:23
[a]Ps. 50:22 [b]Job 27:9; Prov. 1:28
42 [a]Ps. 83:13
...Sam. 3:1; 19:9; ...35:1 [b]2 Sam. ...; Ps. 89:27 [c]Is. 55:5
...Lit., *deceive me*; ...e., give feigned ...ence [a]Ps. 66:3
[1]Lit., *fastnesses* ...37:2 [b]Mic. 7:17
[a]Job 19:25 [b]Ps. 18:2 [c]Ps. 51:14
[a]Ps. 94:1 [b]Ps. ...:43; 47:3; 144:2
...s. 3:7 [b]Ps. 27:6; 59:1 [c]Ps. 11:5
[a]Rom. 15:9 [b]Ps. 108:1
...i.e., victories; lit., ...ations [2]Lit., *seed* ...1:1; 144:10 [b]Ps. 28:8 [c]Ps. 89:4
...1 [a]Ps. 8:1; 50:6; ...1:19, 20 [b]Gen. 1:6, 7
[a]Ps. 74:16 [b]Ps. 139:12
...nother reading is ...*und* [a]Rom. 10:18 [b]Ps. 104:2
[1]Lit., *the* [2]Lit., *the* [a]Ps. 113:3; Eccl. 1:5
...., blameless [a]Ps. ...1:7 [b]Ps. 119:160 ...s. 23:3 [d]Ps. 93:5 [e]Ps. 119:98-100
[a]Ps. 119:128 [b]Ps. ...14 [c]Ps. 12:6 [d]Ps. 36:9
[a]Ps. 119:142 [b]Ps. 119:138

10 They are more desirable than [a]gold, yes, than much fine gold;
[b]Sweeter also than honey and the drippings of the honeycomb.
11 Moreover, by them [a]Thy servant is warned;
In keeping them there is great [b]reward.
12 Who can [a]discern *his* errors? [b]Acquit me of [c]hidden *faults.*
13 Also keep back Thy servant [a]from presumptuous *sins;*
Let them not [b]rule over me;
Then I shall be [1c]blameless,
And I shall be acquitted of [d]great transgression.
14 Let the words of my mouth and [a]the meditation of my heart
Be acceptable in Thy sight,
O LORD, [b]my rock and my [c]Redeemer.

Psalm 20

For the choir director. A Psalm of David

20 May the LORD answer you [a]in the day of trouble!
May the [b]name of the [c]God of Jacob set you *securely* on high!
2 May He send you help [a]from the sanctuary,
And [b]support you from Zion!
3 May He [a]remember all your meal offerings,
And [b]find your burnt offering [1]acceptable! [2]Selah.

4 May He grant you your [a]heart's desire,
And [b]fulfill all your [1]counsel!
5 [1]We will [a]sing for joy over your [2]victory,
And in the name of our God we will [b]set up our banners.
May the LORD [c]fulfill all your petitions.

6 Now [a]I know that the LORD saves His anointed;
He will [b]answer him from His holy heaven,
With the [1c]saving strength of His right hand.
7 Some [1]*boast* in chariots, and some in [a]horses;
But [b]we [2]will boast in the name of the LORD, our God.
8 They have [a]bowed down and fallen;
But we have [b]risen and stood upright.
9 [1a]Save, O LORD;
May the [b]King answer us in the day we call.

Psalm 21

For the choir director. A Psalm of David.

21 O LORD, in Thy strength the king will [a]be glad,
And in Thy [1]salvation how greatly he will rejoice!
2 Thou hast [a]given him his heart's desire,
And Thou hast not withheld the request of his lips. [1]Selah.
3 For Thou [a]dost meet him with the blessings of good things;
Thou dost set a [b]crown of fine gold on his head.
4 He asked life of Thee,
Thou [a]didst give it to him,
[b]Length of days forever and ever.
5 His [a]glory is great through Thy [1]salvation,
[b]Splendor and majesty Thou dost place upon him.
6 For Thou dost make him [1]most [a]blessed forever;
Thou dost make him joyful [b]with gladness in Thy presence.

10 [a]Ps. 119:72 [b]Ps. 119:103
11 [a]Ps. 17:4 [b]
6; Prov. 29:18
12 [a]Ps. 40:12; [b]Ps. 51:1, 2 [c]P
139:23, 24
13 [1]Lit., *compl*
[a]Num. 15:30 [b]P
119:133 [c]Ps. 1
[d]Ps. 25:11
14 [a]Ps. 104:34
18:2 [c]Ps. 31:5;
20:1 [a]Ps. 50:15
91:14 [c]Ps. 46:7
2 [a]Ps. 3:4 [b]Ps.
3 [1]Lit., *fat* [2]*Sel*
mean: *Pause,*
Crescendo or *M*
interlude [a]Acts
[b]Ps. 51:19
4 [1]Or, *purpose*
21:2 [b]Ps. 145:1
5 [1]Or, *Let us sin*
salvation [a]Ps. 9
[b]Ps. 60:4 [c]1 Sar
6 [1]Or, *mighty de*
the victory of His
hand [a]Ps. 41:11
58:9 [c]Ps. 28:8
7 [1]Or, praise *ch*
or, trust, or, are s
through [2]Lit., *ma*
mention of; or, *pr*
the name [a]Ps. 3
[b]2 Chr. 32:8
8 [a]Is. 2:11, 17 [b]P
37:24; Mic. 7:8
9 [1]Or, *O LORD, s*
king; answer us
3:7 [b]Ps. 17:6
21:1 [1]Or, *victory*
59:16, 17
2 [1]*Selah* may me
Pause, Crescend
Musical interlude
20:4; 37:4
3 [a]Ps. 59:10 [b]2 S
12:30
4 [a]Ps. 61:6; 133:3
91:16
5 [1]Or, *victory* [a]Ps
20:5 [b]Ps. 8:5; 96:
6 [1]Lit., *blessings*
[a]1 Chr. 17:27 [b]Ps.

7 For the king [a]trusts in the LORD,
And through the lovingkindness of the Most High [b]he will not
be shaken.
8 Your hand will [a]find out all your enemies;
Your right hand will find out those who hate you.
9 You will make them [a]as a fiery oven in the time [1]of your anger;
The LORD will [b]swallow them up in His wrath,
And [c]fire will devour them.
10 Their [1]offspring Thou wilt destroy from the earth,
And their [2a]descendants from among the sons of men.
11 Though they [1a]intended evil against Thee,
And [b]devised a plot,
They will not succeed.
12 For Thou wilt [a]make them turn their back;
Thou wilt [1]aim [b]with Thy bowstrings at their faces.
13 Be Thou exalted, O LORD, in Thy strength;
We will [a]sing and praise Thy power.

Psalm 22

For the choir director; upon +Aijeleth Hashshahar. A Psalm of David.

22 [a]My God, my God, why hast Thou forsaken me?
[1b]Far from my deliverance are the words of my [2c]groaning.
2 O my God, I [a]cry by day, but Thou dost not answer;
And by night, but [1]I have no rest.
3 Yet [a]Thou art holy,
O Thou who [1]art enthroned upon [b]the praises of Israel.
4 In Thee our fathers [a]trusted;
They trusted, and Thou didst [b]deliver them.
5 To Thee they cried out, and were delivered;
[a]In Thee they trusted, and were not [1]disappointed.

6 But I am a [a]worm, and not a man,
A [b]reproach of men, and [c]despised by the people.
7 All who see me [1a]sneer at me;
They [2]separate with the lip, they [b]wag the head, *saying,*
8 "[1]Commit *yourself* to the LORD; [a]let Him deliver him;
Let Him rescue him, because He delights in him."

9 Yet Thou art He who [a]didst bring me forth from the womb;
Thou didst make me trust *when* upon my mother's breasts.
10 Upon Thee I was cast [a]from [1]birth;
Thou hast been my God from my mother's womb.

11 [a]Be not far from me, for [1]trouble is near;
For there is [b]none to help.
12 Many [a]bulls have surrounded me;
Strong *bulls* of [b]Bashan have encircled me.
13 They [a]open wide their mouth at me,
As a ravening and a roaring [b]lion.
14 I am [a]poured out like water,
And all my [b]bones are out of joint;
My [c]heart is like wax;
It is melted within [1]me.
15 My [a]strength is dried up like a potsherd,

:1 [b]Ps. 112:6
8 [a]Is. 10:10
your presence 4:1 [b]Lam. 2:2 [c]Ps. 50:3
uit [2]Lit., *seed* [a]Ps. 37:28
, *stretched out* :1-3 [b]Ps. 10:2
t., *make ready* [b]Ps. 7:12, 13
Ps. 59:16; 81:1
the hind of the morning
Why art Thou *om helping me, m the words of roaning?* [2]Lit., [a]Matt. 27:46; 5:34 [b]Ps. 10:1 ; Ps. 6:6; 32:3; 38:8
Lit., *there is no ce for me* [a]Ps. 42:3; 88:1
dost inhabit the aises [a]Ps. 99:9 :21; Ps. 148:14
3:53 [b]Ps. 107:6
, *ashamed* [a]Is. 49:23
25:6; Is. 41:14 31:11 [c]Is. 49:7; 53:3
mock me [2]I.e., *e mouths at me* 4; Is. 53:3; Luke 35 [b]Matt. 27:39; Mark 15:29
it., *Roll;* another *is He committed self* [a]Ps. 91:14; Matt. 27:43
9 [a]Ps. 71:5, 6
Lit., *a womb* [a]Is. 46:3; 49:1
Or, *distress* [a]Ps. 2 Kin. 14:26; Ps. 72:12; Is. 63:5
[a]Ps. 22:21; 68:30 32:14; Amos 4:1
[a]Job 16:10; Ps. ; Lam. 2:16; 3:46 [b]Ps. 10:9; 17:12
[1]Lit., *my inward* [a]Job 30:16 [b]Ps. ; Dan. 5:6 [c]Josh. 5; Job 23:16; Ps. 73:26; Nah. 2:10
15 [a]Ps. 38:10

And [b]my tongue cleaves to my jaws;
And Thou dost [c]lay me [1]in the dust of death.
16 For [a]dogs have surrounded me;
[1]A band of evildoers has encompassed me;
[2]They [b]pierced my hands and my feet.
17 I can count all my bones.
[a]They look, they stare at me;
18 They [a]divide my garments among them,
And for my clothing they cast lots.

19 But Thou, O LORD, [a]be not far off;
O Thou my help, [b]hasten to my assistance.
20 Deliver my [1]soul from [a]the sword,
My [b]only *life* from the [2]power of the dog.
21 Save me from the [a]lion's mouth;
And from the horns of the [b]wild oxen Thou dost [c]answer me.

22 I will [a]tell of Thy name to my brethren;
In the midst of the assembly I will praise Thee.
23 [a]You who fear the LORD, praise Him;
All you [1]descendants of Jacob, [b]glorify Him,
And [c]stand in awe of Him, all you [1]descendants of Israel.
24 For He has [a]not despised nor abhorred the affliction of the afflicted;
Neither has He [b]hidden His face from him;
But [c]when he cried to Him for help, He heard.

25 From Thee *comes* [a]my praise in the great assembly;
I shall [b]pay my vows before those who fear Him.
26 The [1]afflicted shall eat and [a]be satisfied;
Those who seek Him will [b]praise the LORD.
Let your [c]heart live forever!
27 All the [a]ends of the earth will remember and turn to the LORD,
And all the [b]families of the nations will worship before [1]Thee.
28 For the [a]kingdom is the LORD's,
And He [b]rules over the nations.
29 All the [1a]prosperous of the earth will eat and worship,
All those who [b]go down to the dust will bow before Him,
Even he who [2c]cannot keep his soul alive.
30 [1a]Posterity will serve Him;
It will be told of the Lord to [b]the *coming* generation.
31 They will come and [a]will declare His righteousness
To a people [b]who will be born, that He has performed *it*.

Psalm 23

A Psalm of David.

23 The LORD is my [a]shepherd,
I [1]shall [b]not want.
2 He makes me lie down in [a]green pastures;
He [b]leads me beside [1c]quiet waters.
3 He [a]restores my soul;
He [b]guides me in the [1c]paths of righteousness
For His name's sake.

15 [1]Lit., *to* [b]J... 19:28 [c]Ps. 10...

16 [1]Or, *An as...* [2]Another readi... *a lion, my . . .* 7 [b]Matt. 27:35 20:25

17 [a]Luke 23:2...

18 [a]Matt. 27:3... 15:24; Luke 23... 19:24

19 [a]Ps. 22:11

20 [1]Or, *life* [2]Li... [a]Ps. 37:14 [b]Ps....

21 [a]Ps. 22:13 22:12 [c]Ps. 34:4... 120:1

22 [a]Ps. 40:10; ...

23 [1]Lit., *seed* ... 135:19, 20 [b]Ps.... [c]Ps. 33:8

24 [a]Ps. 69:33 ... 27:9; 69:17; 102... 31:22; Heb. 5:7

25 [a]Ps. 35:18; ... [b]Ps. 61:8; Eccl. ...

26 [1]Or, *poor* [a]P... 107:9 [b]Ps. 40:1... 69:32

27 [1]Some versi... read *Him* [a]Ps. 2... 82:8 [b]Ps. 86:9

28 [a]Ps. 47:7; Ob... Zech. 14:9; Matt.... [b]Ps. 47:8

29 [1]Lit., *fat ones* ... *did not* [a]Ps. 17:1... 45:12; Hab. 1:16 28:1; Is. 26:19 [c]P... 89:48

30 [1]Lit., *A seed* ... 102:28 [b]Ps. 102:...

31 [a]Ps. 40:9; 71:... [b]Ps. 78:6

23:1 [1]Or, *do* [a]Ps.... 78:52; 80:1; Is. 40... Jer. 31:10; Ezek. 34:11-13; John 10... 1 Pet. 2:25 [b]Ps. 3... 10; Phil. 4:19

2 [1]Lit., *waters of r...* [a]Ps. 65:11-13; Eze... 34:14 [b]Rev. 7:17 36:8; 46:4

3 [1]Lit., *tracks* [a]Ps... 19:7 [b]Ps. 5:8; 31:... 85:13; Prov. 4:11; ...

4 Even though I [a]walk through the [1]valley of the shadow of death,
I [b]fear no [2]evil; for [c]Thou art with me;
Thy [d]rod and Thy staff, they comfort me.
5 Thou dost [a]prepare a table before me in the presence of my
enemies;
Thou [1]hast [b]anointed my head with oil;
My [c]cup overflows.
6 [1]Surely [a]goodness and lovingkindness will follow me all the
days of my life,
And I will [2b]dwell in the house of the LORD [3]forever.

Psalm 24

A Psalm of David.

24 The [a]earth is the LORD's, and [1]all it contains,
The [b]world, and those who dwell in it.
2 For He has [a]founded it upon the seas,
And established it upon the rivers.
3 Who may [a]ascend into the [b]hill of the LORD?
And who may stand in His holy [c]place?
4 He who has [a]clean hands and a [b]pure heart,
Who has not [c]lifted up his soul [1]to falsehood,
And has not [d]sworn deceitfully.
5 He shall receive a [a]blessing from the LORD
And [1b]righteousness from the God of his salvation.
6 [1]This is the generation of those who [a]seek Him,
Who seek Thy face—*even* Jacob. [2]Selah.

7 [a]Lift up your heads, O gates,
And be lifted up, O [1]ancient doors,
That the King of [b]glory may come in!
8 Who is the King of glory?
The LORD [a]strong and mighty,
The LORD [b]mighty in battle.
9 Lift up your heads, O gates,
And lift *them* up, O [1]ancient doors,
That the King of [a]glory may come in!
10 Who is this King of glory?
The LORD of [a]hosts,
He is the King of glory. Selah.

Psalm 25

A Psalm of David.

25 To Thee, O LORD, I [a]lift up my soul.
2 O my God, in Thee [a]I trust,
Do not let me [b]be ashamed;
Do not let my [c]enemies exult over me.
3 Indeed, [a]none of those who wait for Thee will be ashamed;
[1]Those who [b]deal treacherously without cause will be ashamed.

4 [a]Make me know Thy ways, O LORD;
Teach me Thy paths.
5 Lead me in [a]Thy truth and teach me,
For Thou art the [b]God of my salvation;

[1]Or, *valley of deep* ...arkness [2]Or, *harm* [a]Job 10:21, 22; Ps. ...7:14 [b]Ps. 3:6; 27:1 ...16:8; Is. 43:2 [d]Mic. 7:14

...r, *dost anoint* [a]Ps. ...9 [b]Ps. 92:10; Luke 7:46 [c]Ps. 16:5

[1]Or, *Only* [2]Another ...g is *return to* [3]Lit., ...*ength of days* [a]Ps. ...:7, 10 [b]Ps. 27:4-6

...:1 [1]Lit., *its fulness* ... 10:26 [b]Ps. 89:11

...Ps. 104:3, 5; 136:6

[a]Ps. 15:1 [b]Ps. 2:6 [c]Ps. 65:4

[1]Or, *in vain* [a]Job ...:9; Ps. 22:30; 26:6 51:10; 73:1; Matt. ...Ezek. 18:15 [d]Ps. 15:4

[1]I.e., as vindicated ...115:13 [b]Ps. 36:10

[1]Or, *Such* [2]*Selah* ...may mean: *Pause*, ...*scendo* or *Musical* ...*erlude* [a]Ps. 27:4, 8

..., *everlasting* [a]Ps. ...8:20; Is. 26:2 [b]Ps. ..., 9; 97:6; Acts 7:2; 1 Cor. 2:8

...eut. 4:34; Ps. 96:7 15:3, 6; Ps. 76:3-6

..., *everlasting* [a]Ps. 26:8; 57:11

[a]Gen. 32:2; Josh. ...2 Sam. 5:10; Neh. 9:6

[a]Ps. 86:4; 143:8

... 31:1 [b]Ps. 25:20; ...1 [c]Ps. 13:4; 41:11

...r, *Let those . . . be* ...*shamed* [a]Ps. 37:9; ...:1; Is. 49:23 [b]Ps. ...158; Is. 21:2; Hab. 1:13

...33:13; Ps. 27:11; 86:11

... 25:10; 43:3 [b]Ps. 79:9

For Thee I [c]wait all the day.
6 [a]Remember, O LORD, Thy compassion and Thy lovingkindnesses,
For they have been [1b]from of old.
7 Do not remember the [a]sins of my youth or my transgressions;
[b]According to Thy lovingkindness remember Thou me,
For Thy [c]goodness' sake, O LORD.

8 [a]Good and [b]upright is the LORD;
Therefore He [c]instructs sinners in the way.
9 He [a]leads the [1]humble in justice,
And He [b]teaches the [1]humble His way.
10 All the paths of the LORD are [a]lovingkindness and truth
To [b]those who keep His covenant and His testimonies.
11 For [a]Thy name's sake, O LORD,
[b]Pardon my iniquity, for it is great.

12 Who is the man who [a]fears the LORD?
He will [b]instruct him in the way he should choose.
13 His soul will [a]abide in [1]prosperity,
And his [2]descendants will [b]inherit the [3]land.
14 The [1a]secret of the LORD is for those who fear Him,
[2]And He will [b]make them know His covenant.
15 My [a]eyes are continually toward the LORD,
For He will [1b]pluck my feet out of the net.

16 [a]Turn to me and be gracious to me,
For I am [b]lonely and afflicted.
17 [1]The [a]troubles of my heart are enlarged;
Bring me [b]out of my distresses.
18 [a]Look upon my affliction and my [1]trouble,
And [b]forgive all my sins.
19 Look upon my enemies, for they [a]are many;
And they [b]hate me with violent hatred.
20 [a]Guard my soul and deliver me;
Do not let me [b]be ashamed, for I take refuge in Thee.
21 Let [a]integrity and uprightness preserve me,
For [b]I wait for Thee.
22 [a]Redeem Israel, O God,
Out of all his troubles.

Psalm 26

A Psalm of David.

26 [1a]Vindicate me, O LORD, for I have [b]walked in my integrity;
And I have [c]trusted in the LORD [2d]without wavering.
2 [a]Examine me, O LORD, and try me;
[b]Test my [1]mind and my heart.
3 For Thy [a]lovingkindness is before my eyes,
And I have [b]walked in Thy [1]truth.
4 I do not [a]sit with [1]deceitful men,
Nor will I go with [2b]pretenders.
5 I [a]hate the assembly of evildoers,
And I will not sit with the wicked.
6 I shall [a]wash my hands in innocence,
And I will go about [b]Thine altar, O LORD,

5 [c]Ps. 40:1

6 [1]Or, *everlasting* 98:3 [b]Ps. 103:17

7 [a]Job 13:26; 20:1 [b]Ps. 51:1 [c]Ps. 31:1

8 [a]Ps. 86:5 [b]Ps. 9 [c]Ps. 32:8

9 [1]Or, *afflicted* [a]Ps 23:3 [b]Ps. 27:11

10 [a]Ps. 40:11 [b]Ps 103:18

11 [a]Ps. 31:3; 79:9 34:9

12 [a]Ps. 31:19 [b]Ps 25:8; 37:23

13 [1]Lit., *good* [2]Lit *seed* [3]Or, *earth* [a]P 1:33; Jer. 23:6 [b]Ps 37:11; 69:36; Matt.

14 [1]Or, *counsel* or *intimacy* [2]Or, *And covenant, to make know it.* [a]Prov. 3:3 John 7:17 [b]Gen. 1

15 [1]Lit., *bring out* 123:2; 141:8 [b]Ps. 124:7

16 [a]Ps. 69:16 [b]Ps 143:4

17 [1]Some commentators rea *Relieve the trouble my heart* [a]Ps. 40: [b]Ps. 107:6

18 [1]Lit., *toil* [a]2 Sa 16:12; Ps. 31:7 [b]P 103:3

19 [a]Ps. 3:1 [b]Ps.

20 [a]Ps. 86:2 [b]Ps.

21 [a]Ps. 41:12 [b]P

22 [a]Ps. 130:8

26:1 [1]Lit., *Judge do not slide* [a]Ps. [b]2 Kin. 20:3; Prov. [c]Ps. 13:5; 28:7 [d]H 10:23

2 [1]Lit., *kidneys,* figurative for inner [a]Ps. 17:3; 139:23 7:9

3 [1]Or, *faithfulness* 48:9 [b]2 Kin. 20:3; 86:11

4 [1]Or, *worthless* lit., *men of falseho* [2]Or, *dissemblers, hypocrites* [a]Ps. [b]Ps. 28:3

5 [a]Ps. 31:6; 139:

6 [a]Ps. 73:13 [b]Ps 43:3, 4

7 That I may proclaim with the voice of [a]thanksgiving,
And declare all Thy [1]wonders.

8 O LORD, I [a]love the habitation of Thy house,
And the place [1]where Thy [b]glory dwells.
9 [a]Do not [1]take my soul away *along* with sinners,
Nor my life with [b]men of bloodshed,
10 In whose hands is a [a]wicked scheme,
And whose right hand is full of [b]bribes.
11 But as for me, I shall [a]walk in my integrity;
[b]Redeem me, and be gracious to me.
12 [a]My foot stands on a [b]level place;
In the [c]congregations I shall bless the LORD.

Psalm 27

A Psalm of David.

27 The LORD is my [a]light and my [b]salvation;
Whom shall I fear?
The LORD is the [1c]defense of my life;
[d]Whom shall I dread?
2 When evildoers came upon me to [a]devour my flesh,
My adversaries and my enemies, they [b]stumbled and fell.
3 Though a [a]host encamp against me,
My heart will not fear;
Though war arise against me,
In *spite of* this I [1]shall be [b]confident.

4 [a]One thing I have asked from the LORD, that I shall seek:
That I may [b]dwell in the house of the LORD all the days of my life,
To behold [c]the [1]beauty of the LORD,
And to [2d]meditate in His temple.
5 For in the [a]day of trouble He will [b]conceal me in His [1]tabernacle;
In the secret place of His tent He will [c]hide me;
He will [d]lift me up on a rock.
6 And now [a]my head will be lifted up above my enemies
around me;
And I will offer in His tent [b]sacrifices [1]with shouts of joy;
I will [c]sing, yes, I will sing praises to the LORD.

7 [a]Hear, O LORD, when I cry with my voice,
And be gracious to me and [b]answer me.
8 *When Thou didst say,* "[a]Seek My face," my heart said to Thee,
"Thy face, O LORD, [b]I shall seek."
9 [a]Do not hide Thy face from me,
Do not turn Thy servant away in [b]anger;
Thou hast been [c]my help;
[d]Do not abandon me nor [e]forsake me,
O God of my salvation!
10 [1]For my father and [a]my mother have forsaken me,
But [b]the LORD will take me up.

11 [a]Teach me Thy way, O LORD,
And lead me in a [b]level path,
Because of [1]my foes.

12 Do not deliver me over to the [1a]desire of my adversaries;
For [b]false witnesses have risen against me,
And such as [c]breathe out violence.
13 [1]*I would have despaired* unless I had believed that I would see the [a]goodness of the LORD
In the [b]land of the living.
14 [a]Wait for the LORD;
Be [b]strong, and let your heart take courage;
Yes, wait for the LORD.

Psalm 28

A Psalm of David.

28 To Thee, O LORD, I call;
My [a]rock, do not be deaf to me,
Lest, if Thou [b]be silent to me,
I become like those who [c]go down to the pit.
2 Hear the [a]voice of my supplications when I cry to Thee for help,
When I [b]lift up my hands [c]toward [1]Thy holy [d]sanctuary.
3 [a]Do not drag me away with the wicked
And with those who work iniquity;
Who [b]speak peace with their neighbors,
While evil is in their hearts.
4 Requite them [a]according to their work and according to the evil of their practices;
Requite them according to the deeds of their hands;
Repay them their [1]recompense.
5 Because they [a]do not regard the works of the LORD
Nor the deeds of His hands,
He will tear them down and not build them up.

6 Blessed be the LORD,
Because He [a]has heard the voice of my supplication.
7 The LORD is my [a]strength and my [b]shield;
My heart [c]trusts in Him, and I am helped;
Therefore [d]my heart exults,
And with [e]my song I shall thank Him.
8 The LORD is [1]their [a]strength,
And He is a [2b]saving defense to His anointed.
9 [a]Save Thy people, and bless [b]Thine inheritance;
Be their [c]shepherd also, and [d]carry them forever.

Psalm 29

A Psalm of David.

29 [a]Ascribe to the LORD, O [1]sons of the mighty,
Ascribe to the LORD glory and strength.
2 Ascribe to the LORD the glory [1]due to His name;
Worship the LORD [a]in [2]holy array.

3 The [a]voice of the LORD is upon the waters;
The God of glory [b]thunders,
The LORD is over [1c]many waters.
4 The voice of the LORD is [a]powerful,
The voice of the LORD is majestic.

12 [1]Lit., *soul* [b]Deut. 19:18; Matt. 26:60 [c]

13 [1]Or, *Surel believed* [a]Ps. [b]Job 28:13; P. 116:9; 142:5; Jer. 11:19; Ez

14 [a]Ps. 25:3; 40:1; 62:5; 13 20:22; Is. 25:9 31:24

28:1 [a]Ps. 18:2 35:22; 39:12; 8 88:4; 143:7; P

2 [1]Lit., *the inn place of Thy s* [a]Ps. 140:6 [b]Ps 141:2; Lam. 2: 2:8 [c]Ps. 5:7; 1 [d]1 Kin. 6:5

3 [a]Ps. 26:9 [b]P 55:21; 62:4; Je

4 [1]Or, *dealings* 62:12; 2 Tim. 4 18:6; 22:12

5 [a]Is. 5:12

6 [a]Ps. 28:2

7 [a]Ps. 18:2; 59 3:3 [c]Ps. 13:5; [d]Ps. 16:9 [e]Ps. 69:30

8 [1]A few mss. a ancient versions *the strength of people* [2]Or, *ref salvation* [a]Ps. 2 89:17 [b]Ps. 27:1

9 [a]Ps. 106:47 [b] 9:29; 32:9; 1 Kin Ps. 33:12; 106:4 80:1 [d]Deut. 1:31 40:11; 46:3; 63:9

29:1 [1]Or, *sons c* [a]1 Chr. 16:28, 29 96:7-9

2 [1]Lit., *of His na* [2]Or, *the majesty holiness* [a]2 Chr. Ps. 110:3

3 [1]Or, *great* [a]Ps [b]Job 37:4, 5; Ps. [c]Ps. 18:16; 107:2

4 [a]Ps. 68:33

5 The voice of the LORD breaks the cedars;
Yes, the LORD breaks in pieces [a]the cedars of Lebanon.
6 And He makes Lebanon [a]skip like a calf,
And [b]Sirion like a young wild ox.
7 The voice of the LORD hews out [1]flames of fire.
8 The voice of the LORD [1]shakes the wilderness;
The LORD shakes the wilderness of [a]Kadesh.
9 The voice of the LORD makes [a]the deer to calve,
And strips the forests bare,
And [b]in His temple everything says, "Glory!"

10 The LORD sat *as King* at the [a]flood;
Yes, the LORD sits as [b]King forever.
11 [1]The LORD will give [a]strength to His people;
[2]The LORD will bless His people with [b]peace.

Psalm 30

A Psalm; a Song at the Dedication of the House. *A Psalm* of David.

30 I will [a]extol Thee, O LORD, for Thou hast [b]lifted me up,
And hast not let my [c]enemies rejoice over me.
2 O LORD my God,
I [a]cried to Thee for help, and Thou didst [b]heal me.
3 O LORD, Thou hast [a]brought up my soul from [1]Sheol;
Thou hast kept me alive, [2]that I should not [b]go down to the pit.
4 [a]Sing praise to the LORD, you [b]His godly ones,
And [c]give thanks to His holy [1d]name.
5 For [a]His anger is but for a moment,
His [b]favor is for a lifetime;
Weeping may [c]last for the night,
But a shout of joy *comes* in the morning.

6 Now as for me, I said in my prosperity,
"I will [a]never be moved."
7 O LORD, by Thy favor Thou hast made my mountain to stand
strong;
Thou didst [a]hide Thy face, I was dismayed.
8 To Thee, O LORD, I called,
And to the Lord I made supplication:
9 "What profit is there in my blood, if I [a]go down to the pit?
Will the [b]dust praise Thee? Will it declare Thy faithfulness?

10 "[a]Hear, O LORD, and be gracious to me;
O LORD, be Thou my [b]helper."
11 Thou hast turned for me [a]my mourning into dancing;
Thou hast [b]loosed my sackcloth and girded me with [c]gladness;
12 That *my* [1a]soul may sing praise to Thee, and not be silent.
O LORD my God, I will [b]give thanks to Thee forever.

Psalm 31

For the choir director. A Psalm of David.

31 [a]In Thee, O LORD, I have taken refuge;
Let me never [b]be ashamed;
[c]In Thy righteousness deliver me.

g. 9:15; 1 Kin. 04:16; Is. 2:13; 14:8
14:4, 6 [b]Deut. 3:9
[1]I.e., lightning
, *causes . . . to* [a]Num. 13:26
39:1 [b]Ps. 26:8
Gen. 6:17 [b]Ps. 10:16
, *May the LORD*
, *May the LORD*
Ps. 28:8; 68:35; :29 [b]Ps. 37:11; 72:3
:1 [a]Ps. 118:28; 1 [b]Ps. 3:3 [c]Ps. 25:2; 35:19, 24
88:13 [b]Ps. 6:2; 103:3; Is. 53:5
the nether world
mss. read *from*
ng those who go [a]Ps. 86:13 [b]Ps. 28:1
., *memorial* [a]Ps. 1 [b]Ps. 50:5 [c]Ps. 2 [d]Ex. 3:15; Ps. 35:13; Hos. 12:5
103:9; Is. 26:20; [b]Ps. 118:1 [c]Ps. 26:5; 2 Cor. 4:17
[a]Ps. 10:6; 62:2, 6
[a]Deut. 31:17; Ps. 104:29; 143:7
Ps. 28:1 [b]Ps. 6:5
Ps. 4:1; 27:7 [b]Ps. 27:9; 54:4
ccl. 3:4; Jer. 31:4, [b]Is. 20:2 [c]Ps. 4:7
2 [1]Lit., *glory* [a]Ps. ; 57:8; 108:1 [b]Ps. 44:8
31:1 [a]Ps. 31:1-3; -3 [b]Ps. 25:2 [c]Ps. 143:1

2 [a]Incline Thine ear to me, rescue me quickly;
Be Thou to me a [b]rock of [1]strength,
A stronghold to save me.
3 For Thou art my [1]rock and [a]my fortress;
For [b]Thy name's sake Thou wilt lead me and guide me.
4 Thou wilt [a]pull me out of the net which they have secretly laid
for me;
For Thou art my [b]strength.
5 [a]Into Thy hand I commit my spirit;
Thou hast [b]ransomed me, O LORD, [c]God of [1]truth.

6 I hate those who [a]regard [1]vain idols;
But I [b]trust in the LORD.
7 I will [a]rejoice and be glad in Thy lovingkindness,
Because Thou hast [b]seen my affliction;
Thou hast known the troubles of my soul,
8 And Thou hast not [a]given me over into the hand of the enemy;
Thou hast set my feet in a large place.

9 Be gracious to me, O LORD, for [a]I am in distress;
My [b]eye is wasted away from grief, [c]my soul and my body *also*.
10 For my life is spent with [a]sorrow,
And my years with sighing;
My [b]strength has failed because of my iniquity,
And [c]my [1]body has wasted away.
11 Because of all my adversaries, I have become a [a]reproach,
Especially to my [b]neighbors,
And an object of dread to my acquaintances;
Those who see me in the street flee from me.
12 I am [a]forgotten as a dead man, out of mind,
I am like a broken vessel.
13 For I have heard the [1a]slander of many,
[b]Terror is on every side;
While they [c]took counsel together against me,
They [d]schemed to take away my life.

14 But as for me, I trust in Thee, O LORD,
I say, "[a]Thou art my God."
15 My [a]times are in Thy hand;
[b]Deliver me from the hand of my enemies, and from those who
persecute me.
16 Make Thy [a]face to shine upon Thy servant;
[b]Save me in Thy lovingkindness.
17 Let me not be [a]put to shame, O LORD, for I call upon Thee;
Let the [b]wicked be put to shame, let them [c]be silent in [1]Sheol.
18 Let the [a]lying lips be dumb,
Which [b]speak arrogantly against the righteous
With pride and contempt.

19 How great is Thy [a]goodness,
Which Thou hast stored up for those who fear Thee,
Which Thou hast wrought for those who [b]take refuge in Thee,
[c]Before the sons of men!

2 [1]Or, *refuge, protection* [a]Ps. 71:2; 86:1; 102. 18:2; 71:3

3 [1]Or, *crag* [a]Ps [b]Ps. 23:3; 25:11

4 [a]Ps. 25:15 [b]P

5 [1]Or, *faithfulne* [a]Luke 23:46; Ac [b]Ps. 55:18; 71:2 [c]Deut. 32:4; Ps.

6 [1]Lit., *empty v* [a]Jon. 2:8 [b]Ps. 5

7 [a]Ps. 90:14 [b]P

8 [a]Deut. 32:30; 37:33

9 [a]Ps. 66:14; 69 [b]Ps. 6:7 [c]Ps. 63

10 [1]Or, *bones, substance* [a]Ps. [b]Ps. 39:11 [c]Ps. 38:3; 102:3

11 [a]Ps. 69:19 [b] 19:13; Ps. 38:11, 88:8, 18

12 [a]Ps. 88:5

13 [1]Lit., *whisper* [a]Ps. 50:20; Jer. 2 [b]Lam. 2:22 [c]Ps. Matt. 27:1 [d]Ps. 4

14 [a]Ps. 140:6

15 [a]Job 14:5; 24. 143:9

16 [a]Num. 6:25; P 80:3 [b]Ps. 6:4

17 [1]I.e., the nethe world [a]Ps. 25:2, 2 [b]Ps. 25:3 [c]1 Sam Ps. 94:17; 115:17

18 [a]Ps. 109:2; 12 [b]1 Sam. 2:3; Ps. 9 Jude 15

19 [a]Ps. 65:4; 145 64:4; Rom. 2:4; 11 [b]Ps. 5:11 [c]Ps. 23:

20 Thou dost hide them in the [a]secret place of Thy presence from
the [b]conspiracies of man;
Thou dost keep them secretly in a [1]shelter from the [c]strife of
tongues.
21 [a]Blessed be the LORD,
For He has made [b]marvelous His lovingkindness to me in a
besieged [c]city.
22 As for me, [a]I said in my alarm,
"I am [b]cut off from before Thine eyes";
Nevertheless Thou didst [c]hear the voice of my supplications
When I cried to Thee.

23 O love the LORD, all you [a]His godly ones!
The LORD [b]preserves the faithful,
And fully [c]recompenses the proud doer.
24 [a]Be strong, and let your heart take courage,
All you who [1]hope in the LORD.

Psalm 32

A Psalm of David. A [+]Maskil.

32 [a]How blessed is he whose transgression is forgiven,
Whose sin is covered!
2 How blessed is the man to whom the LORD [a]does not impute
iniquity,
And in whose spirit there is [b]no deceit!

3 When [a]I kept silent *about my sin,* [b]my [1]body wasted away
Through my [2c]groaning all day long.
4 For day and night [a]Thy hand was heavy upon me;
My [1b]vitality was drained away *as* with the fever heat of summer.
[2]Selah.

5 I [a]acknowledged my sin to Thee,
And my iniquity I [b]did not hide;
I said, "[c]I will confess my transgressions to the LORD";
And Thou [d]didst forgive the [1]guilt of my sin. Selah.
6 Therefore, let everyone who is godly pray to Thee [1a]in a time
when Thou mayest be found;
Surely [b]in a flood of great waters they shall not reach him.
7 Thou art [a]my hiding place; Thou [b]dost preserve me from trouble;
Thou dost surround me with [1c]songs of deliverance. Selah.

8 I will [a]instruct you and teach you in the way which you
should go;
I will counsel you [b]with My eye upon you.
9 Do not be [a]as the horse or as the mule which have no
understanding,
Whose trappings include bit and bridle to hold them in check,
Otherwise they will not come near to you.
10 Many are the [a]sorrows of the wicked;
But [b]he who trusts in the LORD, lovingkindness shall surround
him.
11 Be [a]glad in the LORD and rejoice, you righteous ones,
And shout for joy, all you who are [b]upright in heart.

pavilion [a]Ps.
s. 37:12 [c]Job
21; Ps. 31:13
8:6 [b]Ps. 17:7
23:7; Ps. 87:5
s. 116:11 [b]Ps.
8:11, 12; Lam.
s. 18:6; 66:19;
145:19
s. 30:4; 37:28;
. 145:20; Rev.
eut. 32:41; Ps.
94:2
r, *wait for* [a]Ps.
27:14
[+]Possibly,
ntemplative, or
actic, or *Skillful*
Psalm
Ps. 85:2; 103:3;
Rom. 4:7, 8
Cor. 5:19 [b]John
1:47
3 [1]Or, *bones,*
ce [2]Lit., *roaring*
2, 3 [b]Ps. 31:10
[c]Ps. 38:8
life juices were
into the drought
ner [2]*Selah* may
mean: *Pause,*
endo or *Musical*
de [a]1 Sam. 5:6;
; 33:7; Ps. 38:2;
9:10 [b]Ps. 22:15
Or, *iniquity* [a]Lev.
[b]Job 31:33 [c]Ps.
:18; Prov. 28:13;
1:9 [d]Ps. 103:12
[1]Lit., *in a time of*
g out [a]Ps. 69:13;
55:6 [b]Ps. 46:1-3;
124:5; 144:7; Is.
43:2
shouts [a]Ps. 9:9;
20; 91:1; 119:114
121:7 [c]Ex. 15:1;
udg. 5:1; Ps. 40:3
. 25:8 [b]Ps. 33:18
9 [a]Prov. 26:3
0 [a]Ps. 16:4; Prov.
21; Rom. 2:9 [b]Ps.
1, 12; Prov. 16:20
[a]Ps. 64:10; 68:3;
2 [b]Ps. 7:10; 64:10

Psalm 33

33 [a]Sing for joy in the LORD, O you righteous ones;
Praise is [b]becoming to the upright.
2 Give thanks to the LORD with the [a]lyre;
Sing praises to Him with a [b]harp of ten strings.
3 Sing to Him a [a]new song;
Play skillfully with [b]a shout of joy.
4 For the word of the LORD [a]is upright;
And all His work is *done* [b]in faithfulness.
5 He [a]loves righteousness and justice;
The [b]earth is full of the lovingkindness of the LORD.

6 By the [a]word of the LORD the heavens were made,
And [b]by the breath of His mouth [c]all their host.
7 He gathers the [a]waters of the sea together [1]as a heap;
He lays up the deeps in storehouses.
8 Let [a]all the earth fear the LORD;
Let all the inhabitants of the world [b]stand in awe of Him.
9 For [a]He spoke, and it was done;
He commanded, and it [1]stood fast.
10 The LORD [a]nullifies the counsel of the nations;
He frustrates the plans of the peoples.
11 The [a]counsel of the LORD stands forever,
The [b]plans of His heart from generation to generation.
12 Blessed is the [a]nation whose God is the LORD,
The people whom He has [b]chosen for His own inheritance.

13 The LORD [a]looks from heaven;
He [b]sees all the sons of men;
14 From [a]His dwelling place He looks out
On all the inhabitants of the earth,
15 He who [a]fashions [1]the hearts of them all,
He who [b]understands all their works.
16 [a]The king is not saved by a mighty army;
A warrior is not delivered by great strength.
17 A [a]horse is a false hope for victory;
Nor does it deliver anyone by its great strength.

18 Behold, [a]the eye of the LORD is on those who fear Him,
On those who [1b]hope for His lovingkindness,
19 To [a]deliver their soul from death,
And to keep them alive [b]in famine.
20 Our soul [a]waits for the LORD;
He is our [b]help and our shield.
21 For our [a]heart rejoices in Him,
Because we trust in His holy name.
22 Let Thy lovingkindness, O LORD, be upon us,
According as we have [1]hoped in Thee.

33:1 [a]Ps. 32:1 ... 3:1; 4:4 [b]Ps. 9...
2 [a]Ps. 71:22; ... [b]Ps. 144:9
3 [a]Ps. 40:3; 9... 144:9; Is. 42:1... 5:9 [b]Ps. 98:4
4 [a]Ps. 19:8 [b]P...
5 [a]Ps. 11:7; 37... 119:64
6 [a]Gen. 1:6; P... Heb. 11:3 [b]Ps. ... [c]Gen. 2:1
7 [1]Some versi... *in a water skin;* ... container [a]Ex. ... Josh. 3:16; Ps. ...
8 [a]Ps. 67:7 [b]P...
9 [1]Or, *stood fo...* [a]Gen. 1:3; Ps. 1...
10 [a]Ps. 2:1-3; I... 19:3
11 [a]Job 23:12; ... 19:21 [b]Ps. 40:5... 139:17; Is. 55:8
12 [a]Ps. 144:15 ... 19:5; Deut. 7:6; ...
13 [a]Job 28:24; ... 14:2 [b]Ps. 11:4
14 [a]1 Kin. 8:39, ... 102:19
15 [1]Or, *their hea... together* [a]Job 10... 119:73 [b]2 Chr. 1... Job 34:21; Jer. 3...
16 [a]Ps. 44:6; 60...
17 [a]Ps. 20:7; 14... Prov. 21:31
18 [1]Or, *wait* [a]Job ... Ps. 32:8; 34:15; 1... 3:12 [b]Ps. 32:10; ...
19 [a]Ps. 56:13; Ac... 12:11 [b]Job 5:20; ... 37:19
20 [a]Ps. 62:1; 130... 8:17 [b]Ps. 115:9
21 [a]Ps. 13:5; 28:7... Zech. 10:7; John 1...
22 [1]Or, *waited fo...*

Psalm 34

A Psalm of David when he [+]feigned madness before [•]Abimelech, who drove him away and he departed.

34 I will [a]bless the LORD at all times;
His [b]praise shall continually be in my mouth.
2 My soul shall [a]make its boast in the LORD;
The [b]humble shall hear it and rejoice.
3 O [a]magnify the LORD with me,
And let us [b]exalt His name together.

4 I [a]sought the LORD, and He answered me,
And [b]delivered me from all my fears.
5 They [a]looked to Him and were radiant,
And their faces shall [b]never be ashamed.
6 This [1]poor man cried and [a]the LORD heard him,
And saved him out of all his troubles.
7 The [a]angel of the LORD encamps around those who fear Him,
And rescues them.

8 O [a]taste and see that the LORD is good;
How [b]blessed is the man who takes refuge in Him!
9 O fear the LORD, you [a]His saints;
For to those who fear Him, there is [b]no want.
10 The young lions do lack and suffer hunger;
But they who seek the LORD shall [a]not be in want of any good thing.
11 [a]Come, you children, listen to me;
[b]I will teach you [c]the fear of the LORD.
12 [a]Who is the man who desires life,
And loves *length of* days that he may [b]see good?
13 Keep [a]your tongue from evil,
And your lips from speaking [b]deceit.
14 [a]Depart from evil, and do good;
Seek peace, and [b]pursue it.

15 The [a]eyes of the LORD are toward the righteous,
And His ears are *open* to their cry.
16 The [a]face of the LORD is against evildoers,
To [b]cut off the memory of them from the earth.
17 *The righteous* [a]cry and the LORD hears,
And delivers them out of all their troubles.
18 The LORD [a]is near to the [b]brokenhearted,
And saves those who are [1c]crushed in spirit.

19 [a]Many are the [b]afflictions of the righteous;
But the LORD [c]delivers him out of them all.
20 He keeps all his bones;
[a]Not one of them is broken.
21 [a]Evil shall slay the wicked;
And those who hate the righteous will be [1]condemned.
22 The LORD [a]redeems the soul of His servants;
And none of those who [b]take refuge in Him will be [1]condemned.

[+]Or, *changed his* [behavior] [•]Possibly a [titl]e of King Achish of Gath. See 1 Sam. 21:10-15

34:1 [a]Eph. 5:20; [1 Th]ess. 5:18 [b]Ps. 71:6

[a]Ps. 44:8; Jer. 9:24; [1 C]or. 1:31 [b]Ps. 69:32

[a]Ps. 35:27; 69:30; [Lu]ke 1:46 [b]Ps. 18:46

[2] Chr. 15:2; Ps. 9:10; Matt. 7:7 [b]Ps. 34:6, 17, 19

[a]Ps. 36:9; Is. 60:5 [b]Ps. 25:3

[1Or,] *afflicted* [a]Ps. 34:4

[P]s. 91:11; Dan. 6:22

[a]Ps. 119:103; Heb. [6:5; 1] Pet. 2:3 [b]Ps. 2:12

[P]s. 31:23 [b]Ps. 23:1

10 [a]Ps. 84:11

[1]1 [a]Ps. 66:16 [b]Ps. 32:8 [c]Ps. 111:10

[P]s. 34:12-16; 1 Pet. [3:]10-12 [b]Eccl. 3:13

[a]Ps. 141:3; Prov. 13:3; James 1:26 [b]1 Pet. 2:22

[a]Ps. 37:27; Is. 1:16, [b]Rom. 14:19; Heb. 12:14

[J]ob 36:7; Ps. 33:18

[a]Lev. 17:10; Jer. [...]1; Amos 9:4 [b]Job [...]7; Ps. 9:6; 109:15; Prov. 10:7

[a]Ps. 34:6; 145:19

[1]Or, *contrite* [a]Ps. [...]18 [b]Ps. 147:3; Is. [...]:1 [c]Ps. 51:17; Is. 57:15

[a]Prov. 24:16 [b]Ps. [3]2 Tim. 3:11f. [c]Ps. 34:4, 6, 17

[a]John 19:33, 36

[1O]r, *held guilty* [a]Ps. [...].23; 140:11; Prov. 24:16

22 [1]V. 21, note 1 [...]n. 1:29; Ps. 71:23 [b]Ps. 37:40

Psalm 35

A Psalm of David.

35 Contend, O LORD, with those who [a]contend with me;
Fight against those who [b]fight against me.
2 Take hold of [1a]buckler and shield,
And rise up for [b]my help.
3 Draw also the spear and [1]the battle-axe to meet those who pursue me;
Say to my soul, "I am [a]your salvation."
4 Let those be [a]ashamed and dishonored who seek my [1]life;
Let those be [b]turned back and humiliated who devise evil against me.
5 Let them be [a]like chaff before the wind,
With the angel of the LORD driving *them* on.
6 Let their way be dark and [a]slippery,
With the angel of the LORD pursuing them.
7 For [a]without cause they [b]hid their net for me;
Without cause they dug a [1]pit for my soul.
8 Let [a]destruction come upon him unawares;
And [b]let the net which he hid catch himself;
Into that very [c]destruction let him fall.

9 And my soul shall [a]rejoice in the LORD;
It shall [b]exult in His salvation.
10 All my [a]bones will say, "LORD, [b]who is like Thee,
Who delivers the afflicted from him [c]who is too strong for him,
And [d]the afflicted and the needy from him who robs him?"
11 [a]Malicious witnesses rise up;
They ask me of things that I do not know.
12 They [a]repay me evil for good,
To the bereavement of my soul.
13 But as for me, [a]when they were sick, my [b]clothing was sackcloth;
I [c]humbled my soul with fasting;
And my [d]prayer kept returning to my bosom.
14 I went about as though it were my friend or brother;
I [a]bowed down [1]mourning, as one who sorrows for a mother.
15 But [a]at my [1]stumbling they rejoiced, and gathered themselves together;
The [2b]smiters whom I did not know gathered together against me,
They [3c]slandered me without ceasing.
16 Like godless jesters at a feast,
They [a]gnashed at me with their teeth.

17 Lord, [a]how long wilt Thou look on?
Rescue my soul [b]from their ravages,
My [c]only *life* from the lions.
18 I will [a]give Thee thanks in the great congregation;
I will [b]praise Thee among a mighty throng.
19 [a]Do not let those who are wrongfully [b]my enemies rejoice over me;
Neither let those [c]who hate me without cause [1d]wink maliciously.
20 For they do not speak peace,

35:1 [a]Ps. 18:43; Is 49:25 [b]Ps. 56:2
2 [1]I.e., small shield [a]Ps. 91:4 [b]Ps. 44:
3 [1]Or, *close up the against those* [a]Ps.
4 [1]Or, *soul* [a]Ps. 7 [b]Ps. 40:14; 129:5
5 [a]Job 21:18; Ps. 83:13; Is. 29:5
6 [a]Ps. 73:18; Jer.
7 [1]*Pit* has been transposed from li above [a]Ps. 69:4; 140:5 [b]Ps. 9:15
8 [a]Ps. 55:23; Is. 4 1 Thess. 5:3 [b]Ps. [c]Ps. 73:18
9 [a]Is. 61:10 [b]Ps. 13:5; Luke 1:47
10 [a]Ps. 51:8 [b]Ex. 15:11; Ps. 86:8; M 7:18 [c]Ps. 18:17 37:14; 109:16
11 [a]Ps. 27:12
12 [a]Ps. 38:20; 10 Jer. 18:20; John 1
13 [a]Job 30:25 [b]P 69:11 [c]Ps. 69:10 10:13; Luke 10:6
14 [1]Or, *dressed i black* [a]Ps. 38:6
15 [1]Or, *limping* [2] *smitten ones* [3]Lit [a]Obad. 12 [b]Job 3 12 [c]Ps. 7:2
16 [a]Job 16:9; Ps. 37:12; Lam. 2:16
17 [a]Ps. 13:1; Hab [b]Ps. 35:7 [c]Ps. 22
18 [a]Ps. 22:22 [b]P 22:25
19 [1]Or, *wink the* [a]Ps. 13:4; 30:1; 3 [b]Ps. 38:19; 69:4 15:25 [d]Prov. 6:1

But they devise [a]deceitful words against those who are quiet in the land.
21 And they [a]opened their mouth wide against me;
They said, "[b]Aha, aha, our eyes have seen it!"

22 [a]Thou hast seen it, O LORD, [b]do not keep silent;
O Lord, [c]do not be far from me.
23 [a]Stir up Thyself, and awake to my right,
And to my cause, my God and my Lord.
24 [a]Judge me, O LORD my God, according to Thy righteousness;
And [b]do not let them rejoice over me.
25 Do not let them say in their heart, "[a]Aha, our desire!"
Do not let them say, "We have [b]swallowed him up!"
26 Let [a]those be ashamed and humiliated altogether who rejoice at my distress;
Let those be [b]clothed with shame and dishonor who [c]magnify themselves over me.

27 Let them [a]shout for joy and rejoice, who favor [b]my vindication;
And [c]let them say continually, "The LORD be magnified,
Who [d]delights in the prosperity of His servant."
28 And [a]my tongue shall declare Thy righteousness
And Thy praise all day long.

Psalm 36

For the choir director. *A Psalm* of David the servant of the LORD.

36 Transgression speaks to the ungodly within [1]his heart;
There is [a]no fear of God before his eyes.
2 For [1]it [a]flatters him in his *own* eyes,
Concerning the discovery of his iniquity *and* the hatred *of it*.
3 The [a]words of his mouth are wickedness and deceit;
He has [b]ceased to [1]be wise *and* to do good.
4 He [a]plans wickedness upon his bed;
He sets himself on a [b]path that is not good;
He [c]does not despise evil.

5 Thy [a]lovingkindness, O LORD, [1]extends to the heavens,
Thy faithfulness *reaches* to the skies.
6 Thy [a]righteousness is like the [1]mountains of God;
Thy [b]judgments are *like* a great deep.
O LORD, Thou [c]preservest man and beast.
7 How [a]precious is Thy lovingkindness, O God!
And the children of men [b]take refuge in the shadow of Thy wings.
8 They [a]drink their fill of the [1]abundance of Thy house;
And Thou dost give them to drink of the [b]river of Thy delights.
9 For with Thee is the [a]fountain of life;
In Thy light we see light.

10 O continue Thy lovingkindness to [a]those who know Thee,
And Thy [b]righteousness to the upright in heart.
11 Let not the foot of pride come upon me,
And let not the hand of the wicked drive me away.

5:21; Jer. 9:8; Mic. 6:12
ob 16:10; Ps. s. 40:15; 70:3
3:7; Ps. 10:14 3:1 [c]Ps. 10:1; ; 38:21; 71:12
Ps. 7:6; 44:23; 59:4; 80:2
9:4; 26:1; 43:1 [b]Ps. 35:19
Ps. 35:21 [b]Ps. :3; Prov. 1:12; Lam. 2:16
Ps. 40:14 [b]Ps. [c]Job 19:5; Ps. 38:16
32:11 [b]Ps. 9:4):16; 70:4 [d]Ps. 147:11; 149:4
1:14; 71:15, 24
nother reading art [a]Rom. 3:18
[1]Or, *he flatters lf* [a]Deut. 29:19; Ps. 10:11; 49:18
nderstand to do [a]Ps. 10:7; 12:2 . 94:8; Jer. 4:22
v. 4:16; Mic. 2:1 65:2 [c]Ps. 52:3; Rom. 12:9
is in [a]Ps. 57:10; 103:11; 108:4
6 [1]Or, *mighty tains* [a]Ps. 71:19 11:8; Ps. 77:19; 11:33 [c]Neh. 9:6; 4:14, 15; 145:16
Ps. 40:5; 139:17 h 2:12; Ps. 17:8; 57:1; 91:4
Lit., *fatness* [a]Ps. 5:4; Is. 25:6; Jer. 2-14 [b]Job 20:17; . 46:4; Rev. 22:1
9 [a]Jer. 2:13
. 22:16 [b]Ps. 24:5

12 There the doers of iniquity have fallen;
They have been thrust down and [a]cannot rise.

Psalm 37

A Psalm of David.

37 [a]Do not fret because of evildoers,
Be not [b]envious toward wrongdoers.
2 For they will [a]wither quickly like the grass,
And [b]fade like the green herb.
3 [a]Trust in the LORD, and do good;
[b]Dwell in the land and [1c]cultivate faithfulness.
4 [a]Delight yourself in the LORD;
And He will [b]give you the desires of your heart.
5 [a]Commit your way to the LORD,
Trust also in Him, and He will do it.
6 And He will bring forth [a]your righteousness as the light,
And your judgment [b]as the noonday.

7 [1]Rest in the LORD and [a]wait [2]patiently for Him;
[b]Do not fret because of him who [c]prospers in his way,
Because of the man who carries out wicked schemes.
8 Cease from anger, and [a]forsake wrath;
Do not fret, *it leads* only to evildoing.
9 For [a]evildoers will be cut off,
But those who wait for the LORD, they will [b]inherit the land.
10 Yet [a]a little while and the wicked man will be no more;
And you will look carefully for [b]his place, and he will not be *there.*
11 But [a]the humble will inherit the land,
And will delight themselves in [b]abundant prosperity.

12 The wicked [a]plots against the righteous,
And [b]gnashes at him with his teeth.
13 The Lord [a]laughs at him;
For He sees [b]his day is coming.
14 The wicked have drawn the sword and [a]bent their bow,
To cast down the [b]afflicted and the needy,
To [c]slay those who are upright in conduct.
15 Their sword will enter their own heart,
And their [a]bows will be broken.

16 [a]Better is the little of the righteous
Than the abundance of many wicked.
17 For the [a]arms of the wicked will be broken;
But the LORD [b]sustains the righteous.
18 The LORD [a]knows the days of the [1]blameless;
And their [b]inheritance will be forever.
19 They will not be ashamed in the time of evil;
And [a]in the days of famine they will have abundance.
20 But the [a]wicked will perish;
And the enemies of the LORD will be like the [1]glory of the pastures,
They vanish—[b]like smoke they vanish away.
21 The wicked borrows and does not pay back,

12 [a]Ps. 140:1… 26:14

37:1 [a]Prov. 23… 24:19 [b]Ps. 73:… 3:31

2 [a]Job 14:2; P… 92:7; James 1:… 129:6

3 [1]Or, *feed se… feed on His fai…* [a]Ps. 62:8 [b]Deu… [c]Is. 40:11; Ezek… 34:13, 14

4 [a]Job 22:26; … 94:19; Is. 58:14… 21:2; 145:19; M…

5 [a]Ps. 55:22; P… 16:3; 1 Pet. 5:7

6 [a]Ps. 97:11; Is… 10; Mic. 7:9 [b]Jo…

7 [1]Or, *Be still* … *longingly* [a]Ps. … 62:5; Lam. 3:26… 37:1, 8 [c]Jer. 12…

8 [a]Eph. 4:31; C…

9 [a]Ps. 37:2, 22… 25:13; Prov. 2:2… 57:13; 60:21; M…

10 [a]Job 24:24 … 7:10; Ps. 37:35, …

11 [a]Matt. 5:5 [b]P…

12 [a]Ps. 31:13, 2… 35:16

13 [a]Ps. 2:4 [b]1 S… 26:10; Job 18:20

14 [a]Ps. 11:2; La… [b]Ps. 35:10; 86:1… 11:2

15 [a]1 Sam. 2:4; …

16 [a]Prov. 15:16; …

17 [a]Job 38:15; P… 10:15; Ezek. 30:2… 71:6; 145:14

18 [1]Lit., *complet… perfect* [a]Ps. 1:6; [b]Ps. 37:27, 29

19 [a]Job 5:20; Ps…

20 [1]I.e., flowers… 73:27 [b]Ps. 68:2; …

But the righteous [a]is gracious and gives.
22 For [a]those blessed by Him will [b]inherit the land;
But those [c]cursed by Him will be cut off.

23 [a]The steps of a man are established by the LORD;
And He [b]delights in his way.
24 When [a]he falls, he shall not be hurled headlong;
Because [b]the LORD is the One [1]who holds his hand.
25 I have been young, and now I am old;
Yet [a]I have not seen the righteous forsaken,
Or [b]his [1]descendants begging bread.
26 All day long [a]he is gracious and lends;
And [b]his [1]descendants are a blessing.

27 [a]Depart from evil, and do good,
[1]So you will abide [b]forever.
28 For the LORD [a]loves [1]justice,
And [b]does not forsake His godly ones;
They are [c]preserved forever;
But the [2d]descendants of the wicked will be cut off.
29 The righteous will [a]inherit the land,
And [b]dwell in it forever.
30 The mouth of the righteous [a]utters wisdom,
And his tongue [b]speaks justice.
31 The [a]law of his God is in his heart;
His [b]steps do not slip.
32 The [a]wicked spies upon the righteous,
And [b]seeks to kill him.
33 The LORD will [a]not leave him in his hand,
Or [b]let him be condemned when he is judged.
34 [a]Wait for the LORD, and keep His way,
And He will exalt you to inherit the land;
When the [b]wicked are cut off, you will see it.

35 I have [a]seen a violent, wicked man
Spreading himself like a [b]luxuriant [1]tree in its native soil.
36 Then [1]he passed away, and lo, he [a]was no more;
I sought for him, but he could not be found.
37 Mark the [1a]blameless man, and behold the [b]upright;
For the man of peace will have a [2c]posterity.
38 But transgressors will be altogether [a]destroyed;
The [1]posterity of the wicked will be [b]cut off.
39 But the [a]salvation of the righteous is from the LORD;
He is their strength [b]in time of trouble.
40 And [a]the LORD helps them, and delivers them;
He [b]delivers them from the wicked, and saves them,
Because they [c]take refuge in Him.

Psalm 38

A Psalm of David, for a memorial.

38 O LORD, [a]rebuke me not in Thy wrath;
And chasten me not in Thy burning anger.
2 For Thine [a]arrows have sunk deep into me,
And [b]Thy hand has pressed down on me.

3 There is [a]no soundness in my flesh [b]because of Thine
indignation;
There is no health [c]in my bones because of my sin.
4 For my [a]iniquities are gone over my head;
As a heavy burden they weigh too much for me.
5 My [1]wounds grow foul *and* fester.
Because of [a]my folly,
6 I am bent over and [a]greatly bowed down;
I [b]go mourning all day long.
7 For my loins are filled with [a]burning;
And there is [b]no soundness in my flesh.
8 I am [a]benumbed and [1]badly crushed;
I [2b]groan because of the [3]agitation of my heart.

9 Lord, all [a]my desire is [1]before Thee;
And my [b]sighing is not hidden from Thee.
10 My heart throbs, [a]my strength fails me;
And the [b]light of my eyes, even [1]that [2]has gone from me.
11 My [1a]loved ones and my friends stand aloof from my plague;
And my kinsmen [b]stand afar off.
12 Those who [a]seek my life [b]lay snares *for me;*
And those who [c]seek to injure me have [1]threatened destruction,
And they [d]devise treachery all day long.

13 But I, like a deaf man, do not hear;
And I am like a [a]dumb man who does not open his mouth.
14 Yes, I am like a man who does not hear,
And in whose mouth are no arguments.
15 For [a]I [1]hope in Thee, O LORD;
Thou [b]wilt answer, O Lord my God.
16 For I said, "May they not rejoice over me,
Who, when my foot slips, [a]would magnify themselves against
me."
17 For I am [a]ready to fall,
And [b]my [1]sorrow is continually before me.
18 For I [1a]confess my iniquity;
I am full of [b]anxiety because of my sin.
19 But my [a]enemies are vigorous *and* [1]strong;
And many are those who [b]hate me wrongfully.
20 And those who [a]repay evil for good,
They [b]oppose me, because I follow what is good.
21 Do not forsake me, O LORD;
O my God, [a]do not be far from me!
22 Make [a]haste to help me,
O Lord, [b]my salvation!

Psalm 39

For the choir director, for [+]Jeduthun. A Psalm of David.

39 I said, "I will [a]guard my ways,
That I [b]may not sin with my tongue;
I will guard [c]my mouth as with a muzzle,
While the wicked are in my presence."
2 I was [a]dumb [1]and silent,
I [2]refrained *even* from good;

3 [a]Is. 1:6 [b]Ps. [c]Job 33:19; Ps 31:10
4 [a]Ezra 9:6; P
5 [1]Or, *stripes*
6 [a]Ps. 35:14 30:28; Ps. 42:9
7 [a]Ps. 102:3 [b]
8 [1]Or, *greatly roar* [3]Lit., *grow* [a]Lam. 1:13, 20f 5:17 [b]Job 3:24 22:1; 32:3
9 [1]Or, *known t* [a]Ps. 10:17 [b]Ps. 102:5
10 [1]Lit., *they h is not with me* 31:10 [b]Ps. 6:7; 88:9
11 [1]Or, *lovers* 31:11; 88:18 [b]L 23:49
12 [1]Lit., *spoken* 54:3 [b]Ps. 140:5 35:4 [d]Ps. 35:20
13 [a]Ps. 39:2, 9
15 [1]Or, *wait for* 39:7 [b]Ps. 17:6
16 [a]Ps. 35:26
17 [1]Lit., *pain* [a]P 35:15 [b]Ps. 13:2
18 [1]Or, *declare* 32:5 [b]2 Cor. 7:9,
19 [1]Or, *numerou* 18:17 [b]Ps. 35:19
20 [a]Ps. 35:12 [b]P 109:5; 1 John 3:1
21 [a]Ps. 22:19; 35
22 [a]Ps. 40:13, 17 27:1
[+]1 Chr. 16:41
39:1 [a]1 Kin. 2:4; 10:31; Ps. 119:9 2:10; Ps. 34:13; J 3:5-12 [c]Ps. 141:3 James 3:2
2 [1]Lit., *with silenc* [2]Lit., *kept silence* 38:13

And my [3]sorrow grew worse.
3 My [a]heart was hot within me;
While I was musing the fire burned;
Then I spoke with my tongue:
4 "LORD, make me to know [a]my end,
And what is the extent of my days,
Let me know how [b]transient I am.
5 "Behold, Thou hast made [a]my days *as* handbreadths,
And my [b]lifetime as nothing in Thy sight,
Surely every man [1]at his best is [2]a mere [c]breath. [3]Selah.
6 "Surely every man [a]walks about as [1]a phantom;
Surely they make an [b]uproar for nothing;
He [c]amasses *riches*, and does not know who will gather them.

7 "And now, Lord, for what do I wait?
My [a]hope is in Thee.
8 "[a]Deliver me from all my transgressions;
Make me not the [b]reproach of the foolish.
9 "I have become [a]dumb, I do not open my mouth,
Because it is [b]Thou who hast done *it*.
10 "[a]Remove Thy plague from me;
Because of [b]the opposition of Thy hand, I am [1]perishing.
11 "With [a]reproofs Thou dost chasten a man for iniquity;
Thou dost [b]consume as a moth what is precious to him;
Surely [c]every man is a mere breath. Selah.

12 "[a]Hear my prayer, O LORD, and give ear to my cry;
Do not be silent [b]at my tears;
For I am [c]a stranger with Thee,
A [d]sojourner like all my fathers.
13 "[a]Turn Thy gaze away from me, that I may [1]smile *again*,
Before I depart and am no more."

Psalm 40

For the choir director. A Psalm of David.

40 I [a]waited [1]patiently for the LORD;
And He inclined to me, and [b]heard my cry.
2 He brought me up out of the [a]pit of destruction, out of the [1]miry clay;
And [b]He set my feet upon a rock [c]making my footsteps firm.
3 And He put a [a]new song in my mouth, a song of praise to our God;
Many will [b]see and fear,
And will trust in the LORD.

4 How [a]blessed is the man who has made the LORD his trust,
And [b]has not [1]turned to the proud, nor to those who [c]lapse into falsehood.
5 Many, O LORD my God, are [a]the wonders which Thou hast done,
And Thy [b]thoughts toward us;
There is none to compare with Thee;
If I would declare and speak of them,
They [c]would be too numerous to count.

2 [3]Lit., *pain*
32:4; Jer. 20:9; Luke 24:32
6:11; Ps. 90:12; :84 [b]Ps. 78:39; 103:14
t., *standing firm* *ltogether vanity* *elah* may mean: *e, Crescendo* or *l interlude* [a]Ps. [b]Ps. 144:4 [c]Job 62:9; Eccl. 6:12
[1]Lit., *an image* or. 7:31; James , 11; 1 Pet. 1:24 27:2; Eccl. 5:17 9:10; Eccl. 2:26; :14; Luke 12:20
7 [a]Ps. 38:15
s. 51:9, 14; 79:9 13; 79:4; 119:22
s. 39:2 [b]2 Sam. 16:10; Job 2:10
Or, *wasting away* 9:34; 13:21 [b]Ps. 32:4
Ezek. 5:15; 2 Pet. [b]Job 13:28; Ps. s. 50:9 [c]Ps. 39:5
[a]Ps. 102:1; 143:1 in. 20:5; Ps. 56:8 Lev. 25:23; 1 Chr. Ps. 119:19; Heb. Pet. 2:11 [d]Gen. 47:9
13 [1]Or, *become heerful* [a]Job 7:19; :20, 21; 14:6; Ps. 102:24
[1]Or, *intently* [a]Ps. ; 27:14; 37:7 [b]Ps. 34:15
t., *mud of the mire* 69:2, 14; Jer. 38:6 s. 27:5 [c]Ps. 37:23
s. 32:7; 33:3 [b]Ps. 52:6; 64:9
[1]Lit., *regard* [a]Ps. 84:12 [b]Job 37:24 [c]Ps. 125:5
[a]Job 5:9; Ps. 136:4 [b]Ps. 139:17; Is. 55:8 [c]Ps. 71:15; 139:18

6 [1a]Sacrifice and meal offering Thou hast not desired;
My ears Thou hast [2]opened;
Burnt offering and sin offering Thou hast not required.
7 Then I said, "Behold, I come;
In the scroll of the book it is [1]written of me;
8 [a]I delight to do Thy will, O my God;
[b]Thy Law is within my heart."

9 I have [a]proclaimed glad tidings of righteousness in the great
congregation;
Behold, I will [b]not restrain my lips,
O LORD, [c]Thou knowest.
10 I have [a]not hidden Thy righteousness within my heart;
I have [b]spoken of Thy faithfulness and Thy salvation;
I have not concealed Thy lovingkindness and Thy truth from the
great congregation.

11 Thou, O LORD, wilt not withhold Thy compassion from me;
[1]Thy [a]lovingkindness and Thy truth will continually
preserve me.
12 For evils beyond number have [a]surrounded me;
My [b]iniquities have overtaken me, so that I am not able to see;
They are [c]more numerous than the hairs of my head;
And my [d]heart has [1]failed me.

13 [a]Be pleased, O LORD, to deliver me;
Make [b]haste, O LORD, to help me.
14 Let those be [a]ashamed and humiliated together
Who [b]seek my [1]life to destroy it;
Let those be turned back and dishonored
Who delight [2]in my hurt.
15 Let those [a]be [1]appalled because of their shame
Who [b]say to me, "Aha, aha!"
16 [a]Let all who seek Thee rejoice and be glad in Thee;
Let those who love Thy salvation [b]say continually,
"The LORD be magnified!"
17 Since [a]I am afflicted and needy,
[1b]Let the Lord be mindful of me;
Thou art my help and my deliverer;
Do not delay, O my God.

Psalm 41

For the choir director. A Psalm of David.

41 How blessed is he who [a]considers the [1]helpless;
The LORD will deliver him [b]in a day of [2]trouble.
2 The LORD will [a]protect him, and keep him alive,
And he shall [1]be called [b]blessed upon the earth;
And [c]do not give him over to the desire of his enemies.
3 The LORD will sustain him upon his sickbed;
In his illness, Thou dost [1]restore him to health.

4 As for me, I said, "O LORD, be gracious to me;
[a]Heal my soul, for [b]I have sinned against Thee."
5 My enemies [a]speak evil against me,

6 [1]I.e., Blood sacrifi [2]Lit., *dug;* or possibly *pierced* [a]1 Sam. 15: Ps. 51:16; Is. 1:11; J 6:20; 7:22, 23; Amos 5:22; Mic. 6:6-8; Heb 10:5-7

7 [1]Or, *prescribed fo*

8 [a]John 4:34 [b]Ps. 37:31; Jer. 31:33; 2 3:3

9 [a]Ps. 22:22, 25 [b]P 119:13 [c]Josh. 22:22 Ps. 139:4

10 [a]Acts 20:20, 27 89:1

11 [1]Or, *May . . . preserve* [a]Ps. 43:3; 57:3; 61:7; Prov. 20:

12 [1]Lit., *forsaken* [a] 18:5; 116:3 [b]Ps. 38 65:3 [c]Ps. 69:4 [d]Ps 73:26

13 [a]Ps. 70:1 [b]Ps. 22:19; 71:12

14 [1]Or, *soul* [2]Or, *to injure me* [a]Ps. 35:4 70:2; 71:13 [b]Ps. 63

15 [1]Or, *desolated* 70:3 [b]Ps. 35:21; 70

16 [a]Ps. 70:4 [b]Ps. 3

17 [1]Or, *The Lord is mindful* [a]Ps. 70:5; 8 109:22 [b]Ps. 40:5; 1 5:7

41:1 [1]Or, *poor* [2]Or *evil* [a]Ps. 82:3, 4; P 14:21 [b]Ps. 27:5; 37

2 [1]Or, *be blessed* 37:28 [b]Ps. 37:22 27:12

3 [1]Lit., *turn all his*

4 [a]Ps. 6:2; 103:3; 147:3 [b]Ps. 51:4

5 [a]Ps. 38:12

"When will he die, and his name perish?"
6 And [1]when he comes to see *me*, he [a]speaks [2]falsehood;
His heart gathers wickedness to itself;
When he goes outside, he tells it.
7 All who hate me whisper together against me;
Against me they [a]devise my hurt, *saying*,
8 "A wicked thing is poured out [1]upon him,
That when he lies down, he will [a]not rise up again."
9 Even my [a]close friend, in whom I trusted,
Who ate my bread,
Has lifted up his heel against me.

10 But Thou, O LORD, be gracious to me, and [a]raise me up,
That I may repay them.
11 By this I know that [a]Thou art pleased with me,
Because [b]my enemy does not shout in triumph over me.
12 As for me, [a]Thou dost uphold me in my integrity,
And Thou dost set me [b]in Thy presence forever.

13 [a]Blessed be the LORD, the God of Israel,
From everlasting to everlasting.
Amen, and Amen.

BOOK 2

Psalm 42

For the choir director. A [+]Maskil of the sons of Korah.

42 As the deer [1]pants for the water brooks,
So my soul [1a]pants for Thee, O God.
2 My soul [a]thirsts for God, for the [b]living God;
When shall I come and [1c]appear before God?
3 My [a]tears have been my food day and night,
While *they* [b]say to me all day long, "Where is your God?"
4 These things I remember, and I [a]pour out my soul within me.
For I [b]used to go along with the throng *and* [1]lead them in procession to the house of God,
With the voice of [c]joy and thanksgiving, a multitude keeping festival.

5 [a]Why are you [1b]in despair, O my soul?
And *why* have you become [c]disturbed within me?
[2d]Hope in God, for I shall [3]again praise [4]Him
For the [5e]help of His presence.
6 O my God, my soul is [1]in despair within me;
Therefore I [a]remember Thee from [b]the land of the Jordan,
And the [2]peaks of [c]Hermon, from Mount Mizar.
7 Deep calls to deep at the sound of Thy waterfalls;
All Thy [a]breakers and Thy waves have rolled over me.
8 The LORD will [a]command His lovingkindness in the daytime;
And His song will be with me [b]in the night,
A prayer to [c]the God of my life.

9 I will say to God [a]my rock, "Why hast Thou forgotten me?

6 [1]Or, *if he* [2]Or, *...ptiness* [a]Ps. 12:2; ...2:4; Prov. 26:24-26
7 [a]Ps. 56:5
8 [1]Or, *within* [a]Ps. 71:10, 11
[a]2 Sam. 15:12; Job ...19; Ps. 55:12, 13, ...er. 20:10; Mic. 7:5; ...26:23; Luke 22:21; John 13:18
10 [a]Ps. 3:3
[a]Ps. 37:23; 147:11 [b]Ps. 25:2
[a]Ps. 18:32; 37:17; [b]Job 36:7; Ps. 21:6
13 [a]Ps. 72:18, 19; ...:52; 106:48; 150:6
[+]Possibly, *Contemplative*, or *Didactic*, or *Skillful Psalm*
...2:1 [1]Lit., *longs for* [a]Ps. 119:131
...me mss. read *see ...e face of God* [a]Ps. ...4:2; 143:6 [b]Josh. ...:10; Ps. 84:2; Jer. ...; Dan. 6:26; Matt. 26:63; Rom. 9:26; ...s. 1:9 [c]Ex. 23:17; Ps. 43:4; 84:7
... 80:5; 102:9 [b]Ps. ...; 115:2; Joel 2:17; Mic. 7:10
...move slowly with [a]1 Sam. 1:15; Job ...6; Ps. 62:8; Lam. [b]Ps. 55:14; 122:1; ...30:29 [c]Ps. 100:4
..., sunk down [2]Or, *Wait for* [3]Or, *still ...e ancient versions ...d Him, the help of countenance and ... God* [5]Or, *saving* [a]Ps. 42:11; 43:5 ...38:6; Matt. 26:38 ...77:3 [d]Ps. 71:14; ...n. 3:24 [e]Ps. 44:3
...sunk down [2]Lit., *...ermons* [a]Ps. 61:2 ...am. 17:22 [c]Deut. 3:8
[a]Ps. 69:1, 2; 88:7; Jon. 2:3
...57:3; 133:3 [b]Job ...0; Ps. 16:7; 63:6; ...49:5 [c]Eccl. 5:18; 8:15
9 [a]Ps. 18:2

Why do I go [b]mourning [1]because of the [c]oppression of the
enemy?"
10 As a shattering of my bones, my adversaries revile me,
While they [a]say to me all day long, "Where is your God?"
11 [a]Why are you [1]in despair, O my soul?
And why have you become disturbed within me?
[2]Hope in God, for I shall yet praise Him,
The [3]help of my countenance, and my God.

Psalm 43

43 [a]Vindicate me, O God, and [b]plead my case against an ungodly
nation;
[1]O deliver me from [c]the deceitful and unjust man!
2 For Thou art the [a]God of my strength; why hast Thou
[b]rejected me?
Why do I go [c]mourning [1]because of the oppression of the
enemy?

3 O send out Thy [a]light and Thy truth, let them lead me;
Let them bring me to Thy [b]holy hill,
And to Thy [c]dwelling places.
4 Then I will go to [a]the altar of God,
To God [1]my exceeding [b]joy;
And upon the [c]lyre I shall praise Thee, O God, my God.

5 [a]Why are you [1]in despair, O my soul?
And why are you disturbed within me?
[2]Hope in God, for I shall [3]again praise Him,
The [4]help of my countenance, and my God.

Psalm 44

For the choir director. A [+]Maskil of the sons of Korah.

44 O God, we have heard with our ears,
Our [a]fathers have told us,
The [b]work that Thou didst in their days,
In the [c]days of old.
2 Thou with Thine own hand didst [a]drive out the nations;
Then Thou didst [b]plant them;
Thou didst [c]afflict the peoples,
Then Thou didst [d]spread them abroad.
3 For by their own sword they [a]did not possess the land;
And their own arm did not save them;
But Thy right hand, and Thine [b]arm, and the [c]light of Thy
presence,
For Thou didst [d]favor them.

4 Thou art [a]my King, O God;
[b]Command [1]victories for Jacob.
5 Through Thee we will [a]push back our adversaries;
Through Thy name we will [b]trample down those who rise up
against us.
6 For I will [a]not trust in my bow,
Nor will my sword save me.
7 But Thou [a]hast saved us from our adversaries,

9 [1]Or, *while the en* *oppresses* [b]Ps. 38 [c]Ps. 17:9

10 [a]Ps. 42:3; Joel

11 [1]Or, *sunk down* *Wait for* [3]Or, *savin* *acts of* [a]Ps. 42:5; 4

43:1 [1]Or, *Mayest* [a]Ps. 26:1; 35:24 [b]1 Sam. 24:15; Ps. [c]Ps. 5:6; 38:12

2 [1]Or, *while the er* *oppresses* [a]Ps. 18 28:7; 31:4 [b]Ps. 44 88:14 [c]Ps. 42:9

3 [a]Ps. 36:9 [b]Ps. 2 3:4; 42:4; 46:4 [c]Ps

4 [1]Lit., *the gladne* *my joy* [a]Ps. 26:6 21:6 [c]Ps. 33:2; 49 57:8; 71:22

5 [1]Or, *sunk down* *Wait for* [3]Or, *still* *saving acts of* [a]Ps 42:5, 11

[+]Possibly, *Contemplative*, or *Didactic*, or *Skillfu* *Psalm*

44:1 [a]Ex. 12:26, 2 Deut. 6:20; Judg. Ps. 78:3 [b]Ps. 78:1 [c]Deut. 32:7; Ps. 7 51:9; 63:9

2 [a]Josh. 3:10; Ne 9:24; Ps. 78:55; 8 [b]Ex. 15:17; 2 Sam Jer. 24:6; Amos 9. [c]Ps. 135:10-12 [d]F 80:9-11; Zech. 2:6

3 [a]Deut. 8:17, 18 24:12 [b]Ps. 77:15 4:6; 89:15 [d]Deut. 7:7, 8; 10:15; Ps.

4 [1]Lit., *salvation* 74:12 [b]Ps. 42:8

5 [a]Deut. 33:17; P 60:12; Dan. 8:4 [b] 108:13; Zech. 10:

6 [a]1 Sam. 17:47; 33:16; Hos. 1:7

7 [a]Ps. 136:24

And Thou hast [b]put to shame those who hate us.
8 In God we have [a]boasted all day long,
And we will [b]give thanks to Thy name forever. [1]Selah.

9 Yet Thou [a]hast rejected *us* and brought us to [b]dishonor,
And [c]dost not go out with our armies.
10 Thou dost cause us to [a]turn back from the adversary;
And those who hate us [b]have taken spoil for themselves.
11 Thou dost give us as [a]sheep [1]to be eaten,
And hast [b]scattered us among the nations.
12 Thou dost [a]sell Thy people [1]cheaply,
And hast not [2]profited by their sale.
13 Thou dost make us a [a]reproach to our neighbors,
A scoffing and a [b]derision to those around us.
14 Thou dost make us [a]a byword among the nations,
A [1b]laughingstock among the peoples.
15 All day long my dishonor is before me,
And [1]my [a]humiliation has overwhelmed me,
16 Because of the voice of him who [a]reproaches and reviles,
Because of the presence of the [b]enemy and the avenger.

17 All this has come upon us, but we have [a]not forgotten Thee,
And we have not [b]dealt falsely with Thy covenant.
18 Our heart has not [a]turned back,
And our steps [b]have not deviated from Thy way,
19 Yet Thou hast [a]crushed us in a place of [b]jackals,
And covered us with [c]the shadow of death.

20 If we had [a]forgotten the name of our God,
Or extended our [1]hands to [b]a strange god;
21 Would not God [a]find this out?
For He knows the secrets of the heart.
22 But [a]for Thy sake we are killed all day long;
We are considered as [b]sheep to be slaughtered.
23 [a]Arouse Thyself, why [b]dost Thou sleep, O Lord?
Awake, [c]do not reject us forever.
24 Why dost Thou [a]hide Thy face,
And [b]forget our affliction and our oppression?
25 For our [a]soul has sunk down into the dust;
Our body cleaves to the earth.
26 [a]Rise up, be our help,
And [b]redeem us for the sake of Thy lovingkindness.

Psalm 45

For the choir director; according to the +Shoshannim.
A •Maskil of the sons of Korah. A Song of Love.

45 My heart [1]overflows with a good theme;
I [2]address my [3]verses to the [4]King;
My tongue is the pen of [a]a ready writer.
2 Thou art fairer than the sons of men;
[a]Grace is poured [1]upon Thy lips;
Therefore God has [b]blessed Thee forever.

3 Gird [a]Thy sword on *Thy* thigh, O [1b]Mighty One,

7 [b]Ps. 53:5
…elah may mean: …, *Crescendo* or …*l interlude* [a]Ps. …34:2 [b]Ps. 30:12
…43:2; 60:1, 10; …; 89:38; 108:11 …:19 [c]Ps. 60:10; 108:11
…ev. 26:17; Josh. … Ps. 89:43 [b]Ps. 89:41
…t., *for food* [a]Ps. …Rom. 8:36 [b]Lev. …:33; Deut. 4:27; …:64; Ps. 106:27; Ezek. 20:23
…it., *for no wealth* …*t a high price on* …*m* [a]Deut. 32:30; …14; 3:8; Is. 52:3, …4; Jer. 15:13
…Deut. 28:37; Ps. …39:41 [b]Ps. 80:6; Ezek. 23:32
…, *shaking of the* …*d* [a]Job 17:6; Ps. …Jer. 24:9 [b]2 Kin. …9:21; Ps. 109:25
…it., *the shame of* …*ace has covered* …2 Chr. 32:21; Ps. 69:7
…s. 74:10 [b]Ps. 8:2
…Ps. 78:7; 119:61, …9, 141, 153, 176 [b]Ps. 78:57
[a]Ps. 78:57 [b]Job …; Ps. 119:51, 157
…51:8; 94:5 [b]Job …29; Is. 13:22; Jer. …Job 3:5; Ps. 23:4
[1]Lit., *palms* [a]Ps. … [b]Deut. 6:14; Ps. 81:9
…Ps. 139:1, 2; Jer. 17:10
[a]Rom. 8:36 [b]Is. 53:7; Jer. 12:3
…s. 7:6 [b]Ps. 78:65 [c]Ps. 77:7
…4 [a]Job 13:24; Ps. …4 [b]Ps. 42:9; Lam. 5:20
25 [a]Ps. 119:25
…Ps. 35:2 [b]Ps. 6:4; 25:22
…Or possibly, *Lilies* •Possibly, *Contemplative*, or …*Didactic*, or *Skillful Psalm*
[1]Lit., *is astir* [2]Lit., …*saying* [3]Lit., *works* [4]Probably refers to …omon as a type of Christ. [a]Ezra 7:6
…Or, *through* [a]Luke 4:22 [b]Ps. 21:6
[1]Or, *warrior* [a]Heb. …Rev. 1:16 [b]Is. 9:6

In Thy splendor and Thy majesty!
4 And in Thy majesty ride on victoriously,
For the cause of truth and [a]meekness *and* righteousness;
Let Thy [b]right hand teach Thee [1]awesome things.
5 Thine [a]arrows are sharp;
The [b]peoples fall under Thee;
Thine arrows are [c]in the heart of the King's enemies.

6 [a]Thy throne, O God, is forever and ever;
A scepter of [b]uprightness is the scepter of Thy kingdom.
7 Thou hast [a]loved righteousness, and hated wickedness;
Therefore God, Thy God, has [b]anointed Thee
With the oil of joy above Thy fellows.
8 All Thy garments are *fragrant with* [a]myrrh and aloes *and* cassia;
Out of ivory palaces [b]stringed instruments have made Thee glad.
9 Kings' daughters are among [a]Thy noble ladies;
At Thy [b]right hand stands the queen in [c]gold from Ophir.

10 Listen, O daughter, give attention and incline your ear;
[a]Forget your people and your father's house;
11 Then the King will desire your beauty;
Because He is your [a]Lord, [b]bow down to Him.
12 And the daughter of [a]Tyre *will come* with a gift;
The [b]rich among the people will entreat your favor.

13 The King's daughter is all glorious within;
Her clothing is [a]interwoven with gold.
14 She will be [a]led to the King [b]in embroidered work;
The [c]virgins, her companions who follow her,
Will be brought to Thee.
15 They will be led forth with gladness and rejoicing;
They will enter into the King's palace.

16 In place of your fathers will be your sons;
You shall make them princes in all the earth.
17 I will cause [a]Thy name to be remembered in all generations;
Therefore the peoples [b]will give Thee thanks forever and ever.

Psalm 46

For the choir director. *A Psalm* of the sons of Korah, +set to Alamoth.
A Song.

46 God is our [a]refuge and strength,
[1]A very [b]present help [c]in [2]trouble.
2 Therefore we will [a]not fear, though [b]the earth should change,
And though [c]the mountains slip into the heart of the [1]sea;
3 Though its [a]waters roar *and* foam,
Though the mountains quake at its swelling pride. [1]Selah.

4 There is a [a]river whose streams make glad the [b]city of God,
The holy [c]dwelling places of the Most High.
5 God is [a]in the midst of her, she will not be moved;
God will [b]help her [1]when morning dawns.
6 The [1]nations [a]made an uproar, the kingdoms tottered;
He [2b]raised His voice, the earth [c]melted.

---

4 [1]Or, *fearful* [a]... 2:3 [b]Ps. 21:8

5 [a]Ps. 18:14; 1... 5:28; 7:13 [b]Ps. ... [c]2 Sam. 18:14

6 [a]Ps. 93:2; He... [b]Ps. 98:9

7 [a]Ps. 11:7; 33... 2:2

8 [a]Song 4:14; J... 19:39 [b]Ps. 150...

9 [a]Song 6:8 [b]1... 2:19 [c]1 Kin. 9:2... 13:12

10 [a]Deut. 21:13... 1:16, 17

11 [a]Gen. 18:12; ... 3:6 [b]Eph. 5:33

12 [a]Ps. 87:4 [b]P... 22:29; 68:29; 72... Is. 49:23

13 [a]Ex. 39:2, 3

14 [a]Song 1:4 [b]J... 5:30; Ezek. 16:1... 45:9

17 [a]Mal. 1:11 [b]P... 138:4

+Possibly, *for sop... voices*

46:1 [1]Or, *Abund... available for help... tight places* [a]Ps. 62:7, 8 [b]Deut. 4:... 145:18 [c]Ps. 9:9

2 [1]Lit., *seas* [a]Ps. 27:1 [b]Ps. 82:5 [c]...

3 [1]*Selah* may me... *Pause, Crescend... Musical interlude* 93:3, 4; Jer. 5:22

4 [a]Ps. 36:8; 65:9; ... 8:6; Rev. 22:1 [b]Ps... 48:1; 87:3; 101:8; ... 60:14; Rev. 3:12 ... 43:3

5 [1]Lit., *at the turni... the morning* [a]Deut... 23:14; Is. 12:6; Eze... 43:7, 9; Hos. 11:9; ... 2:27; Zech. 2:5 [b]P... 37:40; Is. 41:14; Lu... 1:54

6 [1]Or, *Gentiles* [2]L... *gave forth* [a]Ps. 2:1 [b]Ps. 18:13; 68:33; ... 25:30; Joel 2:11; Am... 1:2 [c]Amos 9:5; Mic... Nah. 1:5

7 The LORD of hosts [a]is with us;
The God of Jacob is [b]our stronghold. Selah.

8 Come, [a]behold the works of the LORD,
[1]Who has wrought [b]desolations in the earth.
9 He [a]makes wars to cease to the end of the earth;
He [b]breaks the bow and cuts the spear in two;
He [c]burns the chariots with fire.
10 "[1]Cease *striving* and [a]know that I am God;
I will be [b]exalted among the [2]nations, I will be exalted in the earth."
11 The LORD of hosts is with us;
The God of Jacob is our stronghold. Selah.

Psalm 47

For the choir director. A Psalm of the sons of Korah.

47 O [a]clap your hands, all peoples;
[b]Shout to God with the voice of [1]joy.
2 For the LORD Most High is to be [a]feared,
A [b]great King over all the earth.
3 He [a]subdues peoples under us,
And nations under our feet.
4 He chooses our [a]inheritance for us,
The [b]glory of Jacob whom He loves. [1]Selah.

5 God has [a]ascended [1]with a shout,
The LORD, [1]with the [b]sound of a trumpet.
6 [a]Sing praises to God, sing praises;
Sing praises to [b]our King, sing praises.
7 For God is the [a]King of all the earth;
Sing praises [b]with a [1]skillful psalm.
8 God [a]reigns over the nations,
God [1]sits on [b]His holy throne.
9 The [1a]princes of the people have assembled themselves *as* the [b]people of the God of Abraham;
For the [c]shields of the earth belong to God;
He [2]is [d]highly exalted.

Psalm 48

A Song; a Psalm of the sons of Korah.

48 [a]Great is the LORD, and greatly to be praised,
In the [b]city of our God, His [c]holy mountain.
2 [a]Beautiful in elevation, [b]the joy of the whole earth,
Is Mount Zion *in* the far north,
The [c]city of the great King.
3 God, in her palaces,
Has made Himself known as a [a]stronghold.

4 For, lo, the [a]kings assembled themselves,
They passed by together.
5 They saw *it*, then they were amazed;
They were [a]terrified, they [1]fled in alarm.
6 [1]Panic seized them there,

[a]Num. 14:9; 2 Chr. 3:12 [b]Ps. 9:9; 48:3

[1]Or, *Which He has* ...ught *as desolations* 66:5 [b]Is. 61:4; Jer. 51:43

9 [a]Is. 2:4; Mic. 4:3 Sam. 2:4; Ps. 76:3 [c]Is. 9:5; Ezek. 39:9

0 [1]Or, *Let go, relax* [2]Or, *Gentiles* [a]Ps. 100:3 [b]Is. 2:11, 17

1 [1]Or, *a ringing cry* ...s. 98:8 [b]Ps. 106:47

...eut. 7:21; Neh. 1:5; ...6:3, 5; 68:35 [b]Mal. 1:14

3 [a]Ps. 18:47

[1]*Selah* may mean: ...*use, Crescendo* or *Musical interlude* ...et. 1:4 [b]Amos 6:8; 8:7; Nah. 2:2

...r, *amid* [a]Ps. 68:18 [b]Ps. 98:6

...s. 68:4 [b]Ps. 89:18

...eb., *Maskil* [a]Zech. 14:9 [b]1 Cor. 14:15

[1]Or, *has taken His* [a]1 Chr. 16:31; Ps. 22:28 [b]Ps. 97:2

..., *nobles* [2]Lit., *has* ...*tly exalted Himself* 72:11; 102:22; Is. ...7, 23 [b]Rom. 4:11, ...s. 89:18 [d]Ps. 97:9

[a]1 Chr. 16:25; Ps. ...4; 145:3 [b]Ps. 46:4 ...2:6; 87:1; Is. 2:3; Mic. 4:1; Zech. 8:3

...50:2 [b]Lam. 2:15 [c]Matt. 5:35

3 [a]Ps. 46:7

[a]2 Sam. 10:6-19

[1]Lit., *were hurried away* [a]Ex. 15:15

6 [1]Lit., *Trembling*

Anguish, as of [a]a woman in childbirth.
7 With the [a]east wind
Thou [b]dost break the [c]ships of Tarshish.
8 As we have heard, so have we seen
In the city of the LORD of hosts, in the city of our God;
God will [a]establish her forever. [1]Selah.

9 We have thought on [a]Thy lovingkindness, O God,
In the midst of Thy temple.
10 As is Thy [a]name, O God,
So is Thy [b]praise to the ends of the earth;
Thy [c]right hand is full of righteousness.
11 Let Mount [a]Zion be glad,
Let the [a]daughters of Judah rejoice,
Because of Thy judgments.
12 Walk about Zion, and go around her;
Count her [a]towers;
13 Consider her [a]ramparts;
Go through her palaces;
That you may [b]tell *it* to the next generation.
14 For [1]such is God,
Our God forever and ever;
He will [a]guide us [2]until death.

Psalm 49

For the choir director. A Psalm of the sons of Korah.

49 [a]Hear this, all peoples;
Give ear, all [b]inhabitants of the world,
2 Both [a]low and high,
Rich and poor together.
3 My mouth will [a]speak wisdom;
And the meditation of my heart *will be* [b]understanding.
4 I will incline my ear to [a]a proverb;
[b]I will [1]express my [c]riddle on the harp.

5 Why should I [a]fear in days of adversity,
When the iniquity of my [1]foes surrounds me,
6 Even those who [a]trust in their wealth,
And boast in the abundance of their riches?
7 No man can by any means [a]redeem *his* brother,
Or give to God a [b]ransom for him—
8 For [a]the redemption of [1]his soul is costly,
And he should cease *trying* forever—
9 That he should [a]live on eternally;
That he should not [1b]undergo decay.

10 For he sees *that even* [a]wise men die;
The [b]stupid and the senseless alike perish,
And [c]leave their wealth to others.
11 Their [1a]inner thought is, *that* their houses [b]are forever,
And their dwelling places to all generations;
They have [c]called their lands after their own names.
12 But [a]man in *his* [1]pomp will not endure;
He is like the [2]beasts that [3]perish.

6 [a]Is. 13:8

7 [a]Jer. 18:17 [b]1 Ki 22:48 [c]1 Kin. 10:22 Ezek. 27:25

8 [1]*Selah* may mea *Pause, Crescendo Musical interlude* [a] 87:5

9 [a]Ps. 26:3; 40:10

10 [a]Deut. 28:58; J 7:9; Mal. 1:11 [b]Ps. 2; 100:1 [c]Is. 41:10

11 [a]Ps. 97:8

12 [a]Neh. 3:1, 11, 2

13 [a]Ps. 122:7 [b]Ps 78:5-7

14 [1]Lit., *this* [2]Lit., some mss. and the read *forever.* [a]Ps. Is. 58:11

49:1 [a]Ps. 78:1; Is. Mic. 1:2 [b]Ps. 33:8

2 [a]Ps. 62:9

3 [a]Ps. 37:30 [b]Ps. 119:130

4 [1]Lit., *open up* [a]P 78:2 [b]2 Kin. 3:15 [c]Num. 12:8

5 [1]Lit., *supplanter* [a]Ps. 23:4; 27:1

6 [a]Job 31:24; Ps. Prov. 11:28; Mark

7 [a]Matt. 25:8, 9 [b] 36:18, 19

8 [1]Lit., *their* [a]Mat 16:26

9 [1]Or, *see corrup the pit* [a]Ps. 22:29 16:10; 89:48

10 [a]Eccl. 2:16 [b]P 92:6; 94:8 [c]Ps. 3 Eccl. 2:18, 21; Lu 12:20

11 [1]Some versio read *graves are t houses* [a]Ps. 64:6 10:6 [c]Gen. 4:17; 3:14

12 [1]Lit., *honor* [2]C *animals* [3]Lit., *are destroyed* [a]Ps. 4

13 This is the [a]way of those who are foolish,
And of those after them who [b]approve their words. [1]Selah.
14 As sheep they are appointed [a]for [1]Sheol;
Death shall be their shepherd;
And the [b]upright shall rule over them in the morning;
And their form shall be for [1]Sheol [c]to consume,
[2]So that they have no habitation.
15 But God will [a]redeem my soul from the [1]power of [2]Sheol;
For [b]He will receive me. Selah.

16 Do not be afraid [a]when a man becomes rich,
When the [1]glory of his house is increased;
17 For when he dies he will [a]carry nothing away;
His [1]glory will not descend after him.
18 Though while he lives he [a]congratulates [1]himself—
And though *men* praise you when you do well for yourself—
19 [1]He shall [a]go to the generation of his fathers;
They shall never see [b]the light.
20 [a]Man in *his* [1]pomp, yet without understanding,
Is [b]like the [2]beasts that [3]perish.

Psalm 50

A Psalm of [+]Asaph.

50 [a]The Mighty One, God, the LORD, has spoken,
And summoned the earth [b]from the rising of the sun to its setting.
2 Out of Zion, [a]the perfection of beauty,
God [b]has shone forth.
3 May our God [a]come and not keep silence;
[b]Fire devours before Him,
And it is very [c]tempestuous around Him.
4 He [a]summons the heavens above,
And the earth, to judge His people:
5 "Gather My [a]godly ones to Me,
Those who have made a [b]covenant with Me by [c]sacrifice."
6 And the [a]heavens declare His righteousness,
For [b]God Himself is judge. [1]Selah.

7 "[a]Hear, O My people, and I will speak;
O Israel, I will testify [1]against you;
I am God, [b]your God.
8 "I do [a]not reprove you for your sacrifices,
And your burnt offerings are continually before Me.
9 "I shall take no [a]young bull out of your house,
Nor male goats out of your folds.
10 "For [a]every beast of the forest is Mine,
The cattle on a thousand hills.
11 "I know every [a]bird of the mountains,
And everything that moves in the field is [1]Mine.
12 "If I were hungry, I would not tell you;
For the [a]world is Mine, and [1]all it contains.
13 "Shall I eat the flesh of [1a]bulls,
Or drink the blood of male goats?
14 "Offer to God [a]a sacrifice of thanksgiving,

[1]*Selah* may mean: ause, *Crescendo* or sical interlude [a]Jer. 17:11 [b]Ps. 49:18
14 [1]I.e., the nether ld [2]Lit., *Away from* abitation [a]Ps. 9:17 Dan. 7:18; Mal. 4:3; Cor. 6:2; Rev. 2:26 [c]Job 24:19
Lit., *hand* [a]I.e., the nether world [a]Ps. 16:10; 56:13; Hos. 14 [b]Gen. 5:24; Ps. 16:11; 73:24
:, *wealth* [a]Ps. 37:7
7 [1]Or, *wealth* [a]Ps. 17:14; 1 Tim. 6:7
.it., *his soul* [a]Deut.); Ps. 10:3, 6; Luke 12:19
19 [1]Lit., *You;* or, *It* [a]Gen. 15:15 [b]Job 33:30; Ps. 56:13
0 [1]Lit., *honor* [2]Or, *animals* [3]Lit., *are* *stroyed* [a]Ps. 49:12 [b]Eccl. 3:19
Chr. 15:17; 2 Chr. 29:30
[a]Josh. 22:22 [b]Ps. 113:3
s. 48:2; Lam. 2:15 eut. 33:2; Ps. 80:1; 94:1
[a]Ps. 96:13 [b]Lev. 2; Num. 16:35; Ps. :3; Dan. 7:10 [c]Ps. 18:12, 13
Deut. 4:26; 31:28; 32:1; Is. 1:2
[a]Ps. 30:4; 37:28; [b]Ex. 24:7; 2 Chr. 1; Ps. 25:10 [c]Ps. 50:8
Selah may mean: ise, *Crescendo* or cal interlude [a]Ps. 5; 97:6 [b]Ps. 75:7; 96:13
[1]Or, *to* [a]Ps. 49:1; :8 [b]Ex. 20:2; Ps. 48:14
s. 40:6; 51:16; Is. 1:11; Hos. 6:6
9 [a]Ps. 69:31
10 [a]Ps. 104:24
r, *in My mind;* lit., *h Me* [a]Matt. 6:26
, *its fulness* [a]Ex. Deut. 10:14; Ps. 24:1; 1 Cor. 10:26
[1]Lit., *strong ones* [a]Ps. 50:9
[a]Ps. 27:6; 69:30; :22; 116:17; Hos. Rom. 12:1; Heb. 13:15

And [b]pay your vows to the Most High;
15 And [a]call upon Me in the day of trouble;
I shall [b]rescue you, and you will [c]honor Me."

16 But to the wicked God says,
"What right have you to tell of My statutes,
And to take [a]My covenant in your mouth?
17 "For you [a]hate discipline,
And you [b]cast My words behind you.
18 "When you see a thief, you [1a]are pleased with him,
And [2]you [b]associate with adulterers.
19 "You [1a]let your mouth loose in evil,
And your [b]tongue frames deceit.
20 "You sit and [a]speak against your brother;
You slander your own mother's son.
21 "These things you have done, and [a]I kept silence;
You thought that I was just like you;
I will [b]reprove you, and state *the case* in order before your eyes.

22 "Now consider this, you who [a]forget God,
Lest I [b]tear *you* in pieces, and there be none to deliver.
23 "He who [a]offers a sacrifice of thanksgiving honors Me;
And to him who [1b]orders *his* way *aright*
I shall [c]show the salvation of God."

Psalm 51

For the choir director. A Psalm of David, when +Nathan the prophet came to him, after he had gone in to Bathsheba.

51 [a]Be gracious to me, O God, according to Thy lovingkindness;
According to the greatness of [b]Thy compassion [c]blot out my transgressions.
2 [a]Wash me thoroughly from my iniquity,
And [b]cleanse me from my sin.
3 For [1]I [a]know my transgressions,
And my sin is ever before me.
4 [a]Against Thee, Thee only, I have sinned,
And done what is [b]evil in Thy sight,
So that [c]Thou [1]art justified [2]when Thou dost speak,
And [3]blameless when Thou dost judge.

5 Behold, I was [a]brought forth in iniquity,
And in sin my mother conceived me.
6 Behold, Thou dost desire [a]truth in the [1]innermost being,
And in the hidden part Thou wilt [b]make me know wisdom.
7 [1]Purify me [a]with hyssop, and I shall be clean;
[2]Wash me, and I shall be [b]whiter than snow.
8 [1]Make me to hear [a]joy and gladness,
Let the [b]bones which Thou hast broken rejoice.
9 [a]Hide Thy face from my sins,
And blot out all my iniquities.

10 [a]Create [1]in me a [b]clean heart, O God,
And renew [2]a [c]steadfast spirit within me.

14 [b]Num. 30:2; Deu 23:21; Ps. 22:25; 56 61:8; 65:1; 76:11

15 [a]Ps. 91:15; 107: 13; Zech. 13:9 [b]Ps. 81:7 [c]Ps. 22:23

16 [a]Is. 29:13

17 [a]Prov. 5:12; 12:1 Rom. 2:21, 22 [b]1 K 14:9; Neh. 9:26

18 [1]Some ancient versions read *run together* [2]Lit., *your is with* [a]Rom. 1:32 [b]1 Tim. 5:22

19 [1]Lit., *send* [a]Ps. 10:7 [b]Ps. 36:3; 52:

20 [a]Job 19:18; Mat 10:21

21 [a]Eccl. 8:11; Is. 42:14; 57:11 [b]Ps. 9

22 [a]Job 8:13; Ps. 9 [b]Ps. 7:2

23 [1]Lit., *sets* [a]Ps. 50:14 [b]Ps. 85:13 91:16

+2 Sam. 12:1

51:1 [a]Ps. 4:1; 109 [b]Ps. 69:16; 106:45 51:9; Is. 43:25; 44: Acts 3:19; Col. 2:1

2 [a]Ps. 51:7; Is. 1: 4:4; Jer. 4:14; Acts 22:16; Rev. 1:5 [b]J 33:8; Ezek. 36:33; 9:14; 1 John 1:7, 9

3 [1]Or, *I myself kno* [a]Is. 59:12

4 [1]Or, *mayest be right* [2]Many mss. *in Thy words* [3]Lit. [a]Gen. 20:6; 39:9; 2 Sam. 12:13; Ps. [b]Luke 15:21 [c]Rom

5 [a]Job 14:4; 15:14 58:3; Eph. 2:3

6 [1]Or, *inward part* [a]Job 38:36; Ps. 15 [b]Prov. 2:6; Eccl. 2 James 1:5

7 [1]Or, *Mayest Th purify . . . that I ma clean* [2]Or, *Mayes wash* [a]Ex. 12:22; 14:4; Num. 19:18 9:19 [b]Is. 1:18

8 [1]Or, *Mayest Th make* [a]Is. 35:10; 1:16 [b]Ps. 35:10

9 [a]Jer. 16:17

10 [1]Lit., *for* [2]Or, *upright* [a]Ezek. 18 Eph. 2:10 [b]Ps. 2 Matt. 5:8; Acts 15 [c]Ps. 78:37

11 [a]Do not cast me away from Thy presence,
And do not take Thy [b]Holy Spirit from me.
12 Restore to me the [a]joy of Thy salvation,
And sustain me with a [b]willing spirit.
13 *Then* I will [a]teach transgressors Thy ways,
And sinners will [1]be [b]converted to Thee.

14 Deliver me from [a]bloodguiltiness, O God, Thou [b]God of my salvation;
Then my [c]tongue will joyfully sing of Thy righteousness.
15 O Lord, [1a]open my lips,
That my mouth may [b]declare Thy praise.
16 For Thou [a]dost not delight in sacrifice, otherwise I would give it;
Thou art not pleased with burnt offering.
17 The sacrifices of God are a [a]broken spirit;
A broken and a contrite heart, O God, Thou wilt not despise.

18 [a]By Thy favor do good to Zion;
[1b]Build the walls of Jerusalem.
19 Then Thou wilt delight in [1a]righteous sacrifices,
In [b]burnt offering and whole burnt offering;
Then [2]young bulls will be offered on Thine altar.

Psalm 52

For the choir director. A [+]Maskil of David,
[•]when Doeg the Edomite came and told Saul, and said to him,
"David has come to the house of Ahimelech."

52 Why do you [a]boast in evil, O mighty man?
The [b]lovingkindness of God *endures* all day long.
2 Your tongue devises [a]destruction,
Like a [b]sharp razor, [c]O worker of deceit.
3 You [a]love evil more than good,
[b]Falsehood more than speaking what is right. [1]Selah.
4 You love all words that devour,
O [a]deceitful tongue.

5 [1]But God will break you down forever;
He will snatch you up, and [a]tear you away from *your* tent,
And [b]uproot you from the [c]land of the living. Selah.
6 And the righteous will [a]see and fear,
And will [b]laugh at him, *saying*,
7 "Behold, the man who would not make God his refuge,
But [a]trusted in the abundance of his riches,
And [b]was strong in [1]his *evil* desire."

8 But as for me, I am like a [a]green olive tree in the house of God;
I [b]trust in the lovingkindness of God forever and ever.
9 I will [a]give Thee thanks forever, because Thou hast done *it*,
And I will wait on Thy name, [b]for *it is* good, in the presence of Thy godly ones.

13:23; 24:20; [b]Is. 63:10, 11
5 [b]Ps. 110:3
n back [a]Acts 2 [b]Ps. 22:27
am. 12:9; Ps. Ps. 25:5 [c]Ps. 35:28; 71:15
mayest Thou Ex. 4:15 [b]Ps. 9:14
m. 15:22; Ps. 40:6
17 [a]Ps. 34:18
Mayest Thou [a]Ps. 69:35; Is. 102:16; 147:2
r, sacrifices of ousness [2]Lit., *vill offer young* [a]Ps. 4:5 [b]Ps. 66:13, 15
[+]Possibly, *ntemplative,* or *actic,* or *Skillful* 1 [•]1 Sam. 22:9
[a]Ps. 94:4 [b]Ps. 52:8
5:9 [b]Ps. 57:4; 9:7 [c]Ps. 101:7
lah may mean: , Crescendo or *l interlude* [a]Ps. s. 58:3; Jer. 9:5
4 [a]Ps. 120:3
Also [a]Is. 22:18, Prov. 2:22 [c]Ps. 27:13
7:34; 40:3 [b]Job 22:19
, his destruction 49:6 [b]Ps. 10:6
s. 92:12; 128:3; 11:16 [b]Ps. 13:5
30:12 [b]Ps. 54:6

Psalm 53

For the choir director; according to +Mahalath. A •Maskil of David.

53 [a]The fool has said in his heart, "There is no God,"
They are corrupt, and have committed abominable injustice;
[b]There is no one who does good.
2 God has looked down from heaven upon the sons of men,
To see if there is [a]anyone who [1]understands,
Who [b]seeks after God.
3 [a]Every one of them has turned aside; together they have become corrupt;
There is no one who does good, not even one.

4 Have the workers of wickedness [a]no knowledge,
Who eat up My people *as though* they ate bread,
And have not called upon God?
5 There they were in great [1]fear [a]*where* no [1]fear had been;
For God [b]scattered the bones of [2]him who encamped against you;
You [c]put *them* to shame, because [d]God had rejected them.
6 Oh, that [a]the salvation of Israel [1]would come out of Zion!
When God [2]restores His captive people,
[3]Let Jacob rejoice, let Israel be glad.

Psalm 54

For the choir director; on stringed instruments.
A +Maskil of David, •when the Ziphites came and said to Saul,
"Is not David hiding himself among us?"

54 Save me, O God, by [a]Thy name,
And [1]vindicate me by [b]Thy power.
2 [a]Hear my prayer, O God;
[b]Give ear to the words of my mouth.
3 For strangers have [a]risen against me,
And [b]violent men have [c]sought my [1]life;
They have [d]not set God before them. [2]Selah.

4 Behold, [a]God is my helper;
The Lord is [1]the [b]sustainer of my soul.
5 [1]He will [a]recompense the evil to [2]my foes;
[3b]Destroy them [c]in Thy [4]faithfulness.

6 [1a]Willingly I will sacrifice to Thee;
I will give [b]thanks to Thy name, O LORD, for it is good.
7 For [1]He has [a]delivered me from all [2]trouble;
And my eye has [b]looked *with satisfaction* upon my enemies.

Psalm 55

For the choir director; on stringed instruments. A +Maskil of David.

55 [a]Give ear to my prayer, O God;
And [b]do not hide Thyself from my supplication.
2 Give [a]heed to me, and answer me;
I am restless in my [b]complaint and [1c]am surely distracted,
3 Because of the voice of the enemy,
Because of the [a]pressure of the wicked;

+I.e., sickness tone •Possibl *Contemplative Didactic,* or S *Psalm*

53:1 [a]Ps. 10: 53:1-6 [b]Rom.

2 [1]Or, *acts w* [a]Rom. 3:11 [b]

3 [a]Rom. 3:12

4 [a]Jer. 4:22

5 [1]Or, *dread* possibly, *thos* 26:17, 36; Pro [b]Ps. 141:7; Je Ezek. 6:5 [c]Ps [d]2 Kin. 17:20; Lam. 5:22

6 [1]Lit., *would restores the fc His people* [3]C *will rejoice, Isr glad* [a]Ps. 14:7

+Possibly, *Contemplative Didactic,* or Sk *Psalm* •1 Sam 26:1

54:1 [1]Lit., *judg* 20:1 [b]2 Chr. 2

2 [a]Ps. 17:6; 5 5:1

3 [1]Or, *soul* [2]S mean: *Pause, Crescendo* or *interlude* [a]Ps. [b]Ps. 18:48; 86: 140:1, 4, 11 [c]1 20:1; 25:29; Ps 63:9; 70:2 [d]Ps

4 [1]Lit., *as thos sustain* [a]Ps. 3 37:40; 118:7 [b] 37:17, 24; 41:1 145:14; Is. 41:

5 [1]Lit., *The evi return* [2]Or, *tho lie in wait for m Put to silence* [a]Ps. 94:23 [b]Ps [c]Ps. 89:49; 96: 42:3

6 [1]Or, *With a f offering* [a]Num. 116:17 [b]Ps. 50

7 [1]Or, *it;* i.e., H. [2]Or, *distress* [a]P [b]Ps. 59:10; 92: 118:7

+Possibly, *Contemplative, Didactic,* or *Ski Psalm*

55:1 [a]Ps. 54:2; 86:6 [b]Ps. 27:9

2 [1]Or, *I must m* [a]Ps. 66:19; 86:6 [b]1 Sam. 1:16; Jc Ps. 64:1; 77:3; [c]Is. 38:14; 59:11 7:16

3 [a]Ps. 17:9

For they [b]bring down [1]trouble upon me,
And in anger they [c]bear a grudge against me.

4 My [a]heart is in anguish within me,
And the terrors of [b]death have fallen upon me.
5 Fear and [a]trembling come upon me;
And [1b]horror has overwhelmed me.
6 And I said, "Oh, that I had wings like a dove!
I would fly away and [1a]be at rest.
7 "Behold, I would wander far away,
I would [a]lodge in the wilderness. [1]Selah.
8 "I would hasten to my place of refuge
From the [a]stormy wind *and* tempest."

9 [1]Confuse, O Lord, [a]divide their tongues,
For I have seen [b]violence and strife in the city.
10 Day and night they go around her upon her walls;
And iniquity and mischief are in her midst.
11 [a]Destruction is in her midst;
[b]Oppression and deceit do not depart from her [1]streets.

12 For it is [a]not an enemy who reproaches me,
Then I could bear *it*;
Nor is it one who hates me who [b]has exalted himself against me,
Then I could hide myself from him.
13 But it is you, a man [1]my equal,
My [a]companion and my [2b]familiar friend.
14 We who had sweet [1]fellowship together,
[a]Walked in the house of God in the throng.
15 Let [1]death come [a]deceitfully upon them;
Let them [b]go down alive to [2]Sheol,
For evil is in their dwelling, in their midst.

16 As for me, I shall [a]call upon God,
And the LORD will save me.
17 [a]Evening and [b]morning and at [c]noon, I will complain and
murmur,
And He will hear my voice.
18 He will [a]redeem my soul in peace [1]from the battle *which is*
against me,
For they are [b]many *who strive* with me.
19 God will [a]hear and [1]answer them—
Even the one [b]who [2]sits enthroned from of old— Selah.
With whom there [3]is no change,
And who [c]do not fear God.
20 He has put forth his hands against [a]those who were at peace
with him;
He has [1b]violated his covenant.
21 His [1]speech was [a]smoother than butter,
But his heart was war;
His words were [a]softer than oil,
Yet they were drawn [b]swords.

22 [a]Cast [1]your burden upon the LORD, and He will sustain you;

Or, wickedness
n. 16:7, 8 [c]Ps. 71:11; 143:3

38:8 [b]Ps. 18:4, 5; 116:3

huddering [a]Ps.
[b]Job 21:6; Is. 1:4; Ezek. 7:18

Lit., settle down
[a]Job 3:13

elah may mean:
, Crescendo or
usical interlude
[a]1 Sam. 23:14

4:6; 25:4; 29:6

Lit., Swallow up
11:9 [b]Ps. 11:5; Jer. 6:7

plaza [a]Ps. 5:9
[b]Ps. 10:7; 17:9

41:9 [b]Ps. 35:26

it., according to
y valuation [2]Or,
ntance [a]2 Sam.
[b]Job 19:14; Ps. 41:9

Lit., counsel; or,
macy [a]Ps. 42:4

nother reading is
olations be upon
[2]I.e., the nether
[a]Ps. 64:7; Prov. 47:11; 1 Thess.
[b]Num. 16:30, 33

16 [a]Ps. 57:2, 3

[a]Ps. 141:2; Dan.
cts 3:1; 10:3, 30
5:3; 88:13; 92:2
[c]Acts 10:9

[1]Or, so that none
proach me [a]Ps. 103:4 [b]Ps. 56:2

[1]Or, afflict [2]Or,
from [3]Lit., are no
nges [a]Ps. 78:59
33:27; Ps. 90:2; 93:2 [c]Ps. 36:1

t., profaned [a]Ps.
20:7 [b]Num. 30:2; Ps. 89:34

[1]Lit., mouth [a]Ps.
28:3; Prov. 5:3, 4
[b]Ps. 57:4; 59:7

[1]Or, what He has
en you [a]Ps. 37:5; 1 Pet. 5:7

[b]He will never allow the righteous to [2c]be shaken.
23 But Thou, O God, wilt bring them down to the [1a]pit of destruction;
[b]Men of bloodshed and deceit will [c]not live out half their days.
But I will [d]trust in Thee.

Psalm 56

For the choir director; according to [+]Jonath elem rehokim.
A [•]Mikhtam of David, [Δ]when the Philistines seized him in Gath.

56 Be gracious to me, O God, for man has [1a]trampled upon me;
[2]Fighting all day long he [b]oppresses me.
2 My foes have [1a]trampled upon me all day long,
For [2]they are many who [b]fight proudly against me.
3 [1]When I am [a]afraid,
[2]I will [b]put my trust in Thee.
4 [a]In God, whose word I praise,
In God I have put my trust;
I shall not be afraid.
[b]What can *mere* [1]man do to me?
5 All day long they [1a]distort my words;
All their [2b]thoughts are against me for evil.
6 They [1a]attack, they lurk,
They [b]watch my [2]steps,
As they have [c]waited *to take* my [3]life.
7 Because of wickedness, [1a]cast them forth,
In anger [b]put down the peoples, O God!

8 Thou [a]hast taken account of my wanderings;
Put my [b]tears in Thy bottle;
Are *they* not in [c]Thy book?
9 Then my enemies will [a]turn back [b]in the day when I call;
This I know, [1]that [c]God is for me.
10 In God, *whose* word I praise,
In the LORD, *whose* word I praise,
11 In God I have put my [1]trust, I shall not be afraid.
What can man do to me?
12 Thy [a]vows are *binding* upon me, O God;
I will render thank offerings to Thee.
13 For Thou hast [a]delivered my soul from death,
[1]Indeed [b]my feet from stumbling,
So that I may [c]walk before God
In the [d]light of the [2]living.

Psalm 57

For the choir director; *set to* [+]Al-tashheth.
A [•]Mikhtam of David, [Δ]when he fled from Saul, in the cave.

57 Be gracious to me, O God, be gracious to me,
For my soul [a]takes refuge in Thee;
And in the [b]shadow of Thy wings I will take refuge,
Until destruction [c]passes by.
2 I will cry to God Most High,
To God who [a]accomplishes *all things* for me.
3 He will [a]send from heaven and save me;

22 [2]Or, *totter* 37:24 [c]Ps. 15:

23 [1]Or, *lowest* 73:18; Is. 38:17 28:8 [b]Ps. 5:6 15:32; Prov. 10 25:2; 56:3

[+]Or, *The silent those who are The dove of the terebinths.* [•]Po *Epigrammatic Atonement Psa* [Δ]1 Sam. 21:10,

56:1 [1]Or, *snap* [2]Or, *A fighting r* 57:3 [b]Ps. 17:9

2 [1]Or, *snapped many are fighti* 35:25; 57:3; 12 35:1

3 [1]Lit., *In the d am one who pu* 55:4, 5 [b]Ps. 11

4 [1]Lit., *flesh* [a]P 56:10, 11 [b]Ps. Heb. 13:6

5 [1]Or, *trouble m affairs* [2]Or, *purp* [a]2 Pet. 3:16 [b]Ps

6 [1]Or, *stir up st heels* [3]Lit., *soul* 59:3; 140:2; Is. [b]Ps. 17:11 [c]Ps.

7 [1]Or, *will they escape?* [a]Ps. 3 Prov. 19:5; Ezek Rom. 2:3 [b]Ps. 5

8 [a]Ps. 139:3 [b]2 20:5; Ps. 39:12 3:16

9 [1]Or, *because* 9:3 [b]Ps. 102:2 41:11; 118:6; Ro

11 [1]Or, *trust with*

12 [a]Ps. 50:14

13 [1]Or, *Hast Tho delivered* [2]Or, *lif* 33:19; 49:15; 86: [b]Ps. 116:8 [c]Ps. [d]Job 33:30

[+]Lit., *Do Not Des* [•]Possibly, *Epigra Poem or Atonem Psalm* [Δ]1 Sam. 2 24:3

57:1 [a]Ps. 2:12; 3 [b]Ruth 2:12; Ps. 1 36:7; 63:7; 91:4 26:20

2 [a]Ps. 138:8

3 [a]Ps. 18:16; 144

He reproaches him who [1b]tramples upon me. [2]Selah.
God will send forth His [c]lovingkindness and His [3]truth.

4 My soul is among [a]lions;
I must lie among those who breathe forth fire,
Even the sons of men, whose [b]teeth are spears and arrows,
And their [c]tongue a sharp sword.
5 [a]Be exalted above the heavens, O God;
Let Thy glory *be* above all the earth.
6 They have [1]prepared a [a]net for my steps;
My soul is [b]bowed down;
They [c]dug a pit before me;
They *themselves* have [d]fallen into the midst of it. Selah.

7 [a]My [b]heart is steadfast, O God, my heart is steadfast;
I will sing, yes, I will sing praises!
8 Awake, [a]my glory;
Awake, [b]harp and lyre,
I will awaken the dawn!
9 [a]I will give thanks to Thee, O Lord, among the peoples;
I will sing praises to Thee among the [1]nations.
10 For Thy [a]lovingkindness is great to the heavens,
And Thy [1]truth to the clouds.
11 [a]Be exalted above the heavens, O God;
Let Thy glory *be* above all the earth.

Psalm 58

For the choir director; *set to* +Al-tashheth. A •Mikhtam of David.

58 Do you indeed [1]speak righteousness, O [2]gods?
Do you [a]judge [3]uprightly, O sons of men?
2 No, in heart you [a]work unrighteousness;
On earth you [b]weigh out the violence of your hands.
3 The wicked are estranged [a]from the womb;
These who speak lies [b]go astray from [1]birth.
4 They have venom like the [a]venom of a serpent;
Like a deaf cobra that stops up its ear,
5 So that it [a]does not hear the voice of [1b]charmers,
Or a skillful caster of spells.

6 O God, [a]shatter their teeth in their mouth;
Break out the fangs of the young lions, O LORD.
7 Let them [a]flow away like water that runs off;
When he [1b]aims his arrows, let them be as [2]headless shafts.
8 *Let them be* as a snail which [1]melts away as it goes along,
Like the [a]miscarriages of a woman which never see the sun.
9 Before your [a]pots can feel *the fire of* thorns,
He will [b]sweep them away with a whirlwind, the [1]green and the burning alike.

10 The [a]righteous will rejoice when he [b]sees the vengeance;
He will [c]wash his feet in the blood of the wicked.
11 And men will say, "Surely there is a [1a]reward for the righteous;
Surely there is a God who [b]judges [2]on earth!"

os at [2]Selah ean: *Pause,* o or *Musical* *terlude* [3]Or, ss [b]Ps. 56:2 25:10; 40:11

. 35:17; 58:6 [c]Ps. 55:21; , Prov. 12:18

57:11; 108:5

spread [a]Ps. ; 35:7; 140:5 14 [c]Ps. 7:15 26:27; 28:10; Eccl. 10:8

7-11; 108:1-5 [b]Ps. 112:7

); 30:12 [b]Ps. 150:3

peoples [a]Ps. 108:3

r, faithfulness 03:11; 108:4

s. 57:5; 108:5

o Not Destroy *Epigrammatic* *or Atonement* *Psalm*

other reading *righteousness* *e* [2]Or, *mighty* *or judges* [3]Or, *tly the sons of* *nen* [a]Ps. 82:2

lal. 3:15 [b]Ps. 94:20; Is. 10:1

ne womb [a]Ps. 8:8 [b]Ps. 53:3

eut. 32:33; Ps. 140:3

isperers [a]Jer. 7 [b]Eccl. 10:11

o 4:10; Ps. 3:7

t., *bends* [2]Lit., *they were cut* . 2:11; 7:5; Ps. Is. 13:7; Ezek. 21:7 [b]Ps. 64:3

secretes slime 3:16; Eccl. 6:3

Lit., *living* [a]Ps. Eccl. 7:6 [b]Job s. 83:15; Prov. 10:25

[a]Job 22:19; Ps. ; 64:10; 107:42 2:43; Ps. 91:8; 20; 20:12 [c]Ps. 68:23

Lit., *fruit* [2]Or, *in* 8:20; 19:11; Is. ; Luke 6:23, 35 57:4; 75:7; 94:2

Psalm 59

For the choir director; *set to* [+]Al-tashheth.
A [•]Mikhtam of David, [Δ]when Saul sent *men,*
and they watched the house in order to kill him.

59 [a]Deliver me from my enemies, O my God;
[1b]Set me *securely* on high away from those who rise up
against me.
2 Deliver me from [a]those who do iniquity,
And save me from [b]men of bloodshed.
3 For behold, they [a]have [1]set an ambush for my [2]life;
[3]Fierce men [4a]launch an attack against me,
[b]Not for my transgression nor for my sin, O LORD,
4 [1a]For no guilt of *mine,* they run and set themselves against me.
[b]Arouse Thyself to [2]help me, and see!
5 And Thou, [a]O LORD God of hosts, the God of Israel,
Awake to [1b]punish all the nations;
[c]Do not be gracious to any *who are* treacherous in iniquity. [2]Selah.
6 They [a]return at evening, they howl like a [b]dog,
And go around the city.
7 Behold, they [a]belch forth with their mouth;
[b]Swords are in their lips,
For, *they say,* "[c]Who hears?"
8 But Thou, O LORD, dost [a]laugh at them;
Thou dost [b]scoff at all the nations.

9 *Because of* [1]his [a]strength I will watch for Thee,
For God is my [b]stronghold.
10 [1]My God [a]in His lovingkindness will meet me;
God will let me [b]look *triumphantly* upon [2]my foes.
11 Do not slay them, [a]lest my people forget;
[1b]Scatter them by Thy power, and bring them down,
O Lord, [c]our shield.
12 [1]*On account of* the [a]sin of their mouth *and* the words of their lips,
Let them even be [b]caught in their pride,
And on account of [c]curses and [2]lies which they utter.
13 [1a]Destroy *them* in wrath, [1]destroy *them,* that they may be no
more;
That *men* may [b]know that God [2]rules in Jacob,
To the ends of the earth. Selah.
14 And they [a]return at evening, they howl like a dog,
And go around the city.
15 They [a]wander about [1]for food,
And [2]growl if they are not satisfied.

16 But as for me, I shall [a]sing of Thy strength;
Yes, I shall [b]joyfully sing of Thy lovingkindness in the [c]morning,
For Thou hast been my [d]stronghold,
And a [e]refuge in the day of my distress.
17 [a]O my strength, I will sing praises to Thee;
For God is my [b]stronghold, the [1]God who shows me
lovingkindness.

[+]Lit., *Do Not* [•]Possibly, *Ep... Poem or Ato...* *Psalm* [Δ]1 Sa...

59:1 [1]Or, *Ma... put me in an inaccessibly* [a]Ps. 143:9 [b]P... 69:29

2 [a]Ps. 28:3; ... 53:4; 92:7; 94... 26:9; 139:19; ...

3 [1]Or, *lain in ... soul* [3]Or, *Str... stir up strife* ... [b]1 Sam. 24:11... 4; 69:4

4 [1]Lit., *Witho...* [2]Lit., *meet* [a]P... [b]Ps. 7:6; 35:2...

5 [1]Lit., *visit* [2]... mean: *Pause, Crescendo* or *interlude* [a]Ps. 80:4; 84:8 [b]Ps... 26:14 [c]Is. 2:9; ...

6 [a]Ps. 59:14

7 [a]Ps. 94:4; P... 28 [b]Ps. 57:4; ... 12:18 [c]Job 22... 10:11; 73:11; 9...

8 [a]Ps. 37:13; ... 1:26 [b]Ps. 2:4

9 [1]Many mss. ... some ancient v... read *My streng...* 18:17 [b]Ps. 9:9...

10 [1]Many mss... some ancient v... read *The God ... lovingkindness ... those who lie i... me* [a]Ps. 21:3 ...

11 [1]Or, *Make ... wander* [a]Deut. 6:12 [b]Ps. 106:... 144:6; Is. 33:3

12 [1]Or, *The sir... mouth is the wo... their lips,* [2]Lit., ... [a]Prov. 12:13 [b]2... 3:11 [c]Ps. 10:7

13 [1]Lit., *Bring ... end* [2]Or, *is Rul...* 104:35 [b]Ps. 83...

14 [a]Ps. 59:6

15 [1]Or, *to devo...* [2]Another readin... *all night* [a]Job 1...

16 [a]Ps. 21:13 ... 101:1 [c]Ps. 5:3; ... [d]Ps. 59:9 [e]2 Sa... Ps. 46:1

17 [1]Lit., *God of lovingkindness* ... 59:9 [b]Ps. 59:10...

Psalm 60

For the choir director; according to +Shushan Eduth.
A •Mikhtam of David, to teach; ^when he struggled with Aram-naharaim and with Aram-zobah, and Joab returned,
and smote twelve thousand of Edom in the Valley of Salt.

60 O God, [a]Thou hast rejected us. Thou hast [1b]broken us;
Thou hast been [c]angry; O, [d]restore us.
2 Thou hast made the [1a]land quake, Thou hast split it open;
[b]Heal its breaches, for it totters.
3 Thou hast [1a]made Thy people experience hardship;
Thou hast given us [2]wine to [b]drink that makes us stagger.
4 Thou hast given a [a]banner to those who fear Thee,
That it may be displayed because of the truth. [1]Selah.
5 [a]That Thy [b]beloved may be delivered,
[c]Save with Thy right hand, and answer [1]us!

6 God has spoken in His [1a]holiness:
"I will exult, I will portion out [b]Shechem and measure out the valley of [c]Succoth.
7 "[a]Gilead is Mine, and Manasseh is Mine;
[b]Ephraim also is the [1]helmet of My head;
Judah is My [2c]scepter.
8 "[a]Moab is My washbowl;
Over [b]Edom I shall throw My shoe;
Shout loud, O [c]Philistia, because of Me!"

9 Who will bring me into the besieged city?
Who [1]will lead me to Edom?
10 Hast not Thou Thyself, O God, [a]rejected us?
And [b]wilt Thou not go forth with our armies, O God?
11 O give us help against the adversary,
For [a]deliverance [1]by man is in vain.
12 [1]Through God we shall [a]do valiantly,
And it is He who will [b]tread down our adversaries.

Psalm 61

For the choir director; on a stringed instrument. *A Psalm* of David.

61 [a]Hear my cry, O God;
[b]Give heed to my prayer.
2 From the [a]end of the earth I call to Thee, when my heart is [b]faint;
Lead me to [c]the rock that is higher than I.
3 For Thou hast been a [a]refuge for me,
A [b]tower of strength [1]against the enemy.
4 Let me [1a]dwell in Thy tent forever;
Let me [b]take refuge in the shelter of Thy wings. [2]Selah.

5 For Thou hast heard my [a]vows, O God;
Thou hast given *me* the inheritance of those who [b]fear Thy name.
6 Thou wilt [1a]prolong the king's [2]life;
His years will be as many generations.
7 He will [1]abide [a]before God forever;
Appoint [b]lovingkindness and truth, that they may preserve him.

8 So I will [a]sing praise to Thy name forever,
That I may [b]pay my vows day by day.

Psalm 62

For the choir director; +according to Jeduthun. A Psalm of David.

62 [a]My soul *waits* in silence for God only;
From Him [b]is my salvation.
2 He only is my [a]rock and my salvation,
My [b]stronghold; I shall not be greatly shaken.

3 How long will you assail a man,
That you may murder *him*, all of you,
Like a [a]leaning wall, like a tottering fence?
4 They have counseled only to thrust him down from his high position;
They [a]delight in falsehood;
They [b]bless with [1]their mouth,
But inwardly they curse. [2]Selah.

5 My soul, [a]wait in silence for God only,
For my hope is from Him.
6 He only is [a]my rock and my salvation,
My stronghold; I shall not be shaken.
7 On God my [a]salvation and my glory *rest*;
The rock of my strength, my [b]refuge is in God.
8 [a]Trust in Him at all times, O people;
[b]Pour out your heart before Him;
God is a refuge for us. Selah.

9 Men of [a]low degree are only [b]vanity, and men of rank are a [c]lie;
In the [d]balances they go up;
They are together lighter than breath.
10 [a]Do not trust in oppression,
And do not [1]vainly hope in [b]robbery;
If riches increase, [c]do not set *your* heart *upon them.*

11 [1]Once God has [a]spoken;
[2]Twice I have heard this:
That [b]power belongs to God;
12 And lovingkindness [a]is Thine, O Lord,
For Thou [b]dost recompense a man according to his work.

Psalm 63

A Psalm of David, +when he was in the wilderness of Judah.

63 O God, [a]Thou art my God; I shall seek Thee [1]earnestly;
My soul [b]thirsts for Thee, my flesh [2]yearns for Thee,
In a [c]dry and weary land where there is no water.
2 Thus I have [a]beheld Thee in the sanctuary,
To see Thy power and Thy glory.
3 Because Thy [a]lovingkindness is better than life,
My lips will praise Thee.
4 So I will bless Thee [a]as long as I live;
I will [b]lift up my hands in Thy name.

---

8 [a]Judg. 5:3; 33:2; 71:22 [b] Is. 19:21

+Cf. 1 Chr. 16 Ps. 39 and 77

62:1 [a]Ps. 33:2 37:39

2 [a]Ps. 89:26 59:17; 62:6

3 [a]Is. 30:13

4 [1]Lit., *his* [2]S mean: *Pause, Crescendo* or *interlude* [a]Ps. 28:3; 55:21

5 [a]Ps. 62:1

6 [a]Ps. 62:2

7 [a]Ps. 85:9; Je [b]Ps. 46:1

8 [a]Ps. 37:3, 5; 26:4 [b]1 Sam. 1 42:4; Lam. 2:19

9 [a]Ps. 49:2 [b]Jo Ps. 39:5; Is. 40: 116:11 [d]Is. 40:1

10 [1]Lit., *becom robbery* [a]Is. 30 61:8; Ezek. 22:2 3:1 [c]Job 31:25; 49:6; 52:7; Mark Luke 12:15; 1 T

11 [1]Or, *One thi These two thing heard* [a]Job 33:1 [b]Ps. 59:17; Rev.

12 [a]Ps. 86:5; 1(130:7 [b]Job 34:1 28:4; Jer. 17:10; 16:27; Rom. 2:6 3:8; Rev. 2:23

+1 Sam. 22:5; 23

63:1 [1]Lit., *early faints* [a]Ps. 118:2 42:2; 84:2; Matt. [c]Ps. 143:6

2 [a]Ps. 27:4

3 [a]Ps. 69:16

4 [a]Ps. 104:33; 1 [b]Ps. 28:2; 143:6

5 My soul is [a]satisfied as with [1]marrow and fatness,
And my mouth offers [b]praises with joyful lips.

6 When I remember Thee [a]on my bed,
I meditate on Thee in the [b]night watches,
7 For [a]Thou hast been my help,
And in the [b]shadow of Thy wings I sing for joy.
8 My soul [a]clings [1]to Thee;
Thy [b]right hand upholds me.

9 But those who [a]seek my [1]life, to destroy it,
Will go into the [2b]depths of the earth.
10 [1]They will be [2a]delivered over to the power of the sword;
They will be a [3b]prey for foxes.
11 But the [a]king will rejoice in God;
Everyone who [b]swears by Him will glory,
For the [c]mouths of those who speak lies will be stopped.

Psalm 64

For the choir director. A Psalm of David.

64 Hear my voice, O God, in [a]my [1]complaint;
[b]Preserve my life from dread of the enemy.
2 Hide me from the [a]secret counsel of evildoers,
From the tumult of [b]those who do iniquity,
3 Who [a]have sharpened their tongue like a sword.
They [b]aimed bitter speech *as* their arrow,
4 To [a]shoot [1]from concealment at the blameless;
Suddenly they shoot at him, and [b]do not fear.
5 They [1]hold fast to themselves an evil purpose;
They [2]talk of [a]laying snares secretly;
They say, "[b]Who can see them?"
6 They [1]devise injustices, *saying*,
"We are [2]ready with a well-conceived plot";
For the [3a]inward thought and the heart of a man are [4]deep.

7 But [a]God [1]will shoot at them with an arrow;
Suddenly [2]they will be wounded.
8 So [1]they [2]will [a]make him stumble;
[b]Their own tongue is against them;
All who see them will [c]shake the head.
9 Then all men [1]will [a]fear,
And [2]will [b]declare the work of God,
And [3]will consider [4]what He has done.
10 The righteous man will be [a]glad in the LORD, and will [b]take refuge in Him;
And all the upright in heart will glory.

Psalm 65

For the choir director. A Psalm of David. A Song.

65 There will be silence [1]before Thee, *and* praise in Zion, O God;
And to Thee the [a]vow will be performed.
2 O Thou who dost hear prayer,
To Thee [a]all [1]men come.

[1]Lit., *fat* [a]Ps. 36:8 [b]Ps. 71:23
[a]Ps. 4:4 [b]Ps. 16:7; 42:8; 119:55
[a]Ps. 27:9 [b]Ps. 17:8
8 [1]Lit., *after* [a]Num. ...2; Deut. 1:36; Hos. ... [b]Ps. 18:35; 41:12
...*, soul* [2]Lit., *lowest* ...*es* [a]Ps. 40:14 [b]Ps. 55:15
[1]Lit., *They will pour* ...*ut* [2]Lit., *poured out* [3]Lit., *portion* [a]Jer. 18:21; Ezek. 35:5 [b]Lam. 5:18
[a]Ps. 21:1 [b]Deut. ...3; Is. 45:23; 65:16 ...5:16; Ps. 107:42; Rom. 3:19
[1]Or, *concern* [a]Ps. 55:2 [b]Ps. 140:1
...Ps. 56:6 [b]Ps. 59:2
...s. 140:3 [b]Ps. 58:7
[1]Lit., *in* [a]Ps. 10:8; 11:2 [b]Ps. 55:19
...*, make firm* [2]Lit., ...*f* [a]Ps. 140:5 [b]Job 22:13; Ps. 10:11
...*, search out* [2]Lit., ...*plete* [3]Or, *inward* [4]Or, *unsearchable* [a]Ps. 49:11
...Or, *shot* [2]Or, *they wounded;* lit., *their* ...*ds occurred* [a]Ps. 7:12, 13
...*r, they make their* ...*ue a stumbling for* ...*selves* [2]Or, *made* ...9:3 [b]Prov. 12:13; [c]Ps. 22:7; 44:14; ...8:16; 48:27; Lam. 2:15
[1]Or, *feared* [2]Or, *declared* [3]Or, ...*sidered* [4]Lit., *His* ...*k* [a]Ps. 40:3 [b]Jer. 51:10
...[a]Job 22:19; Ps. ... [b]Ps. 11:1; 25:20
5:1 [1]Lit., *to* [a]Ps. 116:18
...*, flesh* [a]Ps. 86:9; 145:21; Is. 66:23

3 [1a]Iniquities prevail against me;
As for our transgressions, Thou dost [2b]forgive them.
4 How [a]blessed is the one whom Thou dost [b]choose, and bring near *to Thee,*
To dwell in Thy courts.
We will be [c]satisfied with the goodness of Thy house,
Thy holy temple.

5 By [a]awesome *deeds* Thou dost answer us in righteousness, O [b]God of our salvation,
Thou who art the trust of all the [c]ends of the earth and of the farthest [1d]sea;
6 Who dost [a]establish the mountains by His strength,
Being [b]girded with might;
7 Who dost [a]still the roaring of the seas,
The roaring of their waves,
And the [b]tumult of the peoples.
8 And they who dwell in the [a]ends *of the earth* stand in awe of Thy signs;
Thou dost make the [1]dawn and the sunset shout for joy.

9 Thou dost visit the earth, and [a]cause it to overflow;
Thou dost greatly [b]enrich it;
The [1c]stream of God is full of water;
Thou dost prepare their [d]grain, for thus Thou dost prepare [2]the earth.
10 Thou dost water its furrows abundantly;
Thou dost [1]settle its ridges;
Thou dost soften it [a]with showers;
Thou dost bless its growth.
11 Thou hast crowned the year [1]with Thy [2a]bounty,
And Thy [3]paths [b]drip *with* fatness.
12 [a]The pastures of the wilderness drip,
And the [b]hills gird themselves with rejoicing.
13 The meadows are [a]clothed with flocks,
And the valleys are [b]covered with grain;
They [c]shout for joy, yes, they sing.

Psalm 66

For the choir director. A Song. A Psalm.

66 [a]Shout joyfully to God, all the earth;
2 Sing the [a]glory of His name;
Make His [b]praise glorious.
3 Say to God, "How [a]awesome are Thy works!
Because of the greatness of Thy power Thine enemies will [1b]give feigned obedience to Thee.
4 "[a]All the earth will worship Thee,
And will [b]sing praises to Thee;
They will sing praises to Thy name." [1]Selah.

5 [a]Come and see the works of God,
Who is [b]awesome in *His* deeds toward the sons of men.
6 He [a]turned the sea into dry land;
They passed through [b]the river on foot;

3 [1]Lit., *Words of iniquities* [2]Lit., *cove over, atone for* [a]Ps 38:4; 40:12 [b]Ps. 79

4 [a]Ps. 33:12; 84:4 4:3 [c]Ps. 36:8

5 [1]Or, *seas* [a]Ps. 4 66:3 [b]Ps. 85:4 [c]Ps 22:27; 48:10 [d]Ps. 107:23

6 [a]Ps. 95:4 [b]Ps. 9

7 [a]Ps. 89:9; 93:3, 107:29; Matt. 8:26 2:1; 74:23; Is. 17:1

8 [1]Lit., *the outgoir the morning and evening* [a]Ps. 2:8; Is. 24:16

9 [1]Or, *channel* [2]L [a]Lev. 26:4; Job 5:1 68:9; 104:13; 147: 5:24 [b]Ps. 104:24 46:4 [d]Ps. 104:14; 147:14

10 [1]Or, *smooth* [a] 32:2; Ps. 72:6; 14

11 [1]Lit., *of* [2]Or, *goodness* [3]I.e., w tracks [a]Ps. 104:2 [b]Job 36:28; Ps. 14

12 [a]Job 38:26, 27 2:22 [b]Ps. 98:8; Is

13 [a]Ps. 144:13; Is 30:23 [b]Ps. 72:16 98:8; Is. 44:23; 55

66:1 [a]Ps. 81:1; 9 98:4; 100:1

2 [a]Ps. 79:9; Is. 4 [b]Is. 42:12

3 [1]Lit., *deceive* 47:2; 65:5; 145:6 18:44; 81:15

4 [1]*Selah* may me *Pause, Crescenc Musical interlude* 22:27; 67:7; 86:9 Zech. 14:16 [b]Ps

5 [a]Ps. 46:8 [b]Ps

6 [a]Ex. 14:21; Ps [b]Josh. 3:16; Ps.

There let us [c]rejoice in Him!
7 He [a]rules by His might forever;
His [b]eyes keep watch on the nations;
Let not the rebellious [c]exalt themselves. Selah.

8 Bless our God, O peoples,
And [1a]sound His praise abroad,
9 Who [1a]keeps us in life,
And [b]does not allow our feet to [2]slip.
10 For Thou hast [a]tried us, O God;
Thou hast [b]refined us as silver is refined.
11 Thou [a]didst bring us into the net;
Thou didst lay an oppressive burden upon our loins.
12 Thou didst make men [a]ride over our heads;
We went through [b]fire and through water;
Yet Thou [c]didst bring us out into *a place of* abundance.
13 I shall [a]come into Thy house with burnt offerings;
I shall [b]pay Thee my vows,
14 Which my lips uttered
And my mouth spoke when I was [a]in distress.
15 I shall [a]offer to Thee burnt offerings of fat beasts,
With the smoke of [b]rams;
I shall make *an offering of* [1]bulls with male goats. Selah.

16 [a]Come *and* hear, all who [1]fear God,
And I will [b]tell of what He has done for my soul.
17 I cried to Him with my mouth,
And [1]He was [a]extolled with my tongue.
18 If I [1a]regard wickedness in my heart,
The [b]Lord [2]will not [3]hear;
19 But certainly [a]God has heard;
He has given heed to the voice of my prayer.
20 [a]Blessed be God,
Who [b]has not turned away my prayer,
Nor His lovingkindness from me.

Psalm 67

For the choir director; with stringed instruments. A Psalm. A Song.

67 God be gracious to us and [a]bless us,
And [b]cause His face to shine [1]upon us— [2]Selah.
2 That [a]Thy way may be known on the earth,
[b]Thy salvation among all nations.
3 Let the [a]peoples praise Thee, O God;
Let all the peoples praise Thee.
4 Let the [a]nations be glad and sing for joy;
For Thou wilt [b]judge the peoples with uprightness,
And [c]guide the nations on the earth. Selah.
5 Let the [a]peoples praise Thee, O God;
Let all the peoples praise Thee.
6 The [a]earth has yielded its produce;
God, our God, [b]blesses us.
7 God blesses us,
[1]That [a]all the ends of the earth may fear Him.

[c]Ps. 105:43
145:13 [b]Ps. :4 [c]Ps. 140:8
cause to hear of His praise [a]Ps. 98:4
uts our soul in [2]Or, dodder, Ps. 30:3 [b]Ps. 121:3
23:10; Ps. 7:9; 6:2 [b]Is. 48:10; 13:9; Mal. 3:3; 1 Pet. 1:7
m. 1:13; Ezek. 12:13
[a]Is. 51:23 [b]Ps. ; Is. 43:2 [c]Ps. 18:19
[a]Ps. 96:8; Jer. 26 [b]Ps. 22:25; 6:14; Eccl. 5:4
14 [a]Ps. 18:6
[1]Or, cattle [a]Ps. 19 [b]Num. 6:14
Or, revere [a]Ps. [b]Ps. 71:15, 24
[1]Or, praise was my tongue [a]Ps. 30:1
r, had regarded would [3]Or, have Job 36:21; John [b]Job 27:9; Ps. Prov. 1:28; 28:9; :15; James 4:3
s. 18:6; 116:1, 2
[a]Ps. 68:35 [b]Ps. 22:24
Lit., with [2]Selah y mean: Pause, endo or Musical ude [a]Num. 6:25 ; 31:16; 80:3, 7, 19; 119:135
98:2; Acts 18:25; s 2:11 [b]Is. 52:10
3 [a]Ps. 66:4
Ps. 100:1, 2 [b]Ps. ; 96:10, 13; 98:9 [c]Ps. 47:8
5 [a]Ps. 67:3
. 26:4; Ps. 85:12; 34:27; Zech. 8:12 Ps. 29:11; 115:12
Or, And let all . . . rth fear Him [a]Ps. 22:27; 33:8

Psalm 68

For the choir director. A Psalm of David. A Song.

68 [1]Let [a]God arise, [2]let His enemies be scattered;
And [3]let those who hate Him flee before Him.
2 As [a]smoke is driven away, *so* drive *them* away;
As [b]wax melts before the fire,
So let the [c]wicked perish before God.
3 But let the [a]righteous be glad; let them exult before God;
Yes, let them rejoice with gladness.
4 Sing to God, [a]sing praises to His name;
[1b]Lift up *a song* for Him who [c]rides through the deserts,
Whose [d]name is [2]the LORD, and exult before Him.

5 A [a]father of the fatherless and a [b]judge [1]for the widows,
Is God in His [c]holy habitation.
6 God [1a]makes a home for the lonely;
He [b]leads out the prisoners into prosperity,
Only [c]the rebellious dwell in a parched land.

7 O God, when Thou [a]didst go forth before Thy people,
When Thou didst [b]march through the wilderness, [1]Selah.
8 The [a]earth quaked;
The [b]heavens also dropped *rain* at the presence of God;
[1c]Sinai itself *quaked* at the presence of God, the God of Israel.
9 Thou didst [a]shed abroad a plentiful rain, O God;
Thou didst confirm Thine inheritance, when it was [1]parched.
10 Thy creatures settled in it;
Thou didst [a]provide in Thy goodness for the poor, O God.

11 The Lord gives the [1]command;
The [a]women who proclaim the *good* tidings are a great host:
12 "[a]Kings of armies flee, they flee,
And she who remains at home will [b]divide the spoil!"
13 [1]When you lie down [a]among the [2]sheepfolds,
You are like the wings of a dove covered with silver,
And its pinions with glistening gold.
14 When the Almighty [a]scattered the kings [1]there,
It was snowing in [b]Zalmon.

15 A [1a]mountain of God is the mountain of Bashan;
A mountain *of many* peaks is the mountain of Bashan.
16 Why do you look with envy, O mountains with *many* peaks,
At the mountain which God has [a]desired for His abode?
Surely, [b]the LORD will dwell *there* forever.
17 The [a]chariots of God are [1]myriads, [b]thousands upon thousands;
[2]The Lord is among them *as at* Sinai, in holiness.
18 Thou hast [a]ascended on high, Thou hast [b]led captive *Thy* captives;
Thou hast received gifts among men,
Even *among* the rebellious also, that [1]the LORD God may dwell *there*.

19 Blessed be the Lord, who daily [a]bears our burden,

68:1 [1]Or, *Go* [2]Or, *His enem* [3]Or, *those wh shall* [a]Num. 1 12:5; 132:8

2 [a]Ps. 37:20; Hos. 13:3 [b]Ps 97:5; Mic. 1:4 37:20; 80:16

3 [a]Ps. 32:11; 97:12

4 [1]Or, *Cast u* highway [2]Heb [a]Ps. 66:2 [b]Is. 62:10 [c]Deut. 18:10; 68:33; [d]Ex. 6:3; Ps. 8

5 [1]Lit., *of* [a]Ps 146:9 [b]Deut. [c]Deut. 26:15

6 [1]Lit., *makes solitary to dwe house* [a]Ps. 10 113:9 [b]Ps. 69 102:20; 107:10 146:7; Acts 12 [c]Ps. 78:17; 10

7 [1]*Selah* may *Pause, Cresce Musical interlu* 13:21; Ps. 78: 3:13 [b]Judg. 5: 78:52

8 [1]Lit., *This is* which [a]Ex. 19 5:4; 2 Sam. 22 77:18; Jer. 10: 5:4; Ps. 18:9; Is [c]Ex. 19:18; Jud

9 [1]Lit., *weary* 26:4; Deut. 11: 5:10; Ezek. 34:

10 [a]Ps. 65:9; 7 78:20; 107:9

11 [1]Lit., *word* 15:20; 1 Sam.

12 [a]Josh. 10:1 5:19; Ps. 135:1 5:30; 1 Sam. 30

13 [1]Lit., *If* [2]Or, *stones* or *saddl* [a]Gen. 49:14; Ju

14 [1]Lit., *in it* [a]J 10:10 [b]Judg. 9:

15 [1]Or, *mighty mountain is* [a]Ps

16 [a]Deut. 12:5; 87:1, 2; 132:13 132:14

17 [1]Lit., *twice te thousand* [2]Anot reading is *The came from Sina sanctuary* [a]2 Ki Hab. 3:8 [b]Deut. Dan. 7:10

18 [1]Heb., *YAH* 47:5; Eph. 4:8 5:12

19 [a]Ps. 55:22; Is

[b]The God *who* is our salvation. Selah.
20 God is to us a [a]God of deliverances;
And [b]to [1]GOD the Lord belong escapes [2]from death.
21 Surely God will [a]shatter the head of His enemies,
The hairy crown of him who goes on in his guilty deeds.
22 The Lord [1]said, "[a]I will bring *them* back from Bashan.
I will bring *them* back from the depths of the sea;
23 That [1a]your foot may shatter *them* in blood,
The tongue of your [b]dogs *may have* its portion from *your* enemies."

24 They have seen [a]Thy [1]procession, O God,
The [1]procession of my God, my King, [2b]into the sanctuary.
25 The [a]singers went on, the musicians after *them*,
[1]In the midst of the [b]maidens beating tambourines.
26 [a]Bless God in the congregations,
Even the LORD, *you who are* of the [b]fountain of Israel.
27 There is [a]Benjamin, the [1]youngest, [2]ruling them,
The princes of Judah *in* their throng,
The princes of [b]Zebulun, the princes of Naphtali.

28 [1]Your God has [a]commanded your strength;
Show Thyself strong, O God, [b]who hast acted [2]on our behalf.
29 [1]Because of Thy temple at Jerusalem
[a]Kings will bring gifts to Thee.
30 Rebuke the [a]beasts [1]in the reeds,
The herd of [b]bulls with the calves of the peoples,
Trampling under foot the pieces of silver;
He has [c]scattered the peoples who delight in war.
31 Envoys will come out of [a]Egypt;
[1b]Ethiopia will quickly stretch out her hands to God.

32 Sing to God, O [a]kingdoms of the earth;
[b]Sing praises to the Lord, Selah.
33 To Him who [a]rides upon the [1b]highest heavens, which are from ancient times;
Behold, [c]He [2]speaks forth with His voice, a [d]mighty voice.
34 [a]Ascribe strength to God;
His majesty is over Israel,
And [b]His strength is in the [1]skies.
35 [1]O God, *Thou art* [a]awesome from Thy [2]sanctuary.
The God of Israel Himself [b]gives strength and power to the people.
[c]Blessed be God!

Psalm 69

For the choir director; according to [+]Shoshannim. *A Psalm* of David.

69 Save me, O God,
For the [a]waters have [1]threatened my life.
2 I have sunk in deep [a]mire, and there is no foothold;
I have come into deep waters, and a [1b]flood overflows me.
3 I am [a]weary with my crying; my throat is parched;
My [b]eyes fail while I wait for my God.

19 [b]Ps. 65:5
Heb., *YHWH*, ndered *LORD* iew of; lit., *for* 06:43 [b]Deut. 49:15; 56:13
:6; Hab. 3:13
says [a]Num. ; Amos 9:1-3
ome versions ou may *bathe in blood* [a]Ps. [b]1 Kin. 21:19; Jer. 15:3
oings [2]Lit., *in nctuary*; or, *in ss* [a]Ps. 77:13 [b]Ps. 63:2
he *maidens in* [a]1 Chr. 13:8; Ps. 47:6 [b]Ex.); Judg. 11:34
Ps. 22:22, 23; eut. 33:28; Is. 48:1
smallest [2]Or, *r* [a]Judg. 5:14; 1 [b]Judg. 5:18
me mss. read *nd, God* [2]Lit., Ps. 29:11; 44:4 [b]Is. 26:12
[1]Or, *From Thy* [a]1 Kin. 10:10, Chr. 32:23; Ps. 72:10; Is. 18:7
of [a]Job 40:21; :3 [b]Ps. 22:12 . 18:14; 89:10
[1]Lit., *Cush* [a]Is. 21 [b]Is. 45:14; Zeph. 3:10
s. 102:22 [b]Ps. 67:4
[1]Lit., *heaven of ens of old* [2]Lit., *es forth* [a]Deut. s. 18:10; 104:3 t. 10:14; 1 Kin. 46:6 [d]Ps. 29:4
it., *clouds* [a]Ps. :9:1 [b]Ps. 150:1
Or, *Awesome is God from your tuary* [2]Lit., *holy es* [a]Deut. 7:21; ; Ps. 47:2; 66:5 29:11; Is. 40:29 6:20; 2 Cor. 1:3
+ possibly, *Lilies*
Lit., *come to the* [a]Job 22:11; Ps. 42:7; 69:14, 15; Jon. 2:5
, *flowing stream* . 40:2 [b]Jon. 2:3
[a]Ps. 6:6 [b]Deut. 8:32; Ps. 38:10; 2, 123; Is. 38:14

4 Those [a]who hate me without a cause are more than the hairs of my head;
Those who would [1]destroy me [b]are powerful, being wrongfully my enemies,
[c]What I did not steal, I then have to restore.

5 O God, it is Thou who dost know [a]my folly,
And [b]my wrongs are not hidden from Thee.
6 May those who wait for Thee not [a]be ashamed through me, O Lord [1]GOD of hosts;
May those who seek Thee not be dishonored through me, O God of Israel,
7 Because [a]for Thy sake I have borne reproach;
[b]Dishonor has covered my face.
8 I have become [a]estranged [1]from my brothers,
And an alien to my mother's sons.
9 For [a]zeal for Thy house has consumed me,
And [b]the reproaches of those who reproach Thee have fallen on me.
10 When I wept [a]in my soul with fasting,
It became my reproach.
11 When I made [a]sackcloth my clothing,
I became [b]a byword to them.
12 Those who [a]sit in the gate talk about me,
And I *am* the [1b]song of the drunkards.

13 But as for me, my prayer is to Thee, O LORD, [a]at an acceptable time;
O God, in the [b]greatness of Thy lovingkindness,
Answer me with [1]Thy saving truth.
14 Deliver me from the [a]mire, and do not let me sink;
May I be [b]delivered from [1]my foes, and from the [2c]deep waters.
15 May the [1a]flood of water not overflow me,
And may the deep not swallow me up,
And may the [b]pit not shut its mouth on me.

16 Answer me, O LORD, for [a]Thy lovingkindness is good;
[b]According to the greatness of Thy compassion, [c]turn to me,
17 And [a]do not hide Thy face from Thy servant,
For I am [b]in distress; answer me quickly.
18 Oh draw near to my soul *and* [a]redeem it;
[b]Ransom me because of my enemies!
19 Thou dost know my [a]reproach and my shame and my dishonor;
All my adversaries are [1]before Thee.

20 Reproach has [a]broken my heart, and I am so sick.
And [b]I looked for sympathy, but there was none,
And for [c]comforters, but I found none.
21 They also gave me [1a]gall [2]for my food,
And for my thirst they [b]gave me vinegar to drink.

22 May [a]their table before them become a snare;
And [1b]when they are in peace, *may it become* a trap.
23 May their [a]eyes grow dim so that they cannot see,

4 [1]Or, *silenc* 35:19; John 1 35:19; 38:19; 35:11; Jer. 15

5 [a]Ps. 38:5 [b]

6 [1]Heb., *YH* usually rende [a]2 Sam. 12:14

7 [a]Jer. 15:15 44:15; Is. 50:6 51:51

8 [1]Lit., *to* [a]Jo 19:13-15; Ps. 38:11

9 [a]Ps. 119:13 2:17 [b]Ps. 89: Rom. 15:3

10 [a]Ps. 35:13

11 [a]1 Kin. 20: 35:13 [b]1 Kin. 17:6; Ps. 44:14

12 [1]Lit., *songs* 19:1; Ruth 4:1

13 [1]Or, *the fa of Thy salvatio* 32:6; Is. 49:8; 6:2 [b]Ps. 51:1

14 [1]Lit., *those me* [2]Lit., *deep water* [a]Ps. 69: 144:7

15 [1]Lit., *strear* 124:4, 5 [b]Num Ps. 28:1; 141:7

16 [a]Ps. 63:3; 1 [b]Ps. 51:1; 106: 25:16; 86:16

17 [a]Ps. 27:9; 1 143:7 [b]Ps. 31:

18 [a]2 Sam. 4:9 26:11; 49:15 [b]P 119:134

19 [1]Or, known [a]Ps. 22:6; 31:11

20 [a]Jer. 23:9 [b] 142:4; Is. 63:5

21 [1]Or, *poison* [a]Deut. 29:18 [b]M 27:34, 48; Mark 36; Luke 23:36; 19:28-30

22 [1]Lit., *for thos are secure* [a]Ro 10 [b]1 Thess. 5:

23 [a]Is. 6:10

And make their [b]loins shake continually.
24 [a]Pour out Thine indignation on them,
And may Thy burning anger overtake them.
25 May their [1a]camp be desolate;
May none dwell in their tents.
26 For they have [a]persecuted him whom [b]Thou Thyself hast smitten,
And they tell of the pain of those whom [c]Thou hast [1]wounded.
27 Do Thou add [a]iniquity to their iniquity,
And [b]may they not come into [c]Thy righteousness.
28 May they be [a]blotted out of the [b]book of life,
And may they not be [1c]recorded with the righteous.

29 But I am [a]afflicted and in pain;
[1]May Thy salvation, O God, [b]set me *securely* on high.
30 I will [a]praise the name of God with song,
And shall [b]magnify Him with [c]thanksgiving.
31 And it will [a]please the LORD better than an ox
Or a young bull with horns and hoofs.
32 The [a]humble [1]have seen *it and* are glad;
You who seek God, [b]let your heart [2]revive.
33 For [a]the LORD hears the needy,
And [b]does not despise His *who are* prisoners.

34 Let [a]heaven and earth praise Him,
The seas and [b]everything that moves in them.
35 For God will [a]save Zion and [b]build the cities of Judah,
That they may dwell there and [c]possess it.
36 And the [1a]descendants of His servants will inherit it,
And those who love His name [b]will dwell in it.

Psalm 70

For the choir director. *A Psalm* of David; for a memorial.

70 [a]O God, *hasten* to deliver me;
O LORD, hasten to my help!
2 [a]Let those be ashamed and humiliated
Who seek my [1]life;
Let those be turned back and dishonored
Who delight [2]in my hurt.
3 [a]Let those be [1]turned back because of their shame
Who say, "Aha, aha!"

4 Let all who seek Thee rejoice and be glad in Thee;
And let those who love Thy salvation say continually,
"Let God be magnified."
5 But [a]I am afflicted and needy;
[b]Hasten to me, O God!
Thou art my help and my deliverer;
O LORD, do not delay.

Psalm 71

71 [a]In Thee, O LORD, I have taken refuge;
Let me never be ashamed.
2 [a]In Thy righteousness deliver me, and rescue me;

23 [b]Dan. 5:6
[a]Ps. 79:6; Jer. ek. 20:8; Hos. 5:10
encampment
tt. 23:38; Luke :35; Acts 1:20
ierced [a]2 Chr. ech. 1:15 [b]Is. 4 [c]Ps. 109:22
[a]Neh. 4:5; Ps. Rom. 1:28 [b]Is. 0 [c]Ps. 103:17
t., written [a]Ex. 2, 33; Rev. 3:5 4:3; Rev. 13:8; :15 [c]Ps. 87:6; 9; Luke 10:20; Heb. 12:23
Thy salvation, ill set . . . [a]Ps. [b]Ps. 20:1; 59:1
28:7 [b]Ps. 34:3 [c]Ps. 50:14
0:13, 14; 51:16
Some mss. and t versions read [2]Or, live [a]Ps. 4:2 [b]Ps. 22:26
12:5 [b]Ps. 68:6
Ps. 96:11; 98:7; 1-13; Is. 44:23; 9:13 [b]Is. 55:12
Ps. 46:5; 51:18 147:2; Is. 44:26 [c]Obad. 17
[1]Lit., seed [a]Ps. 3; 102:28 [b]Ps. 37:29
[a]Ps. 40:13-17; 70:1-5
Or, soul [2]Or, to e [a]Ps. 35:4, 26
Some mss. read alled [a]Ps. 40:15
0:17 [b]Ps. 141:1
:1 [a]Ps. 25:2, 3; 31:1-3; 71:1-3
2 [a]Ps. 31:1

[b]Incline Thine ear to me, and save me.
3 [a]Be Thou to me a rock of [b]habitation, to which I may continually come;
Thou hast given [c]commandment to save me,
For Thou art [d]my [1]rock and my fortress.
4 [a]Rescue me, O my God, out of the hand of the wicked,
Out of the [1]grasp of the wrongdoer and ruthless man,
5 For Thou art my [a]hope;
O Lord [1]GOD, *Thou art* my [b]confidence from my youth.
6 [1]By Thee I have been [a]sustained from *my* birth;
Thou art He who [b]took me from my mother's womb;
My [c]praise is continually [2]of Thee.

7 I have become a [a]marvel to many;
For Thou art [b]my strong refuge.
8 My [a]mouth is filled with Thy praise,
And with [b]Thy glory all day long.
9 Do not cast me off in the [a]time of old age;
Do not forsake me when my strength fails.
10 For my enemies have spoken [1]against me;
And those who [a]watch for my [2]life [b]have consulted together,
11 Saying, "[a]God has forsaken him;
Pursue and seize him, for there is [b]no one to deliver."

12 O God, [a]do not be far from me;
O my God, [b]hasten to my help!
13 Let those who are adversaries of my soul be [a]ashamed *and* consumed;
Let them be [b]covered with reproach and dishonor, who [c]seek [1]to injure me.
14 But as for me, I will [a]hope continually,
And will [1b]praise Thee yet more and more.
15 My [a]mouth shall tell of Thy righteousness,
And of [b]Thy salvation all day long;
For I [c]do not know the [1]sum *of them.*
16 I will come [a]with the mighty deeds of the Lord [1]GOD;
I will [b]make mention of Thy righteousness, Thine alone.

17 O God, Thou [a]hast taught me from my youth;
And I still [b]declare Thy wondrous deeds.
18 And even when *I am* [a]old and gray, O God, do not forsake me,
Until I [b]declare Thy [1]strength to *this* generation,
Thy power to all who are to come.
19 [1]For Thy [a]righteousness, O God, *reaches* to the [2]heavens,
Thou who hast [b]done great things;
O God, [c]who is like Thee?
20 Thou, who hast [a]shown [1]me many troubles and distresses,
Wilt [b]revive [1]me again,
And wilt bring [1]me up again [c]from the depths of the earth.
21 Mayest Thou increase my [a]greatness,
And turn *to* [b]comfort me.

22 I will also praise Thee with [1a]a harp,
Even Thy [2]truth, O my God;

2 [b]Ps. 17:6

3 [1]Or, *crag* [a]P
3 [b]Deut. 33:27
90:1; 91:9 [c]Ps
42:8 [d]Ps. 18:2

4 [1]Lit., *palm* [a]
140:1, 4

5 [1]Heb., *YHW*
usually render
[a]Ps. 39:7; Jer.
17:7, 13, 17; 5
22:9

6 [1]Lit., *Upon T*
have been sup
[2]Lit., *in* [a]Ps. 22
46:3 [b]Job 10:1
22:9 [c]Ps. 34:1

7 [a]Is. 8:18; 1 C
[b]Ps. 61:3

8 [a]Ps. 35:28; 6
96:6; 104:1

9 [a]Ps. 71:18; 9
46:4

10 [1]Lit., *with re*
to [2]Lit., *soul* [a]P
[b]Ps. 31:13; 83:3
27:1

11 [a]Ps. 3:2 [b]P

12 [a]Ps. 10:1; 2
35:22; 38:21 [b]P
38:22; 40:13; 7

13 [1]Lit., *my inj*
35:4, 26; 40:14
109:29 [c]Esth. 9
71:24

14 [1]Lit., *add up*
Thy praise [a]Ps.
[b]Ps. 71:8

15 [1]Lit., *numbe*
35:28 [b]Ps. 96:2
40:5

16 [1]Heb., *YHW*
usually rendere
[a]Ps. 106:2 [b]Ps.

17 [a]Deut. 4:5; 6
26:7; 40:5; 119:

18 [1]Lit., *arm* [a]P
[b]Ps. 22:31; 78:4

19 [1]Or, *And* [2]Li
height [a]Ps. 36:6
[b]Ps. 126:2; Luke
[c]Deut. 3:24; Ps.

20 [1]Another rea
us [a]Ps. 60:3 [b]P
80:18; 85:6; 119
138:7; Hos. 6:1,
86:13

21 [a]Ps. 18:35 [b]
23:4; 86:17; Is. 1
49:13

22 [1]Lit., *an instr*
of a harp [2]Or,
faithfulness [a]Ps
81:2; 92:1-3; 144

To Thee I will sing praises with the [b]lyre,
O Thou [c]Holy One of Israel.
23 My lips will [a]shout for joy when I sing praises to Thee;
And my [b]soul, which Thou hast redeemed.
24 My [a]tongue also will utter Thy righteousness all day long;
For they are [b]ashamed, for they are humiliated who seek [1]my hurt.

Psalm 72

A Psalm of Solomon.

72 Give the king [a]Thy judgments, O God,
And [b]Thy righteousness to the king's son.
2 [1]May [2]he [a]judge Thy people with righteousness,
And [3b]Thine afflicted with justice.
3 [1]Let the mountains bring [2a]peace to the people,
And the hills in righteousness.
4 [1]May he [a]vindicate the [2]afflicted of the people,
Save the children of the needy,
And crush the oppressor.

5 [1]Let them fear Thee [a]while the sun *endures,*
And [2]as long as the moon, throughout all generations.
6 [1]May he come down [a]like rain upon the mown grass,
Like [b]showers that water the earth.
7 In his days [1]may the [a]righteous flourish,
And [b]abundance of peace till the moon is no more.

8 May he also rule [a]from sea to sea,
And from the River to the ends of the earth.
9 [1]Let [a]the nomads of the desert [b]bow before him;
And his enemies [c]lick the dust.
10 [1]Let the kings of [a]Tarshish and of the [2b]islands bring presents;
The kings of [c]Sheba and [d]Seba [e]offer [3]gifts.
11 [1]And let all [a]kings bow down before him,
All [b]nations serve him.

12 For he will [a]deliver the needy when he cries for help,
The [1]afflicted also, and him who has no helper.
13 He will have [a]compassion on the poor and needy,
And the [1]lives of the needy he will save.
14 He will [1a]rescue their [2]life from oppression and violence;
And their blood will be [b]precious in his sight;
15 So may he live; and may the [a]gold of Sheba be given to him;
And let [1]them pray for him continually;
Let [1]them bless him all day long.

16 May there be abundance of grain in the earth on top of the mountains;
Its fruit will wave like *the cedars of* [a]Lebanon;
And may those from the city flourish like [b]vegetation of the earth.
17 May his [a]name endure forever;
May his name [1]increase [2b]as long as the sun *shines;*
And let *men* [c]bless themselves by him;

…s. 33:2; 147:7 …22; Ps. 78:41; 89:18; Is. 1:4
…s. 5:11; 32:11; …16 [b]Ps. 34:22; 55:18; 103:4
…r, *to injure me* …28 [b]Ps. 71:13
…Kin. 3:9; 1 Chr. …2:13 [b]Ps. 24:5
…r, *He will judge* …f the pronouns …Psalm may be …d *He* since the …reference is to …ssiah. [3]Or, *Thy* …[a]Is. 9:7; 11:2-5; 32:1 [b]Ps. 82:3
…The mountains will bring [2]Or, …*ty* [a]Is. 2:4; 9:5, …, 4; Zech. 9:10
…e will vindicate …umble [a]Is. 11:4
…, *They will fear …efore the moon* …2:17; 89:36, 37
…r, *He will come …wn* [a]Deut. 32:2; …23:4; Hos. 6:3 [b]Ps. 65:10
…e righteous will [a]Ps. 92:12 [b]Is. 2:4
…:31; Zech. 9:10
…he nomads… [a]Ps. 74:14; Is. … [b]Ps. 22:29 [c]Is. 49:23; Mic. 7:17
…r, *The kings… will bring* [2]Or, …*nds* [3]Or, *tribute* …r. 9:21; Ps. 48:7 …7:1; Is. 42:4, 10; …11 [c]1 Kin. 10:1; …; Is. 60:6 [d]Gen. …:7; Is. 43:3 [e]Ps. 45:12; 68:29
…Or, *All kings will …own* [a]Ps. 138:4; …49:23 [b]Ps. 86:9
…r, *humble* [a]Job 29:12; Ps. 72:4
…it., *souls* [a]Prov. 19:17; 28:8
…t., *redeem* [2]Lit., *soul* [a]Ps. 69:18 …Sam. 26:21; Ps. 116:15
…it., *him* [a]Is. 60:6
…Ps. 104:16 [b]Job 5:25
[1]Or, *sprout forth* …, *before the sun* …3:15; Ps. 135:13 …:36 [c]Gen. 12:3; 22:18

[d]Let all nations call him blessed.

18 [a]Blessed be the LORD God, the God of Israel,
Who alone [b]works wonders.
19 And blessed be His [a]glorious name forever;
And may the whole [b]earth be filled with His glory.
[c]Amen, and Amen.

20 The prayers of David the son of Jesse are ended.

BOOK 3

Psalm 73

A Psalm of Asaph.

73 Surely God is [a]good to Israel,
To those who are [b]pure in heart!
2 But as for me, [a]my feet came close to stumbling;
My steps [1]had almost slipped.
3 For I was [a]envious of the [1]arrogant,
As I saw the [b]prosperity of the wicked.
4 For there are no pains in their death;
And their [1]body is fat.
5 They are [a]not [1]in trouble *as other* [2]men;
Nor are they [b]plagued [3]like mankind.
6 Therefore pride is [a]their necklace;
The [b]garment of violence covers them.
7 Their eye [1]bulges from [a]fatness;
The imaginations of *their* heart [2]run riot.
8 They [a]mock, and [1]wickedly speak of oppression;
They [b]speak from on high.
9 They have [a]set their mouth [1]against the heavens,
And their tongue [2]parades through the earth.

10 Therefore [1]his people return to this place;
And waters of [a]abundance are [2]drunk by them.
11 And they say, "[a]How does God know?
And is there knowledge [1]with the Most High?"
12 Behold, [a]these are the wicked;
And always [b]at ease, they have increased *in* wealth.
13 Surely [a]in vain I have [1]kept my heart pure,
And [b]washed my hands in innocence;
14 For I have been stricken [a]all day long,
And [1b]chastened every morning.

15 If I had said, "I will speak thus,"
Behold, I should have betrayed the [a]generation of Thy children.
16 When I [a]pondered to understand this,
It was [1]troublesome in my sight
17 Until I came into the [1a]sanctuary of God;
Then I perceived their [b]end.
18 Surely Thou dost set them in [a]slippery places;
Thou dost cast them down to [1b]destruction.
19 How they are [1a]destroyed in a moment!
They are utterly swept away by [b]sudden terrors!

17 [d]Luke 1:48
18 [a]1 Chr. 29:1 41:13; 89:52; 1 [b]Ex. 15:11; Job 77:14; 86:10; 1
19 [a]Neh. 9:5; [b]Num. 14:21
73:1 [a]Ps. 86:5 24:4; 51:10; Ma
2 [1]Lit., *were ca slip* [a]Ps. 94:18
3 [1]Or, *boasters* 37:1; Prov. 23:1 21:7; Ps. 37:7;
4 [1]Or, *belly*
5 [1]Lit., *in the tr men* [2]Or, *morta with* [a]Job 21:9; 73:12 [b]Ps. 73:1
6 [a]Gen. 41:42; 1:9 [b]Ps. 109:18
7 [1]Lit., *goes for overflow* [a]Job 1 Ps. 17:10; Jer. 5
8 [1]Or, *they spe wickedness; Fro high they speak oppression.* [a]Ps [b]Ps. 17:10; 2 Pe Jude 16
9 [1]Or, *in* [2]Lit., [a]Rev. 13:6
10 [1]Or, *His* [2]Lit *drained out* [a]Ps
11 [1]Lit., *in* [a]Job
12 [a]Ps. 49:6; 52 49:31; Ezek. 23
13 [1]Or, *cleanse heart* [a]Job 21:15 35:3 [b]Ps. 26:6
14 [1]Lit., *my cha* [a]Ps. 38:6 [b]Job 3 Ps. 118:18
15 [a]Ps. 14:5
16 [1]Lit., *labor, tr* [a]Eccl. 8:17
17 [1]Lit., *sanctua* [a]Ps. 27:4; 77:13 37:38
18 [1]Lit., *ruins* [a]P 35:6 [b]Ps. 35:8; 3
19 [1]Lit., *become desolation* [a]Num 16:21; Is. 47:11 18:11

20 Like a [a]dream when one awakes,
O Lord, when [b]aroused, Thou wilt [c]despise their [1]form.

21 When my [a]heart was embittered,
And I was [b]pierced [1]within,
22 Then I was [a]senseless and ignorant;
I was *like* [1]a [b]beast [2]before Thee.
23 Nevertheless [a]I am continually with Thee;
Thou hast taken hold of my right hand.
24 With Thy counsel Thou wilt [a]guide me,
And afterward [b]receive me [1]to glory.

25 [a]Whom have I in heaven *but Thee?*
And [1]besides Thee, I desire nothing on earth.
26 My [a]flesh and my heart may fail,
But God is the [1]strength of my heart and my [b]portion forever.
27 For, behold, [a]those who are far from Thee will [b]perish;
Thou hast [1]destroyed all those who [2c]are unfaithful to Thee.
28 But as for me, [a]the nearness of God is my good;
I have made the Lord [1]GOD my [b]refuge,
That I may [c]tell of all Thy works.

Psalm 74

A [+]Maskil of Asaph.

74 O God, why hast Thou [a]rejected *us* forever?
Why does Thine anger [b]smoke against the [c]sheep of Thy
[1]pasture?
2 Remember Thy congregation, which Thou hast [a]purchased of
old,
Which Thou hast [b]redeemed to be the [c]tribe of Thine inheritance;
And this Mount [d]Zion, where Thou hast dwelt.
3 [1]Turn Thy footsteps toward the [a]perpetual ruins;
The enemy [b]has damaged everything within the sanctuary.
4 Thine adversaries have [a]roared in the midst of Thy meeting
place;
They have set up their [b]own [1]standards [c]for signs.
5 It seems as if one had lifted up
His [1a]axe in a [2]forest of trees.
6 And now [1]all its [a]carved work
They smash with hatchet and [2]hammers.
7 They have [1a]burned Thy sanctuary [2]to the ground;
They have [b]defiled the dwelling place of Thy name.
8 They [a]said in their heart, "Let us [1]completely [2]subdue them."
They have burned all the meeting places of God in the land.
9 We do not see our [a]signs;
There is [b]no longer any prophet,
Nor is there any among us who knows [c]how long.
10 How long, O God, will the adversary [a]revile,
And the enemy [b]spurn Thy name forever?
11 Why [a]dost Thou withdraw Thy hand, even Thy right hand?
From within Thy bosom, [b]destroy *them*!

12 Yet God is [a]my king from of old,
Who works deeds of deliverance in the midst of the earth.

r, *image* [a]Job
:8 [b]Ps. 78:65
[c]1 Sam. 2:30
in my kidneys
16 [b]Acts 2:37
n *animal* [2]Lit.,
ee [a]Ps. 49:10;
[b]Job 18:3; Ps.
:20; Eccl. 3:18
23 [a]Ps. 16:8
ith honor [a]Ps.
8:14; Is. 58:11
:24; Ps. 49:15
with [a]Ps. 16:2;
Phil. 3:8
[1]Lit., *rock* [a]Ps.
0; 40:12; 84:2;
9:81 [b]Ps. 16:5
silenced [2]Lit.,
a whoring from
119:155 [b]Ps.
x. 34:15; Num.
. 106:39; Hos.
4:12; 9:1
[1]Heb., *YHWH,*
rendered LORD
:4; Heb. 10:22;
4:8 [b]Ps. 14:6;
. 40:5; 107:22;
118:17
[+]Possibly,
ntemplative, or
actic, or *Skillful*
Psalm
[1]Or, *pasturing*
:9; 77:7 [b]Deut.
Ps. 18:8; 89:46
13; 95:7; 100:3
x. 15:16; Deut.
[b]Ex. 15:13; Ps.
106:10; Is. 63:9
32:9; Is. 63:17;
:16; 51:19 [d]Ps.
9:11; 68:16
Lift up [a]Is. 61:4
[b]Ps. 79:1
signs [a]Lam. 2:7
n. 2:2 [c]Ps. 74:9
[1]Lit., *axes* [2]Lit.,
cket [a]Jer. 46:22
altogether [2]Or,
[a]1 Kin. 6:18, 29,
32, 35
set on fire [2]Or,
ground they ...
25:9 [b]Ps. 89:39;
Lam. 2:2
altogether [2]Or,
press [a]Ps. 83:4
. 78:43 [b]1 Sam.
Lam. 2:9; Ezek.
Amos 8:11 [c]Ps.
6:3; 79:5; 80:4
Ps. 44:16; 79:12;
9:51 [b]Lev. 24:16
. 2:3 [b]Ps. 59:13
12 [a]Ps. 44:4

13 [1]Thou didst [a]divide the sea by Thy strength;
[1]Thou [b]didst break the heads of the [c]sea monsters [2]in the waters.
14 [1]Thou didst crush the heads of [2a]Leviathan;
[1]Thou didst give him as food for the [3]creatures [b]of the wilderness.
15 [1]Thou didst [a]break open springs and torrents;
[1]Thou didst [b]dry up ever-flowing streams.
16 Thine is the day, Thine also is the night;
[1]Thou hast [a]prepared the [2]light and the sun.
17 [1]Thou hast [a]established all the boundaries of the earth;
[1]Thou hast [2]made [b]summer and winter.

18 Remember this, [1]O LORD, that the enemy has [a]reviled;
And a [b]foolish people has spurned Thy name.
19 Do not deliver the soul of Thy [a]turtledove to the wild beast;
[b]Do not forget the life of Thine afflicted forever.
20 Consider the [a]covenant;
For the [b]dark places of the land are full of the habitations of violence.
21 Let not the [a]oppressed return dishonored;
Let the [b]afflicted and needy praise Thy name.

22 Do arise, O God, *and* [a]plead Thine own cause;
Remember [1]how the [b]foolish man reproaches Thee all day long.
23 Do not forget the voice of Thine [a]adversaries,
The [b]uproar of those who rise against Thee which ascends continually.

Psalm 75

For the choir director; *set to* +Al-tashheth. A Psalm of Asaph, a Song.

75 We [a]give thanks to Thee, O God, we give thanks,
For Thy name is [b]near;
Men declare [c]Thy wondrous works.
2 "When I select an [a]appointed time,
It is I who [b]judge with equity.
3 "The [a]earth and all who dwell in it [1]melt;
It is I who have firmly set its [b]pillars. [2]Selah.
4 "I said to the boastful, 'Do not boast,'
And to the wicked, '[a]Do not lift up the horn;
5 Do not lift up your horn on high,
[a]Do not speak with insolent [1]pride.' "

6 For not from the east, nor from the west,
Nor from the [1a]desert *comes* exaltation;
7 But [a]God is the Judge;
He [b]puts down one, and exalts another.
8 For a [a]cup is in the hand of the LORD, and the wine foams;
It is [1b]well mixed, and He pours out of this;
Surely all the wicked of the earth must drain *and* [c]drink down its dregs.

9 But as for me, I will [a]declare *it* forever;
I will sing praises to the God of Jacob.

13 [1]Or, *Thou* [2]Lit., *on* [a]Ex. 78:13 [b]Is. 51 148:7; Jer. 51

14 [1]Or, *Thou* [2]Or, *sea mons* *people* [a]Job 4 104:26; Is. 27 72:9

15 [1]Or, *Thou* [a]Ex. 17:5, 6; N 20:11; Ps. 78: 105:41; 114:8; [b]Ex. 14:21, 22 2:10; 3:13; Ps.

16 [1]Or, *Thou* [2]Or, *luminary* 1:14-18; Ps. 1 136:7, 8

17 [1]Or, *Thou* [2]Or, *formed* [a]D Acts 17:26 [b]G Ps. 147:16-18

18 [1]Or, *that th has reviled the* [a]Ps. 74:10 [b]De Ps. 14:1; 39:8;

19 [a]Song 2:14 9:18

20 [a]Gen. 17:7; 106:45 [b]Ps. 88

21 [a]Ps. 103:6 35:10; Is. 41:17

22 [1]Lit., *Thy re from the foolish* [a]Ps. 43:1; Is. 3 43:26; Ezek. 20 14:1; 53:1; 74:1

23 [a]Ps. 74:10

+Lit., *Do Not De*

75:1 [a]Ps. 79:13 145:18 [c]Ps. 26 71:17

2 [a]Ps. 102:13 67:4; Is. 11:4

3 [1]Or, *totter* [2]S may mean: *Pau Crescendo* or *M interlude* [a]Ps. 4 24:19 [b]1 Sam. 2

4 [a]Zech. 1:21

5 [1]Lit., *neck* [a]1 2:3; Ps. 94:4

6 [1]Or, *mountain desert* [a]Ps. 3:3

7 [a]Ps. 50:6 [b]1 S 2:7; Ps. 147:6; D

8 [1]Lit., *full of mi* [a]Job 21:20; Ps. 60:3; Jer. 25:15 23:30 [c]Obad. 16

9 [a]Ps. 22:22; 40

10 And all the [a]horns of the wicked [1]He will cut off,
But [b]the horns of the righteous will be lifted up.

Psalm 76

For the choir director; on stringed instruments.
A Psalm of Asaph, a Song.

76 God is [a]known in Judah;
His name is [b]great in Israel.
2 And His [1a]tabernacle is in [b]Salem;
His [c]dwelling place also is in Zion.
3 There He [a]broke the [1]flaming arrows,
The shield, and the sword, and the [2]weapons of war. [3]Selah.

4 Thou art resplendent,
[1]More majestic than the mountains of prey.
5 The [a]stouthearted were plundered;
[1]They sank into sleep;
And none of the [2]warriors could use his hands.
6 At Thy [a]rebuke, O God of Jacob,
Both [1b]rider and horse were cast into a dead sleep.
7 Thou, even Thou, art [a]to be feared;
And [b]who may stand in Thy presence when once [1]Thou art angry?

8 Thou didst cause judgment to be heard from heaven;
The earth [a]feared, and was still,
9 When God [a]arose to judgment,
To save all the humble of the earth. Selah.
10 For the [1a]wrath of man shall praise Thee;
With a remnant of wrath Thou shalt gird Thyself.

11 [a]Make vows to the LORD your God and [b]fulfill *them;*
Let all who are around Him [c]bring gifts to Him who is to be feared.
12 He will cut off the spirit of princes;
He is [1a]feared by the kings of the earth.

Psalm 77

For the choir director; +according to Jeduthun. A Psalm of Asaph.

77 My voice *rises* to God, and I will [a]cry aloud;
My voice *rises* to God, and He will hear me.
2 In the [a]day of my trouble I sought the Lord;
[b]In the night my [c]hand was stretched out [1]without weariness;
My soul [d]refused to be comforted.
3 *When* I remember God, then I am [a]disturbed;
When I [b]sigh, then [c]my spirit grows faint. [1]Selah.
4 Thou hast held my eyelids *open;*
I am so troubled that I [a]cannot speak.
5 I have considered the [a]days of old,
The years of long ago.
6 I will remember my [a]song in the night;
I [b]will meditate with my heart;
And my spirit [1]ponders.

Heb., I [a]Ps. 101:8; 8:25 [b]1 Sam. 2:1; :17; 92:10; 148:14
6:1 [a]Ps. 48:3 [b]Ps. 99:3
[1]Lit., *shelter* [a]Ps. 5; Lam. 2:6 [b]Gen. [c]Ps. 9:11; 132:13; 135:21
[1]Lit., *fiery shafts of* e *bow* [2]Lit., *battle* [3]Selah may mean: use, Crescendo or ical interlude [a]Ps. 46:9
Majestic from the mountains
., *They slumbered* sleep [2]Lit., *men of* nt *have found their* [a]Is. 10:12; 46:12
[1]Lit., *chariot* [a]Ps. [b]Ex. 15:1, 21; Ps. 78:53
it., *Thine anger is* r. 16:25; Ps. 89:7; 4 [b]Ezra 9:15; Ps. :3; Nah. 1:6; Mal. 3:2; Rev. 6:17
Chr. 16:30; 2 Chr. 0:29, 30; Ps. 33:8
[a]Ps. 9:7, 8; 74:22; 82:8
[1]Lit., *wraths* [a]Ex. 9:16; Rom. 9:17
[a]Eccl. 5:4-6 [b]Ps. [c]2 Chr. 32:23; Ps. 68:29
[1]Lit., *awesome to* [a]Ps. 47:2
+1 Chr. 16:41
1 [a]Ps. 3:4; 142:1
and did not grow [a]Ps. 50:15; 86:7 3:6; Is. 26:9 [c]Job ; Ps. 88:9 [d]Gen. 37:35
Selah may mean: se, Crescendo or cal interlude [a]Ps. :5, 11; 43:5 [b]Ps. 142:2 [c]Ps. 61:2; 143:4
4 [a]Ps. 39:9
t. 32:7; Ps. 44:1; 143:5; Is. 51:9
:., *searched* [a]Ps. 42:8 [b]Ps. 4:4

7 Will the Lord [a]reject forever?
And will He [b]never be favorable again?
8 Has His [a]lovingkindness ceased forever?
Has *His* [1b]promise come to an end [2]forever?
9 Has God [a]forgotten to be gracious?
Or has He in anger [1]withdrawn His [b]compassion? Selah.
10 Then I said, "[a]It is my [1]grief,
That the [b]right hand of the Most High has changed."

11 I shall remember the [a]deeds of [1]the LORD;
Surely I will [a]remember Thy wonders of old.
12 I will [a]meditate on all Thy work,
And muse on Thy deeds.
13 Thy way, O God, is [a]holy;
[b]What god is great like our God?
14 Thou art the [a]God who workest wonders;
Thou hast [b]made known Thy strength among the peoples.
15 Thou hast by Thy [1]power [a]redeemed Thy people,
The sons of Jacob and [b]Joseph. Selah.

16 The [a]waters saw Thee, O God;
The waters saw Thee, they were in anguish;
The deeps also trembled.
17 The [a]clouds poured out water;
The skies [b]gave forth a sound;
Thy [c]arrows [1]flashed here and there.
18 The [a]sound of Thy thunder was in the whirlwind;
The [b]lightnings lit up the world;
The [c]earth trembled and shook.
19 Thy [a]way was in the sea,
And Thy paths in the mighty waters,
And Thy footprints may not be known.
20 Thou [a]didst lead Thy people like a flock,
By the hand of [b]Moses and Aaron.

Psalm 78

A [+]Maskil of Asaph.

78 [a]Listen, O my people, to my [1]instruction;
[b]Incline your ears to the words of my mouth.
2 I will [a]open my mouth in a parable;
I will utter [b]dark sayings of old,
3 Which we have heard and known,
And [a]our fathers have told us.
4 We will [a]not conceal them from their children,
But [b]tell to the generation to come the praises of the LORD,
And His strength and His [c]wondrous works that He has done.

5 For He established a [a]testimony in Jacob,
And appointed a [b]law in Israel,
Which He [c]commanded our fathers,
That they should [1d]teach them to their children,
6 [a]That the generation to come might know, *even* [b]the children *yet* to be born,
That they may arise and [c]tell *them* to their children,

7 [a]Ps. 44:9 [b]Ps. 8
8 [1]Lit., *word* [2]Lit., *generation to generation* [a]Ps. 8 [b]2 Pet. 3:9
9 [1]Lit., *shut up* [a]Is 49:15 [b]Ps. 25:6; 4 51:1
10 [1]Or, *infirmity, t years of the right of the Most High* 31:22; 73:14 [b]Ps. 44:2, 3
11 [1]Heb., *YAH* [a]P 105:5; 143:5
12 [a]Ps. 145:5
13 [a]Ps. 63:2; 73: [b]Ex. 15:11; Ps. 71 86:8
14 [a]Ps. 72:18 [b]P 106:8
15 [1]Lit., *arm* [a]Ex Deut. 9:29; Ps. 74 78:42 [b]Ps. 80:1
16 [a]Ex. 14:21; Ps 114:3; Hab. 3:8, 1
17 [1]Lit., *went* [a]J 5:4 [b]Ps. 68:33 [c] 18:14
18 [a]Ps. 18:13; 1 [b]Ps. 97:4 [c]Judg. Ps. 18:7
19 [a]Is. 51:10; Ha
20 [a]Ex. 13:21; 1 Ps. 78:52; 80:1; 63:11-13 [b]Ex. 6: 105:26
[+]Possibly, *Contemplative,* o *Didactic,* or *Skill Psalm*
78:1 [1]Or, *law, te* [a]Is. 51:4 [b]Is. 55:
2 [a]Ps. 49:4; Mat 13:35 [b]Prov. 1:6
3 [a]Ps. 44:1
4 [a]Ex. 12:26; De 11:19; Job 15:18 145:4; Is. 38:19; 1:3 [b]Ex. 13:8, 1 22:30 [c]Job 37:1 26:7; 71:17
5 [1]Lit., *make the known* [a]Ps. 19: Is. 8:20 [b]Ps. 14 [c]Deut. 6:4-9 [d]De
6 [a]Ps. 102:18 [b] 22:31 [c]Deut. 11

7 That they should put their confidence in God,
And [a]not forget the works of God,
But [b]keep His commandments,
8 And [a]not be like their fathers,
A [b]stubborn and rebellious generation,
A generation that [c]did not [1]prepare its heart,
And whose spirit was not [d]faithful to God.

9 The sons of Ephraim [1]were [a]archers equipped with bows,
Yet [b]they turned back in the day of battle.
10 They [a]did not keep the covenant of God,
And refused to [b]walk in His law;
11 And they [a]forgot His deeds,
And His [1]miracles that He had shown them.
12 [a]He wrought wonders before their fathers,
In the land of Egypt, in the [b]field of Zoan.
13 He [a]divided the sea, and caused them to pass through;
And He made the waters stand [b]up like a heap.
14 Then He led them with the cloud by [a]day,
And all the night with a [b]light of fire.
15 He [a]split the rocks in the wilderness,
And gave *them* abundant drink like the ocean depths.
16 He [a]brought forth streams also from the rock,
And caused waters to run down like rivers.

17 Yet they still continued to sin against Him,
To [a]rebel against the Most High in the desert.
18 And in their heart they [a]put God to the test
By asking [b]food according to their desire.
19 Then they spoke against God;
They said, "[a]Can God prepare a table in the wilderness?
20 "Behold, He [a]struck the rock, so that waters gushed out,
And streams were overflowing;
Can He give bread also?
Will He provide [1b]meat for His people?"

21 Therefore the LORD heard and [1]was [a]full of wrath,
And a fire was kindled against Jacob,
And anger also mounted against Israel;
22 Because they [a]did not believe in God,
And did not trust in His salvation.
23 Yet He commanded the clouds above,
And [a]opened the doors of heaven;
24 And He [a]rained down manna upon them to eat,
And gave them [1b]food from heaven.
25 Man did eat the bread of [1]angels;
He sent them [2]food [3a]in abundance.
26 He [a]caused the east wind to blow in the heavens;
And by His [1]power He directed the south wind.
27 When He rained [1]meat upon them like the dust,
Even [a]winged fowl like the sand of the seas,
28 Then He let *them* fall in the midst of [1]their camp,
Round about their dwellings.
29 So they [a]ate and were well filled;

9; 6:12; 8:14 :1, 29; 27:1; Josh. 22:5
right [a]2 Kin. ; 2 Chr. 30:7; 8 [b]Ex. 32:9; 7, 24; 31:27; 2:19; Is. 30:9 3; Ps. 78:37 [d]Ps. 51:10
eing [a]1 Chr. g. 20:39; Ps. 78:57
. 2:20; 1 Kin. 2 Kin. 17:15; s. 119:1; Jer. 23; 44:10, 23
Or, *wonderful* [a]Ps. 106:13
chs. 7-12; Ps. [b]Num. 13:22; 43; Is. 19:11; ; Ezek. 30:14
Ex. 14:21; Ps. 136:13 [b]Ex. 15:8; Ps. 33:7
Ex. 13:21; Ps. 39 [b]Ex. 14:24
x. 17:6; Num. ; Ps. 105:41; 48:21; 1 Cor. 10:4
. 20:8, 10, 11
Deut. 9:22; Is. 10; Heb. 3:16
x. 17:6; Deut. Ps. 78:41, 56; 106:14; 1 Cor. 9 [b]Num. 11:4
x. 16:3; Num. 21:5; Ps. 23:5
., *flesh* [a]Num. Ps. 78:15, 16 [b]Num. 11:18
[1]Or, *became* *ed* [a]Num. 11:1
ut. 1:32; 9:23; Heb. 3:18
7:11; Mal. 3:10
Lit., *grain* [a]Ex. . 105:40; John 6:31
t., *mighty ones* *ovision* [3]Lit., *to* *ation* [a]Ex. 16:3
strength [a]Num. 11:31
Lit., *flesh* [a]Ex. :13; Ps. 105:40
28 [1]Lit., *His*
Num. 11:19, 20

And their desire He gave to them.
30 [1]Before they had satisfied their desire,
[a]While their food was in their mouths,
31 The [a]anger of God rose against them,
And killed [1]some of their [b]stoutest ones,
And [2]subdued the choice men of Israel.
32 In spite of all this they [a]still sinned,
And [b]did not believe in His wonderful works.
33 So He brought [a]their days to an end in [1]futility,
And their years in sudden terror.

34 When He killed them, then they [a]sought Him,
And returned and searched [b]diligently for God;
35 And they remembered that God was their [a]rock,
And the Most High God their [b]Redeemer.
36 But they [a]deceived Him with their mouth,
And [b]lied to Him with their tongue.
37 For their heart was not [a]steadfast toward Him,
Nor were they faithful in His covenant.
38 But He, being [a]compassionate, [1b]forgave *their* iniquity, and did not destroy *them*;
And often He [2c]restrained His anger,
And did not arouse all His wrath.
39 Thus [a]He remembered that they were but [b]flesh,
A [1c]wind that passes and does not return.

40 How often they [a]rebelled against Him in the wilderness,
And [b]grieved Him in the [c]desert!
41 And again and again they [1a]tempted God,
And pained the [b]Holy One of Israel.
42 They [a]did not remember [b]His [1]power,
The day when He [c]redeemed them from the adversary,
43 When He performed His [a]signs in Egypt,
And His [b]marvels in the field of Zoan,
44 And [a]turned their rivers to blood,
And their streams, they could not drink.
45 He sent among them swarms of [a]flies, which devoured them,
And [b]frogs which destroyed them.
46 He gave also their crops to the [a]grasshopper,
And the product of their labor to the [b]locust.
47 He [1]destroyed their vines with [a]hailstones,
And their sycamore trees with frost.
48 He gave over their [a]cattle also to the hailstones,
And their herds to bolts of lightning.
49 He [a]sent upon them His burning anger,
Fury, and indignation, and trouble,
[1]A band of destroying angels.
50 He leveled a path for His anger;
He did not spare their soul from death,
But [a]gave over their life to the plague,
51 And [a]smote all the first-born in Egypt,
The [b]first *issue* of their virility in the tents of [c]Ham.
52 But He [a]led forth His own people like sheep,
And guided them in the wilderness [b]like a flock;

30 [1]Lit., *The estranged fr* 11:33

31 [1]Lit., *amo ones* [2]Lit., *ca bow down* [a]N 34; Job 20:23

32 [a]Num. ch 17 [b]Num. 14 78:11

33 [1]Lit., *vani breath* [a]Num

34 [a]Num. 21 5:15 [b]Ps. 63:

35 [a]Deut. 32 15:13; Deut. 9 74:2; Is. 41:14

36 [a]Ex. 24:7, 33:31 [b]Ex. 32 57:11

37 [a]Ps. 51:10 Acts 8:21

38 [1]Lit., *cove atoned for* [2]Li *away* [a]Ex. 34 14:18-20 [c]Is.

39 [1]Or, *breat* 10:9; Ps. 103: 6:3 [c]Job 7:7, 103:14; James

40 [a]Ps. 95:8, 107:11; Heb. 3 95:10; Is. 63:1 4:30 [c]Ps. 106

41 [1]Or, *put G test* [a]Num. 14 [b]2 Kin. 19:22;

42 [1]Lit., *hand* 8:34 [b]Ps. 44:3 106:10

43 [a]Ps. 105:27 4:21; 7:3

44 [a]Ex. 7:20; P

45 [a]Ex. 8:24; P 105:31 [b]Ex. 8: 105:30

46 [a]1 Kin. 8:37 105:34 [b]Ex. 10

47 [1]Lit., *was k* 9:23-25; Ps. 10

48 [a]Ex. 9:19

49 [1]Lit., *A depu angels of evil* [a]

50 [a]Ex. 12:29,

51 [a]Ex. 12:29; 105:36; 135:8; [b]Gen. 49:3 [c]Ps. 27; 106:22

52 [a]Ex. 15:22 77:20

53 And He led them [a]safely, so that they did not fear;
But [b]the sea engulfed their enemies.

54 So [a]He brought them to His holy [1]land,
To this [2b]hill country [c]which His right hand had gained.
55 He also [a]drove out the nations before them,
And He [b]apportioned them for an inheritance by measurement,
And made the tribes of Israel dwell in their tents.
56 Yet they [1a]tempted and [b]rebelled against the Most High God,
And did not keep His testimonies,
57 But turned back and [a]acted treacherously like their fathers;
They [b]turned aside like a treacherous bow.
58 For they [a]provoked Him with their [b]high places,
And [c]aroused His jealousy with their [d]graven images.
59 When God heard, He [1]was filled with [a]wrath,
And greatly [b]abhorred Israel;
60 So that He [a]abandoned the [b]dwelling place at Shiloh,
The tent [1]which He had pitched among men,
61 And gave up His [a]strength to captivity,
And His glory [b]into the hand of the adversary.
62 He also [a]delivered His people to the sword,
And [1]was filled with wrath at His inheritance.
63 [a]Fire devoured [1]His young men;
And [1]His [b]virgins had no wedding songs.
64 [1]His [a]priests fell by the sword;
And [1]His [b]widows could not weep.

65 Then the Lord [a]awoke as *if from* sleep,
Like a [b]warrior [1]overcome by wine.
66 And He [1a]drove His adversaries backward;
He put on them an everlasting reproach.
67 He also [a]rejected the tent of Joseph,
And did not choose the tribe of Ephraim,
68 But chose the tribe of Judah,
Mount [a]Zion which He loved.
69 And He [a]built His sanctuary like the heights,
Like the earth which He has founded forever.
70 He also [a]chose David His servant,
And took him from the sheepfolds;
71 From [1a]the care of the [2]ewes [b]with suckling lambs He brought him,
To [c]shepherd Jacob His people,
And Israel [d]His inheritance.
72 So he shepherded them according to the [a]integrity of his heart,
And guided them with his skillful hands.

Psalm 79

A Psalm of Asaph.

79 O God, the [a]nations have [1]invaded [b]Thine inheritance;
They have defiled Thy [c]holy temple;
They have [d]laid Jerusalem in ruins.
2 They have given the [a]dead bodies of Thy servants for food to the birds of the heavens,
The flesh of Thy godly ones to the beasts of the earth.

14:19, 20 [b]Ex. 28; Ps. 106:11
54 [1]Lit., *border,* [2]Or, *mountain* :17 [b]Ps. 68:16; 11:9 [c]Ps. 44:3
1. 11:16-23; Ps. osh. 13:7; 23:4; 105:11; 135:12
, put to the test s. 78:18 [b]Judg. 1-13; Ps. 78:40
Ezek. 20:27, 28 [b]Hos. 7:16
eut. 4:25; Judg. ; 1 Kin. 14:9; Is. ev. 26:30; 1 Kin. 2 Kin. 16:4; Jer. Deut. 32:16, 21; 4:22 [d]Ex. 20:4; 26:1; Deut. 4:25
59 [1]Or, *became ed* [a]Deut. 1:34; s. 106:40 [b]Lev. 30; Deut. 32:19; Amos 6:8
[1]Some ancient s read *where He* Sam. 4:11; Ps. 57; Jer. 7:12, 14; 6:6 [b]Josh. 18:1
[a]Ps. 63:2; 132:8 [b]1 Sam. 4:17
62 [1]Or, *became ed* [a]Judg. 20:21; 1 Sam. 4:10
[1]Or, *their* [a]Num. 21:28; Is. 26:11; 48:45 [b]Jer. 7:34; 16:9; Lam. 2:21
Or, *their* [a]1 Sam. 2:18 [b]Job 27:15; Ezek. 24:23
[1]Or, *sobered up* Ps. 44:23; 73:20 [b]Is. 42:13
, smote [a]1 Sam. 5:6
67 [a]Ps. 78:60
[a]Ps. 87:2; 132:13
69 [a]1 Kin. 6:1-38
1 Sam. 16:11, 12
t., *following* [2]Lit., *which gave suck,* [a]2 Sam. 7:8; Is. 0:11 [b]Gen. 33:13 . 5:2; 1 Chr. 11:2; 8:9 [d]1 Sam. 10:1
72 [a]1 Kin. 9:4
1 [1]Lit., *come into* n. 1:10 [b]Ps. 74:2 s. 74:3, 7 [d]2 Kin. 25:9, 10; 2 Chr. 17-19; Jer. 26:18; 2:12-14; Mic. 3:12
[a]Deut. 28:26; Jer. 16:4; 19:7; 34:20

3 They have poured out their blood like water round about
Jerusalem;
And there was [a]no one to bury them.
4 We have become a [a]reproach to our neighbors,
A scoffing and derision to those around us.
5 [a]How long, O LORD? Wilt Thou be angry forever?
Will Thy [b]jealousy [c]burn like fire?
6 [a]Pour out Thy wrath upon the nations which [b]do not know Thee,
And upon the kingdoms which [c]do not call upon Thy name.
7 For they have [a]devoured Jacob,
And [b]laid waste his [1]habitation.

8 [a]Do not remember [1]the iniquities of *our* forefathers against us;
Let Thy compassion come quickly to [b]meet us;
For we are [c]brought very low.
9 [a]Help us, O God of our salvation, for the glory of [b]Thy name;
And deliver us, and [1c]forgive our sins, [d]for Thy name's sake.
10 [a]Why should the nations say, "Where is their God?"
Let there be known among the nations in our sight,
[b]Vengeance for the blood of Thy servants, which has been shed.
11 Let [a]the groaning of the prisoner come before Thee;
According to the greatness of Thy [1]power preserve [2]those who
are [a]doomed to die.
12 And return to our neighbors [a]sevenfold [b]into their bosom
[1]The [c]reproach with which they have reproached Thee, O Lord.
13 So we Thy people and the [a]sheep of Thy [1]pasture
Will [b]give thanks to Thee forever;
To all generations we will [c]tell of Thy praise.

Psalm 80

For the choir director; *set to* [+]El Shoshannim; [•]Eduth. A Psalm of Asaph.

80 Oh, give ear, [a]Shepherd of Israel,
Thou who dost lead [b]Joseph like a flock;
Thou who [c]art enthroned *above* the cherubim, shine forth!
2 Before [a]Ephraim and Benjamin and Manasseh, [b]stir up Thy
power,
And come to save us!
3 O God, [a]restore us,
And [b]cause Thy face to shine *upon us*, [1]and we will be saved.

4 O [a]LORD God *of* hosts,
[b]How long wilt Thou [1]be angry with the prayer of Thy people?
5 Thou hast fed them with the [a]bread of tears,
And Thou hast made them to drink tears in [1]large measure.
6 Thou dost make us [1]an object of contention [a]to our neighbors;
And our enemies laugh among themselves.
7 O God *of* hosts, restore us,
And cause Thy face to shine *upon us*, [1]and we will be saved.

8 Thou didst remove a [a]vine from Egypt;
Thou didst [b]drive out the [1]nations, and didst [c]plant it.
9 Thou didst [a]clear *the ground* before it,
And it [b]took deep root and filled the land.
10 The mountains were covered with its shadow;

3 [a]Jer. 14:16; 1

4 [a]Ps. 44:13; 8
9:16

5 [a]Ps. 13:1; 74
85:5; 89:46 [b]De
29:20; Ezek. 36
38:19 [c]Ps. 89:4
3:8

6 [a]Ps. 69:24; Je
10:25; Ezek. 21
Zeph. 3:8 [b]1 Th
4:5; 2 Thess. 1:
14:4; 53:4

7 [1]Lit., *pasture*
53:4 [b]2 Chr. 36
39:8

8 [1]Or, our *forme*
iniquities [a]Ps. 1
64:9 [b]Ps. 21:3
28:43; Ps. 116:6
Is. 26:5

9 [1]Lit., *cover ov*
atone for [a]2 Chr
[b]Ps. 31:3 [c]Ps. 2
65:3 [d]Jer. 14:7

10 [a]Ps. 42:10;
[b]Ps. 94:1, 2

11 [1]Lit., *arm* [2]Li
children of death
102:20

12 [1]Lit., *Their*
4:15; Lev. 26:21,
12:6; 119:164; P
6:31; 24:16; Is. 3
[b]Ps. 35:13; Is. 65
Jer. 32:18; Luke
[c]Ps. 74:10, 18, 2

13 [1]Or, *pasturin*
74:1; 95:7; 100:3
44:8 [c]Ps. 89:1; I

[+]Possibly, *to the*
[•]Lit., *A testimony*

80:1 [a]Ps. 23:1
77:15; 78:67; Am
5:15 [c]Ex. 25:22;
4:4; 2 Sam. 6:2;

2 [a]Num. 2:18-24
35:23

3 [1]Or, *that we m*
60:1; 80:7, 19; 85
126:1; Lam. 5:21
6:25; Ps. 4:6; 31

4 [1]Lit., *smoke ag*
[a]Ps. 59:5; 84:8 [b]
79:5; 85:5

5 [1]Lit., *a third pa*
[a]Ps. 42:3; 102:9;
30:20

6 [1]Lit., *a strife to*
44:13; 79:4

7 [1]Or, *that we ma*

8 [1]Or, *Gentiles* [a]
80:15; Is. 5:1, 2, 7
2:21; 12:10; Ezek
19:10 [b]Josh. 13:
2 Chr. 20:7; Ps. 4
Acts 7:45 [c]Jer. 1
32:41; Ezek. 17:2
Amos 9:15

9 [a]Ex. 23:28; Jos
24:12; Is. 5:2 [b]H

And [1]the cedars of God with its [a]boughs.
11 It was sending out its branches [a]to the sea,
And its shoots to the River.
12 Why hast Thou [a]broken down its [1]hedges,
So that all who pass *that* way pick its *fruit?*
13 A boar from the forest [a]eats it away,
And whatever moves in the field feeds on it.

14 O God *of* hosts, [a]turn again now, we beseech Thee;
[b]Look down from heaven and see, and take care of this vine,
15 Even the [1a]shoot which Thy right hand has planted,
And on the [2]son whom Thou hast [3]strengthened for Thyself.
16 It is [a]burned with fire, it is cut down;
They perish at the [b]rebuke of Thy countenance.
17 Let [a]Thy hand be upon the man of Thy right hand,
Upon the son of man whom Thou [b]didst make strong for
Thyself.
18 Then we shall not [a]turn back from Thee;
[b]Revive us, and we will call upon Thy name.
19 O LORD God of hosts, [a]restore us;
Cause Thy face to shine *upon us,* [1]and we will be saved.

Psalm 81

For the choir director; [+]on the Gittith. *A Psalm* of Asaph.

81 [a]Sing for joy to God our [b]strength;
Shout [c]joyfully to the [d]God of Jacob.
2 Raise a song, strike [a]the timbrel,
The sweet sounding [b]lyre with the [c]harp.
3 Blow the trumpet at the [a]new moon,
At the full moon, on our [b]feast day.
4 For it is a statute for Israel,
An ordinance of the God of Jacob.
5 He established it for a testimony in Joseph,
When he [1a]went throughout the land of Egypt.
I heard a [b]language that I did not know:

6 "I [1a]relieved his shoulder of the burden,
His hands were freed from the [2]basket.
7 "You [a]called in trouble, and I rescued you;
I [b]answered you in the hiding place of thunder;
I proved you at the [c]waters of Meribah. [1]Selah.
8 "[a]Hear, O My people, and I will [1]admonish you;
O Israel, if you [b]would listen to Me!
9 "Let there be no [a]strange god among you;
Nor shall you worship any foreign god.
10 "[a]I, the LORD, am your God,
Who brought you up from the land of Egypt;
[b]Open your mouth wide and I will [c]fill it.

11 "But My people [a]did not listen to My voice;
And Israel did not [1]obey Me.
12 "So I [a]gave [1]them over to the stubbornness of their heart,
To walk in their own devices.
13 "Oh that My people [a]would listen to Me,

ts boughs are cedars of God [a]Gen. 49:22
11 [a]Ps. 72:8
walls, fences 89:40; Is. 5:5
13 [a]Jer. 5:6
s. 90:13 [b]Ps. 2:19; Is. 63:15
[1]Or, root [2]Or, : branch [3]Or, red [a]Ps. 80:8
Chr. 36:19; Ps. er. 52:13 [b]Ps. 39:11; 76:6
s. 89:21 [b]Ps. 80:15
:5 [b]Ps. 71:20
r, that we may [a]Ps. 80:3
r, according to
. 51:14; 59:16; [b]Ps. 46:1 [c]Ps. 95:2; 98:4 [d]Ps. 84:8
5:20; Ps. 149:3 :3; 98:5; 147:7 s. 108:2; 144:9
m. 10:10 [b]Lev. 23:24
, went out over [b]Deut. 28:49; 114:1; Jer. 5:15
t., removed his from [2]Or, brick [a]Is. 9:4; 10:27
lah may mean: , Crescendo or l interlude [a]Ex. 4:10; Ps. 50:15 :19; 20:18 [c]Ex. um. 20:13; Ps. 95:8
Or, bear witness [a]Ps. 50:7 [b]Ps. 95:7
20:3; Deut. 5:7; 2; Ps. 44:20; Is. 43:12
20:2; Deut. 5:6 9:23 [c]Ps. 37:4; 78:25; 107:9
, yield to [a]Deut. :15; Ps. 106:25
., him [a]Job 8:4; ; Rom. 1:24, 26
[a]Deut. 5:29; Ps. 81:8; Is. 48:18

That Israel would [b]walk in My ways!
14 "I would quickly [a]subdue their enemies,
And [b]turn My hand against their adversaries.
15 "[a]Those who hate the LORD would [b]pretend obedience to Him;
And their time *of punishment* would be forever.
16 "[1]But I would feed you with the [2a]finest of the wheat;
And with [b]honey from the rock I would satisfy you."

Psalm 82

A Psalm of Asaph.

82 God takes His [a]stand in [1]His own congregation;
He [b]judges in the midst of the [2c]rulers.
2 How long will you [a]judge unjustly,
And [b]show partiality to the wicked? [1]Selah.
3 [a]Vindicate the weak and fatherless;
Do justice to the afflicted and destitute.
4 [a]Rescue the weak and needy;
Deliver *them* out of the hand of the wicked.

5 They [a]do not know nor do they understand;
They [b]walk about in darkness;
All the [c]foundations of the earth are shaken.
6 [1]I [a]said, "You are gods,
And all of you are [b]sons of the Most High.
7 "Nevertheless [a]you will die like men,
And fall like *any* [b]one of the princes."
8 [a]Arise, O God, [b]judge the earth!
For it is Thou who dost [c]possess all the nations.

Psalm 83

A Song, a Psalm of Asaph.

83 O God, [a]do not remain quiet;
[b]Do not be silent and, O God, do not be still.
2 For, behold, Thine enemies [a]make an uproar;
And [b]those who hate Thee have [1c]exalted themselves.
3 They [a]make shrewd plans against Thy people,
And [1]conspire together against [b]Thy [2]treasured ones.
4 They have said, "Come, and [a]let us wipe them out [1]as a nation,
That the [b]name of Israel be remembered no more."
5 For they have [1a]conspired together with one mind;
Against Thee do they make a covenant:
6 The tents of [a]Edom and the [b]Ishmaelites;
[c]Moab, and the [d]Hagrites;
7 [a]Gebal, and [b]Ammon, and [c]Amalek;
[d]Philistia with the inhabitants of [e]Tyre;
8 [a]Assyria also has joined with them;
They have become [1]a help to the [b]children of Lot. [2]Selah.

9 Deal with them [a]as with Midian,
As [b]with Sisera *and* Jabin, at the torrent of Kishon,
10 Who were destroyed at En-dor,
Who [a]became as dung for the ground.
11 Make their nobles like [a]Oreb and Zeeb,

13 [b]Ps. 128:1 42:24; Jer. 7:2
14 [a]Ps. 18:47 [b]Amos 1:8
15 [a]Rom. 1:3 18:44; 66:3
16 [1]Lit., *He w him* [2]Lit., *fat* 32:14; Ps. 147 [b]Deut. 32:13
82:1 [1]Lit., *the congregation* [2]Lit., *gods* [a]Is. [b]2 Chr. 19:6; P [c]Ex. 21:6; 22:8
2 [1]*Selah* may *Pause, Cresc Musical interlu* 58:1 [b]Deut. 1 18:5
3 [a]Deut. 24:17 10:18; Is. 11:4 22:16
4 [a]Job 29:12
5 [a]Ps. 14:4; Je Mic. 3:1 [b]Prov 59:9; Jer. 23:1 11:3
6 [1]Lit., *I, on m* [a]Ps. 82:1; John [b]Ps. 89:26
7 [a]Job 21:32; 49:12; Ezek. 3 83:11
8 [a]Ps. 12:5 [b]P 96:13 [c]Ps. 2:8 11:15
83:1 [a]Ps. 28:1 [b]Ps. 109:1
2 [1]Lit., *lifted u head* [a]Ps. 2:1; 17:12 [b]Ps. 81: [c]Judg. 8:28; Ze
3 [1]Or, *consult hidden ones* [a] Is. 29:15 [b]Ps. 31:20
4 [1]Lit., *from* [a] Ps. 74:8; Jer. 4 41:5; Jer. 11:19
5 [1]Or, *consulte* 2:2; Dan. 6:7
6 [a]2 Chr. 20:10 137:7 [b]Gen. 2 [c]2 Chr. 20:10 5:10
7 [a]Josh. 13:5; 27:9 [b]2 Chr. 20 [c]1 Sam. 15:2 4:1; 29:1 [e]Ezek Amos 1:9
8 [1]Lit., *an arm* may mean: *Pa Crescendo* or *interlude* [a]2 Kin [b]Deut. 2:9
9 [a]Judg. 7:1-24 4:7, 15, 21-24
10 [a]Zeph. 1:17
11 [a]Judg. 7:25

And all their princes like [b]Zebah and Zalmunna,
12 Who said, "[a]Let us possess for ourselves
The [b]pastures of God."

13 O my God, make them like the [1a]whirling dust;
Like [b]chaff before the wind.
14 Like [a]fire that burns the forest,
And like a flame that [b]sets the mountains on fire,
15 So pursue them [a]with Thy tempest,
And terrify them with Thy storm.
16 [a]Fill their faces with dishonor,
That they may seek Thy name, O LORD.
17 Let them be [a]ashamed and dismayed forever;
And let them be humiliated and perish,
18 That they may [a]know that [b]Thou alone, whose name is the LORD,
Art the [c]Most High over all the earth.

Psalm 84

For the choir director; [+]on the Gittith. A Psalm of the sons of Korah.

84 How lovely are Thy [a]dwelling places,
O LORD of hosts!
2 My [a]soul longed and even yearned for the courts of the LORD;
My heart and my flesh sing for joy to the [b]living God.
3 The bird also has found a house,
And the swallow a nest for herself, where she may lay her young,
Even Thine [a]altars, O LORD of hosts,
[b]My King and my God.
4 How [a]blessed are those who dwell in Thy house!
They are [b]ever praising Thee. [1]Selah.

5 How blessed is the man whose [a]strength is in Thee;
In [1]whose heart are the [b]highways *to Zion*!
6 Passing through the valley of [1]Baca, they make it a [2]spring,
The [a]early rain also covers it with blessings.
7 They [a]go from strength to strength,
[1]*Every one of them* [b]appears before God in Zion.

8 O [a]LORD God of hosts, hear my prayer;
Give ear, O [b]God of Jacob! Selah.
9 Behold our [a]shield, O God,
And look upon the face of [b]Thine anointed.
10 For [a]a day in Thy courts is better than a thousand *outside*.
I would rather stand at the threshold of the house of my God,
Than dwell in the tents of wickedness.
11 For the LORD God is [a]a sun and [b]shield;
The LORD gives grace and [c]glory;
[d]No good thing does He withhold [1]from those who walk [2]uprightly.
12 O LORD of hosts,
How [a]blessed is the man who trusts in Thee!

11 [b]Judg. 8:12, 21
[a]2 Chr. 20:11 [b]Ps. 132:13
3 [1]Or, *tumbleweed* 17:13 [b]Job 21:18; 35:5; Is. 40:24; Jer. 13:24
s. 9:18 [b]Ex. 19:18; Deut. 32:22
[a]Job 9:17; Ps. 58:9
16 [a]Job 10:15; Ps. 109:29; 132:18
17 [a]Ps. 35:4; 70:2
8 [a]Ps. 59:13 [b]Ps. :10; Is. 45:21 [c]Ps. 9:2; 18:13; 97:9
[+]Or, *according to*
1 [a]Ps. 43:3; 132:5
[a]Ps. 42:1, 2; 63:1 [b]Ps. 42:2
[a]Ps. 43:4 [b]Ps. 5:2
[1]*Selah* may mean: *use, Crescendo* or *ical interlude* [a]Ps. 65:4 [b]Ps. 42:5, 11
it., their [a]Ps. 81:1 86:11; 122:1; Jer. 31:6
obably, Weeping; Balsam trees [2]Or, *ce of springs* [a]Ps. 107:35; Joel 2:23
7 [1]Some ancient *ns read The God ds will be seen in n.* [a]Prov. 4:18; Is. John 1:16; 2 Cor. [b]Ex. 34:23; Deut. 16:16; Ps. 42:2
s. 59:5; 80:4; 84:1 [b]Ps. 81:1
ien. 15:1; Ps. 3:3; 7; 59:11; 115:9-11 am. 16:6; 2 Sam. 1; Ps. 2:2; 132:17
10 [a]Ps. 27:4
it., with regard to with integrity [a]Is. 20; Mal. 4:2; Rev. [b]Gen. 15:1 [c]Ps. 5:9 [d]Ps. 34:9, 10
2 [a]Ps. 2:12; 40:4

Psalm 85

For the choir director. A Psalm of the sons of Korah.

85 O LORD, Thou didst show [a]favor to Thy land;
Thou didst [1b]restore the captivity of Jacob.
2 Thou didst [a]forgive the iniquity of Thy people;
Thou didst [b]cover all their sin. [1]Selah.
3 Thou didst [a]withdraw all Thy fury;
Thou didst [b]turn away from Thy burning anger.

4 [a]Restore us, O God of our salvation,
And [b]cause Thine indignation toward us to cease.
5 Wilt [a]Thou be angry with us forever?
Wilt Thou prolong Thine anger to [1]all generations?
6 Wilt Thou not Thyself [1a]revive us again,
That Thy people may [b]rejoice in Thee?
7 Show us Thy lovingkindness, O LORD,
And [a]grant us Thy salvation.

8 [1]I will hear what God the LORD will say;
For He will [a]speak peace to His people, [2]to His godly ones;
But let them not [b]turn back to [3]folly.
9 Surely [a]His salvation is near to those who [1]fear Him,
That [b]glory may dwell in our land.
10 [a]Lovingkindness and [1]truth have met together;
[b]Righteousness and peace have kissed each other.
11 [1]Truth [a]springs from the earth;
And righteousness looks down from heaven.
12 Indeed, [a]the LORD will give what is good;
And our [b]land will yield its produce.
13 [a]Righteousness will go before Him,
And will make His footsteps into a way.

Psalm 86

A Prayer of David.

86 [a]Incline Thine ear, O LORD, *and* answer me;
For I am [b]afflicted and needy.
2 [a]Do preserve my [1]soul, for I am a [b]godly man;
O Thou my God, save Thy servant who [c]trusts in Thee.
3 Be [a]gracious to me, O Lord,
For [b]to Thee I cry all day long.
4 Make glad the soul of Thy servant,
For to Thee, O Lord, [a]I lift up my soul.
5 For Thou, Lord, art [a]good, and [b]ready to forgive,
And [c]abundant in lovingkindness to all who call upon Thee.
6 [a]Give ear, O LORD, to my prayer;
And give heed to the voice of my supplications!
7 In [a]the day of my trouble I shall call upon Thee,
For [b]Thou wilt answer me.
8 There is [a]no one like Thee among the gods, O Lord;
Nor are there any works [b]like Thine.
9 [a]All nations whom Thou hast made shall come and worship
before Thee, O Lord;
And they shall glorify Thy name.

85:1 [1]*Or, res fortunes* [a]Ps. 106:4 [b]Ezra 14:7; 126:1; J Ezek. 39:25; Joel 3:1
2 [1]*Selah* may *Pause, Cresc Musical interlu* 14:19; 1 Kin. 8 78:38; 103:3; [b]Ps. 32:1
3 [a]Ps. 78:38; [b]Ex. 32:12; De Ps. 106:23; Jo
4 [a]Ps. 80:3,7 9:16
5 [1]Lit., *genera generation* [a]P 79:5; 80:4
6 [1]Or, *bring to* 71:20; 80:18 90:14; 149:2
7 [a]Ps. 106:4
8 [1]Or, *Let me* [2]Lit., *even to* [3]*stupidity* [a]Ps. Hag. 2:9; Zech [b]Ps. 78:57; 2 P
9 [1]Or, *reveren* 34:18; Is. 46:1 84:11; Hag. 2:7 2:5; John 1:14
10 [1]Or, *faithfu* [a]Ps. 25:10; 89: 3:3 [b]Ps. 72:3;
11 [1]Or, *Faithfu* [a]Is. 45:8
12 [a]Ps. 84:11; 1:17 [b]Lev. 26:4 67:6; Ezek. 34: 8:12
13 [a]Ps. 89:14
86:1 [a]Ps. 17:6; 71:2 [b]Ps. 40:17
2 [1]Or, *life* [a]Ps. [b]Ps. 4:3; 50:5 31:14; 56:4
3 [a]Ps. 4:1; 57:1 25:5; 88:9
4 [a]Ps. 25:1; 14
5 [a]Ps. 25:8 [b]Ps [c]Ex. 34:6; Neh. 103:8; 145:8; Jo Jon. 4:2
6 [a]Ps. 55:1
7 [a]Ps. 50:15; 7 17:6
8 [a]Ex. 15:11; 2 7:22; 1 Kin. 8:23 89:6; Jer. 10:6 3:24
9 [a]Ps. 22:27; 66 66:23; Rev. 15:4

10 For Thou art [a]great and [b]doest [1]wondrous deeds;
Thou alone [c]art God.

11 [a]Teach me Thy way, O LORD;
I will walk in Thy truth;
[b]Unite my heart to fear Thy name.
12 I will [a]give thanks to Thee, O Lord my God, with all my heart,
And will glorify Thy name forever.
13 For Thy lovingkindness toward me is great,
And Thou hast [a]delivered my soul from the [1]depths of [2]Sheol.

14 O God, arrogant men have [a]risen up against me,
And [1]a band of violent men have sought my [2]life,
And they have not set Thee before them.
15 But Thou, O Lord, art a God [a]merciful and gracious,
Slow to anger and abundant in lovingkindness and [1]truth.
16 [a]Turn to me, and be gracious to me;
Oh [b]grant Thy strength to Thy servant,
And save the [c]son of Thy handmaid.
17 [a]Show me a sign for good,
That those who hate me may [b]see *it*, and be ashamed,
Because Thou, O LORD, [c]hast helped me and comforted me.

Psalm 87

A Psalm of the sons of Korah. A Song.

87 His [a]foundation is in the holy mountains.
2 The LORD [a]loves the gates of Zion
More than all the *other* dwelling places of Jacob.
3 [a]Glorious things are spoken of you,
O [b]city of God. [1]Selah.
4 "I shall mention [1a]Rahab and Babylon [2]among those who know Me;
Behold, Philistia and [b]Tyre with [3c]Ethiopia:
'This one was born there.' "
5 But of Zion it shall be said, "This one and that one were born in her";
And the Most High Himself will [a]establish her.
6 The LORD shall count when He [a]registers the peoples,
"This one was born there." Selah.
7 Then those who [a]sing as well as those who [1b]play the flutes *shall* say,
"All my [c]springs *of joy* are in you."

Psalm 88

A Song. A Psalm of the sons of Korah. For the choir director; according to Mahalath Leannoth. A •Maskil of Heman +the Ezrahite.

88 O LORD, the [a]God of my salvation,
I have [b]cried out by day and in the night before Thee.
2 Let my prayer [a]come before Thee;
[b]Incline Thine ear to my cry!
3 For my [a]soul has [1]had enough troubles,
And [b]my life has drawn near to [2]Sheol.
4 I am reckoned among those who [a]go down to the pit;

miracles [a]Ps. …Ex. 15:11; Ps. …; 77:14; 136:4 …:4; 32:39; Ps. …37:16; 44:6, 8; …29; 1 Cor. 8:4
…:5 [b]Jer. 32:39
12 [a]Ps. 111:1
…, *lowest Sheol* …e nether world [a]Ps. 30:3
…, *an assembly* …*soul* [a]Ps. 54:3
…Or, *faithfulness* [a]Ps. 86:5
…Ps. 25:16 [b]Ps. …35 [c]Ps. 116:16
…Judg. 6:17; Ps. …22 [b]Ps. 112:10 [c]Ps. 118:13
[a]Ps. 78:69; Is. 28:16
[a]Ps. 78:67, 68
…lah may mean: …, *Crescendo* or …al *interlude* [a]Is. … [b]Ps. 46:4; 48:8
…, Egypt [2]Or, *as* …ush [a]Job 9:13; …10; Is. 19:23-25 …5:12 [c]Ps. 68:31
5 [a]Ps. 48:8
…s. 69:28; Is. 4:3; Ezek. 13:9
[1]Or, *dance* [a]Ps. …; 149:3 [b]2 Sam. …; Ps. 30:11 [c]Ps. 36:9
•Possibly, …ontemplative, or …dactic, or *Skillful* …alm +1 Kin. 4:31; …2:6; Ps. 89: title
[a]Ps. 24:5; 27:9 …22:2; 86:3; Luke 18:7
… 18:6 [b]Ps. 31:2; 86:1
…Or, *been satisfied* … [2]I.e., the nether … [a]Ps. 107:26 [b]Ps. 107:18; 116:3
[a]Ps. 28:1; 143:7

I have become like a man [b]without strength,
5 [1]Forsaken [a]among the dead,
Like the slain who lie in the grave,
Whom Thou dost remember no more,
And they are [b]cut off from Thy hand.
6 Thou hast put me in [a]the lowest pit,
In [b]dark places, in the [c]depths.
7 Thy wrath [a]has rested upon me,
And Thou hast afflicted me with [b]all Thy waves. [1]Selah.
8 Thou hast removed [a]my acquaintances far from me;
Thou hast made me an [1b]object of loathing to them;
I am [c]shut up and cannot go out.
9 My [a]eye has wasted away because of affliction;
I have [b]called upon Thee every day, O LORD;
I have [c]spread out my [1]hands to Thee.

10 Wilt Thou perform wonders for the dead?
Will [a]the [1]departed spirits rise *and* praise Thee? Selah.
11 Will Thy lovingkindness be declared in the grave,
Thy faithfulness in [1]Abaddon?
12 Will Thy wonders be made known in the [a]darkness?
And Thy [1]righteousness in the land of forgetfulness?

13 But I, O LORD, have cried out [a]to Thee for help,
And [b]in the morning my prayer comes before Thee.
14 O LORD, why [a]dost Thou reject my soul?
Why dost Thou [b]hide Thy face from me?
15 I was afflicted and [a]about to die from my youth on;
I suffer [b]Thy terrors; I am [1]overcome.
16 Thy [a]burning anger has passed over me;
Thy terrors have [1b]destroyed me.
17 They have [a]surrounded me [b]like water all day long;
They have [c]encompassed me altogether.
18 Thou hast removed [a]lover and friend far from me;
My acquaintances are *in* darkness.

Psalm 89

A •Maskil of △Ethan +the Ezrahite.

89 I will [a]sing of the lovingkindness of the LORD forever;
To all generations I will [b]make known Thy [c]faithfulness with my mouth.
2 For I have said, "[a]Lovingkindness will be built up forever;
In the heavens Thou wilt establish Thy [b]faithfulness."
3 "I have made a covenant with [a]My chosen;
I have [b]sworn to David My servant,
4 I will establish your [a]seed forever,
And build up your [b]throne to all generations." [1]Selah.

5 And the [a]heavens will praise Thy wonders, O LORD;
Thy faithfulness also [b]in the assembly of the [c]holy ones.
6 For [a]who in the skies is comparable to the LORD?
Who among the [1b]sons of the mighty is like the LORD,
7 A God [a]greatly feared in the council of the [b]holy ones,
And [c]awesome above all those who are around Him?

4 [b]Job 29:12;
5 [1]Lit., *A freed among the de* 31:12 [b]Ps. 31 53:8
6 [a]Ps. 86:13; 3:55 [b]Ps. 143 69:15
7 [1]*Selah* may *Pause, Cresce Musical interlu* 32:4; 39:10 [b]P
8 [1]Lit., *abomir them* [a]Job 19 Ps. 31:11; 142 30:10 [c]Ps. 142 32:2; 36:5
9 [1]Lit., *palms* 31:9 [b]Ps. 22:2 [c]Job 11:13; Ps
10 [1]Or, *ghosts* [a]Ps. 6:5; 30:9
11 [1]I.e., place destruction
12 [1]I.e., faithfu His gracious pr [a]Job 10:21; Ps.
13 [a]Ps. 30:2 [b] 119:147
14 [a]Ps. 43:2; 4 13:24; Ps. 13:1
15 [1]Or, *embarr* [a]Prov. 24:11 [b]J 31:23
16 [1]Or, *silence* [a]2 Chr. 28:11; Is Lam. 1:12 [b]Lan Ezek. 37:11
17 [a]Ps. 118:10- 124:4 [c]Ps. 17:1 22:12, 16
18 [a]Job 19:13; 88:8; 31:11; 38:
•Possibly, *Contemplative, Didactic,* or *Skil Psalm* △1 Kin. 4 +Ps. 88: title
89:1 [a]Ps. 59:16 [b]Ps. 40:10 [c]Ps. 88:11; 89:5, 8, 2 49; 92:2; 119:90 25:1; Lam. 3:23
2 [a]Ps. 103:17 [b] 36:5; 119:90
3 [a]1 Kin. 8:16 [b] 132:11
4 [1]*Selah* may m *Pause, Crescen Musical interlud* [a]2 Sam. 7:16 [b]2 7:13; Is. 9:7; Luk
5 [a]Ps. 19:1; 97:6 149:1 [c]Job 5:1
6 [1]Or, *sons of g* [a]Ps. 86:8; 113:5 29:1; 82:1
7 [a]Ps. 47:2; 68:3 76:7, 11 [b]Ps. 89 96:4

8 O LORD God of hosts, [a]who is like Thee, O mighty [1]LORD?
Thy faithfulness also surrounds Thee.
9 Thou dost rule the swelling of the sea;
When its waves rise, Thou [a]dost still them.
10 Thou Thyself didst crush [1a]Rahab like one who is slain;
Thou didst [b]scatter Thine enemies with [2]Thy mighty arm.

11 The [a]heavens are Thine, the earth also is Thine;
The [b]world and [1]all it contains, Thou hast founded them.
12 The [a]north and the south, Thou hast created them;
[b]Tabor and [c]Hermon [d]shout for joy at Thy name.
13 Thou hast [1]a strong arm;
Thy hand is mighty, Thy [a]right hand is exalted.
14 [a]Righteousness and justice are the foundation of Thy throne;
[b]Lovingkindness and [1]truth go before Thee.
15 How blessed are the people who know the [1a]joyful sound!
O LORD, they walk in the [b]light of Thy countenance.
16 In [a]Thy name they rejoice all the day,
And by Thy righteousness they are exalted.
17 For Thou art the glory of [a]their strength,
And by Thy favor [1]our [b]horn is exalted.
18 For our [a]shield belongs to the LORD,
[1]And our king to the [b]Holy One of Israel.

19 [1]Once Thou didst speak in vision to Thy godly [2]ones,
And didst say, "I have [3]given help to one who is [a]mighty;
I have exalted one [b]chosen from the people.
20 "I have [a]found David My servant;
With My holy [b]oil I have anointed him,
21 With whom [a]My hand will be established;
My arm also will [b]strengthen him.
22 "The enemy will not [1]deceive him,
Nor the [2a]son of wickedness afflict him.
23 "But I shall [a]crush his adversaries before him,
And strike those who hate him.
24 "And My [a]faithfulness and My lovingkindness will be with him,
And in My name his [b]horn will be exalted.
25 "I shall also set his hand [a]on the sea,
And his right hand on the rivers.
26 "He will cry to Me, 'Thou art [a]my Father,
My God, and the [b]rock of my salvation.'
27 "I also shall make him *My* [a]first-born,
The [b]highest of the kings of the earth.
28 "My [a]lovingkindness I will keep for him forever,
And My [b]covenant shall be confirmed to him.
29 "So I will establish his [1a]descendants forever,
And his [b]throne [c]as the days of heaven.

30 "If his sons [a]forsake My law,
And do not walk in My judgments,
31 If they [1]violate My statutes,
And do not keep My commandments,
32 Then I will visit their transgression with the [a]rod,
And their iniquity with stripes.

Heb., *YAH* [a]Ps. 35:10; 71:19
s. 65:7; 107:29
Egypt [2]Lit., *the Thy might* [a]Ps. 30:7; 51:9 [b]Ps. 14; 68:1; 144:6
[1]Lit., *its fulness* 1; 1 Chr. 29:11; 96:5 [b]Ps. 24:1
ob 26:7 [b]Josh. Judg. 4:6; Jer. Deut. 3:8; Josh. 2:1; Ps. 133:3; g 4:8 [d]Ps. 98:8
it., *an arm with ngth* [a]Ps. 98:1; 118:16
Or, *faithfulness* 97:2 [b]Ps. 85:13
[1]Or, *blast of the pet, shout of joy* ev. 23:24; Num.); Ps. 98:6 [b]Ps. 4:3; 67:1; 80:3; 90:8
16 [a]Ps. 105:3
other reading is *u dost exalt our* [a]Ps. 28:8 [b]Ps.); 92:10; 148:14
[1]Or, *Even to the One of Israel our* [a]Ps. 47:9 [b]Ps. 71:22; 78:41
[1]Or, *At that time* e mss. read *one laced help upon* n. 17:10 [b]1 Kin. 11:34; Ps. 78:70
[a]1 Sam. 13:14; 1-12; Acts 13:22 [b]1 Sam. 16:13
Ps. 18:35; 80:17 [b]Ps. 18:32
[1]Or, *exact usury him* [2]Or, *wicked* 2 Sam. 7:10; Ps. 125:3
[a]2 Sam. 7:9; Ps. 18:40
[a]Ps. 89:1 [b]Ps. 132:17
25 [a]Ps. 72:8
Sam. 7:14; 1 Chr. 22:10; Jer. 3:19 . 22:47; Ps. 95:1
Ex. 4:22; Ps. 2:7; :9; Col. 1:15, 18 . 24:7; Ps. 72:11; Rev. 19:16
[a]Ps. 89:33 [b]Ps. 89:3, 34
[1]Lit., *seed* [a]Ps. 89:4, 36 [b]1 Kin. 89:4; 132:12; Is. Jer. 33:17 [c]Deut. 11:21
[a]2 Sam. 7:14; Ps. 119:53
31 [1]Lit., *profane*
2 [a]Job 9:34; 21:9

33 "But I will not break off [a]My lovingkindness from him,
Nor deal falsely in My faithfulness.
34 "My [a]covenant I will not [1]violate,
Nor will I [b]alter [2]the utterance of My lips.
35 "[1]Once I have [a]sworn by My holiness;
I will not lie to David.
36 "His [1a]descendants shall endure forever,
And his [b]throne [c]as the sun before Me.
37 "It shall be established forever [a]like the moon,
And the [b]witness in the sky is faithful." [1]Selah.

38 But Thou hast [a]cast off and [b]rejected,
Thou hast been full of wrath [1]against Thine [c]anointed.
39 Thou hast [a]spurned the covenant of Thy servant;
Thou hast [b]profaned [c]his crown [1]in the dust.
40 Thou hast [a]broken down all his walls;
Thou hast [b]brought his strongholds to ruin.
41 [a]All who pass along the way plunder him;
He has become a [b]reproach to his neighbors.
42 Thou hast [a]exalted the right hand of his adversaries;
Thou hast [b]made all his enemies rejoice.
43 Thou dost also turn back the edge of his sword,
And hast [a]not made him stand in battle.
44 Thou hast made his [1a]splendor to cease,
And cast his throne to the ground.
45 Thou hast [a]shortened the days of his youth;
Thou hast [b]covered him with shame. Selah.

46 [a]How long, O LORD?
Wilt Thou hide Thyself forever?
Will Thy [b]wrath burn like fire?
47 [a]Remember [1]what my span of life is;
For what [b]vanity [2]Thou hast created all the sons of men!
48 What man can live and not [a]see death?
Can he [b]deliver his soul from the [1]power of [2]Sheol? Selah.

49 Where are Thy former lovingkindnesses, O Lord,
Which Thou didst [a]swear to David in Thy faithfulness?
50 Remember, O Lord, the [a]reproach of Thy servants;
[1]How I do bear in my bosom *the reproach of* all the many peoples,
51 With which [a]Thine enemies have reproached, O LORD,
With which they have reproached the footsteps of [b]Thine
anointed.

52 [a]Blessed be the LORD forever!
Amen and Amen.

BOOK 4

Psalm 90

A Prayer of [+]Moses the man of God.

90 LORD, Thou hast been our [1a]dwelling place in all generations.
2 Before [a]the mountains were born,
[1]Or Thou [b]didst give birth to the earth and the world,

33 [a]2 Sam. 7:1
34 [1]Lit., *profar* *that which goes* [a]Deut. 7:9; Jer. 21 [b]Num. 23:1
35 [1]Or, *One th* 60:6; Amos 4:2
36 [1]Lit., *seed* 89:29; Luke 1:3 72:5 [c]Ps. 72:17
37 [1]*Selah* may *Pause, Crescen* *Musical interluc* 72:5 [b]Job 16:1
38 [1]Lit., *with* [a]P [b]Deut. 32:19; 1 28:9 [c]Ps. 20:6; 89:20, 51
39 [1]Lit., *to the* [a]Ps. 78:59; Lam [b]Ps. 74:7 [c]Lam.
40 [a]Ps. 80:12 2:2, 5
41 [a]Ps. 80:12 44:13; 69:9, 19;
42 [a]Ps. 13:2 [b]P
43 [a]Ps. 44:10
44 [1]Lit., *clearne* *luster* [a]Ezek. 28
45 [a]Ps. 102:23 44:15; 71:13; 10
46 [a]Ps. 13:1; 44 [b]Ps. 79:5; 80:4
47 [1]Lit., *of what duration I am* [2]O *Thou . . . men?* 7:7; 10:9; 14:1 [b] 39:5; 62:9; Eccl. 2:11
48 [1]Lit., *hand* [2]I nether world [a]Ps 22:29; 49:9 [b]Ps.
49 [a]2 Sam. 7:15 30:9; Ezek. 34:2
50 [1]Lit., *My bea* *my bosom* [a]Ps. 74:18, 22
51 [a]Ps. 74:10, 1 [b]Ps. 89:38
52 [a]Ps. 41:13; 7 106:48
[+]Deut. 33:1
90:1 [1]Or, *hiding* some ancient ms *place of refuge* [a] 33:27; Ps. 71:3; 9 Ezek. 11:16
2 [1]Or, *And* [a]Job Prov. 8:25 [b]Gen. Ps. 102:25; 104:5

Even [c]from everlasting to everlasting, Thou art God.

3 Thou dost [a]turn man back into dust,
And dost say, "Return, O children of men."
4 For [a]a thousand years in Thy sight
Are like [b]yesterday when it passes by,
[1]Or *as* a [c]watch in the night.
5 Thou [a]hast [1]swept them away like a flood, they [2b]fall asleep;
In the morning they are like [c]grass which [3]sprouts anew.
6 In the morning it [a]flourishes, and [1]sprouts anew;
Toward evening it [b]fades, and [c]withers away.

7 For we have been [a]consumed by Thine anger,
And by Thy wrath we have been [1]dismayed.
8 Thou hast [a]placed our iniquities before Thee,
Our [b]secret *sins* in the light of Thy presence.
9 For [a]all our days have declined in Thy fury;
We have finished our years like a [1]sigh.
10 As for the days of our [1]life, [2]they contain seventy years,
Or if due to strength, [a]eighty years,
Yet their pride is *but* [b]labor and sorrow;
For soon it is gone and we [c]fly away.
11 Who [1]understands the [a]power of Thine anger,
And Thy fury, according to the [b]fear [2]that is due Thee?
12 So [a]teach us to number our days,
That we may [1b]present to Thee a heart of wisdom.

13 Do [a]return, O LORD; [b]how long *will it be*?
And [1]be [c]sorry for Thy servants.
14 O [a]satisfy us in the morning with Thy lovingkindness,
That we may [b]sing for joy and be glad all our days.
15 [a]Make us glad [1]according to the days Thou hast afflicted us,
And the [b]years we have seen [2]evil.
16 Let Thy [a]work appear to Thy servants,
And Thy [b]majesty [1]to their children.
17 And let the [a]favor of the Lord our God be upon us;
And do [1b]confirm for us the work of our hands;
Yes, [1]confirm the work of our hands.

Psalm 91

91 He who dwells in the [a]shelter of the Most High
Will abide in the [b]shadow of the Almighty.
2 I will say to the LORD, "My [a]refuge and my [b]fortress,
My God, in whom I [c]trust!"
3 For it is He who delivers you from the [a]snare of the trapper,
And from the deadly [b]pestilence.
4 He will [a]cover you with His pinions,
And [b]under His wings you may seek refuge;
His [c]faithfulness is a [d]shield and bulwark.

5 You [a]will not be afraid of the [b]terror by night,
Or of the [c]arrow that flies by day;
6 Of the [a]pestilence that [1]stalks in darkness,
Or of the [b]destruction that lays waste at noon.

2; 102:24, 27; Jer. 10:10
ien. 3:19; Job 5; Ps. 104:29
nd [a]2 Pet. 3:8 5 [c]Ex. 14:24; Judg. 7:19
flooded [2]Lit., *e asleep* [3]Or, *es away* [a]Job 6; 27:20 [b]Job 20:8; Ps. 76:5 03:15; Is. 40:6
passes away 4:2 [b]Ps. 92:7; [c]James 1:11
terrified [a]Ps. 39:11
Ps. 50:21; Jer. s. 19:12; Eccl. 12:14
whisper [a]Ps. 78:33
years [2]Lit., *in* [a]2 Kin. 19:35 cl. 12:2-7; Jer. [c]Job 20:8; Ps. 78:39
knows [2]Lit., *of* Ps. 76:7 [b]Neh. 5:9
, gain, bring in 12:29; Ps. 39:4 [b]Prov. 2:1-6
epent in regard 6:4; 80:14 [b]Ps. 10 [c]Ex. 32:12; 36; Ps. 106:45; 4; Amos 7:3, 6; Jon. 3:9
Ps. 36:8; 65:4; Jer. 31:14 [b]Ps. 31:7; 85:6
as many days Or, *trouble* [a]Ps. Deut. 2:14-16; Ps. 31:10
Or, *upon* [a]Deut. Ps. 44:1; 77:12; ab. 3:2 [b]1 Kin. 8:11; Is. 6:3
17 [1]Or, *give* *anence to* [a]Ps. [b]Ps. 37:23; Is. 6:12; 1 Cor. 3:7
Ps. 27:5; 31:20; Ps. 17:8; 121:5; Is. 25:4; 32:2
[a]Ps. 14:6; 91:9; 42:5 [b]Ps. 18:2; Jer. 16:19 [c]Ps. 25:2; 56:4
124:7; Prov. 6:5 37; 2 Chr. 20:9; Ps. 91:6
1:16 [b]Ps. 17:8; 57:1; 63:7 [c]Ps. 40:11 [d]Ps. 35:2
Job 5:19-23; Ps. 27:1 [b]Song 3:8 [c]Ps. 64:4
r, *walks* [a]2 Kin. Ps. 91:10 [b]Job 5:22

7 A thousand may fall at your side,
And ten thousand at your right hand;
But [a]it shall not approach you.
8 You will only look on with your eyes,
And [a]see the recompense of the wicked.
9 [1]For you have made the LORD, [a]my refuge,
Even the Most High, [b]your dwelling place.
10 [a]No evil will befall you,
Nor will any plague come near your [1]tent.

11 For He will give [a]His angels charge concerning you,
To guard you in all your ways.
12 They will [a]bear you up in their hands,
Lest you strike your foot against a stone.
13 You will [a]tread upon the lion and cobra,
The young lion and the [1]serpent you will trample down.

14 "[a]Because he has loved Me, therefore I will deliver him;
I will [b]set him *securely* on high, because he has [c]known My name.
15 "He will [a]call upon Me, and I will answer him;
I will be with him in [1]trouble;
I will rescue him, and [b]honor him.
16 "With [1]a [a]long life I will satisfy him,
And [2b]let him behold My salvation."

Psalm 92

A Psalm, a Song for the Sabbath day.

92 It is [a]good to give thanks to the LORD,
And to [b]sing praises to Thy name, O Most High;
2 To [a]declare Thy lovingkindness in the morning,
And Thy [b]faithfulness [1]by night,
3 [1]With the [a]ten-stringed lute, and [1]with the [a]harp;
[1]With resounding music [2]upon the [a]lyre.
4 For Thou, O LORD, hast made me glad by [1]what Thou [a]hast done,
I will [b]sing for joy at the [c]works of Thy hands.

5 How [a]great are Thy works, O LORD!
Thy [1b]thoughts are very [c]deep.
6 A [a]senseless man has no knowledge;
Nor does a [a]stupid man understand this:
7 That when the wicked [a]sprouted up like grass,
And all [b]who did iniquity flourished,
It *was only* that they might be [c]destroyed forevermore.
8 But Thou, O LORD, art [a]on high forever.
9 For, behold, Thine enemies, O LORD,
For, behold, [a]Thine enemies will perish;
All who do iniquity will be [b]scattered.

10 But Thou hast exalted my [a]horn like *that of* the wild ox;
I have [1]been [b]anointed with fresh oil.
11 And my eye has [a]looked *exultantly* upon [1]my foes,
My ears hear of the evildoers who rise up against me.
12 The [a]righteous man will [1]flourish like the palm tree,
He will grow like a [b]cedar in Lebanon.

7 [a]Gen. 7:23;
14:10

8 [a]Ps. 37:34;

9 [1]Or, *For Th*
LORD art my F
You have mac
Most High you
place. [a]Ps. 91
90:1

10 [1]Or, *dwelli*
12:21

11 [a]Ps. 34:7;
Luke 4:10, 11;

12 [a]Matt. 4:6;

13 [1]Or, *drago.*
14:6; Dan. 6:2
10:19

14 [a]Ps. 145:2
59:1 [c]Ps. 9:10

15 [1]Or, *distres*
12:4; Ps. 50:15
2:30; John 12:

16 [1]Lit., *length*
[2]Or, *cause him*
his eyes on [a]D
Ps. 21:4; Prov.
[b]Ps. 50:23

92:1 [a]Ps. 147:
135:3

2 [1]Lit., *nights*
59:16 [b]Ps. 89:

3 [1]Lit., *Upon* [2]
means of [a]1 S
1 Chr. 13:8; Ne
Ps. 33:2

4 [1]Lit., *Thy wo*
[a]Ps. 40:5; 90:16
106:47 [c]Ps. 8:6
143:5

5 [1]Or, *purpose*
40:5; 111:2; Re
[b]Ps. 33:11; 40:5
139:17 [c]Ps. 36
11:33

6 [a]Ps. 49:10; 7
94:8

7 [a]Job 12:6; Ps
[b]Ps. 94:4 [c]Ps. 3

8 [a]Ps. 83:18; 9
113:5

9 [a]Ps. 37:20 [b]P
89:10

10 [1]Or, *become*
[a]Ps. 75:10; 89:1
112:9 [b]Ps. 23:5;

11 [1]Or, *those w*
wait for me [a]Ps.
91:8

12 [1]Lit., *sprout*
24:6; Ps. 1:3; 52
Jer. 17:8; Hos. 1
[b]Ps. 104:16; Eze

13 [a]Planted in the house of the LORD,
They will flourish [b]in the courts of our God.
14 They will still [1a]yield fruit in old age;
They shall be [2]full of sap and very green,
15 To [1]declare that [a]the LORD is upright;
He is my [b]rock, and there is [c]no unrighteousness in Him.

Psalm 93

93 [a]The LORD [1]reigns, He is [b]clothed with majesty;
The LORD has [c]clothed and girded Himself with strength;
Indeed, the [d]world is firmly established, it will not be moved.
2 Thy [a]throne is established from of old;
Thou [b]art from everlasting.

3 The [a]floods have lifted up, O LORD,
The floods have lifted up their voice;
The floods lift up their pounding waves.
4 More than the sounds of many waters,
Than the mighty breakers of the sea,
The LORD [a]on high is mighty.
5 Thy [a]testimonies are fully confirmed;
[b]Holiness befits Thy house,
O LORD, [1]forevermore.

Psalm 94

94 O LORD, God of [1a]vengeance;
God of [1]vengeance, [2b]shine forth!
2 [a]Rise up, O [b]Judge of the earth;
Render recompense [c]to the proud.
3 How long shall the wicked, O LORD,
How long shall the [a]wicked exult?
4 They pour forth *words,* they [a]speak arrogantly;
All who do wickedness [b]vaunt themselves.
5 They [a]crush Thy people, O LORD,
And [b]afflict Thy heritage.
6 They [a]slay the widow and the [1]stranger,
And murder the orphans.
7 And [a]they have said, "[1]The LORD does not see,
Nor does the God of Jacob pay heed."

8 Pay heed, you [a]senseless among the people;
And when will you understand, [a]stupid ones?
9 He who [a]planted the ear, [1]does He not hear?
He who formed the eye, [1]does He not see?
10 He who [1a]chastens the nations, will He not rebuke,
Even He who [b]teaches man knowledge?
11 The LORD [a]knows the thoughts of man,
[1]That they are a *mere* breath.

12 Blessed is the man whom [a]Thou dost chasten, O [1]LORD,
And [b]dost teach out of Thy law;
13 That Thou mayest grant him [a]relief from the [b]days of adversity,
Until [c]a pit is dug for the wicked.
14 For [a]the LORD will not abandon His people,

[a]Ps. 80:15; Is. ...21 [b]Ps. 100:4; 116:19
...thrive in [2]Lit., ...Prov. 11:30; Is. ...:31; John 15:2; James 3:18
...how forth [a]Job ...s. 25:8 [b]Deut. ...Ps. 18:2; 94:22 [c]Rom. 9:14
..., has assumed ...hip [a]Ps. 96:10; ...9:1 [b]Ps. 104:1 ...; Is. 51:9 [d]Ps. 96:10
...45:6; Lam. 5:19 [b]Ps. 90:2
... 96:11; 98:7, 8
...s. 65:7; 89:6, 9; 92:8
...Lit., *for length of* [a]Ps. 19:7 [b]Ps. ...6:9; 1 Cor. 3:17
[1]Or, *avenging* [2]Or, *has shone* ...Deut. 32:35; Is. ...Nah. 1:2; Rom. [b]Ps. 50:2; 80:1
...:6 [b]Gen. 18:25 [c]Ps. 31:23
3 [a]Job 20:5
...1:18; 75:5 [b]Ps. 10:3; 52:1
... 3:15 [b]Ps. 79:1
...r, *sojourner* [a]Is. 10:2
...Heb., *YAH* [a]Job 22:13; Ps. 10:11
8 [a]Ps. 92:6
..., *can* [a]Ex. 4:11; Prov. 20:12
...Or, *instructs* [a]Ps. ...2 [b]Job 35:11; Is. 28:26
...*For* [a]Job 11:11; 1 Cor. 3:20
...Heb., *YAH* [a]Deut. ...:5; Job 5:17; Ps. ...1; Prov. 3:11, 12; ...Heb. 12:5, 6 [b]Ps. 119:171
[a]Job 34:29; Hab. ...6 [b]Ps. 49:5 [c]Ps. 9:15; 55:23
...Sam. 12:22; Lam. 3:31; Rom. 11:2

Nor will He [b]forsake His inheritance.
15 For [1a]judgment [2]will again be righteous;
And all the upright in heart [3]will follow it.
16 Who will [a]stand up for me against evildoers?
Who will take his stand for me [b]against those who do
wickedness?

17 If [a]the LORD had not been my help,
My soul would soon have dwelt in *the abode of* silence.
18 If I should say, "[a]My foot has slipped,"
Thy lovingkindness, O LORD, will hold me up.
19 When my anxious thoughts [1]multiply within me,
Thy [a]consolations delight my soul.
20 Can a [1a]throne of destruction be allied with Thee,
One [b]which devises [2]mischief by decree?
21 They [a]band themselves together against the [1]life of the righteous,
And [b]condemn [2]the innocent to death.
22 But the LORD has been my [a]stronghold,
And my God the [b]rock of my refuge.
23 And He has [a]brought back their wickedness upon them,
And will [1b]destroy them in their evil;
The LORD our God will [1]destroy them.

Psalm 95

95 O come, let us [a]sing for joy to the LORD;
Let us shout joyfully to [b]the rock of our salvation.
2 Let us [a]come before His presence [b]with [1]thanksgiving;
Let us shout joyfully to Him [c]with [2]psalms.
3 For the LORD is a [a]great God,
And a great King [b]above all gods,
4 In whose hand are the [a]depths of the earth;
The peaks of the mountains are His also.
5 [1]The sea is His, for it was He [a]who made it;
And His hands formed the dry land.

6 Come, let us [a]worship and bow down;
Let us [b]kneel before the LORD our [c]Maker.
7 For He is our God,
And [a]we are the people of His [1b]pasture, and the sheep of His
hand.
[c]Today, [2]if you would hear His voice,
8 Do not harden your hearts, as at [1a]Meribah,
As in the day of [2b]Massah in the wilderness;
9 "When your fathers [a]tested Me,
They tried Me, though they had seen My work.
10 "For [a]forty years I loathed *that* generation,
And said they are a people who err in their heart,
And they do not know My ways.
11 "Therefore I [a]swore in My anger,
Truly they shall not enter into My [b]rest."

Psalm 96

96 [a]Sing to the LORD a [b]new song;
Sing to the LORD, all the earth.

14 [b]Ps. 37:28
15 [1]I.e., admi... of justice [2]Lit. return to righte... [3]Lit., will be af... 97:2; Is. 42:3;
16 [a]Num. 10:... 28:21; 33:10 ... 17:13; 59:2
17 [a]Ps. 124:1
18 [a]Ps. 38:16
19 [1]Or, are m... 57:18; 66:13
20 [1]Or, tribuna... trouble, misfor... [a]Amos 6:3 [b]Ps... 58:2
21 [1]Or, soul [2]... innocent blood... 56:6; 59:3 [b]Ex... Ps. 106:38; Pro... Matt. 27:4
22 [a]Ps. 9:9; 59... 18:2; 71:7
23 [1]Or, silence... 7:16; 140:9, 11 ... 19:15
95:1 [a]Ps. 66:1; [b]Ps. 89:26
2 [1]Or, a song o... thanksgiving [2]O... (with instrumen... accompanimen... 6:6 [b]Ps. 100:4; Jon. 2:9 [c]Ps. 8... 5:19; James 5:1...
3 [a]Ps. 48:1; 13... 145:3 [b]Ps. 96:4
4 [a]Ps. 135:6
5 [1]Lit., Who ha... sea [a]Gen. 1:9, 146:6; Jon. 1:9
6 [a]Ps. 96:9; 99:... [b]2 Chr. 6:13; Da... Phil. 2:10 [c]Ps. ... 149:2; Is. 17:7;
7 [1]Lit., pasturing... that you would ... [a]Ps. 79:13 [b]Ps. ... [c]Heb. 3:7-11, 15
8 [1]Or, place of s... [2]Or, temptation 17:2-7; Num. 20 [b]Ex. 17:7; Deut. ...
9 [a]Num. 14:22; 78:18; 1 Cor. 10:...
10 [a]Acts 7:36; 1... Heb. 3:10, 17
11 [a]Num. 14:23... Deut. 1:35; Heb. [b]Deut. 12:9
96:1 [a]1 Chr. 16:2... [b]Ps. 40:3

2 Sing to the LORD, bless His name;
[a]Proclaim good tidings of His salvation from day to day.
3 Tell of [a]His glory among the nations,
His wonderful deeds among all the peoples.
4 For [a]great is the LORD, and [b]greatly to be praised;
He is to be [c]feared [d]above all gods.
5 For [a]all the gods of the peoples are [1]idols,
But [b]the LORD made the heavens.
6 [a]Splendor and majesty are before Him,
Strength and beauty are in His sanctuary.

7 [1]Ascribe to the LORD, O [a]families of the peoples,
[1b]Ascribe to the LORD glory and strength.
8 [1]Ascribe to the LORD the [a]glory of His name;
Bring an [2b]offering, and come into His courts.
9 [a]Worship the LORD in [1]holy attire;
[b]Tremble before Him, all the earth.
10 Say among the nations, "[a]The LORD reigns;
Indeed, the [a]world is firmly established, it will not be moved;
He will [b]judge the peoples with [1]equity."

11 Let the [a]heavens be glad, and let the [b]earth rejoice;
Let [c]the sea [1]roar, and [2]all it contains;
12 Let the [a]field exult, and all that is in it.
Then all the [b]trees of the forest will sing for joy
13 Before the LORD, [a]for He is coming;
For He is coming to judge the earth.
[b]He will judge the world in righteousness,
And the peoples in His faithfulness.

Psalm 97

97 [a]The LORD [1]reigns; let the [b]earth rejoice;
Let the many [2c]islands be glad.
2 [a]Clouds and thick darkness surround Him;
[b]Righteousness and justice are the foundation of His throne.
3 [a]Fire goes before Him,
And [b]burns up His adversaries round about.
4 His [a]lightnings lit up the world;
The earth saw and [b]trembled.
5 The mountains [a]melted like wax at the presence of the LORD,
At the presence of the [b]Lord of the whole earth.
6 The [a]heavens declare His righteousness,
And [b]all the peoples have seen His glory.

7 Let all those be ashamed who serve [a]graven images,
Who boast themselves of [b]idols;
[1c]Worship Him, all you [2]gods.
8 Zion [1]heard *this* and [a]was glad,
And the daughters of Judah have rejoiced
Because of Thy judgments, O LORD.
9 For Thou art the LORD [a]Most High over all the earth;
Thou art exalted far [b]above all [1]gods.

10 [a]Hate evil, you who love the LORD,

2 [a]Ps. 71:15
3 [a]Ps. 145:12
1; 145:3 [b]Ps. 9:7 [d]Ps. 95:3
, *non-existent* [a]1 Chr. 16:26; [b]Ps. 115:15; Is. 42:5
6 [a]Ps. 104:1
ve [a]Ps. 22:27 16:28, 29; Ps. 29:1, 2
Give [2]Or, *meal* *ring* [a]Ps. 79:9; . 45:12; 72:10
the splendor of [a]1 Chr. 16:29; 0:21; Ps. 29:2; Ps. 33:8; 114:7
Or, *uprightness* 97:1 [b]Ps. 9:8; :11; 67:4; 98:9
under [2]Lit., *its* [a]Ps. 69:34; Is. [b]Ps. 97:1 [c]Ps. 98:7
65:13; Is. 35:1; 2, 13 [b]Is. 44:23
Ps. 98:9 [b]Rev. 19:11
r, *has assumed Kingship* [2]Or, *nds* [a]Ps. 96:10 1 [c]Is. 42:10, 12
9:9; Deut. 4:11; 8:12; Ps. 18:11 [b]Ps. 89:14
18:8; 50:3; Dan. Hab. 3:5 [b]Mal. 4:1; Heb. 12:29
9:16; Ps. 77:18 Ps. 96:9; 104:32
46:6; Amos 9:5; ic. 1:4; Nah. 1:5 [b]Josh. 3:11
19:1; 50:6 [b]Ps. 6:3; 40:5; 66:18
All the gods have shiped Him [2]Or, *ernatural powers* 78:58; Is. 42:17; ; Jer. 10:14 [b]Ps. ; Jer. 50:2; Hab. 2:18 [c]Heb. 1:6
r possibly, hears glad [a]Ps. 48:11; Zeph. 3:14
[1]Or, *supernatural* [a]Ps. 83:18 [b]Ex. 1; Ps. 95:3; 96:4; 135:5
[a]Ps. 34:14; Prov. Amos 5:15; Rom. 12:9

Who [b]preserves the souls of His godly ones;
He [c]delivers them from the hand of the wicked.
11 [a]Light is sown *like seed* for the righteous,
And [b]gladness for the upright in heart.
12 Be [a]glad in the LORD, you righteous ones;
And [b]give thanks [1]to His holy name.

Psalm 98

A Psalm.

98 O sing to the LORD a [a]new song,
For He has done [b]wonderful things,
His [c]right hand and His [d]holy arm have [1]gained the victory for Him.
2 [a]The LORD has made known His salvation;
He has [b]revealed His [1]righteousness in the sight of the nations.
3 He has [a]remembered His lovingkindness and His faithfulness to the house of Israel;
[b]All the ends of the earth have seen the salvation of our God.

4 [a]Shout joyfully to the LORD, all the earth;
[b]Break forth and sing for joy and sing praises.
5 Sing praises to the LORD with the [a]lyre;
With the lyre and the [1b]sound of melody.
6 With [a]trumpets and the sound of the horn
[b]Shout joyfully before [c]the King, the LORD.

7 Let the [a]sea roar and [1]all it contains,
The [b]world and those who dwell in it.
8 Let the [a]rivers clap their hands;
Let the [b]mountains sing together for joy
9 Before the LORD; for He is coming to [a]judge the earth;
He will judge the world with righteousness,
And [b]the peoples with [1]equity.

Psalm 99

99 [a]The LORD reigns, let the peoples tremble;
He [1b]is enthroned *above* the cherubim, let the earth shake!
2 The LORD [1]is [a]great in Zion,
And He is [b]exalted above all the peoples.
3 Let them praise Thy [a]great and awesome name;
[b]Holy is [1]He.
4 And the [1]strength of the King [a]loves [2]justice;
Thou hast established [3b]equity;
Thou hast [c]executed [2]justice and righteousness in Jacob.
5 [1a]Exalt the LORD our God,
And [b]worship at His footstool;
[c]Holy is He.

6 [a]Moses and Aaron were among His [b]priests,
And [c]Samuel was among those who [d]called on His name;
They [e]called upon the LORD, and He answered them.
7 He [a]spoke to them in the pillar of cloud;
They [b]kept His testimonies,
And the statute that He gave them.

---

10 [b]Ps. 31:23; Prov. 2:8 [c]Ps. 3… Jer. 15:21; Dan…

11 [a]Job 22:28; … 112:4; Prov. 4:1… 64:10

12 [1]Lit., *for the … of His holiness* … 32:11 [b]Ps. 30:4…

98:1 [1]Or, *accor… salvation* [a]Ps. 3… [b]Ps. 40:5; 96:3 … 15:6 [d]Is. 52:10

2 [1]I.e., faithfuln… His gracious pro… [a]Is. 52:10 [b]Is. 6… Rom. 3:25

3 [a]Luke 1:54, 7… 22:27

4 [a]Ps. 100:1 [b]Is…

5 [1]Or, *voice of s…* (accompanied b… music) [a]Ps. 92:… 51:3

6 [a]Num. 10:10; … 15:14 [b]Ps. 66:1 … 47:7

7 [1]Lit., *its fulnes…* … 96:11 [b]Ps. 24:1

8 [a]Ps. 93:3; Is. … [b]Ps. 65:12; 89:12

9 [1]Or, *uprightne…* … 96:13 [b]Ps. 96:10

99:1 [1]Lit., *sits* [a]… 97:1 [b]Ex. 25:22; … 4:4; Ps. 80:1

2 [1]Or, *in Zion is …* [a]Ps. 48:1; Is. 12:… 97:9; 113:4

3 [1]Or, *it* [a]Deut. … Ps. 76:1 [b]Lev. 19… Josh. 24:19; 1 Sa… Ps. 22:3; Is. 6:3

4 [1]Or, *Thou hast established in eq… strength of the Ki… loves justice* [2]Or, *judgment* [3]Or, *uprightness* [a]Ps. 33:5 [b]Ps. 17:2; 9… [c]Ps. 103:6; 146:7 … 23:5

5 [1]The verb is pl… [a]Ps. 34:3; 107:32 … 118:28 [b]Ps. 132:… 99:3

6 [a]Jer. 15:1 [b]Ex. 24:6-8; 29:26; 40:… Lev. 8:1-30 [c]1 Sa… 7:9; 12:18; Ps. 22… [d]Ex. 15:25; 32:30

7 [a]Ex. 33:9; Num… [b]Ps. 105:28

8 O LORD our God, Thou didst [a]answer them;
Thou wast a [b]forgiving God to them,
And *yet* an [c]avenger of their *evil* deeds.
9 Exalt the LORD our God,
And worship at His holy hill;
For holy is the LORD our God.

Psalm 100

A Psalm for [+]Thanksgiving.

100 [a]Shout joyfully to the LORD, all the earth.
2 [a]Serve the LORD with gladness;
[b]Come before Him with joyful singing.
3 Know that [a]the LORD [1]Himself is God;
It is He who has [b]made us, and [2]not we ourselves;
We are [c]His people and the sheep of His pasture.

4 Enter His gates [a]with [1]thanksgiving,
And His courts with praise.
Give thanks to Him; [b]bless His name.
5 For [a]the LORD is good;
[b]His lovingkindness is everlasting,
And His [c]faithfulness to all generations.

Psalm 101

A Psalm of David.

101 I will [a]sing of lovingkindness and [1]justice,
To Thee, O LORD, I will sing praises.
2 I will [1a]give heed to the [2]blameless way.
When wilt Thou come to me?
I will walk within my house in the [3b]integrity of my heart.
3 I will set no [a]worthless thing before my eyes;
I hate the [1]work of those who [b]fall away;
It shall not fasten its grip on me.
4 A [a]perverse heart shall depart from me;
I will know no evil.
5 Whoever secretly [a]slanders his neighbor, him I will [1]destroy;
No one who has a [b]haughty look and an arrogant heart will I
endure.

6 My eyes shall be upon the faithful of the land, that they may
dwell with me;
He who walks in a [1a]blameless way is the one who will minister
to me.
7 He who [a]practices deceit shall not dwell within my house;
He who speaks falsehood [b]shall not [1]maintain his position
before me.
8 [a]Every morning I will [1b]destroy all the wicked of the land,
So as to [c]cut off from the [d]city of the LORD all those who do
iniquity.

06:44 [b]Num.
s. 78:38 [c]Ex.
m. 20:12; Ps.
95:11; 107:12

thank offering

. 95:1; 98:4, 6

eut. 12:11, 12;
3:47 [b]Ps. 95:2

e [2]Some mss.
we are [a]Deut.
Kin. 18:39; Ps.
ob 10:3, 8; Ps.
:73 [c]Ps. 74:1,
s. 40:11; Ezek.
34:30, 31

a thank offering
2; 116:17 [b]Ps.
96:2

r. 16:34; 2 Chr.
; Ezra 3:11; Ps.
5; 106:1; 107:1;
Jer. 33:11; Nah.
[b]Ps. 136:1 [c]Ps.
119:90

[1]*Or, judgment*
:14; 89:1; 145:7

ehave prudently
way of integrity
blamelessness
18:5, 14 [b]1 Kin.
9:4

[1]*Or, practice of*
asy [a]Deut. 15:9
h. 23:6; Ps. 40:4

4 [a]Prov. 11:20

[1]*Or, silence* [a]Ps.
20; Jer. 9:4 [b]Ps.
18:27; Prov. 6:17

r, way of integrity
[a]Ps. 119:1

t., be established
ore my eyes [a]Ps.
52:2 [b]Ps. 52:4, 5

[1]*Or, silence* [a]Jer.
2 [b]Ps. 75:10 [c]Ps.
:10-12 [d]Ps. 46:4;
48:2, 8

Psalm 102

A Prayer of the Afflicted, when he is faint,
and +pours out his complaint before the LORD.

102 [a]Hear my prayer, O LORD!
And let my cry for help [b]come to Thee.
2 [a]Do not hide Thy face from me in the day of my distress;
[b]Incline Thine ear to me;
In the day when I call [a]answer me quickly.
3 For my days [a]have been [1]consumed in smoke,
And my [b]bones have been scorched like a hearth.
4 My heart [a]has been smitten like [1]grass and has [b]withered away,
Indeed, I [c]forget to eat my bread.
5 Because of the [1]loudness of my groaning
My [a]bones [2]cling to my flesh.
6 I [1]resemble a [a]pelican of the wilderness;
I have become like an owl of the waste places.
7 I [a]lie awake,
I have become like a lonely bird on a housetop.

8 My enemies [a]have reproached me all day long;
Those who [1b]deride me [2]have used my *name* as a [c]curse.
9 For I have eaten ashes like bread,
And [a]mingled my drink with weeping,
10 [a]Because of Thine indignation and Thy wrath;
For Thou hast [b]lifted me up and cast me away.
11 My days are like a [1a]lengthened shadow;
And [2]I [b]wither away like [3]grass.

12 But Thou, O LORD, dost [1a]abide forever;
And Thy [2b]name to all generations.
13 Thou wilt [a]arise *and* have [b]compassion on Zion;
For [c]it is time to be gracious to her,
For the [d]appointed time has come.
14 Surely Thy servants [1]find pleasure in her stones,
And feel pity for her dust.
15 [1]So the [2a]nations will fear the name of the LORD,
And [b]all the kings of the earth Thy glory.
16 For the LORD has [a]built up Zion;
He has [b]appeared in His glory.
17 He has [a]regarded the prayer of the [1]destitute,
And has not despised their prayer.

18 [1]This will be [a]written for the [b]generation to come;
[2]That [c]a people yet to be created [3]may praise [4]the LORD.
19 For He [a]looked down from His holy height;
[b]From heaven the LORD gazed [1]upon the earth,
20 To hear the [a]groaning of the prisoner;
To [b]set free [1]those who were doomed to death;
21 That *men* may [a]tell of the name of the LORD in Zion,
And His praise in Jerusalem;
22 When [a]the peoples are gathered together,
And the kingdoms, to serve the LORD.

+Ps. 142:2

102:1 [a]Ps. 39 [b]Ex. 2:23; 1 Sa

2 [a]Ps. 69:17

3 [1]Or, *finished* 37:20; James 30:30; Lam. 1:

4 [1]Lit., *herbag* 90:5, 6 [b]Ps. 3 40:7 [c]1 Sam. 2 Sam. 12:17; 10:6; Job 33:2

5 [1]Lit., *voice* [2] *cleaved* [a]Job Lam. 4:8

6 [1]Lit., *have be similar to* [a]Is. 3 Zeph. 2:14

7 [a]Ps. 77:4

8 [1]Or, *made a* [2]Lit., *have swo* [a]Ps. 31:11 [b]Ac [c]2 Sam. 16:5; Is Jer. 29:22

9 [a]Ps. 42:3; 80

10 [a]Ps. 38:3 [b] 27:21; 30:22

11 [1]Lit., *stretch* [2]Or, *as for me,* *herbage* [a]Job 1 109:23 [b]Ps. 10

12 [1]Or, *sit enth* [2]Lit., *memorial* 10:16; Lam. 5:1 3:15; Ps. 135:13

13 [a]Ps. 12:5; 44 60:10; Zech. 1:1 119:126 [d]Ps. 75 8:19

14 [1]Or, *have fo*

15 [1]Or, *And* [2]O *Gentiles, heathe* [a]1 Kin. 8:43; Ps. [b]Ps. 138:4

16 [a]Ps. 147:2 [b] 60:1, 2

17 [1]Or, *naked* [a] 1:6; Ps. 22:24

18 [1]Or, *Let this b written* [2]Or, *And will* [4]Heb., *YAH* 31:19; Rom. 15:4 10:11 [b]Ps. 22:30 48:13 [c]Ps. 22:31

19 [1]Lit., *toward* 26:15; Ps. 14:2; 5 [b]Ps. 33:13

20 [1]Lit., *the sons death* [a]Ps. 79:11 146:7

21 [a]Ps. 22:22

22 [a]Ps. 22:27; 86 49:22, 23; 60:3; Z 8:20-23

23 He has weakened my strength in the way;
He has [a]shortened my days.
24 I say, "O my God, [a]do not take me away in the [1]midst of my days,
Thy [b]years are throughout all generations.
25 "Of old Thou didst [a]found the earth;
And the [b]heavens are the work of Thy hands.
26 "[1]Even they will [a]perish, but Thou dost endure;
And all of them will wear out like a garment;
Like clothing Thou wilt change them, and they will be changed.
27 "But Thou art [1a]the same,
And Thy years will not come to an end.
28 "The [a]children of Thy servants will continue,
And their [1b]descendants will be established before Thee."

Psalm 103

A Psalm of David.

103 [a]Bless the LORD, O my soul;
And all that is within me, *bless* His [b]holy name.
2 Bless the LORD, O my soul,
And [a]forget none of His benefits;
3 Who [a]pardons all your iniquities;
Who [b]heals all your diseases;
4 Who [a]redeems your life from the pit;
Who [b]crowns you with lovingkindness and compassion;
5 Who [a]satisfies your [1]years with good things,
So that your youth is [b]renewed like the eagle.

6 The LORD [a]performs [1]righteous deeds,
And judgments for all who are [b]oppressed.
7 He [a]made known His ways to Moses,
His [b]acts to the sons of Israel.
8 The LORD is [a]compassionate and gracious,
[b]Slow to anger and abounding in lovingkindness.
9 He [a]will not always strive *with us*;
Nor will He [b]keep *His anger* forever.
10 He has [a]not dealt with us according to our sins,
Nor rewarded us according to our iniquities.
11 For as high [a]as the heavens are above the earth,
So great is His lovingkindness toward those who [1]fear Him.
12 As far as the east is from the west,
So far has He [a]removed our transgressions from us.
13 Just [a]as a father has compassion on *his* children,
So the LORD has compassion on those who [1]fear Him.
14 For [a]He Himself knows [1]our frame;
He [b]is mindful that we are *but* [c]dust.

15 As for man, his days are [a]like grass;
As a [b]flower of the field, so he flourishes.
16 When the [a]wind has passed over it, it is no more;
And its [b]place acknowledges it no longer.
17 But the [a]lovingkindness of the LORD is from everlasting to everlasting on those who [1]fear Him,
And His [2]righteousness [b]to children's children,

23 [a]Ps. 39:5
Lit., *half* [a]Ps. ...s. 38:10 [b]Job ...90:2; 102:12; Hab. 1:12
...1:1; Neh. 9:6; ...12 [b]Ps. 96:5
26 [1]Lit., *They* ...*ves* [a]Is. 34:4; ...24:35; 2 Pet. ...0; Rev. 20:11
...*He* [a]Is. 41:4; ...al. 3:6; James 1:17
...it., *seed* [a]Ps. ...:36 [b]Ps. 89:4
[a]Ps. 104:1, 35 ...33:21; 105:3; ...; Ezek. 36:21; 39:7
...eut. 6:12; 8:11
...34:7; Ps. 86:5; Is. 43:25 [b]Ex. ...; Ps. 30:2; Jer. 30:17
...:15 [b]Ps. 5:12
...Or, *desire* [a]Ps. ...:16 [b]Is. 40:31
[1]Or, *deeds of* ...*tion* [a]Ps. 99:4; ...46:7 [b]Ps. 12:5
...3:13; Ps. 99:7; ...19 [b]Ps. 78:11; 106:22
...Ex. 34:6; Num. ...Neh. 9:17; Ps. ...on. 4:2; James ...Ps. 145:8; Joel 2:13; Nah. 1:3
...30:5; Is. 57:16 ...5, 12; Mic. 7:18
...Ezra 9:13; Lam. 3:22
...Or, *revere* [a]Ps. 36:5; 57:10
...Sam. 12:13; Is. ...3:25; Zech. 3:9; Heb. 9:26
...Or, *revere* [a]Mal. 3:17
...e., what we are [a]Is. 29:16 [b]Ps. ...Gen. 3:19; Eccl. 12:7
...s. 90:5; Is. 40:6; ...1:24 [b]Job 14:2; James 1:10, 11
...40:7 [b]Job 7:10; 8:18; 20:9
[1]Or, *revere* [2]I.e., ...ithfulness to His ...s promises [a]Ps. ...[b]Ex. 20:6; Deut. 5:10; Ps. 105:8

18 To [a]those who keep His covenant,
And who remember His precepts to do them.

19 The LORD has established His [a]throne in the heavens;
And His [1b]sovereignty rules over [2]all.
20 Bless the LORD, you [a]His angels,
[b]Mighty in strength, who [c]perform His word,
[d]Obeying the voice of His word!
21 Bless the LORD, all you [a]His hosts,
You [b]who serve Him, doing His will.
22 Bless the LORD, [a]all you works of His,
In all places of His dominion;
Bless the LORD, O my soul!

Psalm 104

104 [a]Bless the LORD, O my soul!
O LORD my God, Thou art very great;
Thou art [b]clothed with splendor and majesty,
2 Covering Thyself with [a]light as with a cloak,
[b]Stretching out heaven like a *tent* curtain.
3 [1]He [a]lays the beams of His upper chambers in the waters;
[1]He makes the [b]clouds His chariot;
[1]He walks upon the [c]wings of the wind;
4 [1]He makes [2a]the winds His messengers,
[3]Flaming [b]fire His ministers.

5 He [a]established the earth upon its foundations,
So that it will not [1]totter forever and ever.
6 Thou [a]didst cover it with the deep as with a garment;
The waters were standing above the mountains.
7 At Thy [a]rebuke they fled;
At the [b]sound of Thy thunder they hurried away.
8 The mountains rose; the valleys sank down
To the [a]place which Thou didst establish for them.
9 Thou didst set a [a]boundary that they may not pass over;
That they may not return to cover the earth.

10 [1]He sends forth [a]springs in the valleys;
They flow between the mountains;
11 They [a]give drink to every beast of the field;
The [b]wild donkeys quench their thirst.
12 [1]Beside them the birds of the heavens [a]dwell;
They [2]lift up *their* voices among the branches.
13 [1]He [a]waters the mountains from His upper chambers;
[b]The earth is satisfied with the fruit of His works.

14 [1]He causes the [a]grass to grow for the [2]cattle,
And [b]vegetation for the [3]labor of man,
So that [4]he may bring forth [5]food [c]from the earth,
15 And [a]wine which makes man's heart glad,
[b]So that he may make *his* face glisten with oil,
And [1]food which [c]sustains man's heart.
16 The trees of the LORD [1]drink their fill,
The cedars of Lebanon which He planted,

---

18 [a]Deut. 7:9
19 [1]Or, *kingd*… *the universe* [b]Ps. 47:2, 8; D… 4:17, 25
20 [a]Ps. 148:2… 29:1; 78:25 [c]… [d]Ps. 91:11; He…
21 [a]1 Kin. 22:… 9:6; Ps. 148:2… 2:13 [b]Ps. 104…
22 [a]Ps. 145:1…
104:1 [a]Ps. 10… 93:1
2 [a]Dan. 7:9 [b]…
3 [1]Lit., *The on*… [a]Amos 9:6 [b]Is. … [c]Ps. 18:10
4 [1]Lit., *Who* [2]… *angels, spirits ministers flame*… [a]Ps. 148:8; Heb… [b]2 Kin. 2:11; 6:1…
5 [1]Or, *move ou*… *place* [a]Job 38:… 24:2
6 [a]Gen. 1:2
7 [a]Ps. 18:15; 1… 50:2 [b]Ps. 29:3;
8 [a]Ps. 33:7
9 [a]Job 38:10, 1… 5:22
10 [1]Lit., *The on*… *sends* [a]Ps. 107… 41:18
11 [a]Ps. 104:13… 39:5
12 [1]Or, *Over, Ab*… [2]Lit., *give forth* [a]… 8:20
13 [1]Lit., *Who* [a]P… 147:8 [b]Jer. 10:1…
14 [1]Lit., *Who* [2]… *beasts* [3]Or, *culti*… *by* or *service of He* [5]Lit., *bread* … 38:27; Ps. 147:8… 1:29 [c]Job 28:5
15 [1]Lit., *bread* [a]… 9:13; Prov. 31:6; 10:19 [b]Ps. 23:5; 141:5; Luke 7:46 18:5; Judg. 19:5,
16 [1]Lit., *are satis*…

17 Where the [a]birds build their nests,
And the [b]stork, whose home is the [1]fir trees.

18 The high mountains are for the [a]wild goats;
The [b]cliffs are a refuge for the [c]rock badgers.
19 He made the moon [a]for the seasons;
The [b]sun knows the place of its setting.
20 Thou [a]dost appoint darkness and it becomes night,
In which all the [b]beasts of the forest [1]prowl about.
21 The [a]young lions roar after their prey,
[1]And [b]seek their food from God.
22 *When* the sun rises they withdraw,
And lie down in their [a]dens.
23 Man goes forth to [a]his work
And to his labor until evening.

24 O LORD, how [a]many are Thy works!
[1]In [b]wisdom Thou hast made them all;
The [c]earth is full of Thy [2]possessions.
25 [1]There is the [a]sea, great and [2]broad,
In which are swarms without number,
Animals both small and great.
26 There the [a]ships move along,
And [1b]Leviathan, which Thou hast formed to sport in it.

27 They all [a]wait for Thee,
To [b]give them their food in [1]due season.
28 Thou dost give to them, they gather *it* up;
Thou [a]dost open Thy hand, they are satisfied with good.
29 Thou [a]dost hide Thy face, they are dismayed;
Thou [b]dost take away their [1]spirit, they expire,
And [c]return to their dust.
30 Thou dost send forth Thy [1a]Spirit, they are created;
And Thou dost renew the face of the ground.

31 Let the [a]glory of the LORD endure forever;
Let the LORD [b]be glad in His works;
32 [1]He [a]looks at the earth, and it [b]trembles;
He [c]touches the mountains, and they smoke.
33 [1]I will sing to the LORD [2a]as long as I live;
[1]I will [b]sing praise to my God [3]while I have my being.
34 Let my [a]meditation be pleasing to Him;
As for me, I shall [b]be glad in the LORD.
35 Let sinners be [a]consumed from the earth,
And let the [b]wicked be no more.
[c]Bless the LORD, O my soul.
[1d]Praise [2]the LORD!

Psalm 105

105 Oh [a]give thanks to the LORD, [b]call upon His name;
[c]Make known His deeds among the peoples.
2 Sing to Him, [a]sing praises to Him;
[1b]Speak of all His [2]wonders.
3 [1]Glory in His holy name;

cypress [a]Ps. 2 [b]Lev. 11:19
b 39:1 [b]Prov. .26 [c]Lev. 11:5
:14 [b]Ps. 19:6
it., *creep* [a]Ps. ; Is. 45:7 [b]Ps. 56:9; Mic. 5:8
., *And to seek* [b]Ps. 145:15; Joel 1:20
22 [a]Job 37:8
23 [a]Gen. 3:19
[1]Or, *With* [2]Or, *ures* [a]Ps. 40:5 :5; Prov. 3:19; 12; 51:15 [c]Ps. 65:9
his [2]Or, *broad dimensions* (lit., [a]Ps. 8:8; 69:34
a sea monster .23; Ezek. 27:9 ; Ps. 74:14; Is. 27:1
., *its appointed* s. 145:15 [b]Job :31; 38:41; Ps. 136:25; 147:9
28 [a]Ps. 145:16
, *breath* [a]Deut. ; Ps. 30:7 [b]Job , 15; Ps. 146:4; 2:7 [c]Gen. 3:19; 10:9; Ps. 90:3
Or, *breath* [a]Job 3:4; Ezek. 37:9
s. 86:12; 111:10 [b]Gen. 1:31
t., *The one who* 5:5; Ps. 97:4, 5; [b]Hab. 3:10 [c]Ex. 19:18; Ps. 144:5
[1]Or, *Let me sing my lifetime* [3]Lit., *le I still am* [a]Ps. 63:4 [b]Ps. 146:2
. 19:14 [b]Ps. 9:2
[1]Or, *Hallelujah!* *YAH* [a]Ps. 59:13 7:10 [c]Ps. 104:1 . 105:45; 106:48
[a]1 Chr. 16:8-22, s. 106:1; Is. 12:4 9:6 [c]Ps. 145:12
[1]Or, *Meditate on* ., *wonderful acts* . 96:1; 98:5 [b]Ps. 2; 119:27; 145:5
3 [1]Or, *Boast*

Let the [a]heart of those who seek the LORD be glad.
4 Seek the LORD and [a]His strength;
[b]Seek His face continually.
5 Remember His [1a]wonders which He has done,
His marvels, and the [b]judgments [2]uttered by His mouth,
6 O seed of [a]Abraham, His servant,
O sons of [b]Jacob, His [c]chosen ones!
7 He is the LORD our God;
His [a]judgments are in all the earth.

8 He has [a]remembered His covenant forever,
The word which He commanded to a [b]thousand generations,
9 *The* [a]*covenant* which He made with Abraham,
And His [b]oath to Isaac.
10 Then He [a]confirmed it to Jacob for a statute,
To Israel as an everlasting covenant,
11 Saying, "[a]To you I will give the land of Canaan
As the [1b]portion of your inheritance,"
12 When they were only a [a]few men in number,
Very few, and [b]strangers in it.
13 And they wandered about from nation to nation,
From *one* kingdom to another people.
14 He [a]permitted no man to oppress them,
And He [b]reproved kings for their sakes:
15 "[a]Do not touch My anointed ones,
And do My prophets no harm."

16 And He [a]called for a famine upon the land;
He [b]broke the whole staff of bread.
17 He [a]sent a man before them,
Joseph, *who* was [b]sold as a slave.
18 They afflicted his [a]feet with fetters,
[1]He himself was laid in irons;
19 Until the time that his [a]word came to pass,
The word of the LORD [1b]tested him.
20 The [a]king sent and released him,
The ruler of peoples, and set him free.
21 He [a]made him lord of his house,
And ruler over all his possessions,
22 To [1]imprison his princes [2a]at will,
That he might teach his elders wisdom.
23 [a]Israel also came into Egypt;
Thus Jacob [b]sojourned in the land of Ham.
24 And He [a]caused His people to be very fruitful,
And made them stronger than their adversaries.

25 He [a]turned their heart to hate His people,
To [b]deal craftily with His servants.
26 He [a]sent Moses His servant,
And [b]Aaron whom He had chosen.
27 They [1a]performed His wondrous acts among them,
And miracles in the land of Ham.
28 He [a]sent darkness and made *it* dark;
And they did not [b]rebel against His words.

3 [a]Ps. 33:21

4 [a]Ps. 63:2 [b]

5 [1]I.e., wonde [2]Lit., *of His mo* 40:5; 77:11 [b]P

6 [a]Ps. 105:42 135:4 [c]1 Chr. 106:5; 135:4

7 [a]Is. 26:9

8 [a]Ps. 105:42; Luke 1:72 [b]De

9 [a]Gen. 12:7; 22:16-18; Gal. [b]Gen. 26:3

10 [a]Gen. 28:1

11 [1]Lit., *meas* [a]Gen. 13:15; 1 [b]Josh. 23:4; Ps

12 [a]Gen. 34:30 7:7 [b]Gen. 23:4 11:9

14 [a]Gen. 20:7; [b]Gen. 12:17; 20

15 [a]Gen. 26:11

16 [a]Gen. 41:54 26:26; Is. 3:1; E

17 [a]Gen. 45:5 37:28, 36; Acts

18 [1]Lit., *His so* *into* [a]Gen. 39:2

19 [1]Or, *refined* 40:20, 21 [b]Ps.

20 [a]Gen. 41:14

21 [a]Gen. 41:40

22 [1]Lit., *bind* [2] *his* [a]Gen. 41:44

23 [a]Gen. 46:6; 7:15 [b]Acts 13:1

24 [a]Ex. 1:7, 9

25 [a]Ex. 1:8; 4:2 1:10; Acts 7:19

26 [a]Ex. 3:10; 4: 4:14; Num. 16:5;

27 [1]Lit., *set the* *of His signs* [a]Ps. 78:43-51; 105:27

28 [a]Ex. 10:21, 2 99:7

29 He [a]turned their waters into blood,
And caused their fish to die.
30 Their land swarmed with [a]frogs
Even in the [b]chambers of their kings.
31 He spoke, and there came a [a]swarm of flies
And [b]gnats in all their territory.
32 He [1]gave them [a]hail for rain,
And flaming fire in their land.
33 He [a]struck down their vines also and their fig trees,
And shattered the trees of their territory.
34 He spoke, and [a]locusts came,
And young locusts, even without number,
35 And ate up all vegetation in their land,
And ate up the fruit of their ground.
36 He also [a]struck down all the first-born in their land,
The [b]first fruits of all their vigor.

37 Then He brought them out with [a]silver and gold;
And among His tribes there was not one who stumbled.
38 Egypt was [a]glad when they departed;
For the [b]dread of them had fallen upon them.
39 He spread a [a]cloud for a [1]covering,
And [b]fire to illumine by night.
40 [1]They [a]asked, and He brought [b]quail,
And satisfied them with the [2c]bread of heaven.
41 He opened the [1]rock, and [a]water flowed out;
[2]It ran in the dry places *like* a river.
42 For He [a]remembered His holy word
With Abraham His servant;
43 And He brought forth His people with joy,
His chosen ones with a joyful [a]shout.
44 He [a]gave them also the lands of the [1]nations,
That they [b]might take possession of *the fruit of* the peoples' labor,
45 So that they might [a]keep His statutes,
And observe His laws,
[1]Praise [2]the LORD!

Psalm 106

106 [1]Praise [2]the LORD!
Oh [a]give thanks to the LORD, for He [b]is good;
For [c]His lovingkindness is everlasting.
2 Who can speak of the [a]mighty deeds of the LORD,
Or can show forth all His praise?
3 How blessed are those who keep [1]justice,
[2]Who [a]practice righteousness at all times!

4 Remember me, O LORD, in *Thy* [a]favor [1]toward Thy people;
Visit me with Thy salvation,
5 That I may see the [a]prosperity of Thy chosen ones,
That I may [b]rejoice in the gladness of Thy nation,
That I may [c]glory with Thine [1]inheritance.

6 [a]We have sinned [1b]like our fathers,
We have committed iniquity, we have behaved wickedly.

[a]Ex. 7:20, 21
. 8:6 [b]Ex. 8:3
Ex. 8:21 [b]Ex. 8:16, 17
nade their rain [a]Ex. 9:23-25
33 [a]Ps. 78:47
[a]Ex. 10:12-15
12:29; 13:15; 135:8; 136:10 [b]Gen. 49:3
[a]Ex. 12:35, 36
Ex. 12:33 [b]Ex. 15:16
r, curtain [a]Ex. Neh. 9:12; Ps. 4:5 [b]Ex. 40:38
One [2]Or, food 6:12; Ps. 78:18 3; Num. 11:31; 27 [c]Ex. 16:15; :15; Ps. 78:24; John 6:31
, boulder [2]Lit., went [a]Ex. 17:6; 0:11; Ps. 78:15; s. 48:21; 1 Cor. 10:4
. 15:13, 14; Ps. 105:8
5:1; Ps. 106:12
Gentiles [a]Josh. 16-23; 13:7; Ps. [b]Deut. 6:10, 11
[1]Or, Hallelujah! eb., YAH [a]Deut. 4:1, 40
[1]Or, Hallelujah! YAH [a]Ps. 105:1; 18:1; 136:1; Jer. 2 Chr. 5:13; 7:3; 3:11; Ps. 100:5 1 Chr. 16:34, 41
145:4, 12; 150:2
udgment [2]Many s. read The one forms [a]Ps. 15:2
it., of [a]Ps. 44:3; 119:132
people [a]Ps. 1:3 8:15 [c]Ps. 105:3
[1]Lit., with [a]1 Kin. ra 9:7; Neh. 1:7; er. 3:25; Dan. 9:5 r. 30:7; Neh. 9:2; 8, 57; Zech. 1:4

7 Our fathers in Egypt did not understand Thy [1]wonders;
They [a]did not remember [2]Thine abundant kindnesses,
But [b]rebelled by the sea, at the [3]Red Sea.
8 Nevertheless He saved them [a]for the sake of His name,
That He might [b]make His power known.
9 Thus He [a]rebuked the [1]Red Sea and it [b]dried up;
And He [c]led them through the deeps, as through the wilderness.
10 So He [a]saved them from the [1]hand of the one who hated *them*,
And [b]redeemed them from the [1]hand of the enemy.
11 And [a]the waters covered their adversaries;
Not one of them was left.
12 Then they [a]believed His words;
They [b]sang His praise.

13 They quickly [a]forgot His works;
They [b]did not wait for His counsel,
14 But [a]craved intensely in the wilderness,
And [1b]tempted God in the desert.
15 So He [a]gave them their request,
But [b]sent a [1]wasting disease among them.

16 When they became [a]envious of Moses in the camp,
And of Aaron, the holy one of the LORD,
17 The [a]earth opened and swallowed up Dathan,
And engulfed the [1]company of Abiram.
18 And a [a]fire blazed up in their [1]company;
The flame consumed the wicked.

19 They [a]made a calf in Horeb,
And worshiped a molten image.
20 Thus they [a]exchanged their glory
For the image of an ox that eats grass.
21 They [a]forgot God their Savior,
Who had done [b]great things in Egypt,
22 [1a]Wonders in the land of Ham,
And awesome things by the [2]Red Sea.
23 Therefore [a]He said that He would destroy them,
Had not [b]Moses His chosen one stood in the breach before Him,
To turn away His wrath from destroying *them*.
24 Then they [a]despised the [b]pleasant land;
They [c]did not believe in His word,
25 But [a]grumbled in their tents;
They did not listen to the voice of the LORD.
26 Therefore He [1a]swore to them,
That He would cast them down in the wilderness,
27 And that He would [a]cast their seed among the nations,
And [b]scatter them in the lands.

28 They [a]joined themselves also to [1]Baal-peor,
And ate [b]sacrifices offered to the dead.
29 Thus they [a]provoked *Him* to anger with their deeds;
And the plague broke out among them.
30 Then Phinehas [a]stood up and interposed;
And so the [b]plague was stayed.

7 [1]I.e., wonde [2]Lit., *the multit* *Thy lovingkind* [3]Lit., *Sea of Re* [a]Judg. 3:7; Ps. 42 [b]Ex. 14:11, 78:17
8 [a]Ezek. 20:9
9 [1]Lit., *Sea of* [a]Ps. 18:15; 78: 50:2; Nah. 1:4 14:21; Is. 51:10 63:11-13
10 [1]Or, *power* 14:30 [b]Ps. 78:
11 [a]Ex. 14:27, Ps. 78:53
12 [a]Ex. 14:31 15:1-21; Ps. 10
13 [a]Ex. 15:24; 17:2 [b]Ps. 107:
14 [1]Or, *put Go* *test* [a]Num. 11:4 78:18; 1 Cor. 10 17:2; 1 Cor. 10:
15 [1]Or, *leannes* *their soul* [a]Num Ps. 78:29 [b]Is. 1
16 [a]Num. 16:1-
17 [1]Or, *assemb* *band* [a]Num. 16 Deut. 11:6
18 [1]Or, *assemb* *band* [a]Num. 16
19 [a]Ex. 32:4; D Acts 7:41
20 [a]Jer. 2:11; R
21 [a]Ps. 78:11; 1 13 [b]Deut. 10:21
22 [1]I.e., Wonde acts [2]Lit., *Sea o* *Reeds* [a]Ps. 105
23 [a]Ex. 32:10; D 9:14; Ezek. 20:8, [b]Ex. 32:11-14; D 9:25-29
24 [a]Num. 14:31 8:7; Jer. 3:19; Ez 20:6 [c]Deut. 1:32 Heb. 3:19
25 [a]Num. 14:2; 1:27
26 [1]Lit., *lifted up* *hand* [a]Num. 14: Ps. 95:11; Ezek. Heb. 3:11
27 [a]Deut. 4:27 [b] 26:33; Ps. 44:11
28 [1]Or, *Baal of P* [a]Num. 25:3; Deut Hos. 9:10 [b]Num.
29 [a]Num. 25:4
30 [a]Num. 25:7 [b] 25:8

31 And it was [a]reckoned to him for righteousness,
To all generations forever.

32 They also [a]provoked *Him* to wrath at the waters of [1]Meribah,
So that it [b]went hard with Moses on their account;
33 Because they [a]were rebellious against [1]His Spirit,
He spoke rashly with his lips.

34 They [a]did not destroy the peoples,
As [b]the LORD commanded them,
35 But [a]they mingled with the nations,
And learned their [1]practices,
36 And [a]served their idols,
[b]Which became a snare to them.
37 They even [a]sacrificed their sons and their daughters to the
[b]demons,
38 And shed [a]innocent blood,
The blood of their [b]sons and their daughters,
Whom they sacrificed to the idols of Canaan;
And the land was [c]polluted with the blood.
39 Thus they became [a]unclean in their [1]practices,
And [b]played the harlot in their deeds.

40 Therefore the [a]anger of the LORD was kindled against His people,
And He [b]abhorred His [1c]inheritance.
41 Then [a]He gave them into the hand of the [1]nations;
And those who hated them ruled over them.
42 Their enemies also [a]oppressed them,
And they were subdued under their [1]power.
43 Many times He would [a]deliver them;
They, however, were rebellious in their [b]counsel,
And *so* [c]sank down in their iniquity.

44 Nevertheless He looked upon their distress,
When He [a]heard their cry;
45 And He [a]remembered His covenant for their sake,
And [1b]relented [c]according to the greatness of His lovingkindness.
46 He also made them [a]*objects* of compassion
In the presence of all their captors.

47 [a]Save us, O LORD our God,
And [b]gather us from among the nations,
To give thanks to Thy holy name,
And [1c]glory in Thy praise.
48 [a]Blessed be the LORD, the God of Israel,
From everlasting even to everlasting.
And let all the people say, "Amen."
[1]Praise [2]the LORD!

BOOK 5

Psalm 107

107 Oh [a]give thanks to the LORD, for [b]He is good;
For His lovingkindness is everlasting.
2 Let [a]the redeemed of the LORD say *so*,

n. 15:6; Num. 25:11-13
, *strife* [a]Num. Ps. 81:7; 95:9 [b]Num. 20:12
s *spirit* [a]Num. 10; Ps. 78:40; 107:11
g. 1:21, 27-36 [b]Deut. 7:2, 16
works [a]Judg. 3:5, 6
g. 2:12 [b]Deut. 7:16
. 12:31; 32:17; ; 17:17; Ezek. ; 1 Cor. 10:20 [b]Lev. 17:7
. 94:21 [b]Deut. Num. 35:33; Is. 24:5; Jer. 3:1, 2
t., *works* [a]Lev. 24; Ezek. 20:18 7; Num. 15:39; 2:17; Hos. 4:12
people [a]Judg. Ps. 78:59 [b]Lev. 30; Deut. 32:19 Deut. 9:29; 32:9
Gentiles [a]Judg. 2:14; Neh. 9:27
t., *hand* [a]Judg. 4:3; 10:12
g. 2:16-18 [b]Ps. 1:12 [c]Judg. 6:6
. 3:9; 6:7; 10:10
[1]Lit., *was sorry* 26:42; Ps. 105:8 2:18 [c]Ps. 69:16
Kin. 8:50; 2 Chr. ; Ezra 9:9; Neh. 1:11; Jer. 42:12
it., *boast* [a]1 Chr. 5, 36 [b]Ps. 147:2 [c]Ps. 47:1
[1]Or, *Hallelujah!* YAH [a]Ps. 41:13; 72:18; 89:52
1 [a]1 Chr. 16:34; 6:1; 118:1; 136:1; :11 [b]2 Chr. 5:13; a 3:11; Ps. 100:5
. 35:9, 10; 62:12; 63:4

Whom He has [b]redeemed from the hand of the adversary,
3 And [a]gathered from the lands,
From the east and from the west,
From the north and from the [1]south.

4 They [a]wandered in the wilderness in a [1]desert region;
They did not find a way to [2]an inhabited [b]city.
5 *They were* hungry [1]and thirsty;
Their [a]soul fainted within them.
6 Then they [a]cried out to the LORD in their trouble;
He delivered them out of their distresses.
7 He led them also by a [1a]straight way,
To go to [2b]an inhabited city.
8 [a]Let them give thanks to the LORD for His lovingkindness,
And for His [1]wonders to the sons of men!
9 For He has [a]satisfied the [1]thirsty soul,
And the [b]hungry soul He has filled with what is good.

10 There were those who [a]dwelt in darkness and in the shadow of death,
[b]Prisoners in [1]misery and [2]chains,
11 Because they had [a]rebelled against the words of God,
And [b]spurned the [c]counsel of the Most High.
12 Therefore He humbled their heart with labor;
They stumbled and there was [a]none to help.
13 Then they [a]cried out to the LORD in their trouble;
He saved them out of their distresses.
14 He [a]brought them out of darkness and the shadow of death,
And [b]broke their bands apart.
15 [a]Let them give thanks to the LORD for His lovingkindness,
And for His [1]wonders to the sons of men!
16 For He has [a]shattered gates of bronze,
And cut bars of iron asunder.

17 Fools, because of [1]their rebellious way,
And [a]because of their iniquities, were afflicted.
18 Their [a]soul abhorred all kinds of food;
And they [b]drew near to the [c]gates of death.
19 Then they cried out to the LORD in their trouble;
He saved them out of their distresses.
20 He [a]sent His word and [b]healed them,
And [c]delivered *them* from their [1]destructions.
21 [a]Let them give thanks to the LORD for His lovingkindness,
And for His [1]wonders to the sons of men!
22 Let them also offer [a]sacrifices of thanksgiving,
And [b]tell of His works with joyful singing.

23 Those who [a]go down to the sea in ships,
Who do business on great waters;
24 They have seen the works of the LORD,
And His [1]wonders in the deep.
25 For He [a]spoke and raised up a [b]stormy wind,
Which [c]lifted up the waves [1]of the sea.
26 They rose up to the heavens, they went down to the depths;

2 [b]Ps. 78:42;

3 [1]Lit., *sea* [a]Neh. 1:9; Ps. 11:12; 43:5; 5 11:17; 20:34

4 [1]Lit., *waste habitable city; of habitation* [a] 14:33; 32:13; 32:10; Josh. 5 [b]Ps. 107:7, 36

5 [1]Lit., *also* [a]

6 [a]Ps. 50:15; 19, 28

7 [1]Or, *level* [2] *habitable city; of habitation* [a] 8:21; Ps. 5:8; [b]Ps. 107:4, 36

8 [1]I.e., wonde [a]Ps. 107:15, 21

9 [1]Or, *parched* 22:26; 34:10; 103:5 [b]Ps. 14 5:6; Luke 1:53

10 [1]Lit., *afflicti irons* [a]Ps. 143 42:7; Mic. 7:8; 1:79 [b]Job 36:8 102:20

11 [a]Ps. 78:40; Lam. 3:42 [b]Nu 2 Chr. 36:16; P Is. 5:24 [c]Ps. 7

12 [a]Ps. 22:11;

13 [a]Ps. 107:6

14 [a]Ps. 86:13; [b]Ps. 116:16; Je 30:8; Nah. 1:13 13:16; Acts 12:

15 [1]I.e., wonde [a]Ps. 107:8, 21,

16 [a]Is. 45:1, 2

17 [1]Lit., *the wa transgression* [a] 7; Jer. 30:14, 15 3:39; Ezek. 24:

18 [a]Job 33:20; 102:4 [b]Job 33: 88:3 [c]Job 38:17 9:13

20 [1]Or, *pits* [a]P 147:15, 18; Mat [b]2 Kin. 20:5; Ps. 103:3; 147:3 [c]J 33:28, 30; Ps. 3 49:15; 56:13; 10

21 [1]I.e., wonder [a]Ps. 107:8, 15, 3

22 [a]Lev. 7:12; P 50:14; 116:17 [b] 73:28; 118:17

23 [a]Is. 42:10; Jo

24 [1]I.e., wonder

25 [1]Lit., *of it* [a]P 105:31, 34 [b]Ps. Jon. 1:4 [c]Ps. 93

Their soul [a]melted away in *their* misery.
27 They reeled and [a]staggered like a drunken man,
And [1]were at their wits' end.
28 Then they cried to the LORD in their trouble,
And He brought them out of their distresses.
29 He [a]caused the storm to be still,
So that the waves [1]of the sea were hushed.
30 Then they were glad because they were quiet;
So He guided them to their desired haven.
31 [a]Let them give thanks to the LORD for His lovingkindness,
And for His [1b]wonders to the sons of men!
32 Let them [a]extol Him also [b]in the congregation of the people,
And [c]praise Him at the seat of the elders.

33 He [1a]changes rivers into a [2]wilderness,
And springs of water into a thirsty ground;
34 A [a]fruitful land into a [b]salt waste,
Because of the wickedness of those who dwell in it.
35 He [1a]changes a [2]wilderness into a pool of water,
And a dry land into springs of water;
36 And there He makes the hungry to dwell,
So that they may establish [1a]an inhabited city,
37 And sow fields, and [a]plant vineyards,
And [1]gather a fruitful harvest.
38 Also He blesses them and they [a]multiply greatly;
And He [b]does not let their cattle decrease.

39 When they are [a]diminished and [b]bowed down
Through oppression, misery, and sorrow,
40 He [a]pours contempt upon [1]princes,
And [b]makes them wander [c]in a pathless waste.
41 But He [a]sets the needy [1]securely on high away from affliction,
And [b]makes *his* families like a flock.
42 The [a]upright see it, and are glad;
But all [b]unrighteousness shuts its mouth.
43 Who is [a]wise? Let him give heed to these things;
And consider the [b]lovingkindnesses of the LORD.

Psalm 108

A Song, a Psalm of David.

108 [a]My heart is steadfast, O God;
I will sing, I will sing praises, even with my [1]soul.
2 Awake, harp and lyre;
I will awaken the dawn!
3 I will give thanks to Thee, O LORD, among the peoples;
And I will sing praises to Thee among the nations.
4 For Thy [a]lovingkindness is great [b]above the heavens;
And Thy truth *reaches* to the skies.
5 [a]Be exalted, O God, above the heavens,
And Thy glory above all the earth.
6 [a]That Thy beloved may be delivered,
Save with Thy right hand, and answer me!

7 God has spoken in His [1]holiness:

22:14; 119:28
l their wisdom owed up [a]Job 2:25; Is. 24:20
of it [a]Ps. 65:7; att. 8:26; Luke 8:24
wonderful acts 8, 15, 21 [b]Ps. 78:4; 111:4
34:3; 99:5; Is. [b]Ps. 22:22, 25 [c]Ps. 35:18
[1]Or, *turns* [2]Or, [a]1 Kin. 17:1, 7; Is. 42:15; 50:2
en. 13:10; 14:3; 25; Deut. 29:23 39:6; Jer. 17:6
[1]Or, *turns* [2]Or, *rt* [a]Ps. 105:41; . 35:6, 7; 41:18
a habitable city; ity of habitation [a]Ps. 107:4, 7
acquire fruits of 2 Kin. 19:29; Is. :21; Amos 9:14
en. 12:2; 17:20; 1:7; Deut. 1:10 [b]Deut. 7:14
in. 10:32; Ezek. 29:15 [b]Ps. 38:6; 44:25; 57:6
Or, *nobles* [a]Job 2:21 [b]Job 12:24 [c]Deut. 32:10
41 [1]Lit., *in an ssibly high place* m. 2:8; Ps. 59:1; [b]Job 21:11; Ps. 78:52; 113:9
[a]Job 22:19; Ps. 6 [b]Job 5:16; Ps. 63:11; Rom. 3:19
s. 64:9; Jer. 9:12; 14:9 [b]Ps. 107:1
[1]Lit., *glory* [a]Ps. 57:7-11; 108:1-5
um. 14:18; Deut. ; Ps. 36:5; 100:5; 18-20 [b]Ps. 113:4
5 [a]Ps. 57:5
60:5-12; 108:6-13
7 [1]Or, *sanctuary*

"I will exult, I will portion out Shechem,
And measure out the valley of Succoth.
8 "Gilead is Mine, Manasseh is Mine;
Ephraim also is the [1]helmet of My head;
[a]Judah is My [2]scepter.
9 "Moab is My washbowl;
Over Edom I shall throw My shoe;
Over Philistia I will shout aloud."

10 [a]Who will bring me into the besieged city?
Who [1]will lead me to Edom?
11 Hast not Thou Thyself, O God, [a]rejected us?
And wilt Thou not go forth with our armies, O God?
12 Oh give us help against the adversary,
For [a]deliverance [1]by man is in vain.
13 [1]Through God we shall do valiantly;
And [a]it is He who will tread down our adversaries.

Psalm 109

For the choir director. A Psalm of David.

109 O [a]God of my praise,
[b]Do not be silent!
2 For they have opened the [1]wicked and [a]deceitful mouth against me;
They have spoken [2]against me with a [b]lying tongue.
3 They have also surrounded me with words of hatred,
And fought against me [a]without cause.
4 In return [a]for my love they act as my accusers;
But [b]I am *in* prayer.
5 Thus they have [1a]repaid me evil for good,
And [b]hatred for my love.

6 Appoint a wicked man over him;
And let an [1a]accuser stand at his right hand.
7 When he is judged, let him [a]come forth guilty;
And let his [b]prayer become sin.
8 Let [a]his days be few;
Let [b]another take his office.
9 Let his [a]children be fatherless,
And his [b]wife a widow.
10 Let his [a]children wander about and beg;
And let them [b]seek *sustenance* [1]far from their ruined homes.
11 Let [a]the creditor [1]seize all that he has;
And let [b]strangers plunder the product of his labor.
12 Let there be none to [1a]extend lovingkindness to him,
Nor [b]any to be gracious to his fatherless children.
13 Let his [a]posterity be [1]cut off;
In a following generation let their [b]name be blotted out.

14 Let [a]the iniquity of his fathers be remembered [1]before the LORD,
And do not let the sin of his mother be [b]blotted out.
15 Let [a]them be before the LORD continually,
That He may [b]cut off their memory from the earth;
16 Because he did not remember to show lovingkindness,

8 [1]Lit., *protect*... *lawgiver* [a]Gen...
10 [1]Or, *has le*... 60:9
11 [a]Ps. 44:9
12 [1]Lit., *of* [a]Is...
13 [1]Or, *In* or *W*... 60:12; 63:1-4
109:1 [a]Deut. 1... [b]Ps. 28:1; 83:1
2 [1]Lit., *wicked*... *and the deceitf*... *with* [a]Ps. 10:7; [b]Ps. 120:2
3 [a]Ps. 35:7; 69... 15:25
4 [a]Ps. 38:20 [b]P... 69:13; 141:5
5 [1]Lit., *laid upo*... [a]Ps. 35:12; 38:2... 7:7; 10:32
6 [1]Or, *adversa*... *Satan* [a]Zech. 3...
7 [a]Ps. 1:5 [b]Pro...
8 [a]Ps. 55:23 [b]A...
9 [a]Ex. 22:24 [b]J...
10 [1]Or, *out of th*... *desolate places*... 4:12; Job 30:5-8... 59:15 [b]Ps. 37:2...
11 [1]Lit., *ensnare*... *at* [a]Neh. 5:7; Jo... 20:15 [b]Is. 1:7; L... Ezek. 7:21
12 [1]Lit., *continue*... 7:28; 9:9 [b]Job 5... 9:17
13 [1]Lit., *for cuttin*... [a]Job 18:19; Ps. 2... 37:28 [b]Ps. 9:5; P... 10:7
14 [1]Lit., *to* [a]Ex. ... Num. 14:18; Is. 6... Jer. 32:18 [b]Neh... Jer. 18:23
15 [a]Ps. 90:8; Jer... 16:17 [b]Job 18:1... 34:16

But persecuted the [a]afflicted and needy man,
And the [b]despondent in heart, to [c]put *them* to death.
17 He also loved cursing, so [a]it came to him;
And he did not delight in blessing, so it was far from him.
18 But he [a]clothed himself with cursing as with his garment,
And it [b]entered into [1]his body like water,
And like oil into his bones.
19 Let it be to him as [a]a garment with which he covers himself,
And for a belt with which he constantly [b]girds himself.
20 [1]Let this be the [a]reward of my accusers from the LORD,
And of those who [b]speak evil against my soul.

21 But Thou, O [1]GOD, the Lord, deal *kindly* with me [a]for Thy name's sake;
Because [b]Thy lovingkindness is good, deliver me;
22 For [a]I am afflicted and needy,
And [1]my heart is [b]wounded within me.
23 I am passing [a]like a shadow when it lengthens;
I am shaken off [b]like the locust.
24 My [a]knees [1]are weak from [b]fasting;
And my flesh has grown lean, without fatness.
25 I also have become a [a]reproach to them;
When they see me, they [b]wag their head.

26 [a]Help me, O LORD my God;
Save me according to Thy lovingkindness.
27 [1]And let them [a]know that this is Thy hand;
Thou, LORD, hast done it.
28 [a]Let them curse, but do Thou bless;
When they arise, they shall be ashamed,
But Thy [b]servant shall be glad.
29 [1]Let [a]my accusers be clothed with dishonor,
And [2]let them [b]cover themselves with their own shame as with a robe.

30 With my mouth I will give thanks abundantly to the LORD;
And in the midst of many [a]I will praise Him.
31 For He stands [a]at the right hand of the needy,
To save him from those who [b]judge his soul.

Psalm 110

A Psalm of David.

110 [a]The LORD says to my Lord:
"[b]Sit at My right hand,
Until I make [c]Thine enemies a footstool for Thy feet."
2 The LORD will stretch forth Thy strong [a]scepter from Zion, *saying,*
"[b]Rule in the midst of Thine enemies."
3 Thy [a]people [1]will volunteer freely in the day of Thy [2]power;
[b]In [3]holy array, from the womb of the dawn,
[4]Thy youth are to Thee *as* the [c]dew.

4 [a]The LORD has sworn and will [b]not [1]change His mind,
"Thou art a [c]priest forever
According to the order of Melchizedek."

Ps. 37:14 [b]Ps. 37:32; 94:6
v. 14:14; Ezek. 35:9; Matt. 7:2
Lit., *his inward* . 73:6; 109:29; 27 [b]Num. 5:22
. 73:6; 109:29; . 7:27 [b]2 Sam. 30:11; Is. 11:5
it., *This is* [a]Ps. 94:23; Is. 3:11; 4:14 [b]Ps. 41:5; 71:10
[1]Heb., *YHWH,* rendered *LORD* :3; 25:11; 79:9; zek. 36:22 [b]Ps. 69:16
2 [1]Lit., *one has my heart within* Ps. 40:17; 86:1 4:12; Ps. 143:4; Prov. 18:14
Ps. 102:11 [b]Ex. 0:19; Job 39:20
Or, *totter* [a]Heb. 2:12 [b]Ps. 35:13
22:6 [b]Ps. 22:7; 3:16; Lam. 2:15; :39; Mark 15:29
26 [a]Ps. 119:86
, *That they may know* [a]Job 37:7
Sam. 16:11, 12 [b]Is. 65:14
Or, *My accusers be* [2]Or, *they will* *er* [a]Job 8:22; Ps. 3 [b]Job 8:22; Ps. 35:26
Ps. 22:22; 35:18; 111:1
[a]Ps. 16:8; 73:23; 21:5 [b]Ps. 37:33
0:1 [a]Matt. 22:44; 2:36; Luke 20:42, ts 2:34, 35; Heb. Matt. 26:64; Eph. ol. 3:1; Heb. 1:3; :12; 12:2 [c]1 Cor. 15:25; Eph. 1:22
45:6; Jer. 48:17; . 19:14 [b]Ps. 2:9; 2:8; Dan. 7:13, 14
it., *will be freewill ferings* [2]Or, *army* r, *the splendor of* ess [4]Or, *The dew hy youth is Thine.* dg. 5:2; Neh. 11:2 r. 16:29; Ps. 96:9 n. 17:12; Mic. 5:7
t., *be sorry* [a]Heb. 7:21 [b]Num. 23:19 ch. 6:13; Heb. 5:6, 10; 6:20; 7:17, 21

5 The Lord is [a]at Thy right hand;
He [1]will [b]shatter kings in the [c]day of His wrath.
6 He will [a]judge among the nations,
He [1]will fill *them* with [b]corpses,
He [2]will [c]shatter the [3]chief men over a broad country.
7 He will [a]drink from the brook by the wayside;
Therefore He will [b]lift up *His* head.

Psalm 111

111 [1]Praise [2]the LORD!
I [a]will give thanks to the LORD with all *my* heart,
In the [b]company of the upright and in the assembly.
2 [a]Great are the works of the LORD;
They are [1b]studied by all who delight in them.
3 [1a]Splendid and majestic is His work;
And [b]His righteousness endures forever.
4 He has made His [1]wonders [2]to be remembered;
The LORD is [a]gracious and compassionate.
5 He has [a]given [1]food to those who [2]fear Him;
He will [b]remember His covenant forever.
6 He has made known to His people the power of His works,
In giving them the heritage of the nations.

7 The works of His hands are [1a]truth and justice;
All His precepts [b]are [2]sure.
8 They are [a]upheld forever and ever;
They are performed in [1b]truth and uprightness.
9 He has sent [a]redemption to His people;
He has [1]ordained His covenant forever;
[b]Holy and [2]awesome is His name.
10 The [1a]fear of the LORD is the beginning of wisdom;
A [b]good understanding have all those who [2]do *His commandments*;
His [c]praise endures forever.

Psalm 112

112 [1]Praise [2]the LORD!
How [a]blessed is the man who [3]fears the LORD,
Who greatly [b]delights in His commandments.
2 His [1a]descendants will be mighty [2]on earth;
The generation of the [b]upright will be blessed.
3 [a]Wealth and riches are in his house,
And his righteousness endures forever.
4 Light arises in the darkness [a]for the upright;
He is [b]gracious and compassionate and righteous.
5 It is well with the man who [a]is gracious and lends;
He will [1]maintain his cause in judgment.
6 For he will [a]never be shaken;
The [b]righteous will be [1]remembered forever.

7 He will not fear [a]evil tidings;
His [b]heart is steadfast, [c]trusting in the LORD.
8 His [a]heart is upheld, he [b]will not fear,
Until he [c]looks *with satisfaction* on his adversaries.

5 [1]Or, *has sha* [a]Ps. 16:8; 109: 68:14; 76:12 [c] 12; Rom. 2:5;

6 [1]Or, *has fille has shattered head over* [a]Is. 3:12; Mic. 4:3 66:24 [c]Ps. 68:

7 [a]Judg. 7:5, 6 27:6

111:1 [1]Or, *Hall will* [2]Heb., *YAH* 35:18; 138:1 [b] 149:1

2 [1]Lit., *sought* 92:5 [b]Ps. 143:5

3 [1]Lit., *Splendo majesty* [a]Ps. 96 145:5 [b]Ps. 112: 119:142

4 [1]I.e., wonderf [2]Lit., *a memoria* 86:5, 15; 103:8;

5 [1]Lit., *prey* [2]O *revere* [a]Matt. 6: [b]Ps. 105:8

7 [1]Or, *faithfulne trustworthy* [a]Re [b]Ps. 19:7; 93:5

8 [1]Or, *faithfulne* 119:160; Is. 40:8 5:18 [b]Ps. 19:9

9 [1]Lit., *comman* [2]I.e., inspiring reverence [a]Luke [b]Ps. 99:3; Luke

10 [1]Or, *reveren* [2]Lit., *do* them [a]J 28:28; Prov. 1:7; Eccl. 12:13 [b]Ps. Prov. 3:4 [c]Ps. 14

112:1 [1]Or, *Halle Blessed* [2]Heb., [3]Or, *reveres* [a]Ps [b]Ps. 1:2; 119:14,

2 [1]Lit., *seed* [2]Or *land* [a]Ps. 102:28 127:4 [b]Ps. 128:4

3 [a]Prov. 3:16; 8: Matt. 6:33

4 [a]Job 11:17; Ps. [b]Ps. 37:26

5 [1]Or, *conduct hi affairs with justice* 37:21

6 [1]Lit., *for an eter remembrance* [a]P 15:5; 55:22 [b]Prov

7 [a]Prov. 1:33 [b]Ps 108:1 [c]Ps. 56:4

8 [a]Heb. 13:9 [b]Ps 56:11; Prov. 1:33; Is. 12:2 [c]Ps. 54:7

9 [1]He [a]has given freely to the poor;
His righteousness endures forever;
His [b]horn will be exalted in honor.

10 The [a]wicked will see it and be [1]vexed;
He will [b]gnash his teeth and [c]melt away;
The [d]desire of the wicked will perish.

Psalm 113

113 [1]Praise [2]the LORD!
[a]Praise, O [b]servants of the LORD.
Praise the name of the LORD.
2 [a]Blessed be the name of the LORD
From this time forth and forever.
3 [a]From the rising of the sun to its setting
The [b]name of the LORD is to be praised.
4 The LORD is [a]high above all nations;
His [b]glory is above the heavens.

5 [a]Who is like the LORD our God,
Who [b]is enthroned on high,
6 Who [1a]humbles Himself to behold
The things that are in heaven and in the earth?
7 He [a]raises the poor from the dust,
And lifts the needy from the ash heap,
8 To make *them* [a]sit with [1]princes,
With the [1]princes of His people.
9 He [a]makes the barren woman abide in the house
As a joyful mother of children.
[1]Praise [2]the LORD!

Psalm 114

114 When Israel went forth [a]from Egypt,
The house of Jacob from a people of [b]strange language,
2 Judah became [a]His sanctuary,
Israel, [b]His dominion.

3 The [a]sea looked and fled;
The [b]Jordan turned back.
4 The mountains [a]skipped like rams,
The hills, like lambs.
5 What [a]ails you, O sea, that you flee?
O Jordan, that you turn back?
6 O mountains, that you skip like rams?
O hills, like lambs?

7 [a]Tremble, O earth, before the Lord,
Before the God of Jacob,
8 Who [a]turned the rock into a [b]pool of water,
The [c]flint into a fountain of water.

Psalm 115

115 [a]Not to us, O LORD, not to us,
But [b]to Thy name give glory

[1]Lit., *He has* ... *he has given* ... Cor. 9:9 [b]Ps. 89:17; 92:10; 148:14

...Or, *angry* [a]Ps. ...7 [b]Ps. 35:16; ...tt. 8:12; 25:30; ...3:28 [c]Ps. 58:7 ...3; Prov. 10:28; 11:7

...Or, *Hallelujah!* ...eb., YAH [a]Ps. ...:1 [b]Ps. 34:22; ...; 79:10; 90:13

...:21; Dan. 2:20

...50:1; Is. 59:19; ...:11 [b]Ps. 18:3; 48:1, 10

...97:9; 99:2 [b]Ps. ...; 57:11; 148:13

...5:11; Ps. 35:10; ...:6 [b]Ps. 103:19

...oks far below in ...vens and on the ...Ps. 11:4; 138:6; Is. 57:15

1 Sam. 2:8; Ps. 107:41

...bles [a]Job 36:7

[1]Or, *Hallelujah!* ...AH [a]1 Sam. 2:5; ...s. 68:6; Is. 54:1

[a]Ex. 12:51; 13:3 [b]Ps. 81:5

...5:17; 29:45, 46; ...8, 69 [b]Ex. 19:6

...14:21; Ps. 77:16 [b]Josh. 3:13, 16

...9:18; Judg. 5:5; ...7; 29:6; Hab. 3:6

5 [a]Hab. 3:8

7 [a]Ps. 96:9

[a]Ex. 17:6; Num. 20:11; Ps. 78:15; ...5:41 [b]Ps. 107:35 [c]Deut. 8:15

[a]Is. 48:11; Ezek. ...2 [b]Ps. 29:2; 96:8

Because of Thy lovingkindness, because of Thy [1]truth.
2 [a]Why should the nations say,
"[b]Where, now, is their God?"
3 But our [a]God is in the heavens;
He [b]does whatever He pleases.
4 Their [a]idols are silver and gold,
The [b]work of man's hands.
5 They have mouths, but they [a]cannot speak;
They have eyes, but they cannot see;
6 They have ears, but they cannot hear;
They have noses, but they cannot smell;
7 [1]They have hands, but they cannot feel;
[2]They have feet, but they cannot walk;
They cannot make a sound with their throat.
8 [a]Those who make them [1]will become like them,
Everyone who trusts in them.

9 O [a]Israel, [b]trust in the LORD;
He is their [c]help and their shield.
10 O house of [a]Aaron, trust in the LORD;
He is their help and their shield.
11 You who [1a]fear the LORD, trust in the LORD;
He is their help and their shield.
12 The LORD [a]has been mindful of us; He will bless *us;*
He will bless the house of Israel;
He will bless the house of Aaron.
13 He will [a]bless those who [1]fear the LORD,
[b]The small together with the great.
14 May the LORD [a]give you increase,
You and your children.
15 May you be blessed of the LORD,
[a]Maker of heaven and earth.

16 The heavens are [a]the heavens of the LORD;
But [b]the earth He has given to the sons of men.
17 The [a]dead do not praise [1]the LORD,
Nor *do* any who go down into [b]silence;
18 But as for us, we will [a]bless [1]the LORD
From this time forth and forever.
[2]Praise [1]the LORD!

Psalm 116

116 [a]I love the LORD, because He [b]hears
My voice *and* my supplications.
2 Because He has [a]inclined His ear to me,
Therefore I shall call *upon Him* as long as I live.
3 The [a]cords of death encompassed me,
And the [1]terrors of [2]Sheol [3]came upon me;
I found distress and sorrow.
4 Then [a]I called upon the name of the LORD:
"O LORD, I beseech Thee, [1b]save my life!"

5 [a]Gracious is the LORD, and [b]righteous;
Yes, our God is [c]compassionate.

115:1 [1]Or, *fa*
2 [a]Ps. 79:10
42:3, 10
3 [a]Ps. 103:19
135:6; Dan. 4
4 [a]Ps. 115:4-
135:15-18; Je
[b]Deut. 4:28; 2
19:18; Is. 37:1
20; Jer. 10:3
5 [a]Jer. 10:5
7 [1]Lit., *Their*
[2]Lit., *Their fee*
8 [1]Or, *are like*
[a]Ps. 135:18; Is
9 [a]Ps. 118:2;
[b]Ps. 37:3; 62:8
33:20
10 [a]Ps. 118:3;
11 [1]Or, *revere*
22:23; 103:11;
12 [a]Ps. 98:3
13 [1]Or, *revere*
103:11; 112:1;
[b]Rev. 11:18; 19
14 [a]Deut. 1:11
15 [a]Gen. 1:1;
Ps. 96:5; 102:2
124:8; 134:3; 14
Acts 14:15; Rev
16 [a]Ps. 89:11
17 [1]Heb., *YAH*
88:10-12; Is. 38
31:17
18 [1]Heb., *YAH*
Hallelujah! [a]Ps.
Dan. 2:20
116:1 [a]Ps. 18:1
6:8; 66:19; Is. 37
Dan. 9:18
2 [a]Ps. 17:6; 31:2
3 [1]Lit., *straits* [2]I
nether world [3]Lit
me [a]Ps. 18:4, 5
4 [1]Or, *deliver my*
[a]Ps. 18:6; 118:5
17:13; 22:20
5 [a]Ps. 86:15; 10
[b]Ezra 9:15; Neh.
Ps. 119:137; 145
Jer. 12:1; Dan. 9:
[c]Ex. 34:6

6 The LORD preserves [a]the simple;
I was [b]brought low, and He saved me.
7 Return to your [a]rest, O my soul,
For the LORD has [b]dealt bountifully with you.
8 For Thou hast [a]rescued my soul from death,
My eyes from tears,
My feet from stumbling.
9 I shall walk before the LORD
In the [1a]land of the living.
10 I [a]believed when I said,
"I am [b]greatly afflicted."
11 I [a]said in my alarm,
"[b]All men are liars."

12 What shall I [a]render to the LORD
For all His [b]benefits [1]toward me?
13 I shall lift up the [a]cup of salvation,
And [b]call upon the name of the LORD.
14 I shall [a]pay my vows to the LORD,
Oh *may it be* [b]in the presence of all His people.
15 [a]Precious in the sight of the LORD
Is the death of His godly ones.
16 O LORD, [1]surely I am [a]Thy servant,
I am Thy servant, the [b]son of Thy handmaid,
Thou hast [c]loosed my bonds.
17 To Thee I shall offer [a]a sacrifice of thanksgiving,
And [b]call upon the name of the LORD.
18 I shall [a]pay my vows to the LORD,
Oh *may it be* in the presence of all His people,
19 In the [a]courts of the LORD's house,
In the midst of you, O [b]Jerusalem.
[1]Praise [2]the LORD!

Psalm 117

117 [a]Praise the LORD, all nations;
Laud Him, all peoples!
2 For His [a]lovingkindness [1]is great toward us,
And the [2b]truth of the LORD is everlasting.
[3]Praise [4]the LORD!

Psalm 118

118 [a]Give thanks to the LORD, for [b]He is good;
For His lovingkindness is everlasting.
2 Oh let [a]Israel say,
"His lovingkindness is everlasting."
3 Oh let the [a]house of Aaron say,
"His lovingkindness is everlasting."
4 Oh let those [a]who [1]fear the LORD say,
"His lovingkindness is everlasting."

5 From *my* [a]distress I called upon [1]the LORD;
[1]The LORD answered me *and* [b]*set me* in a large place.
6 The LORD is [a]for me; I will [b]not fear;
[c]What can man do to me?

:7; Prov. 1:4 . 79:8; 142:6
r. 6:16; Matt. . 13:6; 142:7
49:15; 56:13; 86:13
s [a]Ps. 27:13
or. 4:13 [b]Ps. 88:7
s. 31:22 [b]Ps. 2:9; Rom. 3:4
upon [a]2 Chr. 1 Thess. 3:9 [b]Ps. 103:2
Ps. 16:5 [b]Ps. 80:18; 105:1
50:14; 116:18 [b]Ps. 22:25
5 [a]Ps. 72:14
because [a]Ps. 9:125; 143:12 6 [c]Ps. 107:14
Lev. 7:12; Ps. 4 [b]Ps. 116:13
8 [a]Ps. 116:14
Or, Hallelujah! AH [a]Ps. 92:13; 2 [b]Ps. 102:21
[a]Rom. 15:11
revails over us ithfulness [3]Or, *ah!* [4]Heb., *YAH* 11 [b]Ps. 100:5; 146:6
Chr. 16:8, 34; 6:1; 107:1; Jer. Chr. 5:13; 7:3; 3:11; Ps. 100:5; 136:1-26
2 [a]Ps. 115:9
3 [a]Ps. 115:10
Or, *revere* [a]Ps. 115:11
YAH [a]Ps. 18:6; 20:1 [b]Ps. 18:19
19:27; Ps. 56:9; 13:6 [b]Ps. 23:4; :1 [c]Ps. 56:4, 11

7 The LORD is for me [a]among those who help me;
Therefore I shall [b]look *with satisfaction* on those who hate me.
8 It is [a]better to take refuge in the LORD
Than to trust in man.
9 It is [a]better to take refuge in the LORD
Than to trust in princes.

10 All nations [a]surrounded me;
In the name of the LORD I will surely [b]cut them off.
11 They [a]surrounded me, yes, they surrounded me;
In the name of the LORD I will surely cut them off.
12 They surrounded me [a]like bees;
They were extinguished as a [b]fire of thorns;
In the name of the LORD I will surely cut them off.
13 You [a]pushed me violently so that I [1]was falling,
But the LORD [b]helped me.
14 [1a]The LORD is my strength and song,
And He has become [b]my salvation.

15 The sound of [a]joyful shouting and salvation is in the tents of the righteous;
The [b]right hand of the LORD does valiantly.
16 The [a]right hand of the LORD is exalted;
The right hand of the LORD does valiantly.
17 I [a]shall not die, but live,
And [b]tell of the works of [1]the LORD.
18 [1]The LORD has [a]disciplined me severely,
But He has [b]not given me over to death.

19 [a]Open to me the gates of righteousness;
I shall enter through them, I shall give thanks to [1]the LORD.
20 This is the gate of the LORD;
The [a]righteous will enter through it.
21 I shall give thanks to Thee, for Thou hast [a]answered me;
And Thou hast [b]become my salvation.

22 The [a]stone which the builders rejected
Has become the chief corner *stone*.
23 This is [1]the LORD's doing;
It is marvelous in our eyes.
24 This is the day which the LORD has made;
Let us [a]rejoice and be glad in it.
25 O LORD, [a]do save, we beseech Thee;
O LORD, we beseech Thee, do send [b]prosperity!
26 [a]Blessed is the one who comes in the name of the LORD;
We have [b]blessed you from the house of the LORD.
27 [a]The LORD is God, and He has given us [b]light;
Bind the festival sacrifice with cords [1]to the [c]horns of the altar.
28 [a]Thou art my God, and I give thanks to Thee;
Thou art my God, [b]I extol Thee.
29 [a]Give thanks to the LORD, for He is good;
For His lovingkindness is everlasting.

7 [a]Ps. 54:4 59:10
8 [a]2 Chr. 32 40:4; 108:12 57:13; Jer. 1
9 [a]Ps. 146:3
10 [a]Ps. 3:6; 18:40
11 [a]Ps. 88:1
12 [a]Deut. 1:4 58:9; Nah. 1:
13 [1]Or, *fell* [a] [b]Ps. 86:17
14 [1]Heb., *YA* 15:2; Is. 12:2
15 [a]Ps. 68:3 Ps. 89:13; Lu
16 [a]Ex. 15:6;
17 [1]Heb., *YA* 116:8, 9; Hab. 73:28; 107:22
18 [1]Heb., *YA* 73:14; Jer. 31: 11:32; 2 Cor. 6 86:13
19 [1]Heb., *YA*
20 [a]Ps. 15:1, 140:13; Is. 35: 22:14
21 [a]Ps. 116:1; [b]Ps. 118:14
22 [a]Matt. 21:4 12:10, 11; Luke Acts 4:11; Eph. 1 Pet. 2:7
23 [1]Lit., *from th*
24 [a]Ps. 31:7
25 [a]Ps. 106:47 122:6, 7
26 [a]Matt. 21:9; Mark 11:9; Luke 19:38; John 12: 129:8
27 [1]Lit., *unto* [a] 18:39 [b]Esth. 8:1 18:28; 27:1; 1 P [c]Ex. 27:2
28 [a]Ps. 63:1; 14 [b]Ex. 15:2; Is. 25
29 [a]Ps.118:1

Psalm 119

א Aleph.

119 How blessed are those whose way is [1a]blameless,
Who [b]walk in the law of the LORD.
2 How blessed are those who [a]observe His testimonies,
Who [b]seek Him [c]with all *their* heart.
3 They also [a]do no unrighteousness;
They walk in His ways.
4 Thou hast [1a]ordained Thy precepts,
[2]That we should keep *them* diligently.
5 Oh that my [a]ways may be established
To [b]keep Thy statutes!
6 Then I [a]shall not be ashamed
When I look [1]upon all Thy commandments.
7 I shall [a]give thanks to Thee with uprightness of heart,
When I learn Thy righteous judgments.
8 I shall keep Thy statutes;
Do not [a]forsake me utterly!

ב Beth.

9 How can a young man keep his way pure?
By [a]keeping *it* according to Thy word.
10 With [a]all my heart I have sought Thee;
Do not let me [b]wander from Thy commandments.
11 Thy word I have [a]treasured in my heart,
That I may not sin against Thee.
12 Blessed art Thou, O LORD;
[a]Teach me Thy statutes.
13 With my lips I have [a]told of
All the [b]ordinances of Thy mouth.
14 I have [a]rejoiced in the way of Thy testimonies,
[1]As much as in all riches.
15 I will [a]meditate on Thy precepts,
And [1]regard [b]Thy ways.
16 I shall [1a]delight in Thy statutes;
I shall [b]not forget Thy word.

ג Gimel.

17 [a]Deal bountifully with Thy servant,
That I may live and keep Thy word.
18 Open my eyes, that I may behold
Wonderful things from Thy law.
19 I am a [a]stranger in the earth;
Do not hide Thy commandments from me.
20 My soul is crushed [1a]with longing
After Thine ordinances at all times.
21 Thou dost [a]rebuke the arrogant, [1]the [b]cursed,
Who [c]wander from Thy commandments.
22 [a]Take away reproach and contempt from me,
For I [b]observe Thy testimonies.
23 Even though [a]princes sit and talk against me,
Thy servant [b]meditates on Thy statutes.
24 Thy testimonies also are my [a]delight;
They are [1]my counselors.

:1 [1]Lit., *complete;* *aving integrity* [a]Ps. 1:2, 6; Prov. 11:20; [b]Ps. 128:1; Ezek. 20; 18:17; Mic. 4:2
2 [a]Ps. 25:10; 99:7; 19:22, 168 [b]Deut. Ps. 119:10 [c]Deut. 10:12; 11:13; 13:3; 30:2
[a]1 John 3:9; 5:18
[1]Lit., *commanded* t., *To keep* [a]Deut. 4:13; Neh. 9:13
s. 40:2; Prov. 4:26 . 12:1; 2 Chr. 7:17
Lit., *to* [a]Job 22:26; Ps. 119:80
7 [a]Ps. 119:62
s. 38:21; 71:9, 18
[a]1 Kin. 2:4; 8:25; 2 Chr. 6:16
[a]2 Chr. 15:15; Ps. 145 [b]Ps. 119:21, 118
[a]Ps. 37:31; 40:8; Luke 2:19, 51
2 [a]Ps. 119:26, 64, 08, 124, 135, 171
13 [a]Ps. 40:9 [b]Ps. 119:72
4 [1]Lit., *As over all* [a]Ps. 119:111, 162
r, *look upon* [a]Ps. 19:23, 48, 78, 97, [b]Ps. 25:4; 27:11; Is. 58:2
Lit., *delight myself* 2; 119:24, 35, 47, 77, 92, 143, 174 [b]Ps. 119:93
[a]Ps. 13:6; 116:7
[a]Gen. 47:9; Lev. 1 Chr. 29:15; Ps. :12; 119:54; Heb. 11:13
Lit., *for* [a]Ps. 42:1, 3:1; 84:2; 119:40, 131
[1]Or, *Cursed are* *e who wander . . .* Ps. 68:30 [b]Deut. 6; Ps. 37:22 [c]Ps. 119:10, 118
[a]Ps. 39:8; 119:39 [b]Ps. 119:2
Ps. 119:161 [b]Ps. 119:15
t., *the men of my* *nsel* [a]Ps. 119:16

ד Daleth.

25 My [a]soul cleaves to the dust;
[b]Revive me [c]according to Thy word.
26 I have told of my ways, and Thou hast answered me;
[a]Teach me Thy statutes.
27 Make me understand the way of Thy precepts,
So I will [a]meditate on Thy wonders.
28 My [a]soul [1]weeps because of grief;
[b]Strengthen me according to Thy word.
29 Remove the false way from me,
And graciously grant me Thy law.
30 I have chosen the faithful way;
I have [1]placed Thine ordinances *before me*.
31 I [a]cleave to Thy testimonies;
O LORD, do not put me to shame!
32 I shall run the way of Thy commandments,
For Thou wilt [a]enlarge my heart.

ה He.

33 [a]Teach me, O LORD, the way of Thy statutes,
And I shall observe it to the end.
34 [a]Give me understanding, that I may [b]observe Thy law,
And keep it [c]with all *my* heart.
35 Make me walk in the [a]path of Thy commandments,
For I [b]delight in it.
36 [a]Incline my heart to Thy testimonies,
And not to [b]*dishonest* gain.
37 Turn away my [a]eyes from looking at vanity,
And [b]revive me in Thy ways.
38 [a]Establish Thy [1]word to Thy servant,
[2]As that which produces reverence for Thee.
39 [a]Turn away my reproach which I dread,
For Thine ordinances are good.
40 Behold, I [a]long for Thy precepts;
Revive me through Thy righteousness.

ו Vav.

41 May Thy [a]lovingkindnesses also come to me, O LORD,
Thy salvation [b]according to Thy [1]word;
42 So I shall have an [a]answer for him who [b]reproaches me,
For I trust in Thy word.
43 And do not take the word of truth utterly out of my mouth,
For I [1a]wait for Thine ordinances.
44 So I will [a]keep Thy law continually,
Forever and ever.
45 And I will [a]walk [1]at liberty,
For I [b]seek Thy precepts.
46 I will also speak of Thy testimonies [a]before kings,
And shall not be ashamed.
47 And I shall [1a]delight in Thy commandments,
Which I [b]love.
48 And I shall lift up my hands to Thy commandments,
Which I [a]love;
And I will [b]meditate on Thy statutes.

25 [a]Ps. 44:25 [b]Ps 119:37, 40, 88, 93, 149, 154, 156, 159 143:11 [c]Ps. 119:65

26 [a]Ps. 25:4; 27:1 86:11; 119:12

27 [a]Ps. 105:2; 145

28 [1]Lit., *drops* [a]Ps 22:14; 107:26 [b]Ps 20:2; 1 Pet. 5:10

30 [1]Or, *accounted Thine ordinances*

31 [a]Deut. 11:22

32 [a]1 Kin. 4:29; Is 60:5; 2 Cor. 6:11,

33 [a]Ps. 119:5, 12

34 [a]Ps. 119:27, 7 125, 144, 169 [b]1 22:12; Ezek. 44:24 119:2, 69

35 [a]Ps. 25:4; Is. 4 [b]Ps. 112:1; 119:16

36 [a]1 Kin. 8:58 [b] 33:31; Mark 7:21, Luke 12:15; Heb.

37 [a]Is. 33:15 [b]Ps 71:20; 119:25

38 [1]Or, *promise* *Which is for the fe* *Thee* [a]2 Sam. 7:2

39 [a]Ps. 119:22

40 [a]Ps. 119:20

41 [1]Or, *promise* 119:77 [b]Ps. 119:5 116, 170

42 [a]Prov. 27:11 102:8; 119:39

43 [1]Or, *hope in* 119:49, 74, 81, 1

44 [a]Ps. 119:33

45 [1]Lit., *in a wide place* [a]Prov. 4:12 119:94, 155

46 [a]Matt. 10:18; 26:1, 2

47 [1]Lit., *delight* [a]Ps. 119:16 [b]Ps. 119:97, 127, 159

48 [a]Ps. 119:97, 159 [b]Ps. 119:15

ז Zayin.

49 Remember the word to Thy servant,
[1]In which Thou hast made me hope.
50 This is my [a]comfort in my affliction,
That Thy word has [1]revived me.
51 The arrogant [a]utterly deride me,
Yet I do not [b]turn aside from Thy law.
52 I have [a]remembered Thine ordinances from [1]of old, O LORD,
And comfort myself.
53 Burning [a]indignation has seized me because of the wicked,
Who [b]forsake Thy law.
54 Thy statutes are my songs
In the house of my [a]pilgrimage.
55 O LORD, I [a]remember Thy name [b]in the night,
And keep Thy law.
56 This has become mine,
[1]That I [a]observe Thy precepts.

ח Heth.

57 The LORD is my [a]portion;
I have [1]promised to [b]keep Thy words.
58 I [a]entreated Thy favor [b]with all *my* heart;
[c]Be gracious to me [d]according to Thy [1]word.
59 I [a]considered my ways,
And turned my feet to Thy testimonies.
60 I hastened and did not delay
To keep Thy commandments.
61 The [a]cords of the wicked have encircled me,
But I have [b]not forgotten Thy law.
62 At [a]midnight I shall rise to give thanks to Thee
Because of Thy [b]righteous ordinances.
63 I am a [a]companion of all those who [1]fear Thee,
And of those who keep Thy precepts.
64 [a]The earth is full of Thy lovingkindness, O LORD;
[b]Teach me Thy statutes.

ט Teth.

65 Thou hast dealt well with Thy servant,
O LORD, according to Thy word.
66 Teach me good [1a]discernment and knowledge,
For I believe in Thy commandments.
67 [a]Before I was afflicted I went astray,
But now I keep Thy word.
68 Thou art [a]good and [b]doest good;
[c]Teach me Thy statutes.
69 The arrogant [1]have [a]forged a lie against me;
With all *my* heart I will [b]observe Thy precepts.
70 Their heart is [1a]covered with fat,
But I [b]delight in Thy law.
71 It is [a]good for me that I was afflicted,
That I may learn Thy statutes.
72 The [a]law of Thy mouth is better to me
Than thousands of gold and silver *pieces*.

י Yodh.

73 [a]Thy hands made me and [1]fashioned me;

49 [1]Lit., *On*
...preserved me ...b 6:10; Rom. 15:4
...0:1; Jer. 20:7 ...1; Ps. 44:18; 119:157
...r, *everlasting* [a]Ps. 103:18
...x. 32:19; Ezra ...eh. 13:25; Ps. ...58 [b]Ps. 89:30
...Gen. 47:9; Ps. 119:19
...3:6 [b]Ps. 42:8; ...9:62; Is. 26:9; Acts 16:25
...*Because* [a]Ps. ...19:22, 69, 100
...Lit., *said that I* ...*eep* [a]Ps. 16:5; ...24 [b]Deut. 33:9
...*romise* [a]1 Kin. ...Ps. 119:2 [c]Ps. ...6:1; 57:1 [d]Ps. 119:41
...rk 14:72; Luke 15:17
[a]Job 36:8; Ps. ...s. 119:83, 141, 153, 176
...s. 119:55 [b]Ps. 119:7
...Or, *revere* [a]Ps. 101:6
[a]Ps. 33:5 [b]Ps. 119:12
...*udgment* [a]Phil. 1:9
...119:71, 75; Jer. ...9; Heb. 12:5-11
...Ps. 86:5; 100:5; ...:1; 107:1; Matt. ...17 [b]Deut. 8:16; ...30:5; Ps. 125:4 [c]Ps. 119:12
...Lit., *besmear me* ...s [a]Job 13:4; Ps. ...9:2 [b]Ps. 119:56
...Lit., *gross like fat* ...2:15; Job 15:27; ...10; Is. 6:10; Jer. ...Acts 28:27 [b]Ps. 119:16
[a]Ps. 119:67, 75
...19:10; 119:127; ...Prov. 8:10, 11, 19
[1]Lit., *established* ...10:8; 31:15; Ps. ...38:8; 139:15, 16

[b]Give me understanding, that I may learn Thy commandments.
74 May those who [1]fear Thee [a]see me and be glad,
Because I [2b]wait for Thy word.
75 I know, O LORD, that Thy judgments are [a]righteous,
And that [b]in faithfulness Thou hast afflicted me.
76 O may Thy lovingkindness [1]comfort me,
According to Thy [2]word to Thy servant.
77 May [a]Thy compassion come to me that I may live,
For Thy law is my [b]delight.
78 May [a]the arrogant be ashamed, for they subvert me [b]with a lie;
But I shall [c]meditate on Thy precepts.
79 May those who [1]fear Thee turn to me,
Even those who know Thy testimonies.
80 May my heart be [1a]blameless in Thy statutes,
That I may not [b]be ashamed.

כ Kaph.

81 My [a]soul languishes for Thy salvation;
I [1b]wait for Thy word.
82 My [a]eyes fail *with longing* for Thy [1]word,
[2]While I say, "When wilt Thou comfort me?"
83 Though I have [a]become like a wineskin in the smoke,
I do [b]not forget Thy statutes.
84 How many are the [a]days of Thy servant?
When wilt Thou [b]execute judgment on those who persecute me?
85 The arrogant have [a]dug pits for me,
Men who are not [1]in accord with Thy law.
86 All Thy commandments are [a]faithful;
They have [b]persecuted me with a lie; [c]help me!
87 They almost destroyed me [1]on earth,
But as for me, I [a]did not forsake Thy precepts.
88 Revive me according to Thy lovingkindness,
So that I may keep the testimony of Thy mouth.

ל Lamedh.

89 [a]Forever, O LORD,
Thy word [1]is settled in heaven.
90 Thy [a]faithfulness *continues* [1]throughout all generations;
Thou didst [b]establish the earth, and it [c]stands.
91 They stand this day according to Thine [a]ordinances,
For [b]all things are Thy servants.
92 If Thy law had not been my [a]delight,
Then I would have perished [b]in my affliction.
93 I will [a]never forget Thy precepts,
For by them Thou hast [1b]revived me.
94 I am Thine, [a]save me;
For I have [b]sought Thy precepts.
95 The wicked [a]wait for me to destroy me;
I shall diligently consider Thy testimonies.
96 I have seen [1]a limit to all perfection;
Thy commandment is exceedingly broad.

מ Mem.

97 O how I [a]love Thy law!
It is my [b]meditation all the day.
98 Thy [a]commandments make me wiser than my enemies,

73 [b]Ps. 119:3
74 [1]Or, *reve... hope in* [a]Ps. 35:27; 107:42 119:43
75 [a]Ps. 119:1 12:10
76 [1]Lit., *be fo comfort* [2]Or,
77 [a]Ps. 119:4 119:16
78 [a]Jer. 50:32 119:86 [c]Ps. 1
79 [1]Or, *rever*
80 [1]Lit., *comp having integrit* 119:1 [b]Ps. 119
81 [1]Or, *hope* 84:2 [b]Ps. 119
82 [1]Or, *promi Saying* [a]Ps. 6 119:123; Is. 38 2:11
83 [a]Job 30:30 119:61
84 [a]Ps. 39:4
85 [1]Lit., *accor Thy law* [a]Ps. 7 35:7; 57:6; Jer
86 [a]Ps. 119:13 35:19; 119:78, 109:26
87 [1]Lit., *in the* [a]Is. 58:2
89 [1]Lit., *stands* [a]Ps. 89:2; 119:1 40:8; Matt. 24:3 1:25
90 [1]Lit., *to* [a]Ps 89:1, 2 [b]Ps. 14 [c]Eccl. 1:4
91 [a]Jer. 31:35; [b]Ps. 104:2-4
92 [a]Ps. 119:16 119:50
93 [1]Or, *kept me* [a]Ps. 119:16, 83 119:25
94 [a]Ps. 119:146 119:45
95 [a]Ps. 40:14; I
96 [1]Lit., *an end*
97 [a]Ps. 119:47, 127, 163, 165 [b] 119:15
98 [a]Deut. 4:6; P 119:130

For they are ever [1]mine.
99 I have more insight than all my teachers,
For Thy testimonies are my [a]meditation.
100 I understand [a]more than the aged,
Because I have [b]observed Thy precepts.
101 I have [a]restrained my feet from every evil way,
That I may keep Thy word.
102 I have not [a]turned aside from Thine ordinances,
For Thou Thyself hast taught me.
103 How [a]sweet are Thy [1]words to my [2]taste!
Yes, sweeter than honey to my mouth!
104 From Thy precepts I [a]get understanding;
Therefore I [b]hate every false way.

נ Nun.

105 Thy word is a [a]lamp to my feet,
And a light to my path.
106 I have [a]sworn, and I will confirm it,
That I will keep Thy righteous ordinances.
107 I am exceedingly [a]afflicted;
[1b]Revive me, O LORD, according to Thy word.
108 O accept the [a]freewill offerings of my mouth, O LORD,
And [b]teach me Thine ordinances.
109 My [1a]life is continually [2]in my hand,
Yet I do not [b]forget Thy law.
110 The wicked have [a]laid a snare for me,
Yet I have not [b]gone astray from Thy precepts.
111 I have [a]inherited Thy testimonies forever,
For they are the [b]joy of my heart.
112 I have [a]inclined my heart to perform Thy statutes
Forever, *even* [b]to the end.

ס Samekh.

113 I hate those who are [a]double-minded,
But I love Thy [b]law.
114 Thou art my [a]hiding place and my [b]shield;
I [1c]wait for Thy word.
115 [a]Depart from me, evildoers,
That I may [b]observe the commandments of my God.
116 [a]Sustain me according to Thy [1]word, that I may live;
And [b]do not let me be [2]ashamed of my hope.
117 Uphold me that I may be [a]safe,
That I may [b]have regard for Thy statutes continually.
118 Thou hast [1]rejected all those [a]who wander from Thy statutes,
For their deceitfulness is [2]useless.
119 Thou hast [1]removed all the wicked of the earth *like* [a]dross;
Therefore I [b]love Thy testimonies.
120 My flesh [1a]trembles for fear of Thee,
And I am [b]afraid of Thy judgments.

ע Ayin.

121 I have [a]done justice and righteousness;
Do not leave me to my oppressors.
122 Be [a]surety for Thy servant for good;
Do not let the arrogant [b]oppress me.
123 My [a]eyes fail *with longing* for Thy salvation,

[1]Or, *with me*
9 [a]Ps. 119:15
b 32:7-9 [b]Ps. 119:22, 56
1 [a]Prov. 1:15
. 17:20; Josh. :6; 1 Kin. 15:5
[1]Or, *promises* te [a]Ps. 19:10; :11; 24:13, 14
119:130 [b]Ps. 119:128
)5 [a]Prov. 6:23
6 [a]Neh. 10:29
[1]Or, *Keep me* Ps. 119:25, 50 [b]Ps. 119:25
os. 14:2; Heb. 5 [b]Ps. 119:12
., *soul* [2]I.e., in er [a]Judg. 12:3; 4 [b]Ps. 119:16
s. 91:3; 140:5; :9 [b]Ps. 119:10
Deut. 33:4 [b]Ps. 119:14, 162
s. 119:36 [b]Ps. 119:33
[a]1 Kin. 18:21; es 1:8; 4:8 [b]Ps. 119:47
r, *hope in* [a]Ps. 32:7; 61:4; 91:1 4:9 [c]Ps. 119:74
Ps. 6:8; 139:19; 23 [b]Ps. 119:22
r, *promise* [2]Lit., *shame because* 37:17, 24; 54:4 :2, 20; 31:1, 17; . 5:5; 9:33; Phil. 1:20
[a]Ps. 12:5; Prov. [b]Ps. 119:6, 15
it., *made light of falsehood* [a]Ps. 119:10, 21
[1]Lit., *caused to* se [a]Is. 1:22, 25; . 22:18, 19 [b]Ps. 119:47
[1]Lit., *bristles up* [a]Job 4:14; Hab. 16 [b]Ps. 119:161
2 Sam. 8:15; Job 29:14
[a]Job 17:3; Heb. 22 [b]Ps. 119:134
123 [a]Ps. 119:82

And for Thy righteous [1]word.
124 Deal with Thy servant [a]according to Thy lovingkindness,
And [b]teach me Thy statutes.
125 [a]I am Thy servant; [b]give me understanding,
That I may know Thy testimonies.
126 It is time for the LORD to [a]act,
For they have broken Thy law.
127 Therefore I [a]love Thy commandments
Above gold, yes, above fine gold.
128 Therefore I esteem right all *Thy* [a]precepts concerning everything,
I [b]hate every false way.

פ Pe.

129 Thy testimonies are [a]wonderful;
Therefore my soul [b]observes them.
130 The [a]unfolding of Thy words gives light;
It gives [b]understanding to the simple.
131 I [a]opened my mouth wide and [b]panted,
For I [c]longed for Thy commandments.
132 [a]Turn to me and be gracious to me,
After Thy manner [1]with those who love Thy name.
133 Establish my [a]footsteps in Thy [1]word,
And do not let any iniquity [b]have dominion over me.
134 [a]Redeem me from the oppression of man,
That I may keep Thy precepts.
135 [a]Make Thy face shine upon Thy servant,
And [b]teach me Thy statutes.
136 My eyes [1]shed [a]streams of water,
Because they [b]do not keep Thy law.

צ Tsadhe.

137 [a]Righteous art Thou, O LORD,
And upright are Thy judgments.
138 Thou hast commanded Thy testimonies in [a]righteousness
And exceeding [b]faithfulness.
139 My [a]zeal has [1]consumed me,
Because my adversaries have forgotten Thy words.
140 Thy [1a]word is very [2]pure,
Therefore Thy servant [b]loves it.
141 I am small and [a]despised,
Yet I do not [b]forget Thy precepts.
142 Thy righteousness is an everlasting righteousness,
And [a]Thy law is truth.
143 Trouble and anguish have [1]come upon me;
Yet Thy commandments are my [a]delight.
144 Thy [a]testimonies are righteous forever;
[b]Give me understanding that I may live.

ק Qoph.

145 I cried [a]with all my heart; answer me, O LORD!
I will [b]observe Thy statutes.
146 I cried to Thee; [a]save me,
And I shall keep Thy testimonies.
147 I [1a]rise before dawn and cry for help;
I [2]wait for Thy words.

123 [1]Or, *prom*
124 [a]Ps. 51:1 109:26; 119:88 159 [b]Ps. 119:
125 [a]Ps. 116: 119:27
126 [a]Jer. 18:2 31:11
127 [a]Ps. 19:1
128 [a]Ps. 19:8 119:104
129 [a]Ps. 119:1 119:22
130 [a]Prov. 6:2 19:7
131 [a]Job 29:2 81:10 [b]Ps. 42: 119:20
132 [1]Lit., *to* [a]P 25:16; 106:4
133 [1]Or, *prom.* 17:5 [b]Ps. 19:1 6:12
134 [a]Ps. 119:8 Luke 1:74
135 [a]Num. 6:2 4:6; 31:16; 67:1 7, 19 [b]Ps. 119:
136 [1]Lit., *run d* [a]Jer. 9:1, 18; 14 Lam. 3:48 [b]Ps.
137 [a]Ezra 9:15 9:33; Ps. 116:5; 145:17; Jer. 12: 1:18; Dan. 9:7,
138 [a]Ps. 19:7-9 119:144, 172 [b]P 119:86, 90
139 [1]Lit., *put an* [a]Ps. 69:9; John
140 [1]Or, *promis* *refined* [a]Ps. 12: [b]Ps. 119:47
141 [a]Ps. 22:6 [b] 119:61
142 [a]Ps. 19:9; 1 160
143 [1]Lit., *found* [a]Ps. 119:24
144 [a]Ps. 19:9 [b] 119:27
145 [a]Ps. 119:10 119:22, 55
146 [a]Ps. 3:7
147 [1]Lit., *anticip* *dawn* [2]Or, *hope* 5:3; 57:8; 108:2

148 My eyes anticipate the [a]night watches,
That I may [b]meditate on Thy [1]word.
149 Hear my voice [a]according to Thy lovingkindness;
[b]Revive me, O LORD, according to Thine ordinances.
150 Those who follow after wickedness draw near;
They are far from Thy law.
151 Thou art [a]near, O LORD,
And all Thy commandments are [b]truth.
152 Of old I have [a]known from Thy testimonies,
That Thou hast founded them [b]forever.

ר Resh.

153 [a]Look upon my [b]affliction and rescue me,
For I do not [c]forget Thy law.
154 [a]Plead my cause and [b]redeem me;
Revive me according to Thy [1]word.
155 Salvation is [a]far from the wicked,
For they [b]do not seek Thy statutes.
156 [1a]Great are Thy mercies, O LORD;
Revive me according to Thine ordinances.
157 Many are my [a]persecutors and my adversaries,
Yet I do not [b]turn aside from Thy testimonies.
158 I behold the [a]treacherous and [b]loathe *them*,
Because they do not keep Thy [1]word.
159 Consider how I [a]love Thy precepts;
[b]Revive me, O LORD, according to Thy lovingkindness.
160 The [a]sum of Thy word is [b]truth,
And every one of Thy righteous ordinances [c]is everlasting.

ש Shin.

161 [a]Princes persecute me without cause,
But my heart [b]stands in awe of Thy words.
162 I [a]rejoice at Thy [1]word,
As one who [b]finds great spoil.
163 I [a]hate and despise falsehood,
But I [b]love Thy law.
164 Seven times a day I praise Thee,
Because of Thy [a]righteous ordinances.
165 Those who love Thy law have [a]great peace,
And [1b]nothing causes them to stumble.
166 I [a]hope for Thy salvation, O LORD,
And do Thy commandments.
167 My [a]soul keeps Thy testimonies,
And I [b]love them exceedingly.
168 I [a]keep Thy precepts and Thy testimonies,
For all my [b]ways are before Thee.

ת Tav.

169 Let my [a]cry [1]come before Thee, O LORD;
[b]Give me understanding [c]according to Thy word.
170 Let my [a]supplication come before Thee;
[b]Deliver me according to Thy [1]word.
171 Let my [a]lips utter praise,
For Thou [b]dost teach me Thy statutes.
172 Let my [a]tongue sing of Thy [1]word,
For all Thy [b]commandments are righteousness.

[1]Or, *promise* [a]Ps. 63:6 [b]Ps. 119:15
[a]Ps. 119:124 [b]Ps. 119:25
Ps. 34:18; 145:18; 50:8 [b]Ps. 119:142
[a]Ps. 119:125 [b]Ps. 19:89; Luke 21:33
3 [a]Lam. 5:1 [b]Ps. 9:50 [c]Ps. 119:16; Prov. 3:1; Hos. 4:6
154 [1]Or, *promise* 1 Sam. 24:15; Ps. 5:1; Mic. 7:9 [b]Ps. 119:134
55 [a]Job 5:4 [b]Ps. 119:45, 94
Or, *Many* [a]2 Sam. 24:14
[a]Ps. 7:1; 119:86, 161 [b]Ps. 119:51
[1]Or, *promise* [a]Is. 4:16 [b]Ps. 139:21
[a]Ps. 119:47 [b]Ps. 119:25
[a]Ps. 139:17 [b]Ps. 142 [c]Ps. 119:89, 152
1 [a]1 Sam. 24:11; Ps. 119:23 [b]Ps. 119:120
Or, *promise* [a]Ps. 14, 111 [b]1 Sam. 30:16; Is. 9:3
Ps. 31:6; 119:104, Prov. 13:5 [b]Ps. 119:47
[a]Ps. 119:7, 160
Lit., *they have no* *nbling block* [a]Ps. 11; Prov. 3:2; Is. 2:17 [b]Prov. 3:23; 3:13; 1 John 2:10
[a]Gen. 49:18; Ps. 119:81, 174
Ps. 119:129 [b]Ps. 119:47
[a]Ps. 119:22 [b]Job Ps. 139:3; Prov. 5:21
[1]Lit., *come near* [a]Job 16:18; Ps. 18:6; 102:1 [b]Ps. 119:27, 144 [c]Ps. 119:65, 154
Or, *promise* [a]Ps. 2; 130:2; 140:6; [b]Ps. 22:20; 31:2; 59:1
[a]Ps. 51:15; 63:3 4:12; 119:12; Is. 2:3; Mic. 4:2
Or, *promise* [a]Ps. 14 [b]Ps. 119:138

173 Let Thy [a]hand be [1]ready to help me,
For I have [b]chosen Thy precepts.
174 I [a]long for Thy salvation, O LORD,
And Thy law is my [b]delight.
175 Let my [a]soul live that it may praise Thee,
And let Thine ordinances help me.
176 I have [a]gone astray like a lost sheep; seek Thy servant,
For I do [b]not forget Thy commandments.

Psalm 120

A Song of [+]Ascents.

120 [a]In my trouble I cried to the LORD,
And He answered me.
2 Deliver my soul, O LORD, from [a]lying lips,
From a [b]deceitful tongue.
3 What shall be given to you, and what more shall be done to you,
You [a]deceitful tongue?
4 [a]Sharp arrows of the warrior,
With the *burning* [b]coals of the broom tree.

5 Woe is me, for I sojourn in [a]Meshech,
For I dwell among the [b]tents of [c]Kedar!
6 Too long has my soul had its dwelling
With those who [a]hate peace.
7 I [a]am *for* peace, but when I speak,
They are [b]for war.

Psalm 121

A Song of Ascents.

121 I will [a]lift up my eyes to [b]the mountains;
From whence shall my help come?
2 My [a]help *comes* from the LORD,
Who [b]made heaven and earth.
3 He will not [a]allow your foot to slip;
He who [b]keeps you will not slumber.
4 Behold, He who keeps Israel
Will neither slumber nor sleep.

5 The LORD is your [a]keeper;
The LORD is your [b]shade on your right hand.
6 The [a]sun will not smite you by day,
Nor the moon by night.
7 The LORD will [1a]protect you from all evil;
He will keep your soul.
8 The LORD will [1a]guard your going out and your coming in
[b]From this time forth and forever.

Psalm 122

A Song of Ascents, of David.

122 I was glad when they said to me,
"Let us [a]go to the house of the LORD."
2 Our feet are standing
Within your [a]gates, O Jerusalem,

173 [1]Lit., *to help* [a]Ps. 37:24; 73:23 [b]Josh. 24:22; Luke
174 [a]Ps. 119:166 119:16, 24
175 [a]Is. 55:3
176 [a]Is. 53:6; Jer. Matt. 18:12; Luke [b]Ps. 119:16
[+]Ex. 34:24; 1 Kin.
120:1 [a]Ps. 18:6; 102:2; Jon. 2:2
2 [a]Ps. 109:2; Pro 12:22 [b]Ps. 52:4; 3:13
3 [a]Ps. 52:4; Zeph
4 [a]Ps. 45:5; Prov 25:18; Is. 5:28 [b]P 140:10
5 [a]Gen. 10:2; 1 C 1:5; Ezek. 27:13; 3; 39:1 [b]Song 1:5 [c]Gen. 25:13; Is. 2 60:7; Jer. 2:10; 49 Ezek. 27:21
6 [a]Ps. 35:20
7 [a]Ps. 109:4 [b]Ps
121:1 [a]Ps. 123:1 40:26 [b]Ps. 87:1
2 [a]Ps. 124:8 [b]Ps 115:15
3 [a]1 Sam. 2:9; P [b]Ps. 41:2; 127:1;
5 [a]Ps. 91:4 [b]Ps. 91:1; Is. 25:4
6 [a]Ps. 91:5; Is. 4 Jon. 4:8; Rev. 7:
7 [1]Or, *keep* [a]Ps 91:10-12
8 [1]Or, *keep* [a]De 28:6 [b]Ps. 113:2;
122:1 [a]Ps. 42:4; Mic. 4:2; Zech. 8
2 [a]Ps. 9:14; 87: 116:19; Jer. 7:2

3 Jerusalem, that is [a]built
As a city that is [b]compact together;
4 To which the tribes [a]go up, even the tribes of [1]the LORD—
[2]An ordinance for Israel—
To give thanks to the name of the LORD.
5 For there [a]thrones were set for judgment,
The thrones of the house of David.

6 Pray for the [a]peace of Jerusalem:
"May they prosper who [b]love you.
7 "May peace be within your [a]walls,
And prosperity within your [b]palaces."
8 For the sake of my [a]brothers and my friends,
I will now say, "[b]May peace be within you."
9 For the sake of the house of the LORD our God
I will [a]seek your good.

Psalm 123

A Song of Ascents.

123 To Thee I [a]lift up my eyes,
O Thou who [b]art enthroned in the heavens!
2 Behold, as the eyes of [a]servants *look* to the hand of their master,
As the eyes of a maid to the hand of her mistress;
So our [b]eyes *look* to the LORD our God,
Until He shall be gracious to us.

3 [a]Be gracious to us, O LORD, be gracious to us;
For we are greatly filled [b]with contempt.
4 Our soul is greatly filled
With the [a]scoffing of [b]those who are at ease,
And with the [c]contempt of the proud.

Psalm 124

A Song of Ascents, of David.

124 "[a]Had it not been the LORD who was on our side,"
[b]Let Israel now say,
2 "Had it not been the LORD who was on our side,
When men rose up against us;
3 Then they would have [a]swallowed us alive,
When their [b]anger was kindled against us;
4 Then the [a]waters would have engulfed us,
The stream would have [1]swept over our soul;
5 Then the [a]raging waters would have [1]swept over our soul."

6 Blessed be the LORD,
Who has not given us [1]to be [a]torn by their teeth.
7 Our soul has [a]escaped [b]as a bird out of the [c]snare of the trapper;
The snare is broken and we have escaped.
8 Our [a]help is in the name of the LORD,
Who [b]made heaven and earth.

3 [a]Ps. 48:13; 147:2 [b]2 Sam. 5:9; Neh. 4:6
4 [1]Heb., *YAH* [2]Or, *A testimony* [a]Ex. 23:17; Deut. 16:16; Ps. 84:5
5 [a]Deut. 17:8; 2 Chr. 19:8; Ps. 89:29
6 [a]Ps. 29:11; Jer. 29:7 [b]Ps. 102:14
7 [a]Ps. 51:18; Is. 62:6 [b]Ps. 48:3, 13; Jer. 17:27
8 [a]Ps. 133:1 [b]1 Sam. 25:6; John 20:19
9 [a]Neh. 2:10; Esth. 10:3
123:1 [a]Ps. 121:1; 141:8 [b]Ps. 2:4; 11:4
2 [a]Prov. 27:18; Mal. 1:6 [b]Ps. 25:15
3 [a]Ps. 4:1; 51:1 [b]Neh. 4:4; Ps. 119:22
4 [a]Neh. 2:19; Ps. 79:4 [b]Job 12:5; Is. 32:9, 11; Amos 6:1 [c]Neh. 4:4; Ps. 119:22
124:1 [a]Ps. 94:17 [b]Ps. 129:1
3 [a]Num. 16:30; Ps. 35:25; 56:1; 57:3; Prov. 1:12 [b]Gen. 39:19; Ps. 138:7
4 [1]Or, *passed over* [a]Job 22:11; Ps. 18:16; 32:6; 69:2; 144:7
5 [1]Or, *passed over* [a]Job 38:11
6 [1]Lit., *as a prey to* [a]Job 27:2; Prov. 30:14
7 [a]Ps. 141:10; 2 Cor. 11:33; Heb. 11:34 [b]Prov. 6:5 [c]Ps. 91:3; Hos. 9:8
8 [a]Ps. 121:2 [b]Gen. 1:1; Ps. 134:3

Psalm 125

A Song of Ascents.

125 Those who trust in the LORD
Are as Mount Zion, which [a]cannot be moved, but [b]abides
forever.
2 As the mountains surround Jerusalem,
So [a]the LORD surrounds His people
[b]From this time forth and forever.
3 For the [a]scepter of wickedness shall not rest upon the [1]land of
the righteous;
That the righteous [b]may not put forth their hands to do wrong.

4 [a]Do good, O LORD, to those who are good,
And to those who are [b]upright in their hearts.
5 But as for those who [a]turn aside to their [b]crooked ways,
The LORD will lead them away with the [c]doers of iniquity.
[d]Peace be upon Israel.

Psalm 126

A Song of Ascents.

126 When the LORD [a]brought back [1]the captive ones of Zion,
We were [b]like those who dream.
2 Then our [a]mouth was filled with laughter,
And our [b]tongue with joyful shouting;
Then they said among the nations,
"The LORD has [c]done great things for them."
3 The LORD has done great things for us;
We are [a]glad.

4 Restore our captivity, O LORD,
As the [1a]streams in the [2]South.
5 Those who sow in [a]tears shall reap with [b]joyful shouting.
6 He who goes to and fro weeping, carrying *his* bag of seed,
Shall indeed come again with a shout of joy, bringing his
sheaves *with him.*

Psalm 127

A Song of Ascents, of Solomon.

127 Unless the LORD [a]builds the house,
They labor in vain who build it;
Unless the LORD [b]guards the city,
The watchman keeps awake in vain.
2 It is vain for you to rise up early,
To [1]retire late,
To [a]eat the bread of [2]painful labors;
For He gives to His [b]beloved [c]*even in his* sleep.

3 Behold, [a]children are a [1]gift of the LORD;
The [b]fruit of the womb is a reward.
4 Like arrows in the hand of a [a]warrior,
So are the children of one's youth.
5 How [a]blessed is the man whose quiver is full of them;

125:1 [a]Ps. 46:5 [b]P
61:7; Eccl. 1:4

2 [a]Zech. 2:5 [b]Ps.

3 [1]Lit., *lot* [a]Ps. 89:
Prov. 22:8; Is. 14:5
[b]1 Sam. 24:10; Ps.
55:20; Acts 12:1

4 [a]Ps. 119:68 [b]Ps
7:10; 11:2; 32:11; 3
94:15

5 [a]Job 23:11; Ps.
101:3 [b]Prov. 2:15;
59:8 [c]Ps. 92:7; 94
[d]Ps. 128:6; Gal. 6:

126:1 [1]Or, *those w*
returned to [a]Ps. 8
Jer. 29:14; Hos. 6:
[b]Acts 12:9

2 [a]Job 8:21 [b]Ps.
Is. 35:6 [c]1 Sam. 1
Ps. 71:19; Luke 1:

3 [a]Is. 25:9; Zeph.

4 [1]Lit., *stream-be*
[2]Heb., *Negev* [a]Is.
43:19

5 [a]Ps. 80:5; Jer. 3
16; Lam. 1:2 [b]Is.
51:11; 61:7; Gal. 6

127:1 [a]Ps. 78:69
121:4

2 [1]Lit., *delay sittir*
[2]Lit., *toils* [a]Gen. 3
19 [b]Ps. 60:5 [c]Job
11:18, 19; Prov. 3.
Eccl. 5:12

3 [1]Or, *heritage* [a]
33:5; 48:4; Josh.
4; Ps. 113:9 [b]Deu
7:13; 28:4; Is. 13:

4 [a]Ps. 112:2; 120

5 [a]Ps. 128:2, 3

[b]They shall not be ashamed,
When they [c]speak with their enemies [d]in the gate.

Psalm 128

A Song of Ascents.

128 [a]How blessed is everyone who fears the LORD,
Who [b]walks in His ways.
2 When you shall [a]eat of the [1b]fruit of your hands,
You will be happy and [c]it will be well with you.
3 Your wife shall be like a [a]fruitful vine,
[1]Within your house,
Your children like [b]olive plants
Around your table.
4 Behold, for thus shall the man be blessed
Who fears the LORD.

5 [a]The LORD bless you [b]from Zion,
And may you see the prosperity of Jerusalem all the days of
your life.
6 Indeed, may you see your [a]children's children.
[b]Peace be upon Israel!

Psalm 129

A Song of Ascents.

129 "[1]Many times they have [2a]persecuted me from my [b]youth
up,"
[c]Let Israel now say,
2 "[1]Many times they have [2]persecuted me from my youth up;
Yet they have [a]not prevailed against me.
3 "The plowers plowed upon my back;
They lengthened their furrows."
4 The LORD [a]is righteous;
He has cut in two the [b]cords of the wicked.

5 May all who [a]hate Zion,
Be [b]put to shame and turned backward,
6 Let them be like [a]grass upon the housetops,
Which withers before it [1]grows up;
7 With which the reaper does not fill his [1]hand,
Or the binder of sheaves his [a]bosom;
8 Nor do those who pass by say,
"The [a]blessing of the LORD be upon you;
We bless you in the name of the LORD."

Psalm 130

A Song of Ascents.

130 Out of the [a]depths I have cried to Thee, O LORD.
2 Lord, [a]hear my voice!
Let [b]Thine ears be attentive
To the [c]voice of my supplications.
3 If Thou, [1]LORD, shouldst mark iniquities,
O Lord, who could [a]stand?

ov. 27:11 [c]Is.
:1; Amos 5:12
[d]Gen. 34:20

.1 [a]Ps. 112:1;
:1 [b]Ps. 119:3

abor [a]Is. 3:10
:11; Hag. 2:17
8:12; Eph. 6:3

the innermost
[a]Ezek. 19:10
. 52:8; 144:12

4:3 [b]Ps. 20:2;
135:21

. 48:11; 50:23;
6; Ps. 103:17;
7:6 [b]Ps. 125:5

.it., *Much* [2]Lit.,
hostility toward
; Judg. 3:8; Ps.
[b]Is. 47:12; Jer.
1; Ezek. 16:22;
2:15; 11:1 [c]Ps.
124:1

Lit., *Much* [2]Lit.,
hostility toward
9; 15:20; 20:11;
8; 2 Cor. 4:8, 9

s. 119:137 [b]Ps.
140:5

4:11 [b]Ps. 70:3;
71:13

[1]Lit., *draws out*
19:26; Ps. 37:2;
Is. 37:27

salm [a]Ps. 79:12

1 2:4; Ps. 118:26

[a]Ps. 42:7; 69:2;
Lam. 3:55

Ps. 64:1; 119:149
r. 6:40; Neh. 1:6,
[c]Ps. 28:2; 140:6

., *YAH* [a]Ps. 76:7;
:2; Nah. 1:6; Mal.
3:2; Rev. 6:17

4 But there is [a]forgiveness with Thee,
That Thou mayest be [b]feared.

5 I wait for the LORD, my [a]soul does wait,
And [1b]in His word do I hope.
6 My soul *waits* for the Lord
More than the watchmen [a]for the morning;
Indeed, more than the watchmen for the morning.
7 O Israel, [a]hope in the LORD;
For with the LORD there is [b]lovingkindness,
And with Him is [c]abundant redemption.
8 And He will [a]redeem Israel
From all his iniquities.

Psalm 131

A Song of Ascents, of David.

131 O LORD, my heart is not [a]proud, nor my eyes [1b]haughty;
Nor do I [2]involve myself in [c]great matters,
Or in things [d]too [3]difficult for me.
2 Surely I have [a]composed and quieted my soul;
Like a weaned [b]child *rests* [1]against his mother,
My soul is like a weaned child [1]within me.
3 O Israel, [a]hope in the LORD
[b]From this time forth and forever.

Psalm 132

A Song of Ascents.

132 Remember, O LORD, on David's behalf,
All [a]his affliction;
2 How he swore to the LORD,
And vowed to [a]the Mighty One of Jacob,
3 "Surely I will not [1]enter [a]my house,
Nor [2]lie on my bed;
4 I will not [a]give sleep to my eyes,
Or slumber to my eyelids;
5 Until I find a [a]place for the LORD,
[1]A dwelling place for [b]the Mighty One of Jacob."

6 Behold, we heard of it in [a]Ephrathah;
We found it in the [b]field of [1]Jaar.
7 Let us go into His [1a]dwelling place;
Let us [b]worship at His [c]footstool.
8 [a]Arise, O LORD, to Thy [b]resting place;
Thou and the ark of Thy [c]strength.
9 Let Thy priests be [a]clothed with righteousness;
And let Thy [b]godly ones sing for joy.

10 For the sake of David Thy servant,
Do not turn away the face of Thine [a]anointed.
11 The LORD has [a]sworn to David,
A truth from which He will not turn back;
"[b]Of the fruit of your body I will set upon your throne.
12 "If your sons will keep My covenant,

4 [a]Ex. 34:7; Ps. 86:5; Is. 5 9:9 [b]1 Kin. 8: Jer. 33:8, 9

5 [1]Lit., *for* [a]P 33:20; 40:1; 6 8:17; 26:8 [b]P 119:74, 81

6 [a]Ps. 63:6;

7 [a]Ps. 131:3 103:4 [c]Ps. 11 3:24; Eph. 1:7

8 [a]Ps. 103:3, 1:68; Titus 2:1

131:1 [1]Or, *lo after,* walk [3]C *marvelous* [a]2 22:28; Ps. 10 2:12; Zeph. 3: 30:13; Is. 5:15 45:5; Rom. 12 42:3; Ps. 139:

2 [1]Or, *upon* [a] [b]Matt. 18:3; 1 C

3 [a]Ps. 130:7

132:1 [a]Gen. 4 2 Sam. 16:12

2 [a]Gen. 49:24 49:26; 60:16

3 [1]Lit., *come i tabernacle of up into the cou* [a]Job 21:28

4 [a]Prov. 6:4

5 [1]Lit., *Dwelling* [a]1 Kin. 8:17; 1 C Ps. 26:8; Acts 7 132:2

6 [1]Or, *the wood* 35:19; 1 Sam. 1 [b]1 Sam. 7:1

7 [1]Lit., *dwelling* [a]Ps. 43:3 [b]Ps. 5 [c]1 Chr. 28:2

8 [a]Num. 10:35; 6:41; Ps. 68:1 [b] 132:14 [c]Ps. 78:

9 [a]Job 29:14 [b]P 132:16; 149:5

10 [a]Ps. 2:2; 132

11 [a]Ps. 89:3, 35 [b]2 Sam. 7:12-16, 17:11-14; 2 Chr. Ps. 89:4; Acts 2:

And My testimony which I will teach them,
Their sons also shall [a]sit upon your throne forever."

13 For the LORD has [a]chosen Zion;
He has [b]desired it for His habitation.
14 "This is My [a]resting place forever;
Here I will [b]dwell, for I have desired it.
15 "I will abundantly [a]bless her provision;
I will [b]satisfy her needy with bread.
16 "Her [a]priests also I will clothe with salvation;
And her [a]godly ones will sing aloud for joy.
17 "There I will cause the [a]horn of David to spring forth;
I have prepared a [b]lamp for Mine anointed.
18 "His enemies I will [a]clothe with shame;
But upon himself his [b]crown shall shine."

Psalm 133

A Song of Ascents, of David.

133 Behold, how good and how pleasant it is
For [a]brothers to dwell together in unity!
2 It is like the precious [a]oil upon the head,
Coming down upon the beard,
Even Aaron's beard,
Coming down upon the [b]edge of his robes.
3 It is like the [a]dew of [b]Hermon,
Coming down upon the [c]mountains of Zion;
For there the LORD [d]commanded the blessing—[e]life forever.

Psalm 134

A Song of Ascents.

134 Behold, [a]bless the LORD, all [b]servants of the LORD,
Who [1c]serve [d]by night in the house of the LORD!
2 [a]Lift up your hands to the [b]sanctuary,
And bless the LORD.
3 May the LORD [a]bless you from Zion,
He who [b]made heaven and earth.

Psalm 135

135 [1a]Praise [2]the LORD!
Praise the name of the LORD;
Praise *Him*, O [b]servants of the LORD,
2 You who stand in the house of the LORD,
In the [a]courts of the house of our God!
3 [1]Praise [2]the LORD, for [a]the LORD is good;
[b]Sing praises to His name, [c]for it is lovely.
4 For [1]the LORD has [a]chosen Jacob for Himself,
Israel for His [2b]own possession.

5 For I know that [a]the LORD is great,
And that our Lord is [b]above all gods.
6 [a]Whatever the LORD pleases, He does,
In heaven and in earth, in the seas and in all deeps.
7 [1]He [a]causes the [2]vapors to ascend from the ends of the earth;

32; Acts 2:30
48:1, 2; 78:68 [b]Ps. 68:16
s. 132:8 [b]Ps. 6; Matt. 23:21
. 147:14 [b]Ps. 107:9
Chr. 6:41; Ps. 132:9
x. 29:21; Luke 1. 11:36; 15:4; 9; 2 Chr. 21:7; Ps. 18:28
[a]Job 8:22; Ps. 9:29 [b]Ps. 21:3
en. 13:8; Heb. 13:1
9:7; 30:25, 30; 2 [b]Ex. 28:33; 39:24
v. 19:12; Hos. Mic. 5:7 [b]Deut. :48 [c]Ps. 48:2; 8 [d]Lev. 25:21; 28:8; Ps. 42:8 [e]Ps. 21:4
Lit., *stand* [a]Ps. [b]Ps. 135:1, 2 ut. 10:8; 1 Chr. 0; 2 Chr. 29:11 [d]1 Chr. 9:33
28:2; 1 Tim. 2:8 [b]Ps. 63:2
8:5 [b]Ps. 124:8
[1]Or, *Hallelujah!* YAH [a]Ps. 113:1 [b]Ps. 134:1
. 92:13; 116:19
[1]Or, *Hallelujah!* YAH [a]Ps. 100:5; [b]Ps. 68:4 [c]Ps. 147:1
Heb., *YAH* [2]Or, *treasure* [a]Deut. 0:15; Ps. 105:6 19:5; Mal. 3:17; 2:14; 1 Pet. 2:9
[a]Ps. 48:1; 95:3; 145:3 [b]Ps. 97:9
6 [a]Ps. 115:3
it., *The one who* uds [a]Jer. 10:13; 51:16

Who [b]makes lightnings for the rain;
Who [a]brings forth the wind from His treasuries.

8 [1]He [a]smote the first-born of Egypt,
[2]Both of man and beast.
9 [1]He sent [a]signs and wonders into your midst, O Egypt,
Upon [b]Pharaoh and all his servants.
10 [1a]He [b]smote many nations,
And slew mighty kings,
11 [a]Sihon, king of the Amorites,
And [b]Og, king of Bashan,
And [c]all the kingdoms of Canaan;
12 And He [a]gave their land as a heritage,
A heritage to Israel His people.
13 Thy [a]name, O LORD, is everlasting,
Thy [1]remembrance, O LORD, [2]throughout all generations.
14 For the LORD will [a]judge His people,
And [b]will have compassion on His servants.
15 The [a]idols of the nations are *but* silver and gold,
The work of man's hands.
16 They have mouths, but they do not speak;
They have eyes, but they do not see;
17 They have ears, but they do not hear;
Nor is there any breath at all in their mouths.
18 Those who make them will be like them,
Yes, everyone who trusts in them.

19 O house of [a]Israel, bless the LORD;
O house of Aaron, bless the LORD;
20 O house of Levi, bless the LORD;
You [a]who [1]revere the LORD, bless the LORD.
21 Blessed be the LORD [a]from Zion,
Who [b]dwells in Jerusalem.
[1]Praise [2]the LORD!

Psalm 136

136 [a]Give thanks to the LORD, for [b]He is good;
For [c]His lovingkindness is everlasting.
2 Give thanks to the [a]God of gods,
For His lovingkindness is everlasting.
3 Give thanks to the [a]Lord of lords,
For His lovingkindness is everlasting.
4 To Him who [a]alone does great [1]wonders,
For His lovingkindness is everlasting;
5 To Him who [a]made the heavens [1b]with skill,
For His lovingkindness is everlasting;
6 To Him who [a]spread out the earth above the waters,
For His lovingkindness is everlasting;
7 To Him who [a]made *the* great lights,
For His lovingkindness is everlasting:
8 The [a]sun to rule [1]by day,
For His lovingkindness is everlasting,
9 The [a]moon and stars to rule [1]by night,
For His lovingkindness is everlasting.

7 [a]Jer. 10:13 [b]Job 28:25, 2 26; Zech. 10:

8 [1]Lit., *The o* [2]Lit., *From m beast* [a]Ex. 12 78:51; 105:36

9 [1]Lit., *The o* [a]Ex. 7:10; De Ps. 78:43 [b]Ps

10 [1]Lit., *The* [a]Num. 21:24; 135:10-12; 13 [b]Ps. 44:2

11 [a]Num. 21: Deut. 29:7 [b]N 21:33-35 [c]Jos

12 [a]Deut. 29: 78:55; 136:21,

13 [1]Or, *mem to* [a]Ex. 3:15;

14 [a]Deut. 32: 50:4 [b]Ps. 90:1

15 [a]Ps. 115:4 135:15-18

19 [a]Ps. 115:9

20 [1]Lit., *fear*

21 [1]Or, *Hallel* [2]Heb., *YAH* [a]P 134:3 [b]Ps. 13

136:1 [a]1 Chr. Ps. 106:1; 107 Jer. 33:11 [b]2 C 7:3; Ezra 3:11; 100:5 [c]1 Chr. 1 2 Chr. 20:21; P

2 [a]Deut. 10:17

3 [a]Deut. 10:17

4 [1]I.e., wonder [a]Deut. 6:22; Jo Ps. 72:18

5 [1]Lit., *with understanding* 1:1 [b]Ps. 104:24 3:19; Jer. 10:12

6 [a]Gen. 1:2, 6, 24:2; Is. 42:5; 4 Jer. 10:12

7 [a]Gen. 1:14-18 74:16

8 [1]Or, *over the* 1:16

9 [1]Or, *over the* 1:16

10 To Him who [a]smote [1]the Egyptians in their first-born,
For His lovingkindness is everlasting,
11 And [a]brought Israel out from their midst,
For His lovingkindness is everlasting,
12 With a [a]strong hand and an [b]outstretched arm,
For His lovingkindness is everlasting;
13 To Him who [a]divided the [1]Red Sea [2]asunder,
For His lovingkindness is everlasting,
14 And [a]made Israel pass through the midst of it,
For His lovingkindness is everlasting;
15 But [a]He [1]overthrew Pharaoh and his army in the [2]Red Sea,
For His lovingkindness is everlasting.
16 To Him who [a]led His people through the wilderness,
For His lovingkindness is everlasting;
17 To Him who [a]smote great kings,
For His lovingkindness is everlasting,
18 And [a]slew [1]mighty kings,
For His lovingkindness is everlasting:
19 [a]Sihon, king of the Amorites,
For His lovingkindness is everlasting,
20 And [a]Og, king of Bashan,
For His lovingkindness is everlasting,
21 And [a]gave their land as a heritage,
For His lovingkindness is everlasting,
22 Even a heritage to Israel His [a]servant,
For His lovingkindness is everlasting.

23 Who [a]remembered us in our low estate,
For His lovingkindness is everlasting,
24 And has [a]rescued us from our adversaries,
For His lovingkindness is everlasting;
25 Who [a]gives food to all flesh,
For His lovingkindness is everlasting.
26 Give thanks to the [a]God of heaven,
For His lovingkindness is everlasting.

Psalm 137

137 By the [a]rivers of Babylon,
There we sat down and [b]wept,
When we remembered Zion.
2 Upon the [1a]willows in the midst of it
We [b]hung our [2]harps.
3 For there our captors [1a]demanded of us [2]songs,
And [b]our tormentors mirth, *saying*,
"Sing us one of the songs of Zion."

4 How can we sing [a]the LORD's song
In a foreign land?
5 If I [a]forget you, O Jerusalem,
May my right hand [1]forget *her skill*.
6 May my [a]tongue cleave to the roof of my mouth,
If I do not remember you,
If I do not [1b]exalt Jerusalem
Above my chief joy.

, *Egypt* [a]Ex. 78:51; 135:8
51; 13:3; Ps. 105:43
; 13:9; 1 Kin. eh. 1:10; Ps. r. 32:21 [b]Ex. t. 4:34; 5:15; ; 11:2; 2 Kin. hr. 6:32; Jer. 32:17
Sea of Reeds in parts [a]Ex. s. 66:6; 78:13
22; Ps. 106:9
hook off [2]Lit., *f Reeds* [a]Ex. 78:53; 106:11
13:18; 15:22; 15; Ps. 78:52
s. 135:10-12; 136:17-22
[1]Lit., *majestic* [a]Deut. 29:7
lum. 21:21-24
lum. 21:33-35
1 [a]Josh. 12:1
05:6; Is. 41:8; 44:1; 45:4
. 9:12; 103:14; 106:45
udg. 6:9; Neh. 9:28; Ps. 107:2
104:27; 145:15
24:3, 7; 2 Chr. Ezra 1:2; 5:11; Neh. 1:4
1 [a]Ezek. 1:1, 3 [b]Neh. 1:4
r, *poplars* [2]Lit., [a]Lev. 23:40; Is. [b]Job 30:31; Is. :8; Ezek. 26:13
Lit., *asked* [2]Lit., *ds of song* [a]Ps. 80:6 [b]Is. 49:17
Chr. 29:27; Neh. 12:46
., become lame [a]Is. 65:11
6 [1]Lit., *cause to* [a]Job 29:10; Ps. zek. 3:26 [b]Neh. 2:3

7 Remember, O LORD, against the sons of [a]Edom
The day of Jerusalem,
Who said, "Raze it, raze it,
[b]To its very foundation."
8 O daughter of Babylon, you [1a]devastated one,
How blessed will be the one who [b]repays you
With [2]the recompense with which you have repaid us.
9 How blessed will be the one who seizes and [a]dashes your little ones
Against the rock.

Psalm 138

A Psalm of David.

138 [a]I will give Thee thanks with all my heart;
I will sing praises to Thee before the [b]gods.
2 I will bow down [a]toward Thy holy temple,
And [b]give thanks to Thy name for Thy lovingkindness and Thy [1]truth;
For Thou hast [c]magnified Thy [2]word [3]according to all Thy name.
3 On the day I [a]called Thou didst answer me;
Thou didst make me bold with [b]strength in my soul.

4 [a]All the kings of the earth will give thanks to Thee, O LORD,
When they have heard the words of Thy mouth.
5 And they will [a]sing of the ways of the LORD.
For [b]great is the glory of the LORD.
6 For [a]though the LORD is exalted,
Yet He [b]regards the lowly;
But the [c]haughty He knows from afar.

7 Though I [a]walk in the midst of trouble, Thou wilt [1b]revive me;
Thou wilt [c]stretch forth Thy hand against the wrath of my enemies,
And Thy right hand will [d]save me.
8 The LORD will [a]accomplish what concerns me;
Thy [b]lovingkindness, O LORD, is everlasting;
[c]Do not forsake the [d]works of Thy hands.

Psalm 139

For the choir director. A Psalm of David.

139 O LORD, Thou hast [a]searched me and known *me*.
2 Thou [a]dost know [1]when I sit down and [2]when I rise up;
Thou [b]dost understand my thought from afar.
3 Thou [a]dost [1]scrutinize my [2]path and my lying down,
And art intimately acquainted with all my ways.
4 [1]Even before there is a word on my tongue,
Behold, O LORD, Thou [a]dost know it all.
5 Thou hast [a]enclosed me behind and before,
And [b]laid Thy hand upon me.
6 *Such* [a]knowledge is [b]too wonderful for me;
It is *too* high, I cannot attain to it.

7 [a]Where can I go from Thy Spirit?

7 [a]Ps. 83:4-8 6; Jer. 49:7-2 4:21; Ezek. 2 35:2; Amos 1 10-14 [b]Ps. 7 3:13
8 [1]Or, *devast your recompe* 13:1-22; 47:1- 25:12; 50:1-4 [b]Jer. 50:15; 5 36, 49; Rev. 1
9 [a]2 Kin. 8:12 Hos. 13:16; N
138:1 [a]Ps. 11 95:3; 96:4; 97
2 [1]Or, *faithful. promise* [3]Or, *with* [a]1 Kin. 8. 5:7; 28:2 [b]Ps. [c]Is. 42:21
3 [a]Ps. 118:5 46:1
4 [a]Ps. 72:11;
5 [a]Ps. 145:7
6 [a]Ps. 113:4-7 3:34; Is. 57:15 1:48; James 4 5:5 [c]Ps. 40:4;
7 [1]Or, *keep m* [a]Ps. 23:4; 143 9:8, 9; Ps. 71:2 57:15 [c]Ex. 7:5 Is. 5:25; Jer. 5 Ezek. 6:14; 25 20:6; 60:5
8 [a]Ps. 57:2; Ph [b]Ps. 136:1 [c]Jo Ps. 27:9; 71:9; [d]Job 10:3; 14:1 100:3
139:1 [a]Ps. 17: Jer. 12:3
2 [1]Lit., *my sitti my rising* [a]2 Ki [b]Ps. 94:11; Is. 6 Matt. 9:4
3 [1]Lit., *winnow journeying* [a]Job 31:4
4 [1]Lit., *For ther* [a]Heb. 4:13
5 [a]Ps. 34:7; 12 9:33
6 [a]Rom. 11:33 42:3
7 [a]Jer. 23:24

Or where can I flee from Thy presence?
8 [a]If I ascend to heaven, Thou art there;
If I make my bed in [1]Sheol, behold, [b]Thou art there.
9 If I take the wings of the dawn,
If I dwell in the remotest part of the sea,
10 Even there Thy hand will [a]lead me,
And Thy right hand will lay hold of me.
11 If I say, "Surely the [a]darkness will [1]overwhelm me,
And the light around me will be night,"
12 Even the [a]darkness is not dark [1]to Thee,
And the night is as bright as the day.
[b]Darkness and light are alike *to Thee.*

13 For Thou didst [a]form my [1]inward parts;
Thou didst [b]weave me in my mother's womb.
14 I will give thanks to Thee, for [1]I am fearfully and wonderfully made;
[a]Wonderful are Thy works,
And my soul knows it very well.
15 My [1a]frame was not hidden from Thee,
When I was made in secret,
And skillfully wrought in the [b]depths of the earth.
16 Thine [a]eyes have seen my unformed substance;
And in [b]Thy book they were all written,
The [c]days that were ordained *for me,*
When as yet there was not one of them.

17 How precious also are Thy [a]thoughts to me, O God!
How vast is the sum of them!
18 If I should count them, they would [a]outnumber the sand.
When [b]I awake, I am still with Thee.

19 O that Thou wouldst [a]slay the wicked, O God;
[b]Depart from me, therefore, [c]men of bloodshed.
20 For they [a]speak [1]against Thee wickedly,
And Thine enemies [2b]take *Thy name* in vain.
21 Do I not [a]hate those who hate Thee, O LORD?
And do I not [b]loathe those who rise up against Thee?
22 I hate them with the utmost hatred;
They have become my enemies.

23 [a]Search me, O God, and know my heart;
[b]Try me and know my anxious thoughts;
24 And see if there be any [1a]hurtful way in me,
And [b]lead me in the [c]everlasting way.

Psalm 140

For the choir director. A Psalm of David.

140 [a]Rescue me, O LORD, from evil men;
Preserve me from [b]violent men,
2 Who [a]devise evil things in *their* hearts;
They [b]continually stir up wars.
3 They [a]sharpen their tongues as a serpent;
[b]Poison of a viper is under their lips. [1]Selah.

nether world
-4 [b]Job 26:6; Prov. 15:11
[a]Ps. 23:2, 3
bruise; some entators read *er* [a]Job 22:13
it., *from* [a]Job 22; Dan. 2:22 [b]1 John 1:5
kidneys [a]Ps. s. 44:24 [b]Job 10:11
Some ancient read *Thou art vonderful* [a]Ps. 40:5
t., *bones were* -10; Eccl. 11:5 [b]Ps. 63:9
10:8-10; Eccl. [b]Ps. 56:8 [c]Job 14:5
[a]Ps. 40:5; 92:5
. 40:5 [b]Ps. 3:5
. 11:4 [b]Ps. 6:8; [c]Ps. 5:6; 26:9
of [2]Some mss. *themselves up* Thee [a]Jude 15 20:7; Deut. 5:11
2 Chr. 19:2; Ps. 6 [b]Ps. 119:158
o 31:6; Ps. 26:2 Prov. 17:3; Jer. 20; 1 Thess. 2:4
Lit., *way of pain* 46:9; Prov. 15:9; ; Jer. 25:5; 36:3 5:8; 143:10 [c]Ps. 16:11
[a]Ps. 17:13; 59:2; Ps. 18:48; 86:14; 140:11
7:14; 36:4; 52:2; ov. 6:14; Is. 59:4; s. 7:15 [b]Ps. 56:6
Selah may mean: se, *Crescendo* or *al interlude* [a]Ps. ; 64:3 [b]Ps. 58:4; 3:13; James 3:8

4 [a]Keep me, O LORD, from the hands of the wicked;
[b]Preserve me from violent men,
Who have [1]purposed to [2c]trip up my feet.
5 The proud have [a]hidden a trap for me, and cords;
They have spread a [b]net by the [1]wayside;
They have set [c]snares for me. Selah.

6 I [a]said to the LORD, "Thou art my God;
[b]Give ear, O LORD, to the [c]voice of my supplications.
7 "O [1]GOD the Lord, [a]the strength of my salvation,
Thou hast [b]covered my head in the day of [2]battle.
8 "Do not grant, O LORD, the [a]desires of the wicked;
Do not promote [b]his *evil* device, *lest* they be exalted. Selah.

9 "As for the head of those who surround me,
May the [a]mischief of their lips cover them.
10 "May [a]burning coals fall upon them;
May they be [b]cast into the fire,
Into [1]deep pits from which they [c]cannot rise.
11 "May a [1]slanderer not be established in the earth;
[a]May evil hunt the violent man [2]speedily."

12 I know that the LORD will [a]maintain the cause of the afflicted,
And [b]justice for the poor.
13 Surely the [a]righteous will give thanks to Thy name;
The [b]upright will dwell in Thy presence.

Psalm 141

A Psalm of David.

141 O LORD, I call upon Thee; [a]hasten to me!
[b]Give ear to my voice when I call to Thee!
2 May my prayer be [1]counted as [a]incense before Thee;
The [b]lifting up of my hands as the [c]evening offering.
3 Set a [a]guard, O LORD, [1]over my mouth;
Keep watch over the [b]door of my lips.
4 [a]Do not incline my heart to any evil thing,
To practice deeds [1]of wickedness
With men who [b]do iniquity;
And [c]do not let me eat of their delicacies.

5 Let the [a]righteous smite me [1]in kindness and reprove me;
It is [b]oil upon the head;
Do not let my head refuse it,
[2]For still my prayer [c]is [3]against their wicked deeds.
6 Their judges are [a]thrown down by the sides of the rock,
And they hear my words, for they are pleasant.
7 As when one [a]plows and breaks open the earth,
Our [b]bones have been scattered at the [c]mouth of [1]Sheol.

8 For my [a]eyes are toward Thee, O [1]GOD, the Lord;
In Thee I [b]take refuge; [c]do not [2]leave me defenseless.
9 Keep me from the [1a]jaws of the trap which they have set for me,
And from the [b]snares of those who do iniquity.

4 [1]Or, *devise* ... *push violently* ... 71:4 [b]Ps. 140 ... 36:11

5 [1]Lit., *track* ... Ps. 35:7; 141:... [b]Ps. 31:4; 57:6 ... 1:13 [c]Ps. 141... 8:14; Amos 3:5

6 [a]Ps. 16:2; 3... 143:1 [c]Ps. 116...

7 [1]Heb., *YHWH* ... usually rendered ... [2]Lit., *weapons* ... 28:8; 118:14 ... 144:10

8 [a]Ps. 112:10 ... 9:25; Ps. 10:2, ...

9 [a]Ps. 7:16; P...

10 [1]Lit., *water...* 11:6 [b]Ps. 21:9; ... 3:10 [c]Ps. 36:1...

11 [1]Lit., *man o...* [2]Lit., *thrust upo...* [a]Ps. 34:21

12 [a]1 Kin. 8:45 ... 9:4; 18:27; 82:3 ... 12:5; 35:10

13 [a]Ps. 97:12 ... 11:7; 16:11; 17:...

141:1 [a]Ps. 22:1... 38:22; 70:5 [b]Ps... 143:1

2 [1]Lit., *fixed* [a]E... Luke 1:10; Rev. ... 4 [b]1 Tim. 2:8 [c]... 29:39, 41; 1 Kin... 36; Dan. 9:21

3 [1]Lit., *to* [a]Ps. ... 39:1; Prov. 13:3; ... [b]Mic. 7:5

4 [1]Lit., *in* [a]Ps. 1... [b]Is. 32:6; Hos. 6... 3:15 [c]Prov. 23:6

5 [1]Or, *lovingly* ... *And my prayer* ... *spite of their cala...* [a]Prov. 9:8; 19:25 ... 27:6; Eccl. 7:5; G... [b]Ps. 23:5; 133:2 ... 35:14

6 [a]2 Chr. 25:12

7 [1]I.e., the nethe... [a]Ps. 129:3 [b]Ps. 5... [c]Num. 16:32, 33; ... 88:3-5

8 [1]Heb., *YHWH,* usually rendered ... [2]Lit., *pour out my* ... [a]Ps. 25:15; 123:2 ... 2:12; 11:1 [c]Ps. 2...

9 [1]Lit., *hands of* ... *trap* [a]Ps. 38:12; ... 91:3; 119:110 [b]F...

10 Let the wicked [a]fall into their own nets,
While I pass by [1b]safely.

Psalm 142

[+]Maskil of David, when he was [•]in the cave. A Prayer.

142 I [a]cry aloud with my voice to the LORD;
I [b]make supplication with my voice to the LORD.
2 I [a]pour out my complaint before Him;
I declare my [b]trouble before Him.
3 When [a]my spirit [1]was overwhelmed within me,
Thou didst know my path.
In the way where I walk
They have [b]hidden a trap for me.
4 Look to the right and see;
For there is [a]no one who regards me;
[1]There is no [b]escape for me;
[c]No one cares for my soul.

5 I cried out to Thee, O LORD;
I said, "Thou art [a]my refuge,
My [b]portion in the [c]land of the living.
6 "[a]Give heed to my cry,
For I am [b]brought very low;
Deliver me from my persecutors,
For they are too [c]strong for me.
7 "[a]Bring my soul out of prison,
So that I may give thanks to Thy name;
The righteous will surround me,
For Thou wilt [b]deal bountifully with me."

Psalm 143

A Psalm of David.

143 Hear my prayer, O LORD,
[a]Give ear to my supplications!
Answer me in Thy [b]faithfulness, in Thy [c]righteousness!
2 And [a]do not enter into judgment with Thy servant,
For in Thy sight [b]no man living is righteous.
3 For the enemy has persecuted my soul;
He has crushed my life [a]to the ground;
He [b]has made me dwell in dark places, like those who have long
been dead.
4 Therefore [a]my spirit [1]is overwhelmed within me;
My heart is [2b]appalled within me.

5 I [a]remember the days of old;
I [b]meditate on all Thy doings;
I [c]muse on the work of Thy hands.
6 I [a]stretch out my hands to Thee;
My [b]soul *longs* for Thee, as a [1]parched land. [2]Selah.

7 [a]Answer me quickly, O LORD, my [b]spirit fails;
[c]Do not hide Thy face from me,
Lest I become like [d]those who go down to the pit.

it., *altogether* [a]Ps. 5; 35:8; 57:6 [b]Ps. 124:7
[+]Possibly, *Contemplative*, or *Didactic*, or *Skillful* alm [•]1 Sam. 22:1; 24:3
:1 [a]Ps. 77:1 [b]Ps. 30:8
[a]Ps. 102:title [b]Ps. 77:2
[1]Lit., *fainted* [a]Ps. 143:4 [b]Ps. 140:5
[1]Lit., *Escape has* hed from me [a]Ps. 11; 88:8, 18 [b]Job); Jer. 25:35 [c]Jer. 30:17
[a]Ps. 91:2, 9 [b]Ps. 73:26 [c]Ps. 27:13
s. 17:1 [b]Ps. 79:8; 116:6 [c]Ps. 18:17
Ps. 143:11; 146:7 [b]Ps. 13:6
[a]Ps. 140:6 [b]Ps. 89:1, 2 [c]Ps. 71:2
2 [a]Job 14:3; 22:4 n. 8:46; Job 4:17; ; 25:4; Ps. 130:3; 7:20; Rom. 3:10, 20; Gal. 2:16
44:25 [b]Ps. 88:6; Lam. 3:6
[1]Lit., *faints* [2]Or, *solate* [a]Ps. 77:3; 42:3 [b]Lam. 3:11
77:5, 10, 11 [b]Ps. 77:12 [c]Ps. 105:2
it., *weary* [2]*Selah* ay mean: *Pause*, *cendo* or *Musical* lude [a]Job 11:13; 9 [b]Ps. 42:2; 63:1
[a]Ps. 69:17 [b]Ps. ; 84:2; Jer. 8:18; . 1:22 [c]Ps. 27:9; 102:2 [d]Ps. 28:1; 88:4

8 Let me hear Thy [a]lovingkindness [b]in the morning;
For I trust [c]in Thee;
Teach me the [d]way in which I should walk;
For to Thee I [e]lift up my soul.
9 [a]Deliver me, O LORD, from my enemies;
[1]I take refuge in Thee.

10 [a]Teach me to do Thy will,
For Thou art my God;
Let [b]Thy good Spirit [c]lead me on level [1]ground.
11 [a]For the sake of Thy name, O LORD, [b]revive me.
[c]In Thy righteousness bring my soul out of trouble.
12 And in Thy lovingkindness [1a]cut off my enemies,
And [b]destroy all those who afflict my soul;
For [c]I am Thy servant.

Psalm 144

A Psalm of David.

144 Blessed be the LORD, [a]my rock,
Who [b]trains my hands for war,
And my fingers for battle;
2 My lovingkindness and [a]my fortress,
My [b]stronghold and my deliverer;
My [c]shield and He in whom I take refuge;
Who [d]subdues [1]my people under me.
3 O LORD, [a]what is man, that Thou dost take knowledge of him?
Or the son of man, that Thou dost think of him?
4 [a]Man is like a mere breath;
His [b]days are like a passing shadow.

5 [a]Bow Thy heavens, O LORD, and [b]come down;
[c]Touch the mountains, that they may smoke.
6 Flash forth [a]lightning and scatter them;
Send out Thine [b]arrows and confuse them.
7 Stretch forth Thy hand [a]from on high;
Rescue me and [b]deliver me out of great waters,
Out of the hand of [c]aliens
8 Whose mouths [a]speak deceit,
And whose [b]right hand is a right hand of falsehood.

9 I will sing a [a]new song to Thee, O God;
Upon a [b]harp of ten strings I will sing praises to Thee,
10 Who dost [a]give salvation to kings;
Who [b]dost rescue David His servant from the evil sword.
11 Rescue me, and deliver me out of the hand of [a]aliens,
Whose mouth [b]speaks deceit,
And whose [c]right hand is a right hand of falsehood.

12 Let our sons in their youth be as [a]grown-up plants,
And our daughters as [b]corner pillars [1]fashioned as for a palace;
13 *Let* our [a]garners be full, furnishing every kind of produce,
And our flocks bring forth thousands and ten thousands in our [1]fields;

8 [a]Ps. 90:14 [b]Ps [c]Ps. 25:2 [d]Ps. 27 32:8; 86:11 [e]Ps. 2 86:4

9 [1]Lit., *To Thee h hidden* [a]Ps. 31:15

10 [1]Lit., *land* [a]Ps 5; 119:12 [b]Neh. 9 [c]Ps. 23:3

11 [a]Ps. 25:11 [b]Ps 119:25 [c]Ps. 31:1;

12 [1]Or, *silence* [a] 54:5 [b]Ps. 52:5 [c]P 116:16

144:1 [a]Ps. 18:2 [b]2 Sam. 22:35; Ps

2 [1]Another readir *peoples* [a]Ps. 18:2 91:2 [b]Ps. 59:9 [c] 28:7; 84:9 [d]Ps. 1

3 [a]Job 7:17; Ps. Heb. 2:6

4 [a]Ps. 39:11 [b]Jo 14:2; Ps. 102:11;

5 [a]Ps. 18:9 [b]Is. [c]Ps. 104:32

6 [a]Ps. 18:14 [b]Ps 58:7; Hab. 3:11; Z 9:14

7 [a]Ps. 18:16 [b]Ps 14 [c]Ps. 18:44; 5

8 [a]Ps. 12:2; 41:6 14:22; Deut. 32:4 106:26; Is. 44:20

9 [a]Ps. 33:3; 40:3 33:2

10 [a]Ps. 18:50 [b]2 18:7; Ps. 140:7

11 [a]Ps. 18:44; 5 [b]Ps. 12:2; 41:6 [c] 14:22; Deut. 32:4 106:26; Is. 44:20

12 [1]Lit., *cut after pattern of* [a]Ps. 92:12-14; 128:3 4:4; 7:4

13 [1]Lit., *outside* 3:9, 10

14 *Let our* [a]cattle [1]bear,
Without [2b]mishap and without [3c]loss,
Let there be no [d]outcry in our streets!
15 How blessed are the people who are so situated;
How [a]blessed are the people whose God is the LORD!

Psalm 145

A Psalm of Praise, of David.

145 I will [a]extol Thee, [b]my God, O King;
And I will [c]bless Thy name forever and ever.
2 Every day I will bless Thee,
And I will [a]praise Thy name forever and ever.
3 [a]Great is the LORD, and highly to be praised;
And His [b]greatness is unsearchable.
4 One [a]generation shall praise Thy works to another,
And shall declare Thy mighty acts.
5 On the [a]glorious [1]splendor of Thy majesty,
And [b]on Thy wonderful works, I will meditate.
6 And men shall speak of the [1]power of Thine [a]awesome acts;
And I will [b]tell of Thy greatness.
7 They shall [1]eagerly utter the memory of Thine [a]abundant goodness,
And shall [b]shout joyfully of Thy righteousness.

8 The LORD is [a]gracious and merciful;
Slow to anger and great in lovingkindness.
9 The LORD is [a]good to all,
And His [b]mercies are over all His works.
10 [a]All Thy works shall give thanks to Thee, O LORD,
And Thy [b]godly ones shall bless Thee.
11 They shall speak of the [a]glory of Thy kingdom,
And talk of Thy power;
12 To [a]make known to the sons of men [1]Thy mighty acts,
And the [b]glory of the majesty of [1]Thy kingdom.
13 Thy kingdom is [1]an [a]everlasting kingdom,
And Thy dominion *endures* throughout all generations.

14 The LORD [a]sustains all who fall,
And [b]raises up all who are bowed down.
15 The eyes of all [1]look to Thee,
And Thou [a]dost give them their food in due time.
16 Thou [a]dost open Thy hand,
And dost satisfy the desire of every living thing.

17 The LORD is [a]righteous in all His ways,
And kind in all His deeds.
18 The LORD is [a]near to all who call upon Him,
To all who call upon Him [b]in truth.
19 He will [a]fulfill the desire of those who fear Him;
He will also [b]hear their cry and will save them.
20 The LORD [a]keeps all who love Him;
But all the [b]wicked, He will destroy.
21 My [a]mouth will speak the praise of the LORD;
And [b]all flesh will [c]bless His holy name forever and ever.

Psalm 146

146 [1]Praise [2]the LORD!
[a]Praise the LORD, O my soul!
2 I will praise the LORD [a]while I live;
I will [b]sing praises to my God while I have my being.
3 [a]Do not trust in princes,
In [1]mortal [b]man, in whom there is [c]no salvation.
4 His [a]spirit departs, he [b]returns to [1]the earth;
In that very day his [c]thoughts perish.
5 How [a]blessed is he whose help is the God of Jacob,
Whose [b]hope is in the LORD his God;
6 Who [a]made heaven and earth,
The [b]sea and all that is in them;
Who [c]keeps [1]faith forever;
7 Who [a]executes justice for the oppressed;
Who [b]gives food to the hungry.
The LORD [c]sets the prisoners free.

8 The LORD [a]opens *the eyes of* the blind;
The LORD [b]raises up those who are bowed down;
The LORD [c]loves the righteous;
9 The LORD [1a]protects the [2]strangers;
He [3b]supports the fatherless and the widow;
But He [4]thwarts [c]the way of the wicked.
10 The LORD will [a]reign forever,
Thy God, O Zion, to all generations.
[1]Praise [2]the LORD!

Psalm 147

147 [1]Praise [2]the LORD!
For [a]it is good to sing praises to our God;
For [3]it is pleasant *and* praise is [b]becoming.
2 The LORD [a]builds up Jerusalem;
He [b]gathers the outcasts of Israel.
3 He heals the [a]brokenhearted,
And [b]binds up their [1]wounds.
4 He [a]counts the number of the stars;
He [1b]gives names to all of them.
5 [a]Great is our Lord, and abundant in strength;
His [b]understanding is [1]infinite.
6 The LORD [1a]supports the afflicted;
He brings down the wicked to the ground.

7 [a]Sing to the LORD with thanksgiving;
Sing praises to our God on the lyre,
8 Who [a]covers the heavens with clouds,
Who [b]provides rain for the earth,
Who [c]makes grass to [1]grow on the mountains.
9 He [a]gives to the beast its food,
And to the [b]young ravens which cry.
10 He does not delight in the strength of the [a]horse;
He [b]does not take pleasure in the legs of a man.

146:1 [1]Or, *H*
[2]Heb., *YAH* [a]

2 [a]Ps. 63:4

3 [1]Lit., *a son*
[a]Ps. 118:9 [b]P
Is. 2:22 [c]Ps.
108:12

4 [1]Lit., *his ea*
104:29 [b]Eccl.
33:10; 1 Cor.

5 [a]Ps. 144:15
17:7 [b]Ps. 71:

6 [1]Or, *truth* [a]
115:15; Rev. 1
14:15 [c]Ps. 11

7 [a]Ps. 103:6
107:9; 145:15
68:6; Is. 61:1

8 [a]Matt. 9:30
[b]Ps. 145:14 [c]

9 [1]Or, *keeps*
sojourners [3]O
relieves [4]Lit.,
crooked [a]Ex.
Lev. 19:34 [b]D
10:18; Ps. 68:
147:6

10 [1]Or, *Hallel*
[2]Heb., *YAH* [a]E
Ps. 10:16

147:1 [1]Or, *Ha*
[2]Heb., *YAH* [3]O
gracious [a]Ps.
135:3 [b]Ps. 33

2 [a]Ps. 51:18;
[b]Deut. 30:3; Ps
Is. 11:12; 56:8;
39:28

3 [1]Lit., *sorrow*
34:18; 51:17; I
[b]Job 5:18; Is. 3
Ezek. 34:16

4 [1]Or, *calls the*
their names [a]C
[b]Is. 40:26

5 [1]Lit., *innume*
[a]Ps. 48:1; 145:
40:28

6 [1]Or, *relieves*
37:24; 146:8, 9

7 [a]Ps. 33:2; 95

8 [1]Lit., *spring f*
[a]Job 26:8 [b]Job
38:26; Ps. 104:
38:27; Ps. 104:

9 [a]Ps. 104:27,
145:15 [b]Job 38
Matt. 6:26

10 [a]Ps. 33:17
16:7

11 The LORD [a]favors those who fear Him,
[b]Those who wait for His lovingkindness.

12 Praise the LORD, O Jerusalem!
Praise your God, O Zion!
13 For He has strengthened the [a]bars of your gates;
He has [b]blessed your sons within you.
14 He [a]makes [1]peace in your borders;
He [b]satisfies you with [c]the [2]finest of the wheat.
15 He sends forth His [a]command to the earth;
His [b]word runs very swiftly.
16 He gives [a]snow like wool;
He scatters the [b]frost like ashes.
17 He casts forth His [a]ice as fragments;
Who can stand before His [b]cold?
18 He [a]sends forth His word and melts them;
He [b]causes His wind to blow and the waters to flow.
19 He [a]declares His words to Jacob,
His [b]statutes and His ordinances to Israel.
20 He [a]has not dealt thus with any nation;
And as for His ordinances, they have [b]not known them.
[1]Praise [2]the LORD!

Psalm 148

148 [1]Praise [2]the LORD!
Praise the LORD [a]from the heavens;
Praise Him [b]in the heights!
2 Praise Him, [a]all His angels;
Praise Him, [b]all His hosts!
3 Praise Him, sun and moon;
Praise Him, all stars of light!
4 Praise Him, [1a]highest heavens,
And the [b]waters that are above the heavens!
5 Let them praise the name of the LORD,
For [a]He commanded and they were created.
6 He has also [a]established them forever and ever;
He has made a [b]decree which will not pass away.

7 Praise the LORD from the earth,
[a]Sea monsters and all [b]deeps;
8 [a]Fire and hail, [b]snow and [c]clouds;
[d]Stormy wind, [e]fulfilling His word;
9 [a]Mountains and all hills;
Fruit [b]trees and all cedars;
10 [a]Beasts and all cattle;
[b]Creeping things and winged fowl;
11 [a]Kings of the earth and all peoples;
Princes and all judges of the earth;
12 Both young men and virgins;
Old men and children.

13 Let them praise the name of the LORD,
For His [a]name alone is exalted;
His [b]glory is above earth and heaven.

s. 149:4 [b]Ps. 33:18
3:3; 7:3 [b]Ps. 37:26
your borders [2]Lit., *fat* [a]Ps. 54:13; 60:17, 32:15 [c]Deut. 14; Ps. 81:16
ob 37:12; Ps. :5 [b]Ps. 104:4
[a]Job 37:6; Ps. :8 [b]Job 38:29
ob 37:10 [b]Job 37:9
33:9; 107:20; 5 [b]Ps. 107:25
33:3, 4 [b]Mal. 4:4
Or, *Hallelujah!* AH [a]Deut. 4:7, 4; Rom. 3:1, 2 9:6; Jer. 10:25
Or, *Hallelujah!* AH [a]Ps. 69:34 19; Ps. 102:19; Matt. 21:9
s. 103:20 [b]Ps. 103:21
Lit., *heavens of* s [a]Deut. 10:14; 8:27; Neh. 9:6; 8:33 [b]Gen. 1:7
1:1; Ps. 33:6, 9
[a]Ps. 89:37; Jer. 5, 36; 33:20, 25 [b]Job 38:33
[a]Gen. 1:21; Ps. [b]Gen. 1:2; Deut. 3:13; Hab. 3:10
[a]Ps. 18:12 [b]Ps. [c]Ps. 135:7 [d]Ps. [e]Job 37:12; Ps. 103:20
4:23; 49:13 [b]Is. 55:12
3:20 [b]Hos. 2:18
11 [a]Ps. 102:15
s. 12:4 [b]Ps. 8:1; 113:4

14 And He has [a]lifted up a horn for His people,
[b]Praise for all His godly ones;
Even for the sons of Israel, a people [c]near to Him.
[1]Praise [2]the LORD!

Psalm 149

149 [1]Praise [2]the LORD!
Sing to the LORD a [a]new song,
And His praise [b]in the congregation of the godly ones.
2 Let Israel be glad in [a]his Maker;
Let the sons of Zion rejoice in their [b]King.
3 Let them praise His name with [a]dancing;
Let them sing praises to Him with [b]timbrel and lyre.
4 For the LORD [a]takes pleasure in His people;
He will [b]beautify the afflicted ones with salvation.

5 Let the [a]godly ones exult in glory;
Let them [b]sing for joy on their beds.
6 *Let* the [a]high praises of God *be* in their [1]mouth,
And a [b]two-edged [c]sword in their hand,
7 To [a]execute vengeance on the nations,
And punishment on the peoples;
8 To bind their kings [a]with chains,
And their [b]nobles with fetters of iron;
9 To [a]execute on them the judgment written;
This is an [b]honor for all His godly ones.
[1]Praise [2]the LORD!

Psalm 150

150 [1]Praise [2]the LORD!
Praise God in His [a]sanctuary;
Praise Him in His mighty [3b]expanse.
2 Praise Him for His [a]mighty deeds;
Praise Him according to His excellent [b]greatness.

3 Praise Him with [a]trumpet sound;
Praise Him with [b]harp and lyre.
4 Praise Him with [a]timbrel and dancing;
Praise Him with [b]stringed instruments and [c]pipe.
5 Praise Him with loud [a]cymbals;
Praise Him with resounding cymbals.
6 Let [a]everything that has breath praise [1]the LORD.
[2]Praise [1]the LORD!

14 [1]Or, *Halle* [2]Heb., *YAH* [a]1 Ps. 75:10 [b]D Ps. 109:1; Jer [c]Lev. 10:3; Ep

149:1 [1]Or, *Ha* [2]Heb., *YAH* [a]P [b]Ps. 35:18; 89

2 [a]Ps. 95:6 [b] 8:23; Ps. 47:6

3 [a]2 Sam. 6:1 150:4 [b]Ex. 15 81:2

4 [a]Job 36:11; 35:27; 147:11 132:16; Is. 61:

5 [a]Ps. 132:16 35:10; Ps. 42:8

6 [1]Lit., *throat* 66:17 [b]Heb. 4 4:17

7 [a]Ezek. 25:17 5:15

8 [a]Job 36:8 [b]

9 [1]Or, *Halleluj* [2]Heb., *YAH* [a]D Ezek. 28:26 [b]P 148:14

150:1 [1]Or, *Ha* [2]Heb., *YAH* [3]O *firmament* [a]Ps. 102:19 [b]Ps. 19

2 [a]Ps. 145:12 3:24; Ps. 145:3

3 [a]Ps. 98:6 [b]P

4 [a]Ps. 149:3 [b] Is. 38:20 [c]Gen. Job 21:12

5 [a]2 Sam. 6:5; 13:8; 15:16; Ez Neh. 12:27

6 [1]Heb., *YAH* [2] *Hallelujah!* [3]He [a]Ps. 103:22; 14

of Psalms:

DIVISIONS

	CHAPTER THEMES
	1
	2
	3
	4
	5
	6
	7
	8
	9
	10
	11
	12
	13
	14
	15
	16
	17
	18
	19
	20
	21
	22
	23
	24
	25

Authors:

Purpose:

Key Words:

SEGMENT DIVISIONS

		CHAPTER THEMES
		26
		27
		28
		29
		30
		31
		32
		33
		34
		35
		36
		37
		38
		39
		40
		41
		42
		43
		44
		45
		46
		47
		48
		49
		50

DIVISIONS	CHAPTER THEMES
	51
	52
	53
	54
	55
	56
	57
	58
	59
	60
	61
	62
	63
	64
	65
	66
	67
	68
	69
	70
	71
	72
	73
	74
	75

SEGMENT DIVISIONS

		CHAPTER THEMES
		76
		77
		78
		79
		80
		81
		82
		83
		84
		85
		86
		87
		88
		89
		90
		91
		92
		93
		94
		95
		96
		97
		98
		99
		100

DIVISIONS	CHAPTER THEMES
	101
	102
	103
	104
	105
	106
	107
	108
	109
	110
	111
	112
	113
	114
	115
	116
	117
	118
	119
	120
	121
	122
	123
	124
	125

SEGMENT DIVISIONS

		CHAPTER THEMES
		126
		127
		128
		129
		130
		131
		132
		133
		134
		135
		136
		137
		138
		139
		140
		141
		142
		143
		144
		145
		146
		147
		148
		149
		150

ROVERBS

hen God appeared to King Solomon in a dream, He said, "Ask what you wish Me to give you." non asked for an understanding heart so that he could lead the nation of Israel (*see* 1 Kings 3). In nse to that prayer "God gave Solomon wisdom and very great discernment and breadth of mind, he sand that is on the seashore. And Solomon's wisdom surpassed the wisdom of all the sons of ist and all the wisdom of Egypt. For he was wiser than all men. . . . He also spoke 3,000 proverbs" ngs 4:29-32).

portion of those proverbs has been preserved for us in the book of Proverbs. A proverb is usually a saying or maxim which gives insight on life and human behavior.

e book of Proverbs, which is wisdom literature, is a compilation of true sayings which give om and instruction. However, these maxims cannot be interpreted as prophecies, nor can they be as absolutes. For example, Proverbs says a man's enemies will be at peace with him when his please the Lord. We can accept this as a wise saying which generally proves to be true, but not ys. Our Lord's enemies were not at peace with Him even though He did only those things which ed the Father. Proverbs is full of wise sayings—not promises.

on't rush through Proverbs. Give yourself time for meditation and application. Although Proverbs written between 971 and 686 B.C., the sayings are timeless. They can equip you for life in the home he marketplace.

NGS TO DO

Proverbs uses figurative language—similes and metaphors. Read the section called "Figures of Speech" on page I-61 before you study Proverbs.

Read Proverbs 1:1-7 and note the author, purpose, and theme in the margin of chapter 1. As you look for the purpose, watch the repeated use of *to*. The theme is also repeated in 9:10. Record these insights on the PROVERBS AT A GLANCE chart on page 968.

A wise person appreciates the wisdom of others. Look at PROVERBS AT A GLANCE and note the major segment divisions of this book. You'll see that Solomon respected the wisdom of others. Look up the following verses and note whose words or proverbs follow: Proverbs 10:1; 22:17; 25:1; 30:1; 31:1.

Mark the key words listed on PROVERBS AT A GLANCE. Keep a list of what you learn about wisdom, especially in the first nine chapters. Note how wisdom is personified. (An abstraction, such as wisdom, is personified when it takes on the characteristics of a person. Proverbs 1:20 is an example.)

Watch for and mark the phrase *my son*. Then listen as if it is God the Father speaking to you, His own dear child whom He wants to show the path of life.

Develop a code for marking the subjects covered throughout Proverbs: sexual morality, finances, discipline, the heart, the tongue, the company we keep, etc. As you read through Proverbs repeatedly you'll learn more and more about mankind and you'll find yourself much wiser when it comes to living in the "fear of the Lord." You'll have a collection of insights on the critical issues of life.

Record the theme or themes of each chapter on PROVERBS AT A GLANCE and in the text next to the chapter number. You may find this difficult between chapters 10 through 29 because the proverbs are short and varied. However, simply listing the major topics of each chapter will help you find the major topics at a glance. Color coding or marking each topic throughout the book will help you easily spot what Proverbs teaches about a particular subject. This will be a great help as you share these truths with others or need wisdom on a specific topic.

THINGS TO THINK ABOUT

1. Are you walking in the fear of the Lord? To fear God is to have an awesome respect of who and a reverential trust in His Word and His character—and to live accordingly.
2. Do you rely on your own understanding or do you seek God's wisdom in the matte everyday life?
3. What do you need to do or change in light of the insight and wisdom you've learned from proverbs?
4. Since there are 31 chapters in Proverbs, some people read a chapter a day, month after m This is good as long as you do not neglect other portions of the Word and as long as you yourself adequate time to meditate on these proverbs.
   a. After chapter 9 many proverbs are only two to four lines long. You may want to settle o or two proverbs a day, evaluating your life and relationships in the light of them.
   b. Or you may want to select a theme you marked throughout Proverbs, list what you le from the book as a whole, and then meditate on that theme. For example, you might me on what you learned about diligence versus laziness, or about the tongue.

Chapter 1

To have **knowledge** is to have understanding or information about something. To have **wisdom** is to have the ability to apply knowledge to daily life.

1 The [a]proverbs of Solomon [b]the son of David, king of Israel:
2 To know [a]wisdom and instruction,
To discern the sayings of [b]understanding,
3 To [a]receive instruction in wise behavior,
[b]Righteousness, justice and equity;
4 To give [a]prudence to the [1]naive,
To the youth [b]knowledge and discretion,
5 A wise man will hear and [a]increase in learning,
And a [b]man of understanding will acquire wise counsel,
6 To understand a proverb and a figure,
The words of the wise and their [a]riddles.

7 [a]The fear of the LORD is the beginning of knowledge;
Fools despise wisdom and instruction.

8 [a]Hear, my son, your father's instruction,
And [b]do not forsake your mother's teaching;
9 Indeed, they are a [a]graceful wreath to your head,
And [1b]ornaments about your neck.
10 My son, if sinners [a]entice you,
[b]Do not consent.
11 If they say, "Come with us,
Let us [a]lie in wait for blood,
Let us [b]ambush the innocent without cause;
12 Let us [a]swallow them alive like Sheol,
Even whole, as those who [b]go down to the pit;
13 We shall find all *kinds* of precious wealth,
We shall fill our houses with spoil;
14 Throw in your lot [1]with us,
We shall all have one purse,"
15 My son, [a]do not walk in the way with them.
[b]Keep your feet from their path,
16 For [a]their feet run to evil,

1:1 [a]1 Kin. 4:32 10:1; 25:1; Eccl [b]Eccl. 1:1
2 [a]Prov. 15:33 4:1
3 [a]Prov. 2:1; 19 [b]Prov. 2:9
4 [1]Lit., *simple o* [a]Prov. 8:5, 12 [b] 2:10, 11; 3:21
5 [a]Prov. 9:9 [b]P 14:6; Eccl. 9:11
6 [a]Num. 12:8; F 78:2; Dan. 8:23
7 [a]Job 28:28; P 111:10; Prov. 9:1 15:33; Eccl. 12:1
8 [a]Prov. 4:1 [b]Pr
9 [1]Lit., *necklace* [a]Prov. 4:9 [b]Gen. Dan. 5:29
10 [a]Prov. 16:29 39:7-10; Deut. 1 50:18; Eph. 5:11
11 [a]Prov. 12:6; J 5:26 [b]Ps. 10:8; F 1:18
12 [a]Ps. 124:3 [b]
14 [1]Lit., *in the m of us*
15 [a]Ps. 1:1; Prov [b]Ps. 119:101
16 [a]Prov. 6:17, 1 59:7

And they hasten to shed blood.
17 Indeed, it is [1]useless to spread the net
In the eyes of any [2]bird;
18 But they [a]lie in wait for their own blood;
They ambush their own lives.
19 So are the ways of everyone who [a]gains by violence;
It takes away the life of its possessors.

20 [a]Wisdom shouts in the street,
She [1]lifts her voice in the square;
21 At the head of the noisy *streets* she cries out;
At the entrance of the gates in the city, she utters her sayings:
22 "How long, O [1a]naive ones, will you love [2]simplicity?
And [b]scoffers delight themselves in scoffing,
And fools [c]hate knowledge?
23 "Turn to my reproof,
Behold, I will [a]pour out my spirit on you;
I will make my words known to you.
24 "Because [a]I called, and you [b]refused;
I [c]stretched out my hand, and no one paid attention;
25 And you [a]neglected all my counsel,
And did not [b]want my reproof;
26 I will even [a]laugh at your [b]calamity;
I will mock when your [c]dread comes,
27 When your dread comes like a storm,
And your calamity comes on like a [a]whirlwind,
When distress *and* anguish come on you.
28 "Then they will [a]call on me, but I will not answer;
They will [b]seek me diligently, but they shall not find me,
29 Because they [a]hated knowledge,
And did not choose the fear of the LORD.
30 "They [a]would not accept my counsel,
They spurned all my reproof.
31 "So they shall [a]eat of the fruit of their own way,
And be [b]satiated with their own devices.
32 "For the [a]waywardness of the [1]naive shall kill them,
And the complacency of fools shall destroy them.
33 "But [a]he who listens to me shall [1]live securely,
And shall be at ease from the dread of evil."

Chapter 2

2 My son, if you will [a]receive my sayings,
And [b]treasure my commandments within you,
2 [a]Make your ear attentive to wisdom,
Incline your heart to understanding;
3 For if you cry for discernment,
[1]Lift your voice for understanding;
4 If you seek her as [a]silver,
And search for her as for [b]hidden treasures;
5 Then you will discern the [a]fear of the LORD,
And discover the knowledge of God.
6 For [a]the LORD gives wisdom;
From His mouth *come* knowledge and understanding.
7 He stores up sound wisdom for the upright;

He is a [a]shield to those who walk in integrity,
8 Guarding the paths of justice,
And He [a]preserves the way of His godly ones.
9 Then you will discern [a]righteousness and justice
And equity *and* every [b]good course.
10 For [a]wisdom will enter your heart,
And [b]knowledge will be pleasant to your soul;
11 Discretion will [a]guard you,
Understanding will watch over you,
12 To [a]deliver you from the way of evil,
From the man who speaks [b]perverse things;
13 From those who [a]leave the paths of uprightness,
To walk in the [b]ways of darkness;
14 Who [a]delight in doing evil,
And rejoice in the perversity of evil;
15 Whose paths are [a]crooked,
And who are devious in their ways;
16 To [a]deliver you from the strange woman,
From the [1b]adulteress who flatters with her words;
17 That leaves the [a]companion of her youth,
And forgets the [b]covenant of her God;
18 For [a]her house [1]sinks down to death,
And her tracks *lead* to the [2]dead;
19 None [a]who go to her return again,
Nor do they reach the [b]paths of life.
20 So you will [a]walk in the way of good men,
And keep to the [b]paths of the righteous.
21 For [a]the upright will [1]live in the land,
And [b]the blameless will remain in it;
22 But [a]the wicked will be cut off from the land,
And [b]the treacherous will be [c]uprooted from it.

Chapter 3

3 My son, [a]do not forget my [1]teaching,
But let your heart [b]keep my commandments;
2 For [a]length of days and years of life,
And peace they will add to you.
3 Do not let [a]kindness and truth leave you;
[b]Bind them around your neck,
[c]Write them on the tablet of your heart.
4 So you will [a]find favor and [b]good [1]repute
In the sight of God and man.
5 [a]Trust in the LORD with all your heart,
And [b]do not lean on your own understanding.
6 In all your ways [a]acknowledge Him,
And He will [b]make your paths straight.
7 [a]Do not be wise in your own eyes;
[b]Fear the LORD and turn away from evil.
8 It will be [a]healing to your [1]body,
And [b]refreshment to your bones.
9 [a]Honor the LORD from your wealth,
And from the [b]first of all your produce;
10 So your [a]barns will be filled with plenty,
And your [b]vats will overflow with new wine.

7 [a]Ps. 84:11
8 [a]1 Sam. 2
9 [a]Prov. 8:2 4:18
10 [a]Prov. 14 22:18
11 [a]Prov. 4:6
12 [a]Prov. 28 6:12
13 [a]Prov. 21 82:5; Prov. 4 3:19, 20
14 [a]Prov. 10 11:15
15 [a]Ps. 125: 21:8
16 [1]Lit., *stra woman* [a]Pro [b]Prov. 23:27
17 [a]Mal. 2:14 [b]Gen. 2:24
18 [1]Lit., *bows* [2]Lit., *departed* [a]Prov. 7:27
19 [a]Eccl. 7:2 16:11; Prov. 5
20 [a]Heb. 6:12 4:18
21 [1]Or, *dwell* 29; Prov. 10:3 28:10
22 [a]Ps. 37:38 10:30 [b]Prov. [c]Deut. 28:63;
3:1 [1]Or, *law* 119:61; Prov. 20:6; Deut. 30
2 [a]Ps. 91:16; 3:16; 4:10; 9:1
3 [a]2 Sam. 15 14:22 [b]Deut. 6 Prov. 1:9; 6:21 7:3; Jer. 17:1;
4 [1]Lit., *unders* [a]1 Sam. 2:26; 8:35; Luke 2:5 111:10
5 [a]Ps. 37:3, 5; 22:19 [b]Prov. 2 9:23
6 [a]1 Chr. 28:9; 16:3; Phil. 4:6; 1:5 [b]Is. 45:13;
7 [a]Rom. 12:16 1:1; 28:28; Prov 16:6
8 [1]Lit., *navel* 4:22 [b]Job 21:2
9 [a]Is. 43:23 [b]E Deut. 26:2; Mal.
10 [a]Deut. 28:8 2:24

11 [a]My son, do not reject the [1]discipline of the LORD,
Or loathe His reproof,
12 For [a]whom the LORD loves He reproves,
Even [b]as a father, the son in whom he delights.

13 [a]How blessed is the man who finds wisdom,
And the man who gains understanding.
14 For its [a]profit is better than the profit of silver,
And its gain than fine gold.
15 She is [a]more precious than [1]jewels;
And nothing you desire compares with her.
16 [1a]Long life is in her right hand;
In her left hand are [b]riches and honor.
17 Her [a]ways are pleasant ways,
And all her paths are [b]peace.
18 She is a [a]tree of life to those who take hold of her,
And happy are all who hold her fast.
19 The LORD [a]by wisdom founded the earth;
By understanding He [b]established the heavens.
20 By His knowledge the [a]deeps were broken up,
And the [b]skies drip with dew.
21 My son, [a]let them not depart from your sight;
Keep sound wisdom and discretion,
22 So they will be [a]life to your soul,
And [b]adornment to your neck.
23 Then you will [a]walk in your way securely,
And your foot will not [b]stumble.
24 When you [a]lie down, you will not be afraid;
When you lie down, your sleep will be sweet.
25 [a]Do not be afraid of sudden fear,
Nor of the [1b]onslaught of the wicked when it comes;
26 For the LORD will be [1]your confidence,
And will [a]keep your foot from being caught.

27 [a]Do not withhold good from [1]those to whom it is due,
When it is in your power to do *it*.
28 [a]Do not say to your neighbor, "Go, and come back,
And tomorrow I will give *it*,"
When you have it with you.
29 [a]Do not devise harm against your neighbor,
While he lives in security beside you.
30 [a]Do not contend with a man without cause,
If he has done you no harm.
31 [a]Do not envy a man of violence,
And do not choose any of his ways.
32 For the [a]crooked *man* is an abomination to the LORD;
But [1]He is [b]intimate with the upright.
33 The [a]curse of the LORD is on the house of the wicked,
But He [b]blesses the dwelling of the righteous.
34 Though [a]He scoffs at the scoffers,
Yet [b]He gives grace to the afflicted.
35 [a]The wise will inherit honor,
But fools [1]display dishonor.

r, *instruction* [a]Job 5:17; Heb. 12:5, 6
[a]Rev. 3:19 [b]Deut. 8:5; Prov. 13:24
13 [a]Prov. 8:32, 34
ob 28:15-19; Prov. 8:10, 19; 16:16
[1]Lit., *corals* [a]Job 28:18; Prov. 8:11
it., *Length of days* v. 3:2 [b]Prov. 8:18; 22:4
[a]Matt. 11:29 [b]Ps. 19:165; Prov. 16:7
8 [a]Gen. 2:9; Prov. 13:12; 15:4; Rev. 2:7
[a]Ps. 104:24; Prov. 27 [b]Prov. 8:27, 28
[a]Gen. 7:11 [b]Deut. 33:28; Job 36:28
21 [a]Prov. 4:21
Deut. 32:47; Prov. 3:35; 16:22; 21:21 [b]Prov. 1:9
[a]Prov. 4:12; 10:9 s. 91:12; Is. 5:27; 63:13
ob 11:19; Ps. 3:5; Prov. 1:33; 6:22
[1]Lit., *storm* [a]Ps. ; 1 Pet. 3:14 [b]Job 5:21
[1]Or, *at your side* [a]1 Sam. 2:9
7 [1]Lit., *its owners* m. 13:7; Gal. 6:10
[a]Lev. 19:13; Deut. 24:15
[a]Prov. 6:14; 14:22
Prov. 26:17; Rom. 12:18
s. 37:1; Prov. 24:1
2 [1]Lit., *His private* el is [a]Prov. 11:20 ob 29:4; Ps. 25:14
[a]Lev. 26:14, 16; 11:28; Zech. 5:3, 2:2 [b]Job 8:6; Ps. 1:3
ames 4:6 [b]1 Pet. 5:5
5 [1]Lit., *raise high* [a]Dan. 12:3

Chapter 4

4 Hear, *O* sons, the [a]instruction of a father,
And [b]give attention that you may [1]gain understanding,
2 For I give you [1]sound [a]teaching;
[b]Do not abandon my [2]instruction.
3 When I was a son to my father,
[a]Tender and [b]the only son in the sight of my mother,
4 Then he [a]taught me and said to me,
"Let your heart [b]hold fast my words;
[c]Keep my commandments and live;
5 [a]Acquire wisdom! [b]Acquire understanding!
Do not forget, nor turn away from the words of my mouth.
6 "Do not forsake her, and she will guard you;
[a]Love her, and she will watch over you.
7 "[a]The [1]beginning of wisdom *is:* [b]Acquire wisdom;
And with all your acquiring, get understanding.
8 "[a]Prize her, and she will exalt you;
She will honor you if you embrace her.
9 "She will place [a]on your head a garland of grace;
She will present you with a crown of beauty."

10 Hear, my son, and [a]accept my sayings,
And the [b]years of your life will be many.
11 I have [a]directed you in the way of wisdom;
I have led you in upright paths.
12 When you walk, your [a]steps will not be impeded;
And if you run, you [b]will not stumble.
13 [a]Take hold of instruction; do not let go.
Guard her, for she is your [b]life.
14 [a]Do not enter the path of the wicked,
And do not proceed in the way of evil men.
15 Avoid it, do not pass by it;
Turn away from it and pass on.
16 For they [a]cannot sleep unless they do evil;
And [1]they are robbed of sleep unless they make *someone* stumble.
17 For they [a]eat the bread of wickedness,
And drink the wine of violence.
18 But the [a]path of the righteous is like the [b]light of dawn,
That [c]shines brighter and brighter until the [d]full day.
19 The [a]way of the wicked is like darkness;
They do not know over what they [1b]stumble.

20 My son, [a]give attention to my words;
[b]Incline your ear to my sayings.
21 [a]Do not let them depart from your sight;
[b]Keep them in the midst of your heart.
22 For they are [a]life to those who find them,
And [b]health to all [1]their whole body.
23 Watch over your heart with all diligence,
For [a]from it *flow* the springs of life.
24 Put away from you a [a]deceitful mouth,
And [b]put devious lips far from you.
25 Let your eyes look directly ahead,
And let your [1]gaze be fixed straight in front of you.

4:1 [1]Lit., *know* [a]... 34:11; Prov. 1:8 [b]... 1:2; 2:2
2 [1]Lit., *good* [2]Or, ... [a]Deut. 32:2; Job ... [b]Ps. 89:30; 119:87 ... Prov. 3:1
3 [a]1 Chr. 22:5; 29 ... [b]Zech. 12:10
4 [a]Eph. 6:4 [b]Ps. 119:168 [c]Prov. 7...
5 [a]Prov. 4:7 [b]Pro... 16:16
6 [a]2 Thess. 2:10
7 [1]Or, *the primar... is wisdom* [a]Prov. ... [b]Prov. 23:23
8 [a]1 Sam. 2:30
9 [a]Prov. 1:9
10 [a]Prov. 2:1 [b]P...
11 [a]1 Sam. 12:23
12 [a]Job 18:7; Ps. 18:36 [b]Ps. 91:11 ... 3:23
13 [a]Prov. 3:18 [b]... 3:22; John 6:63
14 [a]Ps. 1:1; Prov...
16 [1]Lit., *their sle... robbed* [a]Ps. 36:4 ... 2:1
17 [a]Prov. 13:2
18 [a]Is. 26:7; Mat... Phil. 2:15 [b]2 Sam ... [c]Dan. 12:3 [d]Job ...
19 [1]Or, *may stum...* [a]Job 18:5, 6; Pro... Is. 59:9, 10; Jer. ... John 12:35 [b]Joh...
20 [a]Prov. 5:1 [b]P...
21 [a]Prov. 3:21 [b]... 7:1, 2
22 [1]Lit., *his* [a]Pro... 3:22 [b]Prov. 3:8; ...
23 [a]Matt. 12:34; ... 19; Mark 7:21; L...
24 [a]Prov. 6:12; ... [b]Prov. 19:1
25 [1]Or, *eyelids*

26 [a]Watch the path of your feet,
And all your [b]ways will be established.
27 [a]Do not turn to the right nor to the left;
[b]Turn your foot from evil.

Chapter 5

5 My son, [a]give attention to my wisdom,
[b]Incline your ear to my understanding;
2 That you may [a]observe discretion,
And your [b]lips may reserve knowledge.
3 For the lips of an [1a]adulteress [b]drip honey,
And [c]smoother than oil is her [2]speech;
4 But in the end she is [a]bitter as wormwood,
[b]Sharp as a two-edged sword.
5 Her feet [a]go down to death,
Her steps lay hold of Sheol.
6 [1]She does not ponder the [a]path of life;
Her ways are [b]unstable, she [c]does not know *it*.

7 [a]Now then, *my* sons, listen to me,
And [b]do not depart from the words of my mouth.
8 [a]Keep your way far from her,
And do not go near the [b]door of her house,
9 Lest you give your vigor to others,
And your years to the cruel one;
10 Lest strangers be filled with your strength,
And your hard-earned goods *go* to the house of an alien;
11 And you groan at your latter end,
When your flesh and your body are consumed;
12 And you say, "How I have [a]hated instruction!
And my heart [b]spurned reproof!
13 "And I have not listened to the voice of my [a]teachers,
Nor inclined my ear to my instructors!
14 "I was almost in utter ruin
In the midst of the assembly and congregation."

15 Drink water from your own cistern,
And [1]fresh water from your own well.
16 Should your [a]springs be dispersed abroad,
Streams of water in the streets?
17 Let them be yours alone,
And not for strangers with you.
18 Let your [a]fountain be blessed,
And [b]rejoice in the [c]wife of your youth.
19 *As* a loving [a]hind and a graceful doe,
Let her breasts satisfy you at all times;
Be [1]exhilarated always with her love.
20 For why should you, my son, be exhilarated with an [1a]adulteress,
And embrace the bosom of a [b]foreigner?
21 For the [a]ways of a man are before the eyes of the LORD,
And He [b]watches all his paths.
22 His [a]own iniquities will capture the wicked,
And he will be held with the cords of his sin.

ov. 5:21; Heb. 13 [b]Ps. 119:5
ut. 5:32; 28:14 1:15; Is. 1:16
ov. 4:20 [b]Prov. 22:17
3:21 [b]Mal. 2:7
trange woman te [a]Prov. 2:16; ; 22:14 [b]Song :11 [c]Ps. 55:21
7:26 [b]Ps. 57:4; Heb. 4:12
5 [a]Prov. 7:27
Lest she watch 6; 5:21 [b]2 Pet. 4 [c]Prov. 30:20
Prov. 7:24 [b]Ps. 119:102
ov. 7:25 [b]Prov. 9:14
Prov. 1:7, 22, 29 Prov. 1:25; 12:1
13 [a]Prov. 1:8
15 [1]Lit., *flowing*
Prov. 5:18; 9:17; Song 4:12, 15
Prov. 9:17; Song 2, 15 [b]Eccl. 9:9 [c]Mal. 2:14
[1]Lit., *intoxicated* 2:9, 17; 4:5; 7:3
20 [1]Lit., *strange oman* [a]Prov. 5:3 . 2:16; 6:24; 7:5; 23:27
[a]Job 14:16; 31:4; 21; Ps. 119:168; 15:3; Jer. 16:17; 9; Hos. 7:2; Heb. 4:13 [b]Prov. 4:26
[a]Num. 32:23; Ps. 9:15; 40:12; Prov. 1:31, 32

23 He will [a]die for lack of instruction,
And in the greatness of his folly he will go astray.

Chapter 6

6 My son, if you have become [a]surety for your neighbor,
Have [1]given a pledge for a stranger,
2 *If* you have been snared with the words of your mouth,
Have been caught with the words of your mouth,
3 Do this then, my son, and deliver yourself;
Since you have come into the [1]hand of your neighbor,
Go, humble yourself, and importune your neighbor.
4 Do not give [a]sleep to your eyes,
Nor slumber to your eyelids;
5 Deliver yourself like a gazelle from *the hunter's* hand,
And like a [a]bird from the hand of the fowler.

6 Go to the [a]ant, O [b]sluggard,
Observe her ways and be wise,
7 Which, having [a]no chief,
Officer or ruler,
8 Prepares her food [a]in the summer,
And gathers her provision in the harvest.
9 How long will you lie down, O sluggard?
When will you arise from your sleep?
10 "[a]A little sleep, a little slumber,
A little folding of the hands to [1]rest"—
11 [a]And your poverty will come in like a [1]vagabond,
And your need like [2]an armed man.

12 A [a]worthless person, a wicked man,
Is the one who walks with a [b]false mouth,
13 Who [a]winks with his eyes, who [1]signals with his feet,
Who [2]points with his fingers;
14 Who *with* [a]perversity in his heart [b]devises evil continually,
Who [1c]spreads strife.
15 Therefore [a]his calamity will come suddenly;
[b]Instantly he will be broken, and there will be [c]no healing.

16 There are six things which the LORD hates,
Yes, seven which are an abomination [1]to Him:
17 [a]Haughty eyes, a [b]lying tongue,
And hands that [c]shed innocent blood,
18 A heart that devises [a]wicked plans,
[b]Feet that run rapidly to evil,
19 A [a]false witness *who* utters lies,
And one who [1b]spreads strife among brothers.

20 [a]My son, observe the commandment of your father,
And do not forsake the [1]teaching of your mother;
21 [a]Bind them continually on your heart;
Tie them around your neck.
22 When you [a]walk about, [1]they will guide you;
When you sleep, [1]they will watch over you;
And when you awake, [1]they will talk to you.

23 [a]Job 4:21;

6:1 [1]Lit., *clap palms* [a]Prov. 17:18; 20:16; 27:13

3 [1]Lit., *palm*

4 [a]Ps. 132:4

5 [a]Ps. 91:3; 1

6 [a]Prov. 30:24 [b]Prov. 6:9; 10:2 20:4; 26:16

7 [a]Prov. 30:27

8 [a]Prov. 10:5

10 [1]Lit., *lie do* 24:33

11 [1]Lit., *one w* [2]Lit., *a man wit shield* [a]Prov. 2

12 [a]Prov. 16:2 4:24; 10:32

13 [1]Lit., *scrape instructs with* [a] 15:12; Ps. 35:1 10:10

14 [1]Lit., *sends* [a]Prov. 17:20 [b]P 3:29; Mic. 2:1 [c] 6:19; 16:28

15 [a]Prov. 24:22 30:13, 14; Jer. 1 [c]2 Chr. 36:16

16 [1]Lit., *of His s*

17 [a]Ps. 18:27; 1 Prov. 21:4; 30:1 31:18; 120:2; Pr 12:22; 17:7 [c]De 19:10; Prov. 28:1 1:15; 59:7

18 [a]Gen. 6:5; P 24:2 [b]Prov. 1:16 59:7; Rom. 3:15

19 [1]Lit., *sends c* 27:12; Prov. 12:1 9; 21:28 [b]Prov. 6

20 [1]Or, *law* [a]Ep

21 [a]Prov. 3:3

22 [1]Lit., *she* [a]Pr

23 For [a]the commandment is a lamp, and the [1]teaching is light;
And reproofs for discipline are the way of life,
24 To [a]keep you from the evil woman,
From the smooth tongue of the [1]adulteress.
25 [a]Do not desire her beauty in your heart,
Nor let her catch you with her [b]eyelids.
26 For [a]on account of a harlot *one is reduced* to a loaf of bread,
And [1]an adulteress [b]hunts for the precious life.
27 Can a man [1]take fire in his bosom,
And his clothes not be burned?
28 Or can a man walk on hot coals,
And his feet not be scorched?
29 So is the one who [a]goes in to his neighbor's wife;
Whoever touches her [b]will not [1]go unpunished.
30 [1]Men do not despise a thief if he steals
To [a]satisfy [2]himself when he is hungry;
31 But when he is found, he must [a]repay sevenfold;
He must give all the [1]substance of his house.
32 The one who commits adultery with a woman is [a]lacking [1]sense;
He who would [b]destroy [2]himself does it.
33 Wounds and disgrace he will find,
And his reproach will not be blotted out.
34 For [a]jealousy [1]enrages a man,
And he will not spare in the [b]day of vengeance.
35 He will not [1]accept any ransom,
Nor will he be [2]content though you give many [3]gifts.

Chapter 7

7 My son, [a]keep my words,
And treasure my commandments within you.
2 [a]Keep my commandments and live,
And my [1]teaching [b]as the [2]apple of your eye.
3 [a]Bind them on your fingers;
[b]Write them on the tablet of your heart.
4 Say to wisdom, "You are my sister,"
And call understanding *your* intimate friend;
5 That they may keep you from an [1]adulteress,
From the foreigner who [2]flatters with her words.

6 For [a]at the window of my house
I looked out [b]through my lattice,
7 And I saw among the [1a]naive,
I discerned among the [2]youths,
A young man [b]lacking [3]sense,
8 Passing through the street near [a]her corner;
And he [1]takes the way to [b]her house,
9 In the [a]twilight, in the [1]evening,
In the [2]middle of the night and *in* the darkness.
10 And behold, a woman *comes* to meet him,
[a]Dressed as a harlot and cunning of heart.
11 She is [a]boisterous and rebellious;
Her [b]feet do not remain at home;
12 *She is* now in the streets, now [a]in the squares,
And [b]lurks by every corner.

Or, *law* [a]Ps. 19:8; 119:105
t., *foreign woman* [a]Prov. 5:3; 7:5, 21
Matt. 5:28 [b]2 Kin. ; Jer. 4:30; Ezek. 23:40
[1]Lit., *a man's wife* Prov. 5:9, 10; 29:3 7:23; Ezek. 13:18
7 [1]Lit., *snatch up*
[1]Lit., *be innocent* Ezek. 18:6; 33:26 [b]Prov. 16:5
., *They do not;* or, *t men . . . ?* [2]Lit., *s soul* [a]Job 38:39
[1]Or, *wealth* [a]Ex. 22:1-4
t., *heart* [2]Lit., *his* Prov. 7:7; 9:4, 16; , 21; 11:12; 12:11 [b]Prov. 7:22, 23
Lit., *is the rage of* v. 27:4; Song 8:6 [b]Prov. 11:4
it., *lift up the face* [2]Lit., *willing* [3]Or, *bribes*
[a]Prov. 2:1; 6:20
Or, *law* [2]Lit., *pupil* 4:4 [b]Deut. 32:10; s. 17:8; Zech. 2:8
[a]Deut. 6:8; 11:18; . 6:21 [b]Prov. 3:3
, *strange woman* [2]Lit., *is smooth*
. 5:28 [b]Song 2:9
[1]Lit., *simple ones* *sons* [3]Lit., *heart* 1:22 [b]Prov. 6:32; 9:4
Lit., *steps* [a]Prov. 7:12 [b]Prov. 7:27
t., *evening of the* [2]Lit., *pupil* (of the eye) [a]Job 24:15
[a]Gen. 38:14, 15; 1 Tim. 2:9
rov. 9:13 [b]1 Tim. 5:13; Titus 2:5
Prov. 9:14 [b]Prov. 23:28

13 So she seizes him and kisses him,
[1]And with a [a]brazen face she says to him:
14 "[1]I was due to offer [a]peace offerings;
Today I have [b]paid my vows.
15 "Therefore I have come out to meet you,
To seek your presence earnestly, and I have found you.
16 "I have spread my couch with [a]coverings,
With colored [b]linens of Egypt.
17 "I have sprinkled my bed
With [a]myrrh, aloes and [b]cinnamon.
18 "Come, let us drink our fill of love until morning;
Let us delight ourselves with caresses.
19 "For [1]the man is not at home,
He has gone on a long journey;
20 He has taken a [a]bag of money [1]with him,
At full moon he will come home."
21 With her many persuasions she entices him;
With her [1a]flattering lips she seduces him.
22 Suddenly he follows her,
As an ox goes to the slaughter,
Or as [1]*one in* fetters to the discipline of a fool,
23 Until an arrow pierces through his liver;
As a [a]bird hastens to the snare,
So he does not know that it *will cost him* his life.

24 Now therefore, *my* sons, [a]listen to me,
And pay attention to the words of my mouth.
25 Do not let your heart [a]turn aside to her ways,
Do not stray into her paths.
26 For many are the [1]victims she has cast down,
And [a]numerous are all her slain.
27 Her [a]house is the way to Sheol,
Descending to the chambers of death.

Chapter 8

8 Does not [a]wisdom call,
And understanding [1]lift up her voice?
2 On top of [a]the heights beside the way,
Where the paths meet, she takes her stand;
3 Beside the [a]gates, at the opening to the city,
At the entrance of the doors, she cries out:
4 "To you, O men, I call,
And my voice is to the sons of men.
5 "O [1a]naive ones, discern prudence;
And, O [b]fools, discern [2]wisdom.
6 "Listen, for I shall speak [a]noble things;
And the opening of my lips *will produce* [b]right things.
7 "For my [a]mouth will utter truth;
And wickedness is an abomination to my lips.
8 "All the utterances of my mouth are in righteousness;
There is nothing [a]crooked or perverted in them.
9 "They are all [a]straightforward to him who understands,
And right to those who [b]find knowledge.
10 "Take my [a]instruction, and not silver,

13 [1]Lit., *She bold her face* [a]Prov. 21:29

14 [1]Lit., *Sac peace offerin me* [a]Lev. 7:1 7:16

16 [a]Prov. 31: 19:9; Ezek. 2

17 [a]Ps. 45:8

19 [1]I.e., my h

20 [1]Lit., *in his* [a]Gen. 42:35

21 [1]Lit., *smoo* 5:3; 6:24

22 [1]Or, *as a s into a trap;* so ancient versio

23 [a]Eccl. 9:12

24 [a]Prov. 5:7

25 [a]Prov. 5:8

26 [1]Lit., *morta wounded* [a]Pro

27 [a]Prov. 2:18 9:18; 1 Cor. 6: Rev. 22:15

8:1 [1]Lit., *give* 1:20, 21; 8:1-3; 1 Cor. 1:24

2 [a]Prov. 9:3, 1

3 [a]Job 29:7

5 [1]Lit., *simple heart* [a]Prov. 1: 1:22, 32; 3:35

6 [a]Prov. 22:20 23:16

7 [a]Ps. 37:30; J 8:14; Rom. 15:8

8 [a]Deut. 32:5; P 2:15; Phil. 2:15

9 [a]Prov. 14:6 [b] 3:13

10 [a]Prov. 3:14,

And knowledge rather than choicest gold.
11 "For wisdom is [a]better than [1]jewels;
And [b]all desirable things can not compare with her.

12 "I, wisdom, [a]dwell with prudence,
And I find [b]knowledge *and* discretion.
13 "The [a]fear of the LORD is to hate evil;
[b]Pride and arrogance and [c]the evil way,
And the [d]perverted mouth, I hate.
14 "[a]Counsel is mine and [b]sound wisdom;
I am understanding, [c]power is mine.
15 "By me [a]kings reign,
And rulers decree justice.
16 "By me princes rule, and nobles,
All who judge rightly.
17 "I [a]love those who love me;
And [b]those who diligently seek me will find me.
18 "[a]Riches and honor are with me,
Enduring [b]wealth and righteousness.
19 "My fruit is [a]better than gold, even pure gold,
And my yield than [b]choicest silver.
20 "I walk in the way of righteousness,
In the midst of the paths of justice,
21 To endow those who love me with wealth,
That I may [a]fill their treasuries.

22 "The LORD possessed me [a]at the beginning of His way,
Before His works [1]of old.
23 "From everlasting I was [1a]established,
From the beginning, [b]from the earliest times of the earth.
24 "When there were no [a]depths I was [1]brought forth,
When there were no springs abounding with water.
25 "[a]Before the mountains were settled,
Before the hills I was [1]brought forth;
26 While He had not yet made the earth and the [1]fields,
Nor the first dust of the world.
27 "When He [a]established the heavens, I was there,
When [b]He inscribed a circle on the face of the deep,
28 When He made firm the skies above,
When the springs of the deep became [1]fixed,
29 When [a]He set for the sea its boundary,
So that the water should not transgress His [1]command,
When He marked out [b]the foundations of the earth;
30 Then [a]I was beside Him, *as* a master workman;
And I was daily *His* delight,
[1]Rejoicing always before Him,
31 [1]Rejoicing in the world, His earth,
And *having* [a]my delight in the sons of men.

32 "Now therefore, *O* sons, [a]listen to me,
For [b]blessed are they who keep my ways.
33 "[a]Heed instruction and be wise,
And do not neglect *it*.
34 "[a]Blessed is the man who listens to me,

., *corals* [a]Job 18; Ps. 19:10 [b]Prov. 3:15
3:5 [b]Prov. 1:4
Prov. 3:7; 16:6 am. 2:3; Prov. . 13:11 [c]Prov. :9 [d]Prov. 6:12
v. 1:25; 19:20; :29; Jer. 32:19 2:7; 3:21; 18:1 ccl. 7:19; 9:16
hr. 1:10; Prov. an. 2:21; Matt. 18; Rom. 13:1
am. 2:30; Prov. n 14:21 [b]Prov. ., 5; John 7:37; James 1:5
Prov. 3:16 [b]Ps. 2:3; Matt. 6:33
ob 28:15; Prov. 4 [b]Prov. 10:20
21 [a]Prov. 24:4
from then [a]Job 28; Ps. 104:24; Prov. 3:19
Or, *consecrated* :1-3 [b]John 17:5
born [a]Gen. 1:2; 15:5; Job 38:16; Prov. 3:20
born [a]Job 15:7; Ps. 90:2
., *outside places*
[a]Prov. 3:19 [b]Job 26:10
28 [1]Lit., *strong*
Lit., *mouth* [a]Job ; Ps. 104:9 [b]Job 38:6; Ps. 104:5
r, *Playing* [a]John 1:2, 3
[1]Or, *Playing* [a]Ps. 16:3; John 13:1
v. 5:7; 7:24 [b]Ps. 1, 2; 128:1; Prov. 29:18; Luke 11:28
33 [a]Prov. 4:1
4 [a]Prov. 3:13, 18

Watching daily at my gates,
Waiting at my doorposts.
35 "For [a]he who finds me finds life,
And [b]obtains favor from the LORD.
36 "But he who [1]sins against me [a]injures himself;
All those who [b]hate me [c]love death."

Chapter 9

9 Wisdom has [a]built her house,
She has hewn out her seven pillars;
2 She has [1a]prepared her food, she has [b]mixed her wine;
She has also [c]set her table;
3 She has [a]sent out her maidens, she [b]calls
From the [c]tops of the heights of the city:
4 "[a]Whoever is [1]naive, let him turn in here!"
To him who [b]lacks [2]understanding she says,
5 "Come, [a]eat of my food,
And drink of the wine I have mixed.
6 "[1]Forsake *your* folly and [a]live,
And [b]proceed in the way of understanding."

7 He who [a]corrects a scoffer gets dishonor for himself,
And he who reproves a wicked man *gets* [1]insults for himself.
8 [a]Do not reprove a scoffer, lest he hate you,
[b]Reprove a wise man, and he will love you.
9 Give *instruction* to a wise man, and he will be still wiser,
Teach a righteous man, and he will [a]increase *his* learning.
10 The [a]fear of the LORD is the beginning of wisdom,
And the knowledge of the Holy One is understanding.
11 For [a]by me your days will be multiplied,
And years of life will be added to you.
12 If you are wise, you are wise [a]for yourself,
And if you [b]scoff, you alone will bear it.

13 The [1]woman of folly is [a]boisterous,
She is [2]naive, and [b]knows nothing.
14 And she sits at the doorway of her house,
On a seat by [a]the high places of the city,
15 Calling to those who pass by,
Who are making their paths straight:
16 "[a]Whoever is [1]naive, let him turn in here,"
And to him who lacks [2]understanding she says,
17 "Stolen water is sweet;
And [a]bread *eaten* in secret is pleasant."
18 But he does not know that the [1]dead are there,
That her guests are in the [a]depths of Sheol.

Chapter 10

10 The [a]proverbs of Solomon.
[b]A wise son makes a father glad,
But [c]a foolish son is a grief to his mother.
2 [1a]Ill-gotten gains do not profit,
But righteousness delivers from death.
3 The LORD [a]will not allow the [1]righteous to hunger,

35 [a]Prov. 4:2 17:3 [b]Prov. 3

36 [1]Or, *miss* [a]Prov. 1:31, 3 [b]Prov. 5:12; 1 21:6

9:1 [a]1 Cor. 3 Eph. 2:20-22;

2 [1]Lit., *slaugh slaughter* [a]Ma [b]Song 8:2 [c]L 14:16, 17

3 [a]Ps. 68:11; 22:3 [b]Prov. 8 [c]Prov. 9:14

4 [1]Lit., *simple heart* [a]Prov. 8 [b]Prov. 6:32

5 [a]Song 5:1; I John 6:27

6 [1]Or, *Forsake simple ones* [a] 8:35; 9:11 [b]Ez 37:24

7 [1]Lit., *a blem* 23:9

8 [a]Prov. 15:12 7:6 [b]Ps. 141:5 10:8

9 [a]Prov. 1:5

10 [a]Job 28:28; 111:10; Prov. 1

11 [a]Prov. 3:16;

12 [a]Job 22:2; F 14:14 [b]Prov. 19

13 [1]Or, *foolish* [2]Lit., *simple* [a]P [b]Prov. 5:6

14 [a]Prov. 9:3

16 [1]Lit., *simple heart* [a]Prov. 9:4

17 [a]Prov. 20:17

18 [1]Lit., *departe spirits* [a]Prov. 7:2

10:1 [a]Prov. 1:1 15:20; 29:3 [c]Pro 17:25; 29:15

2 [1]Lit., *Treasure wickedness* [a]Ps Prov. 11:4; 21:6; 7:19; Luke 12:19

3 [1]Lit., *soul of th righteous* [a]Ps. 3 37:25; Prov. 28:2 6:33

But He [b]will thrust *aside* the craving of the wicked.
4 Poor is he who works with a negligent hand,
But the [a]hand of the diligent makes rich.
5 He who gathers in summer is a son who acts wisely,
But he who sleeps in harvest is a son who acts shamefully.
6 [a]Blessings are on the head of the righteous,
But [b]the mouth of the wicked conceals violence.
7 The [a]memory of the righteous is blessed,
But [b]the name of the wicked will rot.
8 The [a]wise of heart will receive commands,
But [1]a babbling fool will be thrown down.
9 He [a]who walks in integrity walks securely,
But [b]he who perverts his ways will be found out.
10 He [a]who winks the eye causes trouble,
And [1b]a babbling fool will be thrown down.
11 The [a]mouth of the righteous is a fountain of life,
But [b]the mouth of the wicked conceals violence.
12 Hatred stirs up strife,
But [a]love covers all transgressions.
13 On [a]the lips of the discerning, wisdom is found,
But [b]a rod is for the back of him who lacks [1]understanding.
14 Wise men [a]store up knowledge,
But with [b]the mouth of the foolish, ruin is at hand.
15 The [a]rich man's wealth is his [1]fortress,
The [b]ruin of the poor is their poverty.
16 The [1a]wages of the righteous is life,
The income of the wicked, punishment.
17 He [a]is *on* the path of life who heeds instruction,
But he who forsakes reproof goes astray.
18 He [a]who conceals hatred *has* lying lips,
And he who spreads slander is a fool.
19 When there are [a]many words, transgression is unavoidable,
But [b]he who restrains his lips is wise.
20 The tongue of the righteous is *as* [a]choice silver,
The heart of the wicked is *worth* little.
21 The [a]lips of the righteous feed many,
But fools [b]die for lack of [1]understanding.
22 It is the [a]blessing of the LORD that makes rich,
And He adds no sorrow to it.
23 Doing wickedness is like [a]sport to a fool;
And *so is* wisdom to a man of understanding.
24 What [a]the wicked fears will come upon him,
And the [b]desire of the righteous will be granted.
25 When the [a]whirlwind passes, the wicked is no more,
But the [b]righteous *has* an everlasting foundation.
26 Like vinegar to the teeth and smoke to the eyes,
So is the [a]lazy one to those who send him.
27 The [a]fear of the LORD prolongs [1]life,
But the [b]years of the wicked will be shortened.
28 The [a]hope of the righteous is gladness,
But the [b]expectation of the wicked perishes.
29 The [a]way of the LORD is a stronghold to the upright,
But [b]ruin to the workers of iniquity.
30 The [a]righteous will never be shaken,

112:10; Prov. 28:9
ov. 13:4; 21:5
28:20 [b]Prov. :11; Obad. 10
2:6 [b]Ps. 9:5, 13; Eccl. 8:10
the foolish of rov. 9:8; Matt. 7:24
:4; Prov. 3:23; ; Is. 33:15, 16 v. 26:26; Matt. 6; 1 Tim. 5:25
, *the foolish of* s. 35:19; Prov. 3 [b]Prov. 10:8
s. 37:30; Prov. :4 [b]Prov. 10:6
v. 17:9; 1 Cor. ; James 5:20; 1 Pet. 4:8
:, *heart* [a]Prov. ov. 19:29; 26:3
rov. 9:9 [b]Prov. 10; 13:3; 18:7
Lit., *strong city* 1:24; Ps. 52:7; 11 [b]Prov. 19:7
Or, *work* [a]Prov. 11:18, 19
17 [a]Prov. 6:23
8 [a]Prov. 26:24
Job 11:2; Prov. Eccl. 5:3 [b]Prov. ames 1:19; 3:2
20 [a]Prov. 8:19
it., *heart* [a]Prov. Prov. 5:23; Hos. 4:6
n. 24:35; 26:12; 8:18; Prov. 8:21
rov. 2:14; 15:21
Job 15:21; Prov. 27; Is. 66:4 [b]Ps. Prov. 15:8; Matt. 1 John 5:14, 15
[a]Job 21:18; Ps. Prov. 12:7 [b]Ps. Prov. 12:3; Matt. 7:24, 25
26 [a]Prov. 26:6
Lit., *days* [a]Prov. 9:11; 14:27 [b]Job 2, 33; 22:16; Ps. 55:23
Prov. 11:23 [b]Job 11:20; Prov. 11:7
Prov. 13:6 [b]Prov. 21:15
Ps. 37:29; 125:1; Prov. 2:21

But [b]the wicked will not dwell in the land.
31 The [a]mouth of the righteous flows with wisdom,
But the [b]perverted tongue will be cut out.
32 The lips of the righteous bring forth [a]what is acceptable,
But the [b]mouth of the wicked, what is perverted.

Chapter 11

11 A [a]false balance is an abomination to the LORD,
But a [b]just weight is His delight.
2 When [a]pride comes, then comes dishonor,
But with the humble is wisdom.
3 The [a]integrity of the upright will guide them,
But the [b]falseness of the treacherous will destroy them.
4 [a]Riches do not profit in the day of wrath,
But [b]righteousness delivers from death.
5 The [a]righteousness of the blameless will smooth his way,
But [b]the wicked will fall by his own wickedness.
6 The righteousness of the upright will deliver them,
But the treacherous will [a]be caught by *their own* greed.
7 When a wicked man dies, *his* [a]expectation will perish,
And the [b]hope of strong men perishes.
8 The righteous is delivered from trouble,
But the wicked [1]takes his place.
9 With *his* [a]mouth the godless man destroys his neighbor,
But through knowledge the [b]righteous will be delivered.
10 When it [a]goes well with the righteous, the city rejoices,
And when the wicked perish, there is glad shouting.
11 By the blessing of the upright a city is exalted,
But by the mouth of the wicked it is torn down.
12 He who despises his neighbor lacks [1]sense,
But a man of understanding keeps silent.
13 He [a]who goes about as a talebearer reveals secrets,
But he who is [1]trustworthy [b]conceals a matter.
14 Where there is no [a]guidance, the people fall,
But in abundance of counselors there is [1]victory.
15 He who is [a]surety for a stranger will surely suffer for it,
But he who hates [1]going surety is safe.
16 A [a]gracious woman attains honor,
And violent men attain riches.
17 The [a]merciful man does [1]himself good,
But the cruel man [2]does himself harm.
18 The wicked earns deceptive wages,
But he who [a]sows righteousness *gets* a true reward.
19 He who is steadfast in [a]righteousness *will attain* to life,
And [b]he who pursues evil *will bring about* his own death.
20 The perverse in heart are an abomination to the LORD,
But the [a]blameless in *their* [1]walk are His [b]delight.
21 [1]Assuredly, the evil man will not go unpunished,
But the [2]descendants of the righteous will be delivered.
22 *As* a [a]ring of gold in a swine's snout,
So is a beautiful woman who lacks [1]discretion.
23 The desire of the righteous is only good,
But the [a]expectation of the wicked is wrath.
24 There is one who scatters, yet increases all the more,

30 [b]Prov. 2:
31 [a]Ps. 37:3 10:13 [b]Prov.
32 [a]Eccl. 12 2:12; 6:12
11:1 [a]Lev. 1 Deut. 25:13- 20:10, 23; M [b]Prov. 16:11
2 [a]Prov. 16:1 29:23
3 [a]Prov. 13:6 19:3; 22:12
4 [a]Prov. 10:2 7:19; Zeph. 1 7:1
5 [a]Prov. 3:6
6 [a]Ps. 7:15, 1 Eccl. 10:8
7 [a]Prov. 10:2 8:13, 14
8 [1]Lit., *enters*
9 [a]Prov. 16:2 11:6
10 [a]Prov. 28:1
12 [1]Lit., *heart*
13 [1]Lit., *faithf* [a]Lev. 19:16; P 1 Tim. 5:13 [b]P
14 [1]Lit., *delive* [a]Prov. 15:22; 2
15 [1]Lit., *those strike hands* [a] 27:13
16 [a]Prov. 31:2
17 [1]Lit., *good own soul* [2]Lit., *his flesh* [a]Matt 25:34-36
18 [a]Hos. 10:12 6:8, 9; James 3
19 [a]Prov. 10:16 19:23 [b]Prov. 2 Rom. 6:23; Jan
20 [1]Lit., *way* [a] 119:1; Prov. 13 [b]1 Chr. 29:17
21 [1]Lit., *Hand* [2]Lit., *seed*
22 [1]Lit., *taste* [a] 24:47
23 [a]Prov. 10:28 2:8, 9

And there is one who withholds what is justly due, but *it results*
only in want.
25 The [1a]generous man will be [2]prosperous,
And he who [b]waters will himself be watered.
26 He who withholds grain, the [a]people will curse him,
But [b]blessing will be on the head of him who [c]sells *it*.
27 He who diligently seeks good seeks favor,
But [a]he who searches after evil, it will come to him.
28 He who [a]trusts in his riches will fall,
But [b]the righteous will flourish like the *green* leaf.
29 He who [a]troubles his own house will [b]inherit wind,
And [c]the foolish will be servant to the wisehearted.
30 The fruit of the righteous is [a]a tree of life,
And [b]he who is wise [1]wins souls.
31 If [a]the righteous will be rewarded in the earth,
How much more the wicked and the sinner!

Chapter 12

12 Whoever loves [1]discipline loves knowledge,
But he who hates reproof is stupid.
2 A [a]good man will obtain favor from the LORD,
But He will condemn a man [1]who devises evil.
3 A man will [a]not be established by wickedness,
But the root of the [b]righteous will not be moved.
4 An [1a]excellent wife is the crown of her husband,
But she who shames *him* is as [b]rottenness in his bones.
5 The thoughts of the righteous are just,
But the counsels of the wicked are deceitful.
6 The [a]words of the wicked lie in wait for blood,
But the [b]mouth of the upright will deliver them.
7 The [a]wicked are overthrown and are no more,
But the [b]house of the righteous will stand.
8 A man will be praised according to his insight,
But one of perverse [1]mind will be despised.
9 Better is he who is lightly esteemed and has a servant,
Than he who honors himself and lacks bread.
10 A [a]righteous man has regard for the life of his beast,
But the compassion of the wicked is cruel.
11 He [a]who tills his land will have plenty of bread,
But he who pursues vain *things* lacks [1]sense.
12 The [a]wicked desires the [1]booty of evil men,
But the root of the righteous [b]yields *fruit*.
13 [1]An evil man is ensnared by the transgression of his lips,
But the [a]righteous will escape from trouble.
14 A man will be [a]satisfied with good by the fruit of his [1]words,
And the [b]deeds of a man's hands will return to him.
15 The [a]way of a fool is right in his own eyes,
But a wise man is he who listens to counsel.
16 A [a]fool's vexation is known at once,
But a prudent man conceals dishonor.
17 He who [1]speaks truth tells what is right,
But a false witness, deceit.
18 There is one who [a]speaks rashly like the thrusts of a sword,
But the [b]tongue of the wise brings healing.

[1]Lit., *soul of* ...it., *made fat* ...9, 10; 2 Cor. ...7 [b]Matt. 5:7
...24:24 [b]Job ... [c]Gen. 42:6
...sth. 7:10; Ps. ...:15, 16; 57:6
...s. 49:6; Mark ...m. 6:17 [b]Ps. ...12; Jer. 17:8
...15:27 [b]Eccl. ...[c]Prov. 14:19
...*takes* [a]Prov. ...14:25; Dan. ...Cor. 9:19-22; James 5:20
...m. 22:21, 25; ...1; 1 Pet. 4:18
...Or, *instruction*
...*of evil devices* ...[a]Prov. 3:4; 8:35
...v. 11:5 [b]Prov. 10:25
...*irtuous* [a]Prov. ...11; 1 Cor. 11:7 ...:30; Hab. 3:16
...:11, 16 [b]Prov. 14:3
...ob 34:25; Prov. ...[b]Matt. 7:24-27
8 [1]Lit., *heart*
10 [a]Deut. 25:4
...t., *heart* [a]Prov. 28:19
...[1]Lit., *net* [a]Prov. ...0 [b]Prov. 11:30
13 [1]Lit., *In the* ...*ssion of the lips* ...*il snare* [a]Prov. ...1:23; 2 Pet. 2:9
..., *mouth* [a]Prov. ...23; 18:20 [b]Job ...ov. 1:31; 24:12; ...10, 11; Hos. 4:9
...ov. 14:12; 16:2; 21:2
...rov. 14:33; 27:3; 29:11
...7 [1]Lit., *breathes*
...[a]Ps. 57:4 [b]Prov. 4:22; 15:4

19 Truthful lips will be established forever,
But a [a]lying tongue is only for a moment.
20 Deceit is in the heart of those who devise evil,
But counselors of peace have joy.
21 [a]No harm befalls the righteous,
But the wicked are filled with trouble.
22 [a]Lying lips are an abomination to the LORD,
But those who deal faithfully are His delight.
23 A [a]prudent man conceals knowledge,
But the heart of fools proclaims folly.
24 The hand of the diligent will rule,
But the [1]slack *hand* will be [a]put to forced labor.
25 [a]Anxiety in the heart of a man weighs it down,
But a [b]good word makes it glad.
26 The righteous is a guide to his neighbor,
But the way of the wicked leads them astray.
27 A [1]slothful man does not [2]roast his prey,
But the [a]precious possession of a man *is* diligence.
28 [a]In the way of righteousness is life,
And in *its* pathway there is no death.

Chapter 13

13 A [a]wise son *accepts his* father's discipline,
But a [b]scoffer does not listen to rebuke.
2 From the fruit of a man's mouth he [1a]enjoys good,
But the [2]desire of the treacherous is [b]violence.
3 The one who [a]guards his mouth preserves his life;
The one who [b]opens wide his lips [1]comes to ruin.
4 The soul of the sluggard craves and *gets* nothing,
But the soul of the diligent is made fat.
5 A righteous man [a]hates falsehood,
But a wicked man [1b]acts disgustingly and shamefully.
6 Righteousness [a]guards the [1]one whose way is blameless,
But wickedness subverts the [2]sinner.
7 There is one who [a]pretends to be rich, but has nothing;
Another [1]pretends to be [b]poor, but has great wealth.
8 The ransom of a man's life is his riches,
But the poor hears no rebuke.
9 The [a]light of the righteous [1]rejoices,
But the [b]lamp of the wicked goes out.
10 Through presumption [1]comes nothing but strife,
But with those who receive counsel is wisdom.
11 Wealth *obtained* by [1]fraud dwindles,
But the one who gathers [2]by labor increases *it*.
12 Hope deferred makes the heart sick,
But desire [1]fulfilled is a tree of life.
13 The one who [a]despises the word will be [1]in debt to it,
But the one who fears the commandment will be [b]rewarded.
14 The [1]teaching of the wise is a [a]fountain of life,
To turn aside from the [b]snares of death.
15 [a]Good understanding produces favor,
But the way of the treacherous is hard.
16 Every [a]prudent man acts with knowledge,
But a fool [1]displays folly.

19 [a]Ps. 52:4, 19:9
21 [a]Ps. 91:10 Prov. 1:33; 1
22 [a]Rev. 22:1
23 [a]Prov. 10: 13:16; 15:2; 2
24 [1]Lit., *slack* [a]Gen. 49:15; 1 Kin. 9:21
25 [a]Prov. 15: 50:4
27 [1]Lit., *slack* *catch* [a]Prov. 1
28 [a]Deut. 30: 32:46f.; Jer. 21
13:1 [a]Prov. 10 [b]Prov. 9:7, 8; 1
2 [1]Lit., *eats* [2] [a]Prov. 12:14 [b] 1:31; Hos. 10:
3 [1]Lit., *ruin is* 18:21; 21:23; 3:2 [b]Prov. 18:
5 [1]Lit., *causes* *odor and caus* *shame* [a]Col. 3 3:35
6 [1]Lit., *blamel* *of way* [2]Lit., *si* 11:3
7 [1]Lit., *impove* *himself* [a]Prov. Luke 12:20, 21 12:33; 2 Cor. 6 James 2:5
9 [1]I.e., shines [a]Job 29:3; Prov. [b]Job 18:5; Prov.
10 [1]Lit., *gives*
11 [1]Lit., *vanity* *gradually;* lit., *o* *hand*
12 [1]Lit., *coming*
13 [1]Lit., *pledge* [a]Num. 15:31; 2 36:16 [b]Prov. 13
14 [1]Or, *law* [a]Pr 10:11; 14:27 [b]P
15 [a]Ps. 111:10;
16 [1]Lit., *spread* [a]Prov. 12:23

17 A wicked messenger falls into adversity,
But [a]a faithful envoy *brings* healing.
18 Poverty and shame *will come* to him who [a]neglects [1]discipline,
But he who regards reproof will be honored.
19 Desire realized is sweet to the soul,
But it is an abomination to fools to depart from evil.
20 [a]He who walks with wise men will be wise,
But the companion of fools will suffer harm.
21 [a]Adversity pursues sinners,
But the [b]righteous will be rewarded with prosperity.
22 A good man [a]leaves an inheritance to his [1]children's children,
And the [b]wealth of the sinner is stored up for the righteous.
23 [a]Abundant food *is in* the fallow ground of the poor,
But [1]it is swept away by injustice.
24 He who [a]spares his rod hates his son,
But he who loves him [1b]disciplines him diligently.
25 The [a]righteous [1]has enough to satisfy his appetite,
But the stomach of the [b]wicked is in want.

Chapter 14

14 The [a]wise woman builds her house,
But the foolish tears it down with her own hands.
2 He who [a]walks in his uprightness fears the LORD,
But he who is [b]crooked in his ways despises Him.
3 In the mouth of the foolish is a rod [1]for *his* back,
But [a]the lips of the wise will preserve them.
4 Where no oxen are, the manger is clean,
But much increase *comes* by the strength of the ox.
5 A [a]faithful witness will not lie,
But a [b]false witness [1c]speaks lies.
6 A scoffer seeks wisdom, and *finds* none,
But knowledge is easy to him who has understanding.
7 Leave the [a]presence of a fool,
Or you will not [1]discern [2]words of knowledge.
8 The wisdom of the prudent is to understand his way,
But [a]the folly of fools is deceit.
9 Fools mock at [1]sin,
But [a]among the upright there is [2]good will.
10 The heart knows its own [a]bitterness,
And a stranger does not share its joy.
11 The [a]house of the wicked will be destroyed,
But the tent of the upright will flourish.
12 There [a]is a way *which seems* right to a man,
But its [b]end is the way of death.
13 Even in laughter the heart may be in pain,
And the [a]end of joy may be grief.
14 The backslider in heart will have his [a]fill of his own ways,
But a good man will [b]*be satisfied* [1]with his.
15 The [1]naive believes everything,
But the prudent man considers his steps.
16 A wise man [1]is cautious and [a]turns away from evil,
But a fool is arrogant and careless.
17 A quick-tempered man acts foolishly,
And a man of evil devices is hated.

[a]Prov. 25:13
...r, *instruction* ...rov. 15:5, 32
.... 2:20; 15:31
...:10; 54:5; Is. [b]Prov. 11:31; ...3:13; Is. 3:10
...t., *sons' sons* ...12; Ps. 37:25 ...:16, 17; Prov. ...:8; Eccl. 2:26
...ere is what is ... [a]Prov. 12:11
...it., *seeks him with discipline* 19:18; 22:15; ...14; 29:15, 17 ...5; Prov. 3:12; Heb. 12:7
...it., *eats to the ...ion of his soul* 34:10; 103:5; ...15; Prov. 10:3 ...8; Luke 15:14
...uth 4:11; Prov. 31:10-27
...rov. 19:1; 28:6 [b]Prov. 2:15
...*of pride* [a]Prov. 12:6
...t., *breathes out* ...1:5; 3:14 [b]Ex. ...ut. 19:16; Prov. ...:17 [c]Prov. 19:5
...*know* [2]Lit., *lips* [a]Prov. 23:9
8 [a]1 Cor. 3:19
...t., *guilt* [2]Or, *the ...r of God* [a]Prov. 3:34; 11:20
...Sam. 1:10; Job 21:25
11 [a]Job 8:15
...ov. 12:15; 16:25 [b]Rom. 6:21
13 [a]Eccl. 2:1, 2
...Lit., *from himself* ...Prov. 1:31; 12:21 ...rov. 12:14; 18:20
15 [1]Lit., *simple*
[1]Lit., *fears* [a]Job ...; Ps. 34:14; Prov. 3:7; 22:3

18 The [1]naive inherit folly,
But the prudent are crowned with knowledge.
19 The [a]evil will bow down before the good,
And the wicked at the gates of the righteous.
20 The [a]poor is hated even by his neighbor,
But those who love the rich are many.
21 He who [a]despises his neighbor sins,
But [b]happy is he who is gracious to the [1]poor.
22 Will they not go astray who [a]devise evil?
But kindness and truth *will be to* those who devise good.
23 In all labor there is profit,
But [1]mere talk *leads* only to poverty.
24 The [a]crown of the wise is their riches,
But the folly of fools is foolishness.
25 A truthful witness saves lives,
But he who [1a]speaks lies is [2]treacherous.
26 In the [1a]fear of the LORD there is strong confidence,
And [2]his children will have refuge.
27 The [1]fear of the LORD is a fountain of life,
That one may avoid the snares of death.
28 In a multitude of people is a king's glory,
But in the dearth of people is a prince's ruin.
29 He who is [a]slow to anger has great understanding,
But he who is [1]quick-tempered exalts folly.
30 A [a]tranquil heart is life to the body,
But passion is [b]rottenness to the bones.
31 He [a]who oppresses the poor reproaches [b]his Maker,
But he who is gracious to the needy honors Him.
32 The wicked is [a]thrust down by his [1]wrongdoing,
But the [b]righteous has a refuge when he dies.
33 Wisdom rests in the heart of one who has understanding,
But in the [1]bosom of fools it is made known.
34 Righteousness exalts a nation,
But sin is a disgrace to *any* people.
35 The king's favor is toward a [a]servant who acts wisely,
But his anger is toward him who acts shamefully.

Chapter 15

15 A [a]gentle answer turns away wrath,
But a [1b]harsh word stirs up anger.
2 The [a]tongue of the wise makes knowledge [1]acceptable,
But the [b]mouth of fools spouts folly.
3 The [a]eyes of the LORD are in every place,
Watching the evil and the good.
4 A [1]soothing tongue is a tree of life,
But perversion in it [2]crushes the spirit.
5 A fool [1]rejects his father's discipline,
But he who regards reproof is prudent.
6 Much wealth is *in* the house of the [a]righteous,
But trouble is in the income of the wicked.
7 The lips of the wise spread knowledge,
But the hearts of fools are not so.
8 The [a]sacrifice of the wicked is an abomination to the LORD,
But [b]the prayer of the upright is His delight.

18 [1]Lit., *sim*
19 [a]1 Sam. 2 11:29
20 [a]Prov. 19.
21 [1]Or, *afflic* 11:12 [b]Ps. 4 19:17; 28:8
22 [a]Ps. 36:4; 3:29; 12:2; M
23 [1]Lit., *worc*
24 [a]Prov. 10: 21:20
25 [1]Lit., *brea* [2]Lit., *treacher* 14:5
26 [1]Or, *rever* *His* [a]Prov. 18 Is. 33:6
27 [1]Or, *rever*
29 [1]Lit., *short* [a]Prov. 16:32; Eccl. 7:9; Jam
30 [a]Prov. 15:1 12:4; Hab. 3:1
31 [a]Prov. 17:5 25:40; 1 John 31:15; Prov. 22
32 [1]Or, *calam* 6:15; 24:16 [b]G 49:18; Ps. 16:1 37:37; 73:24; 2 5:8; 2 Tim. 4:1
33 [1]Lit., *midst*
35 [a]Matt. 24:4 25:21, 23
15:1 [1]Lit., *pain* [a]Judg. 8:1-3; P 15:18; 25:15 [b] 25:10-13
2 [1]Lit., *good* [a] 15:7 [b]Prov. 12: 13:16; 15:28
3 [a]2 Chr. 16:9; 31:4; Jer. 16:17 4:10; Heb. 4:13
4 [1]Lit., *healing* *the crushing of*
5 [1]Or, *despises*
6 [a]Prov. 8:21
8 [a]Prov. 21:27; 5:1; Is. 1:11; Jer Mic. 6:7 [b]Prov.

9 The way of the wicked is an abomination to the LORD,
But He loves him who [a]pursues righteousness.
10 Stern discipline is for him who forsakes the way;
He who hates reproof will die.
11 [1a]Sheol and [2]Abaddon *lie open* before the LORD,
How much more the [b]hearts of [3]men!
12 A [a]scoffer does not love one who reproves him,
He will not go to the wise.
13 A [a]joyful heart makes a [1]cheerful face,
But [2]when the heart is [b]sad, the [c]spirit is broken.
14 The [a]mind of the intelligent seeks knowledge,
But the mouth of fools feeds on folly.
15 All the days of the afflicted are bad,
But a [1]cheerful heart *has* a continual feast.
16 [a]Better is a little with the [1]fear of the LORD,
Than great treasure and turmoil with it.
17 [a]Better is a [1]dish of [2]vegetables where love is,
Than a [b]fattened ox and hatred with it.
18 A [a]hot-tempered man stirs up strife,
But the [b]slow to anger [c]pacifies contention.
19 The way of the sluggard is as a hedge of thorns,
But the path of the upright is a highway.
20 A [a]wise son makes a father glad,
But a foolish man [b]despises his mother.
21 Folly is joy to him who lacks [1]sense,
But a man of understanding [a]walks straight.
22 Without consultation, plans are frustrated,
But with many counselors they [1]succeed.
23 A [a]man has joy in an [1]apt answer,
And how delightful is a timely [b]word!
24 The [a]path of life *leads* upward for the wise,
That he may keep away from [1]Sheol below.
25 The LORD will [a]tear down the house of the proud,
But He will [b]establish the boundary of the [c]widow.
26 Evil plans are an abomination to the LORD,
But pleasant words are pure.
27 He who [a]profits illicitly troubles his own house,
But he who [b]hates bribes will live.
28 The heart of the righteous [a]ponders how to answer,
But the [b]mouth of the wicked pours out evil things.
29 The LORD is [a]far from the wicked,
But He [b]hears the prayer of the righteous.
30 [1]Bright eyes gladden the heart;
Good news puts fat on the bones.
31 He whose ear listens to the life-giving reproof
Will dwell among the wise.
32 He who [a]neglects discipline [b]despises himself,
But he who [c]listens to reproof acquires [1]understanding.
33 The [1]fear of the LORD is the instruction for wisdom,
And before honor *comes* humility.

Chapter 16 ________________________

16 The [a]plans of the heart belong to man,
But the answer of the tongue is from the LORD.

[a]1 Tim. 6:11
e., the nether [2]I.e., place of
n [3]Lit., *sons*
Job 26:6; Ps.
1 Sam. 16:7;
0; Ps. 44:21;
Acts 1:24
v. 13:1; Amos 5:10
good [2]Lit., *in*
heart [a]Prov.
[b]Prov. 12:25
17:22; 18:14
[a]Prov. 18:15
15 [1]Lit., *good*
verence [a]Ps.
ov. 16:8; Eccl.
4:6; 1 Tim. 6:6
, *portion* [2]Or,
s [a]Prov. 17:1
4; Luke 15:23
16:28; 26:21;
[b]Prov. 14:29
3; Prov. 16:14;
Eccl. 10:4
rov. 10:1; 29:3
[b]Prov. 30:17
., *heart* [a]Prov.
4:8; Eph. 5:15
re established
, *answer of his*
h [a]Prov. 12:14
25:11; Is. 50:4
I.e., the nether
rld [a]Prov. 4:18
ov. 12:7; 14:11
ut. 19:14; Prov.
Ps. 68:5; 146:9
ov. 1:19; 28:25;
6:10 [b]Ex. 23:8;
. 16:19; 1 Sam.
12:3; Is. 33:15
et. 3:15 [b]Prov.
10:32; 15:2
Ps. 18:41; Prov.
[b]Ps. 145:18, 19
The light of the
eyes gladdens
it., *heart* [a]Prov.
3:33 [b]Prov. 8:36
[c]Prov. 15:5
[1]Or, *reverence*
rov. 16:9; 19:21

2 All the ways of a man are clean in his own sight,
But the [a]LORD weighs the [1]motives.
3 [1a]Commit your works to the LORD,
And your plans will be established.
4 The LORD [a]has made everything for [1]its own purpose,
Even the [b]wicked for the day of evil.
5 Everyone who is proud in heart is an abomination to the LORD;
Assuredly, he will not be unpunished.
6 By [a]lovingkindness and truth iniquity is atoned for,
And by the [1b]fear of the LORD one keeps away from evil.
7 When a man's ways are pleasing to the LORD,
He [a]makes even his enemies to be at peace with him.
8 Better is a little with righteousness
Than great income with injustice.
9 The mind of [a]man plans his way,
But [b]the LORD directs his steps.
10 A divine [a]decision is in the lips of the king;
His mouth should not [1]err in judgment.
11 A [a]just balance and scales belong to the LORD;
All the [1]weights of the bag are His [2]concern.
12 It is an abomination for kings to commit wickedness,
For a [a]throne is established on righteousness.
13 Righteous lips are the delight of kings,
And he who speaks right is loved.
14 The wrath of a king is *as* messengers of death,
But a wise man will appease it.
15 In the light of a king's face is life,
And his favor is like a cloud with the [1a]spring rain.
16 How much [a]better it is to get wisdom than gold!
And to get understanding is to be chosen above silver.
17 The [a]highway of the upright is to depart from evil;
He who watches his way preserves his [1]life.
18 [a]Pride *goes* before destruction,
And a haughty spirit before stumbling.
19 It is better to be of a [a]humble spirit with the lowly,
Than to [b]divide the spoil with the proud.
20 He who gives attention to the word shall [a]find good,
And [b]blessed is he who trusts in the LORD.
21 The [a]wise in heart will be called discerning,
And sweetness of [1]speech [b]increases [2]persuasiveness.
22 Understanding is a fountain of life to him who has it,
But the discipline of fools is folly.
23 The [a]heart of the wise teaches his mouth,
And adds [1]persuasiveness to his lips.
24 [a]Pleasant words are a honeycomb,
Sweet to the soul and [b]healing to the bones.
25 [a]There is a way *which seems* right to a man,
But its end is the way of death.
26 A worker's appetite works for him,
For his [1]hunger urges him *on*.
27 A [a]worthless man digs up evil,
While [1]his words are as a [b]scorching fire.
28 A perverse man spreads strife,
And a slanderer separates intimate friends.

2 [1]Lit., *spirit* 16:7; Dan. 5.

3 [1]Lit., *Roll* 55:22; Prov. 5:7

4 [1]Or, *His* Eccl. 3:11 [b]

6 [1]Or, *revere* 4:27; Luke 11 8:13; 14:16

7 [a]Gen. 33:4 17:10

9 [a]Prov. 16:1 [b]Ps. 37:23; P Jer. 10:23

10 [1]Lit., *be u* [a]1 Kin. 3:28

11 [1]Lit., *stone* *work* [a]Prov. 1

12 [a]Prov. 25:

15 [1]Lit., *latter* 29:23

16 [a]Prov. 8:1(

17 [1]Lit., *soul*

18 [a]Prov. 11:2 Jer. 49:16; Ob

19 [a]Prov. 3:34 Is. 57:15 [b]Ex. Judg. 5:30; Pr 1:13, 14

20 [a]Prov. 19:8 2:12; 34:8; Jer.

21 [1]Lit., *lips* [2] *learning* [a]Hos. [b]Prov. 16:23

23 [1]Or, *learnin* 37:30; Prov. 15 12:34

24 [a]Ps. 19:10; 15:26; 24:13, 1 4:22; 17:22

25 [a]Prov. 12:15

26 [1]Lit., *mouth*

27 [1]Lit., *on his* [a]Prov. 6:12, 14, [b]James 3:6

29 A man of violence [a]entices his neighbor,
And leads him in a way that is not good.
30 He who winks his eyes *does so* to devise perverse things;
He who compresses his lips brings evil to pass.
31 A [a]gray head is a crown of glory;
It [b]is found in the way of righteousness.
32 He who is slow to anger is better than the mighty,
And he who rules his spirit, than he who captures a city.
33 The [a]lot is cast into the lap,
But its every [b]decision is from the LORD.

Chapter 17

17 [a]Better is a dry morsel and quietness with it
Than a house full of [1]feasting with strife.
2 A servant who acts wisely will rule over a son who acts
shamefully,
And will share in the inheritance among brothers.
3 The [a]refining pot is for silver and the furnace for gold,
But [b]the LORD tests hearts.
4 An [a]evildoer listens to wicked lips,
A [1]liar pays attention to a destructive tongue.
5 He who mocks the [a]poor reproaches his Maker;
He who [b]rejoices at calamity will not go unpunished.
6 [a]Grandchildren are the crown of old men,
And the [b]glory of sons is their fathers.
7 [1a]Excellent speech is not fitting for a fool;
Much less are [b]lying lips to a prince.
8 A [a]bribe is a [1]charm in the sight of its owner;
Wherever he turns, he prospers.
9 He who [a]covers a transgression seeks love,
But he who repeats a matter [b]separates intimate friends.
10 A rebuke goes deeper into one who has understanding
Than a hundred blows into a fool.
11 A rebellious man seeks only evil,
So a cruel messenger will be sent against him.
12 Let a [a]man meet a [b]bear robbed of her cubs,
Rather than a fool in his folly.
13 He who [a]returns evil for good,
[b]Evil will not depart from his house.
14 The beginning of strife is *like* letting out water,
So [a]abandon the quarrel before it breaks out.
15 He who [a]justifies the wicked, and he who condemns the
righteous,
Both of them alike are an abomination to the LORD.
16 Why is there a price in the hand of a fool to [a]buy wisdom,
When [1]he has no sense?
17 A [a]friend loves at all times,
And a brother is born for adversity.
18 A man lacking in [1]sense [2a]pledges,
And becomes surety in the presence of his neighbor.
19 He who [a]loves transgression loves strife;
He who [b]raises his door seeks destruction.
20 He who has a crooked [1]mind [a]finds no good,
And he who is [b]perverted in his language falls into evil.

[a]Prov. 1:10; 12:26
Prov. 20:29 [b]Prov. 3:1, 2
Prov. 18:18 [b]Prov. 29:26
[1]Lit., *sacrifices of strife* [a]Prov. 15:17
rov. 27:21 [b]1 Chr. 17; Ps. 26:2; Prov. 1; Jer. 17:10; Mal. 3:3
4 [1]Lit., *falsehood* [a]Prov. 14:15
[a]Prov. 14:31 [b]Job 31:29; Prov. 24:17; Obad. 12
[a]Gen. 48:11; Prov. 2 [b]Ex. 20:12; Mal. 1:6
7 [1]Lit., *A lip of dance* [a]Prov. 24:7 31:18; Prov. 12:22
Lit., *stone of favor* ov. 21:14; Is. 1:23; Amos 5:12
rov. 10:12; James 1 Pet. 4:8 [b]Prov. 16:28
rov. 29:9 [b]2 Sam. 17:8; Hos. 13:8
[a]Ps. 35:12; 109:5; er. 18:20 [b]2 Sam. :10; 1 Kin. 21:22; Prov. 13:21
[a]Prov. 20:3; 25:8; 1 Thess. 4:11
[a]Ex. 23:7; Prov. 5; 24:24; Is. 5:23
[1]Lit., *there is no eart* [a]Prov. 23:23
[a]Ruth 1:16; Prov. 18:24
[1]Lit., *heart* [2]Lit., *kes hands* [a]Prov. 6:1; 11:15; 22:26
rov. 29:22 [b]Prov. 16:18; 29:23
Lit., *heart* [a]Prov. 4:20 [b]James 3:8

21 He who [a]begets a fool *does so* to his sorrow,
And the father of a fool has no joy.
22 A [a]joyful heart [1]is good medicine,
But a broken spirit [b]dries up the bones.
23 A wicked man receives a [a]bribe from the bosom
To [b]pervert the ways of justice.
24 Wisdom is in the presence of the one who has understanding,
But the [a]eyes of a fool are on the ends of the earth.
25 A [a]foolish son is a grief to his father,
And [b]bitterness to her who bore him.
26 It is also not good to [a]fine the righteous,
Nor to strike the noble for *their* uprightness.
27 He who [a]restrains his words [1]has knowledge,
And he who has a [b]cool spirit is a man of understanding.
28 Even a fool, when he [a]keeps silent, is considered wise;
When he closes his lips, he is *counted* prudent.

Chapter 18

18 He who separates himself seeks *his own* desire,
He [1a]quarrels against all sound wisdom.
2 A fool does not delight in understanding,
But only [a]in revealing his own [1]mind.
3 When a wicked man comes, contempt also comes,
And with dishonor *comes* reproach.
4 The words of a man's mouth are [a]deep waters;
[1]The fountain of wisdom is a bubbling brook.
5 To [a]show partiality to the wicked is not good,
Nor to [b]thrust aside the righteous in judgment.
6 A fool's lips [1]bring strife,
And his mouth calls for [a]blows.
7 A [a]fool's mouth is his ruin,
And his lips are the snare of his soul.
8 The words of a whisperer are like dainty morsels,
And they go down into the [1]innermost parts of the body.
9 He also who is [a]slack in his work
[b]Is brother to him who destroys.
10 The [a]name of the LORD is a [b]strong tower;
The righteous runs into it and [c]is [1]safe.
11 A [a]rich man's wealth is his strong city,
And like a high wall in his own imagination.
12 [a]Before destruction the heart of man is haughty,
But [b]humility *goes* before honor.
13 He who [a]gives an answer before he hears,
It is folly and shame to him.
14 The [a]spirit of a man can endure his sickness,
But a [b]broken spirit who can bear?
15 The [1a]mind of the prudent acquires knowledge,
And the [b]ear of the wise seeks knowledge.
16 A man's [a]gift makes room for him,
And brings him before great men.
17 The first [1]to plead his case *seems* just,
Until [2]another comes and examines him.
18 The [a]lot puts an end to contentions,
And [1]decides between the mighty.

21 [a]Prov. 10:1; 17 19:13

22 [1]Lit., *causes g healing* [a]Prov. 15: [b]Ps. 22:15

23 [a]Prov. 17:8 [b]E 23:8; Mic. 3:11; 7:

24 [a]Eccl. 2:14

25 [a]Prov. 19:13 [b] 10:1

26 [a]Prov. 17:15;

27 [1]Lit., *knows* [a]P 10:19; James 1:19 [b]Prov. 14:29

28 [a]Job 13:5

18:1 [1]Lit., *breaks* [a]Prov. 3:21; 8:14

2 [1]Lit., *heart* [a]Pro 12:23; 13:16; Eccl

4 [1]Or, *A bubbling a fountain of wisd* [a]Prov. 20:5

5 [a]Lev. 19:15; De 1:17; 16:19; Ps. 8 Prov. 17:15; 24:23 28:21 [b]Ex. 23:2, 6 Prov. 17:26; 31:5; 3:9

6 [1]Lit., *come with* [a]Prov. 19:29

7 [a]Ps. 64:8; 140: Prov. 10:14; 12:13 Eccl. 10:12

8 [1]Lit., *chambers belly*

9 [a]Prov. 10:4 [b]P 28:24

10 [1]Lit., *set on hi* [a]Ex. 3:15 [b]2 Sam 3, 33; Ps. 18:2; 6 91:2; 144:2 [c]Prov

11 [a]Prov. 10:15

12 [a]Prov. 11:2; 1 29:23 [b]Prov. 15:3

13 [a]Prov. 20:25; 7:51

14 [a]Prov. 17:22 15:13

15 [1]Lit., *heart* [a]P 15:14; Eph. 1:17 15:31

16 [a]Gen. 32:20; 25:27

17 [1]Lit., *in his pl* [2]Lit., *his neighbo*

18 [1]Lit., *makes a division* [a]Prov. 1

19 A brother offended *is harder to be won* than a strong city,
And contentions are like the bars of a castle.
20 With the [1a]fruit of a man's mouth his stomach will be satisfied;
[b]He will be satisfied *with* the product of his lips.
21 [a]Death and life are in the [1]power of the tongue,
And those who love it will eat its [b]fruit.
22 He who finds a [a]wife finds a good thing,
And [b]obtains favor from the LORD.
23 The [a]poor man utters supplications,
But the [b]rich man [c]answers roughly.
24 A man of *many* friends *comes* to [1]ruin,
But there is [a]a [2]friend who sticks closer than a brother.

Chapter 19

19 [a]Better is a poor man who [b]walks in his integrity
Than he who is perverse in [1]speech and is a fool.
2 Also it is not good for a person to be without knowledge,
And he who makes [a]haste with his feet [1]errs.
3 The [a]foolishness of man subverts his way,
And his heart [b]rages against the LORD.
4 [a]Wealth adds many friends,
But a poor man is separated from his friend.
5 A [a]false witness will not go unpunished,
And he who [1b]tells lies will not escape.
6 [a]Many will entreat the favor of a [1]generous man,
And every man is a friend to him who [b]gives gifts.
7 All the brothers of a poor man hate him;
How much more do his [a]friends go far from him!
He [b]pursues *them with* words, *but* they are [1]gone.
8 He who gets [1]wisdom loves his own soul;
He who keeps understanding will [a]find good.
9 A [a]false witness will not go unpunished,
And he who [1]tells lies will perish.
10 Luxury is [a]not fitting for a fool;
Much less for a [b]slave to rule over princes.
11 A man's [a]discretion makes him slow to anger,
And it is his glory [b]to overlook a transgression.
12 The [a]king's wrath is like the roaring of a lion,
But his favor is like [b]dew on the grass.
13 A [a]foolish son is destruction to his father,
And the [b]contentions of a wife are a constant dripping.
14 House and wealth are an [a]inheritance from fathers,
But a prudent wife is from the LORD.
15 [a]Laziness casts into a deep sleep,
And an idle [1]man will suffer hunger.
16 He who [a]keeps the commandment keeps his soul,
But he who [1]is careless of his ways will die.
17 He who [a]is gracious to a poor man lends to the LORD,
And He will repay him for his [1b]good deed.
18 [a]Discipline your son while there is hope,
And do not desire [1]his death.
19 *A man of* great anger shall bear the penalty,
For if you rescue *him*, you will only have to do it again.
20 [a]Listen to counsel and accept discipline,

eech [a]Prov. [b]Prov. 14:14
hand [a]Prov. ; Matt. 12:37 3:2; Is. 3:10; Hos. 10:13
n. 2:18; Prov. 14; 31:10-31 [b]Prov. 8:35
19:7 [b]James [c]1 Kin. 12:13; 2 Chr. 10:13
be broken in , *lover* [a]Prov. ohn 15:14, 15
[1]Lit., *his lips* 6 [b]Ps. 26:11; rov. 14:2; 20:7
s [a]Prov. 21:5; 28:20; 29:20
11:3 [b]Is. 8:21
[a]Prov. 14:20
breathes [a]Ex. eut. 19:16-19; ; 21:28 [b]Prov. 6:19
, *noble* [a]Prov. [b]Prov. 18:16; 21:14
not [a]Ps. 38:11 [b]Prov. 18:23
t., *heart* [a]Prov. 16:20
reathes [a]Prov. 9:5; Dan. 6:24
rov. 17:7; 26:1; . 10:6, 7 [b]Prov. 30:22
ov. 14:29; 16:32 5:44; Eph. 4:32; Col. 3:13
ov. 16:14 [b]Gen. Deut. 33:28; Ps. Hos. 14:5; Mic. 5:7
ov. 17:25 [b]Prov. 21:9, 19; 27:15
4 [a]2 Cor. 12:14
[1]Lit., *soul* [a]Prov. 6:9, 10; 24:33
6 [1]Lit., *despises* ov. 13:13; 16:17; uke 10:28; 11:28
, *benefits* [a]Deut. , 8; Prov. 14:31; 27; Eccl. 11:1, 2; att. 10:42; 25:40; 9:6-8; Heb. 6:10 12:14; Luke 6:38
t., *causing him to* rov. 13:24; 23:13; 29:15, 17
[a]Prov. 4:1; 8:33; 12:15

That you may be wise [1]the rest of your days.
21 Many are the [a]plans in a man's heart,
But the [b]counsel of the LORD, it will stand.
22 What is desirable in a man is his [1]kindness,
And *it is* better to be a poor man than a liar.
23 The [1a]fear of the LORD *leads* to life,
So that one may sleep [b]satisfied, [2c]untouched by evil.
24 The [a]sluggard buries his hand [b]in the dish,
And will not even bring it back to his mouth.
25 [a]Strike a scoffer and the [1]naive may become shrewd,
But [b]reprove one who has understanding and he will [2]gain
knowledge.
26 He [a]who assaults *his* father *and* drives *his* mother away
Is a shameful and disgraceful son.
27 Cease listening, my son, to discipline,
And you will stray from the words of knowledge.
28 A rascally witness makes a mockery of justice,
And the mouth of the wicked [1a]spreads iniquity.
29 [1]Judgments are prepared for [a]scoffers,
And [b]blows for the back of fools.

Chapter 20

20 [a]Wine is a mocker, [b]strong drink a brawler,
And whoever [1]is intoxicated by it is not wise.
2 The terror of a king is like the growling of a lion;
He who provokes him to anger [1a]forfeits his own life.
3 [1a]Keeping away from strife is an honor for a man,
But any fool will [2]quarrel.
4 The [a]sluggard does not plow after the autumn,
So he [1]begs during the harvest and has nothing.
5 A plan in the heart of a man is *like* deep water,
But a man of understanding draws it out.
6 Many a man [a]proclaims his own loyalty,
But who can find a [b]trustworthy man?
7 A righteous man who [a]walks in his integrity—
[b]How blessed are his sons after him.
8 [a]A king who sits on the throne of justice
[1]Disperses all evil with his eyes.
9 [a]Who can say, "I have cleansed my heart,
I am pure from my sin"?
10 [1a]Differing weights and differing measures,
Both of them are abominable to the LORD.
11 It is by his deeds that a lad [1a]distinguishes himself
If his conduct is pure and right.
12 The hearing [a]ear and the seeing eye,
The LORD has made both of them.
13 [a]Do not love sleep, lest you become poor;
Open your eyes, *and* you will be satisfied with [1]food.
14 "Bad, bad," says the buyer;
But when he goes his way, then he boasts.
15 There is gold, and an abundance of [1]jewels;
But the lips of knowledge are a more precious thing.
16 Take his garment when he becomes surety for a stranger;
And for foreigners, hold him in pledge.

20 [1]Lit., *in yo end*

21 [a]Prov. 16 33:10, 11; Is.

22 [1]Or, *loyalt*

23 [1]Or, *rever not visited* [a]P 1 Tim. 4:8 [b]P [c]Ps. 91:10; Pr

24 [a]Prov. 26: 26:23; Mark 1

25 [1]Lit., *simp discern* [a]Prov [b]Prov. 9:8

26 [a]Prov. 28:2

28 [1]Or, *swallo* 15:16; 20:12, 1

29 [1]Gr., *Rods* Prov. 9:12 [b]Pr 18:6; 26:3

20:1 [1]Lit., *errs* 9:21; Prov. 23: 28:7; Hos. 4:11 31:4; Is. 5:22;

2 [1]Lit., *sins ag* [a]Num. 16:38; 1 2:23; Prov. 8:36 2:10

3 [1]Lit., *Ceasing burst out* [a]Gen Prov. 17:14

4 [1]Lit., *asks* [a]P 13:4; 21:25

6 [a]Prov. 25:14; 6:2; Luke 18:11 12:1; Luke 18:8

7 [a]Prov. 19:1 [b] 37:26; 112:2

8 [1]Or, *Sifts* [a]Pr 20:26; 25:5

9 [a]1 Kin. 8:46; 6:36; Job 14:4; 7:20; Rom. 3:9; 1:8

10 [1]Lit., *A stone stone, an ephah ephah* [a]Prov. 11 20:23

11 [1]Or, *makes known* [a]Matt. 7:

12 [a]Ex. 4:11; Ps

13 [1]Lit., *bread* 6:9, 10; 19:15; 2

15 [1]Or, *corals*

17 [a]Bread obtained by falsehood is sweet to a man,
But afterward his mouth will be filled with gravel.
18 Prepare [a]plans by consultation,
And [b]make war by wise guidance.
19 He who [a]goes about as a slanderer reveals secrets,
Therefore do not associate with [1b]a gossip.
20 He who [a]curses his father or his mother,
His [b]lamp will go out in [1]time of darkness.
21 An inheritance gained hurriedly at the beginning,
Will not be blessed in the end.
22 [a]Do not say, "I will repay evil";
[b]Wait for the LORD, and He will save you.
23 [1a]Differing weights are an abomination to the LORD,
And a [2b]false scale is not good.
24 [a]Man's steps are *ordained* by the LORD,
How then can man understand his way?
25 It is a snare for a man to say rashly, "It is holy!"
And [a]after the vows to make inquiry.
26 A [a]wise king winnows the wicked,
And [1]drives the [b]*threshing* wheel over them.
27 The [1a]spirit of man is the lamp of the LORD,
Searching all the [2]innermost parts of his being.
28 [1]Loyalty and [a]truth preserve the king,
And he upholds his throne by [1]righteousness.
29 The glory of young men is their strength,
And the [1a]honor of old men is their gray hair.
30 [a]Stripes that wound scour away evil,
And strokes *reach* the [1]innermost parts.

Chapter 21

21 The king's heart is *like* channels of water in the hand of the LORD;
He [a]turns it wherever He wishes.
2 [a]Every man's way is right in his own eyes,
But the LORD [b]weighs the hearts.
3 To do [a]righteousness and justice
Is desired by the LORD rather than sacrifice.
4 Haughty eyes and a proud heart,
The [a]lamp of the wicked, is sin.
5 The plans of the [a]diligent *lead* surely to advantage,
But everyone [b]who is hasty *comes* surely to poverty.
6 The [a]getting of treasures by a lying tongue
Is a fleeting vapor, the [1]pursuit of [b]death.
7 The violence of the wicked will drag them away,
Because they [a]refuse to act with justice.
8 The way of a guilty man is [a]crooked,
But as for the pure, his conduct is upright.
9 It is better to live in a corner of a roof,
Than [1]in a house shared with a contentious woman.
10 The soul of the wicked desires evil;
His [a]neighbor finds no favor in his eyes.
11 When the [a]scoffer is punished, the [1]naive becomes wise;
But when the wise is instructed, he receives knowledge.
12 The righteous one considers the house of the wicked,

[a]Prov. 9:17
1:14; 15:22 Luke 14:31
who opens [a]Prov. 11:13 [b]Prov. 13:3
upil (of eye) 7; Lev. 20:9; 1; Matt. 15:4 ; Prov. 13:9; 24:20
24:29; Matt. n. 12:17, 19; 5:15; 1 Pet. 9 [b]Ps. 27:14
stone and a t., balance of [a]Prov. 20:10 [b]Prov. 11:1
4 [a]Prov. 16:9
[a]Eccl. 5:4, 5
, turns [a]Prov.):8 [b]Is. 28:27
, breath [2]Lit., rs of the body [a]1 Cor. 2:11
Lit., Covenant [a]Prov. 29:14
plendor [a]Prov. 16:31
., chambers of dy [a]Ps. 89:32; 22:15; Is. 53:5; 1 Pet. 2:24
:1 [a]Ezra 6:22
ov. 16:2 [b]Prov. 12; Luke 16:15
m. 15:22; Prov. s. 1:11, 16, 17; 6:6; Mic. 6:7, 8
ov. 24:20; Luke 11:34
Prov. 10:4; 13:4 [b]Prov. 28:22
seekers [a]Prov. :21 [b]Prov. 8:36
os 5:7; Mic. 3:9
8 [a]Prov. 2:15
with a woman of ontentions and a se of association
[a]Ps. 52:3; Prov. 2:14; 14:21
it., simple [a]Prov. 19:25

Turning the [a]wicked to ruin.
13 He who [a]shuts his ear to the cry of the poor
Will also cry himself and not be [b]answered.
14 A [a]gift in secret subdues anger,
And a bribe in the bosom, strong wrath.
15 The execution of justice is joy for the righteous,
But is [a]terror to the workers of iniquity.
16 A man who wanders from the way of understanding
Will [a]rest in the assembly of the [1]dead.
17 He who [a]loves pleasure *will become* a poor man;
He who loves wine and oil will not become rich.
18 The wicked is a [a]ransom for the righteous,
And the [b]treacherous is in the place of the upright.
19 [a]It is better to live in a desert land,
Than with a contentious and vexing woman.
20 There is precious [a]treasure and oil in the dwelling of the wise,
But a foolish man [b]swallows it up.
21 He who [a]pursues righteousness and loyalty
Finds life, righteousness and honor.
22 A [a]wise man scales the city of the mighty,
And brings down the [1]stronghold in which they trust.
23 He who [a]guards his mouth and his tongue,
Guards his soul from troubles.
24 "Proud," "Haughty," "[a]Scoffer," are his names,
Who acts with [b]insolent pride.
25 The [a]desire of the sluggard puts him to death,
For his hands refuse to work;
26 All day long he [1]is craving,
While the righteous [a]gives and does not hold back.
27 The [a]sacrifice of the wicked is an abomination,
How much more when he brings it with evil intent!
28 A [a]false witness will perish,
But the man who listens *to the truth* will speak forever.
29 A wicked man [1a]shows a bold face,
But as for the [b]upright, he makes his way sure.
30 There is [a]no wisdom and no understanding
And no counsel against the LORD.
31 The [a]horse is prepared for the day of battle,
But [b]victory belongs to the LORD.

Chapter 22

22 A [a]*good* name is to be more desired than great riches,
Favor is better than silver and gold.
2 The rich and the poor [1]have a common bond,
The LORD is the [a]maker of them all.
3 The [a]prudent sees the evil and hides himself,
But the [1]naive go on, and are punished for it.
4 The reward of humility *and* the [1]fear of the LORD
Are riches, honor and life.
5 [a]Thorns *and* snares are in the way of the perverse;
He who guards himself will be far from them.
6 [a]Train up a child [1]in the way he should go,
Even when he is old he will not depart from it.
7 The [a]rich rules over the poor,

12 [a]Prov. 14

13 [a]Matt. 18 1 John 3:17 2:13

14 [a]Prov. 18

15 [a]Prov. 10

16 [1]Lit., *dep spirits* [a]Ps. 4

17 [a]Prov. 23.

18 [a]Is. 43:3

19 [a]Prov. 21:

20 [a]Ps. 112:3 8:21; 22:4 [b]J 20:15, 18

21 [a]Prov. 15: 5:6; 1 Cor. 15

22 [1]Lit., *stren trust* [a]2 Sam. Prov. 24:5; Ec 9:15, 16

23 [a]Prov. 12:1 18:21; James

24 [a]Ps. 1:1; P 3:34; 24:9; Is. 16:6; Jer. 48:2

25 [a]Prov. 13:4

26 [1]Lit., *desire* [a]Ps. 37:26; 112 Matt. 5:42; Eph

27 [a]Prov. 15:8 Jer. 6:20; Amos

28 [a]Prov. 19:5

29 [1]Lit., *makes with his face* [a]E [b]Ps. 119:5; Pro

30 [a]Jer. 9:23; A 39; 1 Cor. 3:19,

31 [a]Ps. 20:7; 3 31:1 [b]Ps. 3:8; J 1 Cor. 15:57

22:1 [a]Prov. 10: 7:1

2 [1]Lit., *meet tog* [a]Job 31:15; Prov

3 [1]Lit., *simple* [a] 14:16; 27:12; Is.

4 [1]Or, *reverence*

5 [a]Prov. 15:19

6 [1]Lit., *according way* [a]Eph. 6:4

7 [a]Prov. 18:23; J 2:6

And the borrower *becomes* the lender's slave.
8 He who [a]sows iniquity will reap vanity,
And the [b]rod of his fury will perish.
9 He who [1]is [a]generous will be blessed,
For he [b]gives some of his food to the poor.
10 [a]Drive out the scoffer, and contention will go out,
Even strife and dishonor will cease.
11 He who loves [a]purity of heart
And [1]whose speech is [b]gracious, the king is his friend.
12 The eyes of the LORD preserve knowledge,
But He overthrows the words of the treacherous man.
13 The [a]sluggard says, "There is a lion outside;
I shall be slain in the streets!"
14 The mouth of [1a]an adulteress is a deep pit;
He who is [b]cursed of the LORD will fall [2]into it.
15 Foolishness is bound up in the heart of a child;
The [a]rod of discipline will remove it far from him.
16 He [a]who oppresses the poor to make much for himself
Or who gives to the rich, [b]*will* only *come to* poverty.

17 [a]Incline your ear and hear the words of the wise,
And apply your mind to my knowledge;
18 For it will be [a]pleasant if you keep them within you,
[1]That they may be ready on your lips.
19 So that your [a]trust may be in the LORD,
I have [1]taught you today, even you.
20 Have I not written to you [1a]excellent things
Of counsels and knowledge,
21 To make you [a]know the [1]certainty of the words of truth
That you may [2b]correctly answer to him who sent you?

22 [a]Do not rob the poor because he is poor,
Or [b]crush the afflicted at the gate;
23 For the LORD will [a]plead their case,
And [1]take the life of those who rob them.

24 Do not associate with a man *given* to anger;
Or go with a [a]hot-tempered man,
25 Lest you [a]learn his ways,
And [1]find a snare for yourself.

26 Do not be among those who [a]give [1]pledges,
Among those who become sureties for debts.
27 If you have nothing with which to pay,
Why should he [a]take your bed from under you?

28 [a]Do not move the ancient boundary
Which your fathers have set.

29 Do you see a man skilled in his work?
He will [a]stand before kings;
He will not stand before obscure men.

8 [b]Ps. 125:3
s a good eye 7; 2 Cor. 9:6 [b]Luke 14:13
ien. 21:9, 10; v. 18:6; 26:20
has grace on s. 24:4; Matt. 14:35; 16:13
[a]Prov. 26:13
[1]Lit., *strange* an [2]Lit., *there* 2:16; 5:3; 7:5; 7 [b]Eccl. 7:26
. 13:24; 23:14
cl. 5:8; James [b]Prov. 28:22
17 [a]Prov. 5:1
They together [a]Prov. 2:10
[1]Lit., *made you* now [a]Prov. 3:5
revious [a]Prov. 8:6
[1]Lit., *truth* [2]Lit., *n words of truth* e 1:3, 4 [b]Prov. :13; 1 Pet. 3:15
[a]Ex. 23:6; Job 16; Prov. 22:16 . 7:10; Mal. 3:5
it., *rob the soul* 25:39; Ps. 12:5;); 140:12; Prov. 3:11; Jer. 51:36
24 [a]Prov. 29:22
it., *take* [a]1 Cor. 15:33
it., *strike hands* [a]Prov. 17:18
[a]Ex. 22:26; Prov. 20:16
ut. 19:14; 27:17; 24:2; Prov. 23:10
en. 41:46; 1 Kin. 10:8

Chapter 23

23 When you sit down to dine with a ruler,
Consider carefully [1]what is before you;
2 And put a knife to your throat,
If you are a [a]man of *great* appetite.
3 Do not [a]desire his delicacies,
For it is deceptive food.

4 [a]Do not weary yourself to gain wealth,
[b]Cease from your [1]consideration *of it*.
5 [1]When you set your eyes on it, it is gone.
For [a]*wealth* certainly makes itself wings,
Like an eagle that flies *toward* the heavens.

6 [a]Do not eat the bread of [1]a [b]selfish man,
Or desire his delicacies;
7 For as he [1]thinks within himself, so he is.
He says to you, "Eat and drink!"
But [a]his heart is not with you.
8 You will [a]vomit up [1]the morsel you have eaten,
And waste your [2]compliments.

9 [a]Do not speak in the [1]hearing of a fool,
For he will [b]despise the wisdom of your words.

10 Do not move the ancient boundary,
Or [a]go into the fields of the fatherless;
11 For their [a]Redeemer is strong;
[b]He will plead their case against you.
12 Apply your heart to discipline,
And your ears to words of knowledge.

13 [a]Do not hold back discipline from the child,
Although you [1]beat him with the rod, he will not die.
14 You shall [1]beat him with the rod,
And [a]deliver his soul from Sheol.

15 My son, if your heart is [a]wise,
My own heart also will be glad;
16 And my [1]inmost being will rejoice,
When your lips speak [a]what is right.

17 [a]Do not let your heart envy sinners,
But *live* in the [1b]fear of the LORD [2]always.
18 Surely there is a [1a]future,
And your [b]hope will not be cut off.
19 Listen, my son, and [a]be wise,
And [b]direct your heart in the way.
20 Do not be with [a]heavy drinkers of wine,
Or with [b]gluttonous eaters of meat;
21 For the [a]heavy drinker and the glutton will come to poverty,
And [b]drowsiness will clothe *a man* with rags.

22 [a]Listen to your father who begot you,

23:1 [1]Or, *who*

2 [a]Prov. 23:20

3 [a]Ps. 141:4; 23:6; Dan. 1:5 15, 16

4 [1]Or, *unders* [a]Prov. 15:27; 2 Matt. 6:19; 1 T Heb. 13:5 [b]Pr

5 [1]Lit., *Will yo fly upon it and* [a]Prov. 27:24; 1

6 [1]Lit., *an evil* 141:4 [b]Deut. 28:22

7 [1]Lit., *reckons soul* [a]Prov. 26

8 [1]Lit., *your* [2]L *pleasant words* 25:16

9 [1]Lit., *ears* [a] [b]Prov. 1:7

10 [a]Jer. 22:3; 7:10

11 [a]Job 19:25; 50:34 [b]Prov. 22

13 [1]Lit., *smite* 13:24; 19:18

14 [1]Lit., *smite* 5:5

15 [a]Prov. 23:24 29:3

16 [1]Lit., *kidneys* 8:6

17 [1]Or, *reveren all the day* [a]Ps. Prov. 24:1, 19 [b] 28:14

18 [1]Lit., *latter e* 19:11; 58:11; Pro 24:14 [b]Ps. 9:18

19 [a]Prov. 6:6 [b]P 4:23; 9:6

20 [a]Prov. 20:1; 2 30; Is. 5:22; Matt Luke 21:34; Rom 13:13; Eph. 5:18 21:20; Prov. 28:7

21 [a]Prov. 21:17 6:10, 11

22 [a]Prov. 1:8; Ep

And [b]do not despise your mother when she is old.
23 [a]Buy truth, and do not sell *it,*
Get wisdom and instruction and understanding.

24 The father of the righteous will greatly rejoice,
And [a]he who begets a wise son will be glad in him.
25 Let your [a]father and your mother be glad,
And let her rejoice who gave birth to you.

26 [a]Give me your heart, my son,
And let your eyes [1b]delight in my ways.
27 For a harlot is a [a]deep pit,
And an [1b]adulterous woman is a narrow well.
28 Surely she [a]lurks as a robber,
And increases the [1]faithless among men.

29 Who has [a]woe? Who has sorrow?
Who has contentions? Who has complaining?
Who has wounds without cause?
Who has redness of eyes?
30 Those who [a]linger long over wine,
Those who go to [1]taste [b]mixed wine.
31 Do not look on the wine when it is red,
When it [1]sparkles in the cup,
When it [a]goes down smoothly;
32 At the last it [a]bites like a serpent,
And stings like a [b]viper.
33 Your eyes will see strange things,
And your [1]mind will [a]utter perverse things.
34 And you will be like one who lies down in the [1]middle of the sea,
Or like one who lies down on the top of a [2]mast.
35 "They [a]struck me, *but* I did not become ill;
They beat me, *but* I did not know *it.*
When shall I awake?
I will [b]seek [1]another drink."

Chapter 24

24 Do not be [a]envious of evil men,
Nor desire to [b]be with them;
2 For their [1]minds devise [a]violence,
And their lips [b]talk of trouble.

3 [a]By wisdom a house is built,
And by understanding it is established;
4 And by knowledge the rooms are [a]filled
With all precious and pleasant riches.

5 A [a]wise man is [1]strong,
And a man of knowledge [2]increases power.
6 For [a]by wise guidance you will [1]wage war,
And [b]in abundance of counselors there is victory.

7 Wisdom is [a]too high for a fool,

He does not open his mouth [b]in the gate.

8 He who [a]plans to do evil,
Men will call him a [1]schemer.
9 The [a]devising of folly is sin,
And the scoffer is an abomination to men.

10 If you [a]are slack in the day of distress,
Your strength is limited.

11 [a]Deliver those who are being taken away to death,
And those who are staggering to slaughter, O hold *them* back.
12 If you say, "See, we did not know this,"
Does He not [a]consider *it* [b]who weighs the hearts?
And [c]does He not know *it* who [d]keeps your soul?
And will He not [1e]render to man according to his work?

13 My son, eat [a]honey, for it is good,
Yes, the [b]honey from the comb is sweet to your taste;
14 Know *that* [a]wisdom is thus for your soul;
If you find *it*, then there will be a [1b]future,
And your hope will not be cut off.

15 [a]Do not lie in wait, O wicked man, against the dwelling of the righteous;
Do not destroy his resting place;
16 For a [a]righteous man falls seven times, and rises again,
But the [b]wicked stumble in *time of* calamity.

17 [a]Do not rejoice when your enemy falls,
And do not let your heart be glad when he stumbles;
18 Lest the LORD see *it* and [1]be displeased,
And He turn away His anger from him.

19 [a]Do not fret because of evildoers,
Or be [b]envious of the wicked;
20 For [a]there will be no [1b]future for the evil man;
The [c]lamp of the wicked will be put out.

21 My son, [1a]fear the LORD and the king;
Do not associate with those who are given to change;
22 For their [a]calamity will rise suddenly,
And who knows the ruin *that comes* from both of them?

23 These also are [a]sayings of the wise.
To [1b]show partiality in judgment is not good.
24 He [a]who says to the wicked, "You are righteous,"
[b]Peoples will curse him, nations will abhor him;
25 But [a]to those who rebuke the *wicked* will be delight,
And a good blessing will come upon them.
26 He kisses the lips
Who gives [1]a right answer.

27 Prepare your work outside,

7 [b]Job 5:4; P

8 [1]Or, *devise* [a]Prov. 6:14; 1 1:30

9 [a]Matt. 15:1

10 [a]Deut. 20 Jer. 51:46; He

11 [a]Ps. 82:4;

12 [1]Lit., *bring* [a]Eccl. 5:8 [b]1 Prov. 21:2 [c]P [d]Ps. 121:3-8 34:11; Prov. 1

13 [a]Ps. 19:10 Prov. 25:16; S [b]Prov. 16:24; 2 4:11

14 [1]Lit., *latter* [a]Prov. 2:10 [b]P

15 [a]Ps. 10:9,

16 [a]Job 5:19; 37:24; Mic. 7:8 6:15; 14:32; 24 18:17

17 [a]Job 31:29 35:15, 19; Prov Obad. 12

18 [1]Lit., *it is ev eyes*

19 [a]Ps. 37:1 [b] 23:17; 24:1

20 [1]Lit., *latter e* 15:31 [b]Prov. 2 [c]Job 18:5, 6; 21 Prov. 13:9; 20:2

21 [1]Or, *reverer* [a]Rom. 13:1-7; 1 2:17

22 [a]Prov. 24:16

23 [1]Lit., *regard face* [a]Prov. 1:6; [b]Prov. 18:5; 28:2

24 [a]Prov. 17:15 5:23 [b]Prov. 11:2

25 [a]Prov. 28:23

26 [1]Or, *an hone*

And [a]make it ready for yourself in the field;
Afterwards, then, build your house.

28 Do not be a [a]witness against your neighbor without cause,
And [b]do not deceive with your lips.
29 [a]Do not say, "Thus I shall do to him as he has done to me;
I will [1]render to the man according to his work."

30 I passed by the field of the sluggard,
And by the vineyard of the man [a]lacking [1]sense;
31 And behold, it was completely [a]overgrown with thistles,
Its surface was covered with [1b]nettles,
And its stone [c]wall was broken down.
32 When I saw, I [1]reflected upon it;
I looked, *and* received instruction.
33 "[a]A little sleep, a little slumber,
A little folding of the hands to rest,"
34 Then your poverty will come *as* [1]a robber,
And your want like [2]an armed man.

Chapter 25

25 These also are [a]proverbs of Solomon which the men of Hezekiah, king of Judah, transcribed.
2 It is the glory of God to [a]conceal a matter,
But the glory of [b]kings is to search out a matter.
3 *As* the heavens for height and the earth for depth,
So the heart of kings is unsearchable.
4 Take away the [a]dross from the silver,
And there comes out a vessel for the [b]smith;
5 Take away the [a]wicked *from* before the king,
And his [b]throne will be established in righteousness.
6 Do not claim honor in the presence of the king,
And do not stand in the place of great men;
7 For [a]it is better that it be said to you, "Come up here,"
Than that you should be put lower in the presence of the prince,
Whom your eyes have seen.

8 Do not go out [a]hastily to [1]argue *your case;*
[2]Otherwise, what will you do in [3]the end,
When your neighbor puts you to shame?
9 [1a]Argue your case with your neighbor,
And [b]do not reveal the secret of another,
10 Lest he who hears *it* reproach you,
And the evil report about you not [1]pass away.

11 *Like* apples of gold in settings of silver
Is a [a]word spoken in [1]right circumstances.
12 *Like* [1]an [a]earring of gold and an [b]ornament of [c]fine gold
Is a wise reprover to a [d]listening ear.
13 Like the cold of snow in the [1]time of harvest
Is a [a]faithful messenger to those who send him,
For he refreshes the soul of his masters.
14 *Like* [a]clouds and [b]wind without rain
Is a man who boasts [1]of his gifts falsely.

ov. 27:23-27
25:18 [b]Lev. 1; Eph. 4:25
., *bring back* 2; Matt. 5:39; Rom. 12:17
heart [a]Prov. 6:32
kind of weed 18 [b]Job 30:7 [c]Is. 5:5
set my heart
3 [a]Prov. 6:10
vagabond; lit., *walks* [2]Lit., *a* *n with a shield*
5:1 [a]Prov. 1:1
. 29:29; Rom. :33 [b]Ezra 6:1
. 26:23; Ezek. 8 [b]Mal. 3:2, 3
v. 20:8 [b]Prov. 16:12
[a]Luke 14:7-11
contend [2]Lit., [3]Lit., *its* [a]Prov. :14; Matt. 5:25
Contend [a]Matt. 5 [b]Prov. 11:13
10 [1]Lit., *return*
ts [a]Prov. 15:23
[1]Or, *a nose ring* :2; 35:22; Ezek. 2 [b]2 Sam. 1:24 ob 28:17 [d]Prov. 15:31; 20:12
[1]Lit., *day* [a]Prov. 13:17
[1]Lit., *in a gift of* *ehood* [a]Jude 12 . 5:13; Mic. 2:11

15 By [1a]forbearance a ruler may be persuaded,
And a soft tongue breaks the bone.
16 Have you [a]found honey? Eat *only* [1]what you need,
Lest you have it in excess and vomit it.
17 Let your foot rarely be in your neighbor's house,
Lest he become [1]weary of you and hate you.
18 *Like* a club and a [a]sword and a sharp [b]arrow
Is a man who bears [c]false witness against his neighbor.
19 *Like* a bad tooth and [1]an unsteady foot
Is confidence in a [a]faithless man in time of trouble.
20 *Like* one who takes off a garment on a cold day, *or like* vinegar on [1]soda,
Is he who sings songs to [2]a troubled heart.
21 [a]If [1]your enemy is hungry, give him food to eat;
And if he is thirsty, give him water to drink;
22 For you will [1]heap burning coals on his head,
And [a]the LORD will reward you.
23 The north wind brings forth rain,
And a [1a]backbiting tongue, an angry countenance.
24 It is [a]better to live in a corner of the roof
Than [1]in a house shared with a contentious woman.
25 *Like* cold water to a weary soul,
So is [a]good news from a distant land.
26 *Like* a [a]trampled spring and a [1]polluted well
Is a righteous man who gives way before the wicked.
27 It is not good to eat much honey,
Nor is it glory to [a]search out [1]one's own glory.
28 *Like* a [a]city that is broken into *and* without walls
Is a man [b]who has no control over his spirit.

Chapter 26

26 Like snow in summer and like [a]rain in harvest,
So honor is not [b]fitting for a fool.
2 Like a [a]sparrow in *its* [1]flitting, like a swallow in *its* flying,
So a [b]curse without cause does not [2]alight.
3 A [a]whip is for the horse, a bridle for the donkey,
And a [b]rod for the back of fools.
4 [a]Do not answer a fool according to his folly,
Lest you also be like him.
5 [a]Answer a fool as his folly *deserves*,
Lest he be [b]wise in his own eyes.
6 He cuts off *his own* feet, *and* drinks violence
Who sends a message by the hand of a fool.
7 *Like* the legs *which* hang down from the lame,
So is a proverb in the mouth of fools.
8 Like [1]one who binds a stone in a sling,
So is he who gives honor to a fool.
9 *Like* a thorn *which* [1]falls into the hand of a drunkard,
So is a proverb in the mouth of fools.
10 [1]*Like* an archer who wounds everyone,
So is he who hires a fool or who hires those who pass by.
11 Like [a]a dog that returns to its vomit
Is a fool who [b]repeats [1]his folly.
12 Do you see a man [a]wise in his own eyes?

15 [1]Lit., *leng* [a]Gen. 32:4; 25:24; Eccl.

16 [1]Lit., *you sufficiency* [a]1 Sam. 14:2

17 [1]Lit., *sur*

18 [a]Ps. 57:4 12:18 [b]Jer. 20:16; Prov.

19 [1]Lit., *a sli* [a]Job 6:15; Is.

20 [1]I.e., natr *evil*

21 [1]Lit., *one you* [a]Ex. 23: 6:22; 2 Chr. 2 5:44; Rom. 1

22 [1]Lit., *snat* [a]2 Sam. 16:1 6:4, 6

23 [1]Lit., *tong secrecy* [a]Ps.

24 [1]Lit., *with of contentions house of asso* [a]Prov. 21:9

25 [a]Prov. 15:

26 [1]Lit., *ruine* 32:2; 34:18, 1

27 [1]Lit., *their* 27:2; Luke 14:

28 [a]Prov. 16: 32:5; Neh. 1:3

26:1 [a]1 Sam. [b]Prov. 17:7

2 [1]Lit., *wande come* [a]Prov. 2 16:2 [b]Num. 23 23:5; 2 Sam. 1

3 [a]Ps. 32:9 [b]P 10:13; 19:29

4 [a]Prov. 23:9; 36:21; Matt. 7:6

5 [a]Matt. 16:1-4 21:24-27 [b]Prov 28:11; Rom. 12

8 [1]Lit., *the bind*

9 [1]Lit., *goes up*

10 [1]Or, *A maste workman produ things, But he w a fool is like one hires those who*

11 [1]Lit., *with his* 2:22 [b]Ex. 8:15

12 [a]Prov. 3:7; 2

[b]There is more hope for a fool than for him.
13 The [a]sluggard says, "There is a lion in the road!
A lion is [1]in the open square!"
14 *As* the door turns on its hinges,
So *does* the [a]sluggard on his bed.
15 The [a]sluggard buries his hand in the dish;
He is weary of bringing it to his mouth again.
16 The sluggard is [a]wiser in his own eyes
Than seven men who can [1]give a discreet answer.
17 *Like* one who takes a dog by the ears
Is he who passes by *and* [1]meddles with [a]strife not belonging to him.
18 Like a madman who throws
[a]Firebrands, arrows and death,
19 So is the man who [a]deceives his neighbor,
And says, "[b]Was I not joking?"
20 For lack of wood the fire goes out,
And where there is no [a]whisperer, [b]contention quiets down.
21 *Like* charcoal to hot embers and wood to fire,
So is a [a]contentious man to kindle strife.
22 The [a]words of a whisperer are like dainty morsels,
And they go down into the [1]innermost parts of the body.
23 *Like* an earthen [a]vessel overlaid with silver [b]dross
Are burning lips and a wicked heart.
24 He who [a]hates disguises *it* with his lips,
But he lays up [b]deceit in his [1]heart.
25 When [1]he [a]speaks graciously, do not believe him,
For there are seven abominations in his heart.
26 *Though his* hatred [a]covers itself with guile,
His wickedness will be [b]revealed before the assembly.
27 He who [a]digs a pit will fall into it,
And he who rolls a stone, it will come back on him.
28 A lying tongue hates [1]those it crushes,
And a [a]flattering mouth works ruin.

Chapter 27

27 [a]Do not boast about tomorrow,
For you [b]do not know what a day may bring forth.
2 Let [a]another praise you, and not your own mouth;
A stranger, and not your own lips.
3 A stone is heavy and the sand weighty,
But the provocation of a fool is heavier than both of them.
4 Wrath is fierce and anger is a flood,
But [a]who can stand before jealousy?
5 Better is [a]open rebuke
Than love that is concealed.
6 Faithful are the [a]wounds of a friend,
But [1]deceitful are the [b]kisses of an enemy.
7 A sated [1]man [2]loathes honey,
But to a famished [1]man any bitter thing is sweet.
8 Like a [a]bird that wanders from her nest,
So is a man who [b]wanders from his [1]home.
9 [a]Oil and perfume make the heart glad,
So a [1]man's counsel is sweet to his friend.

2 [b]Prov. 29:20
, *within* [a]Prov. 22:13
14 [a]Prov. 6:9
5 [a]Prov. 19:24
16 [1]Lit., *return* ly [a]Prov. 27:11
[1]Lit., *infuriates self* [a]Prov. 3:30
18 [a]Is. 50:11
ov. 24:28 [b]Eph. 5:4
v. 16:28 [b]Prov. 22:10
ov. 15:18; 29:22
it., *chambers of elly* [a]Prov. 18:8
att. 23:27; Luke :39 [b]Prov. 25:4
[1]Lit., *inward part* 1:6; Prov. 10:18 [b]Prov. 12:20
[1]Lit., *his voice is cious* [a]Ps. 28:3; . 26:23; Jer. 9:8
att. 23:28 [b]Luke 8:17
Esth. 7:10; Prov. 28:10
[1]Lit., *its crushed ones* [a]Prov. 29:5
[a]James 4:13-16 12:19, 20; James 4:14
rov. 25:27; 2 Cor. 10:12, 18; 12:11
rov. 6:34; 1 John 3:12
. 28:23; Gal. 2:14
r, *excessive* [a]Ps. 141:5; Prov. 20:30 [b]Matt. 26:49
7 [1]Lit., *soul* [2]Lit., *tramples on*
[1]Lit., *place* [a]Prov. :2; Is. 16:2 [b]Gen. 21:14
, *soul's* [a]Ps. 23:5; 141:5

10 Do not forsake your own [a]friend or [b]your father's friend,
And do not go to your brother's house in the day of your calamity;
Better is a neighbor who is near than a brother far away.
11 [a]Be wise, my son, and make my heart glad,
That I may [b]reply to him who reproaches me.
12 A prudent man sees evil *and* hides himself,
The [1]naive proceed *and* pay the penalty.
13 [a]Take his garment when he becomes surety for a stranger;
And for an [1]adulterous woman hold him in pledge.
14 [a]He who blesses his friend with a loud voice early in the morning,
It will be reckoned a curse to him.
15 A [a]constant dripping on a day of steady rain
And a contentious woman are alike;
16 He who would [1]restrain her [1]restrains the wind,
And [2]grasps oil with his right hand.
17 Iron sharpens iron,
So one man sharpens another.
18 He who tends the [a]fig tree will eat its fruit;
And he who [b]cares for his master will be honored.
19 As in water face *reflects* face,
So the heart of man *reflects* man.
20 [1a]Sheol and [2]Abaddon are [b]never satisfied,
Nor are the [c]eyes of man ever satisfied.
21 The [a]crucible is for silver and the furnace for gold,
And a man [b]*is tested* by the praise accorded him.
22 Though you [a]pound a fool in a mortar with a pestle along with crushed grain,
Yet his folly will not depart from him.

23 [a]Know well the [1]condition of your flocks,
And pay attention to your herds;
24 For riches are not forever,
Nor does a [a]crown *endure* to all generations.
25 *When* the grass disappears, the new growth is seen,
And the herbs of the mountains are [a]gathered in,
26 The lambs *will be* for your clothing,
And the goats *will bring* the price of a field,
27 And *there will be* goats' milk enough for your food,
For the food of your household,
And sustenance for your maidens.

Chapter 28

28 The wicked [a]flee when no one is pursuing,
But the righteous are [1]bold as a lion.
2 By the transgression of a land [a]many are its princes,
But [b]by a man of understanding *and* knowledge, so it endures.
3 A [a]poor man who oppresses the lowly
Is *like* a driving rain [1]which leaves no food.
4 Those who forsake the law [a]praise the wicked,
But those who keep the law [b]strive with them.
5 Evil men [a]do not understand justice,
But those who seek the LORD [b]understand all things.

10 [a]Prov. 18: 12:6-8; 2 Chr.

11 [a]Prov. 10: 29:3 [b]Ps. 119

12 [1]Lit., *simp*

13 [1]Lit., *stran* 20:16

14 [a]Ps. 12:2

15 [a]Prov. 19:1

16 [1]Lit., *hide(s* *encounters*

18 [a]2 Kin. 18: 8:12; Is. 36:16; 3:8; 9:7; 2 Tim. [b]Luke 12:42-44

20 [1]I.e., The n world [2]I.e., the destruction [a]J Prov. 15:11 [b]P 30:15, 16; Hab [c]Eccl. 1:8; 4:8

21 [a]Prov. 17:3 6:26

22 [a]Prov. 23:35 Jer. 5:3

23 [1]Lit., *face* [a] 31:10; Ezek. 34 John 10:3

24 [a]Job 19:9; P 89:39; Jer. 13:1 5:16; Ezek. 21:2

25 [a]Is. 17:5; Jer 40:10, 12

28:1 [1]Lit., *confi* [a]Lev. 26:17, 36;

2 [a]1 Kin. 16:8-2 15:8-15 [b]Prov. 1

3 [1]Lit., *and there bread* [a]Matt. 18:

4 [a]Ps. 49:18; Ro 1:32 [b]1 Kin. 18:1 13:11, 15; Matt. 3 14:4; Eph. 5:11

5 [a]Ps. 92:6; Is. 6 44:18 [b]Ps. 119:1 Prov. 2:9; John 7: 1 Cor. 2:15; 1 Joh 2:20, 27

6 [a]Better is the poor who walks in his integrity,
Than he who is [1]crooked though he be rich.
7 He who keeps the law is a discerning son,
But he who is a companion of [a]gluttons humiliates his father.
8 He who increases his wealth by [a]interest and usury,
Gathers it [b]for him who is gracious to the poor.
9 He who turns away his ear from listening to the law,
Even his [a]prayer is an abomination.
10 He who leads the upright astray in an evil way
Will [a]himself fall into his own pit,
But the [b]blameless will inherit good.
11 The rich man is [a]wise in his own eyes,
But the poor who has understanding [1]sees through him.
12 When the [a]righteous triumph, there is great glory,
But [b]when the wicked rise, men [1]hide themselves.
13 He who [a]conceals his transgressions will not prosper,
But he who [b]confesses and forsakes *them* will find compassion.
14 How blessed is the man who [a]fears always,
But he who [b]hardens his heart will fall into calamity.
15 *Like* a [a]roaring lion and a rushing bear
Is a [b]wicked ruler over a poor people.
16 A [a]leader who is a great oppressor lacks understanding,
But he who hates unjust gain will prolong *his* days.
17 A man who is [a]laden with the guilt of human blood
Will [1]be a fugitive until death; let no one support him.
18 He who walks blamelessly will be delivered,
But he who is [1a]crooked will fall all at once.
19 [a]He who tills his land will [b]have plenty of food,
But he who follows empty *pursuits* will have poverty in plenty.
20 A [a]faithful man will abound with blessings,
But he who [b]makes haste to be rich will not go unpunished.
21 To [1a]show partiality is not good,
[b]Because for a piece of bread a man will transgress.
22 A man with an [a]evil eye [b]hastens after wealth,
And does not know that want will come upon him.
23 He who [a]rebukes a man will afterward find *more* favor
Than he who [b]flatters with the tongue.
24 He who [a]robs his father or his mother,
And says, "It is not a transgression,"
Is the [b]companion of a man who destroys.
25 An [1]arrogant man [a]stirs up strife,
But he who [b]trusts in the LORD [c]will [2]prosper.
26 He who [a]trusts in his own heart is a fool,
But he who walks wisely will be delivered.
27 He who [a]gives to the poor will never want,
But he who [1]shuts his eyes will have many curses.
28 When the wicked rise, men hide themselves;
But when they perish, the righteous increase.

Chapter 29

29 A man who hardens *his* neck after [a]much reproof
Will [b]suddenly be broken [1]beyond remedy.
2 When the [a]righteous [1]increase, the people rejoice,
But when a wicked man rules, people groan.

erverse of two 's [a]Prov. 19:1
[a]Prov. 23:20
x. 22:25; Lev. o 27:17; Prov. 13:22; 14:31
66:18; 109:7; v. 15:8; 21:27
Ps. 7:15; Prov. att. 6:33; Heb. :12; 1 Pet. 3:9
examines him v. 3:7; 26:5, 12
2 [1]Lit., *will be hed for* [a]Prov. 0; 29:2 [b]Prov. 3; Eccl. 10:5, 6
Job 31:33; Ps. s. 32:5; 1 John 1:9
ov. 23:17 [b]Ps. 95:8; Rom. 2:5
v. 19:12; 1 Pet. Ex. 1:14; Prov. 9:2; Matt. 2:16
10:16; Is. 3:12
..., *flee to the pit* . 9:6; Ex. 21:14
perverse of two vs [a]Prov. 10:27
v. 12:11 [b]Prov. 20:13
Prov. 10:6; Matt. 5; 25:21 [b]Prov. 8:22; 1 Tim. 6:9
[1]Lit., *regard the ce* [a]Prov. 24:23 [b]Ezek. 13:19
rov. 23:6 [b]Prov. 21:5
v. 27:5, 6 [b]Prov. 29:5
ov. 19:26 [b]Prov. 18:9
[1]Lit., *broad soul made fat* [a]Prov. 18 [b]Prov. 29:25; 6:6 [c]Prov. 11:25
26 [a]Prov. 3:5
Lit., *hides* [a]Prov. 11:24; 19:17
[1]Lit., *and there is remedy* [a]1 Sam. Chr. 36:16; Prov. 4-31 [b]Prov. 6:15
Or, *become great* 3:15; Prov. 11:10; 28:12

3 A man who [a]loves wisdom makes his father glad,
But he who [b]keeps company with harlots wastes *his* wealth.
4 The [a]king gives stability to the land by justice,
But a man who takes bribes overthrows it.
5 A man who [a]flatters his neighbor
Is spreading a net for his steps.
6 By transgression an evil man is [a]ensnared,
But the righteous [b]sings and rejoices.
7 The [a]righteous [1]is concerned for the rights of the poor,
The wicked does not understand *such* [2]concern.
8 Scorners [a]set a city aflame,
But [b]wise men turn away anger.
9 When a wise man has a controversy with a foolish man,
[1]The foolish man either rages or laughs, and there is no rest.
10 Men of [a]bloodshed hate the blameless,
But the upright [1]are concerned for his life.
11 A [a]fool [1]always loses his temper,
But a [b]wise man holds it back.
12 If a [a]ruler pays attention to falsehood,
All his ministers *become* wicked.
13 The [a]poor man and the oppressor [1]have this in common:
The LORD gives [b]light to the eyes of both.
14 If a [a]king judges the poor with truth,
His [b]throne will be established forever.
15 The [a]rod and reproof give wisdom,
But a child [1]who gets his own way [b]brings shame to his mother.
16 When the wicked [1]increase, transgression increases;
But the [a]righteous will see their fall.
17 [a]Correct your son, and he will give you comfort;
He will also [1b]delight your soul.
18 Where there is [a]no [1]vision, the people [b]are unrestrained,
But [c]happy is he who keeps the law.
19 A slave will not be instructed by words *alone;*
For though he understands, there will be no response.
20 Do you see a man who is [a]hasty in his words?
There is [b]more hope for a fool than for him.
21 He who pampers his slave from childhood
Will in the end find him to be a son.
22 An [a]angry man stirs up strife,
And a hot-tempered man abounds in transgression.
23 A man's [a]pride will bring him low,
But a [b]humble spirit will obtain honor.
24 He who is a partner with a thief hates his own life;
He [a]hears the oath but tells nothing.
25 The [a]fear of man [1]brings a snare,
But he who [b]trusts in the LORD will be exalted.
26 [a]Many seek the ruler's [1]favor,
But [b]justice for man *comes* from the LORD.
27 An [a]unjust man is abominable to the righteous,
And he who is [b]upright in the way is abominable to the wicked.

Chapter 30

30 The words of Agur the son of Jakeh, the [1]oracle.
The man declares to Ithiel, to Ithiel and Ucal:

3 [a]Prov. 10:1 27:11; 28:7 [b] 6:26; Luke 15

4 [a]2 Chr. 9:8; 8:15; 29:14

5 [a]Ps. 5:9

6 [a]Prov. 22:5 9:12 [b]Ex. 15:

7 [1]Lit., *knows cause* [2]Lit., *k* [a]Job 29:16; Ps Prov. 31:8, 9

8 [a]Prov. 11:11 16:14

9 [1]Lit., *He*

10 [1]Lit., *seek* [a]Gen. 4:5-8; 1

11 [1]Lit., *sends his spirit* [a]Prov 14:33 [b]Prov. 1

12 [a]1 Kin. 12:

13 [1]Lit., *meet* [a]Prov. 22:2 [b]E Ps. 13:3

14 [a]Ps. 72:4; [b]Prov. 16:12; 2

15 [1]Lit., *left to* [a]Prov. 13:24; 2 [b]Prov. 10:1; 17

16 [1]Or, *becom* [a]Ps. 37:34, 36; 91:8; 92:11; Pr

17 [1]Lit., *give o* [a]Prov. 13:24; 2 [b]Prov. 10:1

18 [1]Or, *revela* [a]1 Sam. 3:1; Ps Amos 8:11, 12 32:25 [c]Ps. 1:1, 106:3; 119:2; P John 13:17

20 [a]James 1:1 26:12

22 [a]Prov. 15:18

23 [a]Prov. 11:2; Dan. 4:30, 31; 23:12; James 4 15:33; 18:12; 22 66:2; Luke 14:1 James 4:10

24 [a]Lev. 5:1

25 [1]Lit., *gives* [a] 12:12; 20:2; Luk John 12:42, 43 91:1-16; Prov. 1 28:25

26 [1]Lit., *face* [a]P 19:6 [b]Is. 49:4; 1

27 [a]Ps. 6:8; 139 Prov. 12:8 [b]Ps. Prov. 29:10; Mat 24:9; John 15:18 1 John 3:13

30:1 [1]Or, *burde*

2 Surely I am more [a]stupid than any man,
And I do not have the understanding of a man.
3 Neither have I learned wisdom,
Nor do I have the [a]knowledge of the Holy One.
4 Who has [a]ascended into heaven and descended?
Who has gathered the [b]wind in His fists?
Who has [c]wrapped the waters in [1]His garment?
Who has [d]established all the ends of the earth?
What is His [e]name or His son's name?
Surely you know!

5 Every [a]word of God is tested;
He is a [b]shield to those who take refuge in Him.
6 [a]Do not add to His words
Lest He reprove you, and you be proved a liar.

7 Two things I asked of Thee,
Do not refuse me before I die:
8 Keep deception and [1]lies far from me,
Give me neither poverty nor riches;
Feed me with the [a]food that is my portion,
9 Lest I be [a]full and deny [b]*Thee* and say, "Who is the LORD?"
Or lest I be [c]in want and steal,
And [d]profane the name of my God.

10 Do not slander a slave to his master,
Lest he [a]curse you and you be found guilty.

11 There is a [1]kind of *man* who [a]curses his father,
And does not bless his mother.
12 There is a [1]kind who is [a]pure in his own eyes,
Yet is not washed from his filthiness.
13 There is a [1]kind—oh how [a]lofty are his eyes!
And his eyelids are raised *in arrogance.*
14 There is a [1]kind of *man* whose [a]teeth are *like* swords,
And his [b]jaw teeth *like* knives,
To [c]devour the afflicted from the earth,
And the needy from among men.

15 The leech has two daughters,
"Give," "Give."
There are three things that will not be satisfied,
Four that will not say, "Enough":
16 [1a]Sheol, and the [b]barren womb,
Earth that is never satisfied with water,
And fire that never says, "Enough."
17 The eye that [a]mocks a father,
And [1b]scorns a mother,
The [c]ravens of the valley will pick it out,
And the young [c]eagles will eat it.

18 There are three things which are too wonderful for me,
Four which I do not understand:
19 The way of an [a]eagle in the sky,

. 49:10; 73:22; Prov. 12:1
3 [a]Prov. 9:10
he [a]Ps. 68:18; 3:13; Eph. 4:8 5:10; Ps. 135:7 8; 38:8, 9 [d]Ps. s. 45:18 [e]Rev. 19:12
2:6; 18:30 [b]Ps. 4:11; Prov. 2:7
eut. 4:2; 12:32; Rev. 22:18
[1]Lit., *words of* od [a]Job 23:12; Matt. 6:11
ut. 8:12; 31:20; 9:25; Hos. 13:6 4:27; Job 31:28 6:30 [d]Ex. 20:7
10 [a]Eccl. 7:21
generation [a]Ex. :17; Prov. 20:20
[1]Or, *generation* v. 16:2; Is. 65:5; uke 18:11; Titus 1:15, 16
[1]Or, *generation* 7; Is. 2:11; 5:15
generation [a]Ps. [b]Job 29:17 [c]Ps. 14:4; Amos 8:4
[1]I.e., The nether orld [a]Prov. 27:20 [b]Gen. 30:1
[1]Lit., *despises to* Gen. 9:22 [b]Prov. :20 [c]Deut. 28:26
[a]Deut. 28:49; Jer. 48:40; 49:22

The way of a serpent on a rock,
The way of a ship in the middle of the sea,
And the way of a man with a maid.
20 This is the way of an [a]adulterous woman:
She eats and wipes her mouth,
And says, "I have done no wrong."

21 Under three things the earth quakes,
And under four, it cannot bear up:
22 Under a [a]slave when he becomes king,
And a fool when he is satisfied with food,
23 Under an unloved woman when she gets a husband,
And a maidservant when she supplants her mistress.

24 Four things are small on the earth,
But they are exceedingly wise:
25 The [a]ants are not a strong folk,
But they prepare their food in the summer;
26 The [a]badgers are not mighty folk,
Yet they make their houses in the rocks;
27 The locusts have no king,
Yet all of them go out in [a]ranks;
28 The lizard you may grasp with the hands,
Yet it is in kings' palaces.

29 There are three things which are stately in *their* march,
Even four which are stately when they walk:
30 The lion *which* is [a]mighty among beasts
And does not [1b]retreat before any,
31 The [1]strutting cock, the male goat also,
And a king *when his* army is with him.

32 If you have been foolish in exalting yourself
Or if you have plotted *evil*, [a]*put your* hand on your mouth.
33 For the [1]churning of milk produces butter,
And pressing the nose brings forth blood;
So the [1]churning of [a]anger produces strife.

Chapter 31

31 The words of King Lemuel, the [1]oracle which his mother taught him.
2 What, O my son?
And what, O [a]son of my womb?
And what, O son of my [b]vows?
3 [a]Do not give your strength to women,
Or your ways to that which [b]destroys kings.
4 It is not for [a]kings, O Lemuel,
It is not for kings to [b]drink wine,
Or for rulers to desire strong drink,
5 Lest they drink and forget what is decreed,
And [a]pervert the [1]rights of all the [2]afflicted.
6 Give strong drink to him who is [a]perishing,
And wine to him [1b]whose life is bitter.
7 Let him drink and forget his poverty,

20 [a]Prov. 5:6

22 [a]Prov. 19:10 10:7

25 [a]Prov. 6:6

26 [a]Lev. 11:5; P 104:18

27 [a]Joel 2:7

30 [1]Lit., *turn ba* [a]Judg. 14:18; 2 S 1:23 [b]Mic. 5:8

31 [1]Lit., *girt in th*

32 [a]Job 21:5; 40 7:16

33 [1]Lit., *pressing* [a]Prov. 10:12; 29:2

31:1 [1]Or, *burden*

2 [a]Is. 49:15 [b]1 S 1:11

3 [a]Prov. 5:9 [b]De 17:17; 1 Kin. 11:1 13:26

4 [a]Eccl. 10:17 [b]P 20:1; Is. 5:22; Hos

5 [1]Lit., *judgment sons of affliction* 23:6; Deut. 16:19 17:15

6 [1]Lit., *bitter of s* [a]Job 29:13 [b]Job Is. 38:15

And remember his trouble no more.
8 [a]Open your mouth for the dumb,
For the [1]rights of all the [2]unfortunate.
9 Open your mouth, [a]judge righteously,
And [1]defend the [b]rights of the afflicted and needy.

10 An [a]excellent wife, who can find?
For her worth is far [b]above jewels.
11 The heart of her husband trusts in her,
And he will have no lack of gain.
12 She does him good and not evil
All the days of her life.
13 She looks for wool and flax,
And works with her [1]hands [2]in delight.
14 She is like [a]merchant ships;
She brings her food from afar.
15 She [a]rises also while it is still night,
And [b]gives food to her household,
And [1]portions to her maidens.
16 She considers a field and buys it;
From [1]her earnings she plants a vineyard.
17 She [a]girds [1]herself with strength,
And makes her arms strong.
18 She senses that her gain is good;
Her lamp does not go out at night.
19 She stretches out her hands to the distaff,
And her [1]hands grasp the spindle.
20 She [1a]extends her hand to the poor;
And she stretches out her hands to the needy.
21 She is not afraid of the snow for her household,
For all her household are [a]clothed with scarlet.
22 She makes [a]coverings for herself;
Her clothing is [b]fine linen and [c]purple.
23 Her husband is known [a]in the gates,
When he sits among the elders of the land.
24 She makes [a]linen garments and sells *them*,
And [1]supplies belts to the [2]tradesmen.
25 Strength and [a]dignity are her clothing,
And she smiles at the [1]future.
26 She [a]opens her mouth in wisdom,
And the [1]teaching of kindness is on her tongue.
27 She looks well to the ways of her household,
And does not eat the [a]bread of idleness.
28 Her children rise up and bless her;
Her husband *also*, and he praises her, *saying:*
29 "Many daughters have done nobly,
But you excel them all."
30 Charm is deceitful and beauty is vain,
But a woman who [1a]fears the LORD, she shall be praised.
31 Give her the [1]product of her hands,
And let her works praise her in the gates.

Lit., *judgment* [2]Lit., *ns of passing away* ob 29:12-17; Ps. 82
9 [1]Lit., *judge the flicted* [a]Lev. 19:15; eut. 1:16 [b]Is. 1:17; Jer. 22:16
[a]Ruth 3:11; Prov. 19:14 [b]Job 28:18; Prov. 8:11
3 [1]Lit., *palms* [2]Or, *willingly*
14 [a]Ezek. 27:25
5 [1]Or, *prescribed asks* [a]Prov. 20:13; 2:11 [b]Luke 12:42
Lit., *the fruit of her palms*
17 [1]Lit., *her loins* Kin. 18:46; 2 Kin. 4:29; Job 38:3
19 [1]Lit., *palms*
, *spreads out her* [a]Deut. 15:11; Job 6-20; Prov. 22:9; 12:13; Eph. 4:28
21 [a]2 Sam. 1:24
Prov. 7:16 [b]Gen. 42; Rev. 19:8, 14 8:26; Luke 16:19
eut. 16:18; Ruth 4:1, 11
[1]Lit., *gives* [2]Lit., *ite* [a]Judg. 14:12
[1]Lit., *latter days* [a]1 Tim. 2:9, 10
aw [a]Prov. 10:31
27 [a]Prov. 19:15
[1]Or, *reverences* 12:1; Prov. 22:4
31 [1]Lit., *fruit*

Theme of Proverbs:

Author:

Date:

Purpose:

Key Words:

- wisdom (wise)
- knowledge
- understanding
- fear
- my son
- commandment(s)
- instruction
- tongue
- fool (folly)

SEGMENT DIVISIONS

	MAIN DIVISIONS		CHAPTER THEMES
	THE CRY OF WISDOM, KNOWLEDGE, AND UNDERSTANDING	1	
		2	
		3	
		4	
		5	
		6	
		7	
		8	
		9	
	THE PROVERBS OF SOLOMON AND WISDOM OF WISE MEN	10	
		11	
		12	
		13	
		14	
		15	
		16	
		17	
		18	
		19	
		20	
		21	
		22	
		23	
		24	
	SOLOMON'S PROVERBS TRANSCRIBED	25	
		26	
		27	
		28	
		29	
	WORDS & COUNSEL OF OTHERS	30	
		31	

ECCLESIASTES

e seems inconsistent and unfair at times. Unpredictable. No matter the generation, no matter the n history, the righteous and the wicked have the same experiences, face the same trials, grapple he same problems. And all end up in the grave!

people grow older they look back and see what a breath, what a vapor, life is. It passes so ly . . . and is almost gone. What was its purpose? Was what we strove to attain worth it? Did we s we should have?

/hat advantage does man have in all his work which he does under the sun?" (Ecclesiastes 1:3). what is the conclusion of it all? (*See* Ecclesiastes 12:13.)

IGS TO DO

ral Instructions

A careful observation of Ecclesiastes gives insight into why this book is included in the Bible. So as you begin your study of this book, do the following:

a. Remember all you read must be considered in the context of the whole counsel of God.

b. Read 1:1-3 and 12:13-14 to see how Ecclesiastes begins and ends. Keep these verses in mind as you study.

In the margin of chapter 1, list what you learn about the author:

a. Who and/or what he is; how he describes himself; what he pursued, had, or experienced, and what gain it was to him. This is important. You may want to list your insights on a piece of paper first as you go through Ecclesiastes. Then when you have completed your study, summarize and record them in the margin of chapter 1.

b. As you read the book, observe what the author has seen, come to know, commends, and what he concludes. Mark or note these in a special way as these are important key repeated phrases.

c. After chapter 4, watch for and list in the margin the author's commands and warnings. For example, in 5:1 he tells us to guard our steps when we go into the house of God.

As you read each chapter mark in a distinctive way the key words listed on the ECCLESIASTES AT A GLANCE chart on page 981. List these key words on an index card that you can use as a bookmark while observing this book.

Then when you finish observing each chapter:

a. Look at every reference to God. On a piece of paper list all you learn about Him, what He does, and what we are to do in respect to Him.

b. Also mark the contrasting groups of people: the righteous and the wicked, the wise and the fool. On a separate piece of paper list what you learn about these persons from each chapter.

c. Also mark what you learn about *riches* (wealth) and *labor*.

d. When you have completed your study of the book, summarize in one of the margins what you learned from compiling the above lists.

Record the theme of each chapter on ECCLESIASTES AT A GLANCE and on the line next to the chapter number in the text.

ters 1-8: Exploring Life's Inconsistencies

As you read, mark the key words listed on ECCLESIASTES AT A GLANCE. Also watch for and mark these words: *explore, explored, discover, discovered,* and *directed.*

The words *vanity, futile,* and *futility* are all the Hebrew word *hebel,* which means vapor or breath.

a. *Hebel* appears more in Ecclesiastes than in any other book of the Bible—half of its occurr
are in Ecclesiastes.

b. Except for 11:8 and 12:8, all the occurrences of *vanity* and *futility* appear in this first segm
Ecclesiastes. Therefore after you finish marking each occurrence of these words, list in c
the chapter margins everything you learn from the text about vanity and futility. Reme
that although they are translated two different ways they are the same Hebrew word.

Chapters 9-12: Explaining Life's Inconsistencies

1. Read 9:1 and mark the word *explain*. Do you see how this verse might be used as a pivotal in the book? If so, watch for any explanations the author might give to life's inconsistencies.
2. When you finish observing chapter 10, review each reference to wisdom that you have m. and in the margin list everything you learned about wisdom from Ecclesiastes.
3. As you read 12:1-7, think of the human body and the effects of age on its members. See if you any "pictorial descriptions" of the body and what happens as you get old, i.e., "the grinding which are few" might be a picture of losing some teeth.
4. Complete ECCLESIASTES AT A GLANCE.

THINGS TO THINK ABOUT

1. Where have you been searching for the meaning of life? What have you been pursuing in orc find fulfillment or happiness?
2. Where can the meaning of life be found? Where can't it be found?
3. The author of Ecclesiastes is Solomon, David's son, who was the richest and wisest of men. do you learn from his experience that can help you?
4. Review all you have learned about God from this book. Since God is going to bring every judgment, even those of Christians (2 Corinthians 5:10, Romans 14:10), what are you doing you should continue to do and what do you need to stop doing? Will you?

Chapter 1

1 The words of the [a]Preacher, the son of David, king in Jerusalem.
2 "[1a]Vanity of vanities," says the Preacher,
"[1]Vanity of vanities! All is [2]vanity."

3 [a]What advantage does man have in all his work
Which he does under the sun?
4 A generation goes and a generation comes,
But the [a]earth [1]remains forever.
5 Also, [a]the sun rises and the sun sets;
And [1]hastening to its place it rises there *again*.
6 [1a]Blowing toward the south,
Then turning toward the north,
The wind continues [2]swirling along;
And on its circular courses the wind returns.
7 All the rivers [1]flow into the sea,
Yet the sea is not full.
To the place where the rivers [1]flow,
There they [1]flow again.
8 All things are wearisome;
Man is not able to tell *it*.

1:1 [a]Eccl. 1:12; 12:8-10

2 [1]Or, *Futility o* *futilities* [2]Or, *fut* 39:5, 6; 62:9; 14 Eccl. 12:8; Rom

3 [a]Eccl. 2:11; 3

4 [1]Lit., *stands* 104:5; 119:90

5 [1]Lit., *panting* 19:6

6 [1]Lit., *Going* [2]L *turning* [a]Eccl. 1 John 3:8

7 [1]Lit., *go*

[a]The eye is not satisfied with seeing,
Nor is the ear filled with hearing.
9 [a]That which has been is that which will be,
And that which has been done is that which will be done.
So, there is nothing new under the sun.
10 Is there anything of which one might say,
"See this, it is new"?
Already it has existed for ages
Which were before us.
11 There is [a]no remembrance of [1]earlier things;
And also of the [2]later things which will occur,
There will be for them no remembrance
Among those who will come [2]later *still*.

12 I, the [a]Preacher, have been king over Israel in Jerusalem.
13 And I [a]set my [1]mind to seek and [b]explore by wisdom concerning
all that has been done under heaven. *It* is [2]a grievous [c]task *which* God
has given to the sons of men to be afflicted with.
14 I have seen all the works which have been done under the sun,
and behold, all is [1a]vanity and striving after wind.
15 What is [a]crooked cannot be straightened, and what is lacking
cannot be counted.
16 I [1]said to myself, "Behold, I have magnified and increased [a]wis-
dom more than all who were over Jerusalem before me; and my
[2]mind has observed [3]a wealth of wisdom and knowledge."
17 And I [a]set my [1]mind to know wisdom and to [b]know madness
and folly; I realized that this also is [c]striving after wind.
18 Because [a]in much wisdom there is much grief, and increasing
knowledge *results in* increasing pain.

Chapter 2

2 I said [1]to myself, "Come now, I will test you with [a]pleasure. So
[2]enjoy yourself." And behold, it too was futility.
2 [a]I said of laughter, "It is madness," and of pleasure, "What does
it accomplish?"
3 I explored with my [1]mind *how* to [a]stimulate my body with wine
while my [1]mind was guiding *me* wisely, and how to take hold of
[b]folly, until I could see [c]what good there is for the sons of men [2]to do
under heaven the few [3]years of their lives.
4 I enlarged my works: I [a]built houses for myself, I planted [b]vine-
yards for myself;
5 I made [a]gardens and [b]parks for myself, and I planted in them all
kinds of fruit trees;
6 I made [a]ponds of water for myself from which to irrigate a forest
of growing trees.
7 I bought male and female slaves, and I had [1a]homeborn slaves.
Also I possessed flocks and [b]herds larger than all who preceded me
in Jerusalem.
8 Also, I collected for myself silver and [a]gold, and the treasure of
kings and provinces. I provided for myself [b]male and female singers
and the pleasures of men—many concubines.
9 Then I became [a]great and increased more than all who preceded
me in Jerusalem. My wisdom also stood by me.
10 And [a]all that my eyes desired I did not refuse them. I did not

:20; Eccl. 4:8
l. 1:10; 2:12; 3:15; 6:10
irst or former latter or after ccl. 2:16; 9:5
ccl. 1:1; 7:27; 12:8-10
eart [2]Lit., an l. 1:17 [b]Eccl. 11; 7:25; 8:17 26; 3:10; 4:8
futility [a]Eccl. , 17; 4:4; 6:9
5 [a]Eccl. 7:13
spoke with my ; saying [2]Lit., heart [3]Lit., an dance [a]1 Kin. ; 10:23; Eccl. 2:9
, heart [a]Eccl. 5 [b]Eccl. 2:12; ccl. 1:14; 2:11, 4:4, 6, 16; 6:9
cl. 2:23; 12:12
t., in my heart consider with ess [a]Eccl. 7:4; 8:15
v. 14:13; Eccl. 7:3, 6
it., heart [2]Lit., they do [3]Lit., udg. 9:13; Ps. 5; Eccl. 10:19 25 [c]Eccl. 2:24; 13; 5:18; 6:12; 8:15; 12:13
7:1-12 [b]Song 8:11
Song 4:16; 5:1 [b]Neh. 2:8
. 2:14; 3:15, 16
Lit., sons of the e [a]Gen. 14:14; :3 [b]1 Kin. 4:23
in. 9:28; 10:10, [b]2 Sam. 19:35
hr. 29:25; Eccl. 1:16
10 [a]Eccl. 6:2

withhold my heart from any pleasure, for my heart was pleased
because of all my labor and this was my [b]reward for all my labor.
11 Thus I considered all my activities which my hands had done
and the labor which I had [1]exerted, and behold all was [2a]vanity and
striving after wind and there was [b]no profit under the sun.
12 So I turned to [a]consider wisdom, madness and folly, for what *will*
the man *do* who will come after the king *except* [b]what has already
been done?
13 And I saw that [a]wisdom excels folly as light excels darkness.
14 The wise man's eyes are in his head, but the [a]fool walks in dark-
ness. And yet I know that [b]one fate befalls them both.
15 Then I said [1]to myself, "[a]As is the fate of the fool, it will also
befall me. [b]Why then have I been extremely wise?" So [2]I said to
myself, "This too is vanity."
16 For there is [a]no [1]lasting remembrance of the wise man *as* with the
fool, inasmuch as *in* the coming days all will be forgotten. And [b]how
the wise man and the fool alike die!
17 So I [a]hated life, for the work which had been done under the sun
was [1]grievous to me; because everything is futility and striving after
wind.
18 Thus I hated [a]all the fruit of my labor for which I had labored
under the sun, for I must [b]leave it to the man who will come
after me.
19 And who knows whether he will be a wise man or [a]a fool? Yet he
will have [1]control over all the fruit of my labor for which I have
labored by acting wisely under the sun. This too is [b]vanity.
20 Therefore I [1]completely despaired of all the fruit of my labor for
which I had labored under the sun.
21 When there is a man who has labored with wisdom, knowledge
and [a]skill, then he [b]gives his [1]legacy to one who has not labored with
them. This too is vanity and a great evil.
22 For what does a man get in [a]all his labor and in [1]his striving with
which he labors under the sun?
23 Because all his days his task is painful and [a]grievous; even at
night his [1]mind [b]does not rest. This too is vanity.
24 There is [a]nothing better for a man *than* to eat and drink and [1]tell
himself that his labor is good. This also I have seen, that it is [b]from
the hand of God.
25 For who can eat and who can have enjoyment without [1]Him?
26 For to a person who is good in His sight [a]He has given wisdom
and knowledge and joy, while to the sinner He has given the task of
gathering and collecting so that he may [b]give to one who is good in
God's sight. This too is [c]vanity and striving after wind.

Chapter 3

3 There is an appointed time for everything. And there is a [a]time
for every [1]event under heaven—
2 A time to give birth, and a [a]time to die;
A time to plant, and a time to uproot what is planted.
3 A [a]time to kill, and a time to heal;
A time to tear down, and a time to build up.
4 A time to [a]weep, and a time to [b]laugh;
A time to mourn, and a time to [c]dance.
5 A time to throw stones, and a time to gather stones;

10 [b]Eccl. 3:2

11 [1]Lit., *labo* [2]Or, *futility*, a throughout th [a]Eccl. 1:14; 2 [b]Eccl. 1:3; 3:

12 [a]Eccl. 1:1 1:9, 10; 3:15

13 [a]Eccl. 7:1 9:18; 10:10

14 [a]1 John 2 49:10; Eccl. 7:2; 9:2, 3

15 [1]Lit., *in m* [2]Lit., *I spoke heart* [a]Eccl. 6:8, 11

16 [1]Lit., *fore* 1:11; 9:5 [b]Ec

17 [1]Lit., *evil* 4:2, 3

18 [a]Eccl. 1:3 39:6; 49:10

19 [1]Lit., *dom* [a]1 Kin. 12:13 6:10

20 [1]Lit., *turne my heart to d*

21 [1]Lit., *shar* 4:4 [b]Eccl. 2:1

22 [1]Lit., *the s his heart* [a]Ec

23 [1]Lit., *heart* 14:1; Eccl. 1:1 [b]Ps. 127:2

24 [1]Lit., *caus to see good in* [a]Eccl. 2:3; 3:1 5:18; 6:12; 8:1 56:12; Luke 12 1 Cor. 15:32; 1 6:17 [b]Eccl. 3:1

25 [1]So Gr.; He

26 [a]Job 32:8; [b]Job 27:16, 17 13:22 [c]Eccl. 1

3:1 [1]Lit., *delig* 3:17; 8:6

2 [a]Job 14:5; H

3 [a]Gen. 9:6; 1 2:6; Hos. 6:1, 2

4 [a]Rom. 12:15 126:2 [c]Ex. 15:2

A time to embrace, and a time to shun embracing.
6 A time to search, and a time to give up as lost;
A time to keep, and a time to throw away.
7 A time to tear apart, and a time to sew together;
A time to [a]be silent, and a time to speak.
8 A time to love, and a time to [a]hate;
A time for war, and a time for peace.
9 [a]What profit is there to the worker from that in which he toils?
10 I have seen the [a]task which God has given the sons of men with
which to occupy themselves.
11 He has [a]made everything [1]appropriate in its time. He has also set
eternity in their heart, [2]yet so that man [b]will not find out the work
which God has done from the beginning even to the end.
12 I know that there is [a]nothing better for them than to rejoice and
to do good in one's lifetime;
13 moreover, that every man who eats and drinks sees good in all
his labor—it is the [a]gift of God.
14 I know that everything God does will remain forever; there is
nothing to add to it and there is nothing to take from it, for God has
so worked that men should [1a]fear Him.
15 That [a]which is has been already, and that which will be has
already been, for God seeks what has passed by.
16 Furthermore, I have seen under the sun *that* in the place of jus-
tice there is [a]wickedness, and in the place of righteousness there is
wickedness.
17 I said [1]to myself, "[a]God will judge both the righteous man and
the wicked man," for a [b]time for every [2]matter and for every deed is
there.
18 I said [1]to myself concerning the sons of men, "God has surely
tested them in order for them to see that they are but [a]beasts."
19 [a]For the fate of the sons of men and the fate of beasts [1]is the
same. As one dies so dies the other; indeed, they all have the same
breath and there is no advantage for man over beast, for all is
[2]vanity.
20 All go to the same place. All came from the [a]dust and all return
to the dust.
21 Who knows that the [a]breath of man ascends upward and the
breath of the beast descends downward to the earth?
22 And I have seen that [a]nothing is better than that man should be
happy in his activities, for that is his lot. For who will bring him to
see [b]what will occur after him?

Chapter 4

4 Then I looked again at all the acts of [a]oppression which were
being done under the sun. And behold *I saw* the tears of the
oppressed and *that* they had [b]no one to comfort *them;* and on the side
of their oppressors was power, but they had no one to comfort *them.*
2 So [a]I congratulated the dead who are already dead more than the
living who are still living.
3 But [a]better *off* than both of them is the one who has never ex-
isted, who has never seen the evil activity that is done under the sun.
4 And I have seen that every labor and every [a]skill which is done
is *the result of* rivalry between a man and his neighbor. This too is
[1b]vanity and striving after wind.

7 [a]Amos 5:13
1:3; Prov. 13:5
1:3; 2:11; 5:16
ccl. 1:13; 2:26
, *beautiful* [2]Or, *out which man* 1:31 [b]Job 5:9; 23; 8:17; Rom. 11:33
12 [a]Eccl. 2:24
Eccl. 2:24; 5:19
[1]Or, *be in awe Him* [a]Eccl. 5:7; 8:12, 13; 12:13
[a]Eccl. 1:9; 6:10
ccl. 4:1; 5:8; 8:9
Lit., *in my heart* , *delight* [a]Gen. Ps. 96:13; 98:9; :9; Matt. 16:27; 2:6-10; 2 Thess. [b]Eccl. 3:1; 8:6
[1]Lit., *in my heart* 49:12, 20; 73:22
., *and they have fate* [2]Or, *futility* 9:12; Eccl. 9:12
[a]Gen. 3:19; Ps. 03:14; Eccl. 12:7
21 [a]Eccl. 12:7
Eccl. 2:24 [b]Eccl. 6:12; 8:7; 10:14
b 35:9; Ps. 12:5; 3:16; 5:8; Is. 5:7 r. 16:7; Lam. 1:9
ob 3:11-26; Eccl. 2:17; 7:1
ob 3:11-22; Eccl. 6:3; Luke 23:29
Or, *futility,* and so hroughout the ch. 2:21 [b]Eccl. 1:14

5 The fool [a]folds his hands and [b]consumes his own flesh.
6 One hand full of rest is [a]better than two fists full of labor and
striving after wind.
7 Then I looked again at vanity under the sun.
8 There was a certain man without a [1]dependent, having neither a
son nor a brother, yet there was no end to all his labor. Indeed, [a]his
eyes were not satisfied with riches *and he never asked,* "And [b]for
whom am I laboring and depriving myself of pleasure?" This too is
vanity and it is a [c]grievous task.
9 Two are better than one because they have a good return for
their labor.
10 For if [1]either of them falls, the one will lift up his companion. But
woe to the one who falls when there is not [2]another to lift him up.
11 Furthermore, if two lie down together they [1]keep warm, but
[a]how can one be warm *alone?*
12 And if [1]one can overpower him who is alone, two can resist him.
A cord of three *strands* is not quickly torn apart.
13 A [a]poor, yet wise lad is better than an old and foolish king who
no longer knows *how* to receive [1]instruction.
14 For he has come [a]out of prison to become king, even though he
was born poor in his kingdom.
15 I have seen all the living under the sun throng to the side of the
second lad who [1]replaces him.
16 There is no end to all the people, to all who were before them,
and even the ones who will come later will not be happy with him,
for this too is [a]vanity and striving after wind.

Chapter 5

5 [1a]Guard your steps as you go to the house of God, and draw
near to listen rather than to offer the [b]sacrifice of fools; for they
do not know they are doing evil.
2 [1]Do not be [a]hasty [2]in word or [3]impulsive in thought to bring up a
matter in the presence of God. For God is in heaven and you are on
the earth; therefore let your [b]words be few.
3 For the dream comes through much [1]effort, and the voice of a
[a]fool through many words.
4 When you [a]make a vow to God, do not be late in paying it, for
He takes no delight in fools. [b]Pay what you vow!
5 It is [a]better that you should not vow than that you should vow
and not pay.
6 Do not let your [1]speech cause [2]you to sin and do not say in the
presence of the messenger *of God* that it was a [a]mistake. Why should
God be angry on account of your voice and destroy the work of your
hands?
7 For in many dreams and in many words there is [1]emptiness.
Rather, [2a]fear God.
8 If you see [a]oppression of the poor and [b]denial of justice and
righteousness in the province, do not be [c]shocked at the [1]sight, for
one [2]official watches over another [2]official, and there are higher [3]offi-
cials over them.
9 After all, a king who cultivates the field is an advantage to the
land.
10 [a]He who loves money will not be satisfied with money, nor he
who loves abundance *with its* income. This too is [1]vanity.

5 [a]Prov. 6:10; [b]Is. 9:20

6 [a]Prov. 15:16

8 [1]Lit., *second* 27:20; Eccl. 1:8 [b]Eccl. 2:21 [c]E

10 [1]Lit., *they fa* *second*

11 [1]Lit., *have w* [a]1 Kin. 1:1-4

12 [1]Lit., *he*

13 [1]Or, *warning* 7:19; 9:15

14 [a]Gen. 41:14

15 [1]Lit., *stands* *stead*

16 [a]Eccl. 1:14

5:1 [1]Ch. 4:17 in [a]Ex. 3:5; 30:18- 1:12 [b]1 Sam. 15 Prov. 15:8; 21:2

2 [1]Ch. 5:1 in He *with your mouth* *hurry your heart* 20:25 [b]Prov. 10 Matt. 6:7

3 [1]Lit., *task* [a]Jo Prov. 15:2; Eccl.

4 [a]Num. 30:2; P 50:14; 76:11 [b]Ps 66:13, 14

5 [a]Prov. 20:25;

6 [1]Lit., *mouth* [2]L *your body* [a]Lev. Num. 15:25

7 [1]Lit., *vanity* [2]C *revere* [a]Eccl. 3:1 7:18; 8:12, 13; 12

8 [1]Lit., *delight* [2]L *high one* [3]Lit., *or* [a]Eccl. 4:1 [b]Ezek. [c]1 Pet. 4:12

10 [1]Or, *futility* [a]E 1:8; 2:10, 11; 4:8

11 [a]When good things increase, those who consume them increase.
So what is the advantage to their owners except to [1]look on?
12 The sleep of the working man is [a]pleasant, whether he eats little
or much. But the [1]full stomach of the rich man does not allow him to
sleep.
13 There is a grievous evil *which* I have seen under the sun: [a]riches
being [1]hoarded by their owner to his hurt.
14 When those riches were lost through [1]a bad investment and he
had fathered a son, then there was nothing [2]to support him.
15 [a]As he had come naked from his mother's womb, so will he
return as he came. He will [b]take nothing from the fruit of his labor
that he can carry in his hand.
16 And this also is a grievous evil—exactly as a man [1]is born, thus
will he [2]die. So, [a]what is the advantage to him who [b]toils for the
wind?
17 Throughout his life [a]*he* also eats in darkness with [b]great vexation,
sickness and anger.
18 Here is what I have seen to be [a]good and [1]fitting: to eat, to drink
and [2]enjoy oneself in all one's labor in which he toils under the sun
during the few [3]years of his life which God has given him; for this is
his [4b]reward.
19 Furthermore, as for every man to whom [a]God has given riches
and wealth, He has also [b]empowered him to eat from them and to
receive his [1]reward and rejoice in his labor; this is the [c]gift of God.
20 For he will not often [1]consider the [2]years of his life, because [a]God
keeps [3]him occupied with the gladness of his heart.

Chapter 6

6 There is an [a]evil which I have seen under the sun and it is
prevalent [1]among men—
2 a man to whom God has [a]given riches and wealth and honor so
that his soul [b]lacks nothing of all that he desires, but God has not
empowered him to eat from them, for a foreigner [1]enjoys them. This
is [2]vanity and a severe affliction.
3 If a man fathers a hundred *children* and lives many years, how-
ever many [1]they be, but his soul is not satisfied with good things,
and he does not even have a *proper* [a]burial, *then* I say, "Better [b]the
miscarriage than he,
4 for it comes in futility and goes into obscurity; and its name is
covered in obscurity.
5 "It never sees the sun and it never knows *anything;* [1]it is better off
than he.
6 "Even if the *other* man lives a thousand years twice and does not
[1]enjoy good things—[a]do not all go to one place?"
7 [a]All a man's labor is for his mouth and yet the [1]appetite is not
[2]satisfied.
8 For [a]what advantage does the wise man have over the fool?
What *advantage* does the poor man have, knowing *how* to walk
before the living?
9 What the eyes [a]see is better than what the soul [1]desires. This too
is [b]futility and a striving after wind.
10 Whatever [a]exists has already been named, and it is known what
man is; for he [b]cannot dispute with him who is stronger than he is.

, see with their
yes [a]Eccl. 2:9

satiety [a]Prov. 3:24

guarded [a]Eccl. 6:2

.it., an evil task
.it., in his hand

[a]Job 1:21 [b]Ps.
:17; 1 Tim. 6:7

t., comes [2]Lit.,
l. 1:3; 2:11; 3:9
[b]Prov. 11:29

s. 127:2 [b]Eccl. 2:23

beautiful [2]Lit.,
good [3]Or, days
are [a]Eccl. 2:24
[b]Eccl. 2:10

, share [a]2 Chr.
Eccl. 6:2 [b]Eccl.
6:2 [c]Eccl. 3:13

remember [2]Or,
o with Gr. [a]Ex. 23:25

it., upon [a]Eccl. 5:13

eats from them
ity [a]1 Kin. 3:13
7:14; 73:7; Eccl. 2:10

, the days of his
[a]Is. 14:20; Jer.
2:19 [b]Job 3:16;
Eccl. 4:3

.., more rest has
his one than that

see [a]Eccl. 2:14

, soul [2]Lit., filled
[a]Prov. 16:26

8 [a]Eccl. 2:15

[1]Lit., goes after
11:9 [b]Eccl. 1:14

[a]Eccl. 1:9; 3:15
9:32; 40:2; Prov.
21:30; Is. 45:9

11 For there are many words which increase futility. What *then* is the advantage to a man?
12 For who knows what is good for a man during *his* lifetime, *during* the few [1]years of his futile life? He will [2]spend them like a shadow. For who can tell a man [a]what will be after him under the sun?

Chapter 7

7 A [a]good name is better than a good ointment,
And the [b]day of *one's* death is better than the day of one's birth.
2 It is better to go to a house of mourning
Than to go to a house of feasting,
Because [1]that is the [a]end of every man,
And the living [2b]takes *it* to [3]heart.
3 [a]Sorrow is better than laughter,
For [b]when a face is sad a heart may be happy.
4 The [1]mind of the wise is in the house of mourning,
While the [1]mind of fools is in the house of pleasure.
5 It is better to [a]listen to the rebuke of a wise man
Than for one to listen to the song of fools.
6 For as the [1]crackling of [a]thorn bushes under a pot,
So is the [b]laughter of the fool,
And this too is futility.
7 For [a]oppression makes a wise man mad,
And a [b]bribe [1]corrupts the heart.
8 The [a]end of a matter is better than its beginning;
[b]Patience of spirit is better than haughtiness of spirit.
9 Do not be [1a]eager in your heart to be angry,
For anger resides in the bosom of fools.
10 Do not say, "Why is it that the former days were better than these?"
For it is not from wisdom that you ask about this.
11 Wisdom along with an inheritance is good
And an [a]advantage to those who see the sun.
12 For [a]wisdom is [1]protection *just as* money is [1]protection.
But the advantage of knowledge is that [b]wisdom preserves the lives of its possessors.
13 Consider the [a]work of God,
For who is [b]able to straighten what He has bent?
14 [a]In the day of prosperity be happy,
But [b]in the day of adversity consider—
God has made the one as well as the other
So that man may [c]not discover anything *that will be* after him.
15 I have seen everything during my [1a]lifetime of futility; there is [b]a
righteous man who perishes in his righteousness, and there is [c]a
wicked man who prolongs *his life* in his wickedness.
16 Do not be excessively [a]righteous, and do not [b]be overly wise.
Why should you ruin yourself?
17 Do not be excessively wicked, and do not be a fool. Why should
you [a]die before your time?
18 It is good that you grasp one thing, and also not [1]let go of the
other; for the one who [a]fears God comes forth with [2]both of them.
19 [a]Wisdom strengthens a wise man more than ten rulers who are
in a city.

12 [1]Lit., *days* [a]Eccl. 3:22

7:1 [a]Prov. 22 4:2; 7:8

2 [1]I.e., death *gives* [3]Lit., *his* [a]Eccl. 2:14, 16 6:6; 9:2, 3 [b]Ps

3 [a]Eccl. 2:2 [b]

4 [1]Lit., *heart*

5 [a]Ps.141:5; P 13:18; 15:31, 3 Eccl. 9:17

6 [1]Lit., *voice* 118:12 [b]Eccl.

7 [1]Lit., *destroy* 4:1; 5:8 [b]Ex. 2 16:19; Prov. 17

8 [a]Eccl. 7:1 [b]P 14:29; 16:32; G Eph. 4:2

9 [1]Lit., *hasty in spirit* [a]Prov. 14 James 1:19

11 [a]Prov. 8:10, 2:13

12 [1]Lit., *in a sh* [a]Eccl. 7:19; 9:1 3:18; 8:35

13 [a]Eccl. 3:11; [b]Eccl. 1:15

14 [a]Deut. 26:11 3:22; 9:7; 11:9 8:5; Job 2:10 [c]

15 [1]Lit., *days* [a] 6:12; 9:9 [b]Eccl. [c]Eccl. 8:12, 13

16 [a]Prov. 25:16 3:6 [b]Rom. 12:3

17 [a]Job 22:16; 55:23; Prov. 10:2

18 [1]Lit., *rest yo* [2]Lit., *all* [a]Eccl. 3 8:12, 13; 12:13

19 [a]Eccl. 7:12;

20 Indeed, [a]there is not a righteous man on earth who *continually* does good and who never sins.
21 Also, do not [1]take seriously all words which are spoken, lest you hear your servant [a]cursing you.
22 For [1]you also have realized that you likewise have many times cursed others.
23 I tested all this with wisdom, *and* I said, "I will be wise," [a]but it was far from me.
24 What has been is remote and [a]exceedingly [1]mysterious. [b]Who can discover it?
25 I [1a]directed my [2]mind to know, to investigate, and to seek wisdom and an explanation, and to know the evil of folly and the foolishness of madness.
26 And I discovered more [a]bitter than death the woman whose heart is [b]snares and nets, whose hands are chains. [c]One who is pleasing to God will escape from her, but [d]the sinner will be captured by her.
27 "Behold, I have discovered this," says the Preacher, "*adding* one thing to another to find an explanation,
28 which [1]I am still seeking but have not found. I have found one man among a thousand, but I have not found a [a]woman among all these.
29 "Behold, I have found only this, that [a]God made men upright, but they have sought out many devices."

Chapter 8

8 Who is like the wise man and who knows the interpretation of a matter? A man's wisdom [a]illumines [1]him and causes his [b]stern face to [2]beam.
2 I say, "Keep the [1]command of the king because of the [a]oath [2]before God.
3 "Do not be in a hurry [1a]to leave him. Do not join in an evil matter, for he will do whatever he pleases."
4 Since the word of the king is authoritative, [a]who will say to him, "What are you doing?"
5 He who [a]keeps a *royal* command [b]experiences no [1]trouble, for a wise heart knows the proper time and procedure.
6 For [a]there is a proper time and procedure for every delight, when a man's trouble is heavy upon him.
7 If no one [a]knows what will happen, who can tell him when it will happen?
8 [a]No man has authority to restrain the wind with the wind, or authority over the day of death; and there is no discharge in the time of war, and [b]evil will not deliver [1]those who practice it.
9 All this I have seen and applied my [1]mind to every deed that has been done under the sun wherein a man has exercised [a]authority over *another* man to his hurt.
10 So then, I have seen the wicked buried, those who used to go in and out from the holy place, and they are [a]*soon* forgotten in the city where they did thus. This too is futility.
11 Because the [a]sentence against an evil deed is not executed quickly, therefore [b]the hearts of the sons of men among them are given fully to do evil.
12 Although a sinner does evil a hundred *times* and may [a]lengthen

his *life,* still I know that it will be [b]well for those who fear God, who
fear [1]Him openly.
13 But it will [a]not be well for the evil man and he will not lengthen
his days like a [b]shadow, because he does not fear God.
14 There is futility which is done on the earth, that is, there are
[a]righteous men to whom it [1]happens according to the deeds of the
wicked. On the other hand, there are [b]evil men to whom it [1]happens
according to the deeds of the righteous. I say that this too is futility.
15 So I commended pleasure, for there is nothing good for [a]a man
under the sun except to eat and to drink and to be merry, and this
will stand by him in his [1]toils *throughout* the days of his life which
God has given him under the sun.
16 When I [a]gave my heart to know wisdom and to see the task
which has been done on the earth (even though one should [1b]never
sleep day or night),
17 and I saw every work of God, *I concluded* that [a]man cannot dis-
cover the work which has been done under the sun. Even though
man should seek laboriously, he will not discover; and [b]though the
wise man should say, "I know," he cannot discover.

Chapter 9

9 For I have taken all this to my heart and explain [1]it that right-
eous men, wise men, and their deeds are [a]in the hand of God.
[b]Man does not know whether *it will be* [c]love or hatred; anything
[2]awaits him.
2 [a]It is the same for all. There is [b]one fate for the righteous and for
the wicked; for the good, for the clean, and for the unclean; for the
man who offers a sacrifice and for the one who does not sacrifice. As
the good man is, so is the sinner; as the swearer is, so is the one who
[1]is afraid to swear.
3 This is an evil in all that is done under the sun, that there is [a]one
fate for all men. Furthermore, [b]the hearts of the sons of men are full
of evil, and [c]insanity is in their hearts throughout their lives. After-
wards they *go* to the dead.
4 For whoever is joined with all the living, there is hope; surely a
live dog is better than a dead lion.
5 For the living know they will die; but the dead [a]do not know
anything, nor have they any longer a reward, for their [b]memory is
forgotten.
6 Indeed their love, their hate, and their zeal have already
perished, and they will no longer have a [a]share in all that is done
under the sun.
7 Go *then,* [a]eat your bread in happiness, and drink your wine with
a cheerful heart; for God has already approved your works.
8 Let your [a]clothes be white all the time, and let not [b]oil be lacking
on your head.
9 Enjoy life with the woman whom you love all the days of your
[1a]fleeting life which He has given to you under the sun[2]; for this is
your [b]reward in life, and in your toil in which you have labored
under the sun.
10 Whatever your hand finds to do, verily, [a]do *it* with all your
might; for there is no [b]activity or planning or knowledge or wisdom
in [c]Sheol where you are going.
11 I again saw under the sun that the [a]race is not to the swift, and

12 [1]Lit., *befor* [b]Deut. 4:40; 1: 37:11; Prov. 1 3:10

13 [a]Eccl. 8:8; [b]Job 14:2; Ecc

14 [1]Lit., *strike* 73:14; Eccl. 7: 21:7; Ps. 73:3, 12:1; Mal. 3:15

15 [1]Lit., *labor* 2:24; 3:12, 13;

16 [1]Lit., *see n his eyes* [a]Eccl 14 [b]Eccl. 2:23

17 [a]Eccl. 3:11 73:16; Eccl. 7:2 11:33

9:1 [1]Lit., *all thi before them* [a]D 33:3; Job 12:10 119:109 [b]Eccl. [c]Eccl. 9:6

2 [1]Lit., *fears ar* [a]Job 9:22; Eccl. [b]Eccl. 2:14; 3:19

3 [a]Eccl. 9:2; Je [b]Eccl. 8:11 [c]Ec

5 [a]Job 14:21 [b] 88:12; Eccl. 1:11 8:10; Is. 26:14

6 [a]Eccl. 2:10; 3.

7 [a]Eccl. 2:24; 8

8 [a]Rev. 3:4 [b]Ps

9 [1]Lit., *life of va* [2]Heb. adds *all th of your vanity* [a]E 6:12; 7:15 [b]Eccl

10 [a]Eccl. 11:6; R 12:11; Col. 3:23 9:5 [c]Gen. 37:35 21:13; Is. 38:10

11 [a]Amos 2:14,

the [b]battle is not to the warriors, and neither is bread to the wise, nor
[c]wealth to the discerning, nor favor to men of ability; for time and
[d]chance overtake them all.
12 Moreover, man does not [a]know his time: like fish caught in a
treacherous net, and [b]birds trapped in a snare, so the sons of men are
[c]ensnared at an evil time when it [d]suddenly falls on them.
13 Also this I came to see as wisdom under the sun, and [1]it im-
pressed me.
14 There [a]was a small city with few men in it and a great king came
to it, surrounded it, and constructed large siegeworks against it.
15 But there was found in it a [a]poor wise man and he [1]delivered the
city [b]by his wisdom. Yet [c]no one remembered that poor man.
16 So I said, "[a]Wisdom is better than strength." But the wisdom of
the poor man is despised and his words are not heeded.
17 The [a]words of the wise heard in quietness are *better* than the
shouting of a ruler among fools.
18 [a]Wisdom is better than weapons of war, but [b]one sinner destroys
much good.

Chapter 10

10 Dead flies make a [a]perfumer's oil stink, so a little foolishness
is weightier than wisdom *and* honor.
2 A wise man's heart *directs him* toward the right, but the foolish
[a]man's heart *directs him* toward the left.
3 Even when the fool walks along the road his [1]sense is lacking,
and he [2a]demonstrates to everyone *that* he is a fool.
4 If the ruler's [1]temper rises against you, [a]do not abandon your
position, because [b]composure allays great offenses.
5 There is an evil I have seen under the sun, like an error which
goes forth from the ruler—
6 [a]folly is set in many exalted places while rich men sit in humble
places.
7 I have seen [a]slaves *riding* [b]on horses and princes walking like
slaves on the land.
8 [a]He who digs a pit may fall into it, and a [b]serpent may bite him
who breaks through a wall.
9 He who quarries stones may be hurt by them, and he who splits
logs may be endangered by them.
10 If the [1]axe is dull and he does not sharpen *its* edge, then he must
[2]exert more strength. Wisdom has the advantage of giving success.
11 If the serpent bites [1a]before being charmed, there is no profit for
the charmer.
12 [a]Words from the mouth of a wise man are gracious, while the
lips of a [b]fool consume him;
13 the beginning of [1]his talking is folly, and the end of [2]it is wicked
[a]madness.
14 Yet the [a]fool multiplies words. No man knows what will happen,
and who can tell him [b]what will come after him?
15 The toil of [1]a fool *so* wearies him that he does not *even* know how
to go to a city.
16 Woe to you, O land, whose [a]king is a lad and whose princes
[1]feast in the morning.
17 Blessed are you, O land, whose king is of nobility and whose

Chr. 20:15; Ps.
ch. 4:6 [c]Deut.
8 [d]1 Sam. 6:9
ccl. 8:7 [b]Prov.
[c]Prov. 29:6; Is.
Hos. 9:8 [d]Luke
21:34, 35
it., *great it was*
to me
Sam. 20:16-22
Or, *might have*
ed [a]Eccl. 4:13
1. 20:22 [c]Eccl.
2:16; 8:10
ov. 21:22; Eccl.
7:12, 19
Eccl. 7:5; 10:12
cl. 9:16 [b]Josh.
2 Kin. 21:2-17
0:1 [a]Ex. 30:25
t. 6:33; Col. 3:1
eart [2]Lit., *says*
rov. 13:16; 18:2
spirit [a]Eccl. 8:3
25:24-33; Prov.
25:15
1. 3:1, 5f.; Prov.
28:12; 29:2
v. 19:10 [b]Esth.
6:8-10
[a]Ps. 7:15; Prov.
27 [b]Amos 5:19
[1]Lit., *iron* [2]Lit.,
strengthen
11 [1]Lit., *without*
ment [a]Ps. 58:4,
5; Jer. 8:17
ov. 10:32; 22:11;
22 [b]Prov. 10:14;
18:7; Eccl. 4:5
Lit., *the words of*
mouth [2]Lit., *his*
outh [a]Eccl. 7:25
Prov. 15:2; Eccl.
[b]Eccl. 3:22; 6:12;
7:14; 8:7
15 [1]Lit., *fools*
, *eat* [a]Is. 3:4, 12

princes eat at the appropriate time—for strength, and not for
[a]drunkenness.
18 Through [a]indolence the rafters sag, and through slackness the
house leaks.
19 *Men* prepare a meal for enjoyment, and [a]wine makes life merry,
and [b]money [1]is the answer to everything.
20 Furthermore, [a]in your bedchamber do not [b]curse a king, and in
your sleeping rooms do not curse a rich man, for a bird of the heav-
ens will carry the sound, and the winged creature will make the
matter known.

Chapter 11

11 [a]Cast your bread on the surface of the waters, for you [a]will
find it [1]after many days.
2 [a]Divide your portion to seven, or even to eight, for you do not
know what [b]misfortune may occur on the earth.
3 If the clouds are full, they pour out rain upon the earth; and
whether a tree falls toward the south or toward the north, wherever
the tree falls, there it [1]lies.
4 He who watches the wind will not sow and he who looks at the
clouds will not reap.
5 Just as you do not [a]know [1]the path of the wind and [b]how bones
are formed in the womb of the [2]pregnant woman, so you do not
[c]know the activity of God who makes all things.
6 Sow your seed [a]in the morning, and do not [1]be idle in the eve-
ning, for you do not know whether [2]morning or evening sowing will
succeed, or whether both of them alike will be good.
7 The light is pleasant, and *it is* good for the eyes to [a]see the sun.
8 Indeed, if a man should live many years, let him [a]rejoice in them
all, and let him remember the [b]days of darkness, for they shall be
many. Everything that is to come *will be* futility.
9 Rejoice, young man, during your childhood, and let your heart
be pleasant during the days of young manhood. And follow the
[1]impulses of your heart and the [2a]desires of your eyes. Yet know that
[b]God will bring you to judgment for all these things.
10 So, remove vexation from your heart and put away [1a]pain from
your body, because childhood and the prime of life are fleeting.

Chapter 12

12 [a]Remember also your Creator in the days of your youth,
before the [b]evil days come and the years draw near when you
will say, "I have no delight in them";
2 before the [a]sun, the light, the moon, and the stars are darkened,
and clouds return after the rain;
3 in the day that the watchmen of the house tremble, and mighty
men [a]stoop, the grinding ones stand idle because they are few, and
[b]those who look through [1]windows grow dim;
4 and the doors on the street are shut as the [a]sound of the grinding
mill is low, and one will arise at the sound of the bird, and all the
[b]daughters of song will [1]sing softly.
5 Furthermore, [1]men are afraid of a high place and of terrors on
the road; the almond tree blossoms, the grasshopper drags himself
along, and the caperberry is ineffective. For man goes to his eternal
[a]home while [b]mourners go about in the street.

17 [a]Prov. 31:4

18 [a]Prov. 24:3

19 [1]Lit., *answ* [a]Judg. 9:13; P Eccl. 2:3 [b]Ecc

20 [a]2 Kin. 6:1 12:3 [b]Ex. 22:2 23:5

11:1 [1]Lit., *in, w* [a]Deut. 15:10; F 19:17; Matt. 1C 6:9; Heb. 6:10

2 [a]Ps. 112:9; 5:42; Luke 6:3 6:18, 19 [b]Eccl 12:1

3 [1]Lit., *is*

5 [1]Or, with ma *how the spirit* *bones in the w* [2]Lit., *full* [a]John 139:13-16 [c]Ec 3:10, 11; 8:17

6 [1]Lit., *let dow hand* [2]Lit., *this* [a]Eccl. 9:10

7 [a]Eccl. 6:5; 7:

8 [a]Eccl. 9:7 [b]E

9 [1]Lit., *ways* [2] *sights* [a]Num. 1 Job 31:7; Eccl. [b]Eccl. 3:17; 12: 14:10

10 [1]Lit., *evil* [a]2 7:1; 2 Tim. 2:22

12:1 [a]Deut. 8:1 4:14; Ps. 63:6; [b]Eccl. 11:8

2 [a]Is. 5:30; 13:1 32:7, 8; Joel 3:1 24:29

3 [1]Or, *holes* [a]P 35:14; 38:6 [b]Ge 48:10; 1 Sam. 3

4 [1]Lit., *be broug* [a]Jer. 25:10; Rev [b]2 Sam. 19:35

5 [1]Lit., *they* [a]Jo 30:23 [b]Gen. 50: 9:17

[1]So with Gr.; Heb., ...oved [a]Zech. 4:2, 3

[1]Or, breath [a]Gen. ...:19; Job 34:15; Ps. ...29; Eccl. 3:20 [b]Job ...4; Eccl. 3:21; Luke ...; Acts 7:59 [c]Num. ...2; 27:16; Is. 57:16; Zech. 12:1

8 [a]Eccl. 1:2

9 [a]1 Kin. 4:32 ...Prov. 10:32 [b]Prov. 22:20, 21

...Lit., planted [a]Prov. ...; 22:17; Eccl. 7:5; [b]Acts 2:37 [c]Ezra 9:8; Is. 22:23

...it., making [a]1 Kin. 4:32 [b]Eccl. 1:18

...3 [a]Eccl. 3:14; 5:7; ...; 8:12 [b]Deut. 4:2; 8:5 [c]Deut. 10:12; Mic. 6:8

[a]Eccl. 3:17; 11:9; 10:26; Rom. 2:16; 1 Cor. 4:5

6 *Remember Him* before the silver cord is [1]broken and the [a]golden
bowl is crushed, the pitcher by the well is shattered and the wheel at
the cistern is crushed;
7 then the [a]dust will return to the earth as it was, and the [1b]spirit
will return to [c]God who gave it.
8 "[a]Vanity of vanities," says the Preacher, "all is vanity!"
9 In addition to being a wise man, the Preacher also taught the
people knowledge; and he pondered, searched out and arranged
[a]many proverbs.
10 The Preacher sought to find [a]delightful words and to write
[b]words of truth correctly.
11 The [a]words of wise men are like [b]goads, and masters of *these*
collections are like [1]well-driven [c]nails; they are given by one
Shepherd.
12 But beyond this, my son, be warned: the [1]writing of [a]many books
is endless, and excessive [b]devotion *to books* is wearying to the body.
13 The conclusion, when all has been heard, *is:* [a]fear God and [b]keep
His commandments, because this *applies to* [c]every person.
14 For [a]God will bring every act to judgment, everything which is
hidden, whether it is good or evil.

ECCLESIASTES AT A GLANCE

...of Ecclesiastes:

...DIVISIONS

	CHAPTER THEMES
	1
	2
	3
	4
	5
	6
	7
	8
	9
	10
	11
	12

Author:

Date:

Purpose:

Key Words:
God
vanity (futile, futility)
under the sun (under heaven)
wisdom
righteous (righteousness)
wicked (wickedness)
wise
fool
evil
labor (labored)
riches (wealth)

SONG OF SOLOMON

Song of Solomon is a love story tucked away in the canon of Scripture. On the eighth d Passover the Jews would sing portions of the Song of Solomon, a book they compared to the most place in the temple.

Song of Solomon is a book never quoted by our Lord, but one from which many sing, "I a Beloved's, and He is mine" and "His banner over me is love."

"Many waters cannot quench love,
Nor will rivers overflow it;
If a man were to give all the riches
of his house for love,
It would be utterly despised" (8:7).

THINGS TO DO

1. The Song of Solomon is a unified lyrical poem composed of a variety of songs. There's no book like it in Scripture. Before you begin to analyze its content sit down and read it thr slowly without stopping. Remember, the phrases may seem different or unusual because culture of the eastern people.
2. As you read Song of Solomon notice who is speaking when. The reference notes of the N identify who speaks. If you prefer to identify the speaker yourself, do the following:
   a. Read the book again and mark every time the "woman" speaks and also when the " speaks. Watch for the pronouns *he* and *she* and mark them in a distinctive way.
   b. As you read, you will notice there is a third party referred to in the text as "the daught Jerusalem" and in the reference notes in the margin as "Chorus." Note when "the daught Jerusalem" (the chorus) intervenes. When you see any other parties speaking, mark the well. Note these under "Segment Divisions" on the SONG OF SOLOMON AT A GLA chart on page 992.
3. Now read through the Song of Solomon again. This time do the following:
   a. When you note from the text whose song this is, record it under "Author" on SON SOLOMON AT A GLANCE.
   b. As you read, mark the key words listed on SONG OF SOLOMON AT A GLANCE.
   c. Watch for details about the bride and the bridegroom—their position, family, how they where they met, etc. A careful reading of the book as a whole can help you piece together facts. You might want to write your observations on a piece of paper and then transfer the the margin of the text.
   d. Watch for segment divisions in the book. For instance, note when the courtship ends, whe wedding takes place, and what occurs in the marriage and why. (Watch for the word *wed* Record these divisions on SONG OF SOLOMON AT A GLANCE.
   e. Record the theme of each chapter on SONG OF SOLOMON AT A GLANCE and then o line next to the chapter number. Complete the chart.

THINGS TO THINK ABOUT

1. There are many different interpretations about the meaning of this book. Does Song of Solo speak only about the emotional and physical relationship of love and marriage? Or do symbolize something such as Israel's relationship to God, or the church's relationship to J their heavenly bridegroom, or to the individual's devotion to Christ? If it goes beyond the na

o the spiritual, what would you see that you might apply to your relationship with the Lord esus Christ?

f this book speaks merely of the physical and emotional bonds of marriage, what do you learn rom it that you might apply to your relationship with your mate? Think about the way the bride ınd bridegroom communicated with one another, what they shared, what their physical relationhip was like, what caused problems, and how they solved them.

Vhat can you learn from Song of Solomon that would help you prepare for marriage? For nstance, what can you learn from this book about understanding yourself, your future mate, the mportance of intimacy, purity, and physical oneness?

Vhat do you think an adulterous relationship would do to the intimacy between the bride and he bridegroom? James 4:4 tells us that when we become friends with the world (the world system) we're committing spiritual adultery. What does this do to our intimacy with God? Read 2 Corinthians 11:2-3 and think about it.

Chapter 1

Dr, *Best of the* s [a]1 Kin. 4:32

1 The [1]Song of [a]Songs, which is Solomon's.

E [a]Song 1:4; 4:10

2 "[1]May he kiss me with the kisses of his mouth!
For your [a]love is better than wine.
3 "Your [a]oils have a pleasing fragrance,
Your [b]name is *like* [1]purified oil;
Therefore the [2c]maidens love you.
4 "Draw me after you *and* let us run *together!*
The [a]king has brought me into his chambers."

it., *oil which is tied* (from one another) [2]Or, s [a]Song 4:10; 2:3 [b]Eccl. 7:1 [c]Ps. 45:14

"[1]We will rejoice in you and be glad;
We will [2]extol your [b]love more than wine.
Rightly do they love you."

CHORUS [2]Lit., *ion with praise* :14, 15 [b]Song 1:4; 4:10

5 "[1]I am black but [a]lovely,
O [b]daughters of Jerusalem,
Like the [c]tents of [d]Kedar,
Like the curtains of Solomon.
6 "Do not stare at me because I am [1]swarthy,
For the sun has burned me.
My [a]mother's sons were angry with me;
They made me [b]caretaker of the vineyards,
But I have not taken care of my own vineyard.
7 "Tell me, O you [a]whom my soul loves,
Where do you [b]pasture *your flock,*
Where do you make *it* [c]lie down at noon?
For why should I be like one who [1]veils herself
Beside the flocks of your [d]companions?"

E [a]Song 2:14; [b]Song 2:7; 3:5, 8, 16; 8:4 [c]Ps. 120:5 [d]Is. 60:7

black [a]Ps. 69:8 [b]Song 8:11

e versions read *rs* [a]Song 3:1-4 g 2:16; 6:3 [c]Is. er. 33:12 [d]Song 8:13

8 "[1]If you yourself do not know,
[a]Most beautiful among women,
Go forth on the trail of the flock,
And pasture your young goats
By the tents of the shepherds.

BRIDEGROOM [a]Song 5:9; 6:1

9 "[1]To me, [a]my darling, you are like

have compared [a]Song 1:15; 2:2, 10, 13

My [b]mare among the chariots of Pharaoh.
10 "Your [a]cheeks are lovely with ornaments,
Your neck with strings of [b]beads."

11 "[1]We will make for you ornaments of gold
With beads of silver."

12 "[1]While the king was at his [2]table,
My [3a]perfume gave forth its fragrance.
13 "My beloved is to me a pouch of [a]myrrh
Which lies all night between my breasts.
14 "My beloved is to me a cluster of [a]henna blossoms
In the vineyards of [b]Engedi."

15 "[1,2a]How beautiful you are, my darling,
[2]How beautiful you are!
Your [b]eyes are *like* doves."

16 "[1,2]How handsome you are, [a]my beloved,
And so pleasant!
Indeed, our couch is luxuriant!
17 "The beams of our houses are [a]cedars,
Our rafters, [1b]cypresses.

Chapter 2

2 "[1]I am the [2a]rose of [b]Sharon,
The [c]lily of the valleys."

2 "[1]Like a lily among the thorns,
So is [a]my darling among the [2]maidens."

3 "[1]Like an [2a]apple tree among the trees of the forest,
So is my beloved among the [3]young men.
In his shade I took great delight and sat down,
And his [b]fruit was sweet to my [4]taste.
4 "He has [a]brought me to *his* [1]banquet hall,
And his [b]banner over me is love.
5 "Sustain me with [a]raisin cakes,
Refresh me with [1b]apples,
Because [c]I am lovesick.
6 "*Let* [a]his left hand be under my head
And [a]his right hand [b]embrace me."

7 "[1]I [a]adjure you, O [b]daughters of Jerusalem,
By the [c]gazelles or by the [d]hinds of the field,
[a]That you will not arouse or awaken *my* love,
Until [2]she pleases."

8 "[1]Listen! My beloved!
Behold, he is coming,
Climbing [a]on the mountains,
Leaping on the hills!
9 "My beloved is like a [a]gazelle or a [b]young [1]stag.
Behold, he is standing behind our wall,

9 [b]2 Chr. 1:1

10 [a]Song 5:1 24:53; Is. 61:1

11 [1]CHORUS

12 [1]BRIDE [2] [3]Lit., *nard* [a]So Mark 14:3; Jo

13 [a]Ps. 45:8; 19:39

14 [a]Song 4:1 23:29

15 [1]BRIDEG [2]Lit., *Behold* [a] 1:16; 2:10, 13 6:4, 10 [b]Song

16 [1]BRIDE [2] *Behold* [a]Song 17; 5:2, 5, 6, 8

17 [1]Or, *junipe* 6:9, 10; Jer. 22 [b]2 Chr. 3:5

2:1 [1]BRIDE [2] *crocus* [a]Is. 35 33:9; 35:2 [c]So 7:2; Hos. 14:5

2 [1]BRIDEGR [2]Lit., *daughters* 1:9

3 [1]BRIDE [2]Or [3]Lit., *sons* [4]Lit. [a]Song 8:5 [b]So 16; 8:11, 12

4 [1]Lit., *house* [a]Song 1:4 [b]Ps.

5 [1]Or, *apricots* 6:19; 1 Chr. 16 3:1 [b]Song 7:8 5:8

6 [a]Song 8:3 [b]P

7 [1]BRIDEGRO *it* [a]Song 3:5; 5: [b]Song 1:5 [c]Pro Song 2:9, 17; 3 [d]Gen. 49:21; Ps Hab. 3:19

8 [1]BRIDE [a]So Is. 52:7

9 [1]Lit., *of the st* [a]Prov. 6:5; Song 3:5; 8:14 [b]Song 8:14

He is looking through the windows,
He is peering [c]through the lattice.

10 "My beloved responded and said to me,
'[a]Arise, my darling, my beautiful one,
And come along.
11 'For behold, the winter is past,
The rain is over *and* gone.
12 'The flowers have *already* appeared in the land;
The time has arrived for [1]pruning *the vines*,
And the voice of the [a]turtledove has been heard in our land.
13 'The [a]fig tree has ripened its figs,
And the [b]vines in blossom have given forth *their* fragrance.
Arise, my darling, my beautiful one,
And come along!' "

14 "[1]O [a]my dove, [b]in the clefts of the [2]rock,
In the secret place of the steep [3]pathway,
Let me see your [4]form,
[c]Let me hear your voice;
For your voice is sweet,
And your [4]form is [d]lovely."

15 "[1a]Catch the foxes for us,
The [2]little foxes that are ruining the vineyards,
While our [b]vineyards are in blossom."

16 "[1a]My beloved is mine, and I am his;
He [b]pastures *his flock* among the lilies.
17 "[a]Until [1]the cool of the day when the shadows flee away,
Turn, my beloved, and be like a [b]gazelle
Or a young stag [c]on the mountains of [2]Bether."

Chapter 3

3 "[1]On my bed night after night I sought him
[a]Whom my soul loves;
I [b]sought him but did not find him.
2 '[1]I must arise now and [1]go about the city;
In the [a]streets and in the squares
[2]I must seek him whom my soul loves.'
I sought him but did not find him.
3 "[a]The watchmen who make the rounds in the city found me,
And I said, 'Have you seen him whom my soul loves?'
4 "[a]Scarcely had I [1]left them
When I found him whom my soul loves;
I [b]held on to him and would not let him go,
Until I had [c]brought him to my mother's house,
And into the room of her who conceived me."

5 "[1]I [a]adjure you, O daughters of Jerusalem,
By the [b]gazelles or by the hinds of the field,
That you will not arouse or awaken *my* love,
Until [2]she pleases."

9 [c]Judg. 5:28
10 [a]Song 2:13
singing [a]Gen. 74:19; Jer. 8:7
. 24:32 [b]Song 7:12
RIDEGROOM [3]Or, *cliff* [4]Lit., *nce* [a]Song 5:2; r. 48:28 [c]Song :13 [d]Song 1:5
CHORUS [2]Or, *ng* [a]Ezek. 13:4; 32 [b]Song 2:13
IDE [a]Song 6:3; Song 4:5; 6:2, 3
, *the day blows avage or a kind spice* [a]Song 4:6 g 2:9 [c]Song 2:8
RIDE [a]Song 1:7 [b]Song 5:6
et me arise [2]Or, *e seek* [a]Jer. 5:1
g 5:7; Is. 21:6-8, 11, 12
., *passed* [a]Prov. Prov. 4:13; Rom. 5, 39 [c]Song 8:2
DEGROOM [2]Or, Song 2:7; 5:8; 8:4 [b]Song 2:7

6 "[1,2a]What is this coming up from the wilderness
Like [b]columns of smoke,
Perfumed with [c]myrrh and [d]frankincense,
With all scented powders of the merchant?
7 "Behold, it is the *traveling* couch of Solomon;
Sixty mighty men around it,
Of the mighty men of Israel.
8 "All of them are wielders of the sword,
[a]Expert in war;
Each man has his [b]sword at his side,
Guarding against the [1c]terrors of the night.
9 "King Solomon has made for himself a sedan chair
From the timber of Lebanon.
10 "He made its posts of silver,
Its [1]back of gold
And its seat of purple fabric,
With its interior lovingly fitted out
By the [a]daughters of Jerusalem.
11 "Go forth, O [a]daughters of Zion,
And gaze on King Solomon with the [1]crown
With which his mother has crowned him
On the [b]day of his wedding,
And on the day of his gladness of heart."

Chapter 4

4 "[1,2]How beautiful [a]you are, my darling,
[2]How beautiful you are!
Your [b]eyes are *like* doves [c]behind your veil;
Your [d]hair is like a flock of goats
That have descended from Mount [e]Gilead.
2 "Your [a]teeth are like a flock of *newly* shorn ewes
Which have come up from *their* washing,
All of which bear twins,
And not one among them has [1]lost her young.
3 "Your lips are like a [a]scarlet thread,
And your [b]mouth is lovely.
Your [c]temples are like a slice of a pomegranate
Behind your veil.
4 "Your [a]neck is like the tower of David
Built [1]with rows of stones,
On which are [b]hung a thousand shields,
All the round [c]shields of the mighty men.
5 "Your [a]two breasts are like two fawns,
Twins of a gazelle,
Which [b]feed among the lilies.
6 "[a]Until [1]the cool of the day
When the shadows flee away,
I will go my way to the mountain of [b]myrrh
And to the hill of [b]frankincense.

7 "[a]You are altogether beautiful, my darling,
And there is no blemish in you.
8 "*Come* with me from [a]Lebanon, *my* [b]bride,
May you come with me from Lebanon.

6 [1]CHORUS *Who* [a]Song 8 13:21; Joel 2: 1:13; 4:6, 14; [d]Ex. 30:34; Re

8 [1]Lit., *terror i nights* [a]Jer. 50 45:3 [c]Ps. 91:5

10 [1]Or, *suppo* 1:5

11 [1]Or, *wreath* 3:16, 17; 4:4 [b]

4:1 [1]BRIDEG [2]Lit., *Behold* [a]S 1:15 [b]Song 1: [c]Song 6:7 [d]Sor [e]Mic. 7:14

2 [1]Or, *miscarri* [a]Song 6:6

3 [a]Josh. 2:18 5:16 [c]Song 6:7

4 [1]Or, *for an ar* [a]Song 7:4 [b]Eze 11 [c]2 Sam. 1:21

5 [a]Song 7:3 [b]S 2:16; 6:2, 3

6 [1]Lit., *the day b* [a]Song 2:17 [b]Sor

7 [a]Song 1:15; E

8 [a]1 Kin. 4:33; P 72:16 [b]Song 5:1 62:5

[1]Journey down from the summit of [c]Amana,
From the summit of [d]Senir and Hermon,
From the dens of lions,
From the mountains of leopards.
9 "You have made my heart beat faster, [a]my sister, *my* bride;
You have made my heart beat faster with a single *glance* of your eyes,
With a single strand of your [b]necklace.
10 "[a]How beautiful is your love, my sister, *my* bride!
How much [b]better is your love than wine,
And the [c]fragrance of your oils
Than all *kinds* of [1]spices!
11 "Your lips, *my* bride, [a]drip [b]honey;
Honey and milk are under your tongue,
And the fragrance of your garments is like the [c]fragrance of Lebanon.
12 "A garden locked is my sister, *my* bride,
A [1]rock garden locked, a [a]spring [b]sealed up.
13 "Your shoots are an [1a]orchard of [b]pomegranates
With [c]choice fruits, [d]henna with nard plants,
14 [a]Nard and saffron, calamus and [b]cinnamon,
With all the trees of [c]frankincense,
[d]Myrrh and aloes, along with all the finest [1]spices.
15 "*You are* a garden spring,
A well of [1a]fresh water,
And streams *flowing* from Lebanon."

16 "[1]Awake, O north *wind*,
And come, *wind of* the south;
Make my [a]garden breathe out *fragrance*,
Let its [2]spices [3]be wafted abroad.
May [b]my beloved come into his garden
And eat its [c]choice fruits!"

Chapter 5

5 "[1]I have [a]come into my garden, [b]my sister, *my* bride;
I have gathered my [c]myrrh along with my balsam.
I have eaten my honeycomb [2]and my [d]honey;
I have [e]drunk my wine [2]and my milk.
Eat, [f]friends;
Drink and [3]imbibe deeply, O lovers."

2 "[1]I was asleep, but my heart was awake.
A voice! My beloved was knocking:
'Open to me, [a]my sister, my darling,
[b]My dove, my perfect one!
For my head is [2]drenched with dew,
My [c]locks with the [3]damp of the night.'
3 "I have [a]taken off my dress,
How can I put it on *again?*
I have [b]washed my feet,
How can I dirty them *again?*
4 "My beloved extended his hand through the opening,
And my [1a]feelings were aroused for him.

Look [c]2 Kin. ut. 3:9; 1 Chr. 3; Ezek. 27:5

4:10, 12; 5:1, . 41:42; Prov. k. 16:11; Dan. 5:7

balsam odors [b]Song 1:2, 4 [c]Song 1:3

Prov. 5:3 [b]Ps. 0; Prov. 24:13 27; Hos. 14:6

t., *stone heap* 5:15-18 [b]Gen. 29:3

3 [1]Or, *park* or *dise* [a]Eccl. 2:5 1; 7:12 [c]Song 6; 7:13 [d]Song 1:14

balsam odors 12 [b]Ex. 30:23 4:6 [d]Ps. 45:8; :6; John 19:39

, *living* [a]Zech. 4:8; John 4:10

[1]BRIDE [2]Or, *dors* [3]Lit., *flow* [a]Song 5:1; 6:2 :13; 2:3, 8; 6:2 [c]Song 4:13

BRIDEGROOM *h* [3]Or, *become* ong 6:2 [b]Song Song 1:13; 4:14 4:11 [e]Prov. 9:5; 1 [f]Judg. 14:11, 20; John 3:29

RIDE [2]Lit., *filled* *rops* [a]Song 4:9 2:14; 6:9 [c]Song 5:11

1:7 [b]Gen. 19:2

it., *bowels* [a]Jer. 31:20

5 "I arose to open to my beloved;
And my hands [a]dripped with myrrh,
And my fingers with [1]liquid myrrh,
On the handles of the bolt.
6 "I opened to my beloved,
But my beloved had [a]turned away *and* had gone!
My [1]heart went out *to him* as he [b]spoke.
I [c]searched for him, but I did not find him;
I [d]called him, but he did not answer me.
7 "The [a]watchmen who make the rounds in the city found me,
They struck me *and* wounded me;
The guardsmen of the walls took away my shawl from me.
8 "I [a]adjure you, O daughters of Jerusalem,
If you find my beloved,
As to what you will tell him:
For [b]I am lovesick."

9 "[1,2]What kind of beloved is your beloved,
O [a]most beautiful among women?
[2]What kind of beloved is your beloved,
That thus you adjure us?"

10 "[1]My beloved is dazzling and [a]ruddy,
[2b]Outstanding among ten thousand.
11 "His head is *like* gold, pure gold;
His [a]locks are *like* clusters of dates,
And black as a raven.
12 "His [a]eyes are like doves,
Beside streams of water,
Bathed in milk,
And [1]reposed in *their* [b]setting.
13 "His cheeks are like a [a]bed of balsam,
Banks of sweet-scented herbs;
His lips are [b]lilies,
[c]Dripping with liquid myrrh.
14 "His hands are rods of gold
Set with [a]beryl;
His abdomen is carved ivory
Inlaid with [1b]sapphires.
15 "His legs are pillars of alabaster
Set on pedestals of pure gold;
His appearance is like [a]Lebanon,
Choice as the [b]cedars.
16 "His [1a]mouth is *full of* sweetness.
And he is wholly [b]desirable.
This is my beloved and this is my friend,
O daughters of Jerusalem."

Chapter 6

6 "[1a]Where has your beloved gone,
O [b]most beautiful among women?
Where has your beloved turned,
That we may seek him with you?"

5 [1]Lit., *passin*
5:13

6 [1]Lit., *soul* [a]
[b]Song 5:2 [c]S
[d]Prov. 1:28

7 [a]Song 3:3

8 [a]Song 2:7;
2:5

9 [1]CHORUS
is your belove
than another b
[a]Song 1:8; 6:1

10 [1]BRIDE [2]
up banner [a]1
16:12 [b]Ps. 45

11 [a]Song 5:2

12 [1]Lit., *sitting*
[a]Song 1:15; 4:
25:7

13 [a]Song 6:2
2:1 [c]Song 5:5

14 [1]Lit., *lapis l*
[a]Ex. 28:20; 39:
1:16; Dan. 10:6
24:10; 28:18; J
Is. 54:11

15 [a]Song 7:4 [b]
4:33; Ps. 80:10;
17:23; 31:8

16 [1]Lit., *palate*
7:9 [b]2 Sam. 1:2

6:1 [1]CHORUS
5:6 [b]Song 1:8

2 "[1]My beloved has gone down to his [a]garden,
To the [b]beds of balsam,
To [c]pasture *his flock* in the gardens
And gather [d]lilies.
3 "[a]I am my beloved's and my beloved is mine,
He who [b]pastures *his flock* among the lilies."

E [a]Song 4:16; g 5:13 [c]Song Song 2:1; 5:13
ong 2:16; 7:10 Song 2:16; 4:5

4 "[1a]You are as beautiful as [b]Tirzah, my darling,
As [c]lovely as [d]Jerusalem,
As [e]awesome as an [2]army with banners.
5 "Turn your eyes away from me,
For they have confused me;
[a]Your hair is like a flock of goats
That have descended from Gilead.
6 "[a]Your teeth are like a flock of ewes
Which have come up from *their* washing,
All of which bear twins,
And not one among them has [1]lost her young.
7 "[a]Your temples are like a slice of a pomegranate
Behind your veil.
8 "There are sixty [a]queens and eighty concubines,
And [1b]maidens without number;
9 *But* [a]my dove, my perfect one, is [1]unique:
She is her mother's [1]only *daughter;*
She is the pure *child* of the one who bore her.
The [2b]maidens saw her and called her blessed,
The [c]queens and the concubines *also,* and they praised her,
saying,

RIDEGROOM *bannered ones* g 1:15 [b]1 Kin. Song 1:5 [d]Ps. :2 [e]Song 6:10
5 [a]Song 4:1
[1]Or, *miscarried* [a]Song 4:2
7 [a]Song 4:3
virgins [a]1 Kin. 11:3 [b]Song 1:3
[1]Lit., *one* [2]Lit., *ers* [a]Song 2:14; n. 30:13 [c]1 Kin. 11:3

10 'Who is this that [1]grows like the dawn,
As beautiful as the full [a]moon,
As pure [b]as the sun,
As [c]awesome as [2]an army with banners?'
11 "I went down to the orchard of nut trees
To see the blossoms of the valley,
To see whether [a]the vine had budded
Or the [b]pomegranates had bloomed.
12 "Before I was aware, my soul set me
Over the chariots of [1]my noble people."

Lit., *looks down* *bannered ones* :26 [b]Matt. 17:2; 1:16 [c]Song 6:4
ong 7:12 [b]Song 4:13
nother reading is *Ammi-nadib*

13 "[1,2]Come back, come back, O Shulammite;
Come back, come back, that we may gaze at you!"

"[3]**Why** should you gaze at the Shulammite,
As at the [a]dance of [4b]the two companies?

HORUS [2]Ch. 7:1 in Heb. DEGROOM [4]Or, *Mahanaim* [a]Judg. 1:21 [b]Gen. 32:2; 2 Sam. 17:24

Chapter 7

7 "[1]How beautiful are your [2]feet in sandals,
O [3a]prince's daughter!
The curves of your hips are like [4]jewels,
The work of the hands of an artist.
2 "Your navel is *like* a round goblet
Which never lacks mixed wine;
Your belly is like a heap of wheat

[1]Ch. 7:2 in Heb. t., *footsteps* [3]Or, *nobleman's* [4]Or, *nents* [a]Ps. 45:13

Fenced about with lilies.
3 "Your [a]two breasts are like two fawns,
Twins of a gazelle.
4 "Your [a]neck is like a tower of ivory,
Your eyes *like* the pools in [b]Heshbon
By the gate of Bath-rabbim;
Your nose is like the tower of Lebanon,
Which faces toward Damascus.
5 "Your head [1]crowns you like [a]Carmel,
And the flowing locks of your head are like purple threads;
The king is captivated by *your* tresses.
6 "How [a]beautiful and how delightful you are,
[1]*My* love, with *all* your charms!
7 "[1]Your stature is like a palm tree,
And your breasts are *like its* clusters.
8 "I said, 'I will climb the palm tree,
I will take hold of its fruit stalks.'
Oh, may your breasts be like clusters of the vine,
And the fragrance of your [1]breath like [2a]apples,
9 And your [1a]mouth like the best wine!"

"[2]**It** [b]goes *down* smoothly for my beloved,
Flowing gently *through* the lips of those who fall asleep.

10 "[a]I am my beloved's,
And his [b]desire is for me.
11 "Come, my beloved, let us go out into the [1]country,
Let us spend the night in the villages.
12 "Let us rise early *and go* to the vineyards;
Let us [a]see whether the vine has budded
And its blossoms have opened,
And whether the pomegranates have bloomed.
There I will give you my love.
13 "The [a]mandrakes have given forth fragrance;
And over our doors are all [b]choice *fruits*,
Both new and old,
Which I have saved up for you, my beloved.

Chapter 8

8 "Oh that you were like a brother to me
Who nursed at my mother's breasts.
If I found you outdoors, I would kiss you;
No one would despise me, either.
2 "I would lead you *and* [a]bring you
Into the house of my mother, who used to instruct me;
I would give you spiced wine to drink from the juice of my pomegranates.
3 "Let [a]his left hand be under my head,
And his right hand embrace me."

4 "[1a]I want you to swear, O daughters of Jerusalem,
[2]Do not arouse or awaken *my* love,
Until [3]she pleases."

3 [a]Song 4:5

4 [a]Song 4:4 [b]N
21:26

5 [1]Lit., *is upon*

6 [1]Or, With *love*
your delights [a]S
1:15, 16; 4:10

7 [1]Lit., *This stat*
yours

8 [1]Lit., *nose* [2]O
apricots [a]Song 2

9 [1]Lit., *palate* [2]E
[a]Song 5:16 [b]Pro

10 [a]Song 2:16; 6
[b]Ps. 45:11; Gal. 2

11 [1]Lit., *field*

12 [a]Song 6:11

13 [a]Gen. 30:14 [b]
2:3; 4:13, 16; Mat

8:2 [a]Song 3:4

3 [a]Song 2:6

4 [1]BRIDEGROO
Why should you a
[3]Or, *it* [a]Song 2:7;

5 [1]CHORUS [2]BRIDEGROOM [3]Or, *apricot* [a]Song 3:6 [b]Song 2:3

6 [1]Or, *signet* [2]Or, Its *ardor is as inflexible* [3]Another reading is *A vehement flame* [a]Is. 49:16; Jer. 22:24; Hag. 2:23 [b]Prov. 6:34

7 [a]Prov. 6:35

8 [1]CHORUS [a]Ezek. 16:7

9 [a]1 Kin. 6:15

10 [1]BRIDE [a]Ezek. 16:7

11 [a]Eccl. 2:4 [b]Matt. 21:33 [c]Song 1:6 [d]Is. 7:23 [e]Song 2:3; 8:12

12 [1]Lit., *before me*

13 [1]BRIDEGROOM [a]Song 1:7 [b]Song 2:14

14 [1]BRIDE [2]Lit., *Flee* *of the stags* [a]Song 2:7, 9, 17 [b]Song 4:6

5 "[1a]Who is this coming up from the wilderness,
Leaning on her beloved?"

"[2]**B**eneath the [3b]apple tree I awakened you;
There your mother was in labor with you,
There she was in labor *and* gave you birth.
6 "Put me like a [1]seal over your heart,
Like a [a]seal on your arm.
For love is as strong as death,
[2b]Jealousy is as severe as Sheol;
Its flashes are flashes of fire,
[3]The *very* flame of the LORD.
7 "Many waters cannot quench love,
Nor will rivers overflow it;
[a]If a man were to give all the riches of his house for love,
It would be utterly despised."

8 "[1]We have a little sister,
And she [a]has no breasts;
What shall we do for our sister
On the day when she is spoken for?
9 "If she is a wall,
We shall build on her a battlement of silver;
But if she is a door,
We shall barricade her with [a]planks of cedar."

10 "[1]I was a wall, and [a]my breasts were like towers;
Then I became in his eyes as one who finds peace.
11 "Solomon had a [a]vineyard at Baal-hamon;
He [b]entrusted the vineyard to [c]caretakers;
Each one was to bring a [d]thousand *shekels* of silver for its [e]fruit.
12 "My very own vineyard is [1]at my disposal;
The thousand *shekels* are for you, Solomon,
And two hundred are for those who take care of its fruit."

13 "[1]O you who sit in the gardens,
My [a]companions are listening for your voice—
[b]Let me hear it!"

14 "[1,2]Hurry, my beloved,
And be [a]like a gazelle or a young [3]stag
On the [b]mountains of spices."

Song of Solomon at a Glance

Theme of Song of Solomon:

Author:

Date:

Purpose:

Key Words:

love

beloved

come (coming)

beautiful

Segment Divisions

		Chapter Themes
		1
		2
		3
		4
		5
		6
		7
		8

AIAH

e messages of the Old Testament prophets addressed the people of Israel and Judah who lived ›en the years of 840 to 420 B.C. Isaiah is the first of the major prophets. Isaiah's name, *Yeshayahu,* s "Jehovah Saves" or "Salvation of Jehovah." No other prophet gives more prophecies regarding ›ming Messiah. Isaiah reveals the Christ (Messiah) as the Suffering Servant and the Conquering Under divine inspiration Isaiah announces and declares things that are coming and events which ccur in the future so that God's people might know there is no God besides Him.

›m Isaiah 37:37-38 we know Isaiah lived at least until 681 B.C., the year Esar-Haddon, the son of ıcherib, became king of Assyria after his father's death. Tradition says Isaiah was sawed in two by sseh, the king of Judah who reigned after Hezekiah (2 Kings 21:16). If tradition is correct, Isaiah t be one of the heroes of faith referred to in Hebrews 11:37.

IGS TO DO

e basic structure of Isaiah is easy to remember if it's compared to the Bible's structure. The Bible is ›rised of sixty-six books, thirty-nine in the Old Testament and twenty-seven in the New Testament. ı, which focuses on the Holy One of Israel, has sixty-six chapters which fall into two main ›ons: Isaiah 1 through 39 reveals God's character and judgment, and Isaiah 40 through 66 shows s comfort and redemption. Because Isaiah is a long book filled with discourses and songs, it needs studied segment by segment so that you don't miss the wonder of its promises and prophecies. God to help you understand.

›ral Instructions

As you read through Isaiah one chapter at a time, observe each chapter in the light of the five W's and an H. Ask general questions such as: Who does this chapter focus on? What happens or what is this about? When is this happening? Where will it happen? Why is this going to happen and how?

Isaiah is a set of discourses or songs rather than a historical chronology of events in the life of Israel. Periodically there are historical interludes which are very important. In these interludes God often will tell Isaiah to do something which will act as a sign to the people. For instance, in Isaiah 8:3 Isaiah is to name his son *Maher-shalal-hash-baz,* which means "swift is the booty, speedy is the prey." His name pointed the people to the Assyrian invasion which would come before *Maher-shalal-hash-baz* would learn to say Momma or Daddy. Observe these interludes carefully.

Isaiah recorded many prophecies regarding future events including the captivity, the birth of Messiah, the reign of Messiah, and the last days. Watch for these prophecies and note them in the margin. Also check the reference notes to see where they're fulfilled.

a. As you read some of these prophecies you'll see that the first and second coming of Messiah (Christ) can be prophesied without any indication that there is an interval of time between these comings. For instance, Isaiah 61:1 through 2a covers the first coming of Jesus Christ. As a matter of fact Jesus reads this passage in the synagogue in Nazareth and stops at this point (Luke 4:18-19). Why? Because the next part of the verse, "And the day of vengeance of our God," skips to the day of the Lord, which encompasses His judgment and His second coming.

b. You will find it beneficial to read the section in the introduction of this Bible entitled "Guidelines for Interpreting Predictive Prophecy."

c. On page 997 is a chart called THE PROPHETIC POINTS OF HISTORY. Keeping these prophetic points in mind as you read Isaiah will help you distinguish the time periods to which Isaiah refers. You may want to draw this on a card so you can pull it out and look at it as you study Isaiah.

4. Mark every reference to *the day of the Lord* or *the last days* in a distinctive way, then list observations in the margin and on the chart THE DAY OF THE LORD on page 1878 i appendix. It will become a valuable resource on this critical event in the future. Record the chapter, and verse from which you took your information. Do this all the way through Isaia
5. Babylon plays a significant prophetic role throughout Scripture, even in the day of the Lor what you learn about Babylon in the margin of the text. Then record that information on the WHAT THE BIBLE TEACHES ABOUT BABYLON in the appendix of this Bible (pages 187 1877). When you record your observations on Babylon note the reference (book, chapte verse) from which you took your information. You'll want this for future reference.

Isaiah 1-39: God's Character and Judgment

Chapters 1-12: Discourses Regarding Judah and Jerusalem

1. Read Isaiah 1 to get the spiritual and moral condition and the historical setting of this book.
   a. Examine Isaiah 1 carefully under the scrutiny of the five W's and an H: Who? What? W Where? Why? and How? Ask questions such as: Who wrote this? When was it written? was it written? To whom was it written? What do you learn about them? What are they and why? What will happen? Interrogating the text with such questions will give you insight into what is being said in this chapter. Record your insights in the margin of chapt
   b. To put the book into its chronological setting compare Isaiah 1:1 with the historical ch page 997. Record your insights under "Author" and "Date" on the ISAIAH AT A GL chart on pages 1087 and 1088.
2. As you read Isaiah 2 through 12 one chapter at a time:
   a. Mark the following key words in a distinctive way: *remnant, Israel, Judah, Samaria, Assyri Holy One of Israel,* and *Lord of Hosts* (although these two titles refer to God, it is helpful how each is used, so mark them distinctively).
   b. Also mark every occurrence of *in the last days* and *in that day.* As you mark *in that day* sure you know what day it is referring to. For instance, in Isaiah 2 *in that day* refers to th days. Therefore both can be marked in the same way. However, this may not always b case, so check the context in which "that day" is used.
   c. Write all these key words on an index card that you can use as a bookmark while you Isaiah. Color code them so you can mark them quickly.
   d. Watch for key repeated words or phrases which are not on the list but are distinctive to c chapters.
3. As you read each chapter observe the following and record your insights in the margin.
   a. Notice to whom God is speaking and what He says about their behavior.
   b. Observe the consequences of the behavior.
   c. See if there is an exhortation or plea, followed by a promise of how God will cleanse t bless them, or move on their behalf.
4. Isaiah 6 is a strategic chapter. It records Isaiah's call and commission from the Lord.
   a. To get the historical setting of this chapter read 2 Kings 15. Uzziah is called Azariah in 2 K 15:1 (*see* 2 Chronicles 26:1). On the chart at the beginning of Isaiah, you will notice tha reigns of Uzziah and Jotham overlapped. This is because they served as co-regents for a ti
   b. Observe the progression of events in this chapter and note them in the margin.
5. As you study each chapter, don't forget the "General Instructions." These are an important of the process of carefully observing the text.
6. When you finish observing each chapter record the theme of that chapter on ISAIAH A GLANCE and on the line in the text next to the chapter number.

Chapters 13-23: Oracles Against Various Nations

1. As you read this section chapter by chapter, watch for the following key words:

a. Watch for and mark in a distinctive way the key repeated phrase, *the oracle concerning* ____________. Note who the oracle concerns.

b. Mark the following key words: *the Lord of Hosts, Babylon, day of the Lord,* and *remnant.* Write these on a new card to use as a bookmark.

2. As you observe each chapter, note the following in the margin or mark it in the text.

a. Observe if there's any judgment connected with those to whom the oracle is given and why.

b. Watch where the judgment comes and if there's any effect on Israel.

c. Watch for when something happens. Note this with a clock diagram such as this ⏰.

d. Notice how God's purposes are being worked out in history.

3. Record the theme of each chapter in the same manner you did previously. However, remember that this will not always be easy. The chapter divisions in the Bible are not divinely inspired. Therefore, if you have a hard time summarizing the theme of each chapter, don't be discouraged. When it's not easy to settle on a chapter theme, pick a key verse that the truths of the chapter seem to pivot around, or simply choose some words from the first verse and record these on ISAIAH AT A GLANCE.

apters 24-27: Discourses Regarding "That Day"

1. As you read this segment, mark the following key words: *earth, in that day, salvation,* and *Lord of Hosts.*

2. As you read each chapter observe the following:

a. What happens to the earth and its inhabitants (humans and animals)

b. What the Lord of hosts will do and where He will be

c. What the people's response will be

3. Record the theme of each chapter on ISAIAH AT A GLANCE and in the text.

apters 28-33: Six Woes

1. As you read each chapter watch for and mark the following key words: *woe, the Holy One of Israel, the Lord of Hosts, remnant, Spirit (the* or *My), in that day,* and *salvation.*

2. As you read each of these chapters, note in the margin or mark in the text the following:

a. To whom the woe is given

b. What was done to cause the woe

c. What the Lord will do and what the result will be

3. Record the chapter themes on ISAIAH AT A GLANCE and in the text.

apters 34-35: God's Recompense and Ransom for Zion

1. As you read these two chapters, mark the following key words: *nations* (and any pronouns), *sword, recompense, glory,* and *ransomed.*

2. Look for and list in the margin on whom God's recompense will come, what it will be, and what will follow. Make sure you note what happens to the ransomed, the redeemed. Also note what this will mean to Zion.

3. Record the chapter themes on ISAIAH AT A GLANCE and in the text.

apters 36-39: Historical Account from the Threat of Assyria to the Threat of Babylon

1. Read these chapters and mark the following words: *Assyria, Sennacherib, Rabshakeh, Hezekiah, Isaiah, Babylon, remnant, Lord of Hosts,* and *prayer (prayed).*

2. Now read the chapters again, observing the words you marked. In the margin note what you learn about each of the characters and what they do, what happens as a result, and how God intervenes. List what you learn about God from this chapter. Don't miss what happens to Assyria and Babylon. This is a pivotal point in respect to these two powers and the nation of Israel.

3. Record the chapter themes on ISAIAH AT A GLANCE and in the text.

Isaiah 40-66: God's Comfort and Redemption

Chapters 40-48: Behold the Lord, Your Redeemer

1. Mark the following references to God in a distinctive way: *Lord of Hosts, Holy One of Israel, I a* *Lord (God), no one beside Me (no other God),* and *Redeemer*. Then list in the margin all you see a God that you want to remember for future reference. Note God's character, what He does, a what or whom He is compared.
2. As you do all this don't simply mark these and move on. Meditate on what you see. Thi what these insights can do for your relationship with God. Remember, He is not only Is redeemer but yours also if you have repented and believed in the Lord Jesus Christ.
3. Also mark *servant*. As you read each chapter, check the context (the surrounding verses) in w *servant* is used. This is vital. Note whether *servant* refers to Israel (Jacob) or to the Lord Christ. Record your insights in the margin. If it seems to be a prophetic reference to Jesus, c the reference notes and see if the New Testament verses show how this prophecy was fulfille Jesus. When you make your list in the margin put it under "Israel the Servant" or "Messia Servant."
4. Mark every reference to *redeemed* and *redemption* and list in the margin what you learn abou redeemed. Then once again mark *remnant* (used only one time in this segment), *glory of the* *salvation, nation* and *nations*, and *Babylon*. In the margin record what you learn about each.
5. Put the key words for this segment on a card to use as a bookmark in studying the remaind Isaiah. *Remnant, no God beside me,* and *Babylon* do not appear after this segment.
6. Record your chapter themes as before. Fill in the second line of the segment division for chapters.

Chapters 49-57: Your Redeemer Will Save

1. As you read through this segment, add the following key words to your bookmark: *cove* *Zion,* and *Jerusalem*. Mark *Zion* and *Jerusalem* in the same way. In the margin note what observe from marking these words. Don't forget to delete key words which no longer appear.
2. Do everything you did under numbers 1 through 5 in the previous segment. Watch carefull that the Lord can and will do and note it in the margin. Observe the text carefully to see why segment is titled "Your Redeemer Will Save." Watch for God's instructions and take them to he
3. Watch for prophetic verses which come in the midst of what Isaiah is saying. Give sp attention to 50:6 and 52:13 through 53:12. After you observe Isaiah 53, read it through on knees and substitute your name every time you see *we* or *us*.
4. Look for and record the theme of each chapter. Fill in the second line of the segment divisio these chapters. Then if you think it will be helpful, summarize and list in the margin the points covered in the chapter.

Chapters 58-66: Your Redeemer Will Come

1. Once again mark the key words on your bookmark. Delete *Lord of Hosts* as it's not mentione this segment. Servant becomes *servants* in this segment—don't miss it.
2. There's much in this segment about the events that surround or accompany the Lord's comi reign and what will follow—even in regard to the new heaven and new earth. In the margi what you observe. Also watch for practical lessons and list what you learn in the margin. instance, in Isaiah 58 you'll gain insights on fasting.
3. Once again continue marking everything as you have done in the last two segments u 1 through 5 (Isaiah 40-48).
4. Record your chapter themes and then complete ISAIAH AT A GLANCE. Fill in the second li the segment division for these chapters. Write in any new segment divisions you have seen.

THINGS TO THINK ABOUT

1. God's character never changes; therefore what distressed Him in the days of Isaiah still distre Him. And what He had to judge then, He cannot overlook now. Is there anything in your life

must confess and forsake? And what if you're not willing to do so? Will God be able to overlook it? Think about what you learned about God and His ways.

2. God is sovereign. He ruled over the nations in the days of Israel. Does He do the same today? What, then, can you know? How will your nation fit into all this?

3. Amos says God doesn't do anything without first revealing it to His servants the prophets (Amos 3:7), therefore from studying Isaiah what do you know with an absolute certainty is going to come to pass? If the prophecies regarding the first coming of Jesus Christ literally came to pass (and they did), won't the prophecies regarding His second coming be literally fulfilled? How then are you going to live?

The Prophetic Points of History

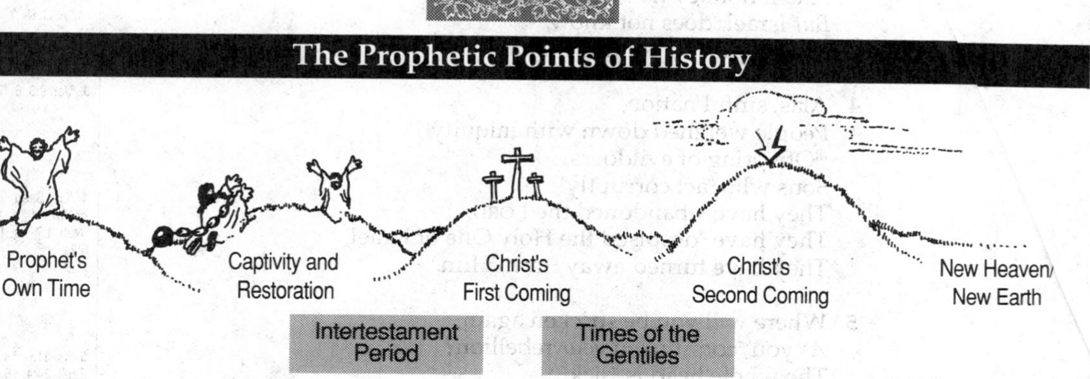

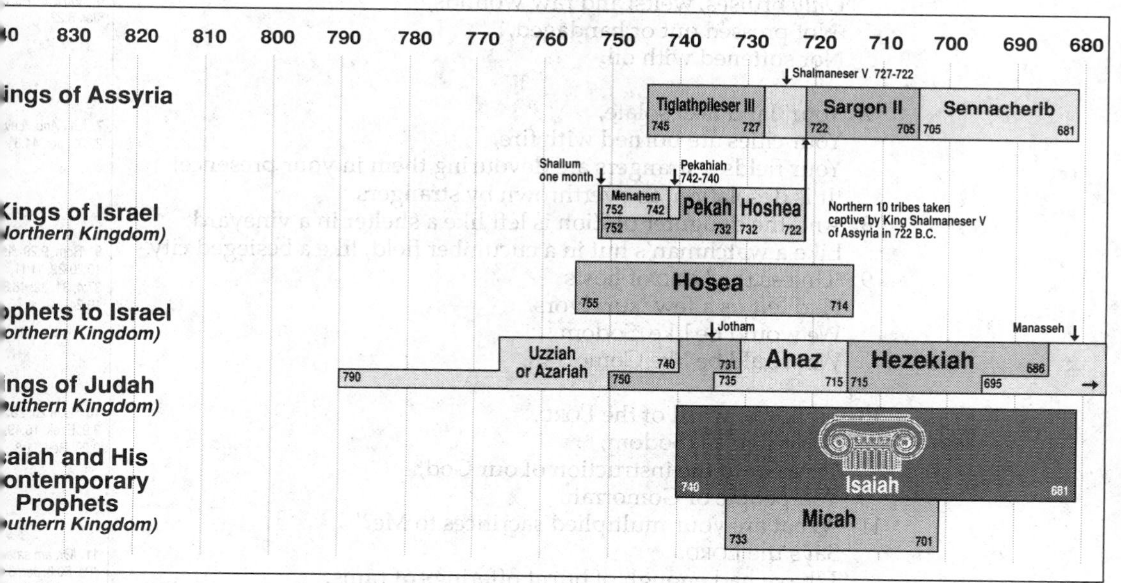

Chapter 1

1 The vision of Isaiah the son of Amoz, concerning [a]Judah and Jerusalem which he saw during the [1]reigns of [b]Uzziah, [c]Jotham, [d]Ahaz, *and* [e]Hezekiah, kings of Judah.

2 [a]Listen, O heavens, and hear, O [b]earth;
For the LORD speaks,
"[c]Sons I have reared and brought up,
But they have [d]revolted against Me.
3 "An ox knows its owner,
And a donkey its master's manger,
But Israel [a]does not know,
My people [b]do not understand."

4 Alas, sinful nation,
People weighed down with iniquity,
[1a]Offspring of evildoers,
Sons who [b]act corruptly!
They have [c]abandoned the LORD,
They have [d]despised the Holy One of Israel,
They have turned away [2]from Him.

5 Where will you be stricken again,
As you [a]continue in *your* rebellion?
The whole head is [b]sick,
And the whole heart is faint.
6 [a]From the sole of the foot even to the head
There is [b]nothing sound in it,
Only bruises, welts, and raw wounds,
[c]Not pressed out or bandaged,
Nor softened with oil.

7 Your [a]land is desolate,
Your cities are burned with fire,
Your fields—strangers are devouring them in your presence;
[1]It is desolation, as overthrown by strangers.
8 And the daughter of Zion is left like a shelter in a vineyard,
Like a watchman's hut in a cucumber field, like a besieged city.
9 [a]Unless the LORD of hosts
Had left us a few [b]survivors,
We would be like [c]Sodom,
We would be like Gomorrah.

10 Hear [a]the word of the LORD,
You rulers of [b]Sodom;
Give ear to the instruction of our God,
You people of Gomorrah.
11 "[a]What are your multiplied sacrifices to Me?"
Says the LORD.
"I [1]have had enough of burnt offerings of rams,
And the fat of fed cattle.
And I take no pleasure in the blood of bulls, lambs, or goats.
12 "When you come [a]to appear before Me,
Who requires [1]of you this trampling of My courts?
13 "Bring your worthless offerings no longer,

1:1 [1]Lit., *days* ... 40:9 [b]2 Kin. 15... 2 Chr. 26:1-23 ... 15:32-38; 2 Ch... [d]2 Kin. 16:1-20 ... 28:1-27; Is. 7:1 ... 18:1-20:21; 2 C... 29:1-32:33

2 [a]Deut. 32:1 ... [c]Jer. 3:22 [d]Is. 3... 65:2

3 [a]Jer. 9:3, 6 [b]...

4 [1]Lit., *Seed* [2]... *backward* [a]Is. ... [b]Neh. 1:7 [c]Is. 1... 5:24

5 [a]Is. 31:6 [b]Is. ... Ezek. 34:4, 16

6 [a]Job 2:7 [b]Ps. ... [c]Jer. 8:22

7 [1]Lit., *And* [a]Le... 26:33; Jer. 44:6

9 [a]Rom. 9:29 [b]... 10:20-22; 11:11, ... 37:4, 31, 32; 46:... 19:24

10 [a]Is. 8:20; 28:... 3:9; Ezek. 16:49... 9:29; Rev. 11:8

11 [1]Or, *am sated* ... [a]Ps. 50:8; Jer. 6:2... Amos 5:21, 22; M...

12 [1]Lit., *of your* ... [a]Ex. 23:17

13 [a]Is. 66:3 [b]1 Chr. 31 [c]Ex. 12:16 [d]Jer. 7:9, 10

[a]Incense is an abomination to Me.
[b]New moon and sabbath, the [c]calling of assemblies—
I cannot [d]endure iniquity and the solemn assembly.
14 "I hate your new moon *festivals* and your [a]appointed feasts,
They have become a burden to Me.
I am [b]weary of bearing *them*.
15 "So when you [a]spread out your hands *in prayer*,
[b]I will hide My eyes from you,
Yes, even though you [c]multiply prayers,
I will not listen.
[d]Your hands are [1]covered with blood.

14 [a]Is. 29:1, 2 [b]Is. 7:13; 43:24

[1]Lit., *full of* [a]1 Kin. :22; Lam. 1:17 [b]Is. 59:2 [c]Mic. 3:4 [d]Is. 59:3

16 "[a]Wash yourselves, [b]make yourselves clean;
[c]Remove the evil of your deeds from My sight.
[d]Cease to do evil,
17 Learn to do good;
[a]Seek justice,
Reprove the ruthless;
[1b]Defend the orphan,
Plead for the widow.

Ps. 26:6 [b]Is. 52:11 [c]Is. 55:7 [d]Jer. 25:5

[1]Or, *Vindicate the* *herless* [a]Jer. 22:3; eph. 2:3 [b]Ps. 82:3

18 "Come now, and [a]let us reason together,"
Says the LORD,
"[b]Though your sins are as scarlet,
They will be as white as snow;
Though they are red like crimson,
They will be like wool.
19 "[a]If you consent and obey,
You will [b]eat the best of the land;
20 "But if you refuse and rebel,
You will be [a]devoured by the sword."
Truly, [b]the mouth of the LORD has spoken.

Is. 41:1, 21; 43:26; . 6:2 [b]Ps. 51:7; Is. ; 44:22; Rev. 7:14

[a]Deut. 28:1; 30:15, 16 [b]Is. 55:2

s. 3:25; 65:12 [b]Is. 5; 58:14; Mic. 4:4; Titus 1:2

21 How the faithful city has become a [a]harlot,
She *who* was full of justice!
Righteousness once lodged in her,
But now murderers.
22 Your silver has become dross,
Your drink diluted with water.
23 Your [a]rulers are rebels,
And companions of thieves;
Everyone [b]loves a bribe,
And chases after rewards.
They [c]do not [1]defend the [2]orphan,
Nor does the widow's plea come before them.

. 57:3-9; Jer. 2:20

Or, *vindicate* [2]Or, *erless* [a]Hos. 5:10; :3 [b]Ex. 23:8; Mic. Is. 10:2; Jer. 5:28; . 22:7; Zech. 7:10

24 Therefore the Lord [1]GOD of hosts,
The [a]Mighty One of Israel declares,
"Ah, I will be relieved of My adversaries,
And [b]avenge Myself on My foes.
25 "I will also turn My hand against you,
And will [a]smelt away your dross as with lye,
And will remove all your alloy.
26 "Then I will restore your [a]judges as at the first,

24 [1]Heb., *YHWH*, ly rendered *LORD* . 132:2; Is. 49:26; [b]Deut. 28:63; Is. 59:18; 61:2; 63:4

[a]Ezek. 22:19-22; Mal. 3:3

26 [a]Is. 60:17

And your counselors as at the beginning;
After that you will be called the [b]city of righteousness,
A faithful city."

27 Zion will be [a]redeemed with justice,
And her [1]repentant ones with righteousness.
28 But [1]transgressors and sinners will be [a]crushed together,
And those who forsake the LORD shall come to an end.
29 Surely, [1]you will be ashamed of the [2a]oaks which you have desired,
And you will be embarrassed at the [b]gardens which you have chosen.
30 For you will be like an [1]oak whose [a]leaf fades away,
Or as a garden that has no water.
31 And the strong man will become tinder,
His work also a spark.
Thus they shall both [a]burn together,
And there will be [b]none to quench *them*.

Chapter 2

2 The word which [a]Isaiah the son of Amoz saw concerning Judah and Jerusalem.
2 Now it will come about that
[a]In the last days,
The [b]mountain of the house of the LORD
Will be established [1]as the chief of the mountains,
And will be raised above the hills;
And [c]all the nations will stream to it.
3 And many peoples will come and say,
"Come, let us go up to the mountain of the LORD,
To the house of the God of Jacob;
That He may teach us [1]concerning His ways,
And that we may walk in His paths."
For the [2]law will go forth [a]from Zion,
And the word of the LORD from Jerusalem.
4 And He will judge between the nations,
And will [1]render decisions for many peoples;
And [a]they will hammer their swords into plowshares, and their spears into pruning hooks.
[b]Nation will not lift up sword against nation,
And never again will they learn war.

5 Come, [a]house of Jacob, and let us walk in the [b]light of the LORD.
6 For Thou hast [a]abandoned Thy people, the house of Jacob,
Because they are filled *with influences* from the east,
And *they are* soothsayers [b]like the Philistines,
And they [c]strike *bargains* with the children of foreigners.
7 Their land has also been filled with silver and gold,
And there is no end to their treasures;
Their land has also been filled with [a]horses,
And there is no end to their chariots.
8 Their land has also been [a]filled with idols;
They worship the [b]work of their hands,
That which their fingers have made.

26 [b]Is. 33:5; 60:14; 62:1, 2; Zech. 8:3

27 [1]Or, *returnees* 35:9f.; 62:12; 63:4

28 [1]Lit., the *crush transgressors and sinners shall be together* [a]Ps. 9:5; 66:24; 2 Thess. 1:8

29 [1]So with some M.T., *they* [2]Or, *terebinths* [a]Is. 57:5; 65:3; 66:17

30 [1]Or, *terebinth* 64:6

31 [a]Is. 5:24; 9:19; 26:11; 33:11-14 [b]I 66:24; Matt. 3:12; 9:43

2:1 [a]Is. 1:1

2 [1]Lit., *on* [a]Mic. 4 [b]Is. 27:13; 66:20 56:7

3 [1]Or, *some of* [2]O *instruction* [a]Is. 51 Luke 24:47

4 [1]Or, *reprove ma* [a]Is. 32:17, 18; Joe [b]Is. 9:5, 7; 11:6-9; 2:18; Zech. 9:10

5 [a]Is. 58:1 [b]Is. 60 19, 20; 1 John 1:5

6 [a]Deut. 31:17 [b]2 1:2 [c]2 Kin. 16:7, 8 Prov. 6:1

7 [a]Deut. 17:16; Is 30:16; 31:1; Mic.

8 [a]Is. 10:11 [b]Ps. 115:4-8; Is. 17:8; 40:19; 44:17

9 So [a]the *common* man has been humbled,
And the man *of importance* has been abased,
But [b]do not forgive them.
10 [a]Enter the rock and hide in the dust
[b]From the terror of the LORD and from the splendor of His majesty.
11 The [1a]proud look of man will be abased,
And the [b]loftiness of man will be humbled,
And the LORD alone will be exalted in that day.

12 For the LORD of hosts will have a day *of reckoning*
Against [a]everyone who is proud and lofty,
And against everyone who is lifted up,
That he may be abased.
13 And *it will be* against all the cedars of Lebanon that are lofty and lifted up,
Against all the [a]oaks of Bashan,
14 Against all the [a]lofty mountains,
Against all the hills that are lifted up,
15 Against every [a]high tower,
Against every fortified wall,
16 Against all the [a]ships of Tarshish,
And against all the beautiful craft.
17 And the pride of man will be humbled,
And the loftiness of men will be abased,
And the LORD alone will be exalted in that day.
18 But the [a]idols will completely vanish.
19 And *men* will [a]go into caves of the rocks,
And into holes of the [1]ground
Before the terror of the LORD,
And before the splendor of His majesty,
When He arises [b]to make the earth tremble.
20 In that day men will [a]cast away to the moles and the [b]bats
Their idols of silver and their idols of gold,
Which they made for themselves to worship,
21 In order to [a]go into the caverns of the rocks and the clefts of the cliffs,
Before the terror of the LORD and the splendor of His majesty,
When He arises to make the earth tremble.
22 [1a]Stop regarding man, whose breath *of life* is in his nostrils;
For [2b]why should he be esteemed?

Chapter 3

3 For behold, the Lord [1]GOD of hosts [a]is going to remove from Jerusalem and Judah
Both [2]supply and support, the whole [2]supply of bread,
And the whole [2]supply of water;
2 [a]The mighty man and the warrior,
The judge and the prophet,
The diviner and the elder,
3 The captain of fifty and the honorable man,
The counselor and the expert artisan,
And the skillful enchanter.
4 And I will make mere [a]lads their princes

[a]Ps. 49:2; 62:9; Is. 5:15 [b]Neh. 4:5
…[a]Is. 2:19, 21; Rev. …5, 16 [b]2 Thess. 1:9
11 [1]Lit., *eyes of the …oftiness of men* [a]Is. …; 37:23 [b]Ps. 18:27; …13:11; 23:9; 2 Cor. 10:5
[a]Job 40:11, 12; Is. 24:4, 21; Mal. 4:1
13 [a]Zech. 11:2
14 [a]Is. 40:4
15 [a]Is. 25:12
…6 [a]1 Kin. 10:22; Is. 23:1, 14; 60:9
[a]Is. 21:9; Mic. 1:7
…[1]Lit., *dust* [a]Is. 2:10 [b]Ps. 18:7; Is. 2:21; …3:13; 24:1, 19, 20; …2:6, 7; Heb. 12:26
…20 [a]Is. 30:22; 31:7 [b]Lev. 11:19
21 [a]Is. 2:19
[1]Lit., *Cease from* [2]Lit., *in what* [a]Ps. …6:3; Jer. 17:5 [b]Ps. …144:3, 4; Is. 40:15, 17; James 4:14
…:1 [1]Heb., *YHWH*, …lly rendered *LORD* …*staff* [a]Lev. 26:26; …; 9:20; Ezek. 4:16
…n. 24:14; Is. 9:14, …5, Ezek. 17:12, 13
4 [a]Eccl. 10:16

[1]capricious children will rule over them,
d the people will be [a]oppressed,
5 ch one by another, and each one by his [b]neighbor;
ne youth will storm against the elder,
And the inferior against the honorable.
When a man [a]lays hold of his brother in his father's house,
saying,
"You have a cloak, you shall be our ruler,
And these ruins will be under your [1]charge,"
7 On that day will he [1]protest, saying,
"I will not be *your* [2a]healer,
For in my house there is neither bread nor cloak;
You should not appoint me ruler of the people."
8 For [a]Jerusalem has stumbled, and Judah has fallen,
Because their [1b]speech and their actions are against the LORD,
To [c]rebel against [2]His glorious presence.
9 [1]The expression of their faces bears witness against them.
And they display their sin like [a]Sodom;
They do not *even* conceal *it*.
Woe to [2]them!
For they have [b]brought evil on themselves.
10 Say to the [a]righteous that *it will go* well *with them,*
For they will eat the fruit of their actions.
11 Woe to the wicked! *It will go* badly *with him,*
For [1a]what he deserves will be done to him.
12 O My people! Their oppressors [1]are [a]children,
And women rule over them.
O My people! [b]Those who guide you lead *you* astray,
And confuse the direction of your paths.

13 [a]The LORD arises to contend,
And stands to judge the people.
14 The LORD [a]enters into judgment with the elders and princes of
His people,
"It is you who have [b]devoured the vineyard;
The [c]plunder of the poor is in your houses.
15 "What do you mean by [a]crushing My people,
And grinding the face of the poor?"
Declares the Lord [1]GOD of hosts.

16 Moreover, the LORD said, "Because the [a]daughters of Zion are
proud,
And walk with [1]heads held high and seductive eyes,
And go along with mincing steps,
And tinkle the bangles on their feet,
17 Therefore the Lord will afflict the scalp of the daughters of Zion
with scabs,
And the LORD will make their foreheads bare."
18 In that day the Lord will take away the beauty of *their* anklets,
headbands, [a]crescent ornaments,
19 dangling earrings, bracelets, veils,
20 [a]headdresses, ankle chains, sashes, perfume boxes, amulets,
21 [1]finger rings, [a]nose rings,
22 festal robes, outer tunics, cloaks, money purses,

4 [1]Lit., *arbitrary pow will rule*

5 [a]Mic. 7:3-6 [b]Is. 9 Jer. 9:3-8

6 [1]Lit., *hand* [a]Is. 4:

7 [1]Lit., *lift up his vo* [2]Lit., *binder of wour* [a]Ezek. 34:4; Hos. 5

8 [1]Lit., *tongue* [2]Lit *eyes of His glory* [a] 1:7; 6:11 [b]Ps. 73:9 Is. 9:17; 59:3 [c]Is. 6

9 [1]Or, *Their partia bears* [2]Lit., *their s* [a]Gen. 13:13; Is. 1: [b]Prov. 8:36; 15:32 6:23

10 [a]Deut. 28:1-14 8:12; Is. 54:17

11 [1]Lit., *the deali his hands* [a]Deut. 28:15-68; Is. 65:6

12 [1]Or, *deal sev* [a]Is. 3:4 [b]Is. 9:16; 28:14, 15

13 [a]Is. 66:16; Ho Mic. 6:2

14 [a]Job 22:4; Ps 143:2; Ezek. 20: [b]Ps. 14:4; Mic. 3 24:9, 14; Ps. 10: 30:14; Is. 10:1, 2 18:12; James 2:

15 [1]Heb., *YHW usually rendere* [a]Ps. 94:5

16 [1]Lit., *outstre necks* [a]Song 3 3:16-4:1, 4; 32:

18 [a]Judg. 8:21

20 [a]Ex. 39:28

21 [1]Or, *signet* [a]Gen. 24:47; E

23 hand mirrors, undergarments, turbans, and veils.
24 Now it will come about that instead of [1]sweet [a]perfume there
will be putrefaction;
Instead of a belt, a rope;
Instead of [b]well-set hair, a [c]plucked-out scalp;
Instead of fine clothes, a [d]donning of sackcloth;
And branding instead of beauty.
25 Your men will [a]fall by the sword,
And your [1]mighty ones in battle.
26 And her [1a]gates will lament and mourn;
And deserted she will [b]sit on the ground.

Chapter 4

4 For seven women will take hold of [a]one man in that day, saying, "We will eat our own bread and wear our own clothes, only let us be called by your name; [b]take away our reproach!"

2 In that day the [a]Branch of the LORD will be beautiful and glorious, and the [b]fruit of the earth *will* be the pride and the adornment of the [c]survivors of Israel.

3 And it will come about that he who is [a]left in Zion and remains in Jerusalem will be called [b]holy—everyone who is [c]recorded for life in Jerusalem.

4 When the Lord has washed away the filth of the [a]daughters of Zion, and [1]purged the [b]bloodshed of Jerusalem from her midst, by the [c]spirit of judgment and the [d]spirit of burning,

5 then the LORD will create over the whole area of Mount Zion and over her assemblies [a]a cloud by day, even smoke, and the brightness of a flaming fire by night; for over all the [b]glory will be a canopy.

6 And there will be a [a]shelter to *give* shade from the heat by day, and refuge and [1]protection from the storm and the rain.

Chapter 5

5 Let me sing now for my well-beloved
A song of my beloved concerning His vineyard.
My well-beloved had a [a]vineyard on [1]a fertile hill.
2 And He dug it all around, removed its stones,
And planted it with [1]the [a]choicest vine.
And He built a tower in the middle of it,
And hewed out a [2]wine vat in it;
Then He [b]expected *it* to produce *good* grapes,
But it produced *only* [3]worthless ones.

3 "And now, O inhabitants of Jerusalem and men of Judah,
[a]Judge between Me and My vineyard.
4 "[a]What more was there to do for My vineyard [1]that I have not
done in it?
Why, when I expected *it* to produce *good* grapes did it produce
[2]worthless ones?
5 "So now let Me tell you what I am going to do to My vineyard:
I will [a]remove its hedge and it will be consumed;
I will [b]break down its wall and it will become [c]trampled ground.
6 "And I will [a]lay it waste;
It will not be pruned or hoed,
But briars and thorns will come up.

24 [1]Or, *balsam oil* ...h. 2:12 [b]1 Pet. 3:3 ...2:12; Ezek. 27:31; ...nos 8:10 [d]Is. 15:3; Lam. 2:10
[1]Lit., *strength* [a]Is. 1:20; 65:12
...t., *entrances* [a]Jer. ...2; Lam. 1:4 [b]Lam. 2:10
[a]Is. 13:12 [b]Gen. 30:23; Is. 54:4
...Is. 11:1; 53:2; Jer. ...; 33:15; Zech. 3:8; ...2 [b]Ps. 72:16 [c]Is. ...0; 37:31, 32; Joel 2:32; Obad. 17
...28:5; 46:3; Rom. ...5 [b]Is. 52:1; 62:12 ...32:32; Ps. 69:28; Luke 10:20
...*rinsed away* [a]Is. ...[b]Is. 1:15 [c]Is. 28:6 ...; 9:19; Matt. 3:11
...13:21, 22; 24:16; ...lum. 9:15-23 [b]Is. 60:1, 2
...it., *a hiding place* ...Ps. 27:5; Is. 25:4; 32:1, 2
[1]Lit., *a horn, the* ...*n of fatness* [a]Ps. ...Jer. 12:10; Matt. ...Mark 12:1; Luke 20:9
[1]Lit., *a bright red* ...[2]Or, *wine press* ...*wild grapes* [a]Jer. ...latt. 21:19; Mark 11:13; Luke 13:6
3 [a]Matt. 21:40
..., *and I have not* [2]Or, *wild grapes* ...36:16; Jer. 2:5; ...5; Mic. 6:3; Matt. 23:37
[a]Ps. 89:40 [b]Ps. ...[c]Is. 10:6; 28:18; ...:15; Luke 21:24; Rev. 11:2
...hr. 36:19-21; Is. ...25; 24:1, 3; Jer. 25:11

l also charge the clouds to [b]rain no rain on it."

7 For the [a]vineyard of the LORD of hosts is the house of Israel,
And the men of Judah His delightful plant.
Thus He looked for justice, but behold, [b]bloodshed;
For righteousness, but behold, a cry of distress.

8 Woe to those who [a]add house to house *and* join field to field,
Until there is no more room,
So that you have to live alone in the midst of the land!
9 In my ears the LORD of hosts *has sworn,* "Surely, [a]many houses shall become [b]desolate,
Even great and fine ones, without occupants.
10 "For [a]ten acres of vineyard will yield *only* one [1]bath *of wine,*
And a [b]homer of seed will yield *but* an [2]ephah of grain."
11 Woe to those who rise early in the morning that they may pursue [a]strong drink;
Who stay up late in the evening that wine may inflame them!
12 And their banquets are *accompanied* by lyre and [a]harp, by tambourine and flute, and by wine;
But they [b]do not pay attention to the deeds of the LORD,
Nor do they consider the work of His hands.

13 Therefore My people go into exile for their [a]lack of knowledge;
And [1]their [b]honorable men are famished,
And their multitude is parched with thirst.
14 Therefore [a]Sheol has enlarged its [1]throat and opened its mouth without measure;
And [2]Jerusalem's splendor, her multitude, her din *of revelry,* and the jubilant within her, descend *into it.*
15 So the *common* man will be humbled, and the man of *importance* abased,
[a]The eyes of the proud also will be abased.
16 But the [a]LORD of hosts will be [b]exalted in judgment,
And the holy God will show Himself [c]holy in righteousness.
17 [a]Then the lambs will graze as in their pasture,
And strangers will eat in the waste places of the [1]wealthy.

18 Woe to those who drag [a]iniquity with the cords of [1]falsehood,
And sin as if with cart ropes;
19 [a]Who say, "Let Him make speed, let Him hasten His work, that we may see *it;*
And let the purpose of the Holy One of Israel draw near
And come to pass, that we may know *it!*"
20 Woe to those who [a]call evil good, and good evil;
Who [1b]substitute darkness for light and light for darkness;
Who [1]substitute bitter for sweet, and sweet for bitter!
21 Woe to those who are [a]wise in their own eyes,
And clever in their own sight!
22 [a]Woe to those who are heroes in drinking wine,
And valiant men in mixing strong drink;
23 [a]Who justify the wicked for a bribe,
And [b]take away the [1]rights of the ones who are in the right!

6 [b]1 Kin. 8:35; 17:1 Jer. 14:1-22
7 [a]Ps. 80:8-11 [b]Is 3:14, 15; 30:12; 59
8 [a]Jer. 22:13-17; M 2:2; Hab. 2:9-12
9 [a]Is. 6:11, 12 [b]M 23:38
10 [1]I.e., Approx. 1 gal. [2]I.e., Approx. bu. [a]Lev. 26:26; Is 7:23; Hag. 1:6; 2:1 [b]Ezek. 45:11
11 [a]Prov. 23:29, 3 Eccl. 10:16, 17; Is 22:13; 28:1, 3, 7, 8
12 [a]Amos 6:5, 6 34:27; Ps. 28:5
13 [1]Lit., *their glor men of famine* [a]Is 27:11; Hos. 4:6 [b]I
14 [1]Or, *appetite her* [a]Prov. 30:16; 2:5
15 [a]Is. 2:11; 10:3
16 [a]Is. 28:17; 30: 61:8 [b]Is. 2:11, 17 10 [c]Is. 8:13; 29:2 1 Pet. 3:15
17 [1]Lit., *the fat* [a] 7:25; Mic. 2:12; Z 2:6
18 [1]Or, *worthless* [a]Is. 59:4-8; Jer. 2
19 [a]Ezek. 12:22 3:4
20 [1]Lit., *set* [a]Pr 17:15; Amos 5:7 17:12; Matt. 6:22 Luke 11:34, 35
21 [a]Prov. 3:7; R 12:16; 1 Cor. 3:1
22 [a]Prov. 23:20; 5:11; 56:12; Hab
23 [1]Lit., *righteo* [a]Ex. 23:8; Is. 1:2 2; Mic. 3:11; 7:3 94:21; James 5

24 Therefore, [a]as a tongue of fire consumes stubble,
And dry grass collapses into the flame,
So their [b]root will become [c]like rot and their blossom [1]blow away as dust;
For they have [d]rejected the law of the LORD of hosts,
And despised the word of the Holy One of Israel.
25 On this account the [a]anger of the LORD has burned against His people,
And He has stretched out His hand against them and struck them down,
And the [b]mountains quaked; and their [c]corpses [1]lay like refuse in the middle of the streets.
[d]For all this His anger [2]is not spent,
But His [e]hand is still stretched out.

26 He will also lift up a [a]standard to the [1]distant nation,
And will [b]whistle for it [c]from the ends of the earth;
And behold, it will [d]come with speed swiftly.
27 [a]No one in it is weary or stumbles,
None slumbers or sleeps;
Nor is the [b]belt at its waist undone,
Nor its sandal strap broken.
28 [1a]Its arrows are sharp, and all its bows are bent;
The hoofs of its horses [2]seem like flint, and its *chariot* [b]wheels like a whirlwind.
29 Its [a]roaring is like a lioness, and it roars like young lions;
It growls as it [b]seizes the prey,
And carries *it* off with [c]no one to deliver *it*.
30 And it shall [a]growl over it in that day like the roaring of the sea.
If one [b]looks to the land, behold, there is darkness *and* distress;
Even the light is darkened by its clouds.

Chapter 6

6 In the year of [a]King Uzziah's death, [b]I saw the Lord sitting on a
throne, lofty and exalted, with the train of His robe filling the
temple.
2 Seraphim stood above Him, [a]each having six wings; with two he
covered his face, and with two he covered his feet, and with two he
flew.
3 And one called out to another and said,
"[a]Holy, Holy, Holy, is the LORD of hosts,
The [1b]whole earth is full of His glory."
4 And the [1]foundations of the thresholds trembled at the voice of
him who called out, while the [2a]temple was filling with smoke.
5 Then I said,
"[a]Woe is me, for I am ruined!
Because I am a man of [b]unclean lips,
And I live among a [c]people of unclean lips;
For my eyes have seen the [d]King, the LORD of hosts."
6 Then one of the seraphim flew to me, with a burning coal in his
hand which he had taken from the [a]altar with tongs.
7 And he [a]touched my mouth *with it* and said, "Behold, this has
touched your lips; and [b]your iniquity is taken away, and your sin is
[1]forgiven."

.it., *ascend* [a]Is.); Joel 2:5 [b]Job [c]Hos. 5:12 [d]Is. , 12; Acts 13:41

were [2]Lit., *has ed away* [a]2 Kin. 13, 17; Is. 66:15 :7; Is. 64:3; Jer. Nah. 1:5 [c]2 Kin. 7; Is. 14:19; Jer. [d]Is. 9:12, 17, 19, 4; Jer. 4:8; Dan. . 7:19; Is. 23:11

6 [1]Lit., *nations;* ably Assyria [a]Is. [b]Is. 7:18; Zech. Deut. 28:49 [d]Is. 13:4, 5 Joel 2:7, 8 [b]Job 12:18

[1]Lit., *Which, its arrows* [2]Lit., *are ed as* [a]Ps. 7:12, :5; Is. 13:18 [b]Is. 21:1; Jer. 4:13

ler. 51:38; Zeph. ; Zech. 11:3 [b]Is. ; 49:24, 25; Mic. 5:8 [c]Is. 42:22

17:12; Jer. 6:23; 21:25 [b]Is. 8:22; 23-28; Joel 2:10; Luke 21:25, 26

Kin. 15:7; 2 Chr. 23; Is. 1:1 [b]John Rev. 4:2, 3; 20:11

2 [a]Rev. 4:8

.it., *fulness of the earth is His glory* :8 [b]Num. 14:21; Ps. 72:19

Lit., *door sockets* *ouse* [a]Rev. 15:8

. 33:20; Luke 5:8 :12, 30 [c]Is. 59:3; 9:3-8 [d]Jer. 51:57

6 [a]Rev. 8:3

, *atoned for* [a]Jer. ; Dan. 10:16 [b]Is. 3:5, 6, 11; 1 John 1:7

8 Then I heard the [a]voice of the Lord, saying, "Whom shall I send, and who will go for Us?" Then [b]I said, "Here am I. Send me!"
9 And He said, "Go, and tell this people:
'Keep on [a]listening, but do not perceive;
Keep on looking, but do not understand.'
10 "[a]Render the hearts of this people [1b]insensitive,
Their ears [2]dull,
And their eyes [3]dim,
[c]Lest they see with their eyes,
Hear with their ears,
Understand with their hearts,
And return and be healed."
11 Then I said, "Lord, [a]how long?" And He answered,
"Until [b]cities are devastated *and* without inhabitant,
Houses are without people,
And the land is utterly desolate,
12 "The LORD has [a]removed men far away,
And the [1b]forsaken places are many in the midst of the land.
13 "Yet there will be a tenth portion in it,
And it will again be *subject* to burning,
Like a terebinth or an [a]oak
Whose stump remains when it is felled.
The [b]holy seed is its stump."

Chapter 7

7 Now it came about in the days of [a]Ahaz, the son of Jotham, the son of Uzziah, king of Judah, that [b]Rezin the king of Aram and [c]Pekah the son of Remaliah, king of Israel, went up to Jerusalem to *wage* war against it, but [d]could not [1]conquer it.
2 When it was reported to the [a]house of David, saying, "The Arameans [1b]have camped in [c]Ephraim," his heart and the hearts of his people shook as the trees of the forest shake [2]with the wind.
3 Then the LORD said to Isaiah, "Go out now to meet Ahaz, you and your son [1]Shear-jashub, at the end of the [a]conduit of the upper pool, on the highway to the [2]fuller's field,
4 and say to him, 'Take care, and be [a]calm, have no [b]fear and [c]do not be fainthearted because of these two stubs of smoldering [d]firebrands, on account of the fierce anger of Rezin and Aram, and the [e]son of Remaliah.
5 'Because [a]Aram, *with* Ephraim and the son of Remaliah, has planned evil against you, saying,
6 "Let us go up against Judah and [1]terrorize it, and make for ourselves a breach in [2]its walls, and set up the son of Tabeel as king in the midst of it,"
7 thus says the Lord [1]GOD, "[a]It shall not stand nor shall it come to pass.
8 "For the head of Aram is [a]Damascus and the head of Damascus is Rezin (now within another 65 years Ephraim will be shattered, *so that it is* no longer a people),
9 and the head of Ephraim is Samaria and the head of Samaria is the son of Remaliah. [a]If you will not believe, you surely shall not [1]last."' "
10 Then the LORD spoke again to Ahaz, saying,

8 [a]Ezek. 10:5; [b]Acts 26:19
9 [a]Is. 43:8; Ma Mark 4:12; Luke John 12:40; Act Rom. 11:8
10 [1]Lit., *fat* [2]Li [3]Lit., *besmeare* 13:15 [b]Deut. 31 32:15 [c]Jer. 5:21
11 [a]Ps. 79:5 [b]L 26:31; Is. 1:7; 3
12 [1]Or, *forsake will be great* [a]D 28:64 [b]Jer. 4:29
13 [a]Job 14:7 [b] 7:6; Ezra 9:2
7:1 [1]Lit., *fight a* [a]2 Kin. 16:1; Is. [b]2 Kin. 15:37 [c]2 15:25; 2 Chr. 28 7:6, 7
2 [1]Lit., *has settl on* [2]Lit., *from be* [a]Is. 7:13; 22:22 8:12 [c]Is. 9:9
3 [1]I.e., a remna return [2]I.e., laundryman's [a]2 18:17; Is. 36:2
4 [a]Ex. 14:13; Is. Lam. 3:26 [b]Is. 1 Matt. 24:6 [c]Deut 1 Sam. 17:32; Is. [d]Amos 4:11; Zec [e]Is. 7:1, 9
5 [a]Is. 7:2
6 [1]Lit., *cause it a sickening dread*
7 [1]Heb., *YHWH*, usually rendered [a]Is. 8:10; 28:18; A 4:25, 26
8 [a]Gen. 14:15; Is
9 [1]Or, *be establis* [a]2 Chr. 20:20; Is. 8:6-8; 30:12-14

11 Shall I not [1]do to Jerusalem and her images
Just as I have done to Samaria and [a]her idols?"
12 So it will be that when the Lord has completed all His [a]work
Mount Zion and on Jerusalem, *He will say,* "I will [1]punish the fruit
the arrogant heart of the king of Assyria and [b]the pomp of [2]h
haughtiness."
13 For [a]he has said,
"By the power of my hand and by my wisdom I did *this,*
For I have understanding;
And I [b]removed the boundaries of the peoples,
And plundered their treasures,
And like a mighty man I brought down [1]*their* inhabitants,
14 And my hand reached to the riches of the peoples like a [a]nest,
And as one gathers abandoned eggs, I gathered all the earth;
And there was not one that flapped its wing or opened *its* beak
or chirped."

15 Is the [a]axe to [b]boast itself over the one who chops with it?
Is the saw to exalt itself over the one who wields it?
That would be like [c]a [1]club wielding those who lift it,
Or like [c]a rod lifting *him who* is not wood.
16 Therefore the Lord, the [1]GOD of hosts, will send a [a]wasting
disease among his [b]stout warriors;
And under his [c]glory a fire will be kindled like a burning flame.
17 And the [a]light of Israel will become a fire and his [b]Holy One a
flame,
And it will [c]burn and devour his thorns and his briars in a single
day.
18 And He will [a]destroy the glory of his forest and of his fruitful
garden, both soul and body;
And it will be as when a sick man wastes away.
19 And the [a]rest of the trees of his forest will be so small in number
That a child could write them down.
20 Now it will come about in that day that the [a]remnant of Israel,
and those of the house of Jacob [b]who have escaped, will never again
rely on the one who struck them, but will truly [c]rely on the LORD, the
Holy One of Israel.
21 A [a]remnant will return, the remnant of Jacob, to the [b]mighty God.
22 For [a]though your people, O Israel, may be like the sand of the
sea,
Only a remnant within them will return;
A [b]destruction is determined, overflowing with righteousness.
23 For a complete destruction, one that is decreed, [a]the Lord [1]GOD of
hosts will execute in the midst of the whole land.
24 Therefore thus says the Lord [1]GOD of hosts, "O My people who
dwell in [a]Zion, [b]do not fear the Assyrian [2]who [c]strikes you with the
rod and lifts up his staff against you, the way Egypt *did.*
25 "For in a very [a]little while [b]My indignation *against you* will be
spent, and My anger *will be directed* to their destruction."
26 And the LORD of hosts will [a]arouse a scourge against him like the
slaughter of [b]Midian at the rock of Oreb; and His [c]staff will be over
the sea, and He will lift it up [d]the way *He did* in Egypt.
27 So it will be in that day, that [1]his [a]burden will be removed from

Lit., *do thus* [a]Is. 2:8

12 [1]Lit., *visit* [2]Lit., ghtiness of his eyes Kin. 19:31; Is. 28:21, 22; 29:14; 65:7 [b]Is. 37:23

3 [1]Or, *those who sit on thrones* [a]2 Kin. 22-24; Is. 37:24-27; zek. 28:4; Dan. 4:30 [b]Hab. 2:6-11

[a]Jer. 49:16; Obad. 4

15 [1]Lit., *staff* [a]Jer. 20 [b]Is. 29:16; 45:9; 1. 9:20, 21 [c]Is. 10:5

16 [1]Heb., *YHWH,* ally rendered LORD Ps. 106:15 [b]Is. 17:4 [c]Is. 8:7; 10:18

[a]Is. 30:33; 31:9 [b]Is. 3 [c]Num. 11:1-3; Is. 7:4; 33:12; Jer. 4:4; 7:20

18 [a]Is. 10:33, 34

19 [a]Is. 21:17

[a]Is. 1:9; 11:11, 16; [b]Is. 4:2; 37:31, 32 r. 14:11; Is. 17:7, 8; 50:10

21 [a]Is. 7:3 [b]Is. 9:6

[a]Rom. 9:27, 28 [b]Is. 2; Dan. 9:27; Rom. 9:28

23 [1]Heb., *YHWH,* ally rendered LORD s. 28:22; Dan. 9:27; Rom. 9:28

24 [1]Heb., *YHWH,* ally rendered LORD Lit., *he* [a]Ps. 87:5, 6 4; 12:2; 37:6 [c]Ex. 5:14-16

[a]Is. 17:14; Hag. 2:6 . 10:5; 26:20; Dan. 11:36

s. 37:36-38 [b]Judg. ; Is. 9:4 [c]Ex. 14:16 [d]Ex. 14:27

[1]I.e., the Assyrian [a]Is. 9:4; 14:25

oulders and his yoke from your neck, and the yoke will be
you because [b]of fatness.
br has come against Aiath,
2 e has passed through [a]Migron;
At [b]Michmash he deposited his [c]baggage.
They have gone through [a]the pass, *saying*,
"[b]Geba will be our lodging place."
[c]Ramah is terrified, and [d]Gibeah of Saul has fled away.
0 Cry aloud with your voice, O daughter of [a]Gallim!
Pay attention, Laishah *and* [1]wretched [b]Anathoth!
31 Madmenah has fled.
The inhabitants of Gebim have sought refuge.
32 Yet today he will halt at [a]Nob;
He [b]shakes his fist at the mountain of the [1c]daughter of Zion, the hill of Jerusalem.

33 Behold, the Lord, the [1]GOD of hosts, will lop off the boughs with a terrible crash;
Those also who are [a]tall in stature will be cut down,
And those who are lofty will be abased.
34 And He will cut down the thickets of the forest with an iron *axe*,
And [a]Lebanon will fall [1]by the Mighty One.

Chapter 11

11 Then a [a]shoot will spring from the [b]stem of Jesse,
And a [c]branch from [d]his roots will bear fruit.
2 And the [a]Spirit of the LORD will rest on Him,
The spirit of [b]wisdom and understanding,
The spirit of counsel and [c]strength,
The spirit of knowledge and the fear of the LORD.
3 And He will delight in the fear of the LORD,
And He will not judge by what His eyes [a]see,
Nor make a decision by what His ears hear;
4 But with [a]righteousness He will judge the [b]poor,
And decide with fairness for the [c]afflicted of the earth;
And He will strike the earth with the [d]rod of His mouth,
And with the [e]breath of His lips He will slay the wicked.
5 Also [a]righteousness will be the belt about His loins,
And [b]faithfulness the belt about His waist.

6 And the [a]wolf will dwell with the lamb,
And the leopard will lie down with the kid,
And the calf and the young lion [1]and the fatling together;
And a little boy will lead them.
7 Also the cow and the bear will graze;
Their young will lie down together;
And the [a]lion will eat straw like the ox.
8 And the nursing child will play by the hole of the cobra,
And the weaned child will put his hand on the viper's den.
9 They will [a]not hurt or destroy in all My holy mountain,
For the [b]earth will be full of the knowledge of the LORD
As the waters cover the sea.

10 Then it will come about in that day

27 [b]Is. 30:23; 55:2

28 [a]1 Sam. 14:2 [b]1 Sam. 13:2, 5 [c]Ju 18:21; 1 Sam. 17:22

29 [a]1 Sam. 13:23 [b]Josh. 21:17; 1 Sam 13:16 [c]Josh. 18:25; 1 Sam. 7:17 [d]1 Sam 10:26

30 [1]An ancient vers reads *Answer her,* (*Anathoth* [a]1 Sam. 25:44 [b]Josh. 21:18 1:1

32 [1]Another readin *house of* [a]1 Sam. 2 22:9 [b]Is. 19:16; Zec 2:9 [c]Is. 1:8; Jer. 6:2

33 [1]Heb., *YHWH,* usually rendered Lo [a]Is. 37:24, 36-38; E 31:3; Amos 2:9

34 [1]Or, *as a mighty one* [a]Is. 2:13; 33:9 37:24

11:1 [a]Is. 4:2; 53:2 9:7; 11:10; Acts 13: [c]Is. 6:13; Jer. 23:5; Zech. 3:8 [d]Rev. 5:5 22:16

2 [a]Is. 42:1; 48:16; Matt. 3:16; John 1: [b]John 16:13; 1 Cor. 1:30; Eph. 1:17, 18 [c]2 Tim. 1:7

3 [a]John 2:25; 7:24

4 [a]Is. 9:7; 16:5; 32 [b]Ps. 72:2, 13, 14; I 3:14 [c]Is. 29:19; 32 61:1 [d]Ps. 2:9; Is. 4 Mal. 4:6 [e]Job 4:9; 30:28, 33; 2 Thess

5 [a]Eph. 6:14 [b]Is.

6 [1]Some versions *will feed together* 65:25

7 [a]Is. 65:25

9 [a]Job 5:23; Is. 6 Ezek. 34:25; Hos. [b]Ps. 98:2, 3; Is. 45 52:10; 66:18-23; H 2:14

That the [a]nations will resort to the [b]root of Jesse,
Who will stand as a [1c]signal for the peoples;
And His [d]resting place will be [2]glorious.

11 Then it will happen on that day that the Lord
Will again recover the second time with His hand
The [a]remnant of His people, who will remain,
From [b]Assyria, [c]Egypt, Pathros, Cush, [d]Elam, Shinar, Hamath,
And from the [1e]islands of the sea.
12 And He will lift up a [a]standard for the nations,
And will [b]assemble the banished ones of Israel,
And will gather the dispersed of Judah
From the four corners of the earth.
13 Then the [a]jealousy of Ephraim will depart,
And those who harass Judah will be cut off;
Ephraim will not be jealous of Judah,
And Judah will not harass Ephraim.
14 And they will [a]swoop down on the slopes of the Philistines on
the [b]west;
Together they will [c]plunder the sons of the east;
[1]They will possess [d]Edom and [e]Moab;
And the sons of Ammon will be [2]subject to them.
15 And the LORD will [1a]utterly destroy
The tongue of the [2]Sea of Egypt;
And He will [b]wave His hand over the [3c]River
With His scorching wind;
And He will strike it into seven streams,
And make *men* walk over [4]dry-shod.
16 And there will be a [a]highway from Assyria
For the [b]remnant of His people who will be left,
Just as there was for Israel
In [c]the day that they came up out of the land of Egypt.

Chapter 12

12 Then you will say on that day,
"[a]I will give thanks to Thee, O LORD;
For [b]although Thou wast angry with me,
Thine anger is turned away,
And Thou dost comfort me.
2 "Behold, [a]God is my salvation,
I will [b]trust and not be afraid;
For [c]the LORD GOD is my strength and song,
And He has become my salvation."
3 Therefore you will joyously [a]draw water
From the [b]springs of salvation.
4 And in that day you will [a]say,
"[b]Give thanks to the LORD, call on His name.
[c]Make known His deeds among the peoples;
[1]Make *them* remember that His name is exalted."
5 [a]Praise the LORD in song, for He has done [1]excellent things;
Let this be known throughout the earth.
6 [a]Cry aloud and shout for joy, O inhabitant of Zion,
For [b]great in your midst is the Holy One of Israel.

[1]Or, *standard* [2]Lit., ...ry [a]Luke 2:32; Acts ...1:18 [b]Is. 11:1; Rom. ...12 [c]Is. 11:12; 49:22; ...2:10; John 3:14, 15; ...:32 [d]Is. 14:3; 28:12; 32:17, 18

[1]Or, *coastlands* [a]Is. ...20-22; 37:4, 31, 32; [b]Is. 19:23-25; Hos. ...11; Zech. 10:10 [c]Is. ...19:21, 22; Mic. 7:12 ...en. 10:22; 14:1 [e]Is. ...24:15; 42:4, 10, 12; ...1; 51:5; 60:9; 66:19

[a]Is. 11:10 [b]Is. 56:8; ...ph. 3:10; Zech. 10:6

[a]Is. 9:21; Jer. 3:18; ...Ezek. 37:16, 17, 22; Hos. 1:11

14 [1]Lit., *Edom and Moab will be the ...utstretching of their hand* [2]Lit., *their ...dience* [a]Jer. 48:40; ...49:22; Hab. 1:8 [b]Is. ...12 [c]Jer. 49:28 [d]Is. ...1; Dan. 11:41; Joel ...19; Amos 9:12 [e]Is. 16:14; 25:10

...Another reading is *dry up the tongue* ...rhaps the Red Sea ...Euphrates [4]Lit., *in ...sandals* [a]Is. 43:16; ...27; 50:2; 51:10, 11 ...9:16 [c]Is. 7:20; 8:7; Rev. 16:12

...6 [a]Is. 19:23; 35:8; ...3; 62:10 [b]Is. 11:11 [c]Ex. 14:26-29

... [a]Ps. 9:1; Is. 25:1 ...s. 30:5; Is. 40:1, 2; 54:7-10

2 [a]Is. 32:2; 45:17; ...2:11 [b]Is. 26:3 [c]Ex. 15:2; Ps. 118:14

...ohn 4:10; 7:37, 38 ...s. 41:18; Jer. 2:13

...; *Proclaim* to them ... [a]Is. 24:15; 42:12; ...0 [b]Ps. 105:1 [c]Ps. 145:4

...Or, *gloriously* [a]Ex. ...Ps. 98:1; Is. 24:14; 42:10, 11; 44:23

...52:9; 54:1; Zeph. ...4 [b]Is. 1:24; 49:26; ...6; Zeph. 3:15-17; Zech. 2:5, 10, 11

Chapter 13

13 The [1a]oracle concerning [b]Babylon which [c]Isaiah the son of
Amoz saw.
2 [a]Lift up a standard on the [1b]bare hill,
Raise your voice to them,
[c]Wave the hand that they may [d]enter the doors of the nobles.
3 I have commanded My consecrated ones,
I have even called My [a]mighty warriors,
My proudly exulting ones,
To *execute* My anger.
4 A [a]sound of tumult on the mountains,
Like that of many people!
A sound of the uproar of kingdoms,
Of nations gathered together!
The LORD of hosts is mustering the army for battle.
5 They are coming from a far country
From the [1a]farthest horizons,
The LORD and His instruments of [b]indignation,
To [c]destroy the whole land.
6 Wail, for the [a]day of the LORD is near!
It will come as [b]destruction from [1]the Almighty.
7 Therefore [a]all hands will fall limp,
And every man's [b]heart will melt.
8 And they will be [a]terrified,
Pains and anguish will take hold of *them;*
They will [b]writhe like a woman in labor,
They will look at one another in astonishment,
Their faces aflame.
9 Behold, [a]the day of the LORD is coming,
Cruel, with fury and burning anger,
To make the land a desolation;
And He will exterminate its sinners from it.
10 For the [a]stars of heaven and their constellations
Will not flash forth their light;
The [b]sun will be dark when it rises,
And the moon will not shed its light.
11 Thus I will [a]punish the world for its evil,
And the [b]wicked for their iniquity;
I will also put an end to the [c]arrogance of the proud,
And abase the [d]haughtiness of the [1e]ruthless.
12 I will make mortal man [1a]scarcer than pure gold,
And mankind than the [b]gold of Ophir.
13 Therefore I shall make the [a]heavens tremble,
And [b]the earth will be shaken from its place
At the fury of the LORD of hosts
In [c]the day of His burning anger.
14 And it will be that like a hunted gazelle,
Or like [a]sheep with none to gather *them,*
They will each turn to his own people,
And each one flee to his own land.
15 Anyone who is found will be [a]thrust through,
And anyone who is captured will fall by the sword.
16 Their [a]little ones also will be dashed to pieces
Before their eyes;

13:1 [1]Or, *burden* 14:28; 15:1 [b]Is. 1… 14:4; 47:1-15; Jer. 50:1-51:64; Matt. … Rev. 14:8 [c]Is. 1:1

2 [1]Or, *wind-swep… mountain* [a]Is. 5:2… 50:2 [b]Jer. 51:25 … 10:32; 19:16 [d]Is. 45:1-3; Jer. 51:58

3 [a]Joel 3:11

4 [a]Is. 5:30; 17:12… 3:14

5 [1]Lit., *end of hea…* [a]Is. 5:26; 7:18 [b]Is. … [c]Is. 24:1

6 [1]Heb., *Shadda…* 2:12; 10:3; 13:9; … 61:2; Ezek. 30:3; … 5:18; Zeph. 1:7 … 10:25; 14:23; Joel

7 [a]Ezek. 7:17 [b]Is. … Ezek. 21:7; Nah. …

8 [a]2 Kin. 19:26; Is… Jer. 46:5 [b]Is. 26:1… 4:31; John 16:21

9 [a]Is. 13:6

10 [a]Is. 5:30; Ezek… Joel 2:10; Matt. 2… Mark 13:24; Luke … Rev. 6:13; 8:12 … 24:23; 50:3; Ezek. … Acts 2:20; Rev. 6:…

11 [1]Or, *tyrants, despots* [a]Is. 26:2… 3:11; 11:4; 14:5 … 2:11; 23:9; Dan. 5… 23 [d]Jer. 48:29 [e]Is… 25:3; 29:5, 20

12 [1]Lit., *more pre…* [a]Is. 4:1; 6:11, 12 … 9:28; Job 28:16; P…

13 [a]Is. 34:4; 51:6… 18:7; Is. 2:19; 24:… 20; Hag. 2:6 [c]Lam…

14 [a]1 Kin. 22:17; … 9:36; Mark 6:34; … 2:25

15 [a]Is. 14:19; Jer. 50:25; 51:3, 4

16 [a]Ps. 137:8, 9; … 13:18; 14:21; Hos… 10:14; Nah. 3:10

Their houses will be plundered
And their wives ravished.

17 Behold, I am going to [a]stir up the Medes against them,
Who will not value silver or [b]take pleasure in gold,
18 And *their* bows will [1]mow down the [a]young men,
They will not even have compassion on the fruit of the womb,
Nor will their [b]eye pity [2]children.
19 And [a]Babylon, the [b]beauty of kingdoms, the glory of the
Chaldeans' pride,
Will be as when God [c]overthrew Sodom and Gomorrah.
20 It will [a]never be inhabited or lived in from generation to
generation;
Nor will the [b]Arab pitch *his* tent there,
Nor will shepherds make *their flocks* lie down there.
21 But [a]desert creatures will lie down there,
And their houses will be full of [1]owls,
Ostriches also will live there, and [2]shaggy goats will frolic there.
22 And [1]hyenas will howl in their fortified towers
And jackals in their luxurious [a]palaces.
Her *fateful* time also [2]will soon come
And her days will not be prolonged.

Chapter 14

14 When the LORD will [a]have compassion on Jacob, and again
[b]choose Israel, and settle them in their own land, then
[c]strangers will join them and attach themselves to the house of Jacob.
2 And the peoples will take them along and bring them to their
place, and the [a]house of Israel will possess them as an inheritance in
the land of the LORD [b]as male servants and female servants; and [1]they
will take their captors captive, and will rule over their oppressors.
3 And it will be in the day when the LORD gives you [a]rest from
your pain and turmoil and harsh service in which you have been
enslaved,
4 that you will [a]take up this [1]taunt against the king of Babylon,
and say,

"How [b]the oppressor has ceased,
And how [2]fury has ceased!
5 "The LORD has broken the staff of the wicked,
The scepter of rulers
6 [a]Which used to strike the peoples in fury with unceasing strokes,
Which [1]subdued the nations in anger with unrestrained
persecution.
7 "The whole earth is at rest *and* is quiet;
They [a]break forth into shouts of joy.
8 "Even the [a]cypress trees rejoice over you, *and* the cedars of
Lebanon, *saying*,
'Since you were laid low, no *tree* cutter comes up against us.'
9 "[a]Sheol from beneath is excited over you to meet you when you
come;
It arouses for you the [1]spirits of the dead, all the [2]leaders of the
earth;
It raises all the kings of the nations from their thrones.
10 "[a]They will all respond and say to you,

7 [a]Jer. 51:11; Dan. :28 [b]Prov. 6:34, 35

[1]Lit., *dash in pieces* , *sons* [a]2 Kin. 8:12; Chr. 36:17 [b]Ezek. 9:5, 10

19 [a]Is. 21:9; 48:14 [b]Dan. 4:30; Rev. 1-16, 19, 21 [c]Gen. 4; Deut. 29:23; Jer. 49:18; Amos 4:11

s. 14:23; 34:10-15; r. 51:37-43 [b]2 Chr. 17:11

21 [1]Or, *howling* *creatures* [2]Or, *goat* *nons* [a]Is. 34:11-15; ph. 2:14; Rev. 18:2

22 [1]Or, *howling* *atures* [2]Lit., *is near to come* [a]Is. 25:2; 32:14; 34:13

:1 [a]Ps. 102:13; Is. 13, 15; 54:7, 8 [b]Is. 41:8, 9; 44:1; 49:7; ch. 1:17; 2:12 [c]Is. :3, 6; Eph. 2:12-19

it., *the captors will* *ome their captives* 45:14; 49:23; 54:3 . 60:10; 61:5; Dan. 7:18, 27

3 [a]Ezra 9:8, 9; Is. 0; 40:2; Jer. 30:10; 46:27

4 [1]Or, *proverb* Amended from the ingless *medhebah* *arhebah* [a]Hab. 2:6 s. 9:4; 16:4; 49:26; 51:13; 54:14

, *ruled* [a]Is. 10:14; 47:6

Ps. 47:1-3; 98:1-9; 126:1-3

5:12; Ezek. 31:16

Or, *shades* (Heb., *pha'im*) [2]Lit., *male goats* [a]Is. 5:14

10 [a]Ezek. 32:21

...n you have been made weak as we,
...u have become like us.
...ur [a]pomp *and* the music of your harps
...lave been brought down to Sheol;
...Maggots are spread out *as your bed* beneath you,
And worms are your covering.'
'How you have [a]fallen from heaven,
O [1b]star of the morning, son of the dawn!
You have been cut down to the earth,
You who have weakened the nations!
13 "But you said in your heart,
'I will [a]ascend to heaven;
I will [b]raise my throne above the stars of God,
And I will sit on the mount of assembly
In the recesses of the north.
14 'I will ascend above the heights of the clouds;
[a]I will make myself like the Most High.'
15 "Nevertheless you [a]will be thrust down to Sheol,
To the recesses of the pit.
16 "Those who see you will gaze at you,
They will [1]ponder over you, *saying,*
'Is this the man who made the earth tremble,
Who shook kingdoms,
17 Who made the world like a [a]wilderness
And overthrew its cities,
Who [b]did not [1]allow his prisoners to *go* home?'
18 "All the kings of the nations lie in glory,
Each in his own [1]tomb.
19 "But you have been [a]cast out of your tomb
Like [1]a rejected branch,
[2]Clothed with the slain who are pierced with a sword,
Who go down to the stones of the [b]pit,
Like a [c]trampled corpse.
20 "You will not be united with them in burial,
Because you have ruined your country,
You have slain your people.
May the [a]offspring of evildoers not be mentioned forever.
21 "Prepare for his sons a place of slaughter
Because of the [a]iniquity of their fathers.
They must not arise and take possession of the earth
And fill the face of the world with cities."
22 "And I will rise up against them," declares the LORD of hosts,
"and will cut off from Babylon [a]name and survivors, [b]offspring and
posterity," declares the LORD.
23 "I will also make it a possession for the [a]hedgehog, and swamps
of water, and I will sweep it with the broom of [b]destruction,"
declares the LORD of hosts.
24 The LORD of hosts has sworn saying, "Surely, [a]just as I have
intended so it has happened, and just as I have planned so it will
stand,
25 to [a]break Assyria in My land, and I will trample him on My
mountains. Then his [b]yoke will be removed from them, and his bur-
den removed from their shoulder.

11 [a]Is. 5:14

12 [1]Heb., *Helel;* i.e. shining one [a]Is. 34... Luke 10:18; Rev. 8... 9:1 [b]2 Pet. 1:19; R... 2:28; 22:16

13 [a]Ezek. 28:2 [b]D... 5:22, 23; 8:10; 2 T... 2:4

14 [a]Is. 47:8; 2 The... 2:4

15 [a]Ezek. 28:8; M... 11:23; Luke 10:15

16 [1]Lit., *show themselves attent...*

17 [1]Lit., *open* [a]Jo... [b]Is. 45:13

18 [1]Lit., *house*

19 [1]Lit., *an abhor... branch* [2]Or, *As th... clothing of those w... are slain* [a]Is. 22:1... [b]Jer. 41:7, 9 [c]Is. 5...

20 [a]Job 18:16, 19... 21:10; 37:28; Is. 1... 31:2

21 [a]Ex. 20:5; Lev... 26:39; Is. 13:16; M... 23:35

22 [a]Prov. 10:7 [b]J... 18:19; Is. 47:9

23 [a]Is. 34:11; Zep... 2:14 [b]1 Kin. 14:1... 13:6

24 [a]Job 23:13; Is... 46:11; 55:8, 9; Ac...

25 [a]Is. 10:12; 30... 31:8 [b]Is. 9:4; 10:... Nah. 1:13

INSIGHT

From 729 B.C. Babylon was part of the Assyrian Empire. The ruler of Assyria assumed the title "King of Babylon." Babylon then became the capital of the Neo-Babylonian Empire which Nebuchadnezzar ruled after the death of his father Naboplassar. Nebuchadnezzar first besieged Jerusalem in 605 B.C. In 586 B.C. he destroyed Jerusalem and the temple.

26 "This is the [a]plan [1]devised against the whole earth; and this i
[b]hand that is stretched out against all the nations.
27 "For [a]the LORD of hosts has planned, and who can frustrate
And as for His stretched-out hand, who can turn it back?"
28 In the [a]year that King Ahaz died this [1b]oracle came:
29 "Do not rejoice, O [a]Philistia, all of you,
Because the rod that [b]struck you is broken;
For from the serpent's root a [c]viper will come out,
And its fruit will be a [d]flying serpent.
30 "And [1]those who are most [a]helpless will eat,
And the needy will lie down in security;
I will [2]destroy your root with [b]famine,
And it will kill off your survivors.
31 "Wail, O [a]gate; cry, O city;
[1]Melt away, O [b]Philistia, all of you;
For smoke comes from the [c]north,
And [d]there is no straggler in his ranks.
32 "How then will one answer the [a]messengers of the nation?
That [b]the LORD has founded Zion,
And [c]the afflicted of His people will seek refuge in it."

Chapter 15

15 The [1]oracle concerning [a]Moab.
Surely in a night [b]Ar of Moab is devastated *and* ruined;
Surely in a night Kir of Moab is devastated *and* ruined.
2 They have gone up to the [1]temple and *to* [a]Dibon, *even* to the high places to weep.
Moab wails over Nebo and Medeba;
Everyone's head is [b]bald *and* every beard is cut off.
3 In their streets they have girded themselves with [a]sackcloth;
[b]On their housetops and in their squares
Everyone is wailing, [1c]dissolved in tears.
4 [a]Heshbon and Elealeh also cry out,
Their voice is heard all the way to Jahaz;
Therefore the [1]armed men of Moab cry aloud;
His soul trembles within him.
5 My heart cries out for Moab;
His fugitives are as far as [a]Zoar *and* Eglath-shelishiyah,
For they go up the [b]ascent of Luhith weeping;
Surely on the road to Horonaim they raise a cry of distress [c]over *their* ruin.
6 For the [a]waters of Nimrim are [1]desolate.
Surely the grass is withered, the tender grass [2]died out,
There is [b]no green thing.
7 Therefore the [a]abundance *which* they have acquired and stored up
They carry off over the brook of [1]Arabim.
8 For the cry of distress has gone around the territory of Moab,
Its wail *goes* as far as Eglaim and its wailing even to Beer-elim.
9 For the waters of Dimon are full of [1]blood;
Surely I will bring added *woes* upon Dimon,
A [a]lion upon the fugitives of Moab and upon the remnant of the land.

6 [1]Lit., *planned* [a]Is. 9; Zeph. 3:6, 8 [b]Ex. 15:12
27 [a]2 Chr. 20:6; Is. 3:13; Dan. 4:31, 35
[1]Or, *burden* [a]2 Kin. 0; 2 Chr. 28:27 [b]Is. 13:1
[a]Is. 2:6; 11:14; Jer. -7; Ezek. 25:15-17; 3:4-8; Amos 1:6-8; Zeph. 2:4-7; Zech. 7 [b]2 Chr. 26:6 [c]Is. 11:8 [d]Is. 30:6
Lit., *the first-born of* elpless [2]Lit., *put to* death [a]Is. 3:14, 15; 22; 11:4 [b]Is. 8:21; 9:20; 51:19
31 [1]Or, *Become* noralized [a]Is. 3:26; 12; 45:2 [b]Is. 14:29 Jer. 1:14 [d]Is. 34:16
[a]Is. 37:9 [b]Ps. 87:1, ; 102:16; Is. 28:16; :28; 54:11 [c]Is. 4:6; 57:13; Zeph. 3:12; . 11:10; James 2:5
[1]Or, *burden of* [a]Is. 4; 25:10; Jer. 48:1; ek. 25:8-11; Amos 2:1-3; Zeph. 2:8-11 [b]Num. 21:28
[1]Lit., *house* [a]Jer. 18, 22 [b]Lev. 21:5; Jer. 48:37
Lit., *going down in* eeping [a]Jon. 3:6-8 er. 48:38 [c]Is. 22:4
Another reading is *the loins of* [a]Num. 8; 32:3; Jer. 48:34
[a]Jer. 48:34 [b]Jer. [c]Is. 59:7; Jer. 4:20
[1]Lit., *desolations* t., *come to an end* 19:5-7; Jer. 48:34 [b]Joel 1:10-12; 2:3
r, *the poplars* [a]Is. 30:6; Jer. 48:36
9 [1]Heb., *dam* (a ay) [a]2 Kin. 17:25; Jer. 50:17

Chapter 16

[a]Send the *tribute* lamb to the ruler of the land,
From [1b]Sela by way of the wilderness to the [c]mountain of the daughter of Zion.
Then, like [1a]fleeing birds *or* scattered [2]nestlings,
The daughters of [b]Moab will be at the fords of the [c]Arnon.
[1]Give *us* advice, make a decision;
[2]Cast your [a]shadow like night [3]at high noon;
[b]Hide the outcasts, do not betray the fugitive.
4 "Let the [1]outcasts of Moab stay with you;
Be a hiding place to them from the destroyer."
For the extortioner has come to an end, destruction has ceased,
[a]Oppressors have completely *disappeared* from the land.
5 A [a]throne will even be established in lovingkindness,
And a judge will sit on it in faithfulness in the tent of [b]David;
Moreover, he will seek justice
And be prompt in righteousness.

6 [a]We have heard of the pride of Moab, an excessive pride;
Even of his arrogance, pride, and fury;
[b]His idle boasts are [1]false.
7 Therefore Moab shall wail; everyone of Moab shall wail.
You shall moan for the [a]raisin cakes of [b]Kir-hareseth
As those who are utterly stricken.
8 For the fields of [a]Heshbon have [1]withered, the vines of [b]Sibmah *as well*;
The lords of the nations have trampled down its choice clusters
Which reached as far as Jazer *and* wandered to the deserts;
[c]Its tendrils spread themselves out *and* passed over the sea.
9 Therefore I will [a]weep bitterly for Jazer, for the vine of Sibmah;
I will drench you with my tears, O [b]Heshbon and Elealeh;
For the shouting over your [c]summer fruits and your harvest has fallen away.
10 And [a]gladness and joy are taken away from the fruitful field;
In the [b]vineyards also there will be no cries of joy or jubilant shouting,
No [c]treader treads out wine in the presses,
For I have made the shouting to cease.
11 Therefore my [1a]heart intones like a harp for Moab,
And my [2]inward feelings for Kir-hareseth.
12 So it will come about when Moab [a]presents himself,
When he [b]wearies himself upon *his* [c]high place,
And comes to his sanctuary to pray,
That he will not prevail.
13 This is the word which the LORD spoke earlier concerning Moab.
14 But now the LORD speaks, saying, "Within three years, as [1a]a
hired man would count them, the glory of [b]Moab will be degraded
along with all *his* great population, and *his* remnant will be very
small *and* [2]impotent."

Chapter 17

17 The [1a]oracle concerning [b]Damascus.
"Behold, Damascus is about to be [c]removed from being a city,

INSIGHT

Moab was a narrow strip of land directly east of the Dead Sea. Its inhabitants were called Moabites.

16:1 [1]I.e., Petra Edom [a]2 Kin. 3:4 7:17 [b]2 Kin. 14:7 42:11 [c]Is. 10:32

2 [1]Or, *fluttering* *nest* [a]Prov. 27:8 48:20, 46 [c]Num. 21:13, 14

3 [1]Lit., *Bring* [2]Li [3]Lit., *in the midst* *noon* [a]Is. 25:4; 3 [b]1 Kin. 18:4

4 [1]So the versio M.T., *My outcast* *Moab* [a]Is. 9:4; 1 49:26; 51:13; 54

5 [a]Is. 9:6, 7; 32: Dan. 7:14; Mic. 4 Luke 1:33 [b]Is. 9

6 [1]Lit., *not so* [a] 48:29; Amos 2:1 3, 4; Zeph. 2:8, 1 48:30

7 [a]1 Chr. 16:3 [b] 3:25; Jer. 48:31

8 [1]Or, *languishe* 15:4 [b]Num. 32:3 48:32

9 [a]Jer. 48:32 [b]I [c]Jer. 40:10, 12; 4

10 [a]Is. 24:8; Jer [b]Judg. 9:27; Is. Amos 5:11, 17 [c] 24:11; Amos 9:1

11 [1]Lit., *entrails* *murmur* [2]Lit., *in* *part* [a]Is. 15:5; 6 Jer. 48:36; Hos. Phil. 2:1

12 [a]Num. 22:39 48:35 [b]1 Kin. 18 15:2

14 [1]Lit., *the yea* *hireling* [2]Lit., *no* *mighty* [a]Job 7:1 Is. 21:16 [b]Is. 25 48:42

17:1 [1]Or, *burde* 13:1 [b]Gen. 14: 2 Kin. 16:9; Jer. Amos 1:3-5; Ze Acts 9:2 [c]Is. 7: 10:9

And it will become a [d]fallen ruin.
2 "The cities [1]of [a]Aroer are forsaken;
They will be for [b]flocks [2]to lie down in,
And there will be [c]no one to frighten *them*.
3 "The [1a]fortified city will disappear from Ephraim,
And [2]sovereignty from Damascus
And the remnant of Aram;
They will be like the [b]glory of the sons of Israel,"
Declares the LORD of hosts.

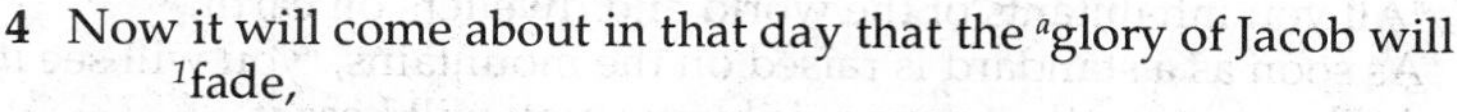

4 Now it will come about in that day that the [a]glory of Jacob will [1]fade,
And [b]the fatness of his flesh will become lean.
5 It will be [a]even like the [1]reaper gathering the standing grain,
As his arm harvests the ears,
Or it will be like one gleaning ears of grain
In the [b]valley of Rephaim.
6 Yet [a]gleanings will be left in it like the [1]shaking of an olive tree,
Two *or* three olives on the topmost bough,
Four *or* five on the branches of a fruitful tree,
Declares the LORD, the God of Israel.
7 In that day man will [a]have regard for his Maker,
And his eyes will look to the Holy One of Israel.
8 And he will not have regard for the [a]altars, the work of his hands,
Nor will he look to that which his [b]fingers have made,
Even the [1c]Asherim and [2]incense stands.
9 In that day [1]their strong cities will be like [2]forsaken places in the forest,
Or like [3]branches which they abandoned before the sons of Israel;
And [4]the land will be a desolation.
10 For [a]you have forgotten the [b]God of your salvation
And have not remembered the [c]rock of your refuge.
Therefore you plant delightful plants
And set them with vine slips of a strange *god*.
11 In the day that you plant *it* you carefully fence *it* in,
And in the [a]morning you bring your seed to blossom;
But the harvest will [b]be a heap
In a day of sickliness and incurable pain.

12 Alas, the uproar of many peoples
[a]Who roar like the roaring of the seas,
And the rumbling of nations
Who rush on like the [b]rumbling of mighty waters!
13 The [a]nations rumble on like the rumbling of many waters,
But He will [b]rebuke them and they will flee far away,
And be chased [c]like chaff in the mountains before the wind,
Or like whirling dust before a gale.
14 At evening time, behold, *there is* terror!
Before morning [a]they are no more.
[1]Such *will be* the portion of those who plunder us,
And the lot of those who pillage us.

[d]Is. 25:2; Jer. 49:2; Mic. 1:6

[1]Gr. reads *forever ever* [2]Lit., *and they will lie down* [a]Num. 32:34 [b]Is. 7:21, 22; Ezek. 25:5; Zeph. 2:6 [c]Mic. 4:4

Or, *fortification* [2]Or, *royal power, kingdom* Is. 7:8, 16; 8:4 [b]Is. 17:4; Hos. 9:11

., *become thin* [a]Is. 10:3 [b]Is. 10:16

Lit., *gathering of the harvest, the standing grain* [a]Is. 17:11; Jer. 33; Joel 3:13; Matt. [b]2 Sam. 5:18, 22

Lit., *striking* [a]Deut. 7; Is. 24:13; 27:12; Obad. 5

s. 10:20; Hos. 3:5; 6:1; Mic. 7:7

8 [1]I.e., wooden symbols of a female deity [2]Or, *sun pillars* Chr. 34:7; Is. 27:9 :8, 20; 30:22; 31:7 . 34:13; Deut. 7:5; Mic. 5:14

9 [1]I.e., man's [2]Gr. reads *the deserted places of the Amorites and the Hivites which they abandoned* [3]Or, *the treetop* [4]Lit., *it*

10 [a]Is. 51:13 [b]Ps. :19; Is. 12:2; 33:2; 1:10; 62:11 [c]Deut. 4, 18, 31; Is. 26:4; 30:29; 44:8

Ps. 90:6 [b]Job 4:8; Hos. 8:7; 10:13

[a]Is. 5:30; Jer. 6:23; 43:2; Luke 21:25 [b]Ps. 18:4

[a]Is. 33:3 [b]Ps. 9:5; 41:11 [c]Job 21:18; :4; 83:13; Is. 29:5; 41:15, 16

[1]Lit., *This* [a]2 Kin. 19:35; Is. 41:12

INSIGHT

Damascus is the capital of Aram.

Chapter 18

18 Alas, oh land of whirring wings
Which lies beyond the rivers of [1a]Cush,
2 Which sends envoys by the sea,
Even in [a]papyrus vessels on the surface of the waters.
Go, swift messengers, to a nation [1b]tall and smooth,
To a people [c]feared [2]far and wide,
A powerful and oppressive nation
Whose land the rivers divide.
3 [a]All you inhabitants of the world and dwellers on earth,
As soon as a standard is raised on the mountains, [b]you will see *it*,
And as soon as the trumpet is blown, you will hear *it*.
4 For thus the LORD has told me,
"I will look [1]from My [a]dwelling place quietly
Like dazzling heat in the [2b]sunshine,
Like a cloud of [c]dew in the heat of harvest."
5 For [a]before the harvest, as soon as the bud [1]blossoms
And the flower becomes a ripening grape,
Then He will cut off the sprigs with pruning knives
And remove *and* cut away the spreading branches.
6 They will be left together for mountain birds [a]of prey,
And for the beasts of the earth;
And the birds of prey will spend the summer *feeding* on them,
And all the beasts of the earth will spend harvest time on them.
7 At that time a gift of homage will be brought to the LORD of hosts
[1]From a [a]people [2]tall and smooth,
Even from a people feared [3]far and wide,
A powerful and oppressive nation,
Whose land the rivers divide—
To the [b]place of the name of the LORD of hosts, *even* Mount Zion.

Chapter 19

19 The [1a]oracle concerning [b]Egypt.
Behold, the LORD is [c]riding on a swift cloud, and is about to come to Egypt;
The [d]idols of Egypt will tremble at His presence,
And the [e]heart of the Egyptians will melt within them.
2 "So I will incite Egyptians against Egyptians;
And they will [a]each fight against his brother, and each against his neighbor,
City against city, *and* kingdom against kingdom.
3 "Then the spirit of the Egyptians will be demoralized within them;
And I will confound their strategy,
So that [a]they will resort to idols and ghosts of the dead,
And to [1]mediums and spiritists.
4 "Moreover, I will deliver the Egyptians into the hand of a [a]cruel master,
And a [1]mighty king will rule over them," declares the Lord [2]GOD of hosts.

5 [a]And the waters from the sea will dry up,
And the river will be parched and dry.

18:1 [1]Or, *Ethiopi* [a]2 Kin. 19:9; Is. 2 Ezek. 30:4, 5, 9; 2:12; 3:10

2 [1]Lit., *drawn ou from it and beyon* 2:3 [b]Is. 18:7 [c]Ge 10:8, 9; 2 Chr. 12 14:9; 16:8

3 [a]Ps. 49:1; Mic. [b]Is. 26:11

4 [1]Lit., *in* [2]Lit., *lig* 26:21; Hos. 5:15 [b]2 Sam. 23:4 [c]Pr 19:12; Is. 26:19; 14:5

5 [1]Lit., *is finishec* 17:10, 11; Ezek.

6 [a]Is. 46:11; 56:9 7:33; Ezek. 32:4- 39:17-20

7 [1]So with some ancient versions DSS; M.T. implies *Consisting of a p* [2]Lit., *drawn out* [3] *from it and beyon* 68:31; Is. 45:14; 3:10; Acts 8:27-3 [b]Zech. 14:16, 17

19:1 [1]Or, *burden* 13:1 [b]Joel 3:19 18:9, 10; 104:3; M 26:64; Rev. 1:7 12:12; Jer. 43:12; [e]Josh. 2:11; Is. 13

2 [a]Judg. 7:22; 1 14:20; 2 Chr. 20:2 Matt. 10:21, 36

3 [1]Or, *ghosts and spirits* [a]1 Chr. 10 8:19; Dan. 2:2

4 [1]Or, *fierce* [2]He *YHWH*, usually rendered *LORD* 20:4; Jer. 46:26; E 29:19

5 [a]Is. 50:2; Jer. 5 Ezek. 30:12

6 And the [1a]canals will emit a stench,
The [2b]streams of Egypt will thin out and dry up;
[c]The reeds and rushes will rot away.
7 The bulrushes by the [a]Nile, by the [1]edge of the Nile
And all the sown fields by the Nile
Will become dry, be driven away, and be no more.
8 And the [a]fishermen will lament,
And all those who cast a [1]line into the Nile will mourn,
And those who spread nets on the waters will [2]pine away.
9 Moreover, the manufacturers of linen made from combed flax
And the weavers of white [a]cloth will be [1]utterly dejected.
10 And [1]the [a]pillars *of Egypt* will be crushed;
All the hired laborers will be grieved in soul.

11 The princes of [1a]Zoan are mere fools;
The advice of Pharaoh's wisest advisers has become [2]stupid.
How can you *men* say to Pharaoh,
"I am a son of the [b]wise, a son of ancient kings"?
12 Well then, where are your wise men?
Please let them tell you,
And let them [1]understand what the LORD of hosts
Has [a]purposed against Egypt.
13 The princes of [1]Zoan have acted foolishly,
The princes of [a]Memphis are deluded;
Those who are the [b]cornerstone of her tribes
Have [2]led Egypt astray.
14 The LORD has mixed within her a spirit of [a]distortion;
[b]They have led Egypt astray in all [1]that it does,
As a [c]drunken man [2]staggers in his vomit.
15 And there will be no work for Egypt
[a]Which *its* head or tail, *its* palm branch or bulrush, may do.
16 In that day the Egyptians will become like women, and they will
tremble and be in [a]dread because of the [b]waving of the hand of the
LORD of hosts, which He is going to wave over them.
17 And the land of Judah will become a [1]terror to Egypt; everyone
[2]to whom it is mentioned will be in dread of it, because of the [a]pur-
pose of the LORD of hosts which He is purposing against them.
18 In that day five cities in the land of Egypt will be speaking the
language of Canaan and [a]swearing *allegiance* to the LORD of hosts;
one will be called the City of [1]Destruction.
19 In that day there will be an [a]altar to the LORD in the midst of the
land of Egypt, and a [b]pillar to the LORD near its border.
20 And it will become a sign and a witness to the LORD of hosts in
the land of Egypt; for they will cry to the LORD because of oppres-
sors, and He will send them a [a]Savior and a [1b]Champion, and He will
deliver them.
21 Thus the LORD will make Himself known to Egypt, and the
Egyptians will know the LORD in that day. They will even worship
with [a]sacrifice and offering, and will make a vow to the LORD and
perform it.
22 And the LORD will strike Egypt, striking but [a]healing; so they
will [b]return to the LORD, and He will respond to them and will heal
them.
23 In that day there will be a [a]highway from Egypt to Assyria, and

[1]Lit., *rivers* [2]Or, *Nile* *...anches;* i.e., the delta [a]Ex. 7:18 [b]Is. 37:25 [c]Ex. 2:3; Job 8:11; Is. 15:6

7 [1]Or, *mouth* [a]Is. 23:3, 10

8 [1]Lit., *hook* [2]Or, *...nguish* [a]Ezek. 47:10; Hab. 1:15

[1]Lit., *ashamed* [a]Prov. 7:16; Ezek. 27:7

...0 [1]Lit., *her pillars* or, *...er weavers* [a]Ps. 11:3

11 [1]Or, *Tanis* [2]Or, *...brutish* [a]Num. 13:22; ...s. 78:12, 43; Is. 30:4 ...Gen. 41:38, 39; 1 Kin. 4:30; Acts 7:22

12 [1]Or, *know* [a]Is. 14:24; Rom. 9:17

[1]Or, *Tanis* [2]Or, *have caused Egypt to stagger* [a]Jer. 2:16; ...:14, 19; Ezek. 30:13 [b]Zech. 10:4

...4 [1]Lit., *its work* [2]Or, *...s astray* [a]Prov. 12:8; ...Matt. 17:17 [b]Is. 3:12; 9:16 [c]Is. 28:7

15 [a]Is. 9:14, 15

...6 [a]2 Cor. 5:11; Heb. 10:31 [b]Is. 11:15

17 [1]Or, *cause of shame* [2]Lit., *who mentions it will be in ...read to it* [a]Is. 14:24; Dan. 4:35

[1]Some ancient mss. ...nd versions read *the ...un* [a]Is. 45:23; 65:16

19 [a]Is. 56:7; 60:7 ...Gen. 28:18; Ex. 24:4; Josh. 22:10, 26, 27

20 [1]Lit., *Mighty One* ...43:3, 11; 45:15, 21; ...:26; 60:16; 63:8 [b]Is. 49:25

...Is. 56:7; 60:7; Zech. 14:16-18

22 [a]Deut. 32:39; Is. 30:26; 57:18; Heb. ...1 [b]Is. 27:13; 45:14; Hos. 14:1

23 [a]Is. 11:16; 35:8; 49:11; 62:10

the Assyrians will come into Egypt and the Egyptians into Assyria,
and the Egyptians will [b]worship with the Assyrians.
24 In that day Israel will be the third *party* with Egypt and Assyria,
a blessing in the midst of the earth,
25 whom the LORD of hosts has blessed, saying, "Blessed is [a]Egypt
My people, and Assyria [b]the work of My hands, and Israel My
inheritance."

Chapter 20

20 In the year that the [1a]commander came to [b]Ashdod, when
Sargon the king of Assyria sent him and he fought against
Ashdod and captured it,
2 at that time the LORD spoke through [a]Isaiah the son of Amoz,
saying, "Go and loosen the [b]sackcloth from your hips, and take your
[c]shoes off your feet." And he did so, going [d]naked and barefoot.
3 And the LORD said, "Even as My servant Isaiah has gone naked
and barefoot three years as a [1a]sign and token against Egypt and
[2b]Cush,
4 so the [a]king of Assyria will lead away the captives of Egypt and
the exiles of Cush, [b]young and old, naked and barefoot with buttocks
uncovered, to the [1]shame of Egypt.
5 "Then they shall be [a]dismayed and ashamed because of Cush
their hope and Egypt their [b]boast.
6 "So the inhabitants of this coastland will say in that day, 'Behold,
such is our hope, where we fled [a]for help to be delivered from the
king of Assyria; and we, [b]how shall we escape?' "

Chapter 21

21 The [1a]oracle concerning the [2b]wilderness of the sea.
As [c]windstorms in the [3]Negev sweep on,
It comes from the wilderness, from a terrifying land.
2 A [a]harsh vision has been shown to me;
The [b]treacherous one still deals treacherously, *and* the destroyer
still destroys.
Go up, [c]Elam, lay siege, Media;
I have made an end of all [1]the groaning she has caused.
3 For this reason my [a]loins are full of anguish;
Pains have seized me like the pains of a [b]woman in labor.
I am so bewildered I cannot hear, so terrified I cannot see.
4 My [1]mind reels, [2]horror overwhelms me;
The twilight I longed for has been [a]turned for me into trembling.
5 They [a]set the table, they [1]spread out the cloth, they eat, they
drink;
"Rise up, captains, oil the shields,"
6 For thus the Lord says to me,
"Go, station the lookout, let him [a]report what he sees.
7 "When he sees [a]riders, horsemen in pairs,
A train of donkeys, a train of camels,
Let him pay close attention, very close attention."
8 Then [1]the lookout called,
"[a]O Lord, I stand continually by day on the watchtower,
And I am stationed every night at my guard post.
9 "Now behold, here comes a troop of riders, horsemen in pairs."
And one answered and said, "[a]Fallen, fallen is Babylon;

23 [b]Is. 27:13

25 [a]Is. 45:14 [b]Ps. 100:3; Is. 29:23; 45: 60:21; 64:8; Eph. 2:

20:1 [1]Heb., *Tartan* [a]2 Kin. 18:17 [b]1 Sa 5:1

2 [a]Is. 1:1; 13:1 [b]Ze 13:4; Matt. 3:4 [c]Ez 24:17, 23 [d]1 Sam. 19:24; Mic. 1:8

3 [1]Or, *wonder* [2]Or, *Ethiopia*, so in vv. 4 [a]Is. 8:18 [b]Is. 37:9;

4 [1]Lit., *nakedness* 19:4 [b]Is. 47:2, 3

5 [a]2 Kin. 18:21; Is. 30:3-5; 31:1; Ezek. 7 [b]Jer. 9:23, 24; 17 1 Cor. 3:21

6 [a]Is. 10:3; 30:7; 3 Jer. 30:1, 7, 15-17; 31:1-3 [b]Matt. 23:3 1 Thess. 5:3; Heb.

21:1 [1]Or, *burden* [2]Or, *sandy wastes*, *country* [3]I.e., Sout country [a]Is. 13:1 13:20-22; 14:23; J 51:42 [c]Zech. 9:14

2 [1]Lit., *her groani* [a]Ps. 60:3 [b]Is. 24:1 33:1 [c]Is. 22:6; Jer.

3 [a]Is. 13:8; 16:11 48:6; Is. 13:8; 26:1 1 Thess. 5:3

4 [1]Lit., *heart has wandered* [2]Lit., *shuddering* [a]Deut

5 [1]Or, *spread out rugs* or possibly, *t arranged the seat* [a]Jer. 51:39, 57; Da 5:1-4

6 [a]2 Kin. 9:17-20

7 [a]Is. 21:9

8 [1]So DSS; M.T., *called like a lion* 2:1

9 [a]Is. 13:19; 47:5 48:14; Jer. 51:8; F 14:8; 18:2

And all the [b]images of her gods [1]are shattered on the ground."
10 O my [a]threshed *people*, and my [1]afflicted of the threshing floor!
What I have heard from the LORD of hosts,
The God of Israel, I make known to you.

11 The [1]oracle concerning [2a]Edom.
One keeps calling to me from [b]Seir,
"Watchman, [3]how far gone is the night?
Watchman, [3]how far gone is the night?"
12 The watchman says,
"Morning comes but also night.
If you would inquire, inquire;
Come back again."

13 The [1]oracle about [a]Arabia.
In the thickets of Arabia you [2]must spend the night,
O caravans of [b]Dedanites.
14 Bring water [1]for the thirsty,
O inhabitants of the land of [a]Tema,
Meet the fugitive with bread.
15 For they have [a]fled from the swords,
From the drawn sword, and from the bent bow,
And from the press of battle.
16 For thus the Lord said to me, "In a [a]year, as [1]a hired man would
count it, all the splendor of [b]Kedar will terminate;
17 and the [a]remainder of the number of bowmen, the mighty men
of the sons of Kedar, will be few; for the LORD God of Israel [b]has
spoken."

Chapter 22

22 The [1]oracle concerning the [a]valley of vision.
What is the matter with you now, that you have all gone up to
the [b]housetops?
2 You who were full of noise,
You boisterous town, you [a]exultant city;
Your slain were [b]not slain with the sword,
Nor [1]did they die in battle.
3 [a]All your rulers have fled together,
And have been captured [1]without the bow;
All of you who were found were taken captive together,
[2]Though they had fled far away.
4 Therefore I say, "Turn your eyes away from me,
Let me [a]weep bitterly,
Do not [1]try to comfort me concerning the destruction of the
daughter of my people."
5 [a]For the Lord [1]GOD of hosts has a [b]day of panic, [c]subjugation,
and confusion
[d]In the valley of vision,
A breaking down of walls
And a crying [2]to the mountain.
6 And [a]Elam took up the quiver
With the chariots, [1]infantry, *and* horsemen;
And [b]Kir uncovered the shield.
7 Then your choicest valleys were full of chariots,

...it., *he has shattered the earth* [b]Is. 46:1; Jer. 50:2; 51:44

10 [1]Lit., *son* [a]Jer. 51:33; Mic. 4:13

...Or, *burden* [2]So the Gr.; Heb., *Dumah,* ...ce [3]Lit., *what is the ...of the night?* [a]Gen. 25:14 [b]Gen. 32:3

...Or, *burden* [2]Or, *will ...end* [a]Jer. 25:23, 24; ... [b]Gen. 10:7; Ezek. 27:15

...[1]Lit., *to meet* [a]Gen. 25:15; Job 6:19

...Is. 13:14, 15; 17:13

...[1]Lit., *the years of a ...ing* [a]Is. 16:14 [b]Ps. 120:5; Song 1:5; Is. ...; 60:7; Ezek. 27:21

...7 [a]Is. 10:19 [b]Num. 23:19; Zech. 1:6

...22:1 [1]Or, *burden of* ... 125:2; Jer. 21:13; ...13:12, 14 [b]Is. 15:3

...[1]Lit., *dead in battle* ...s. 23:7; 32:13 [b]Jer. 14:18; Lam. 2:20

...t., *from a bow* [2]So ...h ancient versions; Heb., *They fled far away* [a]Is. 21:15

...it., *insist* [a]Is. 15:3; ...er. 9:1; Luke 19:41

5 [1]Heb., *YHWH,* ...ally rendered LORD ...*against* [a]Lam. 1:5; [b]Is. 37:3 [c]Is. 10:6; 63:3 [d]Is. 22:1

...it., *man* [a]Is. 21:2; ...49:35 [b]2 Kin. 16:9; Amos 1:5; 9:7

And the horsemen took up fixed positions at the gate.
8 And He removed the [1]defense of Judah.
In that day you [2]depended on the weapons of the [a]house of the forest,
9 And you saw that the breaches
In the *wall* of the city of David were many;
And you [a]collected the waters of the lower pool.
10 Then you counted the houses of Jerusalem,
And you tore down houses to fortify the wall.
11 And you made a reservoir [a]between the two walls
For the waters of the [b]old pool.
But you did not [1]depend on Him who made it,
Nor did you [2]take into consideration Him who planned it long ago.

12 Therefore in that day the Lord [1]GOD of hosts, called *you* to [a]weeping, to wailing,
To [b]shaving the head, and to wearing sackcloth.
13 Instead, there is [a]gaiety and gladness,
Killing of cattle and slaughtering of sheep,
Eating of meat and drinking of wine:
"[b]Let us eat and drink, for tomorrow we may die."
14 But the LORD of hosts revealed Himself [1]to me,
"Surely this [a]iniquity [b]shall not be [2]forgiven you
[c]Until you die," says the Lord [3]GOD of hosts.

15 Thus says the Lord [1]GOD of hosts,
"Come, go to this steward,
To [a]Shebna, who is in charge of the *royal* household,
16 'What right do you have here,
And whom do you have here,
That you have [a]hewn a tomb for yourself here,
You who hew a tomb on the height,
You who carve a resting place for [1]yourself in the rock?
17 'Behold, the LORD is about to hurl you headlong, O man.
And He is about to grasp you firmly,
18 *And* roll you tightly like a ball,
To be [a]cast into a vast country;
There you will die,
And there your splendid chariots will be,
You shame of your master's house.'
19 "And I will [a]depose you from your office,
And [1]I will pull you down from your station.
20 "Then it will come about in that day,
That I will summon My servant [a]Eliakim the son of Hilkiah
21 And I will clothe him with your tunic,
And tie your sash securely about him,
I will entrust him with your [1]authority,
And he will become a [a]father to the inhabitants of Jerusalem and to the house of Judah.
22 "Then I will set [a]the key of the [b]house of David on his shoulder,
When he opens no one will shut,
When he shuts no one will [c]open.
23 "And I will drive him *like* a [a]peg in a firm place,

8 [1]Lit., *screen, covering* [2]Or, *look* ... *considered* [a]1 Kin 10:17

9 [a]2 Kin. 20:20; N... 3:16

11 [1]Or, *look to, consider* [2]Lit., *se*... *Him* [a]2 Kin. 25:4; 39:4 [b]2 Kin. 20:20 2 Chr. 32:3, 4

12 [1]Heb., *YWHW* usually rendered ... [a]Is. 32:11; Joel 1:... 2:17 [b]Mic. 1:16

13 [a]Is. 5:11, 22; ... Luke 17:26-29 [b]I... 56:12; 1 Cor. 15:3...

14 [1]Lit., *in my ea*... [2]Lit., *atoned for* [3]*YHWH*, usually rendered *LORD* [a]... 13:11; 26:21; 30:1... 65:7 [b]1 Sam. 3:1... Ezek. 24:13 [c]Is. ...

15 [1]Heb., *YHWH* usually rendered [a]2 Kin. 18:18, 26, 36:3, 11, 22; 37:2

16 [1]Lit., *himself* [a]2 Sam. 18:18; 2 16:14; Matt. 27:6...

18 [a]Job 18:18; Is...

19 [1]So with man... ancient versions; *He* [a]Job 40:11, ... Ezek. 17:24

20 [a]2 Kin. 18:18; 36:3, 22; 37:2

21 [1]Lit., *rule* [a]Ge... 45:8; Job 29:16

22 [a]Rev. 3:7 [b]Is... 13 [c]Job 12:14

23 [a]Ezra 9:8; Ze...

And he will become a [b]throne of glory to his father's house.
24 "So they will hang on him all the glory of his father's house,
offspring and [1]issue, all the least of vessels, from bowls to all the jars.
25 "In that day," declares the LORD of hosts, "the [a]peg driven in a
firm place will give way; it will even [b]break off and fall, and the load
hanging on it will be cut off, for the [c]LORD has spoken."

Chapter 23

23 The [1]oracle concerning [a]Tyre.
Wail, O [b]ships of [c]Tarshish,
For *Tyre* is destroyed, without house *or* [2d]harbor;
It is reported to them from the land of [3e]Cyprus.
2 [a]Be silent, you inhabitants of the coastland,
You merchants of Sidon;
[1]Your messengers crossed the sea
3 And *were* on many waters.
[a]The grain of the [1b]Nile, the harvest of the River was her revenue;
And she was the [c]market of nations.
4 Be ashamed, O [a]Sidon;
For the sea speaks, the stronghold of the sea, saying,
"I have neither travailed nor given birth,
I have neither brought up young men *nor* reared virgins."
5 When the report *reaches* Egypt,
They will be in [a]anguish at the report of Tyre.
6 Pass over to [a]Tarshish;
Wail, O inhabitants of the coastland.
7 Is this your [a]jubilant *city*,
Whose origin is from antiquity,
Whose feet used to carry her to [1]colonize distant places?

8 Who has planned this against Tyre, [a]the bestower of crowns,
Whose merchants were princes, whose traders were the honored of the earth?
9 [a]The LORD of hosts has planned it to [b]defile the pride of all beauty,
To despise all the [c]honored of the earth.
10 [1]Overflow your land like the Nile, O daughter of Tarshish,
There is no more [2]restraint.
11 He has [a]stretched His hand out [b]over the sea,
He has [c]made the kingdoms tremble;
The LORD has given a command concerning Canaan to [d]demolish its strongholds.
12 And He has said, "[a]You shall exult no more, O crushed virgin daughter of Sidon.
Arise, pass over to [1b]Cyprus; even there you will find no rest."
13 Behold, the land of the Chaldeans—this is the people *which* was
not; [a]Assyria appointed it for [b]desert creatures— they erected their
siege towers, they stripped its palaces, [c]they made it a ruin.
14 Wail, O [a]ships of Tarshish,
For your stronghold is destroyed.
15 Now it will come about in that day that Tyre will be forgotten for
[a]seventy years like the days of one king. At the end of seventy years
it will happen to Tyre as *in* the song of the harlot:
16 Take *your* harp, walk about the city,

Sam. 2:8; Job 36:7
r perhaps, *leaf*
. 22:23 [b]Esth. [c]Is. 46:11; Mic. 4:4
[1]Or, *burden of* ...*ntering* [3]Heb., [a]Josh. 19:29; 5:1; Jer. 25:22; ek. 26:1-27:36; 4-8; Amos 1:9; 9:2-4 [b]Is. 2:16 4; 1 Kin. 10:22 0 [e]Gen. 10:4; 12; Ezek. 27:6
SS; M.T., *Who d over the sea, plenished you.* [a]Is. 47:5
eb., *Shihor* [a]Is. -9 [b]Josh. 13:3; 13:5; Jer. 2:18 [c]Ezek. 27:3-23
Gen. 10:15, 19; :8; Judg. 10:6; :22; 27:3; 47:4; Ezek. 28:21, 22
15:14-16; Josh. 2:9-11
6 [a]Is. 23:1
sojourn afar off [a]Is. 22:2; 32:13
8 [a]Ezek. 28:2
:11; 13:11 [b]Job 1, 12; Dan. 4:37 [c]Is. 5:13; 9:15
[1]Lit., *Pass over* erhaps *girdle* or *shipyard*
14:21; Is. 14:26 . 19:5; 50:2 [c]Is. [d]Is. 25:2; Zech. 9:3, 4
o., *Kittim* [a]Ezek. 3, 14; Rev. 18:22 [b]Is. 23:1
10:5 [b]Is. 13:21; 18:6 [c]Is. 10:7
[a]Is. 2:16; Ezek. 27:25, 26
5 [a]Jer. 25:11, 22

O forgotten harlot;
Pluck the strings skillfully, sing many songs,
That you may be remembered.
17 And it will come about at [a]the end of seventy years that the LORD
will visit Tyre. Then she will go back to her harlot's wages, and will
[b]play the harlot with all the kingdoms [1]on the face of the earth.
18 And her [a]gain and her harlot's wages will be [b]set apart to the
LORD; it will not be stored up or hoarded, but her gain will become
sufficient food and choice attire for those who dwell in the presence
of the LORD.

Chapter 24

24 Behold, the LORD [a]lays the earth waste, devastates it, distorts
its surface, and scatters its inhabitants.
2 And the people will be like the priest, the servant like his master,
the maid like her mistress, the buyer like the seller, the lender like
the borrower, the [a]creditor like the debtor.
3 The earth will be completely laid waste and completely
despoiled, for the LORD has spoken this word.
4 The [a]earth mourns *and* withers, the world fades *and* withers, the
[b]exalted of the people of the earth fade away.
5 The earth is also [a]polluted [1]by its inhabitants, for they trans-
gressed laws, violated statutes, [b]broke the everlasting covenant.
6 Therefore, a [a]curse devours the earth, and those who live in it are
held guilty. Therefore, the [b]inhabitants of the earth are burned, and
few men are left.

7 The [a]new wine mourns,
The vine decays,
All the merry-hearted sigh.
8 The [a]gaiety of tambourines ceases,
The noise of revelers stops,
The gaiety of the harp ceases.
9 They do not drink wine with song;
[a]Strong drink is [b]bitter to those who drink it.
10 The [a]city of chaos is broken down;
[b]Every house is shut up so that none may enter.
11 There is an [a]outcry in the streets concerning the wine;
[b]All joy [1]turns to gloom.
The gaiety of the earth is banished.
12 Desolation is left in the city,
And the [a]gate is battered to ruins.
13 For [a]thus it will be in the midst of the earth among the peoples,
As the [1]shaking of an olive tree,
As the gleanings when the grape harvest is over.
14 [a]They raise their voices, they shout for joy.
They cry out from the [1]west concerning the majesty of the LORD.
15 Therefore [a]glorify the LORD in the [1]east,
The [b]name of the LORD, the God of Israel
In the [2c]coastlands of the sea.
16 From the [a]ends of the earth we hear songs, "[b]Glory to the
Righteous One,"
But I say, "[1c]Woe to me! [1]Woe to me! Alas for me!
The [d]treacherous deal treacherously,
And the treacherous deal very treacherously."

17 [1]Lit., *of the face of* 23:15 [b]Eze Nah. 3:4

18 [a]Ps. 72. 60:5-9; Mic. 28:36; Zech

24:1 [a]Is. 2: 24:19, 20; 3

2 [a]Lev. 25:3 23:19, 20

4 [a]Is. 33:9 24:21

5 [1]Lit., *unde* 3:17; Num. 3 9:17; 10:6 [b]

6 [a]Josh. 23 43:28; Zech. 1:31; 5:24; 9

7 [a]Is. 16:10; 1:10, 12

8 [a]Is. 5:12, 1 26:13; Hos. 2 18:22

9 [a]Is. 5:11, 2

10 [a]Is. 34:11

11 [1]Lit., *is da* [a]Jer. 14:2; 46 16:10; 32:13

12 [a]Is. 14:31;

13 [1]Lit., *striki* 17:6; 27:12

14 [1]Lit., *sea* 48:20; 52:8; 5

15 [1]Lit., *regio* [2]Or, *islands* [a]I [b]Mal. 1:11 [c]Is. 42:4, 10, 12; 4 60:9; 66:19

16 [1]Lit., *Wasti* [a]Is. 11:12; 42:1 28:5; 60:21 [c]L [d]Is. 21:2; 33:1; 5:11

17 [a]Terror and pit and snare
[1]Confront you, O inhabitant of the earth.
18 Then it will be that he who flees the [1]report of disaster will fall
into the pit,
And he who [2]climbs out of the pit will be caught in the snare;
For the [a]windows [3]above are opened, and the [b]foundations of
the earth shake.
19 [a]The earth is broken asunder,
The earth is [b]split through,
The earth is shaken violently.
20 The earth [a]reels to and fro like a drunkard,
And it totters like a [1]shack,
For its [b]transgression is heavy upon it,
And it will fall, [c]never to rise again.
21 So it will happen in that day,
That the LORD will [a]punish the host of [1]heaven, on high,
And the [b]kings of the earth, on earth.
22 And they will be gathered together
Like [a]prisoners in the [1]dungeon,
And will be confined in prison;
And after many days they will [b]be punished.
23 Then the [a]moon will be abashed and the sun ashamed,
For the [b]LORD of hosts will reign on [c]Mount Zion and in
Jerusalem,
And *His* glory will be before His elders.

Chapter 25

25 O LORD, Thou art [a]my God;
I will exalt Thee, I will give thanks to Thy name;
For Thou hast [b]worked wonders,
[c]Plans *formed* long ago, with perfect faithfulness.
2 For Thou hast made a city into a [a]heap,
A [b]fortified city into a ruin;
A [c]palace of strangers is a city no more,
It will never be rebuilt.
3 Therefore a strong people will [a]glorify Thee;
[b]Cities of ruthless nations will revere Thee.
4 For Thou hast been a [a]defense for the helpless,
A defense for the needy in his distress,
A [b]refuge from the storm, a shade from the heat;
For the breath of the [c]ruthless
Is like a *rain* storm *against* a wall.
5 Like heat in drought, Thou dost subdue the [a]uproar of aliens;
Like heat by the shadow of a cloud, the song of the ruthless is
[1]silenced.

6 And [a]the LORD of hosts will prepare a [1]lavish banquet for [b]all
peoples on this mountain;
A banquet of [2]aged wine, [3]choice pieces with marrow,
And [4]refined, aged wine.
7 And on this mountain He will swallow up the [1a]covering which
is over all peoples,
Even the veil which is [2]stretched over all nations.
8 He will [a]swallow up death for all time,

..., *Are upon you* :43; Amos 5:19
sound of terror *oes up from the* *f* [3]Lit., *from the* *ght;* i.e., heaven 7:11 [b]Ps. 18:7; 2:19, 21; 13:13
[a]Is. 24:1 [b]Num. , 32; Deut. 11:6
, hut [a]Is. 19:14; ; 28:7 [b]Is. 1:28; 27; 66:24 [c]Dan. :19; Amos 8:14
Lit., *the height in* *eight* [a]Is. 10:12; 3:11 [b]Ps. 76:12
Lit., *pit* [a]Is. 10:4; :22 [b]Ezek. 38:8; Zech. 9:11, 12
3 [a]Is. 13:10 [b]Is. 0; Zech. 14:6, 7; 1:23; 22:5 [c]Mic. 4:7; Heb. 12:22
:1 [a]Ex. 15:2; Ps. Is. 7:13; 49:4, 5; [b]Ps. 40:5; 98:1 [c]Eph. 1:11
17:1; 26:5; 27:10; [b]Is. 17:3; 25:12 :22; 32:14; 34:13
. 24:15 [b]Is. 13:11
[a]Is. 14:32; 17:10; :5; 33:16 [b]Is. 4:6; s. 29:5, 20; 49:25
Lit., *humbled* [a]Jer. 51:54-56
6 [1]Lit., *feast of fat* *s;* i.e., abundance ., *wine on the lees* t., *fat pieces* [4]Lit., *refined on the lees* 19 [b]Is. 2:2-4; 56:7
7 [1]Lit., *face of the* *vering* [2]Lit., *woven* Cor. 3:15, 16; Eph. 4:18
[a]Hos. 13:14; 1 Cor. 15:54

And the Lord [1]GOD will [b]wipe tears away from all faces,
And He will remove the [c]reproach of His people from all the earth;
For the LORD has spoken.
9 And it will be said in that day,
"Behold, [a]this is our God for whom we have [b]waited that [c]He might save us.
This is the LORD for whom we have waited;
[d]Let us rejoice and be glad in His salvation."
10 For the hand of the LORD will rest on this mountain,
And [a]Moab will be trodden down in his place
As straw is trodden down in the water of a manure pile.
11 And he will [a]spread out his hands in the middle of it
As a swimmer spreads out *his hands* to swim,
But *the Lord* will [b]lay low his pride together with the trickery of his hands.
12 And the [a]unassailable fortifications of your walls He will bring down,
Lay low, *and* cast to the ground, even to the dust.

Chapter 26

26 [a]In that day this song will be sung in the land of Judah:
"We have a [b]strong city;
He sets up walls and ramparts for [1c]security.
2 "Open the [a]gates, that the [b]righteous nation may enter,
The one that [1]remains faithful.
3 "The steadfast of mind Thou wilt keep in perfect [a]peace,
Because he trusts in Thee.
4 "[a]Trust in the LORD forever,
For in [1]GOD the LORD, *we have* an everlasting [b]Rock.
5 "For He has brought low those who dwell on high, the [a]unassailable city;
[b]He lays it low, He lays it low to the ground, He casts it to the dust.
6 "[a]The foot will trample it,
The feet of the [b]afflicted, the steps of the helpless."

7 The [a]way of the righteous is smooth;
O Upright One, [b]make the path of the righteous level.
8 Indeed, *while following* the way of [a]Thy judgments, O LORD,
We have waited for Thee eagerly;
[b]Thy name, even Thy [c]memory, is the desire of *our* souls.
9 [a]At night [1]my soul longs for Thee,
Indeed, [2]my spirit within me [b]seeks Thee diligently;
For when the earth [3]experiences Thy judgments
The inhabitants of the world [c]learn righteousness.
10 *Though* the wicked is shown favor,
He does not [a]learn righteousness;
He [b]deals unjustly in the land of uprightness,
And does not perceive the majesty of the LORD.

11 O LORD, Thy hand is lifted up *yet* they [a]do not see it.
[1]They see [b]*Thy* zeal for the people and are put to shame;
Indeed, [2c]fire will devour Thine enemies.

8 [1]Heb., *YH*... usually rende... [b]Is. 30:19; 35... 65:19; Rev. 7... [c]Ps. 69:9; 89:... 51:7; 54:4; M... 1 Pet. 4:14

9 [a]Is. 35:2; 4... [b]Is. 8:17; 30:1... [c]Is. 33:22; 35:... 26; 60:16 [d]Ps... 35:1, 2, 10; 6...

10 [a]Is. 16:14; ... 48:1-47; Ezek... Amos 2:1-3; Z...

11 [a]Is. 5:25; 1... 40:11; Is. 2:10... 15-17; 16:6, 1...

12 [a]Is. 15:1; 2...

26:1 [1]Or, *salv*... 4:2; 12:1 [b]Is. ... 31:5, 9; 33:5, ... [c]Is. 60:18

2 [1]Lit., *keeps faithfulness* [a]Is... 18; 62:10 [b]Is. ... 54:14, 17; 58:8... 61:3; 62:1, 2

3 [a]Is. 26:12; 2... 57:19; 66:12

4 [1]Heb., YAH, ... rendered *LORD*... 12:2; 50:10; 51... 17:10; 30:29; 4...

5 [a]Is. 25:12 [b]J... 40:11-13

6 [a]Is. 28:3 [b]Is. ... 15; 11:4; 29:19

7 [a]Is. 57:2 [b]Ps... 27:11; Is. 42:16...

8 [a]Is. 51:4; 56:1... 12:4; 24:15; 25:... [c]Ex. 3:15

9 [1]Lit., *with my long* [2]Lit., *with r... . . . I seek* [3]Lit., ... [a]Ps. 63:5, 6; 77:... 119:62; Is. 50:1... 6:12 [b]Ps. 63:1; ... Matt. 6:33 [c]Is. 5... Hos. 5:15

10 [a]Is. 22:12, 1... 7 [b]Hos. 11:7; Jo... 5:37, 38

11 [1]Or, *Let them see . . . and be* ... *the fire for Thine adversaries dev... them* [a]Is. 44:9, 1... 9:7; 37:32; 59:17... 5:24; 9:18, 19; 1... 66:15, 24; Heb. 1...

12 LORD, Thou wilt establish [a]peace for us,
Since Thou hast also performed for us all our works.
13 O LORD our God, [a]other masters besides Thee have ruled us;
But through Thee alone we [1b]confess Thy name.
14 [a]The dead will not live, the [1]departed spirits will not rise;
Therefore Thou hast [b]punished and destroyed them,
And Thou hast wiped out all remembrance of them.
15 [a]Thou hast increased the nation, O LORD,
Thou hast increased the nation, Thou art glorified;
Thou hast [b]extended all the borders of the land.
16 O LORD, they sought Thee [a]in distress;
They [1]could only whisper a prayer,
Thy chastening was upon them.
17 [a]As the pregnant woman approaches *the time* to give birth,
She writhes *and* cries out in her labor pains,
Thus were we before Thee, O LORD.
18 We were pregnant, we writhed *in labor*,
We [a]gave birth, as it were, *only* to wind.
We could not accomplish deliverance for the earth
Nor were [b]inhabitants of the world [1]born.
19 Your [a]dead will live;
[1]Their corpses will rise.
You who lie in the dust, [b]awake and shout for joy,
For your dew is as the dew of the [2]dawn,
And the earth will [3]give birth to the [4]departed spirits.

20 Come, my people, [a]enter into your rooms,
And close your doors behind you;
Hide for a little [1b]while,
Until [c]indignation [2]runs *its* course.
21 For behold, the LORD is about to [a]come out from His place
To [b]punish the inhabitants of the earth for their iniquity;
And the earth will [c]reveal her bloodshed,
And will no longer cover her slain.

Chapter 27

27 In that day [a]the LORD will punish [1b]Leviathan the fleeing serpent,
With His fierce and great and mighty sword,
Even [1]Leviathan the twisted serpent;
And [c]He will kill the dragon who *lives* in the sea.

2 In that day,
"A [1a]vineyard of wine, sing of it!
3 "I, the LORD, am its keeper;
[a]I water it every moment.
Lest anyone [1]damage it,
I [b]guard it night and day.
4 "I have no wrath.
Should [1]someone give Me [a]briars *and* thorns in battle,
Then I would step on them, [b]I would burn them [2]completely.
5 "Or let him [1a]rely on My protection,
Let him make peace with Me,
Let him [b]make peace with Me."

12 [a]Is. 26:3
13 [1]Or, *cause to be* ...*membered* [a]Is. 2:8; 10:11 [b]Is. 63:7
[1]Or, *shades* [a]Deut. ...:28; Ps. 135:17; Is. ... Hab. 2:19 [b]Is. 10:3
[a]Is. 9:3 [b]Is. 33:17; 54:2, 3
[1]Lit., *sound forth a* ...*sper* [a]Is. 37:3; Hos. 5:15
...Is. 13:8; 21:3; John 16:21
18 [1]Lit., *fallen* [a]Is. ...1; 59:4 [b]Ps. 17:14
19 [1]So with some ...ent versions; Heb., ...*y* [2]Lit., *lights* [3]Lit., *cause to fall* [4]Or, ...*es* [a]Is. 25:8; Ezek. 37:1-14; Dan. 12:2; ... 13:14 [b]Eph. 5:14
[1]Lit., *moment* [2]Lit., ...*s over* [a]Ex. 12:22, ...3; Ps. 91:1, 4 [b]Ps. ...; Is. 54:7, 8; 2 Cor. ... [c]Is. 10:5, 25; 13:5; 34:2; 66:14
[a]Mic. 1:3; Jude 14 ...s. 13:11; 30:12-14; ...5:6, 7 [c]Job 16:18; Luke 11:50
[1]Or, *sea monster* ...s. 66:16 [b]Job 3:8; Ps. 74:14; 104:26 [c]Is. 51:9
...Some mss. read *a* ...*ard of delight* [a]Ps. ...8; Is. 5:7; Jer. 2:21
3 [1]Lit., *punish* [a]Is. ...1 [b]1 Sam. 2:9; Is. 31:5; John 10:28
4 [1]Lit., *who* [2]Lit., ...*ltogether* [a]2 Sam. ...3:6; Is. 10:17 [b]Is. ...; Matt. 3:12; Heb. 6:8
..., *take hold of* [a]Is. 25:4 [b]Job 22:21; ...6:3, 12; Rom. 5:1; 2 Cor. 5:20

6 [1]In the days to come Jacob [a]will take root,
Israel will [b]blossom and sprout;
And they will fill the [2]whole world with [c]fruit.

7 Like the striking of Him who has struck them, has [a]He struck them?
Or like the slaughter of His slain, [1]have they been slain?
8 Thou didst contend with them [1]by banishing them, by [a]driving them away.
With His fierce wind He has expelled *them* on the day of the [b]east wind.
9 Therefore through this Jacob's iniquity will be [a]forgiven;
And this will be [1]the full price of the [2b]pardoning of his sin:
When he makes all the [c]altar stones like pulverized chalk stones;
When [3]Asherim and incense altars will not stand.
10 For the fortified city is [a]isolated,
A [1]homestead forlorn and forsaken like the desert;
[b]There the calf will graze,
And there it will lie down and [2]feed on its branches.
11 When its [a]limbs are dry, they are broken off;
Women come *and* make a fire with them.
For they are not a people of [b]discernment,
Therefore [c]their Maker [d]will not have compassion on them.
And their Creator will not be gracious to them.
12 And it will come about in that day, that the LORD [a]will start *His*
threshing from the flowing stream of the [b]Euphrates to the brook of
Egypt; and you will be [c]gathered up one by one, O sons of Israel.
13 It will come about also in that day that a great [a]trumpet will be
blown; and those who were perishing in the land of [b]Assyria and
who were scattered in the land of Egypt will come and [c]worship the
LORD in the holy mountain at Jerusalem.

Chapter 28

28 Woe to the proud crown of the [a]drunkards of [b]Ephraim,
And to the fading flower of its glorious beauty,
Which is at the head of the [1]fertile valley
Of those who are [2]overcome with wine!
2 Behold, the Lord has a strong and [a]mighty *agent;*
As a storm of [b]hail, a tempest of destruction,
Like a storm of [c]mighty overflowing waters,
He has cast *it* down to the earth with *His* hand.
3 The proud crown of the drunkards of Ephraim is [a]trodden under foot.
4 And the fading flower of its glorious beauty,
Which is at the head of the [1]fertile valley,
Will be like the [a]first-ripe fig prior to summer;
Which [2]one sees,
And [3]as soon as it is in his [4]hand,
He swallows it.
5 In that day the [a]LORD of hosts will become a beautiful [b]crown
And a glorious diadem to the remnant of His people;
6 A [a]spirit of justice for him who sits in judgment,
A [b]strength to those who repel the [1]onslaught at the gate.
7 And these also [a]reel with wine and stagger from strong drink:

6 [1]Lit., *Those* [2]Lit., *face of* [a]Is [b]Is. 35:1, 2; Hos 6 [c]Is. 4:2

7 [1]Lit., *he was* 10:12, 17; 30:3 31:8, 9; 37:36-3

8 [1]Some ancie versions read *b measure* [a]Is. 5 54:7 [b]Jer. 4:11; 19:12; Hos. 13:

9 [1]Lit., *all the fr removing* [3]I.e., symbols of a fe deity [a]Is. 1:25; Dan. 11:35 [b]Ro 11:27 [c]Ex. 34:1 12:3; 2 Kin. 10: 17:8

10 [1]Lit., *pastur consume* [a]Is. 3 [b]Is. 17:2

11 [a]Is. 18:5 [b]De 32:28; Is. 1:3; 5 8:7 [c]Deut. 32:18 43:1, 7; 44:2, 21 9:17

12 [a]Is. 11:11; 17 24:13; 56:8 [b]Ge 15:18 [c]Deut. 30 Neh. 1:9

13 [a]Lev. 25:9; 1 15:24; Matt. 24:3 11:15 [b]Is. 19:24, 19:21, 23; 49:7; Zech. 14:16; Heb

28:1 [1]Lit., *valley fatness* [2]Lit., *sm* [a]Is. 28:7; Hos. 7: 9:9

2 [a]Is. 8:7; 40:10 28:17; 30:30; 32: Ezek. 13:11 [c]Is. 30:28; Nah. 1:8

3 [a]Is. 26:6; 28:18

4 [1]Lit., *valley of* [2]Lit., *the one see sees* [3]Lit., *while yet* [4]Lit., *palm* [a]H 9:10; Mic. 7:1; Na

5 [a]Is. 41:16; 45:2 60:1, 19 [b]Is. 62:3

6 [1]Lit., *battle* [a]1 K 3:28; Is. 11:2; 32: John 5:30 [b]2 Chr. 32:6-8; Is. 25:4

7 [a]Is. 5:11, 22; 22 56:12; Hos. 4:11

[b]The priest and [c]the prophet reel with strong drink,
They are confused by wine, they stagger from [d]strong drink;
They reel while [1]having [e]visions,
They totter *when rendering* judgment.
8 For all the tables are full of filthy [a]vomit, without a *single clean*
place.

9 "To [a]whom would He teach knowledge?
And to whom would He interpret the message?
Those *just* [b]weaned from milk?
Those *just* taken from the breast?
10 "For *He says,*
'[1a]Order on order, order on order,
Line on line, line on line,
A little here, a little there.' "
11 Indeed, He will speak to this people
Through [a]stammering lips and a foreign tongue,
12 He who said to them, "Here is [a]rest, give rest to the weary,"
And, "Here is repose," but they would not listen.
13 So the word of the LORD to them will be,
"[1]Order on order, order on order,
Line on line, line on line,
A little here, a little there,"
That they may go and [a]stumble backward, be broken, snared,
and taken captive.
14 Therefore, [a]hear the word of the LORD, O [b]scoffers,
Who rule this people who are in Jerusalem,
15 Because you have said, "We have made a [a]covenant with death,
And with [1]Sheol we have made a [2]pact.
[b]The overwhelming [3]scourge will not reach us when it passes by,
For we have made [c]falsehood our refuge and we have
[d]concealed ourselves with deception."
16 Therefore thus says the Lord [1]GOD,
"[a]Behold, I am laying in Zion a stone, a tested [b]stone,
A costly cornerstone *for* the foundation, [2]firmly placed.
He who believes *in it* will not be [3]disturbed.
17 "And I will make [a]justice the measuring line,
And righteousness the level;
Then [b]hail shall sweep away the refuge of lies,
And the waters shall overflow the secret place.
18 "And your [a]covenant with death shall be [1b]canceled,
And your pact with Sheol shall not stand;
When the [a]overwhelming scourge passes through,
Then you become its [c]trampling *place*.
19 "As [a]often as it passes through, it will [1]seize you.
For [b]morning after morning it will pass through, *anytime* during
the day or night.
And it will be [2]sheer [c]terror to understand [3]what it means."
20 The bed is too short on which to stretch out,
And the [a]blanket is too [1]small to wrap oneself in.
21 For the LORD will rise up as *at* Mount [a]Perazim,
He will be stirred up as in the valley of [b]Gibeon;
To do His [c]task, His [1d]unusual task,
And to work His work, His [2]extraordinary work.

[1]Lit., *seeing* [b]Is. 24:2 ...9:15 [c]Hab. 2:15, 16 [e]Is. 29:11

8 [a]Jer. 48:26

[a]Is. 2:3; 28:26; 30:20; ...:17; 50:4; 54:13 [b]Ps. 131:2

10 [1]Heb., *Sav lasav, sav lasav, Kav lakav, ...av lakav, Ze'er sham, ze'er sham.* These ...ebrew monosyllables, ...itating the babbling of a child, mock the prophet's preaching ...Chr. 36:15; Neh. 9:30

11 [a]Is. 33:19; 1 Cor. 14:21

12 [a]Is. 11:10; 30:15; 32:17, 18; Jer. 6:16; Matt. 11:28, 29

...3 [1]V. 10, note 1. The ...ORD responds to their scoffing by imitating their mockery, to represent the ...nintelligible language of a conqueror. [a]Is. 8:15; Matt. 21:44

[a]Is. 1:10; 28:22 [b]Is. 29:20

15 [1]I.e., the nether ...d [2]So some ancient versions; Heb., *seer* [3]Or, *flood* [a]Is. 28:18 [b]Is. 8:8; 28:2; 30:28; ...Dan. 11:22 [c]Is. 9:15; 30:9; 44:20; 59:3, 4; ...ek. 13:22 [d]Is. 29:15

16 [1]Heb., *YHWH,* ...ually rendered *LORD* ..., *well-laid* [3]Lit., *in a hurry* [a]Rom. 9:33; ...0:11; 1 Pet. 2:6 [b]Ps. 118:22; Is. 8:14, 15; ... 21:42; Mark 12:10; ...ke 20:17; Acts 4:11; Eph. 2:20

17 [a]2 Kin. 21:13; Is. ...; 30:18; 61:8; Amos 7:7-9 [b]Is. 28:2

...8 [1]Lit., *covered over* 28:15 [b]Is. 7:7; 8:10 [c]Is. 28:3; Dan. 8:13

[1]Lit., *take* [2]Lit., *only* ..., *the report,* or, *the ...essage* [a]2 Kin. 24:2 [b]Is. 50:4 [c]Job 6:4; ...:11; 24:17; Ps. 55:4; 88:15; Lam. 2:22

20 [1]Lit., *narrow* [a]Is. 59:6

[1]Lit., *task is strange* [2]Lit., *work is alien* [a]2 Sam. 5:20; 1 Chr. ...1 [b]Josh. 10:10, 12; 2 Sam. 5:25; 1 Chr. ...6 [c]Is. 10:12; 29:14; ...7 [d]Lam. 2:15; 3:33; Luke 19:41-44

22 And now do not carry on as [a]scoffers,
Lest your fetters be made stronger;
For I have heard from the Lord [1]GOD of hosts,
Of decisive [b]destruction on all the earth.

23 Give ear and hear my voice,
Listen and hear my words.
24 Does the [1]farmer plow [2]continually to plant seed?
Does he *continually* [3]turn and harrow the ground?
25 Does he not level its surface,
And sow dill and scatter [a]cummin,
And [1]plant [b]wheat in rows,
Barley in its place, and rye within its [2]area?
26 For his God instructs and teaches him properly.
27 For dill is not threshed with a [a]threshing sledge,
Nor is the cartwheel [1]driven over cummin;
But dill is beaten out with a rod, and cummin with a club.
28 *Grain for* bread is crushed,
Indeed, he does not continue to thresh it forever.
Because the wheel of *his* cart and his horses *eventually* [1]damage *it*,
He does not thresh it longer.
29 This also comes from the LORD of hosts,
Who has made *His* counsel [a]wonderful and *His* wisdom [b]great.

Chapter 29

29 Woe, O [1]Ariel, [1]Ariel the city *where* David *once* [a]camped!
Add year to year, [2b]observe *your* feasts on schedule.
2 And I will bring distress to Ariel,
And she shall be *a city of* lamenting and [a]mourning;
And she shall be like an Ariel to me.
3 And I will [a]camp against you [1]encircling *you*,
And I will set siegeworks against you,
And I will raise up battle towers against you.
4 Then you shall [a]be brought low;
From the earth you shall speak,
And from the dust *where* you are prostrate,
Your words *shall come.*
Your voice shall also be like that of a [1]spirit from the ground,
And your speech shall whisper from the dust.

5 But the multitude of your [1]enemies shall become like fine [a]dust,
And the multitude of the [b]ruthless ones like the chaff which [2]blows away;
And it shall happen [c]instantly, suddenly.
6 From the LORD of hosts you will be [a]punished with [b]thunder and earthquake and loud noise,
With whirlwind and tempest and the flame of a consuming fire.
7 And the [a]multitude of all the nations who wage war against [1]Ariel,
Even all who wage war against her and her stronghold, and who distress her,
Shall be like a dream, a [b]vision of the night.
8 And it will be as when a hungry man dreams—

22 [1]Heb., *YHWH* usually rendered [a]Is. 28:14 [b]Is. 10
24 [1]Lit., *plowma* *all day* [3]Lit., *ope*
25 [1]Lit., *put* [2]Lit *region* [a]Matt. 23 [b]Ex. 9:32
27 [1]Lit., *rolled* [a] 1:3
28 [1]Lit., *discomfi*
29 [a]Is. 9:6 [b]Is. 3 Rom. 11:33
29:1 [1]I.e., Lion of or, Jerusalem [2]Li *your feasts run th round* [a]2 Sam. 5: 1:14; 5:12; 22:12, 29:9, 13
2 [a]Is. 3:26; Lam.
3 [1]Lit., *like a circl* [a]Luke 19:43, 44
4 [1]Or, *ghost* [a]Is. 8
5 [1]Lit., *strangers* *passes away* [a]Is. 41:15, 16 [b]Is. 13:1 25:3; 29:20 [c]Is. 17 30:13; 47:11; 1 Th 5:3
6 [a]Is. 10:3; 26:14, [b]1 Sam. 2:10; Matt. 24:7; Mark 13:8; L 21:11; Rev. 11:13, 16:18
7 [1]V. 1, note 1 [a]Mi 4:11, 12; Zech. 12: [b]Job 20:8; Ps. 73:2 17:14

And behold, he is eating;
But when he awakens, his [1]hunger is not satisfied,
Or as when a thirsty man dreams—
And behold, he is drinking,
But when he awakens, behold, he is faint,
And his [1]thirst is not quenched.
[a]Thus the multitude of all the nations shall be,
Who wage war against Mount Zion.

9 [a]Be delayed and wait.
Blind yourselves and be blind.
They [b]become drunk, but not with wine;
They stagger, but not with strong drink.
10 For the LORD has poured over you a spirit of deep [a]sleep,
He has [b]shut your eyes, the prophets;
And He has covered your heads, the seers.
11 And the entire vision shall be to you like the words of a sealed
[1a]book, which when they give it to the one who [2]is literate, saying,
"Please read this," he will say, "I cannot, for it is sealed."
12 Then the [1]book will be given to the one who [2]is illiterate, saying,
"Please read this." And he will say, "I [3]cannot read."
13 Then the Lord said,
"Because [a]this people draw near with their [1]words
And honor Me with their [2]lip service,
But they remove their hearts far from Me,
And their [3]reverence for Me [4]consists of [5]tradition learned *by rote,*
14 Therefore behold, I will once again deal [a]marvelously with this people, wondrously marvelous;
And [b]the wisdom of their wise men shall perish,
And the discernment of their discerning men shall be concealed."

15 Woe to those who deeply [a]hide their [1]plans from the LORD,
And whose [b]deeds are *done* in a dark place,
And they say, "[c]Who sees us?" or "Who knows us?"
16 You turn *things* around!
Shall the potter be considered [1]as equal with the clay,
That [a]what is made should say to its maker, "He did not make me";
Or what is formed say to him who formed it, "He has no understanding"?

17 Is it not yet just a little while
[1]Before Lebanon will be turned into a [a]fertile field,
And the fertile field will be considered as a forest?
18 And on that day the [a]deaf shall hear [b]words of a book,
And out of *their* gloom and darkness the [c]eyes of the blind shall see.
19 The [a]afflicted also shall increase their gladness in the LORD,
And the [b]needy of mankind shall rejoice in the Holy One of Israel.
20 For the [a]ruthless will come to an end, and the [b]scorner will be finished,
Indeed [c]all who [1]are intent on doing evil will be cut off;

, *soul* [a]Is. 54:17
29:1 [b]Is. 51:17, 21, 22; 63:6
[a]s. 69:23; Is. 6:9, :. 3:6; Rom. 11:8 44:18; 2 Thess. 2:9-12
[1]Or, *scroll* [2]Lit., *books* [a]Is. 8:16; :4, 9; Matt. 13:11
[1]Or, *scroll* [2]Lit., *not know books* *not know books*
[1]Lit., *mouth* [2]Lit., [3]Lit., *fear of Me* [4]Lit., *is* [5]Lit., *andment of rulers* zek. 33:31; Matt. :8, 9; Mark 7:6, 7
s. 6:9, 10; 28:21; 5:7; Hab. 1:5 [b]Is. 25; Jer. 8:9; 49:7; 1 Cor. 1:19
Lit., *counsel* [a]Ps. :11, 13; Is. 28:15; 1 [b]Job 22:13; Is. ; Ezek. 8:12 [c]Ps. 47:10; Mal. 2:17
Lit., *like* [a]Is. 45:9; Jer. 18:1-6; Rom. 9:19-21
t., *And* [a]Ps. 84:6; :33, 35; Is. 32:15
s. 35:5; 42:18, 19; ; Matt. 11:5; Mark 37 [b]Is. 29:11 [c]Ps. 8; Prov. 20:12; Is. 32:3
Ps. 25:9; 37:11; Is. 4; 61:1; Matt. 5:5; :29 [b]Is. 3:14, 15; 4; 14:30, 32; 25:4; Matt. 11:5; James 1:9; 2:5
Lit., *watch evil* [a]Is. 9:5 [b]Is. 28:14 [c]Is. 59:4; Mic. 2:1

21 Who [1]cause a person to be indicted by a word,
And [a]ensnare him who adjudicates at the gate,
And [2b]defraud the one in the right with [3]meaningless arguments.
22 Therefore thus says the LORD, who redeemed [a]Abraham, concerning the house of Jacob,
"Jacob [b]shall not now be ashamed, nor shall his face now turn pale;
23 But when [1]he sees his [a]children, the [b]work of My hands, in his midst,
They will sanctify My name;
Indeed, they will [c]sanctify the Holy One of Jacob,
And will stand in awe of the God of Israel.
24 "And those who [a]err in [1]mind will [b]know [2]the truth,
And those who [3]criticize will [4c]accept instruction.

Chapter 30

30 "Woe to the [a]rebellious children," declares the LORD,
"Who [b]execute a plan, but not Mine,
And [1c]make an alliance, but not of My Spirit,
In order to add sin to sin;
2 Who [a]proceed down to Egypt,
Without [b]consulting [1]Me,
[c]To take refuge in the safety of Pharaoh,
And to seek shelter in the shadow of Egypt!
3 "Therefore the safety of Pharaoh will be [a]your shame,
And the shelter in the shadow of Egypt, your humiliation.
4 "For [a]their princes are at Zoan,
And their ambassadors arrive at Hanes.
5 "Everyone will be [a]ashamed because of a people who cannot profit them,
Who are [b]not for help or profit, but for shame and also for reproach."

6 The [1]oracle concerning the [a]beasts of the [b]Negev.
Through a land of [c]distress and anguish,
From [2]where *come* lioness and lion, viper and [d]flying serpent,
They [e]carry their riches on the [3]backs of young donkeys
And their treasures on [f]camels' humps,
To a people who cannot profit *them;*
7 Even Egypt, whose [a]help is vain and empty.
Therefore, I have called [1]her
"[2b]Rahab who has been exterminated."
8 Now go, [a]write it on a tablet before them
And inscribe it on a scroll,
That it may [1]serve in the time to come
[2]As a witness forever.
9 For this is a [a]rebellious people, [b]false sons,
Sons who [1]refuse to [c]listen
To the [2]instruction of the LORD;
10 Who say to the [a]seers, "You must not see *visions*";
And to the prophets, "You must not [b]prophesy to us what is right,
[c]Speak to us [1]pleasant words,
Prophesy illusions.

21 [1]Lit., *bring a* ... *under condemn*... [2]Lit., *turn aside* ... *confusion* [a]Amo... [b]Is. 32:7; Amos ...

22 [a]Is. 41:8; 51:... 63:16 [b]Is. 45:17... 50:7; 54:4

23 [1]Or, *his child*... *see* [a]Is. 49:20-2... 26:12; 45:11; Ep... [c]Is. 5:16; 8:13

24 [1]Lit., *spirit* [2]L... *understanding* [3]... *murmur* [4]Lit., *lea*... 30:21; Heb. 5:2 ... 41:20; 60:16 [c]Is...

30:1 [1]Lit., *pour* ... *drink offering* [a]Is... 23; 30:9; 65:2 [b]Is... 29:15 [c]Is. 8:11, 1...

2 [1]Lit., *My mouth*... 31:1; Jer. 43:7 [b]I... [c]Is. 36:9

3 [a]Is. 20:5, 6; 36... 42:18, 22

4 [a]Is. 19:11

5 [a]Jer. 2:36 [b]Is. 30:7; 31:3

6 [1]Or, *burden of* ... *them* [3]Lit., *shoul*... [a]Is. 46:1, 2 [b]Gen... [c]Ex. 5:10, 21; Deu... 4:20; 8:15; Is. 5:3... 8:22; Jer. 11:4 [d]D... 8:15; Is. 14:29 [e]Is... 46:1, 2 [f]1 Kin. 10...

7 [1]Lit., *this one* [2]... reads *They are R*... *(or arrogance)*, *to* ... *remain* [a]Is. 30:5 ... 9:13; Ps. 87:4; 89... 51:9

8 [1]Lit., *be* [2]So the... versions; Heb., *Fo*... *and ever* [a]Is. 8:1

9 [1]Lit., *are not wil*... [2]Or, *law* [a]Is. 30:1 ... 28:15; 59:3, 4 [c]Is... 5:24; 24:5

10 [1]Lit., *smooth th*... [a]Is. 29:10 [b]Is. 5:2... 11:21; Amos 2:12; ... [c]1 Kin. 22:8, 13; Je... 6:14; 23:17, 26; E... 13:7; Rom. 16:18; ... 2 Tim. 4:3, 4

11 "Get out of the way, [a]turn aside from the path,
[1b]Let us hear no more about the Holy One of Israel."
12 Therefore thus says the Holy One of Israel,
"[a]Since you have rejected this word,
And have put your trust in [b]oppression and guile, and have
relied on them,
13 Therefore this [a]iniquity will be to you
Like a [b]breach about to fall,
A bulge in a high wall,
Whose collapse comes [c]suddenly in an instant.
14 "And whose collapse is like the smashing of a [a]potter's jar;
[1]So ruthlessly shattered
That a sherd will not be found among its pieces
To [2]take fire from a hearth,
Or to scoop water from a cistern."
15 For thus the Lord [1]GOD, the Holy One of Israel, has said,
"In [2]repentance and [a]rest you shall be saved,
In [b]quietness and trust is your strength."
But you were not willing,
16 And you said, "No, for we will flee on [a]horses,"
Therefore you shall flee!
"And we will ride on swift *horses*,"
Therefore those who pursue you shall be swift.
17 [a]One thousand *shall flee* at the threat of one *man*,
You shall flee at the threat of five;
Until you are left as a [1]flag on a mountain top,
And as a signal on a hill.

18 Therefore the LORD [1a]longs to be gracious to you,
And therefore He [2]waits on [b]high to have compassion on you.
For the LORD is a [c]God of justice;
How blessed are all those who [3d]long for Him.
19 [1]O people in Zion, [a]inhabitant in Jerusalem, you will [b]weep no
longer. He will surely be gracious to you at the sound of your cry;
when He hears it, He will [c]answer you.
20 Although the Lord has given you [a]bread of privation and water
of oppression, *He*, your Teacher will no longer [b]hide Himself, but
your eyes will behold your Teacher.
21 And your ears will hear a word behind you, [1]"This is the [a]way,
walk in it," whenever you [b]turn to the right or to the left.
22 And you will defile your graven [a]images, overlaid with silver,
and your molten [a]images plated with gold. You will scatter them as
an impure thing; *and* say to [1]them, "[b]Be gone!"
23 Then He will [a]give *you* rain for [1]the seed which you will sow in
the ground, and bread *from* the yield of the ground, and it will be
[2]rich and [3]plenteous; on that day [b]your livestock will graze in a
roomy pasture.
24 Also the oxen and the donkeys which work the ground will eat
salted fodder, which [1]has been [a]winnowed with shovel and fork.
25 And on every lofty mountain and on [a]every high hill there will
be [1]streams running with water on the day of the great [b]slaughter,
when the towers fall.
26 And [a]the light of the moon will be as the light of the sun, and the
light of the sun will be seven times *brighter*, like the light of seven

[1]Lit., *Cause to cease from our presence the* [a]Acts 13:8 [b]Job 21:14

12 [a]Is. 5:24; 7:9; 8:6 [b]Is. 3:14, 15; 5:7; 59:13

13 [a]Is. 26:21 [b]1 Kin. 20:30; Ps. 62:4; Is. 58:12 [c]Is. 29:5; 47:11

14 [1]Lit., *Crushed, it will not be spared* [2]Lit., *snatch up* [a]Ps. 2:9; Jer. 19:10, 11

15 [1]Heb., *YHWH*, usually rendered *LORD* [2]Lit., *returning* [a]Ps. 116:7; Is. 28:12 [b]Is. 7:4; 32:17

16 [a]Is. 2:7; 31:1, 3

17 [1]Lit., *pole* [a]Lev. 26:36; Deut. 28:25; 32:30; Josh. 23:10; Prov. 28:1

18 [1]Lit., *waits* [2]Lit., *is on high* [3]Lit., *wait* [a]Is. 42:14, 16; 48:9; Jon. 3:4, 10; 2 Pet. 3:9, 15 [b]Is. 2:11, 17; 33:5 [c]Is. 5:16; 28:17; 61:8 [d]Is. 8:17; 25:9; 26:8; 33:2

19 [1]M.T. reads *A people will inhabit Zion, in Jerusalem.* [a]Is. 65:9; Ezek. 37:25, 28 [b]Is. 25:8; 60:20; 61:1-3 [c]Ps. 50:15; Is. 58:9; 65:24; Matt. 7:7-11

20 [a]1 Kin. 22:27; Ps. 80:5 [b]Ps. 74:9; Amos 8:11

21 [1]Lit., *saying, "This* [a]Is. 25:8, 9; Prov. 3:6; Is. 35:8, 9; 42:16 [b]Is. 29:24

22 [1]Lit., *it "Go out"* [a]Ex. 32:2, 4; Judg. 17:3, 4; Is. 46:6 [b]Matt. 4:10

23 [1]Lit., *your* [2]Lit., *fatness* [3]Lit., *fat* [a]Ps. 65:9-13; 104:13, 14 [b]Ps. 144:13; Is. 32:20; Hos. 4:16

24 [1]Lit., *one winnows* [a]Matt. 3:12; Luke 3:17

25 [1]Lit., *canals, streams of water* [a]Is. 5:6, 7; 41:18; 43:19, 20 [b]Is. 34:2

26 [a]Is. 24:23; 60:19, 20; Rev. 21:23; 22:5

days, on the day [b]the LORD binds up the [c]fracture of His people and
[d]heals the bruise [1]He has inflicted.
27 Behold, [a]the name of the LORD comes from a [1]remote place;
[b]Burning is His anger, and [2]dense is *His* [3]smoke;
His lips are filled with [c]indignation,
And His tongue is like a [d]consuming fire;
28 And His [a]breath is like an overflowing torrent,
Which [b]reaches to the neck,
To [c]shake the nations back and forth in a [1]sieve,
And to *put* in the jaws of the peoples [d]the bridle which [2]leads to ruin.
29 You will have [1]songs as in the night when you keep the festival;
And gladness of heart as when one marches to *the sound of* the flute,
To go to the mountain of the LORD, to the Rock of Israel.
30 And the LORD will cause [1]His voice of authority to be heard.
And the [2]descending of His arm to be seen in fierce anger,
And *in* the flame of a consuming fire,
In cloudburst, downpour, and hailstones.
31 For [a]at the voice of the LORD [b]Assyria will be terrified,
When He strikes with the [c]rod.
32 And every [1]blow of the [2a]rod of punishment,
Which the LORD will lay on him,
Will be with *the music of* [b]tambourines and lyres;
And in battles, [c]brandishing weapons, He will fight them.
33 For [1a]Topheth has long been ready,
Indeed, it has been prepared for the king.
He has made it deep and large,
[2]A pyre of fire with plenty of wood;
The [b]breath of the LORD, like a torrent of [c]brimstone, sets it afire.

Chapter 31

31 Woe to those who go down to [a]Egypt for help,
And [b]rely on horses,
And trust in chariots because they are many,
And in horsemen because they are very strong,
But they do not [c]look to the [d]Holy One of Israel, nor seek the LORD!
2 Yet He also is [a]wise and will [b]bring disaster,
And does [c]not retract His words,
But will arise against the house of [d]evildoers,
And against the help of the [e]workers of iniquity.
3 Now the Egyptians are [a]men, and not God,
And their [b]horses are flesh and not spirit;
So the LORD will [c]stretch out His hand,
And [d]he who helps will stumble
And he who is helped will fall,
And all of them will come to an end together.

4 For thus says the LORD to me,
"As the [a]lion or the young lion growls over his prey,
Against which a band of shepherds is called out,
Will not be terrified at their voice, nor disturbed at their noise,

26 [1]Lit., *of His blo*… [b]Is. 30:… 61:1 [c]Is. 1:6; 30:1… [d]Deut. 32:39; Job … Is. 33:24; Jer. 33:6… 6:1, 2

27 [1]Lit., *distance* [2]Lit., *heaviness* [3]Lit., *uplifting* [a]Is. 59:19… 10:17 [c]Is. 10:5; 13… 66:14 [d]Is. 66:15

28 [1]Lit., *sifting of t*… *worthless* [2]Lit., *misleads* [a]Is. 11:4; 30:33; 2 Thess. 2:8… 8:8 [c]Amos 9:9 [d]2… 19:28; Is. 37:29

29 [1]Lit., *the song*

30 [1]Lit., *the majes*… *His voice* [2]Lit., *des*…

31 [a]Is. 11:4 [b]Is. 10… 14:25; 31:8 [c]Is. 10… 11:4

32 [1]Lit., *passing* [2]L… *staff of foundation* … 10:24 [b]1 Sam. 18:6… Jer. 31:4 [c]Ezek. 32…

33 [1]I.e., the place o… human sacrifice to Molech [2]Lit., *Its pile* [a]2 Kin. 23:10; Jer. 7… 19:6 [b]Is. 11:4; 30:28… [c]Gen. 19:24; Is. 34:9…

31:1 [a]Is. 30:2, 7; 36… [b]Deut. 17:16; Ps. 20… 33:17; Is. 2:7; 30:16… 9:13; Dan. 9:13; Am… 5:4-8 [d]Is. 10:17; 43… Hos. 11:9; Hab. 1:12…

2 [a]Is. 28:29; Rom. 16:27 [b]Is. 45:7 [c]Nu… 23:19; Jer. 44:29 [d]Is… 1:4; 9:17; 14:20 [e]Is. 22:14; 32:6

3 [a]Ezek. 28:9; 2 Th… 2:4 [b]Is. 36:9 [c]Is. 9:… Jer. 15:6; Ezek. 20:3… 34 [d]Is. 30:5, 7; Matt… 15:14

4 [a]Num. 24:9; Hos. 11:10; Amos 3:8

So will the LORD of hosts come down to wage [b]war on Mount
Zion and on its hill."
5 Like [1]flying [a]birds so the LORD of hosts will protect Jerusalem.
He will [b]protect and deliver *it;*
He will pass over and rescue *it.*
6 [a]Return to Him from whom [1]you have [b]deeply defected, O sons
of Israel.
7 For in that day every man will [a]cast away his silver idols and his
gold idols, which your hands have made as [b]a sin.
8 And the [a]Assyrian will fall by a sword not of man,
And a [b]sword not of man will devour him.
So he will [1c]not escape the sword,
And his young men will become [d]forced laborers.
9 "And his [a]rock will pass away because of panic,
And his princes will be terrified at the [b]standard,"
Declares the LORD, whose [c]fire is in Zion and whose furnace is in
Jerusalem.

Chapter 32

32 Behold, a [a]king will reign righteously,
And princes will rule justly.
2 And each will be like a [a]refuge from the wind,
And a shelter from the storm,
Like [1b]streams of water in a dry country,
Like the [a]shade of a [2]huge rock in [3]a parched land.
3 Then [a]the eyes of those who see will not be [1]blinded,
And the ears of those who hear will listen.
4 And the [1]mind of the [a]hasty will discern the [2]truth,
And the tongue of the stammerers will hasten to speak clearly.
5 No longer will the [a]fool be called noble,
Or the rogue be spoken of *as* generous.
6 For a fool speaks nonsense,
And his heart [1a]inclines toward wickedness,
To practice [b]ungodliness and to speak error against the LORD,
To [2c]keep the hungry person unsatisfied
And [3]to withhold drink from the thirsty.
7 As for a rogue, his weapons are evil;
He [a]devises wicked schemes
To [b]destroy *the* afflicted with [1]slander,
[c]Even though *the* needy one speaks [2]what is right.
8 But [a]the noble man devises noble plans;
And by noble plans he stands.

9 Rise up you [a]women who are at ease,
And hear my voice;
[b]Give ear to my word,
You complacent daughters.
10 Within a year and *a few* days,
You will be troubled, O complacent *daughters;*
[a]For the vintage is ended,
And the *fruit* gathering will not come.
11 Tremble, you *women* who are at ease;
[a]Be troubled, you complacent *daughters;*
[b]Strip, undress, and put *sackcloth* on *your* waist,

2:13; Zech. 12:8
hovering [a]Deut. 11; Ps. 91:4 [b]Is. 37:35; 38:6
they [a]Is. 44:22; Jer. 3:10, 14, 22; k. 18:31, 32 [b]Is. 1:2, 5
[a]Is. 2:20; 30:22 [b]1 Kin. 12:30
, *flee* [a]Is. 10:12; ; 30:31-33; 37:7, 8 [b]Is. 66:16 [c]Is. [d]Gen. 49:15; Is. 14:2
ut. 32:31, 37 [b]Is. 5; 13:2; 18:3 [c]Is. 17; 30:33; Zech. 2:5
[a]Ps. 72:1-4; Is. 11:4, 5; Jer. 23:5; .15; Ezek. 37:24; Zech. 9:9
[1]Lit., *canals* [2]Lit., *heavy* [3]Lit., *an hausted* [a]Is. 4:6; [b]Is. 35:6; 41:18; 43:19, 20
turned away [a]Is. 29:18
[1]Lit., *heart* [2]Lit., *wledge* [a]Is. 29:24
5 [a]1 Sam. 25:25
does [2]Lit., *make y the hungry soul he causes to lack* /. 19:3; 24:7-9; Is. 13 [b]Is. 9:17; 10:6 [c]Is. 3:15; 10:2
7 [1]Lit., *words of ehood* [2]Lit., *justly* 5:26-28; Mic. 7:3 :4; 61:1 [c]Is. 5:23
8 [a]Prov. 11:25
s. 47:8; Amos 6:1; h. 2:15 [b]Is. 28:23
5:5, 6; 7:23; 24:7
Is. 22:12 [b]Is. 47:2

12 [a]Beat your breasts for the pleasant fields, for the fruitful vine,
13 [a]For the land of my people *in which* thorns *and* briars shall come up;
Yea, for all the joyful houses, *and for* the [b]jubilant city.
14 Because [a]the palace has been abandoned, the [1]populated [b]city forsaken.
[2]Hill and watch-tower have become [c]caves forever,
A delight for [d]wild donkeys, a pasture for flocks;
15 Until the [a]Spirit is poured out upon us from on high,
And the wilderness becomes a [b]fertile field
And the fertile field is considered as a forest.
16 Then [a]justice will dwell in the wilderness,
And righteousness will abide in the fertile field.
17 And the [a]work of righteousness will be peace,
And the service of righteousness, [b]quietness and [1]confidence forever.
18 Then my people will live in a [a]peaceful habitation,
And in secure dwellings and in undisturbed [b]resting places;
19 And it will [a]hail when the [b]forest comes down,
And [c]the city will be utterly laid low.
20 How [a]blessed will you be, you who sow beside all waters,
Who [1]let out freely the ox and the donkey.

Chapter 33

33 Woe [a]to you, O destroyer,
While you were not destroyed;
And he [b]who is treacherous, while *others* did not deal treacherously with him.
As soon as you shall finish destroying, [c]you shall be destroyed;
As soon as you shall cease to deal treacherously, *others* shall [d]deal treacherously with you.
2 O LORD, [a]be gracious to us; we have [b]waited for Thee.
Be Thou [1]their [2c]strength every morning,
Our salvation also in the [d]time of distress.
3 At the sound of the tumult [a]peoples flee;
At the [b]lifting up of Thyself nations disperse.
4 And your spoil is gathered *as* the caterpillar gathers;
As locusts rushing about, men rush about on it.
5 The LORD is [a]exalted, for He dwells on high;
He has [b]filled Zion with justice and righteousness.
6 And He shall be the [1a]stability of your times,
A [b]wealth of salvation, wisdom, and [c]knowledge;
The [d]fear of the LORD is his treasure.
7 Behold, their brave men cry in [1]the streets,
The [2a]ambassadors of peace weep bitterly.
8 The highways are desolate, [1]the [a]traveler has ceased,
He has [b]broken the covenant, he has despised the cities,
He has no regard for man.
9 [a]The land mourns and pines away,
[b]Lebanon is shamed and withers;
[c]Sharon is like a desert plain,
And Bashan and Carmel [1]lose *their foliage*.

12 [a]Nah. 2:7

13 [a]Is. 5:6, 27:10 [b]Is. 22

14 [1]Lit., *mul* *the* [2]Or, *Oph* 13:22; 25:2; 6:11; 22:2; 24 [c]Is. 13:21; 34 104:11; Jer.

15 [a]Is. 11:2; 59:21; Ezek. 2:28 [b]Ps. 10 29:17; 35:1, 2

16 [a]Is. 33:5;

17 [1]Or, *secu* 72:2, 3; 85:8; Is. 2:4; Rom. James 3:18

18 [a]Is. 26:3, 11:10; 14:3; 3 2:18-23; Zech

19 [a]Is. 28:2, [b]Is. 10:18, 19, 24:10, 12; 26: 29:4

20 [1]Lit., *send* *foot of the ox* 11:1; Is. 30:23

33:1 [a]Is. 10:6 24:16; 48:8 [c]Is 14:25; 31:8; H [d]Jer. 25:12-14

2 [1]Some vers *our* [2]Lit., *arm* 30:18, 19 [b]Is. 40:10; 51:5; 59 37:3

3 [a]Is. 17:13; 2 10:33; 17:13; 5 Jer. 25:30, 31

5 [a]Ps. 97:9 [b]Is 28:6; 32:16

6 [1]Or, *faithfuln* 33:20 [b]Is. 45:1 [c]Is. 11:9 [d]2 Kin Ps. 112:1-3; Is. Matt. 6:33

7 [1]Lit., *the outs* *messengers* [a]2 18:18, 37

8 [1]Lit., *he who* *along the way* [b]Is. 24:5

9 [1]Lit., *shake o* 3:26; 24:4; 29:2 2:13; 10:34 [c]Is. 65:10

10 "Now [a]I will arise," says the LORD,
"Now I will be exalted, now I will be lifted up.
11 "You have [a]conceived [1]chaff, you will give birth to stubble;
[2]My [b]breath will consume you like a fire.
12 "And the peoples will be burned to lime,
[a]Like cut thorns which are burned in the fire.

13 "You who are far away, [a]hear what I have done;
And you who are near, [1]acknowledge My might."
14 [a]Sinners in Zion are terrified;
[b]Trembling has seized the godless.
"Who among us can live with [c]the consuming fire?
Who among us can live with [1]continual [d]burning?"
15 He who [a]walks righteously, and speaks with sincerity,
He who rejects [1]unjust gain,
And shakes his hands so that they hold no bribe;
He who stops his ears from hearing about bloodshed,
And [b]shuts his eyes from looking upon evil;
16 He will dwell on the heights;
[a]His refuge will be the [1]impregnable rock;
[b]His bread will be given *him;*
His water will be sure.

17 Your eyes will see [a]the King in His beauty;
They will behold [b]a far-distant land.
18 Your heart will meditate on [a]terror:
"Where is [b]he who counts?
Where is he who weighs?
Where is he who counts the towers?"
19 You will no longer see a fierce people,
A people of [1a]unintelligible speech [2]which no one comprehends,
Of a stammering tongue [3]which no one understands.
20 [a]Look upon Zion, the city of our appointed feasts;
Your eyes shall see Jerusalem an [b]undisturbed habitation,
[c]A tent which shall not be folded,
Its stakes shall never be pulled up
Nor any of its cords be torn apart.
21 But there the majestic *One,* the LORD, shall be for us
A place of [a]rivers *and* wide canals,
On which no boat with oars shall go,
And on which no mighty ship shall pass—
22 For the LORD is our [a]judge,
The LORD is [b]our lawgiver,
The LORD is [c]our king;
[d]He will save us—
23 Your tackle hangs slack;
It cannot hold the base of its mast firmly,
Nor spread out the sail.
Then the [a]prey of an abundant spoil will be divided;
[b]The lame will take the plunder.
24 And no resident will say, "I am [a]sick";
The people who dwell [1]there will be [b]forgiven *their* iniquity.

0 [a]Ps. 12:5; Is. 2:19, 21
, *dry grass* [2]So ancient version; ads *Your breath* 7:14; Is. 26:18; James 1:15 [b]Is. 1:31
Sam. 23:6, 7; Is. 10:17; 27:4
[1]Lit., *know* [a]Ps. 48:10; Is. 49:1
everlasting [a]Is. 8 [b]Is. 32:11 [c]Is. , 30; Heb. 12:29 9:18, 19; 10:16; 47:14
15 [1]Lit., *gain of* *oners* [a]Ps. 15:2; Is. 58:6-11 [b]Ps. 119:37
.it., *stronghold of* . 25:4 [b]Is. 49:10
7 [a]Is. 6:5; 24:23; 21, 22 [b]Is. 26:15
Is. 17:14 [b]1 Cor. 1:20
[1]Lit., *deepness of* Lit., *from hearing* [3]Lit., *there is no* *rstanding* [a]Deut. 50; Is. 28:11; Jer. 5:15
[a]Ps. 48:12 [b]Ps. 25:1, 2; Is. 32:18 [c]Is. 54:2
41:18; 43:19, 20; 48:18; 66:12
s. 2:4; 11:4; 16:5; [b]Is. 1:10; 51:4, 7; 4:12 [c]Ps. 89:18; 17; Zech. 9:9 [d]Is. ; 35:4; 49:25, 26; 60:16
2 Kin. 7:16 [b]2 Kin. 7:8; Is. 35:6
it., *in it* [a]Is. 30:26; :8; Jer. 30:17 [b]Is. 44:22; Jer. 50:20; . 7:18, 19; 1 John 1:7-9

Chapter 34

34 Draw near, [a]O nations, to hear; and listen, O peoples!
[b]Let the earth and [1]all it contains hear, and the world and all that springs from it.
2 For the LORD's [a]indignation is against all the nations,
And *His* wrath against all their armies;
He has [1b]utterly destroyed them,
He has given them over to [c]slaughter.
3 So their slain will be [a]thrown out,
And their corpses [1]will give off their [b]stench,
And the mountains will [2]be drenched with their [c]blood.
4 And [a]all the host of heaven will [1]wear away,
And the [b]sky will be rolled up like a scroll;
All their hosts will also wither away
As a leaf withers from the vine,
Or as *one* withers from the fig tree.
5 For [a]My sword is satiated in heaven,
Behold it shall descend for judgment upon [b]Edom,
And upon the people whom I have [c]devoted to destruction.
6 The sword of the LORD is filled with blood,
It is [1]sated with fat, with the blood of lambs and goats,
With the fat of the kidneys of rams.
For the LORD has a sacrifice in [a]Bozrah,
And a great slaughter in the land of [b]Edom.
7 [a]Wild oxen shall also [1]fall with them,
And [b]young bulls with strong ones;
Thus their land shall be [c]soaked with blood,
And their dust [2]become greasy with fat.
8 For the LORD has a day of [a]vengeance,
A year of recompense for the [1]cause of Zion.
9 And [1]its streams shall be turned into pitch,
And its loose earth into [a]brimstone,
And its land shall become burning pitch.
10 It shall [a]not be quenched night or day;
Its [b]smoke shall go up forever;
From [c]generation to generation it shall be desolate;
[d]None shall pass through it forever and ever.
11 But [1a]pelican and hedgehog shall possess it,
And [2]owl and raven shall dwell in it;
And He shall stretch over it the [b]line of [3]desolation
And the [4]plumb line of emptiness.
12 Its nobles—there is [a]no one there
Whom they may proclaim king—
And all its princes shall be [b]nothing.
13 And thorns shall come up in its [a]fortified towers,
Nettles and thistles in its fortified cities;
It shall also be a haunt of [b]jackals
And an abode of ostriches.
14 And the desert [a]creatures shall meet with the [1]wolves,
The [2a]hairy goat also shall cry to its kind;
Yes, the [3]night monster shall settle there
And shall find herself a resting place.
15 The tree snake shall make its nest and lay *eggs* there,
And it will hatch and gather *them* under its [1]protection.

34:1 [1]Lit., *its* [a]Ps. 49:1; Is. [b]Deut. 32:1;
2 [1]Lit., *put u ban* [a]Is. 26:2 13:5; 24:1 [c]I 63:6; 65:12
3 [1]Lit., *their go up* [2]Lit., *c* [a]Is. 14:19 [b]J Amos 4:10 [c] 14:19; 35:6;
4 [1]Lit., *rot* [a]I 51:6; Ezek. 3 2:31; Matt. 24 3:10 [b]Rev. 6:
5 [a]Deut. 32:4 46:10; Ezek. 63:1; Jer. 49: Ezek. 25:12-1 35:1-15; Amo Obad. 1-14; [c]Is. 24:6; 43:2
6 [1]Lit., *made* 63:1; Jer. 49:
7 [1]Lit., *go do made fat* [a]Nu Ps. 22:21 [b]Ps Jer. 50:27 [c]Is
8 [1]Or, *contro* 13:6; 35:4; 47 63:4
9 [1]I.e., Edom 29:23; Ps. 11:
10 [a]Is. 1:31; 6 [b]Rev. 14:11; 1 13:20-22; 24:1 34:10-15; Mal. [d]Ezek. 29:11
11 [1]Or, *owl* or [2]Or, *great horr* [3]Or, *formlessn stones of void* 2:14 [b]2 Kin. 2 24:10; Lam. 2:
12 [a]Jer. 27:20 [b]Is. 41:11, 12
13 [a]Is. 13:22; 32:13 [b]Ps. 44 9:11; 10:22
14 [1]Or, *howlin creatures* [2]Or, [3]Heb., *Lilith* [a]Is
15 [1]Lit., *shade*

Yes, [a]the [2]hawks shall be gathered there,
Every one with its kind.

16 Seek from the [a]book of the LORD, and read:
Not one of these will be missing;
None will lack its mate.
For [1b]His mouth has commanded,
And His Spirit has gathered them.
17 And He has cast the [a]lot for them,
And His hand has divided it to them by [b]line.
They shall possess it forever;
From [c]generation to generation they shall dwell in it.

Chapter 35

35 The [a]wilderness and the desert will be glad,
And the [1b]Arabah will rejoice and blossom;
Like the crocus
2 It will [a]blossom profusely
And [b]rejoice with rejoicing and shout of joy.
The [c]glory of Lebanon will be given to it,
The majesty of [d]Carmel and Sharon.
They will see the [e]glory of the LORD,
The majesty of our God.
3 [a]Encourage the [1]exhausted, and strengthen the [2]feeble.
4 Say to those with [a]anxious heart,
"Take courage, fear not.
Behold, your God will come *with* [b]vengeance;
The [c]recompense of God will come,
But He will [d]save you."
5 Then the [a]eyes of the blind will be opened,
And the ears of the deaf will be unstopped.
6 Then the [a]lame will leap like a deer,
And the [b]tongue of the dumb will shout for joy.
For waters will break forth in the [c]wilderness
And streams in the [1]Arabah.
7 And the [1]scorched land will become a pool,
And the thirsty ground [a]springs of water;
In the [b]haunt of jackals, its resting place,
Grass *becomes* reeds and rushes.
8 And [a]a highway will be there, [b]a roadway,
And it will be called the Highway of [c]Holiness.
The unclean will not travel on it,
But it *will* be for him who walks *that* way,
And [d]fools will not wander *on it*.
9 No [a]lion will be there,
Nor will any vicious beast go up on it;
[1]These will not be found there.
But [b]the redeemed will walk *there*,
10 And [a]the ransomed of the LORD will return,
And come with joyful shouting to Zion,
With everlasting joy upon their heads.
They will [1]find gladness and joy,
And [b]sorrow and sighing will flee away.

[2]Or, *kites* [a]Deut. 14:13

o DSS; M.T., *My* 3 [b]Is. 1:20; 40:5; 58:14

s. 17:13, 14; Jer. 5 [b]Is. 34:11 [c]Is. 34:10

[1]Or, *desert* [a]Is. ; 7:21-25; 27:10; 8; 55:12, 13 [b]Is. 41:19; 51:3

. 27:6; 32:15 [b]Is. 35:10; 55:12, 13; 10, 14 [c]Is. 60:13 ong 7:5 [e]Is. 25:9

[1]Lit., *slack hands* t., *tottering knees* 4:3, 4; Heb. 12:12

Is. 32:4 [b]Is. 1:24; :3; 61:2; 63:4 [c]Is. 34:8; 59:18 [d]Ps. 9; Is. 33:22; 35:4

[a]Is. 29:18; 32:3, 4; :7, 16; 50:4; Matt. 11:5; John 9:6, 7

[1]Or, *desert* [a]Matt. ; John 5:8, 9; Acts [b]Matt. 9:32; Luke 4 [c]Is. 35:1; 41:18; 49:10; 51:3; John 7:38

7 [1]Or, *mirage* [a]Is.) [b]Is. 13:22; 34:13

[a]Is. 11:16; 19:23; ; 49:11; 62:10 [b]Is. :21; 51:10 [c]Is. 4:3; 2:1; Matt. 7:13, 14; .1:15, 16 [d]Is. 33:8

t., *It* [a]Is. 5:29; 30:6 51:10; 62:12; 63:4

[1]Lit., *overtake* [a]Is. 27; 51:11 [b]Is. 25:8; 9; 65:19; Rev. 7:17; 21:4

Chapter 36

36 [a]Now it came about in the fourteenth year of King Hezekiah,
[b]Sennacherib king of Assyria came up against all the fortified
cities of Judah and seized them.
2 And the [a]king of Assyria sent Rabshakeh from Lachish to Jerusa-
lem to King Hezekiah with a large army. And he stood by the [b]con-
duit of the upper pool on the highway of the [1]fuller's field.
3 Then [a]Eliakim the son of Hilkiah, who was over the household,
and [b]Shebna the scribe, and Joah the son of Asaph, the recorder,
came out to him.
4 Then [a]Rabshakeh said to them, "Say now to Hezekiah, 'Thus
says the great king, the king of Assyria, "What is this confidence that
you [1]have?
5 "I say, 'Your counsel and strength for the war are only [1]empty
words.' Now on whom do you rely, that [a]you have rebelled
against me?
6 "Behold, you rely on the [a]staff of this crushed reed, *even* on Egypt;
on which if a man leans, it will go into his [1]hand and pierce it. [b]So is
Pharaoh king of Egypt to all who rely on him.
7 "But if you say to me, 'We trust in the LORD our God,' is it not He
[a]whose high places and whose altars Hezekiah has taken away, and
has said to Judah and to Jerusalem, 'You shall worship before this
altar'?
8 "Now therefore, [1]come make a bargain with my master the king
of Assyria, and I will give you two thousand horses, if you are able
on your part to set riders on them.
9 "How then can you [1]repulse one [2]official of the least of my mas-
ter's servants, and [3a]rely on Egypt for chariots and for horsemen?
10 "And have I now come up [1]without the LORD's approval against
this land to destroy it? [a]The LORD said to me, 'Go up against this
land, and destroy it.' " ' "
11 Then Eliakim and Shebna and Joah said to Rabshakeh, "Speak
now to your servants in [a]Aramaic, for we [1]understand *it*; and do not
speak with us in [2b]Judean, in the hearing of the people who are on
the wall."
12 But Rabshakeh said, "Has my master sent me only to your mas-
ter and to you to speak these words, *and* not to the men who sit on
the wall, *doomed* to eat their own dung and drink their own urine
with you?"
13 Then Rabshakeh stood and [a]cried with a loud voice in Judean,
and said, "Hear the words of the great king, the king of Assyria.
14 "Thus says the king, 'Do not let Hezekiah [a]deceive you, for he will
not be able to deliver you;
15 nor let Hezekiah make you [a]trust in the LORD, saying, "The LORD
will surely deliver us, this city shall not be given into the hand of the
king of Assyria."
16 'Do not listen to Hezekiah,' for thus says the king of Assyria,
'[1]Make your peace with me and come out to me, and eat each of his
[a]vine and each of his fig tree and drink each of the [b]waters of his own
cistern,
17 until I come and take you away to a land like your own land, a
land of grain and new wine, a land of bread and vineyards.
18 '*Beware* lest Hezekiah misleads you, saying, "[a]The LORD will

36:1 [a]2 Kin. 18:1 [b]2 Chr. 32:1
2 [1]I.e., launderer [a]2 Kin. 18:17-20:1 2 Chr. 32:9-24; Is. 36:2-38:8 [b]Is. 7:3
3 [a]Is. 22:20 [b]Is. 2
4 [1]Lit., *trust* [a]2 K 18:19
5 [1]Lit., *words of li* [a]2 Kin. 18:7
6 [1]Lit., *palm* [a]Eze 29:6, 7 [b]Ps. 146:3 30:3, 5, 7
7 [a]Deut. 12:2-5; 2 18:4, 5
8 [1]Lit., *please exchange pledges*
9 [1]Lit., *turn away face of* [2]Or, *gover* [3]Lit., *rely on for yo* [a]Is. 20:5; 30:2-5, 7
10 [1]Lit., *without th LORD* [a]1 Kin. 13:1 22:6, 12
11 [1]Lit., *hear* [2]I.e. Hebrew [a]Ezra 4:7 2:4 [b]Is. 36:13
13 [a]2 Chr. 32:18
14 [a]Is. 37:10
15 [a]Is. 36:18, 20; 37:10, 11
16 [1]Lit., *Make with a blessing* [a]1 Kin. Mic. 4:4; Zech. 3:1 [b]Prov. 5:15
18 [a]Is. 36:15

deliver us." Has any one of the gods of the nations delivered his
land from the hand of the king of Assyria?
19 'Where are the gods of [a]Hamath and Arpad? Where are the gods
of [a]Sepharvaim? And when have they [b]delivered Samaria from my
hand?
20 'Who among all the [a]gods of these lands have delivered their
land from my hand, that the [b]LORD should deliver Jerusalem from
my hand?' "
21 But they were silent and [a]answered him not a word; for the
king's commandment was, "Do not answer him."
22 Then [a]Eliakim the son of Hilkiah, who was over the household,
and [b]Shebna the scribe and Joah the son of Asaph, the recorder, came
to Hezekiah with their clothes torn and told him the words of Rab-
shakeh.

Chapter 37

37 And [a]when King Hezekiah heard *it*, he tore his clothes,
covered himself with sackcloth and entered the house of the
LORD.
2 Then he sent [a]Eliakim who was over the household with [b]Shebna
the scribe and the elders of the priests, covered with sackcloth, to
[c]Isaiah the prophet, the son of Amoz.
3 And they said to him, "Thus says Hezekiah, 'This day is a [a]day
of distress, rebuke, and rejection; for [b]children have come to birth,
and there is no strength to [1]deliver.
4 'Perhaps the LORD your God will hear the words of Rabshakeh,
whom his master the king of Assyria has sent to [a]reproach the living
God, and will rebuke the words which the LORD your God has
heard. Therefore, offer a prayer for [b]the remnant that is left.' "
5 So the servants of King Hezekiah came to Isaiah.
6 And Isaiah said to them, "Thus you shall say to your master,
'Thus says the LORD, "[a]Do not be afraid because of the words that
you have heard, with which the servants of the king of Assyria have
blasphemed Me.
7 "Behold, I will put a spirit in him so that he shall [a]hear a rumor
and [b]return to his own land. And I will make him fall by the sword
in his own land." ' "
8 Then Rabshakeh returned and found the king of Assyria fighting
against [a]Libnah, for he had heard that [1]the king had left [b]Lachish.
9 When he [a]heard *them* say concerning Tirhakah king of [1b]Cush,
"He has come out to fight against you," and when he heard *it* he
sent messengers to Hezekiah, saying,
10 "Thus you shall say to Hezekiah king of [1]Judah, '[a]Do not let your
God in whom you trust deceive you, saying, "Jerusalem shall not be
given into the hand of the king of Assyria."
11 '[a]Behold, you have heard what the kings of Assyria have done to
all the lands, destroying them completely. So will you be [1]spared?
12 'Did the gods of [1]those nations which my fathers have destroyed
deliver them, *even* [a]Gozan and [b]Haran and Rezeph and the sons of
Eden who *were* in Telassar?
13 'Where is the king of Hamath, the king of Arpad, the king of the
city of Sepharvaim, *and of* Hena and Ivvah?' "
14 Then Hezekiah took the [1]letter from the hand of the messengers

19 [a]Is. 10:9-11; …-13; Jer. 49:23 [b]2 Kin. 17:6
…1 Kin. 20:23, 28 [b]Is. 36:15
…rov. 9:7, 8; 26:4
…22:20; 36:3 [b]Is. 22:15
…Kin. 19:1-37; Is. 37:1-38
…22:20 [b]Is. 22:15 [c]Is. 1:1; 20:2
…t., *give birth* [a]Is. 26:16; 33:2 [b]Is. …7, 18; 66:9; Hos. 13:13
…36:13-15, 18, 20 …s. 1:9; 10:20-22; 37:31, 32; 46:3
6 [a]Is. 7:4; 35:4
7 [a]Is. 37:9 [b]Is. 37:37, 38
…*he* [a]Num. 33:20; …sh. 10:29 [b]Josh. 10:31, 32
[1]Or, *Ethiopia* [a]Is. …7:7 [b]Is. 18:1; 20:5
…Lit., *Judah, saying* [a]Is. 36:15
[1]Lit., *delivered* [a]Is. 10:9-11; 36:18-20
2 [1]Lit., *the* [a]2 Kin. 17:6; 18:11 [b]Gen. …1; 12:1-4; Acts 7:2
14 [1]Lit., *letters*

and read it, and he went up to the house of the LORD and [2]spread it
out before the LORD.
15 And Hezekiah prayed to the LORD saying,
16 "O LORD of hosts, the God of Israel, [a]who art enthroned *above* the
cherubim, Thou art the [b]God, Thou alone, of all the kingdoms of the
earth. [c]Thou hast made heaven and earth.
17 "[a]Incline Thine ear, O LORD, and hear; open Thine eyes, O LORD,
and see; and [b]listen to all the words of Sennacherib, who sent *them* to
[c]reproach the living God.
18 "Truly, O LORD, the [a]kings of Assyria have devastated all the
countries and their lands,
19 and have cast their gods into the fire, for they were not gods but
the [a]work of men's hands, wood and stone. So they have [b]destroyed
them.
20 "And now, O LORD our God, [a]deliver us from his hand that [b]all the
kingdoms of the earth may know that Thou alone, LORD, [1]art God."
21 Then [a]Isaiah the son of Amoz sent *word* to Hezekiah, saying,
"Thus says the LORD, the God of Israel, 'Because you have prayed to
Me about Sennacherib king of Assyria,
22 this is the word that the LORD has spoken against him:
"She has despised you and mocked you,
The [a]virgin [b]daughter of Zion;
She has [c]shaken *her* head behind you,
The daughter of Jerusalem!
23 "Whom have you [a]reproached and blasphemed?
And against whom have you raised *your* voice,
And [1]haughtily [b]lifted up your eyes?
Against the [c]Holy One of Israel!
24 "Through your servants you have reproached the Lord,
And you have said, 'With my many chariots I came up to the
heights of the mountains,
To the remotest parts of [a]Lebanon;
And I cut down its tall [b]cedars *and* its choice cypresses.
And I will go to its [1]highest peak, its thickest [c]forest.
25 'I dug *wells* and drank waters,
And [a]with the sole of my feet I dried up
All the rivers of [1]Egypt.'
26 "[a]Have you not heard?
Long ago I did it,
From ancient times I [b]planned it.
Now [c]I have brought it to pass,
That [d]you should turn fortified cities into [e]ruinous heaps.
27 "Therefore their inhabitants were short of strength,
They were dismayed and put to shame;
They were *as* the [a]vegetation of the field and *as* the green herb,
As [b]grass on the housetops [1]is scorched before it is grown up.
28 "But I [a]know your sitting down,
And your going out and your coming in,
And your raging against Me.
29 "Because of your raging against Me,
And because your [1a]arrogance has come up to My ears,
Therefore I will put My [b]hook in your nose,
And My [c]bridle in your lips,
And I will turn you back [d]by the way which you came.

14 [2]Lit., *Hezekia*
spread

16 [a]Ex. 25:22; 1
4:4; Ps. 80:1; 99:
[b]Deut. 10:17; Ps.
136:2, 3 [c]Is. 42:5
45:12; Jer. 10:12

17 [a]2 Chr. 6:40;
17:6; Dan. 9:18
74:22 [c]Is. 37:4

18 [a]2 Kin. 15:29;
17:6, 24; 1 Chr. 5

19 [a]Is. 2:8; 17:8;
29 [b]Is. 26:14

20 [1]So DSS and
19:19; M.T. omits
[a]Is. 25:9; 33:22; 3
[b]1 Kin. 18:36, 37;
46:10; Is. 37:16; E
36:23

21 [a]Is. 37:2

22 [a]Jer. 14:17; La
2:13 [b]Ps. 9:14; Z
3:14; Zech. 2:10
16:4

23 [1]Lit., *on high*
37:4 [b]Is. 2:11; 5:1
[c]Ezek. 39:7; Hab.

24 [1]Lit., *farthest h*
[a]Is. 10:33, 34 [b]Is.
[c]Is. 10:18

25 [1]Or, *the besieg*
place [a]Deut. 11:10
1 Kin. 20:10

26 [a]Is. 40:21, 28
2:23; 4:27, 28; 1 P
2:8 [c]Is. 46:11 [d]Is.
[e]Is. 17:1; 25:2

27 [1]So DSS and 2
19:26; M.T., *as a p*
field [a]Is. 40:7 [b]Ps.
129:6

28 [a]Ps. 139:1

29 [1]Lit., *complace*
[a]Is. 10:12 [b]Ezek. 2
38:4 [c]Is. 30:28 [d]Is
37:34

30 "Then this shall be the sign for you: [1]you shall eat this year what
[a]grows of itself, in the second year what springs from the same, and
in the third year sow, reap, plant vineyards, and eat their fruit.
31 "And the [a]surviving [b]remnant of the house of Judah shall again
[c]take root downward and bear fruit upward.
32 "For out of Jerusalem shall go forth a [a]remnant, and out of Mount
Zion [1]survivors. The [b]zeal of the LORD of hosts shall perform this." '
33 "Therefore, thus says the LORD concerning the king of Assyria,
'He shall not come to this city, or shoot an arrow there; neither shall
he come before it with a shield, nor throw up a [a]mound against it.
34 '[a]By the way that he came, by the same he shall return, and he
shall not come to this city,' declares the LORD.
35 'For I will [a]defend this city to save it [b]for My own sake and for
My servant David's sake.' "
36 Then the [a]angel of the LORD went out, and struck 185,000 in the
camp of the Assyrians; and when [1]men arose early in the morning,
behold, all of these were [2]dead.
37 So Sennacherib, king of Assyria, departed and [1]returned *home*,
and lived at [a]Nineveh.
38 And it came about as he was worshiping in the house of Nisroch
his god, that Adrammelech and Sharezer his sons killed him with
the sword; and they escaped into the land of [a]Ararat. And [b]Esar-
haddon his son became king in his place.

Chapter 38

38 [a]In those days Hezekiah became [1]mortally ill. And [b]Isaiah the
prophet the son of Amoz came to him and said to him, "Thus
says the LORD, '[c]Set your house in order, for you shall die and not
live.' "
2 Then Hezekiah turned his face to the wall, and prayed to the
LORD,
3 and said, "[a]Remember now, O LORD, I beseech Thee, how I have
[b]walked before Thee in truth and with a [c]whole heart, and [d]have
done what is good in Thy sight." And Hezekiah [e]wept [1]bitterly.
4 Then the word of the LORD came to Isaiah, saying,
5 "Go and say to Hezekiah, 'Thus says the LORD, the God of your
father David, "I have heard your prayer, I have seen your tears;
behold, I will add [a]fifteen years to your [1]life.
6 "And I will [a]deliver you and this city from the hand of the king of
Assyria; and I will defend this city." '
7 "And this shall be the [a]sign to you from the LORD, that the LORD
will do this thing that He has spoken:
8 "Behold, I will [a]cause the shadow on the stairway, which has gone
down with the sun on the stairway of Ahaz, to go back ten steps." So
the [b]sun's *shadow* went back ten steps on the stairway on which it
had gone down.
9 A writing of Hezekiah king of Judah, after his illness and
[1]recovery:
10 I said, "[a]In the middle of my [1]life
I am to enter the [b]gates of Sheol;
I am to be [c]deprived of the rest of my years."
11 I said, "I shall not see the LORD,
The LORD [a]in the land of the living;
I shall look on man no more among the inhabitants of the world.

30 [1]Lit., *eating* [a]Lev. 25:5, 11
1 [a]Is. 4:2; 10:20 [b]Is. 37:4 [c]Is. 27:6
32 [1]Lit., *those who escape* [a]Is. 37:4 [b]2 Kin. 19:31; Is. 9:7; :17; Joel 2:18; Zech. 1:14
33 [a]Jer. 6:6; 32:24
34 [a]Is. 37:29
[a]2 Kin. 20:6; Is. 31:5; [b]Is. 43:25; 48:9, 11
[1]Lit., *they* [2]Lit., *dead ies* [a]2 Kin. 19:35; Is. 10:12, 33, 34
37 [1]Lit., *went and turned* [a]Gen. 10:11; Jon. 1:2; 3:3; 4:11; Zeph. 2:13
38 [a]Gen. 8:4; Jer. 51:27 [b]Ezra 4:2
8:1 [1]Lit., *sick to the oint of death* [a]2 Kin. 20:1-6, 9-11; 2 Chr. 32:24; Is. 38:1-8 [b]Is. 37:2 [c]2 Sam. 17:23
[1]Lit., *great weeping* [a]Neh. 13:14 [b]2 Kin. , 6; Ps. 26:3 [c]1 Chr. ; 29:19 [d]Deut. 6:18 [e]Ps. 6:6-8
5 [1]Lit., *days* [a]2 Kin. 18:2, 13
6 [a]Is. 31:5; 37:35
7 [a]Judg. 6:17, 21, ; Is. 7:11, 14; 37:30
8 [a]2 Kin. 20:9-11 [b]Josh. 10:12-14
it., *he lived after his illness*
10 [1]Lit., *days* [a]Ps. 102:24 [b]Ps. 107:18 ob 17:11, 15; 2 Cor. 1:9
[a]Ps. 27:13; 116:9

12 "Like a shepherd's [a]tent my dwelling is pulled up and removed
from me;
As a [b]weaver I [c]rolled up my life.
He [d]cuts me off from the loom;
From [e]day until night Thou dost make an end of me.
13 "I composed *my soul* until morning.
[a]Like a lion—so He [b]breaks all my bones,
From [c]day until night Thou dost make an end of me.
14 "[a]Like a swallow, *like* a crane, so I twitter;
I [b]moan like a dove;
My [c]eyes look wistfully to the heights;
O Lord, I am oppressed, be my [d]security.

15 "[a]What shall I say?
[1]For He has spoken to me, and He Himself has done it;
I shall [b]wander about all my years because of the [c]bitterness of
my soul.
16 "O Lord, [a]by *these* things *men* live;
And in all these is the life of my spirit;
[1b]O restore me to health, and [c]let me live!
17 "Lo, for *my own* welfare I had great bitterness;
It is Thou who hast [1a]kept my soul from the pit of [2]nothingness,
For Thou hast [b]cast all my sins behind Thy back.
18 "For [a]Sheol cannot thank Thee,
Death cannot praise Thee;
Those who go down [b]to the pit cannot hope for Thy faithfulness.
19 "It is the [a]living who give thanks to Thee, as I do today;
A [b]father tells his sons about Thy faithfulness.
20 "The LORD will surely save me;
So we will [a]play my songs on stringed instruments
[b]All *the* days of our life [c]at the house of the LORD."

21 Now [a]Isaiah had said, "Let them take a cake of figs, and apply it
to the boil, that he may recover."
22 Then Hezekiah had said, "What is the [a]sign that I shall go up to
the house of the LORD?"

Chapter 39

39 [a]At that time Merodach-baladan son of Baladan, king of Babylon, sent letters and a present to Hezekiah, for he heard that he had been sick and had recovered.
2 And Hezekiah [1]was [a]pleased, and showed them all his treasure house, the [b]silver and the gold and the spices and the precious oil and his whole armory and all that was found in his treasuries. There was nothing in his house, nor in all his dominion, that Hezekiah did not show them.
3 Then Isaiah the [a]prophet came to King Hezekiah and said to him, "What did these men say, and from where have they come to you?" And Hezekiah said, "They have come to me from a far [b]country, from Babylon."
4 And he said, "What have they seen in your house?" So Hezekiah [1]answered, "They have seen all that is in my house; there is nothing among my treasuries that I have not shown them."
5 Then Isaiah said to Hezekiah, "Hear the [a]word of the LORD of hosts,

12 [a]2 Cor. 5:1, 4 1:13, 14 [b]Job 7 1:12 [d]Job 6:9 [e] 4:20; Ps. 73:14

13 [a]Job 10:16 51:8; Dan. 6:24 32:4

14 [a]Job 30:29; P 102:6 [b]Is. 59:11 7:16; Nah. 2:7 [c] 119:123 [d]Job 17 119:122

15 [1]Targum and read *And what s say for He* [a]Ps. [b]1 Kin. 21:27 [c]Jo 10:1; Is. 38:17

16 [1]Lit., *Thou w* 119:71, 75 [b]Ps. [c]Ps. 119:25

17 [1]So some ve Heb., *loved* [2]Or, *destruction* [a]Ps. 86:13; Jon. 2:6 [b] 43:25; Jer. 31:34 7:19

18 [a]Ps. 6:5; 30:9 88:11; Eccl. 9:10 16:33; Ps. 28:1

19 [a]Ps. 118:17; 119:175 [b]Deut. 6 11:19; Ps. 78:5-7

20 [a]Ps. 33:1-3; 68:24-26 [b]Ps. 10 116:2; 146:2 [c]Ps. 116:17-19

21 [a]2 Kin. 20:7, 8

22 [a]Is. 38:7

39:1 [a]2 Kin. 20:12 2 Chr. 32:31; Is. 3

2 [1]Lit., *rejoiced o them* [a]2 Chr. 32:2 Job 31:25 [b]2 Kin. 18:15, 16

3 [a]2 Sam. 12:1; 2 16:7 [b]Deut. 28:49; 5:15

4 [1]Lit., *said*

5 [a]1 Sam. 13:13, 1 15:16

6 'Behold, the days are coming when [a]all that is in your house, and
all that your fathers have laid up in store to this day shall be carried
to Babylon; nothing shall be left,' says the LORD.
7 'And *some* of your sons who shall issue from you, whom you
shall beget, [a]shall be taken away; and [b]they shall become officials in
the palace of the king of Babylon.' "
8 [a]Then Hezekiah said to Isaiah, "The word of the LORD which you
have spoken is good." For he [1]thought, "For there will be peace and
truth [b]in my days."

Chapter 40

40 "[a]Comfort, O comfort My people," says your God.
2 "[a]Speak [1]kindly to Jerusalem;
And call out to her, that her [2b]warfare has ended,
That her [3c]iniquity has been removed,
That she has received of the LORD's hand
[d]Double for all her sins."

3 [a]A voice [1]is calling,
"[b]Clear the way for the LORD in the wilderness;
Make smooth in the desert a highway for our God.
4 "Let every valley be lifted up,
And every mountain and hill be made low;
And let the rough ground become a plain,
And the rugged terrain a broad valley;
5 [1]Then the [a]glory of the LORD will be revealed,
And [b]all flesh will see *it* together;
For the [c]mouth of the LORD has spoken."
6 A voice says, "Call out."
Then [1]he answered, "What shall I call out?"
[a]All flesh is grass, and all its [2]loveliness is like the flower of the field.
7 The [a]grass withers, the flower fades,
[1]When the [b]breath of the LORD blows upon it;
Surely the people are grass.
8 The grass withers, the flower fades,
But [a]the word of our God stands forever.

9 Get yourself up on a [a]high mountain,
O Zion, bearer of [b]good news,
Lift up your voice mightily,
O Jerusalem, bearer of good news;
Lift *it* up, do not fear.
Say to the [c]cities of Judah,
"[d]Here is your God!"
10 Behold, the Lord [1]GOD will come [a]with might,
With His [b]arm ruling for Him.
Behold, His [c]reward is with Him,
And His recompense before Him.
11 Like a shepherd He will [a]tend His flock,
In His arm He will gather the lambs,
And carry *them* in His bosom;
He will gently lead the nursing *ewes*.

[a]2 Kin. 24:13; 13-15; Jer. 20:5
2 Kin. 24:10-16; 10 [b]Dan. 1:1-7
it., *said* [a]2 Chr. 6 [b]2 Chr. 34:28
[a]Is. 12:1; 49:13; , 12; 52:9; 61:2; 3; Jer. 31:10-14; 4-17; 2 Cor. 1:4
., *to the heart of* *ard service* [3]Or, *enalty of iniquity* *epted as paid off* 35:4; Zech. 1:13 41:11-13; 49:25; 5, 17 [c]Is. 33:24; , 11 [d]Jer. 16:18; . 9:12; Rev. 18:6
Or, *of one calling* [a]Matt. 3:3; Mark Luke 3:4-6; John [b]Mal. 3:1; 4:5, 6
, *In order that the* 3; Hab. 2:14 [b]Is. 10; Joel 2:28 [c]Is. :20; 34:16; 58:14
other reading is *I* *d* [2]Or, *constancy* 14:2; Ps. 102:11; 5; 1 Pet. 1:24, 25
Or, *Because* [a]Ps. 6; James 1:10, 11 :9; 41:21; Is. 11:4; 40:24
[a]Is. 55:11; 59:21; Matt. 5:18
[a]Is. 52:7 [b]Is. 61:1 .26 [d]Is. 25:9; 35:2
10 [1]Heb., *YHWH*, ally rendered *LORD* . 9:6, 7 [b]Is. 59:16, . 62:11; Rev. 22:12
[a]Jer. 31:10; Ezek. 12-14, 23, 31; Mic. John 10:11, 14-16

12 Who has [a]measured the [1]waters in the hollow of His hand,
And marked off the heavens by the [2]span,
And [3]calculated the dust of the earth by the measure,
And weighed the mountains in a balance,
And the hills in a pair of scales?
13 [a]Who has [1]directed the Spirit of the LORD,
Or as His [b]counselor has informed Him?
14 [a]With whom did He consult and *who* [b]gave Him understanding?
And *who* taught Him in the path of justice and taught Him knowledge,
And informed Him of the way of understanding?
15 Behold, the [a]nations are like a drop from a bucket,
And are regarded as a speck of [b]dust on the scales;
Behold, He lifts up the [1]islands like fine dust.
16 Even Lebanon is not enough to burn,
Nor its [a]beasts enough for a burnt offering.
17 [a]All the nations are as nothing before Him,
They are regarded by Him as less than nothing and [1]meaningless.

18 [a]To whom then will you liken God?
Or what likeness will you compare with Him?
19 *As for* the [1a]idol, a craftsman casts it,
A goldsmith [b]plates it with gold,
And a silversmith *fashions* chains of silver.
20 He who is too impoverished for *such* an offering
Selects a [a]tree that does not rot;
He seeks out for himself a skillful craftsman
To [1]prepare [2]an idol that [b]will not totter.

21 [a]Do you not know? Have you not heard?
Has it not been declared to you from the beginning?
Have you not understood [b]from the foundations of the earth?
22 It is He who [1]sits above the [2a]vault of the earth,
And its inhabitants are like [b]grasshoppers,
Who [c]stretches out the heavens like a [d]curtain
And spreads them out like a [e]tent to dwell in.
23 He *it is* who reduces [a]rulers to nothing,
Who [b]makes the judges of the earth [1]meaningless.
24 [1]Scarcely have they been planted,
[1]Scarcely have they been sown,
[1]Scarcely has their stock taken root in the earth,
But He merely blows on them, and they wither,
And the [a]storm carries them away like stubble.
25 "[a]To whom then will you liken Me
That I should be *his* equal?" says the Holy One.
26 [a]Lift up your eyes on high
And see [b]who has created these *stars*,
The [c]One who leads forth their host by number,
He calls them all by name;
Because of the [d]greatness of His might and the [1]strength of *His* power
[e]Not one *of them* is missing.

12 [1]DSS reads *of the sea* [2]Or, *cubit;* i.e., 9 in. *contained* or *comprehended* 38:8-11; Ps. 10[illegible] Is. 48:13; Heb. [illegible]

13 [1]Or, *measu[illegible] marked off* [a]Ro[illegible] 11:34; 1 Cor. 2:[illegible] 41:28

14 [a]Job 38:4 [b][illegible] 21:22; Col. 2:3

15 [1]Or, *coastlar[illegible]* [a]Jer. 10:10 [b]Is. [illegible] 29:5

16 [a]Ps. 50:9-11; 6:6, 7; Heb. 10:5

17 [1]Or, *void* [a]Is.

18 [a]Ex. 8:10; 15 1 Sam. 2:2; Is. 4[illegible] 46:5; Mic. 7:18; [illegible] 17:29

19 [1]Or, *graven i[illegible]* [a]Ps. 115:4-8; Is. [illegible] 44:10; Hab. 2:18, [b]Is. 2:20; 30:22

20 [1]Or, *set up* [2][illegible] *graven image* [a]Is 44:14 [b]1 Sam. 5: Is. 41:7; 46:7

21 [a]Ps. 19:1; 50:[illegible] 37:26; Acts 14:17 1:19 [b]Is. 48:13; 5[illegible]

22 [1]Or, *is enthron[illegible]* [2]Or, *circle* [a]Job 2[illegible] Prov. 8:27 [b]Num. [c]Job 9:8; Is. 37:16 44:24 [d]Ps. 104:2 36:29; Ps. 18:11; [illegible]

23 [1]Or, *void* [a]Job 12:21; Ps. 107:40; 34:12 [b]Is. 5:21; Je[illegible] 25:18-27

24 [1]Or, *Not even* 17:13; 41:16

25 [a]Is. 40:18

26 [1]So DSS and ancient versions; M[illegible] *strong* [a]Is. 51:6 [b]Is 42:5; 48:12, 13 [c]Ps 147:4 [d]Ps. 89:11-1[illegible] [e]Is. 34:16; 48:13

27 [a]Why do you say, O Jacob, and assert, O Israel,
"My way is [b]hidden from the LORD,
And the [c]justice due me [1]escapes the notice of [d]my God"?
28 [a]Do you not know? Have you not heard?
The [b]Everlasting God, the LORD, the Creator of the ends of the earth
Does not become weary or tired.
His understanding is [c]inscrutable.
29 He gives strength to the [a]weary,
And to *him who* lacks might He [b]increases power.
30 Though [a]youths grow weary and tired,
And vigorous [b]young men stumble badly,
31 Yet those who [1]wait for the LORD
Will [a]gain new strength;
They will [2b]mount up *with* [3]wings like eagles,
They will run and not get tired,
They will walk and not become weary.

Chapter 41

41 "[a]Coastlands, listen to Me [b]in silence,
And let the peoples [c]gain new strength;
[d]Let them come forward, then let them speak;
[e]Let us come together for judgment.
2 "[a]Who has aroused one from the east
Whom He [b]calls in righteousness to His [1]feet?
He [c]delivers up nations before him,
And subdues kings.
He makes them like [d]dust with his sword,
As the wind-driven [e]chaff with his bow.
3 "He pursues them, passing on in safety,
By a way he had not been [1]traversing with his feet.
4 "[a]Who has performed and accomplished *it*,
Calling forth the generations from the beginning?
'[b]I, the LORD, am the first, and with the last. [c]I am He.' "

5 The [a]coastlands have seen and are afraid;
The [b]ends of the earth tremble;
They have drawn near and have come.
6 Each one helps his neighbor,
And says to his brother, "Be strong!"
7 So the [a]craftsman encourages the [b]smelter,
And he who smooths *metal* with the hammer *encourages* him who beats the anvil,
Saying of the soldering, "It is good";
And he fastens it with nails,
[c]*That* it should not totter.
8 "But you, Israel, [a]My servant,
Jacob whom I have chosen,
Descendant of [b]Abraham My [c]friend,
9 You whom I have [1a]taken from the ends of the earth,
And called from its [b]remotest parts,
And said to you, 'You are [c]My servant,
I have [d]chosen you and not rejected you.
10 'Do not [a]fear, for I am with you;

[1]Lit., passes by my od [a]Is. 49:4, 14 [b]Is. 4:8 [c]Job 27:2; 34:5; uke 18:7, 8 [d]Is. 25:1

28 [a]Is. 40:21 [b]Gen. 21:33; Ps. 90:2 [c]Ps. 147:5; Rom. 11:33

[a]Is. 50:4; Jer. 31:25 [b]Is. 41:10

[a]Jer. 6:11; 9:21 [b]Is. 9:17

1 [1]Or, hope in [2]Or, sprout wings [3]Or, ions [a]Job 17:9; Ps. :5; 2 Cor. 4:8-10, 16 x. 19:4; Deut. 32:11; uke 18:1; 2 Cor. 4:1, Gal. 6:9; Heb. 12:3

:1 [a]Is. 11:11 [b]Hab. :20; Zech. 2:13 [c]Is. :31 [d]Is. 34:1; 48:16 s. 1:18; 43:26; 50:8

Lit., foot [a]Is. 41:25; 1-3; 46:11 [b]Is. 42:6 Chr. 36:23; Ezra 1:2 m. 22:43 [e]Is. 40:24

3 [1]Lit., going

4 [a]Is. 41:26; 44:7; 10 [b]Is. 43:10; 44:6; 1:8, 17; 22:13 [c]Is. 43:13; 46:4; 48:12

41:1; Ezek. 26:15, Josh. 5:1; Ps. 67:7

[a]Is. 44:12, 13 [b]Is. 19 [c]Is. 40:20; 46:7

3 [a]Is. 42:19; 43:10; 1, 2, 21 [b]Is. 29:22; 51:2; 63:16 [c]2 Chr. 20:7; James 2:23

, taken hold of [a]Is. :11 [b]Is. 43:5-7 [c]Is. 1; 44:1 [d]Deut. 7:6; 14:2; Ps. 135:4

[a]Deut. 20:1; 31:6; h. 1:9; Ps. 27:1; Is. , 14; 43:2, 5; Rom. 8:31

Do not anxiously look about you, for I am your God.
I will strengthen you, surely [b]I will help you,
Surely I will uphold you with My righteous [c]right hand.'
11 "Behold, [a]all those who are angered at you will be shamed and dishonored;
[b]Those who contend with you will be as nothing, and will perish.
12 "[a]You will seek those who quarrel with you, but will not find them,
Those who war with you will be as nothing, and non-existent.
13 "For I am the LORD your God, [a]who upholds your right hand,
Who says to you, '[b]Do not fear, I will help you.'
14 "Do not fear, you [a]worm Jacob, you men of Israel;
I will help you," declares the LORD, "[1]and [b]your Redeemer is the Holy One of Israel.
15 "Behold, I have made you a new, sharp threshing sledge with double edges;
[a]You will thresh the [b]mountains, and pulverize *them*,
And will make the hills like chaff.
16 "You will [a]winnow them, and the wind will carry them away,
And the storm will scatter them;
But you will [b]rejoice in the LORD,
You will glory in the Holy One of Israel.

17 "The [1]afflicted and needy are seeking [a]water, but there is none,
And their tongue is parched with thirst;
I, the LORD, [b]will answer them Myself,
As the God of Israel I [c]will not forsake them.
18 "I will open [a]rivers on the bare heights,
And springs in the midst of the valleys;
I will make [b]the wilderness a pool of water,
And the dry land fountains of water.
19 "I will put the cedar in the wilderness,
The acacia, and the [a]myrtle, and the [1]olive tree;
I will place the [a]juniper in the desert,
Together with the box tree and the cypress,
20 That [a]they may see and recognize,
And consider and gain insight as well,
That the [b]hand of the LORD has done this,
And the Holy One of Israel has created it.

21 "[1]Present your case," the LORD says.
"Bring forward your strong *arguments*,"
The [a]King of Jacob says.
22 [a]Let them bring forth and declare to us what is going to take place;
As for the [b]former *events*, declare what they *were*,
That we may consider them, and know their outcome;
Or announce to us what is coming.
23 [a]Declare the things that are going to come afterward,
That we may know that you are gods;
Indeed, [b]do good or evil, that we may anxiously look about us and fear together.
24 Behold, [a]you are of [1]no account,
And [b]your work amounts to nothing;

10 [b]Is. 41:14; 4 49:8 [c]Ps. 89:13

11 [a]Is. 45:24 [b]I 29:5, 7, 8

12 [a]Job 20:7-9; 37:35, 36; Is. 17

13 [a]Is. 42:6; 45 41:10

14 [1]Or, *even yo Redeemer, the H One* [a]Job 25:6; 22:6 [b]Is. 35:10; 44:6, 22-24

15 [a]Mic. 4:13; H 3:12 [b]Is. 42:15; Jer. 9:10; Ezek. 3

16 [a]Jer. 51:2 [b]Is 35:10; 51:3; 61:1

17 [1]Or, *poor* [a]Is. 44:3; 49:10; 55:1 30:19; 65:24 [c]Is. 62:12

18 [a]Is. 30:25; 43 [b]Ps. 107:35; Is. 3

19 [1]Or, *oleaster* 35:1; 55:13; 60:13

20 [a]Is. 40:5; 43:1 [b]Job 12:9; Is. 66:1

21 [1]Lit., *Bring nea* 44:6

22 [a]Is. 44:7; 45:2 46:10 [b]Is. 43:9

23 [a]Is. 42:9; 44:7, 45:3; John 13:19 10:5

24 [1]Lit., *nothing* [a] 115:8; Is. 44:9; 1 C 8:4 [b]Is. 37:19; 41:

He who chooses you is an [c]abomination.
25 "I have aroused [a]one from the north, and he has come;
From the rising of the sun he will call on My name;
And he will come upon rulers as *upon* [b]mortar,
Even as the potter treads clay."
26 Who has [a]declared *this* from the beginning, that we might know?
Or from former times, that we may say, "*He is* right!"?
Surely there was [b]no one who declared,
Surely there was no one who proclaimed,
Surely there was no one who heard your words.
27 "[a]Formerly *I said* to Zion, 'Behold, here they are.'
And to Jerusalem, 'I will give a [b]messenger of good news.'
28 "But [a]when I look, there is no one,
And there is no [b]counselor [1]among them
Who, if I ask, can [c]give an answer.
29 "Behold, all of them are [1]false;
Their [a]works are [b]worthless,
Their molten images are [c]wind and emptiness.

Chapter 42

42 "[a]Behold, My [b]Servant, whom I [1]uphold;
My [c]chosen one *in whom* My [d]soul delights.
I have put My [e]Spirit upon Him;
He will bring forth [f]justice to the [2]nations.
2 "He will not cry out or raise *His voice,*
Nor make His voice heard in the street.
3 "A bruised reed He will not break,
And a dimly burning wick He will not extinguish;
He will faithfully bring forth [a]justice.
4 "He will not be [a]disheartened or crushed,
Until He has established justice in the earth;
And the [b]coastlands will wait expectantly for His [1]law."

5 Thus says God the LORD,
Who [a]created the heavens and [b]stretched them out,
Who spread out the [c]earth and its [1]offspring,
Who [d]gives breath to the people on it,
And spirit to those who walk in it,
6 "I am the LORD, I have [a]called you in righteousness,
I will also [b]hold you by the hand and [c]watch over you,
And I will appoint you as a [d]covenant to the people,
As a [e]light to the nations,
7 To [a]open blind eyes,
To [b]bring out prisoners from the dungeon,
And those who dwell in darkness from the prison.
8 "[a]I am the LORD, that is [b]My name;
I will not give My [c]glory to another,
Nor My praise to [1]graven images.
9 "Behold, the [a]former things have come to pass,
Now I declare [b]new things;
Before they spring forth I proclaim *them* to you."

10 Sing to the LORD a [a]new song,

24 [c]Prov. 3:32; 28:9
5 [a]Is. 41:2; Jer. 50:3 ...Sam. 22:43; Is. 10:6; ...ic. 7:10; Zech. 10:5
26 [a]Is. 41:22; 44:7; ...5:21 [b]Hab. 2:18, 19
...[a]Is. 48:3-8 [b]Is. 40:9; ...:28; 52:7; Nah. 1:15
28 [1]Lit., *out of those* ...Is. 50:2; 59:16; 63:5 ... 40:13, 14 [c]Is. 46:7
[1]Another reading is ...*othing* [a]Is. 2:8; 17:8; ...1:24 [b]Is. 44:9 [c]Jer. 5:13
... [1]Or, *hold fast* [2]Or, *Gentiles* [a]Matt. 12:18-21 [b]Is. 41:8; ...3:10; 49:3-6; 52:13; ...:11; Matt. 12:18-21; ...hil. 2:7 [c]Luke 9:35; 1 Pet. 2:4, 6 [d]Matt. ...17; 17:5; Mark 1:11; Luke 3:22 [e]Is. 11:2; ...21; 61:1; Matt. 3:16; ...ke 4:18, 19, 21 [f]Is. 2:4
[a]Ps. 72:2, 4; 96:13
[1]Or, *instruction* [a]Is. ...8 [b]Is. 11:11; 24:15; ...2:10, 12; 49:1; 51:5; 60:9; 66:19
...Or, *vegetation* [a]Ps. ...02:25, 26; Is. 45:18 ...Ps. 104:2; Is. 40:22 ...24:1, 2; 136:6 [d]Job ...:10; 33:4; Is. 57:16; ...an. 5:23; Acts 17:25
...s. 41:2; Jer. 23:5, 6 ...[b]Is. 41:13; 45:1 [c]Is. ...; 27:3 [d]Is. 49:8 [e]Is. 51:4; 60:1, 3; Luke ...2; Acts 13:47; 26:23
[a]Is. 29:18; 35:5 [b]Is. 49:9; 61:1
[1]Or, *idols* [a]Is. 43:3, ..., 15 [b]Ex. 3:15; Ps. ...:18 [c]Ex. 20:3-5; Is. 48:11
[a]Is. 48:3 [b]Is. 43:19; 48:6
...Ps. 33:3; 40:3; 98:1

Sing His praise from the [b]end of the earth!
[c]You who go down to the sea, and [d]all that is in it.
You [e]islands and those who dwell on them.
11 Let the [a]wilderness and its cities lift up *their voices*,
The settlements where [b]Kedar inhabits.
Let the inhabitants of [c]Sela sing aloud,
Let them shout for joy from the tops of the [d]mountains.
12 Let them [a]give glory to the LORD,
And declare His praise in the [b]coastlands.
13 [a]The LORD will go forth like a warrior,
He will arouse *His* [b]zeal like a man of war.
He will utter a shout, yes, He will raise a war cry.
He will [c]prevail against His enemies.

14 "[a]I have kept silent for a long time,
I have kept still and restrained Myself.
Now like a woman in labor I will groan,
I will both gasp and pant.
15 "I will [a]lay waste the mountains and hills,
And wither all their vegetation;
I will [b]make the rivers into coastlands,
And dry up the ponds.
16 "And I will [a]lead the blind by a way they do not know,
In paths they do not know I will guide them.
I will [b]make darkness into light before them
And [c]rugged places into plains.
These are the things I will do,
And I will [d]not leave them undone."
17 They shall be turned back and be [a]utterly put to shame,
Who trust in [1]idols,
Who say to molten images,
"You are our gods."

18 [a]Hear, you deaf!
And look, you blind, that you may see.
19 Who is blind but My [a]servant,
Or so deaf as My [b]messenger whom I send?
Who is so blind as he that is [1c]at peace *with Me*,
Or so blind as the servant of the LORD?
20 [a]You have seen many things, but you do not observe *them*;
Your ears are open, but none hears.
21 The LORD was pleased for His righteousness' sake
To make the law [a]great and glorious.
22 But this is a people plundered and despoiled;
All of them are [a]trapped in [1]caves,
Or are [b]hidden away in prisons;
They have become a prey with none to deliver *them*,
And a spoil, with none to say, "Give *them* back!"

23 Who among you will give ear to this?
Who will give heed and listen hereafter?
24 Who gave Jacob up for spoil, and Israel to plunderers?
Was it not the LORD, against whom we have sinned,
And in whose ways they [a]were not willing to walk,

10 [b]Is. 49:6; 62 65:5; 107:23 [d]E 20:11; 1 Chr. 16 96:11 [e]Is. 42:4
11 [a]Is. 32:16; 3 [b]Is. 21:16; 60:7 16:1 [d]Is. 52:7;
12 [a]Is. 24:15 [b]
13 [a]Ex. 15:3 [b]Is 26:11; 37:32; 59 66:14-16
14 [a]Ps. 50:21; I
15 [a]Is. 2:12-16; 38:19, 20 [b]Is. 44 50:2; Nah. 1:4-6
16 [a]Is. 29:18; 30 32:3; Jer. 31:8, 9 1:78, 79 [b]Is. 29:1 Eph. 5:8 [c]Is. 40: 3:5 [d]Josh. 1:5; P 94:14; Is. 41:17; 13:5
17 [1]Or, *graven in* [a]Ps. 97:7; Is. 1:29 11; 45:16
18 [a]Is. 29:18; 35
19 [1]Or, *the devot one* [a]Is. 41:8 [b]Is. 44:26 [c]Is. 26:3; 2
20 [a]Rom. 2:21
21 [a]Is. 42:4; 51:4
22 [1]Or, *holes* [a]Is. 24:18 [b]Is. 24:22
24 [a]Is. 30:15

And whose law they did not [b]obey?
25 So He poured out on him the heat of His anger
And the [a]fierceness of battle;
And it set him aflame all around,
Yet he did not recognize *it;*
And it burned him, but he [1b]paid no attention.

Chapter 43

43 But now, thus says the LORD, your [a]Creator, O Jacob,
And He who [b]formed you, O Israel,
"Do not [c]fear, for I have [d]redeemed you;
I have [e]called you by name; you are [f]Mine!
2 "When you [a]pass through the waters, [b]I will be with you;
And through the rivers, they will not overflow you.
When you [c]walk through the fire, you will not be scorched,
Nor will the flame burn you.
3 "For [a]I am the LORD your God,
The Holy One of Israel, your [b]Savior;
I have given Egypt as your ransom,
[1c]Cush and Seba in your place.
4 "Since you are [a]precious in My sight,
Since you are [b]honored and I [c]love you,
I will give *other* men in your place and *other* peoples in exchange for your life.
5 "Do not fear, for [a]I am with you;
I will bring [b]your offspring from the east,
And [c]gather you from the west.
6 "I will say to the [a]north, 'Give *them* up!'
And to the south, 'Do not hold *them* back.'
Bring My [b]sons from afar,
And My daughters from the [c]ends of the earth,
7 Everyone who is [a]called by My name,
And whom I have [b]created for My [c]glory,
[d]Whom I have formed, even whom I have made."

8 Bring out the people who are [a]blind, even though they have eyes,
And the deaf, even though they have ears.
9 All the nations have [a]gathered together
In order that the peoples may be assembled.
Who among them can [b]declare this
And proclaim to us the former things?
Let them present [c]their witnesses [d]that they may be justified,
Or let them hear and say, "It is true."
10 "You are [a]My witnesses," declares the LORD,
"And [b]My servant whom I have chosen,
In order that you may know and believe Me,
And understand that [c]I am He.
[d]Before Me there was no God formed,
And there will be none after Me.
11 "I, even I, am the LORD;
And there is no [a]savior [b]besides Me.
12 "It is I who have declared and saved and proclaimed,
And there was no [a]strange *god* among you;

4 [b]Is. 48:18; 57:17
[1]Lit., *did not lay it to* ...*eart* [a]Is. 5:25; 9:19 ...29:13; 47:7; 57:1; Hos. 7:9
43:1 [a]Is. 43:15 [b]Is. ...:7, 21; 44:2, 21, 24 ...43:5 [d]Is. 44:22, 23; ...20 [e]Gen. 32:28; Is. ...; 45:3, 4 [f]Is. 43:21
...Ps. 66:12; Is. 8:7, 8 ...t. 31:6, 8 [c]Is. 29:6; ...7-29; Dan. 3:25, 27
[1]Or, *Ethiopia* [a]Ex. ...2 [b]Is. 19:20; 43:11; ...5, 21; 49:26; 60:16; 63:8 [c]Is. 20:3-5
...x. 19:5, 6 [b]Is. 49:5 [c]Is. 63:9
[a]Is. 8:10; 43:2 [b]Is. ...:8; 49:12; 61:9 [c]Is. 49:12
[a]Ps. 107:3 [b]2 Cor. 6:18 [c]Is. 45:22
...56:5; 62:2; James 2:7 [b]Ps. 100:3; Is. ...:23; Eph. 2:10 [c]Is. ...23; 46:13 [d]Is. 43:1
...6:9; 42:19; Ezek. 12:2
[a]Is. 34:1; 41:1 [b]Is. ...2, 23, 26 [c]Is. 44:9 [d]Is. 43:26
[a]Is. 44:8 [b]Is. 41:8 ...s. 41:4 [d]Is. 45:5, 6
...1 [a]Is. 43:3; 45:21; ...s. 13:4 [b]Is. 44:6, 8
[a]Deut. 32:16; Ps. 81:9

So you are My witnesses," declares the LORD,
"And I am God.
13 "Even [1a]from eternity [b]I am He;
And there is [c]none who can deliver out of My hand;
[d]I act and who can reverse it?"

14 Thus says the LORD your [a]Redeemer, the Holy One of Israel,
"For your sake I have sent to Babylon,
And will bring them all down as fugitives,
[1]Even the [b]Chaldeans, into the [c]ships [2]in which they rejoice.
15 "I am the LORD, your Holy One,
[a]The Creator of Israel, your [b]King."
16 Thus says the LORD,
Who [a]makes a way through the sea
And a path through the mighty waters,
17 Who brings forth the [a]chariot and the horse,
The army and the mighty man
(They will lie down together *and* not rise again;
They have been [b]quenched *and* extinguished like a wick):
18 "[a]Do not call to mind the former things,
Or ponder things of the past.
19 "Behold, I will do something [a]new,
Now it will spring forth;
Will you not be aware of it?
I will even [b]make a roadway in the wilderness,
Rivers in the desert.
20 "The beasts of the field will glorify Me;
The [a]jackals and the ostriches;
Because I have [b]given waters in the wilderness
And rivers in the desert,
To give drink to My chosen people.
21 "The people whom [a]I formed for Myself,
[b]Will declare My praise.

22 "Yet you have not called on Me, O Jacob;
But you have become [a]weary of Me, O Israel.
23 "You have [a]not brought to Me the sheep of your burnt offerings;
Nor have you [b]honored Me with your sacrifices.
I have not [c]burdened you with [1]offerings,
Nor wearied you with [d]incense.
24 "You have bought Me no [1a]sweet cane with money,
Neither have you [2]filled Me with the fat of your sacrifices;
Rather you have burdened Me with your sins,
You have [b]wearied Me with your iniquities.

25 "I, even I, am the one who [a]wipes out your transgressions [b]for My own sake;
And I will [c]not remember your sins.
26 "[1]Put Me in remembrance; [a]let us argue our case together,
State your *cause,* [b]that you may be proved right.
27 "Your [a]first [1]forefather sinned,
And your [2b]spokesmen have [3]transgressed against Me.
28 "So I will [1]pollute the [2]princes of the sanctuary;
And I will consign Jacob to the [a]ban, and Israel to [b]revilement.

13 [1]So with Gr.; *from the day* [a]Ps Is. 48:16 [b]Is. 41: 50:22 [d]Job 9:12; 14:27

14 [1]Another rea *As for the Chalde their rejoicing* is *into lamentations of their rejoicing* 41:14 [b]Is. 23:13 51:13

15 [a]Is. 43:1 [b]Is. 44:6

16 [a]Ex. 14:21, 2 77:19; Is. 11:15; 50:2; 51:10; 63:1

17 [a]Ex. 15:19 [b] 118:12; Is. 1:31

18 [a]Is. 65:17; Je

19 [a]Is. 42:9; 48: 2 Cor. 5:17 [b]Ex. Num. 20:11; Deu Ps. 78:16; Is. 35 41:18, 19; 49:10

20 [a]Is. 13:22; 35 41:17, 18; 48:21

21 [a]Is. 43:1 [b]Ps 102:18; Is. 42:12 1:74, 75; 1 Pet. 2

22 [a]Mic. 6:3; Ma 3:14

23 [1]Or, *a meal* [a]Amos 5:25 [b]Ze 6; Mal. 1:6-8 [c]Je 7:21-26 [d]Ex. 30 Lev. 2:1; 24:7

24 [1]Or, *calamus saturated* [a]Ex. 3 Jer. 6:20 [b]Ps. 9 1:14; 7:13; Ezek Mal. 2:17

25 [a]Is. 44:22; 5 50:20 [b]Is. 37:35 11; Ezek. 36:22 38:17; Jer. 31:34

26 [1]Or, *Report* [a]Is. 1:18; 41:1; 5 43:9

27 [1]Lit., *father interpreters* [3]Or *rebelled* [a]Is. 51 16:3 [b]Is. 9:15; 2 29:10; Jer. 5:31

28 [1]Or, *pierce* [2]Or, *holy princes* 24:6; 34:5; Jer. 2 Dan. 9:11; Zech [b]Ps. 79:4; Ezek.

Chapter 44

44 "But now listen, O Jacob, My [a]servant;
And Israel, whom I have chosen:
2 Thus says the LORD who made you
And [a]formed you from the womb, who [b]will help you,
'[c]Do not fear, O Jacob My servant;
And you [d]Jeshurun whom I have chosen.
3 'For [a]I will pour out water on [1]the thirsty *land*
And streams on the dry ground;
I will [b]pour out My Spirit on your [c]offspring,
And My blessing on your descendants;
4 And they will spring up [1]among the grass
Like [a]poplars by streams of water.'
5 "This one will say, 'I am the LORD's';
And that one [1]will call on the name of Jacob;
And another will [a]write [2]*on* his hand, 'Belonging to the LORD,'
And will name Israel's name with honor.

6 "Thus says the LORD, the [a]King of Israel
And his [b]Redeemer, the LORD of hosts:
'I am the [c]first and I am the last,
And there is no God [d]besides Me.
7 'And who is like Me? [a]Let him proclaim and declare it;
Yes, let him recount it to Me in order,
[1]From the time that I established the ancient [2]nation.
And let them declare to them the things that are coming
And the events that are going to take place.
8 'Do not tremble and do not be afraid;
[a]Have I not long since announced it to you and declared it?
And [b]you are My witnesses.
Is there any God [c]besides Me,
Or is there any *other* [d]Rock?
I know of none.' "
9 Those who fashion [1]a graven image are all of them futile, and
their precious things are of no profit; even their own witnesses fail to
see or know, so that they will be [a]put to shame.
10 Who has fashioned a god or cast [1]an idol to [a]no profit?
11 Behold, all his companions will be [a]put to shame, for the crafts-
men themselves are mere men. Let them all assemble themselves, let
them stand up, let them tremble, let them together be put to shame.
12 The [a]man shapes iron into a cutting tool, and does his work over
the coals, [1]fashioning it with hammers, and working it with his
strong arm. He also gets hungry and [2]his strength fails; he drinks no
water and becomes weary.
13 [a]*Another* shapes wood, he extends a measuring line; he outlines it
with red chalk. He works it with planes, and outlines it with a com-
pass, and makes it like the form of a man, like the beauty of [b]man, so
that it may sit in a [c]house.
14 Surely he cuts cedars for himself, and takes a [1]cypress or an oak,
and [2]raises *it* for himself among the trees of the forest. He plants a fir,
and the rain makes it grow.
15 Then it becomes *something* for a man to burn, so he takes one of
them and warms himself; he also makes a fire to bake bread. He also

44:1 [a]Is. 41:8; Jer. 30:10; 46:27, 28

2 [a]Is. 44:21, 24 [b]Is. :10 [c]Is. 43:5 [d]Deut. 32:15; 33:5, 26

3 [1]Or, *him who is* *sty* [a]Is. 41:17; Ezek. 34:26; Joel 3:18 [b]Is. 32:15; Joel 2:28 [c]Is. 61:9; 65:23

[1]Another reading is *ke grass among the* *ers* [a]Lev. 23:40; Job 40:22

[1]Another reading is *will be called by the name of Jacob* [2]Or, *with* [a]Ex. 13:9; Neh. 9:38

s. 41:21; 43:15 [b]Is. 41:14; 43:1, 14 [c]Is. ; 43:10; 48:12; Rev. 1:8, 17; 22:13 [d]Is. 1; 44:8; 45:5, 6, 21

7 [1]Lit., *From My establishing of* [2]Or, *eople* [a]Is. 41:22, 26

[a]Is. 42:9; 48:5 [b]Is. 10 [c]Deut. 4:35, 39; Sam. 2:2; Is. 45:5; oel 2:27 [d]Is. 17:10; 26:4; 30:29

9 [1]Or, *an idol* [a]Ps. :7; Is. 42:17; 44:11; 45:16

Or, *a graven image* Is. 41:29; Jer. 10:5; b. 2:18; Acts 19:26

Ps. 97:7; Is. 42:17; 44:9; 45:16

[1]Lit., *and fashions* [2]Lit., *there is no* *ngth* [a]Is. 40:19, 20; 1:6, 7; 46:6, 7; Jer. 10:3-5; Hab. 2:18

13 [a]Is. 41:7 [b]Ps. 5-7 [c]Judg. 17:4, 5; Ezek. 8:10, 11

Or, *holm-oak* [2]Lit., *makes strong*

[a]makes a god and worships it; he makes it a graven image, and [b]falls
down before it.
16 Half of it he burns in the fire; over *this* half he eats meat as he
roasts a roast, and is satisfied. He also warms himself and says,
"Aha! I am warm, I have seen the fire."
17 But the rest of it he [a]makes into a god, his graven image. He falls
down before it and worships; he also [b]prays to it and says, "Deliver
me, for thou art my god."
18 They do not [a]know, nor do they understand, for He has [b]smeared
over their eyes so that they cannot see and their hearts so that they
cannot comprehend.
19 And no one [1]recalls, nor is there [a]knowledge or understanding to
say, "I have burned half of it in the fire, and also have baked bread
over its coals. I roast meat and eat *it*. Then [2]I make the rest of it into
an [b]abomination, [3]I fall down before a block of wood!"
20 He [1a]feeds on ashes; a [b]deceived heart has turned him aside. And
he cannot deliver [2]himself, nor say, "[c]Is there not a lie in my right
hand?"

21 "[a]Remember these things, O Jacob,
And Israel, for you are [b]My servant;
I have formed you, you are My servant,
O Israel, you will [c]not be forgotten by Me.
22 "I have [a]wiped out your transgressions like a thick cloud,
And your sins like a [1]heavy mist.
[b]Return to Me, for I have [c]redeemed you."
23 [a]Shout for joy, O heavens, for the LORD has done *it!*
Shout joyfully, you lower parts of the earth;
[b]Break forth into a shout of joy, you mountains,
O forest, and every tree in it;
For [c]the LORD has redeemed Jacob
And in Israel He [d]shows forth His glory.

24 Thus says the LORD, your [a]Redeemer, and the one who [b]formed
you from the womb,
"I, the LORD, am the maker of all things,
[c]Stretching out the heavens by Myself,
And spreading out the earth [1]all alone,
25 [a]Causing the [1]omens of boasters to fail,
[2]Making fools out of diviners,
[b]Causing wise men to draw back,
And [3]turning their knowledge into foolishness,
26 [a]Confirming the word of His servant,
And [1]performing the purpose of His messengers.
It is I who says of Jerusalem, 'She shall be inhabited!'
And of the [b]cities of Judah, '[c]They shall be built.'
And I will raise up her ruins *again*.
27 "*It is I* who says to the depth of the sea, 'Be dried up!'
And I will make your rivers [a]dry.
28 "*It is I* who says of [a]Cyrus, '*He is* My shepherd!
And he will perform all My desire.'
And [1]he declares of Jerusalem, '[b]She will be built,'
And of the temple, '[2]Your foundation will be laid.' "

15 [a]Is. 44:17 [b]2 C
25:14

17 [a]Is. 44:15 [b]1 K
18:26, 28; Is. 45:2

18 [a]Is. 1:3; Jer. 1
14 [b]Ps. 81:12; Is.
10; 29:10

19 [1]Lit., *returns to*
heart [2]Or, *shall I*
make . . .? [3]Or, *s*
fall . . . ? [a]Is. 5:13
44:18, 19; 45:20
27:15; 1 Kin. 11:5
2 Kin. 23:13, 14

20 [1]Or, *is a comp*
of ashes [2]Lit., *his*
[a]Ps. 102:9 [b]Job
Hos. 4:12; Rom.
22; 2 Thess. 2:11
2 Tim. 3:13 [c]Is. 5
59:3, 4, 13; Rom.

21 [a]Is. 46:8; Zech
[b]Is. 44:1, 2 [c]Is. 4

22 [1]Or, *cloud* [a]P
51:1, 9; Is. 43:25;
3:19 [b]Is. 31:6; 55
43:1; 48:20; 1 Co
1 Pet. 1:18, 19

23 [a]Ps. 69:34; 96
12; Is. 42:10; 49:
[b]Ps. 98:7, 8; 148
Is. 55:12 [c]Is. 43:
49:3; 61:3

24 [1]Or, *who was*
Me? [a]Is. 41:14; 4
[b]Is. 44:2 [c]Is. 40:2
42:5; 45:12, 18; 5

25 [1]Lit., *signs* [2]L
makes [3]Lit., *He*
[a]Is. 47:13 [b]2 Sar
15:31; Job 5:12-
33:10; Is. 29:14;
51:57; 1 Cor. 1:2

26 [1]Lit., *He perf*
[a]Zech. 1:6; Matt.
[b]Is. 40:9 [c]Jer. 32

27 [a]Is. 42:15; 50
50:38; 51:36

28 [1]Lit., *to say*
You will be found
45:1 [b]2 Chr. 36:
Ezra 1:1; Is. 14:
45:13; 54:11

Chapter 45

45 Thus says the LORD to [a]Cyrus His anointed,
Whom I have taken by the right [b]hand,
To [c]subdue nations before him,
And [1]to [d]loose the loins of kings;
To open doors before him so that gates will not be shut:
2 "I will go before you and [a]make the [1]rough places smooth;
I will [b]shatter the doors of bronze, and cut through their iron
[c]bars.
3 "And I will give you the [1a]treasures of darkness,
And hidden wealth of secret places,
In order that you may know that it is I,
The LORD, the God of Israel, who [b]calls you by your name.
4 "For the sake of [a]Jacob My servant,
And Israel My chosen *one*,
I have also [b]called you by your name;
I have given you a title of honor
Though you have [c]not known Me.
5 "I am the LORD, and [a]there is no other;
[b]Besides Me there is no God.
I will [1c]gird you, though you have not known Me;
6 That [1a]men may know from the rising to the setting of the sun
That there is [b]no one besides Me.
I am the LORD, and there is no other,
7 The One [a]forming light and [b]creating darkness,
Causing [1]well-being and [c]creating calamity;
I am the LORD who does all these.

8 "[a]Drip down, O heavens, from above,
And let the clouds pour down righteousness;
Let the [b]earth open up and salvation bear fruit,
[c]And righteousness spring up with it.
I, the LORD, have created it.

9 "Woe to *the one* who [a]quarrels with his [1]Maker—
An earthenware vessel [2]among the vessels of earth!
Will the [b]clay say to the [1]potter, 'What are you doing?'
Or the thing you are making *say*, 'He has no hands'?
10 "Woe to him who says to a father, 'What are you begetting?'
Or to a woman, 'To what are you [1]giving birth?' "

11 Thus says the [a]LORD, the Holy One of Israel, and his [1b]Maker:
"[2c]Ask Me about the things to come [3]concerning My [d]sons,
And you shall commit to Me [e]the work of My hands.
12 "It is I who [a]made the earth, and created man upon it.
I [b]stretched out the heavens with My hands,
And I [1]ordained [c]all their host.
13 "I have aroused him in [a]righteousness,
And I will [b]make all his ways smooth;
He will [c]build My city, and will let My exiles go [d]free,
Without any payment or reward," says the LORD of hosts.

14 Thus says the LORD,
"The [1]products of [a]Egypt and the merchandise of [2b]Cush

45:1 [1]Lit., *I will loose* [a]Is. 44:28 [b]Ps. 73:23; 41:13; 42:6 [c]Is. 41:2, ; Jer. 50:3, 35; 51:11, 20, 24 [d]Job 12:21; Is. 45:5

2 [1]Another reading is *mountains* [a]Is. 40:4 s. 107:16 [c]Jer. 51:30

3 [1]Or, *hoarded treasures* [a]Jer. 41:8; 50:37 [b]Ex. 33:12, 17; Is. 43:1; 49:1

[a]Is. 41:8, 9; 44:1 [b]Is. 43:1 [c]Acts 17:23

5 [1]Or, *arm* [a]Is. 45:6, 14, 18, 21; 46:9 [b]Is. 44:6, 8 [c]Ps. 18:39

6 [1]Lit., *they* [a]Ps. 102:15; Mal. 1:11 [b]Is. 45:5

Or, *peace* [a]Is. 42:16 104:20; 105:28 [c]Is. 1:2; 47:11; Amos 3:6

Ps. 72:6; Hos. 10:12; 14:5; Joel 3:18 [b]Ps. :11 [c]Is. 60:21; 61:11

Lit., *Fashioner* [2]Lit., *th* [a]Job 15:25; 40:8, 9; Ps. 2:2, 3; Prov. 1:30; Jer. 50:24 [b]Is. 9:16; 64:8; Jer. 18:6; Rom. 9:20, 21

[1]Lit., *in labor pains with*

[1]Lit., *Fashioner* [2]Or, *I you ask* [3]Or, *upon* 43:15; 48:17; Ezek. [b]Is. 44:2; 54:5 [c]Is. 8:19 [d]Jer. 31:9 [e]Is. ; 29:23; 60:21; 64:8

2 [1]Or, *commanded* [a]Is. 42:5; 45:18; Jer. 27:5 [b]Ps. 104:2; Is. 5; 44:24 [c]Gen. 2:1; Neh. 9:6

[a]Is. 41:2 [b]Is. 45:2 2 Chr. 36:22, 23; Is. 44:28 [d]Is. 52:3

14 [1]Lit., *labor* [2]Or, *opia* [a]Ps. 68:31; Is. 9:21 [b]Is. 18:1; 43:3

This prophecy regarding Cyrus was given 175 years before his birth. In 539 B.C. Babylon was conquered by Cyrus/Darius of the Medo-Persian Empire.

And the Sabeans, men of stature,
Will [c]come over to you and will be yours;
They will walk behind you, they will come over in [d]chains
And will [e]bow down to you;
They will make supplication to you:
'[3]Surely, [f]God is [4]with you, and [g]there is none else,
No other God.' "
15 Truly, Thou art a God who [a]hides Himself,
O God of Israel, [b]Savior!
16 They will be [a]put to shame and even humiliated, all of them;
The [b]manufacturers of idols will go away together in
humiliation.
17 Israel has been saved by the LORD
With an [a]everlasting salvation;
You [b]will not be put to shame or humiliated
To all eternity.

18 For thus says the LORD, who [a]created the heavens
(He is the God who [b]formed the earth and made it,
He established it and did not create it [1]a [c]waste place,
But formed it to be [d]inhabited),
"I am the LORD, and [e]there is none else.
19 "[a]I have not spoken in secret,
In [1]some dark land;
I did not say to the [2b]offspring of Jacob,
'[c]Seek Me in [3]a waste place';
I, the LORD, [d]speak righteousness
[e]Declaring things that are upright.

20 "[a]Gather yourselves and come;
Draw near together, you fugitives of the nations;
[b]They have no knowledge,
Who [c]carry about [1]their wooden idol,
And [d]pray to a god who cannot save.
21 "[a]Declare and set forth *your case;*
Indeed, let them consult together.
[b]Who has announced this from of old?
Who has long since declared it?
Is it not I, the LORD?
And there is [c]no other God besides Me,
A righteous God and a [d]Savior;
There is none except Me.
22 "[a]Turn to Me, and [b]be saved, all the ends of the earth;
For I am God, and there is no other.
23 "[a]I have sworn by Myself,
The [b]word has gone forth from My mouth in righteousness
And will not turn back,
That to Me [c]every knee will bow, every tongue will [d]swear
allegiance.
24 "They will say of Me, 'Only [a]in the LORD are righteousness and
strength.'
Men will come to Him,
And [b]all who were angry at Him shall be put to shame.

14 [3]Or, *God is wit* *alone* [4]Or, *in* [c]Is. 1 2; 49:23; 54:3 [d]Ps 149:8 [e]Is. 49:23; 6 [f]Jer. 16:19; Zech. 8:20-23; 1 Cor. 14: [g]Is. 45:5

15 [a]Ps. 44:24; Is. 8:17; 57:17 [b]Is. 43

16 [a]Is. 42:17; 44:9 44:11

17 [a]Is. 26:4; 51:6; 11:26 [b]Is. 49:23; 5 54:4

18 [1]Or, *in vain* [a]Is 42:5 [b]Is. 45:12 [c]G 1:2 [d]Gen. 1:26; Ps 115:16 [e]Is. 45:5

19 [1]Lit., *a place o* *land of darkness* *seed* [3]Or, *vain* [a]Is 48:16 [b]Is. 45:25; [c]2 Chr. 15:2; Ps. 7 Jer. 29:13, 14 [d]Ps 19:8; Is. 45:23; 63 43:12; 44:8

20 [1]Lit., *the wood* *their graven imag* 43:9 [b]Is. 44:18, 1 48:5-7 [c]Is. 46:1, 7 10:5 [d]Is. 44:17; 4

21 [a]Is. 41:23; 43: 41:26; 44:7; 48:14 45:5 [d]Is. 43:3, 11

22 [a]Num. 21:8, 9 2 Chr. 20:12; Mic. Zech. 12:10 [b]Is. 3 49:6, 12; 52:10

23 [a]Gen. 22:16; 62:8; Heb. 6:13 [b] 55:11 [c]Rom. 14:1 Phil. 2:10 [d]Deut. Ps. 63:11; Is. 19:1 65:16

24 [a]Jer. 33:16 [b]Is

25 [a]1 Kin. 8:32; Is.
1 [b]Is. 41:16; 60:19

25 "In the LORD all the offspring of Israel
Will be [a]justified, and will [b]glory."

Chapter 46

6:1 [1]Lit., *carried by* [a]Is. 2:18; 21:9; Jer. 50:2-4; 51:44

[1]Or, *their soul has* udg. 18:17, 18, 24; m. 5:21; Jer. 43:12, ; 48:7; Hos. 10:5, 6

46 [a]Bel has bowed down, Nebo stoops over;
Their images are *consigned* to the beasts and the cattle.
The things [1]that you carry are burdensome,
A load for the weary *beast*.
2 They stooped over, they have bowed down together;
They could not rescue the burden,
But [1]have themselves [a]gone into captivity.

[1]Lit., *the belly* [a]Is. 6:12 [b]Is. 10:21, 22 [c]Ps. 71:6; Is. 49:1

3 "[a]Listen to Me, O house of Jacob,
And all [b]the remnant of the house of Israel,
You who have been [c]borne by Me from [1]birth,
And have been carried from the womb;

[1]Lit., *I am He* [2]Lit., *ay hairs* [3]Or, *made ou* [a]Is. 41:4; 43:13; 48:12 [b]Ps. 71:18

4 Even to your old age, [a]I [1]shall be the same,
And even to your [2b]graying years I shall bear *you!*
I have [3]done *it*, and I shall carry *you;*
And I shall bear *you*, and I shall deliver *you*.

5 [a]Is. 40:18, 25

5 "[a]To whom would you liken Me,
And make Me equal and compare Me,
That we should be alike?

6 [a]Is. 40:19; 41:7; 2-17; Jer. 10:4 [b]Is. 44:15, 17

6 "Those who [a]lavish gold from the purse
And weigh silver on the scale
Hire a goldsmith, and he makes it *into* a god;
They [b]bow down, indeed they worship it.

s. 45:20; 46:1; Jer. :5 [b]Is. 40:20; 41:7 s. 41:28 [d]Is. 45:20

7 "They [a]lift it upon the shoulder and carry it;
They set it in its place and it stands *there*.
[b]It does not move from its place.
Though one may cry to it, it [c]cannot answer;
It [d]cannot deliver him from his distress.

it., *firm* [2]Lit., *heart* s. 44:21 [b]Is. 44:19 [c]Is. 50:1

8 "[a]Remember this, and be [1]assured;
[b]Recall it to [2]mind, you [c]transgressors.

eut. 32:7; Is. 42:9; [b]Is. 45:5, 21 [c]Is. 41:26, 27

9 "Remember the [a]former things long past,
For I am God, and there is [b]no other;
I am God, and there is [c]no one like Me,

[a]Ps. 33:11; Prov. 21; Is. 14:24; 25:1; 40:8; Acts 5:39

10 Declaring the end from the beginning
And from ancient times things which have not been done,
Saying, '[a]My purpose will be established,
And I will accomplish all My good pleasure';

[1]Lit., *His* [a]Is. 18:6 41:2 [c]Num. 23:19; Is. 14:24; 37:26

11 Calling a [a]bird of prey from the [b]east,
The man of [1]My purpose from a far country.
Truly I have [c]spoken; truly I will bring it to pass.
I have planned *it, surely* I will do it.

s. 46:3 [b]Ps. 76:5; :4; Zech. 7:11, 12; :13 [c]Ps. 119:150; Is. 48:1; Jer. 2:5

12 "[a]Listen to Me, you [b]stubborn-minded,
Who are [c]far from righteousness.

3 [a]Is. 51:5; 61:11; m. 3:21 [b]Is. 61:3; ; Joel 3:17; 1 Pet. 6 [c]Is. 43:7; 44:23

13 "I [a]bring near My righteousness, it is not far off;
And My salvation will not delay.
And I will grant [b]salvation in Zion,
And My [c]glory for Israel.

Chapter 47

47 "[a]Come down and sit in the dust,
O [b]virgin [c]daughter of Babylon;
Sit on the ground without a throne,
O daughter of the Chaldeans.
For you shall no longer be called [d]tender and delicate.
2 "Take the [a]millstones and [b]grind meal.
Remove your [c]veil, [d]strip off the skirt,
Uncover the leg, cross the rivers.
3 "Your [a]nakedness will be uncovered,
Your shame also will be exposed;
I will [b]take vengeance and will not [1]spare a man."
4 Our [a]Redeemer, the LORD of hosts is His name,
The Holy One of Israel.
5 "[a]Sit silently, and go into [b]darkness,
O daughter of the Chaldeans;
For you will no more be called
The [c]queen of [d]kingdoms.
6 "I was angry with My people,
I profaned My heritage,
And gave them into your hand.
You did not show mercy to them,
On the [a]aged you made your yoke very heavy.
7 "Yet you said, 'I shall be a [a]queen forever.'
These things you did not [b]consider,
Nor remember the [c]outcome of [1]them.

8 "Now, then, hear this, you [a]sensual one,
Who [b]dwells securely,
Who says in [1]your heart,
'[c]I am, and there is no one besides me.
I shall [d]not sit as a widow,
Nor shall I know loss of children.'
9 "But these [a]two things shall come on you [b]suddenly in one day:
Loss of children and widowhood.
They shall come on you in full measure
In spite of your many [c]sorceries,
In spite of the great power of your spells.
10 "And you felt [a]secure in your wickedness and said,
'[b]No one sees me,'
Your [c]wisdom and your knowledge, [1]they have deluded you;
For you have said in your heart,
'[d]I am, and there is no one besides me.'
11 "But [a]evil will come on you
Which you will not know how to charm away;
And disaster will fall on you
For which you cannot atone,
And [b]destruction about which you do not know
Will come on you [c]suddenly.

12 "Stand *fast* now in your [a]spells
And in your many sorceries
With which you have labored from your youth;
Perhaps you will be able to profit,

47:1 [a]Is. 3:26; 48:18 [b]Is. 23:1 Jer. 46:11 [c]Ps Jer. 50:42; 51: 2:7 [d]Deut. 28:

2 [a]Ex. 11:5; Je [b]Job 31:10; Ec Matt. 24:41 [c]G 24:65; Is. 3:23; 11:5 [d]Is. 32:11

3 [1]Lit., *meet* [a] 16:37; Nah. 3:5 34:8; 63:4

4 [a]Is. 41:14

5 [a]Is. 23:2; Jer. Lam. 2:10 [b]Is. [c]Is. 47:7 [d]Is. 13 Dan. 2:37

6 [a]Deut. 28:50

7 [1]Lit., *it* [a]Is. 47 42:25; 57:11 [c]D 32:29; Jer. 5:31; 7:2, 3

8 [1]Lit., *her* [a]Is. 32:9; Jer. 50:11 32:9, 11; Zeph. 2 45:5, 6, 18; 47:1 2:15 [d]Rev. 18:7

9 [a]Is. 13:16, 18; [b]Ps. 73:19; 1 The 5:3; Rev. 18:8, 1 47:13; Nah. 3:4; 18:23

10 [1]Lit., *it has* [a]P 52:7; 62:10; Is. 5 29:15; Ezek. 8:12 [c]Is. 5:21; 44:20 [d]

11 [a]Is. 57:1 [b]Is. Jer. 51:8, 43; Luk 17:27; 1 Thess. 5 47:9

12 [a]Is. 47:9

Perhaps you may cause trembling.
13 "You are [a]wearied with your many counsels;
Let now the [b]astrologers,
Those who prophesy by the stars,
Those who predict by the new moons,
Stand up and [c]save you from what will come upon you.
14 "Behold, they have become [a]like stubble,
[b]Fire burns them;
They cannot deliver themselves from the power of the flame;
There will be [c]no coal to warm by,
Nor a fire to sit before!
15 "So have those become to you with whom you have labored,
Who have [a]trafficked with you from your youth;
Each has wandered in his own [1]way.
There is [b]none to save you.

Chapter 48

48 "[a]Hear this, O house of Jacob, who are named Israel
And who came forth from the [1b]loins of Judah,
Who [c]swear by the name of the LORD
And invoke the God of Israel,
But not in truth nor in [d]righteousness.
2 "For they call themselves after the [a]holy city,
And [b]lean on the God of Israel;
The LORD of hosts is His name.
3 "I [a]declared the former things long ago
And they went forth from My mouth, and I proclaimed them.
[b]Suddenly I acted, and they [c]came to pass.
4 "Because I know that you are [1a]obstinate,
And your [b]neck is an iron sinew,
And your [c]forehead bronze,
5 Therefore I declared *them* to you long ago,
Before [1]they took place I proclaimed *them* to you,
Lest you should say, 'My [a]idol has done them,
And my graven image and my molten image have commanded them.'
6 "You have heard; look at all this.
And you, will you not declare it?
I proclaim to you [a]new things from this time,
Even hidden things which you have not known.
7 "They are created now and not long ago;
And before today you have not heard them,
Lest you should say, 'Behold, I knew them.'
8 "You have not [a]heard, you have not known.
Even from long ago your ear has not been open,
Because I knew that you would deal very treacherously;
And you have been called a [1b]rebel from [2]birth.
9 "[a]For the sake of My name I [b]delay My wrath,
And *for* My praise I restrain *it* for you,
In order not to cut you off.
10 "Behold, I have refined you, but [a]not as silver;
I have tested you in the [b]furnace of affliction.
11 "[a]For My own sake, for My own sake, I will act;
For how can *My name* be profaned?

er. 51:58, 64 [b]Is. 4:25; 47:9; Dan. :2, 10 [c]Is. 47:15
5:24; Nah. 1:10; 1 [b]Is. 10:17; Jer. 32, 58 [c]Is. 44:16
[1]Lit., *side, region* . 18:11 [b]Is. 5:29; 43:13; 46:7
[1]Lit., *waters* [a]Is. 5:12 [b]Num. 24:7; 33:28; Ps. 68:26 t. 6:13; Is. 45:23; [d]Is. 58:2; Jer. 4:2
. 52:1; 64:10 [b]Is. 20; Jer. 7:4; 21:2; . 3:11; Rom. 2:17
41:22; 42:9; 43:9; 7, 8; 45:21; 46:10 9:5; 30:13 [c]Josh. 21:45; Is. 42:9
harsh [a]Ex. 32:9; 31:27; Ezek. 2:4; Chr. 36:13; Prov. Acts 7:51 [c]Ezek. 3:7-9
, *it* [a]Jer. 44:15-18
6 [a]Is. 42:9; 43:19
[1]Or, *transgressor* [2]Lit., *the belly* [a]Is. 25; 47:11; Hos. 7:9 . 9:7, 24; Ps. 58:3; Is. 46:8
48:11 [b]Neh. 9:30, s. 78:38; 103:8-10; Is. 30:18; 65:8
10 [a]Jer. 9:7; Ezek. 18-22 [b]Deut. 4:20; Kin. 8:51; Jer. 11:4
[a]1 Sam. 12:22; Ps. 1; 106:8; Is. 37:35; 25; Jer. 14:7; Ezek. 9, 14, 22, 44; Dan. 9:17-19

And My [b]glory I will not give to another.

12 "Listen to Me, O Jacob, even Israel [1]whom I called;
[a]I am He, [b]I am the first, I am also the last.
13 "Surely My hand [a]founded the earth,
And My right hand spread out the heavens;
When I [b]call to them, they stand together.
14 "[a]Assemble, all of you, and listen!
[b]Who among them has declared these things?
The LORD loves him; he shall [c]carry out His good pleasure on
[d]Babylon,
And His arm *shall be against* the Chaldeans.
15 "I, even I, have spoken; indeed I have [a]called him,
I have brought him, and He will make his ways successful.
16 "[a]Come near to Me, listen to this:
From the first I have [b]not spoken in secret,
[c]From the time it took place, I was there.
And now [d]the Lord [1]GOD has sent Me, and His Spirit."

17 Thus says the LORD, your [a]Redeemer, the Holy One of Israel;
"I am the LORD your God, who teaches you to profit,
Who [b]leads you in the way you should go.
18 "If only you had [a]paid attention to My commandments!
Then your [1b]well-being would have been like a river,
And your [c]righteousness like the waves of the sea.
19 "Your [1a]descendants would have been like the sand,
And [2]your offspring like its grains;
[b]Their name would never be cut off or destroyed from My
presence."

20 [a]Go forth from Babylon! Flee from the Chaldeans!
Declare with the sound of [b]joyful shouting, proclaim this,
[c]Send it out to the end of the earth;
Say, "[d]The LORD has redeemed His servant Jacob."
21 And they did not [a]thirst when He led them through the deserts.
He [b]made the water flow out of the rock for them;
He split the rock, and [c]the water gushed forth.
22 "[a]There is no peace for the wicked," says the LORD.

Chapter 49

49 Listen to Me, O [a]islands,
And pay attention, you peoples from afar.
[b]The LORD called Me from the womb;
From the [1]body of My mother He named Me.
2 And He has made My [a]mouth like a sharp sword;
In the [b]shadow of His hand He has concealed Me,
And He has also made Me a [1]select [c]arrow;
He has hidden Me in His quiver.
3 And He said to Me, "[a]You are My Servant, Israel,
[b]In Whom I will [1]show My glory."
4 But I said, "I have [a]toiled in vain,
I have spent My strength for nothing and vanity;
Yet surely the justice *due* to Me is with the LORD,
And My [b]reward with My God."

11 [b]Deut. 32:2
42:8

12 [1]Lit., *My ca*
[a]Is. 41:4; 43:10
46:4 [b]Is. 44:6;
1:17; 22:13

13 [a]Ex. 20:11;
102:25; Is. 42:5
18; Heb. 1:10-1
40:26

14 [a]Is. 43:9; 45
45:21 [c]Is. 46:1
13:4, 5, 17-19;
50:21-29; 51:24

15 [a]Is. 41:2; 45

16 [1]Heb., *YHW*
usually rendere
[a]Is. 34:1; 41:1; 5
45:19 [c]Is. 43:13
2:9, 11

17 [a]Is. 41:14; 4
49:7, 26; 54:5, 8
32:8; Is. 30:21; 4

18 [1]Or, *peace* [a]
5:29; 32:29; Ps.
81:13-16 [b]Ps. 11
Is. 32:16-18; 66:
45:8; 61:10, 11; 6
Hos. 10:12; Amo

19 [1]Lit., *seed* [2]L
offspring of your
parts [a]Gen. 22:1
10:22; 44:3, 4; 54
33:22 [b]Is. 56:5; 6

20 [a]Jer. 50:8; 51
Zech. 2:6, 7; Rev
[b]Is. 42:10; 49:13;
[c]Is. 62:11; Jer. 31
50:2 [d]Is. 43:1; 52

21 [a]Is. 30:25; 35
41:17, 18; 43:19,
49:10 [b]Ex. 17:6;
78:15, 16 [c]Ps. 78
105:41

22 [a]Is. 57:21

49:1 [1]Lit., *inward*
[a]Is. 42:4 [b]Is. 44:2
46:3; Jer. 1:5

2 [1]Or, *sharpened*
11:4; Heb. 4:12; R
1:16; 2:12, 16 [b]Is.
51:16 [c]Hab. 3:11

3 [1]Or, *glorify Mys*
[a]Zech. 3:8 [b]Is. 44

4 [a]Is. 65:23 [b]Is. 3
59:18

5 And now says [a]the LORD, who formed Me from the womb to be His Servant,
To bring Jacob back to Him, in order that [b]Israel might be gathered to Him
(For I am [c]honored in the sight of the LORD,
And My God is My [d]strength),
6 He says, "It is too [1]small a thing that You should be My Servant
To raise up the tribes of Jacob, and to restore the [a]preserved ones of Israel;
I will also make You a [b]light [2]of the nations
So that My salvation may [3]reach to the [c]end of the earth."
7 Thus says the LORD, the [a]Redeemer of Israel, *and* its Holy One,
To the [b]despised One,
To the One abhorred by the nation,
To the Servant of rulers,
"[c]Kings shall see and arise,
Princes shall also [d]bow down;
Because of the LORD who is faithful, the Holy One of Israel who has chosen You."

8 Thus says the LORD, "In a [a]favorable time I have answered You,
And in a day of salvation I have helped You;
And I will [b]keep You and [c]give You for a covenant of the people,
To [1d]restore the land, to make *them* inherit the desolate heritages;
9 Saying to those who are [a]bound, 'Go forth,'
To those who are in darkness, 'Show yourselves.'
Along the roads they will feed,
And their pasture will be on all [b]bare heights.
10 "They will [a]not hunger or thirst,
Neither will the scorching [b]heat or sun strike them down;
For [c]He who has compassion on them will [d]lead them,
And will guide them to [e]springs of water.
11 "And I will make all [a]My mountains a road,
And My [b]highways will be raised up.
12 "Behold, these shall come [a]from afar;
And lo, these *will come* from the [b]north and from the west,
And these from the land of Sinim."
13 [a]Shout for joy, O heavens! And rejoice, O earth!
Break forth into joyful shouting, O mountains!
For the [b]LORD has comforted His people,
And will [c]have compassion on His afflicted.

14 But Zion said, "The LORD has forsaken me,
And the Lord has forgotten me."
15 "Can a woman forget her nursing child,
And have no compassion on the son of her womb?
Even these may forget, but [a]I will not forget you.
16 "Behold, I have [a]inscribed you on the palms *of My hands;*
Your [b]walls are continually before Me.
17 "Your [1]builders hurry;
Your [a]destroyers and devastators
Will depart from you.
18 "[a]Lift up your eyes and look around;
[b]All of them gather together, [c]they come to you.

Is. 44:2 [b]Is. 11:12; [c]Is. 43:4 [d]Is. 12:2

[1]Lit., *light* [2]Or, *to* ...it., *be* [a]Ps. 37:28; 10 [b]Is. 42:6; 51:4; ...e 2:32; Acts 13:47; 26:23 [c]Is. 48:20

7 [a]Is. 48:17 [b]Ps. ...8; 69:7-9; Is. 53:3 ...:15 [d]Is. 19:21, 23; 27:13; 66:23

...it., *establish* [a]Ps. ...13; 2 Cor. 6:2 [b]Is. ...:3; 27:3; 42:6 [c]Is. 42:6 [d]Is. 44:26

... 42:7; 61:1; Luke 4:18 [b]Is. 41:18

[a]Is. 33:16; 48:21; ... 7:16 [b]Ps. 121:6 ...4:1 [d]Ps. 23:2; Is. ...1 [e]Is. 35:7; 41:17

...s. 40:4 [b]Is. 11:16; ...9:23; 35:8; 62:10

...s. 49:1; 60:4 [b]Is. 43:5, 6

... 44:23 [b]Is. 40:1; ...2 [c]Is. 54:7, 8, 10

15 [a]Is. 44:21

[a]Song 8:6; Hag. ...Ps. 48:12, 13; Is. 62:6, 7

...ancient versions ...DSS; M.T. reads ... [a]Is. 10:6; 37:18

...60:4; John 4:35 ...5; 54:7; 60:4 [c]Is. 49:12

[d]As I live," declares the LORD,
"You shall surely [e]put on all of them as [1]jewels, and bind them on as a bride.
19 "For [a]your waste and desolate places, and your destroyed land—
Surely now you will be [b]too cramped for the inhabitants,
And those who [c]swallowed you will be far away.
20 "The [a]children of [1]whom you were bereaved will yet say in your ears,
'The place is too cramped for me;
Make room for me that I may live *here*.'
21 "Then you will [a]say in your heart,
'Who has begotten these for me,
Since I have been bereaved of my children,
And am [b]barren, an [c]exile and a wanderer?
And who has reared these?
Behold, I was [d]left alone;
[1e]From where did these come?' "

22 Thus says the Lord [1]GOD,
"Behold, I will lift up My hand to the nations,
And set up My [a]standard to the peoples;
And they will [b]bring your sons in *their* bosom,
And your daughters will be carried on *their* shoulders.
23 "And [a]kings will be your guardians,
And their princesses your nurses.
They will [b]bow down to you with their faces to the earth,
And [c]lick the dust of your feet;
And *you* will [d]know that I am the LORD;
Those who hopefully [e]wait for Me will [f]not be put to shame.

24 "[a]Can the prey be taken from the mighty man,
Or the captives of [1]a tyrant be rescued?"
25 Surely, thus says the LORD,
"Even the [a]captives of the mighty man will be taken away,
And the prey of the tyrant will be rescued;
For I will contend with the one who contends with you,
And I will [b]save your sons.
26 "And I will feed your [a]oppressors with their [b]own flesh,
And they will become drunk with their own blood as with sweet wine;
And [c]all flesh will know that I, the LORD, am your [d]Savior,
And your [e]Redeemer, the Mighty One of Jacob."

Chapter 50

50 Thus says the LORD,
"Where is the [a]certificate of divorce,
By which I have [b]sent your mother away?
Or to whom of My creditors did I [c]sell you?
Behold, you were sold for your [d]iniquities,
And for your [e]transgressions your mother [f]was sent away.
2 "Why was there [a]no man when I came?
When I called, *why* was there none to answer?
Is My [b]hand so short that it cannot ransom?
Or have I no power to deliver?

18 [1]Lit., *an o* [d]Is. 45:23; 54 52:1; 61:10

19 [a]Is. 1:7; 3 51:3 [b]Is. 54:1 10:10 [c]Ps. 5

20 [1]Lit., *your bereavement*

21 [1]Lit., *Thes are they?* [a]Is. 54:6, 7 [b]Is. 2 1:1 [c]Is. 5:13 [e]Is. 60:8

22 [1]Heb., *YH* usually render [a]Is. 11:10, 12; 62:10 [b]Is. 14: 60:4

23 [a]Is. 14:1, 2 11 [b]Is. 45:14; [c]Ps. 72:9; Mic. 41:20; 43:10; [e]Ps. 37:9; Is. 2 [f]Ps. 25:3; Is. 4 2:27

24 [1]So ancien and DSS; M.T. *the righteous,* [a]Matt. 12:29; L

25 [a]Is. 10:6; 1 Jer. 50:33, 34 33:22; 35:4

26 [a]Is. 9:4; 14: 51:13; 54:14 [b] [c]Is. 45:6; Ezek. 43:3 [e]Is. 49:7

50:1 [a]Deut. 24 3:8 [b]Is. 54:6, 7 32:30; 2 Kin. 4:1 5:5 [d]Is. 52:3; 5 1:28; 43:27 [f]Jer

2 [a]Is. 41:28; 59 66:4 [b]Gen. 18:1 11:23; Is. 59:1

Behold, I [c]dry up the sea with My rebuke,
I [d]make the rivers a wilderness;
Their fish stink for lack of water,
And die of thirst.
3 "I [a]clothe the heavens with blackness,
And I make sackcloth their covering."

4 The Lord [1]GOD has given Me the tongue of [a]disciples,
That I may know how to [b]sustain the weary one with a word.
He awakens *Me* [c]morning by morning,
He awakens My ear to listen as a disciple.
5 The Lord GOD has [a]opened My ear;
And I was [b]not disobedient,
Nor did I turn back.
6 I [a]gave My back to those who strike *Me*,
And My cheeks to those who pluck out the beard;
I did not cover My face from humiliation and spitting.
7 For the Lord GOD [a]helps Me,
Therefore, I am [b]not disgraced;
Therefore, I have set My face like [c]flint,
And I know that I shall not be ashamed.
8 He who [a]vindicates Me is near;
Who will contend with Me?
Let us [b]stand up to each other;
Who has a case against Me?
Let him draw near to Me.
9 Behold, [a]the Lord GOD helps Me;
[b]Who is he who condemns Me?
Behold, [c]they will all wear out like a garment;
The moth will eat them.
10 Who is among you that fears the LORD,
That obeys the voice of His [a]servant,
That [b]walks in darkness and has no light?
Let him [c]trust in the name of the LORD and rely on his God.
11 Behold, all you who [a]kindle a fire,
Who [1]encircle yourselves with firebrands,
Walk in the light of your fire
And among the brands you have set ablaze.
This you will have from My hand;
And you will [b]lie down in torment.

Chapter 51

51 "[a]Listen to me, you who [b]pursue righteousness,
Who seek the LORD:
Look to the [c]rock from which you were hewn,
And to the [1]quarry from which you were dug.
2 "Look to [a]Abraham your father,
And to Sarah who gave birth to you in pain;
When *he* [b]*was* one I called him,
Then I blessed him and multiplied him."
3 Indeed, [a]the LORD will comfort Zion;
He will comfort all her [b]waste places.
And her [c]wilderness He will make like [d]Eden,
And her desert like the [e]garden of the LORD;

[c]Ex. 14:21; Is. 19:5; 43:16; 44:27 [d]Josh. 3:16; Is. 42:15

[a]Is. 13:10; Rev. 6:12

4 [1]Heb., *YHWH*, ...ally rendered *LORD*, ...nd so throughout the [a]Is. 8:16; 54:13 [b]Is. ...:19; Jer. 31:25 [c]Ps. 5:3; 88:13; 119:147; 143:8

5 [a]Ps. 40:6; Is. 35:5 ...tt. 26:39; John 8:29; 14:31; 15:10; Acts 6:19; Phil. 2:8; Heb. 5:8; 10:7

[a]Matt. 26:67; 27:30; 14:65; 15:19; Luke 22:63

[a]Is. 42:1; 49:8 [b]Is. 45:17; 54:4 [c]Ezek. 3:8, 9

. 45:25; Rom. 8:33, ...s. 1:18; 41:1; 43:26

...s. 41:10 [b]Is. 54:17 ...Job 13:28; Is. 51:8

...0 [a]Is. 49:2, 3; 50:4 9:2; 26:9; Eph. 5:8 [c]Is. 12:2; 26:4

...1 [1]Lit., *gird* [a]Prov. ...18; Is. 9:18; James ...Is. 8:22; 65:13-15; Amos 4:9, 10

[1]Lit., *excavation of ...it* [a]Is. 46:3; 48:12; ... [b]Ps. 94:15; Prov. ...:9 [c]Gen. 17:15-17

2 [a]Is. 29:22; 41:8; [b]Gen. 12:1; 15:5; 1:10; Ezek. 33:24

...s. 40:1; 49:13 [b]Is. ...:9 [c]Is. 35:1; 41:19 ...Gen. 2:8; Joel 2:3 [e]Gen. 13:10

[f]Joy and gladness will be found in her,
Thanksgiving and sound of a melody.

4 "[a]Pay attention to Me, O My people;
And give ear to Me, O My [1]nation;
For a [b]law will go forth from Me,
And I will [2]set My [c]justice for a [d]light of the peoples.
5 "My [a]righteousness is near, My salvation has gone forth,
And My [b]arms will judge the peoples;
The [c]coastlands will wait for Me,
And for My [d]arm they will wait expectantly.
6 "[a]Lift up your eyes to the sky,
Then look to the earth beneath;
For the [b]sky will vanish like smoke,
And the [b]earth will wear out like a garment,
And its inhabitants will die [1]in like manner,
But My [c]salvation shall be forever,
And My righteousness shall not [2]wane.
7 "[a]Listen to Me, you who know righteousness,
A people in whose [b]heart is My law;
Do not fear the [c]reproach of man,
Neither be dismayed at their revilings.
8 "For the [a]moth will eat them like a garment,
And the [b]grub will eat them like wool.
But My [c]righteousness shall be forever,
And My salvation to all generations."

9 [a]Awake, awake, put on strength, O arm of the LORD;
Awake as in the [b]days of old, the generations of long ago.
[c]Was it not Thou who cut Rahab in pieces,
Who pierced the [d]dragon?
10 Was it not Thou who [a]dried up the sea,
The waters of the great deep;
Who made the depths of the sea a pathway
For the [b]redeemed to cross over?
11 So the [a]ransomed of the LORD will return,
And come with joyful shouting to Zion;
And [b]everlasting joy *will be* on their heads.
They will obtain gladness and joy,
And [c]sorrow and sighing will flee away.

12 "I, even I, am He who [a]comforts you.
Who are you that you are afraid of [b]man who dies,
And of the son of man who is made [c]like grass;
13 That you have [a]forgotten the LORD your Maker,
Who [b]stretched out the heavens,
And laid the foundations of the earth;
That you [c]fear continually all day long because of the fury of the oppressor,
As he makes ready to destroy?
But where is the fury of the [d]oppressor?
14 "The [1a]exile will soon be set free, and will not die in the dungeon,
[b]nor will his bread be lacking.

3 [f]Is. 25:9; 41:1… 65:18; 66:10
4 [1]Or, *people* … *cause to rest* [a]… 78:1 [b]Deut. 18:… 2:3; Mic. 4:2 [c]Is… 42:4 [d]Is. 42:6; …
5 [a]Is. 46:13; 54… 40:10 [c]Is. 42:4; [d]Is. 59:16; 63:5
6 [1]Or, *like gnats* … *be broken* [a]Is. 4… [b]Ps. 102:25, 26; … 13:13; 34:4; Ma… Heb. 1:10-12; 2… 3:10 [c]Is. 45:17; …
7 [a]Is. 51:1 [b]Ps. … [c]Is. 25:8; 54:4; M… 5:11; Acts 5:41
8 [a]Is. 50:9 [b]Is. … 66:24 [c]Is. 51:6
9 [a]Is. 51:17; 52:… 6:6; Deut. 4:34 … 26:12; Ps. 89:10 … 30:7 [d]Ps. 74:13; …
10 [a]Is. 11:15, 16… 63:11, 12 [b]Ex. 1… Ps. 106:10; Is. 6…
11 [a]Is. 35:10; Je… 31:11, 12 [b]Is. 60… 61:7 [c]Is. 25:8; 60… 65:19; Rev. 7:17; … 4; 22:3
12 [a]Is. 51:3 [b]Ps… Is. 2:22 [c]Is. 40:6, … 1 Pet. 1:24
13 [a]Deut. 6:12; 8… 17:10 [b]Job 9:8; P… 104:2; Is. 40:22; 4… 18; 48:13 [c]Is. 7:4… 10:24 [d]Is. 49:26; …
14 [1]Lit., *one in ch*… [a]Is. 48:20; 52:2 [b]… 33:6; 49:10

[a]Ps. 107:25; Jer. 31:35

15 "For I am the LORD your God, who [a]stirs up the sea and its waves
roar (the LORD of hosts is His name).

Lit., *plant* [a]Deut. 8; Is. 59:21 [b]Ex. s. 49:2 [c]Is. 66:22

16 "And I have [a]put My words in your mouth, and have [b]covered
you with the shadow of My hand, to [1c]establish the heavens, to
found the earth, and to say to Zion, 'You are My people.' "

., *bowl of the cup* eeling [2]Lit., *drunk* . 51:9; 52:1 [b]Job 20; Is. 29:9; 63:6; 5:15; Rev. 14:10; 16:19

17 [a]Rouse yourself! Rouse yourself! Arise, O Jerusalem,
You who have [b]drunk from the LORD's hand the cup of His
anger;
The [1]chalice of reeling you have [2]drained to the dregs.

Ps. 88:18; 142:4; Is. 49:21

18 There is [a]none to guide her among all the sons she has borne;
Nor is there one to take her by the hand among all the sons she
has reared.

19 These two things have befallen you;
Who will mourn for you?
The [a]devastation and destruction, famine and sword;
How shall I comfort you?

8:21; 9:20; 14:30

20 Your sons have fainted,
They [a]lie *helpless* at the head of every street,
Like an [b]antelope in a net,
Full of the wrath of the LORD,
The [c]rebuke of your God.

s. 5:25; Jer. 14:16 ut. 14:5 [c]Is. 66:15

s. 54:11 [b]Is. 29:9; 51:17; 63:6

21 Therefore, please hear this, you [a]afflicted,
Who are [b]drunk, but not with wine:

t., *bowl of the cup* s. 3:12, 13; 49:25; . 50:34 [b]Is. 51:17

22 Thus says your Lord, the LORD, even your God
Who [a]contends for His people,
"Behold, I have taken out of your hand the [b]cup of reeling;
The [1]chalice of My anger,
You will never drink it again.

Lit., *your soul* [a]Is. Jer. 25:15-17, 26, Zech. 12:2 [b]Josh. 10:24

23 "And I will [a]put it into the hand of your tormentors,
Who have said to [1]you, '[b]Lie down that we may walk over you.'
You have even made your back like the ground,
And like the street for those who walk over *it*."

Chapter 52

[a]Is. 51:9, 17 [b]Ex. , 40; 1 Chr. 16:29; s. 110:3; Is. 49:18; 51:3, 10; Zech. 3:4 Neh. 11:1; Is. 48:2;); Zech. 14:20, 21; , 4:5; Rev. 21:2-27 [d]Is. 35:8

52 [a]Awake, awake,
Clothe yourself in your strength, O Zion;
Clothe yourself in your [b]beautiful garments,
O Jerusalem, the [c]holy city.
For the uncircumcised and the [d]unclean
Will no more come into you.

[a]Is. 29:4 [b]Is. 60:1 9:4; 10:27; 14:25; Zech. 2:7

2 Shake yourself [a]from the dust, [b]rise up,
O captive Jerusalem;
[c]Loose yourself from the chains around your neck,
O captive daughter of Zion.

3 [a]Ps. 44:12; Jer. 3 [b]Is. 1:27; 62:12; 63:4 [c]Is. 45:13

3 For thus says the LORD, "You were [a]sold for nothing and you will
be [b]redeemed [c]without money."

4 [1]Heb., *YHWH*, ally rendered *LORD* [a]Gen. 46:6

4 For thus says the Lord [1]GOD, "My people [a]went down at the first
into Egypt to reside there, then the Assyrian oppressed them
without cause.

[a]Ezek. 36:20, 23; Rom. 2:24

5 "Now therefore, what do I have here," declares the LORD, "seeing
that My people have been taken away without cause?" *Again* the
LORD declares, "Those who rule over them howl, and My [a]name is
continually blasphemed all day long.

6 "Therefore My people shall [a]know My name; therefore in that day
I am the one who is speaking, 'Here I am.'"

7 How lovely on the mountains
Are the feet of him who brings [a]good news,
Who announces [1]peace
And brings good news of [2]happiness,
Who announces salvation,
And says to Zion, "Your [b]God [3]reigns!"
8 Listen! Your watchmen lift up *their* [a]voices,
They shout joyfully together;
For they will see [1]with their own eyes
When the LORD restores Zion.
9 [a]Break forth, shout joyfully together,
You [b]waste places of Jerusalem;
For the LORD has comforted His people,
He has [c]redeemed Jerusalem.
10 The LORD has bared His holy [a]arm
In the sight of all the nations,
[1]That [b]all the ends of the earth may see
The salvation of our God.

11 [a]Depart, depart, go out from there,
[b]Touch nothing unclean;
Go out of the midst of her, [c]purify yourselves,
You who carry the vessels of the LORD.
12 But you will not go out in [a]haste,
Nor will you go [1]as fugitives;
For the [b]LORD will go before you,
And [c]the God of Israel *will be* your rear guard.

13 Behold, My [a]servant will prosper,
He will be high and lifted up, and [1]greatly [b]exalted.
14 Just as many were astonished at you, *My people*,
So His [a]appearance was marred more than any man,
And His form more than the sons of men.
15 Thus He will [a]sprinkle many nations,
Kings will [b]shut their mouths on account of Him;
For [c]what had not been told them they will see,
And what they had not heard they will understand.

Chapter 53

53 [a]Who has believed our message?
And to whom has the arm of the LORD been revealed?
2 For He grew up before Him like a [a]tender [1]shoot,
And like a root out of parched ground;
He has [b]no *stately* form or majesty
That we should look upon Him,
Nor appearance that we should [2]be attracted to Him.
3 He was [a]despised and forsaken of men,
A man of [1]sorrows, and [b]acquainted with [2]grief;
And like one from whom men hide their face,
He was [c]despised, and we did not [d]esteem Him.

4 Surely our [1]griefs He Himself [a]bore,

---

6 [a]Is. 49:23

7 [1]Or, *well-being* *good* [3]Or, *is Kin*[...] 40:9; 61:1; Nah. Rom. 10:15; Eph [b]Ps. 93:1; Is. 24:[...]

8 [1]Lit., *eye to ey*[...] 62:6

9 [a]Ps. 98:4; Is. 4[...] [b]Is. 44:26; 51:3; 6[...] [c]Is. 43:1; 48:20

10 [1]Lit., *And . . . will see* [a]Ps. 98:[...] 51:9; 66:18, 19 [b][...] 45:22; 48:20

11 [a]Is. 48:20; Jer Zech. 2:6, 7; 2 Co 6:17 [b]Num. 19:1[...] [c]Lev. 22:2; Is. 1:1[...]

12 [1]Lit., *in flight* [...] 12:11, 33; Deut. 1 [b]Is. 26:7; 42:16; 4[...] 11 [c]Ex. 14:19, 20 58:8

13 [1]Or, *very high* 42:1; 49:1-7; 53:1[...] 57:15; Phil. 2:9

14 [a]Is. 53:2, 3

15 [a]Num. 19:18-2[...] Ezek. 36:25 [b]Job [c]Rom. 15:21; Eph.

53:1 [a]John 12:38; 10:16

2 [1]Lit., *suckling* [2]L[...] *desire* [a]Is. 11:1 [b]Is 52:14

3 [1]Or, *pains* [2]Or, *sickness* [a]Ps. 22:6 49:7; Luke 18:31-3[...] 53:10 [c]Mark 10:33 [d]John 1:10, 11

4 [1]Or, *sickness* [a]M[...] 8:17

And our [2]sorrows He carried;
Yet we ourselves esteemed Him stricken,
[3]Smitten of [b]God, and afflicted.
5 But He was [1]pierced through for [a]our transgressions,
He was crushed for [b]our iniquities;
The [c]chastening for our [2]well-being *fell* upon Him,
And by [d]His scourging we are healed.
6 All of us like sheep have gone astray,
Each of us has turned to his own way;
But the LORD has caused the iniquity of us all
To [1]fall on Him.

7 He was oppressed and He was afflicted,
Yet He did not [a]open His mouth;
[b]Like a lamb that is led to slaughter,
And like a sheep that is silent before its shearers,
So He did not open His mouth.
8 By oppression and judgment He was taken away;
And as for His generation, who considered
That He was cut off out of the land of the [1]living,
[a]For the transgression of my people to whom the stroke *was due?*
9 His grave was assigned with wicked men,
Yet He was with a [a]rich man in His death,
[b]Because He had [c]done no violence,
Nor was there any deceit in His mouth.

10 But the LORD was pleased
To [a]crush Him, [1b]putting *Him* to grief;
If [2]He would render Himself *as* a guilt [c]offering,
He will see [d]*His* [3]offspring,
He will prolong *His* days,
And the [4]good [e]pleasure of the LORD will prosper in His hand.
11 As a result of the [1]anguish of His soul,
He will [a]see [2]*it* and be satisfied;
By His [b]knowledge the Righteous One,
My Servant, will justify the many,
As He will [c]bear their iniquities.
12 Therefore, I will allot Him a [a]portion with the great,
And He will divide the booty with the strong;
Because He poured out [1b]Himself to death,
And was [c]numbered with the transgressors;
Yet He Himself [d]bore the sin of many,
And interceded for the transgressors.

Chapter 54

54 "[a]Shout for joy, O barren one, you who have borne no *child;*
Break forth into joyful shouting and cry aloud, you who have not travailed;
For the sons of the [b]desolate one *will be* [c]more numerous
Than the sons of the married woman," says the LORD.
2 "[a]Enlarge the place of your tent;
[1]Stretch out the curtains of your dwellings, spare not;
Lengthen your [b]cords,
And strengthen your [b]pegs.

4 [2]Or, *pains* [3]Or, *...ruck down by* [b]John 19:7

[1]Or, *wounded* [2]Or, *...eace* [a]Is. 53:8; Heb. ...28 [b]Is. 53:10; Rom. ...; 1 Cor. 15:3 [c]Deut. ...:2; Heb. 5:8 [d]1 Pet. 2:24, 25

[1]Lit., *encounter Him*

7 [a]Matt. 26:63; ...:12-14; Mark 14:61; ...:5; Luke 23:9; John 9:9 [b]Acts 8:32, 33; Rev. 5:6

...Or, *life* [a]Is. 53:5, 12

...Matt. 27:57-60 [b]Is. 42:1-3 [c]1 Pet. 2:22

[1]Lit., *He made Him* [2]Lit., *His soul* [3]Lit., *...eed* [4]Or, *will of* [a]Is. ...3:5 [b]Is. 53:3, 4 [c]Is. 53:6, 12; John 1:29 ...Ps. 22:30; Is. 54:3; ...9; 66:22 [e]Is. 46:10

[1]Or, *toilsome labor* [2]Another reading is *...ht* [a]John 10:14-18 ...45:25; Rom. 5:18, 19 [c]Is. 53:5, 6

[1]Lit., *His soul* [a]Is. 52:13; Phil. 2:9-11 ...Matt. 26:38, 39, 42 [c]Mark 15:28; Luke ...2:37 [d]Is. 53:6, 11; 2 Cor. 5:21

...:1 [a]Gal. 4:27 [b]Is. ...:4 [c]1 Sam. 2:5; Is. 49:20

..., *Let them stretch* [a]Is. 33:20; 49:19, [b]Ex. 35:18; 39:40

3 "For you will [a]spread abroad to the right and to the left.
And your [1]descendants will [b]possess nations,
And they will [c]resettle the desolate cities.

4 "Fear not, for you will [a]not be put to shame;
Neither feel humiliated, for you will not be disgraced;
But you will forget the [b]shame of your youth,
And the [c]reproach of your widowhood you will remember no more.
5 "For your [a]husband is your Maker,
Whose name is the LORD of hosts;
And your [b]Redeemer is the Holy One of Israel,
Who is called the [c]God of all the earth.
6 "For the LORD has called you,
Like a wife [a]forsaken and grieved in spirit,
Even like a wife of *one's* youth when she is rejected,"
Says your God.
7 "[1]For a [a]brief moment I forsook you,
But with great compassion I will [b]gather you.
8 "In an [1a]outburst of anger
I hid My face from you for a moment;
But with everlasting [b]lovingkindness I will [c]have compassion on you,"
Says the LORD your [d]Redeemer.

9 "For [1]this is like the days of Noah to Me;
When I swore that the waters of Noah
Should [a]not [2]flood the earth again,
So I have sworn that I will [b]not be angry with you,
Nor will I rebuke you.
10 "For the [a]mountains may be removed and the hills may shake,
But My lovingkindness will not be removed from you,
And My [b]covenant of peace will not be shaken,"
Says [c]the LORD who has compassion on you.

11 "O [a]afflicted one, storm-tossed, and [b]not comforted,
Behold, I will set your stones in antimony,
And your foundations I will [c]lay in [1d]sapphires.
12 "Moreover, I will make your battlements of [1]rubies,
And your gates of [2]crystal,
And your entire [3]wall of precious stones.
13 "And [a]all your sons will be [1]taught of the LORD;
And the well-being of your sons will be [b]great.
14 "In [a]righteousness you will be established;
You will be far from [b]oppression, for you will [c]not fear;
And from [d]terror, for it will not come near you.
15 "If anyone fiercely assails *you* it will not be from Me.
[a]Whoever assails you will fall because of you.
16 "Behold, I Myself have created the smith who blows the fire of coals,
And brings out a weapon for its work;
And I have created the destroyer to ruin.
17 "[a]No weapon that is formed against you shall prosper;

3 [1]Lit., *seed* [a](28:14; Is. 43:5, [b]Is. 14:1, 2 [c]Is.

4 [a]Is. 45:17 [b]Je 31:19 [c]Is. 4:1; 2

5 [a]Jer. 3:14; Ho [b]Is. 43:14; 48:17 6:3; 11:9; 65:16

6 [a]Is. 49:14-21; 62:4

7 [1]Lit., *in* [a]Is. 26 11:12; 43:5; 49:1

8 [1]Lit., *overflow* 60:10 [b]Is. 54:10 [c]Is. 49:10, 13 [d]Is

9 [1]Some mss. re *waters of Noah t me* [2]Lit., *cross o* [a]Gen. 9:11 [b]Is. 1 Ezek. 39:29

10 [a]Ps. 102:26; 51:6 [b]2 Sam. 23 89:34; Is. 55:3; 5 61:8 [c]Is. 54:8

11 [1]Or, *lapis lazu* 51:21 [b]Is. 51:18, 14:32; 28:16; 44:2 [d]Job 28:16; Rev. 2

12 [1]I.e., bright re *carbuncles* [3]Lit., *boundary*

13 [1]Or, *disciples* 6:45 [b]Is. 48:18; 6

14 [a]Is. 1:26, 27; 9 62:1 [b]Is. 9:4; 14:4 54:4 [d]Is. 33:18

15 [a]Is. 41:11-16

17 [a]Is. 17:12-14; 2

And [b]every tongue that [1]accuses you in judgment you will
condemn.
This is the heritage of the servants of the LORD,
And their [c]vindication is from Me," declares the LORD.

Chapter 55

55 "Ho! Every one who [a]thirsts, come to the waters;
And you who have [b]no [1]money come, buy and eat.
Come, buy [c]wine and milk
[d]Without money and without cost.
2 "Why do you [1]spend money for what is [a]not bread,
And your wages for what does not satisfy?
Listen carefully to Me, and [b]eat what is good,
And [c]delight yourself in abundance.
3 "[a]Incline your ear and come to Me.
Listen, that [1]you may [b]live;
And I will make [c]an everlasting covenant with you,
According to the [d]faithful mercies [2]shown to David.
4 "Behold, I have made [a]him a witness to the peoples,
A [b]leader and commander for the peoples.
5 "Behold, you will call a [a]nation you do not know,
And a nation which knows you not will [b]run to you,
Because of the LORD your God, even the Holy One of Israel;
For He has [c]glorified you."

6 [a]Seek the LORD while He may be found;
[b]Call upon Him while He is near.
7 [a]Let the wicked forsake his way,
And the unrighteous man his [b]thoughts;
And let him [c]return to the LORD,
And He will have [d]compassion on him;
And to our God,
For He will [e]abundantly pardon.
8 "For My thoughts are not [a]your thoughts,
Neither are [b]your ways My ways," declares the LORD.
9 "For [a]*as* the heavens are higher than the earth,
So are My ways higher than your ways,
And My thoughts than your thoughts.
10 "For as the [a]rain and the snow come down from heaven,
And do not return there without watering the earth,
And making it bear and sprout,
And furnishing [b]seed to the sower and bread to the eater;
11 So shall My [a]word be which goes forth from My mouth;
It shall [b]not return to Me empty,
Without [c]accomplishing what I desire,
And without succeeding *in the matter* for which I sent it.
12 "For you will go out with [a]joy,
And be led forth with [b]peace;
The [c]mountains and the hills will break forth into shouts of joy
before you,
And all the [d]trees of the field will clap *their* hands.
13 "Instead of the [a]thorn bush the [b]cypress will come up;
And instead of the [c]nettle the myrtle will come up;

[1]Lit., *rises against*
. 50:8, 9 [c]Is. 45:24; 46:13

5:1 [1]Lit., *silver* [a]Ps.
1, 2; 63:1; 143:6; Is.
17; 44:3; John 4:14;
7; Rev. 21:6 [b]Lam.
5:4 [c]Song 5:1; Joel
8 [d]Hos. 14:4; Matt.
10:8

Lit., *weigh out silver*
. 6:2; Hos. 8:7 [b]Ps.
26; Is. 1:19; 62:8, 9
[c]Is. 25:6; Jer. 31:14

[1]Lit., *your soul* [2]Lit.,
avid [a]Is. 51:4 [b]Lev.
8:5; Rom. 10:5 [c]Is.
61:8 [d]Acts 13:34

[a]Ps. 18:43; Jer. 30:9;
. 3:5 [b]Ezek. 34:24;
7:24, 25; Dan. 9:25;
Mic. 5:2

5 [a]Is. 45:14, 22-24;
49:6, 12, 23 [b]Zech.
8:22 [c]Is. 60:9

[a]Ps. 32:6; Is. 45:19,
49:8; Amos 5:6 [b]Is.
58:9; 65:24

[a]Is. 1:16, 19; 58:6
2:7; 59:7 [c]Is. 31:6;
:22 [d]Is. 14:1; 54:8,
10 [e]Is. 1:18; 40:2;
43:25; 44:22

Is. 65:2; 66:18 [b]Is.
53:6

9 [a]Ps. 103:11

[a]Is. 30:23 [b]2 Cor.
9:10

11 [a]Is. 45:23; Matt.
5 [b]Is. 44:26; 59:21
[c]Is. 46:10; 53:10

12 [a]Ps. 105:43; Is.
1; 52:9 [b]Is. 54:10,
13; Jer. 29:11 [c]Is.
:23; 49:13 [d]1 Chr.
16:33

Is. 7:19 [b]Is. 60:13
Is. 5:6; 7:24; 32:13

And [1]it will be a [2d]memorial to the LORD,
For an everlasting [e]sign which [f]will not be cut off."

Chapter 56

56 Thus says the LORD,
"[a]Preserve justice, and do righteousness,
For My [b]salvation is about to come
And My righteousness to be revealed.
2 "How [a]blessed is the man who does this,
And the son of man who [b]takes hold of it;
Who [c]keeps from profaning the sabbath,
And keeps his hand from doing any evil."
3 Let not the [a]foreigner who has joined himself to the LORD say,
"The LORD will surely separate me from His people."
Neither let the [b]eunuch say, "Behold, I am a dry tree."
4 For thus says the LORD,
"To the eunuchs who [a]keep My sabbaths,
And choose what pleases Me,
And [b]hold fast My covenant,
5 To them I will give in My [a]house and within My [b]walls a memorial,
And a name better than that of sons and daughters;
I will give [1]them an everlasting [c]name which [d]will not be cut off.

6 "Also the [a]foreigners who join themselves to the LORD,
To minister to Him, and to love the name of the LORD,
To be His servants, every one who [b]keeps from profaning the sabbath,
And holds fast My covenant;
7 Even [a]those I will bring to My [b]holy mountain,
And [c]make them joyful in My house of prayer.
Their burnt offerings and their sacrifices will be acceptable on [d]My altar;
For [e]My house will be called a house of prayer for all the peoples."
8 The Lord [1]GOD, who [a]gathers the dispersed of Israel, declares,
"Yet [b]*others* I will gather to [2]them, to those *already* gathered."

9 All you [a]beasts of the field,
All you beasts in the forest,
Come to eat.
10 His [a]watchmen are [b]blind,
All of them know nothing.
All of them are dumb dogs unable to bark,
[1]Dreamers lying down, who love to slumber;
11 And the dogs are [1a]greedy, they [2]are not satisfied.
And they are shepherds who have [b]no understanding;
They have all [c]turned to their own way,
Each one to his unjust gain, to the last one.
12 "Come," *they say,* "let [1]us get [a]wine, and let us drink heavily of strong drink;
And [b]tomorrow will be like today, only more so."

13 [1]I.e., the transformation desert [2]Lit., *na* 63:12, 14; Jer. 19:20 [f]Is. 56:5

56:1 [a]Is. 1:17; 61:8 [b]Ps. 85:9; 46:13; 51:5

2 [a]Ps. 112:1; 1 [b]Is. 56:4, 6 [c]Ex 20:8-11; 31:13- 56:6; 58:13; Jer 22; Ezek. 20:12

3 [a]Is. 14:1; 56: 23:1; Jer. 38:7;

4 [a]Is. 56:2, 6 [b]

5 [1]So DSS; M.T. *him* [a]Is. 2:2, 3; 66:20 [b]Is. 26:1; [c]Is. 62:2 [d]Is. 48 55:13

6 [a]Is. 56:3; 60:1 [b]Is. 56:2, 4

7 [a]Is. 2:2, 3; 60: 4:1, 2 [b]Is. 11:9; [c]Is. 61:10 [d]Is. 6 [e]Matt. 21:13; Ma 11:17; Luke 19:4

8 [1]Heb., *YHWH*, usually rendered [2]Lit., *him* [a]Is. 11: 60:3-11; 66:18-2 10:16

9 [a]Is. 18:6; 46:11

10 [1]So DSS; M.T. *Ravers* [a]Ezek. 3 29:9-14; Jer. 14:1

11 [1]Lit., *strong o soul/appetite* [2]Lit *not know satisfac* [a]Is. 28:7; Ezek. 1 Mic. 3:5, 11 [b]Is. 57:17; Jer. 22:17

12 [1]So DSS and versions; M. T., *m* 5:11, 12, 22 [b]Ps. Luke 12:19, 20

Chapter 57

57 The righteous man perishes, and no man [a]takes it to heart;
And devout men are taken away, while no one understands.
For the righteous man is taken away from [b]evil,
2 He enters into peace;
They rest in their [1]beds,
Each one who [a]walked in his upright way.
3 "But come here, you sons of a [a]sorceress,
[b]Offspring of an adulterer and [1]a [c]prostitute.
4 "Against whom do you jest?
Against whom do you open wide your mouth
And stick out your tongue?
Are you not children of [a]rebellion,
Offspring of deceit,
5 *Who* inflame yourselves among the [1a]oaks,
[b]Under every luxuriant tree,
Who [c]slaughter the children in the [2]ravines,
Under the clefts of the crags?
6 "Among the [1a]smooth *stones* of the [2]ravine
Is your portion, [3]they are your lot;
Even to them you have [b]poured out a libation,
You have made a grain offering.
Shall I [4c]relent concerning these things?
7 "Upon a [a]high and lofty mountain
You have [b]made your bed.
You also went up there to offer sacrifice.
8 "And behind the door and the doorpost
You have set up your sign;
Indeed, far removed from Me, you have [a]uncovered yourself;
And have gone up and made your bed wide.
And you have made an agreement for yourself with them,
You have loved their [1]bed,
You have looked on *their* [2]manhood.
9 "And you have journeyed to the king with oil
And increased your perfumes;
You have [a]sent your envoys a great distance,
And made *them* go down to [1]Sheol.
10 "You were tired out by the length of your road,
Yet you did not say, '[a]It is hopeless.'
You found [1]renewed strength,
Therefore you did not [2]faint.

11 "Of [a]whom were you worried and fearful,
When you lied, and did [b]not remember Me,
[1]Nor [c]give *Me* a thought?
Was I not silent even for a long time
So you do not fear Me?
12 "I will [a]declare your righteousness and your [b]deeds,
But they will not profit you.
13 "When you cry out, [a]let your collection *of idols* deliver you.
But the wind will carry all of them up,
And a breath will take *them away*.
But he who [b]takes refuge in Me shall [c]inherit the land,
And shall [d]possess My holy mountain."

57:1 [a]Is. 42:25; 47:7 ...Kin. 22:20; Is. 47:11; Jer. 18:11
...e., graves [a]Is. 26:7
So ancient versions; Heb., *she prostitutes herself* [a]Mal. 3:5 [b]Is. Matt. 16:4 [c]Is. 1:21; 57:7-9
4 [a]Is. 48:8
[1]Or, *terebinths* [2]Or, *...dis* [a]Is. 1:29 [b]2 Kin. 16:4; Jer. 2:20; 3:13 [c]2 Kin. 23:10; Ps. ...06:37, 38; Jer. 7:31
6 [1]I.e., symbols of ...ility gods [2]Or, *wadi* [3]Lit., *they, they* [4]Or, *...pent* [a]Jer. 3:9; Hab. ...:19 [b]Jer. 7:18 [c]Jer. 5:9, 29; 9:9
7 [a]Jer. 3:6; Ezek. 16:16 [b]Ezek. 23:41
...Or, *lying down* [2]Lit., *...hand* [a]Ezek. 23:18
...e., the nether world [a]Ezek. 23:16, 40
[1]Lit., *the life of your ...d* [2]Or, *become sick* [a]Jer. 2:25; 18:12
Lit., *You did not set it upon your heart* ...ov. 29:25; Is. 51:12, ...Jer. 2:32; 3:21 [c]Ps. 50:21; Is. 42:14
12 [a]Is. 58:1, 2 [b]Is. ...; 59:6; 65:7; 66:18; Mic. 3:2-4
[a]Jer. 22:20; 30:14 ...Ps. 37:3, 9; Is. 25:4 ...:8; 60:21 [d]Is. 65:9

14 And it shall be said,
"[a]Build up, build up, prepare the way,
Remove *every* obstacle out of the way of My people."
15 For thus says the [a]high and exalted One
Who [1b]lives forever, whose name is Holy,
"I [c]dwell *on* a high and holy place,
And *also* with the [d]contrite and lowly of spirit
In order to [e]revive the spirit of the lowly
And to revive the heart of the contrite.
16 "For I will [a]not contend forever,
[b]Neither will I always be angry;
For the spirit would grow faint before Me,
And the [c]breath *of those whom* I have made.
17 "Because of the iniquity of his [a]unjust gain I was angry and struck him;
I hid *My face* and was angry,
And he went on [b]turning away, in the way of his heart.
18 "I have seen his ways, but I will [a]heal him;
I will [b]lead him and [c]restore comfort to him and to his mourners,
19 Creating the [1a]praise of the lips.
[b]Peace, peace to him who is [c]far and to him who is near,"
Says the LORD, "and I will heal him."
20 But the [a]wicked are like the tossing sea,
For it cannot be quiet,
And its waters toss up refuse and mud.
21 "[a]There is no peace," says [b]my God, "for the wicked."

Chapter 58

58 "[a]Cry loudly, do not hold back;
Raise your voice like a trumpet,
And declare to My people their [b]transgression,
And to the house of Jacob their sins.
2 "Yet they [a]seek Me day by day, and delight to know My ways,
As a nation that has done [b]righteousness,
And [c]has not forsaken the ordinance of their God.
They ask Me *for* just decisions,
They delight [d]in the nearness of God.
3 'Why have we [a]fasted and Thou dost not see?
Why have we humbled ourselves and Thou dost not [1]notice?'
Behold, on the [b]day of your fast you find *your* desire,
And drive hard all your workers.
4 "Behold, you fast for contention and [a]strife and to strike with a wicked fist.
You do not fast like *you do* today to [b]make your voice heard on high.
5 "Is it a fast like this which I choose, a day for a man to humble himself?
Is it for bowing [1]one's head like a reed,
And for spreading out [a]sackcloth and ashes as a bed?
Will you call this a fast, even an [b]acceptable day to the LORD?
6 "Is this not the fast which I choose,
To [a]loosen the bonds of wickedness,
To undo the bands of the yoke,
And to [b]let the oppressed go free,

14 [a]Is. 62:10; Je

15 [1]Or, *dwells in eternity* [a]Is. 52: [b]Deut. 33:27; Is. [c]Is. 33:5; 66:1 [d] 34:18; 51:17; Is. [e]Ps. 147:3; Is. 6

16 [a]Gen. 6:3 [b]P 103:9; Mic. 7:18 42:5

17 [a]Is. 2:7; 56:1 6:13 [b]Is. 1:4; Je 3:14, 22

18 [a]Is. 19:22; 30 53:5 [b]Is. 52:12 61:1-3

19 [1]Lit., *fruit of th* [a]Is. 6:7; 51:16; 59 Heb. 13:15 [b]Is. 2 32:17 [c]Acts 2:39 2:17

20 [a]Job 18:5-14; 3:9, 11

21 [a]Is. 48:22; 59: 49:4

58:1 [a]Is. 40:6 [b]Is 43:27; 50:1; 59:12

2 [a]Is. 1:11; Titus [b]Is. 48:1; Jer. 7:9, [c]Is. 1:4, 28; 59:13 119:151; Is. 29:13 James 4:8

3 [1]Lit., *know* [a]Ma 3:14; Luke 18:12 22:12, 13; Zech. 7

4 [a]Is. 3:14, 15; 59 [b]Is. 1:15; 59:2; Joe 2:12-14

5 [1]Lit., *his* [a]1 Kin. 21:27 [b]Is. 49:8; 61

6 [a]Neh. 5:10-12; J 34:8 [b]Is. 1:17

And [c]break every yoke?
7 "Is it not to [a]divide your bread [1]with the hungry,
And [b]bring the homeless poor into the house;
When you see the [c]naked, to cover him;
And not to [d]hide yourself from your own flesh?
8 "Then your [a]light will break out like the dawn,
And your [b]recovery will speedily spring forth;
And your [c]righteousness will go before you;
The glory of the [d]LORD will be your rear guard.
9 "Then you will [a]call, and the LORD will answer;
You will cry, and He will say, 'Here I am.'
If you [b]remove the yoke from your midst,
The [1c]pointing of the finger, and [d]speaking wickedness,
10 And if you [1a]give yourself to the hungry,
And satisfy the [2]desire of the afflicted,
Then your [b]light will rise in darkness,
And your gloom *will become* like midday.
11 "And the [a]LORD will continually guide you,
And [b]satisfy your [1]desire in scorched places,
And [c]give strength to your bones;
And you will be like a [d]watered garden,
And like a [e]spring of water whose waters do not [2]fail.
12 "And those from among you will [a]rebuild the ancient ruins;
You will [b]raise up the age-old foundations;
And you will be called the repairer of the [c]breach,
The restorer of the [1]streets in which to dwell.

13 "If because of the sabbath, you [a]turn your foot
From doing your *own* pleasure on My holy day,
And call the sabbath a [b]delight, the holy *day* of the LORD
honorable,
And shall honor it, desisting from your [c]*own* ways,
From seeking your *own* pleasure,
And [d]speaking *your own* word,
14 Then you will take [a]delight in the LORD,
And I will make you ride [b]on the heights of the earth;
And I will feed you *with* the heritage of Jacob your father,
For the [c]mouth of the LORD has spoken."

Chapter 59

59 Behold, [a]the LORD's hand is not so short
That it cannot save;
[b]Neither is His ear so dull
That it cannot hear.
2 But your [a]iniquities have made a separation between you and
your God,
And your sins have hidden *His* [1]face from you, so that He does
[b]not hear.
3 For your [a]hands are defiled with blood,
And your fingers with iniquity;
Your lips have spoken [b]falsehood,
Your tongue mutters wickedness.
4 [a]No one sues righteously and [b]no one pleads [1]honestly.
They [c]trust in confusion, and speak lies;

6 [c]Is. 58:9

[1]Lit., *for* [a]Job 31:19, 20; Is. 58:10; Ezek. 8:7, 16 [b]Is. 16:3, 4; . 13:2 [c]Matt. 25:35, 6; Luke 3:11 [d]Deut. :1-4; Luke 10:31, 32

ls. 58:10 [b]Is. 30:26; 24; Jer. 30:17; 33:6 85:13; Is. 62:1 [d]Ex. 14:19; Is. 52:12

9 [1]Lit., *sending out* [a]Ps. 50:15; Is. 55:6; :24 [b]Is. 58:6 [c]Prov. [d]Ps. 12:2; Is. 59:13

0 [1]Lit., *furnish* [2]Or, *soul* [a]Deut. 15:7; Is. 8:7 [b]Job 11:17; Ps. 37:6; Is. 42:16; 58:8

11 [1]Or, *soul* [2]Or, *deceive* [a]Is. 49:10; 7:18 [b]Ps. 107:9; Is. 7 [c]Is. 66:14 [d]Song 4:15; Is. 27:3; Jer. 2 [e]John 4:14; 7:38

Lit., *paths* [a]Is. 49:8; :4; Ezek. 36:10 [b]Is. 28 [c]Is. 30:13; Amos 9:11

Ex. 31:16, 17; 35:2, 3; Is. 56:2, 4, 6; Jer. 17:21-27 [b]Ps. 27:4; ; 84:2, 10 [c]Is. 55:8 [d]Is. 59:13

14 [a]Job 22:26; Is. 61:10 [b]Deut. 32:13; :29; Is. 33:16; Hab. 3:19 [c]Is. 1:20; 40:5

:1 [a]Num. 11:23; Is. 50:2; Jer. 32:17 [b]Is. ; 65:24; Ezek. 8:18

[1]So versions; M. T., *aces* [a]Is. 1:15; 50:1 [b]Is. 58:4

3 [a]Is. 1:15, 21; Jer. :30, 34; Ezek. 7:23; Hos. 4:2 [b]Is. 28:15; 30:9; 59:13

.it., *in truth* [a]Is. 5:7; [b]Is. 59:14, 15 [c]Is. 30:12; Jer. 7:4, 8

They [d]conceive mischief, and bring forth iniquity.
5 They hatch adders' eggs and [a]weave the spider's web;
He who eats of their eggs dies,
And *from* that which is crushed a snake breaks forth.
6 Their webs will not become clothing,
Nor will they [a]cover themselves with their works;
Their [b]works are works of iniquity,
And an [c]act of violence is in their [1]hands.
7 [a]Their feet run to evil,
And they hasten to shed innocent blood;
[b]Their thoughts are thoughts of iniquity;
Devastation and destruction are in their highways.
8 They do not know the [a]way of peace,
And there is [b]no justice in their tracks;
They have made their paths crooked;
[c]Whoever treads on [1]them does not know peace.

9 Therefore, [a]justice is far from us,
And righteousness does not overtake us;
We [b]hope for light, but behold, darkness;
For brightness, but we walk in gloom.
10 We [a]grope along the wall like blind men,
We grope like those who have no eyes;
We [b]stumble at midday as in the twilight,
Among those who are vigorous we are [c]like dead men.
11 All of us growl like bears,
And [a]moan sadly like doves;
We hope for [b]justice, but there is none,
For salvation, *but* it is far from us.
12 For our [a]transgressions are multiplied before Thee,
And our [b]sins [1]testify against us;
For our transgressions are with us,
And [2]we know our iniquities:
13 Transgressing and [a]denying the LORD,
And turning away from our God,
Speaking [b]oppression and revolt,
Conceiving *in* and [c]uttering from the heart lying words.
14 And [a]justice is turned back,
And [b]righteousness stands far away;
For truth has stumbled in the street,
And uprightness cannot enter.
15 Yes, truth is lacking;
And he who turns aside from evil [a]makes himself a prey.

Now the LORD saw,
And it was [1]displeasing in His sight [b]that there was no justice.
16 And He saw that there was [a]no man,
And was astonished that there was no one to intercede;
Then His [b]own arm brought salvation to Him;
And His righteousness upheld Him.
17 And He put on [a]righteousness like a breastplate,
And a [b]helmet of salvation on His head;
And He put on [c]garments of vengeance for clothing,
And wrapped Himself with [d]zeal as a mantle.

4 [d]Job 15:35; P
Is. 33:11

5 [a]Job 8:14

6 [1]Lit., *palms* [a]I
28:20 [b]Is. 57:12
6:7 [c]Is. 58:4; Ez

7 [a]Prov. 1:16; 6.
Rom. 3:15-17 [b]I
66:18; Mark 7:21

8 [1]Lit., *it* [a]Luke
[b]Is. 59:9, 11; Hos
[c]Is. 57:20, 21

9 [a]Is. 59:14 [b]Is.
8:21, 22

10 [a]Deut. 28:29;
5:14 [b]Is. 8:14, 15
28:13 [c]Lam. 3:6

11 [a]Is. 38:14; Eze
7:16 [b]Is. 59:9, 14

12 [1]Lit., *answer*
our iniquities we
them [a]Ezra 9:6; Is
58:1 [b]Is. 3:9; Jer.
Hos. 5:5

13 [a]Josh. 24:27;
30:9; Matt. 10:33;
1:16 [b]Is. 5:7; 30:
9:3, 4 [c]Is. 59:3, 4;
7:21, 22

14 [a]Is. 1:21; 5:7 [b]
46:12; Hab. 1:4

15 [1]Or, *evil* [a]Is. 5:
10:2; 29:21; 32:7
1:21-23

16 [a]Is. 41:28; 63:5
Ezek. 22:30 [b]Ps. 9
Is. 52:10; 63:5

17 [a]Eph. 6:14 [b]Ep
6:17; 1 Thess. 5:8
63:2, 3 [c]Is. 9:7; 37
Zech. 1:14

18 [a]According to *their* [1]deeds, [2]so He will repay,
Wrath to His adversaries, recompense to His enemies;
To the coastlands He will [3]make recompense.
19 So they will fear the name of the LORD from the [a]west
And His glory from the [b]rising of the sun,
For He will [c]come like a [1]rushing stream,
Which the wind of the LORD drives.
20 "And a [a]Redeemer will come to Zion,
And to those who [b]turn from transgression in Jacob," declares
the LORD.
21 "And as for Me, this is My [a]covenant with them," says the LORD:
"My [b]Spirit which is upon you, and My [c]words which I have put in
your mouth, shall not depart from your mouth, nor from the mouth
of your [1]offspring, nor from the mouth of your [1]offspring's off-
spring," says the LORD, "from now and forever."

Chapter 60

60 "[a]Arise, shine; for your [b]light has come,
And the [c]glory of the LORD has risen upon you.
2 "For behold, [a]darkness will cover the earth,
And deep darkness the peoples;
But the LORD will rise upon you,
And His [b]glory will appear upon you.
3 "And [a]nations will come to your light,
And kings to the brightness of your rising.

4 "[a]Lift up your eyes round about, and see;
They all gather together, they [b]come to you.
Your sons will come from afar,
And your [c]daughters will be [1]carried in the arms.
5 "Then you will see and be [a]radiant,
And your heart will [1]thrill and rejoice;
Because the [b]abundance of the sea will be turned to you,
The [c]wealth of the nations will come to you.
6 "A multitude of camels will cover you,
The young camels of Midian and [a]Ephah;
All those from [b]Sheba will come;
They will bring [c]gold and frankincense,
And will [d]bear good news of the praises of the LORD.
7 "All the flocks of [a]Kedar will be gathered together to you,
The rams of Nebaioth will minister to you;
They will go up with acceptance on My [b]altar,
And I shall [1c]glorify My [2]glorious house.
8 "[a]Who are these who fly like a cloud,
And like the doves to their [1]lattices?
9 "Surely the [a]coastlands will wait for Me;
And the [b]ships of Tarshish *will come* first,
To [c]bring your sons from afar,
Their silver and their gold with them,
For the name of the LORD your God,
And for the Holy One of Israel because He has [1d]glorified you.

10 "And [a]foreigners will build up your walls,
And their [b]kings will minister to you;

8 [1]Lit., *recompense* ...it., *accordingly* [3]Lit., ...*epay* [a]Job 34:11; Is. ...6, 7; 66:6; Jer. 17:10

19 [1]Lit., *narrow* [a]Is. ...9:12 [b]Ps. 113:3 [c]Is. 30:28; 66:12

[a]Rom. 11:26 [b]Ezek. ...30, 31; Acts 2:38, 39

21 [1]Lit., *seed* [a]Jer. ...:31-34; Rom. 11:27 ...Is. 11:2; 32:15; 44:3 [c]Is. 55:11

60:1 [a]Is. 52:2 [b]Is. ...0:19, 20 [c]Is. 24:23; 35:2; 58:8

...s. 58:10; Jer. 13:16; Col. 1:13 [b]Is. 4:5

...: 2:3; 45:14, 22-25; 49:23

...it., *nursed upon the* ...*de* [a]Is. 11:12; 49:18 ...49:20-22 [c]Is. 43:6; 49:22

...Lit., *tremble and be* ...*rged* [a]Ps. 34:5 [b]Is. ...:18; 24:14 [c]Is. 61:6

[a]Gen. 25:4 [b]Gen. 25:3; Ps. 72:10 [c]Is. ...60:9; Matt. 2:11 [d]Is. 42:10

... [1]Or, *beautify* [2]Or, ...*autiful* [a]Gen. 25:13 ...Is. 19:19; 56:7 [c]Is. 60:13; Hag. 2:7, 9

8 [1]Or, *dovecotes,* ...*windows* [a]Is. 49:21

...[1]Lit., *beautified* [a]Is. ...11; 24:15; 42:4, 10, ...2; 49:1; 51:5; 66:19 ...48:7; Is. 2:16 [c]Is. ...:2; 43:6; 49:22 [d]Is. 55:5

...0 [a]Is. 14:1, 2; 61:5; ...ch. 6:15 [b]Is. 49:23; Rev. 21:24

For in My [c]wrath I struck you,
And in My favor I have had compassion on you.
11 "And your [a]gates will be open continually;
They will not be closed day or night,
So that *men* may [b]bring to you the wealth of the nations,
With [c]their kings led in procession.
12 "For the [a]nation and the kingdom which will not serve you will
perish,
And the nations will be utterly ruined.
13 "The [a]glory of Lebanon will come to you,
The [b]juniper, the box tree, and the cypress together,
To beautify the place of My sanctuary;
And I shall make the [c]place of My feet glorious.
14 "And the [a]sons of those who afflicted you will come bowing to
you,
And all those who despised you will bow themselves at the
soles of your feet;
And they will call you the [b]city of the LORD,
The [c]Zion of the Holy One of Israel.

15 "Whereas you have been [a]forsaken and [b]hated
With no one passing through,
I will make you an everlasting [c]pride,
A joy from generation to generation.
16 "You will also [a]suck the milk of nations,
And will suck the breast of kings;
Then you will know that I, the LORD, am your [b]Savior,
And your [c]Redeemer, the Mighty One of Jacob.
17 "Instead of bronze I will bring gold,
And instead of iron I will bring silver,
And instead of wood, bronze,
And instead of stones, iron.
And I will make peace your administrators,
And righteousness your overseers.
18 "[a]Violence will not be heard again in your land,
Nor [b]devastation or destruction within your borders;
But you will call your [c]walls salvation, and your [d]gates praise.
19 "No longer will you have the [a]sun for light by day,
Nor for brightness will the moon give you light;
But you will have the [b]LORD for an everlasting light,
And your [c]God for your [1]glory.
20 "Your [a]sun will set no more,
Neither will your moon wane;
For you will have the LORD for an everlasting light,
And the days of your [b]mourning will be finished.
21 "Then all your [a]people *will be* righteous;
They will [b]possess the land forever,
The branch of [1]My planting,
The [c]work of My hands,
That I may be [d]glorified.
22 "The [a]smallest one will become a [1]clan,
And the least one a mighty nation.
I, the LORD, will hasten it in its time."

10 [c]Is. 54:8
11 [a]Is. 26:2; 60 62:10; Rev. 21:2 [b]Is. 60:5 [c]Ps. 1 24:21
12 [a]Is. 14:2; Ze
13 [a]Is. 35:2 [b]Is [c]1 Chr. 28:2; Ps. 132:7
14 [a]Is. 14:1, 2; 23; 49:23; Rev. 1:26 [c]Heb. 12:2
15 [a]Is. 1:7-9; 6: Jer. 30:17 [b]Is. 6 4:2; 65:18
16 [a]Is. 66:11 [b]Is 43:3, 11; 45:15, 63:8 [c]Is. 59:20;
18 [a]Is. 54:14 [b]Is 51:19 [c]Is. 26:1 60:11
19 [1]Or, *beauty* [a] 21:23; 22:5 [b]Is. 2 [c]Is. 41:16; 45:25; 2:5
20 [a]Is. 30:26 [b]Is. 35:10; 65:19; Rev
21 [1]Lit., *His* [a]Is. 25; 52:1 [b]Ps. 37: Is. 57:13; 61:7 [c]Is 19:25; 29:23; 45: 64:8 [d]Is. 61:3
22 [1]Or, *thousand* 10:22; 51:2

Chapter 61

61 The [a]Spirit of the Lord [1]GOD is upon me,
Because the LORD has anointed me
To [b]bring good news to the [2c]afflicted;
He has sent me to [d]bind up the brokenhearted,
To [e]proclaim liberty to captives,
And [3]freedom to prisoners;
2 To [a]proclaim the favorable year of the LORD,
And the [b]day of vengeance of our God;
To [c]comfort all who mourn,
3 To [a]grant those who mourn *in* Zion,
Giving them a garland instead of ashes,
The [b]oil of gladness instead of mourning,
The mantle of praise instead of a spirit of fainting.
So they will be called [1c]oaks of righteousness,
The planting of the LORD, that He may be glorified.

4 Then they will [a]rebuild the ancient ruins,
They will raise up the former devastations,
And they will repair the ruined cities,
The desolations of many generations.
5 And [a]strangers will stand and pasture your flocks,
And [1]foreigners will be your farmers and your vinedressers.
6 But you will be called the [a]priests of the LORD;
You will be spoken of *as* [b]ministers of our God.
You will eat the [c]wealth of nations,
And in their [1]riches you will boast.
7 Instead of your [a]shame *you will have a* [b]double *portion*,
And *instead of* humiliation they will shout for joy over their portion.
Therefore they will possess a double *portion* in their land,
[c]Everlasting joy will be theirs.
8 For I, the LORD, [a]love justice,
I hate robbery [1]in the burnt offering;
And I will faithfully give them their recompense,
And I will make an [b]everlasting covenant with them.
9 Then their offspring will be known among the nations,
And their descendants in the midst of the peoples.
All who see them will recognize them
Because they are the [a]offspring *whom* the LORD has blessed.

10 I will [a]rejoice greatly in the LORD,
My soul will exult in [b]my God;
For He has [c]clothed me with garments of salvation,
He has wrapped me with a robe of righteousness,
As a bridegroom decks himself with a garland,
And [d]as a bride adorns herself with her jewels.
11 For as the [a]earth brings forth its sprouts,
And as a garden causes the things sown in it to spring up,
So the Lord [1]GOD will [b]cause [c]righteousness and praise
To spring up before all the nations.

61:1 [1]Heb., *YHWH*, ually rendered LORD [2]Or, *humble* [3]Lit., *pening to those who are bound* [a]Is. 11:2; 16; Luke 4:18 [b]Matt. 11:5; Luke 7:22 [c]Is. 1:4; 29:19; 32:7 [d]Is. 57:15 [e]Is. 42:7; 49:9

[a]Is. 49:8; 60:10 [b]Is. 12; 13:6; 34:2, 8 [c]Is. :18; Jer. 31:13; Matt. 5:4

[1]Or, *terebinths* [a]Is. :20 [b]Ps. 23:5; 45:7; 4:15 [c]Is. 60:21; Jer. 17:7, 8

s. 49:8; 58:12; Ezek. 36:33; Amos 9:14

5 [1]Lit., *sons of the foreigner* [a]Is. 14:2; 60:10

[1]Or, *glory* [a]Is. 66:21 s. 56:6 [c]Is. 60:5, 11

[a]Is. 54:4 [b]Is. 40:2; ch. 9:12 [c]Ps. 16:11

Or, *with iniquity* [a]Is. 5:16; 28:17; 30:18 n. 17:7; Ps. 105:10; Is. 55:3; Jer. 32:40

9 [a]Is. 44:3

0 [a]Is. 12:1, 2; 25:9; :16; 51:3 [b]Is. 49:4 . 49:18; 52:1 [d]Rev. 21:2

11 [1]Heb., *YHWH*, ally rendered LORD [a]Is. 4:2; 55:10 [b]Is. 45:23, 24; 60:18, 21 [c]Ps. 72:3; 85:11

Chapter 62

62 For Zion's sake I will not keep silent,
And for Jerusalem's sake I will not keep quiet,
Until her [a]righteousness goes forth like brightness,
And her [b]salvation like a torch that is burning.
2 And the [a]nations will see your righteousness,
And all kings your glory;
And you will be called by a new [b]name,
Which the mouth of the LORD will designate.
3 You will also be a [a]crown of beauty in the hand of the LORD,
And a royal [1]diadem in the hand of your God.
4 It will no longer be said to you, "[1a]Forsaken,"
Nor to your land will it any longer be said, "[2]Desolate";
But you will be called, "[3]My delight is in her,"
And your land, "[4b]Married";
For the [c]LORD delights in you,
And *to Him* your land will be married.
5 For *as* a young man marries a virgin,
So your sons will marry you;
And *as* the [1]bridegroom rejoices over the bride,
So your [a]God will rejoice over you.

6 On your walls, O Jerusalem, I have appointed [a]watchmen;
All day and all night they will never keep silent.
You who [b]remind the LORD, take no rest for yourselves;
7 And [a]give Him no rest until He establishes
And makes [b]Jerusalem a praise in the earth.
8 [a]The LORD has sworn by His right hand and by His strong arm,
"I will [b]never again give your grain *as* food for your enemies;
Nor will [1]foreigners drink your new wine, for which you have labored."
9 But those who [a]garner it will eat it, and praise the LORD;
And those who gather it will drink it in the courts of My sanctuary.

10 Go through, [a]go through the gates;
Clear the way [1]for the people;
[b]Build up, build up the [c]highway;
Remove the stones, lift up a [d]standard over the peoples.
11 Behold, the LORD has proclaimed to the [a]end of the earth,
[b]Say to the daughter of Zion, "Lo, your [c]salvation comes;
[d]Behold His reward is with Him, and His recompense before Him."
12 And they will call them, "[a]The holy people,
The [b]redeemed of the LORD";
And you will be called, "Sought out, a city [c]not forsaken."

Chapter 63

63 Who is this who comes from [a]Edom,
With [b]garments of [1]glowing colors from [c]Bozrah,
This One who is majestic in His apparel,
[2]Marching in the greatness of His strength?
"It is I who speak in righteousness, [d]mighty to save."

62:1 [a]Is. 1:26; 61:11 [b]Is. 46:1

2 [a]Is. 60:3 [b]Is. 62:4, 12; 65:15

3 [1]Lit., *turban* Zech. 9:16; 1 T 2:19

4 [1]I.e., Azubah [2]I.e., Shemama Hephzibah [4]I.e Beulah [a]Is. 54: 60:15, 18 [b]Hos 20 [c]Jer. 32:41; 3:17

5 [1]Lit., *exultatio bridegroom* [a]Is.

6 [a]Is. 52:8; Jer. Ezek. 3:17; 33:7 74:2; Jer. 14:21; 5:1, 20

7 [a]Luke 18:1-8 60:18; Jer. 33:9; 3:19, 20

8 [1]Lit., *sons of foreigners* [a]Is. 4 54:9 [b]Lev. 26:16 28:31, 33; Judg. Is. 1:7; Jer. 5:17

9 [a]Is. 65:13, 21-

10 [1]Lit., *of* [a]Is. 2 60:11, 18 [b]Is. 57 11:16; 19:23; 35: 49:11 [d]Is. 11:10, 49:22

11 [a]Is. 42:10; 49: [b]Matt. 21:5; Zech [c]Is. 51:5 [d]Is. 40:1 Rev. 22:12

12 [a]Deut. 7:6; Is. 1 Pet. 2:9 [b]Is. 35: 51:10 [c]Is. 41:17; 62:4

63:1 [1]Or, *crimson Inclining* [a]Ps. 137 34:5, 6; Ezek. 25: 35:1-15; Obad. 1- Mal. 1:2-5 [b]Is. 63: 34:6; Jer. 49:13; A 1:12 [d]Zeph. 3:17

2 Why is Your apparel red,
And Your garments like the one who [a]treads in the wine press?
3 "[a]I have trodden the wine trough alone,
And from the peoples there was no man with Me.
I also [b]trod them in My anger,
And [c]trampled them in My wrath;
And [d]their [1]lifeblood is sprinkled on My garments,
And I [2]stained all My raiment.
4 "For the [a]day of vengeance was in My heart,
And My year of redemption has come.
5 "And I looked, and there was [a]no one to help,
And I was astonished and there was no one to uphold;
So My [b]own arm brought salvation to Me;
And My wrath upheld Me.
6 "And I [a]trod down the peoples in My anger,
And made them [b]drunk in My wrath,
And I [1]poured out their lifeblood on the earth."

7 I shall make mention of the [a]lovingkindnesses of the LORD, the praises of the LORD,
According to all that the LORD has granted us,
And the great [b]goodness toward the house of Israel,
Which He has granted them according to His [c]compassion,
And according to the multitude of His lovingkindnesses.
8 For He said, "Surely, they are [a]My people,
Sons who will not deal falsely."
So He became their [b]Savior.
9 In all their affliction [1a]He was afflicted,
And the [b]angel of His presence saved them;
In His [c]love and in His mercy He [d]redeemed them;
And He [e]lifted them and carried them all the days of old.
10 But they [a]rebelled
And grieved His [b]Holy Spirit;
Therefore, He turned Himself to become their enemy,
He fought against them.
11 Then [a]His people remembered the days of old, of Moses.
Where is [b]He who brought them up out of the sea with the [1]shepherds of His flock?
Where is He who [c]put His Holy Spirit in the midst of [2]them,
12 Who caused His [a]glorious arm to go at the right hand of Moses,
Who [b]divided the waters before them to make for Himself an everlasting name,
13 Who led them through the depths?
Like the horse in the wilderness, they did not [a]stumble;
14 As the cattle which go down into the valley,
The Spirit of the [a]LORD gave [1]them rest.
So didst Thou [b]lead Thy people,
To make for Thyself a glorious name.

15 [a]Look down from heaven, and see from Thy holy and glorious [b]habitation;
Where are Thy [c]zeal and Thy mighty deeds?
The [d]stirrings of Thy heart and Thy compassion are restrained toward me.

2 [a]Rev. 19:13, 15
3 [1]Lit., *juice* [2]Lit., *defiled* [a]Rev. 14:20; 19:15 [b]Is. 22:5; 28:3 Mic. 7:10 [d]Rev. 19:13
[a]Is. 34:8; 35:4; 61:2; Jer. 51:6
[a]Is. 59:16 [b]Ps. 44:3; Is. 40:10; 52:10
6 [1]Lit., *brought down their juice to the earth* [a]Is. 22:5; 34:2; 65:12 [b]Is. 29:9; 51:17, 21
7 [a]Ps. 25:6; 92:2; Is. 4:8, 10 [b]1 Kin. 8:66; 9:25, 35 [c]Ps. 51:1; 86:5, 15; Is. 54:7, 8; Eph. 2:4
8 [a]Ex. 6:7; Is. 3:15; 51:4 [b]Is. 60:16
[1]Another reading is *He was not an adversary.* [a]Judg. 0:16 [b]Ex. 23:20-23; :14, 15 [c]Deut. 7:7, 8 Is. 43:1; 52:9 [e]Deut. 1; 32:10-12; Is. 46:3
[a]Ps. 78:40; 106:33; Acts 7:51; Eph. 4:30 [b]Ps. 51:11; Is. 63:11
1 [1]Some mss. read *shepherd* [2]Lit., *him* [a]Ps. 106:44, 45 [b]Is. 10 [c]Num. 11:17, 25, 29; Hag. 2:5
[a]Ex. 6:6; 15:16 [b]Ex. 14:21, 22; Is. 11:15; 51:10
13 [a]Jer. 31:9
14 [1]Lit., *him* [a]Josh. 4; 23:1 [b]Deut. 32:12
5 [a]Deut. 26:15; Ps. 14 [b]Ps. 68:5; 123:1 Is. 9:7; 26:11; 37:32; 42:13; 59:17 [d]Jer. 31:20; Hos. 11:8

16 For Thou art our [a]Father, though [b]Abraham does not know us,
And Israel does not recognize us.
Thou, O LORD, art our Father,
Our [c]Redeemer from of old is Thy name.
17 Why, O LORD, dost Thou [a]cause us to stray from Thy ways,
And [b]harden our heart from fearing Thee?
[c]Return for the sake of Thy servants, the tribes of Thy heritage.
18 Thy holy people possessed Thy sanctuary for a little while,
Our adversaries have [a]trodden *it* down.
19 We have become *like* those over whom Thou hast never ruled,
Like those who were not called by Thy name.

Chapter 64

64 [1]Oh, that Thou wouldst rend the heavens *and* [a]come down,
That the mountains might [b]quake at Thy presence—
2 [1]As fire kindles the brushwood, *as* fire causes water to boil—
To make Thy name known to Thine adversaries,
That the [a]nations may tremble at Thy presence!
3 When Thou didst [a]awesome things which we did not expect,
Thou didst come down, the mountains quaked at Thy presence.
4 For from of old [a]they have not heard nor perceived by ear,
Neither has the eye seen a God besides Thee,
Who acts in behalf of the one who [b]waits for Him.
5 Thou dost [a]meet him who rejoices in [b]doing righteousness,
Who [c]remembers Thee in Thy ways.
Behold, [d]Thou wast angry, for we sinned,
We continued in them a long time;
And shall we be saved?
6 For all of us have become like one who is [a]unclean,
And all our [b]righteous deeds are like a filthy garment;
And all of us [c]wither like a leaf,
And our [d]iniquities, like the wind, take us away.
7 And there is [a]no one who calls on Thy name,
Who arouses himself to take hold of Thee;
For Thou hast [b]hidden Thy face from us,
And hast [1]delivered us into the power of our iniquities.

8 But now, O LORD, [a]Thou art our Father,
We are the [b]clay, and Thou our potter;
And all of us are the [c]work of Thy hand.
9 Do not be [a]angry beyond measure, O LORD,
[b]Neither remember iniquity forever;
Behold, look now, all of us are [c]Thy people.
10 Thy [a]holy cities have become a [b]wilderness,
Zion has become a wilderness,
Jerusalem a desolation.
11 Our holy and beautiful [a]house,
Where our fathers praised Thee,
Has been burned *by* fire;
And [b]all our precious things have become a ruin.
12 Wilt Thou [a]restrain Thyself at these things, O LORD?
Wilt Thou keep silent and afflict us beyond measure?

16 [a]Is. 1:2; 64:8 29:22; 41:8; 51:2 41:14; 44:6; 60:1
17 [a]Is. 30:28; Ez 14:7-9 [b]Is. 29:13 [c]Num. 10:36
18 [a]Ps. 74:3-7; I
64:1 [1]Ch. 63:19b Heb. [a]Ex. 19:18; 18:9; 144:5; Mic. Hab. 3:13 [b]Judg. Ps. 68:8; Nah. 1:
2 [1]Ch. 64:1 in He [a]Ps. 99:1; Jer. 5:2
3 [a]Ps. 65:5; 66:3 106:22
4 [a]1 Cor. 2:9 [b]Is. 30:18; 40:31
5 [a]Ex. 20:24 [b]Is. [c]Is. 26:13; 63:7 [d]
6 [a]Is. 6:5 [b]Is. 46: 48:1 [c]Ps. 90:5, 6; 1:30 [d]Is. 50:1
7 [1]Reading with t DSS and versions *melted* [a]Is. 59:4; 22:30 [b]Deut. 31:1 1:15; 54:8
8 [a]Is. 63:16 [b]Is. 2 45:9 [c]Ps. 100:3; Is 60:21
9 [a]Is. 57:17; 60:10 43:25; Mic. 7:18 [c] 79:13; Is. 63:8
10 [a]Is. 48:2; 52:1 1:7; 6:11
11 [a]2 Kin. 25:9; Ps 74:5-7; Is. 63:18 [b]L 1:7, 10, 11
12 [a]Ps. 74:10, 11, 19; Is. 42:14; 63:15

Chapter 65

65 "I permitted Myself to be sought by [a]those who did not ask
for Me;
I permitted Myself to be found by those who did not seek Me.
I said, 'Here am I, here am I,'
To a nation which [b]did not call on My name.
2 "[a]I have spread out My hands all day long to a [b]rebellious people,
Who walk *in* the way which is not good, [1]following their own
[c]thoughts,
3 A people who continually [a]provoke Me to My face,
Offering sacrifices in [b]gardens and [c]burning incense on bricks;
4 Who sit among graves, and spend the night in secret places;
Who [a]eat swine's flesh,
And the broth of unclean meat is *in* their pots.
5 "Who say, '[a]Keep to yourself, do not come near me,
For I am holier than you!'
These are smoke in My [1]nostrils,
A fire that burns all the day.
6 "Behold, it is written before Me,
I will [a]not keep silent, but [b]I will repay;
I will even repay into their bosom,
7 Both [1]their own [a]iniquities and the iniquities of their fathers
together," says the LORD.
"Because they have [b]burned incense on the mountains,
And [c]scorned Me on the hills,
Therefore I will [d]measure their former work into their bosom."

8 Thus says the LORD,
"As the new wine is found in the cluster,
And one says, 'Do not destroy it, for there is [1]benefit in it,'
So I will act on behalf of My servants
In order [a]not to destroy [2]all of them.
9 "And I will bring forth [a]offspring from Jacob,
And an [b]heir of My mountains from Judah;
Even [c]My chosen ones shall inherit it,
And [d]My servants shall dwell there.
10 "And [a]Sharon shall be a pasture land for flocks,
And the [b]valley of Achor a resting place for herds,
For My people who [c]seek Me.
11 "But you who [a]forsake the LORD,
Who forget My [b]holy mountain,
Who set a table for [1]Fortune,
And who fill *cups* with mixed wine for [2]Destiny,
12 I will destine you for the [a]sword,
And all of you shall bow down to the [b]slaughter.
Because I called, but you [c]did not answer;
I spoke, but you did not hear.
And you did evil in My sight,
And chose that in which I did not delight."

13 Therefore, thus says the Lord [1]GOD,
"Behold, My servants shall [a]eat, but you shall be [b]hungry.
Behold, My servants shall [c]drink, but you shall be [d]thirsty.
Behold, My servants shall [e]rejoice, but you shall be [f]put to shame.

65:1 [a]Rom. 9:24-26; 0:20 [b]Is. 63:19; Hos. 1:10
2 [1]Lit., *after* [a]Rom. :21 [b]Is. 1:2, 23; 30:1, 9 [c]Ps. 81:11, 12; Is. 59:7; 66:18
[a]Job 1:11; 2:5; Is. 3:8 1:29; 66:17 [c]Is. 66:3
Lev. 11:7; Is. 66:3, 17
5 [1]Lit., *nose* [a]Matt. 1; Luke 7:39; 18:9-12
6 [a]Ps. 50:3, 21; Is. 4; 64:12 [b]Jer. 16:18
[1]Lit., *your* [a]Is. 13:11; :14; 26:21; 30:13, 14 [b]Is. 57:7; Hos. 2:13 Ezek. 20:27, 28 [d]Jer. 5:29; 13:25
[1]Lit., *blessing* [2]Lit., *the whole* [a]Is. 1:9; 10:21, 22; 48:9
9 [a]Is. 45:19, 25; Jer. 31:36, 37 [b]Is. 49:8; 60:21; Amos 9:11-15 [c]Is. 57:13 [d]Is. 32:18
10 [a]Is. 33:9; 35:2 [b]Josh. 7:24, 26; Hos. 2:15 [c]Is. 51:1; 55:6
[1]Heb., *Gad* [2]Heb., *eni* [a]Deut. 29:24, 25; s. 1:4, 28 [b]Is. 2:2, 3; 66:20
12 [a]Is. 27:1; 34:5, 6; 16 [b]Is. 63:6 [c]2 Chr. 5, 16; Prov. 1:24; Is. 1:28; 50:2; 66:4; Jer. 7:13
13 [1]Heb., *YHWH*, ually rendered *LORD* s. 1:19 [b]Is. 8:21 [c]Is. 41:17, 18; 49:10 [d]Is. 5:13 [e]Is. 61:7; 66:14 42:17; 44:9, 11; 66:5

14 "Behold, My servants shall [a]shout joyfully with a glad heart,
But you shall [b]cry out with a [1]heavy heart,
And you shall wail with a broken spirit.
15 "And you will leave your name for a [a]curse to My chosen ones,
And the Lord [1]GOD will slay you.
But [2]My servants will be called by [b]another name.
16 "Because he who [1]is blessed in the earth
Shall [1]be blessed by the [a]God of truth;
And he who swears in the earth
Shall [b]swear by the God of truth;
Because the former troubles are forgotten,
And because they are hidden from My sight!

17 "For behold, I create [a]new heavens and a new earth;
And the [b]former things shall not be remembered or come to
[1]mind.
18 "But be [a]glad and rejoice forever in what I create;
For behold, I create Jerusalem *for* rejoicing,
And her people *for* gladness.
19 "I will also [a]rejoice in Jerusalem, and be glad in My people;
And there will no longer be heard in her
The voice of [b]weeping and the sound of crying.
20 "No longer will there be [1]in it an infant *who lives but a few* days,
Or an old man who does [a]not [2]live out his days;
For the youth will die at the age of one hundred
And the [3b]one who does not reach the age of one hundred
Shall be *thought* accursed.
21 "And they shall [a]build houses and inhabit *them;*
They shall also [b]plant vineyards and eat their fruit.
22 "They shall not build, and [a]another inhabit,
They shall not plant, and another eat;
For [b]as the [1]lifetime of a tree, *so shall be* the days of My people,
And My chosen ones shall [c]wear out the work of their hands.
23 "They shall [a]not labor in vain,
Or bear *children* for calamity;
For they are the [1b]offspring of those blessed by the LORD,
And their descendants with them.
24 "It will also come to pass that before they call, I will [a]answer; and
while they are still speaking, I will hear.
25 "The [a]wolf and the lamb shall graze together, and the [b]lion shall
eat straw like the ox; and [c]dust shall be the serpent's food. They shall
[d]do no evil or harm in all My [e]holy mountain," says the LORD.

Chapter 66

66 Thus says the LORD,
"[a]Heaven is My throne, and the earth is My footstool.
Where then is a [b]house you could build for Me?
And where is a place that [1]I may rest?
2 "For [a]My hand made all these things,
Thus all these things came into being," declares the LORD.
"But to this one I will look,
To him who is humble and [b]contrite of spirit, and who [c]trembles
at My word.

14 [1]Lit., *pain of* [a]Ps. 66:4; Is. 51:11; Jame 5:13 [b]Is. 13:6; Matt.

15 [1]Heb., *YHWH,* usually rendered *LO* [2]So with Gr.; Heb., *H will call His servants* [a]Jer. 24:9; 25:18; Ze 8:13 [b]Is. 62:2

16 [1]Or, *bless(es) himself* [a]Ex. 34:6; P 31:5 [b]Is. 19:18; 45:2

17 [1]Lit., *heart* [a]Is. 66:22; 2 Pet. 3:13; R 21:1 [b]Is. 43:18; Jer.

18 [a]Ps. 98; Is. 12:1, 25:9; 35:10; 41:16; 5 61:10

19 [a]Is. 62:4, 5; Jer. 32:41 [b]Is. 25:8; 30:1 35:10; 51:11; Rev. 7 21:4

20 [1]Lit., *from there* [2]Lit., *fill out* [3]Lit., *on who misses the ma* [a]Deut. 4:40; Job 5:2 Ps. 34:12 [b]Eccl. 8:1 13; Is. 3:11; 22:14

21 [a]Is. 32:18; Amos 9:14 [b]Is. 30:23; 37:3 Jer. 31:5

22 [1]Lit., *days* [a]Is. 6 9 [b]Ps. 92:12-14 [c]P 21:4; 91:16

23 [1]Lit., *seed* [a]Deu 28:3-12; Is. 55:2 [b]Is 61:9; Jer. 32:38, 39; Acts 2:39

24 [a]Ps. 91:15; Is. 5 58:9; Dan. 9:20-23; 10:12

25 [a]Is. 11:6 [b]Is. 11: [c]Gen. 3:14; Mic. 7:1 [d]Is. 11:9; Mic. 4:3 [e] 65:11

66:1 [1]Lit., *is My res place?* [a]1 Kin. 8:27 11:4; Matt. 5:34, 35 23:22 [b]2 Sam. 7:5- Jer. 7:4; John 4:20, Acts 7:48-50

2 [a]Is. 40:26 [b]Ps. 3 Is. 57:15; Matt. 5:3, Luke 18:13, 14 [c]Ps 119:120; Is. 66:5

3 "*But* he who kills an ox is *like* one who slays a man;
He who sacrifices a lamb is *like* the one who breaks a dog's neck;
He who offers a grain offering *is like one who offers* [a]swine's blood;
He who [1b]burns incense is *like* the one who blesses an idol.
As they have chosen their [c]*own* ways,
And their soul delights in their [d]abominations,
4 So I will [a]choose their [1]punishments,
And I will [b]bring on them what they dread.
Because I called, but [c]no one answered;
I spoke, but they did not listen.
And they did [d]evil in My sight,
And chose that in which I did not delight."
5 Hear the word of the LORD, you who [a]tremble at His word:
"Your brothers who [b]hate you, who [c]exclude you for My name's sake,
Have said, 'Let the LORD be glorified, that we may see your joy.'
But [d]they will be put to shame.
6 "A voice of uproar from the city, a voice from the temple,
The voice of the LORD who is [a]rendering recompense to His enemies.

7 "Before she travailed, [a]she brought forth;
Before her pain came, [b]she gave birth to a boy.
8 "[a]Who has heard such a thing? Who has seen such things?
Can a land be [1]born in one day?
Can a nation be brought forth all at once?
As soon as Zion travailed, she also brought forth her sons.
9 "Shall I bring to the point of birth, and [a]not give delivery?" says the LORD.
"Or shall I who gives delivery shut *the womb?*" says your God.
10 "Be [a]joyful with Jerusalem and rejoice for her, all you who [b]love her;
Be exceedingly [c]glad with her, all you who mourn over her,
11 That you may nurse and [a]be satisfied with her comforting breasts,
That you may suck and be delighted with her [b]bountiful bosom."
12 For thus says the LORD, "Behold, I extend [a]peace to her like a river,
And the [b]glory of the nations like an overflowing stream;
And you shall [1]be nursed, you shall be [c]carried on the [2]hip and fondled on the knees.
13 "As one whom his mother comforts, so I will [a]comfort you;
And you shall be comforted in Jerusalem."
14 Then you shall [a]see *this,* and your [b]heart shall be glad,
And your [c]bones shall flourish like the new grass;
And the [d]hand of the LORD shall be made known to His servants,
But He shall be [e]indignant toward His enemies.
15 For behold, the LORD will come in [a]fire
And His [b]chariots like the whirlwind,
To render His anger with fury,
And His rebuke with flames of fire.
16 For the LORD will execute judgment by [a]fire
And by His [b]sword on all flesh,
And those slain by the LORD will be many.

3 [1]Lit., *offers a* ...*norial of incense* ...5:4 [b]Lev. 2:2; Is. ... [c]Is. 57:17; 65:2 [d]Is. 44:19

...it., *ill treatments* ...:31, 32; Is. 65:7 ...ov. 10:24 [c]Prov. ...4; Is. 65:12; Jer. ...2 Kin. 21:2, 6; Is. 65:12; Jer. 7:30

...66:2 [b]Ps. 38:20; ...5 [c]Matt. 5:10-12; ...0:22; John 9:34; ...-20 [d]Luke 13:17

...59:18; 65:6; Joel 3:7

...37:3; 54:1 [b]Rev. 12:5

...it., *travailed with* [a]Is. 64:4

9 [a]Is. 37:3

[a]Deut. 32:43; Is. ...Rom. 15:10 [b]Ps. 122:6 [c]Ps. 137:6

[a]Is. 49:23; 60:16; ...3:18 [b]Is. 60:1, 2; 62:2

[1]Lit., *nurse* [2]Lit., ...*e* [a]Ps. 72:3, 7; Is. ...18 [b]Is. 60:5; 61:6 [c]Is. 60:4

[a]Is. 12:1; 40:1, 2; 51:3; 2 Cor. 1:3, 4

[a]Is. 33:20 [b]Zech. ...0:7 [c]Prov. 3:8; Is. ...11 [d]Ezra 7:9; 8:31 ...s. 10:5; 13:5; 34:2

...10:17; 30:27, 33; ...1:9 [b]Ps. 68:17; Is. 5:28; Hab. 3:8

...6 [a]Is. 30:30; Ezek. ...2 [b]Is. 65:12; Ezek. 38:21

17 "Those who sanctify and purify themselves *to go* to the [a]gardens,
[1]Following one in the center,
Who eat [b]swine's flesh, detestable things, and mice,
Shall [c]come to an end altogether," declares the LORD.
18 "For I [1]know their works and their [a]thoughts; [2]the time is coming
to [b]gather all nations and tongues. And they shall come and see My
glory.
19 "And I will set a [a]sign among them and will send survivors from
them to the nations: [b]Tarshish, [1]Put, [c]Lud, [2]Meshech, Rosh, [d]Tubal,
and [3]Javan, to the distant [e]coastlands that have neither heard My
fame nor seen My glory. And they will [f]declare My glory among the
nations.
20 "Then they shall [a]bring all your brethren from all the nations as a
grain offering to the LORD, on horses, in chariots, in litters, on mules,
and on camels, to My [b]holy mountain Jerusalem," says the LORD,
"just as the sons of Israel bring their grain offering in a [c]clean vessel
to the house of the LORD.
21 "I will also take some of them for [a]priests *and* for Levites," says
the LORD.
22 "For just as the [a]new heavens and the new earth
Which I make will endure before Me," declares the LORD,
"So your [b]offspring and your [c]name will endure.
23 "And it shall be from [a]new moon to new moon
And from sabbath to sabbath,
All [1]mankind will come to [b]bow down before Me," says the
LORD.
24 "Then they shall go forth and look
On the [a]corpses of the men
Who have [1b]transgressed against Me.
For their [c]worm shall not die,
[d]And their fire shall not be quenched;
And they shall be an [e]abhorrence to all [2]mankind."

17 [1]Lit., *After* [a]Is. 65:3 [b]Lev. 11:7; Is 65:4 [c]Is. 1:28, 31

18 [1]So with Gr.; H omits *know* [2]Lit., *coming* [a]Is. 59:7; [b]Is. 45:22-25; Jer.

19 [1]So with Gr.; H *Pul* [2]So with Gr.; *those who draw th bow* [3]I.e., Greece 11:10, 12; 49:22; 6 [b]Is. 2:16; 60:9 [c]Ez 27:10 [d]Gen. 10:2 11:11; 24:15; 60:9 [f]1 Chr. 16:24; Is. 4

20 [a]Is. 43:6; 49:22 60:4 [b]Is. 2:2, 3; 11 56:7; 65:11, 25 [c]Is 52:11

21 [a]Ex. 19:6; Is. 6 1 Pet. 2:5, 9

22 [a]Is. 65:17; Heb 12:26, 27; 2 Pet. 3 Rev. 21:1 [b]Is. 61:8 65:22, 23; John 10:27-29; 1 Pet. 1: [c]Is. 56:5

23 [1]Lit., *flesh* [a]Is. 14; Ezek. 46:1, 6 [b] 19:21, 23; 27:13; 4

24 [1]Or, *rebelled* [2]L *flesh* [a]Is. 5:25; 34: 1:28; 24:20 [c]Is. 14: Mark 9:48 [d]Is. 1:31 Matt. 3:12 [e]Dan. 1

ISAIAH AT A GLANCE

e of Isaiah:

MENT DIVISIONS

		CHAPTER THEMES
DISCOURSES REGARDING JERUSALEM	GOD'S CHARACTER AND JUDGMENT	1
		2
		3
		4
		5
		6
		7
		8
		9
		10
		11
		12
ORACLES		13
		14
		15
		16
		17
		18
		19
		20
		21
		22
		23
DISCOURSES REGARDING THAT DAY		24
		25
		26
		27
WOES		28
		29
		30
		31
		32
		33
HISTORICAL INTERLUDE		34
		35
		36
		37
		38
		39

Author:

Date:

Purpose:

Key Words:

SEGMENT DIVISIONS

			CHAPTER THEMES
	DISCOURSES REGARDING:	GOD'S COMFORT AND REDEMPTION	40
			41
			42
			43
			44
			45
			46
			47
			48
	DISCOURSES REGARDING:		49
			50
			51
			52
			53
			54
			55
			56
			57
	DISCOURSES REGARDING:		58
			59
			60
			61
			62
			63
			64
			65
			66

EREMIAH

Isaiah lived and prophesied one hundred years before the Babylonian captivity; Jeremiah prophe-
ed just before and during Babylon's three sieges of Judah. Between these two great prophets there
as about a thirty-year period when God didn't speak. True prophets were silent, but false prophets
ere very vocal, proclaiming peace rather than judgment. And the people loved it. This occurred
ıring Manasseh's reign, a reign noted for its blasphemy and bloodshed.

Jeremiah was born at this time. However Jeremiah's ministry as a prophet didn't begin until about
7 B.C., the same time that Nabopolassar began his rule of the Neo-Babylonian Empire. Josiah suc-
eded Manasseh as ruler over Judah. Revival came when the Word of the Lord was found in the house
God and Josiah called the people to repentance.

Then, in 612 B.C. Nineveh, the capital of Assyria, fell to the Babylonians. In 605 B.C. as Egypt went to
gage Babylon in battle at Carchemish, Josiah intercepted Necho, King of Egypt, on the plain of
egiddo. Although Necho had warned Josiah not to try to stop him, Josiah did and as a result he was
lled in battle (2 Chronicles 35:20-27).

The revival came to an end, and like her sister Israel, Judah played the harlot again. Egypt was
feated by Babylon at Carchemish, leaving Babylon the predominant world power, God's rod of
dgment for His adulterous wife. And Jeremiah the prophet wept.

HINGS TO DO

apter 1

To understand Jeremiah's message you must understand Jeremiah's call and commission from the
rd. To do so, become thoroughly familiar with Jeremiah 1 before reading the instructions for
emiah 2 through 36.

1. Read the chapter, asking God for insight and understanding. Then read the chapter one more time to become familiar with it as a whole.
2. The first three verses give the historical setting of Jeremiah.
   a. Examine the historical chart at the beginning of Jeremiah on page 1092 in the light of these verses. The "exile of Jerusalem" (1:3) refers to the final siege and destruction of Jerusalem by Nebuchadnezzar, king of Babylon, in 586 B.C.
   b. Jeremiah contains many references to time, such as in Jeremiah 1:1-3. When you encounter one, consult the chart to see who was reigning at the time and what his relationship was to the other kings. The book of Jeremiah is not chronological, so this will help you keep in perspective the timing of events. Mark every reference to time in a distinctive way. You might use a specific color and/or a diagram such as this .
   c. Fill in "Author" and "Date" on the JEREMIAH AT A GLANCE chart on pages 1185 and 1186.
3. Read Jeremiah 1 again. As you do, ask the five W's and an H. Ask questions such as: Who was Jeremiah? What was Jeremiah called to do or be? To whom was he appointed and by whom? When was he called and why? How did he respond? How will he be able to fulfill his appointment? What was he to say? How would the people respond? What was Jeremiah to do? What if the people didn't respond? What would God do?
   a. On a piece of paper, jot down your answers to these questions and any others you think of while observing the text. Don't read anything into the text, but simply let it speak for itself.
   b. In the margin of Jeremiah 1, list all you learn about Jeremiah, his call, and the specifics of his commission. Record what you observed from examining the chapter in light of the five W's and an H. Be as specific as possible. Read the chapter through several more times.

4. Record the theme of this chapter on JEREMIAH AT A GLANCE and in the text next to t chapter number.
5. The rest of Jeremiah revolves around Jeremiah's call and commission. Everything Jeremiah sa and does is rooted in chapter 1. Remember this as you study!

Jeremiah's critical and passionate message consists of discourses and narrative accounts of events Jeremiah's life and in the history of Israel, Judah, and the nations.

Chapters 2-38: Judah's Sin and God's Warning to Return

Read all the instructions before you begin. Every now and then, refresh your memory—Jeremiah long.

1. Study this segment chapter by chapter doing the following:
   a. When Jeremiah spoke he was to do two things: one negative, one positive—in that order. Fir he was to pluck up, break down, destroy, and overthrow. Second, he was to build and pla As you read, observe how Jeremiah does these two things in regard to Judah.
      1) List their sins, their "wickedness" (1:16), which God has to deal with by plucking u tearing down, destroying, and overthrowing. Note their sins by writing them in the margi
      2) Also note any promise of building and planting—restoration. Record in the margin wh God will do on their behalf, when He will do it, and why.

   b. Jeremiah had the assurance God would perform His Word (1:12). As you read, note in t margin what God says will happen to Judah in the way of judgment.
      1) Watch for how God will bring about this judgment. In several places God has Jeremiah some "symbolic" acts in order to get His point across to the people. Watch for these.
      2) Watch for any text which shows that God performed (accomplished or carried out) wh He said He would do. Also note what God has to do because of the covenant (the law) made with them.

   c. Mark all references to time with a clock drawing.
2. Jeremiah was told to speak all God commanded him and that he would be opposed by kin princes, priests, and people.
   a. Note in the margin any opposition that comes Jeremiah's way. You may want to put it unc the heading "Opposition." Observe Jeremiah's struggles and how he handles these. Also nc how God delivers Jeremiah as He said He would in 1:8,18-19. (The height of Jeremiah's phy cal suffering is described in chapters 37 through 38.)
   b. Also note what you learn about the leaders, the shepherds (spiritual), and the prophets.
3. In chapter 21 Nebuchadnezzar, king of Babylon, appears on the scene, for "out of the north t evil will break forth on all the inhabitants of the land" (1:13-14). From this point on, Babylon a Nebuchadnezzar are prominent. You might want to summarize your insights about them in t margin under the heading "Babylon."
4. There are many key repeated words. The following list contains suggestions about which wor to mark—you may want to add to or delete from it. Marking key words is helpful as long as y think about how they contribute to the text and what you learn from their occurrence.
   a. Mark every reference to *nation* or *nations*. Observe which nation it is and make a list in t margin of what you learn about it.
   b. Watch for any words or synonyms that have to do with plucking up, uprooting, destroyi building, planting, or restoring. Mark these in a distinctive way or underline them in the tex
   c. You also might want to mark the following words and their synonyms in a distinctive way you easily can recognize their occurrence in the text: *listen (hear), return (turn, repent), har (adultery, adulteries), wickedness (wicked, iniquity, sin), heart, forsaken (forsake), heal (healing, heale* and *covenant*. Write these on a card, color code them as you want to mark them in your Bib and use the card as a bookmark as you study Jeremiah.

5. As you finish observing each chapter, marking its key words, and putting notes in the margin, record the theme of that chapter on JEREMIAH AT A GLANCE. Also record it in the text on the line next to the chapter number.

hapters 39-45: Jerusalem's Fall and Judah's Uprooting

1. Except for chapter 45, this section is narrative. Therefore as you read each chapter:
   a. Note what happens, when it happens (mark references to time), where it happens, and why.
   b. Note who is involved. Mark in a distinctive way the main characters in each chapter, and then in the margin list who they are and anything significant you want to remember about them.
   c. Mark the key word *listen (hear)* and any other words which are distinctive to each chapter.
2. Record the theme of each chapter as you have done before.

hapters 46-51: Jeremiah's Prophecy Concerning the Nations

1. As you read, note what the Lord says will happen and why. Also note the end result and if the Lord gives any hope for the future. Watch for and mark time phrases.
2. Mark the key words: *concerning, nations, Medes,* and *north*. Also observe what you learn about Israel from these chapters.
3. These chapters contain critical information about Babylon which will help when you study prophecy and/or Revelation. In the margin list what you learn about Babylon. Also list your insights on the chart WHAT THE BIBLE TEACHES ABOUT BABYLON (pages 1876 and 1877).

hapter 52: Judah's Final Days of Exile

1. As you observe this chapter, mark the time phrases and list in the margin what was done to the kings, the city, the temple vessels, and who did it.
2. Record the theme of this chapter on JEREMIAH AT A GLANCE and then complete the chart. Record the segment divisions of Jeremiah.

HINGS TO THINK ABOUT

1. Judah played the harlot. How have you behaved as the bride of Christ? Do you relate to any of Judah's sins? In James 4:4 God calls those who are friends with the world adulterers. What would He call you?
2. How faithful are you to proclaim God's Word to others? What can you learn from Jeremiah's life in this respect? Do you hesitate to share God's Word with others because of fear or because you think they wouldn't listen? Are you dismayed by their faces? What should you do? Think about all the times you marked "listened" in Jeremiah. Judah didn't listen to God—only to those prophets who tickled her ears. How carefully do you listen to God's Word?
3. Would God have relented of the calamity He was about to bring on Judah? Why? What do you learn from this?
4. God uses nations as His rod of judgment and yet He holds them accountable for their actions. What does this tell you about God and about your accountability before Him?

Chapter 1 ____________________________

1 The words of [a]Jeremiah, the son of Hilkiah, of the priests who
were in [b]Anathoth in the land of Benjamin,
2 to whom the word of the LORD came in the days of [a]Josiah, the
son of [b]Amon, king of Judah, in the [c]thirteenth year of his reign.
3 It came also in the days of [a]Jehoiakim, the son of Josiah, king of
Judah, until the end of the eleventh year of [b]Zedekiah, the son of
Josiah, king of Judah, until the exile of Jerusalem in the fifth month.
4 Now the word of the LORD came to me saying,

1:1 [a]2 Chr. 35:25;
2, 21, 22; Ezra 1:1;
an. 9:2; Matt. 2:17;
16:14; 27:9 [b]Josh.
21:18; 1 Kin. 2:26;
Chr. 6:60; Is. 10:30;
Jer. 11:21; 32:7
[a]1 Kin. 13:2; 2 Kin.
4; 22:3; 2 Chr. 34:1;
er. 3:6; 36:2 [b]2 Kin.
1:18, 24 [c]Jer. 25:3
2 Kin. 23:34; 1 Chr.
; 2 Chr. 36:5-8; Jer.
25:1 [b]2 Kin. 24:17;
1 Chr. 3:15; 2 Chr.
36:11-13; Jer. 39:2

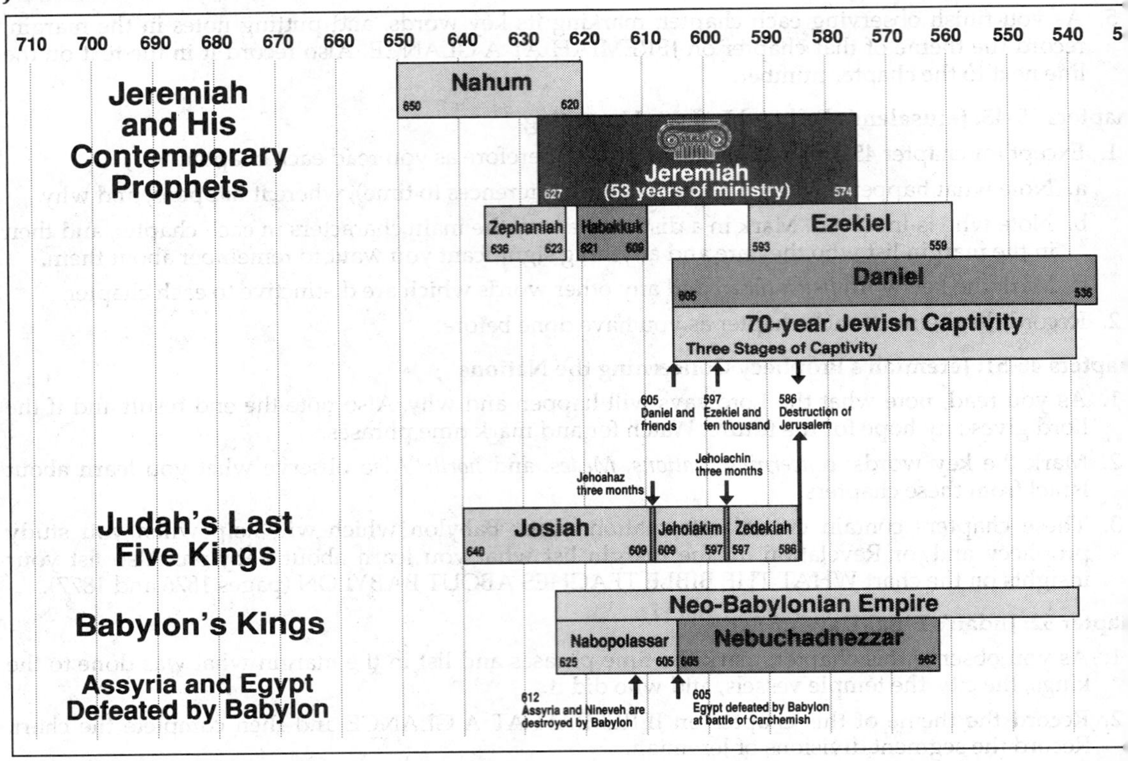

710 700 690 680 670 660 650 640 630 620 610 600 590 580 570 560 550 540 5
Jeremiah and His Contemporary Prophets
Nahum 650 620
Jeremiah (53 years of ministry) 627 574
Zephaniah 636 623
Habakkuk 621 609
Ezekiel 593 559
Daniel 605 536
70-year Jewish Captivity
Three Stages of Captivity
605 Daniel and friends
597 Ezekiel and ten thousand
586 Destruction of Jerusalem
Jehoahaz three months
Jehoiachin three months
Judah's Last Five Kings
Josiah 640 609
Jehoiakim 609 597
Zedekiah 597 586
Babylon's Kings
Neo-Babylonian Empire
Nabopolassar 625 605
Nebuchadnezzar 605 562
Assyria and Egypt Defeated by Babylon
612 Assyria and Nineveh are destroyed by Babylon
605 Egypt defeated by Babylon at battle of Carchemish

INSIGHT

The last kings of Judah:

Josiah
640-609 B.C.

Jehoahaz
(also called Shallum)
609 B.C.

Jehoiakim
(also called Eliakim)
609-597 B.C.

Jehoiachin
(also called Coniah or Jeconiah)
597 B.C.

Zedekiah
(also called Mattaniah)
597-586 B.C.

5 "Before I [a]formed you in the womb I knew you,
And [b]before you were born I consecrated you;
I have [c]appointed you a prophet to the nations."
6 Then [a]I said, "Alas, Lord [1]GOD!
Behold, I do not know how to speak,
Because [b]I am a youth."
7 But the LORD said to me,
"Do not say, 'I am a youth,'
[a]Because everywhere I send you, you shall go,
And [b]all that I command you, you shall speak.
8 "[a]Do not be afraid of them,
For [b]I am with you to deliver you," declares the LORD.
9 Then the LORD stretched out His hand and [a]touched my mouth,
and the LORD said to me,
"Behold, I have [b]put My words in your mouth.
10 "See, [a]I have appointed you this day over the nations and over
the kingdoms,
[b]To pluck up and to break down,
To destroy and to overthrow,
[c]To build and to plant."
11 And the word of the LORD came to me saying, "What do you see,
[a]Jeremiah?" And I said, "I see a rod of an [1]almond tree."
12 Then the LORD said to me, "You have seen well, for [a]I am [1]watch-
ing over My word to perform it."
13 And the word of the LORD came to me a second time saying,

5 [a]Ps. 139:15, 16 49:1, 5; Luke 1:15 1:10; 25:15-26

6 [1]Heb., *YHWH*, usually rendered L [a]Ex. 4:10 [b]1 Kin. 3

7 [a]Ezek. 2:3, 4 [b]N 22:20; Jer. 1:17

8 [a]Ex. 3:12; Deut. Josh. 1:5; Jer. 15:2 [b]Ezek. 2:6

9 [a]Is. 6:7; Mark 7:33-35 [b]Ex. 4:11- Deut. 18:18; Is. 51:

10 [a]Rev. 11:3-6 [b]J 18:7-10; Ezek. 32: 2 Cor. 10:4 [c]Is. 44:26-28; Jer. 24:6 31:28, 40

11 [1]Heb., *shaqed* 24:3; Amos 7:8

12 [1]Heb., *shoqed* 31:28

“[a]What do you see?” And I said, “I see a boiling [b]pot, facing away
from the north.”
14 Then the LORD said to me, “[a]Out of the north the evil [1]will break
forth on all the inhabitants of the land.
15 “For, behold, I am calling [a]all the families of the kingdoms of the
north,” declares the LORD; “and they will come, and they will [b]set
each one his throne at the entrance of the gates of Jerusalem, and
against all its walls round about, and against all the [c]cities of Judah.
16 “And I will [1]pronounce My judgments on them concerning all
their wickedness, whereby they have [a]forsaken Me and have [2b]of-
fered sacrifices to other gods, and worshiped the [c]works of their own
hands.
17 “Now, [a]gird up your loins, and arise, and speak to them all which
I command you. [b]Do not be dismayed before them, lest I dismay you
before them.
18 “Now behold, I have made you today as a fortified city, and as a
pillar of iron and as walls of bronze against the whole land, to the
kings of Judah, to its princes, to its priests and to the people of the
land.
19 “And they will fight against you, but they will not overcome you,
for [a]I am with you to deliver you,” declares the LORD.

Chapter 2

2 Now the word of the LORD came to me saying,
2 “Go and [a]proclaim in the ears of Jerusalem, saying, ‘Thus says
the LORD,

“I remember concerning you the [1b]devotion of your youth,
The love of your betrothals,
[c]Your following after Me in the wilderness,
Through a land not sown.
3 “Israel was [a]holy to the LORD,
The [b]first of His harvest;
[c]All who ate of it became guilty;
Evil came upon them,” declares the LORD.’ ”

4 Hear the word of the LORD, O house of Jacob, and all the families
of the house of Israel.
5 Thus says the LORD,
“[a]What injustice did your fathers find in Me,
That they went far from Me
And walked after [b]emptiness and became empty?
6 “And they did not say, ‘Where is the LORD
Who [a]brought us up out of the land of Egypt,
Who [b]led us through the wilderness,
Through a land of deserts and of pits,
Through a land of drought and of [1]deep darkness,
Through a land that no one crossed
And where no man dwelt?’
7 “And I brought you into the [a]fruitful land,
To eat its fruit and its good things.
But you came and [b]defiled My land,
And My inheritance you made an abomination.
8 “The [a]priests did not say, ‘Where is the LORD?’
And those who handle the law [b]did not know Me;
The [1]rulers also transgressed against Me,

[a]Zech. 4:2 [b]Ezek. 11:3, 7
[1]Lit., *will be opened* :25; Jer. 4:6; 10:22
Jer. 25:9 [b]Is. 22:7; 9:3 [c]Jer. 4:16; 9:11
6 [1]Lit., *speak* [2]Or, *ed incense* [a]Deut. 20 [b]Jer. 7:9; 19:4; 17 [c]Is. 2:8; 37:19; Jer. 10:3-5
[a]1 Kin. 18:46; Job Ezek. 2:6; 3:16-18
um. 14:9; Jer. 1:8; 20:11
Or, *lovingkindness* 58:1; Jer. 7:2; 11:6 k. 16:8; Hos. 2:15 Deut. 2:7; Jer. 2:6
[a]Ex. 19:5, 6; Deut. 4:2 [b]James 1:18; v. 14:4 [c]Is. 41:11; Jer. 30:16; 50:7
[a]Is. 5:4; Mic. 6:3 . 17:15; Jer. 8:19; Rom. 1:21
Or, *the shadow of ath* [a]Ex. 20:2; Is. Deut. 8:15; 32:10
7 [a]Deut. 8:7-9; -12 [b]Ps. 106:38; Jer. 3:2; 16:18
shepherds [a]Jer. [b]Jer. 4:22; Mal. 2:7, 8

And the [c]prophets prophesied by Baal
And walked after [d]things that did not profit.

9 "Therefore I will yet [a]contend with you," declares the LORD,
"And with your sons' sons I will contend.
10 "For [a]cross to the coastlands of [1]Kittim and see,
And send to [b]Kedar and observe closely,
And see if there has been such *a thing* as this!
11 "Has a nation changed gods,
When [a]they were not gods?
But My people have [b]changed their glory
For that which does not profit.
12 "Be appalled, [a]O heavens, at this,
And shudder, be very desolate," declares the LORD.
13 "For My people have committed two evils:
They have forsaken Me,
The [a]fountain of living waters,
To hew for themselves [b]cisterns,
Broken cisterns,
That can hold no water.

14 "Is Israel [a]a slave? Or is he a homeborn servant?
Why has he become a prey?
15 "The young [a]lions have roared at him,
They have [1]roared loudly.
And they have [b]made his land a waste;
His cities have been destroyed, without inhabitant.
16 "Also the [1]men of [a]Memphis and Tahpanhes
Have [2]shaved the [b]crown of your head.
17 "Have you not [a]done this to yourself,
By your forsaking the LORD your God,
When He [a]led you in the way?
18 "But now what are you doing [a]on the road to Egypt,
To drink the waters of the [1b]Nile?
Or what are you doing on the road to Assyria,
To drink the waters of the [2]Euphrates?
19 "[a]Your own wickedness will correct you,
And your [b]apostasies will reprove you;
Know therefore and see that it is evil and [c]bitter
For you to forsake the LORD your God,
And [d]the dread of Me is not in you," declares the Lord [1]GOD of hosts.

20 "For long ago [1a]I broke your yoke
And tore off your bonds;
But you said, 'I will not serve!'
For on every [b]high hill
And under every green tree
You have lain down as a harlot.
21 "Yet I [a]planted you a choice vine,
A completely faithful seed.
How then have you turned yourself before Me
Into the [b]degenerate shoots of a foreign vine?
22 "Although you [a]wash yourself with lye

8 [c]Jer. 23:13 ... 16:19; Hab. 2:...

9 [a]Jer. 2:35; E... 20:35, 36

10 [1]I.e., Cypr... other islands ... [b]Ps. 120:5; Is. ... Jer. 49:28

11 [a]Is. 37:19; ... 16:20 [b]Ps. 10... Rom. 1:23

12 [a]Is. 1:2; Je...

13 [a]Ps. 36:9; J... 17:13; John 4:... 14:3

14 [a]Jer. 5:19; ...

15 [1]Lit., *given* ... *voice* [a]Jer. 50:... 4:7

16 [1]Or, *sons* [2]... *grazed* [a]Is. 19:... 44:1; Hos. 9:6 ... 33:20; Jer. 48:4...

17 [a]Deut. 32:10 ... 4:18

18 [1]Heb., *Shiho...* *River* [a]Is. 30:2 ... 13:3

19 [1]Heb., *YHW...* usually rendere... [a]Is. 3:9; Jer. 4:18 ... 5:5 [b]Jer. 3:6, 8, ... Hos. 11:7 [c]Job 20:12-16; Amos ... [d]Ps. 36:1; Jer. 5:...

20 [1]Or, *you* [a]Le... 26:13 [b]Deut. 12:... 57:5, 7; Jer. 3:2, ...

21 [a]Ex. 15:17; P... 80:8; Is. 5:2 [b]Is. ...

22 [a]Jer. 4:14

[1]Lit., *cause to be great to you* ᵒ., *YHWH*, usually dered *LORD* [b]Job 14:17; Hos. 13:12

And [1]use much soap,
The [b]stain of your iniquity is before Me," declares the Lord [2]GOD.
23 "[a]How can you say, 'I am not defiled,
I have not gone after the [b]Baals'?
Look at your way in the [c]valley!
Know what you have done!
You are a swift young camel [d]entangling her ways,
24 A [a]wild donkey accustomed to the wilderness,
That sniffs the wind in her passion.
In *the time of* her [1]heat who can turn her away?
All who seek her will not become weary;
In her month they will find her.
25 "Keep your feet from being unshod
And your throat from thirst;
But you said, '[a]It is [1]hopeless!
No! For I have [b]loved strangers,
And after them I will walk.'

[a]Prov. 30:12 [b]Jer. 4 [c]Jer. 7:31 [d]Jer. 2:33, 36; 31:22

it., *occasion* [a]Jer. 14:6

r, *desperate* [a]Jer. [b]Deut. 32:16; Jer. 14:10

26 "As the [a]thief is shamed when he is discovered,
So the house of Israel is shamed;
They, their kings, their princes,
And their priests, and their prophets,
27 Who say to a tree, 'You are my father,'
And to a stone, 'You gave me birth.'
For they have turned *their* [a]back to Me,
And not *their* face;
But in the [b]time of their [1]trouble they will say,
'Arise and save us.'
28 "But where are your [a]gods
Which you made for yourself?
Let them arise, if they can [b]save you
In the time of your [1]trouble;
For [c]*according to* the number of your cities
Are your gods, O Judah.

26 [a]Jer. 48:27

r, *evil* [a]Jer. 18:17; [b]Judg. 10:10; Is. 26:16

28 [1]Or, *evil* [a]Deut. 37; Judg. 10:14; Is. 20; Jer. 1:16 [b]Jer. [c]2 Kin. 17:30, 31; Jer. 11:13

29 "Why do you contend with Me?
You have [a]all transgressed against Me," declares the LORD.
30 "[a]In vain I have struck your sons;
They accepted no chastening.
Your [b]sword has devoured your prophets
Like a destroying lion.
31 "O generation, heed the word of the LORD.
Have I been a wilderness to Israel,
Or a [a]land of thick darkness?
Why do My people say, '[b]We *are free to* roam;
We will come no more to Thee'?
32 "Can a virgin forget her ornaments,
Or a bride her attire?
Yet My people have [a]forgotten Me
Days without number.
33 "How well you prepare your way
To seek love!
Therefore even [1]the wicked women
You have taught your ways.

Jer. 5:1; 6:13; Dan. 9:11

30 [a]Is. 1:5; Jer. 5:3; 28 [b]Neh. 9:26; Jer. 6:20-24; Acts 7:52; 1 Thess. 2:15

[a]Is. 45:19 [b]Deut. 32:15; Jer. 2:20, 25

32 [a]Ps. 106:21; Is. 0; Jer. 3:21; 13:25; Hos. 8:14

[1]Or, *in wickedness*

34 "Also on your skirts is found
The [a]lifeblood of the innocent poor;
You did not find them [b]breaking in.
But in spite of all these things,
35 Yet you said, 'I am innocent;
Surely His anger is turned away from me.'
Behold, I will [a]enter into judgment with you
Because you [b]say, 'I have not sinned.'
36 "Why do you [a]go around so much
Changing your way?
Also, [b]you shall be put to shame by Egypt
As you were put to shame by [c]Assyria.
37 "From this *place* also you shall go out
With [a]your hands on your head;
For the LORD has rejected [b]those in whom you trust,
And you shall not prosper with them."

Chapter 3

3 GOD [1]says, "[a]If a husband divorces his wife,
And she goes from him,
And belongs to another man,
Will he still return to her?
Will not that land be completely [2]polluted?
But you [b]are a harlot *with* many [3]lovers;
Yet you [c]turn to Me," declares the LORD.
2 "Lift up your eyes to the [a]bare heights and see;
Where have you not been violated?
By the roads you have [b]sat for them
Like an Arab in the desert,
And you have [c]polluted a land
With your harlotry and with your wickedness.
3 "Therefore the [a]showers have been withheld,
And there has been no spring rain.
Yet you had a [b]harlot's forehead;
You refused to be ashamed.
4 "Have you not just now called to Me,
'[a]My Father, Thou art the [1b]friend of my [c]youth?
5 '[a]Will He be angry forever?
Will He [1]be indignant to the end?'
Behold, you have spoken
And have done evil things,
And you have [2]had your way."
6 Then the LORD said to me in the days of Josiah the king, "Have
you seen what faithless Israel did? She [a]went up on every high hill
and under every green tree, and she was a harlot there.
7 "And [a]I [1]thought, 'After she has done all these things, she will
return to Me'; but she did not return, and her [b]treacherous sister
Judah saw it.
8 "And I saw that for all the adulteries of faithless Israel, I had sent
her away and [a]given her a writ of divorce, yet her [b]treacherous sister
Judah did not fear; but she went and was a harlot also.
9 "And it came about because of the lightness of her harlotry, that
she [a]polluted the land and committed adultery with [b]stones and
trees.

34 [a]2 Kin. 21:16; Ps. 106:38; Jer. 7... 19:4 [b]Ex. 22:2

35 [a]Jer. 25:31 [b]... 28:13; 1 John 1:8

36 [a]Jer. 2:23; 31... Hos. 12:1 [b]Is. 30... [c]2 Chr. 28:16, 20,...

37 [a]2 Sam. 13:19... 14:3, 4 [b]Jer. 37:7

3:1 [1]Lit., *saying* [2]... *alienated* [3]Lit., *companions* [a]Deu... 24:1-4 [b]Jer. 2:20; 16:26, 28, 29 [c]Jer... Zech. 1:3

2 [a]Deut. 12:2; Jer. 3:21; 7:29 [b]Gen. 3... Ezek. 16:25 [c]Jer. ...

3 [a]Lev. 26:19; Jer. 14:3-6 [b]Jer. 6:15; ...

4 [1]Lit., *leader* [a]Jer. 3:19; 31:9 [b]Ps. 71... Prov. 2:17 [c]Jer. 2:2... Hos. 2:15

5 [1]Lit., *keep it* [2]Lit. *been able* [a]Ps. 103... Is. 57:16; Jer. 3:12

6 [a]Jer. 17:2; Ezek. 23:4-10

7 [1]Lit., *said* [a]2 Kin. 17:13 [b]Jer. 3:11; Ez... 16:47

8 [a]Deut. 24:1, 3; Is. 50:1 [b]Ezek. 16:46, 4... 23:11

9 [a]Jer. 2:7; 3:2 [b]Is. 57:6; Jer. 2:27; 10:8

10 "And yet in spite of all this her treacherous sister Judah did not
return to Me with all her heart, but rather in [a]deception," declares
the LORD.
11 And the LORD said to me, "[a]Faithless Israel has proved herself
more righteous than treacherous Judah.
12 "Go, and proclaim these words toward the north and say,

'[a]Return, faithless Israel,' declares the LORD;
'[b]I will not [1]look upon you in anger.
For I am [c]gracious,' declares the LORD;
'I will not be angry forever.
13 'Only [1a]acknowledge your iniquity,
That you have transgressed against the LORD your God
And have [b]scattered your [2]favors to the strangers [c]under every green tree,
And you have not obeyed My voice,' declares the LORD.
14 'Return, O faithless sons,' declares the LORD;
'For I am a [a]master to you,
And I will take you one from a city and two from a family,
And [b]I will bring you to Zion.'

15 "Then I will give you [a]shepherds after My own heart, who will
[b]feed you on knowledge and understanding.
16 "And it shall be in those days when you are multiplied and in-
creased in the land," declares the LORD, "they shall [a]say no more,
'The ark of the covenant of the LORD.' And it shall not come to mind,
nor shall they remember it, nor shall they miss *it*, nor shall it be
made again.
17 "At that time they shall call Jerusalem 'The [a]Throne of the LORD,'
and [b]all the nations will be gathered to it, to Jerusalem, for the [c]name
of the LORD; nor shall they [d]walk anymore after the stubbornness of
their evil heart.
18 "[a]In those days the house of Judah will walk with the house of
Israel, and they will come together [b]from the land of the north to the
[c]land that I gave your fathers as an inheritance.
19 "Then I said,

'How I would set you among [1]My sons,
And give you a pleasant land,
The most [a]beautiful inheritance of the nations!'
And I said, 'You shall call Me, [b]My Father,
And not turn away from following Me.'
20 "Surely, as a woman treacherously departs from her [1]lover,
So you have [a]dealt treacherously with Me,
O house of Israel," declares the LORD.

21 A voice is heard on the [a]bare heights,
The weeping *and* the supplications of the sons of Israel;
Because they have perverted their way,
They have [b]forgotten the LORD their God.
22 "Return, O faithless sons,
[a]I will heal your faithlessness."
"Behold, we come to Thee;
For Thou art the LORD our God.
23 "Surely, [a]the hills are a deception,
A tumult *on* the mountains.
Surely, in the [b]LORD our God

12:2; Hos. 7:14

zek. 16:51, 52; 23:11

[1]Lit., *cause My* *ntenance to fall* 3:14, 22; Ezek. [b]Jer. 3:5 [c]Ps. er. 12:15; 31:20; 33:26

Lit., *know* [2]Lit., [a]Deut. 30:1-3; 5; 14:20; 1 John er. 2:20, 25; 3:2, 6 [c]Deut. 12:2

Jer. 31:32; Hos. 9 [b]Jer. 31:6, 12

Jer. 23:4; 31:10; 34:23; Eph. 4:11 [b]Acts 20:28

16 [a]Is. 65:17

er. 17:12; Ezek. [b]Jer. 3:19; 4:2; 5, 16; 16:19 [c]Is. 60:9 [d]Jer. 11:8

11:13; Jer. 50:4, ; Hos. 1:11 [b]Jer. 31:8 [c]Amos 9:15

it., *the* [a]Ps. 16:6 s. 63:16; Jer. 3:4

, *companion* [a]Is. 48:8

[a]Is. 15:2; Jer. 3:2; 9 [b]Is. 17:10; Jer. 2:32; 13:25

[a]Jer. 30:17; 33:6; Hos. 6:1; 14:4

er. 17:2 [b]Ps. 3:8; Jer. 17:14; 31:7

The people set up their idols on hills (*see* 1 Kings 14:23).

Is the salvation of Israel.
24 "But [a]the shameful thing has consumed the labor of our fathers
since our youth, their flocks and their herds, their sons and their
daughters.
25 "Let us lie down in our [a]shame, and let our humiliation cover us;
for we have sinned against the LORD our God, we and our fathers,
[b]since our youth even to this day. And we have not obeyed the voice
of the LORD our God."

Chapter 4

4 "If you will [a]return, O Israel," declares the LORD,
"*Then* you should return to Me.
And [b]if you will put away your detested things from My
presence,
And will not waver,
2 And you will [a]swear, 'As the LORD lives,'
[b]In truth, in justice, and in righteousness;
Then the [c]nations will bless themselves in Him,
And [d]in Him they will glory."

3 For thus says the LORD to the men of Judah and to Jerusalem,
"[1a]Break up your fallow ground,
And [b]do not sow among thorns.
4 "[a]Circumcise yourselves to the LORD
And remove the foreskins of your heart,
Men of Judah and inhabitants of Jerusalem,
Lest My [b]wrath go forth like fire
And burn with [c]none to quench it,
Because of the evil of your deeds."

5 Declare in Judah and proclaim in Jerusalem, and say,
"[a]Blow the trumpet in the land;
Cry aloud and say,
'[b]Assemble yourselves, and let us go
Into the fortified cities.'
6 "Lift up a [a]standard toward Zion!
Seek refuge, do not stand *still*,
For I am bringing [b]evil from the north,
And great destruction.
7 "A [a]lion has gone up from his thicket,
And a [b]destroyer of nations has set out;
He has gone out from his place
To [c]make your land a waste.
Your cities will be ruins
Without inhabitant.
8 "For this, [a]put on sackcloth,
Lament and wail;
For the [b]fierce anger of the LORD
Has not turned back from us."
9 "And it shall come about in that day," declares the LORD, "that the
[a]heart of the king and the heart of the princes will fail; and the
priests will be appalled, and the [b]prophets will be astounded."
10 Then I said, "Ah, Lord [1]GOD! Surely Thou hast utterly [a]deceived

24 [a]Hos. 9:10

25 [a]Ezra 9:6, 7 22:21

4:1 [a]Jer. 3:22; 1 Joel 2:12 [b]Jer. 7 35:15

2 [a]Deut. 10:20; 45:23; 65:16; Jer [b]Is. 48:1 [c]Gen. 2 Jer. 3:17; 12:15, Gal. 3:8 [d]Is. 45:2 9:24; 1 Cor. 1:31

3 [1]Lit., *Plow for yourselves plowe ground* [a]Hos. 10 [b]Matt. 13:7

4 [a]Deut. 10:16; 3 Jer. 9:25, 26; Ror 2:28, 29; Col. 2:1 30:27, 33; Jer. 21 Zeph. 2:2 [c]Amos Mark 9:43, 48

5 [a]Jer. 6:1; Hos. [b]Josh. 10:20; Jer.

6 [a]Is. 62:10; Jer. 50:2 [b]Jer. 1:14, 1 6:1, 22

7 [a]Jer. 5:6; 25:38; 50:17 [b]Jer. 25:9; 26:7-10 [c]Is. 1:7; 6 Jer. 2:15

8 [a]Is. 22:12; Jer. 6 [b]Is. 5:25; 10:4; Jer

9 [a]Is. 22:3-5; Jer. [b]Is. 29:9, 10; Ezek. 13:9-16

10 [1]Heb., *YHWH*, usually rendered *L* [a]Ezek. 14:9; 2 The 2:11

this people and Jerusalem, saying, '[b]You will have peace'; whereas a
sword touches the [2]throat."
11 In that time it will be said to this people and to Jerusalem, "A
[a]scorching wind from the bare heights in the wilderness in the direc-
tion of the daughter of My people—not to winnow, and not to
cleanse,
12 a wind too strong for [1]this—will come [2]at My command; now I
will also pronounce judgments against them.
13 "Behold, he [a]goes up like clouds,
And his [b]chariots like the whirlwind;
His horses are [c]swifter than eagles.
Woe to us, for [d]we are ruined!"

14 Wash your heart from evil, O Jerusalem,
That you may be saved.
How long will your [a]wicked thoughts
Lodge within you?
15 For a voice declares from [a]Dan,
And proclaims wickedness from Mount Ephraim.
16 "Report *it* to the nations, now!
Proclaim over Jerusalem,
'Besiegers come from a [a]far country,
And [b]lift their voices against the cities of Judah.
17 'Like watchmen of a field they are [a]against her round about,
Because she has [b]rebelled against Me,' declares the LORD.
18 "Your [a]ways and your deeds
Have [1]brought these things to you.
This is your evil. How [b]bitter!
How it has touched your heart!"

19 [a]My [1]soul, my [1]soul! I am in anguish! [2]Oh, my heart!
My [b]heart is pounding in me;
I cannot be silent,
Because [3]you have heard, O my soul,
The [c]sound of the trumpet,
The alarm of war.
20 [a]Disaster on disaster is proclaimed,
For the [b]whole land is devastated;
Suddenly my [c]tents are devastated,
My curtains in an instant.
21 How long must I see the standard,
And hear the sound of the trumpet?
22 "[a]For My people are foolish,
They know Me not;
They are stupid children,
And they have no understanding.
They are shrewd to [b]do evil,
But to do good they do not know."

23 I looked on the earth, and behold, *it was* [1a] formless and void;
And to the heavens, and they had no light.
24 I looked on the mountains, and behold, they were [a]quaking,
And all the hills [1]moved to and fro.
25 I looked, and behold, there was no man,

ife [b]Jer. 5:12; 14:13
r. 13:24; 51:1; 0; Hos. 13:15
t., *these* [2]Lit., *for Me*
19:1; Nah. 1:3 ; 66:15 [c]Lam. b. 1:8 [d]Is. 3:8
Prov. 1:22; Jer. 27; James 4:8
15 [a]Jer. 8:16
39:3; Jer. 5:15 [b]Ezek. 21:22
Kin. 25:1, 4 [b]Is. 0, 23; Jer. 5:23
[1]Lit., *done* [a]Ps. 7; Is. 50:1; Jer. , 19 [b]Jer. 2:19
it., *inward parts* *The walls of my* [3]Or, *I, my soul,* [a]Is. 15:5; 16:11; 2:4; Jer. 9:1, 10; ab. 3:16 [c]Num. 10:9
[a]Ps. 42:7; Ezek. [b]Jer. 4:27 [c]Jer. 10:20
er. 5:4, 21; 10:8; . 1:22 [b]Jer. 9:3; 23; Rom. 16:19; 1 Cor. 14:20
[1]Or, *a waste and* *ness* [a]Gen. 1:2; Is. 24:19
it., *moved lightly* 5:25; Jer. 10:10; Ezek. 38:20

And all the [a]birds of the heavens had fled.
26 I looked, and behold, [1]the [a]fruitful land was a wilderness,
And all its cities were pulled down
Before the LORD, before His fierce anger.

27 For thus says the LORD,
"The [a]whole land shall be a desolation,
Yet I will [b]not execute a complete destruction.
28 "For this the [a]earth shall mourn,
And the [b]heavens above be dark,
Because I have [c]spoken, I have purposed,
And I will not [1]change My mind, nor will I turn from it."
29 At the sound of the horseman and bowman [a]every city flees;
They [b]go into the thickets and climb among the rocks;
[c]Every city is forsaken,
And no man dwells in them.
30 And you, O desolate one, [a]what will you do?
Although you dress in scarlet,
Although you decorate *yourself with* ornaments of gold,
Although you [b]enlarge your eyes with paint,
In vain you make yourself beautiful;
Your [1c]lovers despise you;
They seek your life.
31 For I heard a [1]cry as of a woman in labor,
The anguish as of one giving birth to her first child,
The [1]cry of the daughter of Zion [a]gasping for breath,
[b]Stretching out her [2]hands, *saying*,
"Ah, woe is me, for [3]I faint before murderers."

Chapter 5

5 "[a]Roam to and fro through the streets of Jerusalem,
And look now, and take note.
And seek in her open squares,
If you can [b]find a man,
[c]If there is one who does justice, who seeks [1]truth,
Then I will pardon her.
2 "And [a]although they say, 'As the LORD lives,'
Surely they swear falsely."
3 O LORD, do not [a]Thine eyes look for [1]truth?
Thou hast [b]smitten them,
But they did not [2]weaken;
Thou hast consumed them,
But they [c]refused to take correction.
They have [d]made their faces harder than rock;
They have refused to repent.

4 Then I said, "They are only the poor,
They are foolish;
For they [a]do not know the way of the LORD
Or the ordinance of their God.
5 "I will go to the great
And will speak to them,
For [a]they know the way of the LORD,
And the ordinance of their God."

25 [a]Jer. 9:10; Zeph. 1:3

26 [1]Or, *Carm*
9:10

27 [a]Jer. 12:11 25:11 [b]Jer. 5:1 30:11; 46:28

28 [1]Lit., *be so* 12:4, 11; 14:2; [b]Is. 5:30; 50:3; 2:30, 31 [c]Num Jer. 23:20; 30:2

29 [a]2 Kin. 25:4 2:19-21; Jer. 16 4:7

30 [1]Lit., *param* 10:3; 20:6; Jer. [b]2 Kin. 9:30; Ez 23:40 [c]Jer. 22:2 Lam. 1:2, 19; E 23:9, 10, 22

31 [1]Lit., *sound palms* [3]Lit., *my faints* [a]Is. 42:14 1:15; Lam. 1:17

5:1 [1]Lit., *faithfu* [a]2 Chr. 16:9; Da [b]Ezek. 22:30 [c]G 18:26, 32

2 [a]Is. 48:1; Titus

3 [1]Lit., *faithfulne become sick* [a]2 16:9 [b]Is. 1:5; 9:1 2:30 [c]Jer. 7:28; Zeph. 3:2 [d]Jer. 7 19:15; Ezek. 3:8

4 [a]Is. 27:11; Jer. Hos. 4:6

5 [a]Mic. 3:1

But they too, with one accord, have [b]broken the yoke
And burst the bonds.
6 Therefore [a]a lion from the forest shall slay them,
A [b]wolf of the deserts shall destroy them,
A [c]leopard is watching their cities.
Everyone who goes out of them shall be torn in pieces,
Because their [d]transgressions are many,
Their apostasies are numerous.

7 "Why should I pardon you?
Your sons have forsaken Me
And [a]sworn by those who are [b]not gods.
When I had fed them to the full,
They [c]committed adultery
And trooped to the harlot's house.
8 "They were well-fed lusty horses,
Each one neighing after his [a]neighbor's wife.
9 "Shall I not punish [1]these *people*," declares the LORD,
"And on a nation such as this
[a]Shall I not avenge Myself?

10 "Go up through her vine rows and destroy,
But do not execute a complete destruction;
Strip away her branches,
For they are not the LORD's.
11 "For the [a]house of Israel and the house of Judah
Have dealt very treacherously with Me," declares the LORD.
12 They have [a]lied about the LORD
And said, "[1b]Not He;
Misfortune will [c]not come on us;
And we [d]will not see sword or famine.
13 "And the [a]prophets are *as* wind,
And the word is not in them.
Thus it will be done to them!"

14 Therefore, thus says the LORD, the God of hosts,
"Because you have spoken this word,
Behold, I am [a]making My words in your mouth fire
And this people wood, and it will consume them.
15 "Behold, I am [a]bringing a nation against you from afar, O house of Israel," declares the LORD.
"It is an enduring nation,
It is an ancient nation,
A nation whose [b]language you do not know,
Nor can you understand what they say.
16 "Their [a]quiver is like an [b]open grave,
All of them are mighty men.
17 "And they will [a]devour your harvest and your food;
They will devour your sons and your daughters;
They will devour your flocks and your herds;
They will devour your [b]vines and your fig trees;
They will demolish with the sword your [c]fortified cities in which you trust.

32:25; Ps. 2:3; Jer. 2:20
Jer. 4:7 [b]Ezek. Hab. 1:8; Zeph. Hos. 13:7 [d]Jer. 30:14, 15
Josh. 23:7; Jer. eph. 1:5 [b]Deut. ; Jer. 2:11; Gal. 4:8 [c]Jer. 7:9
er. 13:27; 29:23; Ezek. 22:11
for these things [a]Jer. 9:9
[a]Jer. 3:6, 7, 20
2 [1]Lit., *He is not* hr. 36:16 [b]Prov. er. 14:22; 43:1-4 3:17 [d]Jer. 14:13
b 8:2; Jer. 14:13, 15; 22:22
[a]Is. 24:6; Jer. 1:9; ; Hos. 6:5; Zech. 1:6
[a]Deut. 28:49; Is. er. 4:16 [b]Is. 28:11
5:28; 13:18 [b]Ps. 5:9
[a]Lev. 26:16; Deut. :31, 33; Jer. 8:16; 0:7, 17 [b]Jer. 8:13 [c]Hos. 8:14

18 "Yet even in those days," declares the LORD, "I will not make you
a complete destruction.
19 "And it shall come about [a]when [1]they say, 'Why has the LORD our
God done all these things to us?' then you shall say to them, 'As you
have forsaken Me and served foreign gods in your land, so you shall
[b]serve strangers in a land that is not yours.'
20 "Declare this in the house of Jacob
And proclaim it in Judah, saying,
21 'Hear this, O foolish and [1]senseless people,
Who have [a]eyes, but see not;
Who have ears, but hear not.
22 'Do you not [a]fear Me?' declares the LORD.
'Do you not tremble in My presence?
For I have [b]placed the sand as a boundary for the sea,
An eternal decree, so it cannot cross over it.
Though the waves toss, yet they cannot prevail;
Though they roar, yet they cannot cross over it.
23 'But this people has a [a]stubborn and rebellious heart;
They have turned aside and departed.
24 'They do not say in their heart,
"Let us now fear the LORD our God,
Who [a]gives rain in its season,
Both [b]the autumn rain and the spring rain,
Who keeps for us
The [c]appointed weeks of the harvest."
25 'Your [a]iniquities have turned these away,
And your sins have withheld good from you.
26 'For wicked men are found among My people,
They [a]watch like fowlers [1]lying in wait;
They set a trap,
They catch men.
27 'Like a cage full of birds,
So their houses are full of [a]deceit;
Therefore they have become great and rich.
28 'They are [a]fat, they are sleek,
They also [1]excel in deeds of wickedness;
They do not plead the cause,
The cause of the [2b]orphan, that they may prosper;
And they do not [3]defend the rights of the poor.
29 '[a]Shall I not punish [1]these *people?*' declares the LORD,
'On a nation such as this
Shall I not avenge Myself?'

30 "An appalling and [a]horrible thing
Has happened in the land:
31 The [a]prophets prophesy falsely,
And the priests rule [1]on their *own* authority;
And My people [b]love it so!
But what will you do at the end of it?

Chapter 6 ____________________

6 "Flee for safety, O sons of [a]Benjamin,
From the midst of Jerusalem!
Now blow a trumpet in Tekoa,

19 [1]Or, *you* [a]D
29:24-26; 1 Kin.
Jer. 13:22; 16:1
[b]Deut. 28:48; Je

21 [1]Lit., *without*
[a]Is. 6:9; 43:8; Ez
12:2; Matt. 13:1
8:18; John 12:4
28:26; Rom. 11:

22 [a]Deut. 28:58
119:120; Jer. 2:1
Rev. 15:4 [b]Job
Ps. 104:9; Prov.

23 [a]Deut. 21:18
78:8; Jer. 4:17; 6

24 [a]Ps. 147:8; J
Matt. 5:45; Acts 1
[b]Joel 2:23 [c]Gen.

25 [a]Jer. 2:17; 4:

26 [1]Perhaps, *cr*
down [a]Ps. 10:9;
1:11; Jer. 18:22;
1:15

27 [a]Jer. 9:6

28 [1]Lit., *pass ove*
overlook deeds [2]
fatherless [3]Lit., *ju*
[a]Deut. 32:15 [b]Is.
Jer. 7:6; 22:3; Zec

29 [1]Or, *for these*
[a]Jer. 5:9; Mal. 3:5

30 [a]Jer. 23:14; Ho
6:10

31 [1]Lit., *over their*
hands [a]Ezek. 13:
[b]Mic. 2:11

6:1 [a]Josh. 18:28

And raise a signal over [1b]Beth-haccerem;
For evil looks down from the [c]north,
And a great destruction.
2 "The comely and [a]dainty one, [b]the daughter of Zion, I will cut off.
3 "[a]Shepherds and their flocks will come to her,
They will [b]pitch *their* tents [1]around her,
They will pasture each in his [2]place.
4 "[1a]Prepare war against her;
Arise, and let us [2]attack at [b]noon.
Woe to us, for the day declines,
For the shadows of the evening lengthen!
5 "Arise, and let us [1]attack by night
And [a]destroy her [2]palaces!"
6 For thus says the LORD of hosts,
"[a]Cut down her trees,
And cast up a [b]siege against Jerusalem.
This is the city to be punished,
In whose midst there is only [c]oppression.
7 "[a]As a well [1]keeps its waters fresh,
So she [1]keeps fresh her wickedness.
[b]Violence and destruction are heard in her;
[c]Sickness and wounds are ever before Me.
8 "[a]Be warned, O Jerusalem,
Lest [1b]I be alienated from you;
Lest I make you a desolation,
A land not inhabited."

9 Thus says the LORD of hosts,
"They will [a]thoroughly glean as the vine the [b]remnant of Israel;
Pass your hand again like a grape gatherer
Over the branches."
10 To whom shall I speak and give warning,
That they may hear?
Behold, their [a]ears are [1]closed,
And they cannot listen.
Behold, [b]the word of the LORD has become a reproach to them;
They have no delight in it.
11 But I am [a]full of the wrath of the LORD:
I am [b]weary with holding *it* in.
"[c]Pour *it* out on the children in the street,
And on the [1]gathering of young men together;
For both husband and wife shall be taken,
The aged [2]and the very old.
12 "And their [a]houses shall be turned over to others,
Their fields and their wives together;
For I will [b]stretch out My hand
Against the inhabitants of the land," declares the LORD.
13 "For [a]from the least of them even to the greatest of them,
Everyone is [b]greedy for gain,
And from the prophet even to the priest
Everyone [1]deals falsely.
14 "And they have [a]healed the brokenness of My people
superficially,
Saying, 'Peace, peace,'

.e., house of the yard [b]Neh. 3:14 er. 1:14; 4:6; 6:22

t. 28:56 [b]Is. 1:8; Jer. 4:31

[1]Lit., *against her about* [2]Lit., *hand* :10 [b]2 Kin. 25:1; 4:17; Luke 19:43

Sanctify [2]Lit., *go* er. 6:23; Joel 3:9 r. 15:8; Zeph. 2:4

[1]Lit., *go up* [2]Or, *rtified towers* [a]Is. 32:14; Jer. 52:13

t. 20:19, 20 [b]Jer. 33:4 [c]Jer. 22:17

[1]Lit., *keeps cold* ames 3:11f. [b]Jer. :8; Ezek. 7:11, 23 [c]Jer. 30:12, 13

Lit., *my soul* [a]Jer. :28; 17:23 [b]Ezek. 23:18; Hos. 9:12

[a]Jer. 16:16; 49:9; ad. 5, 6 [b]Jer. 8:3; 11:23

.it., *uncircumcised* er. 5:21; 7:26; Acts 7:51 [b]Jer. 20:8

[1]Lit., *council* [2]Lit., *ith fulness of days* 32:18, 19; Mic. 3:8 er. 15:6; 20:9 [c]Jer. 7:20; 9:21

[a]Deut. 28:30; Jer. 0; 38:22, 23 [b]Jer. 15:6

3 [1]Or, *makes lies* er. 8:10 [b]Is. 56:11; 7; Jer. 8:10; 22:17

4 [a]Jer. 8:11; Ezek. 13:10

But there is no peace.
15 "Were they [a]ashamed because of the abomination they have done?
They were not even ashamed at all;
They did not even know how to blush.
Therefore they shall fall among those who fall;
At the time that I punish them,
They shall be cast down," says the LORD.

16 Thus says the LORD,
"Stand by the ways and see and ask for the [a]ancient paths,
Where the good way is, and walk in it;
And [b]you shall find rest for your souls.
But they said, 'We will not walk *in it*.'
17 "And I set [a]watchmen over you, *saying*,
'Listen to the sound of the trumpet!'
But they said, 'We will not listen.'
18 "Therefore hear, O nations,
And know, O congregation, what is among them.
19 "[a]Hear, O earth: behold, I am bringing disaster on this people,
The [b]fruit of their [1]plans,
Because they have not listened to My words,
And as for My law, they have [c]rejected it also.
20 "[a]For what purpose does [b]frankincense come to Me from Sheba,
And the [1c]sweet cane from a distant land?
[d]Your burnt offerings are not acceptable,
And your sacrifices are not pleasing to Me."
21 Therefore, thus says the LORD,
"Behold, [a]I am [1]laying stumbling blocks before this people.
And they will stumble against them,
[b]Fathers and sons together;
Neighbor and [2]friend will perish."

22 Thus says the LORD,
"Behold, [a]a people is coming from the north land,
And a great nation will be aroused from the [b]remote parts of the earth.
23 "They seize [a]bow and spear;
They are [b]cruel and have no mercy;
Their voice [c]roars like the sea,
And they ride on horses,
Arrayed as a man for the battle
Against you, O daughter of Zion!"
24 We have [a]heard the report of it;
Our hands are limp.
[b]Anguish has seized us,
Pain as of a woman in childbirth.
25 [a]Do not go out into the field,
And [b]do not walk on the road,
For the enemy has a sword,
[c]Terror is on every side.
26 O daughter of my people, [a]put on sackcloth
And [b]roll in ashes;
[1c]Mourn as for an only son,

15 [a]Jer. 3:3; 8:1

16 [a]Is. 8:20; Je 18:15; 31:21; Ma Luke 16:29 [b]Ma

17 [a]Is. 21:11; 58 25:4; Ezek. 3:17 2:1

19 [1]Or, *devices* 1:2; Jer. 19:3, 15 [b]Prov. 1:31 [c]Jer.

20 [1]Lit., *good* [a]P 50:7-9; Is. 1:11; 6 Mic. 6:6 [b]Is. 60:6 30:23 [d]Ps. 40:6; 5:22

21 [1]Lit., *giving* [2] *friend* [a]Is. 8:14; 13:16 [b]Is. 9:14-1 9:21, 22

22 [a]Jer. 1:15; 10 50:41-43 [b]Neh. 1

23 [a]Is. 13:18; Jer [b]Jer. 50:42 [c]Is. 5

24 [a]Is. 28:19; Jer 4:19-21 [b]Is. 21:3; 4:31; 13:21; 30:6; 50:43

25 [a]Jer. 14:18 [b]J 5:6 [c]Jer. 20:10; 4 49:29

26 [1]Lit., *Make for yourself mourning* 4:8 [b]Jer. 25:34; M 1:10 [c]Amos 8:10; 12:10

A lamentation most bitter.
For suddenly the destroyer
Will come upon us.

27 "I have [a]made you an assayer *and* a tester among My people,
That you may know and assay their way."
28 All of them are stubbornly rebellious,
[a]Going about as a talebearer.
They are [b]bronze and iron;
They, all of them, are corrupt.
29 The bellows blow fiercely,
The lead is consumed by the fire;
In vain the refining goes on,
But the [a]wicked are not [1]separated.
30 [a]They call them rejected silver,
Because the [b]LORD has rejected them.

Chapter 7

7 The word that came to Jeremiah from the LORD, saying,
2 "[a]Stand in the gate of the LORD's house and proclaim there this
word, and say, 'Hear the word of the LORD, all you of Judah, who
enter by these gates to worship the LORD!' "
3 Thus says the LORD of hosts, the God of Israel, "[a]Amend your
ways and your deeds, and I will let you dwell in this place.
4 "[a]Do not trust in deceptive words, saying, '[1]This is the temple of
the LORD, the temple of the LORD, the temple of the LORD.'
5 "For [a]if you truly amend your ways and your deeds, if you truly
[b]practice justice between a man and his neighbor,
6 *if* you do not oppress the alien, the [1a]orphan, or the widow, and
do not shed [b]innocent blood in this place, nor [c]walk after other gods
to your own ruin,
7 then I will let you [a]dwell in this place, in the [b]land that I gave to
your fathers forever and ever.
8 "Behold, you are trusting in [a]deceptive words to no avail.
9 "Will you steal, murder, and commit adultery, and swear falsely,
and [1a]offer sacrifices to Baal, and walk after [b]other gods that you
have not known,
10 then [a]come and stand before Me in [b]this house, which is called
by My name, and say, 'We are delivered!'—that you may do all these
abominations?
11 "Has [a]this house, which is called by My name, become a [b]den of
robbers in your sight? Behold, [c]I, even I, have seen *it*," declares the
LORD.
12 "But go now to My place which was in [a]Shiloh, where I [b]made My
name dwell at the first, and [c]see what I did to it because of the
wickedness of My people Israel.
13 "And now, because you have done all these things," declares the
LORD, "and I spoke to you, [a]rising up early and [b]speaking, but you
did not hear, and I [c]called you but you did not answer,
14 therefore, I will do to the [a]house which is called by My name, [b]in
which you trust, and to the place which I gave you and your fathers,
as I [c]did to Shiloh.
15 "And I will [a]cast you out of My sight, as I have cast out all your
brothers, all the [1]offspring of [b]Ephraim.

27 [a]Jer. 1:18; 15:20
28 [a]Jer. 9:4 [b]Ezek. 22:18
[1]Or, *drawn off* [a]Jer. 15:19
30 [a]Ps. 119:119; Is. 22 [b]Jer. 7:29; Hos. 9:17; Zech. 11:8
2 [a]Jer. 17:19; 26:2
Jer. 4:1; 7:5; 18:11; 26:13
[1]Lit., *They are* [a]Jer. 7:8; Mic. 3:11
[a]Is. 1:19; Jer. 4:1, 2 n. 6:12; Jer. 21:12; 22:3
Or, *fatherless* [a]Ex. 22:21-24; Jer. 5:28 . 2:34; 19:4 [c]Deut. 4, 15; 8:19; 11:28; Jer. 13:10
ut. 4:40 [b]Jer. 3:18
8 [a]Jer. 7:4; 28:15
[1]Or, *burn incense* Jer. 11:13, 17 [b]Ex. 20:3; Jer. 7:6; 19:4
[a]Ezek. 23:39 [b]Jer. 7:11, 14, 30; 32:34
11 [a]Is. 56:7 [b]Matt. , Mark 11:17; Luke 19:46 [c]Jer. 29:23
[a]Judg. 18:31; Jer. :6 [b]Josh. 18:1, 10 Sam. 4:10, 11, 22; Ps. 78:60-64
3 [a]Jer. 7:25 [b]Jer. 17 [c]Prov. 1:24; Is. 65:12; 66:4
[a]Deut. 12:5; 1 Kin. Jer. 7:4 [c]Jer. 7:12
5 [1]Lit., *seed* [a]Jer. ; 52:3 [b]Ps. 78:67; s. 7:13; 9:13; 12:1

INSIGHT

Shiloh, the home of the tabernacle, was Israel's religious center for over a century after the conquest of Canaan under Joshua. When they took the ark of the covenant from Shiloh, the Philistines slaughtered 30,000 of Israel's foot soldiers (1 Samuel 4:1-11).

16 "As for you, [a]do not pray for this people, and do not lift up cry or
prayer for them, and do not intercede with Me; for I do not hear you.
17 "Do you not see what they are doing in the cities of Judah and in
the streets of Jerusalem?
18 "The [1]children gather wood, and the fathers kindle the fire, and
the women knead dough to make cakes for the queen of heaven; and
they [a]pour out libations to other gods in order to [b]spite Me.
19 "[a]Do they spite Me?" declares the LORD. "Is it not themselves *they*
spite, to [1]their own [b]shame?"
20 Therefore thus says the Lord [1]GOD, "Behold, My [a]anger and My
wrath will be poured out on this place, on man and on beast and on
the [b]trees of the field and on the fruit of the ground; and it will burn
and not be quenched."
21 Thus says the LORD of hosts, the God of Israel, "Add your [a]burnt
offerings to your sacrifices and [b]eat flesh.
22 "For I did not [a]speak to your fathers, or command them in the day
that I brought them out of the land of Egypt, concerning burnt offer-
ings and sacrifices.
23 "But this is [1]what I commanded them, saying, '[a]Obey My voice,
and [b]I will be your God, and you will be My people; and you will
walk in all the way which I command you, that it may [c]be well with
you.'
24 "Yet they [a]did not obey or incline their ear, but walked in *their own*
counsels *and* in the stubbornness of their evil heart, and [1b]went back-
ward and not forward.
25 "Since the day that your fathers came out of the land of Egypt
until this day, I have [a]sent you all My servants the prophets, daily
rising early and sending *them.*
26 "Yet they did not listen to Me or incline their ear, but [a]stiffened
their neck; they [b]did evil more than their fathers.
27 "And you shall [a]speak all these words to them, but they will not
listen to you; and you shall call to them, but they will [b]not answer
you.
28 "And you shall say to them, 'This is the nation that [a]did not obey
the voice of the LORD their God or accept correction; [1b]truth has per-
ished and has been cut off from their mouth.
29 '[a]Cut off [1]your hair and cast *it* away,
And [b]take up a lamentation on the bare heights;
For the LORD has [c]rejected and forsaken
The generation of His wrath.'
30 "For the sons of Judah have done that which is evil in My sight,"
declares the LORD, "they have [a]set their detestable things in the house
which is called by My name, to defile it.
31 "And they have [a]built the high places of Topheth, which is in the
valley of the son of Hinnom, to [b]burn their sons and their daughters
in the fire, which I [c]did not command, and it did not come into My
[1]mind.
32 "[a]Therefore, behold, days are coming," declares the LORD, "when
it will no more be called Topheth, or the valley of the son of Hinnom,
but the valley of the Slaughter; for they will [b]bury in Topheth [1]be-
cause there is no *other* place.
33 "And the [a]dead bodies of this people will be food for the birds of
the sky, and for the beasts of the earth; and no one will frighten *them*
away.

16 [a]Ex. 32:10; Deut
9:14; Jer. 11:14

18 [1]Lit., *sons* [a]Jer.
19:13 [b]Deut. 32:16,
1 Kin. 14:9; 16:2; Je
11:17; Ezek. 8:17

19 [1]Lit., *their faces*
[a]Job 35:6; 1 Cor. 10
[b]Jer. 9:19; 15:9; 22:

20 [1]Heb., *YHWH,*
usually rendered *Lo*
[a]Is. 42:25; Jer. 6:11
42:18; Lam. 2:3-5;
[b]Jer. 8:13; 11:16

21 [a]Is. 1:11; Jer. 6:
14:12; Amos 5:22
[b]Ezek. 33:25; Hos.

22 [a]1 Sam. 15:22;
51:16; Hos. 6:6

23 [1]Lit., *the word*
which [a]Ex. 15:26;
16:32; Deut. 6:3 [b]
19:5, 6; Lev. 26:12
11:4; 13:11 [c]Is. 3:1
Jer. 38:20; 42:6

24 [1]Lit., *they were*
[a]Deut. 29:19; Ps. 8
Jer. 11:8; Ezek. 20
13, 16, 21 [b]Jer. 15

25 [a]2 Chr. 36:15;
25:4; 29:19; Luke

26 [a]Neh. 9:16; Je
17:23; 19:15 [b]Jer.
16:12; Matt. 23:32

27 [a]Jer. 1:7; 26:2;
2:7 [b]Is. 50:2; 65:1
Zech. 7:13

28 [1]Lit., *faithfulne*
[a]Jer. 6:17; 11:10 [b]
59:14, 15; Jer. 9:5

29 [1]Lit., *your crow*
[a]Job 1:20; Is. 15:2
22:12; Jer. 16:6; M
1:16 [b]Jer. 3:21; 9
18 [c]Jer. 6:30; 14:

30 [a]2 Kin. 21:3f.;
33:3-5, 7; Jer. 32:
Ezek. 7:20; Dan. 9
11:31

31 [1]Lit., *heart* [a]2
23:10; Jer. 19:5; 3
[b]Lev. 18:21; 2 Kin
17:17; Ps. 106:38
[c]Deut. 17:3

32 [1]Or, *until there*
place left [a]Jer. 19
[b]2 Kin. 23:10

33 [a]Deut. 28:26;
79:2; Jer. 12:9; 19

Is. 24:7, 8; Jer. 9; 25:10; Ezek. Hos. 2:11; Rev. [b]Lev. 26:33; Is. 1:7; Jer. 4:27

34 "Then I will make to [a]cease from the cities of Judah and from the
streets of Jerusalem the voice of joy and the voice of gladness, the
voice of the bridegroom and the voice of the bride; for the [b]land will
become a ruin.

Chapter 8

8:1 [a]Ezek. 6:5

8 "At that time," declares the LORD, "they will [a]bring out the bones
of the kings of Judah, and the bones of its princes, and the bones
of the priests, and the bones of the prophets, and the bones of the
inhabitants of Jerusalem from their graves.

2 Kin. 23:5; Jer. Zeph. 1:5; Acts er. 22:19; 36:30 9:37; Ps. 83:10; Jer. 9:22

2 "And they will spread them out to the sun, the moon, and to all
the [a]host of heaven, which they have loved, and which they have
served, and which they have gone after, and which they have
sought, and which they have worshiped. They will not be gathered
[b]or buried; [c]they will be as dung on the face of the ground.

3:21, 22; 7:15, on. 4:3; Rev. 9:6 0:1, 4; Jer. 23:3, 8; 29:14

3 "And [a]death will be chosen rather than life by all the remnant that
remains of this evil family, that remains in all the [b]places to which I
have driven them," declares the LORD of hosts.

4 "And you shall say to them, 'Thus says the LORD,
"Do *men* [a]fall and not get up again?
Does one turn away and not [1]repent?

urn back [a]Prov. ; Amos 5:2; Mic. 7:8

5 "Why then has this people, Jerusalem,
[a]Turned away in continual apostasy?
They [b]hold fast to deceit,
They [c]refuse to return.

. 5:6; 7:24 [b]Jer. 27; 9:6 [c]Jer. 5:3

6 "I [a]have listened and heard,
They have spoken what is not right;
[b]No man repented of his wickedness,
Saying, 'What have I done?'
Everyone turned to his course,
Like a [c]horse charging into the battle.

. 14:2; Mal. 3:16 22:30; Mic. 7:2; 0 [c]Job 39:21-25

7 "Even the stork in the sky
[a]Knows her seasons;
And the [b]turtledove and the swift and the thrush
Observe the time of their [1]migration;
But [c]My people do not know
The ordinance of the LORD.

., *coming* [a]Prov. -8; Is. 1:3 [b]Song 2:12 [c]Jer. 5:4

8 "[a]How can you say, 'We are wise,
And the law of the LORD is with us'?
But behold, the lying pen of the scribes
Has made *it* into a lie.

Job 5:12, 13; Jer. 4:22; Rom. 1:22

9 "The wise men are [a]put to shame,
They are dismayed and caught;
Behold, they have [b]rejected the word of the LORD,
And what kind of wisdom do they have?

. 19:11; Jer. 6:15; r. 1:27 [b]Jer. 6:19

10 "Therefore I will [a]give their wives to others,
Their fields to [1]new owners;
Because from the least even to the greatest
Everyone is [b]greedy for gain;
From the prophet even to the priest
Everyone practices deceit.

[1]Lit., *possessing* [a]Deut. 28:30; Jer. 2, 13; 38:22f. [b]Is. ; 57:17; Jer. 6:13

11 "And they [a]heal the brokenness of the daughter of My people
superficially,

r. 6:14; 14:13, 14; 2:14; Ezek. 13:10

Saying, 'Peace, peace,'
But there is no peace.
12 "Were they [a]ashamed because of the abomination they had done?
They certainly were not ashamed,
And they did not know how to blush;
Therefore they shall [b]fall among those who fall;
At the [c]time of their punishment they shall be brought down,"
Declares the LORD.

13 "I will [a]surely snatch them away," declares the LORD;
"There will be [b]no grapes on the vine,
And [c]no figs on the fig tree,
And the leaf shall wither;
And what I have given them shall pass away." ' "
14 Why are we sitting still?
[a]Assemble yourselves, and let us [b]go into the fortified cities,
And let us perish there,
Because the LORD our God has doomed us
And given us [c]poisoned water to drink,
For [d]we have sinned against the LORD.
15 *We* [a]waited for peace, but no good *came;*
For a time of healing, but behold, terror!
16 From [a]Dan is heard the snorting of his horses;
At the sound of the neighing of his [b]stallions
The whole land quakes;
For they come and [c]devour the land and its fulness,
The city and its inhabitants.
17 "For behold, I am [a]sending serpents against you,
Adders, for which there is [b]no charm,
And they will bite you," declares the LORD.

18 [1]My [a]sorrow is beyond healing,
My [b]heart is faint *within me!*
19 Behold, listen! The cry of the daughter of my people from a
[a]distant land:
"Is the LORD not in Zion? Is her King not within her?"
"Why have they [b]provoked Me with their graven images, with
foreign [1c]idols?"
20 "Harvest is past, summer is ended,
And we are not saved."
21 For the [a]brokenness of the daughter of my people I am broken;
I [b]mourn, dismay has taken hold of me.
22 Is there no [a]balm in Gilead?
Is there no physician there?
[b]Why then has not the [1]health of the daughter of my people
[2]been restored?

Chapter 9

9 [1a]Oh, that my head were waters,
And my eyes a fountain of tears,
That I might weep day and night
For the slain of the [b]daughter of my people!
2 [1a]O that I had in the desert
A wayfarers' lodging place;

12 [a]Ps. 52:1, 7 Jer. 3:3; 6:15; Z [b]Is. 9:14; Jer. 6: 4:5 [c]Deut. 32:3 10:15

13 [a]Jer. 14:12; 22:20, 21 [b]Jer. 7:20; Joel 1:7 [c] 21:19; Luke 13:

14 [a]Jer. 4:5 [b]2 20:6; Jer. 35:11 29:18; Ps. 69:21 9:15; 23:15; Lam Matt. 27:34 [d]Je 14:20

15 [a]Jer. 8:11; 14

16 [a]Judg. 18:29 4:15 [b]Judg. 5:22 3:24; 10:25

17 [a]Num. 21:6; 32:24 [b]Ps. 58:4,

18 [1]So Gr. and versions [a]Is. 22: 1:16, 17 [b]Jer. 23 Lam. 5:17

19 [1]Lit., *vanities* 13:5; 39:3; Jer. 4 9:16 [b]Deut. 32:2 7:19 [c]Ps. 31:6

21 [a]Jer. 4:19; 9:1 14:17 [b]Jer. 14:2; 2:6; Nah. 2:10

22 [1]Or, *healing* *gone up* [a]Gen. 3 Jer. 46:11 [b]Jer. 1 30:13

9:1 [1]Ch. 8:23 in H [a]Is. 22:4; Jer. 8:18 13:17; Lam. 2:18 6:26; 8:21, 22

2 [1]Ch. 9:1 in Heb 55:6, 7; 120:5, 6

That I might leave my people,
And go from them!
For all of them are [b]adulterers,
An assembly of [c]treacherous men.
3 "And they [a]bend their tongue *like* their bow;
Lies and not truth prevail in the land;
For they [b]proceed from evil to evil,
And they [c]do not know Me," declares the LORD.
4 "Let everyone [a]be on guard against his neighbor,
And [b]do not trust any brother;
Because every [c]brother deals [1]craftily,
And every neighbor [d]goes about as a slanderer.
5 "And everyone [a]deceives his neighbor,
And does not speak the truth,
They have taught their tongue to speak lies;
They [b]weary themselves committing iniquity.
6 "Your [a]dwelling is in the midst of deceit;
Through deceit they [b]refuse to know Me," declares the LORD.

7 Therefore thus says the LORD of hosts,
"Behold, I will refine them and [a]assay them;
For [b]what *else* can I do, because of the daughter of My people?
8 "Their [a]tongue is a deadly arrow;
It speaks deceit;
With his mouth one [b]speaks peace to his neighbor,
But inwardly he [c]sets an ambush for him.
9 "[a]Shall I not punish them for these things?" declares the LORD.
"On a nation such as this
Shall I not avenge Myself?

10 "For the [a]mountains I will take up a weeping and wailing,
And for the pastures of the [b]wilderness a dirge,
Because they are [c]laid waste, so that no one passes through,
And the lowing of the cattle is not heard;
Both the [d]birds of the sky and the beasts have fled; they are gone.
11 "And I will make Jerusalem a [a]heap of ruins,
A haunt of [b]jackals;
And I will make the cities of Judah a [c]desolation, without
inhabitant."

12 Who is the [a]wise man that may understand this? And *who is* he
to whom [b]the mouth of the LORD has spoken, that he may declare it?
[c]Why is the land ruined, laid waste like a desert, so that no one
passes through?
13 And the LORD said, "Because they have [a]forsaken My law which
I set before them, and have not obeyed My voice nor walked accord-
ing to it,
14 but have [a]walked after the stubbornness of their heart and after
the [b]Baals, as their [c]fathers taught them,"
15 therefore thus says the LORD of hosts, the God of Israel, "behold,
[a]I will feed them, this people, with wormwood and give them
[b]poisoned water to drink.
16 "And I will [a]scatter them among the nations, whom neither they
nor their fathers have known; and I will send the [b]sword after them
until I have annihilated them."

2 [b]Jer. 5:7, 8; 23:10; Hos. 4:2 [c]Jer. 5:11; 12:1, 6
3 [a]Ps. 64:3; Is. 59:4; Jer. 9:8 [b]Jer. 4:22 [c]Judg. 2:10; 1 Sam. :12; Jer. 4:22; 5:4, 5; os. 4:1; 1 Cor. 15:34
4 [1]I.e., like Jacob (a play on words) [a]Ps. 2:2; Prov. 26:24, 25; Jer. 9:8; Mic. 7:5, 6 r. 12:6 [c]Gen. 27:35 s. 15:3; Prov. 10:18; Jer. 6:28
5 [a]Mic. 6:12 [b]Jer. 12:13; 51:58, 64
6 [a]Ps. 120:5, 6; Jer. 27; 8:5 [b]Job 21:14, 15; Prov. 1:24; Jer. 11:10; 13:10; John 3:19, 20
[a]Is. 1:25; Jer. 6:27; Mal. 3:3 [b]Hos. 11:8
[a]Jer. 9:3 [b]Ps. 28:3 [c]Jer. 5:26
s. 1:24; Jer. 5:9, 29
10 [a]Jer. 4:24; 7:29 [b]Jer. 4:26; Hos. 4:3 Jer. 12:4, 10; Ezek. 14:15; 29:11; 33:28 4:25; 12:4; Hos. 4:3
[a]Is. 25:2; Jer. 51:37 . 13:22; 34:13 [c]Jer. 4:27; 26:9
12 [a]Ps. 107:43; Is. 23; Hos. 14:9 [b]Jer. 9:20; 23:16 [c]Ps. 107:34; Jer. 23:10
3 [a]2 Chr. 7:19; Ps. :30; Jer. 5:19; 22:9
14 [a]Jer. 7:24; 11:8; . 1:21-24 [b]Jer. 2:8, ; 23:27 [c]Gal. 1:14; 1 Pet. 1:18
5 [a]Ps. 80:5 [b]Deut. 8; Jer. 8:14; 23:15; Lam. 3:15
[a]Lev. 26:33; Deut. 64; Jer. 13:24 [b]Jer. 4:27; Ezek. 5:2, 12

17 Thus says the LORD of hosts,
"Consider and call for the [a]mourning women, that they may come;
And send for the [1b]wailing women, that they may come!
18 "And let them make haste, and take up a wailing for us,
That our [a]eyes may shed tears,
And our eyelids flow with water.
19 "For a voice of [a]wailing is heard from Zion,
'[b]How are we ruined!
We are put to great shame,
For we have [c]left the land,
Because they have cast down our dwellings.' "
20 Now hear the word of the LORD, O you [a]women,
And let your ear receive the word of His mouth;
Teach your daughters wailing,
And everyone her neighbor a dirge.
21 For [a]death has come up through our windows;
It has entered our palaces
To cut off the [b]children from the streets,
The young men from the town squares.
22 Speak, "Thus declares the LORD,
'The corpses of men will fall [a]like dung on the open field,
And like the sheaf after the reaper,
But no one will gather *them.*' "
23 Thus says the LORD, "[a]Let not a wise man boast of his wisdom,
and let not the [b]mighty man boast of his might, let not a [c]rich man
boast of his riches;
24 but let him who boasts [a]boast of this, that he understands and
knows Me, that I am the LORD who [b]exercises lovingkindness, justice,
and righteousness on earth; for I [c]delight in these things," declares
the LORD.
25 "Behold, the days are coming," declares the LORD, "that I will
punish all who are circumcised and yet [a]uncircumcised—
26 Egypt, and Judah, and Edom, and the sons of Ammon, and
Moab, and [a]all those inhabiting the desert who clip the hair on their
temples; for all the nations are uncircumcised, and all the house of
Israel are [b]uncircumcised of heart."

Chapter 10

10 Hear the word which the LORD speaks to you, O house of Israel.
2 Thus says the LORD,
"[a]Do not learn the way of the nations,
And do not be terrified by the signs of the heavens
Although the nations are terrified by them;
3 For the customs of the peoples are [1a]delusion;
Because [b]it is wood cut from the forest,
The work of the hands of a craftsman with a cutting tool.
4 "They [a]decorate *it* with silver and with gold;
They [b]fasten it with nails and with hammers
So that it will not totter.
5 "Like a scarecrow in a cucumber field are they,
And they [a]cannot speak;
They must be [b]carried,

17 [1]Lit., *skilled* [a]2 C
35:25; Eccl. 12:5
[b]Amos 5:16

18 [a]Is. 22:4; Jer. 9:1
14:17

19 [a]Jer. 7:29; Ezek.
7:16-18 [b]Deut. 28:2
Jer. 4:13 [c]Jer. 7:15;

20 [a]Is. 32:9

21 [a]2 Chr. 36:17; Je
15:7; 18:21; Ezek. 9
6; Amos 6:9, 10 [b]Je
6:11

22 [a]Ps. 83:10; Is. 5
Jer. 8:2; 16:4; 25:33

23 [a]Eccl. 9:11; Is.
47:10; Ezek. 28:3-7
[b]1 Kin. 20:10, 11; Is
10:8-12 [c]Job 31:24
Ps. 49:6-9

24 [a]Ps. 20:7; 44:8;
41:16; Jer. 4:2; 1 C
1:31; 2 Cor. 10:17;
6:14 [b]Ex. 34:5, 7;
36:5, 7; 51:1 [c]Is. 6
Mic. 7:18

25 [a]Jer. 4:4; Rom.
2:28, 29

26 [a]Jer. 25:23 [b]Le
26:41; Jer. 4:4; 6:1
Ezek. 44:7; Rom. 2

10:2 [a]Lev. 18:3; 2
Deut. 12:30

3 [1]Lit., *vanity* [a]Je
14:22 [b]Is. 44:9-20

4 [a]Is. 40:19 [b]Is. 4
41:7

5 [a]Ps. 115:5; Is. 4
Jer. 10:14; 1 Cor.
[b]Ps. 115:7; Is. 46:

Because they cannot walk!
Do not fear them,
For they [c]can do no harm,
Nor can they do any good."

6 [a]There is none like Thee, O LORD;
Thou art [b]great, and great is Thy name in might.
7 [a]Who would not fear Thee, O [b]King of the nations?
Indeed it is Thy due!
For among all the [c]wise men of the nations,
And in all their kingdoms,
There is none like Thee.
8 But they are altogether [a]stupid and foolish
In their discipline of [1]delusion—[2]their idol is wood!
9 Beaten [a]silver is brought from [b]Tarshish,
And [c]gold from Uphaz,
The work of a craftsman and of the hands of a goldsmith;
Violet and purple are their clothing;
They are all the [d]work of skilled men.
10 But the LORD is the [a]true God;
He is the [b]living God and the [c]everlasting King.
At His wrath the [d]earth quakes,
And the nations cannot [e]endure His indignation.

11 [1]Thus you shall say to them, "The [a]gods that did not make the
heavens and the earth shall [b]perish from the earth and from under
the [2]heavens."

12 *It is* [a]He who made the earth by His power,
Who [b]established the world by His wisdom;
And by His understanding He has [c]stretched out the heavens.
13 When He utters His [a]voice, *there is* a tumult of waters in the heavens,
And He causes the [b]clouds to ascend from the end of the earth;
He makes lightning for the rain,
And brings out the [c]wind from His storehouses.
14 Every man is [a]stupid, devoid of knowledge;
Every goldsmith is put to shame by his [1]idols;
For his molten images are deceitful,
And there is no breath in them.
15 They are [a]worthless, a work of mockery;
In the [b]time of their punishment they will perish.
16 The [a]portion of Jacob is not like these;
For the [1b]Maker of all is He,
And [c]Israel is the tribe of His inheritance;
The [d]LORD of hosts is His name.

17 [a]Pick up your bundle from the ground,
You who dwell under siege!
18 For thus says the LORD,
"Behold, I am [a]slinging out the inhabitants of the land
At this time,
And will cause them distress,
That they may [1]be found."

19 [a]Woe is me, because of my [1]injury!

5 [c]Is. 41:23, 24

6 [a]Ex. 15:11; Deut. ?6; Ps. 86:8, 10; Jer. :16 [b]Ps. 48:1; 96:4; Is. 12:6; Jer. 32:18

7 [a]Rev. 15:4 [b]Ps. :28 [c]Dan. 2:27, 28; 1 Cor. 1:19, 20

.it., *vanities*, or *idols* *it is* [a]Jer. 4:22; 5:4; 10:14

s. 40:19 [b]Ps. 72:10; 3:6 [c]Dan. 10:5 [d]Ps. 115:4

[a]Is. 65:16 [b]Jer. 4:2 . 10:16; 29:10 [d]Jer. 24; 50:46 [e]Ps. 76:7

11 [1]This verse is in Aram. [2]Or, *these* *vens* [a]Ps. 96:5 [b]Is. 2:18; Zeph. 2:11

2 [a]Gen. 1:1, 6; Job 38:4-7; Ps. 136:5; :4, 5; Jer. 51:15, 19 Ps. 78:69; Is. 45:18 [c]Job 9:8; Is. 40:22

3 [a]Ps. 29:3-9 [b]Job 6:27-29 [c]Ps. 135:7

[1]Or, *graven image* Jer. 10:8; 51:17, 18

Is. 41:24; Jer. 8:19; 2 [b]Jer. 8:12; 51:18

.it., *Fashioner* [a]Ps. 73:26; 119:57; Jer. :19; Lam. 3:24 [b]Is. '; Jer. 10:12 [c]Deut. 32:9; Ps. 74:2 [d]Jer. 31:35; 32:18

17 [a]Ezek. 12:3-12

[1]Lit., *find* [a]1 Sam. 25:29

Lit., *breaking* [a]Jer. 4:31

My [b]wound is incurable.
But I said, "Truly this is a sickness,
And I [c]must bear it."
20 My [a]tent is destroyed,
And all my ropes are broken;
My [b]sons have gone from me and are no more.
There is [c]no one to stretch out my tent again
Or to set up my curtains.
21 For the shepherds have become stupid
And [a]have not sought the LORD;
Therefore they have not prospered,
And [b]all their flock is scattered.
22 The sound of a [a]report! Behold, it comes—
A great commotion [b]out of the land of the north—
To [c]make the cities of Judah
A desolation, a haunt of jackals.

23 I know, O LORD, that [a]a man's way is not in himself;
[b]Nor is it in a man who walks to direct his steps.
24 [a]Correct me, O LORD, but with justice;
Not with Thine anger, lest Thou [1]bring me to nothing.
25 [a]Pour out Thy wrath on the nations that [b]do not know Thee,
And on the families that [c]do not call Thy name;
For they have devoured Jacob;
They have [d]devoured him and consumed him,
And have laid waste his [1]habitation.

Chapter 11

11 The word which came to Jeremiah from the LORD, saying,
2 "[a]Hear the words of this [b]covenant, and speak to the men of
Judah and to the inhabitants of Jerusalem;
3 and say to them, 'Thus says the LORD, the God of Israel, "[a]Cursed
is the man who does not heed the words of this covenant
4 which I commanded your forefathers in the [a]day that I brought
them out of the land of Egypt, from the [b]iron furnace, saying, '[c]Listen
to My voice, and [1]do according to all which I command you; so you
shall be [d]My people, and I will be your God,'
5 in order to confirm the [a]oath which I swore to your forefathers,
to give them a land flowing with milk and honey, as *it is* this day." ' "
Then I answered and said, "[b]Amen, O LORD."
6 And the LORD said to me, "[a]Proclaim all these words in the cities
of Judah and in the streets of Jerusalem, saying, '[b]Hear the words of
this covenant and [c]do them.
7 'For I solemnly [a]warned your fathers in the [b]day that I brought
them up from the land of Egypt, even to this day, [1c]warning persis-
tently, saying, "[d]Listen to My voice."
8 'Yet they [a]did not obey or incline their ear, but walked, each one,
in the stubbornness of his evil heart; therefore I brought on them all
the [b]words of this covenant, which I commanded *them* to do, but
they did not.' "
9 Then the LORD said to me, "A [a]conspiracy has been found among
the men of Judah and among the inhabitants of Jerusalem.
10 "They have [a]turned back to the iniquities of their [1]ancestors who
[b]refused to hear My words, and they [c]have gone after other gods to

19 [b]Jer. 14:17 [c]Mic.
20 [a]Jer. 4:20; Lam. [b]Jer. 31:15; Lam. 1:5 [c]Is. 51:18
21 [a]Jer. 2:8 [b]Jer. 23
22 [a]Jer. 4:15 [b]Jer. 1:14; 25:9 [c]Jer. 9:11 49:33
23 [a]Prov. 16:1; 20:2 [b]Is. 26:7
24 [1]Lit., *diminish m* [a]Ps. 6:1; 38:1
25 [1]Or, *pasture* [a]Ps 79:6, 7; Zeph. 3:8 [b] 18:21; 1 Thess. 4:5; 2 Thess. 1:8 [c]Zeph 1:6 [d]Jer. 8:16; 50:7
11:2 [a]Jer. 11:6 [b]Ex 19:5
3 [a]Deut. 27:26; Jer 17:5; Gal. 3:10
4 [1]Lit., *do them* [a]E 24:3-8; Jer. 31:32 [b]Deut. 4:20; 1 Kin. [c]Lev. 26:3; Deut. 11 Jer. 7:23; 26:13 [d]J 24:7; Zech. 8:8
5 [a]Ex. 13:5; Deut. Ps. 105:9; Jer. 32:2 [b]Jer. 28:6
6 [a]Jer. 3:12; 7:2 [b] 11:2 [c]John 13:17; 2:13; James 1:22
7 [1]Lit., *rising early warning* [a]1 Sam. 8 [b]Jer. 11:4 [c]Ex. 15 2 Chr. 36:15; Jer. 7 [d]Jer. 11:7
8 [a]Jer. 7:24; 9:14; 35:15; Ezek. 20:8 26:14-43
9 [a]Ezek. 22:25; H
10 [1]Lit., *former fa* [a]1 Sam. 15:11; Jer 11; Ezek. 20:18 [b] 9:7; Ps. 78:8-10; J 13:10 [c]Judg. 2:11

serve them; the house of Israel and the house of Judah have [d]broken
My covenant which I made with their fathers."
11 Therefore thus says the LORD, "Behold I am [a]bringing disaster on
them which they will [b]not be able to escape; though they will [c]cry to
Me, yet I will not listen to them.
12 "Then the cities of Judah and the inhabitants of Jerusalem will [a]go
and cry to the gods to whom they burn incense, but they surely will
not save them in the time of their disaster.
13 "For your gods are [1a]as many as your cities, O Judah; and [1]as
many as the streets of Jerusalem are the altars you have set up to the
[b]shameful thing, altars to [c]burn incense to Baal.
14 "Therefore [a]do not pray for this people, nor lift up a cry or prayer
for them; for I will [b]not listen when they call to Me because of their
disaster.

15 "What right has My [a]beloved in My house
When [b]she has done many vile deeds?
Can the sacrificial flesh take away from you your disaster,
[1]So *that* you can rejoice?"
16 The LORD called your name,
"A [a]green olive tree, beautiful in fruit and form";
With the [b]noise of a great tumult
He has [c]kindled fire on it,
And its branches are worthless.

17 And the LORD of hosts, who [a]planted you, has [b]pronounced evil
against you because of the evil of the house of Israel and of the
house of Judah, which they have [1]done to provoke Me by [2c]offering
up sacrifices to Baal.

18 Moreover, the LORD [a]made it known to me and I knew it;
Then Thou didst show me their deeds.
19 But I was like a gentle [a]lamb led to the slaughter;
And I did not know that they had [b]devised plots against me,
saying,
"Let us destroy the tree with its [1]fruit,
And [c]let us cut him off from the [d]land of the living,
That his [e]name be remembered no more."
20 But, O LORD of hosts, who [a]judges righteously,
Who [b]tries the [1]feelings and the heart,
Let me see Thy vengeance on them,
For to Thee have I [2]committed my cause.

21 Therefore thus says the LORD concerning the men of [a]Anathoth,
who [b]seek your life, saying, "[c]Do not prophesy in the name of the
LORD, that you might not [d]die at our hand";
22 therefore, thus says the LORD of hosts, "Behold, I am about to
[a]punish them! The [b]young men will die by the sword, their sons and
daughters will die by famine;
23 and a remnant [a]will not be left to them, for I will [b]bring disaster
on the men of Anathoth—[c]the year of their punishment."

Chapter 12

12 [a]Righteous art Thou, O LORD, that I would plead *my* case with
Thee;
Indeed I would [b]discuss matters of justice with Thee:
Why has the [c]way of the wicked prospered?
Why are all those who [d]deal in treachery at ease?

...r. 3:6-11; Ezek. 16:59
...Kin. 22:16; Jer. ...1:17 [b]Is. 24:17; ...:35 [c]Ps. 18:41; ...28; Is. 1:15; Jer. ...4; 14:12; Ezek. ...Mic. 3:4; Zech. 7:13
...)eut. 32:37; Jer. 44:17
..., *the number of* ...23:13; Jer. 2:28 ...r. 3:24 [c]Jer. 7:9
[a]Ex. 32:10; Jer. ...6; 14:11; 1 John [b]Ps. 66:18; Jer. 11:11; Hos. 5:6
[1]Lit., *Then* [a]Jer. ...27 [b]Ezek. 16:25
[a]Ps. 52:8; Rom. ... [b]Ps. 83:2 [c]Ps. ...6; Is. 27:11; Jer. 21:14
17 [1]Or, *done for themselves* [2]Or, *...ing incense* [a]Is. ...2:21; 12:2 [b]Jer. ...5:10; 19:15 [c]Jer. ...7:9; 11:13; 32:29
...Sam. 23:11, 12; ...:9, 10; Ezek. 8:6
... [1]Lit., *bread* [a]Is. ...Jer. 18:18; 20:10 ...3:4; Is. 53:8 [d]Job ...13; Ps. 52:5 [e]Ps. 109:13
...Lit., *kidneys* [2]Lit., ...*led* [a]Gen. 18:25; ...s. 7:8; Jer. 20:12 ...am. 16:7; Ps. 7:9; Jer. 17:10
...er. 1:1 [b]Jer. 12:5, ...0:10 [c]Amos 2:12 [d]Jer. 26:8; 38:4
...Jer. 21:14 [b]2 Chr. 36:17; Jer. 18:21
23 [a]Jer. 6:9 [b]Jer. ...12; Hos. 9:7; Mic. 7:4 [c]Luke 19:44
...:1 [a]Ezra 9:15; Ps. ...; 129:4; Jer. 11:20 ...ob 13:3 [c]Job 12:6; ...5:27, 28; Hab. 1:4; ...3:15 [d]Jer. 3:7, 20; 5:11

2 Thou hast [a]planted them, they have also taken root;
They grow, they have even produced fruit.
Thou art [b]near [1]to their lips
But far from their [2]mind.
3 But Thou [a]knowest me, O LORD;
Thou seest me;
And Thou dost [b]examine my heart's *attitude* toward Thee.
Drag them off like sheep for the slaughter
And [1]set them apart for a [c]day of carnage!
4 How long is the [a]land to mourn
And the [b]vegetation of the countryside to wither?
For the [c]wickedness of those who dwell in it,
[d]Animals and birds have been snatched away,
Because *men* have said, "He will not see our latter [e]ending."

5 "If you have run with footmen and they have tired you out,
Then how can you compete with horses?
If you fall down in a land of peace,
How will you do in the [1a]thicket of the Jordan?
6 "For even your [a]brothers and the household of your father,
Even they have dealt treacherously with you,
Even they have cried aloud after you.
Do not believe them, although they may say [b]nice things to you."

7 "I have [a]forsaken My house,
I have abandoned My inheritance;
I have given the [b]beloved of My soul
Into the hand of her enemies.
8 "My inheritance has become to Me
Like a lion in the forest;
She has [1a]roared against Me;
Therefore I have come to [b]hate her.
9 "Is My inheritance like a speckled bird of prey to Me?
Are the [a]birds of prey against her on every side?
Go, gather all the [b]beasts of the field,
Bring them to devour!
10 "Many [a]shepherds have ruined My [b]vineyard,
They have [c]trampled down My field;
They have made My [d]pleasant field
A desolate wilderness.
11 "[1]It has been made a desolation,
Desolate, it [a]mourns [2]before Me;
The [b]whole land has been made desolate,
Because no man [c]lays it to heart.
12 "On all the [1a]bare heights in the wilderness
Destroyers have come,
For a [b]sword of the LORD is devouring
From one end of the land even to the [2]other;
There is [c]no peace for [3]anyone.
13 "They have [a]sown wheat and have reaped thorns,
They have [b]strained themselves [1]to no profit.
But be ashamed of your [2c]harvest
Because of the [d]fierce anger of the LORD."
14 Thus says the LORD concerning all My [a]wicked neighbors who

2 [1]Lit., *in their* [2]Lit., *kidneys* [a]... 11:17; 45:4; Ez 17:5-10 [b]Is. 29 3:10; Ezek. 33: 1:16

3 [1]Lit., *sanctify* [a]Ps. 139:1-4 [b]P 11:5; Jer. 11:20 17:18; 50:27; J

4 [a]Jer. 4:28; 9: 23:10 [b]Joel 1:1 [c]Ps. 107:34 [d]Je 7:20; 9:10; Hos Hab. 3:17 [e]Jer. Ezek. 7:2

5 [1]Lit., *pride* [a]J 49:19; 50:44

6 [a]Gen. 37:4-11 6:15; Ps. 69:8; J 5 [b]Ps. 12:2; Pro

7 [a]Is. 2:6; Jer. 7 23:39 [b]Jer. 11:1 11:1-8

8 [1]Lit., *raised h* [a]Is. 59:13 [b]Hos. Amos 6:8

9 [a]2 Kin. 24:2; E 23:22-25 [b]Is. 56 7:33; 15:3; 34:20

10 [a]Jer. 6:3; 23: 80:8-16; Is. 5:1-7 63:18 [d]Jer. 3:19

11 [1]Lit., *One has it* [2]Or, *upon* [a]Je 14:2; 23:10 [b]Jer. 27; 25:11 [c]Is. 42

12 [1]Or, *caravan* [2]Lit., *other end of land* [3]Lit., *all fles* 3:2, 21 [b]Is. 34:6; 47:6; Amos 9:4 [c] 16:5; 30:5

13 [1]Lit., *they do profit* [2]Lit., *produ* [a]Lev. 26:16; Deut 28:38; Mic. 6:15; 1:6 [b]Is. 55:2; Jer. [c]Jer. 17:10 [d]Jer. 25:37, 38

14 [a]Jer. 49:1, 7; Z 2:8-10

[b]strike at the inheritance with which I have endowed My people
Israel, "Behold I am about to uproot them from their land and will
[c]uproot the house of Judah from among them.
15 "And it will come about that after I have uprooted them, I will
[a]again have compassion on them; and I will [b]bring them back, each
one to his inheritance and each one to his land.
16 "Then it will come about that if they will really [a]learn the ways of
My people, to [b]swear by My name, 'As the LORD lives,' even as they
taught My people to [c]swear by Baal, then they will be [d]built up in the
midst of My people.
17 "But if they will not listen, then I will [a]uproot that nation, uproot
and destroy it," declares the LORD.

Chapter 13

13 Thus the LORD said to me, "Go and [a]buy yourself a linen
waistband, and put it around your waist, but do not put it in
water."
2 So I bought the waistband in accordance with the [a]word of the
LORD and put it around my waist.
3 Then the word of the LORD came to me a second time, saying,
4 "Take the waistband that you have bought, which is around your
waist, and arise, go to [1]the [a]Euphrates and hide it there in a crevice of
the rock."
5 So I went and hid it by the Euphrates, [a]as the LORD had com-
manded me.
6 And it came about after many days that the LORD said to me,
"Arise, go to the Euphrates and take from there the waistband which
I commanded you to hide there."
7 Then I went to the Euphrates and dug, and I took the waistband
from the place where I had hidden it; and lo, the waistband was
ruined, it was totally worthless.
8 Then the word of the LORD came to me, saying,
9 "Thus says the LORD, 'Just so will I destroy the [a]pride of Judah
and the great pride of Jerusalem.
10 'This wicked people, who [a]refuse to listen to My words, who
[b]walk in the stubbornness of their hearts and have gone after other
gods to serve them and to bow down to them, let them be just like
this waistband, which is totally worthless.
11 'For as the waistband clings to the waist of a man, so I made the
whole household of Israel and the whole household of Judah [a]cling
to Me,' declares the LORD, 'that they might be for Me a people, for
[1b]renown, for [c]praise, and for glory; but they [d]did not listen.'
12 "Therefore you are to speak this word to them, 'Thus says the
LORD, the God of Israel, "Every jug is to be filled with wine."' And
when they say to you, 'Do we not very well know that every jug is to
be filled with wine?'
13 then say to them, 'Thus says the LORD, "Behold I am about to fill
all the inhabitants of this land—the kings that sit for David on his
throne, the priests, the prophets and all the inhabitants of Jerusa-
lem—with [a]drunkenness!
14 "And I will [a]dash them against each other, both the [b]fathers and
the sons together," declares the LORD. "I will [c]not show pity nor be
sorry nor have compassion that I should not destroy them."' "
15 Listen and give heed, do not be [a]haughty,

2:3; 50:11, 12; :8 [c]Deut. 30:3; 47; Is. 11:11-16
48:47; 49:6, 39 [b]Amos 9:14
2:6; 49:6 [b]Jer. eph. 1:5 [c]Josh. 5:7 [d]Jer. 3:17; 4:2; 16:19
:8-12; Is. 60:12
3:1 [a]Jer. 13:11
20:2; Ezek. 2:8
Parah, cf. Josh. , so through v. 7 [a]Jer. 51:63
39:42, 43; 40:16
[a]Lev. 26:19; Is. 10-17; 23:9; Jer. 5-17; Zeph. 3:11
m. 14:11; 2 Chr. 5, 16; Jer. 11:10 9:14; 11:8; 16:12
.it., *a name* [a]Ex. ; Deut. 32:10, 11 32:20 [c]Is. 43:21; 33:9 [d]Ps. 81:11; Jer. 7:13, 24, 26
Ps. 60:3; 75:8; Is. , 63:6; Jer. 25:27; 51:7, 57
[a]Is. 9:20, 21; Jer. 9:9-11 [b]Jer. 6:21; Ezek. 5:10 [c]Deut. 20; Is. 27:11; Jer. 16:5; 21:7
5 [a]Prov. 16:5; Is. 28:14-22

For the LORD has spoken.
16 [a]Give glory to the LORD your God,
Before He brings [b]darkness
And before your [c]feet stumble
On the dusky mountains,
And while you are hoping for light
He makes it into [d]deep darkness,
And turns *it* into gloom.
17 But [a]if you will not listen to it,
My soul will [b]sob in secret for *such* pride;
And my eyes will bitterly weep
And flow down with tears,
Because the [c]flock of the LORD has been taken captive.
18 Say to the [a]king and the queen mother,
"[b]Take a lowly seat,
For your beautiful [c]crown
Has come down from your head."
19 The [a]cities of the Negev have been locked up,
And there is no one to open *them*;
All [b]Judah has been carried into exile,
Wholly carried into exile.

20 "Lift up your eyes and see
Those coming [a]from the north.
Where is the [b]flock that was given you,
Your beautiful sheep?
21 "What will you say when He appoints over you—
And you yourself had taught them—
Former [1a]companions to be head over you?
Will not [b]pangs take hold of you,
Like a woman in childbirth?
22 "And if you [a]say in your heart,
'[b]Why have these things happened to me?'
Because of the [c]magnitude of your iniquity
[d]Your skirts have been removed,
And your heels have [1]been exposed.
23 "[a]Can the Ethiopian change his skin
Or the leopard his spots?
Then you also can [b]do good
Who are accustomed to doing evil.
24 "Therefore I will [a]scatter them like drifting straw
To the desert [b]wind.
25 "This is your [a]lot, the portion measured to you
From Me," declares the LORD,
"Because you have [b]forgotten Me
And trusted in falsehood.
26 "So I Myself have also [a]stripped your skirts off over your face,
That your shame may be seen.
27 "As for your [a]adulteries and your *lustful* neighings,
The [b]lewdness of your prostitution
On the [c]hills in the field,
I have seen your abominations.
Woe to you, O Jerusalem!
[d]How long will you remain unclean?"

16 [a]Josh. 7:19 96:8 [b]Is. 5:30; 59:9; Amos 5:1 [c]Prov. 4:19; Jer [d]Ps. 44:19; 107 Jer. 2:6

17 [a]Mal. 2:2 [b] 119:136; Jer. 9: Luke 19:41, 42 80:1; Jer. 23:1,

18 [a]2 Kin. 24:1 Jer. 22:26 [b]2 C 33:12, 19 [c]Ex. 3:20; Ezek. 24: 44:18

19 [a]Jer. 32:44 20:4; 52:27-30

20 [a]Jer. 1:15; 6 Hab. 1:6 [b]Jer. 1 23:2

21 [1]Or, *chieftai* 2:25; 38:22 [b]Is. Jer. 4:31

22 [1]Or, *sufferec violence* [a]Deut. [b]Jer. 5:19; 16:10 2:17-19; 9:2-9 [d] Ezek. 16:37; Na

23 [a]Prov. 27:22; [b]Jer. 4:22; 9:5

24 [a]Lev. 26:33; 9:16; Ezek. 5:2, 1 4:11; 18:17

25 [a]Job 20:29; P Matt. 24:51 [b]Ps. Jer. 2:32; 3:21

26 [a]Lam. 1:8; Ez 23:29; Hos. 2:10

27 [a]Jer. 5:7, 8 [b]J 11:15 [c]Is. 65:7; J 2:20; Ezek. 6:13 1:22; Hos. 8:5

Chapter 14

14 That which came as the word of the LORD to Jeremiah in regard to the [a]drought:
2 "Judah mourns,
And [a]her gates languish;
They sit on the ground [b]in mourning,
And the [c]cry of Jerusalem has ascended.
3 "And their nobles have [a]sent their [1]servants for water;
They have come to the [b]cisterns and found no water.
They have returned with their vessels empty;
They have been [c]put to shame and humiliated,
And they [d]cover their heads.
4 "Because the [a]ground is [1]cracked,
For there has been [b]no rain on the land;
The [c]farmers have been put to shame,
They have covered their heads.
5 "For even the doe in the field has given birth only to abandon *her young*,
Because there is [a]no grass.
6 "And the [a]wild donkeys stand on the bare heights;
They pant for air like jackals,
Their eyes fail
For there is [b]no vegetation.
7 "Although our [a]iniquities testify against us,
O LORD, act [b]for Thy name's sake!
Truly our [c]apostasies have been many,
We have [d]sinned against Thee.
8 "Thou [a]Hope of Israel,
Its [b]Savior in [c]time of distress,
Why art Thou like a stranger in the land
Or like a traveler who has pitched his *tent* for the night?
9 "Why art Thou like a man dismayed,
Like a mighty man who [a]cannot save?
Yet [b]Thou art in our midst, O LORD,
And we are [c]called by Thy name;
Do not forsake us!"
10 Thus says the LORD to this people, "Even so they have [a]loved to
wander; they have not [b]kept their feet in check. Therefore the LORD
does [c]not accept them; now He will [d]remember their iniquity and call
their sins to account."
11 So the LORD said to me, "[a]Do not pray for the welfare of this
people.
12 "When they fast, I am [a]not going to listen to their cry; and when
they offer [b]burnt offering and grain offering, I am not going to accept
them. Rather I am going to [c]make an end of them by the [d]sword,
famine and pestilence."
13 But, "Ah, Lord [1]GOD!" I said, "Look, the prophets are telling
them, 'You [a]will not see the sword nor will you have famine, but I
will give you [2]lasting [b]peace in this place.' "
14 Then the LORD said to me, "The [a]prophets are prophesying false-
hood in My name. [b]I have neither sent them nor commanded them
nor spoken to them; they are prophesying to you a [c]false vision,
divination, futility and the deception of their own [1]minds.
15 "Therefore thus says the LORD concerning the prophets who are

14:1 [a]Jer. 17:8
[a]Is. 3:26 [b]Jer. 8:21
am. 5:12; Jer. 11:11;
46:12; Zech. 7:13
3 [1]Lit., *little ones*
[a]1 Kin. 18:5 [b]2 Kin.
8:31; Jer. 2:13 [c]Job
; Ps. 40:14 [d]2 Sam.
15:30
Lit., *shattered* [a]Joel
, 20 [b]Jer. 3:3 [c]Joel
1:11
5 [a]Is. 15:6
6 [a]Job 39:5, 6; Jer.
2:24 [b]Joel 1:18
[a]Is. 59:12; Hos. 5:5
's. 25:11; Jer. 14:21
5:6; 8:5 [d]Jer. 3:25;
8:14; 14:20
er. 17:13 [b]Is. 43:3;
3:8 [c]Ps. 9:9; 50:15
um. 11:23; Is. 50:2;
9:1 [b]Ex. 29:45; Ps.
46:5; Jer. 8:19 [c]Is.
63:19; Jer. 15:16
'er. 2:25; 3:13 [b]Ps.
119:101 [c]Jer. 6:20;
Amos 5:22 [d]Jer.
-23; Hos. 8:13; 9:9
x. 32:10; Jer. 7:16;
11:14
Prov. 1:28; Is. 1:15;
11:11; Ezek. 8:18;
lic. 3:4; Zech. 7:13
er. 6:20; 7:21 [c]Jer.
8:13 [d]Jer. 21:9
13 [1]Heb., *YHWH*,
ally rendered *LORD*
[2]Lit., *peace of truth*
. 5:12; 23:17 [b]Jer.
6:14; 8:11
[1]Lit., *hearts* [a]Jer.
23:25 [b]Jer. 23:21
3:16, 26; 27:9, 10;
Ezek. 12:24

prophesying in My name, although it was not I who sent them—yet
they keep saying, 'There shall be no sword or famine in this land'—
[a]by sword and famine those prophets shall [1]meet their end!
16 "The people also to whom they are prophesying will be [a]thrown
out into the streets of Jerusalem because of the famine and the
sword; and there will be no one to [b]bury them—*neither* them, *nor*
their wives, nor their sons, nor their daughters—for I shall [c]pour out
their *own* wickedness on them.
17 "And you will say this word to them,
'[a]Let my eyes flow down with tears night and day,
And let them not cease;
For the virgin [b]daughter of my people has been crushed with a mighty blow,
With a sorely [c]infected wound.
18 'If I [a]go out to the country,
Behold, those [1]slain with the sword!
Or if I enter the city,
Behold, diseases of famine!
For [b]both prophet and priest
Have [2]gone roving about in the land that they do not know.' "

19 Hast Thou completely [a]rejected Judah?
Or hast [1]Thou loathed Zion?
Why hast Thou stricken us so that we [b]are beyond healing?
We [c]waited for peace, but nothing good *came;*
And for a time of healing, but behold, terror!
20 We [a]know our wickedness, O LORD,
The iniquity of our fathers, for [b]we have sinned against Thee.
21 Do not despise *us,* [a]for Thine own name's sake;
Do not disgrace the [b]throne of Thy glory;
Remember *and* do not annul Thy covenant with us.
22 Are there any among the [1a]idols of the nations who [b]give rain?
Or can the heavens grant showers?
Is it not Thou, O LORD our God?
Therefore we [2c]hope in Thee,
For Thou art the one who hast done all these things.

Chapter 15

15 Then the LORD said to me, "Even [a]though [b]Moses and [c]Samuel
were to [d]stand before Me, My [1]heart would not be [2]with this
people; [e]send them away from My presence and let them go!
2 "And it shall be that when they say to you, 'Where should we
go?' then you are to tell them, 'Thus says the LORD:
"Those *destined* [a]for death, to death;
And those *destined* for the sword, to the sword;
And those *destined* for famine, to famine;
And those *destined* for captivity, to captivity." '
3 "And I shall [a]appoint over them four kinds *of doom,*" declares the
LORD: "the sword to slay, the [b]dogs to drag off, and the [c]birds of the
sky and the beasts of the earth to devour and destroy.
4 "And I shall [a]make them an object of horror among all the
kingdoms of the earth because of [b]Manasseh, the son of Hezekiah,
the king of Judah, for what he did in Jerusalem.
5 "Indeed, who will have [a]pity on you, O Jerusalem,

Read 2 Chronicles 33:1-13 to see what Manasseh did.

15 [1]Lit., *be finished* [a]Jer. 23:15; Ezek. 14

16 [a]Ps. 79:2, 3; Jer. 7:33; 15:2, 3 [b]Jer. 8 2 [c]Prov. 1:31; Jer. 13:22-25

17 [a]Jer. 9:1; 13:17; Lam. 1:16 [b]Is. 37:22 Jer. 8:21; Lam. 1:15 2:13 [c]Jer. 10:19; 30

18 [1]Lit., *pierced* [2]O *gone around trading* [a]Jer. 6:25; Lam. 1:2 Ezek. 7:15 [b]Jer. 6:1 8:10

19 [1]Lit., *Thy soul* [a] 6:30; 7:29; 12:7; La 5:22 [b]Jer. 30:13 [c]J 30:26; Jer. 8:15; 1 Thess. 5:3

20 [a]Neh. 9:2; Ps. 3 Jer. 3:25 [b]Jer. 8:14 14:7; Dan. 9:8

21 [a]Ps. 25:11; Jer. [b]Jer. 3:17; 17:12

22 [1]Lit., *vanities* [2](*wait for* [a]Is. 41:29; 10:3 [b]1 Kin. 17:1; 5:24 [c]Lam. 3:26

15:1 [1]Lit., *soul* [2]Li *toward* [a]Ps. 99:6; 14:14, 20 [b]Ex. 32:11-14; Num. 14:13-20; Ps. 99:6; 106:23 [c]1 Sam. 7: 12:23 [d]Jer. 15:19; 18:20; 35:19 [e]2 Ki 17:20; Jer. 7:15; 1(52:3

2 [a]Jer. 14:12; 24:1 43:11; Ezek. 5:2, 1 Zech. 11:9; Rev. 1:

3 [a]Lev. 26:16, 22, Ezek. 14:21 [b]1 Kir 21:23, 24 [c]Deut. 2 Is. 18:6; Jer. 7:33

4 [a]Lev. 26:33; Jer. 29:18; Ezek. 23:46 [b]2 Kin. 21:1-18; 23 27; 24:3, 4; 2 Chr.

5 [a]Ps. 69:20; Is. 5 Jer. 13:14; 21:7

Or who will [b]mourn for you,
Or who will turn aside to ask about your welfare?
6 "You who have [a]forsaken Me," declares the LORD,
"You keep [b]going backward.
So I will [c]stretch out My hand against you and destroy you;
I am [d]tired of relenting!
7 "And I will [a]winnow them with a winnowing fork
At the gates of the land;
I will [b]bereave *them* of children, I will destroy My people;
[c]They did not [1]repent of their ways.
8 "Their [a]widows will be more numerous before Me
Than the sand of the seas;
I will bring against them, against the mother of a young man,
A [b]destroyer at noonday;
I will suddenly bring down on her
Anguish and dismay.
9 "She who [a]bore seven *sons* pines away;
[1]Her breathing is labored.
Her [b]sun has set while it was yet day;
She has been [c]shamed and humiliated.
So I shall [d]give over their survivors to the sword
Before their enemies," declares the LORD.

10 [a]Woe to me, my mother, that you have borne me
As a [b]man of strife and a man of contention to all the land!
I have neither [c]lent, nor have men lent money to me,
Yet everyone curses me.
11 The LORD said, "Surely I will [a]set you free for *purposes of* good;
Surely I will cause the [b]enemy to make supplication to you
In a time of disaster and a time of distress.

12 "Can anyone smash iron,
[a]Iron from the north, or bronze?
13 "Your [a]wealth and your treasures
I will give for booty [b]without cost,
Even for all your sins
And within all your borders.
14 "Then I will cause your enemies to bring [1]*it*
Into a [a]land you do not know;
For a [b]fire has been kindled in My anger,
It will burn upon you."

15 [a]Thou who knowest, O LORD,
Remember me, take notice of me,
And [b]take vengeance for me on my persecutors.
Do *not*, in view of Thy patience, take me away;
Know that [c]for Thy sake I endure reproach.
16 Thy words were found and I [a]ate them,
And Thy [b]words became for me a joy and the delight of my heart;
For I have been [c]called by Thy name,
O LORD God of hosts.
17 I [a]did not sit in the circle of merrymakers,
Nor did I exult.

---

5 [b]Nah. 3:7
r. 6:19; 8:9 [b]Is. 7:24 [c]Jer. 6:12; 1:4 [d]Jer. 6:11; 7:16
turn back from ; Jer. 51:2 [b]Jer. os. 9:12-16 [c]Is. 9:13
Is. 3:25, 26; 4:1 [b]Jer. 22:7
9 [1]Or, *She has* *hed out her soul* am. 2:5; Is. 47:9 r. 6:4; Amos 8:9 50:12 [d]Jer. 21:7
[a]Job 3:1, 3; Jer. 4 [b]Jer. 1:18, 19; 20; 20:7, 8 [c]Ex. ; Lev. 25:36, 37; Deut. 23:19
138:3; Is. 41:10 1:2; 37:3; 38:14; 42:2
12 [a]Jer. 28:14
. 17:3; 20:5 [b]Ps. 44:12; Is. 52:3
14 [1]I. e., your ssessions [a]Deut. 36, 64; Jer. 16:13 . 32:22; Ps. 21:9; Jer. 17:4
5 [a]Jer. 12:3 [b]Jer. 1:20 [c]Ps. 44:22; 69:7-9; Jer. 20:8
[a]Ezek. 3:3 [b]Job Ps. 119:103 [c]Jer. 14:9
Ps. 1:1; Jer. 16:8; 2 Cor. 6:17

Because of Thy hand *upon me* I sat [b]alone,
For Thou didst [c]fill me with indignation.
18 Why has my pain been perpetual
And my [a]wound incurable, refusing to be healed?
Wilt Thou indeed be to me [b]like a deceptive *stream*
With water that is unreliable?

19 Therefore, thus says the LORD,
"[a]If you return, then I will restore you—
[b]Before Me you will stand;
And [c]if you extract the precious from the worthless,
You will become [1]My spokesman.
They for their part may turn to you,
But as for you, you must not turn to them.
20 "Then I will [a]make you to this people
A fortified wall of bronze;
And though they fight against you,
They will not prevail over you;
For [b]I am with you to save you
And deliver you," declares the LORD.
21 "So I will [a]deliver you from the hand of the wicked,
And I will [b]redeem you from the [1]grasp of the violent."

Chapter 16

16 The word of the LORD also came to me saying,
2 "You shall not take a wife for yourself nor have sons or
daughters in this place."
3 For thus says the LORD concerning the sons and daughters born
in this place, and concerning their [a]mothers who bear them, and
their [b]fathers who beget them in this land:
4 "They will [a]die of deadly diseases, they [b]will not be lamented or
buried; they will be as [c]dung on the surface of the ground and come
to an end by sword and famine, and their carcasses will become food
for the [d]birds of the sky and for the beasts of the earth."
5 For thus says the LORD, "Do not enter a house of [1a]mourning, or
go to lament or to console them; for I have [b]withdrawn My peace
from this people," declares the LORD, "*My* [c]lovingkindness and com-
passion.
6 "Both [a]great men and small will die in this land; they will not be
buried, they will not be lamented, nor will anyone [b]gash himself or
[c]shave his head for them.
7 "Neither will men [a]break *bread* in mourning for them, to comfort
anyone for the dead, nor give them a cup of consolation to drink for
anyone's father or mother.
8 "Moreover you shall [a]not go into a house of feasting to sit with
them to eat and drink."
9 For thus says the LORD of hosts, the God of Israel: "Behold, I am
going to [1a]eliminate from this place, before your eyes and in your
time, the voice of rejoicing and the voice of gladness, the voice of the
groom and the voice of the bride.
10 "Now it will come about when you tell this people all these
words that they will say to you, '[a]For what reason has the LORD
declared all this great calamity against us? And what is our iniquity,

17 [b]Ps. 102:7; 13:17; Lam. 3:2 3:24, 25 [c]Jer. 6
18 [a]Job 34:6; J 30:12, 15; Mic. 6:15, 20; Jer. 14
19 [1]Lit., *as My* [a]Jer. 4:1; Zech. [b]1 Kin. 17:1; Jer 35:19 [c]Jer. 6:29 22:26; 44:23
20 [a]Jer. 1:18, 1 3:9 [b]Ps. 46:7; Is Jer. 1:8, 19; 15:1
21 [1]Lit., *palm* [a] 37:40; Is. 49:25; 20:13; 39:11, 12 48:16; Is. 49:26; Jer. 31:11; 50:34
16:3 [a]Jer. 15:8 6:21
4 [a]Jer. 15:2 [b]Je 25:33 [c]Ps. 83:10 9:22; 25:33 [d]Ps. Is. 18:6; Jer. 15:3
5 [1]Or, *banquetin* [a]Ezek. 24:16-23 12:12; 15:1-4 [c]P Is. 27:11; Jer. 13
6 [a]2 Chr. 36:17; 9:6 [b]Deut. 14:1; 41:5; 47:5 [c]Is. 22
7 [a]Deut. 26:14; E 24:17; Hos. 9:4
8 [a]Eccl. 7:2-4; Is. 22:12-14; Jer. 15: Amos 6:4-6
9 [1]Lit., *cause to* [a]Jer. 7:34; 25:10; 26:13; Hos. 2:11; 18:23
10 [a]Deut. 29:24; 9:8; Jer. 5:19; 13:2 22:8

or what is our sin which we have committed against the LORD our
God?'
11 "Then you are to say to them, '*It is* [a]because your forefathers have
forsaken Me,' declares the LORD, 'and have followed [b]other gods and
served them and bowed down to them; but Me they have forsaken
and have not kept My law.
12 'You too have done evil, *even* [a]more than your forefathers; for
behold, you are each one walking according to the [b]stubbornness of
his own [c]evil heart, without listening to Me.
13 'So I will [a]hurl you out of this land into the [b]land which you have
not known, neither you nor your fathers; and there you will [c]serve
other gods day and night, for I shall grant you no favor.'
14 "[a]Therefore behold, days are coming," declares the LORD, "when it
will no longer be said, 'As the LORD lives, who [b]brought up the sons
of Israel out of the land of Egypt,'
15 but, 'As the LORD lives, who brought up the sons of Israel from
the [a]land of the north and from all the countries where He had
banished them.' For I will restore them to their own land which I
gave to their fathers.
16 "Behold, I am going to send for many [a]fishermen," declares the
LORD, "and they will fish for them; and afterwards I shall send for
many hunters, and they will [b]hunt them [c]from every mountain and
every hill, and from the clefts of the rocks.
17 "[a]For My eyes are on all their ways; they are not hidden from My
face, [b]nor is their iniquity concealed from My eyes.
18 "And I will first [a]doubly repay their iniquity and their sin, because they have [b]polluted My land; they have filled My inheritance
with the carcasses of their [c]detestable idols and with their abominations."

19 O LORD, my [a]strength and my stronghold,
And my [b]refuge in the day of distress,
To Thee the [c]nations will come
From the ends of the earth and say,
"Our fathers have inherited nothing but [d]falsehood,
Futility and [1e]things of no profit."
20 Can man make gods for himself?
Yet they are [a]not gods!

21 "Therefore behold, I am going to make them know—
This time I will [a]make them know
My [1]power and My might;
And they shall [b]know that My name is the LORD."

Chapter 17

17 The [a]sin of Judah is written down with an [b]iron stylus;
With a diamond point it is [c]engraved upon the tablet of their heart,
And on the horns of [1]their altars,
2 As they remember their [a]children,
So they *remember* their altars and their [1b]Asherim
By [c]green trees on the high hills.
3 O [a]mountain of Mine in the countryside,
I will [b]give over your wealth and all your treasures for booty,
Your high places for sin throughout your borders.

[a]Deut. 29:25; 1 Kin. 9; 2 Chr. 7:22; Neh. 9:26-29; Jer. 22:9 t. 29:26; 1 Kin. 9:9; Ps. 106:35-41; Jer. 9; 8:2; Ezek. 11:21; 1 Pet. 4:3

[a]Jer. 7:26 [b]1 Sam. 23; Jer. 7:24; 9:14; 10 [c]Eccl. 9:3; Mark 7:21

13 [a]Deut. 4:26, 27; Chr. 7:20; Jer. 15:1 15:14; 17:4 [c]Deut. 28; 28:36; Jer. 5:19

Is. 43:18; Jer. 23:7 . 20:2; Deut. 15:15

15 [a]Ps. 106:47; Is. 11:11-16; 14:1; Jer. 3:18; 23:8; 24:6

[a]Amos 4:2; Hab. 15 [b]1 Sam. 26:20; :2 [c]Is. 2:21; Amos 9:3

[a]2 Chr. 16:9; Job 21; Ps. 90:8; Prov. ; 15:3; Jer. 23:24; ; Zech. 4:10; Luke 2; 1 Cor. 4:5; Heb. 4:13 [b]Jer. 2:22

[a]Jer. 17:18; Rev. [b]Num. 35:33, 34; :7; 3:9 [c]Jer. 7:30; Ezek. 11:18, 21

t., *there is nothing* *able in them* [a]Ps. , 2; Is. 25:4 [b]Nah. Ps. 22:27; Is. 2:2; 17; 4:2 [d]Is. 44:20; b. 2:18 [e]Is. 44:10

[a]Ps. 115:4-8; Is. :19; Jer. 2:11; 5:7; os. 8:4-6; Gal. 4:8

[1]Lit., *hand* [a]Ps. 16 [b]Ps. 83:18; Is. r. 33:2; Amos 5:8

17:1 [1]So ancient rsions; M.T., *your* . 2:22; 4:14 [b]Job Prov. 3:3; 7:3; Is. 49:16; 2 Cor. 3:3

2 [1]I.e., wooden mbols of a female y [a]Jer. 7:18 [b]Ex. :13; 2 Chr. 24:18; Is. 17:8 [c]Jer. 3:6

. 26:18; Mic. 3:12 24:13; Is. 39:4-6; Jer. 15:13; 20:5

4 And you will, even of yourself, [a]let go of your inheritance
That I gave you;
And I will make you serve your [b]enemies
In the [c]land which you do not know;
For you have [d]kindled a fire in My anger
Which will burn forever.

5 Thus says the LORD,
"[a]Cursed is the man who trusts in mankind
And makes [b]flesh his [1]strength,
And whose heart turns away from the LORD.
6 "For he will be like a [a]bush in the desert
And will not see when prosperity comes,
But will live in stony wastes in the wilderness,
A [b]land of salt [1]without inhabitant.
7 "[a]Blessed is the man who trusts in the LORD
And whose [b]trust is the LORD.
8 "For he will be like a [a]tree planted by the water,
That extends its roots by a stream
And will not fear when the heat comes;
But its leaves will be green,
And it will not be anxious in a year of [b]drought
Nor cease to yield fruit.

9 "The [a]heart is more [b]deceitful than all else
And is desperately [c]sick;
Who can understand it?
10 "I, the LORD, [a]search the heart,
I test the [1]mind,
Even [b]to give to each man according to his ways,
According to the [2]results of his deeds.
11 "As a partridge that hatches eggs which it has not laid,
So is he who [a]makes a fortune, but unjustly;
In the midst of his days it will forsake him,
And in [1]the end he will be a [b]fool."

12 [a]A glorious throne on high from the beginning
Is the place of our sanctuary.
13 O LORD, the [a]hope of Israel,
All who [b]forsake Thee will be put to shame.
Those who turn [1]away on earth will be [c]written down,
Because they have forsaken the fountain of living water, even
the LORD.
14 [a]Heal me, O LORD, and I will be healed;
[b]Save me and I will be saved,
For Thou art my [c]praise.
15 Look, they keep [a]saying to me,
"Where is the word of the LORD?
Let it come now!"
16 But as for me, I have not hurried away from *being* a shepherd
after Thee,
Nor have I longed for the woeful day;
[a]Thou Thyself knowest the utterance of my lips
Was in Thy presence.

4 [a]Jer. 12:7; [b]Deut. 28:48; Jer. 15:14; 27 [c]Jer. 16:13 [d]Is Jer. 7:20; 15:1

5 [1]Lit., *arm* [a] Is. 2:22; 30:1; 29:7 [b]2 Chr. 3 31:3

6 [1]Lit., *and is inhabited* [a]Jer [b]Deut. 29:23;

7 [a]Ps. 2:12; 3 84:12; Prov. 16 40:4

8 [a]Ps. 1:3; 92: Ezek. 31:3-9 [b] 14:1-6

9 [a]Eccl. 9:3; M 22 [b]Rom. 7:11 4:22 [c]Is. 1:5, 6 Matt. 13:15; Ma Rom. 1:21

10 [1]Lit., *kidney* *fruit* [a]1 Sam. 1 1 Chr. 28:9; Ps. Prov. 17:3; Jer. 20:12; Rom. 8: 2:23 [b]Ps. 62:12 32:19; Rom. 2:6

11 [1]Lit., *his* [a]Je 8:10; 22:13, 17 12:20

12 [a]Jer. 3:17; 1

13 [1]Lit., *away f* [a]Jer. 14:8; 50:7 1:28 [c]Luke 10:2

14 [a]Jer. 30:17; [b]Ps. 54:1; 60:5 10:21; Ps. 109:1

15 [a]Is. 5:19; 2 P

16 [a]Jer. 12:3

17 Do not be a [a]terror to me;
Thou art my [b]refuge in the day of disaster.
18 Let those who persecute me be [a]put to shame, but as for me, [b]let
me not be put to shame;
Let them be dismayed, but let me not be dismayed.
[c]Bring on them a day of disaster,
And crush them with twofold destruction!
19 Thus the LORD said to me, "Go and stand in the [1]public gate,
through which the kings of Judah come in and go out, as well as in
all the gates of Jerusalem;
20 and say to them, '[a]Listen to the word of the LORD, [b]kings of
Judah, and all Judah, and all inhabitants of Jerusalem, who come in
through these gates:
21 'Thus says the LORD, "[a]Take heed for yourselves, and [b]do not
carry any load on the sabbath day or bring anything in through the
gates of Jerusalem.
22 "And you shall not bring a load out of your houses on the sab-
bath day [a]nor do any work, but keep the sabbath day holy, as I
[b]commanded your [1]forefathers.
23 "Yet they [a]did not listen or incline their ears, but [b]stiffened their
necks in order not to listen or take correction.
24 "But it will come about, if you [a]listen attentively to Me," declares
the LORD, "to [b]bring no load in through the gates of this city on the
sabbath day, [c]but to keep the sabbath day holy by doing no work
on it,
25 [a]then there will come in through the gates of this city kings and
princes [b]sitting on the throne of David, riding in chariots and on
horses, they and their princes, the men of Judah, and the inhabitants
of Jerusalem; and this [c]city will be inhabited forever.
26 "They will come in from the [a]cities of Judah and from the en-
virons of Jerusalem, from the land of Benjamin, from the [b]lowland,
from the hill country, and from the [c]Negev, bringing burnt offerings,
sacrifices, grain offerings and incense, and bringing sacrifices of
thanksgiving to the house of the LORD.
27 "But [a]if you do not listen to Me to keep the sabbath day holy by
not carrying a load and coming in through the gates of Jerusalem on
the sabbath day, then [b]I shall kindle a fire in its gates, and it will
[c]devour the palaces of Jerusalem and [d]not be quenched." ' "

Chapter 18

18 The word which came to Jeremiah from the LORD saying,
2 "Arise and [a]go down to the potter's house, and there I shall
announce My words to you."
3 Then I went down to the potter's house, and there he was,
making something on the [1]wheel.
4 But the vessel that he was making of clay was spoiled in the
hand of the potter; so he remade it into another vessel, as it pleased
the potter to make.
5 Then the word of the LORD came to me saying,
6 "Can I not, O house of Israel, deal with you as this potter *does?*"
declares the LORD. "Behold, like the [a]clay in the potter's hand, so are
you in My hand, O house of Israel.
7 "At one moment I might speak concerning a nation or concerning
a kingdom to [a]uproot, to pull down, or to destroy *it;*

[a]Ps. 88:15 [b]Jer. 16:19; Nah. 1:7

[a]Ps. 35:4, 26; Jer. 20:11 [b]Jer. 1:17 [c]Ps. 35:8

[1]Lit., *gate of the sons of the people*

[a]Ezek. 2:7 [b]Ps. 1, 2; Jer. 19:3, 4

[a]Deut. 4:9, 15, 23; Mark 4:24 [b]Num. 15:32-36; Neh. -21; John 5:9-12

[1]Lit., *fathers* [a]Ex. 20:8-10; Deut. 2-14; Is. 56:2-6; [b]Ex. 31:13-17; 20:12; Zech. 1:4

r. 7:24, 28; 11:10 29:1; Jer. 7:26; 19:15

[a]Ex. 15:26; Deut. 13; Is. 21:7; 55:2 r. 17:21, 22 [c]Ex. -11; Ezek. 20:20

er. 22:4 [b]2 Sam. s. 9:7; Jer. 33:15, ; Luke 1:32 [c]Ps. 3, 14; Heb. 12:22

[a]Jer. 32:44; 33:13 7:7 [c]Ps. 107:22; Jer. 33:11

s. 1:20; Jer. 22:5; 4; Zech. 7:11-14 4:11 [c]2 Kin. 25:9; r. 39:8; Amos 2:5 7:20; Ezek. 20:47

18:2 [a]Jer. 19:1, 2

[1]Lit., *pair of stone discs*

. 45:9; 64:8; Matt. 20:15; Rom. 9:21

7 [a]Jer. 1:10

8 [a]if that nation against which I have spoken turns from its evil, I
will [1b]relent concerning the calamity I planned to bring on it.
9 "Or at another moment I might speak concerning a nation or
concerning a kingdom to [a]build up or to plant *it;*
10 if it does [a]evil in My sight by not obeying My voice, then I will
[1b]think better of the good with which I had promised to [2]bless it.
11 "So now then, speak to the men of Judah and against the in-
habitants of Jerusalem saying, 'Thus says the LORD, "Behold, I am
[a]fashioning calamity against you and devising a plan against you.
Oh [b]turn back, each of you from his evil way, and [1]reform your ways
and your deeds." '
12 "But [a]they will say, 'It's hopeless! For we are going to follow our
own plans, and each of us will act according to the [b]stubbornness of
his evil heart.'

13 "Therefore thus says the LORD,
'[a]Ask now among the nations,
Who ever heard the like of [1]this?
The [b]virgin of Israel
Has done a most [c]appalling thing.
14 'Does the snow of Lebanon forsake the rock of the open country?
Or is the cold flowing water *from* a foreign *land* ever snatched
away?
15 'For [a]My people have forgotten Me,
[b]They burn incense [1]to worthless gods
And they [2]have stumbled [3]from their ways,
[3]From the [c]ancient paths,
To walk in bypaths,
Not on a [d]highway,
16 To make their land a [a]desolation,
An object of perpetual [b]hissing;
Everyone who passes by it will be astonished
And [c]shake his head.
17 'Like an [a]east wind I will [b]scatter them
Before the enemy;
I will [1]show them [c]My back and not *My* face
[d]In the day of their calamity.' "

18 Then they said, "Come and let us [a]devise plans against Jeremiah.
Surely the [b]law is not going to be lost to the priest, nor [c]counsel to the
sage, nor the *divine* [d]word to the prophet! Come on and let us [e]strike
at him with *our* tongue, and let us [f]give no heed to any of his words."

19 Do give heed to me, O LORD,
And listen to [1]what my opponents are saying!
20 [a]Should good be repaid with evil?
For they have [b]dug a pit for [1]me.
Remember how I [c]stood before Thee
To speak good on their behalf,
So as to turn away Thy wrath from them.
21 Therefore, [a]give their children over to famine,
And deliver them up to the [1]power of the sword;
And let their wives become [b]childless and [c]widowed.
Let their men also be smitten to death,
Their [d]young men struck down by the sword in battle.
22 May an [a]outcry be heard from their houses,
When Thou suddenly bringest raiders upon them;

8 [1]Lit., *repent o* 7:3-7; 12:16; Ez 18:21 [b]Ps. 106: 26:3, 13, 19; Ho Joel 2:13, 14; Jo

9 [a]Jer. 1:10; 31 Amos 9:11-15

10 [1]Lit., *repent it good* [a]Ps. 125 7:24-28; Ezek. 3 [b]1 Sam. 2:30; 13

11 [1]Lit., *make g* 5:5; Jer. 4:6; 11: [b]2 Kin. 17:13; Is. 1:16-19; Jer. 4:1 26:20

12 [a]Is. 57:10; Je [b]Deut. 29:19; Jer 16:12

13 [1]Lit., *these* [a] Jer. 2:10, 11 [b]Je 14:17; 31:4 [c]Jer 23:14; Hos. 6:10

15 [1]Lit., *to worthlessness* [2] ancient versions *caused them to* [a]Jer. 2:32; 3:21 65:7; Jer. 7:9; 10 44:17 [c]Jer. 6:16 57:14; 62:10

16 [a]Jer. 25:9; 49 50:13; Ezek. 33: [b]1 Kin. 9:8; Lam. Mic. 6:16 [c]Ps. 2 37:22; Jer. 48:27

17 [1]So ancient versions; M.T. re *look them in the and not in the fac* 48:7 [b]Job 27:21; 13:24 [c]Jer. 2:27; [d]Jer. 46:21

18 [a]Jer. 11:19; 1 [b]Jer. 2:8; Mal. 2:7 5:13; Jer. 8:8 [d]Je [e]Ps. 52:2; Jer. 20 [f]Jer. 43:2

19 [1]Lit., *the voic opponents*

20 [1]Lit., *my soul* 109:4 [b]Ps. 35:7; Jer. 5:26; 18:22 106:23

21 [1]Lit., *hands o* 109:9-20; Jer. 11: 14:16 [b]1 Sam. 15 Is. 13:18 [c]Jer. 15 Ezek. 22:25 [d]Jer. 11:22

22 [a]Jer. 6:26; 25:

[b]For they have dug a pit to capture me
And [c]hidden snares for my feet.
23 Yet Thou, O LORD, knowest
All their [1]deadly designs against me;
[a]Do not [2]forgive their iniquity
Or blot out their sin from Thy sight.
But may they be [3b]overthrown before Thee;
Deal with them in the [c]time of Thine anger!

Chapter 19

19 Thus says the LORD, "Go and buy a [a]potter's earthenware [b]jar, and *take* some of the [c]elders of the people and some of the [1d]senior priests.

2 "Then go out to the [a]valley of Ben-hinnom, which is by the entrance of the potsherd gate; and [b]proclaim there the words that I shall tell you,

3 and say, 'Hear the word of the LORD, O [a]kings of Judah and inhabitants of Jerusalem: thus says the LORD of hosts, the God of Israel, "Behold I am about to bring a [b]calamity upon this place, at which the [c]ears of everyone that hears of it will tingle.

4 "Because they have [a]forsaken Me and have [b]made this an alien place and have burned [1]sacrifices in it to [c]other gods that neither they nor their forefathers nor the kings of Judah had *ever* known, and *because* they have filled this place with the [d]blood of the innocent

5 and have built the [a]high places of Baal to burn their [b]sons in the fire as burnt offerings to Baal, a thing which I never commanded or spoke of, nor did it *ever* enter My [1]mind;

6 therefore, behold, [a]days are coming," declares the LORD, "when this place will no longer be called [b]Topheth or [c]the valley of Ben-hinnom, but rather the valley of Slaughter.

7 "And I shall [a]make void the counsel of Judah and Jerusalem in this place, and [b]I shall cause them to fall by the sword before their enemies and by the hand of those who seek their life; and I shall give over their [c]carcasses as food for the birds of the sky and the beasts of the earth.

8 "I shall also make this city a [a]desolation and an *object of* hissing; [b]everyone who passes by it will be astonished and hiss because of all its [1]disasters.

9 "And I shall make them [a]eat the flesh of their sons and the flesh of their daughters, and they will eat one another's flesh in the siege and in the distress with which their enemies and those who seek their life will distress them." '

10 "Then you are to break the [a]jar in the sight of the men who accompany you

11 and say to them, 'Thus says the LORD of hosts, "Just so shall I [a]break this people and this city, even as one breaks a potter's vessel, which cannot again be repaired; and they will [b]bury in Topheth [1]because there is no *other* place for burial.

12 "This is how I shall treat this place and its inhabitants," declares the LORD, "so as to make this city like Topheth.

13 "And the [a]houses of Jerusalem and the houses of the kings of Judah will be [b]defiled like the place Topheth, because of all the [c]houses on whose rooftops they burned [1]sacrifices to [d]all the heavenly host and [e]poured out libations to other gods." ' "

[b]Jer. 18:20 [c]Ps. 140:5
[1]Lit., *unto death* ... *cover over, atone* ... it., *ones made to* ... *le* [a]Neh. 4:5; Ps. ... 9:14; Is. 2:9 [b]Jer. ... [c]Jer. 7:20; 17:4

9:1 [1]Or, *elders of* ... 18:2 [b]Jer. 19:10 ... um. 11:16 [d]2 Kin. 19:2; Ezek. 8:11
Josh. 15:8; 2 Kin. ... :10; Jer. 7:31, 32; 32:35 [b]Prov. 1:20
[a]Jer. 17:20 [b]Jer. 9; 19:15 [c]1 Sam. 3:11
...r, *incense* [a]Deut. ... 20; Is. 65:11; Jer. ... :13, 17, 19; 17:13 ... 7:22; Dan. 11:31 ... 7:9; 11:13 [d]2 Kin. ... 16; Jer. 2:34; 7:6
[1]Lit., *heart* [a]Num. ... ; Jer. 32:35 [b]Lev. ... ; 2 Kin. 17:17; Ps. 106:37, 38
...er. 7:32 [b]Is. 30:33 [c]Josh. 15:8
[a]Ps. 33:10, 11; Is. ... :17, 18; Jer. 8:8, 9 [b]Lev. 26:17; Deut. ... ; Jer. 15:2, 9 [c]Ps. 79:2; Jer. 16:4
[1]Lit., *blows* [a]Jer. ... 8:16; 49:13; 50:13 ... in. 9:8; 2 Chr. 7:21
[a]Lev. 26:29; Deut. ... 55; Is. 9:20; Lam. 4:10; Ezek. 5:10
10 [a]Jer. 19:1
...Or, *until there is no* ... *ce left to bury* [a]Ps. ... s. 30:14; Lam. 4:2; ... ev. 2:27 [b]Jer. 7:32
[1]Or, *incense* [a]Jer. ... [b]2 Kin. 23:10; Ps. ... 7; 79:1; Ezek. 7:21, ... [c]Jer. 32:29; Zeph. ... [d]Deut. 4:19; 2 Kin. ... 7:16; Jer. 8:2 [e]Jer. 44:18; Ezek. 20:28

14 Then Jeremiah came from Topheth, where the LORD had sent him
to prophesy; and he stood in the [a]court of the LORD's house and said
to all the people:
15 "Thus says the LORD of hosts, the God of Israel, 'Behold, I am
about to bring on this city and all its towns the entire calamity that I
have declared against it, because they have [a]stiffened their necks so
[b]as not to heed My words.' "

Chapter 20

20 When Pashhur the priest, the son of [a]Immer, who was [b]chief
officer in the house of the LORD, heard Jeremiah prophesying
these things,
2 Pashhur had Jeremiah the prophet [a]beaten, and put him in the
[b]stocks that were at the upper [c]Benjamin Gate, which was by the
house of the LORD.
3 Then it came about on the next day, when Pashhur released
Jeremiah from the stocks, that Jeremiah said to him, "Pashhur is not
the name the LORD has [a]called you, but rather [1b]Magor-missabib.
4 "For thus says the LORD, 'Behold, I am going to make you a [a]terror
to yourself and to all your friends; and while [b]your eyes look on,
they will fall by the sword of their enemies. So I shall [c] give over all
Judah to the hand of the king of Babylon, and he will carry them
away as [d]exiles to Babylon and will slay them with the sword.
5 'I shall also give over all the [a]wealth of this city, all its produce,
and all its costly things; even all the treasures of the kings of Judah I
shall give over to the [b]hand of their enemies, and they will plunder
them, take them away, and bring them to Babylon.
6 'And you, [a]Pashhur, and all who live in your house will go into
captivity; and you will enter Babylon, and there you will die, and
there you will be buried, you and all your [b]friends to whom you
have [c]falsely prophesied.' "

7 O LORD, Thou hast deceived me and I was deceived;
Thou hast [a]overcome me and prevailed.
I have become a [b]laughingstock all day long;
Everyone [c]mocks me.
8 For each time I speak, I cry aloud;
I [a]proclaim violence and destruction,
Because for me the [b]word of the LORD has [1]resulted
In reproach and derision all day long.
9 But if I say, "I will not [a]remember Him
Or speak anymore in His name,"
Then in [b]my heart it becomes like a burning fire
Shut up in my bones;
And I am weary of holding *it* in,
And [c]I cannot endure *it*.
10 For [a]I have heard the whispering of many,
"[b]Terror on every side!
[c]Denounce *him*; yes, let us denounce him!"
[1]All my [d]trusted friends,
Watching for my fall, say:
"Perhaps he will be [2]deceived, so that we may [e]prevail
against him
And take our revenge on him."
11 But the [a]LORD is with me like a dread champion;

14 [a]2 Chr. 20:5; 26:2

15 [a]Neh. 9:17, 2 7:26; 17:23 [b]Ps.

20:1 [a]1 Chr. 24:1 Ezra 2:37, 38 [b]2 25:18

2 [a]1 Kin. 22:27; 2 16:10; 24:21; Jer. Amos 7:10-13 [b]J 13:27; 33:11 [c]Jer 37:13; 38:7; Zech

3 [1]I.e., terror on e side [a]Is. 8:3; Hos 9 [b]Jer. 6:25; 20:1

4 [a]Job 18:11-21; 6:25; 46:5; Ezek. [b]Jer. 29:21; 39:6, 21:4-10; 25:9 [d]Je 13:10; 52:27

5 [a]Jer. 15:13; 17:3 [b]2 Kin. 20:17, 18; 36:10; Jer. 27:21,

6 [a]Jer. 20:1 [b]Jer. 29:21 [c]Jer. 14:14, Lam. 2:14

7 [a]Ezek. 3:14 [b]Jo 12:4; Lam. 3:14 [c]P 22:7; Jer. 38:19

8 [1]Lit., *become* [a]J 6:7 [b]2 Chr. 36:16; 6:10

9 [a]1 Kin. 19:3, 4; J 1:2, 3 [b]Job 32:18- Ps. 39:3; Jer. 4:19; Ezek. 3:14; Acts 4: [c]Job 32:18-20

10 [1]Lit., *Every man my peace* [2]Or, *persuaded* [a]Ps. 31: [b]Jer. 6:25 [c]Neh. 6:6 Is. 29:21; Jer. 18:18 [d]Ps. 41:9 [e]1 Kin. 19

11 [a]Jer. 1:8; 15:20; Rom. 8:31

Therefore my [b]persecutors will stumble and not prevail.
They will be utterly ashamed, because they have [1]failed,
With an [c]everlasting disgrace that will not be forgotten.
12 Yet, O LORD of hosts, Thou who dost [a]test the righteous,
Who seest the [1]mind and the heart;
Let me [b]see Thy vengeance on them;
For [c]to Thee I have set forth my cause.
13 [a]Sing to the LORD, praise the LORD!
For He has [b]delivered the soul of the needy one
From the hand of evildoers.

14 Cursed be the [a]day when I was born;
Let the day not be blessed when my mother bore me!
15 Cursed be the man who brought the news
To my father, saying,
"A [1a]baby boy has been born to you!"
And made him very happy.
16 But let that man be like the cities
Which the LORD [a]overthrew without [1]relenting,
And let him hear an [b]outcry in the morning
And a [2]shout of alarm at noon;
17 Because he did not [a]kill me [1]before birth,
So that my mother would have been my grave,
And her womb ever pregnant.
18 Why did I ever come forth from the womb
To [a]look on trouble and sorrow,
So that my [b]days have been spent in [c]shame?

Chapter 21

21 The word which came to Jeremiah from the LORD when [a]King
Zedekiah sent to him [b]Pashhur the son of Malchijah, and
[c]Zephaniah the priest, the son of Maaseiah, saying,
2 "Please [a]inquire of the LORD on our behalf, for [b]Nebuchadnezzar
king of [c]Babylon is warring against us; perhaps the LORD will deal
with us [d]according to all His [1]wonderful acts, that *the enemy* may
withdraw from us."
3 Then Jeremiah said to them, "You shall say to Zedekiah as fol-
lows:
4 'Thus says the LORD God of Israel, "Behold, I am about to [a]turn
back the weapons of war which are in your hands, with which you
are warring against the king of Babylon and the Chaldeans who are
besieging you outside the wall; and I shall [b]gather them into the
center of this city.
5 "And I [a]Myself shall war against you with an [b]outstretched hand
and a mighty arm, even in [c]anger and wrath and great indignation.
6 "I shall also strike down the inhabitants of this city, both man and
beast; they will die of a great [a]pestilence.
7 "Then afterwards," declares the LORD, "[a]I shall give over Zede-
kiah king of Judah and his servants and the people, even those who
survive in this city from the pestilence, the sword, and the famine,
into the hand of Nebuchadnezzar king of Babylon, and into the hand
of their foes, and into the hand of those who seek their lives; and he
will strike them down with the edge of the sword. He [b]will not spare
them nor have pity nor compassion." '

not succeeded; ot acted wisely 32:35, 36; Jer. 20; 17:18 [c]Jer. 23:40
., kidneys [a]Ps. ; 17:3; 139:23; 20; 17:10 [b]Ps. :10; Jer. 11:20 [c]Ps. 62:8
31:7 [b]Ps. 34:6; :33; Jer. 15:21
[a]Job 3:3-6; Jer. 15:10
[1]Lit., male child [a]Gen. 21:6, 7
Lit., being sorry pet blast [a]Gen. :25 [b]Jer. 18:22; 48:3, 4
from the womb ob 3:10, 11, 16; 10:18, 19
3:20; 5:7; 14:1; 15:10; Lam. 3:1 0:9; 102:3 [c]Ps. Jer. 3:25; 1 Cor. 4:9-13
2 Kin. 24:17, 18; ler. 32:1-3; 37:1; 1 Chr. 9:12; Jer. 2 Kin. 25:18; Jer. , 29; 37:3; 52:24
r, miracles [a]Ex. 28; Jer. 37:3, 17; zek. 14:7; 20:1-3 Kin. 25:1 [c]Gen. 2 Kin. 17:24 [d]Ps. 4:1-3; Jer. 32:17
[a]Jer. 32:5; 33:5; 0; 38:2, 3, 17, 18 ; 13:4; Jer. 39:3; 2:5, 7; Zech. 14:2
. 63:10 [b]Ex. 6:6; t. 4:34; Jer. 6:12 . 5:25; Jer. 32:37
Jer. 14:12; 32:24
in. 25:5-7, 18-21; :17; 39:5-9; 52:9 2 Chr. 36:17; Jer. ; Ezek. 7:9; Hab. 1:6-10

8 "You shall also say to this people, 'Thus says the LORD, "Behold, I
[a]set before you the way of life and the way of death.
9 "He who [a]dwells in this city will die by the [b]sword and by famine
and by pestilence; but he who goes out and falls away to the Chalde-
ans who are besieging you will live, and he will have his own life as
booty.
10 "For I have [a]set My face against this city for [1]harm and not for
good," declares the LORD. "It will be [b]given into the hand of the king
of Babylon, and he will [c]burn it with fire." '
11 "Then *say* to the household of the [a]king of Judah, 'Hear the word
of the LORD,
12 O [a]house of David, thus says the LORD:
"[b]Administer justice [1]every [c]morning;
And deliver the *person* who has been robbed from the [2]power of
his oppressor,
[d]That My wrath may not go forth like fire
And [e]burn with none to extinguish *it*,
Because of the evil of their deeds.

13 "Behold, [a]I am against you, O [b]valley dweller,
O [1]rocky plain," declares the LORD,
"You men who say, '[c]Who will come down against us?
Or who will enter into our habitations?'
14 "But I shall punish you [a]according to the [1]results of your deeds,"
declares the LORD,
"And I shall [b]kindle a fire in its forest
That it may devour all its environs." ' "

Chapter 22

22 Thus says the LORD, "Go down to the house of the king of
Judah, and there speak this word,
2 and say, 'Hear the word of the LORD, O king of Judah, who [a]sits
on David's throne, you and your servants and your people who
enter these gates.
3 'Thus says the LORD, "[a]Do justice and righteousness, and deliver
the one who has been robbed from the power of *his* [b]oppressor. Also
[c]do not mistreat *or* do violence to the stranger, the orphan, or the
widow; and do not [d]shed innocent blood in this place.
4 "For if you men will indeed perform this thing, then [a]kings will
enter the gates of this house, sitting [1]in David's place on his throne,
riding in chariots and on horses, *even the king* himself and his ser-
vants and his people.
5 "[a]But if you will not obey these words, I [b]swear by Myself,"
declares the LORD, "that this house will become a desolation." ' "
6 For thus says the LORD concerning the house of the king of
Judah:
"You are *like* [a]Gilead to Me,
Like the summit of Lebanon;
Yet most assuredly I shall make you like a [b]wilderness,
Like cities which are not inhabited.
7 "For I shall set apart [a]destroyers against you,
Each with his weapons;
And they will [b]cut down your choicest cedars
And [c]throw *them* on the fire.

8 [a]Deut. 30:1… 1:19, 20

9 [a]Jer. 38:2, … 39:18; 45:5 [b]J… 24:10

10 [1]Lit., *evil* [a]… 17:10; Jer. 44:… Amos 9:4 [b]Je… 29; 38:3 [c]2 Ch… Jer. 34:2; 37:1… 39:8; 52:13

11 [a]Jer. 17:20

12 [1]Or, *in the hand* [a]Is. 7:2, … 72:1; Is. 1:17; J… 22:3; Zech. 7:9… 101:8; Zeph. 3:… 4:4; 17:4; Ezek… 48; Nah. 1:6 [e]Is… Jer. 7:20

13 [1]Lit., *rock of level place* [a]Je… 23:30-32; Ezek… [b]Ps. 125:2; Is. 2… [c]2 Sam. 5:6, 7; … 49:4; Lam. 4:12… 3, 4

14 [1]Lit., *fruit* [a]Is… 11; Jer. 17:10; 3… [b]2 Chr. 36:19; Is… 18; Jer. 11:16; 1… 52:13; Ezek. 20…

22:2 [a]Is. 9:7; Je… 22:4, 30; Luke 1…

3 [a]Is. 58:6, 7; Je… 23; 21:12; Mic. 6… Zech. 7:9; 8:16; … 23:23 [b]Ps. 72:4… 22:21-24 [c]Jer. 7… 19:4; 22:17

4 [1]Lit., *for David*… 17:25

5 [a]Jer. 17:27; 26… [b]Gen. 22:16; Amo… Heb. 6:13

6 [a]Gen. 37:25; N… 32:1; Song 4:1 [b]P… 107:34; Is. 6:11; J… 7:34; Mic. 3:12

7 [a]Is. 10:3-6; Jer. … [b]Is. 10:33, 34; 37:… [c]Jer. 21:14

8 "And many nations will pass by this city; and they will [a]say to
one another, 'Why has the LORD done thus to this great city?'
9 "Then they will [1]answer, 'Because they [a]forsook the covenant of
the LORD their God and bowed down to other gods and served
them.' "
10 [a]Do not weep for the dead or mourn for him,
But weep continually for the one who goes away;
For [b]he will never return
Or see his native land.
11 For thus says the LORD in regard to [1a]Shallum the son of Josiah,
king of Judah, who became king in the place of Josiah his father, who
went forth from this place, "He will never return there;
12 but in the place where they led him captive, there he will [a]die
and not see this land again.
13 "Woe to him who builds his house [a]without righteousness
And his [1]upper rooms without justice,
Who uses his neighbor's services without pay
And [b]does not give him his wages,
14 Who says, 'I will [a]build myself a roomy house
With spacious [1]upper rooms,
And cut out its windows,
[2]Paneling *it* with [b]cedar and painting *it* [3]bright red.'
15 "Do you become a king because you are competing in cedar?
Did not your father eat and drink,
And [a]do justice and righteousness?
Then it was [b]well with him.
16 "He pled the cause of the [a]afflicted and needy;
Then it was well.
[b]Is not that what it means to know Me?"
Declares the LORD.
17 "But your eyes and your heart
Are *intent* only upon your own [a]dishonest gain,
And on [b]shedding innocent blood
And on practicing oppression and extortion."
18 Therefore thus says the LORD in regard to [a]Jehoiakim the son of
Josiah, king of Judah,
"They will not [b]lament for him:
'[c]Alas, my brother!' or, 'Alas, sister!'
They will not lament for him:
'Alas for the master!' or, 'Alas for his splendor!'
19 "He will be [a]buried with a donkey's burial,
Dragged off and thrown out beyond the gates of Jerusalem.
20 "Go up to Lebanon and cry out,
And lift up your voice in Bashan;
Cry out also from [a]Abarim,
For all your [b]lovers have been crushed.
21 "I spoke to you in your prosperity;
But [a]you said, 'I will not listen!'
[b]This has been your practice [c]from your youth,
That you have not obeyed My voice.
22 "The wind will sweep away all your [a]shepherds,
And your [b]lovers will go into captivity;
Then you will surely be [c]ashamed and humiliated
Because of all your wickedness.

8 [a]Deut. 29:24-26; 1 Kin. 9:8, 9; 2 Chr. 7:20-22; Jer. 16:10
9 [1]Lit., *say* [a]2 Kin. ...7; 2 Chr. 34:25; Jer. 11:3
[a]Eccl. 4:2; Is. 57:1; ...r. 16:7; 22:18 [b]Jer. 25:27; 44:14
11 [1]I.e., Jehoahaz ...n. 23:30-34; 1 Chr. 3:15; 2 Chr. 36:1-4
[a]2 Kin. 23:34; Jer. 22:18
[1]Or, *roof chambers* ...r. 17:11; Mic. 3:10; ...b. 2:9 [b]Lev. 19:13; James 5:4
[1]Or, *roof chambers* [2]Or, *Paneled* [3]Or, *vermilion* [a]Is. 5:8 ...Sam. 7:2; Hag. 1:4
[a]2 Kin. 23:25; Jer. 21:12 [b]Ps. 128:2; Is. 3:10; Jer. 42:6
[a]Ps. 72:1-4, 12, 13 ...hr. 28:9; Jer. 9:24
7 [a]Jer. 6:13; 8:10; ...e 12:15-20 [b]2 Kin. 24:4; Jer. 22:3
[a]2 Kin. 23:36-24:6; 36:5 [b]Jer. 22:10; 34:5 [c]1 Kin. 13:30
[a]1 Kin. 21:23, 24; Jer. 36:30
...Num. 27:12; Deut. 49 [b]Jer. 2:25; 3:1
[a]Jer. 13:10; 19:15 ...r. 3:25 [c]Jer. 3:24; 32:30
2 [a]Jer. 23:1 [b]Jer. 14 [c]Is. 65:13; Jer. 20:11

23 "You who dwell in Lebanon,
Nested in the cedars,
How you will groan when pangs come upon you,
[a]Pain like a woman in childbirth!
24 "As I live," declares the LORD, "even though [1a]Coniah the son of
Jehoiakim king of Judah were a [b]signet *ring* on My right hand, yet I
would pull [1]you [2]off;
25 and I shall [a]give you over into the hand of those who are seeking
your life, yes, into the hand of those whom you dread, even into the
hand of Nebuchadnezzar king of Babylon, and into the hand of the
Chaldeans.
26 "I shall [a]hurl you and your [b]mother who bore you into another
country where you were not born, and there you will die.
27 "But as for the land to which they desire to return, they will not
return to it.
28 "Is this man Coniah a despised, shattered jar?
Or is he an [a]undesirable vessel?
Why have he and his descendants been [b]hurled out
And cast into a [c]land that they had not known?
29 "[a]O land, land, land,
Hear the word of the LORD!
30 "Thus says the LORD,
'Write this man down [a]childless,
A man who will [b]not prosper in his days;
For no man of his [c]descendants will prosper
Sitting on the throne of David
Or ruling again in Judah.' "

Chapter 23

23 "[a]Woe to the shepherds who are [b]destroying and scattering
the [c]sheep of My pasture!" declares the LORD.
2 Therefore thus says the LORD God of Israel concerning the shep-
herds who are [1]tending My people: "You have scattered My flock
and driven them away, and have not attended to them; behold, I am
about to [a]attend to you for the [b]evil of your deeds," declares the
LORD.
3 "Then I Myself shall [a]gather the remnant of My flock out of all the
countries where I have driven them and shall bring them back to
their pasture; and they will be fruitful and multiply.
4 "I shall also raise up [a]shepherds over them and they will [1]tend
them; and they will [b]not be afraid any longer, nor be terrified, [c]nor
will any be missing," declares the LORD.
5 "Behold, *the* [a]days are coming," declares the LORD,
"When I shall raise up for David a righteous [1b]Branch;
And He will [c]reign as king and [2]act wisely
And [d]do justice and righteousness in the land.
6 "In His days Judah will be saved,
And [a]Israel will dwell securely;
And this is His [b]name by which He will be called,
'The [c]LORD our righteousness.'
7 "[a]Therefore behold, *the* days are coming," declares the LORD,
"when they will no longer say, 'As the LORD lives, who brought up
the sons of Israel from the land of Egypt,'
8 [a]but, 'As the LORD lives, who [b]brought up and led back the

23 [a]Jer. 4:31; 6:24

24 [1]I.e., Jehoiach [2]Lit., *off from there* [a]2 Kin. 24:6; 1 Chr 2 Chr. 36:9; Jer. 3 [b]Song 8:6; Is. 49: Hag. 2:23

25 [a]2 Kin. 24:15, Jer. 21:7; 34:20, 2

26 [a]2 Kin. 24:15; 10:18; 16:13 [b]2 K 24:8

28 [a]Ps. 31:12; Je 48:38; Hos. 8:8 [b] 15:1 [c]Jer. 17:4

29 [a]Deut. 4:26; J 6:19; Mic. 1:2

30 [a]1 Chr. 3:17; 1:12 [b]Jer. 2:37; [c]Ps. 94:20; Jer. 3

23:1 [a]Ezek. 13:3 Zech. 11:17 [b]Is. 56:9-12; Jer. 10:2 50:6 [c]Ezek. 34:3

2 [1]Lit., *shepherd* [a]Ex. 32:34 [b]Jer. 44:22

3 [a]Is. 11:11, 12, 31:7, 8; 32:37

4 [1]Or, *shepherd* 3:15; 31:10; Ezek 34:23 [b]Jer. 30:10 46:27, 28 [c]John 10:28; 1 Pet. 1:5

5 [1]Lit., *Sprout* [2]*succeed* [a]Jer. 33 [b]Is. 4:2; 11:1-5; 5 Jer. 30:9; 33:15, Zech. 3:8; 6:12, 9:7; 52:13; Luke 33 [d]Ps. 72:2; Is. 32:1; Dan. 9:24

6 [a]Deut. 33:28; 30:10; Zech. 14: 7:14; 9:6; Matt. 1 [c]Is. 45:24; Jer. 33 Dan. 9:24; Rom. 1 Cor. 1:30

7 [a]Is. 43:18, 19; 16:14, 15

8 [a]Jer. 16:15 [b]Is 6; Ezek. 34:13; A 9:14, 15

descendants of the household of Israel from *the* north land and from all the countries where I had driven them.' Then they will live on their own soil."

9 As for the prophets:
My [a]heart is broken within me,
All my bones tremble;
I have become like a drunken man,
Even like a man overcome with wine,
Because of the LORD
And because of His holy words.
10 For the land is full of [a]adulterers;
For the land [b]mourns because of the curse.
The [c]pastures of the wilderness have dried up.
Their course also is evil,
And their might is not right.
11 "For [a]both prophet and priest are polluted;
Even in My house I have found their wickedness," declares the LORD.
12 "Therefore their way will be like [a]slippery paths to them,
They will be driven away into the [b]gloom and fall down in it;
For I shall bring [c]calamity upon them,
The year of their punishment," declares the LORD.

13 "Moreover, among the prophets of Samaria I saw an [a]offensive thing:
They [b]prophesied by Baal and [c]led My people Israel astray.
14 "Also among the prophets of Jerusalem I have seen a [a]horrible thing:
The committing of [b]adultery and walking in falsehood;
And they strengthen the hands of [c]evildoers,
So that no one has turned back from his wickedness.
All of them have become to Me like [d]Sodom,
And her inhabitants like Gomorrah.
15 "Therefore thus says the LORD of hosts concerning the prophets,
'Behold, I am going to [a]feed them wormwood
And make them drink poisonous water,
For from the prophets of Jerusalem
Pollution has gone forth into all the land.' "

16 Thus says the LORD of hosts,
"[a]Do not listen to the words of the prophets who are prophesying to you.
They are [b]leading you into futility;
They speak a [c]vision of their own [1]imagination,
Not [d]from the mouth of the LORD.
17 "They keep saying to those who [a]despise Me,
'The LORD has said, "[b]You will have peace" ';
And as for everyone who walks in the [c]stubbornness of his own heart,
They say, '[d]Calamity will not come upon you.'
18 "But [a]who has stood in the council of the LORD,
That he should see and hear His word?
Who has given [b]heed to [1]His word and listened?
19 "Behold, the [a]storm of the LORD has gone forth in wrath,

Jer. 8:18; Hab. 3:16
[a]Jer. 9:2; Hos. 4:2, Mal. 3:5 [b]Jer. 12:4 Ps. 107:34; Jer. 9:10
Jer. 6:13; Zeph. 3:4
12 [a]Ps. 35:6; Prov. 4:19; Jer. 13:16 [b]Is. 2; John 12:35 [c]Jer. 11:23
[a]Hos. 9:7, 8 [b]1 Kin. 18:18-21; Jer. 2:8; 23:32 [c]Is. 9:16
14 [a]Jer. 5:30 [b]Jer. [c]Jer. 23:22; Ezek. 2, 23 [d]Gen. 18:20; 32:32; Is. 1:9, 10; 20:16; 49:18; Matt. 11:24
[a]Deut. 29:18; Jer. 8:14; 9:15
6 [1]Lit., *heart* [a]Jer. 10, 14-17; 1 John [b]Matt. 7:15; 2 Cor. 13-15; Gal. 1:8, 9 14:14; Ezek. 13:3, 6 [d]Jer. 9:12, 20
7 [a]Mic. 2:11 [b]Jer. ; Ezek. 13:10 [c]Jer. ; 18:12 [d]Jer. 5:12; mos 9:10; Mic. 3:11
Another reading is [a]Job 15:8, 9; Jer. ; 1 Cor. 2:16 [b]Job 33:31
[a]Jer. 25:32; 30:23; Amos 1:14

Even a whirling tempest;
It will swirl down on the head of the wicked.
20 "The [a]anger of the LORD will not turn back
Until He has [b]performed and carried out the purposes of His
heart;
[c]In the last days you will clearly understand it.
21 "[a]I did not send *these* prophets,
But they ran.
I did not speak to them,
But they prophesied.
22 "But if they had [a]stood in My council,
Then they would have [b]announced My words to My people,
And would have turned them back from their evil way
And from the evil of their deeds.

23 "Am I a God who is [a]near," declares the LORD,
"And not a God far off?
24 "Can a man [a]hide himself in hiding places,
So I do not see him?" declares the LORD.
"[b]Do I not fill the heavens and the earth?" declares the LORD.
25 "I have [a]heard what the prophets have said who [b]prophesy falsely
in My name, saying, 'I had a [c]dream, I had a dream!'
26 "How long? Is there *anything* in the hearts of the prophets who
prophesy falsehood, even *these* prophets of the [a]deception of their
own heart,
27 who intend to [a]make My people forget My name by their dreams
which they relate to one another, just as their fathers [b]forgot My
name because of Baal?
28 "The prophet who has a dream may relate *his* dream, but let him
who has [a]My word speak My word in truth. [b]What does straw have
in common with grain?" declares the LORD.
29 "Is not My word like [a]fire?" declares the LORD, "and like a [b]ham-
mer which shatters a rock?
30 "Therefore behold, [a]I am against the prophets," declares the LORD,
"who steal My words from each other.
31 "Behold, I am against the prophets," declares the LORD, "who use
their tongues and declare, '*The Lord* declares.'
32 "Behold, I am against those who have prophesied [a]false dreams,"
declares the LORD, "and related them, and led My people astray by
their falsehoods and [b]reckless boasting; yet [c]I did not send them or
command them, nor do they [d]furnish this people the slightest
benefit," declares the LORD.
33 "Now when this people or the prophet or a priest asks you
saying, 'What is the [1a]oracle of the LORD?' then you shall say to them,
'What [1]oracle?' The LORD declares, 'I shall [b]abandon you.'
34 "Then as for the prophet or the priest or the people who say, 'The
[a]oracle of the LORD,' I shall bring punishment upon that man and his
household.
35 "Thus shall each of you say to his neighbor and to his brother,
'[a]What has the LORD answered?' or, 'What has the LORD spoken?'
36 "For you will no longer remember the oracle of the LORD, because
every man's own word will become the oracle, and you have [a]per-
verted the words of the [b]living God, the LORD of hosts, our God.

20 [a]2 Kin. 23:26, 27; Jer. 30:24 [b]Is. 55:11 Zech. 1:6 [c]Gen. 49

21 [a]Jer. 14:14; 23:3 27:15

22 [a]Jer. 9:12; 23:18 [b]Jer. 35:15; Zech. 1

23 [a]Ps. 139:1-10

24 [a]Job 22:13, 14; 34:21, 22; Ps. 139: Is. 29:15; Jer. 49:1 Heb. 4:13 [b]1 Kin. 8 2 Chr. 2:6; Is. 66:1

25 [a]Jer. 8:6; 1 Cor. [b]Jer. 14:14 [c]Num. Jer. 23:28, 32; 29:8 Joel 2:28

26 [a]1 Tim. 4:1, 2

27 [a]Deut. 13:1-3; 29:8 [b]Judg. 3:7; 8

28 [a]Jer. 9:12, 20 [b]1 Cor. 3:12, 13

29 [a]Jer. 5:14; 20:9 [b]2 Cor. 10:4, 5

30 [a]Deut. 18:20; 34:16; Jer. 14:14, Ezek. 13:8

32 [a]Deut. 13:1, 2 23:25 [b]Zeph. 3:4 23:21; Lam. 3:37 7:8; Lam. 2:14

33 [1]Or, *burden*, a throughout the ch 13:1; Nah. 1:1; Ha Zech. 9:1; Mal. 1: 12:7; 23:39

34 [a]Lam. 2:14; Z 13:3

35 [a]Jer. 33:3; 42

36 [a]Gal. 1:7, 8; 2 3:16 [b]2 Kin. 19:4 10:10

Jer. 7:14, 15; 23:33; Ezek. 8:18
[a]Jer. 20:11; 42:18; Ezek. 5:14, 15
1 [a]2 Kin. 24:10-16; r. 36:10; Jer. 27:20; 29:1, 2 [b]Amos 8:1
[a]Mic. 7:1; Nah. 3:12
s. 5:4, 7; Jer. 29:17
Jer. 1:11, 13; Amos 8:2; Zech. 4:2
ah. 1:7; Zech. 13:9
[a]Jer. 12:15; 29:10; ; Ezek. 11:17 [b]Jer. 32:41; 33:7; 42:10 [c]Jer. 32:41
7 [a]Deut. 30:6; Jer. 1:33; 32:40; Ezek. ; 36:26 [b]Is. 51:16; 7:23; 30:22; 31:33; 2:38; Ezek. 14:11; ech. 8:8; Heb. 8:10 am. 7:3; Ps. 119:2; Jer. 29:13
[1]Lit., *give up* [a]Jer. [b]Jer. 39:5; Ezek. 2:12, 13 [c]Jer. 39:9 [d]Jer. 44:1, 26-30
[a]Jer. 15:4; 29:18; 7 [b]1 Kin. 9:7; Ps. :13, 14 [c]Is. 65:15
. 51:19; Jer. 21:9; 7:8; Ezek. 5:12-17
1 [a]Jer. 36:1; 46:2 Kin. 24:1, 2; 2 Chr. ; Dan. 1:1, 2 [c]Jer. 32:1
2 [a]Jer. 18:11
Lit., *this* [a]Jer. 1:2 hr. 34:1-3, 8 [c]Jer. 36:2

37 "Thus you will say to *that* prophet, 'What has the LORD answered
you?' and, 'What has the LORD spoken?'
38 "For if you say, 'The oracle of the LORD!' surely thus says the
LORD, 'Because you said this word, "The oracle of the LORD!" I have
also sent to you, saying, "You shall not say, 'The oracle of the
LORD!' " '
39 "Therefore behold, [a]I shall surely forget you and cast you away
from My presence, along with the city which I gave you and your
fathers.
40 "And I will put an everlasting [a]reproach on you and an everlast-
ing humiliation which will not be forgotten."

Chapter 24

24 After [a]Nebuchadnezzar king of Babylon had carried away
captive Jeconiah the son of Jehoiakim, king of Judah, and the
officials of Judah with the craftsmen and smiths from Jerusalem and
had brought them to Babylon, the LORD showed me: behold, two
[b]baskets of figs set before the temple of the LORD!
2 One basket had very good figs, like [a]first-ripe figs; and the other
basket had [b]very bad figs, which could not be eaten due to rotten-
ness.
3 Then the LORD said to me, "[a]What do you see, Jeremiah?" And I
said, "Figs, the good figs, very good; and the bad *figs*, very bad,
which cannot be eaten due to rottenness."
4 Then the word of the LORD came to me, saying,
5 "Thus says the LORD God of Israel, 'Like these good figs, so I will
regard [a]as good the captives of Judah, whom I have sent out of this
place *into* the land of the Chaldeans.
6 'For I will set My eyes on them for good, and I will [a]bring them
again to this land; and I will [b]build them up and not overthrow
them, and I will [c]plant them and not pluck *them* up.
7 'And I will give them a [a]heart to know Me, for I am the LORD; and
they will be [b]My people, and I will be their God, for they will [c]return
to Me with their whole heart.
8 'But like the [a]bad figs which cannot be eaten due to rottenness—
indeed, thus says the LORD—so I will [1]abandon [b]Zedekiah king of
Judah and his officials, and the [c]remnant of Jerusalem who remain in
this land, and the ones who dwell in the land of [d]Egypt.
9 'And I will [a]make them a terror *and an* evil for all the kingdoms
of the earth, as a [b]reproach and a proverb, a taunt and a [c]curse in all
places where I shall scatter them.
10 'And I will send the [a]sword, the famine, and the pestilence upon
them until they are destroyed from the land which I gave to them
and their forefathers.' "

Chapter 25

25 The word that came to Jeremiah concerning all the people of
Judah, in the [a]fourth year of [b]Jehoiakim the son of Josiah, king
of Judah (that was the [c]first year of Nebuchadnezzar king of Baby-
lon),
2 which Jeremiah the prophet spoke to all the [a]people of Judah and
to all the inhabitants of Jerusalem, saying,
3 "From the [a]thirteenth year of [b]Josiah the son of Amon, king of
Judah, even to this day, [1]these [c]twenty-three years the word of the

INSIGHT

Read 2 Kings 24:10-17.

LORD has come to me, and I have spoken to you [2d]again and again,
but you have not listened.
4 "And the LORD has sent to you all His [a]servants the prophets
[1]again and again, but you have not listened nor inclined your ear to
hear,
5 saying, '[a]Turn now everyone from his evil way and from the evil
of your deeds, and dwell on the land which the LORD has given to
you and your forefathers [b]forever and ever;
6 and [a]do not go after other gods to [1]serve them and to [2]worship
them, and do not provoke Me to anger with the work of your hands,
and I will do you no harm.'
7 "Yet you have not listened to Me," declares the LORD, "in order
that you might [a]provoke Me to anger with the work of your hands to
your own harm.
8 "Therefore thus says the LORD of hosts, 'Because you have not
obeyed My words,
9 behold, I will [a]send and take all the families of the north,'
declares the LORD, 'and *I will send* to Nebuchadnezzar king of Baby-
lon, [b]My servant, and will bring them against this land, and against
its inhabitants, and against all these nations round about; and I will
[1]utterly destroy them, and [c]make them a horror, and a hissing, and
an everlasting desolation.
10 'Moreover, I will [1a]take from them the voice of joy and the voice
of gladness, the voice of the bridegroom and the voice of the bride,
the [b]sound of the millstones and the light of the lamp.
11 'And [a]this whole land shall be a desolation and a horror, and
these nations shall serve the king of Babylon [b]seventy years.
12 'Then it will be [a]when seventy years are completed I will [b]punish
the king of Babylon and that nation,' declares the LORD, 'for their
iniquity, and the land of the Chaldeans; and [c]I will make it an ever-
lasting desolation.
13 'And I will bring upon that land all My words which I have
pronounced against it, all that is written in [a]this book, which Jeremi-
ah has prophesied against [b]all the nations.
14 '([1]For [a]many nations and great kings shall make slaves of them,
even them; and I will [b]recompense them according to their deeds,
and according to the work of their hands.)' "
15 For thus the LORD, the God of Israel, says to me, "Take this [a]cup
of the wine of wrath from My hand, and cause all the nations, to
whom I send you, to drink it.
16 "And they shall [a]drink and stagger and go mad because of the
sword that I will send among them."
17 Then I took the cup from the LORD's hand, and [a]made all the
nations drink, to whom the LORD sent me:
18 [a]Jerusalem and the cities of Judah, and its kings *and* its princes,
to make them a ruin, a horror, a hissing, and a curse, as it is this day;
19 [a]Pharaoh king of Egypt, his servants, his princes, and all his
people;
20 and all the [1a]foreign people, all the kings of the [b]land of Uz, all
the kings of the land of the [c]Philistines (even Ashkelon, Gaza, Ekron,
and the remnant of [d]Ashdod);
21 [a]Edom, [b]Moab, and the sons of [c]Ammon;
22 and all the kings of [a]Tyre, all the kings of Sidon, and the kings of
[b]the coastlands which are beyond the sea;

3 [2]Lit., *rising early speaking* [d]Jer. 7:2 11:7; 26:5

4 [1]Lit., *rising early sending* [a]2 Chr. 36 Jer. 26:5

5 [a]2 Kin. 17:13; Is. 7; Jer. 4:1; 35:15; 18:30; Jon. 3:8-10 17:8; Jer. 7:7; 17:2

6 [1]Or, *worship* [2]O *bow down to* [a]Deu 6:14; 8:19; 2 Kin. Jer. 35:15

7 [a]2 Kin. 17:17; 2 Jer. 7:19; 32:30-33

9 [1]Or, *put them u the ban* [a]Jer. 1:15 23 [b]Is. 13:3; Jer. 2 43:10 [c]1 Kin. 9:7, 18:16; 25:18

10 [1]Lit., *cause to perish* [a]Is. 24:8-1 7:34; 16:9; Ezek. Rev. 18:23 [b]Eccl. Is. 47:2

11 [a]Jer. 4:27; 12: [b]2 Chr. 36:21; Jer. 29:10; Dan. 9:2; Z 7:5

12 [a]Ezra 1:1; Jer. 29:10; Dan. 9:2 [b] 13:14; Jer. ch. 50, [c]Is. 13:19

13 [a]Jer. 36:4, 29, [b]Jer. 1:5, 10; 36:2

14 [1]Or, *For they served many nati and great kings* [a] 27:7; 50:9, 41; 51 28 [b]Jer. 51:6, 24,

15 [a]Job 21:20; Ps 75:8; Is. 51:17, 22 51:7

16 [a]Nah. 3:11

17 [a]Jer. 1:10; 25

18 [a]Ps. 60:3; Is.

19 [a]Jer. 46:2-28; 3:8-10

20 [1]Or, *mixed multitude* [a]Jer. 2 50:37; Ezek. 30:5 1:1; Lam. 4:21 [c]J 47:1-7 [d]Is. 20:1

21 [a]Ps. 137:7; Je 49:7-22 [b]Jer. 48: Amos 2:1-3 [c]Jer. 49:1-6; Amos 1:1

22 [a]Jer. 47:4; Ze 9:2-4 [b]Jer. 31:10

23 and [a]Dedan, Tema, [b]Buz, and all who [c]cut the corners *of their hair;*
24 and all the kings of [a]Arabia and all the kings of the [1b]foreign
people who dwell in the desert;
25 and all the kings of Zimri, all the kings of [a]Elam, and all the
kings of [b]Media;
26 and all the kings of the north, near and far, one with another;
and [a]all the kingdoms of the earth which are upon the face of the
ground, and the king of [1b]Sheshach shall drink after them.
27 "And you shall say to them, 'Thus says the LORD of hosts, the God
of Israel, "[a]Drink, be drunk, vomit, fall, and rise no more because of
the [b]sword which I will send among you." '
28 "And it will be, if they [a]refuse to take the cup from your hand to
drink, then you will say to them, 'Thus says the LORD of hosts: "[b]You
shall surely drink!
29 "For behold, I am [a]beginning to work calamity in *this* city which is
[b]called by My name, and shall you be completely free from punish-
ment? You will not be free from punishment; for [c]I am summoning a
sword against all the inhabitants of the earth," declares the LORD of
hosts.'
30 "Therefore you shall prophesy against them all these words, and
you shall say to them,
'The [a]LORD will [b]roar from on high,
And utter His voice from His holy habitation;
He will roar mightily against His [1]fold.
He will shout like those who tread *the grapes,*
Against all the inhabitants of the earth.
31 'A clamor has come to the end of the earth,
Because the LORD has [a]a controversy with the nations.
He is entering into [b]judgment with all flesh;
As for the wicked, He has given them to the sword,' declares the
LORD."

32 Thus says the LORD of hosts,
"Behold, evil is going forth
From [a]nation to nation,
And a great [b]storm is being stirred up
From the remotest parts of the earth.
33 "And those [a]slain by the LORD on that day shall be from one end
of the earth to the [1]other. They shall [b]not be lamented, gathered, or
buried; they shall be like [c]dung on the face of the ground.
34 "Wail, you shepherds, and cry;
And [a]wallow *in ashes,* you masters of the flock;
For the days of your [b]slaughter and your dispersions [1]have
come,
And you shall fall like a choice vessel.
35 "[a]Flight shall perish from the shepherds,
And escape from the masters of the flock.
36 "*Hear* the sound of the cry of the shepherds,
And the wailing of the masters of the flock!
For the LORD is destroying their pasture,
37 "And the peaceful [1a]folds are made silent
Because of the [b]fierce anger of the LORD.
38 "He has left His hiding place [a]like the lion;
For their land has become a horror

21:13; Jer. 49:7, Gen. 22:21 [c]Jer. 9:26; 49:32
24 [1]Or, *mixed* de [a]2 Chr. 9:14 20; 50:37; Ezek. 30:5
[a]Gen. 10:22; Is. ; Jer. 49:34 [b]Is. 7; Jer. 51:11, 28
Cryptic name for bylon [a]Jer. 25:9; 50:9 [b]Jer. 51:41
Jer. 25:16; Hab. 6 [b]Ezek. 21:4, 5
[a]Job 34:33 [b]Jer. 49:12
[a]Prov. 11:31; Is. Jer. 13:13; Ezek. Pet. 4:17 [b]1 Kin. 43 [c]Ezek. 38:21
[1]Or, *pasture* [a]Is. Jer. 25:38 [b]Joel ; 3:16; Amos 1:2
Hos. 4:1; Mic. 6:2 :16; Ezek. 20:35, 36; Joel 3:2
2 [a]2 Chr. 15:6; Is. :2 [b]Is. 30:30; Jer. 23:19
[1]Lit., *other end of earth* [a]Is. 34:2, 3; 16 [b]Ps. 79:3; Jer. zek. 39:4, 17 [c]Is. 5:25
[1]Lit., *are full* [a]Jer. ; Ezek. 27:30 [b]Is. 34:6, 7; Jer. 50:27
5 [a]Job 11:20; Jer. 11:11; Amos 2:14
[1]Or, *pastures* [a]Is. 7:10, 11; Jer. 5:17; 20 [b]Ps. 97:1-3; Is. 66:15; Heb. 12:29
[a]Jer. 4:7; 5:6; Hos. 5:14; 13:7, 8

Because of the fierceness of the [1]oppressing *sword*,
And because of His fierce anger."

Chapter 26

26 In the beginning of the reign of [a]Jehoiakim the son of Josiah,
king of Judah, this word came from the LORD, saying,
2 "Thus says the LORD, '[a]Stand in the court of the LORD's house, and
speak to all the cities of Judah, who have [b]come to worship *in* the
LORD's house, [c]all the words that I have commanded you to speak to
them. [d]Do not omit a word!
3 '[a]Perhaps they will listen and everyone will turn from his evil
way, that [b]I may repent of the calamity which I am planning to do to
them because of the evil of their deeds.'
4 "And you will say to them, 'Thus says the LORD, "[a]If you will not
listen to Me, to [b]walk in My law, which I have set before you,
5 to listen to the words of [a]My servants the prophets, whom I have
been sending to you [1]again and again, but you have not listened;
6 then I will make this house like [a]Shiloh, and this city I will make
a [b]curse to all the nations of the earth." ' "
7 And the [a]priests and the prophets and all the people heard Jere-
miah speaking these words in the house of the LORD.
8 And when Jeremiah finished speaking all that the LORD had
commanded *him* to speak to all the people, the priests and the
prophets and all the people seized him, saying, "[a]You must die!
9 "Why have you prophesied in the name of the LORD saying, 'This
house will be like Shiloh, and this city will be [a]desolate, without
inhabitant'?" And [b]all the people gathered about Jeremiah in the
house of the LORD.
10 And when the [a]princes of Judah heard these things, they came
up from the king's house to the house of the LORD and sat in the
[b]entrance of the New Gate of the LORD's *house*.
11 Then the priests and the prophets [a]spoke to the officials and to
all the people, saying, "A [b]death sentence for this man! For he has
prophesied [c]against this city as you have heard in your hearing."
12 Then Jeremiah spoke to all the officials and to all the people,
saying, "[a]The LORD sent me to prophesy against this house and
against this city all the words that you have heard.
13 "Now therefore [a]amend your ways and your deeds, and obey the
voice of the LORD your God; and the LORD will [1]change His mind
about the misfortune which He has pronounced against you.
14 "But as for me, behold, [a]I am in your hands; do with me as is
good and right in your sight.
15 "Only know for certain that if you put me to death, you will bring
[a]innocent blood on yourselves, and on this city, and on its in-
habitants; for truly the LORD has sent me to you to speak all these
words in your hearing."
16 Then the officials and all the people [a]said to the priests and to the
prophets, "No [b]death sentence for this man! For he has spoken to us
in the name of the LORD our God."
17 Then [a]some of the elders of the land rose up and spoke to all the
assembly of the people, saying,
18 "[1a]Micah of Moresheth prophesied in the days of Hezekiah king
of Judah; and he spoke to all the people of Judah, saying, 'Thus the
LORD of hosts has said,

38 [1]Or, *oppress*

26:1 [a]2 Kin. 23:… 2 Chr. 36:4, 5

2 [a]2 Chr. 24:20, … 7:2; 19:14 [b]Deu… [c]Jer. 1:17; 42:4; … 28:20; Acts 20:2… [d]Deut. 4:2

3 [a]Is. 1:16-19; J… 36:3-7 [b]Jer. 18:8… 3:8

4 [a]Lev. 26:14; 1 … 9:6; Is. 1:20; Jer. 22:5 [b]Jer. 32:23… 44:10, 23

5 [1]Lit., *rising ear… sending* [a]2 Kin. … Ezra 9:11; Jer. 7… 25:3, 4

6 [a]Josh. 18:1; 1 … 4:12; Ps. 78:60, 6… 7:12, 14 [b]2 Kin. … Is. 65:15; Jer. 24… 25:18

7 [a]Jer. 5:31; Mic…

8 [a]Jer. 11:19; 18… Lam. 4:13, 14; Ma… 21:35, 36; 23:34, 27:20

9 [a]Jer. 9:11; 33:1… [b]Acts 3:11; 5:12

10 [a]Jer. 26:21 [b]J… 36:10

11 [a]Jer. 18:23 [b]D… 18:20; Matt. 26:66… 38:4; Acts 6:11-14

12 [a]Jer. 1:17, 18; … Amos 7:15; Acts 4… 5:29

13 [1]Lit., *be sorry* … [a]Jer. 7:3, 5; 18:8, 1… 26:3; 35:15; Joel 2… Jon. 3:9; 4:2

14 [a]Jer. 38:5

15 [a]Num. 35:33; P… 6:16, 17; Jer. 7:6

16 [a]Jer. 26:11; 36… 25; 38:7, 13 [b]Acts 5:34-39; 23:9, 29; … 26:31

17 [a]Acts 5:34

18 [1]Lit., *Micaiah th… Morasthite* [a]Mic. 1

"[b]Zion will be plowed *as* a field,
And Jerusalem will become ruins,
And the [c]mountain of the house as the [2]high places of a forest." '
19 "Did Hezekiah king of Judah and all Judah put him to death? Did
he not [a]fear the LORD and entreat the favor of the LORD, and [b]the LORD
[1]changed His mind about the misfortune which He had pronounced
against them? But we are [c]committing a great evil against ourselves."
20 Indeed, there was also a man who prophesied in the name of the
LORD, Uriah the son of Shemaiah from [a]Kiriath-jearim; and he proph-
esied against this city and against this land words similar to all those
of Jeremiah.
21 When King Jehoiakim and all his mighty men and all the offi-
cials heard his words, then the [a]king sought to put him to death; but
Uriah heard *it*, and he was afraid and [b]fled, and went to Egypt.
22 Then King Jehoiakim sent men to Egypt: [a]Elnathan the son of
Achbor and *certain* men with him *went* into Egypt.
23 And they brought Uriah from Egypt and led him to King Jehoia-
kim, who [a]slew him with a sword, and cast his dead body into the
[1]burial place of the [2]common people.
24 But the hand of [a]Ahikam the son of Shaphan was with Jeremiah,
so that he was [b]not given into the hands of the people to put him to
death.

Chapter 27

27 In the beginning of the reign of [1a]Zedekiah the son of Josiah,
king of Judah, this word came to Jeremiah from the LORD,
saying—
2 thus says the LORD to me—"Make for yourself [a]bonds and [b]yokes
and put them on your neck,
3 and send [1]word to the king of [a]Edom, to the king of [a]Moab, to the
king of the sons of [a]Ammon, to the king of [a]Tyre, and to the king of
[a]Sidon [2]by the messengers who come to Jerusalem to Zedekiah king
of Judah.
4 "And command them *to go* to their masters, saying, 'Thus says the
LORD of hosts, the God of Israel, thus you shall say to your masters,
5 "[a]I have made the earth, the men and the beasts which are on the
face of the earth [b]by My great power and by My outstretched arm,
and I will [c]give it to the one who is [1]pleasing in My sight.
6 "And now I [a]have given all these lands into the hand of Nebu-
chadnezzar king of Babylon, [b]My servant, and I have given him also
the [c]wild animals of the field to serve him.
7 "And [a]all the nations shall serve him, and his son, and his
grandson, [b]until the time of his own land comes; then [c]many nations
and great kings will [1]make him their servant.
8 "And it will be, *that* the nation or the kingdom which [a]will not
serve him, Nebuchadnezzar king of Babylon, and which will not put
its neck under the yoke of the king of Babylon, I will punish that
nation with the [b]sword, with famine, and with pestilence," declares
the LORD, "until I have destroyed [1]it by his hand.
9 "But as for you, [a]do not listen to your prophets, your diviners,
your [1]dreamers, your soothsayers, or your sorcerers, who speak to
you, saying, 'You shall not serve the king of Babylon.'
10 "For they prophesy a [a]lie to you, in order to [b]remove you far from
your land; and I will drive you out, and you will perish.

18 [2]Or, *a wooded height* [b]Neh. 4:2; Ps. 79:1; Jer. 9:11; Mic. 3:12 [c]Is. 2:2, 3; Jer. 26:18; Mic. 4:1; Zech. 8:3

[1]Lit., *was sorry for* [a]2 Chr. 29:6-11; 32:26; Is. 37:1, 4, 15-20 [b]Ex. 32:14; 2 Sam. 24:16 [c]Jer. 44:7; Hab. 2:10

[a]Josh. 9:17; 1 Sam. 6:21; 7:2

[a]2 Chr. 16:10; 24:21; Jer. 36:26; Matt. 14:5 [b]1 Kin. 19:2-4; Matt. 10:23

22 [a]Jer. 36:12

[1]Lit., *graves* [2]Lit., *of the people* [a]Jer. 2:30

24 [a]2 Kin. 22:12-14; Jer. 39:14; 40:5-7 [b]1 Kin. 18:4; Jer. 1:18, 19

[1]Many mss. read *Jehoiakim* [a]2 Kin. 24:18-20; 2 Chr. 36:11-13

2 [a]Jer. 30:8 [b]Jer. 28:10, 13

[1]Lit., *them* [2]Lit., *by the hand of* [a]Jer. 25:21, 22

[1]Or, *upright* [a]Ps. 146:5, 6; Is. 42:5; Jer. 10:12; 51:15 [b]Deut. 9:29; Jer. 32:17; 4:17 [c]Ps. 115:15, 16; Acts 17:26

[a]Jer. 21:7; 22:25; Ezek. 29:18-20 [b]Is. 8; Jer. 25:9; 43:10 [c]. 28:14; Dan. 2:38

[1]Or, *enslave him* [a]2 Chr. 36:20; Jer. 4:30; 46:13 [b]Dan. 5; Zech. 2:8, 9 [c]Is. 14:4-6; Jer. 25:12

8 [1]Lit., *them* [a]Jer. :17-19; 42:15, 16; Ezek. 17:19-21 [b]Jer. ; 27:13; 29:17, 18; Ezek. 14:21

[1]Lit., *dreams* [a]Ex. 2:18; Deut. 18:10; Lev. 19:27; Is. 8:19; Mal. 3:5; Eph. 5:6

[a]Jer. 23:25 [b]Jer. 8:19; 32:31

11 "But the nation which will [a]bring its neck under the yoke of the
king of Babylon and serve him, I will [b]let remain on its land,"
declares the LORD, "and they will till it and dwell in it." ' "
12 And I spoke words like all these to [a]Zedekiah king of Judah,
saying, "Bring your necks under the yoke of the king of Babylon,
and serve him and his people, and live!
13 "Why will you [a]die, you and your people, by the sword, famine,
and pestilence, as the LORD has spoken to that nation which will not
serve the king of Babylon?
14 "So [a]do not listen to the words of the prophets who speak to you,
saying, 'You shall not serve the king of Babylon,' for they prophesy a
[b]lie to you;
15 for [a]I have not sent them," declares the LORD, "but they [b]proph-
esy falsely in My name, in order that I may [c]drive you out, and that
you may perish, [d]you and the prophets who prophesy to you."
16 *Then* I spoke to the priests and to all this people, saying, "Thus
says the LORD: Do not listen to the words of your prophets who
prophesy to you, saying, 'Behold, the [a]vessels of the LORD's house
will now shortly be brought again from Babylon'; for they are proph-
esying a [b]lie to you.
17 "Do not listen to them; serve the king of Babylon, and live! Why
should this city [a]become a ruin?
18 "But [a]if they are prophets, and if the word of the LORD is with
them, let them now [b]entreat the LORD of hosts, that the vessels which
are left in the house of the LORD, in the house of the king of Judah,
and in Jerusalem, may not go to Babylon.
19 "For thus says the LORD of hosts concerning the [a]pillars, concern-
ing the sea, concerning the stands, and concerning the rest of the
vessels that are left in this city,
20 which Nebuchadnezzar king of Babylon did not take when he
[a]carried into exile Jeconiah the son of Jehoiakim, king of Judah, from
Jerusalem to Babylon, and all the nobles of Judah and Jerusalem.
21 "Yes, thus says the LORD of hosts, the God of Israel, concerning
the vessels that are left in the house of the LORD, and in the house of
the king of Judah, and in Jerusalem,
22 'They shall be [a]carried to Babylon, and they shall be there until
the [b]day I visit them,' declares the LORD. 'Then I will [c]bring them
[1]back and restore them to this place.' "

Chapter 28

28 Now it came about in the same year, [a]in the beginning of the
reign of [b]Zedekiah king of Judah, in the fourth year, in the
fifth month, that [c]Hananiah the son of Azzur, the prophet, who was
from [d]Gibeon, spoke to me in the house of the LORD in the presence
of the priests and all the people, saying,
2 "[a]Thus says the LORD of hosts, the God of Israel, 'I have broken
the yoke of the king of Babylon.
3 'Within two years I am going to bring back to this place [a]all the
vessels of the LORD's house, which Nebuchadnezzar king of Babylon
took away from this place and carried to Babylon.
4 'I am [a]also going to bring back to this place [b]Jeconiah the son of
Jehoiakim, king of Judah, and all the [c]exiles of Judah who went to
Babylon,' declares the LORD, 'for I will break the [d]yoke of the king of
Babylon.' "

11 [a]Jer. 27:2, 8, 12 [b]Jer. 21:9; 38:2; 40:9-12; 42:10, 11

12 [a]Jer. 27:3; 28:1; 38:17

13 [a]Prov. 8:36; Jer. 27:8; 38:23; Ezek.

14 [a]Jer. 27:9; 2 Co 11:13-15 [b]Jer. 14:1 23:21; 27:10; 29:8, Ezek. 13:22

15 [a]Jer. 23:21; 29: [b]Jer. 23:25 [c]2 Chr. 25:16; Jer. 27:10 [d] 6:13-15; 14:15, 16

16 [a]2 Kin. 24:13; 2 36:7, 10; Jer. 28:3; 1:2 [b]Jer. 27:10

17 [a]Jer. 7:34

18 [a]1 Kin. 18:24 [b]1 Sam. 7:8; 12:19 Jer. 18:20

19 [a]1 Kin. 7:15; 2 25:13, 17; Jer. 52:

20 [a]2 Kin. 24:12, 2 Chr. 36:10, 18; J 22:28; 24:1

22 [1]Lit., *up* [a]Jer. 3 [b]Jer. 25:11, 12; 29:10; 32:5 [c]Ezra 1:7-11; 5:13-15; 7:

28:1 [a]Jer. 27:1; 4 [b]2 Kin. 24:18-20; 2 36:11-13; Jer. 27:3 [c]Jer. 28:17 [d]Josh. 10:12; 1 Kin. 3:4

2 [a]Jer. 27:12; 28:

3 [a]2 Kin. 24:13; 2 36:10; Jer. 27:16; 1:2

4 [a]Jer. 22:26, 27 [b]2 Kin. 25:27; Jer. 22:24; 24:1 [c]Jer. [d]Jer. 27:8

5 Then the prophet Jeremiah spoke to the prophet Hananiah in the
presence of the priests and in the presence of all the people who
were standing in the [a]house of the LORD,
6 and the prophet Jeremiah said, “[a]Amen! May the LORD do so;
may the LORD [1]confirm your words which you have prophesied to
bring back the vessels of the LORD's house and all the exiles, from
Babylon to this place.
7 “Yet [a]hear now this word which I am about to speak in your
hearing and in the hearing of all the people!
8 “The prophets who were before me and before you from ancient
times [a]prophesied against many lands and against great kingdoms,
of war and of calamity and of pestilence.
9 “The prophet who prophesies of peace, [a]when the word of the
prophet shall come to pass, then that prophet will be known *as* one
whom the LORD has truly sent.”
10 Then Hananiah the prophet took the [a]yoke from the neck of
Jeremiah the prophet and broke it.
11 And Hananiah spoke in the presence of all the people, saying,
“[a]Thus says the LORD, ‘Even so will I break within two full years, the
yoke of Nebuchadnezzar king of Babylon from the neck of all the
nations.’ ” Then the prophet Jeremiah went his way.
12 And the [a]word of the LORD came to Jeremiah, after Hananiah the
prophet had broken the yoke from off the neck of the prophet Jere-
miah, saying,
13 “Go and speak to Hananiah, saying, ‘Thus says the LORD, “You
have broken the yokes of wood, but you have made instead of them
[a]yokes of iron.”
14 ‘For thus says the LORD of hosts, the God of Israel, “I have put a
[a]yoke of iron on the neck of all these nations, that they may serve
Nebuchadnezzar king of Babylon; and they shall [b]serve him. And [c]I
have also given him the beasts of the field.” ’ ”
15 Then Jeremiah the prophet said to Hananiah the prophet, “Lis-
ten now, Hananiah, the LORD has not sent you, and [a]you have made
this people trust in a lie.
16 “Therefore thus says the LORD, ‘[a]Behold, I am about to [1]remove
you from the face of the earth. This year you are going to [b]die,
because you have [2c]counseled rebellion against the LORD.’ ”
17 So Hananiah the prophet died in the same year in the seventh
month.

Chapter 29

29 Now these are the words of the [a]letter which Jeremiah the
prophet sent from Jerusalem to the rest of the elders of the
exile, the priests, the prophets, and all the people whom Nebuchad-
nezzar had taken into exile from Jerusalem to Babylon.
2 (This was after King [a]Jeconiah and the [b]queen mother, the court
officials, the princes of Judah and Jerusalem, the craftsmen and the
smiths had departed from Jerusalem.)
3 *The letter was sent* by the hand of Elasah the son of Shaphan, and
Gemariah the son of [a]Hilkiah, whom Zedekiah king of Judah sent to
Babylon to Nebuchadnezzar king of Babylon, saying,
4 “Thus says the LORD of hosts, the God of Israel, to all the exiles
whom I have [a]sent into exile from Jerusalem to Babylon,

5 [a]Jer. 28:1
6 [1]Or, *fulfill* [a]1 Kin. Ps. 41:13; Jer. 11:5
7 [a]1 Kin. 22:28
ev. 26:14-39; 1 Kin. :15; 17:1; 22:17; Is. -7; Joel 1:20; Amos 1:2; Nah. 1:2
9 [a]Deut. 18:22
10 [a]Jer. 27:2
[a]Jer. 14:14; 27:10; 28:15
12 [a]Jer. 1:2
Ps. 107:16; Is. 45:2
[a]Deut. 28:48; Jer. 8 [b]Jer. 25:11 [c]Jer. 27:6
[a]Jer. 20:6; 29:31; . 2:14; Ezek. 13:2, ; 22:28; Zech. 13:3
16 [1]Lit., *send you away* [2]Lit., *spoken* ien. 7:4; Ex. 32:12; 6:15; 1 Kin. 13:34 . 20:6 [c]Deut. 13:5; Jer. 29:32
:1 [a]2 Chr. 30:1, 6; :20; Jer. 29:25, 29
[a]2 Kin. 24:12-16; Chr. 36:9, 10; Jer. 24-28; 24:1; 27:20 Kin. 24:12, 15; Jer. 13:18; 22:26
3 [a]1 Chr. 6:13
4 [a]Jer. 24:5

INSIGHT

Read 2 Chronicles 36:11-13 and 2 Kings 24:18-25:7.

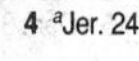

5 '[a]Build houses and live *in them;* and plant gardens, and eat their
[1]produce.
6 'Take [a]wives and [1]become the fathers of sons and daughters, and
take wives for your sons and give your daughters to husbands, that
they may bear sons and daughters; and multiply there and do not
decrease.
7 'And [a]seek the [1]welfare of the city where I have sent you into
exile, and [b]pray to the LORD on its behalf; for in its [1]welfare you will
have [1]welfare.'
8 "For thus says the LORD of hosts, the God of Israel, 'Do not let
your [a]prophets who are in your midst and your diviners [b]deceive
you, and do not listen to [1c]the dreams which [2]they dream.
9 'For they [a]prophesy falsely to you in My name; [b]I have not sent
them,' declares the LORD.
10 "For thus says the LORD, 'When [a]seventy years have been com-
pleted for Babylon, I will visit you and fulfill My [b]good word to you,
to bring you back to this place.
11 'For I know the [a]plans that I [1]have for you,' declares the LORD,
'plans for [b]welfare and not for calamity to give you a future and a
[c]hope.
12 'Then you will [a]call upon Me and come and pray to Me, and I
will [b]listen to you.
13 'And you will [a]seek Me and find *Me,* when you [b]search for Me
with all your heart.
14 'And I will be [a]found by you,' declares the LORD, 'and I will
[b]restore your [1]fortunes and will [c]gather you from all the nations and
from all the places where I have driven you,' declares the LORD, 'and
I will [d]bring you back to the place from where I sent you into exile.'
15 "Because you have said, 'The LORD has raised up [a]prophets for us
in Babylon'—
16 for thus says the LORD concerning the king who sits on the
throne of David, and concerning all the people who dwell in this
city, your brothers who did [a]not go with you into exile—
17 thus says the LORD of hosts, 'Behold, I am sending upon them
the [a]sword, famine, and pestilence, and I will make them like [b]split-
open figs that cannot be eaten due to rottenness.
18 'And I will pursue them with the sword, with famine and with
pestilence; and I will [a]make them a terror to all the kingdoms of the
earth, to be a [b]curse, and a horror, and a [c]hissing, and a reproach
among all the nations where I have driven them,
19 because they have [a]not listened to My words,' declares the LORD,
'which I sent to them again and again by [b]My servants the prophets;
but you did not listen,' declares the LORD.
20 "You, therefore, hear the word of the LORD, all you exiles, whom I
have [a]sent away from Jerusalem to Babylon.
21 "Thus says the LORD of hosts, the God of Israel, concerning Ahab
the son of Kolaiah and concerning Zedekiah the son of Maaseiah,
who are [a]prophesying to you falsely in My name, 'Behold, I will
deliver them into the hand of Nebuchadnezzar king of Babylon, and
he shall slay them before your eyes.
22 'And because of them a [a]curse shall be [1]used by all the exiles
from Judah who are in Babylon, saying, "May the LORD make you
like Zedekiah and like Ahab, whom the king of Babylon [b]roasted in
the fire,

INSIGHT

Why seventy years of captivity? Because for 490 years Israel had not given the land its sabbath rest. See Leviticus 25:1-7; 26:27-35, 40-43; 2 Chronicles 36:20-21.

5 [1]Lit., *fruit* [a]Je

6 [1]Lit., *beget* [a]J 16:2-4

7 [1]Or, *peace* [a]D 4:27; 6:4, 5 [b]Ez 7:23; Dan. 4:19; 2:1, 2

8 [1]Lit., *your* [2]Lit [a]Jer. 27:9; 29:1 14:14; 23:21; 27 28:15; Eph. 5:6 23:25, 27

9 [a]Jer. 27:15; 29 [b]Jer. 29:31

10 [a]2 Chr. 36:21 Jer. 25:12; 27:22 9:2; Zech. 7:5 [b]J 24:6, 7; Zeph. 2:7

11 [1]Lit., *am plan* [a]Ps. 40:5; Jer. 23 30:9, 10 [b]Is. 40:9 Jer. 30:18-22 [c]Je 31:17; Hos. 2:15

12 [a]Ps. 50:15; Je 33:3; Dan. 9:3 [b]P 145:19

13 [a]Deut. 4:29; P 32:6; Matt. 7:7 [b]1 22:19; 2 Chr. 22:9 24:7

14 [1]Or, *captivity* 30:1-10; Ps. 32:6, 55:6 [b]Jer. 30:3; 32:37-41 [c]Is. 43:5 Jer. 23:8; 32:37 3:14; 12:15; 16:15

15 [a]Jer. 29:21, 24

16 [a]Jer. 38:2, 3,

17 [a]Jer. 27:8; 29: 32:24 [b]Jer. 24:3,

18 [a]Deut. 28:25; 29:8; Jer. 15:4; 24 34:17; Ezek. 12:15 65:15; Jer. 42:18 25:9; Lam. 2:15, 1

19 [a]Jer. 6:19 [b]Jer 25:4; 26:5; 35:15

20 [a]Jer. 24:5; Eze 11:9; Mic. 4:10

21 [a]Jer. 14:14, 15; 9; Lam. 2:14; 2 Pet

22 [1]Lit., *taken* [a]Is. 65:15 [b]Dan. 3:6, 2

23 because they have [a]acted foolishly in Israel, and [b]have committed
adultery with their neighbors' wives, and have [c]spoken words in My
name falsely, which I did not command them; and I am He who
[d]knows, and am a witness," declares the LORD.' "
24 And to [a]Shemaiah the Nehelamite you shall speak, saying,
25 "Thus says the LORD of hosts, the God of Israel, 'Because you have
sent [a]letters in your own name to all the people who are in Jerusa-
lem, and to [b]Zephaniah the son of Maaseiah, the priest, and to all the
priests, saying,
26 "The LORD has made you priest instead of Jehoiada the priest, to
be the [1a]overseer in the house of the LORD over every [b]madman who
[c]prophesies, to [d]put him in the stocks and in the iron collar,
27 now then, why have you not rebuked Jeremiah of [a]Anathoth
who prophesies to you?
28 "For he has [a]sent to us in Babylon, saying, '*The exile* will be [b]long;
[c]build houses and live *in them* and plant gardens and eat their [1]pro-
duce.' " ' "
29 And [a]Zephaniah the priest read this letter [1]to Jeremiah the
prophet.
30 Then came the word of the LORD to Jeremiah, saying,
31 "Send to [a]all the exiles, saying, 'Thus says the LORD concerning
[b]Shemaiah the Nehelamite, "Because Shemaiah has [c]prophesied to
you, although I did not send him, and he has [d]made you trust in a
lie,"
32 therefore thus says the LORD, "Behold, I am about to [a]punish
Shemaiah the Nehelamite and his [1]descendants; he shall [b]not have
anyone living among this people, [c]and he shall not see the good that
I am about to do to My people," declares the LORD, "because he has
[2d]preached rebellion against the LORD." ' "

Chapter 30

30 The word which came to Jeremiah from the LORD, saying,
2 "Thus says the LORD, the God of Israel, '[a]Write all the words
which I have spoken to you in a book.
3 'For, behold, [a]days are coming,' declares the LORD, 'when I will
[b]restore the [1]fortunes of My people [c]Israel and Judah.' The LORD says,
'I will also [d]bring them back to the land that I gave to their
forefathers, and they shall possess it.' "
4 Now these are the words which the LORD spoke concerning Isra-
el and concerning Judah,
5 "For thus says the LORD,

'[1]I have heard a sound of [a]terror,
Of dread, and there is no peace.

6 'Ask now, and see,
If a male can give birth.
Why do I see every man
With his hands on his loins, [a]as a woman in childbirth?
And *why* have all faces turned pale?

7 'Alas! for that [a]day is great,
There is [b]none like it;
And it is the time of Jacob's [c]distress,
But he will be [d]saved from it.

8 'And it shall come about on that day,' declares the LORD of hosts,

[a]Gen. 34:7; 2 Sam. :12 [b]Jer. 5:8; 23:14 . 29:8, 9, 21 [d]Prov. 21; Jer. 7:11; 16:17; Mal. 3:5; Heb. 4:13

24 [a]Jer. 29:31, 32

[a]Jer. 29:1 [b]2 Kin. 8; Jer. 21:1; 29:29; 37:3; 52:24

26 [1]Lit., *overseers* . 20:1 [b]2 Kin. 9:11; os. 9:7; Mark 3:21; 10:20; Acts 26:24, 2 Cor. 5:13 [c]Deut. 3:1-5; Zech. 13:1-5 20:1, 2; Acts 16:24

27 [a]Jer. 1:1

Lit., *fruit* [a]Jer. 29:1 r. 29:10 [c]Jer. 29:5

[1]Lit., *in the ears of* [a]Jer. 29:25

[a]Jer. 29:20 [b]Jer. 24 [c]Jer. 14:14, 15; 23; Ezek. 13:8-16, 22, 23 [d]Jer. 28:15

2 [1]Lit., *seed* [2]Lit., *poken* [a]Jer. 36:31 Sam. 2:30-34; Jer. 30 [c]2 Kin. 7:2, 19, 0; Jer. 17:6; 29:10 ut. 13:5; Jer. 28:16

30:2 [a]Is. 30:8; Jer. 5:13; 36:4, 28, 32; Hab. 2:2

[1]Or, *captivity* [a]Jer. :10 [b]Ps. 53:6; Jer. :14; 30:18; 32:44; 39:25; Amos 9:14; h. 3:20 [c]Jer. 3:18 Jer. 16:15; 23:7, 8; Ezek. 20:42; 36:24

[1]Lit., *We* [a]Is. 5:30; . 6:25; 8:16; Amos 5:16-18

. 4:31; 6:24; 22:23

s. 2:12; Hos. 1:11; 2:11; Amos 5:18; 1:14 [b]Lam. 1:12; n. 9:12; 12:1 [c]Jer. 27, 28; 14:8 [d]Jer. 30:10; 50:19

'that I will [a]break his yoke from off [1]their neck, and will tear off [1]their
[b]bonds; and strangers shall no longer [c]make [2]them their slaves.
9 'But they shall serve the LORD their God, and [a]David their king,
whom I will raise up for them.

10 '[a]And fear not, O Jacob My servant,' declares the LORD,
'And do not be dismayed, O Israel;
For behold, I will save you [b]from afar,
And your [1]offspring from the land of their captivity.
And Jacob shall return, and shall be [c]quiet and at ease,
And [d]no one shall make him afraid.
11 'For [a]I am with you,' declares the LORD, 'to save you;
For I will [b]destroy completely all the nations where I have
scattered you,
Only I will [c]not destroy you completely.
But I will [d]chasten you justly,
And will by no means leave you unpunished.'

12 "For thus says the LORD,
'Your wound is incurable,
And your [a]injury is serious.
13 'There is no one to plead your cause;
No healing for *your* sore,
[a]No recovery for you.
14 'All your [a]lovers have forgotten you,
They do not seek you;
For I have [b]wounded you with the wound of an enemy,
With the [c]punishment of a [d]cruel one,
Because your [e]iniquity is great
And your [f]sins are numerous.
15 'Why do you cry out over your injury?
Your pain is incurable.
Because your iniquity is great
And your sins are numerous,
I have done these things to you.
16 'Therefore all who [a]devour you shall be devoured;
And all your adversaries, every one of them, [b]shall go into
captivity;
And those who plunder you shall be for plunder,
And all who prey upon you I will give for prey.
17 'For I will [1]restore you to [2a]health
And I will heal you of your wounds,' declares the LORD,
'Because they have called you an [b]outcast, saying:
"It is Zion; no one [3]cares for her." '

18 "Thus says the LORD,
'Behold, I will [a]restore the [1]fortunes of the tents of Jacob
And [b]have compassion on his dwelling places;
And the [c]city shall be rebuilt on its ruin,
And the [d]palace shall stand on its rightful place.
19 'And from them shall proceed [a]thanksgiving
And the voice of those who [1b]make merry;
And I will [c]multiply them, and they shall not be diminished;
I will also [d]honor them, and they shall not be insignificant.
20 '[1]Their children also shall be as formerly,

8 [1]So Gr.; Heb [2]Lit., *him their* ... 9:4; Jer. 2:20; ... 34:27 [b]Jer. 27 ... 34:27

9 [a]Is. 55:3-5; E... 34:23, 24; 37:2... Hos. 3:5; Luke ... Acts 2:30; 13:2...

10 [1]Lit., *seed* ... 41:13; 43:5; 44 ... 46:27, 28 [b]Is. ... 23:3, 8; 29:14 ... Jer. 33:16; Hos ... [d]Mic. 4:4

11 [a]Jer. 1:8, 19 ... 46:28; Amos 9:8 ... 4:27; 5:10, 18 ... Jer. 10:24

12 [a]2 Chr. 36:1... 15:18; 30:15

13 [a]Jer. 14:19; ...

14 [a]Jer. 22:20, ... 1:2 [b]Lam. 2:4, 5 ... 30:21 [d]Jer. 6:23 [e]Jer. 32:30-35; ... [f]Jer. 5:6

16 [a]Jer. 2:3; 8:1... 10:25 [b]Is. 14:2; ...

17 [1]Lit., *cause t*... [2]Or, *healing* [3]Lit. *seeking* [a]Ex. 15:... 107:20; Is. 30:26 ... 8:22; 33:6 [b]Is. 1... 56:8; Jer. 33:24

18 [1]Or, *captivity* ... 30:3; 31:23 [b]Ps. 102:13 [c]Jer. 31:4... 38-40 [d]1 Chr. 29... Ps. 48:3, 13; 122...

19 [1]Or, *dance* [a]Is. 35:10; 51:3; Jer. 1... 33:11 [b]Ps. 126:1, ... 51:11; Jer. 31:4; Z... 3:14 [c]Jer. 33:22 ... 55:5; 60:9

20 [1]Lit., *His*

And [2]their congregation shall be [a]established before Me;
And I will punish all [2]their oppressors.
21 'And [1]their [a]leader shall be one of them,
And [1]their ruler shall come forth from [1]their midst;
And I will [b]bring him near, and he shall approach Me;
For [2]who would dare to risk his life to [c]approach Me?' declares
the LORD.
22 'And you shall be [a]My people,
And I will be your God.' "

23 Behold, the [a]tempest of the LORD!
Wrath has gone forth,
A [1]sweeping tempest;
It will burst on the head of the wicked.
24 The [a]fierce anger of the LORD will not turn back,
Until He has performed, and until He has accomplished
The intent of His heart;
In the [b]latter days you will understand this.

Chapter 31

31 "At that time," declares the LORD, "I will be the [a]God of all the
[b]families of Israel, and they shall be My people."
2 Thus says the LORD,
"The people who survived the sword
[a]Found grace in the wilderness—
Israel, when it went to [b]find its rest."
3 The LORD appeared to [1]him from afar, *saying,*
"I have [a]loved you with an everlasting love;
Therefore I have drawn you with [b]lovingkindness.
4 "[a]Again I will build you, and you shall be rebuilt,
O virgin of Israel!
Again you shall [1]take up your [b]tambourines,
And go forth to the dances of the [c]merrymakers.
5 "Again you shall [a]plant vineyards
On the [1]hills of Samaria;
The planters shall plant
And shall [2]enjoy *them.*
6 "For there shall be a day when watchmen
On the hills of Ephraim shall call out,
'Arise, and [a]let us go up *to* Zion,
To the LORD our God.' "

7 For thus says the LORD,
"[a]Sing aloud with gladness for Jacob,
And shout among the [1b]chiefs of the nations;
Proclaim, give praise, and say,
'O LORD, [c]save Thy people,
The [d]remnant of Israel.'
8 "Behold, I am [a]bringing them from the north country,
And I will [b]gather them from the remote parts of the earth,
Among them the [c]blind and the [d]lame,
The woman with child and she who is in labor with child,
together;
A great [1]company, they shall return here.

[2]Lit., *his* [a]Is. 54:14

..it., *his* [2]Lit., *who is* ..at gives his heart in ..ge [a]Jer. 30:9; Ezek. ..3, 24; 37:24 [b]Num. ..; Ps. 65:4 [c]Ex. 3:5; Jer. 50:44

[a]Ex. 6:7; Jer. 32:38; ..k. 36:28; Hos. 2:23; Zech. 13:9

..3 [1]Or, *raging* [a]Jer. 23:19

..er. 4:8 [b]Jer. 23:20

[a]Jer. 30:22 [b]Gen. ..8; Is. 41:10; Rom. 11:26-28

[a]Num. 14:20 [b]Ex. ..33:14; Num. 10:33; ..ut. 1:33; Josh. 1:13

..., *me* [a]Deut. 4:37; Mal. 1:2 [b]Ps. 25:6

..r, *be adorned with* ..Jer. 24:6; 33:7 [b]Is. 30:32 [c]Jer. 30:19

..r, *mountains* [2]Lit., ..*le* [a]Ps. 107:37; Is. ..5:21; Ezek. 28:26; Amos 9:14

[a]Is. 2:3; Jer. 31:12; 50:4, 5; Mic. 4:2

[1]Lit., *heads* [a]Ps. ..Jer. 20:13 [b]Deut. ..8:13; Is. 61:9 [c]Ps. ..s. 37:31; Jer. 23:3

..r, *assembly* [a]Jer. 23:8 [b]Deut. 30:4; 43:6; Ezek. 34:13 ..42:16 [d]Is. 40:11; ..ek. 34:16; Mic. 4:6

9 "[a]With weeping they shall come,
And by supplication I will lead them;
I will make them walk by [b]streams of waters,
On a straight path in which they shall [c]not stumble;
For I am a [d]father to Israel,
And Ephraim is [e]My first-born."

10 Hear the word of the LORD, O nations,
And declare in the [a]coastlands afar off,
And say, "He who scattered Israel will [b]gather him,
And keep him as a [c]shepherd keeps his flock."
11 For the LORD has [a]ransomed Jacob,
And redeemed him from the hand of him who was [b]stronger than he.
12 "And they shall [a]come and shout for joy on the [b]height of Zion,
And they shall be [c]radiant over the [1]bounty of the LORD—
Over the [d]grain, and the new wine, and the oil,
And over the young of the [e]flock and the herd;
And their life shall be like a [f]watered garden,
And they shall [g]never languish again.
13 "Then the virgin shall rejoice in the [a]dance,
And the young men and the old, together,
For I will [b]turn their mourning into joy,
And will comfort them, and give them [c]joy for their sorrow.
14 "And I will [1]fill the soul of the priests with [2]abundance,
And My people shall be [a]satisfied with My goodness," declares the LORD.

15 Thus says the LORD,
"[a]A voice is heard in [b]Ramah,
Lamentation *and* bitter weeping.
Rachel is weeping for her children;
She [c]refuses to be comforted for her children,
Because [d]they are no more."
16 Thus says the LORD,
"[a]Restrain your voice from weeping,
And your eyes from tears;
For your [b]work shall be rewarded," declares the LORD,
"And they shall [c]return from the land of the enemy.
17 "And there is [a]hope for your future," declares the LORD,
"And *your* children shall return to their own territory.
18 "I have surely heard Ephraim [a]grieving,
'Thou hast [b]chastised me, and I was chastised,
Like an untrained [c]calf;
[d]Bring me back that I may be restored,
For Thou art the LORD my God.
19 'For after I turned back, I [a]repented;
And after I was instructed, I [b]smote on *my* thigh;
I was [c]ashamed, and also humiliated,
Because I bore the reproach of my youth.'
20 "Is [a]Ephraim My dear son?
Is he a delightful child?
Indeed, as often as I have spoken against him,
I certainly *still* remember him;

9 [a]Ps. 126:5; J
[b]Is. 43:20; 49:1
63:13 [d]Is. 64:8
19 [e]Ex. 4:22

10 [a]Is. 66:19; .
25:22 [b]Jer. 50:
40:11; Ezek. 34

11 [a]Is. 44:23; 4
Jer. 15:21; 50:3
142:6

12 [1]Lit., *goodn*
31:6, 7 [b]Ezek.
[c]Is. 2:2; Mic. 4:1
2:22; Joel 3:18
31:24; 33:12, 1
58:11 [g]Is. 35:1
65:19; John 16:
21:4

13 [a]Judg. 21:2
30:11; Zech. 8:4
61:3 [c]Is. 51:11

14 [1]Lit., *saturat*
fatness [a]Jer. 50

15 [a]Matt. 2:18
18:25; Judg. 4:5
10:29; Jer. 40:1
37:35; Ps. 77:2
5:24; 42:13, 36;
10:20

16 [a]Is. 25:8; 30.
[b]Ruth 2:12; Heb.
[c]Jer. 30:3; Ezek.

17 [a]Jer. 29:11

18 [a]Jer. 3:21 [b]J
5:17; Ps. 94:12
4:16 [d]Ps. 80:3, 7
Jer. 17:14; Lam.
Acts 3:26

19 [a]Ezek. 36:31
12:10 [b]Ezek. 21
Luke 18:13 [c]Jer.

20 [a]Hos. 11:8

Therefore My [1b]heart yearns for him;
I will surely [c]have mercy on him," declares the LORD.

21 "Set up for yourself roadmarks,
Place for yourself guideposts;
[a]Direct your [1]mind to the highway,
The way by which you went.
[b]Return, O virgin of Israel,
Return to these your cities.
22 "How long will you go here and there,
O [a]faithless daughter?
For the LORD has created a new thing in the earth—
A woman will encompass a man."
23 Thus says the LORD of hosts, the God of Israel, "Once again they
will speak this word in the land of Judah and in its cities, when I
[a]restore their [1]fortunes,
'The LORD bless you, O [b]abode of righteousness,
O [c]holy hill!'
24 "And Judah and all its cities will [a]dwell together in it, the farmer
and they who go about with flocks.
25 "[a]For I satisfy the weary ones and [1]refresh everyone who lan-
guishes."
26 At this I [a]awoke and looked, and my [b]sleep was pleasant to me.
27 "Behold, days are coming," declares the LORD, "when I will [a]sow
the house of Israel and the house of Judah with the seed of man and
with the seed of beast.
28 "And it will come about that as I have [a]watched over them to
[b]pluck up, to break down, to overthrow, to destroy, and to bring
disaster, so I will watch over them to [c]build and to plant," declares
the LORD.
29 "In those days they will not say again,
'[a]The fathers have eaten sour grapes,
And the children's teeth are [1]set on edge.'
30 "But [a]everyone will die for his own iniquity; each man who eats
the sour grapes, his teeth will be [1]set on edge.
31 "[a]Behold, days are coming," declares the LORD, "when I will make
a [b]new covenant with the house of Israel and with the house of
Judah,
32 not like the [a]covenant which I made with their fathers in the day
I [b]took them by the hand to bring them out of the land of Egypt, My
[c]covenant which they broke, although I was a husband to them,"
declares the LORD.
33 "But [a]this is the covenant which I will make with the house of
Israel after those days," declares the LORD, "[b]I will put My law
within them, and on their heart I will write it; and [c]I will be their
God, and they shall be My people.
34 "And they shall [a]not teach again, each man his neighbor and each
man his brother, saying, 'Know the LORD,' for they shall all [b]know
Me, from the least of them to the greatest of them," declares the
LORD, "for I will [c]forgive their iniquity, and their [d]sin I will remember
no more."
35 Thus says the LORD,
Who [a]gives the sun for light by day,
And the [1]fixed order of the moon and the stars for light by night,

0 [1]Lit., *inward parts* [b]Gen. 43:30; Judg. 0:16; Is. 63:15; Hos. 1:8 [c]Is. 55:7; 57:18; Hos. 14:4; Mic. 7:18
21 [1]Lit., *heart* [a]Jer. :5 [b]Is. 48:20; 52:11
22 [a]Jer. 3:6; 49:4
[1]Or, *captivity* [a]Jer. 18; 32:44 [b]Is. 1:26; Jer. 50:7 [c]Ps. 48:1; 87:1; Zech. 8:3
[a]Jer. 31:12; Ezek. 36:10; Zech. 8:4-8
[1]Lit., *fill* [a]Ps. 107:9; 31:12, 14; Matt. 5:6; John 4:14
[a]Zech. 4:1 [b]Prov. 3:24
27 [a]Ezek. 36:9, 11; Hos. 2:23
8 [a]Jer. 44:27; Dan. 14 [b]Jer. 1:10; 18:7 [c]Jer. 24:6
[1]Or, *dull* [a]Lam. 5:7; Ezek. 18:2
30 [1]Or, *dull* [a]Deut. 4:16; Is. 3:11; Ezek. 18:4, 20
Jer. 31:31-34; Heb. 8:8-12 [b]Jer. 32:40; 33:14; Ezek. 37:26; Luke 22:20; 1 Cor. 25; 2 Cor. 3:6; Heb. 8:8-12; 10:16, 17
[a]Ex. 19:5; 24:6-8; Deut. 5:2, 3 [b]Deut. :31; Is. 63:12 [c]Jer. 11:7, 8
3 [a]Jer. 32:40; Heb. 6 [b]Ps. 40:8; 2 Cor. 3 [c]Jer. 24:7; 30:22; 32:38
34 [a]1 Thess. 4:9; ohn 2:27 [b]Is. 11:9; 13; Jer. 24:7; Hab. John 6:45; 1 John [c]Jer. 33:8; 50:20; 7:18; Rom. 11:27 43:25; Heb. 10:17
Lit., *statutes* [a]Gen. 18; Deut. 4:19; Ps. 19:1-6; 136:7-9

Who [b]stirs up the sea so that its waves roar;
[c]The LORD of hosts is His name:
36 "[a]If [1]this fixed order departs
From before Me," declares the LORD,
"Then the offspring of Israel also shall [b]cease
From being a nation before Me [2]forever."
37 Thus says the LORD,
"[a]If the heavens above can be measured,
And the foundations of the earth searched out below,
Then I will also [b]cast off all the offspring of Israel
For all that they have done," declares the LORD.

38 "Behold, days are coming," declares the LORD, "when the [a]city shall be rebuilt for the LORD from the [b]Tower of Hananel to the [c]Corner Gate.

39 "And the [a]measuring line shall go out farther straight ahead to the hill Gareb; then it will turn to Goah.

40 "And [a]the whole valley of the dead bodies and of the ashes, and all the fields as far as the brook [b]Kidron, to the corner of the [c]Horse Gate toward the east, shall be [d]holy to the LORD; it shall not be plucked up, or overthrown anymore forever."

Chapter 32

32 The word that came to Jeremiah from the LORD in the [a]tenth year of Zedekiah king of Judah, which was the eighteenth year of Nebuchadnezzar.

2 Now at that time the army of the king of Babylon was besieging Jerusalem, and Jeremiah the prophet was shut up in the [a]court of the guard, which was *in* the house of the king of Judah,

3 because Zedekiah king of Judah had [a]shut him up, saying, "Why do you [b]prophesy, saying, '[c]Thus says the LORD, "Behold, I am about to [d]give this city into the hand of the king of Babylon, and he will take it;

4 and Zedekiah king of Judah shall [a]not escape out of the hand of the Chaldeans, but he shall surely be given into the hand of the king of Babylon, and he shall [b]speak with him [1]face to face, and see him eye to eye;

5 and he shall [a]take Zedekiah to Babylon, and he shall be there until I visit him," declares the LORD. "If you fight against the Chaldeans, you shall [b]not succeed" '?"

Read Leviticus 25:23-28 in regard to redeeming the land.

6 And Jeremiah said, "The word of the LORD came to me, saying,

7 'Behold, Hanamel the son of Shallum your uncle is coming to you, saying, "Buy for yourself my field which is at [a]Anathoth, for you have the [b]right of redemption to buy *it*." '

8 "Then Hanamel my uncle's son came to me in the [a]court of the guard according to the word of the LORD, and said to me, 'Buy my field, please, that is at [b]Anathoth, which is in the land of Benjamin; for you have the right of possession and the redemption is yours; buy *it* for yourself.' Then I knew that this was the [c]word of the LORD.

9 "And I bought the field which was at Anathoth from Hanamel my uncle's son, and I [a]weighed out the silver for him, seventeen [b]shekels of silver.

10 "And I [1a]signed and [b]sealed the deed, and [c]called in witnesses, and weighed out the silver on the scales.

35 [b]Is. 51:15 [c] 10:16; 32:18; 50

36 [1]Lit., *these* [2]Lit., *all the days* 89:36, 37; 148:6 54:9, 10; Jer. 33 [b]Amos 9:8, 9

37 [a]Is. 40:12; J 33:22 [b]Jer. 33:2 Rom. 11:2-5, 26

38 [a]Jer. 30:18; [b]Neh. 3:1; 12:39 14:10 [c]2 Kin. 14 2 Chr. 26:9

39 [a]Zech. 2:1

40 [a]Jer. 7:32; 8: [b]2 Sam. 15:23; 2 23:6, 12; John 1 [c]2 Kin. 11:16; 2 C 23:15; Neh. 3:28 3:17; Zech. 14:2

32:1 [a]2 Kin. 25:1 Jer. 39:1, 2

2 [a]Neh. 3:25; Je 37:21; 38:6; 39:1

3 [a]2 Kin. 6:32 [b]J 26:8, 9 [c]Jer. 21:3 34:2, 3 [d]Jer. 21:4 32:28, 29; 34:2, 3

4 [1]Lit., *mouth to* [a]2 Kin. 25:4-7; Je 37:17; 38:18, 23; [b]Jer. 39:5

5 [a]Jer. 27:22; 39 Ezek. 12:12, 13 17:9, 10, 15

7 [a]Jer. 1:1; 11:21 25:25; Ruth 4:3, 4

8 [a]Jer. 32:2; 33:1 1:1; 32:7 [c]1 Sam. 17; 10:3-7; 1 Kin. Jer. 32:25

9 [a]Gen. 23:16; Ze 11:12 [b]Gen. 24:22 21:32; Neh. 5:15; 4:10

10 [1]Or, *wrote . . . document* [a]Is. 44 32:44 [b]Deut. 32:3 14:17 [c]Ruth 4:1, 8:2

11 "Then I took the deeds of purchase, both the sealed *copy contain-*
ing the [a]terms and conditions, and the open *copy;*
12 and I gave the deed of purchase to [a]Baruch the son of [b]Neriah,
the son of Mahseiah, in the sight of Hanamel my uncle's *son*, and in
the sight of the witnesses who signed the deed of purchase, before
all the Jews who were sitting in the court of the guard.
13 "And I commanded Baruch in their presence, saying,
14 'Thus says the LORD of hosts, the God of Israel, "Take these
deeds, this sealed deed of purchase, and this open deed, and put
them in an earthenware jar, that they may [1]last a long time."
15 'For thus says the LORD of hosts, the God of Israel, "[a]Houses and
fields and vineyards shall again be bought in this land." '
16 "After I had given the deed of purchase to Baruch the son of
Neriah, then I [a]prayed to the LORD, saying,
17 '[a]Ah Lord [1]GOD! Behold, Thou hast [b]made the heavens and the
earth by Thy great power and by Thine outstretched arm! [c]Nothing
is too difficult for Thee,
18 who [a]showest lovingkindness to thousands, but [b]repayest the
iniquity of fathers into the bosom of their children after them, O
[c]great and [d]mighty God. The [e]LORD of hosts is His name;
19 [a]great in counsel and mighty in deed, whose [b]eyes are open to all
the ways of the sons of men, [c]giving to everyone according to his
ways and according to the fruit of his deeds;
20 who hast [a]set signs and wonders in the land of Egypt, *and* even
to this day both in Israel and among mankind; and Thou hast [b]made
a name for Thyself, as at this day.
21 'And Thou didst [a]bring Thy people Israel out of the land of
Egypt with signs and with wonders, and with a strong hand and
with an outstretched arm, and with great terror;
22 and gavest them this land, which Thou didst [a]swear to their
forefathers to give them, a land flowing with milk and honey.
23 'And they [a]came in and took possession of it, but they [b]did not
obey Thy voice or [c]walk in Thy law; they have done nothing of all
that Thou commandedst them to do; therefore Thou hast made [d]all
this calamity come upon them.
24 'Behold, the [a]siege mounds have reached the city to take it; and
the city is [b]given into the hand of the Chaldeans who fight against it,
because of the [c]sword, the famine, and the pestilence; and what Thou
hast spoken has [d]come to pass; and, behold, Thou seest *it*.
25 'And Thou hast said to me, O Lord [1]GOD, "Buy for yourself the
field with money, and call in witnesses"—although the city is given
into the hand of the Chaldeans.' "
26 Then the word of the LORD came to Jeremiah, saying,
27 "Behold, I am the LORD, the [a]God of all flesh; is anything [b]too
difficult for Me?"
28 Therefore thus says the LORD, "Behold, I am about to [a]give this
city into the hand of the Chaldeans and into the hand of Nebuchad-
nezzar king of Babylon, and he shall take it.
29 "And the Chaldeans who are fighting against this city shall enter
and [a]set this city on fire and burn it, with the [b]houses where *people*
have offered incense to Baal on their roofs and poured out libations
to other gods to provoke Me to anger.
30 "Indeed the sons of Israel and the sons of Judah have been doing
only [a]evil in My sight from their youth; for the sons of Israel have

11 [a]Luke 2:27
[a]Jer. 32:16; 36:4, 5, 32; 43:3; 45:1 [b]Jer. 51:59
14 [1]Lit., *stand many days*
[a]Jer. 30:18; 31:5, 12, 32:37, 43, 44; 33:12, 13; Amos 9:14, 15; Zech. 3:10
[a]Gen. 32:9-12; Jer. 12:1; Phil. 4:6, 7
17 [1]Heb., *YHWH*, ...ally rendered *LORD* ...er. 1:6; 4:10 [b]2 Kin. ...9:15; Ps. 102:25; Is. 40:26-29; Jer. 27:5 ...1. 18:14; Jer. 32:27; ...ch. 8:6; Matt. 19:26; ...k 10:27; Luke 1:37; 18:27
[a]Ex. 20:6; 34:6, 7; ...eut. 5:9, 10; 7:9, 10 ...n. 14:9, 10; 16:1-3; ...Matt. 23:32-36 [c]Ps. ...3 [d]Ps. 50:1; Is. 9:6; ...20:11 [e]Jer. 10:16; 31:35
[a]Is. 9:6; 28:29 [b]Job ...21; Jer. 23:24 [c]Ps. ...; Jer. 17:10; 21:14; ...tt. 16:27; John 5:29
[a]Ps. 78:43; 105:27 ...9:16; Is. 63:12, 14; Dan. 9:15
...Ex. 6:6; Deut. 4:34; ...26:8; 2 Sam. 7:23; ...17:21; Ps. 136:11
[a]Ex. 3:8, 17; 13:5; ...1:8; Ps. 105:9-11; Jer. 11:5
[a]Ps. 44:2, 3; 78:54, ...er. 2:7 [b]Neh. 9:26; ...11:8; Dan. 9:10-14 ...Ezra 9:7; Jer. 26:4; ...[d]Lam. 1:18; Dan. 9:11, 12
...4 [a]Jer. 33:4; Ezek. 21:22 [b]Jer. 20:5; ...21:4-7; 32:5 [c]Jer. ...; 29:17, 18; 32:36; ...34:17; Ezek. 14:21 [d]Deut. 4:26; Josh. ...3:15, 16; Zech. 1:6
25 [1]Heb., *YHWH*, ...ally rendered *LORD*
...Num. 16:22; 27:16 ...32:17; Matt. 19:26
...2 Kin. 25:11; 2 Chr. ...7-21; Jer. 19:7-12; ...2:3, 24, 36; 34:2, 3
[a]2 Chr. 36:19; Jer. ...:10; 37:8, 10; 39:8 ...r. 19:13; 44:17-19, 25; 52:13
[a]Deut. 9:7-12; Is. ...); Jer. 2:7; 7:22-26

been only [b]provoking Me to anger by the work of their hands,"
declares the LORD.
31 "Indeed this city has been to Me *a* [a]*provocation of* My anger and
My wrath from the day that they built it, even to this day, that it
should be [b]removed from before My face,
32 because of all the evil of the sons of Israel and the sons of Judah,
which they have done to provoke Me to anger—they, their [a]kings,
their leaders, their priests, their prophets, the men of Judah, and the
inhabitants of Jerusalem.
33 "And they have turned *their* back to Me, and not *their* face; though
I taught them, [1a]teaching again and again, they would not listen [2]and
receive instruction.
34 "But they [a]put their detestable things in the house which is called
by My name, to defile it.
35 "And they built the [a]high places of Baal that are in the valley of
Ben-hinnom to cause their sons and their daughters to pass through
the fire to [b]Molech, which I had not commanded them nor had it
[1]entered My mind that they should do this abomination, to cause
Judah to sin.
36 "Now therefore thus says the LORD God of Israel concerning this
city of which you say, 'It is [a]given into the hand of the king of
Babylon by sword, by famine, and by pestilence.'
37 "Behold, I will [a]gather them out of all the lands to which I have
driven them in My anger, in My wrath, and in great indignation; and
I will bring them back to this place and [b]make them dwell in safety.
38 "And they shall be [a]My people, and I will be their God;
39 and I will [a]give them one heart and one way, that they may fear
Me always, for their own [b]good, and for *the good of* their children
after them.
40 "And I will make an [a]everlasting covenant with them that I will
[b]not turn away from them, to do them good; and I will [c]put the fear
of Me in their hearts so that they will not turn away from Me.
41 "And I will [a]rejoice over them to do them good, and I will [1]faith-
fully [b]plant them in this land with [c]all My heart and with all My
soul.
42 "For thus says the LORD, '[a]Just as I brought all this great disaster
on this people, so I am going to [b]bring on them all the good that I am
promising them.
43 'And [a]fields shall be bought in this land of which you say, "[b]It is a
desolation, without man or beast; it is given into the hand of the
Chaldeans."
44 'Men shall buy fields for money, [1a]sign and seal deeds, and call in
witnesses in the [b]land of Benjamin, in the environs of Jerusalem, in
the cities of Judah, in the cities of the hill country, in the cities of the
lowland, and in the cities of the [2]Negev; for I will [c]restore their
[3]fortunes,' declares the LORD."

Chapter 33

33 Then the word of the LORD came to Jeremiah the second time,
while he was still [1a]confined in the court of the guard, saying,
2 "Thus says [a]the LORD who made [1]*the earth,* the LORD who formed it
to establish it, the [b]LORD is His name,
3 '[a]Call to Me, and I will answer you, and I will tell you [b]great and
mighty things, [c]which you do not know.'

30 [b]Jer. 8:19; 1
25:7

31 [a]1 Kin. 11:7
2 Kin. 21:4-7, 1
5:9-11; 6:6, 7; M
23:37 [b]2 Kin. 2
24:3, 4; Jer. 27:

32 [a]Ezra 9:7; Is
23; Jer. 2:26; 44
Dan. 9:8

33 [1]Lit., *rising u*
and teaching [2]
[a]2 Chr. 36:15, 1
7:13; 25:3; 26:5
John 8:2

34 [a]2 Kin. 21:1-
7:30; 19:4-6; Ez

35 [1]Lit., *come u*
My heart [a]2 Ch
3; 33:6; Jer. 7:3
[b]Lev. 18:21; 20:
1 Kin. 11:7; 2 Ki
Acts 7:43

36 [a]Jer. 32:24

37 [a]Deut. 30:3;
106:47; Is. 11:11
Jer. 16:14, 15; 2
Ezek. 11:17; Hos
Amos 9:14, 15
23:6; Ezek. 34:2
Zech. 14:11

38 [a]Jer. 24:7

39 [a]2 Chr. 30:12
31:33; Ezek. 11:
John 17:21; Acts
[b]Deut. 11:18-21;
37:25

40 [a]Is. 55:3; Jer
34; 50:5; Ezek. 3
[b]Deut. 31:6, 8; E
39:29 [c]Jer. 24:7

41 [1]Or, *truly* [a]D
30:9; Is. 62:5; 65
[b]Jer. 24:6; 31:28
9:15 [c]Hos. 2:19,

42 [a]Jer. 31:28; Z
8:14, 15 [b]Jer. 33

43 [a]Jer. 32:15, 2
Ezek. 37:11-14
33:10

44 [1]Or, *write . . .*
document [2]I.e., S
country [3]Or, *cap*
[a]Jer. 32:10 [b]Jer.
33:13 [c]Jer. 31:23
11, 26

33:1 [1]Lit., *shut u*
32:2, 8; 37:21; 38

2 [1]Lit., *it* [a]Jer. 51
[b]Ex. 3:15; 6:3; 15
10:16

3 [a]Ps. 50:15; 91:
55:6, 7; Jer. 29:12
32:17, 27 [c]Is. 48:

4 "For thus says the LORD God of Israel concerning the [a]houses of this city, and concerning the houses of the kings of Judah, which are broken down *to make a defense* against the [b]siege mounds and against the sword,

5 'While *they* are coming to [a]fight with the Chaldeans, and to fill them with the corpses of men whom I have slain in My anger and in My wrath, and I have [b]hidden My face from this city because of all their wickedness:

6 'Behold, I will bring to it [a]health and healing, and I will heal them; and I will reveal to them an [b]abundance of peace and truth.

7 'And I will [a]restore the [1]fortunes of Judah and the fortunes of Israel, and I will [b]rebuild them as they were at first.

8 'And I will [a]cleanse them from all their iniquity by which they have sinned against Me, and I will pardon all their iniquities by which they have sinned against Me, and by which they have transgressed against Me.

9 'And [1]it shall be to Me a [a]name of joy, praise, and glory before [b]all the nations of the earth, which shall hear of all the [c]good that I do for them, and they shall [d]fear and tremble because of all the good and all the peace that I make for it.'

10 "Thus says the LORD, 'Yet again there shall be heard in this place, of which you say, "It is a [a]waste, without man and without beast," *that is,* in the cities of Judah and in the streets of Jerusalem that are [b]desolate, without man and without inhabitant and without beast,

11 the voice of [a]joy and the voice of gladness, the voice of the bridegroom and the voice of the bride, the voice of those who say,

"[b]Give thanks to the LORD of hosts,
For the LORD is good,
For His lovingkindness is everlasting";

and of those who bring a [c]thank offering into the house of the LORD. For I will restore the [1]fortunes of the land as they were at first,' says the LORD.

12 "Thus says the LORD of hosts, 'There shall again be in this place which is waste, [a]without man or beast, and in all its cities, a [1]habitation of shepherds who rest their [b]flocks.

13 'In the [a]cities of the hill country, in the cities of the lowland, in the cities of the Negev, in the land of Benjamin, in the environs of Jerusalem, and in the cities of Judah, the flocks shall again [b]pass under the hands of the one who numbers them,' says the LORD.

14 'Behold, [a]days are coming,' declares the LORD, 'when I will [b]fulfill the good word which I have spoken concerning the house of Israel and the house of Judah.

15 'In those days and at that time I will cause a [a]righteous Branch of David to spring forth; and He shall execute [b]justice and righteousness on the earth.

16 'In those days [a]Judah shall be saved, and Jerusalem shall dwell in safety; and this is *the name* by which she shall be called: the [b]LORD is our righteousness.'

17 "For thus says the LORD, '[1]David shall [a]never lack a man to sit on the throne of the house of Israel;

18 [1]and the [a]Levitical priests shall never lack a man before Me to offer burnt offerings, to burn grain offerings, and to [b]prepare sacrifices [2]continually.' "

19 And the word of the LORD came to Jeremiah, saying,

[a]Is. 32:13, 14 [b]Jer. 24; Ezek. 4:2; 21:22; Hab. 1:10

er. 21:4-7; 32:5 [b]Is. ; Jer. 21:10; Mic. 3:4

[a]Jer. 17:14; 30:17; 6:1 [b]Is. 66:12; Gal. 5:22, 23

7 [1]Or, *captivity* [a]Ps. 1; Jer. 30:18; 32:44; :26; Amos 9:14 [b]Is. 26; Jer. 30:18; 31:4, 38; Amos 9:14, 15

[a]Ps. 51:2; Is. 44:22; 50:20; Ezek. 36:25, Mic. 7:18, 19; Zech. 13:1; Heb. 9:11-14

9 [1]I.e., this city [a]Is. 62:2, 4, 7; Jer. 13:11 [b]Jer. 3:17, 19; 4:2; 19 [c]Jer. 24:6; 32:42 n. 6:16; Ps. 40:3; Is. 60:5; Hos. 3:5

10 [a]Jer. 32:43 [b]Jer. 26:9; 34:22

1 [1]Or, *captivity* [a]Is. 10; 51:3, 11 [b]1 Chr. 6:8, 34; 2 Chr. 5:13; 7:3; Ezra 3:11; Ps. :4, 5; 106:1; 107:1; ; 136:1 [c]Lev. 7:12, Ps. 107:22; 116:17; . 17:26; Heb. 13:15

[1]Or, *pasture* [a]Jer. 3; 36:29; 51:62 [b]Is. 0; Jer. 31:12; Ezek. 12-15; Zeph. 2:6, 7

[a]Jer. 17:26; 32:44 v. 27:32; Luke 15:4

Jer. 23:5 [b]Is. 32:1, ; Jer. 29:10; 32:42; :9; Ezek. 34:23-25; Hag. 2:6-9

[a]Is. 4:2; 11:1-5; Jer. 6; 30:9; Zech. 3:8; :12, 13 [b]Ps. 72:1-5

[a]Is. 45:17, 22; Jer. [b]Is. 45:24, 25; Jer. 1 Cor. 1:30; 2 Cor. 5:21; Phil. 3:9

Lit., *There shall not be cut off for David* m. 7:16; 1 Kin. 2:4; 5; 1 Chr. 17:11-14; Ps. 89:29-37

Lit., *there shall not be cut off for the* cal priests [2]Lit., *all* ays [a]Num. 3:5-10; t. 18:1; 24:8; Josh. Ezek. 44:15 [b]Ezra 3:5; Heb. 13:15

20 "Thus says the LORD, 'If you can [a]break My covenant for the day,
and My covenant for the night, so that day and night will not be at
their appointed time,
21 then [a]My covenant may also be broken with David My servant
that he shall not have a son to reign on his throne, and with the
Levitical priests, My ministers.
22 'As the [a]host of heaven cannot be counted, and the [b]sand of the
sea cannot be measured, so I will [c]multiply the [1]descendants of
David My servant and the [d]Levites who minister to Me.' "
23 And the word of the LORD came to Jeremiah, saying,
24 "Have you not observed what this people have spoken, saying,
'The [a]two families which the LORD chose, He has [b]rejected them'?
Thus they [c]despise My people, no longer are they as a nation [1]in
their sight.
25 "Thus says the LORD, 'If My [a]covenant *for* day and night *stand* not,
and the [1]fixed patterns of heaven and earth I have [b]not established,
26 then I would [a]reject the [1]descendants of Jacob and David My
servant, [2]not taking from his [1]descendants [b]rulers over the [1]descend-
ants of Abraham, Isaac, and Jacob. But I will [c]restore their [3]fortunes
and will have [d]mercy on them.' "

Chapter 34

34 The word which came to Jeremiah from the LORD, when
[a]Nebuchadnezzar king of Babylon and all his army, with [b]all
the kingdoms of the earth that were under his dominion and all the
peoples, were fighting against Jerusalem and against all its cities,
saying,
2 "Thus says the LORD God of Israel, '[a]Go and speak to Zedekiah
king of Judah and say to him: "Thus says the LORD, 'Behold, [b]I am
giving this city into the hand of the king of Babylon, and [c]he will
burn it with fire.
3 'And [a]you will not escape from his hand, for you will surely be
captured and delivered into his hand; and you will [b]see the king of
Babylon eye to eye, and he will speak with you [1]face to face, and you
will go to Babylon.' " '
4 "Yet hear the word of the LORD, O Zedekiah king of Judah! Thus
says the LORD concerning you, 'You will not die by the sword.
5 'You will die in peace; and as spices were burned for your
fathers, the former kings who were before you, so they will [a]burn
spices for you; and [b]they will lament for you, "Alas, lord!" ' For I
have spoken the word," declares the LORD.
6 Then Jeremiah the prophet spoke [a]all these words to Zedekiah
king of Judah in Jerusalem
7 when the army of the king of Babylon was fighting against Jeru-
salem and against all the remaining cities of Judah, *that is*, [a]Lachish
and [b]Azekah, for they *alone* remained as [c]fortified cities among the
cities of Judah.
8 The word which came to Jeremiah from the LORD, after King
Zedekiah had [a]made a covenant with all the people who were in
Jerusalem to [b]proclaim [1]release to them:
9 that each man should set free his male servant and each man his
female servant, a [a]Hebrew man or a Hebrew woman; so that [b]no one
should keep them, a Jew his brother, in bondage.
10 And all the [a]officials and all the people obeyed, who had entered

20 [a]Ps. 89:37; 104:19-23; Is. 54 Jer. 31:35-37; 33

21 [a]2 Sam. 23:5 7:18; 21:7

22 [1]Lit., *seed* [a](15:5; Jer. 31:37 22:17 [c]Ezek. 37 [d]Is. 66:21; Jer. 33

24 [1]Lit., *to their* [a]Is. 7:17; 11:13; 8, 10, 18; 33:26; 37:22 [b]Jer. 30:1 4:2-4; Esth. 3:6, Ps. 44:13, 14; 83

25 [1]Lit., *statutes* 8:22; Jer. 31:35, 33:20 [b]Ps. 74:16

26 [1]Lit., *seed* [2]L *from taking* [3]Or, *captivity* [a]Jer. 31 [b]Gen. 49:10 [c]Jer [d]Is. 14:1; 54:8; Je 31:20; Ezek. 39:2 Hos. 1:7; 2:23

34:1 [a]2 Kin. 25:1 32:2; 39:1; 52:4 1:15; 27:7; Dan. 2

2 [a]2 Chr. 36:11, 22:1, 2; 37:1, 2 [b] 21:10; 32:3; 34:22 37:8-10 [c]Jer. 32:

3 [1]Lit., *mouth to* [a]2 Kin. 25:4, 5; Je 32:4; 34:21 [b]2 Ki 25:6, 7; Jer. 39:6,

5 [a]2 Chr. 16:14; 2 [b]Jer. 22:18

6 [a]1 Sam. 3:18; 15:16-24

7 [a]Josh. 10:3, 5; 14:19; 18:14; Is. 3 [b]Josh. 10:10; 2 Ch 11:9 [c]2 Chr. 11:5-

8 [1]Or, *liberty* [a]2 K 11:17; 23:2, 3 [b]Ex 21:2; Lev. 25:10, 3 Neh. 5:1-13; Is. 58 Jer. 34:14, 17

9 [a]Gen. 14:13; Ex [b]Lev. 25:39

10 [a]Jer. 26:10, 16

Ex. 24:3, 7, 8; Deut. :2, 3, 27; Jer. 31:32 [b]Ex. 20:2
14 [1]Or, *has sold elf* [a]Ex. 21:2; Deut. 15:12; 1 Kin. 9:22 Sam. 8:7, 8; 2 Kin. 17:13, 14
5 [1]Or, *liberty* [a]Jer. [b]2 Kin. 23:3; Neh. [c]Jer. 7:10f.; 32:34
.it., *caused them to urn* [a]1 Sam. 15:11; 34:11; Ezek. 3:20; :24 [b]Ex. 20:7; Lev. 19:12
7 [1]Or, *liberty* [a]Lev. :34, 35; Esth. 7:10; an. 6:24; Matt. 7:2 32:24; 38:2 [c]Deut. 28:25; Jer. 29:18
[a]Deut. 17:2; Hos. 6:7; 8:1; Rom. 2:8 [b]Gen. 15:10
[a]Jer. 34:10; Ezek. 22:27; Zeph. 3:3, 4
[a]Jer. 11:21; 21:7; 2:25 [b]Deut. 28:26; n. 17:44, 46; 1 Kin. 11; 16:4; Ps. 79:2; er. 7:33; 16:4; 19:7
[a]2 Kin. 25:18-21; 2:3, 4; 39:6; 52:10, 24-27; Ezek. 17:16 [b]Jer. 37:5-11
er. 34:2; 39:1, 2, 8; 13 [b]Jer. 4:7; 9:11 [c]Jer. 33:10; 44:22
[a]2 Kin. 23:34-36; 2 Chr. 36:5-7; Jer. 3; 27:20; Dan. 1:1
Kin. 10:15; 1 Chr. :55 [b]1 Kin. 6:5, 8; 1 Chr. 9:26, 33

into the covenant that each man should set free his male servant and
each man his female servant, so that no one should keep them any
longer in bondage; they obeyed, and set *them free.*
11 But afterward they turned around and took back the male ser-
vants and the female servants, whom they had set free, and brought
them into subjection for male servants and for female servants.
12 Then the word of the LORD came to Jeremiah from the LORD,
saying,
13 "Thus says the LORD God of Israel, 'I [a]made a covenant with your
forefathers in the day that I [b]brought them out of the land of Egypt,
from the house of bondage, saying,
14 "[a]At the end of seven years each of you shall set free his Hebrew
brother, who [1]has been sold to you and has served you six years, you
shall send him out free from you; but your forefathers [b]did not obey
Me, or incline their ear to Me.
15 "Although recently you *had* turned and [a]done what is right in My
sight, each man proclaiming [1]release to his neighbor, and you had
[b]made a covenant before Me [c]in the house which is called by My
name.
16 "Yet you [a]turned and [b]profaned My name, and each man [1]took
back his male servant and each man his female servant, whom you
had set free according to their desire, and you brought them into
subjection to be your male servants and female servants." '
17 "Therefore thus says the LORD, 'You have not obeyed Me in pro-
claiming [1]release each man to his brother, and each man to his neigh-
bor. Behold, I am [a]proclaiming a [1]release to you,' declares the LORD,
'to the [b]sword, to the pestilence, and to the famine; and I will make
you a [c]terror to all the kingdoms of the earth.
18 'And I will give the men who have [a]transgressed My covenant,
who have not fulfilled the words of the covenant which they made
before Me, *when* they [b]cut the calf in two and passed between its
parts—
19 the [a]officials of Judah, and the officials of Jerusalem, the court
officers, and the priests, and all the people of the land, who passed
between the parts of the calf—
20 and I will give them into the hand of their enemies and into the
hand of those who [a]seek their life. And their [b]dead bodies shall be
food for the birds of the sky and the beasts of the earth.
21 'And [a]Zedekiah king of Judah and his officials I will give into the
hand of their enemies, and into the hand of those who seek their life,
and into the hand of the army of the king of Babylon which has
[b]gone away from you.
22 'Behold, I am going to command,' declares the LORD, 'and I will
bring them back to this city; and they shall fight against it and [a]take
it and burn it with fire; and I will make the cities of Judah a [b]desola-
tion [c]without inhabitant.' "

Chapter 35

35 The word which came to Jeremiah from the LORD in the days
of [a]Jehoiakim the son of Josiah, king of Judah, saying,
2 "Go to the house of the [a]Rechabites, and speak to them, and bring
them into the house of the LORD, into one of the [b]chambers, and give
them wine to drink."
3 Then I took Jaazaniah the son of Jeremiah, son of Habazziniah,

and his brothers, and all his sons, and the whole house of the
Rechabites,
4 and I brought them into the house of the LORD, into the chamber
of the sons of Hanan the son of Igdaliah, the [a]man of God, which
was near the chamber of the officials, which was above the chamber
of Maaseiah the son of Shallum, [b]the doorkeeper.
5 Then I set before the [1]men of the house of the Rechabites pitchers
full of wine, and cups; and I said to them, "[a]Drink wine!"
6 But they said, "We will not drink wine, for [a]Jonadab the son of
[b]Rechab, our father, commanded us, saying, 'You shall [c]not drink
wine, you or your sons, forever.
7 'And you shall not build a house, and you shall not sow seed,
and you shall not plant a vineyard or own one; but in [a]tents you
shall dwell all your days, that you may live [b]many days in the land
where you [c]sojourn.'
8 "And we have [a]obeyed the voice of Jonadab the son of Rechab,
our father, in all that he commanded us, not to drink wine all our
days, we, our wives, our sons, or our daughters,
9 nor to build ourselves houses to dwell in; and we [a]do not have
vineyard or field or seed.
10 "We have only [a]dwelt in tents, and have obeyed, and have done
according to all that [b]Jonadab our father commanded us.
11 "But it came about, when [a]Nebuchadnezzar king of Babylon came
up against the land, that we said, 'Come and let us [b]go to Jerusalem
before the army of the Chaldeans and before the army of the Arame-
ans.' So we have dwelt in Jerusalem."
12 Then the word of the LORD came to Jeremiah, saying,
13 "Thus says the LORD of hosts, the God of Israel, 'Go and say to the
men of Judah and the inhabitants of Jerusalem, "[a]Will you not
receive instruction by listening to My words?" declares the LORD.
14 "The [a]words of Jonadab the son of Rechab, which he commanded
his sons not to drink wine, are observed. So they do not drink *wine*
to this day, for they have obeyed their father's command. But I have
spoken to you [1b]again and again; yet you have [c]not listened to Me.
15 "Also I have sent to you all My [a]servants the prophets, sending
them [1]again and again, saying: '[b]Turn now every man from his evil
way, and amend your deeds, and [c]do not go after other gods to
worship them, then you shall [d]dwell in the land which I have given
to you and to your forefathers; but you have not [e]inclined your ear or
listened to Me.
16 'Indeed, the sons of Jonadab the son of Rechab have [a]observed
the command of their father which he commanded them, but this
people has not listened to Me.' " '
17 "Therefore thus says the LORD, the God of hosts, the God of Israel,
'Behold, [a]I am bringing on Judah and on all the inhabitants of Jeru-
salem all the disaster that I have pronounced against them; because I
[b]spoke to them but they did not listen, and I have called them but
they did not answer.' "
18 Then Jeremiah said to the house of the Rechabites, "Thus says
the LORD of hosts, the God of Israel, 'Because you have [a]obeyed the
command of Jonadab your father, kept all his commands, and done
according to all that he commanded you;
19 therefore thus says the LORD of hosts, the God of Israel, "Jonadab

4 [a]Deut. 33:1; 14:6; 1 Kin. 12 1:9-13 [b]1 Chr

5 [1]Lit., *sons* 2:12

6 [a]2 Kin. 10:1 [b]1 Chr. 2:55 [c] Num. 6:2-4; Ju 14; Luke 1:15

7 [a]Gen. 25:27 11:9 [b]Ex. 20:1 6:2, 3 [c]Gen. 3

8 [a]Prov. 1:8, 9 10; 6:20; Eph. 3:20

9 [a]Ps. 37:16; 1 Tim. 6:6

10 [a]Jer. 35:7 [b]

11 [a]2 Kin. 24:1, 1:1, 2 [b]Jer. 4:5

13 [a]Is. 28:9-12; 6:8-10; 32:33

14 [1]Lit., *rising e speaking* [a]Jer. [b]2 Chr. 36:15; Je 25; 11:7; 25:3, 4 30:9; 50:2

15 [1]Lit., *rising e speaking* [a]Jer. 7 25:4; 26:5; 29:1 [b]Is. 1:16, 17; Jer 18:11; 25:5f.; Ez 18:30-32; Acts 2 [c]Deut. 6:14; Jer. 13:10; 25:6 [d]Jer 25:5, 6 [e]Jer. 7:2 11:8; 17:23; 34:1

16 [a]Jer. 35:14;

17 [a]Josh. 23:15; 19:3, 15; 21:4-10 3:12 [b]Prov. 1:24, 65:12; 66:4; Jer. 26, 27; 26:5; Luk 13:34, 35; Rom.

18 [a]Ex. 20:12; E 6:1-3

the son of Rechab [a]shall not lack a man to [b]stand before Me
[1]always."' "

Chapter 36

36 And it came about in the [a]fourth year of Jehoiakim the son of
Josiah, king of Judah, that this word came to Jeremiah from
the LORD, saying,
2 "Take a [1a]scroll and write on it all the [b]words which I have spoken
to you concerning [c]Israel, and concerning Judah, and concerning all
the [d]nations, from the [e]day I *first* spoke to you, from the days of
Josiah, even to this day.
3 "[a]Perhaps the house of Judah will hear all the calamity which I
plan to bring on them, in order that every man will [b]turn from his
evil way; then I will [c]forgive their iniquity and their sin."
4 Then Jeremiah called [a]Baruch the son of Neriah, and Baruch
wrote [1]at the dictation of Jeremiah all the words of the LORD, which
He had spoken to him, on a [2b]scroll.
5 And Jeremiah commanded Baruch, saying, "I am [1a]restricted; I
cannot go into the house of the LORD.
6 "So you go and [a]read from the scroll which you have [b]written [1]at
my dictation the words of the LORD [2]to the people in the LORD's
house on a [c]fast day. And also you shall read them [2]to all *the people of*
Judah who come from their cities.
7 "[a]Perhaps their supplication will [1]come before the LORD, and
everyone will turn from his evil way, for [b]great is the anger and the
wrath that the LORD has pronounced against this people."
8 And Baruch the son of Neriah did according to all that Jeremiah
the prophet commanded him, [a]reading from the book the words of
the LORD in the LORD's house.
9 Now it came about in the [a]fifth year of Jehoiakim the son of
Josiah, king of Judah, in the [b]ninth month, that all the people in
Jerusalem and all the people who [c]came from the cities of Judah to
Jerusalem proclaimed a [d]fast before the LORD.
10 Then Baruch read from the book the words of Jeremiah in the
house of the LORD in the [a]chamber of [b]Gemariah the son of Shaphan
the [c]scribe, in the upper court, at the [d]entry of the New Gate of the
LORD's house, to all the people.
11 Now when [a]Micaiah the son of Gemariah, the son of Shaphan,
had heard all the words of the LORD from the book,
12 he went down to the king's house, into the scribe's chamber.
And, behold, all the officials were sitting there—[a]Elishama the scribe,
and [b]Delaiah the son of Shemaiah, and [c]Elnathan the son of Achbor,
and Gemariah the son of Shaphan, and Zedekiah the son of
Hananiah, and all the *other* officials.
13 And Micaiah [a]declared to them all the words that he had heard,
when Baruch read from the book to the people.
14 Then all the officials sent [a]Jehudi the son of Nethaniah, the son of
Shelemiah, the son of Cushi, to Baruch, saying, "Take in your hand
the scroll from which you have read to the people and come." So
Baruch the son of Neriah [b]took the scroll in his hand and went to
them.
15 And they said to him, "Sit down please, and read it to us." So
Baruch [a]read it to them.
16 Now it came about when they had heard all the words, they

9 [1]Lit., *all the days* ...Chr. 2:55; Jer. 33:17 ... 15:19; Luke 21:36

[a]2 Kin. 24:1; 2 Chr. 36:5-7; Jer. 25:1, 3; 45:1; 46:2; Dan. 1:1

...Lit., *scroll of a book* ... 17:14; Is. 8:1; Jer. ..., 23, 28; Zech. 5:1, [b]Jer. 1:9, 10; 30:2; ...b. 2:2 [c]Jer. 3:3-10; 23:13, 14; 32:30-32 ...er. 1:5, 10; 25:9-29; 47-51 [e]Jer. 1:2, 3; 25:3

...r. 26:3; 36:7; Ezek. ...2:3 [b]Deut. 30:2, 8; ...n. 7:3; Is. 55:7; Jer. ...8:8, 11; 35:15; Jon. ...8 [c]Jon. 3:10; Mark 4:12; Acts 3:19

...Lit., *from the mouth* ...Lit., *scroll of a book* 32:12; 36:18; 43:3; [b]Jer. 36:14; Ezek. 2:9

[1]Lit., *shut up* [a]Jer. ...; 33:1; 2 Cor. 11:23

...Lit., *from my mouth in the ears of,* and so throughout this ...xt [a]Jer. 36:8 [b]Jer. ...4 [c]Jer. 36:9; Zech. 8:19

..., *fall* [a]1 Kin. 8:33; ...Chr. 33:12, 13; Jer. 36:3 [b]Deut. 28:15; ...6, 17; 2 Kin. 22:13, ...er. 4:4; 21:5; Lam. 4:11

8 [a]Jer. 1:17; 36:6

9 [a]Jer. 36:1 [b]Jer. ... [c]Jer. 36:6 [d]Judg. 20:26; 1 Sam. 7:6; ...r. 20:3; Esth. 4:16; ...:14; 2:15; Jon. 3:5

...0 [a]Jer. 35:4 [b]Jer. ..., 25 [c]2 Sam. 8:17; 52:25 [d]Jer. 26:10

11 [a]Jer. 36:13

... [a]Jer. 36:20 [b]Jer. 36:25 [c]Jer. 26:22

13 [a]2 Kin. 22:10

... [a]Jer. 36:21 [b]Jer. ...36:2; Ezek. 2:7-10

15 [a]Jer. 36:21

turned in [a]fear one to another and said to Baruch, "We will surely
[b]report all these words to the king."
17 And they asked Baruch, saying, "Tell us please, [a]how did you
write all these words? *Was it* [1]at his dictation?"
18 Then Baruch said to them, "He [a]dictated all these words to me,
and I wrote them with ink on the book."
19 Then the officials said to Baruch, "Go, [a]hide yourself, you and
Jeremiah, and do not let anyone know where you are."
20 So they went to the [a]king in the court, but they had deposited the
scroll in the chamber of [a]Elishama the scribe, and they reported all
the words to the king.
21 Then the king sent Jehudi to get the scroll, and he took it out of
the chamber of Elishama the scribe. And Jehudi [a]read it to the king
as well as to all the officials who stood beside the king.
22 Now the king was sitting in the [a]winter house in the [b]ninth
month, with *a fire* burning in the brazier before him.
23 And it came about, when Jehudi had read three or four columns,
the king cut it with a scribe's knife and [a]threw *it* into the fire that was
in the brazier, until all the scroll was consumed in the fire that was in
the brazier.
24 Yet the king and all his servants who heard all these words were
[a]not afraid, nor did they [b]rend their garments.
25 Even though Elnathan and Delaiah and Gemariah [a]entreated the
king not to burn the scroll, he would not listen to them.
26 And the king commanded Jerahmeel the king's son, Seraiah the
son of Azriel, and Shelemiah the son of Abdeel to [a]seize Baruch the
scribe and Jeremiah the prophet, but the [b]LORD hid them.
27 Then the word of the LORD came to Jeremiah after the king had
[a]burned the scroll and the words which [b]Baruch had written at the
dictation of Jeremiah, saying,
28 "[a]Take again another scroll and write on it all the former words
that were [b]on the first scroll which Jehoiakim the king of Judah
burned.
29 "And concerning Jehoiakim king of Judah you shall say, 'Thus
says the LORD, "You have [a]burned this scroll, saying, '[b]Why have you
written on it [1]that the [c]king of Babylon shall certainly come and
destroy this land, and shall make man and beast to cease from it?' "
30 'Therefore thus says the LORD concerning Jehoiakim king of
Judah, "He shall have [a]no one to sit on the throne of David, and his
[b]dead body shall be cast out to the heat of the day and the frost of the
night.
31 "I shall also [a]punish him and his [1]descendants and his servants
for their iniquity, and I shall [b]bring on them and the inhabitants of
Jerusalem and the men of Judah all the calamity that I have declared
to them—but they did not listen." ' "
32 Then Jeremiah took another scroll and gave it to Baruch the son
of Neraiah, the scribe, and he [a]wrote on it at the dictation of Jeremiah
all the words of the book which Jehoiakim king of Judah had burned
in the fire; and many [1]similar words were added to them.

Chapter 37

37 Now [a]Zedekiah the son of Josiah whom Nebuchadnezzar
king of Babylon had [b]made king in the land of Judah, reigned
as king in place of [c]Coniah the son of Jehoiakim.

16 [a]Jer. 36:24 24:25 [b]Jer. 13 Amos 7:10, 11
17 [1]Lit., *from* and so through context [a]John 15, 26
18 [a]Jer. 36:4
19 [a]1 Kin. 17: 10; Jer. 26:20-
20 [a]Jer. 36:12
21 [a]2 Kin. 22: 34:18; Ezek. 2
22 [a]Judg. 3:2 3:15 [b]Jer. 36:
23 [a]1 Kin. 22 Prov. 1:30; Is. 28:14, 22; Jer
24 [a]Ps. 36:1; 36:16 [b]Gen. 2 Sam. 1:11; 21:27; 2 Kin. 22:11, 19; Is. 37:1; Jon. 3:6
25 [a]Gen. 37: Acts 5:34-39
26 [a]1 Kin. 19 14; Matt. 23:3 91:1
27 [a]Jer. 36:2 36:4, 18
28 [a]Zech. 1:5 36:4, 23
29 [1]Lit., *sayi* 29:19; Job 15 45:9 [b]Is. 29:2 Jer. 26:9; 32: 25:9-11
30 [a]2 Kin. 24 Jer. 22:30 [b]J
31 [1]Lit., *see* 23:34 [b]Deut. Prov. 29:1; Je 35:17
32 [1]Lit., *like* 4:15, 16; 34:1 18, 23
37:1 [a]2 Kin. 1 Chr. 3:15; 2 36:10 [b]Ezek [c]2 Kin. 24:12 3:16; 2 Chr. 3 Jer. 22:24, 28 52:31

2 But [a]neither he nor his servants nor the people of the land lis-
tened to the words of the LORD which He spoke through Jeremiah
the prophet.
3 Yet [a]King Zedekiah sent Jehucal the son of Shelemiah, and
[b]Zephaniah the son of Maaseiah, the priest, to Jeremiah the prophet,
saying, "[c]Please pray to the LORD our God on our behalf."
4 Now Jeremiah was *still* coming in and going out among the
people, for they had not *yet* [a]put him in the prison.
5 Meanwhile, [a]Pharaoh's army had set out from Egypt; and when
the Chaldeans who had been besieging Jerusalem heard the report
about them, they [b]lifted the *siege* from Jerusalem.
6 Then the word of the LORD came to Jeremiah the prophet, saying,
7 "Thus says the LORD God of Israel, '[a]Thus you are to say to the
king of Judah, who sent you to Me to inquire of Me: "Behold,
[b]Pharaoh's army which has come out for your assistance is going to
return to its own land of Egypt.
8 "The Chaldeans will also [a]return and fight against this city, and
they will capture it and burn it with fire." '
9 "Thus says the LORD, 'Do not [a]deceive yourselves, saying, "The
Chaldeans will surely go away from us," for they will not go.
10 'For [a]even if you had defeated the entire army of Chaldeans who
were fighting against you, and there were *only* wounded men left
among them, each man in his tent, they would rise up and [b]burn this
city with fire.' "
11 Now it happened, when the army of the Chaldeans had lifted *the*
siege from Jerusalem because of Pharaoh's army,
12 that Jeremiah went out from Jerusalem to go to the land of Ben-
jamin in order to [a]take [1]possession of *some* property there among the
people.
13 While he was at the [a]Gate of Benjamin, a captain of the guard
whose name was Irijah, the son of Shelemiah the son of Hananiah
was there; and he [b]arrested Jeremiah the prophet, saying, "You are
[1]going over to the Chaldeans!"
14 But Jeremiah said, "[a]A lie! I am not [1]going over to the Chalde-
ans"; yet he would not listen to him. So Irijah arrested Jeremiah and
brought him to the officials.
15 Then the officials were [a]angry at Jeremiah and beat him, and
they [b]put him in jail in the house of Jonathan the scribe, which they
had made into the prison.
16 For Jeremiah had come into the [1a]dungeon, that is, the vaulted
cell; and Jeremiah stayed there many days.
17 Now King Zedekiah sent and took him *out;* and in his palace the
king [a]secretly asked him and said, "Is there a [b]word from the LORD?"
And Jeremiah said, "There is!" Then he said, "You will be [c]given into
the hand of the king of Babylon!"
18 Moreover Jeremiah said to King Zedekiah, "[a]*In* what *way* have I
sinned against you, or against your servants, or against this people,
that you have put me in prison?
19 "[a]Where then are your prophets who prophesied to you, saying,
'The [b]king of Babylon will not come against you or against this
land'?
20 "But now, please listen, O my lord the king; please let my [a]peti-
tion [1]come before you, and do not make me return to the house of
Jonathan the scribe, that I may not die there."

[a]2 Kin. 24:19, 20; hr. 36:12-16; Prov. 29:12

[a]Jer. 21:1, 2 [b]Jer. 9:25; 52:24 [c]1 Kin. 6; Jer. 2:27; 15:11; 2; 42:1-4, 20; Acts 8:24

Jer. 32:2, 3; 37:15

5 [a]2 Kin. 24:7; Jer. Ezek. 17:15 [b]Jer. 37:11

[a]2 Kin. 22:18; Jer. 21:1, 2; 37:3 [b]Is. ; 31:1-3; Jer. 2:18, ; Lam. 4:17; Ezek. 17:17

[a]Jer. 34:22; 38:23; 39:2-8

ler. 29:8; Obad. 3; . 24:4, 5; Eph. 5:6

[a]Lev. 26:36-38; Is. ; Jer. 21:4, 5 [b]Jer. 37:8

12 [1]Or, *part in a dividing* [a]Jer. 32:8

[1]Lit., *falling* [a]Jer. Zech. 14:10 [b]Jer. 20:10; Luke 23:2; ts 6:11; 24:5-9, 13

[1]Lit., *falling* [a]Ps. 7:12; 52:1, 2; Jer. 4-6; Matt. 5:11, 12

ler. 18:23; 20:1-3; 26:16; Matt. 21:35 Gen. 39:20; 2 Chr. 18:26; Jer. 38:26; Acts 5:18

[1]Lit., *house of the* ern-pit [a]Jer. 38:6

1 Kin. 14:1-4; Jer. 8:5, 14-16, 24-27 22:15, 16; 2 Kin. 1, 12; Jer. 15:11; ; 37:3 [c]Jer. 21:7; Ezek. 12:12, 13; 17:19, 20

Sam. 24:9; 26:18; 6:22; John 10:32; Acts 25:8, 11, 25

[a]Deut. 32:37, 38; n. 3:13; Jer. 2:28 er. 27:14; 28:1-4, 10-17

t., *fall* [a]Jer. 36:7; 38:26

21 Then King Zedekiah gave commandment, and they committed
Jeremiah to the [a]court of the guardhouse and gave him a loaf of
[b]bread daily from the bakers' street, until all the bread in the city was
[c]gone. So Jeremiah remained in the court of the guardhouse.

Chapter 38

38 Now Shephatiah the son of Mattan, and Gedaliah the son of
Pashhur, and Jucal the [a]son of Shelemiah, and [b]Pashhur the
son of Malchijah heard the words that Jeremiah was speaking to all
the people, saying,
2 "Thus says the LORD, 'He who [a]stays in this city will die by the
[b]sword and by famine and by pestilence, but he who goes out to the
Chaldeans will live and have his *own* [c]life as booty and stay alive.'
3 "Thus says the LORD, 'This city will certainly be [a]given into the
hand of the army of the king of Babylon, and he will capture it.' "
4 Then the [a]officials said to the king, "Now let this man be put to
death, inasmuch as he is [1b]discouraging the men of war who are left
in this city and [2]all the people, by speaking such words to them; for
this man [c]is not seeking the well-being of this people, but rather their
harm."
5 So King Zedekiah said, "Behold, he is in your [1]hands; for the
king [a]can *do* nothing against you."
6 Then they took Jeremiah and cast him into the [a]cistern *of* Mal-
chijah the king's son, which was in the court of the guardhouse; and
they let Jeremiah down with ropes. Now in the cistern there was no
water but only [b]mud, and Jeremiah sank into the mud.
7 But [a]Ebed-melech the Ethiopian, [1]a [b]eunuch, while he was in the
king's palace, heard that they had put Jeremiah into the cistern. Now
the king was sitting in the [c]Gate of Benjamin;
8 and Ebed-melech went out from the king's palace and spoke to
the king, saying,
9 "My lord the king, these men have acted wickedly in all that they
have done to Jeremiah the prophet whom they have cast into the
cistern; and he [1]will die right where he is because of the famine, for
there is [a]no more bread in the city."
10 Then the king commanded Ebed-melech the Ethiopian, saying,
"Take thirty men from here [1]under your authority, and bring up
Jeremiah the prophet from the cistern before he dies."
11 So Ebed-melech took the men under his [1]authority and went into
the king's palace to *a place* beneath the storeroom and took from
there worn-out clothes and worn-out rags and let them down by
ropes into the cistern to Jeremiah.
12 Then Ebed-melech the Ethiopian said to Jeremiah, "Now put
these worn-out clothes and rags under your armpits under the
ropes"; and Jeremiah did so.
13 So they pulled Jeremiah up with the ropes and lifted him out of
the cistern, and Jeremiah stayed in the [a]court of the guardhouse.
14 Then King Zedekiah [a]sent and [1]had Jeremiah the prophet
brought to him at the third entrance that is in the house of the LORD;
and the king said to Jeremiah, "I am going to [b]ask you something; do
not hide anything from me."
15 Then Jeremiah said to Zedekiah, "[a]If I tell you, will you not
certainly put me to death? Besides, if I give you advice, you will not
listen to me."

21 [a]Jer. 32:2; [b]1 Kin. 17:6; J Ps. 33:18, 19; [c]2 Kin. 25:3; J 52:6

38:1 [a]Jer. 37: 21:1

2 [a]Jer. 21:9 [b] 34:17; 42:17 [c] 39:18; 45:5

3 [a]Jer. 21:10;

4 [1]Lit., *weaker hands of* [2]Lit., *hands of all* [a]J 26:11, 21; 36:1 5:4; 1 Kin. 18:1 21:20; Neh. 6:9 7:10; Acts 16:2 29:7

5 [1]Lit., *hand* [a] 3:39

6 [a]Jer. 37:16, 2 16:24 [b]Ps. 40:2 14, 15; Jer. 38:2 9:11

7 [1]Or, *an officia* 39:16 [b]Jer. 29:2 8:27 [c]Deut. 21: 29:7; Jer. 37:13 5:10

9 [1]M.T. reads *h* [a]Jer. 37:21; 52:6

10 [1]Lit., *in your*

11 [1]Lit., *hand*

13 [a]Neh. 3:25; J 32:2; 37:21; 38:6 15; Acts 23:35; 2 28:16, 30

14 [1]Lit., *took Jer the prophet to hi* 21:1, 2; 37:17 [b]1 3:17, 18; 1 Kin. 2 Jer. 15:11; 42:2-5

15 [a]Luke 22:67,

16 But King Zedekiah swore to Jeremiah in [a]secret saying, "As the
LORD lives, who made this [1b]life for us, surely I will not put you to
death nor will I give you over to the hand of [c]these men who are
seeking your [1]life."
17 Then Jeremiah said to Zedekiah, "Thus says the LORD [a]God of
hosts, the [b]God of Israel, 'If you will indeed [c]go out to the officers of
the king of Babylon, then [1]you will live, this city will not be burned
with fire, and you and your household will [2]survive.
18 'But if you will [a]not go out to the officers of the king of Babylon,
then this city [b]will be given over to the hand of the Chaldeans; and
they will burn it with fire, and [c]you yourself will not escape from
their hand.' "
19 Then King Zedekiah said to Jeremiah, "I [a]dread the Jews who
have [1b]gone over to the Chaldeans, lest they give me over into their
hand and they [c]abuse me."
20 But Jeremiah said, "They will not give you over. Please [1a]obey
the LORD in what I am saying to you, that it may go [b]well with you
and [2c]you may live.
21 "But if you keep refusing to go out, this is the word which the
LORD has shown me:
22 'Then behold, all of the [a]women who have been left in the palace
of the king of Judah are going to be brought out to the [1]officers of the
king of Babylon; and those women will say,

"[2]Your close friends
Have misled and overpowered you;
While your feet were sunk in the mire,
They turned back."

23 'They will also bring out all your wives and your [a]sons to the
Chaldeans, and [b]you yourself will not escape from their hand, but
will be seized by the hand of the king of Babylon, and [b]this city will
be burned with fire.' "
24 Then Zedekiah said to Jeremiah, "Let no man know about these
words and you will not die.
25 "But if the [a]officials hear that I have talked with you and come to
you and say to you, 'Tell us now what you said to the king, and
what the king said to you; do not hide *it* from us, and we will not
put you to death,'
26 then you are to say to them, 'I was [a]presenting my petition
before the king, not to make me return to the house of Jonathan to
die there.' "
27 Then all the officials came to Jeremiah and questioned him. So he
reported to them in accordance with all these words which the king
had commanded; and they ceased speaking with him, since the [1]con-
versation had not been overheard.
28 So Jeremiah [a]stayed in the court of the guardhouse until the day
that Jerusalem was captured.

Chapter 39

39 [1]Now it came about when Jerusalem was captured [2a]in the
ninth year of Zedekiah king of Judah, in the tenth month,
Nebuchadnezzar king of Babylon and all his army came to Jerusa-
lem and laid siege to it;
2 in the eleventh year of Zedekiah, in the fourth month, in the
ninth *day* of the month, the city *wall* was [a]breached.

16 [1]Lit., *soul* [a]Jer. 7; John 3:2 [b]Num. :22; 27:16; Is. 42:5; 6; Zech. 12:1; Acts 25, 28 [c]Jer. 34:20; 38:4-6

[1]Lit., *your soul* [2]Lit., Ps. 80:7, 14; Amos 5:27 [b]1 Chr. 17:24; 8:4 [c]2 Kin. 24:12; 7-30; Jer. 21:8-10; :12, 17; 38:2; 39:3

[a]Jer. 27:8 [b]2 Kin. 4-10; Jer. 24:8-10; 5; 37:8; 38:3 [c]Jer. 32:4; 34:3

19 [1]Lit., *fallen* [a]Is. 2, 13; 57:11; John 42; 19:12, 13 [b]Jer. 9:9 [c]2 Chr. 30:10; eh. 4:1; Jer. 38:22

[1]Lit., *listen to the of* [2]Lit., *your soul* r. 20:20; Jer. 11:4, 26:13; Dan. 4:27; s 26:29 [b]Jer. 7:23 en. 19:20; Is. 55:3

[1]Or, *princes* [2]Lit., *nen of your peace* r. 6:12; 8:10; 43:6

[a]2 Kin. 25:7; Jer. 41:10 [b]Jer. 38:18

5 [a]Jer. 38:4-6, 27

26 [a]Jer. 37:20

27 [1]Lit., *word*

28 [a]Ps. 23:4; Jer. 20, 21; 37:20, 21; 38:13; 39:13, 14

[1]Ch. 38:28-b in [2]Ch. 39:1 in Heb. Kin. 25:1-12; Jer. 2:4; Ezek. 24:1, 2

n. 25:4; Jer. 52:7

3 Then all the [a]officials of the king of Babylon came in and sat
down at the [b]Middle Gate: Nergal-sar-ezer, Samgar-nebu, Sar-sekim
the [1]Rab-saris, Nergal-sar-ezer *the* [2]Rab-mag, and all the rest of the
officials of the king of Babylon.
4 And it came about, when Zedekiah the king of Judah and all the
men of war saw them, that they [a]fled and went out of the city at
night by way of the king's garden through the gate [b]between the two
walls; and he went out toward the [1]Arabah.
5 But the army of the [a]Chaldeans pursued them and overtook
Zedekiah in the [b]plains of Jericho; and they seized him and brought
him up to Nebuchadnezzar king of Babylon at [c]Riblah in the land of
Hamath, and he passed sentence on him.
6 Then the [a]king of Babylon slew the sons of Zedekiah [b]before his
eyes at Riblah; the king of Babylon also slew all the [c]nobles of Judah.
7 He then [a]blinded Zedekiah's eyes and bound him in [b]fetters of
bronze to bring him to [c]Babylon.
8 The Chaldeans also [a]burned with fire the king's palace and the
houses of the people, and they [b]broke down the walls of Jerusalem.
9 And as for the rest of the people who were left in the city, the
[1a]deserters who had gone over to him and [b]the rest of the people who
remained, [c]Nebuzaradan the [d]captain of the bodyguard carried *them*
into exile in Babylon.
10 But some of the [a]poorest people who had nothing, [a]Nebuzaradan
the captain of the bodyguard left behind in the land of Judah, and
gave them vineyards and fields [1]at that time.
11 Now Nebuchadnezzar king of Babylon gave orders about [a]Jere-
miah through Nebuzaradan the captain of the bodyguard, saying,
12 "Take him and [1]look after him, and [a]do nothing harmful to him;
but rather deal with him just as he tells you."
13 So Nebuzaradan the captain of the bodyguard sent *word,* along
with Nebushazban the [1]Rab-saris, and Nergal-sar-ezer the [2]Rab-mag,
and all the leading officers of the king of Babylon;
14 they even sent and [a]took Jeremiah out of the court of the guard-
house and entrusted him to [b]Gedaliah, the son of [c]Ahikam, the son of
Shaphan, to take him home. So he stayed among the people.
15 Now the word of the LORD had come to Jeremiah while he was
[a]confined in the court of the guardhouse, saying,
16 "Go and speak to [a]Ebed-melech the Ethiopian, saying, 'Thus says
the LORD of hosts, the God of Israel, "Behold, I am about to bring My
words on this city [b]for disaster and not for [1]prosperity; and they will
[c]take place before you on that day.
17 "But I will [a]deliver you on that day," declares the LORD, "and you
shall not be given into the hand of the men whom you dread.
18 "For I will certainly rescue you, and you will not fall by the
sword; but you will have your *own* [a]life as booty, because you have
[b]trusted in Me," declares the LORD.' "

Chapter 40 ____________________

40 The word which came to Jeremiah from the LORD after [a]Nebu-
zaradan captain of the bodyguard had released him from
[b]Ramah, when he had taken him bound in [c]chains, among all the
exiles of Jerusalem and Judah, who were being exiled to Babylon.
2 Now the captain of the bodyguard had taken Jeremiah and said

3 [1]I.e., chief officia [2]I.e., title of a high official [a]Jer. 38:17 21:4

4 [1]I.e., Jordan vall [a]2 Kin. 25:4; Is. 30. Jer. 52:7; Amos 2:1 [b]2 Chr. 32:5

5 [a]Jer. 32:4, 5; 38: 23; 52:8 [b]Josh. 4:1 5:10 [c]2 Kin. 23:33; 52:9, 26, 27

6 [a]2 Kin. 25:7; Jer. 52:10 [b]Deut. 28:34 [c]Jer. 21:7; 24:8-10 34:19-21

7 [a]2 Kin. 25:7; Jer. 52:11; Ezek. 12:13 [b]Judg. 16:21 [c]Jer.

8 [a]2 Kin. 25:9; Jer. 21:10; 38:18; 52:1 [b]2 Kin. 25:10; Neh. Jer. 52:14

9 [1]Lit., *fallers who fallen* [a]Jer. 38:19; 52:15 [b]Jer. 24:8 [c] 25:11, 20; Jer. 39: 40:1; 52:12-16, 26 [d]Gen. 37:36

10 [1]Lit., *on that da* [a]2 Kin. 25:12; Jer.

11 [a]Job 5:15, 16; 1:8; 15:20, 21; Act 24:23

12 [1]Lit., *set your e on* [a]Ps. 105:14, 1 Prov. 16:7; 21:1; 1 3:13

13 [1]I.e., chief offic [2]I.e., title of a high

14 [a]Jer. 38:28; 40 [b]Jer. 40:5 [c]2 Kin. 14; 2 Chr. 34:20; 26:24

15 [a]Jer. 38:28

16 [1]Lit., *good* [a]Je 38:7 [b]Jer. 21:10; 9:12; Zech. 1:6 [c]F 91:8

17 [a]Ps. 41:1, 2; 5

18 [a]Jer. 21:9; 38: 45:5 [b]Ps. 34:22; 17:7, 8

40:1 [a]Jer. 39:9, 1 [b]Jer. 31:15 [c]Acts 7; 21:13; 28:20; E 6:20

to him, "The [a]LORD your God promised this calamity against this
place;
3 and the LORD has brought *it* on and done just as He promised.
Because you *people* [a]sinned against the LORD and did not listen to His
voice, therefore this thing has happened to you.
4 "But now, behold, I am [a]freeing you today from the chains which
are on your hands. If [1]you would prefer to come with me to Babylon,
come *along*, and I will [2]look after you; but if [3]you would prefer not to
come with me to Babylon, [4]never mind. Look, the [b]whole land is
before you; go wherever it seems good and right for you to go."
5 As [1]Jeremiah was still not going back, [2]*he said*, "Go on back then
to [a]Gedaliah the son of Ahikam, the son of Shaphan, whom the king
of Babylon has [b]appointed over the cities of Judah, and stay with
him among the people; or else go anywhere it seems right for you to
go." So the captain of the bodyguard gave him a [c]ration and a [d]gift
and let him go.
6 Then Jeremiah went to [a]Mizpah to [b]Gedaliah the son of Ahikam
and stayed with him among the people who were left in the land.
7 [a]Now all the [1]commanders of the forces that were in the field,
they and their men, heard that the king of Babylon had appointed
Gedaliah the son of Ahikam over the land and that he had put him
in charge of the men, women and [2]children, those of the [b]poorest of
the land who had not been exiled to Babylon.
8 So they came to Gedaliah at Mizpah, along with [a]Ishmael the son
of Nethaniah, and [b]Johanan and Jonathan the sons of Kareah, and
Seraiah the son of Tanhumeth, and the sons of Ephai the [c]Netopha-
thite, and [d]Jezaniah the son of the [e]Maacathite, *both* they and their
men.
9 Then Gedaliah the son of Ahikam, the son of Shaphan, [a]swore to
them and to their men, saying, "[b]Do not be afraid of serving the
Chaldeans; stay in the land and serve the king of Babylon, that it
may go well with you.
10 "Now as for me, behold, I am going to stay at Mizpah to [a]stand *for
you* before the Chaldeans who come to us; but as for you, [b]gather in
wine and [c]summer fruit and oil, and put *them* in your *storage* vessels,
and live in your cities that you have taken over."
11 Likewise also all the Jews who were in [a]Moab and among the
sons of [b]Ammon and in [c]Edom, and who were in all the *other*
countries, heard that the king of Babylon had left a remnant for
Judah and that he had appointed over them Gedaliah the son of
Ahikam, the son of Shaphan.
12 Then all the Jews [a]returned from all the places to which they had
been driven away and came to the land of Judah, to Gedaliah at
Mizpah, and gathered in wine and summer fruit in great abundance.
13 Now Johanan the son of Kareah and all the commanders of the
forces that were in the field came to Gedaliah at Mizpah,
14 and said to him, "Are you well aware that Baalis the king of the
sons of [a]Ammon has sent Ishmael the son of Nethaniah to take your
life?" But Gedaliah the son of Ahikam did not believe them.
15 Then Johanan the son of Kareah spoke secretly to Gedaliah in
Mizpah, saying, "[a]Let me go and kill Ishmael the son of Nethaniah,
and not a man will know! Why should he [b]take your life, so that all
the Jews who are gathered to you should be scattered and the [c]rem-
nant of Judah perish?"

[a]Lev. 26:14-38; Deut. 28:15-68; 29:24-28; 31:17; 32:19-25; Jer. 22:8, 9

[a]Jer. 50:7; Dan. 9:11; Rom. 2:5

[1]Lit., *it is good in your* ...es [2]Lit., *set my eyes* [3]Lit., *it is evil in your* ...s [4]Lit., *refrain!* [a]Jer. ...9:11, 12 [b]Gen. 13:9; 20:15; 47:6

5 [1]Lit., *he* [2]I.e., Nebuzaradan [a]Jer. 39:14 [b]2 Kin. 25:23 52:34 [d]2 Kin. 8:7-9

6 [a]Judg. 20:1; 21:1; ...am. 7:5; 2 Chr. 16:6 [b]Jer. 39:14

7 [1]Or, *princes* [2]Lit., ...*nfants* [a]2 Kin. 25:23 [b]Jer. 39:10; 52:16

8 [a]Jer. 40:14; 41:2 ...er. 40:13, 15; 42:1; [c]2 Sam. 23:28, 29; ...zra 2:22; Neh. 7:26 ...r. 42:1 [e]Deut. 3:14; Josh. 12:5; 2 Sam. 10:6, 8

[a]1 Sam. 20:16, 17; 25:24 [b]Jer. 27:11; 38:17-20

[a]Deut. 1:38; 1 Kin. ...; Jer. 35:19 [b]Deut. ...:13; Jer. 39:10 [c]Is. ...9; Jer. 40:12; 48:32

...Num. 22:1; 25:1, 2; Is. 16:4; Jer. 9:26 1 Sam. 11:1; 12:12 ...Gen. 36:8; Is. 11:14

12 [a]Jer. 43:5

14 [a]1 Sam. 11:1-3; 2 Sam. 10:1-6; Jer. 25:21; 41:10

15 [a]1 Sam. 26:8 ...21:17 [c]Jer. 42:2

16 But Gedaliah the son of Ahikam said to Johanan the son of Kareah, "[a]Do not do this thing, for you are telling a lie about Ishmael."

Chapter 41

41 Now it [a]came about in the seventh month that [b]Ishmael the son of Nethaniah, the son of Elishama, of the royal [1]family and *one* of the chief officers of the king, along with ten men, came to Mizpah to [c]Gedaliah the son of Ahikam. While they [d]were eating bread together there in Mizpah,

2 Ishmael the son of Nethaniah and the ten men who were with him arose and [a]struck down Gedaliah the son of Ahikam, the son of Shaphan, with the sword and [b]put to death the one [c]whom the king of Babylon had appointed over the land.

3 Ishmael also struck down all the Jews who were with him, *that is* with Gedaliah at Mizpah, and the Chaldeans who were found there, the men of war.

4 Now it happened on the [1]next day after the killing of Gedaliah, when no one knew about *it*,

5 that eighty men [a]came from [b]Shechem, from [c]Shiloh, and from [d]Samaria with [e]their beards shaved off and their clothes torn and [1]their bodies [f]gashed, having grain offerings and incense in their hands to bring to the [g]house of the LORD.

6 Then Ishmael the son of Nethaniah went out from Mizpah to meet them, [a]weeping as he went; and it came about as he met them that he said to them, "Come to Gedaliah the son of Ahikam!"

7 Yet it turned out that as soon as they came inside the city, Ishmael the son of Nethaniah and the men that were with him [a]slaughtered them, *and cast them* into the cistern.

8 But ten men who were found among them said to Ishmael, "Do not put us to death; for we have [a]stores of wheat, barley, oil and honey hidden in the field." So he refrained and did not put them to death along with their companions.

9 Now as for the cistern where Ishmael had cast all the corpses of the men whom he had struck down [1]because of Gedaliah, it was the [a]one that King Asa had made on [b]account of Baasha, king of Israel; Ishmael the son of Nethaniah filled it with the slain.

10 Then Ishmael took captive all the [a]remnant of the people who were in Mizpah, the [b]king's daughters and all the people who were left in Mizpah, whom Nebuzaradan the captain of the bodyguard had put under the charge of Gedaliah the son of Ahikam; thus Ishmael the son of Nethaniah took them captive and proceeded to cross over to the sons of [c]Ammon.

11 But Johanan the son of Kareah and all the [a]commanders of the forces that were with him heard of all the evil that Ishmael the son of Nethaniah had done.

12 So they took all the men and went to [a]fight with Ishmael the son of Nethaniah and they found him by the [b]great [1]pool that is in Gibeon.

13 Now it came about, as soon as all the people who were with Ishmael saw Johanan the son of Kareah and the commanders of the forces that were with him, they were glad.

14 So all the people whom Ishmael had taken captive from Mizpah turned around and came back, and went to Johanan the son of Kareah.

---

16 [a]Matt. 10:16 13:5

41:1 [1]Lit., *seed* 25:25 [b]Jer. 40:8 [c]Jer. 39:14; 40:5 41:9; Jer. 40:13,

2 [a]2 Sam. 3:27; 10; 2 Kin. 25:25; 41:9; 109:5; Joh [b]2 Kin. 25:25 [c]Je

4 [1]Or, *second*

5 [1]Lit., *having c* *themselves* [a]2 K 10:13, 14 [b]Gen. 37:12; Judg. 9:1; 12:1, 25 [c]Josh. 1 Judg. 18:31; 1 Sa 3:21; Ps. 78:60 [d] 16:24, 29 [e]Lev. 1 Deut. 14:1 [f]Deut Jer. 16:6 [g]1 Sam 2 Kin. 25:9

6 [a]2 Sam. 3:16; 50:4

7 [a]Ps. 55:23; Is. Ezek. 22:27; 33:2

8 [a]Is. 45:3

9 [1]Or, *by the side* [a]1 Kin. 15:17-22; 2 16:1-6 [b]Judg. 6:2 1 Sam. 13:6; 2 Sa 17:9; Heb. 11:38

10 [a]Jer. 40:11, 12 43:6 [c]Neh. 2:10, 1 4:7; Jer. 40:14

11 [a]Jer. 40:7, 8, 1

12 [1]Lit., *waters* [a](14:14-16; 1 Sam. 30:1-8, 18, 20 [b]2 S 2:13

15 But Ishmael the son of Nethaniah [a]escaped from Johanan with
eight men and went to the sons of Ammon.
16 Then Johanan the son of Kareah and all the commanders of the
forces that were with him took from Mizpah [a]all the remnant of the
people whom he had [1]recovered from Ishmael the son of Nethaniah,
after he had struck down Gedaliah the son of Ahikam, *that is,* the
men who were [2]soldiers, *the* women, *the* [3]children, and *the* eunuchs,
whom he had brought back from Gibeon.
17 And they went and stayed in [1a]Geruth Chimham, which is be-
side Bethlehem, in order to [b]proceed into Egypt
18 because of the Chaldeans; for they were [a]afraid of them, since
Ishmael the son of Nethaniah had struck down Gedaliah the son of
Ahikam, whom [b]the king of Babylon had appointed over the land.

Chapter 42

42 Then all the [1]commanders of the forces, [a]Johanan the son of
Kareah, Jezaniah the son of Hoshaiah, and all the people
[b]both small and great approached
2 and said to Jeremiah the prophet, "Please let our [a]petition [1]come
before you, and [b]pray for us to the LORD your God, *that is* for all this
remnant; because we are left *but* a [c]few out of many, as your own
eyes *now* see us,
3 that the LORD your God may tell us the [a]way in which we should
walk and the thing that we should do."
4 Then Jeremiah the prophet said to them, "I have heard *you.* Be-
hold, I am going to [a]pray to the LORD your God in accordance with
your words; and it will come about that the whole [1]message which
the [b]LORD will answer you I will tell you. I will [c]not keep back a word
from you."
5 Then they said to Jeremiah, "May the [a]LORD be a true and faithful
witness against us, if we do not act in accordance with the whole
[1]message with which the LORD your God will send you to us.
6 "Whether *it* is [1]pleasant or [2]unpleasant, we will [a]listen to the voice
of the LORD our God to whom we are sending you, in order that it
may go [b]well with us when we listen to the voice of the LORD our
God."
7 Now it came about at the [a]end of ten days that the word of the
LORD came to Jeremiah.
8 Then he called for Johanan the son of Kareah, and all the [1]com-
manders of the forces that were with him, and for all the people both
small and great,
9 and said to them, "Thus [a]says the LORD the God of Israel, to
whom you sent me to present your petition before Him:
10 'If you will indeed stay in this land, then I will [a]build you up and
not tear you down, and I will plant you and not uproot you; for I
[1]shall [b]relent concerning the calamity that I have inflicted on you.
11 '[a]Do not be afraid of the king of Babylon, whom you are *now*
fearing; do not be afraid of him,' declares the LORD, 'for [b]I am with
you to save you and deliver you from his hand.
12 'I will also show you compassion, so that [a]he will have compas-
sion on you and restore you to your own soil.
13 'But if you are going to say, "We will [a]not stay in this land," so as
not to listen to the voice of the LORD your God,
14 saying, "No, but we will [a]go to the land of Egypt, where we shall

5 [a]1 Sam. 30:17; 20:20; Job 21:30; Prov. 28:17

Lit., *brought back* men of war [3]Lit., [a]Jer. 42:8; 43:4-7

[1]Or, *the lodging place of Chimham* am. 19:37, 38, 40 [b]Jer. 42:14

51:12, 13; 57:11; 42:11, 16; 43:2, 3; 12:4, 5 [b]Jer. 40:5

[1]Or, *princes* [a]Jer. 3; 41:11, 18 [b]Jer. 8:10; 42:8; 44:12; Acts 8:10

it., *fall* [a]Jer. 36:7; [b]Ex. 8:28; 1 Sam. 2:19; 1 Kin. 13:6; s. 37:4; Jer. 37:3; Acts 8:24; James [c]Lev. 26:22; Deut. ; Is. 1:9; Lam. 1:1

s. 86:11; Prov. 3:6; Jer. 6:16; Mic. 4:2

., *word* [a]Ex. 8:29; am. 12:23 [b]1 Kin. 22:14; Jer. 23:28 Sam. 3:17, 18; Ps. 40:10; Acts 20:20

[1]Lit., *word* [a]Gen. ; Judg. 11:10; Jer. 3:2; Mic. 1:2; Mal. 2:14; 3:5

Lit., *good* [2]Lit., *evil* . 24:7; Deut. 5:27; osh. 24:24 [b]Deut. , 33; 6:3; Jer. 7:23

s. 27:14; Is. 30:18

8 [1]Or, *princes*

[a]2 Kin. 19:4, 6, 20; 22:15

10 [1]Or, *shall have changed my mind* [a]Jer. 24:6; 31:28; ; Ezek. 36:36 [b]Jer. , 8; Hos. 11:8; Joel ; Amos 7:3, 6; Jon. 3:10; 4:2

Jer. 1:8; 27:12, 17; 41:18 [b]Num. 14:9; r. 32:7, 8; Ps. 46:7, ; 118:6; Is. 8:9, 10; 5; Jer. 1:19; 15:20; Rom. 8:31

12 [a]Neh. 1:11; Ps. 106:46; Prov. 16:7

[a]Ex. 5:2; Jer. 44:16

[a]Is. 31:1; Jer. 41:17

not see war or [b]hear the sound of a trumpet or hunger for bread, and we will stay there";

15 then [1]in that case listen to the word of the LORD, O remnant of Judah. Thus says the LORD of hosts, the God of Israel, "If you really set your [2]mind to enter [a]Egypt, and go in to reside there,

16 then it will come about that the [a]sword, which you are afraid of will overtake you there in the land of Egypt; and the famine, about which you are anxious, will follow closely after you there *in* Egypt; and you will die there.

17 "So all the men who set their [1]mind to go to Egypt to reside there will die by the [a]sword, by famine, and by pestilence; and they will [b]have no survivors or refugees from the calamity that I am going to bring on them." ' "

18 For thus says the LORD of hosts, the God of Israel, "As My [a]anger and wrath have been poured out on the inhabitants of Jerusalem, so My wrath will be poured out on you when you enter Egypt. And you will become a [b]curse, an object of horror, an imprecation, and a reproach; and [c]you will see this place no more."

19 The LORD has spoken to you, O remnant of Judah, "Do not [a]go into Egypt!" You should clearly [b]understand that today I have [c]testified against you.

20 For you have *only* [1a]deceived yourselves; for it is you who sent me to the LORD your God, saying, "Pray for us to the LORD our God; and whatever the LORD our God says, tell us so, and we will do it."

21 So, I have [a]told you today, but you have [b]not [1]obeyed the LORD your God, even in whatever He has sent me to *tell* you.

22 Therefore you should now clearly understand that you will [a]die by the sword, by famine, and by pestilence, in the [b]place where you wish to go to reside.

Chapter 43

43 But it came about, as soon as Jeremiah whom the LORD their God had sent, had [a]finished telling all the people all the words of the LORD their God—that is, all these words—

2 that Azariah the [a]son of Hoshaiah, and Johanan the son of Kareah, and all the arrogant men said to Jeremiah, "You are [b]telling a lie! The LORD our God has not sent you to say, 'You are not to enter Egypt to reside there';

3 but [a]Baruch the son of Neriah is inciting you against us to give us over into the hand of the Chaldeans, so they may put us to death or exile us to Babylon."

4 So [a]Johanan the son of Kareah and all the [1]commanders of the forces, and all the people, [b]did not obey the voice of the LORD, so as to [c]stay in the land of Judah.

5 But Johanan the son of Kareah and all the [1]commanders of the forces took the [a]entire remnant of Judah who had returned from all the nations to which they had been driven away, in order to reside in the land of Judah—

6 the men, the women, the [1]children, the [a]king's daughters and [b]every person that Nebuzaradan the captain of the bodyguard had left with Gedaliah the son of Ahikam and [2]grandson of Shaphan, together with [c]Jeremiah the prophet and Baruch the son of Neriah—

7 and they entered the land of Egypt (for they did not obey the voice of the LORD) and went in as far as [a]Tahpanhes.

INSIGHT

Jeremiah's ministry ended sometime after 586 B.C., possibly about 574 B.C. when, according to tradition, he was stoned to death in Egypt. Jeremiah 43:6-7 tells us that Jeremiah's last days were spent in Egypt.

14 [b]Ex. 16:3; N... 11:4; Jer. 4:19, 2...

15 [1]Lit., *now the...* [2]Lit., *face* [a]Deut... Jer. 42:17; 44:12

16 [a]Jer. 44:13, 2... Ezek. 11:8; Amos...

17 [1]Lit., *face* [a]J... 24:10; 38:2; 42:2... 44:13 [b]Jer. 44:1...

18 [a]2 Chr. 36:16... Jer. 7:20; 33:5; 3... [b]Deut. 29:21; Is. ... Jer. 18:16; 24:9; ... 44:12 [c]Jer. 22:1...

19 [a]Deut. 17:16; ... 30:1-7 [b]Ezek. 2:5... [c]Neh. 9:26, 29, 3...

20 [1]Or, *acted err... your souls* [a]Jer. ... Ezek. 14:3

21 [1]Lit., *listened... voice of* [a]Deut. 1... Jer. 43:1; Ezek. 2... Zech. 7:11; Acts 2... 27 [b]Jer. 43:4

22 [a]Jer. 43:11; E... 6:11 [b]Hos. 9:6

43:1 [a]Jer. 26:8; 5...

2 [a]Jer. 42:1 [b]2 C... 36:13; Is. 7:9; Jer. ... 13; 42:5

3 [a]Jer. 36:4, 10, 2... 43:6; 45:1-3

4 [1]Or, *princes* [a]Je... 42:8 [b]2 Chr. 25:16... 42:5, 6; 44:5 [c]Ps. ... Jer. 42:10-12

5 [1]Or, *princes* [a]Je... 40:11

6 [1]Lit., *infants* [2]Lit... *son* [a]Jer. 41:10 [b]J... 39:10; 40:7 [c]Eccl. ... 2; Lam. 3:1

7 [a]Jer. 2:16; 44:1...

8 Then the word of the LORD came to Jeremiah in [a]Tahpanhes,
saying,
9 "Take *some* large stones in your [1]hands and hide them in the
mortar in the [2]brick *terrace* which is at the entrance of Pharaoh's
[3]palace in Tahpanhes, in the sight of [4]some *of the* Jews;
10 and say to them, 'Thus says the LORD of hosts, the God of Israel,
"Behold, I am going to send and get [a]Nebuchadnezzar the king of
Babylon, [b]My servant, and I am going to set his throne *right* over
these stones that I have hidden; and he will spread his [c]canopy over
them.
11 "He will also come and [a]strike the land of Egypt; those who are
meant for death *will be given over* to death, and those for captivity to
captivity, and [b]those for the sword to the sword.
12 "And [1]I shall set fire to the temples of the [a]gods of Egypt, and he
will burn them and take them captive. So he will [b]wrap himself with
the land of Egypt as a shepherd wraps himself with his garment,
and he will depart from there safely.
13 "He will also shatter the [1]obelisks of [2]Heliopolis, which is in the
land of Egypt; and the temples of the gods of Egypt he will burn
with fire."' "

Chapter 44

44 The word that came to Jeremiah for all the Jews living in the
land of Egypt, those who were living in [a]Migdol, [b]Tahpanhes,
[c]Memphis, and the land of [d]Pathros, saying,
2 "Thus says the LORD of hosts, the God of Israel, 'You yourselves
have seen all the calamity that I have brought on Jerusalem and all
the cities of Judah; and behold, this day they are in [a]ruins and no one
lives in them,
3 [a]because of their wickedness which they committed so as to [b]pro-
voke Me to anger by continuing to [c]burn [1]sacrifices *and* to [d]serve
other gods whom they had not known, *neither* they, you, nor your
fathers.
4 'Yet I [a]sent you all My servants the prophets, [1]again and again,
saying, "Oh, do not do this [b]abominable thing which I hate."
5 'But [a]they did not listen or incline their ears to turn from their
wickedness, so as not to burn [1]sacrifices to other gods.
6 'Therefore My [a]wrath and My anger were poured out and
burned in the [b]cities of Judah and in the streets of Jerusalem, so they
have become a ruin and a [c]desolation as it is this day.
7 'Now then thus says the LORD God of hosts, the God of Israel,
"Why are you [a]doing great harm to yourselves, so as to [b]cut off from
you man and woman, child and infant, from among Judah, leaving
yourselves without remnant,
8 [a]provoking Me to anger with the works of your hands, [b]burning
[1]sacrifices to other gods in the land of Egypt, where you are entering
to reside, so that you might be cut off and become a [c]curse and a
reproach among all the nations of the earth?
9 "Have you forgotten the [a]wickedness of your fathers, the wicked-
ness of the kings of Judah, and the wickedness of their wives, your
own wickedness, and the wickedness of your wives, which they
committed in the land of Judah and in the streets of Jerusalem?
10 "But they [a]have not become [1]contrite even to this day, nor have

---

8 [a]Jer. 2:16; 44:1; 46:14; Ezek. 30:18
9 [1]Lit., *hand* [2]Or, *brickwork* [3]Lit., *house* [4]Lit., *men*
10 [a]Jer. 25:9, 11 [b]Is. 44:28; 45:1; Jer. 25:9; 27:6 [c]Ps. 18:11; 27:5; 31:20
11 [a]Is. 19:1-25; Jer. 25:19; 44:13; 46:1, 2, 13-26; Ezek. 29:19, 20 [b]Jer. 15:2
12 [1]Some ancient versions read *He will* [a]Ex. 12:12; Is. 19:1; Jer. 46:25; Ezek. 30:13 [b]Ps. 104:2; 109:18, 19; Is. 49:18
13 [1]Or, *stone pillars* [2]Heb., *Beth-shemesh;* i.e., the house of the sun-god
44:1 [a]Ex. 14:2; Jer. 46:14 [b]Jer. 43:7; Ezek. 30:18 [c]Is. 19:13; Jer. 2:16; 46:14; Ezek. 30:13, 16; Hos. 9:6 [d]Is. 11:11; Ezek. 29:14; 30:14
2 [a]Is. 6:11; Jer. 4:7; 9:11; 34:22; Mic. 3:12
3 [1]Or, *incense* [a]Neh. 9:33; Jer. 2:17-19; 5:23; Ezek. 8:17, 18; Dan. 9:5 [b]Is. 3:8; Jer. 7:19; 32:30-32; 44:8 [c]Jer. 19:4 [d]Deut. 13:6; 29:26; 32:17
4 [1]Lit., *rising early and sending* [a]Jer. 7:13, 25; 26:5; 29:19; 35:15; Zech. 7:7 [b]Jer. 16:18; 32:34, 35; Ezek. 8:10
5 [1]Or, *incense* [a]Jer. 11:8, 10; 13:10
6 [a]Is. 51:17-20; Jer. 42:18; Ezek. 8:18 [b]Jer. 7:17, 34 [c]Jer. 4:27; 34:22
7 [a]Num. 16:38; Jer. 26:19; Ezek. 33:11; Hab. 2:10 [b]Jer. 3:24; 9:21; 51:22
8 [1]Or, *incense* [a]2 Kin. 17:15-17; Jer. 25:6, 7; 44:3; 1 Cor. 10:21, 22 [b]Jer. 7:9; 11:12, 17; 44:3; Hos. 4:13; Hab. 1:16 [c]1 Kin. 9:7, 8; 2 Chr. 7:20; Jer. 42:18
9 [a]Jer. 7:9, 10, 17, 18; 44:17, 21
10 [1]Lit., *crushed* [a]Jer. 6:15; 8:12

they feared nor [b]walked in My law or My statutes, which I have set
before you and before your fathers." '
11 "Therefore thus says the LORD of hosts, the God of Israel, 'Behold,
I am going to [a]set My face against you for [1]woe, even to cut off all
Judah.
12 'And I will [a]take away the remnant of Judah who have set their
[1]mind on entering the land of Egypt to reside there, and they will all
[2b]meet their end in the land of Egypt; they will fall by the sword *and*
meet their end by famine. Both small and great will die by the sword
and famine; and they will become a [c]curse, an object of horror, an
imprecation and a reproach.
13 'And I will [a]punish those who live in the land of Egypt, as I have
punished Jerusalem, with the sword, with famine, and with pes-
tilence.
14 'So there will be [a]no refugees or survivors for the remnant of
Judah who have entered the land of Egypt to reside there and then to
return to the land of Judah, to which they are [1b]longing to return and
live; for none will [c]return except *a few* refugees.' "
15 Then [a]all the men who were aware that their wives were burning
[1]sacrifices to other gods, along with all the women who were stand-
ing by, *as* a large assembly, [2]including all the people who were living
in Pathros in the land of Egypt, responded to Jeremiah, saying,
16 "As for the [1a]message that you have spoken to us in the name of
the LORD, [b]we are not going to listen to you!
17 "But rather we will certainly [a]carry out every word that has pro-
ceeded from our mouths, [1]by burning [2]sacrifices to the [b]queen of
heaven and pouring out libations to her, just as [c]we ourselves, our
forefathers, our kings and our princes did in the cities of Judah and
in the streets of Jerusalem; for *then* we had [d]plenty of [3]food, and were
well off, and saw no [4]misfortune.
18 "But since we stopped burning [1]sacrifices to the queen of heaven
and pouring out libations to her, we have [a]lacked everything and
have [2]met our end by the sword and by famine."
19 "And," *said the women*, "when we were [a]burning [1]sacrifices to the
queen of heaven, and [2]were pouring out libations to her, was it
[b]without our husbands that we made for her *sacrificial* cakes [3]in her
image and poured out libations to her?"
20 Then Jeremiah said to all the people, to the men and women—
even to all the people who were giving him *such* an answer—saying,
21 "As for the [1a]smoking sacrifices that you burned in the cities of
Judah and in the [b]streets of Jerusalem, you and your forefathers,
your kings and your princes, and the people of the land, did not the
LORD [c]remember them, and did not *all this* come into His [2]mind?
22 "So the LORD was [a]no longer able to endure *it*, [b]because of the evil
of your deeds, because of the abominations which you have com-
mitted; thus your land has become a [c]ruin, an object of horror and a
curse, without an inhabitant, as *it is* this day.
23 "Because you have burned [1]sacrifices and have sinned against the
LORD and [a]not obeyed the voice of the LORD or [b]walked in His law,
His statutes or His testimonies, therefore this [c]calamity has befallen
you, as *it has* this day."
24 Then Jeremiah said to all the people, including all the women,
"[a]Hear the word of the LORD, all Judah who are [b]in the land of Egypt,
25 thus says the LORD of hosts, the God of Israel, as follows: 'As for

10 [b]Jer. 26:4; 3
44:23

11 [1]Lit., *evil* [a]L
17:10; 20:5, 6; 2
Jer. 21:10; Amo

12 [1]Lit., *face* [2]
finished [a]Jer. 4
22 [b]Is. 1:28; Je
44:7 [c]Is. 65:15;
18:16; 24:9; 26:
42:18; Zech. 8:1

13 [a]Jer. 11:22;

14 [1]Lit., *lifting u*
soul [a]Jer. 22:10
[b]Jer. 22:26, 27
10:20; Jer. 44:28
9:27

15 [1]Or, *incense*
and [a]Prov. 11:2
1:5; Jer. 5:1-5

16 [1]Lit., *word* [a]
43:2 [b]Prov. 1:24
Jer. 11:8, 10; 13:

17 [1]Or, *so as to*
[2]Or, *incense* [3]Lit
bread [4]Lit., *evil*
30:12; Deut. 23:2
[b]2 Kin. 17:16; Je
[c]Neh. 9:34; Jer. 3
44:21 [d]Ex. 16:3;
2:5-9; Phil. 3:19

18 [1]Or, *incense*
been finished [a]N
11:5, 6; Jer. 40:12
3:13-15

19 [1]Or, *incense*
pour [3]Lit., *to ma*
image of her [a]Je
[b]Num. 30:6, 7; Je

21 [1]Or, *incense*
heart [a]Ezek. 8:10
[b]Jer. 11:13; 44:9,
[c]Ps. 79:8; Is. 64:9
14:10; Hos. 7:2; A
8:7

22 [a]Is. 7:13; 43:2
2:17 [b]Jer. 4:4; 21
30:14 [c]Gen. 19:1
107:33, 34; Jer. 25
18, 38; 29:18; 42:
44:12

23 [1]Or, *incense* [a]
7:13-15; 40:3 [b]Je
44:10; Ps. 119:136
[c]1 Kin. 9:9; Neh. 1
Jer. 44:2; Dan. 9:1

24 [a]Jer. 42:15; 44
[b]Jer. 43:7; 44:15, 2

you and your wives, you have spoken with your mouths and ful-
filled *it* with your hands, saying, "We will [a]certainly perform our
vows that we have vowed, to burn [1]sacrifices to the queen of heaven
and pour out libations to her." [2b]Go ahead and confirm your vows,
and certainly perform your vows!'
26 "[1]Nevertheless hear the word of the LORD, all Judah who are
living in the land of Egypt, 'Behold, I have [a]sworn by My great
name,' says the LORD, '[b]never shall My name be invoked again by the
mouth of any man of Judah in all the land of Egypt, saying, "[c]As the
Lord [2]GOD lives."
27 'Behold, I am watching over them [a]for harm and not for good,
and [b]all the men of Judah who are in the land of Egypt will [1]meet
their end by the sword and by famine until they [2]are completely
gone.
28 '[a]And those who escape the sword will return out of the land of
Egypt to the land of Judah [1b]few in number. Then all the remnant of
Judah who have gone to the land of Egypt to reside there will know
[c]whose word will stand, Mine or theirs.
29 'And this will be the [a]sign to you,' declares the LORD, 'that I am
going to punish you in this place, so that you may know that [b]My
words will surely stand against you for harm.'
30 "Thus says the LORD, 'Behold, I am going to give over [a]Pharaoh
Hophra king of Egypt to the hand of his enemies, to the hand of
those who seek his life, just as I gave over [b]Zedekiah king of Judah to
the hand of Nebuchadnezzar king of Babylon, *who was* his enemy
and was seeking his life.' "

Chapter 45

45 *This is* the message which Jeremiah the prophet spoke to
[a]Baruch the son of Neriah, when he had [b]written down these
words in a book [1]at Jeremiah's dictation, in the [c]fourth year of Jehoia-
kim the son of Josiah, king of Judah, saying:
2 "Thus says the LORD the God of Israel to you, O Baruch:
3 'You said, "Ah, woe is me! For the LORD has added sorrow to my
pain; I am [a]weary with my groaning and have found no rest." '
4 "Thus you are to say to him, 'Thus says the LORD, "Behold, [a]what
I have built I am about to tear down, and what I have planted I am
about to uproot, that is, the whole land."
5 'But you, are you [a]seeking great things for yourself? Do not seek
them; for behold, I am going to [b]bring disaster on all flesh,' declares
the LORD, 'but I will [c]give your life to you as booty in all the places
where you may go.' "

Chapter 46

46 That which came as the word of the LORD to Jeremiah the
prophet [a]concerning the nations.
2 To [a]Egypt, concerning the army of [b]Pharaoh Neco king of Egypt,
which was by the Euphrates River at [c]Carchemish, which Nebuchad-
nezzar king of Babylon defeated in the [d]fourth year of Jehoiakim the
son of Josiah, king of Judah:
3 "[a]Line up the shield and [1]buckler,
And draw near for the battle!
4 "Harness the horses,
And [1]mount the steeds,

…r, *incense* [2]Lit., *…v cause to stand* …4:17; Matt. 14:9; …12 [b]Ezek. 20:39

[1]Lit., *Therefore* … *YHWH*, usually …red LORD [a]Gen. … Deut. 32:40, 41; 22:5; Amos 6:8; …6:13 [b]Ps. 50:16; …:39 [c]Is. 48:1, 2; Jer. 5:2

[1]Lit., *be finished* … *come to an end* …10; 31:28; 39:16 …21:14; Jer. 44:14

28 [1]Lit., *men of* … [a]Jer. 44:14 [b]Is. …9; 27:12, 13 [c]Ps. … Is. 14:27; 46:10, 11; Zech. 1:6

…s. 7:11, 14; 8:18; …4:30; Matt. 24:15, [b]Prov. 19:21; Is. 40:8

…r. 43:9-13; 46:25; …Ezek. 29:3; 30:21 …2 Kin. 25:4-7; Jer. 34:21; 39:5-7

…:1 [1]Lit., *from the …of Jeremiah* [a]Jer. …16; 43:3, 6 [b]Jer. …:4, 18, 32 [c]2 Kin. …2 Chr. 36:5-7; Jer. …; 36:1; 46:2; Dan. 1:1

…. 6:6; 69:3; 2 Cor. 4:1, 16; Gal. 6:9

[a]Is. 5:5; Jer. 1:10; …7; 18:7-10; 31:28

…Kin. 3:9, 11; 2 Kin. …26; Matt. 6:25, 32; 12:16 [b]Is. 66:16; 25:31 [c]Jer. 21:9; 38:2; 39:18

46:1 [a]Jer. 1:10; 25:15-38

[a]Jer. 46:14; Ezek. …chs. 29-32 [b]2 Kin. 23:29, 33-35; Jer. … [c]2 Chr. 35:20; Is. 10:9 [d]Jer. 45:1

…, small shield [a]Is. …:5; Jer. 51:11; Joel …3:9; Nah. 2:1; 3:14

4 [1]Or, *go up, you horsemen*

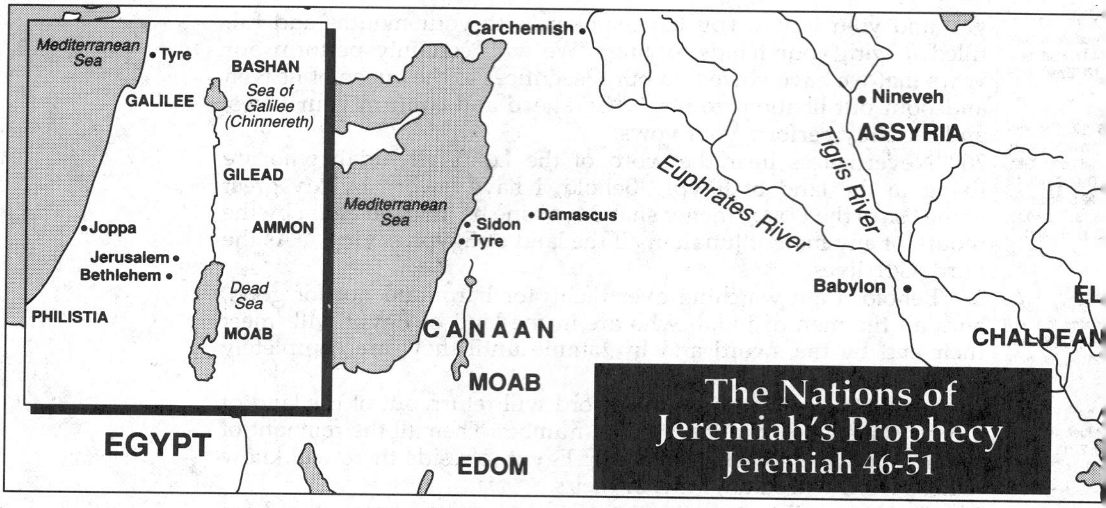

And take your stand with helmets *on!*
[a]Polish the spears,
Put on the [b]scale-armor!
5 "Why have I seen *it?*
They are terrified,
They are [a]drawing back,
And their [b]mighty men are defeated
And have taken refuge in flight,
Without facing back;
[1c]Terror is on every side!"
Declares the LORD.
6 Let not the [a]swift man flee,
Nor the mighty man escape;
In the north beside the river Euphrates
They have [b]stumbled and fallen.
7 Who is this that [a]rises like the Nile,
Like the rivers whose waters surge about?
8 Egypt rises like the Nile,
Even like the rivers whose waters surge about;
And He has said, "I will [a]rise and cover *that* land;
I will surely [b]destroy the city and its inhabitants."
9 Go up, you horses, and [1a]drive madly, you chariots,
That the mighty men may [2]march forward:
Ethiopia and [3b]Put, that handle the shield,
And the [4c]Lydians, that handle *and* bend the bow.
10 For [a]that day belongs to the Lord [1]GOD of hosts,
A day of [b]vengeance, so as to avenge Himself on His foes;
And the [c]sword will devour and be satiated
And [2]drink its fill of their blood;
For there will be a [d]slaughter for the Lord [1]GOD of hosts,
In the land of the north by the river Euphrates.
11 Go [a]up to Gilead and obtain balm,
[b]O virgin daughter of Egypt!
In vain have you multiplied [1]remedies;
There is [c]no healing for you.
12 The nations have heard of your [a]shame,

4 [a]Ezek. 21:9-11 [b]1 Sam. 17:5, 38 26:14; Neh. 4:16 51:3

5 [1]Heb., *Magor-missabib;* Terror is on every [a]Is. 42:17; Jer. 46 [b]Is. 5:25; Ezek. 3 [c]Jer. 6:25; 20:3; 4

6 [a]Is. 30:16 [b]Jer 46:12, 16; Dan. 1

7 [a]Jer. 47:2

8 [a]Is. 37:24 [b]Is.

9 [1]Lit., *act like madmen* [2]Lit., *go* [3]I.e., Libya (or Somaliland) [4]Heb *Ludim* [a]Jer. 47:3; 2:4 [b]Nah. 3:9 [c]Is.

10 [1]Heb., *YHWH,* usually rendered *L* [2]Lit., *be saturated* [a]Joel 1:15 [b]Jer. 5 18 [c]Deut. 32:42; I 31:8; Jer. 12:12 [d] 34:6; Zeph. 1:7

11 [1]Lit., *healings* 8:22 [b]Is. 47:1; Jer 21 [c]Jer. 30:13; Mi Nah. 3:19

12 [a]Jer. 2:36; Nah 3:8-10

And the earth is full of your [b]cry *of distress;*
For one [c]warrior has stumbled over [1]another,
And both of them have fallen down together.

13 *This is* the [1]message which the LORD spoke to Jeremiah the
prophet about the [a]coming of Nebuchadnezzar king of Babylon to
[b]smite the land of Egypt:

14 "Declare in Egypt and proclaim in [a]Migdol,
Proclaim also in Memphis and [b]Tahpanhes;
Say, 'Take your stand and get yourself ready,
For the [c]sword has devoured those around you.'

15 "Why have your [a]mighty ones become prostrate?
They do not stand because the LORD has [b]thrust them down.

16 "They have repeatedly [a]stumbled;
Indeed, they have fallen one against another.
Then they said, 'Get up! And [b]let us go back
To our own people and our native land
Away from the [1c]sword of the oppressor.'

17 "[1]They cried there, 'Pharaoh king of Egypt *is but* [a]a big noise;
He has let the appointed time pass by!'

18 "As I live," declares the [a]King
Whose name is the LORD of hosts,
"Surely one shall come *who looms up* like [b]Tabor among the mountains,
Or like [c]Carmel by the sea.

19 "Make your baggage ready for [a]exile,
O [b]daughter dwelling in Egypt,
For [c]Memphis will become a desolation;
It will even be burned down *and* [1]bereft of inhabitants.

20 "Egypt is a pretty [a]heifer,
But a [1]horsefly is coming [b]from the north—it is coming!

21 "Also her [a]mercenaries in her midst
Are like [1]fattened [b]calves,
For even they too have turned back *and* have fled away together;
They did not stand *their ground*.
For the day of their calamity has come upon them,
The time of their [c]punishment.

22 "Its sound moves along like a serpent;
For they move on [1]like an army
And come to her as woodcutters with axes.

23 "They have cut down her [a]forest," declares the LORD;
"Surely it will no *more* be found,
Even though [1]they are *now* more numerous than [b]locusts
And are without number.

24 "The daughter of Egypt has been put to shame,
Given over to the [1]power of the [a]people of the north."

25 The LORD of hosts, the God of Israel, says, "Behold, I am going to
punish Amon of [a]Thebes, and [b]Pharaoh, and Egypt along with her
[c]gods and her kings, even Pharaoh and those who [d]trust in him.

26 "And I shall give them over to the [1]power of those who are [a]seek-
ing their lives, even into the hand of Nebuchadnezzar king of Baby-
lon and into the hand of his [2]officers. [b]Afterwards, however, it will
be inhabited as in the days of old," declares the LORD.

27 "But as for you, O Jacob My servant, [a]do not fear,
Nor be dismayed, O Israel!

it., *warrior* [b]Jer. 14:2 [c]Is. 19:2
[1]Lit., *word* [a]Jer. :10-13 [b]Is. 19:1
[a]Jer. 44:1 [b]Jer. . 1:20; Jer. 2:30; 46:10; Nah. 2:13
s. 66:15, 16; Jer. [b]Ps. 18:14, 39; 68:1, 2
[1]Lit., *oppressing* [a]Lev. 26:36, 37; . 46:6 [b]Jer. 51:9 [c]Jer. 50:16
[1]Some ancient ons read *Call the of Pharaoh a big se* [a]Ex. 15:9, 10; Kin. 20:10, 11; Is. 19:11-16
[a]Jer. 48:15; Mal. 14 [b]Josh. 19:22; g. 4:6; Ps. 89:12 sh. 12:22; 1 Kin. 18:42
[1]Lit., *without* [a]Is. [b]Jer. 48:18 [c]Jer. :14; Ezek. 30:13
20 [1]Or possibly, *quito* [a]Hos. 10:11 [b]Jer. 1:14; 47:2
[1]Lit., *of the stall* . 10:6; 2 Kin. 7:6; :5 [b]Is. 34:7 [c]Jer. ; Hos. 9:7; Obad. 13; Mic. 7:4
22 [1]Or, *in force*
[1]I.e., trees of the est, the Egyptians 21:14 [b]Judg. 6:5; 7:12; Joel 2:25
., *hand* [a]Jer. 1:15
[a]Ezek. 30:14-16; h. 3:8 [b]Jer. 44:30 12:12; Jer. 43:12, zek. 30:13; Zeph. 2:11 [d]Is. 20:5
6 [1]Lit., *hand* [2]Lit., *vants* [a]Jer. 44:30; zek. 32:11 [b]Ezek. 29:8-14
[a]Is. 41:13, 14; Jer. 30:10, 11

For, see, I am going to [b]save you from afar,
And your descendants from the land of their captivity;
And Jacob shall return and be [c]undisturbed
And secure, with no one making *him* tremble.
28 "O Jacob My servant, do not fear," declares the LORD,
"For [a]I am with you.
For I shall make a full end of all the nations
Where I have driven you,
Yet I shall [b]not make a full end of you;
But I shall [c]correct you properly
And by no means leave you unpunished."

Chapter 47

47 That which came as the word of the LORD to Jeremiah the
prophet concerning the [a]Philistines, before Pharaoh [1]con-
quered [b]Gaza.
2 Thus says the LORD:
"Behold, waters are going to rise from [a]the north
And become an overflowing torrent,
And [b]overflow the land and all its fulness,
The city and those who live in it;
And the men will [c]cry out,
And every inhabitant of the land will wail.
3 "Because of the noise of the [1a]galloping hoofs of his [2]stallions,
The tumult of his chariots, *and* the rumbling of his wheels,
The fathers have not turned back for *their* children,
Because of the limpness of *their* hands,
4 On account of the day that is coming
To [a]destroy all the Philistines,
To cut off from [b]Tyre and Sidon
Every ally that is left;
For the LORD is going to destroy the Philistines,
The remnant of the coastland of [c]Caphtor.
5 "[a]Baldness has come upon Gaza;
[b]Ashkelon has been ruined.
O remnant of their valley,
How long will you [c]gash yourself?
6 "Ah, [a]sword of the LORD,
How long will you not be quiet?
Withdraw into your sheath;
Be at rest and stay still.
7 "How can [1]it be quiet,
When the LORD has [a]given it an order?
Against Ashkelon and against the seacoast—
There He has [b]assigned it."

Chapter 48

48 Concerning [a]Moab.
Thus says the LORD of hosts, the God of Israel,
"Woe to [b]Nebo, for it has been destroyed;
[c]Kiriathaim has been put to shame, it has been captured;
The lofty stronghold has been put to shame and [1]shattered.
2 "There is praise for Moab no longer;
In [a]Heshbon they have devised calamity against her:

27 [b]Is. 11:11; Je 4; 29:14; Mic. 7 23:6; 50:19

28 [a]Ps. 46:7, 11 8:10; 43:2; Jer. [b]Jer. 4:27; Amos [c]Jer. 10:24; Hab

47:1 [1]Lit., *smote* 25:20; Zech. 9:6 10:19; 1 Kin. 4:2 25:20; Amos 1:6 2:4

2 [a]Is. 14:31; Jer 6:22; 46:20, 24 8 [c]Is. 15:2-5; Je

3 [1]Lit., *stamping* [2]Lit., *mighty one* [a]Judg. 5:22; Jer. Nah. 3:2

4 [a]Is. 14:31 [b]Is. Jer. 25:22; Joel 3 Amos 1:9, 10; Ze 9:2-4 [c]Gen. 10:1 Deut. 2:23; Amos

5 [a]Jer. 48:37; Mi [b]Judg. 1:18; Jer. Amos 1:7, 8; Zep 7; Zech. 9:5 [c]Jer 41:5

6 [a]Judg. 7:20; Je 12:12; Ezek. 21:3

7 [1]Lit., *you* [a]Is. 1 Ezek. 14:17 [b]Mic

48:1 [1]Or, *dismay* 15:1; Ezek. 25:9 32:3, 38; Jer. 48:2 [c]Num. 32:37; Jer. Ezek. 25:9

2 [a]Num. 21:25; Je 48:34, 45; 49:3

'Come and let us cut her off from *being* a nation!'
You too, [1]Madmen, will be silenced;
The sword will follow after you.
3 "The sound of an outcry from [a]Horonaim,
'Devastation and great destruction!'
4 "Moab is broken,
Her little ones have sounded out a cry *of distress*.
5 "For by the ascent of [a]Luhith
They will ascend with continual weeping;
For at the descent of Horonaim
They have heard the [1]anguished cry of destruction.
6 "[a]Flee, save your lives,
That you may be like a juniper in the wilderness.
7 "For because of your [a]trust in your own achievements and treasures,
Even you yourself will be captured;
And [b]Chemosh will go off into exile
Together with his priests and his princes.
8 "And a destroyer will come to every city,
So that no city will escape;
The valley also will be ruined,
And the [a]plateau will be destroyed,
As the LORD has said.
9 "Give [1a]wings to Moab,
For she will [2]flee away;
And her cities will become a [b]desolation,
Without inhabitants in them.
10 "[a]Cursed be the one who does the LORD's work [b]negligently,
And cursed be the one who restrains his [c]sword from blood.

11 "Moab has been [a]at ease since his youth;
He has also been [b]undisturbed on his lees,
Neither has he been [c]emptied from vessel to vessel,
Nor has he gone into exile.
Therefore [1]he retains his flavor,
And his aroma has not changed.
12 "Therefore behold, the days are coming," declares the LORD,
"when I shall send to him those who tip *vessels*, and they will tip him
over, and they will empty his vessels and shatter [1]his jars.
13 "And Moab will be [a]ashamed of [b]Chemosh, as the house of Israel
was ashamed of [c]Bethel, their confidence.
14 "How can you say, 'We are [a]mighty warriors,
And men valiant for battle'?
15 "Moab has been destroyed, and [1]men have gone up to [2]his cities;
His choicest [3a]young men have also gone down to the slaughter,"
Declares the [b]King, whose name is the LORD of hosts.
16 "The disaster of Moab will [a]soon come,
And his calamity has swiftly hastened.
17 "Mourn for him, all you who *live* around him,
Even all of you who know his name;
Say, 'How has the mighty [1a]scepter been broken,
A staff of splendor!'
18 "[a]Come down from your glory
And sit [1]on the parched ground,

, a city of Moab
:5; Jer. 48:5, 34
it., *distresses of outcry* [a]Is. 15:5
6 [a]Jer. 51:6
s. 52:7; Is. 59:4; 3 [b]Num. 21:29; Kin. 11:33; Jer. 48:13, 46
osh. 13:9, 17, 21
r, *salt* [2]Or, *fall in* s. 11:1; Is. 16:2; 8:28 [b]Jer. 44:22
Jer. 11:3 [b]1 Kin. 39, 40, 42; 2 Kin. :19 [c]Jer. 47:6, 7
.it., *his flavor has* *ayed in him* [a]Jer. :21; Ezek. 16:49; 1:15 [b]Zeph. 1:12 [c]Nah. 2:2
12 [1]Lit., *their*
3 [a]Is. 45:16; Jer. :39 [b]Judg. 11:24 2:29; Hos. 8:5, 6
14 [a]Ps. 33:16; Is. 10:13-16
Lit., *one has* [2]Lit., [3]I.e., warriors [a]Is. 30, 31; Jer. 50:27 46:18; 51:57; Mal. 1:14
16 [a]Is. 13:22
[1]Or, *rod* [a]Is. 9:4; 14:5
[1]Lit., *in thirst* [a]Is. 47:1

Chemosh was a Moabite god who was believed to provide the people with land. During his reforms King Josiah desecrated a temple built by Solomon for Chemosh (2 Kings 23:13).

O [b]daughter dwelling in [c]Dibon,
For the destroyer of Moab has come up against you,
He has ruined your strongholds.
19 "Stand by the road and keep watch,
O inhabitant of [a]Aroer;
[b]Ask him who flees and her who escapes
And say, 'What has happened?'
20 "Moab has been put to shame, for it has been [1]shattered.
Wail and cry out;
Declare by the [a]Arnon
That Moab has been destroyed.
21 "Judgment has also come upon the plain, upon Holon, [a]Jahzah,
and against [b]Mephaath,
22 against Dibon, Nebo, and Beth-diblathaim,
23 against Kiriathaim, Beth-gamul, and [a]Beth-meon,
24 against [a]Kerioth, Bozrah, and all the cities of the land of Moab,
far and near.
25 "The [a]horn of Moab has been cut off, and his [b]arm broken,"
declares the LORD.
26 "[a]Make him drunk, for he has [1]become [b]arrogant toward the LORD;
so Moab will [2]wallow in his vomit, and he also will become a
laughingstock.
27 "Now was not Israel a [a]laughingstock to you? Or was he [1b]caught
among thieves? For each time you speak about him you [c]shake *your*
head in scorn.
28 "Leave the cities and dwell among the [a]crags,
O inhabitants of Moab,
And be like a [b]dove that nests
Beyond the mouth of the chasm.
29 "[a]We have heard of the pride of Moab—he *is* very proud—
Of his haughtiness, his [b]pride, his arrogance and [1]his
self-exaltation.
30 "I know his [a]fury," declares the LORD,
"But it is futile;
His idle boasts have accomplished nothing.
31 "Therefore I shall [a]wail for Moab,
Even for all Moab shall I cry out;
[1]I will moan for the men of [b]Kir-heres.
32 "More than the [a]weeping for [b]Jazer
I shall weep for you, O vine of Sibmah!
Your tendrils stretched across the sea,
They reached to the sea of Jazer;
Upon your summer fruits and your grape harvest
The destroyer has fallen.
33 "So [a]gladness and joy are taken away
From the fruitful field, even from the land of Moab.
And I have made the wine to [b]cease from the wine presses;
No one will tread *them* with shouting,
The shouting will not be shouts *of joy*.
34 "[a]From the outcry at Heshbon even to [b]Elealeh, even to Jahaz they
have [1]raised their voice, from [c]Zoar even to Horonaim *and to* Eglath-
shelishiyah; for even the waters of Nimrim will become desolate.
35 "And I shall make an end of Moab," declares the LORD, "the one

18 [b]Jer. 46:19 21:30; Josh. 13: Is. 15:2; Jer. 48:

19 [a]Deut. 2:36; 12:2 [b]1 Sam. 4: 14, 16

20 [1]Or, *dismaye* [a]Num. 21:13

21 [a]Num. 21:23 15:4; Jer. 48:34 13:18

23 [a]Josh. 13:17

24 [a]Jer. 48:41; A 2:2

25 [a]Ps. 75:10; Z 1:19-21 [b]Job 22. 10:15

26 [1]Or, *magnifie himself against* [2] *splash into* [a]Jer. [b]Ex. 5:2; Jer. 48: Dan. 5:23

27 [1]Or, *found* [a]L 2:15-17; Mic. 7:8- [b]Jer. 2:26 [c]Job 1 Jer. 18:16

28 [a]Judg. 6:2; Is. Jer. 49:16; Obad. 55:6; Song 2:14

29 [1]Lit., *elevation heart* [a]Is. 16:6; Z 2:8 [b]Job 40:11, 1 138:6

30 [a]Is. 37:28

31 [1]Another read *He* [a]Is. 15:5; 16:7 [b]2 Kin. 3:25; Is. 16 Jer. 48:36

32 [a]Is. 16:8, 9 [b]N 21:32

33 [a]Is. 16:10; Jer. 25:10; Joel 1:12 [b] 5:10; Hag. 2:16

34 [1]Lit., *given fort* 15:4-6 [b]Num. 32: [c]Gen. 13:10; 14:2; 15:5, 6

35 [1]Or, *offers up in* …oke [a]Is. 15:2; 16:12 [b]Jer. 7:9; 11:13

36 [1]Lit., *sounds* [a]Is. 15:5; 16:11 [b]Is. 15:7

37 [a]Is. 15:2; Jer. 16:6; …5; 47:5 [b]Gen. 37:34; Is. 15:3; 20:2

38 [1]Lit., *all of it is* …amentation [a]Is. 22:1 …er. 19:10, 11; 22:28; 25:34

39 [1]Or, *dismayed* [a]Ezek. 26:16

…0 [a]Deut. 28:49; Jer. …9:22; Hos. 8:1; Hab. 1:8 [b]Is. 8:8

41 [a]Jer. 49:22 [b]Is. 3:8; 21:3; Jer. 30:6; Mic. 4:9, 10

42 [1]Or, *magnified* …imself against [a]Ps. 83:4; Jer. 48:2 [b]Is. 37:23; Jer. 48:26

… [a]Is. 24:17, 18; Lam. 3:47

…4 [a]1 Kin. 19:17; Is. …8; Amos 5:19 [b]Jer. 46:21

… [1]Lit., *sons of tumult* …n. 21:28, 29 [b]Num. …:21, 26; Ps. 135:11 [c]Num. 24:17

… [a]Num. 21:29 [b]Judg. …24; 1 Kin. 11:7; Jer. 48:7

… [1]Or, *captivity* [2]Lit., …*d of the days* [a]Jer. 12:14-17; 49:6, 39

… [1]In 1 Kin. 11:5, 33 …Zeph. 1:5, *Milcom* …eut. 23:3, 4; 2 Chr. …:1; Ezek. 21:28-32; …10; Amos 1:13-15; Zeph. 2:8-11

… …Or, *shout of* [a]Num. 10:9; Jer. 4:19

who offers *sacrifice* on the [a]high place and the one who [1b]burns in-
cense to his gods.
36 "Therefore My [a]heart [1]wails for Moab like flutes; My heart also
[1]wails like flutes for the men of Kir-heres. Therefore they have [b]lost
the abundance it produced.
37 "For [a]every head is bald and every beard cut short; there are
gashes on all the hands and [b]sackcloth on the loins.
38 "On all the [a]housetops of Moab and in its streets [1]there is lamenta-
tion everywhere; for I have broken Moab like an undesirable [b]ves-
sel," declares the LORD.
39 "How [1]shattered it is! *How* they have wailed! How Moab has
turned his back—he is ashamed! So Moab will become a laughing-
stock and an [a]object of terror to all around him."

40 For thus says the LORD,
"Behold, one will [a]fly swiftly like an eagle,
And [b]spread out his wings against Moab.
41 "Kerioth has been captured
And the strongholds have been seized,
So the [a]hearts of the mighty men of Moab in that day
Will be like the heart of a [b]woman in labor.
42 "And Moab will be [a]destroyed from *being* a people
Because he has [1]become [b]arrogant toward the LORD.
43 "[a]Terror, pit, and snare are *coming* upon you,
O inhabitant of Moab," declares the LORD.
44 "The one who [a]flees from the terror
Will fall into the pit,
And the one who climbs up out of the pit
Will be caught in the snare;
For I shall bring upon her, *even* upon Moab,
The year of their [b]punishment," declares the LORD.

45 "In the shadow of Heshbon
The fugitives stand without strength;
For a fire has gone forth from Heshbon,
And a [a]flame from the midst of [b]Sihon,
And it has devoured the [c]forehead of Moab
And the scalps of the [1]riotous revelers.
46 "[a]Woe to you, Moab!
The people of [b]Chemosh have perished;
For your sons have been taken away captive,
And your daughters into captivity.
47 "Yet I will [a]restore the [1]fortunes of Moab
In the [2]latter days," declares the LORD.
Thus far the judgment on Moab.

Chapter 49

49 Concerning the sons of [a]Ammon.
Thus says the LORD:
"Does Israel have no sons?
Or has he no heirs?
Why then has [1]Malcam taken possession of Gad
And his people settled in its cities?
2 "Therefore behold, the days are coming," declares the LORD,
"That I shall cause a [1a]trumpet blast of war to be heard

INSIGHT

Malcam, also called Milcom, was the national god of Ammon. When King Solomon was old he worshiped Malcam on the high places he built just outsed Jerusalem. King Josiah desecrated these high places during his reforms (1 Kings 11:1-8, 33; 2 Kings 23:13).

Against [b]Rabbah of the sons of Ammon;
And it will become a desolate heap,
And her [c]towns will be set on fire.
Then Israel will take [d]possession of his possessors,"
Says the LORD.
3 "Wail, O [a]Heshbon, for [b]Ai has been destroyed!
Cry out, O daughters of Rabbah,
[c]Gird yourselves with sackcloth and lament,
And rush back and forth inside the walls;
For [1]Malcam will [d]go into exile
Together with his priests and his princes.
4 "How [a]boastful you are about the valleys!
Your valley is flowing *away*,
O [b]backsliding daughter
Who trusts in her [c]treasures, *saying*,
'[d]Who will come against me?'
5 "Behold, I am going to bring [a]terror upon you,"
Declares the Lord [1]GOD of hosts,
"From all *directions* around you;
And each of you will be [b]driven out [2]headlong,
With no one to gather the [c]fugitives together.
6 "But afterward I will [a]restore
The [1]fortunes of the sons of Ammon,"
Declares the LORD.

7 Concerning [a]Edom.
Thus says the LORD of hosts,
"Is there no longer any [b]wisdom in [c]Teman?
Has good counsel been lost to the prudent?
Has their wisdom decayed?
8 "Flee away, turn back, dwell in the depths,
O inhabitants of [a]Dedan,
For I [1]will bring the [b]disaster of Esau upon him
At the time I [2]punish him.
9 "[a]If grape gatherers came to you,
Would they not leave gleanings?
If thieves *came* by night,
They would destroy *only* [1]until they had enough.
10 "But I have [a]stripped Esau bare,
I have uncovered his hiding places
So that he will not be able to conceal himself;
His [1]offspring has been destroyed along with his [2]relatives
And his neighbors, and [b]he is no more.
11 "Leave your [1a]orphans behind, I will keep *them* alive;
And let your [b]widows trust in Me."
12 For thus says the LORD, "Behold, those [1]who were not sentenced
to drink the [a]cup will certainly drink *it*, and are you the one who will
be [b]completely acquitted? You will not be acquitted, but you will
certainly drink *it*.
13 "For I have [a]sworn by Myself," declares the LORD, "that [b]Bozrah
will become an [c]object of horror, a reproach, a ruin and a curse; and
all its cities will become perpetual ruins."
14 I have [a]heard a message from the LORD,
And an [b]envoy is sent among the nations, *saying*,

2 [b]Deut. 3:11; 11:1; Ezek. 21:2 [c]Josh. 17:11, 16 14:2

3 [1]Cf. v. 1 [a]Jer [b]Josh. 7:2-5; 8: Ezra 2:28 [c]Is. 3 Jer. 48:37 [d]Jer. 48:7

4 [a]Jer. 9:23 [b]J 31:22 [c]Ps. 62:1 28:4, 5; 1 Tim. 6 [d]Jer. 21:13

5 [1]Heb., *YHWH* usually rendered [2]Lit., *before him* 48:43f.; 49:29 [b] 16:16; 46:5 [c]La

6 [1]Or, *captivity* 48:47; 49:39

7 [a]Gen. 25:30; 34:5, 6; Jer. 25:2 Ezek. 25:12; Am Obad. 1-21 [b]Job Jer. 8:9 [c]Gen. 3 15, 34; Jer. 49:2

8 [1]Or, *brought* [2] *punished* [a]Is. 21 Jer. 25:23 [b]Jer. Mal. 1:3, 4

9 [1]Lit., *their suff* [a]Obad. 5

10 [1]Lit., *seed* [2]L *brothers* [a]Jer. 13 [b]Is. 17:14

11 [1]Or, *fatherles* 68:5; Hos. 14:3 68:5; Zech. 7:10

12 [1]Lit., *whose judgment was no* [a]Jer. 25:15 [b]Jer. 29; 1 Pet. 4:17

13 [a]Gen. 22:16; 45:23; Jer. 44:26; 6:8 [b]Gen. 36:33; 1:44; Is. 34:6; 63: Amos 1:12 [c]Is. 34 Jer. 18:16

14 [a]Obad. 1-4 [b] 18:2; 30:4

"[c]Gather yourselves together and come against her,
And rise up for battle!"
15 "For behold, I have made you small among the nations,
Despised among men.
16 "As for the terror of you,
The arrogance of your heart has deceived you,
O you who live in the clefts of [1]the [a]rock,
Who occupy the height of the hill.
Though you make your nest as [b]high as an eagle's,
I will [c]bring you down from there," declares the LORD.
17 "And Edom will become an [a]object of horror; everyone who
passes by it will be horrified and will [b]hiss at all its wounds.
18 "Like the [a]overthrow of Sodom and Gomorrah with its neigh-
bors," says the LORD, "[b]no one will live there, nor will a son of man
reside in it.
19 "[a]Behold, one will come up like a lion from the [1b]thickets of the
Jordan against [2]a perennially watered pasture; for in an instant I
shall make him run away from it, and whoever is [c]chosen I shall
appoint over it. For who is [d]like Me, and who will summon Me *into
court?* And who then is the shepherd [e]who can stand against Me?"
20 Therefore hear the [a]plan of the LORD which He has planned
against Edom, and His purposes which He has purposed against the
inhabitants of Teman: surely they will drag them off, *even* the little
ones of the flock; surely He will make their [1]pasture [b]desolate be-
cause of them.
21 The [a]earth has quaked at the noise of their downfall. There is an
outcry! The noise of it has been heard at the [1]Red Sea.
22 Behold, [1]He will mount up and [a]swoop like an eagle, and spread
out His wings [2]against Bozrah; and the [b]hearts of the mighty men of
Edom in that day will be like the heart of a woman in labor.
23 Concerning [a]Damascus.
"[b]Hamath and [c]Arpad are put to shame,
For they have heard bad news;
They are [d]disheartened.
There is anxiety by the sea,
It [e]cannot be calmed.
24 "Damascus has become helpless;
She has turned away to flee,
And panic has gripped her;
[a]Distress and pangs have taken hold of her
Like a woman in childbirth.
25 "How [1]the [a]city of praise has not been deserted,
The town of My joy!
26 "Therefore, her [a]young men will fall in her streets,
And all the men of war will be [1]silenced in that day," declares
the LORD of hosts.
27 "And I shall [a]set fire to the wall of Damascus,
And it will devour the [1]fortified towers of [b]Ben-hadad."
28 Concerning [a]Kedar and the kingdoms of Hazor, which Nebu-
chadnezzar king of Babylon defeated. Thus says the LORD,
"Arise, go up to Kedar
And devastate the [1b]men of the east.
29 "They will take away their tents and their flocks;
They will carry off for themselves

14 [c]Jer. 50:14

[1]Or, *Sela* [a]2 Kin. ... Jer. 48:28 [b]Job ...:27; Is. 14:13-15 [c]Amos 9:2

...er. 18:16; 49:13; ...0:13; Ezek. 35:7 ...n. 9:8; Jer. 51:37

[a]Gen. 19:24, 25; ...29:23; Jer. 50:40; ...s 4:11; Zeph. 2:9 ...ob 18:15-18; Jer. 49:33

...it., *pride* [2]Or, *an* ...*during habitation* ...):44 [b]Josh. 3:15; 12:5 [c]Num. 16:5 ...x. 15:11; Is. 46:9 [e]Job 41:10

...Or, *habitation* [a]Is. ...24, 27; Jer. 50:45 [b]Mal. 1:3, 4

...it., *Sea of Reeds* [a]Jer. 50:46; Ezek. 26:15, 18

...Or, *one* [2]Or, *over* ...4:13; 48:40; Hos. ...Is. 13:8; Jer. 30:6; 48:41

[a]Gen. 14:15; 15:2; ...5:12; 2 Chr. 16:2; ...3; 17:1; Amos 1:3; ...9:2 [b]Num. 13:21; ...9; Jer. 39:5; Amos 6:2 [c]2 Kin. 18:34; ...9:13; Is. 10:9 [d]Ex. 15; Nah. 2:10 [e]Is. 57:20

24 [a]Is. 13:8

...Or, *deserted is the* ...*praise* [a]Jer. 33:9; 51:41

...Or, *destroyed* [a]Jer. ...; 50:30; Amos 4:10

[1]Or, *palaces* [a]Jer. 43:12; Amos 1:3-5 ...n. 15:18-20; 2 Kin. 13:3

...3 [1]Lit., *sons* [a]Gen. ...5:13; Ps. 120:5; Is. ...1:16, 17; Jer. 2:10; ...ek. 27:21 [b]Job 1:3; Is. 11:14

Their tent [a]curtains, all their goods, and their [b]camels,
And they will call out to one another, '[c]Terror on every side!'
30 "Run away, flee! Dwell in the depths,
O inhabitants of Hazor," declares the LORD;
"For [a]Nebuchadnezzar king of Babylon has formed a plan
against you
And devised a scheme against you.
31 "Arise, go up against a nation which is [a]at ease,
Which lives securely," declares the LORD.
"It has [b]no gates or bars;
They [c]dwell alone.
32 "And their camels will become plunder,
And the multitude of their cattle for booty,
And I shall [a]scatter to all the winds those who [b]cut the corners *of their hair;*
And I shall bring their disaster from every side," declares the
LORD.
33 "And Hazor will become a [a]haunt of jackals,
A desolation forever;
No one will live there,
Nor will a son of man reside in it."

34 That which came as the word of the LORD to Jeremiah the proph-
et concerning [a]Elam, [b]at the beginning of the reign of Zedekiah king
of Judah, saying,

35 "Thus says the LORD of hosts,
'Behold, I am going to [a]break the bow of Elam,
The [1]finest of their might.
36 'And I shall bring upon Elam the [a]four winds
From the four ends of heaven,
And shall [b]scatter them to all these winds;
And there will be no nation
To which the outcasts of Elam will not go.
37 'So I shall [1]shatter Elam before their enemies
And before those who seek their lives;
And I shall [a]bring calamity upon them,
Even My [b]fierce anger,' declares the LORD,
'And I shall [c]send out the sword after them
Until I have consumed them.
38 'Then I shall set My throne in Elam,
And I shall destroy [1]out of it king and princes,'
Declares the LORD.
39 'But it will come about in the last days
That I shall [a]restore the [1]fortunes of Elam,' "
Declares the LORD.

Chapter 50

50 The word which the LORD spoke concerning [a]Babylon, the
land of the Chaldeans, through Jeremiah the prophet:
2 "[a]Declare and proclaim among the nations.
Proclaim it and [b]lift up a standard.
Do not conceal *it but* say,
'[c]Babylon has been captured,
[d]Bel has been put to shame, [1]Marduk has been [2]shattered;

29 [a]Hab. 3:7 [b]1
5:21 [c]Jer. 46:5

30 [a]Jer. 25:9; 2

31 [a]Judg. 18:7;
[b]Is. 42:11 [c]Num.
Deut. 33:28; Mic

32 [a]Ezek. 5:10;
15 [b]Jer. 9:26; 25

33 [a]Is. 13:20-22
9:11; 10:22; 51:3
Zeph. 2:9, 13-15
1:3

34 [a]Gen. 10:22;
Is. 11:11; Jer. 25:
Ezek. 32:24; Dan
[b]2 Kin. 24:17, 18
28:1

35 [1]Lit., *first* [a]Ps
Is. 22:6; Jer. 51:5

36 [a]Dan. 7:2; 8:8
7:1 [b]Jer. 49:32; E
5:10; Amos 9:9

37 [1]Or, *dismay* [a]
6:19 [b]Jer. 30:24
9:16; 48:2

38 [1]Or, *from there*

39 [1]Or, *captivity*
48:47

50:1 [a]Gen. 10:10;
2 Kin. 17:24; Is. 13
47:1; Dan. 1:1; Re

2 [1]Heb., *Merodac*
[2]Or, *dismayed* [a]Je
4:16 [b]Jer. 51:27 [c]
51:31 [d]Is. 46:1

INSIGHT

Marduk and **Bel** were Babylonian deities. Bel was the Babylonian equivalent of Baal, acknowledged as the Lord of heaven.

Her [e]images have been put to shame, her idols have been
shattered.'
3 "For a nation has come up against her out of the [a]north; it will
make her land [b]an object of horror, and there will be [c]no inhabitant in
it. Both man and beast have wandered off, they have gone away!
4 "In those days and at that time," declares the LORD, "the sons of
Israel will come, *both* they and the sons of Judah [a]as well; they will
go along [b]weeping as they go, and it will be [c]the LORD their God they
will seek.
5 "They will [a]ask for the way to Zion, *turning* their faces [1]in its
direction; [2]they [3]will come that they may join themselves to the LORD
in an [b]everlasting covenant that will not be forgotten.

6 "My people have become [a]lost sheep;
[b]Their shepherds have led them astray.
They have made them turn aside *on* the [c]mountains;
They have gone along from mountain to hill
And have forgotten their [d]resting place.
7 "All who came upon them have devoured them;
And their adversaries have said, '[a]We are not guilty,
Inasmuch as they have sinned against the LORD *who is* the
[b]habitation of righteousness,
Even the LORD, the [c]hope of their fathers.'
8 "Wander away from the [a]midst of Babylon,
And [1]go forth from the land of the Chaldeans;
Be also like male goats [2]at the head of the flock.
9 "For behold, I am going to [a]arouse and bring up against Babylon
A horde of great nations from the land of the north,
And they will draw up *their* battle lines against her;
From there she will be taken captive.
Their arrows will be like [1]an expert warrior
Who does not return empty-handed.
10 "And [1a]Chaldea will become plunder;
All who plunder her will have enough," declares the LORD.

11 "Because you are glad, because you are jubilant,
O you who [a]pillage My heritage,
Because you skip about [1]like a threshing [b]heifer
And neigh like [2]stallions,
12 Your [a]mother [1]will be greatly ashamed,
She who gave you birth [1]will be humiliated.
Behold, *she will be* the least of the nations,
A [b]wilderness, a parched land, and a desert.
13 "Because of the indignation of the LORD she will [a]not be inhabited,
But she will be [b]completely desolate;
Everyone who passes by Babylon [c]will be horrified
And will hiss because of all her wounds.
14 "Draw up your battle lines against Babylon on every side,
All you who [1]bend the bow;
Shoot at her, do not be sparing with *your* arrows,
For she has [a]sinned against the LORD.
15 "Raise your battle cry against her on every side!
She has [a]given [1]herself up, her pillars have fallen,
Her [b]walls have been torn down.
For this is the [c]vengeance of the LORD:

2 [e]Jer. 51:47

[a]Is. 13:17; Jer. 50:9; ...1, 27 [b]Is. 14:22, 23; ...er. 50:13 [c]Jer. 9:10, 11; Zeph. 1:3

4 [a]Is. 11:12, 13; Jer. ...8; 31:31; 33:7; Hos. [b]Ezra 3:12, 13; Ps. ...26:5; Jer. 31:9 [c]Hos. 3:5

5 [1]Lit., *hither* [2]M.T. ...*s come ye!* [3]Or, *will* ...*ave come* [a]Is. 35:8; ...6:16 [b]Is. 55:3; Jer. 32:40; Heb. 8:6-10

...s. 53:6; Ezek. 34:15, 16; Matt. 9:36; 10:6 [b]Jer. 23:11-14 [c]Jer. 16; Ezek. 34:6 [d]Jer. 33:12; 50:19

[a]Jer. 2:3; Zech. 11:5 31:23; 40:2, 3 [c]Ps. ...2:4; Jer. 14:8; 17:13

[1]Another reading is ...*hem go forth* [2]Or, *in* ...*nt of* [a]Is. 48:20; Jer. 51:6; Rev. 18:4

[1]So some mss. and ...rsions; M.T. reads *a warrior who makes childless* [a]Jer. 51:1

[1]Or, *the Chaldeans* ...er. 51:24, 35; Ezek. 11:24

[1]Another reading is *in the grass* [2]Lit., *mighty ones* [a]Jer. 12:14 [b]Jer. 46:20

...2 [1]Or, *has become* ...er. 15:9 [b]Jer. 22:6; 51:43

...3 [a]Jer. 34:22 [b]Jer. ... [c]Jer. 18:16; 49:17

[1]Lit., *tread* (in order ...ring) [a]Hab. 2:8, 17

15 [1]Lit., *her hand* 1 Chr. 29:24; 2 Chr. ...0:8; Lam. 5:6 [b]Jer. ...44, 58; 51:58 [c]Jer. 46:10

Take vengeance on her;
[d]As she has done *to others, so* do to her.
16 "Cut off the [a]sower from Babylon,
And the one who wields the sickle at the time of harvest;
From before [1]the [b]sword of the oppressor
[c]They will each turn back to his own people,
And they will each flee to his own land.
17 "Israel is a [a]scattered [1]flock, the [b]lions have driven *them* away. The
first one *who* devoured him was the [c]king of Assyria, and this last
one *who* has broken his bones is [d]Nebuchadnezzar king of Babylon.
18 "Therefore thus says the LORD of hosts, the God of Israel: 'Behold,
I am going to punish the king of Babylon and his land, just as I
[a]punished the king of Assyria.
19 'And I shall [a]bring Israel back to his pasture, and he will graze on
Carmel and Bashan, and his [1]desire will be satisfied in the [b]hill
country of Ephraim and Gilead.
20 'In those days and at that time,' declares the LORD, 'search will be
made for the iniquity of Israel, but [a]there will be none; and for the
sins of Judah, but they will not be found; for I shall pardon those
[b]whom I leave as a remnant.'
21 "Against the land of [1]Merathaim, go up against it,
And against the inhabitants of [2a]Pekod.
Slay and [3]utterly destroy them," declares the LORD,
"And do according to all that I have commanded you.
22 "The [a]noise of battle is in the land,
And great destruction.
23 "How the [a]hammer of the whole earth
Has been cut off and broken!
How Babylon has become
An object of horror among the nations!
24 "I [a]set a snare for you, and you were also [b]caught, O Babylon,
While you yourself were not aware;
You have been found and also seized
Because you have engaged in [c]conflict with the LORD."
25 The LORD has opened His armory
And has brought forth the [a]weapons of His indignation,
For it is a [b]work of the Lord [1]GOD of hosts
In the land of the Chaldeans.
26 Come to her from the [1]farthest border;
[a]Open up her barns,
Pile her up like heaps
And [2b]utterly destroy her,
Let nothing be left to her.
27 [a]Put all her young bulls to the sword;
Let them [b]go down to the slaughter!
Woe be upon them, for their [c]day has come,
The time of their punishment.
28 There is a [a]sound of fugitives and refugees from the land of
Babylon,
To declare in Zion the [b]vengeance of the LORD our God,
Vengeance for His [c]temple.

29 "Summon [1]many against Babylon,
All those who [2]bend the bow:

15 [d]Ps. 137:8; F

16 [1]Or, *the oppr* *sword* [a]Joel 1:11 25:38; 46:16 [c]Is.

17 [1]Lit., *sheep* 3:2 [b]Jer. 2:15; 4 [c]2 Kin. 15:19; 17 18:9-13 [d]2 Kin. 10-12; 25:1-7

18 [a]Is. 10:12; Ez 31:3, 11, 12; Nah 18, 19

19 [1]Lit., *soul* [a]Is. Jer. 31:10; 33:12; 34:13 [b]Jer. 31:6

20 [a]Is. 43:25; Jer 31:34; Mic. 7:19

21 [1]Or, *Double Rebellion* [2]Or, *Punishment* [3]Lit., *under the ban* [a]E 23:23

22 [a]Jer. 4:19-21; 51:54-56

23 [a]Jer. 51:20-24

24 [a]Jer. 48:43, 44 51:31; Dan. 5:30, [c]Job 9:4; 40:2, 9

25 [1]Heb., *YHWH,* usually rendered *L* [a]Is. 13:5 [b]Jer. 50: 51:12, 25, 55

26 [1]Lit., *end* [2]Lit., *under the ban* [a]Is. Jer. 50:10 [b]Is. 14:

27 [a]Is. 34:7 [b]Jer. 48:10 [c]Ps. 37:13; 46:21; 48:44; Ezek.

28 [a]Is. 48:20 [b]Ps. 149:6-9; Jer. 50:15 51:10 [c]Lam. 1:10;

29 [1]Another readir *archers* [2]Lit., *tread* order to string)

Encamp against her on every side,
Let there be no escape[3].
Repay her according to her work;
[a]According to all that she has done, *so* do to her;
For she has become [b]arrogant against the LORD,
Against the Holy One of Israel.
30 "Therefore her [a]young men will fall in her streets,
And all her men of war will be [1b]silenced in that day," declares
the LORD.
31 "Behold, [a]I am against you, O [1]arrogant one,"
Declares the Lord [2]GOD of hosts,
"For your day has come,
The time [3]when I shall punish you.
32 "And the [1a]arrogant one will stumble and fall
With no one to raise him up;
And I shall [b]set fire to his cities,
And it will devour all his environs."

33 Thus says the LORD of hosts,
"The sons of Israel are oppressed,
And the sons of Judah as well;
And [a]all who took them captive have held them fast,
They have refused to let them go.
34 "Their [a]Redeemer is strong, [b]the LORD of hosts is His name;
He will vigorously [c]plead their case,
So that He may [d]bring rest to [1]the earth,
But turmoil to the inhabitants of Babylon.
35 "A [a]sword against the Chaldeans," declares the LORD,
"And against the inhabitants of Babylon,
And against her [b]officials and her [c]wise men!
36 "A sword against the [a]oracle priests, and they will become fools!
A sword against her [b]mighty men, and they will be [1c]shattered!
37 "A sword against [1]their [a]horses and against [1]their chariots,
And against all the [2b]foreigners who are in the midst of her,
And they will become [c]women!
A sword against her treasures, and they will be plundered!
38 "A [1a]drought on her waters, and they will be dried up!
For it is a land of [b]idols,
And they are mad over fearsome idols.
39 "Therefore the [a]desert creatures will live *there* along with the
jackals;
The ostriches also will live in it,
And it will [b]never again be inhabited
Or dwelt in from generation to generation.
40 "As when God overthrew [a]Sodom
And Gomorrah with its neighbors," declares the LORD,
"No man will live there,
Nor will *any* son of man reside in it.

41 "Behold, a people is coming [a]from the north,
And a great nation and many kings
Will be aroused from the remote parts of the earth.
42 "They [a]seize *their* bow and javelin;
They are [b]cruel and have no mercy.

[3]Some mss. add *to her* [a]Ps. 137:8; Jer. 15; 51:56; 2 Thess. 1:6 [b]Ex. 10:3; Jer. 49:16; Dan. 4:37

Or, *made lifeless* or *estroyed* [a]Is. 13:17, '8; Jer. 9:21; 18:21; 6; 51:4 [b]Jer. 51:57

31 [1]Lit., *arrogance* eb., *YHWH*, usually rendered *LORD* nother reading is *of r punishment* [a]Jer. 21:13; Nah. 2:13

Lit., *arrogance* [a]Is. :12-15 [b]Jer. 21:14; 49:27

33 [a]Is. 14:17; 58:6

34 [1]Or, their *land* v. 23:11; Is. 43:14; 15:21; 31:11; Rev. 18:8 [b]Is. 47:4; Jer. 32:18; 51:19 [c]Jer. 51:36; Mic. 7:9 [d]Is. 14:3-7

35 [a]Jer. 47:6; Hos. [b]Dan. 5:1, 2 [c]Dan. 5:7, 8

[1]Or, *dismayed* [a]Is. [b]Jer. 49:22 [c]Nah. 3:13

it., *his* [2]Lit., *mixed itude* [a]Ps. 20:7, 8; er. 51:21, 22 [b]Jer.); Ezek. 30:5 [c]Jer. ; 51:30; Nah. 3:13

Another reading is *ord* [a]Is. 44:27; Jer. 32, 36; Rev. 16:12 [b]Is. 46:1, 6, 7

[a]Is. 13:21; 34:14; v. 18:2 [b]Is. 13:20; Jer. 25:12

Gen. 19:24, 25; Is.); Jer. 49:18; Luke '28-30; 2 Pet. 2:6; Jude 7

. 13:2-5; Jer. 6:22; 50:3, 9; 51:27, 28

42 [a]Jer. 6:23 [b]Is. 13:17, 18; 47:6

Their [c]voice roars like the sea,
And they ride on [d]horses,
[e]Marshalled like a man for the battle
Against you, O daughter of Babylon.
43 "The [a]king of Babylon has heard the report about them,
And his hands hang limp;
[b]Distress has gripped him,
Agony like a woman in childbirth.
44 "[a]Behold, one will come up like a lion from the [1]thicket of the
Jordan to [2]a perennially watered pasture; for in an instant I shall
make them run away from it, and whoever is [b]chosen I shall appoint
over it. For who is [c]like Me, and who will summon Me *into court?*
And who then is the shepherd who can [d]stand before Me?"
45 Therefore hear the [a]plan of the LORD which He has planned
against Babylon, and His purposes which He has purposed against
the land of the Chaldeans: [b]surely they will drag them off, *even* the
little ones of the flock; surely He will make their [1]pasture desolate
because of them.
46 At the [1]shout, "Babylon has been seized!" the [a]earth is shaken,
and an [b]outcry is heard among the nations.

Chapter 51

51 Thus says the LORD:
"Behold, I am going to arouse against Babylon
And against the inhabitants of [1]Leb-kamai
[2]The [a]spirit of a destroyer.
2 "And I shall dispatch [1]foreigners to Babylon that they may
[a]winnow her
And may devastate her land;
For on every side they will be opposed to her
In the day of *her* calamity.
3 "[1]Let not [2]him who [3a]bends his bow [3]bend *it*,
[1]Nor let him rise up in his [b]scale-armor;
So do not spare her young men;
Devote all her army to destruction.
4 "And they will fall down [1]slain in the land of the Chaldeans,
And [a]pierced through in their streets."

5 For [a]neither Israel nor Judah has been [1]forsaken
By his God, the LORD of hosts,
Although their land is [b]full of guilt
[2]Before the Holy One of Israel.
6 [a]Flee from the midst of Babylon,
And each of you save his life!
Do not be [1b]destroyed in her [2]punishment,
For this is the [c]LORD's time of vengeance;
He is going to [d]render recompense to her.
7 Babylon has been a golden [a]cup in the hand of the LORD,
Intoxicating all the earth.
The [b]nations have drunk of her wine;
Therefore the nations are [c]going mad.
8 Suddenly [a]Babylon has fallen and been broken;
[b]Wail over her!
[c]Bring [1]balm for her pain;

42 [c]Is. 5:30 [d]J
47:3; Hab. 1:8
50:9, 14; Joel 2

43 [a]Jer. 51:31
30:6; 49:24

44 [1]Lit., *pride*
enduring habita
[a]Jer. 49:19-21
16:5 [c]Is. 46:9
41:10; Jer. 30:2

45 [1]Or, *habitati*
33:11; Is. 14:24;
51:10, 11 [b]Jer.

46 [1]Lit., *voice*
10:10; 49:21; Ez
26:18; 31:16 [b]Is
15:5; Jer. 46:12;
Ezek. 27:28

51:1 [1]Cryptic na
Chaldea; or, *the*
those who rise u
against Me [2]Or,
destroying wind
4:11, 12; 23:19;
13:15

2 [1]Some versior
winnowers [a]Is. 4
Jer. 15:7; Matt. 3

3 [1]M.T. reads *Ag*
him who [2]I.e., th
Chaldean defend
[3]Lit., *tread(s)* (in
string) [a]Jer. 50:1
[b]Jer. 46:4

4 [1]Or, *wounded*
13:15; 14:19; Jer.
50:30, 37

5 [1]Lit., *widowed*
From [a]Is. 54:7, 8
33:24-26 [b]Hos. 4

6 [1]Or, *silenced* o
lifeless [2]Or, *pena*
iniquity [a]Jer. 50:8
Rev. 18:4 [b]Num.
[c]Jer. 50:15 [d]Jer. 2

7 [a]Jer. 25:15; Hab
2:16; Rev. 14:8; 1
[b]Rev. 14:8; 18:3
25:16

8 [1]Or, *balsam res*
21:9; Jer. 50:2; Re
14:8; 18:2 [b]Is. 13
Rev. 18:9 [c]Jer. 46

Perhaps she may be healed.
9 We applied healing to Babylon, but she was not healed;
Forsake her and [a]let us each go to his own country,
For her judgment has [b]reached to heaven
And [1]towers up to the very skies.
10 The LORD has [a]brought [1]about our vindication;
Come and let us [b]recount in Zion
The work of the LORD our God!

11 [a]Sharpen the arrows, fill the quivers!
The LORD has aroused the spirit of the kings of the Medes,
Because His purpose is against Babylon to destroy it;
For it is the [b]vengeance of the LORD, vengeance for His temple.
12 [a]Lift up a [1]signal against the walls of Babylon;
Post a strong guard,
Station [2]sentries,
Place men in ambush!
For the LORD has both [b]purposed and performed
What He spoke concerning the inhabitants of Babylon.
13 O you who [a]dwell by many waters,
Abundant in [b]treasures,
Your end has come,
The [1]measure of your [2c]end.
14 The [a]LORD of hosts has sworn by Himself:
"Surely I will fill you with a [1]population like [b]locusts,
And they will cry out with [2]shouts of victory over you."

15 *It is* [a]He who made the earth by His power,
Who established the world by His wisdom,
And by His understanding He [b]stretched out the heavens.
16 When He utters His [a]voice, *there is* a tumult of waters in the heavens,
And He causes the [b]clouds to ascend from the end of the earth;
He makes lightning for the rain,
And brings forth the [c]wind from His storehouses.
17 [a]All mankind is stupid, devoid of knowledge;
Every goldsmith is put to shame by his [1]idols,
For his molten images are [b]deceitful,
And there is no breath in them.
18 They are [a]worthless, a work of mockery;
In the time of their punishment they will perish.
19 The [a]portion of Jacob is not like these;
For the [1]Maker of all is He,
And of the [2]tribe of His inheritance;
The [b]LORD of hosts is His name.
20 *He says,* "You are My [1a]war-club, *My* weapon of war;
And with you I [b]shatter nations,
And with you I destroy kingdoms.
21 "And with you I [a]shatter the horse and his rider,
22 And with you I shatter the [a]chariot and its rider,
And with you I shatter [b]man and woman,
And with you I shatter old man and [c]youth,
And with you I shatter young man and virgin,
23 And with you I shatter the shepherd and his flock,

9 [1]Lit., *is lifted* [a]Is. ...4; Jer. 46:16; 50:16 [b]Ezra 9:6; Rev. 18:5
[1]Lit., *forth* [a]Ps. 37:6; ...c. 7:9 [b]Is. 40:2; Jer. 50:28
1 [a]Jer. 46:4, 9; Joel 3:9, 10 [b]Jer. 50:28
[1]Or, *standard* [2]Or, *watchmen* [a]Is. 13:2; ...er. 50:2; 51:27 [b]Jer. 4:28; 23:20; 51:29
13 [1]Lit., *cubit* [2]Lit., ...*g cut off* [a]Rev. 17:1 [b]Is. 45:3 [c]Is. 57:17; Hab. 2:9-11
[1]Or, *mankind* [2]I.e., ...e the song of grape ...eaders [a]Jer. 49:13 ...er. 51:27; Nah. 3:15
15 [a]Gen. 1:1; Jer. 10:12-16; 51:15-19 ...b 9:8; Ps. 146:5, 6; ...32:17; Acts 14:15; Rom. 1:20
6 [a]Job 37:2-6; Ps. ...13 [b]Ps. 135:7; Jer. 10:13 [c]Jon. 1:4
[1]Or, *graven images* ...4:18-20; Jer. 10:14 [b]Hab. 2:18, 19
18 [a]Jer. 18:15
...Lit., *Fashioner* [2]Or, ...*ter*; cf. Num. 24:17 ...s. 73:26; Jer. 10:16 [b]Jer. 50:34
[1]Lit., *shatterer* [a]Is. ...0:5; 41:15, 16; Jer. ...23 [b]Is. 8:9; 41:15, 16; Mic. 4:12, 13
21 [a]Ex. 15:1
[a]Ex. 15:4; Is. 43:17 ...r. 36:17; Is. 13:15, 16 [c]Is. 13:18

And with you I shatter the farmer and his team,
And with you I shatter governors and prefects.
24 "But I will repay Babylon and all the inhabitants of [a]Chaldea for
[b]all their evil that they have done in Zion before your eyes," declares
the LORD.
25 "Behold, [a]I am against you, [b]O destroying mountain,
Who destroys the whole earth," declares the LORD,
"And I will stretch out My hand against you,
And roll you down from the crags
And I will make you a [c]burnt out mountain.
26 "And they will not take from you *even* a stone for a corner
Nor a stone for foundations,
But you will be [a]desolate forever," declares the LORD.

27 [a]Lift up a [1]signal in the land,
Blow a trumpet among the nations!
Consecrate the nations against her,
Summon against her the [b]kingdoms of [c]Ararat, Minni and
[d]Ashkenaz;
Appoint a marshal against her,
Bring up the [e]horses like bristly locusts.
28 Consecrate the nations against her,
The kings of the Medes,
[1]Their governors and all [1]their [2]prefects,
And every land of [3]their dominion.
29 So the [a]land quakes and writhes,
For the purposes of the LORD against Babylon stand,
To make the land of Babylon
[1]A [b]desolation without inhabitants.
30 The [a]mighty men of Babylon have ceased fighting,
They stay in the strongholds;
[b]Their strength is [1]exhausted,
They are becoming [b]*like* women;
Their dwelling places are set on fire,
The [c]bars of her *gates* are broken.
31 One [1a]courier runs to meet [1]another,
And one [2b]messenger to meet [2]another,
To tell the king of Babylon
That his city has been captured from end *to end;*
32 The fords also have been seized,
And they have burned the marshes with fire,
And the men of war are terrified.

33 For thus says the LORD of hosts, the God of Israel:
"The daughter of Babylon is like a [a]threshing floor
At the time [1]it is stamped firm;
Yet in a little while the time of [b]harvest will come for her."

34 "Nebuchadnezzar king of Babylon has [a]devoured me *and*
crushed me,
He has set me down *like* an [b]empty vessel;
He has [c]swallowed me like a monster,
He has filled his stomach with my delicacies;
He has washed me away.

24 [a]Jer. 50:10 [b]Jer. 50:15, 29

25 [a]Jer. 50:31 [b]Is. 13:2; Zech. 4:7 [c]Re 8:8

26 [a]Is. 13:19-22; 5C Jer. 51:29

27 [1]Or, *standard* [a]... 13:2-5; 18:3; Jer. 5C 51:12 [b]Jer. 50:3, 9 [c]Gen. 8:4; 2 Kin. 19 Is. 37:38 [d]Gen. 10: [e]Jer. 50:42

28 [1]Lit., *Her* [2]I.e., lieutenant governor [3]Lit., *his*

29 [1]Or, *An object c horror* [a]Jer. 8:16; 1 50:46; Amos 8:8 [b]I 13:19, 20; 47:11; Je 50:13; 51:26, 43

30 [1]Lit., *dried up* [a] 76:5; Jer. 50:15, 36 [b]Is. 13:7, 8; Nah. 3: [c]Is. 45:1, 2; Lam. 2 Amos 1:5; Nah. 3:1

31 [1]Lit., *runner* [2]Li *announcer* [a]2 Chr. [b]2 Sam. 18:19-31

33 [1]Lit., *of treading* [a]Is. 21:10; 41:15, 1 Mic. 4:13 [b]Is. 17:5 6:11; Joel 3:13; Re 14:15

34 [a]Jer. 50:17 [b]Is. 24:1-3 [c]Job 20:15 51:44

it., *inhabitress* [a]Ps. 137:8

35 "May the [a]violence *done* to me and to my flesh be upon Babylon,"
The [1]inhabitant of Zion will say;
And, "May my blood be upon the inhabitants of Chaldea,"
Jerusalem will say.

oad river [a]Ps. [b]Jer. 51:6, 11; 19 [c]Jer. 50:38

36 Therefore thus says the LORD,
"Behold, I am going to [a]plead your case
And [b]exact full vengeance for you;
And [c]I shall dry up her [1]sea
And make her fountain dry.

8:2 [b]Jer. 25:9

37 "And [a]Babylon will become a heap *of ruins,* a haunt of jackals,
An [b]object of horror and hissing, without inhabitants.

38 [a]Jer. 2:15

38 "They will roar together like [a]young lions,
They will growl like lions' cubs.

. 25:27; 48:26; 1:57 [b]Ps. 76:5

39 "When they become heated up, I shall serve *them* their banquet
And [a]make them drunk, that they may become jubilant
And may [b]sleep a perpetual sleep
And not wake up," declares the LORD.

Or, *young rams* er. 48:15; 50:27

40 "I shall bring them down like [1]lambs [a]to the slaughter,
Like rams together with male goats.

ryptic name for lon [a]Jer. 25:26 [b]Jer. 49:25

41 "How [1a]Sheshak has been captured,
And [b]the praise of the whole earth been seized!
How Babylon has become an object of horror among the nations!

broad river [a]Is. Jer. 51:55; Dan. 9:26

42 "The [1a]sea has come up over Babylon;
She has been engulfed with its tumultuous waves.
43 "Her cities have become an [a]object of horror,
A parched land and a desert,
A land in which [b]no man lives,
And through which no son of man passes.

[a]Jer. 50:12 [b]Is. 13:20; Jer. 2:6

44 "And [a]I shall punish Bel in Babylon,
And I shall make what he has swallowed [b]come out of his mouth;
And the nations will no longer [c]stream to him.
Even the [d]wall of Babylon has fallen down!

. 46:1; Jer. 50:2 ra 1:7, 8 [c]Is. 2:2 Jer. 50:15; 51:58

48:20; Jer. 50:8, ; 51:6; Rev. 18:4 . 19:12-16; Acts 2:40

45 "[a]Come forth from her midst, My people,
And each of you [b]save yourselves
From the fierce anger of the LORD.

., *in the* [2]Lit., *the* :5; Jer. 46:27, 28 . 19:7; Is. 13:3-5 [c]Is. 19:2

46 "Now [a]lest your heart grow faint,
And you be afraid at the [b]report that *will be* heard in the land—
For the report will come [1]one year,
And after that [2]another report in [2]another year,
And violence *will be* in the land
With [c]ruler against ruler—

[a]Is. 21:9; 46:1, 2; 50:2; 51:52 [b]Jer. 50:12, 35-37

47 Therefore behold, days are coming
When I shall punish the [a]idols of Babylon;
And her whole land will be [b]put to shame,
And all her slain will fall in her midst.

[a]Is. 44:23; 48:20; ; Rev. 18:20 [b]Jer. 50:3

48 "Then [a]heaven and earth and all that is in them
Will shout for joy over Babylon,
For [b]the destroyers will come to her from the north,"
Declares the LORD.

9 [a]Ps. 137:8; Jer. 50:29

49 [a]Indeed Babylon is to fall *for* the slain of Israel,

As also for Babylon [b]the slain of all the earth have fallen.
50 You [a]who have escaped the sword,
Depart! Do not stay!
[b]Remember the LORD from afar,
And let Jerusalem [1]come to your mind.
51 [a]We are ashamed because we have heard reproach;
Disgrace has covered our faces,
For [b]aliens have entered
The holy places of the LORD's house.

52 "Therefore behold, the days are coming," declares the LORD,
"When I shall punish her [a]idols,
And the mortally wounded will groan throughout her land.
53 "Though Babylon should [a]ascend to the heavens,
And though she should fortify [1]her lofty stronghold,
From [b]Me destroyers will come to her," declares the LORD.

54 The [a]sound of an outcry from Babylon,
And of great destruction from the land of the Chaldeans!
55 For the LORD is going to destroy Babylon,
And He will make *her* loud [1]noise vanish from her.
And their [a]waves will roar like many waters;
The tumult of their voices [2]sounds forth.
56 For the [a]destroyer is coming against her, against Babylon,
And her mighty men will be captured,
Their [b]bows are shattered;
For the LORD is a God of [c]recompense,
He will fully repay.
57 "And I shall [a]make her princes and her wise men drunk,
Her governors, her prefects, and her mighty men,
That they may sleep a [b]perpetual sleep and not wake up,"
[c]Declares the King, whose name is the LORD of hosts.
58 Thus says the LORD of hosts,
"The broad [a]wall of Babylon will be completely razed,
And her high [b]gates will be set on fire;
So the peoples will [c]toil for nothing,
And the nations become [d]exhausted *only* for fire."
59 The [1]message which Jeremiah the prophet commanded Seraiah
the son of [a]Neriah, the grandson of Mahseiah, when he went with
[b]Zedekiah the king of Judah to Babylon in the fourth year of his
reign. (Now Seraiah was quartermaster.)
60 So Jeremiah [a]wrote in a single [1]scroll all the calamity which
would come upon Babylon, *that is,* all these words which have been
written concerning Babylon.
61 Then Jeremiah said to Seraiah, "As soon as you come to Babylon,
then see that you read all these words aloud,
62 and say, 'Thou, O LORD, hast [1]promised concerning this place to
[a]cut it off, so that there will be [b]nothing dwelling in it, [2]whether man
or beast, but it will be a perpetual desolation.'
63 "And it will come about as soon as you finish reading this [1]scroll,
you will tie a stone to it and [a]throw it into the middle of the
Euphrates,
64 and say, 'Just so shall Babylon sink down and [a]not rise again,

49 [b]Rev. 18:2
50 [1]Lit., *come your heart* [a]Je [b]Deut. 4:29-31 137:6
51 [a]Ps. 44:15 74:3-8; Lam. 1
52 [a]Jer. 50:38
53 [1]Lit., *the he her strength* [a] Job 20:6; Ps. 1 Is. 14:12-14; Je Amos 9:2; Oba 13:3
54 [a]Jer. 48:3-5 50:22, 46
55 [1]Or, *voice given* [a]Ps. 18:4 124:2, 4, 5; Jer.
56 [a]Jer. 51:48, 2:8 [b]Ps. 46:9; 7 [c]Deut. 32:35; Ps 2; Jer. 51:6, 24
57 [a]Jer. 25:27 76:5, 6 [c]Jer. 46 48:15
58 [a]Jer. 50:15 45:1, 2 [c]Hab. 2: 9:5; 51:64; Lam.
59 [1]Lit., *word* [a] 32:12; 36:4; 45:1 28:1; 52:1
60 [1]Or, *book* [a]Is Jer. 30:2, 3; 36:2
62 [1]Lit., *spoken from man even to* [a]Is. 13:19-22; 14: Jer. 50:3, 13, 39, [b]Jer. 51:43; Ezek
63 [1]Or, *book* [a]Je 19:10, 11; Rev. 18
64 [a]Nah. 1:8, 9

because of the calamity that I am going to bring upon her; and they
will become [b]exhausted.' " [c]Thus far are the words of Jeremiah.

Chapter 52

52 [a]Zedekiah was twenty-one years old when he became king,
and he reigned eleven years in Jerusalem; and his mother's
name was [1b]Hamutal the daughter of Jeremiah of [c]Libnah.
2 And he did [a]evil in the sight of the LORD like all that [b]Jehoiakim
had done.
3 For through the [a]anger of the LORD *this* came about in Jerusalem
and Judah until He cast them out from His presence. And Zedekiah
[b]rebelled against the king of Babylon.
4 [a]Now it came about in the ninth year of his reign, on the tenth
day of the tenth month, that Nebuchadnezzar king of Babylon came,
he and all his army, against Jerusalem, camped against it, and built a
[b]siege wall all around [1]it.
5 [a]So the city was under siege until the eleventh year of King
Zedekiah.
6 On the ninth day of the [a]fourth month the [b]famine was so severe
in the city that there was no food for the people of the land.
7 Then the city was [a]broken into, and all the [b]men of war fled and
went forth from the city at night by way of the gate between the two
walls which *was* by the king's garden, though the Chaldeans were
[1c]all around the city. And they went by way of the Arabah.
8 But the army of the Chaldeans pursued the king and [a]overtook
Zedekiah in the [1]plains of Jericho, and all his army was scattered
from him.
9 Then they captured the king and [a]brought him up to the king of
Babylon at [b]Riblah in the land of [c]Hamath; and he [1]passed sentence
on him.
10 And the king of Babylon [a]slaughtered the sons of Zedekiah
before his eyes, and he also slaughtered all the [1]princes of Judah in
Riblah.
11 Then he [a]blinded the eyes of Zedekiah; and the king of Babylon
bound him with bronze fetters and brought him to Babylon, and put
him in prison until the day of his death.
12 [a]Now on the tenth day of the fifth month, which was the [b]nine-
teenth year of King Nebuchadnezzar, king of Babylon, [c]Nebuzara-
dan the captain of the bodyguard, [1]who was in the service of the
king of Babylon, came to Jerusalem.
13 And he [a]burned the house of the LORD, the [b]king's house, and all
the houses of Jerusalem; even every large house he burned with fire.
14 So all the army of the Chaldeans who *were* with the captain of
the guard [a]broke down all the walls around Jerusalem.
15 Then Nebuzaradan the captain of the guard [a]carried away into
exile some of the poorest of the people, the rest of the people who
were left in the city, the [1b]deserters who had deserted to the king of
Babylon, and the rest of the artisans.
16 But [a]Nebuzaradan the captain of the guard left some of the
poorest of the land to be vinedressers and [1]plowmen.
17 Now the bronze [a]pillars which belonged to the house of the LORD
and the [b]stands and the bronze [c]sea, which were in the house of the
LORD, the Chaldeans broke in pieces and carried all their bronze to
Babylon.

64 [b]Jer. 51:58 [c]Job 31:40; Ps. 72:20

1 [1]Another reading is *Hamital* [a]2 Kin. 24:18; 2 Chr. 36:11 [b]2 Kin. 22:31; 24:18 [c]Josh. 10:29; 2 Kin. 8:22; Is. 37:8

[a]1 Kin. 14:22; 2 Kin. 24:19; 2 Chr. 36:12 [b]Jer. 36:30, 31

2 Kin. 24:20; Is. 3:1, 4, 5 [b]2 Chr. 36:13; Ezek. 17:12-16

it., *against it* [a]2 Kin. 5:1; Jer. 39:1; Ezek. 2; Zech. 8:19 [b]Jer. 32:24

5 [a]2 Kin. 25:2

6 [a]Jer. 39:2 [b]2 Kin. :3; Is. 3:1; Jer. 38:9; k. 4:16; 5:16; 14:13

Lit., *against the city* ı *every side* [a]2 Kin. 25:4; Jer. 39:2 [b]Jer. 9:4-7; 51:32 [c]Ezek. 33:21

[1]Lit., *Arabah* [a]Jer. 32:4; 34:21; 37:17; 38:23

9 [1]Lit., *spoke* *gments with* [a]2 Kin. 25:6; Jer. 32:4; 39:5 um. 34:11; Jer. 39:5 ı. 13:21; Josh. 13:5

[1]Or, *commanders* in. 25:7; Jer. 22:30; 39:6

1 [a]Jer. 39:7; Ezek. 12:13

[1]Lit., *stood before the king* [a]2 Kin. 25:8-21; Zech. 7:5; 8:19 [b]2 Kin. 24:12; :8; Jer. 52:29 [c]Jer. 39:9

[a]1 Kin. 9:8; 2 Kin. 9; 2 Chr. 36:19; Ps. 5-8; 79:1; Is. 64:10, Lam. 2:7; Mic. 3:12 [b]Jer. 39:8

[a]2 Kin. 25:10; Neh. 1:3

.it., *fallers who had fallen* [a]2 Kin. 25:11 [b]Jer. 39:9

Or, *unpaid laborers* [a]2 Kin. 25:12; Jer. 39:10; 40:2-6

7 [a]1 Kin. 7:15-22; 2 Kin. 25:13; Jer. 27:19-22; 52:20-23 n. 7:27-37 [c]1 Kin. 7:23-26

18 And they also took away the [a]pots, the shovels, the snuffers, the
basins, the [1]pans, and all the bronze vessels which were used in
temple service.
19 The captain of the guard also took away the [a]bowls, the firepans,
the basins, the pots, the lampstands, the [1]pans and the libation
bowls, what was fine gold and what was fine silver.
20 The two pillars, the one sea, and the twelve bronze bulls that
were under [1]the sea, *and* the stands, which King Solomon had made
for the house of the LORD—the bronze of all these vessels was
[a]beyond weight.
21 As for the pillars, the [a]height of each pillar was eighteen [1]cubits,
and [2]it was twelve cubits in [a]circumference and four fingers in thick-
ness, *and* hollow.
22 Now a [a]capital of bronze was on it; and the height of each capital
was five cubits, with network and [b]pomegranates upon the capital
all around, all of bronze. And the second pillar was like these, in-
cluding pomegranates.
23 And there were ninety-six [1]exposed pomegranates; all [a]the
pomegranates *numbered* a hundred on the network all around.
24 Then the captain of the guard took [a]Seraiah the chief priest and
[b]Zephaniah the second priest, with the three [1c]officers of the temple.
25 He also took from the city one official who was overseer of the
men of war, and seven [1]of the [a]king's advisers who were found in
the city, and the scribe of the commander of the army who mustered
the people of the land, and sixty men of the people of the land who
were found in the midst of the city.
26 And Nebuzaradan the captain of the guard took them and
[a]brought them to the king of Babylon at Riblah.
27 Then the king of Babylon [a]struck them down and put them to
death at Riblah in the land of Hamath. So Judah was [b]led away into
exile from its land.
28 These are the people whom [a]Nebuchadnezzar carried away into
exile: in the [1]seventh year 3,023 Jews;
29 in the eighteenth year of Nebuchadnezzar 832 persons from
Jerusalem;
30 in the twenty-third year of Nebuchadnezzar, [a]Nebuzaradan the
captain of the guard carried into exile 745 Jewish people; there were
4,600 persons in all.
31 [a]Now it came about in the thirty-seventh year of the exile of
Jehoiachin king of Judah, in the twelfth month, on the twenty-fifth of
the month, that [1]Evil-merodach king of Babylon, in the *first* year of
his reign, [2b]showed favor to Jehoiachin king of Judah and brought
him out of prison.
32 [a]Then he spoke kindly to him and set his throne above the
thrones of the kings who *were* with him in Babylon.
33 So [1]Jehoiachin [a]changed his prison clothes, and [2b]had his meals
in [3]the king's presence regularly all the days of his life.
34 And for his allowance, a [a]regular allowance was given him by
the king of Babylon, a daily portion all the days of his life until the
day of his death.

18 [1]Or, *spoons* incense [a]Ex. 2 1 Kin. 7:40, 45; 25:14

19 [1]Or, *spoons* incense [a]1 Kin. 50; 2 Kin. 25:15

20 [1]So Gr. and Heb. omits *the s* [a]1 Kin. 7:47; 2 K

21 [1]I.e., One cu equals approx. 1 [2]Lit., *a line of 12 would encircle it* 7:15; 2 Kin. 25:1 2 Chr. 3:15

22 [a]1 Kin. 7:16; 25:17 [b]1 Kin. 7:

23 [1]Lit., *windwa* [a]1 Kin. 7:20

24 [1]Lit., *keepers door* [a]2 Kin. 25: 1 Chr. 6:14; Ezra [b]2 Kin. 25:18; Je 29:25, 29; 37:3 9:19; Jer. 35:4

25 [1]Lit., *men of seeing the king's* [a]2 Kin. 25:19; Es

26 [a]2 Kin. 25:20

27 [a]2 Kin. 25:21; 8:11-18 [b]Is. 6:11, 27:10; 32:13, 14; 13:19; 20:4; 25:9 39:9; Ezek. 33:28 4:10

28 [1]Or possibly, *seventeenth* [a]2 K 24:2, 3, 12-16; 2 36:20; Ezra 2:1; N 7:6; Dan. 1:1-3

30 [a]2 Kin. 25:11; 39:9

31 [1]Or, *Awil-Marc* ("Man of Marduk") *lifted up the head* [a]2 Kin. 25:27 [b]Ge 40:13, 20; Ps. 3:3;

32 [a]2 Kin. 25:28

33 [1]Lit., *he* [2]Lit., *a* [3]Lit., *his presence* [a]Gen. 41:14, 42; 2 25:29 [b]2 Sam. 9:7 1 Kin. 2:7

34 [a]2 Sam. 9:10; 2 25:30

Jeremiah at a Glance

me of Jeremiah:

ENT DIVISIONS

		Chapter Themes
		1
		2
		3
		4
		5
		6
		7
		8
		9
		10
		11
		12
		13
		14
		15
		16
		17
		18
		19
		20
		21
		22
		23
		24
		25
		26

Author:

Date:

Purpose:

Key Words:

Segment Divisions

		Chapter Themes
		27
		28
		29
		30
		31
		32
		33
		34
		35
		36
		37
		38
		39
		40
		41
		42
		43
		44
		45
		46
		47
		48
		49
		50
		51
		52

[L]AMENTATIONS

[La]mentations is a book of wailings that was read annually by the Jews as a reminder of the fall of [Jerus]alem and destruction of the temple. They were a reminder of an avoidable tragedy caused by [sin...] a reminder of a God who judges but who keeps His covenant forever.

[Th]is expression of grief was written sometime between the destruction of Jerusalem in 586 B.C. and [the r]eturn of the remnant seventy years later. Judah's plight is desperate but not hopeless when they [reme]mber, "The Lord's lovingkindnesses indeed never cease, for His compassions never fail. They are [new] every morning; great is Thy faithfulness" (3:22-23).

[THI]NGS TO DO

[1.] There are five laments in this book; each begins a new chapter. Lamentations is written as poetry. Each chapter, except chapter 3, is twenty-two verses long—a verse for every letter of the Hebrew alphabet. As you read chapter by chapter note how each lament begins and who or what the lament centers on.

[2.] Mark the key words listed on LAMENTATIONS AT A GLANCE on page 1198.

[3.] Note the personification of Jerusalem and Judah. Jerusalem is personified as a woman. The personification is seen in the first lines of Lamentations: "How lonely sits the city . . . she has become like a widow." List what happened to Jerusalem and why—this is key. Note her emotions, the anguish because of her children, the thoughts and memories she has to deal with.

[4.] Carefully observe and list what you learn about God, His character, His judgments, and why He acts as He does. For example, 1:5 states that God caused Judah grief because of Judah's sin. God brought about Judah's captivity because of Judah's transgressions.

[5.] Lamentations gives a more definitive understanding of what took place during the Babylonian siege of Jerusalem. In the margin of the text, list what you learn. For example, 1:10 says the nations entered the sanctuary, the house of God where only Jewish priests were to go. Verse 11 reveals there was a famine—people were seeking bread and giving away precious things in order to get it.

[6.] Determine the theme of the chapter. Write the theme next to the chapter number and on LAMENTATIONS AT A GLANCE.

[7.] Complete LAMENTATIONS AT A GLANCE.

[THI]NGS TO THINK ABOUT

[1.] Have you become more aware of the consequences of sin?

[2.] God's judgment can take many forms. The Sovereign God rules. None can stay His hand or say to Him, "What doest Thou?" for He does according to His will in the army of heaven and among the inhabitants of the earth (Daniel 4:34-35). Do you think you can sin and go unpunished, unchastened by God? Judgment must begin at the house of God. Look at 1 Corinthians 11:31-32.

[3.] Why do you think God deals with sin as He does? How should you respond? Read chapter 3 on your knees, so your dancing needn't be "turned into mourning."

[a]Is. 3:26 [b]Is. 22:2 [c]Is. 54:4

Chapter 1 ________

1 How [a]lonely sits the city
That was [b]full of people!
She has become like a [c]widow

Who was *once* [d]great among the nations!
She who was a princess among the [1]provinces
Has become a [e]forced laborer!
2 She [a]weeps bitterly in the night,
And her tears are on her cheeks;
She has none to comfort her
Among all her [b]lovers.
All her friends have [c]dealt treacherously with her;
They have become her enemies.
3 [a]Judah has gone into exile [1]under affliction,
And [1]under [2]harsh servitude;
She dwells [b]among the nations,
But she has found no rest;
All [c]her pursuers have overtaken her
In the midst of [3]distress.
4 The roads [1]of Zion are in mourning
Because [a]no one comes to the appointed feasts.
All her gates are [b]desolate;
Her priests are groaning,
Her [c]virgins are afflicted,
And she herself [2]is [d]bitter.
5 Her adversaries have become [1]her masters,
Her enemies [2]prosper;
For the LORD has [a]caused her grief
Because of the multitude of her transgressions;
Her little ones have gone away
As captives before the adversary.
6 And all her [a]majesty
Has departed from the daughter of Zion;
Her princes have become like bucks
That have found no pasture;
And they have [1b]fled without strength
Before the pursuer.
7 In the days of her affliction and homelessness
[a]Jerusalem remembers all her precious things
That were from the days of old
When her people fell into the hand of the adversary,
And [b]no one helped her.
The adversaries saw her,
They [c]mocked at her [1]ruin.
8 Jerusalem sinned [a]greatly,
Therefore [b]she has become an unclean thing.
All who honored her despise her
Because they have seen her nakedness;
Even [c]she herself groans and turns away.
9 Her [a]uncleanness was in her skirts;
She [1]did not consider her [b]future;
Therefore she has [2c]fallen astonishingly;
[d]She has no comforter.
"[e]See, O LORD, my affliction,
For the enemy has [f]magnified himself!"
10 The adversary has stretched out his hand
Over all her precious things,
For she has seen the [a]nations enter her sanctuary,

1:1 [1]Or, *distric* 4:21; Ezra 4:20 31:7 [e]2 Kin. 23 40:9

2 [a]Ps. 6:6; 77:2 1:16 [b]Jer. 2:25 22:20-22 [c]Job 14; Ps. 31:11; M

3 [1]Or, *by reaso* [2]Lit., *great* [3]Or, *places* [a]Jer. 13 [b]Lev. 26:39; De 28:64-67 [c]2 Kir

4 [1]Or, *to* [2]Or, *s bitterly* [a]Is. 24:4 2:6, 7 [b]Jer. 9:11 [c]Lam. 2:10, 21 1:8-13

5 [1]Lit., *head* [2]O *ease* [a]Ps. 90:7, Ezek. 8:17, 18; 9

6 [1]Lit., *gone* [a]Je 13:18 [b]2 Kin. 25

7 [1]Lit., *cessation* 42:4; 77:5-9 [b]Jer Lam. 4:17 [c]Ps. 7 Jer. 48:27

8 [a]Is. 59:2-13; La 1:5, 20 [b]Lam. 1:1 [c]Lam. 1:11, 21, 22

9 [1]Lit., *did not remember her lat end* [2]Lit., *come d* [a]Jer. 2:34; Ezek. 2 [b]Deut. 32:29; Is. 4 [c]Is. 3:8; Jer. 13:17 [d]Eccl. 4:1; Jer. 16 [e]Ps. 25:18; 119:15 74:23; Zeph. 2:10

10 [a]Ps. 74:4-8; Is 64:10, 11; Jer. 51

10 [b]Deut. 23:3

11 [1]Lit., *soul* [a]Jer. 38:9; 52:6 [b]1 Sam. 30:12 [c]Jer. 15:19

2 [1]Or, *sorrow* [a]Jer. 18:16; 48:27 [b]Jer. 0:23, 24 [c]Is. 13:13; Jer. 4:8

13 [1]Or, *descended, overthrew* [2]Or, *Sick* ob 30:30; Ps. 22:14; ab. 3:16 [b]Job 19:6; Ps. 66:11 [c]Jer. 44:6

[1]Lit., *stumble* [a]Prov. 5:22; Is. 47:6 [b]Jer. 3, 14 [c]Jer. 32:3, 5; Ezek. 25:4, 7

[1]Or, *feast* [a]Is. 41:2; 13:24; 37:10 [b]Jer. 11; 18:21 [c]Mal. 4:3

6 [1]Lit., *My eye, my* e [a]Jer. 14:17; Lam. , 18; 3:48, 49 [b]Ps. 20; Eccl. 4:1; Lam. 1:2

[a]Is. 1:15; Jer. 4:31 n. 24:2-4; Jer. 12:9 [c]Lam. 1:8

8 [1]Lit., *mouth* [2]Or, *w* [a]Ps. 119:75; Jer. [b]1 Sam. 12:14, 15; er. 4:17 [c]Lam. 1:12 [d]Deut. 28:32, 41

Lit., *their soul* [a]Job 19:13-19; Lam. 1:2 r. 14:15; Lam. 2:20 [c]Lam. 1:11

[1]Lit., *inward parts re in ferment* [2]Lit., *ereaves* [a]Is. 16:11; n. 2:11 [b]Jer. 14:20

The ones whom Thou didst command
That they should [b]not enter into Thy congregation.
11 All her people groan [a]seeking bread;
They have given their precious things for food
To [b]restore their [1]lives themselves.
"See, O LORD, and look,
For I am [c]despised."
12 "Is [a]it nothing to all you who pass this way?
Look and see if there is any [1]pain like my [1]pain
Which was severely dealt out to me,
Which the [b]LORD inflicted on the day of His [c]fierce anger.
13 "From on high He sent fire into my [a]bones,
And it [1]prevailed *over them;*
He has spread a [b]net for my feet;
He has turned me back;
He has made me [c]desolate,
[2]Faint all day long.
14 "The [a]yoke of my transgressions is bound;
By His hand they are knit together;
They have [b]come upon my neck;
He has made my strength [1]fail;
The Lord [c]has given me into the hands
Of *those against whom* I am not able to stand.
15 "The [a]Lord has rejected all my strong men
In my midst;
He has called an appointed [1]time against me
To crush my [b]young men;
The Lord has [c]trodden *as in* a wine press
The virgin daughter of Judah.
16 "For these things I [a]weep;
[1]My eyes run down with water;
Because far from me is a [b]comforter,
One who restores my soul;
My children are desolate
Because the enemy has prevailed."
17 Zion [a]stretches out her hands;
There is no one to comfort her;
The LORD has [b]commanded concerning Jacob
That the ones round about him should be his adversaries;
[c]Jerusalem has become an unclean thing among them.
18 "The LORD is [a]righteous;
For I have [b]rebelled against His [1]command;
Hear now, all peoples,
And [c]behold my [2]pain;
[d]My virgins and my young men
Have gone into captivity.
19 "I [a]called to my lovers, *but* they deceived me;
My [b]priests and my elders perished in the city,
While they sought food to [c]restore [1]their strength themselves.
20 "See, O LORD, for I am in distress;
My [1a]spirit is greatly troubled;
My heart is overturned within me,
For I have been very [b]rebellious.
In the street the sword [2]slays;

In the house it is like death.
21 "They have heard that I [a]groan;
There is no one to comfort me;
All my enemies have heard of my [1]calamity;
They are [b]glad that Thou hast done *it*.
Oh, that Thou wouldst bring the day which Thou hast proclaimed,
That they may become [c]like me.
22 "Let all their wickedness come before Thee;
And [a]deal with them as Thou hast dealt with me
For all my transgressions;
For my groans are many, and my heart is faint."

Chapter 2

2 How the Lord has [a]covered the daughter of Zion
With a cloud in His anger!
He has [b]cast from heaven to earth
The [c]glory of Israel,
And has not remembered His [d]footstool
In the day of His anger.
2 The Lord has [a]swallowed up; He has not spared
All the habitations of Jacob.
In His wrath He has [b]thrown down
The strongholds of the daughter of Judah;
He has [c]brought *them* down to the ground;
He has [d]profaned the kingdom and its princes.
3 In fierce anger He has cut off
[1]All the [a]strength of Israel;
He has [b]drawn back His right hand
From before the enemy.
And He has [c]burned in Jacob like a flaming fire
Consuming round about.
4 He has bent His [a]bow like an enemy,
He has set His right hand like an adversary
And slain all that were [b]pleasant to the eye;
In the tent of the daughter of Zion
He has [c]poured out His wrath like fire.
5 The Lord has become like an [a]enemy.
He has [b]swallowed up Israel;
He has swallowed up all its [c]palaces;
He has destroyed its strongholds
And [d]multiplied in the daughter of Judah
Mourning and moaning.
6 And He has violently treated His [1]tabernacle like a garden *booth;*
He has [a]destroyed His appointed [2]meeting place;
The LORD has [b]caused to be forgotten
The appointed feast and sabbath in Zion,
And He has [c]despised king and priest
In the indignation of His anger.
7 The Lord has [a]rejected His altar,
He has abandoned His sanctuary;
He [b]has delivered into the hand of the enemy
The walls of her palaces.
They have made a [c]noise in the house of the LORD

21 [1]Lit., *evil* [a]La 8, 22 [b]Ps. 35:15; 50:11; Lam. 2:15 14:5, 6; 47:6, 11; 30:16

22 [a]Neh. 4:4, 5; 137:7, 8

2:1 [a]Ezek. 30:18 14:12-15; Ezek. 28:14-16 [c]Is. 64:1 [d]Ps. 99:5; 132:7

2 [a]Ps. 21:9; Lam. [b]Lam. 2:5; Mic. 5: [c]Is. 25:12; 26:5 [d]P 89:39, 40; Is. 43:2

3 [1]Lit., *Every horn* 75:5, 10; Jer. 48:2 [b]Ps. 74:11; Jer. 21 [c]Is. 42:25; Jer. 21:

4 [a]Job 6:4; 16:13; 3:12, 13 [b]Ezek. 24 [c]Is. 42:25; Jer. 7:2

5 [a]Jer. 30:14 [b]La 2:2 [c]Jer. 52:13; La 2:2 [d]Jer. 9:17-20

6 [1]Lit., *booth* [2]Or [a]Jer. 52:13 [b]Jer. 1 Lam. 1:4; Zeph. 3: [c]Lam. 4:16

7 [a]Ps. 78:59-61; 64:11; Ezek. 7:20 [b]Jer. 33:4, 5; 52:1 74:3-8

As in the day of an appointed feast.
8 The LORD [1]determined to destroy
The wall of the daughter of Zion.
He has [a]stretched out a line,
He has not restrained His hand from [2]destroying;
And He has [b]caused rampart and wall to lament;
They have languished together.
9 Her [a]gates have sunk into the ground,
He has destroyed and broken her bars.
Her king and her princes are among the nations;
The [b]law is no more;
Also, her prophets find
[c]No vision from the LORD.
10 The elders of the daughter of Zion
[a]Sit on the ground, they [b]are silent.
They have thrown [c]dust on their heads;
They have girded themselves with [d]sackcloth.
The [e]virgins of Jerusalem
Have bowed their heads to the ground.
11 My [a]eyes fail because of tears,
My [1b]spirit is greatly troubled;
My [2c]heart is poured out on the earth,
[d]Because of the [3]destruction of the daughter of my people,
When [e]little ones and infants faint
In the streets of the city.
12 They say to their mothers,
"[a]Where is grain and wine?"
As they faint like a wounded man
In the streets of the city,
As their [b]life is poured out
On their mothers' bosom.
13 How shall I admonish you?
To what [a]shall I compare you,
O daughter of Jerusalem?
To what shall I liken you as I comfort you,
O [b]virgin daughter of Zion?
For your [1]ruin is as vast as the sea;
Who can [c]heal you?
14 Your [a]prophets have seen for you
False and foolish *visions;*
And they have not [b]exposed your iniquity
So as to restore you from captivity,
But they have [c]seen for you false and misleading [1]oracles.
15 All who pass along the way
[a]Clap their hands *in derision* at you;
They [b]hiss and shake their heads
At the daughter of Jerusalem,
"Is this the city of which they said,
'[c]The perfection of beauty,
[d]A joy to all the earth'?"
16 All [a]your enemies
Have opened their mouths wide against you;
They hiss and [b]gnash *their* teeth.
They say, "We have [c]swallowed *her* up!

[1]Lit., *thought* [2]Lit., *swallowing up* [a]2 Kin. 21:13; Is. 34:11; Amos 7:7-9 [b]Is. 3:26; Jer. 14:2

Neh. 1:3 [b]Hos. 3:4 … 4:14; 23:16; Ezek. 7:26

[a]Job 2:13; Is. 3:26; … 1 [b]Amos 8:3 [c]Job 2; Ezek. 27:30 [d]Is. …; Jon. 3:6-8 [e]Lam. 1:4

[1]Lit., *inward parts are in ferment* [2]Lit., *liver* [3]Lit., *breaking* …am. 1:16; 3:48, 51 …r. 4:19 [c]Job 16:13 …Is. 22:4; Lam. 4:10 …er. 44:7; Lam. 2:19

12 [a]Jer. 5:17 [b]Job …:16; Ps. 42:4; 62:8

13 [1]Lit., *breaking* …m. 1:12 [b]Is. 37:22 Jer. 8:22; 30:12-15

…Lit., *burdens* [a]Jer. …25-29; 29:8, 9 [b]Is. …; Ezek. 23:36; Mic. … [c]Jer. 23:36; Ezek. 22:25, 28

[a]Job 27:23; Ezek. 25:6 [b]Ps. 22:7; Is. …2; Jer. 18:16; 19:8; …ph. 2:15 [c]Ps. 50:2 [d]Ps. 48:2

16 [a]Job 16:10; Ps. …3; Lam. 3:46 [b]Job …; Ps. 35:16; 37:12 …s. 56:2; 124:3; Jer. 51:34

Surely this is the [d]day for which we waited;
We have reached *it*, we have seen *it*."
17 The LORD has [a]done what He purposed;
He has accomplished His word
Which He commanded from days of old.
He has thrown down [b]without sparing,
And He has caused the enemy to [c]rejoice over you;
He has [d]exalted the [1]might of your adversaries.
18 Their [a]heart cried out to the Lord,
"O [b]wall of the daughter of Zion,
Let *your* [c]tears run down like a river day and night;
Give yourself no relief;
Let [1]your eyes have no rest.
19 "Arise, cry aloud in the [a]night
At the beginning of the night watches;
[b]Pour out your heart like water
Before the presence of the Lord;
Lift up your hands to Him
For the [c]life of your little ones
Who are [d]faint because of hunger
At the head of every street."
20 See, O LORD, and look!
With [a]whom hast Thou dealt thus?
Should women [b]eat their [1]offspring,
The little ones who were [2]born healthy?
Should [c]priest and prophet be slain
In the sanctuary of the Lord?
21 On the ground in the streets
Lie [a]young and old,
My [b]virgins and my young men
Have fallen by the sword.
Thou hast slain *them* in the day of Thine anger,
Thou hast slaughtered, [c]not sparing.
22 Thou didst call as in the day of an appointed feast
My [a]terrors on every side;
And there was [b]no one who escaped or survived
In the day of the LORD's anger.
Those [c]whom I [1]bore and reared,
My enemy annihilated them.

Chapter 3

3 I am the man who has [a]seen affliction
Because of the rod of His wrath.
2 He has driven me and made me walk
In [a]darkness and not in light.
3 Surely against me He has [a]turned His hand
Repeatedly all the day.
4 He has caused my [a]flesh and my skin to waste away,
He has [b]broken my bones.
5 He has [a]besieged and encompassed me with [b]bitterness and hardship.
6 In [a]dark places He has made me dwell,
Like those who have long been dead.
7 He has [a]walled *me* in so that I cannot go out;

16 [d]Obad. 12

17 [1]Lit., *horn* 4:28 [b]Lam. 2: Ezek. 5:11; 7:8 [c]Ps. 35:24, 26 14:29 [d]Deut. 2 Lam. 1:5

18 [1]Lit., *the d your eye* [a]Ps. Hos. 7:14 [b]La Hab. 2:11 [c]Ps. Jer. 9:1; Lam. 3:48, 49

19 [a]Ps. 42:3; [b]1 Sam. 1:15; 62:8 [c]Lam. 2:1 51:20

20 [1]Lit., *fruit* [2] *tenderly cared* 32:11; Deut. 9:2 19:9; Lam. 4:10 78:64; Jer. 14:1 23:11, 12

21 [a]2 Chr. 36:1 6:11 [b]Ps. 78:62 [c]Jer. 13:14; Zec

22 [1]Lit., *bore h tenderly cared f* 31:13; Is. 24:17; 6:25 [b]Jer. 11:11 16:2-4; 44:7

3:1 [a]Ps. 88:7, 1

2 [a]Job 30:26; Is Jer. 4:23

3 [a]Ps. 38:2; Is. 5

4 [a]Ps. 31:9, 10; 102:3-5 [b]Ps. 51: 38:13

5 [a]Job 19:8 [b]Je 23:15; Lam. 3:19

6 [a]Ps. 88:5, 6; 14

7 [a]Job 3:23; 19:8

He has made my [1b]chain heavy.
8 Even when I cry out and call for help,
He [a]shuts out my prayer.
9 He has [a]blocked my ways with hewn stone;
He has made my paths crooked.
10 He is to me like a bear lying in wait,
Like a lion in secret places.
11 He has turned aside my ways and [a]torn me to pieces;
He has made me desolate.
12 He [a]bent His bow
And [b]set me as a target for the arrow.
13 He made the [1]arrows of His [a]quiver
To enter into my [2]inward parts.
14 I have become a [a]laughingstock to all my people,
Their *mocking* [b]song all the day.
15 He has [a]filled me with bitterness,
He has made me drunk with wormwood.
16 And He has [a]broken my teeth with [b]gravel;
He has made me cower in the [c]dust.
17 And my soul has been rejected [a]from peace;
I have forgotten [1]happiness.
18 So I say, "My strength has perished,
And *so has* my [a]hope from the LORD."

19 Remember my affliction and my [1]wandering, the [a]wormwood and bitterness.
20 Surely [a]my soul remembers
And is [b]bowed down within me.
21 This I recall to my mind,
Therefore I have [a]hope.
22 The LORD's [a]lovingkindnesses [1]indeed never cease,
[b]For His compassions never fail.
23 *They* are new [a]every morning;
Great is [b]Thy faithfulness.
24 "The LORD is my [a]portion," says my soul,
"Therefore I [b]have hope in Him."
25 The LORD is good to those who [a]wait for Him,
To the [1]person who [b]seeks Him.
26 *It is* good that he [a]waits silently
For the salvation of the LORD.
27 *It is* good for a man that he should bear
The yoke in his youth.
28 Let him [a]sit alone and be silent
Since He has laid *it* on him.
29 Let him [1]put his mouth in the [a]dust,
Perhaps there is [b]hope.
30 Let him give his [a]cheek to [1]the smiter;
Let him be filled with reproach.
31 For the Lord will [a]not reject forever,
32 For if He causes grief,
Then He will have [a]compassion
According to His abundant lovingkindness.
33 For He [a]does not afflict [1]willingly,
Or grieve the sons of men.

it., *bronze piece* [b]Jer. 40:4
30:20; Ps. 22:2
63:17; Hos. 2:6
o 16:12, 13; Jer. 15:3; Hos. 6:1
. 7:12; Lam. 2:4
4; 7:20; Ps. 38:2
[1]Lit., *sons* [2]Lit., *dneys* [a]Jer. 5:16
. 22:6, 7; 123:4; 20:7 [b]Job 30:9; Lam. 3:63
15 [a]Jer. 9:15
3:7; 58:6 [b]Prov. 20:17 [c]Jer. 6:26
7 [1]Lit., *good* [a]Is. 59:11; Jer. 12:12
Job 17:15; Ezek. 37:11
, *bitterness* [a]Jer. :15; Lam. 3:5, 15
b 21:6 [b]Ps. 42:5, 6, 11; 43:5; 44:25
21 [a]Ps. 130:7
Or, *that we are not umed* [a]Ps. 78:38; 3:12; 30:11 [b]Mal. 3:6
ls. 33:2; Zeph. 3:5 [b]Heb. 10:23
4 [a]Ps. 16:5; 73:26 [b]Ps. 33:18
25 [1]Lit., *soul* [a]Ps. ; Is. 25:9 [b]Is. 26:9
26 [a]Ps. 37:7
28 [a]Jer. 15:17
29 [1]Lit., *give* [a]Job ; 40:4 [b]Jer. 31:17
it., *his* [a]Job 16:10; Is. 50:6
Ps. 77:7; 94:14; Is. 54:7-10
32 [a]Ps. 78:38; 06:43-45; Hos. 11:8
[1]Lit., *from His heart* [a]Ps. 119:67, 71, 75; . 33:11; Heb. 12:10

34 To crush under His feet
All the prisoners of the [1]land,
35 To [1]deprive a man of [a]justice
In the presence of the Most High,
36 To [1a]defraud a man in his lawsuit—
Of these things the Lord does not [2]approve.
37 Who is [1]there who speaks and it [a]comes to pass,
Unless the Lord has commanded *it*?
38 *Is it* not from the mouth of the Most High
That [1a]both good and ill go forth?

39 Why should *any* living [1]mortal, or *any* man,
Offer [a]complaint [2]in view of his sins?
40 Let us [a]examine and probe our ways,
And let us return to the LORD.
41 We [a]lift up our heart [1]and hands
Toward God in heaven;
42 We have [a]transgressed and rebelled,
Thou hast [b]not pardoned.
43 Thou hast covered *Thyself* with [a]anger
And [b]pursued us;
Thou hast slain *and* [c]hast not spared.
44 Thou hast [a]covered Thyself with a cloud
So that [b]no prayer can pass through.
45 *Mere* [a]offscouring and refuse Thou hast made us
In the midst of the peoples.
46 All our enemies have [a]opened their mouths against us.
47 [a]Panic and pitfall have befallen us,
Devastation and destruction;
48 My [1a]eyes run down with streams of water
Because of the destruction of the daughter of my people.
49 My eyes pour down [a]unceasingly,
Without stopping,
50 Until the LORD [a]looks down
And sees from heaven.
51 My eyes bring pain to my soul
Because of all the daughters of my city.
52 My enemies [a]without cause
Hunted me down [b]like a bird;
53 They have silenced [1]me [a]in the pit
And have [2b]placed a stone on me.
54 Waters flowed [a]over my head;
I said, "I am cut off!"
55 I [a]called on Thy name, O LORD,
Out of the lowest pit.
56 Thou hast [a]heard my voice,
"[b]Do not hide Thine ear from my *prayer for* relief,
From my cry for help."
57 Thou didst [a]draw near when I called on Thee;
Thou didst say, "[b]Do not fear!"
58 O Lord, Thou didst [a]plead my soul's cause;
Thou hast [b]redeemed my life.
59 O LORD, Thou hast [a]seen my oppression;
[b]Judge my case.

34 [1]Or, *earth*

35 [1]Or, *turn aside man's case* [a]Ps. 140:12; Prov. 17:1

36 [1]Lit., *make cro* [2]Lit., *see* [a]Jer. 22: Hab. 1:13

37 [1]Lit., *this* [a]Ps. 33:9-11

38 [1]Lit., *the evil thi and the good* [a]Job Is. 45:7; Jer. 32:42

39 [1]Or, *human bei* [2]Or, *on the basis of* [a]Jer. 30:15; Mic. 7: Heb. 12:5, 6

40 [a]Ps. 119:59; 13 24; 2 Cor. 13:5

41 [1]Lit., *toward our* [a]Ps. 25:1; 28:2; 141

42 [a]Neh. 9:26; Jer. 14:20; Dan. 9:5 [b]2 24:4; Jer. 5:7, 9

43 [a]Lam. 2:21 [b]Ps 83:15; Lam. 3:66 [c] 2:2, 17, 21

44 [a]Ps. 97:2 [b]Lam Zech. 7:13

45 [a]1 Cor. 4:13

46 [a]Job 30:9, 10; P 22:6-8; Lam. 2:16

47 [a]Is. 24:17, 18; J 48:43, 44

48 [1]Lit., *eye brings* [a]Ps. 119:136; Jer. 9 18; Lam. 1:16; 2:11

49 [a]Ps. 77:2; Jer. 1

50 [a]Ps. 80:14; Is. 63:15; Lam. 5:1

52 [a]Ps. 35:7, 19 [b]1 Sam. 26:20; Ps. 124:7

53 [1]Lit., *my life* [2]O *cast stones* [a]Jer. 3 38:6, 9 [b]Dan. 6:17

54 [a]Ps. 69:2; Jon.

55 [a]Ps. 130:1; Jon

56 [a]Job 34:28 [b]Ps

57 [a]Ps. 145:18 [b]Is 41:10, 14

58 [a]Jer. 50:34 [b]Ps 34:22

59 [a]Jer. 18:19, 20 26:1; 43:1

60 Thou hast seen all their vengeance,
All their [a]schemes against me.
61 Thou hast heard their [a]reproach, O LORD,
All their schemes against me.
62 The [a]lips of my assailants and their whispering
Are against me all day long.
63 Look on their [a]sitting and their rising;
[b]I am their mocking song.
64 Thou wilt [a]recompense them, O LORD,
According to the work of their hands.
65 Thou wilt give them [1a]hardness of heart,
Thy curse will be on them.
66 Thou wilt [a]pursue them in anger and destroy them
From under the [b]heavens of the LORD!

Chapter 4

4 How [a]dark the gold has become,
How the pure gold has changed!
The sacred stones are poured out
At the [1]corner of every street.
2 The precious sons of Zion,
Weighed against fine gold,
How they are regarded as [a]earthen jars,
The work of a potter's hands!
3 Even [a]jackals offer the breast,
They nurse their young;
But the daughter of my people has become [b]cruel
Like [c]ostriches in the wilderness.
4 The [a]tongue of the infant cleaves
To the roof of its mouth because of [b]thirst;
The little ones [c]ask for bread,
But no one breaks *it* for them.
5 Those who ate [a]delicacies
Are desolate in the streets;
Those [1]reared in purple
Embrace ash pits.
6 For the [1]iniquity of the daughter of my people
Is greater than the [2a]sin of Sodom,
Which was [b]overthrown as in a moment,
And no hands were [3]turned toward her.
7 Her [1]consecrated ones were [a]purer than snow,
They were whiter than milk;
They were more ruddy *in* [2]body than corals,
Their polishing *was* like [3b]lapis lazuli.
8 Their appearance is [a]blacker than soot,
They are not recognized in the streets;
Their [b]skin is shriveled on their bones,
It is withered, it has become like wood.
9 Better are those [1a]slain with the sword
Than those [1]slain with hunger;
For they [2b]pine away, being stricken
For lack of the fruits of [3]the field.
10 The hands of compassionate women
[a]Boiled their own children;

60 [a]Jer. 11:19
[a]Ps. 74:18; 89:50; Lam. 5:1; Zeph. 2:8
Ps. 59:7, 12; 140:3; Ezek. 36:3
3 [a]Ps. 139:2 [b]Job 30:9; Lam. 3:14
Ps. 28:4; Jer. 51:6, 24, 56
[1]Or, *insolence* [a]Ex. Deut. 2:30; Is. 6:10
Lam. 3:43 [b]Ps. 8:3
[1]Lit., *head* [a]Ezek. 7:19-22
2 [a]Is. 30:14; Jer. 19:1, 11
. 13:22; 34:13 [b]Is. 5; Ezek. 5:10 [c]Job 39:14-17
s. 22:15 [b]Jer. 14:3 [c]Lam. 2:12
[1]Lit., *established in* on [a]Jer. 6:2; Amos 6:3-7
Or, *punishment for* y [2]Or, *punishment* in [3]Or, *wrung over* Gen. 19:24 [b]Gen. 19:25; Jer. 20:16
Or, *Nazirites* [2]Lit., ones [3]Heb., *sappir* . 51:7 [b]Ex. 24:10; Job 28:16
[a]Job 30:30; Lam. 0 [b]Job 19:20; Ps. 102:3-5
[1]Lit., *pierced* [2]Lit., ow away [3]Lit., *my* s [a]Jer. 16:4 [b]Lev. 26:39; Ezek. 24:23
[a]Lev. 26:29; Deut. 7; 2 Kin. 6:29; Jer. ; Lam. 2:20; Ezek. 5:10

They became [b]food for them
Because of the destruction of the daughter of my people.
11 The LORD has [a]accomplished His wrath,
He has poured out His fierce anger;
And He has [b]kindled a fire in Zion
Which has consumed its foundations.
12 The kings of the earth did not believe,
Nor *did* any of [a]the inhabitants of the world,
That the adversary and the enemy
Could [b]enter the gates of Jerusalem.
13 Because of the sins of her [a]prophets
And the iniquities of her priests,
Who have shed in her midst
The [b]blood of the righteous,
14 They wandered, [a]blind, in the streets;
They were defiled with [b]blood
So that no one could touch their [c]garments.
15 "Depart! [a]Unclean!" [1]they cried of themselves.
"Depart, depart, do not touch!"
So they [b]fled and wandered;
Men among the nations said,
"They shall not continue to dwell *with us*."
16 The presence of the LORD has scattered them;
He will not continue to regard them.
They did not [1a]honor the priests,
They did not favor the elders.
17 Yet our eyes failed;
Looking for [1]help was [a]useless.
In our watching we have watched
For a [b]nation that could not save.
18 They [a]hunted our steps
So that we could not walk in our streets;
Our [b]end drew near,
Our days were [1]finished
For our end had come.
19 Our pursuers were [a]swifter
Than the eagles of the sky.
They chased us on the mountains;
They waited in ambush for us in the wilderness.
20 The [a]breath of our nostrils, the [b]LORD's anointed,
Was [c]captured in their pits,
Of whom we had said, "Under his [d]shadow
We shall live among the nations."
21 Rejoice and be glad, O daughter of [a]Edom,
Who dwells in the land of Uz;
But the [b]cup will come around to you as well,
You will become drunk and make yourself naked.
22 *The punishment* of your iniquity has been [a]completed,
O daughter of Zion;
He will exile you no longer.
But He [b]will punish your iniquity, O daughter of Edom;
He will expose your sins!

10 [b]Deut. 28:

11 [a]Jer. 7:20; 2:17; Ezek. 22 [b]Deut. 32:22;

12 [a]Deut. 29: 21:13

13 [a]Jer. 5:31; Lam. 2:14; Eze 22:26-28 [b]Jer. 26:8, 9; Matt. 2

14 [a]Deut. 28:2 29:10; 56:10; 5 [b]Is. 1:15 [c]Jer.

15 [1]Or, *they (m cried to them* [a] 13:45, 46 [b]Jer.

16 [1]Lit., *lift up t of* [a]Is. 9:14-16; 52:24-27

17 [1]Lit., *our hel* 37:7; Lam. 1:7 29:6, 7, 16

18 [1]Lit., *full* [a]Je [b]Jer. 5:31; Ezek. Amos 8:2

19 [a]Is. 5:26-28; 17; Jer. 4:13; Ha

20 [a]Gen. 2:7 [b]2 1:14; 19:21 [c]Jer. 52:9 [d]Dan. 4:12

21 [a]Ps. 137:7; Je 25:21 [b]Obad. 16

22 [a]Is. 40:2; Jer. 8 [b]Jer. 49:10; Ma

Chapter 5

5 Remember, O LORD, what has befallen us;
Look, and see our [a]reproach!
2 Our inheritance has been turned over to [a]strangers,
Our [b]houses to aliens.
3 We have become orphans [a]without a father,
Our mothers are like widows.
4 [1]We have to pay for our drinking [a]water,
Our wood comes *to us* at a price.
5 [1]Our pursuers are at our necks;
We are worn out, there is [a]no rest for us.
6 We have [1]submitted to [a]Egypt *and* Assyria [2]to get enough bread.
7 Our [a]fathers sinned, *and* are no more;
It is we who have borne their iniquities.
8 [a]Slaves rule over us;
There is [b]no one to deliver us from their hand.
9 We get our bread [1]at the [a]risk of our lives
[2]Because of the sword in the wilderness.
10 Our skin has become as [a]hot as an oven,
Because of [1]the burning heat of famine.
11 They ravished the [a]women in Zion,
The virgins in the cities of Judah.
12 Princes were hung by their hands;
[1a]Elders were not respected.
13 Young men [1a]worked at the grinding mill;
And youths [b]stumbled under *loads* of wood.
14 Elders [1]are gone from the gate,
Young men from their [a]music.
15 The joy of our hearts has [a]ceased;
Our dancing has been turned into mourning.
16 The [a]crown has fallen from our head;
[b]Woe to us, for we have sinned!
17 Because of this our [a]heart is faint;
Because of these things our [b]eyes are dim;
18 Because of [a]Mount Zion which lies desolate,
[b]Foxes prowl in it.

19 [a]Thou, O LORD, dost [1]rule forever;
Thy [b]throne is from generation to generation.
20 Why dost Thou [a]forget us forever;
Why dost Thou forsake us [1]so long?
21 [a]Restore us to Thee, O LORD, that we may be restored;
Renew [b]our days as of old,
22 Unless [a]Thou hast utterly rejected us,
And art exceedingly [b]angry with us.

5:1 [a]Ps. 44:13-16
[a]Is. 1:7; Hos. 8:7, 8 [b]Zeph. 1:13
Ex. 22:24; Jer. 15:8; 18:21
4 [1]Lit., *We drink our* ter for silver [a]Is. 3:1
[1]Lit., *We have been* pursued upon [a]Neh. 9:36, 37
[1]Lit., *given the hand* [2]Lit., *to be satisfied with* [a]Hos. 9:3; 12:1
7 [a]Jer. 14:20; 16:12
Neh. 5:15 [b]Ps. 7:2; Zech. 11:6
9 [1]Lit., *with our soul* In the face of [a]Jer. 40:9-12
[1]Or, *the ravages of hunger* [a]Job 30:30; Lam. 4:8
s. 13:16; Zech. 14:2
2 [1]Lit., *The faces of* lers [a]Is. 47:6; Lam. 4:16
[1]Lit., *carry* [a]Judg. 16:21 [b]Jer. 7:18
[1]Lit., *have ceased* [a]Is. 24:8; Jer. 7:34
[a]Jer. 25:10; Amos 8:10
16 [a]Job 19:9; Ps. :39; Jer. 13:18 [b]Is. 3:9-11
[a]Is. 1:5 [b]Job 17:7; Lam. 2:11
Mic. 3:12 [b]Neh. 4:3
19 [1]Lit., *sit* [a]Ps. 2, 25-27 [b]Ps. 45:6
0 [1]Lit., *to length of* ys [a]Ps. 13:1; 44:24
21 [a]Ps. 80:3; Jer. 1:18 [b]Is. 60:20-22
2 [a]Ps. 60:1, 2; Jer. 7:29 [b]Is. 64:9

Theme of Lamentations:

Author:

Date:

Purpose:

Key Words:
- how
- Zion (Jerusalem, the city)
- anger (wrath)
- transgressions (sin, iniquity, wickedness)
- destroy (destroyed, destruction)
- affliction (afflict)
- desolate

SEGMENT DIVISIONS

		CHAPTER THEMES
		1
		2
		3
		4
		5

ZEKIEL

623 B.C. Buzi was presented with a son: Ezekiel had been born to the priesthood. One year later
ı had a revival under King Josiah.

hen the book of the law was found in the house of the Lord and brought to the king, Josiah wept. ıw the awfulness of Judah's sin and knew that God's wrath burned against them. Although Josiah letermined that Judah would walk after the Lord and keep His commandments, the prophetess ah told him that after his death God would have to bring judgment upon Judah, for they had ken God and burned incense to other gods (*see* 2 Kings 22).

dah's judgment began about four years after King Josiah tried to stop Pharaoh Necho, king of ›t, who was on his way to Carchemish on the Euphrates to block the rising power of Babylon (*see* ronicles 35:20-27). Necho killed Josiah in 609 B.C. on the plain of Megiddo. In 605 B.C. Necho was ıted at Carchemish by Nebuchadnezzar (*see* Jeremiah 46:2).

zekiel was eighteen years old when a handful of the nobles and princes were captured and taken Judah to Babylon. Among them was a boy about fifteen, Daniel, and his three friends, Hananiah, ıael, and Azariah. Ezekiel remained in Judah—at thirty he would be eligible for the priesthood and ld serve God in the temple at Jerusalem. Or so it seemed.

om that time on things were relatively quiet in Judah. The prophets were bringing good news: prophesied peace. The people loved it. They continued in their sin, disturbed only by one lonely ›—Jeremiah's.

hen Jehoiakim, king of Judah, rebelled against Nebuchadnezzar, king of Babylon (2 Kings 23:36- . In 597 B.C. Nebuchadnezzar once again besieged Jerusalem. This time ten thousand were taken ive into Babylon. Ezekiel, who would soon be eligible for the priesthood, was among them. Never n would he see Jerusalem or the temple where he was to serve. Both would be destroyed by uchadnezzar in 586 B.C.

ut Ezekiel would see another temple and another Jerusalem—one which would be called Jehovah nmah, the Lord is there!

.t age thirty, Ezekiel had a vision. . . .

NGS TO DO

ı order to understand the depth and magnitude of Ezekiel, you need to study it again and again. vever, if you will do the following, you will gain a good understanding of the message of Ezekiel.

ıeral Instructions

. Ezekiel has many references to time. These are important and need to be marked in a distinctive way with a color and/or a clock symbol such as this 🕒. Ezekiel 1:1-2 establishes the historical setting of Ezekiel's ministry. The other references to time give you the historical timing of his visions and prophecies.

a. Every time you mark references to time look at the calendar on page 1202 at the beginning of Ezekiel 1 to see what month Ezekiel is referring to.

b. Ezekiel 1:2 is a parenthesis and serves as an explanation of the timing of verse 2. Read 2 Kings 24:8 through 25:21 for a good overview of the historical setting. This will help you understand the timing of Ezekiel's prophecies.

1) As you read, look for Jehoiachin's name, mark it in a distinctive way, and watch when he goes into exile. Also note who is made king when Jehoiachin goes into exile.

2) In the margin record the following information: Jehoiachin was taken captive when Nebuchadnezzar besieged Jerusalem the second time. The first siege is recorded in

2 Kings 24:1-7 and occurred in 605 B.C. The second siege is recorded in 2 Kings 24:10-1 occurred in 597 B.C. Ezekiel was taken captive during the second siege. The third anc siege is recorded in 2 Kings 25:1-21. It began in 588 B.C. and in 586 B.C. the city was cap and destroyed.

3) Read Ezekiel 1:1-3 and record what you learn about Ezekiel under "Author" o EZEKIEL AT A GLANCE chart on pages 1276 and 1277.

4) Now read Numbers 4:3 and observe at what age a man began his priestly service. look at verse 1 and compare this with the way Ezekiel is described and the year he ha first visions from God. Verse 2 tells you what year it was in relationship to the second of Jerusalem, the year when Jehoiachin went into exile.

2. Now that you have the historical setting, as you read the dates of all the other visio prophecies in Ezekiel, you can know that the dates are calculated from the time of Jehoiac and Ezekiel's exile in 597 B.C.

3. Key repeated words and phrases to mark throughout the book are listed on EZEKIEL GLANCE. Write them on a card, color code each in a distinctive way, and then use the carc bookmark while you study Ezekiel.

Chapters 1-3: Ezekiel's Call

1. Read chapters 1 through 3 and mark the key repeated words.
2. As you go through these chapters one at a time, interrogate the text with the five W's and Ask questions such as: What does Ezekiel see? How are they described? Where are they? W is Ezekiel? What is he told to do? Why is he told to do it? When is Ezekiel to speak?
3. In the margin of each chapter record your observations. Note what Ezekiel is called to do how he is to do it. Also note to whom he is sent and why.
4. In summary form list everything you observe from the text about Ezekiel, the people to who was sent, and the glory of the Lord.
5. Record the theme of each chapter on EZEKIEL AT A GLANCE and in the text next to the cha number.

Chapters 4-24: Prophecies about Judah and Jerusalem

1. Read through this segment one chapter at a time. On the first reading of a chapter, mark e reference to the time of a vision. Also mark the key words that are on your bookmark.
   a. Watch for and mark the phrase *know that I am the Lord*. This is a key phrase used throug the remainder of Ezekiel, so add this to your bookmark. Every time you see this phrase, i margin note who is going to know and how they will know it.
   b. When you mark *Spirit, heart,* and *the glory of God,* list in the margin what you learn about from that chapter.
   c. Add *covenant* to your list of key words. When it's used in a chapter, list what you learn abo in the margin. Also watch for additional key repeated words.
2. Now read through the chapter again. Watch for every reference to the "son of man." In margin note God's instructions to Ezekiel, the son of man. Note to whom or to what he wa speak and how. Note whether it was by symbolic acts, messages, visions, parables, or signs. note why he was to speak in that way and the significance of his action. Also notice w Ezekiel's mouth is shut and then later opened. This is important.
3. Record the theme of each chapter as you have done previously.

Chapters 25-32: Prophecies about the Nations

1. Read through this segment one chapter at a time. On the first reading mark the key words. W you mark the phrase *know that I am the Lord,* note in the margin who is going to know and h they will know it.
2. On the second reading of the chapter, identify and record in the margin the nation to whom

prophecy is given and the ruler—if he is mentioned. Also observe and note what will happen to the nation and why.

3. Make sure you note or mark *when* the Word of the Lord came to Ezekiel.

4. Record the theme of each chapter as you have done previously.

apters 33-39: Prophecies about Israel's Restoration

1. Read each chapter and once again:

   a. Mark every reference to time. Don't miss when the visions or prophecies were given to Ezekiel.

   b. Mark every key word. In the margin list what you learn from marking *covenant* and then compare it with what you observed about covenant in Ezekiel 16 and 17.

   c. Continue noting the same observations from marking every occurrence of *know that I am the Lord.* Also list what you learn about the *Spirit, heart,* and *the glory of God.*

2. Read the chapter again. List God's instructions to Ezekiel ("the son of man"). Note to whom or to what he was to speak and what the message was to be. As you look at the prophecy, list what is going to happen, to whom or what it will happen, and when it will happen. Put a clock next to any indication of timing. Also note any symbolic acts he was to perform and why.

3. List the theme of each chapter as before.

apters 40-48: Prophecies about the Temple

1. As you begin observing this final segment, read 40:1-5. In a distinctive way, mark when this final vision is given. Then in the margin list who gives it, how, where, and what Ezekiel is to do.

2. Read each chapter carefully and do the following:

   a. Mark key words as before; however, add to your list *temple (sanctuary, house), holy, offering,* and *gate(s).* The phrase "know that I am the Lord" is not used in this final segment.

   b. Watch for and record the reason for the vision of the temple and its measurements. Also note what you learn about *the glory of the Lord* and the *Spirit,* and their relationship to the temple or sanctuary. Compare this with what you saw in Ezekiel 8 through 11.

   c. Warning—this last segment of Ezekiel may seem a little boring after the first thirty-nine chapters. Don't get bogged down in all the temple measurements. Don't miss the last verse of Ezekiel—it names the city.

   d. In the margin list the main points, instructions, or events of each chapter.

3. Record the theme of these chapters as you have done before. Then complete EZEKIEL AT A GLANCE. Go back to each vision Ezekiel had, note the year when it occurred, and from your calendar on page 1202 record the name of the month and the day. Then transfer this information to the segment division portion of EZEKIEL AT A GLANCE.

INGS TO THINK ABOUT

1. As you think about God's call upon Ezekiel's life, what do you see about Ezekiel's responsibility as a watchman that you could apply to your own life? If the people wouldn't listen, was Ezekiel still to speak (Ezekiel 2, 3, 33)? Remember that the things in the Old Testament were written for our example, encouragement, and perseverance (1 Corinthians 10:6,11 and Romans 15:4).

2. Before Ezekiel ever shared God's message he was told to eat it, to take it to heart, and to listen closely to the Lord (Ezekiel 3). What lessons can you learn from his example? How would what you are doing in this inductive study Bible help you? What do you need to remember as you work your way through this Bible?

3. What have you learned about God and His ways from studying Ezekiel? God took Israel as His wife. Christians are espoused to Jesus Christ, their heavenly bridegroom (2 Corinthians 11:2-3). Have you, like Israel, played the harlot spiritually and hurt God's heart (Ezekiel 6:9, James 4:4)? If so, what do you need to do? If not, what should you do so that you never do?

4. In Ezekiel 20:33 God tells Israel, "As I live, surely with a mighty hand and with an outstre arm and with wrath poured out, I shall be king over you." Think about this verse in the li the character and position of God and in the light of Philippians 2:5-11. Have you gen confessed Jesus Christ as your Lord, your King who has a right to rule over you?
5. Think about what you have observed from marking the word *covenant*. What have you le about the heart of stone and the Spirit dwelling within (Ezekiel 36)? Read 2 Corinthians 3 ar how this parallels what Ezekiel says. Do you have a heart of stone or a heart of flesh? Wh the Spirit of God in relationship to you? Is He within? Read Ezekiel 36:26-27.
6. What have you learned about prophecy from Ezekiel that you could use in sharing God's with the Jews? What about the prophecies of Ezekiel 36 and 37 and the way they alread being fulfilled? And what do you learn about Israel's future in respect to Ezekiel 38 throug This is of great interest to Jews.
7. What have you learned about the holiness of God? What effect will it have on your life?

The Jewish Calendar

Babylonian names (B) for the months are still used today for the Jewish calendar. Canaanite names (C) were used prior to the Babylonian captivity. Four are mentioned in the Old Testament.
Adar-Sheni is an intercalary month used every two to three years or seven times in nineteen years.

1st month	2nd month	3rd month	4th month
Nisan (B) Abib (C) March-April	Iyyar (B) Ziv (C) April-May	Sivan (B) May-June	Tammuz (B) June-July
7th month	*8th month*	*9th month*	*10th month*
5th month	**6th month**	**7th month**	**8th month**
Ab (B) July-August	Elul (B) August-September	Tishri (B) Ethanim (C) September-October	Marcheshvan (B) Bul (C) October-November
11th month	*12th month*	*1st month*	*2nd month*
9th month	**10th month**	**11th month**	**12th month**
Kislev (B) November-December	Tebeth (B) December-January	Shebat (B) January-February	Adar (B) February-March
3rd month	*4th month*	*5th month*	*6th month*

Sacred calendar appears in black • Civil calendar appears in grey

Chapter 1

593 B.C.

INSIGHT

According to Numbers 4:3, men entered the priestly service at the age of thirty.

1 Now it came about in the thirtieth year, on the fifth *day* of the
fourth month, while I was by the [a]river Chebar among the exiles,
the [b]heavens were opened and I saw [1c]visions of God.
2 (On the fifth of the month [1]in the [a]fifth year of King Jehoiachin's
exile,
3 the [a]word of the LORD came expressly to Ezekiel the priest, son of
Buzi, in the [b]land of the Chaldeans by the river Chebar; and there
[c]the hand of the LORD came upon him.)
4 And as I looked, behold, a [a]storm wind was coming from the
north, a great cloud with fire flashing forth continually and a bright
light around it, and in its midst something like [b]glowing metal in the
midst of the fire.
5 And within it there were figures resembling [a]four living beings.
And this was their appearance: they had human [b]form.
6 Each of them had [a]four faces and [b]four wings.
7 And their legs were straight and [1]their feet were like a calf's
hoof, and they gleamed like [a]burnished bronze.

1:1 [1]Some ancie mss. and version *a vision* [a]Ezek. 3 10:15, 20 [b]Matt. Mark 1:10; Luke Acts 7:56; 10:11; 4:1; 19:11 [c]Ex. 2 Num. 12:6; Is. 1:1 Ezek. 8:3; 11:24; Dan. 8:1, 2

2 [1]Lit., *it was* [a]2 24:12-15; Ezek. 8 20:1

3 [a]2 Pet. 1:21 [b]E 12:13 [c]1 Kin. 18:4 2 Kin. 3:15; Ezek. 3:14, 22

4 [a]Is. 21:1; Jer. 2 Ezek. 13:11, 13 [b] 1:27; 8:2

5 [a]Ezek. 10:15, 1 Rev. 4:6-8 [b]Ezek.

6 [a]Ezek. 1:10; 10 21 [b]Ezek. 1:23

7 [1]Lit., *the soles c feet* [a]Dan. 10:6; R 1:15

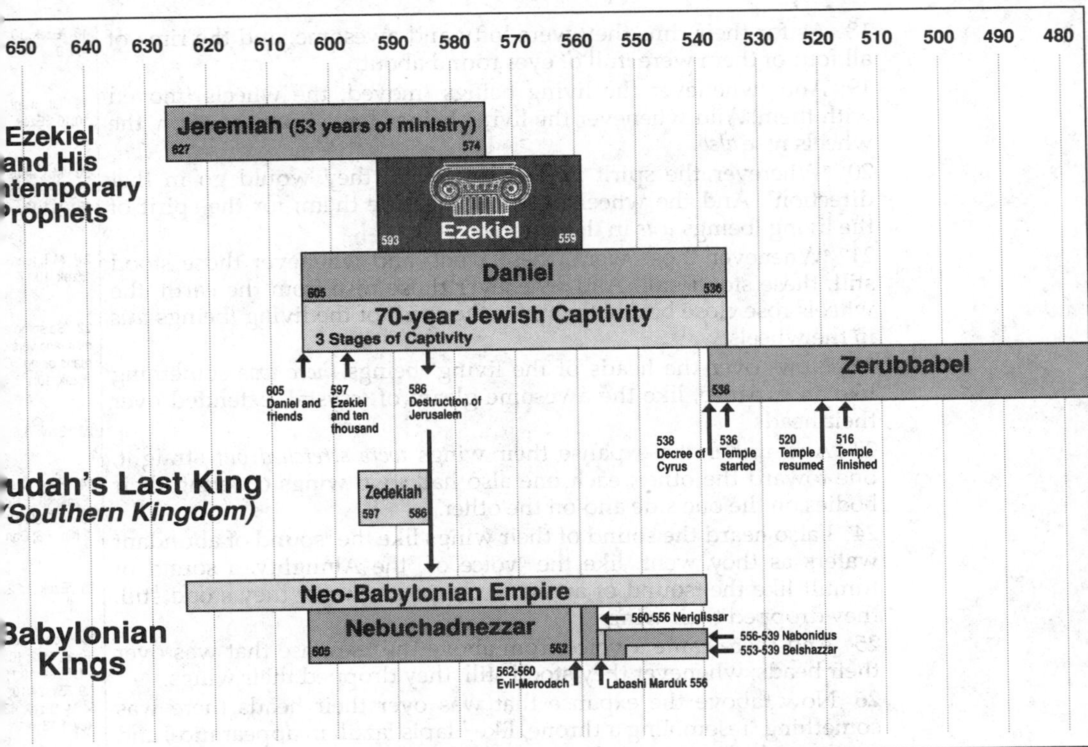

Ezek. 1:17; 10:11 [b]Ezek. 10:8, 21

8 Under their wings on their [a]four sides *were* human [b]hands. As for
the faces and wings of the four of them,

Ezek. 1:17 [b]Ezek. 1:12; 10:22

9 their wings touched one another; their *faces* did [a]not turn when
they moved, each [b]went straight forward.

[1]Lit., *the four of* [a]Rev. 4:7 [b]Ezek. 10:14

10 As for the [a]form of their faces, *each* had the [b]face of a man, [1]all
four had the face of a lion on the right and the face of a bull on the
left, and [1]all four had the face of an eagle.

Is. 6:2; Ezek. 1:23

11 Such were their faces. Their wings were spread out above; each
had two touching another *being*, and [a]two covering their bodies.

Ezek. 1:9 [b]Ezek. 1:20

12 And [a]each went straight forward; [b]wherever the spirit was about
to go, they would go, without turning as they went.

13 [1]So with some ancient versions; Heb., *the likeness of the beings.* [2]Lit., *like the appearance of* [3]Lit., *going out* [a]Ps. 104:4; Rev. 4:5

13 [1]In the midst of the living beings there was something that
looked like burning coals of [a]fire, [2]like torches darting back and forth
among the living beings. The fire was bright, and lightning was
[3]flashing from the fire.

Zech. 4:10 [b]Matt. 24:27; Luke 17:24

14 And the living beings [a]ran to and fro like bolts of [b]lightning.

15 [1]Lit., *for his four faces* [a]Ezek. 1:19-21; 10:9

15 Now as I looked at the living beings, behold, there was one
[a]wheel on the earth beside the living beings, [1]for *each of* the four of
them.

16 [1]Lit., *the look of* [2]Lit., *the wheel in the midst of the wheel* [a]Ezek. 10:9-11 [b]Ezek. 10:9; Dan. 10:6

16 The [a]appearance of the wheels and their workmanship *was* like
[1]sparkling [b]beryl, and all four of them had the same form, their
appearance and workmanship *being* as if [2]one wheel were within
another.

17 [1]Lit., *went* [2]Lit., *sides* [a]Ezek. 1:9, 12; 10:11

17 Whenever they [1]moved, they [1]moved in any of their four [2]direc-
tions, without [a]turning as they [1]moved.

18 As for their rims they were lofty and awesome, and the rims of all four of them were [a]full of eyes round about.

19 And [a]whenever the living beings [1]moved, the wheels [1]moved with them. And whenever the living beings [b]rose from the earth, the wheels rose *also*.

20 [a]Wherever the spirit was about to go, they would go in that direction[1]. And the wheels rose close beside them; for the spirit of the living [2]beings *was* in the wheels.

21 [a]Whenever those went, these went; and whenever those stood still, these stood still. And whenever those rose from the earth, the wheels rose close beside them; for the spirit of the living [1]beings *was* in the wheels.

22 Now [a]over the heads of the living [1]beings *there was* something like an expanse, like the awesome gleam of [2]crystal, extended over their heads.

23 And under the expanse their wings *were stretched out* straight, one toward the other; each one also had [a]two wings covering their bodies on the one side and on the other.

24 I also heard the sound of their wings like the [a]sound of abundant waters as they went, like the [b]voice of [1]the Almighty, a sound of tumult like the [c]sound of an army camp; whenever they stood still, they dropped their wings.

25 And there came a voice from above the [a]expanse that was over their heads; whenever they stood still, they dropped their wings.

26 Now [a]above the expanse that was over their heads there was something [b]resembling a throne, like [1c]lapis lazuli in appearance; and on that which resembled a throne, high up, *was* a figure with the appearance of a [d]man.

27 Then I [1]noticed from the appearance of His loins and upward something [a]like [2]glowing metal that looked like fire all around within it, and from the appearance of His loins and downward I saw something like fire; and *there was* a radiance around Him.

28 As the appearance of the [a]rainbow [1]in the clouds on a rainy day, so *was* the appearance of the surrounding radiance. Such *was* the appearance of the likeness of the [b]glory of the LORD. And when I saw *it*, I [c]fell on my face and heard a voice speaking.

Chapter 2

2 Then He said to me, "Son of man, [a]stand on your feet that I may speak with you!"

2 And as He spoke to me the [a]Spirit entered me and set me on my feet; and I heard *Him* speaking to me.

3 Then He said to me, "Son of man, I am sending you to the sons of Israel, to a rebellious people who have [a]rebelled against Me; [b]they and their fathers have transgressed against Me to this very day.

4 "And I am sending you to them who are [1a]stubborn and obstinate children; and you shall say to them, 'Thus says the Lord [2]GOD.'

5 "As for them, [a]whether they listen or [1]not—for they are a rebellious house—they will [b]know that a prophet has been among them.

6 "And you, son of man, [a]neither fear them nor fear their words, though [b]thistles and thorns are with you and you sit on scorpions; neither fear their words nor be dismayed at their presence, for they are a rebellious house.

18 [a]Ezek. 1 4:6, 8

19 [1]Lit., *we* 10:16 [b]Ezek

20 [1]M.T. ad *to go* [2]M.T. [a]Ezek. 1:12

21 [1]M.T. rea [a]Ezek. 10:17

22 [1]So som mss. and ve reads *being* [a]Ezek. 10:1

23 [a]Ezek. 1:

24 [1]Heb., *Sh* [a]Ezek. 43:2; 19:6 [b]Ezek. [c]2 Kin. 7:6; D

25 [a]Ezek. 1:2

26 [1]Heb., *eb* [a]Ezek. 1:22; 6:1; Ezek. 10 7:9 [c]Ex. 24:1 54:11 [d]Ezek. Rev. 1:13

27 [1]Lit., *saw* *electrum* [a]Ez

28 [1]Lit., *whic in* [a]Gen. 9:13 10:1 [b]Ex. 24: 8:4; 11:22, 23; [c]Gen. 17:3; Ez Dan. 8:17; Re

2:1 [a]Dan. 10: 9:6

2 [a]Ezek. 3:24

3 [a]1 Sam. 8:7, 3:25 [b]Ezek. 2

4 [1]Lit., *the so stiff-faced and hard-hearted* [2]*YHWH*, usually rendered *LORD* 95:8; Is. 48:4; J 6:15; Ezek. 3:7

5 [1]Lit., *forbear* 2:7; 3:11, 27; M 10:12-15; Acts [b]Ezek. 33:33; L 10:10, 11; John

6 [a]Is. 51:12; Je 17; Ezek. 3:9 [b] 23:6, 7; Ezek. 2 Mic. 7:4

7 "But you shall [a]speak My words to them [b]whether they listen or [1]not, for they are rebellious.

8 "Now you, son of man, listen to what I am speaking to you; do not be rebellious like that rebellious house. Open your mouth and [a]eat what I am giving you."

9 Then I looked, behold, a [a]hand was extended to me; and lo, a [1b]scroll *was* in it.

10 When He spread it out before me, it was written on the front and back; and written on it were lamentations, mourning and [a]woe.

Chapter 3

3 Then He said to me, "Son of man, eat what you find; [a]eat this scroll, and go, speak to the house of Israel."

2 So I [a]opened my mouth, and He fed me this scroll.

3 And He said to me, "Son of man, feed your stomach, and [a]fill your [1]body with this scroll which I am giving you." Then I [b]ate it, and it was sweet as [c]honey in my mouth.

4 Then He said to me, "Son of man, [1]go to the house of Israel and speak with My words to them.

5 "For [a]you are not being sent to a people of [1b]unintelligible speech or difficult language, *but* to the house of Israel,

6 nor to many peoples of [1]unintelligible speech or difficult language, whose words you cannot understand. [2]But I have sent you to them [3]who should listen to you;

7 yet the house of Israel will not be willing to listen to you, since they are [a]not willing to listen to Me. Surely the whole house of Israel is [1]stubborn and obstinate.

8 "Behold, I have made your face as hard as their faces, and your forehead as hard as their foreheads.

9 "Like [1]emery harder than flint I have made your forehead. Do not be afraid of them or be dismayed before them, though they are a rebellious house."

10 Moreover, He said to me, "Son of man, take into your heart all My [a]words which I shall speak to you, and listen [1]closely.

11 "And [1]go to the exiles, to the sons of your people, and speak to them and tell them, whether they listen or [2]not, 'Thus says the Lord [3]GOD.'"

12 Then the [a]Spirit lifted me up, and I heard a great [b]rumbling sound behind me, "Blessed be the glory of the LORD [1]in His place."

13 And I *heard* the sound of the wings of the living beings touching one another, and the sound of the [a]wheels beside them, even a great rumbling sound.

14 So the Spirit lifted me up and took me away; and I went embittered in the rage of my spirit, and [a]the hand of the LORD was strong on me.

15 Then I came to the exiles who lived beside the river Chebar at Telabib, and I sat there [a]seven days where they were living, causing consternation among them.

16 Now it came about [a]at the end of seven days that the word of the LORD came to me, saying,

17 "Son of man, I have appointed you a [a]watchman to the house of Israel; whenever you hear a word from My mouth, [b]warn them from Me.

18 "When I say to the wicked, 'You shall surely die'; and you do not

7 [1]Lit., *forbear* [a]Jer. ', 17; Ezek. 3:10, 17 [b]Ezek. 2:5

er. 15:16; Ezek. 3:3; Rev. 10:9

[1]Lit., *scroll of a book* :zek. 8:3 [b]Jer. 36:2; zek. 3:1; Rev. 5:1-5; 10:8-11

[a]Is. 3:11; Rev. 8:13

3:1 [a]Ezek. 2:9

2 [a]Jer. 25:17

3 [1]Lit., *inward parts* Jer. 6:11; 20:9 [b]Jer. 15:16 [c]Ps. 19:10; 9:103; Rev. 10:9, 10

4 [1]Lit., *go, come*

Lit., *deepness of lip and heaviness of gue* [a]Jon. 1:2; Acts 1; 26:17 [b]Is. 28:11; 33:19

Lit., *deepness of lip and heaviness of ue* [2]Or, *If I had sent to them, they would en to you.* [3]Lit., *they*

7 [1]Lit., *of a hard forehead and a stiff heart* [a]1 Sam. 8:7

9 [1]Lit., *corundum*

[1]Lit., *with your ears* ob 22:22; Ezek. 2:8; 3:1-3

Lit., *go, come* [2]Lit., *ear* [3]Heb., *YHWH*, ally rendered *LORD*

2 [1]Or, *from* [a]Ezek. 3:14; 8:3; Acts 8:39 [b]Acts 2:2

13 [a]Ezek. 1:15; 10:16, 17

14 [a]2 Kin. 3:15

15 [a]Job 2:13

16 [a]Jer. 42:7

17 [a]Is. 52:8; 56:10; :6; Jer. 6:17; Ezek. 9 [b]2 Chr. 19:10; Is. 58:1; Hab. 2:1

warn him or speak out to warn the wicked from his wicked way that
he may live, that wicked man shall die in his iniquity, but his [a]blood
I will require at your hand.
19 "Yet if you have [a]warned the wicked, and he does not turn from
his wickedness or from his wicked way, he shall die in his iniquity;
but you have [b]delivered yourself.
20 "Again, [a]when a righteous man turns away from his right-
eousness and commits iniquity, and I place an [b]obstacle before him,
he shall die; since you have not warned him, he shall die in his sin,
and his righteous deeds which he has done shall not be remembered;
but his blood I will require at your hand.
21 "However, if you have [a]warned [1]the righteous man that the right-
eous should not sin, and he does not sin, he shall surely live because
he took warning; and you have delivered yourself."
22 And the hand of the LORD was on me there, and He said to me,
"Get up, go out to the plain, and there I will [a]speak to you."
23 So I got up and went out to the plain; and behold, the [a]glory of
the LORD was standing there, like the glory which [b]I saw by the river
Chebar, and I fell on my face.
24 The [a]Spirit then entered me and made me stand on my feet, and
He spoke with me and said to me, "Go, shut yourself up in your
house.
25 "As for you, son of man, they will [a]put ropes on you and bind you
with them, so that you cannot go out among them.
26 "Moreover, [a]I will make your tongue stick to [1]the roof of your
mouth so that you will be dumb, and cannot be a man who rebukes
them, for they are a rebellious house.
27 "But [a]when I speak to you, I will open your mouth, and you will
say to them, 'Thus says the Lord [1]GOD.' He who hears, let him hear;
and he who refuses, let him refuse; [b]for they are a rebellious house.

Chapter 4

4 "Now you son of man, [a]get yourself a brick, place it before you,
and inscribe a city on it, Jerusalem.
2 "Then [a]lay siege against it, build a siege wall, [1]raise up a ramp,
pitch camps, and place battering rams against it all around.
3 "Then get yourself an iron plate and set it up as an iron wall
between you and the city, and set your face toward it so that [a]it is
under siege, and besiege it. This is a [b]sign to the house of Israel.
4 "As for you, lie down on your left side, and lay the iniquity of the
house of Israel on it; you shall [a]bear their iniquity for the number of
days that you lie on it.
5 "For I have assigned you a number of days corresponding to the
years of their iniquity, three hundred and ninety days; thus [a]you
shall bear the iniquity of the house of Israel.
6 "When you have completed these, you shall lie down a second
time, *but* on your right side, and bear the iniquity of the house of
Judah; I have assigned it to you for forty days, a day for [a]each year.
7 "Then you shall set your face toward the siege of Jerusalem with
your arm bared, and [a]prophesy against it.
8 "Now behold, I will [a]put ropes on you so that you cannot turn
from one side to the other, until you have completed the days of
your siege.
9 "But as for you, take wheat, barley, beans, lentils, millet and

18 [a]Ezek. 3:20
19 [a]2 Kin. 17:1; Ezek. 33:3, 9 [b]E 14:14, 20; Acts 1 Tim. 4:16
20 [a]Ps. 125:5; 18:24; 33:18; Ze [b]Is. 8:14; Jer. 6: Ezek. 14:3, 7-9
21 [1]Lit., *him, the righteous* [a]Acts
22 [a]Acts 9:6
23 [a]Ezek. 1:28; 7:55 [b]Ezek. 1:1
24 [a]Ezek. 2:2
25 [a]Ezek. 4:8
26 [1]Lit., *your pa* [a]Luke 1:20, 22
27 [1]Heb., *YHWH* usually rendered [a]Ezek. 24:27; 33: [b]Ezek. 12:2, 3
4:1 [a]Is. 20:2; Jer. 18:2; 19:1
2 [1]Lit., *cast* [a]Jer. Ezek. 21:22
3 [a]Jer. 39:1, 2; E 5:2 [b]Is. 8:18; 20:3 Ezek. 12:6, 11; 24
4 [a]Lev. 10:17; 16 Num. 18:1
5 [a]Num. 14:34
6 [a]Num. 14:34; D 9:24-26; 12:11, 12 11:2, 3
7 [a]Ezek. 21:2
8 [a]Ezek. 3:25

[a]spelt, put them in one vessel and make them into bread for yourself;
you shall eat it according to the number of the days that you lie on
your side, three hundred and ninety days.
10 "And your food which you eat *shall be* [a]twenty shekels a day by
weight; you shall eat it from time to time.
11 "And the water you drink will be the sixth part of a hin by
measure; you shall drink it from time to time.
12 "And you shall eat it as a barley cake, having baked *it* in their
sight over human [a]dung."
13 Then the LORD said, "Thus shall the sons of Israel eat their bread
[a]unclean among the nations where I shall banish them."
14 But I said, "[a]Ah, Lord [1]GOD! Behold, I have [b]never been defiled;
for from my youth until now I have never eaten what [c]died of itself
or was torn by beasts, nor has any [d]unclean meat ever entered my
mouth."
15 Then He said to me, "See, I shall give you cow's dung in place of
human dung over which you will prepare your bread."
16 Moreover, He said to me, "Son of man, behold, I am going to
[a]break the staff of bread in Jerusalem, and they will eat bread by
[b]weight and with anxiety, and drink water by [c]measure and in hor-
ror,
17 because bread and water will be scarce; and they will be ap-
palled with one another and [a]waste away in their iniquity.

Chapter 5

5 "As for you, son of man, take a [a]sharp sword; take and [1]use it *as*
a barber's razor on your head and beard. Then take [b]scales for
weighing and divide [2]the hair.
2 "One third you shall burn in the fire at the center of the city, when
the [a]days of the siege are completed. Then you shall take one third
and strike *it* with the sword all around [1]the city, and one third you
shall scatter to the wind; and I will [b]unsheathe a sword behind them.
3 "Take also a few in number from [1]them and bind them in the
edges of your *robes*.
4 "And take again some of them and throw them into the fire, and
burn them in the fire; from it a fire will [1]spread to all the house of
Israel.
5 "Thus says the Lord [1]GOD, 'This is [a]Jerusalem; I have set her at the
[b]center of the nations, with lands around her.
6 'But she has rebelled against My ordinances more wickedly than
the nations and against My statutes [a]more than the lands which
surround her; for they have [b]rejected My ordinances and have not
walked [1]in My statutes.'
7 "Therefore, thus says the Lord GOD, 'Because you have [a]more
turmoil than the nations which surround you, and have not walked
in My statutes, nor observed My ordinances, nor observed the or-
dinances of the nations which surround you,'
8 therefore, thus says the Lord GOD, 'Behold, I, even I, am [a]against
you, and I will [b]execute judgments among you in the sight of the
nations.
9 'And because of all your abominations, I will do among you
what I have [a]not done, and the like of which I will never do again.
10 'Therefore, [a]fathers will eat *their* sons among you, and sons will

9:32; Is. 28:25
0 [a]Ezek. 45:12
12 [a]Is. 36:12
n. 1:8; Hos. 9:3
[1]Heb., *YHWH*, rendered *LORD* 1:6; Ezek. 9:8; cts 10:14 [c]Lev. :15; 22:8; Ezek. [d]Deut. 14:3; Is. 65:4; 66:17
v. 26:26; Is. 3:1; zek. 5:16; 14:13 . 4:10, 11; 12:19 [c]Lam. 5:4; Ezek. 12:18, 19
ev. 26:39; Ezek. 24:23; 33:10
.it., *make it pass your head* [2]Lit., *m* [a]Lev. 21:5; Is. :ek. 44:20 [b]Dan. 5:27
, *it* [a]Jer. 39:1, 2; :2-8 [b]Lev. 26:33
3 [1]Lit., *there*
4 [1]Lit., *go out*
5 [1]Heb., *YHWH*, y rendered *LORD*, so throughout the ler. 6:6; Ezek. 4:1 eut. 4:6; Lam. 1:1; Ezek. 16:14
[1]Lit., *in them, My statutes* [a]2 Kin. 3-20; Ezek. 16:47, 1 [b]Neh. 9:16, 17; 78:10; Jer. 11:10; Zech. 7:11
:in. 21:9-11; 2 Chr. 33:9; Jer. 2:10, 11
er. 21:5, 13; Ezek. 7; 21:3; Zech. 14:2 . 24:9; Ezek. 5:15; 11:9
in. 9:12; Amos 3:2; Matt. 24:21
0 [a]Lev. 26:29; Jer. 19:9; Lam. 4:10

eat their fathers; for I will execute judgments on you, and [b]scatter all
your remnant to every wind.
11 'So as I live,' declares the Lord GOD, 'surely, because you have
[a]defiled My sanctuary with all your [b]detestable idols and with all
your abominations, therefore I will also withdraw, and My eye shall
have no pity and I will not spare.
12 'One third of you will die by [a]plague or be consumed by famine
among you, one third will fall by the sword around you, and one
third I will [b]scatter to every wind, and I will [c]unsheathe a sword
behind them.
13 'Thus My anger will be spent, and I will [1]satisfy My wrath on
them, and I shall be [2a]appeased; then they will know that I, the LORD,
have [b]spoken in My zeal when I have spent My wrath upon them.
14 'Moreover, I will make you a desolation and a [a]reproach among
the nations which surround you, in the sight of all who pass by.
15 'So [1]it will be a reproach, a reviling, a [a]warning and an object of
horror to the nations who surround you, when I [b]execute judgments
against you in anger, wrath, and raging rebukes. I, the LORD, have
spoken.
16 'When I send against them the [1]deadly arrows of famine which
[2]were for the destruction of those whom I shall send to destroy you,
then I shall also intensify the famine upon you, and break the staff of
bread.
17 'Moreover, [a]I will send on you famine and wild beasts, and they
will bereave you of children; [b]plague and bloodshed also will pass
through you, and I will bring the sword on you. I, the LORD, have
spoken.' "

Chapter 6

6 And the word of the LORD came to me saying,
2 "Son of man, set your face toward the [a]mountains of Israel, and
prophesy against them,
3 and say, 'Mountains of Israel, listen to the word of the Lord
[1]GOD! Thus says the Lord [1]GOD to the mountains, the hills, the
ravines and the valleys: "Behold, I Myself am going to bring a sword
on you, and [a]I will destroy your high places.
4 "So your [a]altars will become desolate, and your incense altars will
be smashed; and I shall make your slain fall in front of your idols.
5 "I shall also lay the dead bodies of the sons of Israel in front of
their idols; and I shall scatter your [a]bones around your altars.
6 "In all your dwellings, [a]cities will become waste and the high
places will be desolate, that your altars may become waste and
[1]desolate, your [b]idols may be broken and brought to an end, your
incense altars may be cut down, and your works may be blotted out.
7 "And the slain will fall among you, and you will know that I am
the LORD.
8 "However, I shall leave a [a]remnant, for you will have those who
[b]escaped the sword among the nations when you are scattered
among the countries.
9 "Then those of you who escape will [a]remember Me among the
nations to which they will be carried captive, how I have [1b]been hurt
by their adulterous hearts which turned away from Me, and by their
eyes, which played the harlot after their idols; and they will [c]loathe

10 [b]Ps. 44:11; 5:2, 12; 6:8; 12: Amos 9:9; Zech 7:14

11 [a]Jer. 7:9-11; 8:5, 6, 16 [b]Jer. Ezek. 7:20

12 [a]Jer. 15:2; 2 Ezek. 5:17; 6:11 [b]Ezek. 5:2, 10; A 9:9; Zech. 2:6 [c] 43:10, 11; 44:27 5:2; 12:14

13 [1]Lit., *cause t* [2]Lit., *comforted* 1:24 [b]Is. 59:17; 36:5, 6; 38:19

14 [a]Ps. 74:3-10 Ezek. 22:4

15 [1]Ancient vers read *you* [a]Is. 26 22:8, 9; 1 Cor. 1([b]Is. 66:15, 16; Ez 25:17

16 [1]Lit., *evil* [2]Or *destruction, whic send*

17 [a]Lev. 26:22; F 6:8 [b]Ezek. 38:22

6:2 [a]Ezek. 36:1

3 [1]Heb., *YHWH,* usually rendered [a]Lev. 26:30

4 [a]Lev. 26:30; 2 C 14:5; Is. 27:9; Eze

5 [a]2 Kin. 23:14, 1 Jer. 8:1, 2

6 [1]So some ancie versions; Heb., *be their guilt* [a]Lev. 26 6:11; Ezek. 5:14 [b] 6:4; Mic. 1:7; Zech

8 [a]Is. 6:13; Jer. 30 [b]Jer. 44:14, 28; Ez 7:16; 14:22

9 [1]Lit., *been broke broken for Myself t* [a]Deut. 4:29; 30:2; 51:50 [b]Ps. 78:40; 7:13; 43:24; Hos. 1 [c]Job 42:6; Ezek. 20 36:31

themselves in their own sight for the evils which they have com-
mitted, for all their abominations.
10 "Then they will know that I am the LORD; I have not said in vain
[1]that I would inflict this disaster on them." '
11 "Thus says the Lord [1]GOD, 'Clap your hand, [a]stamp your foot, and
say, "[b]Alas, because of all the evil abominations of the house of Isra-
el, which will fall by [c]sword, famine, and plague!
12 "He who is [a]far off will die by the plague, and he who is near will
fall by the sword, and he who remains and is besieged will die by
the famine. Thus shall I [b]spend My wrath on them.
13 "Then you will know that I am the LORD, when their [a]slain are
among their idols around their altars, on [b]every high hill, on all the
tops of the mountains, under every green tree, and under every leafy
oak—the places where they offered soothing aroma to all their idols.
14 "So throughout all their habitations I shall [a]stretch out My hand
against them and make the land more desolate and waste than the
wilderness toward Diblah; thus they will know that I am the
LORD." ' "

Chapter 7

7 Moreover, the word of the LORD came to me saying,
2 "And you, son of man, thus says the Lord [1]GOD to the land of
Israel, 'An [a]end! The end is coming on the four corners of the land.
3 'Now the end is upon you, and I shall send My anger against
you; I shall judge you according to your ways, and I shall bring all
your abominations upon you.
4 'For My eye will have no pity on you, nor shall I spare *you*, but I
shall [a]bring your ways upon you, and your abominations will be
among you; then you will [b]know that I am the LORD!'
5 "Thus says the Lord [1]GOD, 'A [a]disaster, unique disaster, behold it
is coming!
6 'An end is coming; the end has come! It has [a]awakened against
you; behold, it has come!
7 'Your doom has come to you, O inhabitant of the land. The [a]time
has come, the [b]day is near—tumult rather than joyful shouting on
the mountains.
8 'Now I will shortly [a]pour out My wrath on you, and spend My
anger against you, [b]judge you according to your ways, and bring on
you all your abominations.
9 'And My eye will show no pity, nor will I spare. I will [1]repay you
according to your ways, while your abominations are in your midst;
then you will know that I, the LORD, do the smiting.
10 'Behold, the day! Behold, it is coming! *Your* doom has gone forth;
the [a]rod has budded, arrogance has blossomed.
11 'Violence [1]has grown into a rod of [a]wickedness. None of them
shall remain, none of their multitude, none of their [b]wealth, nor any-
thing eminent among them.
12 'The [a]time has come, the day has arrived. Let not the [b]buyer
rejoice nor the seller mourn; for [c]wrath is against all their multitude.
13 'Indeed, the seller will not [1a]regain [2]what he sold as long as [3]they
both live; for the vision regarding all their multitude will not [4]be
averted, nor will any of them maintain his life by his iniquity.
14 'They have [a]blown the trumpet and made everything ready, but

do this evil to
Heb., *YHWH*, ...ndered *LORD* ...:6 [b]Ezek. 9:4 ...ek. 5:12; 7:15
...an. 9:7 [b]Lam. ...22; Ezek. 5:13
... 6:4-7 [b]1 Kin. ...2 Kin. 16:4; Is. ...; Ezek. 20:28; Hos. 4:13
...25; 9:12; Ezek. ...4:13; 20:33, 34
[1]Heb., *YHWH*, rendered *LORD* ...7:3, 5, 6; 11:13; Amos 8:2, 10
...k. 11:21; 22:31; [b]Ezek. 6:7, 14; 7:27
[1]Heb., *YHWH*, rendered *LORD* ...21:12, 13; Nah. 1:9
6 [a]Zech. 13:7
7 [a]Ezek. 7:12; ...25, 28 [b]Is. 22:5
...42:25; Ezek. 9:8; ...Nah. 1:6 [b]Ezek. ...7:3; 33:20; 36:19
9 [1]Lit., *give*
...s. 89:32; Is. 10:5
...t., *has risen* [a]Ps. 125:3; Is. 59:6-8 [b]Zeph. 1:18
[a]Ezek. 7:5-7, 10; ...r. 7:29-31; James ...3, 9 [b]Prov. 20:14; ...or. 7:30 [c]Is. 5:13, ...ek. 6:11, 12; 7:14
...Lit., *return to* [2]Lit., ...*thing sold*, i.e., his ...ed land [3]Lit., *their* ...*e among the living* [4]Lit., *return* [a]Lev. 25:24-28, 31
...Num. 10:9; Jer. 4:5

no one is going to the battle; for My wrath is against all [1]their multi-
tude.
15 'The [a]sword is outside, and the plague and the famine are within.
He who is in the field will die by the sword; famine and the plague
will also consume those in the city.
16 'Even when their survivors [a]escape, they will be on the moun-
tains like [b]doves of the valleys, all of them [1c]mourning, each over his
own iniquity.
17 'All [a]hands will hang limp, and all knees will [1]become like water.
18 'And they will [a]gird themselves with sackcloth, and [b]shuddering
will overwhelm them; and shame *will be* on all faces, and [c]baldness
on all their heads.
19 'They shall [a]fling their silver into the streets, and their gold shall
become an abhorrent thing; their [b]silver and their gold shall not be
able to deliver them in the day of the wrath of the LORD. They cannot
satisfy their [1]appetite, nor can they fill their stomachs, for their iniq-
uity has become an occasion of stumbling.
20 'And they transformed the beauty of His ornaments into pride,
and [a]they made the images of their abominations *and* their detestable
things with it; therefore I will make it an abhorrent thing to them.
21 'And I shall give it into the hands of the [a]foreigners as plunder
and to the wicked of the earth as spoil, and they will profane it.
22 'I shall also turn My [a]face from them, and they will profane My
secret place; then robbers will enter and profane it.
23 '[a]Make the chain, for the land is full of [1b]bloody crimes, and the
city is [c]full of violence.
24 'Therefore, I shall bring the worst of the [a]nations, and they will
possess their houses. I shall also make the [b]pride of the strong ones
cease, and their [c]holy places will be profaned.
25 'When anguish comes, they will seek [a]peace, but there will be
none.
26 '[a]Disaster will come upon disaster, and [b]rumor will be *added* to
rumor; then they will seek a [c]vision from a prophet, but the [d]law will
be lost from the priest and [e]counsel from the elders.
27 'The king will mourn, the prince will be [a]clothed with horror, and
the hands of the people of the land will [1]tremble. According to their
conduct I shall deal with them, and by their judgments I shall judge
them. And they will know that I am the LORD.' "

Chapter 8

592 B.C.

8 And it came about in the sixth year, on the fifth *day* of the sixth
month, as I was sitting in my house with the elders of Judah
sitting before me, that the hand of the Lord [1]GOD fell on me there.
2 Then I looked, and behold, a likeness as the appearance of [1]a
man; from His loins and downward *there was* the [a]appearance of fire,
and from His loins and upward the appearance of brightness, like
the appearance [b]of [2]glowing metal.
3 And He stretched out the form of a hand and caught me by a
lock of my head; and the [a]Spirit lifted me up between earth and
heaven and brought me in the visions of God to Jerusalem, to the
entrance of the [1]north gate of the inner *court*, where the seat of the
idol of jealousy, which [b]provokes to jealousy, was *located*.
4 And behold, the [a]glory of the God of Israel *was* there, like the
appearance which I saw in the plain.

14 [1]Lit., *her*

15 [a]Jer. 14:18; 5:12; 6:11, 12;

16 [1]Lit., *moani* 9:15; Is. 37:31; 6:8; 14:22 [b]Is. [c]Is. 59:11; Nah.

17 [1]Lit., *run wit* [a]Is. 13:7; Ezek. 22:14; Heb. 12:

18 [a]Is. 15:3; Ez 27:31; Amos 8:1 21:6; Ps. 55:5 [c] 27:31

19 [1]Lit., *soul* [a]Is 30:22 [b]Prov. 11. Zeph. 1:18

20 [a]Jer. 7:30

21 [a]2 Kin. 24:13 74:2-8; Jer. 52:1

22 [a]Jer. 18:17; E 39:23, 24

23 [1]Lit., *judgmer blood* [a]Jer. 27:2 9:9; Hos. 4:2 [c]E 8:17

24 [a]Ezek. 21:31; [b]Ezek. 33:28 [c]2 7:20; Ezek. 24:21

25 [a]Ezek. 13:10,

26 [a]Is. 47:11; Jer. [b]Ezek. 21:7 [c]Jer. 37:17 [d]Ps. 74:9; 22:26; Mic. 3:6 [e]J 18:18; Ezek. 11:2

27 [1]Lit., *be terrifie* [a]Job 8:22; Ps. 35: 109:18, 29; Ezek.

8:1 [1]Heb., *YHWH* usually rendered *L*

2 [1]Lit., *fire* [2]Or, *electrum* [a]Ezek. 1 [b]Ezek. 1:4, 27

3 [1]Lit., *facing nort* [a]Ezek. 3:12; 11:1 20:4; Deut. 32:16

4 [a]Ezek. 1:28; 3:2

5 Then He said to me, "Son of man, [a]raise your eyes, now, toward the north." So I raised my eyes toward the north, and behold, to the north of the altar gate *was* this [b]idol of jealousy at the entrance.

6 And He said to me, "Son of man, do you see what they are doing, the great [a]abominations which the house of Israel are committing here, that I should be far from My sanctuary? But yet you will see still greater abominations."

7 Then He brought me to the entrance of the court, and when I looked, behold, a hole in the wall.

8 And He said to me, "Son of man, now [a]dig through the wall." So I dug through the wall, and behold, an entrance.

9 And He said to me, "Go in and see the wicked abominations that they are committing here."

10 So I entered and looked, and behold, every form of creeping things and beasts *and* detestable things, with all the idols of the house of Israel, were carved on the wall all around.

11 And standing in front of them were [a]seventy [b]elders of the house of Israel, with Jaazaniah the son of Shaphan standing among them, each man with his [c]censer in his hand, and the fragrance of the cloud of incense rising.

12 Then He said to me, "Son of man, do you see what the elders of the house of Israel are committing in the dark, each man in the room of his carved images? For they say, '[a]The LORD does not see us; the LORD has [b]forsaken the land.' "

13 And He said to me, "Yet you will see still greater abominations which they are committing."

14 Then He brought me to the entrance of the [a]gate of the LORD's house which *was* toward the north; and behold, women were sitting there weeping for Tammuz.

15 And He said to me, "Do you see *this,* son of man? Yet you will see still greater abominations than these."

16 Then He brought me into the inner court of the LORD's house. And behold, at the entrance to the temple of the LORD, between the porch and the altar, *were* about twenty-five men with their [a]backs to the temple of the LORD and their faces toward the east; and [b]they were [1]prostrating themselves eastward toward the sun.

17 And He said to me, "Do you see *this,* son of man? Is it too light a thing for the house of Judah to commit the abominations which they have committed here, that they have [a]filled the land with violence and [b]provoked Me repeatedly? For behold, they are putting the twig to their nose.

18 "Therefore, I indeed shall deal in wrath. My eye will have no pity nor shall I spare; and [a]though they cry in My ears with a loud voice, yet I shall not listen to them."

Chapter 9

9 Then He cried out in my hearing with a loud [a]voice saying, "Draw near, [1]O executioners of the city, each with his destroying weapon in his hand."

2 And behold, six men came from the direction of the upper gate which faces north, each with his shattering weapon in his hand; and among them was [a]a certain man clothed in linen with a [1]writing case at his loins. And they went in and stood beside the bronze altar.

3 Then the [a]glory of the God of Israel went up from the cherub on

[a]Jer. 3:2; Zech. 5:5 [b]Ps. 78:58; Jer. 7:30; 32:34; Ezek. 8:3

Kin. 23:4, 5; Ezek. 5:11; 8:9, 17

8 [a]Is. 29:15

[a]Num. 11:16, 25; Luke 10:1 [b]Jer. 19:1 [c]Num. 16:17, 35

Ps. 14:1; Is. 29:15; Ezek. 9:9 [b]Ps. 10:11

[a]Ezek. 44:4; 46:9

6 [1]I.e., worshiping Chr. 29:6; Jer. 2:27; Ezek. 23:39 [b]Deut. 4:19; 17:3; Job 1:26-28; Jer. 44:17

Ezek. 7:11, 23; 9:9; Amos 3:10; Mic. 2:2 Jer. 7:18, 19; Ezek. 16:26

Is. 1:15; Jer. 11:11; Mic. 3:4; Zech. 7:13

9:1 [1]Lit., *you who punish* [a]Is. 6:8

[1]Or, *scribal inkhorn* [a]Lev. 16:4

Ezek. 10:4; 11:22, 23

which it had been, to the threshold of the [1]temple. And He called to the man clothed in linen at whose loins was the writing case.

4 And the LORD said to him, "Go through the midst of the city, *even* through the midst of Jerusalem, and put a [a]mark on the foreheads of the men who [b]sigh and groan over all the abominations which are being committed in its midst."

5 But to the others He said in my hearing, "Go through the city after him and strike; do not let your eye have pity, and do not spare.

6 "[1]Utterly [a]slay old men, young men, maidens, little children, and women, but do not [b]touch any man on whom is the mark; and you shall [c]start from My sanctuary." So they started with the [2]elders who *were* before the [3]temple.

7 And He said to them, "[a]Defile the [1]temple and fill the courts with the slain. Go out!" Thus they went out and struck down *the people* in the city.

8 Then it came about as they were striking and I *alone* was left, that I [a]fell on my face and cried out [1]saying, "[b]Alas, Lord [2]GOD! Art Thou destroying the whole remnant of Israel [3]by pouring out Thy wrath on Jerusalem?"

9 Then He said to me, "The iniquity of the house of Israel and Judah is very, very great, and the land is [a]filled with blood, and the city is [b]full of perversion; for [c]they say, 'The LORD has forsaken the land, and the LORD does not see!'

10 "But as for Me, [a]My eye will have no pity nor shall I spare, but [b]I shall bring their conduct upon their heads."

11 Then behold, the man clothed in linen at whose loins was the [1]writing case [2]reported, saying, "I have done just as Thou hast commanded me."

Chapter 10

10 Then I looked, and behold, in the [1a]expanse that was over the heads of the cherubim something like a [b]sapphire stone, in appearance resembling a [c]throne, appeared above them.

2 And He spoke to the man clothed in linen and said, "Enter between the [a]whirling wheels under the [1]cherubim, and fill your hands with [b]coals of fire from between the cherubim, and scatter *them* over the city." And he entered in my sight.

3 Now the cherubim were standing on the right side of the [1]temple when the man entered, and the cloud filled the [a]inner court.

4 Then the [a]glory of the LORD went up from the cherub to the threshold of the temple, and the [b]temple was filled with the cloud, and the court was filled with the [c]brightness of the glory of the LORD.

5 Moreover, the sound of the wings of the cherubim was heard as far as the outer court, like the [a]voice of [1]God Almighty when He speaks.

6 And it came about when He commanded the man clothed in linen, saying, "Take fire from between the whirling wheels, from between the cherubim," he entered and stood beside a wheel.

7 Then the cherub stretched out his hand from between the cherubim to the fire which *was* between the cherubim, took some and put it into the hands of the one clothed in linen, who took *it* and went out.

8 And the cherubim appeared to have the form of a man's hand under their wings.

3 [1]Lit., *house*

4 [a]Ex. 12:7, 13 9:6; 2 Cor. 1:22 2:19; Rev. 7:2, 14:1 [b]Ps. 119:5 Jer. 13:17; Ezek 21:6

6 [1]Lit., To *destr* [2]Or, *old men* [3]L *house* [a]2 Chr. 3 [b]Ex. 12:23; Rev. [c]Jer. 25:29; Am Luke 12:47

7 [1]Lit., *house* [a] 36:17; Ezek. 7:2

8 [1]Lit., *and said* *YHWH*, usually rendered *LORD* *Thy pouring* [a]1 21:16 [b]Ezek. 11 Amos 7:2-6

9 [a]2 Kin. 21:16; 2:34; Ezek. 7:23; 3 [b]Ezek. 22:29; 3:1-3; 7:3 [c]Job 2 Ps. 10:11; 94:7; 29:15; Ezek. 8:12

10 [a]Is. 65:6; Eze 24:14 [b]Ezek. 7:4 Hos. 9:7

11 [1]Or, *inkhorn* *brought back wo*

10:1 [1]Or, *firmam* [a]Ezek. 1:22, 26 [b] 24:10 [c]Rev. 4:2,

2 [1]So with Gr.; H *cherub* [a]Ezek. 1:1 10:13 [b]Ps. 18:10- 6:6; Ezek. 1:13; R

3 [1]Lit., *house*, and throughout the ch. [a]Ezek. 8:3, 16

4 [a]Ezek. 9:3; 11:2 [b]Ex. 40:34, 35; Is. [c]Ezek. 1:28

5 [1]Heb., *El Shado* [a]Job 40:9; Ezek. 1 Rev. 10:3

9 Then I looked, and behold, [a]four wheels beside the cherubim,
one wheel beside each cherub; and the appearance of the wheels *was*
like the gleam of a [1b]Tarshish stone.
10 And as for their appearance, all four of them had the same like-
ness, as if one wheel were within another wheel.
11 When they moved, they went [a]in *any of* their four [1]directions
without turning as they went; but they followed in the direction
which [2]they faced, without turning as they went.
12 And their [a]whole body, their backs, their hands, their wings, and
the [b]wheels were full of eyes all around, the wheels belonging to all
four of them.
13 The wheels were called in my hearing, the whirling wheels.
14 And [a]each one had four faces. The first face *was* the face of a
cherub, the second face *was* the face of a man, the third the face of a
lion, and the fourth the face of an eagle.
15 Then the cherubim rose up. They are the [a]living beings that I saw
by the river Chebar.
16 Now when the cherubim moved, the wheels would go beside
them; also when the cherubim lifted up their wings to rise from the
ground, the wheels would not turn from beside them.
17 When [1]the cherubim [a]stood still, [1]the wheels would stand still;
and when they rose up, [1]the wheels would rise with them; for the
spirit of the living beings *was* in them.
18 Then the glory of the LORD departed from the threshold of the
temple and stood [a]over the cherubim.
19 When [a]the cherubim departed, they lifted their wings and rose
up from the earth in my sight with the wheels beside them; and they
stood still at the entrance of the east gate of the LORD's house. And
the glory of the God of Israel [1]hovered over them.
20 These are the [a]living beings that I saw beneath the God of Israel
by [b]the river Chebar; so I knew that they *were* cherubim.
21 [a]Each one had four faces and each one four wings, and beneath
their wings *was* the form of human hands.
22 As for the likeness of their faces, they were the same faces whose
appearance I had seen by the river Chebar. Each one went straight
ahead.

Chapter 11

11 Moreover, the [a]Spirit lifted me up and brought me to the east
gate of the LORD's house which faced eastward. And behold,
there were twenty-five men at the entrance of the gate, and among
them I saw Jaazaniah son of Azzur and [b]Pelatiah son of Benaiah,
leaders of the people.
2 And He said to me, "Son of man, these are the men who devise
iniquity and [a]give evil advice in this city,
3 who say, '[1]Is not *the time* near to build houses? [2]This [a]*city* is the
pot and we are the flesh.'
4 "Therefore, [a]prophesy against them, son of man, prophesy!"
5 Then the Spirit of the LORD fell upon me, and He said to me,
"Say, 'Thus says the LORD, "So you think, house of Israel, for [a]I know
[1]your [b]thoughts.
6 "You have [a]multiplied your slain in this city, filling its streets with
[1]them."
7 'Therefore, thus says the Lord [1]GOD, "Your [a]slain whom you have

9 [1]Perhaps, *beryl* [a]Ezek. 1:15-17 [b]Dan. 10:6; Rev. 21:20
[1]Lit., *sides* [2]Lit., *the turned* [a]Ezek. 1:17
[a]Rev. 4:6, 8 [b]Ezek. 1:18
14 [a]1 Kin. 7:29, 36; Ezek. 1:6, 10; 10:21; Rev. 4:7
15 [a]Ezek. 1:3, 5
17 [1]Lit., *they* [a]Ezek. 1:21
18 [a]Ps. 18:10
[1]Lit., *over them from above* [a]Ezek. 11:22
[a]Ezek. 1:5, 22, 26; 10:15 [b]Ezek. 1:1
[a]Ezek. 1:6, 8; 10:14; 41:18, 19
1 [a]Ezek. 3:12, 14; 11:24; 43:5 [b]Ezek. 11:13
[a]Ps. 2:1, 2; 52:2; Is. 1; Jer. 5:5; Mic. 2:1
[1]Or, *The time is not* [2]Or, *This is* [a]Jer. 1:13; Ezek. 11:7, 11; 24:3, 6
4 [a]Ezek. 3:4, 17
[1]Lit., *what comes up in your spirit* [a]Jer. 1:20; 17:10 [b]Ezek. 38:10
[1]Lit., *the slain* [a]Is. Ezek. 7:23; 22:2-6, 9, 12, 27
7 [1]Heb., *YHWH*, usually rendered *LORD*, and so throughout the ch.

laid in the midst of [2]the city are the flesh, and this *city* is the pot; but
[3]I shall [b]bring you out of it.
8 "You have [a]feared a sword; so I will [b]bring a sword upon you,"
the Lord GOD declares.
9 "And I shall bring you out of the midst of [1]the city, and I shall
deliver you into the hands of [a]strangers and [b]execute judgments
against you.
10 "You will [a]fall by the sword. I shall judge you to the [b]border of
Israel; so you shall know that I am the LORD.
11 "This *city* will [a]not be a pot for you, nor will you be flesh in the
midst of it, *but* I shall judge you to the border of Israel.
12 "Thus you will know that I am the LORD; for you have not walked
in My statutes nor have you [a]executed My ordinances, but have
acted according to the ordinances of the [b]nations around you." ' "
13 Now it came about as I prophesied, that [a]Pelatiah son of Benaiah
died. Then I fell on my face and cried out with a loud voice and said,
"[b]Alas, Lord GOD! Wilt Thou bring the remnant of Israel to a com-
plete end?"
14 Then the word of the LORD came to me, saying,
15 "Son of man, your brothers, your [1]relatives, [2]your fellow exiles,
and the whole house of Israel, all of them, *are those* to whom the
inhabitants of Jerusalem have said, 'Go far from the LORD; this land
has been given [a]us as a possession.'
16 "Therefore say, 'Thus says the Lord GOD, "Though I had removed
them far away among the nations, and though I had scattered them
among the countries, yet I was a [a]sanctuary for them a little while in
the countries where they had gone." '
17 "Therefore say, 'Thus says the Lord GOD, "I shall [a]gather you from
the peoples and assemble you out of the countries among which you
have been scattered, and I shall give you the land of Israel." '
18 "When they come there, they will [a]remove all its [b]detestable
things and all its abominations from it.
19 "And I shall [a]give them one heart, and shall put a new spirit
within [1]them. And I shall take the [b]heart of stone out of their flesh
and give them a [c]heart of flesh,
20 that they may [a]walk in My statutes and keep My ordinances, and
do them. Then they will be [b]My people, and I shall be their God.
21 "[1]But as for those whose hearts go after their [a]detestable things
and abominations, I shall [b]bring their conduct down on their heads,"
declares the Lord GOD.
22 Then the cherubim [a]lifted up their wings with the wheels beside
them, and [b]the glory of the God of Israel [1]hovered over them.
23 And the [a]glory of the LORD went up from the midst of the city,
and [b]stood over the mountain which is east of the city.
24 And the [a]Spirit lifted me up and brought me in a vision by the
Spirit of God to the exiles [1]in Chaldea. So the vision that I had seen
[2b]left me.
25 Then I [a]told the exiles all the things that the LORD had shown me.

Chapter 12

12 Then the word of the LORD came to me saying,
2 "Son of man, you live in the [a]midst of the [b]rebellious house,
who [c]have eyes to see but do not see, ears to hear but do not hear; for
they are a rebellious house.

7 [2]Lit., *it* [3]So w... Heb., *he will br... out* [a]Ezek. 24:... Mic. 3:2, 3 [b]2 K... 25:18-22; Jer. 5... Ezek. 11:9

8 [a]Prov. 10:24, [b]Job 3:25; Is. 2...

9 [1]Lit., *it* [a]Deut... 49, 50; Ps. 106 [b]Ezek. 5:8; 16:4...

10 [a]Jer. 52:9, 1... [b]2 Kin. 14:25

11 [a]Ezek. 11:3, 24:3, 6

12 [a]Ezek. 18:8, [b]Ezek. 8:10, 14

13 [a]Ezek. 11:1 9:8

15 [1]Lit., *brother...* with Gr. and som... ancient versions *the men of your redemption* [a]Ez... 33:24

16 [a]Ps. 31:20; 9... 91:9; Is. 8:14; Je... 29:7, 11

17 [a]Is. 11:11-16 3:12, 18; 24:5; E... 20:41, 42; 28:25

18 [a]Ezek. 37:23 5:11; 7:20

19 [1]So with Gr. a... many mss.; Heb [a]Jer. 24:7; 32:39; 18:31; 36:26 [b]Ze... 7:12; Rom. 2:4, 5 [c]2 Cor. 3:3

20 [a]Ps. 105:45; ... 36:27 [b]Ezek. 14...

21 [1]Lit., *And to th... heart of their dete... things and their abomination their... goes.* [a]Jer. 16:18 11:18 [b]Ezek. 9:1...

22 [1]Lit., *over the... above* [a]Ezek. 10:... [b]Ezek. 43:2

23 [a]Ezek. 8:4 [b]Z... 14:4

24 [1]I.e., Babyloni... [2]Lit., *went up from* [a]Ezek. 8:3; 11:1; 3... 2 Cor. 12:2-4 [b]Ac... 10:16

25 [a]Ezek. 2:7; 3:4... 17, 27

12:2 [a]Is. 6:5 [b]Ps. 78:40; Is. 1:23; Ez... 2:7, 8 [c]Is. 6:9f.; 43... Jer. 5:21; Matt. 13... 14; Mark 4:12; 8:1... Luke 8:10; John 9:39-41; 12:40; Ac... 28:26f.; Rom. 11:8

3 "Therefore, son of man, prepare for yourself baggage for exile and
go into exile by day in their sight; even go into exile from your place
to another place in their sight. [a]Perhaps they will [1]understand
though they are a rebellious house.
4 "And bring your baggage out by day in their sight, as baggage for
exile. Then you will go out [a]at evening in their sight, as those going
into exile.
5 "Dig a hole through the wall in their sight and [1]go out through it.
6 "Load *the baggage* on *your* shoulder in their sight, *and* carry *it* out
in the dark. You shall [a]cover your face so that you can not see the
land, for I have set you as a [b]sign to the house of Israel."
7 And I [a]did so, as I had been commanded. By day I [b]brought out
my baggage like the baggage of an exile. Then in the evening I dug
through the wall with my hands; I went out in the dark *and* carried
the baggage on *my* shoulder in their sight.
8 And in the morning the word of the LORD came to me, saying,
9 "Son of man, has not the house of Israel, the [a]rebellious house,
said to you, '[b]What are you doing?'
10 "Say to them, 'Thus says the Lord [1]GOD, "This [2a]burden *concerns*
the prince in Jerusalem, as well as all the house of Israel who are [3]in
it." '
11 "Say, 'I am [1]a [a]sign to you. As I have done, so it will be done to
them; they will [b]go into exile, into captivity.'
12 "And the [a]prince who is among them will load *his baggage* on *his*
shoulder in the dark and go out. [1]They will dig a hole through the
wall to bring *it* out. He will cover his face so that he can not see the
land with *his* eyes.
13 "I shall also spread My [a]net over him, and he will be caught in My
snare. And I shall bring him to Babylon in the land of the Chaldeans;
yet he will [b]not see it, though he will die there.
14 "And I shall [a]scatter to every wind all who are around him, his
helpers and all his troops; and I shall draw out a sword after them.
15 "So they will [a]know that I am the LORD when I scatter them
among the nations, and spread them among the countries.
16 "But I shall [1]spare a few of them from the [a]sword, the famine, and
the pestilence that they may tell all their abominations among the
nations where they go, and [2]may [b]know that I am the LORD."
17 Moreover, the word of the LORD came to me saying,
18 "Son of man, [a]eat your bread with trembling, and drink your
water with quivering and anxiety.
19 "Then say to the people of the land, 'Thus says the Lord GOD
concerning the inhabitants of Jerusalem in the land of Israel, "They
will eat their bread with anxiety and drink their water with horror,
because [1]their land will be [2a]stripped of its fulness on account of the
violence of all who live in it.
20 "And the inhabited [a]cities will be laid waste, and the [b]land will be
a desolation. So you will know that I am the LORD." ' "
21 Then the word of the LORD came to me saying,
22 "Son of man, what is this [a]proverb you *people* have concerning the
land of Israel, saying, 'The [b]days are long and every [c]vision fails'?
23 "Therefore say to them, 'Thus says the Lord GOD, "I will make
this proverb cease so that they will no longer use it as a proverb in
Israel." But tell them, "[a]The days draw near as well as the [1]fulfill-
ment of every vision.

Or, *see that they are* 26:3; 36:3, 7; Luke 20:13; 2 Tim. 2:25
4 [a]2 Kin. 25:4; Jer. 39:4; Ezek. 12:12
5 [1]Lit., *bring it out*
[a]1 Sam. 28:8; Ezek. 12:12, 13 [b]Is. 8:18; 3; Ezek. 4:3; 12:11; 24:24
[a]Ezek. 24:18; 37:7, 10 [b]Ezek. 12:3-6
Ezek. 2:5-8; 12:1-3 Ezek. 17:12; 20:49; 24:19
10 [1]Heb., *YHWH*, ally rendered *LORD*, d so throughout the [2]Or, *oracle* [3]Lit., *in midst* [a]2 Kin. 9:25; 13:1; Ezek. 12:3-8
11 [1]Lit., *your sign* ek. 12:6 [b]Jer. 15:2; 28-30; Ezek. 12:3
12 [1]I.e., the king's dants [a]2 Kin. 25:4; r. 39:4; 52:7; Ezek. 12:6
s. 24:17, 18; Ezek. 20; 19:8; Hos. 7:12 [b]Jer. 39:7; 52:11
14 [a]2 Kin. 25:4, 5; Ezek. 5:2; 17:21
15 [a]Ezek. 6:7, 14; 12:16, 20
it., *leave over* [2]Or, *y will know* [a]Ezek. 14:21 [b]Jer. 22:8, 9
[a]Lam. 5:9; Ezek. 4:16
19 [1]Lit., *her* [2]Lit., *solate* [a]Jer. 10:22; ek. 6:6, 7, 14; Mic. 7:13; Zech. 7:14
[a]Is. 3:26; Jer. 4:7; 5:14 [b]Is. 7:23, 24; r. 25:9; Ezek. 36:3
Ezek. 16:44; 18:2, 5:12; Ezek. 11:3; ; Amos 6:3; 2 Pet. 3:4 [c]Ezek. 7:26
3 [1]Lit., *word* [a]Ps. 3; Joel 2:1; Zeph. 1:14

24 "For there will no longer be any [1a]false vision or flattering divina-
tion within the house of Israel.
25 "For I the LORD shall speak, and whatever [a]word I speak will be
performed. It will no longer be delayed, for in [b]your days, O [c]rebel-
lious house, I shall speak the word and perform it," declares the
Lord GOD.' "
26 Furthermore, the word of the LORD came to me saying,
27 "Son of man, behold, the house of Israel is saying, 'The vision that
he sees is for [a]many [1]years *from now,* and he prophesies of times far
off.'
28 "Therefore say to them, 'Thus says the Lord GOD, "None of My
words will be delayed any longer. Whatever word I speak will be
performed," ' " declares the Lord GOD.

Chapter 13

13 Then the word of the LORD came to me saying,
2 "Son of man, prophesy against the [a]prophets of Israel who
prophesy, and say to those who prophesy from their own [1]inspira-
tion, '[b]Listen to the word of the LORD!
3 'Thus says the Lord [1]GOD, "Woe to the [a]foolish prophets who are
following their own spirit and have [b]seen nothing.
4 "O Israel, your prophets have been like foxes among ruins.
5 "You have not [a]gone up into the [b]breaches, nor did you build the
wall around the house of Israel to stand in the battle on the [c]day of
the LORD.
6 "They see [1a]falsehood and lying divination who are saying, 'The
LORD declares,' when the LORD has not sent them; [b]yet they hope for
the fulfillment of *their* word.
7 "[a]Did you not see a false vision and speak a lying divination
when you said, 'The LORD declares,' but it is not I who have
spoken?" ' "
8 Therefore, thus says the Lord GOD, "Because you have spoken
[1]falsehood and seen a lie, therefore behold, [a]I am against you,"
declares the Lord GOD.
9 "So My hand will be against the [a]prophets who see false visions
and utter lying divinations. They will [1]have no place in the council
of My people, [b]nor will they be written down in the register of the
house of Israel, nor will they enter the land of Israel, [2]that you may
know that I am the Lord GOD.
10 "It is definitely because they have [a]misled My people by saying,
'[b]Peace!' when there is [c]no peace. And when anyone builds a wall,
behold, they plaster it over with whitewash;
11 *so* tell those who plaster it over with whitewash, that it will fall.
A [a]flooding rain will come, and you, O hailstones, will fall; and a
violent wind will break out.
12 "Behold, when the wall has fallen, will you not be asked, 'Where
is the plaster with which you plastered *it?*' "
13 Therefore, thus says the Lord GOD, "I will make a violent wind
break out in My wrath. There will also be in My anger a flooding
rain and [a]hailstones to consume *it* in wrath.
14 "So I shall tear down the wall which you plastered over with
whitewash and bring it down to the ground, so that its [a]foundation
is laid bare; and when it falls, you will be [b]consumed in its midst.
And you will [c]know that I am the LORD.

24 [1]Lit., *vain* 14:13-16; Ezek 23; Zech. 13:2
25 [a]Num. 14:2 14:24; Ezek. 6: 12:28 [b]Jer. 16 1:5 [c]Ezek. 12:2
27 [1]Lit., *days* 12:22; Dan. 10:
13:2 [1]Lit., *hear* 9:15; Jer. 37:19 22:25, 28 [b]Is. 1 Amos 7:16
3 [1]Heb., *YHWH* usually rendered and so through ch. [a]Lam. 2:14; 9:7; Zech. 11:15 23:28-32
5 [a]Ps. 106:23; 23:22; Ezek. 22: 58:12 [c]Is. 13:6, 7:19
6 [1]Lit., *vanity* [a]J 29:8; Ezek. 22:2 28:15; 37:19
7 [a]Ezek. 22:28
8 [1]Lit., *vanity* [a]E 5:8; 21:3; Nah. 2:
9 [1]Lit., *not be in* *and you will know* 20:3-6; 28:15-17 69:28; 87:6; Jer. Dan. 12:1
10 [a]Jer. 23:32; 50 [b]Jer. 6:14; 8:11; 14 [c]Ezek. 7:25; 13:16
11 [a]Ezek. 38:22
13 [a]Ex. 9:24, 25; 18:12, 13; Is. 30:30 Rev. 11:19; 16:21
14 [a]Mic. 1:6; Hab. [b]Jer. 6:15; 14:15 13:9

15 "Thus I shall spend My wrath on the wall and on those who have
plastered it over with whitewash; and I shall say to you, 'The wall [1]is
gone and its plasterers are gone,
16 *along with* the prophets of Israel who prophesy to Jerusalem, and
who [a]see visions of peace for her when there is [b]no peace,' declares
the Lord GOD.
17 "Now you, son of man, set your face against the daughters of
your people who are [a]prophesying [b]from their own [1]inspiration.
Prophesy against them,
18 and say, 'Thus says the Lord GOD, "Woe to the women who sew
magic bands on [1]all wrists, and make veils for the heads of *persons* of
every stature to [a]hunt down [2]lives! Will you hunt down the [2]lives of
My people, but preserve the [2]lives *of others* for yourselves?
19 "And [a]for handfuls of barley and fragments of bread, you have
profaned Me to My people to put to death [1]some who should not die
and to [b]keep [1]others alive who should not live, by your lying to My
people who listen to lies."' "
20 Therefore, thus says the Lord GOD, "Behold, I am against your
magic bands by which you hunt [1]lives there as [2]birds, and I will tear
them off your arms; and I will let [1]them go, even those [1]lives whom
you hunt as [2]birds.
21 "I will also tear off your veils and [a]deliver My people from your
hands, and they will no longer be in your hands to be hunted; and
you will know that I am the LORD.
22 "Because you [a]disheartened the righteous with falsehood when I
did not cause him grief, but have [1b]encouraged the wicked not to
[c]turn from his wicked way *and* preserve his life,
23 therefore, you women will no longer see [1a]false visions or practice divination, and I will [b]deliver My people out of your hand. Thus
you will [c]know that I am the LORD."

Chapter 14

14 Then some [a]elders of Israel came to me and [b]sat down
before me.
2 And the word of the LORD came to me saying,
3 "Son of man, these men have [a]set up their idols in their hearts,
and have [b]put right before their faces the stumbling block of their
iniquity. Should I be [c]consulted by them at all?
4 "Therefore speak to them and tell them, 'Thus says the Lord [1]GOD,
"Any man of the house of Israel who sets up his idols in his heart,
puts right before his face the stumbling block of his iniquity, and
then comes to the prophet, I the LORD will be brought to give him an
answer in [2]the matter in view of the [a]multitude of his idols,
5 in order to lay hold of [1a]the hearts of the house of Israel who are
[2b]estranged from Me through all their idols."'
6 "Therefore say to the house of Israel, 'Thus says the Lord GOD,
"[a]Repent and turn away from your idols, and turn your faces away
from all your [b]abominations.
7 "For anyone of the house of Israel or of the [a]immigrants who stay
in Israel who separates himself from Me, sets up his idols in his
heart, puts right before his face the stumbling block of his iniquity,
and *then* comes to the prophet to inquire of Me for himself, [b]I the
LORD will be brought to answer him in My own person.
8 "And I shall [a]set My face against that man and make him a [b]sign

[1]Lit., *is not . . . are not*
16 [a]Jer. 6:14; 8:11; ...k. 13:10 [b]Is. 57:21
[1]Lit., *heart* [a]Judg. ... 2 Kin. 22:14; Luke ...; Acts 21:9 [b]Ezek. 13:2; Rev. 2:20
...Lit., *all joints of the ...d*; M.T. reads *of my hands* [2]Or, *souls* [a]2 Pet. 2:14
... [1]Or, *souls* [a]Prov. ...:21; Mic. 3:5 [b]Jer. 23:14, 17
...0 [1]Lit., *souls* [2]Or, *flying ones*
...1 [a]Ps. 91:3; 124:7
...Lit., *strengthen the ...ds of* [a]Amos 5:12 ...r. 23:14; 34:16, 22 ... 18:21, 27, 30-32; 33:14-16
...Lit., *vanity* [a]Ezek. ...24; 13:6; Mic. 3:6; ...Zech. 13:3 [b]Ezek. ...:21; 34:10 [c]Ezek. 13:9, 21
...[a]2 Kin. 6:32; Ezek. ...1; 20:1 [b]Is. 29:13; Ezek. 33:31, 32
...zek. 20:16 [b]Ezek. 14:4, 7; Zeph. 1:3 ...s. 1:15; Jer. 11:11; Ezek. 20:3, 31
...4 [1]Heb., *YHWH*, ...y rendered *LORD*, ...so throughout the ...ch. [2]Lit., *it* [a]1 Kin. ...24; 2 Kin. 1:16; Is. 66:4
[1]Lit., *their* [2]Or, *all ...stranged from Me ...h their idols* [a]Jer. ...0; Zech. 7:12 [b]Is. ...: 2:11; Zech. 11:8
[a]1 Sam. 7:3; Neh. ...9; Is. 2:20; 30:22; ...:6, 7; Ezek. 18:30 [b]Ezek. 8:6; 14:4
[a]Ex. 12:48; 20:10 [b]Ezek. 14:4
[a]Jer. 44:11; Ezek. ... [b]Is. 65:15; Ezek. 5:15

and [1]a proverb, and I shall cut him off from among My people. So
you will know that I am the LORD.
9 "But if the prophet is [1]prevailed upon to speak a word, it is I, the
LORD, who have [1]prevailed upon that prophet, and I will stretch out
My hand against him and [a]destroy him from among My people
Israel.
10 "And they will bear *the punishment of* their iniquity; as the iniquity
of the inquirer is, so the iniquity of the prophet will be,
11 in order that the house of Israel may no longer [a]stray from Me
and no longer [b]defile themselves with all their transgressions. Thus
they will be [c]My people, and I shall be their God," ' declares the Lord
GOD."
12 Then the word of the LORD came to me saying,
13 "Son of man, if a country sins against Me by [a]committing unfaith-
fulness, and I stretch out My hand against it, [1]destroy its [b]supply of
bread, send famine against it, and cut off from it both man and beast,
14 even [a]*though* these three men, [b]Noah, [c]Daniel, and [d]Job were in its
midst, by their *own* righteousness they could *only* deliver [e]them-
selves," declares the Lord GOD.
15 "If I were to cause [a]wild beasts to pass through the land, and they
[1]depopulated it, and it became desolate so that no one would pass
through it because of the beasts,
16 *though* these three men were in its midst, as I live," declares the
Lord GOD, "they could not deliver either *their* sons or *their* daugh-
ters. [a]They alone would be delivered, but the country would be deso-
late.
17 "Or *if* I should [a]bring a sword on that country and say, 'Let the
sword pass through the country and [b]cut off man and beast from it,'
18 even *though* these three men were in its midst, as I live," declares
the Lord GOD, "they could not deliver either *their* sons or *their*
daughters, but they alone would be delivered.
19 "Or *if* I should send a [a]plague against that country and pour out
My wrath in blood on it, to cut off man and beast from it,
20 even *though* Noah, Daniel, and Job were in its midst, as I live,"
declares the Lord GOD, "they could not deliver either *their* son or
their daughter. They would deliver only themselves by their right-
eousness."
21 For thus says the Lord GOD, "How much more when [a]I send My
four [1]severe judgments against Jerusalem: sword, famine, wild
beasts, and plague to cut off man and beast from it!
22 "Yet, behold, [1]survivors will be left in it who will be brought out,
both sons and daughters. Behold, they are going to come forth to you
and you will [a]see their conduct and actions; then you will be [b]com-
forted for the calamity which I have brought against Jerusalem for
everything which I have brought upon it.
23 "Then they will comfort you when you see their conduct and
actions, for you will know that I have not done [a]in vain whatever I
did [1]to it," declares the Lord GOD.

Chapter 15

15 Then the word of the LORD came to me saying,
2 "Son of man, how is the wood of the [a]vine *better* than any
wood of a branch which is among the trees of the forest?

8 [1]Lit., *prover*

9 [1]Or, *enticed* 6:14, 15; 14:1

11 [a]Ezek. 44: 48:11 [b]Ezek. 37:23 [c]Ezek. 34:30; 36:28

13 [1]Lit., *break* [a]Ezek. 15:8; 20 [b]Lev. 26:26; Is. Ezek. 4:16

14 [a]Jer. 15:1 6:8; 7:1; Heb. 1 [c]Ezek. 28:3; Da 9:21; 10:11 [d]Jo 42:8, 9 [e]Ezek. 20; 18:20

15 [1]Lit., *bereav children* [a]Lev. 2 Num. 21:6; Eze 14:21

16 [a]Gen. 19:29 18:20

17 [a]Lev. 26:25; 5:12; 21:3, 4 [b]E 25:13; Zeph. 1:3

19 [a]Jer. 14:12; E 5:12; 14:21

21 [1]Lit., *evil* [a]Ez 5:17; 33:27; Amo 4:6-10; Rev. 6:8

22 [1]Lit., *escaped* [a]Ezek. 12:16; 36 [b]Ezek. 16:54; 31 32:31

23 [1]Or, *in* [a]Jer. 2

15:2 [a]Ps. 80:8-16 5:1-7; Hos. 10:1

3 "Can wood be taken from it to make [1]anything, or can *men* take a
peg from it on which to hang any vessel?
4 "[1]If it has been put into the [a]fire for fuel, *and* the fire has con-
sumed both of its ends, and its middle part has been charred, is it
then useful for [2]anything?
5 "Behold, while it is intact, it is not made into [1]anything. How
much less, when the fire has consumed it and it is charred, can it still
be made into [1]anything!
6 "Therefore, thus says the Lord [1]GOD, 'As the wood of the vine
among the trees of the forest, which I have given to the fire for fuel,
so have I given up the inhabitants of Jerusalem;
7 and I [a]set My face against them. *Though* they have [b]come out of
the fire, yet the fire will consume them. Then you will know that I
am the LORD, when I set My face against them.
8 'Thus I will make the land desolate, because they have [a]acted
unfaithfully,' " declares the Lord GOD.

Chapter 16

16 Then the word of the LORD came to me saying,
2 "Son of man, [a]make known to Jerusalem her abominations,
3 and say, 'Thus says the Lord [1]GOD to Jerusalem, "Your origin and
your birth are from the land of the Canaanite, your father was an
Amorite and your mother a Hittite.
4 "As for your birth, [a]on the day you were born your navel cord
was not cut, nor were you washed with water for cleansing; you
were not rubbed with salt or even wrapped in cloths.
5 "No eye looked with pity on you to do any of these things for
you, to have compassion on you. Rather you were thrown out into
the [1a]open field, [2]for you were abhorred on the day you were born.
6 "When I passed by you and saw you squirming in your blood, I
said to you *while you were* in your blood, 'Live!' I said to you while
you were in your blood, 'Live!'
7 "I [a]made you [1]numerous like plants of the field. Then you grew
up, became tall, and reached the age for fine ornaments; *your* breasts
were formed and your hair had grown. Yet you were naked and
bare.
8 "Then I passed by you and saw you, and behold, [1]you were at the
time for love; so I [a]spread My skirt over you and covered your
nakedness. I also [b]swore to you and [c]entered into a covenant with
you so that you [d]became Mine," declares the Lord GOD.
9 "Then I bathed you with water, washed off your blood from you,
and [a]anointed you with oil.
10 "I also clothed you with [a]embroidered cloth, and put sandals of
porpoise skin on your feet; and I wrapped you with fine linen and
covered you with silk.
11 "And I adorned you with ornaments, put [a]bracelets on your
hands, and a [b]necklace around your neck.
12 "I also put a [a]ring in your nostril, earrings in your ears, and a
[b]beautiful crown on your head.
13 "Thus you were adorned with [a]gold and silver, and your dress
was of fine linen, silk, and embroidered cloth. You ate fine flour,
honey, and oil; so you were exceedingly beautiful and advanced to
[b]royalty.
14 "Then your [a]fame went forth among the nations on account of

3 [1]Lit., *a work*
Behold [2]Lit., *a*
Is. 27:11; Ezek. 15:6; 19:14
5 [1]Lit., *a work*
[1]Heb., *YHWH*, rendered *LORD*, d so throughout the ch.
[a]Lev. 26:17; Ps. ler. 21:10; Ezek. [b]1 Kin. 19:17; Is. :18; Amos 9:1-4
ek. 14:13; 17:20
[a]Is. 58:1; Ezek. 20:4; 22:2
3 [1]Heb., *YHWH*, rendered *LORD*, nd so throughout the ch.
4 [a]Hos. 2:3
, *surface* [2]Lit., *in e loathing of your soul* [a]Deut. 32:10
it., *a myriad* [a]Ex. 1:7; Deut. 1:10
.it., *your time was* [a]Ruth 3:9; Jer. 2:2 en. 22:16-18 [c]Ex. [d]Ex. 19:5; Ezek. 0:5; Hos. 2:19, 20
9 [a]Ruth 3:3
[a]Ex. 26:36; Ezek. 16:13, 18; 26:16; 27:7, 16
Gen. 24:22, 47; Is. Ezek. 23:42 [b]Gen. 41:42; Prov. 1:9
2 [a]Gen. 24:47; Is. 3:21 [b]Is. 28:5; Jer. 13:18; Ezek. 16:14
13 [a]Ps. 45:13, 14; ek. 16:17 [b]1 Sam. 10:1; 1 Kin. 4:21
14 [a]1 Kin. 10:1, 24

your beauty, for it was [b]perfect because of My splendor which I
bestowed on you," declares the Lord GOD.
15 "But you [a]trusted in your beauty and [b]played the harlot because
of your fame, and you poured out your harlotries on every passer-by
[1]who might be *willing*.
16 "And you took some of your clothes, made for yourself high
places of various colors, and played the harlot on them, [1]which
should never come about nor happen.
17 "You also took your beautiful [1a]jewels *made* of My gold and of My
silver, which I had given you, and made for yourself male images
that you might play the harlot with them.
18 "Then you took your embroidered cloth and covered them, and
offered My oil and My incense before them.
19 "Also [a]My bread which I gave you, fine flour, oil, and honey with
which I fed you, [1]you would offer before them for a soothing aroma;
so it happened," declares the Lord GOD.
20 "Moreover, you took your sons and daughters whom you had
borne to [a]Me, and you [b]sacrificed them to [1]idols to be devoured.
Were your harlotries so small a matter?
21 "You slaughtered [a]My children, and offered them up to [1]idols by
[b]causing them to pass through *the fire*.
22 "And besides all your abominations and harlotries you did not
remember the days of [a]your youth, when you were naked and bare
and squirming in your blood.
23 "Then it came about after all your wickedness ('Woe, woe to you!'
declares the Lord GOD),
24 that you built yourself a [a]shrine and made yourself a [b]high place
in every square.
25 "You built yourself a high place at the top of [a]every street, and
made your beauty abominable; and you spread your legs to every
passer-by to multiply your harlotry.
26 "You also played the harlot with the Egyptians, your [1]lustful
neighbors, and multiplied your harlotry to [a]make Me angry.
27 "Behold now, I have stretched out My hand against you and
diminished your rations. And I delivered you up to the desire of
those who hate you, the [a]daughters of the Philistines, who are
ashamed of your lewd conduct.
28 "Moreover, you played the harlot with the [a]Assyrians because
you were not satisfied; you even played the harlot with them and
still were not satisfied.
29 "You also multiplied your harlotry with the land of merchants,
Chaldea, yet even with this you were not satisfied." ' "
30 "How [a]languishing is your heart," declares the Lord GOD, "while
you do all these things, the actions of a [1b]bold-faced harlot.
31 "When you built your shrine at the beginning of every street and
made your high place in every square, in [a]disdaining money, you
were not like a harlot.
32 "You adulteress wife, who takes strangers instead of her husband!
33 "[1]Men give gifts to all harlots, but you [a]give your gifts to all your
lovers to bribe them to come to you from every direction for your
harlotries.
34 "Thus you are different from those women in your harlotries, in
that no one plays the harlot [1]as you do, because you give money and
no money is given you; thus you are different."

14 [b]Ps. 50:2; L

15 [1]Lit., *to who* *might be* [a]Ezek 27:3 [b]Is. 57:8; J

16 [1]Lit., *things* *had not happen* *will it be*

17 [1]Lit., *articles* *beauty* [a]Ezek. 1

19 [1]Lit., *and you* *offer it* [a]Hos. 2:8

20 [1]Lit., *them* [a]E 13:2, 12; Deut. 2 12 [b]Ps. 106:37, 7:31; Ezek. 20:31

21 [1]Lit., *them* [a]E 13:2 [b]2 Kin. 17:1 19:5

22 [a]Jer. 2:2

24 [a]Jer. 11:13; Ez 16:31, 39; 20:28, [b]Ps. 78:58; Is. 57:

25 [a]Prov. 9:14

26 [1]Lit., *great of fl* [a]Jer. 7:18, 19; Eze

27 [a]Is. 9:12; Ezek.

28 [a]2 Kin. 16:7, 10 2 Chr. 28:16, 20-23 2:18, 36; Ezek. 23: Hos. 10:6

30 [1]Lit., *domineeri* [a]Prov. 9:13; Is. 1:3; 4:22 [b]Is. 3:9; Jer. 3

31 [a]Is. 52:3

33 [1]Lit., *they* [a]Is. 5 Ezek. 16:41; Hos. 8:9, 10

34 [1]Lit., *after you*

35 Therefore, O harlot, hear the word of the LORD.
36 Thus says the Lord GOD, "Because your lewdness was poured
out and your nakedness uncovered through your harlotries with
your lovers and with all your detestable [a]idols, and because of the
blood of your sons which you gave to [1]idols,
37 therefore, behold, I shall [a]gather all your lovers with whom you
took pleasure, even all those whom you loved *and* all those whom
you [b]hated. So I shall gather them against you from every direction
and [c]expose your nakedness to them that they may see all your
nakedness.
38 "Thus I shall [a]judge you, like women who commit adultery or
shed blood are judged; and I shall bring on you the blood of [b]wrath
and jealousy.
39 "I shall also give you into [1]the hands of your lovers, and they will
tear down your shrines, demolish your high places, [a]strip you of
your clothing, take away your [2]jewels, and will leave you naked and
bare.
40 "They will [1]incite a [a]crowd against you, and they will stone you
and cut you to pieces with their swords.
41 "And they will [a]burn your houses with fire and execute judg-
ments on you in the sight of many women. Then I shall [b]stop you
from playing the harlot, and you will also no longer pay [1]your
lovers.
42 "So I [a]shall calm My fury against you, and My jealousy will
depart from you, and I shall be pacified and angry [b]no more.
43 "Because you have [a]not remembered the days of your youth but
[1]have [b]enraged Me by all these things, behold, I in turn will [c]bring
your conduct down on your own head," declares the Lord GOD, "so
that you will not commit this lewdness on top of all your *other*
abominations.
44 "Behold, everyone who quotes [a]proverbs will quote *this* proverb
concerning you, saying, '[1]Like mother, [1]like daughter.'
45 "You are the daughter of your mother, who loathed her husband
and children. You are also the [a]sister of your sisters, who [b]loathed
their husbands and children. Your mother was a Hittite and your
father an Amorite.
46 "Now your [a]older sister is Samaria, who lives [1]north of you with
her [2]daughters; and your younger sister, who lives [3]south of you, is
[b]Sodom with her [2]daughters.
47 "Yet you have not merely walked in their ways or done according
to their abominations; but, as if that were [a]too little, you acted [b]more
corruptly in all your conduct than they.
48 "As I live," declares the Lord GOD, "Sodom, your sister, and her
daughters, have [a]not done as you and your daughters have done.
49 "Behold, this was the guilt of your sister Sodom: she and her
daughters had [a]arrogance, [b]abundant food, and [c]careless ease, but
she did not [1]help the [d]poor and needy.
50 "Thus they were haughty and committed [a]abominations before
Me. Therefore I [b]removed them [1]when I saw *it*.
51 "Furthermore, Samaria did not commit half of your sins, for you
have multiplied your abominations more than they. Thus you have
made your sisters appear [a]righteous by all your abominations which
you have committed.
52 "Also bear your disgrace in that you have [1]made judgment

36 [1]Lit., *them* [a]Jer. Ezek. 20:31; 23:37

37 [a]Jer. 13:22, 26; zek. 23:9, 22; Hos. 2:3, 10; Nah. 3:5, 6 zek. 23:17, 28 [c]Is. 47:3

[a]Ezek. 23:45 [b]Ps. 79:3, 5; Jer. 18:21; . 23:25; Zeph. 1:17

9 [1]Lit., *their hands, they* [2]Lit., *articles auty* [a]Ezek. 23:26; Hos. 2:3

0 [1]Lit., *bring up an nbly* [a]Ezek. 23:47; Hab. 1:6-10

[1]Lit., *a harlot's hire* Kin. 25:9; Jer. 39:8; 2:13 [b]Ezek. 23:48

42 [a]2 Sam. 24:25; 5:13; 21:17; Zech. [b]Is. 40:1, 2; 54:9, 10; Ezek. 39:29

3 [1]So with ancient versions; Heb., *are angry against* [a]Ps. :42; 106:13; Ezek. 2 [b]Is. 63:10; Ezek. Ezek. 11:21; 22:31

[1]Lit., *Her* [a]1 Sam. 3; Ezek. 12:22, 23; 18:2, 3

zek. 23:2 [b]Is. 1:4; k. 23:37-39; Zech. 11:8

6 [1]Lit., *on your left* [2]I.e., environs; so gh v. 55 [3]Lit., *from right* [a]Jer. 3:8-11; Ezek. 23:4 [b]Gen. 0-13; 18:20; Ezek. :48, 49, 53-56, 61

Kin. 16:31 [b]2 Kin. 21:9; Ezek. 5:6; 16:48, 51

48 [a]Matt. 10:15; 11:23, 24

it., *grasp the hand of* [a]Gen. 19:9; Ps. 38:6; Is. 3:9; Ezek. , 17 [b]Gen. 13:10; 22:13; Amos 6:4-6 ke 12:16-20; 16:19 Ezek. 18:7, 12, 16

Many ancient mss. d versions read *as have seen* [a]Gen. 13:13; 18:20; 19:5 [b]Gen. 19:24, 25

51 [a]Jer. 3:8-11

[1]Lit., *mediated for*

favorable for your sisters. Because of your sins in which you acted
[a]more abominably than they, they are more in the right than you.
Yes, be also ashamed and bear your disgrace, in that you made your
sisters appear righteous.
53 "Nevertheless, I will restore their captivity, the captivity of Sodom
and her daughters, the captivity of Samaria and her daughters, and
[1]along with them [2]your own captivity,
54 in order that you may bear your humiliation, and feel [a]ashamed
for all that you have done when you become [b]a consolation to them.
55 "And your sisters, Sodom with her daughters and Samaria with
her daughters, [1]will return to their former state, and you with your
daughters will *also* return to your former state.
56 "As *the name of* your sister Sodom was not heard from your lips in
your day of pride,
57 before your [a]wickedness was uncovered, [1]so now you have be-
come the [b]reproach of the daughters of [2]Edom, and of all who are
around her, of the daughters of the Philistines—those surrounding
you who despise you.
58 "You have [a]borne *the penalty of* your lewdness and abominations,"
the LORD declares.
59 For thus says the Lord GOD, "I will also do with you as you have
done, you who have [a]despised the oath by breaking the covenant.
60 "Nevertheless, I will remember My covenant with you in the days
of your youth, and I will establish an [a]everlasting covenant with you.
61 "Then you will [a]remember your ways and be ashamed when you
receive your sisters, *both* your older and your younger; and I will
give them to you as daughters, but not because of your covenant.
62 "Thus I will [a]establish My covenant with you, and you shall
[b]know that I am the LORD,
63 in order that you may [a]remember and be ashamed, and [b]never
open your mouth anymore because of your humiliation, when I
have [c]forgiven you for all that you have done," the Lord GOD
declares.

Chapter 17

17 Now the word of the LORD came to me saying,
2 "Son of man, propound a riddle, and speak a [a]parable to the
house of Israel,
3 [1]saying, 'Thus says the Lord [2]GOD, "A great [a]eagle with [b]great
wings, long pinions and a full plumage of many colors, came to
[c]Lebanon and took away the top of the cedar.
4 "He plucked off the topmost of its young twigs and brought it to
a land of merchants; he set it in a city of traders.
5 "He also took some of the seed of the land and planted it in
[1a]fertile soil. He [2]placed *it* beside abundant waters; he set it *like* a
[b]willow.
6 "Then it sprouted and became a low, spreading vine with its
branches turned toward him, but its roots remained under it. So it
became a vine, and yielded shoots and sent out branches.
7 "But there was [1]another great eagle with great wings and much
plumage; and behold, this vine bent its roots toward him and sent
out its branches toward him from the beds where it was [a]planted,
that he might water it.

52 [a]Ezek. 16:

53 [1]Lit., *in the* [2]Lit., *the captiv* *captivity*

54 [a]Jer. 2:26 14:22, 23

55 [1]Heb. inclu *return . . . state* Sodom also

57 [1]Lit., *as at t* *of* [2]So with ma and one versio *Aram* [a]Ezek. 1 [b]2 Kin. 16:5-7; 2 28:5, 6, 18-23; 5:14, 15; 22:4

58 [a]Ezek. 23:4

59 [a]Is. 24:5; Ez

60 [a]Is. 55:3; Jer 32:38-41; Ezek.

61 [a]Jer. 50:4, 5; 6:9

62 [a]Ezek. 20:37 37:26 [b]Jer. 24:7 20:43, 44

63 [a]Ezek. 36:31, Dan. 9:7, 8 [b]Ps. Rom. 3:19 [c]Ps. 6 78:38; 79:9

17:2 [a]Ezek. 20:4

3 [1]Lit., *and you s* *say* [2]Heb., *YHWH* usually rendered and so throughou ch. [a]Jer. 48:40; E 17:12; Hos. 8:1 [b] 4:22 [c]Jer. 22:23

5 [1]Lit., *a field of s* [2]Lit., *took* [a]Deut. 8 [b]Is. 44:4

7 [1]So with severa ancient versions; *one* [a]Ezek. 31:4

8 "It was planted in good [1]soil beside abundant waters, that it might yield branches and bear fruit, *and* become a splendid vine." '

9 "Say, 'Thus says the Lord GOD, "Will it thrive? Will he not pull up its roots and cut off its fruit, so that it withers—so that all its sprouting leaves wither? And neither by great [1]strength nor by many people can it be raised from its roots *again*.

10 "Behold, though it is planted, will it thrive? Will it not [a]completely wither as soon as the east wind strikes it—wither on the beds where it grew?" ' "

11 Moreover, the word of the LORD came to me saying,

12 "Say now to the [a]rebellious house, 'Do you not [b]know what these things *mean?'* Say, 'Behold, the [c]king of Babylon came to Jerusalem, took its king and princes, and brought them to him in Babylon.

13 'And he took one of the royal [1a]family and made a covenant with him, [2]putting him under [b]oath. He also took away the [c]mighty of the land,

14 that the kingdom might [a]be [1]in subjection, not exalting itself, *but* keeping his covenant, that it might continue.

15 'But he [a]rebelled against him by sending his envoys to Egypt that they might give him horses and many [1]troops. Will he succeed? Will he who does such things [b]escape? Can he indeed break the covenant and escape?

16 'As I live,' declares the Lord GOD, 'Surely in the [1]country of the king who [2]put him on the throne, whose oath he [a]despised, and whose covenant he broke, [3b]in Babylon he shall die.

17 'And [a]Pharaoh with *his* mighty army and great company will not [1]help him in the war, when they cast up mounds and build siege walls to cut off many lives.

18 'Now he despised the oath by breaking the covenant, and behold, he [1a]pledged his allegiance, yet did all these things; he shall not escape.' "

19 Therefore, thus says the Lord GOD, "As I live, surely My oath which he despised and My covenant which he broke, I will [1]inflict on his head.

20 "And I will spread My [a]net over him, and he will be [b]caught in My snare. Then I will bring him to Babylon and [c]enter into judgment with him there *regarding* the unfaithful act which he has committed against Me.

21 "And all the [1a]choice men in all his troops will fall by the sword, and the survivors will be scattered to every wind; and you will know that I, the LORD, have spoken."

22 Thus says the Lord GOD, "I shall also take *a sprig* from the lofty top of the cedar and set *it* out; I shall pluck from the topmost of its young twigs a tender one, and I shall plant *it* on a [a]high and lofty mountain.

23 "On the high mountain of Israel I shall plant it, that it may bring forth boughs and bear fruit, and become a stately [a]cedar. And birds of every [1]kind will [2]nest under it; they will [2]nest in the shade of its branches.

24 "And all the [a]trees of the field will know that I am the LORD; I bring down the high tree, exalt the low tree, dry up the green tree, and make the dry tree [b]flourish. I am the LORD; I have spoken, and I will perform *it*."

8 [1]Lit., *field*

9 [1]Lit., *arm*

ek. 19:14; Hos. 13:15

:. 2:3-5 [b]Ezek. ; 24:19 [c]2 Kin. 15; Ezek. 1:2; 17:3

seed [2]Lit., *and im to enter into* [a]2 Kin. 24:17; k. 17:5 [b]2 Chr. Kin. 24:15, 16

.it., *low* [a]Ezek. 29:14

people [a]2 Kin. Chr. 36:13; Jer. zek. 17:7 [b]Jer. 8:18, 23; Ezek. 17:18

Lit., *place* [2]Lit., *him king* [3]Lit., *him in Babylon* 4:17, 20; Ezek. 9; 17:13, 18, 19 11; Ezek. 12:13

it., *act with* [a]Is. r. 37:5, 7; Ezek. 29:6, 7

., *gave his hand* [a]1 Chr. 29:24

19 [1]Lit., *give it*

zek. 12:13; 32:3 9:5-7 [c]Jer. 2:35; Ezek. 20:35, 36

So many ancient d versions; M.T., *ves* [a]2 Kin. 25:5, k. 5:2, 10, 12-14

Ps. 72:16; Ezek. 20:40; 37:22

[1]Lit., *wing* [2]Lit., *dwell* [a]Ps. 92:12

4 [a]Ps. 96:12; Is. 5:12 [b]Amos 9:11

Chapter 18

18 Then the word of the LORD came to me saying,
2 "[a]What do you mean by using this proverb concerning the
land of Israel saying,
'[b]The fathers eat the sour grapes,
But the children's teeth [1]are set on edge'?
3 "As I live," declares the Lord [1]GOD, "you are surely not going to
use this proverb in Israel anymore.
4 "Behold, [a]all [1]souls are Mine; the [2]soul of the father as well as the
[2]soul of the son is Mine. The [3]soul who [b]sins will die.
5 "But if a man is righteous, and practices justice and righteousness,
6 and does not [a]eat at the mountain *shrines* or [b]lift up his eyes to
the idols of the house of Israel, or [c]defile his neighbor's wife, or
approach a woman during her menstrual period—
7 if a man does not oppress anyone, but [a]restores to the debtor his
pledge, [b]does not commit robbery, *but* [c]gives his bread to the hungry,
and covers the naked with clothing,
8 if he does not lend *money* on [a]interest or take [b]increase, *if* he
keeps his hand from iniquity, *and* [c]executes true justice between man
and man,
9 *if* he walks in [a]My statutes and My ordinances so as to deal
faithfully—[b]he is righteous *and* will surely [c]live," declares the Lord
GOD.
10 "Then he may [1]have a violent son who sheds blood, and who
does any of these things to a brother
11 (though he himself did not do any of these things), that is, he
even eats at the mountain *shrines*, and [a]defiles his neighbor's wife,
12 oppresses the [a]poor and needy, [b]commits robbery, does not re-
store a pledge, but lifts up his eyes to the idols, *and* [c]commits
abomination,
13 he [a]lends *money* on interest and takes increase; will he live? He
will not live! He has committed all these abominations, he will sure-
ly be put to death; his [b]blood will be [1]on his own head.
14 "Now behold, he [1]has a son who has observed all his father's sins
which he committed, and [a]observing does not do likewise.
15 "He does not eat at the mountain *shrines* or lift up his eyes to the
idols of the house of Israel, or defile his neighbor's wife,
16 or oppress anyone, or retain a pledge, or commit robbery, *but* he
[a]gives his bread to the hungry, and covers the naked with clothing,
17 he keeps his hand from [1]the poor, does not take interest or in-
crease, *but* executes My ordinances, and walks in My statutes; [a]he
will not die for his father's iniquity, he will surely live.
18 "As for his father, because he practiced extortion, robbed *his*
brother, and did what was not good among his people, behold, he
will die for his iniquity.
19 "Yet you say, '[a]Why should the son not bear the punishment for
the father's iniquity?' When the son has practiced [b]justice and right-
eousness, and has observed all My statutes and done them, he shall
surely live.
20 "The person who [a]sins will die. The [b]son will not bear the punish-
ment for the father's iniquity, nor will the father bear the punish-
ment for the son's iniquity; the [c]righteousness of the righteous will
be upon himself, and the wickedness of the wicked will be upon
himself.

18:2 [1]Lit., *bec* [a]Is. 3:15 [b]Jer. Lam. 5:7

3 [1]Heb., *YHW* usually render and so through the ch.

4 [1]Or, *lives* [2]C [3]Or, *person* [a]N 16:22; 27:16; Is 57:16 [b]Ezek. Rom. 6:23

6 [a]Ezek. 6:13; 22:9 [b]Deut. 4: 18:12, 15; 20:2 [c]Ezek. 18:15; 2

7 [a]Deut. 24:13 33:15; Amos 2: 19:13; Amos 3: [c]Deut. 15:11; E 18:16; Matt. 25 Luke 3:11

8 [a]Ex. 22:25; D 23:19, 20 [b]Lev. [c]Zech. 7:9; 8:16

9 [a]Lev. 18:5 [b]P [c]Amos 5:4; Hab Rom. 1:17

10 [1]Lit., *beget*

11 [a]1 Cor. 6:9

12 [a]Amos 4:1; 7:10 [b]Is. 59:6, 7 22:3, 17; Ezek. 18:7, 16, 18 [c]2 21:11; Ezek. 8:6

13 [1]Lit., *on him* 22:25 [b]Ezek. 33

14 [1]Lit., *begets* 29:6-10; 34:21

16 [a]Job 31:16, 2 41:1; Is. 58:7, 10 18:7

17 [1]So M.T.; Gr. *iniquity* as in v. 8 2:7

19 [a]Ex. 20:5; Jer Ezek. 18:2 [b]Ezek 20:18-20; Zech.

20 [a]2 Kin. 14:6; 22:18-20; Ezek. [b]Deut. 24:16; Jer. [c]1 Kin. 8:32; Is. 3 Matt. 16:27; Rom

21 "But if the [a]wicked man turns from all his sins which he has
committed and observes all My statutes and practices justice and
righteousness, he shall surely live; he shall not die.
22 "[a]All his transgressions which he has committed will not be
remembered against him; because of his [b]righteousness which he has
practiced, he will live.
23 "[a]Do I have any pleasure in the death of the wicked," declares the
Lord GOD, "[1]rather than that he should [b]turn from his ways and live?
24 "But when a righteous man [a]turns away from his righteousness,
commits iniquity, and does according to all the abominations that a
wicked man does, will he live? [b]All his righteous deeds which he has
done will not be remembered for his [c]treachery which he has com-
mitted and his sin which he has committed; for them he will die.
25 "Yet you say, '[a]The way of the Lord is not right.' Hear now, O
house of Israel! Is [b]My way not right? Is it not your ways that are not
right?
26 "When a righteous man turns away from his righteousness, com-
mits iniquity, and dies because of it, for his iniquity which he has
committed he will die.
27 "Again, when a wicked man turns away [a]from his wickedness
which he has committed and practices justice and righteousness, he
will save his life.
28 "Because he considered and turned away from all his transgres-
sions which he had committed, he shall surely live; he shall not die.
29 "But the house of Israel says, 'The way of the Lord is not right.'
Are My ways not right, O house of Israel? Is it not your ways that
are not right?
30 "Therefore I will judge you, O house of Israel, each according to
his conduct," declares the Lord GOD. "[a]Repent and turn away from
all your transgressions, so that iniquity may not become a stumbling
block to you.
31 "[a]Cast away from you all your transgressions which you have
committed, and make yourselves a [b]new heart and a new spirit! For
why will you die, O house of Israel?
32 "For I have [a]no pleasure in the death of anyone who dies,"
declares the Lord GOD. "Therefore, repent and live."

Chapter 19

19 "As for you, take up a [a]lamentation for the [b]princes of Israel,
2 and say,

'[1]What was your mother?
A lioness among lions!
She lay down among young lions,
She reared her cubs.
3 'When she brought up one of her cubs,
He became a lion,
And he learned to tear *his* prey;
He devoured men.
4 'Then nations heard about him;
He was captured in their pit,
And they [a]brought him with hooks
To the land of Egypt.
5 'When she saw, as she waited,
That her hope was lost,

[a]Ezek. 18:27, 28; 33:12, 19

22 [a]Is. 43:25; Jer.):20; Ezek. 18:24; 6; Mic. 7:19 [b]Ps. 18:20-24

t., *is it not* [a]Ezek. 18:32; 33:11 [b]Ps. 147:11; Mic. 7:18

4 [a]1 Sam. 15:11; Chr. 24:2, 17-22; zek. 3:20; 18:26; 18 [b]Ezek. 18:22; , 4 [c]Prov. 21:16; zek. 17:20; 20:27

ek. 18:29; 33:17, al. 2:17; 3:13-15 18:25; Jer. 12:1; Zeph. 3:5

7 [a]Is. 1:18; 55:7

zek. 14:6; 33:11; Hos. 12:6

s. 1:16, 17; 55:7 10; Ezek. 11:19; 36:26

ek. 18:23; 33:11

:1 [a]Ezek. 2:10; 2 Kin. 23:29, 30, 24:6, 12; 25:5-7

Dr, *Why did your* er, *a lioness, lie* wn *among lions;* young *lions rear her cubs?*

n. 23:34; 2 Chr. 36:4, 6

She took [1]another of her cubs
And made him a young lion.
6 'And he [a]walked about among the lions;
He became a young lion,
He learned to tear *his* prey;
He devoured men.
7 'And he [1]destroyed their [2]fortified towers
And laid waste their cities;
And the land and its fulness were appalled
Because of the sound of his roaring.
8 'Then [a]nations set against him
On every side from *their* provinces,
And they spread their net over him;
He was captured in their pit.
9 'And [a]they put him in a cage with hooks
And [b]brought him to the king of Babylon;
They brought him in hunting nets
So that his voice should be heard no more
On the mountains of Israel.
10 'Your mother was [a]like a vine in your [1]vineyard,
Planted by the waters;
It was fruitful and full of branches
Because of abundant waters.
11 'And it had [1a]strong branches *fit* for scepters of rulers,
And its [b]height was raised above the clouds
So that it was seen in its height with the mass of its branches.
12 'But it was [a]plucked up in fury;
It was [b]cast down to the ground;
And the [c]east wind dried up its fruit.
Its [1d]strong branch [2]was torn off
So that [3]it withered;
The fire consumed it.
13 'And now it is planted in the [a]wilderness,
In a dry and thirsty land.
14 'And [a]fire has gone out from *its* branch;
It has consumed its shoots *and* fruit,
So that there is not in it a [1]strong branch,
A scepter to rule.' "
This is a lamentation, and has become a lamentation.

Chapter 20

591 B.C.

20 Now it came about in the seventh year, in the fifth *month,* on
the tenth of the month, that [1]certain of the [a]elders of Israel
came to inquire of the LORD, and sat before me.
2 And the word of the LORD came to me saying,
3 "Son of man, speak to the elders of Israel, and say to them, 'Thus
says the Lord [1]GOD, "Do you come to inquire of Me? As I live,"
declares the Lord GOD, "[a]I will not be inquired of by you." '
4 "Will you judge them, will you judge them, son of man? [a]Make
them know the abominations of their fathers;
5 and say to them, 'Thus says the Lord GOD, "On the day when I
[a]chose Israel and [1]swore to the [2]descendants of the house of Jacob
and made Myself known to them in the land of Egypt, when I
[1]swore to them, saying, [b]I am the LORD your God,

5 [1]Lit., *one*

6 [a]2 Kin. 24: 36:9

7 [1]So Targur *knew* [2]Or, *w*

8 [a]2 Kin. 24:

9 [a]2 Chr. 36: 24:15

10 [1]So with s ancient mss.; *blood* [a]Ps. 80

11 [1]Lit., *rods strength* [a]Ps. [b]Ezek. 31:3

12 [1]Lit., *rods strength* [2]So *they were* [3]So *they* [a]Jer. 31:2 2:1; Ezek. 28: 17:10; Hos. 13 27:11; Ezek. 1

13 [a]2 Kin. 24: Ezek. 19:10; 2 Hos. 2:3

14 [1]Lit., *rod of* [a]Ezek. 15:4; 20

20:1 [1]Lit., *men* 8:1, 11, 12

3 [1]Heb., *YHWH* usually rendere and so througho ch. [a]Ezek. 14:3

4 [a]Ezek. 16:2; Matt. 23:32

5 [1]Lit., *lifted up hand,* and so thr the ch. [2]Lit., *see* 6:6-8 [b]Ex. 6:2, 3

6 on that day I swore to them, [a]to bring them out from the land of
Egypt into a land that I had [1]selected for them, [b]flowing with milk
and honey, which is [c]the glory of all lands.
7 "And I said to them, '[a]Cast away, each of you, the detestable
things of his eyes, and [b]do not defile yourselves with the idols of
Egypt; [c]I am the LORD your God.'
8 "But they [a]rebelled against Me and were not willing to listen to
Me; [1]they did not cast away the detestable things of their eyes, nor
did they forsake the [b]idols of Egypt.
Then I [2]resolved to [c]pour out My wrath on them, to accomplish
My anger against them in the midst of the land of Egypt.
9 "But I acted [a]for the sake of My name, that it should [b]not be
profaned in the sight of the nations among whom they *lived*, in
whose sight I made Myself known to them by bringing them out of
the land of Egypt.
10 "So I took them out of the land of Egypt and brought them into
the [a]wilderness.
11 "And I gave them My [a]statutes and informed them of My or-
dinances, by [b]which, if a man [1]observes them, he will live.
12 "And also I gave them My sabbaths to be a [a]sign between Me and
them, that they might know that I am the LORD who sanctifies them.
13 "But the house of Israel [a]rebelled against Me in the wilderness.
They did not walk in My statutes, and they rejected My ordinances,
[b]by which, if a man [1]observes them, he will live; and My [c]sabbaths
they greatly profaned. Then I [2]resolved to [d]pour out My wrath on
them in the wilderness, to annihilate them.
14 "But I acted for the sake of My name, that it should not be
profaned in the sight of the nations, before whose sight I had
brought them out.
15 "And also [a]I swore to them in the wilderness that I would not
bring them into the land which I had given them, flowing with milk
and honey, which is the glory of all lands,
16 because they rejected My ordinances, and as for My statutes,
they did not walk in them; they even profaned My sabbaths, for
their [a]heart continually went after their idols.
17 "Yet My eye spared them rather than destroying them, and I did
not cause their [a]annihilation in the wilderness.
18 "And I said to their [1a]children in the wilderness, '[b]Do not walk in
the statutes of your fathers, or keep their ordinances, or defile your-
selves with their idols.
19 '[a]I am the LORD your God; [b]walk in My statutes, and keep My
ordinances, and [1]observe them.
20 'And [a]sanctify My sabbaths; and they shall be a sign between Me
and you, that you may know that I am the LORD your God.'
21 "But the [a]children rebelled against Me; they did not walk in My
statutes, nor were they careful to observe My ordinances, by which,
if a man observes them, he will live; they profaned My sabbaths. So I
[1]resolved to pour out My wrath on them, to accomplish My anger
against them in the wilderness.
22 "But I [a]withdrew My hand and acted [b]for the sake of My name,
that it should not be profaned in the sight of the nations in whose
sight I had brought them out.
23 "Also I swore to them in the wilderness that I would [a]scatter them
among the nations and disperse them among the lands,

...it., *spied out* [a]Jer. ...22 [b]Ex. 13:5; 33:3 [c]Ps. 48:2
[a]Ex. 20:4, 5; 22:20 [b]Lev. 18:3; Deut. ...29:16-18 [c]Ex. 20:2
...it., *each one* [2]Lit., *said* [a]Deut. 9:7; Is. 63:10 [b]Ex. 32:1-9 [c]Ezek. 5:13; 7:8; 20:13, 21
...x. 32:11-14; Ezek. ...:14, 22; 36:21, 22 [b]Ezek. 39:7
10 [a]Ex. 19:1
...1 [1]Lit., *does* [a]Ex. ...23:33 [b]Lev. 18:5; Ezek. 20:13
...2 [a]Ex. 31:13, 17; Ezek. 20:20
...3 [1]Lit., *does* [2]Lit., [a]Num. 14:11, 12, Ezek. 20:8 [b]Lev. ...5 [c]Is. 56:6; Ezek. [d]Ex. 32:10; Deut. ...:8; Ezek. 20:8, 21
[a]Num. 14:30; Ps. 95:11; 106:26
16 [a]Ezek. 11:21; 14:3-7; 20:8
... [a]Jer. 4:27; 5:18; Ezek. 11:13
[1]Lit., *sons* [a]Num. ...4:31; Deut. 4:3-6 [b]Zech. 1:4
[1]Lit., *do* [a]Ex. 6:7; [b]Deut. 5:32, 33; ...8:1, 2; 11:1; 12:1
20 [a]Jer. 17:22
[1]Lit., *said* [a]Num. 21:5; 25:1-3
[a]Job 13:21; Ps. ...Ezek. 20:17 [b]Is. ...11; Jer. 14:7, 21; Ezek. 20:9, 14
...ev. 26:33; Deut. 4:27; 28:64

24 because they had not observed My ordinances, but had rejected
My statutes, and had profaned My sabbaths, and [a]their eyes were
[1]on the idols of their fathers.
25 "And I also gave them statutes that were [a]not good and ordinan-
ces by which they could not live;
26 and I pronounced them [a]unclean because of their gifts, in that
they [b]caused all [1]their first-born to pass through *the fire* so that I
might make them desolate, in order that they might [c]know that I am
the LORD." '
27 "Therefore, son of man, [a]speak to the house of Israel, and say to
them, 'Thus says the Lord GOD, "Yet in this your fathers have [b]blas-
phemed Me by [c]acting treacherously against Me.
28 "When I had [a]brought them into the land which I swore to give to
them, then they saw every [b]high hill and every leafy tree, and they
offered there their sacrifices, and there they presented the provoca-
tion of their offering. There also they made their soothing aroma,
and there they poured out their libations.
29 "Then I said to them, 'What is the high place to which you go?' So
its name is called [1]Bamah to this day." '
30 "Therefore, say to the house of Israel, 'Thus says the Lord GOD,
"Will you defile yourselves [1]after the manner of your [a]fathers and
play the harlot after their detestable things?
31 "And [1]when you offer your gifts, when you [a]cause your sons to
pass through the fire, you are defiling yourselves with all your idols
to this day. And shall I be inquired of by you, O house of Israel? As I
live," declares the Lord GOD, "I will not be inquired of by you.
32 "And what [a]comes [1]into your mind will not come about, when
you say: 'We will be like the nations, like the tribes of the lands,
[b]serving wood and stone.'
33 "As I live," declares the Lord GOD, "surely with a mighty hand
and with an [a]outstretched arm and with wrath poured out, I shall be
[b]king over you.
34 "And I shall [a]bring you out from the peoples and gather you from
the lands where you are scattered, with a mighty hand and with an
outstretched arm and with [b]wrath poured out;
35 and I shall bring you into the [a]wilderness of the peoples, and
there I shall enter into judgment with you face to face.
36 "As I [a]entered into judgment with your fathers in the [b]wilderness
of the land of Egypt, so I will enter into judgment with you,"
declares the Lord GOD.
37 "And I shall make you [a]pass under the rod, and I shall bring you
into the bond of the covenant;
38 and I shall [a]purge from you the rebels and those who transgress
against Me; I shall bring them out of the land where they sojourn,
but they will [b]not enter the [1]land of Israel. Thus you will know that I
am the LORD.
39 "As for you, O house of Israel," thus says the Lord GOD, "[a]Go,
serve everyone his idols; [1]but later, you will surely listen to Me, and
My holy name you will [b]profane no longer with your gifts and with
your idols.
40 "For on My holy mountain, on the high mountain of Israel," de-
clares the Lord GOD, "there the whole house of Israel, [a]all of them,
will serve Me in the land; there I shall [b]accept them, and there I shall

24 [1]Lit., *after*

25 [a]Ps. 81:12 Rom. 1:21-25

26 [1]Lit., *that w opens the wor* 18:21; 20:2-5; Ezek. 20:30; F [b]Jer. 7:31; 19: [c]Ezek. 6:7; 20

27 [a]Ezek. 2:7; 27 [b]Num. 15:3 2:24 [c]Ezek. 1 39:23, 26

28 [a]Josh. 23:3 Neh. 9:22-26; Jer. 2:7 [b]1 Kin. Ps. 78:58; Is. 5 Jer. 3:6; Ezek.

29 [1]Or, *High P*

30 [1]Lit., *in the* [a]Judg. 2:19; Je 16:12

31 [1]Lit., *in your up* [a]Ps. 106:37 7:31; Ezek. 16:

32 [1]Lit., *upon spirit* [a]Ezek. 11 2:25; 44:17

33 [a]Jer. 21:5 [b] 51:57

34 [a]Is. 27:12, 1 20:38; 34:16 [b]J 42:18; 44:6; Lan

35 [a]Ezek. 19:13 Hos. 2:14

36 [a]Num. 11:1-3 106:15; Ezek. 2 1 Cor. 10:5-10 [b] 32:10

37 [a]Lev. 27:32; 33:13

38 [1]Lit., *ground* [a]Ezek. 34:17-22; 9:9, 10; Zech. 13 Mal. 3:3; 4:1-3 [b] 14:29, 30; Ps. 95 Ezek. 13:9; 20:15 Heb. 4:3

39 [1]Or, *and after if you will not liste Me, but* [a]Jer. 44: [b]Is. 1:13-15; Ezek 23:38, 39; 43:7

40 [a]Is. 66:23; Ez 37:22, 24 [b]Is. 56 60:7; Ezek. 43:12

[1]seek your contributions and the choicest of your gifts, with all your
holy things.
41 "[1]As a soothing aroma I shall accept you, when I [a]bring you out
from the peoples and gather you from the lands where you are scat-
tered; and I shall prove Myself [b]holy among you in the sight of the
nations.
42 "And [a]you will know that I am the LORD, [b]when I bring you into
the land of Israel, into the [c]land which I swore to give to your
forefathers.
43 "And there you will [a]remember your ways and all your deeds,
with which you have defiled yourselves; and you will [b]loathe your-
selves in your own [1]sight for all the evil things that you have done.
44 "Then [a]you will know that I am the LORD when I have dealt with
you [b]for My name's sake, not according to your evil ways or accord-
ing to your corrupt deeds, O house of Israel," declares the Lord
GOD.' "
45 [1]Now the word of the LORD came to me saying,
46 "Son of man, set your face toward [1]Teman, and speak out against
the [a]south, and [b]prophesy against the [c]forest [2]land of the Negev,
47 and say to the forest of the Negev, 'Hear the word of the LORD:
thus says the Lord GOD, "Behold, I am about to [a]kindle a fire in you,
and it shall consume every [1]green tree in you, as well as every dry
tree; the blazing flame will not be quenched, and [2b]the whole surface
from south to north will be burned by it.
48 "And all flesh will see that I, the LORD, have kindled it; it shall
[a]not be quenched." ' "
49 Then I said, "Ah Lord GOD! They are saying of me, 'Is he not *just*
speaking [a]parables?' "

Chapter 21

21 [1]And the word of the LORD came to me saying,
2 "Son of man, [a]set your face toward Jerusalem, and [1b]speak
against the sanctuaries, and prophesy against the land of Israel;
3 and say to the land of Israel, 'Thus says the LORD, "Behold, [a]I am
against you; and I shall draw My sword out of its sheath and cut off
from you the [b]righteous and the wicked.
4 "Because I shall cut off from you the righteous and the wicked,
therefore My sword shall go forth from its sheath against [a]all flesh
from south *to* north.
5 "Thus all flesh will know that I, the LORD, have drawn My sword
out of its sheath. It will [a]not return *to its sheath* again." '
6 "As for you, son of man, groan with breaking [1]heart and bitter
grief, groan in their sight.
7 "And it will come about when they say to you, 'Why do you
groan?' that you will say, 'Because of the [a]news that is coming; and
[b]every heart will melt, all hands will be feeble, every spirit will [1]faint,
and all knees will [2]be weak as water. Behold, it comes and it will
happen,' declares the Lord [3]GOD."
8 Again the word of the LORD came to me saying,
9 "Son of man, prophesy and say, 'Thus says the LORD.' Say,
"[a]A sword, a sword sharpened
And also polished!
10 'Sharpened to make a [a]slaughter,
Polished [1]to flash like lightning!'

40 [1]Or, *require*
41 [1]Lit., *With* [a]Is. ...2, 13; Ezek. 11:17; ...25 [b]Is. 5:16; Ezek. 28:25; 36:23
...Ezek. 36:23; 38:23 ...Ezek. 11:17; 34:13; ...24 [c]Ezek. 20:6, 15
[1]Lit., *faces* [a]Ezek. ...9; 16:61, 63; Hos. ... [b]Jer. 31:18; Ezek. 36:31; Zech. 12:10
...Ezek. 24:24 [b]Ezek. 36:22
[1]Ch. 21:1 in Heb.
...Or, *the South* [2]Lit., ...*field* [a]Jer. 13:19; ...21:4 [b]Ezek. 21:2; ...7:16 [c]Is. 30:6-11
...Lit., *moist* [2]Or, *all* ...*ces* [a]Is. 9:18, 19; ...Jer. 21:14 [b]Is. 13:8
[a]Jer. 7:20; 17:27
...Ezek. 17:2; Matt. ...13:13; John 16:25
[1]Ch. 21:6 in Heb.
[1]Lit., *flow* [a]Ezek. 25:2; 28:21 [b]Job ...9:22; Ezek. 20:46
...21:13; Ezek. 5:8; ...13; 3:5 [b]Is. 57:1
...12:12; Ezek. 7:2; 20:47
...1 Sam. 3:12; Jer. ...20; Ezek. 21:30; Nah. 1:9
6 [1]Lit., *loins*
...Lit., *be dim* [2]Lit., ... [3]Heb., *YHWH*, rendered *LORD*, ...o throughout the ... [a]Ezek. 7:26 [b]Is. 13:7; Nah. 2:10
9 [a]Deut. 32:41
..., *lightning to be* ...*her* [a]Is. 34:5, 6

Or shall we rejoice, the [2]rod of My son [b]despising every tree?
11 "And it is given to be polished, that it may be handled; the sword
is sharpened and polished, to give it into the hand of the slayer.
12 "[a]Cry out and wail, son of man; for it is against My people, it is
against all the [b]officials of Israel. They are delivered over to the
sword with My people, therefore strike *your* thigh.
13 "For *there is* a testing; and what if even the [1]rod which despises
will be no more?" declares the Lord GOD.
14 "You therefore, son of man, prophesy, and clap *your* hands togeth-
er; and let the sword be [a]doubled the third time, the sword for the
slain. It is the sword for the great one slain, which surrounds them,
15 that *their* [a]hearts may melt, and many [b]fall at all their [c]gates. I
have given the glittering sword. Ah! It is made *for striking* like light-
ning, it is wrapped up *in readiness* for slaughter.
16 "[1]Show yourself sharp, go to the right; set yourself; go to the left,
wherever your [2]edge is appointed.
17 "I shall also clap My hands together, and I shall [1a]appease My
wrath; I, the LORD, have spoken."
18 And the word of the LORD came to me saying,
19 "As for you, son of man, [1a]make two ways for the sword of the
king of Babylon to come; both of them will go out of one land. And
[2]make a signpost; [3]make it at the head of the way to the city.
20 "You shall [1]mark a way for the sword to come to [a]Rabbah of the
sons of Ammon, and to Judah into [b]fortified Jerusalem.
21 "For the king of Babylon stands at the [1]parting of the way, at the
head of the two ways, to use [a]divination; he [b]shakes the arrows, he
consults the [2c]household idols, he looks at the liver.
22 "Into his right hand came the divination, 'Jerusalem,' to [a]set bat-
tering rams, to open the mouth [1]for slaughter, to lift up the voice
with a battle cry, to set battering rams against the gates, to cast up
mounds, to build a siege wall.
23 "And it will be to them like a false divination in their eyes; [a]they
have *sworn* solemn oaths. But he [b]brings iniquity to remembrance,
that they may be seized.
24 "Therefore, thus says the Lord GOD, 'Because you have made
your iniquity to be remembered, in that your transgressions are un-
covered, so that in all your deeds your sins appear—because you
have come to remembrance, you will be seized with the hand.
25 'And you, O slain, wicked one, the prince of Israel, whose [a]day
has come, in the time of the [1]punishment of the end,'
26 thus says the Lord GOD, 'Remove the turban, and take off the
[a]crown; this will *be* [1]no more the same. [b]Exalt that which is low, and
abase that which is high.
27 '[a]A ruin, a ruin, a ruin, I shall make it. This also will be no more,
until [b]He comes whose right it is; and I shall give it *to Him.*'
28 "And you, son of man, prophesy and say, 'Thus says the Lord
GOD concerning the sons of Ammon and concerning their [a]reproach,'
and say: 'A sword, a sword is drawn, polished for the slaughter, to
cause it [1]to [b]consume, that it may be like lightning—
29 while they see for you [a]false visions, while they divine lies for
you—to place you on the necks of the wicked who are slain, whose
day has come, in the [b]time of the [1]punishment of the end.
30 '[a]Return *it* to its sheath. In the [b]place where you were created, in
the land of your origin, I shall judge you.

10 [2]Or, *scepter* 110:5, 6; Ezek. 2
12 [a]Ezek. 21:6; 1:13 [b]Ezek. 21:2
13 [1]Or, *scepter*
14 [a]Lev. 26:21, 2 2 Kin. 24:1, 10-1
15 [a]Josh. 2:11; 2 17:10; Ps. 22:14; 21:7 [b]Is. 59:10; J 13:16; 18:15 [c]Je 17:27; Ezek. 21:1
16 [1]Or, *Unite you* [2]Lit., *face*
17 [1]Lit., *cause to* [a]Ezek. 5:13
19 [1]Or, *set for yo* [2]Lit., *cut out a har* [3]Lit., *cut it* [a]Jer. 1 Ezek. 4:1-3
20 [1]Lit., *set* [a]Deu 3:11; Jer. 49:2; Ez 25:5; Amos 1:14 48:12, 13; 125:1,
21 [1]Lit., *mother* *teraphim* [a]Num. 2 23:23 [b]Prov. 16:3 [c]Gen. 31:19, 30; 17:5; 18:17, 20
22 [1]Lit., *in* [a]Ezek 26:9
23 [a]Ezek. 17:16, [b]Num. 5:15; Ezek 21:24; 29:16
25 [1]Or, *iniquity* 37:13; Ezek. 7:2,
26 [1]Lit., *not this* 13:18; Ezek. 16:1 75:7; Ezek. 17:24
27 [a]Hag. 2:21, 2 2:6; 72:7, 10; Jer. 6; Ezek. 34:24; 3
28 [1]Lit., *to finish* 36:15; Zeph. 2:8- 31:8; Jer. 12:12; 46:10, 14
29 [1]Or, *iniquity* 27:9; Ezek. 13:6- 22:28 [b]Ezek. 21 35:5
30 [a]Jer. 47:6, 7 25:5

31 'And I shall [a]pour out My indignation on you; I shall [b]blow on
you with the fire of My wrath, and I shall give you into the hand of
brutal men, [1c]skilled in destruction.
32 'You will be [1a]fuel for the fire; your blood will be in the midst of
the land. You will [b]not be remembered, for I, the LORD, have
spoken.' "

Chapter 22

22 Then the word of the LORD came to me saying,
2 "And you, son of man, will you judge, will you judge the
bloody city? Then cause her to know all her abominations.
3 "And you shall say, 'Thus says the Lord [1]GOD, "A city [a]shedding
blood in her midst, so that her time will come, and that makes idols,
contrary to her *interest*, for defilement!
4 "You have become [a]guilty by [1]the blood which you have shed,
and defiled by your idols which you have made. Thus you have
brought your [2]day near and have come to your years; therefore I
have made you a [b] reproach to the nations, and a mocking to all the
lands.
5 "Those who are near and those who are far from you will mock
you, you of ill repute, full of [a]turmoil.
6 "Behold, the [a]rulers of Israel, each according to his [1]power, have
been in you for the purpose of shedding blood.
7 "They have [a]treated father and mother lightly within you. The
[b]alien they have oppressed in your midst; the [c]fatherless and the
widow they have wronged in you.
8 "You have [a]despised My holy things and [b]profaned My sabbaths.
9 "Slanderous men have been in you for the purpose of shedding
blood, and in you they have eaten at the mountain *shrines*. In your
midst they have [a]committed acts of lewdness.
10 "In you [1]they have [a]uncovered *their* fathers' nakedness; in you
they have humbled her who was [b]unclean in her menstrual impurity.
11 "And one has committed abomination with his [a]neighbor's wife,
and another has lewdly defiled his [b]daughter-in-law. And another in
you has [c]humbled his sister, his father's daughter.
12 "In you they have [a]taken bribes to shed blood; you have taken
[b]interest and profits, and you have injured your neighbors for gain
by [c]oppression, and you have [d]forgotten Me," declares the Lord GOD.
13 "Behold, then, I smite My hand at your [a]dishonest gain which you
have acquired and at [1]the bloodshed which is among you.
14 "Can [a]your heart endure, or can your hands be strong, in the days
that I shall deal with you? [b]I, the LORD, have spoken and shall act.
15 "And I shall [a]scatter you among the nations, and I shall disperse
you through the lands, and I shall [b]consume your uncleanness from
you.
16 "And you will profane yourself in the sight of the nations, and
you will [a]know that I am the LORD." ' "
17 And the word of the LORD came to me saying,
18 "Son of man, the house of Israel has become [a]dross to Me; all of
them are [b]bronze and tin and iron and lead in the [c]furnace; they are
the dross of silver.
19 "Therefore, thus says the Lord GOD, 'Because all of you have be-
come dross, therefore, behold, I am going to gather you into the
midst of Jerusalem.

[1]Or, *artisans of*
:19; 25:7; Nah.
[b]Ps. 18:15; Is.
zek. 22:20, 21;
[c]Jer. 4:7; 6:22,
51:20-23; Hab.
1:6, 10

t., *food* [a]Ezek.
17, 48; Mal. 4:1
[b]Ezek. 25:10

[1]Heb., *YHWH*,
endered *LORD*,
throughout the
Ezek. 22:6, 27;
23:37, 45

your [2]Lit., *days*
n. 21:16; Ezek.
[b]Ps. 44:13, 14;
5:14, 15; 16:57

5 [a]Is. 22:2

, *arm* [a]Is. 1:23;
Ezek. 22:27

0:12; Lev. 20:9;
:16; 27:16 [b]Ex.
21f.; 23:9; Deut.
; Jer. 7:6; Zech.
Ex. 22:22; Ezek.
22:25; Mal. 3:5

k. 22:26 [b]Ezek.
1, 24; 23:38, 39

zek. 23:29; Hos.
4:2, 10, 14

it., *he has* [a]Lev.
ev. 18:19; Ezek.
18:6

ek. 18:11; 33:26
. 18:15 [c]2 Sam.
13:11-14

[a]Ex. 23:8; Deut.
; 27:25; Mic. 7:2,
Lev. 25:36; Deut.
[c]Lev. 19:13 [d]Ps.
:21; Ezek. 23:35

, *your* [a]Is. 33:15;
os 2:6-8; Mic. 2:2

zek. 21:7 [b]Ezek.
17:24

[a]Deut. 4:27; Neh.
zek. 20:23; Zech.
[b]Ezek. 23:27, 48

83:18; Ezek. 6:7

[a]Ps. 119:119; Is.
2; Lam. 4:1 [b]Jer.
0 [c]Prov. 17:3; Is.
48:10

20 'As they gather silver and bronze and iron and lead and tin into the [a]furnace to blow fire on it in order to melt *it,* so I shall gather *you* in My anger and in My wrath, and I shall lay you *there* and melt you.
21 'And I shall gather you and blow on you with the fire of My wrath, and you will be melted in the midst of it.
22 'As silver is melted in the furnace, so you will be melted in the midst of it; and you will know that I, the LORD, have [a]poured out My wrath on you.' "
23 And the word of the LORD came to me saying,
24 "Son of man, say to her, 'You are a land that is [a]not cleansed or rained on in the day of indignation.'
25 "There is a [a]conspiracy of her prophets in her midst, like a roaring lion tearing the prey. They have [b]devoured lives; they have taken treasure and precious things; they have made many [c]widows in the midst of her.
26 "Her [a]priests have done violence to My law and have [b]profaned My holy things; they have made no [c]distinction between the holy and the profane, and they have not taught the difference between the [d]unclean and the clean; and they hide their eyes from My sabbaths, and I am profaned among them.
27 "Her princes within her are like wolves tearing the prey, by shedding blood *and* [a]destroying lives in order to get [b] dishonest gain.
28 "And her prophets have smeared whitewash for them, seeing [a]false visions and divining lies for them, saying, 'Thus says the Lord GOD,' when the LORD has not spoken.
29 "The people of the land have practiced [a]oppression and committed robbery, and they have wronged the poor and needy and have [b]oppressed the sojourner without justice.
30 "And I [a]searched for a man among them who should [b]build up the wall and [c]stand in the gap before Me for the land, that I should not destroy it; but I found [1]no one.
31 "Thus I have poured out My [a]indignation on them; I have consumed them with the fire of My wrath; [b]their way I have brought upon their heads," declares the Lord GOD.

Chapter 23

23 The word of the LORD came to me again saying,
2 "Son of man, there were [a]two women, the daughters of one mother;
3 and they played the harlot in Egypt. They [a]played the harlot in their youth; there their breasts were pressed, and there their virgin bosom was handled.
4 "And their names were Oholah the elder and Oholibah her sister. And they became Mine, and they bore sons and daughters. And *as for* their names, Samaria is Oholah, and Jerusalem is Oholibah.
5 "And Oholah played the harlot [1]while she was Mine; and she lusted after her lovers, after the [a]Assyrians, *her* neighbors,
6 who were clothed in purple, [a]governors and officials, all of them desirable young men, horsemen riding on horses.
7 "And she bestowed her harlotries on them, all of whom *were* the choicest [1]men of Assyria; and with all whom she lusted after, with all their idols she [a]defiled herself.
8 "And she did not forsake her harlotries [a]from *the time in* Egypt; for

20 [a]Is. 1:25
22 [a]Ezek. 20:8; Hos. 5:10
24 [a]Is. 9:13; Je Ezek. 24:13; Z
25 [a]Jer. 11:9; [b]Jer. 2:34; Eze 22:27 [c]Jer. 15: 22:7
26 [a]Jer. 2:8, 26 7:26 [b]1 Sam. 2 22; Ezek. 22:8 10:10; Ezek. 44 [d]Hag. 2:11-14
27 [a]Ezek. 22:2 22:13
28 [a]Jer. 23:25- Ezek. 13:6
29 [a]Is. 5:7; Eze 22:7; Amos 3:1 23:9
30 [1]Lit., *not* [a]Is 63:5; Jer. 5:1 [b] 13:5 [c]Ps. 106:2 15:1
31 [a]Is. 10:5; 13 30:27; Ezek. 22 [b]Ezek. 7:3, 8, 9; 16:43; Rom. 2:8
23:2 [a]Ezek. 16:
3 [a]Lev. 17:7; Je
5 [1]Lit., *under M* [a]2 Kin. 15:19; 16 17:3; Ezek. 16:2 5:13; 8:9, 10
6 [a]Ezek. 23:12,
7 [1]Lit., *sons of A* [a]Ezek. 20:7; 22:3 Hos. 5:3; 6:10
8 [a]Ex. 32:4; 1 Ki 12:28; 2 Kin. 10:2 17:16; Ezek. 23:

in her youth [1]men had lain with her, and they handled her virgin
bosom and poured out their [2]lust on her.
9 "Therefore, I gave her into the hand of her [a]lovers, into the hand
of the [1]Assyrians, after whom she lusted.
10 "They [a]uncovered her nakedness; they took her sons and her
daughters, but they slew her with the sword. Thus she became a
[1]byword among women, and they executed judgments on her.
11 "Now her sister Oholibah saw *this,* yet she was [a]more corrupt in
her lust than she, and her harlotries were more than the harlotries of
her sister.
12 "She lusted after the [1a]Assyrians, governors and officials, the ones
near, magnificently dressed, horsemen riding on horses, all of them
desirable young men.
13 "And I saw that she had defiled herself; they both took [1]the same
way.
14 "So she increased her harlotries. And she saw men [a]portrayed on
the wall, images of the [b]Chaldeans portrayed with vermilion,
15 girded with belts on their loins, with flowing turbans on their
heads, all of them looking like officers, [1]like the [2]Babylonians *in*
Chaldea, the land of their birth.
16 "And [1]when she saw them she [a]lusted after them and sent mes-
sengers to them in Chaldea.
17 "And the [1a]Babylonians came to her to the bed of love, and they
defiled her with their harlotry. And when she had been defiled by
them, [2]she became disgusted with them.
18 "And she [a]uncovered her harlotries and uncovered her naked-
ness; then [1]I became [b]disgusted with her, as [1]I had become disgusted
with her [c]sister.
19 "Yet she multiplied her harlotries, remembering the days of her
youth, when she played the harlot in the land of Egypt.
20 "And she [a]lusted after their paramours, whose flesh is *like* the
flesh of donkeys and whose issue is *like* the issue of horses.
21 "Thus you longed for the [a]lewdness of your youth, when [1]the
Egyptians handled your bosom because of the breasts of your youth.
22 "Therefore, O Oholibah, thus says the Lord [1]GOD, 'Behold I will
arouse your lovers against you, from whom [2]you were alienated,
and I will bring them against you from every side:
23 the [1a]Babylonians and all the [b]Chaldeans, [c]Pekod and Shoa and
Koa, *and* all the [2d]Assyrians with them; desirable young men, gover-
nors and officials all of them, officers and [3]men of renown, all of
them riding on horses.
24 'And they will come against you with weapons, [a]chariots, and
[1]wagons, and with a company of peoples. They will set themselves
against you on every side with buckler and shield and helmet; and I
shall commit the [b]judgment to them, and they will judge you accord-
ing to their customs.
25 'And I will set My [a]jealousy against you, that they may deal with
you in wrath. They will remove your nose and your ears; and your
[1]survivors will fall by the sword. They will take your [b]sons and your
daughters; and your [1]survivors will be consumed by the fire.
26 'They will also [a]strip you of your clothes and take away your
[b]beautiful jewels.
27 'Thus [a]I shall make your lewdness and your harlotry *brought*

8 [1]Lit., *they* [2]Lit., *harlotry*
Lit., *sons of Asshur* Ezek. 16:37; 23:22
[1]Lit., *name* [a]Ezek. 16:37, 41
[a]Jer. 3:8-11; Ezek. 16:51
Lit., *sons of Asshur* [a]2 Kin. 16:7
13 [1]Lit., *one*
Ezek. 8:10 [b]Ezek. 16:29
Lit., *the likeness of* [2]Lit., *sons of Babel*
[1]Lit., *at the sight of* *yes* [a]Ezek. 23:20; Matt. 5:28
Lit., *sons of Babel* Lit., *her soul* [a]2 Kin. 24:17
Lit., *My soul* [a]Jer. 6:12; Ezek. 21:24; 23:10 [b]Ps. 78:59; Jer. 12:8 [c]Ezek. 23:9; Amos 5:21
Ezek. 16:26; 17:15
So two mss.; M.T., *in Egypt* [a]Jer. 3:9; Ezek. 23:3
22 [1]Heb., *YHWH,* *y rendered* LORD, *so throughout the* Lit., *your soul was alienated*
23 [1]Lit., *sons of* *ylon* [2]Lit., *sons of* *ia* [3]Lit., *the called* [a]2 Kin. 20:14-17; 21:19; 23:14-17 n. 24:2; Job 1:17; 23:13 [c]Jer. 50:21 2:14; 25:18; Ezra 6:22
[1]Lit., *wheels* [a]Jer. Ezek. 26:10; Nah. 3, 4 [b]Jer. 39:5, 6; Ezek. 16:38; 23:45
Lit., *remainder* [a]Ex. Ezek. 5:13; 8:17, Zeph. 1:18 [b]Ezek. 23:47; Hos. 2:4
[a]Jer. 13:22; Ezek. 16:39; 23:29 [b]Is. 3:18-23
27 [a]Ezek. 16:41

from the land of Egypt to cease from you, so that you will not lift up
your eyes to them or remember Egypt anymore.'
28 "For thus says the Lord GOD, 'Behold, I will give you into the
hand of those whom you [a]hate, into the hand of those from whom
[1]you were alienated.
29 'And they will [a]deal with you in hatred, take all your property,
and leave you naked and bare. And the nakedness of your harlotries
shall be uncovered, both your lewdness and your harlotries.
30 'These things will be done to you because you have [a]played the
harlot with the nations, because you have defiled yourself with their
idols.
31 'You have walked in the way of your sister; therefore I will give
[a]her cup into your hand.'
32 "Thus says the Lord GOD,
'You will [a]drink your sister's cup,
Which is deep and wide.
[1]You will be [b]laughed at and held in derision;
It contains much.
33 'You will be filled with [a]drunkenness and sorrow,
The cup of horror and desolation,
The cup of your sister Samaria.
34 'And you will [a]drink it and drain it.
Then you will gnaw its fragments
And tear your breasts;
for I have spoken,' declares the Lord GOD.
35 "Therefore, thus says the Lord GOD, 'Because you have [a]forgotten
Me and [b]cast Me behind your back, bear now the *punishment* of your
lewdness and your harlotries.' "
36 Moreover, the LORD said to me, "Son of man, will you [a]judge
Oholah and Oholibah? Then [b]declare to them their abominations.
37 "For they have committed adultery, and blood is on their hands.
Thus they have committed adultery with their idols and even caused
their sons, [a]whom they bore to Me, to pass through *the fire* to [1]them
as food.
38 "Again, they have done this to Me: they have [a]defiled My sanctu-
ary on the same day and have [b]profaned My sabbaths.
39 "For when they had slaughtered their children for their idols,
they entered My [a]sanctuary on the same day to profane it; and lo,
thus they did within My house.
40 "Furthermore, [1]they have even sent for men who come from afar,
to whom a messenger was sent; and lo, they came—for whom you
bathed, [a]painted your eyes, and [b]decorated yourselves with orna-
ments;
41 and you sat on a splendid [a]couch with a [b]table arranged before it,
on which you had set My [c]incense and My [c]oil.
42 "And the sound of a [1a]carefree multitude was with her; and
[b]drunkards were brought from the wilderness with men of the [2]com-
mon sort. And they put [c]bracelets on [3]the hands of the women and
beautiful crowns on their heads.
43 "Then I said concerning her who was [a]worn out by adulteries,
'[1]Will they now commit adultery with her when she is *thus*?'
44 "[1]But they went in to her as they would go in to a harlot. Thus
they went in to Oholah and to Oholibah, the lewd women.
45 "But they, righteous men, will [a]judge them with the judgment of

28 [1]Lit., *your s* *alienated* [a]Jer. 34:20; Ezek. 1 23:17, 22

29 [a]Deut. 28:4 23:25, 26, 45-4

30 [a]Ezek. 6:9

31 [a]2 Kin. 21:1 7:14, 15; Ezek.

32 [1]Or, *It will b* *jesting and der* *because of its* *size* [a]Ps. 60:3 51:17; Jer. 25:1 [b]Ezek. 5:14, 15 22:4, 5

33 [a]Jer. 25:15 Hab. 2:16

34 [a]Ps. 75:8; Is

35 [a]Is. 17:10; J Ezek. 22:12; H 13:6 [b]1 Kin. 14 2:27; 32:33

36 [a]Jer. 1:10; E 20:4; 22:2 [b]Is. Ezek. 16:2; Mic

37 [1]I.e., idols 16:20; 20:26

38 [a]2 Kin. 21:4, Ezek. 5:11; 7:20 17:27; Ezek. 20

39 [a]Jer. 7:9-11

40 [1]Or, *you* (wo [a]2 Kin. 9:30; Jer [b]Is. 3:18-23; Ez 16:13-16

41 [a]Esth. 1:6; Is Amos 6:4 [b]Is. 6 Ezek. 44:16 [c]Je Hos. 2:8

42 [1]Lit., *at ease* *multitude of mar* [3]Lit., *their hands* 16:49; Amos 6:3 51:7 [c]Gen. 24:3 16:11, 12

43 [1]Or, *Now the* *commit adultery* *her, and she with* [a]Ezek. 23:3

44 [1]Or, *And*

45 [a]Ezek. 16:38

adulteresses, and with the judgment of women who shed blood,
because they are adulteresses and blood is on their hands.
46 "For thus says the Lord GOD, 'Bring up a company against them,
and give them over to [a]terror and plunder.
47 'And the company will [a]stone them with stones and cut them
down with their swords; they will slay their sons and their daugh-
ters and [b]burn their houses with fire.
48 'Thus I shall make lewdness cease from the land, that all women
may be admonished and not commit [1]lewdness as you have done.
49 'And your lewdness [1]will be [a]requited upon you, and you will
bear the penalty of *worshiping* your idols; thus you will know that I
am the Lord GOD.' "

Chapter 24

24 And the word of the LORD came to me in the ninth year, in the
tenth month, on the tenth of the month, saying, 588 B.C.
2 "Son of man, write the name of the day, this very day. The king of
Babylon [1]has [a]laid siege to Jerusalem this very day.
3 "And speak a [a]parable to the [b]rebellious house, and say to them,
'Thus says the Lord [1]GOD,

"Put on the [c]pot, put *it* on, and also pour water in it;
4 [1a]Put in it the pieces,
Every good piece, the thigh, and the shoulder;
Fill *it* with choice bones.
5 "Take the [a]choicest of the flock,
And also pile [1]wood under [2]the pot.
Make it boil vigorously.
Also seethe its bones in it."

6 'Therefore, thus says the Lord GOD,
"Woe to the [a]bloody city,
To the pot in which there is rust
And whose rust has not gone out of it!
Take out of it piece after piece,
[1]Without making a choice.
7 "For her blood is in her midst;
She placed it on the bare rock;
She did not [a]pour it on the ground
To cover it with dust.
8 "That it may [a]cause wrath to come up to take vengeance,
I have put her blood on the bare rock,
That it may not be covered."
9 'Therefore, thus says the Lord GOD,
"[a]Woe to the bloody city!
I also shall make the pile great.
10 "Heap on the wood, kindle the fire,
[1]Boil the flesh well,
And mix in the spices,
And let the bones be burned.
11 "Then [a]set it empty on its coals,
So that it may be hot,
And its bronze may [1]glow,
And its [b]filthiness may be melted in it,
Its rust consumed.

6 [a]Jer. 15:4; 24:9; 29:18
[a]Lev. 20:10; Ezek. 16:40 [b]Jer. 39:8
[1]Lit., *according to your lewdness*
[1]Lit., *they will give* ...9:18; Ezek. 7:4, 9; 9:10; 23:35
2 [1]Lit., *leaned on* ...n. 25:1; Jer. 39:1; 52:4
3 [1]Heb., *YHWH*, ...y rendered *LORD*, so throughout the [a]Ps. 78:2; Ezek. ...:2; 20:49 [b]Is. 1:2; ...9; Ezek. 2:3, 6, 8 ...er. 1:13, 14; Ezek. 11:3, 7, 11; 24:6
[1]Lit., *Gather her* ...*eces* [a]Mic. 3:2, 3
...Lit., *bones* [2]Lit., *it* ...9:6; 52:10, 24-27
...No lot has fallen ...it [a]2 Kin. 24:3, 4; ...22:2, 3, 27; Mic. 7:2; Nah. 3:1
...Lev. 17:13; Deut. 12:16
8 [a]Is. 26:21
...24:6; Hab. 2:12
...0 [1]Lit., *Complete*
[1]Lit., *become hot* ...r. 21:10; Mal. 4:1 ...zek. 22:15; 23:27

12 "She has [a]wearied *Me* with toil,
Yet her great rust has not gone from her;
Let her rust *be* in the fire!
13 "In your filthiness is lewdness.
Because I *would* have cleansed you,
Yet you are [a]not clean,
You will not be cleansed from your filthiness again,
Until I have [1b]spent My wrath on you.
14 "I, the LORD, have spoken; it is [a]coming and I shall act. I shall not
relent, and I shall not [b]pity, and I shall not be sorry; [c]according to
your ways and according to your deeds [1]I shall judge you," declares
the Lord GOD.' "
15 And the word of the LORD came to me saying,
16 "Son of man, behold, I am about to take from you the [a]desire of
your eyes with a [b]blow; but you shall not [c]mourn, and you shall not
weep, and your [d]tears shall not come.
17 "Groan silently; make [a]no mourning for the dead. Bind on your
turban, and put your shoes on your feet, and do not cover *your*
mustache, and [b]do not eat the bread of men."
18 So I spoke to the people in the morning, and in the evening my
wife died. And in the morning I did as I was commanded.
19 And the people said to me, "Will you not tell us what these
things that you are doing mean for us?"
20 Then I said to them, "The word of the LORD came to me saying,
21 'Speak to the house of Israel, "Thus says the Lord GOD, 'Behold, I
am about to profane My sanctuary, the pride of your power, the
[a]desire of your eyes, and the delight of your soul; and your [b]sons and
your daughters whom you have left behind will fall by the sword.
22 'And you will do as I have done; you will not cover *your* mus-
tache, and you will not eat the bread of men.
23 'And your turbans will be on your heads and your shoes on your
feet. You [a]will not mourn, and you will not weep; but [b]you will rot
away in your iniquities, and you will groan [1]to one another.
24 'Thus Ezekiel will be a [a]sign to you; according to all that he has
done you will do; when it comes, then you will know that I am the
Lord GOD.' "
25 'As for you, son of man, will *it* not be on the day when I take
from them their [a]stronghold, the joy of their [1]pride, the desire of their
eyes, and [2]their heart's delight, their sons and their daughters,
26 that on that day he who [a]escapes will come to you with informa-
tion for *your* ears?
27 'On that day your [a]mouth will be opened to him who escaped,
and you will speak and be dumb no longer. Thus you will be a sign
to them, and they will know that I am the LORD.' "

Chapter 25

25 And the word of the LORD came to me saying,
2 "Son of man, set your face toward the [a]sons of Ammon, and
prophesy against them,
3 and say to the sons of Ammon, 'Hear the word of the Lord [1]GOD!
Thus says the Lord GOD, "Because you said, '[a]Aha!' against My
sanctuary when it was profaned, and against the land of Israel when
it was made desolate, and against the house of Judah when they
went into exile,

12 [a]Jer. 9:5

13 [1]Lit., *cause* [a]Jer. 6:28-30; E 22:24 [b]Ezek. 5

14 [1]So with se ancient mss. ar versions; M.T., [a]Ps. 33:9; Is. 55 [b]Jer. 13:14; Eze [c]Is. 3:11; Ezek. 36:19

16 [a]Song 7:10; 24:18 [b]Job 23:2 16:5; 22:10 [d]Je

17 [a]Lev. 21:10- 16:7; Hos. 9:4

21 [a]Ps. 27:4; 84 Ezek. 24:16 [b]Je 16:3, 4; Ezek. 2

23 [1]Lit., *a man brother* [a]Job 27 78:64 [b]Lev. 26:3 Ezek. 33:10

24 [a]Ezek. 4:3; L 11:29, 30

25 [1]Or, *beauty lifting up of their* [a]Ps. 48:2; 50:2; 24:21

26 [a]1 Sam. 4:12 1:15-19

27 [a]Ezek. 3:26; 3

25:2 [a]Jer. 49:1-6 1:13-15; Zeph. 2:

3 [1]Heb., *YHWH*, usually rendered and so throughou ch. [a]Ps. 70:2, 3; 21:28; 25:6; 26:2

4 therefore, behold, I am going to give you to the [a]sons of the east
for a possession, and they will set their encampments among you
and make their dwellings among you; they will [b]eat your fruit and
drink your milk.
5 "And I shall make [a]Rabbah a pasture for camels and the sons of
Ammon a resting place for flocks. Thus you will know that I am the
LORD."
6 'For thus says the Lord GOD, "Because you have [a]clapped your
hands and stamped your feet and [b]rejoiced with all the scorn of your
soul against the land of Israel,
7 therefore, behold, I have [a]stretched out My hand against you,
and I shall give you for [b]spoil to the nations. And I shall [c]cut you off
from the peoples and [d]make you perish from the lands; I shall
destroy you. Thus you will [e]know that I am the LORD."
8 'Thus says the Lord GOD, "Because [a]Moab and Seir say, 'Behold,
the house of Judah is like all the nations,'
9 therefore, behold, I am going to [1]deprive the flank of Moab of *its*
cities, of its cities which are on its [2]frontiers, the glory of the land,
[a]Beth-jeshimoth, [b]Baal-meon, and [c]Kiriathaim,
10 and I will give it for a possession, along with the sons of
Ammon, to the [a]sons of the east, that the sons of Ammon may not be
remembered among the nations.
11 "Thus I will execute judgments on Moab, and they will know that
I am the LORD."
12 'Thus says the Lord GOD, "Because [a]Edom has acted against the
house of Judah by taking vengeance, and has incurred grievous
guilt, and avenged themselves upon them,"

6:3, 33; 1 Kin. ...ut. 28:33, 51; Is. 1:7
. 3:11; 2 Sam. ...r. 49:2; Ezek. 21:20
b 27:23; Nah. ...ad. 12; Zeph. 2:8, 10
ek. 25:13, 16; 1:4 [b]Is. 33:4; ... 26:5 [c]Ezek. ...mos 1:14, 15 [e]Ezek. 6:14
5:1; Jer. 48:1; Amos 2:1, 2
...pen [2]Lit., *end* ... 33:49; Josh. ... [b]Num. 32:3, ... 13:17; 1 Chr. ... 48:23 [c]Num. ...sh. 13:19; Jer. 48:1, 23
0 [a]Ezek. 25:4
Chr. 28:17; Ps. ...7; Jer. 49:7-22

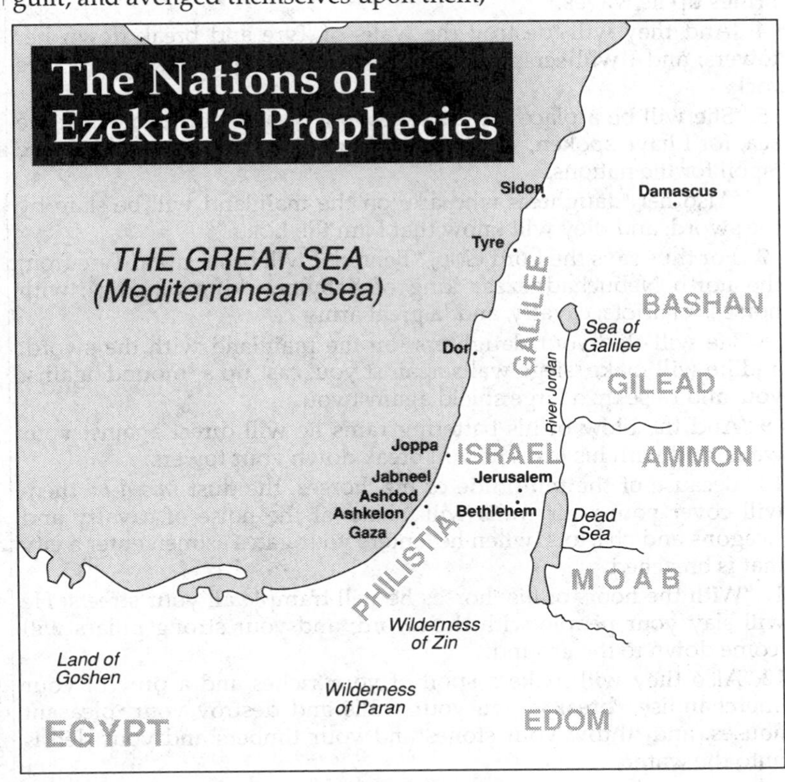

13 therefore, thus says the Lord GOD, "I will also [a]stretch out My
hand against Edom and [b]cut off man and beast from it. And I will lay
it waste; from [c]Teman even to [d]Dedan they will fall by the sword.
14 "And [a]I will lay My vengeance on Edom by the hand of My
people Israel. Therefore, they will act in Edom [b]according to My
anger and according to My wrath; thus they will know My ven-
geance," declares the Lord GOD.
15 'Thus says the Lord GOD, "Because the Philistines have acted in
[a]revenge and have taken vengeance with scorn of soul to destroy
with everlasting enmity,"
16 therefore, thus says the Lord GOD, "Behold, I will [a]stretch out My
hand against the Philistines, even cut off the [b]Cherethites and
destroy the remnant of the seacoast.
17 "And I will execute great vengeance on them with wrathful re-
bukes; and they will [a]know that I am the LORD when I lay My ven-
geance on them." ' "

Chapter 26

587-586 B.C.

26 Now it came about in the eleventh year, on the first of the
month, that the word of the LORD came to me saying,
2 "Son of man, because [a]Tyre has said concerning Jerusalem, 'Aha,
the [b]gateway of the peoples is broken; it has [1c]opened to me. I shall
be filled, *now that* she is laid waste,'
3 therefore, thus says the Lord [1]GOD, 'Behold, I am against you, O
Tyre, and I will bring up [a]many nations against you, as the [b]sea
brings up its waves.
4 'And they will [a]destroy the walls of Tyre and break down her
towers; and I will scrape her debris from her and make her a bare
rock.
5 'She will be a place for the spreading of nets in the midst of the
sea, for I have spoken,' declares the Lord GOD, 'and she will become
[a]spoil for the nations.
6 'Also her [a]daughters who are [1]on the mainland will be slain by
the sword, and they will know that I am the LORD.' "
7 For thus says the Lord GOD, "Behold, I will bring upon Tyre from
the north Nebuchadnezzar king of Babylon, [a]king of kings, with
horses, [b]chariots, cavalry, and [1]a great army.
8 "He will slay your daughters [1]on the mainland with the sword;
and he will make [a]siege walls against you, cast up a [b]mound against
you, and raise up a large shield against you.
9 "And the blow of his battering rams he will direct against your
walls, and with his [1]axes he will break down your towers.
10 "Because of the multitude of his [a]horses, the dust *raised by* them
will cover you; your walls will [b]shake at the noise of cavalry and
[1]wagons and chariots, when he [c]enters your gates as men enter a city
that is breached.
11 "With the hoofs of his [a]horses he will trample all your streets. He
will slay your people with the sword; and your strong pillars will
[b]come down to the ground.
12 "Also they will make a spoil of your riches and a prey of your
[a]merchandise, [b]break down your walls and destroy your [c]pleasant
houses, and [1]throw your stones and your timbers and your debris
[d]into the water.

13 [a]Jer. 49:8, [b]Ezek. 29:8; M [c]Gen. 36:34; J Amos 1:12 [d]J 49:8
14 [a]Is. 11:14 35:11
15 [a]Is. 14:29-3 25:6, 12; Joel 3
16 [a]Jer. 25:20 [b]1 Sam. 30:14;
17 [a]Ps. 9:16
26:2 [1]Lit., *turn* [a]2 Sam. 5:11; Is Jer. 25:22 [b]Is. [c]Ezek. 25:8; 35
3 [1]Heb., *YHW* usually rendere and so through ch. [a]Mic. 4:11 Jer. 50:42; 51:4
4 [a]Is. 23:11; Ez Amos 1:10
5 [a]Ezek. 25:7;
6 [1]Lit., *in the fie* [a]Ezek. 16:46, 5
7 [1]Lit., *an asse even many peo* [a]Ezra 7:12; Is. 1 52:32; Dan. 2:3 [b]Ezek. 23:24; N
8 [1]Lit., *in the fie* 52:4; Ezek. 21:2 32:24
9 [1]Lit., *swords*
10 [1]Lit., *wheels* 4:13; 47:3 [b]Ezek 26:15; 27:28 [c]Je
11 [a]Is. 5:28; Hab [b]Is. 26:5; Jer. 43:
12 [1]Lit., *put* [a]Is. 18; Ezek. 27:3-2 Zech. 9:3 [b]Jer. 5 [c]2 Chr. 32:27; Am 5:11 [d]Ezek. 27:2 34; 28:8

13 "So I will [1]silence the sound of your [a]songs, and the sound of your
[b]harps will be heard no more.
14 "And I will make you a bare rock; you will be a place for the
spreading of nets. You will be [a]built no more, for I the [b]LORD have
spoken," declares the Lord GOD.
15 Thus says the Lord GOD to Tyre, "Shall not the [a]coastlands [b]shake
at the sound of your fall when the wounded groan, when the
slaughter occurs in your midst?
16 "Then all the princes of the sea will [a]go down from their thrones,
remove their robes, and strip off their embroidered garments. They
will [b]clothe themselves with [1]trembling; they will sit on the ground,
[c]tremble every moment, and be appalled at you.
17 "And they will take up a [a]lamentation over you and say to you,

'[b]How you have perished, O inhabited one,
From the seas, O renowned city,
Which was [c]mighty on the sea,
She and her inhabitants,
Who [1]imposed [2]her terror
On all her inhabitants!

18 'Now the [a]coastlands will tremble
On the day of your fall;
Yes, the coastlands which are by the sea
Will be terrified at your [b]passing.'"

19 For thus says the Lord GOD, "When I shall make you a desolate
city, like the cities which are not inhabited, when I shall [a]bring up the
deep over you, and the great waters will cover you,
20 then I shall bring you down with those who [a]go down to the pit,
to the people of old, and I shall make you dwell in the [b]lower parts
of the earth, like the ancient waste places, with those who go down
to the pit, so that you will not [1]be inhabited; but I shall set [c]glory in
the land of the living.
21 "I shall [1]bring [a]terrors on you, and you will be no more; though
you will be sought, [b]you will never be found again," declares the
Lord GOD.

Chapter 27

27 Moreover, the word of the LORD came to me saying,
2 "And you, son of man, [a]take up a lamentation over Tyre;
3 and say to Tyre, [a]who dwells at the [1]entrance to the sea, [b]mer-
chant of the peoples to many coastlands, 'Thus says the Lord [2]GOD,

"O Tyre, you have said, 'I am perfect in beauty.'
4 "Your borders are in the heart of the seas;
Your builders have perfected your beauty.
5 "They have [1]made all *your* planks of fir trees from [a]Senir;
They have taken a cedar from Lebanon to make a mast for you.
6 "Of [a]oaks from [b]Bashan they have made your oars;
With ivory they have [1]inlaid your deck of boxwood from the
coastlands of [c]Cyprus.
7 "Your sail was of fine embroidered linen from Egypt
So that it became your [1]distinguishing mark;
Your [2]awning was [3a]blue and purple from the coastlands of
[b]Elishah.
8 "The inhabitants of Sidon and [a]Arvad were your rowers;
Your [b]wise men, O Tyre, were [1]aboard; they were your pilots.

[1]Lit., *cause to* . 23:16; 24:8, 6:5 [b]Is. 5:12; Rev. 18:22

ut. 13:16; Job Mal. 1:4 [b]Is. 14:27

26:18; 27:35 ; Ezek. 31:16

.it., *tremblings* [b]Job 8:22; Ps. '6; Ezek. 7:27; [c]Ezek. 32:10; Hos. 11:10

put [2]Lit., *their* 19:1, 14; 27:2, 16 [b]Is. 14:12; 50:23 [c]Ezek. 3, 10, 11; 28:2

Is. 41:5; Ezek. :15; 27:35 [b]Is. 23:5-7, 10, 11

, 8; Ezek. 26:3

eturn [a]Is. 14:9, ek. 32:30 [b]Ps. Amos 9:2; Jon. Jer. 33:9; Zech. 2:8

[1]Lit., *give you* [a]Ezek. 26:15, 36 [b]Rev. 18:21

er. 9:10, 17-20; Ezek. 28:12

[1]Lit., *entrances* *YHWH*, usually d *LORD*, and so oughout the ch. . 28:2 [b]Is. 23:3

built [a]Deut. 3:9; 5:23; Song 4:8

made [a]Is. 2:13; ch. 11:2 [b]Num. 33; Is. 2:13; Jer. [c]Gen. 10:4; Is. :1, 12; Jer. 2:10

, *standard* [2]Lit., *ering* [3]Or, *violet* . 25:4; Jer. 10:9 [b]Gen. 10:4

it., *in you* [a]Gen. :18; 1 Chr. 1:16; :11 [b]1 Kin. 9:27

9 "The elders of [a]Gebal and her wise men were with you repairing
your seams;
All the ships of the sea and their sailors were with you in order
to deal in your merchandise.
10 "[a]Persia and [a]Lud and [a]Put were in your army, your men of war.
They hung shield and helmet in you; they set forth your splendor.
11 "The sons of Arvad and your army were on your walls, *all*
around, and the [1]Gammadim were in your towers. They hung their
shields on your walls, *all* around; they perfected your beauty.
12 "Tarshish was your customer because of the abundance of all
kinds of wealth; with silver, iron, tin, and lead, they paid for your
wares.
13 "[a]Javan, [a]Tubal, and [b]Meshech, they were your traders; with the
[c]lives of men and vessels of bronze they paid for your merchandise.
14 "Those from [a]Beth-togarmah gave horses and war horses and
mules for your wares.
15 "The sons of [a]Dedan were your traders. Many coastlands were
[1]your market; [b]ivory tusks and ebony they brought as your payment.
16 "[a]Aram was your customer because of the abundance of your
[1]goods; they paid for your wares with [b]emeralds, purple,
[c]embroidered work, fine linen, coral, and rubies.
17 "Judah and the land of Israel, they were your traders; with the
wheat of [a]Minnith, [1]cakes, honey, oil, and balm they paid for your
merchandise.
18 "[a]Damascus was your customer because of the abundance of your
[1]goods, because of the abundance of all *kinds* of wealth, because of
the wine of Helbon and white wool.
19 "Vedan and Javan paid for your wares [1]from Uzal; wrought iron,
cassia, and [2]sweet cane were among your merchandise.
20 "[a]Dedan traded with you in saddlecloths for riding.
21 "[a]Arabia and all the princes of Kedar, they were [1]your customers
for [b]lambs, rams, and goats; for these they were your customers.
22 "The traders of [a]Sheba and Raamah, they traded with you; they
paid for your wares with the best of all *kinds* of [b]spices, and with all
kinds of precious stones, and gold.
23 "Haran, Canneh, [a]Eden, the traders of Sheba, Asshur, *and* Chil-
mad traded with you.
24 "They traded with you in choice garments, in clothes of [1]blue and
embroidered work, and in carpets of many colors, *and* tightly wound
cords, *which were* among your merchandise.
25 "The [a]ships of Tarshish were [1]the carriers for your merchandise.
And you were filled and were very [2]glorious
In the heart of the seas.

26 "Your rowers have brought you
Into [a]great waters;
The [b]east wind has broken you
In the heart of the seas.
27 "Your wealth, your wares, your merchandise,
Your sailors, and your pilots,
Your repairers of seams, your dealers in merchandise,
And all your men of war who are in you,
With all your company that is in your midst,
Will fall into the heart of the seas

9 [a]Josh. 13:5 5:18

10 [a]Ezek. 30

11 [1]Or, *valorc*

13 [a]Gen. 10:2 66:19; Ezek. 2 [b]Gen. 10:2; Ez 39:1 [c]Joel 3:3 18:13

14 [a]Gen. 10:3 38:6

15 [1]Lit., *the m your hand* [a]Je Ezek. 25:13; 2 [b]1 Kin. 10:22;

16 [1]Lit., *works* 10:6; Is. 7:1-8; 16:57 [b]Ezek. 2 [c]Ezek. 16:13, 1

17 [1]Heb., *pan* [a]Judg. 11:33

18 [1]Lit., *works* 14:15; Is. 7:8; 49:23; Ezek. 47

19 [1]Or, *with ya calamus*

20 [a]Gen. 25:3

21 [1]Lit., *custon your hand* [a]Is. [b]Is. 60:7

22 [a]Gen. 10:7; Ezek. 38:13 [b]G 43:11; 1 Kin. 10

23 [a]2 Kin. 19:12 37:12; Amos 1:5

24 [1]Or, *violet*

25 [1]Lit., *your tra* [2]Lit., *honored* [a]

26 [a]Ezek. 26:19 48:7; Jer. 18:17; 27:14

On the day of your overthrow.
28 "At the sound of the cry of your pilots
The pasture lands will [a]shake.
29 "And all who handle the oar,
The [a]sailors, *and* all the pilots of the sea
Will come down from their ships;
They will stand on the land,
30 And they will [a]make their voice heard over you
And will cry bitterly.
They will [b]cast dust on their heads,
They will [c]wallow in ashes.
31 "Also they will make themselves [a]bald for you
And [b]gird themselves with sackcloth;
And they will [c]weep for you in bitterness of soul
With bitter mourning.
32 "Moreover, in their wailing they will take up a [a]lamentation for you
And lament over you:
'Who is like Tyre,
Like her who is silent in the midst of the sea?
33 'When your wares went out from the seas,
You satisfied many peoples;
With the [a]abundance of your wealth and your merchandise
You enriched the kings of earth.
34 '[1]Now that you are [a]broken by the seas
In the depths of the waters,
Your [b]merchandise and all your company
Have fallen in the midst of you.
35 'All the [a]inhabitants of the coastlands
Are appalled at you,
And their kings are horribly afraid;
They are troubled in countenance.
36 'The merchants among the peoples [a]hiss at you;
You have become [1]terrified,
And you [b]will be no more.' " ' "

Chapter 28

28 The word of the LORD came again to me saying,
2 "Son of man, say to the [1]leader of Tyre, 'Thus says the
Lord [2]GOD,
"Because your heart is lifted up
And you have said, '[a]I am a god,
I sit in the seat of [3]gods,
In the heart of the seas';
Yet you are a [b]man and not God,
Although you make your heart like the heart of God—
3 Behold, you are wiser than [a]Daniel;
There is no secret that is a match for you.
4 "By your wisdom and understanding
You have acquired [a]riches for yourself,
And have acquired gold and silver for your treasuries.
5 "By your great wisdom, by your [a]trade
You have increased your riches,
And your [b]heart is lifted up because of your riches—

Ezek. 26:10, 15, 18
29 [a]Rev. 18:17-19
) [a]Is. 23:1-6; Ezek. 6:17 [b]1 Sam. 4:12; am. 1:2; Lam. 2:10; v. 18:19 [c]Jer. 6:26; Jon. 3:6
31 [a]Is. 15:2; Ezek. 8 [b]Is. 22:12; Ezek. 7:18 [c]Is. 16:9; 22:4
[a]Ezek. 26:17; 27:2; 28:12
[a]Ezek. 27:12, 18; 28:4, 5
34 [1]Lit., *The time* ‹. 26:12; 27:26, 27 [b]Zech. 9:3, 4
23:6; Ezek. 26:16
[1]Lit., *terrors* [a]Jer. 8:16; 19:8; 49:17; 3; Zeph. 2:15 [b]Ps. 37:10, 36
2 [1]Or, *ruler, prince* o., *YHWH*, usually ered *LORD*, and so ghout the ch. [3]Or, *d* [a]Is. 14:14; 47:8; ek. 28:9; 2 Thess. [b]Ps. 9:20; 82:6, 7; s. 31:3; Ezek. 28:9
an. 1:20; 2:20-23, 28; 5:11, 12
Ezek. 27:33; Zech. 9:2, 3
Ezek. 27:12; Hos. 8 [b]Job 31:24, 25; 52:7; Ezek. 28:2; Hos. 13:6

6 Therefore, thus says the Lord GOD,
'Because you have [a]made your heart
Like the heart of God,
7 Therefore, behold, I will bring [a]strangers upon you,
The [b]most ruthless of the nations.
And they will draw their swords
Against the beauty of your wisdom
And defile your splendor.
8 'They will bring you down to the pit,
And you will die the [a]death of those who are slain
In the heart of the seas.
9 'Will you still say, "I am a god,"
In the presence of your slayer,
Although you are a man and not God,
In the hands of those who wound you?
10 'You will die the death of the [a]uncircumcised
By the hand of strangers,
For I have spoken!' declares the Lord GOD!" ' "

11 Again the word of the LORD came to me saying,
12 "Son of man, [a]take up a lamentation over the king of Tyre, and
say to him, 'Thus says the Lord GOD,
"You [1]had the seal of perfection,
Full of wisdom and perfect in beauty.
13 "You were in [a]Eden, the garden of God;
[b]Every precious stone was your covering:
The [c]ruby, the topaz, and the diamond;
The beryl, the onyx, and the jasper;
The lapis lazuli, the turquoise, and the emerald;
And the gold, the workmanship of your [1d]settings and [2]sockets,
Was in you.
On the day that you were created
They were prepared.
14 "You were the [a]anointed cherub who [1]covers,
And I placed you *there*.
You were on the holy [b]mountain of God;
You walked in the midst of the [c]stones of fire.
15 "You were [a]blameless in your ways
From the day you were created,
Until [b]unrighteousness was found in you.
16 "By the [a]abundance of your trade
[1]You were internally [b]filled with violence,
And you sinned;
Therefore I have cast you as profane
From the mountain of God.
And I have destroyed you, O [2]covering cherub,
From the midst of the stones of fire.
17 "Your heart was lifted up because of your [a]beauty;
You [b]corrupted your wisdom by reason of your splendor.
I cast you to the ground;
I put you before [c]kings,
That they may see you.
18 "By the multitude of your iniquities,
In the unrighteousness of your trade,
You profaned your sanctuaries.

6 [a]Ex. 9:17; E

7 [a]Ezek. 26:7
30:11; 31:12; 3
Hab. 1:6-8

8 [a]Ezek. 27:2

10 [a]1 Sam. 17
Ezek. 31:18; 3

12 [1]Lit., were
sealing a patte
19:1; 26:17; 27

13 [1]Or, *tambo*
[2]Or, *flutes* [a]Ge
51:3; Ezek. 31:
36:35 [b]Ezek. 2
[c]Ex. 28:17-20
30:32

14 [1]Or, *guards*
25:17-20; 30:26
Ezek. 28:16 [b]E
20:40; 28:16 [c]E
28:13, 16; Rev.

15 [a]Ezek. 27:3,
28:3-6, 12 [b]Eze
28:17, 18

16 [1]Lit., *They f*
midst [2]Or, *guar*
[a]Ezek. 27:12 [b]E
8:17; Hab. 2:8,

17 [a]Ezek. 27:3,
[b]Is. 19:11 [c]Ezek

Therefore I have brought [a]fire from the midst of you;
It has consumed you,
And I have turned you to [b]ashes on the earth
In the eyes of all who see you.
19 "All who know you among the peoples
Are appalled at you;
You have become [1a]terrified,
And you will be [b]no more." ' "
20 And the word of the LORD came to me saying,
21 "Son of man, [a]set your face toward [b]Sidon, prophesy against her,
22 and say, 'Thus says the Lord GOD,
"Behold, I am against you, O Sidon,
And I shall [1]be glorified in your midst.
Then they will know that I am the LORD, when I [a]execute judgments in her,
And I shall manifest My holiness in her.
23 "For [a]I shall send pestilence to her
And blood to her streets,
And the [b]wounded will [1]fall in her midst
By the sword upon her on every side;
Then they will know that I am the LORD.
24 "And there will be no more for the house of Israel a [a]prickling
brier or a painful thorn from any round about them who scorned
them; then they will know that I am the Lord GOD."
25 'Thus says the Lord GOD, "When I [a]gather the house of Israel
from the peoples among whom they are scattered, and shall manifest
My holiness in them in the sight of the nations, then they will [b]live in
their [1]land which I gave to My servant Jacob.
26 "And they will [a]live in it securely; and they will [b]build houses,
plant vineyards, and live securely, when I [c]execute judgments upon
all who scorn them round about them. Then they will know that I
am the LORD their God." ' "

Chapter 29

587 B.C.

29 In the [a]tenth year, in the tenth *month,* on the twelfth of the
month, the word of the LORD came to me saying,
2 "Son of man, set your face against [a]Pharaoh, king of Egypt, and
prophesy against him and against all [b]Egypt.
3 "Speak and say, 'Thus says the Lord [1]GOD,
"Behold, I am against you, Pharaoh, king of Egypt,
The great [2a]monster that lies in the midst of his [3]rivers,
That [b]has said, 'My Nile is mine, and I myself have made it.'
4 "And I shall put [a]hooks in your jaws,
And I shall make the fish of your [1]rivers cling to your scales.
And I shall bring you up out of the midst of your [1]rivers,
And all the fish of your [1]rivers will cling to your scales.
5 "And I shall [a]abandon you to the wilderness, you and all the fish of your [1]rivers;
You will fall on the [2]open field; you will not be brought together or [3b]gathered.
I have given you for [c]food to the beasts of the earth and to the birds of the sky.
6 "Then all the inhabitants of Egypt will know that I am the LORD,

1:9, 10 [b]Mal. 4:3
errors [a]Ezek. 6 [b]Jer. 51:64
zek. 6:2; 25:2 10:15, 19; Is. 4; Ezek. 27:8
glorify Myself . 28:26; 30:19
[1]Or, *be judged* 22 [b]Jer. 51:52
1. 33:55; Josh. 5. 55:13; Ezek. 2:6
., *ground* [a]Ps. ; Is. 11:12, 13; 7; Ezek. 20:41; 27 [b]Jer. 23:8; 27:11
Jer. 23:6; Ezek. -28; 38:8 [b]Jer. 5, 43, 44; Amos [c]Ezek. 25:11; 28:22
:1 [a]Ezek. 26:1; 29:17; 30:20
[a]Jer. 44:30 [b]Is. 7; Jer. 46:2-26; zek. 30:1-32:32
[1]Heb., *YHWH,* rendered *LORD,* throughout the Lit., *tannim* [3]Or, [a]Is. 27:1; Ezek. zek. 29:9; 30:12
[1]Or, *Nile* [a]2 Kin. 9:28; Ezek. 38:4
Nile [2]Lit., *faces he field* [3]Or, with several mss. and n, *buried* [a]Ezek. [b]Jer. 8:2; 25:33 33; 34:20; Ezek. 39:4

Because they have been *only* a [a]staff *made* of reed to the house of
Israel.
7 "When they took hold of you with the hand,
You [a]broke and tore all their [1]hands;
And when they leaned on you,
You broke and made all their loins [2]quake."
8 'Therefore, thus says the Lord GOD, "Behold, I shall [a]bring upon
you a sword, and I shall cut off from you man and beast.
9 "And the [a]land of Egypt will become a desolation and waste.
Then they will know that I am the LORD.
Because [1]you [b]said, 'The Nile is mine, and I have made *it*,'
10 therefore, behold, I am [a]against you and against your [1]rivers, and
I will make the land of Egypt an utter waste and desolation, from
Migdol *to* Syene and even to the border of [2]Ethiopia.
11 "A man's foot will [a]not pass through it, and the foot of a beast will
not pass through it, and it will not be inhabited for forty years.
12 "So I shall make the land of Egypt a desolation in the [a]midst of
desolated lands. And her cities, in the midst of cities that are laid
waste, will be desolate forty years; and I shall [b]scatter the Egyptians
among the nations and disperse them among the lands."
13 'For thus says the Lord GOD, "At the end of forty years I shall
[a]gather the Egyptians from the peoples [1]among whom they were
scattered.
14 "And I shall turn the fortunes of Egypt and shall make them
return to the land of [a]Pathros, to the land of their origin; and there
they will be a lowly kingdom.
15 "It will be the [a]lowest of the kingdoms; and it will never again lift
itself up above the nations. And I shall make them so small that they
will not [b]rule over the nations.
16 "And it will never again be the [a]confidence of the house of Israel,
[1b]bringing to mind the iniquity of their having turned [2]to Egypt.
Then they will know that I am the Lord GOD." ' "

571 B.C.

17 Now in the [a]twenty-seventh year, in the first *month*, on the first
of the month, the word of the LORD came to me saying,
18 "Son of man, [a]Nebuchadnezzar king of Babylon made his army
labor [1]hard against Tyre; every head was made [b]bald, and every
shoulder was rubbed bare. But he and his army had no wages from
Tyre for the labor that he had [2]performed against it."
19 Therefore, thus says the Lord GOD, "Behold, I [a]shall give the land
of Egypt to Nebuchadnezzar king of Babylon. And he will carry off
her [1b]wealth, and capture her spoil and seize her plunder; and it will
be wages for his army.
20 "I have given him the land of Egypt *for* his labor which he [1a]per-
formed, because they acted for Me," declares the Lord GOD.
21 "On that day I shall make a [a]horn sprout for the house of Israel,
and I shall [1b]open your mouth in their midst. Then they will know
that I am the LORD."

Chapter 30

30 The word of the LORD came again to me saying,
2 "Son of man, prophesy and say, 'Thus says the Lord [1]GOD,
"[a]Wail, 'Alas for the day!'
3 "For the day is near,
Even [a]the day of the LORD is near;

6 [a]2 Kin. 18:2
7 [1]So with so ancient versio *shoulders* [2]Lit [a]2 Kin. 18:21; Ezek. 17:15-1
8 [a]Jer. 46:13; 14:17
9 [1]Lit., *he* [a]Ez 29:10-12; 30:7 13-19 [b]Prov. 18:12; Ezek. 2
10 [1]Or, *Nile* [2] [a]Ezek. 13:8; 2 29:3
11 [a]Jer. 43:11, 46:19; Ezek. 3
12 [a]Jer. 25:15 27:6-11; Ezek. [b]Jer. 46:19; Ez 30:23, 26
13 [1]Lit., *where* 19:22; Jer. 46:
14 [a]Is. 11:11; 15; Ezek. 30:14
15 [a]Ezek. 17:6 30:13; Zech. 1 [b]Ezek. 31:2; 32 3:8-10
16 [1]Lit., *causin remember* [2]Lit *them* [a]Is. 20:5; 31:1; 36:6; Eze 29:6, 7 [b]Is. 64: 14:10; Ezek. 2 Hos. 8:13
17 [a]Ezek. 24:1 29:1; 30:20; 40:1
18 [1]Lit., *a grea* [2]Lit., *labored* [a] 27:6; Ezek. 26:7 [b]Jer. 48:37; Eze
19 [1]Or, *multitu* [a]Ezek. 30:10, 2 32:11 [b]Jer. 43:1 Ezek. 30:14
20 [1]Lit., *labore* 10:6, 7; 45:1-3;
21 [1]Lit., *give yo opening of the r* [a]1 Sam. 2:10; Ps 132:17 [b]Ezek. 3 24:27; 33:22; Am 8; Luke 21:15
30:2 [1]Heb., *YH* usually rendered and so througho ch. [a]Is. 13:6; 15 Ezek. 21:12; Joe 11, 13
3 [a]Ezek. 7:19; 1 Joel 1:15; 2:1; O

It will be a day of [b]clouds,
A time *of doom* for the nations.
4 "And a sword will come upon Egypt,
And anguish will be in [1]Ethiopia,
When the slain fall in Egypt,
They [a]take away her [2]wealth,
And her foundations are torn down.
5 "[1]Ethiopia, Put, Lud, all [2a]Arabia, [3]Libya, and the [4]people of the
land [5]that is in league will fall with them by the sword."
6 'Thus says the LORD,
"Indeed, those who support [a]Egypt will fall,
And the pride of her power will come down;
From Migdol *to* Syene
They will fall within her by the sword,"
Declares the Lord GOD.
7 "And they will be desolate
In the [a]midst of the desolated lands;
And her cities will be
In the midst of the devastated cities.
8 "And they will [a]know that I am the LORD,
When I set a [b]fire in Egypt
And all her helpers are broken.
9 "On that day [a]messengers will go forth from Me in ships to
frighten [b]secure [1]Ethiopia; and [c]anguish will be on them as on the
day of Egypt; for, behold, it comes!"
10 'Thus says the Lord GOD,
"[a]I will also make the [1]multitude of Egypt cease
By the hand of Nebuchadnezzar king of Babylon.
11 "He and his people with him,
[a]The most ruthless of the nations,
Will be brought in to destroy the land;
And they will draw their swords against Egypt
And fill the land with the slain.
12 "Moreover, I will make the [a]Nile canals dry
And [b]sell the land into the hands of evil men.
And I will make the land desolate,
And [1]all that is in it,
By the hand of strangers; I, the LORD, have spoken."

13 'Thus says the Lord GOD,
"I will also [a]destroy the idols
And make the [1]images cease from [2b]Memphis.
And there will no longer be a prince in the land of Egypt;
And I will put fear in the land of Egypt.
14 "And I will make [a]Pathros desolate,
Set a fire in [b]Zoan,
And execute judgments on [1c]Thebes.
15 "And I will pour out My wrath on [1]Sin,
The stronghold of Egypt;
I will also cut off the multitude of [2]Thebes.
16 "And I will set a fire in Egypt;
[1]Sin will writhe in anguish,
[2]Thebes will be breached,
And [3]Memphis *will have* [4]distresses daily.

[b]Ezek. 30:18; 32:7; 34:12
4 [1]Lit., *Cush* [2]Or, *...tude* [a]Ezek. 29:19
...Lit., *Cush* [2]Or, *the ...d people* [3]Or, *Cub* ..., *sons* [5]Lit., *of the ...ant* [a]Jer. 25:20, 24
6 [a]Is. 20:3-6
...er. 25:18-26; Ezek. 29:12
[a]Ps. 58:11; Ezek. 29:6, 9, 16 [b]Ezek. ...; 30:14, 16; Amos 1:4, 7, 10, 12, 14
...t., *Cush* [a]Is. 18:1, ...47:8; Ezek. 38:11; ...6 [c]Is. 19:17; 23:5; Ezek. 32:9, 10
...Or, *wealth* [a]Ezek. 29:19
11 [a]Ezek. 28:7
[1]Lit., *her fulness* ...29:3, 9 [b]Is. 19:4
...r, *futile ones* [2]Or, *...oph* [a]Is. 2:18 [b]Is. ...3; Jer. 2:16; 44:1; ...6:14; Ezek. 30:16
...Or, *No* [a]Is. 11:11; ...er. 44:1, 15; Ezek. ...4 [b]Ps. 78:12, 43; ...s. 19:11, 13 [c]Jer. Ezek. 30:15, 16; Nah. 3:8
15 [1]Or, *Pelusium* [2]Or, *No*
...Or, *Pelusium* [2]Or, ... [3]Or, *Noph* [4]Or, *adversaries*

17 "The young men of [1a]On and of Pi-beseth
Will fall by the sword,
And [2]the women will go into captivity.
18 "And in [a]Tehaphnehes the day will [1]be [b]dark
When I [c]break there the yoke bars of Egypt.
Then the pride of her power will cease in her;
A cloud will cover her,
And her daughters will go into captivity.
19 "Thus I will [a]execute judgments on Egypt,
And they will know that I am the LORD." ' "

587 B.C.

20 And it came about in the [a]eleventh year, in the first *month,* on the
seventh of the month, that the word of the LORD came to me saying,
21 "Son of man, I have [a]broken the arm of Pharaoh king of Egypt;
and, behold, it has not been [b]bound up [1]for healing [2]or wrapped
with a bandage, that it may be strong to hold the sword.
22 "Therefore, thus says the Lord GOD, 'Behold, I am [a]against Pha-
raoh king of Egypt and will break his arms, both the strong and the
[b]broken; and I will make the sword [c]fall from his hand.
23 'And I will [a]scatter the Egyptians among the nations and dis-
perse them among the lands.
24 'For I will [a]strengthen the arms of the king of Babylon and put
[b]My sword in his hand; and I will break the arms of Pharaoh, so that
he will groan before him with the groanings of a wounded man.
25 'Thus I will strengthen the arms of the king of Babylon, but the
arms of Pharaoh will fall. Then they will know that I am the LORD,
when I put My sword into the hand of the king of Babylon and he
[a]stretches it out against the land of Egypt.
26 'When I scatter the Egyptians among the nations and disperse
them among the lands, then they will know that I am the LORD.' "

Chapter 31

587 B.C.

31 And it came about in the [a]eleventh year, in the third *month,* on
the first of the month, that the word of the LORD came to me
saying,
2 "Son of man, say to Pharaoh king of Egypt, and to his [a]multitude,
'Whom are you like in your greatness?
3 'Behold, Assyria *was* a [a]cedar in Lebanon
With beautiful branches and forest shade,
And [1b]very high;
And its top was among the [2]clouds.
4 'The [a]waters made it grow, the [1]deep made it high.
With its rivers it continually [2]extended all around its planting
place,
And it sent out its channels to all the trees of the field.
5 'Therefore [a]its height was loftier than all the trees of the field
And its boughs became many and its branches long
Because of [b]many waters [1]as it spread them out.
6 'All the [a]birds of the heavens nested in its boughs,
And under its branches all the beasts of the field gave birth,
And all great nations lived under its shade.
7 'So it was beautiful in its greatness, in the length of its branches;
For its [1]roots extended to many waters.
8 'The [a]cedars in [b]God's garden [1]could not match it;
The [2]cypresses [1]could not compare with its boughs,

17 [1]Or, *Aven* [2]Lit., *they* [a]Gen. 41:45;

18 [1]So with many and ancient versio M.T., *restrain* [a]Jer. 43:8-13 [b]Ezek. 30 [c]Lev. 26:13; Is. 10: Jer. 27:2; 28:10, 13 30:8; Ezek. 34:27

19 [a]Ps. 9:16; Ezek 15; 25:11; 30:14

20 [a]Ezek. 26:1; 29 17; 31:1

21 [1]Lit., *to give he* [2]Lit., *to put a band to wrap it* [a]Ps. 10: 37:17; Ezek. 30:24 [b]Jer. 30:13; 46:11

22 [a]Jer. 46:25; Ez 29:3 [b]2 Kin. 24:7; 37:7 [c]Jer. 46:21

23 [a]Ezek. 29:12; 18, 26

24 [a]Neh. 6:9; Is. 4 5; Ezek. 30:10, 25 Zech. 10:12 [b]Eze 30:11, 25; Zeph. 2

25 [a]Josh. 8:18; 1 21:16; Is. 5:25

31:1 [a]Jer. 52:5, 6 Ezek. 30:20; 32:1

2 [a]Ezek. 29:19; 3 Nah. 3:9

3 [1]Lit., *high of sta* [2]So Gr.; M.T., *thic boughs* [a]Is. 10:33 Ezek. 17:3, 4, 22; Dan. 4:10, 20-23 10:33; Ezek. 31:5

4 [1]I.e., subterran waters [2]Lit., *was* [a]Ezek. 17:5, 8; Re 17:1, 15

5 [1]Lit., *in its sen forth* [a]Dan. 4:11 1:3; Ezek. 17:5

6 [a]Ezek. 17:23; 3 Dan. 4:12, 21; Ma 13:32

7 [1]Lit., *root was*

8 [1]Lit., *did* [2]Or, *Phoenician junip* [a]Ps. 80:10; Ezek [b]Gen. 2:8, 9; 13:1 51:3; Ezek. 28:13 31:16, 18

And the plane trees [3]could not match its branches.
No tree in [b]God's garden [1]could compare with it in its beauty.
9 'I made it beautiful with the multitude of its branches,
And all the trees of [a]Eden, which were in the [a]garden of God,
were jealous of it.
10 'Therefore, thus says the Lord [1]GOD, "Because [2]it is high in stat-
ure, and it has set its top among the [3]clouds, and its [a]heart is haughty
in its loftiness,
11 therefore, I will give it into the hand of a [1a]despot of the nations;
he will thoroughly deal with it. According to its wickedness I have
[b]driven it away.
12 "And [a]alien [b]tyrants of the nations have cut it down and left it; on
the [c]mountains and in all the valleys its branches have fallen, and its
boughs have been broken in all the ravines of the land. And all the
peoples of the earth have [d]gone down from its shade and left it.
13 "On its ruin all the [a]birds of the heavens will dwell. And all the
beasts of the field will be on its *fallen* branches
14 in order that all the trees by the waters may not be exalted in
their stature, nor set their top among the [1]clouds, nor their [2]well-
watered mighty ones stand *erect* in their height. For they have all
been given over to death, to the [a]earth beneath, among the sons of
men, with those who go down to the pit."
15 'Thus says the Lord GOD, "On the day when it went down to
Sheol I [a]caused lamentations; I closed the [1]deep over it and held back
its rivers. And *its* many waters were stopped up, and I made
Lebanon [2]mourn for it, and all the trees of the field wilted away on
account of it.
16 "I made the nations [a]quake at the sound of its fall when I made it
[b]go down to Sheol with those who go down to the pit; and all the
[1]well-watered trees of Eden, the choicest and best of [c]Lebanon, were
[d]comforted in the earth beneath.
17 "They also [a]went down with it to Sheol to those who were [b]slain
by the sword; and those who were its [1]strength lived [c]under its
shade among the nations.
18 "To which among the trees of Eden are you thus [1]equal in glory
and greatness? Yet you will be brought down with the trees of Eden
to the earth beneath; you will lie in the midst of the [a]uncircumcised,
with those who were slain by the sword. [b]So is Pharaoh and all his
multitude!' " declares the Lord GOD."

Chapter 32

585 B.C.

32 And it came about in the [a]twelfth year, in the twelfth *month*,
on the first of the month, that the word of the LORD came to
me saying,
2 "Son of man, take up a [a]lamentation over Pharaoh king of Egypt,
and say to him,
'You [1]compared yourself to a young [b]lion of the nations,
Yet you are like the [c]monster in the seas;
And you [d]burst forth in your rivers,
And muddied the waters with your feet,
And [2]fouled their rivers.' "
3 Thus says the Lord [1]GOD,
"Now I will [a]spread My net over you
With a company of many peoples,

., *were not like* 8, 9; 13:10; Is. 3; Ezek. 28:13; 31:16, 18
. 2:8, 9; 13:10; 3; Ezek. 28:13; 31:16, 18
[1]Heb., *YHWH*, endered *LORD*, throughout the ., *you are* [3]Or, *oughs* [a]2 Chr. . 10:12; 14:13, ek. 28:17; Dan. 5:20
Or, *mighty one*):10, 11; 32:11, ; Dan. 5:18, 19 3:12; Nah. 3:18
zek. 7:21; 28:7; ab. 1:6 [b]Ezek. 7; 30:11; 32:12 zek. 32:5; 35:8 :17; Dan. 4:14; Nah. 3:17, 18
3:6; Ezek. 29:5; 31:6; 32:4
r, *thick boughs* *rinkers of water* . 16:30, 33; Ps. 9; Ezek. 26:20; 2:24; Amos 9:2; 2:2, 6; Eph. 4:9
., *subterranean waters* [2]Lit., *be ed* [a]Ezek. 32:7; Nah. 2:10
[1]Lit., *drinkers of r* [a]Ezek. 26:15; 8; Hag. 2:7 [b]Is. Ezek. 32:18 [c]Is. ab. 2:17 [d]Ezek. 4:22, 23; 32:31
, *arm* [a]Ps. 9:17 32:20f. [b]Ezek. :3, 6; Dan. 4:12
like [a]Jer. 9:25, k. 28:10; 32:19, [b]Ps. 52:7; Matt. 13:19
1 [a]Ezek. 30:20; :1; 32:17; 33:21
, *were like* [2]Lit., *led by stamping* Ezek. 19:1; 27:2; 32:16 [b]Jer. 4:7; ek. 19:2-6; Nah. [c]Is. 27:1; Ezek. 9:3 [d]Jer. 46:7, 8
[1]Heb., *YHWH*, rendered *LORD*, o throughout the h. [a]Ezek. 12:13

And they shall lift you up in My net.
4 "And I will leave you on the land;
I will cast you on the [1]open field.
And I will cause all the [a]birds of the heavens to dwell on you,
And I will satisfy the beasts of the whole earth [2]with you.
5 "And I will lay your flesh [a]on the mountains,
And fill the valleys with your refuse.
6 "I will also make the land drink the discharge of your [a]blood,
As far as the mountains,
And the ravines shall be full of you.
7 "And when *I* [a]extinguish you,
I will [b]cover the heavens, and darken their [c]stars;
I will cover the [d]sun with a cloud,
And the moon shall not give its light.
8 "All the shining [a]lights in the heavens
I will darken over you
And will set darkness on your land,"
Declares the Lord GOD.
9 "I will also [a]trouble the hearts of many peoples, when I [b]bring
your destruction among the nations, into lands which you have not
known.
10 "And I will make many peoples [a]appalled at you, and their kings
shall be horribly afraid of you when I brandish My sword before
them; and [b]they shall tremble every moment, every man for his own
life, on the day of your fall."
11 For [a]thus says the Lord GOD, "The sword of the king of Babylon
shall come upon you.
12 "By the swords of the mighty ones I will cause your multitude to
fall; all of them are [a]tyrants of the nations,
And they shall [b]devastate the pride of Egypt,
And all its multitude shall be destroyed.
13 "I will also destroy all its cattle from beside many waters;
And [a]the foot of man shall not muddy them anymore,
And the hoofs of beasts shall not muddy them.
14 "Then I will make their waters settle,
And will cause their rivers to run like oil,"
Declares the Lord GOD.
15 "When I make the land of Egypt a [a]desolation,
And the land is destitute of that which filled it,
When I smite all those who live in it,
Then they shall [b]know that I am the LORD.
16 "This is a [a]lamentation and they shall [1]chant it. The daughters of
the nations shall [1]chant it. Over Egypt and over all her multitude
they shall [1]chant it," declares the Lord GOD.

586-585 B.C.

17 And it came about in the [a]twelfth year, on the [a]fifteenth of the
month, that the word of the LORD came to me saying,
18 "Son of man, [a]wail for the multitude of Egypt, and [b]bring it down,
her and the daughters of the powerful nations, to the [c]nether world,
with those who go down to the pit;
19 'Whom do you surpass in beauty?
Go down and make your bed with the [a]uncircumcised.'
20 "They shall fall in the midst of those who are slain by the sword.
[1]She is given over to the sword; they have [a]drawn her and all her
multitudes away.

4 [1]Lit., *surface of field* [2]Lit., *from* [a]Is

5 [a]Ezek. 31:12

6 [a]Ex. 7:17; Is. 34
Ezek. 35:6; Rev. 1

7 [a]Job 18:5, 6; Pr
13:9 [b]Ex. 10:21-2
34:4; Ezek. 30:3,
34:12 [c]Is. 13:10
2:2, 31; 3:15; Amo
Matt. 24:29; Mark
13:24f.; Luke 21:2
Rev. 6:12; 8:12

8 [a]Gen. 1:14

9 [a]Ezek. 27:29-3
28:19; Rev. 18:10
[b]Ex. 15:14-16

10 [a]Ezek. 27:35
26:16

11 [a]Jer. 46:26

12 [a]Ezek. 28:7 [b]
28:19

13 [a]Ezek. 29:11

15 [a]Ps. 107:33,
Ezek. 29:12, 19,
[b]Ex. 7:5; 14:4, 18
9:16; 83:17, 18; E
6:7; 30:19, 26

16 [1]Or, *lament* [a]
1:17; 3:33, 34; 2
35:25; Jer. 9:17;
26:17; 32:2

17 [a]Ezek. 31:1;
33:21

18 [a]Is. 16:9; Eze
32:2, 16; Mic. 1:8
1:10; Ezek. 43:3;
6:5 [c]Ezek. 31:14
18; 32:24

19 [a]Jer. 9:25, 26
31:18; 32:21, 24

20 [1]Or, *The swo
given* [a]Ps. 28:3

21 "The [a]strong among the mighty ones shall speak of him *and* his
helpers from the midst of Sheol, 'They have gone down, they lie still,
the uncircumcised, slain by the sword.'
22 "[a]Assyria is there and all her company; [1]her graves are round
about [2]her. All of them are slain, fallen by the sword,
23 whose [a]graves are set in the remotest parts of the pit, and her
company is round about her grave. All of them are slain, fallen by
the sword, who [1]spread terror in the land of the living.
24 "[a]Elam is there and all her multitude around her grave; all of
them slain, fallen by the sword, who went down uncircumcised to
the [b]lower parts of the earth, who instilled their terror in the [c]land of
the living, and [d]bore their disgrace with those who went down to the
pit.
25 "They have made a [a]bed for her among the slain with all her
multitude. Her graves are around it, they are all uncircumcised, slain
by the sword (although their terror was [1]instilled in the land of the
living), and they bore their disgrace with those who go down to the
pit; [2]they were put in the midst of the slain.
26 "[a]Meshech, [b]Tubal and all their multitude are there; their graves
[1]surround them. All of them were slain by the sword [c]uncircumcised,
though they instilled their terror in the land of the living.
27 "[a]Nor do they lie beside the fallen [1b]heroes of the uncircumcised,
who went down to Sheol with their weapons of war, and whose
swords were laid under their heads; but the punishment for their
[c]iniquity rested on their bones, though the terror of *these* [1]heroes *was*
once in the land of the living.
28 "But in the midst of the uncircumcised you will be broken and lie
with those slain by the sword.
29 "There also is [a]Edom, its kings, and all its [1]princes, who [2]for *all*
their might are laid with those slain by the sword; they will lie with
the uncircumcised, and with those who go down to the pit.
30 "There also are the [1]chiefs of the [a]north, all of them, and all the
[b]Sidonians, who in spite of the terror resulting from their might, in
shame went down with the slain. So they lay down uncircumcised
with those slain by the sword, and bore their disgrace with those
who go down to the pit.
31 "These Pharaoh will see, and he will be [a]comforted for all his
multitude slain by the sword, *even* Pharaoh and all his army,"
declares the Lord GOD.
32 "Though I instilled a terror of him in the land of the living, yet he
will be made to lie down among *the* uncircumcised *along* with those
slain by the sword, *even* Pharaoh and all his multitude," declares the
Lord GOD.

Chapter 33

33 And the word of the LORD came to me saying,
2 "Son of man, speak to the [a]sons of your people, and say to
them, 'If I bring a sword upon a land, and the people of the land take
one man from among them and make him their watchman;
3 and he sees the sword coming upon the land, and he [a]blows on
the trumpet and warns the people,
4 then he who hears the sound of the trumpet and [a]does not take
warning, and a sword comes and takes him away, his [b]blood will be
on his *own* head.

[a]Is. 14:9-12; Ezek. 32:27
[1]Lit., *his* [2]Lit., *him* ...zek. 27:23; 31:3, 16
[1]Lit., *gave*, and so ...ughout the ch. [a]Is. 14:15
[a]Gen. 10:22; 14:1; ... 11:11; Jer. 25:25; ...4-39 [b]Ezek. 26:20; 14, 18; 32:18 [c]Job ...3; Ps. 27:13; 52:5; 42:5; Is. 38:11; Jer. ... [d]Ezek. 16:52, 54; 32:25, 30
...Lit., *given* [2]So with ...ient versions; M.T. *he was* [a]Ps. 139:8
...6 [1]Lit., *are around* [a]Gen. 10:2; Ezek. ...7:13; 38:2, 3; 39:1 ...en. 10:2; Is. 66:19; ...ek. 27:13; 38:2, 3; 39:1 [c]Ezek. 32:19
[1]Or, *mighty ones* ...Is. 14:18, 19 [b]Job ...3-15; Ezek. 32:21 20:11; Ps. 109:18
...Or, *leaders* [2]Or, *in* [a]Is. 34:5-15; Jer. ...7-22; Ezek. 25:13; 35:9, 15
[1]Or, *princes* [a]Jer. 25:26; Ezek. 38:6, 39:2 [b]Jer. 25:22; Ezek. 28:21-23
...zek. 14:22; 31:16
33:2 [a]Ezek. 3:11; ...:12, 17, 30; 37:18
...[a]Neh. 4:18-20; Is. ... Ezek. 33:9; Hos. 8:1; Joel 2:1
...2 Chr. 25:16; Jer. ...Zech. 1:4 [b]Ezek. 33:5, 9; Acts 18:6

The Prophetic Points of History

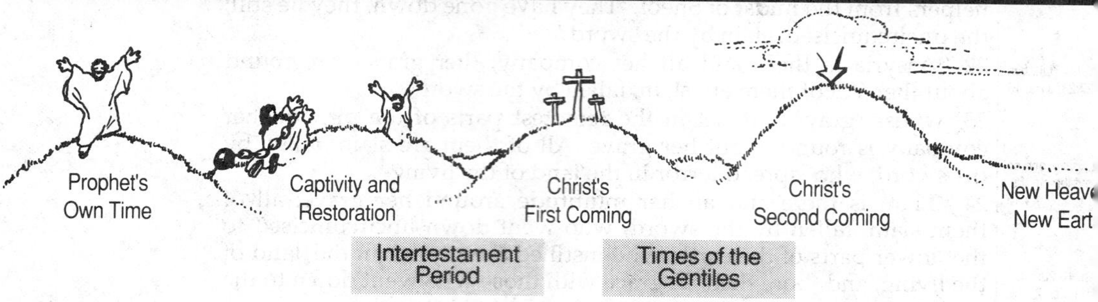

5 'He heard the sound of the trumpet, but did not take warning;
his blood will be on himself. But had he taken warning, he would
have [a]delivered his life.
6 'But if the watchman sees the sword coming and does not blow
the trumpet, and the people are not warned, and a sword comes and
takes a person from them, he is [a]taken away [1]in his iniquity; but his
[b]blood I will require from the watchman's hand.'
7 "Now as for you, son of man, I have [1a]appointed you a watchman
for the house of Israel; so you will hear a [2]message from My mouth,
and give them [b]warning from Me.
8 "When I say to the wicked, 'O wicked man, you shall [a]surely die,'
and you do not speak to warn the wicked from his way, that wicked
man shall die in his iniquity, but his blood I will require from your
hand.
9 "But if you on your part warn a wicked man to turn from his way,
and he [a]does not turn from his way, he will die in his iniquity; but
you have [b]delivered your life.
10 "Now as for you, son of man, say to the house of Israel, 'Thus you
have spoken, saying, "Surely our transgressions and our sins are
upon us, and we are [a]rotting away in them; [b]how then can we [1]sur-
vive?"'
11 "Say to them, '[a]As I live!' declares the Lord [1]GOD, 'I take [b]no
pleasure in the death of the wicked, but rather that the wicked [c]turn
from his way and live. [d]Turn back, turn back from your evil ways!
Why then will you die, O house of Israel?'
12 "And you, son of man, say to [1]your fellow citizens, 'The
[a]righteousness of a righteous man will not deliver him in the day of
his transgression, and as for the wickedness of the wicked, he will
[b]not stumble because of it in the day when he turns from his wicked-
ness; whereas a righteous man will not be able to live [2]by his right-
eousness on the day when he commits sin.'
13 "When I say to the righteous he will surely live, and he *so* trusts
in his righteousness that he [a]commits iniquity, none of his righteous
deeds will be remembered; but in that same iniquity of his which he
has committed he will die.
14 "But when I say to the wicked, 'You will surely die,' and he [a]turns
from his sin and practices [b]justice and righteousness,
15 *if a* wicked man restores a pledge, [a]pays back what he has taken
by robbery, walks by the [b]statutes [1]which ensure life without com-
mitting iniquity, he will surely live; he shall not die.

5 [a]Ex. 9:19-21 11:7

6 [1]Or, *for*, and throughout the [a]Ezek. 18:20, 2 9 [b]Ezek. 3:18,

7 [1]Or, *given* [2] [a]Is. 62:6; Ezek. [b]Jer. 1:17; 26:2 2:7, 8; Acts 5:2

8 [a]Is. 3:11; Eze 13, 18, 20; 33:1

9 [a]Acts 13:40, [b]Ezek. 3:19, 21 20:26

10 [1]Lit., *live* [a]L 26:39; Ezek. 4:1 24:23 [b]Is. 49:14 37:11

11 [1]Heb., *YHW* usually rendere and so througho ch. [a]Is. 49:18; E 5:11 [b]Ezek. 18:2 Hos. 11:8 [c]Jer. 1 Tim. 2:4; 2 Pe [d]Is. 55:6, 7; Jer. Ezek. 18:30, 31 14:1; Acts 3:19

12 [1]Lit., *the son your people* [2]Lit [a]Ezek. 3:18; 18:2 33:20 [b]2 Chr. 7: Ezek. 18:21; 33:

13 [a]Ezek. 18:26 10:38; 2 Pet. 2:2

14 [a]Is. 55:7; Jer. 8; Ezek. 18:27; 3 Hos. 14:1, 4 [b]Mi

15 [1]Lit., *of life* [a] 22:1-4; Lev. 6:4, 19:8 [b]Ps. 119:59 143:8; Ezek. 20:1

6 [a]Is. 1:18; 43:25; Ezek. 18:22

16 "[a]None of his sins that he has committed will be remembered against him. He has practiced justice and righteousness; he will surely live.

7 [1]Lit., *the sons of your people*

17 "Yet [1]your fellow citizens say, 'The way of the Lord is not right,' when it is their own way that is not right.

[1]Lit., *them* [a]Ezek. ; 18:24; 33:12, 13

18 "When the righteous turns from his righteousness and [a]commits iniquity, then he shall die in [1]it.

19 "But when the wicked turns from his wickedness and practices justice and righteousness, he will live by them.

20 [a]Ezek. 18:25

20 "Yet you say, '[a]The way of the Lord is not right.' O house of Israel, I will judge each of you according to his ways."

[1]Or, *refugee* [2]Lit., *itten* [a]Ezek. 31:1; , 17 [b]Jer. 39:1, 2; 2:4-7; Ezek. 24:1, 1. 25:10; Jer. 39:8

21 Now it [a]came about in the [b]twelfth year of our exile, on the fifth of the tenth month, that the [1]refugees from Jerusalem came to me, saying, "[c]The city has been [2]taken."

585 B.C.

Lit., *refugee* [2]Lit., *ntil he came* [3]Or, b [a]Ezek. 1:3; 8:1; [b]Ezek. 3:26, 27; 24:27 [c]Luke 1:64

22 Now the [a]hand of the LORD had been upon me in the evening, before the [1]refugees came. And He [b]opened my mouth [2]at the time *they* came to me in the morning; so my mouth was [c]opened, and I was no longer [3]speechless.

23 Then the word of the LORD came to me saying,

[a]Jer. 39:10; 40:7; . 33:27 [b]Is. 51:2; uke 3:8; Acts 7:5; :12 [c]Ezek. 11:15

24 "Son of man, they who [a]live in these waste places in the land of Israel are saying, '[b]Abraham was *only* one, yet he possessed the land; so to [c]us who are many the land has been given as a possession.'

ev. 17:10, 12, 14; 12:16, 23; 15:23 [b]Jer. 7:9, 10

25 "Therefore, say to them, 'Thus says the Lord GOD, "You eat *meat* with the [a]blood *in it,* lift up your eyes to your idols as you shed blood. [b]Should you then possess the land?

26 "You [1a]rely on your sword, you commit abominations, and each of you defiles his neighbor's wife. Should you then possess the land?"'

[1]Lit., *stand* [a]Mic. 2:1, 2; Zeph. 3:3

27 "Thus you shall say to them, 'Thus says the Lord GOD, "As I live, surely those who are in the waste places will [a]fall by the sword, and whoever is in the [1]open field I will give to the beasts to be devoured, and those who are in the strongholds and in the [b]caves will die of pestilence.

it., *surface of the eld* [a]Jer. 15:2, 3; 2:22; Ezek. 5:12 am. 13:6; Is. 2:19

28 "And I shall [a]make the land a desolation and a waste, and the [b]pride of her power will cease; and the mountains of Israel will be desolate, so that no one will pass through.

Ezek. 5:14; 6:14; :13 [b]Ezek. 7:24; 24:21; 30:6

29 "Then they will know that I am the LORD, when I make the land a desolation and a waste because of all their abominations which they have committed."'

[1]Lit., *the sons of eople* [2]Lit., *word* 3:13; 58:2; Ezek. 14:3; 20:3, 31

30 "But as for you, son of man, [1]your fellow citizens who talk about you by the walls and in the doorways of the houses, speak to one another, each to his brother, saying, '[a]Come now, and hear what the [2]message is which comes forth from the LORD.'

Ps. 78:36, 37; Is. :13; 1 John 3:18 22:13, 27; Luke 12:15

31 "And they come to you as people come, and sit before you *as* My people, and hear your words, but they do not do them, for they do the lustful desires *expressed* by their [a]mouth, *and* their heart goes after their [b]gain.

32 [a]Mark 6:20

32 "And behold, you are to them like a sensual song by one who has a [a]beautiful voice and plays well on an instrument; for they hear your words, but they do not practice them.

[1]Lit., *behold, it is ming* [a]Jer. 28:9; Ezek. 33:29

33 "So when it [a]comes to pass—[1]as surely it will—then they will know that a prophet has been in their midst."

Chapter 34

34 Then the word of the LORD came to me saying,
2 "Son of man, prophesy against the [a]shepherds of Israel.
Prophesy and say to [1]those shepherds, 'Thus says the Lord [2]GOD,
"Woe, shepherds of Israel who have been [3b]feeding themselves!
Should not the shepherds [3c]feed the flock?
3 "You [a]eat the fat and clothe yourselves with the wool, you
[b]slaughter the fat *sheep* without [1]feeding the flock.
4 "Those who are sickly you have not strengthened, the [1]diseased
you have not healed, [a]the broken you have not bound up, the scat-
tered you have not brought back, nor have you [b]sought for the lost;
but with force and with severity you have dominated them.
5 "And they were [a]scattered for lack of a shepherd, and they be-
came [b]food for every beast of the field and were scattered.
6 "My flock [a]wandered through all the mountains and on every
high hill, and [b]My flock was scattered over all the surface of the
earth; and there was [c]no one to search or seek *for them*."'"
7 Therefore, you shepherds, hear the word of the LORD:
8 "As I live," declares the Lord GOD, "surely because My flock has
become a [a]prey, My flock has even become food for all the beasts of
the field for lack of a shepherd, and My shepherds did not search for
My flock, but *rather* the shepherds fed themselves and did not feed
My flock;
9 therefore, you shepherds, hear the word of the LORD:
10 'Thus says the Lord GOD, "Behold, I am [a]against the shepherds,
and I shall demand My [1]sheep [2]from them and make them [b]cease
from feeding [1]sheep. So the shepherds will not [3]feed themselves
anymore, but I shall [c]deliver My flock from their mouth, that they
may not be food for them."'"
11 For thus says the Lord GOD, "Behold, I Myself will [a]search for
My sheep and seek them out.
12 "[a]As a shepherd [1]cares for his herd in the day when he is among
his scattered [2]sheep, so I will [1b]care for My [2]sheep and will deliver
them from all the places to which they were scattered on a [c]cloudy
and gloomy day.
13 "And I will bring them out from the peoples and gather them
from the countries and bring them to their own land; and I will [a]feed
them on the mountains of Israel, by the [b]streams, and in all the
inhabited places of the land.
14 "I will feed them in a [a]good pasture, and their grazing ground
will be on the mountain heights of Israel. There they will lie down in
good grazing ground, and they will feed in [1b]rich pasture on the
mountains of Israel.
15 "I will [a]feed My flock and I will [1]lead them to rest," declares the
Lord GOD.
16 "I will seek the lost, bring back the scattered, bind up the broken,
and strengthen the sick; but the [a]fat and the strong I will destroy. I
will [b]feed them with judgment.
17 "And as for you, My flock, thus says the Lord GOD, 'Behold, I will
[a]judge between one [1]sheep and another, between the rams and the
male goats.
18 'Is it too [a]slight a thing for you that you should feed in the good
pasture, that you must tread down with your feet the rest of your

34:2 [1]Lit., *th* *shepherds* [2] *YHWH*, usua rendered *LO* throughout th *pasturing, pa* 2:8; 3:15; 10: [b]Jer. 23:1; Ez 34:8-10; Mic. [c]Ps. 78:71, 7 Ezek. 34:14, 10:11; 21:15-

3 [1]Lit., *pastu* [a]Zech. 11:16 22:25, 27

4 [1]Lit., *sick* 11:16 [b]Matt. 18:12, 13; Lu

5 [a]Num. 27:1 18:16; Jer. 10 50:6, 7; Matt. 6:34 [b]Ezek. 3

6 [a]Jer. 40:11, 7:16; 1 Pet. 2: 10:16 [c]Ps. 14

8 [a]Acts 20:29

10 [1]Or, (a) *flo* *from their han* *pasture*, and s throughout the 21:13; Ezek. 5 34:2; Zech. 10 [b]1 Sam. 2:29, 52:24-27 [c]Ps. Ezek. 13:23

11 [a]Ezek. 11:1

12 [1]Or, *seek(s* [2]Or, *flock* [a]Jer. [b]Is. 40:11; 56:8 23:3; 31:8; Luk John 10:16 [c]Je Ezek. 30:3; Joe

13 [a]Ezek. 34:2 30; Mic. 7:14 [b]

14 [1]Lit., *fat* [a]P Jer. 31:12-14, 10:9 [b]Ezek. 28 36:29, 30

15 [1]Lit., *cause lie down* [a]Ps. 2 Ezek. 34:23

16 [a]Is. 10:16 [b]

17 [1]Or, *lamb* [a] 20:38; 34:20-22 4:1; Matt. 25:32

18 [a]Num. 16:9, 2 Sam. 7:19; Is.

pastures? Or that you should drink of the clear waters, that you
must [1]foul the rest with your feet?
19 'And as for My flock, they must eat what you tread down with
your feet, and they must drink what you [1]foul with your feet!' "
20 Therefore, thus says the Lord GOD to them, "Behold, I, even I,
will judge between the fat sheep and the lean sheep.
21 "Because you push with side and with shoulder, and [a]thrust at all
the [1]weak with your horns, until you have scattered them [2]abroad,
22 therefore, I will [a]deliver My flock, and they will no longer be a
prey; and I will judge between one sheep and another.
23 "Then I will [a]set over them one [b]shepherd, My servant [c]David,
and he will feed them; he will feed them himself and be their
shepherd.
24 "And I, the LORD, will be their God, and My servant [a]David will
be prince among them; I, the LORD, have spoken.
25 "And I will make a [a]covenant of peace with them and [b]eliminate
harmful beasts from the land, so that they may [c]live securely in the
wilderness and sleep in the woods.
26 "And I will make them and the places around My hill a [a]blessing.
And I will cause [b]showers to come down in their season; they will be
showers of [c]blessing.
27 "Also the tree of the field will yield its fruit, and the earth will
yield its increase, and they will be [a]secure on their land. Then they
will know that I am the LORD, when I have [b]broken the bars of their
yoke and have delivered them from the hand of those who enslaved
them.
28 "And they will no longer be a prey to the nations, and the beasts
of the earth will not devour them; but they will [a]live securely, and no
one will make *them* afraid.
29 "And I will establish for them a [a]renowned planting place, and
they will [b]not again be [1]victims of famine in the land, and they will
not [c]endure the insults of the nations anymore.
30 "Then they will know that [a]I, the LORD their God, am with them,
and that they, the house of Israel, are My people," declares the Lord
GOD.
31 "As for you, My [a]sheep, the [b]sheep of My pasture, you are men,
and I am your God," declares the Lord GOD.

Chapter 35

35 Moreover, the word of the LORD came to me saying,
2 "Son of man, set your face against [a]Mount Seir, and prophe-
sy against it,
3 and say to it, 'Thus says the Lord [1]GOD,

"Behold, I am against you, Mount Seir,
And I will [a]stretch out My hand against you,
And I will make you a [b]desolation and a waste.

4 "I will [a]lay waste your cities,
And you will become a desolation.
Then you will know that I am the LORD.

5 "Because you have had everlasting [a]enmity and have [1]delivered
the sons of Israel to the power of the sword at the time of their
calamity, at the time of the [2b]punishment of the end,
6 therefore, as I live," declares the Lord GOD, "I will [1]give you over

8 [1]Lit., *foul by trampling*
9 [1]Lit., *foul by trampling*
ck [2]Lit., *to the* [a]Deut. 33:17; Luke 13:14-16
72:12-14; Jer. 3; Ezek. 34:10
[a]Rev. 7:17 [b]Is. ...hn 10:11 [c]Jer. ...9; Ezek. 37:24
55:3; Jer. 30:9; 37:24, 25; Hos. 3:5
... 16:60; 20:37; ...ob 5:22, 23; Is. ...-9 [c]Jer. 33:16; ...8:26; 34:27, 28
...en. 12:2; Ezek. ... Deut. 11:13-15; [c]Lev. 25:21; Is. 44:3
[a]Ezek. 38:8, 11 ...:13; Is. 52:2, 3; Jer. 30:8
...er. 30:10; Ezek. 39:26
those gathered ...4:2; 60:21; 61:3 ...34:26, 27; 36:29 [c]Ezek. 36:6, 15
46:7, 11; Ezek. 14:11; 36:28
...Ps. 78:52; 80:1; ...:38 [b]Ps. 100:3; Jer. 23:1
...Gen. 36:8; Ezek. 25:12; 36:5
... [1]Heb., *YHWH*, rendered *LORD*, ...o throughout the [a]Jer. 6:12; 15:6; ...zek. 25:13 [b]Jer. ...7, 18; Ezek. 35:7
... 6:6; 35:9; Mal. 1:3, 4
... Lit., *poured* [2]Or, ...*quity* [a]Ps. 137:7; 25:12, 15; 36:5; ...s 1:11; Obad. 10 ...k. 7:2; 21:25, 29
..., *prepare you for*

to [a]bloodshed, and bloodshed will pursue you; since you have not hated bloodshed, therefore bloodshed will pursue you.

7 "And I will make Mount Seir a waste and a desolation, and I will cut off from it the one who passes through and returns.

8 "And I will [a]fill its mountains with its slain; on your hills and in your valleys and in all your ravines those slain by the sword will [1]fall.

9 "I will make you an everlasting [a]desolation, and your cities will not be inhabited. Then you will know that I am the LORD.

10 "Because you have [a]said, 'These two nations and these two lands will be mine, and we will possess [1]them,' although the [b]LORD was there,

11 therefore, as I live," declares the Lord GOD, "I will deal *with you* [a]according to your anger and according to your envy which you showed because of your hatred against them; so I will [b]make Myself known among them when I judge you.

12 "Then you will know [1]that I, the LORD, have heard all your revilings which you have spoken against the mountains of Israel saying, 'They are laid desolate; they are [a]given to us for food.'

13 "And you have [1a]spoken arrogantly against Me and have multiplied your words against Me; [b]I have heard."

14 'Thus says the Lord GOD, "As all the [a]earth rejoices, I will make you a desolation.

15 "As you [a]rejoiced over the inheritance of the house of Israel because it was desolate, [b]so I will do to you. You will be a [c]desolation, O Mount Seir, and all Edom, all of it. Then they will know that I am the LORD." '

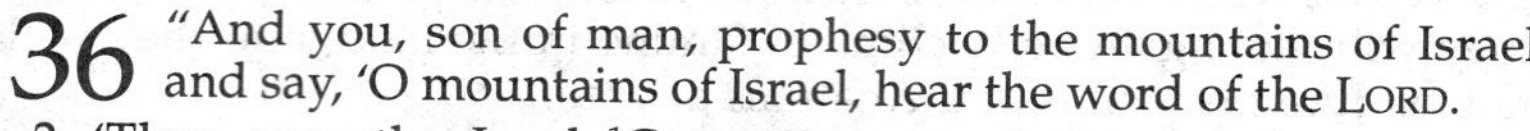

Chapter 36

See the *historical chart of Israel's history* on page I-32. Notice the section from 1948 through the 1990s.

36 "And you, son of man, prophesy to the mountains of Israel and say, 'O mountains of Israel, hear the word of the LORD.

2 'Thus says the Lord [1]GOD, "Because the enemy has spoken against you, 'Aha!' and, 'The everlasting [2a]heights have become our possession,'

3 therefore, prophesy and say, 'Thus says the Lord GOD, "[1]For good cause they have made you [a]desolate and crushed you from every side, that you should become a possession of the rest of the nations, and you have been taken up in the [2b]talk and the whispering of the people." ' "

4 'Therefore, O [a]mountains of Israel, hear the word of the Lord GOD. Thus says the Lord GOD to the mountains and to the hills, to the ravines and to the valleys, to the desolate wastes and to the forsaken cities, which have become a [b]prey and a derision to the rest of the nations which are round about,

5 therefore, thus says the Lord GOD, "Surely in the fire of My [a]jealousy I have spoken against the [b]rest of the nations, and against all Edom, who [1]appropriated My land for themselves as a possession with wholehearted [c]joy *and* with scorn of soul, to drive it out for a prey."

6 'Therefore, prophesy concerning the land of Israel, and say to the mountains and to the hills, to the ravines and to the valleys, "Thus says the Lord GOD, 'Behold, I have spoken in My jealousy and in My wrath because you have [a]endured the insults of the nations.'

6 [a]Is. 63:2-6; 16:38; 32:6

8 [1]Lit., *fall in* 34:5, 6; Ezek. 32:4, 5; 39:4,

9 [a]Jer. 49:13; 25:13

10 [1]Lit., *it* [a]Ps. Ezek. 36:2, 5 48:1-3; 132:13 12:6; Ezek. 48 Zeph. 3:15

11 [a]Ps. 137:7 25:14; Amos 1 9:16; 73:17, 18

12 [1]Or, *that I a LORD: I have h* [a]Jer. 50:7; Eze

13 [1]Lit., *made with your mout* 10:13, 14; 36:2 48:26, 42; Dan [b]Jer. 7:11; 29:2

14 [a]Is. 44:23; Jer. 51:48

15 [a]Jer. 50:11; 4:21 [b]Obad. 15 34:5, 6; Ezek. 3

36:2 [1]Heb., *YH* usually rendere and so through ch. [2]Heb., *Bam* [a]Deut. 32:13; Ps Is. 58:14; Hab. 3

3 [1]Lit., *Becaus the cause* [2]Lit., *the tongue* [a]Jer [b]Ps. 44:13, 14; 18:16; Ezek. 35:

4 [a]Deut. 11:11; 36:1, 6, 8 [b]Ezek 34:8, 28

5 [1]Lit., *gave* [a]Ez 5:13; 36:6; 38:19 25:9, 15-29; Eze [c]Jer. 50:11; Ezek Mic. 7:8

6 [a]Ps. 74:10; 12 Ezek. 34:29

7 "Therefore, thus says the Lord GOD, 'I have [1]sworn that surely the
nations which are around you will themselves endure their insults.
8 'But you, O mountains of Israel, you will [a]put forth your
branches and bear your fruit for My people Israel; for they will soon
come.
9 'For, behold, I am for you, and I will [a]turn to you, and you shall
be [b]cultivated and sown.
10 'And I will multiply men on you, [a]all the house of Israel, all of it;
and the [b]cities will be inhabited, and the waste places will be rebuilt.
11 'And I will multiply on you man and beast; and they will in-
crease and be fruitful; and I will cause you to be inhabited as you
were [a]formerly and will [1]treat you [b]better than at the first. Thus you
will know that I am the LORD.
12 'Yes, I will cause [a]men—My people Israel—to walk on you and
possess you, so that you will become their [b]inheritance and never
again [c]bereave them of children.'
13 "Thus says the Lord GOD, 'Because they say to you, "You are a
[a]devourer of men and have bereaved your [1]nation of children,"
14 therefore, you will no longer devour men, and no longer bereave
your nation of children,' declares the Lord GOD.
15 "And I will not let you hear [a]insults from the nations anymore,
nor will you bear [b]disgrace from the peoples any longer, nor will you
cause your nation to [c]stumble any longer," declares the Lord GOD.' "
16 Then the word of the LORD came to me saying,
17 "Son of man, when the house of Israel was living in their own
land, they [a]defiled it by their ways and their deeds; their way before
Me was like [b]the uncleanness of a woman in her impurity.
18 "Therefore, I [a]poured out My wrath on them for the blood which
they had shed on the land, because they had defiled it with their
idols.
19 "Also I [a]scattered them among the nations, and they were dis-
persed throughout the lands. [b]According to their ways and their
deeds I judged them.
20 "When they came to the nations where they went, they [a]profaned
My holy name, because it was said of them, 'These are the [b]people of
the LORD; yet they have come out of His land.'
21 "But I had [1]concern for My [a]holy name, which the house of Israel
had profaned among the nations where they went.
22 "Therefore, say to the house of Israel, 'Thus says the Lord GOD, "It
is [a]not for your sake, O house of Israel, that I am about to act, but for
My holy name, which you have profaned among the nations where
you went.
23 "And I will [a]vindicate the holiness of My great name which has
been profaned among the nations, which you have profaned in their
midst. Then the [b]nations will know that I am the LORD," declares the
Lord GOD, "when I prove Myself holy among you in their sight.
24 "For I will [a]take you from the nations, gather you from all the
lands, and bring you into your own land.
25 "Then I will [a]sprinkle clean water on you, and you will be clean; I
will cleanse you from all your [b]filthiness and from all your [c]idols.
26 "Moreover, I will give you a [a]new heart and put a new spirit
within you; and I will remove the [b]heart of stone from your flesh and
give you a heart of flesh.

.., *lifted up My hand*
[a]Is. 4:2; 27:6; Ezek. 17:23; 34:26-29
[a]Lev. 26:9 [b]Ezek. 28:26; 34:14; 36:34
[a]Is. 27:6; 49:17-23; ek. 37:21, 22 [b]Jer. 7, 28; 33:12; Ezek. 36:33
[1]Lit., *cause good* 0:18; Ezek. 16:55; . 7:14 [b]Job 42:12; Is. 51:3
2 [a]Ezek. 34:13, 14 . 47:14 [c]Jer. 15:7; Ezek. 22:12, 27
Or, *nations,* and so throughout the ch. [a]Num. 13:32
[a]Is. 60:14; Ezek. ; 36:7 [b]Ps. 89:50; 4; Ezek. 22:4 [c]Is. ; Jer. 13:16; 18:15
er. 2:7 [b]Lev. 15:19
[a]2 Chr. 34:21, 25; n. 2:4; 4:11; Ezek. 22:20, 22
Deut. 28:64; Ezek. ; 22:15; Amos 9:9 zek. 24:14; 39:24; Rom. 2:6
0 [a]Is. 52:5; Ezek. ; Rom. 2:24 [b]Jer. 33:24
[1]Lit., *compassion* s. 74:18; Is. 48:9; Ezek. 20:44
eut. 7:7, 8; 9:5, 6; Ezek. 36:32
3 [a]Is. 5:16; Ezek. 1; 38:23; 39:7, 25 Ps. 102:15; 126:2
[a]Is. 43:5, 6; Ezek. 34:13; 37:21
um. 19:17-19; Ps. Titus 3:5, 6; Heb. 9; 10:22 [b]Is. 4:4; 3:1 [c]Is. 2:18, 20; Hos. 14:3, 8
[a]Ps. 51:10; Ezek. 18:31; John 3:3, Cor. 5:17 [b]Ezek. 11:19; Zech. 7:12

27 "And I will [a]put My Spirit within you and cause you to walk in
My statutes, and you will be careful to observe My ordinances.
28 "And you will live in the land that I gave to your forefathers; so
you will be [a]My people, and I will be your God.
29 "Moreover, I will save you from all your uncleanness; and I will
call for the grain and multiply it, and I [a]will not [1]bring a famine on
you.
30 "And I will [a]multiply the fruit of the tree and the produce of the
field, that you may not receive again the disgrace of famine among
the nations.
31 "Then you will [a]remember your evil ways and your deeds that
were not good, and you will loathe yourselves in your own sight for
your iniquities and your abominations.
32 "I am not doing *this* [a]for your sake," declares the Lord GOD, "let it
be known to you. Be ashamed and confounded for your ways, O
house of Israel!"
33 'Thus says the Lord GOD, "On the day that I cleanse you from all
your iniquities, I will cause the [a]cities to be inhabited, and the [b]waste
places will be rebuilt.
34 "And the desolate land will be cultivated instead of being a
desolation in the sight of everyone who passed by.
35 "And they will say, 'This desolate land has become like the [a]gar-
den of Eden; and the waste, desolate, and ruined cities are fortified
and inhabited.'
36 "Then the nations that are left round about you will know that I,
the LORD, have rebuilt the ruined places *and* planted that which was
desolate; I, the LORD, have spoken and [a]will do it."
37 'Thus says the Lord GOD, "This also I will let the house of Israel
ask Me to do for them: I will increase their men like a flock.
38 "Like the [a]flock [1]for sacrifices, like the flock at Jerusalem during
her appointed feasts, so will the waste cities be filled with [b]flocks of
men. Then they will know that I am the LORD." ' "

Chapter 37

37 The [a]hand of the LORD was upon me, and He [b]brought me out
[1]by the Spirit of the LORD and set me down in the middle of
the [c]valley; and it was full of bones.
2 And He caused me to pass among them round about, and be-
hold, *there were* very many on the surface of the valley; and lo, *they
were* very dry.
3 And He said to me, "Son of man, [a]can these bones live?" And I
answered, "O Lord [1]GOD, [b]Thou knowest."
4 Again He said to me, "[a]Prophesy over these bones, and say to
them, 'O dry bones, [b]hear the word of the LORD.'
5 "Thus says the Lord GOD to these bones, 'Behold, I will cause
[1a]breath to enter you that you may come to life.
6 'And I will put sinews on you, make flesh grow back on you,
cover you with skin, and put breath in you that you may come alive;
and you will [a]know that I am the LORD.' "
7 So I prophesied [a]as I was commanded; and as I prophesied, there
was a [1]noise, and behold, a rattling; and the bones came together,
bone to its bone.
8 And I looked, and behold, sinews were on them, and flesh grew,
and skin covered them; but there was no breath in them.

27 [a]Is. 44:3; Ezek. 37:14; 2:28, 29

28 [a]Ezek. 14 37:23, 27

29 [1]Lit., *put* [a] 34:27, 29; Hos

30 [a]Lev. 26:4; 34:27

31 [a]Ezek. 16: 20:43

32 [a]Deut. 9:5

33 [a]Ezek. 36: 8:7, 8 [b]Is. 58:

35 [a]Is. 51:3; E. Joel 2:3

36 [a]Ezek. 17:2 37:14; Hos. 14:

38 [1]Lit., *of holy* [a]1 Kin. 8:63; 2 C 35:7-9; John 2: 74:1; 100:3; Jer John 10:7, 9, 16

37:1 [1]Or, *in* [a]E 33:22; 40:1 [b]Ez 11:24; 43:5; Act [c]Jer. 7:32-8:2

3 [1]Heb., *YHWH* usually rendere and so througho ch. [a]Ezek. 26:1 32:39; 1 Sam. 2

4 [a]Ezek. 37:9, 22:29; Ezek. 36:

5 [1]Or, *spirit*, and throughout the c [a]Gen. 2:7; Ps. 10 30; Ezek. 37:9,

6 [a]Is. 49:23; Eze 38:23; 39:6; Joel 3:17

7 [1]Lit., *voice*; or, *thunder* [a]Jer. 13

9 Then He said to me, "Prophesy to the breath, prophesy, son of
man, and say to the breath, 'Thus says the Lord GOD, "Come from
the four winds, O breath, and [a]breathe on these slain, that they [b]come
to life."' "
10 So I prophesied as He commanded me, and the [a]breath came
into them, and they came to life, and stood on their feet, an [b]exceed-
ingly great army.
11 Then He said to me, "Son of man, these bones are the [a]whole
house of Israel; behold, they say, 'Our [b]bones are dried up, and our
hope has perished. We are [1]completely [c]cut off.'
12 "Therefore prophesy, and say to them, 'Thus says the Lord GOD,
"Behold, I will open your graves and [a]cause you to come up out of
your graves, My people; and I will bring you into the land of Israel.
13 "Then you will know that I am the LORD, when I have opened
your graves and caused you to come up out of your graves, My
people.
14 "And I will [a]put My [1]Spirit within you, and you will come to life,
and I will place you on your own land. Then you will know that I,
the LORD, have spoken and done it," declares the LORD.' "
15 The word of the LORD came again to me saying,
16 "And you, son of man, take for yourself [a]one stick and write on it,
'For [b]Judah and for the sons of Israel, his companions'; then take
another stick and write on it, 'For [c]Joseph, the stick of Ephraim and
all the house of Israel, his companions.'
17 "Then [a]join them for yourself one to another into one stick, that
they may become one in your hand.
18 "And when the sons of your people speak to you saying, 'Will
you not declare to us [a]what you mean by these?'
19 say to them, 'Thus says the Lord GOD, "Behold, I will take the
stick of Joseph, which is in the hand of Ephraim, and the tribes of
Israel, his companions; and I will put them with it, with the stick of
Judah, and make them one stick, and they will be one in My hand."'
20 "And the sticks on which you write will be in your hand before
their eyes.
21 "And say to them, 'Thus says the Lord GOD, "Behold, I will [a]take
the sons of Israel from among the nations where they have gone, and
I will gather them from every side and bring them into their own
land;
22 and I will make them [a]one nation in the land, on the mountains
of Israel; and [b]one king will be king for all of them; and they will no
longer be two nations, and they will no longer be divided into two
kingdoms.
23 "And they will [a]no longer defile themselves with their idols, or
with their detestable things, or with any of their transgressions; but
[b]I will deliver them from all their [1]dwelling places in which they
have sinned, and will cleanse them. And they will be My people,
and I will be their God.
24 "And My servant [a]David will be king over them, and they will all
have [b]one shepherd; and they will walk in My ordinances, and keep
My statutes, and observe them.
25 "And they shall live on the land that I gave to Jacob My servant,
in which your fathers lived; and they will live on it, they, and their
sons, and their sons' sons, forever; and [a]David My servant shall be
their prince forever.

[a]Ps. 104:30 [b]Hos. 13:14
0 [a]Rev. 11:11 [b]Jer. 30:19; 33:22
11 [1]Lit., *cut off to* *rselves* [a]Jer. 33:24; k. 36:10; 39:25 [b]Ps. 1:7 [c]Ps. 88:5; Lam. 3:54
12 [a]Deut. 32:39; Sam. 2:6; Is. 26:19; 66:14; Hos. 13:14
14 [1]Or, *breath* [a]Is. 32:15; Ezek. 11:19; 5:27; 37:6, 9; 39:29; Joel 2:28, 29; Zech. 12:10
16 [a]Num. 17:2, 3 hr. 10:17; 11:11-17; 9 [c]1 Kin. 12:16-20; 2 Chr. 10:19
Is. 11:13; Jer. 50:4; zek. 37:22-24; Hos. 1:11; Zeph. 3:9
[a]Ezek. 12:9; 17:12; 20:49; 24:19
21 [a]Is. 43:5, 6; Jer. 29:14; Ezek. 36:24; :27; Amos 9:14, 15
[a]Jer. 3:18; 50:4, 5; zek. 36:10 [b]Ezek. 34:23, 24; 37:24
Another reading is *acksliding*s [a]Ezek. 5 [b]Ezek. 36:28, 29
4 [a]Jer. 30:9; Ezek. 24; 37:25; Hos. 3:5 s. 78:71; Is. 40:11; Ezek. 34:23
25 [a]Is. 11:1; Ezek. 37:24; Zech. 6:12

26 "And I will make a [a]covenant of peace with them; it will be an
[b]everlasting covenant with them. And I will [1]place them and [c]multi-
ply them, and will set My [d]sanctuary in their midst forever.
27 "My [a]dwelling place also will be with them; and [b]I will be their
God, and they will be My people.
28 "And the nations will know that I am the LORD [a]who sanctifies
Israel, when My sanctuary is in their midst forever." ' "

Chapter 38

38 And the word of the LORD came to me saying,
2 "Son of man, set your face toward [a]Gog of the land of [b]
Magog, the [1]prince of [c]Rosh, [d]Meshech, and [d]Tubal, and prophesy
against him,
3 and say, 'Thus says the Lord [1]GOD, "Behold, I am against you, O
Gog, [2]prince of Rosh, Meshech, and Tubal.
4 "And I will turn you about, and put hooks into your jaws, and I
will [a]bring you out, and all your army, [b]horses and horsemen, all of
them [1]splendidly attired, a great company *with* buckler and shield,
all of them wielding swords;
5 [a]Persia, [1b]Ethiopia, and [c]Put with them, all of them *with* shield
and helmet;
6 [a]Gomer with all its troops; [b]Beth-togarmah *from* the remote parts
of the north with all its troops—many peoples with you.
7 "[a]Be prepared, and prepare yourself, you and all your companies
that are assembled about you, and be a guard for them.
8 "[a]After many days you will be summoned; in the latter years you
will come into the land that is restored from the sword, *whose in-
habitants* have been [b]gathered from many [1]nations to the [c]mountains
of Israel which had been a continual waste; but [2]its people were
brought out from the [1]nations, and they are [d]living securely, all of
them.
9 "And you will go up, you will come [a]like a storm; you will be like
a [b]cloud covering the land, you and all your troops, and many
peoples with you."
10 'Thus says the Lord GOD, "It will come about on that day, that
[1]thoughts will come into your mind, and you will [a]devise an evil
plan,
11 and you will say, 'I will go up against the land of [1a]unwalled
villages. I will go against those who are [b]at rest, that live securely, all
of them living without walls, and having no bars or gates,
12 to [a]capture spoil and to seize plunder, to turn your hand against
the waste places which are *now* inhabited, and against the people
who are gathered from the nations, who have acquired cattle and
goods, who live at the [1]center of the world.'
13 "[a]Sheba, and [b]Dedan, and the merchants of [c]Tarshish, with all its
[1]villages, will say to you, 'Have you come to capture spoil? Have
you assembled your company to seize plunder, to carry away silver
and gold, to take away cattle and goods, to capture great [d]spoil?' " '
14 "Therefore, prophesy, son of man, and say to Gog, 'Thus says the
Lord GOD, "On that day when My people Israel are [a]living securely,
will you not know *it*?
15 "And [a]you will come from your place out of the remote parts of
the north, you and many peoples with you, all of them riding on
horses, a great assembly and a mighty army;

26 [1]Lit., *give* [a]... 16:62; 20:37; 3... [b]Ps. 89:3, 4; Is. 59:21; Ezek. 16... 30:19; Ezek. 36... 37 [d]Ezek. 20:4...

27 [a]John 1:14; 21:3 [b]Ezek. 37... 2 Cor. 6:16

28 [a]Ex. 31:13; ... 20:12

38:2 [1]Or, *chief* ... *Meshech* [a]Ezek... 14, 16, 18; 39:1... Rev. 20:8 [b]Gen... Ezek. 39:6; Rev... [c]Ezek. 38:3; 39:... [d]Ezek. 27:13; 3...

3 [1]Heb., *YHWH* usually rendered... and so through... ch. [2]Or, *chief pr... Meshech*

4 [1]Or, *clothed in armor* [a]Is. 43:17... 38:15; Dan. 11:4...

5 [1]Lit., *Cush* [a]2... 36:20; Ezra 1:1; 27:10; Dan. 8:20... 10:6-8; Ezek. 30... [c]Ezek. 27:10; 30...

6 [a]Gen. 10:2, 3 10:3; Ezek. 27:1...

7 [a]Is. 8:9

8 [1]Lit., *peoples* ... *was* [a]Is. 24:22 [b]... 11:11; Ezek. 36:2... 37:21; 38:12; 39:... [c]Ezek. 34:13; 36:... [d]Ezek. 38:11, 14;...

9 [a]Is. 5:28; 21:1; 28:2; Jer. 4:13 [b]E... 30:18; 38:16; Joe...

10 [1]Lit., *words* [a]... 36:4; Mic. 2:1

11 [1]Or, *open cou...* [a]Zech. 2:4 [b]Jer. ...

12 [1]Lit., *navel* [a]Is... Ezek. 29:19

13 [1]Or, *young lio...* [a]Ezek. 27:22, 23 25:13; 27:15, 20... 27:12 [d]Is. 10:6; 3... Jer. 15:13

14 [a]Jer. 23:6; Eze... 38:8, 11; Zech. 2:...

15 [a]Ezek. 39:2

16 and you will come up against My people Israel like a cloud to cover the land. It will come about in the last days that I shall bring you against My land, in order that the nations may [a]know Me when I shall be [b]sanctified through you before their eyes, O Gog."

17 'Thus says the Lord GOD, "Are you the one of whom I spoke in former days through My servants the prophets of Israel, who [a]prophesied in those days for *many* years that I would bring you against them?

18 "And it will come about on that day, when Gog comes against the land of Israel," declares the Lord GOD, "that My fury will mount up in My [a]anger.

19 "And in My [a]zeal and in My blazing wrath I declare *that* on that day there will surely be a great [1b]earthquake in the land of Israel.

20 "[a]And the fish of the sea, the birds of the heavens, the beasts of the field, all the creeping things that creep on the earth, and all the men who are on the face of the earth will shake at My presence; the [b]mountains also will be thrown down, the steep pathways will [1]collapse, and every wall will fall to the ground.

21 "And I shall call for a [a]sword against [1]him on all My mountains," declares the Lord GOD. "[b]Every man's sword will be against his brother.

22 "And with pestilence and with blood I shall enter into [a]judgment with him; and I shall rain on him, and on his troops, and on the many peoples who are with him, [1]a torrential rain, with [b]hailstones, fire, and brimstone.

23 "And I shall magnify Myself, sanctify Myself, and [a]make Myself known in the sight of many nations; and they will know that I am the LORD."'

Chapter 39

39 "And [a]you, son of man, prophesy against Gog, and say, 'Thus says the Lord [1]GOD, "Behold, I am against you, O Gog, [2]prince of Rosh, Meshech, and Tubal;

2 and I shall turn you around, drive you on, take you up from the remotest parts of the north, and bring you against the mountains of Israel.

3 "And I shall [a]strike your bow from your left hand, and dash down your arrows from your right hand.

4 "You shall [a]fall on the mountains of Israel, you and all your troops, and the peoples who are with you; I shall give you as [b]food to every [1]kind of predatory bird and beast of the field.

5 "You will fall on the [1]open field; for it is I who have spoken," declares the Lord GOD.

6 "And I shall send [a]fire upon Magog and those who inhabit the [b]coastlands in safety; and they will know that I am the LORD.

7 "And My [a]holy name I shall make known in the midst of My people Israel; and I shall not let My holy name be [b]profaned anymore. And the [c]nations will know that I am the LORD, the [d]Holy One in Israel.

8 "Behold, it is coming and it shall be done," declares the Lord GOD. "That is the day of which I have spoken.

9 "Then those who inhabit the cities of Israel will [a]go out, and make [b]fires with the weapons and burn *them*, both shields and bucklers,

6 [a]Ps. 83:18; Ezek. 23; 38:23 [b]Is. 5:16; 29:23; Ezek. 28:22

[a]Is. 5:26-29; 34:1-6; 1-6; 66:15, 16; Joel 3:9-14

18 [a]Ps. 18:8, 15

Or, *shaking* [a]Deut. ; Ps. 18:7, 8; Ezek. ; 36:5, 6; Nah. 1:2; . 12:29 [b]Joel 3:16; Hag. 2:6, 7, 21

Lit., *fall* [a]Jer. 4:24, 25; Hos. 4:3; Nah. 1:4-6 [b]Zech. 14:4

[1]I.e., Gog [a]Ezek. 14:17 [b]Judg. 7:22; Sam. 14:20; 2 Chr. 20:23; Hag. 2:22

Lit., *an overflowing* . 66:16; Jer. 25:31 11:6; 18:12-14; Is. 28:17

3 [a]Ps. 9:16; Ezek. 37:28; 38:16

:1 [1]Heb., *YHWH*, ly rendered *LORD*, so throughout the [2]Or, *chief prince of shech* [a]Ezek. 38:2

Ps. 76:3; Jer. 21:4, ek. 30:21-24; Hos. 1:5

., *wing* [a]Is. 14:24, 5; Ezek. 39:17-20 zek. 29:5; 32:4, 5; 33:27

5 [1]Lit., *face of the*

[a]Ezek. 30:8, 16; , 22; Amos 1:4, 7, n. 1:6 [b]Ps. 72:10; 66:19; Jer. 25:22

[a]Ezek. 36:20-22; [b]Ex. 20:7; Ezek. :9, 14, 39 [c]Ezek. :16, 23 [d]Is. 12:6; 14; 55:5; 60:9, 14

s. 66:24; Mal. 1:5 sh. 11:6; Ps. 46:9

bows and arrows, war clubs and spears and for seven years they will
make fires of them.
10 "And they will not take wood from the field or gather firewood
from the forests, for they will make fires with the weapons; and they
will take the spoil of those who despoiled them, and seize the
[a]plunder of those who plundered them," declares the Lord GOD.
11 "And it will come about on that day that I shall give Gog a burial
ground there in Israel, the valley of those who pass by east of the
sea, and it will block off the passers-by. So they will bury Gog there
with all his multitude, and they will call *it* the valley of [1]Hamon-gog.
12 "For seven months the house of Israel will be burying them in
order to [a]cleanse the land.
13 "Even all the people of the land will bury *them;* and it will be [1]to
their [a]renown *on* the day that I [b]glorify Myself," declares the Lord
GOD.
14 "And they will set apart men who will constantly pass through
the land, [a]burying those who were passing through, even those left
on the surface of the ground, in order to cleanse it. At the end of
seven months they will make a search.
15 "And as those who pass through the land pass through and
anyone sees a man's bone, then he will [1]set up a marker by it until
the buriers have buried it in the valley of [2]Hamon-gog.
16 "And even *the* name of *the* city will be Hamonah. So they will
cleanse the land." '
17 "And as for you, son of man, thus says the Lord GOD, 'Speak to
every [1]kind of [a]bird and to every [a]beast of the field, "Assemble and
come, gather from every side to My sacrifice which I am going to
[b]sacrifice for you, as a great sacrifice on the mountains of Israel, that
you may eat flesh and drink blood.
18 "You shall [a]eat the flesh of mighty men, and drink the blood of the
princes of the earth, as *though they were* [b]rams, lambs, goats, and
[c]bulls, all of them fatlings of [d]Bashan.
19 "So you will eat fat until you are glutted, and drink blood until
you are drunk, from My sacrifice which I have sacrificed for you.
20 "And you will be glutted at My table with [a]horses and
charioteers, with mighty men and all the men of war," declares the
Lord GOD.
21 "And I shall set My [a]glory among the nations; and all the nations
will see My judgment which I have executed, and My hand which I
have laid on them.
22 "And the house of Israel will [a]know that I am the LORD their God
from that day onward.
23 "And the nations will know that the house of Israel went into
exile for their [a]iniquity because they acted treacherously against Me,
and I [b]hid My face from them; so I gave them into the hand of their
adversaries, and all of them fell by the sword.
24 "[a]According to their uncleanness and according to their transgres-
sions I dealt with them, and I hid My face from them." ' "
25 Therefore thus says the Lord GOD, "Now I shall [1a]restore the
fortunes of Jacob, and have mercy on the whole [b]house of Israel; and
I shall be [c]jealous for My holy name.
26 "And they shall [1a]forget their disgrace and all their treachery
which they [2]perpetrated against Me, when they [b]live securely on
their *own* land with [c]no one to make them afraid.

10 [a]Is. 14:2; 3 5:8; Hab. 2:8
11 [1]Or, *the m* *Gog*
12 [a]Deut. 21:2 39:14, 16
13 [1]Or, *a men them* [a]Jer. 33: 3:19, 20 [b]Ezek
14 [a]Jer. 14:16
15 [1]Lit., *build* *multitude of G*
17 [1]Lit., *wing* Jer. 12:9; Ezek Rev. 19:17, 18 34:6, 7; Jer. 46 Zeph. 1:7
18 [a]Ezek. 29:5 19:18 [b]Jer. 51: 50:27 [d]Ps. 22:1 4:1
20 [a]Ps. 76:5, 6 38:4; Hag. 2:22 19:18
21 [a]Ex. 9:16; Is Ezek. 36:23; 38 39:13
22 [a]Jer. 24:7
23 [a]Jer. 22:8, 9 Ezek. 36:18, 19 1:15; 59:2; Ezek
24 [a]2 Kin. 17:7; 2:17, 19; 4:18; E 36:19
25 [1]Or, *return th captivity* [a]Is. 27: Jer. 33:7; Ezek. [b]Jer. 31:1; Ezek. 37:21, 22; Hos. [c]Ex. 20:5; Nah.
26 [1]Another rea *bear* [2]Lit., *did treacherously* [a]E 16:63; 20:43; 36 [b]1 Kin. 4:25; Eze 34:25-28 [c]Is. 17 4:4

27 “When I [a]bring them back from the peoples and gather them from
the lands of their enemies, then I shall be [b]sanctified [1]through them
in the sight of the many nations.
28 “Then they will know that I am the LORD their God because I
made them go into exile among the nations, and then gathered them
again to their own land; and I will leave none of them there any
longer.
29 “And I will not hide My face from them any longer, for I shall
have [a]poured out My Spirit on the house of Israel,” declares the Lord
GOD.

Chapter 40

40 In the [a]twenty-fifth year of our exile, at the beginning of the
year, on the tenth of the month, in the fourteenth year after
the [b]city was [1]taken, on that same day the [c]hand of the LORD was
upon me and He brought me there.

573 B.C.

2 In the [a]visions of God He brought me into the land of Israel, and
set me on a very [b]high mountain; and on it [c]to the south *there was* a
[d]structure like a city.
3 So He brought me there; and behold, there was a man whose
appearance was like the appearance of [a]bronze, with a [b]line of flax
and a [c]measuring [1]rod in his hand; and he was standing in the
gateway.
4 And the man said to me, “[a]Son of man, [b]see with your eyes, hear
with your ears, and give attention to all that I am going to show you;
for you have been brought here in order to show *it* to you. [c]Declare
to the house of Israel all that you see.”
5 And behold, there was a [a]wall on the outside of the [1]temple all
around, and in the man’s hand was a measuring rod of six cubits,
each of which was a cubit and a [2]handbreadth. So he measured the
thickness of the [3]wall, one rod; and the height, one rod.
6 Then he went to the gate which faced [a]east, went up its steps,
and measured the threshold of the gate, one rod [1]in width; and the
other threshold *was* one rod [1]in width.
7 And the [a]guardroom *was* one rod long and one rod wide; and
there were five cubits between the guardrooms. And the threshold of
the gate by the porch of the gate [1]facing inward *was* one rod.
8 Then he measured the porch of the gate [1]facing inward, one rod.
9 And he measured the porch of the gate, eight cubits; and its side
pillars, two cubits. And the porch of the gate was [1]faced inward.
10 And the guardrooms of the gate toward the east *numbered* three
on each side; the three of them had the same measurement. The side
pillars also had the same measurement on each side.
11 And he measured the width of the [1]gateway, ten cubits, and the
length of the gate, thirteen cubits.
12 And *there was* a [1]barrier *wall* one cubit *wide* in front of the guard-
rooms on each side; and the guardrooms *were* six cubits *square* on
each side.
13 And he measured the gate from the roof of the one guardroom to
the roof of the other, a width of twenty-five cubits from *one* door to
the door opposite.
14 And he made the side pillars sixty cubits *high;* the gate *extended*
round about to the side pillar of the [a]courtyard.

27 [1]Lit., *in* [a]Ezek. 36:24; 37:21 [b]Ezek. 36:23; 38:16, 23
29 [a]Is. 32:15; Ezek. 27; 37:14; Joel 2:28
40:1 [1]Lit., *struck* Ezek. 32:1, 17; 33:21 [b]2 Kin. 25:1-7; Jer. 1-9; 52:4-11; Ezek. 1 [c]Ezek. 1:3; 3:14, 22; 37:1
Ezek. 1:1; 8:3; Dan. 7 [b]Is. 2:2, 3; Ezek. 7:23; 20:40; 37:22; Mic. 4:1; Rev. 21:10 [c]Ps. 48:2; Is. 14:13 [d]1 Chr. 28:12, 19
[1]Lit., *reed*, and so throughout the ch. ek. 1:7; Dan. 10:6; 1:15 [b]Ezek. 47:3; 2:1, 2 [c]Rev. 11:1; 21:15
[a]Ezek. 2:1, 3, 6, 8; 44:5 [b]Ezek. 2:7, 8; 4:5 [c]Is. 21:10; Jer. 26:2; Acts 20:27
[1]Lit., *house* [2]I.e., 4 in. [3]Lit., *building* 26:1; Ezek. 42:20
r, *in depth* [a]Ezek. ; 11:1; 40:20; 43:1
it., *from the house* 40:10-16, 21, 29, 33, 36
it., *from the house*
t., *from the house*
t., *entrance of the gate*
12 [1]Lit., *border*
[a]Ex. 27:9; 1 Chr. s. 100:4; Is. 62:9; Ezek. 8:7; 42:1

15 And *from* the front of the entrance gate to the front of the inner
porch of the gate *was* fifty cubits.
16 And *there were* [1a]shuttered windows *looking* toward the guard-
rooms, and toward their side pillars within the gate all around, and
likewise for the porches. And *there were* windows all around inside;
and on *each* side pillar *were* [b]palm tree ornaments.
17 Then he brought me into the [a]outer court, and behold, *there were*
[b]chambers and a pavement, made for the court all around; thirty
chambers [1]faced the pavement.
18 And the pavement (*that is,* the lower pavement) *was* by the [1]side
of the gates, corresponding to the length of the gates.
19 Then he measured the width from the front of the [a]lower gate to
the front of the exterior of the inner court, a [b]hundred cubits on the
east and on the north.
20 And *as for* the [a]gate of the outer court which faced the north, he
measured its length and its width.
21 And [1]it had three [a]guardrooms on each side; and its [b]side pillars
and its porches [2]had the same measurement as the first gate. Its
length *was* [c]fifty cubits, and the width [d]twenty-five cubits.
22 And its [a]windows, and its porches, and its palm tree ornaments
had the same measurements as the [b]gate which faced toward the east;
and [1]it was reached by seven [c]steps, and its [2]porch *was* in front of
them.
23 And the inner court had a gate opposite the gate on the north as
well as *the gate* on the east; and he measured a [a]hundred cubits from
gate to gate.
24 Then he led me toward the south, and behold, there was a [a]gate
toward the south; and he measured its [b]side pillars and its porches
according to [1]those same measurements.
25 And [1]the gate and its porches had [a]windows all around like
[2]those other windows; the length *was* [b]fifty cubits and the width
twenty-five cubits.
26 And *there were* seven [a]steps going up to it, and its porches *were* in
front of them; and it had [b]palm tree ornaments on its side pillars, one
on each side.
27 And the inner court had a gate toward the [a]south; and he
measured from gate to gate toward the south, a [b]hundred cubits.
28 Then he brought me to the inner court by the south gate; and he
measured the south gate [a]according to those same measurements.
29 Its [a]guardrooms also, its side pillars, and its [b]porches *were* ac-
cording to those same measurements. And [1]the gate and its porches
had [b]windows all around; it *was* [c]fifty cubits long and twenty-five
cubits wide.
30 And *there were* [a]porches all around, twenty-five cubits long and
five cubits wide.
31 And its porches *were* toward the outer court; and [a]palm tree
ornaments *were* on its side pillars, and its stairway had eight [b]steps.
32 And he brought me into the [a]inner court toward the east. And he
measured the gate [b]according to those same measurements.
33 Its [a]guardrooms also, its side pillars, and its porches *were* accord-
ing to those same measurements. And [1]the gate and its porches had
[b]windows all around; it *was* [c]fifty cubits long and twenty-five cubits
wide.
34 And its [a]porches *were* toward the outer court; and [a]palm tree

16 [1]Or, *bevel* *inwards* [a]1 Ki Ezek. 41:16, 2 6:29, 32, 35; 2 Ezek. 40:22, 2 37; 41:18-20,

17 [1]Lit., *to* [a]E 42:1; 46:21; R [b]2 Kin. 23:11; 9:26; 23:28; 2 31:11; Ezek. 4

18 [1]Lit., *shou*

19 [a]Ezek. 40: 46:1, 2 [b]Ezek.

20 [a]Ezek. 40:

21 [1]Lit., *its gu* *were three* [2]Li [a]Ezek. 40:7 [b]E 40:16, 30 [c]Eze [d]Ezek. 40:13

22 [1]Lit., *they v* *going up into it* *porches* [a]Ezek [b]Ezek. 40:6 [c]E 40:26, 31, 34,

23 [a]Ezek. 40:1

24 [1]Lit., *these* *measurements,* throughout the [a]Ezek. 40:6, 20 46:9 [b]Ezek. 40

25 [1]Lit., *it* [2]Lit. *windows* [a]Ezek 22, 29 [b]Ezek. 4

26 [a]Ezek. 40:6, [b]Ezek. 40:16

27 [a]Ezek. 40:2 [b]Ezek. 40:19

28 [a]Ezek. 40:32

29 [1]Lit., *it* [a]Eze 10, 21 [b]Ezek. 4 22, 25 [c]Ezek. 4

30 [a]Ezek. 40:16

31 [a]Ezek. 40:16 40:22, 26, 34, 37

32 [a]Ezek. 40:28 [b]Ezek. 40:28

33 [1]Lit., *it* [a]Ezek 40:29 [b]Ezek. 40 [c]Ezek. 40:21

34 [a]Ezek. 40:16

ornaments *were* on its side pillars, on each side, and its stairway had
eight [b]steps.
35 Then he brought me to the [a]north gate; and he measured *it* ac-
cording to those same measurements,
36 *with* its [a]guardrooms, its side pillars, and its [b]porches. And [1]the
gate had [b]windows all around; the length *was* [c]fifty cubits and the
width twenty-five cubits.
37 And its side pillars *were* toward the outer court; and [a]palm tree
ornaments *were* on its side pillars on each side, and its stairway had
eight [b]steps.
38 And a [a]chamber with its doorway was by the side pillars at the
gates; there they [b]rinse the burnt offering.
39 And in the porch of the gate *were* two [a]tables on each side, on
which to slaughter the [b]burnt offering, the sin offering, and the guilt
offering.
40 And on the outer [1]side, [2]as one went up to the [3]gateway toward
the north, were two tables; and on the other [1]side of the porch of the
gate *were* two tables.
41 Four [a]tables *were* on each side [1]next to the gate; *or,* eight tables on
which they slaughter *sacrifices.*
42 And for the burnt offering *there were* four [a]tables of [b]hewn stone,
a cubit and a half long, a cubit and a half wide, and one cubit high,
on which they lay the instruments with which they slaughter the
[a]burnt offering and the sacrifice.
43 And the double [1]hooks, one handbreadth in length, were in-
stalled [2]in the house all around; and on the tables *was* the flesh of the
offering.
44 And from the outside to the [a]inner gate were [1b]chambers for the
[c]singers in the inner court, *one of* which was at the [2]side of the north
gate, with [3]its front toward the south, and one at the [2]side of the [4]east
gate facing toward the north.
45 And he said to me, "This is the [a]chamber which faces toward the
south, *intended* for the priests who [b]keep charge of the [1] temple;
46 but the [a]chamber which faces toward the north is for the priests
who [b]keep charge of the altar. These are the [c]sons of Zadok, who
from the sons of Levi [d]come near to the LORD to minister to Him."
47 And he measured the court, a *perfect* square, a [a]hundred cubits
long and a hundred cubits wide; and the altar was in front of the
[1]temple.
48 Then he brought me to the [a]porch of the [1]temple and measured
each side pillar of the porch, five cubits on each side; and the width
of the gate was three cubits on each side.
49 The length of the porch was twenty cubits, and the width eleven
cubits; and at the [a]stairway by which it was ascended *were* [b]columns
belonging to the side pillars, one on each side.

Chapter 41

41 Then he [a]brought me to the [1b]nave and measured the [c]side
pillars; six cubits wide on each side *was* the width of the [2]side
pillar.
2 And the width of the entrance *was* ten cubits, and the [1]sides of
the entrance were five cubits on each side. And he measured [2]the
length of the nave, [a]forty cubits, and the width, [a]twenty cubits.
3 Then he went [1a]inside and measured each [b]side pillar of the

34 [b]Ezek. 40:22, 37
35 [a]Ezek. 40:27, 32; 44:4; 47:2
36 [1]Lit., *it* [a]Ezek. 40:7, Ezek. 40:16 [c]Ezek. 40:21
37 Ezek. 40:16 [b]Ezek. 40:34
38 [a]1 Chr. 28:12; Neh. 9; Jer. 35:4; 36:10; Ezek. 40:17; 41:10; 42:13 [b]2 Chr. 4:6
39 [a]Ezek. 40:42 [b]Lev. 1:3-17; Ezek. 46:2
40 [1]Lit., *shoulder* [2]Lit., *to the one going up* ...*ntrance of the gate*
41 [1]Lit., *by the shoulder of* [a]Ezek. 40:39, 40
42 [a]Ezek. 40:39 [b]Ex. 20:25
43 [1]Or, *ledges* [2]Or, *inside*
44 [1]Gr. reads *in two chambers* [2]Lit., ...*der* [3]Lit., *their* [4]Gr. reads *south* [a]Ezek. ...27 [b]Ezek. 40:17, 38 [c]1 Chr. 6:31, 32; 16:41-43; 25:1-7
45 [1]Or, *house* [a]Ezek. ...7, 38 [b]1 Chr. 9:23; Ps. 134:1
46 [a]Ezek. 40:17, 38 ...ev. 6:12, 13; Ezek. 44:15 [c]1 Kin. 2:35; Ezek. 43:19; 48:11 ...v. 10:3; Num. 16:5, Ezek. 42:13; 45:4
47 [1]Lit., *house* [a]Ezek. 40:19, 23, 27
48 [1]Lit., *house* [a]1 Kin. 6:3; 2 Chr. 3:4
49 [a]Ezek. 40:31, 34, ...7 [b]1 Kin. 7:15-22; 2 Chr. 3:17; Jer. ...2:17-23; Rev. 3:12
41:1 [1]I.e., the main inner hall [2]Lit., *tent* [a]Ezek. 40:2, 3, 17 41:21, 23 [c]Ezek. 40:9; 41:3
2 [1]Lit., *shoulders* [2]Lit., *length,* [a]1 Kin. 6:2, 17; 2 Chr. 3:3
3 [1]I.e., of the inner ...*uary* [a]Ezek. 40:16 [b]Ezek. 41:1

doorway, two cubits, and the doorway, six cubits *high;* and the width
of the doorway, seven cubits.
4 And he measured its length, [a]twenty cubits, and the width,
twenty cubits, before the [b]nave; and he said to me, "This is the [c]most
holy *place.*"
5 Then he measured the wall of the [1]temple, six cubits; and the
width of the [a]side chambers, four cubits, all around about the house
on every side.
6 And [a]the side chambers were in three stories, [1]one above another,
and [2]thirty in each story; and [3]the side chambers [b]extended to the
wall which *stood* on [4]their inward side all around, that they might be
fastened, and not be fastened into the wall of the temple *itself.*
7 And the side chambers surrounding the temple were wider at
each successive story. Because the [a]structure surrounding the temple
went upward by stages on all sides of the temple, therefore the
width of the temple *increased* as it went higher; and thus one went up
from the lowest *story* to the highest by way of the [1]second *story.*
8 I saw also that the house had a raised [1]platform all around; the
foundations of the side chambers were a full rod of [a]six [2]long cubits
in height.
9 The [1]thickness of the outer wall of the side chambers was five
cubits. But the [a]free space between the side chambers belonging to
the temple
10 and the *outer* [a]chambers *was* twenty cubits in width all around
the temple on every side.
11 And the [1]doorways of the [2]side chambers toward the [a]free space
consisted of one doorway toward the north and another doorway
toward the south; and the width of the [a]free space was five cubits all
around.
12 And the [a]building that *was* in front of the [b]separate area at the
side toward the west *was* seventy cubits wide; and the wall of the
building was five cubits [1]thick all around, and its length *was* ninety
cubits.
13 Then he measured the temple, a [a]hundred cubits long; the
[b]separate area with the [c]building and its walls *were* also a [a]hundred
cubits long.
14 Also the width of the front of the temple and *that of* the separate
[1]areas along the east *side totaled* a hundred cubits.
15 And he measured the length of the [a]building [1]along the front of
the [b]separate area behind it, with a [2c]gallery on each side, a hundred
cubits; *he* also *measured* the inner nave and the porches of the court.
16 The [a]thresholds, the [1b]latticed windows, and the [2c]galleries round
about their [d]three stories, opposite the threshold, were [e]paneled with
wood all around, and *from* the ground to the windows (but the win-
dows were covered),
17 over the entrance, and to the inner house, and on the outside,
and on all the wall all around inside and outside, by measurement.
18 And it was [1]carved with [a]cherubim and [b]palm trees; and a palm
tree was between cherub and cherub, and every cherub had two
faces,
19 a [a]man's face toward the palm tree on one side, and a young
[a]lion's face toward the palm tree on the other side; they were [1]carved
on all the house all around.

4 [a]1 Kin. 6:20 6:5 [c]Ex. 26:33 1 Kin. 6:16; 7:5 2 Chr. 5:7; Heb

5 [1]Lit., *house,* throughout the [a]1 Kin. 6:5; Eze 41:6-11

6 [1]Lit., *chamb chamber* [2]Lit., *times* [3]Lit., the *coming* [4]Lit., *t of the side cha* [a]1 Kin. 6:5-10 6:6, 10

7 [1]Lit., *middle* 6:8

8 [1]Lit., *height the joint* [a]Ezek

9 [1]Lit., *width* 41:11

10 [a]Ezek. 40:

11 [1]Lit., *doorw side chamber* 41:9

12 [1]Lit., *wide* 41:13, 15; 42: 41:14; 42:10,

13 [a]Ezek. 40: 41:13-15; 42:1 [c]Ezek. 41:12

14 [1]Lit., *area*

15 [1]Lit., *to* [2]C *passageway* 41:12, 13; 42: 41:14; 42:1, 1 [c]Ezek. 41:16;

16 [1]Or, *frame passageways* Ezek. 10:18; 4 41:25 [b]1 Kin. 40:16, 25; 41: 41:15 [d]Ezek. [e]1 Kin. 6:15

18 [1]Lit., *mad* 6:29, 32, 35; 41:20, 25 [b]2 Ezek. 40:16

19 [1]Lit., *mad* 1:10; 10:14

20 From the ground to above the entrance [a]cherubim and [a]palm
trees were [1]carved, as well as *on* the wall of the nave.
21 The [a]doorposts of the [b]nave were square; as for the front of the
sanctuary, the appearance of one doorpost was like that of the other.
22 The [a]altar *was* of wood, three cubits high, and its length two
cubits; its corners, its [1]base, and its [2]sides *were* of wood. And he said
to me, "This is the [b]table that is before the LORD."
23 And the [a]nave and the [b]sanctuary each had a double [c]door.
24 And each of the doors had two leaves, two [1a]swinging leaves;
two *leaves* for one door and two leaves for the other.
25 Also there were [1]carved on them, on the doors of the nave,
[a]cherubim and [a]palm trees like those [1]carved on the walls; and *there*
was a [2b]threshold of wood on the front of the porch outside.
26 And *there were* [1a]latticed windows and [b]palm trees on one side
and on the other, on the sides of the [c]porch; thus *were* the [d]side
chambers of the house and the [2]thresholds.

Chapter 42

42 Then he [a]brought me out into the [b]outer court, the way
[c]toward the north; and he brought me to the [d]chamber which
was opposite the [e]separate area and opposite the [f]building toward the
north.
2 Along the length, *which was* a [a]hundred cubits, *was* the north
door; the width *was* fifty cubits.
3 Opposite the [a]twenty *cubits* which belonged to the inner court,
and opposite the [b]pavement which belonged to the outer court, *was*
[1c]gallery corresponding to [1]gallery in three stories.
4 And before the [a]chambers *was* an inner walk ten cubits wide, a
way of one *hundred* cubits; and their openings *were* on the north.
5 Now the upper chambers *were* [1]smaller because the [2] [a]galleries
took more *space* away from them than from the lower and middle
ones in the building.
6 For they *were* in [a]three stories and had no pillars like the pillars
of the courts; therefore *the upper chambers* were [1]set back from the
ground upward, more than the lower and middle ones.
7 As for the [a]outer wall by the side of the chambers, toward the
outer court facing the chambers, its length *was* fifty cubits.
8 For the length of the chambers which *were* in the outer court *was*
fifty cubits; and behold, *the length of those* facing the temple *was* a
[a]hundred cubits.
9 And below these chambers *was* the [a]entrance on the east side, as
one enters them from the outer court.
10 In the [1]thickness of the [a]wall of the court toward the east, facing
the [b]separate area and facing the building, *there were* [c]chambers.
11 And the [a]way in front of them *was* like the appearance of the
chambers which *were* on the north, according to their length so was
their width; and all their exits *were* both according to their arrange-
ments and openings.
12 And corresponding to the openings of the chambers which were
toward the south was an opening at the head of the way, the way in
front of the [a]wall toward the east, as one enters them.
13 Then he said to me, "The north chambers *and* the south cham-
bers, which are opposite the [a]separate area, they are the [b]holy cham-
bers where the priests who are [c]near to the LORD shall eat the [d]most

, *made* [a]Ezek. 41:18
Kin. 6:33; Ezek. :9, 14, 16; 41:1 [b]Ezek. 41:1
it., *length* [2]Lit., :. 30:1-3; 1 Kin. ; Rev. 8:3 [b]Ex. , 30; Lev. 24:6; 41; 44:16; Mal. 1:7, 12
ek. 41:1 [b]Ezek. [c]1 Kin. 6:31-35
turning [a]1 Kin. 6:34
Lit., *made* [2]Or, *y of wood over* :. 41:18 [b]Ezek. 41:16
Or, *framed* [2]Or, *s* [a]Ezek. 41:16 :. 40:16 [c]Ezek. 48 [d]Ezek. 41:5
Ezek. 40:17, 28, 1 [b]Ezek. 40:17, k. 40:20 [d]Ezek. 17; 42:4 [e]Ezek. 2:10, 13 [f]Ezek. 41:12
2 [a]Ezek. 41:13
Or, *passageway* k. 41:10 [b]Ezek. Ezek. 41:15, 16; 42:5
4 [a]Ezek. 46:19
Lit., *shorter* [2]Or, *ageways* [a]Ezek. 42:3
reduced [a]Ezek. 41:6
[a]Ezek. 42:10, 12
[a]Ezek. 41:13, 14
Ezek. 44:5; 46:19
Lit., *width* [a]Ezek. [b]Ezek. 42:1, 13 [c]Ezek. 40:17
11 [a]Ezek. 42:4
12 [a]Ezek. 42:7
ek. 42:1, 10 [b]Ex. ; Lev. 7:6; 10:13, [c]Lev. 10:3; Deut. zek. 40:46 [d]Lev. 29; 14:13; Num. 18:9, 10

holy things. There they shall lay the most holy things, the grain
offering, the sin offering, and the guilt offering; for the place is holy.
14 "When the priests enter, then they shall not go out into the outer
court from the sanctuary [1]without [a]laying there their [b]garments in
which they minister, for they are holy. They shall put on other gar-
ments; then they shall approach that which is for the people."
15 Now when he had finished measuring the inner house, he
brought me out by the way of the [a]gate which faced toward the east,
and measured it all around.
16 He measured on the east side with the measuring reed five hun-
dred reeds, by the [a]measuring reed.
17 He measured on the north side five hundred reeds by the
measuring reed.
18 On the south side he measured five hundred reeds with the
measuring reed.
19 He turned to the west side, *and* measured five hundred reeds
with the measuring reed.
20 He measured it [1]on the four sides; it had a [a]wall all around, the
[b]length five hundred and the [b]width five hundred, to [c]divide be-
tween the holy and the profane.

Chapter 43

43 Then he led me to the [a]gate, the gate facing toward the east;
2 and behold, the [a]glory of the God of Israel was coming
from the way of the [b]east. And His [c]voice was like the sound of many
waters; and the earth [d]shone with His glory.
3 And *it was* like the appearance of the vision which I saw, like the
[a]vision which I saw when [1]He came to [b]destroy the city. And the
visions *were* like the vision which I saw by the [c]river Chebar; and I
[d]fell on my face.
4 And the glory of the LORD came into the house by the way of the
gate facing toward the [a]east.
5 And the [a]Spirit lifted me up and brought me into the inner court;
and behold, the [b]glory of the LORD filled the house.
6 Then I heard one speaking to me from the house, while a [a]man
was standing beside me.
7 And He said to me, "Son of man, *this is* the place of My [a]throne
and the place of the soles of My feet, where I will [b]dwell among the
sons of Israel forever. And the house of Israel will not again defile
My holy name, neither they nor their kings, by their harlotry and by
the [1c]corpses of their kings [2]when they die,
8 by setting their threshold by My threshold, and their door post
beside My door post, with *only* the wall between Me and them. And
they have [a]defiled My holy name by their abominations which they
have committed. So I have consumed them in My anger.
9 "Now let them [a]put away their harlotry and the [1]corpses of their
kings far from Me; and I will [b]dwell among them forever.
10 "As for you, son of man, [1a]describe the [2]temple to the house of
Israel, that they may be [b]ashamed of their iniquities; and let them
measure the [3c]plan.
11 "And if they are ashamed of all that they have done, make known
to them the [1]design of the house, its structure, its [a]exits, its entrances,
all its designs, all its statutes[2], and all its laws. And write *it* [b]in their

14 [1]Lit., *but th* *shall lay* [a]Ezek [b]Ex. 29:4-9; Le 13; Is. 61:10; Z 3:4, 5

15 [a]Ezek. 40:6

16 [a]Ezek. 40:3

20 [1]Lit., *towar* *winds* [a]Is. 60:1 40:5; Zech. 2:5 45:2; Rev. 21:1 22:26; 44:23; 4

43:1 [a]Ezek. 10 40:6; 42:15; 43 46:1

2 [a]Is. 6:3; Ezek 3:23; 10:18, 19 11:23 [c]Ezek. 1 1:15; 14:2 [d]Eze 10:4; Rev. 18:1

3 [1]So with som and some ancie versions; M.T., 1:4-28 [b]Jer. 1:1 9:1, 5; 32:18 [c]E 10:20 [d]Ezek. 1

4 [a]Ezek. 10:19; 43:2

5 [a]Ezek. 3:14; 8 24; 2 Cor. 12:2- 10:4

6 [a]Ezek. 1:26; 4

7 [1]Or, *monume* Ugaritic [2]Or, *in* *high places* [a]Ps Ezek. 1:26 [b]Eze 37:26, 28 [c]Lev. Ezek. 6:5, 13

8 [a]Ezek. 8:3, 16

9 [1]Or, *monumer* Ugaritic [a]Ezek. 31 [b]Ezek. 37:26 43:7

10 [1]Lit., *declare* *house* [3]Lit., *perf* *or pattern* [a]Ezek [b]Ezek. 16:61, 63 [c]Ezek. 28:12

11 [1]Or, *form(s)* repeats *and all it* *designs* after sta [a]Ezek. 44:5 [b]Eze

sight, so that they may observe its whole [1]design and all its statutes, and [c]do them.

12 "This is the [1]law of the house: its entire [2]area on the top of the [a]mountain all around *shall be* most holy. Behold, this is the [1]law of the house.

13 "And these are the measurements of the [a]altar by cubits (the [b]cubit being a cubit and a handbreadth): the [1]base *shall be* a cubit, and the width a cubit, and its border on its edge round about one span; and this *shall be* the *height of the* [2]base of the altar.

14 "And from the base on the ground to the lower [a]ledge *shall be* two cubits, and the width one cubit; and from the smaller ledge to the larger ledge *shall be* four cubits, and the width [1]one cubit.

15 "And the [1]altar hearth *shall be* four cubits; and from the [1]altar hearth shall extend upwards four [a]horns.

16 "Now the [1]altar hearth *shall be* twelve *cubits* long by twelve wide, [a]square in its four sides.

17 "And the ledge *shall be* fourteen *cubits* long by fourteen wide in its four sides, the border around it *shall be* half a cubit, and its base *shall be* a cubit round about; and its [a]steps shall [1b]face the east."

18 And He said to me, "[a]Son of man, thus says the Lord [1]GOD, 'These are the statutes for the altar on the day it is built, to offer [b]burnt offerings on it and to [c]sprinkle blood on it.

19 'And you shall give to the Levitical priests who are from the offspring of [a]Zadok, who draw [b]near to Me to minister to Me,' declares the Lord GOD, 'a [c]young bull for a [d]sin offering.

20 'And you shall take some of its blood, and put it on its four [a]horns, and on the four corners of the [b]ledge, and on the border round about; thus you shall [c]cleanse it and make atonement for it.

21 'You shall also take the bull for the sin offering; and it *shall be* [a]burned in the appointed place of the house, outside the sanctuary.

22 'And on the second day you shall offer a [a]male goat without blemish for a sin offering; and they shall [b]cleanse the altar, as they cleansed *it* with the bull.

23 'When you have finished cleansing *it*, you shall present a [a]young bull without blemish and a [b]ram without blemish from the flock.

24 'And you shall present them before the LORD, and the priests shall throw [a]salt on them, and they shall offer them up as a burnt offering to the LORD.

25 '[a]For seven days you shall prepare daily a goat for a sin offering; also a young bull and a ram from the flock, without blemish, shall be prepared.

26 'For seven days they shall make atonement for the altar and purify it; so shall they [1]consecrate it.

27 'And when they have completed the days, it shall be that on the [a]eighth day and onward, the priests shall [1]offer your burnt offerings on the altar, and your [b]peace offerings; and I will [c]accept you,' declares the Lord GOD."

Chapter 44

44 Then He brought me back by the way of the [a]outer gate of the sanctuary, which faces the east; and it was shut.

2 And the LORD said to me, "This gate shall be shut; it shall not be opened, and no one shall enter by it, for the [a]LORD God of Israel has entered by it; therefore it shall be shut.

[1]Or, *form(s)* [c]Ezek. 11:20; 36:27

[1]Or, *instruction for border* [a]Ezek. 40:2

[1]Lit., *lap* [2]Or, *back* ...x. 27:1-8; 2 Chr. 4:1 [b]Ezek. 40:5; 41:8

14 [1]Lit., *the* [a]Ezek. 43:17, 20; 45:19

[1]Or, *ariel* shall [a]Ex. ...7:2; Lev. 9:9; 1 Kin. 1:50; Ps. 118:27

[1]Or, *ariel* shall [a]Ex. 27:1

[1]Or, *be on the east* [a]Ex. 20:26 [b]Ezek. 40:6

18 [1]Heb., *YHWH*, ...ally rendered *LORD*, ...d so throughout the ...h. [a]Ezek. 2:1 [b]Ex. ...0:29 [c]Lev. 1:5, 11; Heb. 9:21, 22

[a]1 Kin. 2:35; Ezek. ...0:46; 44:15 [b]Num. 16:5, 40 [c]Lev. 4:3; Ezek. 43:23; 45:18 ...x. 45:19; Heb. 7:27

20 [a]Lev. 8:15; 9:9; ...zek. 43:15 [b]Ezek. ...4, 17 [c]Lev. 16:19; Ezek. 43:22, 26

...1 [a]Ex. 29:14; Lev. 4:12; Heb. 13:11

...zek. 43:25 [b]Ezek. 43:20, 26

...Ex. 29:1, 10; Ezek. 45:18 [b]Ex. 29:1

[a]Lev. 2:13; Num. ...19; Mark 9:49, 50; Col. 4:6

...Ex. 29:35-37; Lev. 8:33, 35

[1]Lit., *fill its hands*

[1]Lit., *make* [a]Lev. ...:1 [b]Lev. 3:1; 17:5 [c]Ezek. 20:40

[a]Ezek. 40:6, 17; 42:14

2 [a]Ezek. 43:2-4

3 "As for the [a]prince, he shall sit in it as prince to [b]eat bread before
the LORD; he shall [c]enter by way of the [d]porch of the gate, and shall
go out [1]by the same way."
4 Then He brought me by way of the [a]north gate to the front of the
house; and I looked, and behold, the [b]glory of the LORD filled the
house of the LORD, and I [c]fell on my face.
5 And the LORD said to me, "Son of man, [1a]mark well, see with
your eyes, and hear with your ears all that I say to you concerning
all the [b]statutes of the house of the LORD and concerning all its laws;
and [1]mark well the entrance of the house, with all exits of the sanc-
tuary.
6 "And you shall say to the [1a]rebellious ones, to the house of Israel,
'Thus says the Lord [2]GOD, "[b]Enough of all your abominations, O
house of Israel,
7 when you brought in [a]foreigners, [b]uncircumcised in heart and
uncircumcised in flesh, to be in My sanctuary to profane it, *even* My
house, when you [c]offered My food, the fat and the blood; for they
[d]made My covenant void—*this* in addition to all your abominations.
8 "And you have not [a]kept charge of My holy things yourselves,
but you have set *foreigners* [1]to keep charge of My sanctuary."
9 'Thus says the Lord GOD, "[a]No foreigner, uncircumcised in heart
and uncircumcised in flesh, of all the foreigners who are among the
sons of Israel, shall enter My sanctuary.
10 "But the Levites who went far from Me, when Israel went astray,
who [a]went astray from Me after their idols, shall [b]bear the punish-
ment for their iniquity.
11 "Yet they shall be [a]ministers in My sanctuary, having [b]oversight at
the gates of the house and [c]ministering in the house; they shall
[d]slaughter the burnt offering and the sacrifice for the people, and
they shall [e]stand before them to minister to them.
12 "Because they ministered to them [a]before their idols and became a
[b]stumbling block of iniquity to the house of Israel, therefore I have
[1c]sworn against them," declares the Lord GOD, "that they shall [d]bear
the punishment for their iniquity.
13 "And they shall [a]not come near to Me to serve as a priest to Me,
nor come near to any of My holy things, to the things that are most
holy; but they shall [b]bear their shame and their abominations which
they have committed.
14 "Yet I will [1]appoint them [2]to [a]keep charge of the house, of all its
service, and of all that shall be done in it.
15 "But the [a]Levitical priests, the sons of [b]Zadok, who [c]kept charge of
My sanctuary when the sons of Israel [d]went astray from Me, shall
come near to Me to minister to Me; and they shall [e]stand before Me
to offer Me the [f]fat and the blood," declares the Lord GOD.
16 "They shall [a]enter My sanctuary; they shall come near to My
[b]table to minister to Me and keep My charge.
17 "And it shall be that when they enter at the gates of the inner
court, they shall be clothed with [a]linen garments; and wool shall not
[1]be on them while they are ministering in the gates of the inner court
and in the house.
18 "Linen [a]turbans shall be on their heads, and [b]linen undergarments
shall be on their loins; they shall not gird themselves with *anything
which makes them* sweat.
19 "And when they go out into the outer court, into the outer court

3 [1]Lit., *by his way* [a]Ezek. 34:24; 37:25 [b]Gen. 31:54; Ex. 24:9-11 [c]Ezek. 46:2 8-10 [d]Ezek. 40:9

4 [a]Ezek. 40:20, 40 6:3, 4; Ezek. 1:28; 3 43:4, 5; Hag. 2:7 [c]E 1:28; 43:3

5 [1]Lit., *set your hea on* [a]Deut. 32:46; E 40:4 [b]Deut. 12:32; Ezek. 43:10, 11

6 [1]Lit., *rebellion* [2]H *YHWH,* usually rendered *LORD,* an throughout the ch. [a]Ezek. 2:5-7; 3:9 [b] 45:9; 1 Pet. 4:3

7 [a]Ex. 12:43-49 [b]L 26:41; Deut. 10:16; 4:4; 9:26 [c]Lev. 22: [d]Gen. 17:14

8 [1]Lit., *as keepers My charge in My* [a] 22:2; Num. 18:7

9 [a]Ezek. 44:7; Joe 3:17; Zech. 14:21

10 [a]2 Kin. 23:8, 9; Ezek. 22:26; 44:12 [b]Num. 18:23

11 [a]Num. 3:5-37; 4:1-33; 18:2-7 [b]1 26:1-19 [c]Ezek. 40 44:14 [d]2 Chr. 29:3 30:17 [e]Num. 16:9

12 [1]Lit., *lifted up M hand* [a]2 Kin. 16:1 [b]Ezek. 14:3, 4 [c]Ez 20:15, 23 [d]Ezek. 4

13 [a]Num. 18:3 [b]E 16:61, 63; 39:26

14 [1]Lit., *give* [2]Lit. *keepers of the cha* [a]Num. 18:4; 1 Chr 23:28-32; Ezek. 4

15 [a]Jer. 33:18-22 [b]Ezek. 40:46; 43:1 48:11 [c]Num. 18:7 Ezek. 40:45 [d]Eze 44:10; 48:11 [e]Zec 7 [f]Lev. 3:16, 17; 1 Ezek. 44:7

16 [a]Num. 18:5, 7 [b]Ezek. 41:22; Mal 1:7, 12

17 [1]Lit., *come up* [a]Ex. 28:42, 43; 39:27-29; Rev. 19

18 [a]Ex. 28:40; Is. Ezek. 24:17, 23 [b] 28:42; Lev. 16:4

to the people, they shall [a]put off their garments in which they have
been ministering and lay them in the holy chambers; then they shall
put on other garments that they may [b]not transmit holiness to the
people with their garments.
20 "Also they shall [a]not shave their heads, yet they shall not [b]let their
locks [1]grow long; they shall only trim *the hair of* their heads.
21 "[a]Nor shall any of the priests drink wine when they enter the
inner court.
22 "And they shall not [1]marry a widow or a [a]divorced woman but
shall [b]take virgins from the offspring of the house of Israel, or a
widow who is the widow of a priest.
23 "Moreover, they shall teach My people *the [a]difference* between the
holy and the profane, and cause them to discern between the un-
clean and the clean.
24 "And in a dispute [a]they shall take their stand to judge; they shall
judge it according to My ordinances. They shall also keep My laws
and My statutes in all My [b]appointed feasts, and [c]sanctify My sab-
baths.
25 "And [1a]they shall not go to a dead person to defile *themselves;*
however, for father, for mother, for son, for daughter, for brother, or
for a sister who has not had a husband, they may defile themselves.
26 "And after he is [a]cleansed, seven days shall [1]elapse for him.
27 "And on the day that he goes into the sanctuary, into the [a]inner
court to minister in the sanctuary, he shall offer his [b]sin offering,"
declares the Lord GOD.
28 "And it shall be with regard to an inheritance for them, *that* [a]I am
their inheritance; and you shall give them no possession in Israel—I
am their possession.
29 "They shall [a]eat the grain offering, the sin offering, and the guilt
offering; and every [1b]devoted thing in Israel shall be theirs.
30 "And the first of all the [a]first fruits of every kind and every [1]con-
tribution of every kind, from all your [1]contributions, shall be for the
priests; you shall also give to the priest the [b]first of your [2]dough to
cause a [c]blessing to rest on your house.
31 "The priests shall not eat any bird or beast that has [a]died a natural
death or has been torn to pieces.

Chapter 45

45 "And when you shall [a]divide by lot the land for inheritance,
you shall offer [1]an [b]allotment to the LORD, a [c]holy portion of
the land; the length shall be the length of 25,000 [d]*cubits,* and the
width shall be [2]10,000. It shall be holy within all its boundary round
about.
2 "Out of this there shall be for the holy place a square round about
[a]five hundred by five hundred *cubits,* and fifty cubits for its [1b]open
space round about.
3 "And from this [1]area you shall measure a length of 25,000 *cubits,*
and a width of 10,000 *cubits;* and in it shall be the sanctuary, the most
holy place.
4 "It shall be the holy portion of the land; it shall be for the [a]priests,
the ministers of the sanctuary, who [b]come near to minister to the
LORD, and it shall be a place for their houses and a holy place for the
sanctuary.
5 "And *an area* [a]25,000 *cubits* in length and 10,000 in width shall be

6:10; 16:4, 23, ek. 42:14 [b]Lev. 27; Ezek. 46:20

[1]Or, *hang loose* 21:5 [b]Num. 6:5

21 [a]Lev. 10:9

, *take as wives emselves* [a]Lev. 14 [b]Lev. 21:13

ev. 10:10; Ezek. ; Hos. 4:6; Mic. Zeph. 3:4; Hag. -13; Mal. 2:6-8

[a]Deut. 17:8, 9; :5; 1 Chr. 23:4; . 19:8-10 [b]Lev. 2, 4, 44 [c]Ezek. 20:12, 20

he [a]Lev. 21:1-4

Lit., *be counted* [a]Num. 19:13-19

ek. 44:17 [b]Lev. 6; Num. 6:9-11

m. 18:20; Deut. 9; 18:1, 2; Josh. 13:33

[1]Or, *dedicated* . 18:9, 14; Josh. [b]Lev. 27:21, 28; Num. 18:14

30 [1]Or, *heave g(s)* [2]Or, *coarse* [a]Num. 18:12, 13; 31:4-6, 10; Neh. 37 [b]Num. 15:20, 21 [c]Mal. 3:10

[a]Lev. 22:8; Deut. 4:21; Ezek. 4:14

Or, *a contribution* with Gr., *20,000* um. 34:13; Josh. 4:3; Ezek. 47:21; 9 [b]Ezek. 48:8, 9 14:20, 21 [d]Ezek. 42:16; 45:2

[1]Or, *pasture land* ek. 42:20 [b]Ezek. 27:28

3 [1]Lit., *measure*

[a]Ezek. 48:10, 11 Num. 16:5; Ezek. 40:45; 43:19

5 [a]Ezek. 48:13

for the Levites, the ministers of the house, *and* for their possession
[1]cities to dwell in.
6 "And you shall give the [a]city possession of *an area* 5,000 *cubits*
wide and 25,000 *cubits* long, alongside the [1]allotment of the holy
portion; it shall be for the whole house of Israel.
7 "And the [a]prince shall have *land* on either side of the holy [1]allot-
ment and the [2]property of the city, adjacent to the holy [1]allotment
and the [2]property of the city, on the west side toward the west and
on the east side toward the east, and in length comparable to one of
the portions, from the west border to the east border.
8 "This shall be his land for a possession in Israel; so My princes
shall no longer [a]oppress My people, but they shall give *the rest of* the
land to the house of Israel [b]according to their tribes."
9 'Thus says the Lord [1]GOD, "[a]Enough, you princes of Israel; put
away [b]violence and destruction, and [c]practice justice and right-
eousness. Stop your [d]expropriations from My people," declares the
Lord GOD.
10 "You shall have [a]just balances, a just [b]ephah, and a just [b]bath.
11 "The ephah and the bath shall be [1]the same quantity, so that the
bath may contain a tenth of a [a]homer, and the ephah a tenth of a
homer; [2]their standard shall be according to the homer.
12 "And the [a]shekel shall be twenty [a]gerahs; twenty shekels, twenty-
five shekels, *and* fifteen shekels shall be your [1]maneh.
13 "This is the offering that you shall offer: a sixth of an ephah from
a homer of wheat; a sixth of an ephah from a homer of barley;
14 and the prescribed portion of oil (*namely,* the bath of oil), a tenth
of a bath from *each* kor (*which is* ten baths *or* a homer, for ten baths
are a homer);
15 and one sheep from *each* flock of two hundred from the watering
places of Israel—for a [a]grain offering, for a burnt offering, and for
peace offerings, to [b]make atonement for them," declares the Lord
GOD.
16 "[a]All the people of the land shall [1]give to this offering for the
[b]prince in Israel.
17 "And it shall be the [a]prince's part *to provide* the [b]burnt offerings,
the grain offerings, and the libations, at the [c]feasts, on the [d]new
moons, and on the sabbaths, at all the appointed feasts of the house
of Israel; he shall provide the sin offering, the grain offering, the
burnt offering, and the [e]peace offerings, to make atonement for the
house of Israel."
18 'Thus says the Lord GOD, "In the [a]first *month,* on the first of the
month, you shall take a young bull [b]without blemish and [c]cleanse
the sanctuary.
19 "And the priest shall take some of the blood from the sin offering
and put *it* on the door posts of the house, on the [a]four corners of the
[b]ledge of the altar, and on the posts of the gate of the inner court.
20 "And thus you shall do on the seventh *day* of the month for
everyone who goes [a]astray or is [1]naive; so you shall make [b]atone-
ment for the house.
21 "In the [a]first *month,* on the fourteenth day of the month, you shall
have the [b]Passover, a feast of seven days; unleavened bread shall be
eaten.
22 "And on that day the prince shall provide for himself and all the
people of the land a [a]bull for a sin offering.

5 [1]So with Gr.; M *twenty chambers*

6 [1]Or, *contributio* [a]Ezek. 48:15-18,

7 [1]Or, *contributio* *possession* [a]Eze 34:24; 37:24; 46:1 48:21

8 [a]Is. 11:3-5; Jer. Ezek. 19:7; 22:27; 46:18 [b]Josh. 11:2

9 [1]Heb., *YHWH,* usually rendered *L* and so throughout ch. [a]Ezek. 44:6 [b] 6:7; Ezek. 7:11, 23 8:17 [c]Jer. 22:3; Ze 8:16 [d]Neh. 5:1-5

10 [a]Lev. 19:36; De 25:15; Prov. 16:11 Amos 8:4-6; Mic. 6 11 [b]Is. 5:10

11 [1]Lit., *one* [2]Lit., *measure* [a]Is. 5:10

12 [1]Or, *mina* [a]Ex. 30:13; Lev. 27:25; 3:47

15 [a]Ezek. 45:17 1:4; 6:30

16 [1]Lit., *be* [a]Ex. 3 15 [b]Is. 16:1

17 [a]Ezek. 46:4-12 [b]1 Kin. 8:64; 1 Chr 2 Chr. 31:3 [c]Lev. 23:1-44; Num. 28:1-29:39 [d]Is. 66 [e]1 Kin. 8:63; Ezek

18 [a]Ex. 12:2 [b]Lev 22:20; Heb. 9:14 16:16, 33; Ezek. 43:22, 26

19 [a]Lev. 16:18-20 Ezek. 43:20 [b]Eze 43:14, 17, 20

20 [1]Lit., *simple* [a] 4:27; Ps. 19:12 [b] 16:20; Ezek. 45:1

21 [a]Num. 28:16f. 12:1-24; Lev. 23:5

22 [a]Lev. 4:14

23 "And *during* the [a]seven days of the feast he shall provide as a
[b]burnt offering to the LORD [c]seven bulls and seven rams without
blemish on every day of the seven days, and a male goat daily for a
sin offering.
24 "And he shall provide as a [a]grain offering an ephah [1]with a bull,
an ephah [1]with a ram, and a hin of oil [1]with an ephah.
25 "In the [a]seventh *month*, on the fifteenth day of the month, at the
feast, he shall provide like this, seven days [1]for the sin offering, the
burnt offering, the grain offering, and the oil."

Chapter 46

46 'Thus says the Lord [1]GOD, "The [a]gate of the [b]inner court facing
east shall be [c]shut the six [d]working days; but it shall be
opened on the [e]sabbath day, and opened on the day of the [f]new
moon.
2 "And the [a]prince shall enter by way of the porch of the gate from
outside and stand by the [b]post of the gate. Then the priests shall
provide his burnt offering and his peace offerings, and he shall wor-
ship at the threshold of the gate and then go out; but the gate shall
not be [c]shut until the evening.
3 "The [a]people of the land shall also worship at the doorway of that
gate before the LORD on the sabbaths and on the [b]new moons.
4 "And the [a]burnt offering which the prince shall offer to the LORD
on the sabbath day shall be [b]six lambs without blemish and a ram
without blemish;
5 and the [a]grain offering shall be an ephah [1]with the ram, and the
grain offering [1]with the lambs [2]as much as he is [b]able to give, and a
hin of oil [1]with an ephah.
6 "And on the day of the [a]new moon *he shall offer* a young bull
without blemish, also six lambs and a ram, *which* shall be without
blemish.
7 "And he shall provide a [a]grain offering, an ephah [1]with the bull,
and an ephah [1]with the ram, and [1]with the lambs as [2]much as he is
[b]able, and a hin of oil [1]with an ephah.
8 "And when the [a]prince enters, he shall go in by way of the porch
of the gate and go out [1]by the same way.
9 "But when the people of the land come [a]before the LORD at the
appointed feasts, he who enters by way of the north gate to worship
shall go out by way of the south gate. And he who enters by way of
the south gate shall go out by way of the north gate. [1]No one shall
return by way of the gate by which he entered but shall go straight
out.
10 "And when they go in, the prince shall go in [a]among them; and
when they go out, [1]he shall go out.
11 "And at the [a]festivals and the appointed feasts the [b]grain offering
shall be an ephah [1]with a bull and an ephah [1]with a ram, and [1]with
the lambs as [2]much as one is able to give, and a hin of oil [1]with an
ephah.
12 "And when the prince provides a [a]freewill offering, a burnt offer-
ing, or peace offerings *as* a freewill offering to the LORD, the gate
facing east shall be [b]opened for him. And he shall provide his burnt
offering and his peace offerings as he does on the [c]sabbath day. Then
he shall go out, and the gate shall be shut after he goes out.
13 "And you shall provide a [a]lamb a year old without blemish for a

.. 23:8 [b]Num. Num. 23:1, 2; Job 42:8
.it., *for* [a]Num. ; Ezek. 46:5-7
.., *according to* 3:33-43; Num. 38; 2 Chr. 5:3; 7:8, 10
[1]Heb., *YHWH*, endered *LORD*, throughout the . [a]Ezek. 45:19 zek. 8:16; 10:3 k. 44:1, 2 [d]Ex. s. 66:23; Ezek. [f]Ezek. 45:18; 46:3, 6
zek. 44:3; 46:8 .. 45:19 [c]Ezek. 46:12
ke 1:10 [b]Ezek. 46:1
.. 45:17 [b]Num. 28:9
or [2]Lit., *a gift of* d [a]Num. 28:12; 45:24; 46:7, 11 [b]Ezek. 46:7
6 [a]Ezek. 46:1
Lit., *for* [2]Lit., *his* an *reach* [a]Ezek. .ev. 14:21; Deut. 6:17; Ezek. 46:5
[1]Lit., *by its way* Ezek. 44:3; 46:2
Lit., *He shall not* 34:23; Ps. 84:7; Mic. 6:6
with many mss. and the ancient rsions; M.T., *they* . 6:14, 15; 1 Chr. 20, 22; 2 Chr. 6:3; 7:4; Ps. 42:4
it., *for* [2]Lit., *a gift* *his hand* [a]Ezek. 7 [b]Ezek. 46:5, 7
Lev. 23:38; 2 Chr. 9:31 [b]Ezek. 44:3; 2, 8 [c]Ezek. 45:17
13 [a]Num. 28:3-5

burnt offering to the LORD daily; [b]morning by morning you shall
provide it.
14 "Also you shall provide a grain offering with it morning by morn-
ing, a [a]sixth of an ephah, and a third of a hin of oil to moisten the fine
flour, a grain offering to the LORD continually by a perpetual [1]or-
dinance.
15 "Thus they shall provide the lamb, the grain offering, and the oil,
morning by morning, for a [a]continual burnt offering."
16 'Thus says the Lord GOD, "If the prince gives a [a]gift *out of* his
inheritance to any of his sons, it shall belong to his sons; it is their
possession by inheritance.
17 "But if he gives a gift from his inheritance to one of his servants, it
shall be his until the [a]year of liberty; then it shall return to the prince.
His inheritance *shall be* only his sons'; it shall belong to them.
18 "And the prince shall [a]not take from the people's inheritance,
[1b]thrusting them out of their possession; he shall give his sons inheri-
tance from his own possession so that My people shall not be scat-
tered, anyone from his possession." ' "
19 Then he brought me through the [a]entrance, which *was* at the side
of the gate, into the holy chambers for the priests, which faced north;
and behold, there *was* a place at the extreme rear toward the west.
20 And he said to me, "This is the place where the priests shall boil
the [a]guilt offering and the sin offering, *and* where they shall [b]bake the
grain offering, in order that they may not bring *them* out into the
outer court to transmit holiness to the people."
21 Then he brought me out into the outer court and led me across
to the four corners of the court; and behold, in every corner of the
court *there was* a *small* court.
22 In the four corners of the court *there were* enclosed courts, forty
cubits long and thirty wide; these four in the corners *were* [1]the same
size.
23 And *there was* a row *of masonry* round about in them, around the
four of them, and boiling places were made under the rows round
about.
24 Then he said to me, "These are the boiling [1]places where the
ministers of the house shall boil the sacrifices of the people."

Chapter 47

47 Then he brought me back to the [a]door of the house; and be-
hold, [b]water was flowing from under the threshold of the
house toward the east, for the house faced east. And the water was
flowing down from under, from the right side of the house, from
south of the altar.
2 And he brought me out by way of the north gate and led me
around [1]on the outside to the outer gate by way of *the gate* that faces
east. And behold, water was trickling from the south side.
3 When the man went out toward the east with a line in his hand,
he measured a thousand cubits, and he led me through the water,
water *reaching* the ankles.
4 Again he measured a thousand and led me through the water,
water *reaching* the knees. Again he measured a thousand and led me
through *the water,* water *reaching* the loins.
5 Again he measured a thousand; *and it was* a river that I could not

13 [b]Is. 50:4
14 [1]Lit., *statut* 28:5
15 [a]Ex. 29:42; 28:6
16 [a]2 Chr. 21:3
17 [a]Lev. 25:10
18 [1]Lit., *oppres* [a]Ezek. 45:8 [b]1 21:19; Ezek. 22 2:1, 2
19 [a]Ezek. 42:9;
20 [a]2 Chr. 35:13 44:29 [b]Lev. 2:4
22 [1]Lit., *one me*
24 [1]Lit., *houses*
47:1 [a]Ezek. 41:2, [b]Ps. 46:4; Is. 30:2 55:1; Jer. 2:13; J 3:18; Zech. 13:1; Rev. 22:1, 17
2 [1]Lit., *by way of*

ˢIs. 11:9; Hab. 2:14
ˡt., and caused me return ᵃEzek. 8:6; 40:4; 44:5
s. 60:13, 21; 61:3; Ezek. 47:12
Lit., healed ᵃDeut. 3:17; Is. 35:6, 7; 7-19; 44:3 ᵇJosh. 3:16
t., two rivers ²Lit., e healed ᵃIs. 12:3; ohn 4:14; 7:37, 38
ᵃMatt. 4:19; 13:47; 5:10 ᵇGen. 14:7; sh. 15:62; 1 Sam. ; 24:1; 2 Chr. 20:2 k. 26:5, 14 ᵈNum. Ps. 104:25; Ezek. 7:15; 48:28 ᵉLuke 5:5-9; John 21:6
¹Lit., healed ²Lit., iven ᵃDeut. 29:23
ᵃEzek. 47:7; Rev. :2 ᵇGen. 2:9 ᶜPs. r. 17:8 ᵈRev. 22:2
13 ¹Heb., YHWH, y rendered LORD, so throughout the h. ᵃNum. 34:2-12 8:5; Ezek. 48:4, 5
it., like his brother lifted up My hand ᵃDeut. 1:8; Ezek. 20:6
Or, Hamath ᵃNum. 34:7-9 ᵇNum. 34:8
¹Or, Zedad ᵃNum. 21; Is. 10:9; Ezek. 7, 20; 48:1; Zech. Gen. 14:15; Ezek. 47:17, 18; 48:1
t., be ᵃNum. 34:9
3 ᵃNum. 34:10-12 37:25; Jer. 50:19 ᶜGen. 13:10, 11
19 ᵃNum. 34:3-5 zek. 48:28 ᶜDeut. 2:51 ᵈNum. 34:5; in. 8:65; Is. 27:12 ᵉEzek. 47:10, 15
0 ¹Or, entrance of math ᵃNum. 34:6 dg. 3:3; 2 Chr. 7:8; 48:1; Amos 6:14

ford, for the water had risen, *enough* water to swim in, a [a]river that
could not be forded.
6 And he said to me, "Son of man, have you [a]seen *this*?" Then he
brought me [1]back to the bank of the river.
7 Now when I had returned, behold, on the bank of the river there
were very many [a]trees on the one side and on the other.
8 Then he said to me, "These waters go out toward the eastern
region and go down into the [a]Arabah; then they go toward the sea,
being made to flow into the [b]sea, and the waters *of the sea* become
[1]fresh.
9 "And it will come about that every living creature which swarms
in every place where the [1]river goes, will live. And there will be very
many fish, for these waters go there, and *the others* [2]become fresh; so
[a]everything will live where the river goes.
10 "And it will come about that [a]fishermen will stand beside it; from
[b]Engedi to Eneglaim there will be a place for the [c]spreading of nets.
Their fish will be according to their kinds, like the fish of the [d]Great
Sea, [e]very many.
11 "But its swamps and marshes will not become [1]fresh; they will be
[2]left for [a]salt.
12 "And [a]by the river on its bank, on one side and on the other, will
grow all *kinds of* [b]trees for food. Their [c]leaves will not wither, and
their fruit will not fail. They will bear every month because their
water flows from the sanctuary, and their fruit will be for food and
their [d]leaves for healing."
13 Thus says the Lord [1]GOD, "This *shall be* the [a]boundary by which
you shall divide the land for an inheritance among the twelve tribes
of Israel; Joseph *shall have* two [b]portions.
14 "And you shall divide it for an inheritance, each one [1]equally
with the other; for I [2a]swore to give it to your forefathers, and this
land shall fall to you [3]as an inheritance.
15 "And this *shall be* the boundary of the land: on the [a]north side,
from the Great Sea *by* the way of Hethlon, to the entrance of [1b]Zedad;
16 [1a]Hamath, Berothah, Sibraim, which is between the border of
[b]Damascus and the border of Hamath; Hazer-hatticon, which is by
the border of Hauran.
17 "And the boundary shall [1]extend from the sea *to* [a]Hazar-enan *at*
the border of Damascus, and on the north
toward the north is the border of Hamath.
This is the north side.
18 "And the [a]east side, from between
Hauran, Damascus, [b]Gilead, and the land of
Israel, *shall be* the [c]Jordan; from the *north*
border to the eastern sea you shall measure.
This is the east side.
19 "And the [a]south side toward the south
shall extend from [b]Tamar as far as the waters
of [c]Meribath-kadesh, to the [d]brook *of Egypt*,
and to the [e]Great Sea. This is the south side
toward the south.
20 "And the [a]west side *shall be* the Great
Sea, from the *south* border to a point opposite
[1b]Lebo-hamath. This is the west side.
21 "So you shall divide this land among
yourselves according to the tribes of Israel.

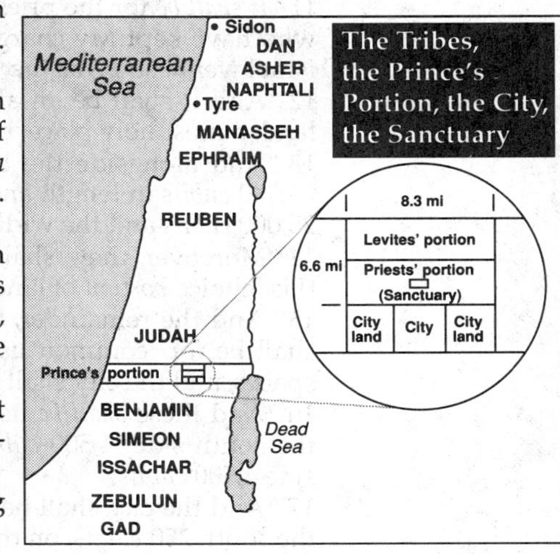

The Tribes, the Prince's Portion, the City, the Sanctuary

22 "And it will come about that you shall divide it by [a]lot for an inheritance among yourselves and among the [b]aliens who stay in your midst, who bring forth sons in your midst. And they shall be to you as the native-born among the sons of Israel; they shall be allotted an [c]inheritance with you among the tribes of Israel.

23 "And it will come about that in the tribe with which the alien stays, there you shall give *him* his inheritance," declares the Lord GOD.

Chapter 48

48 "Now [a]these are the names of the tribes: from the northern extremity, [1]beside the way of Hethlon to [2]Lebo-hamath, *as far as* Hazar-enan *at* the border of Damascus, toward the north [1]beside Hamath, [3]running from east to west, [b]Dan, one *portion*.

2 "And beside the border of Dan, from the east side to the west side, [a]Asher, one *portion*.

3 "And beside the border of Asher, from the east side to the west side, [a]Naphtali, one *portion*.

4 "And beside the border of Naphtali, from the east side to the west side, [a]Manasseh, one *portion*.

5 "And beside the border of Manasseh, from the east side to the west side, [a]Ephraim, one *portion*.

6 "And beside the border of Ephraim, from the east side to the west side, [a]Reuben, one *portion*.

7 "And beside the border of Reuben, from the east side to the west side, [a]Judah, one *portion*.

8 "And beside the border of Judah, from the east side to the west side, shall be the [1]allotment which you shall [2]set apart, 25,000 [3]*cubits* in width, and in length like one of the portions, from the east side to the west side; and the [a]sanctuary shall be in the middle of it.

9 "The allotment that you shall set apart to the LORD *shall be* 25,000 *cubits* in length, and 10,000 in width.

10 "And the holy allotment shall be for these, *namely* for the [a]priests, toward the north 25,000 *cubits in length,* toward the west 10,000 in width, toward the east 10,000 in width, and toward the south 25,000 in length; and the sanctuary of the LORD shall be in its midst.

11 "*It shall be* for the priests who are sanctified of the [a]sons of Zadok, who have kept My charge, who did not go astray when the sons of Israel went astray, as the [b]Levites went astray.

12 "And it shall be an allotment to them from the allotment of the land, a most holy place, by the border of the Levites.

13 "And alongside the border of the priests the Levites *shall have* 25,000 *cubits* in length and 10,000 in width. The whole length *shall be* 25,000 *cubits* and the width 10,000.

14 "Moreover, they [a]shall not sell or exchange any of it, or alienate this [1]choice *portion* of land; for it is holy to the LORD.

15 "And the remainder, 5,000 *cubits* in width and 25,000 [1]in length, shall be for [a]common use for the city, for dwellings and for [2]open spaces; and the city shall be in its midst.

16 "And these *shall be* its measurements: the north side 4,500 *cubits*, the south side [a]4,500 *cubits,* the east side 4,500 *cubits*, and the west side 4,500 *cubits*.

17 "And the city shall have [1]open spaces: on the north 250 *cubits*, on the south 250 *cubits*, on the east 250 *cubits*, and on the west 250 *cubits*.

22 [a]Num. 26:55, 5 14:1; 56:6, 7 [c]Acts 11:18; 15:9; Eph. 2:12-14; 3:6; Col. 3

48:1 [1]Lit., *at the h of* [2]Or, *the entranc Hamath* [3]Lit., *and shall be to it an ea west side* [a]Ex. 1:1 [b]Josh. 19:40-48

2 [a]Josh. 19:24-31

3 [a]Josh. 19:32-39

4 [a]Josh. 13:29-31 17:1-11

5 [a]Josh. 16:5-9; 17:8-10, 14-18

6 [a]Josh. 13:15-21

7 [a]Josh. 15:1-63;

8 [1]Or, *contributio* so throughout the [2]Lit., *offer* [3]Or pos *reeds*, and so throughout the ch 12:6; 33:20-22; E 45:3, 4

10 [a]Ezek. 44:28;

11 [a]Ezek. 40:46; [b]Ezek. 44:10, 12

14 [1]Lit., *first* or *fi fruits* [a]Lev. 25:32 27:10, 28, 33

15 [1]Lit., *in front* *pasture land* [a]Ez 42:20; 45:6

16 [a]Rev. 21:16

17 [1]Or, *pasture l*

18 "And the remainder of the length alongside the holy allotment
shall be 10,000 *cubits* toward the east, and 10,000 toward the west;
and it shall be [1]alongside the holy allotment. And its produce shall
be food for the workers of the city.
19 "And the workers of the city, out of all the tribes of Israel, shall
cultivate it.
20 "The whole allotment *shall be* 25,000 by 25,000 *cubits;* you shall
[1]set apart the holy allotment, a [2]square, with the [3]property of the city.
21 "And the [a]remainder *shall be* for the prince, on the one side and on
the other of the holy allotment and of the [1]property of the city; in
front of the 25,000 *cubits* of the allotment toward the east border and
westward in front of the 25,000 toward the west border, alongside
the portions, *it shall be* for the prince. And the holy allotment and the
sanctuary of the house shall be in the middle of it.
22 "And exclusive of the [1]property of the Levites and the [1]property
of the city, *which* are in the middle of that which belongs to the
prince, *everything* between the border of Judah and the border of
Benjamin shall be for the prince.
23 "As for the rest of the tribes: from the east side to the west side,
[a]Benjamin, one *portion.*
24 "And beside the border of Benjamin, from the east side to the
west side, [a]Simeon, one *portion.*
25 "And beside the border of Simeon, from the east side to the west
side, [a]Issachar, one *portion.*
26 "And beside the border of Issachar, from the east side to the west
side, [a]Zebulun, one *portion.*
27 "And beside the border of Zebulun, from the east side to the west
side, [a]Gad, one *portion.*
28 "And beside the border of Gad, at the south side toward the
south, the border shall be from [a]Tamar to the waters of Meribath-
kadesh, to the brook *of Egypt,* to the [b]Great Sea.
29 "This is the [a]land which you shall divide by lot to the tribes of
Israel for an inheritance, and these are their *several* portions,"
declares the Lord [1]GOD.
30 "And these are the exits of the city: on the [a]north side, 4,500 *cubits*
by measurement,
31 [1]shall be the gates of the city, [2a]named for the tribes of Israel,
three gates toward the north: the gate of Reuben, one; the gate of
Judah, one; the gate of Levi, one.
32 "And on the east side, 4,500 *cubits,* [1]shall be three gates: the gate
of Joseph, one; the gate of Benjamin, one; the gate of Dan, one.
33 "And on the south side, 4,500 *cubits* by measurement, [1]shall be
three gates: the gate of Simeon, one; the gate of Issachar, one; the
gate of Zebulun, one.
34 "On the west side, 4,500 *cubits, shall be* three gates: the gate of
Gad, one; the gate of Asher, one; the gate of Naphtali, one.
35 "*The city shall be* 18,000 *cubits* round about; and the [a]name of the
city from *that* day *shall be,* '[1]The [b]LORD is there.' "

18 [1]Or, *exactly as*
20 [1]Lit., *offer* [2]Lit., ...*h* [3]Or, *possession*
1 [1]Or, *possession* [a]Ezek. 34:24; 45:7; 48:22
2 [1]Or, *possession*
3 [a]Josh. 18:21-28
24 [a]Josh. 19:1-9
5 [a]Josh. 19:17-23
6 [a]Josh. 19:10-16
7 [a]Josh. 13:24-28
[a]Gen. 14:7; 2 Chr. 20:2; Ezek. 47:19 ... 47:10, 15, 19, 20
29 [1]Heb., *YHWH,* ...ly rendered *LORD* [a]Ezek. 47:13-20
[a]Ezek. 48:32-34
31 [1]Lit., *and* [2]Lit., ...*ding to the names of* [a]Rev. 21:12, 13
32 [1]Lit., *and*
33 [1]Lit., *and*
35 [1]Heb., ...*-shammah* [a]Jer. ...; 33:16 [b]Is. 12:6; ...; 24:23; Jer. 3:17; 4:9; Ezek. 35:10; 3:21; Zech. 2:10; Rev. 21:3; 22:3

Ezekiel at a Glance

Theme of Ezekiel:

Author:

Date:

Purpose:

Key Words:

- son of man
- covenant
- vision(s)
- glory
- Spirit (spirit)
- know that I am the Lord
- iniquity
- rebelled (rebellious)
- wrath
- heart
- harlot (harlotries, adultery, adulteries, adulteress)

Segment Divisions

		Chapter Themes
		1
		2
		3
		4
		5
		6
		7
		8
		9
		10
		11
		12
		13
		14
		15
		16
		17
		18
		19
		20
		21
		22
		23
		24

SEGMENT DIVISIONS

		CHAPTER THEMES
		25
		26
		27
		28
		29
		30
		31
		32
		33
		34
		35
		36
		37
		38
		39
		40
		41
		42
		43
		44
		45
		46
		47
		48

DANIEL

Daniel's prophetic ministry began and ended in Babylon. When Nebuchadnezzar first besi
Jerusalem in 605 B.C., Daniel, who was about fifteen years old, was among the captives tak
Babylon.

As Moses predicted, Israel lost its place of supremacy among the nations because they did not
God. Instead of being the head, Israel became the tail to be wagged by the Gentiles (Deuteronomy
Yet, because the gifts and calling of God are irrevocable, when the fullness of the Gentiles come
then all Israel will be saved for the Deliverer will come out of Zion and take away Israel's sir
Romans 11:25-30). All this becomes evident as the prophecies of Daniel unfold.

THINGS TO DO

What the skeleton is to the body, Daniel is to prophecy. All the other prophecies in the Old and
Testament add flesh to Daniel's bones. If you carefully and thoroughly observe Daniel and disc
exactly what the text says, you will find Daniel's prophecies become increasingly clearer and
exciting with every new observation.

General Instructions

Read through Daniel one chapter at a time. Don't hurry. Simply do the following assignmer
each chapter. Record all your notes in the margin of the chapter. As you read, answer the follo
questions and record them in the margin of the text:

1. When do the events of this chapter occur? Mark every reference to time with a clock such as or with a distinctive color so you can see it immediately.
2. What king/kingdom is ruling at the time? Record this in the margin along with a notation o "when" of the chapter. For instance, in the margin of chapter 1, you would put the following:

   Third year of Jehoiakim, king of Judah
   Nebuchadnezzar was king of Babylon
3. Who are the main characters in the chapter?
4. What, in general, is the chapter about?
5. Record the theme or event of the chapter on the DANIEL AT A GLANCE chart on page 1304 on the line in the text next to the chapter number. Then in the margin list the key poin happenings connected with the main event of the chapter.
6. If a vision or dream is recorded, note in the margin who had the vision or dream and wha vision or dream was about. Also, sketch or draw on another piece of paper so you'll b remember and understand the dream or vision.
7. When you finish the above, read "From 722 B.C. Until the Birth of Christ" on page I-33 in section called "Major Events in Israel's History."

Chapters 1-6

1. Read Daniel 1 through 6 again chapter by chapter. This time do the following:
   a. Mark every reference to God in a distinctive way. Watch for the repeated reference to Go the "Most High" and mark this. Then in the margin list what you learn about God f marking those references to Him. Note what He is called, or how He is referred to. T meditate on what you have learned about God and how you can apply these truths to y own life.

   b. In the margins list everything you learn about Daniel: his character, his relationship to and to others, and how he handles and responds to various situations.

c. Mark in a distinctive way the following key repeated words: *kingdom, rules (ruler), dream, mystery (mysteries),* and *Nebuchadnezzar* (including pronouns). Put these on a card and use it as a bookmark. Also watch for and mark key repeated words which appear in individual chapters. If there's room in the margin, summarize what you learn about Nebuchadnezzar.

Study the historical chart on page 1281. In the light of what you have observed in the text and on the chart, see if the first six chapters of Daniel come in chronological order.

ters 7-12

As you prepare to go through these final chapters of Daniel, review what you have observed in chapters 7 through 12 and what you recorded on DANIEL AT A GLANCE. Do you see any difference between the first six chapters of Daniel and the last six?

a. Are the last six chapters chronological?

b. Who had the dreams/visions in each of these major segments?

c. Record your insights to these two questions on DANIEL AT A GLANCE under "Segment Divisions." Show the chronology or lack of it on one line and then on the other write the main theme or emphasis of these two major divisions of Daniel.

Read Daniel 7 through 12 again chapter by chapter. Do the following:

a. As you read each chapter mark the following key words: *vision, kingdom (dominion), horn(s), saints, man of high esteem, end (end time, appointed time, time of the end), covenant, Michael,* and *Gabriel.* Write these on a card you can use as a bookmark.

b. Mark every reference to God in a distinctive way. Then make a list in the margin of everything you learn about Him.

c. List everything you learn about Daniel from observing the text.

erstanding the Visions and Dreams in Daniel

When you come to a vision, observe the details of the vision carefully. See if the text interprets the vision. Read it over and over until you see exactly what the text is saying.

After you observe chapter 7, compare it with chapter 2.

a. If you didn't do a sketch of the vision in chapter 2, stop and do it. Then do a sketch of the vision in chapter 7. What parallels do you see? Which chapter gives more details of the events encompassed in the vision? Pay attention to those details when you sketch out the vision.

b. Mark any references to time with a clock such as this  . In Jewish reckoning "time, times, and half a time" is the equivalent of three-and-a-half years. Note what proceeds a period of time and what brings it to an end.

When you observe chapter 8, list in the margin everything you learn about the ram and the goat. In a distinctive way mark every pronoun which refers to the "rather small horn" of 8:9. Then list everything you observe from the text about this horn. Ask the five W's and an H: Where did it come from? What does it do and where? When does it happen? How long does it last?

When you observe Daniel 9:24-27, follow those verses chronologically.

a. Number from 1 to 6 in the text the six things in Daniel 9:24 which will be accomplished, or list them in the margin.

b. Observe who the seventy weeks pertain to. Read the reference note regarding *weeks.* Then on a piece of paper draw a line and put in the sequence of events. For example:

|Seven weeks|____ (you complete the drawing.)

Decree

Note when the prophecy begins (what starts it) and what happens at each interval of time. Note what happens after the seven weeks and sixty-two weeks and what happens during the last week (the seventieth week) mentioned in 9:27.

c. Observe who destroys the city, the sanctuary, and their relationship to the prince who is to come in 9:27. A historical fact that might help is that Jerusalem was destroyed in A.D. Titus, a Roman general.

5. Read chapters 10 through 12 as one unit and then concentrate on the message and vis chapters 11 through 12.
   a. Mark every reference to time, including the word *then,* which shows the sequence of eve
   b. Chapter 11 is not an easy chapter to understand apart from a grasp of history. It was w years before the fact, but many are not familiar with this period of time. When you read kings of the south and the north, keep in mind that they are so named because o geographical relationship to Israel, the beautiful land.
   c. As you read through the chapter, consult the chart THE HISTORY OF ISRAEL'S RELA SHIP TO THE KINGS OF DANIEL 11 on page 1300. In 11:1-35 there are approximate prophetic statements which have all been fulfilled. The accuracy of Daniel's prophecies re ing the Gentile nations and their relationship to Israel has staggered the minds of theologians. Many even say that because of its historical accuracy, Daniel had to be w sometime after the Maccabean period in the second century B.C. However, the book of I clearly refers to Daniel as the author; so does our Lord Jesus Christ (*see* Matthew 24:15).
   d. If you have not done so, make a list in the margin of everything you learned abo despicable person in Daniel 11:22-35. After Daniel 11:35 list the similarities betwee description of the despicable person of 11:22-35 and Antiochus IV Epiphanes. To da person in history has yet fulfilled the description given in 11:36-45.
   e. Reading *Josephus, the Essential Writings* (Kregel, 1988) will help you understand the testament period, the four hundred silent years from Malachi to Matthew. It also gives i into Rome's role in Israel's history and tells more about the various kings mentioned in I 11:1-35, especially Antiochus IV Epiphanes.
   f. In chapter 12 observe the transition from 11:45 to 12:1 chronologically. Mark all referen time and the events connected with them. Observe this chapter very carefully.
6. When you study the dreams and visions in Daniel, remember that Nebuchadnezzar's dre chapter 2 gives a broad overview and every vision which follows begins to fill in the details. that you have finished observing Daniel, you might want to study the chart A PROPH OVERVIEW OF DANIEL on page 1305 and see how it compares with the text and your u standing of it.
7. Finally, determine how the book of Daniel can be segmented. Note these under "Seg Divisions" on DANIEL AT A GLANCE. Then complete the chart.

THINGS TO THINK ABOUT

1. Keeping in mind the meaning of Daniel's name, "God is my prince" (or judge), think about Daniel lived. Review what you observed of his life and character and determine to be a D You have His promise, "The people who know their God will display strength and take ac (Daniel 11:32b). You have God's spirit; you have His grace (John 14:17, 1 Corinthians 15:10).
2. What did Daniel know about God that would help him accept what happened to him? How this understanding of God help you deal with the situations and circumstances of your life?
3. How does your understanding of future events help you understand and deal with wh happening in history? Have you thought about using Daniel as a tool in sharing the gospel others? Many times prophecy will open the door when nothing else will.

Chapter 1 ____________________________

1 In the third year of the reign of [a]Jehoiakim king of Judah, [b]Nebu-
chadnezzar king of Babylon came to Jerusalem and besieged it.
2 And the [a]Lord gave Jehoiakim king of Judah into his hand, along
with some of the [b]vessels of the house of God; and he brought them

1:1 [a]2 Kin. 24:1; 36:5, 6 [b]Jer. 25: 52:12, 28-30

2 [a]Is. 42:24; Da 38 [b]2 Chr. 36:7; 27:19, 20; Dan. 5

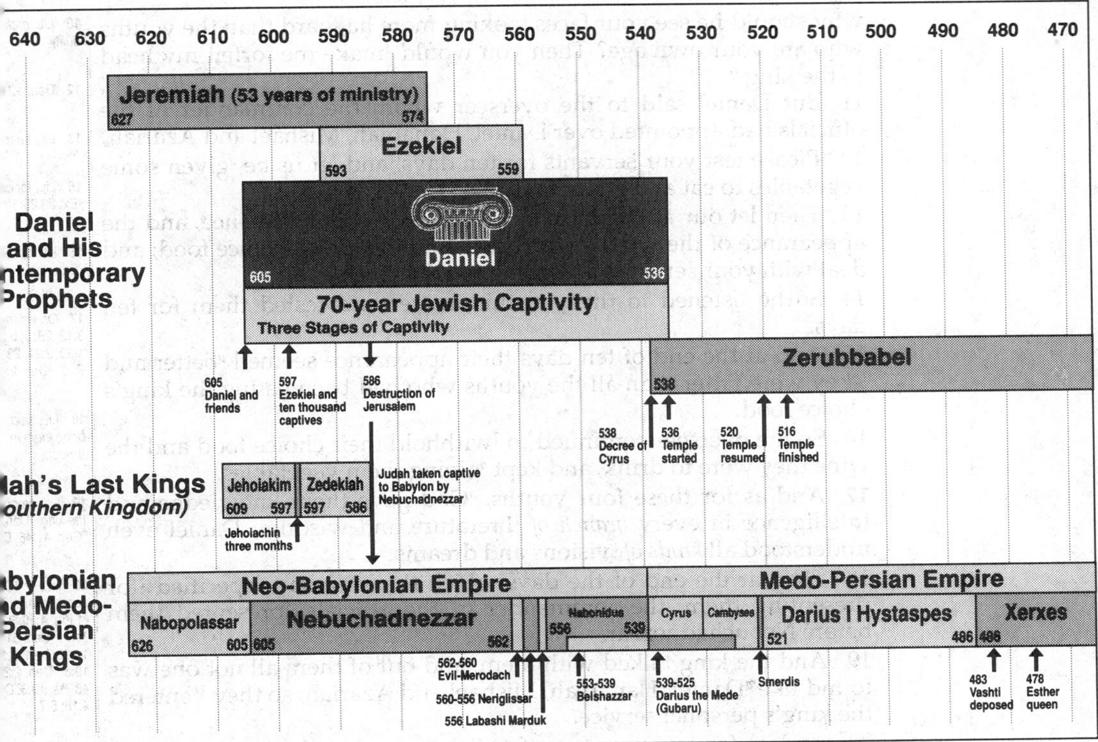

to the land of [c]Shinar, to the house of his [1]god, and he brought the
vessels into the treasury of his [1d]god.
3 Then the king [1]ordered Ashpenaz, the chief of his [2]officials, to
bring in some of the sons of Israel, including some of the [3]royal
[a]family and of the nobles,
4 youths in whom was [a]no defect, who were good-looking, show-
ing [b]intelligence in every *branch of* wisdom, endowed with under-
standing, and discerning knowledge, and who had ability for
[1]serving in the king's [2]court; and *he ordered him* to teach them the
[3]literature and [c]language of the [d]Chaldeans.
5 And the king appointed for them a daily ration from the [a]king's
choice food and from the wine which he drank, and *appointed* that
they should be [1]educated three years, at the end of which they were
to [2b]enter the king's personal service.
6 Now among them from the sons of Judah were [a]Daniel,
Hananiah, Mishael and Azariah.
7 Then the commander of the officials assigned *new* names to
them; and to Daniel he assigned *the name* [a]Belteshazzar, to Hananiah
[b]Shadrach, to Mishael [b]Meshach, and to Azariah [b]Abed-nego.
8 But Daniel [1]made up his mind that he would not [a]defile himself
with the [b]king's choice food or with the [c]wine which he drank; so he
sought *permission* from the commander of the officials that he might
not defile himself.
9 Now God granted Daniel [1a]favor and compassion in the sight of
the commander of the officials,
10 and the commander of the officials said to Daniel, "I am afraid of
my lord the king, who has appointed your food and your drink; for

Or, *gods* [c]Gen. ; 11:2; Is. 11:11; 5:11 [d]Jer. 50:2; 51:44

Or, *said to* [2]Or, *unuchs*, and so out the ch. [3]Lit., *d of the* [a]2 Kin. 24:15; Is. 39:7

, *standing* [2]Lit., *ace* [3]Or, *writing* m. 14:25 [b]Dan. [c]Is. 36:11; Jer. Dan. 2:4 [d]Dan. , 5, 10; 3:8; 4:7; 5:7, 11, 30; 9:1

Or, *reared* [2]Lit., *l before the king* an. 1:8 [b]1 Sam. 16:22; Dan. 1:19

Ezek. 14:14, 20; 28:3; Matt. 24:15

n. 2:26; 4:8; 5:12 [b]Dan. 2:49; 3:12

Lit., *set upon his* ev. 11:47; Ezek. 3, 14; Hos. 9:3, 4 . 141:4; Dan. 1:5 . 32:38; Dan. 5:4

., *lovingkindness* 9:21; 1 Kin. 8:50; Job 5:15, 16; Ps. 06:46; Prov. 16:7

why should he see your faces looking more haggard than the youths
who are your own age? Then you would [1]make me forfeit my head
to the king."
11 But Daniel said to the overseer whom the commander of the
officials had appointed over Daniel, Hananiah, Mishael and Azariah,
12 "Please test your servants for ten days, and let us be [a]given some
vegetables to eat and water to drink.
13 "Then let our appearance be [1]observed in your presence, and the
appearance of the youths who are eating the king's choice food; and
deal with your servants according to what you see."
14 So he listened to them in this matter and tested them for ten
days.
15 And at the end of ten days their appearance seemed [a]better and
[1]they were fatter than all the youths who had been eating the king's
choice food.
16 So the overseer continued to [1]withhold their choice food and the
wine they were to drink, and kept [a]giving them vegetables.
17 And as for these four youths, [a]God gave them knowledge and
intelligence in every *branch of* [1]literature and wisdom; Daniel even
understood all *kinds of* [b]visions and dreams.
18 Then at the end of the days which the king had [1]specified [2]for
presenting them, the commander of the officials [3]presented them
before Nebuchadnezzar.
19 And the king talked with them, and out of them all not one was
found like [a]Daniel, Hananiah, Mishael and Azariah; so they [1b]entered
the king's personal service.
20 And as for every matter of [a]wisdom [1]and understanding about
which the king consulted them, he found them [b]ten times [c]better
than all the [2d]magicians *and* conjurers who *were* in all his realm.
21 And Daniel [1]continued until the [a]first year of Cyrus the king.

Chapter 2

2 Now in the second year of the reign of Nebuchadnezzar, Nebu-
chadnezzar [1a]had dreams; and his spirit was troubled and his
[b]sleep [2]left him.
2 Then the king [1]gave orders to call in the [2a]magicians, the con-
jurers, the sorcerers and the [3]Chaldeans, to tell the king his dreams.
So they came in and stood before the king.
3 And the king said to them, "I [1a]had a dream, and my spirit [2]is
anxious to [3]understand the dream."
4 Then the Chaldeans spoke to the king in [1a]Aramaic: "[b]O king,
live forever! [c]Tell the dream to your servants, and we will declare the
interpretation."
5 The king answered and said to the Chaldeans, "[1]The command
from me is firm: if you do not make known to me the dream and its
interpretation, you will be [2a]torn limb from limb, and your houses
will be made a rubbish heap.
6 "But if you declare the dream and its interpretation, you will
receive from me [a]gifts and a reward and great honor; therefore
declare to me the dream and its interpretation."
7 They answered a second time and said, "Let the king [a]tell the
dream to his servants, and we will declare the interpretation."
8 The king answered and said, "I know for certain that you are

10 [1]Lit., *make guilty*

12 [a]Dan. 1:16

13 [1]Lit., *seen*

15 [1]Lit., *fat of* [a]Ex. 23:25; Pr

16 [1]Lit., *take* [a]Dan. 1:12

17 [1]Or, *writing* 3:12, 28; Job 3 1:20; 2:21, 23; 7:22 [b]Dan. 2:1

18 [1]Lit., *said bring them in brought in*

19 [1]Lit., *stood the king* [a]Dan. [b]Gen. 41:46; D

20 [1]Lit., *of* [2]Or *soothsayer prie* [a]1 Kin. 4:30, 31 1:17 [b]Gen. 31: 14:22; Neh. 4:1 19:3 [c]Dan. 2:2 48 [d]Is. 19:3; Da 4:18; 5:7

21 [1]Lit., *was ur* 6:28; 10:1

2:1 [1]Lit., *dream dreams* [2]Lit., *w upon him* [a]Gen 41:1, 8; Job 33: Dan. 2:3; 4:5 [b]E Dan. 6:18

2 [1]Lit., *said to c soothsayer pries master astrolog so throughout th* [a]Gen. 41:8; Ex. 47:12, 13; Dan. 2:10, 27; 4:6; 5:

3 [1]Lit., *dreamed was troubled* [3]L *know* [a]Gen. 40: 41:15; Dan. 4:5

4 [1]The text is in Aramaic from he through 7:28 [a]Ez Is. 36:11 [b]Dan. 3 5:10 [c]Dan. 2:7

5 [1]Another readi *The word has go me* [2]Lit., *made in limbs* [a]Ezra 6:11 2:12; 3:29

6 [a]Dan. 2:48; 5:7

7 [a]Dan. 2:4

INSIGHT

Daniel was written in Aramaic and Hebrew. The Aramaic portion was from 2:4 through 7:28.

[1]bargaining for time, inasmuch as you have seen that [2]the command
from me is firm,
9 that if you do not make the dream known to me, there is only
[a]one [1]decree for you. For you have agreed together to speak lying
and corrupt [2]words before me until the [3]situation is changed; there-
fore tell me the dream, that I may [b]know that you can declare to me
its interpretation."
10 The Chaldeans answered [1]the king and said, "There is not a man
on earth who could declare the matter [2]for the king, inasmuch as no
great king or ruler has *ever* asked anything like this of any
[3a]magician, conjurer or Chaldean.
11 "Moreover, the thing which the king demands is [1]difficult, and
there is no one else who could declare it [2]to the king except [a]gods,
whose [b]dwelling place is not with *mortal* flesh."
12 Because of this the king became [a]indignant and very furious, and
gave orders to destroy all the wise men of Babylon.
13 So the [1]decree went forth that the wise men should be slain; and
they looked for [a]Daniel and his friends to [2]kill *them*.
14 Then Daniel replied with discretion and discernment to [a]Arioch,
the captain of the king's [1]bodyguard, who had gone forth to slay the
wise men of Babylon;
15 he answered and said to Arioch, the king's commander, "For
what reason is the [1]decree from the king *so* [2]urgent?" Then Arioch
informed Daniel about the matter.
16 So Daniel went in and requested of the king that he would [1]give
him time, in order that he might declare the interpretation to the
king.
17 Then Daniel went to his house and informed his friends, [a]Hana-
niah, Mishael and Azariah, about the matter,
18 in order that they might [a]request compassion from the God of
heaven concerning this mystery, so that Daniel and his friends might
not be [b]destroyed with the rest of the wise men of Babylon.
19 Then the mystery was revealed to Daniel in a night [a]vision. Then
Daniel blessed the God of heaven;
20 Daniel answered and said,

"Let the name of God be [a]blessed forever and ever,
For [b]wisdom and power belong to Him.

21 "And it is He who [a]changes the times and the epochs;
He [b]removes kings and [1]establishes kings;
He gives [c]wisdom to wise men,
And knowledge to [2]men of understanding.

22 "It is He who [a]reveals the profound and hidden things;
[b]He knows what is in the darkness,
And the [c]light dwells with Him.

23 "To Thee, O [a]God of my fathers, I give thanks and praise,
For Thou hast given me [b]wisdom and power;
Even now Thou hast made known to me what we [c]requested of
Thee,
For Thou hast made known to us the king's matter."

24 Therefore, Daniel went in to Arioch, whom the king had ap-
pointed to destroy the wise men of Babylon; he went and spoke to
him as follows: "[a]Do not destroy the wise men of Babylon! Take me
[1]into the king's presence, and I will declare the interpretation to the
king."

, *buying* [2]V. 5, note 1

law [2]Lit., *word*
ne [a]Esth. 4:11;
3:15 [b]Is. 41:23

[1]Lit., *before the*
[3]Or, *soothsayer*
st [a]Dan. 2:2, 27

[1]Or, *rare* [2]Lit.,
e [a]Gen. 41:39;
:11 [b]Ex. 29:45;
Is. 57:15

76:10; Dan. 2:5;
3:13, 19

Or, *law* [2]Lit., *be*
[a]Dan. 1:19, 20

Or, *executioners*
[a]Dan. 2:24

, *law* [2]Or, *harsh*

r, *appoint a time for him*

17 [a]Dan. 1:6

sth. 4:15, 16; Is.
Jer. 33:3; Ezek.
Dan. 2:23 [b]Gen.
18:28; Mal. 3:18

[a]Num. 12:6; Job
5, 16; Dan. 1:17;
7:2, 7, 13

103:1, 2; 113:1,
:18; 145:1, 2, 21
r. 29:11, 12; Job
:13, 16-22; Dan.
2:21-23

Or, *sets up* [2]Lit.,
wers [a]Ps. 31:15;
1. 2:9; 7:25 [b]Job
Ps. 75:6, 7; Dan.
2 [c]1 Kin. 3:9, 10;
4:29; James 1:5

[a]Job 12:22; Ps.
14; Dan. 2:19, 28
26:6; Ps. 139:12;
; Jer. 23:24; Heb.
3 [c]Ps. 36:9; Dan.
14; James 1:17;
1 John 1:5

[a]Gen. 31:42; Ex.
[b]Dan. 1:17; 2:21
1:2, 4; Dan. 2:18,
29, 30

[1]Lit., *in before the*
g [a]Dan. 2:12, 13;
Acts 27:24

25 Then Arioch hurriedly [a]brought Daniel [1]into the king's presence
and spoke to him as follows: "I have found a man among the [2b]exiles
from Judah who can make the interpretation known to the king!"
26 The king answered and said to Daniel, whose name was [a]Belte-
shazzar, "Are you able to make known to me the dream which I
have seen and its interpretation?"
27 Daniel answered before the king and said, "As for the mystery
about which the king has inquired, neither [a]wise men, conjurers,
[1]magicians, *nor* diviners are able to declare *it* to the king.
28 "However, there is a [a]God in heaven who reveals mysteries, and
He has made known to King Nebuchadnezzar what will take place
in the [1b]latter days. This was your dream and the [c]visions [2]in your
mind *while* on your bed.
29 "As for you, O king, *while* on your bed your thoughts [1]turned to
what would take place [2]in the future; and [a]He who reveals mysteries
has made known to you what will take place.
30 "But as for me, this mystery has not been revealed to me for any
[a]wisdom [1]residing in me more than *in* any *other* living man, but for
the purpose of making the interpretation known to the king, and
that you may [2]understand the [b]thoughts of your [3]mind.
31 "You, O king, were looking and behold, there was a single great
statue; that statue, which was large and [1]of extraordinary splendor,
was standing in front of you, and its appearance was [a]awesome.
32 "The [a]head of that statue *was made* of fine gold, its breast and its
arms of silver, its belly and its thighs of bronze,
33 its legs of iron, its feet partly of iron and partly of clay.
34 "You [1]continued looking until a [a]stone was cut out [b]without
hands, and it struck the statue on its feet of iron and clay, and
[c]crushed them.
35 "Then the iron, the clay, the bronze, the silver and the gold were
crushed [1]all at the same time, and became [a]like chaff from the sum-
mer threshing floors; and the wind carried them away so that [b]not a
trace of them was found. But the stone that struck the statue became
a great [c]mountain and filled the whole earth.
36 "This *was* the dream; now we shall tell [a]its interpretation before
the king.
37 "You, O king, are the [a]king of kings, to whom the God of heaven
has given the [1]kingdom, the [b]power, the strength, and the glory;
38 and wherever the sons of men dwell, *or* the [a]beasts of the field, or
the birds of the sky, He has given *them* into your hand and has
caused you to rule over them all. You are the head of gold.
39 "And after you there will arise another kingdom inferior to you,
then another third kingdom of bronze, which will rule over all the
earth.
40 "Then there will be a [a]fourth kingdom as strong as iron; inasmuch
as iron crushes and shatters all things, so, like iron that breaks in
pieces, it will crush and break all these in pieces.
41 "And in that you saw the feet and toes, partly of potter's clay and
partly of iron, it will be a divided kingdom; but it will have in it the
toughness of iron, inasmuch as you saw the iron mixed with [1]com-
mon clay.
42 "And *as* the toes of the feet *were* partly of iron and partly of
pottery, *so* some of the kingdom will be strong and part of it will be
brittle.

25 [1]Lit., *in befo* *king* [2]Lit., *sons* *exile of* [a]Gen. [b]Dan. 1:6; 5:13;

26 [a]Dan. 1:7; 4

27 [1]Or, *soothsa* *priests* [a]Dan. 2 11; 5:7, 8

28 [1]Lit., *end of* *days* [2]Lit., *of yo* [a]Gen. 40:8; 41:1 2:22, 45 [b]Gen. 2:2; Dan. 10:14; 4:1 [c]Dan. 4:5

29 [1]Lit., *came u* *after this* [a]Dan.

30 [1]Lit., *which is* *know* [3]Lit., *hear* 41:16; Dan. 1:17 139:2; Amos 4:1

31 [1]Lit., *its splen* *was surpassing* 1:7

32 [a]Dan. 2:38

34 [1]Lit., *were* [a]D 2:45 [b]Dan. 8:25; 4:6 [c]Ps. 2:9; Is. 6

35 [1]Lit., *like one* 1:4; Is. 17:13; 41: Hos. 13:3 [b]Ps. 3 36 [c]Is. 2:2; Mic. 4

36 [a]Dan. 2:24

37 [1]Or, *sovereig* 47:5; Jer. 27:6, 7; 26:7 [b]Ps. 62:11

38 [a]Ps. 50:10, 11 4:21, 22

40 [a]Dan. 7:23

41 [1]Lit., *clay of m*

43 "And in that you saw the iron mixed with [1]common clay, they
will combine with one another [2]in the seed of men; but they will not
adhere to one another, even as iron does not combine with pottery.
44 "And in the days of those kings the [a]God of heaven will [b]set up a
[c]kingdom which will never be destroyed, and *that* kingdom will not
be [1]left for another people; it will [d]crush and put an end to all these
kingdoms, but it will itself endure forever.
45 "Inasmuch as you saw that a [a]stone was cut out of the mountain
without hands and that it crushed the iron, the bronze, the clay, the
silver, and the gold, the [b]great God has made known to the king
what [c]will take place [1]in the future; so the dream is true, and its
interpretation is trustworthy."
46 Then King Nebuchadnezzar fell on his face and did [a]homage to
Daniel, and gave orders to present to him an offering and [1b]fragrant
incense.
47 The king answered Daniel and said, "Surely [a]your God is a [b]God
of gods and a Lord of kings and a [c]revealer of mysteries, since you
have been able to reveal this mystery."
48 Then the king [1a]promoted Daniel and gave him many great gifts,
and he made him ruler over the whole [b]province of Babylon and
chief [2]prefect over all the wise men of Babylon.
49 And Daniel made request of the king, and he [a]appointed [b]Shad-
rach, Meshach and Abed-nego over the administration of the
province of Babylon, while Daniel *was* at the king's [1c]court.

Chapter 3

3 Nebuchadnezzar the king made an [a]image of gold, the height of
which *was* sixty [1]cubits *and* its width six [1]cubits; he set it up on
the plain of Dura in the [b]province of Babylon.
2 Then Nebuchadnezzar the king sent *word* to assemble the [a]sa-
traps, the prefects and the governors, the counselors, the treasurers,
the judges, the magistrates and all the rulers of the provinces to
come to the dedication of the image that Nebuchadnezzar the king
had set up.
3 Then the satraps, the prefects and the governors, the counselors,
the treasurers, the judges, the magistrates and all the rulers of the
provinces were assembled for the dedication of the image that Nebu-
chadnezzar the king had set up; and they stood before the image
that Nebuchadnezzar had set up.
4 Then the herald loudly proclaimed: "To you [1]the command is
given, [a]O peoples, nations and *men of every* [2]language,
5 that at the moment you [a]hear the sound of the horn, flute, [1]lyre,
[2]trigon, [3]psaltery, bagpipe, and all kinds of music, you are to fall
down and worship the golden image that Nebuchadnezzar the king
has set up.
6 "But whoever does not fall down and worship shall [1]immediately
be [a]cast into the midst of a [b]furnace of blazing fire."
7 Therefore at that time, when all the peoples heard the sound of
the horn, flute, [1]lyre, trigon, psaltery, bagpipe, and all kinds of
music, all the peoples, nations and *men of every* [2]language fell down
and worshiped the golden image that Nebuchadnezzar the king had
set up.
8 For this reason at that time certain [a]Chaldeans came forward and
[1b]brought charges against the Jews.

...., *clay of mud* [2]Or, *with*

passed on to ...8, 37 [b]Is. 9:6, 145:13; Ezek. ...; Dan. 4:3, 34; ..., 27; Mic. 4:7; ..., 33 [d]Ps. 2:9; Dan. 2:34, 35

...*fter this* [a]Dan. [b]Deut. 10:17; ...7:22; Ps. 48:1; 2:18, 19; Dan. ...al. 1:11 [c]Gen. 41:28, 32

...., *sweet odors* ...7; Acts 10:25; ...ev. 19:10; 22:8 ...:31; Ezra 6:10

...Dan. 3:15; 4:25 ...:17; Ps. 136:2, ...n. 11:36 [c]Dan. ..., 30; Amos 3:7

...it., *made great of the prefects* 41:39-43; Dan. 29 [b]Dan. 3:1, 12, 30

...it., *gate* [a]Dan. ...Dan. 1:7 [c]Esth. 21; Amos 5:15

[1]I.e., One cubit ...s approx. 18 in. 12:28; Is. 46:6; ...:20; Dan. 2:31; 8:4; Hab. 2:19 ...Dan. 2:48; 3:30

...n. 3:3, 27; 6:1-7

they command ...*gue* [a]Dan. 3:7; 4:1; 6:25

[1]Or, *zither* [2]I.e., ...*ular lyre* [3]Or, *a* ...*harp* [a]Dan. 3:7, 10, 15

...*n the same hour* ...3:11, 15, 21; 6:7 ...er. 29:22; Ezek. ...22; Matt. 13:42, Rev. 9:2; 14:11

5, notes 1, 2, 3 [2]Lit., *tongue*

...., *ate the pieces* ...Dan. 2:2, 10; 4:7 ...2-16; Esth. 3:8, ...9; Dan. 6:12, 13

For a clear understanding of the empires represented in the statue, consult the charts on pages I-30 through I-32, and the historical account on pages I-33 through I-40.

9 They responded and said to Nebuchadnezzar the king: "[a]O king,
live forever!
10 "You yourself, O king, have [a]made a decree that every man who
hears the sound of the horn, flute, [1]lyre, trigon, psaltery, and bag-
pipe, and all kinds of music, is to [b]fall down and worship the golden
image.
11 "But whoever does not fall down and worship shall be cast into
the midst of a furnace of blazing fire.
12 "There are certain Jews whom you have [a]appointed over the ad-
ministration of the province of Babylon, *namely* Shadrach, Meshach
and Abed-nego. These men, O king, have disregarded you; they do
not serve your gods or worship the golden image which you have
set up."
13 Then Nebuchadnezzar in [a]rage and anger gave orders to bring
Shadrach, Meshach and Abed-nego; then these men were brought
before the king.
14 Nebuchadnezzar responded and said to them, "Is it true, Shad-
rach, Meshach and Abed-nego, that you do not serve [a]my gods or
worship the golden image that I have set up?
15 "Now if you are ready, [a]at the moment you hear the sound of the
horn, flute, [1]lyre, trigon, psaltery, and bagpipe, and all kinds of
music, to fall down and worship the image that I have made, *very
well.* But if you will not worship, you will [2]immediately be [b]cast into
the midst of a furnace of blazing fire; and [c]what god is there who can
deliver you out of my hands?"
16 [a]Shadrach, Meshach and Abed-nego answered and said to the
king, "O Nebuchadnezzar, we do not need to give you an answer
concerning this matter.
17 "[1]If it be *so,* our [a]God whom we serve is able to deliver us from
the furnace of blazing fire; [2]and [b]He will deliver us out of your hand,
O king.
18 "[a]But *even* if *He does* not, [b]let it be known to you, O king, that we
are not going to serve your gods or worship the golden image that
you have set up."
19 Then Nebuchadnezzar was filled with [a]wrath, and his facial ex-
pression was altered toward Shadrach, Meshach and Abed-nego. He
answered [1]by giving orders to heat the furnace seven times more
than it was usually heated.
20 And he commanded certain valiant warriors who *were* in his
army to tie up Shadrach, Meshach and Abed-nego, in order to cast
them into the furnace of blazing fire.
21 Then these men were tied up in their [1a]trousers, their [2]coats, their
caps and their *other* clothes, and were cast into the midst of the
furnace of blazing fire.
22 For this reason, because the king's [1]command *was* [2a]urgent and
the furnace had been made extremely hot, the flame of the fire slew
those men who carried up Shadrach, Meshach and Abed-nego.
23 But these three men, Shadrach, Meshach and Abed-nego, [a]fell
into the midst of the furnace of blazing fire *still* tied up.
24 Then Nebuchadnezzar the king was astounded and stood up in
haste; he responded and said to his high officials, "Was it not three
men we cast bound into the midst of the fire?" They answered and
said to the king, "Certainly, O king."
25 He answered and said, "Look! I see four men loosed *and*

9 [a]Dan. 2:4; 6:6, 21

10 [1]V. 5, note [a]Esth. 3:12-14 3:4-6; 6:12 [b] 7, 15

12 [a]Dan. 2:49

13 [a]Dan. 2:12

14 [a]Is. 46:1; J Dan. 3:1; 4:8

15 [1]V. 5, notes [2]Or, *in the sam* [a]Dan. 3:5 [b]Da [c]Ex. 5:2; Is. 36 Dan. 2:47

16 [a]Dan. 1:7;

17 [1]Or, *If our* (*able* [2]Or, *then* 5:19; Ps. 27:1, 26:3, 4; Jer. 1:8 21 [b]1 Sam. 17 7:7; 2 Cor. 1:10

18 [a]Josh. 24:15 19:14, 18; Is. 5 Dan. 3:28 [b]Heb

19 [1]Lit., *and or* [a]Esth. 7:7; Dan.

21 [1]Or, *leggings* *cloaks* [a]Dan. 3:

22 [1]Lit., *word* [2] *harsh* [a]Ex. 12:3 2:15

23 [a]Is. 43:2

[a]walking *about* in the midst of the fire [1]without harm, and the ap-
pearance of the fourth is like a son of *the* [b]gods!"
26 Then Nebuchadnezzar came near to the door of the furnace of
blazing fire; he responded and said, "Shadrach, Meshach and Abed-
nego, come out, you servants of the [a]Most High God, and come
here!" Then Shadrach, Meshach and Abed-nego [b]came out of the
midst of the fire.
27 And the [a]satraps, the prefects, the governors and the king's high
officials gathered around *and* saw in regard to these men that the
[b]fire had no [1]effect on [2]the bodies of these men nor was the hair of
their head singed, nor were their [3c] trousers [4]damaged, nor had the
smell of fire *even* come upon them.
28 Nebuchadnezzar responded and said, "Blessed be the [a]God of
Shadrach, Meshach and Abed-nego, who has [b]sent His angel and
delivered His servants who put their [c]trust in Him, [1]violating the
king's command, and yielded up their bodies so as [d]not to serve or
worship any god except their own God.
29 "Therefore, I [a]make a decree that any people, nation or tongue
that speaks anything offensive against the God of [b]Shadrach,
Meshach and Abed-nego shall be torn limb from limb and their
[c]houses reduced to a rubbish heap, inasmuch as there is [d]no other
god who is able to deliver in this way."
30 Then the king [a]caused Shadrach, Meshach and Abed-nego to
prosper in the province of Babylon.

Chapter 4

4 [1]Nebuchadnezzar the king to all the peoples, nations, and *men of*
every [2]language that live in all the earth: "May your [3a]peace
abound!
2 "It has seemed good to me to declare the signs and wonders
which the [a]Most High God has done for me.
3 "How great are His [a]signs,
And how mighty are His wonders!
His [b]kingdom is an everlasting kingdom,
And His dominion is from generation to generation.
4 "[1]I, Nebuchadnezzar, was at ease in my house and [a]flourishing in
my palace.
5 "I saw a [a]dream and it made me fearful; and *these* fantasies *as I lay*
on my bed and the [b]visions [1]in my mind kept alarming me.
6 "So I gave orders to [a]bring into my presence all the wise men of
Babylon, that they might make known to me the interpretation of the
dream.
7 "Then the [1a]magicians, the conjurers, the [2]Chaldeans, and the
diviners came in, and I related the dream [3]to them; but they could
not make its [b]interpretation known to me.
8 "But finally Daniel came in before me, whose name is [a]Belte-
shazzar according to the name of my god, and in whom is [1b]a spirit
of the holy gods; and I related the dream [2]to him, *saying*,
9 'O Belteshazzar, [a]chief of the magicians, since I know that [b]a spirit
of the holy gods is in you and [c]no mystery baffles you, [d]tell *me* the
visions of my dream which I have seen, along with its interpretation.
10 'Now *these were* the [a]visions [1]in my mind *as I lay* on my bed: I was
looking, and behold, *there was* a [b]tree in the midst of the [2]earth, and
its height *was* great.

[1]Lit., *there is no* ...*ry in them* [a]Ps. ...9; Is. 43:2 [b]Jer. 1:8, 19; 15:21

[a]Dan. 3:17; 4:2 ...20; 1 Kin. 8:51; Jer. 11:4

...Lit., *power over* ...*heir* [3]Or, *cloaks changed* [a]Dan. 3:2, 3 [b]Is. 43:2; ...:34 [c]Dan. 3:21

...t., *and changed* ...*ng's word* [a]Dan. 5-17 [b]Ps. 34:7, 7:36; Dan. 3:25; ...; Acts 5:19; 12:7 ...s. 22:4, 5; 40:4; ...s. 12:2; 26:3, 4; Jer. 17:7 [d]Dan. 3:16-18

...Dan. 6:26 [b]Dan. ...9; 2:17, 49; 3:12 ...a 6:11; Dan. 2:5 ...Dan. 2:47; 3:15

[a]Dan. 2:49; 3:12

...h. 3:31 in Aram. Lit., *tongue* [3]Or, ...*are or prosperity* ...4:17; Dan. 6:25

...1. 3:26; 4:17, 24, 25, 32, 34

...s. 77:19; 105:27; ...25:1; Dan. 6:27 2:44; 4:34; 6:26

...Ch. 4:1 in Aram. ...30:6; Is. 47:7, 8

[1]Lit., *of my head* ...:3 [b]Dan. 2:1, 28; 4:10, 13

...n. 41:8; Dan. 2:2

[1]Or, *soothsayer priests*, and so ...hout the ch. [2]Or, *astrologers* [3]Lit., [a]Gen. 41:8; Dan. ...7; 5:7 [b]Is. 44:25; ...7:9, 10; Dan. 2:7

[1]Or possibly, *the* ...*t of the holy God*, so throughout the ...Lit., *before* [a]Dan. 2:26; 5:12 [b]Dan. 4:9, 18; 5:11, 14

[a]Dan. 1:20; 2:48; ...Gen. 41:38; Dan. ...Ezek. 28:3; Dan. ...Gen. 41:15; Dan. 2:4, 5

[1]Lit., *of my head* [2]Or, *land*, and so ...hroughout the ch. ...:5 [b]Ezek. 31:3, 6

11 'The tree grew large and became strong,
And its height [a]reached to the sky,
And it *was* visible to the end of the whole earth.
12 'Its foliage *was* [a]beautiful and its fruit abundant,
And in it *was* food for all.
The [b]beasts of the field found [c]shade under it,
And the [d]birds of the sky dwelt in its branches,
And all [1]living creatures fed themselves from it.
13 'I was looking in the [a]visions [1]in my mind *as I lay* on my bed, and
behold, [b]an *angelic* watcher, a [c]holy one, descended from heaven.
14 'He shouted out and spoke as follows:
"[a]Chop down the tree and cut off its branches,
Strip off its foliage and scatter its fruit;
Let the [b]beasts flee from under it,
And the birds from its branches.
15 "Yet [a]leave the stump [1]with its roots in the ground,
But with a band of iron and bronze *around it*
In the new grass of the field;
And let him be drenched with the dew of heaven,
And let [2]him share with the beasts in the grass of the earth.
16 "Let his [1]mind be changed from *that of* a man,
And let a beast's [1]mind be given to him,
And let [a]seven [2]periods of time pass over him.
17 "This sentence is by the decree of the *angelic* watchers,
And the decision is a command of the holy ones,
In order that the living may [a]know
That the Most High is ruler over the realm of mankind,
And [b]bestows it on whom He wishes,
And sets over it the [c]lowliest of men."
18 'This is the dream *which* I, King Nebuchadnezzar, have seen.
Now you, Belteshazzar, tell *me* its interpretation, inasmuch as none
of the [a]wise men of my kingdom is able to make known to me the
interpretation; but you are able, for a [b]spirit of the holy gods is in
you.'
19 "Then Daniel, whose name is Belteshazzar, was appalled for a
while as his [a]thoughts alarmed him. The king responded and said,
'Belteshazzar, do not [b]let the dream or its interpretation alarm you.'
Belteshazzar answered and said, '[c]My lord, *if only* the dream applied
to those who hate you, and its interpretation to [d]your adversaries!
20 'The [a]tree that you saw, which became large and grew strong,
whose height reached to the sky and was visible to all the earth,
21 and whose foliage *was* beautiful and its fruit abundant, and in
which *was* food for all, under which the beasts of the field dwelt and
in whose branches the birds of the sky lodged—
22 it is [a]you, O king; for you have become great and grown strong,
and your [1]majesty has become great and reached to the sky and your
[b]dominion to the end of the earth.
23 'And in that the king saw an *angelic* watcher, a holy one, de-
scending from heaven and saying, "[a]Chop down the tree and
destroy it; yet leave the stump [1]with its roots in the ground, but with
a band of iron and bronze *around it* in the new grass of the field, and
let him be drenched with the dew of heaven, and let [2]him share with
the beasts of the field until [b]seven [3]periods of time pass over him";

11 [a]Deut. 9:1; D
4:21, 22

12 [1]Lit., *flesh* [a]
31:7 [b]Jer. 27:6;
31:6 [c]Lam. 4:20
17:23; Matt. 13:
13:19

13 [1]Lit., *of my h*
[a]Dan. 7:1 [b]Dan.
23 [c]Deut. 33:2;
89:7; Dan. 8:13

14 [a]Ezek. 31:10
Dan. 4:23; Matt.
7:19; Luke 13:7-
[b]Ezek. 31:12, 13
4:12

15 [1]Lit., *of* [2]Lit.,
portion be with [a]
14:7-9

16 [1]Lit., *heart* [2]I
years [a]Dan. 4:23

17 [a]Ps. 9:16; 83:
Dan. 2:21; 5:21 [b]
27:5-7; Dan. 4:25
19 [c]1 Sam. 2:8; I
11:21

18 [a]Gen. 41:8, 15
4:7; 5:8, 15 [b]Dan

19 [a]Jer. 4:19; Da
7:15, 28; 8:27; 10
17 [b]1 Sam. 3:17;
4:4, 5 [c]2 Sam. 18
Dan. 4:24; 10:16
[d]2 Sam. 18:32

20 [a]Dan. 4:10-12

22 [1]Lit., *greatness*
[a]2 Sam. 12:7; Dan
2:37, 38 [b]Jer. 27:6

23 [1]Lit., *of* [2]Lit., *h*
portion be with [3]I.e
years [a]Dan. 4:14,
[b]Dan. 4:16

24 this is the interpretation, O king, and this is the decree of the
Most High, which has [a]come upon my lord the king:
25 that you be [a]driven away from mankind, and your dwelling
place be with the beasts of the field, and you be given grass to eat
like cattle and be drenched with the dew of heaven; and seven
[1]periods of time will pass over you, until you recognize that the
[b]Most High is ruler over the realm of mankind, and [c]bestows it on
whomever He wishes.
26 'And in that it was commanded to [a]leave the stump [1]with the
roots of the tree, your kingdom will be [2]assured to you after you
recognize that *it is* [b]Heaven *that* rules.
27 'Therefore, O king, may my [a]advice be pleasing to you: [1b]break
away now from your sins by *doing* righteousness, and from your
iniquities by [c]showing mercy to *the* poor, in case there may be a
[d]prolonging of your prosperity.'
28 "All *this* [a]happened to Nebuchadnezzar the king.
29 "[a]Twelve months later he was walking on the *roof of* the royal
palace of Babylon.
30 "The king [1]reflected and said, 'Is this not Babylon the [a]great,
which I myself have built as a royal [2]residence by the might of my
power and for the glory of my majesty?'
31 "While the word *was* in the king's mouth, a voice [1]came from
heaven, *saying,* 'King Nebuchadnezzar, to you it is declared: [2]sover-
eignty has been removed from you,
32 and [a]you will be driven away from mankind, and your dwelling
place *will be* with the beasts of the field. You will be given grass to
eat like cattle, and [b]seven [1]periods of time will pass over you, until
you recognize that the [c]Most High is ruler over the realm of man-
kind, and bestows it on whomever He wishes.'
33 "Immediately the word concerning Nebuchadnezzar was ful-
filled; and he was [a]driven away from mankind and began eating
grass like cattle, and his body was drenched with the dew of heaven,
until his hair had grown like eagles' *feathers* and his nails like birds'
claws.
34 "But at the end of [1]that period I, Nebuchadnezzar, raised my eyes
toward heaven, and my [2]reason returned to me, and I blessed the
[a]Most High and praised and honored [b]Him who lives forever;

For His dominion is an [c]everlasting dominion,
And His kingdom *endures* from generation to generation.

35 "And [a]all the inhabitants of the earth are accounted as nothing,
But [b]He does according to His will in the host of heaven
And *among* the inhabitants of earth;
And [c]no one can [1]ward off His hand
Or say to Him, '[d]What hast Thou done?'

36 "At that time my [1a]reason returned to me. And my majesty and
[b]splendor were [2]restored to me for the glory of my kingdom, and my
counselors and my nobles began seeking me out; so I was rees-
tablished in my [3]sovereignty, and surpassing [c]greatness was added
to me.
37 "Now I Nebuchadnezzar praise, exalt, and honor the King of
[a]heaven, for [b]all His works are [1]true and His ways [2]just, and He is
able to humble those who [c]walk in pride."

40:11, 12; Ps. 107:40

years [a]Dan. 1 [b]Ps. 83:18; ; Dan. 4:2, 17 37; 4:17; 5:21

[1]Lit., *of* [2]Lit., *g* [a]Dan. 4:15, 2:18, 19, 28, 37, 44; 4:31

, *redeem now ur sins* [a]Gen. [b]Prov. 28:13; 7; Ezek. 18:7, Acts 8:22 [c]Ps. Is. 58:6, 7, 10 1:29; Jon. 3:9

. 23:19; Zech. 1:6

29 [a]2 Pet. 3:9

nswered [2]Lit., *use* [a]Hab. 2:4

[1]Lit., *fell* [2]Or, *kingdom*

., years [a]Dan. an. 4:16 [c]Dan. 4:17

Dan. 4:25; 5:21

the days [2]Lit., *dge* [a]Dan. 4:2; 5:18, 21 [b]Ps. -27; Dan. 6:26; Rev. 4:10 [c]Ps. er. 10:10; Dan. 4:7; Luke 1:33

, *strike against* 5; Is. 40:15, 17 1; 115:3; 135:6; 7 [c]Job 42:2; Is. 3 [d]Job 9:12; Is. 45:9; Rom. 9:20

[1]Lit., *knowledge* , *returning* [3]Or, [a]2 Chr. 33:12, Dan. 4:34 [b]Dan. Prov. 22:4; Dan. 4:22

[1]Lit., *truth* [2]Lit., *tice* [a]Dan. 4:26; [b]Deut. 32:4; Ps. 5; Is. 5:16 [c]Ex. ; Job 40:11, 12; Dan. 5:20

Chapter 5

5 Belshazzar the king [1]held a great [a]feast for a thousand of his
nobles, and he was drinking wine in the presence of the
thousand.
2 When Belshazzar tasted the wine, he gave orders to bring the
gold and silver [a]vessels which Nebuchadnezzar his [1]father had taken
out of the temple which *was* in Jerusalem, in order that the king and
his nobles, his wives, and his concubines might drink from them.
3 Then they brought the gold vessels that had been taken out of
the temple, the house of God which *was* in Jerusalem; and the king
and his nobles, his wives, and his concubines drank from them.
4 They [a]drank the wine and praised the gods of [b]gold and silver, of
bronze, iron, wood, and stone.
5 Suddenly the fingers of a man's hand emerged and began writ-
ing opposite the lampstand on the plaster of the wall of the king's
palace, and the king saw the [1]back of the hand that did the writing.
6 Then the king's [1a]face grew pale, and his thoughts alarmed him;
and his [b]hip joints went slack, and his [c]knees began knocking
together.
7 The king called aloud to bring in the [a]conjurers, the [1]Chaldeans
and the diviners. The king spoke and said to the wise men of Baby-
lon, "Any man who can read this inscription and explain its inter-
pretation to me will be [b]clothed with purple, and *have* a [c]necklace of
gold around his neck, and have authority as [2d]third *ruler* in the king-
dom."
8 Then all the king's wise men came in, but [a]they could not read
the inscription or make known its interpretation to the king.
9 Then King Belshazzar was greatly [a]alarmed, his [1b]face grew *even*
paler, and his nobles were perplexed.
10 The queen entered the banquet [1]hall because of the words of the
king and his nobles; the queen spoke and said, "[a]O king, live forever!
Do not let your thoughts alarm you or your [2]face be pale.
11 "There is a [a]man in your kingdom in whom is [1]a [b]spirit of the holy
gods; and in the days of your father, illumination, insight, and wis-
dom like the wisdom of the gods were found in him. And King
Nebuchadnezzar, your father, your father [2c]the king, appointed him
chief of the [3]magicians, conjurers, [4]Chaldeans, *and* diviners.
12 "*This was* because an [a]extraordinary spirit, knowledge and in-
sight, interpretation of dreams, explanation of enigmas, and solving
of difficult problems were found in this Daniel, whom the king
named [b]Belteshazzar. Let Daniel now be summoned, and he will
declare the interpretation."
13 Then Daniel was brought in before the king. The king spoke and
said to Daniel, "Are you that Daniel who is one of the [1a]exiles from
Judah, whom my father the king [b]brought from Judah?
14 "Now I have heard about you that [1]a spirit of the gods is in you,
and that illumination, insight, and extraordinary wisdom have been
found in you.
15 "Just now the [a]wise men *and* the conjurers were brought in before
me that they might read this inscription and make its interpretation
known to me, but they [b]could not declare the interpretation of the
[1]message.
16 "But I personally have heard about you, that you are able to give
interpretations and solve difficult problems. Now if you are able to

5:1 [1]Lit., *mac* 1:3; Is. 22:12-

2 [1]Or, *forefat* *throughout the* [a]2 Kin. 24:13; Ezra 1:7-11; D

4 [a]Is. 42:8; Da Rev. 9:20 [b]Ps 135:15; Is. 40: Dan. 3:1; Hab.

5 [1]Or, *palm*

6 [1]Lit., *brightn* *changed for hi* 5:9, 10; 7:28 [b] 69:23 [c]Ezek. 7 21:7; Nah. 2:1(

7 [1]Or, *master astrologers* [2]C *triumvir* [a]Is. 44 47:13; Dan. 4:6 15 [b]Gen. 41:4 Dan. 5:16, 29 16:11 [d]Dan. 2: 29; 6:2, 3

8 [a]Gen. 41:8; D 2:27; 4:7; 5:15

9 [1]Lit., *brightne* *changing upon* [a]Job 18:11; Is. 2 Jer. 6:24; Dan. [b]Is. 13:6-8

10 [1]Lit., *house* *brightness be c* [a]Dan. 3:9; 6:6

11 [1]Or possibly, *Spirit of the holy* [2]Or, *O king* [3]Or, *soothsayer pries* *master astrologe* [a]Gen. 41:11-15; 2:47 [b]Dan. 4:8, 5:14 [c]Dan. 2:48

12 [a]Dan. 5:14; 6 [b]Dan. 1:7; 4:8

13 [1]Lit., *sons of exile* [a]Ezra 4:1; 19, 20; Dan. 2:25 [b]Dan. 1:1, 2

14 [1]Or possibly, *Spirit of God*

15 [1]Lit., *word* [a]D 5:7 [b]Is. 47:12f.; D

read the inscription and make its [a]interpretation known to me, you
will be [b]clothed with purple and *wear* a necklace of gold around your
neck, and you will have authority as the [1]third *ruler* in the king-
dom."
17 Then Daniel answered and said before the king, "[1]Keep your
[a]gifts for yourself, or give your rewards to someone else; however, I
will read the inscription to the king and make the interpretation
known to him.
18 "[1]O king, the [a]Most High God [b]granted [2]sovereignty, [c]grandeur,
glory, and majesty to Nebuchadnezzar your father.
19 "And because of the grandeur which He bestowed on him, all the
peoples, nations, and *men of every* [1]language feared and trembled
before him; [a]whomever he wished he killed, and whomever he
wished he spared alive; and whomever he wished he elevated, and
whomever he wished he humbled.
20 "But when his heart was [a]lifted up and his spirit became so
[1b]proud that he behaved arrogantly, he was [c]deposed from his royal
throne, and *his* glory was taken away from him.
21 "He was also [a]driven away from [1]mankind, and his heart was
made like *that of* beasts, and his dwelling place *was* with the [b]wild
donkeys. He was given grass to eat like cattle, and his body was
drenched with the dew of heaven, until he recognized that the [c]Most
High God is ruler over the realm of mankind, and *that* He sets over it
whomever He wishes.
22 "Yet you, his [1]son, Belshazzar, have [a]not humbled your heart,
[2]even though you knew all this,
23 but you have [a]exalted yourself against the [b]Lord of heaven; and
they have brought the vessels of His house before you, and you and
your nobles, your wives and your concubines have been drinking
wine from them; and you have praised the [c]gods of silver and gold,
of bronze, iron, wood and stone, which do not see, hear or under-
stand. But the God [d]in whose hand are your life-breath and your
[e]ways, you have not glorified.
24 "Then the [1a]hand was sent from Him, and this inscription was
written out.
25 "Now this is the inscription that was written out: '[1]MENĒ,
[1]MENĒ, [2]TEKĒL, [3]UPHARSIN.'
26 "This is the interpretation of the [1]message: 'MENĒ'—God has
numbered your kingdom and [a]put an end to it.
27 " 'TEKĒL'—you have been [a]weighed on the scales and found defi-
cient.
28 " 'PERĒS'—your kingdom has been divided and given over to the
[a]Medes and [1]Persians."
29 Then Belshazzar gave orders, and they [a]clothed Daniel with
purple and *put* a necklace of gold around his neck, and issued a
proclamation concerning him that he *now* had authority as the [1]third
ruler in the kingdom.
30 That same night [a]Belshazzar the Chaldean king was [b]slain.
31 [1]So [a]Darius the Mede received the kingdom at about the age of
sixty-two.

Chapter 6

6 [1]It seemed good to Darius to appoint 120 satraps over the king-
dom, that they should be in charge of the whole kingdom,

[1]Or, *triumvir* [a]Gen. 40:8 [b]Dan. 5:7, 29

[1]Lit., *Let . . . be for* [a]2 Kin. 5:16

8 [1]Lit., *You, O king the kingdom* [a]Dan. 2; 5:21 [b]Dan. 2:37, 38; 4:17 [c]Jer. 25:9; 27:5-7

[1]Lit., *tongue* [a]Dan. 2:12, 13; 3:6; 11:3, 16, 36

0 [1]Lit., *strong* [a]Ex. 9:17; Job 15:25; Is. 3-15; Dan. 4:30, 31 2 Kin. 17:14; 2 Chr. :13 [c]Job 40:11, 12; Jer. 13:18

1 [1]Lit., *the sons of* [a]Job 30:3-7; Dan. 32, 33 [b]Job 39:5-8 9:14-16; Ps. 83:17, ; Ezek. 17:24; Dan. 4:17, 34, 35

2 [1]Or, *descendant* ., *inasmuch as you* 10:3; 2 Chr. 33:23; 36:12

3 [a]2 Kin. 14:10; Is. ; 37:23; Jer. 50:29; . 5:3, 4 [b]Dan. 4:37 115:4-8; Is. 37:19; Hab. 2:18, 19 [d]Job :10 [e]Job 31:4; Ps. 3; Prov. 20:24; Jer. 10:23

4 [1]Lit., *palm of the hand* [a]Dan. 5:5

25 [1]Or, *a mina* (50 kels) from verb "to ber" [2]Or, *a shekel* om verb "to weigh" r, *and half-shekels* .: *peres*) from verb "to divide"

it., *word* [a]Is. 13:6, 7-19; Jer. 50:41-43

Job 31:6; Ps. 62:9

Aram.: *Paras* [a]Is. 3:17; 21:2; 45:1, 2; 5:31; 6:8, 28; Acts 2:9

Or, *triumvir* [a]Dan. 5:7, 16

[a]Dan. 5:1, 2 [b]Is. 9; 47:9; Jer. 51:11, 31, 39, 57

[1]Ch. 6:1 in Aram. [a]Dan. 6:1; 9:1

[1]Ch. 6:2 in Aram.

2 and over them three commissioners (of whom [a]Daniel was one), that these satraps might be accountable to them, and that the king might not suffer [b]loss.

3 Then this Daniel began distinguishing himself [1]among the commissioners and satraps because [2]he possessed an [a]extraordinary spirit, and the king planned to appoint him over the [b]entire kingdom.

4 Then the commissioners and satraps began [a]trying to find a ground of accusation against Daniel in regard to [1]government affairs; but they could find [b]no ground of accusation or *evidence of* corruption, inasmuch as he was faithful, and no negligence or corruption was *to be* found in him.

5 Then these men said, "We shall not find any ground of accusation against this Daniel unless we find *it* against him with regard to the [a]law of his God."

6 Then these commissioners and satraps came [1]by agreement to the king and spoke to him as follows: "King Darius, [a]live forever!

7 "All the [a]commissioners of the kingdom, the prefects and the satraps, the high officials and the governors have [b]consulted together that the king should establish a statute and enforce an injunction that anyone who makes a petition to any god or man besides you, O king, for thirty days, shall [c]be cast into the lions' [1]den.

8 "Now, O king, [a]establish the injunction and sign the document so that it may not be changed, according to the [b]law of the Medes and Persians, which [1]may not be revoked."

9 Therefore King Darius [a]signed the document, that is, the injunction.

10 Now when Daniel knew that the document was signed, he entered his house (now in his roof chamber he had windows open [a]toward Jerusalem); and he continued [b]kneeling on his knees three times a day, [c]praying and [d]giving thanks before his God, [1]as he had been doing previously.

11 Then these men came [1a]by agreement and found Daniel making petition and supplication before his God.

12 Then they approached and [a]spoke before the king about the king's injunction, "Did you not sign an injunction that any man who makes a petition to any god or man besides you, O king, for thirty days, is to be cast into the lions' den?" The king answered and said, "The statement is true, according to the [b]law of the Medes and Persians, which [1]may not be revoked."

13 Then they answered and spoke before the king, "[a]Daniel, who is one of the [1]exiles from Judah, pays [b]no attention to you, O king, or to the injunction which you signed, but keeps making his petition three times a day."

14 Then, as soon as the king heard this statement, he was deeply [a]distressed and set *his* mind on delivering Daniel; and even until sunset he kept exerting himself to rescue him.

15 Then these men came [1]by agreement to the king and said to the king, "Recognize, O king, that it is a [a]law of the Medes and Persians that no injunction or statute which the king establishes may be changed."

16 Then the king gave orders, and Daniel was brought in and [a]cast into the lions' den. The king spoke and said to Daniel, "[1b]Your God whom you constantly serve will Himself deliver you."

17 And a [a]stone was brought and laid over the mouth of the den;

2 [a]Dan. 2:48, 49; 5 29 [b]Ezra 4:22; Est

3 [1]Lit., *above* [2]Lit. *there was in him* [a] 5:12, 14; 9:23 [b]Ge 41:40; Esth. 10:3

4 [1]Lit., *the kingdor* [a]Gen. 43:18; Judg. Jer. 20:10; Dan. 3: Luke 20:20 [b]Dan. Luke 20:26; 23:14, Phil. 2:15; 1 Pet. 2: 3:16

5 [a]Acts 24:13-16,

6 [1]Or, *thronging* [a] 2:3; Dan. 2:4; 5:10

7 [1]Or, *pit,* and so throughout the ch. [a]Dan. 3:2, 27 [b]Ps. 62:4; 64:2-6; 83:1- [c]Ps. 10:9; Dan. 3:6

8 [1]Lit., *does not p away* [a]Esth. 3:12; Is. 10:1 [b]Esth. 1:1 8:8; Dan. 6:12, 15

9 [a]Ps. 118:9; 146:

10 [1]Or, *because* [a]1 Kin. 8:44, 48, 4 5:7; Jon. 2:4 [b]Ps. 55:17; 95:6 [c]Dan. 9:4-19 [d]Ps. 34:1; 4:6; 1 Thess. 5:17

11 [1]Or, *thronging* 37:32, 33; Dan. 6:

12 [1]Lit., *does not away* [a]Dan. 3:8-1 Acts 16:19-21 [b]E 1:19; Dan. 6:8, 15

13 [1]Lit., *sons of t exile* [a]Dan. 2:25; [b]Esth. 3:8; Dan. 3 Acts 5:29

14 [a]Mark 6:26

15 [1]Or, *thronging* [a]Esth. 8:8; Ps. 94: 21; Dan. 6:8, 12

16 [1]Or, *May your God . . . Himself c you* [a]2 Sam. 3:39 38:5; Dan. 6:7 [b]J 5:19; Ps. 37:39, 4 41:10; Dan. 3:17, 6:20; 2 Cor. 1:10

17 [a]Lam. 3:53; M 27:66

and the king sealed it with his own signet ring and with the signet
rings of his nobles, so that nothing might be changed in regard to
Daniel.
18 Then the king went off to his palace and spent the night [a]fasting,
and no entertainment was brought before him; and his [b]sleep fled
from him.
19 Then the king arose with the dawn, at the break of day, and went
in haste to the lions' den.
20 And when he had come near the den to Daniel, he cried out with
a troubled voice. The king spoke and said to Daniel, "Daniel, servant
of the living God, has [a]your God, whom you constantly serve, been
[b]able to deliver you from the lions?"
21 Then Daniel spoke [1]to the king, "[a]O king, live forever!
22 "My God [a]sent His angel and [b]shut the lions' mouths, and they
have not harmed me, inasmuch as [1]I was found innocent before
Him; and also [2]toward you, O king, I have committed no crime."
23 Then the king was very pleased and gave orders for Daniel to be
taken up out of the den. So Daniel was taken up out of the den, and
[a]no injury whatever was found on him, because he had [b]trusted in
his God.
24 The king then gave orders, and they brought those men who had
[1]maliciously accused Daniel, and they [a]cast them, their [b]children, and
their wives into the lions' den; and they had not reached the bottom
of the den before the lions overpowered them and crushed all their
bones.
25 Then Darius the king wrote to all the [a]peoples, nations, and *men*
of every [1]language who were living in all the land: "[b]May your [2]peace
abound!
26 "[1]I [a]make a decree that in all the dominion of my kingdom men
are to fear and tremble before the God of Daniel;

For He is the [b]living God and [c]enduring forever,
And [d]His kingdom is one which will not be destroyed,
And His dominion *will be* [2]forever.

27 "He delivers and rescues and performs [a]signs and wonders
In heaven and on earth,
Who has *also* delivered Daniel from the [1]power of the lions."

28 So this [a]Daniel enjoyed success in the reign of Darius and in the
reign of [b]Cyrus the Persian.

Chapter 7

7 In the first year of Belshazzar king of Babylon Daniel saw a
[a]dream and visions [1]in his mind *as he lay* on his bed; then he
[b]wrote the dream down *and* related the [2]*following* summary of [3]it.
2 Daniel [1]said, "I was [a]looking in my vision by night, and behold,
the [b]four winds of heaven were stirring up the great sea.
3 "And four great [a]beasts were coming up from the sea, different
from one another.
4 "The first *was* [a]like a lion and had *the* wings of an eagle. I kept
looking until its wings were plucked, and it was lifted up from the
ground and made to stand on two feet like a man; a human [1]mind
also was given to it.
5 "And behold, another beast, a second one, resembling a bear. And
it was raised up on one side, and three ribs *were* in its mouth be-
tween its teeth; and thus they said to it, 'Arise, devour much meat!'

Sam. 12:16, 17 . 6:1; Ps. 77:4; Dan. 2:1
[a]Dan. 6:16, 27 en. 18:14; Num. Jer. 32:17; Dan. 3:17
with [a]Dan. 2:4; 6:6
innocence was nd for me [2]Lit., Num. 20:16; Is. Dan. 3:28; Acts Heb. 1:14 [b]Ps. 13; 2 Tim. 4:17; Heb. 11:33
[a]Dan. 3:25, 27 Chr. 5:20; 2 Chr. Ps. 118:8, 9; Is. 3; Dan. 3:17, 28
[1]Lit., *eaten the of Daniel* [a]Deut. 3, 19; Esth. 7:10 ut. 24:16; 2 Kin. 14:6; Esth. 9:10
Lit., *tongue* [2]Or, *are or prosperity* :1, 2; Esth. 3:12; Dan. 4:1 [b]Ezra 4:17; 1 Pet. 1:2
[1]Lit., *From me a is made* [2]Lit., *to nd* [a]Ezra 6:8-12; 3, 21; Dan. 3:29 4:34; 6:20; Hos. , Rom. 9:26 [c]Ps. ; Mal. 3:6 [d]Dan. 3; 7:14, 27; Luke 1:33
[1]Lit., *hand* [a]Dan. 4:2, 3
Dan. 1:21 [b]2 Chr. 22, 23; Dan. 10:1
[1]Lit., *of his head , beginning* [3]Lit., *'s* [a]Job 33:14-16; 1:17; 2:1, 26-28; 9; Joel 2:28 [b]Jer. 36:4, 32
., *spoke and said* 7:7, 13 [b]Rev. 7:1
. 7:17; Rev. 13:1; 17:8
it., *heart* [a]Jer. 4:7

6 "After this I kept looking, and behold, another one, [a]like a
leopard, which had on its [1]back four wings of a bird; the beast also
had [b]four heads, and dominion was given to it.
7 "After this I kept looking in the night visions, and behold, a
[a]fourth beast, dreadful and terrifying and extremely strong; and it
had large iron teeth. It devoured and crushed, and trampled down
the remainder with its feet; and it was different from all the beasts
that were before it, and it had [b]ten horns.
8 "While I was contemplating the horns, behold, [a]another horn, a
little one, came up among them, and three of the first horns were
pulled out by the roots before it; and behold, [1]this horn possessed
eyes like the eyes of a man, and [b]a mouth uttering great *boasts.*
9 "I kept looking
Until [a]thrones were set up,
And the Ancient of Days took *His* seat;
His [b]vesture *was* like white snow,
And the [c]hair of His head like pure wool.
His [d]throne *was* [1]ablaze with flames,
Its [e]wheels *were* a burning fire.
10 "A river of [a]fire was flowing
And coming out from before Him;
[b]Thousands upon thousands were attending Him,
And myriads upon myriads were standing before Him;
The [c]court sat,
And [d]the books were opened.
11 "Then I kept looking because of the sound of the [1]boastful words
which the horn was speaking; I kept looking until the beast was
slain, and its body was destroyed and given to the [a]burning [2]fire.
12 "As for the rest of the beasts, their dominion was taken away, but
an extension of life was granted to them for an appointed period of
time.
13 "I kept looking in the night visions,
And behold, with the clouds of heaven
One like a [a]Son of Man was coming,
And He came up to the Ancient of Days
And was presented before Him.
14 "And to Him was given [a]dominion,
Glory and [1b]a kingdom,
[c]That all the peoples, nations, and *men of every* [2]language
Might serve Him.
[d]His dominion is an everlasting dominion
Which will not pass away;
[e]And His kingdom is one
Which will not be destroyed.
15 "As for me, Daniel, my spirit was distressed [1]within me, and the
[a]visions [2]in my mind kept [b]alarming me.
16 "I approached one of those who were [a]standing by and began
asking him the [1]exact meaning of all this. So he [b]told me and made
known to me the interpretation of these things:
17 'These great beasts, which are four *in number,* are four kings *who*
will arise from the earth.
18 'But the [1a]saints of the Highest One will [b]receive the kingdom
and possess the kingdom forever, [2]for all ages to come.'
19 "Then I desired to know the [1]exact meaning of the [a] fourth beast,

6 [1]Or, *sides* [a]P
[b]Dan. 8:22

7 [a]Dan. 7:19, 2
[b]Rev. 12:3; 13:1

8 [1]Lit., *in this h*
eyes [a]Dan. 8:9
13:5, 6

9 [1]Lit., *flames c*
[a]Rev. 20:4 [b]Ma
[c]Rev. 1:14 [d]Eze
26 [e]Ezek. 10:2,

10 [a]Ps. 18:8; 50
97:3; Is. 30:27, 3
[b]Deut. 33:2; 1 K
22:19; Rev. 5:11
96:11-13; Dan. 7
[d]Dan. 12:1; Rev.
20:11-15

11 [1]Lit., *great* [2]
the fire [a]Rev. 19
20:10

13 [a]Matt. 24:30;
Mark 13:26; 14:6
21:27; Rev. 1:7,
14:14

14 [1]Or, *sovereig*
[2]Lit., *tongue* [a]Da
John 3:35; 1 Cor.
Eph. 1:20-22; Ph
2:9-11; Rev. 1:6;
[b]Dan. 2:37 [c]Ps.
102:22 [d]Mic. 4:7
1:33 [e]Heb. 12:28

15 [1]Lit., *in the mi*
its sheath [2]Lit., *o*
head [a]Dan. 7:1
4:19; 7:28

16 [1]Lit., *truth*
concerning [a]Zech
19; Rev. 5:5; 7:13
[b]Dan. 8:16, 17; 9:

18 [1]Lit., *holy ones*
and unto the age o
ages [a]Dan. 7:22,
27 [b]Ps. 149:5-9;
60:12-14; Dan. 7:
Rev. 2:26, 27; 20:4

19 [1]Lit., *truth*
concerning [a]Dan.

which was different from all [2]the others, exceedingly dreadful, with
its teeth of iron and its claws of bronze, *and which* devoured,
crushed, and trampled down the remainder with its feet,
20 and *the meaning* of the ten horns that *were* on its head, and the
other *horn* which came up, and before which three *of them* fell, name-
ly, that horn which had eyes and a mouth uttering great *boasts*, and
[1]which was larger in appearance than its associates.
21 "I kept looking, and that horn was [a]waging war with the [1]saints
and overpowering them
22 until the Ancient of Days came, and [a]judgment was [1]passed in
favor of the [2]saints of the Highest One, and the time arrived when
the [2]saints took possession of the kingdom.
23 "Thus he said: 'The fourth beast will be a fourth kingdom on the
earth, which will be different from all the *other* kingdoms, and it will
devour the whole earth and tread it down and crush it.
24 'As for the [a]ten horns, out of this kingdom ten kings will arise;
and another will arise after them, and he will be different from the
previous ones and will subdue three kings.
25 'And he will [a]speak [1]out against the [b]Most High and [c]wear down
the [2]saints of the Highest One, and he will intend to make [d]altera-
tions in times and in law; and [3]they will be given into his hand for a
[4e]time, [4]times, and half a [4]time.
26 'But the court will sit *for judgment*, and his dominion will be
[a]taken away, [1]annihilated and destroyed [2]forever.
27 'Then the [1a]sovereignty, the dominion, and the greatness of *all* the
kingdoms under the whole heaven will be given to the people of the
[2]saints of the Highest One; His kingdom *will be* an [b]everlasting king-
dom, and all the dominions will [c]serve and obey Him.'
28 "[1]At this point the revelation ended. As for me, Daniel, my
thoughts were [a]greatly alarming me and my [2]face grew pale, but I
[b]kept the matter [3]to myself."

Chapter 8

8 In the third year of the reign of Belshazzar the king a vision
appeared to me, [1]Daniel, subsequent to the one which appeared
to me [2]previously.
2 And I [a]looked in the vision, and it came about while I was look-
ing, that I was in the citadel of [b]Susa, which is in the province of
[c]Elam; and I looked in the vision, and I myself was beside the Ulai
[1]Canal.
3 Then I lifted my gaze and looked, and behold, a [a]ram which had
two horns was standing in front of the [1]canal. Now the two horns
were [2]long, but one *was* [2]longer than the other, with the [2]longer one
coming up last.
4 I saw the ram [a]butting westward, northward, and southward,
and no *other* beasts could stand before him, nor was there anyone to
rescue from his [1]power; but [b]he did as he pleased and magnified
himself.
5 While I was observing, behold, a male goat was coming from the
west over the surface of the whole earth without touching the
ground; and the [1]goat *had* a [a]conspicuous horn between his eyes.
6 And he came up to the ram that had the two horns, which I had
seen standing in front of the [1]canal, and rushed at him in his mighty
wrath.

[2]Lit., *of them*
its appearance was larger
[1]Lit., *holy ones* Rev. 11:7; 13:7
given for [2]Lit., *...es* [a]Dan. 7:10; 1 Cor. 6:2, 3
7:7; Rev. 17:12
...it., *words* [2]Lit., *...ones* [3]I.e., the ...ts [4]I.e., year(s) ...1:36; Rev. 13:6 ...:26; 4:2, 17, 34 ...:7; 18:24 [d]Dan. ...Dan. 12:7; Rev. 12:14
...it., *to annihilate destroy* [2]Lit., *to ...nd* [a]Rev. 17:14; 19:2
...*, kingdom* [2]Lit., *...ones* [a]Is. 54:3; ...14, 18, 22; Rev. [b]Ps. 145:13; Is. Dan. 2:44; 4:34; Luke 1:33; Rev. ...2:5 [c]Ps. 2:6-12; ...; 72:11; 86:9; Is. 60:12; Rev. 11:1
[1]Lit., *To here the ...of the word* [2]Lit., *brightness was ...g upon me* [3]Lit., *...heart* [a]Dan. 4:19 [b]Luke 2:19, 51
...it., *I, Daniel* [2]Lit., *at the beginning*
...*river* [a]Num. 12:6; ...:2, 15; 8:3 [b]Neh. ...h. 1:2; 2:8 [c]Gen. ...2; 14:1; Is. 11:11; ...:25; Ezek. 32:24
3 [1]Or, *river* [2]Lit., *...gh(er)* [a]Dan. 8:20
[1]Lit., *hand* [a]Deut. ...3:17; 1 Kin. 22:11; ...34:21 [b]Dan. 11:3
...*, buck* [a]Dan. 8:8, 21; 11:3
6 [1]Or, *river*

The map on pages 1898-9 shows the boundaries of the Babylonian, Medo-Persian, Greek, and Roman Empires as they relate to the nations today.

7 And I saw him come beside the ram, and he was enraged at him;
and he struck the ram and shattered his two horns, and the ram had
no strength to withstand him. So he hurled him to the ground and
trampled on him, and there was none to rescue the ram from his
[1]power.
8 Then the male goat magnified *himself* exceedingly. But as soon as
[a]he was mighty, the [b]large horn was broken; and in its place there
came up four conspicuous *horns* toward the [c]four winds of heaven.
9 And out of one of them came forth a rather [a]small horn which
grew exceedingly great toward the south, toward the east, and
toward the [1b]Beautiful *Land*.
10 And it grew up to the host of heaven and caused some of the
host and some of the [a]stars to fall to the earth, and it [b]trampled them
down.
11 It even [a]magnified *itself* [1]to be equal with the [2]Commander of the
host; and it removed the [b]regular sacrifice from Him, and the place
of His sanctuary was thrown down.
12 And on account of transgression the host will be given over *to
the horn* along with the regular sacrifice; and it will [a]fling truth to the
ground and perform *its will* and prosper.
13 Then I heard a [a]holy one speaking, and another holy one said to
that particular one who was speaking, "[b]How long will the vision
about the regular sacrifice apply, [1]while the transgression causes hor-
ror, so as to allow both the holy place and the host [2]to be [c]trampled?"
14 And he said to me, "For [a]2,300 evenings *and* mornings; then the
holy place will be [1]properly restored."
15 And it came about when [a]I, Daniel, had seen the vision, that I
sought [1]to understand it; and behold, standing before me was one
[2]who looked like a [b]man.
16 And I heard the voice of a man between *the banks of* Ulai, and he
called out and said, "[a]Gabriel, give this *man* an understanding of the
vision."
17 So he came near to where I was standing, and when he came I
was frightened and [a]fell on my face; but he said to me, "Son of man,
understand that the vision pertains to the [b]time of the end."
18 Now while he was talking with me, I [a]sank into a deep sleep
with my face to the ground; but he [b]touched me and made me stand
[1]upright.
19 And he said, "Behold, I am going to [a]let you know what will
occur at the final period of the indignation, for *it* pertains to the
appointed time of the end.
20 "The [a]ram which you saw with the two horns represents the kings
of Media and Persia.
21 "And the shaggy [1]goat *represents* the [2]kingdom of Greece, and the
large horn that is between his eyes is the first king.
22 "And the [a]broken *horn* and the four *horns that* arose in its place
represent four kingdoms *which* will arise from *his* nation, although
not with his power.
23 "And in the latter period of their [1]rule,
When the transgressors have [2]run *their course*,
A king will arise
[3]Insolent and skilled in [4]intrigue.
24 "And his power will be mighty, but not by his *own* power,
And he will [1a]destroy to an extraordinary degree

7 [1]Lit., *hand*

8 [a]2 Chr. 26:1
5:20 [b]Dan. 8:2
7:2; Rev. 7:1

9 [1]I.e., Palesti
8:23 [b]Ps. 48:2
11:16, 41

10 [a]Is. 14:13;
48:26; Rev. 12
7:7; 8:7

11 [1]Lit., *up to t*
Prince [a]2 Kin.
23; 2 Chr. 32:1
37:23; Dan. 8:2
37 [b]Ezek. 46:1
11:31; 12:11

12 [a]Is. 59:14

13 [1]Or possibly
transgression th
horrifies [2]Lit., *a*
trampling [a]Dan
23; 1 Pet. 1:12
74:10; 79:5; Is.
Dan. 12:6, 8; Re
[c]Is. 63:18; Jer. 1
Luke 21:24; Heb
Rev. 11:2

14 [1]Lit., *vindica*
[a]Dan. 7:25; 12:7
Rev. 11:2, 3; 12

15 [1]Lit., *unders*
[2]Lit., *like the*
appearance of a
[a]Dan. 8:1 [b]Dan.
10:16, 18

16 [a]Dan. 9:21;
1:19, 26

17 [a]Ezek. 1:28;
Dan. 2:46; Rev.
[b]Dan. 8:19; 11:3

18 [1]Lit., *on my*
standing [a]Dan.
Luke 9:32 [b]Ezek
Dan. 10:10, 16,

19 [a]Dan. 8:15-1

20 [a]Dan. 8:3

21 [1]Lit., *buck* [2]L

22 [a]Dan. 8:8

23 [1]Or, *kingdom*
finished [3]Lit., *Str*
face [4]Or, *ambigu*
speech

24 [1]Or, *corrupt* [a]
8:11-13; 11:36; 12

And prosper and perform *his will;*
He will [1]destroy mighty men and [2]the holy people.
25 "And through his shrewdness
He will cause deceit to succeed by his [1]influence;
And he will magnify *himself* in his heart,
And he will [2]destroy many while *they are* [3]at ease.
He will even [4a]oppose the Prince of princes,
But he will be broken [b]without [1]human agency.
26 "And the vision of the evenings and mornings
Which has been told is [a]true;
But [b]keep the vision secret,
For *it* pertains to many [c]days *in the future.*"
27 Then I, Daniel, was [1a]exhausted and sick for days. Then I got up
again and [b]carried on the king's business; but I was astounded at the
vision, and there was none to [2]explain *it.*

Chapter 9

9 In the first year of [a]Darius the son of Ahasuerus, of Median
descent, who was made king over the kingdom of the Chal-
deans—
2 in the first year of his reign I, Daniel, observed in the books the
number of the years which was *revealed as* the word of the LORD to
[a]Jeremiah the prophet for the completion of the desolations of Jerusa-
lem, *namely,* [a]seventy years.
3 So I [1]gave my attention to the Lord God to seek *Him by* prayer
and supplications, with fasting, sackcloth, and ashes.
4 And I prayed to the LORD my God and confessed and said,
"Alas, O Lord, the [a]great and awesome God, who [b]keeps His cove-
nant and lovingkindness for those who love Him and keep His com-
mandments,
5 [a]we have sinned, committed iniquity, acted wickedly, and [b] rebel-
led, even [c]turning aside from Thy commandments and ordinances.
6 "Moreover, we have not [a]listened to Thy servants the prophets,
who spoke in Thy name to our kings, our princes, our fathers, and
all the people of the land.
7 "[a]Righteousness belongs to Thee, O Lord, but to us [1b]open shame,
as it is this day—to the men of Judah, the inhabitants of Jerusalem,
and all Israel, those who are nearby and those who are far away in
[c]all the countries to which Thou hast driven them, because of their
unfaithful deeds which they have committed against Thee.
8 "[1]Open shame belongs to us, O Lord, to our kings, our princes,
and our fathers, because we have sinned against Thee.
9 "To the Lord our God belong [a]compassion and forgiveness, [1]for
we have [b]rebelled against Him;
10 nor have we obeyed the voice of the LORD our God, to walk in
His [1]teachings which He [a]set before us through His servants the
prophets.
11 "Indeed [a]all Israel has transgressed Thy law and turned aside, not
obeying Thy voice; so the [b]curse has been poured out on us, along
with the oath which is written in the law of Moses the servant of
God, for we have sinned against Him.
12 "Thus He has [a]confirmed His words which He had spoken
against us and against our [1b]rulers who ruled us, to bring on us great

24 [1]Or, *corrupt* [2]Lit., *people of the saints*
25 [1]Lit., *hand* [2]Or, *corrupt* [3]Or, *secure* [4]Lit., *stand against* ...an. 8:11 [b]Job 34:20; Dan. 2:34, 45
... [a]Dan. 10:1 [b]Ezek. 12:27; Dan. 12:4, 9; ...22:10 [c]Dan. 10:14
... [1]Or, *done in* [2]Lit., *make me understand* ...an. 7:28; 8:17; Hab. 3:16 [b]Dan. 2:48
...:1 [a]Dan. 5:31; 11:1
[a]2 Chr. 36:21; Ezra 1:1; Jer. 25:11, 12; 29:10; Zech. 7:5
3 [1]Lit., *set my face*
4 [a]Deut. 7:21; Neh. 9:32 [b]Deut. 7:9
5 [a]1 Kin. 8:48; Neh. 9:33; Ps. 106:6; Is. ...-7; Jer. 14:7 [b]Lam. ...8, 20 [c]Ps. 119:176; Is. 53:6; Dan. 9:11
... [a]2 Chr. 36:16; Jer. 44:4, 5
... [1]Lit., *the shame of ...e* [a]Jer. 23:6; 33:16; ...n. 9:18 [b]Ps. 44:15; Jer. 2:26, 27; 3:25 [c]Deut. 4:27
... [1]Lit., *The shame of face*
... [1]Or, *though* [a]Neh. ...17; Ps. 130:4 [b]Ps. ...:43; Jer. 14:7; Dan. 9:5, 6
... [1]Or, *laws* [a]2 Kin. 17:13-15; 18:12
11 [a]Is. 1:3, 4; Jer. ...0 [b]Deut. 27:15-26
... [1]Lit., *judges who ...dged us* [a]Is. 44:26; 44:2-6; Lam. 2:17; ...h. 1:6 [b]Job 12:17; Ps. 82:2-7; 148:11

calamity; for under the whole heaven there has [c]not been done *anything* like what was done to Jerusalem.

13 "As it is written in the [a]law of Moses, all this calamity has come on us; yet we have [b]not [1]sought the favor of the LORD our God by [c]turning from our iniquity and [2]giving attention to Thy truth.

14 "Therefore, the LORD has [1a]kept the calamity in store and brought it on us; for the LORD our God is [b]righteous with respect to all His deeds which He has done, but we have not obeyed His voice.

15 "And now, O Lord our God, who hast [a]brought Thy people out of the land of Egypt with a mighty hand and hast [b]made a name for Thyself, as it is this day—we have sinned, we have been wicked.

16 "O Lord, in accordance with all Thy [1]righteous acts, let now Thine [a]anger and Thy wrath turn away from Thy city Jerusalem, Thy [b]holy mountain; for because of our sins and the iniquities of our fathers, Jerusalem and Thy people *have become* a [c]reproach to all those around us.

17 "So now, our God, listen to the prayer of Thy servant and to his supplications, and for [1]Thy sake, O Lord, [a]let Thy face shine on Thy [b]desolate sanctuary.

18 "O my God, [a]incline Thine ear and hear! Open Thine eyes and [b]see our desolations and the city which is [c]called by Thy name; for we are not [1d]presenting our supplications before Thee on account of [2]any merits of our own, but on account of Thy great compassion.

19 "O Lord, hear! O Lord, forgive! O Lord, listen and take action! For Thine own sake, O my God, [a]do not delay, because Thy city and Thy people are called by Thy name."

20 Now while I was [a]speaking and praying, and [b]confessing my sin and the sin of my people Israel, and [1]presenting my supplication before the LORD my God in behalf of the holy mountain of my God,

21 while I was still speaking in prayer, then the man [a]Gabriel, whom I had seen in the vision [1]previously, [2]came to me [3]in *my* extreme weariness about the time of the [b]evening offering.

22 And he gave *me* instruction and talked with me, and said, "O Daniel, I have now come forth to give you insight with [a]understanding.

23 "At the [a]beginning of your supplications the [1]command was issued, and I have come to tell *you*, for you are [2b]highly esteemed; so give heed to the message and gain [c]understanding of the vision.

24 "Seventy [1a]weeks have been decreed for your people and your holy city, to [2]finish the transgression, to [3]make an end of sin, to [b]make atonement for iniquity, to bring in [c]everlasting righteousness, to seal up vision and [4]prophecy, and to anoint the most holy *place*.

25 "So you are to know and discern *that* from the issuing of a [1a]decree to restore and rebuild Jerusalem until [2b]Messiah the [c]Prince *there will be* seven weeks and sixty-two weeks; it will be built again, with [3]plaza and moat, even in times of distress.

26 "Then after the sixty-two weeks the [1]Messiah will be [a]cut off and have [2]nothing, and the people of the prince who is to come will [b]destroy the city and the sanctuary. And [3]its end *will come* with a [c]flood; even to the end [4]there will be war; desolations are determined.

27 "And he will make a firm covenant with the many for one week, but in the middle of the week he will put a stop to sacrifice and grain offering; and on the wing of [1a]abominations *will come* one who

12 [c]Lam. 1:12; 2:13 Ezek. 5:9

13 [1]Lit., *softened th face of* [2]Or, *having insight into* [a]Lev. 26:14-45; Deut. 28:15-68; Dan. 9:11 [b]Job 36:13; Is. 9:13; 2:30; 5:3 [c]Jer. 31:18

14 [1]Lit., *watched ov the evil* [a]Jer. 31:28; 44:27 [b]Ps. 51:14; D 9:7

15 [a]Deut. 5:15 [b]Ne 9:10; Jer. 32:20

16 [1]Lit., *righteousnesses* [a]J 32:31, 32 [b]Ps. 87:1 Dan. 9:20; Joel 3:17 Zech. 8:3 [c]Ezek. 5:

17 [1]Lit., *the sake o Lord* [a]Num. 6:24-26 Ps. 80:3, 7, 19 [b]La 5:18

18 [1]Lit., *causing to* [2]Lit., *our righteousnesses* [a]I 37:17 [b]Ps. 80:14 [c] 7:10-12 [d]Jer. 36:7

19 [a]Ps. 44:23; 74:1

20 [1]Lit., *causing to* [a]Ps. 145:18; Is. 58: Dan. 9:3; 10:12 [b]Is

21 [1]Lit., *at the beginning* [2]Lit., *wa reaching;* or, *touchi* [3]Lit., *wearied with weariness* [a]Dan. 8 Luke 1:19, 26 [b]Ex. 29:39; 1 Kin. 18:36 Ezra 9:4

22 [a]Dan. 8:16; 10: Zech. 1:9

23 [1]Lit., *word wen* [2]Lit., *desirable;* or, *precious* [a]Dan. 10 [b]Dan. 10:11, 19 [c]M 24:15

24 [1]Or, *units of se* and so throughout ch. [2]Or, *restrain* [3]Another reading is *up sins* [4]Lit., *proph* [a]Lev. 25:8; Num. 1 Ezek. 4:5, 6 [b]2 Ch 29:24; Is. 53:10; R 5:10 [c]Is. 51:6, 8; 5 Jer. 23:5, 6; Rom. 3:21, 22

25 [1]Lit., *word* [2]Or *anointed one* [3]Or, *streets* [a]Ezra 4:24 6:1-15; Neh. 2:1-8 [b]John 1:41; 4:25 [c] 9:6; Dan. 8:11, 25

26 [1]Or, *anointed* [2]Or, *no one* [3]Or, *h* [4]Or, *war will be de for desolations* [a]Is 53:8; Mark 9:12; L 24:26 [b]Matt. 24:2 13:2; Luke 19:43, [c]Nah. 1:8

27 [1]Or, *detestable things* [a]Dan. 11:3 Matt. 24:15; Mark Luke 21:20

INSIGHT

The word *weeks* in Hebrew is **Shabuim** and means "sevens." There is no indication whether the "sevens" refers to seven days, weeks, months, or years. Seventy sevens (or weeks) is 490. So, if the six things of Daniel 9:24 were not completed within 490 days, weeks, or months, it would be logical to assume that the *sevens* refers to sevens of years. A decree to rebuild and restore Jerusalem was issued by King Artaxerxes of Medo-Persia in 445 B.C. (*see* Nehemiah 1:1-2,8). This began the 490 years.

[2]makes desolate, even until a [b]complete destruction, one that is
decreed, is poured out on the one who [2]makes desolate."

Chapter 10

10 In the third year of [a]Cyrus king of Persia a [1]message was
revealed to [b]Daniel, who was named Belteshazzar; and the
[1c]message was true and *one of* great [2]conflict, but he understood the
[1]message and had an [d]understanding of the vision.
2 In those days I, Daniel, had been [a]mourning for three entire
weeks.
3 I [a]did not eat any [1]tasty food, nor did meat or wine enter my
mouth, nor did I use any ointment at all, until the entire three weeks
were completed.
4 And on the twenty-fourth day of the first month, while I was by
the bank of the great [a]river, that is, the [1]Tigris,
5 I lifted my eyes and looked, and behold, there was a certain man
[a]dressed in linen, whose waist was [b]girded with *a belt of* pure [c]gold of
Uphaz.
6 His body also was like [1]beryl, his face [2]had the appearance of
lightning, [a]his eyes were like flaming torches, his arms and feet like
the gleam of polished bronze, and the sound of his words like the
sound of a [3]tumult.
7 Now I, Daniel, [a]alone saw the vision, while the [b]men who were
with me did not see the vision; nevertheless, a great [c]dread fell on
them, and they ran away to hide themselves.
8 So I was [a]left alone and saw this great vision; yet [b]no strength
was left in me, for my [1]natural color turned to [2]a deathly pallor, and I
retained no strength.
9 But I heard the sound of his words; and as soon as I heard the
sound of his words, I [a]fell into a deep sleep on my face, with my face
to the ground.
10 Then behold, a hand [a]touched me and set me trembling on my
[1]hands and knees.
11 And he said to me, "O [a]Daniel, man of [1]high esteem, [b]understand
the words that I am about to tell you and [c]stand [2]upright, for I have
now been sent to you." And when he had spoken this word to me, I
stood up [d]trembling.
12 Then he said to me, "[a]Do not be afraid, Daniel, for from the first
day that you set your heart on understanding *this* and on [b]humbling
yourself before your God, your words were heard, and I have come
in response [c]to your words.
13 "But the prince of the kingdom of Persia was [1]withstanding me
for twenty-one days; then behold, [a]Michael, one of the chief princes,
came to help me, for I had been left there with the kings of Persia.
14 "Now I have come to [a]give you an understanding of what will
happen to your people in the [1b]latter days, for the vision pertains to
[c]the days yet *future*."
15 And when he had spoken to me according to these words, I
[1]turned my face toward the ground and became [a]speechless.
16 And behold, [1a]one who resembled a human being was [b]touching
my lips; then I opened my mouth and spoke, and said to him who
was standing before me, "O my lord, as a result of the vision [2c]an-
guish has come upon me, and I have retained no strength.
17 "For [a]how can such a servant of my lord talk with such as my

causes horror ...s. 10:23; 28:22
Lit., *word* [2]Or, ...re [a]Dan. 1:21; ...an. 1:7 [c]Dan. ...Dan. 1:17; 2:21
...9:4, 5; Neh. 1:4
[1]Lit., *bread of* ...lity [a]Dan. 6:18
Heb., *Hiddekel* ...x. 1:3; Dan. 8:2
9:2; Dan. 12:6, ...:13; 15:6 [c]Jer. 10:9
6 [1]Or, *yellow* ...entine [2]Lit., *like* ...ing [a]Rev. 1:14; 2:18; 19:12
... 6:17-20 [b]Acts ...7 [c]Ezek. 12:18
..., *splendor* [2]Lit., ...on [a]Gen. 32:24 ...7:28; 8:27; Hab. 3:16
Gen. 15:12; Job 4:13; Dan. 8:18
..., *knees and the* ...*ms of my hands* ...er. 1:9; Dan 8:18
..., *desirability*; or, ...*ciousness* [2]Lit., ...*on your standing* ...):19 [b]Dan. 8:16, [c]Ezek. 2:1 [d]Job 4:14, 15
...41:10, 14; Dan. ...9 [b]Dan. 9:20-23; [c]Acts 10:30, 31
...3 [1]Lit., *standing* ...*site* [a]Dan. 10:21; ...ude 9; Rev. 12:7
... [1]Lit., *end of the* ... [a]Dan. 8:16; 9:22 ...31:29; Dan. 2:28 ...Dan. 8:26; 12:4, 9
[1]Lit., *set* [a]Ezek. 24:27; Luke 1:20
..., *as a likeness of* ...*of man* [2]Lit., *my have* [a]Dan. 8:15 ...:7; Jer. 1:9 [c]Dan. ...:15, 28; 8:17, 27; 10:8, 9
[a]Ex. 24:10, 11; Is. 6:1-5

History of Israel's Relationship to the Kings of Daniel 11

Alexander the Great
336-323 B.C.
The Large Horn of the Shaggy Goat of Greece [8:21]
Twenty-two years after Alexander's death, Greece was divided among four of his generals (8:22):

Lysimachus	**Cassander**	**Ptolemy I Soter**	**Seleucus I Nicator**
took Thrace and Bithynia	took Macedonia	took Egypt	took Syria

Only Ptolemy I Soter and Seleucus I Nicator relate to Israel.

Kings of the South—Egypt		**Kings of the North—Syria**
*1. Ptolemy I Soter, 323-285 B.C. (11:5)		1. Seleucus I Nicator, 312-281 B.C. (11:5)
		2. Antiochus I Soter (not referred to in Daniel)
*2. Ptolemy II Philadelphus, 285-245 B.C. (11:6)	*Marriage*	3. Antiochus II Theos, 262-246 B.C. (11:6)
*3. Ptolemy III Euergetes, 245-221 B.C. (11:7-9)	*2 Wars*	4. Seleucus II Callinicus, 246-226 B.C. (11:7-9)
		5. Seleucus III Ceraunus, 226-223 B.C. (11:10)
*4. Ptolemy IV Philopator, 221-203 B.C. (11:11-12)	*2 Wars*	*6. Antiochus III the Great, 223-187 B.C. (11:10-11, 13, 15-
*5. Ptolemy V Epiphanes, 203-181 B.C. (11:14-15, 17)	*War/Marriage*	*7. Seleucus IV Philopator, 187-175 B.C. (11:20)
6. Ptolemy VI Philometor, 181-145 B.C. (11:25)		*8. **Antiochus IV Epiphanes**, 175-163 B.C. (11:21-35) *(younger son of Antiochus III the Great)*

** These kings ruled Israel*

lord? As for me, there remains just now [b]no strength in me, nor has
any breath been left in me."
18 Then *this* one with human appearance touched me again and
[a]strengthened me.
19 And he said, "O man of [1]high esteem, [a]do not be afraid. Peace
[2]be with you; take [b]courage and be courageous!" Now as soon as he
spoke to me, I received strength and said, "May my lord speak, for
you have [c]strengthened me."
20 Then he said, "Do you [1]understand why I came to you? But I
shall now return to fight against the [2]prince of Persia; so I am going
forth, and behold, the [2a]prince of [3]Greece is about to come.
21 "However, I will tell you what is inscribed in the writing of [a]truth.
Yet there is no one who [1]stands firmly with me against these *forces*
except [b]Michael your prince.

Chapter 11

11 "And in the [a]first year of Darius the Mede, [1]I arose to be [2]an
encouragement and a protection for him.
2 "And now I will tell you the [a]truth. Behold, three more kings are
going to arise [1]in Persia. Then a fourth will gain far more riches than
all *of them;* as soon as he becomes strong through his riches, [2]he will
arouse the whole *empire* against the realm of [3b]Greece.
3 "And a [a]mighty king will arise, and he will rule with great
authority and [b]do as he pleases.
4 "But as soon as he has arisen, his kingdom will be broken up and
parceled out [a]toward the [b]four [1]points of the compass, though not to
his *own* descendants, nor according to his authority which he

17 [b]Dan. 10:8

18 [a]Is. 35:3, 4

19 [1]Lit., *desirab* *preciousness* [2] *you* [a]Judg. 6:23 43:1; Dan. 10:12 1:6, 7, 9; Is. 35:4 138:3; 2 Cor. 12

20 [1]Lit., *know* [2] Satanic angel [3] *Javan* [a]Dan. 8:2

21 [1]Lit., *shows* *strong* [a]Dan. 12 [b]Dan. 10:13; Rev

11:1 [1]Lit., *my sta* *up* was [2]Lit., *for* *strengthener* [a]Da 5:31; 9:1

2 [1]Lit., *for* [2]Or, t *will stir up the rea* *Greece* [3]Heb., *J* [a]Dan. 8:26; 10:1, [b]Dan. 8:21; 10:20

3 [a]Dan. 8:5, 21 5:19; 8:4; 11:16, 3

4 [1]Lit., *winds of t* *heaven* [a]Dan. 8:8 [b]Jer. 49:36; Ezek. Dan. 7:2; 8:8; Zec Rev. 7:1

wielded; for his sovereignty will be [c]uprooted and *given* to others
besides [2]them.
5 "Then the [a]king of the South will grow strong, [1]along with *one* of
his princes [2]who will gain ascendancy over him and obtain
dominion; his domain *will be* a great dominion *indeed*.
6 "And after some years they will form an alliance, and the daugh-
ter of the king of the South will come to the [a]king of the North to
carry out [1]a peaceful arrangement. But she will not retain her [2]posi-
tion of power, nor will he remain with his [3]power, but she will be
given up, along with those who brought her in, and the one who
sired her, as well as he who supported her in *those* times.
7 "But one of the [1]descendants of her line will arise in his place, and
he will come against *their* army and enter the [a]fortress of the king of
the North, and he will deal with them and display *great* strength.
8 "And also their [a]gods with their [1]metal images *and* their precious
vessels of silver and gold he will take into captivity to Egypt, and he
on his part will [2]refrain from *attacking* the king of the North for *some*
years.
9 "Then [1]the latter will enter the realm of the king of the South, but
will return to his *own* land.
10 "And his sons will [1]mobilize and assemble a multitude of great
forces; and one of them will keep on coming and [a]overflow and pass
through, that he may [2]again wage war up to his *very* fortress.
11 "And the [a]king of the South will be enraged and go forth and
fight [1]with the king of the North. Then the latter will raise a great
multitude, but *that* multitude will be given into [2]the hand of the
former.
12 "When the multitude is carried away, his heart will be lifted up,
and he will cause tens of thousands to fall; yet he will not prevail.
13 "For the king of the North will again raise a greater multitude
than the former, and [1]after an [a]interval of some years he will [2]press
on with a great army and much equipment.
14 "Now in those times many will rise up against the king of the
South; the violent ones among your people will also lift themselves
up in order to fulfill the vision, but they will [1]fall down.
15 "Then the king of the North will come, cast up a [a]siege mound,
and capture a well-fortified city; and the forces of the South will not
stand *their ground*, not even [1]their choicest troops, for there will be no
strength to make a stand.
16 "But he who comes against him will [a]do as he pleases, and [b]no
one will *be able to* withstand him; he will also stay *for a time* in the
[1c]Beautiful Land, with destruction in his hand.
17 "And he will [a]set his face to come with the power of his whole
kingdom, [1]bringing with him [2]a proposal of peace which he will put
into effect; he will also give him the daughter of women to ruin it.
But she will not take a stand *for him* or be [3]on his side.
18 "Then he will turn his face to the [a]coastlands and capture many.
But a commander will put a stop to his scorn against him; moreover,
he will [b]repay him for his scorn.
19 "So he will turn his face toward the fortresses of his own land, but
he will [a]stumble and fall and be [b]found no more.
20 "Then in his place one will arise who will [a]send an [1]oppressor
through the [2]Jewel of *his* kingdom; yet within a few days he will be
shattered, though neither in anger nor in battle.

4 [a]I.e., his descendants [c]Jer. 12:15, 17; 18:7

[1]Lit., *and* [2]Lit., *and* [a]Dan. 11:9, 11, 14, 25, 40

6 [1]Or, *an equitable agreement* [2]Lit., *...rength of arm* [3]Lit., *...arm* [a]Dan. 11:7, 13, 15, 40

[1]Lit., *branch of her roots* [a]Dan. 11:19, 38, 39

...3 [1]Lit., *cast images ...r, stand against the* [a]Is. 37:19; 46:1, 2; Jer. 43:12, 13

[1]Lit., *he will*, and so throughout the ch.

[1]Or, *wage war* [2]Or, *...turn and wage* [a]Is. ... Jer. 46:7, 8; 51:42; Dan. 11:26, 40

[1]Lit., *with him, with ...it., his hand* [a]Dan. 11:5

[1]Lit., *at the end of ...e times, years* [2]Or, *...o on coming* [a]Dan. 4:16; 12:7

[1]Lit., *stumble*, and throughout the ch.

[1]Lit., *the people of ... choice ones* [a]Jer. ...6; Ezek. 4:2; 17:17

16 [1]I.e., Palestine ...Dan. 5:19; 11:3, 36 ...sh. 1:5 [c]Dan. 8:9; 11:41

17 [1]Lit., *and* [2]Lit., *...uitable things* [3]Lit., *...for him*; i.e., for her ...ther [a]2 Kin. 12:17; Ezek. 4:3, 7

18 [a]Gen. 10:5; Is. ...9; Jer. 2:10; 31:10; ... 2:11 [b]Hos. 12:14

[a]Ps. 27:2; Jer. 46:6 ...b 20:8; Ps. 37:36; Ezek. 26:21

20 [1]Or, *exactor of ...* [2]Lit., *adornment; ...robably Jerusalem temple* [a]Is. 60:17

21 "And in his place a despicable person will arise, on whom the
honor of kingship has not been conferred, but he will come in a time
of tranquility and [a]seize the kingdom by intrigue.
22 "And the overflowing [a]forces will be flooded away before him
and shattered, and also the prince of the covenant.
23 "And after an alliance is made with him he will practice decep-
tion, and he will go up and gain power with a small *force of* people.
24 "[1]In a time of tranquility he will enter the [a]richest *parts* of the
[2]realm, and he will accomplish what his fathers never did, nor his
[3]ancestors; he will distribute plunder, booty, and possessions among
them, and he will devise his schemes against strongholds, but *only*
for a time.
25 "And he will stir up his strength and [1]courage against the [a]king of
the South with a large army; so the king of the South will mobilize
an extremely large and mighty army for war; but he will not stand,
for schemes will be devised against him.
26 "And those who eat his choice food will [1]destroy him, and his
army will [2a]overflow, but many will fall down slain.
27 "As for both kings, their hearts will be *intent* on [a]evil, and they
will [b]speak lies *to each other* at the same table; but it will not succeed,
for the [c]end is still *to come* at the appointed time.
28 "Then he will return to his land with much [1]plunder; but his heart
will be *set* against the holy covenant, and he will take action and *then*
return to his *own* land.
29 "At the appointed time he will return and come into the South,
but [1]this last time it will not turn out the way it did before.
30 "For ships of [1a]Kittim will come against him; therefore he will be
disheartened, and will return and become enraged at the holy cove-
nant and take action; so he will come back and show regard for
those who forsake the holy covenant.
31 "And forces from him will arise, [a]desecrate the sanctuary fortress,
and do away with the regular sacrifice. And they will set up the
[b]abomination [1]of desolation.
32 "And by [a]smooth *words* he will [1]turn to godlessness those who act
wickedly toward the covenant, but the people who know their God
will display [b]strength and take action.
33 "And [1a]those who have insight among the people will give under-
standing to the many; yet they will [b]fall by sword and by flame, by
captivity and by plunder, for *many* days.
34 "Now when they fall they will be granted a little help, and many
will [a]join with them in [b]hypocrisy.
35 "And some of [1]those who have insight will fall, in order to [a]refine,
[b]purge, and make them [2c]pure, until the [d]end time; because *it is* still
to come at the appointed time.
36 "Then the king will [a]do as he pleases, and he will exalt and [b]mag-
nify himself above every god, and will [c]speak [1]monstrous things
against the [d]God of gods; and he will prosper until the [e]indignation
is finished, for that which is [f]decreed will be done.
37 "And he will show no regard for the [1]gods of his fathers or for the
desire of women, nor will he show regard for any *other* god; for he
will magnify himself above *them* all.
38 "But [1]instead he will honor a god of fortresses, a god whom his
fathers did not know; he will honor *him* with gold, silver, costly
stones, and treasures.

21 [a]2 Sam. 15

22 [a]Dan. 9:26;

24 [1]Lit., *Into tr*
and the richest
will enter [2]Or,
[3]Lit., *fathers' fa*
[a]Num. 13:20; N
Ezek. 34:14

25 [1]Lit., *heart*
11:5

26 [1]Lit., *break*
swept away, an
[a]Dan. 11:10, 40

27 [a]Ps. 52:1; 6
12:2; Jer. 9:3-5;
[c]Dan. 8:19; 11:3
Hab. 2:3

28 [1]Lit., *posses*

29 [1]Lit., *it will n*
happen as the f
as the last

30 [1]I.e., Cyprus
10:4; Num. 24:2
23:1, 12; Jer. 2:1

31 [1]Lit., *that ma*
desolate; or, *tha*
horror [a]Dan. 8:1
12:11 [b]Dan. 9:2
24:15; Mark 13:

32 [1]Or, *pollute t*
[a]Dan. 11:21, 34
5:7-9; Zech. 9:13
10:3-6

33 [1]Or, *instructo*
the people [a]Mal.
[b]Matt. 24:9; John
Heb. 11:36-38

34 [a]Matt. 7:15; A
20:29, 30 [b]Dan.
32; Rom. 16:18

35 [1]Or, *the instru*
[2]Lit., *white* [a]Deut
Prov. 17:3; Dan.
Zech. 13:9; Mal.
[b]John 15:2 [c]Rev.
[d]Dan. 11:27

36 [1]Lit., *extraord*
[a]Dan. 5:19; 11:3,
14:13; Dan. 5:20;
25; 2 Thess. 2:4
13:5, 6 [d]Deut. 10
Ps. 136:2; Dan. 2
[e]Is. 10:25; 26:20;
8:19 [f]Dan. 9:27

37 [1]Or, *God*

38 [1]Lit., *in his pla*

39 "And he will take action against the strongest of fortresses with
the help of a foreign god; he will give great honor to [1]those who
acknowledge *him,* and he will cause them to rule over the many, and
will parcel out land for a price.
40 "And at the [a]end time the [b]king of the South will collide with him,
and the [c]king of the North will [d]storm against him with chariots,
with horsemen, and with many ships; and he will enter countries,
[e]overflow *them,* and pass through.
41 "He will also enter the [1a]Beautiful Land, and many *countries* will
fall; but these will be rescued out of his hand: Edom, [b]Moab and the
foremost of the sons of [c]Ammon.
42 "Then he will stretch out his hand against *other* countries, and the
land of Egypt will not escape.
43 "But he will [1]gain control over the hidden treasures of gold and
silver, and over all the precious things of Egypt; and [a]Libyans and
[b]Ethiopians *will follow* at his [2]heels.
44 "But rumors from the East and from the North will disturb him,
and he will go forth with great wrath to destroy and [1]annihilate
many.
45 "And he will pitch the tents of his royal pavilion between the seas
and the beautiful [a]Holy Mountain; yet he will come to his end, and
no one will help him.

Chapter 12

12 "Now at that time [a]Michael, the great prince who stands
guard over the sons of your people, will arise. And there will
be a [b]time of distress [c]such as never occurred since there was a nation
until that time; and at that time your people, everyone who is found
written in the [d]book, will be rescued.
2 "And [a]many of those who sleep in the dust of the ground will
awake, [b]these to everlasting life, but the others to disgrace *and* ever-
lasting [1]contempt.
3 "And [1]those who have [a]insight will [b]shine brightly like the bright-
ness of the [2]expanse of heaven, and those who [c]lead the many to
righteousness, like the stars forever and ever.
4 "But as for you, Daniel, [a]conceal these words and [b]seal up the
book until the [c]end of time; [d]many will go back and forth, and
knowledge will increase."
5 Then I, Daniel, looked and behold, two others were standing,
one on this bank of the river, and the other on that bank of the river.
6 And [a]one said to the man [b]dressed in linen, who was above the
waters of the river, "[c]How long *will it be* until the end of *these*
wonders?"
7 And I heard the man dressed in linen, who was above the waters
of the river, [1]as he [a]raised his right hand and his left toward heaven,
and swore by [b]Him who lives forever that it would be for a [2c]time,
[2]times, and half *a* [2]*time;* and as soon as [3]they finish [d]shattering the
[4]power of the holy people, all these *events* will be completed.
8 As for me, I heard but could not understand; so I said, "My lord,
what *will be* the [1]outcome of these *events?"*
9 And he said, "Go *your way,* Daniel, for *these* words are concealed
and [a]sealed up until the end time.
10 "[a]Many will be purged, [1]purified and refined; but the [b]wicked will

, *the one who acknowledges*
)an. 11:27, 35; Dan. 11:11, 25 :7, 13, 15 [d]Is. er. 4:13 [e]Dan. 11:10, 26
[1]I.e., Palestine :9; 11:16 [b]Jer. 3:47 [c]Jer. 49:6
rule over [2]Lit., s [a]2 Chr. 12:3; 9 [b]2 Chr. 12:3;):4, 5; Nah. 3:9
[1]Lit., *devote to destruction*
[a]Is. 11:9; 27:13; 25; 66:20; Dan. 9:16, 20
Dan. 10:13, 21; 2:7 [b]Rev. 7:14; Jer. 30:7; Ezek.)an. 9:12; Matt. :21; Mark 13:19)an. 7:10; 10:21
abhorrence [a]Is. Ezek. 37:12-14 latt. 25:46; John 5:28, 29
r, the instructors [2]Or, *firmament* 11:33, 35; 12:10 5:35 [c]Is. 53:11; Dan. 11:33
ı. 8:26; 12:9 [b]Is. ; Dan. 12:9; Rev. Dan. 8:17; 12:9, . 11:9; 29:18, 19; Dan. 11:33
[a]Dan. 8:16; Zech. 2, 13 [b]Ezek. 9:2; 10:5 [c]Dan. 8:13; Matt. 24:3; Mark 13:4
7 [1]Lit., *and* [2]I.e., (s) [3]Lit., *to finish* *and* [a]Ezek. 20:5; 0:5, 6 [b]Dan. 4:34 . 7:25; Rev. 12:14 8:24; Luke 21:24
8 [1]Or, *final end*
9 [a]Dan. 12:4
[1]Lit., *made white* . 13:9 [b]Is. 32:6, 7; Rev. 22:11

act wickedly, and none of the wicked will understand, but [2]those
who [c]have insight will understand.
11 "And from the time that the regular sacrifice is abolished, and the
[1a]abomination of desolation is set up, *there will be* 1,290 days.
12 "How [a]blessed is he who keeps waiting and attains to the [b]1,335
days!
13 "But as for you, go *your way* to the [1]end; then you will enter into
[a]rest and rise *again* for your [b]allotted portion at the end of the [2]age."

10 [2]Or, *the ins* *will* [c]Dan. 12:3 14:9; John 7:17
11 [1]Or, *horrible* *abomination* [a] 9:27; 11:31; Ma Mark 13:14
12 [a]Is. 30:18 8:14; Rev. 11:2 13:5
13 [1]I.e., end of [2]Lit., *days* [a]Is. Rev. 14:13 [b]Ps

DANIEL AT A GLANCE

Theme of Daniel:

Author:

Date:

Purpose:

Key Words:

Segment Divisions		Kings/ Kingdom		Chapter Themes
				1
				2
				3
				4
				5
				6
				7
				8
				9
				10
				11
				12

Prophetic Overview of Daniel

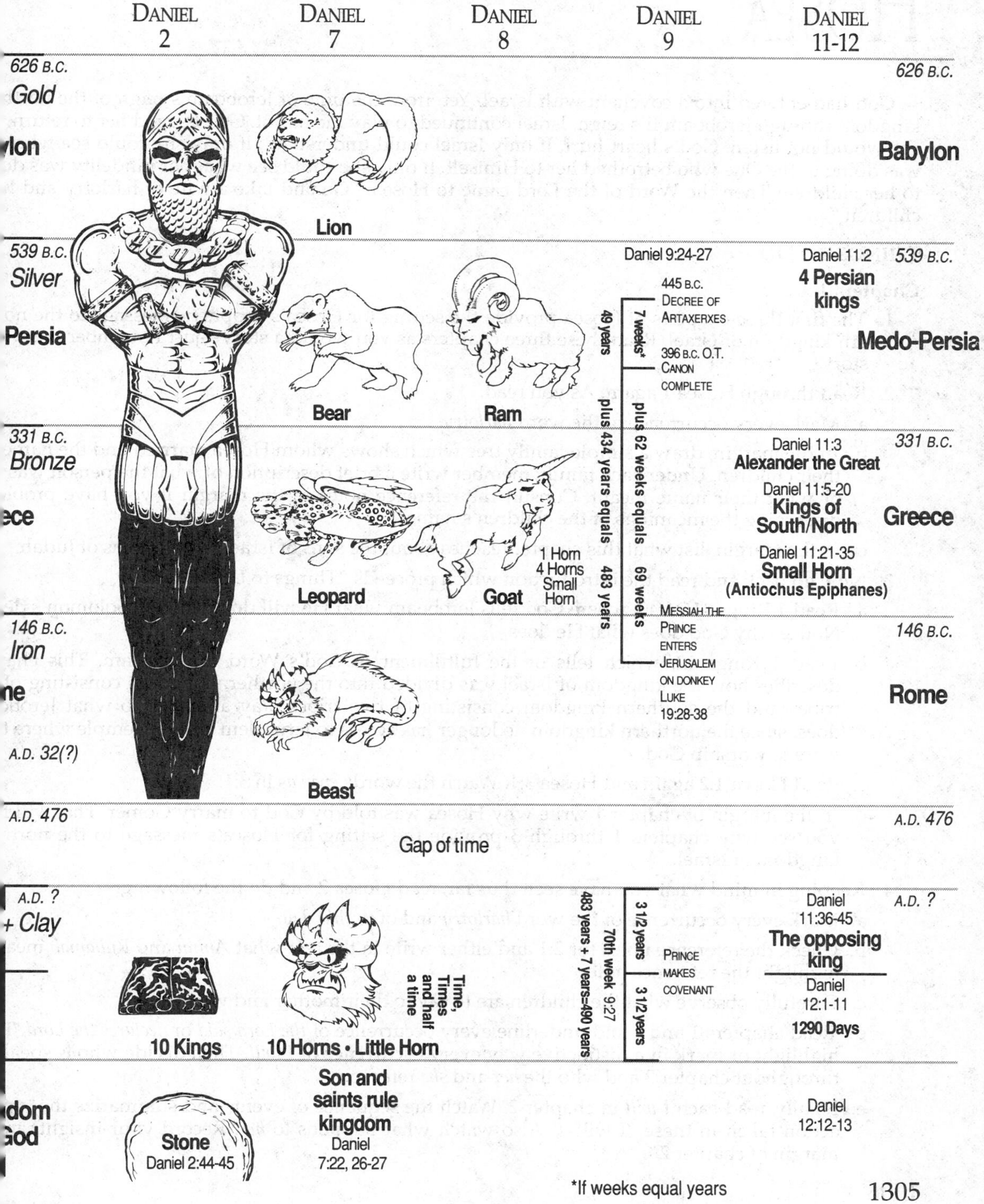

*If weeks equal years

HOSEA

God had entered into a covenant with Israel. Yet, from the time of Jeroboam's reign of the nor kingdom through Jeroboam II's reign, Israel continued to play the harlot. God begged her to retur she would not listen. God's heart hurt. If only Israel could understand; if only she could see wha was doing to the One who betrothed her to Himself. If only she could see what her infidelity was c to her children! Then the Word of the Lord came to Hosea: "Go and take a wife of harlotry and children."

THINGS TO DO

Chapters 1-3

1. The first three chapters of Hosea provide the setting for Hosea's prophetic message to the n ern kingdom of Israel. Read these three chapters as you would a story—just remember it is a story.
2. Read through Hosea 1 again. As you read:
   a. Mark every occurrence of the word *harlotry*.
   b. In the margin, draw a simple family tree which shows whom Hosea married and the nam their children. Under each family member write a brief description of what the person was or what their name meant. Consult the reference notes in the margin if you have prob discerning the meanings of the children's names.
   c. In the margin, list what this chapter teaches about the sons of Israel and the sons of Judah.
3. Now go back and read the introduction which proceeds "Things to Do." Then:
   a. Read 1 Kings 11:26-40, where God tells Jeroboam what He will do after King Solomon's d Notice why God does what He does.
   b. Read 1 Kings 12, which tells of the fulfillment of God's Word to Jeroboam. This cha describes how the kingdom of Israel was divided into the northern kingdom consisting o tribes and the southern kingdom consisting of two tribes. Pay attention to what Jerob does, since the northern kingdom no longer has access to Jerusalem and the temple where were to worship God.
   c. Read Hosea 1:2 again and Hosea 3:1. Watch the words *even as* in 3:1.
   d. In the margin of chapter 1 write why Hosea was told by God to marry Gomer. This will you see why chapters 1 through 3 provide the setting for Hosea's message to the nort kingdom of Israel.
4. Keeping in mind what you have seen thus far, read Hosea 2 and do the following:
   a. Mark every occurrence of the word *harlotry* and of *in that day*.
   b. Check the reference notes for 2:1 and either write in the text what *Ammi* and *Ruhamah* mea highlight the reference note.
   c. Carefully observe what the children are to say to their mother and why.
   d. Read chapters 1 and 2 and underline every occurrence of *the Lord said* or *declares the Lord*. T highlight or mark in a distinctive way every occurrence of *I will*. Then decide who is speal throughout chapter 2 and who the *her* and *she* refer to.
   e. Finally, read each *I will* in chapter 2. Watch the sequence of events and summarize the typ action taken in these "I wills." Also watch what happens to *her*. Record your insights in margin of chapter 2.

f. When you come to 2:23 read the reference notes on this verse and compare this with 1:6,9; 2:1.

5. In the light of all you have seen in chapters 1 and 2, read chapter 3 and do the following:
   a. In a distinctive way mark the word *love.*
   b. In the margin, summarize what God tells Hosea to do and why.
   c. Read 3:5 and mark the reference to *in the last days*, but before you choose how to mark it, see if you find any parallel to *in that day* in chapter 2. If you think any of these references pertain to the day of the Lord, record your insights on the chart THE DAY OF THE LORD in the appendix on pages 1878 and 1879.
6. Write the themes of each of the first three chapters on the HOSEA AT A GLANCE chart on page 1322. Then record the chapter theme next to the chapter number in the text.

apters 4-14

1. Keeping in mind the setting of Hosea 1 through 3, read through Hosea chapter by chapter. As you do:
   a. Mark in a distinctive way the following key words (with their synonyms or pronouns): *harlot* or *harlotry, knowledge, covenant, return, iniquity,* or *sin.* Also mark the phrases *I will, from Me,* and *against Me* (the Lord). Write these words on an index card and use it as a bookmark.
   b. Also mark *Judah, Israel,* and *Ephraim* each in its own distinctive way. As you do, remember Ephraim was one of the ten tribes which comprised the northern kingdom of Israel. After Pekah took the throne in Israel, Tiglath-Pileser, king of Assyria, came against him and took all of the kingdom captive in 733 B.C. except Ephraim and western Manasseh. Ten years later the remainder of the northern kingdom was completely destroyed by the Assyrians in 722 B.C. Thus Ephraim refers to what remained of Israel in those last ten years.
2. After you read a chapter and mark key words and the references to Judah, Israel, and Ephraim, compile your insights on the chart GOD'S RESPONSE TO ISRAEL'S SIN on page 1323.
3. As you read through the remainder of Hosea, remember this is a passionate discourse because of God's relationship to Israel; the relationship of a husband to his wife (Ezekiel 16; Jeremiah 3:6-8); and of a father to His children (Hosea 11:1-3; Jeremiah 31:20). Remember also that because it is passionate, there's quite a bit of repetition, but not without purpose.
4. As you finish reading each chapter, summarize the theme of each one and record it on HOSEA AT A GLANCE and in the text. Also, when you finish the book, decide on its theme and record it on the chart. Then fill in the remainder of the chart.

INGS TO THINK ABOUT

n 2 Corinthians 11:2 Paul wrote, "I am jealous for you with a godly jealousy; for I betrothed you to husband, that to Christ I might present you as a pure virgin."

1. Are there any similarities between your relationship to Jesus Christ and Israel's relationship to God? How are you pleasing your heavenly bridegroom? Are you breaking God's heart in any way?
2. What do you need to do?
3. How do you think God will respond and why?

Chapter 1 ____________________

1 The word of the LORD which came to [a]Hosea the son of Beeri, during the days of [b]Uzziah, [c]Jotham, [d]Ahaz, *and* [e]Hezekiah, kings of Judah, and during the days of [f]Jeroboam the son of Joash, king of Israel.

2 When the LORD first spoke through Hosea, the LORD said to Hosea, "[a]Go, take to yourself a wife of harlotry, and *have* children of

Rom. 9:25 [b]2 Chr. -23; Is. 1:1; Amos :1 [c]2 Kin. 15:5, 7, -38; 2 Chr. 27:1-9 in. 16:1-20; 2 Chr. 27; Is. 1:1; 7:1-17; Mic. 1:1 [e]2 Kin. 18:1-20:21; 2 Chr. :1-32:33; Mic. 1:1 . 13:13; 14:23-29; Amos 1:1

2 [a]Hos. 3:1

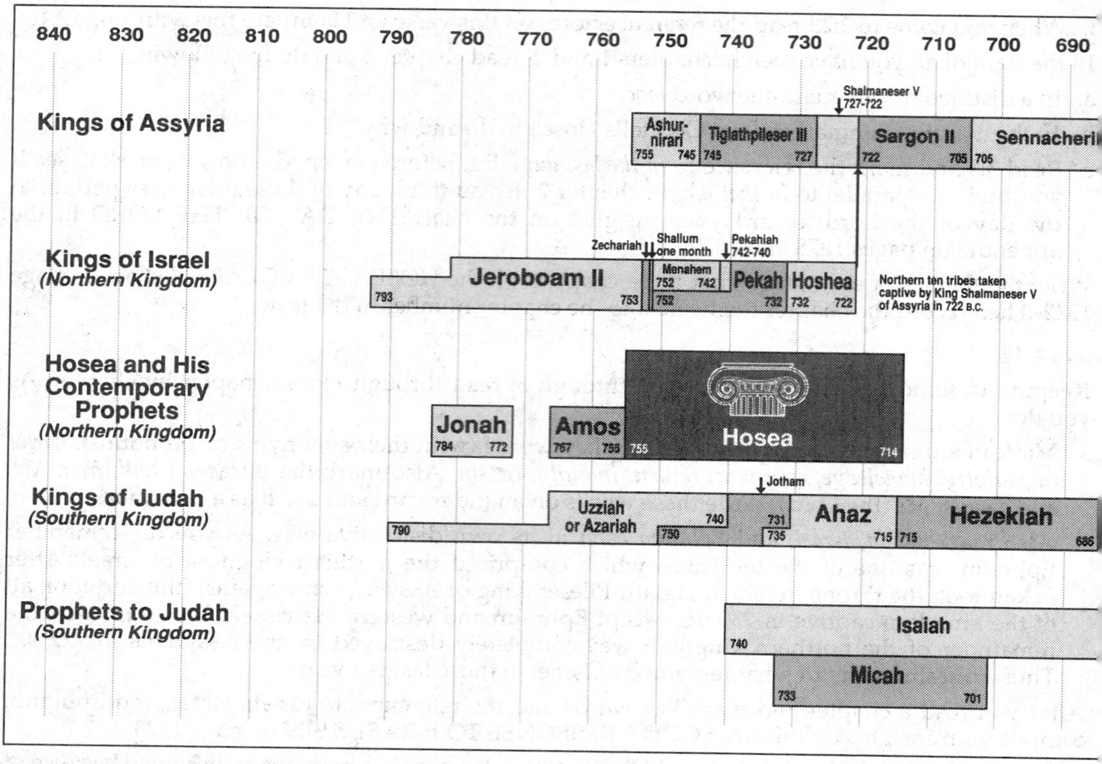

840 830 820 810 800 790 780 770 760 750 740 730 720 710 700 690

Kings of Assyria
Ashur-nirari 755 745 | Tiglathpileser III 745 727 | Shalmaneser V 727-722 | Sargon II 722 705 | Sennacheri 705

Kings of Israel *(Northern Kingdom)*
Jeroboam II 793 753 | Zechariah | Shallum one month | Menahem 752 742 | Pekahiah 742-740 | Pekah 752 732 | Hoshea 732 722
Northern ten tribes taken captive by King Shalmaneser V of Assyria in 722 B.C.

Hosea and His Contemporary Prophets *(Northern Kingdom)*
Jonah 784 772 | Amos 767 755 | Hosea 755 714

Kings of Judah *(Southern Kingdom)*
Uzziah or Azariah 790 740 | Jotham 750 731 | Ahaz 735 715 | Hezekiah 715 686

Prophets to Judah *(Southern Kingdom)*
Isaiah 740 | Micah 733 701

Only one Israelite king, Jeroboam (often referred to as Jeroboam II), is mentioned in Hosea 1:1. Because Hosea mentions the names of the kings of Judah, we can know the other kings who ruled Israel during Hosea's ministry.

harlotry; for [b]the land commits flagrant harlotry, [1]forsaking the
LORD."
3 So he went and took Gomer the daughter of Diblaim, and she
conceived and [a]bore him a son.
4 And the LORD said to him, "Name him [a]Jezreel; for yet a little
while, and [b]I will [1]punish the house of Jehu for the bloodshed of
Jezreel, and [c]I will put an end to the kingdom of the house of Israel.
5 "And it will come about on that day, that I will [a]break the bow of
Israel in the [b]valley of Jezreel."
6 Then she conceived again and gave birth to a daughter. And [1]the
LORD said to him, "Name her [2]Lo-ruhamah, for I will no longer [a]have
compassion on the house of Israel, that I should ever forgive them.
7 "But I will have [a]compassion on the house of Judah and [b]deliver
them by the LORD their God, and will not deliver them by [c]bow,
sword, battle, horses, or horsemen."
8 When she had weaned Lo-ruhamah, she conceived and gave
birth to a son.
9 And [1]the LORD said, "Name him [2]Lo-ammi, for you are not My
people and I am not [3]your God."
10 [1]Yet the number of the sons of Israel
Will be like the [a]sand of the sea,
Which cannot be measured or numbered;
And [b]it will come about that, in the place
Where it is said to them,
"You are [c]not My people,"
It will be said to them,

2 [1]Lit., *from not following after* [b]... 31:16; Jer. 3:1; E... 23:3-21; Hos. 2:5

3 [a]Ezek. 23:4

4 [1]Lit., *visit the bloodshed of Jez... the house of Jeh...* [a]Hos. 2:22 [b]2 Ki... 10:11 [c]2 Kin. 15:...

5 [a]Jer. 49:35; Ez... 39:3 [b]Josh. 17:1... Judg. 6:33

6 [1]Lit., *He* [2]I.e., s... has not obtained compassion [a]Hos...

7 [a]2 Kin. 19:29-3... 30:18 [b]Jer. 25:5, ... Zech. 9:9, 10 [c]Ps... 44:3-7; Zech. 4:6

9 [1]Lit., *He* [2]I.e., n... people [3]Lit., *yours*

10 [1]Ch. 2:1 in Heb... [a]Gen. 22:17; 32:12... 33:22 [b]Rom. 9:26... 65:1; Hos. 1:9

"*You are* the [d]sons of the living God."
11 And the [a]sons of Judah and the sons of Israel will be [b]gathered together,
And they will appoint for themselves [c]one leader,
And they will go up from the land,
For great will be the day of Jezreel.

Chapter 2

2 [1]Say to your brothers, "[2]Ammi," and to your sisters, "[3]Ruhamah."
2 "Contend with your mother, [a]contend,
For she is [b]not my wife, and I am not her husband;
And let her put away her [c]harlotry from her face,
And her adultery from between her breasts,
3 Lest I strip her [a]naked
And expose her as on the [b]day when she was born.
I will also [c]make her like a wilderness,
Make her like desert land,
And slay her with [d]thirst.
4 "Also, I will have no compassion on her children,
Because they are [a]children of harlotry.
5 "For their mother has [a]played the harlot;
She who conceived them has acted shamefully.
For she said, '[a]I will go after my lovers,
Who [b]give *me* my bread and my water,
My wool and my flax, my [c]oil and my drink.'
6 "Therefore, behold, I will [a]hedge up [1]her way with [b]thorns,
And I will build [2]a wall against her so that she cannot find her [c]paths.
7 "And she will [a]pursue her lovers, but she will not overtake them;
And she will seek them, but will not find *them*.
Then she will say, '[b]I will go back to my [c]first husband,
For it was [d]better for me then than now!'

8 "For she does [a]not know that it was [b]I who gave her the grain, the new wine, and the oil,
And lavished on her silver and gold,
Which they [1]used for Baal.
9 "Therefore, I will [a]take back My grain at [1]harvest time
And My new wine in its season.
I will also take away My wool and My flax
Given to cover her nakedness.
10 "And then I will [a]uncover her lewdness
In the sight of her lovers,
And no one will rescue her out of My hand.
11 "I will also [a]put an end to all her gaiety,
Her [b]feasts, her [c]new moons, her sabbaths,
And all her festal assemblies.
12 "And I will [a]destroy her vines and fig trees,
Of which she said, 'These are my wages
Which my lovers have given me.'
And I will [b]make them a forest,
And the [c]beasts of the field will devour them.
13 "And I will punish her for the [a]days of the Baals

0 [d]Is. 63:16; 64:8; ...n 1:12; 1 Pet. 2:10

...11:12 [b]Jer. 23:5, 6; 50:4, 5; Ezek. ...21-24 [c]Jer. 30:21; Hos. 3:5

... [1]Ch. 2:3 in Heb. ..., my people [3]I.e., she has obtained compassion

...Ezek. 23:45; Hos. ...4:5 [b]Is. 50:1 [c]Jer. 3:1, 9, 13

[a]Jer. 13:22; Ezek. ...6:7, 22, 39 [b]Ezek. ...6:4 [c]Is. 32:13, 14; 13:15 [d]Jer. 14:3; Amos 8:11-13

4 [a]Jer. 13:14

...Is. 1:21; Jer. 2:25; ...2; Hos. 3:1 [b]Jer. ...:17, 18; Hos. 2:12 [c]Hos. 2:8

6 [1]So with some ...nt versions; Heb., ...r [2]Lit., *her wall so* ...t [a]Job 19:8; Lam. ...9 [b]Hos. 9:6; 10:8 [c]Jer. 18:15

[a]Hos. 5:13 [b]Luke ...18 [c]Jer. 2:2; 3:1; ...k. 16:8; 23:4 [d]Jer. 14:22; Hos. 13:6

[1]Or, *made into the* ...1:3 [b]Ezek. 16:19

...Lit., *its time* [a]Hos. 8:7; 9:2

10 [a]Ezek. 16:37

... [a]Jer. 7:34; 16:9 ...s. 3:4; Amos 5:21; ...8:10 [c]Is. 1:13, 14

...er. 5:17; 8:13 [b]Is. ...; 7:23 [c]Hos. 13:8

... [a]Hos. 4:13; 11:2

Baal, which meant "lord, owner, possessor, or husband," was the Canaanite god of fertility. **Baal** was part of several compound names for locations where Canaanite deities were worshiped, such as Baal-peor.

When she used to [1b]offer sacrifices to them
And [c]adorn herself with her [2]earrings and jewelry,
And follow her lovers, so that she [d]forgot Me," declares the
LORD.

14 "Therefore, behold, I will allure her,
[a]Bring her into the wilderness,
And speak [1]kindly to her.
15 "Then I will give her her [a]vineyards from there,
And [b]the valley of Achor as a door of hope.
And she will [1c]sing there as in the days of her youth,
As in the [d]day when she came up from the land of Egypt.
16 "And it will come about in that day," declares the LORD,
"That you will call Me [1a]Ishi
And will no longer call Me [2]Baali.
17 "For [a]I will remove the names of the Baals from her mouth,
So that they will be [1]mentioned by their names no more.
18 "In that day I will also make a covenant for them
With the [a]beasts of the field,
The birds of the sky,
And the creeping things of the ground.
And I will [1b]abolish the bow, the sword, and war from the land,
And will make them [c]lie down in safety.
19 "And I will [a]betroth you to Me forever;
Yes, I will betroth you to Me in [b]righteousness and in justice,
In lovingkindness and in compassion,
20 And I will betroth you to Me in faithfulness.
Then you will [a]know the LORD.

21 "And it will come about in that day that [a]I will respond," declares
the LORD.
"I will respond to the heavens, and they will respond to the earth,
22 And the [a]earth will respond to the grain, to the new wine, and to
the oil,
And they will respond to [1]Jezreel.
23 "And I will [a]sow her for Myself in the land.
[b]I will also have compassion on [1]her who had not obtained
compassion,
And [c]I will say to [2]those who were [d]not My people,
'You are My people!'
And [3]they will say, '*Thou art* my God!' "

Chapter 3

3 Then the LORD said to me, "Go again, love a [1]woman *who* is
loved by *her* [2]husband, yet an adulteress, even [a]as the LORD loves
the sons of Israel, though they turn to other gods and love raisin
[b]cakes."
2 So I [a]bought her for myself for fifteen *shekels* of silver and a
homer and a [1]half of barley.
3 Then I said to her, "You shall [a]stay with me for many days. You
shall not play the harlot, nor shall you have a [1]man; so I will also be
toward you."
4 For the sons of Israel will remain for many days [a]without king or

13 [1]Or, *burn* [2]Or, *nose ring* 7:9 [c]Ezek. 16 23:40 [d]Hos. 4 13:6

14 [1]Lit., *upon* [a]Ezek. 20:33-

15 [1]Or, *give a* [a]Ezek. 28:25, 7:26 [c]Jer. 2:1 16:8-14 [d]Hos. 12:9, 13; 13:4

16 [1]I.e., my hu [2]I.e., my maste Baal [a]Is. 54:5;

17 [1]Or, *remem* [a]Ex. 23:13; Jos Ps. 16:4

18 [1]Lit., *break* 5:23; Is. 11:6-9 34:25 [b]Is. 2:4; 39:1-10 [c]Lev. 2 23:6; Ezek. 34:

19 [a]Is. 62:4, 5 1:27; 54:6-8

20 [a]Jer. 31:33, 6:6; 13:4

21 [a]Is. 55:10; Z 8:12; Mal. 3:10,

22 [1]I.e., God so [a]Jer. 31:12; Joel

23 [1]Heb., *Lo-ru* [2]Heb., *Lo-ammi* *he* [a]Jer. 31:27 1:6 [c]Rom. 9:25; 2:10 [d]Hos. 1:9

3:1 [1]I.e., Gomer *companion* [a]Jer. [b]2 Sam. 6:19; 1 C 16:3; Song 2:5

2 [1]Heb., *lethech* 4:10

3 [1]Or, *husband* 21:13

4 [a]Hos. 10:3; 13

prince, [b]without sacrifice or *sacred* [c]pillar, and without [d]ephod or
[1e]household idols.
5 Afterward the sons of Israel will [a]return and seek the LORD their
God and [b]David their king; and [c]they will come trembling to the
LORD and to His goodness in the last days.

Chapter 4

4 [a]Listen to the word of the LORD, O sons of Israel,
For the LORD has a [b]case against the inhabitants of the land,
Because there is [c]no [1]faithfulness or [2]kindness
Or [d]knowledge of God in the land.
2 *There is* [a]swearing, [b]deception, [c]murder, [d]stealing, and [e]adultery.
They employ violence, so that [f]bloodshed [1]follows bloodshed.
3 Therefore the land [a]mourns,
And everyone who lives in it languishes
Along with the beasts of the field and the birds of the sky;
And also the fish of the sea [1]disappear.

4 Yet let no one [1a]find fault, and let none offer reproof;
For your people are like those who [b]contend with the priest.
5 So you will [a]stumble by day,
And the prophet also will stumble with you by night;
And I will destroy your [b]mother.
6 [a]My people are destroyed for lack of knowledge.
Because you have [b]rejected knowledge,
I also will [c]reject you from being My priest.
Since you have [d]forgotten the [e]law of your God,
I also will forget your children.

7 The more they [a]multiplied, the more they sinned against Me;
I will [b]change their glory into shame.
8 They [a]feed on the [1]sin of My people,
And [b]direct their desire toward their iniquity.
9 And it will be, like people, [a]like priest;
So I will [b]punish them for their ways,
And repay them for their deeds.
10 And [a]they will eat, but not have enough;
They will [b]play the harlot, but not increase,
Because they have [1c]stopped giving heed to the LORD.

11 Harlotry, [a]wine, and new wine take away the [1]understanding.
12 My people [a]consult their wooden idol, and their *diviner's* wand
informs them;
For a spirit of harlotry has led *them* astray,
And they have played the harlot, *departing* [1]from their God.
13 They offer sacrifices on the [a]tops of the mountains
And [1b]burn incense on the hills,
[c]Under oak, poplar, and terebinth,
Because their shade is pleasant.
Therefore your daughters play the harlot,
And your [2]brides commit adultery.
14 I will not punish your daughters when they play the harlot
Or your [1]brides when they commit adultery,
For *the men* themselves go apart with harlots

---

4 [1]Heb., *teraphim* [b]Dan. 9:27; 11:31; ...1; Hos. 2:11 [c]Hos. ...:1, 2 [d]Ex. 28:4-12; ...am. 23:9-12 [e]Gen. ...:19, 34; Judg. 17:5; ...4, 17; 1 Sam. 15:23

[a]Jer. 50:4, 5 [b]Jer. ...9; Ezek. 34:24 [c]Is. 2:2, 3; Jer. 31:9

4:1 [1]Or, *truth* [2]Or, ...*ty* [a]Hos. 5:1 [b]Hos. ...; Mic. 6:2 [c]Is. 59:4; Jer. 7:28 [d]Jer. 4:22

...it., *touches* [a]Deut. ...1; Hos. 10:4 [b]Hos. 10:13; 11:12 [c]Gen. ...:8; Hos. 6:9 [d]Deut. ...9; Hos. 7:1 [e]Deut. ...:18; Hos. 7:4 [f]Hos. 6:8; 12:14

...it., *are taken away* ...s. 24:4; 33:9; Amos 5:16; Zeph. 1:3

...it., *contend* [a]Ezek. ...:26; Amos 5:10, 13 [b]Deut. 17:12

...Ezek. 14:3, 7; Hos. ...5 [b]Jer. 15:8; Hos. 2:2, 5

...s. 5:13 [b]Hos. 4:14; ...2:7, 8 [c]Zech. 11:8, 15-17 [d]Hos. 2:13; 13:6 [e]Hos. 8:1, 12

7 [a]Hos. 10:1; 13:6 [b]Hab. 2:16

8 [1]Or, *sin offering* ...s. 10:13 [b]Is. 56:11; Mic. 3:11

[a]Is. 24:2; Jer. 5:31 [b]Hos. 8:13; 9:9

...it., *forsaken giving* ...*d*; or, *forsaken the* ...*to practice* (v. 11) ...*ry*. [a]Lev. 26:26; Is. ...3; Mic. 6:14 [b]Hos. 7:4 [c]Hos. 9:17

[1]Lit., *heart* [a]Prov. 20:1; Is. 5:12; 28:7

...it., *from under* [a]Is. 44:19; Jer. 2:27

...Or, *offer sacrifices* ..., *daughters-in-law* ...er. 3:6 [b]Hos. 2:13; [c]Is. 1:29; Jer. 2:20

..., *daughters-in-law*

And offer sacrifices with [a]temple prostitutes;
So the people without understanding are [2]ruined.

15 Though you, Israel, play the harlot,
Do not let Judah become guilty;
Also do not go to [a]Gilgal,
Or go up to Beth-aven,
[b]And take the oath:
"As the LORD lives!"
16 Since Israel is [a]stubborn
Like a stubborn heifer,
[1]Can the LORD now [b]pasture them
Like a lamb in a large field?
17 Ephraim is joined to [a]idols;
[b]Let him alone.
18 Their liquor gone,
They play the harlot continually;
[a]Their [1]rulers dearly love shame.
19 [a]The wind wraps them in its wings,
And they will be ashamed because of their sacrifices.

Chapter 5

5 Hear this, O priests!
Give heed, O house of Israel!
Listen, O house of the king!
For the judgment applies to you,
For you have been a [a]snare at Mizpah,
And a net spread out on Tabor.
2 And the [a]revolters have [1b]gone deep in depravity,
But I will chastise all of them.
3 I [a]know Ephraim, and Israel is not hidden from Me;
For now, O Ephraim, you have played the harlot,
Israel has defiled itself.
4 Their deeds will not allow them
To return to their God.
For a [a]spirit of harlotry is within them,
And they [b]do not know the LORD.
5 Moreover, the [a]pride of Israel testifies against him,
And Israel and Ephraim stumble in their iniquity;
[b]Judah also has stumbled with them.
6 They will [a]go with their flocks and herds
To seek the LORD, but they will [b]not find *Him*;
He has [c]withdrawn from them.
7 They have [a]dealt treacherously against the LORD,
For they have borne [1b]illegitimate children.
Now the [c]new moon will devour them with their [2]land.

8 [a]Blow the horn in [b]Gibeah,
The trumpet in Ramah.
Sound an alarm at Beth-aven:
"[c]Behind you, Benjamin!"
9 Ephraim will become a [a]desolation in the [b]day of rebuke;
Among the tribes of Israel I [c]declare what is sure.

14 [2]Lit., *thrust d*
[a]Deut. 23:17

15 [a]Hos. 9:15; 1.
[b]Jer. 5:2; 44:26; A
8:14

16 [1]Or, *Now the will pasture . . . fie*
[a]Ps. 78:8 [b]Is. 5:1

17 [a]Hos. 13:2 [b]P
81:12; Hos. 4:4

18 [1]Lit., *shields*
3:11

19 [a]Hos. 12:1; 13

5:1 [a]Hos. 9:8

2 [1]Or, *waded dee slaughter* [a]Hos. 9
[b]Is. 29:15; Hos. 4:

3 [a]Amos 3:2; 5:12

4 [a]Hos. 4:12 [b]Ho
4:6, 14

5 [a]Hos. 7:10 [b]Ez
23:31-35

6 [a]Hos. 8:13; Mic
7 [b]Prov. 1:28; Is.
Jer. 14:12 [c]Ezek.

7 [1]Lit., *strange* [2]
portions [a]Is. 48:8
3:20; Hos. 6:7 [b]H
2:4 [c]Is. 1:14; Hos

8 [a]Joel 2:1 [b]Hos
10:9 [c]Judg. 5:14

9 [a]Is. 28:1-4; Hos
9:11-17 [b]Is. 37:3
46:10; Zech. 1:6

Deut. 19:14; 27:17 zek. 7:8 [c]Ps. 32:6; 93:3, 4

10 The princes of Judah have become like those who [a]move a boundary;
On them I will [b]pour out My wrath [c]like water.

11 [1]Or, with some ent versions, follow othingness [a]Deut. 28:33 [b]Mic. 6:16

11 Ephraim is [a]oppressed, crushed in judgment,
[b]Because he was determined to [1]follow *man's* command.
12 Therefore I am like a [a]moth to Ephraim,
And like rottenness to the house of Judah.

[a]Ps. 39:11; Is. 51:8

13 When Ephraim saw his sickness,
And Judah his [1]wound,
Then Ephraim went to [a]Assyria
And sent to [2b]King Jareb.
But he is [c]unable to heal you,
Or to cure you of your [1]wound.

[1]Or, ulcer [2]Or, the venging king or the at king [a]Hos. 7:11; ; 12:1 [b]Hos. 10:6 [c]Jer. 30:12-15

14 For I *will be* [a]like a lion to Ephraim,
And like a young lion to the house of Judah.
[b]I, even I, will tear to pieces and go away,
I will carry away, and there will be [c]none to deliver.

Ps. 7:2; Hos. 13:7, os 3:4 [b]Ps. 50:22 [c]Mic. 5:8

15 I will go away *and* return to My place
Until they [1a]acknowledge their guilt and seek My face;
In their affliction they will earnestly [b]seek Me.

15 [1]Or, bear their hment [a]Is. 64:7-9; Jer. 3:13, 14 [b]Ps. ; 78:34; Jer. 2:27; Hos. 3:5

Chapter 6

6 "[a]Come, let us return to the LORD.
For [b]He has torn *us,* but [c]He will heal us;
He has [1]wounded *us,* but He will [d]bandage us.
2 "He will [a]revive us after two days;
He will [b]raise us up on the third day
That we may live before Him.
3 "So let us [a]know, let us press on to know the LORD.
His [b]going forth is as certain as the dawn;
And He will come to us like the [c]rain,
Like the spring rain watering the earth."

[1]Lit., struck [a]Jer. 4, 5 [b]Deut. 32:39; 5:14 [c]Jer. 30:17; s. 14:4 [d]Is. 30:26

30:5 [b]1 Cor. 15:4

2:3; Mic. 4:2 [b]Ps. 9:6; Mic. 5:2 [c]Job :23; Ps. 72:6; Joel 2:23

4 What shall I do with you, O [a]Ephraim?
What shall I do with you, O Judah?
For your [1]loyalty is like a [b]morning cloud,
And like the dew which goes away early.
5 Therefore I have [a]hewn *them* in pieces by the prophets;
I have slain them by the [b]words of My mouth;
And the judgments on you are *like* the light that goes forth.
6 For [a]I delight in loyalty [b]rather than sacrifice,
And in the knowledge of God rather than burnt offerings.
7 But [a]like [1]Adam they have [b]transgressed the covenant;
There they have [c]dealt treacherously against Me.
8 [a]Gilead is a city of wrongdoers,
Tracked with [b]bloody *footprints.*
9 And as [a]raiders wait for a man,
So a band of priests [b]murder on the way to Shechem;
Surely they have committed [1c]crime.
10 In the house of Israel I have seen a [a]horrible thing;
Ephraim's [b]harlotry is there, Israel has defiled itself.
11 Also, O Judah, there is a [a]harvest appointed for you,
When I [b]restore the fortunes of My people.

Or, lovingkindness os. 7:1; 11:8 [b]Ps. :34-37; Hos. 13:3

1 Sam. 15:32, 33; r. 1:10; 5:14 [b]Jer. 23:29

att. 9:13; 12:7 [b]Is. 1:11

, men [a]Job 31:33 os. 8:1 [c]Hos. 5:7

. 12:11 [b]Hos. 4:2

, lewdness [a]Hos. Jer. 7:9, 10; Hos. Ezek. 22:9; 23:27; Hos. 2:10

er. 5:30, 31; 23:14 [b]Hos. 5:3

[a]Jer. 51:33; Joel 3:13 [b]Zeph. 2:7

Chapter 7

7 When I [a]would heal Israel,
The iniquity of Ephraim is uncovered,
And the evil deeds of Samaria,
For they deal [b]falsely;
The thief enters in,
[c]Bandits raid outside,
2 And they do not [1]consider in their hearts
That I [a]remember all their wickedness.
Now their [b]deeds are all around them;
They are before My face.
3 [a]With their wickedness they make the [b]king glad,
And the princes with their [c]lies.
4 They are [a]all adulterers
Like an oven heated by the baker,
Who ceases to stir up *the fire*
From the kneading of the dough until it is leavened.
5 On the [1]day of our king, the princes [a]became sick with the heat
of wine;
He stretched out his hand with [b]scoffers,
6 For their hearts are like an [a]oven
As they approach their [1]plotting;
Their [2]anger [3]smolders all night,
In the morning it burns like a flaming fire.
7 All of them are hot like an oven,
And they consume their [a]rulers;
All their kings have fallen.
[b]None of them calls on Me.

8 Ephraim [a]mixes himself with the [1]nations;
Ephraim has become a cake not turned.
9 [a]Strangers devour his strength,
Yet he [b]does not know *it;*
Gray hairs also are sprinkled on him,
Yet he does not know *it.*
10 Though the [a]pride of Israel testifies against him,
Yet [b]they have neither returned to the LORD their God,
Nor have they sought Him, for all this.
11 So [a]Ephraim has become like a silly dove, [b]without [1]sense;
They call to [c]Egypt, they go to [d]Assyria.
12 When they go, I will [a]spread My net over them;
I will bring them down like the birds of the sky.
I will [b]chastise them in accordance with the [1]proclamation to
their assembly.
13 [a]Woe to them, for they have [b]strayed from Me!
Destruction is theirs, for they have rebelled against Me!
I [c]would redeem them, but they speak lies against Me.
14 And [a]they do not cry to Me from their heart
When they wail on their beds;
For the sake of grain and new wine they [1b]assemble themselves,
They [c]turn away from Me.
15 Although I trained *and* strengthened their arms,
Yet they [a]devise evil against Me.
16 They turn, *but* not [1]upward,

7:1 [a]Ezek. 2... 6:4; 7:13; 11:... 4:2 [c]Hos. 6:9

2 [1]Lit., *say to... heart* [a]Ps. 25... 14:10; 17:1; ... 9:9; Amos 8:7... 2:19; 4:18; H...

3 [a]Rom. 1:32... 28:1-4; Hos. 7... 7:3 [c]Hos. 4:2

4 [a]Jer. 9:2; 23...

5 [1]I.e., a festi... occasion [a]Is. ... [b]Is. 28:14

6 [1]Lit., *ambus...* with some anc... versions; M.T.,... [3]Lit., *sleeps* [a]...

7 [a]Hos. 13:10

8 [1]Lit., *people* ... 106:35

9 [a]Is. 1:7; Hos. ... [b]Hos. 4:6

10 [a]Hos. 5:5 [b]...

11 [1]Lit., *heart* ... 11:11 [b]Hos. 4:6... 5:4 [c]Hos. 8:13;... [d]Hos. 5:13; 8:9;...

12 [1]Lit., *report* ... 12:13 [b]Lev. 26... Deut. 28:15

13 [a]Hos. 9:12 ... 14:10; Ezek. 34... 9:17 [c]Jer. 51:9;... 7:1; Matt. 23:37

14 [1]Or, with Gr. ... many ancient ms... *gash themselves* ... 35:9-11; Hos. 8:2... 7:5 [b]Judg. 9:27;... 2:8; Mic. 2:11 [c]H... 13:16

15 [a]Nah. 1:9

16 [1]Or possibly, *Most High*

dignation; or, s. 78:57 [b]Ps. ; 17:10; 73:9; 25; Mal. 3:13, . 23:32; Hos. 9:3, 6

They are like a [a]deceitful bow;
Their princes will fall by the sword
Because of the [2b]insolence of their tongue.
This *will be* their [c]derision in the land of Egypt.

Chapter 8

., palate [a]Jer os. 5:8 [b]Hab. 28:49 [c]Hos. 6:7 [e]Hos. 4:6

8 [a]*Put* the trumpet to your [1]lips!
[b]Like an eagle *the enemy comes* [c]against the house of the LORD,
Because they have [d]transgressed My covenant,
And rebelled against My [e]law.

34; Hos. 7:14 [b]Titus 1:16

2 [a]They cry out to Me,
"My God, [b]we of Israel know Thee!"
3 Israel has rejected the good;
The enemy will pursue him.

.it., he [a]2 Kin. , 17, 25; Hos. 11 [b]Hos. 2:8; 13:1, 2

4 [a]They have set up kings, but not by Me;
They have appointed princes, but I did not know *it*.
With their [b]silver and gold they have made idols for themselves,
That [1]they might be cut off.

Your calf has ted you [a]Hos. 2 [b]Ps. 19:13; Jer. 13:27

5 [1]He has rejected your [a]calf, O Samaria, saying,
"My anger burns against them!"
How long will they be incapable of [b]innocence?
6 For from Israel is even this!

plinters [a]Hos. 13:2

A [a]craftsman made it, so it is not God;
Surely the calf of Samaria will be broken to [1]pieces.
7 For [a]they sow the wind,

t., growth [2]Or, Prov. 22:8 [b]Is. Nah. 1:3 [c]Hos. 2:9

And they reap the [b]whirlwind.
The standing grain has no [1]heads;
It yields [c]no [2]grain.
Should it yield, strangers would swallow it up.

2 Kin. 17:6; Jer. er. 22:28; 25:34

8 Israel is [a]swallowed up;
They are now among the nations
Like a [b]vessel in which no one delights.

it., loves [a]Hos. er. 2:24 [c]Ezek. 16:33, 34

9 For they have gone up to [a]Assyria,
Like [b]a wild donkey all alone;
Ephraim has [c]hired [1]lovers.

[1]Or, suffer for [a]Ezek. 16:37; [b]Jer. 42:2 [c]Is. 10:8

10 Even though they hire *allies* among the nations,
Now I will [a]gather them up;
And they will begin [b]to [1]diminish
Because of the burden of the [c]king of princes.

11 [a]Hos. 10:1

11 Since Ephraim has [a]multiplied altars for sin,
They have become altars of sinning for him.

ut. 4:6, 8 [b]Hos. 4:6

12 Though [a]I wrote for him ten thousand *precepts* of My [b]law,
They are regarded as a strange thing.

. 5:6 [b]Jer. 6:20; Jer. 14:10; Hos. uke 12:2; 1 Cor. 5 [d]Hos. 4:9; 9:7 [e]Hos. 9:3, 6

13 As for My [a]sacrificial gifts,
They [b]sacrifice the flesh and eat *it*,
But the LORD has taken no delight in them.
Now He will [c]remember their iniquity,
And [d]punish *them* for their sins;
They will return to [e]Egypt.

eut. 32:18; Hos. 3; 4:6; 13:6 [b]Is. 9:9, 10

14 For Israel has [a]forgotten his Maker and [b]built palaces;
And Judah has multiplied fortified cities,

But I will send a [c]fire on its cities that it may consume its palatial
dwellings.

Chapter 9

9 [a]Do not rejoice, O Israel, [1]with exultation like the [2]nations!
For you have [b]played the harlot, [3]forsaking your God.
You have loved *harlots'* earnings on [4]every threshing floor.
2 Threshing floor and wine press will [a]not feed them,
And the new wine will fail [1]them.
3 They will not remain in [a]the LORD's land,
But Ephraim will return to [b]Egypt,
And in [c]Assyria they will eat [d]unclean *food*.
4 They will not pour out libations of [a]wine to the LORD,
[b]Their sacrifices will not please Him.
Their bread will [1]*be* like [2]mourners' bread;
All who eat of it will be [c]defiled,
For their bread will be for [3]themselves *alone*;
It will not enter the house of the LORD.
5 [a]What will you do on the day of the appointed festival
And on the day of the [b]feast of the LORD?
6 For behold, they will go because of destruction;
Egypt will gather them up, [a]Memphis will bury them.
Weeds will take over their treasures of silver;
[b]Thorns *will be* in their tents.

7 The days of [a]punishment have come,
The days of [b]retribution have come;
[1]Let Israel know *this*!
The prophet is a [c]fool,
The [2]inspired man is [d]demented,
Because of the grossness of your [e]iniquity,
And *because* your hostility is *so* great.
8 Ephraim *was* a watchman with my God, a prophet;
Yet the snare of a bird catcher is in all his ways,
And there is *only* hostility in the house of his God.
9 They have gone [a]deep [1]in depravity
As in the days of [b]Gibeah;
He will [c]remember their iniquity,
He will punish their sins.

10 I found Israel like [a]grapes in the wilderness;
I saw your forefathers as the [b]earliest fruit on the fig tree in its
first *season*.
But they came to [c]Baal-peor and devoted themselves to [1d]shame,
And they became as [e]detestable as that which they loved.
11 As for Ephraim, their [a]glory will fly away like a bird—
No birth, no pregnancy, and no conception!
12 Though they bring up their children,
Yet I will bereave them [1]until not a man is left.
Yes, [a]woe to them indeed when I depart from them!
13 Ephraim, as I have seen,
Is planted in a pleasant meadow like [a]Tyre;
But Ephraim will bring out his children for slaughter.
14 Give them, O LORD—what wilt Thou give?

14 [c]Jer. 17:

9:1 [1]Lit., *to* ... *peoples* [3]Lit ... *from your G* ... *threshing flo* ... [a]Is. 22:12, 13 ... 10:5 [b]Hos. 4

2 [1]Lit., *her* ...

3 [a]Lev. 25:2 ... [b]Hos. 7:16; 8 ... 7:11 [d]Ezek. 4

4 [1]Lit., be *to* ... *bread of misf* ... [3]Lit., *their app* ... 29:40 [b]Jer. 6 ... 8:13 [c]Hag. 2.

5 [a]Is. 10:3; Je ... [b]Hos. 2:11; Jo

6 [a]Is. 19:13; ... 44:1; 46:14, 1 ... 30:13, 16 [b]Is. ... Hos. 10:8

7 [1]Or, *Israel w* ... *it* [2]Lit., *man o* ... [a]Is. 10:3; Jer. ... Mic. 7:4; Luke ... [b]Is. 34:8; Jer. ... 25:14 [c]Lam. 2 ... Ezek. 13:3, 10 ... 44:25 [e]Ezek. 1

9 [1]Lit., *they ha* ... *corrupted* [a]Is. ... [b]Judg. 19:12, 1 ... Hos. 10:9 [c]Hos ... 8:13

10 [1]I.e., Baal ... [b]Jer. 24:2 [c]Num ... 25:1-5; Ps. 106 ... [d]Jer. 11:13; Hos ... [e]Ps. 115:8; Eze

11 [a]Hos. 4:7; 1

12 [1]Lit., *withou* ... [a]Deut. 31:17; Ho

13 [a]Ezek. 26:1-

Give them a [a]miscarrying womb and dry breasts.

15 All their evil is at [a]Gilgal;
Indeed, I came to hate them there!
Because of the [b]wickedness of their deeds
I will drive them out of My house!
I will love them no more;
All their princes are [c]rebels.
16 [a]Ephraim is stricken, their root is dried up,
They will bear [b]no fruit.
Even though they bear children,
I will slay the [c]precious ones of their womb.
17 My God will cast them away
Because they have [a]not listened to Him;
And they will be [b]wanderers among the nations.

Chapter 10

10 Israel is a [1]luxuriant [a]vine;
He produces fruit for himself.
The more his fruit,
The more altars he [b]made;
The [2]richer his land,
The better [3]he made the *sacred* [c]pillars.
2 Their heart is [1a]faithless;
Now they must bear their [b]guilt.
[2]The LORD will [c]break down their altars
And destroy their *sacred* pillars.

3 Surely now they will say, "We have [a]no king,
For we do not revere the LORD.
As for the king, what can he do for us?"
4 They speak *mere* words,
[1]With [a]worthless oaths they make covenants;
And [b]judgment sprouts like poisonous weeds in the furrows of
the field.
5 The inhabitants of Samaria will fear
For the [1a]calf of [b]Beth-aven.
Indeed, its people will mourn for it,
And its [c]idolatrous priests [2]will cry out over it,
Over its [d]glory, since it has departed from it.
6 The thing itself will be carried to [a]Assyria
As tribute to [1b]King Jareb;
Ephraim will [2]be [c]seized with shame,
And Israel will be ashamed of its [d]own counsel.
7 Samaria will be [a]cut off *with* her king,
Like a stick on the surface of the water.
8 Also the [a]high places of Aven, the [b]sin of Israel, will be
destroyed;
[c]Thorn and thistle will grow on their altars,
Then they will [d]say to the mountains,
"Cover us!" And to the hills, "Fall on us!"
9 From the days of Gibeah you have sinned, O Israel;
There they stand!

14 [a]Hos. 9:11

…5 [a]Hos. 4:15; 12:11 …4:9; 7:2; 12:2 [c]Is. 1:23; Hos. 5:2

…6 [a]Hos. 5:11 [b]Hos. 8:7 [c]Ezek. 24:21

…[a]Hos. 4:10 [b]Hos. 7:13

1 [1]Or, *degenerate* …r, *better* [3]Lit., *they* …5:1-7; Ezek. 15:1-6 …er. 2:28; Hos. 8:11; …2:11 [c]1 Kin. 14:23; Hos. 3:4

[1]Lit., *smooth* [2]Lit., …Kin. 18:21; Zeph. … [b]Hos. 13:16 [c]Hos. 10:8; Mic. 5:13

[a]Ps. 12:4; Is. 5:19

…, *Swearing falsely* …*making a covenant* …ek. 17:13-19; Hos. … [b]Deut. 31:16, 17; 17:3, 4; Amos 5:7

5 [1]So with some …ent versions; Heb., … [2]Or, *who used to* …*ce over* [a]Hos. 8:5, 6 [b]Hos. 4:15; 5:8 …. 23:5 [c]Hos. 9:11

[1]Or, *the avenging* …*g or the great king* …it., *receive shame* …s. 11:5 [b]Hos. 5:13 …4:7 [d]Is. 30:3; Jer. 7:24

7 [a]Hos. 13:11

[a]Hos. 4:13 [b]1 Kin. …:28-30; 13:34 [c]Is. …13; Hos. 9:6; 10:2 …2:19; Luke 23:30; Rev. 6:16

Will not the battle against the sons of iniquity overtake them in
Gibeah?
10 When it is My [a]desire, I will [1b]chastise them;
And [c]the peoples will be gathered against them
When they are bound for their double guilt.

11 And Ephraim is a trained [a]heifer that loves to thresh,
But I will [b]come over her fair neck *with a yoke*;
I will harness Ephraim,
Judah will plow, Jacob will harrow for himself.
12 [a]Sow with a view to righteousness,
Reap in accordance with [1]kindness;
[b]Break up your fallow ground,
For it is time to [c]seek the LORD
Until He [d]comes to [2e]rain righteousness on you.
13 You have [a]plowed wickedness, you have reaped injustice,
You have eaten the fruit of [b]lies.
Because you have trusted in your way, in your [c]numerous
warriors,
14 Therefore, a tumult will arise among your people,
And all your [a]fortresses will be destroyed,
As Shalman destroyed Beth-arbel on the day of battle,
When [b]mothers were dashed in pieces with *their* children.
15 Thus it will be done to you at Bethel because of your great
wickedness.
At dawn the king of Israel will be completely cut off.

Chapter 11

11 When Israel *was* a youth I loved him,
And [a]out of Egypt I [b]called My son.
2 The more [1a]they called them,
The more they went from [1]them;
They kept [b]sacrificing to the Baals
And [c]burning incense to idols.
3 Yet it is I who taught Ephraim to walk,
[1]I [a]took them in My arms;
But they did not know that I [b]healed them.
4 I [a]led them with cords of a man, with bonds of love,
And [b]I became to them as one who lifts the yoke from their jaws;
And I bent down *and* [c]fed them.

5 [1]They will not return to the land of Egypt;
But Assyria—he will be [2]their king,
Because they [a]refused to return *to Me.*
6 And the [a]sword will whirl against [1]their cities,
And will demolish [1]their gate bars
And [b]consume *them* because of their [c]counsels.
7 So My people are bent on [a]turning from Me.
Though [1]they call [2]them to *the One* on high,
None at all exalts *Him.*

8 [a]How can I give you up, O Ephraim?
How can I surrender you, O Israel?
How can I [1]make you like [b]Admah?

10 [1]Or, *bind* [a]
5:13 [b]Hos. 4:9
16:16

11 [a]Jer. 50:11;
4:16; Mic. 4:13
28:14

12 [1]Or, *loyalty*
teach [a]Prov. 1
[b]Jer. 4:3 [c]Hos.
[d]Hos. 6:3 [e]Is.

13 [a]Job 4:8; P
Gal. 6:7, 8 [b]Ho
7:3; 11:12 [c]Ps

14 [a]Is. 17:3 [b]

11:1 [a]Hos. 2:1
13; 13:4 [b]Ex.
Matt. 2:15

2 [1]I.e., God's
[a]2 Kin. 17:13-1
2:13; 4:13 [c]Is.
18:15

3 [1]So ancient
Heb., *He . . .* H
1:31; 32:10, 11
107:20; Jer. 30

4 [a]Jer. 31:2, 3
26:13 [c]Ex. 16:
78:25

5 [1]Lit., *He* [2]Li
[a]Hos. 7:16

6 [1]Lit., *his* [a]H
[b]Lam. 2:9 [c]Ho

7 [1]I.e., God's
[2]Lit., *him;* i.e.,
[a]Jer. 3:6, 7; 8:

8 [1]Lit., *give* [a]
7:1 [b]Gen. 14:
29:23

How can I treat you like [b]Zeboiim?
My heart is turned over within Me,
[2]All My compassions are kindled.
9 I will [a]not execute My fierce anger;
I will not destroy Ephraim [b]again.
For [c]I am God and not man, the [d]Holy One in your midst,
And I will not come in [1]wrath.
10 They will [a]walk after the LORD,
He will [b]roar like a lion;
Indeed He will roar,
And *His* sons will come [c]trembling from the west.
11 They will come trembling like birds from [a]Egypt,
And like [b]doves from the land of [a]Assyria;
And I will [c]settle them in their houses, declares the LORD.

12 [1]Ephraim surrounds Me with [a]lies,
And the house of Israel with deceit;
Judah is also unruly against God,
Even against the Holy One who is faithful.

Chapter 12

12 [1]Ephraim feeds on [a]wind,
And pursues the [b]east wind continually;
He multiplies lies and violence.
Moreover, [2]he makes a covenant with Assyria,
And oil is carried to Egypt.
2 The LORD also has a [a]dispute with Judah,
And will punish Jacob [b]according to his ways;
He will repay him according to his deeds.
3 In the womb he [a]took his brother by the heel,
And in his maturity he [b]contended with God.
4 Yes, he wrestled with the angel and prevailed;
He wept and [a]sought His favor.
He found Him at [b]Bethel,
And there He spoke with us,
5 Even the LORD, the God of hosts;
The LORD is His [1a]name.
6 Therefore, [a]return to your God,
[b]Observe [1]kindness and justice,
And [c]wait for your God continually.
7 A [1]merchant, in whose hands are false [a]balances,
He loves to oppress.
8 And Ephraim said, "Surely I have become [a]rich,
I have found wealth for myself;
In all my labors they will find in me
[b]No iniquity, which *would be* sin."
9 But I *have been* the LORD your God since the land of Egypt;
I will make you [a]live in tents again,
As in the days of the appointed festival.
10 I have also spoken to the [a]prophets,
And I [1]gave numerous visions;
And through the prophets I gave [b]parables.
11 Is there iniquity *in* Gilead?
Surely they are worthless.

ogether [b]Gen. 8; Deut. 29:23

.it., *excitement* :17 [b]Jer. 26:3; um. 23:19 [d]Is. 12:6; 41:14, 16

3:5; 6:1-3 [b]Is. oel 3:16; Amos 1:2 [c]Is. 66:2, 5

1:11 [b]Is. 60:8; [c]Ezek. 28:25, 26; 34:27, 28

:h. 12:1 in Heb. [a]Hos. 4:2; 7:3

:h. 12:2 in Heb. *hey make* [a]Jer. ien. 41:6; Ezek. 17:10

os. 4:1; Mic. 6:2 [b]Hos. 4:9; 7:2

en. 25:26 [b]Gen. 32:28

en. 32:26 [b]Gen. 13-19; 35:10-15

, *memorial* [a]Ex. 3:15

Or, *loyalty* [a]Hos. 10:12 [b]Mic. 6:8 [c]Mic. 7:7

Canaanite [a]Prov. os 8:5; Mic. 6:11

62:10; Hos. 13:6; . 3:17 [b]Hos. 4:8; 14:1

9 [a]Lev. 23:42

Lit., *multiplied the* on [a]2 Kin. 17:13; 7:25 [b]Ezek. 17:2; 20:49

In Gilgal they sacrifice bulls,
Yes, [a]their altars are like the stone heaps
Beside the furrows of the field.

12 Now [a]Jacob fled to the [1]land of Aram,
And [b]Israel worked for a wife,
And for a wife he kept *sheep.*
13 But by a [a]prophet the LORD brought Israel from Egypt,
And by a prophet he was kept.
14 [a]Ephraim has provoked to bitter anger;
So his Lord will leave his [b]bloodguilt on him,
And bring back his [c]reproach to him.

Chapter 13

13 [a]When Ephraim [1]spoke, *there was* trembling.
He [b]exalted himself in Israel,
But through [c]Baal he [2]did wrong and died.
2 And now they sin more and more,
And make for themselves [a]molten images,
Idols [1b]skillfully made from their silver,
All of them the [c]work of craftsmen.
They say of them, "Let the [2]men who sacrifice kiss the [d]calves!"
3 Therefore, they will be like the [a]morning cloud,
And like dew which [1]soon disappears,
Like [b]chaff which is blown away from the threshing floor,
And like [c]smoke from a [2]chimney.

4 Yet I *have been* the [a]LORD your God
Since the land of Egypt;
And you were not to know [b]any god except Me,
For there is no savior [c]besides Me.
5 I [1a]cared for you in the wilderness,
[b]In the land of drought.
6 As *they had* their pasture, they became [a]satisfied,
And being satisfied, their [b]heart became proud;
Therefore, they [c]forgot Me.
7 So I will be [a]like a lion to them;
Like a [b]leopard I will [1]lie in wait by the wayside.
8 I will encounter them [a]like a bear robbed of her cubs,
And I will tear open [1]their chests;
There I will also [b]devour them like a lioness,
As a wild beast would tear them.

9 *It is* your destruction, O Israel,
[1]That *you are* [a]against Me, against your [b]help.
10 Where now is your [a]king
That he may save you in all your cities,
And your [b]judges of whom you [1]requested,
"Give me a king and princes"?
11 I [a]gave you a king in My anger,
And [b]took him away in My wrath.

12 The iniquity of Ephraim is bound up;
His sin is [a]stored up.

11 [a]Hos. 8:11;

12 [1]Lit., *field* 28:5 [b]Gen. 29

13 [a]Ex. 14:19 63:11-14

14 [a]2 Kin. 17:7 [b]Ezek. 18:10-1 11:18; Mic. 6:1

13:1 [1]Or, *spok trembling* [2]Or, *guilty* [a]Job 29: [b]Judg. 8:1; 12:1 2:8-17; 11:2

2 [1]Or, *accordin own understan* [2]Lit., *sacrificers (among) manki* 46:6; Jer. 10:4; 2:8 [b]Is. 44:17-2 8:6 [d]Hos. 8:5, 6

3 [1]Lit., *goes aw early* [2]Lit., *wind* [a]Hos. 6:4 [b]Ps. 1 17:13; Dan. 2:35 68:2

4 [a]Hos. 12:9 [b]E 2 Kin. 18:35 [c]Is. 45:21, 22

5 [1]Or, *knew* [a]D 32:10 [b]Deut. 8:1

6 [a]Deut. 8:12, 1 32:13-15; Jer. 5: 7:14 [c]Hos. 2:13; 8:14

7 [1]Or, *watch* [a]La 3:10; Hos. 5:14 [b]

8 [1]Lit., *the enclo their heart* [a]2 Sa 17:8 [b]Ps. 50:22

9 [1]Or, *But in Me help* [a]Jer. 2:17, 1 1:12, 13 [b]Deut. 33:26, 29

10 [1]Lit., *said* [a]2 K 17:4; Hos. 8:4 [b]1 8:5, 6

11 [a]1 Sam. 8:7; 10:17-24 [b]1 Sam. 15:26; 1 Kin. 14:7- Hos. 10:7

12 [a]Deut. 32:34, Job 14:17; Rom. 2

13 The pains of [a]childbirth come upon him;
He is [b]not a wise son,
For [1]it is not the time that he should [c]delay at the opening of the womb.
14 Shall I [a]ransom them from the [1]power of Sheol?
Shall I redeem them from death?
[b]O Death, where are your thorns?
O Sheol, where is your sting?
[c]Compassion will be hidden from My sight.

15 Though he [a]flourishes among the [1]reeds,
An [b]east wind will come,
The wind of the LORD coming up from the wilderness;
And his fountain will [c]become dry,
And his spring will be dried up;
It will [d]plunder *his* treasury of every precious article.
16 [1]Samaria will be held [a]guilty,
For she has [b]rebelled against her God.
[c]They will fall by the [d]sword,
Their little ones will be [e]dashed in pieces,
And their pregnant [f]women will be ripped open.

Chapter 14

14 [1a]Return, O Israel, to the LORD your God,
For you have stumbled [2]because of your [b]iniquity.
2 Take words with you and return to the LORD.
Say to Him, "[a]Take away all iniquity,
And [1]receive *us* graciously,
That we may [b]present [2]the fruit of our lips.
3 "Assyria will not save us,
We will [a]not ride on horses;
Nor will we say again, '[b]Our god,'
To the [c]work of our hands;
For in [d]Thee the [1]orphan finds mercy."

4 I will [a]heal their apostasy,
I will [b]love them freely,
For My anger has [c]turned away from them.
5 I will be like the [a]dew to Israel;
He will blossom like the [b]lily,
And he will [1]take root like *the cedars of* [c]Lebanon.
6 His shoots will [1]sprout,
And his [2]beauty will be like the [a]olive tree,
And his fragrance like *the cedars of* [b]Lebanon.
7 Those who [a]live in his shadow
Will [1]again raise [b]grain,
And they will blossom like the vine.
His renown *will be* like the wine of Lebanon.

8 O Ephraim, what more have I to do with [a]idols?
It is I who answer and look after [1]you.
I am like a luxuriant [b]cypress;
From [c]Me comes your fruit.

Lit., *it is the time* *should not tarry* *breaking forth of* *en* [a]Is. 13:8; Mic. 10 [b]Deut. 32:6; 4 [c]Is. 37:3; 66:9

[1]Lit., *hand* [a]Ps. Ezek. 37:12, 13 Cor. 15:55 [c]Jer. 20:16; 31:35-37

brothers [a]Gen. Hos. 10:1 [b]Gen. :6; Jer. 4:11, 12; :10; 19:12 [c]Jer. 51:36 [d]Jer. 20:5

Ch. 14:1 in Heb. 10:2 [b]Hos. 7:14 8:12 [d]Hos. 11:6 os. 10:14 [f]2 Kin. 15:16

Ch. 14:2 in Heb. [a]Hos. 6:1; 10:12; Joel 2:13 [b]Hos. 4:8; 5:5; 9:7

ccept that which *s good* [2]So with t versions; M.T., *s as bulls* [a]Mic. [b]Ps. 51:16, 17; 6:6; Heb. 13:15

fatherless [a]Ps. ; Is. 31:1 [b]Hos. 13:2 [c]Hos. 4:12 [d]Ps. 10:14; 68:5

57:18; Hos. 6:1 n. 3:17 [c]Is. 12:1

strike his roots 19:12; Is. 26:19 g 2:1; Matt. 6:28 [c]Is. 35:2

6 [1]Lit., *go* [2]Or, *ndor* [a]Jer. 11:16 [b]Song 4:11

return, they will *se grain* [a]Ezek. [b]Hos. 2:21, 22

aim [a]Job 34:32; 14:3 [b]Is. 41:19 [c]Ezek. 17:23

9 [a]Whoever is wise, let him understand these things;
Whoever is discerning, let him know them.
For the [b]ways of the LORD are right,
And the [c]righteous will walk in them,
But [d]transgressors will stumble in them.

9 [a]Ps. 107:43; ... 9:12 [b]Ps. 111:7 ... 10:29; Zeph. 3:5 ... 26:7 [d]Is. 1:28

HOSEA AT A GLANCE

Theme of Hosea:

Author:

Date:

Purpose:

Key Words:

SEGMENT DIVISIONS

		CHAPTER THEMES
		1
		2
		3
		4
		5
		6
		7
		8
		9
		10
		11
		12
		13
		14

God's Response to Israel's Sin

Their Iniquity	The Immediate or Long-Range Consequences

Their Future or Hope

JOEL

Although we know nothing about Joel, nor of the time of his writing other than what we read i
short prophetic book, Joel's message is significant. When Peter preached on Pentecost, he expl
Pentecost in the light of a prophecy in Joel (Acts 2:14-21; Joel 2:28-32).

Joel uses a present-day plague to call God's people to repentance. As he does this, Joel, like the
prophets, warns them of the coming day of the Lord—a day that is as sure as the promises of God.

THINGS TO DO

1. Read through Joel and mark the key words listed on the JOEL AT A GLANCE chart on page
2. To correctly interpret Joel, you must pay attention to the time when certain events occur. switches from the present to the future. To pick this up, watch for and mark the words *the* *now*. Put a clock such as this next to any references to time. Also, watch the sequen events.
3. As you read through Joel note the following and record what you learn in the appropriate se on the JOEL OBSERVATIONS CHART on page 1331.
   a. What is going to happen to the people, the land, the nations, and the animals and who or is going to do it.
   b. What the people are to do and why.
   c. How God will respond and the effect it will have on the people.
   d. When applicable, note when any of the above will happen.
4. Record the theme of each chapter on JOEL AT A GLANCE as well as in the text next t chapter number. Then fill in the rest of the chart. Be sure to record the theme or message of Jo
5. The day of the Lord is an important day prophetically. In the appendix of this Bible you will the chart THE DAY OF THE LORD (page 1878). Record your insights from Joel on "the day o Lord." As you do so, note the reference (book, chapter, and verse) you took your informa from so you can find it later.

THINGS TO THINK ABOUT

1. What do you see happening in the world, in your nation? Could it be the judgment of the L What could you and others learn from Joel's exhortations? What could you do?
2. Have you failed God in any way? According to what you have seen in Joel, is there a chan return to Him? What could you do? How can you apply the message of Joel to your life? Wha you think would happen if your church "collectively" repented and returned to the Lord in manner? Think about it and ask God what to do.

Chapter 1 ______________________

1 The [a]word of the LORD that came to [b]Joel, the son of Pethuel.
2 [a]Hear this, O [b]elders,
And listen, all inhabitants of the land.
[c]Has *anything like* this happened in your days
Or in your fathers' days?
3 [a]Tell your sons about it,
And *let* your sons *tell* their sons,
And their sons the next generation.

1:1 [a]Jer. 1:2; Eze Hos. 1:1 [b]Acts 2:

2 [a]Hos. 4:1; 5:1 8:8; Joel 1:14 [c]Je 30:7; Joel 2:2

3 [a]Ex. 10:2; Ps.

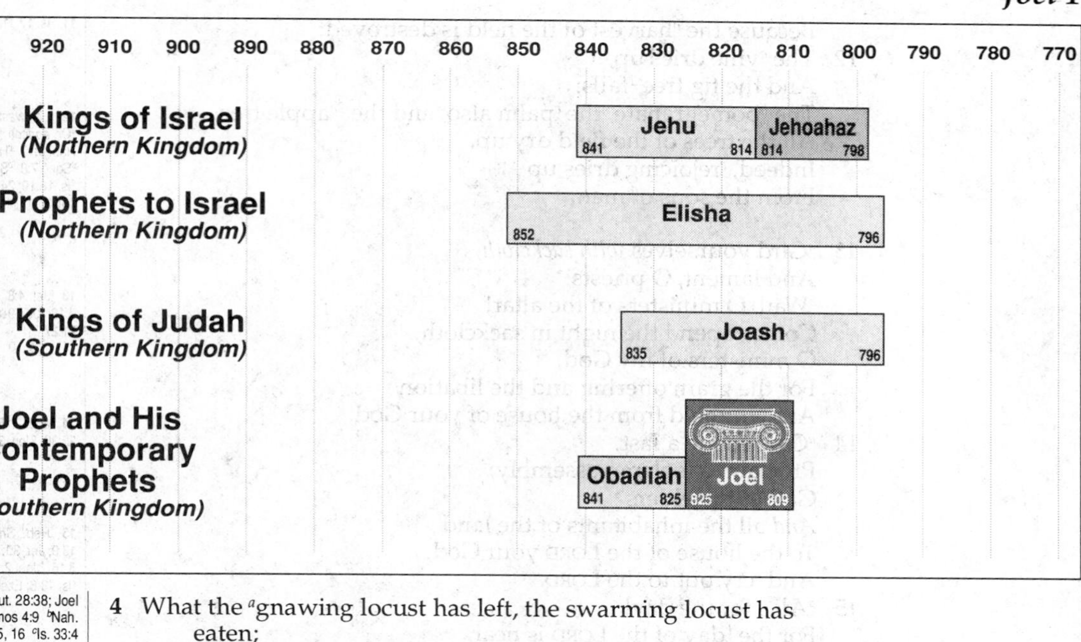

[a]Deut. 28:38; Joel ; Amos 4:9 [b]Nah. 3:15, 16 [c]Is. 33:4

4 What the [a]gnawing locust has left, the swarming locust has
eaten;
And what the [b]swarming locust has left, the creeping locust has
eaten;
And what the creeping locust has left, the [c]stripping locust has
eaten.

oel 3:3 [b]Is. 32:10

5 Awake, [a]drunkards, and weep;
And wail, all you wine drinkers,
On account of the sweet wine
That is [b]cut off from your mouth.

6 [1]Lit., *come up* *inst* [a]Joel 2:2, 11, 25 [b]Rev. 9:8

6 For a [a]nation has [1]invaded my land,
Mighty and without number;
[b]Its teeth are the teeth of a lion,
And it has the fangs of a lioness.

a stump [a]Is. 5:6; Amos 4:9

7 It has [a]made my vine a waste,
And my fig tree [1]splinters.
It has stripped them bare and cast *them* away;
Their branches have become white.

22:12 [b]Joel 1:13; Amos 8:10

8 [a]Wail like a virgin [b]girded with sackcloth
For the bridegroom of her youth.

os. 9:4; Joel 1:13; 2:14 [b]Joel 2:17

9 The [a]grain offering and the libation are cut off
From the house of the LORD.
The [b]priests mourn,
The ministers of the LORD.

Lit., *wastes away* 4:4, 7 [b]Jer. 12:11

10 The field is [a]ruined,
[b]The land mourns,
For the grain is ruined,
The new wine dries up,
Fresh oil [1]fails.

, *The farmers are ashamed, The* *ressers wail* [a]Jer. 14:4; Amos 5:16

11 [1a]Be ashamed, O farmers,
Wail, O vinedressers,
For the wheat and the barley;

Because the [b]harvest of the field is destroyed.
12 The [a]vine dries up,
And the fig tree [1]fails;
The [b]pomegranate, the [c]palm also, and the [2d]apple tree,
All the trees of the field dry up.
Indeed, [e]rejoicing dries up
From the sons of men.

13 [a]Gird yourselves *with sackcloth,*
And lament, O priests;
[b]Wail, O ministers of the altar!
Come, [c]spend the night in sackcloth,
O ministers of my God,
For the grain offering and the libation
Are withheld from the house of your God.
14 [a]Consecrate a fast,
Proclaim a [b]solemn assembly;
Gather the elders
And all the inhabitants of the land
To the house of the LORD your God,
And [c]cry out to the LORD.
15 [a]Alas for the day!
For the [b]day of the LORD is near,
And it will come as [c]destruction from the [1]Almighty.
16 Has not [a]food been cut off before our eyes,
Gladness and [b]joy from the house of our God?
17 The [1a]seeds shrivel under their [2]clods;
The storehouses are desolate,
The barns are torn down,
For the grain is dried up.
18 How [a]the beasts groan!
The herds of cattle wander aimlessly
Because there is no pasture for them;
Even the flocks of sheep [1]suffer.
19 [a]To Thee, O LORD, I cry;
For [b]fire has devoured the pastures of the wilderness,
And the flame has burned up all the trees of the field.
20 Even the beasts of the field [1a]pant for Thee;
For the [b]water brooks are dried up,
And fire has devoured the pastures of the wilderness.

Chapter 2

2 [a]Blow a trumpet in Zion,
And sound an alarm on My holy mountain!
Let all the inhabitants of the land tremble,
For the [b]day of the LORD is coming;
Surely it is near,
2 A day of [a]darkness and gloom,
A day of clouds and thick darkness.
As the dawn is spread over the mountains,
So there is a [b]great and mighty people;
There has [c]never been *anything* like it,
Nor will there be again after it
To the years of many generations.

11 [b]Is. 17:11;

12 [1]Lit., *waste* [2]Or, *apricot* [a]J Hab. 3:17 [b]Ha [c]Song 7:8 [d]Sc [e]Is. 16:10; 24:1 48:33

13 [a]Jer. 4:8; E 7:18 [b]Jer. 9:10 21:27

14 [a]Joel 2:15, 23:36 [c]Jon. 3:8

15 [1]Heb., *Sha* 13:9; Jer. 30:7; 5:16 [b]Joel 2:1, [c]Is. 13:6; Ezek.

16 [a]Is. 3:7; Am [b]Deut. 12:7; Ps.

17 [1]Or, *dried fig* *shovels* [a]Is. 17:

18 [1]Lit., *bear punishment* [a]1 K Jer. 12:4; 14:5, 6 4:3

19 [a]Ps. 50:15; M [b]Jer. 9:10; Amos

20 [1]Lit., *long for* 104:21; 147:9; Jo 1:18 [b]1 Kin. 17:7

2:1 [a]Jer. 4:5; Joe Zeph. 1:16 [b]Joel 2:11, 31; 3:14; Ob 15; Zeph. 1:14

2 [a]Joel 2:10, 31; 5:18; Zeph. 1:15 1:6; 2:11, 25 [c]Lar 1:12; Dan. 9:12; 1 Joel 1:2

3 A [a]fire consumes before them,
And behind them a flame burns.
The land is [b]like the garden of Eden before them,
But a [c]desolate wilderness behind them,
And nothing at all escapes them.
4 Their [a]appearance is like the appearance of horses;
And like war horses, so they run.
5 [1]With a [a]noise as of chariots
They leap on the tops of the mountains,
Like the [2]crackling of a [b]flame of fire consuming the stubble,
Like a mighty people arranged for battle.
6 Before them the people are in [a]anguish;
All [b]faces [1]turn pale.
7 They run like mighty men;
They climb the wall like soldiers;
And they each [a]march [1]in line,
Nor do they deviate from their paths.
8 They do not crowd each other;
They march everyone in his path.
When they [1]burst through the [2]defenses,
They do not break ranks.
9 They rush on the city,
They run on the wall;
They climb into the [a]houses,
They [b]enter through the windows like a thief.
10 Before them the earth [a]quakes,
The heavens tremble,
The [b]sun and the moon grow dark,
And the stars lose their brightness.
11 And the LORD [a]utters His voice before [b]His army;
Surely His camp is very great,
For [c]strong is he who carries out His word.
The [d]day of the LORD is indeed great and very awesome,
And [e]who can endure it?
12 "Yet even now," declares the LORD,
"[a]Return to Me with all your heart,
And with [b]fasting, weeping, and mourning;
13 And [a]rend your heart and not [b]your garments."
Now return to the LORD your God,
For He is [c]gracious and compassionate,
Slow to anger, abounding in lovingkindness,
And [d]relenting of evil.
14 Who knows [a]whether He will *not* turn and relent,
And leave a [b]blessing behind Him,
Even [c]a grain offering and a libation
For the LORD your God?
15 [a]Blow a trumpet in Zion,
[b]Consecrate a fast, proclaim a solemn assembly,
16 Gather the people, [a]sanctify the congregation,
Assemble the elders,
Gather the children and the nursing infants.
Let the [b]bridegroom come out of his room
And the bride out of her *bridal* chamber.
17 Let the priests, the LORD's ministers,

[a]Ps. 97:3; Is. 9:18, 9 [b]Is. 51:3; Ezek. [c]Ex. 10:5, 15; Ps. 34, 35; Zech. 7:14
4 [a]Rev. 9:7
, *Like the noise of* *hariots* [2]Lit., *noise* Rev. 9:9 [b]Is. 5:24; 30:30
r, *become flushed* s. 13:8; Nah. 2:10 [b]Jer. 30:6
[1]Lit., *in his ways* [a]Prov. 30:27
8 [1]Lit., *fall* [2]Lit., n, probably *javelin*
x. 10:6 [b]Jer. 9:21; John 10:1
s. 18:7; Joel 3:16; ah. 1:5 [b]Is. 13:10; 4; Jer. 4:23; Ezek. 8; Joel 2:31; 3:15; . 24:29; Rev. 8:12
Ps. 46:6; Is. 13:4; . 25:30; Joel 3:16 2:25 [c]Jer. 50:34; . 18:8 [d]Jer. 30:7; :15; 2:1, 31; 3:14; ph. 1:14, 15; Rev. Ezek. 22:14; Mal. 3:2
eut. 4:29; Jer. 4:1, Ezek. 33:11; Hos. 12:6 [b]Dan. 9:3
[a]Ps. 34:18; 51:17; :15 [b]Gen. 37:34; n. 1:11; Job 1:20; er. 41:5 [c]Ex. 34:6 8:8; 42:10; Amos 7:3, 6
ler. 26:3; Jon. 3:9 :19 [c]Joel 1:9, 13
Num. 10:3; 2 Kin. 10:20 [b]Joel 1:14
Sam. 16:5; 2 Chr. 29:5 [b]Ps. 19:5

Weep [a]between the porch and the altar,
And let them say, "[b]Spare Thy people, O LORD,
And do not make Thine inheritance a [c]reproach,
A byword among the nations.
Why should they among the peoples say,
'[d]Where is their God?' "

18 Then the LORD [1]will be [a]zealous for His land,
And [2]will have [b]pity on His people.
19 And the LORD [1]will answer and say to His people,
"Behold, I am going to [a]send you grain, new wine, and oil,
And you will be satisfied *in full* with [2]them;
And I will [b]never again make you a reproach among the nations.
20 "But I will remove the [a]northern *army* far from you,
And I will drive it into a parched and desolate land,
And its vanguard into the [b]eastern sea,
And its rear guard into the [c]western sea.
And its [d]stench will arise and its foul smell will come up,
For it has done great things."

21 [a]Do not fear, O land, rejoice and be glad,
For the LORD has done [b]great things.
22 Do not fear, beasts of the field,
For the [a]pastures of the wilderness have turned green,
For the tree has borne its fruit,
The fig tree and the vine have yielded [1]in full.
23 So rejoice, O [a]sons of Zion,
And [b]be glad in the LORD your God;
For He has [c]given you [1]the early rain for *your* vindication.
And He has poured down for you the rain,
The [2]early and [3d]latter rain [4]as before.
24 And the threshing floors will be full of grain,
And the vats will [a]overflow with the new wine and oil.
25 "Then I will make up to you for the years
That the swarming [a]locust has eaten,
The creeping locust, the stripping locust, and the gnawing locust,
My great army which I sent among you.
26 "And you shall have plenty to [a]eat and be satisfied,
And [b]praise the name of the LORD your God,
Who has [c]dealt wondrously with you;
Then My people will [d]never be put to shame.
27 "Thus you will [a]know that I am in the midst of Israel,
And that I am the LORD your God
And there is [b]no other;
And My people will never be [c]put to shame.

28 "[1a]And it will come about after this
That I will [b]pour out My Spirit on all [2c]mankind;
And your sons and daughters will prophesy,
Your old men will dream dreams,
Your young men will see visions.
29 "And even on the [a]male and female servants
I will pour out My Spirit in those days.

17 [a]2 Chr. 8:1
8:16 [b]Ex. 32:1
37:20; Amos 7
44:13; 74:10
42:10; 79:10; 1

18 [1]Or, *was z*
[2]Or, *had pity* [a]
1:14; 8:2 [b]Is. 6
63:9, 15

19 [1]Or, *answe*
said [2]Lit., *it* [a]J
Hos. 2:21, 22;
Mal. 3:10 [b]Eze
36:15

20 [a]Jer. 1:14, 1
[b]Zech. 14:8 [c]D
11:24 [d]Is. 34:3,
4:10

21 [a]Is. 54:4; Je
Zeph. 3:16, 17
126:3; Joel 2:26

22 [1]Lit., *their w*
[a]Ps. 65:12, 13

23 [1]I.e., autumn
possibly, *the tea*
righteousness
autumn [3]I.e., sp
[4]So with ancient
versions; Heb.,
first [a]Ps. 149:2
12:2-6 [c]Deut. 11
41:16; Jer. 5:24;
3:18; Zech. 10:7
26:4; Hos. 6:3; Z
10:1

24 [a]Lev. 26:10;
9:13; Mal. 3:10

25 [a]Joel 1:4-7; 2

26 [a]Lev. 26:5; D
11:15; Is. 62:9 [b]D
12:7; Ps. 67:5-7
126:2, 3; Is. 25:1
45:17

27 [a]Lev. 26:11, 1
3:17, 21 [b]Is. 45:5
49:23

28 [1]Ch. 3:1 in He
[2]Lit., *flesh* [a]Acts
2:17-21 [b]Is. 32:15
44:3; Ezek. 39:29
12:10 [c]Is. 40:5; 4

29 [a]1 Cor. 12:13;
3:28

tt. 24:29; Mark
5; Luke 21:11,
, 26; Acts 2:19

:10; 34:4; Joel
5; Matt. 24:29;
4; Luke 21:25;
; Rev. 6:12, 13
Zeph. 1:14-16;
Mal. 4:1, 5

3:3; Acts 2:21;
:13 [b]Is. 46:13;
11:26 [c]Is. 4:2;
. 17 [d]Is. 11:11;
Mic. 4:7; Rom.
9:27

Ch. 4:1 in Heb.
:3; Ezek. 38:14
[b]Jer. 16:15

YHWH judges
6:18; Mic. 4:12;
4:2 [b]Joel 3:12,
[c]Is. 66:16; Jer.
31; Ezek. 38:22
:17; Ezek. 34:6
k. 35:10; 36:1-5

, *Given* [a]Obad.
3:10 [b]Amos 2:6

. 23:1-18; Amos
10; Zech. 9:2-4;
11:21, 22; Luke
4 [b]Is. 14:29-31;
er. 47:1-7; Ezek.
17; Amos 1:6-8;
9:5-7 [c]Is. 34:8;
59:18

t., *goodly things*
in. 12:18; 2 Chr.
21:16, 17

t., *sons of Javan*
[a]Ezek. 27:13

3:5, 6; Jer. 23:8;
Zech. 9:13

4:2; 60:14 [b]Job
Ps. 72:10; Ezek.
38:13

. 51:27 [b]Jer. 6:4;
8:7; Mic. 3:5 [c]Is.
, 10; Jer. 46:3, 4;
Zech. 14:2, 3

[a]Is. 2:4; Mic. 4:3
[b]Zech. 12:8

11 [1]Or, *Lend aid*
ek. 38:15, 16 [b]Is.
13:3

e., YHWH judges
3:2, 14 [b]Ps. 7:6;
98:9; Is. 2:4; 3:13

ev. 14:14-19 [b]Jer.
; Hos. 6:11 [c]Rev.
19, 20; 19:15 [d]Is.
Lam. 1:15 [e]Gen.
18:20

30 "And I will [a]display wonders in the sky and on the earth,
Blood, fire, and columns of smoke.
31 "The [a]sun will be turned into darkness,
And the moon into blood,
Before the [b]great and awesome day of the LORD comes.
32 "And it will come about that [a]whoever calls on the name of the
LORD
Will be delivered;
For [b]on Mount Zion and in Jerusalem
There will be those who [c]escape,
As the LORD has said,
Even among the [d]survivors whom the LORD calls.

Chapter 3

3 "[1]For behold, [a]in those days and at that time,
When I [b]restore the fortunes of Judah and Jerusalem,
2 I will [a]gather all the nations,
And bring them down to the [b]valley of [1]Jehoshaphat.
Then I will [c]enter into judgment with them there
On behalf of My people and My inheritance, Israel,
Whom they have [d]scattered among the nations;
And they have [e]divided up My land.
3 "They have also [a]cast lots for My people,
[1b]Traded a boy for a harlot,
And sold a girl for wine that they may drink.
4 "Moreover, what are you to Me, O [a]Tyre, Sidon, and all the
regions of [b]Philistia? Are you rendering Me a recompense? But if you
do recompense Me, swiftly and speedily I will [c]return your recom-
pense on your head.
5 "Since you have [a]taken My silver and My gold, brought My pre-
cious [1]treasures to your temples,
6 and sold the [a]sons of Judah and Jerusalem to the [1]Greeks in order
to remove them far from their territory,
7 behold, I am going to [a]arouse them from the place where you
have sold them, and return your recompense on your head.
8 "Also I will [a]sell your sons and your daughters into the hand of
the sons of Judah, and they will sell them to the [b]Sabeans, to a dis-
tant nation," for the LORD has spoken.
9 [a]Proclaim this among the nations:
[b]Prepare a war; [c]rouse the mighty men!
Let all the soldiers draw near, let them come up!
10 [a]Beat your plowshares into swords,
And your pruning hooks into spears;
[b]Let the weak say, "I am a mighty man."
11 [1a]Hasten and come, all you surrounding nations,
And gather yourselves there.
Bring down, O LORD, Thy [b]mighty ones.
12 Let the nations be aroused
And come up to the [a]valley of [1]Jehoshaphat,
For there I will sit to [b]judge
All the surrounding nations.
13 [a]Put in the sickle, for the [b]harvest is ripe.
Come, [c]tread, for the [d]wine press is full;
The vats overflow, for their [e]wickedness is great.

INSIGHT

Sabeans are the descendants of Seba, the son of Cush or possibly of Sheba, the son of Raamah (see Genesis 10:7). Sabeans destroyed Job's flocks, herds, and servants. They were known as traveling merchants. The term *Sabeans* could have been adapted to refer to foreign or nomadic merchants.

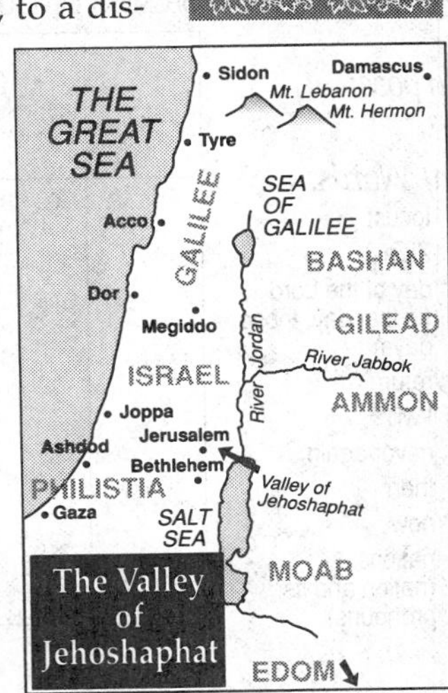

The Valley of Jehoshaphat

14 [a]Multitudes, multitudes in the [b]valley of [1]decision!
For the [c]day of the LORD is near in the valley of [1]decision.
15 The [a]sun and moon grow dark,
And the stars lose their brightness.
16 And the LORD [a]roars from Zion
And [b]utters His voice from Jerusalem,
And the [c]heavens and the earth tremble.
But the LORD is a [d]refuge for His people
And a [e]stronghold to the sons of Israel.
17 Then you will [a]know that I am the LORD your God,
Dwelling in Zion My [b]holy mountain.
So Jerusalem will be [c]holy,
And [d]strangers will pass through it no more.

18 And it will come about in that day
That the [a]mountains will drip with [1]sweet wine,
And the hills will [b]flow with milk,
And all the [c]brooks of Judah will flow with water;
And a [d]spring will go out from the house of the LORD,
To water the valley of [2]Shittim.
19 Egypt will become a waste,
And Edom will become a desolate wilderness,
Because of the [a]violence [1]done to the sons of Judah,
In whose land they have shed innocent blood.
20 But Judah will be [a]inhabited forever,
And Jerusalem for all generations.
21 And I will [a]avenge their blood which I have not avenged,
For the LORD dwells in Zion.

14 [1]I.e., God's [a]Is. 34:2-8 [b]Joe 12 [c]Joel 1:15; 11, 31

15 [a]Joel 2:10,

16 [a]Hos. 11:10 1:2 [b]Joel 2:11 38:19; Joel 2:10 2:6 [d]Ps. 61:3; I Jer. 17:17 [e]Jer. Nah. 1:7

17 [a]Joel 2:27 56:7; Ezek. 20: 4:3; Obad. 17 [d] Nah. 1:15

18 [1]Lit., *freshly out grape juice acacias* [a]Amos [b]Ex. 3:8 [c]Is. 30: 35:6 [d]Ezek. 47:

19 [1]Lit., *of the s* [a]Obad. 10

20 [a]Ezek. 37:25 9:15

21 [a]Is. 4:4

JOEL AT A GLANCE

Theme of Joel:

Author:

Date:

Purpose:

Key Words:
- locust
- Zion
- day of the Lord (in that day, those days)
- return
- I will
- never again
- then
- now
- nations (nation and its pronouns)

SEGMENT DIVISIONS

		CHAPTER THEMES
		1
		2
		3

JOEL OBSERVATIONS CHART

What Happens to the People	What the People Are to Do	What Is the Effect on People

What Happens to the Land Before and During Judgment	What Happens to the Land After Judgment

What Will Happen to the Animals

What Happens to the Nations and Why

How Will God Respond

AMOS

While the cows of Bashan (the best of breeds raised in Canaan) grazed and were pampered i northern Transjordan, the Israelites of the northern kingdom went up to worship at Bethel. Th Bethel the higher echelon would burn incense and present their sacrifices at the altar.

Bethel was the place where Jeroboam I, the first king of Israel (the northern kingdom), had set u golden calves (1 Kings 12-13). He felt he had to. When the twelve tribes divided into two kingd those of the northern kingdom were cut off from Jerusalem. Jerusalem now belonged to the two t of the southern kingdom, Judah and Benjamin. If Jeroboam's people went to celebrate the feas Jerusalem at the temple as God commanded, they might defect to the southern kingdom.

So Jeroboam commissioned his own priests and instituted his own feast. The people would wo as they pleased, where they pleased. Those who did not go to Bethel could go to Gilgal, an principal place of worship. In Gilgal they could present their thank offerings with leaven, proc their free-will offerings, and even worship other gods.

Israel became prosperous, politically secure. Jeroboam I died and Jeroboam II reigned. It w golden era. Surely God was pleased with Israel—or that's what they supposed until a shepherd the small city of Tekoa just ten miles south of Jerusalem appeared on the scene.

Then the Word of the Lord came.

THINGS TO DO

General Instructions

In order to understand the historical setting of Amos, do the following:

1. Read Amos 1:1 and then record what you learn about Amos on the AMOS AT A GLANCE c on page 1345 under "Author." Then under "Date" record the information that gives you a cl to the time of these visions (*see* Zechariah 14:5). Under "Purpose" fill in Amos's reason for wr (*see* Amos 1:1).
2. Study the historical chart on page 1334 which shows Amos's relationship to the kings of Is and Judah. Remember Amos is a prophet to the northern kingdom.
3. Read 2 Chronicles 26:1-23 and 2 Kings 14:23 through 15:7. When you come across Aza remember this is another name for King Uzziah, who ruled over the southern kingdom.

As you read through Amos, you'll find three key phrases which divide the book into t segments. Therefore your instructions will be divided accordingly.

Chapters 1-2

1. Read Amos 1 and 2 and mark each occurrence of the phrase *Thus says the Lord, for three trans sions of* _________ *and for four.* Note whose transgressions God is going to deal with in e incident.
2. Read what follows each of the statements you have marked. Look for another key repea phrase, then mark or color it in a distinctive way.
3. Then observe why God will not revoke their punishment and what the punishment will be. N their punishment by marking each occurrence of *I will.*
4. In 2:4,6 God deals with the southern kingdom, Judah, and with the northern kingdom, Israel understand why God speaks to them separately, look at Amos 1:1 and notice to whom Amos sent as a prophet. (This information is also on the historical chart on page 1334 under Am name.) It's important to keep this in mind as you study the rest of Amos.

5. Record the theme of the first two chapters on AMOS AT A GLANCE and in the text next to the chapter numbers.

apters 3-6

1. The second key repeated phrase is *hear this word*. Read Amos 3 through 6 and distinctively mark each occurrence of this phrase. Also mark every *Israel* (and every reference to Israel throughout Amos). Then list in the margin all you learn from marking *Israel*.
2. Read Amos 3 through 6 a second time, chapter by chapter. As you read these messages from the Lord, ask the five W's and an H. Ask questions such as: Who is speaking? To whom? What is being said? What is going to happen? When will it happen? Where will it take place? Why will it happen? How will it happen? (Remember, you won't always find answers to every question.)
3. Mark in a distinctive way key repeated words or phrases. For instance, marking every *I will* as it refers to God and asking the five W's and an H will help you see what God is going to do. Watch for *yet* in chapter 4 and *seek* in chapter 5. Mark every reference to *the day of the Lord*. Then in the margin list everything you learn about this day.
4. In the margin list important insights about God, Israel, what the people are doing wrong, and what they don't like.
5. When you finish studying a chapter, decide on the theme or topic of that chapter and record it on AMOS AT A GLANCE and in the text next to the chapter number.

apters 7-9

1. The key repeated phrase which sets off the last segment of Amos is *thus the Lord God showed me*. Read these last three chapters and distinctively mark each occurrence of this phrase.
2. As you read through this final segment of Amos, watch what Amos was shown, and how he responds. Also observe the response to Amos's prophecy and how Amos deals with this.
3. In chapter 8 you see one final *hear this*. Pay careful attention to what God is going to do. Compare 8:8 with 1:1.
4. Although the phrase *thus the Lord God showed me* is not used in 9:1, can you see that *I saw the Lord . . . and He said* could be Amos's fifth vision, which parallels those you marked in chapters 7 through 9? If so, mark it as you did the others.
5. Mark the *I wills* of God and any other key words or phrases.
6. In the chapter margins record your insights about God and Israel.
7. Record the chapter themes as you did before and complete AMOS AT A GLANCE. Make sure you also record the theme of Amos.
8. In the appendix of this Bible you will find the chart called THE DAY OF THE LORD (page 1878). Record your insights from Amos on the day of the Lord on this chart. As you do, note the reference (book, chapter, and verse) from which you took your information so you can find it later.
9. Finally, watch the closing words of Amos. What is God's promise? Remember any reference to the land. Has this promise regarding the land of Israel been fulfilled? Think of Israel's history. In the section called "Major Events in Israel's History," read "From Christ to the 1990s" on page I-42. Then answer the question.

INGS TO THINK ABOUT

1. Has wealth, the ease of life, the possession of things, the pursuit of happiness led to complacency in your worship? Are you worshiping God His way or your way?
2. As you review the list of Israel's sins, are you guilty of any? According to what you read in Amos, could Israel or the other nations sin and not reap the consequences? Can you?
3. What is the purpose of God's judgments? When God decides to judge, what can we do? What can we expect?

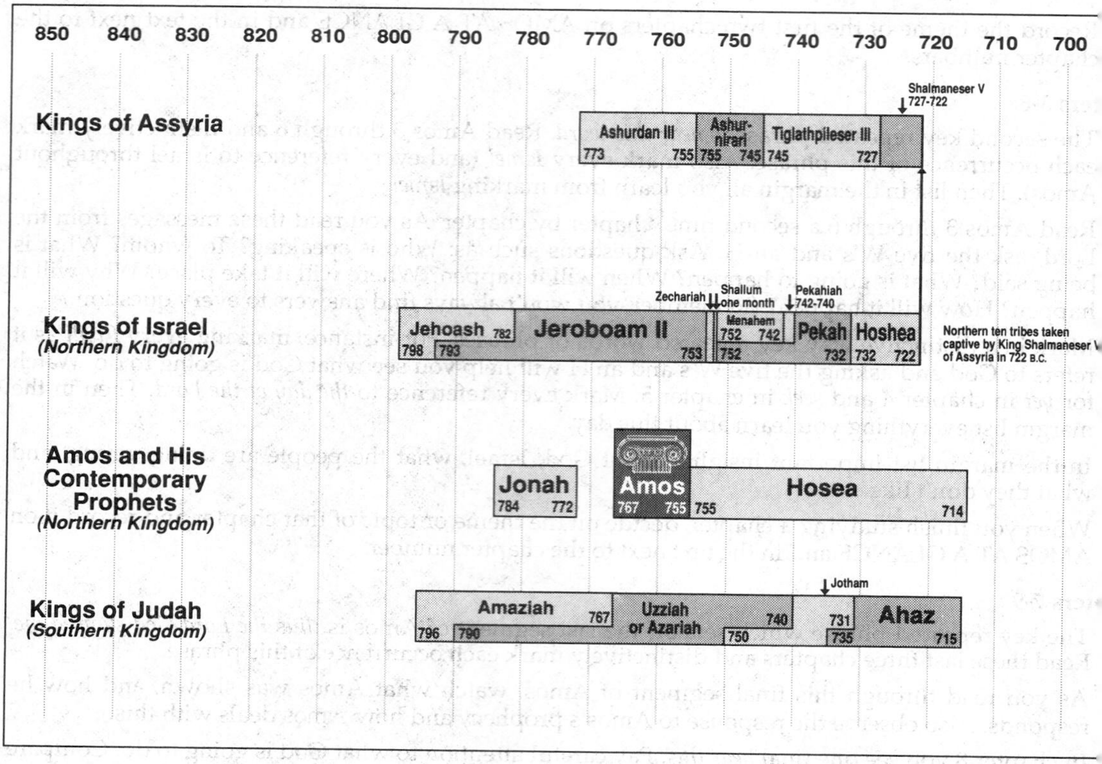

Chapter 1

1 The words of Amos, who was among the [a]sheepherders from
[b]Tekoa, which he [1]envisioned in visions concerning Israel in the
days of [c]Uzziah king of Judah, and in the days of [d]Jeroboam son of
Joash, king of Israel, two years before the [e]earthquake.

2 And he said,
"The [a]LORD roars from Zion,
And from Jerusalem He utters His voice;
And the shepherds' [b]pasture grounds mourn,
And the [1c]summit of Carmel dries up."

3 Thus says the LORD,
"For [a]three transgressions of [b]Damascus and for four
I will not [1]revoke its *punishment*,
Because they threshed Gilead with *implements* of sharp iron.
4 "So I will send fire upon the house of Hazael,
And it will consume the citadels of [a]Ben-hadad.
5 "I will also [a]break the *gate* bar of Damascus,
And cut off the inhabitant from the [1]valley of Aven,
And him who holds the scepter, from Beth-eden;
So the people of Aram will go exiled to [b]Kir,"
Says the LORD.

6 Thus says the LORD,
"For three transgressions of [a]Gaza and for four
I will not revoke its *punishment*,

1:1 [1]Lit., *saw concerning* [a]Am 7:14 [b]2 Sam. 14 6:1 [c]2 Chr. 26:1- 1:1 [d]2 Kin. 14:23 Hos. 1:1; Amos 7 11 [e]Zech. 14:5

2 [1]Lit., *head* [a]Is Jer. 25:30; Joel 3 [b]Jer. 12:4; Joel 1 [c]Amos 9:3

3 [1]Lit., *cause it to back*, and so thro the ch. [a]Amos 2: [b]Is. 8:4; 17:1-3; J 49:23-27; Zech. 9

4 [a]1 Kin. 20:1; 2 6:24

5 [1]Possibly, *Baal* [a]Jer. 51:30; Lam. [b]2 Kin. 16:9; Amo

6 [a]1 Sam. 6:17; J 47:1, 5; Zeph. 2:4

zek. 35:5; Obad. 11

Because they deported an entire population
To [b]deliver *it* up to Edom.
7 "So I will send fire upon the wall of Gaza,
And it will consume her citadels.
8 "I will also cut off the inhabitant from [a]Ashdod,
And him who holds the scepter, from [b]Ashkelon;
I will even [1]unleash My [2]power upon Ekron,
And the remnant of the [c]Philistines will perish,"
Says the Lord [3]GOD.

Lit., *cause to return* [2]Lit., *hand* [3]Heb., *YHWH*, usually ıered *LORD* [a]2 Chr. 6; Amos 3:9; Zech. 6 [b]Jer. 47:5; Zeph. [c]Is. 14:29-31; Jer. 7:1-7; Ezek. 25:16; 3:4-8; Zeph. 2:4-7; Zech. 9:5-7

9 Thus says the LORD,
"For three transgressions of [a]Tyre and for four
I will not revoke its *punishment*,
Because they delivered up an entire population to
Edom
And did not remember *the* covenant of [1b]brotherhood.
10 "So I will [a]send fire upon the wall of Tyre,
And it will consume her citadels."

[1]Lit., *brothers* [a]Is. 23:1-18; Jer. 25:22; 26:2-4; Joel 3:4-8; 9:1-4; Matt. 11:21, 22; Luke 10:13, 14 [b]1 Kin. 9:11-14

10 [a]Zech. 9:4

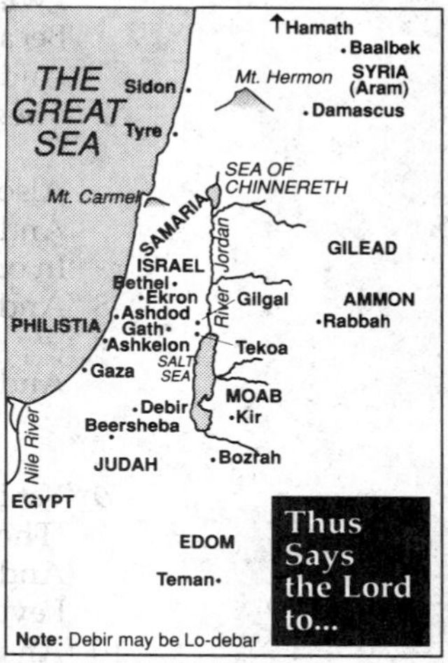

11 Thus says the LORD,
"For three transgressions of [a]Edom and for four
I will not revoke its *punishment*,
Because he [b]pursued his brother with the sword,
While he [1]stifled his compassion;
His anger also [c]tore continually,
And he maintained his fury forever.
12 "So I will send fire upon [a]Teman,
And it will consume the citadels of Bozrah."

[1]Lit., *corrupted* [a]Is. 34:5, 6; 63:1-6; Jer. 49:7-22; Ezek. 25:12-14; 35:1-15; ıd. 1-14; Mal. 1:2-5 n. 20:14-21; 2 Chr. ; Obad. 10-12 [c]Is. 57:16; Mic. 7:18

12 [a]Jer. 49:7, 20; Obad. 9

13 Thus says the LORD,
"For three transgressions of the sons of [a]Ammon and for four
I will not revoke its *punishment*,
Because they [b]ripped open the pregnant women of Gilead
In order to [c]enlarge their borders.
14 "So I will kindle a fire on the wall of [a]Rabbah,
And it will consume her citadels
Amid [1b]war cries on the day of battle
And a [c]storm on the day of tempest.
15 "Their [a]king will go into exile,
He and his princes together," says the LORD.

[a]Jer. 49:1-6; Ezek. 3-32; 25:2-7; Zeph. 8, 9 [b]2 Kin. 15:16; Hos. 13:16 [c]Is. 5:8; Ezek. 35:10

[1]Or, *shouts* [a]Deut. 1; 1 Chr. 20:1; Jer. 49:2 [b]Ezek. 21:22; Amos 2:2 [c]Is. 29:6; 30:30

15 [a]Jer. 49:3

Chapter 2

2 Thus says the LORD,
"For three transgressions of [a]Moab and for four
I will not [1]revoke its *punishment*,
Because he [b]burned the bones of the king of Edom to lime.
2 "So I will send fire upon Moab,
And it will consume the citadels of [a]Kerioth;
And Moab will die amid [b]tumult,
With [1]war cries and the sound of a trumpet.
3 "I will also cut off the [1a]judge from her midst,
And slay all her [b]princes with him," says the LORD.

4 Thus says the LORD,

Lit., *cause it to turn* and so throughout ch. [a]Is. 15:1-16:14; 0-12; Jer. 48:1-47; Ezek. 25:8-11; Zeph. 9 [b]2 Kin. 3:26, 27

[1]Or, *shouts* [a]Jer. 24, 41 [b]Jer. 48:45

r, *executive officer* 2:10; 141:6; Amos 5:7, 12; 6:12 [b]Job 12:21; Is. 40:23

"For three transgressions of [a]Judah and for four
I will not revoke its *punishment*,
Because they [b]rejected the law of the LORD
And have not kept His statutes;
Their [1c]lies also have led them astray,
Those after which their [d]fathers walked.
5 "So I will [a]send fire upon Judah,
And it will consume the citadels of Jerusalem."

6 Thus says the LORD,
"For three transgressions of [a]Israel and for four
I will not revoke its *punishment*,
Because they [b]sell the righteous for money
And the needy for a pair of sandals.
7 "These who [1]pant after the *very* dust of the earth on the head of the [a]helpless
Also [b]turn aside the way of the humble;
And a [c]man and his father [2]resort to the same [3]girl
In order to profane My holy name.
8 "And on garments [a]taken as pledges they stretch out beside [b]every altar,
And in the house of their God they [c]drink the wine of those who have been fined.

9 "Yet it was I who destroyed the [a]Amorite before them,
[1]Though his [b]height *was* like the height of cedars
And he *was* strong as the oaks;
I even destroyed his [c]fruit above and his root below.
10 "And it was I who [a]brought you up from the land of Egypt,
And I led you in the wilderness [b]forty years
[1]That you might take possession of the land of the [c]Amorite.
11 "Then I [a]raised up some of your sons to be prophets
And some of your young men to be [b]Nazirites.
Is this not so, O sons of Israel?" declares the LORD.
12 "But you made the Nazirites drink wine,
And you commanded the prophets saying, 'You [a]shall not prophesy!'
13 "Behold, I am [1a]weighted down beneath you
As a wagon [2]is weighted down when filled with sheaves.
14 "[1a]Flight will perish from the swift,
And the stalwart will not strengthen his power,
Nor the [b]mighty man save his [2]life.
15 "He who [a]grasps the bow will not stand *his ground*,
The swift of foot will not escape,
Nor will he who rides the [b]horse save his [1]life.
16 "Even the [1]bravest among the warriors will [a]flee naked in that day," declares the LORD.

Chapter 3

3 Hear this word which the LORD has spoken against you, sons of
Israel, against the entire [1a]family which [2]He brought up from the
land of Egypt,
2 "[a]You only have I [1]chosen among all the families of the earth;
Therefore, I will [2b]punish you for all your iniquities."

4 [1]Or, *false g* [a]2 Kin. 17:19; Amos 3:2 [b]Ju 2:17-20; 2 Kin 22:11-17; Jer. [c]Is. 9:15, 16; 2 16:19; Hab. 2 9:14; 16:11, 1 20:18, 24, 30

5 [a]Jer. 17:27; Hos. 8:14

6 [a]2 Kin. 18:11 [b]Joel 3:3; Amo 12; 8:6

7 [1]Or, *trample at the head of helpless on the* [2]Lit., *go* [3]Poss harlot, or a tem prostitute [a]Am Mic. 2:2, 9 [b]Ar [c]Hos. 4:14

8 [a]Ex. 22:26 [b] 3:14 [c]Amos 4:

9 [1]Lit., *Whose* [a]Num. 21:23-25 10:12 [b]Num. 1 [c]Ezek. 17:9; Ma

10 [1]Lit., *To pos* [a]Ex. 12:51; 20:2 3:1; 9:7 [b]Deut. 3:8

11 [a]Deut. 18:18 7:25 [b]Num. 6:2, Judg. 13:5

12 [a]Is. 30:10; Je 11:21; Amos 7:1 Mic. 2:6

13 [1]Or, *tottering totters* [a]Is. 1:14

14 [1]Or, *A place refuge* [2]Lit., *sou* 30:16, 17 [b]Ps. 3 Jer. 9:23

15 [1]Lit., *soul* [a]Je 51:56; Ezek. 39:3 31:3

16 [1]Lit., *stout of* [a]Judg. 4:17

3:1 [1]I.e., nation [a]Jer. 8:3; 13:11

2 [1]Lit., *known* [2]L *visit* [a]Gen. 18:19; 19:5, 6; Deut. 4:32 7:6 [b]Jer. 14:10; E 20:36; Dan. 9:12; 2:9

3 Do two men walk together unless they have made an
[1]appointment?
4 Does a [a]lion roar in the forest when he has no prey?
Does a young lion [1]growl from his den unless he has captured
something?
5 Does a bird fall into a trap on the ground when there is no [1]bait
in it?
Does a trap spring up from the earth when it captures nothing
at all?
6 If a [a]trumpet is blown in a city will not the people tremble?
If a [b]calamity occurs in a city has not the LORD done it?
7 [1]Surely the Lord [2]GOD does nothing
Unless He [a]reveals His secret counsel
To His servants the prophets.
8 A [a]lion has roared! Who will not fear?
The [b]Lord [1]GOD has spoken! [c]Who can but prophesy?
9 Proclaim on the citadels in [a]Ashdod and on the citadels in the
land of Egypt and say, "Assemble yourselves on the [b]mountains of
Samaria and see *the* great tumults within her and *the* [c]oppressions in
her midst.
10 "But they [a]do not know how to do what is right," declares the
LORD, "these who [b]hoard up [1]violence and devastation in their
citadels."
11 Therefore, thus says the Lord GOD,
"An [a]enemy, even one surrounding the land,
Will pull down your [1]strength from you
And your [b]citadels will be looted."
12 Thus says the LORD,
"Just as the shepherd [1a]snatches from the lion's mouth a couple of
legs or a piece of an ear,
So will the sons of Israel dwelling in Samaria be [2]snatched
away—
With *the* [b]corner of a bed and *the* [3c]cover of a couch!
13 "Hear and [a]testify against the house of Jacob,"
Declares the Lord GOD, the God of hosts.
14 "For on the day that I punish Israel's transgressions,
I will also punish the altars of [a]Bethel;
The horns of the altar will be cut off,
And they will fall to the ground.
15 "I will also smite the [1a]winter house together with the [b]summer
house;
The houses of [2c]ivory will also perish
And the [d]great houses will come to an end,"
Declares the LORD.

Chapter 4

4 Hear this word, you cows of [a]Bashan who are on the [b]mountain
of Samaria,
Who [c]oppress the poor, who crush the needy,
Who say to [1]your husbands, "Bring now, that we may [d]drink!"
2 The Lord [1]GOD has [a]sworn by His [b]holiness,
"Behold, the days are coming upon you
When [2]they will take you away with [c]meat hooks,
And the last of you with [d]fish hooks.

Or, *agreement*

give his voice 21; Hos. 5:14; 11:10

striker-bar set

:5, 19, 21; 6:1; 5:8; Zeph. 1:16 14:24-27; 45:7

[1]Or, *For* [2]Heb., *YH* [a]Gen. 6:13; Jer. 23:22; Dan. 22; John 15:15

[1]Heb., *YHWH*, rendered *LORD*, throughout the Amos 1:2 [b]Jon. :1-3 [c]Jer. 20:9; Acts 4:20

am. 5:1 [b]Amos [c]Amos 5:11; 8:6

, the booty from [a]Ps. 14:4; Jer. Amos 5:7; 6:12 8-10; Zeph. 1:9; Zech. 5:3, 4

[1]Or, *stronghold* 6:14 [b]Amos 2:5

Or, *delivers* [2]Or, *ed* [3]Lit., *damask* 1. 17:34-37 [b]Ps. [c]Esth. 1:6; 7:8; Amos 6:4

13 [a]Ezek. 2:7

Kin. 23:15; Hos. -8, 14, 15; Amos ; 5:5, 6; 7:10, 13

Or, *autumn* [2]I.e., inlay [a]Jer. 36:22 udg. 3:20 [c]1 Kin. ; Ps. 45:8 [d]Amos 2:5; 6:11

1 [1]Lit., *their lords* 2:12; Ezek. 39:18 s 3:9; 6:1 [c]Amos 6 [d]Amos 2:8; 6:6

2 [1]Heb., *YHWH*, y rendered *LORD*, so throughout the it., *he* [a]Amos 6:8; :7 [b]Ps. 89:35 [c]Is. ; Ezek. 38:4 [d]Jer. ; Ezek. 29:4; Hab. 1:15

3 "You will [a]go out *through* breaches *in the walls,*
Each one straight before her,
And you [1]will be cast to Harmon," declares the LORD.

4 "Enter Bethel and transgress;
In Gilgal multiply transgression!
[a]Bring your sacrifices every morning,
Your tithes every three days.
5 "[1]Offer a [a]thank offering also from that which is leavened,
And proclaim [b]freewill offerings, make them known.
For so you [c]love *to do,* you sons of Israel,"
Declares the Lord GOD.

6 "But I gave you also [a]cleanness of teeth in all your cities
And lack of bread in all your places,
Yet you have [b]not returned to Me," declares the LORD.
7 "And furthermore, I [a]withheld the rain from you
While *there were* still three months until harvest.
Then I would send rain on one city
And on [b]another city I would not send rain;
One part would be rained on,
While the part not rained on would dry up.
8 "So two or three cities would stagger to another city to drink
[a]water,
But would [b]not be satisfied;
Yet you have [c]not returned to Me," declares the LORD.
9 "I [a]smote you with scorching *wind* and mildew;
And the [b]caterpillar was devouring
Your many gardens and vineyards, fig trees and olive trees;
Yet you have [c]not returned to Me," declares the LORD.
10 "I sent a [a]plague among you after the manner of Egypt;
I [b]slew your young men by the sword along with your [c]captured
horses,
And I made the [d]stench of your camp rise up in your nostrils;
Yet you have [e]not returned to Me," declares the LORD.
11 "I overthrew you as [a]God overthrew Sodom and Gomorrah,
And you were like a [b]firebrand snatched from a blaze;
Yet you have [c]not returned to Me," declares the LORD.
12 "Therefore, thus I will do to you, O Israel;
Because I shall do this to you,
Prepare to [a]meet your God, O Israel."
13 For behold, He who [a]forms mountains and [b]creates the wind
And [c]declares to man what are His thoughts,
He who [d]makes dawn into darkness
And [e]treads on the high places of the earth,
[f]The LORD God of hosts is His name.

Chapter 5

5 Hear this word which I take up for you as a [a]dirge, O house of
Israel.
2 She has fallen, she will [a]not rise again—
The [b]virgin Israel.
She *lies* neglected on her land;
There is [c]none to raise her up.

3 [1]So Gr.; M.T. *will cast* [a]Jer.

4 [a]Num. 28:3; 5:21, 22

5 [1]Lit., *Offer up smoke* [a]Lev. 7: 22:18-21 [c]Jer. Hos. 9:1, 10

6 [a]Is. 3:1; Jer. [b]Is. 9:13; Jer. 5 2:17

7 [a]Deut. 11:17; 7:13; Is. 5:6 [b]E 26; 10:22, 23

8 [a]1 Kin. 18:5; 14:4 [b]Ezek. 4:1 Hag. 1:6 [c]Jer. 3

9 [a]Deut. 28:22; 2:17 [b]Joel 1:4, 7 7:1, 2 [c]Jer. 3:10

10 [a]Ex. 9:3; Lev. Deut. 28:27, 60; 78:50 [b]Jer. 11:22 18:21; 48:15 [c]2 13:3, 7 [d]Joel 2:2 9:13

11 [a]Gen. 19:24, Deut. 29:23; Is. 1 [b]Zech. 3:2 [c]Jer. 2

12 [a]Is. 32:11; 64: 5:22

13 [a]Job 38:4-7; P 65:6; Is. 40:12 [b]P 135:7; Jer. 10:13 2:28, 30 [d]Jer. 13: Joel 2:2; Amos 5:8 [e]Mic. 1:3 [f]Is. 47:4 10:16; Amos 5:8,

5:1 [a]Jer. 7:29; 9:1 Ezek. 19:1

2 [a]Amos 8:14 [b]J 14:17 [c]Is. 51:18; 50:32

3 For thus says the Lord [1]GOD,
"The city which goes forth a thousand *strong*
Will have a [a]hundred left,
And the one which goes forth a hundred *strong*
Will have [b]ten left to the house of Israel."

4 For thus says the LORD to the house of Israel,
"[a]Seek Me [b]that you may live.
5 "But do not [1]resort to [a]Bethel,
And do not come to [b]Gilgal,
Nor cross over to [c]Beersheba;
For Gilgal will certainly go into captivity,
And Bethel will [2]come to trouble.
6 "[a]Seek the LORD that you may live,
Lest He break forth like a [b]fire, [1]O house of Joseph,
And it consume with none to quench *it* for Bethel,
7 *For* those who turn [a]justice into wormwood
And [1]cast righteousness down to the earth."

8 He who made the [a]Pleiades and Orion
And [b]changes deep darkness into morning,
[1]Who also [c]darkens day *into* night,
Who [d]calls for the waters of the sea
And pours them out on the surface of the earth,
The [e]LORD is His name.
9 It is He who [a]flashes forth *with* destruction upon the strong,
So that [b]destruction comes upon the fortress.

10 They hate him who [a]reproves in the [1]gate,
And they [b]abhor him who speaks *with* integrity.
11 Therefore, because you [1]impose heavy rent on the poor
And exact a tribute of grain from them,
Though you have built [a]houses of well-hewn stone,
Yet you will not live in them;
You have planted pleasant vineyards, yet you will [b]not drink
their wine.
12 For I know your transgressions are many and your sins are
great,
You who [a]distress the righteous *and* accept bribes,
And [1]turn aside the poor in the [2]gate.
13 Therefore, at [1]such a time the prudent person [a]keeps silent, for it
is an evil time.

14 Seek good and not evil, that you may live;
And thus may the LORD God of hosts be with you,
[a]Just as you have said!
15 [a]Hate evil, love good,
And establish justice in the [1]gate!
Perhaps the LORD God of hosts
[b]May be gracious to the [c]remnant of Joseph.

16 Therefore, thus says the LORD God of hosts, the Lord,
"There is [a]wailing in all the plazas,
And in all the streets they say, 'Alas! Alas!'

3 [1]Heb., *YHWH*, ...ally rendered *LORD*, ...d so throughout the ... [a]Is. 6:13 [b]Amos 6:9

[a]Deut. 4:29; 32:46, Jer. 29:13 [b]Is. 55:3

5 [1]Lit., *seek* [2]Or, ...*ome iniquity* [a]1 Kin. ...:28, 29; Amos 3:14; ...4; 7:10, 13 [b]1 Sam. ...7:16; 11:14 [c]Gen. ...1:31-33; Amos 8:14

...Or, *in the house* [a]Is. ...5:3, 6, 7; Amos 5:14 [b]Deut. 4:24

[1]Lit., *they have put* ...*wn* [a]Amos 2:3; 5:12; 6:12

8 [1]Lit., *And He darkened* [a]Job 9:9; 38:31 [b]Job 12:22; ...8:12; Is. 42:16 [c]Ps. ...04:20 [d]Ps. 104:6-9; ...nos 9:6 [e]Amos 4:13

[a]Is. 29:5; Amos 2:14 [b]Mic. 5:11

10 [1]I.e., the place ...here court was held ...s. 29:21; Amos 5:15 ...Kin. 22:8; Is. 59:15; Jer. 17:16-18

[1]Another reading is ...*ample upon* [a]Amos ...15; 6:11 [b]Mic. 6:15

[1]Lit., *they turn* [2]I.e., ...e place where court ...eld [a]Is. 1:23; 5:23; Amos 2:6

...Lit., *that time* [a]Eccl. 3:7; Hos. 4:4

14 [a]Mic. 3:11

15 [1]I.e., the place ...here court was held ...s. 97:10; Rom. 12:9 ...2:14 [c]Mic. 5:3, 7, 8

...6 [a]Jer. 9:10, 18-20; Amos 8:3

They also call the [b]farmer to mourning
And [1c]professional mourners to lamentation.
17 "And in all the [a]vineyards *there is* wailing,
Because I shall pass through the midst of you," says the LORD.

18 Alas, you who are longing for the [a]day of the LORD,
For what purpose *will* the day of the LORD *be* to you?
It *will be* [b]darkness and not light;
19 As when a man [a]flees from a lion,
And a bear meets him,
[1]Or goes home, leans his hand against the wall,
And a snake bites him.
20 *Will* not the day of the LORD *be* [a]darkness instead of light,
Even gloom with no brightness in it?

21 "I hate, I [a]reject your festivals,
Nor do I [1b]delight in your solemn assemblies.
22 "Even though you [a]offer up to Me burnt offerings and your grain offerings,
I will not accept *them;*
And I will not *even* look at the [b]peace offerings of your fatlings.
23 "Take away from Me the noise of your songs;
I will not even listen to the sound of your harps.
24 "But let [a]justice roll down like waters
And righteousness like an ever-flowing stream.
25 "[1a]Did you present Me with sacrifices and grain offerings in the
wilderness for forty years, O house of Israel?
26 "[a]You also carried along [1]Sikkuth your king and [2]Kiyyun, your
images, [3]the star of your gods which you made for yourselves.
27 "Therefore, I will make you go into exile beyond Damascus," says
the LORD, whose name is the God of hosts.

Chapter 6

6 [a]Woe to those who are at ease in Zion,
And to those who *feel* secure in the mountain of Samaria,
The [b]distinguished men of the foremost of nations,
To whom the house of Israel comes.
2 Go over to [a]Calneh and look,
And go from there to [b]Hamath the great,
Then go down to [c]Gath of the Philistines.
Are [1]they better than these kingdoms,
Or is their territory greater than yours?
3 Do you [a]put off the day of calamity,
And would you [b]bring near the seat of violence?

4 Those who recline on beds of ivory
And sprawl on their [a]couches,
And [b]eat lambs from the flock
And calves from the midst of the stall,
5 Who improvise to the sound of the harp,
And like David have [1]composed [a]songs for themselves,
6 Who [a]drink wine from [1]sacrificial bowls
While they anoint themselves with the finest of oils,
Yet they have not [b]grieved over the ruin of Joseph.

16 [1]Lit., *those know lamenta* ... 1:11 [c]2 Chr. 3... 9:17

17 [a]Is. 16:10; ...

18 [a]Is. 5:19; J... Joel 1:15; 2:1, ... [b]Is. 5:30; Joel 2...

19 [1]Or, *Then* ... 20:24; Is. 24:17... 15:2, 3; 48:44

20 [a]Is. 13:10; ... 1:15

21 [1]Lit., *like to* ... [a]Is. 1:11-16; 66... 4:4, 5; 8:10 [b]Le... Jer. 14:12; Hos...

22 [a]Is. 66:3; Mi... [b]Lev. 7:11-15; A...

24 [a]Jer. 22:3; E... 45:9; Mic. 6:8

25 [1]Or, *You pre... Me with the sac... and a grain offe...* [a]Deut. 32:17; Jo... 24:14; Neh. 9:18... Acts 7:42, 43

26 [1]Or, *Sakkuth (Saturn) or shrin... your Moloch* [2]O... *Kaiwan (Saturn)... stands of* [3]Or, *y... gods* [a]Acts 7:43

6:1 [a]Is. 32:9-11; ... 1:12; Luke 6:24 ... 19:5; Amos 3:2

2 [1]Or, *you* [a]Gen... Is. 10:9 [b]1 Kin. 8... 2 Kin. 18:34; Is. ... [c]1 Sam. 5:8; 2 Ch...

3 [a]Is. 56:12; Am... 9:10 [b]Amos 3:10

4 [a]Amos 3:12 [b]E... 34:2, 3

5 [1]Or, *invented m... instruments* [a]1 C... 15:16; 23:5; Is. 5:...

6 [1]Lit., *sprinkling basins* [a]Amos 2:8 [b]Ezek. 9:4

7 Therefore, they will now [a]go into exile at the head of the exiles,
And the [b]sprawlers' [1]banqueting will [2]pass away.

8 The Lord [1]GOD has [a]sworn by Himself, the LORD God of hosts
has declared:
"I [b]loathe the arrogance of Jacob,
And I [2]detest his [c]citadels;
Therefore, I will [d]deliver up *the* city and [3]all it contains."
9 And it will be, if [a]ten men are left in one house, they will die.
10 Then one's [1]uncle, or his [2a]undertaker, will lift him up to carry
out *his* bones from the house, and he will say to the one who is in the
innermost part of the house, "Is anyone else with you?" And that
one will say, "No one." Then he will [3]answer, "[b]Keep quiet. For [4]the
name of the LORD is [c]not to be mentioned."
11 For behold, the LORD is going to [a]command that the [b]great house
be smashed to pieces and the small house to fragments.
12 Do horses run on rocks?
Or does one plow [1]them with oxen?
Yet you have turned [a]justice into poison,
And the fruit of righteousness into [2]wormwood,
13 You who rejoice in [1a]Lo-debar,
[2]And say, "Have we not [b]by our *own* strength taken [3]Karnaim for
ourselves?"
14 "For behold, [a]I am going to raise up a nation against you,
O house of Israel," declares the LORD God of hosts,
"And they will afflict you from the [b]entrance of Hamath
To the [b]brook of the Arabah."

Chapter 7

7 Thus the Lord [1]GOD showed me, and behold, He was forming a
[a]locust-swarm [2]when the spring crop began to sprout. And be-
hold, the spring crop *was* after the king's [3]mowing.
2 And it came about, [1]when it had [a]finished eating the vegetation
of the land, that I said,
"[b]Lord GOD, please pardon!
[2]How can Jacob stand,
For he is [c]small?"
3 The LORD [1a]changed His mind about this.
"It shall not be," said the LORD.
4 Thus the Lord GOD showed me, and behold, the Lord GOD was
calling to contend *with them* by [a]fire, and it consumed the great deep
and began to consume the [1]farm land.
5 Then I said,
"[a]Lord GOD, please stop!
[b]How can Jacob stand, for he is small?"
6 The LORD [1a]changed His mind about this.
"This too shall not be," said the Lord GOD.
7 Thus He showed me, and behold, the Lord was standing [1]by a
[2]vertical wall, with a plumb line in His hand.
8 And the LORD said to me, "[a]What do you see, Amos?" And I said,
"A plumb line." Then the Lord said,
"Behold I am about to put a [b]plumb line
In the midst of My people Israel.
I will [1c]spare them no longer.

…, *cultic feasts* [2]Lit., *aside* [a]Amos 7:11, …7 [b]1 Kin. 20:16-21; Dan. 5:4-6, 30

8 [1]Heb., *YHWH*, …ally rendered *LORD* [2]Lit., *hate* [3]Lit., *its …lness* [a]Gen. 22:16; …22:5; 51:14; Amos …2; 8:7 [b]Lev. 26:30; …32:19; Ps. 106:40; …5:21 [c]Amos 3:10, 11 [d]Hos. 11:6

9 [a]Amos 5:3

…0 [1]Or, *beloved one* …Lit., *one who burns* [3]Lit., *say* [4]Lit., *not …ake mention of the …e of* [a]1 Sam. 31:12 …nos 5:13; 8:3 [c]Jer. 44:26; Ezek. 20:39

… [a]Is. 55:11 [b]2 Kin. …9; Amos 3:15; 5:11

[1]Another reading is …sea with oxen [2]I.e., bitterness [a]1 Kin. …7-13; Is. 59:13, 14; …os. 10:4; Amos 5:7, 11, 12

13 [1]Lit., *a thing of …ng* [2]Lit., *Who* [3]Lit., *pair of horns* [a]Job …15; Ps. 2:2-4; Luke …9, 20 [b]Ps. 75:4, 5; Is. 28:14, 15

… [a]Jer. 5:15 [b]Num. …34:7, 8; 1 Kin. 8:65; 2 Kin. 14:25

7:1 [1]Heb., *YHWH*, …ally rendered *LORD*, …d so throughout the …ch. [2]Lit., *at the …nning of the coming …o of* [3]Or, *shearings* Joel 1:4; Amos 4:9; Nah. 3:15

…Lit., *if* [2]Lit., *As who* …x. 10:15 [b]Jer. 14:7, …1; Ezek. 9:8; 11:13 [c]Is. 37:4; Jer. 42:2

…Or, *relented* [a]Deut. …46; Jer. 26:19; Hos. …8; Amos 5:15; Jon. 3:10

…Lit., *portion* [a]Deut. …2:22; Is. 66:15, 16; Amos 2:5

…Ps. 85:4; Joel 2:17 [b]Amos 7:2

[1]Or, *relented* [a]Ps. …45; Amos 7:3; Jon. 3:10

…Or, *upon* [2]Lit., *wall of a plumb line*

… [1]Lit., *pass him by* …Jer. 1:11; Amos 8:2 …n. 21:13; Is. 28:17; …:11; Lam. 2:8 [c]Jer. Ezek. 7:4-9; Amos 8:2

9 "The [a]high places of Isaac will be desolated
And the [b]sanctuaries of Israel laid waste.
Then shall I [c]rise up against the house of Jeroboam with the
sword."
10 Then Amaziah, the [a]priest of Bethel, sent *word* to [b]Jeroboam, king
of Israel, saying, "Amos has [c]conspired against you in the midst of
the house of Israel; the land is unable to endure all his words.
11 "For thus Amos says, 'Jeroboam will die by the sword and Israel
will certainly go from its land into exile.' "
12 Then Amaziah said to Amos, "[a]Go, you seer, flee away to the
land of Judah, and there eat bread and there do your prophesying!
13 "But [a]no longer prophesy at Bethel, for it is a [b]sanctuary of the
king and a royal [1]residence."
14 Then Amos answered and said to Amaziah, "I am not a prophet,
nor am I the [a]son of a prophet; for I am a herdsman and a [1]grower of
sycamore figs.
15 "But the LORD took me from [1]following the flock and the LORD
said to me, 'Go [a]prophesy to My people Israel.'
16 "And now hear the word of the LORD: you are saying, 'You [a]shall
not prophesy against Israel [b]nor shall you [1]speak against the house
of Isaac.'
17 "Therefore, thus says the LORD, 'Your [a]wife will become a harlot in
the city, your [b]sons and your daughters will fall by the sword, your
land will be parceled up by a *measuring* line, and you yourself will
die [1]upon [c]unclean soil. Moreover, Israel will certainly go from its
land into exile.' "

Chapter 8

8 Thus the Lord [1]GOD showed me, and behold, *there was* a basket
of summer fruit.
2 And He said, "What do you see, Amos?" And [a]I said, "A basket
of summer fruit." Then the LORD said to me, "The [b]end has come for
My people Israel. I will [1c]spare them no longer.
3 "[1]The [a]songs of the palace will turn to [b]wailing in that day,"
declares the Lord GOD. "Many *will be* the [c]corpses; in every place
[2]they will cast them forth [3]in silence."
4 Hear this, you who [1a]trample the needy, to do away with the
humble of the land,
5 saying,
"When will the [a]new moon [1]be over,
So that we may sell grain,
And the [b]sabbath, that we may open the wheat *market*,
To make the [2]bushel smaller and the shekel bigger,
And to [c]cheat with [3]dishonest scales,
6 So as to [a]buy the helpless for [1]money
And the needy for a pair of sandals,
And *that* we may sell the refuse of the wheat?"

7 The LORD has [a]sworn by the [b]pride of Jacob,
"Indeed, I will [c]never forget any of their deeds.
8 "Because of this will not the land [a]quake
And everyone who dwells in it [b]mourn?
Indeed, all of it will [c]rise up like the Nile,
And it will be tossed about,

9 [a]Gen. 46:1; 10:8; Mic. 1:5 26:31; Is. 63:1 51:51; Amos 7 [c]2 Kin. 15:8-10 7:11

10 [a]1 Kin. 12: 13:33 [b]2 Kin. [c]Jer. 26:8-11;

12 [a]Matt. 8:34

13 [1]Lit., *house* 2:12; Acts 4:18 12:29, 32; Amo

14 [1]Or, *nipper* 20:35; 2 Kin. 2 4:38; 2 Chr. 19

15 [1]Lit., *behin* 1:7; Ezek. 2:3,

16 [1]Lit., *flow* [a] 2:12; 7:13 [b]De Ezek. 20:46; 21

17 [1]Or, *in an u land* [a]Hos. 4:13 [b]Jer. 14:16 [c]2 K Ezek. 4:13; Hos

8:1 [1]Heb., *YHW* usually rendere and so through the ch.

2 [1]Lit., *pass hin* [a]Jer. 24:3 [b]Ezek 6 [c]Amos 7:8

3 [1]Or, *They will the palace song he has thrown* [3] *hush!* [a]Amos 5: 5; 8:10 [b]Amos 5 [c]Amos 6:8-10

4 [1]Or, *snap at* [a] 14:4; Prov. 30:14 2:7; 5:11, 12

5 [1]Lit., *pass by ephah* [3]Lit., *bala deception* [a]Num 2 Kin. 4:23 [b]Ex. 31:13-17; Neh. 1 [c]Hos. 12:7; Mic. 6

6 [1]Lit., *silver* [a]Ar

7 [a]Amos 4:2 [b]De 33:26, 29; Ps. 68 Amos 6:8 [c]Ps. 10 Hos. 7:2; 8:13

8 [a]Ps. 18:7; 60:2; 5:25 [b]Hos. 4:3 [c]J 46:7, 8; Amos 9:5

And subside like the Nile of Egypt.
9 "And it will come about in that day," declares the Lord GOD,
"That I shall make the [a]sun go down at noon
And [b]make the earth dark in [1]broad daylight.
10 "Then I shall [a]turn your festivals into mourning
And all your songs into [1]lamentation;
And I will bring [b]sackcloth on everyone's loins
And baldness on every head.
And I will make it [c]like *a time of* mourning for an only son,
And the end of it will be like a bitter day.

11 "Behold, days are coming," declares the Lord GOD,
"When I will send a famine on the land,
Not a famine for bread or a thirst for water,
But rather [a]for hearing the words of the LORD.
12 "And people will stagger from sea to sea,
And from the north even to the east;
They will go to and fro to [a]seek the word of the LORD,
But they will not find *it*.
13 "In that day the beautiful [a]virgins
And the young men will [b]faint from thirst.
14 "*As for* those who swear by the [1a]guilt of Samaria,
Who say, 'As your god lives, O [b]Dan,'
And, 'As the way of [c]Beersheba lives,'
They will fall and [d]not rise again."

Chapter 9

9 I saw the Lord standing beside the [a]altar, and He said,
"Smite the capitals so that the [b]thresholds will shake,
And [c]break them on the heads of them all!
Then I will [d]slay the rest of them with the sword;
They will [e]not have a fugitive who will flee,
Or a refugee who will escape.
2 "Though they dig into [a]Sheol,
From there shall My hand take them;
And though they [b]ascend to heaven,
From there will I bring them down.
3 "And though they hide on the summit of Carmel,
I will [a]search them out and take them from there;
And though they [b]conceal themselves from My sight on the
floor of the sea,
From there I will command the [c]serpent and it will bite them.
4 "And though they go into [a]captivity before their enemies,
From there I will command the sword that it slay them,
And I will [b]set My eyes against them for evil and not for good."

5 And the Lord [1]GOD of hosts,
The One who [a]touches the land so that it melts,
And [b]all those who dwell in it mourn,
And all of it rises up like the Nile
And subsides like the Nile of Egypt;
6 The One who builds His [1a]upper chambers in the heavens,
And has founded His vaulted dome over the earth,
He who [b]calls for the waters of the sea

[1]Lit., *a day of light* 5:14; Is. 13:10; Jer. Mic. 3:6 [b]Is. 59:9, 10; Amos 4:13; 5:8

[1]Or, *a dirge* [a]Job 23; Amos 5:21 [b]Is. 15:2, 3; Jer. 48:37; k. 7:18; 27:31 [c]Jer. 6:26; Zech. 12:10

[a]1 Sam. 3:1; 2 Chr. :3; Ps. 74:9; Ezek. 7:26; Mic. 3:6

12 [a]Ezek. 20:3, 31

3 [a]Lam. 1:18; 2:21 [b]Is. 41:17; Hos. 2:3

r, *Ashimah* [a]Hos. 5 [b]1 Kin. 12:28, 29 os 5:5 [d]Amos 5:2

mos 3:14 [b]Zeph. 4 [c]Ps. 68:21; Hab. [d]Amos 7:17 [e]Jer. 11:11

2 [a]Ps. 139:8 [b]Jer. 51:53; Obad. 4

[a]Jer. 16:16 [b]Job Ps. 139:9, 10 [c]Is. 27:1

[a]Lev. 26:33 [b]Lev. Jer. 21:10; 39:16; 44:11

5 [1]Heb., *YHWH*, ly rendered *LORD*, so throughout the Ps. 104:32; 144:5; ; Mic. 1:4 [b]Amos 8:8

6 [1]Or, *stairs* [a]Ps. :3, 13 [b]Amos 5:8

And [c]pours them out on the face of the earth,
[d]The LORD is His name.

7 "Are you not as the sons of [a]Ethiopia to Me,
O sons of Israel?" declares the LORD.
"Have I not brought up Israel from the land of Egypt,
And the [b]Philistines from Caphtor and the [c]Arameans from [d]Kir?
8 "Behold, the [a]eyes of the Lord GOD are on the sinful kingdom,
And I will [b]destroy it from the face of the earth;
Nevertheless, I will [c]not totally destroy the house of Jacob,"
Declares the LORD.
9 "For behold, I am commanding,
And I will [a]shake the house of Israel among all nations
As *grain* is shaken in a sieve,
But not a [1]kernel will fall to the ground.
10 "All the [a]sinners of My people will die by the sword,
Those who say, '[b]The calamity will not overtake or confront us.'
11 "In that day I will [a]raise up the fallen [1b]booth of David,
And wall up its [c]breaches;
I will also raise up its ruins,
And rebuild it as in the [d]days of old;
12 [a]That they may possess the remnant of [b]Edom
And all the [1]nations who are [c]called by My name,"
Declares the LORD who does this.

13 "Behold, days are coming," declares the LORD,
"When the [a]plowman will overtake the reaper
And the treader of grapes him who sows seed;
When the [b]mountains will drip sweet [c]wine,
And all the hills will be dissolved.
14 "Also I will [a]restore the [1]captivity of My people Israel,
And they will [b]rebuild the ruined cities and live *in them*,
They will also [c]plant vineyards and drink their wine,
And make gardens and eat their fruit.
15 "I will also plant them on their land,
And [a]they will not again be rooted out from their land
Which I have given them,"
Says the LORD your God.

6 [c]Ps. 104:6
4:13

7 [a]2 Chr. 14:9
20:4; 43:3 [b]D
Jer. 47:4 [c]Am
[d]2 Kin. 16:9; Is

8 [a]Jer. 44:27;
9:4 [b]Amos 7:1
[c]Jer. 5:10; 30:1
36; Joel 2:32;
3:12; Obad. 17

9 [1]Or, *pebble*
30:28; Luke 22

10 [a]Is. 33:14;
13:8 [b]Amos 6:

11 [1]Or, *shelter*
tabernacle [a]Ac
15:16-18 [b]Is. 1
80:12 [d]Is. 63:11
46:26

12 [1]Or, *Gentile*
[a]Obad. 19 [b]Nu
Is. 11:14 [c]Is. 43

13 [a]Lev. 26:5 [b]
3:18 [c]Gen. 49:1

14 [1]Or, *fortunes*
53:6; Is. 60:4; Je
18 [b]Is. 61:4; 65:
24:6; 31:28

15 [a]Is. 60:21; Ez
34:28; 37:25

e of Amos:

DIVISIONS

	CHAPTER THEMES
	1
	2
	3
	4
	5
	6
	7
	8
	9

Author:

Date:

Purpose:

Key Words:

OBADIAH

God said that whoever touched Israel, touched the apple (pupil) of His eye. According to Ob 1:10-14, Edom had touched God's eye.

Scholars are divided about whether the incident referred to in these verses occurred during the of Jehoram (853-841 B.C.) when the Philistines and the Arabs invaded Jerusalem, or during Baby sieges of Jerusalem (between 605 and 586 B.C.). However, the exact date is not critical to the messa the book. What we do know is that in both instances Edom did not respond as God wanted, thus c this report from the Lord. It came as a word through "the Lord's servant," which is the meani Obadiah's name.

THINGS TO DO

1. Read this book once without stopping to get an overview of Obadiah's message.
2. Read through Obadiah again and in a distinctive way mark the key words listed or OBADIAH AT A GLANCE chart on page 1349.
3. Remember Jacob and Esau were brothers, born to Rebekah and Isaac. If you want to refresh memory, read Genesis 27:1 through 28:9, 32 through 33; Romans 9:10-13; and Numbers 20:1 Genesis 36 gives the genealogy of Esau and says, "Esau is Edom." It also names Esau as the f of the Edomites.

   Although the people of Edom (descendants of Esau) and Israel (descendants of Jacob) are rel (Amos 1:11-12), biblical history records many conflicts between them. Look at the map on 1348 and notice the proximity of Edom to Israel. Edom was a constant threat to Israel, repeat thwarting the nation and blocking Judean access to the Gulf of Aqaba.
4. Now read through Obadiah again, asking the five W's and an H. Ask questions such as: W writing? To whom? Why? What is being written about? What is going to happen? To wh How? Summarize your observations in the margin of the text.
5. Look at the map and find the Negev and the other places mentioned at the end of Obadiah. T are real lands, real people, and what God says will happen to them *will* happen.
6. Since Obadiah is just one chapter, record the theme (subject) of each paragraph on OBADIAH A GLANCE and then fill in the rest of the chart, including the theme of Obadiah.
7. The day of the Lord is an important day prophetically. In the appendix of this Bible you will a chart titled THE DAY OF THE LORD (page 1878). Record your insights on the day of the l on this chart. As you do so, note the reference (book, chapter, and verse) you took your infor tion from so you can find it later.

THINGS TO THINK ABOUT

1. Sometimes when tragic and unjust things happen, we wonder where God is. If He is righte just, and omnipotent, why doesn't He intervene? What do you learn from Obadiah that h answer these questions? What do you learn from this for your own life?
2. How should we respond to the tragedies of others, the dark hours of our enemies? What c God think when we use their tragedy to our advantage?

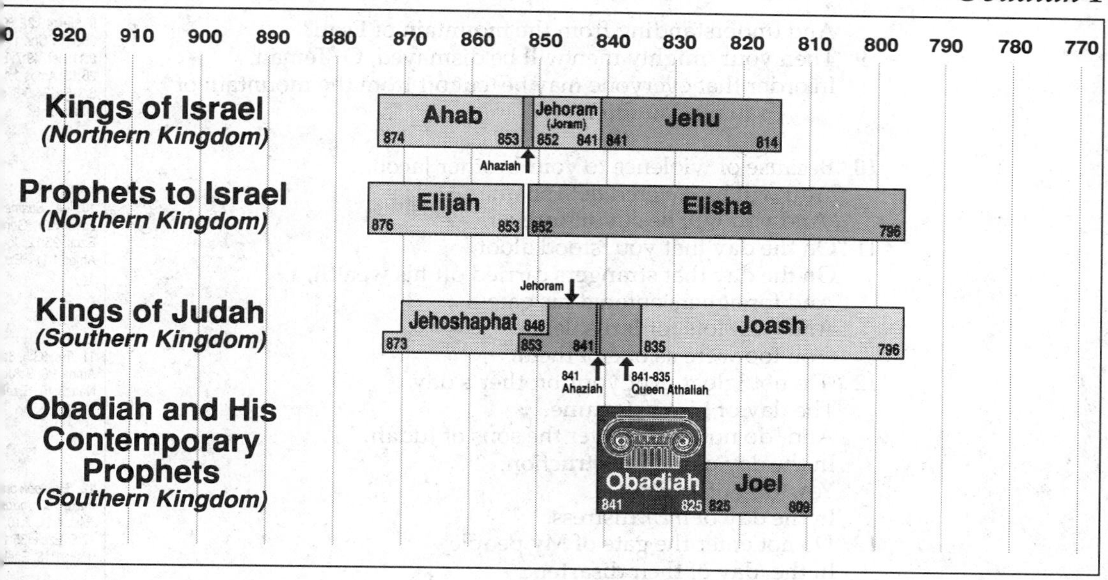

Chapter 1

1 The vision of Obadiah.
Thus says the Lord [1]God concerning [a]Edom—
[b]We have heard a report from the LORD,
And an [c]envoy has been sent among the nations saying,
"[d]Arise and let us go against her for battle"—
2 "Behold, I will make you [a]small among the nations;
You are greatly despised.
3 "The [a]arrogance of your heart has deceived you,
You who live in the clefts of [1]the [b]rock,
In the loftiness of your dwelling place,
Who say in your heart,
'[c]Who will bring me down to earth?'
4 "Though you [a]build high like the eagle,
Though you set your nest among the [b]stars,
From there I will bring you down," declares the LORD.
5 "If [a]thieves came to you,
If [1]robbers by night—
O how you will be ruined!—
Would they not steal *only* [2]until they had enough?
If grape gatherers came to you,
[b]Would they not leave *some* gleanings?
6 "O how Esau will be [a]ransacked,
And his hidden treasures searched out!
7 "All the [a]men [1]allied with you
Will send you forth to the border,
And the men at peace with you
Will deceive you and overpower you.
They who eat your [b]bread
Will set an ambush for you.
(There is [c]no understanding [2]in him.)
8 "Will I not on that day," declares the LORD,
"[a]Destroy wise men from Edom

1 [1]Heb., *YHWH*, ...y rendered LORD ...:7; Is. 21:11, 12; ...-17; 63:1-6; Jer. 49:7-22; Ezek. ...2-14; 35:15; Joel ...; Amos 1:11, 12; ... [b]Jer. 49:14-16; ...ad. 1-4 [c]Is. 18:2; 30:4 [d]Jer. 6:4, 5

...n. 24:18; Is. 23:9

...; *Sela* [a]Is. 16:6; ...16 [b]2 Kin. 14:7; ...Chr. 25:11f. [c]Is. ...3-15; Rev. 18:7

...ob 20:6, 7; Hab. ...:9 [b]Is. 14:12-15

..., *devastators of night* [2]Lit., *their ...iency* [a]Jer. 49:9 [b]Deut. 24:21

6 [a]Jer. 49:10

7 [1]Lit., *of your ...nt* [2]I.e., in Esau; ...Jer. 30:14 [b]Ps. 19:11; Jer. 49:7

...12-14; Is. 29:14

And understanding from the mountain of Esau?
9 "Then your [a]mighty men will be dismayed, O [b]Teman,
In order that everyone may be [c]cut off from the mountain of
Esau by slaughter.

10 "Because of [a]violence to your brother Jacob,
[1]You will be covered *with* shame,
[b]And you will be cut off forever.
11 "On the day that you [a]stood aloof,
On the day that strangers carried off his wealth,
And foreigners entered his gate
And [b]cast lots for Jerusalem—
[c]You too were as one of them.
12 "[a]Do not [1]gloat over your brother's day,
The day of his misfortune.
And [b]do not rejoice over the sons of Judah
In the day of their destruction;
Yes, [c]do not [2]boast
In the day of *their* distress.
13 "Do not enter the gate of My people
In the [a]day of their disaster.
Yes, you, do not [1]gloat over their calamity
In the day of their disaster.
And do not [b]loot their wealth
In the day of their disaster.
14 "And do not [a]stand at the fork of the road
To cut down their fugitives;
And do not imprison their survivors
In the day of their distress.

15 "For the [a]day of the LORD draws near on all the nations.
[b]As you have done, it will be done to you.
Your [c]dealings will return on your own head.
16 "Because just as you [a]drank on [b]My holy mountain,
All the nations [c]will drink continually.
They will drink and [1]swallow,
And become as if they had never existed.
17 "But on Mount [a]Zion there will be those who escape,
And it will be holy.
And the house of Jacob will [b]possess their possessions.
18 "Then the house of Jacob will be a [a]fire
And the house of Joseph a flame;
But the house of Esau *will be* as stubble.
And they will set [1]them on fire and consume [1]them,
So that there will be [b]no survivor of the house of
Esau,"
For the LORD has spoken.
19 Then *those of* the [1]Negev will [a]possess the mountain of
Esau,
And *those of* the [2]Shephelah the [b]Philistine *plain*;
Also, they will [c]possess the territory of Ephraim and
the territory of Samaria,
And Benjamin *will possess* Gilead.
20 And the exiles of this host of the sons of Israel,

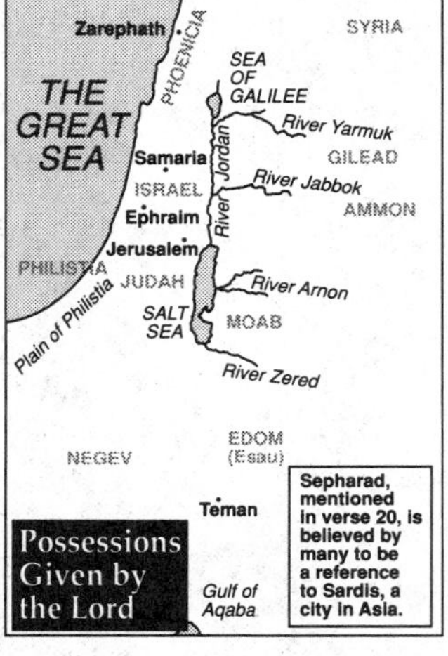

Possessions Given by the Lord

Sepharad, mentioned in verse 20, is believed by many to be a reference to Sardis, a city in Asia.

9 [a]Jer. 49:2… 36:11; 1 Chr. 2:11; Jer. 49… 25:13; Amos 3:3 [c]Is. 34:5… Obad. 5

10 [1]Lit., *Sha… cover you* [a]… Ezek. 25:12… Amos 1:11

11 [a]Ps. 83:5… Amos 1:6, 9… Nah. 3:10 [c]…

12 [1]Lit., *loo… make your r…* [a]Mic. 4:11; 7… 17:5; Ezek. … [c]Ps. 31:18; …

13 [1]Lit., *loo…* 35:5 [b]Ezek. 36:2, 3

14 [a]Is. 16:3…

15 [a]Ezek. 3… 1:15; 2:1, 11… 5:18, 20 [b]Je… 51:56; Hab. 35:11

16 [1]Or, *stag…* 49:12 [b]Joel… 51:22, 23; J…

17 [a]Is. 4:2, … 2; Amos 9:1…

18 [1]I.e., the… Esau [a]Is. 5:… 19; Zech. 12… 11:23; Amos…

19 [1]I.e., So… [2]I.e., the foo… 11:14; Amos… 11:14 [c]Jer. …

20 [a]1 Kin. 17:9; Luke
26 [b]Jer. 32:44; 33:13

21 [a]Neh. 9:27 [b]Ps. 22:28; 47:7-9; 67:4; ...ch. 14:9; Rev. 11:15

Who are *among* the Canaanites as far as [a]Zarephath,
And the exiles of Jerusalem who are in Sepharad
Will possess the [b]cities of the Negev.
21 The [a]deliverers will ascend Mount Zion
To judge the mountain of Esau,
And the [b]kingdom will be the LORD's.

OBADIAH AT A GLANCE

...e of Obadiah:

...T DIVISIONS

		PARAGRAPH THEMES
		VERSES 1-9
		VERSES 10-14
		VERSES 15-21

Author:

Date:

Purpose:

Key Words:
the day
Esau (Edom)
Jacob (Judah)
the nations
Mount Zion (My holy mountain)
the Lord spoke (or any phrase having to do with the Lord speaking, declaring, or reporting)

JONAH

Just before God commissioned Amos and then Hosea as prophets to the northern kingdom to
Israel of the impending invasion by the Assyrians, He appointed the prophet Jonah to go to Nin
the capital of Assyria. Fifty years later in 722 B.C., Assyria would take the northern kingdor
captivity.

God knew what Assyria would do. Why then did He bother to send Jonah to the wicked c
Nineveh? Because of who He is. The focus of Jonah is not a man trapped in the belly of a great fis
focus is people engraved on the heart of God.

THINGS TO DO

1. Before you read through Jonah, look up 2 Kings 14:23-27, which mentions Jonah and his mi during the reign of Jeroboam II, king of Israel. At that time Shalmaneser IV was king of Assy
2. In the margin of each chapter list everything you learn about God. Note His character and as well as His response to a sinful people and a "wrong-way" prophet.
3. In a distinctive way mark the key words listed on the JONAH AT A GLANCE chart on page
4. Record the theme of each chapter on JONAH AT A GLANCE and in the text next to the ch number. Then fill in the rest of the chart.
5. Contrast Jonah's heart with God's heart. Record your insights in the margin of chapter 4.

THINGS TO THINK ABOUT

1. What or who evokes compassion in your heart? How does your heart compare with God's? it long for the same things? Why?
2. Is there something that you know God wants you to do that you haven't done? What can learn from Jonah's life?
3. How did Jesus view the story of Jonah? Read Matthew 12:39-41,16:4. Will you accept as t what Jesus accepted as fact—or did Jesus compare His resurrection to a mythological tale?

Chapter 1 ______

1 The word of the LORD came to [a]Jonah the son of Amittai saying,
2 "Arise, go to [a]Nineveh the great city, and [b]cry against it, for
their [c]wickedness has come up before Me."
3 But Jonah rose up to flee to [a]Tarshish [b]from the presence of the
LORD. So he went down to [c]Joppa, found a ship which was going to
Tarshish, paid the fare, and went down into
it to go with them to Tarshish from the
presence of the LORD.
4 And the [a]LORD hurled a great wind on
the sea and there was a great storm on the
sea so that the ship was about to [1]break up.
5 Then the sailors became afraid, and
every man cried to [a]his god, and they
[b]threw the [1]cargo which was in the ship
into the sea to lighten *it* [2]for them. But
Jonah had gone below into the hold of the
ship, lain down, and fallen sound asleep.

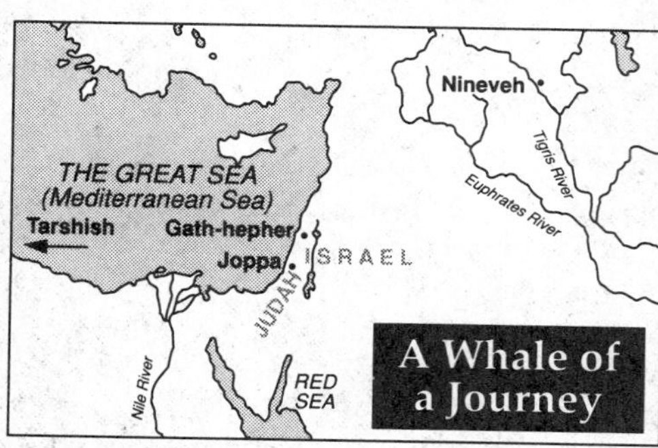

1:1 [a]2 Kin. 14:25 12:39-41; 16:4; L 11:29, 30, 32

2 [a]Gen. 10:11; 2 19:36; Is. 37:37; 1:1; Zeph. 2:13 [b] 58:1 [c]Gen. 18:20 7:2

3 [a]Is. 23:1, 6, 10; 10:9 [b]Gen. 4:16; 139:7, 9, 10 [c]Jos 19:46; 2 Chr. 2:16 3:7; Acts 9:36, 43

4 [1]Lit., *be broken* 107:23-28; 135:6,

5 [1]Lit., *vessels* [2] *from upon them* [a] 18:26 [b]Acts 27:18 19, 38

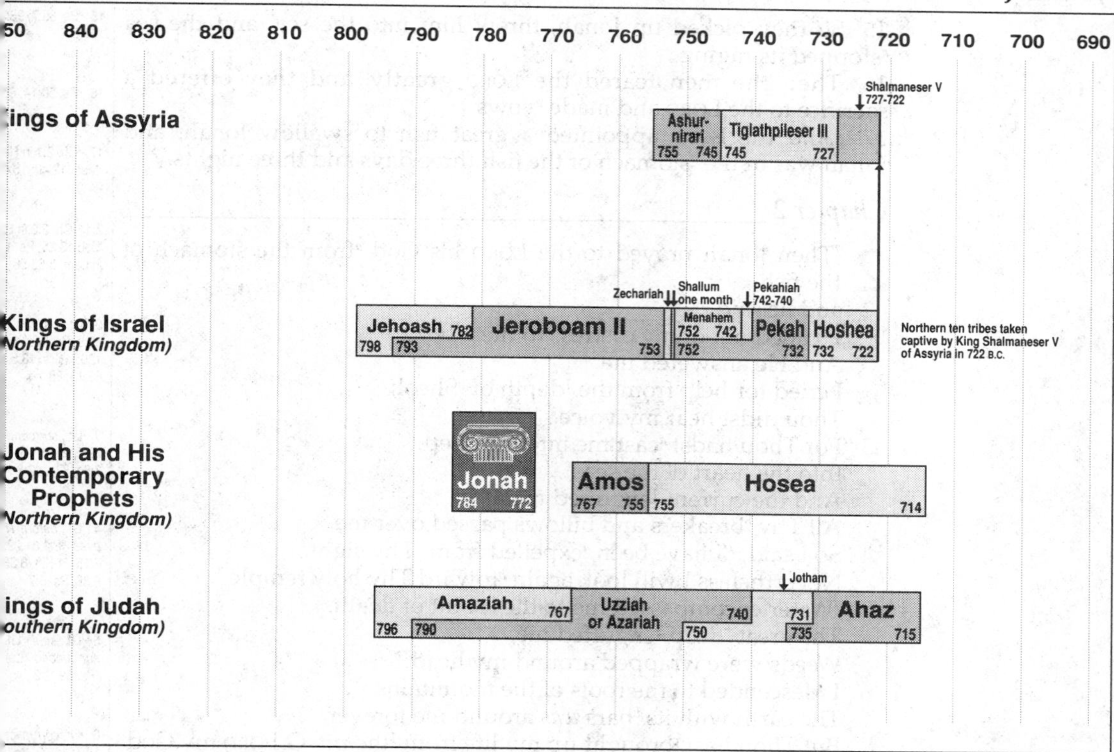

. 107:28 [b]2 Sam. ; Amos 5:15; Jon. 3:9

Lit., *know* [a]Josh. 18; 1 Sam. 10:20, ; 14:41, 42; Acts 26 [b]Num. 32:23; Prov. 16:33

osh. 7:19; 1 Sam. 4:43 [b]Gen. 47:3; 1 Sam. 30:13

[a]Gen. 14:13; Ex. :15; 2:13 [b]2 Kin. 28, 32, 33 [c]Ezra 1:2; Neh. 1:4; Ps. 36:26; Dan. 2:18 eh. 9:6; Ps. 95:5; 146:6

[1]Lit., *What is this have done* [a]Job 27:22; Jon. 1:3

.it., *from upon us*

t., *from upon you* am. 24:17; 1 Chr. 21:17

it., *dug their oars into the water*

[a]Ps. 107:28; Jon. Ps. 115:3; 135:6; Dan. 4:34, 35

6 So the captain approached him and said, "How is it that you are
sleeping? Get up, [a]call on your god. Perhaps *your* [b]god will be con-
cerned about us so that we will not perish."
7 And each man said to his mate, "Come, let us [a]cast lots so we
may [1]learn on whose account this calamity *has struck* us." So they
cast lots and the [b]lot fell on Jonah.
8 Then they said to him, "[a]Tell us, now! On whose account *has* this
calamity *struck* us? What is your [b]occupation? And where do you
come from? What is your country? From what people are you?"
9 And he said to them, "I am a [a]Hebrew, and I [b]fear the LORD [c]God
of heaven who [d]made the sea and the dry land."
10 Then the men became extremely frightened and they said to
him, "[1]How could you do this?" For the men knew that he was
[a]fleeing from the presence of the LORD, because he had told them.
11 So they said to him, "What should we do to you that the sea may
become calm [1]for us?"—for the sea was becoming increasingly
stormy.
12 And he said to them, "Pick me up and throw me into the sea.
Then the sea will become calm [1]for you, for I know that [a]on account
of me this great storm *has come* upon you."
13 However, the men [1]rowed *desperately* to return to land but they
could not, for the sea was becoming *even* stormier against them.
14 Then they called on the [a]LORD and said, "We earnestly pray, O
LORD, do not let us perish on account of this man's life and do not
put innocent blood on us; for [b]Thou, O LORD, hast done as Thou hast
pleased."

15 So they picked up Jonah, threw him into the sea, and the sea
[a]stopped its raging.
16 Then the men feared the LORD greatly, and they offered a
sacrifice to the LORD and made [a]vows.
17 [1]And the LORD appointed a great fish to swallow Jonah, and
Jonah was in the [a]stomach of the fish three days and three nights.

Chapter 2

2 [1]Then Jonah prayed to the LORD his God [a]from the stomach of
the fish,
2 and he said,
"I [a]called out of my distress to the LORD,
And He answered me.
I cried for help from the [1]depth of [b]Sheol;
Thou didst hear my voice.
3 "For Thou hadst [a]cast me into the deep,
Into the heart of the seas,
And the current [1]engulfed me.
All Thy [b]breakers and billows passed over me.
4 "So I said, 'I have been [a]expelled from [1]Thy sight.
Nevertheless I will look again [b]toward Thy holy temple.'
5 "[a]Water encompassed me to the [1]point of death.
The great [b]deep [2]engulfed me,
Weeds were wrapped around my head.
6 "I [a]descended to the roots of the mountains.
The earth with its [b]bars *was* around me forever,
But Thou hast [c]brought up my life from [1]the pit, O LORD my God.
7 "While [1]I was [a]fainting away,
I [b]remembered the LORD;
And my [c]prayer came to Thee,
Into [d]Thy holy temple.
8 "Those who [a]regard [1]vain idols
Forsake their faithfulness,
9 But I will [a]sacrifice to Thee
With the voice of thanksgiving.
That which I have vowed I will [b]pay.
[c]Salvation is from the LORD."
10 Then the LORD commanded the [a]fish, and it vomited Jonah up
onto the dry land.

Chapter 3

3 Now the word of the LORD came to Jonah the second time,
saying,
2 "Arise, go to [a]Nineveh the great city and [b]proclaim to it the
proclamation which I am going to tell you."
3 So Jonah arose and went to Nineveh according to the word of
the LORD. Now Nineveh was [1]an [a]exceedingly great city, a three days'
walk.
4 Then Jonah began to go through the city one day's walk; and he
[a]cried out and said, "Yet forty days and Nineveh will be over-
thrown."
5 Then the people of Nineveh believed in God; and they called a
[a]fast and put on sackcloth from the greatest to the least of them.
6 When the word reached the king of Nineveh, he arose from his

15 [a]Ps. 65:7; 107:29
16 [a]Ps. 50:1
17 [1]Ch. 2:1 i [a]Matt. 12:40;
2:1 [1]Ch. 2:2 [a]Job 13:15; P 2; Lam. 3:53-
2 [1]Lit., *belly* 30:6; Ps. 18:4 120:1 [b]Ps. 18 86:13; 88:1-7
3 [1]Lit., *surrou* 69:1, 2, 14, 15 3:54 [b]Ps. 42:
4 [1]Lit., *before eyes* [a]Ps. 31: 7:15 [b]1 Kin. 8 6:38; Ps. 5:7
5 [1]Lit., *soul* [2] *surrounded* [a] [b]Ps. 69:1, 2
6 [1]Or, *corrupt* 18:5; 116:3 [b]Is Matt. 16:18 [c]J Ps. 16:10; 30:3
7 [1]Lit., *my sou within me* [a]Ps. [b]Ps. 77:10, 11; [c]2 Chr. 30:27; [d]Ps. 11:4; 65:4 Mic. 1:2; Hab.
8 [1]Lit., *empty* [a]2 Kin. 17:15; F Jer. 10:8
9 [a]Ps. 50:14, 2 33:11; Hos. 14: 22:27; Eccl. 5:4 3:8; Is. 45:17
10 [a]Jon. 1:17
3:2 [a]Zeph. 2:13 1:17; Ezek. 2:7
3 [1]Lit., *a great God* [a]Jon. 1:2;
4 [a]Matt. 12:41; 11:32
5 [a]Dan. 9:3; Jo

throne, laid aside his robe from him, [a]covered *himself* with sackcloth,
and sat on the [1]ashes.
7 And he issued a [a]proclamation and it said, "In Nineveh by the
decree of the king and his nobles: Do not let man, beast, herd, or
flock taste a thing. Do not let them eat or drink water.
8 "But both man and beast must be covered with sackcloth; and let
[1]men [a]call on God earnestly that each may [b]turn from his wicked
way and from the violence which is in [2]his hands.
9 "[a]Who knows, God may turn and relent, and withdraw His burn-
ing anger so that we shall not perish?"
10 When God saw their deeds, that they [a]turned from their wicked
way, then [b]God relented concerning the calamity which He had de-
clared He would [1]bring upon them. And He did not do *it.*

Chapter 4

4 But it greatly displeased Jonah, and he became [a]angry.
2 And he [a]prayed to the LORD and said, "Please LORD, was not
this [1]what I said while I was still in my *own* country? Therefore, [2]in
order to forestall this I [b]fled to Tarshish, for I knew that Thou art a
[c]gracious and compassionate God, slow to anger and abundant in
lovingkindness, and one who relents concerning calamity.
3 "Therefore now, O LORD, please [a]take my [1]life from me, for death
is [b]better to me than life."
4 And the LORD said, "Do you have good reason to be angry?"
5 Then Jonah went out from the city and sat east of [1]it. There he
made a shelter for himself and [a]sat under it in the shade until he
could see what would happen in the city.
6 So the LORD God appointed a [1]plant and it grew up over Jonah to
be a shade over his head to deliver him from his discomfort. And
Jonah was [2]extremely happy about the [1]plant.
7 But God appointed a worm when dawn came the next day, and
it attacked the plant and it [a]withered.
8 And it came about when the sun came up that God appointed a
scorching [a]east wind, and the [b]sun beat down on Jonah's head so
that he became faint and begged with *all* his soul to die, saying,
"[c]Death is better to me than life."
9 Then God said to Jonah, "Do you have good reason to be angry
about the plant?" And he said, "I have good reason to be angry, even
to death."
10 Then the LORD said, "You had compassion on the plant for which
you did not work, and *which* you did not cause to grow, which [1]came
up overnight and perished [2]overnight.
11 "And should I not [a]have compassion on Nineveh, the great city in
which there are more than 120,000 persons who do not [b]know *the
difference* between their right and left hand, as well as many
[c]animals?"

6 [1]Or, *dust* [a]Esth. [4]:1-4; Jer. 6:26; Ezek. 27:30, 31
7 [a]2 Chr. 20:3; Ezra 8:21; Jon. 3:5
[8 1]Lit., *them* [2]Lit., *their* [a Ps]. 130:1; Jon. 1:6, 14 [b Is. 59]:16-19; 55:6, 7; Jer. 18:11
[9] [a]2 Sam. 12:22; Joel 2:14
10 [1]Lit., *do* [a]1 Kin. 21:27-29; Jer. 31:18 [b]Ex. 32:14; Jer. 18:8; Amos 7:3, 6
1 [a]Jon. 4:4, 9; Matt. 20:15; Luke 15:28
[2 1]Lit., *my word* [2]Lit., *I was beforehand in [fleei]ng* [a]Jer. 20:7 [b]Jon. [1]:3 [c]Ex. 34:6; Num. [14:1]8; Ps. 86:5, 15; Joel 2:13
3 [1]Lit., *soul* [a]1 Kin. [1]9:4; Job 6:8, 9 [b]Job 7:15, 16; Eccl. 7:1
[5 1]Lit., *the city* [a]1 Kin. 19:9, 13
[6 1]Probably a castor oil [plan]t, and so in vv. 7, 9 [a]nd 10 [2]Lit., *greatly*
7 [a]Joel 1:12
[8] [a]Ezek. 19:12; Hos. [1]3:15 [b]Ps. 121:6; Is. 49:10 [c]Jon. 4:3
[10 1]Lit., *was a son of a [ni]ght* [2]Lit., *a son of a night*
[11] [a]Jon. 3:10 [b]Deut. [1:39;] Is. 7:16 [c]Ps. 36:6

Theme of Jonah:

Author:

Date:

Purpose:

Key Words:
compassion (compassionate)
relent(s)
turn (turned)
pray (prayer)
perish
Lord
called on the Lord (called out to the Lord)

SEGMENT DIVISIONS

		CHAPTER THEMES
		1
		2
		3
		4

MICAH

Micah knew his calling and was ready to fulfill it, for Micah knew his God. What a contrast he is to prophet Jonah! Micah, whose name means "who is like Jehovah," reminds a rebellious people "the l is coming forth from *His* place."

NGS TO DO

. Micah 1:1 gives the historical setting of Micah. Read it carefully and answer as many of the five W's and an H as you can concerning the who, when, where, why, what, and how of this book. Consult the historical chart at the beginning of Micah to see the book in context.

You will note that the reign of the three kings of Judah covers the years 750-686 B.C. Remember that Assyria conquered the northern kingdom in 722 B.C. and Babylon conquered the southern kingdom in 586 B.C.

. For the historical background of the kings of Judah mentioned in Micah 1:1, read 2 Kings 15:32 through 20:21 and 2 Chronicles 27:1 through 33:20.

. Read one chapter at a time. As you observe the text of each chapter:

a. Mark the key words listed on the MICAH AT A GLANCE chart on page 1365. You will find it helpful to record these on a card that you can use as a bookmark while you study Micah.

b. Watch for references to time, such as *when, then, in that day, in the last days*. You might want to draw a clock or note in some other way the references to time.

c. Since Micah's prophecy concerns Samaria (representing the northern kingdom of Israel) and Jerusalem (representing the southern kingdom of Judah), next to the word *Samaria* in Micah 1:1 put "NK" for northern kingdom. Next to the word *Jerusalem* put "SK" for southern kingdom.

As you observe the text, watch which kingdom Micah is referring to. Observe what is said regarding their sins, the consequences of their sin, their future, and the remnant. If it will help, list your insights in the margin.

d. Watch what God is going to do and to whom. Always note to whom Micah is referring.

e. In the margin list everything you learn about Micah and what he is to do.

f. Record the theme or subject of each chapter on the line next to the chapter number in the text and on MICAH AT A GLANCE. When you finish the last chapter of Micah, complete the chart.

In the appendix of this Bible you will find a chart titled THE DAY OF THE LORD (page 1878). Record your insights from Micah on the last days if you think these pertain to the day of the Lord. As you do so, note the reference (book, chapter, and verse) from which you took your information so you can find it later.

NGS TO THINK ABOUT

Review what you have learned about God the Father and the Son in this book. Meditate on these truths. Tell God you want to know Him more intimately and ask Him to open the eyes of your understanding. Ask Him to show you how to live in light of who He is.

Micah 4:12 says the nations do not know the thoughts of the Lord nor do they understand His purpose. They didn't know—but the child of God can know through studying His Word. Remember Amos said, "Surely the Lord GOD does nothing unless He reveals His secret counsel to His servants the prophets" (3:7). God's secret counsel and His plan for the future is in the Word of God. Are you ordering your life in such a way that you take time to study His Word?

What have you learned about the unchanging love and compassion of our God in pardoning your sins? Are you living accordingly?

4. Although you may not be able to trust in others, can you trust in God? Are you? Can H
you? In Micah 6:6-8 God tells you how to approach Him and what He requires. Will yo
accordingly?

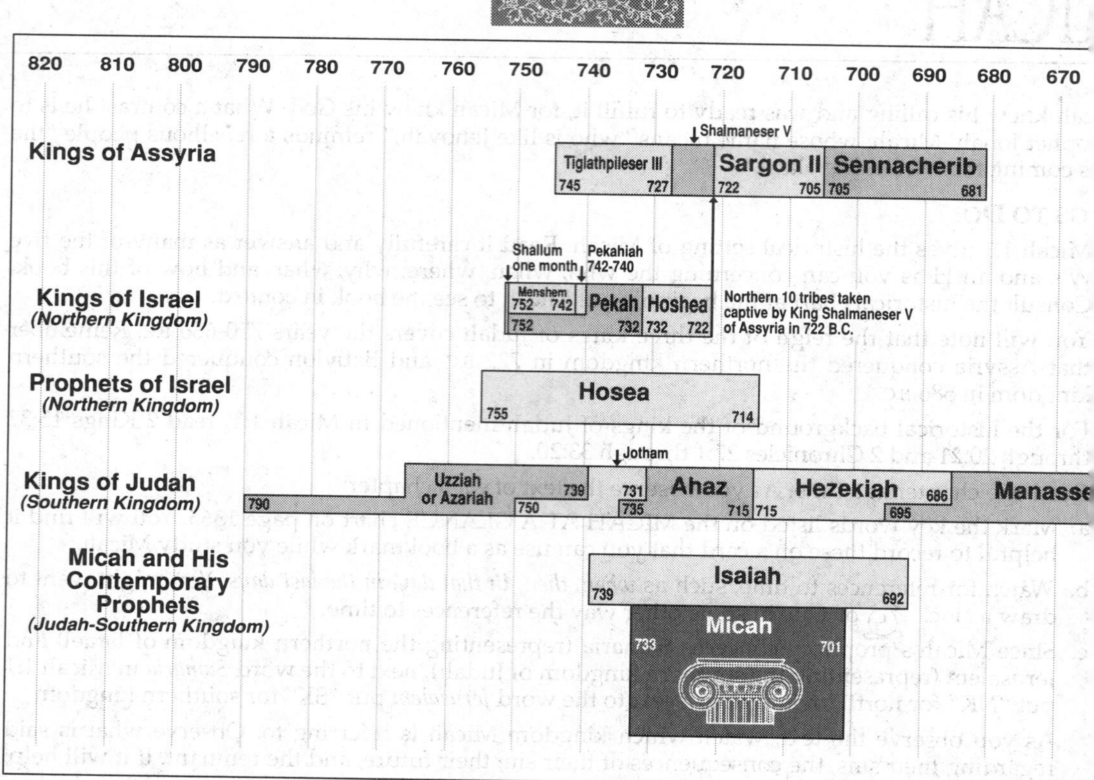

Chapter 1

1 The [a]word of the LORD which came *to* [b]Micah of Moresheth in the
days of [c]Jotham, [d]Ahaz, *and* [e]Hezekiah, kings of Judah, which he
saw concerning Samaria and Jerusalem.

2 Hear, O peoples, all of [1]you;
[a]Listen, O earth and [2]all it contains,
And let the Lord [3]GOD be a [b]witness against you,
The Lord from His holy temple.
3 For behold, the LORD is [a]coming forth from His place.
He will come down and [b]tread on the high places of the [1]earth.
4 [a]The mountains will melt under Him,
And the valleys will be split,
Like wax before the fire,
Like water poured down a steep place.
5 All this is for the rebellion of Jacob
And for the sins of the house of Israel.
What is the [a]rebellion of Jacob?
Is it not [b]Samaria?
What is the [c]high [1]place of Judah?
Is it not Jerusalem?
6 For I will make Samaria a [a]heap of ruins [1]in the open country,

1:1 [a]2 Pet. 1:2
26:18 [c]2 Kin. 1
32-38; 2 Chr. 2
1:1; Hos. 1:1 [d]
16:1-20; 2 Chr.
Is. 7:1-12 [e]2 K
18:1-20; 2 Chr.

2 [1]Lit., *them* [2]
fulness [3]Heb.,
usually rendere
[a]Jer. 6:19; 22:2
50:7

3 [1]Or, *land* [a]Is.
[b]Amos 4:13

4 [a]Ps. 97:5; Is.
Nah. 1:5

5 [1]Lit., *places* [a]
2:19 [b]Is. 7:9; Ar
8:14 [c]2 Chr. 34

6 [1]Lit., *of the fie*
[a]2 Kin. 19:25; M

[b]Planting places for a vineyard.
I will [c]pour her stones down into the valley,
And will [d]lay bare her foundations.
7 All of her [a]idols will be smashed,
All of her earnings will be burned with fire,
And all of her images I will make desolate,
For she collected *them* from a [b]harlot's earnings,
And to the earnings of a harlot they will return.

8 Because of this I must lament and wail,
I must go [a]barefoot and naked;
I must make a lament like the [b]jackals
And a mourning like the ostriches.
9 For her [1a]wound is incurable,
For [b]it has come to Judah;
It has reached the [c]gate of my people,
Even to Jerusalem.
10 [a]Tell it not in Gath,
Weep not at all.
At [1]Beth-le-aphrah roll yourself in the dust.
11 [1]Go on your way, inhabitant of [2]Shaphir, in [a]shameful nakedness.
The inhabitant of [3b]Zaanan does not [4]escape.
The lamentation of [5]Beth-ezel: "He will take from you its [6]support."
12 For the inhabitant of [1]Maroth
Becomes weak [a]waiting for good,
Because a calamity has come down from the LORD
To the [b]gate of Jerusalem.
13 Harness the chariot to the team of horses,
O inhabitant of [a]Lachish—
She was the beginning of sin
To the daughter of Zion—
Because in you were found
The [b]rebellious acts of Israel.
14 Therefore, you will give parting [a]gifts
On behalf of Moresheth-gath;
The houses of [b]Achzib *will* become a [c]deception
To the kings of Israel.
15 Moreover, I will bring on you
The one who takes possession,
O inhabitant of [1a]Mareshah.
The glory of Israel will enter [b]Adullam.
16 Make yourself [a]bald and cut off your hair,
Because of the children of your delight;
Extend your baldness like the eagle,
For they will [b]go from you into exile.

Chapter 2

2 Woe to those who [a]scheme iniquity,
Who work out evil on their beds!
[1b]When morning comes, they do it,
For it is in the [c]power of their hands.
2 They [a]covet fields and then [b]seize *them*,

…r. 31:5; Amos 5:11 …4:1 [d]Ezek. 13:14

[a]Deut. 9:21; 2 Chr. … [b]Deut. 23:18; Is. 23:17

8 [a]Is. 32:11 [b]Is. 13:21, 22

[1]Lit., *wounds* [a]Is. …26; Jer. 30:12, 15 …1. 18:13; Is. 8:7, 8 [c]Mic. 1:12

…e., house of dust [a]2 Sam. 1:20

11 [1]I.e., Go into captivity [2]I.e., …easantness [3]I.e., …g out [4]Lit., *go out* …house of removal …t., *standing place* …zek. 23:29 [b]Josh. 15:37

…e., bitterness [a]Is. …9:9-11; Jer. 14:19 [b]Mic. 1:9

…Josh. 10:3; 2 Kin. …Is. 36:2 [b]Mic. 1:5

…Kin. 16:8 [b]Josh. …15:44 [c]Jer. 15:18

[1]I.e., possession …sh. 15:44 [b]Josh. …5; 15:35; 2 Sam. 23:13

[a]Is. 22:12 [b]2 Kin. …6; Amos 7:11, 17

…Lit., *In the light of …orning* [a]Ps. 36:4; …32:7; Nah. 1:11 …Mos. 7:6, 7 [c]Gen. …:29; Deut. 28:32; Prov. 3:27

…Jer. 22:17; Amos 8:4 [b]Is. 5:8

And houses, and take *them* away.
They [1c]rob a man and his house,
A man and his inheritance.
3 Therefore, thus says the LORD,
"Behold, I am [a]planning against this [b]family a calamity
From which you [c]cannot remove your necks;
And you will not walk [d]haughtily,
For it will be an [e]evil time.
4 "On that day they will [a]take up against you a [1]taunt
And [2b]utter a bitter lamentation *and* say,
'We are completely [c]destroyed!
He exchanges the portion of my people;
How He removes it from me!
To the apostate He [d]apportions our fields.'
5 "Therefore, you will have no one [1a]stretching a measuring line
For you by lot in the assembly of the LORD.

6 '[a]Do not [1]speak out,' *so* they [1]speak out.
But if [2]they do [b]not [1]speak out concerning these things,
[c]Reproaches will not be turned back.
7 "Is it being said, O house of Jacob:
'Is the Spirit of the LORD [a]impatient?
Are these His doings?'
Do not My words [b]do good
To the one [c]walking uprightly?
8 " [1]Recently My people have arisen as an [a]enemy—
You [b]strip the [2]robe off the garment,
From [c]unsuspecting passers-by,
From those returned from war.
9 "The women of My people you [a]evict,
Each *one* from her pleasant house.
From her children you take My [b]splendor forever.
10 "Arise and go,
For this is no place [a]of rest
Because of the [b]uncleanness that brings on destruction,
A painful destruction.
11 "If a man walking after wind and [a]falsehood
Had told lies *and said,*
'I will [1]speak out to you concerning [b]wine and liquor,'
He would be [2]spokesman to [c]this people.

12 "I will surely [a]assemble all of you, Jacob,
I will surely gather the [b]remnant of Israel.
I will put them together like sheep in the fold;
Like a flock in the midst of its pasture
They will be noisy with men.
13 "The breaker goes up before them;
They break out, pass through the gate, and go out by it.
So their king goes on before them,
And the LORD at their head."

Chapter 3

3 And I said,
"[a]Hear now, heads of Jacob

2 [1]Lit., *oppre*
21:1-15

3 [a]Deut. 28:4
18:11 [b]Jer. 8
3:1, 2 [c]Lam.
[d]Is. 2:11, 12

4 [1]Or, *prover*
lament [a]Hab.
9:10, 17-21; M
[c]Is. 6:11; 24:3
[d]Jer. 6:12; 8:1

5 [1]Lit., *casting*
34:13, 16-29;
32:8; Josh. 18

6 [1]Lit., *flow* [2]
prophets [a]Is. 3
Amos 2:12; 7:1
29:10; Mic. 3:6
6:16

7 [a]Is. 50:2; 59:
119:65, 68, 116
15:16 [c]Ps. 15:

8 [1]Lit., *And yes*
[2]Or, *ornaments*
12:8 [b]Mic. 3:2,
[c]Ps. 120:6, 7

9 [a]Jer. 10:20 [b]
39:21; Hab. 2:1

10 [a]Deut. 12:9
106:38

11 [1]Lit., *flow* [2]L
who flows oracle
5:31 [b]Is. 28:7 [c]
30:10, 11

12 [a]Mic. 4:6, 7
5:7, 8; 7:18

3:1 [a]Is. 1:10; Mic

And rulers of the house of Israel.
Is it not for you to [b]know justice?
2 "You who hate good and love evil,
Who [a]tear off their skin from them
And their flesh from their bones,
3 And who [a]eat the flesh of my people,
Strip off their skin from them,
Break their bones,
And [b]chop *them* up as for the pot
And as meat in a kettle."
4 Then they will [a]cry out to the LORD,
But He will not answer them.
Instead, He will [b]hide His face from them at that time,
Because they have [c]practiced evil deeds.

5 Thus says the LORD concerning the prophets
Who [a]lead my people astray;
When they have *something* to bite with their teeth,
They [b]cry, "Peace,"
But against him who puts nothing in their mouths,
They declare holy war.
6 Therefore *it will be* [a]night for you—without vision,
And darkness for you—without divination.
The [b]sun will go down on the prophets,
And the day will become dark over them.
7 The seers will be [a]ashamed
And the [b]diviners will be embarrassed.
Indeed, they will all [c]cover *their* [1]mouths
Because there is [d]no answer from God.
8 On the other hand [a]I am filled with power—
With the Spirit of the LORD—
And with justice and courage
To [b]make known to Jacob his rebellious act,
Even to Israel his sin.
9 Now hear this, [a]heads of the house of Jacob
And rulers of the house of Israel,
Who [b]abhor justice
And twist everything that is straight,
10 Who [a]build Zion with bloodshed
And Jerusalem with violent injustice.
11 Her leaders pronounce [a]judgment for a bribe,
Her [b]priests instruct for a price,
And her prophets divine for money.
Yet they lean on the LORD saying,
"[c]Is not the LORD in our midst?
Calamity will not come upon us."
12 Therefore, on account of you,
[a]Zion will be plowed as a field,
[b]Jerusalem will become a heap of ruins,
And the [c]mountain of the [1]temple *will become* high places of a forest.

Ps. 82:1-5; Jer. 5:5
2 [a]Ps. 53:4; Ezek. :27; Mic. 2:8; 7:2, 3
s. 14:4; 27:2; Zeph. 3 [b]Ezek. 11:3, 6, 7
4 [a]Ps. 18:41; Prov. Is. 1:15; Jer. 11:11 eut. 31:17; Is. 59:2 [c]Is. 3:11; Mic. 7:13
[a]Is. 3:12; 9:15, 16; :14, 15 [b]Jer. 6:14
6 [a]Is. 8:20-22; 9:10-12 [b]Is. 59:10
7 [1]Lit., *mustache* h. 13:4 [b]Is. 44:25; 7:12-14 [c]Mic. 7:16 am. 28:6; Mic. 3:4
. 61:1, 2; Jer. 1:18 [b]Is. 58:1
Mic. 1:1 [b]Ps. 58:1, 2; Is. 1:23
er. 22:13, 17; Hab. 2:12
[a]Is. 1:23; Mic. 7:3 Jer. 6:13 [c]Is. 48:2
[1]Lit., *house* [a]Jer. 18 [b]Ps. 79:1; Jer. 9:11 [c]Mic. 4:1

Chapter 4

4 And it will come about in the [a]last days
That the [b]mountain of the house of the LORD
Will be established [1]as the chief of the mountains.
It will be raised above the hills,
And the [c]peoples will stream to it.
2 And [a]many nations will come and say,
"[b]Come and let us go up to the mountain of the LORD
And to the house of the God of Jacob,
That [c]He may teach us about His ways
And that we may walk in His paths."
For [d]from Zion will go forth the law,
Even the word of the LORD from Jerusalem.
3 And He will [a]judge between many peoples
And render decisions for mighty, [1]distant nations.
Then they will hammer their swords [b]into plowshares
And their spears into pruning hooks;
Nation will not lift up sword against nation,
And never again will they [2]train for war.
4 And each of them will [a]sit under his vine
And under his fig tree,
With [b]no one to make *them* afraid,
For the [c]mouth of the LORD of hosts has spoken.
5 Though all the peoples walk
Each in the [a]name of his god,
As for us, [b]we will walk
In the name of the [c]LORD our God forever and ever.

6 "In that day," declares the LORD,
"I will assemble the [a]lame,
And [b]gather the outcasts,
Even those whom I have afflicted.
7 "I will make the lame a [a]remnant,
And the outcasts a strong nation,
And the [b]LORD will reign over them in Mount Zion
From now on and forever.
8 "And as for you, [1a]tower of the flock,
[2]Hill of the daughter of Zion,
To you it will come—
Even the [b]former dominion will come,
The kingdom of the daughter of Jerusalem.

9 "Now, why do you [a]cry out loudly?
Is there no king among you,
Or has your [b]counselor perished,
That agony has gripped you like a woman in childbirth?
10 "[a]Writhe and labor to give birth,
Daughter of Zion,
Like a woman in childbirth,
For now you will [b]go out of the city,
Dwell in the field,
And go to Babylon.
[c]There you will be rescued;
[d]There the LORD will redeem you

4:1 [1]Lit., *on* [a]Is. 2 Dan. 2:28; 10:14; 3:5 [b]Ezek. 43:12; 3:12; Zech. 8:3 [c]P 22:27; 86:9; Jer. 3

2 [a]Zech. 2:11; 14: [b]Is. 2:3; Jer. 31:6 25:8, 9, 12; Is. 54: [d]Is. 42:1-4; Zech.

3 [1]Lit., *at a distan* [2]Lit., *learn* [a]Is. 2:4 11:3-5 [b]Joel 3:10

4 [a]1 Kin. 4:25; Ze 3:10 [b]Lev. 26:6; J 30:10 [c]Is. 1:20; 4

5 [a]2 Kin. 17:29 [b] 10:12 [c]Josh. 24:1 26:8, 13

6 [a]Zeph. 3:19 [b]P 147:2; Ezek. 34:1 37:21

7 [a]Mic. 5:7, 8; 7:1 24:23

8 [1]Heb., *Migdal-* [2]Heb., *Ophel of* 48:3, 12; 61:3; Mi 2:12 [b]Is. 1:26; Ze 9:10

9 [a]Jer. 8:19 [b]Is.

10 [a]Mic. 5:3 [b]2 20:18; Hos. 2:14 43:14; 45:13; Mic 7:8-12 [d]Is. 48:20 52:9-12

[1]Lit., *look on* [a]Is. 5:25-30; 17:12-14

From the hand of your enemies.
11 "And now [a]many nations have been assembled against you
Who say, 'Let her be polluted,
And let our eyes [1]gloat over Zion.'

12 [a]Ps. 147:19, 20

12 "But they do not [a]know the thoughts of the LORD,
And they do not understand His purpose;
For He has gathered them like sheaves to the threshing floor.
13 "Arise and [a]thresh, daughter of Zion,

13 [a]Is. 41:15 [b]Jer. 51:20-23 [c]Is. 60:9

For your horn I will make iron
And your hoofs I will make bronze,
That you may [b]pulverize many peoples,
That you may [c]devote to the LORD their unjust gain
And their wealth to the Lord of all the earth.

Chapter 5

[1]Ch. 4:14 in Heb. it., *He has* [a]1 Kin. 4; Job 16:10; Lam. 3:30

5 "[1]Now muster yourselves in troops, daughter of troops;
[2]They have laid siege against us;
With a rod they will [a]smite the judge of Israel on the cheek.
2 " [1]But as for [a]you, Bethlehem Ephrathah,

h. 5:1 in Heb. [2]Or, *s appearances are om long ago, from days of old* [a]Gen. 9; 48:7; Ruth 4:11; 2:6 [b]Is. 11:1; Luke 4; John 7:42 [c]Jer. 21; Zech. 9:9 [d]Ps. :25; Prov. 8:22, 23

Too little to be among the clans of Judah,
From [b]you One will go forth for Me to be [c]ruler in Israel.
[2]His goings forth are [d]from long ago,
From the days of eternity."
3 Therefore, He will [a]give them *up* until the time
When she [b]who is in labor has borne a child.
Then the [c]remainder of His brethren
Will return to the sons of Israel.
4 And He will arise and [a]shepherd *His flock*

s. 11:8; Mic. 4:10; [b]Mic. 4:9, 10 [c]Is. :20-22; Mic. 5:7, 8

In the strength of the LORD,
In the majesty of the name of the LORD His God.
And they will [1]remain,
Because [2]at that time He will be great
To the [b]ends of the earth.
5 And this One [a]will be *our* peace.

[1]Or, *live* in safety t., *now* [a]Is. 40:11; 9; Ezek. 34:13-15, 24; Mic. 7:14 [b]Is. 45:22; 52:10

When the [b]Assyrian invades our land,
When he tramples on our [1]citadels,
Then we will raise against him
Seven shepherds and eight leaders of men.
6 And they will [a]shepherd the land of Assyria with the sword,

palaces [a]Is. 9:6; e 2:14; Eph. 2:14; l. 1:20 [b]Is. 8:7, 8; 10:24-27

The land of [b]Nimrod at its entrances;
And He will [c]deliver *us* from the Assyrian
When he attacks our land
And when he tramples our territory.

7 Then the [a]remnant of Jacob

ah. 2:11-13; Zeph. Gen. 10:8-11 [c]Is. 14:25; 37:36, 37

Will be among many peoples
Like [b]dew from the LORD,
Like [c]showers on vegetation
Which do not wait for man
Or delay for the sons of men.
8 And the remnant of Jacob

lic. 2:12; 4:7; 5:3; [b]Deut. 32:2; Ps. 3; Hos. 14:5 [c]Ps. 72:6; Is. 44:3

Will be among the nations,
Among many peoples

[a]Like a lion among the beasts of the forest,
Like a young lion among flocks of sheep,
Which, if he passes through,
[b]Tramples down and [c]tears,
And there is [d]none to rescue.
9 Your hand will be [a]lifted up against your adversaries,
And all your enemies will be cut off.

10 "And it will be in that day," declares the LORD,
"[a]That I will cut off your [b]horses from among you
And destroy your chariots.
11 "I will also cut off the [a]cities of your land
And tear down all your [b]fortifications.
12 "I will cut off [a]sorceries from your hand,
And you will have fortunetellers no more.
13 "[a]I will cut off your carved images
And your *sacred* pillars from among you,
So that you will no longer bow down
To the work of your hands.
14 "I will root out your [1a]Asherim from among you
And destroy your cities.
15 "And I will [a]execute vengeance in anger and wrath
On the nations which have not obeyed."

Chapter 6

6 Hear now what the LORD is saying,
"Arise, plead your case [1]before the mountains,
And let the hills hear your voice.
2 "Listen, you mountains, to the indictment of the LORD,
And you enduring [a]foundations of the earth,
Because the [b]LORD has a case against His people;
Even with Israel He will dispute.
3 "[a]My people, [b]what have I done to you,
And [c]how have I wearied you? Answer Me.
4 "Indeed, I [a]brought you up from the land of Egypt
And [b]ransomed you from the house of slavery,
And I sent before you [c]Moses, Aaron, and [d]Miriam.
5 "My people, remember now
What [a]Balak king of Moab counseled
And what Balaam son of Beor answered him,
And from [b]Shittim to [c]Gilgal,
In order [1]that you might know the [d]righteous acts of the LORD."

6 [a]With what shall I come to the LORD
And bow myself before the God on high?
Shall I come to Him with [b]burnt offerings,
With yearling calves?
7 Does the LORD take delight in [a]thousands of rams,
In ten thousand rivers of oil?
Shall I present my [b]first-born *for* my rebellious acts,
The fruit of my body for the sin of my soul?
8 He has [a]told you, O man, what is good;
And [b]what does the LORD require of you
But to [c]do justice, to [d]love [1]kindness,

8 [a]Gen. 49:9; Nu 24:9 [b]Ps. 44:5; Is 41:15, 16; Mic. 4: Zech. 10:5 [c]Hos. [d]Ps. 50:22

9 [a]Ps. 10:12; 21: 26:11

10 [a]Zech. 9:10 [b] 17:16; Is. 2:7; Ho

11 [a]Is. 1:7; 6:11 2:12-17; Hos. 10: Amos 5:9

12 [a]Deut. 18:10- 2:6; 8:19

13 [a]Is. 2:18; 17:8 6:9

14 [1]I.e., wooden symbols of a fem deity [a]Ex. 34:13; 17:8; 27:9

15 [a]Is. 1:24; 65:

6:1 [1]Lit., *with*

2 [a]2 Sam. 22:16 104:5 [b]Is. 1:18; 4:1; 12:2

3 [a]Ps. 50:7 [b]Jer [c]Is. 43:22, 23

4 [a]Ex. 12:51; 20 [b]Deut. 7:8 [c]Ex. 4 Ps. 77:20 [d]Ex. 1

5 [1]Lit., *to know* 22:5, 6 [b]Num. 2 Josh. 2:1; 3:1 [c]J 4:19; 5:9, 10 [d]1 12:7; Is. 1:27

6 [a]Ps. 40:6-8 [b]P 51:16, 17

7 [a]Ps. 50:9; Is. 40:16 [b]Lev. 18:2 20:1-5; 2 Kin. 16 7:31

8 [1]Or, *loyalty* [a]D 30:15 [b]Deut. 10 56:1; Jer. 22:3 [c]

And to walk [2e]humbly with your God?

9 The voice of the LORD will call to the city—
And it is sound wisdom to fear Thy name:
"Hear, O tribe. Who has appointed [1]its time?
10 "Is there yet a man in the wicked house,
Along with treasures of [a]wickedness,
And a [1b]short measure *that is* cursed?
11 "Can I justify wicked [a]scales
And a bag of deceptive weights?
12 "For the rich men of *the* [1]city are full of [a]violence,
Her residents speak [b]lies,
And their [c]tongue is deceitful in their mouth.
13 "So also I will make *you* [a]sick, striking you down,
[b]Desolating *you* because of your sins.
14 "You will eat, but you will [a]not be satisfied,
And your [1]vileness will be in your midst.
You will *try to* remove *for safekeeping*,
But you will [b]not preserve *anything*,
And what you do preserve I will give to the sword.
15 "You will sow but you will [a]not reap.
You will tread the olive but will not anoint yourself with oil;
And the grapes, but you will [b]not drink wine.
16 "The statutes of [a]Omri
And all the works of the house of [b]Ahab are observed;
And in their devices you [c]walk.
Therefore, I will give you up for [d]destruction
And [1]your inhabitants for [e]derision,
And you will bear the [f]reproach of My people."

Chapter 7

7 Woe is me! For I am
Like the fruit pickers and the [a]grape gatherers.
There is not a cluster of grapes to eat,
Or a [b]first-ripe fig *which* [1]I crave.
2 The [1]godly person has [a]perished from the land,
And there is no upright *person* among men.
All of them lie in wait for [b]bloodshed;
Each of them hunts the other with a [c]net.
3 Concerning evil, both hands do it [a]well.
The prince asks, also the judge, for a [b]bribe,
And a great man speaks the desire of his soul;
So they weave it together.
4 The best of them is like a [a]briar,
The most upright like a [b]thorn hedge.
The day when you post a watchman,
Your [c]punishment will come.
Then their [d]confusion will occur.
5 Do not [a]trust in a neighbor;
Do not have confidence in a friend.
From her who lies in your bosom
Guard [1]your lips.
6 For [a]son treats father contemptuously,
Daughter rises up against her mother,

circumspectly
s. 57:15; 66:2

9 [1]Lit., *it*

Lit., *shrunken*
[a]Jer. 5:26, 27;
[b]Ezek. 45:9,
10; Amos 8:5

v. 19:36; Hos.
12:7

her [a]Is. 1:23;
os 6:3, 4; Mic.
[b]Jer. 9:2-6, 8;
:13; Amos 2:4
[c]Is. 3:8

c. 1:9 [b]Is. 1:7;
6:11

4 [1]Or possibly,
or *excreta* [a]Is.
9:20 [b]Is. 30:6

. 28:38-40; Jer.
3 [b]Amos 5:11;
Zeph. 1:13

Lit., *her* [a]1 Kin.
5:25, 26 [b]1 Kin.
9-33 [c]Jer. 7:24
18:16; Mic. 6:13
. 19:8; 25:9, 18;
[f]Ps. 44:13; Jer.
:51; Hos. 12:14

.it., *my soul* [a]Is.
[b]Is. 28:4; Hos.
9:10

r, *loyal* [a]Is. 57:1
; Mic. 3:10 [c]Jer.
5:26; Hos. 5:1

[a]Prov. 4:16, 17
s 5:12; Mic. 3:11

Ezek. 2:6; 28:24
h. 1:10 [c]Is. 10:3;
os. 9:7 [d]Is. 22:5

openings of your
mouth [a]Jer. 9:4

t. 10:21, 35; Luke
12:53

Daughter-in-law against her mother-in-law;
[b]A man's enemies are the men of his own household.

7 But as for me, I will [a]watch expectantly for the LORD;
I will [b]wait for the God of my salvation.
My [c]God will hear me.
8 [a]Do not rejoice over me, O [b]my enemy.
Though I fall I will [c]rise;
Though I dwell in darkness, the LORD is a [d]light for me.

9 I will bear the indignation of the LORD
Because I have sinned against Him,
Until He [a]pleads my case and executes justice for me.
He will bring me out to the [b]light,
And I will see His [1c]righteousness.
10 Then my enemy will see,
And shame will cover her who [a]said to me,
"Where is the LORD your God?"
My eyes will look on her;
[1]At that time she will [2]be [b]trampled down,
Like mire of the streets.
11 *It will be* a day for [a]building your walls.
On that day will your boundary be extended.
12 It *will be* a day when [1]they will [a]come to you
From Assyria and the cities of Egypt,
From Egypt even to the [2]Euphrates,
Even from sea to sea and mountain to mountain.
13 And the earth will become [a]desolate because of her inhabitants,
On account of the [b]fruit of their deeds.

14 [a]Shepherd Thy people with Thy [b]scepter,
The flock of Thy [1]possession
Which dwells by itself in the woodland,
In the midst of [2]a fruitful field.
Let them feed in [c]Bashan and Gilead
[d]As in the days of old.
15 "As in the days when you came out from the land of Egypt,
I will show [1a]you miracles."
16 Nations [a]will see and be ashamed
Of all their might.
They will [b]put *their* hand on *their* mouth,
Their ears will be deaf.
17 They will [a]lick the dust like a serpent,
Like [b]reptiles of the earth.
They will come [c]trembling out of their [1]fortresses;
To the LORD our God they will come in [d]dread,
And they will be afraid before Thee.
18 Who is a God like Thee, who [a]pardons iniquity
And passes over the rebellious act of the [b]remnant of His [1]possession?
He does not [c]retain His anger forever,
Because He [d]delights in [2]unchanging love.
19 He will again have compassion on us;
[a]He will tread our iniquities under foot.

6 [b]Matt. 10:3

7 [a]Hab. 2:1
Is. 25:9 [c]Ps.

8 [a]Prov. 24:1
12 [b]Mic. 7:10
9:11 [d]Is. 9:2

9 [1]I.e., right
[a]Jer. 50:34 [b]
Is. 42:7, 16 [c]
56:1

10 [1]Lit., *Now become a tra*
place [a]Joel 2:
51:23; Zech.

11 [a]Is. 54:11;

12 [1]Lit., *he* [2]L
[a]Is. 19:23-25;

13 [a]Jer. 25:11
6:13 [b]Is. 3:10,
3:4

14 [1]Or, *inherit*
Carmel [a]Ps. 9
40:11; 49:10; M
[b]Lev. 27:32; Ps
[c]Jer. 50:19 [d]Ar

15 [1]Lit., *him* [a]
34:10; Ps. 78:1

16 [a]Is. 26:11 [b]

17 [1]Lit., *fastnes*
[a]Ps. 72:9; Is. 49
[b]Deut. 32:24 [c]P
18:45 [d]Is. 25:3;

18 [1]Or, *inherita*
lovingkindness
34:7, 9; Is. 43:25
2:12; 4:7; 5:7, 8
103:8, 9, 13 [d]Je

19 [a]Jer. 50:20

[1]Several ancient [versions] read *our* [b]Is. [...]; 43:25; Jer. 31:34

[20] [1]Or, *faithfulness* [2]Or, *lovingkindness* [a]Gen. 24:27; 32:10 [b]Deut. 7:8, 12

Yes, Thou wilt [b]cast all [1]their sins
Into the depths of the sea.
20 Thou wilt give [1a]truth to Jacob
And [2]unchanging love to Abraham,
Which Thou didst [b]swear to our forefathers
From the days of old.

Micah at a Glance

[Theme] of Micah:

Divisions

	Chapter Themes
	1
	2
	3
	4
	5
	6
	7

Author:

Date:

Purpose:

Key Words:
Samaria
Jerusalem
Jacob
Israel
Judah
Zion
Assyrian
destroy(ed, destruction)
remnant
in that day (in the last days)
My (Thy, His) people

NAHUM

One hundred years had passed since Jonah went to Nineveh to proclaim its destruction. N another prophet, Nahum, proclaims his vision from God regarding Nineveh, the capital of Ass What a sharp contrast between Nahum's prophetic message and the meaning of his name—comfor

Assyria sat smugly on her throne. Under Sargon II, Assyria had conquered Israel in 722 B.C. In B.C. under Sennacherib's rule the Assyrians had invaded Judah. Rabshakeh, Sennacherib's general, boasted to Judah that no gods of the nations they had conquered had been able to deliver their pec To Hezekiah, king of Judah, he proclaimed, "Do not let your God in whom you trust deceive saying, 'Jerusalem shall not be given into the hand of the king of Assyria.' Behold, you have h what the kings of Assyria have done to all the lands, destroying them completely. So will you spared?" (2 Kings 19:10-11).

God spared Judah. Sennacherib, king of Assyria, returned to Nineveh and died there.

But that wasn't the end of the story. God had a message for Nineveh, the capital of Assyria, wh the time of Nahum's prophecy sat at the pinnacle of wealth and power, secure behind her impregn walls. Or so she thought.

THINGS TO DO

1. If you have time, read Jonah to see what God said to the people of Nineveh one hundred y earlier and how they responded.
2. Read Nahum and as you read, mark the key words listed on the NAHUM AT A GLANCE c on page 1371.
3. Study the historical chart on page 1367 to see the context of the book.
4. Now read Nahum chapter by chapter and do the following:
   a. Nahum tells us much about God. Carefully observe the text and then in the margin summa what you learn about God. For instance, in 1:4 it says God rules over nature. Write that in y list in the margin under the title "God."
   b. Observe all you can about Nineveh. Watch for the repeated use of *Nineveh* and the pron which refer to Nineveh, such as *you* and *your*. Mark any reference to Nineveh that you mis Then in the margin list what you learn about "Nineveh's Sin."
   c. Make a third list in the margin, "What Will Happen to Nineveh?"
5. Record the theme or subject of each chapter on NAHUM AT A GLANCE and in the text or line next to the chapter number. Also record the theme of the book and complete any c information requested on the chart.

THINGS TO THINK ABOUT

1. What do you learn about the justice of God and the certainty of His Word from this book? Is the kind of God you can trust? Why?
2. Is there anything that can stop God from doing what He says or plans?
3. Can compassionate people deliver this kind of a message? What if you were impressed by Go bring this kind of warning to others? Would you? What would motivate you or hinder you the way, remember the meaning of Nahum's name.

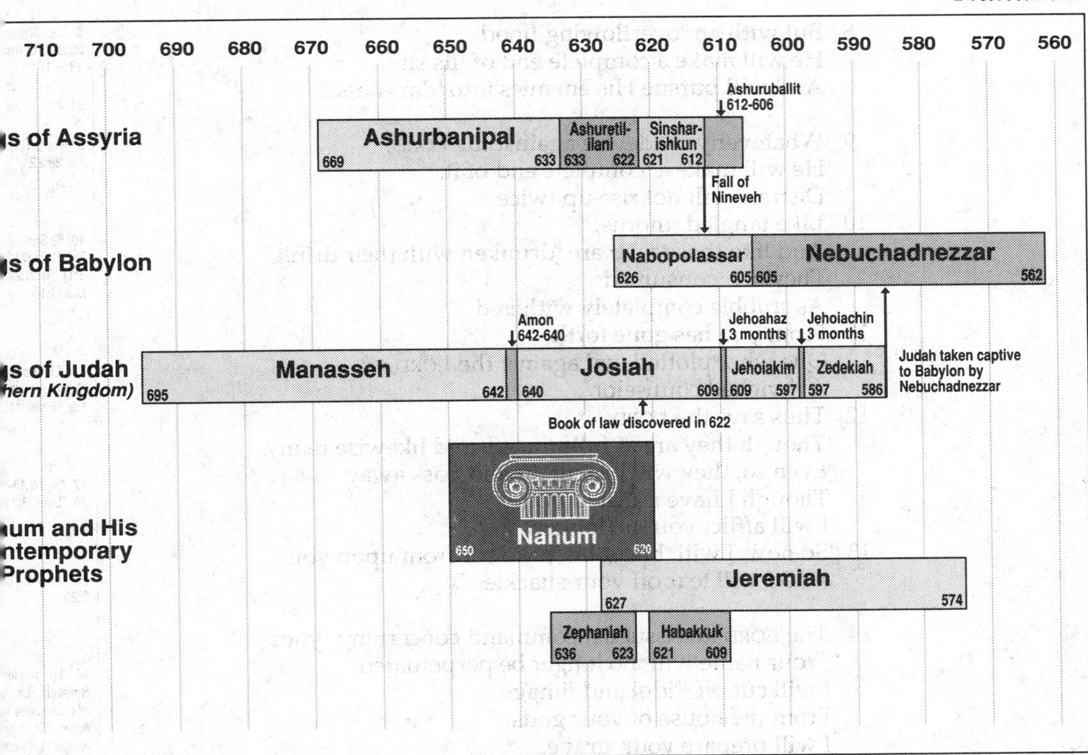

Chapter 1

1 The [1a]oracle of [b]Nineveh. The book of the vision of Nahum the
Elkoshite.
2 A [a]jealous and avenging God is the LORD;
The LORD is [b]avenging and [1]wrathful.
The LORD takes [c]vengeance on His adversaries,
And He reserves wrath for His enemies.
3 The LORD is [a]slow to anger and great in power,
And the LORD will by no means leave *the guilty* unpunished.
In [b]whirlwind and storm is His way,
And [c]clouds are the dust beneath His feet.
4 He [a]rebukes the sea and makes it dry;
He dries up all the rivers.
[b]Bashan and Carmel wither;
The blossoms of Lebanon wither.
5 Mountains [a]quake because of Him,
And the hills [b]dissolve;
Indeed the earth is [c]upheaved by His presence,
The [d]world and all the inhabitants in it.
6 [a]Who can stand before His indignation?
Who can endure the [b]burning of His anger?
His [c]wrath is poured out like fire,
And the [d]rocks are broken up by Him.
7 The LORD is [a]good,
A stronghold in the day of trouble,
And [b]He knows those who take refuge in Him.

Or, *burden* [a]Is. 9:1; Jer. 23:33, 1:1; Zech. 9:1; [b]2 Kin. 19:36; 1:2; Nah. 2:8; Zeph. 2:13

a possessor of Ex. 20:5; Josh. Deut. 32:35, 41 [c]Ps. 94:1

x. 34:6, 7; Neh. Ps. 103:8 [b]Ex. 6; Is. 29:6 [c]Ps. 104:3; Is. 19:1

sh. 3:15, 16; Ps. ; Is. 50:2; Matt. 8:26 [b]Is. 33:9

. 19:18; 2 Sam. 18:7 [b]Mic. 1:4 1, 20 [d]Ps. 98:7

10:10; Mal. 3:2 3:13 [c]Is. 66:15 [d]1 Kin. 19:11

25:8; 37:39, 40; 33:11 [b]Ps. 1:6; :14; 2 Tim. 2:19

8 But with an [a]overflowing flood
He will make a complete end of [1]its site,
And will pursue His enemies into [b]darkness.

9 Whatever you [a]devise against the LORD,
He will make a [b]complete end of it.
Distress will not rise up twice.
10 Like tangled [a]thorns,
And like those who are [b]drunken with their drink,
They are [c]consumed
As stubble completely withered.
11 From you has gone forth
One who [a]plotted evil against the LORD,
A [1b]wicked counselor.
12 Thus says the LORD,
"Though they are at full *strength* and likewise many,
Even so, they will be [a]cut off and pass away.
Though I have afflicted you,
I will afflict you [b]no longer.
13 "So now, I will [a]break his yoke bar from upon you,
And I will tear off your shackles."

14 The LORD has issued a command concerning [1]you:
"[2]Your name will [a]no longer be perpetuated.
I will cut off [3b]idol and [4]image
From the house of your gods.
I will prepare your [c]grave,
For you are contemptible."

15 [1]Behold, [a]on the mountains the feet of him who brings good news,
Who announces peace!
[b]Celebrate your feasts, O Judah;
Pay your vows.
For [c]never again will the [2]wicked one pass through you;
He is [d]cut off completely.

Chapter 2

2 [1]The one who [a]scatters has come up against [2]you.
Man the fortress, watch the road;
[3]Strengthen your back, [4]summon all *your* strength.
2 For the LORD will restore the [a]splendor of Jacob
[b]Like the splendor of Israel,
Even though devastators have devastated them
And [c]destroyed their vine branches.

3 The shields of [1]his mighty men are *colored* red,
The warriors are dressed in [a]scarlet,
The chariots are *enveloped* in [2]flashing steel
[3]When he is prepared *to march*,
And the cypress [b]*spears* are brandished.
4 The [a]chariots race madly in the streets,
They rush wildly in the [1]squares,
Their appearance is like torches,

8 [1]I.e., Ninev[...] 28:2, 17f.; Am[...] 13:9, 10

9 [a]Ps. 2:1; Na[...] [b]Is. 28:22

10 [a]2 Sam. 2[...] 7:4 [b]Is. 56:12[...] 3:11 [c]Is. 5:24[...] Mal. 4:1

11 [1]Or, *worthl[...] Belial* [a]Is. 10:7[...] 1:9 [b]Ezek. 11[...]

12 [a]Is. 10:16-[...] 34 [b]Lam. 3:31

13 [a]Is. 9:4; 10 2:20

14 [1]I.e., the kin[...] Nineveh [2]Lit., [...] *of your name v[...] sown* [3]Or, *a gr[...] image* [4]Lit., *ca[...] image* [a]Job 18 109:13; Is. 14:2[...] 46:1, 2; Mic. 5:[...] [c]Ezek. 32:22, 2[...]

15 [1]Ch. 2:1 in [...] [2]Or, *worthless c[...]* Heb., *Belial* [a]Is 52:7; Rom. 10:[...] 23:2, 4 [c]Is. 52:[...] 3:17 [d]Is. 29:7, [...]

2:1 [1]Ch. 2:2 in [...] [2]Lit., *your face [...] Make strong yo[...]* [4]Lit., *strengthen[...] greatly* [a]Jer. 51

2 [a]Is. 60:15 [b]E[...] 37:21-23 [c]Ps. 8[...]

3 [1]I.e., those at[...] Nineveh [2]Lit., *fi[...] steel* [3]Lit., *On th[...] of his preparatio[...]* [a]Ezek. 23:14, 15 39:23

4 [1]Lit., *broad pla[...]* [a]Is. 66:15; Jer. 4 Ezek. 26:10; Nah[...]

They dash to and fro like lightning flashes.
5 He remembers his [a]nobles;
They [b]stumble in their march,
They hurry to her wall,
And the [1]mantelet is set up.
6 The gates of the rivers are opened,
And the palace is dissolved.
7 And it is fixed:
She is stripped, she is carried away,
And her handmaids are [a]moaning like the sound of doves,
[b]Beating on their [1]breasts.

8 Though Nineveh *was* like a pool of water throughout her days,
Now they are fleeing;
"Stop, stop,"
But [a]no one turns back.
9 Plunder the silver!
Plunder the [a]gold!
For there is no limit to the treasure—
Wealth from every kind of desirable object.
10 She is [a]emptied! Yes, she is desolate and waste!
[b]Hearts are melting and knees knocking!
Also anguish is in [1]the whole body,
And all their [c]faces are grown pale!
11 Where is the den of the lions
And the feeding place of the [a]young lions,
Where the lion, lioness, and lion's cub prowled,
With nothing to disturb *them*?
12 The lion tore enough for his cubs,
[1]Killed *enough* for his lionesses,
And filled his lairs with prey
And his dens with torn flesh.
13 "Behold, [a]I am against you," declares the LORD of hosts. "I will
[b]burn up her chariots in smoke, a sword will devour your young
lions, I will [c]cut off your prey from the land, and no longer will the
voice of your messengers be heard."

Chapter 3

3 [a]Woe to the bloody city, completely full of lies *and* pillage;
Her prey never departs.
2 The [a]noise of the whip,
The noise of the rattling of the wheel,
Galloping horses,
And [1]bounding chariots!
3 Horsemen charging,
Swords flashing, [a]spears gleaming,
[b]Many slain, a mass of corpses,
And [1c]countless dead bodies—
They stumble over [2]the dead bodies!
4 *All* because of the [a]many harlotries of the harlot,
The charming one, the [b]mistress of sorceries,
Who [c]sells nations by her harlotries
And families by her sorceries.
5 "Behold, [a]I am against you," declares the LORD of hosts;

ering used in
e [a]Nah. 3:18
[b]Jer. 46:12

t., *hearts* [a]Is.
11 [b]Is. 32:12

er. 46:5; 47:3

ev. 18:12, 16

ll the loin [a]Is.
4:10-13; Nah.
2:14; Is. 13:7,
21:7 [c]Joel 2:6

11 [a]Is. 5:29

[1]Lit., *Strangled*

r. 21:13; Ezek.
ah. 3:5 [b]Josh.
; Ps. 46:9 [c]Is.
4, 25; Nah. 3:1

[a]Ezek. 24:6, 9

skipping [a]Job
2-25; Jer. 47:3;
Nah. 2:3, 4

there is no end
Lit., *their* [a]Hab.
[b]Is. 34:3; 66:16
:36; Ezek. 39:4

Is. 23:17; Ezek.
29; Rev. 17:1, 2
:9, 12, 13 [c]Rev.
18:3

er. 50:31; Ezek.
26:3; Nah. 2:13

"And I will [1b]lift up your skirts over your face,
And [c]show to the nations your nakedness
And to the kingdoms your disgrace.
6 "I will [a]throw [1]filth on you
And [b]make you vile,
And set you up as a [c]spectacle.
7 "And it will come about that all who see you
Will [1]shrink from you and say,
'Nineveh is devastated!
[a]Who will grieve for her?'
Where will I seek comforters for you?"

INSIGHT

No-amon refers to **Thebes,** the Greek name for No, the capital of Egypt. Since Nahum reminds Nineveh of the fall of No-amon (Thebes), his prophecy had to come after 663 B.C. and before Nineveh was destroyed in 612 B.C. by the Babylonians, Medes, and Scythians.

8 Are you better than [1a]No-amon,
Which was situated by the [b]waters of the Nile,
With water surrounding her,
Whose rampart *was* [2]the sea,
Whose wall *consisted* of [2]the sea?
9 [a]Ethiopia was *her* might,
And Egypt too, without limits.
[b]Put and [c]Lubim were among [1]her helpers.
10 Yet she [a]became an exile,
She went into captivity;
Also her [b]small children were dashed to pieces
[c]At the head of every street;
They [d]cast lots for her honorable men,
And all her great men were bound with fetters.
11 You too will become [a]drunk,
You will be [b]hidden.
You too will search for a refuge from the enemy.
12 All your fortifications are [a]fig trees with [1b]ripe fruit—
When shaken, they fall into the eater's mouth.
13 Behold, your people are [a]women in your midst!
The gates of your land are [b]opened wide to your enemies;
Fire consumes your gate bars.
14 [a]Draw for yourself water for the siege!
[b]Strengthen your fortifications!
Go into the clay and tread the mortar!
Take hold of the brick mold!
15 There [a]fire will consume you,
The sword will cut you down;
It will [b]consume you as the locust *does*.

Multiply yourself like the creeping locust,
Multiply yourself like the swarming locust.
16 You have increased your [a]traders more than the stars of
heaven—
The creeping locust [1]strips and flies away.
17 Your [1a]guardsmen are like the swarming locust.
Your [b]marshals are like hordes of grasshoppers
Settling in the stone walls on a cold day.
The sun rises and they flee,
And the place where they are is not known.
18 Your shepherds are [a]sleeping, O [b]king of Assyria;
Your [c]nobles are lying down.

5 [1]Lit., *uncov* [b]Is. 47:2, 3; Je [c]Ezek. 16:37

6 [1]Lit., *detest things* [a]Job 9 30:8; Mal. 2:9 14:16; Jer. 51

7 [1]Lit., *flee* [a]I Jer. 15:5

8 [1]I.e., the city Thebes [2]I.e., [a]Jer. 46:25; Ez 30:14-16 [b]Is.

9 [1]Lit., *your* [a] [b]Jer. 46:9; Eze 30:5; 38:5 [c]2 C 16:8

10 [a]Is. 19:4; 2 137:9; Is. 13:16 13:16 [c]Lam. 2 3:3; Obad. 11

11 [a]Is. 49:26; J 25:27; Nah. 1:1 2:10, 19; Hos.

12 [1]Lit., *first fru* [a]Rev. 6:13 [b]Is.

13 [a]Is. 19:16; J 50:37; 51:30 [b]Is 2; Nah. 2:6

14 [a]2 Chr. 32:3 [b]Nah. 2:1

15 [a]Is. 66:15, 1 2:13; 3:13 [b]Joel

16 [1]I.e., strips vegetation; or, *m* [a]Is. 23:8

17 [1]Or, *officials* 9:7 [b]Jer. 51:27

18 [a]Ps. 76:5, 6; 56:10; Jer. 51:57 50:18 [c]Nah. 2:5

[d]1 Kin. 22:17; Is. 13:14

Your people are [d]scattered on the mountains,
And there is no one to regather *them*.
19 There is [a]no relief for your breakdown,
Your [b]wound is incurable.
All who hear [1]about you
Will [c]clap *their* hands over you,
For on whom has not your evil passed continually?

[1]Lit., *your report*
er. 46:11; Mic. 1:9
0:12 [c]Job 27:23; Lam. 2:15

Nahum at a Glance

of Nahum:

Chapter Themes
1
2
3

Author:

Date:

Purpose:

Key Words:
I am against you

I will

Nineveh
(Assyria)

Judah
(Jacob, Israel)

HABAKKUK

"The righteous will live by his faith." This verse, which pierced Martin Luther's heart and br about a reformation, is from Habakkuk (2:4). Paul will echo it in Romans and Galatians, but its are in the Old Testament, where God affirms that salvation has always been by faith and faith alon

And what is the setting of the verse that unshackled Luther from the chains of religion and br him into a vital relationship with the living God? You will discover this as you study Habakkuk, a which ends with a crescendo of faith in anticipation of Judah's darkest of hours.

THINGS TO DO

General Instructions

As you read Habakkuk it's critical for you to know whether God is speaking or Habakk speaking. Since the book is only three chapters long, read through Habakkuk and note in the m when God speaks or when Habakkuk speaks. Try it on your own, then look at the HABAKKUK GLANCE chart on page 1378 for the segment divisions which show who is speaking when.

Chapter 1

1. An oracle can be translated "a burden." What is Habakkuk's burden—what is bothering Note this in the margin of chapter 1 where it is described.
2. Read through Habakkuk 1 and mark every reference to *God* (*God, the Holy One, Lord,* etc. every personal pronoun which refers to Him. Then in the margin list everything you learn God as a personality and note what He is going to do.
3. The Chaldeans, another name for the Babylonians, invaded the southern kingdom of Judah times. In 605 B.C. Daniel and many nobles were taken captive. Then in 597 B.C. Ezekiel was captive. The third and final siege occurred in 586 B.C. when Jerusalem and the temple destroyed. List in the margin everything you learn about the Chaldeans—what they will dc what will happen to them.
4. Study the historical chart on page 1373 and notice the relationship between the tin Habakkuk's writing and the Babylonian invasion.

Chapter 2

1. Mark every reference, including pronouns, to the *proud* or *haughty man.* Then, in the margi what he is like and with whom he is contrasted.
2. Mark each use of the word *woe* and then observe to whom the woe is going to come, why it come, and what will happen when it comes. If you want to, summarize this in the margin.
3. List in the margin what you learn about God.

Chapter 3

1. Habakkuk's prayer is written in a poetic form which is intensely emotional. A statement is n and then followed by a similar statement which heightens the meaning or repeats the tru another way. Read the prayer again, keeping its form in mind.
2. As you read, ask the five W's and an H: Who is doing what? To whom or what? When will done? Why will it be done? What specifically is going to happen? How? In the margin everything you learn about God from this chapter.
3. What does this chapter say about Habakkuk and his relationship to God? List it in the ma Then compare what you write with 2:4. How is Habakkuk going to live? Have his circumsta changed?

Fill in the appropriate sections of HABAKKUK AT A GLANCE, recording the theme of each paragraph, each chapter, and of the book itself. Fill in any other information asked for on the chart. Also record the theme of each chapter on the line in the text next to the chapter number.

GS TO THINK ABOUT

What do you learn about God? His ways, His Word, His character? If He is the same yesterday, today, and forever, how would such insight into God influence your relationship to Him and to His Word? How would this affect your response to your circumstances?

What have you learned about the haughty or proud? God says in James 4 that He resists the proud. Can you understand why? Can you see any element of pride or haughtiness in your life which you need to deal with?

Review what you learned about the woes pronounced by God. Ask God to search your heart. Would these woes be applicable to you because of your lifestyle? Do you need to confess anything to God and receive His forgiveness and cleansing (*see* 1 John 1:9)?

As you look at how Habakkuk begins and ends, think about what brought about the difference in Habakkuk and then apply it to your own life. Are you questioning, doubting God and His ways, and is it causing despair? What do you need to do?

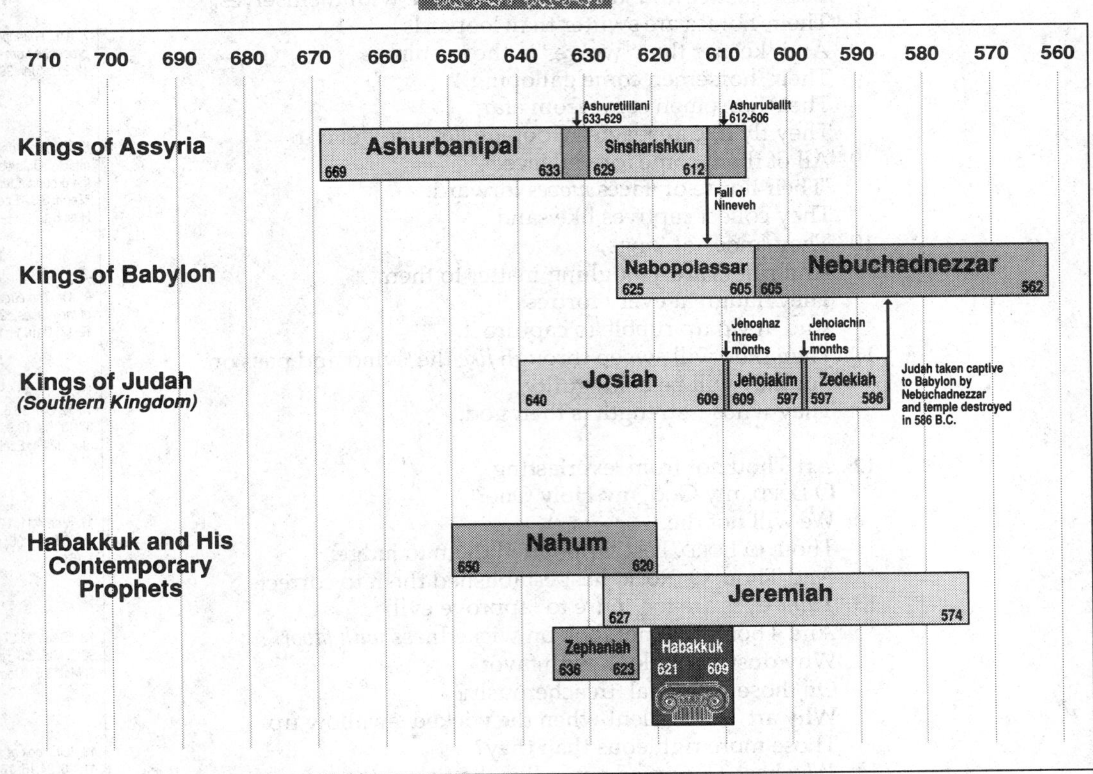

[1]Or, *burden* [a]Is. 13:1; Nah. 1:1

. 13:1, 2; 22:1, 2 [b]Jer. 14:9

Chapter 1 ______________________

1 The [1a]oracle which Habakkuk the prophet saw.
2 [a]How long, O LORD, will I call for help,
And Thou wilt not hear?
I cry out to Thee, "Violence!"
Yet Thou dost [b]not save.

3 Why dost Thou make me [a]see iniquity,
And cause *me* to look on wickedness?
Yes, [b]destruction and violence are before me;
[c]Strife exists and contention arises.
4 Therefore, the [a]law is [1]ignored
And justice [2]is never upheld.
For the wicked [b]surround the righteous;
Therefore, justice comes out [c]perverted.

5 "[a]Look among the nations! Observe!
Be astonished! [b]Wonder!
Because *I* am doing [c]something in your days—
You would not believe if [1]you were told.
6 "For behold, I am [a]raising up the Chaldeans,
That [1]fierce and impetuous people
Who march [2]throughout the earth
To [3b]seize dwelling places which are not theirs.
7 "They are dreaded and [a]feared.
Their [b]justice and [1]authority [2]originate with themselves.
8 "Their [a]horses are swifter than leopards
And [1]keener than [b]wolves in the evening.
Their [2]horsemen come galloping,
Their horsemen come from afar;
They fly like an [c]eagle swooping *down* to devour.
9 "All of them come for violence.
[1]Their horde of [a]faces *moves* forward.
They collect captives like sand.
10 "They [a]mock at kings,
And rulers are a laughing matter to them.
They [b]laugh at every fortress,
And [c]heap up rubble to capture it.
11 "Then they will sweep through *like* the [a]wind and pass on.
But they will be held [b]guilty,
They whose [c]strength is their god."

12 Art Thou not from [a]everlasting,
O LORD, my God, my Holy One?
We will not die.
Thou, O LORD, hast [b]appointed them to judge;
And Thou, O [c]Rock, hast established them to correct.
13 *Thine* eyes are too [a]pure to [1]approve evil,
And Thou canst not look on wickedness *with favor.*
Why dost Thou [b]look with favor
On those who deal [c]treacherously?
Why art Thou [d]silent when the wicked [e]swallow up
Those more righteous than they?
14 *Why* hast Thou made men like the fish of the sea,
Like creeping things without a ruler over them?
15 *The Chaldeans* [a]bring all of them up with a hook,
[b]Drag them away with their net,
And gather them together in their fishing net.
Therefore, they rejoice and are glad.
16 Therefore, they offer a sacrifice to their net.
And [1]burn incense to their fishing net;

3 [a]Ps. 55:9-11 20:18 [b]Jer. 20 15:10

4 [1]Or, *ineffect* *numbered* [2]Lit., *goes forth* [a]Ps 119:126; Is. 59 [b]Ps. 22:12; Is. [c]Is. 5:20; Ezek.

5 [1]Lit., *it* [a]Acts [b]Is. 29:9 [c]Is. 2 Ezek. 12:22-28

6 [1]Lit., *bitter* [2]*breadth of* [3]Lit. *possession of* 24:2; Jer. 4:11- 8:10

7 [1]Lit., *eminen* *proceeds from* 18:2, 7 [b]Jer. 39

8 [1]Or, *more ea* attack [2]Or, *stee* the ground [a]Jer [b]Zeph. 3:3 [c]Eze Hos. 8:1

9 [1]Or, *The eag of their faces* [a]2 12:17; Dan. 11:1

10 [a]2 Chr. 36:6, 37:13 [b]Is. 10:9; [c]Jer. 32:24; Eze

11 [a]Jer. 4:11, 12 2:3 [c]Dan. 4:30; 1:16

12 [a]Deut. 33:27 90:2; Mal. 3:6 [b]I 6; Mal. 3:5 [c]Deu

13 [1]Lit., *look at* 11:4-6; 34:15, 16 12:1, 2 [c]Is. 24:16 50:21 [e]Ps. 35:25

15 [a]Jer. 16:16; A 4:2 [b]Ps. 10:9

16 [1]Or, *sacrifice*

Because through [a]these things their [2]catch is [3]large,
And their food is [4]plentiful.
17 Will they therefore empty their [a]net
And continually [b]slay nations without sparing?

Chapter 2

2 I will [a]stand on my guard post
And station myself on the rampart;
And I will [b]keep watch to see [c]what He will speak to me,
And how I may reply [1]when I am reproved.
2 Then the LORD answered me and said,
"[a]Record the vision
And inscribe *it* on tablets,
That [1]the one who [2]reads it may run.
3 "For the vision is yet for the [a]appointed time;
It [1]hastens toward the goal, and it will not [2]fail.
Though it tarries, [b]wait for it;
For it will certainly come, it [c]will not delay.

4 "Behold, as for the [a]proud one,
His soul is not right within him;
But the [b]righteous will live by his [1]faith.
5 "Furthermore, [a]wine betrays the [b]haughty man,
So that he does not [c]stay at home.
He [d]enlarges his appetite like Sheol,
And he is like death, never satisfied.
He also gathers to himself all nations
And collects to himself all peoples.

6 "Will not all of these [a]take up a taunt-song against him,
Even mockery *and* insinuations against him,
And say, '[b]Woe to him who increases what is not his—
For how long—
And makes himself [1]rich with loans?'
7 "Will not [1]your creditors [a]rise up suddenly,
And those who [2]collect from you awaken?
Indeed, you will become plunder for them.
8 "Because you have [a]looted many nations,
All the remainder of the peoples will loot you—
Because of human bloodshed and violence [1]done to the land,
To the town and all its inhabitants.

9 "Woe to him who gets [a]evil gain for his house
To [b]put his nest on high
To be delivered from the hand of calamity!
10 "You have devised a [a]shameful thing for your house
By cutting off many peoples;
So you are [b]sinning against yourself.
11 "Surely the [a]stone will cry out from the wall,
And the rafter will answer it from the [1]framework.

12 "Woe to him who [a]builds a city with bloodshed
And founds a town with [1]violence!
13 "Is it not indeed from the LORD of hosts

portion [3]Lit., ...tiful [4]Lit., the ...n [a]Jer. 44:17
...8 [b]Is. 14:5, 6
[1]Lit., upon my [a]Is. 21:8 [b]Ps. 5:3 [c]Ps. 85:8
...ne may read it ...ently [2]Or, is to ...t [a]Deut. 27:8; ...5:4; Rev. 1:19
...pants [2]Or, lie ...:17, 19; 10:14 ...27:14 [c]Ezek. ...25; Heb. 10:37
...thfulness [a]Ps. ...13:11 [b]Rom. ...Gal. 3:11; Heb. 10:38
...ov. 20:1 [b]Prov. ... [c]2 Kin. 14:10 ...7:20; 30:16; Is. 5:11-15
Lit., heavy [a]Is. ...-10; Jer. 50:13 ...-29; Hab. 2:12
those who bite ... [2]Lit., violently ...ou [a]Prov. 29:1
of the land [a]Is. 27:7; Zech. 2:8
...er. 22:13; Ezek. ...:27 [b]Jer. 49:16
...Kin. 9:26; Nah. ...Hab. 2:16 [b]Jer. 26:19
...it., wood [a]Josh. ...:27; Luke 19:40
..., injustice [a]Mic. 3:10; Nah. 3:1

That peoples [a]toil for fire,
And nations grow weary for nothing?
14 "For the earth will be [a]filled
With the knowledge of the glory of the LORD,
As the waters cover the sea.

15 "Woe to you who make [1]your neighbors drink,
Who mix in your venom even to make *them* drunk
So as to look on their nakedness!
16 "You will be filled with disgrace rather than honor.
Now you yourself [a]drink and [1]expose your *own* nakedness.
The [b]cup in the LORD's right hand will come around to you,
And [c]utter disgrace *will come* upon your glory.
17 "For the [a]violence [1]done to Lebanon will [2]overwhelm you,
And the devastation of *its* beasts [3]by which you terrified them,
[b]Because of human bloodshed and [c]violence [4]done to the land,
To the town and all its inhabitants.

18 "What [a]profit is the [1]idol when its maker has carved it,
Or [2]an image, a [b]teacher of falsehood?
For *its* maker [c]trusts in his *own* handiwork
When he fashions speechless idols.
19 "Woe to him who [a]says to a *piece of* wood, '[b]Awake!'
To a dumb stone, 'Arise!'
And that is *your* teacher?
Behold, it is overlaid with [c]gold and silver,
And there is [d]no breath at all inside it.
20 "But the [a]LORD is in His holy temple.
[1]Let all the earth [b]be silent before Him."

Chapter 3

3 A prayer of Habakkuk the prophet, according to [1]Shigionoth.
2 LORD, I have [a]heard [1]the report about Thee *and* [2]I [b]fear.
O LORD, [c]revive [d]Thy work in the midst of the years,
In the midst of the years make it known;
In wrath remember [3e]mercy.

3 God comes from [a]Teman,
And the Holy One from Mount [b]Paran. Selah.
His [c]splendor covers the heavens,
And the [d]earth is full of His praise.
4 *His* [a]radiance is like the sunlight;
He has rays *flashing* from His hand,
And there is the hiding of His [b]power.
5 Before Him goes [a]pestilence,
And [b]plague comes [1]after Him.
6 He stood and surveyed the earth;
He looked and [a]startled the nations.
Yes, the perpetual mountains were shattered,
The ancient hills [1]collapsed.
His ways are [b]everlasting.
7 I saw the tents of Cushan under [a]distress,
The tent curtains of the land of [b]Midian were trembling.

13 [a]Is. 50:11

14 [a]Ps. 22:27 Zech. 14:9

15 [1]Lit., *his r*

16 [1]Lit., *show uncircumcise stagger;* so D ancient versio 4:21 [b]Jer. 25 [c]Nah. 3:6

17 [1]Lit., *of Le* [2]Lit., *cover* [3]L *terrified them the land* [a]Joe Zech. 11:1 [b]P Hab. 2:8 [c]Jer Hab. 2:8

18 [1]Or, *a grav* [2]Lit., *a cast me image* [a]Is. 42 Jer. 2:27, 28 14; Zech. 10:2 115:4, 8

19 [a]Jer. 2:27, [b]1 Kin. 18:26-2 135:15-18; Jer 14 [d]Ps. 135:1

20 [1]Lit., *Hush Him, all the ea* 1:2 [b]Zeph. 1:7 2:13

3:1 [1]I.e., a hig emotional poe

2 [1]Or, *Thy rep stand in awe o work, O LORD; midst of the ye it,* [3]Or, *compas* [a]Job 42:5 [b]Ps. Jer. 10:7 [c]Ps. 85:6 [d]Ps. 44:1 1:5 [e]Num. 14:1 2 Sam. 24:15-1 54:8

3 [a]Jer. 49:7; Ar 1:12; Obad. 9 21:21; Deut. 33 113:4; 148:13 48:10

4 [a]Ps. 18:12 [b]

5 [1]Lit., *at His fe* 12:29, 30; Num. 16:46-49 [b]Num Ps. 18:12, 13

6 [1]Lit., *bowed; down* [a]Job 21:1 35:5 [b]Hab. 1:12

7 [a]Ex. 15:14-16 31:7, 8; Judg. 7 8:12

8 Did the LORD rage against the [a]rivers,
Or *was* Thine anger against the rivers,
Or *was* Thy wrath against the [b]sea,
That Thou didst [c]ride on Thy horses,
On Thy [d]chariots of salvation?
9 Thy [a]bow was made bare,
The rods of [1]chastisement were sworn. Selah.
Thou didst [b]cleave the earth with rivers.
10 The mountains saw Thee *and* quaked;
The downpour of waters swept by.
The deep [a]uttered forth its voice,
It lifted high its hands.
11 [a]Sun *and* moon stood in their places;
They went away at the [b]light of Thine arrows,
At the radiance of Thy gleaming spear.
12 In indignation Thou didst [a]march through the earth;
In anger Thou didst [1b]trample the nations.
13 Thou didst go forth for the [a]salvation of Thy people,
For the salvation of Thine [b]anointed.
Thou didst strike the [c]head of the house of the evil
To lay him open from [1]thigh to neck. Selah.
14 Thou didst pierce with his [a]own [1]spears
The head of his [2]throngs.
They [b]stormed in to scatter [3]us;
Their exultation *was* like those
Who [c]devour the oppressed in secret.
15 Thou didst [a]tread on the sea with Thy horses,
On the [b]surge of many waters.

16 I heard and my [1]inward parts [a]trembled,
At the sound my lips quivered.
Decay enters my [b]bones,
And in my place I tremble.
Because I must [c]wait quietly for the day of distress,
[2]For the [d]people to arise *who* will invade us.
17 Though the [a]fig tree should not blossom,
And there be no [1]fruit on the vines,
Though the yield of the [b]olive should fail,
And the fields produce no food,
Though the [c]flock should be cut off from the fold,
And there be [d]no cattle in the stalls,
18 Yet I will [a]exult in the LORD,
I will [b]rejoice in the [c]God of my salvation.
19 The Lord [1]GOD is my [a]strength,
And [b]He has made my feet like hinds' *feet*,
And makes me walk on my [c]high places.

For the choir director, on my stringed instruments.

Ex. 7:19, 20; Josh. 3:16; Is. 50:2 [b]Ex. 6, 21; Ps. 114:3, 5 33:26; Ps. 18:10; . 3:15 [d]Ps. 68:17

., *word* [a]Ps. 7:12, 3; Hab. 3:11 [b]Ps. 78:16; 105:41

[a]Ps. 93:3; 98:7, 8

[a]Josh. 10:12-14 [b]Ps. 18:14

[1]Or, *thresh* [a]Ps. 7 [b]Is. 41:15; Jer. 51:33; Mic. 4:13

[1]Lit., *foundation* 5:2; 2 Sam. 5:20; 19, 20 [b]Ps. 20:6; [c]Ps. 68:21; 110:6

[1]Lit., *shafts* [2]Or, *rriors* or *villagers* , *me* [a]Judg. 7:22 11:40; Zech. 9:14 [c]Ps. 10:8; 64:2-5

. 77:19; Hab. 3:8 [b]Ex. 15:8

.it., *belly* [2]Or, *To upon the people will* [a]Dan. 10:8; 3:2 [b]Job 30:17, Jer. 23:9 [c]Luke 21:19 [d]Jer. 5:15

., *produce* [a]Joel 0-12; Amos 4:9; 4:8, 9 [b]Mic. 6:15 1:18 [d]Jer. 5:17

[a]Ex. 15:1, 2; Job , Is. 61:10; Rom. Ps. 46:1-5; Phil. s. 25:5; 27:1; Is. 12:2

[1]Heb., *YHWH*, rendered *LORD* 18:32, 33; 27:1; . 45:24 [b]2 Sam. 34 [c]Deut. 33:29

Theme of Habakkuk:

Author:

Date:

Purpose:

Key Words:

SEGMENT DIVISIONS	WHO IS SPEAKING	PARAGRAPH THEMES
	HABAKKUK SPEAKS	1:1-4
	GOD SPEAKS	1:5-11
	HABAKKUK SPEAKS	1:12-17
	GOD SPEAKS	2:1-3
		2:4-5
		2:6-8
		2:9-11
		2:12-14
		2:15-17
		2:18-20
	HABAKKUK PRAYS	3:1-2
		3:3-7
		3:8-15
		3:16-19

ZEPHANIAH

During the latter years of King Josiah's reign, Israel was a spiritual oasis which was surrounded by ostasy—an abandonment of faith.

We do not know exactly when Zephaniah's prophecy came, although it was during Josiah's reign 40-609 B.C.). However, some argument can be made from the text that Zephaniah prophesied before reforms Josiah made sometime between 622 and 621 B.C. Whenever it came, it came full gale, a rmy blast calling God's people to humility and righteousness in the face of the day of the Lord's ger.

IINGS TO DO

1. Zephaniah 1:1 gives the genealogy of Zephaniah and also the historical setting of the book. Record your insights about the author on the ZEPHANIAH AT A GLANCE chart on page 1385. If you want a more thorough picture of the historical setting of Zephaniah, read 2 Kings 22:1 through 23:30 and 2 Chronicles 34:1 through 35:27.
2. Consult the historical chart on page 1380 to see the relationship of his prophecy to the Babylonian captivity and the destruction of Nineveh.
3. Read Zephaniah paragraph by paragraph, watching carefully for the references to the different peoples and places. Mark these references and note what is said about each one.
   a. Be careful to note when there is a change of subject. Watch carefully what happens in 3:1. Although Jerusalem is not mentioned by name at the beginning of chapter 3, the prophecy changes from Nineveh (the Assyrian capital) to Jerusalem.
   b. Decide on the theme or subject covered in each paragraph and record this under "Paragraph Themes" on ZEPHANIAH AT A GLANCE.
4. Now read Zephaniah chapter by chapter and mark the key words listed on ZEPHANIAH AT A GLANCE.
   a. Watch for any other key words as you read chapter by chapter and mark these.
   b. As you mark *the day* or *that day* notice what will happen in that day and how it relates, if at all, to the day of the Lord. (Remember, prophecy can have a near and a distant fulfillment. If you are not familiar with interpreting prophecy, you can read "Guidelines for Interpreting Predictive Prophecy" in the front of the Bible on page I-58.)
   c. In the margin of each chapter list what you learn from the key words you marked. Note what God will do, to whom, and why. Also note what effect it will have on Israel.
5. In the appendix is the chart titled THE DAY OF THE LORD (*see* page 1878) on which you can record what you learn about the day of the Lord. Note the reference (book, chapter, and verse) you took your information from so you can find it later.
6. Fill in ZEPHANIAH AT A GLANCE. Record the theme of each chapter and of the book in the designated spaces. Then record the chapter theme in the text next to the chapter number.

INGS TO THINK ABOUT

1. The day of the Lord is also mentioned in the New Testament. One such reference is in 1 Thessalonians 5:1-11. If the day of the Lord is yet future, what should you be doing to prepare for the time of its approaching?
2. What do you learn about the nation of Israel and its future? Are you using these truths in sharing the good news of Jesus Christ with God's people, the Jews?

3. Think about what you have learned about God from Zephaniah and how such knowledge sho
affect the way you live.

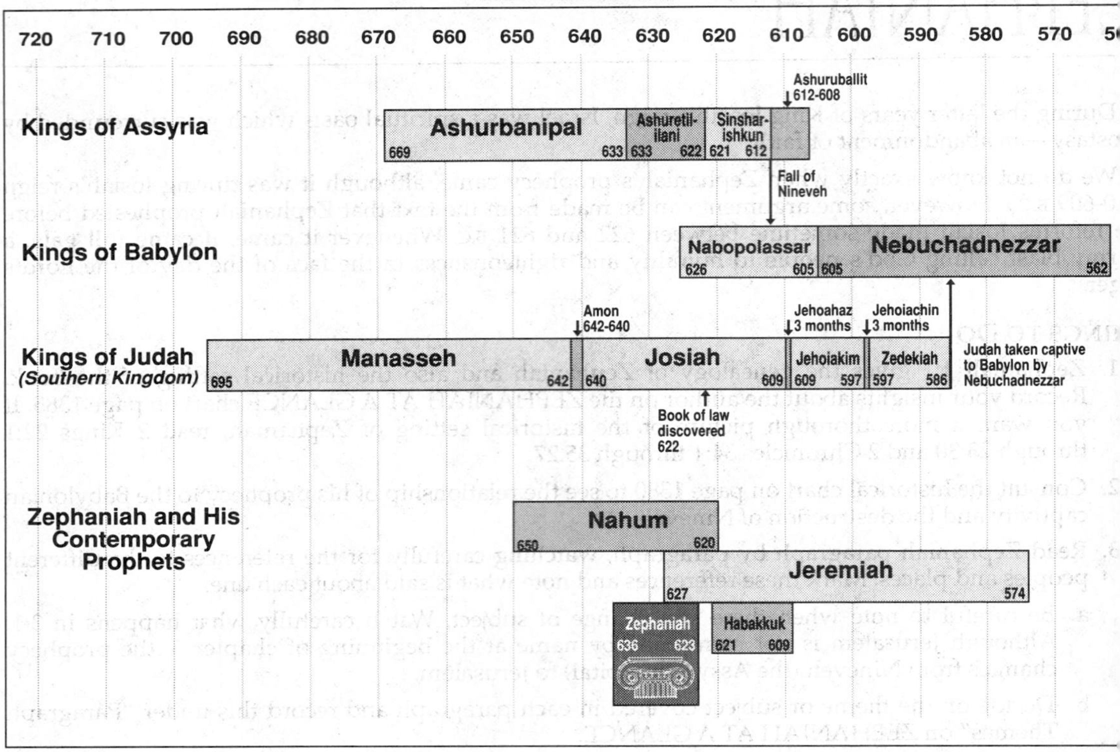

Chapter 1 ____________________

1 The word of the LORD which came to Zephaniah son of Cushi,
son of Gedaliah, son of Amariah, son of Hezekiah, in the days of
[a]Josiah son of [b]Amon, king of Judah,
2 "I will completely [a]remove all *things*
From the face of the [1]earth," declares the LORD.
3 "I will remove [a]man and beast;
I will remove the [b]birds of the sky
And the fish of the sea,
And the [1c]ruins along with the wicked;
And I will cut off man from the face of the [2]earth," declares the
LORD.
4 "So I will [a]stretch out My hand against Judah
And against all the inhabitants of Jerusalem.
And I will [b]cut off the remnant of Baal from this place,
And the names of the [c]idolatrous priests along with the priests.
5 "And those who bow down on the [a]housetops to the host of
heaven,
And those who bow down *and* [b]swear to the LORD and *yet* swear
by [1c]Milcom,
6 And those who have [a]turned back from following the LORD,
And those who have [b]not sought the LORD or inquired of Him."

1:1 [a]2 Kin. 22:1, 2; 2 Chr. 34:1-33; Jer. 22:11 [b]2 Kin. 21:18; 2 Chr. 33:20-25

2 [1]*Lit., ground* [a]Ge 6:7; Jer. 7:20; Ezek 33:27, 28

3 [1]*Or, stumbling b* [2]*Lit., ground* [a]Is. 6: 12 [b]Jer. 4:25; 9:10 [c]Ezek. 7:19; 14:3,

4 [a]Jer. 6:12; Ezek. 6:14 [b]Mic. 5:13 [c]2 23:5; Hos. 10:5

5 [1]*Or, their king;* M *Malcam*, probably variant spelling of Milcom [a]2 Kin. 23: Jer. 19:13 [b]Jer. 5:2 7:9, 10 [c]1 Kin. 11:5 Jer. 49:1

6 [a]Is. 1:4; Hos. 7:1 [b]Is. 9:13

7 [1a]Be silent before the Lord [2]GOD!
For the [b]day of the LORD is near,
For the LORD has prepared a [c]sacrifice,
He has [d]consecrated His guests.
8 "Then it will come about on the day of the LORD's sacrifice,
That I will [a]punish the princes, the king's sons,
And all who clothe themselves with [b]foreign garments.
9 "And I will punish on that day all who leap on the *temple*
threshold,
Who fill the house of their [1]lord with [a]violence and deceit.
10 "And on that day," declares the LORD,
"There will be the sound of a cry from the [a]Fish Gate,
A wail from the [1b]Second Quarter,
And a loud crash from the [c]hills.
11 "Wail, O inhabitants of the [1]Mortar,
For all the [2]people of [a]Canaan will be silenced;
All who weigh out [b]silver will be cut off.
12 "And it will come about at that time
That I will [a]search Jerusalem with lamps,
And I will punish the men
Who are [1b]stagnant in spirit,
Who say in their hearts,
'The LORD will [c]not do good or evil!'
13 "Moreover, their wealth will become [a]plunder,
And their houses desolate;
Yes, [b]they will build houses but not inhabit *them*,
And plant vineyards but not drink their wine."

14 Near is the [a]great [b]day of the LORD,
Near and coming very quickly;
Listen, the day of the LORD!
[1]In it the warrior [c]cries out bitterly.
15 A day of wrath is that day,
A day of [a]trouble and distress,
A day of destruction and desolation,
A day of [b]darkness and gloom,
A day of clouds and thick darkness,
16 A day of [a]trumpet and battle cry,
Against the [b]fortified cities
And the high corner towers.
17 And I will bring [a]distress on men,
So that they will walk [b]like the blind,
Because they have sinned against the LORD;
And their [c]blood will be poured out like dust,
And their [d]flesh like dung.
18 Neither their [a]silver nor their gold
Will be able to deliver them
On the day of the LORD's wrath;
And [b]all the earth will be devoured
In the fire of His jealousy,
For He will [c]make a complete end,
Indeed a terrifying one,
Of all the inhabitants of the earth.

Hush [2]Heb., HWH, usually d *LORD* [a]Hab. . 2:13 [b]Zeph. [c]Is. 34:6; Jer. Sam. 16:5; Is. 13:3

.21; Hab. 1:10 [b]Is. 2:6

ord [a]Jer. 5:27; Amos 3:10

e., a district of salem [a]2 Chr. eh. 3:3; 12:39 34:22 [c]Ezek. 6:13

e., a district of erusalem [2]Or, *ant people will* 5; Zech. 14:21 6, 17; Hos. 9:6

, *thickening on* es [a]Jer. 16:16, . 9:4-11; Amos r. 48:11; Amos Ezek. 8:12; 9:9

er. 15:13; 17:3 5:11; Mic. 6:15

it., *There* [a]Jer. el 2:11; Mal. 4:5 k. 7:7, 12; 30:3; 15; 3:14; Zeph. [c]Ezek. 7:16-18

22:5 [b]Joel 2:2, ; Amos 5:18-20

27:13; Jer. 4:19 [b]Is. 2:12-15

er. 10:18 [b]Deut. [c]Ezek. 24:7, 8 [d]Jer. 8:2; 9:22

ek. 7:19 [b]Zeph. Gen. 6:7; Ezek. 7:5-7

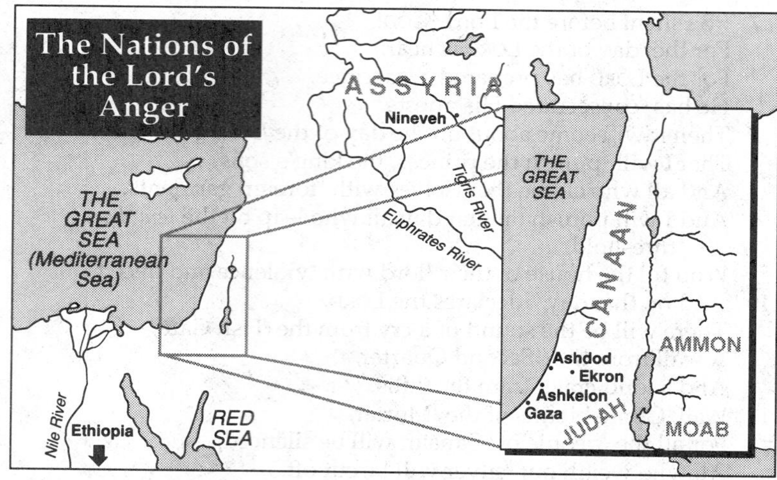

Chapter 2

2 Gather yourselves together, yes, [a]gather,
O nation [b]without [1]shame,
2 Before the decree [1]takes effect—
The day passes [a]like the chaff—
Before the [b]burning anger of the LORD comes upon you,
Before the [c]day of the LORD's anger comes upon you.
3 [a]Seek the LORD,
All you [b]humble of the [1]earth
Who have carried out His [2]ordinances;
[c]Seek righteousness, seek humility.
Perhaps you will be [d]hidden
In the day of the LORD's anger.

4 For [a]Gaza will be abandoned,
And Ashkelon a desolation;
[a]Ashdod will be driven out at noon,
And [a]Ekron will be uprooted.
5 Woe to the inhabitants of the seacoast,
The nation of the [1a]Cherethites!
The word of the LORD is [b]against you,
O [c]Canaan, land of the Philistines;
And I will [d]destroy you,
So that there will be [e]no inhabitant.
6 So the seacoast will be [a]pastures,
With [1]caves for shepherds and folds for flocks.
7 And the coast will be
For the [a]remnant of the house of Judah,
They will [b]pasture on it.
In the houses of Ashkelon they will lie down at evening;
For the LORD their God will [c]care for them
And [d]restore their fortune.

8 "I have heard the [1a]taunting of Moab
And the [b]revilings of the sons of Ammon,
With which they have [2]taunted My people

The **Cherethites** were probably paid soldiers of the Philistines. David used some of these soldiers as personal bodyguards. Both Ezekiel and Zephaniah pronounced judgment on them.

2:1 [1]Or, *longi*
20:4; Joel 1:14
3:3; 6:15

2 [1]Lit., *is born*
17:13; Hos. 13
4:11; Nah. 1:6
1:18

3 [1]Or, *land* [2]C
[a]Ps. 105:4; Am
[b]Ps. 22:26; Is.
[c]Amos 5:14, 15
57:1; Is. 26:20

4 [a]Amos 1:7, 8
9:5-7

5 [1]I.e., a segm
Philistines with
Crete [a]Ezek. 2
[b]Amos 3:1 [c]Ze
[d]Is. 14:29, 30

6 [1]Or, *meadow*
wells [a]Is. 5:17;

7 [a]Is. 11:16 [b]Is
[c]Ex. 4:31; Ps. 8
[d]Jer. 32:44; Zep

8 [1]Lit., *reproac*
reproached [a]E
25:8 [b]Ezek. 25:

And [3c]become arrogant against their territory.
9 "Therefore, as I live," declares the LORD of hosts,
The God of Israel,
"Surely [a]Moab will be like [b]Sodom,
And the sons of [c]Ammon like [d]Gomorrah—
A place possessed by nettles and salt pits,
And a perpetual desolation.
The remnant of My people will [e]plunder them,
And the remainder of My nation will inherit them."
10 This they will have in return for their [a]pride, because they have
[1b]taunted and [2]become arrogant against the people of the LORD of
hosts.
11 The LORD will be [a]terrifying to them, for He will [1]starve [b]all the
gods of the earth; and all the [c]coastlands of the nations will [d]bow
down to Him, everyone from his *own* place.
12 "You also, O [a]Ethiopians, will be slain by My sword."
13 And He will [a]stretch out His hand against the north
And destroy [b]Assyria,
And He will make [c]Nineveh a desolation,
Parched like the wilderness.
14 And flocks will lie down in her midst,
[1]All beasts which range in herds;
Both the [2a]pelican and the hedgehog
Will lodge in [3]the tops of her pillars;
[4]Birds will sing in the window,
Desolation *will be* on the threshold;
For He has laid bare the cedar work.
15 This is the [a]exultant city
Which [b]dwells securely,
Who says in her heart,
"[c]I am, and there is no one besides me."
How she has become a [d]desolation,
A resting place for beasts!
[e]Everyone who passes by her will hiss
And wave his hand *in contempt*.

Chapter 3

3 Woe to her who is [a]rebellious and [b]defiled,
The [c]tyrannical city!
2 She [a]heeded no voice;
She [b]accepted no instruction.
She did not [c]trust in the LORD;
She did not [d]draw near to her God.
3 Her [a]princes within her are roaring lions,
Her judges are [b]wolves at evening;
They leave nothing for the morning.
4 Her prophets are [a]reckless, treacherous men;
Her [b]priests have profaned the sanctuary.
They have done violence to the law.
5 The LORD is [a]righteous [b]within her;
He will [c]do no injustice.
[d]Every morning He brings His justice to light;
He does not fail.
But the unjust [e]knows no shame.

8 [3]Lit., *made themselves great* [c]Amos 1:13

9 [a]Is. 15:1-9; Jer. .1-47; Amos 2:1-3 [b]Gen. 19:24 [c]Jer. -6; Ezek. 25:1-10 . 29:23 [e]Is. 11:14

[1]Lit., *reproached* *made* themselves [a]Is. 16:6 [b]Zeph. 2:8

[1]Lit., *make lean* l 2:11 [b]Zeph. 1:4 :15 [d]Ps. 72:8-11; Zeph. 3:9

s. 18:1-7; 20:4, 5; Ezek. 30:4-9

[a]Is. 14:26; Zeph. s. 10:16; Mic. 5:6 [c]Nah. 3:7

[1]Or, *All* kinds of *sts in crowds;* lit., kind of *beast of a* *ation* [2]Or, *owl* or ackdaw [3]Lit., *her* *tals* [4]Lit., *A voice* [a]Is. 14:23; 34:11

s. 22:2 [b]Is. 32:9, [c]Is. 47:8; Ezek. [d]Is. 32:14 [e]Jer. 18:16; 19:8

Jer. 5:23 [b]Ezek. 23:30 [c]Jer. 6:6

er. 7:23-28 [b]Jer. ; 5:3; 2 Tim. 3:16 78:22; Jer. 13:25 [d]Ps. 73:28

zek. 22:27 [b]Jer. 5:6; Hab. 1:8

udg. 9:4 [b]Ezek. 2:26; Mal. 2:7, 8

eut. 32:4 [b]Zeph. 5, 17 [c]Ps. 92:15 7:18 [e]Zeph. 2:1

6 "I have cut off nations;
Their corner towers are in ruins.
I have made their streets [a]desolate,
With no one passing by;
Their [b]cities are laid waste,
Without a man, [c]without an inhabitant.
7 "I said, 'Surely you will revere Me,
[a]Accept instruction.'
So her dwelling will [b]not be cut off
According to all that I have appointed concerning her.
But they were eager to [c]corrupt all their deeds.

8 "Therefore, [a]wait for Me," declares the LORD,
"For the day when I rise up to the prey.
Indeed, My decision is to [b]gather nations,
To assemble kingdoms,
To pour out on them My indignation,
All My burning anger;
For [c]all the earth will be devoured
By the fire of My zeal.
9 "For then I will [1]give to the peoples [a]purified lips,
That all of them may [b]call on the name of the LORD,
To serve Him [2]shoulder to shoulder.
10 "From beyond the rivers of [a]Ethiopia
My [1]worshipers, [2]My dispersed ones,
Will [b]bring My offerings.
11 "In that day you will [a]feel no shame
Because of all your deeds
By which you have rebelled against Me;
For then I will remove from your midst
Your [b]proud, exulting ones,
And you will never again be haughty
On My [c]holy mountain.
12 "But I will leave among you
A [a]humble and lowly people,
And they will [b]take refuge in the name of the LORD.
13 "The [a]remnant of Israel will [b]do no wrong
And [c]tell no lies,
Nor will a deceitful tongue
Be found in their mouths;
For they shall [d]feed and lie down
With no one to make them tremble."

14 Shout for joy, O daughter of Zion!
[a]Shout *in triumph,* O Israel!
Rejoice and exult with all *your* heart,
O daughter of Jerusalem!
15 The LORD has taken away [a]*His* judgments against you,
He has cleared away your enemies.
The King of Israel, the LORD, is [b]in your midst;
You will [c]fear disaster no more.
16 [a]In that day it will be said to Jerusalem:
"[b]Do not be afraid, O Zion;
[c]Do not let your hands fall limp.

6 [a]Jer. 9:12; Zech Matt. 23:38 [b]Lev. Is. 6:11 [c]Zeph. 2:5

7 [a]Job 36:10; Ps. 1 Tim. 1:5 [b]Jer. 7 [c]Hos. 9:9

8 [a]Ps. 27:14; Is. 3 Hab. 2:3 [b]Ezek. 38:14-23; Joel 3:2 [c]Zeph. 1:18

9 [1]Lit., *change* [2]*with one shoulder* [a]... 19:18; 57:19 [b]Ps 22:27; 86:9; Hab. Zeph. 2:11

10 [1]Or, *suppliant* *the daughter of M* [2]*dispersed ones* [a]... 68:31; Is. 18:1 [b]Is 60:6, 7

11 [a]Is. 45:17; 54: 2:26, 27 [b]Is. 2:12 [c]Is. 11:9; 56:7; Ez 20:40

12 [a]Is. 14:30 [b]Is 14:32; 50:10; Nah Zech. 13:8, 9

13 [a]Is. 10:20-22; 4:7; Zeph. 2:7 [b]P 119:3; Jer. 31:33; 3:5 [c]Zech. 8:3, 1 14:5 [d]Ezek. 34:1

14 [a]Zech. 9:9

15 [a]Ps. 19:9; Jo 5:30; Rev. 18:20 37:26-28; Zeph. 54:14

16 [a]Is. 25:9 [b]Is. 4 [c]Job 4:3; Heb.

[1]Lit., *A warrior who* ...es [2]Or, with some ...nt versions, *renew* ... in [a]Zeph. 3:5, 15 [b]Is. 63:1 [c]Is. 62:5

17 "The LORD your God is [a]in your midst,
A [1b]victorious warrior.
He will [c]exult over you with joy,
He will [2]be quiet in His love,
He will rejoice over you with shouts of joy.

...Lit., *were* [2]Lit., *her* ... 42:2-4; Ezek. 9:4

18 "I will gather those who [a]grieve about the appointed feasts—
They [1]came from you, *O Zion;*
The reproach *of exile* is a burden on [2]them.

...[a]Is. 60:14 [b]Ezek. ...; Mic. 4:6 [c]Ezek. ...27, 57 [d]Is. 60:18; ...62:7; Zech. 8:23

19 "Behold, I am going to deal at that time
With all your [a]oppressors,
I will save the [b]lame
And gather the outcast,
And I will turn their [c]shame into [d]praise and renown
In all the earth.

[a]Ezek. 37:12, 21 ...eut. 26:18, 19; Is. ...6:22 [c]Jer. 29:14; ...oel 3:1; Zeph. 2:7

20 "At that time I will [a]bring you in,
Even at the time when I gather you together;
Indeed, I will give you [b]renown and praise
Among all the peoples of the earth,
When I [c]restore your fortunes before your eyes,"
Says the LORD.

ZEPHANIAH AT A GLANCE

...eme of Zephaniah:

...ENT
...IONS

Paragraph Themes		Chapter Themes
1:1-6		
1:7-13		
1:14-18		
2:1-3		
2:4-7		
2:8-11		
2:12-15		
3:1-7		
3:8-13		
3:14-20		

Author:

Date:

Purpose:

Key Words:
I will
(the Lord will,
He will)

the day of the
Lord
(the day, in or
on that day)

remnant

HAGGAI

Discouragement reigned. Only a remnant returned to Jerusalem after the seventy years of ex small remnant in comparison to the number of people taken captive. Many Jews were reluctant to Babylon to return to Jerusalem. The land of their captors had become home. The Babylonian allowed them to establish businesses. They had built their houses. Their children, while born i tivity, were secure. Why should they leave?

A small remnant returned to rebuild the temple . . . soon a discouraging task. Their zeal dwi What was enthusiastically begun was forgotten before God's house was completed. For about s years the temple stood unfinished and ignored.

Then around 520 B.C. the Word of the Lord came to Haggai.

THINGS TO DO

1. Read Haggai in one sitting in order to familiarize yourself with the pattern of the book. A read, note or do the following:

   a. In a distinctive way, mark every reference to time throughout the book so you can s immediately. You could draw a clock in the margin or in the text.

   b. Study the two charts at the beginning of Zechariah on page 1392. The first gives the hist setting of Haggai and Zechariah, since they were contemporaries. As you look at the hist chart, see who Darius is. The second chart is a Jewish calendar which will help you di when Haggai (and Zechariah) received their messages from the Lord.

   c. Mark every use of the phrases, *the Word of the Lord came by the prophet Haggai* and *the Word Lord came by Haggai the prophet saying*. Each occurrence of these phrases begins a messag will help you see the structure of Haggai.

2. As you read Haggai a second time, concentrate on one message at a time and do the followi

   a. As you read chapter 1, mark 1:13 the same way you marked the other phrases saying th Word of the Lord came by Haggai, the prophet. Scholars debate whether this shou considered a separate message from the first part of the chapter. If so, the book would co five messages rather than four. See what you think.

   b. As you read each message (which begins with "the Word of the Lord came"), watch fo mark in a distinctive way the key repeated words used throughout Haggai. These are list the HAGGAI AT A GLANCE chart on page 1389. Mark any other key words you observe.

   c. After you have read each message and marked key words, observe the content of each sage by asking the five W's and an H. Ask: To whom was the message given? What w about? What is going to happen? Who is responsible? Why was it given? What are th believe or do? When are they to do it? How are they to do it? How will it happen? Reco you learn about each message in the section for "Paragraph Themes" on HAGGAI A GLANCE.

3. Now, go back through Haggai and list the truths you learned from the key words which marked. Also, list everything you learned about God, especially what He controls or determ Record these lists in the margins of Haggai.

4. Complete HAGGAI AT A GLANCE. Record the paragraph themes and the theme of each ch in the appropriate places. Then record the chapter theme in the text next to the chapter nu Finally, write out the theme of the book and fill in any other information needed.

INGS TO THINK ABOUT

.. Have you given too much attention and time to your personal affairs and needs but neglected the things of God that are important for the spreading of the gospel or the furtherance of His work?

. What might God be trying to say when cataclysmic events take place? Do you take advantage of these things to turn people's attention and thoughts to God?

. When discouraged in your service to God, do you quit, or do you courageously persevere, determined to be faithful and to leave the outcome to God?

Chapter 1

1 In the [a]second year of Darius the king, on the first day of the
sixth month, the word of the LORD came by the prophet [b]Haggai
to [c]Zerubbabel the son of Shealtiel, [d]governor of Judah, and to
[e]Joshua the son of Jehozadak, the high priest saying,
2 "Thus says the LORD of [1]hosts, 'This people says, "The time has
not come, *even* the time for the house of the LORD to be rebuilt." ' "
3 Then the word of the LORD came by Haggai the prophet saying,
4 "Is it time for you yourselves to dwell in your paneled houses
while this house [a]*lies* desolate?"
5 Now therefore, thus says the LORD of hosts, "[1]Consider your
ways!
6 "You have [a]sown much, but [1]harvest little; *you* eat, but *there is* not
enough to be satisfied; *you* drink, but *there is* [2]not *enough* to become
drunk; *you* put on clothing, but no one is warm *enough*; and he who
earns, earns wages *to put* into a purse with holes."
7 Thus says the LORD of hosts, "[1]Consider your ways!
8 "Go up to the [1]mountains, bring wood and [a]rebuild the [2]temple,
that I may be [b]pleased with it and be [c]glorified," says the LORD.
9 "[a]*You* look for much, but behold, *it comes* to little; when you bring
it home, I [b]blow it *away*. Why?" declares the LORD of hosts, "Because
of My house which [c]*lies* desolate, while each of you runs to his own
house.
10 "Therefore, because of you the [a]sky has withheld [1]its dew, and the
earth has withheld its produce.
11 "And I called for a [a]drought on the land, on the mountains, on the
grain, on the new wine, on the oil, on what the ground produces, on
[b]men, on cattle, and on [c]all the labor of [1]your hands."
12 Then [a]Zerubbabel the son of Shealtiel, and [b]Joshua the son of
Jehozadak, the high priest, with all the remnant of the people,
[c]obeyed the voice of the LORD their God and the words of Haggai the
prophet, as the LORD their God had sent him. And the people
[1d]showed reverence for the LORD.
13 Then Haggai, the [a]messenger of the LORD, spoke [1]by the commis-
sion of the LORD to the people saying, " '[b]I am with you,' declares the
LORD."
14 So the LORD stirred up the spirit of [a]Zerubbabel the son of Sheal-
tiel, [a]governor of Judah, and the spirit of Joshua the son of Jeho-
zadak, the high priest, and the spirit of all the [b]remnant of the
people; and they came and [c]worked on the house of the LORD of
hosts, their God,
15 on the twenty-fourth day of the sixth month in the second year
of Darius the king.

[a]Ezra 4:24 [b]Ezra 5:14; Hag. 1:3, 12, 2:1, 10, 20 [c]Ezra ...eh. 7:7; Hag. 1:12, 4; Zech. 4:6; Matt. 13 [d]1 Kin. 10:15; ...a 5:3 [e]Zech. 6:11

Lit., *hosts, saying*

...r. 33:10, 12; Hag. 1:9

Set your heart on

bring in [2]Lit., *not* ...*ing drunk* [a]Deut. ...3:38-40; Hos. 8:7; ... 1:9, 10; 2:16, 17

Set your heart on

..., *mountain* [2]Lit., ... [a]1 Kin. 6:1 [b]Ps. ..., 14 [c]Hag. 2:7, 9

Prov. 27:20; Eccl. ...s. 40:7 [c]Hag. 1:4

...0 [1]Lit., *from dew* ...28:23, 24; 1 Kin. 7:1; Joel 1:18-20

..., *the palms* [a]Jer. ...2-6; Mal. 3:9, 11 ...28:22 [c]Hag. 2:17

...it., *feared before* 1:1 [b]Hag. 1:14; ...s. 1:19; 1 Thess. [d]Deut. 31:12, 13; ... 112:1; Is. 50:10

Or, *the message* ...4:26; Ezek. 3:17; ...; 3:1 [b]Ps. 46:11; Is. 41:10; 43:2

Hag. 1:1; 2:2, 21 1:12 [c]Ezra 5:2; Neh. 4:6

Chapter 2

2 On the twenty-first of the seventh month, the word of the LORD
came by [a]Haggai the prophet saying,
2 "Speak now to [a]Zerubbabel the son of Shealtiel, [a]governor of
Judah, and to [a]Joshua the son of Jehozadak, the high priest, and to
the [b]remnant of the people saying,
3 'Who is [a]left among you who saw this [1]temple in its [b]former
glory? And how do you see it now? Does it not [2]seem to you like
nothing [3]in comparison?
4 'But now [1a]take courage, Zerubbabel,' declares the LORD, 'take
courage also, Joshua son of Jehozadak, the high priest, and all you
people of the land take courage,' declares the LORD, 'and work; for [b]I
am with you,' says the LORD of hosts.
5 'As for the [1a]promise which I [2]made you when you came out of
Egypt, [3]My [b]Spirit is abiding in your midst; [c]do not fear!'
6 "For thus says the LORD of hosts, '[a]Once more [1]in a [b]little while, I
am going to [c]shake the heavens and the earth, the sea also and the
dry land.
7 'And I will shake [a]all the nations; and [1]they will come with the
[b]wealth of all nations; and I will [c]fill this house with glory,' says the
LORD of hosts.
8 'The [a]silver is Mine, and the gold is Mine,' declares the LORD of
hosts.
9 'The latter [a]glory of this house will be greater than the [b]former,'
says the LORD of hosts, 'and in this place I shall give [c]peace,' declares
the LORD of hosts."
10 On the [a]twenty-fourth of the ninth *month*, in the second year of
Darius, the word of the LORD came to Haggai the prophet saying,
11 "Thus says the LORD of hosts, '[a]Ask now the priests *for* a [1]ruling:
12 'If a man carries [a]holy meat in the [1]fold of his garment, and
touches bread with [2]this fold, or cooked food, wine, oil, or any *other*
food, will it become holy?' " And the priests answered and said,
"No."
13 Then Haggai said, "[a]If one who is unclean from a [1]corpse
touches any of these, will *the latter* become unclean?" And the priests
answered and said, "It will become unclean."
14 Then Haggai answered and said, " '[a]So is this people. And so is
this nation before Me,' declares the LORD, 'and so is every work of
their hands; and what they offer there is unclean.
15 'But now, do [1a]consider from this day [2]onward: before one [b]stone
was placed on another in the temple of the LORD,
16 [1]from that time *when* one came to a *grain* heap of twenty
measures, there would be only ten; and *when* one came to the wine
vat to draw fifty [2]measures, there would be *only* twenty.
17 'I smote you *and* every work of your hands with [a]blasting wind,
mildew, and hail; [1]yet you *did* not *come back* to Me,' declares the
LORD.
18 'Do [1a]consider from this day [2]onward, from the [b]twenty-fourth
day of the ninth *month*; from the day when the temple of the LORD
was [c]founded, [1]consider:
19 'Is the seed still in the barn? Even including the vine, the fig tree,
the pomegranate, and the olive tree, it has not borne *fruit*. Yet from
this day on I will [a]bless *you*.' "

2:1 [a]Hag. 1:1

2 [a]Hag. 1:1

3 [1]Lit., *house* ... *your eyes* [3]L... [a]Ezra 3:12 [b]H...

4 [1]Lit., *be str*... 31:23; 1 Chr. 28:20; Zech. 6:10 [b]2 Sam. 7:9

5 [1]Lit., *word* ... *with* [3]Or, *wh*... *standing* [a]Ex. 29:45, 46; 33 34:8-10 [b]Neh 63:11, 14 [c]Is. Zech. 8:13

6 [1]Lit., *it is a* ... 12:26 [b]Is. 10 [c]Hag. 2:21

7 [1]Or, *the de*... *nations will c*... 2:44; Joel 3:9 60:4-9 [c]1 Kin 60:7

8 [a]1 Chr. 29: 60:17

9 [a]Zech. 2:5 [c]Is. 9:6, 7; 66

10 [a]Hag. 2:2

11 [1]Lit., *law* 17:8-11; Mal.

12 [1]Lit., *wing* *wing* [a]Ex. 29 6:27, 29; 7:6; 44:19; Matt.

13 [1]Lit., *sou*... 22:4-6; Num.

14 [a]Prov. 15 1:11-15

15 [1]Lit., *set* ... [2]Or, *backwa*... 1:5, 7; 2:18 4:24

16 [1]Lit., *sinc*... *were* [2]Or, *tro*...

17 [1]Or, *but* ... *have in com*... [a]Deut. 28:22 8:37; Amos 4

18 [1]Lit., *set* [2]Or, *backwa*... 32:29; Hag. 2:10 [c]Ezra 5 8:9, 12

19 [a]Ps. 128 31:12, 14; M...

20 [a]Hag. 2:10

21 [a]Ezra 5:2; Hag. 1:1; . 4:6-10 [b]Hag. 2:6; Heb. 12:26, 27

22 [1]Or, *Gentiles* [a]Ezek. 6; Zeph. 3:8 [b]Mic. 6 [c]Ps. 46:9; Ezek. ; Mic. 5:10 [d]Amos [e]Judg. 7:22; 2 Chr. 20:23

23 [1]Or, *seal* [a]Song 8:6; er. 22:24 [b]Is. 42:1; 43:10

20 Then the word of the LORD came a second time to Haggai on the
[a]twenty-fourth *day* of the month saying,
21 "Speak to [a]Zerubbabel governor of Judah saying, 'I am going to
[b]shake the heavens and the earth.
22 'And I will [a]overthrow the thrones of kingdoms and destroy the
[b]power of the kingdoms of the [1]nations; and I will [c]overthrow the
chariots and their riders, and the [d]horses and their riders will go
down, [e]everyone by the sword of another.'
23 'On that day,' declares the LORD of hosts, 'I will take you, Zerub-
babel, son of Shealtiel, My servant,' declares the LORD, 'and I will
make you like a [1a]signet *ring*, for [b]I have chosen you,' " declares the
LORD of hosts.

HAGGAI AT A GLANCE

e of Haggai:

s

PARAGRAPH THEMES	CHAPTER THEMES
1:1-12	1
1:13-15	
2:1-9	2
2:10-19	
2:20-23	

Author:

Date:

Purpose:

Key Words:

day of the month

the word of the Lord came

house (temple)

remnant

consider

shake

ZECHARIAH

The earth was peaceful and quiet. All the nations, except for Israel, were at rest. From Is perspective, it looked as if God had abandoned His people and forgotten His holy city, Jerus Jerusalem's walls were torn down, Solomon's temple had been destroyed, and now a partially r temple stood on its site. Even if this temple were completed, it wouldn't begin to equal Solomon's.

The majority of God's people had settled in their land of exile and were reluctant to retu Jerusalem. Only a remnant had come back, and they were a discouraged lot who soon abandone rebuilding of the house of God until the Word of the Lord first came through Haggai and Zechariah.

Born in Babylon, Zechariah was among the remnant who returned to Jerusalem under the le ship of Zerubbabel and Joshua. Although Zechariah belonged to the priestly line he, like Hagg predecessor, was to be God's prophet to the returned and discouraged remnant.

And so, about 520 to 519 B.C., the Word of the Lord came to Zechariah—a needed word, an enco ing word.

THINGS TO DO

General Instructions

If you are going to have a good understanding of Zechariah, it will help to put it into its hist context. Although this will take extra study, it will be worthwhile.

Ezra gives the historical setting of Zechariah, therefore if you haven't studied Ezra, read it b you start Zechariah. Ezra, like Zechariah, is a post-exilic book, which simply means it was written the Jews were sent into exile under the Babylonians (Chaldeans) in 586 B.C. Ezra records the retur remnant to Jerusalem under the reign and decree of Cyrus, a Persian king who ruled from 5 530 B.C. The Babylonians conquered Judah, then the Medes and Persians conquered the Babylonian

1. As you read Ezra, observe what is said regarding rebuilding the temple, since the temple pl key role in Ezra and in Zechariah. Also watch for any reference to Zerubbabel and to Jeshua, is called Joshua in Zechariah. Joshua is also called Jeshua in Nehemiah, another post-exilic which focuses on rebuilding the walls of Jerusalem.
2. If you haven't studied Haggai, study it next, as Haggai and Zechariah are contemporaries.

Chapters 1-8

1. The book of Zechariah divides into two segments: chapters 1 through 8 and chapters 9 thr 14. As you read the first segment, mark every occurrence of the phrase *the Word of the Lord* There will be slight variations to the wording (i.e. *the Word of the Lord of hosts came*). How mark each occurrence the same way. Then in the margin, note the main point of the Lo message. Also, if the text tells you when the word came, draw a time clock such as this (L) in text. Consult the historical chart on page 1392 for the chronological setting of these messages.
2. As you read, also watch for the phrases, *what do you see?*, *the Lord showed me*, *I saw*, or *I lifted u eyes.* In the margin write "Vision," and then note briefly what the vision was. As you do you'll see many correlations between *the Word of the Lord* and the vision.
3. Watch for and mark in a distinctive way the following key words or phrases, along with synonyms or pronouns: *listen (stop their ears from hearing)*, *return*, *again*, *temple (house of the L* *nations*, *Judah*, *Jerusalem*, *I will dwell in your midst (I will be the glory in her midst* or any referen the Lord's coming), and *seventy years*.

   Record these key words and phrases on a card and use it as a bookmark as you study Zecha You'll find it helpful to color or mark these phrases in the same way you'll mark them in the t

Zechariah contains many prophecies regarding the Messiah's first and final comings, the nation of Israel and Jerusalem, and the future of the nations. Therefore, as you read Zechariah chapter by chapter, watch for these prophecies and note them under the appropriate columns on the chart ZECHARIAH'S PROPHETIC REVELATIONS on page 1406.

God's name, Jehovah-sabbaoth, Lord of Hosts is used repeatedly. Mark these occurrences. Then as you study Zechariah, on a separate piece of paper keep a list of all you learn about God. When you finish Zechariah, record this list in the margin of Zechariah.

After you study each chapter, record its theme (subject) on the ZECHARIAH AT A GLANCE chart on page 1407 under the appropriate chapter number and then in the text next to the chapter number.

ters 9-14

As you read through this segment, watch for the same key words and/or phrases you marked in chapters 1 through 8, but add to your list *in that day* and any reference to the Lord as *King*.

Also mark the phrase *the burden of the Word of the Lord*. The occurrences of this phrase divide these final chapters of Zechariah into segments.

After you mark the key words and phrases in this segment, list in the margin or on the chart ZECHARIAH'S PROPHETIC REVELATIONS what you learn about each. If you believe *that day* refers to the day of the Lord, also record your insights on the chart THE DAY OF THE LORD in the appendix (page 1878).

When you read chapter 13, watch what will happen to the two parts and *the third*. Watch the pronouns *they* and *them*, and then list in the margin all you learn about *the third*—the remnant that survives.

In chapter 14 you'll see a reference to the *Feast of Booths*. In the front of your Bible, you'll find a chart called THE FEASTS OF ISRAEL (pages I-48 and I-49). As you look at the chart, note the significance of the Feast of Booths, or tabernacles as it is sometimes referred to.

Record the theme of each chapter as you did previously. Then when you finish, write the theme of Zechariah on ZECHARIAH AT A GLANCE. Record the main theme of the two major segment divisions and fill in the other information called for on the chart.

Since Haggai and Zechariah were contemporaries, it would be interesting to note how the messages given by the Lord to these two prophets correlate in time. After you've studied both books, look at the "time clocks" in both books and note when the messages came in relationship to one another. List the messages in the order of their occurrence.

NGS TO THINK ABOUT

As you've studied Zechariah, have you been touched by the awesomeness of God's sovereignty? What does it mean to you personally to realize that God reigns supreme over the nations? That He has declared things before they have come to pass, and that as He has purposed so it shall be? If He can handle nations, can He handle your life?

Do you take time to listen—really listen—to what God says in His Word? If you haven't listened, God's invitation "to return to Him" is still there in Zechariah for you. Believe Him . . . and return.

How can you apply the truth of Zechariah 4:6-7 to your own life? Remember the things that were written in the Old Testament were written for our encouragement and perseverance. They're not simply historical records; they are the bread of life by which we live.

God said, "The Lord is coming; He'll dwell in our midst." Are you prepared? According to 1 John 3:2-3 the coming of the Lord is a purifying hope. What do you need to do in order not to be ashamed at His coming?

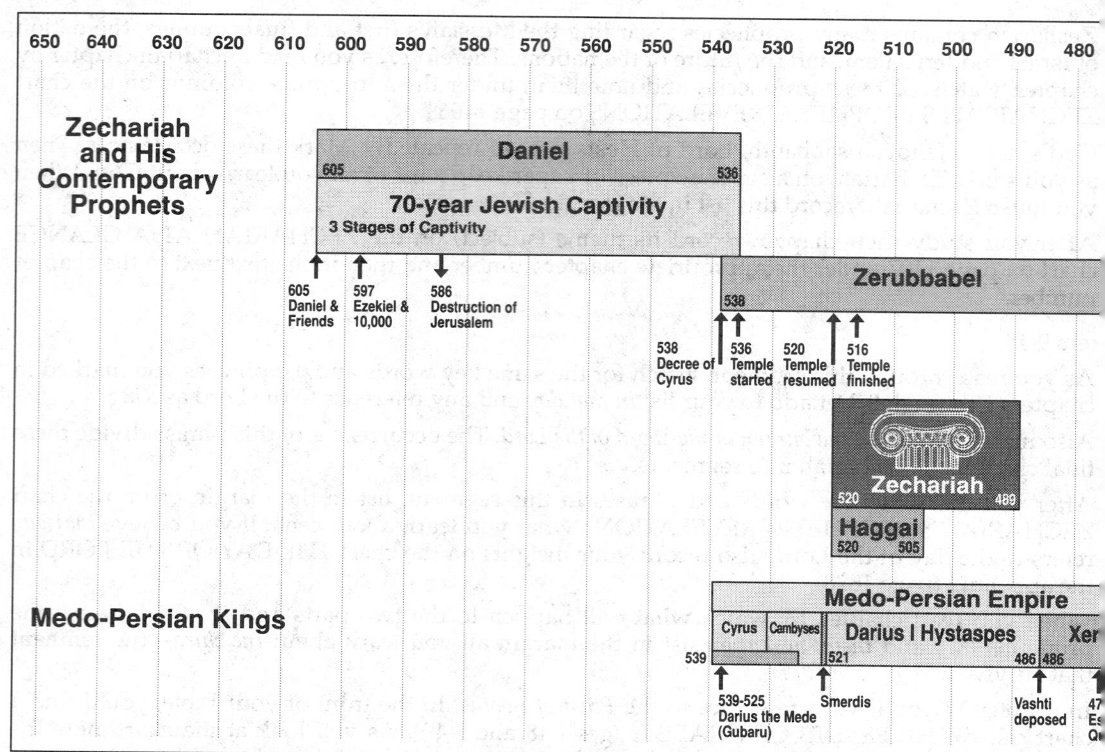

The Jewish Calendar

Babylonian names (B) for the months are still used today for the Jewish calendar. Canaanite names (C) were used prior to the Babylonian captivity. Four are mentioned in the Old Testament.
Adar-Sheni is an intercalary month used every two to three years or seven times in nineteen years.

1st month	2nd month	3rd month	4th month
Nisan (B) Abib (C) March-April	Iyyar (B) Ziv (C) April-May	Sivan (B) May-June	Tammuz (B) June-July
7th month	*8th month*	*9th month*	*10th month*
5th month	**6th month**	**7th month**	**8th month**
Ab (B) July-August	Elul (B) August-September	Tishri (B) Ethanim (C) September-October	Marcheshvan (B) Bul (C) October-November
11th month	*12th month*	*1st month*	*2nd month*
9th month	**10th month**	**11th month**	**12th month**
Kislev (B) November-December	Tebeth (B) December-January	Shebat (B) January-February	Adar (B) February-March
3rd month	*4th month*	*5th month*	*6th month*

Sacred calendar appears in black • Civil calendar appears in grey

Chapter 1

1 In the eighth month of the second year of [a]Darius, the word of
the LORD came to [b]Zechariah the prophet, the son of Berechiah,
the son of [c]Iddo saying,
2 "The LORD was very [a]angry with your fathers.
3 "Therefore say to them, 'Thus says the LORD of hosts, "[a]Return to

1:1 [a]Ezra 4:24; Hag. 1:15; 2:10; 1:7; 7:1 [b]Ezra 5: Zech. 7:1; Matt. Luke 11:51 [c]Ne

2 [a]2 Chr. 36:16; Ezek. 8:18; Zech

3 [a]Is. 31:6; 44:2 3:7

[a]Ps. 78:8; 106:6, 7 . 24:19; 36:15 [c]Is. 19; Jer. 4:1; Ezek. [d]Jer. 6:17; 11:7, 8

Me," declares the LORD of hosts, "that I may return to you," says the
LORD of hosts.
4 "Do not be [a]like your fathers, to whom the [b]former prophets pro-
claimed, saying, 'Thus says the LORD of hosts, "[c]Return now from
your evil ways and from your evil deeds." ' But they did [d]not listen
or give heed to Me," declares the LORD.

m. 5:7 [b]John 8:52

5 "Your [a]fathers, where are they? And the [b]prophets, do they live
forever?

. 12:16, 17; 44:28, Amos 9:10 [b]Lam. 2:17

6 "But did not My words and My statutes, which I commanded My
servants the prophets, [a]overtake your fathers? Then they repented
and said, '[b]As the LORD of hosts purposed to do to us in accordance
with our ways and our deeds, so He has dealt with us.' " ' "

:ech. 6:2; Rev. 6:4 eh. 8:15; Is. 41:19; 13; Zech. 1:10, 11 'ech. 6:3; Rev. 6:2

7 On the twenty-fourth day of the eleventh month, which is the
month Shebat, in the second year of Darius, the word of the LORD
came to Zechariah the prophet, the son of Berechiah, the son of Iddo,
as follows:

Zech. 1:19; 4:4, 5, :4 [b]Zech. 2:3; 5:5

8 I saw at night, and behold, a man was riding on a [a]red horse, and
he was standing among the [b]myrtle trees which were in the ravine,
with red, sorrel, and [c]white horses behind him.

) [1]Lit., *walk about* *h* [a]Job 1:7; Zech. 1:11; 4:10; 6:5-8

9 Then I said, "My [a]lord, what are these?" And the [b]angel who was
speaking with me said to me, "I will show you what these are."
10 And the man who was standing among the myrtle trees
answered and said, "These are those whom the LORD has sent to
[1a]patrol the earth."

Lit., *walked about* *rough* [2]Lit., *sitting* . 1:8, 10 [b]Is. 14:7

11 So they answered the angel of the LORD who was [a]standing
among the myrtle trees, and said, "We have [1]patrolled the earth, and
behold, [b]all the earth is [2]peaceful and quiet."

2 [a]Ps. 74:10; Jer. :4; Hab. 1:2 [b]Ps. 3; Jer. 30:18 [c]Ps.); Jer. 15:17 [d]Jer. ; 29:10; Dan. 9:2; Zech. 7:5

12 Then the angel of the LORD answered and said, "O LORD of hosts,
[a]how long wilt Thou [b]have no compassion for Jerusalem and the
cities of Judah, with which Thou hast been [c]indignant these [d]seventy
years?"

[1]Lit., *good* [a]Zech. ; 4:1 [b]Is. 40:1, 2; 57:18

13 And the LORD answered the [a]angel who was speaking with me
with [1]gracious words, [b]comforting words.

[a]Is. 40:2, 6; Zech. 1:17 [b]Zech. 8:2

14 So the angel who was speaking with me said to me, "[a]Proclaim,
saying, 'Thus says the LORD of hosts, "I am [b]exceedingly jealous for
Jerusalem and Zion.

it., *helped for evil* 1. 1:2 [b]Ps. 123:4; 48:11 [c]Amos 1:11

15 "But I am very [a]angry with the nations who are [b]at ease; for while
I was only a little angry, they [1c]furthered the disaster."

Is. 54:8-10; Zech. 1 [b]Ezra 6:14, 15; . 4:9 [c]Jer. 31:39; Zech. 2:2, 4

16 'Therefore, thus says the LORD, "I will [a]return to Jerusalem with
compassion; My [b]house will be built in it," declares the LORD of
hosts, "and a measuring [c]line will be stretched over Jerusalem." '

. 44:26; 61:4 [b]Is. 51:3 [c]Zech. 2:12

17 "Again, proclaim, saying, 'Thus says the LORD of hosts, "My
[a]cities will again overflow with prosperity, and the LORD will again
[b]comfort Zion and again [c]choose Jerusalem." ' "

[1]Ch. 2:1 in Heb.

18 [1]Then I lifted up my eyes and looked, and behold, *there were* four
horns.

[a]1 Kin. 22:11; Ps. 5; Amos 6:13 mg.

19 So I said to the angel who was speaking with me, "What are
these?" And he answered me, "These are the [a]horns which have
scattered Judah, Israel, and Jerusalem."

[a]Is. 44:12; 54:16

20 Then the LORD showed me four [a]craftsmen.

[a]Zech. 1:19 [b]Ps. 75:10

21 And I said, "What are these coming to do?" And he said, "These
are the [a]horns which have scattered Judah, so that no man lifts up his
head; but these *craftsmen* have come to terrify them, to [b]throw down

the horns of the nations who have lifted up *their* horns against the
land of Judah in order to scatter it."

Chapter 2

2 [1]Then I lifted up my eyes and looked, and behold, *there was* a
man with a [a]measuring line in his hand.
2 So I said, "Where are you going?" And he said to me, "To
[a]measure Jerusalem, to see how wide it is and how long it is."
3 And behold, the [a]angel who was speaking with me was going
out, and another angel was coming out to meet him,
4 and said to him, "Run, speak to that [a]young man, saying, '[b]Jeru-
salem will be inhabited [1c]without walls, because of the [d]multitude of
men and cattle within it.
5 'For I,' declares the LORD, 'will be a [a]wall of fire [1]around her, and I
will be the [b]glory in her midst.' "
6 "[1]Ho there! [a]Flee from the land of the north," declares the LORD,
"for I have [b]dispersed you as the four winds of the heavens,"
declares the LORD.
7 "Ho, Zion! [a]Escape, you who are living with the daughter of Bab-
ylon."
8 For thus says the LORD of hosts, "After [1a]glory He has sent me
against the nations which plunder you, for he who touches you,
touches the [2b]apple of His eye.
9 "For behold, I will [a]wave My hand over them, so that they will be
[b]plunder for their slaves. Then you will know that the LORD of hosts
has sent Me.
10 "[a]Sing for joy and be glad, O daughter of Zion; for behold I am
coming and I will [b]dwell in your midst," declares the LORD.
11 "And [a]many nations will join themselves to the LORD in that day
and will become My people. Then I will [b]dwell in your midst, and
you will [c]know that the LORD of hosts has sent Me to you.
12 "And the LORD will [1a]possess Judah as His portion in the holy
land, and will again [b]choose Jerusalem.
13 "[1a]Be silent, all flesh, before the LORD; for He is [b]aroused from His
holy habitation."

Chapter 3

3 Then he showed me [a]Joshua the high priest standing before the
angel of the LORD, and [1b]Satan standing at his right hand to
accuse him.
2 And the LORD said to Satan, "[a]The LORD rebuke you, Satan! In-
deed, the LORD who has [b]chosen Jerusalem rebuke you! Is this not a
[c]brand plucked from the fire?"
3 Now Joshua was clothed with [a]filthy garments and standing
before the angel.
4 And he spoke and said to those who were standing before him
saying, "[a]Remove the filthy garments from him." Again he said to
him, "See, I have [b]taken your iniquity away from you and [1]will
[c]clothe you with festal robes."
5 Then I said, "Let them put a clean [a]turban on his head." So they
put a clean turban on his head and clothed him with garments,
while the angel of the LORD was standing by.
6 And the angel of the LORD admonished Joshua saying,
7 "Thus says the LORD of hosts, 'If you will [a]walk in My ways, and

2:1 [1]Ch. 2:5 in He [a]Jer. 31:39; Ezek. 47:3; Zech. 1:16
2 [a]Jer. 31:39; Eze 40:3; Rev. 21:15-1
3 [a]Zech. 1:9
4 [1]Lit., like *unwall villages;* or, like *op country* [a]Jer. 1:6; 1:4; 1 Tim. 4:12 [b]Z 1:17; 8:4 [c]Ezek. 3 [d]Is. 49:20; Jer. 30: 33:22
5 [1]Lit., *to her* [a]Is. 26:1; 60:18 [b]Hag. Zech. 2:10, 11
6 [1]Lit., *Ho! ho!* [a]J 3:18 [b]Jer. 31:10; 11:16
7 [a]Is. 48:20; Jer.
8 [1]Or, *the glory* [2] *pupil* [a]Is. 60:7-9 32:10; Ps. 17:8
9 [a]Is. 19:16 [b]Is.
10 [a]Is. 65:18, 19; 9:9 [b]Zech. 2:5; 8:
11 [a]Mic. 4:2 [b]Zec 10 [c]Zech. 2:9
12 [1]Or, *inherit* [a]D 32:9; Ps. 33:12; J 10:16 [b]2 Chr. 6:6 132:13, 14; Zech.
13 [1]Lit., *Hush* [a]H 2:20; Zeph. 1:7 [b] 78:65; Is. 51:9
3:1 [1]Or, the *Adve* or *Accuser* [a]Ezra Hag. 1:1; Zech. 6 [b]1 Chr. 21:1; Job Ps. 109:6; Rev. 1
2 [a]Mark 9:25; Ju [b]Zech. 2:12 [c]Am 4:11; Jude 23
3 [a]Ezra 9:15; Is. 64:6
4 [1]Lit., *to clothe* 43:25; Ezek. 36:2 [b]Mic. 7:18, 19; Ze 3:9 [c]Is. 52:1; 61:1
5 [a]Job 29:14; Is.
7 [a]1 Kin. 3:14

if you will perform My service, then you will also [b]govern My house
and also have charge of My [c]courts, and I will grant you [1]free access
among these who are standing *here*.
8 'Now listen, Joshua the high priest, you and your friends who
are sitting in front of you—indeed they are men who are a [a]symbol,
for behold, I am going to bring in My servant the [1b]Branch.
9 'For behold, the stone that I have set before Joshua; on one stone
are [a]seven eyes. Behold, I will engrave an inscription on it,' declares
the LORD of hosts, 'and I will [b]remove the iniquity of that land in one
day.
10 'In that day,' declares the LORD of hosts, 'every one of you will
invite his neighbor to *sit* under *his* [a]vine and under *his* fig tree.' "

Chapter 4

4 Then [a]the angel who was speaking with me returned, and
[b]roused me as a man who is awakened from his sleep.
2 And he said to me, "[a]What do you see?" And I said, "I see, and
behold, a [b]lampstand all of gold with its bowl on the top of it, and its
[c]seven lamps on it with seven spouts belonging to each of the lamps
which are on the top of it;
3 also [a]two olive trees by it, one on the right side of the bowl and
the other on its left side."
4 Then I answered and said to the angel who was speaking with
me saying, "What are these, [a]my lord?"
5 So [a]the angel who was speaking with me answered and said to
me, "[b]Do you not know what these are?" And I said, "No, my lord."
6 Then he answered and [1]said to me, "This is the word of the LORD
to [a]Zerubbabel saying, '[b]Not by might nor by power, but by My
[c]Spirit,' says the LORD of hosts.
7 'What are you, O great [a]mountain? Before Zerubbabel *you will
become* a plain; and he will bring forth the top stone with [b]shouts of
"Grace, grace to it!" ' "
8 Also the word of the LORD came to me saying,
9 "The hands of Zerubbabel have [a]laid the foundation of this house,
and his hands will [b]finish *it*. Then you will know that the LORD of
hosts has sent me to [1]you.
10 "For who has despised the day of [a]small things? [1]But these [b]seven
will be glad when they see the [2c]plumb line in the hand of Zerubba-
bel—*these are* the [d]eyes of the LORD which [e]range to and fro through-
out the earth."
11 Then I answered and said to him, "What are these [a]two olive
trees on the right of the lampstand and on its left?"
12 And I answered the second time and said to him, "What are the
two olive [1]branches which are beside the two golden pipes, which
empty the golden *oil* from themselves?"
13 So he answered me saying, "[a]Do you not know what these are?"
And I said, "No, [b]my lord."
14 Then he said, "These are the two [1a]anointed ones, who are
[b]standing by the [c]Lord of the whole earth."

Chapter 5

5 Then I lifted up my eyes again and looked, and behold, *there was*
a flying [a]scroll.

t., *goings* [b]Deut. 7:9, 12 [c]Is. 62:9
Sprout [a]Is. 8:18; Ezek. 12:11 [b]Is. ; 53:2; Jer. 23:5; 3:15; Zech. 6:12
[a]Zech. 4:10 [b]Jer. 50:20; Zech. 3:4
[a]1 Kin. 4:25; Is. 36:16; Mic. 4:4
Zech. 1:9 [b]1 Kin. 9:5-7; Jer. 31:26
: 1:13; Zech. 5:2 x. 25:31, 37; Jer. 52:19 [c]Rev. 4:5
. 4:11; Rev. 11:4
ech. 1:9; 4:5, 13; 6:4
[a]Zech. 1:9; 4:1 [b]Zech. 4:13
[1]Lit., *said to me,* [a]Ezra 5:2; Hag. [b]Is. 11:2-4; 30:1; [c]2 Chr. 32:7, 8; Eph. 6:17
14:4, 6; Is. 40:4; 51:25; Nah. 1:5; h. 14:4, 5 [b]Ezra 0, 11; Ps. 84:11
[1]Lit., *you* (plural) 8-10; 5:16; Hag. [b]Ezra 6:14, 15; Zech. 6:12, 13
Or, *But they will when they see . . rubbabel. These are the eyes of* o [2]Lit., *plummet* ne [a]Neh. 4:2-4; 7:2, 5; Hag. 2:3 ch. 3:9; Rev. 8:2 s 7:7, 8 [d]2 Chr. Prov. 15:3; Jer. Zech. 1:10; Rev. 5:6
h. 4:3; Rev. 11:4
12 [1]Or, *clusters*
ech. 4:5 [b]Zech. 4:4, 5
t., *sons of fresh* Ex. 29:7; 40:15; 16:1, 12, 13; Is. 3; Dan. 9:24-26 :1-7 [c]Mic. 4:13
Jer. 36:2; Ezek. 2:9; Rev. 5:1

2 And he said to me, "[a]What do you see?" And I answered, "I see a
flying scroll; its length is twenty [1]cubits and its width ten cubits."
3 Then he said to me, "This is the [a]curse that is going forth over
the face of the whole [1]land; surely everyone who [b]steals will be
purged away according to [2]the writing on one side, and everyone
who [c]swears will be purged away according to [2]the writing on the
other side.
4 "I will [a]make it go forth," declares the LORD of hosts, "and it will
[b]enter the house of the [c]thief and the house of the one who swears
falsely by My name; and it will spend the night within that house
and [d]consume it with its timber and stones."
5 Then [a]the angel who was speaking with me went out, and said
to me, "Lift up now your eyes, and see what this is, going forth."
6 And I said, "What is it?" And he said, "This is the [1a] ephah going
forth." Again he said, "This is their [2]appearance in all the [3]land
7 (and behold, a lead cover was lifted up); and this is a woman
sitting inside the ephah."
8 Then he said, "This is [a]Wickedness!" And he threw her down
into the middle of the ephah and cast the lead weight on its [1]open-
ing.
9 Then I lifted up my eyes and looked, and there two women were
coming out with the wind in their wings; and they had wings like
the wings of a [a]stork, and they lifted up the ephah between the earth
and the heavens.
10 And I said to the angel who was speaking with me, "Where are
they taking the ephah?"
11 Then he said to me, "To build a [1]temple for her in the land of
[a]Shinar; and when it is prepared, she will be set there on her own
pedestal."

Chapter 6

6 Now I lifted up my eyes again and looked, and behold, [a]four
chariots were coming forth from between the two mountains;
and the mountains *were* bronze mountains.
2 With the first chariot *were* [a]red horses, with the second chariot
[b]black horses,
3 with the third chariot [a]white horses, and with the fourth chariot
strong [b]dappled horses.
4 Then I spoke and said to the angel who was speaking with me,
"[a]What are these, my lord?"
5 And the angel answered and said to me, "These are the [a]four
spirits of heaven, going forth after standing before the Lord of all the
earth,
6 with one of which the black horses are going forth to the [a]north
country; and the white ones go forth after them, while the dappled
ones go forth to the [b]south country.
7 "When the strong ones went out, they [1]were eager to go to [2a]patrol
the earth." And He said, "Go, [2]patrol the earth." So they [3]patrolled
the earth.
8 Then He cried out to me and spoke to me saying, "See, those
who are going to the land of the north have [1a]appeased My wrath in
the land of the north."
9 The [a]word of the LORD also came to me saying,
10 "[a]Take *an offering* from the exiles, from Heldai, Tobijah, and

2 [1]I.e., One c equals appro: [a]Zech. 4:2

3 [1]Or, *earth* 24:6; 43:28; J [b]Ex. 20:15; L Mal. 3:8, 9 [c] Is. 48:1; Jer. 5:4

4 [a]Mal. 3:5 3 [c]Jer. 2:26 14:34, 35; Jo

5 [a]Zech. 1:9

6 [1]I.e., Appro [2]Lit., *eye;* so versions rea [3]Or, *earth* [a]L Amos 8:5

8 [1]Lit., *mout* 12:7; Amos 8 6:11

9 [a]Lev. 11:1 104:17; Jer.

11 [1]Lit., *hou* 10:10; 11:2; 11:11; Dan.

6:1 [a]Dan. 7. Zech. 1:18; 6

2 [a]Zech. 1:8 [b]Rev. 6:5

3 [a]Rev. 6:2

4 [a]Zech. 1:9

5 [a]Jer. 49:3 37:9; Dan. 7 Matt. 24:31;

6 [a]Jer. 1:14 6:1; 25:9; 46 1:4 [b]Is. 43:6

7 [1]Lit., *soug* [2]Lit., *walk a through* [3]Lit *about throug* 1:10

8 [1]Lit., *caus to rest in* [a]E 24:13; Zech

9 [a]Zech. 1:

10 [a]Ezra 7. 8:26-30; Je

Jedaiah; and you go the same day and enter the house of Josiah the
son of Zephaniah, where they have arrived from Babylon.
11 "And take silver and gold, make an *ornate* [a]crown, and set *it* on
the head of [b]Joshua the son of Jehozadak, the high priest.
12 "Then say to him, 'Thus says the LORD of hosts, "Behold, a man
whose name is [1a]Branch, for He will [2b]branch out from where He is;
and He will [c]build the temple of the LORD.
13 "Yes, it is He who will build the temple of the LORD, and He who
will [a]bear the honor and sit and [b]rule on His throne. Thus, He will be
a [c]priest on His throne, and the counsel of peace will be between the
two [1]offices." '
14 "Now the [a]crown will become a reminder in the temple of the
LORD to Helem, Tobijah, Jedaiah, and [1]Hen the son of Zephaniah.
15 "And [a]those who are far off will come and [1]build the temple of the
LORD." Then you will [b]know that the LORD of hosts has sent me to
you. And it will take place, if you completely [c]obey the LORD your
God.

Chapter 7

7 Then it came about in the fourth year of King Darius, that the
word of the LORD came to Zechariah on the fourth *day* of the
ninth month, *which is* [a]Chislev.
2 Now *the town of* Bethel had sent Sharezer and Regemmelech and
[1]their men to [2a]seek the favor of the LORD,
3 speaking to the [a]priests who belong to the house of the LORD of
hosts, and to the prophets saying, "Shall I weep in the [b]fifth month
[1]and abstain, as I have done these many years?"
4 Then the word of the LORD of hosts came to me saying,
5 "Say to all the people of the land and to the priests, 'When you
fasted and mourned in the fifth and seventh months [1]these [a]seventy
years, was it actually for [b]Me that you fasted?
6 'And when you eat and drink, [1]do you not eat for yourselves and
do you not drink for yourselves?
7 'Are not *these* the words which the LORD [a]proclaimed by the
former prophets, when Jerusalem was inhabited and [1b]prosperous
with its cities around it, and the [2c]Negev and the [3]foothills were
inhabited?' "
8 Then the word of the LORD came to Zechariah saying,
9 "Thus has the LORD of hosts said, '[a]Dispense true justice, and
practice [b]kindness and compassion each to his brother;
10 and [a]do not oppress the widow or the [1]orphan, the [2]stranger or
the poor; and do [b]not devise evil in your hearts against one another.'
11 "But they [a]refused to pay attention, and [1b]turned a stubborn
shoulder and [2c]stopped their ears from hearing.
12 "And they made their [a]hearts *like* [1b]flint [2]so that they could not
hear the law and the [c]words which the LORD of hosts had sent by His
Spirit through the [d]former prophets; therefore great [e]wrath came
from the LORD of hosts.
13 "And it came about that just as [a]He called and they would not
listen, so [b]they called and I would not listen," says the LORD of hosts;
14 "but I [1a]scattered them with a [b]storm wind among all the nations
whom they have not known. Thus the land is [c]desolated behind
them, [2]so that [d]no one went back and forth, for they [e]made the
pleasant land desolate."

Chapter 8

8 Then the word of the LORD of hosts came saying,

2 "Thus says the LORD of hosts, 'I am [a]exceedingly jealous for Zion, yes, with great wrath I am jealous for her.'

3 "Thus says the LORD, 'I will return to Zion and will [a]dwell in the midst of Jerusalem. Then Jerusalem will be called the City of [b]Truth, and the mountain of the LORD of hosts *will be called* the Holy Mountain.'

4 "Thus says the LORD of hosts, '[a]Old men and old women will again sit in the [1]streets of Jerusalem, each man with his staff in his hand because of [2]age.

5 'And the [1]streets of the city will be filled with [a]boys and girls playing in its [1]streets.'

6 "Thus says the LORD of hosts, 'If it is [1a]too difficult in the sight of the remnant of this people in those days, will it also be [1b]too difficult in My sight?' declares the LORD of hosts.

7 "Thus says the LORD of hosts, 'Behold, I am going to save My people from the land of the [1a]east and from the land of the [2]west;

8 and I will [a]bring them *back*, and they will [b]live in the midst of Jerusalem, and they will be [c]My people and I will be their God in [1]truth and righteousness.'

9 "Thus says the LORD of hosts, 'Let your hands be [a]strong, you who are listening in these days to these words from the mouth of the [b]prophets, *those* who *spoke* in the day that the foundation of the house of the LORD of hosts was laid, to the end that the temple might be built.

10 'For before those days there was [a]no wage for man or any wage for animal; and for him who went out or came in there was no [1b]peace because of [2]his enemies, and I [c]set all men one against another.

11 'But now I will [a]not [1]treat the remnant of this people as in the former days,' declares the LORD of hosts.

12 'For *there will be* [a]peace for the seed: the vine will yield its fruit, the land will yield its produce, and the heavens will give their [b]dew; and I will cause the remnant of this people to inherit [c]all these *things*.

13 'And it will come about that just as you were a [a]curse among the nations, O house of Judah and house of Israel, so I will save you that you may become a [b]blessing. Do not fear; let your [c]hands be strong.'

14 "For thus says the LORD of hosts, 'Just as I [a]purposed to do harm to you when your fathers provoked Me to wrath,' says the LORD of hosts, 'and I have not [b]relented,

15 so I have again purposed in these days to [a]do good to Jerusalem and to the house of Judah. [b]Do not fear!

16 'These are the things which you should do: speak the [a]truth to one another; [b]judge with truth and judgment for peace in your [1]gates.

17 'Also let none of you [a]devise evil in your heart against another, and do not love [1b]perjury; for all these are what I [c]hate,' declares the LORD."

18 Then the word of the LORD of hosts came to me saying,

19 "Thus says the LORD of hosts, 'The fast of the [a]fourth, the fast of the [b]fifth, the fast of the [c]seventh, and the fast of the [d]tenth *months* will become [e]joy, gladness, and [1]cheerful feasts for the house of Judah; so [f]love truth and peace.'

8:2 [a]Zech. 1:1

3 [a]Zech. 2:10, [b]Zech. 8:16, 1

4 [1]Or, *squares* *multitude of da* 65:20

5 [1]Or, *squares* 30:19, 20; 31:1

6 [1]Or, *wonder* 118:23; 126:1- 32:17, 27

7 [1]Lit., *rising* *setting sun* [a]Ps Is. 11:11; 27:12

8 [1]Or, *faithfuln* [a]Zeph. 3:20; Ze 10:10 [b]Jer. 3:1 37:25 [c]Ezek. 1 36:28; Zech. 2:

9 [a]1 Chr. 22:13 35:4; Hag. 2:4 5:1; 6:14

10 [1]Or, *safety* *adversary* [a]Hag 2:15-19 [b]2 Chr. [c]Is. 19:2; Amos

11 [1]Lit., *be to t* 103:9; Is. 12:1; 2:19

12 [a]Lev. 26:3-6 27:28; Deut. 33 Hos. 13:3 [c]Is. 6 Obad. 17

13 [a]Jer. 29:18; 9:11 [b]Ps. 72:17 19:24, 25; Ezek. Zech. 14:11 [c]Ze

14 [a]Jer. 31:28 4:28; Ezek. 24:1

15 [a]Jer. 29:11; 7:18-20 [b]Zech.

16 [1]I.e., the pla where court was [a]Ps. 15:2; Prov. 12:17-19; Zech. Eph. 4:25 [b]Is. 9: 5; Zech. 7:9

17 [1]Lit., *false oa* [a]Prov. 3:29; Jer. Zech. 7:10 [b]Zec Mal. 3:5 [c]Prov. 6 Hab. 1:13

19 [1]Or, *goodly* 25:3, 4; Jer. 39:2 7:3, 5 [c]2 Kin. 25 Zech. 7:5 [d]Jer. 5 [e]Ps. 30:11; Is. 12 [f]Zech. 8:16; Luke 1:74, 75

20 "Thus says the LORD of hosts, '*It will* yet *be* that [a]peoples will
come, even the inhabitants of many cities.
21 'And the inhabitants of one will go to another saying, "Let us go
at once to [a]entreat the favor of the LORD, and to seek the LORD of
hosts; [1]I will also go."
22 'So [a]many peoples and mighty nations will come to seek the
LORD of hosts in Jerusalem and to [b]entreat the favor of the LORD.'
23 "Thus says the LORD of hosts, 'In those days ten men from all the
[1]nations will [2a]grasp the [3]garment of a Jew saying, "Let us go with
you, for we have heard that God is with you." ' "

Chapter 9

9 The [1]burden of the word of the LORD is against the land of
Hadrach, with [a]Damascus as its resting place (for the eyes of
men, especially of all the tribes of Israel, are toward the LORD),

2 And [a]Hamath also, which borders on it;
[b]Tyre and [c]Sidon, [1]though [2]they are [b]very wise.
3 For Tyre built herself a [a]fortress
And [b]piled up silver like dust,
And [c]gold like the mire of the streets.
4 Behold, the Lord will [a]dispossess her
And cast her wealth into the sea;
And she will be [b]consumed with fire.
5 Ashkelon will see *it* and be afraid.
Gaza too will writhe in great pain;
Also Ekron, for her expectation has been confounded.
Moreover, the king will perish from Gaza,
And Ashkelon will not be inhabited.
6 And a [1]mongrel race will dwell in [a]Ashdod,
And I will cut off the pride of the Philistines.
7 And I will remove their blood from their mouth,
And their detestable things from between their teeth.
Then they also will be a remnant for our God,
And be like a [1]clan in Judah,
And Ekron like a Jebusite.
8 But I will camp around My house [1]because of an army,
Because of [a]him who passes by and returns;

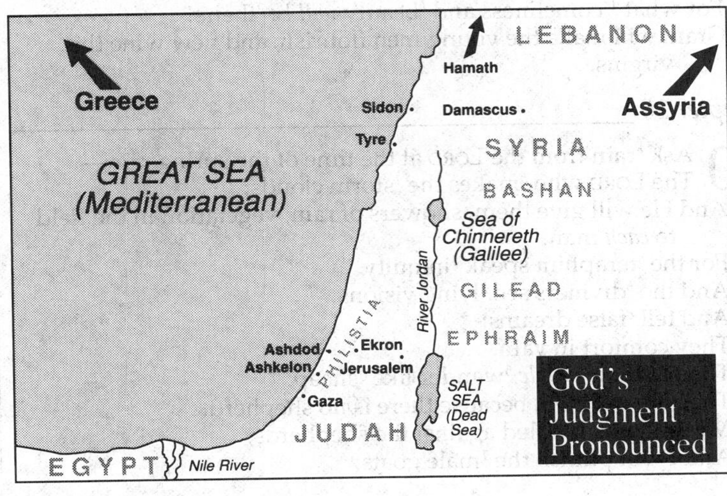

Ps. 117:1; Jer. 4:2, 3; Zech. 2:11; 14:16
let me go too [a]Zech. 7:2
s. 2:2, 3; 25:7; 2, 23; 60:3-12 [b]Zech. 8:21
, languages of ns [2]Lit., grasp, will grasp [3]Or, of the garment 5:14, 24; 60:14
Or, oracle [a]Is. Jer. 49:23-27; Amos 1:3-5
because [2]I.e., , they are [a]Jer. [b]Ezek. 28:2-5, 2 [c]Ezek. 28:21
. 19:29; 2 Sam. ob 27:16; Ezek. 28:4, 5 [c]1 Kin. 10:21, 27
. 26:3-5 [b]Ezek. 28:18
Lit., bastard will s 1:8; Zeph. 2:4
7 [1]Or, chief
, as a guard, so one will go back d forth [a]Is. 52:1

And [b]no oppressor will pass over them anymore,
For now I have seen with My eyes.
9 [a]Rejoice greatly, O daughter of Zion!
Shout *in triumph*, O daughter of Jerusalem!
Behold, your [b]king is coming to you;
He is [1c]just and [d]endowed with salvation,
[e]Humble, and mounted on a donkey,
Even on a [f]colt, the [2]foal of a donkey.
10 And I will [a]cut off the chariot from Ephraim,
And the [b]horse from Jerusalem;
And the [c]bow of war will be cut off.
And He will speak [d]peace to the nations;
And His [e]dominion will be from sea to sea,
And from the [1]River to the ends of the earth.

11 As for you also, because of the [a]blood of *My* covenant with you,
I have set your [b]prisoners free from the [1]waterless pit.
12 Return to the [1a]stronghold, O prisoners [2]who have the [b]hope;
This very day I am declaring that I will restore [c]double to you.
13 For I will [a]bend Judah [1]as My bow,
I will fill the bow with Ephraim.
And I will stir up your sons, O Zion, against your sons,
O [b]Greece;
And I will make you like a [c]warrior's sword.
14 Then the LORD will appear [a]over them,
And His [b]arrow will go forth like lightning;
And the Lord [1]GOD will blow the [c]trumpet,
And will march in the [d]storm winds of the south.
15 [a]The LORD of hosts will defend them.
And they will [b]devour, and trample on the [c]sling stones;
And they will drink, *and* be [d]boisterous as with wine;
And they will be filled like a *sacrificial* basin,
Drenched like the [e]corners of the altar.
16 And the LORD their God will [a]save them in that day
As the flock of His people;
For *they are as* the stones of a [b]crown,
[1]Sparkling in His land.
17 For what [1a]comeliness and [b]beauty *will be* [2]theirs!
Grain will make the young men flourish, and new wine the
virgins.

Chapter 10

10 Ask [a]rain from the LORD at the time of the spring rain—
The LORD who [b]makes the [1]storm clouds;
And He will give them [c]showers of rain, vegetation in the field
to *each* man.
2 For the [a]teraphim speak [1]iniquity,
And the [b]diviners see [2]lying visions,
And tell [c]false dreams;
They comfort in vain.
Therefore *the people* [3]wander like [d]sheep,
They are afflicted, because there is no shepherd.
3 "My [a]anger is kindled against the shepherds,
And I will punish the [1]male goats;

8 [b]Is. 54:14;

9 [1]Or, *vindic* *victorious* [2]L *female donk* 3:14, 15; Zec [b]Ps. 110:1; Is Jer. 23:5, 6; John 12:15 [d]Is. 43:3, 11 [f]Judg. 10:4; I

10 [1]I.e., Eup [a]Hos. 1:7 [b]M [c]Hos. 2:18 [d]I Mic. 4:2-4 [e]P 60:12

11 [1]Lit., *ciste* *there is no wa* 24:8; Heb. 10 24:22; 51:14

12 [1]Or, *Stron* [2]Lit., *of the ho* 16:19; Joel 3: 14:8; 17:13; H 19 [c]Is. 61:7

13 [1]Lit., *for M* 51:20 [b]Joel 3: 45:3

14 [1]Heb., *YH* usually render [a]Is. 31:5; Zech 18:14; Hab. 3: 27:13 [d]Is. 21:1

15 [a]Is. 37:35; 12:8 [b]Zech. 12 41:28 [d]Ps. 78: 27:2

16 [1]Or, *Display* [a]Jer. 31:10, 11

17 [1]Lit., *goodn* *his* [a]Jer. 31:12, 27:4; Is. 33:17

10:1 [1]Or, *thund* [a]Joel 2:23 [b]Jer. [c]Is. 30:23

2 [1]Or, *futility* [2]L [3]Lit., *journey* [a]E 21:21; Hos. 3:4 27:9 [c]Jer. 23:32 34:5, 8; Matt. 9:3 6:34

3 [1]I.e., leaders 25:34-36

3 [b]Ezek. 34:12

For the LORD of hosts has [b]visited His flock, the house of Judah,
And will make them like His majestic horse in battle.

4 [1]Lit., *him* [2]Or, ...sor [a]Luke 20:17; ... 2:20; 1 Pet. 2:6 ...1:20; Zech. 9:10

4 "From [1]them will come the [a]cornerstone,
From [1]them the tent peg,
From [1]them the bow of [b]battle,
From [1]them every [2]ruler, *all* of them together.

5 [a]2 Sam. 22:43 ...s 2:15; Hag. 2:22

5 "And they will be as mighty men,
[a]Treading down *the enemy* in the mire of the streets in battle;
And they will fight, for the LORD *will be* with them;
And the [b]riders on horses will be put to shame.

[1]Or, *make them ...well* [a]Zech. 10:12 ...8:7; 9:16 [c]Zech. ...[d]Is. 54:8; Zech. ...[e]Is. 54:4 [f]Zech. 13:9

6 "And I shall [a]strengthen the house of Judah,
And I shall [b]save the house of Joseph,
And I shall [1c]bring them back,
Because I have had [d]compassion on them;
And they will be as though I had [e]not rejected them,
For I am the LORD their God, and I will [f]answer them.

...Or, *Let their heart* [a]Is. 54:13; Ezek. 37:25

7 "And Ephraim will be like a mighty man,
And their heart will be glad as if *from* wine;
Indeed, their [a]children will see *it* and be glad,
[1]Their heart will rejoice in the LORD.

...*were numerous* ...6; 7:18, 19 [b]Jer. ...2; Rev. 7:9 [c]Jer. ...:20; Ezek. 36:11

8 "I will [a]whistle for them to gather them together,
For I have redeemed them;
And they will be as [b]numerous as they [1c]were before.

...Lit., *sow* [a]1 Kin. ...47, 48; Ezek. 6:9

9 "When I [1]scatter them among the peoples,
They will [a]remember Me in far countries,
And they with their children will live and come back.

..., *And* [a]Is. 11:11 ...19 [c]Is. 49:19, 20

10 "I will [a]bring them back from the land of Egypt,
And gather them from Assyria;
And I will bring them into the land of [b]Gilead and Lebanon,
[1]Until [c]no *room* can be found for them.

[a]Is. 51:9, 10 [b]Is. ...5-7 [c]Zeph. 2:13 [d]Ezek. 30:13

11 "And He will pass through the [a]sea *of* distress,
And strike the waves in the sea,
So that all the depths of the [b]Nile will dry up;
And the pride of [c]Assyria will be brought down,
And the scepter of [d]Egypt will depart.

...Zech. 10:6 [b]Mic. 4:5

12 "And I shall [a]strengthen them in the LORD,
And in His name [b]they will walk," declares the LORD.

Chapter 11

...1:1 [a]Jer. 22:6, 7 [b]Ezek. 31:3

11 Open your doors, O Lebanon,
That a [a]fire may feed on your [b]cedars.

...uniper [2]Another ...ng is *forest of the vintage*

2 Wail, O [1]cypress, for the cedar has fallen,
Because the glorious *trees* have been destroyed;
Wail, O oaks of Bashan,
For the [2]impenetrable forest has come down.

[1]Or, *jungle* [a]Jer. ...34-36 [b]Jer. 2:15; 50:44

3 There is a sound of the shepherds' [a]wail,
For their glory is ruined;
There is a [b]sound of the young lions' roar,
For the [1]pride of the Jordan is ruined.

...4:22; Zech. 11:7

4 Thus says the LORD my God, "Pasture the flock *doomed* to
[a]slaughter.

...Lit., *are not held* [a]Jer. 50:7 [b]Hos. ...Tim. 6:9 [c]Ezek. 34:2, 3

5 "Those who buy them slay them and [1]go [a]unpunished, and *each of*
those who sell them says, 'Blessed be the LORD, for [b]I have become
rich!' And their [c]own shepherds have no pity on them.

6 "For I shall [a]no longer have pity on the inhabitants of the land,"
declares the LORD; "but behold, I shall [b]cause the men to [1]fall, each
into another's [2]power and into the [2]power of his king; and they will
strike the land, and I shall [c]not deliver *them* from their [2]power."
7 So I [a]pastured the flock *doomed* to slaughter, [1]hence the [b]afflicted
of the flock. And I took for myself two [c]staffs: the one I called
[2d]Favor, and the other I called [3e]Union; so I pastured the flock.
8 Then I annihilated the three shepherds in [a]one month, for my
soul was impatient with them, and their soul also [1]was weary of me.
9 Then I said, "I will not pasture you. What is to [a]die, [1]let it die,
and what is to be annihilated, [2]let it be annihilated; and [3]let those
who are left eat one another's flesh."
10 And I took my staff, [1a]Favor, and cut it in pieces, to [2b]break my
covenant which I had made with all the peoples.
11 So it was [1]broken on that day, and [2]thus the [a]afflicted of the flock
who were watching me realized that it was the word of the LORD.
12 And I said to them, "If it is good in your sight, give *me* my
[a]wages; but if not, [1]never mind!" So they weighed out [b]thirty *shekels*
of silver as my wages.
13 Then the LORD said to me, "Throw it to the [a]potter, *that* mag-
nificent price at which I was valued by them." So I took the thirty
shekels of silver and threw them to the potter in the house of the
LORD.
14 Then I cut my second staff, [1a]Union, in pieces, to [b]break the
brotherhood between Judah and Israel.
15 And the LORD said to me, "Take again for yourself the equipment
of a [1a]foolish shepherd.
16 "For behold, I am going to raise up a shepherd in the land who
will [a]not care for the perishing, seek the scattered, heal the broken, or
sustain the one standing, but will [b]devour the flesh of the fat *sheep*
and tear off their hoofs.
17 "[a]Woe to the worthless shepherd
Who leaves the flock!
A [b]sword will be on his arm
And on his right eye!
His [c]arm will be totally withered,
And his right eye will be [1]blind."

Chapter 12

12 The [1]burden of the word of the LORD concerning Israel.
Thus declares the LORD who [a]stretches out the heavens, [b]lays
the foundation of the earth, and [c]forms the spirit of man within him,
2 "Behold, I am going to make Jerusalem a [a]cup [1]that causes reeling
to all the peoples around; and when the siege is against Jerusalem, it
will also be against [b]Judah.
3 "And it will come about in that day that I will make Jerusalem a
heavy [a]stone for all the peoples; all who lift it will be [b]severely [1]in-
jured. And all the [c]nations of the earth will be gathered against it.
4 "In that day," declares the LORD, "I will strike every horse with
bewilderment, and his rider with madness. But I will [1]watch over
the house of Judah, while I strike every horse of the peoples with
blindness.
5 "Then the clans of Judah will say in their hearts, '[1]A strong

6 [1]Lit., *find* [a]Jer. 13:14 Mic. 7:2-6; [c]Ps. 50:22;

7 [1]Another *for the shee* [2]Or, *Pleasa* *Cords* [a]Zec 39:10; Zeph [c]Ezek. 37:16 90:17; Zech 133:1; Ezek Zech. 11:14

8 [1]Or, *detes* 5:7

9 [1]Or, *will d* *be annihilate* *those . . . wi* 15:2

10 [1]Or, *Plea* [2]Or, *annul* [b]Ps. 89:39; J

11 [1]Or, *annu* [2]Another rea *sheep deale* [a]Zeph. 3:12

12 [1]Lit., *ceas* 5:6; Mal. 3:5 37:28; Ex. 21 26:15; 27:9,

13 [a]Matt. 27: 1:18, 19

14 [1]Or, *Cord* 11:7 [b]Is. 9:21 11:6

15 [1]Or, *usele* 6:10-12; Zech

16 [a]Jer. 23:2 34:2-6

17 [1]Lit., *comp* *dimmed* [a]Jer. Zech. 10:2; 11 50:35-37 [c]Eze 30:21, 22

12:1 [1]Or, *orac* 42:5; 44:24; Je [b]Job 26:7; Ps. 26; Heb. 1:10- 57:16; Heb. 12

2 [1]Lit., *of reeli* 75:8; Is. 51:22, [b]Zech. 14:14

3 [1]Lit., *scratch* 2:34, 35, 44, 45 21:44 [c]Zech. 1

4 [1]Lit., *open M*

5 [1]Lit., *My stre*

support for us are the inhabitants of Jerusalem through the LORD of hosts, their God.'

6 "In that day I will make the clans of Judah like a [a]firepot among pieces of wood and a flaming torch among sheaves, so they will consume on the right hand and on the left all the surrounding peoples, while the [b]inhabitants of Jerusalem again dwell on their own sites in Jerusalem.

7 "The LORD also will [a]save the tents of Judah first in order that the glory of the house of [b]David and the glory of the inhabitants of Jerusalem may not be magnified above Judah.

8 "In that day the LORD will [a]defend the inhabitants of Jerusalem, and the one who [1b]is feeble among them in that day will be like David, and the house of David *will be* like [c]God, like the [d]angel of the LORD before them.

9 "And it will come about in that day that I will [1a]set about to destroy all the nations that come against Jerusalem.

10 "And I will [a]pour out on the house of David and on the inhabitants of Jerusalem, [1]the Spirit of grace and of supplication, so that they will look on Me whom they have [b]pierced; and they will mourn for Him, as one [c]mourns for an only son, and they will weep bitterly over Him, like the bitter weeping over a first-born.

11 "In that day there will be great [a]mourning in Jerusalem, like the mourning of Hadadrimmon in the [1]plain of [2]Megiddo.

12 "And the land will mourn, every family by itself; the family of the house of David by itself, and their wives by themselves; the family of the house of Nathan by itself, and their wives by themselves;

13 the family of the house of Levi by itself, and their wives by themselves; the family of the Shimeites by itself, and their wives by themselves;

14 all the families that remain, every family by itself, and their wives by themselves.

Chapter 13

13 "In that day a [a]fountain will be opened for the house of David and for the inhabitants of Jerusalem, for [b]sin and for [c]impurity.

2 "And it will come about in that day," declares the LORD of hosts, "that I will [a]cut off the names of the idols from the land, and they will no longer be remembered; and I will also remove the [b]prophets and the [c]unclean spirit from the land.

3 "And it will come about that if anyone still [a]prophesies, then his father and mother who gave birth to him will say to him, 'You shall [b]not live, for you have spoken [c]falsely in the name of the LORD'; and his [d]father and mother who gave birth to him will pierce him through when he prophesies.

4 "Also it will come about in that day that the prophets will each be [a]ashamed of his vision when he prophesies, and they will not put on a [b]hairy robe in order to deceive;

5 but he will say, 'I am [a]not a prophet; I am a tiller of the ground, for a man [1]sold me as a slave in my youth.'

6 "And one will say to him, 'What are these wounds [a]between your [1]arms?' Then he will say, '*Those* with which I was wounded in the house of [2]my friends.'

7 "Awake, O [a]sword, against My [b]Shepherd,

17, 18; Obad. . 11:1 [b]Zech. 2:4; 8:3-5
30:18 [b]Amos 9:11
tumbles [a]Joel Zech. 9:14, 15 3; Josh. 23:10; [c]Ps. 8:5; 82:6 Ex. 14:19; 33:2
seek to [a]Zech. 14:2, 3
Or, *a spirit* [a]Is. ek. 39:29; Joel 9 [b]John 19:37; 1:7 [c]Jer. 6:26; Amos 8:10
e., broad valley *egiddon* [a]Matt. 24:30; Rev. 1:7
Jer. 2:13; 17:13 , 7; Is. 1:16-18; 9 [c]Num. 19:17; 4; Ezek. 36:25
3:13; Hos. 2:17 3:14, 15 [c]1 Kin. Ezek. 36:25, 29
er. 23:34 [b]Deut. Ezek. 14:9 [c]Jer. [d]Deut. 13:6-11; Matt. 10:37
r. 6:15; 8:9; Mic. Kin. 1:8; Is. 20:2; Matt. 3:4
, *caused another me* [a]Amos 7:14
[1]Lit., *hands* [2]Lit., *ose who love me* [a]2 Kin. 9:24
[a]Jer. 47:6; Ezek. [b]Is. 40:11; Ezek. 3, 24; 37:24; Mic. 5:2, 4

And against the man, My [c]Associate,"
Declares the LORD of hosts.
"[d]Strike the Shepherd that the sheep may be scattered;
And I will [e]turn My hand [1]against the little ones.
8 "And it will come about in all the land,"
Declares the LORD,
"That [a]two parts in it will be cut off *and* perish;
But the third will be left in it.
9 "And I will bring the third part through the [a]fire,
Refine them as silver is refined,
And test them as gold is tested.
They will [b]call on My name,
And I will [c]answer them;
I will say, 'They are [d]My people,'
And they will say, 'The LORD is my God.' "

Chapter 14

14 Behold, a [a]day is coming for the LORD when [b]the spoil taken from you will be divided among you.
2 For I will [a]gather all the nations against Jerusalem to battle, and the city will be captured, the [b]houses plundered, the women ravished, and half of the city exiled, but the rest of the people will not be cut off from the city.
3 Then the LORD will go forth and [a]fight against those nations, as [1]when He fights on a day of battle.
4 And in that day His feet will [a]stand on the Mount of Olives, which is in front of Jerusalem on the east; and the Mount of Olives will be [b]split in its middle from east to west by a very large valley, so that half of the mountain will move toward the north and the other half toward the south.
5 And you will flee by the valley of My mountains, for the valley of the mountains will reach to Azel; yes, you will flee just as you fled before the [a]earthquake in the days of Uzziah king of Judah. [b]Then the LORD, my God, will come, *and* all the holy ones with [1]Him!
6 And it will come about in that day that there will be [a]no light; the [1]luminaries will dwindle.
7 For it will be [a]a unique day which is [b]known to the LORD, neither day nor night, but it will come about that at [c]evening time there will be light.
8 And it will come about in that day that [a]living waters will flow out of Jerusalem, half of them toward the eastern sea and the other half toward the western sea; it will be in summer as well as in winter.
9 And the LORD will be [a]king over all the earth; in that day the LORD will be *the only* [b]one, and His name *the only* one.
10 All the land will be changed into a plain from [a]Geba to [b]Rimmon south of Jerusalem; but [1]Jerusalem will [c]rise and [d]remain on its site from [e]Benjamin's Gate as far as the place of the First Gate to the [f]Corner Gate, and from the [g]Tower of Hananel to the king's wine presses.
11 And [1]people will live in it, and there will be [a]no more curse, for Jerusalem will [b]dwell in security.
12 Now this will be the plague with which the LORD will strike all the peoples who have gone to war against Jerusalem; their flesh will

7 [1]Or, *upon* Jer. 23:5, 6 [d] 10; Matt. 26:3 14:27 [e]Is. 1:2

8 [a]Is. 6:13; E 5:2-4, 12

9 [a]Is. 48:10; [b]Ps. 34:15-17 Zech. 12:10 65:24; Jer. 29 Zech. 10:6 [d]H

14:1 [a]Is. 13:6 2:1; Mal. 4:1 14:14

2 [a]Zech. 12:2 13:16

3 [1]Lit., *His da fighting* [a]Zech

4 [a]Ezek. 11:23 64:1, 2; Ezek. Mic. 1:3, 4; Ha Zech. 4:7; 14:8

5 [1]So the vers Heb., *Thee* [a]Is Amos 1:1 [b]Ps. Is. 66:15, 16; M 16:27; 25:31

6 [1]Lit., *glorious will congeal* [a]Is Jer. 4:23; Ezek Joel 2:30, 31; A 2:16, 19

7 [a]Jer. 30:7; Ar [b]Is. 45:21; Acts [c]Is. 58:10; Rev.

8 [a]Ezek. 47:1- 3:18; John 7:38 22:1, 2

9 [a]Is. 2:24; 45:2 9:9; 14:16, 17 [b] 6:4; Is. 45:21-24

10 [1]Lit., *it* [a]1 Ki 15:22 [b]Josh. 15 Judg. 20:45, 47 Amos 9:11 [d]Jer Zech. 12:6 [e]Jer. 38:7 [f]2 Kin. 14:1 31:38

11 [1]Lit., *they* [a]Z 8:13; Rev. 22:3 23:5, 6; Ezek. 34

[a]rot while they stand on their feet, and their eyes will rot in their
sockets, and their tongue will rot in their mouth.
13 And it will come about in that day that a great panic from the
LORD will [1]fall on them; and they will [a]seize one another's hand, and
the hand of one will [2]be lifted against the hand of another.
14 And [a]Judah also will fight at Jerusalem; and the [b]wealth of all the
surrounding nations will be gathered, gold and silver and garments
in great abundance.
15 So also like this [a]plague, will be the plague on the horse, the
mule, the camel, the donkey, and all the cattle that will be in those
camps.
16 Then it will come about that any who are left of all the nations
that went against Jerusalem will [a]go up from year to year to worship
the King, the LORD of hosts, and to celebrate the [b]Feast of Booths.
17 And it will be that whichever of the families of the earth does
not go up to Jerusalem to worship the [a]King, the LORD of hosts, there
will be [b]no rain on them.
18 And if the family of Egypt does not go up or enter, then no *rain*
will fall on them; it will be the [a]plague with which the LORD smites
the nations who do not go up to celebrate the Feast of Booths.
19 This will be the [1]punishment of Egypt, and the [1]punishment of
all the nations who do not go up to celebrate the Feast of Booths.
20 In that day there will *be inscribed* on the bells of the horses,
"[a]HOLY TO THE LORD." And the [b]cooking pots in the LORD's house
will be like the bowls before the altar.
21 And every cooking pot in Jerusalem and in Judah will be [a]holy
to the LORD of hosts; and all who sacrifice will come and take of
them and boil in them. And there will no longer be a [1b]Canaanite in
the house of the LORD of hosts in that day.

[a]Lev. 26:16; Deut. 28:21, 22

3 [1]Lit., *be among* t., *rise up against* [a]Zech. 11:6

Zech. 12:2, 5 [b]Is. 23:18; Zech. 14:1

15 [a]Zech. 14:12

16 [a]Is. 60:6-9; :18-21, 23 [b]Lev. 23:34-44

[a]Zech. 14:9, 16 14:3-6; Amos 4:7

[a]Zech. 14:12, 15

19 [1]Lit., *sin*

20 [a]Ex. 28:36-38 [b]Ezek. 46:20

1 [1]Or, *merchant* 8:10; Rom. 14:6, or. 10:31 [b]Zeph. 1:11

ZECHARIAH'S PROPHETIC REVELATIONS

Concerning Messiah, Judah, and Jerusalem	Concerning the Nations	Concerning Messiah, the Savior and King

ZECHARIAH AT A GLANCE

e of Zechariah:

DIVISIONS

	CHAPTER THEMES
	1
	2
	3
	4
	5
	6
	7
	8
	9
	10
	11
	12
	13
	14

Author:

Date:

Purpose:

Key Words:

MALACHI

Because they hadn't obeyed the Word of the Lord, in 586 B.C. the children of Israel were take captivity. The nation that was once the head became the tail—just as God had spoken throug prophet Moses. And just as God had spoken through Jeremiah the prophet, the children of I captivity lasted for seventy years.

In 538 B.C. Cyrus, king of Persia, issued a decree allowing the children of Israel to return to Jeru and rebuild their temple. It was just as God had said when Isaiah gave this prophecy 175 years Cyrus was born. In 516 B.C. Zerubbabel finished the temple just as God promised. In 445 B.C. the P King Artaxerxes permitted Nehemiah to return to Jerusalem and rebuild its walls—just as Dani prophesied.

Over and over the children of Israel saw that God stood by His Word. Just as Solomon wr Proverbs, the hearts of kings were in God's hands and He could turn them wherever He wanted then did the remnant of Israel think they could live and worship any way they wanted once the returned from their seventy years of exile and had settled again in Israel? Had they grown ti waiting for the fulfillment of the prophesies which promised the Messiah would reign as king o the earth? Had God abandoned them as He had Esau's descendants? Did they think He would the heathen nations who had come against them to go unpunished? Or were they enterta thoughts that God really did not love them, that He would not keep His covenant promises?

Whatever it was, once again the remnant became apathetic in their relationship with God. S spoke one more time through Malachi, whose name means "my messenger." It was sometime a 433 B.C.

THINGS TO DO

1. Since Malachi is a short book, read it without interruption so you can get a perspective c book before you observe it chapter by chapter. As you read, catch the atmosphere of this Remember, this was written to people who had been sent into exile because of disobedienc then had returned to their land just as God had promised.
2. Now read through Malachi one chapter at a time, doing the following:
   a. In a distinctive way or color mark the key words listed on the MALACHI AT A GLA chart on page 1413. Write these key words on a card you can use as a bookmark while study Malachi.
   b. Note in the margin who God is upset with, why He is upset, and what He tells them to c what He is going to do as a result.
   c. As you mark every reference to *you say* or *said*, watch what the people say and how answers.
   d. Take note of what will happen to those who fear His name and to those who do not. Re your insights in the margin.
   e. Note God's call to return to Him, how they are to return, and what will happen if they do.
3. When you finish each chapter, decide what the main subject or theme of that chapter is and record it on MALACHI AT A GLANCE and next to the chapter number in the text.
4. As you read the final chapter of Malachi, read Deuteronomy 28 through 30, which speaks o blessings or curses upon those who obey or disobey the law given by Moses.
5. God was silent for four hundred years after He spoke through His prophet Malachi. His sil was broken when an angel appeared to Zacharias with the news that he and Elizabeth w give birth to a son. Read Luke 1:5-17 and Matthew 11:2-15 and see how these passages rela

God's final promise in Malachi. Record the essence of that promise in the margin of Malachi 4 and then write next to it the cross-references in Luke and Matthew.

In the appendix is a chart called THE DAY OF THE LORD (page 1878). Record on it what you learn from Malachi about that day. Note the reference (book, chapter, and verse) you took your information from so you can find it later.

:GS TO THINK ABOUT

What do you learn from God's Word to the priests that you can apply to your own life? Read through the list you compiled on "the priests" and remember that if you belong to the Lord Jesus Christ you are part of a kingdom of priests unto God. What kind of a priest are you? In principle do you think God expects anything less of you as a Christian? For instance, what do you offer the Lord of your time and talents, your tithe and offering? Do you give others instructions according to the Word of the Lord or according to the current philosophy of the world? What about your covenant relationship with your mate?

Are you tired of serving God? Do you fear Him? If so, what is God's promise to you?

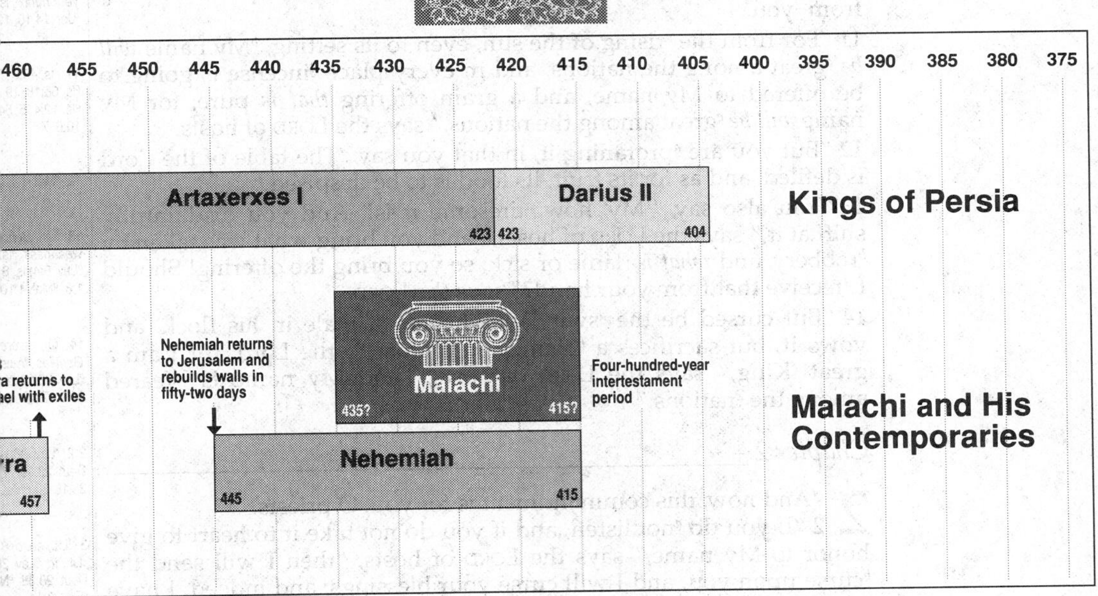

Lit., *burden* [2]Or, *messenger* [a]Is. h. 1:1; Hab. 1:1; . 9:1 [b]Mal. 2:11

. 4:37; 7:8; 23:5; 1:8, 9; Jer. 31:3; ;:12 [b]Rom. 9:13

er. 49:10, 16-18; 35:3, 4, 7, 8, 15

rebuild the ruins [2]Lit., *border of* *ness* [3]Or, *whom* *ORD has cursed* 5:17 [b]Is. 9:9, 10 s 3:15; 5:11; 6:11 . 35:9; Obad. 10

will be great [2]Or, *itory* [a]Ps. 35:27; Mic. 5:4

[a]Ex. 20:12; Prov. 30:11, 17

Chapter 1

1 The [1a]oracle of the word of the LORD to [b]Israel through [2]Malachi.
2 "I have [a]loved you," says the LORD. But you say, "How hast
Thou loved us?" "*Was* not Esau Jacob's brother?" declares the LORD.
"Yet I [b]have loved Jacob;
3 but I have hated Esau, and I have [a]made his mountains a desola-
tion, and *appointed* his inheritance for the jackals of the wilderness."
4 Though Edom says, "We have been [a]beaten down, but we will
[1b]return and build up the ruins"; thus says the LORD of hosts, "They
may [c]build, but I will tear down; and *men* will call them the [2]wicked
territory, and the people [3]toward whom the LORD is indignant [d]for-
ever."
5 And your eyes will see this and you will say, "[a]The LORD [1]be
magnified beyond the [2]border of Israel!"
6 " 'A son [a]honors *his* father, and a servant his master. Then if I am a

[b]father, where is My honor? And if I am a master, where is My
[1]respect?' says the LORD of hosts to you, O [c]priests who despise My
name. But you say, 'How have we despised Thy name?'
7 "*You* are presenting [a]defiled [1b]food upon My altar. But you say,
'How have we defiled Thee?' In that you say, 'The [c]table of the LORD
is to be despised.'
8 "But when you present the [a]blind for sacrifice, is it not evil? And
when you present the lame and sick, is it not evil? [1]Why not offer it
to your [b]governor? Would he be pleased with you? Or would he
receive you kindly?" says the LORD of hosts.
9 "But now [1]will you not [a]entreat God's favor, that He may be gra-
cious to us? [2]With such an offering on your part, will He [b]receive any
of you kindly?" says the LORD of hosts.
10 "Oh that there were one among you who would [a]shut the [1]gates,
that you might not uselessly kindle *fire on* My altar! I am not pleased
with you," says the LORD of hosts, "[b]nor will I accept an offering
from [2]you.
11 "For from the [a]rising of the sun, even to its setting, [b]My name *will*
be [c]great among the nations, and in every place [d]incense is going to
be offered to My name, and a grain offering *that is* pure; for My
name *will be* [e]great among the nations," says the LORD of hosts.
12 "But you are [a]profaning it, in that you say, 'The table of the Lord
is defiled, and as for its fruit, its food is to be despised.'
13 "You also say, '[1]My, how [a]tiresome it is!' And you disdainfully
sniff at it," says the LORD of hosts, "and you bring what was taken by
[b]robbery, and *what is* [c]lame or sick; so you bring the offering! Should
I [d]receive that from your hand?" says the LORD.
14 "But cursed be the [a]swindler who has a male in his flock, and
vows it, but sacrifices a [b]blemished animal to the Lord, for I am a
great [c]King," says the LORD of hosts, "and My name is [1d]feared
among the [2]nations."

Chapter 2

2 "And now, this commandment is for you, O priests.
2 "If you do [a]not listen, and if you do not take it to heart to give
honor to My name," says the LORD of hosts, "then I will send the
[b]curse upon you, and I will curse your blessings; and indeed, I have
[c]cursed them *already*, because you are not taking *it* to heart.
3 "Behold, I am going to [a]rebuke your [1]offspring, and I will [b]spread
[2]refuse on your faces, the [2]refuse of your [c]feasts; and you will be
taken away [3]with it.
4 "Then you will know that I have sent this commandment to you,
[1]that My [a]covenant may [2]continue with Levi," says the LORD of hosts.
5 "My covenant with him was *one of* life and [a]peace, and I gave
them to him *as an object of* [1]reverence; so he [2b]revered Me, and stood
in awe of My name.
6 "[1a]True instruction was in his mouth, and unrighteousness was
not found on his lips; he walked [b]with Me in peace and uprightness,
and he [c]turned many back from iniquity.
7 "For the lips of a priest should preserve [a]knowledge, and [1]men
should [b]seek [2]instruction from his mouth; for he is the [c]messenger of
the LORD of hosts.
8 "But as for you, you have turned aside from the way; you have

6 [1]Lit., *fear* 1:31; Is. 1:2; Mal. 2:10 [c]Z Mal. 2:1-9

7 [1]Lit., *bread* 13 [b]Lev. 3:11 [c]Mal. 1:12

8 [1]Lit., *Offer* [a]Lev. 22:22; 15:21 [b]Hag.

9 [1]Lit., *entrea* [2]Lit., *This has your hand* [a]J Joel 2:12-14 5:22

10 [1]Or, *doors* *your hand* [a]Is [b]Jer. 14:10, 1

11 [a]Is. 45:6 [c]Is. 66:18, 19 [e]Is. 12:4, 5; 54 10:6, 7

12 [a]Mal. 1:7

13 [1]Lit., *Beho weariness* [a]Is [b]Lev. 6:4; Is. 6 1:8 [d]Mal. 1:10

14 [1]Or, *revere* *Gentiles* [a]Acts [b]Lev. 22:18-20 14:9 [d]Zeph. 2:

2:2 [a]Lev. 26:1 Deut. 28:15 [b]D 28:16-20 [c]Mal

3 [1]Lit., *seed* [2]([3]Lit., *to* [a]Lev. 2 Deut. 28:38 [b]N [c]Ex. 29:14

4 [1]Or, *to be My covenant with* [a]Num. 3:11-13, 18:21; Neh. 13: 3:1

5 [1]Or, *fear* [2]Or [a]Num. 25:12 [b]N 25:7, 8, 13

6 [1]Or, *Law of tr* 119:142, 151, 16 [b]Deut. 33:8, 9; P 37:37 [c]Jer. 23:2

7 [1]Lit., *they* [2]Or [a]Lev. 10:11; Neh [b]Num. 27:21; De 17:8-11; Jer. 18: Ezek. 7:26 [c]Hag caused many to [a]stumble [1]by the instruction; you have [2b] corrupted the covenant of Levi," says the LORD of hosts.

9 "So [a]I also have made you despised and [b]abased [1]before all the people, just as you are not keeping My ways, but are showing [c]partiality in the [2]instruction.

10 "Do we not all have [a]one father? [b]Has not one God created us? Why do we deal [c]treacherously each against his brother so as to profane the [d]covenant of our fathers?

11 "Judah has dealt [a]treacherously, and an abomination has been committed in Israel and in Jerusalem; for Judah has [b]profaned the sanctuary of the LORD [1]which He loves, and has married the daughter of a foreign god.

12 "*As* for the man who does this, may the [a]LORD cut off from the tents of Jacob *everyone* who awakes and answers, or who [b]presents [1]an offering to the LORD of hosts.

13 "And this is [1]another thing you do: you cover the altar of the LORD with tears, with weeping and with groaning, because He [a]no longer regards the [2]offering or accepts *it with* favor from your hand.

14 "Yet you say, 'For what reason?' Because the LORD has been a witness between you and the [a]wife of your youth, against whom you have dealt [b]treacherously, though she is your companion and your wife by covenant.

15 "[1]But not one has [a]done *so* who has a remnant of the Spirit. And [2]what did *that* one *do* while he was seeking a [b]godly [3]offspring? Take heed then, to your spirit, and let no one deal [c]treacherously against the wife of your youth.

16 "For [1]I hate [2a]divorce," says the LORD, the God of Israel, "and [3]him who covers his garment with [4b]wrong," says the LORD of hosts. "So take heed to your spirit, that you do not deal treacherously."

17 You have [a]wearied the LORD with your words. Yet you say, "How have we wearied *Him*?" In that you say, "[b]Everyone who does evil is good in the sight of the LORD, and He [c]delights in them," or, "[d]Where is the God of [e]justice?"

Chapter 3

3 "[a]Behold, I am going to send [b]My [1]messenger, and he will [2c]clear the way before Me. And the Lord, whom you seek, will suddenly come to His temple; [3]and the [1d]messenger of the covenant, in whom you delight, behold, He is coming," says the LORD of hosts.

2 "But who can [a]endure the day of His coming? And who can stand when He appears? For He is like a [b]refiner's fire and like [1]fullers' soap.

3 "And He will sit as a smelter and purifier of silver, and He will [a]purify the sons of Levi and refine them like gold and silver, so that they may [b]present to the LORD [1]offerings in righteousness.

4 "Then the [1]offering of Judah and Jerusalem will be [a]pleasing to the LORD, as in the [b]days of old and as in former years.

5 "Then I will draw near to you for judgment; and I will be a swift witness against the [a]sorcerers and against the [b]adulterers and against those who [c]swear falsely, and against those who oppress the [d]wage earner in his wages, the [e]widow and the [1]orphan, and those who turn aside the [2f]alien, and do not [3]fear Me," says the LORD of hosts.

6 "For [1]I, the LORD, [a]do not change; therefore you, O sons of Jacob, [2]are not consumed.

Or, *in the law* [2]Or, *olated* [a]Jer. 18:15 n. 25:12, 13; Neh. 3:29; Ezek. 44:10

[1]Lit., *to* [2]Or, *law* . 3:6 [b]Ezek. 7:26 ut. 1:17; Mic. 3:11

. 63:16; 64:8; Jer. ; 1 Cor. 8:6; Eph. Acts 17:24f. [c]Jer. [d]Ex. 19:4-6; 24:3, 7, 8

[1]Or, *in that he has and married* [a]Jer. 3:7-9 [b]Ezra 9:1, 2

r, *a grain offering* 24:21; Hos. 9:12 [b]Mal. 1:10, 13

[1]Lit., *second* [2]Or, *rain offering* [a]Jer. 11:14; 14:12

Is. 54:6 [b]Jer. 9:2; Mal. 3:5

5 [1]Or, *Did He not one, although He the remnant* [2]Or, *one? He sought a dly offspring* [3]Lit., [a]Gen. 2:24; Matt. :4, 5 [b]Ruth 4:12; 2:20 [c]Ex. 20:14; Lev. 20:10

t., *He hates* [2]Lit., *ing away* [3]Lit., *he ers* [4]Or, *violence* 24:1; Matt. 5:31; 6-8 [b]Ps. 73:6; Is. 59:6

[a]Is. 43:22, 24 [b]Is. Zeph. 1:12 [c]Job 4 [d]2 Pet. 3:4 [e]Is. 5:19; Jer. 17:15

[1]Or, *angel* [2]Or, *repare* [3]Or, *even* t. 11:10, 14; Mark ; Luke 1:76; 7:27 1:13; John 1:6, 7 Is. 40:3 [d]Is. 63:9

Lit., *laundrymen's* :14; Ezek. 22:14; :17 [b]Zech. 13:9; t. 3:10-12; 1 Cor. 3:13-15

r, *grain offerings* 1:25; Dan. 12:10 [b]Ps. 4:5; 51:19

[1]Or, *grain offering* 51:17-19 [b]2 Chr. 7:1-3, 12

r, *fatherless* [2]Or, *urner* [3]Or, *revere* 18:10; Jer. 27:9, ek. 22:9-11 [c]Jer. ; Zech. 5:4 [d]Lev. 13 [e]Ex. 22:22-24 [f]Deut. 27:19

I am the LORD; I not [2]Or, *have not to an end* [a]Num. 3:19; James 1:17

7 "From the [a]days of your fathers you have turned aside from My
statutes, and have not kept *them*. [b]Return to Me, and I will return to
you," says the LORD of hosts. "But you say, 'How shall we return?'
8 "Will a man [1]rob God? Yet you are robbing Me! But you say, 'How
have we robbed Thee?' In [a]tithes and [2]offerings.
9 "You are [a]cursed with a curse, for you are [1]robbing Me, the whole
nation *of you*!
10 "[a]Bring the whole tithe into the storehouse, so that there may be
[1]food in My house, and test Me now in this," says the LORD of hosts,
"if I will not [b]open for you the windows of heaven, and [c]pour out for
you a blessing until [2d]it overflows.
11 "Then I will rebuke the [a]devourer for you, so that it may not
[1]destroy the fruits of the ground; nor will your vine in the field cast
its grapes," says the LORD of hosts.
12 "And [a]all the nations will call you blessed, for you shall be a
[b]delightful land," says the LORD of hosts.
13 "Your words have been [1]arrogant against Me," says the LORD.
"Yet you say, 'What have we spoken against Thee?'
14 "You have said, 'It is [a]vain to serve God; and what [b]profit is it that
we have kept His charge, and that we have walked in mourning
before the LORD of hosts?
15 'So now we [a]call the arrogant blessed; not only are the doers of
wickedness built up, but they also test God and [b]escape.' "
16 Then those who [1]feared the LORD spoke to one another, and the
LORD [a]gave attention and heard *it*, and a [b]book of remembrance was
written before Him for those who [1]fear the LORD and who esteem
His name.
17 "And they will be [a]Mine," says the LORD of hosts, "on the [b]day
that I [1]prepare *My* [2c]own possession, and I will [3]spare them as a man
[3d]spares his own son who serves him."
18 So you will again [a]distinguish between the righteous and the
wicked, between one who serves God and one who does not serve
Him.

Chapter 4

4 "[1]For behold, the day is coming, [a]burning like a furnace; and all
the arrogant and every evildoer will be [b]chaff; and the day that is
coming will [c]set them ablaze," says the LORD of hosts, "so that it will
leave them neither root nor branch."
2 "But for you who [1]fear My name the [a]sun of righteousness will
rise with [b]healing in its wings; and you will go forth and [c]skip about
like calves from the stall.
3 "And you will [a]tread down the wicked, for they shall be [b]ashes
under the soles of your feet [c]on the day [1]which I am preparing," says
the LORD of hosts.
4 "[1a]Remember the law of Moses My servant, *even the* statutes and
ordinances which I commanded him in Horeb for all Israel.
5 "Behold, I am going to send you [a]Elijah the prophet before the
coming of the great and terrible day of the LORD.
6 "And he will [1a]restore the hearts of the fathers to *their* children,
and the hearts of the children to their fathers, lest I come and [b]smite
the land with a [2]curse."

7 [a]Jer. 7:25, 2
12 [b]Zech. 1:3

8 [1]Or, *defraud*
heave offerings
13:11, 12

9 [1]Or, *defraud*
2:2

10 [1]Lit., *prey*
is not room *en*
[a]Lev. 27:30; Nu
18:21-24; Deu
14:22-29; Neh.
[b]Ps. 78:23-29
34:26 [c]Lev. 26

11 [1]Lit., *ruin* [a]
2:25

12 [a]Is. 61:9 [b]

13 [1]Lit., *strong*

14 [a]Jer. 2:25;
[b]Is. 58:3

15 [a]Is. 2:22; M
[b]Jer. 7:10

16 [1]Or, *revere*
34:15; Jer. 31:
4:3; Dan. 12:1

17 [1]Lit., *make*
special treasur
have (has) cor
on [a]Is. 43:1 [b]
[c]Ex. 19:5; Deu
43:21; 1 Pet. 2
103:13

18 [a]Gen. 18:2
5:15

4:1 [1]Ch. 3:19
[a]Ps. 21:9; Nah
Mal. 3:2, 3; 2 P
[b]Is. 5:24; Obad
9:18, 19

2 [1]Or, *revere*
23:4; Is. 30:26
[b]Jer. 30:17; 33
35:6

3 [1]Or, *when I*
40:12; Is. 26:6
[b]Ezek. 28:18 [c]

4 [1]Ch. 3:22 in
[a]Deut. 4:23; 8:

5 [a]Matt. 11:14;
17:10-13; Mark
Luke 1:17; Joh

6 [1]Or, *turn* [2]O
destruction [a]L
[b]Is. 11:4; Rev.

MALACHI AT A GLANCE

ne of Malachi:

NT
ONS

CHAPTER THEMES
1
2
3
4

Author:

Date:

Purpose:

Key Words:

Lord of hosts

but you say
(yet you say)

in that you say
(you say)

profane
(profaned)

My
(or Thy name)

priest(s)

sacrifice(s)
(offering)

curse

THE NEW TESTAMENT

NEW AMERICAN STANDARD BIBLE

ATTHEW

od promised Abraham that through his seed all the nations of the earth would be blessed (Genesis 15:1-6). Where was this son of Abraham?

od promised Isaiah that a child would be born, a son would be given, and the government would on His shoulders. His name would be Wonderful Counselor, Mighty God, Eternal Father, Prince of e. There would be no end to the increase of His government or of peace. He would occupy the ne of David (Isaiah 9:6-7). Where was this son of David?

o one knew until a baby's cry went up from Bethlehem Ephrathah. The Magi from the East arrived rusalem saying, "Where is He who has been born King of the Jews?" The One who was to be ruler rael (Micah 5:2), the son of David, the son of Abraham, had been born. Matthew tells us about Him, King of the Jews.

NGS TO DO

From the first verse Matthew's purpose is clear: to show that Jesus was the long-awaited king, the son of David, the Messiah whose coming was prophesied throughout the Old Testament.

Matthew presents certain facts concerning the person and work of Jesus, then Matthew follows with an account of Jesus' teaching, which he brings to an end with the phrase, "And when Jesus had finished these words" (or "giving instructions" or "parables"). This pattern then repeats itself and divides the Gospel into six segments, each (except the last) ending with this phrase.

Therefore before you read through Matthew chapter by chapter, mark in a distinctive way each occurrence of this dividing phrase in 7:28; 11:1; 13:53; 19:1; and 26:1. Remember this phrase concludes that particular teaching. Then the cycle begins again.

Now read Matthew chapter by chapter, keeping in mind these six segments. As you read:

a. In a distinctive way mark the key words listed on the MATTHEW AT A GLANCE chart on page 1466.

   1) List in the margin what you learn about the kingdom in the references you marked *king* and *the kingdom of heaven/God*.

   2) In addition to these key words, watch for other key words or phrases. If you haven't read the instructions "How to Observe the Bible Chapter by Chapter" you need to do so. They begin on page I-13.

b. Using the same color pen each time, underline when the author either refers to or quotes from an Old Testament prophecy which shows Jesus as the promised King. Then, note in the margin how Jesus fulfills that prophecy. (You can spot the Old Testament quotes because the NASB prints them in small capital letters.)

c. Watch for the events, works, or facts which demonstrate who Jesus Christ is. You may want to note these in the margin.

d. When you read Jesus' teaching on a particular subject, in the margin make a list of the main points covered in His teaching. If it is a prophetic teaching, pay attention to time phrases or indicators including *then* and *when*. Watch for the progression of events.

e. Record the main theme or event of each chapter on MATTHEW AT A GLANCE.

Chapters 26 through 28 give an account of the final events in the life of Jesus. Record the progression of events on the appropriate charts in the appendix of this Bible: THE ARREST, TRIAL, AND CRUCIFIXION OF JESUS CHRIST (page 1882) and/or THE ACCOUNT OF JESUS' RESURRECTION (page 1883). It would be wise to first record these insights on notebook paper and then transfer them to the charts.

a. When you record the circumstances surrounding the resurrection of Jesus Christ, also no post-resurrection appearances which are recorded in Matthew. After you do this for al Gospels you will have comprehensive notes on all that took place.

b. As you do this, remember, Luke gives the chronological order of events; therefore, it bec the chronological plumbline for the other Gospel records.

4. A chart titled WHAT THE GOSPELS TEACH ABOUT THE KINGDOM OF GOD, KINGDOM OF HEAVEN is on pages 1880 and 1881. List and consolidate everything you from Matthew about the kingdom on a piece of notebook paper. Then transfer this to the cha

5. Complete MATTHEW AT A GLANCE. Under "Segment Divisions," record the theme of segment of Matthew. There's also a blank line for any other segment divisions you might see

THINGS TO THINK ABOUT

1. Have you bowed your knee to Jesus as King in your life? Read Matthew 7:21-27 and think the difference between merely hearing something and hearing and living accordingly. Which describes you?

2. Can you explain from Scripture to another person why Jesus is the King of the promised dom?

3. Do you realize that Jesus' final words to His disciples in Matthew 28:19-20 are your responsi also? What are you doing in order to fulfill His Great Commission? As you go, are you ma disciples? Are you teaching them to observe all that He has commanded?

Chapter 1 ______________________

See **The Genealogy of Jesus Christ** on page 1874.

1 The book of the genealogy of Jesus Christ, [a]the son of David, [b]the
son of Abraham.
2 To Abraham was born Isaac; and to Isaac, Jacob; and to Jacob,
[1]Judah and his brothers;
3 and to Judah were born Perez and Zerah by Tamar; and to [a]Perez
was born Hezron; and to Hezron, [1]Ram;
4 and to Ram was born Amminadab; and to Amminadab, Nah-
shon; and to Nahshon, Salmon;
5 and to Salmon was born Boaz by Rahab; and to Boaz was born
Obed by Ruth; and to Obed, Jesse;
6 and to Jesse was born David the king.
And to David [a]was born Solomon by her *who had been the wife* of
Uriah;
7 and to Solomon [a]was born Rehoboam; and to Rehoboam, Abijah;
and to Abijah, [1]Asa;
8 and to Asa was born Jehoshaphat; and to Jehoshaphat, [1]Joram;
and to Joram, Uzziah;
9 and to Uzziah was born [1]Jotham; and to Jotham, Ahaz; and to
Ahaz, Hezekiah;
10 and to Hezekiah was born Manasseh; and to Manasseh, [1]Amon;
and to Amon, Josiah;
11 and to Josiah were born [1]Jeconiah and his brothers, at the time of
the [a]deportation to Babylon.
12 And after the [a]deportation to Babylon, to Jeconiah was born
[1]Shealtiel; and to Shealtiel, Zerubbabel;
13 and to Zerubbabel was born [1]Abihud; and to Abihud, Eliakim;
and to Eliakim, Azor;
14 and to Azor was born Zadok; and to Zadok, Achim; and to
Achim, Eliud;

1:1 [a]2 Sam. 7:
Ps. 89:3f.; 132:
9:6f.; 11:1; Matt
Luke 1:32, 69;
7:42; Acts 13:2
1:3; Rev. 22:16
1:1-6: *Luke 3:3*
Gen. 22:18; Gal

2 [1]Gr., *Judas.*
of Old Testamen
characters will b
in their Old Test
form.

3 [1]Gr., *Aram* [a]
4:18-22; 1 Chr.
Matt. 1:3-6

6 [a]2 Sam. 11:27

7 [1]Gr., *Asaph* [a]
3:10ff.

8 [1]Gr., *Jehoram*

9 [1]Gr., *Joatham*

10 [1]Gr., *Amos*

11 [1]Or, *Jehoiach*
[a]2 Kin. 24:14f.; J
27:20; Matt. 1:17

12 [1]Gr., *Salathie*
[a]2 Kin. 24:14f.; J
27:20; Matt. 1:17

13 [1]Gr., *Abiud*

15 and to Eliud was born Eleazar; and to Eleazar, Matthan; and to
Matthan, Jacob;
16 and to Jacob was born Joseph the husband of Mary, by whom
was born Jesus, [a]who is called [1]Christ.
17 Therefore all the generations from Abraham to David are four-
teen generations; and from David to the [a]deportation to Babylon
fourteen generations; and from the [a]deportation to Babylon to *the
time of* [1]Christ fourteen generations.
18 Now the birth of Jesus Christ was as follows. When His [a]mother
Mary had been betrothed to Joseph, before they came together she
was [b]found to be with child by the Holy Spirit.
19 And Joseph her husband, being a righteous man, and not want-
ing to disgrace her, desired [1a]to put her away secretly.
20 But when he had considered this, behold, an angel of the Lord
appeared to him in a dream, saying, "[a]Joseph, son of David, do not
be afraid to take Mary as your wife; for that which has been [1]con-
ceived in her is of the Holy Spirit.
21 "And she will bear a Son; and [a]you shall call His name Jesus, for it
is He who [b]will save His people from their sins."
22 Now all this [1]took place that what was [a]spoken by the Lord
through the prophet might be fulfilled, saying,
23 "[a]BEHOLD, THE VIRGIN SHALL BE WITH [b]CHILD, AND SHALL BEAR A SON,
AND THEY SHALL CALL HIS NAME [1]IMMANUEL," which translated means,
"[c]GOD WITH US."
24 And Joseph arose from his sleep, and did as the angel of the
Lord commanded him, and took *her* as his wife,
25 and [1]kept her a virgin until she [a]gave birth to a Son; and [b]he
called His name Jesus.

Chapter 2

2 Now after Jesus was [a]born in Bethlehem of Judea in the days of
[b]Herod the king, behold, [1]magi from the east arrived in Jerusa-
lem, saying,
2 "Where is He who has been born [a]King of the Jews? For we saw
[b]His star in the east, and have come to worship Him."
3 And when Herod the king heard it, he was troubled, and all
Jerusalem with him.
4 And gathering together all the chief priests and scribes of the
people, he *began* to inquire of them where [1]the Christ was to be born.
5 And they said to him, "[a]In Bethlehem of Judea, for so it has been
written [1]by the prophet,
6 '[a]AND YOU, BETHLEHEM, LAND OF JUDAH,
ARE BY NO MEANS LEAST AMONG THE LEADERS OF JUDAH;
FOR OUT OF YOU SHALL COME FORTH A RULER,
WHO WILL [b]SHEPHERD MY PEOPLE ISRAEL.'"
7 Then Herod secretly called the magi, and ascertained from them
[1]the time [a]the star appeared.
8 And he sent them to Bethlehem, and said, "Go and make careful
search for the Child; and when you have found *Him*, report to me,
that I too may come and worship Him."
9 And having heard the king, they went their way; and lo, the star,
which they had seen in the east, went on before them, until it came
and stood over where the Child was.

[1]I.e., the Messiah . 27:17, 22; Luke 2:11; John 4:25

[1]I.e., the Messiah Kin. 24:14f.; Jer. 20; Matt. 1:11, 12

Matt. 12:46; Luke 1:27 [b]Luke 1:35

Or, *to divorce her* 22:20-24; 24:1-4; John 8:4, 5

20 [1]Lit., *begotten* [a]Luke 2:4

[a]Luke 1:31; 2:21 e 2:11; John 1:29; 4:12; 5:31; 13:23, , 39; Col. 1:20-23

22 [1]Or, *has taken* *lace* [a]Luke 24:44; Rom. 1:2-4

Or, *Emmanuel* [a]Is. Is. 9:6, 7 [c]Is. 8:10

25 [1]Lit., *was not* *ing her* [a]Luke 2:7 tt. 1:21; Luke 2:21

2:1 [1]Pronounced -ji, a caste of wise en specializing in ogy, medicine and ural science [a]Mic. Luke 2:4-7 [b]Luke 1:5

23:5; 30:9; Zech. Matt. 27:11; Luke 23:38; John 1:49 [b]Num. 24:17

[1]I.e., the Messiah

t., *through* [a]John 7:42

ic. 5:2; John 7:42 [b]John 21:16

t., *the time of the aring star* [a]Num. 24:17

10 And when they saw the star, they rejoiced exceedingly with
great joy.
11 And they came into the house and saw the Child with [a]Mary His
mother; and they fell down and [b]worshiped Him; and opening their
treasures they presented to Him gifts of gold and frankincense and
myrrh.
12 And having been [a]warned *by God* [b]in a dream not to return to
Herod, they departed for their own country by another way.
13 Now when they had departed, behold, an [a]angel of the Lord
*[b]appeared to Joseph in a dream, saying, "Arise and take the Child
and His mother, and flee to Egypt, and remain there until I tell you;
for Herod is going to search for the Child to destroy Him."
14 And he arose and took the Child and His mother by night, and
departed for Egypt;
15 and was there until the death of Herod, that what was spoken by
the Lord through the prophet might be fulfilled, saying, "[a]OUT OF
EGYPT DID I CALL [b]MY SON."
16 Then when Herod saw that he had been tricked by [a]the magi, he
became very enraged, and sent and [b]slew all the male children who
were in Bethlehem and in all its environs, from two years old and
under, according to the time which he had ascertained from the
magi.
17 Then that which was spoken through Jeremiah the prophet was
fulfilled, saying,
18 "[a]A VOICE WAS HEARD IN RAMAH,
WEEPING AND GREAT MOURNING,
RACHEL WEEPING FOR HER CHILDREN;
AND SHE REFUSED TO BE COMFORTED,
BECAUSE THEY WERE NO MORE."
19 But when Herod was dead, behold, an angel of the Lord *[a]ap-
peared in a dream to Joseph in Egypt, saying,
20 "Arise and take the Child and His mother, and go into the land of
Israel; for those who sought the Child's life are dead."
21 And he arose and took the Child and His mother, and came into
the land of Israel.
22 But when he heard that Archelaus was reigning over Judea in
place of his father Herod, he was afraid to go there. And being
[a]warned *by God* in a dream, he departed for the regions of Galilee,
23 and came and resided in a city called [a]Nazareth, that what was
spoken through the prophets might be fulfilled, "He shall be called a
[b]Nazarene."

Chapter 3

3 Now [a]in those days [b]John the Baptist *[1]came, [2]preaching in the
[c]wilderness of Judea, saying,
2 "[a]Repent, for [b]the kingdom of [1]heaven [2]is at hand."
3 For this is the [a]one referred to [1]by Isaiah the prophet, saying,
"[b]THE VOICE OF ONE CRYING IN THE WILDERNESS,
'[c]MAKE READY THE WAY OF THE LORD,
MAKE HIS PATHS STRAIGHT!' "
4 Now John himself had [1a]a garment of camel's hair, and a leather
belt about his waist; and his food was [b]locusts and wild honey.
5 Then Jerusalem [a]was going out to him, and all Judea, and all [b]the
district around the Jordan;

11 [a]Matt. 1:1 [b]Matt. 14:33
12 [a]Matt. 2:1 Luke 2:26; Ac Heb. 8:5; 11:7 33:15, 16; Ma
13 [a]Acts 5:19 12:7-11 [b]Matt
15 [a]Hos. 11:1 24:8 [b]Ex. 4:2
16 [a]Matt. 2:1
18 [a]Jer. 31:15
19 [a]Matt. 1:20 13, 22
22 [a]Matt. 2:12
23 [a]Luke 1:26 John 1:45, 46 1:24; John 18:
3:1 [1]Or, *arrive* *proclaiming as* [a]Matt. 3:1-12; *1:3-8; Luke 3:2* 1:6-8, 19-28 [b] 11:11-14; 16:14 15:61; Judg. 1:
2 [1]Lit., *the hea* [2]Lit., *has come* [a]Matt. 4:17 [b]Da Matt. 4:17, 23; 10:7; Mark 1:15 10:9f.; 11:20; 2
3 [1]Lit., *through* 1:17, 76 [b]Is. 40 1:23
4 [1]Lit., *his garm* [a]2 Kin. 1:8; Zech Matt. 11:8; Mark [b]Lev. 11:22
5 [a]Mark 1:5 [b]L

6 and they were being [a]baptized by him in the Jordan River, as
they confessed their sins.
7 But when he saw many of the [a]Pharisees and [b]Sadducees coming
for baptism, he said to them, "You [c]brood of vipers, who warned you
to flee from [d]the wrath to come?
8 "[a]Therefore bring forth fruit [b]in keeping with repentance;
9 and do not suppose that you can say to yourselves, '[a]We have
Abraham for our father'; for I say to you, that God is able from these
stones to raise up children to Abraham.
10 "And [a]the axe is already laid at the root of the trees; [b]every tree
therefore that does not bear good fruit is cut down and thrown into
the fire.
11 "As for me, [a]I baptize you [1]with water for repentance, but He who
is coming after me is mightier than I, and I am not fit to remove His
sandals; [b]He will baptize you [1]with the Holy Spirit and fire.
12 "And His [a]winnowing fork is in His hand, and He will thorough-
ly clear His threshing floor; and He will [b]gather His wheat into the
barn, but He will burn up the [c]chaff with [d]unquenchable fire."
13 [a]Then Jesus *arrived [b]from Galilee at the Jordan *coming* to John,
to be baptized by him.
14 But John tried to prevent Him, saying, "I have need to be bap-
tized by You, and do You come to me?"
15 But Jesus answering said to him, "Permit *it* at this time; for in
this way it is fitting for us [a]to fulfill all righteousness." Then he
*permitted Him.
16 And after being baptized, Jesus went up immediately from the
water; and behold, the heavens were opened, and [1a]he saw the Spirit
of God descending as a dove, *and* coming upon Him,
17 and behold, a voice out of the heavens, saying, "[a]This is [1]My
beloved Son, in whom I am well-pleased."

Chapter 4

4 [a]Then Jesus was led up by the Spirit into the wilderness [b]to be
tempted by the devil.
2 And after He had [a]fasted forty days and forty nights, He [1]then
became hungry.
3 And [a]the tempter came and said to Him, "If You are the [b]Son of
God, command that these stones become [1]bread."
4 But He answered and said, "It is written, '[a]MAN SHALL NOT LIVE
ON BREAD ALONE, BUT ON EVERY WORD THAT PROCEEDS OUT OF THE MOUTH
OF GOD.'"
5 Then the devil *took Him into [a]the holy city; and he had Him
stand on the pinnacle of the temple,
6 and *said to Him, "If You are the Son of God throw Yourself
down; for it is written,

'[a]HE WILL GIVE HIS ANGELS CHARGE CONCERNING YOU';
and
'ON *their* HANDS THEY WILL BEAR YOU UP,
LEST YOU STRIKE YOUR FOOT AGAINST A STONE.'"

7 Jesus said to him, "[1]On the other hand, it is written, '[a]YOU SHALL
NOT [2]PUT THE LORD YOUR GOD TO THE TEST.'"
8 [a]Again, the devil *took Him to a very high mountain, and
*showed Him all the kingdoms of the world, and their glory;

att. 3:11, 13-16; John 1:25, 26; s 1:5; 2:38-41; 10:37
16:1ff.; 23:13, att. 22:23; Acts ; 23:6ff. [c]Matt. 3:33 [d]1 Thess. 1:10
3:8; Eph. 5:8, 9 [b]Acts 26:20
uke 3:8; 16:24; 3, 39, 53; Acts om. 4:1; 9:7, 8; Gal. 3:29
[a]Luke 3:9 [b]Ps. 14; Matt. 7:19; John 15:2
he Gr. here can ated *in, with* or rk 1:4, 8; Luke ohn 1:26f.; Acts 8:36, 38; 11:16 33; Acts 2:3, 4; Titus 3:5
s. 30:24; 41:16; 5:7; 51:2; Luke att. 13:30 [c]Ps. 6:24; Jer. 7:20; 3:41, 42; Mark 9:43, 48
3:13-17: *Mark Luke 3:21, 22;* 1:31-34 [b]Matt. 2:22
s. 40:7, 8; John 4:34; 8:29
He [a]Mark 1:10; 3:22; John 1:32; Acts 7:56
Lit., *My Son, the* ved [a]Ps. 2:7; Is. att. 12:18; 17:5; 9:7; Luke 9:35; John 12:28
att. 4:1-11: *Mark 13; Luke 4:1-13* 15; James 1:14
, *later, afterward* 4:28; 1 Kin. 19:8
3 [1]Lit., *loaves* hess. 3:5 [b]Matt. 6:63; Mark 3:11; Luke 1:35; 4:41; 34, 49; Acts 9:20
4 [a]Deut. 8:3
h. 11:1, 18; Dan. 9:24; Matt. 27:53
6 [a]Ps. 91:11, 12
[1]Lit., *Again* [2]Or, *t . . . God* [a]Deut. 6:16
att. 16:26; 1 John 2:15-17

9 and he said to Him, "[a]All these things will I give You, if You fall
down and worship me."
10 Then Jesus *said to him, "Begone, Satan! For it is written, '[a]YOU
SHALL WORSHIP THE LORD YOUR GOD, AND [1]SERVE HIM ONLY.' "
11 Then the devil *left Him; and behold, [a]angels came and *began* to
minister to Him.
12 Now when He heard that [a]John had [1]been taken into custody,
[b]He withdrew into Galilee;
13 and leaving Nazareth, He came and [a]settled in Capernaum,
which is by the sea, in the region of Zebulun and Naphtali.
14 *This was* to fulfill what was spoken through Isaiah the prophet,
saying,
15 "[a]THE LAND OF ZEBULUN AND THE LAND OF NAPHTALI,
[1]BY THE WAY OF THE SEA, BEYOND THE JORDAN, GALILEE OF THE
[2]GENTILES—
16 "[a]THE PEOPLE WHO WERE SITTING IN DARKNESS SAW A GREAT LIGHT,
AND TO THOSE WHO WERE SITTING IN THE LAND AND SHADOW OF
DEATH,
UPON THEM A LIGHT DAWNED."

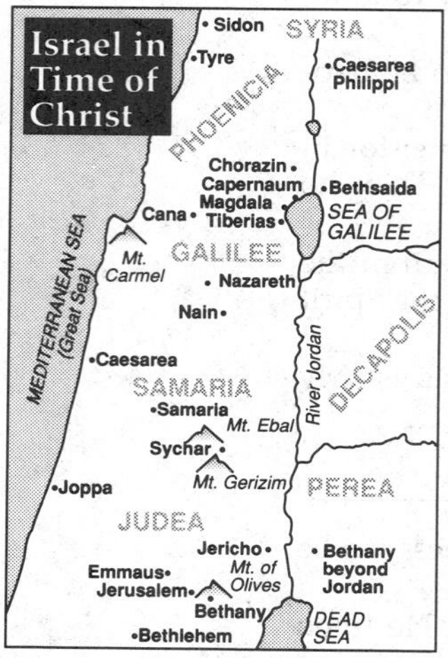

17 [a]From that time Jesus began to [1]preach and say, "[b]Re-
pent, for the kingdom of heaven is at hand."
18 [a]And walking by [b]the Sea of Galilee, He saw two
brothers, [c]Simon who was called Peter, and Andrew his
brother, casting a net into the sea; for they were fishermen.
19 And He *said to them, "[1]Follow Me, and I will make
you fishers of men."
20 And they immediately left the nets, and followed Him.
21 And going on from there He saw two other brothers,
[1a]James the *son* of Zebedee, and [2]John his brother, in the
boat with Zebedee their father, mending their nets; and He
called them.
22 And they immediately left the boat and their father,
and followed Him.
23 And *Jesus* was going about [a]in all Galilee, [b]teaching in
their synagogues, and [c]proclaiming the [1]gospel of the
kingdom, and [d]healing every kind of disease and every
kind of sickness among the people.
24 And the news about Him went out [a]into all Syria; and they
brought to Him all who were ill, taken with various diseases and
pains, [b]demoniacs, [1c]epileptics, [d]paralytics; and He healed them.
25 And great multitudes [a]followed Him from Galilee and [b]Decapo-
lis and Jerusalem and Judea and *from* [c]beyond the Jordan.

Chapter 5

5 [a]And when He saw the multitudes, He went up on [b]the [1]moun-
tain; and after He sat down, His disciples came to Him.
2 And [a]opening His mouth He *began* to teach them, saying,
3 "[a]Blessed are the poor in spirit, for [b]theirs is the kingdom of
heaven.
4 "Blessed are [a]those who mourn, for they shall be comforted.
5 "Blessed are [a]the [1]gentle, for they shall inherit the earth.
6 "Blessed are [a]those who hunger and thirst for righteousness, for
they shall be satisfied.
7 "Blessed are [a]the merciful, for they shall receive mercy.

9 [a]1 Cor. 10:
10 [1]Or, *fulfill duty to Him* [a] 10:20
11 [a]Matt. 26: 22:43; Heb. 1
12 [1]Lit., *been up* [a]Matt. 14: 1:14; Luke 3: 3:24 [b]Mark 1: 4:14; John 1:
13 [a]Matt. 11: 1:21; 2:1; Luk John 2:12; 4:
15 [1]Or, *Towa* [2]Or, *nations* [a]
16 [a]Is. 9:2; 60 2:32
17 [1]Or, *procla* 1:14, 15 [b]Mat
18 [a]Matt. 4:18 *1:16-20;* Luke John 1:40-42 15:29; Mark 7: 5:1; John 6:1 10:2; 16:18; Jo 1:40-42
19 [1]Lit., *Come after Me*
21 [1]Or, *Jacob Joannes,* Heb. *Johanan* [a]Matt 20:20
23 [1]Or, *good n* [a]Mark 1:39; Lu 44 [b]Matt. 9:35 Mark 1:21; 6:2; Luke 4:15; 6:6; John 6:59; 18: 3:2; 9:35; 24:14 1:14; Luke 4:43 16:16; Acts 20: 28:31 [d]Matt. 8 14:14; 15:30; 1 21:14; Mark 1:3 Luke 4:40; 7:21 10:38
24 [1]Lit., *moon-* [a]Mark 7:26; Luk Acts 15:23; 18: 21:3; Gal. 1:21 8:16, 28, 33; 9: 12:22; 15:22; M 5:15, 16, 18; Lu John 10:21 [c]Ma 17:15 [d]Matt. 8: Mark 2:3-5, 9; L
25 [a]Mark 3:7, 8 6:17 [b]Mark 5:2 [c]Matt. 4:15
5:1 [1]Or, *hill* [a]M 5-7; Luke 6:20-4 [b]Mark 3:13; Luk 9:28; John 6:3,
2 [a]Matt. 13:35; 8:35; 10:34; 18:
3 [a]Matt. 5:3-12; 6:20-23 [b]Matt. 5 19:14; 25:34; Ma 10:14; Luke 6:20
4 [a]Is. 61:2; John Rev. 7:17
5 [1]Or, *humble, r* [a]Ps. 37:11
6 [a]Is. 55:1, 2; Jo 4:14; 6:48ff.; 7:3
7 [a]Prov. 11:17; M 6:14, 15; 18:33-3

8 "Blessed are [a]the pure in heart, for [b]they shall see God.
9 "Blessed are the peacemakers, for [a]they shall be called sons of God.
10 "Blessed are those who have been [a]persecuted for the sake of righteousness, for [b]theirs is the kingdom of heaven.
11 "Blessed are you when *men* [a]cast insults at you, and persecute you, and say all kinds of evil against you falsely, on account of Me.
12 "Rejoice, and be glad, for your reward in heaven is great, for [a]so they persecuted the prophets who were before you.
13 "You are the salt of the earth; but [a]if the salt has become tasteless, how will it be made salty *again*? It is good for nothing anymore, except to be thrown out and trampled under foot by men.
14 "You are [a]the light of the world. A city set on a [1]hill cannot be hidden.
15 "[a]Nor do *men* light a lamp, and put it under the peck-measure, but on the lampstand; and it gives light to all who are in the house.
16 "Let your light shine before men in such a way that they may [a]see your good works, and [b]glorify your Father who is in heaven.
17 "Do not think that I came to abolish the [a]Law or the Prophets; I did not come to abolish, but to fulfill.
18 "For truly I say to you, [a]until heaven and earth pass away, not [1]the smallest letter or stroke shall pass away from the Law, until all is accomplished.
19 "Whoever then annuls one of the least of these commandments, and so teaches [1]others, shall be called least [a]in the kingdom of heaven; but whoever [2]keeps and teaches *them*, he shall be called great in the kingdom of heaven.
20 "For I say to you, that unless your [a]righteousness surpasses *that* of the scribes and Pharisees, you shall not enter the kingdom of heaven.
21 "[a]You have heard that [1]the ancients were told, '[b]YOU SHALL NOT COMMIT MURDER' and 'Whoever commits murder shall be [2]liable to [c]the court.'
22 "But I say to you that everyone who is angry with his brother[1] shall be [2]guilty before [a]the court; and whoever shall say to his brother, '[3]Raca,' shall be [2]guilty before [4b]the supreme court; and whoever shall say, 'You fool,' shall be [2]guilty *enough to go* into the [5c]fiery hell.
23 "If therefore you are [a]presenting your [1]offering at the altar, and there remember that your brother has something against you,
24 leave your [1]offering there before the altar, and go your way; first be [a]reconciled to your brother, and then come and present your [1]offering.
25 "[a]Make friends quickly with your opponent at law while you are with him on the way, in order that your opponent may not deliver you to the judge, and the judge to the officer, and you be thrown into prison.
26 "Truly I say to you, [a]you shall not come out of there, until you have paid up the last [1]cent.
27 "[a]You have heard that it was said, '[b]YOU SHALL NOT COMMIT ADULTERY';
28 but I say to you, that everyone who looks on a woman [a]to lust for her has committed adultery with her already in his heart.
29 "And [a]if your right eye makes you [1]stumble, tear it out, and throw

Ps. 24:4 [b]Heb. John 3:2; Rev. 22:4
Matt. 5:45; Luke :35; Rom. 8:14
et. 3:14 [b]Matt. 4; 25:34; Mark e 6:20; 22:29f.
11 [a]1 Pet. 4:14
hr. 36:16; Matt. 3:37; Acts 7:52; ess. 2:15; Heb. ff.; James 5:10
Mark 9:50; Luke 14:34f.
[1]Or, *mountain* :18; John 8:12; 9:5; 12:36
Mark 4:21; Luke 1:33; Phil. 2:15
Pet. 2:12 [b]Matt. 9:8
17 [a]Matt. 7:12
one iota (yodh) *e projection of a er* (serif) [a]Matt. :35; Luke 16:17
, *the men* [2]Lit., *es* [a]Matt. 11:11
[a]Luke 18:11, 12
t., *it was said to ients* [2]Or, *guilty* [a]Matt. 5:27, 33, Ex. 20:13; Deut. 7 [c]Deut. 16:18; 2 Chr. 19:5f.
ome mss. insert *hout cause* [2]Or, *le to* [3]Aram. for *head or good for nothing* [4]Lit., *the Sanhedrin* [5]Lit., *na of fire* [a]Deut. 18; 2 Chr. 19:5f. att. 10:17; 26:59; 3:9; 14:55; 15:1; :66; John 11:47; 4:15; 5:21; 6:12; 2:30; 23:1; 24:20 att. 5:29f.; 10:28; 23:15, 33; Mark 43ff.; Luke 12:5; James 3:6
, *gift* [a]Matt. 5:24
[1]Or, *gift* [a]Rom. 12:17, 18
Prov. 25:8f.; Luke 12:58
6 [1]Lit., *quadrans* aling two lepta or es); i.e., 1/64 of a rius [a]Luke 12:59
Matt. 5:21, 33, 38, [b]Ex. 20:14; Deut. 5:18
Sam. 11:2-5; Job 31:1; Matt. 15:19; James 1:14, 15
[1]I.e., cause to sin . 18:9; Mark 9:47

it from you; for it is better for you that one of the parts of your body
perish, [2]than for your whole body to be thrown into [3b]hell.
30 "And [a]if your right hand makes you [1]stumble, cut it off, and
throw it from you; for it is better for you that one of the parts of your
body perish, [2]than for your whole body to go into [3b]hell.
31 "And it was said, '[a]WHOEVER SENDS HIS WIFE AWAY, LET HIM GIVE HER
A CERTIFICATE OF DIVORCE';
32 [a]but I say to you that everyone who [1]divorces his wife, except for
the cause of unchastity, makes her commit adultery; and whoever
marries a [2]divorced woman commits adultery.
33 "Again, [a]you have heard that [1]the ancients were told, '[2b]YOU SHALL
NOT [3]MAKE FALSE VOWS, BUT SHALL FULFILL YOUR [4]VOWS TO THE LORD.'
34 "But I say to you, [a]make no oath at all, either by heaven, for it is
[b]the throne of God,
35 or by the earth, for it is the [a]footstool of His feet, or [1]by Jerusa-
lem, for it is [b]THE CITY OF THE GREAT KING.
36 "Nor shall you make an oath by your head, for you cannot make
one hair white or black.
37 "But let your statement be, 'Yes, yes' *or* 'No, no'; and anything
beyond these is [1]of [a]evil.
38 "[a]You have heard that it was said, '[b]AN EYE FOR AN EYE, AND A
TOOTH FOR A TOOTH.'
39 "But I say to you, do not resist him who is evil; but [a]whoever
slaps you on your right cheek, turn to him the other also.
40 "And if anyone wants to sue you, and take your [1]shirt, let him
have your [2]coat also.
41 "And whoever shall force you to go one mile, go with him two.
42 "[a]Give to him who asks of you, and do not turn away from him
who wants to borrow from you.
43 "[a]You have heard that it was said, '[b]YOU SHALL LOVE YOUR NEIGH-
BOR, [c]and hate your enemy.'
44 "But I say to you, [a]love your enemies, and pray for those who
persecute you
45 in order that you may [1]be [a]sons of your Father who is in heaven;
for He causes His sun to rise on *the* evil and *the* good, and sends rain
on *the* righteous and *the* unrighteous.
46 "For [a]if you love those who love you, what reward have you? Do
not even the [1]tax-gatherers do the same?
47 "And if you greet your brothers only, what do you do more *than
others*? Do not even the Gentiles do the same?
48 "Therefore [a]you are to be perfect, as your heavenly Father is
perfect.

Chapter 6

6 "Beware of practicing your righteousness before men [a]to be
noticed by them; otherwise you have no reward with your
Father who is in heaven.
2 "When therefore you [1]give alms, do not sound a trumpet before
you, as the hypocrites do in the synagogues and in the streets, that
they [a]may be honored by men. [b]Truly I say to you, they have their
reward in full.
3 "But when you give alms, do not let your left hand know what
your right hand is doing

29 [2]Lit., *not yo*
body [3]Gr., *Ge*
[b]Matt. 5:22

30 [1]I.e., cause
[2]Lit., *not your v*
body [3]Gr., *Ge*
[a]Matt. 18:8; Ma
[b]Matt. 5:22

31 [a]Deut. 24:1
3:1; Matt. 19:7;
10:4

32 [1]Or, *sends*
[2]Or, *sent away*
19:9; Mark 10:1
16:18; 1 Cor. 7:

33 [1]Lit., *it was*
the ancients [2]*y*
your are singula
[3]Or, *break your*
[4]Lit., *oaths* [a]Ma
27, 38, 43; 23:1
[b]Lev. 19:12; Nu
Deut. 23:21, 23

34 [a]James 5:1
66:1; Matt. 23:2

35 [1]Or, *toward*
66:1; Acts 7:49
48:2

37 [1]Or, *from th*
one [a]Matt. 6:13
38; John 17:15;
2 Thess. 3:3; 1
2:13f.; 3:12; 5:1

38 [a]Matt. 5:21,
43 [b]Ex. 21:24;
24:20; Deut. 19:

39 [a]Matt. 5:39-4
6:29, 30; 1 Cor.

40 [1]Or, *tunic*; i.e
garment worn ne
the body [2]Or, *cl*
outer garment

42 [a]Deut. 15:7-1
6:34f.; 1 Tim. 6:

43 [a]Matt. 5:21, 2
38 [b]Lev. 19:18
23:3-6

44 [a]Luke 6:27f.;
Acts 7:60; Rom.

45 [1]Or, *show
yourselves to be*
5:9; Luke 6:35; A
14:17

46 [1]I.e., Collecto
Roman taxes for
[a]Luke 6:32

48 [a]Lev. 19:2; D
18:13; 2 Cor. 7:1;
3:12-15

6:1 [a]Matt. 6:5, 1

2 [1]Or, *do an act*
charity [a]Matt. 6:5
23:5 [b]Matt. 6:5, 1
Luke 6:24

4 that your [1]alms may be in secret; and [a]your Father who sees in
secret will repay you.
5 "And when you pray, you are not to be as the hypocrites; for they
love to [a]stand and pray in the synagogues and on the street corners,
[1b]in order to be seen by men. [c]Truly I say to you, they have their
reward in full.
6 "But you, when you pray, [a]go into your inner room, and when
you have shut your door, pray to your Father who is in secret, and
[b]your Father who sees in secret will repay you.
7 "And when you are praying, do not use meaningless repetition,
as the Gentiles do, for they suppose that they will be heard for their
[a]many words.
8 "Therefore do not be like them; for [a]your Father knows what you
need, before you ask Him.
9 "[a]Pray, then, in this way:
'Our Father who art in [1]heaven,
Hallowed be Thy name.
10 '[a]Thy kingdom come.
[b]Thy will be done,
On earth as it is in heaven.
11 '[a]Give us this day [1]our daily bread.
12 'And [a]forgive us our debts, as we also have forgiven our debtors.
13 'And do not lead us into temptation, but [a]deliver us from [1b]evil.
[2][For Thine is the kingdom, and the power, and the glory,
forever. Amen.]'
14 "[a]For if you forgive men for their transgressions, your heavenly
Father will also forgive you.
15 "But [a]if you do not forgive men, then your Father will not forgive
your transgressions.
16 "And [a]whenever you fast, do not put on a gloomy face as the
hypocrites *do,* for they [1]neglect their appearance in order to be seen
fasting by men. [b]Truly I say to you, they have their reward in full.
17 "But you, when you fast, [a]anoint your head, and wash your face
18 so that you may not be seen fasting by men, but by your Father
who is in secret; and your [a]Father who sees in secret will repay you.
19 "[a]Do not lay up for yourselves treasures upon earth, where moth
and rust destroy, and where thieves break in and steal.
20 "But lay up for yourselves [a]treasures in heaven, where neither
moth nor rust destroys, and where thieves do not break in or steal;
21 for [a]where your treasure is, there will your heart be also.
22 "[a]The lamp of the body is the eye; if therefore your eye is [1]clear,
your whole body will be full of light.
23 "But if [a]your eye is bad, your whole body will be full of darkness.
If therefore the light that is in you is darkness, how great is the
darkness!
24 "[a]No one can serve two masters; for either he will hate the one
and love the other, or he will hold to one and despise the other. You
cannot serve God and [1b]mammon.
25 "[a]For this reason I say to you, [1]do not be [b]anxious for your life, *as
to* what you shall eat, or what you shall drink; nor for your body, *as
to* what you shall put on. Is not life more than food, and the body
than clothing?
26 "[a]Look at the birds of the [1]air, that they do not sow, neither do

eds of charity :10; Matt. 6:6, 18; Heb. 4:13

o be apparent [a]Mark 11:25; :11, 13 [b]Matt. [c]Matt. 6:2, 16; Luke 6:24

s. 26:20; Matt. -39; Acts 9:40 [b]Matt. 6:4, 18

[a]1 Kin. 18:26f.

8:9; 69:17-19; 32; Luke 12:30

., *the heavens* t. 6:9-13: *Luke 11:2-4*

Matt. 3:2; 4:17 tt. 26:42; Luke 42; Acts 21:14

r, *our bread for ning day* or *our il bread* [a]Prov. ls. 33:16; Luke 11:3

34:7; Ps. 32:1; latt. 9:2; 26:28; 7; 1 John 1:7-9

Or, *the evil one* ause omitted in est mss. [a]John 5; 1 Cor. 10:13; ess. 3:3; 2 Tim. Pet. 2:9; 1 John :18 [b]Matt. 5:37

Matt. 7:2; Mark Eph. 4:32; Col. 3:13

15 [a]Matt. 18:35

Lit., *render their unrecognizable* 58:5 [b]Matt. 6:2

Ruth 3:3; 2 Sam. 12:20

18 [a]Matt. 6:4, 6

Prov. 23:4; Matt. Luke 12:21, 33; 2; 1 Tim. 6:9, 10; 13:5; James 5:2

Matt. 19:21; Luke 2:33; 1 Tim. 6:19

21 [a]Luke 12:34

r, *healthy* [a]Matt. 3: *Luke 11:34, 35*

Matt. 20:15; Mark 7:22

Or, *riches* [a]1 Kin. Luke 16:13; Gal. James 4:4 [b]Luke 16:9, 11, 13

5 [1]Or, *stop being* s [a]Matt. 6:25-33: *e 12:22-31* [b]Matt. 28, 31, 34; Luke 1; 12:11, 22; Phil. 4:6; 1 Pet. 5:7

Lit., *heaven* [a]Job 35:11; 38:41; Ps. 104:27, 28; Matt. :29ff.; Luke 12:24

they reap, nor gather into barns, and *yet* your heavenly Father feeds
them. Are you not worth much more than they?
27 "And which of you by being [a]anxious can [b]add a *single* [1]cubit to
his [2]life's span?
28 "And why are you [a]anxious about clothing? Observe how the
lilies of the field grow; they do not toil nor do they spin,
29 yet I say to you that even [a]Solomon in all his glory did not clothe
himself like one of these.
30 "But if God so arrays the [a]grass of the field, which is *alive* today
and tomorrow is thrown into the furnace, *will He* not much more *do
so for* you, [b]O men of little faith?
31 "Do not be [a]anxious then, saying, 'What shall we eat?' or 'What
shall we drink?' or 'With what shall we clothe ourselves?'
32 "For all these things the Gentiles eagerly seek; for [a]your heavenly
Father knows that you need all these things.
33 "But [1]seek first [2]His kingdom and His righteousness; and [a]all
these things shall be [3]added to you.
34 "Therefore do not be [a]anxious for tomorrow; for tomorrow will
[1]care for itself. *Each* day has enough trouble of its own.

Chapter 7

7 "[a]Do not judge lest you be judged.
2 "For in the way you judge, you will be judged; and [1a]by your
standard of measure, it will be measured to you.
3 "And why do you [a]look at the speck that is in your brother's eye,
but do not notice the log that is in your own eye?
4 "[a]Or how [1]can you say to your brother, 'Let me take the speck out
of your eye,' and behold, the log is in your own eye?
5 "You hypocrite, first take the log out of your own eye, and then
you will see clearly to take the speck out of your brother's eye.
6 "[a]Do not give what is holy to dogs, and do not throw your pearls
before swine, lest they trample them under their feet, and turn and
tear you to pieces.
7 "[1a]Ask, and [b]it shall be given to you; [2]seek, and you shall find;
[3]knock, and it shall be opened to you.
8 "For everyone who asks receives, and he who seeks finds, and to
him who knocks it shall be opened.
9 "Or what man is there among you, [1]when his son shall ask him
for a loaf, [2]will give him a stone?
10 "Or [1]if he shall ask for a fish, he will not give him a snake,
will he?
11 "If you then, being evil, know how to give good gifts to your
children, [a]how much more shall your Father who is in heaven give
what is good to those who ask Him!
12 "[a]Therefore, however you want people to treat you, [1]so treat
them, for [b]this is the Law and the Prophets.
13 "[a]Enter by the narrow gate; for the gate is wide, and the way is
broad that leads to destruction, and many are those who enter by it.
14 "For the gate is small, and the way is narrow that leads to life,
and few are those who find it.
15 "Beware of the [a]false prophets, who come to you in sheep's cloth-
ing, but inwardly are [b]ravenous wolves.
16 "You will [1a]know them by their fruits. [2]Grapes are not gathered
from thorn *bushes*, nor figs from thistles, are they?

27 [1]I.e., One equals appro [2]Or, *height* [a] 28, 31, 34; L 12:11, 22; Ph 1 Pet. 5:7 [b]P

28 [a]Matt. 6:2 34; Luke 10: 22; Phil. 4:6;

29 [a]1 Kin. 10 9:4-6, 20-22

30 [a]James 1 1 Pet. 1:24 [b] 14:31; 16:8

31 [a]Matt. 6:2 34; Luke 10:4 22; Phil. 4:6;

32 [a]Matt. 6:8

33 [1]Or, *conti seek* [2]Or, *the* [3]Or, *provided* 19:28; Mark 1 Luke 18:29f.;

34 [1]Or, *will w itself* [a]Matt. 6 28, 31; Luke 1 12:11, 22; Phi 1 Pet. 5:7

7:1 [a]Matt. 7:1 *6:37f., 41f.*; R 14:10, 13

2 [1]Lit., *by wh measure you* [a]Mark 4:24; L

3 [a]Rom. 2:1

4 [1]Lit., *will* [a]L

6 [a]Matt. 15:26

7 [1]Or, *Keep a* [2]Or, *keep seek keep knocking* 7:7-11: *Luke 1* [b]Matt. 18:19; 2 Mark 11:24; Jo 15:7, 16; 16:23 1:5f.; 1 John 3

9 [1]Lit., *whom will not give hi stone, will he?*

10 [1]Lit., *also*

11 [a]Ps. 84:11; Rom. 8:32; Ja

12 [1]Or, *you, to for* [a]Luke 6:31 22:40; Rom. 13 5:14

13 [a]Luke 13:24

15 [a]Matt. 24:11 Mark 13:22; Lu Acts 13:6; 2 Pe 1 John 4:1; Rev 19:20; 20:10 [b]E 22:27; John 10: 20:29

16 [1]Or, *recogn They do not ga* [a]Matt. 7:20; 12: 6:44; James 3:

17 "Even so, [a]every good tree bears good fruit; but the bad tree bears
bad fruit.
18 "A good tree cannot produce bad fruit, nor can a bad tree produce
good fruit.
19 "[a]Every tree that does not bear good fruit is cut down and thrown
into the fire.
20 "So then, you will [1]know them [a]by their fruits.
21 "[a]Not everyone who says to Me, 'Lord, Lord,' will enter the king-
dom of heaven; but he who does the will of My Father who is in
heaven.
22 "[a]Many will say to Me on [b]that day, 'Lord, Lord, did we not
prophesy in Your name, and in Your name cast out demons, and in
Your name perform many [1]miracles?'
23 "And then I will declare to them, 'I never knew you; [a]DEPART FROM
ME, YOU WHO PRACTICE LAWLESSNESS.'
24 "Therefore [a]everyone who hears these words of Mine, and [1]acts
upon them, [2]may be compared to a wise man, who built his house
upon the rock.
25 "And the rain descended, and the [1]floods came, and the winds
blew, and burst against that house; and *yet* it did not fall, for it had
been founded upon the rock.
26 "And everyone who hears these words of Mine, and does not [1]act
upon them, will be like a foolish man, who built his house upon the
sand.
27 "And the rain descended, and the [1]floods came, and the winds
blew, and burst against that house; and it fell, and great was its fall."
28 [1a]The result was that when Jesus had finished these words, [b]the
multitudes were amazed at His teaching;
29 for He was teaching them as *one* having authority, and not as
their scribes.

Chapter 8

8 And when He had come down from the mountain, great multi-
tudes followed Him.
2 And behold, [a]a leper came to Him, and [1b]bowed down to Him,
saying, "Lord, if You are willing, You can make me clean."
3 And He stretched out His hand and touched him, saying, "I am
willing; be cleansed." And immediately his [a]leprosy was cleansed.
4 And Jesus *said to him, "[a]See that you tell no one; but [b]go, [c]show
yourself to the priest, and present the [1]offering that Moses com-
manded, for a testimony to them."
5 And [a]when He had entered Capernaum, a centurion came to
Him, entreating Him,
6 and saying, "[1]Lord, my [2]servant is [3]lying [a]paralyzed at home,
[4]suffering great pain."
7 And He *said to him, "I will come and heal him."
8 But the centurion answered and said, "[1]Lord, I am not worthy
for You to come under my roof, but just [2]say the word, and my
[3]servant will be healed.
9 "For I, too, am a man under [a]authority, with soldiers under me;
and I say to this one, 'Go!' and he goes, and to another, 'Come!' and
he comes, and to my slave, 'Do this!' and he does *it*."
10 Now when Jesus heard *this*, He marveled, and said to those who

[a]Matt. 12:33, 35
Matt. 3:10; Luke :7; John 15:2, 6
[1]Or, *recognize* 16; 12:33; Luke 44; James 3:12
21 [a]Luke 6:46
works of power tt. 25:11f.; Luke 5ff. [b]Matt. 10:15
[a]Ps. 6:8; Matt. :41; Luke 13:27
, *does* [2]Lit., *will* *npared to* [a]Matt. 7: *Luke 6:47-49*; t. 16:18; James 1:22-25
25 [1]Lit., *rivers*
26 [1]Lit., *do*
27 [1]Lit., *rivers*
., *And it came to* Matt. 11:1; 13:53; :1 [b]Matt. 13:54; ; Mark 1:22; 6:2; Luke 4:32; John 7:46
2 [1]Or, *worshiped* Matt. 8:2-4: *Mark 44; Luke 5:12-14* Matt. 9:18; 15:25; 20:20; John 9:38; Acts 10:25
. 11:5; Luke 4:27
, *gift* [a]Matt. 9:30; 17:9; Mark 1:44; ; 5:43; 7:36; 8:30; Luke 4:41; 8:56; [b]Mark 1:44; Luke 7:14 [c]Lev. 13:49; 14:2ff.
Matt. 8:5-13: *Luke 7:1-10*
[1]Or, *Sir* [2]Lit., *boy* it., *throwing* [4]Lit., *earfully tormented* [a]Matt. 4:24
Sir [2]Lit., *say with a word* [3]Lit., *boy*
ark 1:27; Luke 9:1

were following, "Truly I say to you, I have not found such great faith
[1]with anyone in Israel.
11 "And I say to you, that many [a]shall come from east and west, and
[1]recline *at the table* with Abraham, and Isaac, and Jacob, in the king-
dom of heaven;
12 but [a]the sons of the kingdom shall be cast out into [b]the outer
darkness; in that place [c]there shall be weeping and gnashing of
teeth."
13 And Jesus said to the centurion, "Go your way; let it be done to
you [a]as you have believed." And the [1]servant was healed that *very*
hour.
14 [a]And when Jesus had come to Peter's [1]home, He saw his mother-
in-law lying sick in bed with a fever.
15 And He touched her hand, and the fever left her; and she arose,
and [1]waited on Him.
16 And when evening had come, they brought to Him many [a]who
were demon-possessed; and He cast out the spirits with a word, and
[b]healed all who were ill
17 in order that what was spoken through Isaiah the prophet might
be fulfilled, saying, "[a]HE HIMSELF TOOK OUR INFIRMITIES, AND [1]CARRIED
AWAY OUR DISEASES."
18 Now when Jesus saw a crowd around Him, [a]He gave orders to
depart to the other side.
19 [a]And a certain scribe came and said to Him, "Teacher, I will
follow You wherever You go."
20 And Jesus *said to him, "The foxes have holes, and the birds of
the [1]air *have* [2]nests; but [a]the Son of Man has nowhere to lay His
head."
21 And another of the disciples said to Him, "Lord, permit me first
to go and bury my father."
22 But Jesus *said to him, "[a]Follow Me; and allow the dead to bury
their own dead."
23 [a]And when He got into the boat, His disciples followed Him.
24 And behold, there arose [1]a great storm in the sea, so that the boat
was covered with the waves; but He Himself was asleep.
25 And they came to *Him,* and awoke Him, saying, "[a]Save *us,* Lord;
we are perishing!"
26 And He *said to them, "Why are you timid, [a]you men of little
faith?" Then He arose, and rebuked the winds and the sea; and [1]it
became perfectly calm.
27 And the men marveled, saying, "What kind of a man is this, that
even the winds and the sea obey Him?"
28 [a]And when He had come to the other side into the country of the
Gadarenes, two men who were [b]demon-possessed met Him as they
were coming out of the tombs; *they were* so exceedingly violent that
no one could pass by that road.
29 And behold, they cried out, saying, "[a]What do we have to do
with You, Son of God? Have You come here to torment us before [1]the
time?"
30 Now there was at a distance from them a herd of many swine
feeding.
31 And the demons *began* to entreat Him, saying, "If You are *going
to* cast us out, send us into the herd of swine."
32 And He said to them, "Begone!" And they came out, and went

10 [1]Some mss ... *not even in Isra...*
11 [1]Or, *dine* [a]Is. 59:19; Mal. 1:11 ... 13:29
12 [a]Matt. 13:38 ... 22:13; 25:30 [c]M... 13:42, 50; 22:13 ... 25:30; Luke 13:...
13 [1]Lit., *boy* [a]... 9:22, 29
14 [1]Or, *house* ... 8:14-16: *Mark 1... Luke 4:38-41*
15 [1]Or, *served*
16 [a]Matt. 4:24 ... 4:23; 8:33
17 [1]Or, *remove...* 53:4
18 [a]Mark 4:35; ... 8:22
19 [a]Matt. 8:19-2... *9:57-60*
20 [1]Or, *sky* [2]Or *roosting places* 7:13; Matt. 9:6; ... 40; 13:41; 16:13 ... 17:9; 19:28; 26:6... 8:38; Luke 12:8; ... 21:36; John 1:51 ... 6:27; 12:34; Acts...
22 [a]Matt. 9:9; M... 2:14; Luke 9:59, ... John 1:43; 21:19
23 [a]Matt. 8:23-2... *4:36-41; Luke 8:2...*
24 [1]Lit., *a shakin...*
25 [a]Matt. 8:2; 9:1...
26 [1]Lit., *a great c... occurred* [a]Matt. 6... 14:31; 16:8; 17:20
28 [a]Matt. 8:28-34 ... *5:1-17; Luke 8:26...* [b]Matt. 4:24
29 [1]I.e., the appo... time of judgment ... 11:12; 2 Sam. 16:... 19:22; 1 Kin. 17:1... 2 Kin. 3:13; 2 Chr. ... 35:21; Mark 1:24; ... Luke 4:34; 8:28; J... 2:4

into the swine, and behold, the whole herd rushed down the steep
bank into the sea and perished in the waters.
33 And the herdsmen ran away, and went to the city, and reported
everything, [1]including the *incident* of the [a]demoniacs.
34 And behold, the whole city came out to meet Jesus; and when
they saw Him, [a]they entreated *Him* to depart from their region.

Chapter 9

9 And getting into a boat, He crossed over, and came to [a]His own
city.
2 [a]And behold, they were bringing to Him a [b]paralytic, lying on a
bed; and Jesus seeing their faith said to the paralytic,
"[c]Take courage, My [1]son, [d]your sins [2]are forgiven."
3 And behold, some of the scribes said [1]to themselves,
"This *fellow* [a]blasphemes."
4 And Jesus [a]knowing their thoughts said, "Why are you
thinking evil in your hearts?
5 "For which is easier, to say, '[a]Your sins [1]are forgiven,' or
to say, 'Rise, and walk'?
6 "But in order that you may know that [a]the Son of Man
has authority on earth to forgive sins"—then He *said to
the [b]paralytic—"Rise, take up your bed, and go home."
7 And he rose, and [1]went home.
8 But when the multitudes saw *this*, they were [1]filled
with awe, and [a]glorified God, who had given such
authority to men.
9 [a]And as Jesus passed on from there, He saw a man,
called [b]Matthew, sitting [1]in the tax office; and He *said to
him, "[c]Follow Me!" And he rose, and followed Him.
10 And it happened that as He was reclining *at the table* in the
house, behold many [1]tax-gatherers and [2]sinners came and [3]were
dining with Jesus and His disciples.
11 And when the Pharisees saw *this*, they said to His disciples,
"[a]Why is your Teacher eating with the tax-gatherers and sinners?"
12 But when He heard this, He said, "*It is* not [a]those who are
healthy who need a physician, but those who are sick.
13 "But go and learn [a]what *this* means, '[b]I DESIRE [1]COMPASSION, [2]AND
NOT SACRIFICE,' for [c]I did not come to call the righteous, but sinners."
14 Then the disciples of John *came to Him, saying, "Why do we
and [a]the Pharisees fast, but Your disciples do not fast?"
15 And Jesus said to them, "The [1]attendants of the bridegroom can-
not mourn as long as the bridegroom is with them, can they? But the
days will come when the bridegroom is taken away from them, and
then they will fast.
16 "But no one puts [1]a patch of unshrunk cloth on an old garment;
for [2]the patch pulls away from the garment, and a worse tear results.
17 "Nor do *men* put new wine into old [1]wineskins; otherwise the
wineskins burst, and the wine pours out, and the wineskins are
ruined; but they put new wine into fresh wineskins, and both are
preserved."
18 [a]While He was saying these things to them, behold, there came
[1]a *synagogue* [2]official, and [3b]bowed down before Him, saying, "My
daughter has just died; but come and lay Your hand on her, and she
will live."

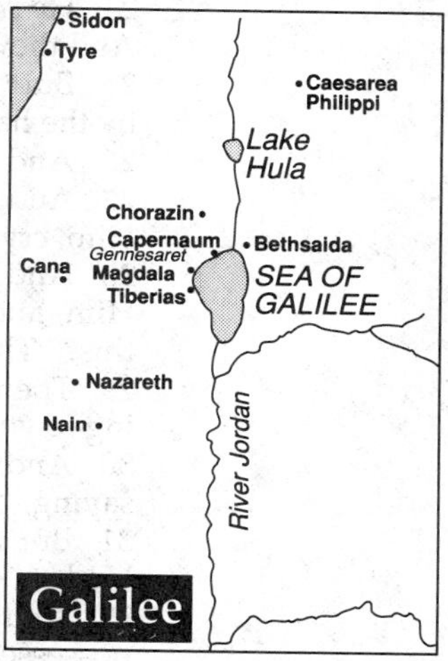

…t., *and* [a]Matt. 4:24
[a]Amos 7:12; Acts 16:39
[a]Matt. 4:13; Mark 5:21
…Lit., *child* [2]Lit., *are …ng forgiven* [a]Matt. …2-8: *Mark 2:3-12; …ke 5:18-26* [b]Matt. …4; 9:6 [c]Matt. 9:22; Mark 6:50; 10:49; 16:33; Acts 23:11 …2:5, 9; Luke 5:20, 23; 7:48
…Lit., *among* [a]Mark 3:28, 29
[a]Matt. 12:25; Luke 6:8; 9:47
5 [1]Lit., *are being …ven* [a]Matt. 9:2, 6; …2:5, 9; Luke 5:20, 23; 7:48
[a]Matt. 8:20; John …7 [b]Matt. 4:24; 9:2
7 [1]Or, *departed*
[1]Or, *afraid* [a]Matt. 15:31; Mark 2:12; …ke 2:20; 5:25, 26; …16; 13:13; 17:15; …; John 15:8; Acts …:21; 11:18; 21:20; …r. 9:13; Gal. 1:24
…, *at the tax booth* …latt. 9:9-17: *Mark …22; Luke 5:27-38* …10:3; Mark 2:14; …; Luke 6:15; Acts …1:13 [c]Matt. 8:22
…I.e., Collectors of …an taxes for profit …, irreligious Jews …Lit., *reclined with*
…Matt. 11:19; Mark …; Luke 5:30; 15:2
[a]Mark 2:17; Luke 5:31
[1]Or, *mercy* [2]I.e., …than [a]Matt. 12:7 …6:6 [c]Mark 2:17; …5:32; 1 Tim. 1:15
14 [a]Luke 18:12
[1]Lit., *sons of the bridal-chamber*
…Lit., *that which is* [2]Lit., *that which fills up*
…., skins used as bottles
…, *one* [2]Lit., *ruler …orshiped* [a]Matt. …: *Mark 5:22-43; …41-56* [b]Matt. 8:2

19 And Jesus rose and *began* to follow him, and *so did* His disciples.
20 And behold, a woman who had been suffering from a hemor-
rhage for twelve years, came up behind Him and touched [a]the fringe
of His [1]cloak;
21 for she was saying [1]to herself, "If I only [a]touch His garment, I
shall [2]get well."
22 But Jesus turning and seeing her said, "Daughter, [a]take courage;
[b]your faith has [1]made you well." And [2]at once the woman was [1]made
well.
23 And when Jesus came into the [1]official's house, and saw [a]the
flute-players, and the crowd in noisy disorder,
24 He *began* to say, "Depart; for the girl [a]has not died, but is asleep."
And they *began* laughing at Him.
25 But [a]when the crowd had been put out, He entered and [b]took her
by the hand; and the girl [1]arose.
26 And [a]this news went out into all that land.
27 And as Jesus passed on from there, two blind men followed
Him, crying out, and saying, "Have mercy on us, [a]Son of David!"
28 And after He had come into the house, the blind men came up to
Him, and Jesus *said to them, "Do you believe that I am able to do
this?" They *said to Him, "Yes, Lord."
29 Then He touched their eyes, saying, "Be it done to you [a]accord-
ing to your faith."
30 And their eyes were opened. And Jesus [a]sternly warned them,
saying, "See *here,* let no one know *about this*!"
31 But they went out, and [a]spread the news about Him in all that
land.
32 And as they were going out, behold, [a]a dumb man, [b]demon-
possessed, [1]was brought to Him.
33 And after the demon was cast out, the dumb man spoke; and the
multitudes marveled, saying, "[a]Nothing like this [1]was ever seen in
Israel."
34 But the Pharisees were saying, "He [a]casts out the demons by the
ruler of the demons."
35 And Jesus was going about all the cities and the villages, [a]teach-
ing in their synagogues, and proclaiming the gospel of the kingdom,
and healing every kind of disease and every kind of sickness.
36 And [a]seeing the multitudes, He felt compassion for them,
[b]because they were [1]distressed and [2]downcast like sheep [3]without a
shepherd.
37 Then He *said to His disciples, "[a]The harvest is plentiful, but the
workers are few.
38 "Therefore beseech the Lord of the harvest to send out workers
into His harvest."

Chapter 10

10 And [a]having summoned His twelve disciples, He gave them
authority over unclean spirits, to cast them out, and to [b]heal
every kind of disease and every kind of sickness.
2 [a]Now the names of the twelve apostles are these: The first,
[b]Simon, who is called Peter, and [b]Andrew his brother; and [1c]James
the *son* of Zebedee, and [2]John his brother;
3 [a]Philip and [1]Bartholomew; [b]Thomas and [c]Matthew the tax-
gatherer; [2d]James the *son* of Alphaeus, and [e]Thaddaeus;

20 [1]Or, *outer* [a]Num. 15:38; 22:12; Matt. 1

21 [1]Lit., *in he be saved* [a]Ma Mark 3:10; Luk

22 [1]Lit., *save* [2]Lit., *from that* [a]Matt. 9:2 [b]Ma 15:28; Mark 5: Luke 7:50; 8:4 18:42

23 [1]Lit., *ruler's* 35:25; Jer. 9:1 Ezek. 24:17

24 [a]John 11:1 20:10

25 [1]Or, *was ra* [a]Acts 9:40 [b]Ma

26 [a]Matt. 4:24; 14:1; Mark 1:28 Luke 4:14, 37;

27 [a]Matt. 1:1; 15:22; 20:30, 3 15; 22:42; Mark 48; 12:35; Luke 39; 20:41f.

29 [a]Matt. 8:13;

30 [a]Matt. 8:4

31 [a]Matt. 4:24; 14:1; Mark 1:28 Luke 4:14, 37; 5

32 [1]Lit., *they br* [a]Matt. 12:22, 24 4:24

33 [1]Lit., *ever ap* [a]Mark 2:12

34 [a]Matt. 12:24 3:22; Luke 11:15 7:20f.

35 [a]Matt. 4:23; 1:14

36 [1]Or, *harasse thrown down* [3]L *having* [a]Matt. 14 15:32; Mark 6:34 [b]Num. 27:17; Ez 34:5; Zech. 10:2 6:34

37 [a]Luke 10:2

10:1 [a]Mark 3:13 6:7 [b]Matt. 9:35;

2 [1]Or, *Jacob* [2]G *Joannes,* Heb., *Johanan* [a]Matt. *Mark 3:16-19; Lu 6:14-16; Acts 1:1* [b]Matt. 4:18 [c]Mat

3 [1]I.e., son of Ta (Aram.) [2]Or, *Jac* [a]John 1:43ff. [b]Jo 11:16; 14:5; 20:2 21:2 [c]Matt. 9:9 15:40 [e]Mark 3:1 6:16; Acts 1:13

4 Simon the [1]Zealot, and [a]Judas Iscariot, the one who betrayed Him.

5 [a]These twelve Jesus sent out after instructing them, saying, "Do not [1]go in *the* way of *the* Gentiles, and do not enter *any* city of the [b]Samaritans;

6 but rather [1]go to [a]the lost sheep of the house of Israel.

7 "And as you [1]go, [2]preach, saying, '[a]The kingdom of heaven [3]is at hand.'

8 "Heal *the* sick, raise *the* dead, cleanse *the* lepers, cast out demons; freely you received, freely give.

9 "[a]Do not acquire gold, or silver, or copper [1]for your money belts,

10 or a [1]bag for *your* journey, or even two [2]tunics, or sandals, or a staff; for [a]the worker is worthy of his [3]support.

11 "And into whatever city or village you enter, inquire who is worthy in it; and abide there until you go away.

12 "And as you enter the [1]house, [a]give it your greeting.

13 "And if the house is worthy, let your *greeting of* peace come upon it; but if it is not worthy, let your *greeting of* peace return to you.

14 "And whoever does not receive you, nor heed your words, as you go out of that house or that city, [a]shake off the dust of your feet.

15 "Truly I say to you, [a]it will be more tolerable for *the* land of [b]Sodom and Gomorrah in [c]the day of judgment, than for that city.

16 "[a]Behold, I send you out as sheep in the midst of wolves; therefore [1]be [b]shrewd as serpents, and [c]innocent as doves.

17 "But beware of men; for they will deliver you up to *the* [a]courts, and scourge you [b]in their synagogues;

18 and you shall even be brought before governors and kings for My sake, as a testimony to them and to the Gentiles.

19 "[a]But when they deliver you up, [b]do not become anxious about how or what you will speak; for it shall be given you in that hour what you are to speak.

20 "For [a]it is not you who speak, but *it is* the Spirit of your Father who speaks in you.

21 "[a]And brother will deliver up brother to death, and a father *his* child; and [b]children will rise up against parents, and [1]cause them to be put to death.

22 "And [a]you will be hated by all on account of My name, but [b]it is the one who has endured to the end who will be saved.

23 "But whenever they [a]persecute you in this city, flee to [1]the next; for truly I say to you, you shall not finish *going through* the cities of Israel, [b]until the Son of Man comes.

24 "[a]A [1]disciple is not above his teacher, nor a slave above his master.

25 "It is enough for the disciple that he become as his teacher, and the slave as his master. [a]If they have called the head of the house [1b]Beelzebul, how much more the members of his household!

26 "Therefore do not [a]fear them, [b]for there is nothing covered that will not be revealed, and hidden that will not be known.

27 "[a]What I tell you in the darkness, speak in the light; and what you hear *whispered* in *your* ear, proclaim [b]upon the housetops.

28 "And do not fear those who kill the body, but are unable to kill the soul; but rather [a]fear Him who is able to destroy both soul and body in [1b]hell.

29 "[a]Are not two sparrows sold for a [1]cent? And *yet* not one of them will fall to the ground apart from your Father.

Cananaean
4; Luke 22:3;
:71; 13:2, 26

off to [a]Mark
e 9:2 [b]2 Kin.
.; Luke 9:52;
16; John 4:9,
48; Acts 8:25

oceed [a]Matt.
15:24

proceed [2]Or,
aim [3]Lit., has
ar [a]Matt. 3:2

., into [a]Matt.
Mark 6:8-11;
3-5; 10:4-12;
Luke 22:35

knapsack or
ag [2]Or, inner
arments [3]Lit.,
ment [a]1 Cor.
4; 1 Tim. 5:18

Or, household
am. 25:6; Ps.
122:7, 8

4 [a]Acts 13:51

Matt. 11:22, 24
24; 2 Pet. 2:6;
7 [c]Matt. 7:22;
4; 12:36; Acts
1 Thess. 5:4;
25; 2 Pet. 2:9;
n 4:17; Jude 6

16 [1]Or, show
es to be [a]Luke
Gen. 3:1; Matt.
5; Rom. 16:19
[c]Hos. 7:11

tt. 5:22 [b]Matt.
ark 13:9; Luke
ts 5:40; 22:19;
26:11

Matt. 10:19-22:
13:11-13; Luke
17 [b]Matt. 6:25;
Luke 12:11, 12

uke 12:12; Acts
3:9; 2 Cor. 13:3

Or, put them to
Matt. 10:35, 36;
13:12 [b]Mic. 7:6

Matt. 24:9; Luke
7; John 15:18ff.
13; Mark 13:13

[1]Lit., the other
tt. 23:34 [b]Matt.
16:27f.

Or, pupil [a]Luke
hn 13:16; 15:20

[1]Or, Beezebul;
read Beelzebub
:34 [b]2 Kin. 1:2;
12:24, 27; Mark
ke 11:15, 18, 19

[a]Matt. 10:26-33:
ke 12:2-9 [b]Mark
Luke 8:17; 12:2;
1 Cor. 4:5

uke 12:3 [b]Matt.
24:17; Acts 5:20

8 [1]Gr., Gehenna
eb. 10:31 [b]Matt.
5:22; Luke 12:5

Gr., assarion, the
llest copper coin
[a]Luke 12:6

30 "But [a]the very hairs of your head are all numbered.
31 "Therefore do not fear; [a]you are of more value than many spar-
rows.
32 "[a]Everyone therefore who shall confess [1]Me before men, I will
also confess [2]him before My Father who is in heaven.
33 "But [a]whoever shall deny Me before men, I will also deny him
before My Father who is in heaven.
34 "[a]Do not think that I came to [1]bring peace on the earth; I did not
come to bring peace, but a sword.
35 "For I came to [a]SET A MAN AGAINST HIS FATHER, AND A DAUGHTER
AGAINST HER MOTHER, AND A DAUGHTER-IN-LAW AGAINST HER MOTHER-IN-
LAW;
36 and [a]A MAN'S ENEMIES WILL BE THE MEMBERS OF HIS HOUSEHOLD.
37 "[a]He who loves father or mother more than Me is not worthy of
Me; and he who loves son or daughter more than Me is not worthy
of Me.
38 "And [a]he who does not take his cross and follow after Me is not
worthy of Me.
39 "[a]He who has found his [1]life shall lose it, and he who has lost his
[1]life for My sake shall find it.
40 "[a]He who receives you receives Me, and [b]he who receives Me
receives Him who sent Me.
41 "[a]He who receives a prophet in *the* name of a prophet shall receive
a prophet's reward; and he who receives a righteous man in the
name of a righteous man shall receive a righteous man's reward.
42 "And [a]whoever in the name of a disciple gives to one of these
[1]little ones even a cup of cold water to drink, truly I say to you he
shall not lose his reward."

Chapter 11

11 [a]And it came about that when Jesus had finished [1]giving in-
structions to His twelve disciples, He departed from there [b]to
teach and [2]preach in their cities.
2 [a]Now when [b]John in prison heard of the works of Christ, he sent
word by his disciples,
3 and said to Him, "Are You [a]the [1]Expected One, or shall we look
for someone else?"
4 And Jesus answered and said to them, "Go and report to John
what you hear and see:
5 [a]*the* BLIND RECEIVE SIGHT and *the* lame walk, *the* lepers are cleansed
and *the* deaf hear, and *the* dead are raised up, and *the* [b]POOR HAVE THE
[1]GOSPEL PREACHED TO THEM.
6 "And blessed is he [1]who [a]keeps from [2]stumbling over Me."
7 And as these were going *away,* Jesus began to speak to the multi-
tudes about John, "What did you go out into [a]the wilderness to look
at? A reed shaken by the wind?
8 "[1]But what did you go out to see? A man dressed in soft *clothing?*
Behold, those who wear soft *clothing* are in kings' [2]palaces.
9 "[1]But why did you go out? To see [a]a prophet? Yes, I say to you,
and one who is more than a prophet.
10 "This is the one about whom it [1]is written,
'[a]BEHOLD, I SEND MY MESSENGER BEFORE YOUR FACE,
WHO WILL PREPARE YOUR WAY BEFORE YOU.'
11 "Truly, I say to you, among those born of women there has not

30 [a]1 Sam. 1... 2 Sam. 14:11 1:52; Luke 2... 27:34
31 [a]Matt. 12:...
32 [1]Lit., *in M... him* [a]Luke 12...
33 [a]Mark 8:3... 9:26; 2 Tim. 2...
34 [1]Lit., *cast* 10:34, 35: *Lu...*
35 [a]Mic. 7:6; ... 10:21; Luke 1...
36 [a]Mic. 7:6; ...
37 [a]Deut. 33:... 14:26
38 [a]Matt. 16:2... 8:34; Luke 9:2...
39 [1]Or, *soul* [a]... 16:25; Mark 8:... 9:24; 17:33; Jo...
40 [a]Matt. 18:5... 10:16; John 13... 4:14 [b]Mark 9:3... 9:48; John 12:...
41 [a]Matt. 25:4...
42 [1]I.e., humb... 25:40; Mark 9:...
11:1 [1]Or, *com...* [2]Or, *proclaim* [a]... 7:28 [b]Matt. 9:3... 23:5
2 [a]Matt. 11:2-1... *7:18-35;* Matt. 4... [b]Matt. 14:3; Ma... Luke 9:7ff.
3 [1]Lit., *Coming* [a]Ps. 118:26; Ma... John 6:14; 11:2... 10:37
5 [1]Or, *good ne...* 35:5f.; Matt. 8:3... [b]Is. 61:1; Luke 4...
6 [1]Lit., *whoever taking offense a...* 5:29; 13:57; 24:1... 26:31; Mark 6:3... 6:61; 16:1
7 [a]Matt. 3:1
8 [1]Or, *Well then... houses*
9 [1]Or, *Well then,* ... 14:5; 21:26; Luke... 20:6
10 [1]Lit., *has bee... written* [a]Mal. 3:1 1:2

arisen *anyone* greater than John the Baptist; yet he who is [1]least in the
kingdom of heaven is greater than he.
12 "And [a]from the days of John the Baptist until now the kingdom of
heaven [1]suffers violence, and violent men [2]take it by force.
13 "For all the prophets and the Law prophesied until John.
14 "And if you care to accept *it*, he himself is [a]Elijah, who [1]was to
come.
15 "[a]He who has ears to hear, let him hear.
16 "But to what shall I compare this generation? It is like children
sitting in the market places, who call out to the other *children*,
17 and say, 'We played the flute for you, and you did not dance; we
sang a dirge, and you did not [1]mourn.'
18 "For John came neither [a]eating nor [b]drinking, and they say, '[c]He
has a demon!'
19 "The Son of Man came eating and drinking, and they say, 'Be-
hold, a gluttonous man and a [1]drunkard, [a]a friend of [2]tax-gatherers
and sinners!' [3]Yet wisdom is vindicated by her deeds."
20 Then He began to reproach the cities in which most of His
[1a]miracles were done, because they did not repent.
21 "[a]Woe to you, Chorazin! Woe to you, [b]Bethsaida! For if the
[1]miracles had occurred in [c]Tyre and [c]Sidon which occurred in you,
they would have repented long ago in [d]sackcloth and ashes.
22 "Nevertheless I say to you, [a]it shall be more tolerable for Tyre and
Sidon in [b]*the* day of judgment, than for you.
23 "And you, [a]Capernaum, will not be exalted to heaven, will you?
You shall [1b]descend to [c]Hades; for if the [2]miracles had occurred in
[d]Sodom which occurred in you, it would have remained to this day.
24 "Nevertheless I say to you that [a]it shall be more tolerable for the
land of [b]Sodom in *the* day of judgment, than for you."
25 [a]At that [1]time Jesus answered and said, "I [2]praise Thee, O
[b]Father, Lord of heaven and earth, that [c]Thou didst hide these things
from *the* wise and intelligent and didst reveal them to babes.
26 "Yes, [a]Father, for thus it was well-pleasing in Thy sight.
27 "[a]All things [1]have been handed over to Me by My Father; and no
one [2]knows the Son, except the Father; nor does anyone [2]know the
Father, [b]except the Son, and anyone to whom the Son wills to reveal
Him.
28 "[a]Come to Me, all [1]who are weary and heavy-laden, and I will
give you rest.
29 "Take My yoke upon you, and [a]learn from Me, for I am gentle and
humble in heart; and [b]YOU SHALL FIND REST FOR YOUR SOULS.
30 "For [a]My yoke is [1]easy, and My load is light."

Chapter 12

12 [a]At that [1]time Jesus went on the Sabbath through the grain-
fields, and His disciples became hungry and began to [b]pick
the heads *of grain* and eat.
2 But when the Pharisees saw it, they said to Him, "Behold, Your
disciples do what [a]is not lawful to do on a Sabbath."
3 But He said to them, "Have you not read what David did, when
he became hungry, he and his companions;
4 how he entered the house of God, and [a]they ate the [1]consecrated
bread, which was not lawful for him to eat, nor for those with him,
but for the priests alone?

11 [1]Or, *less*
[1]Or, *is forcibly* [2]Or, *seize it for*
s [a]Luke 16:16
[1]Or, *is to come* [a]Mal. 4:5; Matt. Mark 9:11-13; :17; John 1:21
[a]Matt. 13:9, 43; , 23; Luke 8:8; ev. 2:7, 11, 17, .6, 13, 22; 13:9
beat the breast
Matt. 3:4 [b]Luke Matt. 9:34; John :48f., 52; 10:20
Or, *wine-drinker* ., Collectors of taxes for profit *nd* [a]Matt. 9:11; e 5:29-32; 15:2
works of power [a]Luke 10:13-15
works of power 11:21-23: *Luke 15* [b]Mark 6:45; uke 9:10; John 4; 12:21 [c]Matt. 5:21; Mark 3:8; , 31; Luke 4:26; Acts 12:20; 27:3 [d]Rev. 11:3
att. 10:15; 11:24 tt. 10:15; 12:36; Rev. 20:11, 12
ne mss. read *be ught down* [2]Or, *of power* [a]Matt. 3 [b]Is. 14:13, 15; k. 26:20; 31:14; 24 [c]Matt. 16:18; :15; 16:23; Acts ; Rev. 1:18; 6:8; 3f. [d]Matt. 10:15
att. 10:15; 11:22 [b]Matt. 10:15
r, *occasion* [2]Or, *nowledge to Thy* [a]Matt. 11:25-27: *10:21, 22* [b]Luke :42; 23:34; John ; 12:27, 28 [c]Ps. 3:2; 1 Cor. 1:26ff.
ke 22:42; 23:34; 11:41; 12:27, 28
[1]Lit., *were given ver* [2]Or, *perfectly (s)* [a]Matt. 28:18; 3:35; 13:3; 17:2 :29; 10:15; 17:25
[1]Or, *who work to stion* [a]Jer. 31:25; John 7:37
John 13:15; Eph. ; Phil. 2:5; 1 Pet. , 1 John 2:6 [b]Jer. 6:16
30 [1]Or, *kindly or sant* [a]1 John 5:3
:1 [1]Or, *occasion* Matt. 12:1-8: *Mark 23-28; Luke 6:1-5* [b]Deut. 23:25
Matt. 12:10; Luke ; 14:3; John 5:10; 7:23; 9:16
Or, *showbread*; lit., *es of presentation* [a]1 Sam. 21:6

5 "Or have you not read in the Law, that on the Sabbath the priests
in the temple [1]break the Sabbath, and are innocent?
6 "But I say to you, that something [a]greater than the temple is here.
7 "But if you had known what this [1]means, '[a]I DESIRE [2]COMPASSION,
AND NOT A SACRIFICE,' you would not have condemned the innocent.
8 "For [a]the Son of Man is Lord of the Sabbath."
9 [a]And departing from there, He went into their synagogue.
10 And behold, *there was* a man with a withered hand. And they
questioned Him, saying, "[a]Is it lawful to heal on the Sabbath?"—in
order that they might accuse Him.
11 And He said to them, "[a]What man shall there be [1]among you,
who shall have one sheep, and if it falls into a pit on the Sabbath,
will he not take hold of it, and lift it out?
12 "Of [a]how much more value then is a man than a sheep! So then, it
is lawful to do [1]good on the Sabbath."
13 Then He *said to the man, "Stretch out your hand!" And [a]he
stretched it out, and it was restored to [1]normal, like the other.
14 But the Pharisees went out, and [a]counseled together against
Him, *as to* how they might destroy Him.
15 But Jesus, [1]aware of *this,* withdrew from there. And many fol-
lowed Him, and [a]He healed them all,
16 and [a]warned them not to [1]make Him known,
17 in order that what was spoken through Isaiah the prophet, might
be fulfilled, saying,
18 "[a]BEHOLD, MY [1]SERVANT WHOM I [2]HAVE CHOSEN;
[b]MY BELOVED IN WHOM MY SOUL [3]IS WELL-PLEASED;
[c]I WILL PUT MY SPIRIT UPON HIM,
[a]AND HE SHALL PROCLAIM [4]JUSTICE TO THE [5]GENTILES.
19 "[a]HE WILL NOT QUARREL, NOR CRY OUT;
NOR WILL ANYONE HEAR HIS VOICE IN THE STREETS.
20 "[a]A BATTERED REED HE WILL NOT BREAK OFF,
AND A SMOLDERING WICK HE WILL NOT PUT OUT,
UNTIL HE [1]LEADS [2]JUSTICE TO VICTORY.
21 "[a]AND IN HIS NAME THE [1]GENTILES WILL HOPE."
22 [a]Then there was brought to Him a [b]demon-possessed man *who*
was blind and dumb, and He healed him, so that the dumb man
spoke and saw.
23 And all the multitudes were amazed, and *began* to say, "This *man*
cannot be the [a]Son of David, can he?"
24 But when the Pharisees heard it, they said, "This man [a]casts out
demons only by [1]Beelzebul the ruler of the demons."
25 [a]And [b]knowing their thoughts He said to them, "[1]Any kingdom
divided against itself is laid waste; and [1]any city or house divided
against itself shall not stand.
26 "And if [a]Satan casts out Satan, he [1]is divided against himself; how
then shall his kingdom stand?
27 "And if I [a]by [1]Beelzebul cast out demons, [b]by whom do your sons
cast them out? Consequently they shall be your judges.
28 "But [a]if I cast out demons by the Spirit of God, then the kingdom
of God has come upon you.
29 "Or how can anyone enter the strong man's house and carry off
his property, unless he first binds the strong *man*? And then he will
plunder his house.

5 [1]Or, *profane*
6 [a]2 Chr. 6:18 2; Matt. 12:41,
7 [1]Lit., *is* [2]Or, [a]Hos. 6:6; Matt
8 [a]Matt. 8:20;
9 [a]Matt. 12:9-1 *3:1-6; Luke 6:6*
10 [a]Matt. 12:2; 13:14; 14:3; Jo 7:23; 9:16
11 [1]Lit., *of* [a]Lu
12 [1]Lit., *well* [a] 10:31; Luke 14
13 [1]Lit., *health* 8:3; Acts 28:8
14 [a]Matt. 26:4; 14:1; Luke 22:2 7:30, 44; 8:59; 1 39; 11:53
15 [1]Lit., *knowin* 4:23
16 [1]Or, *reveal w* *was* [a]Matt. 8:4; 17:9
18 [1]Lit., *Child* [2] *chose* [3]Or, *took pleasure* [4]Or, *ju* [5]Or, *nations* [a]Is. [b]Matt. 3:17; 17:5 4:18; John 3:34
19 [a]Is. 42:2
20 [1]Or, *puts fort* *judgment* [a]Is. 42
21 [1]Or, *nations* 15:12
22 [a]Matt. 12:22, *Luke 11:14, 15;* M 9:32, 34 [b]Matt. 4 2 Thess. 2:9
23 [a]Matt. 9:27
24 [1]Or, *Beezebul* others read *Beelz* [a]Matt. 9:34
25 [1]Lit., *Every* [a]M 12:25-29: *Mark 3:* *Luke 11:17-22* [b]M
26 [1]Lit., *was* [a]Ma 4:10; 13:19
27 [1]V. 24, note 1 9:34 [b]Acts 19:13
28 [a]1 John 3:8

30 "[a]He who is not with Me is against Me; and he who does not
gather with Me scatters.
31 "[a]Therefore I say to you, any sin and blasphemy shall be forgiven
men, but blasphemy against the Spirit shall not be forgiven.
32 "[a]And whoever shall speak a word against the Son of Man, it
shall be forgiven him; but whoever shall speak against the Holy
Spirit, it shall not be forgiven him, either in [b]this age, or in the *age* to
come.
33 "Either make the tree good, and its fruit good; or make the tree
bad, and its fruit bad; for [a]the tree is known by its fruit.
34 "[a]You brood of vipers, how can you, being evil, speak [1]what is
good? [b]For the mouth speaks out of that which fills the heart.
35 "[a]The good man out of *his* good treasure brings forth [1]what is
good; and the evil man out of *his* evil treasure brings forth [2]what is
evil.
36 "And I say to you, that every [1]careless word that men shall speak,
they shall render account for it in [a]the day of judgment.
37 "For [1]by your words you shall be justified, and [1]by your words
you shall be condemned."
38 Then some of the scribes and Pharisees answered Him, saying,
"Teacher, [a]we want to see a [1]sign from You."
39 But He answered and said to them, "[a]An evil and adulterous
generation craves for a [1]sign; and *yet* no [1]sign shall be given to it but
the [1]sign of Jonah the prophet;
40 for just as [a]JONAH WAS THREE DAYS AND THREE NIGHTS IN THE BELLY OF
THE SEA MONSTER, so shall [b]the Son of Man be [c]three days and three
nights in the heart of the earth.
41 "[a]The men of Nineveh shall stand up with this generation at the
judgment, and shall condemn it because [b]they repented at the
preaching of Jonah; and behold, [c]something greater than Jonah is
here.
42 "[a]*The* Queen of *the* South shall rise up with this generation at the
judgment and shall condemn it, because she came from the ends of
the earth to hear the wisdom of Solomon; and behold, [b]something
greater than Solomon is here.
43 "[a]Now when the unclean spirit goes out of a man, it passes
through waterless places, seeking rest, and does not find *it*.
44 "Then it says, 'I will return to my house from which I came'; and
when it comes, it finds it unoccupied, swept, and put in order.
45 "Then it goes, and takes along with it seven other spirits more
wicked than itself, and they go in and live there; and [a]the last state of
that man becomes worse than the first. That is the way it will also be
with this evil generation."
46 [a]While He was still speaking to the multitudes, behold, His
[b]mother and [c]brothers were standing outside, seeking to speak to
Him.
47 And someone said to Him, "Behold, Your mother and Your
brothers are standing outside seeking to speak to You."
48 But He answered the one who was telling Him and said, "Who
is My mother and who are My brothers?"
49 And stretching out His hand toward His disciples, He said, "Be-
hold, My mother and My brothers!
50 "For whoever does the will of My Father who is in heaven, he is
My brother and sister and mother."

k 9:40; Luke 9:50; 11:23
att. 12:31, 32; :28-30; Luke 12:10
12:10 [b]Matt. ; Mark 10:30; 18:30; 20:34, . 1:21; 1 Tim. n. 4:10; Titus :12; Heb. 6:5
7:16-18; Luke ; John 15:4-7
., *good things* ; 23:33; Luke am. 24:13; Is. att. 12:34, 35; ke 6:45; Eph. James 3:2-12
:., *good things things* [a]Prov. 21; 25:11, 12; 3:52; Col. 4:6
useless [a]Matt. 10:15
in accordance with
[1]Or, *attesting le* [a]Matt. 16:1; 8:11, 12; Luke ohn 2:18; 6:30; 1 Cor. 1:22
[1]Or, *attesting miracle* [a]Matt. 12:39-42: *Luke -32;* Matt. 16:4
on. 1:17 [b]Matt. 0 [c]Matt. 16:21
. 1:2 [b]Jon. 3:5 [c]Matt. 12:6, 42
in. 10:1; 2 Chr. [b]Matt. 12:6, 41
[a]Matt. 12:43-45: *Luke 11:24-26*
[a]Mark 5:9; Luke eb. 6:4-8; 2 Pet. 2:20
[a]Matt. 12:46-50: *k 3:31-35; Luke -21* [b]Matt. 1:18; 1ff.; 13:55; Luke 3; 2:33f., 48, 51; 1, 5, 12; 19:25f.; 4 [c]Matt. 13:55; 6:3; John 2:12; 5, 10; Acts 1:14; or. 9:5; Gal. 1:19

Chapter 13

13 On that day Jesus went out of [a]the house, and was sitting [b]by
the sea.
2 And great multitudes gathered to Him, so that [a]He got into a
boat and sat down, and the whole multitude was standing on the
beach.
3 And He spoke many things to them in [a]parables, saying, "Be-
hold, the sower went out to sow;
4 and as he sowed, some *seeds* fell beside the road, and the birds
came and ate them up.
5 "And others fell upon the rocky places, where they [1]did not have
much soil; and immediately they sprang up, because they had no
depth of soil.
6 "But when the sun had risen, they were scorched; and because
they had no root, they withered away.
7 "And others fell [1]among the thorns, and the thorns came up and
choked them out.
8 "And others fell on the good soil, and *yielded a crop, some a
[a]hundredfold, some sixty, and some thirty.
9 "[a]He who has ears, let him hear."
10 And the disciples came and said to Him, "Why do You speak to
them in parables?"
11 And He answered and said to them, "[a]To you it has been granted
to know the mysteries of the kingdom of heaven, but to them it has
not been granted.
12 "[a]For whoever has, to him shall *more* be given, and he shall have
an abundance; but whoever does not have, even what he has shall be
taken away from him.
13 "Therefore I speak to them in parables; because while [a]seeing they
do not see, and while hearing they do not hear, nor do they under-
stand.
14 "And [1]in their case the prophecy of Isaiah is being fulfilled, which
says,
'[2a]YOU WILL KEEP ON HEARING, [3]BUT WILL NOT UNDERSTAND;
AND [4]YOU WILL KEEP ON SEEING, BUT WILL NOT PERCEIVE;
15 [a]FOR THE HEART OF THIS PEOPLE HAS BECOME DULL,
AND WITH THEIR EARS THEY SCARCELY HEAR,
AND THEY HAVE CLOSED THEIR EYES
LEST THEY SHOULD SEE WITH THEIR EYES,
AND HEAR WITH THEIR EARS,
AND UNDERSTAND WITH THEIR HEART AND RETURN,
AND I SHOULD HEAL THEM.'
16 "[a]But blessed are your eyes, because they see; and your ears, be-
cause they hear.
17 "For truly I say to you, that [a]many prophets and righteous men
desired to see what you see, and did not see *it*; and to hear what you
hear, and did not hear *it*.
18 "[a]Hear then the parable of the sower.
19 "When anyone hears [a]the word of the kingdom, and does not
understand it, [b]the evil *one* comes and snatches away what has been
sown in his heart. This is the one on whom seed was sown beside
the road.
20 "And the one on whom seed was sown on the rocky places, this is
the man who hears the word, and immediately receives it with joy;

13:1 [a]Matt. [b]Matt. 13:1- *4:1-12; Luke* Mark 2:13
2 [a]Luke 5:3
3 [a]Matt. 13:1 4:2ff.
5 [1]Lit., *were*
7 [1]Lit., *upon*
8 [a]Gen. 26:1 13:23
9 [a]Matt. 11:1 11, 17, 29; 3:6
11 [a]Matt. 19: John 6:65; 1 C Col. 1:27; 1 Jo 2:20, 27
12 [a]Matt. 25: 4:25; Luke 8:1
13 [a]Deut. 29: 42:19, 20; Jer. Ezek. 12:2
14 [1]Lit., *for th* *With a hearing* *hear* [3]Lit., *and* *seeing you wil* 6:9; Mark 4:12 8:10; John 12: 28:26, 27; Rom 11:8
15 [a]Is. 6:10; P Zech. 7:11; Lu John 8:43, 44; 4:4; Heb. 5:11
16 [a]Matt. 13:1 *Luke 10:23, 24* 16:17; John 20
17 [a]John 8:56; 11:13; 1 Pet. 1:1
18 [a]Matt. 13:18 *Mark 4:13-20; L* *8:11-15*
19 [a]Matt. 4:23 5:37

21 yet he has no *firm* root in himself, but is *only* temporary, and
when affliction or persecution arises because of the word, immedi-
ately he [1a]falls away.
22 "And the one on whom seed was sown among the thorns, this is
the man who hears the word, and the worry of [a]the [1]world, and the
[b]deceitfulness of riches choke the word, and it becomes unfruitful.
23 "And the one on whom seed was sown on the good soil, this is
the man who hears the word and understands it; who indeed bears
fruit, and brings forth, some [a]a hundredfold, some sixty, and some
thirty."
24 He presented another parable to them, saying, "[a]The kingdom of
heaven [1]may be compared to a man who sowed good seed in his
field.
25 "But while men were sleeping, his enemy came and sowed [1]tares
also among the wheat, and went away.
26 "But when the [1]wheat sprang up and bore grain, then the tares
became evident also.
27 "And the slaves of the landowner came and said to him, 'Sir, did
you not sow good seed in your field? [1]How then does it have tares?'
28 "And he said to them, 'An [1]enemy has done this!' And the slaves
*said to him, 'Do you want us, then, to go and gather them up?'
29 "But he *said, 'No; lest while you are gathering up the tares, you
may root up the wheat with them.
30 'Allow both to grow together until the harvest; and in the time of
the harvest I will say to the reapers, "First gather up the tares and
bind them in bundles to burn them up; but [a]gather the wheat into
my barn." ' "
31 He presented another parable to them, saying, "[a]The kingdom of
heaven is like [b]a mustard seed, which a man took and sowed in his
field;
32 and this is smaller than all *other* seeds; but when it is full grown,
it is larger than the garden plants, and becomes a tree, so that [a]THE
BIRDS OF THE [1]AIR come and NEST IN ITS BRANCHES."
33 He spoke another parable to them, "[a]The kingdom of heaven is
like leaven, which a woman took, and hid in [b]three [1]pecks of meal,
until it was all leavened."
34 All these things Jesus spoke to the multitudes in parables, and
He did not speak to them [a]without a parable,
35 so that what was spoken through the prophet might be fulfilled,
saying,

"[a]I WILL OPEN MY MOUTH IN PARABLES;
I WILL UTTER THINGS HIDDEN SINCE THE FOUNDATION OF THE WORLD."

36 Then He left the multitudes, and went into [a]the house. And His
disciples came to Him, saying, "[b]Explain to us the parable of the
[1]tares of the field."
37 And He answered and said, "The one who sows the good seed is
[a]the Son of Man,
38 and the field is the world; and *as for* the good seed, these are [a]the
sons of the kingdom; and the tares are [b]the sons of [c]the evil *one;*
39 and the enemy who sowed them is the devil, and the harvest is
[a]the [1]end of the age; and the reapers are angels.
40 "Therefore just as the tares are gathered up and burned with fire,
so shall it be at [a]the [1]end of the age.
41 "[a]The Son of Man [b]will send forth His angels, and they will gather

is caused to e [a]Matt. 11:6
r, *age* [a]Matt. 9; Mark 4:19; ; 1 Cor. 1:20; 8; 2 Cor. 4:4; 1:4; Eph. 2:2 3; 1 Tim. 6:9, 10, 17
3 [a]Matt. 13:8
'as compared 13:31, 33, 45, 3; 20:1; 22:2; Mark 4:26-30; uke 13:18, 20
'arnel, a weed embling wheat
26 [1]Lit., *grass*
., *From where*
., *enemy man*
30 [a]Matt. 3:12
Matt. 13:31, 32: *4:30-32; Luke 19;* Matt. 13:24 :20; Luke 17:6
Or, *sky* [a]Ezek. 23; Ps. 104:12; 31:6; Dan. 4:12
Gr., *sata* [a]Matt. *ke 13:21;* Matt. en. 18:6; Judg. 9; 1 Sam. 1:24
Mark 4:34; John 10:6; 16:25
35 [a]Ps. 78:2
darnel, a weed sembling wheat :1 [b]Matt. 15:15
37 [a]Matt. 8:20
Matt. 8:12 [b]John ts 13:10; 1 John 3:10 [c]Matt. 5:37
, *consummation* 2:32; 13:22, 40, :3; 28:20; 1 Cor. 10:11; Heb. 9:26
, *consummation* 2:32; 13:22, 39, :3; 28:20; 1 Cor. 10:11; Heb. 9:26
Matt. 8:20 [b]Matt. 24:31

out of His kingdom [1]all [c]stumbling blocks, and those who commit
lawlessness,
42 and [a]will cast them into the furnace of fire; in that place [b]there
shall be weeping and gnashing of teeth.
43 "[a]Then THE RIGHTEOUS WILL SHINE FORTH AS THE SUN in the kingdom
of their Father. [b]He who has ears, let him hear.
44 "[a]The kingdom of heaven is like a treasure hidden in the field,
which a man found and hid; and from joy over it he goes and [b]sells
all that he has, and buys that field.
45 "Again, [a]the kingdom of heaven is like a merchant seeking fine
pearls,
46 and upon finding one pearl of great value, he went and sold all
that he had, and bought it.
47 "Again, [a]the kingdom of heaven is like a dragnet cast into the sea,
and gathering *fish* of every kind;
48 and when it was filled, they drew it up on the beach; and they
sat down, and gathered the good *fish* into containers, but the bad
they threw away.
49 "So it will be at [a]the [1]end of the age; the angels shall come forth,
and [2]take out the wicked from among the righteous,
50 and [a]will cast them into the furnace of fire; [b]there shall be weep-
ing and gnashing of teeth.
51 "Have you understood all these things?" They *said to Him,
"Yes."
52 And He said to them, "Therefore every scribe who has become a
disciple of the kingdom of heaven is like a head of a household, who
brings forth out of his treasure things new and old."
53 [a]And it came about that when Jesus had finished these parables,
He departed from there.
54 [a]And coming to [1]His home town He [2b]*began* teaching them in
their synagogue, so that [c]they became astonished, and said, "Where
did this man *get* this wisdom, and *these* [3]miraculous powers?
55 "Is not this the carpenter's son? Is not [a]His mother called Mary,
and His [a]brothers, James and Joseph and Simon and Judas?
56 "And [a]His sisters, are they not all with us? Where then *did* this
man *get* all these things?"
57 And they [1]took [a]offense at Him. But Jesus said to them, "[b]A
prophet is not without honor except in his [2]home town, and in his
own household."
58 And He did not do many [1]miracles there because of their un-
belief.

Chapter 14

14 [a]At that [1]time [b]Herod the tetrarch heard the news about Jesus,
2 and said to his servants, "[a]This is John the Baptist; [1]he has
risen from the dead; and that is why miraculous powers are at work
in him."
3 For when [a]Herod had John arrested, he bound him, and put him
[b]in prison on account of [c]Herodias, the wife of his brother Philip.
4 For John had been saying to him, "[a]It is not lawful for you to
have her."
5 And although he wanted to put him to death, he feared the
multitude, because [1]they regarded him as [a]a prophet.

41 [1]Or, *eve* *is offensive*
42 [a]Matt. 13 8:12
43 [a]Dan. 12 11:15
44 [a]Matt. 13 13:46
45 [a]Matt. 13
47 [a]Matt. 13
49 [1]Or, *cons* [2]Or, *separate* 13:39, 40
50 [a]Matt. 13: 8:12
53 [a]Matt. 7:2
54 [1]Or, *His o* *the country* [2](*teaching* [3]Or, [a]Matt. 13:54-5 *6:1-6* [b]Matt. 4 7:28
55 [a]Matt. 12:4
56 [a]Mark 6:3
57 [1]Lit., *were* *made to stumb* *own part of the* [a]Matt. 11:6 [b]M Luke 4:24; Joh
58 [1]Or, *works*
14:1 [1]Or, *occa* [a]Matt. 14:1-12: *6:14-29;* Matt. *Luke 9:7-9* [b]Ma Luke 3:1, 19; 8. 23:7f., 11f., 15; 4:27; 12:1
2 [1]Or, *he, hims* [a]Matt. 16:14; Ma Luke 9:7
3 [a]Matt. 14:1-12 *6:14-29;* Mark 8 Luke 3:1, 19; 8:3 23:7f., 11f., 15; A 4:27; 12:1 [b]Mat 11:2 [c]Matt. 14:6 6:17, 19, 22; Luk
4 [a]Lev. 18:16; 2
5 [1]Lit., *they wer* *holding* [a]Matt. 1

6 But when Herod's birthday [1]came, the daughter of [a]Herodias
danced [2]before *them* and pleased [b]Herod.
7 Thereupon he promised with an oath to give her whatever she
asked.
8 And having been prompted by her mother, she *said, "Give me
here on a platter the head of John the Baptist."
9 And although he was grieved, the king commanded *it* to be
given because of his oaths, and because of [1]his dinner guests.
10 And he sent and had John beheaded in the prison.
11 And his head was brought on a platter and given to the girl; and
she brought *it* to her mother.
12 And his disciples came and took away the body and buried [1]it;
and they went and reported to Jesus.
13 [a]Now when Jesus heard *it*, He withdrew from there in a boat, to
a lonely place by Himself; and when the multitudes heard *of this*,
they followed Him on foot from the cities.
14 And when He went [1]ashore, He [a]saw a great multitude, and felt
compassion for them, and [b]healed their sick.
15 And when it was evening, the disciples came to Him, saying,
"The place is desolate, and the time is already past; so send the
multitudes away, that they may go into the villages and buy food for
themselves."
16 But Jesus said to them, "They do not need to go away; you give
them *something* to eat!"
17 And they *said to Him, "We have here only [a]five loaves and two
fish."
18 And He said, "Bring them here to Me."
19 And ordering the multitudes to recline on the grass, He took the
five loaves and the two fish, and looking up toward heaven, He
[a]blessed *the food*, and breaking the loaves He gave them to the disci-
ples, and the disciples *gave* to the multitudes,
20 and they all ate, and were satisfied. And they picked up what
was left over of the broken pieces, twelve full [a]baskets.
21 And there were about five thousand men who ate, aside from
women and children.
22 [a]And immediately He [1]made the disciples get into the boat, and
go ahead of Him to the other side, while He sent the multitudes
away.
23 And after He had sent the multitudes away, [a]He went up to the
mountain by Himself to pray; and when it was evening, He was
there alone.
24 But the boat was already many [1]stadia away from the land, [2]bat-
tered by the waves; for the wind was contrary.
25 And in [a]the [1]fourth watch of the night He came to them, walking
on the sea.
26 And when the disciples saw Him walking on the sea, they were
[1]frightened, saying, "It is [a]a ghost!" And they cried out for fear.
27 But immediately Jesus spoke to them, saying, "[a]Take courage, it
is I; [b]do not be afraid."
28 And Peter answered Him and said, "Lord, if it is You, command
me to come to You on the water."
29 And He said, "Come!" And Peter got out of the boat, and
walked on the water and came toward Jesus.

...rred [2]Lit., *in* [a]Matt. 14:3; ...19, 22; Luke ...[b]att. 14:1-12: ...*:14-29;* Mark ...3:1, 19; 8:3; ...:7f., 11f., 15; ...ts 4:27; 12:1
...t., *those who* ...he table *with him*
12 [1]Lit., *him*
...att. 14:13-21: ...*6:32-44; Luke* ...*John 6:1-13;* ...att. 15:32-38
...it., *out* [a]Matt. ...6 [b]Matt. 4:23
7 [a]Matt. 16:9
...m. 9:13; Matt. ...26; Mark 6:41; ...2; Luke 24:30; ...35; Rom. 14:6
...att. 16:9; Mark ...19; Luke 9:17; John 6:13
...Lit., *compelled* ...4:22-33: *Mark* ...*; John 6:15-21*
...ark 6:46; Luke ...:28; John 6:15
[1]A stadion was ...600 feet [2]Lit., *tormented*
...3-6 a.m. [a]Matt. ...43; Mark 13:35
troubled [a]Luke 24:37
...Matt. 9:2 [b]Matt. ...; 28:5, 10; Mark ...; Luke 1:13, 30; ...10; 12:32; John 6:20; Rev. 1:17

30 But seeing the wind, he became afraid, and beginning to sink, he
cried out, saying, "Lord, save me!"
31 And immediately Jesus stretched out His hand and took hold of
him, and *said to him, "[a]O you of little faith, why did you doubt?"
32 And when they got into the boat, the wind stopped.
33 And those who were in the boat worshiped Him, saying, "You
are certainly [a]God's Son!"
34 [a]And when they had crossed over, they came to [1]land at
[b]Gennesaret.
35 And when the men of that place [1]recognized Him, they sent into
all that surrounding district and brought to Him all who were sick;
36 and they *began* to entreat Him that they might just touch [a]the
fringe of His cloak; and as many as [b]touched *it* were cured.

Chapter 15

15 [a]Then some Pharisees and scribes *came to Jesus [b]from Jerusa-
lem, saying,
2 "Why do Your disciples transgress the tradition of the elders? For
they [a]do not wash their hands when they eat bread."
3 And He answered and said to them, "And why do [1]you your-
selves transgress the commandment of God for the sake of your
tradition?
4 "For God said, '[a]HONOR YOUR FATHER AND MOTHER,' and, '[b]HE WHO
SPEAKS EVIL OF FATHER OR MOTHER, LET HIM [1]BE PUT TO DEATH.'
5 "But you say, 'Whoever shall say to *his* father or mother, "Any-
thing of mine you might have been helped by has been [1]given *to
God*,"
6 he is not to honor his father [1]or his mother[2].' And *thus* you in-
validated the [3]word of God for the sake of your tradition.
7 "You hypocrites, rightly did Isaiah prophesy of you, saying,
8 '[a]THIS PEOPLE HONORS ME WITH THEIR LIPS,
BUT THEIR HEART IS FAR AWAY FROM ME.
9 'BUT IN VAIN DO THEY WORSHIP ME,
TEACHING AS [a]DOCTRINES THE PRECEPTS OF MEN.' "
10 And after He called the multitude to Him, He said to them,
"Hear, and understand.
11 "[a]Not what enters into the mouth defiles the man, but what pro-
ceeds out of the mouth, this defiles the man."
12 Then the disciples *came and *said to Him, "Do You know that
the Pharisees were [1]offended when they heard this statement?"
13 But He answered and said, "[a]Every plant which My heavenly
Father did not plant shall be rooted up.
14 "Let them alone; [a]they are blind guides [1]of the blind. And [b]if a
blind man guides a blind man, both will fall into a pit."
15 And Peter answered and said to Him, "[a]Explain the parable to
us."
16 And He said, "Are you still lacking in understanding also?
17 "Do you not understand that everything that goes into the mouth
passes into the [1]stomach, and is [2]eliminated?
18 "But [a]the things that proceed out of the mouth come from the
heart, and those defile the man.
19 "[a]For out of the heart come evil thoughts, murders, adulteries,
[1]fornications, thefts, false witness, slanders.

31 [a]Matt. 6 16:8
33 [a]Matt. 4
34 [1]Lit., *the* 14:34-36: *M* John 6:24, 2 6:53; Luke 5
35 [1]Or, *kne*
36 [a]Matt. 9: 9:21; Mark 3 8:22; Luke 6
15:1 [a]Matt. *Mark 7:1-23* 3:22; 7:1; Jo Acts 25:7
2 [a]Luke 11:3
3 [1]Or, *you a*
4 [1]Lit., *die th* [a]Ex. 20:12; D [b]Ex. 21:17; L
5 [1]Or, *a gift,*
6 [1]Many mss contain *or his* [2]I.e., by suppo with it [3]Some *law*
8 [a]Is. 29:13
9 [a]Col. 2:22
11 [a]Matt. 15:1 10:14, 15; 1 Ti
12 [1]Lit., *caus stumble*
13 [a]Is. 60:21; John 15:2; 1 C
14 [1]Some mss contain *of the* [a]Matt. 23:16, 2 6:39
15 [a]Matt. 13:3
17 [1]Lit., *belly out into the latr*
18 [a]Matt. 12:34 7:20
19 [1]I.e., sexual immorality [a]Ga

20 "These are the things which defile the man; but to eat with un-
washed hands does not defile the man."
21 [a]And Jesus went away from there, and withdrew into the district
of [b]Tyre and [b]Sidon.
22 And behold, a Canaanite woman came out from that region, and
began to cry out, saying, "Have mercy on me, O Lord, [a]Son of David;
my daughter is cruelly [b]demon-possessed."
23 But He did not answer her a word. And His disciples came to
Him and kept asking Him, saying, "Send her away, for she is shout-
ing out after us."
24 But He answered and said, "I was sent only to [a]the lost sheep of
the house of Israel."
25 But she came and [a]*began* [1]to bow down before Him, saying,
"Lord, help me!"
26 And He answered and said, "It is not [1]good to take the children's
bread and throw it to the dogs."
27 But she said, "Yes, Lord; [1]but even the dogs feed on the crumbs
which fall from their masters' table."
28 Then Jesus answered and said to her, "O woman, [a]your faith is
great; be it done for you as you wish." And her daughter was healed
[1]at once.
29 [a]And departing from there, Jesus went along by [b]the Sea of
Galilee, and having gone up to the mountain, He was sitting there.
30 And great multitudes came to Him, bringing with them *those
who were* lame, crippled, blind, dumb, and many others, and they
laid them down at His feet; and [a]He healed them,
31 so that the multitude marveled as they saw the dumb speaking,
the crippled [1]restored, and the lame walking, and the blind seeing;
and they [a]glorified the God of Israel.
32 [a]And Jesus called His disciples to Him, and said, "[b]I feel compas-
sion for the multitude, because they [1]have remained with Me now
three days and have nothing to eat; and I do not wish to send them
away hungry, lest they faint on the way."
33 And the disciples *said to Him, "Where would we get so many
loaves in a desolate place to satisfy such a great multitude?"
34 And Jesus *said to them, "How many loaves do you have?" And
they said, "Seven, and a few small fish."
35 And He directed the multitude to [1]sit down on the ground;
36 and He took the seven loaves and the fish; and [a]giving thanks,
He broke them and started giving them to the disciples, and the
disciples *in turn,* to the multitudes.
37 And they all ate, and were satisfied, and they picked up what
was left over of the broken pieces, seven large [a]baskets full.
38 And those who ate were four thousand men, besides women
and children.
39 And sending away the multitudes, He got into [a]the boat, and
came to the region of [b]Magadan.

Chapter 16

16 [a]And the [b]Pharisees and Sadducees came up, and testing Him
[c]asked Him to show them a [1]sign from heaven.
2 But He answered and said to them, [1]"[a]When it is evening, you
say, '*It will be* fair weather, for the sky is red.'
3 "And in the morning, '*There will be* a storm today, for the sky is

[a]Matt. 15:21-28: ...rk *7:24-30* [b]Matt. 11:21
[a]Matt. 9:27 [b]Matt. 4:24
24 [a]Matt. 10:6
...5 [1]Or, *to worship* [a]Matt. 8:2
26 [1]Or, *proper*
27 [1]Lit., *for*
...it., *from that hour* [a]Matt. 9:22
[a]Matt. 15:29-31; ...k 7:31-37 [b]Matt. 4:18
30 [a]Matt. 4:23
...r, *healthy* [a]Matt. 9:8
...it., *are remaining* ... 15:32-39: *Mark* ...; Matt. 14:13-21 [b]Matt. 9:36
35 [1]Lit., *recline*
...att. 14:19; 26:27; ... 22:17, 19; John ..., 23; Acts 27:35; Rom. 14:6
...att. 16:10; Mark ...:8, 20; Acts 9:25
[a]Mark 3:9 [b]Mark 8:10
...:1 [1]Or, *attesting* ... [a]Matt. 16:1-12: ...k *8:11-21* [b]Matt. ...:6, 11, 12 [c]Matt. ...2:38; Luke 11:16
... earliest mss. do ...tain the rest of v. 3. [a]Luke 12:54f.

red and threatening.' [a]Do you know how to discern the [1]appearance
of the sky, but cannot *discern* the signs of the times?
4 "[a]An evil and adulterous generation seeks after a [1]sign; and a
[1]sign will not be given it, except the sign of Jonah." And He left
them, and went away.
5 And the disciples came to the other side and had forgotten to
take bread.
6 And Jesus said to them, "Watch out and [a]beware of the [1]leaven of
the [b]Pharisees and Sadducees."
7 And they began to discuss among themselves, saying, "*It is* be-
cause we took no bread."
8 But Jesus, aware of this, said, "[a]You men of little faith, why do
you discuss among yourselves that you have no bread?
9 "Do you not yet understand or remember [a]the five loaves of the
five thousand, and how many baskets you took up?
10 "Or [a]the seven loaves of the four thousand, and how many large
baskets you took up?
11 "How is it that you do not understand that I did not speak to you
concerning bread? But [a]beware of the [1]leaven of the [b]Pharisees and
Sadducees."
12 Then they understood that He did not say to beware of the
leaven of bread, but of the teaching of the [a]Pharisees and Sadducees.
13 [a]Now when Jesus came into the district of [b]Caesarea Philippi, He
began asking His disciples, saying, "Who do people say that [c]the Son
of Man is?"
14 And they said, "Some *say* [a]John the Baptist; and others, [1b]Elijah;
but still others, [2]Jeremiah, or one of the prophets."
15 He *said to them, "But who do you say that I am?"
16 And Simon Peter answered and said, "Thou art [1a]the Christ, [b]the
Son of [c]the living God."
17 And Jesus answered and said to him, "Blessed are you, [a]Simon
[1]Barjona, because [b]flesh and blood did not reveal *this* to you, but My
Father who is in heaven.
18 "And I also say to you that you are [1a]Peter, and upon this [2]rock I
will build My church; and the gates of [b]Hades shall not overpower it.
19 "I will give you [a]the keys of the kingdom of heaven; and
[b]whatever you shall bind on earth [1]shall be bound in heaven, and
whatever you shall loose on earth [1]shall be loosed in heaven."
20 [a]Then He [1]warned the disciples that they should tell no one that
He was [2b]the Christ.
21 [a]From that time Jesus Christ began to show His disciples that He
must go to Jerusalem, and [b]suffer many things from the elders and
chief priests and scribes, and be killed, and be raised up on the third
day.
22 And Peter took Him aside and began to rebuke Him, saying,
"[1]God forbid *it*, Lord! This shall never [2]happen to You."
23 But He turned and said to Peter, "Get behind Me, [a]Satan! You are
a stumbling block to Me; for you are not setting your mind on
[1]God's interests, but man's."
24 Then Jesus said to His disciples, "If anyone wishes to come after
Me, let him deny himself, and [a]take up his cross, and follow Me.
25 "For [a]whoever wishes to save his [1]life shall lose it; but whoever
loses his [1]life for My sake shall find it.
26 "For what will a man be profited, if he gains the whole world,

3 [1]Lit., *face* [a]Luk
4 [1]Or, *attesting m* [a]Matt. 12:39; Luk
6 [1]Or, *yeast* [a]Ma 8:15; Luke 12:1 3:7
8 [a]Matt. 6:30; 8:2 14:31
9 [a]Matt. 14:17-2
10 [a]Matt. 15:34-
11 [1]Or, *yeast* [a]M 16:6; Mark 8:15; 12:1 [b]Matt. 3:7;
12 [a]Matt. 3:7; 5:2
13 [a]Matt. 16:13- *Mark 8:27-29; Lu 9:18-20* [b]Mark 8 [c]Matt. 8:20; 16:2
14 [1]Gr., *Elias* [2]G *Jeremias* [a]Matt. [b]Matt. 17:10; Ma Luke 9:8; John 1
16 [1]I.e., the Mes [a]Matt. 1:16; 16:2 11:27 [b]Matt. 4:3 42:2; Matt. 26:63 14:15; Rom. 9:26 3:3; 6:16; 1 Thes 1 Tim. 3:15; 4:10 3:12; 9:14; 10:31 Rev. 7:2
17 [1]I.e., son of J [a]John 1:42; 21:1 [b]1 Cor. 15:50; Ga Eph. 6:12; Heb.
18 [1]Gr., *Petros*, stone [2]Gr., *petra* rock, bed-rock [a] 4:18 [b]Matt. 11:2
19 [1]Or, *shall ha been* [a]Is. 22:22; 1:18; 3:7 [b]Matt. John 20:23
20 [1]Or, *strictly admonished* [2]I.e Messiah [a]Matt. Mark 8:30; Luke [b]Matt. 1:16; 16:1 11:27
21 [a]Matt. 16:21- *Mark 8:31-9:1; L 9:22-27* [b]Matt. 1 17:9, 12, 22f.; 20 27:63; Mark 9:12 Luke 17:25; 18:3 John 2:19
22 [1]Lit., (God be *merciful to You*
23 [1]Lit., *the thin God* [a]Matt. 4:10
24 [a]Matt. 10:38; 14:27
25 [1]Or, *soul* [a]M 10:39

and forfeits his soul? Or what will a man give in exchange for his
soul?
27 "For the [a]Son of Man [b]is going to come in the glory of His Father
with His angels; and [c]WILL THEN RECOMPENSE EVERY MAN ACCORDING TO
HIS [1]DEEDS.
28 "Truly I say to you, there are some of those who are standing here
who shall not taste death until they see the [a]Son of Man [b]coming in
His kingdom."

Chapter 17

17 [a]And six days later Jesus *took with Him [b]Peter and [1]James
and John his brother, and *brought them up to a high moun-
tain by themselves.
2 And He was transfigured before them; and His face shone like
the sun, and His garments became as white as light.
3 And behold, Moses and Elijah appeared to them, talking with
Him.
4 And Peter answered and said to Jesus, "Lord, it is good for us to
be here; if You wish, [a]I will make three [1]tabernacles here, one for You,
and one for Moses, and one for Elijah."
5 While he was still speaking, behold, a bright cloud over-
shadowed them; and behold, [a]a voice out of the cloud, saying, "[b]This
is My beloved Son, with whom I am well-pleased; listen to Him!"
6 And when the disciples heard *this,* they fell on their faces and
were much afraid.
7 And Jesus came to *them* and touched them and said, "Arise, and
[a]do not be afraid."
8 And lifting up their eyes, they saw no one, except Jesus Himself
alone.
9 [a]And as they were coming down from the mountain, Jesus com-
manded them, saying, "[b]Tell the vision to no one until [c]the Son of
Man has [d]risen from the dead."
10 And His disciples asked Him, saying, "Why then do the scribes
say that [a]Elijah must come first?"
11 And He answered and said, "Elijah is coming and will restore all
things;
12 but I say to you, that Elijah already came, and they did not
recognize him, but did [1]to him whatever they wished. So also [a]the
Son of Man is going to suffer [2]at their hands."
13 Then the disciples understood that He had spoken to them about
John the Baptist.
14 [a]And when they came to the multitude, a man came up to Him,
falling on his knees before Him, and saying,
15 "[1]Lord, have mercy on my son, for he is a [a]lunatic, and is very ill;
for he often falls into the fire, and often into the water.
16 "And I brought him to Your disciples, and they could not cure
him."
17 And Jesus answered and said, "O unbelieving and perverted
generation, how long shall I be with you? How long shall I put up
with you? Bring him here to Me."
18 And Jesus rebuked him, and the demon came out of him, and
the boy was cured [1]at once.
19 Then the disciples came to Jesus privately and said, "Why could
we not cast it out?"

doing [a]Matt. 10:23; 24:3, 26:64; Mark Luke 21:27; 2; Acts 1:11; 23; 1 Thess. 2 Thess. 1:7, James 5:7f.; :16; 3:4, 12; :28; Rev. 1:7 Prov. 24:12; 14:12; 1 Cor. r. 5:10; Eph. l. 3:25; Rev. 20:12; 22:12

. 8:20 [b]Matt. 3, 27, 37, 39; 8:38; 13:26; ; John 21:22; 1 Cor. 15:23; s. 1:10; 4:16; :7, 10; 2:1, 8; .; 2 Pet. 1:16; ; 1 John 2:28; Rev. 1:7

Jacob [a]Matt. 3: *Mark 9:2-8;* *:28-36* [b]Matt. ark 5:37; 13:3

, sacred tents 9:5; Luke 9:33

ark 1:11; Luke Pet. 1:17f. [b]Is. tt. 3:17; 12:18

7 [a]Matt. 14:27

17:9-13: *Mark* att. 8:4 [c]Matt. 7:12, 22 [d]Matt. 16:21

[a]Mal. 4:5; Matt. 11:14; 16:14

n him; or, *in his* [2]Lit., *by them* . 8:20; 17:9, 22

[a]Matt. 17:14-19: *k 9:14-28;* Matt. 8: *Luke 9:37-42*

Sir [a]Matt. 4:24

., from that hour

20 And He *said to them, "Because of the littleness of your faith; for
truly I say to you, [a]if you have faith as [b]a mustard seed, you shall say
to [c]this mountain, 'Move from here to there,' and it shall move; and
[d]nothing shall be impossible to you.
21 ["[1a]But this kind does not go out except by prayer and fasting."]
22 [a]And while they were gathering together in Galilee, Jesus said to
them, "The Son of Man is going to be [1]delivered into the hands of
men;
23 and [a]they will kill Him, and He will be raised on the third day."
And they were deeply grieved.
24 And when they had come to Capernaum, those who collected
[a]the [1]two-drachma *tax* came to Peter, and said, "Does your teacher
not pay [a]the [1]two-drachma *tax*?"
25 He *said, "Yes." And when he came into the house, Jesus [1]spoke
to him first, saying, "What do you think, Simon? From whom do the
kings of the earth collect [a]customs or [b]poll-tax, from their sons or
from strangers?"
26 And upon his saying, "From strangers," Jesus said to him, "Con-
sequently the sons are [1]exempt.
27 "But, lest we [1a]give them offense, go to the sea, and throw in a
hook, and take the first fish that comes up; and when you open its
mouth, you will find a [2]stater. Take that and give it to them for you
and Me."

Chapter 18

18 [a]At that [1]time the disciples came to Jesus, saying, "[b]Who then
is [2]greatest in the kingdom of heaven?"
2 And He called a child to Himself and set him [1]before them,
3 and said, "Truly I say to you, unless you [1]are converted and
[a]become like children, you shall not enter the kingdom of heaven.
4 "Whoever then humbles himself as this child, he is the greatest in
the kingdom of heaven.
5 "And whoever receives one such child in My name receives Me;
6 but [a]whoever [b]causes one of these little ones who believe in Me
to stumble, it is better for him that a [1]heavy millstone be hung
around his neck, and that he be drowned in the depth of the sea.
7 "Woe to the world because of *its* stumbling blocks! For [a]it is in-
evitable that stumbling blocks come; but woe to that man through
whom the stumbling block comes!
8 "And [a]if your hand or your foot causes you to stumble, cut it off
and throw it from you; it is better for you to enter life crippled or
lame, than having two hands or two feet, to be cast into the eternal
fire.
9 "And [a]if your eye causes you to stumble, pluck it out, and throw
it from you. It is better for you to enter life with one eye, than having
two eyes, to be cast into the [1b]fiery hell.
10 "See that you do not despise one of these little ones, for I say to
you, that [a]their angels in heaven continually behold the face of My
Father who is in heaven.
11 ["[1a]For the Son of Man has come to save that which was lost.]
12 "What do you think? [a]If any man [1]has a hundred sheep, and one
of them has gone astray, does he not leave the ninety-nine on the
mountains and go and search for the one that is straying?

20 [a]Matt. 21 11:23f.; Luke [b]Matt. 13:31; [c]Matt. 17:9; 1 [d]Mark 9:23; J

21 [1]Many m contain this v 9:29

22 [1]Or, *betra* 17:22, 23: *Ma* *9:30-32; Luke*

23 [a]Matt. 16:

24 [1]Equivale denarii or two wages paid a tax [a]Ex. 30:1

25 [1]Or, *antici what he was say,* [a]Rom. 1 22:17, 19

26 [1]Or, *free*

27 [1]Lit., *cause stumble* [2]Or, s worth four dra [a]Matt. 5:29, 30 9; Mark 9:42, 4 Luke 17:2; Joh 1 Cor. 8:13

18:1 [1]Lit., *hou greater* [a]Matt. *Mark 9:33-37; 9:46-48* [b]Luke

2 [1]Lit., *in their*

3 [1]Lit., *are turr* [a]Matt. 19:14; M 10:15; Luke 18 1 Cor. 14:20; 1

6 [1]Lit., *millston by a donkey* [a]M 9:42; Luke 17:2 8:12 [b]Matt. 17:

7 [a]Luke 17:1; 1 11:19; 1 Tim. 4:

8 [a]Matt. 5:30; M

9 [1]Lit., *Gehenn* [a]Matt. 5:29; Mar [b]Matt. 5:22

10 [a]Luke 1:19; 12:15; Rev. 8:2

11 [1]Most ancien do not contain th [a]Luke 19:10

12 [1]Or, *comes t* [a]Matt. 18:12-14: *15:4-7*

13 "And if it turns out that he finds it, truly I say to you, he rejoices over it more than over the ninety-nine which have not gone astray.

14 "Thus it is not *the* will [1]of your Father who is in heaven that one of these little ones perish.

15 "And [a]if your brother sins[1], go and reprove him [2]in private; if he listens to you, you have won your brother.

16 "But if he does not listen *to you*, take one or two more with you, so that [a]BY THE MOUTH OF TWO OR THREE WITNESSES EVERY [1]FACT MAY BE CONFIRMED.

17 "And if he refuses to listen to them, [a]tell it to the church; and if he refuses to listen even to the church, [b]let him be to you as [1]a Gentile and [1]a [2]tax-gatherer.

18 "Truly I say to you, [a]whatever you shall [1]bind on earth [2]shall be bound in heaven; and whatever you [3]loose on earth [2]shall be loosed in heaven.

19 "Again I say to you, that if two of you agree on earth about anything that they may ask, [a]it shall be done for them [1]by My Father who is in heaven.

20 "For where two or three have gathered together in My name, [a]there I am in their midst."

21 Then Peter came and said to Him, "Lord, [a]how often shall my brother sin against me and I forgive him? Up to [b]seven times?"

22 Jesus *said to him, "I do not say to you, up to seven times, but up to [a]seventy times seven.

23 "For this reason [a]the kingdom of heaven may be compared to a certain king who wished to [b]settle accounts with his slaves.

24 "And when he had begun to settle *them*, there was brought to him one who owed him [1]ten thousand talents.

25 "But since he [1a]did not have *the means* to repay, his lord commanded him [b]to be sold, along with his wife and children and all that he had, and repayment to be made.

26 "The slave therefore falling down, [a]prostrated himself before him, saying, 'Have patience with me, and I will repay you everything.'

27 "And the lord of that slave felt compassion and released him and [a]forgave him the [1]debt.

28 "But that slave went out and found one of his fellow slaves who owed him a hundred [1]denarii; and he seized him and *began* to choke *him*, saying, 'Pay back what you owe.'

29 "So his fellow slave fell down and *began* to entreat him, saying, 'Have patience with me and I will repay you.'

30 "He was unwilling however, but went and threw him in prison until he should pay back what was owed.

31 "So when his fellow slaves saw what had happened, they were deeply grieved and came and reported to their lord all that had happened.

32 "Then summoning him, his lord *said to him, 'You wicked slave, I forgave you all that debt because you entreated me.

33 '[a]Should you not also have had mercy on your fellow slave, even as I had mercy on you?'

34 "And his lord, moved with anger, handed him over to the torturers until he should repay all that was owed him.

35 "[a]So shall My heavenly Father also do to you, if each of you does not forgive his brother from [1]your heart."

[1]Lit., *before*

...any mss. add ...nst you [2]Lit., *you and him* ... 19:17; Luke ...6:1; 2 Thess. ...; James 5:19

...*word* [a]Deut. ...19:15; ...18:17; 2 Cor. ...m. 5:19; Heb. 10:28

...Lit., *the* [2]I.e., ...ctor of Roman ...profit [a]1 Cor. ...hess. 3:6, 14f.

...*bid* [2]Or, *shall* ...*en* [3]Or, *permit* ...9; John 20:23

...*om* [a]Matt. 7:7

...) [a]Matt. 28:20

... 18:15 [b]Luke 17:4

22 [a]Gen. 4:24

...t. 13:24 [b]Matt. 25:19

...ut $10,000,000 ...ver content but ...much more in buying power

...*was unable to* ...7:42 [b]Ex. 21:2; ...5:39; 2 Kin. 4:1; Neh. 5:5

26 [a]Matt. 8:2

...*oan* [a]Luke 7:42

...e denarius was ...ent to one day's wage

...Matt. 6:12; Eph. 4:32

[1]Lit., *your hearts* [a]Matt. 6:14

Chapter 19

19 [a]And it came about that when Jesus had finished these words,
He departed from Galilee, and [b]came into the region of Judea
beyond the Jordan;
2 and great multitudes followed Him, and [a]He healed them there.

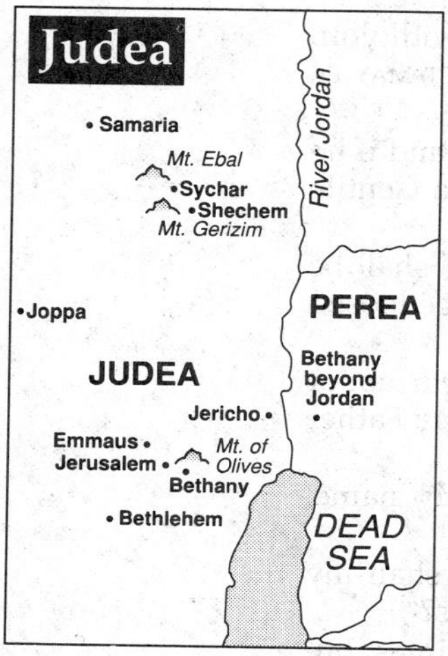

3 And *some* Pharisees came to Him, testing Him, and
saying, "[a]Is it lawful *for a man* to [1]divorce his wife for any
cause at all?"
4 And He answered and said, "Have you not read, [a]that
He who created *them* from the beginning MADE THEM MALE
AND FEMALE,
5 and said, '[a]FOR THIS CAUSE A MAN SHALL LEAVE HIS FATHER
AND MOTHER, AND SHALL CLEAVE TO HIS WIFE; AND [b]THE TWO
SHALL BECOME ONE FLESH'?
6 "Consequently they are no longer two, but one flesh.
What therefore God has joined together, let no man
separate."
7 They *said to Him, "[a]Why then did Moses command to
GIVE HER A CERTIFICATE OF DIVORCE AND SEND *her* AWAY?"
8 He *said to them, "[1]Because of your hardness of heart,
Moses permitted you to [2]divorce your wives; but from the
beginning it has not been this way.
9 "And I say to you, [a]whoever [1]divorces his wife, except
for [2]immorality, and marries another woman [3]commits adultery[4]."
10 The disciples *said to Him, "If the relationship of the man with
his wife is like this, it is better not to marry."
11 But He said to them, "[a]Not all men *can* accept this statement, but
[b]*only* those to whom it has been given.
12 "For there are eunuchs who were born that way from their
mother's womb; and there are eunuchs who were made eunuchs by
men; and there are *also* eunuchs who made themselves eunuchs for
the sake of the kingdom of heaven. He who is able to accept *this*, let
him accept *it*."
13 [a]Then *some* children were brought to Him so that He might lay
His hands on them and pray; and the disciples rebuked them.
14 But Jesus said, "[1a]Let the children alone, and do not hinder them
from coming to Me; for [b]the kingdom of heaven belongs to such as
these."
15 And after laying His hands on them, He departed from there.
16 [a]And behold, one came to Him and said, "Teacher, what good
thing shall I do that I may obtain [b]eternal life?"
17 And He said to him, "Why are you asking Me about what is
good? There is *only* One who is good; but [a]if you wish to enter into
life, keep the commandments."
18 He *said to Him, "Which ones?" And Jesus said, "[a]YOU SHALL
NOT COMMIT MURDER; YOU SHALL NOT COMMIT ADULTERY; YOU SHALL NOT
STEAL; YOU SHALL NOT BEAR FALSE WITNESS;
19 [a]HONOR YOUR FATHER AND MOTHER; and [b]YOU SHALL LOVE YOUR
NEIGHBOR AS YOURSELF."
20 The young man *said to Him, "All these things I have kept; what
am I still lacking?"
21 Jesus said to him, "If you wish to be [1]complete, go *and* [a]sell your
possessions and give to *the* poor, and you shall have [b]treasure in
heaven; and come, follow Me."

19:1 [a]Matt. 19:1-9: *Mark*
2 [a]Matt. 4:2
3 [1]Or, *send* [a]Matt. 5:31
4 [a]Gen. 1:27
5 [a]Gen. 2:24 5:31 [b]1 Cor.
7 [a]Deut. 24:1 5:31
8 [1]Or, *With r* *to* [2]Or, *send*
9 [1]Or, *sends* [2]I.e., sexual in [3]Some early m *makes her co* *adultery* [4]Sor mss. add *and marries a divo woman comm adultery* [a]Mat
11 [a]1 Cor. 7:7 13:11
13 [a]Matt. 19:1 *Mark 10:13-16 18:15-17*
14 [1]Or, *Permi children* [a]Matt. Mark 10:15; Lu 1 Cor. 14:20; 1 [b]Matt. 5:3
16 [a]Matt. 19:16 *Mark 10:17-30, 18:18-30;* Luke 10:25-28 [b]Matt
17 [a]Lev. 18:5; 9:29; Ezek. 20:
18 [a]Ex. 20:13- 5:17-20
19 [a]Ex. 20:12; 5:16 [b]Lev. 19:1
21 [1]Or, *perfect* 12:33; 16:9; Acts 4:34f. [b]Matt. 6:2

22 But when the young man heard this statement, he went away
grieved; for he was one who owned much property.
23 And Jesus said to His disciples, "Truly I say to you, [a]it is hard for
a rich man to enter the kingdom of heaven.
24 "And again I say to you, [a]it is easier for a camel to go through the
eye of a needle, than for a rich man to enter the kingdom of God."
25 And when the disciples heard *this,* they were very astonished
and said, "Then who can be saved?"
26 And looking upon *them* Jesus said to them, "[a]With men this is
impossible, but with God all things are possible."
27 Then Peter answered and said to Him, "Behold, we have left
everything and followed You; what then will there be for us?"
28 And Jesus said to them, "Truly I say to you, that you who have
followed Me, in the regeneration when [a]the Son of Man will sit on
[1]His glorious throne, [b]you also shall sit upon twelve thrones, judging
the twelve tribes of Israel.
29 "And [a]everyone who has left houses or brothers or sisters or
father or mother[1] or children or farms for My name's sake, shall
receive [2]many times as much, and shall inherit eternal life.
30 "[a]But many *who are* first will be last; and *the* last, first.

Chapter 20

20 "For [a]the kingdom of heaven is like [1]a landowner who went
out early in the morning to hire laborers [2]for his [b]vineyard.
2 "And when he had agreed with the laborers for a [1]denarius for
the day, he sent them into his vineyard.
3 "And he went out about the [1]third hour and saw others standing
idle in the market place;
4 and to those he said, 'You too go into the vineyard, and
whatever is right I will give you.' And *so* they went.
5 "Again he went out about the [1]sixth and the ninth hour, and did
[2]the same thing.
6 "And about the [1]eleventh *hour* he went out, and found others
standing; and he *said to them, 'Why have you been standing here
idle all day long?'
7 "They *said to him, 'Because no one hired us.' He *said to them,
'You too go into the vineyard.'
8 "And when [a]evening had come, the [1]owner of the vineyard *said
to his [b]foreman, 'Call the laborers and pay them their wages, begin-
ning with the last *group* to the first.'
9 "And when those *hired* about the eleventh hour came, each one
received a [1]denarius.
10 "And when those *hired* first came, they thought that they would
receive more; and they also received each one a denarius.
11 "And when they received it, they grumbled at the landowner,
12 saying, 'These last men have worked *only* one hour, and you
have made them equal to us who have borne the burden and the
[a]scorching heat of the day.'
13 "But he answered and said to one of them, '[a]Friend, I am doing
you no wrong; did you not agree with me for a denarius?
14 'Take what is yours and go your way, but I wish to give to this
last man the same as to you.
15 'Is it not lawful for me to do what I wish with what is my own?
Or is your [a]eye [1]envious because I am [2]generous?'

13:22; Mark ; Luke 18:24
10:25; Luke 18:25
n. 18:14; Job 32:17; Zech. 10:27; Luke 1:37; 18:27
the throne of [a]Matt. 25:31 30; Rev. 3:21; 4; 11:16; 20:4
y mss. add *or* y mss. read *a* *edfold* [a]Matt. 10:29f.; Luke 18:29f.
t. 20:16; Mark 1; Luke 13:30
[1]Lit., *a man, a* *wner* [2]Lit., *into* . 13:24 [b]Matt. 21:28, 33
e denarius was nt to one day's wage
3 [1]I.e., 9 a.m.
e., Noon and 3 [2]Lit., *similarly*
6 [1]I.e., 5 p.m.
rd [a]Lev. 19:13; 4:15 [b]Luke 8:3
e denarius was ent to one day's wage
[a]Jon. 4:8; Luke 55; James 1:11
att. 22:12; 26:50
, *evil* [2]Lit., *good* 15:9; Matt. 6:23; Mark 7:22

16 "Thus [a]the last shall be first, and the first last."
17 [a]And as Jesus was about to go up to Jerusalem, He took the
twelve *disciples* aside by themselves, and on the way He said to
them,
18 "Behold, we are going up to Jerusalem; and the Son of Man [a]will
be [1]delivered to the chief priests and scribes, and they will condemn
Him to death,
19 and [a]will deliver Him to the Gentiles to mock and scourge and
crucify *Him,* and on [b]the third day He will be raised up."
20 [a]Then the mother of [b]the sons of Zebedee came to Him with her
sons, [c]bowing down, and making a request of Him.
21 And He said to her, "What do you wish?" She *said to Him,
"Command that in Your kingdom these two sons of mine [a]may sit,
one on Your right and one on Your left."
22 But Jesus answered and said, "You do not know what you are
asking for. Are you able [a]to drink the cup that I am about to drink?"
They *said to Him, "We are able."
23 He *said to them, "[a]My cup you shall drink; but to sit on My
right and on *My* left, this is not Mine to give, [b]but it is for those for
whom it has been [c]prepared by My Father."
24 And hearing *this,* the ten became indignant with the two
brothers.
25 [a]But Jesus called them to Himself, and said, "You know that the
rulers of the Gentiles lord it over them, and *their* great men exercise
authority over them.
26 "It is not so among you, [a]but whoever wishes to become great
among you shall be your servant,
27 and whoever wishes to be first among you shall be your slave;
28 just as [a]the Son of Man [b]did not come to be served, but to serve,
and to give His [1]life a ransom for many."
29 [a]And as they were going out from Jericho, a great multitude
followed Him.
30 And behold, two blind men sitting by the road, hearing that
Jesus was passing by, cried out, saying, "Lord, [a]have mercy on us,
[b]Son of David!"
31 And the multitude sternly told them to be quiet; but they cried
out all the more, saying, "Lord, have mercy on us, [a]Son of David!"
32 And Jesus stopped and called them, and said, "What do you
want Me to do for you?"
33 They *said to Him, "Lord, *we want* our eyes to be opened."
34 And moved with compassion, Jesus touched their eyes; and im-
mediately they regained their sight and followed Him.

Chapter 21

21 "[a]And when they had approached Jerusalem and had come
to Bethphage, to [b]the Mount of Olives, then Jesus sent two
disciples,
2 saying to them, "Go into the village opposite you, and immedi-
ately you will find a donkey tied *there* and a colt with her; untie *them,*
and bring *them* to Me.
3 "And if anyone says something to you, you shall say, 'The Lord
has need of them,' and immediately he will send them."
4 [a]Now this took place that what was spoken through the prophet
might be fulfilled, saying,

16 [a]Matt. 19
10:31; Luke

17 [a]Matt. 20
Mark 10:32-
18:31-33

18 [1]Or, *betr*
16:21

19 [a]Matt. 27
2:23; 3:13; 4
[b]Matt. 16:21;
Luke 18:32f.

20 [a]Matt. 20
Mark 10:35-4
4:21; 10:2 [c]M

21 [a]Matt. 19

22 [a]Is. 51:17
49:12; Matt. 2
Luke 22:42; J

23 [a]Acts 12:2
[b]Matt. 13:11 [c]
25:34

25 [a]Matt. 20:2
Luke 22:25-27

26 [a]Matt. 23:1
9:35; 10:43; Lu

28 [1]Or, *soul* [a]
8:20 [b]Matt. 26
13:13ff.; 2 Cor.
2:7; 1 Tim. 2:6
2:14; Heb. 9:28

29 [a]Matt. 20:2
Mark 10:46-52,
18:35-43; Matt.

30 [a]Matt. 20:31
9:27

31 [a]Matt. 9:27

21:1 [a]Matt. 21:
Mark 11:1-10; L
19:29-38 [b]Matt.
26:30; Mark 11:
14:26; Luke 19:
21:37; 22:39; Jo
Acts 1:12

4 [a]Matt. 21:4-9:
11:7-10; Luke 1
John 12:12-15

. 62:11; Zech. 9:9
7 [1]Lit., *on them*
8 [a]2 Kin. 9:13
[a]Matt. 9:27 [b]Ps. 18:26 [c]Luke 2:14
Matt. 21:26; Mark 5; Luke 7:16, 39; 24:19; John 1:21, 4:19; 6:14; 7:40; ; Acts 3:22f.; 7:37 [b]Matt. 2:23
2 [1]Lit., *the doves* t. 21:12-16: *Mark 11:15-18; Luke* 5-47; Matt. 21:12, ohn 2:13-16 [b]Ex. 3 [c]Lev. 1:14; 5:7; 12:8
t., *cave* [a]Is. 56:7 [b]Jer. 7:11
14 [a]Matt. 4:23
15 [a]Matt. 9:27
. 8:2; Matt. 11:25
Matt. 26:6; Mark 1, 12; 14:3; Luke 24:50; John 11:1, 18; 12:1
[a]Matt. 21:18-22: *11:12-14, 20-24*
19 [a]Luke 13:6-9
latt. 17:20; Mark 1:23; Luke 17:6; James 1:6
22 [a]Matt. 7:7
[a]Matt. 21:23-27: *k 11:27-33; Luke* 1-8 [b]Matt. 26:55

From Bethany, Bethphage Across the Mount of Olives into Jerusalem

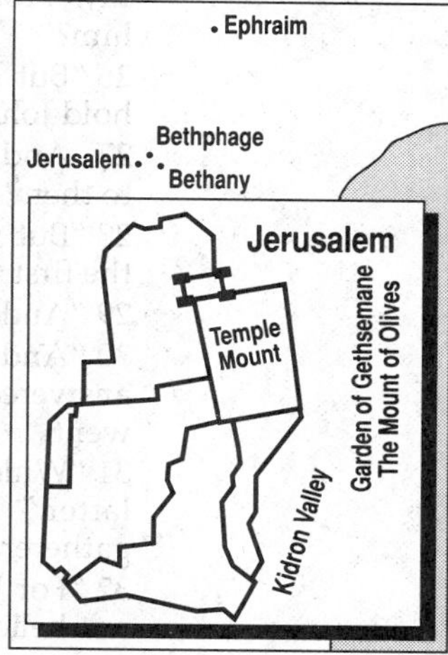

5 "[a]SAY TO THE DAUGHTER OF ZION,
'BEHOLD YOUR KING IS COMING TO YOU,
GENTLE, AND MOUNTED ON A DONKEY,
EVEN ON A COLT, THE FOAL OF A BEAST OF BURDEN.' "

6 And the disciples went and did just as Jesus had directed them,

7 and brought the donkey and the colt, and laid on them their garments, [1]on which He sat.

8 And most of the multitude [a]spread their garments in the road, and others were cutting branches from the trees, and spreading them in the road.

9 And the multitudes going before Him, and those who followed after were crying out, saying,
"Hosanna to the [a]Son of David;
[b]BLESSED IS HE WHO COMES IN THE NAME OF THE LORD;
Hosanna [c]in the highest!"

10 And when He had entered Jerusalem, all the city was stirred, saying, "Who is this?"

11 And the multitudes were saying, "This is [a]the prophet Jesus, from [b]Nazareth in Galilee."

12 [a]And Jesus entered the temple and cast out all those who were buying and selling in the temple, and overturned the tables of the [b]moneychangers and the seats of those who were selling [1c]doves.

13 And He *said to them, "It is written, '[a]MY HOUSE SHALL BE CALLED A HOUSE OF PRAYER'; but you are making it a [b]ROBBERS' [1]DEN."

14 And *the* blind and *the* lame came to Him in the temple, and [a]He healed them.

15 But when the chief priests and the scribes saw the wonderful things that He had done, and the children who were crying out in the temple and saying, "Hosanna to the [a]Son of David," they became indignant,

16 and said to Him, "Do You hear what these are saying?" And Jesus *said to them, "Yes; have you never read, '[a]OUT OF THE MOUTH OF INFANTS AND NURSING BABES THOU HAST PREPARED PRAISE FOR THYSELF'?"

17 And He left them and went out of the city to [a]Bethany, and lodged there.

18 [a]Now in the morning, when He returned to the city, He became hungry.

19 And seeing a lone [a]fig tree by the road, He came to it, and found nothing on it except leaves only; and He *said to it, "No longer shall there ever be *any* fruit from you." And at once the fig tree withered.

20 And seeing *this*, the disciples marveled, saying, "How did the fig tree wither at once?"

21 And Jesus answered and said to them, "Truly I say to you, [a]if you have faith, and do not doubt, you shall not only do what was done to the fig tree, but even if you say to this mountain, 'Be taken up and cast into the sea,' it shall happen.

22 "And [a]all things you ask in prayer, believing, you shall receive."

23 [a]And when He had come into the temple, the chief priests and the elders of the people came to Him [b]as He was teaching, and said, "By what authority are You doing these things, and who gave You this authority?"

24 And Jesus answered and said to them, "I will ask you one [1]thing
too, which if you tell Me, I will also tell you by what authority I do
these things.
25 "The baptism of John was from what *source*, from heaven or from
men?" And they *began* reasoning among themselves, saying, "If we
say, 'From heaven,' He will say to us, 'Then why did you not believe
him?'
26 "But if we say, 'From men,' we fear the multitude; for they all
hold John to be [a]a prophet."
27 And answering Jesus, they said, "We do not know." He also said
to them, "Neither will I tell you by what authority I do these things.
28 "But what do you think? A man had two [1]sons, and he came to
the first and said, '[2]Son, go work today in the [a]vineyard.'
29 "And he answered and said, '[1]I will, sir'; and he did not go.
30 "And he came to the second and said [1]the same thing. But he
answered and said, '[2]I will not'; *yet* he afterward regretted *it* and
went.
31 "Which of the two did the will of his father?" They *said, "The
latter." Jesus *said to them, "Truly I say to you that [a]the [1]tax-
gatherers and harlots [2]will get into the kingdom of God before you.
32 "For John came to you in the way of righteousness and you did
not believe him; but [a]the tax-gatherers and harlots did believe him;
and you, seeing this, did not even feel remorse afterward so as to
believe him.
33 "Listen to another parable. [a]There was a [1]landowner who
[b]PLANTED A [c]VINEYARD AND PUT A WALL AROUND IT AND DUG A WINE PRESS
IN IT, AND BUILT A TOWER, and rented it out to [2]vine-growers, and
[d]went on a journey.
34 "And when the [1]harvest time approached, he [a]sent his slaves to
the vine-growers to receive his produce.
35 "And the vine-growers took his slaves and beat one, and killed
another, and stoned a third.
36 "Again he [a]sent another group of slaves larger than the first; and
they did [1]the same thing to them.
37 "But afterward he sent his son to them, saying, 'They will respect
my son.'
38 "But when the vine-growers saw the son, they said among them-
selves, 'This is the heir; come, let us kill him, and seize his inheri-
tance.'
39 "And they took him, and threw him out of the vineyard, and
killed him.
40 "Therefore when the [1]owner of the vineyard comes, what will he
do to those vine-growers?"
41 They *said to Him, "He will bring those wretches to a wretched
end, and [a]will rent out the vineyard to other vine-growers, who will
pay him the proceeds at the *proper* seasons."
42 Jesus *said to them, "Did you never read in the Scriptures,

'[a]THE STONE WHICH THE BUILDERS REJECTED,
THIS BECAME THE CHIEF CORNER *stone*;
THIS CAME ABOUT FROM THE LORD,
AND IT IS MARVELOUS IN OUR EYES'?

43 "Therefore I say to you, the kingdom of God will be taken away
from you, and be given to a nation producing the fruit of it.

24 [1]Lit., *wor*
26 [a]Matt. 11 6:20
28 [1]Lit., *chil* *Child* [a]Matt.
29 [1]Some m *will not'; yet h afterward reg went*
30 [1]Lit., *likew* [2]Some mss. r *and he did no*
31 [1]I.e., Colle Roman taxes [2]Or, *are gettin* [a]Luke 7:29, 3
32 [a]Luke 3:12
33 [1]Lit., *a ma householder* [2] *farmers,* also v 38, 40 [a]Matt. 2 *Mark 12:1-12; 20:9-19* [b]Is. 5: [c]Matt. 20:1; 21 [d]Matt. 25:14
34 [1]Lit., *the se the fruits* [a]Matt
36 [1]Lit., *likewis* 22:4
40 [1]Lit., *lord*
41 [a]Matt. 8:11f. 13:46; 18:6; 28:
42 [a]Ps. 118:22f 4:11; Rom. 9:33 2:7

44 "And [a]he who falls on this stone will be broken to pieces; but on
whomever it falls, it will scatter him like dust."
45 And when the chief priests and the Pharisees heard His
parables, they understood that He was speaking about them.
46 And when they sought to seize Him, they [a]feared the multitudes,
because they held Him to be a [b]prophet.

Chapter 22

22 And Jesus answered and spoke to them again in parables,
saying,
2 "[a]The kingdom of heaven may be compared to [1]a king, who [2]gave
a [b]wedding feast for his son.
3 "And he [a]sent out his slaves to call those who had been invited to
the wedding feast, and they were unwilling to come.
4 "Again he [a]sent out other slaves saying, 'Tell those who have been
invited, "Behold, I have prepared my dinner; my oxen and my fattened livestock are *all* butchered and everything is ready; come to
the wedding feast."'
5 "But they paid no attention and went their way, one to his own
[1]farm, another to his business,
6 and the rest seized his slaves and mistreated them and killed
them.
7 "But the king was enraged and sent his armies, and destroyed
those murderers, and set their city on fire.
8 "Then he *said to his slaves, 'The wedding is ready, but those who
were invited were not worthy.
9 'Go therefore to [a]the main highways, and as many as you find
there, invite to the wedding feast.'
10 "And those slaves went out into the streets, and gathered together
all they found, both evil and good; and the wedding hall was filled
with [1]dinner guests.
11 "But when the king came in to look over the dinner guests, he
saw there [a]a man not dressed in wedding clothes,
12 and he *said to him, '[a]Friend, how did you come in here [1]without
wedding clothes?' And he was speechless.
13 "Then the king said to the servants, 'Bind him hand and foot, and
cast him into [a]the outer darkness; in that place there shall be weeping and gnashing of teeth.'
14 "For many are [1a]called, but few *are* [a]chosen."
15 [a]Then the Pharisees went and counseled together how they
might trap Him [1]in what He said.
16 And they *sent their disciples to Him, along with the [a]Herodians,
saying, "Teacher, we know that You are truthful and teach the way
of God in truth, and [1]defer to no one; for You are not partial to any.
17 "Tell us therefore, what do You think? Is it [1]lawful to give a [a]poll-tax to [b]Caesar, or not?"
18 But Jesus perceived their [1]malice, and said, "Why are you testing
Me, you hypocrites?
19 "Show Me the [a]coin *used* for the poll-tax." And they brought Him
a [1]denarius.
20 And He *said to them, "Whose likeness and inscription is this?"
21 They *said to Him, "Caesar's." Then He *said to them, "[a]Then
render to Caesar the things that are Caesar's; and to God the things
that are God's."

44 [a]Is. 8:14, 15
Matt. 21:26 [b]Matt. 21:11
2:2 [1]Lit., *a man, a* [2]Lit., *made* [a]Matt. :24; 22:2-14; Luke 6-24 [b]Luke 12:36; John 2:2
3 [a]Matt. 21:34
4 [a]Matt. 21:36
5 [1]Or, *field*
9 [a]Ezek. 21:21; Obad. 14
.it., *those reclining at the table*
Kin. 10:22; Zech. 3:3, 4
2 [1]Lit., *not having* Matt. 20:13; 26:50
[a]Matt. 8:12; 25:30; Luke 13:28
[1]Or, *invited* [a]Matt. ; 2 Pet. 1:10; Rev. 17:14
.it., *in word* [a]Matt. 22:15-22; *Mark 17; Luke 20:20-26*
[1]I.e., you court no s favor [a]Mark 3:6; 8:15; 12:13
7 [1]Or, *permissible* 17:25 [b]Luke 2:1; 3:1
[1]Or, *wickedness*
The denarius was alent to one day's vage [a]Matt. 17:25
[a]Mark 12:17; Luke 20:25; Rom. 13:7

22 And hearing *this,* they marveled, and [a]leaving Him, they went
away.
23 [a]On that day *some* [b]Sadducees (who say [c]there is no resurrection)
came to Him and questioned Him,
24 saying, "Teacher, Moses said, '[a]IF A MAN DIES, HAVING NO CHILDREN,
HIS BROTHER AS NEXT OF KIN SHALL MARRY HIS WIFE, AND RAISE UP AN
OFFSPRING TO HIS BROTHER.'
25 "Now there were seven brothers with us; and the first married
and died, and having no offspring left his wife to his brother;
26 so also the second, and the third, down to the seventh.
27 "And last of all, the woman died.
28 "In the resurrection therefore whose wife of the seven shall she
be? For they all had her."
29 But Jesus answered and said to them, "You are mistaken, [a]not
[1]understanding the Scriptures, or the power of God.
30 "For in the resurrection they neither [a]marry, nor are given in mar-
riage, but are like angels[1] in heaven.
31 "But regarding the resurrection of the dead, have you not read
that which was spoken to you by God, saying,
32 '[a]I AM THE GOD OF ABRAHAM, AND THE GOD OF ISAAC, AND THE GOD
OF JACOB'? He is not the God of the dead but of the living."
33 And when the multitudes heard *this,* [a]they were astonished at
His teaching.
34 [a]But when the Pharisees heard that He had put [b]the Sadducees to
silence, they gathered themselves together.
35 And one of them, [1a]a lawyer, asked Him *a question,* testing Him,
36 "Teacher, which is the great commandment in the Law?"
37 And He said to him, " '[a]YOU SHALL LOVE THE LORD YOUR GOD WITH
ALL YOUR HEART, AND WITH ALL YOUR SOUL, AND WITH ALL YOUR MIND.'
38 "This is the great and [1]foremost commandment.
39 "The second is like it, '[a]YOU SHALL LOVE YOUR NEIGHBOR AS YOUR-
SELF.'
40 "[a]On these two commandments depend the whole Law and the
Prophets."
41 [a]Now while the Pharisees were gathered together, Jesus asked
them a question,
42 saying, "What do you think about [1]the Christ, whose son is He?"
They *said to Him, "[a]*The son* of David."
43 He *said to them, "Then how does David [1a]in the Spirit call Him
'Lord,' saying,
44 '[a]THE LORD SAID TO MY LORD,
"SIT AT MY RIGHT HAND,
UNTIL I PUT THINE ENEMIES BENEATH THY FEET" '?
45 "If David then calls Him 'Lord,' how is He his son?"
46 And [a]no one was able to answer Him a word, nor did anyone
dare from that day on to ask Him another question.

Chapter 23

23 [a]Then Jesus spoke to the multitudes and to His disciples,
2 saying, "[a]The scribes and the Pharisees have seated them-
selves in the chair of Moses;
3 therefore all that they tell you, do and observe, but do not do
according to their deeds; for they say *things,* and do not do *them.*
4 "And [a]they tie up heavy loads, and lay them on men's shoulders;

22 [a]Mark 12
23 [a]Matt. 22 *Mark 12:18-* *20:27-40* [b]M [c]Acts 23:8
24 [a]Deut. 25
29 [1]Or, *know* 20:9
30 [1]Other m *God* [a]Matt. 2 17:27
32 [a]Ex. 3:6
33 [a]Matt. 7:2
34 [a]Matt. 22: *Mark 12:28-3* 10:25-37 [b]Ma
35 [1]I.e., an ex Mosaic Law [a] 7:30; 10:25; 1 52; 14:3; Titus
37 [a]Deut. 6:5
38 [1]Or, *first*
39 [a]Lev. 19:18 19:19; Gal. 5:1
40 [a]Matt. 7:12
41 [a]Matt. 22:4 *Mark 12:35-37,* *20:41-44*
42 [1]I.e., the Me [a]Matt. 9:27
43 [1]Or, *by insp* [a]2 Sam. 23:2; R 4:2
44 [a]Ps. 110:1; M 26:64; Mark 16: 2:34f.; 1 Cor. 15 Heb. 1:13; 10:13
46 [a]Mark 12:34 14:6; 20:40
23:1 [a]Matt. 23: *Mark 12:38, 39;* *20:45, 46*
2 [a]Deut. 33:3f.; 7:6, 25; Neh. 8:4
4 [a]Luke 11:46; A 15:10

but they themselves are unwilling to move them with *so much as* a
finger.
5 "But they do all their deeds [a]to be noticed by men; for they
[b]broaden their [1]phylacteries, and lengthen [c]the tassels *of their*
garments.
6 "And they [a]love the place of honor at banquets, and the chief seats
in the synagogues,
7 and respectful greetings in the market places, and being called
by men, [a]Rabbi.
8 "But [a]do not be called [b]Rabbi; for One is your Teacher, and you are
all brothers.
9 "And do not call *anyone* on earth your father; for [a]One is your
Father, He who is in heaven.
10 "And do not be called [1]leaders; for One is your Leader, *that is,*
Christ.
11 "[a]But the greatest among you shall be your servant.
12 "And [a]whoever exalts himself shall be humbled; and whoever
humbles himself shall be exalted.
13 "[a]But woe to you, scribes and Pharisees, hypocrites, [b]because you
shut off the kingdom of heaven [1]from men; for you do not enter in
yourselves, nor do you allow those who are entering to go in.
14 ["[1]Woe to you, scribes and Pharisees, hypocrites, because [a]you
devour widows' houses, even while for a pretense you make long
prayers; therefore you shall receive greater condemnation.]
15 "Woe to you, scribes and Pharisees, hypocrites, because you
travel about on sea and land to make one [1a]proselyte; and when he
becomes one, you make him twice as much a son of [2b]hell as your-
selves.
16 "Woe to you, [a]blind guides, who say, '[b]Whoever swears by the
[1]temple, that is nothing; but whoever swears by the gold of the
[1]temple, he is obligated.'
17 "You fools and blind men; [a]which is [1]more important, the gold, or
the [2]temple that sanctified the gold?
18 "And, 'Whoever swears by the altar, *that* is nothing, but whoever
swears by the [1]offering upon it, he is obligated.'
19 "You blind men, [a]which is [1]more important, the [2]offering or the
altar that sanctifies the [2]offering?
20 "Therefore he who swears by the altar, swears *both* by the altar
and by everything on it.
21 "And he who swears by the [1]temple, swears *both* by [2]the temple
and by Him who [a]dwells within it.
22 "And he who swears by heaven, [a]swears *both* by the throne of
God and by Him who sits upon it.
23 "[a]Woe to you, scribes and Pharisees, hypocrites! For you tithe
mint and dill and [1]cummin, and have neglected the weightier
provisions of the law: justice and mercy and faithfulness; but these
are the things you should have done without neglecting the others.
24 "You [a]blind guides, who strain out a gnat and swallow a camel!
25 "Woe to you, scribes and Pharisees, hypocrites! For [a]you clean the
outside of the cup and of the dish, but inside they are full [1]of robbery
and self-indulgence.
26 "You blind Pharisee, first [a]clean the inside of the cup and of the
dish, so that the outside of it may become clean also.
27 "[a]Woe to you, scribes and Pharisees, hypocrites! For you are like

[1]I.e., small boxes ntaining Scripture worn for religious ses [a]Matt. 6:1, 5, x. 13:9; Deut. 6:8; 11:18 [c]Matt. 9:20

[a]Luke 11:43; 14:7; 20:46

Matt. 23:8; 26:25, ; Mark 9:5; 10:51; 21; John 1:38, 49; 6; 4:31; 6:25; 9:2; 11:8; 20:16

James 3:1 [b]Matt. '; 26:25, 49; Mark :51; 11:21; 14:45; 1:38, 49; 3:2, 26; 1; 6:25; 9:2; 11:8; 20:16

9 [a]Matt. 6:9; 7:11

10 [1]Or, *teachers*

11 [a]Matt. 20:26

uke 14:11; 18:14

3 [1]Lit., *in front of* 23:15, 16, 23, 25, 29 [b]Luke 11:52

his v. not found in liest mss. [a]Mark 2:40; Luke 20:47

Or, *convert* [2]Gr., *enna* [a]Acts 2:10; 3:43 [b]Matt. 5:22

6 [1]Or, *sanctuary* att. 15:14; 23:24 [b]Matt. 5:33-35

Lit., *greater* [2]Or, *tuary* [a]Ex. 30:29

18 [1]Or, *gift*

Lit., *greater* [2]Or, *gift* [a]Ex. 29:37

sanctuary [2]Lit., . 8:13; Ps. 26:8; 132:14

66:1; Matt. 5:34

milar to caraway ds [a]Matt. 23:13; Luke 11:42

24 [a]Matt. 23:16

Or, *as a result of* 7:4; Luke 11:39f.

[a]Mark 7:4; Luke 11:39f.

Luke 11:44; Acts 23:3

whitewashed tombs which on the outside appear beautiful, but in-
side they are full of dead men's bones and all uncleanness.
28 "Even so you too outwardly appear righteous to men, but in-
wardly you are full of hypocrisy and lawlessness.
29 "[a]Woe to you, scribes and Pharisees, hypocrites! For you build the
tombs of the prophets and adorn the monuments of the righteous,
30 and say, 'If we had been *living* in the days of our fathers, we
would not have been partners with them in *shedding* the blood of the
prophets.'
31 "Consequently you bear witness against yourselves, that you [a]are
[1]sons of those who murdered the prophets.
32 "[1]Fill up then the measure *of the guilt* of your fathers.
33 "You serpents, [a]you brood of vipers, how shall you escape the
[1]sentence of [2b]hell?
34 "[a]Therefore, behold, [b]I am sending you prophets and wise men
and scribes; some of them you will kill and crucify, and some of
them you will [c]scourge in your synagogues, and [d]persecute from city
to city,
35 that upon you may fall *the guilt of* all the righteous blood shed on
earth, from the blood of righteous
[a]Abel to the blood of Zechariah, the
[b]son of Berechiah, whom [c]you mur-
dered between the [1]temple and the
altar.
36 "Truly I say to you, all these
things shall come upon [a]this
generation.
37 "[a]O Jerusalem, Jerusalem, who
[b]kills the prophets and stones those
who are sent to her! How often I
wanted to gather your children
together, [c]the way a hen gathers
her chicks under her wings, and
you were unwilling.
38 "Behold, [a]your house is being
left to you [1]desolate!
39 "For I say to you, from now on
you shall not see Me until you say,
'[a]BLESSED IS HE WHO COMES IN THE
NAME OF THE LORD!' "

The Temple Mount

Chapter 24

24 [a]And Jesus [b]came out from the temple and was going away
[1]when His disciples came up to point out the temple build-
ings to Him.
2 And He answered and said to them, "Do you not see all these
things? Truly I say to you, [a]not one stone here shall be left upon
another, which will not be torn down."
3 And as He was sitting on [a]the Mount of Olives, the disciples
came to Him privately, saying, "Tell us, when will these things be,
and what *will be* the sign of [b]Your coming, and of the [1]end of the
age?"
4 And Jesus answered and said to them, "[a]See to it that no one
misleads you.

29 [a]Luke 1

31 [1]Or, *des* [a]Matt. 23:34 7:51f.

32 [1]Lit., *An*

33 [1]Or, *judg* *Gehenna* [a]M Luke 3:7 [b]M

34 [a]Matt. 23 Luke 11:49-5 36:15, 16 [c]M [d]Matt. 10:23

35 [1]Or, *sanc* [a]Gen. 4:8ff.; [b]Zech. 1:1 [c]

36 [a]Matt. 10

37 [a]Matt. 23 *Luke 13:34,* 3 5:12 [c]Ruth 2

38 [1]Some ms contain *deso* 9:7f.; Jer. 22:5

39 [a]Ps. 118:2 21:9

24:1 [1]Lit., *and* 24:1-51: *Mark* *21:5-36* [b]Matt

2 [a]Luke 19:44

3 [1]Or, *consum* [a]Matt. 21:1 [b]M 16:27f.; 24:27,

4 [a]Jer. 29:8

5 "For [a]many will come in My name, saying, 'I am the [1]Christ,' and will mislead many.
6 "And you will be hearing of [a]wars and rumors of wars; see that you are not frightened, for *those things* must take place, but *that* is not yet the end.
7 "For [a]nation will rise against nation, and kingdom against kingdom, and in various places there will be [b]famines and earthquakes.
8 "[a]But all these things are *merely* the beginning of birth pangs.
9 "[a]Then they will deliver you to tribulation, and will kill you, and [b]you will be hated by all nations on account of My name.
10 "And at that time many will [1a]fall away and will deliver up one another and hate one another.
11 "And many [a]false prophets will arise, and will mislead many.
12 "And because lawlessness is increased, [1]most people's love will grow cold.
13 "[a]But the one who endures to the end, he shall be saved.
14 "And this [a]gospel of the kingdom [b]shall be preached in the whole [1c]world for a witness to all the nations, and then the end shall come.
15 "Therefore when you see the [a]ABOMINATION OF DESOLATION which was spoken of through Daniel the prophet, standing in [b]the holy place ([c]let the reader understand),
16 then let those who are in Judea flee to the mountains;
17 let him who is on [a]the housetop not go down to get the things out that are in his house;
18 and let him who is in the field not turn back to get his cloak.
19 "But [a]woe to those who are with child and to those who nurse babes in those days!
20 "But pray that your flight may not be in the winter, or on a Sabbath;
21 for then there will be a [a]great tribulation, such as has not occurred since the beginning of the world until now, nor ever shall.
22 "And unless those days had been cut short, no [1]life would have been saved; but for [a]the sake of the [2]elect those days shall be cut short.
23 "[a]Then if anyone says to you, 'Behold, here is the [1]Christ,' or '[2]There *He is*,' do not believe *him*.
24 "For false Christs and [a]false prophets will arise and will show great [1b]signs and wonders, so as to mislead, if possible, even [c]the [2]elect.
25 "Behold, I have told you in advance.
26 "If therefore they say to you, 'Behold, He is in the wilderness,' do not go forth, *or*, 'Behold, He is in the inner rooms,' do not believe *them*.
27 "[a]For just as the lightning comes from the east, and flashes even to the west, so shall the [b]coming of the [c]Son of Man be.
28 "[a]Wherever the corpse is, there the [1]vultures will gather.
29 "But immediately after the [a]tribulation of those days [b]THE SUN WILL BE DARKENED, AND THE MOON WILL NOT GIVE ITS LIGHT, AND [c]THE STARS WILL FALL from [1]the sky, and the powers of [1]the heavens will be shaken,
30 and then [a]the sign of the Son of Man will appear in the sky, and then all the tribes of the earth will mourn, and they will see [b]the SON OF MAN COMING ON THE CLOUDS OF THE SKY with power and great glory.

., Messiah [a]Matt. 1, 24; Acts 5:36f.; 1 John 2:18; 4:3
6 [a]Rev. 6:4
Chr. 15:6; Is. 19:2; Rev. 6:8, 12 [b]Acts 11:28; Rev. 6:5, 6
att. 24:8-20; Luke 21:12-24
Matt. 10:17; John [b]Matt. 10:22; John 15:18ff.
[1]Lit., *be caused to* *mble* [a]Matt. 11:6
[a]Matt. 7:15; 24:24
2 [1]Lit., *the love of many*
13 [a]Matt. 10:22
t., *inhabited earth* Matt. 4:23 [b]Rom. 0:18; Col. 1:6, 23 uke 2:1; 4:5; Acts 3; 17:6, 31; 19:27; ; 10:18; Heb. 1:6; ; Rev. 3:10; 16:14
[a]Dan. 9:27; 11:31; :11 [b]Mark 13:14; 1:20; John 11:48; Acts 6:13f.; 21:28 k 13:14; Rev. 1:3
17 [a]1 Sam. 9:25; 2 Sam. 11:2; Matt. ; Luke 5:19; 12:3; 17:31; Acts 10:9
19 [a]Luke 23:29
an. 12:1; Joel 2:2; Matt. 24:29
2 [1]Lit., *flesh* [2]Or, *osen ones* [a]Matt. ; 24:24, 31; Luke 18:7
e., Messiah [2]Lit., *ere* [a]Luke 17:23f.
24 [1]Or, *attesting* *cles* [2]Or, *chosen* [a]Matt. 7:15; 24:11 hn 4:48; 2 Thess. Matt. 22:14; 24:22, 31; Luke 18:7
uke 17:24 [b]Matt. 7, 39 [c]Matt. 8:20
[1]Or, *eagles* [a]Job :30; Ezek. 39:17; . 1:8; Luke 17:37
Or, *heaven* [a]Matt. [b]Is. 13:10; 24:23; . 32:7; Joel 2:10, :15f.; Amos 5:20; Zeph. 1:15; Matt. 29-35; Acts 2:20; 6:12-17; 8:12 [c]Is. 34:4; Rev. 6:13
[a]Matt. 24:3; Rev. [b]Dan. 7:13; Matt. 6:27; 24:3, 37, 39

31 "And [a]He will send forth His angels with [b]A GREAT TRUMPET and THEY WILL GATHER TOGETHER His [1c]elect from [d]the four winds, from one end of the sky to the other.

32 "Now learn the parable from the fig tree: when its branch has already become tender, and puts forth its leaves, you know that summer is near;

33 even so you too, when you see all these things, [1]recognize that [2]He is near, *right* [a]at the [3]door.

34 "Truly I say to you, [a]this [1]generation will not pass away until all these things take place.

35 "[a]Heaven and earth will pass away, but My words shall not pass away.

36 "But [a]of that day and hour no one knows, not even the angels of heaven, nor the Son, but the Father alone.

37 "For [1]the [a]coming of the Son of Man will be [b]just like the days of Noah.

38 "For as in those days which were before the flood they were eating and drinking, they were [a]marrying and giving in marriage, until the day that [b]Noah entered the ark,

39 and they did not [1]understand until the flood came and took them all away; so shall the [a]coming of the Son of Man be.

40 "Then there shall be two men in the field; one [1]will be taken, and one [1]will be left.

41 "[a]Two women *will be* grinding at the [1b]mill; one [2]will be taken, and one [2]will be left.

42 "Therefore [a]be on the alert, for you do not know which day your Lord is coming.

43 "But [1]be sure of this, that [a]if the head of the house had known [b]at what time of the night the thief was coming, he would have been on the alert and would not have allowed his house to be [2]broken into.

44 "For this reason [a]you be ready too; for [b]the Son of Man is coming at an hour when you do not think *He will.*

45 "[a]Who then is the [b]faithful and [c]sensible slave whom his [1]master [d]put in charge of his household to give them their food at the proper time?

46 "Blessed is that slave whom his [1]master finds so doing when he comes.

47 "Truly I say to you, that [a]he will put him in charge of all his possessions.

48 "But if that evil slave says in his heart, 'My [1]master [2]is not coming for a long time,'

49 and shall begin to beat his fellow slaves and eat and drink with [1]drunkards;

50 the [1]master of that slave will come on a day when he does not expect *him* and at an hour which he does not know,

51 and shall [1]cut him in pieces and [2]assign him a place with the hypocrites; [a]weeping shall be there and the gnashing of teeth.

Chapter 25 ______________________

25 "Then [a]the kingdom of heaven will be comparable to ten virgins, who took their [b]lamps, and went out to meet the bridegroom.

2 "And five of them were foolish, and five were [a]prudent.

31 [1]Or, *chosen c* [a]Matt. 13:41 [b]Ex Deut. 30:4; Is. 27 Zech. 9:14; 1 Cor 15:52; 1 Thess. 4 Heb. 12:19; Rev. 11:15 [c]Matt. 24:2 [d]Dan. 7:2; Zech. Rev. 7:1

33 [1]Lit., *know* [2]C [3]Lit., *doors* [a]Jam Rev. 3:20

34 [1]Or, *race* [a]Ma 10:23; 16:28; 23:

35 [a]Matt. 5:18; M 13:31; Luke 21:3

36 [a]Mark 13:32; 1:7

37 [1]Lit., *just as . were the days* [a]M 16:27; 24:3, 30, 3 [b]Gen. 6:5; 7:6-23 17:26f.

38 [a]Matt. 22:30 7:7

39 [1]Lit., *know* [a]M 16:27; 24:3, 30, 3

40 [1]Lit., *is*

41 [1]I.e., handmil *is* [a]Luke 17:35 [b] 11:5; Deut. 24:6;

42 [a]Matt. 24:43, 25:10, 13; Luke 1 21:36

43 [1]Lit., *know th dug through* [a]Ma 24:42, 44; 25:10, Luke 12:39f.; 21: [b]Matt. 14:25; Ma 13:35; Luke 12:3

44 [a]Matt. 24:42, 25:10, 13; Luke 1 21:36 [b]Matt. 24:

45 [1]Or, *lord* [a]Ma 24:45-51: *Luke 12:42-46* [b]Matt. 23; Luke 16:10 [c] 7:24; 10:16; 25:2 [d]Matt. 25:21, 23

46 [1]Or, *lord*

47 [a]Matt. 25:21,

48 [1]Or, *lord* [2]Lit.

49 [1]Lit., *those w drunk*

50 [1]Or, *lord*

51 [1]Or, *severely scourge him* [2]Lit *appoint his portic* [a]Matt. 8:12

25:1 [a]Matt. 13:2 [b]John 18:3; Acts Rev. 4:5; 8:10

2 [a]Matt. 7:24; 10 25:2ff.

3 "For when the foolish took their lamps, they took no oil with
them,
4 but the [a]prudent took oil in flasks along with their lamps.
5 "Now while the bridegroom was delaying, they all got drowsy
and *began* to sleep.
6 "But at midnight there was a shout, 'Behold, the bridegroom!
Come out to meet *him.*'
7 "Then all those virgins rose, and trimmed their lamps.
8 "And the foolish said to the prudent, 'Give us some of your oil,
for our lamps are going out.'
9 "But the [a]prudent answered, saying, 'No, there will not be enough
for us and you *too;* go instead to the dealers and buy *some* for your-
selves.'
10 "And while they were going away to make the purchase, the
bridegroom came, and those who were [a]ready went in with him to
[b]the wedding feast; and [c]the door was shut.
11 "And later the other virgins also came, saying, '[a]Lord, lord, open
up for us.'
12 "But he answered and said, 'Truly I say to you, I do not know
you.'
13 "[a]Be on the alert then, for you do not know the day nor the hour.
14 "[a]For *it is* just like a man [b]*about* to go on a journey, who called his
own slaves, and entrusted his possessions to them.
15 "And to one he gave five [1a]talents, to another, two, and to another,
one, each according to his own ability; and he [b]went on his journey.
16 "Immediately the one who had received the five [a]talents went and
traded with them, and gained five more talents.
17 "In the same manner the one who *had received* the two *talents*
gained two more.
18 "But he who received the one *talent* went away and dug in the
ground, and hid his [1]master's money.
19 "Now after a long time the master of those slaves *came and
*[a]settled accounts with them.
20 "And the one who had received the five [a]talents came up and
brought five more talents, saying, 'Master, you entrusted five talents
to me; see, I have gained five more talents.'
21 "His master said to him, 'Well done, good and [a]faithful slave; you
were faithful with a few things, I will [b]put you in charge of many
things, enter into the joy of your [1]master.'
22 "The one also who *had received* the two [a]talents came up and said,
'Master, you entrusted to me two talents; see, I have gained two
more talents.'
23 "His master said to him, 'Well done, good and [a]faithful slave; you
were faithful with a few things, I will put you in charge of many
things; enter into the joy of your master.'
24 "And the one also who had received the one [a]talent came up and
said, 'Master, I knew you to be a hard man, reaping where you did
not sow, and gathering where you scattered no *seed*.
25 'And I was afraid, and went away and hid your talent in the
ground; see, you have what is yours.'
26 "But his master answered and said to him, 'You wicked, lazy
slave, you knew that I reap where I did not sow, and gather where I
scattered no *seed*.

[a]Matt. 7:24; 10:16; 25:2ff.
[a]Matt. 7:24; 10:16; 25:2ff.
10 [a]Matt. 24:42ff. uke 12:35f. [c]Matt. 7:21ff.; Luke 13:25
[a]Matt. 7:21ff.; Luke 13:25
13 [a]Matt. 24:42ff.
4 [a]Matt. 25:14-30; e 19:12-27 [b]Matt. 21:33
talent was $1,000 ver content, much e in buying power. [a]Matt. 18:24; Luke 9:13 [b]Matt. 21:33
[a]Matt. 18:24; Luke 19:13
18 [1]Or, *lord's*
19 [a]Matt. 18:23
[a]Matt. 18:24; Luke 19:13
1 [1]Or, *lord* [a]Matt. , 47; 25:23 [b]Luke 22:29; Rev. 3:21; 21:7
[a]Matt. 18:24; Luke 19:13
[a]Matt. 24:45, 47; 25:21
[a]Matt. 18:24; Luke 19:13

27 'Then you ought to have put my money [1]in the bank, and on my
arrival I would have received my *money* back with interest.
28 'Therefore take away the talent from him, and give it to the one
who has the ten talents.'
29 "[a]For to everyone who has shall *more* be given, and he shall have
an abundance; but from the one who does not have, even what he
does have shall be taken away.
30 "And cast out the worthless slave into [a]the outer darkness; in that
place there shall be weeping and gnashing of teeth.
31 "But when [a]the Son of Man comes in His glory, and all the angels
with Him, then [b]He will sit on His glorious throne.
32 "And all the nations will be [a]gathered before Him; and He will
separate them from one another, [b]as the shepherd separates the
sheep from the goats;
33 and He will put the sheep [a]on His right, and the goats [b]on the
left.
34 "Then the King will say to those on His right, 'Come, you who are
blessed of My Father, [a]inherit the kingdom prepared for you [b]from
the foundation of the world.
35 'For [a]I was hungry, and you gave Me *something* to eat; I was
thirsty, and you gave Me drink; [b]I was a stranger, and you invited
Me in;
36 [a]naked, and you clothed Me; I was sick, and you [b]visited Me; [c]I
was in prison, and you came to Me.'
37 "Then the righteous will answer Him, saying, 'Lord, when did we
see You hungry, and feed You, or thirsty, and give You drink?
38 'And when did we see You a stranger, and invite You in, or
naked, and clothe You?
39 'And when did we see You sick, or in prison, and come to You?'
40 "And [a]the King will answer and say to them, 'Truly I say to you,
[b]to the extent that you did it to one of these brothers of Mine, *even*
the least *of them*, you did it to Me.'
41 "Then He will also say to those on His left, '[a]Depart from Me,
accursed ones, into the [b]eternal fire which has been prepared for [c]the
devil and his angels;
42 for I was hungry, and you gave Me *nothing* to eat; I was thirsty,
and you gave Me nothing to drink;
43 I was a stranger, and you did not invite Me in; naked, and you
did not clothe Me; sick, and in prison, and you did not visit Me.'
44 "Then they themselves also will answer, saying, 'Lord, when did
we see You hungry, or thirsty, or a stranger, or naked, or sick, or in
prison, and did not [1]take care of You?'
45 "Then He will answer them, saying, 'Truly I say to you, to the
extent that you did not do it to one of the least of these, you did not
do it to Me.'
46 "And these will go away into [a]eternal punishment, but the right-
eous into [b]eternal life."

Chapter 26

26 [a]And it came about that when Jesus had finished all these
words, He said to His disciples,
2 "[a]You know that after two days [b]the Passover is coming, and the
Son of Man is *to be* [c]delivered up for crucifixion."

27 [1]Lit., *to the*

29 [a]Matt. 13:1
4:25; Luke 8:1
15:2

30 [a]Matt. 8:12
Luke 13:28

31 [a]Matt. 16:2
1 Thess. 4:16;
1:7; Heb. 9:28;
Rev. 1:7 [b]Matt

32 [a]Matt. 13:4
5:10 [b]Ezek. 34

33 [a]1 Kin. 2:19
45:9 [b]Eccl. 10

34 [a]Matt. 5:3; 1
Luke 12:32; 1 C
15:50; Gal. 5:21
2:5 [b]Matt. 13:3
11:50; John 17:
1:4; Heb. 4:3; 9
1 Pet. 1:20; Rev
17:8

35 [a]Is. 58:7; Ez
16; James 2:15,
[b]Job 31:32; Heb

36 [a]Is. 58:7; Ez
16; James 2:15,
[b]James 1:27 [c]2
1:16f.

40 [a]Matt. 25:34
19:38; Rev. 17:1
19:16 [b]Prov. 19
Matt. 10:42; Heb

41 [a]Matt. 7:23
9:48; Luke 16:24
7 [c]Matt. 4:10; Re

44 [1]Or, *serve*

46 [a]Dan. 12:2; J
5:29; Acts 24:15
19:29; John 3:15
5:24; 6:27, 40, 47
17:2f.; Acts 13:46
Rom. 2:7; 5:21; 6
Gal. 6:8; 1 John 5

26:1 [a]Matt. 7:28

2 [a]Matt. 26:2-5:
14:1, 2; Luke 22:1
[b]John 11:55; 13:1
10:4

3 [a]Then the chief priests and the elders of the people were
gathered together in [b]the court of the high priest, named [c]Caiaphas;
4 and they [a]plotted together to seize Jesus by stealth, and kill *Him*.
5 But they were saying, "Not during the festival, [a]lest a riot occur
among the people."
6 [a]Now when Jesus was in [b]Bethany, at the home of Simon the
leper,
7 [a]a woman came to Him with an alabaster vial of very costly
perfume, and she poured it upon His head as He reclined *at the table*.
8 But the disciples were indignant when they saw *this*, and said,
"Why this waste?
9 "For this *perfume* might have been sold for a high price and *the
money* given to the poor."
10 But Jesus, aware of this, said to them, "Why do you bother the
woman? For she has done a good deed to Me.
11 "For [a]the poor you have with you always; but you do not always
have Me.
12 "For when she poured this perfume upon My body, she did it [a]to
prepare Me for burial.
13 "Truly I say to you, [a]wherever this gospel is preached in the
whole world, what this woman has done shall also be spoken of in
memory of her."
14 [a]Then one of the twelve, named [b]Judas Iscariot, went to the chief
priests,
15 and said, "What are you willing to give me [1]to [2a]deliver Him up
to you?" And [b]they weighed out to him thirty [3]pieces of silver.
16 And from then on he *began* looking for a good opportunity to
[1]betray Him.
17 [a]Now on the first *day* of [b]Unleavened Bread the disciples came to
Jesus, saying, "Where do You want us to prepare for You to eat the
Passover?"
18 And He said, "Go into the city to [a]a certain man, and say to him,
'The Teacher says, "[b]My time is at hand; I *am to* keep the Passover at
your house with My disciples."'"
19 And the disciples did as Jesus had directed them; and they pre-
pared the Passover.
20 [a]Now when evening had come, He was reclining *at the table* with
the twelve disciples.
21 And as they were eating, He said, "[a]Truly I say to you that one of
you will betray Me."
22 And being deeply grieved, they [1]each one began to say to Him,
"Surely not I, Lord?"
23 And He answered and said, "[a]He who dipped his hand with Me
in the bowl is the one who will betray Me.
24 "The Son of Man *is to* go, [a]just as it is written of Him; but woe to
that man by whom the Son of Man is betrayed! [b]It would have been
good [1]for that man if he had not been born."
25 And [a]Judas, who was betraying Him, answered and said, "Sure-
ly it is not I, [b]Rabbi?" He *said to him, "[c]You have said *it* yourself."
26 [a]And while they were eating, Jesus took *some* bread, and [1b]after a
blessing, He broke *it* and gave *it* to the disciples, and said, "Take, eat;
this is My body."
27 And when He had taken a cup and given thanks, He gave *it* to
them, saying, "Drink from it, all of you;

ohn 11:47 [b]Matt. 3, 69; 27:27; Mark 4, 66; 15:16; Luke 22:55; John 18:15 . 26:57; Luke 3:2; 11:49; 18:13, 14, 24, 28; Acts 4:6

4 [a]Matt. 12:14

5 [a]Matt. 27:24

att. 26:6-13: *Mark -9;* Luke 7:37-39; hn 12:1-8 [b]Matt. 21:17

7 [a]Luke 7:37f.

Deut. 15:11; Mark 14:7; John 12:8

12 [a]John 19:40

13 [a]Mark 14:9

[a]Matt. 26:14-16: *k 14:10, 11; Luke 2:3-6* [b]Matt. 10:4; 5, 47; 27:3; John 12:4; 13:26; Acts 1:16

it., *and I will* [2]Or, *betray* [3]Or, *silver ekels* [a]Matt. 10:4 1:32; Zech. 11:12

r, *deliver Him up*

[a]Matt. 26:17-19: *k 14:12-16; Luke 13* [b]Ex. 12:18-20

Mark 14:13; Luke 2:10 [b]John 7:6, 8

[a]Matt. 26:20-24: *Mark 14:17-21*

[a]Luke 22:21-23; John 13:21f.

22 [1]Or, *one after another*

[a]Ps. 41:9; John 13:18, 26

Lit., *for him if that ad not been born* att. 26:31, 54, 56; Mark 9:12; Luke 4:25-27, 46; Acts f.; 26:22f.; 1 Cor. 5:3; 1 Pet. 1:10f. 18:7; Mark 14:21

att. 26:14 [b]Matt. 3:7; 26:49 [c]Matt. 7:11; Luke 22:70

26 [1]Lit., *having blessed* [a]Matt. 26:26-29: *Mark 14:22-25; Luke 22:17-20;* 1 Cor. -25; 1 Cor. 10:16 [b]Matt. 14:19

INSIGHT

See the chart ***The Feasts of Israel*** located on pages I-48 and I-49.

28 for [a]this is My blood of the covenant, which is poured out for
[b]many for forgiveness of sins.
29 "But I say to you, I will not drink of this fruit of the vine from
now on until that day when I drink it new with you in My Father's
kingdom."
30 [a]And after singing a hymn, they went out to [b]the Mount of
Olives.
31 Then Jesus *said to them, "You will all [1a]fall away because of Me
this night, for it is written, '[b]I WILL STRIKE DOWN THE SHEPHERD, AND THE
SHEEP OF THE FLOCK SHALL BE [c]SCATTERED.'
32 "But after I have been raised, [a]I will go before you to Galilee."
33 But Peter answered and said to Him, "*Even* though all may [1]fall
away because of You, I will never fall away."
34 Jesus said to him, "[a]Truly I say to you that [b]this *very* night, before
a cock crows, you shall deny Me three times."
35 Peter *said to Him, "[a]Even if I have to die with You, I will not
deny You." All the disciples said the same thing too.
36 [a]Then Jesus *came with them to a place called [b]Gethsemane, and
*said to His disciples, "Sit here while I go over there and pray."
37 And He took with Him [a]Peter and the two sons of Zebedee, and
began to be grieved and distressed.
38 Then He *said to them, "[a]My soul is deeply grieved, to the point
of death; remain here and [b]keep watch with Me."
39 And He went a little beyond *them,* and fell on His face and
prayed, saying, "My Father, if it is possible, let [a]this cup pass from
Me; [b]yet not as I will, but as Thou wilt."
40 And He *came to the disciples and *found them sleeping, and
*said to Peter, "So, you *men* could not [a]keep watch with Me for one
hour?
41 "[a]Keep watching and praying, that you may not enter into
temptation; [b]the spirit is willing, but the flesh is weak."
42 He went away again a second time and prayed, saying, "My
Father, if this [a]cannot pass away unless I drink it, [b]Thy will be done."
43 And again He came and found them sleeping, for their eyes
were heavy.
44 And He left them again, and went away and prayed a third time,
saying the same thing once more.
45 Then He *came to the disciples, and *said to them, "[1]Are you still
sleeping and taking your rest? Behold, [a]the hour is at hand and the
Son of Man is being betrayed into the hands of sinners.
46 "Arise, let us be going; behold, the one who betrays Me is at
hand!"
47 [a]And while He was still speaking, behold, [b]Judas, one of the
twelve, came up, [1]accompanied by a great multitude with swords
and clubs, from the chief priests and elders of the people.
48 Now he who was betraying Him gave them a sign, saying,
"Whomever I shall kiss, He is the one; seize Him."
49 And immediately he went to Jesus and said, "Hail, [a]Rabbi!" and
kissed Him.
50 And Jesus said to him, "[a]Friend, *do* what you have come for."
Then they came and laid hands on Jesus and seized Him.
51 And behold, [a]one of those who were with Jesus [1]reached and
drew out his [b]sword, and struck the [a]slave of the high priest, and [2]cut
off his ear.

28 [a]Ex. 24:8; [b]Matt. 20:28
30 [a]Matt. 26: *Mark 14:26-3 22:31-34* [b]Ma
31 [1]Or, *stum* 11:6 [b]Zech. 1 16:32
32 [a]Matt. 28; Mark 16:7
33 [1]Or, *stumb*
34 [a]Matt. 26:7 13:38 [b]Mark 1
35 [a]John 13:3
36 [a]Matt. 26:3 *Mark 14:32-42 22:40-46* [b]Ma Luke 22:39; Jo
37 [a]Matt. 4:21 Mark 5:37
38 [a]John 12:27 26:40, 41
39 [a]Matt. 20:22 26:42; Mark 14 22:42; John 6:3
40 [a]Matt. 26:38
41 [a]Matt. 26:38 14:38
42 [a]Matt. 20:22 26:39; Mark 14: 22:42; John 6:3
45 [1]Or, *Keep o sleeping therefo* [a]Mark 14:41; Jo 12:27; 13:1
47 [1]Lit., *and wit* [a]Matt. 26:47-56: *14:43-50; Luke 22:47-53; John 1* [b]Matt. 26:14
49 [a]Matt. 23:7; 2
50 [a]Matt. 20:13;
51 [1]Lit., *extende hand* [2]Lit., *took c* [a]Mark 14:47; Luk 22:50; John 18:1 [b]Luke 22:38

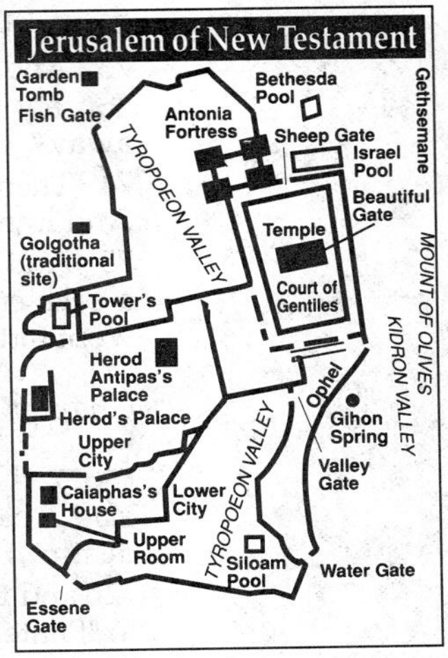

Gen. 9:6; Rev. 13:10

52 Then Jesus *said to him, "Put your sword back into its
place; for [a]all those who take up the sword shall perish by
the sword.

legion equaled ...ps [a]Mark 5:9, ...ke 8:30 [b]Matt. 4:11

53 "Or do you think that I cannot appeal to My Father, and
He will at once put at My disposal more than twelve
[1a]legions of [b]angels?

...4 [a]Matt. 26:24

54 "How then shall [a]the Scriptures be fulfilled, that it must
happen this way?"

...k 12:35; 14:49; ...20; 19:47; 20:1; John 7:14, 28; 8:2, 20; 18:20

55 At that time Jesus said to the multitudes, "Have you
come out with swords and clubs to arrest Me as against a
robber? [a]Every day I used to sit in the temple teaching and
you did not seize Me.

...56 [a]Matt. 26:24

56 "But all this has taken place that [a]the Scriptures of the
prophets may be fulfilled." Then all the disciples left Him
and fled.

[a]Matt. 26:57-68: *14:53-65; John ...f., 19-24* [b]Matt. 26:3

57 [a]And those who had seized Jesus led Him away to
[b]Caiaphas, the high priest, where the scribes and the elders
were gathered together.

servants [a]John ...:15 [b]Matt. 26:3 ...5:25; John 7:32, ...6; Acts 5:22, 26

58 But [a]Peter also was following Him at a distance as far as the
[b]courtyard of the high priest, and entered in, and sat down with the
[1c]officers to see the outcome.

[1]Or, *Sanhedrin* [a]Matt. 5:22

59 Now the chief priests and the whole [1a]Council kept trying to
obtain false testimony against Jesus, in order that they might put
Him to death;

60 [a]Deut. 19:15

60 and they did not find *any*, even though many false witnesses
came forward. But later on [a]two came forward,

..., *sanctuary* [2]Or, ...Matt. 27:40; Mark ...5:29; John 2:19; Acts 6:14

61 and said, "This man stated, '[a]I am able to destroy the [1]temple of
God and to rebuild it [2]in three days.'"

62 And the high priest stood up and said to Him, "Do You make no
answer? What is it that these men are testifying against You?"

[1]Or, *charge You ...er oath* [2]I.e., the ...ah [a]Matt. 27:12, John 19:9 [b]Matt. 26:63-66; Luke ...:67-71 [c]Lev. 5:1 ...16:16 [e]Matt. 4:3

63 But [a]Jesus kept silent. [b]And the high priest said to Him, "I [1c]ad-
jure You by [d]the living God, that You tell us whether You are [2]the
Christ, [e]the Son of God."

[1]Or, *from now on* ...26:25 [b]Ps. 110:1; ...4:62 [c]Dan. 7:13; Matt. 16:27f.

64 Jesus *said to him, "[a]You have said it *yourself*; nevertheless I tell
you, [1]hereafter you shall see [b]THE SON OF MAN SITTING AT THE RIGHT
HAND OF POWER, and [c]COMING ON THE CLOUDS OF HEAVEN."

...r, *outer garments* ...14:6; Mark 14:63; Acts 14:14

65 Then the high priest [a]tore his [1]robes, saying, "He has blas-
phemed! What further need do we have of witnesses? Behold, you
have now heard the blasphemy;

[a]Lev. 24:16; John 19:7

66 what do you think?" They answered and said, "[a]He is deserving
of death!"

[1]Or possibly, *beat ...ith rods* [a]Is. 50:6; ...t. 26:67, 68; Luke ...63-65; John 18:22 ...27:30; Mark 10:34

67 [a]Then they [b]spat in His face and beat Him with their fists; and
others [1]slapped Him,

[1]I.e., the Messiah ...14:65; Luke 22:64

68 and said, "[a]Prophesy to us, You [1]Christ; who is the one who hit
You?"

...9 [a]Matt. 26:69-75: ...ark 14:66-72; Luke 22:55-62; John ...-18, 25-27 [b]Matt. 26:3

69 [a]Now Peter was sitting outside in the [b]courtyard, and a certain
servant-girl came to him and said, "You too were with Jesus the
Galilean."

70 But he denied *it* before them all, saying, "I do not know what
you are talking about."

71 And when he had gone out to the gateway, another *servant-girl*
saw him and *said to those who were there, "This man was with
Jesus of Nazareth."

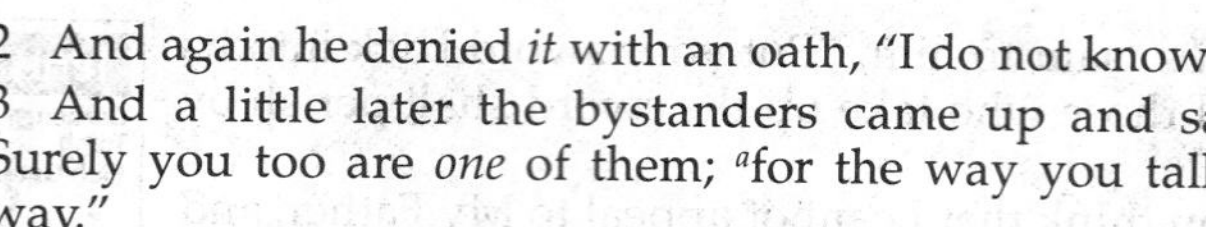

72 And again he denied *it* with an oath, "I do not know the man."
73 And a little later the bystanders came up and said to Peter,
"Surely you too are *one* of them; [a]for the way you talk [1]gives you
away."
74 Then he began to curse and swear, "I do not know the man!"
And immediately a cock crowed.
75 And Peter remembered the word which Jesus had said, "[a]Before
a cock crows, you will deny Me three times." And he went out and
wept bitterly.

Chapter 27

27 [a]Now when morning had come, all the chief priests and the
elders of the people took counsel against Jesus to put Him to
death;
2 and they bound Him, and led Him away, and [a]delivered Him up
to [b]Pilate the governor.
3 Then when [a]Judas, who had betrayed Him, saw that He had
been condemned, he felt remorse and returned [b]the thirty [1]pieces of
silver to the chief priests and elders,
4 saying, "I have sinned by betraying innocent blood." But they
said, "What is that to us? [a]See *to that* yourself!"
5 And he threw the pieces of silver into [a]the sanctuary and
departed; and [b]he went away and hanged himself.
6 And the chief priests took the pieces of silver and said, "It is not
lawful to put them into the temple treasury, since it is the price of
blood."
7 And they counseled together and with [1]the money bought the
Potter's Field as a burial place for strangers.
8 [a]For this reason that field has been called the Field of Blood to
this day.
9 Then that which was spoken through Jeremiah the prophet was
fulfilled, saying, "[a]AND [1]THEY TOOK THE THIRTY PIECES OF SILVER, THE
PRICE OF THE ONE WHOSE PRICE HAD BEEN SET by the sons of Israel;
10 [a]AND [1]THEY GAVE THEM FOR THE POTTER'S FIELD, AS THE LORD
DIRECTED ME."
11 [a]Now Jesus stood before the governor, and the governor ques-
tioned Him, saying, "Are You the [b]King of the Jews?" And Jesus said
to him, "[c]*It is as* you say."
12 And while He was being accused by the chief priests and elders,
[a]He made no answer.
13 Then Pilate *said to Him, "Do You not hear how many things
they testify against You?"
14 And [a]He did not answer him with regard to even a *single*
[1]charge, so that the governor was quite amazed.
15 [a]Now at *the* feast the governor was accustomed to release for the
multitude *any* one prisoner whom they wanted.
16 And they were holding at that time a notorious prisoner, called
Barabbas.
17 When therefore they were gathered together, Pilate said to them,
"Whom do you want me to release for you? Barabbas, or Jesus [a]who
is called Christ?"
18 For he knew that because of envy they had delivered Him up.

73 [1]Lit., *make evident* [a]Mark Luke 22:59; J

75 [a]Matt. 26:3

27:1 [a]Mark 15 22:66; John 18

2 [a]Matt. 20:19 3:1; 13:1; 23:1 3:13; 4:27; 1 T

3 [1]Or, *silver sh* [a]Matt. 26:14 [b]M 26:15

4 [a]Matt. 27:24

5 [a]Matt. 26:61; 1:9, 21 [b]Acts 1

7 [1]Lit., *them*

8 [a]Acts 1:19

9 [1]Some mss. *took* [a]Zech. 11:

10 [1]Some mss. *gave* [a]Zech. 11:

11 [a]Matt. 27:11- *Mark 15:2-5; Lu 3; John 18:29-3* 2:2 [c]Matt. 26:25

12 [a]Matt. 26:63; 19:9

14 [1]Lit., *word* [a]M 27:12; Mark 15:5 23:9; John 19:9

15 [a]Matt. 27:15- *Mark 15:6-15; Lu 23:[17]-25;* John 18:39-19:16

17 [a]Matt. 1:16; 2

19 And [a]while he was sitting on the judgment seat, his wife sent to
him, saying, "Have nothing to do with that [b]righteous Man; for [1]last
night I suffered greatly [c]in a dream because of Him."
20 But the chief priests and the elders persuaded the multitudes to
[a]ask for Barabbas, and to put Jesus to death.
21 But the governor answered and said to them, "Which of the two
do you want me to release for you?" And they said, "Barabbas."
22 Pilate *said to them, "Then what shall I do with Jesus [a]who is
called Christ?" They all *said, "Let Him be crucified!"
23 And he said, "Why, what evil has He done?" But they kept
shouting all the more, saying, "Let Him be crucified!"
24 And when Pilate saw that he was accomplishing nothing, but
rather that [a]a riot was starting, he took water and [b]washed his hands
in front of the multitude, saying, "I am innocent of [1c]this Man's
blood; [d]see *to that* yourselves."
25 And all the people answered and said, "[a]His blood *be* on us and
on our children!"
26 Then he released Barabbas [1]for them; but after having Jesus
[a]scourged, he delivered Him to be crucified.
27 [a]Then the soldiers of the governor took Jesus into [b]the
Praetorium and gathered the whole *Roman* [1c]cohort around Him.
28 And they stripped Him, and [a]put a scarlet robe on Him.
29 [a]And after weaving a crown of thorns, they put it on His head,
and a [1]reed in His right hand; and they kneeled down before Him
and mocked Him, saying, "[b]Hail, King of the Jews!"
30 And [a]they spat on Him, and took the reed and *began* to beat Him
on the head.
31 [a]And after they had mocked Him, they took His robe off and put
His garments on Him, and led Him away to crucify *Him*.
32 [a]And as they were coming out, they found a man of [b]Cyrene
named Simon, [1]whom they pressed into service to bear His cross.
33 [a]And when they had come to a place called [b]Golgotha, which
means Place of a Skull,
34 [a]they gave Him [b]wine to drink mingled with gall; and after tast-
ing *it*, He was unwilling to drink.
35 And when they had crucified Him, [a]they divided up His gar-
ments among themselves, casting [1]lots;
36 and sitting down, they *began* to [a]keep watch over Him there.
37 And they put up above His head the charge against Him [1]which
read, "[a]THIS IS JESUS THE KING OF THE JEWS."
38 At that time two robbers *were crucified with Him, one on the
right and one on the left.
39 And those passing by were [1]hurling abuse at Him, [a]wagging
their heads,
40 and saying, "[a]You who *are going to* destroy the temple and
rebuild it in three days, save Yourself! [b]If You are the Son of God,
come down from the cross."
41 In the same way the chief priests also, along with the scribes and
elders, were mocking *Him*, and saying,
42 "[a]He saved others; [1]He cannot save Himself. [b]He is the King of
Israel; let Him now come down from the cross, and we shall believe
in Him.
43 "[a]HE TRUSTS IN GOD; LET HIM DELIVER *Him* NOW, IF HE TAKES PLEASURE
IN HIM; for He said, 'I am the Son of God.' "

today [a]John ; Acts 12:21; 25:6, 10, 17 27:24 [c]Gen. ; Num. 12:6; 5; Matt. 1:20; 2:12f., 19, 22
0 [a]Acts 3:14
2 [a]Matt. 1:16
nss. read *the this righteous* . 26:5 [b]Deut. [c]Matt. 27:19 [d]Matt. 27:4
sh. 2:19; Acts 5:28
o *them* [a]Mark e 23:16; John 19:1
attalion [a]Matt. 7:27-31: *Mark* 0 [b]Matt. 26:3; 8:28, 33; 19:9 [c]Acts 10:1
rk 15:17; John 19:2
taff (made of a [a]Mark 15:17; [b]Mark 15:18; John 19:3
tt. 26:67; Mark 4; 14:65; 15:19
1 [a]Mark 15:20
this one [a]Matt. *ark 15:21; Luke :26; John 19:17* :10; 6:9; 11:20; 13:1
[a]Matt. 27:34-44: *15:22-32; Luke 23:33-43; John* 24 [b]Luke 23:33; John 19:17
s. 69:21 [b]Mark 15:23
a lot [a]Ps. 22:18
36 [a]Matt. 27:54
t., *written* [a]Mark uke 23:38; John 19:19
Or, *blaspheming* b 16:4; Ps. 22:7; Lam. 2:15; Mark 15:29
Matt. 26:61; John 2:19 [b]Matt. 27:42
2 [1]Or, *can He not ve Himself* [a]Mark 5:31; Luke 23:35 Matt. 27:37; Luke John 1:49; 12:13
43 [a]Ps. 22:8

44 [a]And the robbers also who had been crucified with Him were
casting the same insult at Him.
45 [a]Now from the [1]sixth hour darkness [2]fell upon all the land until
the [3]ninth hour.
46 And about the ninth hour Jesus cried out with a loud voice,
saying, "[a]ELI, ELI, LAMA SABACHTHANI?" that is, "MY GOD, MY GOD,
WHY HAST THOU FORSAKEN ME?"
47 And some of those who were standing there, when they heard it,
began saying, "This man is calling for Elijah."
48 And [a]immediately one of them ran, and taking a sponge, he
filled it with sour wine, and put it on a reed, and gave Him a drink.
49 But the rest *of them* said, "[1]Let us see whether Elijah will come to
save Him."[2]
50 And Jesus [a]cried out again with a loud voice, and yielded up *His*
spirit.
51 [a]And behold, [b]the veil of the temple was torn in two from top to
bottom, and [c]the earth shook; and the rocks were split,
52 and the tombs were opened; and many bodies of the [1]saints who
had [a]fallen asleep were raised;
53 and coming out of the tombs after His resurrection they entered
[a]the holy city and appeared to many.
54 [a]Now the centurion, and those who were with him [b]keeping
guard over Jesus, when they saw [c]the earthquake and the things that
were happening, became very frightened and said, "Truly this was
[1d]the Son of God!"
55 [a]And many women were there looking on from a distance, who
had followed Jesus from Galilee, [1b]ministering to Him,
56 among whom was [a]Mary Magdalene, *along with* Mary the
mother of James and Joseph, and [b]the mother of the sons of Zebedee.
57 [a]And when it was evening, there came a rich man from
Arimathea, named Joseph, who himself had also become a disciple
of Jesus.
58 This man went to Pilate and asked for the body of Jesus. Then
Pilate ordered *it* to be given over *to him*.
59 And Joseph took the body and wrapped it in a clean linen cloth,
60 and laid it in his own new tomb, which he had hewn out in the
rock; and he rolled [a]a large stone against the entrance of the tomb
and went away.
61 And [a]Mary Magdalene was there, and the other Mary, sitting
opposite the grave.
62 Now on the next day, which is *the one* after [a]the preparation, the
chief priests and the Pharisees gathered together with Pilate,
63 and said, "Sir, we remember that when He was still alive that
deceiver said, '[a]After three days I *am to* rise again.'
64 "Therefore, give orders for the grave to be made secure until the
third day, lest the disciples come and steal Him away and say to the
people, 'He has risen from the dead,' and the last deception will be
worse than the first."
65 Pilate said to them, "You have a [a]guard; go, make it *as* secure as
you know how."
66 And they went and made the grave secure, and along with [a]the
guard they set a [b]seal on [c]the stone.

44 [a]Luke 23
45 [1]I.e., noo *occurred* [3]I.e [a]Matt. 27:45- *15:33-41; Lu*
46 [a]Ps. 22:1
48 [a]Ps. 69:2 15:36; Luke 2 19:29
49 [1]Lit., *Perm see* [2]Some e add *And anot spear and pie side, and the. out water and* John 19:34)
50 [a]Mark 15: 23:46; John 1
51 [a]Matt. 27:5 *Mark 15:38-4* 23:47-49 [b]Ex. Mark 15:38; L Heb. 9:3 [c]Ma
52 [1]Or, *holy o* 7:60
53 [a]Matt. 4:5
54 [1]Or possib *of God* or *a so god* [a]Mark 15: 23:47 [b]Matt. 2 [c]Matt. 27:51 [d]M 27:43
55 [1]Or, *waiting* [a]Mark 15:40f.; L 23:49; John 19 [b]Mark 15:41; L
56 [a]Matt. 28:1; 15:40, 47; 16:9, 8:2; John 19:25 18 [b]Matt. 20:20
57 [a]Matt. 27:57 *Mark 15:42-47; 23:50-56; John*
60 [a]Matt. 27:66 Mark 16:4
61 [a]Matt. 27:56
62 [a]Mark 15:42 23:54; John 19: 31, 42
63 [a]Matt. 16:21; 20:19; Mark 8:31 10:34; Luke 9:22 18:31-33
65 [a]Matt. 27:66;
66 [a]Matt. 27:65; [b]Dan. 6:17 [c]Mat 28:2; Mark 16:4

8:1 [a]Matt. 28:1-8; *Mark 16:1-8; Luke 1-10;* John 20:1-8 [b]Matt. 27:56, 61
[a]Luke 24:4; John):12 [b]Matt. 27:66; Mark 16:4
n. 7:9; 10:6; Mark ; John 20:12; Acts 1:10
5 [1]Or, *Stop being raid* [a]Matt. 14:27; 28:10; Rev. 1:17
Matt. 12:40; 16:21; 27:63
latt. 26:32; 28:10, 16; Mark 16:7
[1]Lit., *saying hello*
0 [1]Or, *Stop being raid* [a]Matt. 14:27; John 20:17; Rom. 29; Heb. 2:11f., 17 att. 26:32; 28:7, 16
[a]Matt. 27:65, 66
.it., *make you free n care* [a]Matt. 27:2
[a]Matt. 9:31; Mark 1:45 [b]Matt. 27:8
Matt. 26:32; 28:7, Mark 15:41; 16:7
17 [a]Mark 16:11
Dan. 7:13f.; Matt. 1:27; 26:64; Rom. Eph. 1:20-22; Phil. .; Col. 2:10; 1 Pet. 3:22
ark 16:15f. [b]Matt. 2; Acts 1:8; 14:21 Matt. 25:32; Luke [d]Acts 2:38; 8:16; 1. 6:3; 1 Cor. 1:13, 15ff.; Gal. 3:27
[1]Lit., *all the days* 18:20; Acts 18:10 [b]Matt. 13:39

Chapter 28

28 [a]Now after the Sabbath, as it began to dawn toward the first
day of the week, [b]Mary Magdalene and the other Mary came
to look at the grave.
2 And behold, a severe earthquake had occurred, for [a]an angel of
the Lord descended from heaven and came and rolled away [b]the
stone and sat upon it.
3 And [a]his appearance was like lightning, and his garment as
white as snow;
4 and the guards shook for fear of him, and became like dead men.
5 And the angel answered and said to the women, "[1a]Do not be
afraid; for I know that you are looking for Jesus who has been
crucified.
6 "He is not here, for He has risen, [a]just as He said. Come, see the
place where He was lying.
7 "And go quickly and tell His disciples that He has risen from the
dead; and behold, He is going before you [a]into Galilee, there you
will see Him; behold, I have told you."
8 And they departed quickly from the tomb with fear and great
joy and ran to report it to His disciples.
9 And behold, Jesus met them [1]and greeted them. And they came
up and took hold of His feet and worshiped Him.
10 Then Jesus *said to them, "[1a]Do not be afraid; go and take word
to [b]My brethren to leave [c]for Galilee, and there they shall see Me."
11 Now while they were on their way, behold, some of [a]the guard
came into the city and reported to the chief priests all that had hap-
pened.
12 And when they had assembled with the elders and counseled
together, they gave a large sum of money to the soldiers,
13 and said, "You are to say, 'His disciples came by night and stole
Him away while we were asleep.'
14 "And if this should come to [a]the governor's ears, we will win him
over and [1]keep you out of trouble."
15 And they took the money and did as they had been instructed;
and this story was widely [a]spread among the Jews, *and is* [b]to this day.
16 But the eleven disciples proceeded [a]to Galilee, to the mountain
which Jesus had designated.
17 And when they saw Him, they worshiped *Him;* but [a]some were
doubtful.
18 And Jesus came up and spoke to them, saying, "[a]All authority
has been given to Me in heaven and on earth.
19 "[a]Go therefore and [b]make disciples of [c]all the nations, [d]baptizing
them in the name of the Father and the Son and the Holy Spirit,
20 teaching them to observe all that I commanded you; and lo, [a]I
am with you [1]always, even to [b]the end of the age."

MATTHEW AT A GLANCE

Theme of Matthew:

Author:

Date:

Purpose:

Key Words:
King (kingdom, kingdom of heaven, kingdom of God)

fulfilled

mark every reference to the devil or demons with a red pitchfork

covenant

SEGMENT DIVISIONS		CHAPTER THEMES
		1
		2
		3
		4
		5
		6
		7
		8
		9
		10
		11
		12
		13
		14
		15
		16
		17
		18
		19
		20
		21
		22
		23
		24
		25
		26
		27
		28

ɅARK

ⱯYes, Jesus was born to be King of the Jews, as Matthew so clearly points out. However, the gospel ; not just for the Jews; it was for the world. Before Jesus would reign as King of kings, He would be ·ant of all by dying for mankind. Mark tells of the works and authority of the One who came not to ·erved but to serve and to give His life as a ransom for many.

INGS TO DO

Mark is a fast-paced Gospel which emphasizes the works of Jesus rather than the teachings of Jesus. nough Jesus is referred to as a teacher a number of times, Mark shows Jesus' power and authority ough the works He does as He goes about His Father's business.

As you read Mark you will notice the repeated use of the word *immediately* as Mark takes his reader n one event in the life of Jesus to another. These events and the works of Jesus show the reader us' power and authority as the servant of God and man.

apters 1-13

. Although the emphasis in the Gospel of Mark is on the works of Jesus that show His divine power, Mark opens his Gospel by declaring the deity of Jesus Christ. He also gives an account of the events that took place prior to and in preparation for Jesus' ministry. Read Mark 1:1-13 and list in the margin of the text the following:

   a. The facts that declare the divinity of Jesus Christ

   b. The events that took place in Jesus' life prior to His public ministry

.. As you read Mark chapter by chapter, in a distinctive way mark the key words listed on the MARK AT A GLANCE chart on page 1499.

   a. Record these key words on a card and use it as a bookmark while you study this Gospel.

   b. Also underline in the text each geographical location, whether it is a city, a region, or a place such as the temple or the synagogue. Noting these will help in your overall understanding of these events in Jesus' life.

. In the margin list the main events covered in that chapter. These events (including healings and miracles) demonstrate Jesus' authority.

   a. As you look at each event, note how it demonstrates Jesus' authority, how the people respond, and what Jesus has authority over.

   b. Record your insights in the margin. List the event. Then under that event note how the people, religious leaders, disciples, and so on responded. For instance:

   Healing on Sabbath

   Pharisees counsel to destroy Him

   c. After you have recorded these demonstrations and responses, be sure you note the scope of Jesus' authority. For example, next to the illustration above, you would write: "authority over Sabbath." Watch for Jesus' power over nature, demons, disease, and so on. Ask God to show you how this demonstration of Jesus' power declares His divinity. Also, notice how these events portray Jesus as a servant.

   d. Throughout these chapters, Jesus faces the accusations and rejection of the Jewish religious leaders of His day. Each time the scribes, Pharisees, or Sadducees accuse Jesus, He reasons with them. Note that conflict in the margin.

. Also list in the margin the main points of Jesus' teachings, whether the teaching comes as a result of healing, casting out demons, a miracle, or in response to a question from either the discip the multitude. Also note the response of those who hear the teaching.

5. Mark each reference to the kingdom of God and watch for the following:
   a. When does Jesus increase His emphasis on the kingdom of God? Note this in the margin.
   b. Underline every prediction of Jesus' death and resurrection and note how it coincides Jesus' emphasis on the kingdom of God.
   c. Observe that in the first part of Mark Jesus defines the kingdom of God, then at chapter emphasis shifts to how to enter into the kingdom.
   d. In the appendix is a chart titled WHAT THE GOSPELS TEACH ABOUT THE KINGDO GOD/THE KINGDOM OF HEAVEN (pages 1880 and 1881). Compile the *main* teachings Mark about the kingdom of God on this chart. It would be good to do this on notebook first and then consolidate your insights and transfer them to the chart in the appendix.

Chapters 14-16

1. When you read Mark's account of the trial, death, burial, and resurrection of Jesus Christ, r the progression of events on the appropriate charts in the appendix: THE ARREST, TRIAL, CRUCIFIXION OF JESUS CHRIST (page 1882) and THE ACCOUNT OF JE RESURRECTION (page 1883). Once again, do this on notebook paper before transferrin information to the chart.
   a. When you record the circumstances surrounding the resurrection of Jesus Christ, also not post-resurrection appearances recorded in Mark. After you do this for all four Gospels you have comprehensive notes on everything that took place at this time in our Lord's life.
   b. As you do this, remember that because Luke gives the chronological order of events, it i chronological plumbline for the other Gospel records.
2. After you finish reading and marking each chapter, record the theme of that chapter on M AT A GLANCE. Also record it in the text on the line next to the chapter number.
3. Complete MARK AT A GLANCE. Fill in any segment divisions you've seen from studyin book.

Things to Think About

1. People often say that Mark shows the servant aspect of Jesus' ministry. Although the word *se* is only used four times, Mark 10:45 says Jesus "did not come to be served, but to serve, ar give His life a ransom for many." How like your Lord are you in that respect? Would ot regard you as a servant? Or do they see you as having to be "number one"? What is it t "number one" in God's eyes?
2. Jesus talks about discipleship in this Gospel. According to Jesus, what is required of disci Can you consider yourself a true disciple of Jesus Christ? Why? Think about Mark 8:34-36 10:28-31.
3. Can you say with Peter, "Thou art the Christ, the Son of the Living God?" And will you liste Him, to Jesus, as the Father commands?

Chapter 1

1 The beginning of the gospel of Jesus Christ, [1a]the Son of God.
2 [a]As it is written in Isaiah the prophet,
"[b]BEHOLD, I SEND MY MESSENGER BEFORE YOUR FACE,
WHO WILL PREPARE YOUR WAY;
3 [a]THE VOICE OF ONE CRYING IN THE WILDERNESS,
'MAKE READY THE WAY OF THE LORD,
MAKE HIS PATHS STRAIGHT.' "

1:1 [1]Many mss. contain *the Son* [a]Matt. 4:3

2 [a]Mark 1:2-8: *M 3:1-11; Luke 3:2-* [b]Mal. 3:1; Matt. 1 Luke 7:27

3 [a]Is. 40:3; Matt. Luke 3:4; John 1:

4 John the Baptist appeared in the wilderness [1a]preaching a bap-
tism of repentance for the [b]forgiveness of sins.
5 And all the country of Judea was going out to him, and all the
people of Jerusalem; and they were being baptized by him in the
Jordan River, confessing their sins.
6 And John was clothed with camel's hair and *wore* [a]a leather belt
around his waist, and [1]his diet was locusts and wild honey.
7 And he was [1]preaching, and saying, "After me One is coming
who is mightier than I, and I am not fit to stoop down and untie the
thong of His sandals.
8 "I baptized you [1]with water; but He will baptize you [1]with the
Holy Spirit."
9 [a]And it came about in those days that Jesus [b]came from Nazareth
in Galilee, and was baptized by John in the Jordan.
10 And immediately coming up out of the water, He saw the heav-
ens [1]opening, and the Spirit like a dove descending upon Him;
11 and a voice came out of the heavens: "[a]Thou art My beloved Son,
in Thee I am well-pleased."
12 [a]And immediately the Spirit *impelled Him *to go* out into the
wilderness.
13 And He was in the wilderness forty days being tempted by
[a]Satan; and He was with the wild beasts, and the angels were minis-
tering to Him.
14 [a]And after John had been [1]taken into custody, Jesus came into
Galilee, [2]bpreaching the gospel of God,
15 and saying, "[a]The time is fulfilled, and the kingdom of God is at
hand; [b]repent and [1]believe in the gospel."
16 [a]And as He was going along by the Sea of Galilee, He saw Simon
and Andrew, the brother of Simon, casting a net in the sea; for they
were fishermen.
17 And Jesus said to them, "Follow Me, and I will make you be-
come fishers of men."
18 And they immediately left the nets and followed Him.
19 And going on a little farther, He saw [1]James the *son* of Zebedee,
and John his brother, who were also in the boat mending the nets.
20 And immediately He called them; and they left their father Zebe-
dee in the boat with the hired servants, and went away [1]to follow
Him.
21 [a]And they *went into Capernaum; and immediately on the Sab-
bath [b]He entered the synagogue and *began* to teach.
22 And [a]they were amazed at His teaching; for He was teaching
them as *one* having authority, and not as the scribes.
23 And just then there was in their synagogue a man with an un-
clean spirit; and he cried out,
24 saying, "[a]What do we have to do with You, Jesus [1]of [b]Nazareth?
Have You come to destroy us? I know who You are—[c]the Holy One
of God!"
25 And Jesus rebuked him, saying, "Be quiet, and come out of
him!"
26 And throwing him into convulsions, the unclean spirit cried out
with a loud voice, and came out of him.
27 And they were all [a]amazed, so that they debated among them-
selves, saying, "What is this? A new teaching with authority! He
commands even the unclean spirits, and they obey Him."

4 [1]Or, *proclaiming*
13:24 [b]Luke 1:77
Lit., *he was eating*
[a]2 Kin. 1:8
7 [1]Or, *proclaiming*
he Gr. here can be
lated *in, with* or *by*
Mark 1:9-11: *Matt.*
-17; Luke 3:21, 22
tt. 2:23; Luke 2:51
[1]Or, *being parted*
[a]Ps. 2:7; Is. 42:1;
3:17; 12:18; Mark
9:7; Luke 3:22
2 [a]Mark 1:12, 13:
1-11; Luke 4:1-13
13 [a]Matt. 4:10
[1]Lit., *delivered up*
roclaiming [a]Matt.
4:12 [b]Matt. 4:23
r, put your trust in
al. 4:4; Eph. 1:10;
Tim. 2:6; Titus 1:3
tt. 3:2; Acts 20:21
ark 1:16-20: *Matt.*
3-22; Luke 5:2-11;
John 1:40-42
19 [1]Or, *Jacob*
20 [1]Lit., *after Him*
ark 1:21-28: *Luke*
31-37 [b]Matt. 4:23;
Mark 1:39; 10:1
22 [a]Matt. 7:28
Lit., *the Nazarene*
8:29 [b]Matt. 2:23;
0:47; 14:67; 16:6;
4:34; 24:19; Acts
[c]Luke 1:35; 4:34;
n 6:69; Acts 3:14
[a]Mark 10:24, 32;
16:5, 6

28 And immediately the news about Him went out everywhere into
all the surrounding district of Galilee.
29 [a]And immediately [1]after they had come [b]out of the synagogue,
they came into the house of Simon and Andrew, with [2]James and
John.
30 Now Simon's mother-in-law was lying sick with a fever; and
immediately they *spoke to Him about her.
31 And He came to her and raised her up, taking her by the hand,
and the fever left her, and she [1]waited on them.
32 [a]And [b]when evening had come, [b]after the sun had set, they *began*
bringing to Him all who were ill and those who were [c]demon-
possessed.
33 And the whole [a]city had gathered at the door.
34 And He [a]healed many who were ill with various diseases, and
cast out many demons; and He was not permitting the demons to
speak, because they [1]knew who He was.
35 [a]And in the early morning, while it was still dark, He arose and
went out and departed to a lonely place, and [b]was praying there.
36 And Simon and his companions hunted for Him;
37 and they found Him, and *said to Him, "Everyone is looking for
You."
38 And He *said to them, "Let us go somewhere else to the towns
nearby, in order that I may [1]preach there also; for that is what I came
out for."
39 [a]And He went into their synagogues throughout all Galilee,
[1]preaching and casting out the demons.
40 [a]And a leper *came to Him, beseeching Him and [b]falling on his
knees before Him, and saying to Him, "If You are willing, You can
make me clean."
41 And moved with compassion, He stretched out His hand, and
touched him, and *said to him, "I am willing; be cleansed."
42 And immediately the leprosy left him and he was cleansed.
43 And He sternly warned him and immediately sent him away,
44 and He *said to him, "[a]See that you say nothing to anyone; but
[a]go, show yourself to the priest and [b]offer for your cleansing what
Moses commanded, for a testimony to them."
45 But he went out and began to [a]proclaim it freely and to [a]spread
the news about, to such an extent that [1]Jesus could no longer public-
ly enter a city, but [2]stayed out in unpopulated areas; and [b]they were
coming to Him from everywhere.

Chapter 2

2 And when He had come back to Capernaum several days after-
ward, it was heard that He was at home.
2 And [a]many were gathered together, so that there was no longer
room, even near the door; and He was speaking the word to them.
3 [a]And they *came, bringing to Him a [b]paralytic, carried by four
men.
4 And being unable to [1]get to Him because of the crowd, they
[a]removed the roof [2]above Him; and when they had dug an opening,
they let down the pallet on which the [b]paralytic was lying.
5 And Jesus seeing their faith *said to the paralytic, "My [1]son,
[a]your sins are forgiven."

29 [1]Some mss. re *after He had come* He came [2]Or, Jac [a]Mark 1:29-31: Ma *8:14, 15; Luke 4:3* [b]Mark 1:21, 23

31 [1]Or, *served*

32 [a]Mark 1:32-34 *8:16, 17; Luke 4:4* [b]Matt. 8:16; Luke [c]Matt. 4:24

33 [a]Mark 1:21

34 [1]Some mss. r *knew Him to be C* [a]Matt. 4:23

35 [a]Mark 1:35-38 *4:42, 43* [b]Matt. 1 Luke 5:16

38 [1]Or, *proclaim*

39 [1]Or, *proclaim* [a]Matt. 4:23; 9:35; 1:23; 3:1

40 [a]Mark 1:40-44 *8:2-4; Luke 5:12-* [b]Matt. 8:2; Mark 1 Luke 5:12

44 [a]Matt. 8:4 [b]Le 14:1-32

45 [1]Lit., *He* [2]Lit. [a]Matt. 28:15; Luk [b]Mark 2:2, 13; 3:7 5:17; John 6:2

2:2 [a]Mark 1:45;

3 [a]Mark 2:3-12: *9:2-8; Luke 5:18-* [b]Matt. 4:24

4 [1]Lit., *bring to* [2] *where He was* [a] 5:19 [b]Matt. 4:24

5 [1]Lit., *child* [a]Ma

6 But there were some of the scribes sitting there and reasoning in
their hearts,
7 "Why does this man speak that way? He is blaspheming; [a]who
can forgive sins [1]but God alone?"
8 And immediately Jesus, aware [1]in His spirit that they were
reasoning that way within themselves, *said to them, "Why are you
reasoning about these things in your hearts?
9 "Which is easier, to say to the [a]paralytic, 'Your sins are forgiven';
or to say, 'Arise, and take up your pallet and walk'?
10 "But in order that you may know that the Son of Man has
authority on earth to forgive sins"—He *said to the paralytic—
11 "I say to you, rise, take up your pallet and go home."
12 And he rose and immediately took up the pallet and went out in
the sight of all; so that they were all amazed and [a]were glorifying
God, saying, "[b]We have never seen anything like this."
13 And He went out again by the seashore; and [a]all the multitude
were coming to Him, and He was teaching them.
14 [a]And as He passed by, He saw [b]Levi the *son* of Alphaeus sitting
in the tax office, and He *said to him, "[c]Follow Me!" And he rose and
followed Him.
15 And it [1]came about that He was reclining *at the table* in his house,
and many [2]tax-gatherers and sinners [3]were dining with Jesus and
His disciples; for there were many of them, and they were following
Him.
16 And when [a]the scribes of the Pharisees saw that He was eating
with the sinners and tax-gatherers, they *began* saying to His disci-
ples, "[b]Why is He eating and drinking with tax-gatherers and sin-
ners?"
17 And hearing this, Jesus *said to them, "[a]*It is* not those who are
healthy who need a physician, but those who are sick; I did not come
to call the righteous, but sinners."
18 [a]And John's disciples and the Pharisees were fasting; and they
*came and *said to Him, "Why do John's disciples and the disciples
of the Pharisees fast, but Your disciples do not fast?"
19 And Jesus said to them, "While the bridegroom is with them,
[1]the attendants of the bridegroom do not fast, do they? So long as
they have the bridegroom with them, they cannot fast.
20 "But the [a]days will come when the bridegroom is taken away
from them, and then they will fast in that day.
21 "No one sews [1]a patch of unshrunk cloth on an old garment;
otherwise [2]the patch pulls away from it, the new from the old, and a
worse tear results.
22 "And no one puts new wine into old [1]wineskins; otherwise the
wine will burst the skins, and the wine is lost, and the skins *as well;*
but *one puts* new wine into fresh wineskins."
23 [a]And it came about that He was passing through the grainfields
on the Sabbath, and His disciples began to make their way along
while [b]picking the heads *of grain.*
24 And the Pharisees were saying to Him, "See here, [a]why are they
doing what is not lawful on the Sabbath?"
25 And He *said to them, "Have you never read what David did
when he was in need and became hungry, he and his companions:
26 how he entered the house of God in the time of [a]Abiathar *the*
high priest, and ate the [1]consecrated bread, which [b]is not lawful for

if not one, God [a]Is. 43:25
8 [1]Lit., *by*
9 [a]Matt. 4:24
Matt. 9:8 [b]Matt. 9:33
13 [a]Mark 1:45
k 2:14-17: *Matt. 3; Luke 5:27-32* 9:9 [c]Matt. 8:22
it., *comes* [2]I.e., ectors of Roman s for profit [3]Lit., *re reclining with*
[a]Luke 5:30; Acts 23:9 [b]Matt. 9:11
. 9:12, 13; Luke 5:31, 32
k 2:18-22: *Matt. 7; Luke 5:33-38*
[1]Lit., *sons of the bridal-chamber*
Matt. 9:15; Luke 17:22
.it., *that which is* [2]Lit., *that which fills up*
., skins used as bottles
k 2:23-28: *Matt. 2:1-8; Luke 6:1-5* [b]Deut. 23:25
24 [a]Matt. 12:2
showbread; lit., *s of presentation* m. 21:1; 2 Sam. Chr. 24:6 [b]Lev. 24:9

anyone to eat except the priests, and he gave *it* also to those who
were with him?"
27 And He was saying to them, "[a]The Sabbath [1]was made [2]for man,
and [b]not man [2]for the Sabbath.
28 "Consequently, the Son of Man is Lord even of the Sabbath."

Chapter 3

3 [a]And He [b]entered again into a synagogue; and a man was there
with a withered hand.
2 And [a]they were watching Him *to see* if He would heal him on the
Sabbath, [b]in order that they might accuse Him.
3 And He *said to the man with the withered hand, "[1]Rise and
come forward!"
4 And He *said to them, "Is it lawful on the Sabbath to do good or
to do harm, to save a life or to kill?" But they kept silent.
5 And after [a]looking around at them with anger, grieved at their
hardness of heart, He *said to the man, "Stretch out your hand." And
he stretched it out, and his hand was restored.
6 And the Pharisees went out and immediately *began* [1]taking coun-
sel with the [a]Herodians against Him, *as to* how they might destroy
Him.
7 [a]And Jesus withdrew to the sea with His disciples; and [b]a great
multitude from Galilee followed; and *also* from Judea,
8 and from Jerusalem, and from [a]Idumea, and beyond the Jordan,
and the vicinity of [b]Tyre and Sidon, a great multitude heard of all
that He was doing and came to Him.
9 [a]And He told His disciples that a boat should stand ready for
Him because of the multitude, in order that they might not crowd
Him;
10 for He had [a]healed many, with the result that all those who had
[b]afflictions pressed about Him in order to [c]touch Him.
11 And whenever the unclean spirits beheld Him, they would fall
down before Him and cry out, saying, "You are [a]the Son of God!"
12 And He [a]earnestly warned them not to [1]make Him known.
13 And He *went up to [a]the mountain and *[b]summoned those
whom He Himself wanted, and they came to Him.
14 And He appointed twelve[1], that they might be with Him, and
that He might send them out to preach,
15 and to have authority to cast out the demons.
16 And He appointed the twelve: [a]Simon (to whom He gave the
name Peter),
17 and [1]James, the *son* of Zebedee, and John the brother of [1]James
(to them He gave the name Boanerges, which means, "Sons of
Thunder");
18 and Andrew, and Philip, and Bartholomew, and Matthew, and
Thomas, and [1]James the *son* of Alphaeus, and Thaddaeus, and Simon
the [2]Zealot;
19 and Judas Iscariot, who also betrayed Him.
20 And He *came [1a]home, and the [b]multitude *gathered again, [c]to
such an extent that they could not even eat [2]a meal.
21 And when [a]His own [1]people heard *of this,* they went out to take
custody of Him; for they were saying, "[b]He has lost His senses."
22 And the scribes who came down [a]from Jerusalem were saying,

27 [1]Or, *ca* *being* [2]Lit., *of* [a]Ex. 23: 5:14 [b]Col.

3:1 [a]Mark *12:9-14; Lu* [b]Mark 1:21,

2 [a]Luke 6:7 20:20 [b]Mat Luke 6:7; 11

3 [1]Lit., *Aris* *midst*

5 [a]Luke 6:1

6 [1]Lit., *givir* 22:16; Mark

7 [a]Mark 3:7 *12:15, 16; L* [b]Matt. 4:25;

8 [a]Josh. 15: 35:15; 36:5

9 [a]Mark 4:1;

10 [a]Matt. 4:2 5:29, 34; Luk [c]Matt. 9:21; 1 6:56; 8:22

11 [a]Matt. 4:3

12 [1]Or, *revea* *was* [a]Matt. 8:

13 [a]Matt. 5:1; 6:12 [b]Matt. 1 6:7; Luke 9:1

14 [1]Some ea add *whom He* *apostles*

16 [a]Mark 3:16 *10:2-4; Luke 6* Acts 1:13

17 [1]Or, *Jacob*

18 [1]Or, *Jacob* *Cananaean*

20 [1]Lit., *into a* [2]Lit., *bread* [a]M 7:17; 9:28 [b]Ma 3:7 [c]Mark 6:31

21 [1]Or, *kinsme* 3:31f. [b]John 10 26:24

22 [a]Matt. 15:1

"He is possessed by [1b]Beelzebul," and "[c]He casts out the demons by
the ruler of the demons."
23 [a]And He called them to Himself and began speaking to them in
[b]parables, "How can [c]Satan cast out Satan?
24 "And if a kingdom is divided against itself, that kingdom cannot
stand.
25 "And if a house is divided against itself, that house will not be
able to stand.
26 "And if [a]Satan has risen up against himself and is divided, he
cannot stand, but [1]he is finished!
27 "[a]But no one can enter the strong man's house and plunder his
property unless he first binds the strong man, and then he will
plunder his house.
28 "[a]Truly I say to you, all sins shall be forgiven the sons of men, and
whatever blasphemies they utter;
29 but [a]whoever blasphemes against the Holy Spirit never has for-
giveness, but is guilty of an eternal sin"—
30 because they were saying, "He has an unclean spirit."
31 [a]And His mother and His brothers *arrived, and standing out-
side they sent *word* to Him, and called Him.
32 And a multitude was sitting around Him, and they *said to Him,
"Behold, Your mother and Your brothers[1] are outside looking for
You."
33 And answering them, He *said, "Who are My mother and My
brothers?"
34 And looking about on those who were sitting around Him, He
*said, "[a]Behold, My mother and My brothers!
35 "For whoever [a]does the will of God, he is My brother and sister
and mother."

Chapter 4

4 [a]And He began to teach again [b]by the sea. And such a very great
multitude [1]gathered to Him that [c]He got into a boat in the sea
and sat down; and the whole multitude was by the sea on the land.
2 And He was teaching them many things in [a]parables, and was
saying to them in His teaching,
3 "Listen *to this*! Behold, the sower went out to sow;
4 and it came about that as he was sowing, some *seed* fell beside
the road, and the birds came and ate it up.
5 "And other *seed* fell on the rocky *ground* where it did not have
much soil; and immediately it sprang up because it had no depth of
soil.
6 "And after the sun had risen, it was scorched; and because it had
no root, it withered away.
7 "And other *seed* fell among the thorns, and the thorns came up
and choked it, and it yielded no crop.
8 "And other *seeds* fell into the good soil and as they grew up and
increased, they yielded a crop and produced thirty, sixty, and a hun-
dredfold."
9 And He was saying, "[a]He who has ears to hear, let him hear."
10 And as soon as He was alone, [1]His followers, along with the
twelve, *began* asking Him *about* the parables.
11 And He was saying to them, "To you has been given the mystery

See the section on *Parables*, under **"Figures of Speech,"** on page I-63.

22 [1]Or, *Beezebul;* ...rs read *Beelzebub* [b]Matt. 10:25; 11:18 [c]Matt. 9:34

...ark 3:23-27: *Matt. 12:25-29; Luke* ...7-22 [b]Matt. 13:3ff.; ...k 4:2ff. [c]Matt. 4:10

...Lit., *he has an end* [a]Matt. 4:10

27 [a]Is. 49:24, 25

... [a]Matt. 12:31, 32; ...ark 3:28-30; Luke 12:10

29 [a]Luke 12:10

...ark 3:31-35: *Matt.* ...*-50; Luke 8:19-21*

...ater mss. add *and Your sisters*

34 [a]Matt. 12:49

...5 [a]Eph. 6:6; Heb. ...1 Pet. 4:2; 1 John 2:17

[1]Lit., *is gathered* ...ark 4:1-12: *Matt.* ...*1-15; Luke 8:4-10* ...k 2:13; 3:7 [c]Luke 5:1-3

...att. 13:3ff.; Mark 3:23; 4:2ff.

...Matt. 11:15; Mark ...ev. 2:7, 11, 17, 29

[1]Lit., *those about Him*

of the kingdom of God; but [a]those who are outside get everything [b]in
parables,
12 in order that [a]WHILE SEEING, THEY MAY SEE AND NOT PERCEIVE; AND
WHILE HEARING, THEY MAY HEAR AND NOT UNDERSTAND LEST THEY RETURN
AND BE FORGIVEN."
13 [a]And He *said to them, "Do you not understand this parable?
And how will you understand all the parables?
14 "The sower sows the word.
15 "And these are the ones who are beside the road where the word
is sown; and when they hear, immediately [a]Satan comes and takes
away the word which has been sown in them.
16 "And in a similar way these are the ones on whom seed was
sown on the rocky *places,* who, when they hear the word, immedi-
ately receive it with joy;
17 and they have no *firm* root in themselves, but are *only* tem-
porary; then, when affliction or persecution arises because of the
word, immediately they [1]fall away.
18 "And others are the ones on whom seed was sown among the
thorns; these are the ones who have heard the word,
19 and the worries of [a]the [1]world, and the [b]deceitfulness of riches,
and the desires for other things enter in and choke the word, and it
becomes unfruitful.
20 "And those are the ones on whom seed was sown on the good
soil; and they hear the word and accept it, and [a]bear fruit, thirty,
sixty, and a hundredfold."
21 And He was saying to them, "[a]A lamp is not brought to be put
under a peck-measure, is it, or under a bed? Is it not *brought* to be
put on the lampstand?
22 "[a]For nothing is hidden, except to be revealed; nor has *anything*
been secret, but that it should come to light.
23 "[a]If any man has ears to hear, let him hear."
24 And He was saying to them, "Take care what you listen to. [1a]By
your standard of measure it shall be measured to you; and more
shall be given you besides.
25 "[a]For whoever has, to him shall *more* be given; and whoever does
not have, even what he has shall be taken away from him."
26 And He was saying, "The kingdom of God is like a man who
casts seed upon the soil;
27 and goes to bed at night and gets up by day, and the seed
sprouts up and grows—how, he himself does not know.
28 "The soil produces crops by itself; first the blade, then the head,
then the mature grain in the head.
29 "But when the crop permits, he immediately [1a]puts in the sickle,
because the harvest has come."
30 [a]And He said, "How shall we [1b]picture the kingdom of God, or
by what parable shall we present it?
31 "*It is* like a mustard seed, which, when sown upon the soil,
though it is smaller than all the seeds that are upon the soil,
32 yet when it is sown, grows up and becomes larger than all the
garden plants and forms large branches; so that [a]THE BIRDS OF THE [1]AIR
can NEST UNDER ITS SHADE."
33 And with many such parables He was speaking the word to
them as they were able to hear it;

11 [a]1 Cor. 5:1… 4:5; 1 Thess. … 1 Tim. 3:7 [b]M… 4:2

12 [a]Is. 6:9f.; … 5:21; Ezek. 12… 13:14; Luke 8… 12:40; Rom. …

13 [a]Mark 4:13… *13:18-23; Luk…*

15 [a]Matt. 4:10… 5:8; Rev. 20:2…

17 [1]Lit., *are ca… stumble*

19 [1]Or, *age* [a]M… 13:22; Rom. 12… 2:2; 6:12 [b]Prov… 1 Tim. 6:9, 10, …

20 [a]John 15:2f… 7:4

21 [a]Matt. 5:15; … 8:16; 11:33

22 [a]Matt. 10:26… 8:17; 12:2

23 [a]Matt. 11:15… 43; Mark 4:9; Lu… 14:35; Rev. 3:6, … 13:9

24 [1]Lit., *By wha… measure you me…* [a]Matt. 7:2; Luke …

25 [a]Matt. 13:12; … Luke 8:18; 19:26…

29 [1]Lit., *sends fo…* [a]Joel 3:13

30 [1]Lit., *compare…* [a]Mark 4:30-32: *M… 13:31, 32; Luke … 19* [b]Matt. 13:24

32 [1]Or, *sky* [a]Eze… 17:23; Ps. 104:12… Ezek. 31:6; Dan. …

34 and He did not speak to them [a]without a parable; but He was
[b]explaining everything privately to His own disciples.
35 [a]And on that day, when evening had come, He *said to them,
"Let us go over to the other side."
36 And [1]leaving the multitude, they *took Him along with them,
just as He was, [a]in the boat; and other boats were with Him.
37 And there *arose a fierce gale of wind, and the waves were
breaking over the boat so much that the boat was already filling up.
38 And He Himself was in the stern, asleep on the cushion; and
they *awoke Him and *said to Him, "Teacher, do You not care that
we are perishing?"
39 And being aroused, [a]He rebuked the wind and said to the sea,
"Hush, be still." And the wind died down and [1]it became perfectly
calm.
40 And He said to them, "Why are you so timid? [a]How is it that
you have no faith?"
41 And they became very much afraid and said to one another,
"Who then is this, that even the wind and the sea obey Him?"

Chapter 5

5 [a]And they came to the other side of the sea, into the country of
the Gerasenes.
2 And when He had come out of [a]the boat, immediately a man
from the tombs [b]with an unclean spirit met Him,
3 and he had his dwelling among the tombs. And no one was able
to bind him anymore, even with a chain;
4 because he had often been bound with shackles and chains, and
the chains had been torn apart by him, and the shackles broken in
pieces, and no one was strong enough to subdue him.
5 And constantly night and day, among the tombs and in the
mountains, he was crying out and gashing himself with stones.
6 And seeing Jesus from a distance, he ran up and bowed down
before Him;
7 and crying out with a loud voice, he *said, "[a]What do I have to
do with You, Jesus, [b]Son of [c]the Most High God? I implore You by
God, do not torment me!"
8 For He had been saying to him, "Come out of the man, you
unclean spirit!"
9 And He was asking him, "What is your name?" And he *said to
Him, "My name is [a]Legion; for we are many."
10 And he *began* to entreat Him earnestly not to send them out of
the country.
11 Now there was a big herd of swine feeding there on the moun-
tain.
12 And *the demons* entreated Him, saying, "Send us into the swine
so that we may enter them."
13 And He gave them permission. And coming out, the unclean
spirits entered the swine; and the herd rushed down the steep bank
into the sea, about two thousand *of them*; and they [1]were drowned in
the sea.
14 And their herdsmen ran away and reported it in the city and *out*
in the country. And *the people* came to see what it was that had
happened.
15 And they *came to Jesus and *observed the man who had been

Matt. 13:34; John :25 [b]Luke 24:27

rk 4:35-41: *Matt. 8:18, 23-27; Luke 8:22, 25*

Or, *sending away* 3:9; 4:1; 5:2, 21

Lit., *a great calm* urred [a]Ps. 65:7; 7:29; Matt. 8:26; Luke 8:24

Matt. 14:31; Luke 8:25

ark 5:1-17: *Matt. 34; Luke 8:26-37*

Mark 3:9; 4:1, 36; 5:21 [b]Mark 1:23

Matt. 8:29 [b]Matt. [c]Luke 8:28; Acts 16:17; Heb. 7:1

Matt. 26:53; Mark 5:15; Luke 8:30

, *were drowning*

[a]demon-possessed sitting down, [b]clothed and [c]in his right mind, the
very man who had had the "[d]legion"; and they became frightened.
16 And those who had seen it described to them how it had hap-
pened to the [a]demon-possessed man, and *all* about the swine.
17 And they began to [a]entreat Him to depart from their region.
18 [a]And as He was getting into the boat, the man who had been
[b]demon-possessed was entreating Him that he might [1]accompany
Him.
19 And He did not let him, but He *said to him, "[a]Go home to your
people and report to them [1]what great things the Lord has done for
you, and *how* He had mercy on you."
20 And he went away and began to [a]proclaim in [b]Decapolis [1]what
great things Jesus had done for him; and everyone marveled.
21 [a]And when Jesus had crossed over again in [b]the boat to the other
side, a great multitude gathered about Him; and He [1]stayed [c]by the
seashore.
22 [a]And one of [b]the synagogue [1]officials named Jairus *came up,
and upon seeing Him, *fell at His feet,
23 and *entreated Him earnestly, saying, "My little daughter is at
the point of death; *please* come and [a]lay Your hands on her, that she
may [1]get well and live."
24 And He went off with him; and a great multitude was following
Him and pressing in on Him.
25 And a woman who had had a hemorrhage for twelve years,
26 and had endured much at the hands of many physicians, and
had spent all that she had and was not helped at all, but rather had
grown worse,
27 after hearing about Jesus, came up in the crowd behind *Him,* and
touched His [1]cloak.
28 For she [1]thought, "If I just touch His garments, I shall [2]get well."
29 And immediately the flow of her blood was dried up; and she
felt in her body that she was healed of her [a]affliction.
30 And immediately Jesus, perceiving in Himself that [a]the power
proceeding from Him had gone forth, turned around in the crowd
and said, "Who touched My garments?"
31 And His disciples said to Him, "You see the multitude pressing
in on You, and You say, 'Who touched Me?' "
32 And He looked around to see the woman who had done this.
33 But the woman fearing and trembling, aware of what had hap-
pened to her, came and fell down before Him, and told Him the
whole truth.
34 And He said to her, "Daughter, [a]your faith has [1]made you well;
[b]go in peace, and be healed of your [c]affliction."
35 While He was still speaking, they *came from the *house of* the
[a]synagogue official, saying, "Your daughter has died; why trouble
the Teacher anymore?"
36 But Jesus, overhearing what was being spoken, *said to the
[a]synagogue official, "[b]Do not be afraid *any longer,* only [1]believe."
37 And He allowed no one to follow with Him, except [a]Peter and
[1]James and John the brother of [1]James.
38 And they *came to the house of the [a]synagogue official; and He
*beheld a commotion, and *people* loudly weeping and wailing.
39 And entering in, He *said to them, "Why make a commotion
and weep? The child has not died, but is asleep."

15 [a]Matt. 4 5:16, 18 [b]L [c]Luke 8:35
16 [a]Matt. 4 5:15
17 [a]Matt. 8: 16:39
18 [1]Lit., *be* [a]Mark 5:18-2 *8:38, 39* [b]M Mark 5:15, 1
19 [1]Or, *ever* [a]Luke 8:39
20 [1]Or, *ever* [a]Ps. 66:16 [b] Mark 7:31
21 [1]Lit., *was* Luke 8:40 [b]M [c]Mark 4:1
22 [1]Or, *rulers* 5:22-43: *Matt* *Luke 8:41-56* 9:18; Mark 5: Luke 8:49; 13 13:15; 18:8, 1
23 [1]Lit., *be sa* [a]Mark 6:5; 7:3 16:18; Luke 4: Acts 6:6; 9:17;
27 [1]Or, *outer*
28 [1]Lit., *was s* [2]Lit., *be saved*
29 [a]Mark 3:10
30 [a]Luke 5:17
34 [1]Lit., *saved* [a]Matt. 9:22 [b]Lu 8:48; Acts 16:3 2:16 [c]Mark 3:1
35 [a]Mark 5:22
36 [1]Or, *keep or believing* [a]Mark [b]Luke 8:50
37 [1]Or, *Jacob* 17:1; 26:37
38 [a]Mark 5:22

40 And they *began* laughing at Him. But putting them all out, He *took along the child's father and mother and His own companions, and *entered *the room* where the child was.
41 And taking the child by the hand, He *said to her, "Talitha kum!" (which translated means, "Little girl, [a]I say to you, arise!").
42 And immediately the girl rose and *began* to walk; for she was twelve years old. And immediately they were completely astounded.
43 And He [a]gave them strict orders that no one should know about this; and He said that *something* should be given her to eat.

Chapter 6

6 [a]And He went out from there, and He *came into [1b]His home town; and His disciples *followed Him.
2 And when the Sabbath had come, He began [a]to teach in the synagogue; and the [b]many listeners were astonished, saying, "Where did this man *get* these things, and what is *this* wisdom given to Him, and such [1]miracles as these performed by His hands?
3 "Is not this [a]the carpenter, [b]the son of Mary, and brother of [1]James, and Joses, and Judas, and Simon? Are not [c]His sisters here with us?" And they [2]took [d]offense at Him.
4 And Jesus said to them, "[a]A prophet is not without honor except in [1b]his home town and among his *own* relatives and in his *own* household."
5 And He could do no [1]miracle there except that He [a]laid His hands upon a few sick people and healed them.
6 And He wondered at their unbelief.
[a]**And** He was going around the villages teaching.
7 [a]And [b]He *summoned the twelve and began to send them out [c]in pairs; and He was giving them authority over the unclean spirits;
8 [a]and He instructed them that they should take nothing for *their* journey, except a mere staff; no bread, no [1]bag, no money in their belt;
9 but [1]*to* wear sandals; and *He added*, "Do not put on two [2]tunics."
10 And He said to them, "Wherever you enter a house, stay there until you [1]leave town.
11 "And any place that does not receive you or listen to you, as you go out from there, [a]shake off the dust [1]from the soles of your feet for a testimony against them."
12 [a]And they went out and [1]preached that *men* should repent.
13 And they were casting out many demons and [a]were anointing with oil many sick people and healing them.
14 [a]And King Herod heard *of it*, for His name had become well known; and *people* were saying, "[b]John the Baptist has risen from the dead, and that is why these miraculous powers are at work in Him."
15 But others were saying, "He is [a]Elijah." And others were saying, "He is [b]a prophet, like one of the prophets *of old*."
16 But when Herod heard *of it*, he kept saying, "John, whom I beheaded, has risen!"
17 For Herod himself had sent and had John arrested and bound in prison on account of [a]Herodias, the wife of his brother Philip, because he had married her.
18 For John had been saying to Herod, "[a]It is not lawful for you to have your brother's wife."

ke 7:14; Acts 9:40
43 [a]Matt. 8:4
Or, *His own part of the country* [a]Mark 6: *Matt. 13:54-58* t. 13:54, 57; Luke 4:16, 23
r, *works of power* . 4:23; Mark 10:1 [b]Matt. 7:28
Jacob [2]Lit., *were made to stumble* Matt. 13:55 [b]Matt. 2:46 [c]Matt. 13:56 [d]Matt. 11:6
Or, *his own part of the country* [a]Matt. John 4:44 [b]Mark 6:1
Or, *work of power* [a]Mark 5:23
[a]Matt. 9:35; Mark 10:1; Luke 13:22
Mark 6:7-11: *Matt.* *, 9-14; Luke 9:1, 3-5;* Luke 10:4-11 att. 10:1, 5; Mark ; Luke 9:1 [c]Luke 10:1
[1]Or, *knapsack or* *ggar's bag* [a]Matt. 10:10
, *being shod with* r, *inner garments*
[1]Lit., *go out from there*
, *under your feet* 0:14; Acts 13:51
proclaimed as a [a]Matt. 11:1; Luke 9:6
13 [a]James 5:14
rk 6:14-29: *Matt.* *2;* Mark 6:14-16: *:7-9* [b]Matt. 14:2; Luke 9:19
Matt. 16:14; Mark :28 [b]Matt. 21:11
[a]Matt. 14:3; Luke 3:19
18 [a]Matt. 14:4

19 And [a]Herodias had a grudge against him and wanted to put him
to death and could not *do so;*
20 for [a]Herod was afraid of John, knowing that he was a righteous
and holy man, and kept him safe. And when he heard him, he was
very perplexed; [1]but he [2]used to enjoy listening to him.
21 And a strategic day came when Herod on his birthday [a]gave a
banquet for his lords and [1]military commanders and the leading
men [b]of Galilee;
22 and when the daughter of [a]Herodias herself came in and danced,
she pleased Herod and [1]his dinner guests; and the king said to the
girl, "Ask me for whatever you want and I will give it to you."
23 And he swore to her, "Whatever you ask of me, I will give it to
you; up to [a]half of my kingdom."
24 And she went out and said to her mother, "What shall I ask for?"
And she said, "The head of John the Baptist."
25 And immediately she came in haste before the king and asked,
saying, "I want you to give me right away the head of John the
Baptist on a platter."
26 And although the king was very sorry, *yet* because of his oaths
and because of [1]his dinner guests, he was unwilling to refuse her.
27 And immediately the king sent an executioner and commanded
him to bring *back* his head. And he went and had him beheaded in
the prison,
28 and brought his head on a platter, and gave it to the girl; and the
girl gave it to her mother.
29 And when his disciples heard *about this,* they came and took
away his body and laid it in a tomb.
30 [a]And the [b]apostles *gathered together with Jesus; and they re-
ported to Him all that they had done and taught.
31 And He *said to them, "Come away by yourselves to a lonely
place and rest a while." (For there were many *people* coming and
going, and [a]they did not even have time to eat.)
32 [a]And they went away in [b]the boat to a lonely place by them-
selves.
33 And *the people* saw them going, and many recognized *them,* and
they ran there together on foot from all the cities, and got there
ahead of them.
34 And when He went [1]ashore, He [a]saw a great multitude, and He
felt compassion for them because [b]they were like sheep without a
shepherd; and He began to teach them many things.
35 And when it was already quite late, His disciples came up to
Him and *began* saying, "The place is desolate and it is already quite
late;
36 send them away so that they may go into the surrounding
countryside and villages and buy themselves [1]something to eat."
37 But He answered and said to them, "You give them *something* to
eat!" [a]And they *said to Him, "Shall we go and spend two hundred
[1b]denarii on bread and give them *something* to eat?"
38 And He *said to them, "How many loaves do you have? Go
look!" And when they found out, they *said, "Five and two fish."
39 And He commanded them all to recline by groups on the green
grass.
40 And they reclined in companies of hundreds and of fifties.
41 And He took the five loaves and the two fish, and looking up

19 [a]Matt. 14:3

20 [1]Lit., *and hearing him g*
[a]Matt. 21:26

21 [1]I.e., chilia
command of a
troops [a]Esth.
[b]Luke 3:1

22 [1]Lit., *those reclined at the him* [a]Matt. 14:

23 [a]Esth. 5:3,

26 [1]Lit., *those at the table*

30 [a]Luke 9:10
10:2; Mark 3:14
6:13; 9:10; 17:5
24:10; Acts 1:2,

31 [a]Mark 3:20

32 [a]Mark 6:32-4
14:13-21; Luke
John 6:5-13; Ma
8:2-9 [b]Mark 3:9;
6:45

34 [1]Lit., *out* [a]Ma
9:36 [b]Num. 27:1
1 Kin. 22:17; 2 C
18:16; Zech. 10:2

36 [1]Lit., *what the eat*

37 [1]The denariu
equivalent to one
wage [a]John 6:7
18:28; Luke 7:41

toward heaven, He [a]blessed *the food* and broke the loaves and He
kept giving *them* to the disciples to set before them; and He divided
up the two fish among them all.
42 And they all ate and were satisfied.
43 And they picked up twelve full [a]baskets of the broken pieces,
and also of the fish.
44 And there were [a]five thousand men who ate the loaves.
45 [a]And immediately He made His disciples get into [b]the boat and
go ahead of *Him* to the other side to [c]Bethsaida, while He Himself
was sending the multitude away.
46 And after [a]bidding them farewell, He departed [b]to the mountain
to pray.
47 And when it was evening, the boat was in the midst of the sea,
and He *was* alone on the land.
48 And seeing them [1]straining at the oars, for the wind was against
them, at about the [2a]fourth watch of the night, He *came to them,
walking on the sea; and He intended to pass by them.
49 But when they saw Him walking on the sea, they supposed that
it was a ghost, and cried out;
50 for they all saw Him and were [1]frightened. But immediately He
spoke with them and *said to them, "[a]Take courage; it is I, [b]do not be
afraid."
51 And He got into [a]the boat with them, and the wind stopped; and
they were greatly astonished,
52 for [a]they [1]had not gained any insight from the *incident of* the
loaves, but [2]their heart [b]was hardened.
53 [a]And when they had crossed over they came to land at Gen-
nesaret, and moored to the shore.
54 And when they had come out of the boat, immediately *the people*
recognized Him,
55 and ran about that whole country and began to carry about on
their pallets those who were sick, to [1]the place they heard He was.
56 And wherever He entered villages, or cities, or countryside, they
were laying the sick in the market places, and entreating Him that
they might just [a]touch [b]the fringe of His cloak; and as many as
touched it were being cured.

Chapter 7

7 [a]And the Pharisees and some of the scribes gathered together
around Him when they had come [b]from Jerusalem,
2 and had seen that some of His disciples were eating their bread
with [a]impure hands, that is, unwashed.
3 (For the Pharisees and all the Jews do not eat unless they [1]care-
fully wash their hands, *thus* observing the [a]traditions of the elders;
4 and *when they come* from the market place, they do not eat unless
they [1]cleanse themselves; and there are many other things which
they have received in order to observe, such as the [2]washing of [a]cups
and pitchers and copper pots.)
5 And the Pharisees and the scribes *asked Him, "Why do Your
disciples not walk according to the [a]tradition of the elders, but eat
their bread with [b]impure hands?"
6 And He said to them, "Rightly did Isaiah prophesy of you hypo-
crites, as it is written,
'[a]THIS PEOPLE HONORS ME WITH THEIR LIPS,

[a]Matt. 14:19
[a]Matt. 14:20
[a]Matt. 14:21
:45-51: *Matt.* John 6:15-21 ‹ 6:32 [c]Matt. :1; Mark 8:22
cts 18:18, 21; [b]Matt. 14:23
., *harassed in* [2]I.e., 3-6 a.m. 3; Mark 13:35
oubled [a]Matt. [b]Matt. 14:27
1 [a]Mark 6:32
[1]Lit., *had not* *d on the basis* *heir mind was* *, made dull, or* *ensible* [a]Mark ff. [b]Rom. 11:7
6:53-56: *Matt.* John 6:24, 25
Or, *where they* *hearing that He* *was*
ark 3:10 [b]Matt. 9:20
rk 7:1-23: *Matt.* -20 [b]Matt. 15:1
15:2; Mark 7:5; 38; Acts 10:14, :8; Rom. 14:14; :29; Rev. 21:27
Lit., *with the fist* 5, 8, 9, 13; Gal. 1:14
r, sprinkle [2]Lit., *ng* [a]Matt. 23:25
ark 7:3, 8, 9, 13; 1:14 [b]Mark 7:2
6 [a]Is. 29:13

But their heart is far away from Me.
7 '[a]But in vain do they worship Me,
Teaching as doctrines the precepts of men.'
8 "Neglecting the commandment of God, you hold to the [a]tradition
of men."
9 He was also saying to them, "You nicely set aside the command-
ment of God in order to keep your [a]tradition.
10 "For Moses said, '[a]Honor your father and your mother'; and,
'[b]He who speaks evil of father or mother, let him [1]be put to death';
11 but you say, 'If a man says to *his* father or *his* mother, anything of
mine you might have been helped by is [a]Corban (that is to say,
[1]given *to God*),'
12 you no longer permit him to do anything for *his* father or *his*
mother;
13 *thus* invalidating the word of God by your [a]tradition which you
have handed down; and you do many things such as that."
14 And after He called the multitude to Him again, He *began* saying
to them, "Listen to Me, all of you, and understand:
15 there is nothing outside the man which going into him can defile
him; but the things which proceed out of the man are what defile the
man.
16 ["[1]If any man has ears to hear, let him hear."]
17 And when leaving the multitude, He had entered [a]the house,
[b]His disciples questioned Him about the parable.
18 And He *said to them, "Are you so lacking in understanding
also? Do you not understand that whatever goes into the man from
outside cannot defile him;
19 because it does not go into his heart, but into his stomach, and [1]is
eliminated?" (*Thus He* declared [a]all foods [b]clean.)
20 And He was saying, "[a]That which proceeds out of the man, that
is what defiles the man.
21 "For from within, out of the heart of men, proceed the evil
thoughts, [1]fornications, thefts, murders, adulteries,
22 deeds of coveting *and* wickedness, *as well as* deceit, sensuality,
[1a]envy, slander, [2]pride *and* foolishness.
23 "All these evil things proceed from within and defile the man."
24 [a]And from there He arose and went away to the region of [b]Tyre[1].
And when He had entered a house, He wanted no one to know *of it*;
[2]yet He could not escape notice.
25 But after hearing of Him, a woman whose little daughter had an
unclean spirit, immediately came and fell at His feet.
26 Now the woman was a [1]Gentile, of the Syrophoenician race. And
she kept asking Him to cast the demon out of her daughter.
27 And He was saying to her, "Let the children be satisfied first, for
it is not [1]good to take the children's bread and throw it to the dogs."
28 But she answered and *said to Him, "Yes, Lord, *but* even the
dogs under the table feed on the children's crumbs."
29 And He said to her, "Because of this [1]answer go your way; the
demon has gone out of your daughter."
30 And going back to her home, she found the child [1]lying on the
bed, the demon having departed.
31 [a]And again He went out from the region of [b]Tyre, and came
through Sidon to [c]the Sea of Galilee, within the region of [d]Decapolis.

7 [a]Is. 29:13
8 [a]Mark 7:3, Gal. 1:14
9 [a]Mark 7:3, Gal. 1:14
10 [1]Lit., *die th* [a]Ex. 20:12; De [b]Ex. 21:17; Le
11 [1]Or, *a gift, offering* [a]Lev. 27:6
13 [a]Mark 7:3, Gal. 1:14
16 [1]Many mss contain this ve
17 [a]Mark 2:1; 9:28 [b]Matt. 15
19 [1]Lit., *goes* *the latrine* [a]Ro 14:1-12; Col. 2 [b]Luke 11:41; Ac 11:9
20 [a]Matt. 15:18 7:23
21 [1]I.e., acts of immorality
22 [1]Lit., *an evil* [2]Or, *arrogance* 6:23; 20:15
24 [1]Some early add *and Sidon and* [a]Mark 7:24 *Matt. 15:21-28* 11:21; Mark 7:31
26 [1]Lit., *Greek*
27 [1]Or, *proper*
29 [1]Lit., *word*
30 [1]Lit., *thrown*
31 [a]Mark 7:31-3 *15:29-31* [b]Matt. Mark 7:24 [c]Matt. [d]Matt. 4:25; Mark

32 [a]Mark 5:23

32 And they *brought to Him one who was deaf and spoke with
difficulty, and they *entreated Him to [a]lay His hand upon him.

33 [a]Mark 8:23

33 And [a]He took him aside from the multitude by himself, and put
His fingers into his ears, and after [a]spitting, He touched his tongue
with the saliva;

34 [a]Mark 8:12

34 and looking up to heaven with a deep [a]sigh, He *said to him,
"Ephphatha!" that is, "Be opened!"

)r, bond [2]Lit., was loosed

35 And his ears were opened, and the [1]impediment of his tongue
[2]was removed, and he *began* speaking plainly.
36 And [a]He gave them orders not to tell anyone; but the more He
ordered them, the more widely they [b]continued to proclaim it.

[a]Matt. 8:4 [b]Mark 1:45

37 And they were utterly astonished, saying, "He has done all
things well; He makes even the deaf to hear, and the dumb to
speak."

[a]Mark 8:1-9: *Matt.* *-39;* Mark 6:34-44

Chapter 8

8 In those days again, when there was a great multitude and they
had nothing to eat, [a]He called His disciples and *said to them,

t. 9:36; Mark 6:34

2 "[a]I feel compassion for the multitude because they have remained
with Me now three days, and have nothing to eat;
3 and if I send them away hungry to their home, they will faint on
the way; and some of them have come from a distance."

4 [1]Lit., *loaves*

4 And His disciples answered Him, "Where will anyone be able to
find enough to satisfy these men with [1]bread here in a desolate
place?"

, *recline* [2]Lit., *set before*

5 And He was asking them, "How many loaves do you have?"
And they said, "Seven."

, *set before them* [a]Matt. 14:19

6 And He *directed the multitude to [1]sit down on the ground; and
taking the seven loaves, He gave thanks and broke them, and started
giving them to His disciples to [2]serve to them, and they served them
to the multitude.

Matt. 15:37; Mark 8:20

7 They also had a few small fish; and [a]after He had blessed them,
He ordered these to be [1]served as well.
8 And they ate and were satisfied; and they picked up seven large
[a]baskets full of what was left over of the broken pieces.

10 [a]Matt. 15:39

9 And about four thousand were *there;* and He sent them away.
10 And immediately He entered the boat with His disciples, and
came to the district of [a]Dalmanutha.

The exact location of Dalmanutha is unknown. However, it is believed to be another name for Magdala or the name for a nearby region.

11 [1]Or, *attesting* *acle* [2]Lit., *testing* *n* [a]Mark 8:11-21: *t.* 16:1-12 [b]Matt. 12:38

11 [a]And the Pharisees came out and began to argue with
Him, [b]seeking from Him a [1]sign from heaven, [2]to test Him.

, *to Himself* [2]Or, *g miracle* [3]Lit., *if* *gn shall be given* :34 [b]Matt. 12:39

12 And [a]sighing deeply [1]in His spirit, He *said, "Why
does this generation seek for a [2]sign? Truly I say to you,
[3b]no [2]sign shall be given to this generation."
13 And leaving them, He again embarked and went away
to the other side.

were not having

14 And they had forgotten to take bread; and [1]did not
have more than one loaf in the boat with them.
15 And He was giving orders to them, saying, "[a]Watch
out! Beware of the leaven of the Pharisees and the leaven of
[b]Herod."

Matt. 16:6; Luke Matt. 14:1; 22:16

16 And they *began* to discuss with one another *the fact* that
they had no bread.

, *dull, insensible* [a]Mark 6:52

17 And Jesus, aware of this, *said to them, "Why do you
discuss *the fact* that you have no bread? [a]Do you not yet see
or understand? Do you have a [1]hardened heart?

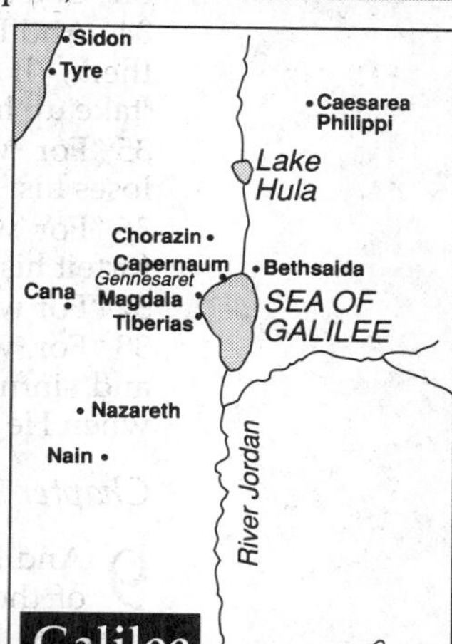

18 "[a]HAVING EYES, DO YOU NOT SEE? AND HAVING EARS, DO YOU NOT HEAR? And do you not remember,

19 when I broke [a]the five loaves for the five thousand, how many [b]baskets full of broken pieces you picked up?" They *said to Him, "Twelve."

20 "And when *I broke* [a]the seven for the four thousand, how many large [b]baskets full of broken pieces did you pick up?" And they *said to Him, "Seven."

21 And He was saying to them, "[a]Do you not yet understand?"

22 And they *came to [a]Bethsaida. And they *brought a blind man to Him, and *entreated Him to [b]touch him.

23 And taking the blind man by the hand, He [a]brought him out of the village; and after [a]spitting on his eyes, and [b]laying His hands upon him, He asked him, "Do you see anything?"

24 And he [1]looked up and said, "I see men, for [2]I am seeing *them* like trees, walking about."

25 Then again He laid His hands upon his eyes; and he looked intently and was restored, and *began* to see everything clearly.

26 And He sent him to his home, saying, "Do not even enter [a]the village."

27 [a]And Jesus went out, along with His disciples, to the villages of [b]Caesarea Philippi; and on the way He questioned His disciples, saying to them, "Who do people say that I am?"

28 [a]And they told Him, saying, "John the Baptist; and others *say* Elijah; but others, one of the prophets."

29 And He *continued* by questioning them, "But who do you say that I am?" [a]Peter *answered and *said to Him, "Thou art [1]the Christ."

30 And [a]He [1]warned them to tell no one about Him.

31 [a]And He began to teach them that [b]the Son of Man must suffer many things and be rejected by the elders and the chief priests and the scribes, and be killed, and after three days rise again.

32 And He was stating the matter [a]plainly. And Peter took Him aside and began to rebuke Him.

33 But turning around and seeing His disciples, He rebuked Peter, and *said, "Get behind Me, [a]Satan; for you are not setting your mind on [1]God's interests, but man's."

34 And He summoned the multitude with His disciples, and said to them, "If anyone wishes to come after Me, let him deny himself, and [a]take up his cross, and follow Me.

35 "For [a]whoever wishes to save his [1]life shall lose it; but whoever loses his [1]life for My sake and the gospel's shall save it.

36 "For what does it profit a man to gain the whole world, and forfeit his soul?

37 "For what shall a man give in exchange for his soul?

38 "For [a]whoever is ashamed of Me and My words in this adulterous and sinful generation, [b]the Son of Man will also be ashamed of him when He [c]comes in the glory of His Father with the holy angels."

Chapter 9 ________________

9 And He was saying to them, "[a]Truly I say to you, there are some of those who are standing here who shall not taste death until they see the kingdom of God after it has come with power."

2 [a]And six days later, Jesus *took with Him [b]Peter and [1]James and

18 [a]Jer. 5:21; 12:2; Mark 4:1
19 [a]Mark 6:41 [b]Matt. 14:20
20 [a]Mark 8:6- 8:8
21 [a]Mark 6:52
22 [a]Matt. 11:2 6:45 [b]Mark 3:
23 [a]Mark 7:33 5:23
24 [1]Or, *gained* [2]Or, *they look*
26 [a]Mark 8:23
27 [a]Mark 8:27 *16:13-16; Luke* [b]Matt. 16:13
28 [a]Mark 6:14; 9:7, 8
29 [1]I.e., the Me [a]John 6:68, 69
30 [1]Or, *strictly admonished* [a]M 16:20; Luke 9:2
31 [a]Mark 8:31- *Matt. 16:21-28; 9:22-27* [b]Matt.
32 [a]John 10:24 16:25, 29; 18:20
33 [1]Lit., *the thin God* [a]Matt. 4:10
34 [a]Matt. 10:38; 14:27
35 [1]Or, *soul* [a]M 10:39; Luke 17:3 12:25
38 [a]Matt. 10:33; 9:26; Heb. 11:16 8:20 [c]Matt. 16:27 13:26; Luke 9:26
9:1 [a]Matt. 16:28; 13:26; Luke 9:27
2 [1]Or, *Jacob* [a]M 9:2-8: *Matt. 17:1- 9:28-36* [b]Mark 5:

John, and *brought them up to a high mountain by themselves. And
He was transfigured before them;
3 and [a]His garments became radiant and exceedingly white, as no
launderer on earth can whiten them.
4 And Elijah appeared to them along with Moses; and they were
talking with Jesus.
5 And Peter answered and *said to Jesus, "[a]Rabbi, it is good for us
to be here; and [b]let us make three [1]tabernacles, one for You, and one
for Moses, and one for Elijah."
6 For he did not know what to answer; for they became terrified.
7 Then a cloud [1]formed, overshadowing them, and [a]a voice [1]came
out of the cloud, "[b]This is My beloved Son, [2]listen to Him!"
8 And all at once they looked around and saw no one with them
anymore, except Jesus alone.
9 [a]And as they were coming down from the mountain, He [b]gave
them orders not to relate to anyone what they had seen, [1]until the
Son of Man should rise from the dead.
10 And they [1]seized upon [2]that statement, discussing with one
another [3]what rising from the dead might mean.
11 And they asked Him, saying, "*Why is it* that the scribes say that
[a]Elijah must come first?"
12 And He said to them, "Elijah does first come and restore all
things. And *yet* how is it written of [a]the Son of Man that [b]He should
suffer many things and be treated with contempt?
13 "But I say to you, that Elijah has [1]indeed come, and they did to
him whatever they wished, just as it is written of him."
14 [a]And when they came *back* to the disciples, they saw a large
crowd around them, and *some* scribes arguing with them.
15 And immediately, when the entire crowd saw Him, they were
[a]amazed, and *began* running up to greet Him.
16 And He asked them, "What are you discussing with them?"
17 And one of the crowd answered Him, "Teacher, I brought You
my son, possessed with a spirit which makes him mute;
18 and [1]whenever it seizes him, it [2]dashes him *to the ground* and he
foams *at the mouth*, and grinds his teeth, and [3]stiffens out. And I told
Your disciples to cast it out, and they could not *do it*."
19 And He *answered them and *said, "O unbelieving generation,
how long shall I be with you? How long shall I put up with you?
Bring him to Me!"
20 And they brought [1]the boy to Him. And when he saw Him,
immediately the spirit threw him into a convulsion, and falling to
the ground, he *began* rolling about and foaming *at the mouth*.
21 And He asked his father, "How long has this been happening to
him?" And he said, "From childhood.
22 "And it has often thrown him both into the fire and into the water
to destroy him. But if You can do anything, take pity on us and help
us!"
23 And Jesus said to him, "'If You can!' [a]All things are possible to
him who believes."
24 Immediately the boy's father cried out and *began* saying, "I do
believe; help my unbelief."
25 And when Jesus saw that [a]a crowd was [1]rapidly gathering, He
rebuked the unclean spirit, saying to it, "You deaf and dumb spirit, I
[2]command you, come out of him and do not enter him [3]again."

3 [a]Matt. 28:3
[1]Or, *sacred tents* 23:7 [b]Matt. 17:4; Luke 9:33
Or, *occurred* [2]Or, *ve constant heed* Pet. 1:17f. [b]Matt. Mark 1:11; Luke 3:22
Lit., *except when* ark 9:9-13: *Matt. 9-13* [b]Matt. 8:4; 5:43; 7:36; 8:30
10 [1]Or, *kept to selves* [2]Lit., *the ment* [3]Lit., *what e rising from the dead*
4:5; Matt. 11:14
lark 9:31 [b]Matt. 16:21; 26:24
13 [1]Lit., *also*
k 9:14-28: *Matt. 9; Luke 9:37-42*
k 14:33; 16:5, 6
, *wherever* [2]Or, *im* [3]Or, *withers away*
20 [1]Lit., *him*
att. 17:20; John 11:40
25 [1]Or, *running er* [2]Or, *I Myself mand* [3]Or, *from on* [a]Mark 9:15

26 And after crying out and throwing him into terrible convulsions,
it came out; and *the boy* became so much like a corpse that most *of*
them said, "He is dead!"
27 But Jesus took him by the hand and raised him; and he got up.
28 And when He had come [a]into *the* house, His disciples *began*
questioning Him privately, "Why could we not cast it out?"
29 And He said to them, "This kind cannot come out by anything
but prayer[1]."
30 [a]And from there they went out and *began* to go through Galilee,
and He was unwilling for anyone to know *about it*.
31 For He was teaching His disciples and telling them, "[a]The Son of
Man is to be [1]delivered into the hands of men, and they will kill
Him; and when He has been killed, He will rise three days later."
32 But [a]they [1]did not understand *this* statement, and they were
afraid to ask Him.
33 [a]And they came to Capernaum; and when He [1]was in [b]the house,
He *began* to question them, "What were you discussing on the way?"
34 But they kept silent, for on the way [a]they had discussed with one
another which *of them was* the greatest.
35 And sitting down, He called the twelve and *said to them, "[a]If
anyone wants to be first, [1]he shall be last of all, and servant of all."
36 And taking a child, He set him [1]before them, and taking him in
His arms, He said to them,
37 "[a]Whoever receives [1]one child like this in My name receives Me;
and whoever receives Me does not receive Me, but Him who sent
Me."
38 [a]John said to Him, "Teacher, we saw someone casting out
demons in Your name, and [b]we tried to hinder him because he was
not following us."
39 But Jesus said, "Do not hinder him, for there is no one who shall
perform a miracle in My name, and be able soon afterward to speak
evil of Me.
40 "[a]For he who is not against us is [1]for us.
41 "For [a]whoever gives you a cup of water to drink [1]because of your
name as *followers* of Christ, truly I say to you, he shall not lose his
reward.
42 "And [a]whoever causes one of these [1]little ones who believe to
stumble, it [2]would be better for him if, with a heavy millstone hung
around his neck, he [3]had been cast into the sea.
43 "And [a]if your hand causes you to stumble, cut it off; it is better for
you to enter life crippled, than having your two hands, to go into
[1b]hell, into the [c]unquenchable fire,
44 [[1]where THEIR WORM DOES NOT DIE, AND THE FIRE IS NOT QUENCHED.]
45 "And if your foot causes you to stumble, cut it off; it is better for
you to enter life lame, than having your two feet, to be cast into
[1a]hell,
46 [[1]where THEIR WORM DOES NOT DIE, AND THE FIRE IS NOT QUENCHED.]
47 "And [a]if your eye causes you to stumble, cast it out; it is better for
you to enter the kingdom of God with one eye, than having two
eyes, to be cast into [1b]hell,
48 [a]where THEIR WORM DOES NOT DIE, AND [b]THE FIRE IS NOT QUENCHED.
49 "For everyone will be salted with fire.
50 "Salt is good; but [a]if the salt becomes unsalty, with what will you

28 [a]Mark 2:
29 [1]Many m *fasting*
30 [a]Mark 9: *17:22, 23; Lu*
31 [1]Or, *betr* 16:21; Mark
32 [1]Lit., *wer knowing* [a]Lu 9:45; 18:34;
33 [1]Lit., *had* [a]Mark 9:33-3 *18:1-5; Luke* [b]Mark 3:19
34 [a]Matt. 18 9:50; Luke 22
35 [1]Or, *let hi* [a]Matt. 20:26; Mark 10:43, 4 22:26
36 [1]Lit., *in the*
37 [1]Lit., *one children* [a]Mat Luke 10:16; J
38 [a]Mark 9:38 *9:49, 50* [b]Num
40 [1]Or, *on ou* [a]Matt. 12:30; L
41 [1]Lit., *in a n you are Christ* 10:42
42 [1]I.e., humb *better for him i millstone turne donkey is hung has been cast* 18:6; Luke 17:2 8:12
43 [1]Gr., *Gehe* [a]Matt. 5:30; 18 5:22 [c]Matt. 3:1
44 [1]Vv. 44 and which are ident v. 48, are not fo the best ancien
45 [1]Gr., *Gehen* [a]Matt. 5:22
46 [1]V. 44, note
47 [1]Gr., *Gehen* [a]Matt. 5:29; 18:9 5:22
48 [a]Is. 66:24 [b] 3:12; 25:41
50 [a]Matt. 5:13; 14:34f.

[1]make it salty *again*? [b]Have salt in yourselves, and [c]be at peace with
one another."

Chapter 10

10 [a]And rising up, He *went from there to the region of Judea,
and beyond the Jordan; and crowds *gathered around Him
again, and, [b]according to His custom, He once more *began* to teach
them.
2 And *some* Pharisees came up to Him, testing Him, and *began* to
question Him whether it was lawful for a man to [1]divorce a wife.
3 And He answered and said to them, "What did Moses command
you?"
4 And they said, "[a]Moses permitted *a man* TO WRITE A CERTIFICATE OF
DIVORCE AND [1]SEND *her* AWAY."
5 But Jesus said to them, "[1a]Because of your hardness of heart he
wrote you this commandment.
6 "But [a]from the beginning of creation, *God* [b]MADE THEM MALE AND
FEMALE.
7 "[a]FOR THIS CAUSE A MAN SHALL LEAVE HIS FATHER AND MOTHER,[1]
8 [a]AND THE TWO SHALL BECOME ONE FLESH; consequently they are no
longer two, but one flesh.
9 "What therefore God has joined together, let no man separate."
10 And in the house the disciples *began* questioning Him about this
again.
11 And He *said to them, "[a]Whoever [1]divorces his wife and marries
another woman commits adultery against her;
12 and [a]if she herself [1]divorces her husband and marries another
man, she is committing adultery."
13 [a]And they were bringing children to Him so that He might touch
them; and the disciples rebuked them.
14 But when Jesus saw this, He was indignant and said to them,
"Permit the children to come to Me; do not hinder them; [a]for the
kingdom of God belongs to such as these.
15 "Truly I say to you, [a]whoever does not receive the kingdom of
God like a child shall not enter it *at all*."
16 And He [a]took them in His arms and *began* blessing them, laying
His hands upon them.
17 [a]And as He was setting out on a journey, a man ran up to Him
and [b]knelt before Him, and *began* asking Him, "Good Teacher, what
shall I do to [c]inherit eternal life?"
18 And Jesus said to him, "Why do you call Me good? No one is
good except God alone.
19 "You know the commandments, '[a]DO NOT MURDER, DO NOT COMMIT
ADULTERY, DO NOT STEAL, DO NOT BEAR FALSE WITNESS, Do not defraud,
HONOR YOUR FATHER AND MOTHER.'"
20 And he said to Him, "Teacher, I have kept [a]all these things from
my youth up."
21 And looking at him, Jesus felt a love for him, and said to him,
"One thing you lack: go and sell all you possess, and give to the
poor, and you shall have [a]treasure in heaven; and come, follow Me."
22 But at these words [1]his face fell, and he went away grieved, for
he was one who owned much property.
23 And Jesus, looking around, *said to His disciples, "[a]How hard it
will be for those who are wealthy to enter the kingdom of God!"

...it., *season it* [b]Col. ...[c]Mark 9:34; Rom. ...2:18; 2 Cor. 13:11; 1 Thess. 5:13

...1 [a]Mark 10:1-12: ...*Matt. 19:1-9* [b]Matt. 26:55; Mark 1:21; ...13; 4:2; 6:2, 6, 34; 12:35; 14:49

2 [1]Or, *send away*

...[1]Or, *divorce* her ...24:1, 3; Matt. 5:31

...Or, *With reference to* [a]Matt. 19:8

...Mark 13:19; 2 Pet. ...4 [b]Gen. 1:27; 5:2

...me mss. add *and cleave to his wife* [a]Gen. 2:24

8 [a]Gen. 2:24

[1]Or, *sends away* [a]Matt. 5:32

[1]Or, *sends away* [a]1 Cor. 7:11, 13

[a]Mark 10:13-16: ...*t. 19:13-15; Luke 18:15-17*

14 [a]Matt. 5:3

...Matt. 18:3; 19:14; ...uke 18:17; 1 Cor. 14:20; 1 Pet. 2:2

16 [a]Mark 9:36

[a]Mark 10:17-31: ...*t. 19:16-30; Luke* ...*8-30* [b]Mark 1:40 ...Matt. 25:34; Luke ...0:25; 18:18; Acts ...Eph. 1:18; 1 Pet. 1:4

...20:12-16; Deut. 5:16-20

20 [a]Matt. 19:20

21 [a]Matt. 6:20

[1]Or, *he became gloomy*

23 [a]Matt. 19:23

24 And the disciples [a]were amazed at His words. But Jesus
*answered again and *said to them, "Children, how hard it is [1]to
enter the kingdom of God!
25 "[a]It is easier for a camel to go through the eye of [1]a needle than for
a rich man to enter the kingdom of God."
26 And they were even more astonished and said [1]to Him, "[2]Then
who can be saved?"
27 Looking upon them, Jesus *said, "[a]With men it is impossible, but
not with God; for all things are possible with God."
28 [a]Peter began to say to Him, "Behold, we have left everything and
followed You."
29 Jesus said, "Truly I say to you, [a]there is no one who has left
house or brothers or sisters or mother or father or children or farms,
for My sake and for the gospel's sake,
30 but that he shall receive a hundred times as much now in [1]the
present age, houses and brothers and sisters and mothers and
children and farms, along with persecutions; and in [a]the age to come,
eternal life.
31 "But [a]many *who are* first, will be last; and the last, first."
32 [a]And they were on the road, going up to Jerusalem, and Jesus
was walking on ahead of them; and they [b]were amazed, and those
who followed were fearful. And again He took the twelve aside and
began to tell them what was going to happen to Him,
33 *saying,* "Behold, we are going up to Jerusalem, and [a]the Son of
Man will be [1]delivered to the chief priests and the scribes; and they
will condemn Him to death, and will [2]deliver Him to the Gentiles.
34 "And they will mock Him and [a]spit upon Him, and scourge Him,
and kill *Him,* and three days later He will rise again."
35 [a]And [1]James and John, the two sons of Zebedee, *came up to
Him, saying to Him, "Teacher, we want You to do for us whatever
we ask of You."
36 And He said to them, "What do you want Me to do for you?"
37 And they said to Him, "[1]Grant that we [a]may sit in Your glory,
one on Your right, and one on *Your* left."
38 But Jesus said to them, "You do not know what you are asking
for. Are you able [a]to drink the cup that I drink, or [b]to be baptized
with the baptism with which I am baptized?"
39 And they said to Him, "We are able." And Jesus said to them,
"The cup that I drink [a]you shall drink; and you shall be baptized
with the baptism with which I am baptized.
40 "But to sit on My right or on *My* left, this is not Mine to give; [a]but
it is for those for whom it has been prepared."
41 [a]And hearing this, the ten began to feel indignant with [1]James
and John.
42 And calling them to Himself, Jesus *said to them, "You know
that those who are recognized as rulers of the Gentiles lord it over
them; and their great men exercise authority over them.
43 "But it is not so among you, [a]but whoever wishes to become great
among you shall be your servant;
44 and whoever wishes to be first among you shall be slave of all.
45 "For even the Son of Man [a]did not come to be served, but to serve,
and to give His [1]life a ransom for many."
46 [a]And they *came to Jericho. And [b]as He was going out from

24 [1]Later ms *for those who* *wealth* [a]Mark

25 [1]Lit., *the* [a] 19:24

26 [1]Later mss *one another* [2]

27 [a]Matt. 19:2

28 [a]Matt. 4:20

29 [a]Matt. 6:33 Luke 18:29f.

30 [1]Lit., *this tir* 12:32

31 [a]Matt. 19:30 Luke 13:30

32 [a]Mark 10:32 *Matt. 20:17-19; 18:31-33* [b]Mark

33 [1]Or, *betraye* *betray* [a]Mark 8

34 [a]Matt. 16:21 27:30; Mark 9:3

35 [1]Or, *Jacob* 10:35-45: *Matt.*

37 [1]Lit., *Give to* [a]Matt. 19:28

38 [a]Matt. 20:22 12:50

39 [a]Acts 12:2; R

40 [a]Matt. 13:11

41 [1]Or, *Jacob* [a] 10:42-45; Luke 2

43 [a]Matt. 20:26; Mark 9:35; Luke

45 [1]Or, *soul* [a]Ma 20:28

46 [a]Mark 10:46-5 *Matt. 20:29-34; L* *18:35-43* [b]Luke 19:1

Jericho with His disciples and a great multitude, a blind beggar
named Bartimaeus, the son of Timaeus, was sitting by the road.
47 And when he heard that it was Jesus the [a]Nazarene, he began to
cry out and say, "Jesus, [b]Son of David, have mercy on me!"
48 And many were sternly telling him to be quiet, but he kept
crying out all the more, "[a]Son of David, have mercy on me!"
49 And Jesus stopped and said, "Call him *here.*" And they *called
the blind man, saying to him, "[a]Take courage, arise! He is calling for
you."
50 And casting aside his cloak, he jumped up, and came to Jesus.
51 And answering him, Jesus said, "What do you want Me to do for
you?" And the blind man said to Him, "[1a]Rabboni, *I want* to regain
my sight!"
52 And Jesus said to him, "Go your way; [a]your faith has [1]made you
well." And immediately he regained his sight and *began* following
Him on the road.

Chapter 11

11 [a]And as they *approached Jerusalem, at Bethphage and [b]Bethany, near [c]the Mount of Olives, He *sent two of His disciples,
2 and *said to them, "Go into the village opposite you, and imme-
diately as you enter it, you will find a colt tied *there,* on which no one
yet has ever sat; untie it and bring it *here.*
3 "And if anyone says to you, 'Why are you doing this?'
you say, 'The Lord has need of it'; and immediately he [1]will
send it back here."
4 And they went away and found a colt tied at the door
outside in the street; and they *untied it.
5 And some of the bystanders were saying to them,
"What are you doing, untying the colt?"
6 And they spoke to them just as Jesus had told *them,*
and they gave them permission.
7 [a]And they *brought the colt to Jesus and put their gar-
ments on it; and He sat upon it.
8 And many spread their garments in the road, and
others *spread* leafy branches which they had cut from the
fields.
9 And those who went before, and those who followed
after, were crying out,
"Hosanna!
[a]BLESSED IS HE WHO COMES IN THE NAME OF THE LORD;
10 Blessed *is* the coming kingdom of our father David;
Hosanna [a]in the highest!"
11 And [a]He entered Jerusalem *and came* into the temple;
and after looking all around, [b]He departed for Bethany
with the twelve, since it was already late.
12 [a]And on the next day, when they had departed from Bethany, He
became hungry.
13 And seeing at a distance a fig tree in leaf, He went *to see* if
perhaps He would find anything on it; and when He came to it, He
found nothing but leaves, for it was not the season for figs.
14 And He answered and said to it, "May no one ever eat fruit from
you again!" And His disciples were listening.
15 [a]And they *came to Jerusalem. And He entered the temple and

From Bethany, Bethphage Across the Mount of Olives into Jerusalem

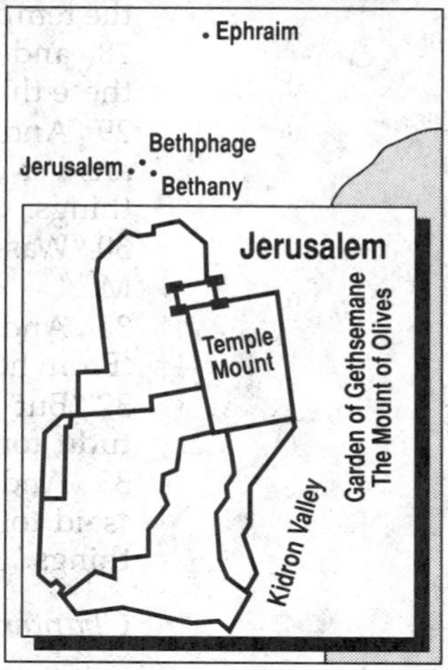

[a]Mark 1:24 [b]Matt. 9:27
48 [a]Matt. 9:27
49 [a]Matt. 9:2
[1]I.e., My Master 23:7; John 20:16
[1]Lit., *saved you* [a]Matt. 9:22
1 [a]Mark 11:1-10: *Matt. 21:1-9; Luke* -38 [b]Matt. 21:17 [c]Matt. 21:1
3 [1]Lit., *sends*
ark 11:7-10: *Matt.* ; *Luke 19:35-38; John 12:12-15*
Ps. 118:26; Matt. 21:9
10 [a]Matt. 21:9
att. 21:12 [b]Matt. 21:17
[a]Mark 11:12-14, : *Matt. 21:18-22*
[a]Mark 11:15-18: *21:12-16; Luke* 47; John 2:13-16

began to cast out those who were buying and selling in the temple, and overturned the tables of the moneychangers and the seats of those who were selling [1]doves;
16 and He would not permit anyone to carry [1]goods through the temple.
17 And He *began* to teach and say to them, "Is it not written, '[a]MY HOUSE SHALL BE CALLED A HOUSE OF PRAYER FOR ALL THE NATIONS'? [b]But you have made it a ROBBERS' [1]DEN."
18 And the chief priests and the scribes heard *this*, and [a]*began* seeking how to destroy Him; for they were afraid of Him, for [b]all the multitude was astonished at His teaching.
19 And [a]whenever evening came, [1]they would go out of the city.
20 [a]And as they were passing by in the morning, they saw the fig tree withered from the roots *up*.
21 And being reminded, Peter *said to Him, "[a]Rabbi, behold, the fig tree which You cursed has withered."
22 And Jesus *answered saying to them, "[a]Have faith in God.
23 "[a]Truly I say to you, whoever says to this mountain, 'Be taken up and cast into the sea,' and does not doubt in his heart, but believes that what he says is going to happen, it shall be *granted* him.
24 "Therefore I say to you, [a]all things for which you pray and ask, believe that you have received them, and they shall be *granted* you.
25 "And whenever you [a]stand praying, [b]forgive, if you have anything against anyone; so that your Father also who is in heaven may forgive you your transgressions.
26 ["[1a]But if you do not forgive, neither will your Father who is in heaven forgive your transgressions."]
27 And they *came again to Jerusalem. [a]And as He was walking in the temple, the chief priests, and scribes, and elders *came to Him,
28 and *began* saying to Him, "By what authority are You doing these things, or who gave You this authority to do these things?"
29 And Jesus said to them, "I will ask you one question, and you answer Me, and *then* I will tell you by what authority I do these things.
30 "Was the baptism of John from heaven, or from men? Answer Me."
31 And they *began* reasoning among themselves, saying, "If we say, 'From heaven,' He will say, 'Then why did you not believe him?'
32 "But [1]shall we say, 'From men'?"—they were afraid of the multitude, for all considered John to have been a prophet indeed.
33 And answering Jesus, they *said, "We do not know." And Jesus *said to them, "Neither [1]will I tell you by what authority I do these things."

Chapter 12

12 [a]And He began to speak to them in parables: "[b]A man [c]PLANTED A VINEYARD, AND PUT A [1]WALL AROUND IT, AND DUG A VAT UNDER THE WINE PRESS, AND BUILT A TOWER, and rented it out to [2]vine-growers and went on a journey.
2 "And at the *harvest* time he sent a slave to the vine-growers, in order to receive *some* of the produce of the vineyard from the vine-growers.
3 "And they took him, and beat him, and sent him away empty-handed.

15 [1]Lit., *the c*

16 [1]Lit., *a ves* receptacle or of any kind

17 [1]Lit., *cave* [b]Jer. 7:11

18 [a]Matt. 21:4 12:12; Luke 2 7:1 [b]Matt. 7:2

19 [1]I.e., Jesus disciples [a]Ma Mark 11:11; Lu

20 [a]Mark 11:1 20-24: *Matt. 2*

21 [a]Matt. 23:7

22 [a]Matt. 17:2

23 [a]Matt. 17:2 13:2

24 [a]Matt. 7:7f.

25 [a]Matt. 6:5 [b] 6:14

26 [1]Many mss. contain this v. [a] 6:15; 18:35

27 [a]Mark 11:27 *Matt. 21:23-27;* *20:1-8*

32 [1]Or, *if we sa*

33 [1]Lit., *do I tell*

12:1 [1]Or, *fence* *tenant farmers, a* 2, 7, 9 [a]Mark 3:2 4:2ff. [b]Mark 12:1 *Matt. 21:33-46;* *20:9-19* [c]Is. 5:1,

4 "And again he sent them another slave, and they wounded him in the head, and treated him shamefully.

5 "And he sent another, and that one they killed; and *so with* many others, beating some, and killing others.

6 "He had one more *to send,* a beloved son; he sent him last *of all* to them, saying, 'They will respect my son.'

7 "But those vine-growers said to one another, 'This is the heir; come, let us kill him, and the inheritance will be ours!'

8 "And they took him, and killed him, and threw him out of the vineyard.

9 "What will the [1]owner of the vineyard do? He will come and destroy the vine-growers, and will give the vineyard to others.

10 "Have you not even read this Scripture:

'[a]THE STONE WHICH THE BUILDERS REJECTED,
THIS BECAME THE CHIEF CORNER *stone;*

11 [a]THIS CAME ABOUT FROM THE LORD,
AND IT IS MARVELOUS IN OUR EYES'?"

12 And [a]they were seeking to seize Him; and *yet* they feared the multitude; for they understood that He spoke the parable against them. And *so* [b]they left Him, and went away.

13 [a]And they *sent some of the Pharisees and [b]Herodians to Him, in order to [c]trap Him in a statement.

14 And they *came and *said to Him, "Teacher, we know that You are truthful, and [1]defer to no one; for You are not partial to any, but teach the way of God in truth. Is it [2]lawful to pay a poll-tax to Caesar, or not?

15 "Shall we pay, or shall we not pay?" But He, knowing their hypocrisy, said to them, "Why are you testing Me? Bring Me a [1]denarius to look at."

16 And they brought *one.* And He *said to them, "Whose likeness and inscription is this?" And they said to Him, "Caesar's."

17 And Jesus said to them, "[a]Render to Caesar the things that are Caesar's, and to God the things that are God's." And they [1]were amazed at Him.

18 [a]And *some* Sadducees (who say that there is no resurrection) *came to Him, and *began* questioning Him, saying,

19 "Teacher, Moses wrote for us that [a]IF A MAN'S BROTHER DIES, and leaves behind a wife, AND LEAVES NO CHILD, HIS BROTHER SHOULD TAKE THE WIFE, AND RAISE UP OFFSPRING TO HIS BROTHER.

20 "There were seven brothers; and the first took a wife, and died, leaving no offspring.

21 "And the second one took her, and died, leaving behind no offspring; and the third likewise;

22 and *so* [1]all seven left no offspring. Last of all the woman died also.

23 "In the resurrection, [1]when they rise again, which one's wife will she be? For [2]all seven had her as wife."

24 Jesus said to them, "Is this not the reason you are mistaken, that you do not [1]understand the Scriptures, or the power of God?

25 "For when they rise from the dead, they neither marry, nor are given in marriage, but are like angels in heaven.

26 "But [1]regarding the fact that the dead rise again, have you not read in the book of Moses, [a]in the *passage about the burning* bush, how

9 [1]Lit., *lord*
10 [a]Ps. 118:22
11 [a]Ps. 118:23
ark 11:18 [b]Matt. 22:22
[a]Mark 12:13-17: . 22:15-22; Luke -26 [b]Matt. 22:16 [c]Luke 11:54
4 [1]Lit., *it is not a em to You about e;* i.e., You court nan's favor [2]Or, *permissible*
he denarius was ent to one day's wage
Or, *were greatly ing* [a]Matt. 22:21
[a]Mark 12:18-27: , 22:23-33; Luke 27-38; Acts 23:8
19 [a]Deut. 25:5
[1]Lit., *the seven*
ost ancient mss. ot contain *when again* [2]Lit., *the seven*
24 [1]Or, *know*
concerning the d, that they rise 0:37; Rom. 11:2

God spoke to him, saying, '[b]I AM THE GOD OF ABRAHAM, AND THE GOD
OF ISAAC, AND THE GOD OF JACOB'?
27 "[a]He is not the God [1]of the dead, but of the living; you are greatly
mistaken."
28 [a]And one of the scribes came and heard them arguing, and
[b]recognizing that He had answered them well, asked Him, "What
commandment is the [1]foremost of all?"
29 Jesus answered, "The foremost is, '[a]HEAR, O ISRAEL! THE LORD
OUR GOD IS ONE LORD;
30 [a]AND YOU SHALL LOVE THE LORD YOUR GOD WITH ALL YOUR HEART,
AND WITH ALL YOUR SOUL, AND WITH ALL YOUR MIND, AND WITH ALL YOUR
STRENGTH.'
31 "The second is this, '[a]YOU SHALL LOVE YOUR NEIGHBOR AS YOURSELF.'
There is no other commandment greater than these."
32 And the scribe said to Him, "Right, Teacher, You have truly
stated that [a]HE IS ONE; AND THERE IS NO ONE ELSE BESIDES HIM;
33 [a]AND TO LOVE HIM WITH ALL THE HEART AND WITH ALL THE UNDER-
STANDING AND WITH ALL THE STRENGTH, AND TO LOVE ONE'S NEIGHBOR AS
HIMSELF, [b]is much more than all burnt offerings and sacrifices."
34 And when Jesus saw that he had answered intelligently, He said
to him, "You are not far from the kingdom of God." [a]And after that,
no one would venture to ask Him any more questions.
35 [a]And Jesus answering *began* to say, as He [b]taught in the temple,
"How *is it that* the scribes say that [1]the Christ is the [c]son of David?
36 "David himself said [1]in the Holy Spirit,

'[a]THE LORD SAID TO MY LORD,
"SIT AT MY RIGHT HAND,
UNTIL I PUT THINE ENEMIES BENEATH THY FEET." '

37 "David himself calls Him 'Lord'; and *so* in what sense is He his
son?" And [a]the great crowd [1]enjoyed listening to Him.
38 [a]And in His teaching He was saying: "Beware of the scribes who
like to walk around in long robes, and *like* [b]respectful greetings in the
market places,
39 and chief seats in the synagogues, and places of honor at ban-
quets,
40 [a]who devour widows' houses, and for appearance's sake offer
long prayers; these will receive greater condemnation."
41 [a]And He sat down opposite [b]the treasury, and *began* observing
how the multitude were [c]putting [1]money into the treasury; and
many rich people were putting in large sums.
42 And a poor widow came and put in two [1]small copper coins,
which amount to a [2]cent.
43 And calling His disciples to Him, He said to them, "Truly I say
to you, this poor widow put in more than all [1]the contributors to the
treasury;
44 for they all put in out of their [1]surplus, but she, out of her pover-
ty, put in all she owned, [2]all she had [a]to live on."

Chapter 13

See the illustration of Herod's temple on page I-22.

13 [a]And as He was going out of the temple, one of His disciples
*said to Him, "Teacher, behold [1]what wonderful stones and
[1]what wonderful buildings!"
2 And Jesus said to him, "Do you see these great buildings? [a]Not
one stone shall be left upon another which will not be torn down."

26 [b]Ex. 3:6
27 [1]Or, *of co*
[a]Matt. 22:32;
28 [1]Or, *first*
12:28-34: *Ma*
22:34-40; Lu
10:25-28; 20
22:34; Luke
29 [a]Deut. 6:4
30 [a]Deut. 6:5
31 [a]Lev. 19:1
32 [a]Deut. 4:3
33 [a]Deut. 6:5
15:22; Hos. 6
6:6-8; Matt. 9
34 [a]Matt. 22:
35 [1]I.e., the M
[a]Mark 12:35-3
22:41-46; Luk
20:41-44 [b]Ma
Mark 10:1 [c]M
36 [1]Or, *by* [a]P
37 [1]Lit., *was g*
hearing Him
38 [a]Mark 12:3
Matt. 23:1-7; L
20:45-47 [b]Ma
Luke 11:43
40 [a]Luke 20:4
41 [1]I.e., coppe
[a]Mark 12:41-4
21:1-4 [b]John 8
[c]2 Kin. 12:9
42 [1]Gr., *lepta*
quadrans; i.e.,
denarius
43 [1]Lit., *those*
were putting in
44 [1]Or, *abunda*
[2]Lit., *her whole*
livelihood [a]Luke
15:12, 30; 21:4
13:1 [1]Lit., *how*
[a]Mark 13:1-37:
Luke 21:5-36
2 [a]Luke 19:44

3 And as He was sitting on [a]the Mount of Olives opposite the
temple, [b]Peter and [1]James and John and Andrew were questioning
Him privately,
4 "Tell us, when will these things be, and what *will be* the [1]sign
when all these things are going to be fulfilled?"
5 And Jesus began to say to them, "See to it that no one misleads
you.
6 "Many will come in My name, saying, '[a]I am *He!*' and will mis-
lead many.
7 "And when you hear of wars and rumors of wars, do not be
frightened; *those things* must take place; but *that is* not yet the end.
8 "For nation will arise against nation, and kingdom against king-
dom; there will be earthquakes in various places; there will *also* be
famines. These things are *merely* the beginning of birth pangs.
9 "But [1]be on your guard; for they will [a]deliver you to *the* [2]courts,
and you will be flogged [b]in *the* synagogues, and you will stand
before governors and kings for My sake, as a testimony to them.
10 "[a]And the gospel must first be preached to all the nations.
11 "[a]And when they [1]arrest you and deliver you up, do not be
anxious beforehand about what you are to say, but say whatever is
given you in that hour; for it is not you who speak, but *it is* the Holy
Spirit.
12 "And brother will deliver brother to death, and a father *his* child;
and children will rise up against parents and [1]have them put to
death.
13 "And [a]you will be hated by all on account of My name, but the
one who endures to the end, he shall be saved.
14 "But [a]when you see the [b]ABOMINATION OF DESOLATION standing
where it should not be (let the reader understand), then let those
who are in Judea flee to the mountains.
15 "[a]And let him who is on the housetop not go down, or enter in, to
get anything out of his house;
16 and let him who is in the field not turn back to get his cloak.
17 "But woe to those who are with child and to those who nurse
babes in those days!
18 "But pray that it may not happen in the winter.
19 "For those days will be a *time of* tribulation such as has not oc-
curred [a]since the beginning of the creation which God created, until
now, and never shall.
20 "And unless the Lord had shortened *those* days, no [1]life would
have been saved; but for the sake of the [2]elect whom He chose, He
shortened the days.
21 "And then if anyone says to you, 'Behold, here is [1]the Christ'; or,
'Behold, *He is* there'; do not believe *him;*
22 for false Christs and [a]false prophets will arise, and will show
[1b]signs and [b]wonders, in order, if possible, to lead the elect astray.
23 "But take heed; behold, I have told you everything in advance.
24 "But in those days, after that tribulation, [a]THE SUN WILL BE
DARKENED, AND THE MOON WILL NOT GIVE ITS LIGHT,
25 [a]AND THE STARS WILL BE FALLING from heaven, and the powers that
are in [1]the heavens will be shaken.
26 "And then they will see [a]THE SON OF MAN [b]COMING IN CLOUDS with
great power and glory.
27 "And then He will send forth the angels, and [a]will gather together

[1]Or, *Jacob* [a]Matt. 21:1 [b]Matt. 17:1
, *attesting miracle*
6 [a]John 8:24
9 [1]Lit., *look to yourselves* [2]Or, ...nhedrin *or council* [a]Matt. 10:17
10 [a]Matt. 24:14
[1]Lit., *lead* [a]Mark 13:11-13: *Matt.* ...2; *Luke 21:12-17*
[1]Lit., *put them to death*
...Matt. 10:22; John 15:21
...att. 24:15f. [b]Dan. ...:27; 11:31; 12:11
15 [a]Luke 17:31
[a]Dan. 12:1; Mark 10:6
...0 [1]Lit., *flesh* [2]Or, *chosen ones*
[1]I.e., the Messiah
22 [1]Or, *attesting* ...acles [a]Matt. 7:15 24:24; John 4:48
[a]Is. 13:10; Ezek. ...:7; Joel 2:10, 31; 3:15; Rev. 6:12
[1]Or, *heaven* [a]Is. 34:4; Rev. 6:13
...an. 7:13; Rev. 1:7 16:27; Mark 8:38
27 [a]Deut. 30:4

His [1]elect from the four winds, [b]from the farthest end of the earth, to
the farthest end of heaven.
28 "Now learn the parable from the fig tree: when its branch has
already become tender, and puts forth its leaves, you know that
summer is near.
29 "Even so, you too, when you see these things happening, [1]recog-
nize that [2]He is near, *right* at the [3]door.
30 "Truly I say to you, this [1]generation will not pass away until all
these things take place.
31 "Heaven and earth will pass away, but My words will not pass
away.
32 "[a]But of that day or hour no one knows, not even the angels in
heaven, nor the Son, but the Father *alone.*
33 "Take heed, [a]keep on the alert; for you do not know when the
appointed time is.
34 "[a]*It is* like a man, away on a journey, *who* upon leaving his house
and [1]putting his slaves in charge, *assigning* to each one his task, also
commanded the doorkeeper to stay on the alert.
35 "Therefore, [a]be on the alert—for you do not know when the
[1]master of the house is coming, whether in the evening, at midnight,
at [b]cockcrowing, or [c]in the morning—
36 lest he come suddenly and find you [a]asleep.
37 "And what I say to you I say to all, '[a]Be on the alert!' "

Chapter 14

14 [a]Now [b]the Passover and Unleavened Bread was two days off;
and the chief priests and the scribes [c]were seeking how to
seize Him by stealth, and kill *Him;*
2 for they were saying, "Not during the festival, lest there be a riot
of the people."
3 [a]And while He was in [b]Bethany at the home of Simon the leper,
and reclining *at the table,* there came a woman with an alabaster vial
of very [c]costly perfume of pure nard; *and* she broke the vial and
poured it over His head.
4 But some were indignantly *remarking* to one another, "Why has
this perfume been wasted?
5 "For this perfume might have been sold for over three hundred
[1]denarii, and *the money* given to the poor." And they were scolding
her.
6 But Jesus said, "Let her alone; why do you bother her? She has
done a good deed to Me.
7 "For [a]the poor you always have with you, and whenever you
wish, you can do them good; but you do not always have Me.
8 "She has done what she could; [a]she has anointed My body before-
hand for the burial.
9 "And truly I say to you, [a]wherever the gospel is preached in the
whole world, that also which this woman has done shall be spoken
of in memory of her."
10 [a]And Judas Iscariot, [b]who was one of the twelve, went off to the
chief priests, in order to [1]betray Him to them.
11 And they were glad when they heard *this,* and promised to give
him money. And he *began* seeking how to betray Him at an oppor-
tune time.
12 [a]And on the first day of [b]Unleavened Bread, when [1]the Passover

27 [1]Or, *cho*... [b]Zech. 2:6
29 [1]Lit., *kno*... [3]Lit., *doors*
30 [1]Or, *race*
32 [a]Matt. 24...
33 [a]Eph. 6:1...
34 [1]Lit., *givi*... *authority to* [a]... 12:36-38
35 [1]Lit., *lord* ... 24:42; Mark 1... [b]Mark 14:30 ... 14:25; Mark 6...
36 [a]Rom. 13:...
37 [a]Matt. 24:... 13:35
14:1 [a]Mark 14... *Matt. 26:2-5; L*... 2 [b]Ex. 12:1-27... 14:12; John 1... [c]Matt. 12:14
3 [a]Mark 14:3-... *26:6-13;* Luke ... John 12:1-8 [b]... 21:17 [c]Matt. 2... John 12:3
5 [1]The denari... equivalent to o... wage
7 [a]Deut. 15:11;... 26:11; John 12:...
8 [a]John 19:40
9 [a]Matt. 26:13
10 [1]Or, *deliver* ... [a]Mark 14:10, 11 ... *26:14-16; Luke*... [b]John 6:71
12 [1]Lit., *they we*... *sacrificing* [a]Mar... 14:12-16: *Matt.* ... *26:17-19; Luke*... [b]Matt. 26:17

lamb was being [c]sacrificed, His disciples *said to Him, "Where do
You want us to go and prepare for You to eat the Passover?"
13 And He *sent two of His disciples, and *said to them, "Go into
the city, and a man will meet you carrying a pitcher of water; follow
him;
14 and wherever he enters, say to the owner of the house, 'The
Teacher says, "Where is My [a]guest room in which I may eat the
Passover with My disciples?" '
15 "And he himself will show you a large upper room furnished *and*
ready; and prepare for us there."
16 And the disciples went out, and came to the city, and found *it*
just as He had told them; and they prepared the Passover.
17 [a]And when it was evening He *came with the twelve.
18 And as they were reclining *at the table* and eating, Jesus said,
"Truly I say to you that one of you will [1]betray Me—[2]one who is
eating with Me."
19 They began to be grieved and to say to Him one by one, "Surely
not I?"
20 And He said to them, "*It is* one of the twelve, [1]one who dips
with Me in the bowl.
21 "For the Son of Man *is to* go, just as it is written of Him; but woe
to that man [1]by whom the Son of Man is betrayed! *It would have been*
good [2]for that man if he had not been born."
22 [a]And while they were eating, He took *some* bread, and [1]after a
[b]blessing He broke *it*; and gave *it* to them, and said, "Take *it*; this is
My body."
23 And when He had taken a cup, *and* given thanks, He gave *it* to
them; and they all drank from it.
24 And He said to them, "This is My [a]blood of the [b]covenant, which
is poured out for many.
25 "Truly I say to you, I shall never again drink of the fruit of the
vine until that day when I drink it new in the kingdom of God."
26 [a]And after singing a hymn, they went out to [b]the Mount of
Olives.
27 [a]And Jesus *said to them, "You will all [1]fall away, because it is
written, '[b]I WILL STRIKE DOWN THE SHEPHERD, AND THE SHEEP SHALL BE
SCATTERED.'
28 "But after I have been raised, [a]I will go before you to Galilee."
29 But Peter said to Him, "*Even* though all may [1]fall away, yet I will
not."
30 And Jesus *said to him, "Truly I say to you, that you yourself
[1a]this very night, before [b]a cock crows twice, shall three times deny
Me."
31 But *Peter* kept saying insistently, "*Even* if I have to die with You, I
will not deny You!" And they all were saying the same thing, too.
32 [a]And they *came to a place named Gethsemane; and He *said to
His disciples, "Sit here until I have prayed."
33 And He *took with Him Peter and [1]James and John, and began
to be very [a]distressed and troubled.
34 And He *said to them, "[a]My soul is deeply grieved to the point
of death; remain here and keep watch."
35 And He went a little beyond *them*, and [1]fell to the ground, and
began to pray that if it were possible, [a]the hour might [2]pass Him by.
36 And He was saying, "[a]Abba! Father! All things are possible for

[c]Deut. 16:5; Mark
Luke 22:7; 1 Cor.
5:7
14 [a]Luke 22:11
[a]Mark 14:17-21:
tt. 26:20-24; Luke
2:14, 21-23; John
13:18ff.
[1]Or, *deliver Me up*
[2]Or, *the one*
20 [1]Or, *the one*
[1]Or, *through* [2]Lit.,
*m if that man had
not been born*
22 [1]Lit., *having
blessed* [a]Mark
14:22-25: *Matt.
26:26-29; Luke
22:17-20;* 1 Cor.
3-25; Mark 10:16
[b]Matt. 14:19
4 [a]Ex. 24:8 [b]Jer.
31:31-34
latt. 26:30 [b]Matt.
21:1
r, *stumble* [a]Mark
14:27-31: *Matt.
-35* [b]Zech. 13:7
28 [a]Matt. 28:16
29 [1]Or, *stumble*
.it., *today, on this
ight* [a]Matt. 26:34
< 14:68, 72; John
13:38
[a]Mark 14:32-42:
*t. 26:36-46; Luke
22:40-46*
Or, *Jacob* [a]Mark
9:15; 16:5, 6
Matt. 26:38; John
12:27
[1]Lit., *was falling*
., *pass from Him*
6:45; Mark 14:41
m. 8:15; Gal. 4:6

Thee; remove this cup from Me; [b]yet not what I will, but what Thou wilt."
37 And He *came and *found them sleeping, and *said to Peter, "Simon, are you asleep? Could you not keep watch for one hour?
38 "[a]Keep watching and praying, that you may not come into temptation; the spirit is willing, but the flesh is weak."
39 And again He went away and prayed, saying the same [1]words.
40 And again He came and found them sleeping, for their eyes were very heavy; and they did not know what to answer Him.
41 And He *came the third time, and *said to them, "[1]Are you still sleeping and taking your rest? It is enough; [a]the hour has come; behold, the Son of Man is being [2]betrayed into the hands of sinners.
42 "Arise, let us be going; behold, the one who betrays Me is at hand!"
43 [a]And immediately while He was still speaking, Judas, one of the twelve, *came up, [1]accompanied by a multitude with swords and clubs, from the chief priests and the scribes and the elders.
44 Now he who was betraying Him had given them a signal, saying, "Whomever I shall kiss, He is the one; seize Him, and lead Him away [1]under guard."
45 And after coming, he immediately went to Him, saying, "[a]Rabbi!" and kissed Him.
46 And they laid hands on Him, and seized Him.
47 But a certain one of those who stood by drew his sword, and struck the slave of the high priest, and [1]cut off his ear.
48 And Jesus answered and said to them, "Have you come out with swords and clubs to arrest Me, as against a robber?
49 "Every day I was with you [a]in the temple teaching, and you did not seize Me; but [1]*this has happened* that the Scriptures might be fulfilled."
50 And they all left Him and fled.
51 And a certain young man was following Him, wearing *nothing but* a linen sheet over *his* naked *body;* and they *seized him.
52 But he left the linen sheet behind, and escaped naked.
53 [a]And they led Jesus away to the high priest; and all the chief priests and the elders and the scribes *gathered together.
54 And Peter had followed Him at a distance, [a]right into [b]the courtyard of the high priest; and he was sitting with the [1]officers, and [c]warming himself at the [2]fire.
55 Now the chief priests and the whole [1a]Council kept trying to obtain testimony against Jesus to put Him to death; and they were not finding any.
56 For many were giving false testimony against Him, and *yet* their testimony was not consistent.
57 And some stood up and *began* to give false testimony against Him, saying,
58 "We heard Him say, '[a]I will destroy this [1]temple made with hands, and in three days I will build another made without hands.'"
59 And not even in this respect was their testimony consistent.
60 And the high priest stood up *and came* forward and questioned Jesus, saying, "Do You make no answer? [1]What is it that these men are testifying against You?"
61 [a]But He kept silent, and made no answer. [b]Again the high priest

36 [b]Matt. 26
38 [a]Matt. 26.
39 [1]Lit., *word*
41 [1]Or, *Keep sleeping there* delivered up 14:35
43 [1]Lit., *and* [a]Mark 14:43-5 *26:47-56; Luk 22:47-53; Joh*
44 [1]Lit., *safely*
45 [a]Matt. 23:7
47 [1]Lit., *took o*
49 [1]Or possibl *Scriptures be f* [a]Mark 12:35; L 19:47; 21:37
53 [a]Mark 14:53 *Matt. 26:57-68; 18:12f., 19-24*
54 [1]Or, *servan light* [a]Mark 14: [b]Matt. 26:3 [c]Ma 14:67; John 18.
55 [1]Or, *Sanhed* [a]Matt. 5:22
58 [1]Or, *sanctua* [a]Matt. 26:61; Ma 15:29; John 2:19
60 [1]Or, *what do testify?*
61 [a]Matt. 26:63 14:61-63: *Matt. Luke 22:67-71*

was questioning Him, and [1]saying to Him, "Are You [2]the Christ, the Son of the Blessed *One?*"

62 And Jesus said, "I am; and you shall see [a]THE SON OF MAN SITTING AT THE RIGHT HAND OF POWER, and [b]COMING WITH THE CLOUDS OF HEAVEN."

63 And [a]tearing his clothes, the high priest *said, "What further need do we have of witnesses?

64 "You have heard the [a]blasphemy; how does it seem to you?" And they all condemned Him to be deserving of death.

65 And some began to [a]spit at Him, and [1b]to blindfold Him, and to beat Him with their fists, and to say to Him, "[c]Prophesy!" And the officers [2]received Him with [3]slaps *in the face*.

66 [a]And as Peter was below in [b]the courtyard, one of the servant-girls of the high priest *came,

67 and seeing Peter [a]warming himself, she looked at him, and *said, "You, too, were with Jesus the [b]Nazarene."

68 But he denied *it*, saying, "I neither know nor understand what you are talking about." And he [a]went out onto the [1]porch.[2]

69 And the maid saw him, and began once more to say to the bystanders, "This is *one* of them!"

70 But again [a]he was denying it. And after a little while the bystanders were again saying to Peter, "Surely you are *one* of them, [b]for you are a Galilean too."

71 But he began to [1]curse and swear, "I do not know this man you are talking about!"

72 And immediately a cock crowed a second time. And Peter remembered how Jesus had made the remark to him, "Before [a]a cock crows twice, you will deny Me three times." [1]And he began to weep.

Chapter 15

15 [a]And early in the morning the chief priests with the elders and scribes, and the whole [1b]Council, immediately held a consultation; and binding Jesus, they led Him away, and delivered Him up to Pilate.

2 [a]And Pilate questioned Him, "Are You the King of the Jews?" And answering He *said to him, "*It is as* you say."

3 And the chief priests *began* to accuse Him [1]harshly.

4 And Pilate was questioning Him again, saying, "Do You make no answer? See how many charges they bring against You!"

5 But Jesus [a]made no further answer; so that Pilate was amazed.

6 [a]Now at *the* feast he used to release for them *any* one prisoner whom they requested.

7 And the man named Barabbas had been imprisoned with the insurrectionists who had committed murder in the insurrection.

8 And the multitude went up and began asking him *to do* as he had been accustomed to do for them.

9 And Pilate answered them, saying, "Do you want me to release for you the King of the Jews?"

10 For he was aware that the chief priests had delivered Him up because of envy.

11 But the chief priests stirred up the multitude [a]*to ask* him to release Barabbas for them instead.

...it., *says* [2]I.e., the Messiah

[a]Ps. 110:1; Mark 3:26 [b]Dan. 7:13

[a]Num. 14:6; Matt. 26:65; Acts 14:14

64 [a]Lev. 24:16

...r, *cover over His* [2]Or, *treated* [3]Or ...ssibly, *blows with* ...Matt. 26:67; Mark [b]Esth. 7:8 [c]Matt. ...6:68; Luke 22:64

[a]Mark 14:66-72: ...26:69-75; Luke 22:56-62; John 18, 25-27 [b]Mark 14:54

...ark 14:54 [b]Mark 1:24

...8 [1]Or, *forecourt, ...way* [2]Later mss. ...*d a cock crowed* [a]Mark 14:54

...ark 14:68 [b]Matt. ...6:73; Luke 22:59

[1]Or, *put himself under a curse*

Thinking of this, ...egan weeping or ...ng out, he began weeping [a]Mark 14:30, 68

[1]Or, *Sanhedrin* ...27:1 [b]Matt. 5:22

...ark 15:2-5: Matt. ...14; Luke 23:2, 3; John 18:29-38

..., *of many things*

5 [a]Matt. 27:12

...k 15:6-15: Matt. 27:15-26; Luke 23:18-25; John 18:39-19:16

11 [a]Acts 3:14

12 And answering again, Pilate was saying to them, "Then what
shall I do with Him whom you call the King of the Jews?"
13 And they shouted [1]back, "Crucify Him!"
14 But Pilate was saying to them, "Why, what evil has He done?"
But they shouted all the more, "Crucify Him!"
15 And wishing to satisfy the multitude, Pilate released Barabbas
for them, and after having Jesus [a]scourged, he delivered *Him* to be
crucified.
16 [a]And the soldiers took Him away into [b]the [1]palace (that is, the
Praetorium), and they *called together the whole *Roman* [2c]cohort.
17 And they *dressed Him up in [1]purple, and after weaving a
crown of thorns, they put it on Him;
18 and they began to acclaim Him, "Hail, King of the Jews!"
19 And they kept beating His head with a [1]reed, and spitting at
Him, and kneeling and bowing before Him.
20 And after they had mocked Him, they took the purple off Him,
and put His garments on Him. And they *led Him out to crucify
Him.
21 [a]And they *pressed into service a passer-by coming from the
country, Simon of Cyrene (the father of Alexander and [b]Rufus), to
bear His cross.
22 [a]And they *brought Him to the place [b]Golgotha, which is trans-
lated, Place of a Skull.
23 And they tried to give Him [a]wine mixed with myrrh; but He did
not take it.
24 And they *crucified Him, and *[a]divided up His garments among
themselves, casting [1]lots for them, *to decide* [2]what each should take.
25 And it was the [1a]third hour [2]when they crucified Him.
26 And the inscription of the charge against Him [1]read, "[a]THE
KING OF THE JEWS."
27 And they *crucified two robbers with Him, one on His right and
one on His left.
28 [[1]And the Scripture was fulfilled which says, "And He was num-
bered with transgressors."]
29 And those passing by were [1]hurling abuse at Him, [a]wagging
their heads, and saying, "Ha! You who *are going to* [b]destroy the
temple and rebuild it in three days,
30 save Yourself, and come down from the cross!"
31 In the same way the chief priests also, along with the scribes,
were mocking *Him* among themselves and saying, "[a]He saved
others; [1]He cannot save Himself.
32 "Let *this* Christ, [a]the King of Israel, now come down from the
cross, so that we may see and believe!" And [b]those who were
crucified with Him were casting the same insult at Him.
33 [a]And when the [1b]sixth hour had come, darkness [2]fell over the
whole land until the [3b]ninth hour.
34 And at the [a]ninth hour Jesus cried out with a loud voice, "[b]ELOI,
ELOI, LAMA SABACHTHANI?" which is translated, "MY GOD, MY GOD,
WHY HAST THOU FORSAKEN ME?"
35 And when some of the bystanders heard it, they *began* saying,
"Behold, He is calling for Elijah."
36 And someone ran and filled a sponge with sour wine, put it on a
reed, and gave Him a drink, saying, "[1]Let us see whether Elijah will
come to take Him down."

13 [1]Or, *agai*
15 [a]Matt. 27
16 [1]Or, *cour battalion* [a]M 15:16-20: *Ma 27:27-31* [b]M 27:27 [c]Acts
17 [1]A term fo varying from purple
19 [1]Or, *staff* reed)
21 [a]Mark 15: *27:32; Luke 2* [b]Rom. 16:13
22 [a]Mark 15: *Matt. 27:33-4 23:33-43; Joh 19:17-24* [b]Lu John 19:17
23 [a]Matt. 27:3
24 [1]Lit., *a lot who should ta* [a]Ps. 22:18; Jo
25 [1]I.e., 9 a.m *and* [a]Mark 15:
26 [1]Lit., *had b inscribed* [a]Ma
28 [1]Many mss contain this v.
29 [1]Or, *blasph* [a]Ps. 22:7; 109: 27:39 [b]Mark 14 John 2:19
31 [1]Or, *can He save Himself?* 27:42; Luke 23:
32 [a]Matt. 27:42 15:26 [b]Matt. 27 Mark 15:27; Lu 23:39-43
33 [1]I.e., noon [2] *occurred* [3]I.e., 3 [a]Mark 15:33-41: *27:45-56; Luke 23:44-49* [b]Matt. Mark 15:25; Luk
34 [a]Matt. 27:45 15:25; Luke 23: 22:1; Matt. 27:46
36 [1]Lit., *Permit see;* or, *Hold off, see*

37 [a]And Jesus uttered a loud cry, and breathed His last.
38 [a]And the veil of the temple was torn in two from top to bottom.
39 [a]And when the centurion, who was standing [1]right in front of
Him, saw [2]the way He breathed His last, he said, "Truly this man
was [3]the Son of God!"
40 [a]And there were also *some* women looking on from a distance,
among whom *were* Mary Magdalene, and Mary the mother of [1]James
[b]the [2]Less and Joses, and [c]Salome.
41 And when He was in Galilee, they used to follow Him and
[1a]minister to Him; and *there were* many other women who had come
up with Him to Jerusalem.
42 [a]And when evening had already come, because it was [b]the
preparation day, that is, the day before the Sabbath,
43 Joseph of Arimathea came, a [a]prominent member of the Council,
who himself was [b]waiting for the kingdom of God; and he [c]gathered
up courage and went in before Pilate, and asked for the body of
Jesus.
44 And Pilate wondered if He was dead by this time, and summon-
ing the centurion, he questioned him as to whether He was already
dead.
45 And ascertaining this from [a]the centurion, he granted the body
to Joseph.
46 And *Joseph* bought a linen cloth, took Him down, wrapped Him
in the linen cloth, and laid Him in a tomb which had been hewn out
in the rock; and he rolled a stone against the entrance of the tomb.
47 And [a]Mary Magdalene and Mary the *mother* of Joses were look-
ing on *to see* where He was laid.

Chapter 16

16 [a]And when the Sabbath was over, [b]Mary Magdalene, and
Mary the *mother* of [1]James, and Salome, [c]bought spices, that
they might come and anoint Him.
2 And very early on the first day of the week, they *came to the
tomb when the sun had risen.
3 And they were saying to one another, "Who will roll away [a]the
stone for us from the entrance of the tomb?"
4 And looking up, they *saw that the stone had been rolled away,
[1]although it was extremely large.
5 And [a]entering the tomb, they saw a young man sitting at the
right, wearing a white robe; and they [b]were amazed.
6 And he *said to them, "[a]Do not be amazed; you are looking for
Jesus the [b]Nazarene, who has been crucified. [c]He has risen; He is not
here; behold, *here is* the place where they laid Him.
7 "But go, tell His disciples and Peter, '[a]He is going before you into
Galilee; there you will see Him, just as He said to you.' "
8 And they went out and fled from the tomb, for trembling and
astonishment had gripped them; and they said nothing to anyone,
for they were afraid.
9 [[1]Now after He had risen early on the first day of the week, He
first appeared to [a]Mary Magdalene, from whom He had cast out
seven demons.
10 [a]She went and reported to those who had been with Him, while
they were mourning and weeping.

. 27:50; Luke
3; John 19:30

5:31-33; Matt.
1; Luke 23:45

opposite Him
t He thus [3]Or
a son of God
a god [a]Matt.
15:45; Luke
23:47

r, Jacob [2]Lit.,
r in stature or
ark 15:40, 41:
27:55f.; Luke
9; John 19:25
3 [c]Mark 16:1

wait on [a]Matt.
27:55f.

Mark 15:42-47:
27:57-61; Luke
23:50-56; John
2 [b]Matt. 27:62

tt. 27:57; Luke
51; Acts 13:50;
[b]Matt. 27:57;
25, 38; 23:51;
8 [c]John 19:38

5 [a]Mark 15:39

tt. 27:56; Mark
15:40; 16:1

, Jacob [a]Mark
3: Matt. 28:1-8;
24:1-10; John
8 [b]Mark 15:47
ke 23:56; John
19:39f.

att. 27:60; Mark
15:46; 16:4

4 [1]Lit., *for*

[a]John 20:11, 12
[b]Mark 9:15

ark 9:15 [b]Mark
Matt. 28:6; Luke
24:6

att. 26:32; Mark
14:28

me of the oldest
not contain vv.
att. 27:56; John
20:14

10 [a]John 20:18

11 And when they heard that He was alive, and had been seen by
her, [a]they refused to believe it.
12 And after that, [a]He appeared in a different form [b]to two of them,
while they were walking along on their way to the country.
13 And they went away and reported it to the others, but they [a]did
not believe them either.
14 And afterward [a]He appeared [b]to the eleven themselves as they
were reclining *at the table;* and He reproached them for their [c]unbelief
and hardness of heart, because they had not believed those who had
seen Him after He had risen.
15 And He said to them, "[a]Go into all the world and preach the
gospel to all creation.
16 "[a]He who has believed and has been baptized shall be saved; but
he who has disbelieved shall be condemned.
17 "And these [1]signs will accompany those who have believed: [a]in
My name they will cast out demons, they will [b]speak with new
tongues;
18 they will [a]pick up serpents, and if they drink any deadly *poison*,
it shall not hurt them; they will [b]lay hands on the sick, and they will
recover."
19 So then, when the Lord Jesus had [a]spoken to them, He [b]was
received up into heaven, and [c]sat down at the right hand of God.
20 And they went out and preached everywhere, while the Lord
worked with them, and confirmed the word by the [1]signs that fol-
lowed.[2]]

[[3]*And they promptly reported all these instructions to Peter and his companions. And after that, Jesus Himself sent out through them from east to west the sacred and imperishable proclamation of eternal salvation.*]

11 [a]Mat
16:13, 1
41; John
12 [a]Mar
21:1, 14
13 [a]Mat
16:11, 14
41; John
14 [a]Mar
21:1, 14
John 20:
15:5 [c]Ma
16:11, 13
41; John
15 [a]Matt
16 [a]John
16:31
17 [1]Or, a
miracles
Luke 10:
8:7; 16:1
2:4; 10:4
12:10, 28
18 [a]Luke
28:3-5 [b]
19 [a]Acts
9:51; 24:5
20:17; Ac
1 Tim. 3:1
Luke 22:6
Rom. 8:3
Col. 3:1;
10:12; 12
20 [1]Or, a
miracles
add *Ame*
mss. and
contain th
usually af
have it at

of Mark:

IVISIONS

CHAPTER THEMES
1
2
3
4
5
6
7
8
9
10
11
12
13
14
15
16

Author:

Date:

Purpose:

Key Words:

immediately

authority

kingdom of God

mark every reference to the devil or demons with a red pitchfork

covenant

LUKE

In Matthew we see Jesus, King of the Jews. In Mark, we behold the servant who came to give a ransom for many. Then Luke walks us, chronologically, through the days of the Son of Man. book we see the fulfillment of the things written about Him in the law of Moses, the prophets, a psalms . . . things which no other Gospel tells us.

THINGS TO DO

1. Luke's purpose in writing is stated in Luke 1:1-4. Read it and then record it on the LUKE GLANCE chart on page 1553.
2. As you read chapter by chapter, be sure to do the following:
   a. Mark the key words listed on LUKE AT A GLANCE.
   b. Mark references to time with a symbol such as this . The references will come in different forms, from the mention of actual days or years to the naming of a Jewish chief priest, or a king. This part of your study will keep before you the timing and seque the events in Jesus' life. These are critical to Luke's purpose.
   c. It is also important to note where each event takes place. Underline any reference to cities, or regions. Locate these on the map on page 1509. Note in the margin *where* som occurs, along with *when* it occurs.
   d. List in the margin the main points covered in each chapter.
      1) As you list each event in the margin of the text, color code or mark it in a distinctive it can be recognized as an event. This will help you see at a glance the chronology of in Luke. You can also consult the chart on page 1554.
      2) As you note each event or teaching, pay attention to the setting and the response of who are listening or participating in what is happening. In the margin, note their res Watch where Jesus is, His relationships to people, what social events He's involved i what He expects from people.
   e. If Jesus tells a parable or tells of an incident such as the rich man and Lazarus dying (Lu note what provokes Jesus to do so.
   f. Record the theme of each chapter on the line next to the chapter number and on LUKE GLANCE.
3. Record the facts concerning Jesus' betrayal, arrest, trial, crucifixion, resurrection, resurrection appearances, and ascension on the appropriate charts in the appendix of this THE ARREST, TRIAL, AND CRUCIFIXION OF JESUS CHRIST (page 1882) and/or ACCOUNT OF JESUS' RESURRECTION (page 1883). Do this on notebook paper befor write it in your Bible. After you do this for all four Gospels you will have comprehensive no what took place at this time in our Lord's life.
4. In the appendix you will find a chart WHAT THE GOSPELS TEACH ABOUT THE KING OF GOD/THE KINGDOM OF HEAVEN (pages 1880 and 1881). Record on a piece of pap information you glean from marking every reference to *the kingdom of God* in Luke. Then solidate your findings and record them on the chart in your Bible. After you study a Gospels, you'll have an overview of what the Gospels teach about the kingdom of God.

THINGS TO THINK ABOUT

1. Have you been slow of heart to believe all that Moses and the prophets wrote about Jesus C

Do you see Jesus as the Son of Man, the fulfillment of prophecy, the Christ, the Son of God? Have you bowed to Him as Lord of your life?

. Jesus reached out to the hurting, the sinners, and the outcasts. He visited in their homes. He was available, accessible. What about you? Do you have compassion on these people? Are you wasting your life on self or are you investing in others? What did you learn from watching His response to others that you can apply to your life?

. If Jesus needed to withdraw often to a lonely place to pray, what about you? Is prayer a priority in your life? Do you understand and incorporate the principles of prayer that Jesus taught in the Gospel of Luke?

Chapter 1 ____________________

1 Inasmuch as many have undertaken to compile an account of
the things [1a]accomplished among us,
2 just as those who [a]from the beginning [1]were [b]eyewitnesses and
[2c]servants of [d]the [3]word have handed them down to us,
3 it seemed fitting for me as well, [a]having [1]investigated everything
carefully from the beginning, to write *it* out for you [b]in consecutive
order, [c]most excellent [d]Theophilus;
4 so that you might know the exact truth about the things you
have been [1a]taught.
5 [a]In the days of Herod, king of Judea, there [1]was a certain priest
named [2]Zacharias, of the [b]division of [3]Abijah; and he had a wife
[4]from the daughters of Aaron, and her name was Elizabeth.
6 And they were both [a]righteous in the sight of God, walking
[b]blamelessly in all the commandments and requirements of the Lord.
7 And they had no child, because Elizabeth was barren, and they
were both advanced in [1]years.
8 Now it came about, while [a]he was performing his priestly ser-
vice before God in the *appointed* order of his division,
9 according to the custom of the priestly office, he was chosen by
lot [a]to enter the temple of the Lord and burn incense.
10 And the whole multitude of the people were in prayer [a]outside
at the hour of the incense offering.
11 And [a]an angel of the Lord appeared to him, standing to the right
of the altar of incense.
12 And Zacharias was troubled when he saw *him,* and [a]fear
[1]gripped him.
13 But the angel said to him, "[a]Do not be afraid, Zacharias, for your
petition has been heard, and your wife Elizabeth will bear you a son,
and [b]you will [1]give him the name John.
14 "And you will have joy and gladness, and many will rejoice at his
birth.
15 "For he will be great in the sight of the Lord, and he will [a]drink no
wine or liquor; and he will be filled with the Holy Spirit, [1]while yet
in his mother's womb.
16 "And he will [a]turn back many of the sons of Israel to the Lord
their God.
17 "And it is he who will [a]go *as a forerunner* before Him in the spirit
and power of [b]Elijah, [c]TO TURN THE HEARTS OF THE FATHERS BACK TO THE
CHILDREN, and the disobedient to the attitude of the righteous; so as
to [a]make ready a people prepared for the Lord."

...r, *on which there* ...*conviction* [a]Rom. ...21; 14:5; Col. 2:2; ...12; 1 Thess. 1:5; ... 4:17; Heb. 6:11; 10:22

...Lit., *became* [2]Or, ...*sters* [3]I.e., gospel ...15:27; Acts 1:21f. ...1:16; 1 John 1:1 ...26:16; 1 Cor. 4:1; ... 2:3 [d]Mark 4:14; ...; Acts 8:4; 14:25; 16:6; 17:11

...*followed* [a]1 Tim. ...[b]Acts 11:4; 18:23 ...Acts 23:26; 24:3; 26:25 [d]Acts 1:1

..., *orally instructed* ...Acts 18:25; Rom. ... Cor. 14:19; Gal. 6:6

..., *came into being* ..., Zechariah [3]Gr., ...a [4]I.e., of priestly ...escent [a]Matt. 2:1 [b]1 Chr. 24:10

...n. 7:1; Acts 2:25; [b]Phil. 2:15; 3:6; 1 Thess. 3:13

7 [1]Lit., *days*

...Chr. 24:19; 2 Chr. 8:14; 31:2

9 [a]Ex. 30:7f.

10 [a]Lev. 16:17

...ke 2:9; Acts 5:19

..., *fell upon* [a]Luke 2:9

...Lit., *call his name* ...14:27; Luke 1:30 [b]Luke 1:60, 63

... [1]Lit., *even from* ... 6:3; Judg. 13:4; ...11:18; Luke 7:33

...Matt. 3:2, 6; Luke 3:3

...Luke 1:76 [b]Matt. 11:14 [c]Mal. 4:6

18 And Zacharias said to the angel, "How shall I know this *for*
certain? For [a]I am an old man, and my wife is advanced in [1]years."
19 And the angel answered and said to him, "I am [a]Gabriel, who
[1b]stands in the presence of God; and I have been sent to speak to you,
and to bring you this good news.
20 "And behold, you shall be silent and unable to speak until the
day when these things take place, because you did not believe my
words, which shall be fulfilled in their proper time."
21 And the people were waiting for Zacharias, and were wondering
at his delay in the temple.
22 But when he came out, he was unable to speak to them; and they
realized that he had seen a vision in the temple; and he [a]kept
[1]making signs to them, and remained mute.
23 And it came about, when the days of his priestly service were
ended, that he went back home.
24 And after these days Elizabeth his wife became pregnant; and
she [1]kept herself in seclusion for five months, saying,
25 "This is the way the Lord has dealt with me in the days when He
looked *with favor* upon *me*, to [a]take away my disgrace among men."
26 Now in the sixth month the angel [a]Gabriel was sent from God to
a city in Galilee, called [b]Nazareth,
27 to [a]a virgin engaged to a man whose name was Joseph, [b]of the
[1]descendants of David; and the virgin's name was Mary.
28 And coming in, he said to her, "Hail, [1]favored one! The Lord [2]*is*
with you."[3]
29 But she [a]was greatly troubled at *this* statement, and kept ponder-
ing what kind of salutation this might be.
30 And the angel said to her, "[a]Do not be afraid, Mary; for you have
found favor with God.
31 "And behold, you will conceive in your womb, and bear a son,
and you [a]shall name Him Jesus.
32 "He will be great, and will be called the Son of [a]the Most High;
and the Lord God will give Him [b]the throne of His father David;
33 [a]and He will reign over the house of Jacob forever; [b]and His
kingdom will have no end."
34 And Mary said to the angel, "How [1]can this be, since I [2]am a
virgin?"
35 And the angel answered and said to her, "[a]The Holy Spirit will
come upon you, and the power of [b]the Most High will overshadow
you; and for that reason [c]the [1]holy offspring shall be called [d]the Son
of God.
36 "And behold, even your relative Elizabeth has also conceived a
son in her old age; and [1]she who was called barren is now in her
sixth month.
37 "For [1a]nothing will be impossible with God."
38 And [1]Mary said, "Behold, the [2]bondslave of the Lord; be it done
to me according to your word." And the angel departed from her.
39 Now [1]at this time Mary arose and went with haste to [a]the hill
country, to a city of Judah,
40 and entered the house of Zacharias and greeted Elizabeth.
41 And it came about that when Elizabeth heard Mary's greeting,
the baby leaped in her womb; and Elizabeth was [a]filled with the
Holy Spirit.

18 [1]Lit., *days* 17:17

19 [1]Lit., *stan* [a]Dan. 8:16; 9 1:26 [b]Matt. 1

22 [1]Or, *beck nodding to* [a]L

24 [1]Lit., *was*

25 [a]Gen. 30:2 25:8

26 [a]Luke 1:19 2:23

27 [1]Lit., *hous* 1:18 [b]Matt. 1 Luke 2:4

28 [1]Or, *O wor blessed* [2]Or, b mss. add *you blessed amon*

29 [a]Luke 1:12

30 [a]Matt. 14:2 1:13

31 [a]Is. 7:14; M 25; Luke 2:21

32 [a]Mark 5:7; 1:35, 76; 6:35; 7:48 [b]2 Sam. 7 16; Is. 9:7

33 [a]Matt. 1:1 7:13, 16; Ps. 89 Dan. 2:44; 7:14 Matt. 28:18

34 [1]Lit., *shall know no man*

35 [1]Lit., *the ho begotten* [a]Matt [b]Luke 1:32 [c]Ma [d]Matt. 4:3; John 49; 20:31

36 [1]Lit., *this is month to her wh*

37 [1]Lit., *not any* [a]Gen. 18:14; Je Matt. 19:26

38 [1]Gr., *Mariam* Miriam; so throu Luke [2]I.e., fema

39 [1]Lit., *in these* [a]Josh. 20:7; 21:1 1:65

41 [a]Luke 1:67; 4:8; 9:17

42 And she cried out with a loud voice, and said, "Blessed among
women *are* you, and blessed *is* the fruit of your womb!
43 "And [1]how has it *happened* to me, that the mother of [a]my Lord
should come to me?
44 "For behold, when the sound of your greeting reached my ears,
the baby leaped in my womb for joy.
45 "And [a]blessed *is* she who believed [1]that there would be a fulfill-
ment of what had been spoken to her [2]by the Lord."
46 And Mary said:
"[a]My soul [1b]exalts the Lord,
47 And [a]my spirit has rejoiced in [b]God my Savior.
48 "For [a]He has had regard for the humble state of His [1]bondslave;
For behold, from this time on all generations will count me
[b]blessed.
49 "For the Mighty One has done great things for me;
And holy is His name.
50 "[a]AND HIS MERCY IS [1]UPON GENERATION AFTER GENERATION
TOWARD THOSE WHO FEAR HIM.
51 "[a]He has done [1]mighty deeds with His arm;
He has scattered *those who were* proud in the [2]thoughts of their
heart.
52 "He has brought down rulers from *their* thrones,
And has [a]exalted those who were humble.
53 "[a]HE HAS FILLED THE HUNGRY WITH GOOD THINGS;
And sent away the rich empty-handed.
54 "He has given help to Israel His servant,
[1]In remembrance of His mercy,
55 [a]As He spoke to our fathers,
[b]To Abraham and his [1]offspring forever."
56 And Mary stayed with her about three months, and *then*
returned to her home.
57 Now the time [1]had come for Elizabeth to give birth, and she
brought forth a son.
58 And her neighbors and her relatives heard that the Lord had
[1a]displayed His great mercy toward her; and they were rejoicing
with her.
59 And it came about that on [a]the eighth day they came to circum-
cise the child, and they were going to call him Zacharias, [1]after his
father.
60 And his mother answered and said, "No indeed; but [a]he shall be
called John."
61 And they said to her, "There is no one among your relatives who
is called by that name."
62 And they [a]made signs to his father, as to what he wanted him
called.
63 And he asked for a tablet, and wrote as follows, "[a]His name is
John." And they were all astonished.
64 [a]And at once his mouth was opened and his tongue *loosed*, and
he *began* to speak in praise of God.
65 And fear came on all those living around them; and all these
matters were being talked about in all [a]the hill country of Judea.
66 And all who heard them kept them in mind, saying, "What then
will this child *turn out to* be?" For [a]the hand of the Lord was certainly
with him.

Lit., *whence this to me* [a]Luke 2:11
45 [1]*Or possibly,* ...*cause there will be* [2]Lit., *from* [a]Luke 1:20, 48
[1]Lit., *makes great* ...ke 1:46-53: *1 Sam. 2:1-10* [b]Ps. 34:2f.
...s. 35:9; Hab. 3:18 ...Tim. 1:1; 2:3; Titus 2:10; 3:4; Jude 25
[1]I.e., female slave ...138:6 [b]Luke 1:45
50 [1]Lit., *unto generations and* ...*tions* [a]Ps. 103:17
[1]Lit., *might* [2]Lit., ...*ught, attitude* [a]Ps. 98:1; 118:15
52 [a]Job 5:11
53 [a]Ps. 107:9
54 [1]Lit., *So as to remember*
[1]Lit., *seed* [a]Gen. ...; Ps. 132:11; Gal. 3:16 [b]Gen. 17:7
[1]Lit., *was fulfilled*
...8 [1]Lit., *magnified* [a]Gen. 19:19
...it., *after the name* [a]Gen. 17:12; Lev. ...ke 2:21; Phil. 3:5
...0 [a]Luke 1:13, 63
62 [a]Luke 1:22
...3 [a]Luke 1:13, 60
64 [a]Luke 1:20
65 [a]Luke 1:39
66 [a]Acts 11:21

67 And his father Zacharias [a]was filled with the Holy Spirit, and [b]prophesied, saying:

68 "[a]Blessed *be* the Lord God of Israel,
For He has visited us and accomplished [b]redemption for His people,
69 And has raised up a [a]horn of salvation for us
In the house of David [b]His servant—
70 [a]As He spoke by the mouth of His holy prophets [b]from of old—
71 [1a]Salvation [b]FROM OUR ENEMIES,
And FROM THE HAND OF ALL WHO HATE US;
72 [a]To show mercy toward our fathers,
[b]And to remember His holy covenant,
73 [a]The oath which He swore to Abraham our father,
74 To grant us that we, being delivered from the hand of our enemies,
Might serve Him without fear,
75 [a]In holiness and righteousness before Him all our days.
76 "And you, child, will be called the [a]prophet of [b]the Most High;
For you will go on [c]BEFORE THE LORD TO [d]PREPARE HIS WAYS;
77 To give to His people *the* knowledge of salvation
[1]By [a]the forgiveness of their sins,
78 Because of the tender mercy of our God,
With which [a]the Sunrise from on high shall visit us,
79 [a]TO SHINE UPON THOSE WHO SIT IN DARKNESS AND THE SHADOW OF DEATH,
To guide our feet into the [b]way of peace."

80 [a]And the child continued to grow, and to become strong in spirit, and he lived in the deserts until the day of his public appearance to Israel.

Chapter 2

2 Now it came about in those days that a decree went out from [a]Caesar Augustus, that a census be taken of [b]all [1]the inhabited earth.

2 [1]This was the first census taken while [2]Quirinius was governor of [a]Syria.

3 And all were proceeding to register for the census, everyone to his own city.

4 And Joseph also went up from Galilee, from the city of Nazareth, to Judea, to the city of David, which is called Bethlehem, because [a]he was of the house and family of David,

5 in order to register, along with Mary, who was engaged to him, and was with child.

6 And it came about that while they were there, the days were completed for her to give birth.

7 And she [a]gave birth to her first-born son; and she wrapped Him in cloths, and laid Him in a [1]manger, because there was no room for them in the inn.

8 And in the same region there were *some* shepherds staying out in the fields, and keeping watch over their flock by night.

9 And [a]an angel of the Lord suddenly [b]stood before them, and the glory of the Lord shone around them; and they were terribly frightened.

67 [a]Luke 1:4 8; 9:17 [b]Joe
68 [a]1 Kin. 1: 41:13; 72:18; [b]Luke 1:71; 2 9:12
69 [a]1 Sam. 2 18:2; 89:17; 1 Ezek. 29:21
70 [a]Rom. 1:2 3:21
71 [1]Or, *Delive* [a]Luke 1:68 [b]F
72 [a]Mic. 7:20 105:8f., 42; 10
73 [a]Gen. 22:1 6:13
75 [a]Eph. 4:24
76 [a]Matt. 11:9 1:32 [c]Mal. 3:1; 11:10; Mark 1: 7:27 [d]Luke 1:1
77 [1]Or, *Consis* [a]Jer. 31:34; Ma
78 [a]Mal. 4:2; E 2 Pet. 1:19
79 [a]Is. 9:2 [b]Is. Matt. 4:16
80 [a]Luke 2:40
2:1 [1]I.e., the Ro empire [a]Matt. 2 Luke 3:1 [b]Matt.
2 [1]Or, *This took as a first census Kyrenios* [a]Matt.
4 [a]Luke 1:27
7 [1]Or, *feeding tr* [a]Matt. 1:25
9 [a]Luke 1:11; Ac [b]Luke 24:4; Acts

10 And the angel said to them, "[a]Do not be afraid; for behold, I
bring you good news of a great joy which shall be for all the people;
11 for today in the city of David there has been born for you a
[a]Savior, who is [1b]Christ [c]the Lord.
12 "And [a]this *will be* a sign for you: you will find a baby wrapped in
cloths, and lying in a [1]manger."
13 And suddenly there appeared with the angel a multitude of the
heavenly host praising God, and saying,
14 "[a]Glory to God in the highest,
And on earth peace among men [1b]with whom He is pleased."
15 And it came about when the angels had gone away from them
into heaven, that the shepherds *began* saying to one another, "Let us
go straight to Bethlehem then, and see this thing that has happened
which the Lord has made known to us."
16 And they came in haste and found their way to Mary and
Joseph, and the baby as He lay in the [1]manger.
17 And when they had seen this, they made known the statement
which had been told them about this Child.
18 And all who heard it wondered at the things which were told
them by the shepherds.
19 But Mary [a]treasured up all these things, pondering them in her
heart.
20 And the shepherds went back, [a]glorifying and praising God for
all that they had heard and seen, just as had been told them.
21 And when [a]eight days were completed [1]before His circumcision,
[b]His name was *then* called Jesus, the name given by the angel before
He was conceived in the womb.
22 [a]And when the days for their purification according to the law of
Moses were completed, they brought Him up to Jerusalem to present
Him to the Lord
23 (as it is written in the Law of the Lord, "[a]EVERY *first-born* MALE
THAT OPENS THE WOMB SHALL BE CALLED HOLY TO THE LORD"),
24 and to offer a sacrifice according to what was said in the Law of
the Lord, "[a]A PAIR OF TURTLEDOVES, OR TWO YOUNG PIGEONS."
25 And behold, there was a man in Jerusalem whose name was
Simeon; and this man was [a]righteous and devout, [b]looking for the
consolation of Israel; and the Holy Spirit was upon him.
26 And [a]it had been revealed to him by the Holy Spirit that he
would not [b]see death before he had seen the Lord's [1]Christ.
27 And he came in the Spirit into the temple; and when the parents
brought in the child Jesus, [1a]to carry out for Him the custom of the
Law,
28 then he took Him into his arms, and blessed God, and said,
29 "Now Lord, Thou dost let Thy bond-servant depart
In peace, [a]according to Thy word;
30 For my eyes have [a]seen Thy salvation,
31 Which Thou hast prepared in the presence of all peoples,
32 [a]A LIGHT [1]OF REVELATION TO THE GENTILES,
And the glory of Thy people Israel."
33 And His father and [a]mother were amazed at the things which
were being said about Him.
34 And Simeon blessed them, and said to Mary [a]His mother, "Be-
hold, this *Child* is appointed for [b]the fall and [1]rise of many in Israel,
and for a sign to be opposed—

10 [a]Matt. 14:27
..., Messiah [a]Matt. ...; John 4:42; Acts ... Matt. 1:16; 16:16, ...John 11:27 [c]Luke ... Acts 2:36; 10:36
...Or, *feeding trough* ... Sam. 2:34; 2 Kin. 20:8f.; Is. 7:11, 14
14 [1]Lit., *of good* ...*re;* or possibly, *of* ... *will* [a]Matt. 21:9; ...9:38 [b]Luke 3:22; ...oh. 1:9; Phil. 2:13
...Or, *feeding trough*
19 [a]Luke 2:51
20 [a]Matt. 9:8
21 [1]Lit., *so as to* ...*ncise Him* [a]Gen. ...; Lev. 12:3; Luke ... [b]Matt. 1:21, 25; Luke 1:31
22 [a]Lev. 12:6-8
...x. 13:2, 12; Num. 3:13; 8:17
[a]Lev. 5:11; 12:8
[a]Luke 1:6 [b]Mark ... Luke 2:38; 23:51
Messiah [a]Matt. ... [b]Ps. 89:48; John 8:51; Heb. 11:5
...it., *to do for Him* ...*ng to* [a]Luke 2:22
29 [a]Luke 2:26
...s. 119:166, 174; ...52:10; Luke 3:6
[1]Or, *for* [a]Is. 9:2; ...:6; 49:6, 9; 51:4; Matt. 4:16; Acts 13:47; 26:23
33 [a]Matt. 12:46
[1]Or, *resurrection* ...att. 12:46 [b]Matt. ...:44; 1 Cor. 1:23; ...2:16; 1 Pet. 2:8

35 and a sword will pierce even your own soul—to the end that
thoughts from many hearts may be revealed."
36 And there was a [a]prophetess, [1]Anna the daughter of Phanuel, of
[b]the tribe of Asher. She was advanced in [2]years, [c]having lived with a
husband seven years after her [3]marriage,
37 and then as a widow to the age of eighty-four. And she never left
the temple, serving night and day with [a]fastings and prayers.
38 And at that very [1]moment she came up and *began* giving thanks
to God, and continued to speak of Him to all those who were [a]look-
ing for the redemption of Jerusalem.
39 And when they had performed everything according to the Law
of the Lord, they returned to Galilee, to [a]their own city of Nazareth.
40 [a]And the Child continued to grow and become strong, [1]increas-
ing in wisdom; and the grace of God was upon Him.
41 And His parents used to go to Jerusalem every year at [a]the Feast
of the Passover.
42 And when He became twelve, they went up *there* according to
the custom of the Feast;
43 and as they were returning, after spending the [a]full number of
days, the boy Jesus stayed behind in Jerusalem. And His parents
were unaware of it,
44 but supposed Him to be in the caravan, and went a day's jour-
ney; and they *began* looking for Him among their relatives and ac-
quaintances.
45 And when they did not find Him, they returned to Jerusalem,
looking for Him.
46 And it came about that after three days they found Him in the
temple, sitting in the midst of the teachers, both listening to them,
and asking them questions.
47 And all who heard Him [a]were amazed at His understanding and
His answers.
48 And when they saw Him, they were astonished; and [a]His
mother said to Him, "[1]Son, why have You treated us this way? Be-
hold, [b]Your father and I [2]have been anxiously looking for You."
49 And He said to them, "Why is it that you were looking for Me?
Did you not know that [a]I had to be in My Father's [1]*house?"*
50 And [a]they did not understand the statement which He [1]had
made to them.
51 And He went down with them, and came to [a]Nazareth; and He
continued in subjection to them; and [b]His mother [1c]treasured all *these*
[2]things in her heart.
52 And Jesus kept increasing in wisdom and [1]stature, and in [a]favor
with God and men.

Chapter 3

3 Now in the fifteenth year of the reign of Tiberius Caesar, when
[a]Pontius Pilate was governor of Judea, and [b]Herod was tetrarch
of Galilee, and his brother Philip was tetrarch of the region of Ituraea
and Trachonitis, and Lysanias was tetrarch of Abilene,
2 in the high priesthood of [a]Annas and [b]Caiaphas, [c]the word of
God came to John, the son of Zacharias, in the wilderness.
3 And he came into all [a]the district around the Jordan, preaching a
baptism of repentance for the forgiveness of sins;
4 as it is written in the book of the words of Isaiah the prophet,

36 [1]Or, *Har* *days* [3]Lit., [a]Luke 2:38; [b]Josh. 19:24
37 [a]Luke 5. 13:3; 14:23
38 [1]Lit., *ho* 1:68; 2:25
39 [a]Matt. 2 1:26; 2:51;
40 [1]Lit., *be* *of* [a]Luke 1:
41 [a]Ex. 12 Deut. 16:1-
43 [a]Ex. 12
47 [a]Matt. 7 22:33; Mark 11:18; Luke 7:15
48 [1]Lit., *Ch* *looking* [a]M [b]Luke 2:49;
49 [1]Or, *affa* *the things* [a]John 4:34;
50 [1]Lit., *ha* [a]Mark 9:32 18:34
51 [1]Lit., *w* [2]Lit., *words* [b]Matt. 12:4
52 [1]Or, *ag*
3:1 [a]Matt. 14:1
2 [a]John 18 4:6 [b]Matt. 3:3-10: *Ma* *Mark 1:3-5*
3 [a]Matt. 3:

Herod's Family Tree

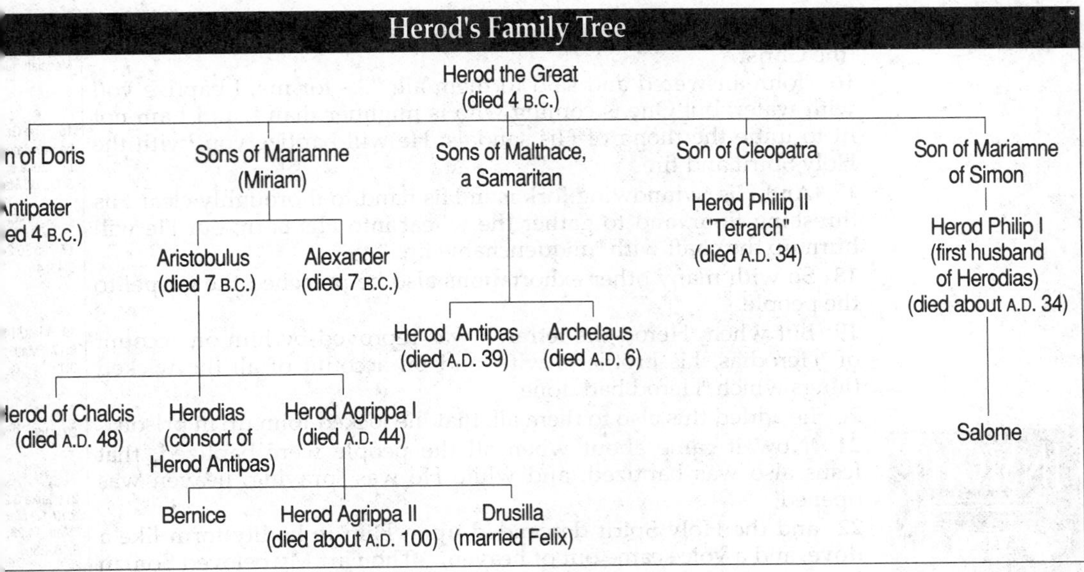

"[a]THE VOICE OF ONE CRYING IN THE WILDERNESS,
'MAKE READY THE WAY OF THE LORD,
MAKE HIS PATHS STRAIGHT.
5 '[a]EVERY RAVINE SHALL BE FILLED UP,
AND EVERY MOUNTAIN AND HILL SHALL BE [1]BROUGHT LOW;
AND THE CROOKED SHALL BECOME STRAIGHT,
AND THE ROUGH ROADS SMOOTH;
6 [a]AND ALL [1]FLESH SHALL [b]SEE THE SALVATION OF GOD.' "
7 He therefore *began* saying to the multitudes who were going out
to be baptized by him, "[a]You brood of vipers, who warned you to
flee from the wrath to come?
8 "Therefore bring forth fruits in keeping with repentance, and [a]do
not begin to say [1]to yourselves, '[b]We have Abraham for our father,'
for I say to you that God is able from these stones to raise up
children to Abraham.
9 "And also the axe is already laid at the root of the trees; [a]every
tree therefore that does not bear good fruit is cut down and thrown
into the fire."
10 And the multitudes were questioning him, saying, "[a]Then what
shall we do?"
11 And he would answer and say to them, "Let the man who has
two tunics [a]share with him who has none; and let him who has food
do likewise."
12 And *some* [1a]tax-gatherers also came to be baptized, and they said
to him, "Teacher, what shall we do?"
13 And he said to them, "[1]Collect no more than what you have been
ordered to."
14 And *some* [1]soldiers were questioning him, saying, "And *what
about* us, what shall we do?" And he said to them, "Do not take
money from anyone by force, or [a]accuse *anyone* falsely, and [b]be con-
tent with your wages."
15 Now while the people were in a state of expectation and all were

4 [a]Is. 40:3
eled [a]Is. 40:4
mankind [a]Is. :5 [b]Luke 2:30
t. 12:34; 23:33
in [a]Luke 5:21; 26; 14:9 [b]John 8:33
latt. 7:19; Luke 13:6-9
3:12, 14; Acts 2:37, 38
Is. 58:7; 1 Tim. James 2:14-20
e., Collectors of taxes for profit [a]Luke 7:29
13 [1]Or, *Exact*
., men in active ary service [a]Ex. 23:1 [b]Phil. 4:11

[1]wondering in their hearts about John, [a]as to whether he might be
[2]the Christ,
16 [a]John answered and said to them all, "As for me, I baptize you
with water; but One is coming who is mightier than I, and I am not
fit to untie the thong of His sandals; He will baptize you [1]with the
Holy Spirit and fire.
17 "And His [a]winnowing fork is in His hand to thoroughly clear His
threshing floor, and to gather the wheat into His barn; but He will
burn up the chaff with [b]unquenchable fire."
18 So with many other exhortations also he preached the gospel to
the people.
19 But when [a]Herod the tetrarch was reproved by him on account
of [a]Herodias, his brother's wife, and on account of all the wicked
things which [b]Herod had done,
20 he added this also to them all, that [a]he locked John up in prison.
21 [a]Now it came about when all the people were baptized, that
Jesus also was baptized, and while He was [b]praying, heaven was
opened,
22 and the Holy Spirit descended upon Him in bodily form like a
dove, and a voice came out of heaven, "[a]Thou art My beloved Son, in
Thee I am well-pleased."
23 And [a]when He began His ministry, Jesus Himself was about
thirty years of age, [1]being supposedly *the* son of [b]Joseph, the *son* of
[2]Eli,
24 the *son* of Matthat, the *son* of Levi, the *son* of Melchi, the *son* of
Jannai, the *son* of Joseph,
25 the *son* of Mattathias, the *son* of Amos, the *son* of Nahum, the *son*
of [1]Hesli, the *son* of Naggai,
26 the *son* of Maath, the *son* of Mattathias, the *son* of Semein, the *son*
of Josech, the *son* of Joda,
27 the *son* of Joanan, the *son* of Rhesa, [a]the *son* of Zerubbabel, the
son of [1]Shealtiel, the *son* of Neri,
28 the *son* of Melchi, the *son* of Addi, the *son* of Cosam, the *son* of
Elmadam, the *son* of Er,
29 the *son* of [1]Joshua, the *son* of Eliezer, the *son* of Jorim, the *son* of
Matthat, the *son* of Levi,
30 the *son* of Simeon, the *son* of [1]Judah, the *son* of Joseph, the *son* of
Jonam, the *son* of Eliakim,
31 the *son* of Melea, the *son* of Menna, the *son* of Mattatha, the *son* of
Nathan, the *son* of David,
32 [a]the *son* of Jesse, the *son* of Obed, the *son* of Boaz, the *son* of
[1]Salmon, the *son* of [2]Nahshon,
33 the *son* of Amminadab, the *son* of Admin, the *son* of [1]Ram, the
son of Hezron, the *son* of Perez, the *son* of Judah,
34 the *son* of Jacob, the *son* of Isaac, [a]the *son* of Abraham, the *son* of
Terah, the *son* of Nahor,
35 the *son* of Serug, the *son* of [1]Reu, the *son* of Peleg, the *son* of
[2]Heber, the *son* of Shelah,
36 the *son* of Cainan, the *son* of Arphaxad, the *son* of Shem, [a]the *son*
of Noah, the *son* of Lamech,
37 the *son* of Methuselah, the *son* of Enoch, the *son* of Jared, the *son*
of Mahalaleel, the *son* of Cainan,
38 the *son* of Enosh, the *son* of Seth, the *son* of Adam, the *son* of God.

INSIGHT

See **The Genealogy of Jesus Christ** on page 1874.

15 [1]O... *debatir...* Messia...

16 [1]Th... be tran... *by* [a]Lu... *3:11, 1...*

17 [a]Is. 9:43, 48...

19 [a]Ma... 6:17 [b]M... 3:1

20 [a]Joh...

21 [a]Luk... *3:13-17,* [b]Matt. 14... 9:18, 28...

22 [a]Ps. Matt. 3:1... 1:11; Luk... 1:17

23 [1]Lit., *thought Heli* [a]Ma... 1:1 [b]Ma... 3:23-27

25 [1]Also...

27 [1]Gr., ... [a]Matt. 1:1...

29 [1]Gr., ...

30 [1]Gr., ...

32 [1]Gr., S... *Naasson* 3:32-34: ...

33 [1]Gr., A...

34 [a]Luke... *11:26-30;* ...

35 [1]Gr., R... *Eber*

36 [a]Luke 3... *5:3-32; 1C...*

:1 [1]Or, *under the* *nfluence of;* lit., *in* .uke 4:1-13: *Matt.* *11; Mark 1:12, 13* [b]Luke 3:3
34:28; 1 Kin. 19:8
4 [a]Deut. 8:3
Lit., *the inhabited* *rth* [a]Matt. 4:8-10 [b]Matt. 24:14
their (referring to ıgdoms) [a]1 John 5:19
7 [1]Or, *bow down*
eut. 6:13; 10:20; Matt. 4:10
9 [a]Matt. 4:5-7
10 [a]Ps. 91:11
11 [a]Ps. 91:12
)r, *tempt . . . God* [a]Deut. 6:16
Matt. 4:12 [b]Matt. 9:26; Luke 4:37
15 [a]Matt. 4:23
6 [a]Luke 2:39, 51 13:54; Mark 6:1f. [c]Acts 13:14-16
17 [1]Or, *scroll*
61:1; Matt. 11:5; 12:18; John 3:34
61:2; Lev. 25:10
'Or, *scroll* [a]Luke 17 [b]Matt. 26:55
21 [1]Lit., *ears*
, *testifying* [2]Lit., *roceeding out of* *th* [a]Matt. 13:55; k 6:3; John 6:42

Chapter 4

4 [a]And Jesus, full of the Holy Spirit, [b]returned from the Jordan and
was led about [1]by the Spirit in the wilderness
2 for [a]forty days, being tempted by the devil. And He ate nothing
during those days; and when they had ended, He became hungry.
3 And the devil said to Him, "If You are the Son of God, tell this
stone to become bread."
4 And Jesus answered him, "It is written, '[a]MAN SHALL NOT LIVE ON
BREAD ALONE.' "
5 [a]And he led Him up and showed Him all the kingdoms of [1b]the
world in a moment of time.
6 And the devil said to Him, "I will give You all this domain and
[1]its glory; [a]for it has been handed over to me, and I give it to
whomever I wish.
7 "Therefore if You [1]worship before me, it shall all be Yours."
8 And Jesus answered and said to him, "It is written, '[a]YOU SHALL
WORSHIP THE LORD YOUR GOD AND SERVE HIM ONLY.' "
9 [a]And he led Him to Jerusalem and had Him stand on the pin-
nacle of the temple, and said to Him, "If You are the Son of God,
throw Yourself down from here;
10 for it is written,

'[a]HE WILL GIVE HIS ANGELS CHARGE CONCERNING YOU TO GUARD YOU,'

11 and,

'[a]ON *their* HANDS THEY WILL BEAR YOU UP,
LEST YOU STRIKE YOUR FOOT AGAINST A STONE.' "

12 And Jesus answered and said to him, "It is said, '[a]YOU SHALL NOT
[1]PUT THE LORD YOUR GOD TO THE TEST.' "
13 And when the devil had finished every temptation, he departed
from Him until an opportune time.
14 And [a]Jesus returned to Galilee in the power of the Spirit; and
[b]news about Him spread through all the surrounding district.
15 And He *began* [a]teaching in their synagogues and was praised by
all.
16 And He came to [a]Nazareth, where He had been brought up; and
as was His custom, [b]He entered the synagogue on the Sabbath, and
[c]stood up to read.
17 And the [1]book of the prophet Isaiah was handed to
Him. And He opened the [1]book, and found the place
where it was written,
18 "[a]THE SPIRIT OF THE LORD IS UPON ME,
BECAUSE HE ANOINTED ME TO PREACH THE GOSPEL TO THE
POOR.
HE HAS SENT ME TO PROCLAIM RELEASE TO THE CAPTIVES,
AND RECOVERY OF SIGHT TO THE BLIND,
TO SET FREE THOSE WHO ARE DOWNTRODDEN,
19 [a]TO PROCLAIM THE FAVORABLE YEAR OF THE LORD."
20 And He [a]closed the [1]book, and gave it back to the at-
tendant, and [b]sat down; and the eyes of all in the syna-
gogue were fixed upon Him.
21 And He began to say to them, "Today this Scripture
has been fulfilled in your [1]hearing."
22 And all were [1]speaking well of Him, and wondering at
the gracious words which [2]were falling from His lips; and
they were saying, "[a]Is this not Joseph's son?"

23 And He said to them, "No doubt you will quote this proverb to Me, 'Physician, heal yourself! Whatever we heard was done [a]at Capernaum, do here in [b]your home town as well.' "

24 And He said, "Truly I say to you, [a]no prophet is welcome in his home town.

25 "But I say to you in truth, there were many widows in Israel [a]in the days of Elijah, when the sky was shut up for three years and six months, when a great famine came over all the land;

26 and yet Elijah was sent to none of them, but [a]only to [1]Zarephath, *in the land* of [b]Sidon, to a woman who was a widow.

27 "And there were many lepers in Israel in the time of Elisha the prophet; and none of them was cleansed, but [a]only Naaman the Syrian."

28 And all in the synagogue were filled with rage as they heard these things;

29 and they rose up and [a]cast Him out of the city, and led Him to the brow of the hill on which their city had been built, in order to throw Him down the cliff.

30 But [a]passing through their midst, He went His way.

31 And [a]He came down to [b]Capernaum, a city of Galilee. And He was teaching them on the Sabbath;

32 and [a]they were amazed at His teaching, for [b]His [1]message was with authority.

33 And there was a man in the synagogue [1]possessed by the spirit of an unclean demon, and he cried out with a loud voice,

34 "[1]Ha! [a]What do we have to do with You, Jesus [2]of [b]Nazareth? Have You come to destroy us? I know who You are—[b]the Holy One of God!"

35 And Jesus [a]rebuked him, saying, "Be quiet and come out of him!" And when the demon had thrown him down in *their* midst, he came out of him without doing him any harm.

36 And amazement came upon them all, and they *began* discussing with one another saying, "What is [1]this message? For [a]with authority and power He commands the unclean spirits, and they come out."

37 And [a]the report about Him was getting out into every locality in the surrounding district.

38 [a]And He arose and *left* the synagogue, and entered Simon's home. Now Simon's mother-in-law was [b]suffering from a high fever; and they made request of Him on her behalf.

39 And standing over her, He [a]rebuked the fever, and it left her; and she immediately arose and [1]waited on them.

40 [a]And while [b]the sun was setting, all who had any sick with various diseases brought them to Him; and [c]laying His hands on every one of them, He was [d]healing them.

41 And demons also were coming out of many, crying out and saying, "You are [a]the Son of God!" And [b]rebuking them, He would [c]not allow them to speak, because they knew Him to be [1]the Christ.

42 [a]And when day came, He departed and went to a lonely place; and the multitudes were searching for Him, and came to Him, and tried to keep Him from going away from them.

43 But He said to them, "I must preach the kingdom of God to the other cities also, [a]for I was sent for this purpose."

44 And He kept on preaching in the synagogues [a]of [1]Judea.

23 [a]Matt. 4:13; 1:21ff.; 2:1ff.; Luk 4:35ff.; John 4:46 [b]Mark 6:1; Luke 51; 4:16
24 [a]Matt. 13:57; 6:4; John 4:44
25 [a]1 Kin. 17:1; James 5:17
26 [1]Gr., *Sarepta* [a]1 Kin. 17:9 [b]Ma
27 [a]2 Kin. 5:1-14
29 [a]Num. 15:35; 7:58; Heb. 13:12
30 [a]John 10:39
31 [a]Luke 4:31-3 *1:21-28* [b]Matt. 4 Luke 4:23
32 [1]Lit., *word* [a]M 7:28 [b]Luke 4:36 7:46
33 [1]Lit., *having*
34 [1]Or possibly, *alone* [2]Lit., *the Nazarene* [a]Matt [b]Mark 1:24
35 [a]Matt. 8:26; 4:39; Luke 4:39,
36 [1]Or, *this word with authority . . out?* [a]Luke 4:32
37 [a]Luke 4:14
38 [a]Luke 4:38, *8:14, 15; Mark 1* [b]Matt. 4:24
39 [1]Or, *served* 4:35, 41
40 [a]Luke 4:40, *8:16, 17; Mark 1* [b]Mark 1:32 [c]Ma [d]Matt. 4:23
41 [1]I.e., the Mes [a]Matt. 4:3 [b]Luke [c]Matt. 8:16; Mar
42 [a]Luke 4:42, *Mark 1:35-38*
43 [a]Mark 1:38
44 [1]I.e., the cou the Jews (includ Galilee); some r read *Galilee* [a]M

Chapter 5

5 [a]Now it came about that while the multitude were pressing
around Him and listening to the word of God, He was standing
by [b]the lake of Gennesaret;
2 and He saw two boats lying at the edge of the lake; but the
fishermen had gotten out of them, and were washing their nets.
3 And [a]He got into one of the boats, which was Simon's, and asked
him to put out a little way from the land. And He sat down and
began teaching the multitudes from the boat.
4 And when He had finished speaking, He said to Simon, "Put out
into the deep water and [a]let down your nets for a catch."
5 And Simon answered and said, "[a]Master, [b]we worked hard all
night and caught nothing, but at Your [1]bidding I will let down the
nets."
6 And when they had done this, [a]they enclosed a great quantity of
fish; and their nets *began* to break;
7 and they signaled to their partners in the other boat, for them to
come and help them. And they came, and filled both of the boats, so
that they began to sink.
8 But when Simon Peter saw *that,* he fell down at Jesus' [1]feet,
saying, "Depart from me, for I am a sinful man, O Lord!"
9 For amazement had seized him and all his companions because
of the catch of fish which they had taken;
10 and so also [1]James and John, sons of Zebedee, who were
partners with Simon. And Jesus said to Simon, "[a]Do not fear, from
now on you will be [b]catching men."
11 And when they had brought their boats to land, [a]they left every-
thing and followed Him.
12 [a]And it came about that while He was in one of the cities, be-
hold, *there was* a man full of leprosy; and when he saw Jesus, he fell
on his face and implored Him, saying, "Lord, if You are willing, You
can make me clean."
13 And He stretched out His hand, and touched him, saying, "I am
willing; be cleansed." And immediately the leprosy left him.
14 And He ordered him to tell no one, "But go and [a]show yourself
to the priest, and make an offering for your cleansing, just as Moses
commanded, for a testimony to them."
15 But [a]the news about Him was spreading even farther, and great
multitudes were gathering to hear *Him* and to be healed of their
sicknesses.
16 But He Himself would *often* slip away [1]to the [2]wilderness and
[a]pray.
17 And it came about [1]one day that He was teaching; and [a]there
were *some* Pharisees and [b]teachers of the law sitting *there,* who had
[c]come from every village of Galilee and Judea and *from* Jerusalem;
and [d]the power of the Lord was *present* for Him to perform healing.
18 [a]And behold, *some* men *were* carrying on a [1]bed a man who was
paralyzed; and they were trying to bring him in, and to set him
down in front of Him.
19 And not finding any *way* to bring him in because of the crowd,
they went up on [a]the roof and let him down [b]through the tiles with
his stretcher, right in the center, in front of Jesus.
20 And seeing their faith, He said, "[1]Friend, [a]your sins are forgiven
you."

1 [a]Matt. 4:18-22; ark 1:16-20; Luke -11; John 1:40-42 Num. 34:11; Deut. Josh. 12:3; 13:27; Matt. 4:18
tt. 13:2; Mark 3:9, 10; 4:1
4 [a]John 21:6
word [a]Luke 8:24; 49; 17:13 [b]John 21:3
6 [a]John 21:6
8 [1]Lit., *knees*
[1]Or, *Jacob* [a]Matt. 4:27 [b]2 Tim. 2:26
[a]Matt. 4:20, 22; 9; Mark 1:18, 20; Luke 5:28
ke 5:12-14: *Matt.* 2-4; *Mark 1:40-44*
.ev. 13:49; 14:2ff.
15 [a]Matt. 9:26
.it., *in* [2]Or, *lonely* ces [a]Matt. 14:23; 1:35; Luke 6:12
Lit., *on one of the* Matt. 15:1 [b]Luke Mark 1:45 [d]Mark ; Luke 6:19; 8:46
, *stretcher* [a]Luke 8-26: *Matt. 9:2-8; Mark 2:3-12*
att. 24:17 [b]Mark 2:4
., *Man* [a]Matt. 9:2

21 And the scribes and the Pharisees [a]began to reason, saying,
"[b]Who is this *man* who speaks blasphemies? [c]Who can forgive sins,
but God alone?"
22 But Jesus, [1]aware of their reasonings, answered and said to them,
"Why are you reasoning in your hearts?
23 "Which is easier, to say, 'Your sins have been forgiven you,' or to
say, 'Rise and walk'?
24 "But in order that you may know that the Son of Man has
authority on earth to forgive sins,"—He said to the [a]paralytic—"I say
to you, rise, and take up your stretcher and go home."
25 And at once he rose up before them, and took up what he had
been lying on, and went home, [a]glorifying God.
26 And they were all seized with astonishment and *began* [a]glorify-
ing God; and they were filled [b]with fear, saying, "We have seen
remarkable things today."
27 [a]And after that He went out, and noticed a [1]tax-gatherer named
[b]Levi, sitting in the tax office, and He said to him, "Follow Me."
28 And he [a]left everything behind, and rose and *began* to follow
Him.
29 And [a]Levi gave a big [1]reception for Him in his house; and there
was a great crowd of [b]tax-gatherers and other *people* who were reclin-
ing *at the table* with them.
30 And [a]the Pharisees and their scribes *began* grumbling at His dis-
ciples, saying, "Why do you eat and drink with the tax-gatherers
and sinners?"
31 And Jesus answered and said to them, "[a]*It is* not those who are
well who need a physician, but those who are sick.
32 "I have not come to call the righteous but sinners to repentance."
33 And they said to Him, "[a]The disciples of John often fast and offer
prayers; the *disciples* of the Pharisees also do [1]the same; but Yours eat
and drink."
34 And Jesus said to them, "You cannot make the [1]attendants of the
bridegroom fast while the bridegroom is with them, can you?
35 "[a]But *the* days will come; and when the bridegroom is taken away
from them, then they will fast in those days."
36 And He was also telling them a parable: "No one tears a piece
from a new [1]garment and puts it on an old [1]garment; otherwise he
will both tear the new, and the piece from the new will not match the
old.
37 "And no one puts new wine into old [1]wineskins; otherwise the
new wine will burst the [1]skins, and it will be spilled out, and the
[1]skins will be ruined.
38 "But new wine must be put into fresh wineskins.
39 "And no one, after drinking old *wine* wishes for new; for he says,
'The old is good *enough*.'"

Chapter 6

6 [a]Now it came about that on a *certain* [1]Sabbath He was passing
through *some* grainfields; and His disciples [b]were picking and
eating the heads *of grain,* rubbing them in their hands.
2 But some of the Pharisees said, "Why do you do what [a]is not
lawful on the Sabbath?"
3 And Jesus answering them said, "Have you not even read [a]what
David did when he was hungry, he and those who were with him,

21 [a]Luke 3:8 7:49 [c]Is. 43:2
22 [1]Or, perce
24 [a]Matt. 4:2
25 [a]Matt. 9:8
26 [a]Matt. 9:8 1:65; 7:16
27 [1]I.e., Colle Roman taxes [a]Luke 5:27-39 *9:9-17; Mark 2* [b]Matt. 9:9
28 [a]Luke 5:11
29 [1]Or, *banqu* 9:9 [b]Luke 15:1
30 [a]Mark 2:16 15:2; Acts 23:9
31 [a]Matt. 9:12, Mark 2:17
33 [1]Or, *likewis* 9:14; Mark 2:18
34 [1]Lit., *sons o bridal-chamber*
35 [a]Matt. 9:15; 2:20; Luke 17:22
36 [1]Or, *cloak*
37 [1]I.e., skins us bottles
6:1 [1]Many mss. *the second-first Sabbath;* i.e., the second Sabbath the first [a]Luke 6: *Matt. 12:1-8; Ma 2:23-28* [b]Deut. 2
2 [a]Matt. 12:2
3 [a]1 Sam. 21:6

4 how he entered the house of God, and took and ate the [1]consecrated bread which [a]is not lawful for any to eat except the priests alone, and gave it to his companions?"

5 And He was saying to them, "The Son of Man is Lord of the Sabbath."

6 [a]And it came about [b]on another Sabbath, that He entered [c]the synagogue and was teaching; and there was a man there [1]whose right hand was withered.

7 And the scribes and the Pharisees [a]were watching Him closely, *to see* if He healed on the Sabbath, in order that they might find *reason* to accuse Him.

8 But He [a]knew [1]what they were thinking, and He said to the man with the withered hand, "Rise and [2]come forward!" And he rose and [3]came forward.

9 And Jesus said to them, "I ask you, is it lawful on the Sabbath to do good, or to do harm, to save a life, or to destroy it?"

10 And after [a]looking around at them all, He said to him, "Stretch out your hand!" And he did *so;* and his hand was restored.

11 But they themselves were filled with [1]rage, and discussed together what they might do to Jesus.

12 And it was [1]at this time that He went off to [a]the mountain to [b]pray, and He spent the whole night in prayer to God.

13 And when day came, [a]He called His disciples to Him; and chose twelve of them, whom He also named as [b]apostles:

14 Simon, whom He also named Peter, and Andrew his brother; and [1]James and John; and Philip and Bartholomew;

15 and [a]Matthew and Thomas; James *the son* of Alphaeus, and Simon who was called the Zealot;

16 Judas *the son* of James, and Judas Iscariot, who became a traitor.

17 And He [a]descended with them, and stood on a level place; and *there was* [b]a great multitude of His disciples, and a great throng of people from all Judea and Jerusalem and the coastal region of [c]Tyre and Sidon,

18 [1]who had come to hear Him, and to be healed of their diseases; and those who were troubled with unclean spirits were being cured.

19 And all the multitude were trying to [a]touch Him, for [b]power was coming from Him and healing *them* all.

20 And turning His gaze on His disciples, He *began* to say, "[a]Blessed *are* you *who are* poor, for [b]yours is the kingdom of God.

21 "Blessed *are* you who hunger now, for you shall be satisfied. Blessed *are* you who weep now, for you shall laugh.

22 "[a]Blessed are you when men hate you, and [b]ostracize you, and cast insults at you, and spurn your name as evil, for the sake of the Son of Man.

23 "Be glad in that day, and [a]leap *for joy,* for behold, your reward is great in heaven; for [b]in the same way their fathers used to [1]treat the prophets.

24 "But woe to [a]you who are rich, for [b]you are receiving your comfort in full.

25 "Woe to you who [1]are well-fed now, for you shall be hungry. Woe *to you* who laugh now, for you shall mourn and weep.

26 "Woe *to you* when all men speak well of you, for in the same way their fathers used to [1]treat the [a]false prophets.

)r, *showbread;* lit., *es of presentation* [a]Lev. 24:9

.it., *and his* [a]Luke 11: Matt. *12:9-14;* *k 3:1-6* [b]Luke 6:1 [c]Matt. 4:23

7 [a]Mark 3:2

.it., *their thoughts* *., stand;* or, *stood* *to the midst* [3]Lit., *stood* [a]Matt. 9:4

10 [a]Mark 3:5

11 [1]Lit., *folly*

Lit., *in these days* 5:1 [b]Matt. 14:23; ıke 5:16; 9:18, 28

ıke 6:13-16: *Matt.* *-4; Mark 3:16-19;* *1:13* [b]Mark 6:30

)r, *Jacob,* also vv. 15 and 16

15 [a]Matt. 9:9

[a]Luke 6:12 [b]Matt. Mark 3:7, 8 [c]Matt. 11:21

18 [1]Most English rsions begin v. 18 th *and those who*

Matt. 9:21; 14:36; 3:10 [b]Luke 5:17

Matt. 5:3-12; Luke :20-23 [b]Matt. 5:3

Pet. 4:14 [b]John 9:22; 16:2

Lit., *do to* [a]Mal. 4 36:16; Acts 7:52

ıke 16:25; James 5:1 [b]Matt. 6:2

[1]Lit., *having been filled*

[1]Lit., *do to* [a]Matt. 7:15

27 "But I say to you who hear, [a]love your enemies, do good to those who hate you,
28 bless those who curse you, [a]pray for those who [1]mistreat you.
29 "[a]Whoever hits you on the cheek, offer him the other also; and whoever takes away your [1]coat, do not withhold your [2]shirt from him either.
30 "Give to everyone who asks of you, and whoever takes away what is yours, do not demand it back.
31 "[a]And just as you want people to [1]treat you, [1]treat them in the same way.
32 "And [a]if you love those who love you, what credit is *that* to you? For even sinners love those who love them.
33 "And if you do good to those who do good to you, what credit is *that* to you? For even sinners do the same.
34 "[a]And if you lend to those from whom you expect to receive, what credit is *that* to you? Even sinners lend to sinners, in order to receive back the same *amount*.
35 "But [a]love your enemies, and do good, and lend, [1]expecting nothing in return; and your reward will be great, and you will be [b]sons of [c]the Most High; for He Himself is kind to ungrateful and evil *men*.
36 "[1]Be merciful, just as your Father is merciful.
37 "[a]And do not judge and you will not be judged; and do not condemn, and you will not be condemned; [1b]pardon, and you will be pardoned.
38 "Give, and it will be given to you; [a]good measure, pressed down, shaken together, running over, they will pour [b]into your lap. For by your standard of measure it will be measured to you in return."
39 And He also spoke a parable to them: "[a]A blind man cannot guide a blind man, can he? Will they not both fall into a pit?
40 "[a]A [1]pupil is not above his teacher; but everyone, after he has been fully trained, will [2]be like his teacher.
41 "And why do you look at the speck that is in your brother's eye, but do not notice the log that is in your own eye?
42 "Or how can you say to your brother, 'Brother, let me take out the speck that is in your eye,' when you yourself do not see the log that is in your own eye? You hypocrite, first take the log out of your own eye, and then you will see clearly to take out the speck that is in your brother's eye.
43 "[a]For there is no good tree which produces bad fruit; nor, [1]on the other hand, a bad tree which produces good fruit.
44 "[a]For each tree is known by its own fruit. For men do not gather figs from thorns, nor do they pick grapes from a briar bush.
45 "[a]The good man out of the good [1]treasure of his heart brings forth what is good; and the evil *man* out of the evil *treasure* brings forth what is evil; [b]for his mouth speaks from [2]that which fills his heart.
46 "And [a]why do you call Me, 'Lord, Lord,' and do not do what I say?
47 "[a]Everyone who comes to Me, and hears My words, and [1]acts upon them, I will show you whom he is like:
48 he is like a man building a house, who [1]dug deep and laid a foundation upon the rock; and when a flood rose, the [2]torrent burst against that house and could not shake it, because it had been well built.
49 "But the one who has heard, and has not acted *accordingly*, is like

27 [a]Matt. 5:4 6:35
28 [1]Or, *revile* 5:44; Luke 6:
29 [1]Or, *cloak* garment [2]Or, garment worn body [a]Luke 6 *Matt. 5:39-42*
31 [1]Lit., *do to* 7:12
32 [a]Matt. 5:46
34 [a]Matt. 5:42
35 [1]Or, *not de at all* [a]Luke 6: 5:9 [c]Luke 1:32
36 [1]Or, *Becom*
37 [1]Lit., *releas* 6:37-42: *Matt. 7* [b]Matt. 6:14; Luk Acts 3:13
38 [a]Mark 4:24 79:12; Is. 65:6, 32:18
39 [a]Matt. 15:14
40 [1]Or, *disciple reach his teache level* [a]Matt. 10:2 13:16; 15:20
43 [1]Lit., *again* 6:43, 44: *Matt. 7. 18, 20*
44 [a]Matt. 7:16; 1
45 [1]Or, *treasury, storehouse* [2]Lit., *abundance of* [a]M 12:35 [b]Matt. 12:3
46 [a]Mal. 1:6; Ma
47 [1]Lit., *does* [a]L 6:47-49: *Matt. 7:* James 1:22ff.
48 [1]Lit., *dug and deep* [2]Lit., *river*

a man who built a house upon the ground without any foundation;
and the [1]torrent burst against it and immediately it collapsed, and
the ruin of that house was great."

Chapter 7

7 [a]When He had completed all His discourse in the hearing of the
people, [b]He went to Capernaum.
2 And a certain centurion's slave, [1]who was highly regarded by
him, was sick and about to die.
3 And when he heard about Jesus, [a]he sent some [1]Jewish elders
asking Him to come and [2]save the life of his slave.
4 And when they had come to Jesus, they earnestly entreated Him,
saying, "He is worthy for You to grant this to him;
5 for he loves our nation, and it was he who built us our syna-
gogue."
6 Now Jesus *started* on His way with them; and when He was
already not far from the house, the centurion sent friends, saying to
Him, "[1]Lord, do not trouble Yourself further, for I am not worthy for
You to come under my roof;
7 for this reason I did not even consider myself worthy to come to
You, but *just* [1]say the word, and my [2]servant will be healed.
8 "For I, too, am a man under authority, with soldiers under me;
and I say to this one, 'Go!' and he goes; and to another, 'Come!' and
he comes; and to my slave, 'Do this!' and he does it."
9 Now when Jesus heard this, He marveled at him, and turned
and said to the multitude that was following Him, "I say to you, [a]not
even in Israel have I found such great faith."
10 And when those who had been sent returned to the house, they
found the slave in good health.
11 And it came about [1]soon afterwards, that He went to a city called
Nain; and His disciples were going along with Him, [2]accompanied
by a large multitude.
12 Now as He approached the gate of the city, behold, [1]a dead man
was being carried out, the [2]only son of his mother, and she was a
widow; and a sizeable crowd from the city was with her.
13 And when [a]the Lord saw her, He felt compassion for her, and
said to her, "[1]Do not weep."
14 And He came up and touched the coffin; and the bearers came to
a halt. And He said, "Young man, I say to you, arise!"
15 And the [1]dead man sat up, and began to speak. And *Jesus* gave
him back to his mother.
16 And [a]fear gripped them all, and they *began* [b]glorifying God,
saying, "A great [c]prophet has arisen among us!" and, "God has
[1]visited His people!"
17 [a]And this report concerning Him went out all over Judea, and in
all the surrounding district.
18 [a]And the disciples of John reported to him about all these things.
19 And summoning [1]two of his disciples, John sent them to [a]the
Lord, saying, "Are You the [2]Expected One, or do we look for [3]some-
one else?"
20 And when the men had come to Him, they said, "John the Bap-
tist has sent us to You, saying, 'Are You the [1]Expected One, or do we
look for someone else?' "

9 [1]Lit., *river*
7:28 [b]Luke *Matt. 8:5-13*
hom he was honorable
elders of the , bring safely escue [a]Matt. 8:5
6 [1]Or, *Sir*
y with a word [2]Or, *boy*
10; Luke 7:50
mss. read *on day* [2]Lit., *and*
one who had only begotten
Stop weeping 19; 10:1; 11:1, 2; 13:15; 17:5, 6; 19:8; 22:61; John 4:1; 6:23; 11:2
5 [1]Or, *corpse*
ared for [a]Luke Matt. 9:8 [c]Matt. :11; Luke 7:39
17 [a]Matt. 9:26
7:18-35: Matt. *11:2-19*
t., a certain two t., Coming One early mss. read *who is different* 7:13; 10:1; 11:1, 42; 13:15; 17:5, 3:6; 19:8; 22:61; ; John 4:1; 6:23; 11:2
it., Coming One

21 At that [1]very time He [a]cured many *people* of diseases and [b]afflic-
tions and evil spirits; and He granted sight to many *who were* blind.
22 And He answered and said to them, "Go and report to John
what you have seen and heard: *the* [a]BLIND RECEIVE SIGHT, *the* lame
walk, *the* lepers are cleansed, and *the* deaf hear, *the* dead are raised
up, *the* [b]POOR HAVE THE GOSPEL PREACHED TO THEM.
23 "And blessed is he [1]who keeps from stumbling over Me."
24 And when the messengers of John had left, He began to speak to
the multitudes about John, "What did you go out into the wilderness
to look at? A reed shaken by the wind?
25 "[1]But what did you go out to see? A man dressed in soft [2]cloth-
ing? Behold, those who are splendidly clothed and live in luxury are
found in royal palaces.
26 "But what did you go out to see? A prophet? Yes, I say to you, and
one who is more than a prophet.
27 "This is the one about whom it [1]is written,
'[a]BEHOLD, I SEND MY MESSENGER BEFORE YOUR FACE,
WHO WILL PREPARE YOUR WAY BEFORE YOU.'
28 "I say to you, among those born of women, there is no one greater
than John; yet he who is [1]least in the kingdom of God is greater than
he."
29 And when all the people and the [1]tax-gatherers heard *this,* they
[2]acknowledged [a]God's justice, [b]having been baptized with [c]the bap-
tism of John.
30 But the Pharisees and the [1a]lawyers rejected God's purpose for
themselves, not having been baptized by [2]John.
31 "To what then shall I compare the men of this generation, and
what are they like?
32 "They are like children who sit in the market place and call to one
another; and they say, 'We played the flute for you, and you did not
dance; we sang a dirge, and you did not weep.'
33 "For John the Baptist has come [a]eating no bread and drinking no
wine; and you say, 'He has a demon!'
34 "The Son of Man has come eating and drinking; and you say,
'Behold, a gluttonous man, and a [1]drunkard, a friend of [2]tax-
gatherers and sinners!'
35 "[1]Yet wisdom [a]is vindicated by all her children."
36 Now one of the Pharisees was requesting Him to [1]dine with him.
And He entered the Pharisee's house, and reclined *at the table.*
37 [a]And behold, there was a woman in the city who was a [1]sinner;
and when she learned that He was reclining *at the table* in the
Pharisee's house, she brought an alabaster vial of perfume,
38 and standing behind *Him* at His feet, weeping, she began to wet
His feet with her tears, and kept wiping them with the hair of her
head, and kissing His feet, and anointing them with the perfume.
39 Now when the Pharisee who had invited Him saw this, he said
[1]to himself, "If this man were [2a]a prophet He would know who and
what sort of person this woman is who is touching Him, that she is a
[3]sinner."
40 And Jesus answered and said to him, "Simon, I have something
to say to you." And he [1]replied, "Say it, Teacher."
41 "A certain moneylender had two debtors: one owed five hundred
[1a]denarii, and the other fifty.

21 [1]Lit., *hou*
4:23 [b]Mark

22 [a]Is. 35:5

23 [1]Lit., *who*

25 [1]Or, *Well*
[2]Or, *garment*

27 [1]Lit., *has*
written [a]Mal.
11:10; Mark 1

28 [1]Or, *less*

29 [1]I.e., Colle
Roman taxes
[2]Or, *justified*
7:35 [b]Matt. 2
3:12 [c]Acts 18

30 [1]I.e., expe
Mosaic Law [2]
[a]Matt. 22:35

33 [a]Luke 1:15

34 [1]Or, *wine-*
[2]I.e., Collectors
Roman taxes f

35 [1]Lit., *And*

36 [1]Lit., *eat*

37 [1]I.e., an imr
woman [a]Matt.
Mark 14:3-9; Lu
7:37-39; John 1

39 [1]Lit., *to hims*
saying [2]Some
read *the prophe*
an immoral wor
[a]Luke 7:16; Joh

40 [1]Lit., *says*

41 [1]The denariu
equivalent to on
wage [a]Matt. 18:
Mark 6:37

42 "When they [a]were unable to repay, he graciously forgave them
both. Which of them therefore will love him more?"
43 Simon answered and said, "I suppose the one whom he forgave
more." And He said to him, "You have judged correctly."
44 And turning toward the woman, He said to Simon, "Do you see
this woman? I entered your house; you [a]gave Me no water for My
feet, but she has wet My feet with her tears, and wiped them with
her hair.
45 "You [a]gave Me no kiss; but she, since the time I came in, [1]has not
ceased to kiss My feet.
46 "[a]You did not anoint My head with oil, but she anointed My feet
with perfume.
47 "For this reason I say to you, her sins, which are many, have been
forgiven, for she loved much; but he who is forgiven little, loves
little."
48 And He said to her, "[a]Your sins have been forgiven."
49 And those who were reclining *at the table* with Him began to say
[1]to themselves, "[a]Who is this *man* who even forgives sins?"
50 And He said to the woman, "[a]Your faith has saved you; [b]go in
peace."

Chapter 8

8 And it came about soon afterwards, that He *began* going about
from one city and village to another, [a]proclaiming and preaching
the kingdom of God; and the twelve were with Him,
2 and *also* [a]some women who had been healed of evil spirits and
sicknesses: [b]Mary who was called Magdalene, from whom seven
demons had gone out,
3 and Joanna the wife of Chuza, [a]Herod's [b]steward, and Susanna,
and many others who were contributing to their support out of their
private means.
4 [a]And when a great multitude were coming together, and those
from the various cities were journeying to Him, He spoke by way of
a parable:
5 "The sower went out to sow his seed; and as he sowed, some fell
beside the road; and it was trampled under foot, and the birds of the
[1]air ate it up.
6 "And other *seed* fell on rocky *soil*, and as soon as it grew up, it
withered away, because it had no moisture.
7 "And other *seed* fell among the thorns; and the thorns grew up
with it, and choked it out.
8 "And other *seed* fell into the good soil, and grew up, and
produced a crop a hundred times as great." As He said these things,
He would call out, "[a]He who has ears to hear, let him hear."
9 [a]And His disciples *began* questioning Him as to what this parable
might be.
10 And He said, "[a]To you it has been granted to know the mysteries
of the kingdom of God, but to the rest *it is* in parables, in order that
[b]SEEING THEY MAY NOT SEE, AND HEARING THEY MAY NOT UNDERSTAND.
11 "Now the parable is this: [a]the seed is the word of God.
12 "And those beside the road are those who have heard; then the
devil comes and takes away the word from their heart, so that they
may not believe and be saved.
13 "And those on the rocky *soil are* those who, when they hear,

Matt. 18:25
. 18:4; 19:2; Judg. 19:21; 1 Tim. 5:10
Lit., *was not*
2 Sam. 15:5
ı. 12:20; Ps. cl. 9:8; Dan. 10:3
:2; Mark 2:5, uke 5:20, 23
mong [a]Luke 5:21
tt. 9:22; Luke 18:42 [b]Mark 34; Luke 8:48
1 [a]Matt. 4:23
t. 27:55; Mark ; Luke 23:49, t. 27:56; Mark 16:9
tt. 14:1 [b]Matt. 20:8
ke 8:4-8: *Matt.* 2-9; *Mark 4:1-9*
5 [1]Lit., *heaven*
att. 11:15; Mark ıke 14:35; Rev. 17, 29; 3:6, 13, 22; 13:9
ke 8:9-15: *Matt.* 3; *Mark 4:10-20*
. 13:11 [b]Is. 6:9; 3:14; Acts 28:26
11 [a]1 Pet. 1:23

receive the word with joy; and these have no *firm* root; [1]they believe
for a while, and in time of temptation fall away.
14 "And the *seed* which fell among the thorns, these are the ones who
have heard, and as they go on their way they are choked with wor-
ries and riches and pleasures of *this* life, and bring no fruit to
maturity.
15 "And the *seed* in the good soil, these are the ones who have heard
the word in an honest and good heart, and hold it fast, and bear fruit
with [1]perseverance.
16 "Now [a]no one after lighting a lamp covers it over with a con-
tainer, or puts it under a bed; but he puts it on a lampstand, in order
that those who come in may see the light.
17 "[a]For nothing is hidden that shall not become evident, nor *any-
thing* secret that shall not be known and come to light.
18 "Therefore take care how you listen; [a]for whoever has, to him
shall *more* be given; and whoever does not have, even what he
[1]thinks he has shall be taken away from him."
19 [a]And His mother and brothers came to Him, and they were un-
able to get to Him because of the crowd.
20 And it was reported to Him, "Your mother and Your brothers are
standing outside, wishing to see You."
21 But He answered and said to them, "My mother and My
brothers are these [a]who hear the word of God and do it."
22 [a]Now it came about on one of *those* days, that He and His disci-
ples got into a boat, and He said to them, "Let us go over to the other
side of [b]the lake." And they launched out.
23 But as they were sailing along He fell asleep; and a fierce gale of
wind descended upon [a]the lake, and they *began* to be swamped and
to be in danger.
24 And they came to Him and woke Him up, saying, "[a]Master,
Master, we are perishing!" And being aroused, He [b]rebuked the
wind and the surging waves, and they stopped, and [1]it became calm.
25 And He said to them, "Where is your faith?" And they were
fearful and amazed, saying to one another, "Who then is this, that
He commands even the winds and the water, and they obey Him?"
26 [a]And they sailed to the country of the [1]Gerasenes, which is op-
posite Galilee.
27 And when He had come out onto the land, He was met by a
certain man from the city who was possessed with demons; and who
had not put on any clothing for a long time, and was not living in a
house, but in the tombs.
28 And seeing Jesus, he cried out and fell before Him, and said in a
loud voice, "[a]What do I have to do with You, Jesus, Son of [b]the Most
High God? I beg You, do not torment me."
29 For He [1]had been commanding the unclean spirit to come out of
the man. For it had seized him many times; and he was bound with
chains and shackles and kept under guard; and *yet* he would burst
his fetters and be driven by the demon into the desert.
30 And Jesus asked him, "What is your name?" And he said, "[a]Le-
gion"; for many demons had entered him.
31 And they were entreating Him not to command them to depart
into [a]the abyss.
32 Now there was a herd of many swine feeding there on the

13 [1]Lit., *who*

15 [1]Or, *stea*

16 [a]Matt. 5:1
4:21; Luke 11

17 [a]Matt. 10:
4:22; Luke 12

18 [1]Or, *seem*
[a]Matt. 13:12;
Luke 19:26

19 [a]Luke 8:19
12:46-50; Mar

21 [a]Luke 11:2

22 [a]Luke 8:22
8:23-27; Mark
[b]Luke 5:1f.; 8:2

23 [a]Luke 5:1f.;

24 [1]Lit., *a calm*
occurred [a]Luke
[b]Luke 4:39

26 [1]Other mss.
Gergesenes or
Gadarenes [a]Lu
8:26-37: *Matt. 8*
Mark 5:1-17

28 [a]Matt. 8:29
5:7

29 [1]Or, *was*
commanding

30 [a]Matt. 26:53

31 [a]Rom. 10:7;
9:1f., 11; 11:7; 17
20:1, 3

mountain; and *the demons* entreated Him to permit them to enter [1]the
swine. And He gave them permission.
33 And the demons came out from the man and entered the swine;
and the herd rushed down the steep bank into [a]the lake, and were
drowned.
34 And when the herdsmen saw what had happened, they ran
away and reported it in the city and *out* in the country.
35 And *the people* went out to see what had happened; and they
came to Jesus, and found the man from whom the demons had gone
out, sitting down [a]at the feet of Jesus, clothed and in his right mind;
and they became frightened.
36 And those who had seen it reported to them how the man who
was [a]demon-possessed had been [1]made well.
37 And all the people of the country of the [1]Gerasenes and the
surrounding district asked Him to depart from them; for they were
gripped with great fear; and He got into a boat, and returned.
38 [a]But the man from whom the demons had gone out was begging
Him that he might [1]accompany Him; but He sent him away, saying,
39 "Return to your house and describe what great things God has
done for you." And he went away, proclaiming throughout the
whole city what great things Jesus had done for him.
40 [a]And as Jesus returned, the multitude welcomed Him, for they
had all been waiting for Him.
41 [a]And behold, there came a man named Jairus, and he was an
[1b]official of the synagogue; and he fell at Jesus' feet, and *began* to
entreat Him to come to his house;
42 for he had an [1]only daughter, about twelve years old, and she
was dying. But as He went, the multitudes were pressing against
Him.
43 And a woman who had a hemorrhage for twelve years, [1]and
could not be healed by anyone,
44 came up behind Him, and touched the fringe of His [1]cloak; and
immediately her hemorrhage stopped.
45 And Jesus said, "Who is the one who touched Me?" And while
they were all denying it, Peter said,[1] "[a]Master, the multitudes are
crowding and pressing upon You."
46 But Jesus said, "Someone did touch Me, for I was aware that
[a]power had gone out of Me."
47 And when the woman saw that she had not escaped notice, she
came trembling and fell down before Him, and declared in the pres-
ence of all the people the reason why she had touched Him, and
how she had been immediately healed.
48 And He said to her, "Daughter, [a]your faith has [1]made you well;
[b]go in peace."
49 While He was still speaking, someone *came from *the house of*
[a]the synagogue official, saying, "Your daughter has died; do not
trouble the Teacher anymore."
50 But when Jesus heard *this,* He answered him, "[a]Do not be afraid
any longer; only believe, and she shall be [1]made well."
51 And when He had come to the house, He did not allow anyone
to enter with Him, except Peter and John and James, and the girl's
father and mother.
52 Now they were all weeping and [a]lamenting for her; but He said,
"Stop weeping, for she has not died, but [b]is asleep."

[1]Lit., *them*
e 5:1f.; 8:22
[a]Luke 10:39
aved [a]Matt. 4:24
er mss. read
ergesenes or
Gadarenes
e with [a]Luke
Mark 5:18-20
:1; Mark 5:21
., *ruler* [a]Luke
Matt. 9:18-26;
:22-43 [b]Mark
22; Luke 8:49
only begotten
ome mss. add
d spent all her
on physicians
outer garment
ome early mss.
those with him
[a]Luke 5:5
46 [a]Luke 5:17
[1]Or, *saved you*
22 [b]Mark 5:34;
Luke 7:50
49 [a]Luke 8:41
Or, *saved* [a]Mark
5:36
Matt. 11:17; Luke
27 [b]John 11:13

53 And they *began* laughing at Him, knowing that she had died.
54 He, however, took her by the hand and called, saying, "Child, arise!"
55 And her spirit returned, and she rose immediately; and He gave orders for *something* to be given her to eat.
56 And her parents were amazed; but He [a]instructed them to tell no one what had happened.

Chapter 9

9 [a]And He called the twelve together, and gave them power and authority over all the demons, and to heal diseases.
2 And He sent them out to [a]proclaim the kingdom of God, and [1]to perform healing.
3 And He said to them, "[a]Take nothing for *your* journey, [b]neither a staff, nor a [1]bag, nor bread, nor money; and do not *even* have [2]two tunics apiece.
4 "And whatever house you enter, stay there, and take your leave from there.
5 "And as for those who do not receive you, as you go out from that city, [a]shake off the dust from your feet as a testimony against them."
6 And departing, they *began* going about [1]among the villages, [a]preaching the gospel, and healing everywhere.
7 [a]Now [b]Herod the tetrarch heard of all that was happening; and he was greatly perplexed, because it was said by some that [c]John had risen from the dead,
8 and by some that [a]Elijah had appeared, and by others, that one of the prophets of old had risen again.
9 And Herod said, "I myself had John beheaded; but who is this man about whom I hear such things?" And [a]he kept trying to see Him.
10 [a]And when the apostles returned, they gave an account to Him of all that they had done. [b]And taking them with Him, He withdrew by Himself to a city called [c]Bethsaida.
11 But the multitudes were aware of this and followed Him; and welcoming them, He *began* speaking to them about the kingdom of God and curing those who had need of healing.
12 And the day began to decline, and the twelve came and said to Him, "Send the multitude away, that they may go into the surrounding villages and countryside and find lodging and get [1]something to eat; for here we are in a desolate place."
13 But He said to them, "You give them *something* to eat!" And they said, "We have no more than five loaves and two fish, unless perhaps we go and buy food for all these people."
14 (For there were about five thousand men.) And He said to His disciples, "Have them recline *to eat* [a]in groups of about fifty each."
15 And they did so, and had them all recline.
16 And He took the five loaves and the two fish, and looking up to heaven, He blessed them, and broke *them*, and kept giving *them* to the disciples to set before the multitude.
17 And they all ate and were satisfied; and [1]the broken pieces which they had left over were picked up, twelve [a]baskets *full*.
18 [a]And it came about that while He was [b]praying alone, the disciples were with Him, and He questioned them, saying, "Who do the multitudes say that I am?"

56 [a]Matt. 8
9:1 [a]Matt. 1... 6:7
2 [1]Some ms... *heal the sick*
3 [1]Or, *knaps... beggar's bag... garment* [a]Lu... *Matt. 10:9-1...* *6:8-11;* Luke 22:35 [b]Matt. ... Mark 6:8; Lu...
5 [a]Luke 10:1... 13:51
6 [1]Or, *from v... village* [a]Mark... Luke 8:1
7 [a]Luke 9:7-9... *14:1, 2;* Mark... [b]Matt. 14:1; Lu... 13:31; 23:7 [c]...
8 [a]Matt. 16:14
9 [a]Luke 23:8
10 [a]Mark 6:30... 9:10-17: *Matt. Mark 6:32-44;* ... *6:5-13* [c]Matt. 1...
12 [1]Lit., *provis...*
14 [a]Mark 6:39
17 [1]Lit., *that wh... left over to them broken pieces w...* [a]Matt. 14:20
18 [a]Luke 9:18-... *16:13-16; Mark...* [b]Matt. 14:23; Lu... 9:28

19 And they answered and said, "John the Baptist, and others *say*
Elijah; but others, that one of the prophets of old has risen again."
20 And He said to them, "But who do you say that I am?" And
Peter answered and said, "[a]The [1]Christ of God."
21 But He [1a]warned them, and instructed *them* not to tell this to
anyone,
22 [a]saying, "[b]The Son of Man must suffer many things, and be
rejected by the elders and chief priests and scribes, and be killed, and
be raised up on the third day."
23 And He was saying to *them* all, "[a]If anyone wishes to come after
Me, let him deny himself, and take up his cross daily, and follow Me.
24 "For [a]whoever wishes to save his [1]life shall lose it, but whoever
loses his [1]life for My sake, he is the one who will save it.
25 "For what is a man profited if he gains the whole world, and
[a]loses or forfeits himself?
26 "[a]For whoever is ashamed of Me and My words, of him will the
Son of Man be ashamed when He comes in His glory, and *the glory* of
the Father and of the holy angels.
27 "But I say to you truthfully, [a]there are some of those standing here
who shall not taste death until they see the kingdom of God."
28 [a]And some eight days after these sayings, it came about that He
took along [b]Peter and John and James, and [c]went up to the mountain
[d]to pray.
29 And while He was [a]praying, the appearance of His face [b]became
different, and His clothing *became* white *and* [1]gleaming.
30 And behold, two men were talking with Him; and they were
Moses and Elijah,
31 who, appearing in [1]glory, were speaking of His [a]departure which
He was about to accomplish at Jerusalem.
32 Now Peter and his companions [a]had been overcome with sleep;
but when they were fully awake, they saw His glory and the two
men standing with Him.
33 And it came about, as [1]these were parting from Him, Peter said
to Jesus, "[a]Master, it is good for us to be here; and [b]let us make three
[2]tabernacles: one for You, and one for Moses, and one for Elijah"—
[c]not realizing what he was saying.
34 And while he was saying this, a cloud [1]formed and *began* to
overshadow them; and they were afraid as they entered the cloud.
35 And [a]a voice came out of the cloud, saying, "[b]This is My Son, *My*
Chosen One; listen to Him!"
36 And when the voice [1]had spoken, Jesus was found alone. And
[a]they kept silent, and reported to no one in those days any of the
things which they had seen.
37 [a]And it came about on the next day, that when they had come
down from the mountain, a great multitude met Him.
38 And behold, a man from the multitude shouted out, saying,
"Teacher, I beg You to look at my son, for he is my [1]only *boy*,
39 and behold, a spirit seizes him, and he suddenly screams, and it
throws him into a convulsion with foaming *at the mouth*, and as it
mauls him, it scarcely leaves him.
40 "And I begged Your disciples to cast it out, and they could not."
41 And Jesus answered and said, "O unbelieving and perverted
generation, how long shall I be with you, and put up with you?
Bring your son here."

42 And while he was still approaching, the demon [1]dashed him *to*
the ground, and threw him into a convulsion. But Jesus rebuked the
unclean spirit, and healed the boy, and gave him back to his father.
43 And they were all amazed at the [1a]greatness of God.
[b]**B**ut while everyone was marveling at all that He was doing, He
said to His disciples,
44 "Let these words sink into your ears; [a]for the Son of Man is going
to be [1]delivered into the hands of men."
45 But [a]they [1]did not understand this statement, and it was con-
cealed from them so that they might not perceive it; and they were
afraid to ask Him about this statement.
46 [a]And an argument [1]arose among them as to which of them might
be the greatest.
47 But Jesus, [a]knowing [1]what they were thinking in their heart, took
a child and stood him by His side,
48 and said to them, "[a]Whoever receives this child in My name
receives Me; and whoever receives Me receives Him who sent Me;
[b]for he who is [1]least among you, this is the one who is great."
49 [a]And John answered and said, "[b]Master, we saw someone cast-
ing out demons in Your name; and we tried to hinder him because
he does not follow along with us."
50 But Jesus said to him, "Do not hinder *him;* [a]for he who is not
against you is [1]for you."
51 And it came about, when the days were approaching for [a]His
[1]ascension, that He resolutely set His face [b]to go to Jerusalem;
52 and He sent messengers on ahead of Him. And they went, and
entered a village of the [a]Samaritans, to [1]make arrangements for Him.
53 And they did not receive Him, [a]because [1]He was journeying
with His face toward Jerusalem.
54 And when His disciples [a]James and John saw *this,* they said,
"Lord, do You want us to [b]command fire to come down from heaven
and consume them[1]?"
55 But He turned and rebuked them, [[1]and said, "You do not know
what kind of spirit you are of;
56 for the Son of Man did not come to destroy men's lives, but to
save them."] And they went on to another village.
57 And [a]as they were going along the road, [b]someone said to Him,
"I will follow You wherever You go."
58 And Jesus said to him, "The foxes have holes, and the birds of
the [1]air *have* [2]nests, but [a]the Son of Man has nowhere to lay His
head."
59 And He said to another, "[a]Follow Me." But he said, "[1]Permit me
first to go and bury my father."
60 But He said to him, "Allow the dead to bury their own dead; but
as for you, go and [a]proclaim everywhere the kingdom of God."
61 And another also said, "I will follow You, Lord; but [a]first permit
me to say good-bye to those at home."
62 But Jesus said to him, "[a]No one, after putting his hand to the
plow and looking back, is fit for the kingdom of God."

Chapter 10

10 Now after this [a]the Lord appointed [1]seventy [b]others, and sent
them [c]two and two ahead of Him to every city and place
where He Himself was going to come.

42 [1]Or, *tore*
43 [1]Or, *maje*
1:16 [b]Luke 9
Matt. 17:22f.;
9:30-32
44 [1]Or, *betra*
9:22
45 [1]Lit., *were*
knowing [a]Ma
46 [1]Lit., *enter*
[a]Luke 9:46-48
18:1-5; Mark 9
Luke 22:24
47 [1]Lit., *the re*
or, *argument*
48 [1]Or, *lowlie*
10:40; Luke 10
13:20 [b]Luke 2
49 [a]Luke 9:49,
Mark 9:38-40
5:5; 9:33
50 [1]Or, *on you*
[a]Matt. 12:30; L
51 [1]Lit., *taking*
[a]Mark 16:19 [b]L
13:22; 17:11; 1
19:11, 28
52 [1]Or, *prepare*
10:5; Luke 10:3
John 4:4
53 [1]Lit., *His fa*
proceeding tow
[a]John 4:9
54 [1]Some mss.
Elijah did [a]Mark
[b]2 Kin. 1:9-16
55 [1]Many mss.
contain bracket
portion
57 [a]Luke 9:51
9:57-60: *Matt. 8*
58 [1]Or, *sky* [2]Or,
roosting-places
8:20
59 [1]Some mss.
Lord [a]Matt. 8:22
60 [a]Matt. 4:23
61 [a]1 Kin. 19:20
62 [a]Phil. 3:13
10:1 [1]Some mss
seventy-two [a]Lu
7:13 [b]Luke 9:1f.,
[c]Mark 6:7

2 And He was saying to them, "[a]The harvest is plentiful, but the
laborers are few; therefore beseech the Lord of the harvest to send
out laborers into His harvest.
3 "Go your ways; [a]behold, I send you out as lambs in the midst of
wolves.
4 "[a]Carry no purse, no [1]bag, no shoes; and greet no one on the way.
5 "And whatever house you enter, first say, 'Peace *be* to this house.'
6 "And if a [1]man of peace is there, your peace will rest upon him;
but if not, it will return to you.
7 "And stay in [1]that house, eating and drinking [2]what they give
you; for [a]the laborer is worthy of his wages. Do not keep moving
from house to house.
8 "And whatever city you enter, and they receive you, [a]eat what is
set before you;
9 and heal those in it who are sick, and say to them, '[a]The kingdom
of God has come near to you.'
10 "But whatever city you enter and they do not receive you, go out
into its streets and say,
11 '[a]Even the dust of your city which clings to our feet, we wipe off
in protest against you; yet [1]be sure of this, that [b]the kingdom of God
has come near.'
12 "I say to you, [a]it will be more tolerable in that day for [b]Sodom,
than for that city.
13 "[a]Woe to you, [b]Chorazin! Woe to you, [b]Bethsaida! For if the
[1]miracles had been performed in [b]Tyre and Sidon which occurred in
you, they would have repented long ago, sitting in [c]sackcloth and
ashes.
14 "But it will be more tolerable for [a]Tyre and Sidon in the judgment,
than for you.
15 "And you, [a]Capernaum, will not be exalted to heaven, will you?
You will be brought down to Hades!
16 "[a]The one who listens to you listens to Me, and [b]the one who
rejects you rejects Me; and he who rejects Me rejects the One who
sent Me."
17 And the [1]seventy returned with joy, saying, "Lord, even [a]the
demons are subject to us in Your name."
18 And He said to them, "I was watching [a]Satan fall from heaven
like lightning.
19 "Behold, I have given you authority to [a]tread upon serpents and
scorpions, and over all the power of the enemy, and nothing shall
injure you.
20 "Nevertheless do not rejoice in this, that the spirits are subject to
you, but rejoice that [a]your names are recorded in heaven."
21 [a]At that very [1]time He rejoiced greatly in the Holy Spirit, and
said, "I [2]praise Thee, O Father, Lord of heaven and earth, that Thou
didst hide these things from *the* wise and intelligent and didst reveal
them to babes. Yes, Father, for thus it was well-pleasing in Thy sight.
22 "[a]All things have been handed over to Me by My Father, and [b]no
one knows who the Son is except the Father, and who the Father is
except the Son, and anyone to whom the Son wills to reveal *Him*."
23 [a]And turning to the disciples, He said privately, "Blessed *are* the
eyes which see the things you see,
24 for I say to you, that many prophets and kings wished to see the

tt. 9:37, 38; John 4:35
3 [a]Matt. 10:16
[1]Or, *knapsack* or *gar's bag* [a]Matt. 14; Mark 6:8-11; ke 9:3-5; 10:4-12
6 [1]Lit., *son*
; the house itself *., the things from* *em* [a]Matt. 10:10; 9:14; 1 Tim. 5:18
8 [a]1 Cor. 10:27
t. 3:2; 10:7; Luke 10:11
Lit., *know* [a]Matt. Mark 6:11; Luke cts 13:51 [b]Matt. ; 10:7; Luke 10:9
[a]Gen. 19:24-28; latt. 10:15; 11:24 [b]Matt. 10:15
, works of power e 10:13-15: *Matt.* *-23* [b]Is. 23:1-18; 26:1-28:26; Joel latt. 11:21 [c]Rev. 11:3
14 [a]Matt. 11:21
. 14:13-15; Matt. 4:13; 11:23
latt. 10:40; Mark Luke 9:48; John Gal. 4:14 [b]John .48; 1 Thess. 4:8
Some mss. read *venty-two* [a]Mark 16:17
18 [a]Matt. 4:10
[a]Ps. 91:13; Mark 16:18
) [a]Ex. 32:32; Ps. 28; Is. 4:3; Ezek. ; Dan. 12:1; Phil. Heb. 12:23; Rev. 3:8; 17:8; 20:12, 15; 21:27
[1]Lit., *hour* [2]Or, *nowledge to Thy* [a]Luke 10:21, 22: *Matt. 11:25-27*
John 3:35 [b]John 10:15
[a]Luke 10:23, 24: *Matt. 13:16, 17*

things which you see, and did not see *them*, and to hear the things
which you hear, and did not hear *them*."
25 [a]And behold, a certain [1b]lawyer stood up and put Him to the test,
saying, "Teacher, what shall I do to inherit eternal life?"
26 And He said to him, "What is written in the Law? How [1]does it
read to you?"
27 And he answered and said, "[a]YOU SHALL LOVE THE LORD YOUR GOD
WITH ALL YOUR HEART, AND WITH ALL YOUR SOUL, AND WITH ALL YOUR
STRENGTH, AND WITH ALL YOUR MIND; AND YOUR NEIGHBOR AS YOURSELF."
28 And He said to him, "You have answered correctly; [a]DO THIS, AND
YOU WILL LIVE."
29 But wishing [a]to justify himself, he said to Jesus, "And who is my
neighbor?"
30 Jesus replied and said, "A certain man was [a]going down from
Jerusalem to Jericho; and he fell among robbers, and they stripped
him and [1]beat him, and went off leaving him half dead.
31 "And by chance a certain priest was going down on that road,
and when he saw him, he passed by on the other side.
32 "And likewise a Levite also, when he came to the place and saw
him, passed by on the other side.
33 "But a certain [a]Samaritan, who was on a journey, came upon him;
and when he saw him, he felt compassion,
34 and came to him, and bandaged up his wounds, pouring oil and
wine on *them;* and he put him on his own beast, and brought him to
an inn, and took care of him.
35 "And on the next day he took out two [1]denarii and gave them to
the innkeeper and said, 'Take care of him; and whatever more you
spend, when I return, I will repay you.'
36 "Which of these three do you think proved to be a neighbor to the
man who fell into the robbers' *hands?*"
37 And he said, "The one who showed mercy toward him." And
Jesus said to him, "Go and do [1]the same."
38 Now as they were traveling along, He entered a certain village;
and a [1]woman named [a]Martha welcomed Him into her home.
39 And she had a sister called [a]Mary, who moreover was listening
to the Lord's word, [b]seated at His feet.
40 But [a]Martha was distracted with [1]all her preparations; and she
came up *to Him,* and said, "Lord, do You not care that my sister has
left me to do all the serving alone? Then tell her to help me."
41 But the Lord answered and said to her, "[a]Martha, Martha, you
are [b]worried and bothered about so many things;
42 [1a]but *only* a few things are necessary, [2]really *only* one, for [b]Mary
has chosen the good part, which shall not be taken away from her."

Chapter 11

11 And it came about that while He was praying in a certain
place, after He had finished, one of His disciples said to Him,
"Lord, teach us to pray just as John also taught his disciples."
2 And He said to them, "[a]When you pray, say:
'[1]Father, hallowed be Thy name.
Thy kingdom come.
3 'Give us [a]each day our [1]daily bread.
4 'And forgive us our sins,
For we ourselves also forgive everyone who [a]is indebted to us.

25 [1]I.e., an
Mosaic Law
10:25-28: M
22:34-40; M
12:28-31; M
19:16-19 [b]M

26 [1]Lit., *do*

27 [a]Deut. 6
19:18

28 [a]Lev. 18
20:11; Matt.

29 [a]Luke 16

30 [1]Lit., *laid*
upon [a]Luke
19:28

33 [a]Matt. 10
9:52

35 [1]The den
equivalent to
wage

37 [1]Or, *likew*

38 [1]Lit., *certa*
[a]Luke 10:40f.
11:1, 5, 19ff.,
12:2

39 [a]Luke 10:4
11:1f., 19f., 28
12:3 [b]Luke 8:
22:3

40 [1]Lit., *much*
[a]Luke 10:38, 4
11:1, 5, 19ff., 3
12:2

41 [a]Luke 10:3
John 11:1, 5, 1
39; 12:2 [b]Matt

42 [1]Some mss
but one thing is
necessary [2]Lit
27:4; John 6:27
10:39; John 11
28, 31f., 45; 12

11:2 [1]Some m
phrases from M
6:9-13 to make
passages close
similar [a]Luke 1
Matt. 6:9-13

3 [1]Or, *bread fo*
coming day or r
bread [a]Acts 17:

4 [a]Luke 13:4 m

And lead us not into temptation.' "
5 And He said to them, "[1]Suppose one of you shall have a friend,
and shall go to him at midnight, and say to him, 'Friend, lend me
three loaves;
6 for a friend of mine has come to me from a journey, and I have
nothing to set before him';
7 and from inside he shall answer and say, 'Do not bother me; the
door has already been shut and my children [1]and I are in bed; I
cannot get up and give you *anything*.'
8 "I tell you, even though he will not get up and give him *anything*
because he is his friend, yet [a]because of his [1]persistence he will get
up and give him as much as he needs.
9 "And I say to you, [1a]ask, and it shall be given to you; [2]seek, and
you shall find; [3]knock, and it shall be opened to you.
10 "For everyone who asks, receives; and he who seeks, finds; and to
him who knocks, it shall be opened.
11 "Now [1]suppose one of you fathers is asked by his son for a [2]fish;
he will not give him a snake instead of a fish, will he?
12 "Or *if* he is asked for an egg, he will not give him a scorpion,
will he?
13 "[a]If you then, being evil, know how to give good gifts to your
children, how much more shall *your* [1]heavenly Father give the Holy
Spirit to those who ask Him?"
14 [a]And He was casting out a demon, and it was dumb; and it came
about that when the demon had gone out, the dumb man spoke; and
the multitudes marveled.
15 But some of them said, "He casts out demons [a]by [1b]Beelzebul, the
ruler of the demons."
16 And others, [1]to test *Him*, [a]were demanding of Him a [2]sign from
heaven.
17 [a]But He knew their thoughts, and said to them, "[1]Any kingdom
divided against itself is laid waste; and a house *divided* against [2]itself
falls.
18 "And if [a]Satan also is divided against himself, how shall his king-
dom stand? For you say that I cast out demons by [b]Beelzebul.
19 "And if I by [a]Beelzebul cast out demons, by whom do your sons
cast them out? Consequently they shall be your judges.
20 "But if I cast out demons by the [a]finger of God, then [b]the kingdom
of God has come upon you.
21 "When [1]a strong *man*, fully armed, guards his own homestead, his
possessions are [2]undisturbed;
22 but when someone stronger than he attacks him and overpowers
him, he takes away from him all his armor on which he had relied,
and distributes his plunder.
23 "[a]He who is not with Me is against Me; and he who does not
gather with Me, scatters.
24 "[a]When the unclean spirit goes out of [1]a man, it passes through
waterless places seeking rest, and not finding any, it says, 'I will
return to my house from which I came.'
25 "And when it comes, it finds it swept and put in order.
26 "Then it goes and takes *along* seven other spirits more evil than
itself, and they go in and live there; and the last state of that man
becomes worse than the first."
27 And it came about while He said these things, one of the women

ich one of you
[1]Lit., *with me*
hamelessness [a]Luke 18:1-5
ep asking [2]Or, king [3]Or, keep nocking [a]Luke 3: Matt. 7:7-11
which of you, a [1]I ask the father arly mss. insert vill not give him will he, or for a
.it., *Father from* ven [a]Matt. 7:11; Luke 18:7f.
Luke 11:14, 15: 12:22, 24; Matt. 9:32-34
ere and in vv. 18 some mss. read ebul [a]Matt. 9:34 [b]Matt. 10:25
Lit., *were testing* attesting miracle 2:38; 16:1; Mark 8:11
.it., *every* [2]Lit., *a* [a]Luke 11:17-22: 12:25-29; Mark 3:23-27
Matt. 4:10 [b]Matt. 10:25
19 [a]Matt. 10:25
x. 8:19 [b]Matt. 3:2
[1]Lit., *the* [2]Lit., *in peace*
[a]Matt. 12:30; Mark 9:40
4 [1]Lit., *the* [a]Luke 26: Matt. 12:43-45

in the crowd raised her voice, and said to Him, "[a]Blessed is the
womb that bore You, and the breasts at which You nursed."
28 But He said, "On the contrary, blessed are [a]those who hear the
word of God, and observe it."
29 And as the crowds were increasing, He began to say, "[a]This
generation is a wicked generation; it [b]seeks for a [1]sign, and *yet* no
[1]sign shall be given to it but the [1]sign of Jonah.
30 "For just as [a]Jonah became a [1]sign to the Ninevites, so shall the
Son of Man be to this generation.
31 "The [a]Queen of the South shall rise up with the men of this
generation at the judgment and condemn them, because she came
from the ends of the earth to hear the wisdom of Solomon; and
behold, something greater than Solomon is here.
32 "The men of Nineveh shall stand up with this generation at the
judgment and condemn it, because [a]they repented at the preaching
of Jonah; and behold, something greater than Jonah is here.
33 "[a]No one, after lighting a lamp, puts it away in a cellar, nor under
a peck-measure, but on the lampstand, in order that those who enter
may see the light.
34 "[a]The lamp of your body is your eye; when your eye is [1]clear,
your whole body also is full of light; but when it is bad, your body
also is full of darkness.
35 "Then watch out that the light in you may not be darkness.
36 "If therefore your whole body is full of light, with no dark part in
it, it shall be wholly illumined, as when the lamp illumines you with
its rays."
37 Now when He had spoken, a Pharisee *asked Him to have lunch
with him; and He went in, and reclined *at the table.*
38 And when the Pharisee saw it, he was surprised that He had not
first [1a]ceremonially washed before the [2]meal.
39 But [a]the Lord said to him, "Now [b]you Pharisees clean the outside
of the cup and of the platter; but [1]inside of you, you are full of
robbery and wickedness.
40 "[a]You foolish ones, did not He who made the outside make the
inside also?
41 "But [a]give that which is within as charity, and [1]then all things are
[b]clean for you.
42 "[a]But woe to you Pharisees! For you [b]pay tithe of mint and rue
and every *kind of* garden herb, and *yet* disregard justice and the love
of God; but these are the things you should have done without
neglecting the others.
43 "Woe to you Pharisees! For you [a]love the front seats in the syna-
gogues, and the respectful greetings in the market places.
44 "[a]Woe to you! For you are like [1]concealed tombs, and the people
who walk over *them* are unaware *of it.*"
45 And one of the [1a]lawyers *said to Him in reply, "Teacher, when
You say this, You insult us too."
46 But He said, "Woe to you [a]lawyers as well! For [b]you weigh men
down with burdens hard to bear, [1]while you yourselves will not
even touch the burdens with one of your fingers.
47 "[a]Woe to you! For you build the [1]tombs of the prophets, and *it was*
your fathers *who* killed them.
48 "Consequently, you are witnesses and approve the deeds of your

27 [a]Luke 2
28 [a]Luke 8:
29 [1]Or, *atte* *miracle* [a]Lu Matt. 12:39- 16:4; Mark 8 12:38; Luke
30 [1]Or, *atte* *miracle* [a]Jor
31 [a]1 Kin. 1 2 Chr. 9:1-12
32 [a]Jon. 3:5
33 [a]Matt. 5:1 4:21; Luke 8:
34 [1]Or, *heal* 11:34, 35: *Ma*
38 [1]Lit., *bapt* *lunch* [a]Matt. 7:3f.
39 [1]Lit., *your* *full* [a]Luke 7:1 23:25f.
40 [a]Luke 12:2 15:36
41 [1]Lit., *beho* 12:33; 16:9 [b] Titus 1:15
42 [a]Matt. 23:2 27:30; Luke 18
43 [a]Matt. 23:6 12:38f.; Luke 1
44 [1]Or, *indisti* *unseen* [a]Matt.
45 [1]I.e., exper Mosaic Law [a] 22:35; Luke 11:
46 [1]Lit., *and* [a] 22:35; Luke 11: [b]Matt. 23:4
47 [1]Or, *monum* [a]Matt. 23:29ff.

fathers; because it was they who killed them, and you build *their* tombs.

49 "For this reason also [a]the wisdom of God said, '[b]I will send to them prophets and apostles, and *some* of them they will kill and *some* they will [1]persecute,

50 in order that the blood of all the prophets, shed [a]since the foundation of the world, may be [1]charged against this generation,

51 from [a]the blood of Abel to [b]the blood of Zechariah, who perished between the altar and the house *of God;* yes, I tell you, it shall be [1]charged against this generation.'

52 "Woe to you [1a]lawyers! For you have taken away the key of knowledge; [b]you did not enter in yourselves, and those who were entering in you hindered."

53 And when He left there, the scribes and the Pharisees began to be very hostile and to question Him closely on many subjects,

54 [a]plotting against Him, [b]to catch [1]*Him* in something He might say.

Chapter 12

12 Under these circumstances, after [1]so many thousands of the multitude had gathered together that they were stepping on one another, He began saying to His disciples first *of all,* "[a]Beware of the leaven of the Pharisees, which is hypocrisy.

2 "[a]But there is nothing covered up that will not be revealed, and hidden that will not be known.

3 "Accordingly, whatever you have said in the dark shall be heard in the light, and what you have [1]whispered in the inner rooms shall be proclaimed upon [a]the housetops.

4 "And I say to you, [a]My friends, do not be afraid of those who kill the body, and after that have no more that they can do.

5 "But I will [1]warn you whom to fear: [a]fear the One who after He has killed has authority to cast into [2b]hell; yes, I tell you, fear Him!

6 "Are not [a]five sparrows sold for two [1]cents? And *yet* not one of them is forgotten before God.

7 "[a]Indeed, the very hairs of your head are all numbered. Do not fear; you are of more value than many sparrows.

8 "And I say to you, everyone who [a]confesses Me before men, the Son of Man shall confess him also before the angels of God;

9 but [a]he who denies Me before men shall be denied [b]before the angels of God.

10 "[a]And everyone who will speak a word against the Son of Man, it shall be forgiven him; but he who blasphemes against the Holy Spirit, it shall not be forgiven him.

11 "And when they bring you before [a]the synagogues and the rulers and the authorities, do not become [b]anxious about how or what you should speak in your defense, or what you should say;

12 for [a]the Holy Spirit will teach you in that very hour what you ought to say."

13 And someone [1]in the crowd said to Him, "Teacher, tell my brother to divide the *family* inheritance with me."

14 But He said to him, "[a]Man, who appointed Me a judge or arbiter over you?"

15 And He said to them, "[a]Beware, and be on your guard against every form of greed; for not *even* when one has an abundance does his life consist of his possessions."

49 [1]*Or, drive out* ...Cor. 1:24, 30; Col. ...3 [b]Matt. 23:34-36
...**0** [1]*Or, required of* [a]Matt. 25:34
...**1** [1]*Or, required of* [a]Gen. 4:8 [b]2 Chr. 24:20, 21
...i.e., experts in the ...osaic Law [a]Matt. ...45; Luke 11:45, 46 [b]Matt. 23:13
...it., *something out ...mouth* [a]Mark 3:2; ...20:20; Acts 23:21 [b]Mark 12:13
...**2:1** [1]Lit., *myriads* ...t. 16:6, 11f.; Mark 8:15
...uke 12:2-9: *Matt. ...6-33;* Matt. 10:26; ...k 4:22; Luke 8:17
...Lit., *spoken in the* ...Matt. 10:27; 24:17
...**4** [a]John 15:13-15
...**5** [1]*Or, show* [2]Gr., ...*enna* [a]Heb. 10:31 [b]Matt. 5:22
...[1]Gr., *assaria,* the ...mallest of copper ...oins [a]Matt. 10:29
7 [a]Matt. 10:30
...Matt. 10:32; Luke 15:10; Rom. 10:9
...Matt. 10:33; Luke ...9:26 [b]Luke 15:10
...[a]Matt. 12:31, 32; Mark 3:28-30
...Matt. 10:17 [b]Matt. ...0:19; Mark 13:11; ...uke 12:22; 21:14
...Matt. 10:20; Luke 21:15
13 [1]Lit., *out of*
...ic. 6:8; Rom. 2:1, 3; 9:20
15 [a]1 Tim. 6:6-10

16 And He told them a parable, saying, "The land of a certain rich
man was very productive.
17 "And he began reasoning to himself, saying, 'What shall I do,
since I have no place to store my crops?'
18 "And he said, 'This is what I will do: I will tear down my barns
and build larger ones, and there I will store all my grain and my
goods.
19 'And I will say to my soul, "Soul, [a]you have many goods laid up
for many years *to come;* take your ease, eat, drink *and* be merry." '
20 "But God said to him, '[a]You fool! This *very* night [1b]your soul is
required of you; and [c]*now* who will own what you have prepared?'
21 "So is the man who [a]lays up treasure for himself, and is not rich
toward God."
22 And He said to His disciples, "[a]For this reason I say to you, do
not be anxious for *your* [1]life, *as to* what you shall eat; nor for your
body, *as to* what you shall put on.
23 "For life is more than food, and the body than clothing.
24 "Consider the [a]ravens, for they neither sow nor reap; and they
have no storeroom nor [b]barn; and *yet* God feeds them; how much
more valuable you are than the birds!
25 "And which of you by being anxious can add a *single* [1a]cubit to his
[2]life's span?
26 "If then you cannot do even a very little thing, why are you
anxious about other matters?
27 "Consider the lilies, how [1]they grow; they neither toil nor spin;
but I tell you, even [a]Solomon in all his glory did not clothe himself
like one of these.
28 "But if God so arrays the grass in the field, which is *alive* today
and tomorrow is thrown into the furnace, how much more *will He*
clothe you, [a]O men of little faith!
29 "And do not seek what you shall eat, and what you shall drink,
and do not [a]keep worrying.
30 "For [1]all these things the nations of the world eagerly seek; but
your Father knows that you need these things.
31 "But seek for His kingdom, and [a]these things shall be added to
you.
32 "[a]Do not be afraid, [b]little flock, for [c]your Father has chosen gladly
to give you the kingdom.
33 "[a]Sell your possessions and give to charity; make yourselves
purses which do not wear out, [b]an unfailing treasure in heaven,
where no thief comes near, nor moth destroys.
34 "For [a]where your treasure is, there will your heart be also.
35 "[1a]Be dressed in [b]readiness, and *keep* your lamps alight.
36 "And be like men who are waiting for their master when he
returns from the wedding feast, so that they may immediately open
the door to him when he comes and knocks.
37 "Blessed are those slaves whom the master shall find [a]on the alert
when he comes; truly I say to you, that [b]he will gird himself *to serve,*
and have them recline *at the table,* and will come up and wait on
them.
38 "[a]Whether he comes in the [1]second watch, or even in the [2]third,
and finds *them* so, blessed are those *slaves.*
39 "[a]And [1]be sure of this, that if the head of the house had known at

19 [a]Eccl. 11:9
20 [1]Lit., *they a demanding you from you* [a]Jer. Luke 11:40 [b]Jo [c]Ps. 39:6
21 [a]Luke 12:33
22 [1]Or, *soul* [a]L 12:22-31: *Matt.*
24 [a]Job 38:41 12:18
25 [1]I.e., One c equals approx. [2]Or, *height* [a]Ps
27 [1]Some mss *they grow* [a]1 K 10:4-7; 2 Chr. 9
28 [a]Matt. 6:30
29 [a]Matt. 6:31
30 [1]Or, *these t the nations of t*
31 [a]Matt. 6:33
32 [a]Matt. 14:2 21:15-17 [c]Eph
33 [a]Matt. 19:2 11:41; 18:22 [b] 6:20; Luke 12:2
34 [a]Matt. 6:21
35 [1]Lit., *Let yo be girded* [a]Ma [b]Eph. 6:14; 1 P
37 [a]Matt. 24:4 17:8; John 13:4
38 [1]I.e., 9 p.m. midnight [2]I.e., to 3 a.m. [a]Matt
39 [1]Lit., *know* 12:39, 40: *Matt 24:43, 44*

what hour the thief was coming, he would not have allowed his
house to be [2b]broken into.
40 "[a]You too, be ready; for the Son of Man is coming at an hour that
you do not [1]expect."
41 And Peter said, "Lord, are You addressing this parable to us, or
[a]to everyone *else* as well?"
42 And [a]the Lord said, "[b]Who then is the faithful and sensible
[c]steward, whom his master will put in charge of his [1]servants, to give
them their rations at the proper time?
43 "Blessed is that [a]slave whom his [1]master finds so doing when he
comes.
44 "Truly I say to you, that he will put him in charge of all his
possessions.
45 "But if that slave says in his heart, 'My master [1]will be a long time
in coming,' and begins to beat the slaves, *both* men and women, and
to eat and drink and get drunk;
46 the master of that slave will come on a day when he does not
expect *him,* and at an hour he does not know, and will cut him in
pieces, and assign him a place with the unbelievers.
47 "And that slave who knew his master's will and did not get ready
or act in accord with his will, shall [a]receive many lashes,
48 but the one who did not [a]know *it,* and committed deeds worthy
of [1]a flogging, will receive but few. [b]And from everyone who has
been given much shall much be required; and to whom they
entrusted much, of him they will ask all the more.
49 "I [1]have come to cast fire upon the earth; and [2]how I wish it were
already kindled!
50 "But I have a [a]baptism to [1]undergo, and how distressed I am until
it is accomplished!
51 "[a]Do you suppose that I came to grant peace on earth? I tell you,
no, but rather division;
52 for from now on five *members* in one household will be divided,
three against two, and two against three.
53 "They will be divided, [a]father against son, and son against father;
mother against daughter, and daughter against mother; mother-in-law against daughter-in-law, and daughter-in-law against mother-in-law."
54 And He was also saying to the multitudes, "[a]When you see a
cloud rising in the west, immediately you say, 'A shower is coming,'
and so it turns out.
55 "And when *you see* a south wind blowing, you say, 'It will be a
[a]hot day,' and it turns out *that way.*
56 "You hypocrites! [a]You know how to analyze the appearance of the
earth and the sky, but [1]why do you not analyze this present time?
57 "And [a]why do you not even on your own initiative judge what is
right?
58 "For [a]while you are going with your opponent to appear before
the magistrate, on *your* way *there* make an effort to [1]settle with him,
in order that he may not drag you before the judge, and the judge
turn you over to the constable, and the constable throw you into
prison.
59 "I say to you, you shall not get out of there until you have paid
the very last [1a]cent."

[2]Lit., *dug through* [b]Matt. 6:19
..., *think, suppose* ...3:33; Luke 21:36
[a]Luke 12:47, 48
..., *service* [a]Luke ... [b]Luke 12:42-46: *24:45-51* [c]Matt. ...:45; Luke 16:1ff.
[1]Or, *lord* [a]Luke 12:42
...it., *is delaying to come*
...eut. 25:2; James 4:17
[1]Lit., *blows* [a]Lev. ...17; Num. 15:29f. [b]Matt. 13:12
[1]Or, *came* [2]Lit., *do I wish if . . . ?*
[1]Lit., *be baptized with* [a]Mark 10:38
[a]Luke 12:51-53: *Matt. 10:34-36*
...7:6; Matt. 10:21
54 [a]Matt. 16:2f.
55 [a]Matt. 20:12
...*how* [a]Matt. 16:3
57 [a]Luke 21:30
[1]Lit., *be released* ...*im* [a]Luke 12:58, ...9: *Matt. 5:25, 26*
[1]Gr., *lepton;* i.e., ...28 of a denarius [a]Mark 12:42

Chapter 13

13 Now on the same occasion there were some present who reported to Him about the Galileans, whose blood [a]Pilate had [1]mingled with their sacrifices.

2 And He answered and said to them, "[a]Do you suppose that these Galileans were *greater* sinners than all *other* Galileans, because they suffered this *fate?*

3 "I tell you, no, but unless you [1]repent, you will all likewise perish.

4 "Or do you suppose that those eighteen on whom the tower in [a]Siloam fell and killed them, were *worse* [1b]culprits than all the men who live in Jerusalem?

5 "I tell you, no, but unless you repent, you will all likewise perish."

6 And He *began* telling this parable: "A certain man had [a]a fig tree which had been planted in his vineyard; and he came looking for fruit on it, and did not find any.

7 "And he said to the vineyard-keeper, 'Behold, for three years I have come looking for fruit on this fig tree [1]without finding any. [a]Cut it down! Why does it even use up the ground?'

8 "And he answered and said to him, 'Let it alone, sir, for this year too, until I dig around it and put in fertilizer;

9 and if it bears fruit next year, *fine;* but if not, cut it down.' "

10 And He was [a]teaching in one of the synagogues on the Sabbath.

11 And behold, there was a woman who for eighteen years had had [a]a sickness caused by a spirit; and she was bent double, and could not straighten up at all.

12 And when Jesus saw her, He called her over and said to her, "Woman, you are freed from your sickness."

13 And He [a]laid His hands upon her; and immediately she was made erect again, and *began* [b]glorifying God.

14 And [a]the synagogue official, indignant because Jesus [b]had healed on the Sabbath, *began* saying to the multitude in response, "[c]There are six days in which work should be done; therefore come during them and get healed, and not on the Sabbath day."

15 But [a]the Lord answered him and said, "You hypocrites, [b]does not each of you on the Sabbath untie his ox or his donkey from the stall, and lead him away to water *him?*

16 "And this woman, [a]a daughter of Abraham as she is, whom [b]Satan has bound for eighteen long years, should she not have been released from this bond on the Sabbath day?"

17 And as He said this, all His opponents were being humiliated; and [a]the entire multitude was rejoicing over all the glorious things being done by Him.

18 Therefore [a]He was saying, "[b]What is the kingdom of God like, and to what shall I compare it?

19 "It is like a mustard seed, which a man took and threw into his own garden; and it grew and became a tree; and [a]THE BIRDS OF THE [1]AIR NESTED IN ITS BRANCHES."

20 And again He said, "[a]To what shall I compare the kingdom of God?

21 "[a]It is like leaven, which a woman took and hid in [b]three [1]pecks of meal, until it was all leavened."

22 And He was passing through from one city and village to another, teaching, and [a]proceeding on His way to Jerusalem.

13:1 [1]Or, *s*... *with* [a]Matt.

2 [a]John 9:2

3 [1]Or, *are r*...

4 [1]Lit., *debt*... 3:15; Is. 8:6; 11 [b]Matt. 6:1... 11:4

6 [a]Matt. 21:...

7 [1]Lit., *and I*... [a]Matt. 3:10; 7... 3:9

10 [a]Matt. 4:2...

11 [a]Luke 13:...

13 [a]Mark 5:2... 9:8

14 [a]Mark 5:2... 12:2; Luke 14:... 20:9; Deut. 5:...

15 [a]Luke 7:13... 14:5

16 [a]Luke 19:9... 4:10; Luke 13:...

17 [a]Luke 18:43

18 [a]Luke 13:18... *Matt. 13:31, 32, 4:30-32* [b]Matt. ... Luke 13:20

19 [1]Or, *sky* [a]E... 17:23

20 [a]Matt. 13:24... 13:18

21 [1]Gr., *sata* [a]L... 13:20, 21: *Matt.* ... [b]Matt. 13:33

22 [a]Luke 9:51

23 And someone said to Him, "Lord, are there *just* a few who are
being saved?" And He said to them,
24 "[a]Strive to enter by the narrow door; for many, I tell you, will seek
to enter and will not be [1]able.
25 "Once the head of the house gets up and [a]shuts the door, and you
begin to stand outside and knock on the door, saying, '[b]Lord, open
up to us!' [1]then He will answer and say to you, '[c]I do not know
where you are from.'
26 "Then you will [a]begin to say, 'We ate and drank in Your presence,
and You taught in our streets';
27 and He will say, 'I tell you, [a]I do not know where you are from;
[b]DEPART FROM ME, ALL YOU EVILDOERS.'
28 "[a]There will be weeping and gnashing of teeth there when you
see Abraham and Isaac and Jacob and all the prophets in the king-
dom of God, but yourselves being cast out.
29 "And they [a]will come from east and west, and from north and
south, and will recline *at the table* in the kingdom of God.
30 "And behold, [a]*some* are last who will be first and *some* are first
who will be last."
31 Just at that time some Pharisees came up, saying to Him, "Go
away and depart from here, for [a]Herod wants to kill You."
32 And He said to them, "Go and tell that fox, 'Behold, I cast out
demons and perform cures today and tomorrow, and the third *day* I
[1a]reach My goal.'
33 "Nevertheless [a]I must journey on today and tomorrow and the
next *day;* for it cannot be that a [b]prophet should perish outside of
Jerusalem.
34 "[a]O Jerusalem, Jerusalem, *the city* that kills the prophets and
stones those sent to her! How often I wanted to gather your children
together, [b]just as a hen *gathers* her brood under her wings, and you
would not *have it!*
35 "Behold, your house is left to you [1]*desolate;* and I say to you, you
shall not see Me until *the time* comes when you say, '[a]BLESSED IS HE
WHO COMES IN THE NAME OF THE LORD!' "

Chapter 14

14 And it came about when He went into the house of one of the
[1]leaders of the Pharisees on *the* Sabbath to eat bread, that
[a]they were watching Him closely.
2 And [1]there, in front of Him was a certain man suffering from
dropsy.
3 And Jesus answered and spoke to the [1a]lawyers and Pharisees,
saying, "[b]Is it lawful to heal on the Sabbath, or not?"
4 But they kept silent. And He took hold of him, and healed him,
and sent him away.
5 And He said to them, "[a]Which one of you shall have a [1]son or an
ox fall into a well, and will not immediately pull him out on a
Sabbath day?"
6 [a]And they could make no reply to this.
7 And He *began* speaking a parable to the invited guests when He
noticed how [a]they had been picking out the places of honor *at the
table;* saying to them,
8 "When you are invited by someone to a wedding feast, [a]do not

[1]Or, *able, once* [a]Matt. 7:13
[1]Lit., *and* [a]Matt. 5:10 [b]Matt. 7:22; 5:11 [c]Matt. 7:23; 5:12; Luke 13:27
26 [a]Luke 3:8
[a]Luke 13:25 [b]Ps. 6:8; Matt. 25:41
[a]Matt. 8:12; 22:13; 25:30
29 [a]Matt. 8:11
[a]Matt. 19:30; 20:16; Mark 10:31
[a]Matt. 14:1; Luke 3:1; 9:7; 23:7
[1]Or possibly, *am* ...*cted* [a]Heb. 2:10; 5:9; 7:28
[a]John 11:9 [b]Matt. 21:11
[a]Luke 13:34, 35: ...*t. 23:37-39;* Luke ...:41 [b]Matt. 23:37
[1]Later mss. add ...*late* [a]Ps. 118:26; 21:9; Luke 19:38
[1]I.e., members of ...hedrin [a]Mark 3:2
2 [1]Lit., *behold*
3 [1]I.e., experts in ...osaic Law [a]Matt. [b]Matt. 12:2; Luke 13:14
...ome ancient mss. ...ad *donkey* [a]Matt. 12:11; Luke 13:15
[a]Matt. 22:46; Luke 20:40
7 [a]Matt. 23:6
8 [a]Prov. 25:6, 7

[1]take the place of honor, lest someone more distinguished than you may have been invited by him,

9 and he who invited you both shall come and say to you, 'Give place to this man,' and then [a]in disgrace you [1]proceed to occupy the last place.

10 "But when you are invited, go and recline at the last place, so that when the one who has invited you comes, he may say to you, 'Friend, [a]move up higher'; then you will have honor in the sight of all who [1]are at the table with you.

11 "[a]For everyone who exalts himself shall be humbled, and he who humbles himself shall be exalted."

12 And He also went on to say to the one who had invited Him, "When you give a luncheon or a dinner, do not invite your friends or your brothers or your relatives or rich neighbors, lest they also invite you in return, and repayment come to you.

13 "But when you give a [1]reception, invite *the* poor, *the* crippled, *the* lame, *the* blind,

14 and you will be [1]blessed, since they [2]do not have *the means* to repay you; for you will be repaid at [a]the resurrection of the righteous."

15 And when one of those who were reclining *at the table* with Him heard this, he said to Him, "[a]Blessed is everyone who shall eat bread in the kingdom of God!"

16 But He said to him, "[a]A certain man was giving a big dinner, and he invited many;

17 and at the dinner hour he sent his slave to say to those who had been invited, 'Come; for everything is ready now.'

18 "But they all alike began to make excuses. The first one said to him, 'I have bought a [1]piece of land and I need to go out and look at it; [2]please consider me excused.'

19 "And another one said, 'I have bought five yoke of oxen, and I am going to try them out; [1]please consider me excused.'

20 "And another one said, '[a]I have married a wife, and for that reason I cannot come.'

21 "And the slave came *back* and reported this to his master. Then the head of the household became angry and said to his slave, 'Go out at once into the streets and lanes of the city and bring in here the poor and crippled and blind and lame.'

22 "And the slave said, 'Master, what you commanded has been done, and still there is room.'

23 "And the master said to the slave, 'Go out into the highways and along the hedges, and compel *them* to come in, that my house may be filled.

24 'For I tell you, none of those men who were invited shall taste of my dinner.' "

25 Now great multitudes were going along with Him; and He turned and said to them,

26 "[a]If anyone comes to Me, and does not [1]hate his own father and mother and wife and children and brothers and sisters, yes, and even his own life, he cannot be My disciple.

27 "Whoever does not [a]carry his own cross and come after Me cannot be My disciple.

28 "For which one of you, when he wants to build a tower, does not

8 [1]Lit., *recli*

9 [1]Lit., *begi*

10 [1]Lit., *recl* table [a]Prov.

11 [a]2 Sam. 2 29:23; Matt. 2 1:52; 18:14; J

13 [1]Or, *banq*

14 [1]Or, *happy* *unable to* [a]Jo Acts 24:15; Re

15 [a]Rev. 19:9

16 [a]Matt. 22:2 14:16-24

18 [1]Or, *field* [2]L *request you*

19 [1]Lit., *I reque*

20 [a]Deut. 24:5; 7:33

26 [1]I.e., by com of his love for Me 10:37

27 [a]Matt. 10:38; Mark 8:34; Luke

first sit down and calculate the cost, to see if he has enough to
complete it?
29 "Otherwise, when he has laid a foundation, and is not able to
finish, all who observe it begin to ridicule him,
30 saying, 'This man began to build and was not able to finish.'
31 "Or what king, when he sets out to meet another king in battle,
will not first sit down and take [a]counsel whether he is strong enough
with ten thousand *men* to encounter the one coming against him
with twenty thousand?
32 "Or else, while the other is still far away, he sends [1]a delegation
and asks terms of peace.
33 "So therefore, no one of you can be My disciple who [a]does not
give up all his own possessions.
34 "Therefore, salt is good; but [a]if even salt has become tasteless,
with what will it be seasoned?
35 "It is useless either for the soil or for the manure pile; [1]it is thrown
out. [a]He who has ears to hear, let him hear."

Chapter 15

15 Now all the [1a]tax-gatherers and the [2]sinners were coming near
Him to listen to Him.
2 And both the Pharisees and the scribes *began* to [1]grumble,
saying, "This man receives sinners and [a]eats with them."
3 And He told them this parable, saying,
4 "[a]What man among you, if he has a hundred sheep and has lost
one of them, does not leave the ninety-nine in the [1]open pasture, and
go after the one which is lost, until he finds it?
5 "And when he has found it, he lays it on his shoulders, rejoicing.
6 "And when he comes home, he calls together his friends and his
neighbors, saying to them, 'Rejoice with me, for I have found my
sheep which was lost!'
7 "I tell you that in the same way, there will be *more* joy in heaven
over one sinner who repents, than over ninety-nine righteous per-
sons who need no repentance.
8 "Or what woman, if she has ten [1]silver coins and loses one coin,
does not light a lamp and sweep the house and search carefully until
she finds it?
9 "And when she has found it, she calls together her [1]friends and
neighbors, saying, 'Rejoice with me, for I have found the coin which
I had lost!'
10 "In the same way, I tell you, there is joy [a]in the presence of the
angels of God over one sinner who repents."
11 And He said, "A certain man had two sons;
12 and the younger of them said to his father, 'Father, give me [a]the
share of the estate that falls to me.' And he divided his [1b]wealth
between them.
13 "And not many days later, the younger son gathered everything
together and went on a journey into a distant country, and there he
squandered his estate with loose living.
14 "Now when he had spent everything, a severe famine occurred in
that country, and he began to be in need.
15 "And he went and [1]attached himself to one of the citizens of that
country, and he sent him into his fields to feed swine.

[a]Prov. 20:18
an embassy
; Heb. 11:26
t. 5:13; Mark 9:50
, they throw it [a]Matt. 11:15
, Collectors of axes for profit , irreligious or acticing Jews [a]Luke 5:29
umble among es [a]Matt. 9:11
.it., *wilderness* 8:12-14; Luke 15:4-7
drachmas, one was equivalent a day's wages
women friends and neighbors
att. 10:32; Luke 15:7
.it., *living* [a]Deut. 17 [b]Mark 12:44; Luke 15:30
.it., *was joined to*

16 "And he was longing [1]to fill his [2]stomach with the [3]pods that the swine were eating, and no one was giving *anything* to him.

17 "But when he came to [1]his senses, he said, 'How many of my father's hired men have more than enough bread, but I am dying here with hunger!

18 'I will get up and go to my father, and will say to him, "Father, I have sinned against heaven, and [1]in your sight;

19 "I am no longer worthy to be called your son; make me as one of your hired men." '

20 "And he got up and came to [1]his father. But while he was still a long way off, his father saw him, and felt compassion *for him,* and ran and [2a]embraced him, and [3]kissed him.

21 "And the son said to him, 'Father, I have sinned against heaven and in your sight; I am no longer worthy to be called your son.[1]'

22 "But the father said to his slaves, 'Quickly bring out [a]the best robe and put it on him, and [b]put a ring on his hand and sandals on his feet;

23 and bring the fattened calf, kill it, and let us eat and be merry;

24 for this son of mine was [a]dead, and has come to life again; he was lost, and has been found.' And they began to be merry.

25 "Now his older son was in the field, and when he came and approached the house, he heard music and dancing.

26 "And he summoned one of the servants and *began* inquiring what these things might be.

27 "And he said to him, 'Your brother has come, and your father has killed the fattened calf, because he has received him back safe and sound.'

28 "But he became angry, and was not willing to go in; and his father came out and *began* entreating him.

29 "But he answered and said to his father, 'Look! For so many years I have been serving you, and I have never [1]neglected a command of yours; and *yet* you have never given me a [2]kid, that I might be merry with my friends;

30 but when this son of yours came, who has devoured your [1a]wealth with harlots, you killed the fattened calf for him.'

31 "And he said to him, '*My* child, you [1]have always been with me, and all that is mine is yours.

32 'But [1]we had to be merry and rejoice, for this brother of yours was [a]dead and *has begun* to live, and *was* lost and has been found.' "

Chapter 16

16 Now He was also saying to the disciples, "There was a certain rich man who had a steward, and this *steward* was [1]reported to him as [a]squandering his possessions.

2 "And he called him and said to him, 'What is this I hear about you? Give an account of your stewardship, for you can no longer be steward.'

3 "And the steward said to himself, 'What shall I do, since my [1]master is taking the stewardship away from me? I am not strong enough to dig; I am ashamed to beg.

4 'I [1]know what I shall do, so that when I am removed from the stewardship, they will receive me into their homes.'

5 "And he summoned each one of his [1]master's debtors, and he *began* saying to the first, 'How much do you owe my master?'

16 [1]Some m... *be satisfied* ... *belly* [3]I.e., o... tree

17 [1]Lit., *hims...*

18 [1]Lit., *befo...*

20 [1]Lit., *his* ... *fell on his ne...* *kissed him a...* *again* [a]Gen. ... 46:29; Acts 2...

21 [1]Some an... add *make me* ... *your hired me...*

22 [a]Zech. 3:4 ... 6:11 [b]Gen. 41...

24 [a]Matt. 8:22... 9:60; 15:32; R... 11:15; Eph. 2:1... Col. 2:13; 1 Ti...

29 [1]Or, *disobe...* *young goat*

30 [1]Lit., *living* ... 29:3; Luke 15:1...

31 [1]Lit., *are al...* *with me*

32 [1]Lit., *it was* *necessary* [a]Luk...

16:1 [1]Or, *accus...* [a]Luke 15:13

3 [1]Or, *lord*

4 [1]Lit., *have co...* *the knowledge o...*

5 [1]Or, *lord's*

6 "And he said, 'A hundred [1]measures of oil.' And he said to him,
'Take your bill, and sit down quickly and write fifty.'
7 "Then he said to another, 'And how much do you owe?' And he
said, 'A hundred [1]measures of wheat.' He *said to him, 'Take your
bill, and write eighty.'
8 "And his [1]master praised the unrighteous steward because he had
acted shrewdly; for the sons of [a]this age are more shrewd in relation
to their own [2]kind than the [b]sons of light.
9 "And I say to you, [a]make friends for yourselves by means of the
[1b]mammon of unrighteousness; that when it fails, [c]they may receive
you into the eternal dwellings.
10 "[a]He who is faithful in a very little thing is faithful also in much;
and he who is unrighteous in a very little thing is unrighteous also
in much.
11 "If therefore you have not been faithful in the *use of* unrighteous
[1a]mammon, who will entrust the true *riches* to you?
12 "And if you have not been faithful in *the use of* that which is
another's, who will give you that which is [1]your own?
13 "[a]No [1]servant can serve two masters; for either he will hate the
one, and love the other, or else he will hold to one, and despise the
other. You cannot serve God and [2b]mammon."
14 Now the Pharisees, who were [a]lovers of money, were listening to
all these things, and they [b]were scoffing at Him.
15 And He said to them, "You are those who [a]justify yourselves [1]in
the sight of men, but [b]God knows your hearts; for that which is
[2]highly esteemed among men is detestable [3]in the sight of God.
16 "[a]The Law and the Prophets *were proclaimed* until John; since then
[b]the gospel of the kingdom of God is preached, and everyone is
forcing his way into it.
17 "[a]But it is easier for heaven and earth to pass away than for one
[1]stroke of a letter of the Law to fail.
18 "[a]Everyone who [1]divorces his wife and marries another commits
adultery; and he who marries one who is [2]divorced from a husband
commits adultery.
19 "Now there was a certain rich man, and he habitually dressed in
purple and fine linen, gaily living in splendor every day.
20 "And a certain poor man named Lazarus [a]was laid at his gate,
covered with sores,
21 and longing to be fed with the *crumbs* which were falling from
the rich man's table; besides, even the dogs were coming and licking
his sores.
22 "Now it came about that the poor man died and he was carried
away by the angels to [a]Abraham's bosom; and the rich man also died
and was buried.
23 "And in [a]Hades [1]he lifted up his eyes, being in torment, and *saw
Abraham far away, and Lazarus in his bosom.
24 "And he cried out and said, '[a]Father Abraham, have mercy on me,
and send Lazarus, that he may dip the tip of his finger in water and
cool off my tongue; for I am in agony in [b]this flame.'
25 "But Abraham said, 'Child, remember that [a]during your life you
received your good things, and likewise Lazarus bad things; but
now he is being comforted here, and you are in agony.
26 'And [1]besides all this, between us and you there is a great chasm

baths, one bath
between 8 and 9
gal.

r., *kors*, one kor
between 10 and
12 bu.

3 [1]Or, *lord* [2]Lit.,
generation [a]Matt.
:32; Luke 20:34
12:36; Eph. 5:8;
1 Thess. 5:5

Or, *riches* [a]Matt.
:21; Luke 11:41;
Matt. 6:24; Luke
, 13 [c]Luke 16:4

[a]Matt. 25:21, 23

Or, *riches* [a]Luke
16:9

Some mss. read
our own

, *house-servant*
ches [a]Matt. 6:24
[b]Luke 16:9

Tim. 3:2 [b]Luke
23:35

[1]Lit., *before men*
igh [3]Lit., *before*
uke 10:29; 18:9,
Sam. 16:7; Prov.
Acts 1:24; Rom.
8:27

tt. 11:12f. [b]Matt.
4:23

., projection of a
erif) [a]Matt. 5:18

[1]Or, *sends away*
ent away [a]Matt.
; 1 Cor. 7:10, 11

20 [a]Acts 3:2

John 1:18; 13:23

Lit., *having lifted*
up [a]Matt. 11:23

[a]Luke 3:8; 16:30;
9:9 [b]Matt. 25:41

25 [a]Luke 6:24

[1]Lit., *in all these*
things

fixed, in order that those who wish to come over from here to you
may not be able, and *that* none may cross over from there to us.'
27 "And he said, 'Then I beg you, Father, that you send him to my
father's house—
28 for I have five brothers—that he may [a]warn them, lest they also
come to this place of torment.'
29 "But Abraham *said, 'They have [a]Moses and the Prophets; let
them hear them.'
30 "But he said, 'No, [a]Father Abraham, but if someone goes to them
from the dead, they will repent!'
31 "But he said to him, 'If they do not listen to Moses and the
Prophets, neither will they be persuaded if someone rises from the
dead.' "

Chapter 17

17 And He said to His disciples, "[a]It is inevitable that [1]stumbling
blocks should come, but woe to him through whom they
come!
2 "[a]It would be better for him if a millstone were hung around his
neck and he were thrown into the sea, than that he should cause one
of these [1]little ones to stumble.
3 "[1]Be on your guard! [a]If your brother sins, rebuke him; and if he
repents, forgive him.
4 "And if he sins against you [a]seven times a day, and returns to you
seven times, saying, 'I repent,' [1]forgive him."
5 And [a]the apostles said to [b]the Lord, "Increase our faith!"
6 And [a]the Lord said, "If you had faith like [b]a mustard seed, you
would say to this [c]mulberry tree, 'Be uprooted and be planted in the
sea'; and it would [1]obey you.
7 "But which of you, having a slave plowing or tending sheep, will
say to him when he has come in from the field, 'Come immediately
and [1]sit down to eat'?
8 "But will he not say to him, '[a]Prepare something for me to eat, and
properly [1]clothe yourself and serve me until I have eaten and drunk;
and [2]afterward you will eat and drink'?
9 "He does not thank the slave because he did the things which
were commanded, does he?
10 "So you too, when you do all the things which are commanded
you, say, 'We are unworthy slaves; we have done *only* that which we
ought to have done.' "
11 And it came about while He was [a]on the way to Jerusalem, that
[b]He was passing [1]between Samaria and Galilee.
12 And as He entered a certain village, ten leprous men who [a]stood
at a distance met Him;
13 and they raised their voices, saying, "Jesus, [a]Master, have mercy
on us!"
14 And when He saw them, He said to them, "[a]Go and show your-
selves to the priests." And it came about that as they were going,
they were cleansed.
15 Now one of them, when he saw that he had been healed, turned
back, [a]glorifying God with a loud voice,
16 and he fell on his face at His feet, giving thanks to Him. And he
was a [a]Samaritan.

28 [a]Acts 2: 10:42; 18:5 23:11; 28:2 Eph. 4:17; 2:11; 4:6

29 [a]Luke 4 5:45-47; Ac

30 [a]Luke 3: 19:9

17:1 [1]Or, *te sin* [a]Matt. 18 11:19; 1 Tim.

2 [1]I.e., humb 18:6; Mark 9 8:12

3 [1]Lit., *Take yourselves* [a]

4 [1]Lit., *you s forgive* [a]Matt.

5 [a]Mark 6:30 7:13

6 [1]Or, *have o* [a]Luke 7:13 [b]M 13:31; 17:20; Luke 13:19 [c]L

7 [1]Lit., *recline*

8 [1]Lit., *gird* [2]L *these things* [a]L 12:37

11 [1]Lit., *throug midst of;* or, *alo borders of* [a]Luk [b]Luke 9:52ff.; Jo

12 [a]Lev. 13:45f

13 [a]Luke 5:5

14 [a]Lev. 14:1-3 8:4; Luke 5:14

15 [a]Matt. 9:8

16 [a]Matt. 10:5

17 And Jesus answered and said, "Were there not ten cleansed? But
the nine—where are they?
18 "[1]Was no one found who turned back to [a]give glory to God, ex-
cept this foreigner?"
19 And He said to him, "Rise, and go your way; [a]your faith [1]has
made you well."
20 Now having been questioned by the Pharisees [a]as to when the
kingdom of God was coming, He answered them and said, "The
kingdom of God is not coming with [1b]signs to be observed;
21 nor will [a]they say, 'Look, here *it is!*' or, 'There *it is!*' For behold,
the kingdom of God is [1]in your midst."
22 And He said to the disciples, "[a]The days shall come when you
will long to see one of the days of the Son of Man, and you will not
see it.
23 "[a]And they will say to you, 'Look there! Look here!' Do not go
away, and do not run after *them*.
24 "[a]For just as the lightning, when it flashes out of one part [1]of the
sky, shines to the other part [1]of the sky, so will the Son of Man be in
His day.
25 "[a]But first He must suffer many things and be rejected by this
generation.
26 "[a]And just as it happened [b]in the days of Noah, so it shall be also
in the days of the Son of Man:
27 they were eating, they were drinking, they were marrying, they
were being given in marriage, until the day that Noah entered the
ark, and the flood came and destroyed them all.
28 "[1]It was the same as happened in [a]the days of Lot: they were
eating, they were drinking, they were buying, they were selling, they
were planting, they were building;
29 but on the day that Lot went out from Sodom it rained fire and
[1]brimstone from heaven and destroyed them all.
30 "It will be [1]just the same on the day that the Son of Man [a]is
revealed.
31 "On that day, let not the one who is [a]on the housetop and whose
goods are in the house go down to take them away; and likewise let
not the one who is in the field turn back.
32 "[a]Remember Lot's wife.
33 "[a]Whoever seeks to keep his [1]life shall lose it, and whoever loses
his life shall preserve it.
34 "I tell you, on that night there will be two men in one bed; one
will be taken, and the other will be left.
35 "[a]There will be two women grinding at the same place; one will
be taken, and the other will be left.
36 ["[1a]Two men will be in the field; one will be taken and the other
will be left."]
37 And answering they *said to Him, "Where, Lord?" And He said
to them, "[a]Where the body *is*, there also will the [1]vultures be
gathered."

Chapter 18

18 Now He was telling them a parable to show that at all times
they [a]ought to pray and not to [b]lose heart,
2 saying, "There was in a certain city a judge who did not fear
God, and did not [a]respect man.

Were there not *ose who* [a]Matt. 9:8
has saved you :22; Luke 18:42
Lit., *observation* 19:11; Acts 1:6 [b]Luke 14:1
[1]Or, *within you* [a]Luke 17:23
Matt. 9:15; Mark 2:20; Luke 5:35
att. 24:23; Mark 3:21; Luke 21:8
., *under heaven* [a]Matt. 24:27
att. 16:21; Luke 9:22
Luke 17:26, 27: *24:37-39* [b]Gen. 6:5-8; 7
Lit., *In the same* *vay as* [a]Gen. 19
29 [1]Or, *sulphur*
.it., *according to* *ne things* [a]Matt. ; 1 Cor. 1:7; Col. ness. 1:7; 1 Pet. :13; 1 John 2:28
Matt. 24:17, 18; 15f.; Luke 21:21
32 [a]Gen. 19:26
[1]Or, *soul* [a]Matt. 10:39
35 [a]Matt. 24:41
any mss. do not ain this v. [a]Matt. 24:40
r, *eagles* [a]Matt. 24:28
1 [a]Luke 11:5-10 [b]2 Cor. 4:1
uke 18:4; 20:13; Heb. 12:9

3 "And there was a widow in that city, and she kept coming to him,
saying, '[1]Give me legal protection from my opponent.'
4 "And for a while he was unwilling; but afterward he said to him-
self, 'Even though I do not fear God nor [a]respect man,
5 yet [a]because this widow bothers me, I will [1]give her legal protec-
tion, lest by continually coming she [2b]wear me out.' "
6 And [a]the Lord said, "Hear what the unrighteous judge *said;
7 now shall not God [a]bring about justice for His [b]elect, who cry to
Him day and night, [1]and will He [c]delay long over them?
8 "I tell you that He will bring about justice for them speedily.
However, when the Son of Man comes, [a]will He find [1]faith on the
earth?"
9 And He also told this parable to certain ones who [a]trusted in
themselves that they were righteous, and [b]viewed others with con-
tempt:
10 "Two men [a]went up into the temple to pray, one a Pharisee, and
the other a [1]tax-gatherer.
11 "The Pharisee [a]stood and was praying thus to himself, 'God, I
thank Thee that I am not like other people: swindlers, unjust, adul-
terers, or even like this [1]tax-gatherer.
12 'I [a]fast twice a week; I [b]pay tithes of all that I get.'
13 "But the [1]tax-gatherer, [a]standing some distance away, [b]was even
unwilling to lift up his eyes to heaven, but [c]was beating his breast,
saying, 'God, be [2]merciful to me, the sinner!'
14 "I tell you, this man went down to his house justified rather than
the other; [a]for everyone who exalts himself shall be humbled, but he
who humbles himself shall be exalted."
15 [a]And they were bringing even their babies to Him so that He
might touch them, but when the disciples saw it, they *began* rebuk-
ing them.
16 But Jesus called for them, saying, "Permit the children to come to
Me, and do not hinder them, for the kingdom of God belongs to
such as these.
17 "Truly I say to you, [a]whoever does not receive the kingdom of
God like a child shall not enter it *at all*."
18 [a]And a certain ruler questioned Him, saying, "Good Teacher,
what shall I do to inherit eternal life?"
19 And Jesus said to him, "Why do you call Me good? No one is
good except God alone.
20 "You know the commandments, '[a]DO NOT COMMIT ADULTERY, DO
NOT MURDER, DO NOT STEAL, DO NOT BEAR FALSE WITNESS, HONOR YOUR
FATHER AND MOTHER.' "
21 And he said, "All these things I have kept from *my* youth."
22 And when Jesus heard *this*, He said to him, "One thing you still
lack; [a]sell all that you possess, and distribute it to the poor, and you
shall have [b]treasure in heaven; and come, follow Me."
23 But when he had heard these things, he became very sad; for he
was extremely rich.
24 And Jesus looked at him and said, "[a]How hard it is for those
who are wealthy to enter the kingdom of God!
25 "For [a]it is easier for a camel to [1]go through the eye of a needle,
than for a rich man to enter the kingdom of God."
26 And they who heard it said, "[1]Then who can be saved?"

3 [1]Lit., *Do*

4 [a]Luke 18 Heb. 12:9

5 [1]Lit., *do* [2]Lit., *hit me eye* [a]Luke 9:27

6 [a]Luke 7:

7 [1]Or, *and long-sufferi them* [a]Rev. 24:22; Rom 3:12; 2 Tim. 1:1 [c]2 Pet.

8 [1]Lit., *the f* 17:26ff.

9 [a]Luke 16: 14:3, 10

10 [1]I.e., Col Roman taxes [a]1 Kin. 10:5; 8; Acts 3:1

11 [1]V. 10, nc 6:5; Mark 11: 22:41

12 [a]Matt. 9:1 11:42

13 [1]V. 10, no *propitious* [a]M Mark 11:25; L [b]Ezra 9:6 [c]Lu

14 [a]Matt. 23: 14:11

15 [a]Luke 18: *Matt. 19:13-15 10:13-16*

17 [a]Matt. 18:3 Mark 10:15; 1 14:20; 1 Pet. 2

18 [a]Luke 18:1 *Matt. 19:16-29 10:17-30;* Luke

20 [a]Ex. 20:12- 5:16-20

22 [a]Matt. 19:21 12:33 [b]Matt. 6:

24 [a]Matt. 19:23 10:23f.

25 [1]Lit., *enter* 19:24; Mark 10:

26 [1]Lit., *And*

27 But He said, "[a]The things impossible with men are possible with
God."
28 And Peter said, "Behold, [a]we have left [1]our own *homes*, and fol-
lowed You."
29 And He said to them, "Truly I say to you, [a]there is no one who
has left house or wife or brothers or parents or children, for the sake
of the kingdom of God,
30 who shall not receive many times as much at this time and in
[a]the age to come, eternal life."
31 [a]And He took the twelve aside and said to them, "Behold, [b]we
are going up to Jerusalem, and [c]all things which are written through
the prophets about the Son of Man will be accomplished.
32 "[a]For He will be [1]delivered to the Gentiles, and will be mocked
and mistreated and spit upon,
33 and after they have scourged Him, they will kill Him; and the
third day He will rise again."
34 And [a]they understood none of these things, and this saying was
hidden from them, and they did not comprehend the things that
were said.
35 [a]And it came about that [b]as He was approaching Jericho, a cer-
tain blind man was sitting by the road, begging.
36 Now hearing a multitude going by, he *began* to inquire what this
might be.
37 And they told him that Jesus of Nazareth was passing by.
38 And he called out, saying, "Jesus, [a]Son of David, have mercy on
me!"
39 And those who led the way were sternly telling him to be quiet;
but he kept crying out all the more, "[a]Son of David, have mercy on
me!"
40 And Jesus [1]stopped and commanded that he be brought to Him;
and when he had come near, He questioned him,
41 "What do you want Me to do for you?" And he said, "Lord, *I want*
to regain my sight!"
42 And Jesus said to him, "[1]Receive your sight; [a]your faith has
[2]made you well."
43 And immediately he regained his sight, and *began* following
Him, [a]glorifying God; and when [b]all the people saw it, they gave
praise to God.

Chapter 19

19 And He [a]entered and was passing through Jericho.
2 And behold, there was a man called by the name of Zac-
cheus; and he was a chief [1]tax-gatherer, and he was rich.
3 And he was trying to see who Jesus was, and he was unable
because of the crowd, for he was small in stature.
4 And he ran on ahead and climbed up into a [1a]sycamore tree in
order to see Him, for He was about to pass through that way.
5 And when Jesus came to the place, He looked up and said to
him, "Zaccheus, hurry and come down, for today I must stay at your
house."
6 And he hurried and came down, and received Him [1]gladly.
7 And when they saw it, they all *began* to [1]grumble, saying, "He
has gone [2]to be the guest of a man who is a sinner."
8 And Zaccheus [1]stopped and said to [a]the Lord, "Behold, Lord,

27 [a]Matt. 19:26
t., *our own things* [a]Luke 5:11
Matt. 6:33; 19:29; Mark 10:29f.
30 [a]Matt. 12:32
[a]Luke 18:31-33: t. 20:17-19; Mark 32-34 [b]Luke 9:51 [c]Ps. 22; Is. 53
, *betrayed* [a]Matt. 16:21
[a]Mark 9:32; Luke 9:45
[a]Luke 18:35-43: t. 20:29-34; Mark -52 [b]Matt. 20:29; 10:46; Luke 19:1
[a]Matt. 9:27; Luke 18:39
39 [a]Luke 18:38
40 [1]Lit., *stood*
[1]Or, *Regain* [2]Or, *d you* [a]Matt. 9:22
[a]Matt. 9:8 [b]Luke :43; 13:17; 19:37
9:1 [a]Luke 18:35
[1]I.e., Collector of an taxes for profit
[1]I.e., fig-mulberry Kin. 10:27; 1 Chr. 2 Chr. 1:15; 9:27; 47; Is. 9:10; Luke 17:6
6 [1]Lit., *rejoicing*
, *grumble among elves* [2]Or, *to find lodging*
stood [a]Luke 7:13

half of my possessions I will give to the poor, and if I have [b]de-
frauded anyone of anything, I will give back [c]four times as much."
9 And Jesus said to him, "Today salvation has come to this house,
because he, too, is [a]a son of Abraham.
10 "For [a]the Son of Man has come to seek and to save that which was
lost."
11 And while they were listening to these things, He went on to tell
a parable, because [a]He was near Jerusalem, and they supposed that
[b]the kingdom of God was going to appear immediately.
12 He said therefore, "[a]A certain nobleman went to a distant
country to receive a kingdom for himself, and *then* return.
13 "And he called ten of his slaves, and gave them ten [1]minas, and
said to them, 'Do business *with this* [2]until I come *back.*'
14 "But his citizens hated him, and sent [1]a delegation after him,
saying, 'We do not want this man to reign over us.'
15 "And it came about that when he returned, after receiving the
kingdom, he ordered that these slaves, to whom he had given the
money, be called to him in order that he might know what business
they had done.
16 "And the first appeared, saying, '[1]Master, your [2]mina has made
ten minas more.'
17 "And he said to him, 'Well done, good slave, because you have
been [a]faithful in a very little thing, be in authority over ten cities.'
18 "And the second came, saying, 'Your [1]mina, [2]master, has made
five minas.'
19 "And he said to him also, 'And you are to be over five cities.'
20 "And another came, saying, 'Master, behold your mina, which I
kept put away in a handkerchief;
21 for I was afraid of you, because you are an exacting man; you
take up what you did not lay down, and reap what you did not sow.'
22 "He *said to him, '[1]By your own words I will judge you, you
worthless slave. Did you know that I am an exacting man, taking up
what I did not lay down, and reaping what I did not sow?
23 '[1]Then why did you not put the money in the bank,
and having come, I would have collected it with interest?'
24 "And he said to the bystanders, 'Take the mina away
from him, and give it to the one who has the ten minas.'
25 "And they said to him, 'Master, he has ten minas *al-
ready.*'
26 "[a]I tell you, that to everyone who has shall *more* be
given, but from the one who does not have, even what he
does have shall be taken away.
27 "But [a]these enemies of mine, who did not want me to
reign over them, bring them here and [b]slay them in my
presence."
28 And after He had said these things, He [a]was going on
ahead, [b]ascending to Jerusalem.
29 And it came about that [a]when He approached Beth-
phage and [b]Bethany, near the [1]mount that is called [2c]Olivet,
He sent two of the disciples,
30 saying, "Go into the village opposite *you,* in which as
you enter you will find a colt tied, on which no one yet has
ever sat; untie it, and bring it *here.*
31 "And if anyone asks you, 'Why are you untying it?'
thus shall you speak, 'The Lord has need of it.' "

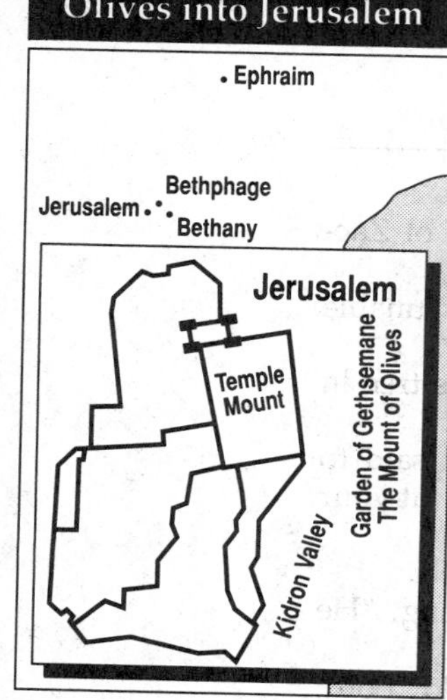

From Bethany, Bethphage Across the Mount of Olives into Jerusalem

8 [b]Luke 3:14 Lev. 6:5; Nur 2 Sam. 12:6
9 [a]Luke 3:8; Rom. 4:16; G
10 [a]Matt. 18
11 [a]Luke 9:5 17:20
12 [a]Matt. 25: Luke 19:12-27
13 [1]A mina is about 100 day [2]Lit., *while I ar*
14 [1]Or, *an em*
16 [1]Lit., *Lord* note 1
17 [a]Luke 16:10
18 [1]V. 13, note *lord*
22 [1]Lit., *Out of own mouth*
23 [1]Lit., *And*
26 [a]Matt. 13:12 4:25; Luke 8:18
27 [a]Luke 19:14 22:7; Luke 20:16
28 [a]Mark 10:32 9:51
29 [1]Or, *hill* [2]Or, *Grove* [a]Luke 19: *Matt. 21:1-9; Mar 11:1-10* [b]Matt. 21 [c]Luke 21:37; Acts

32 And those who were sent went away and found it just as He had
told them.
33 And as they were untying the colt, its [1]owners said to them,
"Why are you untying the colt?"
34 And they said, "The Lord has need of it."
35 And they brought it to Jesus, [a]and they threw their garments on
the colt, and put Jesus *on it*.
36 And as He was going, they were spreading their garments in the
road.
37 And as He was now approaching, near the descent of [a]the
Mount of Olives, the whole multitude of the disciples began to
[b]praise God [1]joyfully with a loud voice for all the [2]miracles which
they had seen,
38 saying,

"[a]BLESSED IS THE [b]KING WHO COMES IN THE NAME OF THE LORD;
Peace in heaven and [c]glory in the highest!"

39 [a]And some of the Pharisees [1]in the multitude said to Him,
"Teacher, rebuke Your disciples."
40 And He answered and said, "I tell you, if these become silent,
[a]the stones will cry out!"
41 And when He approached, He saw the city and [a]wept over it,
42 saying, "If you had known in this day, even you, the things
which make for peace! But now they have been hidden from your
eyes.
43 "For the days shall come upon you [1]when your enemies will
[a]throw up a [2]bank before you, and [b]surround you, and hem you in
on every side,
44 and will level you to the ground and your children within you,
and [a]they will not leave in you one stone upon another, because you
did not recognize [b]the time of your visitation."
45 [a]And He entered the temple and began to cast out those who
were selling,
46 saying to them, "It is written, '[a]AND MY HOUSE SHALL BE A HOUSE
OF PRAYER,' [b]but you have made it a ROBBERS' [1]DEN."
47 And [a]He was teaching daily in the temple; but the chief priests
and the scribes and the leading men among the people [b]were trying
to destroy Him,
48 and they could not find [1]anything that they might do, for all the
people were hanging upon [2]His words.

Chapter 20

20 [a]And it came about on one of the days while [b]He was teaching
the people in the temple and [c]preaching the gospel, that the
chief priests and the scribes with the elders [d]confronted *Him*,
2 and they spoke, saying to Him, "Tell us by what authority You
are doing these things, or who is the one who gave You this
authority?"
3 And He answered and said to them, "I shall also ask you a
[1]question, and you tell Me:
4 "Was the baptism of John from heaven or from men?"
5 And they reasoned among themselves, saying, "If we say, 'From
heaven,' He will say, 'Why did you not believe him?'
6 "But if we say, 'From men,' all the people will stone us to death,
for they are convinced that John was a [a]prophet."

33 [1]Lit., *lords*

[a]Luke 19:35-38: [M]att. 21:4-9; Mark [...]0; John 12:12-15

[...]Lit., *as they were* [...]ng [2]Or, *works of* [a]Matt. 21:1; Luke [...]:29 [b]Luke 18:43

[...]s. 118:26 [b]Matt. [...]5:34 [c]Matt. 21:9; Luke 2:14

[1]Lit., *from* [a]Matt. 21:15f.

40 [a]Hab. 2:11

[a]Luke 13:34, 35

[...], *and* [2]I.e., a dirt mound for siege [...]oses [a]Eccl. 9:14; [...]; 37:33; Jer. 6:6; [...] 4:2; 26:8 [b]Luke 21:20

[a]Matt. 24:2; Mark [...] Luke 21:6 [b]1 Pet. 2:12

[a]Luke 19:45, 46: [...]. 21:12, 13; Mark [...]17; John 2:13-16

[...], *cave* [a]Is. 56:7; [...]7:11; Matt. 21:13; [...] 11:17 [b]Jer. 7:11

[...]Matt. 26:55; Luke [...]:37 [b]Luke 20:19

[4]8 [1]Lit., *what they* [mi]*ght do* [2]Lit., *Him, listening*

[2]0:1 [a]Luke 20:1-8: [Ma]tt. 21:23-27; Mark [...]7-33 [b]Matt. 26:55 [Lu]ke 8:1 [d]Acts 4:1; 6:12

3 [1]Lit., *word*

[a]Matt. 11:9; Luke 7:29, 30

7 And they answered that they did not know where *it came* from.
8 And Jesus said to them, "Neither [1]will I tell you by what
authority I do these things."
9 [a]And He began to tell the people this parable: "A man planted a
vineyard and rented it out to [1]vine-growers, and went on a journey
for a long time.
10 "And at the *harvest* time he sent a slave to the vine-growers, in
order that they might give him *some* of the produce of the vineyard;
but the vine-growers beat him and sent him away empty-handed.
11 "And he proceeded to send another slave; and they beat him also
and treated him shamefully, and sent him away empty-handed.
12 "And he proceeded to send a third; and this one also they
wounded and cast out.
13 "And the [1]owner of the vineyard said, 'What shall I do? I will
send my beloved son; perhaps they will [a]respect him.'
14 "But when the vine-growers saw him, they reasoned with one
another, saying, 'This is the heir; let us kill him that the inheritance
may be ours.'
15 "And they threw him out of the vineyard and killed him. What,
therefore, will the [1]owner of the vineyard do to them?
16 "He will come and [a]destroy these vine-growers and will give the
vineyard to others." And when they heard it, they said, "[b]May it
never be!"
17 But He looked at them and said, "What then is this that is writ-
ten,

'[a]THE STONE WHICH THE BUILDERS REJECTED,
THIS BECAME [b]THE CHIEF CORNER *stone*'?

18 "[a]Everyone who falls on that stone will be broken to pieces; but
on whomever it falls, it will scatter him like dust."
19 And the scribes and the chief priests [a]tried to lay hands on Him
that very hour, and they feared the people; for they understood that
He spoke this parable against them.
20 [a]And they watched Him, and sent spies who [1]pretended to be
righteous, in order [b]that they might [2]catch Him in some statement, so
as to deliver Him up to the rule and the authority of [c]the governor.
21 And they questioned Him, saying, "Teacher, we know that You
speak and teach correctly, and You [1]are not partial to any, but teach
the way of God in truth.
22 "Is it [1]lawful for us [a]to pay taxes to Caesar, or not?"
23 But He detected their trickery and said to them,
24 "Show Me a [1]denarius. Whose [2]likeness and inscription does it
have?" And they said, "Caesar's."
25 And He said to them, "Then [a]render to Caesar the things that are
Caesar's, and to God the things that are God's."
26 And they were unable to [1a]catch Him in a saying in the presence
of the people; and marveling at His answer, they became silent.
27 [a]Now there came to Him some of the [b]Sadducees (who say that
there is no resurrection),
28 and they questioned Him, saying, "Teacher, Moses wrote for us
that [a]IF A MAN'S BROTHER DIES, having a wife, AND HE IS CHILDLESS, HIS
BROTHER SHOULD TAKE THE WIFE AND RAISE UP OFFSPRING TO HIS BROTHER.
29 "Now there were seven brothers; and the first took a wife, and
died childless;
30 and the second

8 [1]Lit., *do I*

9 [1]Or, *tena*... also vv. 10, [a]Luke 20:9-... *21:33-46; M*...

13 [1]Lit., *lord*

15 [1]Lit., *lord*

16 [a]Matt. 21... 12:9; Luke 1... 3:4, 6, 31; 6:... 13; 9:14; 11:... 6:15; Gal. 2:1... 6:14

17 [a]Ps. 118:... 2:20; 1 Pet. 2...

18 [a]Matt. 21:...

19 [a]Luke 19:...

20 [1]Lit., *feign themselves* [2]... *hold of His w*... 20:20-26: *Ma*... *22:15-22; Mar*... *12:13-17;* Mar... [b]Luke 11:54; 2... [c]Matt. 27:2

21 [1]Lit., *do no*... *a face*

22 [1]Or, *permis*... [a]Matt. 17:25; L...

24 [1]The denari... equivalent to o... wage [2]Lit., *ima*...

25 [a]Matt. 22:21... 12:17

26 [1]Lit., *take h*... *saying* [a]Luke 1...

27 [a]Luke 20:27-... *Matt. 22:23-33;* ... *12:18-27* [b]Acts ...

28 [a]Deut. 25:5

31 and the third took her; and in the same way [1]all seven [2]died, leaving no children.
32 "Finally the woman died also.
33 "In the resurrection therefore, which one's wife will she be? For [1]all seven had her as wife."
34 And Jesus said to them, "The sons of [a]this age marry and are given in marriage,
35 but those who are considered worthy to attain to [a]that age and the resurrection from the dead, neither marry, nor are given in marriage;
36 for neither can they die anymore, for they are like angels, and are [a]sons of God, being sons of the resurrection.
37 "But that the dead are raised, even Moses showed, in [a]the *passage about the burning* bush, where he calls the Lord [b]THE GOD OF ABRAHAM, AND THE GOD OF ISAAC, AND THE GOD OF JACOB.
38 "[a]Now He is not the God of the dead, but of the living; for [b]all live to Him."
39 And some of the scribes answered and said, "Teacher, You have spoken well."
40 For [a]they did not have courage to question Him any longer about anything.
41 [a]And He said to them, "How *is it that* they say [1]the Christ is [b]David's son?
42 "For David himself says in the book of Psalms,
'[a]THE LORD SAID TO MY LORD,
"SIT AT MY RIGHT HAND,
43 [a]UNTIL I MAKE THINE ENEMIES A FOOTSTOOL FOR THY FEET." '
44 "David therefore calls Him 'Lord,' and how is He his son?"
45 [a]And while all the people were listening, He said to the disciples,
46 "Beware of the scribes, [a]who like to walk around in long robes, and love respectful greetings in the market places, and chief seats in the synagogues, and places of honor at banquets,
47 who devour widows' houses, and for appearance's sake offer long prayers; these will receive greater condemnation."

Chapter 21

21 [a]And He looked up and saw the rich putting their gifts into the treasury.
2 And He saw a certain poor widow putting [1]in [a]two [2]small copper coins.
3 And He said, "Truly I say to you, this poor widow put in more than all *of them;*
4 for they all out of their [1]surplus put into the [2]offering; but she out of her poverty put in all [3]that she had [a]to live on."
5 [a]And while some were talking about the temple, that it was adorned with beautiful stones and votive gifts, He said,
6 "*As for* these things which you are looking at, the days will come in which [a]there will not be left one stone upon another which will not be torn down."
7 And they questioned Him, saying, "Teacher, when therefore will these things be? And what *will be* the [1]sign when these things are about to take place?"
8 And He said, "See to it that you be not misled; for many will

t., *the seven also* ., *left no children, and died*
33 [1]Lit., *the*
Matt. 12:32; Luke 16:8
Matt. 12:32; Luke 16:8
m. 8:16f.; 1 John 3:1, 2
k 12:26 [b]Ex. 3:6
Matt. 22:32; Mark 2:27 [b]Rom. 14:8
Matt. 22:46; Luke 14:6
I.e., the Messiah
e 20:41-44: *Matt. 22:41-46; Mark 5-37* [b]Matt. 9:27
42 [a]Ps. 110:1
43 [a]Ps. 110:1
[a]Luke 20:45-47: *att. 23:1-7; Mark 12:38-40*
Luke 11:43; 14:7
1 [a]Luke 21:1-4: *Mark 12:41-44*
Or, *therein* [2]Gr., *ota* [a]Mark 12:42
abundance [2]Lit., *t., the living that ad* [a]Mark 12:44
e 21:5-36: *Matt. 24; Mark 13*
6 [a]Luke 19:44
attesting miracle

See the illustration of Herod's temple on page I-22.

come in My name, saying, '[a]I am *He*,' and, 'The time is at hand'; [b]do
not go after them.
9 "And when you hear of wars and disturbances, do not be ter-
rified; for these things must take place first, but the end *does* not
follow immediately."
10 Then He continued by saying to them, "Nation will rise against
nation, and kingdom against kingdom,
11 and there will be great earthquakes, and in various places
plagues and famines; and there will be terrors and great [1]signs from
heaven.
12 "But before all these things, [a]they will lay their hands on you and
will persecute you, delivering you to the synagogues and prisons,
[1]bringing you before kings and governors for My name's sake.
13 "[a]It will lead to [1]an opportunity for your testimony.
14 "[a]So make up your minds not to prepare beforehand to defend
yourselves;
15 for [a]I will give you [1]utterance and wisdom which none of your
opponents will be able to resist or refute.
16 "But you will be delivered up even by parents and brothers and
relatives and friends, and they will put *some* of you to death,
17 and you will be hated by all on account of My name.
18 "Yet [a]not a hair of your head will perish.
19 "[a]By your endurance you will gain your [1]lives.
20 "But when you see Jerusalem [a]surrounded by armies, then [1]recog-
nize that her desolation is at hand.
21 "Then let those who are in Judea flee to the mountains, and let
those who are in the midst of [1]the city depart, and [a]let not those who
are in the country enter [1]the city;
22 because these are [a]days of vengeance, in order that all things
which are written may be fulfilled.
23 "Woe to those who are with child and to those who nurse babes in
those days; for [a]there will be great distress upon the [1]land, and wrath
to this people,
24 and they will fall by [a]the edge of the sword, and will be led
captive into all the nations; and [b]Jerusalem will be [c]trampled under
foot by the Gentiles until [d]the times of the Gentiles be fulfilled.
25 "And there will be [1]signs in sun and moon and stars, and upon
the earth dismay among nations, in perplexity at the roaring of the
sea and the waves,
26 men fainting from fear and the expectation of the things which
are coming upon the [1]world; for the powers of [2]the heavens will be
shaken.
27 "And [a]then they will see [b]THE SON OF MAN COMING IN A CLOUD with
power and great glory.
28 "But when these things begin to take place, straighten up and lift
up your heads, because [a]your redemption is drawing near."
29 And He told them a parable: "Behold the fig tree and all the
trees;
30 as soon as they put forth *leaves*, you see it and [a]know for your-
selves that summer is now near.
31 "Even so you, too, when you see these things happening, [1]recog-
nize that [a]the kingdom of God is near.
32 "Truly I say to you, this [1]generation will not pass away until all
things take place.

8 [a]John 8:24 17:23

11 [1]Or, *attesti* *miracles*

12 [1]Lit., *being* [a]Luke 21:12-17 *10:19-22; Mark*

13 [1]Lit., *a testi* *you* [a]Phil. 1:12

14 [a]Luke 12:11

15 [1]Lit., *a mou* 12:12

18 [a]Matt. 10:30 12:7

19 [1]Or, *soul* [a]M 10:22; 24:13; Ro 5:3f.; Heb. 10:36 James 1:3; 2 Pe

20 [1]Lit., *know* 19:43

21 [1]Lit., *her* [a]Lu 17:31

22 [a]Is. 63:4; Da 9:24-27; Hos. 9:

23 [1]Or, *earth* 8:19; 1 Cor. 7:26

24 [a]Gen. 34:26 17:13; Heb. 11:3 63:18; Dan. 8:1 11:2 [d]Rom. 11:2

25 [1]Or, *attestin* *miracles*

26 [1]Lit., *inhabit* [2]Or, *heaven*

27 [a]Matt. 16:27 26:64; Mark 13: [b]Dan. 7:13; Rev

28 [a]Luke 18:7

30 [a]Luke 12:57

31 [1]Lit., *know*

32 [1]Or, *race*

33 "[a]Heaven and earth will pass away, but My words will not pass
away.
34 "[a]Be on guard, that your hearts may not be weighted down with
dissipation and drunkenness and the worries of life, and that day
come on you suddenly like a trap;
35 for it will come upon all those who dwell on the face of all the
earth.
36 "But [a]keep on the alert at all times, praying in order that you may
have strength to escape all these things that are about to take place,
and to [b]stand before the Son of Man."
37 Now [1]during the day He was [a]teaching in the temple, but [2b]at
evening He would go out and spend the night on [3c]the mount that is
called [4]Olivet.
38 And all the people would get up [a]early in the morning *to come* to
Him in the temple to listen to Him.

Chapter 22

22 [a]Now the Feast of Unleavened Bread, which is called the
[b]Passover, was approaching.
2 And the chief priests and the scribes [a]were seeking how they
might put Him to death; for they were afraid of the people.
3 [a]And [b]Satan entered into Judas who was called Iscariot, [1]belong-
ing to the number of the twelve.
4 And he went away and discussed with the chief priests and
[a]officers how he might betray Him to them.
5 And they were glad, and agreed to give him money.
6 And he consented, and *began* seeking a good opportunity to
betray Him to them [1]apart from the multitude.
7 [a]Then came the *first* day of Unleavened Bread on which [b]the
Passover *lamb* had to be sacrificed.
8 And He sent [a]Peter and John, saying, "Go and prepare the Pass-
over for us, that we may eat it."
9 And they said to Him, "Where do You want us to prepare it?"
10 And He said to them, "Behold, when you have entered the city, a
man will meet you carrying a pitcher of water; follow him into the
house that he enters.
11 "And you shall say to the owner of the house, 'The Teacher says
to you, "Where is the guest room in which I may eat the Passover
with My disciples?"'
12 "And he will show you a large, furnished, upper room; prepare it
there."
13 And they departed and found *everything* just as He had told
them; and they prepared the Passover.
14 [a]And when the hour had come He reclined *at the table,* and [b]the
apostles with Him.
15 And He said to them, "I have earnestly desired to eat this Pass-
over with you before I suffer;
16 for I say to you, I shall never again eat it [a]until it is fulfilled in the
kingdom of God."
17 [a]And when He had taken a cup *and* [b]given thanks, He said,
"Take this and share it among yourselves;
18 for [a]I say to you, I will not drink of the fruit of the vine from now
on until the kingdom of God comes."
19 And when He had taken *some* bread *and* [a]given thanks, He broke

[a]Matt. 5:18; Luke 16:17
[a]Matt. 24:42-44; :19; Luke 12:40, ;5; 1 Thess. 5:2ff.
lark 13:33; Luke [b]Luke 1:19; Rev. 7:9; 8:2; 11:4
[1]Lit., *days* [2]Lit., [3]Or, *the hill* [4]Or, *ve Grove* [a]Matt. :55; Luke 19:47 :19 [c]Matt. 21:1
38 [a]John 8:2
[a]Luke 22:1, 2: *:2-5; Mark 14:1,* 12:1-27 [b]John 11:55; 13:1
2 [a]Matt. 12:14
being of [a]Luke *Matt. 26:14-16; 4:10, 11* [b]Matt.); John 13:2, 27
Chr. 9:11; Neh. uke 22:52; Acts 4:1; 5:24, 26
[1]Or, *without a disturbance*
22:7-13: *Matt. 26:17-19; Mark 6* [b]Mark 14:12
ts 3:1, 11; 4:13, ; 8:14; Gal. 2:9
att. 26:20; Mark :17 [b]Mark 6:30
e 14:15; 22:18, 30; Rev. 19:9
Luke 22:17-20: *26:26-29; Mark 4:22-25;* 1 Cor. 5; 1 Cor. 10:16 [b]Matt. 14:19
att. 26:29; Mark 14:25
9 [a]Matt. 14:19

it, and gave *it* to them, saying, "This is My body [1]which is given for
you; do this in remembrance of Me."
20 And in the same way *He took* the cup after they had eaten,
saying, "This cup which is [a]poured out for you is the [b]new covenant
in My blood.
21 "[a]But behold, the hand of the one betraying Me is with Me on the
table.
22 "For indeed, the Son of Man is going [a]as it has been determined;
but woe to that man by whom He is betrayed!"
23 And they began to discuss among themselves which one of them
it might be who was going to do this thing.
24 And there arose also [a]a dispute among them *as to* which one of
them was regarded to be greatest.
25 [a]And He said to them, "The kings of the Gentiles lord it over
them; and those who have authority over them are called 'Benefac-
tors.'
26 "But not so with you, [a]but let him who is the greatest among you
become as [b]the youngest, and the leader as the servant.
27 "For [a]who is greater, the one who reclines *at the table,* or the one
who serves? Is it not the one who reclines *at the table*? But [b]I am
among you as the one who serves.
28 "And you are those who have stood by Me in My [a]trials;
29 and just as My Father has granted Me a [a]kingdom, I grant you
30 that you may [a]eat and drink at My table in My [b]kingdom, and
[c]you will sit on thrones judging the twelve tribes of Israel.
31 "Simon, Simon, behold, [a]Satan has [1]demanded *permission* to [b]sift
you like wheat;
32 but I [a]have prayed for you, that your faith may not fail; and you,
when once you have turned again, [b]strengthen your brothers."
33 [a]And he said to Him, "Lord, with You I am ready to go both to
prison and to death!"
34 And He said, "I say to you, Peter, the cock will not crow today
until you have denied three times that you know Me."
35 And He said to them, "[a]When I sent you out without purse and
bag and sandals, you did not lack anything, did you?" And they
said, "*No,* nothing."
36 And He said to them, "But now, let him who has a purse take it
along, likewise also a bag, and let him who has no sword sell his
[1]robe and buy one.
37 "For I tell you, that this which is written must be fulfilled in Me,
'[a]AND HE WAS NUMBERED WITH TRANSGRESSORS'; for [b]that which refers to
Me has *its* fulfillment."
38 And they said, "Lord, look, here are two [a]swords." And He said
to them, "It is enough."
39 [a]And He came out and proceeded [b]as was His custom to [c]the
Mount of Olives; and the disciples also followed Him.
40 [a]And when He arrived at the place, He said to them, "[b]Pray that
you may not enter into temptation."
41 And He withdrew from them about a stone's throw, and He
[a]knelt down and *began* to pray,
42 saying, "Father, if Thou art willing, remove this [a]cup from Me;
[b]yet not My will, but Thine be done."
43 [1]Now an [a]angel from heaven appeared to Him, strengthening
Him.

19 [1]Some do not cont remainder any of v. 20
20 [a]Matt. 2 14:24 [b]Ex. 31:31; 1 Co 2 Cor. 3:6; 9:15
21 [a]Luke 2 *Matt. 26:21 14:18-21;* P John 13:18,
22 [a]Acts 2: 10:42; 17:31
24 [a]Mark 9: 9:46
25 [a]Luke 22 *Matt. 20:25- 10:42-45*
26 [a]Matt. 23 9:35; Luke 9 5:5
27 [a]Luke 12 20:28; John
28 [a]Heb. 2:1
29 [a]Matt. 5:3 2:12
30 [a]Luke 22: 5:3; 2 Tim. 2: 19:28
31 [1]Or, *obtai asking* [a]Job 2:1-6; Matt. 4 9:9
32 [a]John 17: [b]John 21:15-1
33 [a]Luke 22: *Matt. 26:33-3 14:29-31; Joh*
35 [a]Matt. 10: 6:8; Luke 9:3ff
36 [1]Or, *outer*
37 [a]Is. 53:12 17:4; 19:30
38 [a]Luke 22:3
39 [a]Matt. 26:3 14:26; John 18 21:37 [c]Matt. 2
40 [a]Luke 22:4 *Matt. 26:36-46 14:32-42* [b]Mat Luke 22:46
41 [a]Matt. 26:3 14:35; Luke 18
42 [a]Matt. 20:2 26:39
43 [1]Some anc do not contain and 44 [a]Matt.

44 And [a]being in agony He was praying very fervently; and His
sweat became like drops of blood, falling down upon the ground.
45 And when He rose from prayer, He came to the disciples and
found them sleeping from sorrow,
46 and said to them, "Why are you sleeping? Rise and [a]pray that
you may not enter into temptation."
47 [a]While He was still speaking, behold, a multitude *came,* and the
one called Judas, one of the twelve, was preceding them; and he
approached Jesus to kiss Him.
48 But Jesus said to him, "Judas, are you betraying the Son of Man
with a kiss?"
49 And when those who were around Him saw what was going to
happen, they said, "Lord, shall we strike with the [a]sword?"
50 And a certain one of them struck the slave of the high priest and
cut off his right ear.
51 But Jesus answered and said, "[1]Stop! No more of this." And He
touched his ear and healed him.
52 And Jesus said to the chief priests and [a]officers of the temple and
elders who had come against Him, "Have you come out with
swords and clubs [b]as against a robber?
53 "While I was with you daily in the temple, you did not lay hands
on Me; but [1]this hour and the power of darkness are yours."
54 [a]And having arrested Him, they led Him *away,* and brought Him
to the house of the high priest; but [b]Peter was following at a distance.
55 [a]And after they had kindled a fire in the middle of [b]the courtyard
and had sat down together, Peter was sitting among them.
56 And a certain servant-girl, seeing him as he sat in the firelight,
and looking intently at him, said, "This man was with Him too."
57 But he denied *it,* saying, "Woman, I do not know Him."
58 And a little later, [a]another saw him and said, "You are *one* of
them too!" But Peter said, "Man, I am not!"
59 And after about an hour had passed, another man *began* to insist,
saying, "Certainly this man also was with Him, [a]for he is a Galilean
too."
60 But Peter said, "Man, I do not know what you are talking
about." And immediately, while he was still speaking, a cock
crowed.
61 And [a]the Lord turned and looked at Peter. And Peter remem-
bered the word of the Lord, how He had told him, "[b]Before a cock
crows today, you will deny Me three times."
62 And he went out and wept bitterly.
63 [a]And the men who were holding [1]Jesus in custody were mocking
Him, and beating Him,
64 and they blindfolded Him and were asking Him, saying,
"[a]Prophesy, who is the one who hit You?"
65 And they were saying many other things against Him, [a]blas-
pheming.
66 [a]And when it was day, [b]the [1]Council of elders of the people as-
sembled, both chief priests and scribes, and they led Him away to
their [c]council *chamber,* saying,
67 "[a]If You are the [1]Christ, tell us." But He said to them, "If I tell you,
you will not believe;
68 and if I ask a question, you will not answer.

44 [a]Heb. 5:7
46 [a]Luke 22:40
[a]Luke 22:47-53: *. 26:47-56; Mark* *50; John 18:3-11*
49 [a]Luke 22:38
"Let Me at least and He touched
Luke 22:4 [b]Luke 22:37
[1]Lit., *this is your our and power of darkness*
Matt. 26:57; Mark 53 [b]Matt. 26:58; 4:54; John 18:15
[a]Luke 22:55-62: *. 26:69-75; Mark 14:66-72; John 18, 25-27* [b]Matt. 26:3
58 [a]John 18:26
Matt. 26:73; Mark 14:70
Luke 7:13 [b]Luke 22:34
[1]Lit., *Him* [a]Matt. 67f.; Mark 14:65; John 18:22f.
Matt. 26:68; Mark 14:65
65 [a]Matt. 27:39
[1]Or, *Sanhedrin* 7:1f.; Mark 15:1; 8:28 [b]Acts 22:5 [c]Matt. 5:22
Messiah [a]Matt. 26:63-66; Mark 14:61-63; Luke ; John 18:19-21

69 "[a]But from now on [b]THE SON OF MAN WILL BE SEATED AT THE RIGHT
HAND of the power OF GOD."
70 And they all said, "Are You [a]the Son of God, then?" And He said
to them, "[1b]Yes, I am."
71 And they said, "What further need do we have of testimony? For
we have heard it ourselves from His own mouth."

Chapter 23

23 Then the whole body of them arose and [a]brought Him before
Pilate.
2 [a]And they began to accuse Him, saying, "We found this man
[b]misleading our nation and [c]forbidding to pay taxes to Caesar, and
saying that He Himself is [1]Christ, a King."
3 And Pilate asked Him, saying, "Are You the King of the Jews?"
And He answered him and said, "[a]*It is as* you say."
4 And Pilate said to the chief priests and the multitudes, "[a]I find
no guilt in this man."
5 But they kept on insisting, saying, "He stirs up the people, teach-
ing all over Judea, [a]starting from Galilee, even as far as this place."
6 But when Pilate heard it, he asked whether the man was a
Galilean.
7 And when he learned that He belonged to Herod's jurisdiction,
he sent Him to [a]Herod, who himself also was in Jerusalem [1]at that
time.
8 Now Herod was very glad when he saw Jesus; for [a]he had
wanted to see Him for a long time, because he had been hearing
about Him and was hoping to see some [1]sign performed by Him.
9 And he questioned Him [1]at some length; but [a]He answered him
nothing.
10 And the chief priests and the scribes were standing there, accus-
ing Him vehemently.
11 And Herod with his soldiers, after treating Him with contempt
and mocking Him, [a]dressed Him in a gorgeous robe and sent Him
back to Pilate.
12 Now [a]Herod and Pilate became friends with one another that
very day; for before they had been at enmity with each other.
13 And Pilate summoned the chief priests and the [a]rulers and the
people,
14 and said to them, "You brought this man to me as one
who [a]incites the people to rebellion, and behold, having
examined Him before you, I [b]have found no guilt in this
man regarding the charges which you make against Him.
15 "No, nor has [a]Herod, for he sent Him back to us; and
behold, nothing deserving death has been done by Him.
16 "I will therefore [a]punish Him and release Him."
17 [[1]Now he was obliged to release to them at the feast
one prisoner.]
18 But they cried out all together, saying, "[a]Away with
this man, and release for us Barabbas!"
19 (He was one who had been thrown into prison for a
certain insurrection made in the city, and for murder.)
20 And Pilate, wanting to release Jesus, addressed them
again,
21 but they kept on calling out, saying, "Crucify, crucify
Him!"

Jerusalem of New Testament

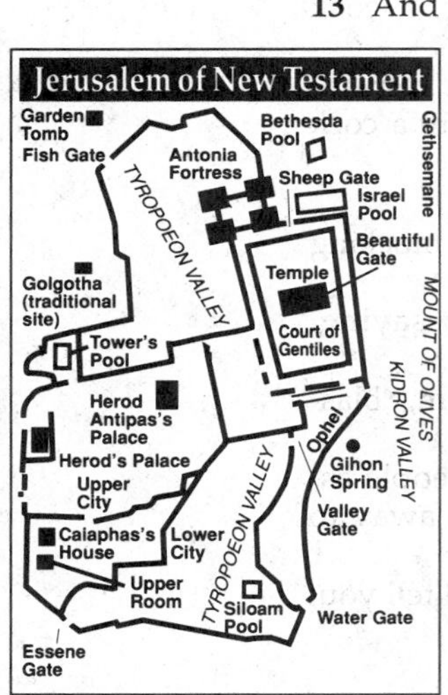

69 [a]Matt. 26
14:62; 16:19
70 [1]Lit., *You
am* [a]Matt. 4:
26:64; 27:11;
23:1 [a]Matt. 2
15:1; John 18
2 [1]I.e., Mess
23:2, 3: *Matt.
Mark 15:2-5;
18:29-37* [b]Lu
[c]Luke 20:22;
18:33ff.; 19:1
3 [a]Luke 22:7
4 [a]Matt. 27:2
15:14; Luke 2
John 18:38;
5 [a]Matt. 4:12
7 [1]Lit., *in the*
[a]Matt. 14:1;
Luke 3:1; 9:7
8 [1]Or, *attest*
[a]Luke 9:9
9 [1]Lit., *in ma*
[a]Matt. 27:12,
15:5; John 1
11 [a]Matt. 27
12 [a]Acts 4:2
13 [a]Luke 23
7:26, 48; 12:
3:17; 4:5, 8;
14 [a]Luke 23
23:4
15 [a]Luke 9:
16 [a]Matt. 27
15:15; Luke
19:1; Acts 16
17 [1]Many m
contain this
18 [a]Luke 23
*Matt. 27:15-
15:6-15*; Joh
18:39-19:16

22 And he said to them the third time, "Why, what evil has this man done? I have found in Him no guilt *demanding* death; I will therefore [a]punish Him and release Him."
23 But they were insistent, with loud voices asking that He be crucified. And their voices *began* to prevail.
24 And Pilate pronounced sentence that their demand should be granted.
25 And he released the man they were asking for who had been thrown into prison for insurrection and murder, but he delivered Jesus to their will.
26 [a]And when they led Him away, they laid hold of one Simon of [b]Cyrene, coming in from the country, and placed on him the cross to carry behind Jesus.
27 And there were following Him a great multitude of the people, and of women who were [1a]mourning and lamenting Him.
28 But Jesus turning to them said, "Daughters of Jerusalem, stop weeping for Me, but weep for yourselves and for your children.
29 "For behold, the days are coming when they will say, '[a]Blessed are the barren, and the wombs that never bore, and the breasts that never nursed.'
30 "Then they will begin TO [a]SAY TO THE MOUNTAINS, 'FALL ON US,' AND TO THE HILLS, 'COVER US.'
31 "For if they do these things in the green tree, what will happen in the dry?"
32 [a]And two others also, who were criminals, were being led away to be put to death with Him.
33 [a]And when they came to the place called [1]The Skull, there they crucified Him and the criminals, one on the right and the other on the left.
34 [1]But Jesus was saying, "[a]Father, forgive them; for they do not know what they are doing." [b]And they cast lots, dividing up His garments among themselves.
35 And the people stood by, looking on. And even the [a]rulers were sneering at Him, saying, "He saved others; [b]let Him save Himself if this is the [1]Christ of God, His Chosen One."
36 And the soldiers also mocked Him, coming up to Him, [a]offering Him sour wine,
37 and saying, "[a]If You are the King of the Jews, save Yourself!"
38 Now there was also an inscription above Him, "[a]THIS IS THE KING OF THE JEWS."
39 [a]And one of the criminals who were hanged *there* was [1]hurling abuse at Him, saying, "Are You not the [2]Christ? [b]Save Yourself and us!"
40 But the other answered, and rebuking him said, "Do you not even fear God, since you are under the same sentence of condemnation?
41 "And we indeed justly, for we are receiving [1]what we deserve for our deeds; but this man has done nothing wrong."
42 And he was saying, "Jesus, remember me when You come [1]in Your kingdom!"
43 And He said to him, "Truly I say to you, today you shall be with Me in [a]Paradise."
44 [a]And it was now about [1b]the sixth hour, and darkness [2]fell over the whole land until [3]the ninth hour,

22 [a]Luke 23:16
.uke 23:26: *Matt.* *Mark 15:21;* John :17 [b]Matt. 27:32
[1]Lit., *beating the* *reast* [a]Luke 8:52
Matt. 24:19; Luke 11:27; 21:23
s. 10:8; Is. 2:19, 20; Rev. 6:16
Matt. 27:38; Mark 5:27; John 19:18
Lat., *Calvarius;* *, Calvary* [a]Luke 23:33-43: *Matt. 27:33-44; Mark* *2; John 19:17-24*
ome mss. do not *But Jesus was . . . doing.* [a]Matt. .uke 22:42 [b]Ps. 2:18; John 19:24
Messiah [a]Luke 13 [b]Matt. 27:43
36 [a]Matt. 27:48
37 [a]Matt. 27:43
att. 27:37; Mark :26; John 19:19
Or, *blaspheming* Messiah [a]Matt. ark 15:32; Luke 23:39-43 [b]Luke 23:35, 37
t., *things worthy* *at we have done*
42 [1]Or, *into*
r. 12:4; Rev. 2:7
., 12 noon [2]Or, *red* [3]I.e., 3 p.m. 23:44-49: *Matt. 27:45-56; Mark* *41* [b]John 19:14

45 the sun [1]being obscured; and [a]the veil of the temple was torn [2]in two.
46 And Jesus, [a]crying out with a loud voice, said, "Father, [b]INTO THY HANDS I COMMIT MY SPIRIT." And having said this, He breathed His last.
47 [a]Now when the centurion saw what had happened, he *began* [b]praising God, saying, "Certainly this man was [1]innocent."
48 And all the multitudes who came together for this spectacle, when they observed what had happened, *began* to return, [a]beating their breasts.
49 [a]And all His acquaintances and [a]the women who accompanied Him from Galilee, were standing at a distance, seeing these things.
50 [a]And behold, a man named Joseph, who was a [b]member of the Council, a good and righteous man
51 (he had not consented to their plan and action), *a man* from Arimathea, a city of the Jews, who was [a]waiting for the kingdom of God;
52 this man went to Pilate and asked for the body of Jesus.
53 And he took it down and wrapped it in a linen cloth, and laid Him in a tomb cut into the rock, where no one had ever lain.
54 And it was [a]the preparation day, and the Sabbath was about to [1]begin.
55 Now [a]the women who had come with Him out of Galilee followed after, and saw the tomb and how His body was laid.
56 And they returned and [a]prepared spices and perfumes.
And [b]on the Sabbath they rested according to the commandment.

Chapter 24

24 [a]But on the first day of the week, at early dawn, they came to the tomb, bringing the spices which they had prepared.
2 And they found the stone rolled away from the tomb,
3 but when they entered, they did not find the body of [a]the Lord Jesus.
4 And it happened that while they were perplexed about this, behold, [a]two men suddenly [b]stood near them in dazzling apparel;
5 and as *the women* were terrified and bowed their faces to the ground, *the men* said to them, "Why do you seek the living One among the dead?
6 "[1]He is not here, but He [a]has [2]risen. Remember how He spoke to you [b]while He was still in Galilee,
7 saying that [a]the Son of Man must be delivered into the hands of sinful men, and be crucified, and the third day rise again."
8 And [a]they remembered His words,
9 and returned from the tomb and reported all these things to the eleven and to all the rest.
10 Now they were [a]Mary Magdalene and Joanna and Mary the *mother* of James; also the other women with them were telling these things to [b]the apostles.
11 And these words appeared [1]to them as nonsense, and they [a]would not believe them.
12 [[1]But Peter arose and [a]ran to the tomb; stooping and looking in, he *saw the linen wrappings [2]only; and he went away [b]to his home, marveling at that which had happened.]

45 [1]Lit., *fai*
the middle
26:31-33; M

46 [a]Matt. 2
15:37; John
31:5

47 [1]Lit., *rig*
[a]Matt. 27:54
15:39 [b]Matt

48 [a]Luke 8:

49 [a]Matt. 27
15:40f.; Luke
19:25

50 [a]Luke 23
Matt. 27:57-
15:42-47; Jo
19:38-42 [b]M

51 [a]Mark 15
2:25

54 [1]Lit., *daw*
27:62; Mark

55 [a]Luke 23:

56 [a]Mark 16
24:1 [b]Ex. 20:
5:14

24:1 [a]Luke 2
Matt. 28:1-8;
16:1-8; John

3 [a]Luke 7:13;

4 [a]John 20:12
2:9; Acts 12:7

6 [1]Some anci
do not contain
here, but He h
[2]Or, *been raise*
16:6 [b]Matt. 17
Mark 9:30f.; Lu
24:44

7 [a]Matt. 16:21
24:46

8 [a]John 2:22

10 [a]Matt. 27:5
6:30

11 [1]Lit., *in thei*
[a]Mark 16:11

12 [1]Some anci
do not contain v
[2]Or, *by themsel*
[a]John 20:3-6 [b]
20:10

13 And behold, [a]two of them were going that very day to a village
named Emmaus, which was [1]about seven miles from Jerusalem.
14 And they were conversing with each other about all these things
which had taken place.
15 And it came about that while they were conversing and discuss-
ing, Jesus Himself approached, and *began* traveling with them.
16 But [a]their eyes [1]were prevented from recognizing Him.
17 And He said to them, "What are these words that you are ex-
changing with one another as you are walking?" And they stood
still, looking sad.
18 And one of them, named Cleopas, answered and said to Him,
"Are You [1]the only one visiting Jerusalem and unaware of the things
which have happened here in these days?"
19 And He said to them, "What things?" And they said to Him,
"The things about [a]Jesus the Nazarene, who was a [b]prophet mighty
in deed and word in the sight of God and all the people,
20 and how the chief priests and our [a]rulers delivered Him up to
the sentence of death, and crucified Him.
21 "But we were hoping that it was He who was going to [a]redeem
Israel. Indeed, besides all this, it is the third day since these things
happened.
22 "But also some women among us amazed us. [a]When they were at
the tomb early in the morning,
23 and did not find His body, they came, saying that they had also
seen a vision of angels, who said that He was alive.
24 "And some of those who were with us went to the tomb and
found it just exactly as the women also had said; but Him they did
not see."
25 And He said to them, "O foolish men and slow of heart to
believe in all that [a]the prophets have spoken!
26 "[a]Was it not necessary for the [1]Christ to suffer these things and to
enter into His glory?"
27 And beginning [1]with [a]Moses and [1]with all the [b]prophets, He
explained to them the things concerning Himself in all the Scrip-
tures.
28 And they approached the village where they were going, and
[a]He acted as though He would go farther.
29 And they urged Him, saying, "Stay with us, for it is *getting*
toward evening, and the day [1]is now nearly over." And He went in
to stay with them.
30 And it came about that when He had reclined *at the table* with
them, He took the bread and [a]blessed *it*, and breaking *it*, He *began*
giving *it* to them.
31 And their [a]eyes were opened and they recognized Him; and He
vanished from [1]their sight.
32 And they said to one another, "[1]Were not our hearts burning
within us while He was speaking to us on the road, while He [a]was
[2]explaining the Scriptures to us?"
33 And they arose that very hour and returned to Jerusalem, and
[a]found gathered together the eleven and [b]those who were with them,
34 saying, "[a]The Lord has really risen, and [b]has appeared to
Simon."
35 And they *began* to relate [1]their experiences on the road and how
[a]He was recognized by them in the breaking of the bread.

e., 60 stadia, one n was about 600 ft. [a]Mark 16:12
[1]Lit., *were being* ted [a]Luke 24:31; John 20:14; 21:4
18 [1]Or, *visiting Jerusalem alone*
Mark 1:24 [b]Matt. 21:11
20 [a]Luke 23:13
21 [a]Luke 1:68
22 [a]Luke 24:1ff.
25 [a]Matt. 26:24
, Messiah [a]Luke 44ff.; Heb. 2:10; 1 Pet. 1:11
[1]Lit., *from* [a]Gen. 12:3; Num. 21:9 :14]; Deut. 18:15 1:45]; John 5:46 [b]2 Sam. 7:12-16; 7:14 [Matt. 1:23]; :1f. [Matt. 4:15f.]; 1 [Matt. 12:18ff.]; 53:4 [Matt. 8:17; 22:37]; Dan. 7:13 t. 24:30] Mic. 5:2 tt. 2:6]; Zech. 9:9 21:5]; Acts 13:27
28 [a]Mark 6:48
29 [1]Lit., *has now declined*
30 [a]Matt. 14:19
[1]Lit., *them* [a]Luke 24:16
[1]Lit., *Was not our* art [2]Lit., *opening* [a]Luke 24:45
lark 16:13 [b]Acts 1:14
uke 24:6 [b]1 Cor. 15:5
[1]Lit., *the things* [a]Luke 24:30f.

36 And while they were telling these things, [a]He Himself stood in
their midst.[1]
37 But they were startled and frightened and thought that they
were seeing [a]a spirit.
38 And He said to them, "Why are you troubled, and why do
doubts arise in your [1]hearts?
39 "[a]See My hands and My feet, that it is I Myself; [b]touch Me and see,
for a spirit does not have flesh and bones as you see that I have."
40 [[1]And when He had said this, He showed them His hands and
His feet.]
41 And while they still [1a]could not believe *it* for joy and were mar-
veling, He said to them, "[b]Have you anything here to eat?"
42 And they gave Him a piece of a broiled fish;
43 and He took it and [a]ate *it* before them.
44 Now He said to them, "[a]These are My words which I spoke to
you while I was still with you, that all things which are written
about Me in the [b]Law of Moses and the Prophets and [c]the Psalms
must be fulfilled."
45 Then He [a]opened their [1]minds to understand the Scriptures,
46 and He said to them, "[a]Thus it is written, that the [1]Christ should
suffer and [b]rise again from the dead the third day;
47 and that [a]repentance [1]for forgiveness of sins should be pro-
claimed [2]in His name to [b]all the nations, beginning from Jerusalem.
48 "You are [a]witnesses of these things.
49 "And behold, [a]I am sending forth the promise of My Father upon
you; but [b]you are to stay in the city until you are clothed with power
from on high."
50 And He led them out as far as [a]Bethany, and He lifted up His
hands and blessed them.
51 And it came about that while He was blessing them, He parted
from them.[1]
52 And they[1] returned to Jerusalem with great joy,
53 and were continually in the temple, [1]praising God.

36 [1]Some ancien… insert *And He sa…* *them, "Peace be…* *you."* [a]Mark 16:14
37 [a]Matt. 14:26; … 6:49
38 [1]Lit., *heart*
39 [a]John 20:20, … [b]John 20:27; 1 Jo…
40 [1]Many mss. d… contain this v.
41 [1]Lit., *were disbelieving* [a]Luk… 24:11 [b]John 21:5
43 [a]Acts 10:41
44 [a]Luke 9:22, 4… 18:31-34; 22:37 … 24:27 [c]Ps. 2:7ff. … 13:33]; Ps. 16:10 … 2:27]; Ps. 22:1-18 … 27:34-46]; Ps. 69 … [John 19:28ff.]; P… 110:1 [Matt. 22:4… 118:22f. [Matt. 21…
45 [1]Lit., *mind* [a]L… 24:32; Acts 16:14 1 John 5:20
46 [1]I.e., Messiah … 24:26, 44 [b]Luke…
47 [1]Some mss. r… *and forgiveness* … *the basis of* [a]Act… 10:43; 13:38; 26:… [b]Matt. 28:19
48 [a]Acts 1:8, 22; … 3:15; 4:33; 5:32; … 41; 13:31; 1 Pet. …
49 [a]John 14:26 … 1:4
50 [a]Matt. 21:17; … 1:12
51 [1]Some mss. … *and was carried* … *heaven*
52 [1]Some mss. … *worshiped Him,* …
53 [1]Lit., *blessing*

of Luke:

IVISIONS

	CHAPTER THEMES
	1
	2
	3
	4
	5
	6
	7
	8
	9
	10
	11
	12
	13
	14
	15
	16
	17
	18
	19
	20
	21
	22
	23
	24

Author:

Date:

Purpose:

Key Words:

kingdom of God

Son of Man

mark every reference to the devil or demons with a red pitchfork

covenant

PREPARATION | PUBLIC MINISTRY | SACRIFICE

OBSCURITY (VANISHING)

POPULARITY (DECLINING)

OPPOSITION (INCREASING)

Period	Event / Reference	Duration	Region
	BIRTH		
	John 1:19ff		
	JOHN INTRODUCES JESUS		
OPENING EVENTS		4 months	
	John 2:13ff		
	JESUS CLEANSES TEMPLE		
EARLY MINISTRIES		8 months	EARLY JUDEAN
	Mark 1:14		
	JESUS RETURNS TO GALILEE		
EXTENDED MINISTRIES		4 months	EARLY GALILEAN
	Luke 6:12ff		
	JESUS ORDAINS THE TWELVE		
EXTENDED MINISTRIES		10 months	MIDDLE GALILEAN
	Matthew 15:21		
	TO TYRE AND SIDON		
SPECIALIZED MINISTRIES		6 months	LATER GALILEAN
	John 7:10		
	TO FEAST OF TABERNACLES		
CONCLUDING MINISTRIES		3 months	LATER JUDEAN
	John 10:40		
	BEYOND JORDAN		
CONCLUDING MINISTRIES		3 months	PEREAN
	Matthew 21:1		
	TRIUMPHAL ENTRY		
	DEATH	2 months	
	RESURRECTION		
	40 days		
	ASCENSION		

5 B.C. — FIRST YEAR — SECOND YEAR — THIRD YEAR

ANNUAL PASSOVERS	John 2:13	John 5:1	John 6:4	John 11:55

Luke	Luke 1	Luke 4:13	Luke 4:14	Luke 6:12	Luke 9:17	Luke 9:18	Luke 9:51	Luke 13:22	Luke 19:28	Luke 24

Used by permission. Jensen, Irving L. Luke: *A Self-Study Guide*. Chicago: Moody Press, 1970.

)HN

d in the flesh! What would He be like? What would He do? How would He live in relationship to .ther once He came to earth? How would people know He was God? Would He force people to e in Him? And what about those who refused to believe He is God?

d what of those who believed, who followed Him? What would God in the flesh expect from And what if they failed?

d in the flesh. It would be hard for some to believe, but their belief or unbelief would be a matter and death.

ree other Gospels had been written. Years had passed. One more Gospel was needed, one which l answer these questions and more. One which would illuminate shadows of doubt. So the e John sat down to write a fourth and final Gospel to explain the one who came to explain the r. It was about A.D. 85.

GS TO DO

Although the author of John is not identified by name, tradition holds that it was the apostle John. Read John 21:20-25 and note how the author identifies himself. You might want to put this reference or information under "Author" on the JOHN AT A GLANCE chart on page 1596.

To understand the purpose of John read John 20:30-31. Record John's purpose on JOHN AT A GLANCE.

ters 1-12

Carefully read this segment chapter by chapter, observing what the author includes to accomplish his purpose.

a. As you read these chapters, look for and mark the following key words and their synonyms: *believe, life, sign, signs, judge, judgment, witness, true, truth, king,* and *kingdom.*

b. You will find it helpful to write down the key words on a card to use as a bookmark. Mark the words on the card in the same way you want to mark them in your Bible.

c. Also mark any repeated key words that are pertinent to the message of the chapter.

As you read each of the first twelve chapters, ask the five W's and an H: Who? What? Where? When? Why? and How? Look specifically for the following, recording whatever facts you find in each chapter in the margin. As you move your findings to the margin, use the headings set in italics below as your headings in the margins and/or fill in the chart on page 1595.

a. *Events:* What is happening? For example, "Nicodemus came to Jesus by night."

b. *Geographic locations:* Where is this event taking place? For example, John was baptizing at Bethany beyond the Jordan.

c. *Timing of events:* When is this event taking place? For example, "on the third day," or "before the feast of the Passover." In the text, mark these mentions of time by drawing a clock such as this . Also, when you read of Jesus attending a feast, consult the chart THE FEASTS OF ISRAEL in the front of this Bible (pages I-48 and I-49).

d. *Portrayals of Christ:* How is Jesus pictured or described? For example: "the Word" and "the Lamb of God."

e. *Signs and Miracles:* The signs that John recorded were for the purpose of leading people to believe that Jesus is the Christ, the Son of God. Look for these signs or miracles. For example, Jesus turned water into wine. The text says, "This was the beginning of His signs."

f. *References that show the deity of Jesus (where and how it shows that Jesus is God):* Look for verses that show Jesus is God. For example, John 10:33 says, "For a good work we do not ston[e] but for blasphemy; and because You, being a man, make Yourself out to be God."

g. *Witnesses:* Throughout his Gospel, John refers to those who bear witness to Jesus. Wh[o are] these witnesses and what is their witness? For example, John said, "I have seen, and [have] borne witness that this is the Son of God" (John 1:34).

3. Determine the main subject or theme of each chapter and then record it next to the ch[apter] number and on JOHN AT A GLANCE.

Chapters 13-17

1. This segment brings a change in Jesus' ministry as He draws away with the disciples in or[der to] prepare them for what is to come. Make a new list of key words on a bookmark: *believe*, *works, commandments, fruit, abide, ask, truth, true, truly, devil, Satan,* and *ruler of this world*. (Go [back] to chapter 12 and mark the references to *Satan*.)
2. Mark in a distinctive way all references, including pronouns, to God, Jesus, and the Holy S[pirit]. Then list in the margin everything you learn about the Holy Spirit. This is especially import[ant in] chapters 14 through 16.
3. List in the chapter margins any specific instructions or commandments Jesus gives the discip[les].
4. Record the main theme of each chapter as you did before.

Chapters 18-21

1. The final chapters of John give an account of the events surrounding the arrest, trial, crucif[ixion,] resurrection, and the post-resurrection appearances of Jesus Christ. As you read each chapter[:]
   a. Mark the following key words and their synonyms: *witness, believe, love, truth, true, life,* and *kingdom*.
   b. In the appendix you'll find two charts: THE ARREST, TRIAL, AND CRUCIFIXION OF J[ESUS] CHRIST (page 1882) and THE ACCOUNT OF JESUS' RESURRECTION (page 1883). Reco[rd on] the appropriate chart the progression of events from Jesus' arrest through His resurrectio[n and] post-resurrection appearances. (It would be good to do this on notebook paper before re[cord]ing it on the chart.) Also remember since Luke gives the chronological order of eve[nts, it] becomes the chronological plumbline for the other Gospel records.
2. Once again determine the theme of each chapter and record it as you have done previously.
3. In the appendix you will find a chart WHAT THE GOSPELS TEACH ABOUT THE KING[DOM] OF GOD/THE KINGDOM OF HEAVEN (pages 1880 and 1881). Compile what John te[aches] about the King and the kingdom on this chart. John 3 contains the only two references t[o the] kingdom. The other references to Jesus as the king are in the first and last segments of [John.] Compile your information on notebook paper before you write it on the chart.
4. Complete JOHN AT A GLANCE by doing the following:
   a. Review your chapter themes of John and determine the theme of the book. Record this i[n the] appropriate place on JOHN AT A GLANCE.
   b. You'll notice a section called "Segment Divisions" and then two lines where you can re[cord] "Signs and Miracles" and "Portrayals of Christ." Review the information you have reco[rded] on WRITTEN THAT YOU MIGHT BELIEVE. Record your observations on the approp[riate] segment division line. For example, in chapter 1 Jesus is referred to as "the Lamb of G[od."] Simply record that fact under chapter 1 under "Portrayals of Christ." This will give y[ou a] visual picture of the structure of John.

THINGS TO THINK ABOUT

1. Do you really believe Jesus is God? Do you live accordingly?
2. Do you know how to take another person through the Scriptures to show them that Jesus is G[od?]
3. Do all men know you are a disciple of Jesus Christ because of your love for others and bec[ause] you have continued in His Word?

Are you relying on the Spirit of God to comfort you, help you, bear witness through you, do the work of God through you, and guide you into all truth? Are you sharing Him with others?

Do you look at other Christians and wonder why God deals differently with you than He does with them? Do you need to hear His words to Peter in John 21:22, "If I want him to remain until I come, what is that to you? You follow Me!"? Are you willing to follow Jesus wherever He leads, even if you have to do it alone? Are you telling others about Him?

Chapter 1

1 [a]In the beginning was [b]the Word, and the Word was [c]with God,
and [d]the Word was God.
2 [1]He was in the beginning with God.
3 [a]All things came into being [1]by Him, and apart from Him noth-
ing came into being that has come into being.
4 [a]In Him was life, and the life was [b]the light of men.
5 And [a]the light shines in the darkness, and the darkness did not
[1]comprehend it.
6 There [1]came a man, sent from God, whose name was [a]John.
7 [1]He came [a]for a witness, that he might bear witness of the light,
[b]that all might believe through him.
8 [1a]He was not the light, but *came* that he might bear witness of the
light.
9 There was [a]the true light [1]which, coming into the world, en-
lightens every man.
10 He was in the world, and [a]the world was made through Him,
and the world did not know Him.
11 He came to His [1]own, and those who were His own did not
receive Him.
12 But as many as received Him, to them He gave the right to
become [a]children of God, *even* [b]to those who believe in His name,
13 [a]who were [1]born not of [2]blood, nor of the will of the flesh, nor of
the will of man, but of God.
14 And [a]the Word [b]became flesh, and [1c]dwelt among us, and [d]we
beheld His glory, glory as of [2]the only begotten from the Father, full
of [e]grace and [f]truth.
15 John *[a]bore witness of Him, and cried out, saying, "This was He
of whom I said, '[b]He who comes after me [1]has a higher rank than I,
[c]for He existed before me.' "
16 For of His [a]fulness [1]we have all received, and [2]grace upon grace.
17 For [a]the Law was given through Moses; [b]grace and [c]truth were
realized through Jesus Christ.
18 [a]No man has seen God at any time; [b]the only begotten [1]God, who
is [c]in the bosom of the Father, [d]He has explained *Him*.
19 And this is [a]the witness of John, when [b]the Jews sent to him
priests and Levites [c]from Jerusalem to ask him, "Who are you?"
20 And he confessed, and did not deny, and he confessed, "[a]I am
not [1]the Christ."
21 And they asked him, "What then? Are you [a]Elijah?" And he
*said, "I am not." "Are you [b]the Prophet?" And he answered, "No."
22 They said then to him, "Who are you, so that we may give an
answer to those who sent us? What do you say about yourself?"

en. 1:1; Col.
n 1:1 [b]John
19:13 [c]John
nn 1:2 [d]Phil.
2:6
.it., *This one*
rough [a]John
Cor. 8:6; Col.
.16; Heb. 1:2
5:26; 11:25;
hn 8:12; 9:5;
12:46
r, overpower
[a]John 3:19
ne into being
[a]Matt. 3:1
is one [a]John
2; 3:26; 5:33
2; Acts 19:4;
Gal. 3:26
at one [a]John
1:20
ch enlightens
n coming into
[a]1 John 2:8
Cor. 8:6; Col.
:16; Heb. 1:2
, own things,
sions, domain
n 11:52; Gal.
ohn 1:7; 3:18;
hn 3:23; 5:13
egotten [2]Lit.,
s [a]John 3:5f.;
3; 1 Pet. 1:23;
ohn 2:29; 3:9
, tabernacled
e, only one of
[a]Rev. 19:13
1:3; Gal. 4:4;
.; 1 Tim. 3:16;
; 1 John 1:1f.;
John 7 [c]Rev.
ke 9:32; John
:22, 24; 2 Pet.
hn 1:1 [e]John
m. 5:21; 6:14
2; 14:6; 18:37
.it., *is become*
me [a]John 1:7
11; John 1:27,
30 [c]John 1:30
we all received
race for grace
23; 3:19; 4:13;
Col. 1:19; 2:9
n 7:19 [b]John
m. 5:21; 6:14
2; 14:6; 18:37
ome later mss.
on [a]Ex. 33:20;
:46; Col. 1:15;
. 6:16; 1 John
John 3:16, 18;
[c]Luke 16:22;
23 [d]John 3:11
ohn 1:7 [b]John
5:10, 15f., 18;
7:1, 11, 13, 15,
22, 48, 52, 57;
; 10:24, 31, 33
[c]Matt. 15:1

20 [1]I.e., the Messiah [a]Luke 3:15f.; John 3:28 **21** [a]Matt. 11:14; 16:14 [b]Deut. 18:15, 18; Matt. 21:11; John 1:25

23 He said, "I am [a]A VOICE OF ONE CRYING IN THE WILDERNESS, 'MAKE
STRAIGHT THE WAY OF THE LORD,' as Isaiah the prophet said."
24 Now they had been sent from the Pharisees.
25 And they asked him, and said to him, "Why then are you baptiz-
ing, if you are not the [1]Christ, nor Elijah, nor [a]the Prophet?"
26 John answered them saying, "[a]I baptize [1]in water, *but* among you
stands One whom you do not know.
27 "*It is* [a]He who comes after me, the [b]thong of whose sandal I am
not worthy to untie."
28 These things took place in Bethany [a]beyond the Jordan, where
John was baptizing.
29 The next day he *saw Jesus coming to him, and *said, "Behold,
[a]the Lamb of God who [b]takes away the sin of the world!
30 "This is He on behalf of whom I said, '[a]After me comes a Man
who [1]has a higher rank than I, [b]for He existed before me.'
31 "And I did not recognize [1]Him, but in order that He might be
manifested to Israel, I came baptizing [2]in water."
32 And John [a]bore witness saying, "[b]I have beheld the Spirit de-
scending as a dove out of heaven, and He remained upon Him.
33 "And I did not recognize [1]Him, but He who sent me to baptize [2]in
water said to me, 'He upon whom you see the Spirit descending and
remaining upon Him, [a]this is the one who baptizes [2]in the Holy
Spirit.'
34 "And I have seen, and have borne witness that this is [a]the Son of
God."
35 Again [a]the next day John was standing [1]with two of his disciples,
36 and he looked upon Jesus as He walked, and *said, "Behold, [a]the
Lamb of God!"
37 And the two disciples heard him speak, and they followed Jesus.
38 And Jesus turned, and beheld them following, and *said to them,
"What do you seek?" And they said to Him, "[a]Rabbi (which trans-
lated means Teacher), where are You staying?"
39 He *said to them, "Come, and you will see." They came there-
fore and saw where He was staying; and they stayed with Him that
day, for it was about the [1]tenth hour.
40 [a]One of the two who heard John *speak,* and followed Him, was
Andrew, Simon Peter's brother.
41 He *found first his own brother Simon, and *said to him, "We
have found the [a]Messiah" (which translated means [1]Christ).
42 He brought him to Jesus. Jesus looked at him, and said, "You are
Simon the son of [1a]John; you shall be called [b]Cephas" (which is trans-
lated [2c]Peter).
43 [a]The next day He purposed to go forth into [b]Galilee, and He
*found [c]Philip. And Jesus *said to him, "[d]Follow Me."
44 Now [a]Philip was from [b]Bethsaida, of the city of Andrew and
Peter.
45 [a]Philip *found [b]Nathanael and *said to him, "We have found
Him of whom [c]Moses in the Law and *also* [c]the Prophets wrote, Jesus
of [d]Nazareth, [e]the son of Joseph."
46 And Nathanael *said to him, "[a]Can any good thing come out of
Nazareth?" [b]Philip *said to him, "Come and see."
47 Jesus saw Nathanael coming to Him, and *said of him, "Behold,
an [a]Israelite indeed, in whom is no guile!"
48 Nathanael *said to Him, "How do You know me?" Jesus

23 [a]Is. 40:3 Mark 1:3; Lu
25 [1]I.e., Me [a]Deut. 18:15 21:11; John
26 [1]The Gr. be translate *by* [a]Matt. 3: 1:8; Luke 3:1
27 [a]Matt. 3: 1:30 [b]Matt. 1:7; Luke 3:1
28 [a]John 3:2
29 [a]Is. 53:7; Acts 8:32; 1 Rev. 5:6, 8, [b]Matt. 1:21;
30 [1]Lit., *has before me* [a] John 1:27 [b]
31 [1]I.e., as t Messiah [2]Th can be trans *with* or *by*
32 [a]John 1:7 3:16; Mark 1 3:22
33 [1]I.e., as th Messiah [2]Th can be transl *with*, or *by* [a]M Mark 1:8; Luk Acts 1:5
34 [a]Matt. 4:3
35 [1]Lit., *and*
36 [a]John 1:2
38 [a]Matt. 23 1:49
39 [1]Perhaps (Roman time)
40 [a]Matt. 4:1 1:16-20; Luke John 1:40-42
41 [1]Gr., *Anoi* [a]Dan. 9:25; Jo
42 [1]Gr., *Joan* Rock or Stone 16:17; John 2 [b]1 Cor. 1:12; 3 15:5; Gal. 1:1 14 [c]Matt. 16:1
43 [a]John 1:2 [b]Matt. 4:12; Jo 2:11 [c]Matt. 10 1:44-48; 6:5, 7 14:8f. [d]Matt. 8
44 [a]Matt. 10:3 1:44-48; 6:5, 7 14:8f. [b]Matt. 1
45 [a]Matt. 10:3 1:44-48; 6:5, 7 14:8f. [b]John 1 21:2 [c]Luke 24 [d]Matt. 2:23 [e]L 3:23; 4:22; Joh
46 [a]John 7:41 [b]Matt. 10:3; Jo 1:44-48; 6:5, 7 14:8f.
47 [a]Rom. 9:4

answered and said to him, "Before [a]Philip called you, when you
were under the fig tree, I saw you."
49 Nathanael answered Him, "[a]Rabbi, You are [b]the Son of God; You
are the [c]King of Israel."
50 Jesus answered and said to him, "Because I said to you that I
saw you under the fig tree, do you believe? You shall see greater
things than these."
51 And He *said to him, "Truly, truly, I say to you, you shall see [a]the
heavens opened, and [b]the angels of God ascending and descending
on [c]the Son of Man."

Chapter 2

2 And on [a]the third day there was a wedding in [b]Cana of Galilee,
and the [c]mother of Jesus was there;
2 and Jesus also was invited, and His [a]disciples, to the wedding.
3 And when the wine gave out, the mother of Jesus *said to Him,
"They have no wine."
4 And Jesus *said to her, "[a]Woman, [1b]what do I have to do with
you? [c]My hour has not yet come."
5 His [a]mother *said to the servants, "Whatever He says to you,
do it."
6 Now there were six stone waterpots set there [a]for the Jewish
custom of purification, containing [1]twenty or thirty gallons each.
7 Jesus *said to them, "Fill the waterpots with water." And they
filled them up to the brim.
8 And He *said to them, "Draw *some* out now, and take it to the
[1]headwaiter." And they took it *to him.*
9 And when the headwaiter tasted the water [a]which had become
wine, and did not know where it came from (but the servants who
had drawn the water knew), the headwaiter *called the bridegroom,
10 and *said to him, "Every man serves the good wine first, and
when *men* [a]have [1]drunk freely, *then* that which is poorer; you have
kept the good wine until now."
11 This beginning of *His* [1a]signs Jesus did in Cana of [b]Galilee, and
manifested His [c]glory, and His disciples believed in Him.
12 After this He went down to [a]Capernaum, He and His [b]mother,
and *His* [b]brothers, and His [c]disciples; and there they stayed a few
days.
13 And [a]the Passover of the Jews was at hand, and Jesus
[b]went up to Jerusalem.
14 [a]And He found in the temple those who were selling
oxen and sheep and doves, and the moneychangers seated.
15 And He made a scourge of cords, and drove *them* all
out of the temple, with the sheep and the oxen; and He
poured out the coins of the moneychangers, and over-
turned their tables;
16 and to those who were selling [a]the doves He said,
"Take these things away; stop making [b]My Father's house
a house of merchandise."
17 His [a]disciples remembered that it was written, "[b]ZEAL
FOR THY HOUSE WILL CONSUME ME."
18 [a]The Jews therefore answered and said to Him, "[b]What
sign do You show to us, seeing that You do these things?"
19 Jesus answered and said to them, "[a]Destroy this
[1]temple, and in three days I will raise it up."

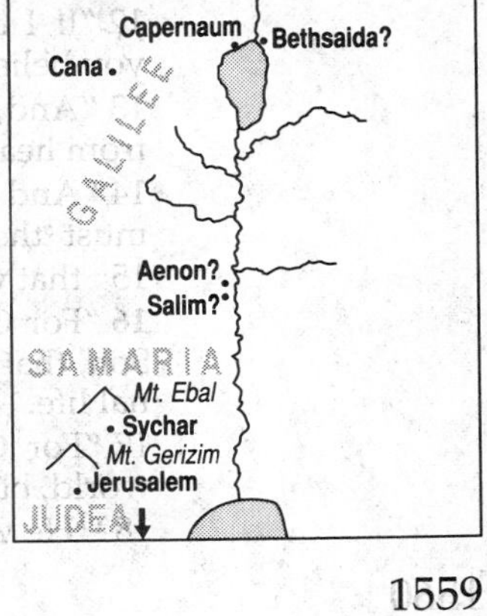

Jesus Ministers from Capernaum to Jerusalem

10:3; John
, 7; 12:21f.;
14:8f.
1:38 [b]John
2:2; 27:42;
John 12:13
k. 1:1; Matt.
e 3:21; Acts
; Rev. 19:11
[c]Matt. 8:20
1:29, 35, 43
; 4:46; 21:2
[c]Matt. 12:46
40-49; 2:12,
2; 4:2, 8, 27;
22, 24, 60f.,
66; 7:3; 8:31
at to Me and
u (a Hebrew
[a]John 19:26
9 [c]John 7:6,
8, 30; 8:20
[a]Matt. 12:46
Two or three
[a]Mark 7:3f.;
John 3:25
[1]Or, *steward*
9 [a]John 4:46
ave become
[a]Matt. 24:49;
45; Acts 2:15;
1; Eph. 5:18;
ess. 5:7; Rev.
17:2, 6
[1]Or, *attesting*
e., one which
points to the
ural power of
in redeeming
hn 2:23; 3:2;
2, 14, 26, 30;
10:41; 11:47;
20:30 [b]John
3 [c]John 1:14
t. 4:13 [b]Matt.
46 [c]John 2:2
16:1-6; John
11:55 [b]Luke
41; John 2:23
2:14-16: *Matt.*
Mark 11:15, 17;
45f.; Mal. 3:1ff.
21:12 [b]Luke
2:49
2:2 [b]Ps. 69:9
n 1:19 [a]Matt.
12:38
[1]Or, *sanctuary*
26:61; 27:40;
58; 15:29; Acts
6:14

20 [a]The Jews therefore said, "It took [b]forty-six years to build this
[1]temple, and will You raise it up in three days?"
21 But He was speaking of [a]the [1]temple of His body.
22 When therefore He was raised from the dead, His [a]disciples [b]re-
membered that He said this; and they believed [c]the Scripture, and
the word which Jesus had spoken.
23 Now when He was in Jerusalem at [a]the Passover, during the
feast, many believed in His name, [b]beholding His signs which He
was doing.
24 But Jesus, on His part, was not entrusting Himself to them, for
[a]He knew all men,
25 and because He did not need anyone to bear witness concerning
man [a]for He Himself knew what was in man.

Chapter 3

3 Now there was a man of the Pharisees, named [a]Nicodemus, a
[b]ruler of the Jews;
2 this man came to Him by night, and said to Him, "[a]Rabbi, we
know that You have come from God *as* a teacher; for no one can do
these [1b]signs that You do unless [c]God is with him."
3 Jesus answered and said to him, "Truly, truly, I say to you, unless
one [a]is born [1]again, he cannot see [b]the kingdom of God."
4 Nicodemus *said to Him, "How can a man be born when he is
old? He cannot enter a second time into his mother's womb and be
born, can he?"
5 Jesus answered, "Truly, truly, I say to you, unless one is born of
[a]water and the Spirit, he cannot enter into [b]the kingdom of God.
6 "[a]That which is born of the flesh is flesh, and that which is born of
the Spirit is spirit.
7 "Do not marvel that I said to you, 'You must be born [1]again.'
8 "[a]The wind blows where it wishes and you hear the sound of it,
but do not know where it comes from and where it is going; so is
everyone who is born of the Spirit."
9 Nicodemus answered and said to Him, "How can these things
be?"
10 Jesus answered and said to him, "Are you [a]the teacher of Israel,
and do not understand these things?
11 "Truly, truly, I say to you, [a]we speak that which we know, and
[b]bear witness of that which we have seen; and [b]you do not receive
our witness.
12 "If I told you earthly things and you do not believe, how shall
you believe if I tell you heavenly things?
13 "And [a]no one has ascended into heaven, but [b]He who descended
from heaven, *even* [c]the Son of Man.[1]
14 "And as [a]Moses lifted up the serpent in the wilderness, even so
must [b]the Son of Man [c]be lifted up;
15 that whoever [1]believes may [a]in Him have eternal life.
16 "For God so [a]loved the world, that He [b]gave His [1c]only begotten
Son, that whoever [d]believes in Him should not perish, but have eter-
nal life.
17 "For God [a]did not send the Son into the world [b]to judge the
world, but that the world should be saved through Him.
18 "[a]He who believes in Him is not judged; he who does not believe

20 [1]Or, *sar* [a]John 1:19
21 [1]Or, *sar* [a]1 Cor. 6:19
22 [a]John 2 24:8; John 14:26 [c]Ps. 24:26f.; Joh 13:33
23 [a]John 2 2:11
24 [a]Acts 1:
25 [a]Matt. 9: 1:42, 47; 6:6
3:1 [a]John 7 [b]Luke 23:13 7:26, 48
2 [1]Or, *attes miracles* [a]M John 3:26 [b] [c]John 9:33; 14:10f.; Acts
3 [1]Or, *from* [a]2 Cor. 5:17; [b]Matt. 19:24; Mark 9:47; 1 3:5
5 [a]Ezek. 36: 5:26; Titus 3 19:24; 21:31; 10:14f.; John
6 [a]John 1:13 15:50
7 [1]Or, *from a*
8 [a]Ps. 135:7; Ezek. 37:9
10 [a]Luke 2:4 Acts 5:34
11 [a]John 1:1 8:26, 28; 12:4 [b]John 3:32
13 [1]Later ms *is in heaven* 30:12; Prov. 3 2:34; Rom. 10 4:9 [b]John 3:3 42 [c]Matt. 8:2
14 [a]Num. 21: 8:20 [c]John 8:
15 [1]Some ms *believes in Hi have eternal li* 20:31; 1 John
16 [1]Or, *uniqu one of His kin* 5:8; Eph. 2:4; 2:16; 1 John 4 1:5 [b]Rom. 8:3 4:9 [c]John 1:1 1 John 4:9 [d]Jo 6:40; 11:25f.
17 [a]John 3:34 6:29, 38, 57; 7 10:36; 11:42; 1 18, 21, 23, 25; [b]Luke 19:10; J 12:47; 1 John 4
18 [a]Mark 16:1 5:24

has been judged already, because he has not believed in the name of
[b]the [1]only begotten Son of God.
19 "And this is the judgment, that [a]the light is come into the world,
and men loved the darkness rather than the light; for [b]their deeds
were evil.
20 "[a]For everyone who does evil hates the light, and does not come
to the light, lest his deeds should be exposed.
21 "But he who [a]practices the truth comes to the light, that his deeds
may be manifested as having been wrought in God."
22 After these things Jesus and His [a]disciples came into the land of
Judea, and there He was spending time with them and [b]baptizing.
23 And John also was baptizing in Aenon near Salim, because there
was [1]much water there; and they were coming and were being bap-
tized.
24 For [a]John had not yet been thrown into prison.
25 There arose therefore a discussion on the part of John's disciples
with a Jew about [a]purification.
26 And they came to John and said to him, "[a]Rabbi, He who was
with you [b]beyond the Jordan, to whom you [c]have borne witness,
behold, He is baptizing, and all are coming to Him."
27 John answered and said, "[a]A man can receive nothing, unless it
[b]has been given him from heaven.
28 "You yourselves bear me witness, that I said, '[a]I am not the
[1]Christ,' but, 'I have been sent before Him.'
29 "He who has the bride is [a]the bridegroom; but the friend of the
bridegroom, who stands and hears him, rejoices greatly because of
the bridegroom's voice. And so this [b]joy of mine has been made full.
30 "He must increase, but I must decrease.
31 "[a]He who comes from above is above all, [b]he who is of the earth is
from the earth and speaks of the earth. [a]He who comes from heaven
is above all.
32 "What He has seen and heard, of that He [a]bears witness; and [a]no
man receives His witness.
33 "He who has received His witness [a]has set his seal to *this*, that
God is true.
34 "For He whom God has [a]sent speaks the words of God; [1b]for He
gives the Spirit without measure.
35 "[a]The Father loves the Son, and [b]has given all things into His
hand.
36 "He who [a]believes in the Son has eternal life; but he who [b]does
not [1]obey the Son shall not see life, but the wrath of God abides on
him."

Chapter 4

4 When therefore [a]the Lord knew that the Pharisees had heard that
Jesus was making and [b]baptizing more disciples than John
2 (although [a]Jesus Himself was not baptizing, but His [b]disciples
were),
3 He left [a]Judea, and departed [b]again into Galilee.
4 And He had to pass through [a]Samaria.
5 So He *came to a city of [a]Samaria, called Sychar, near [b]the parcel
of ground that [c]Jacob gave to his son Joseph;
6 and Jacob's well was there. Jesus therefore, being wearied from

unique, only kind [b]John ; 1 John 4:9
:4; 8:12; 9:5; 6 [b]John 7:7
20, 21; Eph. 5:11, 13
[a]1 John 1:6
ın 2:2 [b]John 4:1, 2
many waters
tt. 4:12; 14:3; 7; Luke 3:20
25 [a]John 2:6
tt. 23:7; John n 1:28 [c]John 1:7
Cor. 4:7; Heb. [b]James 1:17
essiah [a]John 1:20, 23
att. 9:15; 25:1 15:11; 16:24; il. 2:2; 1 John 1:4; 2 John 12
tt. 28:18; John ; 8:23 [b]1 Cor. 47; 1 John 4:5
32 [a]John 3:11
hn 6:27; Rom. 28; 1 Cor. 9:2; :22; Eph. 1:13; Tim. 2:19; Rev. 7:3-8
or He does not ve the Spirit by ure [a]John 3:17 :18; Luke 4:18; Acts 1:2; 10:38
att. 28:18; John 2 [b]Matt. 11:27; Luke 10:22
, believe [a]John Acts 14:2; Heb. 3:18
uke 7:13 [b]John 26; 1 Cor. 1:17
3:22, 26; 1 Cor. 1:17 [b]John 2:2
ohn 3:22 [b]John 2:11f.
4 [a]Luke 9:52
uke 9:52 [b]Gen. :19; Josh. 24:32 48:22; John 4:12

INSIGHT

It is difficult to pinpoint who the Samaritans are racially. However, it is believed that after the Assyrians conquered the northern kingdom, they "imported" people into Samaria. Some of the Samaritan Jews married the importees. When the Jews returned after the captivity, the Samaritans wanted a share in rebuilding the temple but were rejected because of their pagan practices. The enmity continued through the time of Jesus (see 2 Kings 17:33 and Ezra 4:2-3).

His journey, was sitting thus by the well. It was about [1]the sixth
hour.
7 There *came a woman of Samaria to draw water. Jesus *said to
her, "Give Me a drink."
8 For His [a]disciples had gone away into [b]the city to buy food.
9 The [a]Samaritan woman therefore *said to Him, "How is it that
You, being a Jew, ask me for a drink since I am a Samaritan
woman?" (For [b]Jews have no dealings with Samaritans.)
10 Jesus answered and said to her, "If you knew the gift of God,
and who it is who says to you, 'Give Me a drink,' you would have
asked Him, and He would have given you [a]living water."
11 She *said to Him, "[1]Sir, You have nothing to draw with and the
well is deep; where then do You get that [a]living water?
12 "You are not greater than our father Jacob, are You, who [a]gave us
the well, and drank of it himself, and his sons, and his cattle?"
13 Jesus answered and said to her, "Everyone who drinks of this
water shall thirst again;
14 but whoever drinks of the water that I shall give him [a]shall never
thirst; but the water that I shall give him shall become in him a well
of water springing up to [b]eternal life."
15 The woman *said to Him, "[1]Sir, [a]give me this water, so I will not
be thirsty, nor come all the way here to draw."
16 He *said to her, "Go, call your husband, and come here."
17 The woman answered and said, "I have no husband." Jesus
*said to her, "You have well said, 'I have no husband';
18 for you have had five husbands, and the one whom you now
have is not your husband; this you have said truly."
19 The woman *said to Him, "[1]Sir, I perceive that You are [a]a
prophet.
20 "[a]Our fathers worshiped in [b]this mountain, and you *people* say
that [c]in Jerusalem is the place where men ought to worship."
21 Jesus *said to her, "Woman, believe Me, [a]an hour is coming when
[b]neither in this mountain, nor in Jerusalem, shall you worship the
Father.
22 "[a]You worship that which you do not know; we worship that
which we know, for [b]salvation is from the Jews.
23 "But [a]an hour is coming, and now is, when the true worshipers
shall worship the Father [b]in spirit and truth; for such people the
Father seeks to be His worshipers.
24 "God is [1]spirit, and those who worship Him must worship [a]in
spirit and truth."
25 The woman *said to Him, "I know that [a]Messiah is coming ([b]He
who is called Christ); when that One comes, He will declare all
things to us."
26 Jesus *said to her, "[a]I who speak to you am *He*."
27 And at this point His [a]disciples came, and they marveled that He
had been speaking with a woman; yet no one said, "What do You
seek?" or, "Why do You speak with her?"
28 So the woman left her waterpot, and went into the city, and *said
to the men,
29 "Come, see a man [a]who told me all the things that I *have* done;
[b]this is not [1]the Christ, is it?"
30 They went out of the city, and were coming to Him.

6 [1]Perhaps (Roman time
8 [a]John 2:2 4:5, 39
9 [a]Luke 9:52 4:3-6, 11ff.; M John 8:48; Ac
10 [a]Jer. 2:13 4:14; 7:37f.; 21:6; 22:1, 17
11 [1]Or, *Lord* John 4:14; 7: 7:17; 21:6; 22
12 [a]John 4:6
14 [a]John 6:3 [b]Matt. 25:46;
15 [1]Or, *Lord*
19 [1]Or, *Lord* 21:11; Luke 7: 24:19; John 6. 9:17
20 [a]Gen. 33:2 4:12 [b]Deut. 11 Josh. 8:33 [c]L
21 [a]John 4:23 16:2, 32 [b]Mal. 1 Tim. 2:8
22 [a]2 Kin. 17:2 2:3; Rom. 3:1f.
23 [a]John 4:21; 16:2, 32 [b]Phil.
24 [1]Or, *a Spirit* 3:3
25 [a]Dan. 9:25; 1:41 [b]Matt. 1:1 22; Luke 2:11
26 [a]John 8:24, 9:37; 13:19
27 [a]John 4:8
29 [1]I.e., the Me [a]John 4:17f. [b]M 12:23; John 7:2

31 In the meanwhile the disciples were requesting Him, saying,
"[a]Rabbi, eat."
32 But He said to them, "I have food to eat that you do not know
about."
33 The [a]disciples therefore were saying to one another, "No one
brought Him *anything* to eat, did he?"
34 Jesus *said to them, "My food is to [a]do the will of Him who sent
Me, and to [b]accomplish His work.
35 "Do you not say, 'There are yet four months, and *then* comes the
harvest'? Behold, I say to you, lift up your eyes, and look on the
fields, that they are white [a]for harvest.
36 "Already he who reaps is receiving [a]wages, and is gathering [b]fruit
for [c]life eternal; that he who sows and he who reaps may rejoice
together.
37 "For in this *case* the saying is true, '[a]One sows, and another reaps.'
38 "I sent you to reap that for which you have not labored; others
have labored, and you have entered into their labor."
39 And from [a]that city many of the Samaritans believed in Him
because of the word of the woman who testified, "[b]He told me all the
things that I *have* done."
40 So when the Samaritans came to Him, they were asking Him to
stay with them; and He stayed there two days.
41 And many more believed because of His word;
42 and they were saying to the woman, "It is no longer because of
what you said that we believe, for we have heard for ourselves and
know that this One is indeed [a]the Savior of the world."
43 And after [a]the two days He went forth from there into Galilee.
44 For Jesus Himself testified that [a]a prophet has no honor in his
own country.
45 So when He came to Galilee, the Galileans received Him, [a]having
seen all the things that He did in Jerusalem at the feast; for they
themselves also went to the feast.
46 He came therefore again to [a]Cana of Galilee [b]where He had made
the water wine. And there was a certain royal official, whose son
was sick at [c]Capernaum.
47 When he heard that Jesus had come [a]out of Judea into Galilee, he
went to Him, and was requesting *Him* to come down and heal his
son; for he was at the point of death.
48 Jesus therefore said to him, "Unless you *people* see [1a]signs and
[a]wonders, you *simply* will not believe."
49 The royal official *said to Him, "[1]Sir, come down before my child
dies."
50 Jesus *said to him, "[a]Go your way; your son lives." The man
believed the word that Jesus spoke to him, and he started off.
51 And as he was now going down, *his* slaves met him, saying that
his [1]son was living.
52 So he inquired of them the hour when he began to get better.
They said therefore to him, "Yesterday at the [1]seventh hour the fever
left him."
53 So the father knew that *it was* at that hour in which Jesus said to
him, "Your son lives"; and he himself believed, and [a]his whole
household.
54 This is again a [a]second [1]sign that Jesus performed, when He had
[b]come out of Judea into Galilee.

3:7; 26:25, 9:5; 11:21; n 1:38, 49; 5; 9:2; 11:8
3-16; John :40-49; 2:2
i 5:30; 6:38 5:36; 17:4; 19:28, 30
7, 38; Luke 10:2
1:18; 1 Cor. [b]Rom. 1:13 ; John 3:36; ; Rom. 2:7; 6:23
8; Mic. 6:15
5, 30 [b]John 4:29
. 1:21; Luke in 1:29; Acts 1 Tim. 4:10; 1 John 4:14
[a]John 4:40
13:57; Mark 4; Luke 4:24
5 [a]John 2:23
nn 2:1 [b]John ke 4:23; John 2:12
[a]John 4:3, 54
[1]Or, *attesting* s [a]Dan. 4:2f.; 24:24; Mark 2:19, 22, 43; 12; 6:8; 7:36; ; 15:12; Rom. ; 1 Cor. 1:22; 2:12; 2 Thess. 2:9; Heb. 2:4
49 [1]Or, *Lord*
50 [a]Matt. 8:13
51 [1]Or, *boy*
Perhaps 7 p.m. (Roman time)
53 [a]Acts 11:14
[1]Or, *attesting* cle [a]John 2:11 [b]John 4:45f.

Chapter 5

5 After these things there was [1a]a feast of the Jews, and Jesus went
up to Jerusalem.
2 Now there is in Jerusalem by [a]the sheep *gate* a pool, which is
called [b]in [1]Hebrew [2]Bethesda, having five porticoes.
3 In these lay a multitude of those who were sick, blind, lame, and
withered, [[1]waiting for the moving of the waters;
4 for an angel of the Lord went down at certain seasons into the
pool, and stirred up the water; whoever then first, after the stirring
up of the water, stepped in was made well from whatever disease
with which he was afflicted.]
5 And a certain man was there, who had been thirty-eight years in
his sickness.
6 When Jesus saw him lying there, and knew that he had already
been a long time *in that condition,* He *said to him, "Do you wish to
get well?"
7 The sick man answered Him, "Sir, I have no man to put me into
the pool when [a]the water is stirred up, but while I am coming,
another steps down before me."
8 Jesus *said to him, "[a]Arise, take up your pallet, and walk."
9 And immediately the man became well, and took up his pallet
and *began* to walk.
[a]**N**ow it was the Sabbath on that day.
10 Therefore [a]the Jews were saying to him who was cured, "It is the
Sabbath, and [b]it is not permissible for you to carry your pallet."
11 But he answered them, "He who made me well was the one who
said to me, 'Take up your pallet and walk.' "
12 They asked him, "Who is the man who said to you, 'Take up
your pallet, and walk'?"
13 But he who was healed did not know who it was; for Jesus had
slipped away while there was a crowd in *that* place.
14 Afterward Jesus *found him in the temple, and said to him, "Be-
hold, you have become well; do not [a]sin anymore, [b]so that nothing
worse may befall you."
15 The man went away, and told [a]the Jews that it was Jesus who
had made him well.
16 And for this reason [a]the Jews were persecuting Jesus, because He
was doing these things on the Sabbath.
17 But He answered them, "My Father is working until now, and I
Myself am working."
18 For this cause therefore [a]the Jews [b]were seeking all the more to
kill Him, because He not only was breaking the Sabbath, but also
was calling God His own Father, [c]making Himself equal with God.
19 Jesus therefore answered and was saying to them, "Truly, truly, I
say to you, [a]the Son can do nothing of Himself, unless *it is* something
He sees the Father doing; for whatever *the Father* does, these things
the Son also does in like manner.
20 "[a]For the Father loves the Son, and shows Him all things that He
Himself is doing; and [b]greater works than these will He show Him,
that you may marvel.
21 "For just as the Father raises the dead and [a]gives them life, even
so [b]the Son also gives life to whom He wishes.
22 "For not even the Father judges anyone, but [a]He has given all
judgment to the Son,

5:1 [1]Many mss *the feast;* i.e., th Passover [a]Deu John 2:13

2 [1]I.e., Jewish [2]Many mss. rea *Bethsaida* or *Be* [a]Neh. 3:1, 32; 1 [b]John 19:13, 17 20:16; Acts 21:4 9:11; 16:16

3 [1]Many mss. contain the rem v. 3, nor v. 4

7 [a]John 5:4

8 [a]Matt. 9:6; Ma Luke 5:24

9 [a]John 9:14

10 [a]John 1:19; 18 [b]Neh. 13:19 17:21f.; Matt. 12 6:2; John 7:23;

14 [a]Mark 2:5; J 8:11 [b]Ezra 9:14

15 [a]John 1:19;

16 [a]John 1:19; 15, 18

18 [a]John 1:19; [b]John 5:16; 7:1 10:33; 19:7

19 [a]Matt. 26:39 5:30; 6:38; 8:28 14:10

20 [a]Matt. 3:17; 3:35; 2 Pet. 1:1 14:12

21 [a]Rom. 4:17 [b]John 11:25

22 [a]John 5:27; Acts 10:42; 17:

23 in order that all may honor the Son, even as they honor the
Father. [a]He who does not honor the Son does not honor the Father
who sent Him.
24 "Truly, truly, I say to you, he who hears My word, and [a]believes
Him who sent Me, has eternal life, and [b]does not come into judg-
ment, but has [c]passed out of death into life.
25 "Truly, truly, I say to you, [a]an hour is coming and now is, when
[b]the dead shall hear the voice of the Son of God; and those who [c]hear
shall live.
26 "For just as the Father has life in Himself, even so He [a]gave to the
Son also to have life in Himself;
27 and He gave Him authority to [a]execute judgment, because He is
[1]*the* Son of Man.
28 "Do not marvel at this; for [a]an hour is coming, in which [b]all who
are in the tombs shall hear His voice,
29 and shall come forth; [a]those who did the good *deeds* to a resur-
rection of life, those who committed the evil *deeds* to a resurrection of
judgment.
30 "[a]I can do nothing on My own initiative. As I hear, I judge; and
[b]My judgment is just, because I do not seek My own will, but [c]the
will of Him who sent Me.
31 "[a]If I *alone* bear witness of Myself, My testimony is not [1]true.
32 "There is [a]another who bears witness of Me, and I know that the
testimony which He bears of Me is true.
33 "You have sent to John, and he [a]has borne witness to the truth.
34 "But [a]the witness which I receive is not from man, but I say these
things that you may be saved.
35 "He was [a]the lamp that was burning and was shining and you
[b]were willing to rejoice for a while in his light.
36 "But the witness which I have is greater than *that of* John; for [a]the
works which the Father has given Me [b]to accomplish, the very works
that I do, bear witness of Me, that the Father [c]has sent Me.
37 "And the Father who sent Me, [a]He has borne witness of Me. You
have neither heard His voice at any time, nor seen His form.
38 "And you do not have [a]His word abiding in you, for you do not
believe Him whom He [b]sent.
39 "[1a]You search the Scriptures, because you think that in them you
have eternal life; and it is [b]these that bear witness of Me;
40 and you are unwilling to come to Me, that you may have life.
41 "[a]I do not receive glory from men;
42 but I know you, that you do not have the love of God in your-
selves.
43 "I have come in My Father's name, and you do not receive Me; [a]if
another shall come in his own name, you will receive him.
44 "How can you believe, when you [a]receive [1]glory from one
another, and you do not seek [b]the [1]glory that is from [c]the *one and* only
God?
45 "Do not think that I will accuse you before the Father; the one
who accuses you is [a]Moses, in whom you have set your hope.
46 "For if you believed Moses, you would believe Me; for [a]he wrote
of Me.
47 "But [a]if you do not believe his writings, how will you believe My
words?"

ıke 10:16; 1 John 2:23
John 3:18; 12:44;):31; 1 John 5:13 :18 [c]1 John 3:14
hn 4:21, 23; 5:28 uke 15:24 [c]John 30; 8:43, 47; 9:27
[a]John 1:4; 6:57
Or, *a son of man* 9:39; Acts 10:42; 17:31
John 4:21 [b]John :24; 1 Cor. 15:52
[a]Dan. 12:2; Matt. 5:46; Acts 24:15
John 5:19 [b]John [c]John 4:34; 6:38
e., admissible as evidence [a]John 8:14
32 [a]John 5:37
John 1:7, 15, 19, 32; 3:26-30
ohn 5:32; 1 John 5:9
[a]2 Sam. 21:17; 1:19 [b]Mark 1:5
Matt. 11:4; John 10:25, 38; 14:11; 5:24 [b]John 4:34 [c]John 3:17
Matt. 3:17; Mark uke 3:22; 24:27; 8:18; 1 John 5:9
ohn 2:14 [b]John 3:17
Or, (a command) *h the Scriptures!* John 7:52; Rom. Luke 24:25, 27; Acts 13:27
John 5:44; 7:18; 1 Thess. 2:6
43 [a]Matt. 24:5
r, *honor* or *fame* :41 [b]Rom. 2:29 7:3; 1 Tim. 1:17
John 9:28; Rom. 2:17ff.
46 [a]Luke 24:27
[a]Luke 16:29, 31

Chapter 6

See the chart ***The Feasts of Israel*** located on pages I-48 and I-49.

6 After these things [a]Jesus went away to the other side of [b]the Sea of Galilee (or [c]Tiberias).

2 And a great multitude was following Him, because they were seeing the [1a]signs which He was performing on those who were sick.

3 And [a]Jesus went up on the mountain, and there He sat with His disciples.

4 Now [a]the Passover, the feast of the Jews, was at hand.

5 Jesus therefore lifting up His eyes, and seeing that a great multitude was coming to Him, *said to [a]Philip, "Where are we to buy bread, that these may eat?"

6 And this He was saying to [a]test him; for He Himself knew what He was intending to do.

7 [a]Philip answered Him, "[b]Two hundred [1]denarii worth of bread is not sufficient for them, for everyone to receive a little."

8 One of His [a]disciples, [b]Andrew, Simon Peter's brother, *said to Him,

9 "There is a lad here who has five barley loaves and two [a]fish, but what are these for so many people?"

10 Jesus said, "Have the people [1]sit down." Now there was [a]much grass in the place. So the men [1]sat down, in number about [b]five thousand.

11 Jesus therefore took the loaves; and [a]having given thanks, He distributed to those who were seated; likewise also of the [b]fish as much as they wanted.

12 And when they were filled, He *said to His [a]disciples, "Gather up the leftover fragments that nothing may be lost."

13 And so they gathered them up, and filled twelve [a]baskets with fragments from the five barley loaves, which were left over by those who had eaten.

14 When therefore the people saw the [1]sign which He had performed, they said, "This is of a truth the [a]Prophet who is to come into the world."

15 Jesus therefore perceiving that they were [1]intending to come and take Him by force, [a]to make Him king, [b]withdrew again to [c]the mountain by Himself alone.

16 Now when evening came, His [a]disciples went down to the sea,

17 and after getting into a boat, they *started to* cross the sea [a]to Capernaum. And it had already become dark, and Jesus had not yet come to them.

18 And the sea *began* to be stirred up because a strong wind was blowing.

19 When therefore they had rowed about [1]three or four miles, they *beheld Jesus walking on the sea and drawing near to the boat; and they were frightened.

20 But He *said to them, "It is I; [1a]do not be afraid."

21 They were willing therefore to receive Him into the boat; and immediately the boat was at the land to which they were going.

22 The next day [a]the multitude that stood on the other side of the sea saw that there was no other small boat there, except one, and that Jesus [b]had not entered with His disciples into the boat, but *that* His disciples had gone away alone.

23 There came other small boats from [a]Tiberias near to the place where they ate the bread after the [b]Lord [c]had given thanks.

6:1 [a]John 6: *14:13-21; M Luke 9:10-1* 4:18; Luke 5 6:23; 21:1

2 [1]Or, *attest miracles* [a]Jo 23; 3:2; 6:14, 12:18, 37; 20

3 [a]Matt. 5:1; Luke 6:12; 9 6:15

4 [a]Deut. 16:1

5 [a]John 1:43

6 [a]2 Cor. 13:

7 [1]The dena equivalent to wage [a]John [b]Mark 6:37

8 [a]John 2:2

9 [a]John 6:11; 10, 13

10 [1]Lit., *reclin* [a]Mark 6:39 [b]M

11 [a]Matt. 15:3 6:23 [b]John 6: 10, 13

12 [a]John 2:2

13 [a]Matt. 14:2

14 [1]Or, *attesti miracle* [a]Matt. 21:11; John 1:

15 [1]Or, *about* 18:36f. [b]John *Matt. 14:22-33 6:45-51* [c]John

16 [a]John 2:2

17 [a]Mark 6:45 6:24, 59

19 [1]I.e., 25 or 3

20 [1]Or, *stop fe* [a]Matt. 14:27

22 [a]John 6:2 [b] 6:15ff.

23 [a]John 6:1 [b] 7:13 [c]John 6:1

att. 14:34; Mark
3; John 6:17, 59
25 [a]Matt. 23:7
ohn 6:24 [b]John
6:2, 14, 30
[a]Is. 55:2 [b]John
; 4:14; 6:40, 47,
28; 17:2f. [c]Matt.
); John 6:53, 62
[d]John 3:33
[a]1 Thess. 1:3;
es 2:22; 1 John
Rev. 2:26 [b]John
3:17
att. 12:38 [b]John
6:2, 14, 26
Ex. 16:4, 15, 21;
11:8; John 6:49,
78:24; Ex. 16:4,
; Neh. 9:15; Ps.
105:40
He who comes
[a]John 6:41, 50
34 [a]John 4:15
[a]John 6:48, 51
[b]John 4:14
36 [a]John 6:26
n 6:39; 17:2, 24
ohn 3:13 [b]Matt.
John 4:34; 5:30
[d]John 6:29
n 6:37; 17:2, 24
ohn 17:12; 18:9
:15; John 6:40,
44, 54; 11:24
n 12:45; 14:17,
ohn 3:16 [c]Matt.
; John 6:39, 44,
54; 11:24
John 1:19; 6:52
hn 6:33, 51, 58
ke 4:22 [b]John
[c]John 6:38, 62
[a]Jer. 31:3; Hos.
ohn 6:65; 12:32
[b]John 6:39
cts 7:42; 13:40;
3:11 [b]Is. 54:13;
:34 [c]Phil. 3:15;
ess. 4:9; 1 John
2:27
46 [a]John 1:18
ohn 3:36; 5:24;
6:51, 58; 11:26
[a]John 6:35, 51

24 When the multitude therefore saw that Jesus was not there, nor
His disciples, they themselves got into the small boats, and [a]came to
Capernaum, seeking Jesus.
25 And when they found Him on the other side of the sea, they said
to Him, "[a]Rabbi, when did You get here?"
26 Jesus answered them and said, "Truly, truly, I say to you, you
[a]seek Me, not because you saw [b]signs, but because you ate of the
loaves, and were filled.
27 "Do not [a]work for the food which perishes, but for the food which
endures to [b]eternal life, which [c]the Son of Man shall give to you, for
on Him the Father, *even* God, [d]has set His seal."
28 They said therefore to Him, "What shall we do, that we may
work the works of God?"
29 Jesus answered and said to them, "This is [a]the work of God, that
you believe in Him whom He [b]has sent."
30 They said therefore to Him, "[a]What then do You do for a [b]sign,
that we may see, and believe You? What work do You perform?
31 "[a]Our fathers ate the manna in the wilderness; as it is written, '[b]HE
GAVE THEM BREAD OUT OF HEAVEN TO EAT.' "
32 Jesus therefore said to them, "Truly, truly, I say to you, it is not
Moses who has given you the bread out of heaven, but it is My
Father who gives you the true bread out of heaven.
33 "For the bread of God is [1]that which [a]comes down out of heaven,
and gives life to the world."
34 They said therefore to Him, "Lord, evermore [a]give us this
bread."
35 Jesus said to them, "[a]I am the bread of life; he who comes to Me
shall not hunger, and he who believes in Me [b]shall never thirst.
36 "But [a]I said to you, that you have seen Me, and yet do not believe.
37 "[a]All that the Father gives Me shall come to Me, and the one who
comes to Me I will certainly not cast out.
38 "For [a]I have come down from heaven, [b]not to do My own will, but
[c]the will of Him who [d]sent Me.
39 "And this is the will of Him who sent Me, that of [a]all that He has
given Me I [b]lose nothing, but [c]raise it up on the last day.
40 "For this is the will of My Father, that everyone who [a]beholds the
Son and [b]believes in Him, may have eternal life; and I Myself will
[c]raise him up on the last day."
41 [a]The Jews therefore were grumbling about Him, because He
said, "I am the bread that [b]came down out of heaven."
42 And they were saying, "[a]Is not this Jesus, the son of Joseph,
whose father and mother [b]we know? How does He now say, '[c]I have
come down out of heaven'?"
43 Jesus answered and said to them, "Do not grumble among your-
selves.
44 "No one can come to Me, unless the Father who sent Me [a]draws
him; and I will [b]raise him up on the last day.
45 "It is written [a]in the prophets, '[b]AND THEY SHALL ALL BE [c]TAUGHT OF
GOD.' Everyone who has heard and learned from the Father, comes
to Me.
46 "[a]Not that any man has seen the Father, except the One who is
from God; He has seen the Father.
47 "Truly, truly, I say to you, he who believes [a]has eternal life.
48 "[a]I am the bread of life.

49 "[a]Your fathers ate the manna in the wilderness, and they died.
50 "This is the bread which [a]comes down out of heaven, so that one
may eat of it and [b]not die.
51 "[a]I am the living bread that [b]came down out of heaven; if anyone
eats of this bread, [c]he shall live forever; and the bread also which I
shall give [d]for the life of the world is [e]My flesh."
52 [a]The Jews therefore [b]*began* to argue with one another, saying,
"How can this man give us *His* flesh to eat?"
53 Jesus therefore said to them, "Truly, truly, I say to you, unless
you eat the flesh of [a]the Son of Man and drink His blood, you have
no life in yourselves.
54 "He who eats My flesh and drinks My blood has eternal life, and I
will [a]raise him up on the last day.
55 "For My flesh is true food, and My blood is true drink.
56 "He who eats My flesh and drinks My blood [a]abides in Me, and I
in him.
57 "As the [a]living Father [b]sent Me, and I live because of the Father, so
he who eats Me, he also shall live because of Me.
58 "This is the bread which [a]came down out of heaven; not as [b]the
fathers ate, and died, he who eats this bread [c]shall live forever."
59 These things He said [a]in the synagogue, as He taught [b]in Caper-
naum.
60 Many therefore of His [a]disciples, when they heard *this* said,
"[b]This is a difficult statement; who can listen to it?"
61 But Jesus, [a]conscious that His disciples grumbled at this, said to
them, "Does this [b]cause you to stumble?
62 "*What* then if you should behold [a]the Son of Man [b]ascending
where He was before?
63 "[a]It is the Spirit who gives life; the flesh profits nothing; [b]the
words that I have spoken to you are spirit and are life.
64 "But there are [a]some of you who do not believe." For Jesus [b]knew
from the beginning who they were who did not believe, and [c]who it
was that would [1]betray Him.
65 And He was saying, "For this reason I have [a]said to you, that no
one can come to Me, unless [b]it has been granted him from the
Father."
66 As a result of this many of His [a]disciples [b]withdrew, and were
not walking with Him anymore.
67 Jesus said therefore to [a]the twelve, "You do not want to go away
also, do you?"
68 [a]Simon Peter answered Him, "Lord, to whom shall we go? You
have [b]words of eternal life.
69 "And we have believed and have come to know that You are [a]the
Holy One of God."
70 Jesus answered them, "[a]Did I Myself not choose you, [b]the twelve,
and *yet* one of you is [c]a devil?"
71 Now He meant Judas [a]*the son* of Simon Iscariot, for he, [b]one of
[c]the twelve, [1]was going to betray Him.

Chapter 7

7 And after these things Jesus [a]was walking in Galilee; for He was
unwilling to walk in Judea, because [b]the Jews [c]were seeking to
kill Him.
2 Now the feast of the Jews, [a]the Feast of Booths, was at hand.

49 [a]John 6:
50 [a]John 6:
3:36; 5:24; 6
11:26
51 [a]John 6:
[b]John 6:41,
3:36; 5:24; 6
11:26 [d]John
3:14f.; Heb.
1 John 4:10
6:53-56
52 [a]John 1:1
[b]John 9:16;
53 [a]Matt. 8:2
6:27, 62
54 [a]John 6:3
56 [a]John 15
1 John 2:24;
57 [a]Matt. 16:
5:26 [b]John 3
6:29, 38
58 [a]John 6:3
[b]John 6:31, 4
3:36; 5:24; 6:
11:26
59 [a]Matt. 4:2
6:24
60 [a]John 2:2
[b]John 6:52
61 [a]John 6:6
11:6
62 [a]Matt. 8:2
6:27, 53 [b]Mar
John 3:13
63 [a]2 Cor. 3:6
6:68
64 [1]Or, *delive*
[a]John 6:60, 66
2:25 [c]Matt. 10
6:71; 13:11
65 [a]John 6:37
[b]Matt. 13:11; J
66 [a]John 2:2;
[b]John 6:60, 64
67 [a]Matt. 10:2
2:2; 6:70f.; 20:
68 [a]Matt. 16:1
6:63; 12:49f.; 1
69 [a]Mark 1:24
Luke 9:20
70 [a]John 15:16
[b]Matt. 10:2; Jo
6:71; 20:24 [c]Jo
13:2, 27; 17:12
71 [1]Or, *was int*
to [a]John 12:4;
[b]Mark 14:10 [c]M
10:2; John 2:2;
20:24
7:1 [a]John 4:3;
11:54 [b]John 1:1
13, 15, 35 [c]Joh
7:19; 8:37, 40;
2 [a]Lev. 23:34; D
16:13, 16; Zech
14:16-19

3 His [a]brothers therefore said to Him, "Depart from here, and go
into Judea, that Your [b]disciples also may behold Your works which
You are doing.
4 "For no one does anything in secret, [1]when he himself seeks to be
known publicly. If You do these things, show Yourself to the world."
5 For not even His [a]brothers were believing in Him.
6 Jesus therefore *said to them, "[a]My time is not yet at hand, but
your time is always opportune.
7 "[a]The world cannot hate you; but it hates Me because I testify of
it, that [b]its deeds are evil.
8 "Go up to the feast yourselves; I do not go up[1] to this feast be-
cause [a]My time has not yet fully come."
9 And having said these things to them, He stayed in Galilee.
10 But when His [a]brothers had gone up to the feast, then He Him-
self also went up, not publicly, but as it were, in secret.
11 [a]The Jews therefore [b]were seeking Him at the feast, and were
saying, "Where is He?"
12 And there was much grumbling among the multitudes concern-
ing Him; [a]some were saying, "He is a good man"; others were
saying, "No, on the contrary, He leads the multitude astray."
13 Yet no one was speaking openly of Him for [a]fear of the Jews.
14 But when it was now the midst of the feast Jesus went up into
the temple, and *began to* [a]teach.
15 [a]The Jews therefore were marveling, saying, "How has this man
[b]become learned, having never been educated?"
16 Jesus therefore answered them, and said, "[a]My teaching is not
Mine, but His who sent Me.
17 "[a]If any man is willing to do His will, he shall know of the teach-
ing, whether it is of God, or *whether* I speak from Myself.
18 "He who speaks from himself [a]seeks his own glory; but He who is
seeking the glory of the One who sent Him, He is true, and there is
no unrighteousness in Him.
19 "[a]Did not Moses give you the Law, and *yet* none of you carries out
the Law? Why do you [b]seek to kill Me?"
20 The multitude answered, "[a]You [1]have a demon! Who seeks to
kill You?"
21 Jesus answered and said to them, "I did [a]one [1]deed, and you all
marvel.
22 "On this account [a]Moses has given you circumcision (not because
it is from Moses, but from [b]the fathers), and on *the* Sabbath you
circumcise a man.
23 "[a]If a man receives circumcision on *the* Sabbath that the Law of
Moses may not be broken, are you angry with Me because I made an
entire man well on *the* Sabbath?
24 "Do not [a]judge according to appearance, but [1]judge with right-
eous judgment."
25 Therefore some of the people of Jerusalem were saying, "Is this
not the man whom they are seeking to kill?
26 "And look, He is speaking publicly, and they are saying nothing
to Him. [a]The rulers do not really know that this is [1]the Christ, do
they?
27 "However, [a]we know where this man is from; but whenever the
Christ may come, no one knows where He is from."
28 Jesus therefore cried out in the temple, [a]teaching and saying,

12:46; Mark
John 7:5, 10
[b]John 6:60
4 [1]Lit., *and*
12:46; Mark
John 7:3, 10
26:18; John
2:4; 7:8, 30
5:18f. [b]John
3:19f.
e authorities
et [a]John 7:6
12:46; Mark
; John 7:3, 5
7:13, 15, 35
[b]John 11:56
John 7:40-43
9:22; 12:42;
19:38; 20:19
. 26:55; John
7:28
:19; 7:11, 13,
5 [b]Acts 26:24
6 [a]John 3:11
5:9, 14; Prov.
. 12:10; John
3:21; 8:43f.
5:41; 8:50, 54;
12:43
in 1:17 [b]Mark
1:18; John 7:1
are demented
tt. 11:18; John
48f., 52; 10:20
Or, *work* [a]John
5:2-9, 16; 7:23
ev. 12:3 [b]Gen.
; 21:4; Acts 7:8
Matt. 12:2; John
5:9, 10
[1]Lit., *judge the*
eous judgment
19:15; Is. 11:3;
7:9; John 8:15
e., the Messiah
23:13; John 3:1
hn 6:42; 7:41f.;
9:29
28 [a]John 7:14

"[b]You both know Me and know where I am from; and [c]I have not
come of Myself, but He who sent Me is true, whom you do not
know.
29 "[a]I know Him; because [b]I am from Him, and [c]He sent Me."
30 They [a]were seeking therefore to seize Him; and no man laid his
hand on Him, because His [b]hour had not yet come.
31 But [a]many of the multitude believed in Him; and they were
saying, "[b]When [1]the Christ shall come, He will not perform more
[2c]signs than those which this man has, will He?"
32 The Pharisees heard the multitude muttering these things about
Him; and the chief priests and the Pharisees sent [a]officers to [b]seize
Him.
33 Jesus therefore said, "[a]For a little while longer I am with you,
then [b]I go to Him who sent Me.
34 "[a]You shall seek Me, and shall not find Me; and where I am, you
cannot come."
35 [a]The Jews therefore said to one another, "[b]Where does this man
intend to go that we shall not find Him? He is not intending to go to
[c]the Dispersion among [d]the Greeks, and teach the Greeks, is He?
36 "What is this statement that He said, '[a]You will seek Me, and will
not find Me; and where I am, you cannot come'?"
37 Now on [a]the last day, the great *day* of the feast, Jesus stood and
cried out, saying, "[b]If any man is thirsty, [1]let him come to Me and
drink.
38 "He who believes in Me, [a]as the Scripture said, 'From [1]his inner-
most being shall flow rivers of [b]living water.' "
39 But this He spoke [a]of the Spirit, whom those who believed in
Him were to receive; [1]for [b]the Spirit was not yet *given*, because Jesus
was not yet [c]glorified.
40 *Some* of the multitude therefore, when they heard these words,
were saying, "This certainly is [a]the Prophet."
41 Others were saying, "This is [1]the Christ." Still others were
saying, "[a]Surely [1]the Christ is not going to come from Galilee, is He?
42 "Has not the Scripture said that the Christ comes from [a]the off-
spring of David, and from Bethlehem, the village where David
was?"
43 So [a]there arose a division in the multitude because of Him.
44 And [a]some of them wanted to seize Him, but no one laid hands
on Him.
45 The [a]officers therefore came to the chief priests and Pharisees,
and they said to them, "Why did you not bring Him?"
46 The [a]officers answered, "[b]Never did a man speak the way this
man speaks."
47 The Pharisees therefore answered them, "[a]You have not also
been led astray, have you?
48 "[a]No one of [b]the rulers or Pharisees has believed in Him, has he?
49 "But this multitude which does not know the Law is accursed."
50 [a]Nicodemus *said to them (he who came to Him before, being
one of them),
51 "[a]Our Law does not judge a man, unless it first hears from him
and knows what he is doing, does it?"
52 They answered and said to him, "[a]You are not also from Galilee,
are you? Search, and see that no prophet arises out of Galilee."
53 [[1]And everyone went to his home.

28 [b]John 6 9:29 [c]John

29 [a]Matt. 11 8:55; 17:25 [c]John 3:17

30 [a]Matt. 21 7:32, 44; 10 7:6; 8:20

31 [1]I.e., the [2]Or, *attesting* [a]John 2:23; 11:45; 12:11 7:26 [c]John

32 [a]Matt. 26 7:45f. [b]Matt.

33 [a]John 12 14:19; 16:16 14:12, 28; 16 28; 20:17

34 [a]John 7:3 13:33

35 [a]John 7:1 8:22 [c]Ps. 14 11:12; 56:8; Z James 1:1; 1 [d]John 12:20; 17:4; 18:4; R

36 [a]John 7:3 13:33

37 [1]I.e., let h coming to Me him keep drin 23:36; Num. Neh. 8:18 [b]Jo 14; 6:35

38 [1]Lit., *out o* [a]Is. 44:3; 55:1 [b]John 4:10

39 [1]Other ms *the Holy Spirit yet given* [a]Jo John 1:33 [b]Jo Acts 1:4f.; 2:4 [c]John 12:16, 2 16:14; 17:1

40 [a]Matt. 21:1 1:21

41 [1]I.e., the M [a]John 1:46; 7:5

42 [a]Ps. 89:4; Matt. 1:1; 2:5f. 2:4ff.

43 [a]John 9:16

44 [a]John 7:30

45 [a]John 7:32

46 [a]John 7:32 7:28

47 [a]John 7:12

48 [a]John 12:42 23:13; John 7:2

50 [a]John 3:1;

51 [a]Ex. 23:1; D 17:6; 19:15; Pro Acts 23:3

52 [a]John 1:46;

53 [1]John 7:53- not found in mo old mss.

Chapter 8

8 But Jesus went to [a]the Mount of Olives.
2 And early in the morning He came again into the temple, and
all the people were coming to Him; and [a]He sat down and *began* to
teach them.
3 And the scribes and the Pharisees *brought a woman caught in
adultery, and having set her in the midst,
4 they *said to Him, "Teacher, this woman has been caught in
adultery, in the very act.
5 "Now in the Law [a]Moses commanded us to stone such women;
what then do You say?"
6 And they were saying this, [a]testing Him, [b]in order that they
might have grounds for accusing Him. But Jesus stooped down, and
with His finger wrote on the ground.
7 But when they persisted in asking Him, [a]He straightened up,
and said to them, "[b]He who is without sin among you, let him *be the*
[c]first to throw a stone at her."
8 And again He stooped down, and wrote on the ground.
9 And when they heard it, they *began* to go out one by one, begin-
ning with the older ones, and He was left alone, and the woman,
where she was, in the midst.
10 And [a]straightening up, Jesus said to her, "Woman, where are
they? Did no one condemn you?"
11 And she said, "No one, [1]Lord." And Jesus said, "[a]Neither do I
condemn you; go your way. From now on [b]sin no more."]
12 Again therefore Jesus spoke to them, saying, "[a]I am the light of
the world; [b]he who follows Me shall not walk in the darkness, but
shall have the light of life."
13 The Pharisees therefore said to Him, "[a]You are bearing witness of
Yourself; Your witness is not [1]true."
14 Jesus answered and said to them, "[a]Even if I bear witness of
Myself, My witness is true; for I know [b]where I came from, and
where I am going; but [c]you do not know where I come from, or
where I am going.
15 "[a]You people judge [1]according to the flesh; [b]I am not judging
anyone.
16 "But even [a]if I do judge, My judgment is true; for I am not alone *in*
it, but I and [1]He who sent Me.
17 "Even in [a]your law it has been written, that the testimony of [b]two
men is [1]true.
18 "I am He who bears witness of Myself, and [a]the Father who sent
Me bears witness of Me."
19 And so they were saying to Him, "Where is Your Father?" Jesus
answered, "You know neither Me, nor My Father; [a]if you knew Me,
you would know My Father also."
20 These words He spoke in [a]the treasury, as [b]He taught in the
temple; and no one seized Him, because [c]His hour had not yet come.
21 He said therefore again to them, "I go away, and [a]you shall seek
Me, and [b]shall die in your sin; where I am going, you cannot come."
22 Therefore [a]the Jews were saying, "Surely He will not kill Him-
self, will He, since He says, '[b]Where I am going, you cannot come'?"
23 And He was saying to them, "[a]You are from below, I am from
above; [b]you are of this world, [c]I am not of this world.

8:1 [a]Matt. 21:1
att. 26:55; John 8:20
ev. 20:10; Deut. 22:22f.
Matt. 16:1; 19:3; , 35; Mark 8:11; 15; Luke 10:25; 1:16 [b]Mark 3:2
ohn 8:10 [b]Matt. om. 2:1 [c]Deut. 17:7
10 [a]John 8:7
Sir [a]John 3:17 [b]John 5:14
[a]John 1:4; 9:5; :35 [b]Matt. 5:14
alid [a]John 5:31
hn 18:37; Rev. 14 [b]John 8:42; 28 [c]John 7:28; 9:29
[1]I.e., a carnal [a]1 Sam. 16:7; :24 [b]John 3:17
y ancient mss. *the Father who Me* [a]John 5:30
7 [1]I.e., valid or le [a]Deut. 17:6; 5 [b]Matt. 18:16
hn 5:37; 1 John 5:9
ohn 7:28; 8:55; 14:7, 9; 16:3
Mark 12:41, 43; :1 [b]John 7:14; 8:2 [c]John 7:30
hn 7:34 [b]John 8:24
1:19; 8:48, 52, 57 [b]John 7:35
n 3:31 [b]1 John John 17:14, 16

24 "I said therefore to you, that you [a]shall die in your sins; for unless
you believe that [1b]I am *He*, [a]you shall die in your sins."
25 And so they were saying to Him, "Who are You?" Jesus said to
them, "[1]What have I been saying to you *from* the beginning?
26 "I have many things to speak and to judge concerning you, but
[a]He who sent Me is true; and [b]the things which I heard from Him,
these I speak to the world."
27 They did not realize that He had been speaking to them about
the Father.
28 Jesus therefore said, "When you [a]lift up the Son of Man, then
you will know that [1b]I am *He*, and [c]I do nothing on My own initia-
tive, but I speak these things as the Father taught Me.
29 "And He who sent Me is with Me; [a]He [1]has not left Me alone, for
[b]I always do the things that are pleasing to Him."
30 As He spoke these things, [a]many came to believe in Him.
31 Jesus therefore was saying to those Jews who had believed Him,
"[a]If you abide in My word, *then* you are truly [b]disciples of Mine;
32 and [a]you shall know the truth, and [b]the truth shall make you
free."
33 They answered Him, "[a]We are Abraham's offspring, and have
never yet been enslaved to anyone; how is it that You say, 'You shall
become free'?"
34 Jesus answered them, "Truly, truly, I say to you, [a]everyone who
commits sin is the slave of sin.
35 "And [a]the slave does not remain in the house forever; [b]the son
does remain forever.
36 "If therefore the Son [a]shall make you free, you shall be free in-
deed.
37 "I know that you are [a]Abraham's offspring; yet [b]you seek to kill
Me, because My word [1]has no place in you.
38 "I speak the things which I have seen [1]with *My* Father; therefore
you also do the things which you heard from [a]*your* father."
39 They answered and said to Him, "Abraham is [a]our father." Jesus
*said to them, "[b]If you are Abraham's children, do the deeds of
Abraham.
40 "But as it is, [a]you are seeking to kill Me, a man who has [b]told you
the truth, which I heard from God; this Abraham did not do.
41 "You are doing the deeds of [a]your father." They said to Him, "We
were not born of fornication; [b]we have one Father, *even* God."
42 Jesus said to them, "If God were your Father, [a]you would love
Me; [b]for I proceeded forth and have come from God, for I have [c]not
even come on My own initiative, but [1d]He sent Me.
43 "Why do you not understand [1a]what I am saying? *It is* because
you cannot [b]hear My word.
44 "[a]You are of [b]*your* father the devil, and [c]you want to do the desires
of your father. [d]He was a murderer from the beginning, and does not
stand in the truth, because [e]there is no truth in him. Whenever he
speaks [1]a lie, he [f]speaks from his own *nature;* for he is a liar, and the
father of [2]lies.
45 "But because [a]I speak the truth, you do not believe Me.
46 "Which one of you convicts Me of sin? If [a]I speak truth, why do
you not believe Me?
47 "[a]He who is of God hears the words of God; for this reason you
do not hear *them,* because you are not of God."

24 [1]Most autho
associate this w
3:14, *I AM WH*
[a]John 8:21 [b]Ma
Mark 13:6; Luk
John 4:26; 8:28
13:19

25 [1]Or, *That w
have been say
from the beginn*

26 [a]John 3:33;
[b]John 8:40; 12:

28 [1]Lit., *I AM* (
note) [a]John 3:1
12:32 [b]Matt. 2
13:6; Luke 21:8
4:26; 8:24, 58;
[c]John 3:11; 5:1

29 [1]Or, *did not*
[a]John 8:16; 16:
[b]John 4:34

30 [a]John 7:31

31 [a]John 15:7;
9 [b]John 2:2

32 [a]John 1:14,
[b]John 8:36; Ro
2 Cor. 3:17; Ga
James 2:12; 1

33 [a]Matt. 3:9;
John 8:37, 39

34 [a]Rom. 6:16
2:19

35 [a]Gen. 21:1
4:30 [b]Luke 15:

36 [a]John 8:32

37 [1]Or, *makes
progress* [a]Mat
John 8:39 [b]Jo
8:40

38 [1]Or, *in the
of* [a]John 8:41,

39 [a]Matt. 3:9;
8:37 [b]Rom. 9:

40 [a]John 7:1;
[b]John 8:26

41 [a]John 8:38,
[b]Deut. 32:6; Is.
64:8

42 [1]Lit., *that O*
[a]1 John 5:1 [b]J
16:28, 30; 17:8
7:28 [d]John 3:1

43 [1]Or, *My m
speaking* [a]Joh
39, 41 [b]John 5

44 [1]Lit., *the li*
[a]1 John 3:8 [b]J
41 [c]John 7:17
3:4; 1 John 3:8
[e]1 John 2:4

45 [a]John 18:3

46 [a]John 18:3

47 [a]1 John 4:

48 [a]The Jews answered and said to Him, "Do we not say rightly
that You are a [b]Samaritan and [c]have a demon?"
49 Jesus answered, "I do not [a]have a demon; but I honor My Father,
and you dishonor Me.
50 "But [a]I do not seek My glory; there is One who seeks and judges.
51 "Truly, truly, I say to you, if anyone [a]keeps My word he shall
never [b]see death."
52 [a]The Jews said to Him, "Now we know that You [b]have a demon.
Abraham died, and the prophets *also*; and You say, 'If anyone [c]keeps
My word, he shall never [d]taste of death.'
53 "Surely You [a]are not greater than our father Abraham, who died?
The prophets died too; whom do You make Yourself out *to be*?"
54 Jesus answered, "[a]If I glorify Myself, My glory is nothing; [b]it is
My Father who glorifies Me, of whom you say, 'He is our God';
55 and [a]you have not come to know Him, [b]but I know Him; and if I
say that I do not know Him, I shall be [c]a liar like you, [b]but I do know
Him, and [d]keep His word.
56 "[a]Your father Abraham [b]rejoiced [1]to see My day, and he saw *it* and
was glad."
57 [a]The Jews therefore said to Him, "You are not yet fifty years old,
and have You seen Abraham?"
58 Jesus said to them, "Truly, truly, I say to you, before Abraham
[1]was born, [a]I am."
59 Therefore they [a]picked up stones to throw at Him; but Jesus [1b]hid
Himself, and went out of the temple[2].

Chapter 9

9 And as He passed by, He saw a man blind from birth.
2 And His disciples asked Him, saying, "[a]Rabbi, who sinned,
[b]this man or his [c]parents, that he should be born blind?"
3 Jesus answered, "*It was* neither *that* this man sinned, nor his
parents; but *it was* in order [a]that the works of God might be dis-
played in him.
4 "We must work the works of Him who sent Me, [a]as long as it is
day; night is coming, when no man can work.
5 "While I am in the world, I am [a]the light of the world."
6 When He had said this, He [a]spat on the ground, and made clay
of the spittle, and applied the clay to his eyes,
7 and said to him, "Go, wash in [a]the pool of Siloam" (which is
translated, Sent). And so he went away and [b]washed, and [c]came *back*
seeing.
8 The neighbors therefore, and those who previously saw him as a
beggar, were saying, "Is not this the one who used to [a]sit and beg?"
9 Others were saying, "This is he," *still* others were saying, "No,
but he is like him." He kept saying, "I am the one."
10 Therefore they were saying to him, "How then were your eyes
opened?"
11 He answered, "The man who is called Jesus made clay, and
anointed my eyes, and said to me, 'Go to [a]Siloam, and wash'; so I
went away and washed, and I received sight."
12 And they said to him, "Where is He?" He *said, "I do not know."
13 They *brought to the Pharisees him who was formerly blind.
14 [a]Now it was a Sabbath on the day when Jesus made the clay, and
opened his eyes.

ohn 1:19 [b]Matt. John 4:9 [c]John 7:20
49 [a]John 7:20
John 5:41; 8:54
ohn 8:55; 14:23; 20; 17:6 [b]Matt. Luke 2:26; John ; Heb. 2:9; 11:5
ohn 1:19 [b]John ohn 8:55; 14:23; 7:6 [d]John 8:51
53 [a]John 4:12
ohn 8:50 [b]John 7:39
ohn 8:19; 15:21 :29 [c]John 8:44 ohn 8:51; 15:10
in order that he ee [a]John 8:37, att. 13:17; Heb. 11:13
57 [a]John 1:19
[1]Lit., *came into* [a]Ex. 3:14; John 1:1; 17:5, 24
it., *was hidden* e mss. add *and* *ough the midst* *n went His way* *d so passed by* att. 12:14; John 8 [b]John 12:36
att. 23:7 [b]Luke John 9:34; Acts 28:4 [c]Ex. 20:5
3 [a]John 11:4
ohn 7:33; 11:9; 2:35; Gal. 6:10
5:14; John 1:4; 8:12; 12:46
Mark 7:33; 8:23
. 3:15; Is. 8:6; 3:4; John 9:11 3f. [c]Is. 29:18; 2:7; Matt. 11:5; John 11:37
[a]Acts 3:2, 10
11 [a]John 9:7
14 [a]John 5:9

15 [a]Again, therefore, the Pharisees also were asking him how he
received his sight. And he said to them, "He applied clay to my eyes,
and I washed, and I see."
16 Therefore some of the Pharisees were saying, "This man is not
from God, because He [a]does not keep the Sabbath." But others were
saying, "How can a man who is a sinner perform such [1b]signs?" And
[c]there was a division among them.
17 They *said therefore to the blind man [a]again, "What do you say
about Him, since He opened your eyes?" And he said, "He is a
[b]prophet."
18 [a]The Jews therefore did not believe *it* of him, that he had been
blind, and had received sight, until they called the parents of the
very one who had received his sight,
19 and questioned them, saying, "Is this your son, who you say was
born blind? Then how does he now see?"
20 His parents answered them and said, "We know that this is our
son, and that he was born blind;
21 but how he now sees, we do not know; or who opened his eyes,
we do not know. Ask him; he is of age, he shall speak for himself."
22 His parents said this because they [a]were afraid of the Jews; for
the Jews [b]had already agreed, that if anyone should confess Him to
be [1]Christ, [c]he should be put out of the synagogue.
23 For this reason his parents said, "[a]He is of age; ask him."
24 So a second time they called the man who had been blind, and
said to him, "[a]Give glory to God; we know that [b]this man is a sin-
ner."
25 He therefore answered, "Whether He is a sinner, I do not know;
one thing I do know, that, whereas I was blind, now I see."
26 They said therefore to him, "What did He do to you? How did
He open your eyes?"
27 He answered them, "[a]I told you already, and you did not [b]listen;
why do you want to hear *it* again? You do not want to become His
disciples too, do you?"
28 And they reviled him, and said, "You are His disciple, but [a]we
are disciples of Moses.
29 "We know that God has spoken to Moses; but as for this man, [a]we
do not know where He is from."
30 The man answered and said to them, "Well, here is an amazing
thing, that you do not know where He is from, and *yet* He opened
my eyes.
31 "We know that [a]God does not hear sinners; but if anyone is God-
fearing, and does His will, He hears him.
32 "[1]Since the beginning of time it has never been heard that anyone
opened the eyes of a person born blind.
33 "[a]If this man were not from God, He could do nothing."
34 They answered and said to him, "[a]You were born entirely in sins,
and are you teaching us?" And they [b]put him out.
35 Jesus heard that they had [a]put him out; and finding him, He
said, "Do you believe in the [b]Son of Man?"
36 He answered and said, "And [a]who is He, [1]Lord, that I may
believe in Him?"
37 Jesus said to him, "You have both seen Him, and [a]He is the one
who is talking with you."
38 And he said, "Lord, I believe." And he [a]worshiped Him.

15 [a]John 9

16 [1]Or, *atte*
miracles [a]M
Luke 13:14;
7:23 [b]John
6:52; 7:12, 4

17 [a]John 9:
18:15; Matt.

18 [a]John 1:

22 [1]I.e., the
[a]John 7:13
7:45-52 [c]Luk
John 12:42;

23 [a]John 9:2

24 [a]Josh. 7:
10:11; Rev. 1
9:16

27 [a]John 9:1
5:25

28 [a]John 5:4
2:17

29 [a]John 8:1

31 [a]Job 27:8f
Ps. 34:15f.; 66
145:19; Prov.
28:9; Is. 1:15;
5:16ff.

32 [1]Lit., *From*
it was not hea

33 [a]John 3:2;

34 [a]John 9:2
9:22, 35; 3 Joh

35 [a]John 9:22,
3 John 10 [b]Ma

36 [1]Or, *Sir* [a]R

37 [a]John 4:26

38 [a]Matt. 8:2

39 And Jesus said, "[a]For judgment I came into this world, that
[b]those who do not see may see; and that [c]those who see may become
blind."
40 Those of the Pharisees who were with Him heard these things,
and said to Him, "[a]We are not blind too, are we?"
41 Jesus said to them, "[a]If you were blind, you would have no sin;
but since you say, '[b]We see,' your sin remains.

Chapter 10

10 "Truly, truly, I say to you, he who does not enter by the door
into the fold of the sheep, but climbs up some other way, he is
[a]a thief and a robber.
2 "But he who enters by the door is [a]a shepherd of the sheep.
3 "To him the doorkeeper opens, and the sheep hear [a]his voice, and
he calls his own sheep by name, and [b]leads them out.
4 "When he puts forth all his own, he goes before them, and the
sheep follow him because they know [a]his voice.
5 "And a stranger they simply will not follow, but will flee from
him, because they do not know [a]the voice of strangers."
6 This [a]figure of speech Jesus spoke to them, but they did not
understand what those things were which He had been saying to
them.
7 Jesus therefore said to them again, "Truly, truly, I say to you, I
am [a]the door of the sheep.
8 "All who came before Me are [a]thieves and robbers, but the sheep
did not hear them.
9 "[a]I am the door; if anyone enters through Me, he shall be saved,
and shall go in and out, and find pasture.
10 "The thief comes only to steal, and kill, and destroy; I came that
they [a]might have life, and might [1]have *it* abundantly.
11 "[a]I am the good shepherd; the good shepherd [b]lays down His life
for the sheep.
12 "He who is a hireling, and not a [a]shepherd, who is not the owner
of the sheep, beholds the wolf coming, and leaves the sheep, and
flees, and the wolf snatches them, and scatters *them*.
13 "*He flees* because he is a hireling, and is not concerned about the
sheep.
14 "[a]I am the good shepherd; and [b]I know My own, and My own
know Me,
15 even as [a]the Father knows Me and I know the Father; and [b]I lay
down My life for the sheep.
16 "And I have [a]other sheep, which are not of this fold; I must bring
them also, and they shall hear My voice; and they shall become [b]one
flock *with* [c]one shepherd.
17 "For this reason the Father loves Me, because I [a]lay down My life
that I may take it again.
18 "[a]No one [1]has taken it away from Me, but I [b]lay it down on My
own initiative. I have authority to lay it down, and I have authority
to take it up again. [c]This commandment I received from My Father."
19 [a]There arose a division again among the Jews because of these
words.
20 And many of them were saying, "He [a]has a demon and [b]is in-
sane. Why do you listen to Him?"

hn 3:19; 5:22, 27 [b]Luke 4:18 [c]Matt. 13:13; 15:14
40 [a]Rom. 2:19
[a]John 15:22, 24 [b]Prov. 26:12
10:1 [a]John 10:8
2 [a]John 10:11f.
hn 10:4f., 16, 27 [b]John 10:9
ohn 10:5, 16, 27
ohn 10:4, 16, 27
[a]John 16:25, 29; 2 Pet. 2:22
7 [a]John 10:1f., 9
Jer. 23:1f.; Ezek. 34:2ff.; John 10:1
9 [a]John 10:1f., 9
10 [1]Or, *have* *ance* [a]John 5:40
[a]Is. 40:11; Ezek. :11-16, 23; John):14; Heb. 13:20; et. 5:4; Rev. 7:17 hn 10:15, 17, 18; :13; 1 John 3:16
12 [a]John 10:2
ohn 10:11 [b]John 10:27
Matt. 11:27; Luke .22 [b]John 10:11, 17, 18
[a]Is. 56:8 [b]John 52; 17:20f.; Eph. 3-18; 1 Pet. 2:25 ek. 34:23; 37:24
ohn 10:11, 15, 18
ny Gr. mss. read *es* [a]Matt. 26:53; 2:19; 5:26 [b]John 11, 15, 17 [c]John ; 15:10; Phil. 2:8; Heb. 5:8
[a]John 7:43; 9:16
John 7:20 [b]Mark 3:21

21 Others were saying, "These are not the sayings of one [a]demon-
possessed. [b]A demon cannot open the eyes of the blind, can he?"
22 At that time the Feast of the Dedication took place at Jerusalem;
23 it was winter, and Jesus was walking in the temple in the portico
of [a]Solomon.
24 [a]The Jews therefore gathered around Him, and were saying to
Him, "How long will You keep us in suspense? If You are [1]the
Christ, tell us [b]plainly."
25 Jesus answered them, "[a]I told you, and you do not believe; [b]the
works that I do in My Father's name, these bear witness of Me.
26 "But you do not believe, because [a]you are not of My sheep.
27 "My sheep [a]hear My voice, and [b]I know them, and they fol-
low Me;
28 and I give [a]eternal life to them, and they shall never perish; and
[b]no one shall snatch them out of My hand.
29 "[1]My Father, who has given *them* to Me, is greater than all; and no
one is able to snatch *them* out of the Father's hand.
30 "[a]I and the Father are [1]one."
31 The Jews [a]took up stones again to stone Him.
32 Jesus answered them, "I showed you many good works from the
Father; for which of them are you stoning Me?"
33 The Jews answered Him, "For a good work we do not stone You,
but for [a]blasphemy; and because You, being a man, [b]make Yourself
out *to be* God."
34 Jesus answered them, "Has it not been written in [a]your [b]Law, '[c]I
SAID, YOU ARE GODS'?
35 "If he called them gods, to whom the word of God came (and the
Scripture cannot be broken),
36 do you say of Him, whom the Father [a]sanctified and [b]sent into
the world, 'You are blaspheming,' because I said, '[c]I am the Son of
God'?
37 "[a]If I do not do the works of My Father, do not believe Me;
38 but if I do them, though you do not believe Me, believe [a]the
works, that you may [1]know and understand that [b]the Father is in
Me, and I in the Father."
39 Therefore [a]they were seeking again to seize Him, and [b]He eluded
their grasp.
40 And He went away [a]again beyond the Jordan to the place where
John was first baptizing, and He was staying there.
41 And many came to Him and were saying, "While John per-
formed no [a]sign, yet [b]everything John said about this man was true."
42 And [a]many believed in Him there.

Chapter 11

11 Now a certain man was sick, Lazarus of [a]Bethany, the village
of Mary and her sister [b]Martha.
2 And it was the Mary who [a]anointed [b]the Lord with ointment,
and wiped His feet with her hair, whose brother Lazarus was sick.
3 The sisters therefore sent to Him, saying, "[a]Lord, behold, [b]he
whom You love is sick."
4 But when Jesus heard it, He said, "This sickness is not unto
death, but for [a]the glory of God, that the Son of God may be glorified
by it."
5 Now Jesus loved [a]Martha, and her sister, and Lazarus.

21 [a]Matt. 4 4:11; John 9
23 [a]Acts 3:
24 [1]I.e., the [a]John 1:19; [b]Luke 22:67
25 [a]John 8: [b]John 5:36;
26 [a]John 8:
27 [a]John 10 [b]John 10:14
28 [a]John 17 2:25; 5:11 [b]J 6:37, 39
29 [1]Some ea read *What M has given Me than all*
30 [1]Lit., (neu *unity;* or, *one* [a]John 17:21ff
31 [a]John 8:5
33 [a]Lev. 24:1 5:18
34 [a]John 8:17 12:34; 15:25; 3:19; 1 Cor. 14 82:6
36 [a]Jer. 1:5; J [b]John 3:17 [c]Jo 10:30
37 [a]John 10:2
38 [1]Lit., *know continue know* 10:25; 14:11 [b]J 14:10f., 20; 17:
39 [a]John 7:30 4:30; John 8:59
40 [a]John 1:28
41 [a]John 2:11 1:27, 30, 34; 3:2
42 [a]John 7:31
11:1 [a]Matt. 21:1 11:18 [b]Luke 10: John 11:5, 19ff.
2 [a]Luke 7:38; Jo 12:3 [b]Luke 7:13 11:3, 21, 32; 13:1
3 [a]Luke 7:13; Jo 11:2, 21, 32; 13:1 [b]John 11:5, 11, 3
4 [a]John 9:3; 10: 11:40
5 [a]John 11:1

6 When therefore He heard that he was sick, He stayed then two
days *longer* in the place where He was.
7 Then after this He *said to the disciples, "[a]Let us go to Judea
again."
8 The disciples *said to Him, "[a]Rabbi, the Jews were just now seek-
ing [b]to stone You, and are You going there again?"
9 Jesus answered, "[a]Are there not twelve hours in the day? If
anyone walks in the day, he does not stumble, because he sees the
light of this world.
10 "But if anyone walks in the night, he stumbles, because the light
is not in him."
11 This He said, and after that He *said to them, "Our [a]friend
Lazarus [b]has fallen asleep; but I go, that I may awaken him out of
sleep."
12 The disciples therefore said to Him, "Lord, if he has fallen
asleep, he will [1]recover."
13 Now [a]Jesus had spoken of his death, but they thought that He
was speaking of [1]literal sleep.
14 Then Jesus therefore said to them plainly, "Lazarus is dead,
15 and I am glad for your sakes that I was not there, so that you
may believe; but let us go to him."
16 [a]Thomas therefore, who is called [1b]Didymus, said to *his* fellow
disciples, "Let us also go, that we may die with Him."
17 So when Jesus came, He found that he had already been in the
tomb [a]four days.
18 Now [a]Bethany was near Jerusalem, about [1]two miles off;
19 and many of [a]the Jews had come to [b]Martha and Mary, [c]to con-
sole them concerning *their* brother.
20 [a]Martha therefore, when she heard that Jesus was coming, went
to meet Him; but [a]Mary still sat in the house.
21 Martha therefore said to Jesus, "[a]Lord, [b]if You had been here, my
brother would not have died.
22 "Even now I know that [a]whatever You ask of God, God will give
You."
23 Jesus *said to her, "Your brother shall rise again."
24 Martha *said to Him, "[a]I know that he will rise again in the
resurrection on the last day."
25 Jesus said to her, "[a]I am the resurrection and the life; he who
believes in Me shall live even if he dies,
26 and everyone who lives and believes in Me [a]shall never die. Do
you believe this?"
27 She *said to Him, "Yes, Lord; I have believed that You are [1a]the
Christ, the Son of God, *even* [2b]He who comes into the world."
28 And when she had said this, she [a]went away, and called Mary
her sister, saying secretly, "[b]The Teacher is here, and is calling for
you."
29 And when she heard it, she *arose quickly, and was coming to
Him.
30 Now Jesus had not yet come into the village, but [a]was still in the
place where Martha met Him.
31 [a]The Jews then who were with her in the house, and [b]consoling
her, when they saw that Mary rose up quickly and went out, fol-
lowed her, supposing that she was going to the tomb to [1]weep there.
32 Therefore, when Mary came where Jesus was, she saw Him, and

fell at His feet, saying to Him, "[a]Lord, [b]if You had been here, my
brother would not have died."
33 When Jesus therefore saw her [1]weeping, and [a]the Jews who came
with her, *also* [1]weeping, He [b]was deeply moved in spirit, and [2c]was
troubled,
34 and said, "Where have you laid him?" They *said to Him, "Lord,
come and see."
35 Jesus [a]wept.
36 And so [a]the Jews were saying, "Behold how He [1b]loved him!"
37 But some of them said, "Could not this man, who [a]opened the
eyes of him who was blind, [1]have kept this man also from dying?"
38 Jesus therefore again being deeply moved within, *came to the
tomb. Now it was a [a]cave, and a stone was lying against it.
39 Jesus *said, "Remove the stone." Martha, the sister of the
deceased, *said to Him, "Lord, by this time [1]there will be a stench,
for he has been *dead* [a]four days."
40 Jesus *said to her, "[a]Did I not say to you, if you believe, you will
see the glory of God?"
41 And so they removed the [a]stone. And Jesus [b]raised His eyes, and
said, "[c]Father, I thank Thee that Thou heardest Me.
42 "And I knew that Thou hearest Me always; but [a]because of the
people standing around I said it, that they may believe that [b]Thou
didst send Me."
43 And when He had said these things, He cried out with a loud
voice, "Lazarus, come forth."
44 He who had died came forth, [a]bound hand and foot with wrap-
pings; and [b]his face was wrapped around with a cloth. Jesus *said to
them, "Unbind him, and let him go."
45 [a]Many therefore of the Jews, [b]who had come to Mary and [c]beheld
what He had done, believed in Him.
46 But some of them went away to the [a]Pharisees, and told them the
things which Jesus had done.
47 Therefore [a]the chief priests and the Pharisees [b]convened a [c]coun-
cil, and were saying, "What are we doing? For this man is perform-
ing many [1d]signs.
48 "If we let Him *go on* like this, all men will believe in Him, and the
Romans will come and take away both our [a]place and our nation."
49 But a certain one of them, [a]Caiaphas, [b]who was high priest that
year, said to them, "You know nothing at all,
50 nor do you take into account that [a]it is expedient for you that one
man should die for the people, and that the whole nation should not
perish."
51 Now this he did not say [1]on his own initiative; but [a]being high
priest that year, he prophesied that Jesus was going to die for the
nation,
52 and not for the nation only, but that He might also [a]gather
together into one the children of God who are scattered abroad.
53 So from that day on they [a]planned together to kill Him.
54 Jesus therefore [a]no longer continued to walk publicly among the
Jews, but went away from there to the country near the wilderness,
into a city called [b]Ephraim; and there He stayed with the disciples.
55 Now [a]the Passover of the Jews was at hand, and many went up
to Jerusalem out of the country before the Passover, [b]to purify them-
selves.

32 [a]J 11:21
33 [1]L *troubl* 11:19 [c]John
35 [a]L 11:33
36 [1]L [a]John
37 [1]Li *that th die* [a]J
38 [a]M 15:46; 20:1
39 [1]Li [a]John 1
40 [a]Jo
41 [a]Ma 15:46; 20:1 [b] 7:55 [c]
42 [a]Jo [b]John 3
44 [a]Joh 20:7
45 [a]Joh 11:19; 1 2:23
46 [a]Joh
47 [1]Or, *miracles* 45; 11:57 [c]Matt. 5:
48 [a]Matt
49 [a]Matt 11:51; 18
50 [a]John
51 [1]Lit., [a]John 18:
52 [a]John
53 [a]Matt.
54 [a]John 13:19 mg.
55 [a]Matt. 14:1; Luke 2:13; 12:1; 9:10; 2 Ch John 18:28

56 Therefore they [a]were seeking for Jesus, and were saying to one
another, as they stood in the temple, "What do you think; that He
will not come to the feast at all?"
57 Now [a]the chief priests and the Pharisees had given orders that if
anyone knew where He was, he should report it, that they might
seize Him.

Chapter 12

12 [a]Jesus, therefore, six days before [b]the Passover, came to [c]Beth-
any where Lazarus was, whom Jesus had raised from the
dead.
2 So they made Him a supper there, and [a]Martha was
serving; but Lazarus was one of those reclining *at the table*
with Him.
3 [a]Mary therefore took a pound of very costly [b]perfume
of pure nard, and anointed the feet of Jesus, and wiped His
feet with her hair; and the house was filled with the
fragrance of the perfume.
4 But [a]Judas Iscariot, one of His disciples, who was in-
tending to [1]betray Him, *said,
5 "Why was this perfume not sold for [1]three hundred
denarii, and given to poor *people*?"
6 Now he said this, not because he was concerned about
the poor, but because he was a thief, and as he [a]had the
money box, he used to pilfer [b]what was put into it.
7 Jesus therefore said, "Let her alone, in order that she
may keep [1]it for [a]the day of My burial.
8 "[a]For the poor you always have with you, but you do
not always have Me."
9 The [a]great multitude therefore of the Jews learned that
He was there; and they came, not for Jesus' sake only, but
that they might also see Lazarus, [b]whom He raised from
the dead.
10 But the chief priests took counsel that they might put
Lazarus to death also;
11 because [a]on account of him [b]many of the Jews were going away,
and were believing in Jesus.
12 On the next day [1a]the great multitude who had come to [b]the
feast, when they heard that Jesus was coming to Jerusalem,
13 took the branches of the palm trees, and went out to meet Him,
and *began* to cry out, "[a]Hosanna! BLESSED IS HE WHO COMES IN THE
NAME OF THE LORD, even the [b]King of Israel."
14 And Jesus, finding a young donkey, sat on it; as it is written,
15 "[a]FEAR NOT, DAUGHTER OF ZION; BEHOLD, YOUR KING IS COMING,
SEATED ON A DONKEY'S COLT."
16 [a]These things His disciples did not understand at the first; but
when Jesus [b]was glorified, then they remembered that these things
were written of Him, and that they had done these things to Him.
17 And so [a]the multitude who were with Him when He called
Lazarus out of the tomb, and raised him from the dead, were bearing
Him witness.
18 [a]For this cause also the multitude went and met Him, [b]because
they heard that He had performed this [1]sign.

From Bethany, Bethphage Across the Mount of Olives into Jerusalem

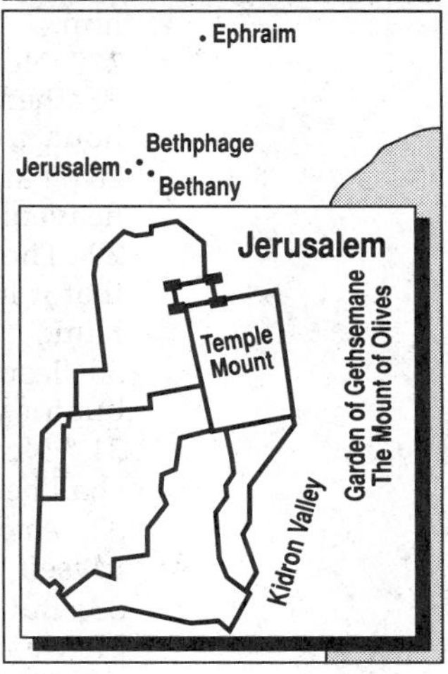

56 [a]John 7:11
57 [a]John 11:47
2:1 [a]John 12:1-8: att. 26:6-13; Mark 3-9; Luke 7:37-39 ohn 11:55; 12:20 Matt. 21:17; John 11:43f.
2 [a]Luke 10:38
Luke 7:37f.; John 11:2 [b]Mark 14:3
Dr, *deliver Him up* [a]John 6:71
[1]Equivalent to 11 months' wages
ohn 13:29 [b]Luke 8:3
e., The custom of nointing for burial [a]John 19:40
Deut. 15:11; Matt. 26:11; Mark 14:7
Mark 12:37; John 12:12 mg. [b]John 11:43f.; 12:1, 17f.
ohn 11:45f.; 12:18 [b]John 7:31; 11:42
[1]Or, *the common* [a]John 12:12-15: *Matt. 21:4-9; Mark 0; Luke 19:35-38* [b]John 12:1
Ps. 118:26 [b]John 1:49
15 [a]Zech. 9:9
[a]Mark 9:32; John 4:26 [b]John 7:39; 12:23
17 [a]John 11:42
18 [1]Or, *attesting acle* [a]Luke 19:37; 2:12 [b]John 12:11

19 The Pharisees therefore said to one another, "You see that you
are not doing any good; look, the world has gone after Him."
20 Now there were certain [a]Greeks among those who were going
up to worship at [b]the feast;
21 these therefore came to [a]Philip, who was from [b]Bethsaida of Gali-
lee, and *began to* ask him, saying, "Sir, we wish to see Jesus."
22 Philip *came and *told [a]Andrew; Andrew and Philip *came, and
they *told Jesus.
23 And Jesus *answered them, saying, "[a]The hour has come for the
Son of Man to [b]be glorified.
24 "Truly, truly, I say to you, [a]unless a grain of wheat falls into the
earth and dies, it remains by itself alone; but if it dies, it bears much
fruit.
25 "[a]He who loves his [1]life loses it; and he who [b]hates his [1]life in this
world shall keep it to life eternal.
26 "If anyone serves Me, let him follow Me; and [a]where I am, there
shall My servant also be; if anyone serves Me, the Father will [b]honor
him.
27 "[a]Now My soul has become troubled; and what shall I say,
'[b]Father, save Me from [c]this hour'? But for this purpose I came to this
hour.
28 "[a]Father, glorify Thy name." There came therefore a [b]voice out of
heaven: "I have both glorified it, and will glorify it again."
29 The multitude therefore, who stood by and heard it, were saying
that it had thundered; others were saying, "[a]An angel has spoken to
Him."
30 Jesus answered and said, "[a]This voice has not come for My sake,
but for your sakes.
31 "[a]Now judgment is upon this world; now [b]the ruler of this world
shall be cast out.
32 "And I, if I [a]be lifted up from the earth, will [b]draw all men to
Myself."
33 But He was saying this [a]to indicate the kind of death by which
He was to die.
34 The multitude therefore answered Him, "We have heard out of
[a]the Law that [1b]the Christ is to remain forever; and how can You say,
'The [c]Son of Man must be [d]lifted up'? Who is this [c]Son of Man?"
35 Jesus therefore said to them, "[a]For a little while longer [b]the light
is among you. [c]Walk while you have the light, that darkness may not
overtake you; he who [d]walks in the darkness does not know where
he goes.
36 "While you have the light, [a]believe in the light, in order that you
may become [b]sons of light."

These things Jesus spoke, and He departed and [1c]hid Himself
from them.
37 But though He had performed so many [1]signs before them, *yet*
they were not believing in Him;
38 that the word of Isaiah the prophet might be fulfilled, which he
spoke, "[a]LORD, WHO HAS BELIEVED OUR REPORT? AND TO WHOM HAS THE
ARM OF THE LORD BEEN REVEALED?"
39 For this cause they could not believe, for Isaiah said again,
40 "[a]HE HAS BLINDED THEIR EYES, AND HE [b]HARDENED THEIR HEART; LEST
THEY SEE WITH THEIR EYES, AND PERCEIVE WITH THEIR HEART, AND [1]BE
CONVERTED, AND I HEAL THEM."

20 [a]John 7:3
12:1
21 [a]John 1:4
11:21
22 [a]John 1:4
23 [a]Matt. 26
14:35, 41; Jo
17:1 [b]John 7
13:32
24 [a]Rom. 14
15:36
25 [1]Or, *soul*
10:39; 16:25;
Luke 9:24; 17
14:26
26 [a]John 14:3
2 Cor. 5:8; Ph
1 Thess. 4:17
2:30; Ps. 91:1
12:37
27 [a]Matt. 26:3
14:34; John 11
[b]Matt. 11:25 [c]
28 [a]Matt. 11:2
3:17; 17:5; Ma
9:7; Luke 3:22
29 [a]Acts 23:9
30 [a]John 11:42
31 [a]John 3:19;
16:11 [b]John 14
16:11; 2 Cor. 4:
2:2; 6:12; 1 Joh
5:19
32 [a]John 3:14;
12:34 [b]John 6:4
33 [a]John 18:32
34 [1]I.e., the Me
[a]John 10:34 [b]Ps
Is. 9:7; Ezek. 37
Dan. 7:14 [c]Matt
[d]John 3:14; 8:28
35 [a]John 7:33;
[b]John 12:46; 1 J
2:10 [c]Gal. 6:10;
5:8 [d]1 John 1:6;
36 [1]Lit., *was hid*
[a]John 12:46 [b]Lu
16:8; John 8:12
8:59
37 [1]Or, *attesting*
miracles
38 [a]Is. 53:1; Rom
40 [1]Lit., *should b*
turned; i.e., turn a
[a]Is. 6:10; Matt. 13
[b]Mark 6:52

41 These things Isaiah said, because [a]he saw His glory, and [b]he spoke of Him.

42 Nevertheless [a]many even of [b]the rulers believed in Him, but [c]because of the Pharisees they were not confessing *Him,* lest they should be [1d]put out of the synagogue;

43 [a]for they loved the approval of men rather than the approval of God.

44 And Jesus cried out and said, "[a]He who believes in Me does not believe in Me, but in Him who sent Me.

45 "And [a]he who beholds Me beholds the One who sent Me.

46 "[a]I have come *as* light into the world, that everyone who believes in Me may not remain in darkness.

47 "And if anyone hears My sayings, and does not keep them, I do not judge him; for [a]I did not come to judge the world, but to save the world.

48 "[a]He who rejects Me, and does not receive My sayings, has one who judges him; [b]the word I spoke is what will judge him at [c]the last day.

49 "[a]For I did not speak [1]on My own initiative, but the Father Himself who sent Me [b]has given Me commandment, what to say, and what to speak.

50 "And I know that [a]His commandment is eternal life; therefore the things I speak, I speak [b]just as the Father has told Me."

Chapter 13

13 Now before the Feast of [a]the Passover, Jesus knowing that [b]His hour had come that He should depart out of this world [c]to the Father, having loved His own who were in the world, He loved them [1]to the end.

2 And during supper, [a]the devil having already put into the heart of [b]Judas Iscariot, *the son* of Simon, to betray Him,

3 *Jesus,* [a]knowing that the Father had given all things into His hands, and that [b]He had come forth from God, and was going back to God,

4 *rose from supper, and *laid aside His garments; and taking a towel, He [a]girded Himself about.

5 Then He *poured water into the basin, and began to [a]wash the disciples' feet, and to wipe them with the towel with which He was girded.

6 And so He *came to Simon Peter. He *said to Him, "Lord, do You wash my feet?"

7 Jesus answered and said to him, "What I do you do not realize now, but you shall understand [a]hereafter."

8 Peter *said to Him, "Never shall You wash my feet!" Jesus answered him, "[a]If I do not wash you, [b]you have no part with Me."

9 Simon Peter *said to Him, "Lord, not my feet only, but also my hands and my head."

10 Jesus *said to him, "He who has bathed needs only to wash his feet, but is completely clean; and [a]you are clean, but not all *of you.*"

11 For [a]He knew the one who was betraying Him; for this reason He said, "Not all of you are clean."

12 And so when He had washed their feet, and [a]taken His garments, and reclined *at the table* again, He said to them, "Do you know what I have done to you?

[a]Is. 6:1ff. [b]Luke 24:27

42 [1]I.e., ...unicated [a]John ...48; 12:11 [b]Luke ...3:13 [c]John 7:13 [d]John 9:22

...3 [a]John 5:41, 44

...Matt. 10:40; John 5:24

45 [a]John 14:9

[a]John 1:4; 3:19; ...3:12; 9:5; 12:35f.

...John 3:17; 8:15f.

...ke 10:16 [b]Deut. ...8f.; John 5:45ff.; ...Matt. 10:15; John ...cts 17:31; 1 Pet. ...Pet. 3:3, 7; Heb. 10:25

...9 [1]Lit., *of Myself* ...3:11; 7:16; 8:26, 14:10, 24 [b]John 14:31; 17:8

...John 6:68 [b]John 5:19; 8:28

13:1 [1]Lit., *to the ...most;* or, *eternally* ...13; 11:55 [b]John ...John 13:3; 16:28

...John 6:70; 13:27 [b]John 6:71

...John 3:35 [b]John 8:42

...Luke 12:37; 17:8

[a]Gen. 18:4; 19:2; ...24; Judg. 19:21; ...7:44; 1 Tim. 5:10

7 [a]John 13:12ff.

...s. 51:2, 7; Ezek. ...6:25; Acts 22:16; ...6:11; Heb. 10:22 ...t. 12:12; 2 Sam. ...0:1; 1 Kin. 12:16

[a]John 15:3; Eph. 5:26

[a]John 6:64; 13:2

12 [a]John 13:4

13 "You call Me [a]Teacher and [b]Lord; and [1]you are right, for *so* I am.
14 "If I then, [a]the Lord and the Teacher, washed your feet, you also
ought to wash one another's feet.
15 "For I gave you [a]an example that you also should do as I did to
you.
16 "Truly, truly, I say to you, [a]a slave is not greater than his master;
neither *is* [b]one who is sent greater than the one who sent him.
17 "If you know these things, you are [a]blessed if you do them.
18 "[a]I do not speak of all of you. I know the ones I have [b]chosen; but
it is [c]that the Scripture may be fulfilled, '[d]HE WHO EATS MY BREAD HAS
LIFTED UP HIS HEEL AGAINST ME.'
19 "From now on [a]I am telling you before *it* comes to pass, so that
when it does occur, you may believe that [b]I am *He*.
20 "Truly, truly, I say to you, [a]he who receives whomever I send
receives Me; and he who receives Me receives Him who sent Me."
21 When Jesus had said this, He [a]became troubled in spirit, and
testified, and said, "Truly, truly, I say to you, that [b]one of you will
[1]betray Me."
22 The disciples *began* looking at one another, [a]at a loss *to know* of
which one He was speaking.
23 There was reclining on [a]Jesus' breast one of His disciples, [b]whom
Jesus loved.
24 Simon Peter therefore *gestured to him, and *said to him, "Tell
us who it is of whom He is speaking."
25 He, [a]leaning back thus on Jesus' breast, *said to Him, "Lord, who
is it?"
26 Jesus therefore *answered, "That is the one for whom I shall dip
the morsel and give it to him." So when He had dipped the morsel,
He *took and *gave it to Judas, [a]*the son* of Simon Iscariot.
27 And after the morsel, [a]Satan then [b]entered into him. Jesus there-
fore *said to him, "What you do, do quickly."
28 Now no one of those reclining *at the table* knew for what purpose
He had said this to him.
29 For some were supposing, because Judas [a]had the money box,
that Jesus was saying to him, "Buy the things we have need of [b]for
the feast"; or else, that he should [c]give something to the poor.
30 And so after receiving the morsel he went out immediately; and
[a]it was night.
31 When therefore he had gone out, Jesus *said, "Now [1]is [a]the Son
of Man [b]glorified, and [c]God [1]is glorified in Him;
32 [1]if God is glorified in Him, [a]God will also glorify Him in Him-
self, and will glorify Him immediately.
33 "[a]Little children, I am with you [b]a little while longer. [c]You shall
seek Me; and as I said to the Jews, I now say to you also, 'Where I am
going, you cannot come.'
34 "A [a]new commandment I give to you, [b]that you love one another,
[c]even as I have loved you, that you also love one another.
35 "[a]By this all men will know that you are My disciples, if you have
love for one another."
36 Simon Peter *said to Him, "Lord, where are You going?" Jesus
answered, "[a]Where I go, you cannot follow Me now; but [b]you shall
follow later."
37 Peter *said to Him, "Lord, why can I not follow You right now?
[a]I will lay down my life for You."

13 [1]Lit., *yo*
[a]John 11:28
1 Cor. 12:3;

14 [a]John 1
12:3; Phil. 2

15 [a]1 Pet. 5

16 [a]Matt. 1
6:40; John 1
[b]2 Cor. 8:23

17 [a]Matt. 7
11:28; Jame

18 [a]John 13
6:70; 15:16,
15:25; 17:12
19:24, 36 [d]
Matt. 26:21ff
14:18f.; Luke
John 13:21,

19 [a]John 14
[b]John 8:24

20 [a]Matt. 10
9:37; Luke 9
Gal. 4:14

21 [1]Or, *deliv*
[a]John 11:33
26:21f.; Mark
Luke 22:21ff.
13:18, 22, 26

22 [a]Matt. 26
14:18ff.; Luke
John 13:18, 2

23 [a]John 1:1
19:26; 20:2; 2

25 [a]John 21:

26 [a]John 6:7

27 [a]Matt. 4:1
22:3; John 13

29 [a]John 12:6
13:1 [c]John 12

30 [a]Luke 22:5

31 [1]Or, *was*
8:20 [b]John 7:
14:13; 17:4; 1

32 [1]Some anc
do not contain
phrase [a]John

33 [a]1 John 2:1
7:33 [c]John 7:3

34 [a]John 15:12
1 John 2:7f.; 3:
2 John 5 [b]Lev.
Matt. 5:44; Gal.
1 Thess. 4:9; H
1 Pet. 1:22; 1 J
[c]Eph. 5:2; 1 Jo

35 [a]1 John 3:1

36 [a]John 13:33
16:5 [b]John 21:
2 Pet. 1:14

37 [a]John 13:37
Matt. 26:33-35;
14:29-31; Luke

38 Jesus *answered, "Will you lay down your life for Me? Truly,
truly, I say to you, [a]a cock shall not crow, until you deny Me three
times.

Chapter 14

14 "[a]Let not your heart be troubled; [1]believe in God, believe also
in Me.
2 "In My Father's house are many dwelling places; if it were not so,
I would have told you; for [a]I go to prepare a place for you.
3 "And if I go and prepare a place for you, [a]I will come again, and
receive you to Myself; that [b]where I am, *there* you may be also.
4 "[1]And you know the way where I am going."
5 [a]Thomas *said to Him, "Lord, we do not know where You are
going, how do we know the way?"
6 Jesus *said to him, "I am [a]the way, and [b]the truth, and [c]the life; no
one comes to the Father, but through Me.
7 "[a]If you had known Me, you would have known My Father also;
from now on you [b]know Him, and have [c]seen Him."
8 [a]Philip *said to Him, "Lord, show us the Father, and it is enough
for us."
9 Jesus *said to him, "Have I been so long with you, and *yet* you
have not come to know Me, Philip? [a]He who has seen Me has seen
the Father; how do you say, 'Show us the Father'?
10 "Do you not believe that [a]I am in the Father, and the Father is in
Me? [b]The words that I say to you I do not speak on My own initia-
tive, but the Father abiding in Me does His works.
11 "Believe Me that [a]I am in the Father, and the Father in Me; other-
wise [b]believe on account of the works themselves.
12 "Truly, truly, I say to you, he who believes in Me, the works that I
do shall he do also; and [a]greater *works* than these shall he do; be-
cause [b]I go to the Father.
13 "And [a]whatever you ask in My name, that will I do, that [b]the
Father may be glorified in the Son.
14 "If you ask Me anything [a]in My name, I will do *it*.
15 "[a]If you love Me, you will keep My commandments.
16 "And I will ask the Father, and He will give you another [1a]Helper,
that He may be with you forever;
17 *that is* [a]the Spirit of truth, [b]whom the world cannot receive, be-
cause it does not behold Him or know Him, *but* you know Him
because He abides with you, and will be in you.
18 "I will not leave you as orphans; [a]I will come to you.
19 "[1a]After a little while [b]the world will behold Me no more; but you
will behold Me; [c]because I live, you shall live also.
20 "[a]In that day you shall know that [b]I am in My Father, and you in
Me, and I in you.
21 "[a]He who has My commandments and keeps them, he it is who
loves Me; and [b]he who loves Me shall be loved by My Father, and I
will love him, and will [c]disclose Myself to him."
22 [a]Judas (not Iscariot) *said to Him, "Lord, what then has hap-
pened [b]that You are going to disclose Yourself to us, and not to the
world?"
23 Jesus answered and said to him, "[a]If anyone loves Me, he will
[b]keep My word; and [c]My Father will love him, and We [d]will come to
him, and make Our abode with him.

ark 14:30; John 18:27
r, *you believe in* od [a]John 14:27; 16:22, 24
[a]John 13:33, 36
[a]John 14:18, 28 [b]John 12:26
[1]Many ancient orities read *And* e *I go you know,* e *way you know*
5 [a]John 11:16
10:9; Rom. 5:2; :18; Heb. 10:20 1:14 [c]John 1:4; :25; 1 John 5:20
hn 8:19 [b]1 John 2:13 [c]John 6:46
8 [a]John 1:43
ohn 1:14; 12:45; l. 1:15; Heb. 1:3
hn 10:38; 14:11, ohn 5:19; 14:24
hn 10:38; 14:10, 20 [b]John 5:36
ohn 4:37f.; 5:20 ohn 7:33; 14:28
Matt. 7:7 [b]John 13:31
n 15:16; 16:23f.
John 14:21, 23; :10; 1 John 5:3; 2 John 6
Gr., *Paracletos,* led alongside to ; or, *Intercessor* ohn 7:39; 14:26; 6:7; Rom. 8:26; 1 John 2:1
hn 15:26; 16:13; 4:6; 5:7 [b]1 Cor. 2:14
[a]John 14:3, 28
., *Yet a little and* orld [a]John 7:33 16:16, 22 [c]John 6:57
[a]John 16:23, 26 ohn 10:38; 14:11
John 14:15, 23; :10; 1 John 5:3; 6 [b]John 14:23; 27 [c]Ex. 33:18f.; Prov. 8:17
[a]Luke 6:16; Acts [b]Acts 10:40, 41
John 14:15, 21; :10; 1 John 5:3; n 6 [b]John 8:51; 2:5 [c]John 14:21 6:16; Eph. 3:17; 2:24; Rev. 3:20; 21:3

24 "He who does not love Me [a]does not keep My words; and [b]the
word which you hear is not Mine, but the Father's who sent Me.
25 "These things I have spoken to you, while abiding with you.
26 "But the [a]Helper, the Holy Spirit, [b]whom the Father will send in
My name, [c]He will teach you all things, and [d]bring to your
remembrance all that I said to you.
27 "[a]Peace I leave with you; My peace I give to you; not as the world
gives, do I give to you. [b]Let not your heart be troubled, nor let it be
fearful.
28 "[a]You heard that I said to you, 'I go away, and [b]I will come to
you.' If you loved Me, you would have rejoiced, because [c]I go to the
Father; for [d]the Father is greater than I.
29 "And now [a]I have told you before it comes to pass, that when it
comes to pass, you may believe.
30 "I will not speak much more with you, for [a]the ruler of the world
is coming, and he has nothing in Me;
31 but that the world may know that I love the Father, and as [a]the
Father gave Me commandment, even so I do. Arise, [b]let us go from
here.

Chapter 15

15 "[a]I am the true vine, and My Father is the [b]vinedresser.
2 "Every branch in Me that does not bear fruit, He takes
away; and every *branch* that bears fruit, He [1]prunes it, that it may
bear more fruit.
3 "[a]You are already clean because of the word which I have spoken
to you.
4 "[a]Abide in Me, and I in you. As the branch cannot bear fruit of
itself, unless it abides in the vine, so neither *can* you, unless you
abide in Me.
5 "I am the vine, you are the branches; he who abides in Me, and I
in him, he [a]bears much fruit; for apart from Me you can do nothing.
6 "If anyone does not abide in Me, he is [a]thrown away as a branch,
and dries up; and they gather them, and cast them into the fire, and
they are burned.
7 "If you abide in Me, and My words abide in you, [a]ask whatever
you wish, and it shall be done for you.
8 "[a]By this is My Father glorified, [1]that you bear much fruit, and *so*
[b]prove to be My disciples.
9 "Just as [a]the Father has loved Me, I have also loved you; abide in
My love.
10 "[a]If you keep My commandments, you will abide in My love; just
as [b]I have kept My Father's commandments, and abide in His love.
11 "[a]These things I have spoken to you, that My joy may be in you,
and *that* your [b]joy may be made full.
12 "This is [a]My commandment, that you love one another, just as I
have loved you.
13 "[a]Greater love has no one than this, that one [b]lay down his life for
his friends.
14 "You are My [a]friends, if [b]you do what I command you.
15 "No longer do I call you slaves, for the slave does not know what
his master is doing; but I have called you friends, for [a]all things that I
have heard from My Father I have made known to you.
16 "[a]You did not choose Me, but I chose you, and appointed you,

24 [a]John 1
7:16; 14:10

26 [a]John 14
24:49; John
16:7; Acts 2
16:13f.; 1 Jo
[d]John 2:22

27 [a]John 16
Phil. 4:7; Co
[b]John 14:1

28 [a]John 14
14:3, 18 [c]Jo
[d]John 10:29;

29 [a]John 13

30 [a]John 12

31 [a]John 10
[b]John 13:1; 1

15:1 [a]Ps. 80
5:1ff.; Ezek.
Matt. 21:33ff.
15:13; Rom.
1 Cor. 3:9

2 [1]Lit., *cleans*

3 [a]John 13:10
Eph. 5:26

4 [a]John 6:56;
1 John 2:6

5 [a]John 15:16

6 [a]John 15:2

7 [a]Matt. 7:7; J

8 [1]Another rea
*that you bear m
and become M
disciples* [a]Matt
[b]John 8:31

9 [a]John 3:35;
24, 26

10 [a]John 14:15
8:29

11 [a]John 17:13
3:29

12 [a]John 13:34
1 John 3:23; 2 J

13 [a]Rom. 5:7f.
10:11

14 [a]Luke 12:4
12:50

15 [a]John 8:26;

16 [a]John 6:70;
15:19

that you should go and [b]bear fruit, and *that* your fruit should remain,
that [c]whatever you ask of the Father in My name, He may give to
you.
17 "This [a]I command you, that you love one another.
18 "[a]If the world hates you, [1]you know that it has hated Me before *it*
hated you.
19 "If you were of the world, the world would love its own; but
because you are not of the world, but [a]I chose you out of the world,
[b]therefore the world hates you.
20 "Remember the word that I said to you, '[a]A slave is not greater
than his master.' If they persecuted Me, [b]they will also persecute
you; if they [c]kept My word, they will keep yours also.
21 "But all these things they will do to you [a]for My name's sake,
[b]because they do not know the One who sent Me.
22 "[a]If I had not come and spoken to them, they would not have [1]sin,
but now they have no excuse for their sin.
23 "He who hates Me hates My Father also.
24 "[a]If I had not done among them [b]the works which no one else did,
they would not have [1]sin; but now they have both seen and hated
Me and My Father as well.
25 "But *they have done this* in order that the word may be fulfilled that
is written in their [a]Law, '[b]THEY HATED ME WITHOUT A CAUSE.'
26 "When the [1a]Helper comes, [b]whom I will send to you from the
Father, *that is* [c]the Spirit of truth, who proceeds from the Father, [d]He
will bear witness of Me,
27 [1]and [a]you *will* bear witness also, because you have been with Me
[b]from the beginning.

Chapter 16

16 "[a]These things I have spoken to you, that you may be kept
from [b]stumbling.
2 "[1]They will [a]make you outcasts from the synagogue, but [b]an hour
is coming for everyone [c]who kills you to think that he is offering
service to God.
3 "And these things they will do, [a]because they have not known the
Father, or Me.
4 "But these things I have spoken to you, [a]that when their hour
comes, you [1]may remember that I told you of them. And these things
I did not say to you [b]at the beginning, because I was with you.
5 "But now [a]I am going to Him who sent Me; and none of you asks
Me, '[b]Where are You going?'
6 "But because I have said these things to you, [a]sorrow has filled
your heart.
7 "But I tell you the truth, it is to your advantage that I go away; for
if I do not go away, the [1a]Helper shall not come to you; but if I go, [b]I
will send Him to you.
8 "And He, when He comes, will convict the world concerning sin,
and righteousness, and judgment;
9 concerning sin, [a]because they do not believe in Me;
10 and concerning [a]righteousness, because [b]I go to the Father, and
you no longer behold Me;
11 [a]and concerning judgment, because the ruler of this world has
been judged.

15:5 [c]John 15:7; 16:23
John 15:12
mperative) [a]John 7:7; [b]John 3:13
5:16 [b]Matt. John 17:14
10:24; John 1 Cor. 4:12; 2 Tim. 3:12 [c]John 8:51
10:22; 24:9; Luke 21:12, s 4:17; 5:41; 1 Pet. 4:14; [b]John 8:19, 17:25; Acts ; 1 John 3:1
guilt [a]John 9:41; 15:24
guilt [a]John [b]John 5:36; 10:37
n 10:34 [b]Ps. 35:19; 69:4
, *Paracletos*, alongside to , *Intercessor* 14:16 [b]John [c]John 14:17 [d]1 John 5:7
, (imperative) *itness* [a]Luke ; John 19:35; ohn 1:2; 4:14 [b]Luke 1:2
ohn 15:18-27 [b]Matt. 11:6
hey will make ommunicated 2 [b]John 4:21; [c]Is. 66:5; Acts 9-11; Rev. 6:9
19, 55; 15:21; s 3:17; 1 John 3:1
nay remember , that I told you 3:19 [b]Luke 1:2
:33; 16:10, 17, hn 13:36; 14:5
hn 14:1; 16:22
Paracletos, one ongside to help; *ercessor* [a]John 6 [b]John 14:26
[a]John 15:22, 24
Acts 3:14; 7:52; :31; 1 Pet. 3:18 [b]John 16:5
11 [a]John 12:31

12 "I have many more things to say to you, but you cannot bear *them* now.

13 "But when He, [a]the Spirit of truth, comes, He will [b]guide you into all the truth; for He will not speak on His own initiative, but whatever He hears, He will speak; and He will disclose to you what is to come.

14 "He shall [a]glorify Me; for He shall take of Mine, and shall disclose *it* to you.

15 "[a]All things that the Father has are Mine; therefore I said, that He takes of Mine, and will disclose *it* to you.

16 "[a]A little while, and [b]you will no longer behold Me; and again a little while, and [c]you will see Me."

17 *Some* of His disciples therefore said to one another, "What is this thing He is telling us, '[a]A little while, and you will not behold Me; and again a little while, and you will see Me'; and, 'because [b]I go to the Father'?"

18 And so they were saying, "What is this that He says, 'A little while'? We do not know what He is talking about."

19 [a]Jesus knew that they wished to question Him, and He said to them, "Are you deliberating together about this, that I said, 'A little while, and you will not behold Me, and again a little while, and you will see Me'?

20 "Truly, truly, I say to you, that [a]you will weep and lament, but the world will rejoice; you will be sorrowful, but [b]your sorrow will be turned to joy.

21 "[a]Whenever a woman is in travail she has sorrow, because her hour has come; but when she gives birth to the child, she remembers the anguish no more, for joy that a [1]child has been born into the world.

22 "Therefore [a]you too now have sorrow; but [b]I will see you again, and your heart will rejoice, and no one takes your joy away from you.

23 "And [a]in that day [b]you will [1]ask Me no question. Truly, truly, I say to you, [c]if you shall ask the Father for anything, He will give it to you in My name.

24 "[a]Until now you have asked for nothing in My name; ask, and you will receive, that your [b]joy may be made full.

25 "These things I have spoken to you in [1a]figurative language; [b]an hour is coming when I will speak no more to you in [1]figurative language, but will tell you plainly of the Father.

26 "[a]In that day [b]you will ask in My name, and I do not say to you that I will request the Father on your behalf;

27 for [a]the Father Himself loves you, because you have loved Me, and [b]have believed that [c]I came forth from the Father.

28 "[a]I came forth from the Father, and have come into the world; I am leaving the world again, and [b]going to the Father."

29 His disciples *said, "Lo, now You are speaking plainly, and are not using [a]a [1]figure of speech.

30 "Now we know that You know all things, and have no need for anyone to question You; by this we [a]believe that You [b]came from God."

31 Jesus answered them, "Do you now believe?

32 "Behold, [a]an hour is coming, and has *already* come, for [b]you to be

13 [a]John 1
14:26

14 [a]John 7

15 [a]John 1

16 [a]John 7.
14:18-24; 1
[c]John 16:22

17 [a]John 16
16:5

19 [a]Mark 9:
6:61

20 [a]Mark 16
23:27 [b]John

21 [1]Lit., *hum*
[a]Is. 13:8; 21:
66:7; Hos. 13
4:9; 1 Thess.

22 [a]John 16:
16:16

23 [1]Lit., *ques*
nothing [a]Joh
16:26 [b]John
[c]John 15:16

24 [a]John 14:
3:29; 15:11

25 [1]Lit., *prove*
figures of spee
13:34; John 10
[b]John 16:2

26 [a]John 14:2
[b]John 16:19, 3

27 [a]John 14:2
[b]John 2:11; 16:
8:42

28 [a]John 8:42;
[b]John 13:1, 3;
10, 17

29 [1]Lit., *prover*
13:34; John 10:

30 [a]John 2:11;
[b]John 8:42; 16:2

32 [a]John 4:23;
[b]Zech. 13:7; Ma

9:27 [d]John 8:29
4:27 [b]John . [c]Matt. 9:2 2 Cor. 2:14; ; Rev. 3:21; 12:11
[a]John 11:41 :39; 13:31f.
esh [2]Lit., *all h Thou hast to them He* [b]John 6:37, 9, 24 [c]John 10:28
5:44 [b]John 3, 21, 23, 25
13:31 [b]Luke 7; John 4:34
17:1 [b]John :24; Phil. 2:6
17:26 [b]John 9; 17:2, 9, 24) [d]John 8:51
16:68; 12:49 15; 17:14, 26 42; 16:27, 30 7; 17:18, 21, 23, 25
22:32; John [b]Luke 23:34; 17:20f. [c]John 9; 17:2, 6, 24 [d]John 17:6
[a]John 16:15
n 13:1 [b]John ; 17:13 [c]John ohn 17:6; Phil. . 19:12 [e]John om. 12:5; Gal. 3:28
17:6; Phil. 2:9; 2 [b]John 6:39; ohn 6:70 [d]Ps. 9; John 13:18
hn 7:33; 17:11 11 [c]John 3:29
n 15:19 [b]John 8:23; 17:16
ut of the power *evil* [a]Matt. 5:37
6 [a]John 17:14
17 [a]John 15:3
n 3:17; 17:3, 8, 25 [b]Matt. 10:5; ohn 4:38; 20:21
hn 15:13 [b]John Cor. 7:14; Col. :6; 1 John 3:18
21 [a]John 10:38; 17:11, 23

scattered, each to [c]his own *home,* and to leave Me alone; and *yet* [d]I am
not alone, because the Father is with Me.
33 "These things I have spoken to you, that [a]in Me you may have
peace. [b]In the world you have tribulation, but [c]take courage; [d]I have
overcome the world."

Chapter 17

17 These things Jesus spoke; and [a]lifting up His eyes to heaven,
He said, "Father, the hour has come; [b]glorify Thy Son, that the
Son may glorify Thee,
2 even as [a]Thou gavest Him authority over all [1]mankind, that [b]to
[2]all whom Thou hast given Him, [c]He may give eternal life.
3 "And this is eternal life, that they may know Thee, [a]the only true
God, and Jesus Christ whom [b]Thou hast sent.
4 "[a]I glorified Thee on the earth, [b]having accomplished the work
which Thou hast given Me to do.
5 "And now, [a]glorify Thou Me together with Thyself, Father, with
the glory which I had [b]with Thee before the world was.
6 "[a]I manifested Thy name to the men whom [b]Thou gavest Me out
of the world; [c]Thine they were, and Thou gavest them to Me, and
they have [d]kept Thy word.
7 "Now they have come to know that everything Thou hast given
Me is from Thee;
8 for [a]the words which Thou gavest Me [b]I have given to them; and
they received *them,* and truly understood that [c]I came forth from
Thee, and they believed that [d]Thou didst send Me.
9 "[a]I ask on their behalf; [b]I do not ask on behalf of the world, but of
those whom [c]Thou hast given Me; for [d]they are Thine;
10 and [a]all things that are Mine are Thine, and Thine are Mine; and
I have been glorified in them.
11 "And I am no more in the world; and *yet* [a]they themselves are in
the world, and [b]I come to Thee. [c]Holy Father, keep them in Thy
name, *the name* [d]which Thou hast given Me, that [e]they may be one,
even as We *are.*
12 "While I was with them, I was keeping them in Thy name [a]which
Thou hast given Me; and I guarded them, and [b]not one of them
perished but [c]the son of perdition, that the [d]Scripture might be ful-
filled.
13 "But now [a]I come to Thee; and [b]these things I speak in the world,
that they may have My [c]joy made full in themselves.
14 "I have given them Thy word; and [a]the world has hated them,
because [b]they are not of the world, even as I am not of the world.
15 "I do not ask Thee to take them out of the world, but to keep them
[1]from [2a]the evil *one.*
16 "[a]They are not of the world, even as I am not of the world.
17 "[a]Sanctify them in the truth; Thy word is truth.
18 "As [a]Thou didst send Me into the world, [b]I also have sent them
into the world.
19 "And for their sakes I [a]sanctify Myself, that they themselves also
may be [b]sanctified [c]in truth.
20 "I do not ask in behalf of these alone, but for those also who
believe in Me through their word;
21 that they may all be one; [a]even as Thou, Father, *art* in Me, and I

in Thee, that they also may be in Us; [b]that the world may
[1]believe that [c]Thou didst send Me.
22 "And the [a]glory which Thou hast given Me I have given
to them; that they may be one, just as We are one;
23 [a]I in them, and Thou in Me, that they may be perfected
[1]in unity, that the world may [2]know that [b]Thou didst send
Me, and didst [c]love them, even as Thou didst love Me.
24 "Father, [1]I desire that [a]they also, whom Thou hast given
Me, [b]be with Me where I am, in order that they may behold
My [c]glory, which Thou hast given Me; for Thou didst love
Me before [d]the foundation of the world.
25 "O [a]righteous Father, [1]although [b]the world has not
known Thee, [1]yet I have known Thee; and these have
known that [c]Thou didst send Me;
26 and [a]I have made Thy name known to them, and will
make it known; that [b]the love wherewith Thou didst love
Me may be in them, and I in them."

Chapter 18

18 When Jesus had spoken these words, [a]He went forth with His
disciples over [b]the [1]ravine of the Kidron, where there was [c]a
garden, into which He Himself entered, and His disciples.
2 Now Judas also, who was [1]betraying Him, knew the place; for
Jesus had [a]often met there with His disciples.
3 [a]Judas then, having received [b]the *Roman* [1]cohort, and [c]officers
from the chief priests and the Pharisees, *came there with lanterns
and [d]torches and weapons.
4 Jesus therefore, [a]knowing all the things that were coming upon
Him, went forth, and *said to them, "[b]Whom do you seek?"
5 They answered Him, "Jesus the Nazarene." He *said to them, "I
am *He*." And Judas also who was betraying Him, was standing with
them.
6 When therefore He said to them, "I am *He*," they drew back, and
fell to the ground.
7 Again therefore He asked them, "[a]Whom do you seek?" And
they said, "Jesus the Nazarene."
8 Jesus answered, "I told you that I am *He*; if therefore you seek
Me, let these go their way,"
9 that the word might be fulfilled which He spoke, "[a]Of those
whom Thou hast given Me I lost not one."
10 Simon Peter therefore [a]having a sword, drew it, and struck the
high priest's slave, and cut off his right ear; and the slave's name
was Malchus.
11 Jesus therefore said to Peter, "Put the sword into the sheath; [a]the
cup which the Father has given Me, shall I not drink it?"
12 [a]So [b]the *Roman* [1]cohort and the [2]commander, and the [b]officers of
the Jews, arrested Jesus and bound Him,
13 and led Him to [a]Annas first; for he was father-in-law of [b]Caia-
phas, who was high priest that year.
14 Now Caiaphas was the one who had advised the Jews that [a]it
was expedient for one man to die on behalf of the people.
15 And [a]Simon Peter was following Jesus, and *so was* another disci-
ple. Now that disciple was known to the high priest, and entered
with Jesus into [b]the court of the high priest,

21 [1]Gr. tens *continually b* [b]John 17:8 17:3, 8, 18,

22 [a]John 1:

23 [1]Lit., *into* tense indica *continually k* 10:38; 17:11 3:17; 17:3, 8 [c]John 16:27

24 [1]Some m *that which T given Me, I c where I am, may be with* [a]John 17:2 12:26 [c]John 17:22 [d]Matt. John 17:5

25 [1]Lit., *and* 17:11; 1 John 7:29; 15:21 17:3, 8, 18, 2

26 [a]John 17: 15:9

18:1 [1]Lit., *winter-torrent* 26:30, 36; Ma 32; Luke 22:3 15:23; 1 Kin. 15:13; 2 Kin. 2 Chr. 15:16; 30:14; Jer. 31 26:36; Mark 1 18:26

2 [1]Or, *deliveri up* [a]Luke 21:3

3 [1]Normally 6 *battalion* [a]Joh *Matt. 26:47-56 14:43-50; Luke 22:47-53* [b]Joh Acts 10:1 [c]Joh 18:12, 18 [d]Ma

4 [a]John 6:64; [b]John 18:7

7 [a]John 18:4

9 [a]John 17:12

10 [a]Matt. 26:5 14:47

11 [a]Matt. 20:22 Mark 14:36; Luk

12 [1]Or, *battalio* chiliarch, in com a thousand troo [a]John 18:12f.: *M 26:57ff.* [b]John 1

13 [a]Luke 3:2; J 18:24 [b]Matt. 26 11:49, 51

14 [a]John 11:50

15 [a]Matt. 26:58 14:54; Luke 22:5 [b]Matt. 26:3; John 18:24, 28

16 [a]but Peter was standing at the door outside. So the other disciple,
who was known to the high priest, went out and spoke to the door-
keeper, and brought in Peter.
17 [a]The slave-girl therefore who kept the door *said to Peter, "[b]You
are not also *one* of this man's disciples, are you?" He *said, "I am
not."
18 Now the slaves and the [a]officers were standing *there*, having
made [b]a charcoal fire, for it was cold and they were [c]warming them-
selves; and Peter also was with them, standing and warming him-
self.
19 [a]The high priest therefore questioned Jesus about His disciples,
and about His teaching.
20 Jesus answered him, "I [a]have spoken openly to the world; I al-
ways [b]taught in [1]synagogues, and [c]in the temple, where all the Jews
come together; and I spoke nothing in secret.
21 "Why do you question Me? Question those who have heard what
I spoke to them; behold, these know what I said."
22 And when He had said this, one of the [a]officers standing by
[b]gave Jesus a blow, saying, "Is that the way You answer the high
priest?"
23 [a]Jesus answered him, "If I have spoken wrongly, bear witness of
the wrong; but if rightly, why do you strike Me?"
24 [a]Annas therefore sent Him bound to [a]Caiaphas the high priest.
25 [a]Now [b]Simon Peter was standing and warming himself. They
said therefore to him, "[c]You are not also *one* of His disciples, are
you?" He denied *it*, and said, "I am not."
26 One of the slaves of the high priest, being a relative of the one
[a]whose ear Peter cut off, *said, "Did I not see you in [b]the garden with
Him?"
27 Peter therefore denied *it* again; and immediately [a]a cock crowed.
28 [a]They *led Jesus therefore from [b]Caiaphas into [c]the [1]Praetorium,
and it was early; and they themselves did not enter into [c]the [1]Prae-
torium in order that [d]they might not be defiled, but might eat the
Passover.
29 [a]Pilate therefore went out to them, and *said, "What accusation
do you bring against this Man?"
30 They answered and said to him, "If this Man were not an evil-
doer, we would not have delivered Him up to you."
31 Pilate therefore said to them, "Take Him yourselves, and judge
Him according to your law." The Jews said to him, "We are not
permitted to put anyone to death,"
32 that [a]the word of Jesus might be fulfilled, which He spoke, sig-
nifying by what kind of death He was about to die.
33 Pilate therefore [a]entered again into the Praetorium, and sum-
moned Jesus, and said to Him, "[b]Are You the King of the Jews?"
34 Jesus answered, "Are you saying this [1]on your own initiative, or
did others tell you about Me?"
35 Pilate answered, "I am not a Jew, am I? Your own nation and the
chief priests delivered You up to me; what have You done?"
36 Jesus answered, "[a]My kingdom [1]is not of this world. If My king-
dom were of this world, then My servants would be fighting, that I
might not be delivered up to the Jews; but as it is, My kingdom is
not [2]of this realm."
37 Pilate therefore said to Him, "So You are a king?" Jesus

1 18:16-18: :69f.; Mark e 22:55-57
2:13 [b]John 18:25
18:3 [b]John k 14:54, 67
n 18:19-24: 59-68; Mark ke 22:63-71
synagogue 8:26 [b]Matt. 6:59 [c]Matt. 26:55
18:3 [b]John 19:3
tt. 5:39; Acts 23:2-5
[a]John 18:13
hn 18:25-27: :71-75; Mark :69-72; Luke [b]John 18:18 [c]John 18:17
18:10 [b]John 18:1
[a]John 13:38
e., governor's dence [a]Matt. rk 15:1; Luke [b]John 18:13 t. 27:27; John 3; 19:9 [d]John :55; Acts 11:3
ohn 18:29-38: 7:11-14; Mark ; Luke 23:2, 3
tt. 20:19; 26:2; 10:33f.; Luke hn 3:14; 8:28; 12:32f.
ohn 18:28, 29; ike 23:3; John 19:12
., from yourself
, is not derived [2]Lit., from here att. 26:53; Luke 7:21; John 6:15

answered, "[a]You say *correctly* that I am a king. For this I have been
born, and for this I have come into the world, [b]to bear witness to the
truth. [c]Everyone who is of the truth hears My voice."
38 Pilate *said to Him, "What is truth?"
And when he had said this, he [a]went out again to the Jews, and
*said to them, "[b]I find no guilt in Him.
39 "[a]But you have a custom, that I should release someone [1]for you
at the Passover; do you wish then that I release [1]for you the King of
the Jews?"
40 Therefore they cried out again, saying, "[a]Not this Man, but
Barabbas." Now Barabbas was a robber.

Chapter 19

19 Then Pilate therefore took Jesus, and [1a]scourged Him.
2 [a]And the soldiers wove a crown of thorns and put it on His
head, and arrayed Him in a purple robe;
3 and they *began* to come up to Him, and say, "[a]Hail, King of the
Jews!" and to [b]give Him blows *in the face*.
4 And Pilate [a]came out again, and *said to them, "Behold, I am
bringing Him out to you, that you may know that [b]I find no guilt in
Him."
5 Jesus therefore came out, [a]wearing the crown of thorns and the
purple robe. And *Pilate* *said to them, "Behold, the Man!"
6 When therefore the chief priests and the [a]officers saw Him, they
cried out, saying, "Crucify, crucify!" Pilate *said to them, "Take Him
yourselves, and crucify Him, for [b]I find no guilt in Him."
7 The Jews answered him, "[a]We have a law, and by that law He
ought to die because He [b]made Himself out *to be* the Son of God."
8 When Pilate therefore heard this statement, he was the more
afraid;
9 and he [a]entered into the [1]Praetorium again, and *said to Jesus,
"Where are You from?" But [b]Jesus gave him no answer.
10 Pilate therefore *said to Him, "You do not speak to me? Do You
not know that I have authority to release You, and I have authority
to crucify You?"
11 Jesus answered, "[a]You would have no authority [1]over Me, unless
it had been given you from above; for this reason [b]he who delivered
Me up to you has *the* greater sin."
12 As a result of this Pilate [1]made efforts to release Him, but the
Jews cried out, saying, "[a]If you release this Man, you are no friend of
Caesar; everyone who makes himself out *to be* a king [2]opposes
Caesar."
13 When Pilate therefore heard these words, he brought Jesus out,
and [a]sat down on the judgment seat at a place called [1]The Pavement,
but [b]in [2]Hebrew, Gabbatha.
14 Now it was [a]the day of preparation for the Passover; it was about
the [1b]sixth hour. And he *said to the Jews, "Behold, [c]your King!"
15 They therefore cried out, "[a]Away with *Him*, away with *Him*,
crucify Him!" Pilate *said to them, "Shall I crucify your King?" The
chief priests answered, "We have no king but Caesar."
16 So he then [a]delivered Him to them to be crucified.
17 [a]They took Jesus therefore, and He went out, [1b]bearing His own
cross, to the place called [c]the Place of a Skull, which is called [d]in
[2]Hebrew, Golgotha.

37 [a]Matt.
15:2; Luke
[b]John 1:14
[c]John 8:47

38 [a]John
[b]Luke 23:4,

39 [1]Or, *to*
18:39-19:16
27:15-26;
Luke 23:18

40 [a]Acts 3:

19:1 [1]Or, *h*
scourged [a]

2 [a]Matt. 27
15:16-19

3 [a]Matt. 27:
15:18 [b]John

4 [a]John 18:
[b]Luke 23:4;
19:6

5 [a]John 19:

6 [a]Matt. 26:
18:3 [b]Luke
18:38; 19:4

7 [a]Lev. 24:1
26:63-66 [b]Jo
10:33

9 [1]I.e., gover
official reside
18:33 [b]Matt.
27:12, 14; Jo

11 [1]Lit., *agai*
13:1 [b]John 1
28ff.; Acts 3:1

12 [1]Lit., *was*
[2]Or, *speaks a*
[a]Luke 23:2; J

13 [1]Gr., *The*
Lithostrotos [2]
Jewish Arama
27:19 [b]John 5
19:17, 20

14 [1]Perhaps 6
(Roman time)
27:62; John 19
[b]Matt. 27:45; M
15:25 [c]John 1

15 [a]Luke 23:1

16 [a]Matt. 27:2
15:15; Luke 23

17 [1]Lit., *bearin*
cross for Himse
Jewish Aramaic
19:17-24: *Matt.*
27:33-44; Mark
15:22-32; Luke
23:33-43 [b]Matt
Mark 15:21; Lu
23:26 [c]Luke 23
[d]John 19:13

18 There they crucified Him, and with Him [a]two other men, one on
either side, and Jesus in between.
19 And Pilate wrote an inscription also, and put it on the cross. And
it was written, "[a]JESUS THE NAZARENE, [b]THE KING OF THE
JEWS."
20 Therefore this inscription many of the Jews read, for the place
where Jesus was crucified was near the city; and it was written [a]in
[1]Hebrew, Latin, *and* in Greek.
21 And so the chief priests of the Jews were saying to Pilate, "Do
not write, '[a]The King of the Jews'; but that He said, 'I am [a]King of the
Jews.' "
22 Pilate answered, "[a]What I have written I have written."
23 [a]The soldiers therefore, when they had crucified Jesus, took His
outer garments and made [b]four parts, a part to every soldier and *also*
the [1]tunic; now the tunic was seamless, woven [2]in one piece.
24 They said therefore to one another, "[a]Let us not tear it, but cast
lots for it, *to decide* whose it shall be"; [b]that the Scripture might be
fulfilled, "THEY [c]DIVIDED MY OUTER GARMENTS AMONG THEM, AND FOR
MY CLOTHING THEY CAST [1]LOTS."
25 Therefore the soldiers did these things. [a]But there were standing
by the cross of Jesus [b]His mother, and His mother's sister, Mary the
wife of Clopas, and [c]Mary Magdalene.
26 When Jesus therefore saw His mother, and [a]the disciple whom
He loved standing nearby, He *said to His mother, "[b]Woman, behold,
your son!"
27 Then He *said to the disciple, "Behold, your mother!" And from
that hour the disciple took her into [a]his own *household*.
28 After this, Jesus, [a]knowing that all things had already been ac-
complished, [b]in order that the Scripture might be fulfilled, *said, "[c]I
am thirsty."
29 A jar full of sour wine was standing there; so [a]they put a sponge
full of the sour wine upon *a branch of* hyssop, and brought it up to
His mouth.
30 When Jesus therefore had received the sour wine, He said, "[a]It is
finished!" And He bowed His head, and [b]gave up His spirit.
31 The Jews therefore, because it was [a]the day of preparation, so
that [b]the bodies should not remain on the cross on the Sabbath ([1]for
that Sabbath was a [c]high *day*), asked Pilate that their legs might be
broken, and *that* they might be taken away.
32 The soldiers therefore came, and broke the legs of the first man,
and of the other man who was [a]crucified with Him;
33 but coming to Jesus, when they saw that He was already dead,
they did not break His legs;
34 but one of the soldiers pierced His side with a spear, and imme-
diately there came out [a]blood and water.
35 And he who has seen has [a]borne witness, and his witness is true;
and he knows that he is telling the truth, so that you also may
believe.
36 For these things came to pass, [a]that the Scripture might be ful-
filled, "[b]NOT A BONE OF HIM SHALL BE [1]BROKEN."
37 And again another Scripture says, "[a]THEY SHALL LOOK ON HIM
WHOM THEY PIERCED."
38 [a]And after these things Joseph of Arimathea, being a disciple of
Jesus, but a [b]secret *one*, for [c]fear of the Jews, asked Pilate that he

Luke 23:32
7:37; Mark
Luke 23:38
n 19:14, 21
i.e., Jewish
John 19:13
n 19:14, 19
13:14; Esth. 4:16
, *khiton*, the
worn next to
[2]Lit., *woven*
e upper part
gh the whole
27:35; Mark
Luke 23:34
[b]Acts 12:4
t., *a lot* [a]Ex.
27:35; Mark
; Luke 23:34
28, 36f. [c]Ps. 22:18
27:55f.; Mark
; Luke 23:49
6 [c]Luke 8:2;
John 20:1, 18
13:23 [b]John 2:4
e 18:28; John
32; Acts 21:6
hn 13:1; 17:4
:24, 36f. [c]Ps. 69:21
ohn 19:29, 30:
7:48, 50; Mark
6f.; Luke 23:36
nn 17:4 [b]Matt.
rk 15:37; Luke 23:46
, *for the day of*
bath was great
:14, 42 [b]Deut.
23; Josh. 8:29;
26f. [c]Ex. 12:16
2 [a]John 19:18
[a]1 John 5:6, 8
nn 15:27; 21:24
[1]Or, *crushed* or
d [a]John 19:24,
Ex. 12:46; Num.
9:12; Ps. 34:20
ech. 12:10; Rev. 1:7
[a]John 19:38-42:
27:57-61; Mark
15:42-47; Luke
56 [b]Mark 15:43
[c]John 7:13

might take away the body of Jesus; and Pilate granted permission.
He came therefore, and took away His body.
39 And [a]Nicodemus came also, who had first come to Him by
night; [b]bringing a [1]mixture of [c]myrrh and aloes, about a [d]hundred
[2]pounds *weight*.
40 And so they took the body of Jesus, and [a]bound it in [b]linen
wrappings with the spices, as is the burial custom of the Jews.
41 Now in the place where He was crucified there was a garden;
and in the garden a [a]new tomb, [b]in which no one had yet been laid.
42 Therefore on account of the Jewish day of [a]preparation, because
the tomb was [b]nearby, they laid Jesus there.

Chapter 20

20 [a]Now on the first *day* of the week [b]Mary Magdalene *came
early to the tomb, while it *was still dark, and *saw [c]the stone
already taken away from the tomb.
2 And so she *ran and *came to Simon Peter, and to the other
[a]disciple whom Jesus [1]loved, and *said to them, "[b]They have taken
away the Lord out of the tomb, and we do not know where they
have laid Him."
3 [a]Peter therefore went forth, and the other disciple, and they were
going to the tomb.
4 And the two were running together; and the other disciple ran
ahead faster than Peter, and came to the tomb first;
5 and [a]stooping and looking in, he *saw the [b]linen wrappings lying
there; but he did not go in.
6 Simon Peter therefore also *came, following him, and entered the
tomb; and he *beheld the linen wrappings lying *there,*
7 and [a]the face-cloth, which had been on His head, not lying with
the [b]linen wrappings, but rolled up in a place by itself.
8 So the other disciple who [a]had first come to the tomb entered
then also, and he saw and believed.
9 For as yet [a]they did not understand the Scripture, [b]that He must
rise again from the dead.
10 So the disciples went away again [a]to their own homes.
11 [a]But Mary was standing outside the tomb weeping; and so, as
she wept, she [b]stooped and looked into the tomb;
12 and she *beheld [a]two angels in white sitting, one at the head, and
one at the feet, where the body of Jesus had been lying.
13 And they *said to her, "[a]Woman, why are you weeping?" She
*said to them, "Because [b]they have taken away my Lord, and I do
not know where they have laid Him."
14 When she had said this, she turned around, and *[a]beheld Jesus
standing *there,* and [b]did not know that it was Jesus.
15 Jesus *said to her, "[a]Woman, why are you weeping? Whom are
you seeking?" Supposing Him to be the gardener, she *said to Him,
"Sir, if you have carried Him away, tell me where you have laid
Him, and I will take Him away."
16 Jesus *said to her, "Mary!" She *turned and *said to Him [a]in
[1]Hebrew, "[b]Rabboni!" (which means, Teacher).
17 Jesus *said to her, "Stop clinging to Me, for I have not yet
ascended to the Father; but go to [a]My brethren, and say to them, 'I
[b]ascend to My Father and your Father, and My God and your God.' "

39 [1]Anot *package* litras (12 [a]John 3:1 [c]Ps. 45:8; Song 4:14 [d]John 12:

40 [a]Matt. 14:8; John 24:12; Joh

41 [a]Matt. 23:53

42 [a]John [b]John 19:2

20:1 [a]John *Matt. 28:1- 16:1-8; Luk* [b]John 19:2 [c]Matt. 27:6 Mark 15:46 24:2; John

2 [1]Lit., *was* [a]John 13:23 20:13

3 [a]Luke 24: 20:3-10

5 [a]John 20: 19:40

7 [a]John 11: 19:40

8 [a]John 20:

9 [a]Matt. 22:2 2:22 [b]Luke 2

10 [a]Luke 24

11 [a]Mark 16 20:5

12 [a]Matt. 28: 16:5; Luke 24

13 [a]John 20: 20:2

14 [a]Matt. 28: 16:9 [b]John 2

15 [a]John 20:1

16 [1]I.e., Jewis Aramaic [a]Joh [b]Matt. 23:7; M

17 [a]Matt. 28:1 12:26; 16:19; J

18 [a]Mary Magdalene *came, [b]announcing to the disciples, "I have
seen the Lord," and *that* He had said these things to her.
19 When therefore it was evening, on that day, the first *day* of the
week, and when the doors were shut where the disciples were, for
[a]fear of the Jews, Jesus came and stood in their midst, and *said to
them, "[1b]Peace *be* with you."
20 And when He had said this, [a]He showed them both His hands
and His side. The disciples therefore [b]rejoiced when they saw the
Lord.
21 Jesus therefore said to them again, "[a]Peace *be* with you; [b]as the
Father has sent Me, I also send you."
22 And when He had said this, He breathed on them, and *said to
them, "Receive the Holy Spirit.
23 "[a]If you forgive the sins of any, *their sins* [1]have been forgiven
them; if you retain the *sins* of any, they have been retained."
24 But [a]Thomas, one of [b]the twelve, called [1a]Didymus, was not with
them when Jesus came.
25 The other disciples therefore were saying to him, "We have seen
the Lord!" But he said to them, "Unless I shall see in [a]His hands the
imprint of the nails, and put my finger into the place of the nails,
and put my hand into His side, [b]I will not believe."
26 And [1]after eight days again His disciples were inside, and
Thomas with them. Jesus *came, the doors having been [2]shut, and
stood in their midst, and said, "[a]Peace *be* with you."
27 Then He *said to Thomas, "[a]Reach here your finger, and see My
hands; and reach here your hand, and put it into My side; and be not
unbelieving, but believing."
28 Thomas answered and said to Him, "My Lord and my God!"
29 Jesus *said to him, "Because you have seen Me, have you
believed? [a]Blessed *are* they who did not see, and *yet* believed."
30 [a]Many other [1b]signs therefore Jesus also performed in the pres-
ence of the disciples, which are not written in this book;
31 but these have been written [a]that you may believe that Jesus is
[1]the Christ, [b]the Son of God; and that [c]believing you may have life in
His name.

Chapter 21

21 After these things Jesus [1a]manifested Himself [b]again to the
disciples at the [c]Sea of Tiberias, and He manifested *Himself* in
this way.
2 There were together Simon Peter, and [a]Thomas called [1]Didymus,
and [b]Nathanael of [c]Cana in Galilee, and [d]the *sons* of Zebedee, and
two others of His disciples.
3 Simon Peter *said to them, "I am going fishing." They *said to
him, "We will also come with you." They went out, and got into the
boat; and [a]that night they caught nothing.
4 But when the day was now breaking, Jesus stood on the beach;
yet the disciples did not [a]know that it was Jesus.
5 Jesus therefore *said to them, "Children, [a]you do not have [1]any
fish, do you?" They answered Him, "No."
6 And He said to them, "[a]Cast the net on the right-hand side of the
boat, and you will find *a catch*." They cast therefore, and then they
were not able to haul it in because of the great number of fish.
7 [a]That disciple therefore whom Jesus [1]loved *said to Peter, "It is

20:1 [b]Mark
ke 24:10, 23

Peace to you
7:13 [b]Luke
John 14:27;
20:21, 26

ke 24:39, 40;
19:34 [b]John
16:20, 22

24:36; John
9, 26 [b]John
17:18

3 [1]I.e., have
viously been
[a]Matt. 16:19;
18:18

e Twin [a]John
6 [b]John 6:67

20:20 [b]Mark
16:11

, a week later
locked [a]Luke
; John 14:27;
20:19, 21

e 24:40; John
20:25

29 [a]1 Pet. 1:8

[1]Or, *attesting*
s [a]John 21:25
[b]John 2:11

., the Messiah
9:35 [b]Matt. 4:3
[c]John 3:15

made Himself
e [a]Mark 16:12;
n 21:14 [b]John
, 26 [c]John 6:1

the Twin [a]John
6 [b]John 1:45ff.
2:1 [d]Matt. 4:21;
1:19; Luke 5:10

3 [a]Luke 5:5

uke 24:16; John
20:14

something eaten
ad [a]Luke 24:41

6 [a]Luke 5:4ff.

[1]Lit., *was loving*
ohn 13:23; 21:20

the Lord." And so when Simon Peter heard that it was the Lord, he
put his outer garment on (for he was stripped *for work*), and threw
himself into the sea.
8 But the other disciples came in the little boat, for they were not
far from the land, but about [1]one hundred yards away, dragging the
net *full* of fish.
9 And so when they got out upon the land, they *saw a charcoal
[a]fire *already* laid, and [b]fish placed on it, and bread.
10 Jesus *said to them, "Bring some of the [a]fish which you have
now caught."
11 Simon Peter went up, and drew the net to land, full of large fish,
a hundred and fifty-three; and although there were so many, the net
was not torn.
12 Jesus *said to them, "Come *and* have [a]breakfast." None of the
disciples ventured to question Him, "Who are You?" knowing that it
was the Lord.
13 Jesus *came and *took [a]the bread, and *gave them, and the [b]fish
likewise.
14 This is now the [a]third time that Jesus [1]was manifested to the
disciples, after He was raised from the dead.
15 So when they had [a]finished breakfast, Jesus *said to Simon Peter,
"Simon, [1]*son* of John, do you [2b]love Me more than these?" He *said to
Him, "Yes, Lord; You know that I [3]love You." He *said to him, "Tend
[c]My lambs."
16 He *said to him again a second time, "Simon, *son* of John, do you
[1]love Me?" He *said to Him, "Yes, Lord; You know that I [2]love You."
He *said to him, "[a]Shepherd My sheep."
17 He *said to him the third time, "Simon, *son* of John, do you [1]love
Me?" Peter was grieved because He said to him [a]the third time, "Do
you [1]love Me?" And he said to Him, "Lord, [b]You know all things;
You know that I [1]love You." Jesus *said to him, "[c]Tend My sheep.
18 "Truly, truly, I say to you, when you were younger, you used to
gird yourself, and walk wherever you wished; but when you grow
old, you will stretch out your hands, and someone else will gird you,
and bring you where you do not wish to *go*."
19 Now this He said, [a]signifying by [b]what kind of death he would
glorify God. And when He had spoken this, He *said to him,
"[c]Follow Me!"
20 Peter, turning around, *saw the [a]disciple whom Jesus loved fol-
lowing *them;* the one who also had [b]leaned back on His breast at the
supper, and said, "Lord, who is the one who betrays You?"
21 Peter therefore seeing him *said to Jesus, "Lord, and what about
this man?"
22 Jesus *said to him, "If I want him to remain [a]until I come, what *is*
that to you? You [b]follow Me!"
23 This saying therefore went out among [a]the brethren that that
disciple would not die; yet Jesus did not say to him that he would
not die, but *only*, "If I want him to remain [b]until I come, what *is that*
to you?"
24 This is the disciple who [a]bears witness of these things, and wrote
these things; and we know that his witness is true.
25 And there are also [a]many other things which Jesus did, which if
they *were written in detail, I suppose that even the world itself
*would not contain the books which *were written.

8 [1]Lit., *200*

9 [a]John 18:
6:9, 11; 21:

10 [a]John 6:
21:9, 13

12 [a]John 21

13 [a]John 21
6:9, 11; 21:9,

14 [1]Or, *mad*
visible [a]John

15 [1]Here and
and 17 some
son of Jonas
agapao [3]Gr.,
[a]John 21:12
26:33; Mark
13:37 [c]Luke

16 [1]Gr., *agap*
phileo [a]Matt.
20:28; 1 Pet.
7:17

17 [1]Gr., *phile*
13:38 [b]John 1
[c]John 21:15, 1

19 [a]John 12:3
[b]2 Pet. 1:14 [c]M
16:24; John 21

20 [a]John 21:7
13:25

22 [a]Matt. 16:27
4:5; 11:26; Jam
Rev. 2:25 [b]Mat
16:24; John 21

23 [a]Acts 1:15
16:27f.; 1 Cor. 4
11:26; James 5:
2:25

24 [a]John 15:27

25 [a]John 20:30

...RITTEN THAT YOU MIGHT BELIEVE—JOHN 1 THROUGH 12

Geographic Locations	Timing of Events	Portrayals of Christ	Signs	Deity of Christ	Witnesses

Theme of John:

Author:

Date:

Purpose:

Key Words:

SEGMENT DIVISIONS

	PORTRAYALS OF JESUS CHRIST	SIGNS AND MIRACLES	MINISTRY	CHAPTER THEMES
			TO ISRAEL	1
				2
				3
				4
				5
				6
				7
				8
				9
				10
				11
			TO DISCIPLES	12
				13
				14
				15
				16
				17
			TO ALL MANKIND	18
				19
				20
			TO DISCIPLES	21

CTS

ı going away."

eleven heard nothing else. The promise of another Helper, the Holy Spirit, fell on deaf ears. The ıt that they could do the works that Jesus had done—and even greater—must have seemed ıterous.

ıs had died. He was buried. But He had risen! For over forty days the disciples saw, heard, and ·d the Word of Life as He spoke with them of things concerning the kingdom of God.

d then once again He was gone, taken away before their very eyes! He left with the promise to ne Spirit and commissioned them to reach the world.

·n came Pentecost and the acts of the apostles. Luke had to write Theophilus all about it. It was ɔly about A.D. 63.

GS TO DO

ers 1-2

the first two chapters of the book of Acts, Luke gives an account of Christ's ascension and the Spirit's coming.

Read chapter 1, looking for Jesus' instructions and promises to the apostles.

a. In a distinctive way mark every occurrence of the key words (along with their synonyms and pronouns) listed on the ACTS AT A GLANCE chart on page 1650. Record these key words on a card that you can use as a bookmark while studying Acts.

b. In the chapter margin list everything you learn from the references to the Holy Spirit.

c. In the margin list the instructions and the promises that Jesus gives to the apostles.

d. Note the main events that occur in this chapter by either marking these events within the text or listing them in the margin.

The key verse for Acts is found in chapter 1. This verse also gives an outline for the book. See if you can identify it. When you do, put a box around it and in the margin write: "Key verse of Acts."

As you read chapter 2:

a. Keep in mind that in the NASB any scripture printed in small caps indicates that the scripture is either an Old Testament quotation or an allusion to an Old Testament text. Observe how much is taken from the Old Testament.

b. List in the margin the main events that occur. As you note them, ask the five W's and an H: Who? What? When? Where? Why? and How? Ask: Who was present on the day of Pentecost? What happened? Whom did it affect? What was their response? Why did they respond as they did? How did they hear? And so on.

c. Mark key words. Also mark every reference to the Holy Spirit and to Jesus, including their synonyms or pronouns. Then list in the margin what you learn about each from this chapter. Watch the word *promise* and note its relationship to the Spirit. Compare this with Acts 1:4-5.

d. Mark every reference to time with a clock such as this . Do this throughout the book of Acts whether the time is indicated by an event, such as a feast or the death of Herod, or through mentioning a certain period of months or years.

e. List in the margin or mark in some way the main points in Peter's sermon on the day of Pentecost. Note what he emphasized in his sermon and the result.

4. Determine the theme of each of these chapters. Then record the themes on ACTS AT A GL and on the line next to the chapter number in the text.

Chapters 3-7

1. As you study, do the following:
   a. Read each chapter in the light of the five W's and an H. Then in the margin note: happens in that chapter? Where and when did it happen? Who is involved? How are done or said?
   b. Mark every reference to the Holy Spirit and then list what you learn about the Holy Spi ministry, and the results. Also mark the other key words listed on ACTS AT A GLANCE.
   c. If a message is proclaimed in these chapters, list in the margin the main points of that me Also note the effect of the message on those who hear it.
2. Determine the theme of each chapter and then record the theme as before.

Chapters 8-12

1. Read Acts 8:1-8 and then Acts 1:8. What do you see happening in Acts 8 that is a change fro first seven chapters? Note this in the margin of chapter 8.
2. Read chapters 8 through 11 carefully as significant events occur in these chapters. As you re
   a. List the main events in each chapter. Who does what? When? Where is it done? What is What is the result? Who is affected? How does it happen? Don't add to the text, but s observe it and list in the margin what you learn.
   b. Mark key words and list everything you learn about the Holy Spirit in the margin o chapter. This is crucial to chapters 8, 10, and 11. Note to whom the Holy Spirit comes.
   c. Record the theme of each chapter in the text and on ACTS AT A GLANCE.
3. As you read and study chapter 12, keep in mind that this chapter is pivotal. At this poi focus of the book turns from Peter's ministry to Paul's (Saul).

Chapters 13-28

1. Included in these chapters is an account of Paul's missionary journeys: Paul's first missi journey in 13 through 14; Paul's second missionary journey in 15:36 through 18:22; and third missionary journey in 18:23 through 21:17.

   For easy reference, write and color code in the margin where each journey begins.
2. As you study these chapters, mark the key repeated words. Add the word *synagogue* to you Also keep in mind what you learned from Acts 1:8 and watch carefully the work of the throughout these chapters. In the margin note your insights.
   a. Examine each chapter with the five W's and an H. Note in the text who accompanies where they go, and what happens. There's a map on page 1623 on which you can trace ea Paul's journeys. Mark each journey in a different color.
   b. Carefully observe each time the gospel is proclaimed, whether to an individual or a g Watch how Paul reasons with Jews and Gentiles. Also note what their response is and Paul handles it.
3. In several instances you will notice Paul giving his testimony. It would be beneficial to com each of these instances along with Acts 9 and the account of his conversion. It will give y more complete picture of all that happened on that significant day.
4. Record the theme of each chapter on ACTS AT A GLANCE and in the text. Then determin main subject for the book of Acts and record it. Then complete the chart. Record the ways might segment the book of Acts according to its themes.

THINGS TO THINK ABOUT

1. What have you learned from Acts about the Holy Spirit and your responsibility to be a wi for the Lord Jesus Christ?

Based on what you saw in the sermons that were preached and the personal witnesses which were given, what would you include in your witness? Where would the emphasis be?

As you studied the lives of the early apostles and the commitment of the early church, how has God spoken to your heart? Stop and think about how they lived, and then think about how you are living. Do you have the Holy Spirit living inside you? Isn't He the same today, yesterday, and forever? If you are filled with the Holy Spirit and are not quenching Him, what should be happening?

Chapter 1

1 The first account I [1]composed, [a]Theophilus, about all that Jesus
[b]began to do and teach,
2 until the day when He [a]was taken up, after He [b]had [1]by the Holy
Spirit given orders to [c]the apostles whom He had [d]chosen.
3 To [1]these [a]He also presented Himself alive, after His suffering, by
many convincing proofs, appearing to them over *a period of* forty
days, and speaking of [b]the things concerning the kingdom of God.
4 And [1]gathering them together, He commanded them [a]not to
leave Jerusalem, but to wait for [2b]what the Father had promised,
"Which," *He said*, "you heard of from Me;
5 for [a]John baptized with water, but you shall be baptized [1]with
the Holy Spirit [2b]not many days from now."
6 And so when they had come together, they were asking Him,
saying, "Lord, [a]is it at this time You are restoring the kingdom to
Israel?"
7 He said to them, "It is not for you to know times or epochs
which [a]the Father has fixed by His own authority;
8 but you shall receive power [a]when the Holy Spirit has come
upon you; and you shall be [b]My witnesses both in Jerusalem, and in
all Judea and [c]Samaria, and even to [d]the remotest part of the earth."
9 And after He had said these things, [a]He was lifted up while they
were looking on, and a cloud received Him out of their sight.
10 And as they were gazing intently into [1]the sky while He was
departing, [2]behold, [a]two men in white clothing stood beside them;
11 and they also said, "[a]Men of Galilee, why do you stand looking
into [1]the sky? This Jesus, who [b]has been taken up from you into
heaven, will [c]come in just the same way as you have watched Him
go into heaven."
12 Then they [a]returned to Jerusalem from the [1b]mount called
[2]Olivet, which is near Jerusalem, a Sabbath day's journey away.
13 And when they had entered, they went up to [a]the upper room,
where they were staying; [b]that is, Peter and John and [1]James and
Andrew, Philip and Thomas, Bartholomew and Matthew, [1]James *the
son* of Alphaeus, and Simon the Zealot, and [c]Judas *the* [2]*son* of [1]James.
14 These all with one mind [a]were continually devoting themselves
to prayer, along with [1b]*the* women, and Mary the [c]mother of Jesus,
and with His [c]brothers.
15 And [1]at this time Peter stood up in the midst of [a]the brethren (a
gathering of about one hundred and twenty [2]persons was there
together), and said,
16 "Brethren, [a]the Scripture had to be fulfilled, which the Holy Spirit
foretold by the mouth of David concerning Judas, [b]who became a
guide to those who arrested Jesus.

.it., *made* [a]Luke 1:3 [b]Luke 3:23
, through [a]Mark Acts 1:9, 11, 22 att. 28:19f.; Mark ohn 20:21f.; Acts Mark 6:30 [d]John 3:18; Acts 10:41
it., *whom* [a]Matt. Mark 16:12, 14; 24:34, 36; John 19, 26; 21:1, 14; 5-7 [b]Acts 8:12; 19:8; 28:23, 31
r, *eating with;* or bly, *lodging with* e *promise of the* her [a]Luke 24:49 14:16, 26; 15:26; Acts 2:33
in [2]Lit., *not long* hese many days 3:11; Mark 1:8; 3:16; John 1:33; 1:16 [b]Acts 2:1-4
Matt. 17:11; Mark ike 17:20; 19:11
Matt. 24:36; Mark 13:32
cts 2:1-4 [b]Luke ohn 15:27 [c]Acts 14 [d]Matt. 28:19; 15; Rom. 10:18; Col. 1:23
24:50, 51; Acts 1:2
eaven [2]Lit., *and* Luke 24:4; John 20:12
r, *heaven* [a]Acts 31 [b]Mark 16:19; ts 1:9, 22 [c]Matt. 6:27f.; Acts 3:21
r, *hill* [2]Or, *Olive* ove [a]Luke 24:52 [b]Matt. 21:1
[1]Or, *Jacob* [2]Or *, brother* [a]Mark Luke 22:12; Acts 20:8 [b]Acts 1:13: att. 10:2-4; Mark 19; Luke 6:14-16 [c]John 14:22
, certain women 2:42; 6:4; Rom. ; Eph. 6:18; Col. Luke 8:2f. [c]Matt. 12:46
t., *in these days* es [a]John 21:23; 6:3; 9:30; 10:23; 2, 26, 29; 12:17; , 3, 22, 23, 32f., 40; 17:6, 10, 14; ; 21:7, 17; 22:5; 14f.; Rom. 1:13
hn 13:18; 17:12; 20 [b]Matt. 26:47; 43; Luke 22:47; John 18:3

17 "For he was [a]counted among us, and received his portion in [b]this
ministry."
18 (Now this man [a]acquired a field with [b]the price of his wicked-
ness; and falling headlong, he burst open in the middle and all his
bowels gushed out.
19 And it became known to all who were living in Jerusalem; so
that in [a]their own language that field was called [1]Hakeldama, that is,
Field of Blood.)
20 "For it is written in the book of Psalms,

'[a]LET HIS HOMESTEAD BE MADE DESOLATE,
AND LET NO MAN DWELL IN IT';

and,

'[b]HIS [1]OFFICE LET ANOTHER MAN TAKE.'

21 "It is therefore necessary that of the men who have accompanied
us all the time that [a]the Lord Jesus went in and out [1]among us—
22 [a]beginning [1]with the baptism of John, until the day that He [b]was
taken up from us—one of these should become a [c]witness with us of
His resurrection."
23 And they put forward two men, Joseph called Barsabbas (who
was also called Justus), and [a]Matthias.
24 And they [a]prayed, and said, "Thou, Lord, [b]who knowest the
hearts of all men, show which one of these two Thou hast chosen
25 to [1]occupy [a]this ministry and [b]apostleship from which Judas
turned aside to go to his own place."
26 And they [1a]drew lots for them, and the lot fell [2]to [b]Matthias; and
he was [3]numbered with [c]the eleven apostles.

Chapter 2

2 And when [a]the day of Pentecost [1]had come, they were all
together in one place.
2 And suddenly there came from heaven a noise like a violent,
rushing wind, and it filled [a]the whole house where they were sitting.

17 [a]John 6:70f. 1:25; 20:24; 21:

18 [a]Matt. 27:3- [b]Matt. 26:14f.

19 [1]Some early read *Hakeldama* [a]Matt. 27:8; Acts

20 [1]Lit., *positio* *overseer* [a]Ps. 6 [b]Ps. 109:8

21 [1]Lit., *to us* [a] 24:3

22 [1]Lit., *from* 3:16; Mark 1:1-4 Luke 3:21 [b]Mar Acts 1:2 [c]Acts

23 [a]Acts 1:26

24 [a]Acts 6:6; 1 14:23 [b]1 Sam. Jer. 17:10; Acts Rom. 8:27

25 [1]Lit., *take th* *of* [a]Acts 1:17 [b] 1:5; 1 Cor. 9:2;

26 [1]Lit., *gave* [2] *upon* [3]Lit., *chos* [a]Lev. 16:8; Josh 1 Sam. 14:41f.; 10:34; 11:1; Pro [b]Acts 1:23 [c]Acts

2:1 [1]Lit., *was b* *fulfilled* [a]Lev. 23 Acts 20:16; 1 C

2 [a]Acts 4:31

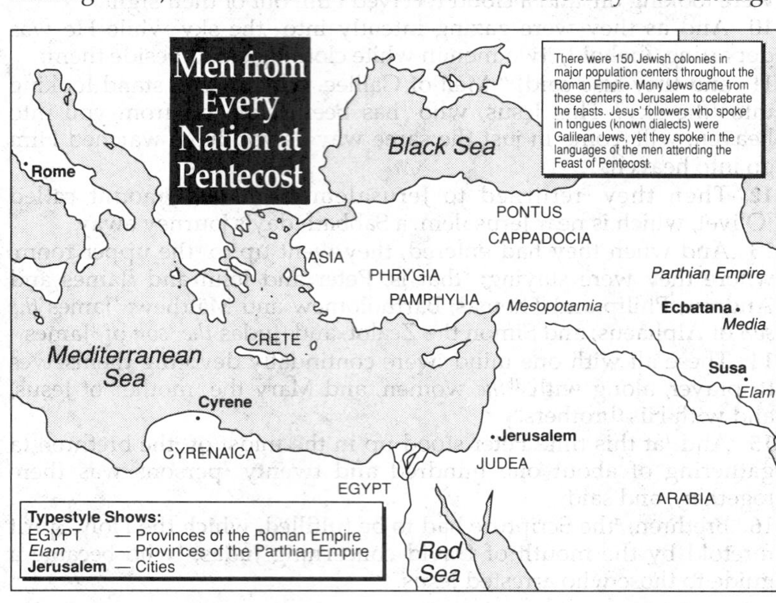

3 And there appeared to them tongues as of fire [1]distributing
themselves, and [2]they [3]rested on each one of them.
4 And they were all [a]filled with the Holy Spirit and began to
[b]speak with other tongues, as the Spirit was giving them [1]utterance.
5 Now there were Jews living in Jerusalem, [a]devout men, from
every nation under heaven.
6 And when [a]this sound occurred, the multitude came together,
and were bewildered, because they were each one hearing them
speak in his own [1]language.
7 And [a]they were amazed and marveled, saying, "[1]Why, are not all
these who are speaking [b]Galileans?
8 "And how is it that we each hear *them* in our own [1]language [2]to
which we were born?
9 "Parthians and Medes and Elamites, and residents of Mesopo-
tamia, Judea and [a]Cappadocia, [b]Pontus and [1c]Asia,
10 [a]Phrygia and [b]Pamphylia, Egypt and the districts of Libya
around [c]Cyrene, and [1d]visitors from Rome, both Jews and
[2e]proselytes,
11 Cretans and Arabs—we hear them in our *own* tongues speaking
of the mighty deeds of God."
12 And [a]they all continued in amazement and great perplexity,
saying to one another, "What does this mean?"
13 But others were mocking and saying, "[a]They are full of [1]sweet
wine."
14 But Peter, [1]taking his stand with [a]the eleven, raised his voice and
declared to them: "Men of Judea, and all you who live in Jerusalem,
let this be known to you, and give heed to my words.
15 "For these men are not drunk, as you suppose, [a]for it is *only* the
[1]third hour of the day;
16 but this is what was spoken of through the prophet Joel:
17 '[a]AND IT SHALL BE IN THE LAST DAYS,' God says,
'THAT I WILL POUR FORTH OF MY SPIRIT UPON ALL [1]MANKIND;
AND YOUR SONS AND YOUR DAUGHTERS SHALL PROPHESY,
AND YOUR YOUNG MEN SHALL SEE VISIONS,
AND YOUR OLD MEN SHALL DREAM DREAMS;
18 EVEN UPON MY BONDSLAVES, BOTH MEN AND WOMEN,
I WILL IN THOSE DAYS POUR FORTH OF MY SPIRIT
And they shall prophesy.
19 'AND I WILL GRANT WONDERS IN THE SKY ABOVE,
AND SIGNS ON THE EARTH BENEATH,
BLOOD, AND FIRE, AND VAPOR OF SMOKE.
20 'THE SUN SHALL BE TURNED INTO DARKNESS,
AND THE MOON INTO BLOOD,
BEFORE THE GREAT AND GLORIOUS DAY OF THE LORD SHALL COME.
21 'AND IT SHALL BE, THAT [a]EVERYONE WHO CALLS ON THE NAME OF THE
LORD SHALL BE SAVED.'
22 "Men of Israel, listen to these words: [a]Jesus the Nazarene, [b]a man
[1]attested to you by God with [2]miracles and [c]wonders and [3]signs
which God performed through Him in your midst, just as you your-
selves know—
23 this *Man*, delivered up by the [a]predetermined plan and fore-
knowledge of God, [b]you nailed to a cross by the hands of [1]godless
men and put *Him* to death.

To understand the significance of Pentecost, see the chart ***The Feasts of Israel*** located on pages I-48 and I-49.

...g distributed ...it., it [3]Or, sat

...bility to speak ...t. 10:20; Acts ...:8, 31; 6:3, 5; ...; 9:17; 11:15; [b]Mark 16:17; ...12:10f.; 14:21

...2:25; Acts 8:2

...lect [a]Acts 2:2

...Behold [a]Acts ...tt. 26:73; Acts 1:11

...dialect [2]Lit., in

...e., west coast ...of Asia Minor ...:1 [b]Acts 18:2; ...1:1 [c]Acts 6:9; ...0; 20:4; 21:27; ...:2; Rom. 16:5; ...:19; 2 Cor. 1:8; ...1:15; Rev. 1:4

...the sojourning ...s [2]I.e., Gentile ...erts to Judaism ...6; 18:23 [b]Acts ...; 14:24; 15:38; ...tt. 27:32 [c]Acts ...:1 [e]Matt. 23:15

12 [a]Acts 2:7

[1]Or, new wine [a]1 Cor. 14:23

... [1]Or, being put ...as spokesman [a]Acts 1:26

15 [1]I.e., 9 a.m. [a]1 Thess. 5:7

[1]Lit., flesh [a]Joel 2:28-32

21 [a]Rom. 10:13

[1]Or, exhibited or ...dited [2]Or, works ...ver [3]Or, attesting ...racles [a]Acts 3:6; ...10:38 [b]John 3:2 ...48; Acts 2:19, 43

..., men without the ...aw; i.e., heathen ...22:22; Acts 3:18; ...Pet. 1:20 [b]Matt. ...Mark 15:24; Luke ...3:33; 24:20; John ...19:18; Acts 3:13

24 "[1]And [a]God raised Him up again, putting an end to the [2]agony of
death, since it [b]was impossible for Him to be held in its power.
25 "For David says of Him,
'[a]I WAS ALWAYS BEHOLDING THE LORD IN MY PRESENCE;
FOR HE IS AT MY RIGHT HAND, THAT I MAY NOT BE SHAKEN.
26 'THEREFORE MY HEART WAS GLAD AND MY TONGUE EXULTED;
MOREOVER MY FLESH ALSO WILL ABIDE IN HOPE;
27 BECAUSE THOU WILT NOT ABANDON MY SOUL TO [a]HADES,
[b]NOR [1]ALLOW THY [2]HOLY ONE TO [3]UNDERGO DECAY.
28 'THOU HAST MADE KNOWN TO ME THE WAYS OF LIFE;
THOU WILT MAKE ME FULL OF GLADNESS WITH THY PRESENCE.'
29 "[1]Brethren, I may confidently say to you regarding the [a]patriarch
David that he both [b]died and [c]was buried, and [d]his tomb is [2]with us
to this day.
30 "And so, because he was [a]a prophet, and knew that [b]GOD HAD
SWORN TO HIM WITH AN OATH TO SEAT *one* [1]OF HIS DESCENDANTS UPON HIS
THRONE,
31 he looked ahead and spoke of the resurrection of [1]the Christ, that
[a]HE WAS NEITHER ABANDONED TO HADES, NOR DID His flesh [2]SUFFER
DECAY.
32 "This Jesus [a]God raised up again, to which we are all [b]witnesses.
33 "Therefore having been exalted [1a]to the right hand of God, and
[b]having received from the Father [c]the promise of the Holy Spirit, He
has [d]poured forth this which you both see and hear.
34 "For it was not David who ascended into [1]heaven, but he himself
says:
'[a]THE LORD SAID TO MY LORD,
"SIT AT MY RIGHT HAND,
35 UNTIL I MAKE THINE ENEMIES A FOOTSTOOL FOR THY FEET." '
36 "Therefore let all the [a]house of Israel know for certain that God
has made Him both [b]Lord and [1]Christ—this Jesus [c]whom you
crucified."
37 Now when they heard *this*, they were [1]pierced to the heart, and
said to Peter and the rest of the apostles, "[2]Brethren, [a]what shall we
do?"
38 And Peter *said* to them, "[a]Repent, and let each of you be [b]bap-
tized in the name of Jesus Christ for the forgiveness of your sins; and
you shall receive the gift of the Holy Spirit.
39 "For [a]the promise is for you and your children, and for all who
are [b]far off, as many as the Lord our God shall call to Himself."
40 And with many other words he solemnly [a]testified and kept on
exhorting them, saying, "[1]Be saved from this [b]perverse generation!"
41 So then, those who had received his word were baptized; and
there were added that day about three thousand [1a]souls.
42 And they were [a]continually devoting themselves to the apostles'
teaching and to fellowship, to [b]the breaking of bread and [1a]to prayer.
43 And [1]everyone kept feeling a sense of awe; and many [a]wonders
and [2]signs were taking place through the apostles[3].
44 And all those who had believed [1]were together, and [a]had all
things in common;
45 and they [a]*began* selling their property and possessions, and were
sharing them with all, as anyone might have need.
46 [a]And day by day continuing with one mind in the temple, and

24 [1]Lit., *Wh* *raised up* [2]L *pangs* [a]Matt Mark 16:6; L Acts 2:32; 3: 5:30; 10:40; 37; 17:31; R 8:11; 10:9; 1 15:15; 2 Cor. 1:1; Eph. 1:2 1 Thess. 1:1 1 Pet. 1:21 [b]

25 [a]Ps. 16:8

27 [1]Lit., *give* or *pious* [3]Lit. *corruption* [a]M Acts 2:31 [b]A

29 [1]Lit., *Men* [2]Lit., *among* Heb. 7:4 [b]Ac [c]1 Kin. 2:10 [d]

30 [1]Lit., *of th* *loins* [a]Matt. 2 132:11; 2 San 89:3f.

31 [1]I.e., the M [2]Lit., *see corr* 11:23; Acts 2:

32 [a]Acts 2:24 4:10; 5:30; 10: 33, 34, 37; 17 4:24; 6:4; 8:11 1 Cor. 6:14; 15 4:14; Gal. 1:1; Col. 2:12; 1 Th Heb. 13:20; 1 [b]Acts 1:8

33 [1]Or, *by* [a]M Acts 5:31 [b]Act [c]John 7:39; Ga [d]Acts 2:17; 10:

34 [1]Lit., *the he* 110:1; Matt. 22

36 [1]I.e., Messi 36:22, 32, 37; 4 2:11 [c]Acts 2:23

37 [1]Or, *smitten* *conscience* [2]Li *brothers* [a]Luke 12, 14

38 [a]Mark 1:15; 24:47; Acts 3:19 20:21 [b]Mark 16 8:12, 16; 22:16

39 [a]Is. 44:3; 54 Joel 2:32; Rom. 2:12 [b]Eph. 2:13

40 [1]Or, *Escape* 16:28 [b]Deut. 32 17:17; Phil. 2:15

41 [1]I.e., persons 3:23; 7:14; 27:37 13:1; 1 Pet. 3:20

42 [1]Lit., *the pra* [a]Acts 1:14 [b]Luke Acts 2:46; 20:7; 10:16

43 [1]Lit., *fear was* *occurring to eve* [2]Or, *attesting mi* [3]Some ancient m *in Jerusalem; an* *fear was upon al* 2:22

44 [1]Some ancien do not contain we 4:32, 37; 5:2

45 [a]Matt. 19:21;

46 [a]Acts 5:42

[b]breaking bread [1]from house to house, they were taking their [2]meals
together with gladness and [3]sincerity of heart,
47 praising God, and [a]having favor with all the people. And the
Lord [b]was adding [1]to their number day by day [c]those who were
being saved.

Chapter 3

3 Now [a]Peter and John were going up to the temple at the [1]ninth
hour, [b]the hour of prayer.
2 And [a]a certain man who had been lame from his mother's womb
was being carried along, whom they [b]used to set down every day at
the gate of the temple which is called Beautiful, [c]in order to beg
[1]alms of those who were entering the temple.
3 And when he saw [a]Peter and John about to go into the temple,
he *began* asking to receive alms.
4 And Peter, along with John, [a]fixed his gaze upon him and said,
"Look at us!"
5 And he *began* to give them his attention, expecting to receive
something from them.
6 But Peter said, "I do not possess silver and gold, but what I do
have I give to you: [a]In the name of Jesus Christ the Nazarene—
walk!"
7 And seizing him by the right hand, he raised him up; and imme-
diately his feet and his ankles were strengthened.
8 [a]And [1]with a leap, he stood upright and *began* to walk; and he
entered the temple with them, walking and leaping and praising
God.
9 And [a]all the people saw him walking and praising God;
10 and they were taking note of him as being the one who used to
[a]sit at the Beautiful Gate of the temple to *beg* alms, and they were
filled with wonder and amazement at what had happened to him.
11 And while he was clinging to [a]Peter and John, all the people ran
together to them at the so-called [1b]portico of Solomon, full of amaze-
ment.
12 But when Peter saw *this,* he replied to the people, "Men of Israel,
why do you marvel at this, or why do you gaze at us, as if by our
own power or piety we had made him walk?
13 "[a]The God of Abraham, Isaac, and Jacob, [b]the God of our fathers,
has glorified His [1c]servant Jesus, *the one* whom [d]you delivered up,
and disowned in the presence of [e]Pilate, when he had [f]decided to
release Him.
14 "But you disowned [a]the Holy and Righteous One, and [b]asked for
a murderer to be granted to you,
15 but put to death the [1a]Prince of life, *the one* whom [b]God raised
from the dead, *a fact* to which we are [c]witnesses.
16 "And on the basis of faith [a]in His name, *it is* the name of [1]Jesus
which has strengthened this man whom you see and know; and the
faith which *comes* through Him has given him this perfect health in
the presence of you all.
17 "And now, brethren, I know that you acted [a]in ignorance, just as
your [b]rulers did also.
18 "But the things which [a]God announced beforehand by the mouth
of all the prophets, [b]that His [1]Christ should suffer, He has thus ful-
filled.

the various ...omes [2]Lit., ...r, *simplicity* ...; Acts 2:42; ...Cor. 10:16

...ether [a]Acts ...s 2:41; 4:4; ...7; 9:31, 35, ...4; 14:1, 21; ...1 Cor. 1:18

...p.m. [a]Luke ...ts 3:3, 4, 11 ...Matt. 27:45; ...Acts 10:30

...*ift of charity* ...Luke 16:20 ...8; Acts 3:10

...:8; Acts 3:1, 4, 11

... [a]Acts 10:4

...2; 3:16; 4:10

...*ng up* [a]Acts 14:10

...Acts 4:16, 21

...9:8; Acts 3:2

...*r, colonnade* ...8; Acts 3:3, 4 ...23; Acts 5:12

Child [a]Matt. ...Ex. 3:13, 15; ...; 7:32; 22:14 ...3:26; 4:27, 30 ... 20:19; John ...s 2:23 [e]Matt. ...2 [f]Luke 23:4

...ark 1:24; Acts ...2; 2 Cor. 5:21 ... 27:20; Mark ...uke 23:18, 25

Author [a]Acts ...eb. 2:10; 12:2 ...4 [c]Luke 24:48

His [a]Acts 3:6

...ke 23:34; John ...ts 13:27; 26:9; ...3 [b]Luke 23:13

Anointed One; ...Messiah [a]Acts ...ke 24:27; Acts 17:3; 26:23

19 "[a]Repent therefore and return, that your sins may be wiped away,
in order that [b]times of refreshing may come from the presence of the
Lord;
20 and that He may send Jesus, the [1]Christ appointed for you,
21 [a]whom heaven must receive until *the* [1]period of [b]restoration of all
things about which [c]God spoke by the mouth of His holy prophets
from ancient time.
22 "Moses said, '[a]THE LORD GOD SHALL RAISE UP FOR YOU A PROPHET
[1]LIKE ME FROM YOUR BRETHREN; TO HIM YOU SHALL GIVE HEED in every-
thing He says to you.
23 '[a]And it shall be that every [b]soul that does not heed that prophet
[c]shall be utterly destroyed from among the people.'
24 "And likewise, [a]all the prophets who have spoken, from Samuel
and *his* successors onward, also announced these days.
25 "It is you who are [a]the sons of the prophets, and of the [b]covenant
which God [1]made with your fathers, saying to Abraham, '[c]AND IN
YOUR SEED ALL THE FAMILIES OF THE EARTH SHALL BE BLESSED.'
26 "For you [a]first, God [b]raised up His [1]Servant, and sent Him to bless
you by turning every one *of you* from your wicked ways."

Chapter 4

4 And as they were speaking to the people, the priests and [a]the
captain of the temple *guard,* and [b]the Sadducees, [c]came upon
them,
2 being greatly disturbed because they were teaching the people
and proclaiming [1a]in Jesus the resurrection from the dead.
3 And they laid hands on them, and [a]put them in jail until the next
day, for it was already evening.
4 But many of those who had heard the [1]message believed; and
[a]the number of the men came to be about five thousand.
5 And it came about on the next day, that their [a]rulers and elders
and scribes were gathered together in Jerusalem;
6 and [a]Annas the high priest *was there,* and [b]Caiaphas and John
and Alexander, and all who were of high-priestly descent.
7 And when they had placed them in the center, they *began to*
inquire, "By what power, or in what name, have you done this?"
8 Then Peter, [1a]filled with the Holy Spirit, said to them, "[2b]Rulers
and elders of the people,
9 if we are on trial today for [a]a benefit done to a sick man, [1]as to
how this man has been made well,
10 let it be known to all of you, and to all the people of Israel, that
[1a]by the name of Jesus Christ the Nazarene, whom you crucified,
whom [b]God raised from the dead—[1]by [2]this *name* this man stands
here before you in good health.
11 "[1a]He is the [b]STONE WHICH WAS [c]REJECTED by you, THE BUILDERS, *but*
WHICH BECAME THE VERY CORNER *stone.*
12 "And there is salvation in [a]no one else; for there is no other name
under heaven that has been given among men, by which we must be
saved."
13 Now as they observed the [a]confidence of [b]Peter and John, and
understood that they were uneducated and untrained men, they
were marveling, and [c]*began* to recognize them [1]as having been with
Jesus.

19 [a]Acts
[b]2 Thess.

20 [1]Or, *A*
i.e., Messi

21 [1]Lit., *p*
[a]Acts 1:11
Rom. 8:21

22 [1]Or, *as*
me [a]Deut.
Acts 7:37

23 [a]Deut.
2:41 [c]Lev.

24 [a]Luke 2
17:3; 26:23

25 [1]Lit., *co*
[a]Acts 2:39
[c]Gen. 22:18

26 [1]Or, *Ch*
15:24; John
13:46; Rom
[b]Acts 2:24

4:1 [a]Luke 2
3:7 [c]Luke 2
6:12

2 [1]Or, *in the*
[a]Acts 3:15; 1

3 [a]Acts 5:18

4 [1]Or, *word*

5 [a]Luke 23:1

6 [a]Luke 3:2

8 [1]Or, *having*
filled [2]Or, *Ru*
people and e
2:4; 13:9 [b]Lu
Acts 4:5

9 [1]Or, *by wh*
3:7f.

10 [1]Or, *in* [2]C
[a]Acts 2:22; 3:
2:24

11 [1]Lit., *This*
[a]Matt. 21:42
118:22 [c]Mark

12 [a]Matt. 1:21
10:43; 1 Tim. 2

13 [1]Lit., *that t*
been [a]Acts 4:
22:8; Acts 4:19
7:15

14 And seeing the man who had been healed standing with them,
they had nothing to say in reply.
15 But when they had ordered them to go aside out of the [1a]Council,
they *began* to confer with one another,
16 saying, "[a]What shall we do with these men? For the fact that a
[b]noteworthy [1]miracle has taken place through them is apparent to all
who live in Jerusalem, and we cannot deny it.
17 "But in order that it may not spread any further among the
people, let us warn them to speak no more to any man [a]in this
name."
18 And when they had summoned them, they [a]commanded them
not to speak or teach at all [1]in the name of Jesus.
19 But [a]Peter and John answered and said to them, "[b]Whether it is
right in the sight of God to give heed to you rather than to God, you
be the judge;
20 for [a]we cannot stop speaking what we have seen and heard."
21 And when they had threatened them further, they let them go
(finding no basis on which they might punish them) [a]on account of
the people, because they were all [b]glorifying God for what had hap-
pened;
22 for the man was more than forty years old on whom this
[1]miracle of healing had been performed.
23 And when they had been released, they went to their own *com-
panions,* and reported all that the chief priests and the elders had said
to them.
24 And when they heard *this,* they lifted their voices to God with
one accord and said, "O [1]Lord, it is Thou who [a]DIDST MAKE THE HEAV-
EN AND THE EARTH AND THE SEA, AND ALL THAT IS IN THEM,
25 who [a]by the Holy Spirit, *through* the mouth of our father David
Thy servant, didst say,

'[b]WHY DID THE [1]GENTILES RAGE,
AND THE PEOPLES DEVISE FUTILE THINGS?
26 '[a]THE KINGS OF THE EARTH [1]TOOK THEIR STAND,
AND THE RULERS WERE GATHERED TOGETHER
AGAINST THE LORD, AND AGAINST HIS [2b]CHRIST.'

27 "For truly in this city there were gathered together against Thy
holy [1a]servant Jesus, whom Thou didst anoint, both [b]Herod and
[c]Pontius Pilate, along with [d]the [2]Gentiles and the peoples of Israel,
28 to do whatever Thy hand and [a]Thy purpose predestined to
occur.
29 "And [1]now, Lord, take note of their threats, and grant that Thy
bond-servants may [a]speak Thy word with all [b]confidence,
30 while Thou dost extend Thy hand to heal, and [1a]signs and
wonders take place through the name of Thy holy [2b]servant Jesus."
31 And when they had prayed, the [a]place where they had gathered
together was shaken, and they were all [b]filled with the Holy Spirit,
and *began* to [c]speak the word of God with [d]boldness.
32 And the [1]congregation of those who believed were of one heart
and soul; and not one *of them* [2]claimed that anything belonging to
him was his own; but [a]all things were common property to them.
33 And [a]with great power the apostles were giving [b]witness to the
resurrection of the Lord Jesus[1], and abundant grace was upon them
all.
34 For there was not a needy person among them, for all who were

5 [1]Or, *Sanhedrin* [a]Matt. 5:22
6 [1]Or, *sign* [a]John :47 [b]Acts 3:7-10
17 [a]John 15:21
Or, *on the basis of* [a]Acts 5:28f.
[a]Acts 4:13 [b]Acts 5:28f.
20 [a]1 Cor. 9:16
ts 5:26 [b]Matt. 9:8
22 [1]Or, *sign*
[1]Or, *Master* [a]Ex. :11; Neh. 9:6; Ps. 146:6
Or, *nations* [a]Acts 1:16 [b]Ps. 2:1
[1]Or, *approached* *nointed One;* i.e., h [a]Ps. 2:2 [b]Dan. ; Luke 4:18; Acts 10:38; Heb. 1:9
7 [1]Or, *Child* [2]Or, *tions* [a]Acts 3:13; [b]Matt. 14:1; Luke 7-11 [c]Matt. 27:2; 15:1; Luke 23:1, 2; John 18:28, 29 [d]Matt. 20:19
28 [a]Acts 2:23
29 [1]Or, *as for the nt situation* [a]Phil. 4 [b]Acts 4:13, 31; 14:3
30 [1]Or, *attesting racles* [2]Or, *Child* 4:48 [b]Acts 3:13; 4:27
cts 2:1 [b]Acts 2:4 1:14 [d]Acts 4:13; 14:3
r, *multitude* [2]Lit., *aying* [a]Acts 2:44
[1]Some mss. add [a]Acts 1:8 [b]Luke 24:48

owners of land or houses [a]would sell them and bring the [1]proceeds
of the sales,
35 and [a]lay them at the apostles' feet; and they would be
[b]distributed to each, as any had need.
36 And Joseph, a Levite of [a]Cyprian birth, who was also called
[b]Barnabas by the apostles (which translated means, Son of [1c]Encour-
agement),
37 and who owned a tract of land, sold it and brought the money
and [a]laid it at the apostles' feet.

Chapter 5

5 But a certain man named Ananias, with his wife Sapphira, sold a
piece of property,
2 and [a]kept back *some* of the price for himself, with his wife's [1]full
knowledge, and bringing a portion of it, he [b]laid it at the apostles'
feet.
3 But Peter said, "Ananias, why has [a]Satan filled your heart to lie
[b]to the Holy Spirit, and to [c]keep back *some* of the price of the land?
4 "While it remained *unsold,* did it not remain your own? And after
it was sold, was it not [1]under your control? Why is it that you have
[2]conceived this deed in your heart? You have not lied to men, but [a]to
God."
5 And as he heard these words, Ananias [a]fell down and breathed
his last; and [b]great fear came upon all who heard of it.
6 And the [1]young men arose and [a]covered him up, and after carry-
ing him out, they buried him.
7 Now there elapsed an interval of about three hours, and his wife
came in, not knowing what had happened.
8 And Peter responded to her, "Tell me whether you sold the land
[1a]for such and such a price?" And she said, "Yes, [1]that was the price."
9 Then Peter *said* to her, "Why is it that you have agreed together
to [a]put [b]the Spirit of the Lord to the test? Behold, the feet of those
who have buried your husband are at the door, and they shall carry
you out *as well.*"
10 And she [a]fell immediately at his feet, and breathed her last; and
the young men came in and found her dead, and they carried her
out and buried her beside her husband.
11 And [a]great fear came upon the whole church, and upon all who
heard of these things.
12 And [1]at the hands of the apostles many [a]signs and wonders were
taking place among the people; and they were all with one accord in
[b]Solomon's portico.
13 But none of the rest dared to associate with them; however, [a]the
people [1]held them in high esteem.
14 And all the more [a]believers in the Lord, multitudes of men and
women, were constantly [b]added to *their number;*
15 to such an extent that they even carried the sick out into the
streets, and laid them on cots and pallets, so that when Peter came
by, [a]at least his shadow might fall on any one of them.
16 And also the [1]people from the cities in the vicinity of Jerusalem
were coming together, bringing people who were sick [2]or afflicted
with unclean spirits; and they were all being healed.
17 But the high priest rose up, along with all his associates (that is
[a]the sect of [b]the Sadducees), and they were filled with jealousy;

34 [1]Lit., *the price the things being s* [a]Matt. 19:21; Acts

35 [a]Acts 4:37; 5: [b]Acts 2:45; 6:1

36 [1]Or, *Exhortati Consolation* [a]Ac 11:19f.; 13:4; 15: 21:3, 16; 27:4 [b]A 9:27; 11:22, 30; 1 13:1, 2, 7; 1 Cor. Gal. 2:1, 9, 13; C 4:10 [c]Acts 2:40; 13:15; 1 Cor. 14: 1 Thess. 2:3

37 [a]Acts 4:35; 5:

5:2 [1]Or, *collusio* 5:3 [b]Acts 4:35, 3

3 [a]Matt. 4:10; Lu 22:3; John 13:2, [b]Acts 5:4, 9 [c]Act

4 [1]Or, *in your au* [2]Or, *placed* [a]Acts

5 [a]Ezek. 11:13; 5:10 [b]Acts 2:43;

6 [1]Lit., *younger* 19:40

8 [1]Lit., *for so mu* [a]Acts 5:2

9 [a]Acts 15:10 [b]A 5:3, 4

10 [a]Ezek. 11:13; 5:5

11 [a]Acts 2:43; 5:

12 [1]Lit., *through* 4:48 [b]John 10:23 3:11

13 [1]Lit., *were ho* [a]Acts 2:47; 4:21

14 [a]2 Cor. 6:15 2:47; 11:24

15 [a]Acts 19:12

16 [1]Lit., *multitud and*

17 [a]Acts 15:5 [b] 3:7; Acts 4:1

18 and they laid hands on the apostles, and [a]put them in a public jail.

19 But [a]an angel of the Lord during the night opened the gates of the prison, and taking them out he said,

20 "Go your way, stand and [1]speak to the people in the temple [2a]the whole message of this Life."

21 And upon hearing *this,* they entered into the temple [a]about daybreak, and *began* to teach. Now when [b]the high priest and his associates had come, they called [c]the [1]Council together, even all the Senate of the sons of Israel, and sent *orders* to the prison house for them to be brought.

22 But [a]the officers who came did not find them in the prison; and they returned, and reported back,

23 saying, "We found the prison house locked quite securely and the guards standing at the doors; but when we had opened up, we found no one inside."

24 Now when [a]the captain of the temple *guard* and the chief priests heard these words, they were greatly perplexed about them as to what [1]would come of this.

25 But someone came and reported to them, "Behold, the men whom you put in prison are standing in the temple and teaching the people!"

26 Then [a]the captain went along with [b]the officers and *proceeded* to bring them *back* without violence (for [c]they were afraid of the people, lest they should be stoned).

27 And when they had brought them, they stood them [1]before [a]the Council. And the high priest questioned them,

28 saying, "We gave you [a]strict orders not to continue teaching in this name, and behold, you have filled Jerusalem with your teaching, and [b]intend to bring this man's blood upon us."

29 But Peter and the apostles answered and said, "[a]We must obey God rather than men.

30 "[a]The God of our fathers [b]raised up Jesus, [1]whom you had [c]put to death by hanging Him on a [2]cross.

31 "[a]He is the one whom God exalted [1]to His right hand as a [2b]Prince and a [c]Savior, to grant [d]repentance to Israel, and forgiveness of sins.

32 "And we are [a]witnesses[1] of these things; and [b]*so is* the Holy Spirit, whom God has given to those who obey Him."

33 But when they heard this, they were [a]cut [1]to the quick and were intending to slay them.

34 But a certain Pharisee named [a]Gamaliel, a [b]teacher of the Law, respected by all the people, stood up in [c]the Council and gave orders to put the men outside for a short time.

35 And he said to them, "Men of Israel, take care what you propose to do with these men.

36 "For some time ago Theudas rose up, [a]claiming to be somebody; and a group of about four hundred men joined up with him. [1]And he was slain; and all who [2]followed him were dispersed and came to nothing.

37 "After this man Judas of Galilee rose up in the days of [a]the census, and drew away *some* people after him, he too perished, and all those who [1]followed him were scattered.

38 "And so in the present case, I say to you, stay away from these

18 [a]Acts 4:3

[a]Matt. 1:20, 24; , 19; 28:2; Luke ; 2:9; Acts 8:26; ; 12:7, 23; 27:23

[1]*Or, continue to* *eak* [2]*Lit., all the* [a]John 6:63, 68

[1]*Or, Sanhedrin* n 8:2 [b]Acts 4:6 5:22; Acts 5:27, 34, 41

att. 26:58; Acts 5:26

[1]*Lit., this would* [a]Acts 4:1; 5:26

cts 5:24 [b]Acts [c]Acts 4:21; 5:13

in [a]Matt. 5:22; cts 5:21, 34, 41

cts 4:18 [b]Matt. 7:25; Acts 2:23, 36; 3:14f.; 7:52

29 [a]Acts 4:19

, on whom you *d violent hands* *ood* [a]Acts 3:13 24 [c]Acts 10:39; al. 3:13; 1 Pet. 2:24

by [2]*Or, Leader* :33 [b]Acts 3:15 1 [d]Luke 24:47; Acts 2:38

me mss. add *in* *r of Him* [a]Luke ohn 15:26; Acts om. 8:16; Heb. 2:4

, in their hearts Acts 2:37; 7:54

cts 22:3 [b]Luke :17 [c]Acts 5:21

Who was slain *, were obeying* 9; Gal. 2:6; 6:3

, were obeying [a]Luke 2:2

men and let them alone, for if this plan or [1]action should [a]be of men,
it will be overthrown;
39 but if it is of God, you will not be able to overthrow them; or else
you may even be found [a]fighting against God."
40 And they [1]took his advice; and after calling the apostles in, they
[a]flogged them and ordered them to [2]speak no more in the name of
Jesus, and *then* released them.
41 So they went on their way from the presence of the [1a]Council,
[b]rejoicing that they had been considered worthy to suffer shame [c]for
[2]*His* name.
42 [a]And every day, in the temple and [1]from house to house, they
[2]kept right on teaching and [3b]preaching Jesus *as* the [4]Christ.

Chapter 6

6 Now [1]at this time while the [a]disciples were [b]increasing *in number,*
a complaint arose on the part of the [2c]Hellenistic *Jews* against the
native [d]Hebrews, because their [e]widows were being overlooked in
[f]the daily serving *of food.*
2 And the twelve summoned the [1]congregation of the disciples
and said, "It is not desirable for us to neglect the word of God in
order to serve tables.
3 "But select from among you, [a]brethren, seven men of good reputa-
tion, [b]full of the Spirit and of wisdom, whom we may put in charge
of this task.
4 "But we will [a]devote ourselves to prayer, and to the [1]ministry of
the word."
5 And the statement found approval with the whole [1]congrega-
tion; and they chose [a]Stephen, a man [b]full of faith and of the Holy
Spirit, and [c]Philip, Prochorus, Nicanor, Timon, Parmenas and
[2]Nicolas, a [3d]proselyte from [e]Antioch.
6 And these they brought before the apostles; and after [a]praying,
they [b]laid their hands on them.
7 And [a]the word of God kept on spreading; and [b]the number of the
disciples continued to increase greatly in Jerusalem, and a great
many of the priests were becoming obedient to [c]the faith.
8 And Stephen, full of grace and power, was performing great
[a]wonders and [1]signs among the people.
9 But some men from what was called the Synagogue of the Freed-
men, *including* both [a]Cyrenians and [b]Alexandrians, and some from
[c]Cilicia and [1d]Asia, rose up and argued with Stephen.
10 And *yet* they were unable to cope with the wisdom and the
Spirit with which he was speaking.
11 Then they secretly induced men [1]to say, "We have heard him
speak blasphemous words against Moses and *against* God."
12 And they stirred up the people, the elders and the scribes, and
they [a]came upon him and dragged him away, and brought him
[1]before [b]the [2]Council.
13 And they put forward [a]false witnesses who said, "This man in-
cessantly speaks against this [b]holy place, and the Law;
14 for we have heard him say that [a]this Nazarene, Jesus, will
destroy this place and alter [b]the customs which Moses handed down
to us."
15 And fixing their gaze on him, all who were sitting in the
[1a]Council saw his face like the face of an angel.

38 [1]Or, *work* [a]... 11:30

39 [a]Prov. 21:30 ... 11:17

40 [1]Lit., *were persuaded by h... not be speaking* ... 10:17

41 [1]Or, *Sanhe...* the *name* (par excellence) [a]A... [b]1 Pet. 4:14, 16 ... 15:21

42 [1]Or, *in the v... private homes* ... *were not ceasin...* [3]Or, *telling the ... news of* [4]I.e., M... [a]Acts 2:46 [b]Act... 11:20; 17:18; G...

6:1 [1]Lit., *in the...* [2]I.e., non-Pales... Jews who norm... spoke Greek [a]... 11:26 [b]Acts 2:4... [c]Acts 9:29; 11:2... [d]2 Cor. 11:22; P... [e]Acts 9:39, 41; ... 5:3 [f]Acts 4:35; ...

2 [1]Or, *multitud...*

3 [a]John 21:23; ... 1:15 [b]Acts 2:4

4 [1]Or, *service* ... 1:14

5 [1]Lit., *multitud...* *Nikolaos* [3]I.e., ... convert to Juda... [a]Acts 6:8ff.; 11:... 22:20 [b]Acts 6:3... [c]Acts 8:5ff.; 21:... 23:15 [e]Acts 11...

6 [a]Acts 1:24 [b]... 8:10; 27:18; De... Mark 5:23; Acts ... 9:17; 13:3; 19:6 ... 4:14; 2 Tim. 1:6 ... 6:2

7 [a]Acts 12:24; ... [b]Acts 6:1 [c]Acts ... 14:22; Gal. 1:23 ... Jude 3, 20

8 [1]Or, *attesting miracles* [a]John ...

9 [1]I.e., west co... province of Asia ... [a]Matt. 27:32; Ac... [b]Acts 18:24 [c]A... 15:23, 41; 21:3... 23:34; 27:5; Ga... [d]Acts 16:6; 19:1... 21:27; 24:18

11 [1]Lit., *saying*

12 [1]Lit., *into* [2]... *Sanhedrin* [a]Lu... Acts 4:1 [b]Matt. ...

13 [a]Matt. 26:59 ... Acts 7:58 [b]Mat... Acts 21:28; 25:...

14 [a]Matt. 26:61 ... 15:1; 21:21; 26

15 [1]Or, *Sanhe...* [a]Matt. 5:22

Chapter 7

7 And the high priest said, "Are these things so?"
2 And he said, "Hear me, [a]brethren and fathers! [b]The God of
glory [c]appeared to our father Abraham when he was in
Mesopotamia, before he lived in [1]Haran,
3 and said to him, '[a]DEPART FROM YOUR COUNTRY AND YOUR RELATIVES,
AND COME INTO THE LAND THAT I WILL SHOW YOU.'
4 "[a]Then he departed from the land of the Chaldeans, and settled in
[1]Haran. And [b]from there, after his father died, *God* removed him into
this country in which you are now living.
5 "And He gave him no inheritance in it, not even a foot of ground;
and *yet,* even when he had no child, [a]He promised that HE WOULD
GIVE IT TO HIM AS A POSSESSION, AND TO HIS OFFSPRING AFTER HIM.
6 "But [a]God spoke to this effect, that his OFFSPRING WOULD BE ALIENS
IN A FOREIGN LAND, AND THAT THEY WOULD [1]BE ENSLAVED AND MISTREATED
FOR FOUR HUNDRED YEARS.
7 " 'AND WHATEVER NATION TO WHICH THEY SHALL BE IN BONDAGE I
MYSELF WILL JUDGE,' said God, 'AND [a]AFTER THAT THEY WILL COME OUT
AND [1]SERVE ME IN THIS PLACE.'
8 "And He [a]gave him [1]the covenant of circumcision; and so
[b]*Abraham* became the father of Isaac, and circumcised him on the
eighth day; and [c]Isaac *became the father of* Jacob, and [d]Jacob *of* the
twelve [e]patriarchs.
9 "And the patriarchs [a]became jealous of Joseph and sold him into
Egypt. And *yet* God was with him,
10 and rescued him from all his afflictions, and [a]granted him favor
and wisdom in the sight of Pharaoh, king of Egypt; and he made
him governor over Egypt and all his household.
11 "Now [a]a famine came over all Egypt and Canaan, and great afflic-
tion *with it;* and our fathers [1]could find no [2]food.
12 "But [a]when Jacob heard that there was grain in Egypt, he sent our
fathers *there* the first time.
13 "And on the second *visit* [a]Joseph [1]made himself known to his
brothers, and [b]Joseph's family was disclosed to Pharaoh.
14 "And [a]Joseph sent *word* and invited Jacob his father and all his
relatives to come to him, [b]seventy-five [c]persons *in all.*
15 "And [a]Jacob went down to Egypt and *there* passed away, he and
our fathers.
16 "And *from there* they were removed to [1a]Shechem, and laid in the
tomb which Abraham had purchased for a sum of money from the
sons of [2]Hamor in [1]Shechem.
17 "But as the [a]time of the promise was approaching which God had
assured to Abraham, [b]the people increased and multiplied in Egypt,
18 until [a]THERE AROSE ANOTHER KING OVER EGYPT WHO KNEW NOTHING
ABOUT JOSEPH.
19 "It was he who took [a]shrewd advantage of our race, and
mistreated our fathers so that they would [1b]expose their infants and
they would not survive.
20 "And it was at this time that [a]Moses was born; and he was lovely
[1]in the sight of God; and he was nurtured three months in his
father's home.
21 "And after he had been [1]exposed, [a]Pharaoh's daughter [2]took him
away, and nurtured him as her own son.

ir., *Kharran* [a]Acts [b]Ps. 29:3; 1 Cor. [c]Gen. 11:31; 15:7
3 [a]Gen. 12:1
r., *Kharran* [a]Gen. 11:31; 15:7 [b]Gen. 12:4, 5
Gen. 12:7; 13:15; 15:18; 17:8
Lit., *enslave them and mistreat them* [a]Gen. 15:13f.
Or, *worship* [a]Ex. 3:12
a [a]Gen. 17:10ff. en. 21:2-4 [c]Gen. 6 [d]Gen. 29:31ff.; ff.; 35:23ff. [e]Acts 2:29
. 37:11, 28; 39:2, 21f.; 45:4
10 [a]Gen. 39:21; 40-46; Ps. 105:21
11 [1]Lit., *were not* ding [2]Or, *fodder* Gen. 41:54f.; 42:5
12 [a]Gen. 42:2
3 [1]Or, *was made* wn [a]Gen. 45:1-4 [b]Gen. 45:16
Gen. 45:9, 10, 17, Gen. 46:26f.; Ex. eut. 10:22 [c]Acts 2:41
n. 46:1-7; 49:33; Ex. 1:6
r., *Sychem* [2]Gr., nor [a]Gen. 23:16; :19; 50:13; Josh. 24:32
Gen. 15:13 [b]Ex. 1:7f.
18 [a]Ex. 1:8
Or, *put out to die* 1:10f., 16ff. [b]Ex. 1:22
Lit., *to God* [a]Ex. 2:2; Heb. 11:23
Or, *put out to die* dopted him [a]Ex. 2:5f., 10

22 "And Moses was educated in all [a]the learning of the Egyptians, and he was a man of power in words and deeds.

23 "But when he was approaching the age of forty, [a]it entered his [1]mind to visit his brethren, the sons of Israel.

24 "And when he saw one *of them* being treated unjustly, he defended him and took vengeance for the oppressed by striking down the Egyptian.

25 "And he [1]supposed that his brethren understood that God was granting them [2]deliverance [3]through him; but they did not understand.

26 "[a]And on the following day he appeared to them as they were fighting together, and he tried to reconcile them in peace, saying, 'Men, you are brethren, why do you injure one another?'

27 "But the one who was injuring his neighbor pushed him away, saying, '[a]WHO MADE YOU A RULER AND JUDGE OVER US?

28 '[a]YOU DO NOT MEAN TO KILL ME AS YOU KILLED THE EGYPTIAN YESTERDAY, DO YOU?'

29 "And at this remark [a]MOSES FLED, AND BECAME AN ALIEN IN THE LAND OF [1]MIDIAN, where he [b]became the father of two sons.

30 "And after forty years had passed, [a]AN ANGEL APPEARED TO HIM IN THE WILDERNESS OF MOUNT Sinai, IN THE FLAME OF A BURNING THORN BUSH.

31 "And when Moses saw it, he *began* to marvel at the sight; and as he approached to look *more* closely, there came the voice of the Lord:

32 '[a]I AM THE GOD OF YOUR FATHERS, THE GOD OF ABRAHAM AND ISAAC AND JACOB.' And Moses shook with fear and would not venture to look.

33 "[a]BUT THE LORD SAID TO HIM, '[b]TAKE OFF THE SANDALS FROM YOUR FEET, FOR THE PLACE ON WHICH YOU ARE STANDING IS HOLY GROUND.

34 '[a]I HAVE CERTAINLY SEEN THE OPPRESSION OF MY PEOPLE IN EGYPT, AND HAVE HEARD THEIR GROANS, AND I HAVE COME DOWN TO DELIVER THEM; [1b]COME NOW, AND I WILL SEND YOU TO EGYPT.'

35 "This Moses whom they [a]disowned, saying, 'WHO MADE YOU A RULER AND A JUDGE?' is the one whom God [1]sent *to be* both a ruler and a deliverer with the [2]help of the angel who appeared to him in the thorn bush.

36 "[a]This man led them out, performing [b]wonders and [1]signs in the land of Egypt and in the Red Sea and in the [c]wilderness for forty years.

37 "This is the Moses who said to the sons of Israel, '[a]GOD SHALL RAISE UP FOR YOU A PROPHET [1]LIKE ME FROM YOUR BRETHREN.'

38 "This is the one who was in [a]the [1]congregation in the wilderness together with [b]the angel who was speaking to him on Mount Sinai, and *who was* with our fathers; and he received [c]living [d]oracles to pass on to you.

39 "And our fathers were unwilling to be obedient to him, but [a]repudiated him and in their hearts turned back to Egypt,

40 [a]SAYING TO AARON, 'MAKE FOR US GODS WHO WILL GO BEFORE US; FOR THIS MOSES WHO LED US OUT OF THE LAND OF EGYPT—WE DO NOT KNOW WHAT HAPPENED TO HIM.'

41 "And [1]at that time [a]they made a [2]calf and brought a sacrifice to the idol, and were rejoicing in [b]the works of their hands.

42 "But God [a]turned away and delivered them up to [1]serve the [2]host of heaven; as it is written in the book of the prophets, '[b]IT WAS NOT TO

22 [a]1 Kin. 4:3

23 [1]Lit., *hear* 2:11f.; Heb. 11

25 [1]Lit., *was* [2]Or, *salvation through his ha*

26 [a]Ex. 2:13f.

27 [a]Ex. 2:14;

28 [a]Ex. 2:14

29 [1]Gr., *Madia* 2:15, 22 [b]Ex. 1

30 [a]Ex. 3:1f.; I

32 [a]Ex. 3:6; M

33 [a]Ex. 3:5 [b]J

34 [1]Lit., *and no hither!* [a]Ex. 3:7 3:10

35 [1]Lit., *has se hand* [a]Ex. 2:14 7:27

36 [1]Or, *attestin miracles* [a]Ex. 1 33:1; Heb. 8:9 14:21; John 4:4 16:35; Num. 14. 95:8-10; Acts 7: 13:18; Heb. 3:8f

37 [1]Or, *as* He ra *me* [a]Deut. 18:15 Acts 3:22

38 [1]Or, *church; ekklesia* [a]Ex. 19 [b]Acts 7:53 [c]Deu Heb. 4:12 [d]Rom Heb. 5:12; 1 Pet.

39 [a]Num. 14:3f.

40 [a]Ex. 32:1, 23

41 [1]Lit., *in those* [2]Or, *young bull* [a] 32:4, 6 [b]Rev. 9:2

42 [1]Or, *worship* heavenly bodies 24:20; Is. 63:10; 19:13; Ezek. 20:3 [b]Amos 5:25

ME THAT YOU OFFERED VICTIMS AND SACRIFICES [c]FORTY YEARS IN THE
WILDERNESS, WAS IT, O HOUSE OF ISRAEL?
43 '[a]YOU ALSO TOOK ALONG THE TABERNACLE OF MOLOCH AND THE STAR
OF THE GOD [1]ROMPHA, THE IMAGES WHICH YOU MADE TO WORSHIP THEM. I
ALSO WILL REMOVE YOU BEYOND BABYLON.'
44 "Our fathers had [a]the tabernacle of testimony in the wilderness,
just as He who spoke to Moses directed *him* to make it [b]according to
the pattern which he had seen.
45 "And having received it in their turn, our fathers [a]brought it in
with [1]Joshua upon dispossessing the [2]nations whom God drove out
before our fathers, until the time of David.
46 "And [a]*David* found favor in God's sight, and [b]asked that he might
find a dwelling place for the [1]God of Jacob.
47 "But it was [a]Solomon who built a house for Him.
48 "However, [a]the Most High does not dwell in *houses* made by
human hands; as the prophet says:
49 '[a]HEAVEN IS MY THRONE,
AND EARTH IS THE FOOTSTOOL OF MY FEET;
WHAT KIND OF HOUSE WILL YOU BUILD FOR ME?' says the Lord;
'OR WHAT PLACE IS THERE FOR MY REPOSE?
50 '[a]WAS IT NOT MY HAND WHICH MADE ALL THESE THINGS?'
51 "You men who are [a]stiff-necked and uncircumcised in heart and
ears are always resisting the Holy Spirit; you are doing just as your
fathers did.
52 "[a]Which one of the prophets did your fathers not persecute? And
they killed those who had previously announced the coming of [b]the
Righteous One, whose betrayers and murderers [c]you have now be-
come;
53 you who received the law as [a]ordained by angels, and *yet* did not
keep it."
54 Now when they heard this, they were [a]cut [1]to the quick, and they
began gnashing their teeth at him.
55 But being [a]full of the Holy Spirit, he [b]gazed intently into heaven
and saw the glory of God, and Jesus standing [c]at the right hand of
God;
56 and he said, "Behold, I see the [a]heavens opened up and [b]the Son
of Man standing at the right hand of God."
57 But they cried out with a loud voice, and covered their ears, and
they rushed upon him with one impulse.
58 And when they had [a]driven him out of the city, they *began* ston-
ing *him*, and [b]the witnesses [c]laid aside their robes at the feet of [d]a
young man named Saul.
59 And they went on stoning Stephen as he [a]called upon *the Lord*
and said, "Lord Jesus, receive my spirit!"
60 And [a]falling on his knees, he cried out with a loud voice, "Lord,
[b]do not hold this sin against them!" And having said this, he [1c]fell
asleep.

Chapter 8 ____________________

8 And [a]Saul was in hearty agreement with putting him to death.
And on that day a great persecution arose against [b]the church in
Jerusalem; and they were all [c]scattered throughout the regions of
Judea and [d]Samaria, except the apostles.

[c]Acts 7:36
...ss. spell it: ...mphan, or ... Raiphan, ...an [a]Amos 5:26, 27
...3, 9; 38:21 [b]Ex. 25:40
...Jesus [2]Or, ...eut. 32:49; ...18:1; 23:9; ...; Ps. 44:2f.
...arliest mss. ...e instead of Septuagint ...d [a]2 Sam. ...2:1-5; Acts ...am. 7:1-16; ...hr. 17:1-14
...1-38; 8:20; ...Chr. 3:1-17
[a]Luke 1:32
Matt. 5:34f.
...50 [a]Is. 66:2
...2:9; 33:3, 5; ...Num. 27:14; ...r. 6:10; 9:26
...6:15f.; Matt. ...31, 37 [b]Acts ...; 1 John 2:1 ...s 3:14; 5:28
...t. 33:2; Acts ...19; Heb. 2:2
...their hearts [a]Acts 5:33
...ts 2:4 [b]John [c]Mark 16:19
...1:51 [b]Matt. 8:20
...ev. 24:14, 16; [b]Deut. 13:9f.; ...ts 6:13 [c]Acts ...ts 8:1; 22:20; 26:10
...Acts 9:14, 21; ...om. 10:12-14; ...2; 2 Tim. 2:22
...expired [a]Luke ...att. 5:44; Luke ...an. 12:2; Matt. ...n 11:11f.; Acts ...Cor. 15:6, 18, ...Thess. 4:13ff.; 2 Pet. 3:4
...ts 7:58; 22:20; ...cts 9:31 [c]Acts ...:19 [d]Acts 1:8; 8:5, 14; 9:31

2 And *some* devout men buried Stephen, and made loud lamentation over him.
3 But [a]Saul *began* ravaging the church, entering house after house; and [b]dragging off men and women, he would put them in prison.
4 Therefore, those [a]who had been scattered went about [1b]preaching the word.
5 And [a]Philip went down to the city of Samaria and *began* proclaiming [1]Christ to them.
6 And the multitudes with one accord were giving attention to what was said by Philip, as they heard and saw the [1]signs which he was performing.
7 For *in the case of* many who had [a]unclean spirits, they were coming out *of them* shouting with a loud voice; and many who had been [b]paralyzed and lame were healed.
8 And there was [a]much rejoicing in that city.
9 Now there was a certain man named Simon, who formerly was practicing [a]magic in the city, and astonishing the people of Samaria, [b]claiming to be someone great;
10 and they all, from smallest to greatest, were giving attention to him, saying, "[a]This man is what is called the Great Power of God."
11 And they were giving him attention because he had for a long time astonished them with his [a]magic arts.
12 But when they believed Philip [a]preaching the good news about the kingdom of God and the name of Jesus Christ, they were being [b]baptized, men and women alike.
13 And even Simon himself believed; and after being baptized, he continued on with Philip; and as he observed [a]signs and [b]great miracles taking place, he was constantly amazed.
14 Now when [a]the apostles in Jerusalem heard that Samaria had received the word of God, they sent them [b]Peter and John,
15 who came down and prayed for them, [a]that they might receive the Holy Spirit.
16 For He had [a]not yet fallen upon any of them; they had simply been [b]baptized [1]in the name of the Lord Jesus.
17 Then they [a]*began* laying their hands on them, and they were [b]receiving the Holy Spirit.
18 Now when Simon saw that the Spirit was bestowed through the laying on of the apostles' hands, he offered them money,
19 saying, "Give this authority to me as well, so that everyone on whom I lay my hands may receive the Holy Spirit."
20 But Peter said to him, "May your silver perish with you, because you thought you could [a]obtain the gift of God with money!
21 "You have [a]no part or portion in this [1]matter, for your heart is not [b]right before God.
22 "Therefore repent of this wickedness of yours, and pray the Lord that [a]if possible, the intention of your heart may be forgiven you.
23 "For I see that you are in the gall of bitterness and in [a]the [1]bondage of iniquity."
24 But Simon answered and said, "[a]Pray to the Lord for me yourselves, so that nothing of what you have said may come upon me."
25 And so, when they had solemnly [a]testified and spoken [b]the word of the Lord, they started back to Jerusalem, and were [c]preaching the gospel to many villages of the [d]Samaritans.
26 But [a]an angel of the Lord spoke to [b]Philip saying, "Arise and go

INSIGHT

See the insight box about the **Samaritans** on page 1562.

3 [a]Acts 9: 22:4, 19; 2 15:9; Gal. 3:6; 1 Tim. 2:6
4 [1]Or, *brin tidings of* [b]Acts 8:12;
5 [1]I.e., the [a]Acts 6:5; 8
6 [1]Or, *atte*
7 [a]Mark 16 4:24
8 [a]John 4:4 8:39
9 [a]Acts 8:1 [b]Acts 5:36
10 [a]Acts 14
11 [a]Acts 8:9
12 [a]Acts 1:3 2:38
13 [a]Acts 8:6 19:11
14 [a]Acts 8:1
15 [a]Acts 2:3
16 [1]Lit., *into* 28:19; Acts 1 2:38; 10:48
17 [a]Mark 5:2 6:6 [b]Acts 2:4
20 [a]2 Kin. 5: Dan. 5:17; Ma Acts 2:38
21 [1]Or, *teach word* [a]Deut. 12:12; Eph. 5: 78:37
22 [a]Is. 55:7
23 [1]Or, *fetter*
24 [a]Gen. 20:7 Num. 21:7; Ja
25 [a]Luke 16:2 13:12 [c]Acts 8: 10:5
26 [a]Acts 5:19 [b]Acts 8:5

south to the road that descends from Jerusalem to [c]Gaza." ([1]This is a
desert *road*.)
27 And he arose and went; and behold, [a]there was an Ethiopian
eunuch, a court official of Candace, queen of the Ethiopians, who
was in charge of all her treasure; and he [b]had come to Jerusalem to
worship.
28 And he was returning and sitting in his [1]chariot, and was reading the prophet Isaiah.
29 And [a]the Spirit said to Philip, "Go up and join this [1]chariot."
30 And when Philip had run up, he heard him reading Isaiah the
prophet, and said, "Do you understand what you are reading?"
31 And he said, "Well, how could I, unless someone guides me?"
And he invited Philip to come up and sit with him.
32 Now the passage of Scripture which he was reading was this:
"[a]HE WAS LED AS A SHEEP TO SLAUGHTER;
AND AS A LAMB BEFORE ITS SHEARER IS SILENT,
SO HE DOES NOT OPEN HIS MOUTH.
33 "[a]IN HUMILIATION HIS JUDGMENT WAS TAKEN AWAY;
WHO SHALL [1]RELATE HIS [2]GENERATION?
FOR HIS LIFE IS REMOVED FROM THE EARTH."
34 And the eunuch answered Philip and said, "Please *tell me*, of
whom does the prophet say this? Of himself, or of someone else?"
35 And Philip [a]opened his mouth, and [b]beginning from this Scripture he [c]preached Jesus to him.
36 And as they went along the road they came to some water; and
the eunuch *said, "Look! Water! [a]What prevents me from being baptized?"
37 [[1]And Philip said, "If you believe with all your heart, you may."
And he answered and said, "I believe that Jesus Christ is the Son of
God."]
38 And he ordered the [1]chariot to stop; and they both went down
into the water, Philip as well as the eunuch; and he baptized him.
39 And when they came up out of the water, [a]the Spirit of the Lord
snatched Philip away; and the eunuch saw him no more, but went
on his way rejoicing.
40 But Philip [1]found himself at [2a]Azotus; and as he passed through
he [b]kept preaching the gospel to all the cities, until he came to
[c]Caesarea.

Chapter 9

9 [a]Now Saul, still [b]breathing [1]threats and murder against the disciples of the Lord, went to the high priest,
2 and asked for [a]letters from him to [b]the synagogues at [c]Damascus,
so that if he found any belonging to [d]the Way, both men and women,
he might bring them bound to Jerusalem.
3 And it came about that as he journeyed, he was approaching
Damascus, and [a]suddenly a light from heaven flashed around him;
4 and [a]he fell to the ground, and heard a voice saying to him,
"Saul, Saul, why are you persecuting Me?"
5 And he said, "Who art Thou, Lord?" And He *said*, "I am Jesus
whom you are persecuting,
6 but rise, and enter the city, and [a]it shall be told you what you
must do."

This city is [c]Gen. 10:19
31; 87:4; Is. Kin. 8:41f.; John 12:20
Or, carriage
riage [a]Acts 11:12; 13:2; 0:23; 21:11; 25; Heb. 3:7
32 [a]Is. 53:7
escribe [2]Or, gin [a]Is. 53:8
tt. 5:2 [b]Luke 17:2; 18:28; 3 [c]Acts 5:42
[a]Acts 10:47
mss. do not contain this v.
[1]Or, carriage
18:12; 2 Kin. zek. 3:12, 14; 1:1, 24; 43:5; 2 Cor. 12:2
Or, was found shdod [a]Josh. am. 5:1 [b]Acts cts 9:30; 10:1, 12:19; 18:22; 16; 23:23, 33; 25:1, 4, 6, 13
, threat [a]Acts 1-22; 22:3-16; -18 [b]Acts 8:3; 9:13-21
9:14, 21; 22:5; [b]Matt. 10:17 . 14:15; 2 Cor. al. 1:17 [d]John s 18:25f.; 19:9, 22:4; 24:14, 22
3 [a]1 Cor. 15:8
cts 22:7; 26:14
6 [a]Acts 9:16

7 And the men who traveled with him [a]stood speechless, [b]hearing
the [1]voice, but seeing no one.
8 And Saul got up from the ground, and [a]though his eyes were
open, he [1]could see nothing; and leading him by the hand, they
brought him into [b]Damascus.
9 And he was three days without sight, and neither ate nor drank.
10 Now there was a certain disciple at [a]Damascus, named [b]Ananias;
and the Lord said to him in [c]a vision, "Ananias." And he said, "Be-
hold, *here am* I, Lord."
11 And the Lord *said* to him, "Arise and go to the street called
Straight, and inquire at the house of Judas for a man from [a]Tarsus
named Saul, for behold, he is praying,
12 and he has seen [1]in a vision a man named Ananias come in and
[a]lay his hands on him, so that he might regain his sight."
13 But Ananias answered, "Lord, I have heard from many about
this man, [a]how much harm he did to [b]Thy [1]saints at Jerusalem;
14 and here he [a]has authority from the chief priests to bind all who
[b]call upon Thy name."
15 But the Lord said to him, "Go, for [a]he is a chosen [1]instrument of
Mine, to bear My name before [b]the Gentiles and [c]kings and the sons
of Israel;
16 for [a]I will show him how much he must suffer for My name's
sake."
17 And Ananias departed and entered the house, and after [a]laying
his hands on him said, "[b]Brother Saul, the Lord Jesus, who appeared
to you on the road by which you were coming, has sent me so that
you may regain your sight, and be [c]filled with the Holy Spirit."
18 And immediately there fell from his eyes something like scales,
and he regained his sight, and he arose and was baptized;
19 and he took food and was strengthened.
Now [a]for several days he was with [b]the disciples who were at
Damascus,
20 and immediately he *began* to proclaim Jesus [a]in the synagogues,
[1]saying, "He is [b]the Son of God."
21 And all those hearing him continued to be amazed, and were
saying, "Is this not he who in Jerusalem [a]destroyed those who [b]called
on this name, and *who* had come here for the purpose of bringing
them bound before the chief priests?"
22 But Saul kept increasing in strength and confounding the Jews
who lived at Damascus by proving that this *Jesus* is the [1]Christ.
23 And when [a]many days had elapsed, [b]the Jews plotted together to
do away with him,
24 but [a]their plot became known to Saul. And [b]they were also
watching the gates day and night so that they might put him to
death;
25 but his disciples took him by night, and let him down through
an opening in the wall, lowering him in a large basket.
26 And [a]when he had come to Jerusalem, he was trying to associate
with the disciples; and they were all afraid of him, not believing that
he was a disciple.
27 But [a]Barnabas took hold of him and brought him to the apostles
and described to them how he had [b]seen the Lord on the road, and
that He had talked to him, and how [c]at Damascus he had [d]spoken
out boldly in the name of Jesus.

7 [1]Or, *sou* 26:14 [b]Joh Acts 22:9

8 [1]Lit., *was* [a]Acts 9:18; 14:15; 2 Co 1:17

10 [a]Gen. 1 11:32; Gal. 22:12 [c]Acts 19; 11:5; 12 18:9

11 [a]Acts 9: 21:39; 22:3

12 [1]Some n contain *in a* [a]Mark 5:23; 9:17

13 [1]Or, *holy* 8:3 [b]Acts 9: 26:10; Rom. 26, 31; 16:2, 1:2

14 [a]Acts 9:2 7:59

15 [1]Or, *vess* 13:2; Rom. 1 Gal. 1:15; Ep [b]Acts 22:21; Rom. 1:5; 11 Gal. 1:16; 2:7 3:1, 8; 1 Tim. 4:17 [c]Acts 2 32; 2 Tim. 4:1

16 [a]Acts 20:2 11, 13; 2 Cor. 11:23-27; 1 T

17 [a]Mark 5:2 6:6; 9:12 [b]Ac [c]Acts 2:4

19 [a]Acts 26:2 9:26, 38; 11:2

20 [1]Lit., *that* 13:5, 14; 14:1; 17:2, 10; 18:4, [b]Matt. 4:3; Act 13:33

21 [a]Acts 8:3; 1:13, 23 [b]Acts

22 [1]I.e., Mess

23 [a]Gal. 1:17, [b]1 Thess. 2:16

24 [a]Acts 20:3, 23:12, 30; 25:3 11:32f.

26 [a]Acts 22:17 26:20

27 [a]Acts 4:36 9:3-6 [c]Acts 9:2 [d]Acts 4:13, 29;

28 And he was with them [1]moving about freely in Jerusalem,
[a]speaking out boldly in the name of the Lord.
29 And he was talking and arguing with the [a]Hellenistic *Jews;* but
they were attempting to put him to death.
30 But when [a]the brethren learned *of it,* they brought him down to
[b]Caesarea and [c]sent him away to [d]Tarsus.
31 So [a]the church throughout all Judea and Galilee and Samaria
[1]enjoyed peace, being built up; and, going on in the fear of the Lord
and in the comfort of the Holy Spirit, it continued to increase.
32 Now it came about that as Peter was traveling through all *those*
parts, he came down also to [a]the [1]saints who lived at [2b]Lydda.
33 And there he found a certain man named Aeneas, who had been
bedridden eight years, for he was paralyzed.
34 And Peter said to him, "Aeneas, Jesus Christ heals you; arise,
and make your bed." And immediately he arose.
35 And all who lived at [1a]Lydda and [b]Sharon saw him, and they
[c]turned to the Lord.
36 Now in [a]Joppa there was a certain disciple named Tabitha
(which translated *in Greek* is called [1]Dorcas); this woman was
abounding with deeds of kindness and charity, which she continual-
ly did.
37 And it came about [1]at that time that she fell sick and died; and
when they had washed her body, they laid it in an [a]upper room.
38 And since Lydda was near [a]Joppa, [b]the disciples, having heard
that Peter was there, sent two men to him, entreating him, "Do not
delay to come to us."
39 And Peter arose and went with them. And when he had come,
they brought him into the [a]upper room; and all the [b]widows stood
beside him weeping, and showing all the [1]tunics and garments that
Dorcas used to make while she was with them.
40 But Peter [a]sent them all out and [b]knelt down and prayed, and
turning to the body, he said, "[c]Tabitha, arise." And she opened her
eyes, and when she saw Peter, she sat up.
41 And he gave her his hand and raised her up; and calling [a]the
[1]saints and [b]widows, he presented her alive.
42 And it became known all over [a]Joppa, and [b]many believed in the
Lord.
43 And it came about that he stayed many days in [a]Joppa with [b]a
certain tanner, Simon.

Chapter 10

10 Now *there was* a certain man at [a]Caesarea named Cornelius, a
centurion of what was [b]called the Italian [1]cohort,
2 a devout man, and [a]one who feared God with all his household,
and [b]gave many [1]alms to the *Jewish* people, and prayed to God con-
tinually.
3 About [a]the [1]ninth hour of the day he clearly saw [b]in a vision [c]an
angel of God who had *just* come in to him, and said to him, "Cor-
nelius!"
4 And [a]fixing his gaze upon him and being much alarmed, he said,
"What is it, Lord?" And he said to him, "Your prayers and [1]alms
[b]have ascended [c]as a memorial before God.
5 "And now dispatch *some* men to [a]Joppa, and send for a man
named Simon, who is also called Peter;

6 he [1]is staying with a certain tanner *named* [a]Simon, whose house is
by the sea."
7 And when the angel who was speaking to him had departed, he
summoned two of his [1]servants and a devout soldier of those who
were in constant attendance upon him,
8 and after he had explained everything to them, he sent them to
[a]Joppa.
9 And on the next day, as they were on their way, and approaching
the city, [a]Peter went up on [b]the housetop about [c]the [1]sixth hour to
pray.
10 And he became hungry, and was desiring to eat; but while they
were making preparations, he [a]fell into a trance;
11 and he *beheld [a]the [1]sky opened up, and a certain [2]object like a
great sheet coming down, lowered by four corners to the ground,
12 and there were in it all *kinds of* four-footed animals and [1]crawling
creatures of the earth and birds of the [2]air.
13 And a voice came to him, "Arise, Peter, [1]kill and eat!"
14 But Peter said, "By no means, [a]Lord, for [b]I have never eaten
anything [1]unholy and unclean."
15 And again a voice *came* to him a second time, "[a]What God has
cleansed, no *longer* consider [1]unholy."
16 And this happened three times; and immediately the [1]object was
taken up into the [2]sky.
17 Now while Peter was greatly perplexed [1]in mind as to what [a]the
vision which he had seen might be, behold, [b]the men who had been
sent by Cornelius, having asked directions for Simon's house, ap-
peared at the gate;
18 and calling out, they were asking whether Simon, who was also
called Peter, was [1]staying there.
19 And while Peter was reflecting on [a]the vision, [b]the Spirit said to
him, "Behold, [1]three men are looking for you.
20 "But arise, go downstairs, and [a]accompany them [1]without misgiv-
ings; for I have sent them Myself."
21 And Peter went down to the men and said, "Behold, I am the
one you are looking for; what is the reason for which you have
come?"
22 And they said, "Cornelius, a centurion, a righteous and [a]God-
fearing man well spoken of by the entire nation of the Jews, [b]was
divinely directed by a [c]holy angel to send for you *to come* to his house
and hear [1d]a message from you."
23 And so he invited them in and gave them lodging.
And on the next day he arose and went away with them, and
[a]some of [b]the brethren from [c]Joppa accompanied him.
24 And on the following day he entered [a]Caesarea. Now Cornelius
was waiting for them, and had called together his relatives and close
friends.
25 And when it came about that Peter entered, Cornelius met him,
and fell at his feet and [1a]worshiped *him.*
26 But Peter raised him up, saying, "[a]Stand up; I too am *just* a
man."
27 And as he talked with him, he entered, and [1]found [a]many people
assembled.
28 And he said to them, "You yourselves know how [a]unlawful it is
for a man who is a Jew to associate with a foreigner or to visit him;

6 [1]Or, *is lo*
9:43
7 [1]Or, *hous*
8 [a]Acts 9:3
9 [1]I.e., noo
10:9-32; 11:
19:13; 32:29
Matt. 24:17
Acts 10:3
10 [a]Acts 11
11 [1]Or, *hea*
vessel [a]Joh
12 [1]Or poss
reptiles [2]Or,
13 [1]Or, *sacr*
14 [1]Or, *prof.*
common [a]M
John 4:11ff.;
22:8 [b]Lev. 1
Deut. 14:4-2
4:14; Dan. 1:
10:28
15 [1]Lit., *com*
[a]Matt. 15:11;
Rom. 14:14;
10:25ff.; 1 Ti
Titus 1:15
16 [1]Or, *vess*
heaven
17 [1]Lit., *hims*
10:3 [b]Acts 1
18 [1]Or, *lodgi*
19 [1]One earl
reads *two* [a]A
[b]Acts 8:29
20 [1]Lit., *doub*
nothing [a]Acts
22 [1]Lit., *word*
10:2 [b]Matt. 2:
8:38; Luke 9:2
14:10 [d]Acts 1
23 [a]Acts 10:4
[b]Acts 1:15 [c]A
24 [a]Acts 8:40
25 [1]Or, *prostr*
himself in reve
[a]Matt. 8:2
26 [a]Acts 14:15
19:10; 22:8f.
27 [1]Lit., *finds*
10:24
28 [a]John 4:9;
Acts 11:3

and *yet* [b]God has shown me that I should not call any man [1]unholy
or unclean.
29 "That is why I came without even raising any objection when I
was sent for. And so I ask for what reason you have sent for me."
30 And Cornelius said, "[a]Four days ago to this hour, I was praying
in my house during [b]the [1]ninth hour; and behold, [c]a man stood
before me in shining garments,
31 and he *said, 'Cornelius, your prayer has been heard and your
[1]alms have been remembered before God.
32 'Send therefore to [a]Joppa and invite Simon, who is also called
Peter, to come to you; he is [1]staying at the house of Simon *the* tanner
by the sea.'
33 "And so I sent to you immediately, and you have [1]been kind
enough to come. Now then, we are all here present before God to
hear all that you have been commanded by the Lord."
34 And [a]opening his mouth, Peter said:
"I most certainly understand *now* that [b]God is not one to show
partiality,
35 but [a]in every nation the man who [1b]fears Him and [2]does what is
right, is welcome to Him.
36 "[1]The word which He sent to the sons of Israel, [a]preaching [2b]peace
through Jesus Christ (He is [c]Lord of all)—
37 you yourselves know the thing which took place throughout all
Judea, starting from Galilee, after the baptism which John
proclaimed.
38 "[1]*You know of* [a]Jesus of Nazareth, how God [b]anointed Him with
the Holy Spirit and with power, [2c]and *how* He went about doing
good, and healing all who were oppressed by the devil; for [d]God
was with Him.
39 "And we are [a]witnesses of all the things He did both in the [1]land
of the Jews and in Jerusalem. And they also [b]put Him to death by
hanging Him on a [2]cross.
40 "[a]God raised Him up on the third day, and granted that He
should become visible,
41 [a]not to all the people, but to [b]witnesses who were chosen before-
hand by God, *that is,* to us, [c]who ate and drank with Him after He
arose from the dead.
42 "And He [a]ordered us to [1]preach to the people, and solemnly to
[b]testify that this is the One who has been [c]appointed by God as
[d]Judge of the living and the dead.
43 "Of Him [a]all the prophets bear witness that through [b]His name
everyone who believes in Him receives forgiveness of sins."
44 While Peter was still speaking these words, [a]the Holy Spirit fell
upon all those who were listening to the [1]message.
45 And [a]all the [1]circumcised believers who had come with Peter
were amazed, because the gift of the Holy Spirit had been [b]poured
out upon the Gentiles also.
46 For they were hearing them [a]speaking with tongues and exalting
God. Then Peter answered,
47 "[a]Surely no one can refuse the water for these to be baptized who
[b]have received the Holy Spirit just as we *did,* can he?"
48 And he [a]ordered them to be baptized [b]in the name of Jesus
Christ. Then they asked him to stay on for a few days.

profane; lit., [b]Acts 10:14f., 35; 15:9
.., 3 to 4 p.m. 9, 22f. [b]Acts [c]Acts 10:3-6, 30-32
eds of charity
odging [a]John 28; Acts 11:3
, done well in coming
tt. 5:2 [b]Deut. r. 19:7; Rom. 2:6; Eph. 6:9; 5; 1 Pet. 1:17
r, reverences [2]Lit., *works usness* [a]Acts 28 [b]Acts 10:2
ne mss. read, *nt the word to the gospel of e* [a]Acts 13:32 9; 2:14; Rom. h. 2:17 [c]Matt. cts 2:36; Rom. 10:12
possibly, *How inted Jesus of reth* [2]Lit., *who* cts 2:22 [b]Acts att. 4:23 [d]John 3:2
Or, countryside [a]Luke 24:48; :41 [b]Acts 5:30
40 [a]Acts 2:24
ohn 14:19, 22; ike 24:48; Acts ike 24:43; Acts 1:4 mg.
proclaim [a]Acts ke 16:28 [c]Luke [d]John 5:22, 27; :31; 2 Tim. 4:1; 1 Pet. 4:5
cts 3:18 [b]Luke Acts 2:38; 4:12
Lit., *word* [a]Acts 11:15; 15:8
, believers from ne circumcision; wish Christians cts 10:23 [b]Acts 2:33, 38
Mark 16:17; Acts 2:4; 19:6
Acts 8:36 [b]Acts 44f.; 11:17; 15:8
[a]1 Cor. 1:14-17 2:38; 8:16; 19:5

Chapter 11

11 Now the apostles and [a]the brethren who were throughout
Judea heard that the Gentiles also had received the word of
God.
2 And when Peter came up to Jerusalem, [1a]those who were circum-
cised took issue with him,
3 saying, "[a]You [1]went to uncircumcised men and ate with them."
4 But Peter began *speaking* and *proceeded* to explain to them [a]in
orderly sequence, saying,
5 "[a]I was in the city of Joppa praying; and in a trance I saw [b]a
vision, a certain [1]object coming down like a great sheet lowered by
four corners from [2]the sky; and it came right down to me,
6 and when I had fixed my gaze upon it and was observing it [1]I
saw the four-footed animals of the earth and the wild beasts and the
[2]crawling creatures and the birds of the [3]air.
7 "And I also heard a voice saying to me, 'Arise, Peter; [1]kill and
eat.'
8 "But I said, 'By no means, Lord, for nothing [1]unholy or unclean
has ever entered my mouth.'
9 "But a voice from heaven answered a second time, '[a]What God
has cleansed, no longer [1]consider unholy.'
10 "And this happened three times, and everything was drawn back
up into [1]the sky.
11 "And behold, at that moment three men appeared before the
house in which we were *staying*, having been sent to me from
[a]Caesarea.
12 "And [a]the Spirit told me to go with them [1b]without misgivings.
And [c]these six brethren also went with me, and we entered the
man's house.
13 "And he reported to us how he had seen the angel [1]standing in
his house, and saying, 'Send to Joppa, and have Simon, who is also
called Peter, brought here;
14 and he shall speak [a]words to you by which you will be saved,
you and [b]all your household.'
15 "And as I began to speak, [a]the Holy Spirit fell upon them, just [b]as
He did upon us at the beginning.
16 "And I remembered the word of the Lord, how He used to say,
'[a]John baptized with water, but you shall be baptized [1]with the Holy
Spirit.'
17 "If [a]God therefore gave to them the same gift as *He gave* to us also
after believing in the Lord Jesus Christ, [b]who was I that I could
[1]stand in God's way?"
18 And when they heard this, they [1]quieted down, and [a]glorified
God, saying, "Well then, God has granted to the Gentiles also the
[b]repentance *that leads* to life."
19 [a]So then those who were scattered because of the [1]persecution
that arose in connection with Stephen made their way [2]to [b]Phoenicia
and [c]Cyprus and [d]Antioch, speaking the word to no one except to
Jews alone.
20 But there were some of them, men of [a]Cyprus and [b]Cyrene, who
came to [c]Antioch and *began* speaking to the [1d]Greeks also, [2e]preaching
the Lord Jesus.
21 And [a]the hand of the Lord was with them, and [b]a large number
who believed turned to the Lord.

11:1 [a]Acts
2 [1]Lit., thos circumcision Jewish Chris 10:45
3 [1]Or, enter house of [a]M Acts 10:28;
4 [a]Luke 1:3
5 [1]Or, vesse heaven [a]Act 11:5-14 [b]Act
6 [1]Lit., and possibly, rep heaven
7 [1]Or, sacrifi
8 [1]Or, profan common
9 [1]Lit., make [a]Acts 10:15
10 [1]Or, heav
11 [a]Acts 8:40
12 [1]Or, witho any distinction 8:29 [b]Acts 15 3:22 [c]Acts 10
13 [1]Or, after stood in his h said
14 [a]Acts 10:2 4:53; Acts 10: 31-34; 18:8; 1
15 [a]Acts 10:4 2:4
16 [1]Or, in [a]Ac
17 [1]Or, prever [a]Acts 10:45, 47 5:39
18 [1]Lit., becam [a]Matt. 9:8 [b]2 C
19 [1]Or, tribulat as far as [a]Acts [b]Acts 15:3; 21:2 4:36 [d]Acts 6:5; 22, 27; 13:1; 14 15:22f., 30, 35; Gal. 2:11
20 [1]Some mss. Greek-speaking [2]Or, bringing the news of [a]Acts 4 [b]Matt. 27:32; Ac 6:9; 13:1 [c]Acts 11:19, 22, 27; 1 14:26; 15:22f., 3 18:22; Gal. 2:11 7:35 [e]Acts 5:42
21 [a]Luke 1:66 2:47

22 And the [1]news about them [2]reached the ears of the church at
Jerusalem, and they sent [a]Barnabas off [3]to [b]Antioch.
23 Then when he had come and [1]witnessed [a]the grace of God, he
rejoiced and *began* to encourage them all with [2]resolute heart to
remain *true* to the Lord;
24 for he was a good man, and [a]full of the Holy Spirit and of faith.
And [b]considerable [1]numbers were [2]brought to the Lord.
25 And he left for [a]Tarsus to look for Saul;
26 and when he had found him, he brought him to [a]Antioch. And it
came about that for an entire year they [1]met with the church, and
taught considerable [2]numbers; and [b]the disciples were first called
[c]Christians in [a]Antioch.
27 Now [1]at this time [a]some prophets came down from Jerusalem to
[b]Antioch.
28 And one of them named [a]Agabus stood up and *began* to indicate
[1]by the Spirit that there would certainly be a great famine [b]all over
the [2]world. And this took place in the *reign* of [c]Claudius.
29 And in the proportion that any of [a]the disciples had means, each
of them determined to send *a contribution* for the [1]relief of [b]the
brethren living in Judea.
30 [a]And this they did, sending it [1]in charge of [b]Barnabas and Saul to
the [c]elders.

Chapter 12

12 Now about that time [1]Herod the king laid hands on some
who belonged to the church, in order to mistreat them.
2 And he [a]had James the brother of John [b]put to death with a
sword.
3 And when he saw that it [a]pleased the Jews, he proceeded to
arrest Peter also. Now [1]it was during [b]the days of Unleavened Bread.
4 And when he had seized him, he put him in prison, delivering
him to four [1a]squads of soldiers to guard him, intending after [b]the
Passover to bring him out before the people.
5 So Peter was kept in the prison, but prayer for him was being
made fervently by the church to God.
6 And on the very night when Herod was about to bring him
forward, Peter was sleeping between two soldiers, [a]bound with two
chains; and guards in front of the door were watching over the
prison.
7 And behold, [a]an angel of the Lord suddenly [b]appeared, and a
light shone in the cell; and he struck Peter's side and roused him,
saying, "Get up quickly." And [c]his chains fell off his hands.
8 And the angel said to him, "Gird yourself and [1]put on your
sandals." And he did so. And he *said to him, "Wrap your cloak
around you and follow me."
9 And he went out and continued to follow, and he did not know
that what was being done by the angel was real, but thought he was
seeing [a]a vision.
10 And when they had passed the first and second guard, they
came to the iron gate that leads into the city, which [a]opened for them
by itself; and they went out and went along one street; and immedi-
ately the angel departed from him.
11 And when Peter [a]came to himself, he said, "Now I know for sure

...rd [2]Lit., was
...Lit., *as far as*
...36 [b]Acts 6:5;
20, 27; 13:1;
22; Gal. 2:11
...., *seen* [2]Lit.,
...*f heart* [a]Acts
14:26; 15:40;
20:24, 32
...t., *multitudes*
...*led* [a]Acts 2:4
...7; 5:14; 11:21
...25 [a]Acts 9:11
...*vere gathered*
...Lit., *multitude*
11:20, 22, 27
...2:2; Acts 1:15
...8; 1 Pet. 4:16
in these days
...49; Acts 2:17;
...or. 12:10, 28f.
11:20, 22, 26;
...6; 15:22f., 30,
...:22; Gal. 2:11
through [2]Lit.,
...*d earth* [a]Acts
[b]Matt. 24:14
[c]Acts 18:2
service [a]John
...cts 1:15; 6:1f.;
26, 38; 11:26;
...; 14:20, 22, 28
[b]Acts 11:1
...it., *through the*
...*of* [a]Acts 12:25
...6 [c]Acts 14:23;
...4, 6, 22f.; 16:4;
...; 21:18; 1 Tim.
..., 19; Titus 1:5;
...:14; 1 Pet. 5:1;
...hn 1; 3 John 1
...:1 [1]I.e., Herod
Agrippa I
...att. 4:21; 20:23
[b]Mark 10:39
..., *they were the*
...cts 24:27; 25:9
15; 23:15; Acts
20:6
...*uaternions*; one
...on is composed
soldiers [a]John
...3 [b]Ex. 12:1-27;
14:1; Acts 12:3
6 [a]Acts 21:33
...5:19 [b]Luke 2:9;
...4:4 [c]Acts 16:26
8 [1]Lit., *bind*
9 [a]Acts 9:10
...Acts 5:19; 16:26
11 [a]Luke 15:17

that [b]the Lord has sent forth His angel and rescued me from the
hand of Herod and from all [1]that the Jewish people were expecting."
12 And when he realized *this,* he went to the house of Mary, the
mother of [a]John who was also called Mark, where many were
gathered together and [b]were praying.
13 And when he knocked at the door of the gate, [a]a servant-girl
named Rhoda came to answer.
14 And when she recognized Peter's voice, [a]because of her joy she
did not open the gate, but ran in and announced that Peter was
standing in front of the gate.
15 And they said to her, "You are out of your mind!" But she kept
insisting that it was so. And they kept saying, "It is [a]his angel."
16 But Peter continued knocking; and when they had opened *the*
door, they saw him and were amazed.
17 But [a]motioning to them with his hand to be silent, he described
to them how the Lord had led him out of the prison. And he said,
"Report these things to [1b]James and [c]the brethren." And he departed
and went to another place.
18 Now when day came, there was no small disturbance among the
soldiers *as to* [1]what could have become of Peter.
19 And when Herod had searched for him and had not found him,
he examined the guards and ordered that they [a]be led away *to execu-*
tion. And he went down from Judea to [b]Caesarea and was spending
time there.
20 Now he was very angry with the people of [a]Tyre and Sidon; and
with one accord they came to him, and having won over Blastus the
king's chamberlain, they were asking for peace, because [b]their
country was fed by the king's country.
21 And on an appointed day Herod, having put on his royal ap-
parel, took his seat on the [1]rostrum and *began* delivering an address
to them.
22 And the people kept crying out, "The voice of a god and not of a
man!"
23 And immediately [a]an angel of the Lord struck him because he
did not give God the glory, and he was eaten by worms and [1]died.
24 But [a]the word of the Lord continued to grow and to be multi-
plied.
25 And [a]Barnabas and [a]Saul returned [1]from Jerusalem [b]when they
had fulfilled their [2]mission, taking along with *them* [c]John, who was
also called Mark.

Chapter 13

13 Now there were at [a]Antioch, in the [b]church that was *there,*
[c]prophets and [d]teachers: [e]Barnabas, and Simeon who was
called Niger, and Lucius of [f]Cyrene, and Manaen who had been
brought up with [g]Herod the tetrarch, and Saul.
2 And while they were ministering to the Lord and fasting, [a]the
Holy Spirit said, "Set apart for Me [b]Barnabas and Saul for [c]the work
to which I have called them."
3 Then, when they had fasted and [a]prayed and [b]laid their hands on
them, [c]they sent them away.
4 So, being [a]sent out by the Holy Spirit, they went down to
Seleucia and from there they sailed to [b]Cyprus.
5 And when they reached Salamis, they *began* to proclaim the

11 [1]Lit., *the ... of the peop... Jews* [b]Dan...
12 [a]Acts 12... 13; 15:37, 3... 2 Tim. 4:11; 1 Pet. 5:13
13 [a]John 18...
14 [a]Luke 24...
15 [a]Matt. 18...
17 [1]Or, *Jac...* 13:16; 19:33 [b]Mark 6:3; A... 21:18; 1 Cor. 1:19; 2:9, 12
18 [1]Lit., *wha... had become*
19 [a]Acts 16:... [b]Acts 8:40
20 [a]Matt. 11:... 5:11; Ezra 3:7... 27:17
21 [1]Or, *judgm...*
23 [1]Lit., *brea... last* [a]2 Sam. ... 2 Kin. 19:35; ...
24 [a]Acts 6:7; ...
25 [1]Some anc... read *to Jerusa... ministry* [a]Acts 13:1ff. [b]Acts 1... [c]Acts 12:12
13:1 [a]Acts 11:... 11:26 [c]Acts 11... 15:32; 19:6; 21... 11:4f.; 13:2, 8f... 32, 37 [d]Rom. ... 1 Cor. 12:28f.; ... 4:11; James 3:... 4:36 [f]Matt. 27:... 11:20 [g]Matt. 1...
2 [a]Acts 8:29; ... [b]Acts 4:36 [c]Ac...
3 [a]Acts 1:24 [b]... [c]Acts 13:4; 14:2...
4 [a]Acts 13:2f. ... 4:36

word of God in [a]the synagogues of the Jews; and they also had [b]John
as their helper.
6 And when they had gone through the whole island as far as
Paphos, they found a certain [a]magician, a Jewish [b]false prophet
whose name was Bar-Jesus,
7 who was with the [a]proconsul, Sergius Paulus, a man of intel-
ligence. This man summoned Barnabas and Saul and sought to hear
the word of God.
8 But Elymas the [a]magician (for thus his name is translated) was
opposing them, seeking to turn the [b]proconsul away from [c]the faith.
9 But Saul, who was also *known as* Paul, [1a]filled with the Holy
Spirit, fixed his gaze upon him,
10 and said, "You who are full of all deceit and fraud, you [a]son of
the devil, you enemy of all righteousness, will you not cease to make
crooked [b]the straight ways of the Lord?
11 "And now, behold, [a]the hand of the Lord is upon you, and you
will be blind and not see the sun for a time." And immediately a
mist and a darkness fell upon him, and he went about seeking those
who would lead him by the hand.
12 Then the [a]proconsul believed when he saw what had happened,
being amazed at [b]the teaching of the Lord.
13 Now Paul and his companions put out to sea from [a]Paphos and
came to [b]Perga in [c]Pamphylia; and [d]John left them and returned to
Jerusalem.
14 But going on from Perga, they arrived at [a]Pisidian [b]Antioch, and
on [c]the Sabbath day they went into [d]the synagogue and sat down.
15 And after [a]the reading of the Law and [b]the Prophets [c]the syna-
gogue officials sent to them, saying, "Brethren, if you have any word
of exhortation for the people, say it."
16 And Paul stood up, and [a]motioning with his hand, he said,
"Men of Israel, and [b]you who fear God, listen:
17 "The God of this people Israel [a]chose our fathers, and [1b]made the
people great during their stay in the land of Egypt, and with an
uplifted arm [c]He led them out from it.
18 "And for [a]a period of about forty years [b]He [1]put up with them in
the wilderness.
19 "And [a]when He had destroyed [b]seven nations in the land of
Canaan, He [c]distributed their land as an inheritance—*all of which took*
[d]about four hundred and fifty years.
20 "And after these things He [a]gave *them* judges until [b]Samuel the
prophet.
21 "And then they [a]asked for a king, and God gave them [b]Saul the
son of Kish, a man of the tribe of Benjamin, for forty years.
22 "And after He had [a]removed him, He raised up David to be their
king, concerning whom He also testified and said, '[b]I HAVE FOUND
DAVID the son of Jesse, A MAN AFTER MY HEART, who will do all My
[1]will.'
23 "[a]From the offspring of this man, [b]according to promise, God has
brought to Israel [c]a Savior, Jesus,
24 after [a]John had proclaimed before [1]His coming a [b]baptism of
repentance to all the people of Israel.
25 "And while John [a]was completing his course, [b]he kept saying,
'What do you suppose that I am? I am not *He*. But behold, one is
coming after me the sandals of whose feet I am not worthy to untie.'

s 9:20; 13:14 [b]Acts 12:12
9 [b]Matt. 7:15
:8, 12; 18:12; 19:38
9 [b]Acts 13:7, ; 19:38 [c]Acts 6:7
ving just been [a]Acts 2:4; 4:8
t. 13:38; John s. 14:9; 2 Pet. 2:15
x. 9:3; 1 Sam. Job 19:21; Ps. 4; Heb. 10:31
13:7, 8; 18:12; 38 [b]Acts 8:25; 35f.; 19:10, 20
cts 13:6 [b]Acts 25 [c]Acts 2:10; 4; 15:38; 27:5 [d]Acts 12:12
s 14:24 [b]Acts 21; 2 Tim. 3:11 :42, 44; 16:13; :4 [d]Acts 9:20; 13:5
s 15:21; 2 Cor. 4f. [b]Acts 13:27 [c]Mark 5:22
ts 12:17 [b]Acts 10:2; 13:26
r, *exalted* [a]Ex. 3:14, 16; Deut. cts 7:17ff. [b]Ex. 1:7 [c]Ex. 12:51
ne ancient mss. *bore them up in* *ns as a nurse in* *derness* [a]Num. cts 7:36 [b]Deut. 1:31
cts 7:45 [b]Deut. sh. 14:1; 19:51; 5 [d]Judg. 11:26; 1 Kin. 6:1
g. 2:16 [b]1 Sam. 3:20; Acts 3:24
21 [a]1 Sam. 8:5 n. 9:1f.; 10:1, 21
t., *wills* [a]1 Sam. 26, 28; 16:1, 13 Sam. 13:14; Ps. 89:20; Acts 7:46
[a]Matt. 1:1 [b]Acts 32f. [c]Luke 2:11; John 4:42
., *the face of His* *ing* [a]Mark 1:1-4; :22; 19:4 [b]Luke 3:3
cts 20:24 [b]Matt. ; Mark 1:7; Luke 6; John 1:20, 27

26 "Brethren, sons of Abraham's family, and those among you who fear God, to us the word of [a]this salvation is sent out.
27 "For those who live in Jerusalem, and their [a]rulers, [b]recognizing neither Him nor the [1]utterances of [c]the prophets which are [d]read every Sabbath, fulfilled *these* by condemning *Him*.
28 "And though they found no ground for *putting Him to* death, they [a]asked Pilate that He be [1]executed.
29 "And when they had [a]carried out all that was written concerning Him, [b]they took Him down from [c]the [1]cross and [d]laid Him in a tomb.
30 "But God [a]raised Him from the dead;
31 and for many days [a]He appeared to those who came up with Him from Galilee to Jerusalem, the very ones who are now [b]His witnesses to the people.
32 "And we [a]preach to you the good news of [b]the promise made to the fathers,
33 that God has fulfilled this *promise* [1]to our children in that He [a]raised up Jesus, as it is also written in the second Psalm, '[b]THOU ART MY SON; TODAY I HAVE BEGOTTEN THEE.'
34 "*And as for the fact* that He [a]raised Him up from the dead, no more to return to decay, He has spoken in this way: '[b]I WILL GIVE YOU THE HOLY *and* SURE *blessings* OF DAVID.'
35 "Therefore He also says in another *Psalm*, '[a]THOU WILT NOT [1]ALLOW THY [2]HOLY ONE TO [3]UNDERGO DECAY.'
36 "For [a]David, after he had [1]served [b]the purpose of God in his own generation, [c]fell asleep, and was laid among his fathers, and [2]underwent decay;
37 but He whom God [a]raised did not [1]undergo decay.
38 "Therefore let it be known to you, brethren, that [a]through [1]Him forgiveness of sins is proclaimed to you,
39 and through Him [a]everyone who believes is [1]freed[2] from all things, from which you could not be [1]freed through the Law of Moses.
40 "Take heed therefore, so that the thing spoken of [a]in the Prophets may not come upon *you*:
41 '[a]BEHOLD, YOU SCOFFERS, AND MARVEL, AND [1]PERISH;
FOR I AM ACCOMPLISHING A WORK IN YOUR DAYS,
A WORK WHICH YOU WILL NEVER BELIEVE, THOUGH SOMEONE SHOULD DESCRIBE IT TO YOU.' "
42 And as [1]Paul and Barnabas were going out, [2]the people kept begging that these [3]things might be spoken to them the next [a]Sabbath.
43 Now when *the meeting of* the synagogue had broken up, many of the Jews and of the [a]God-fearing [1b]proselytes followed Paul and Barnabas, who, speaking to them, were urging them to continue in [c]the grace of God.
44 And the next [a]Sabbath nearly the whole city assembled to hear the word of [1]God.
45 But when [a]the Jews saw the crowds, they were filled with jealousy, and *began* contradicting the things spoken by Paul, and were [1]blaspheming.
46 And Paul and Barnabas spoke out boldly and said, "It was necessary that the word of God should be spoken to you [a]first; since you repudiate it, and judge yourselves unworthy of eternal life, behold, [b]we are turning to the Gentiles.

26 [a]John 6:
4:12; 5:20; 1

27 [1]Lit., *voi*
23:13 [b]Acts
24:27 [d]Acts

28 [1]Lit., *des*
[a]Matt. 27:22,
15:13, 14; Lu
23:21-23; Jo
Acts 3:14

29 [1]Lit., *woo*
26:22 [b]Luke
[c]Acts 5:30 [d]
27:57-61; Ma
15:42-47; Lu
23:50-56; Jo

30 [a]Acts 2:2
34, 37

31 [a]Acts 1:3
24:48

32 [a]Acts 5:4
[b]Acts 13:23;
1:2; 4:13; 9:4

33 [1]Some m
us their child
2:24; 13:30, 3
2:7

34 [a]Acts 2:24
33, 37 [b]Is. 55

35 [1]Lit., *give*
Devout or *Pio*
see corruption
16:10; Acts 2:

36 [1]Or, *serve*
generation by
purpose of Go
saw corruptio
2:29 [b]Acts 13
20:27 [c]1 Kin.
8:1

37 [1]Lit., *see c*
[a]Acts 2:24; 13:

38 [1]Lit., *this C*
24:47; Acts 2:3

39 [1]Lit., *justifie*
Gr. text the ren
this v. is part o
[a]Acts 10:43; R
10:4

40 [a]Luke 24:4
6:45; Acts 7:42

41 [1]Lit., *disapp*
[a]Hab. 1:5

42 [1]Lit., *they w*
they [3]Lit., *word*
13:14

43 [1]I.e., Gentil
converts to Jud
[a]Acts 13:50; 16
17:4, 17; 18:7
23:15 [c]Acts 11:

44 [1]Some anci
read *the Lord* [a]
13:14

45 [1]Or, *reviling*
13:50; 14:2, 4, 5
1 Thess. 2:16

46 [a]Acts 3:26; 9
13:5, 14 [b]Acts 1
19:9; 22:21; 26:2

47 "For thus the Lord has commanded us,
'[a]I HAVE PLACED YOU AS A [b]LIGHT FOR THE GENTILES,
THAT YOU SHOULD [1]BRING SALVATION TO THE END OF THE EARTH.' "
48 And when the Gentiles heard this, they *began* rejoicing and
glorifying [a]the word of [1]the Lord; and as many as [b]had been ap-
pointed to eternal life believed.
49 And [a]the word of the Lord was being spread through the whole
region.
50 But [a]the Jews aroused the [1b]devout women [c]of prominence and
the leading men of the city, and instigated a persecution against Paul
and Barnabas, and drove them out of their [2]district.
51 But [a]they shook off the dust of their feet *in protest* against them
and went to [b]Iconium.
52 And the disciples were continually [a]filled with joy and with the
Holy Spirit.

Chapter 14

14 And it came about that in [a]Iconium [b]they entered the syna-
gogue of the Jews together, and spoke in such a manner [c]that
a great multitude believed, both of Jews and of [d]Greeks.
2 But [a]the Jews who [1b]disbelieved stirred up the [2]minds of the
Gentiles, and embittered them against [c]the brethren.
3 Therefore they spent a long time *there* [a]speaking boldly *with*

7 [1]Lit., *be for*
ion [a]Is. 42:6;
6 [b]Luke 2:32

ancient mss.
[a]Acts 13:12
. 8:28ff.; Eph.
1:4f., 11

[a]Acts 13:12

Or, *worshiping*
ndaries [a]Acts
14:2, 4, 5, 19;
2:14ff. [b]Acts
:14; 17:4, 17;
[c]Mark 15:43

t. 10:14; Mark
ke 9:5; 10:11;
6 [b]Acts 14:1,
:2; 2 Tim. 3:11

52 [a]Acts 2:4

[a]Acts 13:51;
1; 16:2; 2 Tim.
cts 13:5 [c]Acts
ohn 7:35; Acts
18:4

sobeyed [2]Lit.,
Acts 13:45, 50;
, 19; 1 Thess.
ff. [b]John 3:36
[c]Acts 1:15

4:29f.; 20:32;
Heb. 2:4

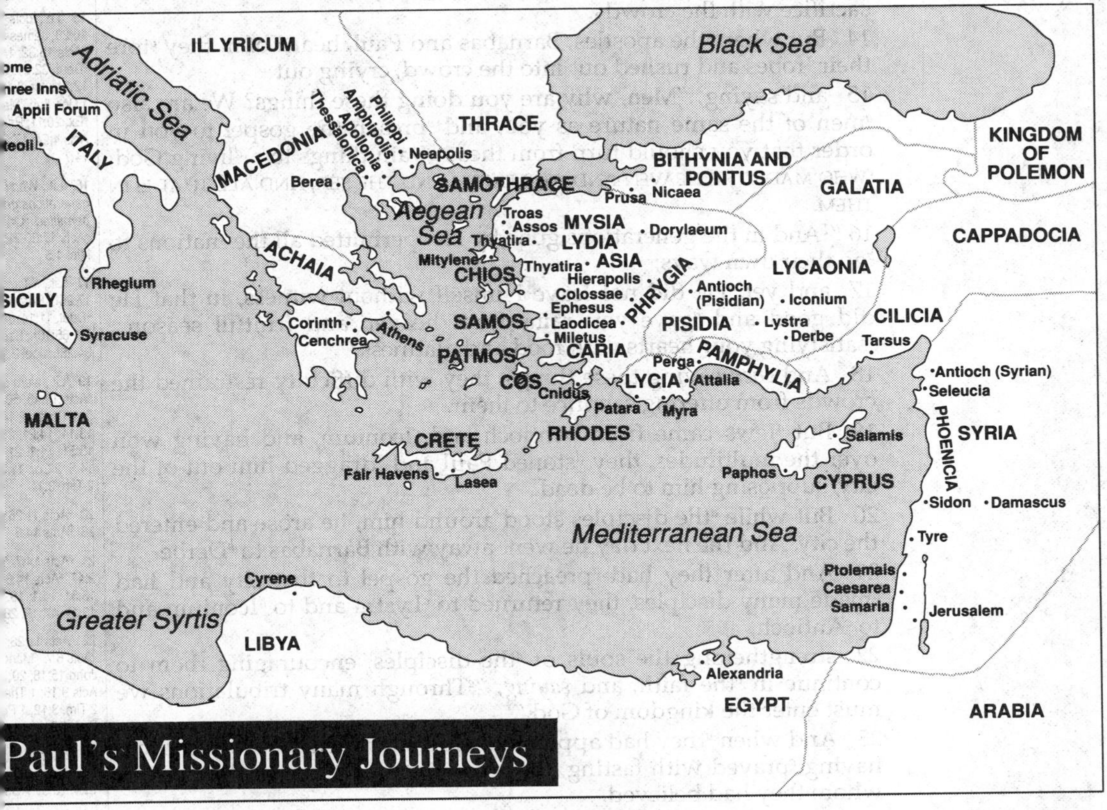

Paul's Missionary Journeys

reliance upon the Lord, who was bearing witness to the word of His
grace, granting that [1b]signs and wonders be done by their hands.
4 [a]But the multitude of the city was divided; and some [1]sided with
[b]the Jews, and some with [c]the apostles.
5 And when an attempt was made by both the Gentiles and [a]the
Jews with their rulers, to mistreat and to [b]stone them,
6 they became aware of it and fled to the cities of [a]Lycaonia,
[b]Lystra and [c]Derbe, and the surrounding region;
7 and there they continued to [a]preach the gospel.
8 And at [a]Lystra there was sitting [b]a certain man, without strength
in his feet, lame from his mother's womb, who had never walked.
9 This man was listening to Paul as he spoke, who, [a]when he had
fixed his gaze upon him, and had seen that he had [b]faith to be [1]made
well,
10 said with a loud voice, "Stand upright on your feet." [a]And he
leaped up and *began* to walk.
11 And when the multitudes saw what Paul had done, they raised
their voice, saying in the [a]Lycaonian language, "[b]The gods have be-
come like men and have come down to us."
12 And they *began* calling Barnabas, [1]Zeus, and Paul, [2]Hermes, be-
cause he was [3]the chief speaker.
13 And the priest of Zeus, whose *temple* was [1]just outside the city,
brought oxen and garlands to the gates, and [a]wanted to offer
sacrifice with the crowds.
14 But when [a]the apostles, Barnabas and Paul, heard of it, they [b]tore
their [1]robes and rushed out into the crowd, crying out
15 and saying, "Men, why are you doing these things? We are also
[a]men of the same nature as you, and [b]preach the gospel to you in
order that you should turn from these [1c]vain things to a [d]living God,
[e]WHO MADE THE HEAVEN AND THE EARTH AND THE SEA, AND ALL THAT IS IN
THEM.
16 "[1]And in the generations gone by He [a]permitted all the [2]nations to
[b]go their own ways;
17 and yet [a]He did not leave Himself without witness, in that He
did good and [b]gave you rains from heaven and fruitful seasons,
[1]satisfying your hearts with food and gladness."
18 And *even* saying these things, they with difficulty restrained the
crowds from offering sacrifice to them.
19 But [a]Jews came from [b]Antioch and [c]Iconium, and having won
over the multitudes, they [d]stoned Paul and [1]dragged him out of the
city, supposing him to be dead.
20 But while [a]the disciples stood around him, he arose and entered
the city. And the next day he went away with Barnabas to [b]Derbe.
21 And after they had [a]preached the gospel to that city and had
[b]made many disciples, they returned to [c]Lystra and to [d]Iconium and
to [e]Antioch,
22 strengthening the souls of [a]the disciples, encouraging them to
continue in [b]the faith, and *saying*, "[c]Through many tribulations we
must enter the kingdom of God."
23 And when [a]they had appointed [b]elders for them in every church,
having [c]prayed with fasting, they [d]commended them to the Lord in
whom they had believed.
24 And they passed through [a]Pisidia and came into [b]Pamphylia.

3 [1]Or, *attest* *miracles* [b]Jo
4 [1]Lit., *were* 17:4f.; 19:9; 2 [b]Acts 13:45, 5 19; 1 Thess. [c]Acts 14:14
5 [a]Acts 13:45 4, 19; 1 Thes [b]Acts 14:19
6 [a]Acts 14:11 14:8, 21; 16: 3:11 [c]Acts 14 20:4
7 [a]Acts 14:15
8 [a]Acts 14:6, 2 Tim. 3:11 [b]
9 [1]Lit., *saved* 10:4 [b]Matt. 9
10 [a]Acts 3:8
11 [a]Acts 14:6 8:10; 28:6
12 [1]Lat., *Jupi* *Mercurius* [3]Li *leader of the s*
13 [1]Lit., *in fro* [a]Dan. 2:46
14 [1]Or, *outer* [a]Acts 14:4 [b]N Matt. 26:65; M
15 [1]I.e., idols 10:26; James [b]Acts 13:32; 14 [c]Deut. 32:21; 1 12:21; Jer. 8:19 1 Cor. 8:4 [d]Ma [e]Ex. 20:11; Ps. Acts 4:24; 17:2 14:7
16 [1]Lit., *Who i* *generations go* *permitted* [2]Or, [a]Acts 17:30 [b]P Mic. 4:5
17 [1]Lit., *filling* 17:26f.; Rom. 1 [b]Deut. 11:14; Jo Ps. 65:10f.; Eze 34:26f.; Joel 2:2
19 [1]Lit., *were* [a]Acts 13:45, 50 5; 1 Thess. 2:14 13:14; 14:21, 26 13:51; 14:1, 21 14:5; 2 Cor. 11:2 2 Tim. 3:11
20 [a]Acts 11:26; 28 [b]Acts 14:6
21 [a]Acts 14:7 [b] 2:47 [c]Acts 14:6 13:51; 14:1, 19 13:14; 14:19, 26
22 [a]Acts 11:26; [b]Acts 6:7 [c]Mark John 15:18, 20; Acts 9:16; 1 The 2 Tim. 3:12; 1 Pe Rev. 1:9
23 [a]2 Cor. 8:19; 1:5 [b]Acts 11:30 1:24; 13:3 [d]Acts
24 [a]Acts 13:14 13:13

25 And when they had spoken the word in [a]Perga, they went down
to Attalia;
26 and from there they sailed to [a]Antioch, from [b]which they had
been [c]commended to the grace of God for the work that they had
[1]accomplished.
27 And when they had arrived and gathered the church together,
they *began* to [a]report all things that God had done with them and
[1]how He had opened a [b]door of faith to the Gentiles.
28 And they spent [1]a long time with [a]the disciples.

Chapter 15

15 And [a]some men came down from Judea and *began* teaching
[b]the brethren, "Unless you are [c]circumcised according to [d]the
custom of Moses, you cannot be saved."
2 And when Paul and Barnabas had [1]great dissension and [a]debate
with them, [2b]*the brethren* determined that Paul and Barnabas and
certain others of them should go up to Jerusalem to the [c]apostles and
elders concerning this issue.
3 Therefore, being [a]sent on their way by the church, they were
passing through both [b]Phoenicia and Samaria, [c]describing in detail
the conversion of the Gentiles, and were bringing great joy to all [d]the
brethren.
4 And when they arrived at Jerusalem, they were received by the
church and [a]the apostles and the elders, and they [b]reported all that
God had done with them.
5 But certain ones of [a]the sect of the [b]Pharisees who had believed,
stood up, saying, "It is necessary to [c]circumcise them, and to direct
them to observe the Law of Moses."
6 And [a]the apostles and the elders came together to [1]look into this
[2]matter.
7 And after there had been much [a]debate, Peter stood up and said
to them, "Brethren, you know that [1]in the early days [b]God made a
choice among you, that by my mouth the Gentiles should hear the
word of [c]the gospel and believe.
8 "And God, [a]who knows the heart, bore witness to them, [b]giving
them the Holy Spirit, just as He also did to us;
9 and [a]He made no distinction between us and them, [b]cleansing
their hearts by faith.
10 "Now therefore why do you [a]put God to the test by placing upon
the neck of the disciples a yoke which [b]neither our fathers nor we
have been able to bear?
11 "But we believe that we are saved through [a]the grace of the Lord
Jesus, in the same way as they also are."
12 And all the multitude kept silent, and they were listening to
Barnabas and Paul as they were [a]relating what [b]signs and wonders
God had done through them among the Gentiles.
13 And after they had stopped speaking, [1a]James answered, saying,
"Brethren, listen to me.
14 "[a]Simeon has related how God first concerned Himself about
taking from among the Gentiles a people for His name.
15 "And with this the words of [a]the Prophets agree, just as it is
written,
16 '[a]AFTER THESE THINGS [b]I will return,
AND I WILL REBUILD THE [1]TABERNACLE OF DAVID WHICH HAS FALLEN,

[a]Acts 13:13
ulfilled [a]Acts s 13:3 [c]Acts 11:23; 15:40
t., *that* [a]Acts 4, 12; 21:19 . 16:9; 2 Cor. 4:3; Rev. 3:8
it., *not a little* 11:26; 14:22
15:24 [b]Acts 22, 32 [c]Lev. s 15:5; 1 Cor. Gal. 2:11, 14; f. [d]Acts 6:14
a little [2]Or, *it rmined* [a]Acts ial. 2:2 [c]Acts 5:4, 6, 22, 23; 16:4
s 20:38; 21:5; ; 1 Cor. 16:6, or. 1:16; Titus John 6 [b]Acts s 14:27; 15:4, :15; 15:22, 32
:30; 15:6, 22, [b]Acts 14:27; 15:12
5:17; 24:5, 14; 22 [b]Matt. 3:7; [c]1 Cor. 7:18; 2:11, 14; 5:2f.
ee about [2]Lit., ts 11:30; 15:4, 22, 23; 16:4
om days of old cts 15:2 [b]Acts f. [c]Acts 20:24
:24 [b]Acts 2:4; 10:44, 47
Acts 10:28, 34; 2 [b]Acts 10:43
Acts 5:9 [b]Matt. 23:4; Gal. 5:1
om. 3:24; 5:15; :14; Eph. 2:5-8
14:27; 15:3, 4 [b]John 4:48
Or, *Jacob* [a]Acts 12:17
15:7; 2 Pet. 1:1
15 [a]Acts 13:40
Or, *tent* [a]Amos :11 [b]Jer. 12:15

AND I WILL REBUILD ITS RUINS,
AND I WILL RESTORE IT,
17 [a]IN ORDER THAT THE REST OF [1]MANKIND MAY SEEK THE LORD,
AND ALL THE GENTILES [2b]WHO ARE CALLED BY MY NAME,'
18 [a]SAYS THE LORD, WHO [1b]MAKES THESE THINGS KNOWN FROM OF OLD.
19 "Therefore it is [a]my judgment that we do not trouble those who
are turning to God from among the Gentiles,
20 but that we write to them that they abstain from [1a]things con-
taminated by idols and from [b]fornication and from [c]what is strangled
and from blood.
21 "For [a]Moses from ancient generations has in every city those who
preach him, since he is read in the synagogues every Sabbath."
22 Then it seemed good to [a]the apostles and the elders, with the
whole church, to choose men from among them to send to [b]Antioch
with Paul and Barnabas—Judas called Barsabbas, and [c]Silas, leading
men among [d]the brethren,
23 and they [1]sent this letter by them,

"[a]The apostles and the brethren who are elders, to [b]the brethren
in [c]Antioch and [d]Syria and [e]Cilicia who are from the Gentiles,
[f]greetings.

24 "Since we have heard that [a]some [1]of our number to whom we
gave no instruction have [b]disturbed you with *their* words, un-
settling your souls,
25 [a]it seemed good to us, having [1]become of one mind, to select
men to send to you with our beloved Barnabas and Paul,
26 men who have [1a]risked their lives for the name of our Lord
Jesus Christ.
27 "Therefore we have sent [a]Judas and [b]Silas, who themselves will
also report the same things by word *of mouth*.
28 "For [a]it seemed good to [b]the Holy Spirit and to [c]us to lay upon
you no greater burden than these essentials:
29 that you abstain from [a]things sacrificed to idols and from
[a]blood and from [a]things strangled and from [a]fornication; [1]if
you keep yourselves free from such things, you will do well.
Farewell."

30 So, when they were sent away, [a]they went down to Antioch; and
having gathered the [1]congregation together, they delivered the letter.
31 And when they had read it, they rejoiced because of its [1]en-
couragement.
32 And [a]Judas and [b]Silas, also being [c]prophets themselves, [1]encour-
aged and strengthened [d]the brethren with a lengthy message.
33 And after they had spent time *there*, they were sent away from
the brethren [a]in peace to those who had [b]sent them out.
34 [[1]But it seemed good to Silas to remain there.]
35 But [a]Paul and Barnabas stayed in Antioch, teaching and [b]preach-
ing, with many others also, [c]the word of the Lord.
36 And after some days Paul said to Barnabas, "Let us return and
visit the brethren in [a]every city in which we proclaimed [b]the word of
the Lord, *and see* how they are."
37 And Barnabas was desirous of taking [a]John, called Mark, along
with them also.
38 But Paul kept insisting that they should not take him along who
had [a]deserted them [1]in Pamphylia and had not gone with them to
the work.

17 [1]Lit., *me upon whom called* [a]Amo [b]Deut. 28:10 Jer. 14:9; Da James 2:7

18 [1]Or, *doe things which known* [a]Am 45:21

19 [a]Acts 15

20 [1]Lit., *the of* [a]Ex. 34:1 1:8; Acts 15: 8:7, 13; 10:7 Rev. 2:14, 20 18:6-23 [c]Ge 3:17; 7:26; 1 19:26; Deut. 15:23; 1 Sam

21 [a]Acts 13: 3:14f.

22 [a]Acts 15: 11:20 [c]Acts 40; 16:19, 25 10, 14f.; 18:5 1:19; 1 Thess 2 Thess. 1:1; 5:12 [d]Acts 15

23 [1]Lit., *wro hand* [a]Acts 1 15:1 [c]Acts 11 4:24; Acts 15 1:21 [e]Acts 6: 23:26; James 2 John 10f.

24 [1]Lit., *from* 15:1 [b]Gal. 1:

25 [1]Or, *met t* [a]Acts 15:28

26 [1]Lit., *giver* [a]Acts 9:23ff.; 1

27 [a]Acts 15:2 [b]Acts 15:22

28 [a]Acts 15:2 5:32; 15:8 [c]Ac 15:19, 25

29 [1]Lit., *from keeping yours free* [a]Acts 15:

30 [1]Or, *multit* 15:22f.

31 [1]Or, *exhort*

32 [1]Or, *exhort* 15:22, 27 [b]Ac [c]Acts 13:1 [d]Ac

33 [a]Mark 5:34 16:36; 1 Cor. 1 Heb. 11:31 [b]A

34 [1]Many mss contain this v.

35 [a]Acts 12:25 8:4 [c]Acts 13:12

36 [a]Acts 13:4, 51; 14:6, 24f. [b] 13:12

37 [a]Acts 12:12

38 [1]Lit., *from* 13:13

39 And there arose such a sharp disagreement that they separated
from one another, and Barnabas took [a]Mark with him and sailed
away to [b]Cyprus.
40 But Paul chose [a]Silas and departed, being [b]committed by the
brethren to the grace of the Lord.
41 And he was traveling through [a]Syria and [b]Cilicia, strengthening
the churches.

Chapter 16

16 And he came also to [a]Derbe and to [a]Lystra. And behold, a
certain disciple was there, named [b]Timothy, the son of a
[c]Jewish woman who was a believer, but his father was a Greek,
2 and he was well spoken of by [a]the brethren who were in [b]Lystra
and [c]Iconium.
3 Paul wanted this man to [1]go with him; and he [a]took him and
circumcised him because of the Jews who were in those parts, for
they all knew that his father was a Greek.
4 Now while they were passing through the cities, they were
delivering [a]the decrees, which had been decided upon by [b]the
apostles and [c]elders who were in Jerusalem, for them to observe.
5 So [a]the churches were being strengthened [1]in the faith, and were
[b]increasing in number daily.
6 And they passed through the [1a]Phrygian and [b]Galatian region,
having been forbidden by the Holy Spirit to speak the word in
[2c]Asia;
7 and when they had come to [a]Mysia, they were trying to go into
[b]Bithynia, and the [c]Spirit of Jesus did not permit them;
8 and passing [1]by [a]Mysia, they came down to [b]Troas.
9 And [a]a vision appeared to Paul in the night: [1]a certain man of
[b]Macedonia was standing and appealing to him, and saying, "Come
over to Macedonia and help us."
10 And when he had seen [a]the vision, immediately [b]we sought to
[1]go into Macedonia, concluding that God had called us to [c]preach
the gospel to them.
11 [1]Therefore putting out to sea from [a]Troas, we ran [b]a straight
course to Samothrace, and on the day following to Neapolis;
12 and from there to [a]Philippi, which is a leading city of the district
of [b]Macedonia, [c]a *Roman* colony; and we were staying in this city for
some days.
13 And on [a]the Sabbath day we went outside the gate to a riverside,
where we were supposing that there would be a place of prayer; and
we sat down and began speaking to the women who had assembled.
14 And a certain woman named Lydia, from the city of [a]Thyatira, a
seller of purple fabrics, [b]a worshiper of God, was listening; [1]and the
Lord [c]opened her heart to respond to the things spoken by Paul.
15 And when she and [a]her household had been baptized, she urged
us, saying, "If you have judged me to be faithful to the Lord, come
into my house and stay." And she prevailed upon us.
16 And it happened that as we were going to [a]the place of prayer, a
certain slave-girl having [b]a spirit of divination met us, who was
bringing her masters much profit by fortunetelling.
17 Following after Paul and us, she kept crying out, saying, "These
men are bond-servants of [a]the Most High God, who are proclaiming
to you [1]the way of salvation."

Sum-BIBAZO
Together - to cause to
come

Voices speak out of
person

cts 12:12; 15:37;
. 4:10 [b]Acts 4:36
Acts 15:22 [b]Acts
11:23; 14:26
[a]Matt. 4:24; Acts
15:23 [b]Acts 6:9
[a]Acts 14:6 [b]Acts
14f.; 18:5; 19:22;
om. 16:21; 1 Cor.
16:10; 2 Cor. 1:1,
hil. 1:1; 2:19; Col.
hess. 1:1; 3:2, 6;
s. 1:1; 1 Tim. 1:2,
6:20; 2 Tim. 1:2;
m. 1; Heb. 13:23
[c]2 Tim. 1:5; 3:15
Acts 16:40 [b]Acts
14:6 [c]Acts 13:51
go out [a]Gal. 2:3
cts 15:28f. [b]Acts
15:2 [c]Acts 11:30
Or, *in faith* [a]Acts
9:31 [b]Acts 2:47
Phrygia and the
tian region [2]I.e.,
coast province of
Minor [a]Acts 2:10;
:23 [b]Acts 18:23;
r. 16:1; Gal. 1:2;
Tim. 4:10; 1 Pet.
1:1 [c]Acts 2:9
cts 16:8 [b]1 Pet.
Luke 24:49; Acts
om. 8:9; Gal. 4:6;
1:19; 1 Pet. 1:11
r, *through* [a]Acts
cts 16:11; 20:5f.;
2:12; 2 Tim. 4:13
Or, *A man* [a]Acts
[b]Acts 16:10, 12;
9:21f., 29; 20:1,
7:2; Rom. 15:26
it., *go out* [a]Acts
9:10 [b][we] Acts
:10-17; 20:5-15;
-18; 27:1-28:16
[c]Acts 14:7
me ancient mss.
And [a]Acts 16:8;
:5f.; 2 Cor. 2:12;
4:13 [b]Acts 21:1
s 20:6; Phil. 1:1;
2:2 [b]Acts 16:9,
8:5; 19:21f., 29;
1, 3; 27:2; Rom.
:26 [c]Acts 16:21
13 [a]Acts 13:14
it., *whose heart*
d opened [a]Rev.
; 2:18, 24 [b]Acts
3:7 [c]Luke 24:45
15 [a]Acts 11:14
cts 16:13 [b]Lev.
20:6, 27; Deut.
1 Sam. 28:3, 7;
Kin. 21:6; 1 Chr.
10:13; Is. 8:19
t., *a way* [a]Mark
5:7

18 And she continued doing this for many days. But Paul was
greatly annoyed, and turned and said to the spirit, "I command you
[a]in the name of Jesus Christ to come out of her!" And it came out at
that very [1]moment.
19 But when her masters saw that their hope of [a]profit was [1]gone,
they seized [b]Paul and Silas and [c]dragged them into the market place
before the authorities,
20 and when they had brought them to the chief magistrates, they
said, "These men are throwing our city into confusion, being Jews,
21 and [a]are proclaiming customs which it is not lawful for us to
accept or to observe, being [b]Romans."
22 And the crowd rose up together against them, and the chief
magistrates tore their [1]robes off them, and proceeded to order [2]*them*
to be [a]beaten with rods.
23 And when they had inflicted many blows upon them, they
threw them into prison, commanding [a]the jailer to guard them
securely;
24 [1]and he, having received such a command, threw them into the
inner prison, and fastened their feet in [a]the stocks.
25 But about midnight [a]Paul and Silas were praying and [b]singing
hymns of praise to God, and the prisoners were listening to them;
26 and suddenly [a]there came a great earthquake, so that the founda-
tions of the prison house were shaken; and immediately [b]all the
doors were opened, and everyone's [c]chains were unfastened.
27 And when [a]the jailer had been roused out of sleep and had seen
the prison doors opened, he drew his sword and was about [b]to kill
himself, supposing that the prisoners had escaped.
28 But Paul cried out with a loud voice, saying, "Do yourself no
harm, for we are all here!"
29 And he called for lights and rushed in and, trembling with fear,
he fell down before [a]Paul and Silas,
30 and after he brought them out, he said, "Sirs, [a]what must I do to
be saved?"
31 And they said, "[a]Believe in the Lord Jesus, and you shall be
saved, you and [b]your household."
32 And they spoke the word of [1]the Lord to him together with all
who were in his house.
33 And he took them [a]that *very* hour of the night and washed their
wounds, and immediately he was baptized, he and all his *household*.
34 And he brought them into his house and set [1]food before them,
and rejoiced [2]greatly, having believed in God with [a]his whole house-
hold.
35 Now when day came, the chief magistrates sent their policemen,
saying, "Release those men."
36 And [a]the jailer reported these words to Paul, *saying*, "The chief
magistrates have sent to release you. Now therefore, come out and
go [b]in peace."
37 But Paul said to them, "They have beaten us in public without
trial, [a]men who are Romans, and have thrown us into prison; and
now are they sending us away secretly? No indeed! But let them
come themselves and bring us out."
38 And the policemen reported these words to the chief
magistrates. And [a]they were afraid when they heard that they were
Romans,

18 [1]Lit., *hour* [a]M
16:17
19 [1]Lit., *gone ou*
16:16; 19:25f. [b]A
15:22, 40; 16:25,
[c]Acts 8:3; 17:6f.;
James 2:6
21 [a]Esth. 3:8 [b]A
16:12
22 [1]Or, *outer ga*
[2]Lit., *to beat with*
[a]2 Cor. 11:25; 1 T
2:2
23 [a]Acts 16:27,
24 [1]Lit., *who, ha*
received [a]Job 1
33:11; Jer. 20:2f.
25 [a]Acts 16:19
5:19
26 [a]Acts 4:31 [b]
12:10 [c]Acts 12:7
27 [a]Acts 16:23,
[b]Acts 12:19
29 [a]Acts 16:19
30 [a]Acts 2:37; 2
31 [a]Mark 16:16
11:14; 16:15
32 [1]Some ancie
read *God*
33 [a]Acts 16:25
34 [1]Lit., *a table*
greatly with his
household, havi
believed in God
11:14; 16:15
36 [a]Acts 16:27
15:33
37 [a]Acts 22:25-
38 [a]Acts 22:29

39 and they came and appealed to them, and when they had
brought them out, they kept begging them [a]to leave the city.
40 And they went out of the prison and entered *the house of* [a]Lydia,
and when they saw [b]the brethren, they [1]encouraged them and de-
parted.

Chapter 17

17 Now when they had traveled through Amphipolis and Apol-
lonia, they came to [a]Thessalonica, where there was a syna-
gogue of the Jews.
2 And [a]according to Paul's custom, he went to them, and for three
[b]Sabbaths reasoned with them from [c]the Scriptures,
3 [1]explaining and [2]giving evidence that the [3]Christ [a]had to suffer
and [b]rise again from the dead, and *saying,* "[c]This Jesus whom I am
proclaiming to you is the [3]Christ."
4 [a]And some of them were persuaded and joined [b]Paul and Silas,
[1]along with a great multitude of the [c]God-fearing [d]Greeks and [2]a
number of the [e]leading women.
5 But [a]the Jews, becoming jealous and taking along some wicked
men from the market place, formed a mob and set the city in an
uproar; and coming upon the house of [b]Jason, they were seeking to
bring them out to the people.
6 And when they did not find them, they *began* [a]dragging Jason
and some brethren before the city authorities, shouting, "These men
who have upset [1b]the world have come here also;
7 [1]and Jason [a]has welcomed them, and they all act [b]contrary to the
decrees of Caesar, saying that there is another king, Jesus."
8 And they stirred up the crowd and the city authorities who
heard these things.
9 And when they had received a [1]pledge from [a]Jason and the
others, they released them.
10 And [a]the brethren immediately sent [b]Paul and Silas away by
night to [c]Berea; [1]and when they arrived, they went into [d]the syna-
gogue of the Jews.
11 Now these were more noble-minded than those in [a]Thessalonica,
[1]for they received the word with [2]great eagerness, examining the
Scriptures daily, *to see* whether these things were so.
12 [a]Many of them therefore believed, [1]along with a number of
[b]prominent Greek [c]women and men.
13 But when the Jews of [a]Thessalonica found out that the word of
God had been proclaimed by Paul in [b]Berea also, they came there
likewise, agitating and stirring up the crowds.
14 And then immediately [a]the brethren sent Paul out to go as far as
the sea; and [b]Silas and [c]Timothy remained there.
15 Now [a]those who conducted Paul brought him as far as [b]Athens;
and receiving a command for [c]Silas and Timothy to [d]come to him as
soon as possible, they departed.
16 Now while Paul was waiting for them at [a]Athens, his spirit was
being provoked within him as he was beholding the city full of idols.
17 So he was reasoning [a]in the synagogue with the Jews and [b]the
God-fearing *Gentiles,* and in the market place every day with those
who happened to be present.
18 And also some of the Epicurean and Stoic philosophers were
[1]conversing with him. And some were saying, "What would [a]this

[2]idle babbler wish to say?" Others, "He seems to be a proclaimer of
strange [3]deities,"—because he was preaching [b]Jesus and the resur-
rection.
19 And they [a]took him and brought him [1]to the [2b]Areopagus,
saying, "May we know what [c]this new teaching is [3]which you are
proclaiming?
20 "For you are bringing some strange things to our ears; we want to
know therefore what these things mean."
21 (Now all the Athenians and the strangers [a]visiting there used to
spend their time in nothing other than telling or hearing something
new.)
22 And Paul stood in the midst of the [1]Areopagus and said, "Men
of [a]Athens, I observe that you are very [b]religious in all respects.
23 "For while I was passing through and examining the [a]objects of
your worship, I also found an altar with this inscription, 'TO AN
UNKNOWN GOD.' What therefore [b]you worship in ignorance, this I
proclaim to you.
24 "[a]The God who made the world and all things in it, since He is
[b]Lord of heaven and earth, does not [c]dwell in temples made with
hands;
25 neither is He served by human hands, [a]as though He needed
anything, since He Himself gives to all life and breath and all things;
26 and [a]He made from [1]one, every nation of mankind to live on all
the face of the earth, having [b]determined *their* appointed times, and
the boundaries of their habitation,
27 that they should seek God, if perhaps they might grope for Him
and find Him, [a]though He is not far from each one of us;
28 for [a]in Him we live and move and [1]exist, as even some of your
own poets have said, 'For we also are His offspring.'
29 "Being then the offspring of God, we [a]ought not to think that the
Divine Nature is like gold or silver or stone, an image formed by the
art and thought of man.
30 "Therefore having [a]overlooked [b]the times of ignorance, God is
[c]now declaring to men that all everywhere should repent,
31 because He has fixed [a]a day in which [b]He will judge [1c]the world
in righteousness through a Man whom He has [d]appointed, having
furnished proof to all men [2]by [e]raising Him from the dead."
32 Now when they heard of [a]the resurrection of the dead, some
began to sneer, but others said, "We shall hear you [1]again concerning
this."
33 So Paul went out of their midst.
34 But some men joined him and believed, among whom also were
Dionysius the [a]Areopagite and a woman named Damaris and others
with them.

Chapter 18

18 After these things he left [a]Athens and went to [b]Corinth.
2 And he found a certain Jew named [a]Aquila, a native of
[b]Pontus, having recently come from [c]Italy with his wife [a]Priscilla,
because [d]Claudius had commanded all the Jews to leave Rome. He
came to them,
3 and because he was of the same trade, he stayed with them and
[a]they were working; for by trade they were tent-makers.

18 [2]I.e., or makes his l picking up s *demons* [b]A 17:31f.

19 [1]Or, *bef of Ares,* goc *which is bei by you* [a]Ac [b]Acts 17:22

21 [a]Acts 2:

22 [1]Or poss Council of th Areopagus [b]Acts 25:19

23 [a]2 Thess 4:22

24 [a]Is. 42:5; [b]Deut. 10:14 115:16; Matt [c]1 Kin. 8:27;

25 [a]Job 22:2 50:10-12

26 [1]Some la read *one blo* 2:10 [b]Deut. 12:23

27 [a]Deut. 4:7 23:23f.; Acts

28 [1]Lit., *are* 12:10; Dan. 5

29 [a]Is. 40:18 1:23

30 [a]Acts 14:1 3:25 [b]Acts 17 24:47; Acts 26 2:11f.

31 [1]Lit., *the ir earth* [2]Or, *wh raised* [a]Matt. [b]Ps. 9:8; 96:13 John 5:22, 27; 10:42 [c]Matt. 2 17:6 [d]Luke 22 2:24

32 [1]Lit., *also a* [a]Acts 17:18, 31

34 [a]Acts 17:19

18:1 [a]Acts 17: 18:8; 19:1; 1 C 2 Cor. 1:1, 23; 2 Tim. 4:20

2 [a]Acts 18:18, 16:3; 1 Cor. 16 2 Tim. 4:19 [b]A [c]Acts 27:1, 6; H 13:24 [d]Acts 11

3 [a]Acts 20:34; 4:12; 9:14f.; 2 C 12:13; 1 Thess. 4:11; 2 Thess. 3

4 And he was reasoning [a]in the synagogue every [b]Sabbath and
trying to persuade [c]Jews and Greeks.
5 But when [a]Silas and Timothy [b]came down from [c]Macedonia, Paul
began devoting himself completely to the word, solemnly [d]testifying
to the Jews that [e]Jesus was the [1]Christ.
6 And when they resisted and blasphemed, he [a]shook out his gar-
ments and said to them, "Your [b]blood *be* upon your own heads! I am
clean. From now on I shall go [c]to the Gentiles."
7 And he departed from there and went to the house of a certain
man named [1]Titius Justus, [a]a worshiper of God, whose house was
next to the synagogue.
8 And [a]Crispus, [b]the leader of the synagogue, believed in the Lord
[c]with all his household, and many of the [d]Corinthians when they
heard were believing and being baptized.
9 And the Lord said to Paul in the night by [a]a vision, "Do not be
afraid *any longer*, but go on speaking and do not be silent;
10 for I am with you, and no man will attack you in order to harm
you, for I have many people in this city."
11 And he settled *there* a year and six months, teaching the word of
God among them.
12 But while Gallio was [a]proconsul of [b]Achaia, [c]the Jews with one
accord rose up against Paul and brought him before [d]the judgment
seat,
13 saying, "This man persuades men to worship God contrary to
[a]the law."
14 But when Paul was about to [a]open his mouth, Gallio said to the
Jews, "If it were a matter of wrong or of vicious crime, O Jews, it
would be reasonable for me to put up with you;
15 but if there are [a]questions about words and names and your own
law, look after it yourselves; I am unwilling to be a judge of these
matters."
16 And he drove them away from [a]the judgment seat.
17 And they all took hold of [a]Sosthenes, [b]the leader of the syna-
gogue, and *began* beating him in front of [c]the judgment seat. And
Gallio was not concerned about any of these things.
18 And Paul, having remained many days longer, [a]took leave of
[b]the brethren and put out to sea for [c]Syria, and with him were
[d]Priscilla and [d]Aquila. In [e]Cenchrea [1]he [f]had his hair cut, for he was
keeping a vow.
19 And they came to [a]Ephesus, and he left them there. Now he
himself entered [b]the synagogue and reasoned with the Jews.
20 And when they asked him to stay for a longer time, he did not
consent,
21 but [a]taking leave of them and saying, "I will return to you again
[b]if God wills," he set sail from [c]Ephesus.
22 And when he had landed at [a]Caesarea, he went up and greeted
the church, and went down to [b]Antioch.
23 And having spent some time *there*, he departed and passed suc-
cessively through the [a]Galatian region and Phrygia, strengthening all
the disciples.
24 Now a certain Jew named [a]Apollos, an [b]Alexandrian by birth,
[1]an eloquent man, came to [c]Ephesus; and he was mighty in the Scrip-
tures.
25 This man had been instructed in [a]the way of the Lord; and being

fervent in spirit, he was speaking and teaching accurately the things
concerning Jesus, being acquainted only with [b]the baptism of John;
26 and he began to speak out boldly in the synagogue. But when
[a]Priscilla and Aquila heard him, they took him aside and explained
to him [b]the way of God more accurately.
27 And when he wanted to go across to [a]Achaia, [b]the brethren encouraged him and wrote to [c]the disciples to welcome him; and when
he had arrived, he [1]helped greatly those who had believed through
grace;
28 for he powerfully refuted the Jews in public, demonstrating [a]by
the Scriptures that [b]Jesus was the [1]Christ.

Chapter 19

19 And it came about that while [a]Apollos was at [b]Corinth, Paul
having passed through the [c]upper country came to [d]Ephesus,
and found some disciples,
2 and he said to them, "[a]Did you receive the Holy Spirit when you
believed?" And they *said* to him, "No, [b]we have not even heard
whether [1]there is a Holy Spirit."
3 And he said, "Into what then were you baptized?" And they
said, "[a]Into John's baptism."
4 And Paul said, "[a]John baptized with the baptism of repentance,
telling the people [b]to believe in Him who was coming after him, that
is, in Jesus."
5 And when they heard this, they were [a]baptized [1]in the name of
the Lord Jesus.
6 And when Paul had [a]laid his hands upon them, the Holy Spirit
came on them, and they *began* [b]speaking with tongues and
[c]prophesying.
7 And there were in all about twelve men.
8 And he entered [a]the synagogue and continued speaking out
boldly for three months, reasoning and [1]persuading *them* [b]about the
kingdom of God.
9 But when [a]some were becoming hardened and disobedient,
speaking evil of [b]the Way before the multitude, he withdrew from
them and took away [c]the disciples, reasoning daily in the school of
Tyrannus.
10 And this took place for [a]two years, so that all who lived in [1b]Asia
heard [c]the word of the Lord, both Jews and Greeks.
11 And God was performing [a]extraordinary [1]miracles by the hands
of Paul,
12 [a]so that handkerchiefs or aprons were even carried from his
body to the sick, and the diseases left them and [b]the evil spirits went
out.
13 But also some of the Jewish [a]exorcists, who went from place to
place, attempted to name over those who had the evil spirits the
name of the Lord Jesus, saying, "I adjure you by Jesus whom Paul
preaches."
14 And seven sons of one Sceva, a Jewish chief priest, were doing
this.
15 And the evil spirit answered and said to them, "I recognize
Jesus, and I know about Paul, but who are you?"
16 And the man, in whom was the evil spirit, leaped on them and

25 [b]Luke 7
26 [a]Acts 1 18:25
27 [1]Or, *he* *through gra* *who had be* 18:12; 19:1 18:18 [c]Act
28 [1]I.e., Me 8:35 [b]Acts
19:1 [a]Acts 1:12; 3:5, 6, 16:12; Titus 18:1 [c]Acts 18:21, 24; 1 34f.; 20:16f. 1 Cor. 15:32 1:1; 1 Tim. 1 1:18; 4:12;
2 [1]Or, *the H* *has been gi* 8:15f.; 11:16 7:39
3 [a]Luke 7:2
4 [a]Matt. 3:11 7, 8; Luke 3: 1:26, 27; Act [b]John 1:7
5 [1]Lit., *into* 16; 10:48
6 [a]Acts 6:6; 16:17; Acts 2 [c]Acts 13:1
8 [1]Some anc read *persuad* *the things ab* 9:20; 18:26
9 [a]Acts 14:4 19:23 [c]Acts
10 [1]I.e., west province of As [a]Acts 19:8; 20 16:6; 19:22, 2 [c]Acts 13:12; 1
11 [1]Or, *works* [a]Acts 8:13
12 [a]Acts 5:15 16:17
13 [a]Matt. 12:2 11:19

subdued all of them and overpowered them, so that they fled out of
that house naked and wounded.
17 And this became known to all, both Jews and Greeks, who lived
in [a]Ephesus; and fear fell upon them all and the name of the Lord
Jesus was being magnified.
18 Many also of those who had believed kept coming, confessing
and disclosing their practices.
19 And many of those who practiced magic brought their books
together and *began* burning them in the sight of all; and they counted
up the price of them and found it [1]fifty thousand [a]pieces of silver.
20 So [1a]the word of the Lord [b]was growing mightily and prevailing.
21 Now after these things were finished, Paul purposed in the
[1]spirit to [a]go to Jerusalem [b]after he had passed through [c]Macedonia
and [d]Achaia, saying, "After I have been there, [e]I must also see
Rome."
22 And having sent into [a]Macedonia two of [b]those who ministered
to him, [c]Timothy and [d]Erastus, he himself stayed in [1e]Asia for a
while.
23 And about that time there arose no small disturbance concerning
[a]the Way.
24 For a certain man named Demetrius, a silversmith, who made
silver shrines of [1]Artemis, [a]was bringing no little [2]business to the
craftsmen;
25 these he gathered together with the workmen of similar *trades,*
and said, "Men, you know that our prosperity [1]depends upon this
business.
26 "And you see and hear that not only in [a]Ephesus, but in almost all
of [1b]Asia, this Paul has persuaded and turned away a considerable
number of people, saying that [2c]gods made with hands are no gods
at all.
27 "And not only is there danger that this trade of ours fall into
disrepute, but also that the temple of the great goddess [1]Artemis be
regarded as worthless and that she whom all of [2a]Asia and [b]the
[3]world worship should even be dethroned from her magnificence."
28 And when they heard *this* and were filled with rage, they *began*
crying out, saying, "Great is [1]Artemis of the [a]Ephesians!"
29 And the city was filled with the confusion, and they rushed with
one accord into the theater, [1]dragging along [a]Gaius and [b]Aristarchus,
Paul's traveling [c]companions from [d]Macedonia.
30 And when Paul wanted to go into the [1]assembly, [a]the disciples
would not let him.
31 And also some of the [1]Asiarchs who were friends of his sent to
him and repeatedly urged him not to [2]venture into the theater.
32 [a]So then, some were shouting one thing and some another, for
the [1]assembly was in confusion, and the majority did not know [2]for
what cause they had come together.
33 And some of the crowd [1]concluded *it was* Alexander, since the
Jews had put him forward; and having [a]motioned with his hand,
Alexander was intending to make a defense to the [2]assembly.
34 But when they recognized that he was a Jew, a *single* outcry
arose from them all as they shouted for about two hours, "Great is
[1]Artemis of the Ephesians!"
35 And after quieting the multitude, the town clerk *said, "Men of
[a]Ephesus, what man is there after all who does not know that the

Acts 18:19
obably, fifty and Greek A drachma ted a day's [a]Luke 15:8
rding to the he Lord the as growing [b]Acts 6:7; 12:24
Spirit [a]Acts 1:15; Rom. 1:16 [b]Acts 16:5 [c]Acts 2, 29; Rom. Thess. 1:7f. 8:12 [e]Acts 1. 15:24, 28
west coast Asia Minor 9; 19:21, 29 13:5; 19:29; 8:19 [c]Acts Rom. 16:23; [e]Acts 19:10
[a]Acts 19:9
Diana [2]Or, 16:16, 19f.
[1]Lit., *is from*
note 1 [2]Lit., [a]Acts 18:19 [c]Deut. 4:28; s. 44:10-20; Acts 17:29; 10:19; Rev. 9:20
iana [2]V. 22, e 1 [3]Lit., *the earth* [a]Acts [b]Matt. 24:14
Diana [a]Acts 18:19
[1]Lit., *having* d [a]Acts 20:4 4; 27:2; Col. m. 24 [c]Acts 19:22; 20:34; [d]Acts 16:9; 19:22
people [a]Acts 19:9
e., political or fficials of the of Asia [2]Lit., *give himself*
ekklesia [2]Or, hose account [a]Acts 21:34
Or, *instructed* [2]Lit., *people* [a]Acts 12:17
[1]Lat., *Diana*
[a]Acts 18:19

city of the Ephesians is guardian of the temple of the great [1]Artemis,
and of the *image* which fell down from [2]heaven?
36 "Since then these are undeniable facts, you ought to keep calm
and to do nothing rash.
37 "For you have brought these men *here* who are neither [a]robbers of
temples nor blasphemers of our goddess.
38 "So then, if Demetrius and the craftsmen who are with him have a
complaint against any man, the courts are in session and [1a]procon-
suls are *available*; let them bring charges against one another.
39 "But if you want anything beyond this, it shall be settled in the
[1]lawful [2]assembly.
40 "For indeed we are in danger of being accused of a riot in connec-
tion with today's affair, since there is no *real* cause *for it*; and in this
connection we shall be unable to account for this disorderly gather-
ing."
41 And after saying this he dismissed the [1]assembly.

Chapter 20

20 And after the uproar had ceased, Paul sent for [a]the disciples
and when he had exhorted them and taken his leave of them,
he departed [b]to go to [c]Macedonia.
2 And when he had gone through those districts and had given
them much exhortation, he came to Greece.
3 And *there* he spent three months, and when [a]a plot was formed
against him by the Jews as he was about to set sail for [b]Syria, he
determined to return through [c]Macedonia.
4 And [1]he was accompanied by Sopater of [a]Berea, *the son* of Pyr-
rhus; and by [b]Aristarchus and Secundus of the [c]Thessalonians; and
[b]Gaius of [d]Derbe, and [e]Timothy; and [f]Tychicus and [g]Trophimus of
[2h]Asia.
5 But these had gone on ahead and were waiting for [a]us at [b]Troas.
6 And [a]we sailed from [b]Philippi after [c]the days of Unleavened
Bread, and came to them at [d]Troas within five days; and there we
stayed seven days.
7 And on [a]the first day of the week, when [b]we were gathered
together to [c]break bread, Paul *began* talking to them, intending to
depart the next day, and he prolonged his [1]message until midnight.
8 And there were many [a]lamps in the [b]upper room where we were
gathered together.
9 And there was a certain young man named Eutychus sitting [1]on
the window sill, sinking into a deep sleep; and as Paul kept on
talking, he was overcome by sleep and fell down from the third
floor, and was picked up dead.
10 But Paul went down and [a]fell upon him and after embracing
him, he [b]said, "[1]Do not be troubled, for his life is in him."
11 And when he had gone *back* up, and had [a]broken the bread and
[1]eaten, he talked with them a long while, until daybreak, and so
departed.
12 And they took away the boy alive, and were [1]greatly comforted.
13 But [a]we, going ahead to the ship, set sail for Assos, intending
from there to take Paul on board; for thus he had arranged it, intend-
ing himself to go [1]by land.
14 And when he met us at Assos, we took him on board and came
to Mitylene.

35 [1]Lat., *D*
Zeus; or, *J*

37 [a]Rom. 2

38 [1]Or, *pro*
governors

39 [1]Or, *reg*
ekklesia

41 [1]Gr., *ek*

20:1 [a]Acts
19:21 [c]Acts

3 [a]Acts 9:2
[b]Matt. 4:24
20:1

4 [1]Lit., *there*
accompanie
west coast p
Asia Minor
[b]Acts 19:29
[d]Acts 14:6 [e]
[f]Eph. 6:21; C
2 Tim. 4:12;
[g]Acts 21:29;
4:20 [h]Acts
20:16, 18

5 [a]Acts 16:1
[b]Acts 16:8

6 [a]Acts 16:1
[b]Acts 16:12
[d]Acts 16:8

7 [1]Lit., *word,*
[a]1 Cor. 16:2;
[b]Acts 16:10;
[c]Acts 2:42; 20

8 [a]Matt. 25:1

9 [1]Or, *at the*

10 [1]Or, *Stop*
troubled [a]1 K
2 Kin. 4:34 [b]M
9:23f.; Mark 5

11 [1]Lit., *taste*
2:42; 20:7

12 [1]Lit., *not m*

13 [1]Or, *on foo*
16:10; 20:5-15

15 And sailing from there, we arrived the following day opposite
Chios; and the next day we crossed over to Samos; and [1]the day
following we came to [a]Miletus.
16 For Paul had decided to sail past [a]Ephesus in order that he might
not have to spend time in [1b]Asia; for he was hurrying [c]to be in Jerusa-
lem, if possible, [d]on the day of Pentecost.
17 And from Miletus he sent to [a]Ephesus and called to him [b]the
elders of the church.
18 And when they had come to him, he said to them,
"You yourselves know, [a]from the first day that I set foot in [1]Asia,
how I was with you the whole time,
19 serving the Lord with all humility and with tears and with trials
which came upon me through [a]the plots of the Jews;
20 how I [a]did not shrink from declaring to you anything that was
profitable, and teaching you publicly and [1]from house to house,
21 solemnly [a]testifying to both Jews and Greeks of [b]repentance
toward God and [c]faith in our Lord Jesus Christ.
22 "And now, behold, bound in [1]spirit, [a]I am on my way to Jerusa-
lem, not knowing what will happen to me there,
23 except that [a]the Holy Spirit solemnly [b]testifies to me in every city,
saying that [c]bonds and afflictions await me.
24 "But [a]I do not consider my life of any account as dear to myself, in
order that I may [b]finish my course, and [c]the ministry which I
received from the Lord Jesus, to [d]testify solemnly of the gospel of
[e]the grace of God.
25 "And now, behold, I know that all of you, among whom I went
about [a]preaching the kingdom, will see my face no more.
26 "Therefore I [1]testify to you this day, that [a]I am [2]innocent of the
blood of all men.
27 "For I [a]did not shrink from declaring to you the whole [b]purpose of
God.
28 "Be on guard for yourselves and for all [a]the flock, among which
the Holy Spirit has made you [1]overseers, to shepherd [b]the church of
[2]God which [c]He [3]purchased with His own blood.
29 "I know that after my departure [a]savage wolves will come in
among you, not sparing [b]the flock;
30 and from among your own selves men will arise, speaking per-
verse things, to draw away [a]the disciples after them.
31 "Therefore be on the alert, remembering that night and day for a
period of [a]three years I did not cease to admonish each one [b]with
tears.
32 "And now I [a]commend you to [1]God and to [b]the word of His grace,
which is able to [c]build *you* up and to give *you* [d]the inheritance among
all those who are sanctified.
33 "[a]I have coveted no one's silver or gold or clothes.
34 "You yourselves know that [a]these hands ministered to my *own*
needs and to the [b]men who were with me.
35 "In everything I showed you that by working hard in this manner
you must help the weak and remember the words of the Lord Jesus,
that He Himself said, 'It is more blessed to give than to receive.'"
36 And when he had said these things, he [a]knelt down and prayed
with them all.
37 And [1]they *began* to weep aloud and [2a]embraced Paul, and
repeatedly kissed him,

ater mss. add *'ter staying at 'lium, the day* [a]Acts 20:17; 2 Tim. 4:20
e., west coast of Asia Minor 9 [b]Acts 16:6; [c]Acts 19:21; 2; 1 Cor. 16:8 [d]Acts 2:1
s 18:19 [b]Acts 11:30
note 1 [a]Acts , 10; 20:4, 16
19 [a]Acts 20:3
in the various homes [a]Acts 20:27
ke 16:28; Acts):23, 24 [b]Acts 3; 26:20 [c]Acts 18; Eph. 1:15; 2:5; Philem. 5
ne Spirit [a]Acts 17:16; 20:16
cts 8:29 [b]Luke ts 18:5; 20:21, cts 9:16; 21:33
s 21:13 [b]Acts Tim. 4:7 [c]Acts ke 16:28; Acts 4 [e]Acts 11:23; 20:32
Matt. 4:23; Acts 28:31
[1]Or, *call you to* [2]Lit., *pure from* [a]Acts 18:6
ts 20:20 [b]Acts 13:36
ishops [2]Some mss. read *the* [3]Lit., *acquired* ke 12:32; John 17; Acts 20:29; et. 5:2f. [b]Matt. 8; Rom. 16:16;):32 [c]Eph. 1:7, tus 2:14; 1 Pet. 9; 2:9; Rev. 5:9
ek. 22:27; Matt. ke 12:32; John 17; Acts 20:28; 1 Pet. 5:2f.
30 [a]Acts 11:26
[a]Acts 19:8, 10; 17 [b]Acts 20:19
ne ancient mss. *the Lord* [a]Acts :23 [b]Acts 14:3; Acts 9:31 [d]Acts Eph. 1:14; 5:5; 1:12; 3:24; Heb. 9:15; 1 Pet. 1:4
[a]1 Cor. 9:4-18; 2 Cor. 11:7-12; 3; 1 Thess. 2:5f.
Acts 18:3 [b]Acts 19:22
[a]Acts 9:40; 21:5; Luke 22:41
, a considerable g of all occurred ll on Paul's neck [a]Luke 15:20

38 [1]grieving especially over [a]the word which he had spoken, that they should see his face no more. And they were [b]accompanying him to the ship.

Chapter 21

21 And when it came about that [a]we had parted from them and had set sail, we ran [b]a straight course to Cos and the next day to Rhodes and from there to Patara;

2 and having found a ship crossing over to [a]Phoenicia, we went aboard and set sail.

3 And when we had come in sight of [a]Cyprus, leaving it on the left, we kept sailing to [b]Syria and landed at [c]Tyre; for [d]there the ship was to unload its cargo.

4 And after looking up [a]the disciples, we stayed there seven days; and they kept telling Paul [1b]through the Spirit not to set foot in Jerusalem.

5 And when it came about that [1]our days there were ended, we departed and started on our journey, while they all, with wives and children, [a]escorted us until *we were* out of the city. And after [b]kneeling down on the beach and praying, we said farewell to one another.

6 Then we went on board the ship, and they returned [a]home again.

7 And when we had finished the voyage from [a]Tyre, we arrived at Ptolemais; and after greeting [b]the brethren, we stayed with them for a day.

8 And on the next day we departed and came to [a]Caesarea; and entering the house of [b]Philip the [c]evangelist, who was [b]one of the seven, we stayed with him.

9 Now this man had four virgin daughters who were [a]prophetesses.

10 And as we were staying there for some days, a certain prophet named [a]Agabus came down from Judea.

11 And coming to us, he [a]took Paul's belt and bound his own feet and hands, and said, "This [b]is what the Holy Spirit says: 'In this way the Jews at Jerusalem will [c]bind the man who owns this belt and [d]deliver him into the hands of the Gentiles.' "

12 And when we had heard this, we as well as the local residents *began* begging him [a]not to go up to Jerusalem.

13 Then Paul answered, "What are you doing, weeping and breaking my heart? For [a]I am ready not only to be bound, but even to die at Jerusalem for [b]the name of the Lord Jesus."

14 And since he would not be persuaded, we fell silent, remarking, "[a]The will of the Lord be done!"

15 And after these days we got ready and [a]started on our way up to Jerusalem.

16 And *some* of [a]the disciples from [b]Caesarea also came with us, taking us to Mnason of [c]Cyprus, a [d]disciple of long standing with whom we were to lodge.

17 And when we had come to Jerusalem, [a]the brethren received us gladly.

18 And now the following day Paul went in with us to [1a]James, and all [b]the elders were present.

19 And after he had greeted them, he [a]*began* to relate one by one the things which God had done among the Gentiles through his [b]ministry.

38 [1]Lit., *suf*
[a]Acts 20:25

21:1 [a][we] A
21:1-18 [b]Ac

2 [a]Acts 11:1

3 [a]Acts 4:36
[b]Matt. 4:24 [c]
21:7 [d]Acts 2

4 [1]I.e., beca
impressions
the Spirit [a]Ac
21:16 [b]Acts 2

5 [1]Lit., *we ha*
completed th
[a]Acts 15:3 [b]L
Acts 9:40; 20

6 [a]John 19:2

7 [a]Acts 12:20
[b]Acts 1:15; 21

8 [a]Acts 8:40;
[b]Acts 6:5; 8:5
4:11; 2 Tim. 4:

9 [a]Luke 2:36;
1 Cor. 11:5

10 [a]Acts 11:28

11 [a]1 Kin. 22:1
20:2; Jer. 13:1-
11; John 18 [b]A
[c]Acts 9:16; 21:
20:19

12 [a]Acts 21:15

13 [a]Acts 20:24
5:41; 9:16

14 [a]Luke 22:42

15 [a]Acts 21:12

16 [a]Acts 21:4
8:40 [c]Acts 4:36
[d]Acts 15:7

17 [a]Acts 1:15; 2

18 [1]Or, *Jacob* [a]
12:17 [b]Acts 11:

19 [a]Acts 14:27
1:17

20 And when they heard it they *began* [a]glorifying God; and they
said to him, "You see, brother, how many [1]thousands there are
among the Jews of those who have believed, and they are all
[b]zealous for the Law;
21 and they have been told about you, that you are [a]teaching all the
Jews who are among the Gentiles to forsake Moses, telling them [b]not
to circumcise their children nor to walk according to [c]the customs.
22 "What, then, is *to be done*? They will certainly hear that you have
come.
23 "Therefore do this that we tell you. We have four men who [1a]are
under a vow;
24 take them and [a]purify yourself along with them, and [1]pay their
expenses in order that they may [b]shave their [2]heads; and all will
know that there is nothing to the things which they have been told
about you, but that you yourself also walk orderly, keeping the Law.
25 "But concerning the Gentiles who have believed, we wrote, [a]hav-
ing decided that they should abstain from [1]meat sacrificed to idols
and from blood and from what is strangled and from fornication."
26 Then Paul [1]took the men, and the next day, [a]purifying himself
along with them, [b]went into the temple, giving notice of the comple-
tion of the days of purification, until the sacrifice was offered for
each one of them.
27 And when [a]the seven days were almost over, [b]the Jews from
[1c]Asia, upon seeing him in the temple, *began* to stir up all the multi-
tude and laid hands on him,
28 crying out, "Men of Israel, come to our aid! [a]This is the man who
preaches to all men everywhere against our people, and the Law,
and this place; and besides he has even brought Greeks into the
temple and has [b]defiled this holy place."
29 For they had previously seen [a]Trophimus the [b]Ephesian in the
city with him, and they supposed that Paul had brought him into the
temple.
30 And all the city was aroused, and [1]the people rushed together;
and taking hold of Paul, they [a]dragged him out of the temple; and
immediately the doors were shut.
31 And while they were seeking to kill him, a report came up to the
[1]commander of the [a]*Roman* [2]cohort that all Jerusalem was in con-
fusion.
32 And at once he [a]took along *some* soldiers and centurions, and ran
down to them; and when they saw the [1]commander and the soldiers,
they stopped beating Paul.
33 Then the [1]commander came up and took hold of him, and or-
dered him to be [a]bound with [b]two chains; and he *began* asking who
he was and what he had done.
34 But among the crowd [a]some were shouting one thing *and* some
another, and when he could not find out the [1]facts on account of the
uproar, he ordered him to be brought into [b]the barracks.
35 And when he got to [a]the stairs, it so happened that he was car-
ried by the soldiers because of the violence of the [1]mob;
36 for the multitude of the people kept following behind, crying
out, "[a]Away with him!"
37 And as Paul was about to be brought into [a]the barracks, he said
to the [1]commander, "May I say something to you?" And he *said,
"Do you know Greek?

...thousands [b]Acts 15:1; ...n. 10:2; Gal. 1:14
21:28 [b]Acts ...1 Cor. 7:18f. [c]Acts 6:14
...ve a vow on ...um. 6:13-21; Acts 18:18
...end on them [a]John 11:55; 24:18 [b]Acts 18:18
...thing [a]Acts 15:19f., 29
...ook the men ...ext day, and ...mself [a]John ...; Acts 21:24; ...n. 6:13; Acts 24:18
..., west coast of Asia Minor ...13-20 [b]Acts ...8 [c]Acts 16:6
...s 6:13 [b]Matt. ...s 6:13f.; 24:6
...s 20:4 [b]Acts 18:19
...it., *a running of the people* [a]2 Kin. 11:15; 16:19; 26:21
..., chiliarch, in ...mand of one ...d troops [2]Or, ...on [a]Acts 10:1
note 1 [a]Acts 23:27
note 1 [a]Acts 21:11; 22:29; ...20; Eph. 6:20; ...16; 2:9 [b]Acts 12:6
...ertainty [a]Acts ... [b]Acts 21:37; 23:10, 16, 32
...ultitude [a]Acts 21:40
...ke 23:18; John ...15; Acts 22:22
..., note 1 [a]Acts ...; 22:24; 23:10, 16, 32

38 "Then you are not [a]the Egyptian who some [1]time ago stirred up a revolt and led the four thousand men of the Assassins out [b]into the wilderness?"
39 But Paul said, "[a]I am a Jew of Tarsus in [b]Cilicia, a citizen of no insignificant city; and I beg you, allow me to speak to the people."
40 And when he had given him permission, Paul, standing on [a]the stairs, [b]motioned to the people with his hand; and when there [1]was a great hush, he spoke to them in the [2c]Hebrew dialect, saying,

Chapter 22

22 "[a]Brethren and fathers, hear my defense which I now *offer* to you."
2 And when they heard that he was addressing them in the [1a]Hebrew dialect, they became even more quiet; and he *said,
3 "[a]I am [b]a Jew, born in [c]Tarsus of [d]Cilicia, but brought up in this city, educated [1]under [e]Gamaliel, [2f]strictly according to the law of our fathers, being zealous for God, just as [g]you all are today.
4 "And [a]I persecuted this [b]Way to the death, binding and putting both men and women into prisons,
5 as also [a]the high priest and all [b]the Council of the elders [1]can testify. From them I also [c]received letters to [d]the brethren, and started off for [c]Damascus in order to bring even those who were there to Jerusalem [2]as prisoners to be punished.
6 "[a]And it came about that as I was on my way, approaching Damascus about noontime, a very bright light suddenly flashed from heaven all around me,
7 and I fell to the ground and heard a voice saying to me, 'Saul, Saul, why are you persecuting Me?'
8 "And I answered, 'Who art Thou, Lord?' And He said to me, 'I am [a]Jesus the Nazarene, whom you are persecuting.'
9 "And those who were with me [a]beheld the light, to be sure, but [b]did not [1]understand the voice of the One who was speaking to me.
10 "And I said, '[a]What shall I do, Lord?' And the Lord said to me, 'Arise and go on into Damascus; and there you will be told of all that has been appointed for you to do.'
11 "But since I [a]could not see because of the [1]brightness of that light, I was led by the hand by those who were with me, and came into Damascus.
12 "And a certain [a]Ananias, a man who was devout by the standard of the Law, *and* [b]well spoken of by all the Jews who lived there,
13 came to me, and standing near said to me, '[a]Brother Saul, receive your sight!' And [1b]at that very time I looked up at him.
14 "And he said, '[a]The God of our fathers has [b]appointed you to know His will, and to [c]see the [d]Righteous One, and to hear an [1]utterance from His mouth.
15 'For you will be [a]a witness for Him to all men of [b]what you have seen and heard.
16 'And now why do you delay? [a]Arise, and be baptized, and [b]wash away your sins, [c]calling on His name.'
17 "And it came about when I [a]returned to Jerusalem and was praying in the temple, that I [b]fell into a trance,
18 and I saw Him saying to me, '[a]Make haste, and get out of Jerusalem quickly, because they will not accept your testimony about Me.'
19 "And I said, 'Lord, they themselves understand that in one

38 [1]Lit., *da* 5:36 [b]Matt
39 [a]Acts 9. [b]Acts 6:9
40 [1]Lit., *oc* Jewish Aran 21:35 [b]Acts [c]John 5:2; A 22:2; 26:14
22:1 [a]Acts
2 [1]I.e., Jew [a]Acts 21:40
3 [1]Lit., *at th* [2]Lit., *accord strictness o ancestral la* 9:1-22; 22:3 26:9-18 [b]Ac [c]Acts 9:11 [d] [e]Acts 5:34 26:5; Phil. 3 21:20
4 [a]Acts 8:3; 26:9-11 [b]Ac
5 [1]Lit., *testi* [2]Lit., *having bound* [a]Acts 22:66; Acts 5 4:14 [c]Acts 9 2:29; 3:17; 1 28:17, 21; R
6 [a]Acts 22:6 *9:3-8; 26:12-*
8 [a]Acts 26:9
9 [1]Or, *hear* comprehensi 26:13 [b]Acts 9
10 [a]Acts 16:3
11 [1]Or, *glory*
12 [a]Acts 9:10 6:3; 10:22
13 [1]Or, *instar that very hou* 9:17 [b]Acts 9:
14 [1]Or, *mess voice* [a]Acts 3 9:15; 26:16 [c] 26:16; 1 Cor. [d]Acts 7:52
15 [a]Acts 23:1 [b]Acts 22:14
16 [a]Acts 9:18 2:38; 1 Cor. 6: 5:26; Heb. 10: 7:59
17 [a]Acts 9:26 [b]Acts 10:10
18 [a]Acts 9:29

synagogue after another [a]I used to imprison and [b]beat those who
believed in Thee.
20 'And [a]when the blood of Thy witness Stephen was being shed, I
also was standing by approving, and watching out for the cloaks of
those who were slaying him.'
21 "And He said to me, 'Go! For I will send you far away [a]to the
Gentiles.'"
22 And they listened to him up to this statement, and *then* they
raised their voices and said, "[a]Away with such a fellow from the
earth, for [b]he should not be allowed to live!"
23 And as they were crying out and [a]throwing off their cloaks and
[b]tossing dust into the air,
24 the [1]commander ordered him to be brought into [a]the barracks,
stating that he should be [b]examined by scourging so that he might
find out the reason why they were shouting against him that way.
25 And when they stretched him out [1]with thongs, Paul said to the
centurion who was standing by, "Is it lawful for you to scourge [a]a
man who is a Roman and uncondemned?"
26 And when the centurion heard *this,* he went to the [1]commander
and told him, saying, "What are you about to do? For this man is a
Roman."
27 And the [1]commander came and said to him, "Tell me, are you a
Roman?" And he said, "Yes."
28 And the [1]commander answered, "I acquired this citizenship with
a large sum of money." And Paul said, "But I was actually born *a
citizen.*"
29 Therefore those who were about to [a]examine him immediately
[1]let go of him; and the [2]commander also [b]was afraid when he found
out that he was a Roman, and because he had [3c]put him in chains.
30 But on the next day, [a]wishing to know for certain why he had
been accused by the Jews, he [b]released him and ordered the chief
priests and all [c]the [1]Council to assemble, and brought Paul down
and set him before them.

Chapter 23

23 And Paul, looking intently at [a]the [1]Council, said, "[b]Brethren, [c]I
have [2]lived my life with a perfectly good conscience before
God up to this day."
2 And the high priest [a]Ananias commanded those standing beside
him [b]to strike him on the mouth.
3 Then Paul said to him, "God is going to strike you, [a]you white-
washed wall! And do you [b]sit to try me according to the Law, and in
violation of the Law order me to be struck?"
4 But the bystanders said, "Do you revile God's high priest?"
5 And Paul said, "I was not aware, brethren, that he was high
priest; for it is written, '[a]YOU SHALL NOT SPEAK EVIL OF A RULER OF YOUR
PEOPLE.'"
6 But perceiving that one part were [a]Sadducees and the other
Pharisees, Paul *began* crying out in [b]the [1]Council, "[c]Brethren, [d]I am a
Pharisee, a son of Pharisees; I am on trial for [e]the hope and resurrec-
tion of the dead!"
7 And as he said this, there arose a dissension between the
Pharisees and Sadducees; and the assembly was divided.

9 [a]Acts 8:3; 22:4 10:17; Acts 26:11
[a]Acts 7:58f.; 8:1; 26:10
21 [a]Acts 9:15
22 [a]Acts 21:36; hess. 2:16 [b]Acts 25:24
cts 7:58 [b]2 Sam. 16:13
[1]I.e., chiliarch, in command of one and troops [a]Acts 1:34 [b]Acts 22:29
it., *for the thongs* [a]Acts 16:37
26 [1]V. 24, note 1
27 [1]V. 24, note 1
28 [1]V. 24, note 1
Or, *withdrew from* 24, note 1 [3]Lit., *him* [a]Acts 22:24 6:38 [c]Acts 21:33
[1]Or, *Sanhedrin* Acts 23:28 [b]Acts 21:33 [c]Matt. 5:22
[1]Or, *Sanhedrin* *conducted myself as a citizen* [a]Acts 23:6, 15, 20, 28 2:5 [c]Acts 24:16; 1:12; 2 Tim. 1:3
[a]Acts 24:1 [b]John 18:22
Matt. 23:27 [b]Lev. Deut. 25:2; John 7:51
5 [a]Ex. 22:28
Sanhedrin [a]Matt. 23 [b]Acts 22:30; 15, 20, 28 [c]Acts [d]Acts 26:5; Phil. [e]Acts 24:15, 21; 26:8

8 For [a]the Sadducees say that there is no resurrection, nor an angel, nor a spirit; but the Pharisees acknowledge them all.

9 And there arose a great uproar; and some of [a]the scribes of the Pharisaic party stood up and *began* to argue heatedly, saying, "[b]We find nothing wrong with this man; [c]suppose a spirit or an angel has spoken to him?"

10 And as a great dissension was developing, the [1]commander was afraid Paul would be torn to pieces by them and ordered the troops to go down and take him away from them by force, and bring him into [a]the barracks.

11 But on [a]the night *immediately* following, the Lord stood at his side and said, "[b]Take courage; for [c]as you have [d]solemnly witnessed to My cause at Jerusalem, so you must witness at Rome also."

12 And when it was day, [a]the Jews formed a [1]conspiracy and [b]bound themselves under an oath, saying that they would neither eat nor drink until they had killed Paul.

13 And there were more than forty who formed this plot.

14 And they came to the chief priests and the elders, and said, "We have [a]bound ourselves under a solemn oath to taste nothing until we have killed Paul.

15 "Now, therefore, you [1]and [a]the [2]Council notify the [3]commander to bring him down to you, as though you were going to determine his case by a more thorough investigation; and we for our part are ready to slay him before he comes near *the place*."

16 But the son of Paul's sister heard of their ambush, [1]and he came and entered [a]the barracks and told Paul.

17 And Paul called one of the centurions to him and said, "Lead this young man to the [1]commander, for he has something to report to him."

18 So he took him and led him to the [1]commander and *said, "Paul [a]the prisoner called me to him and asked me to lead this young man to you since he has something to tell you."

19 And the [1]commander took him by the hand and stepping aside, *began* to inquire of him privately, "What is it that you have to report to me?"

20 And he said, "[a]The Jews have agreed to ask you to bring Paul down tomorrow to [b]the [1]Council, as though they were going to inquire somewhat more thoroughly about him.

21 "So do not [1]listen to them, for more than forty of them are [a]lying in wait for him who have [b]bound themselves under a curse not to eat or drink until they slay him; and now they are ready and waiting for the promise from you."

22 Therefore the [1]commander let the young man go, instructing him, "Tell no one that you have notified me of these things."

23 And he called to him two of the centurions, and said, "Get two hundred soldiers ready by [1]the third hour of the night to proceed to [a]Caesarea, [2]with seventy horsemen and two hundred [3]spearmen."

24 *They were* also to provide mounts to put Paul on and bring him safely to [a]Felix the governor.

25 And he wrote a letter having this form:

26 "Claudius Lysias, to the [a]most excellent governor Felix, [b]greetings.

27 "When this man was arrested by the Jews and was about to be

8 [a]Matt. 22:23; M… 12:18; Luke 20:2…

9 [a]Mark 2:16; Lu… 5:30 [b]Acts 23:29… 12:29; Acts 22:6…

10 [1]I.e., chiliarch… command of one thousand troops … 21:34; 23:16, 32

11 [a]Acts 18:9 [b]… 9:2 [c]Acts 19:21 … 16:28; Acts 28:2…

12 [1]Or, *mob* [a]A… 9:23; 23:30; 1 Th… 2:16 [b]Acts 23:14…

14 [a]Acts 23:12, …

15 [1]Lit., *with* [2]O… *Sanhedrin* [3]V. 1… 1 [a]Acts 22:30; 2… 20, 28

16 [1]Or, *having b… present* with ther… *he entered* [a]Act… 23:10, 32

17 [1]V. 10, note 1…

18 [1]V. 10, note 1… 3:1

19 [1]V. 10, note 1…

20 [1]Or, *Sanhedr…* [a]Acts 23:14f. [b]A… 22:30; 23:1, 6, 1…

21 [1]Lit., *be pers… by them* [a]Luke 1… [b]Acts 23:12, 14

22 [1]V. 10, note 1…

23 [1]I.e., 9 p.m. … *and* [3]Or, *slinger… bowmen* [a]Acts 8… 23:33

24 [a]Acts 23:26, … 24:1, 3, 10; 25:14…

26 [a]Luke 1:3; Ac… 26:25 [b]Acts 15:2…

slain by them, [a]I came upon them with the troops and rescued
him, [b]having learned that he was a Roman.
28 "And [a]wanting to ascertain the charge for which they were
accusing him, I [b]brought him down to their [1c]Council;
29 and I found him to be accused over [a]questions about their
Law, but [1]under [b]no accusation deserving death or [2]imprison-
ment.
30 "And when I was [a]informed that there would be [b]a plot against
the man, I sent him to you at once, also instructing [c]his ac-
cusers to [1]bring charges against him before you.[2]"
31 So the soldiers, in accordance with their orders, took Paul and
brought him by night to Antipatris.
32 But the next day, leaving [a]the horsemen to go on with him, they
returned to [b]the barracks.
33 And when these had come to [a]Caesarea and delivered the letter
to [b]the governor, they also presented Paul to him.
34 And when he had read it, he asked from what [a]province he was;
and when he learned that [b]he was from Cilicia,
35 he said, "I will give you a hearing after your [a]accusers arrive
also," giving orders for him to be [b]kept in Herod's [1]Praetorium.

Chapter 24

24 And after [a]five days the high priest [b]Ananias came down with
some elders, [1]with a certain [2]attorney *named* Tertullus; and
they [3]brought charges to [c]the governor against Paul.
2 And after *Paul* had been summoned, Tertullus began to accuse
him, saying *to the governor*,
"**S**ince we have through you attained much peace, and since by
your providence reforms are being carried out for this nation,
3 we acknowledge *this* in every way and everywhere, [a]most excel-
lent Felix, with all thankfulness.
4 "But, that I may not weary you any further, I beg you [1]to grant us,
by your kindness, a brief hearing.
5 "For we have found this man a real pest and a fellow who stirs up
dissension among all the Jews throughout [1]the world, and a
ringleader of the [a]sect of the Nazarenes.
6 "And he even tried to [a]desecrate the temple; and [1]then we ar-
rested him. [[2]And we wanted to judge him according to our own
Law.
7 "But Lysias the commander came along, and with much violence
took him out of our hands,
8 ordering his accusers to come before you.] And by examining
him yourself concerning all these matters, you will be able to ascer-
tain the things of which we accuse him."
9 And [a]the Jews also joined in the attack, asserting that these
things were so.
10 And when [a]the governor had nodded for him to speak, Paul
responded:
"**K**nowing that for many years you have been a judge to this
nation, I cheerfully make my defense,
11 since you can take note of the fact that no more than [a]twelve
days ago I went up to Jerusalem to worship.
12 "And [a]neither in the temple, nor in the synagogues, nor in the city

itself did they find me carrying on a discussion with anyone or [b]causing [1]a riot.
13 "[a]Nor can they prove to you *the charges* of which they now accuse me.
14 "But this I admit to you, that according to [a]the Way which they call a [b]sect I do serve [1c]the God of our fathers, [d]believing everything that is in accordance with the Law, and that is written in the Prophets;
15 having a hope in God, which [a]these men cherish themselves, that there shall certainly be a resurrection of both the righteous and the wicked.
16 "In view of this, [a]I also [1]do my best to maintain always a blameless conscience *both* before God and before men.
17 "Now [a]after several years I [b]came to bring [1]alms to my nation and to present offerings;
18 in which they found me *occupied* in the temple, having been [a]purified, without *any* [b]crowd or uproar. But *there were* certain [c]Jews from [1]Asia—
19 who ought to have been present before you, and to [a]make accusation, if they should have anything against me.
20 "Or else let these men themselves tell what misdeed they found when I stood before [a]the [1]Council,
21 other than for this one statement which [a]I shouted out while standing among them, 'For the resurrection of the dead I am on trial before you today.' "
22 But Felix, having a more exact knowledge about [a]the Way, put them off, saying, "When Lysias the [1]commander comes down, I will decide your case."
23 And he gave orders to the centurion for him to be [a]kept in custody and *yet* [b]have *some* freedom, and not to prevent any of [c]his friends from ministering to him.
24 But some days later, Felix arrived with Drusilla, his [1]wife who was a Jewess, and sent for Paul, and heard him *speak* about [a]faith in Christ Jesus.
25 And as he was discussing [a]righteousness, [b]self-control and [c]the judgment to come, Felix became frightened and said, "Go away for the present, and when I find time, I will summon you."
26 At the same time too, he was hoping that [a]money would be given him by Paul; therefore he also used to send for him quite often and converse with him.
27 But after two years had passed, Felix [1]was succeeded by Porcius [a]Festus; and [b]wishing to do the Jews a favor, Felix left Paul [c]imprisoned.

Chapter 25

25 Festus therefore, having arrived in [a]the province, three days later went up to Jerusalem from [b]Caesarea.
2 And the chief priests and the leading men of the Jews [a]brought charges against Paul; and they were urging him,
3 requesting a [1]concession against [2]Paul, that he might [3]have him brought to Jerusalem (*at the same time,* [a]setting an ambush to kill him on the way).
4 Festus then [a]answered that Paul [b]was being kept in custody at [c]Caesarea and that he himself was about to leave shortly.

12 [1]Lit., *a* *mob* [b]Act
13 [a]Acts
14 [1]Lit., *t* *god* [a]Acts [b]Acts 15:5 3:13 [d]Acts 22f.; 28:23
15 [a]Dan. 5:28f.; 11:
16 [1]Lit., *pr* *myself* [a]A
17 [1]Or, *gif* [a]Acts 20:3 11:29f.; Ro 1 Cor. 16:1 8:1-4; 9:1, 2:10
18 [1]I.e., we province of [a]Acts 21:26 24:12 [c]Acts
19 [a]Acts 23
20 [1]Or, *Sar* [a]Matt. 5:22
21 [a]Acts 23
22 [1]I.e., chi command of thousand tro 24:14
23 [a]Acts 23 28:16 [c]Acts
24 [1]Lit., *own* 20:21
25 [a]Titus 2:1 5:23; Titus 1: 1:6 [c]Acts 10:
26 [a]Acts 24:1
27 [1]Lit., *rece* *successor, Po* *Festus* [a]Acts 12; 26:24f., 32 12:3; 25:9 [c]A 25:14
25:1 [a]Acts 23 8:40; 25:4, 6,
2 [a]Acts 24:1;
3 [1]Or, *favor* [3]Lit., *send for h* *Jerusalem* [a]A
4 [a]Acts 25:16 24:23 [c]Acts 8: 6, 13

down [2]Lit., [3]Or, *accuse*

5 "Therefore," he *said, "let the influential men among you [1]go
there with me, and if there is anything wrong [2]about the man, let
them [3]prosecute him."

:40; 25:1, 4, 27:19; Acts 25:10, 17

6 And after he had spent not more than eight or ten days among
them, he went down to [a]Caesarea; and on the next day he took his
seat on [b]the tribunal and ordered Paul to be brought.

24:5f. [b]Acts 24:13

7 And after he had arrived, the Jews who had come down from
Jerusalem stood around him, bringing [a]many and serious charges
against him [b]which they could not prove;

6:13; 24:12; 28:17

8 while Paul said in his own defense, "[a]I have committed no of-
fense either against the Law of the Jews or against the temple or
against Caesar."

judged [a]Acts [b]Acts 25:20

9 But Festus, [a]wishing to do the Jews a favor, answered Paul and
said, "[b]Are you willing to go up to Jerusalem and [1]stand trial before
me on these *charges*?"

tt. 27:19; Acts 25:6, 17

10 But Paul said, "I am standing before Caesar's [a]tribunal, where I
ought to be tried. I have done no wrong to *the* Jews, as you also very
well know.

cts 25:21, 25; 26:32; 28:19

11 "If then I am a wrongdoer, and have committed anything worthy
of death, I do not refuse to die; but if none of those things is *true* of
which these men accuse me, no one can hand me over to them. I
[a]appeal to Caesar."

different body mentioned in :15 and 24:20

12 Then when Festus had conferred with [1]his council, he answered,
"You have appealed to Caesar, to Caesar you shall go."

[1]Lit., *greeting* *us* [a]Acts 8:40; 25:1, 4, 6

13 Now when several days had elapsed, King Agrippa and Bernice
arrived at [a]Caesarea, [1]and paid their respects to Festus.
14 And while they were spending many days there, Festus laid
Paul's case before the king, saying, "There is a certain man [a]left a
prisoner by Felix;

4 [a]Acts 24:27

15 and when I was at Jerusalem, the chief priests and the elders of
the Jews [a]brought charges against him, asking for a sentence of con-
demnation upon him.

Acts 24:1; 25:2

ts 25:4f. [b]Acts 23:30

16 "And I [a]answered them that it is not the custom of the Romans to
hand over any man before [b]the accused meets his accusers face to
face, and has an opportunity to make his defense against the
charges.

att. 27:19; Acts 25:6, 10

17 "And so after they had assembled here, I made no delay, but on
the next day took my seat on [a]the tribunal, and ordered the man to
be brought.
18 "And when the accusers stood up, they *began* bringing charges
against him not of such crimes as I was expecting;

Or, *superstition* cts 18:15; 23:29 [b]Acts 17:22

19 but they *simply* had some [a]points of disagreement with him
about their own [1b]religion and about a certain dead man, Jesus,
whom Paul asserted to be alive.

it., *these* [a]Acts 25:9

20 "And [a]being at a loss how to investigate [1]such matters, I asked
whether he was willing to go to Jerusalem and there stand trial on
these matters.

., *the Augustus'* this case Nero) [a]Acts 25:11f.

21 "But when Paul [a]appealed to be held in custody for [1]the
Emperor's decision, I ordered him to be kept in custody until I send
him to Caesar."

22 [a]Acts 9:15

22 And [a]Agrippa *said* to Festus, "I also would like to hear the man
myself." "Tomorrow," he *said, "you shall hear him."

Lit., *and Bernice* cts 25:13; 26:30

23 And so, on the next day when [a]Agrippa had come [1]together with
[a]Bernice, amid great pomp, and had entered the auditorium

[2]accompanied by the [3]commanders and the prominent men of the
city, at the command of Festus, Paul was brought in.
24 And Festus *said, "King Agrippa, and all you gentlemen here
present with us, you behold this man about whom [a]all the people of
the Jews appealed to me, both at Jerusalem and here, loudly declar-
ing that [b]he ought not to live any longer.
25 "But I found that he had committed [a]nothing worthy of death;
and since he himself [b]appealed to [1]the Emperor, I decided to send
him.
26 "[1]Yet I have nothing definite about him to write to my lord. There-
fore I have brought him before you *all* and especially before you,
King Agrippa, so that after the investigation has taken place, I may
have something to write.
27 "For it seems absurd to me in sending a prisoner, not to indicate
also the charges against him."

Chapter 26

26 And [a]Agrippa said to Paul, "You are permitted to speak for
yourself." Then Paul stretched out his hand and *proceeded* to
make his defense:
2 "In regard to all the things of which I am accused by the Jews, I
consider myself fortunate, King Agrippa, that I am about to make
my defense before you today;
3 [1]especially because you are an expert in all [a]customs and [2]ques-
tions among *the* Jews; therefore I beg you to listen to me patiently.
4 "So then, all Jews know [a]my manner of life from my youth up,
which from the beginning was spent among my *own* nation and at
Jerusalem;
5 since they have known about me for a long time previously, if
they are willing to testify, that I lived *as* a [a]Pharisee [b]according to the
strictest [c]sect of our religion.
6 "And now I am [1]standing trial [a]for the hope of [b]the promise made
by God to our fathers;
7 *the promise* [a]to which our twelve tribes hope to attain, as they
earnestly serve *God* night and day. And for this [b]hope, O King, I am
being [c]accused by Jews.
8 "Why is it considered incredible among you *people* [a]if God does
raise the dead?
9 "So then, [a]I thought to myself that I had to do many things hostile
to [b]the name of Jesus of Nazareth.
10 "And this is [1]just what I [a]did in Jerusalem; not only did I lock up
many of the [2]saints in prisons, having [b]received authority from the
chief priests, but also when they were being put to death I [c]cast my
vote against them.
11 "And [a]as I punished them often in all the synagogues, I tried to
force them to blaspheme; and being [b]furiously enraged at them, I
kept pursuing them [c]even to [1]foreign cities.
12 "[1]While thus engaged [a]as I was journeying to Damascus with the
authority and commission of the chief priests,
13 at midday, O King, I saw on the way a light from heaven,
[1]brighter than the sun, shining all around me and those who were
journeying with me.

23 [2]Lit., *and* chiliarchs, i[n] of one thous[and]
24 [a]Acts 25 22:22
25 [1]V. 21, n 23:4; Acts 2[3] 25:11f.
26 [1]Lit., *Abo[ut] have nothing*
26:1 [a]Acts 9
3 [1]Or, *becau[se] especially ex[pert] controversial* [a]Acts 6:14; 2[5]
4 [a]Gal. 1:13f
5 [a]Acts 23:6; [b]Acts 22:3 [c]A
6 [1]Lit., *being* [a]Acts 24:15; 2 [b]Acts 13:32
7 [a]James 1:1 24:15; 28:20
8 [a]Acts 23:6
9 [a]John 16:2; 1:13 [b]John 15
10 [1]Lit., *also* *ones* [a]Acts 8:3 [b]Acts 9:1f. [c]Ac
11 [1]Or, *outlying* 10:17; Acts 22: 9:1 [c]Acts 22:5
12 [1]Lit., *In whic[h]* [a]Acts 26:12-18: *22:6-11*
13 [1]Lit., *above brightness of*

14 "And when we had [a]all fallen to the ground, I heard a voice saying to me in the [1b]Hebrew dialect, 'Saul, Saul, why are you persecuting Me? It is hard for you to kick against the goads.'

15 "And I said, 'Who art Thou, Lord?' And the Lord said, 'I am Jesus whom you are persecuting.

16 'But arise, and [a]stand on your feet; for this purpose I have appeared to you, to [b]appoint you a [c]minister and [d]a witness not only to the things which you have [1]seen, but also to the things in which I will appear to you;

17 [a]delivering you [b]from the *Jewish* people and from the Gentiles, to whom I am sending you,

18 to [a]open their eyes so that they may turn from [b]darkness to light and from the dominion of [c]Satan to God, in order that they may receive [d]forgiveness of sins and an [e]inheritance among those who have been sanctified by [f]faith in Me.'

19 "Consequently, King Agrippa, I did not prove disobedient to the heavenly vision,

20 but *kept* declaring both [a]to those of Damascus first, and *also* [b]at Jerusalem and *then* throughout all the region of Judea, and *even* [c]to the Gentiles, that they should [d]repent and turn to God, performing deeds [e]appropriate to repentance.

21 "For this reason *some* Jews [a]seized me in the temple and tried [b]to put me to death.

22 "And so, having obtained help from God, I stand to this day [a]testifying both to small and great, stating nothing but what [b]the Prophets and Moses said was going to take place;

23 [1a]that [2]the Christ was [3]to suffer, *and* [1]that [b]by reason of *His* resurrection from the dead He should be the first to proclaim [c]light both to the *Jewish* people and to the Gentiles."

24 And while *Paul* was saying this in his defense, Festus *said in a loud voice, "Paul, you are out of your mind! [1]*Your* great [a]learning is [2]driving you mad."

25 But Paul *said, "I am not out of my mind, [a]most excellent Festus, but I utter words [1]of sober truth.

26 "For the king [1a]knows about these matters, and I speak to him also with confidence, [2]since I am persuaded that none of these things escape his notice; for this has not been done in a corner.

27 "King Agrippa, do you believe the Prophets? I know that you [1]do."

28 And Agrippa *replied* to Paul, "[1]In a short time you [2]will persuade me to [3]become a [a]Christian."

29 And Paul *said*, "[1]I would to God, that whether [2]in a short or long time, not only you, but also all who hear me this day, might become such as I am, except for these [a]chains."

30 And [a]the king arose and the governor and Bernice, and those who were sitting with them,

31 and when they had drawn aside, they *began* talking to one another, saying, "[a]This man is not doing anything worthy of death or [1]imprisonment."

32 And Agrippa said to Festus, "This man might have been [a]set free if he had not [b]appealed to Caesar."

[1]I.e., Jewish
c [a]Acts 9:7
[b]Acts 21:40

e early mss.
Me [a]Ezek.
10:11 [b]Acts
e 1:2 [d]Acts
22:15

, 19 [b]1 Chr.
5; Acts 9:15

5; 42:7, 16;
8; Col. 1:13;
9 [b]John 1:5;
; Col. 1:12f.;
5; 1 Pet. 2:9
[d]Luke 24:47;
[e]Acts 20:32
[f]Acts 20:21

9:19ff. [b]Acts
17-20 [c]Acts
6 [d]Acts 3:19
3:8; Luke 3:8

cts 21:27, 30
[b]Acts 21:31

16:28 [b]Acts
10:43; 24:14

whether [2]I.e.,
Messiah [3]Lit.,
ct to suffering
24; Acts 3:18
5:20, 23; Col.
1:5 [c]Is. 42:6;
e 2:32; 2 Cor.
4:4

it., The many
t., turning you
s [a]John 7:15;
2 Tim. 3:15

t., of truth and
[a]Acts 23:26;
24:3

, understands
for [a]Acts 26:3

7 [1]Lit., believe

Vith a little [2]Or,
convince [3]Lit.,
ke [a]Acts 11:26

I would pray to
h a little or with
ch [a]Acts 21:33

30 [a]Acts 25:23

t., bonds [a]Acts
23:29

cts 28:18 [b]Acts
25:11

Chapter 27

27 And when it was decided that [a]we [b]should sail for [c]Italy, they
proceeded to deliver Paul and some other prisoners to a cen-
turion of the Augustan [1d]cohort named Julius.

Paul: Caesarea to Rome

2 And embarking in an Adramyttian
ship, which was about to sail to the regions
along the coast of [1a]Asia, we put out to sea,
accompanied by [b]Aristarchus, a [c]Mace-
donian of [d]Thessalonica.
3 And the next day we put in at [a]Sidon;
and Julius [b]treated Paul with consideration
and [c]allowed him to go to his friends and
receive care.
4 And from there we put out to sea and
sailed under the shelter of [a]Cyprus because
[b]the winds were contrary.
5 And when we had sailed through the sea along the coast of
[a]Cilicia and [b]Pamphylia, we landed at Myra in Lycia.
6 And there the centurion found an [a]Alexandrian ship sailing for
[b]Italy, and he put us aboard it.
7 And when we had sailed slowly for a good many days, and with
difficulty had arrived off Cnidus, [a]since the wind did not permit us
to go farther, we sailed under the shelter of [b]Crete, off Salmone;
8 and with difficulty [a]sailing past it we came to a certain place
called Fair Havens, near which was the city of Lasea.
9 And when considerable time had passed and the voyage was
now dangerous, since even [a]the [1]fast was already over, Paul *began* to
admonish them,
10 and said to them, "Men, I perceive that the voyage will certainly
be *attended* with [a]damage and great loss, not only of the cargo and
the ship, but also of our lives."
11 But the centurion was more persuaded by the [a]pilot and the
[1]captain of the ship, than by what was being said by Paul.
12 And because the harbor was not suitable for wintering, the
majority reached a decision to put out to sea from there, if somehow
they could reach Phoenix, a harbor of [a]Crete, facing [1]southwest and
northwest, and spend the winter *there*.
13 And [1]when a moderate south wind came up, supposing that
they had gained their purpose, they weighed anchor and *began* [a]sail-
ing along [b]Crete, close *inshore*.
14 But before very long there [a]rushed down from [1]the land a violent
wind, called [2]Euraquilo;
15 and when the ship was caught *in it*, and could not face the wind,
we gave way *to it*, and let ourselves be driven along.
16 And running under the shelter of a small island called [1]Clauda,
we were scarcely able to get the *ship's* boat under control.
17 And after they had hoisted it up, they used [1]supporting cables in
undergirding the ship; and fearing that they might [a]run aground on
the shallows of Syrtis, they let down the [2]sea anchor, and so let them-
selves be driven along.
18 The next day as we were being violently storm-tossed, [1]they
began to [a]jettison the cargo;
19 and on the third day they threw the ship's tackle overboard with
their own hands.

27:1 [1]Or, *b* [a][we] Acts 1 27:1-28 [b]Ac 25 [c]Acts 18 [d]Acts 10:1

2 [1]I.e., wes province of [a]Acts 2:9 [b]A [c]Acts 16:9

3 [a]Matt. 11: 27:43 [c]Acts

4 [a]Acts 4:36

5 [a]Acts 6:9

6 [a]Acts 28:1 18:2; 27:1

7 [a]Acts 27:4 2:11; 27:12f., 1:5, 12

8 [a]Acts 27:1

9 [1]I.e., Day o Atonement in September o [a]Lev. 16:29-3 23:27-29; Nu.

10 [a]Acts 27:2

11 [1]Or, *owne* 18:17

12 [1]Or possib *northeast and southeast* [a]A 27:13, 21; Tit

13 [1]Lit., *a sou having gently* [a]Acts 27:8 [b]A 27:12f., 21; Tit

14 [1]Lit., *it* [2]I.e northeaster

16 [1]Some anc read *Cauda*

17 [1]Lit., *helps* possibly, *sail* 27:26, 29

18 [1]Lit., *they w doing a throwin* [a]Jon. 1:5; Acts

20 And since neither sun nor stars appeared for many days, and no
small storm was assailing *us,* from then on all hope of our being
saved was gradually abandoned.
21 And [1]when they had gone a long time without food, then Paul
stood up in their midst and said, "[a]Men, you ought to have [2]fol-
lowed my advice and not to have set sail from [b]Crete, and [3]incurred
this [a]damage and loss.
22 "And *yet* now I urge you to [a]keep up your courage, for there shall
be no loss of life among you, but *only* of the ship.
23 "For this very night [a]an angel of the God to whom I belong and
[b]whom I serve [c]stood before me,
24 saying, 'Do not be afraid, Paul; [a]you must stand before Caesar;
and behold, God has granted you [b]all those who are sailing with
you.'
25 "Therefore, [a]keep up your courage, men, for I believe God, that [1]it
will turn out exactly as I have been told.
26 "But we must [a]run aground on a certain [b]island."
27 But when the fourteenth night had come, as we were being
driven about in the Adriatic Sea, about midnight the sailors *began* to
surmise that [1]they were approaching some land.
28 And they took soundings, and found *it to be* twenty fathoms;
and a little farther on they took another sounding and found *it to be*
fifteen fathoms.
29 And fearing that we might [a]run aground somewhere on the
[1]rocks, they cast four anchors from the stern and [2]wished for
daybreak.
30 And as the sailors were trying to escape from the ship, and had
let down [a]the *ship's* boat into the sea, on the pretense of intending to
lay out anchors from the bow,
31 Paul said to the centurion and to the soldiers, "Unless these men
remain in the ship, you yourselves cannot be saved."
32 Then the soldiers cut away the [a]ropes of the *ship's* boat, and let it
fall away.
33 And until the day was about to dawn, Paul was encouraging
them all to take some food, saying, "Today is the fourteenth day that
you have been constantly watching and going without eating,
having taken nothing.
34 "Therefore I encourage you to take some food, for this is for your
preservation; for [a]not a hair from the head of any of you shall
perish."
35 And having said this, he took bread and [a]gave thanks to God in
the presence of all; and he broke it and began to eat.
36 And all [a]of them [1]were encouraged, and they themselves also
took food.
37 And all of us in the ship were two hundred and seventy-six
[1a]persons.
38 And when they had eaten enough, they *began* to lighten the ship
by [a]throwing out the wheat into the sea.
39 And when day came, [a]they [1]could not recognize the land; but
they [2]did observe a certain bay with a beach, and they [3]resolved to
[4]drive the ship onto it if they could.
40 And casting off [a]the anchors, they [1]left them in the sea while at
the same time they were loosening the ropes of the rudders, and
hoisting the foresail to the wind, they were heading for the beach.

there being nence from obeyed me ained [a]Acts [b]Acts 27:7
ts 27:25, 36
5:19 [b]Rom. 18:9; 23:11; 2 Tim. 4:17
23:11 [b]Acts 7:31, 42, 44
will be [a]Acts 27:22, 36
cts 27:17, 29 [b]Acts 28:1
me land was baching them
rough places were praying become day cts 27:17, 26
[a]Acts 27:16
2 [a]John 2:15
[a]Matt. 10:30
[a]Matt. 14:19
[1]Lit., *became* Acts 27:22, 25
t., *souls* [a]Acts 2:41
1:5; Acts 27:18
[1]Or, *were not* *izing* [2]Or, *were* *ving* [3]Or, *were* *solving* [4]Some mss. read *bring* *p safely ashore* [a]Acts 28:1
Or, *were leaving* [a]Acts 27:29

41 But striking a [1]reef where two seas met, they ran the vessel
aground; and the prow stuck fast and remained immovable, but the
stern *began* to be broken up by the force *of the waves.*
42 And the soldiers' plan was to [a]kill the prisoners, that none *of*
them should swim away and escape;
43 but the centurion, [a]wanting to bring Paul safely through, kept
them from their intention, and commanded that those who could
swim should [1]jump overboard first and get to land,
44 and the rest *should follow*, some on planks, and others on various
things from the ship. And thus it happened that [a]they all were
brought safely to land.

Chapter 28

28 And when [a]they had been brought safely through, [b]then we
found out that [c]the island was called [1]Malta.
2 And [a]the [1]natives showed us extraordinary kindness; for because
of the rain that had set in and because of the cold, they kindled a fire
and [b]received us all.
3 But when Paul had gathered a bundle of sticks and laid them on
the fire, a viper came out [1]because of the heat, and fastened on his
hand.
4 And when [a]the [1]natives saw the creature hanging from his hand,
they *began* saying to one another, "[b]Undoubtedly this man is a mur-
derer, and though he has been saved from the sea, [2]justice has not
allowed him to live."
5 However [a]he shook the creature off into the fire and suffered no
harm.
6 But they were expecting that he was about to swell up or sud-
denly fall down dead. But after they had waited a long time and had
seen nothing unusual happen to him, they changed their minds and
[a]*began* to say that he was a god.
7 Now in the neighborhood of that place were lands belonging to
the leading man of the island, named Publius, who welcomed us
and entertained us courteously three days.
8 And it came about that the father of Publius was lying *in bed*
afflicted with *recurrent* fever and dysentery; and Paul went in *to see*
him and after he had [a]prayed, he [b]laid his hands on him and healed
him.
9 And after this had happened, the rest of the people on the island
who had diseases were coming to him and getting cured.
10 And they also honored us with many [1]marks of respect; and
when we were setting sail, they [2]supplied *us* with [3]all we needed.
11 And at the end of three months we set sail on [a]an Alexandrian
ship which had wintered at the island, and which had [1]the Twin
Brothers for its figurehead.
12 And after we put in at Syracuse, we stayed there for three days.
13 And from there we [1]sailed around and arrived at Rhegium, and
a day later a south wind sprang up, and on the second day we came
to Puteoli.
14 [1]There we found *some* [a]brethren, and were invited to stay with
them for seven days; and thus we came to Rome.
15 And the [a]brethren, when they heard about us, came from there
as far as the [1]Market of Appius and [2]Three Inns to meet us; and
when Paul saw them, he thanked God and took courage.

41 [1]Lit., *pla*

42 [a]Acts 12

43 [1]Lit., *cas* *themselves*

44 [a]Acts 27

28:1 [1]Or, *M* mss. read *M* [a][we] Acts 16 [b]Acts 27:39

2 [1]Lit., *barba* [a]Acts 28:4; R 1 Cor. 14:11; [b]Rom. 14:1

3 [1]Or, *from t*

4 [1]Lit., *barba* personificatio goddess [a]Act [b]Luke 13:2, 4

5 [a]Mark 16:1

6 [a]Acts 14:11

8 [a]Acts 9:40; 5:14f. [b]Matt. 9 5:23; 6:5

10 [1]Lit., *hono* *put on board* *things pertaini* *needs*

11 [1]Gr., the Di i.e., Castor and twin sons of Ze 27:6

13 [1]Some earl read *weighed a*

14 [1]Lit., *where* 21:23; Acts 1:1 9:30; Rom. 1:1

15 [1]Lat., *Appii* station about 4 from Rome [2]La *Tabernae*, a sta about 33 miles Rome [a]Acts 1:1 10:23; 11:1, 12, 12:17

16 And when we entered Rome, Paul was [a]allowed to stay by him-
self, with the soldier who was guarding him.
17 And it happened that after three days he called together those
who were [a]the leading men of the Jews, and when they had come
together, he *began* saying to them, "[b]Brethren, [c]though I had done
nothing against our people, or [d]the customs of our [1]fathers, yet I was
delivered prisoner from Jerusalem into the hands of the Romans.
18 "And when they had [a]examined me, they [b]were willing to release
me because there was [c]no ground [1]for putting me to death.
19 "But when the Jews [1]objected, I was forced to [a]appeal to Caesar;
not that I had any accusation against my nation.
20 "For this reason therefore, I [1]requested to see you and to speak
with you, for I am wearing [a]this chain for [b]the sake of the hope of
Israel."
21 And they said to him, "We have neither received letters from
Judea concerning you, nor have any of [a]the brethren come here and
reported or spoken anything bad about you.
22 "But we desire to hear from you what [1]your views are; for con-
cerning this [a]sect, it is known to us that [b]it is spoken against
everywhere."
23 And when they had set a day for him, they came to him at [a]his
lodging in large numbers; and he was explaining to them by solemn-
ly [b]testifying about the kingdom of God, and trying to persuade
them concerning Jesus, [c]from both the Law of Moses and from the
Prophets, from morning until evening.
24 And [a]some were being persuaded by the things spoken, but
others would not believe.
25 And when they did not agree with one another, they *began* leav-
ing after Paul had spoken one *parting* word, "The Holy Spirit rightly
spoke through Isaiah the prophet to your fathers,
26 saying,
'[a]GO TO THIS PEOPLE AND SAY,
"[1b]YOU WILL KEEP ON HEARING, [2]BUT WILL NOT UNDERSTAND;
AND [3]YOU WILL KEEP ON SEEING, BUT WILL NOT PERCEIVE;
27 [a]FOR THE HEART OF THIS PEOPLE HAS BECOME DULL,
AND WITH THEIR EARS THEY SCARCELY HEAR,
AND THEY HAVE CLOSED THEIR EYES;
LEST THEY SHOULD SEE WITH THEIR EYES,
AND HEAR WITH THEIR EARS,
AND UNDERSTAND WITH THEIR HEART AND RETURN,
AND I SHOULD HEAL THEM." '
28 "Let it be known to you therefore, that [a]this salvation of God has
been sent [b]to the Gentiles; they will also listen."
29 [[1]And when he had spoken these words, the Jews departed,
having a great dispute among themselves.]
30 And he stayed two full years [1]in his own rented quarters, and
was welcoming all who came to him,
31 [1a]preaching the kingdom of God, and teaching concerning the
Lord Jesus Christ [b]with all openness, unhindered.

[a]Acts 24:23
forefathers 25:2 [b]Acts 25:8 [c]Acts 6:14
death in me 22:24 [b]Acts [c]Acts 23:29; 25:25; 26:31
oke against 5:11, 21, 25; 26:32
vited you to d speak with 21:33 [b]Acts 26:6f.
s 3:17; 22:5; 4; Rom. 9:3
u think [a]Acts [b]1 Pet. 2:12; :16; 4:14, 16
m. 22 [b]Luke cts 1:3; 23:11 [c]Acts 8:35
24 [a]Acts 14:4
vith a hearing [3]Lit., *seeing ll see* [a]Is. 6:9 [b]Matt. 13:14f.
27 [a]Is. 6:10
:3; Luke 2:30; 26 [b]Acts 9:15; 13:46
ny mss. do not contain this v.
[1]Or, *at his own expense*
Or, *proclaiming* 23; Acts 20:25; 23 [b]2 Tim. 2:9

ACTS AT A GLANCE

Theme of Acts:

Author:

Date:

Purpose:

Key Words:

believe (believed)

baptized (baptism)

Spirit

witness (witnesses)

word (word of God)

saved

church

SEGMENT DIVISIONS			CHAPTER THEMES	
			1	
			2	
			3	
			4	
			5	
			6	
			7	
			8	
			9	
			10	
			11	
			12	
			13	
			14	
			15	
			16	
			17	
			18	
			19	
			20	
			21	
			22	
			23	
			24	
			25	
			26	
			27	
			28	

OMANS

e gospel Paul preached, justification by faith alone, was under siege. While many directly sed this gospel, others twisted it to suit their own preferences. The Judaizers said salvation might grace but the believer is "kept" by the law. They insisted that circumcision was necessary for ion. At the other extreme, the antinomians taught that once you were saved by grace you could ny way you wanted—even continue in sin—and be assured of eternal life.

ly a clear explanation of the gospel could refute such errors. Eager to prove the gospel's power to and sanctify both Jew and Gentile, Paul, like a wise lawyer, calls the gospel to the witness stand xamines it from every angle. The result is the book of Romans, a theological masterpiece written d A.D. 56 or 57.

IGS TO DO

Romans is the constitution of the Christian faith. If you understand Romans you'll have a plumbline for correctly interpreting any teaching on the gospel. It's a book you need to observe until you are so familiar with the text its meaning is obvious.

a. Read Romans in one sitting before you begin your study. If that's not possible, read it a chapter at a time. Every time you see the word *gospel,* mark it in a distinctive way so you can easily spot it in the text.

b. Paul gives his reasons for writing Romans in the first and the last two chapters. Record these reasons in the appropriate place on the OBSERVATIONS CHART on page 1673.

c. Watch for references to the recipients of this letter and record on the OBSERVATIONS CHART what you learn about them. Note whether Paul is writing to Gentiles, Jews, or both. Also as you read, find out as much as you can about Paul. Record your insights on the chart.

The book of Romans can be divided into four segments, each building on the previous one: chapters 1 through 5, 6 through 8, 9 through 11, and 12 through 16. Instructions for each segment follow. As you complete each one, return to these instructions so you can see what to do in the next.

pters 1-5

Read Romans 1 through 5 a chapter at a time, observing and marking the text. Complete instructions on how to observe the text are in the front of your Bible in the section, "How to Observe the Bible Chapter by Chapter" (page I-13).

a. Mark each of the following key words and their synonyms: *grace, faith, law, justified (justify, just), righteous (righteousness), wrath, judge (judgment), gospel, believe, sin, Gentiles, God, Jesus Christ*, and *Spirit.*

b. List these words on a card to use as a bookmark when you study Romans. As you come to each new segment of Romans, add the next group of key words to your card. Mark or color code them on the card in the same way you plan to mark them in your Bible.

c. Each chapter has key words or phrases which are unique to that chapter. Mark the following:

   1) In chapter 1 mark *exchanged the* and *God gave them over.* Note the progression of events as you observe what the people did and how God responded.

   2) In chapter 4 mark and observe *reckoned.*

   3) In chapter 5 mark and observe *gift.*

   4) Mark any other key words that are pertinent to a chapter or to the book.

2. List in the margin what you learn from the text about each key word. For example, *sin* is word. What do you learn from the text about *sin*? About *wrath*? About *righteousness*? And sc
3. From chapters 3 through 11 of Romans, Paul periodically asks an important question an answers it. Mark each of Paul's questions. You might put a cloud like this a each and then color each the same throughout the book. Carefully read each question an how Paul answers it.
4. Watch for the word *therefore* and see what it's "there for." Several chapters have it in th verse. When Paul uses *therefore* he is making a point you won't want to miss.
5. When you finish observing each chapter, record the theme of that chapter in the text next chapter number and on the ROMANS AT A GLANCE chart on page 1674.
6. What do you see as the theme in this first segment of Romans? Write it (in pencil) on ROM AT A GLANCE in the first space under "Segment Divisions."

Chapters 6-8

1. Follow the same procedure as you did in the previous segment. Continue to mark the key you marked in chapters 1 through 5, and in these chapters also mark the following word their synonyms: *flesh, dead, died, death, life, reign, master, slave,* and *freed from sin.*
2. If it's significant, list in the margin what you learn from marking the prominent key words segment of Romans.
3. Don't forget to mark Paul's questions. Then observe how he answers each one.
4. Record the theme of each chapter and of this segment as you did before.
5. On the OBSERVATIONS CHART on page 1673 is a place to record everything you learn chapters 5 through 8 regarding our position in Adam (before we were saved) and our posit Christ (after we were saved). Don't read anything into the text, but simply record what you

Chapters 9-11

1. Follow the same pattern you used in the first segment and mark the same key words you m in chapters 1 through 8. Also mark the following key words in this segment of Romans: *forek predestined**, *choice (chosen), Israel* (and its pronouns), *unbelief, saved, salvation* (go back and m in Romans 1:16), and *mercy.*

   *These words also are used in Romans 8:29-30. Go back and mark them, and in the margin what you learn from the text.
2. In this section it is critical that you follow Paul's reasoning by marking each question and noting *how* Paul answers each question. Don't read into the text meanings that aren't ther God speak as you listen. Meditate on Romans 11:33-36.
3. Note chapter and segment themes as before.

Chapters 12-16

1. At this point, Paul makes a transition and changes from explaining the doctrinal aspect o gospel to describing how to live it out practically. As Paul turns from doctrine to duty, not *therefore* and how it would relate to what has been written in the first eleven chapters of Ron Think about what Paul is asking you to do. Is it reasonable? Why? What do you need to do?
2. Read Romans chapters 12 through 16 and identify the main topic or subject of each chapter. the following key words: *love, authority (rulers), brethren (brother), Lord, Gentiles, minister (se serving, servant), judge (judgment), weak (weaknesses), worker,* and *worked.*
3. Complete ROMANS AT A GLANCE. Fill in the chapter and segment themes and then recor theme of Romans. (Don't forget to record your chapter themes in the text, too.)

THINGS TO THINK ABOUT

1. Suppose someone accused you of not being a Christian. What proof could you give of the that you are a true child of God?

Do you know how to share the gospel with someone? How?

From your study of Romans, how is a person saved?

How will your relationships to those in authority over you and to those who are your brothers and sisters in the faith change as you apply the truth of Romans to your life?

Are you ready to defend the gospel? Can you refute modern-day Judaizers and/or antinomians?

Chapter 1

1 Paul, a bond-servant of Christ Jesus, [1a]called *as* an apostle, [b]set
apart for [c]the gospel of God,
2 which He [a]promised beforehand through His [b]prophets in the
holy Scriptures,
3 concerning His Son, who was born [a]of a [1]descendant of David
[b]according to the flesh,
4 who was declared [a]the Son of God with power [1]by the resurrec-
tion from the dead, according to the [2]Spirit of holiness, Jesus Christ
our Lord,
5 through whom we have received grace and [a]apostleship [1]to
bring about *the* [b]obedience of faith among [c]all the Gentiles, for His
name's sake,
6 among whom you also are the [a]called of Jesus Christ;
7 to all who are [a]beloved of God in Rome, called *as* [1b]saints: [c]Grace
to you and peace from God our Father and the Lord Jesus Christ.
8 First, [a]I thank my God through Jesus Christ for you all, because
[b]your faith is being proclaimed throughout the whole world.
9 For [a]God, whom I [b]serve in my spirit in the *preaching of the* gospel
of His Son, is my witness *as to* how unceasingly [c]I make mention of
you,
10 always in my prayers making request, if perhaps now at last by
[a]the will of God I may succeed in coming to you.
11 For [a]I long to see you in order that I may impart some spiritual
gift to you, that you may be established;
12 that is, that I may be encouraged together with you *while* among
you, each of us by the other's faith, both yours and mine.
13 And [a]I do not want you to be unaware, [b]brethren, that often I
[c]have planned to come to you (and have been prevented thus far) in
order that I might obtain some [d]fruit among you also, even as among
the rest of the Gentiles.
14 [a]I am [1]under obligation both to Greeks and to [b]barbarians, both
to the wise and to the foolish.
15 Thus, for my part, I am eager to [a]preach the gospel to you also
who are in Rome.
16 For I am not [a]ashamed of the gospel, for [b]it is the power of God
for salvation to everyone who believes, to the [c]Jew first and also to
[d]the Greek.
17 For in it [a]*the* righteousness of God is revealed [1]from faith to faith;
as it is written, "[2b]BUT THE RIGHTEOUS *man* SHALL LIVE BY FAITH."
18 For [a]the wrath of God is revealed from heaven against all ungod-
liness and unrighteousness of men, who [b]suppress the truth [1]in un-
righteousness,
19 because [a]that which is known about God is evident [1]within
them; for God made it evident to them.
20 For [a]since the creation of the world His invisible attributes, His

1:1 [1]Lit., *a called* [a]1 Cor. 1:1; 9:1; . 1:1 [b]Acts 9:15; Gal. 1:15 [c]Mark 1:14; Rom. 15:16
[a]Titus 1:2 [b]Luke Rom. 3:21; 16:26
, seed [a]Matt. 1:1 1:14; Rom. 4:1; 3, 5; 1 Cor. 10:18
Or, *as a result of* *, spirit* [a]Matt. 4:3
it., *for obedience* ts 1:25; Gal. 1:16 6:7; Rom. 16:26 [c]Acts 9:15
de 1; Rev. 17:14
holy ones [a]Rom. 8:39 [b]Acts 9:13; :28ff.; 1 Cor. 1:2, m. 6:25f.; 1 Cor. Cor. 1:2; Gal. 1:3; :2; Phil. 1:2; Col. :2; 1 Thess. 1:1; 2 Thess. 1:2
[a]1 Cor. 1:4; Eph. .; Phil. 1:3f.; Col. Thess. 1:2; 2:13 3:22; Rom. 16:19
[a]Rom. 9:1 [b]Acts 2 Tim. 1:3 [c]Eph. 1:16; Phil. 1:3f.
Acts 18:21; Rom. 15:32
Acts 19:21; Rom. 15:23
om. 11:25; 1 Cor. 12:1; 2 Cor. 1:8; hess. 4:13 [b]Acts Rom. 7:1; 1 Cor.); 14:20, 26; Gal. Acts 19:21; Rom. :22f. [d]John 4:36; 6; Phil. 1:22; Col. 1:6
t., *debtor* [a]1 Cor. 9:16 [b]Acts 28:2
15 [a]Rom. 15:20
Mark 8:38; 2 Tim. 16 [b]1 Cor. 1:18, [c]Acts 3:26; Rom. 2:9 [d]John 7:35
r., *by* [2]Or, *But he righteous by faith live.* [a]Rom. 3:21;); Phil. 3:9 [b]Hab. ; Gal. 3:11; Heb. 10:38
Or, *by* [a]Rom. 5:9; Eph. 5:6; Col. 3:6 [b]2 Thess. 2:6f.
Or, *among* [a]Acts 14:17; 17:24ff.
20 [a]Mark 10:6

eternal power and divine nature, have been clearly seen, [b]being un-
derstood through what has been made, so that they are without
excuse.
21 For even though they knew God, they did not [1]honor Him as
God, or give thanks; but they became [a]futile in their speculations,
and their foolish heart was darkened.
22 [a]Professing to be wise, they became fools,
23 and [a]exchanged the glory of the incorruptible God for an image
in the form of corruptible man and of birds and four-footed animals
and [1]crawling creatures.
24 Therefore [a]God gave them over in the lusts of their hearts to
impurity, that their bodies might be [b]dishonored among them.
25 For they exchanged the truth of God for [1]a [a]lie, and worshiped
and served the creature rather than the Creator, [b]who is blessed
[2]forever. Amen.
26 For this reason [a]God gave them over to [b]degrading passions; for
their women exchanged the natural function for that which is [1]un-
natural,
27 and in the same way also the men abandoned the natural func-
tion of the woman and burned in their desire toward one another,
[a]men with men committing [1]indecent acts and receiving in [2]their
own persons the due penalty of their error.
28 And just as they did not see fit [1]to acknowledge God any longer,
[a]God gave them over to a depraved mind, to do those things which
are not proper,
29 being filled with all unrighteousness, wickedness, greed, evil;
full of envy, murder, strife, deceit, malice; *they are* [a]gossips,
30 slanderers, [1a]haters of God, insolent, arrogant, boastful, inventors
of evil, [b]disobedient to parents,
31 without understanding, untrustworthy, [a]unloving, unmerciful;
32 and, although they know the ordinance of God, that those who
practice such things are worthy of [a]death, they not only do the same,
but also [b]give hearty approval to those who practice them.

Chapter 2

2 Therefore you are [a]without excuse, [b]every man *of you* who passes
judgment, for in that [c]you judge another, you condemn yourself;
for you who judge practice the same things.
2 And we know that the judgment of God [1]rightly falls upon those
who practice such things.
3 And do you suppose this, [a]O man, [1]when you pass judgment
upon those who practice such things and do the same *yourself*, that
you will escape the judgment of God?
4 Or do you think lightly of [a]the riches of His [b]kindness and [c]for-
bearance and [d]patience, not knowing that the kindness of God leads
you to repentance?
5 But [1]because of your stubbornness and unrepentant heart [a]you
are storing up wrath for yourself [b]in the day of wrath and revelation
of the righteous judgment of God,
6 [a]who WILL RENDER TO EVERY MAN ACCORDING TO HIS DEEDS:
7 to those who by [a]perseverance in doing good seek for [b]glory and
honor and [c]immortality, [d]eternal life;
8 but to those who are [a]selfishly ambitious and [b]do not obey the
truth, but obey unrighteousness, wrath and indignation.

20 [b]Job 12:7-9; 19:1-6; Jer. 5:21f

21 [1]Lit., *glorify* [a]17:15; Jer. 2:5; E 4:17f.

22 [a]Jer. 10:14; 1 1:20

23 [1]Or possibly, *reptiles* [a]Deut. 4 Ps. 106:20; Jer. 2 Acts 17:29

24 [a]Rom. 1:26, 2 Eph. 4:19 [b]Eph.

25 [1]Lit., *the lie* [2]*unto the ages* [a]Is 44:20; Jer. 10:14 16:19 [b]Rom. 9:5 11:31

26 [1]Lit., *against* [a]Rom. 1:24 [b]1 Th 4:5

27 [1]Lit., *the shar deed* [2]Lit., *thems* [a]Lev. 18:22; 20:1 1 Cor. 6:9

28 [1]Lit., *to have knowledge* [a]Ror

29 [a]2 Cor. 12:20

30 [1]Or, *hateful t* [a]Ps. 5:5 [b]2 Tim.

31 [a]2 Tim. 3:3

32 [a]Rom. 6:21 11:48; Acts 8:1; 2

2:1 [a]Rom. 1:20 12:14; Rom. 2:3; [c]2 Sam. 12:5-7; 7:1; Luke 6:37; R 14:22

2 [1]Lit., *is accord truth against*

3 [1]Lit., *who pass judgment* [a]Luke Rom. 2:1; 9:20

4 [a]Rom. 9:23; 11 2 Cor. 8:2; Eph. 2:7; Phil. 4:19; C 1:27; 2:2; Titus 3 [b]Rom. 11:22 [c]Ro 3:25 [d]Ex. 34:6; F 9:22; 1 Tim. 1:16 3:20; 2 Pet. 3:9,

5 [1]Or, *in accorda with* [a]Deut. 32:3 Prov. 1:18 [b]Ps. 1 2 Cor. 5:10; 2 Th 1:5; Jude 6

6 [a]Ps. 62:12; Pr 24:12; Matt. 16:2

7 [a]Luke 8:15; He 10:36 [b]Rom. 2:1 2:7; 1 Pet. 1:7 [c]1 15:42, 50, 53f.; E 6:24; 2 Tim. 1:10 25:46

8 [a]2 Cor. 12:20; 5:20; Phil. 1:17; 2 James 3:14, 16 [b]2 Thess. 2:12

9 *There will be* [a]tribulation and distress [1]for every soul of man who
does evil, of the Jew [b]first and also of the Greek,
10 but [a]glory and honor and peace to every man who does good, to
the Jew [b]first and also to the Greek.
11 For [a]there is no partiality with God.
12 For all who have sinned [1a]without the Law will also perish
[1]without the Law; and all who have sinned [2]under the Law will be
judged [3]by the Law;
13 for [a]not the hearers [1]of the Law are [2]just before God, but the
doers [1]of the Law will be justified.
14 For when Gentiles who do not have [1]the Law do [2a]instinctively
the things of the Law, these, not having [1]the Law, are a law to them-
selves,
15 in that they show [a]the work of the Law written in their hearts,
their conscience bearing witness, and their thoughts alternately ac-
cusing or else defending them,
16 on the day when, [a]according to my gospel, [b]God will judge the
secrets of men through Christ Jesus.
17 But if you bear the name "Jew," and [a]rely [1]upon the Law, and
boast in God,
18 and know *His* will, and [1a]approve the things that are essential,
being instructed out of the Law,
19 and are confident that you yourself are a guide to the blind, a
light to those who are in darkness,
20 a [1]corrector of the foolish, a teacher of [2]the immature, having in
the Law [a]the embodiment of knowledge and of the truth,
21 you, therefore, [a]who teach another, do you not teach yourself?
You who [1]preach that one should not steal, do you steal?
22 You who say that one should not commit adultery, do you com-
mit adultery? You who abhor idols, do you [a]rob temples?
23 You who [a]boast [1]in the Law, through your breaking the Law, do
you dishonor God?
24 For "[a]THE NAME OF GOD IS BLASPHEMED AMONG THE GENTILES
[b]BECAUSE OF YOU," just as it is written.
25 For indeed circumcision is of value, if you [a]practice [1]the Law; but
if you are a transgressor [2]of the Law, [b]your circumcision has become
uncircumcision.
26 [a]If therefore [b]the [1]uncircumcised man [c]keeps the requirements of
the Law, will not his uncircumcision be regarded as circumcision?
27 And will not [a]he who is physically uncircumcised, if he keeps
the Law, will he not [b]judge you who [1]though having the letter *of the*
Law and circumcision are a transgressor [2]of the Law?
28 For [a]he is not a Jew who is one outwardly; neither is circum-
cision that which is outward in the flesh.
29 But [a]he is a Jew who is one inwardly; and [b]circumcision is that
which is of the heart, by the [c]Spirit, not by the letter; [d]and his praise
is not from men, but from God.

Chapter 3

3 Then what [1]advantage has the Jew? Or what is the benefit of
circumcision?
2 Great in every respect. First of all, that [a]they were entrusted with
the [b]oracles of God.

upon [a]Rom. 3:26; Rom. ; 1 Pet. 4:17
:7; Heb. 2:7; [b]Rom. 2:9
10:17; Acts 10:34
out law [2]Or, [3]*Or, by law* ; 1 Cor. 9:21
, of law [2]Or, [a]Matt. 7:21, ; John 13:17; es 1:22f., 25
law [2]Lit., *by* [a]Acts 10:35; m. 1:19; 2:15
Rom. 2:14, 27
16:25; 1 Cor. 1:11; 1 Tim. im. 2:8 [b]Acts 31; Rom. 3:6; 14:10
pon law [a]Mic. n 5:45; Rom. 2:23; 9:4
Or, distinguish een the things fer [a]Phil. 1:10
nstructor [2]Lit., *s* [a]Rom. 3:31; 2 Tim. 1:13
roclaim [a]Matt. 23:3ff.
22 [a]Acts 19:37
Or, in law [a]Mic. ohn 5:45; Rom. 2:17; 9:4
Is. 52:5; Ezek. 20ff. [b]2 Pet. 2:2
law [2]*Or, of law* 2:13f., 27 [b]Jer. 4:4; 9:25f.
uncircumcision Cor. 7:19 [b]Rom. ph. 2:11 [c]Rom. 2:25, 27; 8:4
Lit., *through the* Or, *of law* [a]Rom. Eph. 2:11 [b]Matt. 12:41
John 8:39; Rom. 7; 9:6; Gal. 6:15
hil. 3:3; Col. 2:11 0:6 [c]Rom. 2:27; 2 Cor. 3:6 [d]John 2:43; 1 Cor. 4:5; 2 Cor. 10:18
3:1 [1]Lit., *is the antage of the Jew*
2 [a]Deut. 4:8; Ps. ; Rom. 9:4 [b]Acts 7:38

3 What then? If [a]some [1]did not believe, their [2]unbelief will not
nullify the faithfulness of God, will it?
4 [a]May it never be! Rather, let God be found true, though every
man *be found* [b]a liar, as it is written,

"[c]THAT THOU MIGHTEST BE JUSTIFIED IN THY WORDS,
AND MIGHTEST PREVAIL WHEN THOU [1]ART JUDGED."

5 But if our unrighteousness [1a]demonstrates the righteousness of
God, [b]what shall we say? The God who inflicts wrath is not un-
righteous, is He? ([c]I am speaking in human terms.)
6 [a]May it never be! For otherwise how will [b]God judge the world?
7 But if through my lie [a]the truth of God abounded to His glory,
[b]why am I also still being judged as a sinner?
8 And why not *say* (as we are slanderously reported and as some
affirm that we say), "[a]Let us do evil that good may come"? [1]Their
condemnation is just.
9 What then? [1a]Are we better than they? Not at all; for we have
already charged that both [b]Jews and [c]Greeks are [d]all under sin;
10 as it is written,

"[a]THERE IS NONE RIGHTEOUS, NOT EVEN ONE;
11 THERE IS NONE WHO UNDERSTANDS,
THERE IS NONE WHO SEEKS FOR GOD;
12 ALL HAVE TURNED ASIDE, TOGETHER THEY HAVE BECOME USELESS;
THERE IS NONE WHO DOES GOOD,
THERE IS NOT EVEN ONE."
13 "[a]THEIR THROAT IS AN OPEN GRAVE,
WITH THEIR TONGUES THEY KEEP DECEIVING,"
"[b]THE POISON OF ASPS IS UNDER THEIR LIPS";
14 "[a]WHOSE MOUTH IS FULL OF CURSING AND BITTERNESS";
15 "[a]THEIR FEET ARE SWIFT TO SHED BLOOD,
16 DESTRUCTION AND MISERY ARE IN THEIR PATHS,
17 AND THE PATH OF PEACE HAVE THEY NOT KNOWN."
18 "[a]THERE IS NO FEAR OF GOD BEFORE THEIR EYES."

19 Now we know that whatever the [a]Law says, it speaks to [b]those
who are [1]under the Law, that every mouth may be closed, and [c]all
the world may become accountable to God;
20 because [a]by the works [1]of the Law no flesh will be justified in
His sight; for [2b]through the Law *comes* the knowledge of sin.
21 But now apart [1]from the Law [a]*the* righteousness of God has been
manifested, being [b]witnessed by the Law and the Prophets,
22 even *the* [a]righteousness of God through [b]faith [c]in Jesus Christ for
[d]all those who believe; for [e]there is no distinction;
23 for [1]all [a]have sinned and fall short of the glory of God,
24 being justified as a gift [a]by His grace through [b]the redemption
which is in Christ Jesus;
25 whom God displayed publicly as [a]a [1]propitiation [2b]in His blood
through faith. *This was* to demonstrate His righteousness, [3]because in
the [c]forbearance of God He [d]passed over the sins previously com-
mitted;
26 for the demonstration, *I say*, of His righteousness at the present
time, that He might be just and the justifier of the one who [1]has faith
in Jesus.
27 Where then is [a]boasting? It is excluded. By [b]what kind of law? Of
works? No, but by a law of faith.

3 [1]Or, *were* [2]Or, *unfaith* [a]Rom. 10:1

4 [1]Or, *dost judgment* [a] Rom. 3:6, 3 116:11; Rom 51:4

5 [1]Or, *comm* [a]Rom. 5:8; 2 7:11 [b]Rom. 8:31; 9:14, 3 6:19; 1 Cor. Gal. 3:15

6 [a]Luke 20: 3:4, 31 [b]Ror

7 [a]Rom. 3:4

8 [1]Lit., *Whos* 6:1

9 [1]Or possib *worse* [a]Rom [b]Rom. 2:1-29 1:18-32 [d]Ro 11:32; Gal. 3.

10 [a]Ps. 14:1-

13 [a]Ps. 5:9

14 [a]Ps. 10:7

15 [a]Is. 59:7f.

18 [a]Ps. 36:1

19 [1]Lit., *in* [a]J [b]Rom. 2:12 [c]

20 [1]Or, *of law through law* [a] Acts 13:39; Ga [b]Rom. 4:15; 5

21 [1]Or, *from la* 1:17; 9:30 [b]Ac Rom. 1:2

22 [a]Rom. 1:17 [b]Rom. 4:5 [c]Ac Gal. 2:16, 20; 3 3:12 [d]Rom. 4: 10:4 [e]Rom. 10 3:28; Col. 3:11

23 [1]Or, *all sinn* [a]Rom. 3:9

24 [a]Rom. 4:4f., Eph. 2:8 [b]1 Co Eph. 1:7; Col. 1 Heb. 9:15

25 [1]Or, *a propi sacrifice* [2]Or, *b because of the over of the sins previously comr the forbearance* [a]1 John 2:2; 4:1 [b]1 Cor. 5:7; Heb 28; 1 Pet. 1:19; 1:5 [c]Rom. 2:4 [d] 14:16; 17:30

26 [1]Lit., *is of the Jesus.*

27 [a]Rom. 2:17, 1 Cor. 1:29ff. [b]R 9:31

28 [1]For [a]we maintain that a man is justified by faith apart from
works [2]of the Law.
29 Or [a]is God *the God* of Jews only? Is He not *the God* of Gentiles
also? Yes, of Gentiles also,
30 since indeed [a]God [b]who will justify the [1]circumcised [2]by faith
and the [3]uncircumcised through faith [c]is one.
31 Do we then nullify [1]the Law through faith? [a]May it never be! On
the contrary, we [b]establish the Law.

Chapter 4

4 What then shall we say that Abraham, [1]our forefather [a]according
to the flesh, has found?
2 For if Abraham was justified by works, he has something to
boast about; but [a]not [1]before God.
3 For what does the Scripture say? "[a]AND ABRAHAM BELIEVED GOD,
AND IT WAS RECKONED TO HIM AS RIGHTEOUSNESS."
4 Now to the one who [a]works, his wage is not reckoned as a favor,
but as what is due.
5 But to the one who does not work, but [a]believes in Him who
justifies the ungodly, his faith is reckoned as righteousness,
6 just as David also speaks of the blessing upon the man to whom
God reckons righteousness apart from works:
7 "[a]BLESSED ARE THOSE WHOSE LAWLESS DEEDS HAVE BEEN FORGIVEN,
AND WHOSE SINS HAVE BEEN COVERED.
8 "[a]BLESSED IS THE MAN WHOSE SIN THE LORD WILL NOT [1b]TAKE INTO
ACCOUNT."
9 Is this blessing then upon [1a]the circumcised, or upon [2]the uncir-
cumcised also? For [b]we say, "[c]FAITH WAS RECKONED TO ABRAHAM AS
RIGHTEOUSNESS."
10 How then was it reckoned? While he was [1]circumcised, or [2]un-
circumcised? Not while [1]circumcised, but while [2]uncircumcised;
11 and he [a]received the sign of circumcision, [b]a seal of the right-
eousness of the faith which [1]he had while uncircumcised, that he
might be [c]the father of [d]all who believe without being circumcised,
that righteousness might be reckoned to them,
12 and the father of circumcision to those who not only are of the
circumcision, but who also follow in the steps of the faith of our
father Abraham which [1]he had while uncircumcised.
13 For [a]the promise to Abraham or to his [1]descendants [b]that he
would be heir of the world was not [2]through the Law, but through
the righteousness of faith.
14 For [a]if those who are [1]of the Law are heirs, faith is made void
and the promise is nullified;
15 for [a]the Law brings about wrath, but [b]where there is no law,
neither is there violation.
16 For this reason *it is* [1]by faith, that *it might be* in accordance with
[a]grace, in order that the promise may be certain to [b]all the [2]descend-
ants, not only to [3]those who are of the Law, but also to [3c]those who
are of the faith of Abraham, who is [d]the father of us all,
17 (as it is written, "[a]A FATHER OF MANY NATIONS HAVE I MADE YOU") in
the sight of Him whom he believed, *even* God, [b]who gives life to the
dead and [1c]calls into being [d]that which does not exist.
18 In hope against hope he believed, in order that he might become

[a]a father of many nations, according to that which had been spoken,
"[b]SO SHALL YOUR [1]DESCENDANTS BE."
19 And without becoming weak in faith he contemplated his own
body, now [a]as good as dead since [b]he was about a hundred years old,
and [c]the deadness of Sarah's womb;
20 yet, with respect to the promise of God, he did not waver in
unbelief, but grew strong in faith, [a]giving glory to God,
21 and [a]being fully assured that [b]what He had promised, He was
able also to perform.
22 Therefore also [a]IT WAS RECKONED TO HIM AS RIGHTEOUSNESS.
23 Now [a]not for his sake only was it written, that it was reckoned to
him,
24 but for our sake also, to whom it will be reckoned, as those [a]who
believe in Him who [b]raised Jesus our Lord from the dead,
25 *He* who was [a]delivered up because of our transgressions, and
was [b]raised because of our justification.

Chapter 5

5 [a]Therefore having been justified by faith, [1b]we have peace with
God through our Lord Jesus Christ,
2 through whom also we have [a]obtained our introduction by faith
into this grace [b]in which we stand; and [1]we exult in hope of the glory
of God.
3 [a]And not only this, but [1]we also [b]exult in our tribulations, know-
ing that tribulation brings about [c]perseverance;
4 and [a]perseverance, [b]proven character; and proven character,
hope;
5 and hope [a]does not disappoint, because the love of God has been
[b]poured out within our hearts through the Holy Spirit who was
given to us.
6 For while we were still [a]helpless, [b]at the right time [c]Christ died
for the ungodly.
7 For one will hardly die for a righteous man; though perhaps for
the good man someone would dare even to die.
8 But God [a]demonstrates [b]His own love toward us, in that while
we were yet sinners, [c]Christ died for us.
9 Much more then, having now been justified [1a]by His blood, we
shall be saved [b]from the wrath *of God* through Him.
10 For if while we were [a]enemies, we were reconciled to God
through the death of His Son, much more, having been reconciled,
we shall be saved [1b]by His life.
11 [a]And not only this, [1]but we also exult in God through our Lord
Jesus Christ, through whom we have now received [b]the reconcilia-
tion.
12 Therefore, just as through [a]one man sin entered into the world,
and [b]death through sin, and [c]so death spread to all men, because all
sinned—
13 for [1]until the Law sin was in the world; but [a]sin is not imputed
when there is no law.
14 Nevertheless death reigned from Adam until Moses, even over
those who had not sinned [a]in the likeness of the offense of Adam,
who is a [1b]type of Him who was to come.
15 But [1]the free gift is not like the transgression. For if by the trans-
gression of [a]the one [b]the many died, much more did the grace of God

18 [1]Lit., se
4:17 [b]Gen
19 [a]Heb. 1
17:17 [c]Ge
20 [a]Matt. 9
21 [a]Rom.
18:14; Heb.
22 [a]Gen. 1
23 [a]Rom. 1
9:9f.; 10:11;
24 [a]Rom. 1
1:21 [b]Acts 2
25 [a]Is. 53:4
5:6, 8; 8:32;
Eph. 5:2 [b]R
1 Cor. 15:17
5:1 [1]Some
mss. read *le*
[a]Rom. 3:28
2 [1]Or, *let us*
2:18; 3:12; H
1 Pet. 3:18
3 [1]Or, *let us*
[a]Rom. 5:11;
2 Cor. 8:19
James 1:2f.
4 [a]Luke 21:1
2:22; James
5 [a]Ps. 119:11
9:33; Heb. 6:
2:33; 10:45; (
Titus 3:6
6 [a]Rom. 5:8,
4:4 [c]Rom. 4:2
8:32; Gal. 2:2
8 [a]Rom. 3:5
3:16; 15:13; F
[c]Rom. 4:25; 5
Gal. 2:20; Eph
9 [1]Or, *in* [a]Ro
[b]Rom. 1:18; 1
1:10
10 [1]Or, *in* [a]R
2 Cor. 5:18f.; E
Col. 1:21f. [b]R
Heb. 7:25; 1 J
11 [1]Lit., *but al*
exulting [a]Rom
8:23; 9:10; 2 C
[b]Rom. 5:10; 11
2 Cor. 5:18f.
12 [a]Gen. 2:17;
Rom. 5:15-17;
15:21f. [b]Rom.
1 Cor. 15:56; Ja
1:15 [c]Rom. 5:1
21; 1 Cor. 15:22
13 [1]Or, *until la*
4:15
14 [1]Or, *foresha*
[a]Hos. 6:7 [b]1 Co
15 [1]Lit., *not as*
trespass, so als
free gift [a]Rom.
19 [b]Rom. 5:19

and the gift by [c]the grace of the one Man, Jesus Christ, abound to the
many.
16 And the gift is not like *that which came* through the one who
sinned; for on the one hand [a]the judgment *arose* from one *transgres-
sion* [1]resulting in condemnation, but on the other hand the free gift
arose from many transgressions [2]resulting in justification.
17 For if by the transgression of the one, death reigned [a]through the
one, much more those who receive the abundance of grace and of
the gift of righteousness will [b]reign in life through the One, Jesus
Christ.
18 So then as through [a]one transgression [1]there resulted condemna-
tion to all men, even so through one [b]act of righteousness [2]there
resulted [c]justification of life to all men.
19 For as through the one man's disobedience [a]the many [b]were
made sinners, even so through [c]the obedience of the One [a]the many
will be made righteous.
20 And [1a]the Law came in that the transgression might increase; but
where sin increased, [b]grace abounded all the more,
21 that, as [a]sin reigned in death, even so [b]grace might reign through
righteousness to eternal life through Jesus Christ our Lord.

Chapter 6

6 [a]What shall we say then? Are we to [b]continue in sin that grace
might increase?
2 [a]May it never be! How shall we who [b]died to sin still live in it?
3 Or do you not know that all of us who have been [a]baptized into
[b]Christ Jesus have been baptized into His death?
4 Therefore we have been [a]buried with Him through baptism into
death, in order that as Christ was [b]raised from the dead through the
[c]glory of the Father, so we too might walk in [d]newness of life.
5 For [a]if we have become [1]united with *Him* in the likeness of His
death, certainly we shall be also [2]*in the likeness* of His resurrection,
6 knowing this, that our [a]old [1]self was [b]crucified with *Him*, that our
[c]body of sin might be [2]done away with, that we should no longer be
slaves to sin;
7 for [a]he who has died is [1]freed from sin.
8 Now [a]if we have died with Christ, we believe that we shall also
live with Him,
9 knowing that Christ, having been [a]raised from the dead, is never
to die again; [b]death no longer is master over Him.
10 For the death that He died, He died to sin, once for all; but the
life that He lives, He lives to God.
11 Even so consider yourselves to be [a]dead to sin, but alive to God
in Christ Jesus.
12 Therefore do not let sin [a]reign in your mortal body that you
should obey its lusts,
13 and do not go on [a]presenting [1]the members of your body to sin
as [2]instruments of unrighteousness; but [b]present yourselves to God
as those alive from the dead, and your members *as* [2]instruments of
righteousness to God.
14 For [a]sin shall not [b]be master over you, for [c]you are not under law,
but [d]under grace.
15 What then? [a]Shall we sin because we are not under law but
under grace? [b]May it never be!

Acts 15:11
16 [1]Lit., *to*
on [2]Lit., *to*
teousness
Cor. 11:32
7; 3:6, 19;
12, 15, 16;
1f. [b]2 Tim.
; Rev. 22:5
18 [1]Lit., *to*
ion [2]Lit., *to*
Rom. 5:12,
3:25 [c]Rom.
4:25
m. 5:15, 18
11:32 [c]Phil.
2:8
law [a]Rom.
.; Gal. 3:19
1 Tim. 1:14
om. 5:12, 14
; Rom. 6:23
. 3:5 [b]Rom.
3:8; 6:15
20:16; Rom.
6:11; 7:4, 6;
ol. 2:20; 3:3;
1 Pet. 2:24
28:19 [b]Acts
6; 19:5; Gal.
3:27
2 [b]Acts 2:24;
[c]John 11:40;
4 [d]Rom. 7:6;
7; Gal. 6:15;
23f.; Col. 3:10
nited with the
ess [2]Or, *with*
0; Phil. 3:10f.;
Col. 2:12; 3:1
an [2]Or, *made*
s [a]Eph. 4:22;
:9 [b]Gal. 2:20;
4 [c]Rom. 7:24
quitted [a]1 Pet.
4:1
m. 6:4; 2 Cor.
0; 2 Tim. 2:11
2:24; Rom. 6:4
[b]Rev. 1:18
om. 6:2; 7:4, 6;
Col. 2:20; 3:3;
1 Pet. 2:24
12 [a]Rom. 6:14
your members
[2]Or, *weapons*
1. 6:16, 19; 7:5;
:5 [b]Rom. 12:1;
4f.; 1 Pet. 2:24
[a]Rom. 8:2, 12
12 [c]Rom. 5:18;
ial. 4:21 [d]Rom.
5:17, 21
Rom. 6:1 [b]Luke
20:16; Rom. 6:2

16 Do you not [a]know that when you present yourselves to someone
as [b]slaves for obedience, you are slaves of the one whom you obey,
either of [c]sin [1]resulting in death, or of obedience [2]resulting in right-
eousness?
17 But [a]thanks be to God that [1]though you were slaves of sin, you
became obedient from the heart to that [b]form of teaching to which
you were committed,
18 and having been [a]freed from sin, you became slaves of right-
eousness.
19 [a]I am speaking in human terms because of the weakness of your
flesh. For just [b]as you presented your members *as* slaves to impurity
and to lawlessness, [1]resulting in *further* lawlessness, so now present
your members *as* slaves to righteousness, [2]resulting in sanctification.
20 For [a]when you were slaves of sin, you were free in regard to
righteousness.
21 Therefore what [1a]benefit were you then [2]deriving [3]from the
things of which you are now ashamed? For the outcome of those
things is [b]death.
22 But now having been [a]freed from sin and [b]enslaved to God, you
[1]derive your [2c]benefit, [3]resulting in sanctification, and [d]the outcome,
eternal life.
23 For the wages of [a]sin is death, but the free gift of God is [b]eternal
life in Christ Jesus our Lord.

Chapter 7

7 Or do you not know, [a]brethren (for I am speaking to those who
know the law), that the law has jurisdiction over a person as
long as he lives?
2 For [a]the married woman is bound by law to her husband while
he is living; but if her husband dies, she is released from the law
concerning the husband.
3 So then if, while her husband is living, she is joined to another
man, she shall be called an adulteress; but if her husband dies, she is
free from the law, so that she is not an adulteress, though she is
joined to another man.
4 Therefore, my brethren, you also were [a]made to die [b]to the Law
[c]through the body of Christ, that you might be joined to another, to
Him who was raised from the dead, that we might bear fruit for
God.
5 For while we were [a]in the flesh, the sinful passions, which were
[b]*aroused* by the Law, were at work [c]in [1]the members of our body to
bear fruit for death.
6 But now we have been [a]released from the Law, having [b]died to
that by which we were bound, so that we serve in [c]newness of [d]the
[1]Spirit and not in oldness of the letter.
7 [a]What shall we say then? Is the Law sin? [b]May it never be! On
the contrary, [c]I would not have come to know sin except [1]through the
Law; for I would not have known about [2]coveting if the Law had not
said, "[d]YOU SHALL NOT [2]COVET."
8 But sin, [a]taking opportunity [b]through the commandment, pro-
duced in me [1]coveting of every kind; for [c]apart [2]from the Law sin *is*
dead.
9 And I was once alive apart [1]from the Law; but when the com-
mandment came, sin became alive, and I died;

16 [1]Lit., *to*
to righteou
11:2; 1 Cor.
6:2, 3, 9, 1
9:13, 24 [b]J
2 Pet. 2:19
6:21, 23

17 [1]Lit., *yo*
slaves . . . b
became [a]R
2 Cor. 2:14

18 [a]John 8:
6:22; 8:2

19 [1]Lit., *to I*
[2]Lit., *to sanc*
[a]Rom. 3:5 [b]

20 [a]Matt. 6:
6:16

21 [1]Lit., *frui*
having [3]Lit.,
12:13; Ezek.
Rom. 7:5 [b]R
5:12; 6:16, 2
Gal. 6:8

22 [1]Lit., *hav*
[3]Lit., *to sanct*
[a]John 8:32; R
8:2 [b]1 Cor. 7
2:16 [c]Rom. 7
1:9

23 [a]Rom. 1:3
6:16, 21; 8:6,
6:8 [b]Matt. 25
5:21; 8:38, 39

7:1 [a]Rom. 1:1

2 [a]1 Cor. 7:39

4 [a]Rom. 6:2;
8:2; Gal. 2:19;
[c]Col. 1:22

5 [1]Lit., *our me*
bear [a]Rom. 8:
10:3 [b]Rom. 7:
6:13, 21, 23

6 [1]Or, *spirit* [a]F
[b]Rom. 6:2 [c]Ro
[d]Rom. 2:29

7 [1]Or, *through*
lust [a]Rom. 3:5
20:16 [c]Rom. 3
5:20 [d]Ex. 20:1
5:21

8 [1]Or, *lust* [2]Or,
law [a]Rom. 7:11
3:20; 7:11 [c]1 C

9 [1]Or, *from law*

10 and this commandment, which was [1a]to result in life, proved [2]to
result in death for me;
11 for sin, [a]taking opportunity [b]through the commandment,
[c]deceived me, and through it killed me.
12 [a]So then, the Law is holy, and the commandment is holy and
righteous and good.
13 Therefore did that which is good become *a cause of* death for me?
[a]May it never be! Rather it was sin, in order that it might be shown to
be sin by effecting my death through that which is good, that
through the commandment sin might become utterly sinful.
14 For we know that the Law is [a]spiritual; but I am [a]of flesh, [b]sold
[1c]into bondage to sin.
15 For that which I am doing, [a]I do not understand; for I am not
practicing [b]what I *would* like to *do,* but I am doing the very thing I
hate.
16 But if I do the very thing I do not wish *to do,* I agree with [a]the
Law, *confessing* that it is good.
17 So now, [a]no longer am I the one doing it, but sin which in-
dwells me.
18 For I know that nothing good dwells in me, that is, in my [a]flesh;
for the wishing is present in me, but the doing of the good *is* not.
19 For [a]the good that I wish, I do not do; but I practice the very evil
that I do not wish.
20 But if I am doing the very thing I do not wish, [a]I am no longer
the one doing it, but sin which dwells in me.
21 I find then [a]the [1]principle that evil is present in me, the one who
wishes to do good.
22 For I joyfully concur with the law of God [1]in [a]the inner man,
23 but I see [a]a different law in [1]the members of my body, waging
war against the [b]law of my mind, and making me a prisoner [2]of [c]the
law of sin which is in my members.
24 Wretched man that I am! Who will set me free from [1a]the body of
this [b]death?
25 [a]Thanks be to God through Jesus Christ our Lord! So then, on the
one hand I myself with my mind am serving the law of God, but on
the other, with my flesh [b]the law of sin.

Chapter 8

8 There is therefore now no [a]condemnation for those who are [b]in
[c]Christ Jesus.
2 For [a]the law of the Spirit of life [1]in [b]Christ Jesus [c]has set [2]you free
from the law of sin and of death.
3 For [a]what the Law could not do, [1b]weak as it was through the
flesh, God *did:* sending His own Son in [c]the likeness of [2]sinful flesh
and *as an offering* for sin, He condemned sin in the flesh,
4 in order that the [a]requirement of the Law might be fulfilled in us,
who [b]do not walk according to the flesh, but according to the Spirit.
5 For those who are according to the flesh set their minds on [a]the
things of the flesh, but those who are according to the Spirit, [b]the
things of the Spirit.
6 [a]For the mind set on the flesh is [b]death, but the mind set on the
Spirit is life and peace,
7 because the mind set on the flesh is [a]hostile toward God; for it

life [2]Lit., *to*
18:5; Luke
. 10:5; Gal.
3:12
7:8 [b]Rom.
[c]Gen. 3:13
7:16; 1 Tim.
1:8
[a]Luke 20:16
., *under sin*
3:1 [b]1 Kin.
Kin. 17:17;
6:6; Gal. 4:3
[c]Rom. 3:9
5:15 [b]Rom.
9; Gal. 5:17
7:12; 1 Tim.
1:8
[a]Rom. 7:20
nn 3:6; Rom.
7:25; 8:3
[a]Rom. 7:15
[a]Rom. 7:17
., *law* [a]Rom.
7:23, 25; 8:2
r, *concerning*
6; Eph. 3:16;
1 Pet. 3:4
my members
[a]Rom. 6:19;
7; James 4:1;
1 [b]Rom. 7:25
. 7:21, 25; 8:2
Or, *this body of*
Rom. 6:6; Col.
:11 [b]Rom. 8:2
. 15:57 [b]Rom.
7:21, 23; 8:2
om. 5:16; 8:34
9f. [c]Rom. 8:2,
11, 39; 16:3
as set you free
Jesus [2]Some
mss. read *me*
. 15:45 [b]Rom.
39; 16:3 [c]John
Rom. 6:14, 18;
7:4
wherein it was
Lit., *flesh of sin*
cts 13:39; Heb.
f. [b]Rom. 7:18f.;
7:18 [c]Phil. 2:7;
. 2:14, 17; 4:15
1:6; Rom. 2:26
[b]Gal. 5:16, 25
l. 5:19-21 [b]Gal.
5:22-25
6:8 [b]Rom. 6:21;
8:13
7 [a]James 4:4

does not subject itself to the law of God, for it is not even able *to do so;*

8 and those who are [a]in the flesh cannot please God.

9 However, you are not [a]in the flesh but in the Spirit, if indeed the Spirit of God [b]dwells in you. But [c]if anyone does not have the Spirit of Christ, he does not belong to Him.

10 And [a]if Christ is in you, though the body is dead because of sin, yet the spirit is [1]alive because of righteousness.

11 But if the Spirit of Him who [a]raised Jesus from the dead dwells in you, [b]He who raised [c]Christ Jesus from the dead will also give life to your mortal bodies [1]through His Spirit who indwells you.

12 So then, brethren, we are under obligation, not to the flesh, to live according to the flesh—

13 for [a]if you are living according to the flesh, you [1]must die; but if by the Spirit you are [b]putting to death the deeds of the body, you will live.

14 For all who are [a]being led by the Spirit of God, these are [b]sons of God.

15 For you [a]have not received a spirit of slavery [1]leading to fear again, but you [b]have received [2]a spirit of adoption as sons by which we cry out, "[c]Abba! Father!"

16 The Spirit Himself [a]bears witness with our spirit that we are [b]children of God,

17 and if children, [a]heirs also, heirs of God and fellow heirs with Christ, [b]if indeed we suffer with *Him* in order that we may also be glorified with *Him*.

18 For I consider that the sufferings of this present time [a]are not worthy to be compared with the [b]glory that is to be revealed to us.

19 For the [a]anxious longing of the creation waits eagerly for [b]the revealing of the [c]sons of God.

20 For the creation [a]was subjected to [b]futility, not of its own will, but [c]because of Him who subjected it, [1]in hope

21 that [a]the creation itself also will be set free from its slavery to corruption into the freedom of the glory of the children of God.

22 For we know that the whole creation [a]groans and suffers the pains of childbirth together until now.

23 [a]And not only this, but also we ourselves, having [b]the first fruits of the Spirit, even we ourselves [c]groan within ourselves, [d]waiting eagerly for *our* adoption as sons, [e]the redemption of our body.

24 For [a]in hope we have been saved, but [b]hope that is seen is not hope; for [1]why does one also hope for what he sees?

25 But [a]if we hope for what we do not see, with perseverance we wait eagerly for it.

26 And in the same way the Spirit also helps our weakness; for [a]we do not know how to pray as we should, but [b]the Spirit Himself intercedes for *us* with groanings too deep for words;

27 and [a]He who searches the hearts knows what [b]the mind of the Spirit is, because He [c]intercedes for the [1]saints according to *the will of* God.

28 And we know that [1]God causes [a]all things to work together for good to those who love God, to those who are [b]called according to *His* purpose.

29 For whom He [a]foreknew, He also [b]predestined *to become*

8 [a]Rom. 7:
9 [a]Rom. 7:
Rom. 8:11;
6:19; 2 Cor.
Phil. 1:19; 2
1 John 4:13
10 [1]Lit., *life*
Gal. 2:20; E
1:27
11 [1]Some a
read *becaus*
2:24; Rom. 6
5:21 [c]Rom.
16:3
13 [1]Or, *are*
[a]Rom. 8:6 [b]
14 [a]Gal. 5:1
Matt. 5:9; Jo
8:16, 19; 9:8
6:18; Gal. 3:
3:1; Rev. 21:
15 [1]Lit., *for*
[2]Or, *the Spir*
Heb. 2:15 [b]F
Gal. 4:5f. [c]M
Gal. 4:6
16 [a]Acts 5:3
Matt. 5:9; Joh
8:14, 19; 9:8,
6:18; Gal. 3:2
3:1; Rev. 21:7
17 [a]Acts 20:3
4:7; Eph. 3:6;
Heb. 1:14; Re
[b]2 Cor. 1:5, 7;
Col. 1:24; 2 T
1 Pet. 4:13
18 [a]2 Cor. 4:1
4:13 [b]Col. 3:4
1 Pet. 1:5; 5:1
19 [a]Phil. 1:20
8:18; 1 Cor. 1
1 Pet. 1:7, 13;
[c]Hos. 1:10; M
1:12; Rom. 8:1
26; 2 Cor. 6:18
1 John 3:1; Re
20 [1]Some anc
read *in hope;*
creation [a]Gen
[b]Ps. 39:5f.; Ec
[c]Gen. 3:17; 5:2
21 [a]Acts 3:21;
3:13; Rev. 21:1
22 [a]Jer. 12:4,
23 [a]Rom. 5:3
8:16; 2 Cor. 1:2
5:2, 4 [d]Rom. 8
Gal. 5:5 [e]Rom.
24 [1]Some anc
read *who hope*
he sees? [a]Ror
1 Thess. 5:8; T
[b]Rom. 4:18; 2 C
Heb. 11:1
25 [a]1 Thess. 1
26 [a]Matt. 20:22
12:8 [b]John 14:
8:15f.; Eph. 6:18
27 [1]Or, *holy on*
139:1f.; Luke 16
1:24; Rev. 2:23
8:6 [c]Rom. 8:34
28 [1]Some ancie
read *all things w*
together for goo
8:32 [b]Rom. 8:3
11:29; 1 Cor. 1:9
15; 5:8; Eph. 1:1
2 Thess. 2:14; H
1 Pet. 2:9; 3:9
29 [a]Rom. 11:2;
2 Tim. 1:9; 1 Pet
[b]Rom. 9:23; 1 C
Eph. 1:5, 11

[c]conformed to the image of His Son, that He might be the [d]first-born
among many brethren;
30 and whom He [a]predestined, these He also [b]called; and whom He
called, these He also [c]justified; and whom He justified, these He also
[d]glorified.
31 [a]What then shall we say to these things? [b]If God *is* for us, who *is*
against us?
32 He who [a]did not spare His own Son, but [b]delivered Him up for
us all, how will He not also with Him freely give us all things?
33 Who will bring a charge against [a]God's elect? [b]God is the one
who justifies;
34 who is the one who [a]condemns? Christ Jesus is He who [b]died,
yes, rather who was [1c]raised, who is [d]at the right hand of God, who
also [e]intercedes for us.
35 Who shall separate us from [a]the love of [1]Christ? Shall [b]tribula-
tion, or distress, or [c]persecution, or [c]famine, or [c]nakedness, or [c]peril,
or sword?
36 Just as it is written,

"[a]FOR THY SAKE WE ARE BEING PUT TO DEATH ALL DAY LONG;
WE WERE CONSIDERED AS SHEEP TO BE SLAUGHTERED."

37 But in all these things we overwhelmingly [a]conquer through
[b]Him who loved us.
38 For I am convinced that neither [a]death, nor life, nor [b]angels, nor
principalities, nor [a]things present, nor things to come, nor powers,
39 nor height, nor depth, nor any other created thing, shall be able
to separate us from [a]the love of God, which is [b]in Christ Jesus our
Lord.

Chapter 9

9 [a]I am telling the truth in Christ, I am not lying, my conscience
bearing me witness in the Holy Spirit,
2 that I have great sorrow and unceasing grief in my heart.
3 For [a]I could [1]wish that I myself were [b]accursed, *separated* from
Christ for the sake of my brethren, my kinsmen [c]according to the
flesh,
4 who are [a]Israelites, to whom belongs [b]the adoption as sons and
[c]the glory and [d]the covenants and [e]the giving of the Law and [f]the
temple service and [g]the promises,
5 whose are [a]the fathers, and [b]from whom is [1]the Christ according
to the flesh, [c]who is over all, [d]God [e]blessed [2]forever. Amen.
6 But *it is* not as though [a]the word of God has failed. [b]For they are
not all Israel who are *descended* from Israel;
7 neither are they all children [a]because they are Abraham's [1]de-
scendants, but: "[b]THROUGH ISAAC YOUR [1]DESCENDANTS WILL BE NAMED."
8 That is, it is not the children of the flesh who are [a]children of
God, but the [b]children of the promise are regarded as [1]descendants.
9 For this is a word of promise: "[a]AT THIS TIME I WILL COME, AND
SARAH SHALL HAVE A SON."
10 [a]And not only this, but there was [b]Rebekah also, when she had
conceived *twins* by one man, our father Isaac;
11 for though *the twins* were not yet born, and had not done any-
thing good or bad, in order that [a]God's purpose according to *His*
choice might stand, not because of works, but because of Him who
calls,

or. 15:49; Phil. Col. 1:18; Heb. 1:6
m. 9:23; 11:29; 7; Eph. 1:5, 11 28; 9:24; 1 Cor. al. 1:6, 15; 5:8; Eph. 1:11; 3:11; ess. 2:14; Heb. 1 Pet. 2:9; 3:9 or. 6:11 [d]John om. 8:21; 9:23
3:5; 4:1 [b]Ps. 8:6; Matt. 1:23
hn 3:16; Rom. :8 [b]Rom. 4:25
Luke 18:7 [b]Is. 50:8f.
e ancient mss. raised from the
om. 8:1 [b]Rom. cts 2:24 [d]Mark om. 8:27; Heb. 7:25
e ancient mss. d [a]Rom. 8:37f. 2:9; 2 Cor. 4:8 or. 4:11; 2 Cor. 11:26f.
Ps. 44:22; Acts :24; 1 Cor. 4:9; 30f.; 2 Cor. 1:9; 10f.; 6:9; 11:23
n 16:33; 1 Cor. Gal. 2:20; Eph. 5:2; Rev. 1:5
or. 3:22 [b]1 Cor. oh. 1:21; 1 Pet. 3:22
5:8 [b]Rom. 8:1
Cor. 11:10; Gal. :20; 1 Tim. 2:7
ray [a]Ex. 32:32 2:3; 16:22; Gal. om. 1:3; 11:14; Eph. 6:5
eut. 7:6; 14:1f.; 9:6 [b]Ex. 4:22; :15 [c]Ex. 40:34; 11; Ezek. 1:28; :5 [d]Gen. 17:2; :14; Luke 1:72; 3:25; Eph. 2:12 Deut. 4:13f.; Ps. 19 [f]Heb. 9:1, 6 39; 13:32; Eph. 2:12
e., the Messiah , *unto the ages* 13; Rom. 11:28 1-16; Rom. 1:3 6-19 [d]John 1:1 [e]Rom. 1:25
n. 23:19 [b]John om. 2:28f.; Gal. 6:16
it., *seed* [a]John 3, 39; Gal. 4:23 :12; Heb. 11:18
t., *seed* [a]Rom. Rom. 4:13, 16; :29; 4:28; Heb. 11:11
9 [a]Gen. 18:10
Rom. 5:3 [b]Gen. 25:21
Rom. 4:17; 8:28

12 it was said to her, "[a]THE OLDER WILL SERVE THE YOUNGER."
13 Just as it is written, "[a]JACOB I LOVED, BUT ESAU I HATED."
14 [a]What shall we say then? [b]There is no injustice with God, is
there? [c]May it never be!
15 For He says to Moses, "[a]I WILL HAVE MERCY ON WHOM I HAVE MERCY,
AND I WILL HAVE COMPASSION ON WHOM I HAVE COMPASSION."
16 So then it *does* not *depend* on the man who wills or the man who
[a]runs, but on [b]God who has mercy.
17 For the Scripture says to Pharaoh, "[a]FOR THIS VERY PURPOSE I
RAISED YOU UP, TO DEMONSTRATE MY POWER IN YOU, AND THAT MY NAME
MIGHT BE PROCLAIMED [1]THROUGHOUT THE WHOLE EARTH."
18 So then He has mercy on whom He desires, and He [a]hardens
whom He desires.
19 [a]You will say to me then, "[b]Why does He still find fault? For
[c]who resists His will?"
20 On the contrary, who are you, [a]O man, who [b]answers back to
God? [c]The thing molded will not say to the molder, "Why did you
make me like this," will it?
21 Or does not the potter have a right over the clay, to make from
the same lump one vessel [1]for honorable use, and another [2]for com-
mon use?
22 What if God, although willing to demonstrate His wrath and to
make His power known, endured with much [a]patience vessels of
wrath [b]prepared for destruction?
23 And *He did so* in order that He might make known [a]the riches of
His glory upon [b]vessels of mercy, which He [c]prepared beforehand
for glory,
24 *even* us, whom He also [a]called, [b]not from among Jews only, but
also from among Gentiles.
25 As He says also in Hosea,
"[a]I WILL CALL THOSE WHO WERE NOT MY PEOPLE, 'MY PEOPLE,'
AND HER WHO WAS NOT BELOVED, 'BELOVED.' "
26 "[a]AND IT SHALL BE THAT IN THE PLACE WHERE IT WAS SAID TO THEM,
'YOU ARE NOT MY PEOPLE,'
THERE THEY SHALL BE CALLED SONS OF [b]THE LIVING GOD."
27 And Isaiah cries out concerning Israel, "[a]THOUGH THE NUMBER OF
THE SONS OF ISRAEL BE [b]AS THE SAND OF THE SEA, IT IS [c]THE REMNANT THAT
WILL BE SAVED;
28 [a]FOR THE LORD WILL EXECUTE HIS WORD UPON THE EARTH, [1]THOROUGH-
LY AND [2]QUICKLY."
29 And just as Isaiah foretold,
"[a]EXCEPT [b]THE LORD OF [1]SABAOTH HAD LEFT TO US A [2]POSTERITY,
[c]WE WOULD HAVE BECOME AS SODOM, AND WOULD HAVE [3]RESEMBLED
GOMORRAH."
30 [a]What shall we say then? That Gentiles, who did not pursue
righteousness, attained righteousness, even [b]the righteousness which
is [1]by faith;
31 but Israel, [a]pursuing a law of righteousness, did not [b]arrive at
that law.
32 Why? Because *they did* not *pursue it* [1]by faith, but as though *it*
were [1]by works. They stumbled over [a]the stumbling stone,
33 just as it is written,
"[a]BEHOLD, I LAY IN ZION [b]A STONE OF STUMBLING AND A ROCK OF
OFFENSE,

12 [a]Gen. 25:23
13 [a]Mal. 1:2f.
14 [a]Rom. 3:5 19:7; Rom. 2:1 20:16
15 [a]Ex. 33:19
16 [a]Gal. 2:2 [b]
17 [1]Lit., *in* [a]Ex
18 [a]Ex. 4:21; 7 10:20, 27; 11:1 17; Deut. 2:30; 11:20; John 12: 11:7, 25
19 [a]Rom. 11:19 15:35; James 2 [b]Rom. 3:7 [c]2 C Job 9:12; Dan.
20 [a]Rom. 2:1 33:13 [c]Is. 29:1 64:8; Jer. 18:6; 9:22f.; 2 Tim. 2
21 [1]Lit., *for hon* *for dishonor*
22 [a]Rom. 2:4 16:4; 1 Pet. 2:8
23 [a]Rom. 2:4; 3:16 [b]Acts 9:15 8:29f.
24 [a]Rom. 8:28 3:29
25 [a]Hos. 2:23; 2:10
26 [a]Hos. 1:10 16:16
27 [a]Is. 10:22 [b] 22:17; Hos. 1:1 11:5
28 [1]Lit., *finishin* [2]Lit., *cutting it s* 10:23
29 [1]I.e., Hosts *seed* [3]Lit., *bee* *like* [a]Is. 1:9 [b]Ja 5:4 [c]Deut. 29:2 13:19; Jer. 49:1 Amos 4:11
30 [1]Lit., *out of* 9:14 [b]Rom. 1:1 10:6; Gal. 2:16; Phil. 3:9; Heb. 1
31 [a]Is. 51:1; Ro 10:2f., 20; 11:7
32 [1]Lit., *out of* 1 Pet. 2:6, 8
33 [a]Is. 28:16 [b]

[c]AND HE WHO BELIEVES IN HIM [d]WILL NOT BE [1]DISAPPOINTED."

Chapter 10

10 Brethren, my heart's desire and my prayer to God for them is
for *their* salvation.
2 For I bear them witness that they have [a]a zeal for God, but not in
accordance with knowledge.
3 For not knowing about [a]God's righteousness, and [b]seeking to
establish their own, they did not subject themselves to the right-
eousness of God.
4 For [a]Christ is the [1]end of the law for righteousness to [b]everyone
who believes.
5 For Moses writes that the man who practices the righteousness
which is [1]based on law [a]shall live [2]by that righteousness.
6 But [a]the righteousness [1]based on faith speaks thus, "[b]DO NOT SAY
IN YOUR HEART, 'WHO WILL ASCEND INTO HEAVEN?' (that is, to bring
Christ down),
7 or 'WHO WILL DESCEND INTO THE [a]ABYSS?' (that is, to [b]bring Christ
up from the dead)."
8 But what does it say? "[a]THE WORD IS NEAR YOU, IN YOUR MOUTH AND
IN YOUR HEART"—that is, the word of faith which we are preaching,
9 [1]that [a]if you confess with your mouth Jesus *as* Lord, and [b]believe
in your heart that [c]God raised Him from the dead, you shall be
saved;
10 for with the heart man believes, [1]resulting in righteousness, and
with the mouth he confesses, [2]resulting in salvation.
11 For the Scripture says, "[a]WHOEVER BELIEVES IN HIM WILL NOT BE
[1]DISAPPOINTED."
12 For [a]there is no distinction between Jew and Greek; for the same
Lord is [b]Lord of [c]all, abounding in riches for all who call upon Him;
13 for "[a]WHOEVER WILL CALL UPON THE NAME OF THE LORD WILL BE
SAVED."
14 How then shall they call upon Him in whom they have not
believed? And how shall they believe in Him [a]whom they have not
heard? And how shall they hear without [b]a preacher?
15 And how shall they preach unless they are sent? Just as it is
written, "[a]HOW BEAUTIFUL ARE THE FEET OF THOSE WHO [1b]BRING GLAD
TIDINGS OF GOOD THINGS!"
16 However, they [a]did not all heed the [1]glad tidings; for Isaiah says,
"[b]LORD, WHO HAS BELIEVED OUR REPORT?"
17 So faith *comes* from [a]hearing, and hearing by [b]the word [1]of Christ.
18 But I say, surely they have never heard, have they? Indeed they
have;

"[a]THEIR VOICE HAS GONE OUT INTO ALL THE EARTH,
AND THEIR WORDS TO THE ENDS OF THE [1]WORLD."

19 But I say, surely Israel did not know, did they? At the first Moses
says,

"[a]I WILL [b]MAKE YOU JEALOUS BY THAT WHICH IS NOT A NATION,
BY A NATION WITHOUT UNDERSTANDING WILL I ANGER YOU."

20 And Isaiah is very bold and says,

"[a]I WAS FOUND BY THOSE WHO SOUGHT ME NOT,
I BECAME MANIFEST TO THOSE WHO DID NOT ASK FOR ME."

21 But as for Israel He says, "[a]ALL THE DAY LONG I HAVE STRETCHED
OUT MY HANDS TO A DISOBEDIENT AND OBSTINATE PEOPLE."

...t., *put to shame*
...0:11 [d]Rom. 5:5
...0:2 [a]Acts 21:20
...1:17 [b]Is. 51:1; ...10:2f., 20; 11:7
[1]Or, *goal* [a]Rom. ...4; Gal. 3:24; 4:5 [b]Rom. 3:22
...Lit., *out of, from* ...*by it* [a]Lev. 18:5; ...29; Ezek. 20:11, ...21; Rom. 7:10
...Lit., *out of, from* ...30 [b]Deut. 30:12
...uke 8:31 [b]Heb. 13:20
8 [a]Deut. 30:14
...*because* [a]Matt. ...uke 12:8; Rom. ...Cor. 12:3; Phil. ...cts 16:31; Rom. ...4:24 [c]Acts 2:24
10 [1]Lit., *to* ...*ousness* [2]Lit., *to salvation*
...t., *put to shame* ...8:16; Rom. 9:33
[a]Rom. 3:22, 29 ...36 [c]Rom. 3:29
...2:32; Acts 2:21
[a]Eph. 2:17; 4:21 ...s 8:31; Titus 1:3
[1]Or, *preach the* ...[a]Is. 52:7 [b]Rom. 1:15; 15:20
..., *gospel* [a]Rom. ...3:1; John 12:38
[1]Or, *concerning* ...Gal. 3:2, 5 [b]Col. 3:16
..., *inhabited earth* ...19:4; Rom. 1:8; ...23; 1 Thess. 1:8
...ut. 32:21 [b]Rom. 11:11, 14
...65:1; Rom. 9:30
21 [a]Is. 65:2

Chapter 11

11 I say then, God has not [a]rejected His people, has He? [b]May it
never be! For [c]I too am an Israelite, [1]a descendant of Abraham,
of the tribe of Benjamin.
2 God [a]has not rejected His people whom He [b]foreknew. [c]Or do
you not know what the Scripture says in *the passage about* Elijah, how
he pleads with God against Israel?
3 "Lord, [a]THEY HAVE KILLED THY PROPHETS, THEY HAVE TORN DOWN
THINE ALTARS, AND I ALONE AM LEFT, AND THEY ARE SEEKING MY LIFE."
4 But what [1]is the divine response to him? "[a]I HAVE KEPT for Myself
SEVEN THOUSAND MEN WHO HAVE NOT BOWED THE KNEE TO BAAL."
5 In the same way then, there has also come to be at the present
time [a]a remnant according to *God's* [1]gracious choice.
6 But [a]if it is by grace, it is no longer on the basis of works, other-
wise grace is no longer grace.
7 What then? That which [a]Israel is seeking for, it has not obtained,
but [1]those who were chosen obtained it, and the rest were [b]hardened;
8 just as it is written,
"[a]GOD GAVE THEM A SPIRIT OF STUPOR,
EYES TO SEE NOT AND EARS TO HEAR NOT,
DOWN TO THIS VERY DAY."
9 And David says,
"[a]LET THEIR TABLE BECOME A SNARE AND A TRAP,
AND A STUMBLING BLOCK AND A RETRIBUTION TO THEM.
10 "[a]LET THEIR EYES BE DARKENED TO SEE NOT,
AND BEND THEIR BACKS FOREVER."
11 [a]I say then, they did not stumble so as to fall, did they? [b]May it
never be! But by their transgression [c]salvation *has come* to the Gen-
tiles, to [d]make them jealous.
12 Now if their transgression be riches for the world and their
failure be riches for the Gentiles, how much more will their [1a]fulfill-
ment be!
13 But I am speaking to you who are Gentiles. Inasmuch then as [a]I
am an apostle of Gentiles, I magnify my ministry,
14 if somehow I might [a]move to jealousy [b]my [1]fellow countrymen
and [c]save some of them.
15 For if their rejection be the [a]reconciliation of the world, what will
their acceptance be but [b]life from the dead?
16 And if the [a]first piece *of dough* be holy, the lump is also; and if the
root be holy, the branches are too.
17 But if some of the [a]branches were broken off, and [b]you, being a
wild olive, were grafted in among them and became partaker with
them of the [1]rich root of the olive tree,
18 do not be arrogant toward the branches; but if you are arrogant,
remember that [a]it is not you who supports the root, but the root *sup-*
ports you.
19 [a]You will say then, "Branches were broken off so that I might be
grafted in."
20 Quite right, they were broken off for their unbelief, but you
[a]stand by your faith. [b]Do not be conceited, but fear;
21 for if God did not spare the natural branches, neither will He
spare you.
22 Behold then the kindness and severity of God; to those who fell,

11:1 [1]Lit., *of the* *Abraham* [a]1 Sa 12:22; Jer. 31:3 33:24-26 [b]Luke [c]2 Cor. 11:22; P

2 [a]Ps. 94:14 [b]R 8:29 [c]Rom. 6:1

3 [a]1 Kin. 19:10,

4 [1]Lit., *says* [a]1 19:18

5 [1]Lit., *choice o* [a]2 Kin. 19:4; Ro

6 [a]Rom. 4:4

7 [1]Lit., *the elec* [a]Rom. 9:31 [b]Ma Rom. 9:18; 11:2 3:14

8 [a]Deut. 29:4; I Matt. 13:13f.

9 [a]Ps. 69:22

10 [a]Ps. 69:23

11 [a]Rom. 11:1 20:16 [c]Acts 28: [d]Rom. 11:14

12 [1]Or, *fulness* 11:25

13 [a]Acts 9:15

14 [1]Lit., *flesh* [a] 11:11 [b]Gen. 29: 2 Sam. 19:12f.; 9:3 [c]1 Cor. 1:21 9:22; 1 Tim. 1:15 2 Tim. 1:9; Titus

15 [a]Rom. 5:11 15:24, 32

16 [a]Num. 15:18 10:37; Ezek. 44:

17 [1]Lit., *root of* *fatness* [a]Jer. 11: John 15:2 [b]Eph.

18 [a]John 4:22

19 [a]Rom. 9:19

20 [a]Rom. 5:2; 1 10:12; 2 Cor. 1:2 [b]Rom. 12:16; 1 T 6:17; 1 Pet. 1:17

severity, but to you, God's [a]kindness, [b]if you continue in His kind-
ness; otherwise you also [c]will be cut off.
23 And they also, [a]if they do not continue in their unbelief, will be
grafted in; for God is able to graft them in again.
24 For if you were cut off from what is by nature a wild olive tree,
and were grafted contrary to nature into a cultivated olive tree, how
much more shall these who are the natural *branches* be grafted into
their own olive tree?
25 For [a]I do not want you, brethren, to be uninformed of this
[b]mystery, lest you be [c]wise in your own estimation, that a partial
[d]hardening has happened to Israel until the [e]fulness of the Gentiles
has come in;
26 and thus all Israel will be saved; just as it is written,

"[a]THE DELIVERER WILL COME FROM ZION,
HE WILL REMOVE UNGODLINESS FROM JACOB."

27 "[a]AND THIS IS [1]MY COVENANT WITH THEM,
[b]WHEN I TAKE AWAY THEIR SINS."

28 [1]From the standpoint of the gospel they are [a]enemies for your
sake, but [2]from the standpoint of *God's* choice they are beloved for
[b]the sake of the fathers;
29 for the gifts and the [a]calling of God [b]are irrevocable.
30 For just as you once were disobedient to God, but now have
been shown mercy because of their disobedience,
31 so these also now have been disobedient, in order that because
of the mercy shown to you they also may now be shown mercy.
32 For [a]God has shut up all in disobedience that He might show
mercy to all.
33 Oh, the depth of [a]the riches [1]both of the [b]wisdom and knowledge
of God! [c]How unsearchable are His judgments and unfathomable
His ways!
34 For [a]WHO HAS KNOWN THE MIND OF THE LORD, OR WHO BECAME HIS
COUNSELOR?
35 Or [a]WHO HAS FIRST GIVEN TO HIM [1]THAT IT MIGHT BE PAID BACK TO HIM
AGAIN?
36 For [a]from Him and through Him and to Him are all things. [b]To
Him *be* the glory [1]forever. Amen.

Chapter 12

12 [a]I urge you therefore, brethren, by the mercies of God, to [b]pre-
sent your bodies a living and holy sacrifice, [1]acceptable to
God, *which is* your [2]spiritual service of worship.
2 And do not [a]be conformed to [b]this [1]world, but be transformed by
the [c]renewing of your mind, that you may [d]prove what the will of
God is, that which is good and [2]acceptable and perfect.
3 For through [a]the grace given to me I say to every man among
you [b]not to think more highly of himself than he ought to think; but
to think so as to have sound judgment, as God has allotted to [c]each a
measure of faith.
4 For [a]just as we have many members in one body and all the
members do not have the same function,
5 so we, [a]who are many, are [b]one body in Christ, and individually
members one of another.
6 And since we have gifts that [a]differ according to the grace given

to us, *let each exercise them accordingly*: if [b]prophecy, according to the
proportion of his faith;
7 if [1a]service, in his serving; or he who [b]teaches, in his teaching;
8 or he who [a]exhorts, in his exhortation; he who gives, with
[1b]liberality; [c]he who [2]leads, with diligence; he who shows mercy,
with [d]cheerfulness.
9 Let [a]love be without hypocrisy. [b]Abhor what is evil; cling to what
is good.
10 Be [a]devoted to one another in brotherly love; [1]give preference to
one another [b]in honor;
11 not lagging behind in diligence, [a]fervent in spirit, [b]serving the
Lord;
12 [a]rejoicing in hope, [b]persevering in tribulation, [c]devoted to prayer,
13 [a]contributing to the needs of the [1]saints, [2b]practicing hospitality.
14 [a]Bless those who persecute [1]you; bless and curse not.
15 [a]Rejoice with those who rejoice, and weep with those who weep.
16 [a]Be of the same mind toward one another; [b]do not be haughty in
mind, but [1]associate with the lowly. [c]Do not be wise in your own
estimation.
17 [a]Never pay back evil for evil to anyone. [1b]Respect what is right in
the sight of all men.
18 If possible, [a]so far as it depends on you, [b]be at peace with all
men.
19 [a]Never take your own revenge, beloved, but [1]leave room for the
wrath *of God*, for it is written, "[b]VENGEANCE IS MINE, I WILL REPAY," says
the Lord.
20 "[a]BUT IF YOUR ENEMY IS HUNGRY, FEED HIM, AND IF HE IS THIRSTY, GIVE
HIM A DRINK; FOR IN SO DOING YOU WILL HEAP BURNING COALS UPON HIS
HEAD."
21 Do not be overcome by evil, but overcome evil with good.

Chapter 13

13 Let every [1a]person be in [b]subjection to the governing
authorities. For [c]there is no authority except [2]from God, and
those which exist are established by God.
2 Therefore he who resists authority has opposed the ordinance of
God; and they who have opposed will receive condemnation upon
themselves.
3 For [a]rulers are not a cause of fear for [1]good behavior, but for evil.
Do you want to have no fear of authority? Do what is good, and you
will have praise from the same;
4 for it is a minister of God to you for good. But if you do what is
evil, be afraid; for it does not bear the sword for nothing; for it is a
minister of God, an [a]avenger who brings wrath upon the one who
practices evil.
5 Wherefore it is necessary to be in subjection, not only because of
wrath, but also [a]for conscience' sake.
6 For because of this you also pay taxes, for *rulers* are servants of
God, devoting themselves to this very thing.
7 [a]Render to all what is due them: [b]tax to whom tax *is due;* [c]custom
to whom custom; fear to whom fear; honor to whom honor.
8 Owe nothing to anyone except to love one another; for [a]he who
loves [1]his neighbor has fulfilled *the* law.
9 For this, "[a]YOU SHALL NOT COMMIT ADULTERY, YOU SHALL NOT

6 [b]Acts 1
12:10
7 [1]Or, *off*
[a]Acts 6:1;
28 [b]Acts
12:28; 14
8 [1]Or, *sin*
gives aid
11:23; 13:
8:2; 9:11,
12:28; 1 T
[d]2 Cor. 9:7
9 [a]2 Cor.
1:5 [b]1 The
10 [1]Or, *ou*
another in
honor [a]Jo
1 Thess. 4
2 Pet. 1:7
Phil. 2:3; 1
11 [a]Acts 1
20:19
12 [a]Rom.
10:32, 36
13 [1]Or, *hol*
pursuing [a]
1 Cor. 16:1
Heb. 6:10
1 Tim. 3:2
14 [1]Some
do not conta
[a]Matt. 5:44;
1 Cor. 4:12
15 [a]Job 30
13:3
16 [1]Or, *acc*
yourself to l
[a]Rom. 15:5;
13:11; Phil.
1 Pet. 3:8 [b]
12:3 [c]Prov.
11:25
17 [1]Lit., *Tak*
for [a]Prov. 20
Rom. 12:19
18 [a]Rom. 1:
9:50; Rom. 1
19 [1]Lit., *give*
[a]Prov. 20:22;
Rom. 12:17
32:35; Ps. 94
1 Thess. 4:6;
20 [a]2 Kin. 6:2
25:21f.; Matt.
6:27
13:1 [1]Or, *sou*
[a]Acts 2:41 [b]T
1 Pet. 2:13f.
4:17; John 19
3 [1]Lit., *good w*
[a]1 Pet. 2:14
4 [a]1 Thess. 4
5 [a]Eccl. 8; 1 P
2:13, 19
7 [a]Matt. 22:21
12:17; Luke 20
[b]Luke 20:22; 2
[c]Matt. 17:25
8 [1]Lit., *the oth*
7:12; 22:39f.; J
13:34; Rom. 13
5:14; James 2:
9 [a]Ex. 20:13ff.;
5:17ff.

MURDER, YOU SHALL NOT STEAL, YOU SHALL NOT COVET," and if there is
any other commandment, it is summed up in this saying, "[b]YOU
SHALL LOVE YOUR NEIGHBOR AS YOURSELF."
10 Love [1]does no wrong to a neighbor; [a]love therefore is the fulfill-
ment of *the* law.
11 And this *do*, knowing the time, that it is [a]already the hour for you
to [b]awaken from sleep; for now [1]salvation is nearer to us than when
we believed.
12 [a]The night is almost gone, and [b]the day is at hand. Let us there-
fore lay aside [c]the deeds of darkness and put on [d]the armor of light.
13 Let us [1a]behave properly as in the day, [b]not in carousing and
drunkenness, not in sexual promiscuity and sensuality, not in strife
and jealousy.
14 But [a]put on the Lord Jesus Christ, and make no provision for the
flesh [b]in regard to *its* lusts.

Chapter 14

14 Now [a]accept the one who is [b]weak in faith, *but* not for *the*
purpose of passing judgment on his opinions.
2 [a]One man has faith that he may eat all things, but he who is
[b]weak eats vegetables *only*.
3 Let not him who eats [a]regard with contempt him who does not
eat, and let not him who does not eat [b]judge him who eats, for God
has [c]accepted him.
4 [a]Who are you to judge the [1]servant of another? To his own
[2]master he stands or falls; and stand he will, for the Lord is able to
make him stand.
5 [a]One man [1]regards one day above another, another regards every
day *alike*. Let each man be [b]fully convinced in his own mind.
6 He who observes the day, observes it for the Lord, and he who
eats, [1]does so for the Lord, for he [a]gives thanks to God; and he who
eats not, for the Lord he does not eat, and gives thanks to God.
7 For not one of us [a]lives for himself, and not one dies for himself;
8 for if we live, we live for the Lord, or if we die, we die for the
Lord; therefore [a]whether we live or die, we are the Lord's.
9 For to this end [a]Christ died and lived *again*, that He might be
[b]Lord both of the dead and of the living.
10 But you, why do you judge your brother? Or you again, why do
you [a]regard your brother with contempt? For [b]we shall all stand
before the judgment seat of God.
11 For it is written,

"[a]AS I LIVE, SAYS THE LORD, [b]EVERY KNEE SHALL BOW TO ME,
AND EVERY TONGUE SHALL [1]GIVE PRAISE TO GOD."

12 So then [a]each one of us shall give account of himself to God.
13 Therefore let us not [a]judge one another anymore, but rather
determine this—[b]not to put an obstacle or a stumbling block in a
brother's way.
14 I know and am convinced in the Lord Jesus that [a]nothing is
unclean in itself; but to him who [b]thinks anything to be unclean, to
him it is unclean.
15 For if because of food your brother is hurt, you are no longer
[a]walking according to love. [b]Do not destroy with your food him for
whom Christ died.

16 Therefore [a]do not let what is for you a good thing be [1]spoken of
as evil;
17 for the kingdom of God [a]is not eating and drinking, but right-
eousness and [b]peace and [b]joy in the Holy Spirit.
18 For he who in this *way* [a]serves Christ is [b]acceptable to God and
approved by men.
19 So then [1]let us [a]pursue the things which make for peace and the
[b]building up of one another.
20 [a]Do not tear down the work of God for the sake of food. [b]All
things indeed are clean, but [c]they are evil for the man who eats [1]and
gives offense.
21 [a]It is good not to eat meat or to drink wine, or *to do anything* by
which your brother stumbles.
22 The faith which you have, have [1]as your own conviction before
God. Happy is he who [a]does not condemn himself in what he ap-
proves.
23 But [a]he who doubts is condemned if he eats, because *his eating is*
not from faith; and whatever is not from faith is sin.

Chapter 15

15 Now we who are strong ought to bear the weaknesses of
[a]those without strength and not *just* please ourselves.
2 Let each of us [a]please his neighbor [1]for his good, to his [b]edifica-
tion.
3 For even [a]Christ did not please Himself; but as it is written,
"[b]THE REPROACHES OF THOSE WHO REPROACHED THEE FELL UPON ME."
4 For [a]whatever was written in earlier times was written for our
instruction, that through perseverance and the encouragement of the
Scriptures we might have hope.
5 Now may the [a]God [1]who gives perseverance and encouragement
grant you [b]to be of the same mind with one another according to
Christ Jesus;
6 that with one accord you may with one [1]voice glorify [a]the God
and Father of our Lord Jesus Christ.
7 Wherefore, [a]accept one another, just as Christ also accepted [1]us to
the glory of God.
8 For I say that Christ has become a servant to [a]the circumcision on
behalf of the truth of God to confirm [b]the promises *given* to the
fathers,
9 and for [a]the Gentiles to [b]glorify God for His mercy; as it is written,
"[c]THEREFORE I WILL [1]GIVE PRAISE TO THEE AMONG THE GENTILES,
AND I WILL SING TO THY NAME."
10 And again he says,
"[a]REJOICE, O GENTILES, WITH HIS PEOPLE."
11 And again,
"[a]PRAISE THE LORD ALL YOU GENTILES,
AND LET ALL THE PEOPLES PRAISE HIM."
12 And again Isaiah says,
"[a]THERE SHALL COME [b]THE ROOT OF JESSE,
AND HE WHO ARISES TO RULE OVER THE GENTILES,
[c]IN HIM SHALL THE GENTILES HOPE."
13 Now may the God of hope fill you with all [a]joy and peace in
believing, that you may abound in hope [b]by the power of the Holy
Spirit.

16 [1]Lit., *bl* [a]1 Cor. 10:
17 [a]1 Cor. 15:13; Gal.
18 [a]Rom. 1 8:21; Phil. 4 2:12
19 [1]Many a read *we pu* 34:14; Rom 1 Cor. 7:15; Heb. 12:14 1 Cor. 10:23 2 Cor. 12:19 4:12, 29
20 [1]Lit., *with* [a]Rom. 14:15 10:15; Rom. [c]1 Cor. 8:9-1
21 [a]1 Cor. 8
22 [1]Lit., *acc* *yourself* [a]1 J
23 [a]Rom. 14
15:1 [a]Rom. 1 6:2; 1 Thess.
2 [1]Lit., *for wh* *to edification* 9:22; 10:24, 3 13:9 [b]Rom. 1 1 Cor. 10:23; 2 Cor. 12:19; 4:12, 29
3 [a]2 Cor. 8:9
4 [a]Rom. 4:23f 3:16
5 [1]Lit., *of pers* [a]2 Cor. 1:3 [b]R
6 [1]Lit., *mouth*
7 [1]Some mss. *you* [a]Rom. 14:1
8 [a]Matt. 15:24; 3:26 [b]Rom. 4:1 1:20
9 [1]Or, *confess* 3:29; 11:30f. [b]M [c]2 Sam. 22:50; P
10 [a]Deut. 32:43
11 [a]Ps. 117:1
12 [a]Is. 11:10 [b]R 22:16 [c]Matt. 12:
13 [a]Rom. 14:17 15:19; 1 Cor. 2:4; 1 Thess. 1:5

14 And concerning you, my brethren, I myself also am convinced
that you yourselves are full of [a]goodness, filled with [b]all knowledge,
and able also to admonish one another.
15 But I have written very boldly to you on some points, so as to
remind you again, because of [a]the grace that was given me [1]from
God,
16 to be [a]a minister of Christ Jesus to the Gentiles, ministering as a
priest the [b]gospel of God, that *my* [c]offering of the Gentiles might
become acceptable, sanctified by the Holy Spirit.
17 Therefore in Christ Jesus I have found [a]reason for boasting in
[b]things pertaining to God.
18 For I will not presume to speak of anything [1]except what [a]Christ
has accomplished through me, [2]resulting in the obedience of the
Gentiles by word and deed,
19 in the power of [1a]signs and wonders, [b]in the power of the Spirit;
so that [c]from Jerusalem and round about as [d]far as Illyricum I have
[2]fully preached the gospel of Christ.
20 And thus I aspired to [a]preach the gospel, not where Christ was
already named, [b]that I might not build upon another man's founda-
tion;
21 but as it is written,
"[a]THEY WHO HAD NO NEWS OF HIM SHALL SEE,
AND THEY WHO HAVE NOT HEARD SHALL UNDERSTAND."
22 For this reason [a]I have often been hindered from coming to you;
23 but now, with no further place for me in these regions, and since
I [a]have had for many years a longing to come to you
24 whenever I [a]go to Spain—for I hope to see you in passing, and to
be [b]helped on my way there by you, when I have first [c]enjoyed your
company [1]for a while—
25 but now, [a]I am going to Jerusalem [b]serving the [1]saints.
26 For [a]Macedonia and [b]Achaia have been pleased to make a con-
tribution for the poor among the [1]saints in Jerusalem.
27 Yes, they were pleased *to do so,* and they are indebted to them.
For [a]if the Gentiles have shared in their spiritual things, they are
indebted to minister to them also in material things.
28 Therefore, when I have finished this, and [a]have [1]put my seal on
this fruit of theirs, I will [b]go on by way of you to Spain.
29 And I know that when [a]I come to you, I will come in the fulness
of the blessing of Christ.
30 Now I urge you, brethren, by our Lord Jesus Christ and by [a]the
love of the Spirit, to [b]strive together with me in your prayers to God
for me,
31 that I may be [a]delivered from those who are disobedient in
Judea, and *that* my [b]service for Jerusalem may prove acceptable to
the [1c]saints;
32 so that [a]I may come to you in joy by [b]the will of God and find
refreshing rest in your company.
33 Now [a]the God of peace be with you all. Amen.

Chapter 16

16 I [a]commend to you our sister Phoebe, who is a [1]servant of the
church which is at [b]Cenchrea;
2 that you [a]receive her in the Lord in a manner worthy of the
[1b]saints, and that you help her in whatever matter she may have

...h. 5:9; 2 Thess. ...Cor. 1:5; 8:1, 7, 10; 12:8; 13:2
...ne mss. read *by ...God* [a]Rom. 12:3
...Acts 9:15; Rom. ...Rom. 1:1; 15:19, ...Rom. 12:1; Eph. 5:2; Phil. 2:17
[a]Phil. 3:3 [b]Heb. 2:17; 5:1
...Or, *which Christ ...ot accomplished ...the obedience* ...ts 15:12; 21:19; ... 1:5; 2 Cor. 3:5
...9 [1]Or, *attesting ...es* [2]Lit., *fulfilled* ...hn 4:48 [b]Rom. ...5:13; 1 Cor. 2:4; ...hess. 1:5 [c]Acts ...21 [d]Acts 20:1f.
...m. 1:15; 10:15; ...6 [b]1 Cor. 3:10; 2 Cor. 10:15f.
21 [a]Is. 52:15
22 [a]Rom. 1:13; 1 Thess. 2:18
...cts 19:21; Rom. ...:10f.; 15:29, 32
..., *in part* [a]Rom. ...:28 [b]Acts 15:3 [c]Rom. 1:12
...*oly ones* [a]Acts ...21 [b]Acts 24:17
...5, note 1 [a]Acts ...or. 16:5; 2 Cor. ...3; 7:5; 8:1; 9:2, 11:9; Phil. 4:15; ...ess. 1:7f.; 4:10; ...:3 [b]Acts 18:12; 19:21
27 [a]1 Cor. 9:11
...*sealed to them ...ruit* [a]John 3:33 [b]Rom. 15:24
...ts 19:21; Rom. ...:10f.; 15:23, 32
...5:22; Col. 1:8 1:11; Col. 4:12
[1]V. 25, note 1 1:10; 2 Thess. ...Tim. 3:11; 4:17 15:25f.; 2 Cor. [c]Acts 9:13, 15
...n. 15:23 [b]Acts ...:21; Rom. 1:10
... 16:20; 2 Cor. ...3:11; Phil. 4:9; 5:23; 2 Thess. 16; Heb. 13:20
...Or, *deaconess* ...:1 [b]Acts 18:18
...*oly ones* [a]Phil. [b]Acts 9:13, 15

need of you; for she herself has also been a helper of many, [2]and of
myself as well.
3 Greet [a]Prisca and Aquila, my fellow workers [b]in [c]Christ Jesus,
4 who for my life risked their own necks, to whom not only do I
give thanks, but also all the churches of the Gentiles;
5 also *greet* [a]the church that is in their house. Greet Epaenetus, my
beloved, who is the [b]first convert to Christ from [1c]Asia.
6 Greet Mary, who has worked hard for you.
7 Greet Andronicus and [1]Junias, my [a]kinsmen, and my [b]fellow
prisoners, who are outstanding among the apostles, who also were
[c]in Christ before me.
8 Greet Ampliatus, my beloved in the Lord.
9 Greet Urbanus, our fellow worker [a]in Christ, and Stachys my
beloved.
10 Greet Apelles, the approved [a]in Christ. Greet those who are of
the *household* of Aristobulus.
11 Greet Herodion, my [a]kinsman. Greet those of the *household* of
Narcissus, who are in the Lord.
12 Greet Tryphaena and Tryphosa, workers in the Lord. Greet Per-
sis the beloved, who has worked hard in the Lord.
13 Greet [a]Rufus, a choice man in the Lord, also his mother and
mine.
14 Greet Asyncritus, Phlegon, Hermes, Patrobas, Hermas and the
brethren with them.
15 Greet Philologus and Julia, Nereus and his sister, and Olympas,
and all [a]the [1]saints who are with them.
16 [a]Greet one another with a holy kiss. All the churches of Christ
greet you.
17 Now I urge you, brethren, keep your eye on those who cause
dissensions and [1]hindrances [a]contrary to the teaching which you
learned, and [b]turn away from them.
18 For such men are [a]slaves, not of our Lord Christ but of [b]their own
[1]appetites; and by their [c]smooth and flattering speech they deceive
the hearts of the unsuspecting.
19 For the report of your obedience [a]has reached to all; therefore I
am rejoicing over you, but [b]I want you to be wise in what is good,
and innocent in what is evil.
20 And [a]the God of peace will soon crush [b]Satan under your feet.
[c]The grace of our Lord Jesus be with you.
21 [a]Timothy my fellow worker greets you, and *so do* [b]Lucius and
[c]Jason and [d]Sosipater, my [e]kinsmen.
22 I, Tertius, who [a]write this letter, greet you in the Lord.
23 [a]Gaius, host to me and to the whole church, greets you. [b]Erastus,
the city treasurer greets you, and Quartus, the brother.
24 [[1]The grace of our Lord Jesus Christ be with you all. Amen.]
25 [a]Now to Him who is able to establish you [b]according to my
gospel and the preaching of Jesus Christ, according to the revelation
of [c]the mystery which has been kept secret for [d]long ages past,
26 but now is manifested, and by [a]the Scriptures of the prophets,
according to the commandment of the eternal God, has been made
known to all the nations, *leading* to [b]obedience of faith;
27 to the only wise God, through Jesus Christ, [a]be the glory forever.
Amen.

2 [2]Lit., *an*
myself

3 [a]Acts 18
8:11ff.; 16:
2 Cor. 5:17
1:22 [c]Rom

5 [1]I.e., we
province of
[a]1 Cor. 16:
Philem. 2
[c]Acts 16:6

7 [1]Or, *Juni*
[a]Rom. 9:3;
[b]Col. 4:10;
[c]Rom. 8:11
10; 2 Cor. 5
Gal. 1:22

9 [a]Rom. 8:
10; 2 Cor. 5
Gal. 1:22

10 [a]Rom. 8
7, 9; 2 Cor.
Gal. 1:22

11 [a]Rom. 9

13 [a]Mark 1

15 [1]V. 2, no
16:2, 14

16 [a]1 Cor. 1
13:12; 1 The
1 Pet. 5:14

17 [1]Lit., *occ*
stumbling [a]
6:3 [b]Matt. 7
1:8f.; 2 Thes
Titus 3:10; 2

18 [1]Lit., *bell*
14:18 [b]Phil.
2:4; 2 Pet. 2:

19 [a]Rom. 1:
4:22; Matt. 1
14:20

20 [a]Rom. 15
4:10 [c]1 Cor.
2 Cor. 13:14;
Phil. 4:23; 1 T
5:28; 2 Thess
Rev. 22:21

21 [a]Acts 16:1
13:1 [?] [c]Acts
[d]Acts 20:4 [?]
9:3; 16:7, 11

22 [a]1 Cor. 16
6:11; Col. 4:18
3:17; Philem.

23 [a]Acts 19:2
[?]; 1 Cor. 1:14
19:22; 2 Tim.

24 [1]Many ms
contain this v.

25 [a]Eph. 3:20
[b]Rom. 2:16 [c]M
13:35; Rom. 1
1 Cor. 2:1, 7; 4
1:9; 3:3, 9; 6:1
1:26f.; 2:2; 4:3
3:16 [d]2 Tim. 1
1:2

26 [a]Rom. 1:2

27 [a]Rom. 11:3

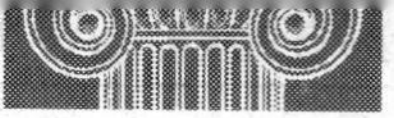

Romans Observations Chart

out Paul

Why He Wrote

out the Recipients

In Adam *(According to the flesh)*	**In Christ** *(According to the Spirit)*

ROMANS AT A GLANCE

Theme of Romans:

Author:

Date:

Purpose:

Key Words:

SEGMENT DIVISIONS			CHAPTER THEMES
			1
			2
			3
			4
			5
			6
			7
			8
			9
			10
			11
			12
			13
			14
			15
			16

CORINTHIANS

n abounded in the cosmopolitan city of Corinth, the chief city of Greece. Corinth overlooked the ›w isthmus that connected the Greek mainland with Peloponnesus and received ships in its two ›rs. At one time it was home of at least twelve heathen temples. The Corinthians were intrigued by k philosophy and captivated by the disciplined training and athletic events held at the Isthmus. desperately needed to hear the good news of Jesus Christ, the one crucified for sinners.

ie worship ceremonies carried out by some one thousand temple prostitutes connected with the ›le of Aphrodite, the goddess of love, bred blatant immorality throughout Corinth—so much so he Greek verb "to Corinthianize" meant to practice sexual immorality.

ostitutes openly plied their wares and meat markets thrived on sales from the sacrifices offered in emples. The Corinthians ate well, satisfied their sexual urges without condemnation, flirted with visdom of men, and did all they could to keep their bodies as beautiful as those of the Greek gods. loved to listen to great orators. For the 250,000 citizens there were almost two slaves per person. t more did Corinth need? Freedom. Freedom from sin and death. God met that need by blocking at every hand on his second missionary journey until he received the Macedonian call, "Come and us."

ter establishing the Corinthian church Paul eventually went to Ephesus where he stayed for three . From there he wrote his first epistle to the Corinthian believers who so desperately needed help orrection.

NGS TO DO

ral Instructions

vo things prompted Paul to write to the Corinthians, and it is these two things which cause a al division in his epistle to the Corinthians.

Read 1 Corinthians 1:10-11 to discover Paul's first reason for writing and record it on the 1 CORINTHIANS AT A GLANCE chart on page 1697 in the first space under "Major Segment Division."

The second division is noted by a phrase which will be repeated throughout the last segment of 1 Corinthians: *now concerning*. Read 7:1 and notice the transition. From this point on Paul deals with matters the Corinthians had questions on or issues that they needed to be instructed in.

Write the first half of 7:1 as the segment division for the second half of 1 Corinthians on the chart 1 CORINTHIANS AT A GLANCE.

As you read, look for and note on the OBSERVATIONS CHART on page 1696 what you learn about the Corinthians, any commands directed to them, and the warnings Paul gives them.

ters 1-6

In chapter 1 note what Paul commends and list this in the margin under "Commendations."

Read chapters 1 through 6, one chapter at a time. As you read, keep in mind what you read in the introduction to this book. Do the following:

a. Note the problems Paul deals with. You can see these problems several ways.

   1) As you read ask the five W's and an H (Who? What? When? Where? Why? and How?), especially concentrating on the problems, subjects, or people mentioned. Why would Paul mention by name these people in this chapter? Who is causing this problem? How did the Corinthians get this way? Why does Paul say what he does about himself or his ministry?

2) As you read each of the first six chapters, in the margin under the heading "Proble the problems Paul deals with in each chapter.

b. Mark key words. Key words help you see the main topics in a chapter. They indicate w problems are and what the solution is. Make a list in the margin of what is taught abo of the words or subjects unless you already have covered the subject under "Problems."

Write the following key words for this segment on a card and use it as a bookmark wh study chapters 1 through 6. They are: *God, Jesus (Christ, Lord), Spirit, divisions (divided* (note whose spirit or what spirit), *power, mind, wise, wisdom, preach, body,* and *church* or *ch*

3. As you finish each chapter, summarize the theme (subject) of that chapter and recor 1 CORINTHIANS AT A GLANCE and in the text next to the chapter number.

Chapters 7-16

1. Look for every occurrence of the phrases *now concerning* and *now I make known to you.* phrases divide this last segment into the issues Paul needs to address. Note what issu addresses when he uses these phrases. As you come to each one, record it on the second the "Segment Divisions" on 1 CORINTHIANS AT A GLANCE.
2. Mark the key words as you read each chapter or group of chapters covering one broad s These words will help you tie the chapters together. Make a new list of key words to u bookmark in this segment.

   The key words are: *God, Jesus (Christ, Lord), Spirit, body, unbelieving* or *unbelievers, thin thinking, church* or *churches, idols (idolaters, idolatry), knowledge, preach,* and *gospel. Divisio factions* each are used one time in chapter 11, but it is significant as Paul again deal problems as he gives further instruction to the church.
3. Using the five W's and an H, ask questions such as: Why does the church have this quest problem? How are they behaving? What is their thinking? What are Paul's instructions reg this subject? Why are they to do this? What are the consequences if they don't?
4. As you read each chapter, keep in mind that since the church at Corinth is divided i opinion of Paul, he continues to explain his position and/or ministry. Watch for his explan Also note how they relate to the issue he is dealing with.
5. In the margin of the text, note the main points covered in each chapter.
6. Record the theme of each chapter in the text next to the chapter number and on 1 CORINTH AT A GLANCE.
7. When you finish studying 1 Corinthians chapter by chapter, think about all you have obs about this book. Then record the theme of 1 Corinthians on 1 CORINTHIANS AT A GL and fill out any other information requested on the chart.

THINGS TO THINK ABOUT

1. Are you having any of the same problems in your own life or in your church that the Corin had? Do you think this letter has the answers for your problems or questions? How ca apply what you have learned?
2. According to the context of 1 Corinthians 3, what does it mean to be a carnal or fleshly Chri Remember, context is king and rules over all accurate interpretation.
3. Are you untaught—ignorant—concerning spiritual gifts? Do you know about one or two of but not the others? Have you believed or even taught others in accord with what the counsel of God has to say on the subject, or have you merely gone by your experien reasoning? Do you appreciate others' gifts even though they may be different from yours?
4. On what do you base your beliefs about marriage, divorce, and remarriage? What did you from 1 Corinthians about these topics? Did this change your belief?
5. Is the preaching of the cross foolishness to you, or is it a demonstration of the power of God?

Chapter 1

1 Paul, [a]called *as* an apostle of Jesus Christ [1]by [b]the will of God,
and [c]Sosthenes our [d]brother,
2 to [a]the church of God which is at [b]Corinth, to those who have
been sanctified in Christ Jesus, [1]saints [c]by calling, with all who in
every place [d]call upon the name of our Lord Jesus Christ, their *Lord*
and ours:
3 [a]Grace to you and peace from God our Father and the Lord Jesus
Christ.
4 [a]I thank [1]my God always concerning you, for the grace of God
which was given you in Christ Jesus,
5 that in everything you were [a]enriched in Him, in all [b]speech and
[b]all knowledge,
6 even as [a]the testimony concerning Christ was confirmed [1]in you,
7 so that you are not lacking in any gift, [a]awaiting eagerly the
revelation of our Lord Jesus Christ,
8 [a]who shall also confirm you to the end, blameless in [b]the day of
our Lord Jesus Christ.
9 [a]God is faithful, through whom you were [b]called into [c]fellowship
with His Son, Jesus Christ our Lord.
10 Now [a]I exhort you, [b]brethren, by the name of our Lord Jesus
Christ, that you all [1]agree, and there be no [2c]divisions among you,
but you be [3]made complete in [d]the same mind and in the same
judgment.
11 For I have been informed concerning you, my brethren, by
Chloe's *people*, that there are quarrels among you.
12 Now I mean this, that [a]each one of you is saying, "I am of Paul,"
and "I of [b]Apollos," and "I of [c]Cephas," and "I of Christ."
13 [1]Has Christ been divided? Paul was not crucified for you, was
he? Or were you [a]baptized [2]in the name of Paul?
14 [1]I thank God that I [a]baptized none of you except [a]Crispus and
[b]Gaius,
15 that no man should say you were baptized [1]in my name.
16 Now I did baptize also the [a]household of Stephanas; beyond
that, I do not know whether I baptized any other.
17 [a]For Christ did not send me to baptize, but to preach the gospel,
[b]not in [1]cleverness of speech, that the cross of Christ should not be
made void.
18 For the word of the cross is to [a]those who [1]are perishing [b]foolish-
ness, but to us who [2]are being saved it is [c]the power of God.
19 For it is written,

"[a]I WILL DESTROY THE WISDOM OF THE WISE,
AND THE CLEVERNESS OF THE CLEVER I WILL SET ASIDE."

20 [a]Where is the wise man? Where is the scribe? Where is the
debater of [b]this age? Has not God [c]made foolish the wisdom of [d]the
world?
21 For since in the wisdom of God [a]the world through its wisdom
did not *come to* know God, [b]God was well-pleased through the
[c]foolishness of the [1]message preached to [d]save those who believe.
22 For indeed [a]Jews ask for [1]signs, and Greeks search for wisdom;
23 but we preach [1a]Christ crucified, [b]to Jews a stumbling block, and
to Gentiles [c]foolishness,

[1]Lit., *through* [b]Rom. 1:10; [c]Acts 18:17 [d]Acts 1:15
...Or, *holy ones* ...10:32 [b]Acts ...om. 1:7; 8:28 [d]Acts 7:59
3 [a]Rom. 1:7
...ancient mss. ...ot contain *my* [a]Rom. 1:8
...9:11 [b]Rom. ...4; 2 Cor. 8:7
... [1]Or, *among* ...1:10; 1 Tim. ...1:8; Rev. 1:2
...17:30; Rom. ...23; Phil. 3:20; 2 Pet. 3:12
...:19; Phil. 1:6; ...Thess. 3:13; ...ke 17:24, 30; ...; 2 Cor. 1:14; ...1:6, 10; 2:16; ...5:2; 2 Thess. 2:2
...7:9; Is. 49:7; 10:13; 2 Cor. ...Thess. 5:24; ...s. 3:3 [b]Rom. ...8 [c]1 John 1:3
...Lit., *speak the* ...me thing [2]Lit., ...s [3]Or, *united* ...1 [b]Rom. 1:13 ...11:18 [d]Rom. ...:16; Phil. 1:27
...Matt. 23:8-10; ... [b]Acts 18:24; ...2 [c]John 1:42; ...3:22; 9:5; 15:5
...hrist has been ...d! or, *Christ is* ...ded! [2]Lit., *into* ...:19; Acts 2:38
...e ancient mss. ...ve thanks that ... [b]Rom. 16:23
15 [1]Lit., *into*
...Cor. 16:15, 17
...wisdom [a]John 10:48 [b]1 Cor. ...; 2 Cor. 10:10; 11:6
...erish [2]Or, *are* ...ed [a]Acts 2:47; ...Cor. 2:15; 4:3; ...s. 2:10 [b]1 Cor. ...25; 2:14; 4:10 ...16; 1 Cor. 1:24
19 [a]Is. 29:14
[a]Job 12:17; Is. ...; 33:18 [b]Matt. ...; 1 Cor. 2:6, 8; ... [c]Rom. 1:20ff. ...n 12:31; 1 Cor. ...27f.; 6:2; 11:32; James 4:4
[1]Lit., *preaching* ...n 12:31; 1 Cor. ...27f.; 6:2; 11:32; ...4 [b]Luke 12:32; ...1:15; Col. 1:19 ...r. 1:18, 23, 25; ... [d]Rom. 11:14; James 5:20
...2 [1]Or, *attesting* ...es [a]Matt. 12:38
... [1]I.e., Messiah ...r. 2:2; Gal. 3:1; ...ike 2:34; 1 Pet. ...or. 1:18, 21, 25; 2:14; 4:10

24 but to those who are [a]the called, both Jews and Greeks, Christ [b]the power of God and [c]the wisdom of God.

25 Because the [a]foolishness of God is wiser than men, and [b]the weakness of God is stronger than men.

26 For [1]consider your [a]calling, brethren, that there were [b]not many wise according to [2]the flesh, not many mighty, not many noble;

27 but [a]God has chosen the foolish things of [b]the world to shame the wise, and God has chosen the weak things of [b]the world to shame the things which are strong,

28 and the base things of [a]the world and the despised, God has chosen, [b]the things that are not, that He might [c]nullify the things that are,

29 that [a]no [1]man should boast before God.

30 But [1]by His doing you are in [a]Christ Jesus, who became to us [b]wisdom from God, [2]and [c]righteousness and [d]sanctification, and [e]redemption,

31 that, just as it is written, "[a]LET HIM WHO BOASTS, BOAST IN THE LORD."

Chapter 2

2 And when I came to you, brethren, I [a]did not come with superiority of speech or of wisdom, proclaiming to you [b]the [1]testimony of God.

2 For I determined to know nothing among you except [a]Jesus Christ, and Him crucified.

3 And I was with you in [a]weakness and in [b]fear and in much trembling.

4 And my [1]message and my preaching were [a]not in persuasive words of wisdom, but in demonstration of [b]the Spirit and of power,

5 that your faith should not [1]rest on the wisdom of men, but on [a]the power of God.

6 Yet we do speak wisdom among those who are [a]mature; a wisdom, however, not of [b]this age, nor of the rulers of [b]this age, who are [c]passing away;

7 but we speak God's wisdom in a [a]mystery, the hidden *wisdom,* which God [b]predestined before the [c]ages to our glory;

8 *the wisdom* [a]which none of the rulers of [b]this age has understood; for if they had understood it, they would not have crucified [c]the Lord of glory;

9 but just as it is written,

"[a]THINGS WHICH EYE HAS NOT SEEN AND EAR HAS NOT HEARD,
AND *which* HAVE NOT ENTERED THE HEART OF MAN,
ALL THAT GOD HAS PREPARED FOR THOSE WHO LOVE HIM."

10 [1a]For to us God revealed *them* [b]through the Spirit; for the Spirit searches all things, even the [c]depths of God.

11 For who among men knows the *thoughts* of a man except the [a]spirit of the man, which is in him? Even so the *thoughts* of God no one knows except the Spirit of God.

12 Now we [a]have received, not the spirit of [b]the world, but the Spirit who is from God, that we might know the things freely given to us by God,

13 which things we also speak, [a]not in words taught by human wisdom, but in those taught by the Spirit, [1]combining spiritual *thoughts* with spiritual *words.*

24 [a]Rom. 8 1:16; 1 Cor. 11:49; 1 Co

25 [a]1 Cor. 2:14; 4:10

26 [1]Lit., *see human stan* [a]Rom. 11:29 11:25; 1 Cor

27 [a]James 1:20

28 [a]1 Cor. 1 4:17 [c]Job 3 2:6; 2 Thess 2:14

29 [1]Lit., *fles*

30 [1]Lit., *of H both* [a]Rom. 4:15 [b]1 Cor. 23:5f.; 33:16 5:21; Phil. 3: 1:2; 6:11; 1 T [e]Rom. 3:24; 14; Col. 1:14

31 [a]Jer. 9:23 10:17

2:1 [1]Some a mss. read *my* [a]1 Cor. 1:17; [b]1 Cor. 2:7

2 [a]1 Cor. 1:2

3 [a]1 Cor. 4:1 11:30; 12:5, 9 [b]Is. 19:16; 2 C Eph. 6:5

4 [1]Lit., *word* 1:17; 2:1, 13 15:19; 1 Cor.

5 [1]Lit., *be* [a]2 6:7; 12:9

6 [a]Eph. 4:13; Heb. 5:14; 6:1 13:22; 1 Cor. [c]1 Cor. 1:28

7 [a]Rom. 11:25 1 Cor. 2:1 [b]Ro [c]Heb. 1:2; 11:3

8 [a]1 Cor. 1:26 [b]Matt. 13:22; 1 1:20 [c]Acts 7:2 2:1

9 [a]Is. 64:4; 65

10 [1]Some anc use *But* [a]Matt. 13:11; 16:17; G Eph. 3:3, 5 [b]Jo 14:26 [c]Rom. 1

11 [a]Prov. 20:27

12 [a]Rom. 8:15 1:27

13 [1]Or, *interpre spiritual* things *spiritual* men [a] 1:17; 2:1, 4

14 But [1]a [a]natural man [b]does not accept the things of the Spirit of God; for they are [c]foolishness to him, and he cannot understand them, because they are spiritually [2]appraised.

15 But he who is [a]spiritual appraises all things, yet he himself is appraised by no man.

16 For [a]WHO HAS KNOWN THE MIND OF THE LORD, THAT HE SHOULD INSTRUCT HIM? But [b]we have the mind of Christ.

Chapter 3

3 And I, brethren, could not speak to you as to [a]spiritual men, but as to [b]men of flesh, as to [c]babes in Christ.

2 I gave you [a]milk to drink, not solid food; for you [b]were not yet able *to receive it*. Indeed, even now you are not yet able,

3 for you are still fleshly. For since there is [a]jealousy and strife among you, are you not fleshly, and are you not walking [1b]like mere men?

4 For when [a]one says, "I am of Paul," and another, "I am of Apollos," are you not *mere* [b]men?

5 What then is Apollos? And what is Paul? [a]Servants through whom you believed, even [b]as the Lord gave *opportunity* to each one.

6 [a]I planted, [b]Apollos watered, but [c]God was causing the growth.

7 So then neither the one who plants nor the one who waters is anything, but God who causes the growth.

8 Now he who plants and he who waters are one; but each will [a]receive his own [1]reward according to his own labor.

9 For we are God's [a]fellow workers; you are God's [1b]field, God's [c]building.

10 According to [a]the grace of God which was given to me, as a wise master builder [b]I laid a foundation, and [c]another is building upon it. But let each man be careful how he builds upon it.

11 For no man can lay a [a]foundation other than the one which is laid, which is Jesus Christ.

12 Now if any man builds upon the foundation with gold, silver, [1]precious stones, wood, hay, straw,

13 [a]each man's work will become evident; for [b]the day will show it, because it is *to be* revealed with fire; and the fire itself will test [1]the quality of each man's work.

14 If any man's work which he has built upon it remains, he shall [a]receive a reward.

15 If any man's work is burned up, he shall suffer loss; but he himself shall be saved, yet [a]so as through fire.

16 [a]Do you not know that [b]you are a [1]temple of God, and *that* the Spirit of God dwells in you?

17 If any man destroys the [1]temple of God, God will destroy him, for the [1]temple of God is holy, and [2]that is what you are.

18 [a]Let no man deceive himself. [b]If any man among you thinks that he is wise in [c]this age, let him become foolish that he may become wise.

19 For [a]the wisdom of this world is foolishness before God. For it is written, "*He is* [b]THE ONE WHO CATCHES THE WISE IN THEIR CRAFTINESS";

20 and again, "[a]THE LORD KNOWS THE REASONINGS of the wise, THAT THEY ARE USELESS."

Or, *an unspiritual* ... *xamined* [a]1 Cor. 46; James 3:15; de 19 mg. [b]John :17 [c]1 Cor. 1:18

Cor. 3:1; 14:37; Gal. 6:1

[a]Is. 40:13; Rom. :34 [b]John 15:15

Cor. 2:15; 14:37; 6:1 [b]Rom. 7:14; 2:14 [c]1 Cor. 2:6; 4:14; Heb. 5:13

eb. 5:12f.; 1 Pet. 2:2 [b]John 16:12

Lit., *according to* an [a]Rom. 13:13; Cor. 1:10f.; 11:18 [b]1 Cor. 3:4

Cor. 1:12 [b]1 Cor. 3:3

m. 15:16; 2 Cor. 6; 4:1; 5:18; 6:4; n. 3:7; Col. 1:25; :12 [b]Rom. 12:6; 1 Cor. 3:10

1 Cor. 4:15; 9:1; 1; 2 Cor. 10:14f. 18:24-27; 1 Cor. 2 [c]1 Cor. 15:10

, *wages* [a]1 Cor. 5; 9:17; Gal. 6:4

, *cultivated land* 6:20; 2 Cor. 6:1 1:3; Matt. 15:13 Cor. 3:16; Eph. Col. 2:7; 1 Pet. 2:5

om. 12:3; 1 Cor. 0 [b]Rom. 15:20; 3:11f. [c]1 Thess. 3:2

[a]Is. 28:16; Eph. :20; 1 Pet. 2:4ff.

12 [1]Or, *costly*

Lit., *of what sort h man's work is* :5 [b]Matt. 10:15; or. 1:8; 2 Thess. 2 Tim. 1:12, 18; 4:8

[a]1 Cor. 3:8; 4:5; 9:17; Gal. 6:4

[a]Job 23:10; Ps. 10, 12; Jude 23

[1]Or, *sanctuary* :16 [b]Rom. 8:9; 19; 2 Cor. 6:16; Eph. 2:21f.

sanctuary [2]Lit., *which you are*

:21 [b]1 Cor. 8:2; :3 [c]1 Cor. 1:20

Cor. 1:20 [b]Job 5:13

20 [a]Ps. 94:11

21 So then [a]let no one boast in men. For [b]all things belong to you,
22 [a]whether Paul or Apollos or Cephas or the world or [b]life or death
or things present or things to come; all things belong to you,
23 and [a]you belong to Christ; and [b]Christ belongs to God.

Chapter 4

4 Let a man regard us in this manner, as [a]servants of Christ, and
[b]stewards of [c]the mysteries of God.
2 In this case, moreover, it is required [1]of stewards that one be
found trustworthy.
3 But to me it is a very small thing that I should be examined by
you, or by *any* human [1]court; in fact, I do not even examine myself.
4 For I [a]am conscious of nothing against myself, yet I am not by
this [b]acquitted; but the one who examines me is the Lord.
5 Therefore [a]do not go on [1]passing judgment before [2]the time, *but*
wait [b]until the Lord comes who will both [c]bring to light the things
hidden in the darkness and disclose the motives of *men's* hearts; and
then each man's [d]praise will come to him from God.
6 Now these things, brethren, I have figuratively applied to myself
and Apollos for your sakes, that in us you might learn not to exceed
[a]what is written, in order that no one of you might [b]become [1]arrogant
[c]in behalf of one against the other.
7 For who regards you as superior? And [a]what do you have that
you did not receive? But if you did receive it, why do you boast as if
you had not received it?
8 You are [a]already filled, you have already become rich, you have
become kings without us; and *I* would indeed that you had become
kings so that we also might reign with you.
9 For, I think, God has exhibited us apostles last of all, as men
[a]condemned to death; because we [b]have become a spectacle to the
world, [1]both to angels and to men.
10 We are [a]fools for Christ's sake, but [b]you are prudent in Christ;
[c]we are weak, but you are strong; you are distinguished, but we are
without honor.
11 To this present hour we are both [a]hungry and thirsty, and are
poorly clothed, and are roughly treated, and are homeless;
12 and we toil, [a]working with our own hands; when we are
[b]reviled, we bless; when we are [c]persecuted, we endure;
13 when we are slandered, we try to [1]conciliate; we have [a]become
as the scum of the world, the dregs of all things, *even* until now.
14 I do not write these things to [a]shame you, but to admonish you
as my beloved [b]children.
15 For if you were to have countless [a]tutors in Christ, yet *you would*
not *have* many fathers; for in [b]Christ Jesus I [c]became your father
through the [d]gospel.
16 I exhort you therefore, be [a]imitators of me.
17 For this reason I [a]have sent to you [b]Timothy, who is my [c]beloved
and faithful child in the Lord, and he will remind you of my ways
which are in Christ, [d]just as I teach everywhere in every church.
18 Now some have become [1a]arrogant, as though I were not [b]com-
ing to you.
19 But I [a]will come to you soon, [b]if the Lord wills, and I shall find
out, not the [1]words of those who are [c]arrogant, but their power.

21 [a]1 Cor. 4 8:32
22 [a]1 Cor. 1 [b]Rom. 8:38
23 [a]1 Cor. 1 10:7; Gal. 3: 11:3; 15:28
4:1 [a]Luke 1 9:17; Titus 1 4:10 [c]Rom.
2 [1]Lit., *in*
3 [1]Lit., *day*
4 [a]Acts 23:1 1:12 [b]Ps. 14 2:13
5 [1]Lit., *judgi anything* [2]I.e. appointed tim judgment [a]M Rom. 2:1 [b]Jo Rom. 2:16 [c] [d]Rom. 2:29; 2 Cor. 10:18
6 [1]Lit., *puffe* [a]1 Cor. 1:19, [b]1 Cor. 4:18f. [c]1 Cor. 1:12;
7 [a]John 3:27 12:3, 6; 1 Pet
8 [a]Rev. 3:17f
9 [1]Or, *and to and to men* [a] 1 Cor. 15:31; 11:23 [b]Heb.
10 [a]Acts 17: 1 Cor. 1:18 [b] 1:19f.; 3:18; 2 11:19 [c]1 Cor. 13:9
11 [a]Rom. 8:3 11:23-27
12 [a]Acts 18:3 3:9 [c]John 15: 8:35
13 [1]Or, *cons* 3:45
14 [a]1 Cor. 6:5 [b]2 Cor. 6:13; 1 Thess. 2:11; 2:1; 3 John 4
15 [a]Gal. 3:24 1:30; [c]Num. 1 1 Cor. 3:8; Gal Philem. 10 [d]1 14, 18, 23; 15:
16 [a]1 Cor. 11: 3:17; 4:9; 1 Th 2 Thess. 3:9
17 [a]1 Cor. 16: 16:1 [c]1 Cor. 4 1 Tim. 1:2, 18; 1:2 [d]1 Cor. 7: 16:1; Titus 1:5
18 [1]Lit., *puffed* [a]1 Cor. 4:6 [b]1
19 [1]Lit., *word* 19:21; 20:2; 1 11:34; 16:5f.; 1 2 Cor. 1:15f. [b] 18:21 [c]1 Cor. 4

20 For the kingdom of God does [a]not consist in [1]words, but in
power.
21 What do you desire? [a]Shall I come to you with a rod or with love
and a spirit of gentleness?

Chapter 5

5 It is actually reported that there is immorality among you, and
immorality of such a kind as does not exist even among the
Gentiles, that someone has [a]his father's wife.
2 And [1]you [a]have become [2]arrogant, and [3]have not [b]mourned in-
stead, in order that the one who had done this deed might be
[c]removed from your midst.
3 For I, on my part, though [a]absent in body but present in spirit,
have already judged him who has so committed this, as though I
were present.
4 [a]In the name of our Lord Jesus, when you are assembled, and [1]I
with you in spirit, [b]with the power of our Lord Jesus,
5 *I have decided* to [a]deliver such a one to [b]Satan for the destruction
of his flesh, that his spirit may be saved in [c]the day of the Lord
[1]Jesus.
6 [a]Your boasting is not good. [b]Do you not know that [c]a little leaven
leavens the whole lump *of dough*?
7 Clean out the old leaven, that you may be a new lump, just as
you are *in fact* unleavened. For Christ our [a]Passover also has been
sacrificed.
8 Let us therefore celebrate the feast, [a]not with old leaven, nor with
the leaven of malice and wickedness, but with the unleavened bread
of sincerity and truth.
9 I wrote you in my letter [a]not to associate with immoral people;
10 I *did* not at all *mean* with the immoral people of this world, or
with the covetous and swindlers, or with [a]idolaters; for then you
would have to go out of the world.
11 But [1]actually, I wrote to you not to associate [2]with any so-called
[a]brother if he should be an immoral person, or covetous, or [b]an
idolater, or a reviler, or a drunkard, or a swindler—not even to eat
with such a one.
12 For what have I to do with judging [a]outsiders? [b]Do you not
judge those who are within *the church*?
13 But those who are outside, God [1]judges. [a]REMOVE THE WICKED MAN
FROM AMONG YOURSELVES.

Chapter 6

6 Does any one of you, when he has a [1]case against his neighbor,
dare to go to law before the unrighteous, and [a]not before the
[2]saints?
2 Or [a]do you not know that [b]the [1]saints will judge [c]the world? And
if the world is judged by you, are you not competent *to* [2]*constitute* the
smallest law courts?
3 [a]Do you not know that we shall judge angels? How much more,
matters of this life?
4 If then you have law courts dealing with matters of this life, [1]do
you appoint them as judges who are of no account in the church?
5 [a]I say *this* to your shame. *Is it* so, *that* there is not among you one
wise man who will be able to decide between his [b]brethren,

it., *word* [a]1 Cor. 2:4
Cor. 1:23; 2:1, 3; 12:20; 13:2, 10
[a]Lev. 18:8; Deut. 22:30; 27:20
, *have you . . . ?* , *puffed up* [3]Or, *ou . . . ?* [a]1 Cor. 6 [b]2 Cor. 7:7-10 [c]1 Cor. 5:13
ol. 2:5; 1 Thess. 2:17
t., *my spirit, with power* [a]2 Thess. hn 20:23; 2 Cor. 2:10; 13:3, 10
me ancient mss. ot contain *Jesus* rov. 23:14; Luke 2:31; 1 Tim. 1:20 4:10 [c]1 Cor. 1:8
Cor. 5:2; James Rom. 6:16 [c]Hos. tt. 16:6, 12; Gal. 5:9
ark 14:12; 1 Pet. 1:19
[a]Ex. 12:19; 13:7; Deut. 16:3
Cor. 6:14; Eph. 11; 2 Thess. 3:6
10 [a]1 Cor. 10:27
[1]Or, *now I write* *ether if any man* *a brother should* s 1:15; 2 Thess. or. 10:7, 14, 20f.
ark 4:11 [b]1 Cor. 5:3-5; 6:1-4
3 [1]Or, *will judge* t. 13:5; 17:7, 12; 22:21; 1 Cor. 5:2
[1]Lit., *matter* [2]Or, *es* [a]Matt. 18:17
, note 2 [2]Or, *try* *al cases?* [a]Rom. an. 7:18, 22, 27; :28 [c]1 Cor. 1:20
3 [a]Rom. 6:16
appoint them . . . church.
Cor. 4:14; 15:34 :15; 9:13; 1 Cor. 6:1

6 but brother goes to law with brother, and that before [a]unbelievers?

7 Actually, then, it is already a defeat for you, that you have lawsuits with one another. [a]Why not rather be wronged? Why not rather be defrauded?

8 On the contrary, you yourselves wrong and defraud, and that *your* [a]brethren.

9 Or [a]do you not know that the unrighteous shall not [b]inherit the kingdom of God? [c]Do not be deceived; [d]neither fornicators, nor idolaters, nor adulterers, nor [1]effeminate, nor homosexuals,

10 nor thieves, nor *the* covetous, nor drunkards, nor revilers, nor swindlers, shall [a]inherit the kingdom of God.

11 And [a]such were some of you; but you were [b]washed, but you were [c]sanctified, but you were [d]justified in the name of the Lord Jesus Christ, and in the Spirit of our God.

12 [a]All things are lawful for me, but not all things are profitable. All things are lawful for me, but I will not be mastered by anything.

13 [a]Food is for the [1]stomach, and the [1]stomach is for food; but God will [b]do away with both [2]of them. Yet the body is not for immorality, but [c]for the Lord; and [d]the Lord is for the body.

14 Now God has not only [a]raised the Lord, but [b]will also raise us up through His power.

15 [a]Do you not know that [b]your bodies are members of Christ? Shall I then take away the members of Christ and make them members of a harlot? [c]May it never be!

16 Or [a]do you not know that the one who joins himself to a harlot is one body *with her*? For He says, "[b]THE TWO WILL BECOME ONE FLESH."

17 But the one who joins himself to the Lord is [a]one spirit *with Him*.

18 [a]Flee immorality. Every *other* sin that a man commits is outside the body, but the [1]immoral man sins against his own body.

19 Or [a]do you not know that [b]your body is a [1]temple of the Holy Spirit who is in you, whom you have from [2]God, and that [c]you are not your own?

20 For [a]you have been bought with a price: therefore glorify God in [b]your body.

Chapter 7

7 Now concerning the things about which you wrote, it is [a]good for a man not to touch a woman.

2 But because of immoralities, let each man have his own wife, and let each woman have her own husband.

3 Let the husband [1]fulfill his duty to his wife, and likewise also the wife to her husband.

4 The wife does not have authority over her own body, but the husband *does*; and likewise also the husband does not have authority over his own body, but the wife *does*.

5 [a]Stop depriving one another, except by agreement for a time that you may devote yourselves to prayer, and [1]come together again lest [b]Satan tempt you because of your lack of self-control.

6 But this I say by way of concession, [a]not of command.

7 [1]Yet I wish that all men were [a]even as I myself am. However, [b]each man has his own gift from God, one in this manner, and another in that.

6 [a]2 Cor. 6:1 5:8
7 [a]Matt. 5:3
8 [a]1 Thess.
9 [1]I.e., effem perversion [b]Acts 20:32; 15:50; Gal. 5 5:5 [c]Luke 21 15:33; Gal. 6 1:16; 1 John 13:13; 1 Cor. 5:19-21; Eph 1 Tim. 1:10; 22:15
10 [a]Acts 20: 15:50; Gal. 5 5:5
11 [a]1 Cor. 12 2:2f.; Col. 3:5 3:3-7 [b]Acts 2 5:26 [c]1 Cor. [d]Rom. 8:30
12 [a]1 Cor. 10
13 [1]Lit., *belly and them* [b]Col. 2:22 19 [d]Gal. 5:24
14 [a]Acts 2:24 6:39f.; 1 Cor.
15 [a]1 Cor. 6: 12:5; 1 Cor. 6 Eph. 5:30
16 [a]1 Cor. 6: 2:24; Matt. 19 10:8; Eph. 5:3
17 [a]John 17: Rom. 8:9-11; 6:15; Gal. 2:20
18 [1]Or, *one w practices imm* [a]1 Cor. 6:9; 2 12:21; Eph. 5: 3:5; Heb. 13:4
19 [1]Or, *sanct. God? And you* [a]1 Cor. 6:3 1 Cor. 3:16; 2 [c]Rom. 14:7f.
20 [a]Acts 20:28 7:23; 1 Pet. 1:1 2 Pet. 2:1; Rev [b]Rom. 12:1; Ph
7:1 [a]1 Cor. 7:8
3 [1]Lit., *render*
5 [1]Lit., *be* [a]Ex 1 Sam. 21:5
6 [a]2 Cor. 8:8
7 [1]Some ancie read *For* [a]1 Co 9:5 [b]Matt. 19:1 12:6; 1 Cor. 12:

8 But I say to the unmarried and to widows that it is [a]good for
them if they remain [b]even as I.
9 But if they do not have self-control, [a]let them marry; for it is
better to marry than to [1]burn.
10 But to the married I give instructions, [a]not I, but the Lord, that
the wife should not [1]leave her husband
11 (but if she does leave, let her remain unmarried, or else be recon-
ciled to her husband), and that the husband should not [1]send his
wife away.
12 But to the rest [a]I say, not the Lord, that if any brother has a wife
who is an unbeliever, and she consents to live with him, let him not
[1]send her away.
13 And a woman who has an unbelieving husband, and he con-
sents to live with her, let her not [1]send her husband away.
14 For the unbelieving husband is sanctified through his wife, and
the unbelieving wife is sanctified through [1]her believing husband;
for otherwise your children are unclean, but now they are [a]holy.
15 Yet if the unbelieving one leaves, let him leave; the brother or the
sister is not under bondage in such *cases,* but God has called [1]us [2a]to
peace.
16 For how do you know, O wife, whether you will [a]save your
husband? Or how do you know, O husband, whether you will save
your wife?
17 Only, [a]as the Lord has assigned to each one, as God has called
each, in this manner let him walk. And [b]thus I direct in [c]all the
churches.
18 Was any man called *already* circumcised? Let him not become
uncircumcised. Has anyone been called in uncircumcision? [a]Let him
not be circumcised.
19 [a]Circumcision is nothing, and uncircumcision is nothing, but
what matters is [b]the keeping of the commandments of God.
20 [a]Let each man remain in that [1]condition in which he was called.
21 Were you called while a slave? [1]Do not worry about it; but if you
are able also to become free, rather [2]do that.
22 For he who was called in the Lord while a slave, is [a]the Lord's
freedman; likewise he who was called while free, is [b]Christ's slave.
23 [a]You were bought with a price; do not become slaves of men.
24 Brethren, [a]let each man remain with God in that *condition* in
which he was called.
25 Now concerning virgins I have [a]no command of the Lord, but I
give an opinion as one who [1b]by the mercy of the Lord is trustwor-
thy.
26 I think then that this is good in view of the [1]present [a]distress, that
[b]it is good for a man [2]to remain as he is.
27 Are you bound to a wife? Do not seek to be released. Are you
released from a wife? Do not seek a wife.
28 But if you should marry, you have not sinned; and if a virgin
should marry, she has not sinned. Yet such will have [1]trouble in this
life, and I am trying to spare you.
29 But this I say, brethren, [a]the time has been shortened, so that
from now on those who have wives should be as though they had
none;
30 and those who weep, as though they did not weep; and those

8 [a]1 Cor. 7:1, 26 [b]1 Cor. 7:7; 9:5
9 [1]I.e., burn with ...ion [a]1 Tim. 5:14
[1]Lit., *depart from* ...2:16; Matt. 5:32; ...9; Mark 10:2-12; ...6:18; 1 Cor. 7:6
...r, *leave his wife*
12 [1]Or, *leave her* ...7:6; 2Cor. 11:17
13 [1]Or, *leave her husband*
[1]Lit., *the brother* ...ra 9:2; Mal. 2:15
...ne ancient mss. [2]Lit., *in* [a]Rom. 14:19
...m. 11:14; 1 Pet. 3:1
...m. 12:3 [b]1 Cor. 7 [c]1 Cor. 11:16; ...33; 2 Cor. 8:18; ...1:28; Gal. 1:22; ... 2:14; 2 Thess. 1:4
18 [a]Acts 15:1ff.
...1. 2:27, 29; Gal. ...; 5:6; 6:15; Col. ...:11 [b]Rom. 2:25
..., *calling* [a]1 Cor. 7:24
..., *Let it not be a* ...*o you* [2]Lit., *use*
[a]John 8:32, 36; ...1. 16 [b]Eph. 6:6; ...:24; 1 Pet. 2:16
23 [a]1 Cor. 6:20
24 [a]1 Cor. 7:20
...has had mercy ...n on him by the ...o be trustworthy ...7:6 [b]2 Cor. 4:1; 1 Tim. 1:13, 16
...mpending [2]Lit., ...e [a]Luke 21:23; ...ss. 2:2 [b]1 Cor. 7:1, 8
...it., *tribulation in the flesh*
[a]Rom. 13:11f.; 1 Cor. 7:31

who rejoice, as though they did not rejoice; and those who buy, as
though they did not possess;
31 and those who use the world, as though they did not [a]make full
use of it; for [b]the form of this world is passing away.
32 But I want you to be free from concern. One who is [a]unmarried
is concerned about the things of the Lord, how he may please the
Lord;
33 but one who is married is concerned about the things of the
world, how he may please his [1]wife,
34 and *his interests* are divided. And the woman who is unmarried,
and the virgin, is concerned about the things of the Lord, that she
may be holy both in body and spirit; but one who is married is
concerned about the things of the world, how she may please her
husband.
35 And this I say for your own benefit; not to put a restraint upon
you, but [1]to promote what is seemly, and *to secure* undistracted devo-
tion to the Lord.
36 But if any man thinks that he is acting unbecomingly toward his
virgin *daughter,* if she should be of full age, and if it must be so, let
him do what he wishes, he does not sin; let [1]her marry.
37 But he who stands firm in his heart, [1]being under no constraint,
but has authority [2]over his own will, and has decided this in his own
heart, to keep his own virgin *daughter,* he will do well.
38 So then both he who gives his own virgin *daughter* in marriage
does well, and he who does not give her in marriage will do better.
39 [a]A wife is bound as long as her husband lives; but if her husband
[1]is dead, she is free to be married to whom she wishes, only [b]in the
Lord.
40 But [a]in my opinion she is happier if she remains as she is; and I
think that I also have the Spirit of God.

Chapter 8

8 Now concerning [a]things sacrificed to idols, we know that we all
have [b]knowledge. Knowledge [1c]makes arrogant, but love
[d]edifies.
2 [a]If anyone supposes that he knows anything, he has not yet
[b]known as he ought to know;
3 but if anyone loves God, he [a]is known by Him.
4 Therefore concerning the eating of [a]things sacrificed to idols, we
know that [1]there is [b]no such thing as an idol in the world, and that
[c]there is no God but one.
5 For even if [a]there are so-called gods whether in heaven or on
earth, as indeed there are many gods and many lords,
6 yet for us [a]there is *but* one God, [b]the Father, [c]from whom are all
things, and we *exist* for Him; and [d]one Lord, Jesus Christ, [e]by whom
are all things, and we *exist* through Him.
7 However not all men [a]have this knowledge; but [b]some, being
accustomed to the idol until now, eat *food* as if it were sacrificed to an
idol; and their conscience being weak is defiled.
8 But [a]food will not [1]commend us to God; we are neither [2]the
worse if we do not eat, nor [3]the better if we do eat.
9 But [a]take care lest this [1]liberty of yours somehow become a stum-
bling block to the [b]weak.
10 For if someone sees you, who have [a]knowledge, dining in an

31 [a]1 Cor. 9:18 7:29; 1 John 2:1
32 [a]1 Tim. 5:5
33 [1]Some mss. *wife. And there i difference also b the wife and the One who is unm concerned...*
35 [1]Lit., *for wha seemly*
36 [1]Lit., *them*
37 [1]Lit., *having necessity* [2]Lit., *pertaining to*
39 [1]Lit., *has fal asleep* [a]Rom. 7 [b]2 Cor. 6:14
40 [a]1 Cor. 7:6,
8:1 [1]Lit., *puffs u* 15:20; 1 Cor. 8: [b]Rom. 15:14; 1 10; 10:15 [c]1 Co [d]Rom. 14:19
2 [a]1 Cor. 3:18 13:8-12; 1 Tim.
3 [a]Ps. 1:6; Jer. Amos 3:2; Rom 11:2; Gal. 4:9
4 [1]I.e., has no r existence [a]Acts 1 Cor. 8:1, 7, 10 14:15; 1 Cor. 10 4:8 [c]Deut. 4:35 1 Cor. 8:6
5 [a]2 Thess. 2:4
6 [a]Deut. 4:35, Is. 46:9; Jer. 10 1 Cor. 8:4 [b]Mal Eph. 4:6 [c]Rom [d]John 13:13; 1 Eph. 4:5; 1 Tim [e]John 1:3; Col.
7 [a]1 Cor. 8:4ff. 14:14, 22f.
8 [1]Or, *present lacking* [3]Lit., *abounding* [a]Ro
9 [1]Lit., *right* [a]F 14:13, 21; 1 Co Gal. 5:13 [b]Ron 1 Cor. 8:10f.
10 [a]1 Cor. 8:4f

idol's temple, will not his conscience, if he is weak, be strengthened
to eat [b]things sacrificed to idols?
11 For through [a]your knowledge he who is weak [b]is ruined, the
brother for whose sake Christ died.
12 [a]And thus, by sinning against the brethren and wounding their
conscience when it is weak, you sin [b]against Christ.
13 Therefore, [a]if food causes my brother to stumble, I will never eat
meat again, that I might not cause my brother to stumble.

Chapter 9

9 Am I not [a]free? Am I not an [b]apostle? Have I not [c]seen Jesus our
Lord? Are you not [d]my work in the Lord?
2 If to others I am not an apostle, at least I am to you; for you are
the [a]seal of my [b]apostleship in the Lord.
3 My defense to those who examine me is this:
4 [1a]Do we not have a right to eat and drink?
5 [1a]Do we not have a right to take along a [2]believing wife, even as
the rest of the apostles, and the [b]brothers of the Lord, and [c]Cephas?
6 Or do only [1a]Barnabas and I not have a right to refrain from
working?
7 Who at any time serves [a]as a soldier at his own expense? Who
[b]plants a vineyard, and does not eat the fruit of it? Or who tends a
flock and does not [1]use the milk of the flock?
8 I am not speaking these things [a]according to [1]human judgment,
am I? Or does not the Law also say these things?
9 For it is written in the Law of Moses, "[a]YOU SHALL NOT MUZZLE
THE OX WHILE HE IS THRESHING." God is not concerned about [b]oxen, is
He?
10 Or is He speaking altogether for our sake? Yes, [a]for our sake it
was written, because [b]the plowman ought to plow in hope, and the
thresher *to thresh* in hope of sharing *the crops.*
11 [a]If we sowed spiritual things in you, is it too much if we should
reap material things from you?
12 If others share the right over you, do we not more? Nevertheless,
we [a]did not use this right, but we endure all things, [b]that we may
cause no hindrance to the [c]gospel of Christ.
13 [a]Do you not know that those who [b]perform sacred services eat
the *food* of the temple, *and* those who attend regularly to the altar
have their share with the altar?
14 So also [a]the Lord directed those who proclaim the [b]gospel to [c]get
their living from the gospel.
15 But I have [a]used none of these things. And I am not writing these
things that it may be done so in my case; for it would be better for
me to die than have any man make [b]my boast an empty one.
16 For if I preach the gospel, I have nothing to boast of, for [a]I am
under compulsion; for woe is me if I do not preach [b]the gospel.
17 For if I do this voluntarily, I have a [a]reward; but if against my
will, I have a [b]stewardship entrusted to me.
18 What then is my [a]reward? That, when I preach the gospel, I may
offer the gospel [b]without charge, so as [c]not to make full use of my
right in the gospel.
19 For though I am [a]free from all *men,* I have made myself [b]a slave
to all, that I might [c]win the more.
20 And [a]to the Jews I became as a Jew, that I might win Jews; to

ts 15:20; 1 Cor. 8:1, 4, 7
or. 8:4ff. [b]Rom. 14:15, 20
latt. 18:6; Rom. 20 [b]Matt. 25:45
n. 14:21; 1 Cor. Cor. 6:3; 11:29
Cor. 9:19; 10:29 4:14; Rom. 1:1; 12:12; 1 Thess. Tim. 2:7; 2 Tim. ts 9:3, 17; 18:9; 8; 23:11; 1 Cor. 1 Cor. 3:6; 4:15
ohn 3:33; 2 Cor. 3:2f. [b]Acts 1:25
It is not that we right to eat and ? [a]1 Cor. 9:14; 1 Thess. 2:6, 9; 2 Thess. 3:8f.
It is not that we no right to take . Cephas, is it? ., sister, as wife Cor. 7:7f. [b]Matt. latt. 8:14; John 1:42
I and Barnabas [a]Acts 4:36
, eat of [a]2 Cor. m. 1:18; 2 Tim. eut. 20:6; Prov. 8; 1 Cor. 3:6, 8
man [a]Rom. 3:5
ut. 25:4; 1 Tim. [b]Deut. 22:1-4; Prov. 12:10
0 [a]Rom. 4:23f. [b]2 Tim. 2:6
n. 15:27; 1 Cor. 9:14
cts 18:3; 20:33; :15, 18 [b]2 Cor. 2 [c]1 Cor. 4:15; , 18, 23; 2 Cor. 2:12
om. 6:16 [b]Lev. , 26; 7:6, 31ff.; 9f.; 18:8-20, 31; Deut. 18:1
att. 10:10; Luke 0:7; 1 Tim. 5:18 4:15; 9:12, 16, 23; 2 Cor. 2:12 10:8; 1 Cor. 9:4
cts 18:3; 20:33; :12, 18 [b]2 Cor. 11:10
cts 9:15; Rom. Cor. 4:15; 9:12, 23; 2 Cor. 2:12
hn 4:36; 1 Cor. 18 [b]1 Cor. 4:1; Eph. 3:2; Phil. 1:16; Col. 1:25
hn 4:36; 1 Cor. 17 [b]Acts 18:3; Cor. 11:7; 12:13 Cor. 7:31; 9:12
Cor. 9:1 [b]2 Cor. al. 5:13 [c]Matt. 8:15; 1 Pet. 3:1
20 [a]Acts 16:3; 26; Rom. 11:14

those who are under [1]the Law, as under [1]the Law, though [b]not being
myself under [1]the Law, that I might win those who are under [1]the
Law;
21 to those who are [a]without law, [b]as without law, though not being
without the law of God but [c]under the law of Christ, that I might
win those who are without law.
22 To the [a]weak I became weak, that I might win the weak; I have
become [b]all things to all men, [c]that I may by all means save some.
23 And I do all things for the sake of the gospel, that I may become
a fellow partaker of it.
24 [a]Do you not know that those who run in a race all run, but *only*
one receives [b]the prize? [c]Run in such a way that you may win.
25 And everyone who [a]competes in the games exercises self-control
in all things. They then *do it* to receive a perishable [b]wreath, but we
an imperishable.
26 Therefore I [a]run in such a way, as not without aim; I box in such
a way, as not [b]beating the air;
27 but I [1]buffet [a]my body and make it my slave, lest possibly, after I
have preached to others, I myself should be disqualified.

Chapter 10

10 For [a]I do not want you to be unaware, brethren, that our
fathers were all [b]under the cloud, and all [c]passed through the
sea;
2 and all [1]were [a]baptized into Moses in the cloud and in the sea;
3 and all [a]ate the same spiritual food;
4 and all [a]drank the same spiritual drink, for they were drinking
from a spiritual rock which followed them; and the rock was [1]Christ.
5 Nevertheless, with most of them God was not well-pleased; for
[a]they were laid low in the wilderness.
6 Now these things happened as [a]examples for us, that we should
not crave evil things, as [b]they also craved.
7 And do not be [a]idolaters, as some of them were; as it is written,
"[b]THE PEOPLE SAT DOWN TO EAT AND DRINK, AND STOOD UP TO [c]PLAY."
8 Nor let us act immorally, as [a]some of them [1]did, and [b]twenty-
three thousand fell in one day.
9 Nor let us try the Lord, as [a]some of them [1]did, and were
destroyed by the serpents.
10 Nor [a]grumble, as some of them [1]did, and [b]were [2]destroyed by the
[c]destroyer.
11 Now these things happened to them as an [a]example, and [b]they
were written for our instruction, upon whom [c]the ends of the ages
have come.
12 Therefore let him who [a]thinks he stands take heed lest he fall.
13 No temptation has overtaken you but such as is common to
man; and [a]God is faithful, who will not allow you to be [b]tempted
beyond what you are able, but with the temptation will provide the
way of escape also, that you may be able to endure it.
14 Therefore, my [a]beloved, flee from [b]idolatry.
15 I speak as to wise men; you judge what I say.
16 Is not the [a]cup of blessing which we bless a sharing in the blood
of Christ? Is not the [1b]bread which we break a sharing in the body of
Christ?

20 [1]Or, *law* [b]Ga

21 [a]Rom. 2:12, [b]Gal. 2:3; 3:2 [c]1 7:22; Gal. 6:2

22 [a]Rom. 14:1; 2 Cor. 11:29 [b]1 10:33 [c]Rom. 11

24 [a]1 Cor. 9:13 3:14; Col. 2:18 2:2; 2 Tim. 4:7; 12:1

25 [a]Eph. 6:12; 6:12; 2 Tim. 2:5 [b]2 Tim. 4:8; Jam 1 Pet. 5:4; Rev. 3:11

26 [a]Gal. 2:2; 2 Heb. 12:1 [b]1 C

27 [1]Lit., *bruise* 8:13

10:1 [a]Rom. 1:1 13:21; Ps. 105: 14:22, 29; Neh. Ps. 66:6

2 [1]Some ancie read *received b* [a]Rom. 6:3; 1 Co Gal. 3:27

3 [a]Ex. 16:4, 35 8:3; Neh. 9:15, 78:24f.; John 6

4 [1]I.e., the Mes [a]Ex. 17:6; Num Ps. 78:15

5 [a]Num. 14:29 26:65; Heb. 3:1

6 [a]1 Cor. 10:11 11:4, 34; Ps. 10

7 [a]Ex. 32:4; 1 10:14 [b]Ex. 32: 32:19

8 [1]Lit., *acted ir* [a]Num. 25:1ff. 25:9

9 [1]Lit., *made t* [a]Num. 21:5f.

10 [1]Lit., *grumb being destroye* 16:41; 17:5, 10 16:49 [c]Ex. 12: 2 Sam. 24:16; 21:15; Heb. 11

11 [a]1 Cor. 10:6 4:23 [c]Rom. 13

12 [a]Rom. 11:2 3:17

13 [a]1 Cor. 1:9 2:9

14 [a]Heb. 6:9 10:7, 19f.; 1 Jo

16 [1]Lit., *loaf* [a] 26:27f.; Mark 1 Luke 22:20; 1 11:25 [b]Matt. 2 Luke 22:19; Ac 1 Cor. 11:23f.

17 Since there is one [1]bread, we [a]who are many are one body; for we
all partake of the one [1]bread.
18 Look at [1]the nation [a]Israel; are not those who [b]eat the sacrifices
sharers in the altar?
19 What do I mean then? That a thing sacrificed to idols is any-
thing, or [a]that an idol is anything?
20 *No,* but *I say* that the things which the Gentiles sacrifice, they
[a]sacrifice to demons, and not to God; and I do not want you to
become sharers in demons.
21 [a]You cannot drink the cup of the Lord and the cup of demons;
you cannot partake of the table of the Lord and [b]the table of demons.
22 Or do we [a]provoke the Lord to jealousy? We are not [b]stronger
than He, are we?
23 [a]All things are lawful, but not all things are profitable. All things
are lawful, but not all things [b]edify.
24 Let no one [a]seek his own *good,* but that of his [1]neighbor.
25 [a]Eat anything that is sold in the meat market, without asking
questions for conscience' sake;
26 [a]FOR THE EARTH IS THE LORD'S, AND [1]ALL IT CONTAINS.
27 If [a]one of the unbelievers invites you, and you wish to go, [b]eat
anything that is set before you, without asking questions for con-
science' sake.
28 But [a]if anyone should say to you, "This is meat sacrificed to
idols," do not eat *it,* for the sake of the one who informed *you,* and
for conscience' sake;
29 I mean not your own conscience, but the other *man's;* for [a]why is
my freedom judged by another's conscience?
30 If I partake with thankfulness, [a]why am I slandered concerning
that for which I [b]give thanks?
31 Whether, then, you eat or drink or [a]whatever you do, do all to
the glory of God.
32 [a]Give no offense either to Jews or to Greeks or to [b]the church of
God;
33 just as I also [a]please all men in all things, [b]not seeking my own
profit, but the *profit* of the many, [c]that they may be saved.

Chapter 11

11 [a]Be imitators of me, just as I also am of Christ.
2 Now [a]I praise you because you [b]remember me in every-
thing, and [c]hold firmly to the traditions, just as I delivered them to
you.
3 But I want you to understand that [1]Christ is the [a]head of every
man, and [b]the man is the head of a woman, and God is the [c]head of
[1]Christ.
4 Every man who has *something* on his head while praying or
[a]prophesying, disgraces his head.
5 But every [a]woman who has her head uncovered while praying
or prophesying, disgraces her head; for she is one and the same with
her [1]whose head is [b]shaved.
6 For if a woman does not cover [1]her head, let her also [2]have her
hair cut off; but if it is disgraceful for a woman to [2]have her hair cut
off or [1]her head shaved, let her cover [1]her head.
7 For a man ought not to have his head covered, since he is the
[a]image and glory of God; but the woman is the glory of man.

8 For [a]man [1]does not originate from woman, but woman from man;
9 for indeed man was not created for the woman's sake, but [a]woman for the man's sake.
10 Therefore the woman ought to have *a symbol of* authority on her head, because of the angels.
11 However, in the Lord, neither is woman [1]independent of man, nor is man [1]independent of woman.
12 For as the woman [1]originates from the man, so also the man *has his birth* through the woman; and [a]all things [2]originate [b]from God.
13 [a]Judge [1]for yourselves: is it proper for a woman to pray to God *with head* uncovered?
14 Does not even nature itself teach you that if a man has long hair, it is a dishonor to him,
15 but if a woman has long hair, it is a glory to her? For her hair is given to her for a covering.
16 But if one is inclined to be contentious, [a]we have no [1]other practice, nor have [b]the churches of God.
17 But in giving this instruction, [a]I do not praise you, because you come together not for the better but for the worse.
18 For, in the first place, when you come together [1]as a church, I hear that [2a]divisions exist among you; and in part, I believe it.
19 For there [a]must also be factions among you, [b]in order that those who are approved may have become [1]evident among you.
20 Therefore when you meet together, it is not to eat the Lord's Supper,
21 for in your eating each one takes his own supper first; and one is hungry and [a]another is drunk.
22 What! Do you not have houses in which to eat and drink? Or do you despise the [a]church of God, and [b]shame those who have nothing? What shall I say to you? Shall [c]I praise you? In this I will not praise you.
23 For [a]I received from the Lord that which I also delivered to you, that [b]the Lord Jesus in the night in which He was betrayed took bread;
24 and when He had given thanks, He broke it, and said, "This is My body, which [1]is for you; do this in remembrance of Me."
25 In the same way *He took* [a]the cup also, after supper, saying, "This cup is the [b]new covenant in My blood; do this, as often as you drink *it*, in remembrance of Me."
26 For as often as you eat this bread and drink the cup, you proclaim the Lord's death [a]until He comes.
27 Therefore whoever eats the bread or drinks the cup of the Lord in an unworthy manner, shall be [a]guilty of the body and the blood of the Lord.
28 But let a man [a]examine himself, and so let him eat of the bread and drink of the cup.
29 For he who eats and drinks, eats and drinks judgment to himself, if he does not judge the body rightly.
30 For this reason many among you are weak and sick, and a number [a]sleep.
31 But if we judged ourselves rightly, we should not be judged.
32 But when we are judged, we are [a]disciplined by the Lord in order that we may not be condemned along with [b]the world.

8 [1]Lit., *is not* [a]Gen. 2:21-23; 2:13
9 [a]Gen. 2:18
11 [1]Lit., *withou*
12 [1]Lit., *is* [2]Lit [a]2 Cor. 5:18 [b]R 11:36
13 [1]Lit., *in* [a]Lu
16 [1]Lit., *such* 4:5; 9:1-3, 6 [b]
17 [a]1 Cor. 11:
18 [1]Lit., *in chu* *schisms* [a]1 Co 3:3
19 [1]Or, *manife* 18:7; Luke 17:1 4:1; 2 Pet. 2:1 13:3; 1 John 2:
21 [a]Jude 12
22 [a]1 Cor. 10:3 [b]James 2:6 [c]1 11:2, 17
23 [a]1 Cor. 15:3 1:12; Col. 3:24 11:23-25: *Matt. 26:26-28; Mark 14:22-24; Luke 22:17-20;* 1 Co
24 [1]Some anci read *is broken*
25 [a]1 Cor. 10:1 24:6-8; Luke 22 2 Cor. 3:6
26 [a]John 21:22 4:5
27 [a]Heb. 10:29
28 [a]Matt. 26:2 13:5; Gal. 6:4
30 [a]Acts 7:60
32 [a]2 Sam. 7: 94:12; Heb. 12 Rev. 3:19 [b]1 C

[a]1 Cor. 11:21
r. 11:22 [c]1 Cor.
7; 16:1 [d]1 Cor.
4:19

Cor. 12:4; 14:1
[b]Rom. 1:13

Cor. 6:11; Eph.
:11f.; 1 Pet. 4:3
hess. 1:9 [c]Ps.
5; Is. 46:7; Jer.
0:5; Hab. 2:18f.

3 [1]Or, in [2]Gr.,
a [a]Matt. 22:43;
4:2f.; Rev. 1:10
3 [c]John 13:13;
Rom. 10:9

1. 12:6f.; 1 Cor.
Eph. 4:4ff., 11;
Heb. 2:4

or. 15:28; Eph.
1:23; 4:6

Cor. 12:12-30;
4:26; Eph. 4:12

Cor. 2:6; 2 Cor.
[b]Rom. 15:14;
2:11, 16; 2 Cor.
4; 4:6; 8:7; 11:6

[2]Lit., healings
or. 13:2; 2 Cor.
Cor. 12:28, 30

it., effects [2]Or,
of power [3]Lit.,
ishings [a]1 Cor.
al. 3:5 [b]1 Cor.
13:2, 8 [c]1 Cor.
ohn 4:1 [d]Mark
Cor. 12:28, 30;
14:2ff. [e]1 Cor.
12:30; 14:26

1 [a]1 Cor. 12:4

1. 12:4f.; 1 Cor.
[b]1 Cor. 12:27

; in [a]Eph. 2:18
3:22; Gal. 3:28;
3-18; Col. 3:11
[c]John 7:37-39

[a]1 Cor. 12:20

[1]Lit., not a part

[1]Lit., not a part

r. 12:28 [b]Rom.
6; 1 Cor. 12:11

Cor. 12:12, 14

[1]Lit., to a much
ater degree the
members

[1]Or, think to be

33 So then, my brethren, when you come together to eat, wait for
one another.
34 If anyone is [a]hungry, let him eat [b]at home, so that you may not
come together for judgment. And the remaining matters I shall [c]ar-
range [d]when I come.

Chapter 12

12 Now concerning [a]spiritual *gifts*, brethren, [b]I do not want you
to be unaware.
2 [a]You know that when you were pagans, *you were* [b]led astray to
the [c]dumb idols, however you were led.
3 Therefore I make known to you, that no one speaking [1a]by the
Spirit of God says, "Jesus is [2b]accursed"; and no one can say, "Jesus is
[c]Lord," except [1a]by the Holy Spirit.
4 Now there are [a]varieties of gifts, but the same Spirit.
5 And there are varieties of ministries, and the same Lord.
6 And there are varieties of effects, but the same [a]God who works
all things in all *persons*.
7 But to each one is given the manifestation of the Spirit [a]for the
common good.
8 For to one is given the word of [a]wisdom through the Spirit, and
to another the word of [b]knowledge according to the same Spirit;
9 to another [a]faith [1]by the same Spirit, and to another [b]gifts of
[2]healing [1]by the one Spirit,
10 and to another the [1]effecting of [2a]miracles, and to another
[b]prophecy, and to another the [3c]distinguishing of spirits, to another
various [d]kinds of tongues, and to another the [e]interpretation of ton-
gues.
11 But one and the same Spirit works all these things, [a]distributing
to each one individually just as He wills.
12 For even [a]as the body is one and *yet* has many members, and all
the members of the body, though they are many, are one body, [b]so
also is Christ.
13 For [1a]by one Spirit we were all baptized into one body, whether
[b]Jews or Greeks, whether slaves or free, and we were all made to
[c]drink of one Spirit.
14 For [a]the body is not one member, but many.
15 If the foot should say, "Because I am not a hand, I am not *a part*
of the body," it is not for this reason [1]any the less *a part* of the body.
16 And if the ear should say, "Because I am not an eye, I am not *a*
part of the body," it is not for this reason [1]any the less *a part* of the
body.
17 If the whole body were an eye, where would the hearing be? If
the whole were hearing, where would the sense of smell be?
18 But now God has [a]placed the members, each one of them, in the
body, [b]just as He desired.
19 And if they were all one member, where would the body be?
20 But now [a]there are many members, but one body.
21 And the eye cannot say to the hand, "I have no need of you"; or
again the head to the feet, "I have no need of you."
22 On the contrary, [1]it is much truer that the members of the body
which seem to be weaker are necessary;
23 and those *members* of the body, which we [1]deem less honorable,

[2]on these we bestow more abundant honor, and our unseemly *mem-*
bers come to have more abundant seemliness,
24 whereas our seemly *members* have no need *of it*. But God has *so*
composed the body, giving more abundant honor to that *member*
which lacked,
25 that there should be no [1]division in the body, but *that* the mem-
bers should have the same care for one another.
26 And if one member suffers, all the members suffer with it; if *one*
member is [1]honored, all the members rejoice with it.
27 Now you are [a]Christ's body, and [b]individually members of it.
28 And God has [1a]appointed in [b]the church, first [c]apostles, second
[d]prophets, third [e]teachers, then [2f]miracles, then [g]gifts of healings,
helps, [h]administrations, *various* [i]kinds of tongues.
29 All are not apostles, are they? All are not prophets, are they? All
are not teachers, are they? All are not *workers of* [1]miracles, are they?
30 All do not have gifts of healings, do they? All do not speak with
tongues, do they? All do not [a]interpret, do they?
31 But [a]earnestly desire the greater gifts.
And I show you a still more excellent way.

Chapter 13

13 If I speak with the [a]tongues of men and of [b]angels, but do not
have love, I have become a noisy gong or a [c]clanging cymbal.
2 And if I have *the gift of* [a]prophecy, and know all [b]mysteries and
all [c]knowledge; and if I have [d]all faith, so as to [e]remove mountains,
but do not have love, I am nothing.
3 And if I [a]give all my possessions to feed *the poor*, and if I [b]deliver
my body [1]to be burned, but do not have love, it profits me nothing.
4 Love [a]is patient, love is kind, *and* [b]is not jealous; love does not
brag *and* is not [c]arrogant,
5 does not act unbecomingly; it [a]does not seek its own, is not pro-
voked, [b]does not take into account a wrong *suffered*,
6 [a]does not rejoice in unrighteousness, but [b]rejoices with the truth;
7 [1a]bears all things, believes all things, hopes all things, endures all
things.
8 Love never fails; but if *there are gifts of* [1a]prophecy, they will be
done away; if *there are* [b]tongues, they will cease; if *there is* knowledge,
it will be done away.
9 For we [a]know in part, and we prophesy in part;
10 but when the perfect comes, the partial will be done away.
11 When I was a child, I used to speak as a child, think as a child,
reason as a child; when I became a man, I did away with childish
things.
12 For now we [a]see in a mirror [1]dimly, but then [b]face to face; now I
know in part, but then I shall know fully just as I also [c]have been
fully known.
13 But now abide faith, hope, love, these three; but the [1]greatest of
these is [a]love.

Chapter 14

14 [a]Pursue love, yet [b]desire earnestly [c]spiritual *gifts*, but especial-
ly that you may [d]prophesy.
2 For one who [a]speaks in a tongue does not speak to men, but to
God; for no one [1]understands, but [2]in *his* spirit he speaks [b]mysteries.

23 [2]Or, *the* *with*
25 [1]Lit., *sc*
26 [1]Lit., *glo*
27 [a]1 Cor. Eph. 1:23; 1:18, 24; 2: 12:5; Eph.
28 [1]Lit., *se* [2]Or, *works* [a]1 Cor. 12: 10:32 [c]Eph 13:1; Eph. 2 [e]Acts 13:1 12:10, 29 [g] 30 [h]Rom. 1 12:10
29 [1]Or, *wor*
30 [a]1 Cor. 1
31 [a]1 Cor.
13:1 [a]1 Cor. [b]2 Cor. 12:4 [c]Ps. 150:5
2 [a]Matt. 7:2 1 Cor. 11:4; 39 [b]1 Cor. 1 [c]Rom. 15:14 12:9 [e]Matt. 21:21; Mark
3 [1]Some an read *that I m* [a]Matt. 6:2 [b]D
4 [a]Prov. 10:1 1 Thess. 5:14 4:8 [b]Acts 7:9
5 [a]1 Cor. 10: 2:21 [b]2 Cor.
6 [a]2 Thess. 2 [b]2 John 4; 3 J
7 [1]Or, *covers* 9:12
8 [1]Lit., *proph* [a]1 Cor. 13:2
9 [a]1 Cor. 8:2;
12 [1]Lit., *in a r* [a]2 Cor. 5:7; Ph James 1:23 [b]G 32:30; Num. 1 1 John 3:2 [c]1
13 [1]Lit., *greate* 5:6
14:1 [a]1 Cor. 1 [b]1 Cor. 12:31; [c]1 Cor. 12:1 [d]1
2 [1]Lit., *hears* *the Spirit* [a]Mar 1 Cor. 12:10, 2 13:1; 14:18ff. 13:2

3 But one who prophesies speaks to men for [a]edification and [b]exhortation and consolation.

4 One who [a]speaks in a tongue [b]edifies himself; but one who [c]prophesies [b]edifies the church.

5 Now I wish that you all [a]spoke in tongues, but [b]*even* more that you would prophesy; and greater is one who prophesies than one who [a]speaks in tongues, unless he interprets, so that the church may receive [c]edifying.

6 But now, brethren, if I come to you speaking in tongues, what shall I profit you, unless I speak to you either by way of [a]revelation or of [b]knowledge or of [c]prophecy or of [d]teaching?

7 Yet *even* lifeless things, either flute or harp, in producing a sound, if they do not produce a distinction in the tones, how will it be known what is played on the flute or on the harp?

8 For if [a]the [1]bugle produces an indistinct sound, who will prepare himself for battle?

9 So also you, unless you utter by the tongue speech that is clear, how will it be known what is spoken? For you will be [a]speaking into the air.

10 There are, perhaps, a great many kinds of [1]languages in the world, and no *kind* is without meaning.

11 If then I do not know the meaning of the language, I shall be to the one who speaks a [1a]barbarian, and the one who speaks will be a [1]barbarian [2]to me.

12 So also you, since you are zealous of [1]spiritual *gifts,* seek to abound for the [a]edification of the church.

13 Therefore let one who speaks in a tongue pray that he may interpret.

14 For if I pray in a tongue, my spirit prays, but my mind is unfruitful.

15 [a]What is *the outcome* then? I shall pray with the spirit and I shall pray with the mind also; I shall [b]sing with the spirit and I shall sing with the mind also.

16 Otherwise if you bless [1]in the spirit *only,* how will the one who fills the place of the [2]ungifted say [a]the "Amen" at your [b]giving of thanks, since he does not know what you are saying?

17 For you are giving thanks well enough, but the other man is not [a]edified.

18 I thank God, I speak in tongues more than you all;

19 however, in the church I desire to speak five words with my mind, that I may instruct others also, rather than ten thousand words in a tongue.

20 [a]Brethren, [b]do not be children in your thinking; yet in evil [c]be babes, but in your thinking be mature.

21 In [a]the Law it is written, "[b]BY MEN OF STRANGE TONGUES AND BY THE LIPS OF STRANGERS I WILL SPEAK TO THIS PEOPLE, AND EVEN SO THEY WILL NOT LISTEN TO ME," says the Lord.

22 So then tongues are for a sign, not to those who believe, but to unbelievers; but [a]prophecy *is for a sign,* not to unbelievers, but to those who believe.

23 If therefore the whole church should assemble together and all speak in tongues, and [1]ungifted men or unbelievers enter, will they not say that [a]you are mad?

m. 14:19; 1 Cor. 2, 17, 26 [b]Acts 4:36

ark 16:17; 1 Cor. 10, 28, 30; 13:1; 8ff., 26f. [b]Rom. 1 Cor. 14:5, 12, 26 [c]1 Cor. 13:2

ark 16:17; 1 Cor. 10, 28, 30; 13:1; 8ff., 26f. [b]Num. 9 [c]Rom. 14:19; 14:4, 12, 17, 26

Cor. 14:26; Eph. 17 [b]1 Cor. 12:8 3:2 [d]Acts 2:42; 17; 1 Cor. 14:26

trumpet [a]Num. Jer. 4:19; Ezek. 33:3-6; Joel 2:1

9 [a]1 Cor. 9:26

10 [1]Lit., *voices*

oreigner [2]Or, *in* stimation [a]Acts 28:2

t., *spirits* [a]Rom. ; 1 Cor. 14:4, 5, 17, 26

cts 21:22; 1 Cor. [b]Eph. 5:19; Col. 3:16

r, *with the* [2]I.e., ersed in spiritual [a]Deut. 27:15-26; 6:36; Neh. 5:13; Ps. 106:48; Jer. 28:6; Rev. 5:14; 12 [b]Matt. 15:36

m. 14:19; 1 Cor. 14:4, 5, 12, 26

om. 1:13 [b]Eph. Heb. 5:12f. [c]Ps. Matt. 18:3; Rom. 16:19; 1 Pet. 2:2

hn 10:34; 1 Cor. 4:34 [b]Is. 28:11f.

22 [a]1 Cor. 14:1

6, note 2 [a]Acts 2:13

24 But if all [a]prophesy, and an unbeliever or an [1]ungifted man enters, he is [b]convicted by all, he is called to account by all;
25 [a]the secrets of his heart are disclosed; and so he will [b]fall on his face and worship God, [c]declaring that God is certainly among you.
26 [a]What is *the outcome* then, [b]brethren? When you assemble, [c]each one has a [d]psalm, has a [e]teaching, has a [e]revelation, has a [f]tongue, has an [g]interpretation. Let [h]all things be done for edification.
27 If anyone speaks in a [a]tongue, *it should be* by two or at the most three, and *each* in turn, and let one [b]interpret;
28 but if there is no interpreter, let him keep silent in the church; and let him speak to himself and to God.
29 And let two or three [a]prophets speak, and let the others [b]pass judgment.
30 But if a revelation is made to another who is seated, let the first keep silent.
31 For you can all prophesy one by one, so that all may learn and all may be exhorted;
32 and the spirits of prophets are subject to prophets;
33 for God is not *a God* of [a]confusion but of [1]peace, as in [b]all the churches of the [c]saints.
34 Let the women [a]keep silent in the churches; for they are not permitted to speak, but [b]let them subject themselves, just as [c]the Law also says.
35 And if they desire to learn anything, let them ask their own husbands at home; for it is [1]improper for a woman to speak in church.
36 [1]Was it from you that the word of God *first* went forth? Or has it come to you only?
37 [a]If anyone thinks he is a prophet or [b]spiritual, let him recognize that the things which I write to you [c]are the Lord's commandment.
38 But if anyone [1]does not recognize *this,* he is not recognized.
39 Therefore, my brethren, [a]desire earnestly to [b]prophesy, and do not forbid to speak in tongues.
40 But [a]let all things be done properly and in an orderly manner.

Chapter 15

15 Now [a]I make known to you, brethren, the [b]gospel which I preached to you, which also you received, [c]in which also you stand,
2 by which also you are saved, [a]if you hold fast [1]the word which I preached to you, [b]unless you believed in vain.
3 For [a]I delivered to you [1]as of first importance what I also received, that Christ died [b]for our sins [c]according to the Scriptures,
4 and that He was buried, and that He was [a]raised on the third day [b]according to the Scriptures,
5 and that [a]He appeared to [b]Cephas, then [c]to the twelve.
6 After that He appeared to more than five hundred brethren at one time, most of whom remain until now, but some [a]have fallen asleep;
7 then He appeared to [1a]James, then to [b]all the apostles;
8 and last of all, as it were [1]to one untimely born, [a]He appeared to me also.
9 For I am [a]the least of the apostles, who am not fit to be called an apostle, because I [b]persecuted the church of God.

24 [1]V. 16, r [a]1 Cor. 14:1
25 [a]John 4: 17:16 [c]Is. 4 2:47; Zech. 4:13
26 [a]1 Cor. 1:13 [c]1 Cor. [d]Eph. 5:19 [f]1 Cor. 14:2 12:10; 14:5, [h]Rom. 14:19
27 [a]1 Cor. 1 12:10; 14:5,
29 [a]1 Cor. 37 [b]1 Cor. 1
33 [1]Or, *peac . . . saints, le* 14:40 [b]1 Co 7:17 [c]Acts 9
34 [a]1 Cor. 1 [b]1 Tim. 2:11f [c]1 Cor. 14:21
35 [1]Or, *disg*
36 [1]Lit., *Or w*
37 [a]2 Cor. 10 2:15 [c]1 John
38 [1]Some ar read *is ignora be ignorant*
39 [a]1 Cor. 12 [b]1 Cor. 13:2;
40 [a]1 Cor. 14
15:1 [a]Rom. 2 1:11 [b]Rom. 2 3:6; 4:15 [c]Ro 11:20; 2 Cor.
2 [1]Lit., *to wha* [a]Rom. 11:22
3 [1]Lit., *among* [a]1 Cor. 11:23 1:29; Gal. 1:4; 3; 1 Pet. 2:24 53:5-12; Matt. Luke 24:25-27 8:32f.; 17:2f.;
4 [a]Matt. 16:21 2:20ff.; Acts 2 16:8ff.; Acts 2
5 [a]Luke 24:34 1:12 [c]Mark 16 24:36; John 20
6 [a]Acts 7:60; 1 15:18, 20
7 [1]Or, *Jacob* 12:17 [b]Luke 24 Acts 1:3f.
8 [1]Lit., *to an un birth* [a]Acts 9:3- 22:6-11; 26:12- 1 Cor. 9:1
9 [a]2 Cor. 12:11 3:8; 1 Tim. 1:15 8:3

10 But by [a]the grace of God I am what I am, and His grace toward
me did not prove vain; but I [b]labored even more than all of them, yet
[c]not I, but the grace of God with me.
11 Whether then *it was* I or they, so we preach and so you believed.
12 Now if Christ is preached, that He has been raised from the
dead, how do some among you say that there [a]is no resurrection of
the dead?
13 But if there is no resurrection of the dead, not even Christ has
been raised;
14 and [a]if Christ has not been raised, then our preaching is vain,
your faith also is vain.
15 Moreover we are even found *to be* false witnesses of God, be-
cause we witnessed [1]against God that He [a]raised [2]Christ, whom He
did not raise, if in fact the dead are not raised.
16 For if the dead are not raised, not even Christ has been raised;
17 and if Christ has not been raised, your faith is worthless; [a]you
are still in your sins.
18 Then those also who [a]have fallen asleep in Christ have perished.
19 If we have hoped in Christ in this life only, we are [a]of all men
most to be pitied.
20 But now Christ [a]has been raised from the dead, the [b]first fruits of
those who [c]are asleep.
21 For since [a]by a man *came* death, by a man also *came* the resurrec-
tion of the dead.
22 For [a]as in Adam all die, so also in [1]Christ all shall be made alive.
23 But each in his own order: Christ [a]the first fruits, after that [b]those
who are Christ's at [c]His coming,
24 then *comes* the end, when He delivers up [a]the kingdom to the
[b]God and Father, when He has abolished [c]all rule and all authority
and power.
25 For He must reign [a]until He has put all His enemies under His
feet.
26 The last enemy that will be [a]abolished is death.
27 For [a]HE HAS PUT ALL THINGS IN SUBJECTION UNDER HIS FEET. But
when He says, "[b]All things are put in subjection," it is evident that
He is excepted who put all things in subjection to Him.
28 And when [a]all things are subjected to Him, then the Son Himself
also will be subjected to the One who subjected all things to Him,
that [b]God may be all in all.
29 Otherwise, what will those do who are baptized for the dead? If
the dead are not raised at all, why then are they baptized for them?
30 Why are we also [a]in danger every hour?
31 I protest, brethren, by the boasting in you, which I have in Christ
Jesus our Lord, [a]I die daily.
32 If [1]from human motives I [a]fought with wild beasts at [b]Ephesus,
what does it profit me? If the dead are not raised, [c]LET US EAT AND
DRINK, FOR TOMORROW WE DIE.
33 [a]Do not be deceived: "Bad company corrupts good morals."
34 [a]Become sober-minded [1]as you ought, and stop sinning; for some
have [b]no knowledge of God. [c]I speak *this* to your shame.
35 But [a]someone will say, "How are [b]the dead raised? And with
what kind of body do they come?"
36 [a]You fool! That which you [b]sow does not come to life unless it
dies;

37 and that which you sow, you do not sow the body which is to be, but a bare grain, perhaps of wheat or of [1]something else.

38 But God gives it a body just as He wished, and [a]to each of the seeds a body of its own.

39 All flesh is not the same flesh, but there is one *flesh* of men, and another flesh of beasts, and another flesh of birds, and another of fish.

40 There are also heavenly bodies and earthly bodies, but the glory of the heavenly is one, and the *glory* of the earthly is another.

41 There is one glory of the sun, and another glory of the moon, and another glory of the stars; for star differs from star in glory.

42 [a]So also is the resurrection of the dead. It is sown [1b]a perishable *body,* it is raised [2c]an imperishable *body;*

43 it is sown in dishonor, it is raised in [a]glory; it is sown in weakness, it is raised in power;

44 it is sown a [a]natural body, it is raised a [b]spiritual body. If there is a natural body, there is also a spiritual *body.*

45 So also it is written, "The first [a]MAN, Adam, BECAME A LIVING SOUL." The [b]last Adam *became* a [c]life-giving spirit.

46 However, the spiritual is not first, but the natural; then the spiritual.

47 The first man is [a]from the earth, [1b]earthy; the second man is from heaven.

48 As is the earthy, so also are those who are earthy; and as is the heavenly, [a]so also are those who are heavenly.

49 And just as we have [a]borne the image of the earthy, [1]we [b]shall also bear the image of the heavenly.

50 Now I say this, brethren, that [a]flesh and blood cannot [b]inherit the kingdom of God; nor does [1]the perishable inherit [2c]the imperishable.

51 Behold, I tell you a [a]mystery; we shall not all sleep, but we shall all be [b]changed,

52 in a moment, in the twinkling of an eye, at the last trumpet; for [a]the trumpet will sound, and [b]the dead will be raised [1]imperishable, and [c]we shall be changed.

53 For this [1]perishable must put on [2a]the imperishable, and this [b]mortal must put on immortality.

54 But when this [1]perishable will have put on [2]the imperishable, and this mortal will have put on immortality, then will come about the saying that is written, "[a]DEATH IS SWALLOWED UP in victory.

55 "[a]O DEATH, WHERE IS YOUR VICTORY? O DEATH, WHERE IS YOUR STING?"

56 The sting of [a]death is sin, and [b]the power of sin is the law;

57 but [a]thanks be to God, who gives us the [b]victory through our Lord Jesus Christ.

58 [a]Therefore, my beloved brethren, be steadfast, immovable, always abounding in [b]the work of the Lord, knowing that your toil is not *in* vain in the Lord.

Chapter 16

16 Now concerning [a]the collection for [b]the saints, as [c]I directed the churches of [d]Galatia, so do you also.

2 On [a]the first day of every week let each one of you [1]put aside and save, as he may prosper, that [b]no collections be made when I come.

37 [1]Lit., *so*
38 [a]Gen. 1
42 [1]Lit., *in*
[2]Lit., *in inc*
[a]Dan. 12:3
[b]Rom. 8:21
15:50; Gal.
2:7
43 [a]Phil. 3
44 [a]1 Cor.
15:50
45 [a]Gen. 2
5:14 [c]John
Rom. 8:2
47 [1]Lit., *ma*
[a]John 3:31
3:19
48 [a]Phil. 3:2
49 [1]Some a
read *let us a*
5:3 [b]Rom. 8
50 [1]Lit., *cor*
[2]Lit., *incorru*
16:17; John
[b]1 Cor. 6:9 [c]
51 [a]1 Cor. 1
5:2, 4
52 [1]Lit., *inco*
[a]Matt. 24:31
5:28 [c]1 Thes
53 [1]Lit., *corr*
[2]Lit., *incorrup*
2:7 [b]2 Cor. 5
54 [1]V. 53, no
53, note 2 [a]Is
55 [a]Hos. 13:1
56 [a]Rom. 5:1
3:20; 4:15; 7:8
57 [a]Rom. 7:2
2:14 [b]Rom. 8:
2:14f.; 1 John
21:4
58 [a]2 Pet. 3:1
16:10
16:1 [a]Acts 24
15:25f. [b]Acts 9
[c]1 Cor. 4:17 [d]A
2 [1]Lit., *put by*
[a]Acts 20:7 [b]2 C

3 And when I arrive, [a]whomever you may approve, I shall send
them with letters to carry your gift to Jerusalem;
4 and if it is fitting for me to go also, they will go with me.
5 But I [a]shall come to you after I go through [b]Macedonia, for I [c]am
going through Macedonia;
6 and perhaps I shall stay with you, or even spend the winter, that
you may [a]send me on my way wherever I may go.
7 For I do not wish to see you now [a]*just* in passing; for I hope to
remain with you for some time, [b]if the Lord permits.
8 But I shall remain in [a]Ephesus until [b]Pentecost;
9 for a [a]wide door [1]for effective *service* has opened to me, and
[b]there are many adversaries.
10 Now if [a]Timothy comes, see that he is with you without [1]cause to
be afraid; for he is doing [b]the Lord's work, as I also am.
11 [a]Let no one therefore despise him. But [b]send him on his way [c]in
peace, so that he may come to me; for I expect him with the brethren.
12 But concerning [a]Apollos our brother, I encouraged him greatly to
come to you with the brethren; and it was not at all *his* desire to
come now, but he will come when he has opportunity.
13 [a]Be on the alert, [b]stand firm in the faith, [c]act like men, [d]be strong.
14 Let all that you do be done [a]in love.
15 Now I urge you, brethren (you know the [a]household of
Stephanas, that [1]they were the [b]first fruits of [c]Achaia, and that they
have devoted themselves for [d]ministry to [e]the saints),
16 that [a]you also be in subjection to such men and to everyone who
helps in the work and labors.
17 And I rejoice over the [1a]coming of Stephanas and Fortunatus and
Achaicus; because they have [2]supplied [b]what was lacking on your
part.
18 For they [a]have refreshed my spirit and yours. Therefore [b]ac-
knowledge such men.
19 The churches of [a]Asia greet you. [b]Aquila and Prisca greet you
heartily in the Lord, with [c]the church that is in their house.
20 All the brethren greet you. [a]Greet one another with a holy kiss.
21 The greeting is in [a]my own hand—[1]Paul.
22 If anyone does not love the Lord, let him be [1a]accursed.
[2b]Maranatha.
23 [a]The grace of the Lord Jesus be with you.
24 My love be with you all in Christ Jesus. Amen.

3:1; 8:18f.
19 [b]Rom.
Acts 19:21
5:3; 1 Cor.
16:11
15f. [b]Acts
18:21
[b]Acts 2:1
and [a]Acts
[b]Acts 19:9
; *for* [a]Acts
:17; 2 Cor.
Cor. 15:58
4:12; Titus
5:3; 1 Cor.
Acts 15:33
3:24; 1 Cor.
1:12; 3:5f.
:42 [b]1 Cor.
al. 5:1; Phil.
Thess. 3:8;
15 [c]1 Sam.
10:12 [d]Ps.
3:16; 6:10;
Col. 1:11
[a]1 Cor. 14:1
was [a]1 Cor.
16:5 [c]Acts
Rom. 15:31
[e]1 Cor. 16:1
. 5:12; Heb.
13:17
esence [2]Or,
up for your
[a]2 Cor. 7:6f.
:9; Phil. 2:30
:13; Philem.
[b]Phil. 2:29;
Thess. 5:12
s 16:6 [b]Acts
[c]Rom. 16:5
[a]Rom. 16:16
Paul's [a]Rom.
al. 6:11; Col.
Thess. 3:17;
Philem. 19
r., *anathema*
, O [our] Lord
m. 9:3 [b]Phil.
5; Rev. 22:20
[a]Rom. 16:20

1 Corinthians Observations Chart

Description of the Corinthians

Commands to the Corinthians

Warnings to the Corinthians

orinthians:

CHAPTER THEMES	
1	
2	
3	
4	
5	
6	
7	
8	
9	
10	
11	
12	
13	
14	
15	
16	

Author:

Date:

Purpose:

Key Words:

2 CORINTHIANS

Paul, the apostle to the Gentiles, was taught and appointed by Jesus Christ. Strong in faitl dent, and greatly used by God, Paul was loved by multitudes and hated by thousands. Dete that the grace of God would not be given in vain, he worked harder than anyone.

However, Paul's labor was not without cost. He endured conflicts without and fears within. persevered. What were his conflicts, his fears, his sufferings? Were they similar to yours? And h he endure? What held him? As Paul writes his second epistle to the Corinthians from Mac probably in the winter of A.D. 55, he lets us see the answers to these questions.

THINGS TO DO

General Instructions

1. Second Corinthians is different from Paul's other epistles. Watch the atmosphere or tone epistle. Paul is defending himself, which is unusual for Paul. As you read through the boo the issues Paul addresses and what he says to the Corinthians, and you'll understand wh is up against.
   a. Study the OBSERVATIONS CHART on page 1713 and see what you'll need to observe study 2 Corinthians chapter by chapter. Make a duplicate of this chart so you can use worksheet. When you've completed it, record the information on the chart in your Bible.
   b. As you read each chapter, list everything you learn about Paul. Be sure to note the aff he endured: What must he do in respect to the Corinthians? What has been done to him Corinthians? Ask God to show you Paul's character, his heart, his joys, and his sorrows.
   c. Note what you learn about the Corinthians. Remember to ask the five W's and an H: W they like? What is their relationship with Paul like? What is going on in the Corinthian at this time? What have they said about Paul? What problems has Paul had to deal v respect to them?
   d. What is Paul's desire or goal for the Corinthians?
   e. Titus is mentioned several times in this letter. Record what you learn about him 2 Corinthians.
2. As you read 2 Corinthians chapter by chapter, do the following:
   a. Mark in a distinctive way the key words (and their synonyms and pronouns) listed 2 CORINTHIANS AT A GLANCE chart on page 1714. Write these on a card that you c as a bookmark while you study 2 Corinthians. (Hint: If you mark every reference to Sata a red pitchfork, it will be easy to spot.)
   b. As you come to specific chapters you will notice other key words which are not list 2 CORINTHIANS AT A GLANCE. Mark these also.
   c. If there are several truths you learn from the use of the key word within a chapter, list margin what you learn from that word. For example, you might list all you learn *affliction* and *suffering*. Record this heading in the margin of each chapter where you these key words and mark it in a distinctive way so you can spot its recurrence throu 2 Corinthians: "Affliction/Suffering." Then under it list what you learn from that chapter.
3. Look for the theme (subject) of each chapter and record it next to the chapter number in th and under "Chapter Themes" on 2 CORINTHIANS AT A GLANCE.

rs 1-7

. the midst of this very personal letter, Paul gives some insights on several subjects. In the argin where they appear, list what you learn about each subject.

Chapter 3 mentions the new covenant (which is grace) and the old covenant (which is law). These are described as ministries and then the ministries are contrasted according to the result of each, i.e. condemnation or righteousness. List in the margin what you learn about each from the text.

In chapter 5 Paul talks about what will happen to our earthly bodies when we die. He also discusses the judgment seat of Christ and our ministry of reconciliation. Identify how these relate to one another and what you learn about each from the text. Write your observations in the margins.

In chapter 7 Paul deals with two kinds of sorrow and what they produce. Don't miss this. Take notes in the margin.

Vhat is Paul writing about in chapters 1 through 7? Is there a theme which runs through these hapters? Remember that key words reveal the themes. What key words are repeated the most in iis segment?

Iow does Paul begin and end this segment?

Record the theme for chapters 1 through 7 on 2 CORINTHIANS AT A GLANCE under "Segment Divisions."

ers 8-9

Vhat subject is Paul talking about in chapters 8 and 9? Note the use of the words *ministry, work,* nd *service*. What ministry or work or service is he referring to?

Record this subject as the theme of this segment in the appropriate space on 2 CORINTHIANS AT A GLANCE.

ers 10-13

Notice when the key word *boast* first appears in the text and what happens when it appears. Note vhat or whom the boasting is in and what you learn.

In the margin of chapter 11 list what you learn about Satan and spiritual warfare from these four chapters.

What does Paul seem to be doing in chapters 10 through 13? What opposition is there to Paul, and what is the opposition saying about him? What is his response to this opposition? Record the theme of this segment under "Segment Divisions" and complete the chart.

GS TO THINK ABOUT

What is the purpose of affliction? When you need to be comforted, do you run to men or to God?

Is it wrong to feel sorrow, to be hurt, or to have a broken heart? Is it wrong to cause sorrow, to hurt, or to break another's heart?

How do you deal with those who oppose you? How do you minister to those who are caught in the middle of a conflict and don't know who to believe?

Paul was human just like us; he had feelings just like we do. What can we learn from him about how we are to live and respond in spite of our feelings? When is the time to give a defense of one's self, of one's ministry?

Are you prepared to stand before the judgment seat of Christ?

What place does the ministry of giving play in your life?

If you were to examine yourself, would you find your Christianity genuine?

Chapter 1

1 Paul, [a]an apostle of [b]Christ Jesus [c]by the will of God, and
[d]Timothy *our* brother, to [e]the church of God which is at [f]Corinth
with all the [1]saints who are throughout [g]Achaia:
2 [a]Grace to you and peace from God our Father and the Lord Jesus
Christ.
3 [a]Blessed *be* the God and Father of our Lord Jesus Christ, the
Father of mercies and [b]God of all comfort;
4 who [a]comforts us in all our affliction so that we may be able to
comfort those who are in any affliction with the comfort with which
we ourselves are comforted by God.
5 For just [a]as the sufferings of Christ are [1]ours in abundance, so
also our comfort is abundant through Christ.
6 But if we are afflicted, it is [a]for your comfort and salvation; or if
we are comforted, it is for your comfort, which is effective in the
patient enduring of the same sufferings which we also suffer;
7 and our hope for you is firmly grounded, knowing that [a]as you
are sharers of our sufferings, so also you are *sharers* of our comfort.
8 For [a]we do not want you to be unaware, brethren, of our [b]afflic-
tion which came *to us* in [1c]Asia, that we were burdened excessively,
beyond our strength, so that we despaired even of life;
9 [1]indeed, we had the sentence of death within ourselves in order
that we should not trust in ourselves, but in God who raises the
dead;
10 who [a]delivered us from so great a *peril of* death, and will deliver
us, [1]He [b]on whom we have set our hope. And He will yet deliver us,
11 you also joining in [a]helping us through your prayers, that thanks
may be given by [b]many persons on our behalf for the favor bestowed
upon us through *the prayers of* many.
12 For our [1]proud confidence is this, the testimony of [a]our con-
science, that in holiness and [b]godly sincerity, [c]not in fleshly wisdom
but in the grace of God, we have conducted ourselves in the world,
and especially toward you.
13 For we write nothing else to you than what you read and under-
stand, and I hope you will understand [a]until the end;
14 just as you also partially did understand us, that we are your
reason to be proud as you also are ours, in [a]the day of our Lord
Jesus.
15 And in this confidence I intended at first to [a]come to you, that
you might [1]twice receive a [2b]blessing;
16 [1]that is, to [a]pass [2]your way into [b]Macedonia, and again from
Macedonia to come to you, and by you to be [c]helped on my journey
to Judea.
17 Therefore, I was not vacillating when I intended to do this, was
I? Or that which I purpose, do I purpose [a]according to the flesh, that
with me there should be yes, yes and no, no *at the same time*?
18 But as [a]God is faithful, [b]our word to you is not yes and no.
19 For [a]the Son of God, Christ Jesus, who was preached among you
by us—by me and [b]Silvanus and [c]Timothy—was not yes and no, but
is yes [d]in Him.
20 For [a]as many as may be the promises of God, [b]in Him they are
yes; wherefore also by Him is [c]our Amen to the glory of God
through us.

1:1 [1]Or, *ho* [a]Rom. 1:1; Eph. 1:1; C 2 Tim. 1:1; [b]Gal. 3:26 [d]Acts 16:1; 2 Cor. 1:19 10:32 [f]Acts 18:12
2 [a]Rom. 1:
3 [a]Eph. 1:3 [b]Rom. 15:5
4 [a]Is. 51:12 2 Cor. 7:6, 7
5 [1]Lit., *to us* 4:10; Phil. 3: 1:24
6 [a]2 Cor. 4: Eph. 3:1, 13
7 [a]Rom. 8:1
8 [1]I.e., west province of A [a]Rom. 1:13 19:23; 1 Cor. [c]Acts 16:6
9 [1]Lit., *but w*
10 [1]Or, *on w have set our He will also* 15:31 [b]1 Tim
11 [a]Rom. 15 1:19; Philem. 4:15; 9:11f.
12 [1]Lit., *boas* 23:1; 1 Thess Heb. 13:18 [b]2 2:17 [c]1 Cor. 1 James 3:15
13 [a]1 Cor. 1:8
14 [a]1 Cor. 1:8
15 [1]Lit., *have grace* [2]Some mss. read *joy* 4:19 [b]Rom. 1:
16 [1]Lit., *and* [2] *through you in* 19:21; 1 Cor. 1 [b]Acts 19:21; Ro 15:26 [c]Acts 15 16:6, 11
17 [a]2 Cor. 10:2
18 [a]1 Cor. 1:9 2:17
19 [a]Matt. 4:3; 1 26:63 [b]Acts 15 1 Thess. 1:1; 2 1:1; 1 Pet. 5:12 18:5; 2 Cor. 1:1 13:8
20 [a]Rom. 15:8 13:8 [c]1 Cor. 14 3:14

21 Now He who [a]establishes us with you in Christ and [b]anointed us
is God,
22 who also [a]sealed us and [b]gave *us* the Spirit in our hearts as a
[1]pledge.
23 But [a]I call God as witness [1]to my soul, that [b]to spare you I came
no more to [c]Corinth.
24 Not that we [a]lord it over your faith, but are workers with you for
your joy; for in your faith you are [b]standing firm.

Chapter 2

2 But I determined this [1]for my own sake, that I [a]would not come
to you in sorrow again.
2 For if I [a]cause you sorrow, who then makes me glad but the one
whom I made sorrowful?
3 And this is the very thing I [a]wrote you, lest, [b]when I came, I
should have sorrow from those who ought to make me rejoice;
having [c]confidence in you all, that my joy would be *the joy* of you all.
4 For out of much affliction and anguish of heart I [a]wrote to you
with many tears; not that you should be made sorrowful, but that
you might know the love which I have especially for you.
5 But [a]if any has caused sorrow, he has caused sorrow not to me,
but in some degree—[1]in order not to say too much—to all of you.
6 Sufficient for such a one is [a]this punishment which was *inflicted*
by the majority,
7 so that on the contrary you should rather [a]forgive and comfort
him, lest somehow such a one be overwhelmed by excessive sorrow.
8 Wherefore I urge you to reaffirm *your* love for him.
9 For to this end also [a]I wrote that I might [1b]put you to the test,
whether you are [c]obedient in all things.
10 But whom you forgive anything, I *forgive* also; for indeed what I
have forgiven, if I have forgiven anything, *I did it* for your sakes [a]in
the presence of Christ,
11 in order that no advantage be taken of us by [a]Satan; for [b]we are
not ignorant of his schemes.
12 Now when I came to [a]Troas for the [b]gospel of Christ and when a
[c]door was opened for me in the Lord,
13 I [a]had no rest for my spirit, not finding [b]Titus my brother; but
[c]taking my leave of them, I went on to [d]Macedonia.
14 [a]But thanks be to God, who always [b]leads us in His triumph in
Christ, and manifests through us the [c]sweet aroma of the
[d]knowledge of Him in every place.
15 For we are a [a]fragrance of Christ to God among [b]those who are
being saved and among those who are perishing;
16 [a]to the one an aroma from death to death, to the other an aroma
from life to life. And who is [b]adequate for these things?
17 For we are not like many, [1a]peddling the word of God, but [b]as
from sincerity, but as from God, we speak in Christ [c]in the sight of
God.

Chapter 3

3 Are we beginning to [a]commend ourselves again? Or do we need,
as some, [b]letters of commendation to you or from you?
2 [a]You are our letter, written in our hearts, known and read by all
men;

r. 1:8 [b]1 John 2:20, 27
[1]own payment
3 [b]Rom. 8:16; 5:5; Eph. 1:14
, upon [a]Rom. . 1:20 [b]1 Cor. ; 2 Cor. 2:1, 3 [c]2 Cor. 1:1
or. 4:5; 11:20; [b]Rom. 11:20; 1 Cor. 15:1
as far as I am
[a]1 Cor. 4:21; 2 Cor. 12:21
2 [a]2 Cor. 7:8
or. 2:9; 7:8, 12
r. 4:21; 2 Cor. 21 [c]Gal. 5:10; :4; Philem. 21
or. 2:9; 7:8, 12
., that I be not some [a]1 Cor. 5:1f.
r. 5:4f.; 2 Cor. 7:11
6:1; Eph. 4:32
know the proof
u [a]2 Cor. 2:3f. 8:2; Phil. 2:22 Cor. 7:15; 10:6
Cor. 5:4; 2 Cor. 4:6
tt. 4:10 [b]Luke Cor. 4:4; 1 Pet. 5:8
ts 16:8 [b]Rom. r. 4:3, 4; 8:18; 10:14; 11:4, 7; 2 [c]Acts 14:27
or. 7:5 [b]2 Cor. f.; 8:6, 16, 23; 8; Gal. 2:1, 3; 4:10; Titus 1:4 [d]Rom. 15:26
om. 1:8; 6:17; 15:57; 2 Cor. :15 [b]Col. 2:15 ; Ezek. 20:41; 5:2; Phil. 4:18 [d]1 Cor. 12:8
ong 1:3; Ezek. Eph. 5:2; Phil. 3 [b]1 Cor. 1:18
ke 2:34; John . 2:7f. [b]2 Cor. 3:5f.
[1]Or, corrupting
4:2; Gal. 1:6-9 8; 2 Cor. 1:12; ss. 2:4; 1 Pet. [c]2 Cor. 12:19
or. 5:12; 10:12, 1 [b]Acts 18:27; 1 Cor. 16:3
2 [a]1 Cor. 9:2

3 being manifested that you are a letter of Christ, [1a]cared for by us,
written not with ink, but with the Spirit of [b]the living God, not on
[c]tablets of stone, but on [d]tablets of [2e]human hearts.
4 And such [a]confidence we have through Christ toward God.
5 Not that we are adequate in ourselves to consider anything as
coming from ourselves, but [a]our adequacy is from God,
6 who also made us adequate *as* [a]servants of a [b]new covenant, not
of [c]the letter, but of the Spirit; for the letter kills, but [d]the Spirit gives
life.
7 But if the [a]ministry of death, [b]in letters engraved on stones, came
[1]with glory, [c]so that the sons of Israel could not look intently at the
face of Moses because of the glory of his face, fading *as* it was,
8 how shall the ministry of the Spirit fail to be even more with
glory?
9 For if [a]the ministry of condemnation has glory, much more does
the [b]ministry of righteousness abound in glory.
10 For indeed what had glory, in this case has no glory on account
of the glory that surpasses *it*.
11 For if that which fades away *was* [1]with glory, much more that
which remains *is* in glory.
12 [a]Having therefore such a hope, [b]we use great boldness in *our*
speech,
13 and *are* not as Moses, [a]*who* used to put a veil over his face that
the sons of Israel might not look intently at the end of what was
fading away.
14 But their minds were [a]hardened; for until this very day at the
[b]reading of [c]the old covenant the same veil [1]remains unlifted, be-
cause it is removed in Christ.
15 But to this day whenever Moses is read, a veil lies over their
heart;
16 [a]but whenever a man turns to the Lord, the veil is taken away.
17 Now the Lord is the Spirit; and where [a]the Spirit of the Lord is,
[b]*there* is liberty.
18 But we all, with unveiled face [a]beholding as in a mirror the
[b]glory of the Lord, are being [c]transformed into the same image from
glory to glory, just as from [d]the Lord, the Spirit.

Chapter 4

4 Therefore, since we have this [a]ministry, as we [b]received mercy,
we [c]do not lose heart,
2 but we have renounced the [a]things hidden because of shame, not
walking in craftiness or [b]adulterating the word of God, but by the
manifestation of truth [c]commending ourselves to every man's con-
science in the sight of God.
3 And even if our [a]gospel is [b]veiled, it is veiled [1]to [c]those who are
perishing,
4 in whose case [a]the god of [b]this [1]world has [c]blinded the minds of
the unbelieving, [2]that they might not see the [d]light of the gospel of
the [e]glory of Christ, who is the [f]image of God.
5 For we [a]do not preach ourselves but Christ Jesus as Lord, and
ourselves as your bond-servants [1]for Jesus' sake.
6 For God, who said, "[a]Light shall shine out of darkness," is the
One who has [b]shone in our hearts to give the [c]light of the knowledge
of the glory of God in the face of Christ.

3 [1]Lit., *serve* *hearts of fles* 3:6 [b]Matt. 16 24:12; 31:18; 2 Cor. 3:7 [d]P 7:3; Jer. 17:1 31:33; Ezek. 36:26

4 [a]Eph. 3:12

5 [a]1 Cor. 15:

6 [a]1 Cor. 3:5 31:31; Luke 2 [c]Rom. 2:29 [d] Rom. 7:6

7 [1]Or, *in glor* 4:15; 5:20; 7: 3:9; Gal. 3:10 24:12; 31:18; 2 Cor. 3:3 [c]E 34:29-35; 2 C

9 [a]Deut. 27:2 3:7; Heb. 12: [b]Rom. 1:17; 3

11 [1]Lit., *throu*

12 [a]2 Cor. 7: 4:13, 29; 2 Co Eph. 6:19; 1 T

13 [a]Ex. 34:33 2 Cor. 3:7

14 [1]Or, *rema* *being reveale* *done away in* [a]Rom. 11:7; 2 [b]Acts 13:15 [c]

16 [a]Ex. 34:34 11:23

17 [a]Is. 61:1f.; [b]John 8:32; G

18 [a]1 Cor. 13 17:22, 24; 2 C [c]Rom. 8:29 [d]

4:1 [a]1 Cor. 3: 7:25 [c]Luke 1 4:16; Gal. 6:9 3:13; 2 Thess

2 [a]Rom. 6:21 4:5 [b]2 Cor. 2: 5:11f.

3 [1]Lit., *in* [a]2 [b]1 Cor. 2:6ff.; 3:14 [c]1 Cor. 1 2 Cor. 2:15

4 [1]Lit., *age* [2] *the light . . . in* *God, should r* *upon them* [a]J 12:31 [b]Matt. [c]2 Cor. 3:14 [d] 26:18; 2 Cor. [e]2 Cor. 3:18; 4 1:18; Phil. 2:6 1:15; Heb. 1:3

5 [1]Or, *throug* [a]1 Cor. 4:15f.; 2:6f.

6 [a]Gen. 1:3 [b] 1:19 [c]Acts 26 4:4

7 But we have this treasure in [a]earthen vessels, that the surpassing
greatness of [b]the power may be of God and not from ourselves;
8 *we are* [a]afflicted in every way, but not [b]crushed; [c]perplexed, but
not despairing;
9 [a]persecuted, but not [b]forsaken; [c]struck down, but not destroyed;
10 [a]always carrying about in the body the dying of Jesus, that [b]the
life of Jesus also may be manifested in our body.
11 For we who live are constantly being delivered over to death for
Jesus' sake, that the life of Jesus also may be manifested in our mor-
tal flesh.
12 So death works in us, but life in you.
13 But having the same [a]spirit of faith, according to what is written,
"[b]I BELIEVED, THEREFORE I SPOKE," we also believe, therefore also we
speak;
14 knowing that He who [a]raised the Lord Jesus [b]will raise us also
with Jesus and will [c]present us with you.
15 For all things *are* [a]for your sakes, that the grace which is [1b]spread-
ing to more and more people may cause the giving of thanks to
abound to the glory of God.
16 Therefore we [a]do not lose heart, but though our outer man is
decaying, yet our [b]inner man is [c]being renewed day by day.
17 For momentary, [a]light affliction is producing for us an eternal
weight of glory far beyond all comparison,
18 while we [a]look not at the things which are seen, but at the things
which are not seen; for the things which are seen are temporal, but
the things which are not seen are eternal.

Chapter 5

5 For we know that if [1]the [a]earthly [b]tent which is our house is torn
down, we have a building from God, a house [c]not made with
hands, eternal in the heavens.
2 For indeed in this *house* we [a]groan, longing to be [b]clothed with
our dwelling from heaven;
3 inasmuch as we, having put it on, shall not be found naked.
4 For indeed while we are in this tent, we [a]groan, being burdened,
because we do not want to be unclothed, but to be [b]clothed, in order
that what is [c]mortal may be swallowed up by life.
5 Now He who prepared us for this very purpose is God, who
[a]gave to us the Spirit as a [1]pledge.
6 Therefore, being always of good courage, and knowing that
[a]while we are at home in the body we are absent from the Lord—
7 for [a]we walk by faith, not by [1]sight—
8 we are of good courage, I say, and [a]prefer rather to be absent
from the body and [b]to be at home with the Lord.
9 Therefore also we have as our ambition, whether at home or
absent, to be [a]pleasing to Him.
10 For we must all appear before [a]the judgment seat of Christ, that
each one may be recompensed for [1]his deeds in the body, according
to what he has done, whether good or bad.
11 Therefore knowing the [a]fear of the Lord, we persuade men, but
we are made manifest to God; and I hope that we are [b]made manifest
also in your consciences.
12 We are not [a]again commending ourselves to you but *are* giving

:19; 10:9; 33:6; 4:2; 2 Cor. 5:1; :20 [b]Judg. 7:2; 1 Cor. 2:5
[a]2 Cor. 1:8; 7:5 6:12 [c]Gal. 4:20
hn 15:20; Rom. Ps. 129:2; Heb. Ps. 37:24; Prov. 24:16; Mic. 7:8
[a]Rom. 6:5; 8:36; 6:17 [b]Rom. 6:8
Cor. 12:9 [b]Ps. 116:10
14 [a]Acts 2:24 ess. 4:14 [c]Luke Eph. 5:27; Col. 1:22; Jude 24
being multiplied rough the many 8:28; 2 Cor. 1:6 :19; 2 Cor. 1:11
Cor. 4:1 [b]Rom. . 40:29, 31; Col. 3:10
17 [a]Rom. 8:18
om. 8:24; 2 Cor. 7; Heb. 11:1, 13
[1]Lit., *our earthly of the tent* [a]Job 9; 1 Cor. 15:47; :7 [b]2 Pet. 1:13f. 4:58; Acts 7:48; Heb. 9:11, 24
om. 8:23; 2 Cor. [b]1 Cor. 15:53f.; 2 Cor. 5:4
Cor. 5:2 [b]1 Cor. 5:53f.; 2 Cor. 5:2 [c]1 Cor. 15:54
; down payment 3:23; 2 Cor. 1:22
6 [a]Heb. 11:13f.
[1]Or, *appearance* or. 13:12; 2 Cor. 4:18
Phil. 1:23 [b]John 12:26; Phil. 1:23
Rom. 14:18; Col. 10; 1 Thess. 4:1
[1]Lit., *the things the body* [a]Matt. Acts 10:42; Rom. :10, 12; Eph. 6:8
eb. 10:31; 12:29; e 23 [b]2 Cor. 4:2
12 [a]2 Cor. 3:1

you an [b]occasion to be proud of us, that you may have *an answer* for
those who take pride in appearance, and not in heart.
13 For if we [1]are [a]beside ourselves, it is for God; if we are of sound
mind, it is for you.
14 For the love of Christ [a]controls us, having concluded this, that
[b]one died for all, therefore all died;
15 and He died for all, that they who live should no longer [a]live for
themselves, but for Him who died and rose again on their behalf.
16 Therefore from now on we recognize no man [1a]according to the
flesh; even though we have known Christ [1]according to the flesh, yet
now we know *Him thus* no longer.
17 Therefore if any man is [a]in Christ, [1]*he is* [b]a new creature; [c]the old
things passed away; behold, new things have come.
18 Now [a]all *these* things are from God, [b]who reconciled us to Him-
self through Christ, and gave us the [c]ministry of reconciliation,
19 namely, that [a]God was in Christ reconciling the world to Him-
self, [b]not counting their trespasses against them, and [1]He has [2]com-
mitted to us the word of reconciliation.
20 Therefore, we are [a]ambassadors for Christ, [b]as though God were
entreating through us; we beg you on behalf of Christ, be [c]reconciled
to God.
21 He made Him who [a]knew no sin *to be* [b]sin on our behalf, that we
might become the [c]righteousness of God in Him.

Chapter 6

6 And [a]working together *with Him,* [b]we also urge you not to
receive [c]the grace of God in vain—
2 for He says,

"[a]AT THE ACCEPTABLE TIME I LISTENED TO YOU,
AND ON THE DAY OF SALVATION I HELPED YOU";

behold, now is "THE ACCEPTABLE TIME," behold, now is "THE DAY OF
SALVATION"—
3 [a]giving no cause for offense in anything, in order that the minis-
try be not discredited,
4 but in everything [a]commending ourselves as [1b]servants of God,
[c]in much endurance, in afflictions, in hardships, in distresses,
5 in [a]beatings, in imprisonments, in [b]tumults, in labors, in sleep-
lessness, in [c]hunger,
6 in purity, in [a]knowledge, in [b]patience, in kindness, in the [c]Holy
Spirit, in [d]genuine love,
7 in [a]the word of truth, in [b]the power of God; by [c]the weapons of
righteousness for the right hand and the left,
8 by glory and [a]dishonor, by [b]evil report and good report; *regarded*
as [c]deceivers and yet [d]true;
9 as unknown yet well-known, as [a]dying yet behold, [b]we live; as
[1]punished yet not put to death,
10 as [a]sorrowful yet always [a]rejoicing, as [b]poor yet making many
rich, as [c]having nothing yet possessing [d]all things.
11 [a]Our mouth [1]has spoken freely to you, O Corinthians, our [b]heart
is opened wide.
12 You are not restrained [1]by us, but [a]you are restrained in your
own [2]affections.
13 Now in a like [a]exchange—I speak as to [b]children—open wide *to
us* also.

12 [b]2 Cor. 1:14
1:26
13 [1]Lit., *were*
3:21; 2 Cor. 11:
12:11
14 [a]Acts 18:5
5:15; 6:6f.; Gal.
Col. 3:3
15 [a]Rom. 14:7
16 [1]I.e., by wh
the flesh [a]John
2 Cor. 11:18; P
17 [1]Or, there is
creation [a]Rom
[b]John 3:3; Rom
Gal. 6:15 [c]Is. 4
65:17; Eph. 4:2
21:4f.
18 [a]1 Cor. 11:1
5:10; Col. 1:20
3:5
19 [1]Lit., *having*
placed in us [a]C
[b]Rom. 4:8; 1 Co
20 [a]Mal. 2:7; E
[b]2 Cor. 6:1 [c]Ro
Col. 1:20
21 [a]Acts 3:14;
4:15; 7:26; 1 Pe
1 John 3:5 [b]Ro
4:25; 8:3; Gal. 3
[c]Rom. 1:17; 3:2
1 Cor. 1:30
6:1 [a]1 Cor. 3:9
5:20 [c]Acts 11:2
2 [a]Is. 49:8
3 [a]1 Cor. 8:9, 1
4 [1]Or, *ministers*
3:5 [b]1 Cor. 3:5;
2:24f. [c]Acts 9:1
4:8-11; 6:4ff.; 11
12:10
5 [a]Acts 16:23
19:23ff. [c]1 Cor.
6 [a]1 Cor. 12:8;
11:6 [b]2 Cor. 1:2
13:10 [c]1 Cor. 2
1 Thess. 1:5 [d]R
7 [a]2 Cor. 2:17;
[b]1 Cor. 2:5 [c]Ro
13:12; 2 Cor. 10
6:11ff.
8 [a]1 Cor. 4:10
3:8; 1 Cor. 4:13;
12:16 [c]Matt. 27
[d]2 Cor. 1:18; 4:2
1 Thess. 2:3f.
9 [1]Or, *discipline*
[a]Rom. 8:36 [b]2 C
10; 4:11
10 [a]John 16:22
7:4; Phil. 2:17; 4
1:24; 1 Thess. 1
[b]1 Cor. 1:5; 2 Co
[c]Acts 3:6 [d]Rom
1 Cor. 3:21
11 [1]Lit., *is open*
[a]Ezek. 33:22; Ep
[b]Is. 60:5; 2 Cor.
12 [1]Or, *in us* [a]L
inward parts [a]2
13 [a]Gal. 4:12 [b]
4:14

14 [a]Do not be [1]bound together with [b]unbelievers; for what [c]partner-
ship have righteousness and lawlessness, or what fellowship has
light with darkness?
15 Or what [a]harmony has Christ with [1]Belial, or [2]what has a
[b]believer in common with an [c]unbeliever?
16 Or [a]what agreement has the temple of God with idols? For we
are [b]the temple of [c]the living God; just as God said,

"[d]I WILL [e]DWELL IN THEM AND [f]WALK AMONG THEM;
AND I WILL BE THEIR GOD, AND THEY SHALL BE MY PEOPLE.

17 "[a]Therefore, [b]COME OUT FROM THEIR MIDST AND BE SEPARATE," says
the Lord.
"AND DO NOT TOUCH WHAT IS UNCLEAN;
And I will welcome you.
18 "[a]And I will be a father to you,
And you shall be [b]sons and daughters to Me,"
Says the Lord Almighty.

Chapter 7

7 Therefore, having these promises, [a]beloved, [b]let us cleanse our-
selves from all defilement of flesh and spirit, perfecting holiness
in the fear of God.
2 [a]Make room for us *in your hearts;* we wronged no one, we cor-
rupted no one, we took advantage of no one.
3 I do not speak to condemn you; for I have said [a]before that you
are [b]in our hearts to die together and to live together.
4 Great is my [a]confidence [1]in you, great is my [b]boasting on your
behalf; I am filled with [c]comfort. I am overflowing with [d]joy in all
our affliction.
5 For even when we came into [a]Macedonia our flesh had no rest,
but we were [b]afflicted on every side: [c]conflicts without, fears within.
6 But [a]God, who comforts the [1]depressed, [b]comforted us by the
coming of [c]Titus;
7 and not only by his coming, but also by the comfort with which
he was comforted in you, as he reported to us your longing, your
mourning, your zeal for me; so that I rejoiced even more.
8 For though I [a]caused you sorrow by my letter, I do not regret it;
though I did regret it—*for* I see that that letter caused you sorrow,
though only for a while—
9 I now rejoice, not that you were made sorrowful, but that you
were made sorrowful to *the point of* repentance; for you were made
sorrowful according to *the will of* God, in order that you might not
suffer loss in anything through us.
10 For the sorrow that is according to *the will of* God produces a
[a]repentance [1]without regret, *leading* to salvation; but the sorrow of
the world produces death.
11 For behold what earnestness this very thing, this [1]godly sorrow,
has produced in you: what vindication of yourselves, what indigna-
tion, what fear, what [a]longing, what zeal, what [b]avenging of wrong!
In everything you [c]demonstrated yourselves to be innocent in the
matter.
12 So although [a]I wrote to you *it was* not for the sake of [b]the of-
fender, nor for the sake of the one offended, but that your earnest-
ness on our behalf might be made known to you in the sight of God.
13 For this reason we have been [a]comforted.

, *unequally* eut. 22:10; [b]1 Cor. 6:6 1 John 1:6

Beliar [2]Lit., *s a believer* *ı unbeliever* 0:21 [b]Acts :21 [c]1 Cor. 6:6

1 Cor. 10:21 6:19 [e]Matt. 29:45; Lev. 31:1; Ezek. . 25:8; John 23 [f]Rev. 2:1

[b]Rev. 18:4

7:14; 1 Chr. s. 43:6; Hos. [b]Rom. 8:14

. 6:9 [b]1 Pet. 1:15f.

6:12f.; 12:15

. 6:11f. [b]Phil. 1:7

[a]2 Cor. 3:12 4; 8:24; 9:2f.; 0:8; Phil. 1:26; s. 1:4 [c]2 Cor. 4 [d]2 Cor. 6:10

. 15:26; 2 Cor. or. 4:8 [c]Deut. 32:25

umble [a]2 Cor. 3f. [b]2 Cor. 7:13 or. 2:13; 7:13f.

8 [a]2 Cor. 2:2

Or, leading *to a* *n without regret* [a]Acts 11:18

11 [1]Lit., *sorrow* *ccording to God* 7:7 [b]2 Cor. 2:6 [c]Rom. 3:5

2 Cor. 2:3, 9; 7:8 [b]1 Cor. 5:1f.

13 [a]2 Cor. 7:6

And besides our comfort, we rejoiced even much more for the
joy of [b]Titus, because his [c]spirit has been refreshed by you all.
14 For if in anything I have [a]boasted to him about you, I was not
put to shame; but as we spoke all things to you in truth, so also our
boasting before [b]Titus proved to be *the* truth.
15 And his [1]affection abounds all the more toward you, as he
remembers the [a]obedience of you all, how you received him with
[b]fear and trembling.
16 I rejoice that in everything [a]I have confidence in you.

Chapter 8

8 Now, brethren, we *wish to* make known to you the grace of God
which has been [a]given in the churches of [b]Macedonia,
2 that in a great ordeal of affliction their abundance of joy and
their deep poverty overflowed in the [a]wealth of their liberality.
3 For I testify that [a]according to their ability, and beyond their
ability *they gave* of their own accord,
4 begging us with much entreaty for the [a]favor of participation in
the [1b]support of the [2]saints,
5 and *this,* not as we had [1]expected, but they first [a]gave themselves
to the Lord and to us by [b]the will of God.
6 Consequently we [a]urged [b]Titus that as he had previously [c]made a
beginning, so he would also complete in you [d]this gracious work as
well.
7 But just as you [a]abound [b]in everything, in faith and utterance
and knowledge and in all earnestness and in the [1]love we inspired in
you, *see* that you [a]abound in this gracious work also.
8 I [a]am not speaking *this* as a command, but as proving through
the earnestness of others the sincerity of your love also.
9 For you know [a]the grace of our Lord Jesus Christ, that [b]though
He was rich, yet for your sake He became poor, that you through His
poverty might become rich.
10 And I [a]give *my* opinion in this matter, for this is to your ad-
vantage, who were the first to begin [b]a year ago not only to do *this,*
but also to desire *to do it.*
11 But now finish [1]doing it also; that just as *there was* the [a]readiness
to desire it, so *there may be* also the completion of it by your ability.
12 For if the readiness is present, it is acceptable [a]according to what
a man has, not according to what he does not have.
13 For *this* is not for the ease of others *and* for your affliction, but by
way of equality—
14 at this present time your abundance *being a supply* for [a]their
want, that their abundance also may become *a supply* for [a]your want,
that there may be equality;
15 as it is written, "[a]HE WHO *gathered* MUCH DID NOT HAVE TOO MUCH,
AND HE WHO *gathered* LITTLE HAD NO LACK."
16 But [a]thanks be to God, who [b]puts the same earnestness on your
behalf in the heart of [c]Titus.
17 For he not only accepted our [a]appeal, but being himself very
earnest, he has gone to you of his own accord.
18 And we have sent along with him [a]the brother whose fame in *the
things of* the [b]gospel *has spread* through [c]all the churches;
19 [a]and not only *this,* but he has also been [b]appointed by the
churches to travel with us in [c]this gracious work, which is being

13 [b]2 Cor. [c]1 Cor. 16:
14 [a]2 Cor. 9:2f.; 10:8; 2 Thess. 1: 2:13; 7:6, 1
15 [1]Lit., *in* [a]2 Cor. 2:9 Phil. 2:12
16 [a]2 Cor.
8:1 [a]2 Cor. 16:9
2 [a]Rom. 2:4
3 [a]1 Cor. 16 8:11
4 [1]Lit., *serv saints* [2]Or, *h* [a]Acts 24:17; 15:25f. [b]Ror 2 Cor. 8:19f.;
5 [1]Lit., *hope* 8:1 [b]1 Cor.
6 [a]2 Cor. 8:1 [b]2 Cor. 2:13; [c]2 Cor. 8:10 24:17; Rom.
7 [1]Lit., *love f you;* some an read *your lov* [a]2 Cor. 9:8 [b]F 15:14; 1 Cor.
8 [a]1 Cor. 7:6
9 [a]2 Cor. 13: 20:28; 2 Cor. 2:6f.
10 [a]1 Cor. 7:2 [b]1 Cor. 16:2f.;
11 [1]Lit., *the d* [a]2 Cor. 8:12, 1
12 [a]Mark 12:4 21:3, 4; 2 Cor.
14 [a]Acts 4:34; 9:12
15 [a]Ex. 16:18
16 [a]2 Cor. 2:14 17:17 [c]2 Cor. 2 8:6, 23
17 [a]2 Cor. 8:6;
18 [a]1 Cor. 16:3; 12:18 [b]2 Cor. 2 [c]1 Cor. 4:17; 7:1
19 [a]Rom. 5:3 [b] 14:23; 1 Cor. 16 [c]2 Cor. 8:4, 6

administered by us for the glory of the Lord Himself, and *to show* our
[d]readiness,
20 [1]taking precaution that no one should discredit us in our ad-
ministration of this generous gift;
21 for we [a]have regard for what is honorable, not only in [b]the sight
of the Lord, but also in the sight of men.
22 And we have sent with them our brother, whom we have often
tested and found diligent in many things, but now even more
diligent, because of *his* great confidence in you.
23 As for [a]Titus, *he is* my [b]partner and fellow worker [1]among you; as
for our [c]brethren, *they are* [2d]messengers of the churches, [e]a glory to
Christ.
24 Therefore [1]openly before the churches [2]show them the proof of
your love and of our [a]reason for boasting about you.

Chapter 9

9 For [a]it is superfluous for me to write to you about this [b]ministry
to the [1]saints;
2 for I know your readiness, of which I [a]boast about you to the
[b]Macedonians, *namely,* that [c]Achaia has been prepared since [d]last
year, and your zeal has stirred up most of them.
3 But I have sent the brethren, that our [a]boasting about you may
not be made empty in this case, that, [b]as I was saying, you may be
prepared;
4 lest if any [a]Macedonians come with me and find you un-
prepared, we (not to speak of you) should be put to shame by this
confidence.
5 So I thought it necessary to urge the [a]brethren that they would
go on ahead to you and arrange beforehand your previously
promised [1b]bountiful gift, that the same might be ready as a [1c]bounti-
ful gift, and not [2d]affected by covetousness.
6 Now this *I say,* [a]he who sows sparingly shall also reap sparingly;
and he who sows [1]bountifully shall also reap [1]bountifully.
7 Let each one *do* just as he has purposed in his heart; not [a]grudg-
ingly or under compulsion; for [b]God loves a cheerful giver.
8 And [a]God is able to make all grace abound to you, that always
having all sufficiency in everything, you may have an abundance for
every good deed;
9 as it is written,

"[a]HE SCATTERED ABROAD, HE GAVE TO THE POOR,
HIS RIGHTEOUSNESS ABIDES FOREVER."

10 Now He who supplies [a]seed to the sower and bread for food,
will supply and multiply your seed for sowing and [b]increase the
harvest of your righteousness;
11 you will be [a]enriched in everything for all liberality, which
through us is producing [b]thanksgiving to God.
12 For the ministry of this service is not only fully supplying [a]the
needs of the [1]saints, but is also overflowing [b]through many
thanksgivings to God.
13 Because of the proof given by this [a]ministry they will [b]glorify
God for *your* obedience to your [c]confession of the [d]gospel of Christ,
and for the liberality of your [1]contribution to them and to all,

or. 8:11, 12; 9:2
it., *avoiding this*
m. 12:17 [b]Prov. 3:4; Rom. 14:18
it., *for you* [2]Lit., *stles* [a]2 Cor. 8:6 lem. 17 [c]2 Cor. 2 [d]John 13:16; 25 [e]1 Cor. 11:7
t., *in the face of ches* [2]Or, *show the proof . . . for g to them about you* [a]2 Cor. 7:4
[1]Or, *holy ones* 4:9 [b]2 Cor. 8:4
Cor. 7:4 [b]Rom. :26 [c]Acts 18:12 [d]2 Cor. 8:10
Cor. 7:4 [b]1 Cor. 16:2
4 [a]Rom. 15:26
., *blessing* [2]Lit., *s covetousness* :3 [b]Gen. 33:11; 1:15; 2 Cor. 9:6 hil. 4:17 [d]2 Cor. 12:17f.
., *with blessings* :24f.; 22:9; Gal. 6:7, 9
ut. 15:10; 1 Chr. om. 12:8; 2 Cor. 8:12 [b]Ex. 25:2
8 [a]Eph. 3:20
9 [a]Ps. 112:9
[a]Is. 55:10 [b]Hos. 10:12
Cor. 1:5 [b]2 Cor. 1:11
2 [1]Or, *holy ones* :14 [b]2 Cor. 1:11
[1]Or, *sharing with m* [a]Rom. 15:31; or. 8:4 [b]Matt. 9:8 6:12f.; Heb. 3:1; :23 [d]2 Cor. 2:12

14 while they also, by prayer on your behalf, yearn for you because
of the surpassing grace of God in you.
15 [a]Thanks be to God for His indescribable [b]gift!

Chapter 10

10 Now [a]I, Paul, myself [b]urge you by the [c]meekness and gentle-
ness of Christ—I who [d]am [1]meek when face to face with you,
but bold toward you when absent!
2 I ask that [a]when I am present I may not be bold with the con-
fidence with which I propose to be courageous against [b]some, who
regard us as if we walked [c]according to the flesh.
3 For though we walk in the flesh, we do not war [a]according to the
flesh,
4 for the [a]weapons of our warfare are not of the flesh, but [1]divinely
powerful [b]for the destruction of fortresses.
5 *We are* destroying speculations and every [a]lofty thing raised up
against the knowledge of God, and *we are* taking every thought cap-
tive to the [b]obedience of Christ,
6 and we are ready to punish all disobedience, whenever [a]your
obedience is complete.
7 [1a]You are looking at [2]things as they are outwardly. [b]If anyone is
confident in himself that he is Christ's, let him consider this again
within himself, that just as he is Christ's, [c]so also are we.
8 For even if [a]I should boast somewhat [1]further about our
[b]authority, which the Lord gave for building you up and not for
destroying you, I shall not be put to shame,
9 [1]for I do not wish to seem as if I would terrify you by my letters.
10 For they say, "His letters are weighty and strong, but his [1]per-
sonal presence is [a]unimpressive, and [b]his speech contemptible."
11 Let such a person consider this, that what we are in word by
letters when absent, such persons *we are* also in deed when present.
12 For we are not bold to class or compare ourselves with [1]some of
those who [a]commend themselves; but when they measure them-
selves by themselves, and compare themselves with themselves,
they are without understanding.
13 But we will not boast [a]beyond *our* measure, but [1b]within the
measure of the sphere which God apportioned to us as a measure, to
reach even as far as you.
14 For we are not overextending ourselves, as if we did not reach to
you, for [a]we were the first to come even as far as you in the [b]gospel
of Christ;
15 not boasting [a]beyond *our* measure, *that is,* in [b]other men's labors,
but with the hope that as [c]your faith grows, we shall be, [1]within our
sphere, [d]enlarged even more by you,
16 so as to [a]preach the gospel even to [b]the regions beyond you, *and*
not to boast [1c]in what has been accomplished in the sphere of
another.
17 But [a]HE WHO BOASTS, LET HIM BOAST IN THE LORD.
18 For not he who [a]commends himself is approved, but [b]whom the
Lord commends.

Chapter 11

11 I wish that you would [a]bear with me in a little [b]foolishness;
but [1]indeed you are bearing with me.

15 [a]2 Cor. 2:1... 5:15f.

10:1 [1]Lit., *low...* 5:2; Eph. 3:1; ... [b]Rom. 12:1 [c]M... 11:29; 1 Cor. 4... 4:5 [d]1 Cor. 2:3... 10:10

2 [a]1 Cor. 4:21; 13:2, 10 [b]1 Co... [c]Rom. 8:4; 2 C...

3 [a]Rom. 8:4; 2...

4 [1]Or, *mighty t... God* [a]1 Cor. 9:... 6:7; 1 Tim. 1:18 1:10; 2 Cor. 10...

5 [a]Is. 2:11f. [b]2...

6 [a]2 Cor. 2:9

7 [1]Or, *Look at you look at . . . what is before face* [a]John 7:2... 5:12 [b]1 Cor. 1:... 14:37 [c]1 Cor. ... 2 Cor. 11:23; G...

8 [1]Or, *more ab...* [a]2 Cor. 7:4 [b]2 ...

9 [1]Lit., *that I m... seem*

10 [1]Lit., *bodily presence is we...* [a]1 Cor. 2:3; 2 C... Gal. 4:13f. [b]1 C... 2 Cor. 11:6

12 [1]Or, *any* [a]2... 10:18

13 [1]Lit., *accord... the measure* [a]2... 10:15 [b]Rom. 1... 2 Cor. 10:15f.

14 [a]1 Cor. 3:6 2:12

15 [1]Lit., *accord... our sphere* [a]2 ... 10:13 [b]Rom. 1... [c]2 Thess. 1:3 [d]...

16 [1]Lit., *to the ... prepared in the...* 11:7 [b]Acts 19:2... 15:20

17 [a]Jer. 9:24; 1... 1:31

18 [a]2 Cor. 10:1... 2:29; 1 Cor. 4:5

11:1 [1]Or, *do in... bear with me* [a]... 17:17; 2 Cor. 11... 19f. [b]2 Cor. 5:1... 11:17, 21

2 For I am jealous for you with a godly jealousy; for I [a]betrothed
you to one husband, that to Christ I might [b]present you *as* a pure
virgin.
3 But I am afraid, lest as the [a]serpent deceived Eve by his crafti-
ness, your minds should be led astray from the simplicity and purity
of devotion to Christ.
4 For if one comes and preaches [a]another Jesus whom we have not
preached, or you receive a [b]different spirit which you have not re-
ceived, or a [c]different gospel which you have not accepted, you [d]bear
this [e]beautifully.
5 For I consider myself [a]not in the least inferior to the [1]most
eminent apostles.
6 But even if I am [a]unskilled in speech, yet I am not *so* in
[b]knowledge; in fact, in every way we have [c]made *this* evident to you
in all things.
7 Or [a]did I commit a sin in humbling myself that you might be
exalted, because I preached the [b]gospel of God to you [c]without
charge?
8 I robbed other churches, [a]taking wages *from them* to serve you;
9 and when I was present with you and was in need, I was [a]not a
burden to anyone; for when [b]the brethren came from [c]Macedonia,
they fully supplied my need, and in everything I kept myself from
[a]being a burden to you, [1]and will continue to do so.
10 [a]As the truth of Christ is in me, [b]this boasting of mine will not be
stopped in the regions of [c]Achaia.
11 Why? [a]Because I do not love you? [b]God knows *I do!*
12 But what I am doing, I will continue to do, [a]that I may cut off
opportunity from those who desire an opportunity to be [1]regarded
just as we are in the matter about which they are boasting.
13 For such men are [a]false apostles, [b]deceitful workers, disguising
themselves as apostles of Christ.
14 And no wonder, for even [a]Satan disguises himself as an [b]angel of
light.
15 Therefore it is not surprising if his servants also disguise them-
selves as servants of righteousness; [a]whose end shall be according to
their deeds.
16 [a]Again I say, let no one think me foolish; but if *you do,* receive me
even as foolish, that I also may boast a little.
17 That which I am speaking, I am not speaking [1a]as the Lord
would, but as [b]in foolishness, in this confidence of boasting.
18 Since [a]many boast [b]according to the flesh, I will boast also.
19 For you, [a]being *so* wise, bear with the foolish gladly.
20 For you bear with anyone if he [a]enslaves you, if he [b]devours you,
if he [c]takes advantage of you, if he [d]exalts himself, if he [e]hits you in
the face.
21 To *my* [a]shame I *must* say that we have been [b]weak *by comparison.*
But in whatever respect anyone *else* [c]is bold (I [d]speak in foolishness),
I am just as bold myself.
22 Are they [a]Hebrews? [b]So am I. Are they [c]Israelites? [c]So am I. Are
they [1d]descendants of Abraham? [e]So am I.
23 Are they [a]servants of Christ? (I speak as if insane) I more so; in
[1b]far more labors, in [1c]far more imprisonments, [2d]beaten times
without number, often in [e]danger of death.
24 Five times I received from the Jews [a]thirty-nine *lashes.*

Hos. 2:19f.; Eph. 26f. [b]2 Cor. 4:14
en. 3:4, 13; John 44; 1 Thess. 3:5; Tim. 2:14; Rev. 12:9, 15
Cor. 3:11 [b]Rom. Gal. 1:6 [d]2 Cor. 11:1 [e]Mark 7:9
, super-apostles . 12:11; Gal. 2:6
Cor. 1:17 [b]1 Cor. Eph. 3:4 [c]2 Cor. 4:2
or. 12:13 [b]Rom. Cor. 2:12 [c]Acts 18:3; 1 Cor. 9:18 r. 4:12; 9:6; Phil. 4:15, 18
., and I will keep Cor. 12:13f., 16 Acts 18:5 [c]Rom. 26; Phil. 4:15-18
[a]Rom. 1:9; 9:1; . 1:23; Gal. 2:20 :15 [c]Acts 18:12
or. 12:15 [b]Rom. Cor. 2:17; 11:31; 12:2f.
t., found [a]1 Cor. 9:12
[a]Acts 20:30; Gal. Phil. 1:15; Titus ; 2 Pet. 2:1; Rev. 2:2 [b]Phil. 3:2
[a]Matt. 4:10; Eph. ; Col. 1:13 [b]Col. 1:12
5 [a]Rom. 2:6; 3:8
16 [a]2 Cor. 11:1
., in accordance the Lord [a]1 Cor. 25 [b]2 Cor. 11:21
Phil. 3:3f. [b]2 Cor. 5:16
19 [a]1 Cor. 4:10
2 Cor. 1:24; Gal. :3, 9; 5:1 [b]Mark :40 [c]2 Cor. 11:3; :16 [d]2 Cor. 10:5 [e]1 Cor. 4:11
Cor. 6:8 [b]2 Cor. :10 [c]2 Cor. 10:2 [d]2 Cor. 11:17
[1]*Lit., seed* [a]Acts [b]Phil. 3:5 [c]Rom. Gal. 3:16 [e]Rom. 11:1
23 [1]*Lit., more abundant* [2]*Lit., edingly in stripes* . 3:5; 2 Cor. 3:6; :7 [b]1 Cor. 15:10 6:5 [d]Acts 16:23; 6:5 [e]Rom. 8:36
24 [a]Deut. 25:3

25 Three times I was [a]beaten with rods, once I was [b]stoned, three
times I was shipwrecked, a night and a day I have spent in the deep.
26 *I have been* on frequent journeys, in dangers from rivers, dangers
from robbers, dangers from *my* [a]countrymen, dangers from the [b]Gen-
tiles, dangers in the [c]city, dangers in the wilderness, dangers on the
sea, dangers among [d]false brethren;
27 *I have been* in [a]labor and hardship, [1]through many sleepless
nights, in [b]hunger and thirst, often [c]without food, in cold and [2d]ex-
posure.
28 Apart from *such* [1]external things, there is the daily pressure upon
me *of* concern for [a]all the churches.
29 Who is [a]weak without my being weak? Who is [1]led into sin
[2]without my intense concern?
30 If I have to boast, I will boast of what pertains to my [a]weakness.
31 The God and Father of the Lord Jesus, [a]He who is blessed
forever, [b]knows that I am not lying.
32 In [a]Damascus the ethnarch under Aretas the king was [b]guarding
the city of the Damascenes in order to seize me,
33 and I was let down in a basket [a]through a window [1]in the wall,
and *so* escaped his hands.

Chapter 12

12 [a]Boasting is necessary, though it is not profitable; but I will go
on to visions and [b]revelations [1]of the Lord.
2 I know a man [a]in Christ who fourteen years ago—whether in the
body I do not know, or out of the body I do not know, [b]God knows—
such a man was [c]caught up to the [d]third heaven.
3 And I know how such a man—whether in the body or apart
from the body I do not know, [a]God knows—
4 was [a]caught up into [b]Paradise, and heard inexpressible words,
which a man is not permitted to speak.
5 [a]On behalf of such a man will I boast; but on my own behalf I
will not boast, except in regard to *my* [b]weaknesses.
6 For if I do wish to boast I shall not be [a]foolish, [b]for I shall be
speaking the truth; but I refrain *from this,* so that no one may credit
me with more than he sees *in* me or hears from me.
7 And because of the surpassing greatness of the [a]revelations, for
this reason, to keep me from exalting myself, there was given me a
[b]thorn in the flesh, a [c]messenger of Satan to buffet me—to keep me
from exalting myself!
8 Concerning this I entreated the Lord [a]three times that it might
depart from me.
9 And He has said to me, "My grace is sufficient for you, for
[1a]power is perfected in weakness." Most gladly, therefore, I will
rather [b]boast about my weaknesses, that the power of Christ may
dwell in me.
10 Therefore [a]I am well content with weaknesses, with [1]insults,
with [b]distresses, with [c]persecutions, with [b]difficulties, [d]for Christ's
sake; for [e]when I am weak, then I am strong.
11 I have become [a]foolish; you yourselves compelled me. Actually I
should have been commended by you, for [b]in no respect was I in-
ferior to the [1]most eminent apostles, even though [c]I am a nobody.
12 The [1a]signs [2]of a true apostle were performed among you with all
perseverance, by [1]signs and wonders and [3]miracles.

25 [a]Acts 14:19
26 [a]Acts 9 50; 14:5; 18:12; 20: 23:10, 12; 1 Thess. 2 14:5, 19; [c]Acts 21:3
27 [1]Lit., *o wakefulne nakedness clothing* [a] 2 Thess. 3 4:11; Phil. 6:5 [d]1 Cor
28 [1]Or, *the unmention* 7:17
29 [1]Lit., *m stumble* [2]L *not burn* [a] 9:22
30 [a]1 Cor.
31 [a]Rom. 11:11
32 [a]Acts 9:
33 [1]Lit., *thr* 9:25
12:1 [1]Or *pc* [a]2 Cor. 11:1 12:5, 9 [b]1 C 2 Cor. 12:7; 2:2; Eph. 3:3
2 [a]Rom. 16: 11:11 [c]Ezek 8:39; 2 Cor. 1 Thess. 4:1 12:5 [d]Deut. 148:4; Eph. 4:14
3 [a]2 Cor. 11:
4 [a]Ezek. 8:3 2 Cor. 12:2; 1 4:17; Rev. 12 23:43
5 [a]2 Cor. 12: 2:3; 2 Cor. 12
6 [a]2 Cor. 5:1 12:11 [b]2 Cor.
7 [a]2 Cor. 12: 33:55; Ezek. 2 Hos. 2:6 [c]Job 4:10; 1 Cor. 5:
8 [a]Matt. 26:44
9 [1]Later mss. *power* [a]1 Cor. 3:16; Phil. 4:13 2:3; 2 Cor. 12:
10 [1]Or, *mistre* [a]Rom. 5:3; 8:3 6:4 [c]2 Thess. 2 Tim. 3:11 [d]2 5:15, 20 [e]2 Co
11 [1]Or, *super-a* [a]2 Cor. 5:13; 11 12:6 [b]1 Cor. 15 2 Cor. 11:5 [c]1 13:2; 15:9
12 [1]Or, *attestin miracles* [2]Lit., *c apostle* [3]Or, *wo power* [a]John 4. Rom. 15:19; 1 C

13 For in what respect were you treated as inferior to the rest of the churches, except that [a]I myself did not become a burden to you? Forgive me [b]this wrong!

14 Here [a]for this third time I am ready to come to you, and I [b]will not be a burden to you; for I [c]do not seek what is yours, but [d]you; for [e]children are not responsible to save up for *their* parents, but [f]parents for *their* children.

15 And I will [a]most gladly spend and be expended for your souls. If [b]I love you the more, am I to be loved the less?

16 But be that as it may, I [a]did not burden you myself; nevertheless, crafty fellow that I am, I [b]took you in by deceit.

17 [a]*Certainly* I have not taken advantage of you through any of those whom I have sent to you, have I?

18 I [a]urged [b]Titus *to go,* and sent [c]the brother with him. Titus did not take any advantage of you, did he? Did we not [1]conduct ourselves [2]in the same [d]spirit *and walk* [e]in the same steps?

19 All this time [1]you have been thinking that we are defending ourselves to you. *Actually,* [a]it is in the sight of God that we have been speaking in Christ; and [b]all for your upbuilding, [c]beloved.

20 For I am afraid that perhaps [a]when I come I may find you to be not what I wish and may be found by you to be not what you wish; that perhaps *there may be* [b]strife, jealousy, [c]angry tempers, [d]disputes, [e]slanders, [f]gossip, [g]arrogance, [h]disturbances;

21 I am afraid that when I come again my God may humiliate me before you, and I may mourn over many of those who have [a]sinned in the past and not repented of the [b]impurity, [1]immorality and sensuality which they have practiced.

Chapter 13

13 [a]This is the third time I am coming to you. [b]EVERY [1]FACT [2]IS TO BE CONFIRMED BY THE [3]TESTIMONY OF TWO OR THREE WITNESSES.

2 I have previously said when present the second time, and though now absent I say in advance to those who have [a]sinned in the past and to all the rest as well, that [b]if I come again, I will not [c]spare *anyone,*

3 since you are [a]seeking for proof of the [b]Christ who speaks in me, and who is not weak toward you, but [c]mighty in you.

4 For indeed He was [a]crucified because of weakness, yet He lives [b]because of the power of God. For we also are [c]weak [1]in Him, yet [d]we shall live with Him because of the power of God *directed* toward you.

5 [a]Test yourselves *to see* if you are in the faith; [b]examine yourselves! Or do you not recognize this about yourselves, that Jesus Christ is in you—unless indeed you [1c]fail the test?

6 But I trust that you will realize that we ourselves [1]do not fail the test.

7 Now we pray to God that you do no wrong; not that we ourselves may appear approved, but that you may do what is right, even though we should [1]appear unapproved.

8 For we can do nothing against the truth, but *only* for the truth.

9 For we rejoice when we ourselves are [a]weak but you are strong; this we also pray for, [1]that you be [b]made complete.

[a]1 Cor. 9:12, 18; 2 Cor. 11:9; 12:14 [b]2 Cor. 11:7

…Cor. 1:15; 13:1, 2 …9:12, 18; 2 Cor. …9; 12:13 [c]1 Cor. …33 [d]1 Cor. 9:19 …4:14f.; Gal. 4:19 …9:14; Ezek. 34:2

[a]Rom. 9:3; 2 Cor. …6; Phil. 2:17; Col. …24; 1 Thess. 2:8; …Tim. 2:10 [b]2 Cor. 11:11

…Cor. 11:9 [b]2 Cor. 11:20

17 [a]2 Cor. 9:5

…Lit., *walk* [2]Or, *by …me Spirit* [a]2 Cor. …Cor. 2:13 [c]2 Cor. …8:18 [d]1 Cor. 4:21 [e]Rom. 4:12

…r, *have you been …king . . . ?* [a]Rom. …Cor. 2:17 [b]Rom. …4:19; 2 Cor. 10:8; …s. 5:11 [c]Heb. 6:9

…Cor. 4:21; 2 Cor. [b]1 Cor. 1:11; 3:3 …5:20 [d]Rom. 2:8; …Cor. 11:19 [e]Rom. …ames 4:11; 1 Pet. …om. 1:29 [g]1 Cor. …5, 18; 5:2 [h]1 Cor. 14:33

21 [1]I.e., sexual …ality [a]2 Cor. 13:2 …Cor. 6:9, 18; Gal. 5:19; Col. 3:5

[1]Lit., *word* [2]Lit., *…ill be* [3]Lit., *mouth* …Cor. 12:14 [b]Deut. …9:15; Matt. 18:16

…or. 12:21 [b]1 Cor. …4:21; 2 Cor. 13:10 …2 Cor. 1:23; 10:11

[a]2 Cor. 10:1, 10 …10:20; 1 Cor. 5:4; [c]2 Cor. 9:8; 10:4

[1]Some early mss. …d *with Him* [a]Phil. …Pet. 3:18 [b]Rom. …4; 6:4; 1 Cor. 6:14 …r. 2:3; 2 Cor. 13:9 [d]Rom. 6:8

…, *are unapproved* …6:6 [b]1 Cor. 11:28 [c]1 Cor. 9:27

6 [1]Lit., *are not unapproved*

7 [1]Lit., *be as*

…, *your completion* …2 Cor. 12:10; 13:4 …Cor. 1:10; 2 Cor. 13:11; Eph. 4:12; 1 Thess. 3:10

10 For this reason I am writing these things while absent, in order
that when present [a]I may not use [b]severity, in accordance with the
[c]authority which the Lord gave me, for building up and not for
tearing down.
11 [a]Finally, brethren, [1]rejoice, [2b]be made complete, be comforted, [c]be
like-minded, [d]live in peace; and [e]the God of love and peace shall be
with you.
12 [a]Greet one another with a holy kiss.
13 [a]All the [1]saints greet you.
14 [a]The grace of the Lord Jesus Christ, and the [b]love of God, and the
[c]fellowship of the Holy Spirit, be with you all.

10 [a]2 Cor. 2:3
1:13 [c]1 Cor. 5:4
10:8
11 [1]Or possibly
farewell [2]Or, *pu*
yourselves in or
[a]1 Thess. 4:1; 2
3:1 [b]1 Cor. 1:10
13:9; Eph. 4:12
1 Thess. 3:10 [c]
12:16 [d]Mark 9:
[e]Rom. 15:33; Ep
12 [a]Rom. 16:16
13 [1]Or, *holy on*
4:22
14 [a]Rom. 16:20
8:9 [b]Rom. 5:5;
[c]Phil. 2:1

2 Corinthians Observations Chart

Paul

His character	His afflictions	His conflict with the Corinthians

The Corinthians

Their strengths	Their weaknesses	Their problems with Paul

ul's desire for the Corinthians	Insights on Titus

2 Corinthians at a Glance

Theme of 2 Corinthians:

Author:

Date:

Purpose:

Key Words:
comfort (comforted)
afflicted (affliction, suffer, sufferings)
sorrow(ful)
boast (boasting or glory, as both are from same Greek root word)
confidence
commend(ing)
death
life
heart
joy (rejoice, rejoicing, rejoiced)
ministry
grace
Titus
mark references to enemy (warfare, serpent, Satan, as well as relative pronouns and synonyms) all with a red pitchfork

Segment Divisions		Chapter Themes
		1
		2
		3
		4
		5
		6
		7
		8
		9
		10
		11
		12
		13

ALATIANS

ıe gospel introduced the Jews to a new way of life—that of grace rather than law. The old covenant all of its regulations was made obsolete by the new covenant (Hebrews 8:13). This transition was ːult for some Jewish believers to handle, and a group called the Judaizers sprung up. The Judaizers ʻaced Christianity but said that some of the old covenant rites, including circumcision, still must be rved.

s Paul, God's apostle to the Gentiles, went on his missionary journeys sharing the gospel of grace, y of these Judaizers followed him, teaching the necessity of keeping the law to one degree or ıer. They even went to Galatia. That's why Paul wrote what he did to the churches in Galatia.

ıere is some uncertainty about whether Galatians was written after Paul's first or second mission- ɔurney and so the exact date of his writing is not known. The debate centers on whether Paul was ng to the northern or southern churches of Galatia. If Paul wrote to the northern churches the le would have been written sometime between A.D. 53 and 57, but if the letter was written to the ıern churches it would have been between A.D. 48 and 49.

owever, the date does not affect the message of this critical letter. The truths in this epistle will ate you to walk in that glorious freedom of a righteous life in the Spirit—truths you can glean ıgh careful observation. Therefore, devote your energies to discovering these truths rather than to ting when Galatians was written.

ıe more you read and observe the text of this book, the more you'll understand Paul's words: "It is nger I who live, but Christ lives in me; and the life which I now live in the flesh I live by faith in on of God, who loved me, and delivered Himself up for me" (Galatians 2:20).

NGS TO DO

Read Acts 13 and 14 and then look at the map on page 1717 to acquaint yourself with the cities in this area. Also review the chart on page 1716 showing the sequence of events in Paul's life after his conversion.

As you read mark the key words (and their synonyms and pronouns) that are listed on the GALATIANS AT A GLANCE chart on page 1724. Mark any other key words you see as you read.

a. The key words will help you see the theme of this epistle. The best way to see and absorb the book's message is to read through Galatians as many times as possible. Familiarity with the text and careful observation of what is being said is crucial when you study the Bible.

b. After you mark the key words, list in the margin everything you learn from the text about the key words.

c. Jesus Christ is mentioned thirty-eight times in Galatians. List everything you learn about Him from this book.

Record the chapter themes on GALATIANS AT A GLANCE and in the text. Record the theme of the book and complete the chart.

As you read through the book, note Paul's emphasis in the first two chapters and then how the focus changes in chapter 3.

a. Look for the questions Paul asks the recipients of this letter. Watch for words such as: *brethren, you,* and *foolish Galatians*. Make a list of these things on the chart PAUL'S CONCERN FOR THE CHURCHES AT GALATIA on page 1723. (You may want to list these on scrap paper before you write them in your Bible.)

b. Think about why Paul said all he did about himself in those first two chapters. What does this have to do with what follows in the rest of his epistle?

c. Notice the progression of events in Paul's life as presented in these chapters. (There's a the chronology of these events on this page.)

5. In chapter 3 mark *promise*. Note what the promise is; the text will tell you.
6. Fill in the segment divisions on GALATIANS AT A GLANCE.

THINGS TO THINK ABOUT

1. Are you living under grace or law? Have you accepted the grace of God for your salvat still put yourself under the law?
2. According to Galatians 5:16-21, if you live under grace, under the control of the Spirit of G will not be able to live a life habitually controlled by the flesh, producing the works of th Evaluate your walk according to these verses.
3. What do you boast in?
4. As you look at Paul's life, what do you learn for your own life?

Sequence of Events in Paul's Life after His Conversion*

There are differing opinions on these dates; however, for continuity's sake this will be the basis for all dates.

Year A.D.	Event
33-34	Conversion, time in Damascus
35-47	Some silent years except we know:
	1. Spent time in Arabia and Damascus
	2. Made first visit to Jerusalem
	3. Went to Tarsus, Syria-Cilicia area
	4. Was with Barnabas in Antioch
	5. With Barnabas took relief to brethren in Judea—Paul's second visit to Jerusalem
	6. Returns to Antioch; sent out with Barnabas by church at Antioch
47-48	First missionary journey: *Galatians written(?)*
49	Apostolic Council at Jerusalem—Paul visits Jerusalem (compare Acts 15 with Galatians 2
49-51	Second missionary journey: *1 and 2 Thessalonians written*
52-56	Third missionary journey: *1 and 2 Corinthians and Romans written*
56	Paul goes to Jerusalem and is arrested; held at Caesarea
57-59	Appearance before Felix and Drusilla; before Festus; before Agrippa
59-60	Appeals to Caesar, sent from Caesarea to Rome
60-62	First Roman imprisonment: *Ephesians, Philemon, Colossians, and Philippians written*
62	Paul's release; possible trip to Spain
62	Paul in Macedonia: *1 Timothy written*
62	Paul goes to Crete: *Titus written*
63-64	Paul taken to Rome and imprisoned: *2 Timothy written*
64	Paul is absent from the body and present with the Lord—hallelujah!
	(Others put Paul's conversion about A.D. 35, his death in A.D. 68.)

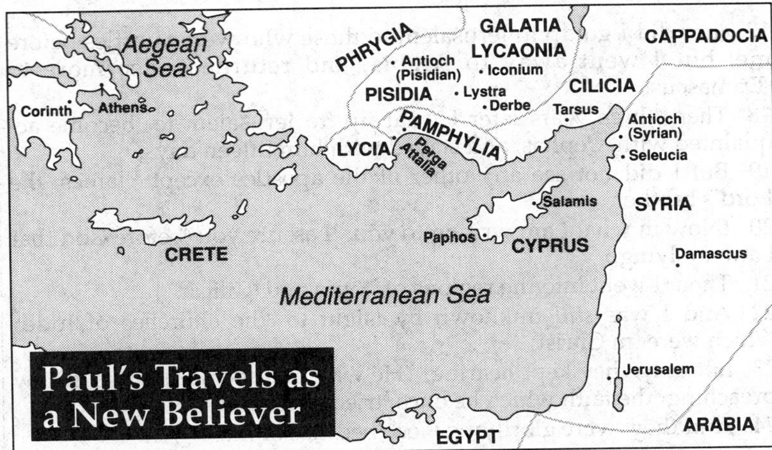

Paul's Travels as a New Believer

Chapter 1

1 Paul, [a]an apostle ([b]not *sent* from men, nor through the agency of
man, but [c]through Jesus Christ, and God the Father, who [d]raised
Him from the dead),
2 and all [a]the brethren who are with me, to [b]the churches of
Galatia:
3 [a]Grace to you and peace from [1]God our Father, and the Lord
Jesus Christ,
4 who [a]gave Himself for our sins, that He might deliver us out of
[b]this present evil [1]age, according to the will of [c]our God and Father,
5 [a]to whom *be* the glory forevermore. Amen.
6 I am amazed that you are so quickly deserting [a]Him who called
you [1]by the grace of Christ, for a [b]different gospel;
7 which is *really* not another; only there are some who are [a]disturb-
ing you, and want to distort the gospel of Christ.
8 But even though we, or [a]an angel from heaven, should preach to
you a gospel [1]contrary to that which we have preached to you, let
him be [2b]accursed.
9 As we [a]have said before, so I say again now, [b]if any man is
preaching to you a gospel [1]contrary to that which you received, let
him be [2c]accursed.
10 For am I now [a]seeking the favor of men, or of God? Or am I
striving to please men? If I were still trying to please men, I would
not be a [b]bond-servant of Christ.
11 For [a]I would have you know, brethren, that the gospel which
was preached by me is [b]not according to man.
12 For [a]I neither received it from man, nor was I taught it, but *I
received it* through a [b]revelation of Jesus Christ.
13 For you have heard of [a]my former manner of life in Judaism,
how I [b]used to persecute [c]the church of God beyond measure, and
[d]tried to destroy it;
14 and I [a]was advancing in Judaism beyond many of my contem-
poraries among my [1]countrymen, being more extremely zealous for
my [b]ancestral traditions.
15 But when He who had set me apart, *even* from my mother's
womb, and [a]called me through His grace, was pleased
16 to reveal His Son in me, that I might [a]preach Him among the
Gentiles, [b]I did not immediately consult with [1c]flesh and blood,

or. 1:1 [b]Gal.
ts 9:15; Gal.
. [d]Acts 2:24
. 4:21 [b]Acts
; 1 Cor. 16:1
e early mss.
d the Father,
r Lord Jesus
st [a]Rom. 1:7
d [a]Gal. 2:20
; Rom. 12:2;
4 [c]Phil. 4:20
[a]Rom. 11:36
[a]Rom. 8:28;
; 5:8 [b]2 Cor.
:7, 11; 2:2, 7;
14; 1 Tim. 1:3
:24; Gal. 5:10
er than, more
Gr., *anathema*
14 [b]Rom. 9:3
er than, more
Gr., *anathema*
18:23 [b]Rom.
:17 [c]Rom. 9:3
[a]1 Cor. 10:33;
:4 [b]Rom. 1:1;
Phil. 1:1
n. 2:16; 1 Cor.
1 Cor. 3:4; 9:8
or. 11:23; Gal.
or. 2:10; 2 Cor.
; Gal. 1:16; 2:2
ts 26:4f. [b]Acts
22:4, 5 [c]1 Cor.
:32 [d]Acts 9:21
Lit., *race* [a]Acts
Jer. 9:14; Matt.
rk 7:3; Col. 2:8
9:1, 5; Jer. 1:5;
9:15; Rom. 1:1;
Gal. 1:6
, human beings
s 9:15; Gal. 2:9
20 [c]Matt. 16:17

17 [a]nor did I go up to Jerusalem to those who were apostles before
me; but I went away to Arabia, and returned once more to
[b]Damascus.
18 Then [a]three years later I went up [b]to Jerusalem to [1]become ac-
quainted with [c]Cephas, and stayed with him fifteen days.
19 But I did not see any other of the apostles except [1a]James, the
Lord's brother.
20 (Now in what I am writing to you, [1]I assure you [a]before God that
I am not lying.)
21 Then [a]I went into the regions of [b]Syria and [c]Cilicia.
22 And I was *still* unknown by [1]sight to [a]the churches of Judea
which were [b]in Christ;
23 but only, they kept hearing, "He who once persecuted us is now
preaching [a]the faith which he once [b]tried to destroy."
24 And they [a]were glorifying God [1]because of me.

Chapter 2

2 Then after an interval of fourteen years I [a]went up again to Jeru-
salem with [b]Barnabas, taking [c]Titus along also.
2 And [1]it was because of a [a]revelation that I went up; and I sub-
mitted to them the [b]gospel which I preach among the Gentiles, but *I*
did so in private to those who were of reputation, for fear that I might
be [c]running, or had run, in vain.
3 But not even [a]Titus who was with me, though he was a Greek,
was [b]compelled to be circumcised.
4 But *it was* because of the [a]false brethren who [b]had sneaked in to
spy out our [c]liberty which we have in Christ Jesus, in order to [d]bring
us into bondage.
5 But we did not yield in subjection to them for even an hour, so
that [a]the truth of the gospel might remain with you.
6 But from those who [1]were of high [a]reputation (what they were
makes no difference to me; [b]God [2]shows no partiality)—well, those
who were of reputation contributed nothing to me.
7 But on the contrary, seeing that I had been [a]entrusted with the
[b]gospel [1]to the uncircumcised, just as [c]Peter *had been* [2]to the circum-
cised
8 (for He who effectually worked for Peter in *his* [a]apostleship [1]to
the circumcised effectually worked for me also to the Gentiles),
9 and recognizing [a]the grace that had been given to me, [1b]James
and [c]Cephas and John, who were [d]reputed to be [e]pillars, gave to me
and [f]Barnabas the [g]right [2]hand of fellowship, that we *might* [h]*go* to the
Gentiles, and they to the circumcised.
10 *They* only *asked* us to remember the poor—[a]the very thing I also
was eager to do.
11 But when [a]Cephas came to [b]Antioch, I opposed him to his face,
because he [1]stood condemned.
12 For prior to the coming of certain men from [1a]James, he used to
[b]eat with the Gentiles; but when they came, he *began* to withdraw
and hold himself aloof, [c]fearing [2]the party of the circumcision.
13 And the rest of the Jews joined him in hypocrisy, with the result
that even [a]Barnabas was carried away by their hypocrisy.
14 But when I saw that they [a]were not [1]straightforward about [b]the
truth of the gospel, I said to [c]Cephas in the presence of all, "If you,

17 [a]Acts 9 9:2
18 [1]Or, *vis* [a]Acts 9:22f [c]John 1:42 11, 14
19 [1]Or, *Ja* 12:46; Acts
20 [1]Lit., *be God* [a]Rom 1:23; 11:31
21 [a]Acts 9 15:23, 41
22 [1]Lit., *fac* 7:17; 1 The [b]Rom. 16:7
23 [a]Acts 6: [b]Acts 9:21
24 [1]Lit., *in*
2:1 [a]Acts 1 4:36; Gal. 2 [c]2 Cor. 2:13
2 [1]Lit., *acc revelation I* [a]Acts 15:2; [b]Gal. 1:6 [c]F 1 Cor. 9:24ff Phil. 2:16; 2 Heb. 12:1
3 [a]2 Cor. 2: [b]Acts 16:3;
4 [a]Acts 15: 11:13, 26; G [b]2 Pet. 2:1; J 5:1, 13; Jam [d]Rom. 8:15;
5 [a]Gal. 1:6; 1:5
6 [1]Lit., *seem something* [2] *not receive a* [a]2 Cor. 11:5; 2:9; 6:3 [b]Act
7 [1]Lit., *of the uncircumcisi the circumcis* 9:17; 1 Thess 1 Tim. 1:11 Gal. 1:16 [c]Ga 2:9, 11, 14
8 [1]Lit., *of the circumcision*
9 [1]Or, *Jacob hands* [a]Rom. 12:17; Gal. 2: 22:8; Gal. 1:18 14 [e]2 Cor. 11: Gal. 2:2, 6; 6:3 3:15; Rev. 3:1 4:36; Gal. 2:1, 10:15 [h]Gal. 1:
10 [a]Acts 24:1
11 [1]Or, *was to condemned;* li *who was cond was self-conde* [a]Gal. 1:18; 2:7, [b]Acts 11:19; 15
12 [1]Or, *Jacob* converts *from* *circumcised;* lit *from the circum* [a]Acts 12:17; Ga [b]Acts 11:3 [c]Ac
13 [a]Acts 4:36; 2:1, 9
14 [1]Or, *progre toward;* lit., *wal straightly* [a]Heb. [b]Gal. 1:6; 2:5; C [c]Gal. 1:18; 2:7,

being a Jew, [d]live like the Gentiles and not like the Jews, how *is it that*
you compel the Gentiles to live like Jews?[2]
15 "We *are* [a]Jews by nature, and not [b]sinners from among the Gen-
tiles;
16 nevertheless knowing that [a]a man is not justified by the works of
[1]the Law but through faith in Christ Jesus, even we have believed in
Christ Jesus, that we may be justified by [b]faith in Christ, and not by
the works of [1]the Law; since [c]by the works of [1]the Law shall no [2]flesh
be justified.
17 "But if, while seeking to be justified in Christ, we ourselves have
also been found [a]sinners, is Christ then a minister of sin? [b]May it
never be!
18 "For if I rebuild what I have *once* destroyed, I [a]prove myself to be
a transgressor.
19 "For through [1]the Law I [a]died to [1]the Law, that I might live to
God.
20 "I have been [a]crucified with Christ; and it is no longer I who live,
but [b]Christ lives in me; and [1]the *life* which I now live in the flesh I
live by faith in [c]the Son of God, who [d]loved me, and [e]delivered
Himself up for me.
21 "I do not nullify the grace of God; for [a]if righteousness *comes*
through [1]the Law, then Christ died needlessly."

Chapter 3

3 [1]You foolish [a]Galatians, who has bewitched you, before whose
eyes Jesus Christ [b]was publicly portrayed *as* crucified?
2 This is the only thing I want to find out from you: did you
receive the Spirit by the works of [1]the Law, or by [2a]hearing with
faith?
3 Are you so foolish? Having begun [1]by the Spirit, are you now
[2]being perfected by the flesh?
4 Did you suffer so many things in vain—[a]if indeed it was in vain?
5 Does He then, who [a]provides you with the Spirit and [b]works
[1]miracles among you, do it by the works of [2]the Law, or by [3c]hearing
with faith?
6 [1]Even so [a]Abraham [b]BELIEVED GOD, AND IT WAS RECKONED TO HIM AS
RIGHTEOUSNESS.
7 Therefore, [1]be sure that [a]it is those who are of faith who are [b]sons
of Abraham.
8 And the Scripture, foreseeing that God [1]would justify the [2]Gen-
tiles by faith, preached the gospel beforehand to Abraham, *saying*,
"[a]ALL THE NATIONS SHALL BE BLESSED IN YOU."
9 So then [a]those who are of faith are blessed with [1]Abraham, the
believer.
10 For as many as are of the works of [1]the Law are under a curse;
for it is written, "[a]CURSED IS EVERYONE WHO DOES NOT ABIDE BY ALL
THINGS WRITTEN IN THE BOOK OF THE LAW, TO PERFORM THEM."
11 Now that [a]no one is justified [1]by [2]the Law before God is evident;
for, "[3b]THE RIGHTEOUS MAN SHALL LIVE BY FAITH."
12 [1]However, the Law is not [2]of faith; on the contrary, "[a]HE WHO
PRACTICES THEM SHALL LIVE [3]BY THEM."
13 Christ [a]redeemed us from the curse of the Law, having become a
curse for us—for it is written, "[b]CURSED IS EVERYONE WHO HANGS ON [c]A
[1]TREE"—

ome close the quotation here, tend it through cts 10:28; Gal. 2:12
. 3:4f. [b]1 Sam. :18; Luke 24:7
aw [2]Or, *mortal* cts 13:39; Gal. om. 3:22; 9:30 3:2; Rom. 3:20
al. 2:15 [b]Luke 0:16; Gal. 3:21
18 [a]Rom. 3:5
aw [a]Rom. 6:2; 7:4; 1 Cor. 9:20
Or, *insofar as I* 6:6; Gal. 5:24; m. 8:10 [c]Matt. om. 8:37 [e]Gal. 1:4
law [a]Gal. 3:21
it., *O* [a]Gal. 1:2 1:23; Gal. 5:11
r, *law* [2]Lit., *the of faith* [a]Rom. 10:17
ith [2]Or, *ending with*
4 [a]1 Cor. 15:2
works of power r, *law* [3]Lit., *the of faith* [a]2 Cor. il. 1:19 [b]1 Cor. 0 [c]Rom. 10:17
Just as [a]Rom. 4:3 [b]Gen. 15:6
t., *know* [a]Rom. Gal. 3:9 [b]Luke 19:9; Gal. 6:16
., *justifies* [2]Lit., *ons* [a]Gen. 12:3
t., *the believing aham* [a]Gal. 3:7
[1]Or, *law* [a]Deut. 27:26
n [2]Or, *law* [3]Or, *who is righteous shall live.* [a]Gal. Hab. 2:4; Rom. :17; Heb. 10:38
And [2]Or, *based* r, *in* [a]Lev. 18:5; Rom. 10:5
cross; lit., *wood* 5 [b]Deut. 21:23 [c]Acts 5:30

14 in order that [a]in Christ Jesus the blessing of Abraham might [1]come to the Gentiles, so that we [b]might receive [c]the promise of the Spirit through faith.

15 [a]Brethren, [b]I speak [1]in terms of human relations: [c]even though it is *only* a man's [2]covenant, yet when it has been ratified, no one sets it aside or adds [3]conditions to it.

16 Now the promises were spoken [a]to Abraham and to his seed. He does not say, "And to seeds," as *referring* to many, but *rather* to one, "[b]And to your seed," that is, Christ.

17 What I am saying is this: the Law, which came [a]four hundred and thirty years later, does not invalidate a covenant previously ratified by God, so as to nullify the promise.

18 For [a]if the inheritance is [1]based on law, it is no longer [1]based on a promise; but [b]God has granted it to Abraham by means of a promise.

19 [a]Why the Law then? It was added [1]because of transgressions, having been [b]ordained through angels [c]by the [2]agency of a mediator, until [d]the seed should come to whom the promise had been made.

20 Now [a]a mediator is not [1]for one *party only*; whereas God is *only* one.

21 Is the Law then contrary to the promises of God? [a]May it never be! For [b]if a law had been given which was able to impart life, then righteousness [1]would indeed have been [2]based on law.

22 But the Scripture has [a]shut up all [1]men under sin, that the promise by faith in Jesus Christ might be given to those who believe.

23 But before faith came, we were kept in custody under the law, [a]being shut up to the faith which was later to be revealed.

24 Therefore the Law has become our [1a]tutor *to lead us* to Christ, that [b]we may be justified by faith.

25 But now that faith has come, we are no longer under a [1a]tutor.

26 For you are all [a]sons of God through faith in [b]Christ Jesus.

27 For all of you who were [a]baptized into Christ have [b]clothed yourselves with Christ.

28 [a]There is neither Jew nor Greek, there is neither slave nor free man, there is [1]neither male nor female; for [b]you are all one in [c]Christ Jesus.

29 And if [a]you [1]belong to Christ, then you are Abraham's [2]offspring, heirs according to [b]promise.

Chapter 4

4 Now I say, as long as the heir is a [1]child, he does not differ at all from a slave although he is [2]owner of everything,

2 but he is under guardians and [1]managers until the date set by the father.

3 So also we, while we were children, were held [a]in bondage under the [1b]elemental things of the world.

4 But when [a]the fulness of the time came, God sent forth His Son, [b]born of a woman, born [c]under [1]the Law,

5 in order that He might redeem those who were under [1]the Law, that we might receive the adoption as [a]sons.

6 And because you are sons, [a]God has sent forth the Spirit of His Son into our hearts, crying, "[b]Abba! Father!"

7 Therefore you are no longer a slave, but a son; and [a]if a son, then an heir [1]through God.

---

14 [1]Or, *oc*... 4:9, 16; Ga... 3:2 [c]Acts 2...

15 [1]Lit., *ac*... *man* [2]Or, *w*... *testament* [a]Acts 1:15; Gal. 6:18 [b]... [c]Heb. 6:16

16 [a]Luke 1... 4:13, 16; 9...

17 [a]Gen. 1... 12:40; Acts...

18 [1]Lit., *ou*... [a]Rom. 4:14

19 [1]Or, *for*... *defining* [2]Li... [a]Rom. 5:20 [c]Ex. 20:19; I... [d]Gal. 3:16

20 [1]Lit., *of c*... 2:5; Heb. 8:6...

21 [1]Or, *wou*... *be* [2]Lit., *out*... [a]Luke 20:16; [b]Gal. 2:21

22 [1]Lit., *thin*... 11:32

23 [a]Rom. 11...

24 [1]Lit., *chil*... [a]1 Cor. 4:15

25 [1]Lit., *chil*... [a]1 Cor. 4:15

26 [a]Rom. 8:... [b]Rom. 8:1; G... 4:14; 5:6, 24; Phil. 1:1; Col. 1:12; 2 Tim. 1...

27 [a]Matt. 28:... 6:3; 1 Cor. 10... 13:14

28 [1]Lit., *not n*... *female* [a]Rom... 1 Cor. 12:13; ... [b]John 17:11; E... [c]Rom. 8:1; Ga... 4:14; 5:6, 24; ... Phil. 1:1; Col. 1:12; 2 Tim. 1:...

29 [1]Lit., *are C*... [2]Lit., *seed* [a]Ro... 1 Cor. 3:23 [b]R... Gal. 3:18; 4:28

4:1 [1]Or, *minor*

2 [1]Or, *steward*...

3 [1]Or, *rudimen*... *teachings* or *pr*... [a]Gal. 2:4; 4:8f., [b]Gal. 4:9; Col. ... Heb. 5:12

4 [1]Or, *law* [a]Ma... [b]John 1:14; Ro... 8:3; Phil. 2:7 [c]... 2:21f., 27

5 [1]Or, *law* [a]Ro... Gal. 3:26

6 [a]Acts 16:7; R... 8:9, 16; 2 Cor. 3... [b]Mark 14:36; Ro...

7 [1]I.e., through... gracious act of... 8:17

8 However at that time, [a]when you did not know God, you were
[b]slaves to [c]those which by nature are no gods.
9 But now that you have come to know God, or rather to be
[a]known by God, [b]how is it that you turn back again to the weak and
worthless [1c]elemental things, to which you desire to be enslaved all
over again?
10 You [a]observe days and months and seasons and years.
11 I fear for you, that perhaps I have labored [1]over you in vain.
12 I beg of you, [a]brethren, [b]become as I *am*, for I also *have become* as
you *are*. You have done me no wrong;
13 but you know that it was because of a [1]bodily illness that I
preached the gospel to you the [2]first time;
14 and that which was a [1]trial to you in my [2]bodily condition you
did not despise or [3]loathe, but [a]you received me as an angel of God,
as [b]Christ Jesus *Himself*.
15 Where then is [1]that sense of blessing you had? For I bear you
witness, that if possible, you would have plucked out your eyes and
given them to me.
16 Have I therefore become your enemy [a]by [1]telling you the truth?
17 They eagerly seek you, not commendably, but they wish to shut
you out, in order that you may seek them.
18 But it is good always to be eagerly sought in a commendable
manner, and [a]not only when I am present with you.
19 [a]My children, with whom [b]I am again in labor until [c]Christ is
formed in you—
20 but I could wish to be present with you now and to change my
tone, for [a]I am perplexed about you.
21 Tell me, you who want to be under law, do you not [a]listen to the
law?
22 For it is written that Abraham had two sons, [a]one by the bond-
woman and [b]one by the free woman.
23 But [a]the son by the bondwoman was born according to the flesh,
and [b]the son by the free woman through the promise.
24 [1a]This is allegorically speaking: for these *women* are two cove-
nants, one *proceeding* from [b]Mount Sinai bearing children [2]who are to
be [c]slaves; [3]she is Hagar.
25 Now this Hagar is Mount Sinai in Arabia, and corresponds to
the present Jerusalem, for she is in slavery with her children.
26 But [a]the Jerusalem above is free; [1]she is our mother.
27 For it is written,

"[a]REJOICE, BARREN WOMAN WHO DOES NOT BEAR;
BREAK FORTH AND SHOUT, YOU WHO ARE NOT IN LABOR;
FOR MORE ARE THE CHILDREN OF THE DESOLATE
THAN OF THE ONE WHO HAS A HUSBAND."

28 And you brethren, [a]like Isaac, are [b]children of promise.
29 But as at that time [a]he who was born according to the flesh
[b]persecuted him *who was born* according to the Spirit, [c]so it is now
also.
30 But what does the Scripture say?

"[a]CAST OUT THE BONDWOMAN AND HER SON,
FOR [b]THE SON OF THE BONDWOMAN SHALL NOT BE AN HEIR WITH THE
SON OF THE FREE WOMAN."

31 So then, brethren, we are not children of a bondwoman, [1]but of
the free woman.

Cor. 1:21; Eph. 2; 1 Thess. 4:5; s. 1:8 [b]Gal. 4:3 13:9; Is. 37:19; 11; 1 Cor. 8:4f.; 10:20

Or, *rudimentary* gs *or principles* 8:3 [b]Col. 2:20 [c]Gal. 4:3

Rom. 14:5; Col. 2:16

11 [1]Or, *for*

al. 6:18 [b]2 Cor. 6:11, 13

t., *weakness of* esh [2]Or, *former*

emptation [2]Lit., [3]Lit., *spit out at* 10:40; 1 Thess. 2:13 [b]Gal. 3:26

15 [1]Lit., *the* ongratulation of yourselves

16 [1]Or, *dealing* uthfully with you [a]Amos 5:10

18 [a]Gal. 4:13f.

ohn 2:1 [b]1 Cor. 4:15 [c]Eph. 4:13

20 [a]2 Cor. 4:8

21 [a]Luke 16:29

en. 16:15 [b]Gen. 21:2

[a]Rom. 9:7; Gal. [b]Gen. 17:16ff.; 21:1; Gal. 4:28; Heb. 11:11

Lit., *Which* [2]Lit., *very* [3]Lit., *which* or. 10:11 [b]Deut. 33:2 [c]Gal. 4:3

it., *which* [a]Heb. 2:22; Rev. 3:12; 21:2, 10

27 [a]Is. 54:1

Gal. 4:23 [b]Rom. 9:7ff.; Gal. 3:29

Gal. 4:23 [b]Gen. 21:9 [c]Gal. 5:11

[a]Gen. 21:10, 12 [b]John 8:35

[1]V. 5:1, note 1

Chapter 5 ______________________________

5 [1a]It was for freedom that Christ set us free; therefore [b]keep stand-
ing firm and do not be subject again to a [c]yoke of slavery.
2 Behold I, [a]Paul, say to you that if you receive [b]circumcision,
Christ will be of no benefit to you.
3 And I [a]testify again to every man who receives [b]circumcision,
that he is under obligation to [c]keep the whole Law.
4 You have been severed from Christ, you who [1]are seeking to be
justified by law; you have [a]fallen from grace.
5 For we through the Spirit, by faith, are [a]waiting for the hope of
righteousness.
6 For in [a]Christ Jesus [b]neither circumcision nor uncircumcision
means anything, but [c]faith working through love.
7 You were [a]running well; who hindered you from obeying the
truth?
8 This persuasion *did* not *come* from [a]Him who calls you.
9 [a]A little leaven leavens the whole lump *of dough*.
10 [a]I have confidence [1]in you in the Lord, that you [b]will adopt no
other view; but the one who is [c]disturbing you shall bear his judg-
ment, whoever he is.
11 But I, brethren, if I still preach circumcision, why am I still [a]per-
secuted? Then [b]the stumbling block of the cross has been abolished.
12 Would that [a]those who are troubling you would even [1b]mutilate
themselves.
13 For you were called to [a]freedom, brethren; [b]only *do* not *turn* your
freedom into an opportunity for the flesh, but through love [c]serve
one another.
14 For [a]the whole Law is fulfilled in one word, in the *statement*,
"[b]YOU SHALL LOVE YOUR NEIGHBOR AS YOURSELF."
15 But if you [a]bite and devour one another, take care lest you be
consumed by one another.
16 But I say, [a]walk by the Spirit, and you will not carry out [b]the
desire of the flesh.
17 For [a]the flesh [1]sets its desire against the Spirit, and the Spirit
against the flesh; for these are in opposition to one another, [b]so that
you may not do the things that you [2]please.
18 But if you are [a]led by the Spirit, [b]you are not under the Law.
19 Now the deeds of the flesh are evident, which are: [1a]immorality,
impurity, sensuality,
20 idolatry, [a]sorcery, enmities, [b]strife, jealousy, outbursts of anger,
[c]disputes, dissensions, [1d]factions,
21 envying, [a]drunkenness, carousing, and things like these, of
which I forewarn you just as I have forewarned you that those who
practice such things shall not [b]inherit the kingdom of God.
22 But [a]the fruit of the Spirit is [b]love, joy, peace, patience, kindness,
goodness, faithfulness,
23 gentleness, [a]self-control; against such things [b]there is no law.
24 Now those who [1]belong to [a]Christ Jesus have [b]crucified the flesh
with its passions and [c]desires.
25 If we live by the Spirit, let us also [1]walk [a]by the Spirit.
26 Let us not become [a]boastful, challenging one another, envying
one another.

5:1 [1]Some prefer to joi[n] and render *freedom of* *woman Ch*[rist] *free* [a]John Rom. 8:15; Gal. 2:4; 5: 16:13 [c]Acts 2:4

2 [a]2 Cor. 1[0] 15:1; Gal. 5

3 [a]Luke 16 15:1; Gal. 5 [c]Rom. 2:25

4 [1]Or, *woul*[d] 12:15; 2 Pe[t]

5 [a]Rom. 8:2

6 [a]Gal. 3:26 7:19; Gal. 6: 1:4f.; 1 Thes James 2:18,

7 [a]Gal. 2:2

8 [a]Rom. 8:2

9 [a]1 Cor. 5:6

10 [1]Lit., *tow* 2:3 [b]Gal. 5:7 [c]Gal. 1:7; 5:1

11 [a]Gal. 4:29 [b]Rom. 9:33;

12 [1]Or, *cut* *off* [a]Gal. 2:4; [b]Deut. 23:1

13 [a]Gal. 5:1 8:9; 1 Pet. 2: 9:19; Eph. 5:2

14 [a]Matt. 7:1 Rom. 13:8, 10 [b]Lev. 19:18; M John 13:34

15 [a]Gal. 5:20;

16 [a]Rom. 8:4 Gal. 5:24f. [b]R 13:14; Eph. 2:

17 [1]Lit., *lusts* [2]Lit., *wish* [a]Ro 23; 8:5ff. [b]Ror

18 [a]Rom. 8:14 6:14; 7:4; 1 Tim

19 [1]I.e., sexua immorality [a]1 18; 2 Cor. 12:2

20 [1]Or, *heresie* 21:8 [b]2 Cor. 12 [c]Rom. 2:8; Jam 3:14ff. [d]1 Cor.

21 [a]Rom. 13:13 6:9

22 [a]Matt. 7:16f 5:9 [b]Rom. 5:1- 13:4; Col. 3:12-

23 [a]Acts 24:25 5:18

24 [1]Lit., *are of* *Jesus* [a]Gal. 3:2 [b]Rom. 6:6; Gal. 6:14 [c]Gal. 5:16f

25 [1]Or, *follow th* [a]Gal. 5:16

26 [a]Phil. 2:3

Chapter 6

6 [a]Brethren, even if a man is caught in any trespass, you who are
[b]spiritual, [c]restore such a one [d]in a spirit of gentleness; *each one*
looking to yourself, lest you too be tempted.
2 [a]Bear one another's burdens, and thus fulfill [b]the law of Christ.
3 For [a]if anyone thinks he is something when he is nothing, he
deceives himself.
4 But let each one [a]examine his own work, and then he will have
reason for [b]boasting in regard to himself alone, and not in regard to
another.
5 For [a]each one shall bear his own load.
6 And [a]let the one who is taught [b]the word share all good things
with him who teaches.
7 [a]Do not be deceived, [b]God is not mocked; for [c]whatever a man
sows, this he will also reap.
8 [a]For the one who sows to his own flesh shall from the flesh reap
[b]corruption, but [c]the one who sows to the Spirit shall from the Spirit
reap eternal life.
9 And [a]let us not lose heart in doing good, for in due time we shall
reap if we [b]do not grow weary.
10 So then, [1a]while we have opportunity, let us do good to all men,
and especially to those who are of the [b]household of [c]the faith.
11 See with what large letters I [1]am writing to you [a]with my own
hand.
12 Those who desire [a]to make a good showing in the flesh try to
[b]compel you to be circumcised, simply that they [c]may not be per-
secuted [1]for the cross of Christ.
13 For those who [1]are circumcised do not even [a]keep [2]the Law
themselves, but they desire to have you circumcised, that they may
[b]boast in your flesh.
14 But [a]may it never be that I should boast, [b]except in the cross of
our Lord Jesus Christ, [c]through [1]which the world has been crucified
to me, and [d]I to the world.
15 For [a]neither is circumcision anything, nor uncircumcision, but a
[b]new [1]creation.
16 And those who will [1]walk by this rule, peace and mercy *be* upon
them, and upon the [a]Israel of God.
17 From now on let no one cause trouble for me, for I bear on my
body the [a]brand-marks of Jesus.
18 [a]The grace of our Lord Jesus Christ be [b]with your spirit,
[c]brethren. Amen.

6:18; 1 Thess.
or. 2:15 [c]2 Cor.
ess. 3:15; Heb.
3; James 5:19f.
[d]1 Cor. 4:21
m. 15:1 [b]Rom.
or. 9:21; James
2:12; 2 Pet. 3:2
cts 5:36; 1 Cor.
8; 2 Cor. 12:11
or. 11:28 [b]Phil.
1:26
rov. 9:12; Rom.
4:12; 1 Cor. 3:8
[a]1 Cor. 9:11, 14
[b]2 Tim. 4:2
. 6:9 [b]Job 13:9
[c]2 Cor. 9:6
o 4:8; Hos. 8:7;
n. 6:21 [b]1 Cor.
42 [c]Rom. 8:11;
James 3:18
r. 15:58; 2 Cor.
att. 10:22; Heb.
5; James 5:7f.
as [a]Prov. 3:27;
35 [b]Eph. 2:19;
3:6; 1 Pet. 2:5;
s 6:7; Gal. 1:23
Or, *have written*
[a]1 Cor. 16:21
[1]Or, *because of*
t. 23:27f. [b]Acts
15:1 [c]Gal. 5:11
ne ancient mss.
have been [2]Or,
om. 2:25 [b]Phil.
3:3
r, *whom* [a]Luke
Gal. 2:17; 3:21
2:2 [c]Gal. 2:20;
) [d]Rom. 6:2, 6;
Gal. 2:19f.; 5:24
creature [a]Rom.
28; 1 Cor. 7:19;
6 [b]2 Cor. 5:17;
), 15; 4:24; Col.
3:10
follow this rule
:6; Gal. 3:7, 29;
Phil. 3:3
44:5; Ezek. 9:4;
:10; 11:23; Rev.
13:16
8 [a]Rom. 16:20
:22 [c]Acts 1:15;
1:13; Gal. 3:15;
4:12, 28, 31

PAUL'S CONCERN FOR THE CHURCHES AT GALATIA

GALATIANS AT A GLANCE

Theme of Galatians:

Author:

Date:

Purpose:

Key Words:
Paul
(and pronouns relating to him)
gospel
grace
law
Spirit
faith
promise
covenant
Christ (Jesus)
free (freedom)

SEGMENT DIVISIONS

		CHAPTER THEMES
		1
		2
		3
		4
		5
		6

ᐳHESIANS

ᐳhesus, the fourth-largest city in the Roman Empire, was the home of the temple of the goddess nis, sometimes referred to as Diana. Of all the deities in Asia, none was more sought after than nis.

ıt by the time of Paul, Ephesus's position as a center of trade was lost because the harbor became vigable. From that point on, the worship of Artemis became the city's means of economic survival. tourist and pilgrim trade associated with Artemis made many in Ephesus wealthy. Silversmiths their living selling images of this goddess and her temple. Innkeepers and restaurant owners rich from the large influx of worshipers who traveled great distances to see the temple of Artemis, of the seven wonders of the world. Even the temple treasury served as a bank, loaning large sums oney to many, including kings. And since Artemis was the patroness of sex, prostitutes sold their es without condemnation in the two-story brothel on Marble Road.

lthough Artemis was the main attraction, all sorts of magic and sorcery were conjured up and then mented. This documentation would later be referred to as *Ephesia grammata*.

ıen God sent Paul to live in Ephesus and called out for Himself a church, a light to illumine the ltic darkness of this city.

ıis brief glimpse into the historical and cultural setting of Ephesians should help you understand Paul wrote what he did to the church in Ephesus. The message of this epistle is needed as much y as it was in A.D. 60 to 62 when Paul wrote it as a prisoner in Rome.

NGS TO DO

eral Instructions

Read Ephesians in one sitting before examining it chapter by chapter.

When you finish, read Acts 18:18-21 (Paul's first visit to Ephesus was on his second missionary journey). Then read Acts 19 for an account of Paul's second visit on his third missionary journey. This passage will help you understand why Ephesians deals with warfare and our position in Christ more extensively than any other epistle.

pters 1-3

ead Ephesians 1 through 3 one chapter at a time, doing the following:

Mark each reference to God, and in the margin list everything God does.

Mark distinctively each use of *in Christ* or *in Him* so you easily can spot it in the text. Then on the OBSERVATIONS CHART on page 1734, under the heading "Our Wealth and Position in Christ," list what believers have *in Christ*. Pay particular attention to the phrase *in the heavenly places*, which is key to warfare. Note the chapter and verse the information comes from when you make your list, e.g. 1:13. (You may want to list this information on scrap paper before you record it in your Bible.)

Mark each reference to the Spirit or Holy Spirit. On the OBSERVATIONS CHART, under the heading "Our Relationship with the Holy Spirit," list what is taught about the person and work of the Holy Spirit.

Mark distinctively each occurrence of *rich* or *riches*. Then in the margin list what you learn about these riches. Remember to ask the five W's and an H: Who is rich and in what? How are these riches described? What is done with the riches? And so on.

Mark each use of *former* or *formerly*. Then on the same chart under the heading "Our Former Lifestyle and Walk," list what Ephesians says about how believers used to live before salvation.

6. Mark the other key words (with their synonyms and pronouns) listed on the EPHESIANS GLANCE chart on page 1733. Put these on a card and use it as a bookmark. Then in the m list what is said about each key word. Just record the facts.

Chapters 4-6

1. Read Ephesians 4 through 6 chapter by chapter, doing the following:
   a. Mark each occurrence of *walk*. Then on the OBSERVATIONS CHART, under the heading Walk in Christ," list what is taught about the lifestyle of a believer. Also go back to 2:2,1 mark and list what these verses teach about the believer's lifestyle. Then ask yourself: Ho I to live? Why am I able to live this way?
   b. Continue to mark the key words on your bookmark. Also list what you learn from the u *former(ly)* in this section of Ephesians. Note the contrast between our former lifestyle an walk in Christ.
   c. Mark the following: *Holy Spirit, in Christ,* and *in the Lord*. Then list what you learn and about it. This will help you see how to walk in Him.
2. Record any other observations you have of the text as instructed in "How to Observe the Chapter by Chapter," which is in the front of this Bible (page I-13).
3. On EPHESIANS AT A GLANCE:
   a. Record the theme of the book and of each chapter in the appropriate spaces. (Remember back and record each chapter's theme in the text next to the chapter number.)
   b. As you have seen, there's a change of emphasis between chapters 3 and 4. Write down "Segment Division" what best summarizes the content of chapters 1 through 3 and chapters 4 through 6.

THINGS TO THINK ABOUT

1. Stop and review all you observed and listed about your position as a child of God. Go th chapter 1 again and note everything God has done for you. Watch for the personal pronou Also note the phrase *according to* and the word *will*. Think about what God has done for yo why. Then thank Him and tell Him you want to live accordingly.
2. Ephesians 2:8-10 are such important verses. Think about what God is saying to you and as to show you whether you are trusting in His grace or in your works to get you to heave don't stop there. Think about the relationship of good works to the life of a believer. How a walking? Memorize these verses.
3. In your home do you live according to Ephesians 5:18 through 6:4?
4. Are you able to stand firm or are you defeated by the devil's schemes? Don't forget where seated. Think about the armor of God. Do you have it on and are you standing firm in righteousness, peace, salvation, and faith? Are you able to use the Word of God as your offe weapon?

Chapter 1 ______

1 Paul, [a]an apostle of [b]Christ Jesus [1c]by the will of God, to the
[2d]saints who are [3]at [e]Ephesus, and [f]*who are* faithful in [b]Christ
Jesus:
2 [a]Grace to you and peace from God our Father and the Lord Jesus
Christ.
3 [a]Blessed *be* the God and Father of our Lord Jesus Christ, who has
blessed us with every spiritual blessing in [b]the heavenly *places* in
Christ,
4 just as [a]He chose us in Him before [b]the foundation of the world,
that we should be [c]holy and blameless before [1]Him. [d]In love

1:1 [1]Lit., *throu* *holy ones* [3]Sc ancient mss. c contain *at Eph* [a]2 Cor. 1:1 [b]R [c]1 Cor. 1:1 [d]A [e]Acts 18:19 [f]C

2 [a]Rom. 1:7

3 [a]2 Cor. 1:3 1:20; 2:6; 3:10

4 [1]Or, *Him, in* [a]Eph. 2:10; 2 T 2:13f. [b]Matt. 2 [c]Eph. 5:27; Co [d]Eph. 4:2, 15,

5 [1]He [a]predestined us to [b]adoption as sons through Jesus Christ to
Himself, [c]according to the [2]kind intention of His will,
6 [a]to the praise of the glory of His grace, which He freely bestowed
on us in [b]the Beloved.
7 [a]In [1]Him we have [b]redemption [c]through His blood, the [d]forgive-
ness of our trespasses, according to [e]the riches of His grace,
8 which He [1]lavished upon [2]us. In all wisdom and insight
9 He [1a]made known to us the mystery of His will, [b]according to
His [2]kind intention which He [c]purposed in Him
10 with a view to an administration [1]suitable to [a]the fulness of the
times, *that is,* [b]the summing up of all things in Christ, things [2]in the
heavens and things upon the earth. In Him
11 [1]also we [2a]have obtained an inheritance, having been [b]predes-
tined [c]according to His purpose who works all things [d]after the
counsel of His will,
12 to the end that we who were the first to hope in [1]Christ should
be [a]to the praise of His glory.
13 In [1]Him, you also, after listening to [a]the message of truth, the
gospel of your salvation—having also [2]believed, you were [b]sealed in
[1]Him with [c]the Holy Spirit of promise,
14 who is [1a]given as a pledge of [b]our inheritance, with a view to the
[c]redemption of [d]*God's own* possession, [e]to the praise of His glory.
15 For this reason I too, [a]having heard of the faith in the Lord Jesus
which *exists* among you, and [1]your love for [b]all the [2]saints,
16 [a]do not cease giving thanks for you, [b]while making mention *of*
you in my prayers;
17 that the [a]God of our Lord Jesus Christ, [b]the Father of glory, may
give to you a spirit of [c]wisdom and of [d]revelation in the [1]knowledge
of Him.
18 *I pray that* [a]the eyes of your heart [1]may be enlightened, so that
you may know what is the [b]hope of His [c]calling, what are [d]the riches
of the glory of [e]His inheritance in [f]the [2]saints,
19 and what is the surpassing greatness of His power toward us
who believe. [a]*These are* in accordance with the working of the
[b]strength of His might
20 which He brought about in Christ, when He [a]raised Him from
the dead, and [b]seated Him at His right hand in [c]the heavenly *places,*
21 far above [a]all rule and authority and power and dominion, and
every [b]name that is named, not only in [c]this age, but also in the one
to come.
22 And He [a]put all things in subjection under His feet, and gave
Him as [b]head over all things to the church,
23 which is His [a]body, the [b]fulness of Him who [c]fills [d]all in all.

Chapter 2

2 And you [1]were [a]dead [2]in your trespasses and sins,
2 in which you [a]formerly walked according to the [1]course of
[b]this world, according to [c]the prince of the power of the air, of the
spirit that is now working in [d]the sons of disobedience.
3 Among them we too all [a]formerly lived in [b]the lusts of our flesh,
[1]indulging the desires of the flesh and of the [2]mind, and were [c]by
nature [d]children of wrath, [e]even as the rest.
4 But God, being [a]rich in mercy, because of [b]His great love with
which He loved us,

5 [1]Lit., *having*
ned [2]Lit., *good*
e [a]Acts 13:48;
. 8:29f. [b]Rom.
Phil. 2:13; Col.
1:19
1:12, 14 [b]Matt.
3:17
om [a]Col. 1:14
24; 1 Cor. 1:30;
4 [c]Acts 20:28;
:25 [d]Acts 2:38
Eph. 1:18; 2:7;
3:8, 16
made abundant
d [2]Or, *us, in all*
om and insight
making known
good pleasure
11:25; Eph. 3:3
1:21; Gal. 1:15
3:28; Eph. 1:11
, *of* [2]Lit., *upon*
15 [b]Eph. 3:15;
; Col. 1:16, 20
, *in whom also*
r, were made a
ge [a]Deut. 4:20;
:14; Titus 2:14
[c]Rom. 8:28f.;
1 [d]Rom. 9:11;
Heb. 6:17
., the Messiah
[a]Eph. 1:6, 14
.it., *whom* [2]Or,
Him, you were
Eph. 4:21; Col.
:30 [c]Acts 2:33
down payment
22 [b]Acts 20:32
1:7 [d]Eph. 1:11
[e]Eph. 1:6, 12
y ancient mss.
ntain *your love*
ote 2 [a]Col. 1:4;
[b]Eph. 1:1; 3:18
. 1:8f.; Col. 1:9
[b]Rom. 1:9
true knowledge
:17; Rom. 15:6
Cor. 2:8 [c]Col.
.9 [d]1 Cor. 14:6
being [2]Or, *holy*
ts 26:18; 2 Cor.
. 6:4 [b]Eph. 4:4
1:29 [e]Eph. 1:7
1:11 [f]Col. 1:12
. 3:7; Col. 1:29
[b]Eph. 6:10
cts 2:24 [b]Mark
6:19 [c]Eph. 1:3
att. 28:18; Col.
[b]Phil. 2:9; Rev.
2 [c]Matt. 12:32
.6; 1 Cor. 15:27
1:3; Eph. 4:15;
Col. 1:18
Cor. 12:27; Eph.
1:18, 24 [b]John
ph. 3:19 [c]Eph.
4:10 [d]Col. 3:11
, *being* [2]Or, *by*
[a]Eph. 2:5; Col.
2:13
ge [a]1 Cor. 6:11;
2:3 [b]Eph. 1:21
2:31; Eph. 6:12
[d]Eph. 5:6
.it., *doing* [2]Lit.,
[a]Eph. 2:2 [b]Gal.
Rom. 2:14; Gal.
[d]Rom. 5:9; Col.
et. 2:14 [e]Rom.
5:12
1:7 [b]John 3:16

5 even when we were [a]dead [1]in our transgressions, made us alive
together [2]with Christ ([b]by grace you have been saved),
6 and [a]raised us up with Him, and [b]seated us with Him in [c]the
heavenly *places,* in [d]Christ Jesus,
7 in order that in the ages to come He might show the surpassing
[a]riches of His grace in [b]kindness toward us in Christ Jesus.
8 For [a]by grace you have been saved [b]through faith; and [1]that not
of yourselves, *it is* [c]the gift of God;
9 [a]not as a result of works, that [b]no one should boast.
10 For we are His workmanship, [a]created in [b]Christ Jesus for [c]good
works, which God [d]prepared beforehand, that we should [e]walk in
them.
11 Therefore remember, that [a]formerly [b]you, the Gentiles in the
flesh, who are called "[c]Uncircumcision" by the so-called "[c]Cir-
cumcision," *which is* performed in the flesh by human hands—
12 *remember* that you were at that time separate from Christ, [1a]ex-
cluded from the commonwealth of Israel, and strangers to [b]the cove-
nants of promise, having [c]no hope and [d]without God in the world.
13 But now in [a]Christ Jesus you who [b]formerly were [c]far off [1]have
[c]been brought near [2d]by the blood of Christ.
14 For He Himself is [a]our peace, [b]who made both *groups into* one,
and broke down the [1]barrier of the dividing wall,
15 [1]by [a]abolishing in His flesh the enmity, *which is* [b]the Law of com-
mandments *contained* in ordinances, that in Himself He might [2c]make
the two into [d]one new man, *thus* establishing [e]peace,
16 and might [a]reconcile them both in [b]one body to God through the
cross, [1]by it having [c]put to death the enmity.
17 AND [a]HE CAME AND PREACHED [b]PEACE TO YOU WHO WERE [c]FAR AWAY,
AND PEACE TO THOSE WHO WERE [c]NEAR;
18 for through Him we both have [a]our access in [b]one Spirit to [c]the
Father.
19 So then you are no longer [a]strangers and aliens, but you are
[b]fellow citizens with the [1]saints, and are of [c]God's household,
20 having been [a]built upon [b]the foundation of [c]the apostles and
prophets, [d]Christ Jesus Himself being the [e]corner *stone,*
21 [a]in whom the whole building, being fitted together is growing
into [b]a holy [1]temple in the Lord;
22 in whom you also are being [a]built together into a [b]dwelling of
God in the Spirit.

Chapter 3

3 For this reason I, Paul, [a]the prisoner of [b]Christ Jesus [c]for the sake
of you [d]Gentiles—
2 if indeed you have heard of the [a]stewardship of God's grace
which was given to me for you;
3 [a]that [b]by revelation there was [c]made known to me [d]the mystery,
[e]as I wrote before in brief.
4 [1]And by referring to this, when you read you can understand
[a]my insight [2]into the [b]mystery of Christ,
5 which in other generations was not made known to the sons of
men, as it has now been revealed to His holy [a]apostles and prophets
[1]in the Spirit;

5 [1]Or, *by* [2]Some an
read *in Ch*
2:1 [b]Acts
6 [a]Col. 2:1
1:20 [c]Eph
1:1; 2:10,
7 [a]Rom. 2
[b]Titus 3:4
8 [1]I.e., tha
[a]Acts 15:11
[b]1 Pet. 1:5
9 [a]Rom. 3
1:9 [b]1 Cor.
10 [a]Eph. 2
Col. 3:10 [b]
13 [c]Titus 2
1:4 [e]Eph. 4
11 [a]Eph. 2
12:2; Eph. 5
2:28f.; Col.
12 [1]Or, *alie*
[a]Rom. 9:4;
[b]Gal. 3:17;
[c]1 Thess. 4:
4:8; 1 Thess
13 [1]Lit., *be*
were made
[a]Eph. 1:1; 2.
2:2 [c]Is. 57:1
2:39; Eph. 2
3:25; Col. 1:
14 [1]Lit., *the*
wall of the b
9:6; Eph. 2:1
3:15 [b]1 Cor.
3:28; Col. 3:
15 [1]Or, *the e*
abolishing in
the Law [2]Lit.
[a]Eph. 2:16; C
[b]Col. 2:14, 20
3:28; Eph. 2:
3:10, 11 [d]Ga
3:10f. [e]Is. 9:6
2:14; Col. 3:1
16 [1]Or, *in Hi*
[a]2 Cor. 5:18;
22 [b]1 Cor. 10
4:4 [c]Eph. 2:1
17 [a]Is. 57:19;
10:14 [b]Acts 1
2:14 [c]Eph. 2:
18 [a]Rom. 5:2
3:12 [b]1 Cor. 1
Eph. 4:4 [c]Col.
19 [1]Or, *holy c*
[a]Eph. 2:12; He
1 Pet. 2:11 [b]P
Heb. 12:22f. [c]
20 [a]1 Cor. 3:9
16:18; 1 Cor. 3
21:14 [c]1 Cor.
Eph. 3:5 [d]1 Co
[e]Ps. 118:22; Lu
21 [1]Or, *sanctu*
[a]Eph. 4:15f.; C
[b]1 Cor. 3:16f.
22 [a]1 Cor. 3:9,
2 Cor. 6:16 [b]Ep
3:1 [a]Acts 23:18
4:1; 2 Tim. 1:8;
1, 9, 23 [b]Gal. 5
[c]2 Cor. 1:6; Eph
[d]Eph. 3:8
2 [a]Eph. 1:10; 3
1:25; 1 Tim. 1:4
3 [a]Acts 22:17,
26:16ff. [b]Gal. 1
[c]Eph. 1:9; 3:4, 6
[d]Rom. 11:25; 16
Eph. 3:4, 9; 6:19
1:26f.; 4:3 [e]Eph
Heb. 13:22; 1 P

4 [1]Lit., *To which, when you read* [2]Lit., *in* [a]2 Cor. 11:6 [b]Rom. 11:25; 16:25; Eph. 3:3, 9; 6:19; Col. 1:26f.; 4:3 **5** [1]Or, *by* [a]1 Cor. 12:28; Eph. 2:20

6 *to be specific,* that the Gentiles are [a]fellow heirs and [b]fellow mem-
bers of the body, and [c]fellow partakers of the promise in [d]Christ Jesus
through the gospel,
7 [a]of which I was made a [b]minister, according to the gift of [c]God's
grace which was given to me [d]according to the working of His
power.
8 To me, [a]the very least of all [1]saints, this grace was given, to
[b]preach to the Gentiles the unfathomable [c]riches of Christ,
9 and to [1]bring to light what is the administration of the [a]mystery
which for ages has been [b]hidden in God, [c]who created all things;
10 in order that the manifold [a]wisdom of God might now be [b]made
known through the church to the [c]rulers and the authorities in [d]the
heavenly *places.*
11 *This was* in [a]accordance with the [1]eternal purpose which He [2]car-
ried out in [b]Christ Jesus our Lord,
12 in whom we have boldness and [1a]confident [b]access through faith
[2]in Him.
13 Therefore I ask [1]you not [a]to lose heart at my tribulations [b]on your
behalf, [2]for they are your glory.
14 For this reason, I [a]bow my knees before the Father,
15 from whom [1]every family in heaven and on earth derives its
name,
16 that He would grant you, according to [a]the riches of His glory, to
be [b]strengthened with power through His Spirit in [c]the inner man;
17 so that [a]Christ may dwell in your hearts through faith; *and* that
you, being [b]rooted and [c]grounded in love,
18 may be able to comprehend with [a]all the [1]saints what is [b]the
breadth and length and height and depth,
19 and to know [a]the love of Christ which [b]surpasses knowledge,
that you may be [c]filled up to all the [d]fulness of God.
20 [a]Now to Him who is [b]able to do exceeding abundantly beyond
all that we ask or think, [c]according to the power that works
within us,
21 [a]to Him *be* the glory in the church and in Christ Jesus to all
generations [1]forever and ever. Amen.

Chapter 4

4 I, therefore, [a]the prisoner of the Lord, [b]entreat you to [c]walk in a
manner worthy of the [d]calling with which you have been [e]called,
2 with all [a]humility and gentleness, with patience, showing for-
bearance to one another [b]in love,
3 being diligent to preserve the unity of the Spirit in the [a]bond of
peace.
4 *There is* [a]one body and one Spirit, just as also you were called in
one [b]hope of your calling;
5 [a]one Lord, one faith, one baptism,
6 one God and Father of all [a]who is over all and through all and in
all.
7 But [a]to each one of us [b]grace was given [c]according to the measure
of Christ's gift.
8 Therefore [1]it says,

"[a]WHEN HE ASCENDED ON HIGH,
HE [b]LED CAPTIVE A HOST OF CAPTIVES,
AND HE GAVE GIFTS TO MEN."

ial. 3:29 [b]Eph.
Eph. 5:7 [d]Gal.
5:24
23, 25 [b]1 Cor.
cts 9:15; Rom.
Eph. 3:2 [d]Eph.
1:19; 3:20
[1]Or, *holy ones*
5:9 [b]Acts 9:15;
1f. [c]Rom. 2:4;
Eph. 1:7; 3:16
e ancient mss.
make all know
. 11:25; 16:25;
3, 4; 6:19; Col.
; 4:3 [b]Col. 3:3
[c]Rev. 4:11
n. 11:33; 1 Cor.
ph. 1:23; 1 Pet.
ph. 1:21; 6:12;
), 15 [d]Eph. 1:3
purpose of the
formed [a]Eph.
5:24; Eph. 3:1
[1]Lit., *access in*
ce [2]Lit., *of Him*
3:4; Heb. 4:16;
5; 1 John 2:28;
:21 [b]Eph. 2:18
, that I may not
[2]Lit., *which are*
. 4:1 [b]Eph. 3:1
14 [a]Phil. 2:10
[1]Or, *the whole*
[a]Eph. 1:18; 3:8
5:13; Phil. 4:13;
11 [c]Rom. 7:22
n 14:23; Rom.
Cor. 13:5; Eph.
1 Cor. 3:6; Col.
2:7 [c]Col. 1:23
3, note 1 [a]Eph.
:15 [b]Job 11:8f.
[a]Rom. 8:35, 39
4:7 [c]Col. 2:10
[d]Eph. 1:23
. 16:25 [b]2 Cor.
9:8 [c]Eph. 3:7
t., *of the age of*
es [a]Rom. 11:36
Eph. 3:1 [b]Rom.
Eph. 2:10; Col.
; 1 Thess. 2:12
n. 11:29 [e]Rom.
8:28f.
:12f. [b]Eph. 1:4
3 [a]Col. 3:14f.
or. 12:4ff.; Eph.
18 [b]Eph. 1:18
5 [a]1 Cor. 8:6
6 [a]Rom. 11:36
[a]1 Cor. 12:7, 11
3:2 [c]Rom. 12:3
He [a]Ps. 68:18
[b]Col. 2:15

9 (Now this *expression,* "He [a]ascended," what [1]does it mean except that He also [2]had descended into [b]the lower parts of the earth?

10 He who descended is Himself also He who ascended [a]far above all the heavens, that He might [b]fill all things.)

11 And He [a]gave [b]some *as* apostles, and some *as* prophets, and some *as* [c]evangelists, and some *as* pastors and [d]teachers,

12 [a]for the equipping of the [1]saints for the work of service, to the building up of [b]the body of Christ;

13 until we all attain to [a]the unity of the faith, and of the [1b]knowledge of the Son of God, to a [c]mature man, to the measure of the stature [2]which belongs to the [d]fulness of Christ.

14 [1]As a result, we are [a]no longer to be children, [b]tossed here and there by waves, and carried about by every wind of doctrine, by the trickery of men, by [c]craftiness [2]in [d]deceitful scheming;

15 but [1]speaking the truth [a]in love, we [2]are to [b]grow up in all *aspects* into Him, who is the [c]head, *even* Christ,

16 from whom [a]the whole body, being fitted and held together [1]by that which every joint supplies, according to the [2]proper working of each individual part, causes the growth of the body for the building up of itself [b]in love.

17 [a]This I say therefore, and affirm together with the Lord, [b]that you walk no longer just as the Gentiles also walk, in the [c]futility of their mind,

18 being [a]darkened in their understanding, [1b]excluded from the life of God, because of the [c]ignorance that is in them, because of the [d]hardness of their heart;

19 and they, having [a]become callous, [b]have given themselves over to [c]sensuality, [1]for the practice of every kind of impurity with greediness.

20 But you did not [a]learn [1]Christ in this way,

21 if indeed you [a]have heard Him and have [b]been taught in Him, just as truth is in Jesus,

22 that, in reference to your former manner of life, you [a]lay aside the [b]old [1]self, which is being corrupted in accordance with the [c]lusts of deceit,

23 and that you be [a]renewed in the spirit of your mind,

24 and [a]put on the [b]new [1]self, which [2c]in *the likeness of* God has been created in righteousness and holiness of the truth.

25 Therefore, [a]laying aside falsehood, [b]SPEAK TRUTH, EACH ONE *of you,* WITH HIS NEIGHBOR, for we are [c]members of one another.

26 [a]BE ANGRY, AND *yet* DO NOT SIN; do not let the sun go down on your anger,

27 and do not [a]give the devil [1]an opportunity.

28 Let him who steals steal no longer; but rather [a]let him labor, [b]performing with his own hands what is good, [c]in order that he may have *something* to share with him who has need.

29 Let no [1a]unwholesome word proceed from your mouth, but only such *a word* as is good for [b]edification [2]according to the need *of the moment,* that it may give grace to those who hear.

30 And [a]do not grieve the Holy Spirit of God, [1]by whom you were [b]sealed for the day of redemption.

9 [1]Lit., *is it*
[2]Some anci
read *had fir*
descended
[b]Is. 44:23
10 [a]Eph. 1:
4:14; 7:26
11 [a]Eph. 4:
13:1; 1 Cor.
21:8 [d]Acts
12 [1]Or, *holy*
[a]2 Cor. 13:9
12:27; Eph.
13 [1]Or, *true*
[2]Lit., *of the*
[a]Eph. 4:3, 5
Eph. 1:17; P
[c]1 Cor. 14:2
Heb. 5:14
Eph. 1:23
14 [1]Lit., *tha*
longer be
regard to th
of deceit [a]1
[b]James 1:6;
[c]1 Cor. 3:19
11:3 [d]Eph.
15 [1]Or, *holc*
walking in [2]
grow up [a]E
[b]Eph. 2:21
16 [1]Lit., *thr*
joint of the s
working in m
[a]Rom. 12:4f.
[b]Eph. 1:4
17 [a]Col. 2:4
4:22 [c]Rom.
2:18; 1 Pet.
2:18
18 [1]Or, *alie*
[a]Rom. 1:21
12 [c]Acts 3:1
1 Cor. 2:8; H
1 Pet. 1:14
Rom. 11:7, 2
3:14
19 [1]Or, *gree*
practice of e
impurity [a]1 T
[b]Rom. 1:24
20 [1]I.e., the
[a]Matt. 11:29
21 [a]Rom. 10
1:13; 2:17; C
[b]Col. 2:7
22 [1]Lit., *mar*
4:25, 31; Col
12:1; James
2:1 [b]Rom. 6
11:3; Heb. 3
23 [a]Rom. 12
24 [1]Lit., *mar*
according to
[a]Rom. 13:14
7:6; 12:2; 2 C
Col. 3:10 [c]E
25 [a]Eph. 4:2
3:8; Heb. 12
1:21; 1 Pet. 2
8:16; Eph. 4
3:9 [c]Rom. 12
26 [a]Ps. 4:4
27 [1]Lit., *a pl*
12:19; James
28 [a]Acts 20:
4:12; Gal. 6:1
[b]1 Thess. 4:1
3:8, 11f.; Titu
[c]Luke 3:11; 1
4:12

29 [1]Lit., *rotten* [2]Lit., *of the need* [a]Matt. 12:34; Eph. 5:4; Col. 3:8 [b]Eccl. 10:12; Rom. 14:19; Col. 4:6 **30** [1]Lit., *in* [a]Is. 63:10; 1 Thess. 5:19 [b]John 3:33; Eph. 1:13

31 [a]Let all bitterness and wrath and anger and clamor and slander
be [b]put away from you, along with all [c]malice.
32 And [a]be kind to one another, tender-hearted, forgiving each
other, [b]just as God in Christ also has forgiven [1]you.

Chapter 5

5 [a]Therefore be imitators of God, as beloved children;
2 and [a]walk in love, just as Christ also [b]loved [1]you, and [c]gave
Himself up for us, an [d]offering and a sacrifice to God [2]as a [e]fragrant
aroma.
3 But do not let [a]immorality [1]or any impurity or greed even be
named among you, as is proper among [2]saints;
4 and *there must be no* [a]filthiness and silly talk, or coarse jesting,
which [b]are not fitting, but rather [c]giving of thanks.
5 For this you know with certainty, that [a]no [1]immoral or impure
person or covetous man, who is an idolater, has an inheritance in the
kingdom [b]of Christ and God.
6 [a]Let no one deceive you with empty words, for because of these
things [b]the wrath of God comes upon [c]the sons of disobedience.
7 Therefore do not be [a]partakers with them;
8 for [a]you were formerly [b]darkness, but now you are light in the
Lord; walk as [c]children of light
9 (for [a]the fruit of the light *consists* in all [b]goodness and right-
eousness and truth),
10 [1a]trying to learn what is pleasing to the Lord.
11 And [a]do not participate in the unfruitful [b]deeds of [c]darkness, but
instead even [1d]expose them;
12 for it is disgraceful even to speak of the things which are done
by them in secret.
13 But all things become visible [a]when they are [1]exposed by the
light, for everything that becomes visible is light.
14 For this reason [1]it says,
"[a]Awake, sleeper,
And arise from [b]the dead,
And Christ [c]will shine on you."
15 Therefore [1]be careful how you [a]walk, not [b]as unwise men, but as
wise,
16 [1a]making the most of your time, because [b]the days are evil.
17 So then do not be foolish, but [a]understand what the will of the
Lord is.
18 And [a]do not get drunk with wine, [1]for that is [b]dissipation, but be
[c]filled with the Spirit,
19 [a]speaking to [1]one another in [b]psalms and [c]hymns and spiritual
[d]songs, [e]singing and making melody with your heart to the Lord;
20 [a]always giving thanks for all things in the name of our Lord
Jesus Christ to [1b]God, even the Father;
21 [1a]and be subject to one another in the [2b]fear of Christ.
22 [a]Wives, *[b]be subject* to your own husbands, [c]as to the Lord.
23 For [a]the husband is the head of the wife, as Christ also is the
[b]head of the church, He Himself [c]*being* the Savior of the body.
24 But as the church is subject to Christ, so also the wives *ought to be*
to their husbands in everything.
25 [a]Husbands, love your wives, just as Christ also loved the church
and [b]gave Himself up for her;

Rom. 3:14; Col.
, 19 [b]Eph. 4:22
[c]1 Pet. 2:1
ne ancient mss.
s [a]1 Cor. 13:4;
:12f.; 1 Pet. 3:8
4f.; 2 Cor. 2:10
Matt. 5:48; Luke
6:36; Eph. 4:32
ne ancient mss.
us [2]Lit., *for an*
dor of fragrance
4:15; Col. 3:14
3:34; Rom. 8:37
:51; Rom. 4:25;
2:20; Eph. 5:25
27; 9:14; 10:10,
[e]Ex. 29:18, 25;
2 Cor. 2:14
nd all [2]Or, *holy*
ones [a]Col. 3:5
att. 12:34; Eph.
Col. 3:8 [b]Rom.
:28 [c]Eph. 5:20
[1]I.e., one who
commits sexual
lity [a]1 Cor. 6:9;
. 3:5 [b]Col. 1:13
:8 [b]Rom. 1:18;
l. 3:6 [c]Eph. 2:2
7 [a]Eph. 3:6
[a]Eph. 2:2 [b]Acts
ol. 1:12f. [c]John
36; Rom. 13:12
Gal. 5:22 [b]Rom.
15:14
t., *proving what*
[a]Rom. 12:2
reprove [a]1 Cor.
Cor. 6:14 [b]Rom.
Acts 26:18; Col.
2f. [d]1 Tim. 5:20
reproved [a]John
3:20f.
, *He* [a]Is. 26:19;
2:1; 60:1; Rom.
Eph. 2:1 [c]Luke
1:78f.
t., *look carefully*
h. 5:2 [b]Col. 4:5
, *redeeming the*
[a]Col. 4:5 [b]Gal.
1:4; Eph. 6:13
Rom. 12:2; Col.
:9; 1 Thess. 4:3
[1]Lit., *in which is*
v. 20:1; 23:31f.;
:13; 1 Cor. 5:11;
. 5:7 [b]Titus 1:6;
4:4 [c]Luke 1:15
[1]Or, *yourselves*
ol. 3:16 [b]1 Cor.
26 [c]Acts 16:25
9 [e]1 Cor. 14:15
it., *the God and*
[a]Rom. 1:8; Eph.
ol. 3:17 [b]1 Cor.
15:24
t., *being subject*
everence [a]Gal.
Phil. 2:3; 1 Pet.
5:5 [b]2 Cor. 5:11
h. 5:22-6:9: *Col.*
[b]1 Cor. 14:34f.;
s 2:5; 1 Pet. 3:1
[c]Eph. 6:5
Cor. 11:3 [b]Eph.
22 [c]1 Cor. 6:13
h. 5:28, 33; Col.
1 Pet. 3:7 [b]Eph.
5:2

26 [a]that He might sanctify her, having [b]cleansed her by the [c]washing
of water with [d]the word,
27 that He might [a]present to Himself the church [1]in all her glory,
having no spot or wrinkle or any such thing; but that she should be
[b]holy and blameless.
28 So husbands ought also to [a]love their own wives as their own
bodies. He who loves his own wife loves himself;
29 for no one ever hated his own flesh, but nourishes and cherishes
it, just as Christ also *does* the church,
30 because we are [a]members of His [b]body.
31 [a]FOR THIS CAUSE A MAN SHALL LEAVE HIS FATHER AND MOTHER, AND
SHALL CLEAVE TO HIS WIFE; AND THE TWO SHALL BECOME ONE FLESH.
32 This mystery is great; but I am speaking with reference to Christ
and the church.
33 Nevertheless let each individual among you also [a]love his own
wife even as himself; and *let* the wife *see to it* that she [1b]respect her
husband.

Chapter 6

6 [a]Children, obey your parents in the Lord, for this is right.
2 [a]HONOR YOUR FATHER AND MOTHER (which is the first command-
ment with a promise),
3 THAT IT MAY BE WELL WITH YOU, AND THAT YOU MAY LIVE LONG ON THE
EARTH.
4 And, [a]fathers, do not provoke your children to anger; but [b]bring
them up in the discipline and instruction of the Lord.
5 [a]Slaves, be obedient to those who are your [1]masters according to
the flesh, with [b]fear and trembling, in the sincerity of your heart, [c]as
to Christ;
6 [a]not [1]by way of eyeservice, as [b]men-pleasers, but as [c]slaves of
Christ, [d]doing the will of God from the [2]heart.
7 With good will [1]render service, [a]as to the Lord, and not to men,
8 [a]knowing that [b]whatever good thing each one does, this he will
receive back from the Lord, [c]whether slave or free.
9 And, masters, do the same things to them, and [a]give up threaten-
ing, knowing that [b]both their Master and yours is in heaven, and
there is [c]no partiality with Him.
10 Finally, [a]be strong in the Lord, and in [b]the strength of His might.
11 [a]Put on the full armor of God, that you may be able to stand firm
against the [b]schemes of the devil.
12 For our [a]struggle is not against [1b]flesh and blood, but [c]against the
rulers, against the powers, against the [d]world forces of this [e]dark-
ness, against the [f]spiritual *forces* of wickedness in [g]the heavenly
places.
13 Therefore, take up [a]the full armor of God, that you may be able
to [b]resist in [c]the evil day, and having done everything, to stand firm.
14 Stand firm therefore, [a]HAVING GIRDED YOUR LOINS WITH TRUTH, and
HAVING [b]PUT ON THE BREASTPLATE OF RIGHTEOUSNESS,
15 and having [a]shod YOUR FEET WITH THE PREPARATION OF THE GOSPEL
OF PEACE;
16 [1]in addition to all, taking up the [a]shield of faith with which you
will be able to extinguish all the [b]flaming missiles of [c]the evil *one*.
17 And take [a]THE HELMET OF SALVATION, and the [b]sword of the Spirit,
which is [c]the word of God.

26 [a]Titus 2 10:10, 14, [b]2 Pet. 1:9 1 Cor. 6:11 [d]John 15:3 10:8f.; Eph

27 [1]Lit., *glo* [a]2 Cor. 4:14 1:22 [b]Eph.

28 [a]Eph. 5 1 Pet. 3:7

30 [a]1 Cor. [b]Eph. 1:23

31 [a]Gen. 2 19:5; Mark

33 [1]Lit., *fea* 5:25, 28; 1 P [b]1 Pet. 3:2, 5

6:1 [a]Prov. 6 Col. 3:20

2 [a]Ex. 20:12

4 [a]Col. 3:21 18:19; Deut. Ps. 78:4; Pro 2 Tim. 3:15

5 [1]I.e., earth with fear [a]Co 1 Tim. 6:1; T [b]1 Cor. 2:3 [c]

6 [1]Lit., *accor* [2]Lit., *soul* [a]C [b]Gal. 1:10 [c]1 [d]Mark 3:35

7 [1]Lit., *rende* 3:23

8 [a]Col. 3:24 16:27; 2 Cor. 3:24f. [c]1 Cor. Col. 3:11

9 [a]Lev. 25:43 31:13ff.; John Col. 4:1 [c]Deut Acts 10:34; Co

10 [a]1 Cor. 16 2:1 [b]Eph. 1:19

11 [a]Rom. 13:1 6:13 [b]Eph. 4:1

12 [1]Lit., *blood flesh* [a]1 Cor. 9 [b]Matt. 16:17 [c]E 2:2; 3:10 [d]John [e]Acts 26:18; Co [f]Eph. 3:10 [g]Ep

13 [a]Eph. 6:11 4:7 [c]Eph. 5:16

14 [a]Is. 11:5; Lu 12:35; 1 Pet. 1: 59:17; Rom. 13 6:13; 1 Thess. 5

15 [a]Is. 52:7; Ro

16 [1]Lit., *in all* [a] 5:8 [b]Ps. 7:13; 1 [c]Matt. 5:37

17 [a]Is. 59:17 [b]Is Hos. 6:5; Heb. 4 [c]Eph. 5:26; Heb.

18 With all [a]prayer and petition [1b]pray at all times [c]in the Spirit, and
with this in view, [2d]be on the alert with all [e]perseverance and [f]peti-
tion for all the saints,
19 and [a]*pray* on my behalf, that utterance may be given to me [b]in the
opening of my mouth, to make known with [c]boldness [d]the mystery
of the gospel,
20 for which I am an [a]ambassador [b]in [1]chains; that [2]in *proclaiming* it I
may speak [c]boldly, [d]as I ought to speak.
21 [a]But that you also may know about my circumstances, how I am
doing, [b]Tychicus, [c]the beloved brother and faithful minister in the
Lord, will make everything known to you.
22 [1]And [a]I have sent him to you for this very purpose, so that you
may know [2]about us, and that he may [b]comfort your hearts.
23 [a]Peace be to the brethren, and [b]love with faith, from God the
Father and the Lord Jesus Christ.
24 Grace be with all those who love our Lord Jesus Christ [1]with *a
love* incorruptible.

t., *praying* [2]Lit., [a]Phil. 4:6 [b]Luke 1; Col. 1:3; 4:2; ss. 5:17 [c]Rom. 6f. [d]Mark 13:33 1:14 [f]1 Tim. 2:1 ol. 4:3; 1 Thess. 25 [b]2 Cor. 6:11 3:12 [d]Eph. 3:3 *a chain* [2]Some nss. read *I may it boldly* [a]2 Cor. ; Philem. 9 mg. 33; 28:20; Eph. hil. 1:7; Col. 4:3 . 3:12 [d]Col. 4:4 n. 6:21, 22: *Col.* cts 20:4; 2 Tim. 4:12 [c]Col. 4:7 ., *Whom I have to you* [2]Lit., *the about us* [a]Col. 8 [b]Col. 2:2; 4:8 om. 15:33; Gal. ; 2 Thess. 3:16; 5:14 [b]Gal. 5:6; 1 Thess. 5:8 , *in incorruption*

EPHESIANS AT A GLANCE

of Ephesians:

Author:

Date:

Purpose:

Key Words:
- every reference to God,
- in Christ (in Him, in the Lord)
- the (Holy) Spirit
- rich(es)
- in the heavenly places
- former(ly)
- grace
- power (strength)
- body (church)
- redemption
- walk
- mark every reference to the devil (including powers, rulers, authorities, etc.) all with a red pitchfork

DIVISIONS

	CHAPTER THEMES
	1
	2
	3
	4
	5
	6

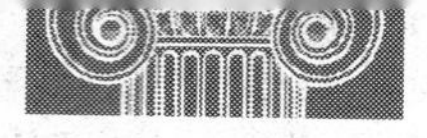

Ephesians Observations Chart

Our Wealth and Position in Christ

Our Relationship with the Holy Spirit

Our Former Lifestyle and Walk

Our Walk in Christ

HILIPPIANS

ocked by the Spirit of God from going into Asia and Bithynia, Paul had a vision of a man from donia asking him to come to Macedonia and help the churches there.

nfident that God had given him direction, Paul sailed with Timothy and Luke from Troas on a d missionary journey. Philippi, in Macedonia, basked in the fact that it was also a Roman colony 1 ensured its citizens all the benefits of Roman citizenship.

was his custom, when Paul reached a city he sought out the Jews. While there were not enough living in Philippi to form a synagogue, the Jews there met for prayer on the Sabbath. Little did realize he'd end up in prison. God knew there was a Roman jailer and his family who needed

e events of that day inaugurated the beginning of the church at Philippi . . . the church Paul ssed as he took pen in hand around the year A.D. 61 or 62.

GS TO DO

Familiarize yourself with the message of Philippians by reading the entire book in one sitting. As you read, look for the verses in chapters 1 and 4 which tell where Paul is as he writes.

To understand the historical setting of Philippians, read Acts 15:35 through 17:1, which records Paul's first visit to Philippi. After his third missionary journey, Paul went to Jerusalem where he was arrested. From there Paul was taken by a Roman guard to Caesarea, the Mediterranean seaport where the Roman consulate often went to escape the heat and confines of Jerusalem. After remaining a prisoner in Caesarea for over two years, Paul, who as a Roman citizen had appealed to Caesar, was sent to Rome where he lived under house arrest. Read Acts 28:14-31 and note how long Paul remained a prisoner at Rome. How does this compare with where Paul was when he wrote Philippians?

As you read Philippians chapter by chapter, do the following.

a. Under "Author" on your OBSERVATIONS CHART on page 1741 note where Paul is, why he's there, and what his attitude is in the midst of his difficult circumstances.

b. In a distinctive way, mark each key word (and its synonyms and pronouns) that is listed on the PHILIPPIANS AT A GLANCE chart on page 1742. This will help you discover the themes (main subjects) of each chapter and of the book itself. Watch for other key words which are not listed but which may be emphasized in a particular chapter of Philippians.

c. In the margin list what you learn from the text about each of the key words in Philippians.

d. Record any other observations as instructed and demonstrated in "How to Observe the Bible Chapter by Chapter" in the front of the Bible (page I-13).

e. List each of the instructions Paul gives to the Philippian saints on the chart PAUL'S INSTRUCTIONS TO THE PHILIPPIANS on page 1742. As you list these instructions, evaluate your life in the light of each one.

On PHILIPPIANS AT A GLANCE:

a. Fill in the theme for the book and for each chapter. Be sure you also record the chapter theme in the text next to the chapter number.

b. Under "Segment Divisions" record what you see to be Paul's example in each chapter. Remember, in Philippians 3:17 Paul tells them to follow his example.

c. On the next line under "Segment Divisions" write down what each chapter says about who or what Jesus Christ is in relationship to the believer.

d. For another segment division, record a command to believers that correlates with each theme.

THINGS TO THINK ABOUT

1. What have you learned from Philippians about your relationship to suffering as a Ch How is it going to affect the way you respond?
2. Can you say with Paul, "For to me, to live is Christ, and to die is gain"? If you can't, thin what has replaced Christ's rightful place in your life.
3. What have you learned from Jesus' example for your own life? Do you have the attitude o in respect to God and others? Do you regard others as more important than yourself?
4. Do you allow your circumstances to affect your peace? What is keeping you from His After reading Philippians 4 do you see any way to handle life's anxieties?
5. What have you learned about your own needs and sharing with others in need?

Chapter 1 ______________________________

1 [a]Paul and [b]Timothy, [c]bond-servants of [d]Christ Jesus, to [e]all the
[1f]saints in Christ Jesus who are in [g]Philippi, including the [h]over-
seers and [i]deacons:
2 [a]Grace to you and peace from God our Father and the Lord Jesus
Christ.
3 [a]I thank my God in all my remembrance of you,
4 always offering prayer with joy in [a]my every prayer for you all,
5 in view of your [1a]participation in the [b]gospel [c]from the first day
until now.
6 *For I am* confident of this very thing, that He who began a good
work in you will perfect it until [a]the day of Christ Jesus.
7 [1]For [a]it is only right for me to feel this way about you all, because
I [b]have you in my heart, since both in my [2c]imprisonment and in the
[d]defense and confirmation of the [e]gospel, you all are partakers of
grace with me.
8 For [a]God is my witness, how I long for you all with the [1]affection
of [b]Christ Jesus.
9 And this I pray, that [a]your love may abound still more and more
in [b]real knowledge and all discernment,
10 so that you may [1a]approve the things that are excellent, in order
to be sincere and blameless [2]until [b]the day of Christ;
11 having been filled with the [a]fruit of righteousness which *comes*
through Jesus Christ, to the glory and praise of God.
12 Now I want you to know, brethren, that my circumstances [a]have
turned out for the greater progress of the [b]gospel,
13 so that my [1a]imprisonment in *the cause of* Christ has become well
known throughout the whole [2]praetorian guard and to [b]everyone
else,
14 and that most of the [1]brethren, trusting in the Lord because of
my [2a]imprisonment, have [b]far more courage to speak the word of
God without fear.
15 [a]Some, to be sure, are preaching Christ even from envy and
strife, but some also from good will;
16 [1]the latter *do it* out of love, knowing that I am appointed for the
defense of the [a]gospel;
17 the former proclaim Christ [a]out of selfish ambition, [1]rather than

1:1 [1]Or, *ho* [a]2 Cor. 1:1 [c]Rom. 1:1; [d]Gal. 3:26 Col. 1:2 [f]A [g]Acts 16:12 20:28; 1 Ti 1:7 [i]1 Tim.
2 [a]Rom. 1:
3 [a]Rom. 1:
4 [a]Rom. 1:
5 [1]Or, *shar preaching* [a]Acts 2:42; [b]Phil. 1:7; 2 [c]Acts 16:12 2:12; 4:15
6 [a]1 Cor. 1: 2:16
7 [1]Lit., *Just* [2]Lit., *bonds* 1:13 [b]2 Cor 21:33; Eph. 1:13f., 17 [d] [e]Phil. 1:5, 12 2:22; 4:3, 15
8 [1]Lit., *inwa* [a]Rom. 1:9 [b]
9 [a]1 Thess. 1:9
10 [1]Or, *disti between the which differ* [a]Rom. 2:18 Phil. 1:6; 2:1
11 [a]James 3
12 [a]Luke 21 1:5, 7, 16, 27 4:3, 15
13 [1]Lit., *bon governor's p* 1:7; 2 Tim. 2: 28:30
14 [1]Or, *breth Lord, trusting of my bonds bonds* [a]Phil. 2:9 [b]Acts 4:3 3:12; 7:4; Phi
15 [a]2 Cor. 11
16 [1]Some la reverse the o 16 and 17 [a]P 12, 27; 2:22; 4
17 [1]Lit., *not s* [a]Rom. 2:8; Ph

from pure motives, thinking to cause me distress in my [2b]imprison-
ment.
18 What then? Only that in every way, whether in pretense or in
truth, Christ is proclaimed; and in this I rejoice, yes, and I will
rejoice.
19 For I know that this shall turn out for my [1]deliverance [a]through
your [2]prayers and the provision of [b]the Spirit of Jesus Christ,
20 according to my [a]earnest expectation and [b]hope, that I shall not
be put to shame in anything, but *that* with [c]all boldness, Christ shall
even now, as always, be [d]exalted in my body, [e]whether by life or by
death.
21 For to me, [a]to live is Christ, and to die is gain.
22 [1]But if *I am* to live *on* in the flesh, this *will mean* [a]fruitful labor for
me; and I do not know [2]which to choose.
23 But I am hard-pressed from both *directions,* having the [a]desire to
depart and [b]be with Christ, for *that* is very much better;
24 yet to remain on in the flesh is more necessary for your sake.
25 And [a]convinced of this, I know that I shall remain and continue
with you all for your progress and joy in the faith,
26 so that your [a]proud confidence in me may abound in Christ
Jesus through my coming to you again.
27 Only conduct yourselves in a manner [a]worthy of the [b]gospel of
Christ; so that whether I come and see you or remain absent, I may
hear of you that you are [c]standing firm in [d]one spirit, with one [1]mind
[e]striving together for the faith of the gospel;
28 in no way alarmed by *your* opponents—which is a [a]sign of
destruction for them, but of salvation for you, and that *too,* from
God.
29 For to you [a]it has been granted for Christ's sake, not only to
believe in Him, but also to [b]suffer for His sake,
30 experiencing the same [a]conflict which [b]you saw in me, and now
hear *to be* in me.

Chapter 2

2 If therefore there is any encouragement in Christ, if there is any
consolation of love, if there is any [a]fellowship of the Spirit, if any
[1b]affection and compassion,
2 [a]make my joy complete [1]by [b]being of the same mind, maintaining
the same love, united in spirit, intent on one purpose.
3 Do nothing from [1a]selfishness or [b]empty conceit, but with
humility of mind let [c]each of you regard one another as more impor-
tant than himself;
4 [a]do not *merely* look out for your own personal interests, but also
for the interests of others.
5 [a]Have this attitude [1]in yourselves which was also in [b]Christ
Jesus,
6 who, although He [a]existed in the [b]form of God, [c]did not regard
equality with God a thing to be grasped,
7 but [1a]emptied Himself, taking the form of a [b]bond-servant, *and*
[c]being made in the likeness of men.
8 And being found in appearance as a man, [a]He humbled Himself
by becoming [b]obedient to the point of death, even [c]death [1]on a cross.
9 [a]Therefore also God [b]highly exalted Him, and bestowed on Him
[c]the name which is above every name,

., *bonds* [b]Phil. 1:7; 2 Tim. 2:9
salvation [2]Lit., *ication* [a]2 Cor. :11 [b]Acts 16:7
n. 8:19 [b]Rom. et. 4:16 [c]Acts Cor. 3:12; 7:4; 4 [d]1 Cor. 6:20 [e]Rom. 14:8
21 [a]Gal. 2:20
But if to live in sh, this will be or for me, then it., *what I shall se* [a]Rom. 1:13
Cor. 5:8; 2 Tim. 6 [b]John 12:26
25 [a]Phil. 2:24
Cor. 5:12; 7:4; Phil. 2:16
soul [a]Eph. 4:1 [c]1 Cor. 16:13; :1 [d]Acts 4:32 [e]Jude 3
[a]2 Thess. 1:5
Matt. 5:11, 12 [b]Acts 14:22
Col. 1:29; 2:1; ss. 2:2; 1 Tim. Tim. 4:7; Heb. 2; 12:1 [b]Acts 40; Phil. 1:13
, *inward parts* 14 [b]Col. 3:12
., *that you be* 1 3:29 [b]Rom. 2:16; Phil. 4:2
ntentiousness 2:8; Phil. 1:17 [c]Rom. 12:10; Eph. 5:21
[a]Rom. 15:1f.
among [a]Matt. n. 15:3 [b]Phil. 1:1
1 [b]2 Cor. 4:4 10:33; 14:28
aid aside His s [a]2 Cor. 8:9 20:28 [c]John 8:3; Gal. 4:4; Heb. 2:17
of [a]2 Cor. 8:9 . 26:39; John n. 5:19; Heb. 8 [c]Heb. 12:2
b. 1:9 [b]Matt. ts 2:33; Heb. 9 [c]Eph. 1:21

10 that at the name of Jesus [a]EVERY KNEE SHOULD BOW, of [b]those who
are in heaven, and on earth, and under the earth,
11 and that every tongue should confess that Jesus Christ is [a]Lord,
to the glory of God the Father.
12 So then, my beloved, [a]just as you have always obeyed, not as in
my presence only, but now much more in my absence, work out
your [b]salvation with [c]fear and trembling;
13 for it is [a]God who is at work in you, both to will and to work [b]for
His good pleasure.
14 Do all things without [a]grumbling or disputing;
15 that you may [1]prove yourselves to be [a]blameless and innocent,
[b]children of God above reproach in the midst of a [c]crooked and
perverse generation, among whom you [2d]appear as [3]lights in the
world,
16 holding [1]fast the word of life, so that in [a]the day of Christ I may
have cause to glory because I did not [b]run in vain nor [c]toil in vain.
17 But even if I am being [a]poured out as a drink offering upon [b]the
sacrifice and service of your faith, I rejoice and share my joy with
you all.
18 And you too, *I urge you,* rejoice in the same way and share your
joy with me.
19 But I hope [1]in the Lord Jesus to [a]send [b]Timothy to you shortly, so
that I also may be encouraged when I learn of your condition.
20 For I have no one *else* [a]of kindred spirit who will genuinely be
concerned for your welfare.
21 For they all [a]seek after their own interests, not those of Christ
Jesus.
22 But you know [a]of his proven worth that [b]he served with me in
the furtherance of the gospel [c]like a child *serving* his father.
23 [a]Therefore I hope to send him immediately, as soon as I see how
things *go* with me;
24 and [a]I trust in the Lord that I myself also shall be coming shortly.
25 But I thought it necessary to send to you [a]Epaphroditus, my
brother and [b]fellow worker and [c]fellow soldier, who is also your
[1d]messenger and [e]minister to my need;
26 because he was longing [1]for you all and was distressed because
you had heard that he was sick.
27 For indeed he was sick to the point of death, but God had mercy
on him, and not on him only but also on me, lest I should have
sorrow upon sorrow.
28 Therefore I have sent him all the more eagerly in order that
when you see him again you may rejoice and I may be less con-
cerned *about you.*
29 Therefore [a]receive him in the Lord with all joy, and [b]hold men
like him in high regard;
30 because he came close to death [a]for the work of Christ, risking
his life to [b]complete [1]what was deficient in your service to me.

Chapter 3

3 Finally, my brethren, [a]rejoice in the Lord. To write the same
things *again* is no trouble to me, and it is a safeguard for you.
2 Beware of the [a]dogs, beware of the [b]evil workers, beware of the
[1]false circumcision;

10 [a]Is. 45:2 14:11 [b]Eph
11 [a]John 1 10:9; 14:9
12 [a]Phil. 1: [b]Heb. 5:9 [c]
13 [a]Rom. 1 12:6; 15:10; [b]Eph. 1:5
14 [a]1 Cor. 4:9
15 [1]Or, *bec* *shine* [3]Or, *l* *stars* [a]Luke 3:6 [b]Matt. 5 5:1 [c]Deut. 3 2:40 [d]Matt.
16 [1]Or, *fort* [b]Gal. 2:2 [c]Is 4:11; 1 Thes
17 [a]2 Cor. 1 4:6 [b]Num. 2 Rom. 15:16
19 [1]Or, *trus* 2:23 [b]Phil. 1
20 [a]1 Cor. 1 3:10
21 [a]1 Cor. 1 Phil. 2:4
22 [a]Rom. 5: 16:2 [b]Acts 1 16:10; 2 Tim [c]1 Cor. 4:17
23 [a]Phil. 2:1
24 [a]Phil. 1:2
25 [1]Lit., *apo* 4:18 [b]Rom. Phil. 4:3; Phi [c]Philem. 2 [d] 2 Cor. 8:23
26 [1]Some ar read *to see y*
29 [a]Rom. 16 16:18
30 [1]Lit., *your* *of service* [a]A [b]1 Cor. 16:17;
3:1 [a]Phil. 2:1
2 [1]Lit., *mutila* *katatome* [a]Ps 20; Gal. 5:15; 22:15 [b]2 Cor.

3 for [a]we are the *true* [1]circumcision, who [b]worship in the Spirit of
God and [c]glory in [d]Christ Jesus and put no confidence in the flesh,
4 although [a]I myself might have confidence even in the flesh. If
anyone else has a mind to put confidence in the flesh, I far more:
5 [a]circumcised the eighth day, of the [b]nation of Israel, of the [c]tribe
of Benjamin, a [b]Hebrew of Hebrews; as to the Law, [d]a Pharisee;
6 as to zeal, [a]a persecutor of the church; as to the [b]righteousness
which is in the Law, found [c]blameless.
7 But [a]whatever things were gain to me, those things I have
counted as loss for the sake of Christ.
8 More than that, I count all things to be loss in view of the sur-
passing value of [1a]knowing [b]Christ Jesus my Lord, for whom I have
suffered the loss of all things, and count them but rubbish in order
that I may gain Christ,
9 and may be found in Him, not having [a]a righteousness of my
own derived from *the* Law, but that which is through faith in Christ,
[b]the righteousness which *comes* from God on the basis of faith,
10 that I may [a]know Him, and [b]the power of His resurrection and
[1c]the fellowship of His sufferings, being [d]conformed to His death;
11 [1]in order that I may [a]attain to the resurrection from the dead.
12 Not that I have already [a]obtained *it*, or have already [b]become
perfect, but I press on [1]in order that I may [c]lay hold of that [2]for which
also I [d]was laid hold of by [e]Christ Jesus.
13 Brethren, I do not regard myself as having laid hold of *it* yet; but
one thing *I do*: [a]forgetting what *lies* behind and reaching forward to
what *lies* ahead,
14 I [a]press on toward the goal for the prize of the [b]upward call of
God in [c]Christ Jesus.
15 Let us therefore, as many as are [1a]perfect, have this attitude; and
if in anything you have a [b]different attitude, [c]God will reveal that
also to you;
16 however, let us keep [1a]living by that same *standard* to which we
have attained.
17 Brethren, [a]join in following my example, and observe those who
walk according to the [b]pattern you have in us.
18 For [a]many walk, of whom I often told you, and now tell you
even [b]weeping, *that they are* enemies of [c]the cross of Christ,
19 whose end is destruction, whose god is *their* [1a]appetite, and
whose [b]glory is in their shame, who [c]set their minds on earthly things.
20 For [a]our [1]citizenship is in heaven, from which also we eagerly
[b]wait for a Savior, the Lord Jesus Christ;
21 who will [a]transform [1]the body of our humble state into [b]confor-
mity with [2]the [c]body of His glory, [d]by the exertion of the power that
He has even to [e]subject all things to Himself.

Chapter 4

4 Therefore, my beloved brethren [1]whom I [a]long *to see*, my joy and
crown, so [b]stand firm in the Lord, my beloved.
2 I urge Euodia and I urge Syntyche to [1a]live in harmony in the
Lord.
3 Indeed, true comrade, I ask you also to help these women who
have shared my struggle in *the cause of* the gospel, together with
Clement also, and the rest of my [a]fellow workers, whose [b]names are
in the book of life.

ritome [a]Rom. 9:6; Gal. 6:15 [c]Rom. 15:17; 4 [d]Rom. 8:39; Phil. 1:1; 3:12
or. 5:16; 11:18
e 1:59 [b]Rom. ; 2 Cor. 11:22 1 [d]Acts 22:3; 23:6; 26:5
s 8:3; 22:4, 5; hil. 3:9 [c]Phil. 2:15
[a]Luke 14:33
he knowledge r. 9:23f.; John ph. 4:13; Phil. et. 1:3 [b]Rom. Phil. 1:1; 3:12
10:5; Phil. 3:6 0; 1 Cor. 1:30
articipation in 3f.; John 17:3; 4:13; Phil. 3:8; 13 [b]Rom. 6:5 7 [d]Rom. 6:5; :36; Gal. 6:17
., *if somehow* 1 Cor. 15:23; Rev. 20:5f.
if I may even because also 9:24f.; 1 Tim. [b]1 Cor. 13:10 :12, 19 [d]Acts m. 8:39; Phil. 1:1; 3:3, 8
3 [a]Luke 9:62
or. 9:24; Heb. 8:28; 11:29; 1:9 [c]Phil. 3:3
nature [a]Matt. Cor. 2:6 [b]Gal. hn 6:45; Eph. ; 1 Thess. 4:9
., *following in ne* [a]Gal. 6:16
or. 4:16; 11:1; 9 [b]1 Pet. 5:3
. 11:13 [b]Acts 31 [c]Gal. 6:14
, *belly* [a]Rom. 1:12 [b]Rom. de 13 [c]Rom. 8:5f.; Col. 3:2
Lit., *common-* ph. 2:19; Phil. Col. 3:1; Heb. 2 [b]1 Cor. 1:7
ur lowly body glorious body 43-53 [b]Rom. l. 3:4 [c]1 Cor. 9 [d]Eph. 1:19 [e]1 Cor. 15:28
., *and longed* l. 1:8 [b]1 Cor. 13; Phil. 1:27
e of the same ind [a]Phil. 2:2
l. 2:25 [b]Luke 10:20

4 [a]Rejoice in the Lord always; again I will say, rejoice!
5 Let your forbearing *spirit* be known to all men. [a]The Lord is
[1]near.
6 [a]Be anxious for nothing, but in everything by [b]prayer and suppli-
cation with thanksgiving let your requests be made known to God.
7 And [a]the peace of God, which surpasses all [1]comprehension,
shall [b]guard your hearts and your [c]minds in [d]Christ Jesus.
8 Finally, brethren, [a]whatever is true, whatever is honorable, what-
ever is right, whatever is pure, whatever is [1]lovely, whatever is [2]of
good repute, if there is any excellence and if anything worthy of
praise, [3]let your mind dwell on these things.
9 The things you have learned and received and heard and seen
[a]in me, practice these things; and [b]the God of peace shall be with
you.
10 But I rejoiced in the Lord greatly, that now at last [a]you have
revived your concern for me; indeed, you were concerned *before*, but
you lacked opportunity.
11 Not that I speak [1]from want; for I have learned to be [2a]content in
whatever circumstances I am.
12 I know how to get along with humble means, and I also know
how to live in prosperity; in any and every circumstance I have
learned the secret of being filled and going [a]hungry, both of having
abundance and [b]suffering need.
13 I can do all things [1]through Him who [a]strengthens me.
14 Nevertheless, you have done well to [a]share *with me* in my afflic-
tion.
15 And you yourselves also know, Philippians, that at the [1a]first
preaching of the gospel, after I departed from [b]Macedonia, no church
[c]shared with me in the matter of giving and receiving but you alone;
16 for even in [a]Thessalonica you sent *a gift* more than once for my
needs.
17 [a]Not that I seek the gift itself, but I seek for the [1]profit which
increases to your account.
18 But I have received everything in full, and have an abundance; I
am [1]amply supplied, having received from [a]Epaphroditus [2]what you
have sent, [3b]a fragrant aroma, an acceptable sacrifice, well-pleasing
to God.
19 And [a]my God shall supply [1]all your needs according to His
[b]riches in glory in Christ Jesus.
20 Now to [a]our God and Father [b]*be* the glory [1]forever and ever.
Amen.
21 Greet every [1]saint in Christ Jesus. [a]The brethren who are with me
greet you.
22 [a]All the [1b]saints greet you, especially those of Caesar's
household.
23 [a]The grace of the Lord Jesus Christ [b]be with your spirit.

4 [a]Phil. 3:
5 [1]Or, *at h* 16:22 mg. James 5:8
6 [a]Matt. 6 6:18; 1 Tir
7 [1]Lit., *mi* John 14:2 Col. 3:15 [c]2 Cor. 10 4:19, 21
8 [1]Or, *lov* *gracious* [3]Lit., *pond* *things* [a]R 1 Pet. 2:12
9 [a]Phil. 3 15:33
10 [a]2 Cor 2:30
11 [1]Lit., *a* [2]Or, *self-s* [a]2 Cor. 9:8 8; Heb. 13
12 [a]1 Cor 11:9
13 [1]Lit., *i* Eph. 3:16
14 [a]Heb.
15 [1]Lit., *b* [a]Phil. 1:5 [c]2 Cor. 11
16 [a]Acts 2:9
17 [1]Lit., *f* 9:11f.; 2 C
18 [1]Lit., *r* *the things* [3]Lit., *an o* *fragrance* [b]Ex. 29:18 Eph. 5:2
19 [1]Or, *e* *yours* [a]2 [b]Rom. 2:4
20 [1]Lit., *t* *the ages* [b]Rom. 11
21 [1]Or, *h* 1:2
22 [1]V. 21 [a]2 Cor. 13
23 [a]Rom [b]2 Tim. 4

PHILIPPIANS OBSERVATIONS CHART

ook for both pronouns and direct references.

pients: *Look for* the saints, brethren, beloved, you, *or any other ways Paul addresses those to whom he is writing. (Remember to ng the five W's and an H: How does Paul describe the Philippians? What are their problems? What is his concern for them? Why ting to the Philippians?)*

PAUL'S INSTRUCTIONS TO THE PHILIPPIANS

PHILIPPIANS AT A GLANCE

Theme of Philippians:

Author:

Date:

Purpose:

Key Words:
Christ Jesus

joy
(rejoice)

mind
(attitude)

gospel

SEGMENT DIVISIONS

COMMAND TO:	JESUS IS:	PAUL'S EXAMPLE	CHAPTER THEMES
	1:21 MY LIFE		1
			2
3:17 FOLLOW PAUL'S EXAMPLE			3
		4:1 LEARNED TO BE CONTENT IN HIS CIRCUMSTANCES	4

OLOSSIANS

lossae was located twelve miles from Laodicea and about one hundred miles east of Ephesus in alley of the Lycus River in the southern part of ancient Phrygia, the adopted home of Oriental cism. Many Jews, Phrygians, and Greeks came to Colossae because it was on a main trade route. nixture of backgrounds made the city an interesting cultural center where all sorts of new ideas octrines from the East were discussed and considered.

th all these ungodly influences, it is no wonder the church at Colossae was on Paul's heart during nprisonment in Rome. He may never have seen their faces, but they belonged to his Christ and he ne with them in Spirit. Physically he might be bound by chains, but he could reach them by letter. was one way he could protect them from the wolves who were out to devour God's flock.

ıl wrote sometime around A.D. 62. This letter to the faithful saints at Colossae was one whose ge would be needed down through the ages. Maybe that's one of the reasons God didn't let Paul r this message in person.

GS TO DO

As you read Colossians chapter by chapter, learn all you can from the text about the author and the recipients and discover why the author writes what he does to this particular church. This will give you the key to understanding Colossians. Following this simple procedure will help:

a. As you read, ask the five W's and an H: Who? What? Where? Why? When? and How? Ask questions such as: Who wrote this? Where were they? To whom? What were these people like? What were their situations? What were their problems? When was this written? What seemed to be going on? Why did the author say what he did?

Asking questions like these—answered only from what the text says—gives insight into a book of the Bible and helps you to understand the context and purpose of the book and to keep its teachings and truths in their proper context.

b. As you read, watch for every reference to the author(s) (including names and pronouns such as *I, my, we, us*). Keep asking the five W's and an H and record your insights on the OBSERVATIONS CHART on page 1749.

c. Look for pronouns such as *you* and note the relationship between the author and the recipients. Ask questions such as: How did the gospel get to the Colossians? Who preached the gospel to them? What was the author's main concern for the Colossians? The answers will help you understand why this letter was written. Record your insights on the OBSERVATIONS CHART.

Now read through Colossians again, a chapter at a time. As you read:

a. Mark the key words and phrases that are listed on the COLOSSIANS AT A GLANCE chart on page 1750. Be sure to mark the synonyms and pronouns for each key word also and mark every reference to Jesus: i.e. *with Him, by Him, for Him, through Him,* and so on.

b. In the margin list what you learn from marking *in Him,* and from marking other key words.

c. Also record any other observations of the text as instructed in "How to Observe the Bible Chapter by Chapter" in the front of your Bible (page I-13).

When you get to chapter 2 note the warnings in this chapter by looking for the words *see to it, let,* and *no one.*

a. Record these warnings along with any instructions on the OBSERVATIONS CHART.

b. With these warnings in mind read the section called "Understanding Gnosticism" in the front of your Bible (page I-57).

4. Proceed through chapters 3 and 4, adding pertinent information to your OBSERVA
CHART.
5. On the COLOSSIANS AT A GLANCE chart, be sure to record the theme of the book and
chapter. Remember to record the chapter theme in the text next to the chapter number.
out the date the book was written, the name of the author, and his purpose for writing.

THINGS TO THINK ABOUT

1. What are you pursuing? Does it have eternal value? Is it drawing you to God or keepi
from time alone with God in prayer and in studying the Word? Are you seeking things a
earthly things?
2. Are you being deluded with any modern-day philosophies or traditions which contra
Word or aren't in the Word? Any legalistic rules which are not clearly taught in th
Testament? Any mystical teachings or prophecies that can't be supported in the Word of
that have a tendency to add something which isn't there or which seem to be only for
group of people?
3. Inductive Bible study is not easy. The enemy will do all he can to keep you from knowi
and His Word intimately for it is your major defense and offense in spiritual warfare. A
going to make it your goal to let the Word of Christ richly dwell within you and to wal
precepts?
4. Are you proclaiming the Lord Jesus Christ and holding to all He is and all that you have
as He is presented in Colossians?
5. As you have studied Colossians, have you seen any areas in your life in which you are
short or simply walking in disobedience to God's Word? What are you going to do (no
what happens)?

Chapter 1 ____________________

1 [a]Paul, [b]an apostle of Jesus Christ [1c]by the will of God, and
[d]Timothy [2]our brother,
2 to the [1a]saints and faithful brethren in Christ *who are* at Colossae:
[b]Grace to you and peace from God our Father.

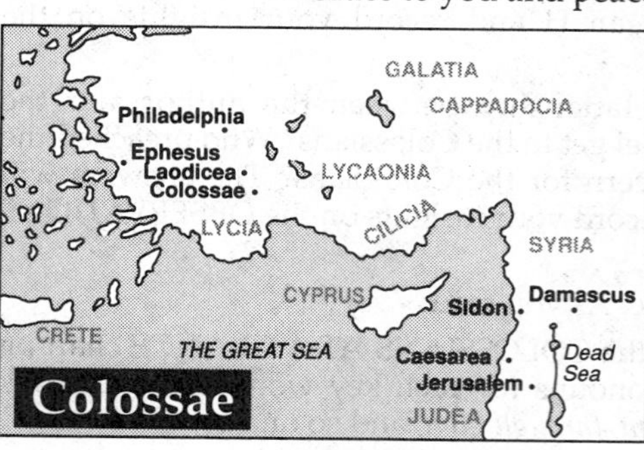

3 [a]We give thanks to God, [b]the Father of
our Lord Jesus Christ, praying always for
you,
4 [a]since we heard of your faith in Christ
Jesus and the [b]love which you have [1]for [c]all
the [2]saints;
5 because of the [a]hope [b]laid up for you in
[1]heaven, of which you previously [c]heard in
the word of truth, [2]the gospel,
6 which has come to you, just as [1a]in all
the world also it is constantly bearing [b]fruit
and [2]increasing, even as *it has been doing* in
you also since the day you [c]heard *of it* and [3]understood the grace of
God in truth;
7 just as you learned *it* from [a]Epaphras, our [b]beloved fellow bond-
servant, who is a faithful servant of Christ on [1]our behalf,
8 and he also informed us of your [a]love in the Spirit.
9 For this reason also, [a]since the day we heard *of it*, [b]we have not
ceased to pray for you and to ask that you may be filled with the
[1c]knowledge of His will in all spiritual [d]wisdom and understanding,
10 so that you may [a]walk in a manner worthy of the Lord, [1b]to

1:1 [1]Lit., *th* *the* [a]Phil. 1: 1:1 [c]1 Cor. 1:1; 1 Thess

2 [1]Or, *holy* 9:13 [b]Rom.

3 [a]Rom. 1:8 15:6; 2 Cor.

4 [1]Or, *towa* *ones* [a]Eph. 5:6 [c]Eph. 6:

5 [1]Lit., *the h* [2]Or, *of the g* 23:6 [b]2 Tim. 1:13

6 [1]Or, *it is in* [2]Or, *spreadi* [3]Or, *came re* *know* [a]Rom. [b]Rom. 1:13

7 [1]Some late read *your* [a]C [b]Col. 4:7

8 [a]Rom. 15:

9 [1]Or, *real k* [a]Col. 1:4 [b]E [c]Phil. 1:9 [d]E

10 [1]Lit., *unto* *pleasing* [a]Ep [b]Eph. 5:10

please *Him* in all respects, [c]bearing fruit in every good work and
[2]increasing in the [3]knowledge of God;
11 [a]strengthened with all power, according to [1]His glorious might,
[2]for the attaining of all steadfastness and [3]patience; [b]joyously
12 giving thanks to [a]the Father, who has qualified us [1]to share in
[b]the inheritance of the [2]saints in [c]light.
13 For He delivered us from the [1a]domain of darkness, and trans-
ferred us to the kingdom of [2b]His beloved Son,
14 [a]in whom we have redemption, the forgiveness of sins.
15 And He is the [a]image of the [b]invisible God, the [c]first-born of all
creation.
16 For [1a]by Him all things were created, [a]*both* in the heavens and on
earth, visible and invisible, whether [b]thrones or dominions or rulers
or authorities—[c]all things have been created [2]by Him and for Him.
17 And He [1a]is before all things, and in Him all things [2]hold
together.
18 He is also [a]head of [b]the body, the church; and He is [c]the begin-
ning, [d]the first-born from the dead; so that He Himself might come
to have first place in everything.
19 For [1]it was [a]the *Father's* good pleasure for all [b]the [2]fulness to
dwell in Him,
20 and through Him to [a]reconcile all things to Himself, having
made [b]peace through [c]the blood of His cross; through Him, *I say,*
[d]whether things on earth or things in [1]heaven.
21 And although you were [a]formerly alienated and hostile in mind,
engaged in evil deeds,
22 yet He has now [a]reconciled you in His fleshly [b]body through
death, in order to [c]present you before Him [d]holy and blameless and
beyond reproach—
23 if indeed you continue in [1]the faith firmly [a]established and stead-
fast, and not moved away from the [b]hope of the gospel that you have
heard, which was proclaimed [c]in all creation under heaven, [d]and of
which I, Paul, [2]was made a [3e]minister.
24 [a]Now I rejoice in my sufferings for your sake, and in my flesh [b]I
[1]do my share on behalf of [c]His body (which is the church) in filling
up that which is lacking [2]in Christ's afflictions.
25 [a]Of *this church* I [1]was made a minister according to the
[b]stewardship from God bestowed on me for your benefit, that I
might [2]fully carry out the *preaching of* the word of God,
26 *that is,* [a]the mystery which has been hidden from the *past* ages
and generations; but has now been manifested to His [1]saints,
27 to whom [a]God willed to make known what is [b]the riches of the
glory of this mystery among the Gentiles, which is [c]Christ in you, the
[d]hope of glory.
28 And we proclaim Him, [a]admonishing every man and teaching
every man [1]with all [b]wisdom, that we may [c]present every man
[2d]complete in Christ.
29 And for this purpose also I [a]labor, [b]striving [c]according to His
[1]power, which [2]mightily works within me.

Chapter 2

2 For I want you to know how great a [a]struggle I have on your
behalf, and for those who are at [b]Laodicea, and for all those who
have not [1]personally seen my face,

growing by the
edge [3]Or, *real*
ige [b]Eph. 5:10
[c]Rom. 1:13
he might of His
., unto all [3]Or,
tience with joy
5:13 [b]Eph. 4:2
nto the portion
ly ones [a]Eph.
ts 20:32 [c]Acts
26:18
authority [2]Lit.,
Son of His love
5:12 [b]Eph. 1:6
4 [a]Rom. 3:24
Cor. 4:4 [b]John
8 [c]Rom. 8:29
1 [2]Or, *through*
[b]Eph. 1:20f.;
15 [c]John 1:3;
:36; 1 Cor. 8:6
)r, has existed
o [2]Or, *endure*
John 1:1; 8:58
h. 1:22 [b]Eph.
Col. 1:24; 2:19
4 [d]Acts 26:23
all the fulness
eased to dwell
ulness of deity
:5 [b]John 1:16
, the heavens
:18; Eph. 2:16
5:1; Eph. 2:14
:13 [d]Col. 1:16
om. 5:10; Eph.
2:3, 12
Cor. 5:18; Eph.
om. 7:4 [c]Eph.
:28 [d]Eph. 1:4
omit, the [2]Lit.,
[3]Or, *servant*
3:17; Col. 2:7
[c]Mark 16:15;
Col. 1:6 [d]Eph.
. 1:25 [e]1 Cor.
3:5
presentatively
fill up [2]Lit., *of*
17; 2 Cor. 1:5;
:15; Phil. 2:17
:8; 2:10 [c]Col.
1:18
became [2]Lit.,
ull the word of
ol. 1:23 [b]Eph.
3:2
[1]Or, *holy ones*
. 16:25f.; Eph.
.; Col. 2:2; 4:3
. 13:11 [b]Eph.
3; 3:16 [c]Rom.
0 [d]1 Tim. 1:1
n [2]Or, *perfect*
:31; Col. 3:16
2:6f.; Col. 2:3
2 [d]Matt. 5:48;
Eph. 4:13
working [2]Lit.,
[a]1 Cor. 15:10
:1; 4:12 [c]Eph.
:19; Col. 2:12
it., in the flesh
29; 4:12 [b]Col.
15f.; Rev. 1:11

2 that their [a]hearts may be encouraged, having been [b]knit together
in love, and *attaining* to all [c]the wealth [1]that comes from the full
assurance of understanding, *resulting* in a [d]true knowledge of [e]God's
mystery, *that is,* Christ *Himself,*
3 in whom are hidden all [a]the treasures of wisdom and
knowledge.
4 [a]I say this in order that no one may delude you with [b]persuasive
argument.
5 For even though I am [a]absent in body, nevertheless I am with
you in spirit, rejoicing [1]to see [2]your [b]good discipline and the [c]stability
of your faith in Christ.
6 As you therefore have received [a]Christ Jesus the Lord, *so* [1b]walk
in Him,
7 having been firmly [a]rooted *and now* being [b]built up in Him and
[c]established [1]in your faith, just as you [d]were instructed, *and* over-
flowing [2]with gratitude.
8 [a]See to it that no one takes you captive through [b]philosophy and
empty deception, according to the tradition of men, according to the
[c]elementary principles of the world, [1]rather than according to Christ.
9 For in Him all the [a]fulness of Deity dwells in bodily form,
10 and in Him you have been [a]made [1]complete, and [b]He is the head
[2]over all [c]rule and authority;
11 and in Him [a]you were also circumcised with a circumcision
made without hands, in the removal of [b]the body of the flesh by the
circumcision of Christ;
12 having been [a]buried with Him in baptism, in which you were
also [b]raised up with Him through faith in the working of God, who
[c]raised Him from the dead.
13 And when you were [a]dead [1]in your transgressions and the uncir-
cumcision of your flesh, He [b]made you alive together with Him,
having forgiven us all our transgressions,
14 having canceled out [a]the certificate of debt consisting of decrees
against us *and* which was hostile to us; and [b]He has taken it out of
the way, having nailed it to the cross.
15 When He had [1a]disarmed the [b]rulers and authorities, He [a]made a
public display of them, having [c]triumphed over them through [2]Him.
16 Therefore let no one [1a]act as your judge in regard to [b]food or
[b]drink or in respect to a [c]festival or a [d]new moon or a [e]Sabbath [2]day—
17 things which are [a]a *mere* shadow of what is to come; but the
[1]substance [2]belongs to Christ.
18 Let no one keep [1a]defrauding you of your prize by [b]delighting in
[2]self-abasement and the worship of the angels, taking his stand on
visions he has seen, [c]inflated without cause by his [d]fleshly mind,
19 and not holding fast to [a]the head, from whom [b]the entire body,
being supplied and held together by the joints and [1]ligaments, grows
with a growth [2]which is from God.
20 [a]If you have died with Christ [1]to the [b]elementary principles of
the world, [c]why, as if you were living in the world, do you submit
yourself to [d]decrees, such as,
21 "Do not handle, do not taste, do not touch!"
22 (which all *refer* [a]*to* things destined to perish [1]with the using)—in
accordance with the [b]commandments and teachings of men?
23 These are matters which have, to be sure, the appearance of

2 [1]Lit., *of t* *assurance* 14:31; Eph 4:8 [b]Col. 2 1:7, 18; 3:1 13:11 [e]Ror Eph. 3:3f.;
3 [a]Is. 11:2;
4 [a]Eph. 4: 16:18
5 [1]Lit., *and* *your ordere* [a]1 Cor. 5:3 14:40 [c]1 P
6 [1]Or, *leac* [a]Gal. 3:26
7 [1]Or, *by* read *in it w* 3:17 [b]1 Co 2:20 [c]1 Co 4:21
8 [1]Lit., *an* 8:9; 10:12; Heb. 3:12 Col. 2:23; [c]Gal. 4:3; (
9 [a]2 Cor. 5
10 [1]Or, *ful* [a]Eph. 3:19 [c]1 Cor. 15: Col. 2:15
11 [a]Rom. 2:11 [b]Ron Gal. 5:24;
12 [a]Rom. 6:5; Eph. 2 3:1 [c]Acts
13 [1]Or, *by* [a]Eph. 2:1 Col. 2:12
14 [a]Eph. 2:20 [b]1 Pe
15 [1]Or, *di* *Himself of* the cross [b]John 12:3 15:24; Eph 2:10 [c]2 C
16 [1]Lit., *ju* *days* [a]Ro 7:19; Rom 9:10 [c]Lev. 14:5 [d]1 C 2 Chr. 31: [e]Mark 2:27
17 [1]Lit., *b* *Christ* [a]H
18 [1]Or, *gi* *against yo* *humility* Phil. 3:14 [c]1 Cor. 4:6
19 [1]Lit., *b* *God* [a]Eph 1:23; 4:16
20 [1]Lit., *fr* 6:2 [b]Col. [d]Col. 2:14,
22 [1]Or, *b* *consumed* [b]Is. 29:13; Titus 1:14

wisdom in [1a]self-made religion and self-abasement and [b]severe treat-
ment of the body, *but are* of no value against [c]fleshly indulgence.

Chapter 3

3 If then you have been [a]raised up with Christ, keep seeking the
things above, where Christ is, [b]seated at the right hand of God.
2 [1a]Set your mind on the things above, not on the things that are on
earth.
3 For you have [a]died and your life is hidden with Christ in God.
4 When Christ, [a]who is our life, is revealed, [b]then you also will be
revealed with Him in glory.
5 [a]Therefore [1]consider [b]the members of your earthly body as dead
to [2c]immorality, impurity, passion, evil desire, and greed, which
[3]amounts to idolatry.
6 For it is on account of these things that [a]the wrath of God will
come[1],
7 and [a]in them you also once walked, when you were living in
them.
8 But now you also, [a]put them all aside: [b]anger, wrath, malice,
slander, *and* [c]abusive speech from your mouth.
9 [1a]Do not lie to one another, since you [b]laid aside the old [2]self with
its *evil* practices,
10 and have [a]put on the new [1]self who is being [2b]renewed to a true
knowledge [c]according to the image of the One who [d]created him
11 —*a renewal* in which [a]there is no *distinction between* Greek and
Jew, [b]circumcised and uncircumcised, [c]barbarian, Scythian, [d]slave
and freeman, but [e]Christ is all, and in all.
12 And so, as those who have been [a]chosen of God, holy and
beloved, [b]put on a [c]heart of compassion, kindness, [d]humility, gentle-
ness and [1e]patience;
13 [a]bearing with one another, and [b]forgiving each other, whoever
has a complaint against anyone; [b]just as the Lord forgave you, so
also should you.
14 And beyond all these things *put on* love, which is [1a]the perfect
bond of [b]unity.
15 And let [a]the peace of Christ [1]rule in your hearts, to which [2]in-
deed you were called in [b]one body; and [3]be thankful.
16 Let [a]the word of [1]Christ richly dwell within you, [2]with all wis-
dom [b]teaching and admonishing one another [c]with psalms *and*
hymns *and* spiritual songs, [d]singing [3]with thankfulness in your
hearts to God.
17 And [a]whatever you do in word or deed, *do* all in the name of the
Lord Jesus, [b]giving thanks through Him to God the Father.
18 [a]Wives, [b]be subject to your husbands, as is fitting in the Lord.
19 [a]Husbands, love your wives, and do not be embittered against
them.
20 [a]Children, be obedient to your parents in all things, for this is
well-pleasing [1]to the Lord.
21 [a]Fathers, do not [1]exasperate your children, that they may not lose
heart.
22 [a]Slaves, in all things obey those who are your masters [1]on earth,
[b]not with [2]external service, as those who *merely* please men, but with
sincerity of heart, fearing the Lord.

23 Whatever you do, do your work [1]heartily, [a]as for the Lord [2]rather
than for men;
24 [a]knowing that from the Lord you will receive the reward [1]of [b]the
inheritance. It is the Lord Christ whom you [c]serve.
25 For [a]he who does wrong will receive the consequences of the
wrong which he has done, and [1b]that without partiality.

Chapter 4

4 Masters, grant to your slaves justice and fairness, [a]knowing that
you too have a Master in heaven.
2 [a]Devote yourselves to prayer, keeping alert in it with *an attitude
of* thanksgiving;
3 praying at the same time [a]for us as well, that God may open up
to us a [b]door for [c]the word, so that we may speak forth [d]the mystery
of Christ, for which I have also [e]been imprisoned;
4 in order that I may make it clear [a]in the way I ought to speak.
5 [1a]Conduct yourselves with wisdom toward [b]outsiders, [2c]making
the most of the opportunity.
6 [a]Let your speech always be [1]with grace, seasoned, *as it were*, with
[b]salt, so that you may know how you should [c]respond to each per-
son.
7 [a]As to all my affairs, [b]Tychicus, *our* [c]beloved brother and faithful
servant and fellow bond-servant in the Lord, will bring you informa-
tion.
8 [a]For I have sent him to you for this very purpose, that you may
know *about* our circumstances and that he may [b]encourage your
hearts;
9 [1]and with him [a]Onesimus, *our* faithful and [b]beloved brother,
[c]who is one of your *number.* They will inform you about the whole
situation here.
10 [a]Aristarchus, my [b]fellow prisoner, sends you his greetings; and
also [c]Barnabas' cousin Mark (about whom you received [1]instructions:
[d]if he comes to you, welcome him);
11 and *also* Jesus who is called Justus; these are the only [a]fellow
workers for the kingdom of God [b]who are from the circumcision;
and they have proved to be an encouragement to me.
12 [a]Epaphras, [b]who is one of your number, a bondslave of Jesus
Christ, sends you his greetings, always [c]laboring earnestly for you in
his prayers, that you may [1]stand [2d]perfect and [3]fully assured in all
the will of God.
13 For I bear him witness that he has [1]a deep concern for you and
for those who are in [a]Laodicea and Hierapolis.
14 [a]Luke, the beloved physician, sends you his greetings, and *also*
[b]Demas.
15 Greet the brethren who are in [a]Laodicea and also [1]Nympha and
[b]the church that is in [2]her house.
16 And [a]when [1]this letter is read among you, have it also read in the
church of the Laodiceans; and you, for your part [a]read [1]my letter *that
is coming* from [b]Laodicea.
17 And say to [a]Archippus, "Take heed to the [b]ministry which you
have received in the Lord, that you may [1]fulfill it."
18 [1]I, Paul, [a]write this greeting with my own hand. [b]Remember my
[2c]imprisonment. [d]Grace be with you.

23 [1]L [2]Lit., a
24 [1]L [a]Eph. 1 Pet.
25 [1]L *partial* [b]Deut. 10:34;
4:1 [a]E
2 [a]Ac
3 [a]Ep 14:27 3:3, 4;
4 [a]Eph
5 [1]Lit., *redeer* [a]Eph. 5 [c]Eph. 5
6 [1]Or, 4:29 [b] 3:15
7 [a]Col *6:21, 2* 2 Tim. Col. 1:7
8 [a]Eph
9 [1]Lit., *Onesin* [b]Col. 1:
10 [1]Or, 19:29; [b]Rom. 12:12, [d]2 Tim.
11 [a]Ror 11:2
12 [1]Or, *complet* [3]Or, *ma* [a]Col. 1:7 [b]Col. 4:9 [d]Col. 1:2
13 [1]Or, *great pa* 4:15f.
14 [a]2 Ti 24 [b]2 Ti Philem.
15 [1]Or, (masc.) mss. rea 2:1; 4:13
16 [1]Lit., 5:27; 2 T [b]Col. 2:1;
17 [1]Or, *fulfill,* [a]Ph 4:5
18 [1]Lit., *my hand bonds* [a]1 [b]Heb. 13: Col. 4:3 2 Tim. 4:2 Heb. 13:2

Colossians Observations Chart

thor

cipients

rnings and Instructions

Colossians at a Glance

Theme of Colossians:

Author:

Date:

Purpose:

Key Words:

wisdom
knowledge
understanding
fullness
all
complete
faith
mystery
in Him
(or before Him,
through Him,
etc.)

Segment Divisions	Chapter Themes
	1
	2
	3
	4

THESSALONIANS

mothy joined Paul and Silas (Silvanus) while they were in Lystra on Paul's second missionary .ey. Since his father was a Greek, Timothy hadn't been circumcised. There was no sense in causing ınnecessary conflicts with the Jews who were in those parts, so Paul had Timothy circumcised. ;s went smoothly until Paul had his vision of a man from Macedonia appealing to him to come ıelp them.

lieving this call was of God, the three went to Philippi—and the persecution began. Paul and Silas beaten with rods and thrown into prison. Undaunted, convinced of their heavenly commission, io traveled on through Amphipolis and Appollonia and came to Thessalonica. There they found a h synagogue where for three Sabbaths Paul reasoned with the Thessalonians from the Scripture. and Greeks, including a number of leading women, heard and believed. The other Jews became ıs. Once again there was opposition, but this time the persecution was not directed only to the)ut also to those who had believed.

)nsequently, the Thessalonian believers sent Paul, Silas, and Timothy to Berea by night where the gospel bore fruit. When the Jews of Thessalonica heard what happened in Berea, they ln't bear it. They went to Berea to persecute the men who were upsetting the world.

om Berea Paul went to Athens, and from Athens to Corinth. But the church at Thessalonica was on eart. How were they doing in the midst of such adamant opposition? Paul had to find out. So t A.D. 51, while in Corinth, Paul sat down to write his first epistle to the church at Thessalonica.

ıGS TO DO

Read 1 Thessalonians chapter by chapter. Record the following information on the OBSERVATIONS CHART on page 1757. (Be sure to take your answers from the text.)

a. List what you learn about the author(s). Look for the relationship of the author(s) to the recipients. In chapter 2, what comparisons are drawn to show how the author(s) feel about those to whom they are writing? Don't miss it.

b. List everything you learn about the recipients. Who had they been serving? What happened when they heard and believed the gospel? What were they enduring, etc.?

c. Note the different problems or concerns that are addressed in the letter.

Go through the book and mark the key words (along with their synonyms and pronouns) listed on the 1 THESSALONIANS AT A GLANCE chart on page 1758. As you observe the key words, list in the margin everything you learn from the text about each word. List what you learn about *the coming of the Lord* in one place in the margin.

In chapters 4 and 5 are several truths about those "who have fallen asleep" and those "who are alive and remain." List what you observe from the text about each of these on the second page of the OBSERVATIONS CHART. As you do, note the progression of events in 1 Thessalonians 4:13-18. Ask the five W's and an H of the text: Who is involved? What will happen? Where will they meet the Lord? When? Why are they not to sorrow? How will all this happen?

Watch what you learn about "the day of the Lord" in chapter 5. Record this information on the chart THE DAY OF THE LORD in the appendix (page 1878).

On 1 THESSALONIANS AT A GLANCE, record the theme of the book. Then record the theme of each chapter on the chart and in the text next to the chapter number. Fill in any additional information under author, date, purpose, etc.

Often you will be able to note a turning point in the book because the subject being addressed

will change. These topical changes divide the book into segments. Think through the fo
questions to see if you can determine a segment division in 1 Thessalonians.

a. Where does the main subject of the book change?

b. What is the topic in the first three chapters of the book?

c. What does the subject become in the last two chapters?

d. Title each segment of the book by thinking of the theme or subject discussed in the fir chapters and then in the last two. Record your segment divisions on 1 THESSALONIA A GLANCE.

THINGS TO THINK ABOUT

1. In this book Paul pours his life into other men who could carry on the work of the gosp you spending time imparting the things God has done in your life to another who can, i minister to others?
2. It is sometimes hard to give thanks in all things, yet that is the will of God. Go back over few days and think of the things that have happened in your life for which you have no thanks. Determine in your heart to obey this command.
3. Are the circumstances in your life difficult? How are you responding? What will others say your response? Can people imitate your walk with God?
4. Are you abstaining from sexual immorality? Are you defrauding others sexually in any all? Do you realize that if you're acting on your sexual passions in a way contrary to God' that God will act as the avenger against you?
5. Do you pray without ceasing (5:17) for those in your life who don't know our Lord? I storm the throne for answers to your problems? Do you pray consistently for others. convicting command, isn't it?

Chapter 1

1 [a]Paul and [b]Silvanus and [c]Timothy to the [d]church of the Thes-
salonians in God the Father and the Lord Jesus Christ: [e]Grace to
you and peace.
2 [a]We give thanks to God always for all of you, [b]making mention *of*
you in our prayers;
3 constantly bearing in mind your [a]work of faith and labor of [b]love
and [1c]steadfastness of hope [2]in our Lord Jesus Christ in the presence
of [d]our God and Father,
4 knowing, [a]brethren beloved by God, [b]*His* choice of you;
5 for our [a]gospel did not come to you in word only, but also [b]in
power and in the Holy Spirit and with [c]full conviction; just as you
know [d]what kind of men we [1]proved to be among you for your sake.
6 You also became [a]imitators of us and of the Lord, [b]having
received [c]the word in much tribulation with the [d]joy of the Holy
Spirit,
7 so that you became an example to all the believers in [a]Macedonia
and in [b]Achaia.
8 For [a]the word of the Lord has [b]sounded forth from you, not only
in [c]Macedonia and [d]Achaia, but also [e]in every place your faith
toward God has gone forth, so that we have no need to say anything.
9 For they themselves report about us what kind of a [1a]reception
we had [2]with you, and how you [b]turned to God [c]from [3]idols to serve
[4d]a living and true God,
10 and to [a]wait for His Son from [1]heaven, whom He [b]raised from
the dead, *that is* Jesus, who [c]delivers us from [d]the wrath to come.

1:1 [a]2 Thes [b]2 Cor. 1:19 [d]Acts 17:1
2 [a]Rom. 1:8 1:3 [b]Rom. 1
3 [1]Or, *perse* [2]Lit., *of* [a]Joh [b]1 Cor. 13:1 8:25; 15:4
4 [a]Rom. 1:7 2:13 [b]2 Pet.
5 [1]Lit., *beca* 9:14 [b]Rom. [c]Luke 1:1; C [d]1 Thess. 2:
6 [a]1 Cor. 4:1 [b]Acts 17:5-1 4:2 [d]Acts 13 6:10; Gal. 5:
7 [a]Rom. 15: 18:12
8 [a]Col. 3:16; 3:1 [b]Rom. 1 15:26 [d]Acts [e]Rom. 1:8; 1 2:14
9 [1]Lit., *entra* to [3]Or, *the id* *the* [a]1 Thess 14:15 [c]1 Cor [d]Matt. 16:16
10 [1]Lit., *the* [a]Matt. 16:27f. 1:7 [b]Acts 2:2 5:9 [d]Matt. 3:7 2:16; 5:9

Chapter 2

2 For you yourselves know, brethren, that our [1a]coming to you
[b]was not in vain,
2 but after we had already suffered and been [a]mistreated in
[b]Philippi, as you know, we had the boldness in our God [c]to speak to
you the [d]gospel of God amid much [1e]opposition.
3 For our [a]exhortation does not *come* from [b]error or [c]impurity or
[1]by way of [d]deceit;
4 [a]but just as we have been approved by God to be [b]entrusted with
the gospel, so we speak, [c]not as pleasing men but God, who
[1d]examines our hearts.
5 For we never came [1]with flattering speech, as you know, nor
with [a]a pretext for greed—[b]God is witness—
6 nor did we [a]seek glory from men, either from you or from others,
even though as [b]apostles of Christ we might have [1]asserted our
authority.
7 But we [1]proved to be [2a]gentle [3]among you, [b]as a nursing *mother*
[4]tenderly cares for her own children.
8 Having thus a fond affection for you, we were well-pleased to
[a]impart to you not only the [b]gospel of God but also our own [1]lives,
because you had become [2]very dear to us.
9 For you recall, brethren, our [a]labor and hardship, *how* [b]working
night and day so as not to be a [c]burden to any of you, we proclaimed
to you the [d]gospel of God.
10 You are witnesses, and *so is* [a]God, [b]how devoutly and uprightly
and blamelessly we [1]behaved toward you [2]believers;
11 just as you know how we *were* [a]exhorting and encouraging and
[1b]imploring each one of you as [c]a father *would* his own children,
12 so that you may [a]walk in a manner worthy of the God who [b]calls
you into His own kingdom and [c]glory.
13 And for this reason we also constantly [a]thank God that when
you received from us the [b]word of God's message, you accepted *it*
[c]not *as* the word of men, but *for* what it really is, the word of God,
[d]which also performs its work in you who believe.
14 For you, brethren, became [a]imitators of [b]the churches of God in
Christ Jesus that are [c]in Judea, for [d]you also endured the same suffer-
ings at the hands of your own countrymen, [e]even as they *did* from
the Jews,
15 [a]who both killed the Lord Jesus and [b]the prophets, and [1]drove us
out. [2]They are not pleasing to God, [2]but hostile to all men,
16 [a]hindering us from speaking to the Gentiles [b]that they might be
saved; with the result that they always [c]fill up the measure of their
sins. But [d]wrath has come upon them [1]to the utmost.
17 But we, brethren, having been bereft of you for a [1]short while—
[a]in [2]person, not in [3]spirit—were all the more eager with great desire
[b]to see your face.
18 [1]For [a]we wanted to come to you—I, Paul, [2b]more than once—and
yet [c]Satan [d]thwarted us.
19 For who is our hope or [a]joy or crown of exultation? Is it not even
you, in the presence of our Lord Jesus at His [1b]coming?
20 For you are [a]our glory and joy.

[1]Lit., *entrance* . 1:9 [b]2 Thess. 1:10
truggle, conflict 14:5; 16:19-24; Phil. 1:30 [b]Acts 4 [c]Acts 17:1-9 1:1 [e]Phil. 1:30
in deceit [a]Acts [b]2 Thess. 2:11 4:7 [d]2 Cor. 4:2
proves [a]2 Cor. [b]Gal. 2:7 [c]Gal. 10 [d]Rom. 8:27
it., *in a word of y* [a]Acts 20:33; 2:3 [b]Rom. 1:9; 1 Thess. 2:10
6 [1]Or, *been ensome* [a]John , 44; 2 Cor. 4:5 [b]1 Cor. 9:1f.
became gentle e ancient mss. *bes* [3]Lit., *in the dst of you* [4]Or, *es* [a]2 Tim. 2:24 ; 1 Thess. 2:11
Or, *souls* [2]Lit., [a]2 Cor. 12:15; :16 [b]Rom. 1:1 4:16; 2 Thess. ts 18:3 [c]1 Cor. or. 11:9 [d]Rom. 1:1
, *became* [2]Or, *ieve* [a]1 Thess. 5 [b]2 Cor. 1:12; 1 Thess. 1:5
[1]Or, *testifying* ss. 5:14 [b]Luke 8; 1 Thess. 4:6 4:14; 1 Thess. 2:7
ph. 4:1 [b]Rom. 1 Thess. 5:24; s. 2:14 [c]2 Cor. 4:6; 1 Pet. 5:10
1. 1:8; 1 Thess. m. 10:17; Heb. att. 10:20; Gal. 14 [d]Heb. 4:12
[a]1 Thess. 1:6 or. 7:17; 10:32 22 [d]Acts 17:5; s. 3:4; 2 Thess. [e]Heb. 10:33f.
persecuted us d [a]Luke 24:20; 23 [b]Matt. 5:12; Acts 7:52
[1]Or, *forever* or *ner* [a]Acts 9:23; 50; 14:2, 5, 19; 18:12; 21:21f., 25:2, 7 [b]1 Cor. 3 [c]Gen. 15:16; 23; Matt. 23:32 [d]1 Thess. 1:10
occasion of an [2]Lit., *face* [3]Lit., *art* [a]1 Cor. 5:3 [b]1 Thess. 3:10
Because [2]Lit., *once and twice* n. 15:22 [b]Phil. tt. 4:10 [d]Rom. 1:13; 15:22
resence [a]Phil. tt. 16:27; Mark 8; John 21:22; :13; 4:15; 5:23
0 [a]2 Cor. 1:14

Chapter 3

3 Therefore [a]when we could endure *it* no longer, we thought it
best to be left behind at [b]Athens alone;
2 and we sent [a]Timothy, our brother and God's fellow worker in
the gospel of Christ, to strengthen and encourage you as to your
faith,
3 so that no man may be [1]disturbed by these afflictions; for you
yourselves know that [a]we have been destined for this.
4 For indeed when we were with you, we *kept* telling you in ad-
vance that we were going to suffer affliction; [1a]and so it came to pass,
[2]as you know.
5 For this reason, [a]when I could endure *it* no longer, I also [b]sent to
[1]find out about your faith, for fear that [c]the tempter might have
tempted you, and [d]our labor should be in vain.
6 But now that [a]Timothy has come to us from you, and has
brought us good news of [b]your faith and love, and that you always
[c]think kindly of us, longing to see us just as we also long to see you,
7 for this reason, brethren, in all our distress and affliction we
were comforted about you through your faith;
8 for now we *really* live, if you [a]stand firm in the Lord.
9 For [a]what thanks can we render to God for you in return for all
the joy with which we rejoice before our God on your account,
10 as we [a]night and day keep praying most earnestly that we may
[b]see your face, and may [c]complete what is lacking in your faith?
11 [a]Now may [b]our God and Father [c]Himself and Jesus our Lord
[d]direct our way to you;
12 and may the Lord cause you to increase and [a]abound in love for
one another, and for all men, just as we also *do* for you;
13 so that He may [a]establish your hearts [b]unblamable in holiness
before [c]our God and Father at the [1d]coming of our Lord Jesus [e]with
all His [2]saints.

Chapter 4

4 [a]Finally then, [b]brethren, we request and exhort you in the Lord
Jesus, that, as you received from us *instruction* as to how you
ought to [1c]walk and [d]please God (just as you actually do [1]walk), that
you may [e]excel still more.
2 For you know what commandments we gave you [1]by *the
authority of* the Lord Jesus.
3 For this is the will of God, your sanctification; *that is,* that you
[a]abstain from [1]sexual immorality;
4 that [a]each of you know how to [1]possess his own [2b]vessel in
sanctification and [c]honor,
5 not in [1a]lustful passion, like the Gentiles who [b]do not know God;
6 *and* that no man transgress and [a]defraud his brother [b]in the mat-
ter because [c]the Lord is *the* avenger in all these things, just as we also
[d]told you before and solemnly warned *you.*
7 For [a]God has not called us for [b]the purpose of impurity, but [1]in
sanctification.
8 Consequently, he who rejects *this* is not rejecting man but the
God who [a]gives His Holy Spirit to you.
9 Now as to the [a]love of the brethren, you [b]have no need for *anyone*

3:1 [a]1 The
17:15f.
2 [a]2 Cor. 1
3 [1]Or, *dec*
9:16; 14:22
4 [1]Lit., *just*
and [a]1 The
5 [1]Or, *to kn*
ascertain [a]
1 Thess. 3:
3:2 [c]Matt. 4
6:1; Phil. 2:
6 [a]Acts 18.
1:3 [c]1 Cor.
8 [a]1 Cor. 1
9 [a]1 Thess
10 [a]2 Tim.
[b]1 Thess. 2:
13:9
11 [a]2 Thess
1:4; 1 Thess
[c]1 Thess. 4:
2 Thess. 2:
Rev. 21:3 [d]
12 [a]Phil. 1:
4:1, 10; 2 Th
13 [1]Or, *pres*
holy ones [a]
1 Thess. 3:2
[c]Gal. 1:4; 1
[d]1 Thess. 2:
25:31; Mark
1 Thess. 4:1
1:7
4:1 [1]Or, *con*
yourselves
13:11; 2 The
[b]Gal. 6:1; 1
2 Thess. 1:3
13 [c]Eph. 4:1
5:9 [e]Phil. 1:
3:12; 4:10; 2
2 [1]Lit., *throu*
3 [1]Or, *fornic*
[a]1 Cor. 6:18
4 [1]Or, *acqui*
body; or poss
[a]1 Cor. 7:2, 9
4:7; 1 Pet. 3:
1:24
5 [1]Lit., *pass*
[a]Rom. 1:26 [b]
6 [a]1 Cor. 6:8
7:11 [c]Rom.
Heb. 13:4 [d]L
1 Thess. 2:11
7 [1]I.e., in the
sphere of [a]1
[b]1 Thess. 2:3
8 [a]Rom. 5:5;
1:22; Gal. 4:6
3:24
9 [a]John 13:3
12:10 [b]2 Cor
1 Thess. 5:1

to write to you, for you yourselves are [c]taught by God to love one
another;
10 for indeed [a]you do practice it toward all the brethren who are in
all Macedonia. But we urge you, brethren, to [b]excel still more,
11 and to make it your ambition [a]to lead a quiet life and [b]attend to
your own business and [c]work with your hands, just as we com-
manded you;
12 so that you may [1a]behave properly toward [b]outsiders and [2c]not
be in any need.
13 But [a]we do not want you to be uninformed, brethren, about
those who [b]are asleep, that you may not grieve, as do [c]the rest who
have [d]no hope.
14 For if we believe that Jesus died and rose again, [a]even so God
will bring with Him [b]those who have fallen asleep [1]in Jesus.
15 For this we say to you [a]by the word of the Lord, that [b]we who are
alive, [1]and remain until [c]the coming of the Lord, shall not precede
[d]those who have fallen asleep.
16 For the Lord [a]Himself [b]will descend from heaven with a [1c]shout,
with the voice of [d]*the* archangel, and with the [e]trumpet of God; and
[f]the dead in Christ shall rise first.
17 Then [a]we who are alive [1]and remain shall be [b]caught up together
with them [c]in the clouds to meet the Lord in the air, and thus we
shall always [d]be with the Lord.
18 Therefore comfort one another with these words.

Chapter 5

5 Now as to the [a]times and the epochs, brethren, you [b]have no
need of anything to be written to you.
2 For you yourselves know full well that [a]the day of the Lord [1]will
come [b]just like a thief in the night.
3 While they are saying, "[a]Peace and safety!" then [1b]destruction
[2]will come upon them suddenly like [c]birth pangs upon a woman
with child; and they shall not escape.
4 But you, brethren, are not in [a]darkness, that the day should over-
take you [1b]like a thief;
5 for you are all [a]sons of light and sons of day. We are not of night
nor of [b]darkness;
6 so then let us not [a]sleep as [1b]others do, but let us be alert and
[2c]sober.
7 For those who sleep do their sleeping at night, and those who
get drunk get [a]drunk at night.
8 But since [a]we are of *the* day, let us [b]be [1]sober, having put on the
[c]breastplate of [d]faith and love, and as a [e]helmet, the [f]hope of salva-
tion.
9 For God has not destined us for [a]wrath, but for [b]obtaining salva-
tion through our Lord Jesus Christ,
10 [a]who died for us, that whether we are awake or asleep, we may
live together with Him.
11 Therefore [1]encourage one another, and [a]build up one another,
just as you also are doing.
12 But we request of you, brethren, that you [1a]appreciate those [b]who
diligently labor among you, and [c]have charge over you in the Lord
and give you [2]instruction,

13 and that you esteem them very highly in love because of their
work. [a]Live in peace with one another.
14 And we urge you, brethren, admonish [a]the [1]unruly, encourage
[b]the fainthearted, help [c]the weak, be [d]patient with all men.
15 See that [a]no one repays another with evil for evil, but always
[b]seek after that which is good for one another and for all men.
16 [a]Rejoice always;
17 [a]pray without ceasing;
18 in everything [a]give thanks; for this is God's will for you in Christ
Jesus.
19 [a]Do not quench the Spirit;
20 do not despise [a]prophetic [1]utterances.
21 But [a]examine everything *carefully*; [b]hold fast to that which is
good;
22 abstain from every [1]form of evil.
23 Now [a]may the God of peace [b]Himself sanctify you entirely; and
may your [c]spirit and soul and body be preserved complete, [d]without
blame at [e]the coming of our Lord Jesus Christ.
24 [a]Faithful is He who [b]calls you, and He also will bring it to pass.
25 Brethren, [a]pray for us[1].
26 [a]Greet all the brethren with a holy kiss.
27 I adjure you by the Lord to [a]have this letter read to all the
[b]brethren.
28 [a]The grace of our Lord Jesus Christ be with you.

13 [a]Mark 9
14 [1]Or, *un*
[a]2 Thess. 3
35:4 [c]Rom
1 Cor. 8:7ff
[d]1 Cor. 13:
15 [a]Matt. 5
12:17; 1 Pe
12:9; Gal. 6
1 Thess. 5:
16 [a]Phil. 4
17 [a]Eph. 6
18 [a]Eph. 5
19 [a]Eph. 4
20 [1]Or, *gift*
1 Cor. 14:3
21 [a]1 Cor.
1 John 4:1
Gal. 6:10; 1
22 [1]Or, *app*
23 [a]Rom.
[b]1 Thess. 3
1:46f.; Heb.
[d]James 1:4
[e]1 Thess. 2:
24 [a]1 Cor.
3:3 [b]1 Thes
25 [1]Some r
also [a]Eph.
2 Thess. 3:
26 [a]Rom. 1
27 [a]Col. 4:
28 [a]Rom. 1
2 Thess. 3:1

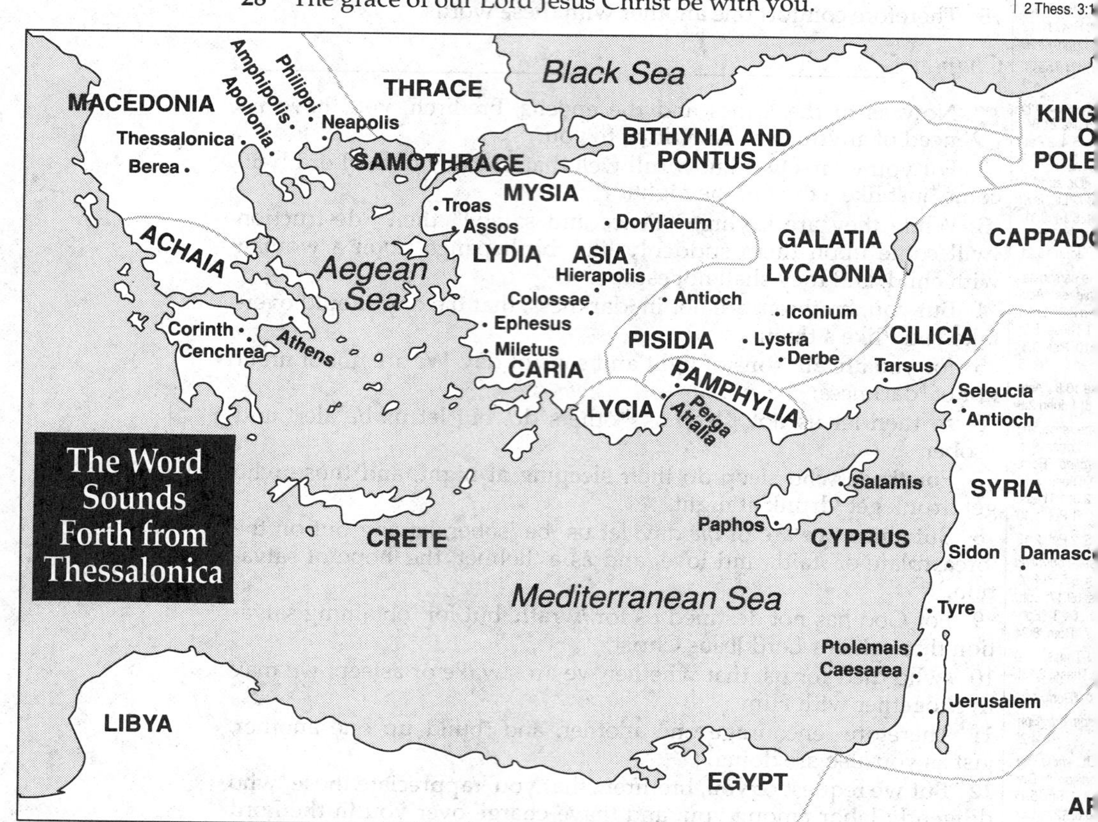

The Word Sounds Forth from Thessalonica

1 Thessalonians Observations Chart

r

Who wrote 1 Thessalonians?

What relationship did these men have to one another?

Had they worked together before? If so, where? How? Why?

Describe the ministry these men had among the recipients

Recipients

Who are they?

What was their relationship to the author(s)?

What was their condition when the author(s) first ministered to them? Who were they serving?

What conditions were they in when the letter was written?

How strongly did the author(s) feel about the recipients?

Did they think of them often? How do you know?

What comparisons shows the kind of love the author(s) feel for them?

What had the recipients become?

lems/Concerns/Struggles

(continued)

1 Thessalonians 4:13-18

Those who have fallen asleep	Those who are alive and remain	Progression of eve

1 Thessalonians at a Glance

Theme of 1 Thessalonians:

Author:

Date:

Purpose:

Key Words:

gospel (word)

faith

love

hope

Lord Jesus Christ (any reference to Jesus)

God

Holy Spirit

affliction (tribulation, sufferings)

of the Lord

day of the Lord

Segment Divisions	Chapter Themes
	1
	2
	3
	4
	5

THESSALONIANS

ad been four to six months since Paul wrote in A.D. 51 his first epistle to the church at .onica. Their persecution had not subsided, but much to Paul's joy, his labor had not been in ey had withstood the attacks of the tempter.

vever, Paul was concerned about some things in the church. Once again, during his second nary journey, he had to take time to write with his own hand—he couldn't dictate this letter to a The church had to know without a doubt it was from him.

GS TO DO

: you haven't studied 1 Thessalonians, you should before you begin 2 Thessalonians. However, if ou've worked through 1 Thessalonians, then read it once again. Observe what Paul says about ie coming of the Lord Jesus. Also give special attention to 1 Thessalonians 4:13 through 5:11.

Jow read 2 Thessalonians. Watch how 1 Thessalonians ties in with 2 Thessalonians. Look for the ›llowing information and record it on the OBSERVATIONS CHART on page 1763.

. What do you learn about the author and the recipients of this letter? What are the circumstances of the recipients? Have things changed since Paul's day?

. Paul addresses several problems which need correction. List these in the margin and on the chart. This will help you see the author's purpose in writing. Then note the instructions or commands related to each problem addressed. List these on your OBSERVATIONS CHART.

. Paul also praises the Thessalonians and encourages them about the things they are doing well. List the exhortations he includes in his letter.

ı. Be certain you record what happens to those who do not obey the gospel.

. From what you have observed about the author and the recipients, why do you think Paul wrote this book? Record this on 2 THESSALONIANS AT A GLANCE on page 1762 under "Purpose."

Read through 2 Thessalonians again, a chapter at a time, doing the following.

ı. Mark the key words (including their synonyms and pronouns) listed on 2 THESSALONIANS AT A GLANCE. Also watch for any words you feel are key but aren't listed.

›. Now go back through the key words and in the margin make a list of what you have learned. Make one list for each word. In other words, you will have one list of everything these three chapters teach about *the coming of Christ*, one list for *affliction and suffering*, one list for *the day of the Lord*, and so on.

On the OBSERVATIONS CHART are two more headings: "When the Day of the Lord Comes" and "When the Man of Lawlessness Is Revealed."

ı. Carefully read 2 Thessalonians 2:1-12 and list everything the chapter says must happen before the day of the Lord can come.

›. Do the same for the revelation of the man of lawlessness.

:. Record your insights on the chart THE DAY OF THE LORD in the appendix (page 1878).

Think through each chapter and record its theme on 2 THESSALONIANS AT A GLANCE and in the appropriate place in the text. Also record the theme of the book, author, date, and purpose.

GS TO THINK ABOUT

How do you react in trials? How do you respond to persecution? Does your response glorify God? Do people see your faith? Is His love evident?

2. Do you lead a disciplined life? Does your lifestyle encourage laziness in others? Or can "Follow my example"? Are you doing your share for the furtherance of the kingdom, or just waiting for Jesus to come back?

3. When the good you do doesn't seem appreciated—or even noticed—how do you feel? Fo are you doing it? Will you persevere?

4. Does what you believe about prophecy or any other doctrine come from a careful, person of God's Word or is it from what others teach you? Are you holding fast to what you kno Word of God—or are you easily persuaded by "faddish" teaching?

Chapter 1 ______________________________

1 [a]Paul and [b]Silvanus and [c]Timothy to the [d]church of the Thes-
salonians in God our Father and the Lord Jesus Christ:
2 [a]Grace to you and peace from God the Father and the Lord Jesus
Christ.
3 We ought always [a]to give thanks to God for you, [b]brethren, as is
only fitting, because your faith is greatly enlarged, and the [c]love of
each one of you toward one another grows *ever* greater;
4 therefore, we ourselves [a]speak proudly of you among [b]the
churches of God for your [1]perseverance and faith [b]in the midst of all
your persecutions and afflictions which you endure.
5 *This is* a [a]plain indication of God's righteous judgment so that
you may be [b]considered worthy of the kingdom of God, for which
indeed you are suffering.
6 [1]For after all [a]it is *only* just [2]for God to repay with affliction those
who afflict you,
7 and *to give* relief to you who are afflicted [1]and to us as well
[2a]when the Lord Jesus shall be revealed [b]from heaven [c]with [3]His
mighty angels [d]in flaming fire,
8 dealing out retribution to those who [a]do not know God and to
those who [b]do not obey the gospel of our Lord Jesus.
9 And these will pay the penalty of [a]eternal destruction, [b]away
from the presence of the Lord and from the glory of His power,
10 when He comes to be [a]glorified [1]in His [2]saints on that [b]day, and
to be marveled at among all who have believed—for our [c]testimony
to you was believed.
11 To this end also we [a]pray for you always that our God may
[1b]count you worthy of your [c]calling, and fulfill every desire for
[d]goodness and the [e]work of faith with power;
12 in order that the [a]name of our Lord Jesus may be glorified in
you, and you in Him, according to the grace of our God and [1]the
Lord Jesus Christ.

Chapter 2 ______________________________

2 Now we request you, [a]brethren, with regard to the [1b]coming of
our Lord Jesus Christ, and our [c]gathering together to Him,
2 that you may not be quickly shaken from your [1]composure or be
disturbed either by a [a]spirit or a [2b]message or a [c]letter as if from us, to
the effect that [d]the day of the Lord [e]has come.
3 [a]Let no one in any way deceive you, for *it will not come* unless the
[1b]apostasy comes first, and the [c]man of [2]lawlessness is revealed, the
[d]son of destruction,
4 who opposes and exalts himself above [1a]every so-called god or

1:1 [a]1 The [b]2 Cor. 1:1 [d]Acts 17:1
2 [a]Rom. 1
3 [a]Rom. 1 1 Thess. 1 2:13 [b]1 Th 2 Thess. 2 3:12
4 [1]Or, *stea* [a]2 Cor. 7:4 2:19 [b]1 Co 1 Thess. 2
5 [a]Phil. 1:2 20:35; 2 Th
6 [1]Lit., *If ir the sight o* Col. 3:25; I
7 [1]Lit., *alo* [2]Lit., *at the the Lord Je angels of H* [a]Luke 17:3 4:16 [c]Jude 19:18; Is. 6 1:13; Dan. 25:41; 1 Co 10:27; 12:2 Jude 7; Rev
8 [a]Gal. 4:8
9 [a]Phil. 3:1 5:3 [b]Is. 2:1 2 Thess. 2:
10 [1]Or, *in t of* [2]Or, *holy* 49:3; John 1 1 Thess. 2:1 2:11ff.; 1 Co [c]1 Cor. 1:6;
11 [1]Or, *ma* [b]2 Thess. 1: 11:29 [d]Rom [e]1 Thess. 1:
12 [1]Or omit 24:15; 66:5; Phil. 2:9ff.
2:1 [1]Or, *pre* [a]2 Thess. 1: 2:19 [c]Mark 1 Thess. 4:1
2 [1]Lit., *mino* [a]1 Cor. 14:3 4:1 [b]1 Thess 2 Thess. 2:1 3:17 [d]1 Cor. 7:26
3 [1]Or, *falling the faith* [2]So mss. read *si* 5:6 [b]1 Tim. 4 7:25; 8:25; 1 2 Thess. 2:8 13:5ff. [d]John
4 [1]Or, *all tha God* [a]1 Cor.

object of worship, so that he takes his seat in the temple of God,
[b]displaying himself as being God.
5 Do you not remember that [a]while I was still with you, I was
telling you these things?
6 And you know [a]what restrains him now, so that in his time he
may be revealed.
7 For [a]the mystery of lawlessness is already at work; only [b]he who
now restrains *will do so* until he is taken out of the way.
8 And then that lawless one [a]will be revealed whom the Lord will
slay [b]with the breath of His mouth and bring to an end by the [c]ap-
pearance of His [1]coming;
9 *that is,* the one whose [1]coming is in accord with the activity of
[a]Satan, with all power and [2b]signs and false wonders,
10 and with [1]all the deception of wickedness for [a]those who perish,
because they did not receive the love of [b]the truth so as to be saved.
11 And for this reason [a]God [1]will send upon them [2]a [b]deluding
influence so that they might believe [3]what is false,
12 in order that they all may be [1]judged who [a]did not believe the
truth, but [2b]took pleasure in wickedness.
13 [a]But we should always give thanks to God for you, [b]brethren
beloved by the Lord, because [c]God has chosen you [1]from the begin-
ning [d]for salvation [2e]through sanctification [3]by the Spirit and faith in
the truth.
14 And it was for this He [a]called you through [b]our gospel, [1]that you
may gain the glory of our Lord Jesus Christ.
15 So then, brethren, [a]stand firm and [b]hold to the traditions which
you were taught, whether [c]by word *of mouth* or [c]by letter [1]from us.
16 [a]Now may our Lord Jesus Christ [a]Himself and God our Father,
who has [b]loved us and given us eternal comfort and [c]good hope by
grace,
17 [a]comfort and [b]strengthen your hearts in every good work and
word.

Chapter 3 __________

3 [a]Finally, brethren, [b]pray for us that [c]the word of the Lord may
[1]spread rapidly and be glorified, just as *it did* also with you;
2 and that we may be [a]delivered from [1]perverse and evil men; for
not all have [2]faith.
3 But [a]the Lord is faithful, and [1]He will strengthen and protect you
[2]from [b]the evil *one.*
4 And we have [a]confidence in the Lord concerning you, that you
[b]are doing and will *continue to* do what we command.
5 And may the Lord [a]direct your hearts into the love of God and
into the steadfastness of Christ.
6 Now we command you, brethren, [a]in the name of our Lord Jesus
Christ, that you [1b]keep aloof from every brother who [2]leads an [3c]un-
ruly life and not according to [d]the tradition which [4]you received
from us.
7 For you yourselves know how you ought to [1a]follow our ex-
ample, because we did not act in an undisciplined manner among
you,
8 nor did we [a]eat [1]anyone's bread [2]without paying for it, but with
[b]labor and hardship we *kept* [c]working night and day so that we
might not be a burden to any of you;

14; Ezek. 28:2
[a]1 Thess. 3:4
[a]2 Thess. 2:7
[a]Rev. 17:5, 7 [b]2 Thess. 2:6
resence [a]Dan. 5; 8:25; 11:36; hess. 2:3; Rev. [b]Is. 11:4; Rev. 19:15 [c]1 Tim. n. 1:10; 4:1, 8; Titus 2:13
presence [2]Or, esting miracles att. 4:10 [b]Matt. :24; John 4:48
10 [1]Or, *every* n [a]1 Cor. 1:18 hess. 2:12, 13
sends [2]Lit., *an* error [3]Or, *the* n. 22:22; Rom. [b]1 Thess. 2:3; 2 Tim. 4:4
Or, *condemned* proved [a]Rom. n. 1:32; 1 Cor. 13:6
e ancient mss. t fruits [2]Lit., *in* [a]2 Thess. 1:3 ess. 1:4 [c]Eph. [d]1 Cor. 1:21; ess. 2:12; 5:9; 1:5 [e]1 Thess. 4:7; 1 Pet. 1:2
to the gaining [a]1 Thess. 2:12 [b]1 Thess. 1:5
Lit., *of* [a]1 Cor. 3 [b]1 Cor. 11:2; 3:6 [c]2 Thess. 2:2
[a]1 Thess. 3:11 :16 [c]Titus 3:7; 1 Pet. 1:3
Thess. 3:2, 13 [b]2 Thess. 3:3
run [a]1 Thess. [b]1 Thess. 5:25 [c]1 Thess. 1:8
improper [2]Or, n [a]Rom. 15:31
, will [2]Or, *from* vil [a]1 Cor. 1:9; ss. 5:24 [b]Matt. 5:37
2:3 [b]1 Thess. 4:10
[a]1 Thess. 3:11
oid [2]Lit., *walks disorderly* [3]Or, ciplined [4]Many mss. read *they* Cor. 5:4 [b]Rom. 17; 1 Cor. 5:11; 3:14 [c]1 Thess. Thess. 3:7, 11 11:2; 2 Thess. 2:15
[1]Lit., *imitate us* . 1:6; 2 Thess. 3:9
., from anyone ely [a]1 Cor. 9:4 ess. 2:9 [c]Acts 8:3; Eph. 4:28

9 not because we do not have [a]the right *to this,* but in order to offer
ourselves [b]as a model for you, that you might [1]follow our example.
10 For even [a]when we were with you, we used to give you this
order: [b]if anyone will not work, neither let him eat.
11 For we hear that some among you are [a]leading an undisciplined
life, doing no work at all, but acting like [b]busybodies.
12 Now such persons we command and [a]exhort in the Lord Jesus
Christ to [b]work in quiet fashion and eat their own bread.
13 But as for you, [a]brethren, [b]do not grow weary of doing good.
14 And if anyone does not obey our [1]instruction [2a]in this letter, take
special note of that man [3b]and do not associate with him, so that he
may be [c]put to shame.
15 And *yet* [a]do not regard him as an enemy, but [1b]admonish him as
a [c]brother.
16 Now [a]may the Lord of peace [b]Himself continually grant you
peace in every [1]circumstance. [c]The Lord be with you all!
17 [1]I, Paul, write this greeting [a]with my own hand, and this is a
distinguishing mark in every letter; this is the way I write.
18 [a]The grace of our Lord Jesus Christ be with you all.

9 [1]Lit., *imitate* [a]1 Cor. 9:4ff. 3:7
10 [a]1 Thess. [b]1 Thess. 4:11
11 [a]2 Thess. [b]1 Tim. 5:13;
12 [a]1 Thess. [b]1 Thess. 4:11
13 [a]1 Thess. [b]2 Cor. 4:1; G
14 [1]Lit., *word through* [3]Lit., *associate* [a]C [b]2 Thess. 3:6 4:14
15 [1]Or, *keep admonishing* [b]1 Thess. 5:14 [c]2 Thess. 3:6,
16 [1]Lit., *way* 15:33 [b]1 Thes [c]Ruth 2:4
17 [1]Lit., *The my hand of P* 16:21
18 [a]Rom. 16: 1 Thess. 5:28

2 Thessalonians at a Glance

Author:

Date:

Purpose:

Key Words:
- affliction
- suffering (persecutions)
- coming of Jesus Christ (or synonymous references)
- God
- Spirit
- glory (glorified)
- man of lawlessness
- undisciplined (unruly)
- day of the Lord (and relative pronouns)
- truth

Theme of 2 Thessalonians:

Segment Divisions

	Chapter Themes
	1
	2
	3

2 Thessalonians Observations Chart

Recipients

Those Who Do Not Obey the Gospel

ems/Concerns

Instructions

Exhortations

hen the Day of the Lord Comes

When the Man of Lawlessness Is Revealed

1 TIMOTHY

Thirty years of labor for the gospel had taken its toll on Paul. His body bore the brand-mar servant of Jesus Christ (Galatians 6:17). However, the intensity of his sufferings was minor comp the intensity of his love and concern for the churches etched upon his heart.

Undaunted by two years of house arrest in Rome, Paul pressed on toward the prize of th calling in Christ Jesus. He intended to visit Asia, Macedonia, and possibly Spain. Spain had been heart before he became a prisoner of Rome.

He also was concerned about the church at Ephesus. Timothy, his faithful co-laborer, was pas that strategically important church. Possibly concerned that he might be delayed and that Ti might need something in writing to set before others as an ever-present reminder, Paul took qui ink, spread out the parchment, and wrote his first epistle to his beloved son, an epistle which become a legacy for the church and a pillar and support of the truth. It was around A.D. 62.

THINGS TO DO

1. Read 1 Timothy. Note 1:3 and 3:14-15 to see why Paul wrote this epistle. Keep this in mind read the book and then on the 1 TIMOTHY AT A GLANCE chart on page 1770, reco purpose for writing.
2. Read 1 Timothy again, one chapter at a time. On your OBSERVATIONS CHART on page 17
   a. Record how Paul describes himself. Note how he refers to himself, stating his posit authority which qualifies him to instruct Timothy in the matters described in this letter.
   b. Note how Paul describes Timothy, where Timothy is when the letter is written, and wh relationship is to Paul.
   c. Write down the commands and instructions Paul gives about specific groups of peo practices. Record what you learn about overseers (elders) and deacons. Also record wh see about general groups of believers (i.e.: men, women) in the church. There is a desig space for each of these groups on the OBSERVATIONS CHART.
   d. Record the specific charges Paul gives Timothy as his representative in Ephesus and as t who is organizing and instructing the church there.
3. As you read, look for the key words (and their synonyms and pronouns) that are list 1 TIMOTHY AT A GLANCE. These key words give clues about the most important and often-mentioned instructions.
4. In the margin of the chapter, list everything you learn from the text about these key word can learn much about what was important to the health of the church.
5. What do you think is the theme of 1 Timothy? Are there any problems or concerns the must address? How does the theme relate to these concerns? Record the theme of the bo 1 TIMOTHY AT A GLANCE and then list the theme of each chapter on the chart and also text. Finally, fill in any additional information under author, purpose, and so on.

THINGS TO THINK ABOUT

1. Do I operate in my own church according to these principles?
2. How do I esteem my local church leadership?
3. Do I pray on behalf of all men, including those in authority?

Chapter 1

1 Paul, [a]an apostle of [b]Christ Jesus [c]according to the command-
ment of [c]God our Savior, and of [b]Christ Jesus, *who is* our [d]hope;
2 to [a]Timothy, [a]*my* true child in *the* faith: [b]Grace, mercy *and* peace
from God the Father and [c]Christ Jesus our Lord.
3 As I urged you [1]upon my departure for [a]Macedonia, [2]remain on
at [b]Ephesus, in order that you may instruct certain men not to [c]teach
strange doctrines,
4 nor to [1]pay attention to [a]myths and end-
less [b]genealogies, which give rise to mere
[c]speculation rather than [d]*furthering* [2]the ad-
ministration of God which is by faith.
5 But the goal of our [1a]instruction is love
[b]from a pure heart and a [c]good conscience
and a sincere [d]faith.
6 For some men, straying from these
things, have turned aside to [a]fruitless
discussion,
7 [a]wanting to be [b]teachers of the Law,
even though they do not understand either what they are saying or
the matters about which they make confident assertions.
8 But we know that [a]the Law is good, if one uses it lawfully,
9 realizing the fact that [a]law is not made for a righteous man, but
for those who are lawless and [b]rebellious, for the [c]ungodly and sin-
ners, for the unholy and [d]profane, for those who kill their fathers or
mothers, for murderers
10 [1]and [2a]immoral men [1]and [b]homosexuals [1]and [c]kidnappers [1]and
[d]liars [1]and [e]perjurers, and whatever else is contrary to [f]sound teach-
ing,
11 according to [a]the glorious gospel of [b]the blessed God, with which
I have been [c]entrusted.
12 I thank [a]Christ Jesus our Lord, who has [b]strengthened me, be-
cause He considered me faithful, [c]putting me into service;
13 even though I was formerly a blasphemer and a [a]persecutor and
a violent aggressor. And yet I was [b]shown mercy, because [c]I acted
ignorantly in unbelief;
14 and the [a]grace of our Lord was more than abundant, with the
[b]faith and love which are *found* in Christ Jesus.
15 [a]It is a trustworthy statement, deserving full acceptance, that
[b]Christ Jesus came into the world to [c]save sinners, among whom [d]I
am foremost *of all*.
16 And yet for this reason I [a]found mercy, in order that in me as the
foremost, Jesus Christ might [b]demonstrate His perfect patience, as an
example for those [1]who would believe in Him for eternal life.
17 Now to the [a]King [1]eternal, [b]immortal, [c]invisible, the [d]only God,
[e]*be* honor and glory [2]forever and ever. Amen.
18 This [a]command I entrust to you, Timothy, [b]my [1]son, in accord-
ance with the [c]prophecies previously made concerning you, that by
them you may [d]fight the good fight,
19 keeping [a]faith and a good conscience, which some have rejected
and suffered shipwreck in regard to [1b]their faith.
20 [1]Among these are [a]Hymenaeus and [b]Alexander, whom I have
[c]delivered over to Satan, so that they may be [d]taught not to blas-
pheme.

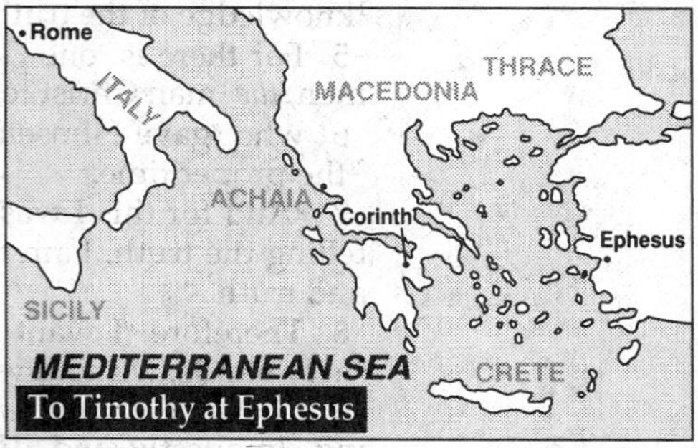
Rome
ITALY
THRACE
MACEDONIA
ACHAIA
Corinth
Ephesus
SICILY
MEDITERRANEAN SEA
CRETE
To Timothy at Ephesus

or. 1:1 [b]1 Tim.
Titus 1:3 [d]Col.
1:27
im. 1:2 [b]Rom.
Tim. 1:2; Titus
4 [c]1 Tim. 1:12
while departing
remain [a]Rom.
6 [b]Acts 18:19
. 16:17; 2 Cor.
al. 1:6f.; 1 Tim.
6:3
4 [1]*Or, occupy*
lves with [2]*Lit.,*
vision [a]1 Tim.
Tim. 4:4; Titus
et. 1:16 [b]Titus
m. 2:23 [d]Eph.
3:2
commandment
. 1:18 [b]2 Tim.
Tim. 1:19; 3:9;
3; 1 Pet. 3:16,
21 [d]2 Tim. 1:5
6 [a]Titus 1:10
nes 3:1 [b]Luke
2:46
Rom. 7:12, 16
23 [b]Titus 1:6,
et. 4:18; Jude
Tim. 4:7; 6:20;
Heb. 12:16
[1]Lit., *for* [2]Or,
rs [a]1 Cor. 6:9
22 [c]Ex. 21:16;
3 [d]Rev. 21:8,
5 [e]Matt. 5:33
:6; 6:3; 2 Tim.
1:9, 13; 2:1, 2
or. 4:4 [b]1 Tim.
6:15 [c]Gal. 2:7
al. 3:26 [b]Acts
il. 4:13; 2 Tim.
17 [c]Acts 9:15
cts 8:3 [b]1 Cor.
25 [c]Acts 26:9
n. 5:20; 1 Cor.
Cor. 4:15; Gal.
[b]1 Thess. 1:3;
15; 4:12; 6:11;
13; 2:22; Titus
2:2
Tim. 3:1; 4:9;
2:11; Titus 3:8
; Luke 15:2ff.;
[c]Rom. 11:14
15:9; Eph. 3:8
Or, destined to
r. 7:25; 1 Tim.
:13 [b]Eph. 2:7
t., of the ages
he ages of the
es [a]Rev. 15:3
16 [c]Col. 1:15
; 1 Tim. 6:15;
Rom. 2:7, 10;
1:36; Heb. 2:7
child [a]1 Tim.
n. 1:2 [c]1 Tim.
[d]2 Cor. 10:4;
; 2 Tim. 2:3f.;
4:7
, the [a]1 Tim.
Tim. 6:12, 21;
2 Tim. 2:18
it., *Of* [a]2 Tim.
[b]2 Tim. 4:14
or. 5:5 [d]1 Cor.
; Heb. 12:5ff.

Chapter 2

2 First of all, then, I urge that [a]entreaties *and* prayers, petitions *and*
thanksgivings, be made on behalf of all men,
2 [a]for kings and all who are in [1]authority, in order that we may
lead a tranquil and quiet life in all godliness and [2]dignity.
3 This is good and acceptable in the sight of [a]God our Savior,
4 [a]who desires all men to be [b]saved and to [c]come to the
[1]knowledge of the truth.
5 For there is [a]one God, *and* [b]one mediator also between God and
men, *the* [c]man Christ Jesus,
6 who [a]gave Himself as a ransom for all, the [b]testimony [1]*borne* at
[2c]the proper time.
7 [a]And for this I was appointed a [1]preacher and [b]an apostle ([c]I am
telling the truth, I am not lying) as a teacher of [d]the Gentiles in faith
and truth.
8 Therefore [a]I want the men [b]in every place to pray, [c]lifting up
[d]holy hands, without wrath and dissension.
9 Likewise, *I want* [a]women to adorn themselves with proper cloth-
ing, [1]modestly and discreetly, not with braided hair and gold or
pearls or costly garments;
10 but rather by means of good works, as befits women making a
claim to godliness.
11 [a]Let a woman quietly receive instruction with entire submissive-
ness.
12 [a]But I do not allow a woman to teach or exercise authority over a
man, but to remain quiet.
13 [a]For it was Adam who was first [1]created, *and* then Eve.
14 And *it was* not Adam *who* was deceived, but [a]the woman being
quite deceived, fell into transgression.
15 But *women* shall be [1]preserved through the bearing of children if
they continue in [a]faith and love and sanctity with [2]self-restraint.

Chapter 3

3 [a]It is a trustworthy statement: if any man aspires to the [b]office of
[1]overseer, it is a fine work he desires *to do.*
2 [1a]An overseer, then, must be above reproach, [b]the husband of one
wife, [c]temperate, prudent, respectable, [d]hospitable, [e]able to teach,
3 [a]not addicted to wine [1]or pugnacious, but gentle, uncontentious,
[b]free from the love of money.
4 *He must be* one who [a]manages his own household well, keeping
his children under control with all dignity
5 (but if a man does not know how to manage his own household,
how will he take care of [a]the church of God?);
6 *and* not a new convert, lest he become [a]conceited and fall into the
[b]condemnation [1]incurred by the devil.
7 And he must [a]have a good reputation with [b]those outside *the
church,* so that he may not fall into reproach and [c]the snare of the
devil.
8 [a]Deacons likewise *must be* men of dignity, not [1]double-tongued,
[2b]or addicted to much wine [2c]or fond of sordid gain,
9 [a]*but* holding to the mystery of the faith with a clear conscience.
10 And [a]let these also first be tested; then let them serve as deacons
if they are beyond reproach.

2:1 [a]Eph
2 [1]Or, *a* [2]Or, *seric* 6:10; Ror
3 [a]Luke 1:1; 4:10
4 [1]Or, *re* [a]Ezek. 18 3:17; 1 Ti 2:11; 2 Pe 11:14 [c]2 Titus 1:1;
5 [a]Rom. 1 Cor. 8:4 Gal. 3:20 Rom. 1:3
6 [1]Or, to *its own tir* 20:28; Ga 1:6 [c]Mark 4:4; 1 Tim 1:3
7 [1]Or, *he* 1 Tim. 1:1 [b]1 Cor. 9:1 [d]Acts 9:15
8 [a]Phil. 1: 5:14; Titus 4:21; 1 Co 2:14; 1 Th 63:4; Luke 24:4; Jam
9 [1]Lit., *wi* [a]1 Pet. 3:3
11 [a]1 Cor. 2:5
12 [a]1 Cor. 2:5
13 [1]Or, *for* 2:7, 22; 3:1 11:8ff.
14 [a]Gen. 3 11:3
15 [1]Lit., *sa discretion*
3:1 [1]Or, *bis* 1:15 [b]Acts 1:1
2 [1]Lit., *The* 3:2-4; Titus 2:36f.; 1 Tin 1:6 [c]1 Tim. Titus 2:2 [d]F Titus 1:8; H 1 Pet. 4:9 [e]
3 [1]Lit., *not* [b]1 Tim. 3:8; 1:7; Heb. 13
4 [a]1 Tim. 3:
5 [a]1 Cor. 10 3:15
6 [1]Lit., *of th* [a]1 Tim. 6:4; [b]1 Tim. 3:7
7 [a]2 Cor. 8:2 4:11 [c]1 Tim. 2:26
8 [1]Or, *given double-talk* [a]Phil. 1:1; 1 T [b]1 Tim. 5:23; [c]1 Tim. 3:3; T 1 Pet. 5:2
9 [a]1 Tim. 1:5
10 [a]1 Tim. 5

11 [1]Women *must* likewise *be* dignified, [a]not malicious gossips, but
[b]temperate, faithful in all things.
12 Let [a]deacons be [b]husbands of *only* one wife, *and* [1c]good managers
of *their* children and their own households.
13 For those who have served well as deacons [a]obtain for them-
selves a [1]high standing and great confidence in the faith that is in
Christ Jesus.
14 I am writing these things to you, hoping to come to you before
long;
15 but [1]in case I am delayed, *I write* so that you may know how [2]one
ought to conduct himself in [a]the household of God, which is the
[b]church of [c]the living God, the [d]pillar and support of the truth.
16 And by common confession great is [a]the mystery of godliness:
[1]He who was [b]revealed in the flesh,
Was [2c]vindicated [3]in the Spirit,
[d]Beheld by angels,
[e]Proclaimed among the nations,
[f]Believed on in the world,
[g]Taken up in glory.

Chapter 4

4 But [a]the Spirit explicitly says that [b]in later times some will fall
away from the faith, paying attention to [c]deceitful spirits and
[d]doctrines of demons,
2 by means of the hypocrisy of liars [a]seared in their own con-
science as with a branding iron,
3 *men* who [a]forbid marriage *and advocate* [b]abstaining from foods,
which [c]God has created to be [d]gratefully shared in by those who
believe and know the truth.
4 For [a]everything created by God is good, and nothing is to be
rejected, if it is [b]received with gratitude;
5 for it is sanctified by means of [a]the word of God and prayer.
6 In pointing out these things to [a]the brethren, you will be a good
[b]servant of Christ Jesus, *constantly* nourished on the words of the
faith and of the [1c]sound doctrine which you [d]have been following.
7 But have nothing to do with [a]worldly [b]fables fit only for old
women. On the other hand, discipline yourself for the purpose of
[c]godliness;
8 for [a]bodily discipline is only of little profit, but [b]godliness is
profitable for all things, since it [c]holds promise for the [d]present life
and *also* for the *life* to come.
9 [a]It is a trustworthy statement deserving full acceptance.
10 For it is for this we labor and strive, because we have fixed [a]our
hope on [b]the living God, who is [c]the Savior of all men, especially of
believers.
11 [1a]Prescribe and teach these things.
12 [a]Let no one look down on your youthfulness, but *rather* in
speech, conduct, [b]love, faith *and* purity, show yourself [c]an example
[1]of those who believe.
13 [a]Until I come, give attention to the *public* [b]reading *of Scripture,* to
exhortation and teaching.
14 Do not neglect the spiritual gift within you, which was bestowed
upon you through [a]prophetic utterance with [b]the laying on of hands
by the [1c]presbytery.

deacons' conesses ; Titus 2:3 1 Tim. 3:2
aging well 1 Tim. 3:8 [c]1 Tim. 3:4
ood [a]Matt. 25:21
delay [2]Or, *to conduct* Cor. 3:16; Eph. 2:21f.; 17 [b]1 Tim. :16; 1 Tim. 2:9; 2 Tim. 2:19
later mss. Or, *justified* Rom. 16:25 1 Pet. 1:20; 5, 8 [c]Rom. 2:13; 24:4; :12 [e]Rom. . 1:19; Col. Thess. 1:10 9; Acts 1:9
16:13; Acts 1:11; 1 Cor. hess. 2:3ff.; ; 2 Pet. 3:3; [c]1 John 4:6 James 3:15
[a]Eph. 4:19
. 13:4 [b]Col. [c]Gen. 1:29; 14:6; 1 Cor. .; 1 Tim. 4:4
0:26 [b]Rom. Cor. 10:30f.; 1 Tim. 4:3
25, 31; Heb. 11:3
good [a]Acts 2 Cor. 11:23 0 [d]Luke 1:3; 0, 22; 2 Tim. 3:10
. 1:9 [b]1 Tim. . 4:8; 6:3, 5f.; 2 Tim. 3:5
2:23 [b]1 Tim. 5f.; 2 Tim. 3:5 7:9, 11; Prov. :4; Matt. 6:33 ; 12:32; Mark 10:30
[a]1 Tim. 1:15
. 1:10; 1 Tim. [b]1 Tim. 3:15 42; 1 Tim. 2:4
11 [1]Or, *Keep* *nmanding and* 1 Tim. 5:7; 6:2
[1]Or, *to* [a]1 Cor. :11; Titus 2:15 14 [c]Titus 2:7; 1 Pet. 5:3
. 3:14 [b]2 Tim. 3:15ff.
board of elders :18 [b]Acts 6:6; :22; 2 Tim. 1:6 [c]Acts 11:30

15 Take pains with these things; be *absorbed* in them, so that your
progress may be evident to all.
16 [a]Pay close attention to yourself and to your teaching; persevere
in these things; for as you do this you will [1b]insure salvation both for
yourself and for those who hear you.

Chapter 5

5 [a]Do not sharply rebuke an [b]older man, but *rather* appeal to *him* as
a father, *to* [c]the younger men as brothers,
2 the older women as mothers, *and* the younger women as sisters,
in all purity.
3 Honor widows who are [a]widows indeed;
4 but if any widow has children or grandchildren, [a]let them first
learn to practice piety in regard to their own family, and to [1]make
some return to their parents; for this is [b]acceptable in the sight of
God.
5 Now she who is a [a]widow indeed, and who has been left alone
[b]has fixed her hope on God, and continues in [c]entreaties and prayers
night and day.
6 But she who [a]gives herself to wanton pleasure is [b]dead even
while she lives.
7 [1a]Prescribe these things as well, so that they may be above re-
proach.
8 But if anyone does not provide for his own, and especially for
those of his household, he has [a]denied the faith, and is worse than an
unbeliever.
9 Let a widow be [a]put on the list only if she is not less than sixty
years old, *having been* [b]the wife of one man,
10 having a reputation for [a]good works; *and* if she has brought up
children, if she has [b]shown hospitality to strangers, if she [c]has
washed the [1]saints' feet, if she has [d]assisted those in distress, *and* if
she has devoted herself to every good work.
11 But refuse *to put* younger widows *on the list*, for when they feel
[a]sensual desires in disregard of Christ, they want to get married,
12 *thus* incurring condemnation, because they have set aside their
previous [1]pledge.
13 And at the same time they also learn *to be* idle, as they go around
from house to house; and not merely idle, but also [a]gossips and
[b]busybodies, talking about [c]things not proper *to mention*.
14 Therefore, I want younger *widows* to get [a]married, bear children,
[b]keep house, *and* [c]give the enemy no occasion for reproach;
15 for some [a]have already turned aside to follow [b]Satan.
16 If any woman who is a believer [a]has *dependent* widows, let her
[b]assist them, and let not the church be burdened, so that it may assist
those who are [c]widows indeed.
17 Let [a]the elders who [b]rule well be considered worthy of double
honor, especially those who [c]work hard [1]at preaching and teaching.
18 For the Scripture says, "[a]YOU SHALL NOT MUZZLE THE OX WHILE HE IS
THRESHING," and "[b]The laborer is worthy of his wages."
19 Do not receive an accusation against an [a]elder except on the basis
of [b]two or three witnesses.
20 Those who continue in sin, [a]rebuke in the presence of all, [b]so that
the rest also may be fearful *of sinning*.
21 [a]I solemnly charge you in the presence of God and of Christ

16 [1]Lit., *yourself* [a]Acts 20:
5:1 [a]Lev. 2:2 [c]Titu
3 [a]Acts 6 1 Tim. 5:5
4 [1]Lit., *gi recomper* 6:2 [b]1 Tir
5 [a]Acts 6 1 Tim. 5:3 7:34; 1 Pe 2:37; 1 Tir 1:3
6 [a]James 15:24; 2 T 3:1
7 [1]Or, *Kee command* 4:11
8 [a]2 Tim. 1:16; 2 Pet
9 [a]1 Tim. 5 3:2
10 [1]Or, *ho* 9:36; 1 Tim 2:7; 3:8; 1 P [b]1 Tim. 3:2 John 13:14
11 [a]Rev. 18
12 [1]Lit., *fai*
13 [a]3 John [b]2 Thess. 3 1:11
14 [a]1 Cor. 7 4:3 [b]Titus 2 6:1
15 [a]1 Tim. 1 4:10
16 [a]1 Tim. 5 5:10 [c]1 Tim.
17 [1]Lit., *in w* 11:30; 1 Tim. [b]Rom. 12:8 5:12
18 [a]Deut. 25 9:9 [b]Lev. 19: 24:15; Matt. 1 10:7; 1 Cor. 9
19 [a]Acts 11:3 4:14; 5:17 [b]D 19:15; Matt. 1
20 [a]Gal. 2:14 5:11; 2 Tim. 4 7:11
21 [a]Luke 9:26 6:13; 2 Tim. 2

Jesus and of *His* chosen angels, to maintain these *principles* without
bias, doing nothing in a *spirit of* partiality.
22 [a]Do not lay hands upon anyone *too* hastily and [1]thus share
[b]*responsibility for* the sins of others; keep yourself [2]free from sin.
23 No longer drink water *exclusively,* but [a]use a little wine for the
sake of your stomach and your frequent ailments.
24 The sins of some men are quite evident, going before them to
judgment; for others, their *sins* [a]follow after.
25 Likewise also, deeds that are good are quite evident, and [a]those
which are otherwise cannot be concealed.

Chapter 6

6 [a]Let all who are under the yoke as slaves regard their own
masters as worthy of all honor so [b]that the name of God and *our*
doctrine may not be spoken against.
2 And let those who have believers as their masters not be dis-
respectful to them because they are [a]brethren, but let them serve
them all the more, because those who [1]partake of the benefit are
believers and beloved. [b]Teach and [2]preach these *principles.*
3 If anyone [a]advocates a different doctrine, and does not [1]agree
with [b]sound words, those of our Lord Jesus Christ, and with the
doctrine [c]conforming to godliness,
4 he is [a]conceited *and* understands nothing; but he [1]has a morbid
interest in [b]controversial questions and [c]disputes about words, out of
which arise envy, strife, abusive language, evil suspicions,
5 and constant friction between [a]men of depraved mind and de-
prived of the truth, who [b]suppose that [1]godliness is a means of gain.
6 [a]But godliness *actually* is a means of [b]great gain, when accom-
panied by [c]contentment.
7 For [a]we have brought nothing into the world, [1]so we cannot take
anything out of it either.
8 And if we [a]have food and covering, with these we shall be con-
tent.
9 [a]But those who want to get rich fall into temptation and [b]a snare
and many foolish and harmful desires which plunge men into ruin
and destruction.
10 For [a]the love of money is a root of all [1]sorts of evil, and some by
longing for it have [b]wandered away from the faith, and pierced
themselves with many a pang.
11 But [a]flee from these things, you [b]man of God; and pursue right-
eousness, godliness, [c]faith, [d]love, [1]perseverance *and* gentleness.
12 [a]Fight the good fight of [b]faith; [c]take hold of the eternal life [d]to
which you were called, and you made the good [e]confession in the
presence of [f]many witnesses.
13 [a]I charge you in the presence of God, who [1]gives life to all things,
and of [b]Christ Jesus, who testified the [c]good confession [d]before Pon-
tius Pilate,
14 that you keep the commandment without stain or reproach until
the [a]appearing of our Lord Jesus Christ,
15 which He will [1]bring about at [a]the proper time—He who is [b]the
blessed and [c]only Sovereign, [d]the King of [2]kings and [e]Lord of [3]lords;
16 [a]who alone possesses immortality and [b]dwells in unapproach-
able light; [c]whom no man has seen or can see. [d]To Him *be* honor and
eternal dominion! Amen.

do not share [a]1 Tim. 3:10; ı. 5:11; 1 Tim. 3:2-7
3 [a]1 Tim. 3:8
4 [a]Rev. 14:13
5 [a]Prov. 10:9
6:5; Titus 2:9; 18 [b]Titus 2:5
enefit by their [2]Lit., *exhort,* cts 1:15; Gal. 28; Philem. 16 [b]1 Tim. 4:11
., *come to;* or, th [a]1 Tim. 1:3 :10 [c]Titus 1:1
, *is sick about* 6 [b]1 Tim. 1:4 5; 2 Tim. 2:14
ligion [a]2 Tim. ıs 1:15 [b]Titus :11; 2 Pet. 2:3
uke 12:15-21; :6-10 [b]1 Tim. hil. 4:11; Heb. 13:5
mss. read *it is* at [a]Job 1:21; Eccl. 5:15
8 [a]Prov. 30:8
v. 15:27; 23:4;); Luke 12:21; 7 [b]1 Tim. 3:7
he evils [a]Col. Tim. 3:3; 6:9 [b]James 5:19
steadfastness . 2:22 [b]2 Tim. [c]1 Tim. 1:14 [d]2 Tim. 3:10
or. 9:25f.; Phil. 0; 1 Tim. 1:18 9 [c]Phil. 3:12; 19 [d]Col. 3:15 r. 9:13; 1 Tim. [f]1 Tim. 4:14; 2 Tim. 2:2
reserves alive 21 [b]Gal. 3:26; . 1:12, 15; 2:5 r. 9:13; 1 Tim. att. 27:2; John 18:37
[a]2 Thess. 2:8
it., *show* [2]Lit., *who reign as* Lit., *those who lords* [a]1 Tim. . 1:11 [c]1 Tim. ut. 10:17; Rev. 16 [e]Ps. 136:3
Tim. 1:17 [b]Ps. ; James 1:17; 5 [c]John 1:18

17 Instruct those who are rich in [a]this present world [b]not to be con-
ceited or to [c]fix their hope on the uncertainty of riches, but on God,
[d]who richly supplies us with all things to enjoy.
18 *Instruct them* to do good, to be rich in [a]good [1]works, [b]to be
generous and ready to share,
19 [a]storing up for themselves the treasure of a good foundation for
the future, so that they may [b]take hold of that which is life indeed.
20 O [a]Timothy, guard [b]what has been entrusted to you, avoiding
[c]worldly *and* empty chatter *and* the opposing arguments of what is
falsely called "knowledge"—
21 which some have professed and thus [a]gone astray [1]from [b]the
faith.

[c]Grace be with you.

17 [a]Matt. 12
4:10; Titus 2
62:10; Luke
Rom. 11:20;
[c]1 Tim. 4:10

18 [1]Or, *dee*
5:10 [b]Rom.
4:28

19 [a]Matt. 6:2
6:12

20 [a]1 Tim. 1
1:12, 14 [c]1 T
2 Tim. 2:16

21 [1]Lit., *conc*
[a]2 Tim. 2:18
1:19 [c]Col. 4:

1 Timothy at a Glance

Theme of 1 Timothy:

Author:

Date:

Purpose:

Key Words:

teach

faith

doctrine

godliness

Segment Divisions	Chapter Themes
	1
	2
	3
	4
	5
	6

1 TIMOTHY OBSERVATIONS CHART

ul **Timothy** **The Rich** **Women**

erseers (Elders) **Deacons** **Men**

Widows

Slaves

ayer **Charges and Instructions to Timothy**

2 TIMOTHY

Paul now found himself in a new set of circumstances. It was about A.D. 64 (some say A.D. Timothy was heavy on his heart. Paul had to write one last letter to his disciple, reminding Tim crucial matters concerning the ministry and urging him to make every effort to come quickly— winter.

THINGS TO DO

1. Read through 2 Timothy to get the flow of the book and to see the thrust of the letter personal nature.
2. Read 2 Timothy again. In chapters 1 and 2, and then in chapter 4, Paul refers to his circums where he is and what is about to take place in his life. To help set the context of the letter, on the OBSERVATIONS CHART on page 1777 what you learn about Paul's circumstances.
3. As you read 2 Timothy you probably noticed the many commands and/or instructions Pa Timothy. These are easy to spot because the verb usually comes first in the sentence a "you" is implied. An example of this is seen in 1:6: "Kindle afresh the gift."
   a. List the instructions and/or commands Paul gives Timothy throughout the letter OBSERVATIONS CHART. (Be sure to note the chapter and verse in which you find each.
   b. As you look for these instructions and/or commands, mark the key words (an synonyms and pronouns) that are listed on the 2 TIMOTHY AT A GLANCE chart o 1778. Be sure to mark any reference to the gospel (*sound words, Word, Scripture, sacred w* etc.) and to suffering (*persecution, hardship,* etc.).
4. Think back over the list of instructions and/or commands Paul gives Timothy and keep i the emphasis Paul places on the gospel. What do you think Paul's main message is to Tim this second epistle? Record this as the theme of the book on 2 TIMOTHY AT A GLANCE.
5. Look at the book one chapter at a time and summarize the main teaching or theme o chapter and then record it on 2 TIMOTHY AT A GLANCE and in the text next to the c number. (Note: The theme of each chapter should relate to the general theme of the book.)
6. At the bottom of 2 TIMOTHY AT A GLANCE, you'll see space to trace two themes, " Example" and "God's Provision," which run throughout the book. Doing this will giv additional insight into the practicality of 2 Timothy for your own life. Examine each cha the light of these two themes and record your insights on the appropriate space on the chart

THINGS TO THINK ABOUT

1. What is your responsibility toward the gospel? To what lengths will you go in order to car this responsibility?
2. What are you doing to make sure you handle the Word of God accurately? Do you simply what you have been taught or are you carefully studying the Word systematically? (Wi *International Inductive Study Bible* there's no excuse not to!)
3. Are you willing to suffer for the sake of those who would come to know the Lord Jesus and receive salvation?
4. What kind of men and women do you need to beware of in these last days?
5. How are you living? Are you a coward or have you fought the good fight of faith?
6. Are you ready to die? How will you feel when you see Jesus Christ face to face?

Chapter 1

1 Paul, [a]an apostle of [b]Christ Jesus [1c]by the will of God, according
to the promise of [d]life in Christ Jesus,
2 to [a]Timothy, my beloved [1b]son: [c]Grace, mercy *and* peace from
God the Father and Christ Jesus our Lord.
3 [a]I thank God, whom I [b]serve with a [c]clear conscience [1]the way
my forefathers did, [d]as I constantly remember you in my [2]prayers
night and day,
4 [a]longing to see you, [b]even as I recall your tears, so that I may be
filled with joy.
5 [1]For I am mindful of the [a]sincere faith within you, which first
dwelt in your grandmother Lois, and [b]your mother Eunice, and I am
sure that *it is* in you as well.
6 And for this reason I remind you to kindle afresh [a]the gift of God
which is in you through [a]the laying on of my hands.
7 For God has not given us a [a]spirit of timidity, but of power and
love and [1]discipline.
8 Therefore [a]do not be ashamed of the [b]testimony of our Lord, or of
me [c]His prisoner; but join with *me* in [d]suffering for the [e]gospel ac-
cording to the power of God,
9 who has [a]saved us, and [b]called us with a holy [c]calling, [d]not ac-
cording to our works, but according to His own [b]purpose and grace
which was granted us in [e]Christ Jesus from [f]all eternity,
10 but [a]now has been revealed by the [b]appearing of our Savior
[c]Christ Jesus, who [d]abolished death, and brought life and immor-
tality to light through the gospel,
11 [a]for which I was appointed a preacher and an apostle and a
teacher.
12 For this reason I also suffer these things, but [a]I am not ashamed;
for I know [b]whom I have believed and I am convinced that He is
able to [c]guard what I have entrusted to Him [1]until [d]that day.
13 [1a]Retain the [b]standard of [c]sound words [d]which you have heard
from me, in the [e]faith and love which are in [f]Christ Jesus.
14 Guard, through the Holy Spirit who [a]dwells in us, the [1b]treasure
which has been entrusted to *you*.
15 You are aware of the fact that all who are in [1a]Asia [b]turned away
from me, among whom are Phygelus and Hermogenes.
16 The Lord grant mercy to [a]the house of Onesiphorus for he often
refreshed me, and [b]was not ashamed of my [1c]chains;
17 but when he was in Rome, he eagerly searched for me, and
found me—
18 the Lord grant to him to find mercy from the Lord on [a]that day—
and you know very well what services he rendered at [b]Ephesus.

Chapter 2

2 You therefore, my [1a]son, [b]be strong in the grace that is in [c]Christ
Jesus.
2 And the things [a]which you have heard from me in the presence
of [b]many witnesses, these [c]entrust to [d]faithful men, who will be [e]able
to teach others also.
3 [a]Suffer hardship with *me*, as a good [b]soldier of [c]Christ Jesus.
4 No soldier in active service [a]entangles himself in the affairs of

[1]Lit., *through*
1:1 [b]Gal. 3:26
1 [d]1 Tim. 6:19
ild [a]Acts 16:1;
2 [b]1 Tim. 1:2;
. 2:1; Titus 1:4
[c]Rom. 1:7
[1]Lit., *from my*
refathers [2]Or,
ons [a]Rom. 1:8
14 [c]Acts 23:1;
im. 1:5 [d]Rom.
1:9
4:9, 21 [b]Acts
20:37
Lit., *Receiving*
membrance of
:5 [b]Acts 16:1;
2 Tim. 3:15
6 [a]1 Tim. 4:14
ound judgment
27; Rom. 8:15
ark 8:38; Rom.
2 Tim. 1:12, 16
1:6 [c]Eph. 3:1;
6 [d]2 Tim. 2:3,
Tim. 1:10; 2:8
. 11:14 [b]Rom.
. [c]Rom. 11:29
:9 [e]2 Tim. 1:1
5:25; Eph. 1:4;
Titus 1:2
[a]Rom. 16:26
ss. 2:8; 2 Tim.
4, 8; Titus 2:11
m. 1:1 [d]1 Cor.
26; Heb. 2:14f.
11 [a]1 Tim. 2:7
or [a]2 Tim. 1:8,
us 3:8 [c]1 Tim.
20; 2 Tim. 1:14
8; 3:13; 2 Tim.
1:18; 4:8
[1]Or, *Hold the*
[a]2 Tim. 3:14;
9 [b]Rom. 2:20;
7 [c]1 Tim. 1:10
m. 2:2 [e]1 Tim.
14 [f]2 Tim. 1:1
, *good deposit*
[b]1 Tim. 6:20;
2 Tim. 1:12
he province of
ts 2:9 [b]2 Tim.
4:10, 11, 16
chain [a]2 Tim.
Tim. 1:8 [c]Eph.
6:20
Cor. 1:8; 3:13;
:12; 4:8 [b]Acts
:19; 1 Tim. 1:3
, *child* [a]2 Tim.
. 6:10 [c]2 Tim.
1:1
. 1:13 [b]1 Tim.
2 [c]1 Tim. 1:18
. 1:12 [e]2 Cor.
2:14ff.; 3:5
m. 1:8 [b]1 Cor.
. 1:18 [c]2 Tim.
1:1
4 [a]2 Pet. 2:20

everyday life, so that he may please the one who enlisted him as a
soldier.
5 And also if anyone [a]competes as an athlete, he [1]does not win the
prize unless he competes according to the rules.
6 [a]The hard-working farmer ought to be the first to receive his
share of the crops.
7 Consider what I say, for the Lord will give you understanding in
everything.
8 Remember Jesus Christ, [a]risen from the dead, [b]descendant of
David, [c]according to my gospel,
9 [1]for which I [a]suffer hardship even to [b]imprisonment as a
[c]criminal; but [d]the word of God [e]is not imprisoned.
10 For this reason [a]I endure all things for [b]the sake of those who are
chosen, [c]that they also may obtain the [d]salvation which is in [e]Christ
Jesus *and* with *it* [f]eternal glory.
11 [a]It is a trustworthy statement:
For [b]if we died with Him, we shall also live with Him;
12 If we endure, [a]we shall also reign with Him;
If we [1b]deny Him, He also will deny us;
13 If we are faithless, [a]He remains faithful; for [b]He cannot deny
Himself.
14 Remind *them* of these things, and solemnly [a]charge *them* in the
presence of God not to [b]wrangle about words, which is useless, *and*
leads to the ruin of the hearers.
15 Be diligent to [a]present yourself approved to God as a workman
who does not need to be ashamed, handling accurately [b]the word of
truth.
16 But [a]avoid [b]worldly *and* empty chatter, for [1]it will lead to further
ungodliness,
17 and their [1]talk will spread like [2]gangrene. Among them are
[a]Hymenaeus and Philetus,
18 *men* who have gone astray from the truth saying that [a]the resur-
rection has already taken place, and thus they upset [b]the faith of
some.
19 Nevertheless, the [a]firm foundation of God stands, having this
[b]seal, "[c]The Lord knows those who are His," and, "[d]Let everyone
who names the name of the Lord abstain from wickedness."
20 Now in a large house there are not only gold and silver vessels,
but also vessels of wood and of earthenware, and [a]some to honor
and some to dishonor.
21 Therefore, if a man cleanses himself from [a]these *things,* he will be
a vessel for honor, sanctified, useful to the Master, [b]prepared for
every good work.
22 Now [a]flee from youthful lusts, and pursue righteousness, [b]faith,
love *and* peace, with those who [c]call on the Lord [d]from a pure heart.
23 But refuse foolish and ignorant [a]speculations, knowing that they
[b]produce [1]quarrels.
24 And [a]the Lord's bond-servant must not be quarrelsome, but be
kind to all, [b]able to teach, patient when wronged,
25 [a]with gentleness correcting those who are in opposition, [b]if per-
haps God may grant them repentance leading to [c]the knowledge of
the truth,
26 and they may come to their senses *and escape* from [a]the snare of
the devil, having been [b]held captive [1]by him to do his will.

5 [1]Lit., *is no* [a]1 Cor. 9:25
6 [a]1 Cor. 9:
8 [a]Acts 2:24 [c]Rom. 2:16
9 [1]Lit., *in wh* 1:8; 2:3 [b]Ph [c]Luke 23:32 1:8 [e]Acts 28 4:17
10 [a]Col. 1:2 18:7; Titus 1 1:6; 1 Thess [d]1 Cor. 1:21 2:1, 3 [f]2 Co 1 Pet. 5:10
11 [a]1 Tim. 1 6:8; 1 Thess
12 [1]Lit., *sha* [a]Matt. 19:28; 22:29; Rom. [b]Matt. 10:33; 1 Tim. 5:8
13 [a]Rom. 3 1:9 [b]Num. 2 1:2
14 [a]1 Tim. 5 4:1 [b]1 Tim. 2:23; Titus 3
15 [a]Rom. 6 1:12 [b]Eph. 1:18
16 [1]Lit., *they further progr ungodliness* [b]1 Tim. 1:9;
17 [1]Lit., *wor cancer* [a]1 Ti
18 [a]1 Cor. 1 [b]1 Tim. 1:19;
19 [a]Is. 28:16 3:15 [b]John 3 10:14; 1 Cor. 13:27; 1 Cor.
20 [a]Rom. 9:
21 [a]1 Tim. 6 2:16-18 [b]2 C Eph. 2:10; 2
22 [a]1 Tim. 6 1:14 [c]Acts 7 1:5
23 [1]Lit., *figh* [a]1 Tim. 6:4; 2 Titus 3:9 [b]Ti James 4:1
24 [a]1 Tim. 3 1:7 [b]1 Tim. 3
25 [a]Gal. 6:1; 1 Pet. 3:15 [b] [c]1 Tim. 2:4
26 [1]Or *possi to do His will* 3:7 [b]Luke 5:

Chapter 3

3 But realize this, that [a]in the last days difficult times will come.
2 For men will be [a]lovers of self, [b]lovers of money, [c]boastful,
[c]arrogant, [d]revilers, [c]disobedient to parents, [e]ungrateful, [f]unholy,
3 [a]unloving, irreconcilable, [b]malicious gossips, without self-
control, brutal, [1c]haters of good,
4 [a]treacherous, [b]reckless, [c]conceited, [d]lovers of pleasure rather than
lovers of God;
5 holding to a form of [1a]godliness, although they have [b]denied its
power; and [c]avoid such men as these.
6 For among them are those who [1a]enter into households and cap-
tivate [b]weak women weighed down with sins, led on by [c]various
impulses,
7 always learning and never able to [a]come to the [1]knowledge of
the truth.
8 And just as [a]Jannes and Jambres [b]opposed Moses, so these *men*
also oppose the truth, [c]men of depraved mind, rejected as regards
the faith.
9 But they will not make further progress; for their [a]folly will be
obvious to all, [b]as also that of those *two* came to be.
10 But you [a]followed my teaching, conduct, purpose, faith,
patience, [b]love, [1]perseverance,
11 [a]persecutions, *and* [b]sufferings, such as happened to me at [c]Anti-
och, at [d]Iconium *and* at [e]Lystra; what [f]persecutions I endured, and out
of them all [g]the Lord delivered me!
12 And indeed, all who desire to live godly in Christ Jesus [a]will be
persecuted.
13 But evil men and impostors [a]will proceed *from bad* to worse,
[b]deceiving and being deceived.
14 You, however, [a]continue in the things you have learned and be-
come convinced of, knowing from whom you have learned *them*;
15 and that [a]from childhood you have known [b]the sacred writings
which are able to [c]give you the wisdom that leads to [d]salvation
through faith which is in [e]Christ Jesus.
16 [1a]All Scripture is [2]inspired by God and profitable for teaching,
for reproof, for correction, for [3]training in righteousness;
17 that [a]the man of God may be adequate, [b]equipped for every good
work.

Chapter 4

4 [a]I solemnly charge *you* in the presence of God and of Christ
Jesus, who is to [b]judge the living and the dead, and by His
[c]appearing and His kingdom:
2 preach [a]the word; be ready in season *and* out of season; [b]reprove,
rebuke, exhort, with [1]great [c]patience and instruction.
3 For [a]the time will come when they will not endure [b]sound
doctrine; but *wanting* to have their ears tickled, they will accumulate
for themselves teachers in accordance to their own desires;
4 and [a]will turn away their ears from the truth, and [b]will turn aside
to myths.
5 But you, [a]be sober in all things, [b]endure hardship, do the work of
an [c]evangelist, fulfill your [d]ministry.

:1 [a]1 Tim. 4:1
il. 2:21 [b]Luke
Tim. 3:3; 6:10
. 1:30 [d]2 Pet.
2 [e]Luke 6:35
[f]1 Tim. 1:9
ot loving good
. 1:31 [b]1 Tim.
:11 [c]Titus 1:8
ts 7:52 [b]Acts
im. 3:6 [d]Phil.
3:19
eligion [a]1 Tim.
im. 5:8 [c]Matt.
; 2 Thess. 3:6
ep into [a]Jude
. 5:6; Titus 3:3
[c]Titus 3:3
Or, recognition
[a]2 Tim. 2:25
:11 [b]Acts 13:8
[c]1 Tim. 6:5
:11 [b]Ex. 7:11,
12; 8:18; 9:11
steadfastness
:20, 22; 1 Tim.
6 [b]1 Tim. 6:11
[a]2 Cor. 12:10
r. 1:5, 7 [c]Acts
, 45, 50 [d]Acts
:1-7, 19 [e]Acts
4:8-20 [f]2 Cor.
[g]Rom. 15:31
hn 15:20; Acts
22; 2 Cor. 4:9f.
m. 2:16 [b]Titus
3:3
im. 1:13; Titus
1:9
im. 1:5 [b]John
om. 2:27 [c]Ps.
f. [d]1 Cor. 1:21
[e]2 Tim. 1:1
ossibly, Every
ure inspired by
also profitable
God-breathed
ing which is in
m. 4:23f.; 15:4;
2 Pet. 1:20f.
. 6:11 [b]2 Tim.
21; Heb. 13:21
m. 5:21; 2 Tim.
4 [b]Acts 10:42
ss. 2:8; 2 Tim.
1:10; 4:8
., all [a]Gal. 6:6;
3; 1 Thess. 1:6
:20; Titus 1:13;
5 [c]2 Tim. 3:10
m. 3:1 [b]1 Tim.
10; 2 Tim. 1:13
ss. 2:11; Titus
.14 [b]1 Tim. 1:4
t. 1:13 [b]2 Tim.
cts 21:8 [d]Eph.
4:12; Col. 4:17

6 For I am already being [a]poured out as a drink offering, and the
time of [b]my departure has come.
7 [a]I have fought the good fight, I have finished [b]the course, I have
kept [c]the faith;
8 in the future there [a]is laid up for me [b]the crown of righteousness,
which the Lord, the righteous Judge, will award to me on [c]that day;
and not only to me, but also to [d]all who have loved His [e]appearing.
9 [a]Make every effort to come to me soon;
10 for [a]Demas, having loved [b]this present [1]world, has deserted me
and gone to [c]Thessalonica; Crescens *has gone* to [2d]Galatia, [e]Titus to
Dalmatia.
11 [a]Only [b]Luke is with me. Pick up [c]Mark and bring him with you,
[d]for he is useful to me for service.
12 But [a]Tychicus I have sent to [b]Ephesus.
13 When you come bring the cloak which I left at [a]Troas with Car-
pus, and the books, especially the parchments.
14 [a]Alexander the coppersmith did me much harm; [b]the Lord will
repay him according to his deeds.
15 Be on guard against him yourself, for he vigorously opposed our
[1]teaching.
16 At my first defense no one supported me, but all deserted me;
[a]may it not be counted against them.
17 But the Lord stood with me, and [a]strengthened me, in order that
through me [b]the proclamation might [1]be [c]fully accomplished, and
that all [d]the Gentiles might hear; and I was [e]delivered out of [f]the
lion's mouth.
18 The Lord will deliver me from every evil deed, and will [1a]bring
me safely to His [b]heavenly kingdom; [c]to [2]Him *be* the glory forever
and ever. Amen.
19 Greet Prisca and [a]Aquila, and [b]the household of Onesiphorus.
20 [a]Erastus remained at [b]Corinth, but [c]Trophimus I left sick at [d]Mile-
tus.
21 [a]Make every effort to come before [b]winter. Eubulus greets you,
also Pudens and Linus and Claudia and all the brethren.
22 [a]The Lord be with your spirit. [b]Grace be with you.

6 [a]Phil. 2:17
1:23; 2 Pet. 1
7 [a]1 Cor. 9:2
1:30; 1 Tim. 1
[b]Acts 20:24;
[c]2 Tim. 3:10
8 [a]Col. 1:5; 1
[b]1 Cor. 9:25;
James 1:12
1:12 [e]Phil. 3:
4:1
9 [a]2 Tim. 1:4
Titus 3:12
10 [1]Or, *age*
ancient mss.
[a]Col. 4:14 [b]1
[c]Acts 17:1 [d]A
[e]2 Cor. 2:13;
2:3; Titus 1:4
11 [a]2 Tim. 1:
4:14; Philem.
12:12, 25; 15
Col. 4:10 [d]2
12 [a]Acts 20:4
6:21, 22; Col.
[b]Acts 18:19
13 [a]Acts 16:8
14 [a]Acts 19:3
1:20 [b]Ps. 62:
2:6; 12:19
15 [1]Lit., *word*
16 [a]Acts 7:60
13:5
17 [1]Or, *be ful*
[a]1 Tim. 1:12; 2
[b]Titus 1:3 [c]2
[d]Acts 9:15; Ph
[e]Rom. 15:31;
3:11 [f]1 Sam.
22:21
18 [1]Or, *save r*
[2]Lit., *Whom*
1:21 [b]1 Cor. 1
2 Tim. 4:1; He
12:22 [c]Rom.
2 Pet. 3:18
19 [a]Acts 18:2
1:16
20 [a]Acts 19:22
16:23 [b]Acts 1
20:4; 21:29 [d]A
21 [a]2 Tim. 4:9
3:12
22 [a]Gal. 6:18;
4:23; Philem. 2
4:18

2 Timothy Observations Chart

Where is he?

Why is he there?

Who is with him?

What is about to happen?

How is he going to handle it?

Paul's Instructions to Timothy

2 Timothy at a Glance

Theme of 2 Timothy:

Author:

Date:

Purpose:

Key Words:
- gospel
- word
- suffer (suffering[s], persecutions)
- endure(d)
- faith
- ashamed

Segment Divisions

God's Provision	Paul's Example	Chapter Themes
		1
		2
Delivered Paul Out of Persecutions	Endured Persecutions	3
		4

TUS

n Paul sailed past Crete on his way to Rome he was not the master of his own ship. He was prisoner. How wise the centurion guard would have been had he followed Paul's urging to put in Crete! Despite the winds, they sailed on under much duress. As Paul had predicted, the ship t in Malta, the island fifty-eight miles south of Sicily.

's ship sank to the bottom of the sea; Crete sank to the depths of sin. Broken to pieces morally by essant pounding of a godless lifestyle, Crete needed the good news of the gospel. Unlike the owever, it was not beyond redemption.

ther Crete was on Paul's heart before his two years' house arrest in Rome, we don't know. We ow that once Paul was free from Rome's chains he apparently went with Titus to Crete and left ere.

Paul wrote Titus, it was about A.D. 62. He didn't know he'd return to Rome for one final onment.

GS TO DO

ead through Titus without stopping so that you understand the general content and thrust of he letter.

ead Titus again, one chapter at a time.

. As you read each chapter, look for the information about the author: who he is, how he describes himself, where he is, etc. Record your insights on the OBSERVATIONS CHART on page 1783. Note the chapter and verse in which you find your information; it helps when you want to find something later.

. Mark the key words listed on the TITUS AT A GLANCE chart on page 1782. Be sure also to mark the synonyms and pronouns.

. In the margin of your Bible, list the truths you learn from the text about each key word.

The commands, warnings, and instructions Paul includes in his letter to Titus help define Paul's purpose for writing. Read Titus again chapter by chapter and note each command, warning, or nstruction Paul gives Titus. List these on the OBSERVATIONS CHART under "Instructions to Titus."

Note on the OBSERVATIONS CHART what you learn about Titus and his relationship to Paul. In chapter 1 Paul clearly tells us where Titus is and why he is there.

In his letter Paul mentions various groups of people. List what you learn about each of these groups under the designated heading on your OBSERVATIONS CHART.

Listing Paul's commands, warnings, and instructions to Titus probably has helped you see the dominant subject of Titus. There are two verses, one in chapter 2 and one in chapter 3, which summarize the thrust of Paul's letter. These will help you determine the theme of the epistle. Record it on TITUS AT A GLANCE.

a. Now summarize the theme or main message of each chapter and record these on TITUS AT A GLANCE and in the text next to the chapter number.

b. Fill in author, date, and purpose on the same chart.

GS TO THINK ABOUT

The world's lifestyle denies God. By your lifestyle and attitudes, do you deny ungodliness and worldly desires, or do you indulge the desires of your flesh?

It's difficult always to be considerate to everyone, isn't it? When did you last fail in this area?

Have you determined afresh to be gentle and uncontentious even in the most difficult si
with the most difficult person? Your actions often will speak louder than your words ever

3. Your salvation was not based on performance but upon the mercy and grace of God. W
your heavenly Father saved you from? Think on His goodness that brought you from dea
life and brought you out of the kingdom of darkness into the kingdom of His glorious ligh
you thanked Him lately for His mercy and grace? Why not do it now? Pray for those close
who have yet to experience the saving grace of God.

Chapter 1

1 Paul, [a]a bond-servant of God, and an [b]apostle of Jesus Christ, [1]for
the faith of those [c]chosen of God and [d]the knowledge of the truth
which is [e]according to godliness,
2 in [a]the hope of eternal life, which God, [b]who cannot lie,
[c]promised [1d]long ages ago,
3 but [a]at the proper time manifested, *even* His word, in [b]the procla-
mation [c]with which I was entrusted [d]according to the commandment
of [e]God our Savior;
4 to [a]Titus, [b]my true child [1]in a [c]common faith: [d]Grace and peace
from God the Father and [e]Christ Jesus our Savior.
5 For this reason I left you in [a]Crete, that you might set in order
what remains, and [b]appoint [c]elders in every city as I directed you,

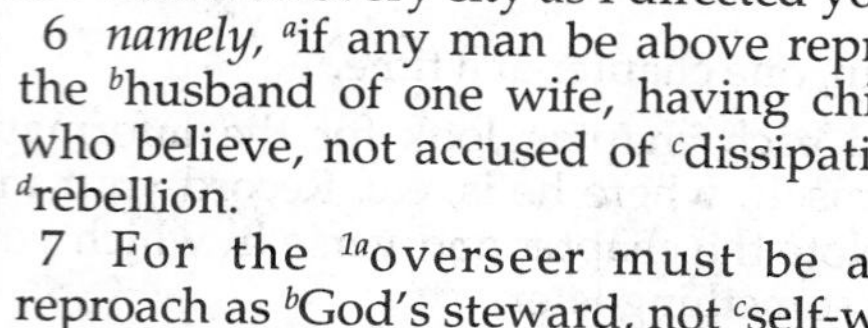

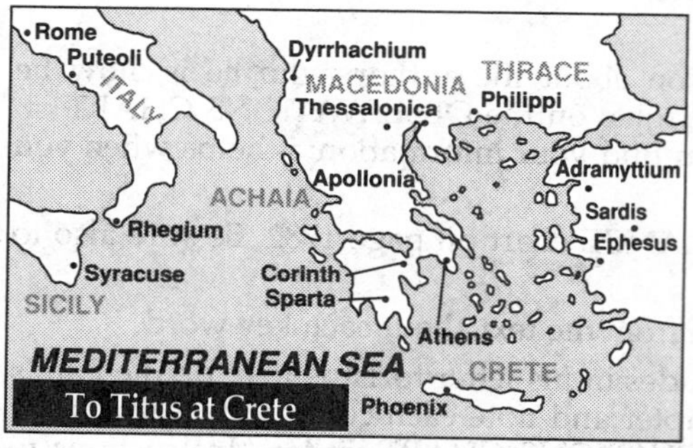

To Titus at Crete

6 *namely,* [a]if any man be above reproach,
the [b]husband of one wife, having children
who believe, not accused of [c]dissipation or
[d]rebellion.
7 For the [1a]overseer must be above
reproach as [b]God's steward, not [c]self-willed,
not quick-tempered, not [d]addicted to wine,
not pugnacious, [e]not fond of sordid gain,
8 but [a]hospitable, [b]loving what is good,
sensible, just, devout, self-controlled,
9 [a]holding fast the faithful word which is
in accordance with the teaching, that he
may be able both to exhort in [b]sound doctrine and to refute those
who contradict.
10 [a]For there are many [b]rebellious men, [c]empty talkers and
deceivers, especially [d]those of the circumcision,
11 who must be silenced because they are upsetting [a]whole
families, teaching [b]things they should not *teach,* [c]for the sake of sor-
did gain.
12 One of themselves, a prophet of their own, said, "[a]Cretans are
always liars, evil beasts, lazy gluttons."
13 This testimony is true. For this cause [a]reprove them [b]severely
that they may be [c]sound in the faith,
14 not paying attention to Jewish [a]myths and [b]commandments of
men who [c]turn away from the truth.
15 [a]To the pure, all things are pure; but [b]to those who are defiled
and unbelieving, nothing is pure, but both their [c]mind and their
conscience are defiled.
16 [a]They profess to know God, but by *their* deeds they [b]deny *Him,*
being [c]detestable and [d]disobedient, and [e]worthless [f]for any good
deed.

1:1 [1]Or, *ac* [a]Rom. 1:1; Rev. 1:1 [b]2 [c]Luke 18:7 [e]1 Tim. 6:3

2 [1]Lit., *befo* *eternal* [a]2 T Titus 3:7 [b]2 Heb. 6:18 [c] [d]2 Tim. 1:9

3 [a]1 Tim. 2: 16:25; 2 Tim [c]1 Tim. 1:11 [e]Luke 1:47; 1 Titus 2:10; 3

4 [1]Lit., *acco* [a]2 Cor. 2:13; 2:3; 2 Tim. 4: 1:2 [c]2 Pet. 1 1:7 [e]1 Tim. 1:1

5 [a]Acts 27:7 [b]Acts 14:23

6 [a]1 Tim. 3:2 1:6-8 [b]1 Tim 5:18 [d]Titus 1

7 [1]Or, *bishop* 3:2 [b]1 Cor. 4 2:10 [d]1 Tim. [e]1 Tim. 3:3, 8

8 [a]1 Tim. 3:2 3:3

9 [a]2 Thess. 2 1:19; 2 Tim. 1 [b]1 Tim. 1:10;

10 [a]2 Cor. 11 1:6 [c]1 Tim. 1: 11:2

11 [a]1 Tim. 5:4 3:6 [b]1 Tim. 5: [c]1 Tim. 6:5

12 [a]Acts 2:11;

13 [a]1 Tim. 5:2 4:2; Titus 2:15 13:10 [c]Titus 2

14 [a]1 Tim. 1:4 2:22 [c]2 Tim. 4

15 [a]Luke 11:4 14:20 [b]Rom. 1 [c]1 Tim. 6:5

16 [a]1 John 2:4 5:8 [c]Rev. 21:8 3:3 [e]2 Tim. 3:8 3:17; Titus 3:1

Chapter 2

2 But as for you, speak the things which are fitting for [a]sound doctrine.
2 [a]Older men are to be [b]temperate, dignified, sensible, [c]sound [d]in faith, in love, in [1]perseverance.
3 Older women likewise are to be reverent in their behavior, [a]not malicious gossips, nor [b]enslaved to much wine, teaching what is good,
4 that they may [1]encourage the young women to love their husbands, to love their children,
5 *to be* sensible, pure, [a]workers at home, kind, being [b]subject to their own husbands, [c]that the word of God may not be dishonored.
6 Likewise urge [a]the young men to be [1]sensible;
7 in all things show yourself to be [a]an example of good deeds, *with* [1]purity in doctrine, dignified,
8 sound *in* speech which is beyond reproach, in order [a]that the opponent may be put to shame, having nothing bad to say about us.
9 *Urge* [a]bondslaves to be subject to their own masters in everything, to be well-pleasing, not [1]argumentative,
10 not pilfering, but showing all good faith that they may adorn the doctrine of [a]God our Savior in every respect.
11 For the grace of God has [a]appeared, [1b]bringing salvation to all men,
12 [1]instructing us to deny ungodliness and [a]worldly desires and [b]to live sensibly, righteously and godly [c]in the present age,
13 looking for the blessed hope and the [a]appearing of the glory of [1b]our great God and Savior, Christ Jesus;
14 who [a]gave Himself for us, [b]that He might redeem us from every lawless deed and [c]purify for Himself a [d]people for His own possession, [e]zealous for good deeds.
15 These things speak and [a]exhort and [a]reprove with all [1]authority. [b]Let no one disregard you.

Chapter 3

3 [a]Remind them [b]to be subject to rulers, to authorities, to be obedient, to be [c]ready for every good deed,
2 to malign no one, [a]to be uncontentious, [a]gentle, [b]showing every consideration for all men.
3 [a]For we also once were foolish ourselves, [b]disobedient, [c]deceived, [d]enslaved to [e]various lusts and pleasures, spending our life in [f]malice and [f]envy, hateful, hating one another.
4 But when the [a]kindness of [b]God our Savior and *His* love for mankind [c]appeared,
5 [a]He saved us, [b]not on the basis of deeds which we have done in righteousness, but [c]according to His mercy, by the [d]washing of regeneration and [e]renewing by the Holy Spirit,
6 [a]whom He poured out upon us [b]richly through Jesus Christ our Savior,
7 that being justified by His grace we might be made [a]heirs [1]according to *the* hope of eternal life.
8 [a]This is a trustworthy statement; and concerning these things I [b]want you to speak confidently, so that those who have [c]believed

2:1 [a]Titus 1:9
steadfastness
9 [b]1 Tim. 3:2
s 1:13 [d]1 Tim. 1:2, 14
ı. 3:11 [b]1 Tim. 3:8
4 [1]*Or, train*
m. 5:14 [b]Eph.
22 [c]1 Tim. 6:1
, sensible in all
ɔw [a]1 Tim. 5:1
soundness; lit.,
ɔtness [a]1 Tim. 4:12
ss. 3:14; 1 Pet. 2:12
, contradicting
6:5; 1 Tim. 6:1
10 [a]Titus 1:3
[1]*Or, to all men,*
g [a]2 Tim. 1:10;
3:4 [b]1 Tim. 2:4
Or, disciplining
. 6:9; Titus 3:3
ı. 3:12 [c]1 Tim. 6:17
the great God and our Savior
ss. 2:8 [b]1 Tim.
Tim. 1:2; Titus 1:4; 2 Pet. 1:1
Tim. 2:6 [b]Ps.
8; 1 Pet. 1:18f.
7:23; Heb. 1:3;
John 1:7 [d]Ex.
Deut. 4:20; 7:6;
ph. 1:11; 1 Pet.
Eph. 2:10; Titus
3:8; 1 Pet. 3:13
[1]*Lit., command*
Tim. 4:13; 5:20;
.2 [b]1 Tim. 4:12
m. 2:14 [b]Rom.
:1 [c]2 Tim. 2:21
Tim. 3:3; 1 Pet.
8 [b]2 Tim. 2:25
11:30; Col. 3:7
us 1:16 [c]2 Tim.
[d]Rom. 6:6, 12
3:6; Titus 2:12
[f]Rom. 1:29
ı. 2:4; Eph. 2:7;
2:3 [b]Titus 2:10
[c]Titus 2:11
n. 11:14; 2 Tim.
Eph. 2:9 [c]Eph.
Pet. 1:3 [d]John
ph. 5:26; 1 Pet.
.21 [e]Rom. 12:2
5:5 [b]Rom. 2:4;
1 Tim. 6:17
Or, of eternal life
cording to hope
att. 25:34; Mark
Rom. 8:17, 24;
Titus 1:2
m. 1:15 [b]1 Tim.
:8 [c]2 Tim. 1:12

God may be careful to [d]engage in good deeds. These things are good
and profitable for men.
9 But [a]shun [b]foolish controversies and [c]genealogies and strife and
[d]disputes about the Law; for they are [e]unprofitable and worthless.
10 [a]Reject a [b]factious man [c]after a first and second warning,
11 knowing that such a man is [a]perverted and is sinning, being
self-condemned.
12 When I send Artemas or [a]Tychicus to you, [b]make every effort to
come to me at Nicopolis, for I have decided to [c]spend the winter
there.
13 Diligently help Zenas the [a]lawyer and [b]Apollos on their way so
that nothing is lacking for them.
14 And let [a]our *people* also learn to [b]engage in good [1]deeds to meet
[c]pressing needs, that they may not be [d]unfruitful.
15 [a]All who are with me greet you. Greet those who love us [b]in *the*
faith.
[c]Grace be with you all.

8 [d]Titus 2:7, 1

9 [a]2 Tim. 2:16 1:4; 2 Tim. 2:2 1:4 [d]James 4: 2:14

10 [a]2 John 10 16:17 [c]Matt. 1

11 [a]Titus 1:14

12 [a]Acts 20:4, 6:21f.; Col. 4:7 4:12 [b]2 Tim. 4 [c]2 Tim. 4:21

13 [a]Matt. 22:3 18:24; 1 Cor. 1

14 [1]Or, *occup* [a]Titus 2:8 [b]Tit [c]Rom. 12:13; F [d]Matt. 7:19; Ph Col. 1:10

15 [a]Acts 20:3 1:2 [c]Col. 4:18

TITUS AT A GLANCE

Theme of Titus:

Author:

Date:

Purpose:

Key Words:
God
Jesus Christ
doctrine
truth
grace
deeds

SEGMENT DIVISIONS	PARAGRAPH THEMES
	1:1-4
	1:5-9
	1:10-16
	2:1-15
	3:1-15A
	3:15B

TITUS OBSERVATIONS CHART

	Titus	Instructions to Titus
re is he?	Where is he? Why?	
does he describe himself?	What is his relationship to Paul?	

rs (Overseers)	Older Men	Older Women
	Young Men	Young Women
ans	Bondslaves	

PHILEMON

Slavery was a fact of life in Paul's day—a fact Paul couldn't change. But Paul could show slav masters how they were to behave toward one another as those redeemed by Jesus, who had bec bondservant on their behalf. In his epistles Paul shared these principles.

Now, however, something else had come up. Paul had to appeal to Philemon, a believer Colossae, about a very personal matter—one of Philemon's slaves had run away, and accord Roman law, could be put to death by his master. So, about the same time he wrote Colossians wrote to Philemon from his rented quarters where he, a prisoner of Rome, also could be put to de was about A.D. 61 or 62.

THINGS TO DO

1. Philemon is only one short chapter. Read it to gain an understanding of why this lette written.
   a. When you finish reading, go back and note everything you learn about Paul o OBSERVATIONS CHART on page 1786. Also watch for Paul's reason for writing and h goes about achieving his purpose. Then record the reasons on the PHILEMON AT A GL chart also on page 1786.
   b. Also note everything you learn about the recipients of Paul's letter and record this inforn in the appropriate section of the OBSERVATIONS CHART.
   c. Record on the OBSERVATIONS CHART everything you learn about Onesimus.
2. Carefully read the book again, marking each of the key words (with their synonym pronouns) listed on the PHILEMON AT A GLANCE chart. Then in the margin list the trut learn about each of these words from the text.
3. Record the theme of Philemon on PHILEMON AT A GLANCE and also in the text. Be Philemon is only one chapter, it is divided into paragraphs on the chart. Read the book para by paragraph and record on the chart the theme of each paragraph. Then fill in the rest chart.

THINGS TO THINK ABOUT

1. Are you willing to appeal to someone on behalf of another—to assume the role of an advoca
2. What can you learn from Paul's example in the way he appealed to Philemon?
3. Is there someone whom you need to forgive and offer restoration?
4. Can someone appeal to you to do the right thing on the basis of your character, or do they h force your hand through rules, regulations, or some sort of "bribe"?

Chapter 1 ______

1 [a]Paul, [b]a prisoner of [c]Christ Jesus, and [d]Timothy [1]our brother, to
Philemon our beloved *brother* and [e]fellow worker,
2 and to Apphia [1a]our sister, and to [b]Archippus our [c]fellow soldier,
and to [d]the church in your house:
3 [a]Grace to you and peace from God our Father and the Lord Jesus
Christ.
4 [a]I thank my God always, making mention of you in my prayers,

1:1 [1]Lit., *the* [b]Eph. 3:1 [c]Ga [d]2 Cor. 1:1; Co [e]Phil. 2:25; Ph

2 [1]Lit., *the* [a]F [b]Col. 4:17 [c]Ph 2 Tim. 2:3 [d]R

3 [a]Rom. 1:7

4 [a]Rom. 1:8f.

5 because I [a]hear of your love, and of the faith which you have
toward the Lord Jesus, and toward all the [1]saints;
6 *and I pray* that the fellowship of your faith may become effective
[1]through the [a]knowledge of every good thing which is in [2]you [3]for
Christ's sake.
7 For I have come to have much [a]joy and comfort in your love,
because the [1]hearts of the [2]saints have been [b]refreshed through you,
brother.
8 Therefore, [a]though I have [1]enough confidence in Christ to order
you *to do* that which is [b]proper,
9 yet for love's sake I rather [a]appeal *to you*—since I am such a
person as Paul, [1]the [b]aged, and now also [c]a prisoner of [d]Christ
Jesus—
10 I [a]appeal to you for my [b]child, whom I have begotten in my
[1]imprisonment, [2c]Onesimus,
11 who formerly was useless to you, but now is useful both to you
and to me.
12 And I have sent him back to you in person, that is, *sending* my
very heart,
13 whom I wished to keep with me, that in your behalf he might
minister to me in my [1a]imprisonment for the gospel;
14 but without your consent I did not want to do anything, that
your goodness should [a]not be as it were by compulsion, but of your
own free will.
15 For perhaps [a]he was for this reason parted *from you* for a while,
that you should have him back forever,
16 [a]no longer as a slave, but more than a slave, [b]a beloved brother,
especially to me, but how much more to you, both [c]in the flesh and
in the Lord.
17 If then you regard me a [a]partner, accept him as *you would* me.
18 But if he has wronged you in any way, or owes you anything,
charge that to my account;
19 [a]I, Paul, am writing this with my own hand, I will repay it ([b]lest I
should [1]mention to you that you owe to me even your own self as
well).
20 Yes, brother, let me benefit from you in the Lord; [a]refresh my
heart in Christ.
21 [a]Having confidence in your obedience, I write to you, since I
know that you will do even more than what I say.
22 And at the same time also prepare me a [a]lodging; for [b]I hope that
through [c]your prayers [d]I shall be given to you.
23 [a]Epaphras, my [b]fellow prisoner in Christ Jesus, greets you,
24 *as do* [a]Mark, [b]Aristarchus, [c]Demas, [c]Luke, my [d]fellow workers.
25 [a]The grace of the Lord Jesus Christ be [b]with your spirit.[1]

PHILEMON OBSERVATIONS CHART

The Author	The Recipients	Onesimus

PHILEMON AT A GLANCE

Theme of Philemon:

Author:

Date:

Purpose:

Key Words:
love

appeal

slave

SEGMENT DIVISIONS	PARAGRAPH THEMES
	VERSES 1-3
	VERSES 4-7
	VERSES 8-20
	VERSES 21-22
	VERSES 23-25

EBREWS

ːsecution increased as the gospel spread. The persecution was especially intense for Jewish ers because they had turned their back on the world and its ways and had abandoned the ances of the law which Jews had embraced since the time of Moses. This left them in a no-man's Jews as well as Gentiles who did not believe in the Lord Jesus Christ could not understand —nor would many tolerate their newfound faith without challenge or attack.

agine yourself in a similar situation. What if you were wrong about Jesus Christ? What if He were ally the Messiah? And what about the new covenant? What if it didn't replace the old covenant? if you really did need a blood sacrifice for your sins? *What if?*

that we could be secure in our faith, God moved an unknown author to take up pen and ment and write the book we call Hebrews. No other book in the New Testament gives us what ·ws gives us—the assurance that we have a high priest who is touched with the feeling of our nesses, one who ever lives to make intercession for us.

brews probably was written before A.D. 70 as the temple still was standing and the priests still making religious sacrifices.

IGS TO DO

Before you begin your study of Hebrews, read Hebrews 13:22 to discover the author's purpose for writing. Record this on the HEBREWS AT A GLANCE chart on page 1805.

In order to grasp the truth of this book, it's necessary to understand to whom the book is written. So, as you read Hebrews chapter by chapter, make sure:

a. You learn all you can about the recipients of this letter (epistle). Look for and mark the words *we, you, beloved,* and *brethren*. Then record what you learn about the recipients on the OBSERVATIONS CHART on page 1804 under "Recipients."

b. Note on the OBSERVATIONS CHART what you learn from the text about the author.

c. As you read, keep in mind the author's purpose for writing. Throughout the book you will see him exhorting his readers. Most of his exhortations begin with "let us." Mark each *let us* and then list each exhortation on the OBSERVATIONS CHART.

d. Throughout the book, the author periodically warns his readers about certain things.

   1) Note each warning on the OBSERVATIONS CHART. An example of a warning is found in 2:1: "We must pay much closer attention to what we have heard, lest we drift away from it."

   2) As you note the warning, watch for the consequences of not heeding the warning. Also remember to whom the book is addressed. Let the text speak for itself. Don't read into it—just let it say what it says.

As you study each chapter, do the following:

a. Mark the key words (including their synonyms and pronouns) listed on the HEBREWS AT A GLANCE chart. Then write the same key words on an index card and mark them in the same distinctive way you mark them in the text. Use this card as a reminder of what you are looking for as you study the book of Hebrews.

b. List in the margin what you learn from each key word.

c. As you finish reading a chapter, decide on the theme or subject of that chapter and record it next to the chapter number in the text and on HEBREWS AT A GLANCE.

For a deeper study of Hebrews, you can make some additional charts (these charts are not included in this Bible.)

a. Look back through your work and note all the times you marked *Jesus* and the pr referring to Him. Also look for the phrase *better than*. Then make a chart on THE SUPRE OF JESUS and list what you learn from Hebrews about our Lord. (Or record this infor in the margin of your Bible.)

b. There's much in Hebrews about the priesthood and about Jesus as our high priest. chart entitled THE PRIESTHOOD AND JESUS and break your information into three co "Insights into Priests and the Priesthood," "Insights into Jesus, Our Great High Pries "How This Applies to Me." Record your insights into the proper columns. (Or list thi mation in the margin of your Bible.)

c. Review what you learn from marking *covenant* and note what the text says on a chart y A COMPARISON OF THE TWO COVENANTS: LAW AND GRACE AS TAUG HEBREWS. (Or in the margin next to chapters 8 through 10, list what you learn about covenant and law and the new covenant and grace.)

5. Complete HEBREWS AT A GLANCE by doing the following:

   a. Look at each of your chapter themes and record it in the proper place on the chart and text. Determine the theme of Hebrews and record it.

   b. Fill in the section titled "Segment Division."

      1) Segment divisions indicate a change in the thrust or topic of the book. One cha emphasis occurs at Hebrews 10:19, where the author stops dealing with the do aspects of the truth he is sharing and begins to address the practical aspects. Reco segment division on the chart in the appropriate space.

      2) Look again at the chapter themes and see if there are any other divisions you can rec so, record them on the chart. Completing this exercise will help you find where a s truth is covered in Hebrews.

THINGS TO THINK ABOUT

1. Meditate on the truths you learned about Jesus. Do you see Him as "better than . . . "? supreme is He in your life?
2. As you press on to Christian maturity, are you noticing a new sense of confidence in your G your faith being strengthened? Are you drawing near to God? Do you think Jesus unders what you're going through? Can He really help?
3. Are you laying aside every encumbrance (every weighty thing that is slowing you dow every sin, and running with endurance the race set before you? If not, what is holding you b
4. How are your morals? Do you believe and live in the light of the fact that God will fornicators and adulterers?
5. Are you continually offering up the sacrifice of praise? What are some things you can than for today?

Chapter 1 ______

1 God, after He [a]spoke long ago to the fathers in [b]the prophets in
many portions and [c]in many ways,
2 [1a]in these last days [b]has spoken to us in [c]*His* Son, whom He
appointed [d]heir of all things, [e]through whom also He made the
[2f]world.
3 [1]And He is the radiance of His glory and the exact [a]representa-
tion of His nature, and [2b]upholds all things by the word of His
power. When He had made [c]purification of sins, He [d]sat down at the
right hand of the [e]Majesty on high;

1:1 [a]John 9:2 Heb. 2:2f.; 3:5; 11:18; 12:25 [b] 3:21 [c]Num. 12 Joel 2:28

2 [1]Or, *at the e these days* [2]L [a]Matt. 13:39; 1 1:20 [b]John 9:2 5:26, 27; Heb. 7:28 [d]Ps. 2:8; 28:18; Mark 12 8:17; Heb. 2:8 1:3; 1 Cor. 8:6; 1:16 [f]1 Cor. 2: 11:3

3 [1]Lit., *Who being* [2]Lit., *upholding* [a]2 Cor. 4:4 [b]Col. 1:17 [c]Titus 2:14; Heb. 9:14 [d]Mark 16:19; Heb. 8:1; 10:12; 12:2 [e]2 Pet. 1:17

4 having become as much better than the angels, as He has in-
herited a more excellent [a]name than they.
5 For to which of the angels did He ever say,
"[a]THOU ART MY SON,
TODAY I HAVE BEGOTTEN THEE"?
And again,
"[b]I WILL BE A FATHER TO HIM
AND HE SHALL BE A SON TO ME"?
6 And [1]when He again [a]brings the first-born into [2b]the world, He
says,
"[c]AND LET ALL THE ANGELS OF GOD WORSHIP HIM."
7 And of the angels He says,
"[a]WHO MAKES HIS ANGELS WINDS,
AND HIS MINISTERS A FLAME OF FIRE."
8 But of the Son *He says,*
"[a]THY THRONE, O GOD, IS FOREVER AND EVER,
AND THE RIGHTEOUS SCEPTER IS THE SCEPTER OF [1]HIS KINGDOM.
9 "[a]THOU HAST LOVED RIGHTEOUSNESS AND HATED LAWLESSNESS;
[b]THEREFORE GOD, THY GOD, HATH [c]ANOINTED THEE
WITH THE OIL OF GLADNESS ABOVE THY COMPANIONS."
10 And,
"[a]THOU, LORD, IN THE BEGINNING DIDST LAY THE FOUNDATION OF THE
EARTH,
AND THE HEAVENS ARE THE WORKS OF THY HANDS;
11 [a]THEY WILL PERISH, BUT THOU REMAINEST;
[b]AND THEY ALL WILL BECOME OLD AS A GARMENT,
12 [a]AND AS A MANTLE THOU WILT ROLL THEM UP;
AS A GARMENT THEY WILL ALSO BE CHANGED.
BUT THOU ART [b]THE SAME,
AND THY YEARS WILL NOT COME TO AN END."
13 But to which of the angels has He ever said,
"[a]SIT AT MY RIGHT HAND,
[b]UNTIL I MAKE THINE ENEMIES
A FOOTSTOOL FOR THY FEET"?
14 Are they not all [a]ministering spirits, sent out to render service for
the sake of those who will [b]inherit [c]salvation?

Chapter 2

2 For this reason we must pay much closer attention to [1]what we
have heard, lest [a]we drift away *from it.*
2 For if the word [a]spoken through [b]angels proved [1]unalterable, and
[c]every transgression and disobedience received a just [d]recompense,
3 [a]how shall we escape if we neglect so great a [b]salvation? [1]After it
was at the first [c]spoken through the Lord, it was [d]confirmed to us by
those who heard,
4 God also bearing witness with them, both by [a]signs and wonders
and by [b]various [1]miracles and by [2c]gifts of the Holy Spirit [d]according
to His own will.
5 For He did not subject to angels [1a]the world to come, concerning
which we are speaking.
6 But one has testified [a]somewhere, saying,
"[b]WHAT IS MAN, THAT THOU REMEMBEREST HIM?
OR THE SON OF MAN, THAT THOU ART CONCERNED ABOUT HIM?
7 "[a]THOU HAST MADE HIM [1]FOR A LITTLE WHILE LOWER THAN THE ANGELS;

Eph. 1:21
cts 13:33; Sam. 7:14
when He [2]Lit., *the* arth [a]Heb. 4:14 [c]Ps. 97:7
[a]Ps. 104:4
mss. read [a]Ps. 45:6
5:7 [b]John . 2:9; Heb. [c]Is. 61:1, 3
Ps. 102:25
102:26 [b]Is. ; Heb. 8:13
102:26, 27 [b]Heb. 13:8
110:1; Matt. 1:3 [b]Josh. Heb. 10:13
3:20f.; Dan. 25:34; Mark us 3:7; Heb. Rom. 11:14; 1; Heb. 2:3; 5:9; 9:28
e things that heard [a]Prov. 3:21
adfast [a]Heb. s 7:53 [c]Heb. [d]Heb. 10:35; 11:26
., *Which was* 10:29; 12:25 11:14; 1 Cor. eb. 1:14; 5:9; b. 1:1 [d]Mark e 1:2; 1 John 1:1
orks of power outions [a]John 6:14 [c]1 Cor. ph. 4:7 [d]Eph. 1:5
, the inhabited tt. 24:14; Heb. 6:5
. 4:4 [b]Ps. 8:4
ttle lower [a]Ps. 8:5, 6

THOU HAST CROWNED HIM WITH GLORY AND HONOR,
[2]AND HAST APPOINTED HIM OVER THE WORKS OF THY HANDS;
8 [a]"THOU HAST PUT ALL THINGS IN SUBJECTION UNDER HIS FEET."
For in subjecting all things to him, He left nothing that is not subject
to him. But now [b]we do not yet see all things subjected to him.
9 But we do see Him who has been [a]made [1]for a little while lower
than the angels, *namely,* Jesus, [b]because of the suffering of death
[c]crowned with glory and honor, that [d]by the grace of God He might
[e]taste death [f]for everyone.
10 For [a]it was fitting for Him, [b]for whom are all things, and through
whom are all things, in bringing many sons to glory, to [c]perfect the
[1d]author of their salvation through sufferings.
11 For both He who [a]sanctifies and those who [b]are [1]sanctified are all
[c]from one *Father*; for which reason He is not ashamed to call them
[d]brethren,
12 saying,
"[a]I WILL PROCLAIM THY NAME TO MY BRETHREN,
IN THE MIDST OF THE [1]CONGREGATION I WILL SING THY PRAISE."
13 And again,
"[a]I WILL PUT MY TRUST IN HIM."
And again,
"[b]BEHOLD, I AND THE CHILDREN WHOM GOD HAS GIVEN ME."
14 Since then the children share in [1a]flesh and blood, [b]He Himself
likewise also partook of the same, that [c]through death He might
render powerless [d]him who had the power of death, that is, the
devil;
15 and might deliver those who through [a]fear of death were subject
to slavery all their lives.
16 For assuredly He does not [1]give help to angels, but He gives
help to the [2]descendant of Abraham.
17 Therefore, He [1]had [a]to be made like His brethren in all things,
that He might [b]become a merciful and faithful [c]high priest in [d]things
pertaining to God, to [e]make propitiation for the sins of the people.
18 For since He Himself was [a]tempted in that which He has suf-
fered, He is able to come to the aid of those who are tempted.

Chapter 3

3 Therefore, [a]holy brethren, partakers of a [b]heavenly calling, con-
sider Jesus, [c]the Apostle and [d]High Priest of our [e]confession.
2 [1]He was faithful to Him who [2]appointed Him, as [a]Moses also
was in all His house.
3 [a]For He has been counted worthy of more glory than Moses, by
just so much as the builder of the house has more honor than the
house.
4 For every house is built by someone, but the builder of all things
is God.
5 Now [a]Moses was faithful in all His house as [b]a servant, [c]for a
testimony of those things [d]which were to be spoken later;
6 but Christ *was faithful* as [a]a Son over His house [b]whose house we
are, [c]if we hold fast our [d]confidence and the boast of our [e]hope firm
until the end.
7 Therefore, just as [a]the Holy Spirit says,
"[b]TODAY IF YOU HEAR HIS VOICE,
8 [a]DO NOT HARDEN YOUR HEARTS AS [1]WHEN THEY PROVOKED ME,

7 [2]Some do not con[...] *hands*

8 [a]Ps. 8:6 [b]1 Cor. 15[...]

9 [1]Or, *a li*[...] [a]Heb. 2:7 [...] Heb. 1:9 [...] 3:13; 1 Pe[...] 3:16 [e]Matt[...] 8:52 [f]Heb.[...]

10 [1]Or, *lea*[...] 24:26 [b]Ro[...] [c]Heb. 5:9; [...] 3:15; 5:31

11 [1]Or, *be*[...] [a]Heb. 13:12 [...] 10:10 [c]Act[...] [d]Matt. 25:40 [...] 3:34f.; John[...]

12 [1]Or, *chu*[...] 22:22

13 [a]Is. 8:17

14 [1]Lit., *blo*[...] *flesh* [a]Matt.[...] [b]John 1:14 [...] 15:54-57; 2 [...] [d]John 12:31

15 [a]Rom. 8[...]

16 [1]Lit., *tak*[...] *angels, but* [...] *hold of* [2]Lit.,[...]

17 [1]Lit., *was* [...] *to be* [a]Phil. [...] 2:14 [b]Heb. [...] [c]Heb. 3:1; 4:[...] 10; 6:20; 7:2[...] 3; 9:11; 10:2[...] 15:17; Heb. [...] 9:24; 1 John

18 [a]Heb. 4:1[...]

3:1 [a]Acts 1:1[...] 2:11; 3:12; 10[...] [b]Phil. 3:14 [c]J[...] [d]Heb. 2:17; 4[...] 10; 6:20; 7:26 [...] 3; 9:11; 10:21 [...] 9:13; Heb. 4:1[...]

2 [1]Lit., *Being* [2]Or, *made* [a]E[...] Num. 12:7; H[...]

3 [a]2 Cor. 3:7-[...]

5 [a]Ex. 40:16; [...] 12:7; Heb. 3:2 [...] 14:31; Num. 1[...] [c]Deut. 18:18f.

6 [a]Heb. 1:2 [b][...] 3:16; 1 Tim. 3[...] 11:22; Heb. 3[...] [d]Eph. 3:12; He[...] 10:19, 35 [e]He[...] 7:19; 10:23; 11 [...] 1:3

7 [a]Acts 28:25; [...] 10:15 [b]Ps. 95[...] 3:15; 4:7

8 [1]Lit., *in the provocation* [a]P[...]

As in the day of trial in the wilderness,
9 [a]Where your fathers tried *Me* by testing *Me*,
And saw My works for [b]forty years.
10 "[a]Therefore I was angry with this generation,
And said, 'They always go astray in their heart;
And they did not know My ways';
11 [a]As I swore in My wrath,
'They shall not enter My rest.'"
12 [a]Take care, brethren, lest there should be in any one of you an
evil, unbelieving heart, in falling away from [b]the living God.
13 But [a]encourage one another day after day, as long as it is *still*
called "Today," lest any one of you be hardened by the [b]deceitfulness
of sin.
14 For we have become partakers of Christ, [a]if we hold fast the
beginning of our [b]assurance firm until the end;
15 while it is said,
"[a]Today if you hear His voice,
Do not harden your hearts, as [1]when they provoked Me."
16 For who [a]provoked *Him* when they had heard? Indeed, [b]did not
all those who came out of Egypt *led* by Moses?
17 And with whom was He angry for forty years? Was it not with
those who sinned, [a]whose bodies fell in the wilderness?
18 And to whom did He swear [a]that they should not enter His rest,
but to those who were [b]disobedient?
19 And *so* we see that they were not able to enter because of [a]un-
belief.

Chapter 4

4 Therefore, let us fear lest, while a promise remains of entering
His rest, any one of you should seem to have [a]come short of it.
2 For indeed we have had good news preached to us, just as they
also; but [a]the word [1]they heard did not profit them, because [2]it was
not united by faith in those who heard.
3 [1]For we who have believed enter that rest, just as He has said,
"[a]As I swore in My wrath,
They shall not enter My rest,"
although His works were finished [b]from the foundation of the world.
4 For He has thus said [a]somewhere concerning the seventh *day*,
"[b]And God [c]rested on the seventh day from all His works";
5 and again in this *passage*, "[a]They shall not enter My rest."
6 Since therefore it remains for some to enter it, and those who
formerly had good news preached to them failed to enter because of
[a]disobedience,
7 He again fixes a certain day, "Today," saying [1]through David
after so long a time just [a]as has been said before,
"[b]Today if you hear His voice,
Do not harden your hearts."
8 For [a]if [1]Joshua had given them rest, He would not have spoken
of another day after that.
9 There remains therefore a Sabbath rest for the people of God.
10 For the one who has entered His rest has himself also [a]rested
from his works, as [b]God did from His.
11 Let us therefore be diligent to enter that rest, lest anyone fall
through *following* the same [a]example of [b]disobedience.

11 [b]Acts 7:36
[a]Ps. 95:10
:11; Heb. 4:3, 5
2:8; Heb. att. 16:16; 31; 12:22
:4f. [b]Eph. 4:22
Heb. 11:1
Lit., *in the* Ps. 95:7f.; b. 3:7; 4:7
29; 44:3, 8 :2, 11, 30; :35, 36, 38
:29; 1 Cor. 10:5
4:23; Deut. 4:2 [b]Rom. Heb. 4:6, 11
in 3:18, 36; 3; Heb 3:12
or. 6:1; Gal. Heb. 12:15
earing [2]Or, *. . faith with eard* [a]Rom. 17; Gal. 3:2; Thess. 2:13
ancient mss. *erefore* [a]Ps. . 3:11 [b]Matt. 25:34
:6 [b]Gen. 2:2 20:11; 31:17
11; Heb. 3:11
eb. 3:18; 4:11
n [a]Heb. 3:7f. [b]Ps. 95:7f.
Jesus [a]Josh. 22:4
. 14:13 [b]Gen. 2:2; Heb. 4:4
et. 2:6 [b]Heb. 3:18; 4:6

12 For [a]the word of God is [b]living and [c]active and sharper than any two-edged [d]sword, and piercing as far as the division of [e]soul and [e]spirit, of both joints and marrow, and [f]able to judge the thoughts and intentions of the heart.

13 And [a]there is no creature hidden from His sight, but all things are [b]open and laid bare to the eyes of Him with whom we have to do.

14 Since then we have a great [a]high priest who has [b]passed through the heavens, Jesus [c]the Son of God, let us hold fast our [d]confession.

15 For we do not have [a]a high priest who cannot sympathize with our weaknesses, but One who has been [b]tempted in all things as *we are, yet* [c]without sin.

16 Let us therefore [a]draw near with [b]confidence to the throne of grace, that we may receive mercy and may find grace to help in time of need.

Chapter 5

5 For every high priest [a]taken from among men is appointed on behalf of men in [b]things pertaining to God, in order to [c]offer both gifts and sacrifices [d]for sins;

2 [1a]he can deal gently with the [b]ignorant and [c]misguided, since he himself also is [2d]beset with weakness;

3 and because of it he is obligated to offer *sacrifices* [a]for sins, [b]as for the people, so also for himself.

4 And [a]no one takes the honor to himself, but *receives it* when he is called by God, even [b]as Aaron was.

5 So also Christ [a]did not glorify Himself so as to become a [b]high priest, but He who [c]said to Him,

"[d]THOU ART MY SON,
TODAY I HAVE BEGOTTEN THEE";

6 just as He says also in another *passage*,

"[a]THOU ART A PRIEST FOREVER
ACCORDING TO [b]THE ORDER OF MELCHIZEDEK."

7 In the days of His flesh, [1a]He offered up both prayers and supplications with [b]loud crying and tears to the One [c]able to save Him [2]from death, and He [3]was heard because of His [d]piety.

8 Although He was [a]a Son, He learned [b]obedience from the things which He suffered.

9 And having been made [a]perfect, He became to all those who obey Him the source of eternal salvation,

10 being designated by God as [a]a high priest according to [b]the order of Melchizedek.

11 Concerning [1]him we have much to say, and *it is* hard to explain, since you have become dull of hearing.

12 For though [1]by this time you ought to be teachers, you have need again for someone to teach you [a]the [2b]elementary principles of the [c]oracles of God, and you have come to need [d]milk and not solid food.

13 For everyone who partakes *only* of milk is not accustomed to the word of righteousness, for he is a [a]babe.

14 But solid food is for [a]the mature, who because of practice have their senses [b]trained to [c]discern good and evil.

12 [a]Jer. 5:26; Heb 1:23 [b]Ac [c]1 Thess. 6:17 [e]1 T [f]John 12:4 14:24f.

13 [a]2 Chr 33:13-15

14 [a]Heb. 4:10; Heb. 9:24 [c]Mat 1:2; 6:6; 7 [d]Heb. 3:1

15 [a]Heb. 2:18 [c]2 Co 7:26

16 [a]Heb. 7

5:1 [a]Ex. 2 2:17 [c]Heb. 9:9; 10:11 Heb. 7:27;

2 [1]Lit., *bei* [2]Or, *subjec weakness* 4:15 [b]Eph. 9:7 mg. [c]Ja 1 Pet. 2:25

3 [a]1 Cor. 15 7:27; 10:12 16:6; Heb. 7

4 [a]Num. 16 2 Chr. 26:18 1 Chr. 23:13

5 [a]John 8:5 2:17; 5:10 [c] [d]Ps. 2:7

6 [a]Ps. 110:4 [b]Heb. 5:10; 6 7:11, 17

7 [1]Lit., *who offered up* [2] [3]Lit., *having* [a]Matt. 26:39, Mark 14:36, 22:41, 44 [b]M 50; Mark 15:3 Luke 23:46 [c] 14:36 [d]Heb.

8 [a]Heb. 1:2

9 [a]Heb. 2:10

10 [a]Heb. 2:17 [b]Heb. 5:6

11 [1]Or, *Him o*

12 [1]Lit., *beca time* [2]Lit., *eler the beginning* [b]Heb. 6:1 [c]Ac [d]1 Cor. 3:2; 1 P

13 [a]1 Cor. 3:1 1 Pet. 2:2

14 [a]1 Cor. 2:6 4:13; Heb. 6:1 4:7 [c]Rom. 14:

Chapter 6

6 Therefore [a]leaving [b]the [1]elementary teaching about the [2]Christ,
let us press on to [3c]maturity, not laying again a foundation of
repentance from [d]dead works and of faith toward God,
2 of [a]instruction about washings, and [b]laying on of hands, and the
[c]resurrection of the dead, and [c]eternal judgment.
3 And this we shall do, [a]if God permits.
4 For in the case of those who have once been [a]enlightened and
have tasted of [b]the heavenly gift and have been made [c]partakers of
the Holy Spirit,
5 and [a]have tasted the good [b]word of God and the powers of [c]the
age to come,
6 and *then* have fallen away, it is [a]impossible to renew them again
to repentance, [1b]since they again crucify to themselves the Son of
God, and put Him to open shame.
7 For ground that drinks the rain which often [1]falls upon it and
brings forth vegetation useful to those [a]for whose sake it is also
tilled, receives a blessing from God;
8 but if it yields thorns and thistles, it is worthless and [a]close [1]to
being cursed, and [2]it ends up being burned.
9 But, [a]beloved, we are convinced of better things concerning you,
and things that [1]accompany salvation, though we are speaking in
this way.
10 For [a]God is not unjust so as to forget [b]your work and the love
which you have shown toward His name, in having [c]ministered and
in still ministering to the [1]saints.
11 And we desire that each one of you show the same diligence [1]so
as to realize the [a]full assurance of [b]hope until the end,
12 that you may not be sluggish, but [a]imitators of those who
through [b]faith and patience [c]inherit the promises.
13 For [a]when God made the promise to Abraham, since He could
swear by no one greater, He [b]swore by Himself,
14 saying, "[a]I WILL SURELY BLESS YOU, AND I WILL SURELY MULTIPLY YOU."
15 And thus, [a]having patiently waited, he obtained the promise.
16 [a]For men swear by one greater *than themselves*, and with them [b]an
oath *given* as confirmation is an end of every dispute.
17 [1]In the same way God, desiring even more to show to [a]the heirs
of the promise [b]the unchangeableness of His purpose, [2]interposed
with an oath,
18 in order that by two unchangeable things, in which [a]it is impos-
sible for God to lie, we may have strong encouragement, we who
have fled for refuge in laying hold of [b]the hope set before us.
19 [1]This [a]hope we have as an anchor of the soul, a *hope* both sure
and steadfast and one which [b]enters [2]within the veil,
20 [a]where Jesus has entered as a forerunner for us, having become a
[b]high priest forever according to the order of Melchizedek.

Chapter 7

7 For this [a]Melchizedek, king of Salem, priest of the [b]Most High
God, who met Abraham as he was returning from the slaughter
of the kings and blessed him,
2 to whom also Abraham apportioned a tenth part of all *the spoils*,

was first of all, by the translation *of his name*, king of righteousness, and then also king of Salem, which is king of peace.

3 Without father, without mother, [a]without genealogy, having neither beginning of days nor end of life, but made like [b]the Son of God, he abides a priest perpetually.

4 Now observe how great this man was to whom Abraham, the [a]patriarch, [b]gave a tenth of the choicest spoils.

5 And those indeed of [a]the sons of Levi who receive the priest's office have commandment [1]in the Law to collect [2]a tenth from the people, that is, from their brethren, although these [3]are descended from Abraham.

6 But the one [a]whose genealogy is not traced from them [b]collected [1]a tenth from Abraham, and [b]blessed the one who [c]had the promises.

7 But without any dispute the lesser is blessed by the greater.

8 And in this case mortal men receive tithes, but in that case one *receives them*, [a]of whom it is witnessed that he lives on.

9 And, so to speak, through Abraham even Levi, who received tithes, paid tithes,

10 for he was still in the loins of his father when Melchizedek met him.

11 [a]Now if perfection was through the Levitical priesthood (for on the basis of it [b]the people received the Law), what further need *was there* for another priest to arise [c]according to the order of Melchizedek, and not be designated according to the order of Aaron?

12 For when the priesthood is changed, of necessity there takes place a change of law also.

13 For [a]the one concerning whom [b]these things are spoken belongs to another tribe, from which no one has officiated at the altar.

14 For it is evident that our Lord [1]was [a]descended from Judah, a tribe with reference to which Moses spoke nothing concerning priests.

15 And this is clearer still, if another priest arises according to the likeness of Melchizedek,

16 who has become *such* not on the basis of a law of [a]physical requirement, but according to the power of [b]an indestructible life.

17 For it is witnessed *of Him*,

"[a]THOU ART A PRIEST FOREVER
ACCORDING TO THE ORDER OF MELCHIZEDEK."

18 For, on the one hand, there is a setting aside of a former commandment [a]because of its weakness and uselessness

19 (for [a]the Law made nothing perfect), and on the other hand there is a bringing in of a better [b]hope, through which we [c]draw near to God.

20 And inasmuch as *it was* not without an oath

21 (for they indeed became priests without an oath, but He with an oath through the One who said to Him,

"[a]THE LORD HAS SWORN
AND [b]WILL NOT CHANGE HIS MIND,
'THOU ART A PRIEST [c]FOREVER' ");

22 so much the more also Jesus has become the [a]guarantee of [b]a better covenant.

23 And the *former* priests, on the one hand, existed in greater numbers, because they were prevented by death from continuing,

3 [a]Heb. 7 Heb. 7:1,
4 [a]Acts 2: [b]Gen. 14:2
5 [1]Lit., *acc* [2]Or, *tithes come out c* [a]Num. 18:2 31:4f.
6 [1]Or, *tithe* [b]Heb. 7:1f.
8 [a]Heb. 5:6
11 [a]Heb. 7. [b]Heb. 9:6; 1 5:6; 7:17
13 [a]Heb. 7: 7:11
14 [1]Lit., *rose* [a]Num. 24:17 Mic. 5:2; Ma 5:5
16 [a]Heb. 9:1 9:14
17 [a]Ps. 110:4 6:20; 7:21
18 [a]Rom. 8:3 3:21; Heb. 7:1
19 [a]Acts 13:3 3:20; 7:7f.; Ga 3:21; Heb. 9:9 [b]Heb. 3:6 [c]Lar Heb. 4:16; 7:2 22; James 4:8
21 [a]Ps. 110:4; 7:17 [b]Num. 23 1 Sam. 15:29; 11:29 [c]Heb. 7:
22 [a]Ps. 119:12 38:14 [b]Heb. 8:

24 but He, on the other hand, because He abides [a]forever, holds His
priesthood permanently.
25 Hence, also, He is able to [a]save [1]forever those who [b]draw near to
God through Him, since He always lives to [c]make intercession for
them.
26 For it was fitting that we should have such a [a]high priest, [b]holy,
[c]innocent, undefiled, separated from sinners and [d]exalted above the
heavens;
27 who does not need daily, like those high priests, to [a]offer up
sacrifices, [b]first for His own sins, and then for the *sins* of the people,
because this He did [c]once for all when He [d]offered up Himself.
28 For the Law appoints men as high priests [a]who are weak, but the
word of the oath, which came after the Law, *appoints* [b]a Son, [c]made
perfect forever.

Chapter 8

8 Now the main point in what has been said *is this*: we have such a
[a]high priest, who has taken His seat at [b]the right hand of the
throne of the [b]Majesty in the heavens,
2 a [a]minister [1]in the sanctuary, and [1]in the [b]true [2]tabernacle, which
the Lord [c]pitched, not man.
3 For every [a]high priest is appointed [b]to offer both gifts and sacri-
fices; hence it is necessary that this *high priest* also have something to
offer.
4 Now if He were on earth, He would not be a priest at all, since
there are those who [a]offer the gifts according to the Law;
5 who serve [a]a copy and [b]shadow of the heavenly things, just as
Moses [1]was [c]warned *by God* when he was about to erect the [2]taber-
nacle; for, "[d]SEE," He says, "THAT YOU MAKE all things ACCORDING TO
THE PATTERN WHICH WAS SHOWN YOU ON THE MOUNTAIN."
6 But now He has obtained a more excellent ministry, by as much
as He is also the [a]mediator of [b]a better covenant, which has been
enacted on better promises.
7 For [a]if that first *covenant* had been faultless, there would have
been no occasion sought for a second.
8 For finding fault with them, He says,
"[a]BEHOLD, DAYS ARE COMING, SAYS THE LORD,
[1]WHEN I WILL EFFECT [b]A NEW COVENANT
WITH THE HOUSE OF ISRAEL AND WITH THE HOUSE OF JUDAH;
9 [a]NOT LIKE THE COVENANT WHICH I MADE WITH THEIR FATHERS
ON THE DAY WHEN I TOOK THEM BY THE HAND
TO LEAD THEM OUT OF THE LAND OF EGYPT;
FOR THEY DID NOT CONTINUE IN MY COVENANT,
AND I DID NOT CARE FOR THEM, SAYS THE LORD.
10 "[a]FOR THIS IS THE COVENANT THAT I WILL MAKE WITH THE HOUSE OF
ISRAEL
AFTER THOSE DAYS, SAYS THE LORD:
I WILL PUT MY LAWS INTO THEIR MINDS,
AND I WILL WRITE THEM [b]UPON THEIR HEARTS.
AND I WILL BE THEIR GOD,
AND THEY SHALL BE MY PEOPLE.
11 "[a]AND THEY SHALL NOT TEACH EVERYONE HIS FELLOW CITIZEN,
AND EVERYONE HIS BROTHER, SAYING, 'KNOW THE LORD,'
FOR [b]ALL SHALL KNOW ME,

n 12:34; :23f., 28
mpletely
Heb. 7:19
Heb. 9:24
7 [b]2 Cor.
5 [c]1 Pet.
Heb. 4:14
[b]Lev. 9:7;
Heb. 9:12,
[d]Eph. 5:2;
10:10, 12
[b]Heb. 1:2
Heb. 2:10
3:1; Heb.
Ps. 110:1;
Heb. 1:3
Or, *sacred*
):11 [b]Heb.
[c]Ex. 33:7
:17 [b]Rom.
Gal. 2:20;
eb. 5:1; 8:4
; 7:27; 8:3;
9:9; 10:11
[2]Or, *sacred*
9:23 [b]Col.
10:1 [c]Matt.
11:7; 12:25
[d]Ex. 25:40
. 2:5 [b]Luke
b. 7:22; 8:8;
9:15; 12:24
[a]Heb. 7:11
[a]Jer. 31:31
); 2 Cor. 3:6;
:6, 13; 9:15;
12:24
19:5; 24:6-8;
3; Jer. 31:32
31:33; Rom.
; Heb. 10:16
[b]2 Cor. 3:3
er. 31:34 [b]Is.
3; John 6:45;
1 John 2:27

FROM THE LEAST TO THE GREATEST OF THEM.
12 "[a]FOR I WILL BE MERCIFUL TO THEIR INIQUITIES,
[b]AND I WILL REMEMBER THEIR SINS NO MORE."
13 [1]When He said, "[a]A new *covenant*," He has made the first obsolete. [b]But whatever is becoming obsolete and growing old is [2]ready to disappear.

Inside of the Tabernacle

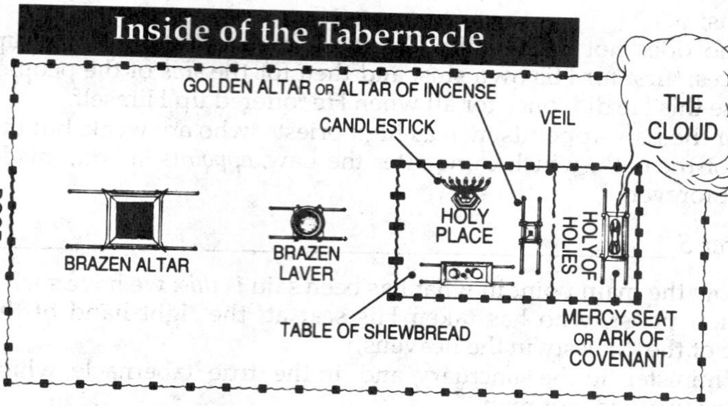

Chapter 9

9 Now even the first *covenant* had [a]regulations of divine worship and [b]the earthly sanctuary.

2 For there was [a]a [1]tabernacle prepared, the [2]outer one, in which *were* [b]the lampstand and [c]the table and [d]the [3]sacred bread; this is called the holy place.

3 And behind [a]the second veil, there was a [1]tabernacle which is called the [b]Holy of Holies,

4 having a golden [1a]altar of incense and [b]the ark of the covenant covered on all sides with gold, in which *was* [c]a golden jar holding the manna, and [d]Aaron's rod which budded, and [e]the tables of the covenant.

5 And above it *were* the [a]cherubim of glory [b]overshadowing the mercy seat; but of these things we cannot now speak in detail.

6 Now when these things have been thus prepared, the priests [a]are continually entering the [1]outer [2]tabernacle, performing the divine worship,

7 but into [a]the second only [b]the high priest *enters*, [c]once a year, [d]not without *taking* blood, which he [e]offers for himself and for the [1f]sins of the people committed in ignorance.

8 [a]The Holy Spirit *is* signifying this, [b]that the way into the holy place has not yet been disclosed, while the [1]outer tabernacle is still standing,

9 which *is* a symbol for the present time. Accordingly [a]both gifts and sacrifices are offered which [b]cannot make the worshiper perfect in conscience,

10 since they *relate* only to [a]food and [b]drink and various [c]washings, [d]regulations for the [1]body imposed until [e]a time of reformation.

11 But when Christ appeared *as* a [a]high priest of the [b]good things [1]to come, *He entered* through [c]the greater and more perfect [2]tabernacle, [d]not made with hands, that is to say, [e]not of this creation;

12 and not through [a]the blood of goats and calves, but [b]through His

12 [a]Is. 4 31:34; 50 19 [b]Heb.

13 [1]Or, *I* [2]Or, *near* 2 Cor. 3:6 8:6, 8; 9:1 [b]2 Cor. 5:1

9:1 [a]Heb. 25:8; Heb

2 [1]Or, *sac* *first* [3]Lit., *presentati* 9; 26:1-30 25:31-39 [d]Ex. 25:30 Matt. 12:4

3 [1]Or, *sac* 26:31-33; 4 26:33

4 [1]Or, *cens* 30:1-5; 37: 25:10ff.; 37: 16:32f. [d]Nu [e]Ex. 25:16; 32:15; Deut 10:3-5

5 [a]Ex. 25:1 25:17, 20; L 1 Kin. 8:7

6 [1]Lit., *first tent* [a]Num.

7 [1]Lit., *ignor* *people* [a]Heb 16:12ff. [c]Ex. 16:34; Heb. 16:11, 14 [e]H [f]Num. 15:25;

8 [1]Lit., *first* [b]John 14:6; H

9 [a]Heb. 5:1

10 [1]Lit., *flesh* 11:2ff.; Col. 2: 6:3 [c]Lev. 11:2 19:13; Mark 7 7:16 [e]Heb. 7:

11 [1]Some anc read *that have* [2]Or, *sacred ter* 2:17 [b]Heb. 10 8:2; 9:24 [d]Mar 2 Cor. 5:1 [e]2 C Heb. 12:27; 13

12 [a]Lev. 4:3; Heb. 9:19 [b]He 13:12

own blood, He [c]entered the holy place [d]once for all, [1]having obtained
[e]eternal redemption.
13 For if [a]the blood of goats and bulls and [b]the ashes of a heifer
sprinkling those who have been defiled, sanctify for the [1]cleansing of
the flesh,
14 how much more will [a]the blood of Christ, who through [1b]the
eternal Spirit [c]offered Himself without blemish to God, [d]cleanse
[2]your conscience from [e]dead works to serve [f]the living God?
15 And for this reason [a]He is the [b]mediator of a [c]new covenant, in
order that since a death has taken place for the redemption of the
transgressions that were *committed* under the first covenant, those
who have been [d]called may [e]receive the promise of [f]the eternal inher-
itance.
16 For where a [1]covenant is, there must of necessity [2]be the death of
the one who made it.
17 For a [1]covenant is valid *only* when [2]men are dead, [3]for it is never
in force while the one who made it lives.
18 Therefore even the first *covenant* was not inaugurated without
blood.
19 For when every commandment had been [a]spoken by Moses to
all the people according to the Law, [b]he took the [c]blood of the calves
and the goats, with [d]water and scarlet wool and hyssop, and
sprinkled both [e]the book itself and all the people,
20 saying, "[a]THIS IS THE BLOOD OF THE COVENANT WHICH GOD COM-
MANDED YOU."
21 And in the same way he [a]sprinkled both the [1]tabernacle and all
the vessels of the ministry with the blood.
22 And according to the [1]Law, *one may* [a]almost *say,* all things are
cleansed with blood, and [b]without shedding of blood there is no
forgiveness.
23 Therefore it was necessary for the [a]copies of the things in the
heavens to be cleansed with these, but [a]the heavenly things them-
selves with better sacrifices than these.
24 For Christ [a]did not enter a holy place made with hands, a *mere*
copy of [b]the true one, but into [c]heaven itself, now [d]to appear in the
presence of God for us;
25 nor was it that He should offer Himself often, as [a]the high priest
enters [b]the holy place [a]year by year with blood not his own.
26 Otherwise, He would have needed to suffer often since [a]the
foundation of the world; but now [b]once at [c]the consummation of the
ages He has been [d]manifested to put away sin [1e]by the sacrifice of
Himself.
27 And inasmuch as [a]it is [1]appointed for men to die once and after
this [b]*comes* judgment,
28 so Christ also, having been [a]offered once to [b]bear the sins of
many, shall appear [c]a second time for [d]salvation [e]without *reference to*
sin, to those who [f]eagerly await Him.

Chapter 10

10 For the Law, since it has *only* [a]a shadow of [b]the good things to
come *and* not the very [1]form of things, [2]can [c]never by the same
sacrifices year by year, which they offer continually, [d]make perfect
those who draw near.
2 Otherwise, would they not have ceased to be offered, because

the worshipers, having once been cleansed, would no longer have
had [a]consciousness of sins?
3 But [a]in [1]those *sacrifices* there is a reminder of sins year by year.
4 For it is [a]impossible for the [b]blood of bulls and goats to take
away sins.
5 Therefore, [a]when He comes into the world, He says,
"[b]SACRIFICE AND OFFERING THOU HAST NOT DESIRED,
BUT [c]A BODY THOU HAST PREPARED FOR ME;
6 [a]IN WHOLE BURNT OFFERINGS AND *sacrifices* FOR SIN THOU HAST TAKEN
NO PLEASURE.
7 "[a]THEN I SAID, 'BEHOLD, I HAVE COME
(IN [b]THE ROLL OF THE BOOK IT IS WRITTEN OF ME)
TO DO THY WILL, O GOD.' "
8 After saying above, "[a]SACRIFICES AND OFFERINGS AND [b]WHOLE BURNT
OFFERINGS AND *sacrifices* [c]FOR SIN THOU HAST NOT DESIRED, NOR HAST
THOU TAKEN PLEASURE *in them*" (which are offered according to the
Law),
9 then He said, "[a]BEHOLD, I HAVE COME TO DO THY WILL." He takes
away the first in order to establish the second.
10 By [1]this will we have been [a]sanctified through [b]the offering of
[c]the body of Jesus Christ [d]once for all.
11 And every priest stands daily ministering and [a]offering time
after time the same sacrifices, which [b]can never take away sins;
12 but He, having offered one sacrifice [a]for [1]sins [b]for all time, [c]SAT
DOWN AT THE RIGHT HAND OF GOD,
13 waiting from that time onward [a]UNTIL HIS ENEMIES BE MADE A
FOOTSTOOL FOR HIS FEET.
14 For by one offering He has [a]perfected [b]for all time those who are
[1]sanctified.
15 And [a]the Holy Spirit also bears witness to us; for after saying,
16 "[a]THIS IS THE COVENANT THAT I WILL MAKE WITH THEM
AFTER THOSE DAYS, SAYS THE LORD:
I WILL PUT MY LAWS UPON THEIR HEART,
AND UPON THEIR MIND I WILL WRITE THEM,"
He then says,
17 "[a]AND THEIR SINS AND THEIR LAWLESS DEEDS
I WILL REMEMBER NO MORE."
18 Now where there is forgiveness of these things, there is no
longer *any* offering for sin.
19 Since therefore, brethren, we [a]have confidence to [b]enter the holy
place by the blood of Jesus,
20 by [a]a new and living way which He inaugurated for us through
[b]the veil, that is, His flesh,
21 and since *we have* [a]a great priest [b]over the house of God,
22 let us [a]draw near with a [1]sincere heart in [b]full assurance of faith,
having our hearts [c]sprinkled *clean* from an evil conscience and our
bodies [d]washed with pure water.
23 Let us hold fast the [a]confession of our [b]hope without wavering,
for [c]He who promised is faithful;
24 and let us consider how [a]to stimulate one another to love and
[b]good deeds,
25 not forsaking our own [a]assembling together, as is the habit of
some, but [b]encouraging *one another*; and all the more, as you see [c]the
day drawing near.

2 [a]1 Pet.
3 [1]Lit., *th* [a]Heb. 9:7
4 [a]Heb. 1 9:12f.
5 [a]Heb. 1 [c]Heb. 2:14 2:24
6 [a]Ps. 40:
7 [a]Ps. 40: 6:2; Jer. 36 3:1f.
8 [a]Ps. 40: [b]Mark 12:3
9 [a]Ps. 40:7
10 [1]Lit., *w* 17:19; Eph. 2:11; 10:14 [b]John 6:51; Heb. 7:27; 10:12 [c]Heb 1 Pet. 2:24
11 [a]Heb. 5: 6:6-8; Heb.
12 [1]Or, *sins down* [a]Heb 10:14 [c]Ps. 1:3
13 [a]Ps. 110
14 [1]Or, *bein sanctified* [a] [b]Heb. 10:12
15 [a]Heb. 3:7
16 [a]Jer. 31:3 8:10
17 [a]Jer. 31:3 8:12
19 [a]Heb. 3:6 [b]Heb. 9:25
20 [a]Heb. 9:8 6:19; 9:3
21 [a]Heb. 2:17 3:15; Heb. 3:6
22 [1]Lit., *true* 7:19; 10:1 [b]H [c]Ezek. 36:25; 12:24; 1 Pet. 1 22:16; 1 Cor. 6 5:26; Titus 3:5 3:21
23 [a]Heb. 3:1 [c]1 Cor. 1:9; 10 11:11
24 [a]Heb. 13:1
25 [a]Acts 2:42 3:13 [c]1 Cor. 3

26 For if we go on [a]sinning willfully after receiving [b]the knowledge
of the truth, there no longer remains a sacrifice for sins,
27 but a certain terrifying expectation of [a]judgment, and [b]THE FURY
OF A FIRE WHICH WILL CONSUME THE ADVERSARIES.
28 [a]Anyone who has set aside the Law of Moses dies without mercy
on *the testimony of* two or three witnesses.
29 [a]How much severer punishment do you think he will deserve
[b]who has trampled under foot the Son of God, and has regarded as
unclean [c]the blood of the covenant [d]by which he was sanctified, and
has [e]insulted the Spirit of grace?
30 For we know Him who said, "[a]VENGEANCE IS MINE, I WILL REPAY."
And again, "[b]THE LORD WILL JUDGE HIS PEOPLE."
31 It is a [a]terrifying thing to fall into the hands of the [b]living God.
32 But remember [a]the former days, [1]when, after being [b]enlightened,
you endured a great [c]conflict of sufferings,
33 partly, by being [a]made a public spectacle through reproaches
and tribulations, and partly by becoming [b]sharers with those who
were so treated.
34 For you [a]showed sympathy to the prisoners, and accepted [b]joy-
fully the seizure of your property, knowing that you have for your-
selves [c]a better possession and an abiding one.
35 Therefore, do not throw away your [a]confidence, which has a
great [b]reward.
36 For you have need of [a]endurance, so that when you have [b]done
the will of God, you may [c]receive [1]what was promised.
37 [a]FOR YET IN A VERY LITTLE WHILE,
[b]HE WHO IS COMING WILL COME, AND WILL NOT DELAY.
38 [a]BUT MY RIGHTEOUS ONE SHALL LIVE BY FAITH;
AND IF HE SHRINKS BACK, MY SOUL HAS NO PLEASURE IN HIM.
39 But [1]we are not of those who shrink back to destruction, but of
those who have faith to the [2]preserving of the soul.

Chapter 11

11 Now faith is the [1a]assurance of *things* [b]hoped for, the [2]convic-
tion of [c]things not seen.
2 For by it the [a]men of old [1b]gained approval.
3 By faith we understand that the [1a]worlds were prepared [b]by the
word of God, so that what is seen [c]was not made out of things which
are visible.
4 By faith [a]Abel offered to God a better sacrifice than Cain,
through which he [b]obtained the testimony that he was righteous,
God testifying [1]about his [c]gifts, and through [2]faith, though [d]he is
dead, he still speaks.
5 By faith [a]Enoch was taken up so that he should not [b]see death;
AND HE WAS NOT FOUND BECAUSE GOD TOOK HIM UP; for he obtained the
witness that before his being taken up he was pleasing to God.
6 And without faith it is impossible to please *Him*, for he who
[a]comes to God must believe that He is, and *that* He is a rewarder of
those who seek Him.
7 By faith [a]Noah, being [b]warned *by God* about [c]things not yet seen,
[1d]in reverence [e]prepared an ark for the salvation of his household, by
which he condemned the world, and became an heir of [f]the right-
eousness which is according to faith.
8 By faith [a]Abraham, when he was called, obeyed by going out to

a place which he was to [b]receive for an inheritance; and he went out,
not knowing where he was going.
9 By faith he lived as an alien in [a]the land of promise, as in a
foreign *land*, [b]dwelling in tents with Isaac and Jacob, [c]fellow heirs of
the same promise;
10 for he was looking for [a]the city which has [b]foundations, [c]whose
architect and builder is God.
11 By faith even [a]Sarah herself received [1]ability to conceive, even
beyond the proper time of life, since she considered Him [b]faithful
who had promised;
12 therefore, also, there was born of one man, and [a]him as good as
dead [1]at that, *as many descendants* [b]AS THE STARS OF HEAVEN IN NUMBER,
AND INNUMERABLE AS THE SAND WHICH IS BY THE SEASHORE.
13 [a]All these died in faith, [b]without receiving the promises, but
[c]having seen them and having welcomed them from a distance, and
[d]having confessed that they were strangers and exiles on the earth.
14 For those who say such things make it clear that they are seeking
a country of their own.
15 And indeed if they had been [1]thinking of that *country* from
which they went out, [a]they would have had opportunity to return.
16 But as it is, they desire a better *country*, that is a [a]heavenly one.
Therefore [b]God is not [1]ashamed to be [c]called their God; for [d]He has
prepared a city for them.
17 By faith [a]Abraham, when he was tested, offered up Isaac; and he
who had [b]received the promises was offering up his only begotten
son;
18 *it was he* to whom it was said, "[a]IN ISAAC YOUR [1]DESCENDANTS
SHALL BE CALLED."
19 [1]He considered that [a]God is able to raise *men* even from the dead;
from which he also received him back [2]as a [b]type.
20 By faith [a]Isaac blessed Jacob and Esau, even regarding things to
come.
21 By faith [a]Jacob, as he was dying, blessed each of the sons of
Joseph, and [b]worshiped, *leaning* on the top of his staff.
22 By faith [a]Joseph, when he was dying, made mention of the ex-
odus of the sons of Israel, and gave orders concerning his bones.
23 By faith [a]Moses, when he was born, was hidden for three months
by his parents, because they saw he was a beautiful child; and they
were not afraid of the [b]king's edict.
24 By faith Moses, [a]when he had grown up, refused to be called the
son of Pharaoh's daughter;
25 choosing rather to [a]endure ill-treatment with the people of God,
than to enjoy the passing pleasures of sin;
26 [a]considering the reproach of [1]Christ greater riches than the
treasures of Egypt; for he was looking to the [b]reward.
27 By faith he [a]left Egypt, not [b]fearing the wrath of the king; for he
endured, as [c]seeing Him who is unseen.
28 By faith he [a]kept the Passover and the sprinkling of the blood, so
that [b]he who destroyed the first-born might not touch them.
29 By faith they [a]passed through the Red Sea as though *they were
passing* through dry land; and the Egyptians, when they attempted
it, were [1]drowned.
30 By faith [a]the walls of Jericho fell down, [b]after they had been
encircled for seven days.

8 [b]Gen. 12
9 [a]Acts 7:5 13:3, 18; 18 6:17
10 [a]Heb. 1 [b]Rev. 21:14 11:16
11 [1]Lit., *po laying dowr* [a]Gen. 17:19 21:2 [b]Heb.
12 [1]Lit., *in* [a]Rom. 4:19 22:17; 32:12
13 [a]Matt. 13 11:39 [c]John 11:27 [d]Gen. 1 Chr. 29:15 Eph. 2:19; 1 2:11
15 [1]Or, *rem* [a]Gen. 24:6-8
16 [1]Lit., *ash them, to be* 4:18 [b]Mark 2:11 [c]Gen. 2 28:13; Ex. 3 [d]Heb. 11:10;
17 [a]Gen. 22 James 2:21
18 [1]Lit., *see* 21:12; Rom.
19 [1]Lit., *Con* [2]Or, *figurative speaking;* lit., *parable* [a]Ror [b]Heb. 9:9
20 [a]Gen. 27:
21 [a]Gen. 48: 20 [b]Gen. 47: 1:47
22 [a]Gen. 50: 13:19
23 [a]Ex. 2:2 [b] 1:16, 22
24 [a]Ex. 2:10,
25 [a]Heb. 11:3
26 [1]I.e., the M [a]Luke 14:33; F [b]Heb. 2:2
27 [a]Ex. 2:15; 13:17f. [b]Ex. 2 10:28f. [c]Col. 1 11:1, 13
28 [a]Ex. 12:21f 12:23, 29f.; 1 C
29 [1]Lit., *swallo* [a]Ex. 14:22-29
30 [a]Josh. 6:20 6:15f.

31 By faith [a]Rahab the harlot did not perish along with those who
were disobedient, after she had welcomed the spies [1]in peace.
32 And what more shall I say? For time will fail me if I tell of
[a]Gideon, [b]Barak, [c]Samson, [d]Jephthah, of [e]David and [f]Samuel and the
prophets,
33 who by faith [a]conquered kingdoms, [b]performed *acts of* righteous-
ness, [c]obtained promises, [d]shut the mouths of lions,
34 [a]quenched the power of fire, [b]escaped the edge of the sword,
from weakness were made strong, [c]became mighty in war, [c]put
foreign armies to flight.
35 [a]Women received *back* their dead by resurrection; and others
were tortured, not accepting their [1]release, in order that they might
obtain a better resurrection;
36 and others [1]experienced mockings and scourgings, yes, also
[a]chains and imprisonment.
37 They were [a]stoned, they were [b]sawn in two, [1]they were tempted,
they were [c]put to death with the sword; they went about [d]in
sheepskins, in goatskins, being destitute, afflicted, [e]ill-treated
38 (*men* of whom the world was not worthy), [a]wandering in deserts
and mountains and caves and holes [1]in the ground.
39 And all these, having [1a]gained approval through their faith, [b]did
not receive [2]what was promised,
40 because God had [1]provided [a]something better for us, so that
[b]apart from us they should not be made perfect.

Chapter 12

12 Therefore, since we have so great a cloud of witnesses sur-
rounding us, let us also [a]lay aside every encumbrance, and
the sin which so easily entangles us, and let us [b]run with [c]endurance
the race that is set before us,
2 [1]fixing our eyes on Jesus, the [2a]author and perfecter of faith, who
for the joy set before Him [b]endured the cross, [c]despising the shame,
and has [d]sat down at the right hand of the throne of God.
3 For [a]consider Him who has endured such hostility by sinners
against Himself, so that you may not grow weary [1b]and lose heart.
4 [a]You have not yet resisted [1b]to the point of shedding blood in
your striving against sin;
5 and you have forgotten the exhortation which is addressed to
you as sons,

"[a]MY SON, DO NOT REGARD LIGHTLY THE DISCIPLINE OF THE LORD,
NOR [b]FAINT WHEN YOU ARE REPROVED BY HIM;
6 [a]FOR THOSE [b]WHOM THE LORD LOVES HE DISCIPLINES,
AND HE SCOURGES EVERY SON WHOM HE RECEIVES."

7 It is for discipline that you endure; [a]God deals with you as with
sons; for what son is there whom *his* father does not discipline?
8 But if you are without discipline, [a]of which all have become
partakers, then you are illegitimate children and not sons.
9 Furthermore, we had [1]earthly fathers to discipline us, and we
[a]respected them; shall we not much rather be subject to [b]the Father of
[2]spirits, and [c]live?
10 For they [1]disciplined us for a short time as seemed best to them,
but He *disciplines us* for *our* good, [a]that we may share His holiness.
11 All discipline [a]for the moment seems not to be joyful, but

with [a]Josh.
James 2:25
Jdg. ch. 6-8
4, 5 [c]Judg.
Judg. ch. 11,
m. 16:1, 13
Sam. 1:20
ch. 4, 7, 11,
m. 5:17-20;
12 [b]1 Sam.
2 Sam. 8:15
:11f. [d]Judg.
am. 17:34ff.;
Dan. 6:22
3:23ff. [b]Ex.
Sam. 18:11;
Kin. ch. 19;
; Ps. 144:10
; 15:8, 15f.;
51f.; 2 Sam.
1-6; 10:15ff.
redemption
17:23; 2 Kin.
4:36f.
received the
Gen. 39:20;
22:27; 2 Chr.
20:2; 37:15
mss. do not
in they were
1 Kin. 21:13;
:21 [b]2 Sam.
; 1 Chr. 20:3
0; Jer. 26:23
3, 19; 2 Kin.
.; Zech. 13:4
. 11:25; 13:3
[a]1 Kin. 18:4,
13; 19:9
., *obtained a*
ony [2]Lit., *the*
e [a]Heb. 11:2
10:36; 11:13
eseen [a]Heb.
6 [b]Rev. 6:11
. 13:12; Eph.
or. 9:24; Gal.
[c]Heb. 10:36
oking to [2]Or,
er [a]Heb. 2:10
:8f.; Heb. 2:9
:18, 23; Heb.
13 [d]Heb. 1:3
ainting in your
Rev. 2:3 [b]Gal.
:9; Heb. 12:5
s far as blood
0:32ff.; 13:13
[b]Phil. 2:8
17; Prov. 3:11
[b]Heb. 12:3
rov. 3:12 [b]Ps.
75; Rev. 3:19
t. 8:5; 2 Sam.
13:24; 19:18;
23:13f.
8 [a]1 Pet. 5:9
fathers of our
[2]Or, *our spirits*
e 18:2 [b]Num.
:16; Rev. 22:6
[c]Is. 38:16
10 [1]Lit., *were*
ng [a]2 Pet. 1:4
11 [a]1 Pet. 1:6

sorrowful; yet to those who have been trained by it, afterwards it
yields the [b]peaceful fruit of righteousness.
12 Therefore, [1a]strengthen the hands that are weak and the knees
that are feeble,
13 and [a]make straight paths for your feet, so that *the limb* which is
lame may not be put out of joint, but rather [b]be healed.
14 [a]Pursue peace with all men, and the [b]sanctification without
which no one will [c]see the Lord.
15 See to it that no one [a]comes short of the grace of God; that no
[b]root of bitterness springing up causes trouble, and by it many be
[c]defiled;
16 that *there be* no [a]immoral or [b]godless person like Esau, [c]who sold
his own birthright for a *single* meal.
17 For you know that even afterwards, [a]when he desired to inherit
the blessing, he was rejected, for he found no place for repentance,
though he sought for it with tears.
18 [a]For you have not come to [b]*a mountain* that may be touched and
to a blazing fire, and to darkness and gloom and whirlwind,
19 and to the [a]blast of a trumpet and the [b]sound of words which
sound was such that those who heard [c]begged that no further word
should be spoken to them.
20 For they could not bear the command, "[a]IF EVEN A BEAST TOUCHES
THE MOUNTAIN, IT WILL BE STONED."
21 And so terrible was the sight, *that* Moses said, "[a]I AM FULL OF FEAR
and trembling."
22 But [a]you have come to Mount Zion and to [b]the city of [c]the living
God, [d]the heavenly Jerusalem, and to [e]myriads of [1]angels,
23 to the general assembly and [a]church of the first-born who [b]are
enrolled in heaven, and to God, [c]the Judge of all, and to the [d]spirits
of righteous men made perfect,
24 and to Jesus, the [a]mediator of a new covenant, and to the
[b]sprinkled blood, which speaks better than [c]*the blood* of Abel.
25 [a]See to it that you do not refuse Him who is [b]speaking. For [c]if
those [1]did not escape when they [d]refused him who [e]warned *them* on
earth, much [2]less *shall* we *escape* who turn away from Him who
[e]*warns* from heaven.
26 And [a]His voice shook the earth then, but now He has promised,
saying, "[b]YET ONCE MORE I WILL SHAKE NOT ONLY THE EARTH, BUT ALSO
THE HEAVEN."
27 And this *expression*, "Yet once more," denotes [a]the removing of
those things which can be shaken, as of created things, in order that
those things which cannot be shaken may remain.
28 Therefore, since we receive a [a]kingdom which cannot be shaken,
let us [1]show gratitude, by which we may [b]offer to God an acceptable
service with reverence and awe;
29 for [a]our God is a consuming fire.

Chapter 13

13 Let [a]love of the brethren continue.
2 Do not neglect to [a]show hospitality to strangers, for by this
some have [b]entertained angels without knowing it.
3 [a]Remember [b]the prisoners, as though in prison with them, and
those who are ill-treated, since you yourselves also are in the body.

11 [b]Is. 32:1
4:8; James
12 [1]Lit., *ma*
[a]Is. 35:3
13 [a]Prov. 4
2:14 [b]Gal. 6
5:16
14 [a]Rom. 1
6:22; Heb. 1
5:8; Heb. 9:
15 [a]2 Cor. 6
Heb. 4:1 [b]D
[c]Titus 1:15
16 [a]Heb. 13
1:9 [c]Gen. 2
17 [a]Gen. 27
18 [a]2 Cor. 3
12:18ff. [b]Ex.
16ff.; 20:18;
5:22
19 [a]Ex. 19:1
20:18; Matt.
19:19; Deut.
20:19; Deut.
20 [a]Ex. 19:1
21 [a]Deut. 9:
22 [1]Or, *ange*
assembly, ar
church [a]Rev.
[b]Eph. 2:19; P
Heb. 11:10; F
[c]Heb. 3:12 [d]
Heb. 11:16 [e]
23 [a]Ex. 4:22
[b]Luke 10:20
18:25; Ps. 50
[d]Heb. 11:40;
24 [a]1 Tim. 2:
8:6; 9:15 [b]He
10:22; 1 Pet.
4:10; Heb. 11
25 [1]Lit., *were*
escaping [2]Lit
[a]Heb. 3:12 [b]H
[c]Heb. 2:2f.; 10
[d]Heb. 12:19 [e]
Heb. 8:5; 11:7
26 [a]Ex. 19:18
5:4f. [b]Hag. 2:
27 [a]Is. 34:4; 5
65:17; Rom. 8
1 Cor. 7:31; H
28 [1]Lit., *have*
2:44 [b]Heb. 13
29 [a]Deut. 4:24
33:14; 2 Thess
Heb. 10:27, 31
13:1 [a]Rom. 12
1 Thess. 4:9; 1
2 [a]Matt. 25:35
12:13; 1 Pet. 4
18:1ff.; 19:1f.
3 [a]Col. 4:18 [b]
25:36; Heb. 10

4 [a]*Let* marriage *be held* in honor among all, and let the *marriage* bed
be undefiled; [b]for fornicators and adulterers God will judge.
5 Let your character be [a]free from the love of money, [b]being con-
tent with what you have; for He Himself has said, "[c]I WILL NEVER
DESERT YOU, NOR WILL I EVER FORSAKE YOU,"
6 so that we confidently say,
"[a]THE LORD IS MY HELPER, I WILL NOT BE AFRAID.
WHAT SHALL MAN DO TO ME?"
7 Remember [a]those who led you, who spoke [b]the word of God to
you; and considering the [1]result of their conduct, [c]imitate their faith.
8 [a]Jesus Christ *is* the same yesterday and today, *yes* and forever.
9 [a]Do not be carried away by varied and strange teachings; for it is
good for the heart to [b]be strengthened by grace, not by [c]foods,
[d]through which those who [1]were thus occupied were not benefited.
10 We have an altar, [a]from which those [b]who serve the [1]tabernacle
have no right to eat.
11 For [a]the bodies of those animals whose blood is brought into the
holy place by the high priest *as an offering* for sin, are burned outside
the camp.
12 Therefore Jesus also, [a]that He might sanctify the people [b]through
His own blood, suffered [c]outside the gate.
13 Hence, let us go out to Him outside the camp, [a]bearing His
reproach.
14 For here [a]we do not have a lasting city, but we are seeking [b]*the
city* which is to come.
15 [a]Through Him then, let us continually offer up a [b]sacrifice of
praise to God, that is, [c]the fruit of lips that [1]give thanks to His name.
16 And do not neglect doing good and [a]sharing; for [b]with such
sacrifices God is pleased.
17 [a]Obey your leaders, and submit *to them*; for [b]they keep watch
over your souls, as those who will give an account. [1]Let them do this
with joy and not [2]with grief, for this would be unprofitable for you.
18 [a]Pray for us, for we are sure that we have a [b]good conscience,
desiring to conduct ourselves honorably in all things.
19 And I urge *you* all the more to do this, [a]that I may be restored to
you the sooner.
20 Now [a]the God of peace, who [b]brought up from the dead the
[c]great Shepherd of the sheep [1]through [d]the blood of the [e]eternal cove-
nant, *even* Jesus our Lord,
21 [a]equip you in every good thing to do His will, [b]working in us
that [c]which is pleasing in His sight, through Jesus Christ, [d]to whom
be the glory forever and ever. Amen.
22 But [a]I urge you, [b]brethren, [1]bear with [2]this [b]word of exhortation,
for [c]I have written to you briefly.
23 Take notice that [a]our brother Timothy has been released, with
whom, if he comes soon, I shall see you.
24 Greet [a]all of your leaders and all the [1b]saints. Those from [c]Italy
greet you.
25 [a]Grace be with you all.

HEBREWS OBSERVATIONS CHART

Author

Recipients

Exhortations

Warnings/Consequences

HEBREWS AT A GLANCE

Hebrews:

SIONS

	CHAPTER THEMES
1	
2	
3	
4	
5	
6	
7	
8	
9	
10	
11	
12	
13	

Author:
unknown

Date:

Purpose:

Key Words:
Jesus (Son)

God

angels

priest (priests, priesthood)

therefore

faith (faithful)

greater

better (better than)

let us

perfect

mark the reference to the devil with a red pitchfork

JAMES

What a turnaround from the day James told his half-brother what to do if He wanted to be publicly! Full of unbelief, convinced that Jesus was nothing more than his eldest brother, Jam Jesus to take His disciples and go up to the Feast of Booths and do His works there. He migl more disciples there, but James was not to be numbered as one of them—until Jesus rose from th (1 Corinthians 15:7).

Convinced from that point on that Jesus was the Christ, James would lay claim not to his p relationship to Jesus but to his spiritual relationship as a bondservant of the Lord Jesus Christ.

James became a pillar of the church, a leader of the council of Jerusalem, and a friend of Pet Paul. But most of all he was a friend of Jesus, a covenant friend for whom he'd be martyred a A.D. 62.

Sometime before A.D. 50 or in the early A.D. 50s, James would write his one epistle to be inclu the pages of Holy Scripture, an epistle that would show what the gospel is like when it's lived shoe leather.

Things to Do

1. Read James in one sitting to familiarize yourself with the book as a whole. James structu writing distinctly. Once you see the pattern he uses, you will better understand the flow book.
   a. First, James introduces a subject by making a statement or giving an instruction. For exa in James 1:2 he says to consider it all joy when you encounter various trials.
   b. He then usually follows with more instructions concerning that particular subject, *or* he an illustration pertaining to the subject, *or* he gives an explanation of it.
2. As you read back through James, mark the key words (and their synonyms and pronouns) on the JAMES AT A GLANCE chart on page 1812. (Key words help you see the subjects book.)
   a. Mark every use of *say (says)* and *works* in chapter 2.
   b. Don't miss marking *tongue* and its pronouns in chapter 3.
   c. You may find other key words which are not listed for you. Mark these and also mark and any reference to the devil (as you have done throughout your Bible).
3. Read James chapter by chapter looking for this pattern:
   a. List the subject introduced by the author on the JAMES SUBJECT BY SUBJECT chart on 1812 and 1813. Be sure to include the chapter and verse from which you took the informa
   b. Next, if the author gives instructions or illustrations regarding that particular subject, r that information in the appropriate column. See JAMES SUBJECT BY SUBJECT for an exa of how to do this.
4. After you list the subjects in each chapter, determine the theme of each chapter and record themes on JAMES AT A GLANCE and in the text by each chapter number.
5. Finally, look for the theme of James. From the information gathered, determine if one sub more predominate than the others or if there is a common denominator between the subject more dominant or common subject will be the theme of James and points to the author's r for writing. Record the theme of James on JAMES AT A GLANCE.

Things to Think About

1. How are you handling the trials in your life?

are you a doer of the Word or a hearer only?

Do you show partiality in dealing with people? Are you a respecter of persons?

s your faith seen by your works?

Are you a friend of the world?

Chapter 1

1 [1a]James, a [b]bond-servant of God and [c]of the Lord Jesus Christ, to
[d]the twelve tribes who are [2e]dispersed abroad, [f]greetings.
2 [a]Consider it all joy, my brethren, when you encounter [b]various
[1]trials,
3 knowing that [a]the testing of your [b]faith produces [1c]endurance.
4 And let [1a]endurance have *its* perfect [2]result, that you may be
[3b]perfect and complete, lacking in nothing.
5 But if any of you [a]lacks wisdom, let him ask of God, who gives to
all men generously and [1]without reproach, and [b]it will be given to
him.
6 But let him [a]ask in faith [b]without any doubting, for the one who
doubts is like the surf of the sea [c]driven and tossed by the wind.
7 For let not that man expect that he will receive anything from the
Lord,
8 *being* a [1a]double-minded man, [b]unstable in all his ways.
9 [a]But let the [1]brother of humble circumstances glory in his high
position;
10 and *let* the rich man *glory* in his humiliation, because [a]like
[1]flowering grass he will pass away.
11 For the sun rises with [1a]a scorching wind, and [b]withers the grass;
and its flower falls off, and the beauty of its appearance is destroyed;
so too the rich man in the midst of his pursuits will fade away.
12 [a]Blessed is a man who perseveres under trial; for once he has
[1]been approved, he will receive [b]the crown of life, which *the Lord* [c]has
promised to those who [d]love Him.
13 Let no one say when he is tempted, "[a]I am being tempted [1]by
God"; for God cannot be tempted [2]by evil, and He Himself does not
tempt anyone.
14 But each one is tempted when he is carried away and enticed by
his own lust.
15 Then [a]when lust has conceived, it gives birth to sin; and when
[b]sin is accomplished, it brings forth death.
16 [a]Do not be deceived, [b]my beloved brethren.
17 Every good thing bestowed and every perfect gift is [a]from above,
coming down from [b]the Father of lights, [c]with whom there is no
variation, or [1]shifting shadow.
18 In the exercise of [a]His will He [b]brought us forth by [c]the word of
truth, so that we might be, [1]as it were, the [d]first fruits [2]among His
creatures.
19 [1]*This* [a]you know, [b]my beloved brethren. But let everyone be quick
to hear, [c]slow to speak *and* [d]slow to anger;
20 for [a]the anger of man does not achieve the righteousness of God.
21 Therefore [a]putting aside all filthiness and *all* [1]that remains of
wickedness, in [2]humility receive [b]the word implanted, which is able
to save your souls.

acob [2]Lit., *in* ersion [a]Acts s 1:1 [c]Rom. 22:30 [e]John [f]Acts 15:23
temptations James 1:12; [b]1 Pet. 1:6
eadfastness [b]Heb. 6:12 [c]Luke 21:19
note 1 [2]Lit., [3]Or, *mature*
21:19 [b]Matt. 48; Col. 4:12
Lit., *does not* [a]1 Kin. 3:9ff.; 7 [b]Matt. 7:7
21:21 [b]Mark 10:20 [c]Matt. 31; Eph. 4:14
Or, *doubting,* [a]James 4:8 [b]2 Pet. 2:14
urch member [a]Luke 14:11
the flower of [a]1 Cor. 7:31; 1 Pet. 1:24
it., *the* [a]Matt. 102:4, 11; Is. 40:7f.
assed the test James 5:11; 4:14 [b]1 Cor. 20:6; James Cor. 2:9; 8:3
from [2]Lit., *of* s [a]Gen. 22:1 ob 15:35; Ps. 59:4 [b]Rom. 5:12; 6:23
Cor. 6:9 [b]Acts ames 1:2, 19; 3:1, 10; 4:11; 5:12, 19
it., *shadow of* ng [a]John 3:3; 3:15, 17 [b]Ps. ohn 1:5 [c]Mal. 3:6
a certain first [2]Lit., *of* [a]John [b]James 1:15; 3, 23 [c]2 Cor. n. 1:13; 2 Tim. 2:3; Rev. 14:4
[1]Or, *Know* this hn 2:21 [b]Acts James 1:2, 16; 3:1, 10; 4:11; [c]Prov. 10:19; [d]Prov. 16:32; Eccl. 7:9
att. 5:22; Eph. 4:26
abundance of Or, *gentleness* 22; 1 Pet. 2:1 3; 1 Pet. 1:22f.

22 [a]But prove yourselves doers of the word, and not merely hearers who delude themselves.

23 For if anyone is a hearer of the word and not a doer, he is like a man who looks at his [1]natural face [a]in a mirror;

24 for *once* he has looked at himself and gone away, [1]he has immediately forgotten what kind of person he was.

25 But one who looks intently at the perfect law, [a]the *law* of liberty, and abides by it, not having become a forgetful hearer but [1]an effectual doer, this man shall be [b]blessed in [2]what he does.

26 If anyone thinks himself to be religious, and yet does not [a]bridle his tongue but deceives his *own* heart, this man's religion is worthless.

27 This is pure and undefiled religion [a]in the sight of *our* God and Father, to [b]visit [c]orphans and widows in their distress, *and* to keep oneself unstained [1]by [d]the world.

Chapter 2

2 [a]My brethren, [b]do not hold your faith in our [c]glorious Lord Jesus Christ with *an attitude of* [d]personal favoritism.

2 For if a man comes into your [1]assembly with a gold ring and dressed in [2a]fine clothes, and there also comes in a poor man in [b]dirty clothes,

3 and you [1]pay special attention to the one who is wearing the [a]fine clothes, and say, "You sit here in a good place," and you say to the poor man, "You stand over there, or sit down by my footstool,"

4 have you not made distinctions among yourselves, and become judges [a]with evil [1]motives?

5 Listen, [a]my beloved brethren: did not [b]God choose the poor [1]of this world *to be* [c]rich in faith and [d]heirs of the kingdom which He [e]promised to those who love Him?

6 But you have dishonored the poor man. Is it not the rich who oppress you and [1]personally [a]drag you into [2]court?

7 [a]Do they not blaspheme the fair name [1]by which you have been called?

8 If, however, you [a]are fulfilling the [1]royal law, according to the Scripture, "[b]YOU SHALL LOVE YOUR NEIGHBOR AS YOURSELF," you are doing well.

9 But if you [a]show partiality, you are committing sin *and* are convicted by the [1]law as transgressors.

10 For whoever keeps the whole [1]law and yet [a]stumbles in one *point,* he has become [b]guilty of all.

11 For He who said, "[a]DO NOT COMMIT ADULTERY," also said, "[b]DO NOT COMMIT MURDER." Now if you do not commit adultery, but do commit murder, you have become a transgressor of the [1]law.

12 So speak and so act, as those who are to be judged by [a]*the* law of liberty.

13 For [a]judgment *will be* merciless to one who has shown no mercy; mercy [1]triumphs over judgment.

14 [a]What use is it, [b]my brethren, if a man says he has faith, but he has no works? Can [1]that faith save him?

15 [a]If a brother or sister is without clothing and in need of daily food,

16 and one of you says to them, "[a]Go in peace, be warmed and be

22 [a]Matt. 7 6:46-49; Ro James 1:22

23 [1]Lit., *the birth;* or, *na* 13:12

24 [1]Lit., *an*

25 [1]Lit., *a c work* [2]Lit., [a]John 8:32; Gal. 2:4; 6:2 2:12; 1 Pet. 13:17

26 [a]Ps. 39: James 3:2-1

27 [1]Lit., *fro* 2:13; Gal. 3: 25:36 [c]Deut 31:16, 17, 2 Is. 1:17, 23 12:32; Eph. 2:12; James 1:4; 2:20; 1

2:1 [a]James 12:2 [c]Acts 7 2:8 [d]Acts 10 2:9

2 [1]Or, *synag bright* [a]Luke James 2:3 [b]

3 [1]Lit., *look* 23:11

4 [1]Lit., *reaso* [a]Luke 18:6; J

5 [1]Lit., *to the* 1:16 [b]Job 34 1:27f. [c]Luke 2:9 [d]Matt. 5: [e]James 1:12

6 [1]Lit., *they themselves* *courts* [a]Acts

7 [1]Lit., *which called upon y* 11:26; 1 Pet.

8 [1]Or, *law of* [a]Matt. 7:12 [b]L

9 [1]Or, *Law* [a] James 2:1

10 [1]Or, *Law* 3:2; 2 Pet. 1:1 24 [b]Matt. 5:19

11 [1]Or, *Law* Deut. 5:18 [b]E Deut. 5:17

12 [a]James 1:

13 [1]Lit., *boas* [a]Prov. 21:13; 18:32-35; Luke

14 [1]Lit., *the* [a] 1:22ff. [b]James

15 [a]Matt. 25:3 3:11

16 [a]1 John 3:

filled," and yet you do not give them what is necessary for *their*
body, what use is that?
17 Even so [a]faith, if it has no works, is dead, *being* by itself.
18 [a]But someone [1]may *well* say, "You have faith, and I have works;
show me your [b]faith without the works, and I will [c]show you my
faith [d]by my works."
19 You believe that [1a]God is one. [b]You do well; [c]the demons also
believe, and shudder.
20 But are you willing to recognize, [a]you foolish fellow, that [b]faith
without works is useless?
21 [a]Was not Abraham our father justified by works, when he of-
fered up Isaac his son on the altar?
22 You see that [a]faith was working with his works, and [1]as a result
of the [b]works, faith was [2]perfected;
23 and the Scripture was fulfilled which says, "[a]AND ABRAHAM
BELIEVED GOD, AND IT WAS RECKONED TO HIM AS RIGHTEOUSNESS," and he
was called [b]the friend of God.
24 You see that a man is justified by works, and not by faith alone.
25 And in the same way was not [a]Rahab the harlot also justified by
works, [b]when she received the messengers and sent them out by
another way?
26 For just as the body without *the* spirit is dead, so also [a]faith
without works is dead.

Chapter 3

3 [a]Let not many *of you* become teachers, [b]my brethren, knowing
that as such we shall incur a [1]stricter judgment.
2 For we all [a]stumble in many *ways*. [b]If anyone does not stumble in
[1]what he says, he is a [c]perfect man, able to [d]bridle the whole body as
well.
3 Now [a]if we put the bits into the horses' mouths so that they may
obey us, we direct their entire body as well.
4 Behold, the ships also, though they are so great and are driven
by strong winds, are still directed by a very small rudder, wherever
the inclination of the pilot desires.
5 So also the tongue is a small part of the body, and *yet* it [a]boasts of
great things. [b]Behold, how great a forest is set aflame by such a small
fire!
6 And [a]the tongue is a fire, the *very* world of iniquity; the tongue is
set among our members as that which [b]defiles the entire body, and
sets on fire the course of *our* [1]life, and is set on fire by [2c]hell.
7 For every [1]species of beasts and birds, of reptiles and creatures of
the sea, is tamed, and has been tamed by the human [1]race.
8 But no one can tame the tongue; *it is* a restless evil *and* full of
[a]deadly poison.
9 With it we bless [a]*our* Lord and Father; and with it we curse men,
[b]who have been made in the likeness of God;
10 from the same mouth come *both* blessing and cursing. My
brethren, these things ought not to be this way.
11 Does a fountain send out from the same opening *both* [1]fresh and
bitter *water*?
12 [a]Can a fig tree, my brethren, produce olives, or a vine produce
figs? Neither *can* salt water produce [1]fresh.

ial. 5:6; James 2:20, 26
Lit., *will* [a]Rom. Rom. 3:28; 4:6; 11:33 [c]James att. 7:16f.; Gal. 5:6
Or, *there is one* Deut. 6:4; Mark 29 [b]James 2:8 29; Mark 1:24; Luke 4:34; Acts 19:15
m. 9:20; 1 Cor. ial. 5:6; James 2:17, 26
1. 22:9, 10, 12, 16-18
, *by the deeds* *mpleted* [a]John 29; Heb. 11:17 [b]1 Thess. 1:3
en. 15:6; Rom. . 20:7; Is. 41:8
. 11:31 [b]Josh. 2:4, 6, 15
ial. 5:6; James 2:17, 20
1 [1]Or, *greater* *mnation* [a]Matt. 3; Rom. 2:20f.; [b]James 1:16; 3:10
word [a]James Matt. 12:34-37; :2-12 [c]James [d]James 1:26
3 [a]Ps. 32:9
s. 12:3f.; 73:8f. [b]Prov. 26:20f.
xistence, origin *Gehenna* [a]Ps. 3; Prov. 16:27 12:36f.; 15:11, 8f. [c]Matt. 5:22
7 [1]Lit., *nature*
s. 140:3; Eccl. 11; Rom. 3:13
es 1:27 [b]Gen. 26; 1 Cor. 11:7
11 [1]Lit., *sweet*
note 1 [a]Matt. 7:16

13 Who among you is wise and understanding? [a]Let him show by
his [b]good behavior his deeds in the gentleness of wisdom.
14 But if you have bitter [a]jealousy and [1]selfish ambition in your
heart, do not be arrogant and *so* lie against [b]the truth.
15 This wisdom is not that which comes down [a]from above, but is
[b]earthly, [1c]natural, [d]demonic.
16 For where [a]jealousy and [1]selfish ambition exist, there is disorder
and every evil thing.
17 But the wisdom [a]from above is first [b]pure, then [c]peaceable,
[d]gentle, [1]reasonable, [e]full of mercy and good fruits, [f]unwavering,
without [g]hypocrisy.
18 And the [1a]seed whose fruit is righteousness is sown in peace [2]by
those who make peace.

Chapter 4

4 What is the source of quarrels and [a]conflicts among you? [2]Is not
the source your pleasures that wage [b]war in your members?
2 You lust and do not have; *so* you [a]commit murder. And you are
envious and cannot obtain; *so* you fight and quarrel. You do not have
because you do not ask.
3 You ask and [a]do not receive, because you ask [1]with wrong mo-
tives, so that you may spend *it* [2]on your pleasures.
4 You [a]adulteresses, do you not know that friendship with [b]the
world is [c]hostility toward God? [d]Therefore whoever wishes to be a
friend of the world makes himself an enemy of God.
5 Or do you think that the Scripture [a]speaks to no purpose: "[1]He
[2]jealously desires [b]the Spirit which He has made to dwell in us"?
6 But [a]He gives a greater grace. Therefore *it* says, "[b]GOD IS OPPOSED
TO THE PROUD, BUT GIVES GRACE TO THE HUMBLE."
7 [a]Submit therefore to God. [b]Resist the devil and he will flee from
you.
8 [a]Draw near to God and He will draw near to you. [b]Cleanse your
hands, you sinners; and [c]purify your hearts, you [d]double-minded.
9 [a]Be miserable and mourn and weep; let your laughter be turned
into mourning, and your joy to gloom.
10 [a]Humble yourselves in the presence of the Lord, and He will
exalt you.
11 [a]Do not speak against one another, [b]brethren. He who speaks
against a brother, or [c]judges his brother, speaks against [d]the law, and
judges the law; but if you judge the law, you are not [e]a doer of the
law, but a judge *of it*.
12 There is *only* one [a]Lawgiver and Judge, the One who is [b]able to
save and to destroy; but [c]who are you who judge your neighbor?
13 [a]Come now, you who say, "[b]Today or tomorrow, we shall go to
such and such a city, and spend a year there and engage in business
and make a profit."
14 [1]Yet you do not know [2]what your life will be like tomorrow. [a]You
are *just* a vapor that appears for a little while and then vanishes
away.
15 [1]Instead, *you ought* to say, "[a]If the Lord wills, we shall live and
also do this or that."
16 But as it is, you boast in your [1]arrogance; [a]all such boasting is
evil.

13 [a]James 2:
2:12
14 [1]Or, *strife*
2:8; 2 Cor. 12
3:16 [b]1 Tim. 2
1:18; 5:19
15 [1]Or, *unspi*
[a]James 1:17
2:6; 3:19 [c]2 C
Jude 19 [d]2 T
1 Tim. 4:1; Re
16 [1]V. 14, not
[a]Rom. 2:8; 2 C
James 3:14
17 [1]Or, *willing*
[a]James 1:17
7:11; James 4
5:9; Heb. 12:1
3:2 [e]Luke 6:3
2:13 [f]James 2
12:9; 2 Cor. 6
18 [1]Lit., *fruit*
righteousness
[a]Prov. 11:18; I
Hos. 10:12; A
Gal. 6:8; Phil.
4:1 [1]Lit., *Whe*
and whence f
[2]Lit., Are they
from your [a]Ti
[b]Rom. 7:23
2 [a]James 5:6
3:15
3 [1]Lit., *wicke*
in [a]1 John 3:2
4 [a]Jer. 2:2; E
16:32 [b]James
[c]Rom. 8:7; 1 J
[d]Matt. 6:24; J
5 [1]Or, *The Sp*
He has made
us jealously c
[2]Lit., *desires t*
[a]Num. 23:19
6:19; 2 Cor. 6
6 [a]Is. 54:7f.;
13:12 [b]Ps. 13
3:34; Matt. 23
5:5
7 [a]1 Pet. 5:6
4:27; 6:11f.; 1
8 [a]2 Chr. 15:2
1:3; Mal. 3:7;
[b]Job 17:9; Is.
1 Tim. 2:8 [c]Je
James 3:17; 1
1 John 3:3 [d]J
9 [a]Neh. 8:9;
14:13; Luke 6
10 [a]Job 5:11;
21:26; Luke 1
James 4:6
11 [a]2 Cor. 12
James 5:9; 1
[b]James 1:16;
[c]Matt. 7:1; Ro
[d]James 2:8 [e]
12 [a]Is. 33:22
5:9 [b]Matt. 10
14:4
13 [a]James 5
27:1; Luke 12
14 [1]Lit., *Who*
[2]Some mss. r
morrow; for w
life is yours [a]
Ps. 39:5; 102
15 [1]Lit., *Inste*
saying [a]Acts
16 [1]Or, *prete*
[a]1 Cor. 5:6

17 Therefore, [a]to one who knows *the* [1]right thing to do, and does not
do it, to him it is sin.

Chapter 5

5 [a]Come now, [b]you rich, [c]weep and howl for your miseries which
are coming upon you.
2 [a]Your riches have rotted and your garments have become moth-
eaten.
3 Your gold and your silver have rusted; and their rust will be a
witness against you and will consume your flesh like fire. It is [a]in the
last days that you have stored up your treasure!
4 Behold, [a]the pay of the laborers who mowed your fields, *and*
which has been withheld by you, cries out *against you;* and [b]the
outcry of those who did the harvesting has reached the ears of [c]the
Lord of [1]Sabaoth.
5 You have [a]lived luxuriously on the earth and led a life of wanton
pleasure; you have [1]fattened your hearts in [b]a day of slaughter.
6 You have condemned and [1a]put to death [b]the righteous *man;* he
does not resist you.
7 Be patient, therefore, [a]brethren, [b]until the coming of the Lord.
[c]Behold, the farmer waits for the precious produce of the soil, being
patient about it, until [1]it gets [d]the early and late rains.
8 [a]You too be patient; [b]strengthen your hearts, for [c]the coming of
the Lord is [d]at hand.
9 [a]Do not [1]complain, [b]brethren, against one another, that you your-
selves may not be judged; behold, [c]the Judge is standing [2d]right at
the [3]door.
10 As an example, [a]brethren, of suffering and patience, take [b]the
prophets who spoke in the name of the Lord.
11 Behold, we count those [a]blessed who endured. You have heard of
[b]the [1]endurance of Job and have seen [c]the [2]outcome of the Lord's
dealings, that [d]the Lord is full of compassion and *is* merciful.
12 But above all, [a]my brethren, [b]do not swear, either by heaven or
by earth or with any other oath; but [1]let your yes be yes, and your
no, no; so that you may not fall under judgment.
13 Is anyone among you [a]suffering? [b]Let him pray. Is anyone cheer-
ful? Let him [c]sing praises.
14 Is anyone among you sick? Let him call for [a]the elders of the
church, and let them pray over him, [1b]anointing him with oil in the
name of the Lord;
15 and the [a]prayer [1]offered in faith will [2b]restore the one who is sick,
and the Lord will [c]raise him up, and if he has committed sins, [3]they
will be forgiven him.
16 Therefore, [a]confess your sins to one another, and pray for one
another, so that you may be [b]healed. [c]The effective [1]prayer of a right-
eous man can accomplish much.
17 Elijah was [a]a man with a nature like ours, and [b]he prayed
[1]earnestly that it might not rain; and it did not rain on the earth for
[c]three years and six months.
18 And he [a]prayed again, and [b]the [1]sky [2]poured rain, and the earth
produced its fruit.
19 My brethren, [a]if any among you strays from [b]the truth, and one
turns him back,

)r, *good* [a]Luke
hn 9:41; 2 Pet. 2:21

es 4:13 [b]Luke
1 Tim. 6:9 [c]Is.
5:3; Ezek. 30:2

13:28; Is. 50:9; Matt. 6:19f.

[a]James 5:7, 8

e., Hosts [a]Lev.
ob 24:10f.; Jer.
; Mal. 3:5 [b]Ex.
eut. 24:15; Job
3f. [c]Rom. 9:29

[1]Lit., *nourished*
k. 16:49; Luke
Tim. 5:6; 2 Pet.
ler. 12:3; 25:34

[1]Or, *murdered*
mes 4:2 [b]Heb.
38; 1 Pet. 4:18

e [a]James 4:11;
) [b]John 21:22;
2:19 [c]Gal. 6:9
1:14; Jer. 5:24; Joel 2:23

8 [a]Luke 21:19
ss. 3:13 [c]John
; 1 Thess. 2:19
3:11, 12; 1 Pet. 4:7

it., *groan* [2]Lit.,
ore [3]Lit., *doors*
s 4:11 [b]James
10 [c]1 Cor. 4:5;
4:12; 1 Pet. 4:5
33; Mark 13:29

nes 4:11; 5:7, 9
[b]Matt. 5:12

steadfastness
end of the Lord
10; 1 Pet. 3:14
21f.; 2:10 [c]Job
[d]Ex. 34:6; Ps. 103:8

et yours be the
es, and the no,
es 1:16 [b]Matt. 5:34-37

mes 5:10 [b]Ps.
[c]1 Cor. 14:15; Col. 3:16

4 [1]Lit., *having*
ed [a]Acts 11:30
ark 6:13; 16:18

t., *of* [2]Or, *save*
, *it* [a]James 1:6
or. 1:21; James
hn 6:39; 2 Cor. 4:14

it., *supplication*
. 3:6; Mark 1:5;
8 [b]Heb. 12:13;
et. 2:24 [c]Gen.
-32; John 9:31

Lit., *with prayer*
s 14:15 [b]1 Kin.
8:1 [c]Luke 4:25

, *heaven* [2]Lit.,
e [a]1 Kin. 18:42
[b]1 Kin. 18:45

att. 18:15; Gal.
1 [b]James 3:14

20 let him know that he who turns a sinner from the error of his
way will [a]save his soul from death, and will [b]cover a multitude of
sins.

20 [a]Rom. 11:1 1:21; James 1: 10:12; 1 Pet. 4

JAMES AT A GLANCE

Theme of James:

Author:

Date:

Purpose:

Key Words:
brethren

faith

perfect (perfected)

judge(s), (judged, judgment)

law

SEGMENT DIVISIONS	CHAPTER THEMES
	1
	2
	3
	4
	5

JAMES SUBJECT BY SUBJECT

Subject	Instruction	Illustration/Explanation
Trials (1:2-8)	—consider it all joy	
	—let endurance have its	—when you endure trials you will be made mor
	perfect result	(mature), complete, lacking nothing
	—ask God for wisdom	
	—ask in faith, not doubting	—doubter like surf of sea
		—doubter will not receive anything from the Lor

JAMES SUBJECT BY SUBJECT

ject	Instruction	Illustration/Explanation

1 PETER

The hour had come for the Shepherd to be smitten and for the sheep to be scattered. So, Jesu to spend his final hours with his eleven, preparing them for the tribulation that would come.

Yet after Jesus' resurrection and ascension, the tribulation seemed to be relatively mild. T gruntled Pharisees wanted to shut up the men who were turning Jerusalem upside down wi teaching and miracles, but nothing seemed life-threatening.

Then the first stone was thrown. Stephen, the first martyr, was brought to the ground. Un Saul watched him die. In hearty agreement with Stephen's death, Saul went to the high priest permission to round up those of the Way who were spreading this gospel. Saul's purge was lived. Jesus saved Saul on the road to Damascus and changed his name to Paul. But the persecu Christians continued. Herod the king became the adversary of believers, and Jews who had c know Jesus as the Messiah were scattered abroad to other Roman provinces.

However, it wasn't until Nero that the persecution of Christians reached beyond the conf Judah. Rumor had it that Nero had burned Rome so he could rebuild it as he wanted. Nee scapegoat to divert attention from himself, Nero blamed the fire on the Christians and beg systematic persecution of God's children.

Jesus had prepared Peter for the world's tribulation; now Peter would prepare others. Peter his first epistle on the eve of Nero's persecution, about A.D. 63 or 64.

Nero died in A.D. 68, but not before Rome put Peter to death.

THINGS TO DO

1. Read through 1 Peter and do the following:
   a. In the initial verses of the book Peter describes himself and states to whom he is writin in the last verses of the book, he tells why he wrote this epistle. Record your insights ab author and his purpose in writing on the 1 PETER AT A GLANCE chart on page 1820.
   b. Pay close attention to what you see about the recipients of 1 Peter. What is their con What is going on in their midst? Record what you learn about them on the OBSERVA CHART on page 1821.
2. Read 1 Peter chapter by chapter, looking for and marking in a distinctive way the key word their synonyms and pronouns) that are listed on 1 PETER AT A GLANCE. Also remem mark the words such as *grace* and references to the devil which you are marking throughou Bible. In the margin list the truths you learn from every mention of these key words. T imperative if you want to understand 1 Peter.
3. Peter gives the reader many commands or instructions about things to do. You notice these construction of the sentence. The verb usually comes first and the "you" is implied. An ex is seen in 1:13: "Gird your minds for action."
   a. Underline the instructions or commands that Peter gives throughout the book. Then list under "General Instructions" on the OBSERVATIONS CHART.
   b. If you'll evaluate these instructions and commands you'll see that 1 Peter was written no for the recipients but also for you. Think about how these apply to your own life.
4. Peter also gives instructions to specific groups of people such as servants, wives, husband List his instructions to each group under the proper heading on the OBSERVATIONS CHAR
5. From what you have read, why do you think the believers are to do these things? In other w what future event is the motivation for living life in accordance with Peter's exhortations?
6. Finally, summarize the theme of each chapter and record these themes on 1 PETER

GLANCE and in the text next to the chapter number. Don't forget to record the overall theme of 1 Peter.

IGS TO THINK ABOUT

What have you learned about the way you are to live? How are you to respond to others—even when they are not living properly or treating you properly? What is Jesus' example in 1 Peter 2:21-25? Will you follow it?

As you think about what those believers were suffering, should you be surprised if you undergo the same? What will suffering accomplish in your life?

Even if you don't have a Nero in your life, is your adversary, the devil, still prowling about like a lion, seeking whom he may devour? What are you to do, according to 1 Peter?

When our Lord Jesus Christ returns, will you be found standing firm in the true grace that has been provided you? What must you do or change in order to be prepared to see Him face to face?

Chapter 1

1 [a]Peter, an apostle of Jesus Christ, to those who reside as [b]aliens,
[c]scattered throughout [d]Pontus, [e]Galatia, [d]Cappadocia, [d]Asia, and
[f]Bithynia, [g]who are chosen
2 according to the [a]foreknowledge of God the Father, [b]by the
sanctifying work of the Spirit, [1]that you may [c]obey Jesus Christ and
be [d]sprinkled with His blood: [e]May grace and peace [2]be yours in
fullest measure.
3 [a]Blessed be the God and Father of our Lord Jesus Christ, who
[b]according to His great mercy [c]has caused us to be born again to [d]a
living hope through the [e]resurrection of Jesus Christ from the dead,
4 to *obtain* an [a]inheritance *which is* imperishable and undefiled and
[b]will not fade away, [c]reserved in heaven for you,
5 who are [a]protected by the power of God [b]through faith for [c]a
salvation ready [d]to be revealed in the last time.
6 [a]In this you greatly rejoice, even though now [b]for a little while, [c]if
necessary, you have been distressed by [d]various [1]trials,
7 that the [1a]proof of your faith, *being* more precious than gold
which [2]is perishable, [b]even though tested by fire, [c]may be found to
result in praise and glory and honor at [d]the revelation of Jesus
Christ;
8 and [a]though you have not seen Him, you [b]love Him, and though
you do not see Him now, but believe in Him, you greatly rejoice with
joy inexpressible and [1]full of glory,
9 obtaining as [a]the outcome of your faith the salvation of [1]your
souls.
10 [a]As to this salvation, the prophets who [b]prophesied of the [c]grace
that *would come* to you made careful search and inquiry,
11 [1]seeking to know what person or time [a]the Spirit of Christ within
them was indicating as He [b]predicted the sufferings of Christ and the
glories [2]to follow.
12 It was revealed to them that they were not serving themselves,
but you, in these things which now have been announced to you
through those who [a]preached the gospel to you by [b]the Holy Spirit
sent from heaven—things into which [c]angels long to [1]look.
13 Therefore, [a]gird [1]your minds for action, [2b]keep sober *in spirit*, fix
your [c]hope completely on the [d]grace [3]to be brought to you at [e]the
revelation of Jesus Christ.

et. 1:1 [b]1 Pet.
nes 1:1 [d]Acts
cts 16:6 [f]Acts
tt. 24:22; Luke
18:7
nto obedience
ıkling [2]Lit., *be*
ltiplied for you
29; 1 Pet. 1:20
. 2:13 [c]1 Pet.
[d]Heb. 10:22;
24 [e]2 Pet. 1:2
Cor. 1:3 [b]Gal.
is 3:5 [c]James
t. 1:23 [d]1 Pet.
5, 15; 1 John
. 15:20; 1 Pet.
3:21
s 20:32; Rom.
. 3:24 [b]1 Pet.
:4 [c]2 Tim. 4:8
0:28; Phil. 4:7
[c]1 Cor. 1:21;
. 2:13 [d]1 Pet.
4:13; 5:1
r, temptations
2 [b]1 Pet. 5:10
3:17 [d]James
:2; 1 Pet. 4:12
, genuineness
ishes [a]James
r. 3:13 [c]Rom.
17:30; 1 Pet.
1:13; 4:13
lorified [a]John
29 [b]Eph. 3:19
e ancient mss.
ot contain your
[a]Rom. 6:22
tt. 13:17; Luke
[b]Matt. 26:24
[c]1 Pet. 1:13
inquiring [2]Lit.,
e [a]2 Pet. 1:21
[b]Matt. 26:24
r, gain a clear
[a]1 Pet. 1:25;
2:2-4 [c]1 Tim.
3:16
it., the loins of
mind [2]Lit., *be*
[3]Or, *which is*
ed [a]Eph. 6:14
5:6, 8; 2 Tim.
1 Pet. 4:7; 5:8
3 [d]1 Pet. 1:10
[e]1 Pet. 1:7

14 As [1a]obedient children, do not [2b]be conformed to the former lusts
which were yours in your [c]ignorance,
15 but [1a]like the Holy One who called you, [2b]be holy yourselves also
[c]in all *your* behavior;
16 because it is written, "[a]YOU SHALL BE HOLY, FOR I AM HOLY."
17 And if you [a]address as Father the One who [b]impartially [c]judges
according to each man's work, conduct yourselves [d]in fear during
the time of your [e]stay *upon earth;*
18 knowing that you were not [1a]redeemed with perishable things
like silver or gold from your [b]futile way of life inherited from your
forefathers,
19 but with precious [a]blood, as of a [b]lamb unblemished and spot-
less, *the blood* of Christ.
20 For He was [a]foreknown before [b]the foundation of the world, but
has [c]appeared [1]in these last times [d]for the sake of you
21 who through Him are [a]believers in God, who raised Him from
the dead and [b]gave Him glory, so that your faith and [c]hope are in
God.
22 Since you have [a]in obedience to the truth [b]purified your souls for
a [1c]sincere love of the brethren, fervently love one another from [2]the
heart,
23 for you have been [a]born again [b]not of seed which is perishable
but imperishable, *that is,* through the living and abiding [c]word of
God.
24 For,

"[a]ALL FLESH IS LIKE GRASS,
AND ALL ITS GLORY LIKE THE FLOWER OF GRASS.
THE GRASS WITHERS,
AND THE FLOWER FALLS OFF,

25 [a]BUT THE WORD OF THE LORD ABIDES FOREVER."
And this is [b]the word which was [1]preached to you.

Chapter 2

2 Therefore, [a]putting aside all [1]malice and all guile and [2]hypocrisy
and [2]envy and all [2b]slander,
2 [a]like newborn babes, long for the [1b]pure [2]milk of the word, that
by it you may [c]grow [3]in respect to salvation,
3 if you have [a]tasted [1b]the kindness of the Lord.
4 And coming to Him as to a living stone, [a]rejected by men, but
[1]choice and precious in the sight of God,
5 [a]you also, as living stones, [1]are being built up as a [b]spiritual
house for a holy [c]priesthood, to [d]offer up spiritual sacrifices accept-
able to God through Jesus Christ.
6 For *this* is contained in [1]Scripture:

"[a]BEHOLD I LAY IN ZION A CHOICE STONE, A [b]PRECIOUS CORNER *stone,*
AND HE WHO BELIEVES IN [2]HIM SHALL NOT BE [3]DISAPPOINTED."

7 [a]This precious value, then, is for you who believe. But for those
who disbelieve,

"[b]THE STONE WHICH THE BUILDERS [c]REJECTED,
THIS BECAME THE VERY CORNER *stone,*"

8 and,

"[a]A STONE OF STUMBLING AND A ROCK OF OFFENSE";

[b]for they stumble because they are disobedient to the word, [c]and to
this *doom* they were also appointed.

14 [1]Lit., *childr* *obedience* [2]O *yourselves* [a]1 [b]Rom. 12:2; 1 [c]Eph. 4:18
15 [1]Lit., *accor* [2]Or, *become* 4:7; 1 John 3:3 7:1 [c]James 3:
16 [a]Lev. 11:44 20:7
17 [a]Ps. 89:26 3:19; Matt. 6:9 10:34 [c]Matt. 1 [d]2 Cor. 7:1; He 1 Pet. 3:15 [e]1
18 [1]Or, *ranso* 52:3; 1 Cor. 6: 2:14; Heb. 9:1 4:17
19 [a]Acts 20:2 1:2 [b]John 1:29
20 [1]Lit., *at the* *the times* [a]Ac Eph. 1:4; 1 Pe Rev. 13:8 [b]Ma [c]Heb. 9:26 [d]H
21 [a]Rom. 4:24 [b]John 17:5, 24 3:16; Heb. 2:9 1:3
22 [1]Lit., *unhyp* [2]Some mss. re *clean heart* [a]1 [b]James 4:8 [c]J 13:34; Rom. 1 Heb. 13:1; 1 P 3:8
23 [a]John 3:3; 1:3 [b]John 1:1 4:12
24 [a]Is. 40:6ff. 1:10f.
25 [1]Lit., *preac* *good news to* 40:8 [b]Heb. 6:5
2:1 [1]Or, *wicke* [2]plural nouns 4:22, 25, 31; J 1:21 [b]James 4
2 [1]Or, *unadul* [2]Or, *spiritual* (*logikos) milk* *salvation* [a]Ma 19:14; Mark 1 18:17; 1 Cor. [b]1 Cor. 3:2 [c]E
3 [1]Lit., *that th* *kind* [a]Heb. 6:5 34:8; Titus 3:4
4 [1]Lit., *chose* *elect* [a]1 Pet. 2
5 [1]Or, *allow y* *to be built up* *yourselves up* 3:9 [b]Gal. 6:10 3:15 [c]Is. 61:6 1 Pet. 2:9; Re [d]Rom. 15:16;
6 [1]Or, *a script* *it* [3]Or, *put to s* 28:16; Rom. 9 10:11; 1 Pet. 2 2:20
7 [a]2 Cor. 2:16 2:7, 8 [b]Ps. 11 Matt. 21:42; L [c]1 Pet. 2:4
8 [a]Is. 8:14 [b]1 Gal. 5:11 [c]Ro

9 But you are [a]A CHOSEN RACE, A royal [b]PRIESTHOOD, A [c]HOLY NATION,
[d]A PEOPLE FOR *God's* OWN POSSESSION, that you may proclaim the excel-
lencies of Him who has called you [e]out of darkness into His mar-
velous light;
10 [a]for you once were NOT A PEOPLE, but now you are THE PEOPLE OF
GOD; you had NOT RECEIVED MERCY, but now you have RECEIVED MERCY.
11 [a]Beloved, [b]I urge you as [c]aliens and strangers to abstain from
[d]fleshly lusts, which wage [e]war against the soul.
12 [a]Keep your behavior excellent among the Gentiles, so that in the
thing in which they [b]slander you as evildoers, they may [1]on account
of your good deeds, as they observe *them,* [c]glorify God [d]in the day of
[2]visitation.
13 [a]Submit yourselves for the Lord's sake to every human institu-
tion, whether to a king as the one in authority,
14 or to governors as sent [1]by him [a]for the punishment of evildoers
and the [b]praise of those who do right.
15 For [a]such is the will of God that by doing right you may [b]silence
the ignorance of foolish men.
16 *Act* as [a]free men, and do not use your freedom as a covering for
evil, but *use it* as [b]bondslaves of God.
17 [a]Honor all men; [b]love the brotherhood, [c]fear God, [d]honor the
[1]king.
18 [a]Servants, be submissive to your masters with all respect, not
only to those who are good and [b]gentle, but also to those who are
[1]unreasonable.
19 For this *finds* [1]favor, if for the sake of [a]conscience toward God a
man bears up under sorrows when suffering unjustly.
20 For what credit is there if, when you sin and are harshly treated,
you endure it with patience? But if [a]when you do what is right and
suffer *for it* you patiently endure it, this *finds* [1]favor with God.
21 For [a]you have been called for this purpose, [b]since Christ also
suffered for you, leaving you [c]an example for you to follow in His
steps,
22 WHO [a]COMMITTED NO SIN, NOR WAS ANY DECEIT FOUND IN HIS MOUTH;
23 [1]and while being [a]reviled, He [2]did not revile in return; while
suffering, He uttered no threats, but kept entrusting *Himself* to Him
who judges righteously;
24 and He Himself [1a]bore our sins in His body on the [2b]cross, that
we [c]might die to [3]sin and live to righteousness; for [d]by His [4]wounds
you were [e]healed.
25 For you were [a]continually straying like sheep, but now you have
returned to the [b]Shepherd and [1]Guardian of your souls.

Chapter 3

3 [a]In the same way, you wives, [b]be submissive to your own hus-
bands so that even if any *of them* are disobedient to the word,
they may be [c]won without a word by the behavior of their wives,
2 as they observe your chaste and [1]respectful behavior.
3 [a]And let not your adornment be *merely* external—braiding the
hair, and wearing gold jewelry, or putting on dresses;
4 but *let it be* [a]the hidden person of the heart, with the imperishable
quality of a gentle and quiet spirit, which is precious in the sight of
God.
5 For in this way in former times the holy women also, [a]who

20f.; Deut. 1:6; 66:21; v. 1:6 [c]Ex. t. 7:6 [d]Ex. 4:20; 14:2; 4 [e]Is. 9:2; Acts 26:18; 2 Cor. 4:6
1:10; 2:23; 9:25; 10:19
6:9; 1 Pet. 12:1 [c]Lev. 39:12; Eph. 1:13; 1 Pet. 13:14; Gal. [e]James 4:1
s a result of st's coming in judgment ; Phil. 2:15; 1 Pet. 2:15; 8:22 [c]Matt. John 13:31; 6 [d]Is. 10:3; Luke 19:44
[a]Rom. 13:1
ugh [a]Rom. [b]Rom. 13:3
3:17 [b]1 Pet. 2:12
3:32; James 6:22; 1 Cor. 7:22
eror [a]Rom. 13:7 [b]1 Pet. [c]Prov. 24:21 ; 1 Pet. 2:13
verse [a]Eph. [b]James 3:17
race [a]Rom. et. 3:14, 16f.
V. 19, note 1 [a]1 Pet. 3:17
14:22; 1 Pet. et. 3:18; 4:1, 11:29; 16:24
; 2 Cor. 5:21
ho [2]Lit., was ing [a]Is. 53:7; :3; 1 Pet. 3:9
ried . . . up to s [2]Lit., wood [4]Lit., wound; [a]Is. 53:4, 11; :3; Heb. 9:28 0 [c]Rom. 6:2, s. 53:5 [e]Heb. ; James 5:16
[1]Or, Bishop, seer [a]Is. 53:6 :11; 1 Pet. 5:4
Pet. 3:7 [b]Eph. . 3:18 [c]1 Cor. 9:19
[1]Lit., with fear
3ff.; 1 Tim. 2:9
4 [a]Rom. 7:22
5:5; 1 Pet. 1:3

hoped in God, used to adorn themselves, being submissive to their
own husbands.
6 Thus Sarah obeyed Abraham, [a]calling him lord, and you have
become her children if you do what is right [1b]without being
frightened by any fear.
7 [a]You husbands likewise, live with *your wives* in an under-
standing way, as with a weaker [b]vessel, since she is a woman; and
grant her honor as a fellow heir of the grace of life, so that your
prayers may not be hindered.
8 [1]To sum up, [a]let all be harmonious, sympathetic, [b]brotherly,
[c]kindhearted, and [d]humble in spirit;
9 [a]not returning evil for evil, or [b]insult for insult, but [1]giving a
[c]blessing instead; for [d]you were called for the very purpose that you
might [e]inherit a blessing.
10 For,

"[a]LET HIM WHO MEANS TO LOVE LIFE AND SEE GOOD DAYS
REFRAIN HIS TONGUE FROM EVIL AND HIS LIPS FROM SPEAKING GUILE.
11 "[a]AND LET HIM TURN AWAY FROM EVIL AND DO GOOD;
LET HIM SEEK PEACE AND PURSUE IT.
12 "[a]FOR THE EYES OF THE LORD ARE UPON THE RIGHTEOUS,
AND HIS EARS ATTEND TO THEIR PRAYER,
BUT THE FACE OF THE LORD IS AGAINST THOSE WHO DO EVIL."

13 And [a]who is there to harm you if you prove zealous for what is
good?
14 But even if you should [a]suffer for the sake of righteousness, [b]*you
are* blessed. [c]AND DO NOT FEAR THEIR [1]INTIMIDATION, AND DO NOT BE
TROUBLED,
15 but [1]sanctify [a]Christ as Lord in your hearts, always *being* ready
[b]to make a defense to everyone who asks you to give an account for
the [a]hope that is in you, yet [c]with gentleness and [2d]reverence;
16 [1]and keep a [a]good conscience so that in the thing in which [b]you
are slandered, those who revile your good behavior in Christ may be
put to shame.
17 For [a]it is better, [b]if [1]God should will it so, that you suffer for
doing what is right rather than for doing what is wrong.
18 For [a]Christ also died for sins [b]once for all, *the* just for *the* unjust,
in order that He might [c]bring us to God, having been put to death [d]in
the flesh, but made alive [e]in the [1]spirit;
19 in [1]which also He went and [a]made proclamation to the spirits
now in prison,
20 who once were disobedient, when the [a]patience of God [b]kept
waiting in the days of Noah, during the construction of [c]the ark, in
which a few, that is, [d]eight [e]persons, were brought safely through *the*
water.
21 [a]And corresponding to that, baptism now saves you—[b]not the
removal of dirt from the flesh, but an appeal to God for a [c]good
conscience—through [d]the resurrection of Jesus Christ,
22 [a]who is at the right hand of God, [b]having gone into heaven, [c]after
angels and authorities and powers had been subjected to Him.

Chapter 4

4 Therefore, since [a]Christ has [1]suffered in the flesh, [b]arm your-
selves also with the same purpose, because [c]he who has [1]suf-
fered in the flesh has ceased from sin,

6 [1]Lit., *anc* [a]Gen. 18:1

7 [a]Eph. 5:2 [b]1 Thess. 4

8 [1]Or, *Fina* 12:16 [b]1 P [c]Eph. 4:32 Phil. 2:3; 1

9 [1]Lit., *bles* [a]Rom. 12:1 5:15 [b]1 Co 2:23 [c]Luke 12:14; 1 Co [d]1 Pet. 2:21 Heb. 6:14;

10 [a]Ps. 34:

11 [a]Ps. 34:

12 [a]Ps. 34:

13 [a]Prov. 1

14 [1]Lit., *fea* 5:10; 1 Pet. 4:15f. [b]Jam 8:12f.; 1 Pet

15 [1]I.e., set *fear* [a]1 Pet. 4:6 [c]2 Tim. 1:17

16 [1]Lit., *hav* [a]1 Tim. 1:5; 1 Pet. 3:21 2:12, 15

17 [1]Lit., *the* [a]1 Pet. 2:20; [b]Acts 18:21; 2:15; 4:19

18 [1]Or, *Spiri* 2:21 [b]Heb. 9 10:10 [c]Rom. 3:12 [d]Col. 1 4:1 [e]1 Pet. 4

19 [1]Or, *whor* 4:6

20 [a]Rom. 2:4 6:3, 5, 13f. [d]Gen. 8:18; 2 [e]Acts 2:41; 1 22; 2:25; 4:19

21 [a]Acts 16:3 3:5 [b]Heb. 9:1 [c]1 Tim. 1:5; H 1 Pet. 3:16 [d]1

22 [a]Mark 16: 4:14; 6:20 [c]R Heb. 1:6

4:1 [1]I.e., suff death [a]1 Pet. [b]Eph. 6:13 [c]R

2 [a]so as to live [b]the rest of the time in the flesh no longer for the
lusts of men, but for the [c]will of God.
3 For [a]the time already past is sufficient *for you* to have carried out
the desire of the Gentiles, [b]having pursued a course of sensuality,
lusts, drunkenness, carousals, drinking parties and [1]abominable
idolatries.
4 And in *all* this, they are surprised that you do not run with *them*
into the same excess of [a]dissipation, and they [b]malign *you;*
5 but they shall give account to Him who is ready to judge [a]the
living and the dead.
6 For [a]the gospel has for this purpose been preached even to those
who are dead, that though they are judged in the flesh as men, they
may live in the spirit according to *the will of* God.
7 [a]The end of all things [1]is at hand; therefore, [b]be of sound judg-
ment and sober *spirit* for the purpose of [2]prayer.
8 Above all, [a]keep fervent in your love for one another, because
[b]love covers a multitude of sins.
9 [a]Be hospitable to one another without [b]complaint.
10 [a]As each one has received a *special* gift, employ it in serving one
another, as good [b]stewards of the manifold grace of God.
11 [a]Whoever speaks, *let him speak,* as it were, the [b]utterances of God;
whoever serves, *let him do so* as [1c]by the strength which God supplies;
so that [d]in all things God may be glorified through Jesus Christ, [e]to
whom belongs the glory and dominion forever and ever. Amen.
12 [a]Beloved, do not be surprised at the [b]fiery ordeal among you,
which comes upon you for your testing, as though some strange
thing were happening to you;
13 but to the degree that you [a]share the sufferings of Christ, keep on
rejoicing; so that also at the [b]revelation of His glory, [c]you may rejoice
with exultation.
14 If you are reviled [1a]for the name of Christ, [b]you are blessed,
[c]because the Spirit of glory and of God rests upon you.
15 By no means [a]let any of you suffer as a murderer, or thief, or
evildoer, or a [1b]troublesome meddler;
16 but if *anyone suffers* as a [a]Christian, let him not feel ashamed, but
in that name let him [b]glorify God.
17 For *it is* time for judgment [a]to begin [1]with [b]the household of God;
and if *it* [c]*begins* with us first, what *will be* the outcome for those [d]who
do not obey the [e]gospel of God?
18 [a]AND IF IT IS WITH DIFFICULTY THAT THE RIGHTEOUS IS SAVED, [1]WHAT
WILL BECOME OF THE [b]GODLESS MAN AND THE SINNER?
19 Therefore, let those also who suffer according to [a]the will of God
entrust their souls to a faithful Creator in doing what is right.

Chapter 5 ______________________________

5 [a]Therefore, I exhort the elders among you, as *your* [b]fellow elder
and [c]witness of the sufferings of Christ, and a [d]partaker also of
the glory that is to be revealed,
2 shepherd [a]the flock of God among you, exercising oversight [b]not
under compulsion, but voluntarily, according to *the will of* God; and
[c]not for sordid gain, but with eagerness;
3 nor yet as [a]lording it over [1]those allotted to your charge, but
[2]proving to be [b]examples to the flock.

. 6:2; Col. 3:3
4 [c]Mark 3:35
wless [a]1 Cor.
n. 13:13; Eph.
2:2; 4:17ff.
. 5:18 [b]1 Pet.
3:16
s 10:42; Rom.
4:9; 2 Tim. 4:1
Pet. 1:12; 3:19
as come near
rayers [a]Rom.
. 9:26; James
1 2:18 [b]1 Pet.
1:13
t. 1:22 [b]Prov.
1 Cor. 13:4ff.;
James 5:20
Tim. 3:2; Heb.
3:2 [b]Phil. 2:14
12:6f. [b]1 Cor.
4:1
om [a]1 Thess.
2:1, 15; Heb.
cts 7:38 [c]Eph.
; 6:10 [d]1 Cor.
31; 1 Pet. 2:12
. 11:36; 1 Pet.
Rev. 1:6; 5:13
. 2:11 [b]1 Pet.
1:6f.
n. 8:17; 2 Cor.
:10; Phil. 3:10
7; 5:1 [c]2 Tim.
2:12
[a]John 15:21;
26; 1 Pet. 4:16
11; Luke 6:22;
s 5:41 [c]2 Cor.
4:10f., 16
[1]Lit., *one who*
others' affairs
et. 2:19f.; 3:17
4:11; 2 Thess.
1; 1 Tim. 5:13
s 5:41; 28:22;
7 [b]1 Pet. 4:11
it., *from* [a]Jer.
ek. 9:6; Amos
im. 3:15; Heb.
et. 2:5 [c]Rom.
[d]2 Thess. 1:8
[e]Rom. 1:1
Lit., *where will*
[a]Prov. 11:31;
31 [b]1 Tim. 1:9
9 [a]1 Pet. 3:17
1 [a]Acts 11:30
hn 1; 3 John 1
48; Heb. 12:1
, 7; 4:13; Rev.
1:9
hn 21:16; Acts
8 [b]Philem. 14
[c]1 Tim. 3:8
the allotments
oming [a]Ezek.
; Matt. 20:25f.
15; Phil. 3:17;
. 1:7; 2 Thess.
im. 4:12; Titus
2:7

4 And when the Chief [a]Shepherd appears, you will receive the
[b]unfading [1c]crown of glory.
5 [a]You younger men, likewise, [b]be subject to your elders; and all of
you, clothe yourselves with [c]humility toward one another, for [d]GOD
IS OPPOSED TO THE PROUD, BUT GIVES GRACE TO THE HUMBLE.
6 [a]Humble yourselves, therefore, under the mighty hand of God,
that He may exalt you at the proper time,
7 casting all your [a]anxiety upon Him, because He cares for you.
8 [a]Be of sober *spirit*, [b]be on the alert. Your adversary, [c]the devil,
prowls about like a roaring [d]lion, seeking someone to devour.
9 [1a]But resist him, [b]firm in *your* faith, knowing that [c]the same ex-
periences of suffering are being accomplished by your [2]brethren who
are in the world.
10 And after you have suffered [a]for a little while, the [b]God of all
grace, who [c]called you to His [d]eternal glory in Christ, will Himself
[e]perfect, [f]confirm, strengthen *and* establish you.
11 [a]To Him *be* dominion forever and ever. Amen.
12 Through [a]Silvanus, our faithful brother [1](for so I regard *him*), [b]I
have written to you briefly, exhorting and testifying that this is [c]the
true grace of God. [d]Stand firm in it!
13 [1]She who is in Babylon, chosen together with you, sends you
greetings, and *so does* my son, [a]Mark.
14 [a]Greet one another with a kiss of love.
[b]Peace be to you all who are in Christ.

4 [1]Lit., *wreath* 2:25 [b]1 Pet. 1 9:25
5 [a]Luke 22:26 5:1 [b]Eph. 5:2 3:8 [d]Prov. 3:3 4:6
6 [a]Matt. 23:12 14:11; 18:14; 4:10
7 [a]Ps. 55:22;
8 [a]1 Pet. 1:13 24:42 [c]James [d]2 Tim. 4:17
9 [1]Lit., *whom* [2]Lit., *brotherh* [a]James 4:7 [b] [c]Acts 14:22
10 [a]1 Pet. 1:6 4:10 [c]1 Cor. 1 1 Thess. 2:12 4:17; 2 Tim. 2 [e]1 Cor. 1:10; H 13:21 [f]Rom. 1 2 Thess. 2:17;
11 [a]Rom. 11:3 4:11
12 [1]Lit., *(as I* [a]2 Cor. 1:19 [b] 13:22 [c]Acts 1 1 Pet. 1:13; 4: 15:1
13 [1]Some ms *The church w* 12:12, 25; 15: Col. 4:10; Phil
14 [a]Rom. 16: 6:23

1 PETER AT A GLANCE

Theme of 1 Peter:

Author:

Date:

Purpose:

Key Words:
suffering
(and all its synonyms)
grace
glory
salvation
Jesus Christ
God
Holy Spirit
called
chosen
holy

SEGMENT DIVISIONS	CHAPTER THEMES
	1
	2
	3
	4
	5

1 Peter Observations Chart

hor

Recipients

eral Instructions

tructions to

rvants

Wives

Husbands

lders

Younger men

2 PETER

A fisherman by trade, Peter had been captured and transformed by a Shepherd. Is it any w that even in Peter's darkest hour, the welfare of God's sheep was uppermost in his mind?

Ever since the day he stood with Jesus by a fire, the morning air full of the aroma of roasti Peter had known the way he would die. But Peter would be faithful. His concern about his dea the way he would die would not override his concern for his Lord's sheep, the sheep Jes commissioned him to feed and shepherd. And so, sometime around A.D. 63 or 64, Peter writes "t who have received a faith of the same kind as ours."

In A.D. 64, according to tradition, Peter was crucified upside down for the Lord he once knowing. My, how Peter had grown in the grace and knowledge of his God!

THINGS TO DO

1. To familiarize yourself with 2 Peter, read the book without stopping or taking notes. The m of this short book is easily seen in each of the paragraphs, so as you read, notice the con each. You will see that Peter contrasts certain things. Based on this first reading, what contrast is Peter making in this book?
2. Read 2 Peter again, looking for facts concerning the author (pronouns such as *I, we, us*) a recipients (pronouns such as *you, your*). Mark these in a distinctive way in the text. Then OBSERVATIONS CHART on page 1827 record the answers to the following questions: Wha the author say about himself? When in his life is he writing? Who are the recipients? H they described?
3. In a distinctive way, mark the key words (and their synonyms and pronouns) which are lis the 2 PETER AT A GLANCE chart on page 1826. Then list in the margin the truths you le marking these key words. Be as thorough as possible because the lists will help you see th of the book.
4. Read through 2 Peter again and look for specific instructions that Peter gives the readers co ing their behavior and belief. Record these on the OBSERVATIONS CHART under "Instruct Also look for and note any people or groups of people of which Peter warns them to beware
5. In this book, Peter states specifically why he is writing. Look for and underline any ve which Peter says, *"I am writing to you."* Also, underline any other verses that indicate his pu in writing. Record his purpose for writing on 2 PETER AT A GLANCE.
6. Summarize the message of each paragraph and record its theme on 2 PETER AT A GLA Then determine the chapter themes and the book theme and record these in the appro places on the chart and in the text.

THINGS TO THINK ABOUT

1. What would it take to live your life so that you may be found spotless and blameless coming?
2. Is there a danger today that false teachers will arise among the brethren as in Peter's day? do you need to know to be able to detect them?
3. How can you keep from falling from your own steadfastness? Practically, what do you need in order to grow in the grace and knowledge of Jesus Christ?

Chapter 1

1 [1]Simon Peter, a [a]bond-servant and [b]apostle of Jesus Christ, to
those who have received [c]a faith of the same [2]kind as ours, [3]by
[d]the righteousness of [e]our God and Savior, Jesus Christ:
2 [a]Grace and peace be multiplied to you in [b]the knowledge of God
and of Jesus our Lord;
3 seeing that His [a]divine power has granted to us everything per-
taining to life and godliness, through the true [b]knowledge of Him
who [c]called us [1]by His own glory and [2]excellence.
4 [1]For by these He has granted to us His precious and magnificent
[a]promises, in order that by them you might become [b]partakers of *the*
divine nature, having [c]escaped the [d]corruption that is in [e]the world
by lust.
5 Now for this very reason also, applying all diligence, in your
faith [a]supply [b]moral [1]excellence, and in *your* moral excellence,
[c]knowledge;
6 and in *your* knowledge, [a]self-control, and in *your* self-control,
[b]perseverance, and in *your* perseverance, [c]godliness;
7 and in *your* godliness, [a]brotherly kindness, and in *your* brotherly
kindness, love.
8 For if these *qualities* are yours and are increasing, they render
you neither useless nor [a]unfruitful in the true [b]knowledge of our
Lord Jesus Christ.
9 For he who lacks these *qualities* is [a]blind *or* short-sighted, having
forgotten *his* [b]purification from his former sins.
10 Therefore, brethren, be all the more diligent to make certain
about His [a]calling and [b]choosing you; for as long as you practice
these things, you will never [c]stumble;
11 for in this way the entrance into [a]the eternal kingdom of our
[b]Lord and Savior Jesus Christ will be [c]abundantly [d]supplied to you.
12 Therefore, [a]I shall always be ready to remind you of these things,
even though you *already* know *them,* and have been established in
[b]the truth which is present with *you.*
13 And I consider it [a]right, as long as I am in [b]this *earthly* dwelling,
to [c]stir you up by way of reminder,
14 knowing that [a]the laying aside of my *earthly* dwelling is im-
minent, [b]as also our Lord Jesus Christ has made clear to me.
15 And I will also be diligent that at any time after my [a]departure
you may be able to call these things to mind.
16 For we did not follow cleverly devised [a]tales when we made
known to you the [b]power and coming of our Lord Jesus Christ, but
we were [c]eyewitnesses of His majesty.
17 For when He received honor and glory from God the Father,
such an [1a]utterance as this was [2]made to Him by the [b]Majestic Glory,
"This is My beloved Son with whom I am well-pleased"—
18 and we ourselves heard this [1]utterance made from heaven when
we were with Him on the [a]holy mountain.
19 [1]And *so* we have [a]the prophetic word *made* more [b]sure, to which
you do well to pay attention as to [c]a lamp shining in a dark place,
until the [d]day dawns and the [e]morning star arises [f]in your hearts.
20 But [a]know this first of all, that [b]no prophecy of Scripture is *a
matter* of one's own interpretation,
21 for [a]no prophecy was ever made by an act of human will, but
men [b]moved by the Holy Spirit spoke from God.

Chapter 2

2 But [a]false prophets also arose among the people, just as there
will also be [b]false teachers [c]among you, who will [d]secretly intro-
duce [e]destructive heresies, even [f]denying the [g]Master who [h]bought
them, bringing swift destruction upon themselves.
2 And many will follow their [a]sensuality, and because of them [b]the
way of the truth will be [c]maligned;
3 and in *their* [a]greed they will [b]exploit you with [c]false words; [d]their
judgment from long ago is not idle, and their destruction is not
asleep.
4 For [a]if God did not spare angels when they sinned, but cast them
into hell and [b]committed them to pits of darkness, reserved for judg-
ment;
5 and did not spare [a]the ancient world, but preserved [b]Noah, a
[1]preacher of righteousness, with seven others, when He brought a
[c]flood upon the world of the ungodly;
6 and *if* He [a]condemned the cities of Sodom and Gomorrah to
destruction by reducing *them* to ashes, having made them an
[b]example to those who would [c]live ungodly thereafter;
7 and *if* He [a]rescued righteous Lot, oppressed by the [b]sensual con-
duct of [c]unprincipled men
8 (for by what he saw and heard *that* [a]righteous man, while living
among them, felt *his* righteous soul tormented day after day with
their lawless deeds),
9 [a]*then* the Lord knows how to rescue the godly from [1]temptation,
and to keep the unrighteous under punishment for the [b]day of judg-
ment,
10 and especially those who [1a]indulge the flesh in *its* corrupt desires
and [b]despise authority. Daring, [c]self-willed, they do not tremble
when they [b]revile angelic [2]majesties,
11 [a]whereas angels who are greater in might and power do not
bring a reviling judgment against them before the Lord.
12 But [a]these, like unreasoning animals, [b]born as creatures of
instinct to be captured and killed, reviling where they have no
knowledge, will in [1]the destruction of those creatures also be
destroyed,
13 suffering wrong as [a]the wages of doing wrong. They count it a
pleasure to [b]revel in the [c]daytime. They are stains and blemishes,
[b]reveling in their [1]deceptions, as they [d]carouse with you,
14 having eyes full of adultery and that never cease from sin, [a]entic-
ing [b]unstable souls, having a heart trained in [c]greed, [d]accursed
children;
15 forsaking [a]the right way they have gone astray, having followed
[b]the way of Balaam, the *son* of Beor, who loved [c]the wages of un-
righteousness,
16 but he received a rebuke for his own transgression; [a]*for* a dumb
donkey, speaking with a voice of a man, restrained the madness of
the prophet.
17 These are [a]springs without water, and mists driven by a storm,
[b]for whom the [1]black darkness has been reserved.
18 For speaking out [a]arrogant *words* of [b]vanity they [c]entice by flesh-
ly desires, by [d]sensuality, those who barely [e]escape from the ones
who live in error,

2:1 [a]Deut. 6:13 [b]2 Co
[c]Matt. 7:15 [d]Gal. 2:4; [e]1 Cor. 11: [f]Jude 4 [g]F [h]1 Cor. 6:2

2 [a]Gen. 19 2:7, 18; Ju 16:17; 22:4 [c]Rom. 2:24

3 [a]1 Tim. 6 2:14; Jude 2:17; 1 The [c]Rom. 16:1 1:16 [d]Deut

4 [a]Jude 6

5 [1]Or, *hera* 26:20; 2 Pe 6:8, 9; 1 Pe [c]2 Pet. 3:6

6 [a]Gen. 19 [b]Is. 1:9; Ma 11:23; Rom 7 [c]Jude 15

7 [a]Gen. 19 [b]Gen. 19:5ff 18; Jude 4

8 [a]Heb. 11:

9 [1]Or, *trial* 10:13; Rev. 10:15; Jude

10 [1]Lit., *go* *glories* [a]2 P 16, 18 [b]Ex. 8 [c]Titus 1:7

11 [a]Jude 9

12 [1]Lit., *thei* *destruction a* 10 [b]Jer. 12:3

13 [1]Some a read *love fea* 2:15 [b]Rom. [c]1 Thess. 5:7 11:21; Jude

14 [a]2 Pet. 2: 1:8; 2 Pet. 3: 2:3 [d]Eph. 2:3

15 [a]Acts 13: 22:5, 7; Deut. 13:2; Jude 11 2:14 [c]2 Pet. 2

16 [a]Num. 22 30ff.

17 [1]Lit., *black* *darkness* [a]Ju [b]Jude 13

18 [a]Jude 16 4:17 [c]2 Pet. 2 [d]2 Pet. 2:2 [e]2 2:20

19 promising them freedom while they themselves are slaves of
corruption; for [a]by what a man is overcome, by this he is enslaved.
20 For if after they have [a]escaped the defilements of the world by
[b]the knowledge of the [c]Lord and Savior Jesus Christ, they are again
[d]entangled in them and are overcome, [e]the last state has become
worse for them than the first.
21 [a]For it would be better for them not to have known the way of
righteousness, than having known it, to turn away from [b]the holy
commandment [c]delivered to them.
22 It has happened to them according to the true proverb, "[a]A DOG
RETURNS TO ITS OWN VOMIT," and, "A sow, after washing, *returns* to
wallowing in the mire."

Chapter 3

3 This is now, [a]beloved, the second letter I am writing to you in
which I am [b]stirring up your sincere mind by way of reminder,
2 that you should [a]remember the words spoken beforehand by [b]the
holy prophets and [c]the commandment of the Lord and Savior *spoken*
by your apostles.
3 [a]Know this first of all, that [b]in the last days [c]mockers will come
with *their* mocking, [d]following after their own lusts,
4 and saying, "[a]Where is the promise of His [b]coming? For *ever*
since the fathers [c]fell asleep, all continues just as it was [d]from the
beginning of creation."
5 For [1]when they maintain this, it escapes their notice that [a]by the
word of God *the* heavens existed long ago and *the* earth was [b]formed
out of water and by water,
6 through which [a]the world at that time was [b]destroyed, being
flooded with water.
7 But [a]the present heavens and earth by His word are being
reserved for [b]fire, kept for [c]the day of judgment and destruction of
ungodly men.
8 But do not let this one *fact* escape your notice, [a]beloved, that with
the Lord one day is as a thousand years, and [b]a thousand years as
one day.
9 [a]The Lord is not slow about His promise, as some count slow-
ness, but [b]is patient toward you, [c]not wishing for any to perish but
for all to come to repentance.
10 But [a]the day of the Lord [b]will come like a thief, in which [c]the
heavens [d]will pass away with a roar and the [e]elements will be
destroyed with intense heat, and [f]the earth and [1]its works will be
[2]burned up.
11 Since all these things are to be destroyed in this way, what sort of
people ought you to be in holy conduct and godliness,
12 [a]looking for and hastening the coming of the day of God, on
account of which [b]the heavens will be destroyed by burning, and the
[c]elements will melt with intense heat!
13 But according to His [a]promise we are looking for [b]new heavens
and a new earth, [c]in which righteousness dwells.
14 [a]Therefore, [b]beloved, since you look for these things, be diligent
to be [c]found by Him in peace, [d]spotless and blameless,
15 and regard the [a]patience of our Lord *to be* salvation; just as also
[b]our beloved brother Paul, [c]according to the wisdom given him,
wrote to you,

16 as also in all *his* letters, speaking in them of [a]these things, [b]in
which are some things hard to understand, which the untaught and
[c]unstable distort, as *they do* also [d]the rest of the Scriptures, to their
own destruction.
17 You therefore, [a]beloved, knowing this beforehand, [b]be on your
guard lest, being carried away by [c]the error of [d]unprincipled men,
you [e]fall from your own steadfastness,
18 but grow in the grace and [a]knowledge of our [b]Lord and Savior
Jesus Christ. [c]To Him *be* the glory, both now and to the day of eternity. Amen.

16 [a]2 Pet. 3: 5:11 [c]2 Pet. [d]2 Pet. 3:2

17 [a]2 Pet. 3: 10:12 [c]2 Pet [d]2 Pet. 2:7 [e]

18 [a]2 Pet. 1: 1:11; 2:20 [c]F 2 Tim. 4:18;

2 Peter at a Glance

Theme of 2 Peter:

Author:

Date:

Purpose:

Key Words:
prophecy (prophet, prophetic)
knowledge (know, knowing, known)
remind (reminder)
true (truth)
diligent (diligence)
false
destroyed
promise

Segment Divisions	Paragraph Themes
	1:1-4
	1:5-11
	1:12-21
	2:1-22
	3:1-7
	3:8-13
	3:14-18

2 Peter Observations Chart

er **Recipients**

ructions

rnings

1 JOHN

As a boy, John thought of Jesus as just a cousin, one of the sons of Aunt Mary, his mother S[illegible] sister. Little did he realize that someday he'd be chosen by God to be one of His twelve apostles.

He had been known as a "son of thunder" (Mark 3:17); but a transformation had taken pl[illegible] was called "the disciple whom Jesus loved"—and that he was.

Even though John's name is not mentioned in this epistle, there's much evidence he's the John had been with Jesus. He had seen Him, heard Him, touched Him, and had been filled w[illegible] love. This is evident as you hear John's fatherly heart for those who belong to Jesus. He lo[illegible] fathers, the young men, the dear children. Yet, as he writes about the antichrists and deceivers, [illegible] hear the rumble of thunder in the background.

We don't know when John wrote this first epistle. It may have been between A.D. 85 and 95 w[illegible] was in Ephesus before being exiled to the isle of Patmos. Love—and thunder—compelled him t[illegible] He had to protect his children from a deception that could darken their understanding if they w[illegible] warned about the brewing storm of gnosticism—a teaching which could keep them from fellowship with him (1 John 1:3).

THINGS TO DO

1. If you want to handle a passage of Scripture accurately you must always interpret it in th[illegible] of its context. Context simply means that which goes "with" (*con*) the "text." Context must [illegible] rule when it comes to interpretation. Identifying the author's purpose for writing will he[illegible] discern the context of a passage. What the author says, he says in the light of his purp[illegible] writing.

   In this particular letter the author tells us his purpose in seven different verses: 1:4; 2:1, 12[illegible] and 26. Then in 1 John 5:13, he concludes by summarizing his purpose for writing. Rea[illegible] verses and record his reasons for writing on the chart I AM WRITING TO YOU on pag[illegible] Then read 1 John 5:13 and record on the 1 JOHN AT A GLANCE chart on page 1835 the a[illegible] purpose for writing.

2. One of the major heresies the church would face was gnosticism. Gnosticism wasn't in full in John's time but the seeds had been sown. Understanding gnosticism will help you understand why John concentrated on the truths contained in his writing. Therefore, befo[illegible] go any further, read the article "Understanding Gnosticism" in the front of your Bible (page

3. Now read 1 John chapter by chapter and observe the text using the instructions outlined in to Observe the Bible Chapter by Chapter" in the front of this Bible (page I-13).

   a. Mark in a distinctive way each of the key words (and their synonyms and pronouns) lis[illegible] 1 JOHN AT A GLANCE. When you finish marking these words, go to the chart 1 JOH[illegible] WORDS on page 1834 and record the number of times each word is used in each chapter add them up to see the number of times each word is used in 1 John. Doing this will he[illegible] see the main themes of 1 John.

   b. John uses a number of contrasts in order to make his point: light/darkness; child[illegible] God/children of the devil, etc. Watch for these contrasts and in the margin next to wher[illegible] are found list what you learn from them.

   c. When you finish your observations on each chapter:

      1) List in the margin the truths you learn from each of the key words.

      2) Remember, 1 John was written "in order that you may know." When you finish readi[illegible] five chapters, trace throughout 1 John the repeated use of the word *know* and record

you learn from the text on the chart WHAT I CAN KNOW and HOW I CAN KNOW IT on pages 1834 and 1835. As you make this list, watch the matters John deals with in respect to wrong behavior or wrong belief.

3) Keep a running list of everything you learn about God, Jesus Christ, and the Spirit from this book. Record it in the margin.

Record the theme of each chapter on 1 JOHN AT A GLANCE. Fill in any remaining information called for on the chart. Also, record the theme of each chapter next to the chapter number within the text.

GS TO THINK ABOUT

Based on the criteria given in this book, how can you know whether or not you have eternal life?

What have you learned about sin from 1 John? Do you practice sin or righteousness?

Do you love the things of the world? Are you caught up in the pride of life, in boasting, or in desiring whatever your eyes see?

According to 1 John 3, what are you to do when your heart condemns you?

Does your belief about Jesus Christ match what 1 John teaches about Him?

Chapter 1

1 What was [a]from the beginning, what we have [b]heard, what we
have [c]seen with our eyes, what we [d]beheld and our hands
[e]handled, concerning the [f]Word of Life—
2 and [a]the life was manifested, and we have [b]seen and [c]bear wit-
ness and proclaim to you [d]the eternal life, which was [e]with the
Father and was [a]manifested to us—
3 what we have [a]seen and [b]heard we proclaim to you also, that you
also may have fellowship with us; and indeed our [c]fellowship is
with the Father, and with His Son Jesus Christ.
4 And [a]these things we write, so that our [b]joy may be made com-
plete.
5 And [a]this is the message we have heard from Him and announce
to you, that [b]God is light, and in Him there is no darkness at all.
6 [a]If we say that we have fellowship with Him and *yet* walk in the
darkness, we [b]lie and [c]do not practice the truth;
7 but if we [a]walk in the light as [b]He Himself is in the light, we have
fellowship with one another, and [c]the blood of Jesus His Son clean-
ses us from all sin.
8 [a]If we say that we have no sin, we are deceiving ourselves, and
the [b]truth is not in us.
9 [a]If we confess our sins, He is faithful and righteous to forgive us
our sins and [b]to cleanse us from all unrighteousness.
10 [a]If we say that we have not sinned, we [b]make Him a liar, and
[c]His word is not in us.

Chapter 2

2 [a]My little children, I am [b]writing these things to you that you
may not sin. And if anyone sins, [c]we have an [1d]Advocate with
the Father, Jesus Christ the righteous;
2 and He Himself is [a]the [1]propitiation for our sins; and not for ours
only, but also [b]for *those of* the whole world.
3 And [a]by this we know that we have come to [b]know Him, if we
[c]keep His commandments.

1:1f.; 1 John 4 [b]Acts 4:20; [c]John 19:35; 6; 1 John 1:2 4; 1 John 4:14 e 24:39; John [f]John 1:1, 4
4; 1 John 3:5, [b]John 19:35; [c]John 15:27; n 4:14 [d]John ; 17:3; 1 John 13, 20 [e]John 1:1
19:35; 2 Pet. ohn 1:1 [b]Acts ohn 1:1 [c]John 21; 1 Cor. 1:9
hn 2:1 [b]John 3:29
1:19; 1 John [b]1 Tim. 6:16; James 1:17
8:12; 1 John 8:55; 1 John 0 [c]John 3:21
[b]1 Tim. 6:16 [c]Titus 2:14
15:14; Prov. Rom. 3:10ff.; 2 [b]John 8:44; 1 John 2:4
s. 32:5; Prov. 3 [b]Titus 2:14
15:14 [b]John 3; 1 John 5:10 [c]1 John 2:14
r., *Paracletos*, d alongside to n 13:33; Gal. ohn 2:12, 28; , 18; 4:4; 5:21 [c]Rom. 8:34; :5; Heb. 7:25; [d]John 14:16
r, *satisfaction* 25; Heb. 2:17; [b]John 4:42; ; 1 John 4:14
ohn 2:5; 3:24; [b]1 John 2:4; [c]John 14:15; ohn 3:22, 24; . 12:17; 14:12

4 The one who says, "[a]I have come to [b]know Him," and does not
keep His commandments, is a [c]liar, and [d]the truth is not in him;
5 but whoever [a]keeps His word, in him the [b]love of God has truly
been perfected. [c]By this we know that we are in Him:
6 the one who says he [a]abides in Him [b]ought himself to walk in the
same manner as He walked.
7 [a]Beloved, I am [b]not writing a new commandment to you, but an
old commandment which you [1]have had [c]from the beginning; the
old commandment is the word which you have heard.
8 [1]On the other hand, I am writing [a]a new commandment to you,
which is true in Him and in you, because [b]the darkness is passing
away, and [c]the true light is already shining.
9 The one who says he is in the light and *yet* [a]hates his [b]brother is
in the darkness until now.
10 [a]The one who loves his brother abides in the light and there is no
cause for stumbling in him.
11 But the one who [a]hates his brother is in the darkness and [b]walks
in the darkness, and does not know where he is going because the
darkness has [c]blinded his eyes.
12 I am writing to you, [a]little children, because [b]your sins are for-
given you for His name's sake.
13 I am writing to you, fathers, because you know Him [a]who has
been from the beginning. I am writing to you, young men, because
[b]you have overcome [c]the evil one. I have written to you, children,
because [d]you know the Father.
14 I have written to you, fathers, because you know Him [a]who has
been from the beginning. I have written to you, young men, because
you are [b]strong, and the [c]word of God abides in you, and [d]you have
overcome the evil one.
15 Do not love [a]the world, nor the things in the world. [b]If anyone
loves the world, the love of the Father is not in him.
16 For all that is in the world, [a]the lust of the flesh and [b]the lust of
the eyes and [c]the boastful pride of life, is not from the Father, but is
from the world.
17 And [a]the world is passing away, and *also* its lusts; but the one
who [b]does the will of God abides forever.
18 Children, [a]it is the last hour; and just as you heard that [b]antichrist
is coming, [c]even now many antichrists have arisen; from this we
know that it is the last hour.
19 [a]They went out from us, but they were not *really* of us; for if they
had been of us, they would have remained with us; but *they went out*,
[b]in order that [1]it might be shown that they all are not of us.
20 [1]But you have an [a]anointing from [b]the Holy One, and [2c]you all
know.
21 I have not written to you because you do not know the truth, but
[a]because you do know it, and [1]because no lie is [b]of the truth.
22 Who is the liar but [a]the one who denies that Jesus is the [1]Christ?
This is [b]the antichrist, the one who denies the Father and the Son.
23 [a]Whoever denies the Son does not have the Father; the one who
confesses the Son has the Father also.
24 As for you, let that abide in you which you heard [a]from the
beginning. If what you heard from the beginning abides in you, you
also [b]will abide in the Son and in the Father.

4 [a]Titus 1:10 3:6; 4:7f. [c]1 J [d]1 John 1:8

5 [a]John 14:2 4:12 [c]1 John 4:13; 5:2

6 [a]John 15:4 13:15; 15:10;

7 [1]Lit., *were* [a]Heb. 6:9; 1 J 21; 4:1, 7, 11 13:34; 1 John 4:21; 2 John 5 2:24; 3:11; 2 J

8 [1]Lit., *Again* 13:34 [b]Rom. Eph. 5:8; 1 Th [c]John 1:9

9 [a]1 John 2:1 4:20 [b]Acts 1: 3:10, 16; 4:20

10 [a]John 11:9 2:10, 11

11 [a]1 John 2: 4:20 [b]John 1 1 John 1:6 [c]2 2 Pet. 1:9

12 [a]1 John 2 13:38; 1 Cor.

13 [a]1 John 1: 16:33; 1 John 5:4f.; Rev. 2:7 5:37; 1 John 2 5:18f. [d]John 1 John 2:3

14 [a]1 John 1: 6:10 [c]John 5: 1 John 1:10 2:13

15 [a]Rom. 12 1:27 [b]James

16 [a]Rom. 13 2:3; 1 Pet. 2:1 27:20 [c]James

17 [a]1 Cor. 7: 3:35

18 [a]Rom. 13: 4:1; 1 Pet. 4:7 24:5, 24; 1 Jo 4:3; 2 John 7 13:22; 1 John

19 [1]Lit., *they made manifes* 20:30 [b]1 Cor.

20 [1]Lit., *And* ancient mss. *know all thing* 1:21; 1 John 2 1:24; Acts 10: 28:5; Matt. 13 14:26; 1 Cor. 1 John 2:27

21 [1]Or, *know* [a]James 1:19; 1:12; Jude 5 8:44; 18:37; 1

22 [1]I.e., Mes [a]1 John 4:3; 2 [b]Matt. 24:5, 24 2:18; 4:3; 2 Jo

23 [a]John 8:1 17:3; 1 John 4 2 John 9

24 [a]1 John 2 14:23; 1 John 2 John 9

25 And [a]this is the promise which He Himself [1]made to us: eternal
life.
26 These things I have written to you concerning those who are
trying to [a]deceive you.
27 And as for you, the [a]anointing which you received from Him
abides in you, and you have no need for anyone to teach you; but as
His anointing [b]teaches you about all things, and is [c]true and is not a
lie, and just as it has taught you, [1]you abide in Him.
28 And now, [a]little children, abide in Him, so that when He [b]ap-
pears, we may have [c]confidence and [d]not [1]shrink away from Him in
shame [2]at His [e]coming.
29 If you know that [a]He is righteous, you know that everyone also
who practices righteousness [b]is [1]born of Him.

Chapter 3

3 See [1a]how great a love the Father has bestowed upon us, that we
should be called [b]children of God; and *such* we are. For this
reason the world does not know us, because [c]it did not know Him.
2 [a]Beloved, now we are [b]children of God, and [c]it has not appeared
as yet what we shall be. We know that, when He [d]appears, we shall
be [e]like Him, because we shall [f]see Him just as He is.
3 And everyone who has this [a]hope *fixed* on Him [b]purifies himself,
just as He is pure.
4 Everyone who practices sin also practices lawlessness; and [a]sin is
lawlessness.
5 And you know that He [a]appeared in order to [b]take away sins;
and [c]in Him there is no sin.
6 No one who abides in Him [a]sins; no one who sins has seen Him
or [1b]knows Him.
7 [a]Little children, let no one [b]deceive you; [c]the one who practices
righteousness is righteous, just as He is righteous;
8 the one who practices sin is [a]of the devil; for the devil [1]has
sinned from the beginning. [b]The Son of God [c]appeared for this pur-
pose, [d]that He might destroy the works of the devil.
9 No one who is [1a]born of God [b]practices sin, because His seed
abides in him; and he cannot sin, because he is [1]born of God.
10 By this the [a]children of God and the [b]children of the devil are
obvious: anyone who does not practice righteousness is not of God,
nor the one who [c]does not love his [d]brother.
11 [a]For this is the message [b]which you have heard from the begin-
ning, [c]that we should love one another;
12 not as [a]Cain, *who* was of [b]the evil one, and slew his brother. And
for what reason did he slay him? Because [c]his deeds were evil, and
his brother's were righteous.
13 Do not marvel, brethren, if [a]the world hates you.
14 We know that we have [a]passed out of death into life, [b]because we
love the brethren. He who does not love abides in death.
15 Everyone who [a]hates his brother is a murderer; and you know
that [b]no murderer has eternal life abiding in him.
16 We know love by this, that [a]He laid down His life for us; and [b]we
ought to lay down our lives for the [c]brethren.
17 But [a]whoever has the world's goods, and beholds his brother in
need and [b]closes his [1]heart [2]against him, [c]how does the love of God
abide in him?

18 [a]Little children, let us not love with word or with tongue, but in
deed and [b]truth.
19 We shall know by this that we are [a]of the truth, and shall [1]assure
our heart [2]before Him,
20 in whatever our heart condemns us; for God is greater than our
heart, and knows all things.
21 [a]Beloved, if our heart does not condemn us, we have [b]confidence
[1]before God;
22 and [a]whatever we ask we receive from Him, because we [b]keep
His commandments and do [c]the things that are pleasing in His sight.
23 And this is His commandment, that we [1a]believe in [b]the name of
His Son Jesus Christ, and love one another, just as [c]He [2]com-
manded us.
24 And the one who [a]keeps His commandments [b]abides in Him,
and He in him. And [c]we know by this that [d]He abides in us, by the
Spirit whom He has given us.

Chapter 4

4 [a]Beloved, do not believe every [b]spirit, but test the spirits to see
whether they are from God; because [c]many false prophets have
gone out into the world.
2 By this you know the Spirit of God: [a]every spirit that [b]confesses
that [c]Jesus Christ has come in the flesh is from God;
3 and every spirit that [a]does not confess Jesus is not from God; and
this is the *spirit* of the [b]antichrist, of which you have heard that it is
coming, and [c]now it is already in the world.
4 You are from God, [a]little children, and [b]have overcome them;
because [c]greater is He who is in you than [d]he who is in the world.
5 [a]They are from the world; therefore they speak *as* from the
world, and the world listens to them.
6 [a]We are from God; [b]he who knows God listens to us; [c]he who is
not from God does not listen to us. By this we know [d]the spirit of
truth and [e]the spirit of error.
7 [a]Beloved, let us [b]love one another, for love is from God; and
[c]everyone who loves is [1d]born of God and [e]knows God.
8 The one who does not love does not know God, for [a]God is love.
9 By this the love of God was manifested [1a]in us, that [b]God has sent
His [2]only begotten Son into the world so that we might live through
Him.
10 In this is love, [a]not that we [1]loved God, but that [b]He loved us and
sent His Son *to be* [c]the propitiation for our sins.
11 [a]Beloved, if God so loved us, [b]we also ought to love one another.
12 [a]No one has beheld God at any time; if we love one another, God
abides in us, and His [b]love is perfected in us.
13 [a]By this we know that we abide in Him and He in us, because He
has given us of His Spirit.
14 And we have beheld and [a]bear witness that the Father has [b]sent
the Son *to be* the Savior of the world.
15 [a]Whoever confesses that [b]Jesus is the Son of God, God [c]abides in
him, and he in God.
16 And [a]we have come to know and have believed the love which
God has [1b]for us. [c]God is love, and the one who [d]abides in love
abides in God, and God abides in him.
17 By this, [a]love is perfected with us, that we may have [b]confidence

18 [a]1 Joh [b]2 John 1;
19 [1]Or, *pe* *before Hin* *our heart*
21 [1]Lit., *to* 3:2 [b]1 Joh
22 [a]Job 2: 7:7; 21:22; [b]1 John 2: Heb. 13:21
23 [1]Or, *be* *name* [2]Or, *commandr* 6:29 [b]John 3:18 [c]John 15:12; 1 Jo
24 [a]1 John 6:56; 10:38 24; 4:15 [c]J Rom. 8:9, 1 Thess. 4: 4:13 [d]1 Joh
4:1 [a]3 John 29:8; 1 Cor. 1 Thess. 5: 2 Thess. 2: 14:14; 2 Pet 2:18
2 [a]1 Cor. 12 2:23 [c]John 1:2
3 [a]1 John 2 7 [b]1 John 2 [c]2 Thess. 2: 2:18
4 [a]1 John 2: 2:13 [c]Rom. 1 John 3:20
5 [a]John 15:
6 [a]John 8:2 4:4 [b]John 8: 18:37 [c]1 Co [d]John 14:17
7 [1]Or, *begot* [a]1 John 2:7 3:11 [c]1 John [d]1 John 2:29 8:3; 1 John 2
8 [a]1 John 4:
9 [1]Or, *in our* *unique,* only kind [a]John 9 4:16 [b]John 3 1 John 4:10;
10 [1]Some ms *had loved* [a]R 10; 1 John 4: 3:16f.; 1 John [c]1 John 2:2
11 [a]1 John 2: 4:7
12 [a]John 1:18 6:16; 1 John 4 [b]1 John 2:5; 4
13 [a]Rom. 8:9; 3:24
14 [a]John 15:2 1:2 [b]John 3:1 1 John 2:2
15 [a]1 John 2:2 10:9; 1 John 3 5:1, 5 [c]1 John
16 [1]Lit., *in* [a]Jo [b]John 9:3; 1 Jo [c]1 John 4:7, 8 4:12f.
17 [a]1 John 2:5 [b]1 John 2:28

in [c]the day of judgment; because [d]as He is, so also are we in this world.

18 There is no fear in love; but [a]perfect love casts out fear, because fear [1]involves punishment, and the one who fears is not [b]perfected in love.

19 [a]We love, because He first loved us.

20 [a]If someone says, "I love God," and [b]hates his brother, he is a [c]liar; for [d]the one who does not love his brother whom he has seen, [1e]cannot love God whom he has not seen.

21 And [a]this commandment we have from Him, that the one who loves God [b]should love his brother also.

Chapter 5

5 [a]Whoever believes that Jesus is the [1]Christ is [2b]born of God; and whoever loves the [3]Father [c]loves the *child* [2]born of Him.

2 [a]By this we know that [b]we love the children of God, when we love God and [1]observe His commandments.

3 For [a]this is the love of God, that we [b]keep His commandments; and [c]His commandments are not burdensome.

4 For whatever is [1a]born of God [b]overcomes the world; and this is the victory that has overcome the world—our faith.

5 And who is the one who overcomes the world, but he who [a]believes that Jesus is the Son of God?

6 This is the one who came [a]by water and blood, Jesus Christ; not [1]with the water only, but [1]with the water and [1]with the blood.

7 And it is [a]the Spirit who bears witness, because the Spirit is the truth.

8 For there are [a]three that bear witness, [1]the Spirit and the water and the blood; and the three are [2]in agreement.

9 [a]If we receive the witness of men, the witness of God is greater; for the witness of God is this, that [b]He has borne witness concerning His Son.

10 The one who believes in the Son of God [a]has the witness in himself; the one who does not believe God has [b]made Him a liar, because he has not believed in the witness that God has borne concerning His Son.

11 And the witness is this, that God has given us [a]eternal life, and [b]this life is in His Son.

12 [a]He who has the Son has the life; he who does not have the Son of God does not have the life.

13 [a]These things I have written to you who [b]believe in the name of the Son of God, in order that you may know that you have [c]eternal life.

14 And this is [a]the confidence which we have [1]before Him, that, [b]if we ask anything according to His will, He hears us.

15 And if we know that He hears us *in* whatever we ask, [a]we know that we have the requests which we have asked from Him.

16 If anyone sees his brother [1]committing a sin not *leading* to death, [a]he shall ask and *God* will for him give life to those who commit sin not *leading* to death. [b]There is a sin *leading* to death; [c]I do not say that he should make request for this.

17 [a]All unrighteousness is sin, and [b]there is a sin not *leading* to death.

18 [a]We know that [b]no one who is [1]born of God sins; but He who
was [1]born of God [c]keeps him and [d]the evil one does not [e]touch him.
19 [a]We know that [b]we are of God, and [c]the whole world lies in *the
power of* the evil one.
20 And [a]we know that [b]the Son of God has come, and has [c]given us
understanding, in order that we might know [d]Him who is true, and
we [e]are in Him who is true, in His Son Jesus Christ. [f]This is the true
God and [g]eternal life.
21 [a]Little children, guard yourselves from [b]idols.

18 [1]Or, b
[a]1 John 5
[b]1 John 3
1:27; Jude
2:13 [e]Joh
19 [a]1 Joh
[b]1 John 4:
12:31; 17:
20 [a]1 Joh
[b]John 8:42
[c]Luke 24:4
17:3; Rev.
1:18; 14:9;
Rev. 3:7 [f]1
[g]1 John 5:1
21 [a]1 John
10:7, 14; 1

I Am Writing to You

1:4	
2:1	
2:12	
2:13	
2:14	
2:21	
2:26	

1 John Key Words

Chapter	Fellowship	Abide	Sin	Know	Love	Born of God	Write	Light	Tr
1									
2									
3									
4									
5									
Total									

What I Can Know	How I Can Know It

What I Can Know	How I Can Know It

1 John at a Glance

f 1 John:

Chapter Themes
1
2
3
4
5

Author:

Date:

Purpose:

Key Words:
fellowship
abide
sin
know
love
born of God
light
truth (true)
write
mark every reference to the devil (or evil one) with a red pitchfork

2 JOHN

A caring father can't ignore something that threatens his children. Thus, around A.D. 90, the p
apostle John sits down to write yet another epistle. It's short, to the point, and needful—even too

THINGS TO DO

1. Read through 2 John as you would a letter you had just received. Then read it again and:
   a. Mark the key words listed on the 2 JOHN AT A GLANCE chart on page 1837.
   b. List in the margin all you learn about the recipients of this letter. Note John's feelings them, his instructions (or commandments) to them, and his warnings. Note also the rea his warning.
2. Record the theme of 2 John in the appropriate space on 2 JOHN AT A GLANCE. Then rec theme of each paragraph and fill in any other pertinent information.

THINGS TO THINK ABOUT

1. What does this book say about someone who does not abide in the teaching of Christ? know someone who could fit that description? What should you do?
2. You probably noted that verse 4 says "some" of your children are walking in truth. A careful to walk in all the truth you know? Do you realize that before God you are respon live out the truth that has been entrusted to you?
3. According to this little epistle, what does it mean to walk in love? Are you doing this?

Chapter 1 ______________________

1 [a]The elder to the [b]chosen [c]lady and her children, whom I [d]love in
truth; and not only I, but also all who [e]know the truth,
2 for [a]the sake of the truth which abides [b]in us and will be [c]with us
forever:
3 [a]Grace, mercy *and* peace will be with us, from God the Father
and from Jesus Christ, the Son of the Father, in truth and love.
4 [a]I was very glad to find *some* of your children walking in truth,
just as we have received commandment *to do* from the Father.
5 And now I ask you, lady, [a]not as writing to you a new command-
ment, but the one which we have had [a]from the beginning, that we
[b]love one another.
6 And [a]this is love, that we walk according to His commandments.
This is the commandment, [b]just as you have heard [c]from the begin-
ning, that you should walk in it.
7 For [a]many deceivers have [b]gone out into the world, those who
[c]do not acknowledge Jesus Christ *as* coming in the flesh. This is [a]the
deceiver and the [d]antichrist.
8 [a]Watch yourselves, [b]that you might not lose what [1]we have ac-
complished, but that you may receive a full reward.
9 Anyone who [1]goes too far and [a]does not abide in the teaching of
Christ, does not have God; the one who abides in the teaching, he
has both the Father and the Son.

1:1 [a]Acts 1 5:1; 3 John 16:13; 1 Pet 2 John 13 [d]1 John 3:18 3 John 1 [e]Jo 1 Tim. 2:4

2 [a]2 Pet. 1:1 1:8 [c]John 14

3 [a]Rom. 1:7

4 [a]3 John 3f.

5 [a]1 John 2: 13:34, 35; 15 1 John 3:11;

6 [a]1 John 2:5 [b]1 John 2:24

7 [a]1 John 2:2 2:19; 4:1 [c]1 J [d]1 John 2:18

8 [1]Some anc read *you* [a]Ma [b]1 Cor. 3:8; H

9 [1]Lit., *goes* [a]John 7:16; 8: 2:23

13:16f.; Rom. Thess. 3:6, 14; Titus 3:10
10 If anyone comes to you and does not bring this teaching, [a]do not
receive him into *your* house, and do not give him a greeting;
h. 5:11; 1 Tim. 5:22; Jude 23
11 for the one who gives him a greeting [a]participates in his evil
deeds.
e ancient mss. *ur* [a]3 John 13, n 3:29; 1 John 1:4
12 [a]Having many things to write to you, I do not want to *do so* with
paper and ink; but I hope to come to you and speak face to face, that
[1]your [b]joy may be made full.
13 [a]2 John 1
13 The children of your [a]chosen sister greet you.

2 John at a Glance

of 2 John:

Paragraph Themes
-3
-11
2-13

Author:

Date:

Purpose:

Key Words:

truth

love

commandment(s)

teaching

walk

abide(s)

deceiver

3 JOHN

Love cares about the individual. Love encourages. Love rebukes. Love walks in truth. And
love, John wrote a third epistle before he was exiled to Patmos, where he wrote Revelation.
around A.D. 90.

THINGS TO DO

1. Read this short letter through once. Then read the book again, marking each of the key listed on the 3 JOHN AT A GLANCE chart on page 1839. List in the margin what you lear the key words.
2. To whom is the book written? List in the margin everything you learn about him from this
3. Other names are mentioned. Who is named and what is said about each? List this informa the margin of the text. What do you learn as you observe the contrast between these people
4. Make a list of the instructions and warnings John gives in this short epistle.
5. Complete 3 JOHN AT A GLANCE.

THINGS TO THINK ABOUT

1. What is your testimony before others? Are you known for your love of others or for your yourself? Do you share what you have with others? Do you listen to others? Do you hav first?
2. According to what John says in this epistle, what does the way you live have to do wit relationship to God?
3. Are you quick to love, to exhort, and to stand for truth? What do you need to do?

Chapter 1

1 [a]The elder to the beloved [b]Gaius, whom I [c]love in truth.
2 Beloved, I pray that in all respects you may prosper and be in
good health, just as your soul prospers.
3 For I [1a]was very glad when [b]brethren came and bore witness to
your truth, *that is,* how you [a]are walking in truth.
4 I have no greater joy than [1]this, to hear of [a]my children [b]walking
in the truth.
5 Beloved, you are acting faithfully in whatever you accomplish
for the [a]brethren, and especially *when they are* [b]strangers;
6 and they bear witness to your love before the church; and you
will do well to [a]send them on their way in a manner [b]worthy of God.
7 For they went out for the sake of [a]the Name, [b]accepting nothing
from the Gentiles.
8 Therefore we ought to [1]support such men, that we may be fellow
workers [2]with the truth.
9 I wrote something to the church; but Diotrephes, who loves to
[a]be first among them, does not accept [1]what we say.
10 For this reason, [a]if I come, I will call attention to his deeds which
he does, unjustly accusing us with wicked words; and not satisfied

1:1 [a]2 John 1 19:29; 20:4; F 16:23; 1 Cor. [c]1 John 3:18;

3 [1]Or, *am ve when brethre and bear witn* [a]2 John 4 [b]Ac Gal. 6:10; 3 J

4 [1]Lit., *these that I hear* [a]1 4:14f.; 2 Cor. 6 4:19; 1 Thess. 1 Tim. 1:2; 2 T Philem. 10; 1 [b]2 John 4

5 [a]Acts 1:15; 3 John 3, 10 [b] 12:13; Heb. 13

6 [a]Acts 15:3; [b]Col. 1:10; 1 T

7 [a]John 15:21 5:41; Phil. 2:9 20:33, 35

8 [1]Or, *receive men as guests*

9 [1]Lit., *us* [a]2 J

10 [a]2 John 12

hn 10; 3 John :15; Gal. 6:10; 5 [d]John 9:34 . 34:14; 37:27 hn 2:29; 3:10 [c]1 John 3:6 cts 6:3; 1 Tim. ı 19:35; 21:24 13 [a]2 John 12 20:19, 21, 26; 23; 1 Pet. 5:14 [b]John 10:3

with this, neither does he himself [b]receive the [c]brethren, and he for-
bids those who desire *to do so,* and [d]puts *them* out of the church.
11 Beloved, [a]do not imitate what is evil, but what is good. [b]The one
who does good is of God; [c]the one who does evil has not seen God.
12 Demetrius [a]has received a *good* testimony from everyone, and
from the truth itself; and we also bear witness, and [b]you know that
our witness is true.
13 [a]I had many things to write to you, but I am not willing to write
them to you with pen and ink;
14 but I hope to see you shortly, and we shall speak face to face.
[a]Peace *be* to you. The friends greet you. Greet the friends [b]by name.

3 John at a Glance

f 3 John:

Paragraph Themes
2-4
5-8
9-12
13-14

Author:

Date:

Purpose:

Key Words:

truth

witness

good

evil

JUDE

Jude had to speak up. He intended to write one thing, but was compelled to write anoth wasn't an apostle. He wasn't a pillar in the church like his brother James. And although he w half-brother of the Lord Jesus Christ, Jude did not claim any relationship to Jesus Christ other th of being His bondservant.

Initially, Jude didn't believe in Jesus (John 7:5), but finally he saw Jesus as He was—the God—and then he understood. Jude had grown up in the presence of the One who came to sa people from their sins (Matthew 1:21). No wonder Jude had to write what he did.

THINGS TO DO

1. Though only one chapter in length, Jude is a pertinent book. Read it to familiarize yourse the content.
2. Now read it again. This time find out what you can about the author, the recipients, and reason for writing. Mark in a distinctive way every reference to the recipients (*beloved, you*).
   a. In the margin of your Bible, list what you learn about Jude and the recipients. As you d how Jude and the recipients are described. At this point *don't* list what the recipients are instead, list only how they are described.
   b. When you discover Jude's purpose for writing, put it on the JUDE AT A GLANCE ch page 1842. If you don't see his reason immediately, don't panic; you will by the time yo finished Jude.
3. Now read through Jude again:
   a. Mark every occurrence of *these men* and *these* in the same way but do not mark *these* in v Then in the margin of Jude, list everything Jude says about *these men*.
   b. Who are "these men"? Read verse 4. If you think "these men" refers back to "certain pe in verse 4, then mark *certain persons* in the same way you marked *these* and *these men* what you learn from verse 4 to your list that describes "these men."
4. Read Jude again. Mark *condemnation, destroyed,* and *judgment*. Leave out *destroyed* in verse 1C the literal meaning is "corrupted" and is different from the meaning of the other words.
5. Mark every use of *ungodly*. There is a pattern in this letter. First Jude refers to "these un men," then he uses Old Testament examples or illustrations to make a point. Read through again, and watch for this pattern.
6. If you want to study Jude further, look up the cross references in the margin to the Old Testa characters and illustrations and see what you learn from each. This will deepen your insigh "these ungodly men."
7. In the margin, list Jude's instructions to the "beloved" and also list everything God is going for "the called, the beloved in God the Father" (verse 1).
8. Finally, write down the theme of Jude on JUDE AT A GLANCE. Now look at Jude paragra paragraph, choose a theme for each paragraph, and then record it in the designated place o chart. Fill in any other information requested.

THINGS TO THINK ABOUT

1. Think about the promises to the "beloved in God." Spend time in prayer, praising God for He will do on your behalf. Then think of the responsibilities that are yours and talk with about how you are to fulfill these within the sphere of your life.

Review the characteristics of the ungodly. Do you know of anyone who fits this description? How did God tell you to respond to these ungodly persons in verses 22 and 23? Are you willing to do so? Talk with God about it.

Chapter 1

1 [1a]Jude, a [b]bond-servant of Jesus Christ, and brother of [2]James, to
[c]those who are the called, beloved in God the Father, and [d]kept
for Jesus Christ:
2 [a]May mercy and peace and love [b]be multiplied to you.
3 [a]Beloved, while I was making every effort to write you about our
[b]common salvation, I felt the necessity to write to you appealing that
you [c]contend earnestly for [d]the faith which was once for all
[e]delivered to [f]the [1]saints.
4 For certain persons have [a]crept in unnoticed, those who were
long beforehand [1b]marked out for this condemnation, ungodly per-
sons who turn [c]the grace of our God into [d]licentiousness and [e]deny
our only Master and Lord, Jesus Christ.
5 Now I desire to [a]remind you, though [b]you know all things once
for all, that [1]the Lord, [c]after saving a people out of the land of Egypt,
[2]subsequently destroyed those who did not believe.
6 And [a]angels who did not keep their own domain, but aban-
doned their proper abode, He has [b]kept in eternal bonds under dark-
ness for the judgment of the great day.
7 Just as [a]Sodom and Gomorrah and the [b]cities around them, since
they in the same way as these indulged in gross immorality and
[c]went after strange flesh, are exhibited as an [1d]example, in undergo-
ing the [e]punishment of eternal fire.
8 Yet in the same manner these men, also by dreaming, [a]defile the
flesh, and reject authority, and revile [1]angelic majesties.
9 But [a]Michael [b]the archangel, when he disputed with the devil
and argued about [c]the body of Moses, did not dare pronounce
against him a railing judgment, but said, "[d]The Lord rebuke you."
10 But [a]these men revile the things which they do not understand;
and [b]the things which they know by instinct, [a]like unreasoning ani-
mals, by these things they are [1]destroyed.
11 Woe to them! For they have gone [a]the way of Cain, and for pay
[1]they have rushed headlong into [b]the error of Balaam, and [c]perished
in the rebellion of Korah.
12 These men are those who are [1]hidden reefs [a]in your love feasts
when they feast with you [b]without fear, caring for themselves;
[c]clouds without water, [d]carried along by winds; autumn trees
without fruit, [2]doubly dead, [e]uprooted;
13 [a]wild waves of the sea, casting up [b]their own [1]shame like foam;
wandering stars, [c]for whom the [2]black darkness has been reserved
forever.
14 And about these also [a]Enoch, *in* the seventh *generation* from
Adam, prophesied, saying, "[b]Behold, the Lord came with [1]many
thousands of His holy ones,
15 [a]to execute judgment upon all, and to convict all the ungodly of
all their ungodly deeds which they have done in an ungodly way,
and of all the harsh things which [b]ungodly sinners have spoken
against Him."
16 These are [a]grumblers, finding fault, [b]following after their *own*

r., *Judas* [2]Or, [a]Matt. 13:55; 3; [Luke 6:16; 22; Acts 1:13] 1 [c]Rom. 1:6f. 1f.; 1 Pet. 1:5; Jude 21
:16; 1 Tim. 1:2 1:2; 2 Pet. 1:2
ly ones [a]Heb. Jude 1, 17, 20 4 [c]1 Tim. 6:12 s 6:7; Jude 20 :21 [f]Acts 9:13
, *written about* 2:4; 2 Tim. 3:6 :8 [c]Acts 11:23 [e]2 Tim. 2:12; :16; 2 Pet. 2:1; 1 John 2:22
e ancient mss. *esus* [2]Lit., *the* *d time* [a]2 Pet. ; 3:1f. [b]1 John . 12:51; 1 Cor. 10; Heb. 3:16f.
2:4 [b]2 Pet. 2:9
Or, *example of eternal fire, in* *ng punishment* 19:24f.; 2 Pet. ut. 29:23; Hos. et. 2:2 [d]2 Pet. 6 [e]Matt. 25:41; 1:8f.; 2 Pet. 3:7
glories [a]2 Pet. 2:10
0:13, 21; 12:1; 12:7 [b]1 Thess. et. 2:11 [c]Deut. 4:6 [d]Zech. 3:2
[1]Lit., *corrupted* :12 [b]Phil. 3:19
[1]Lit., *they have themselves out* 3-8; Heb. 11:4; hn 3:12 [b]Num. Pet. 2:15; Rev. [c]Num. 16:1-3, 31-35
Or, *stains* [2]Lit., [a]1 Cor. 11:20ff.; t. 2:13 and mg. zek. 34:2, 8, 10 v. 25:14; 2 Pet. ph. 4:14 [e]Matt. 15:13
[1]Or, *shameless* [2]Lit., *blackness* *ness*; or, *nether* [a]Is. 57:20 [b]Phil. 9 [c]2 Pet. 2:17; Jude 6
Lit., *His holy ten* *nds* [a]Gen. 5:18, Deut. 33:2; Dan. Matt. 16:27; Heb. 12:22
et. 2:6ff. [b]1 Tim. 1:9
Num. 16:11, 41; r. 10:10 [b]2 Pet. 2:10; Jude 18

lusts; [1]they speak [c]arrogantly, flattering people [d]for the sake of *gain-*
ing an advantage.
17 But you, [a]beloved, [b]ought to remember the words that were
spoken beforehand by [c]the apostles of our Lord Jesus Christ,
18 that they were saying to you, "[a]In the last time there shall be
mockers, [b]following after their own ungodly lusts."
19 These are the ones who cause divisions, [1a]worldly-minded,
[2]devoid of the Spirit.
20 But you, [a]beloved, [b]building yourselves up on your most holy
[a]faith; [c]praying in the Holy Spirit;
21 keep yourselves in the love of God, [a]waiting anxiously for the
mercy of our Lord Jesus Christ to eternal life.
22 And [1]have mercy on some, who are doubting;
23 save others, [a]snatching them out of the fire; and on some have
mercy with fear, [b]hating even the garment polluted by the flesh.
24 [a]Now to Him who is able to keep you from stumbling, and to
[b]make you stand in the presence of His glory blameless with [c]great
joy,
25 to the [a]only [b]God our Savior, through Jesus Christ our Lord, [c]*be*
glory, majesty, dominion and authority, [d]before all time and now and
[1]forever. Amen.

16 [1]Lit., *the* *speaks* [c]2 [d]2 Pet. 2:3
17 [a]Jude 3 [c]Heb. 2:3
18 [a]Acts 2 4:1; 2 Tim. 2 Pet. 3:3
19 [1]Or, *me* [2]Lit., *not ha* 2:14f.; Jam
20 [a]Jude 3 1 Thess. 5:
21 [a]Titus 2 9:28; 2 Pet.
22 [1]Some read *convin*
23 [a]Amos 3:2; 1 Cor. 3:3f.; Rev. 3
24 [a]Rom. 4:14 [c]1 Pet
25 [1]Lit., *to* [a]John 5:44; [b]Luke 1:47 11:36 [d]Heb

Jude at a Glance

Theme of Jude:

Author:

Date:

Purpose:

Key Words:

Segment Divisions	Paragraph Themes
	1-2
	3-4
	5-16
	17-23
	24-25

EVELATION

n, one of the sons of Zebedee, identifies himself throughout his Gospel not by his name, but as ne whom Jesus loved." John walked in faith, taking Jesus at His word, and was secure in His

erefore, when John was banished to the isle of Patmos and, according to tradition, submerged in a ron of hot oil, he remained steadfast in Jesus' love. He was faithful to his calling even in the midst o's persecutions of Christians in A.D. 54 through 68 and then Domitian's in A.D. 81 through 96.

ile John was on Patmos, God unveiled to him the coming of the Lord Jesus Christ and what soon l come to pass—a revelation unparalleled, the last to be given. It was about A.D. 95. With John's tion the New Testament canon of Scripture would be complete. The church could be secure. prophecy would be fulfilled . . . just as God had said.

GS TO DO

ters 1-3

To familiarize yourself with the first two segments of the book of Revelation, carefully read 1:1 through 4:1 in one sitting. (By the way, *revelation* is a translation of the Greek word *apokalupsis,* which means unveiling.)

Mark the following key words (along with their synonyms and pronouns) in chapter 1, and then in the margin list everything you learn from the text about these words: *Jesus Christ, God (the Father), Spirit (seven Spirits),* and *write.* Then transfer this information to the chart WHAT REVELATION TEACHES ABOUT GOD, JESUS, AND THE HOLY SPIRIT on page 1869.

Revelation 1:19 gives an outline of the book of Revelation.

a. List the three things John was to write:

   1) ______________________

   2) ______________________

   3) ______________________

b. Now look at Revelation 4:1 and note how it relates to 1:19. Revelation 4 begins the third segment of Revelation. Chapter 1 describes what John saw, and chapters 2 and 3 are "the things which are." What is the third segment that begins in 4:1?

c. Using the terminology found in Revelation 1:19, record these three segments in the space for segment divisions on the REVELATION AT A GLANCE chart on page 1871. (The lines to divide the book into these sections already are drawn.)

Read Revelation 1 through 3 and do the following:

a. Watch for key repeated phrases or words listed on REVELATION AT A GLANCE. Mark these in a distinctive way so you can spot them immediately. In Jesus' messages to the churches, watch for a pattern as Jesus addresses each church.

b. Now concentrate on Jesus' messages to the churches, one church at a time. Record what you learn about each church on the chart JESUS' MESSAGES TO THE CHURCHES on page 1868. When you see what is said regarding those who overcome, note how John describes overcomers in 1 John 5:4-5. Add what you learn to the chart.

Record the main theme of each chapter in the text next to the chapter number and on REVELATION AT A GLANCE.

Chapters 4-22

1. In the last nineteen chapters of Revelation Jesus shows John "the things which must shor place." Read Revelation 4 through 22 one chapter at a time, and for each chapter do the fol
   a. As you read ask the five W's and an H: Who? What? Why? When? Where? and Ho example, if it's an event ask: What is happening? Who is involved? When will this happ where? Why is this happening? How will it happen? If it's a person: Who is this? Wha person like? What does he do? When? Where? Why? What are the consequences? How accomplish it?
   b. Mark key repeated words (along with their synonyms and pronouns—*he, she, it, we, t* and *you*) in a distinctive way. Some key words are listed on REVELATION AT A GL Since it's a long list, write these on a card, color code the words as you intend to mark t the text, and use the card as a bookmark.
   c. As you go through Revelation chapter by chapter, let the text speak for itself. Remembe is revealed gradually, so don't become impatient. Simply observe what is being said v adding your own interpretation. Stay in an attitude of prayer, asking God to open the your understanding.
2. Babylon plays a prominent role throughout the Word of God. Therefore, in the appendix c Bible under WHAT THE BIBLE TEACHES ABOUT BABYLON (pages 1876 and 1877), what you learn about Babylon. When you record your observations note the reference so th can find the information in your Bible later.
3. List on the chart WHAT REVELATION TEACHES ABOUT GOD, JESUS, AND THE SPIRIT everything you learn about the Godhead.
4. Mark every reference to time with a clock such as this or in some other significan References to time will be important when you do an in-depth study of prophecy.
5. There is a separate chart on page 1870 called THE SEVEN SEALS, TRUMPETS, AND BC Fill in this chart as you read this segment.
6. When you finish going through Revelation, record the chapter themes in the text a REVELATION AT A GLANCE, along with other pertinent information called for on the cha
7. Finally, see how various chapters of the book group according to events, places, or person your chapter themes as a guide to see when these groupings occur. Record these groupings "Segments Divisions" on REVELATION AT A GLANCE, placing them under the chapter bers in which they occur.

THINGS TO THINK ABOUT

Chapters 1-3

1. As you look at the Lord's message to each church, do you think the message could be f church today? Look back through Jesus' messages to the churches in chapters 2 and 3 anc what the Spirit is saying to him who has "an ear." To whom is the Spirit speaking? What do want you to hear? To do?
2. Think about what you have learned about Jesus Christ from these three chapters and then some time worshiping Him for who and what He is.
3. Are you an overcomer? How does it show? Is there anything you need to do that you'r doing so that when Jesus appears you won't be ashamed?

Chapters 4-22

1. Revelation gives insight into the judgment of God upon the wicked because of what they ship. It also gives a glimpse of the way the righteous worship. How would you compare worship with the worship described in Revelation? You might want to go back thr Revelation and look at the scenes where God is worshiped and use them as a pattern for wo
2. Now that you have a better understanding of the wrath to come upon the unbeliever,

priority needs to be placed on sharing the gospel? Is witnessing a priority in your church? Is witnessing a priority in your personal life?

Are you sure that you are a child of God? If not, will you acknowledge the Lord Jesus Christ as God, receive His forgiveness for your sins, and let Him take full control of your life? Surely you have seen that He is worthy—and trustworthy.

What have you learned about your God? In the light of this, are you living in anticipation of Jesus' coming?

Chapter 1

1 The Revelation of Jesus Christ, which [a]God gave Him to [b]show
to His bond-servants, [c]the things which must shortly take place;
and He sent and [1]communicated *it* [d]by His angel to His bond-servant
[e]John,
2 who bore witness to [a]the word of God and to [b]the testimony of
Jesus Christ, *even* to all that he saw.
3 [a]Blessed is he who reads and those who hear the words of the
prophecy, and [1]heed the things which are written in it; [b]for the time
is near.
4 [a]John to [b]the seven churches that are in [c]Asia: [d]Grace to you and
peace, from [e]Him who is and who was and who is to come; and from
[f]the seven Spirits who are before His throne;
5 and from Jesus Christ, [a]the faithful witness, the [b]first-born of the
dead, and the [c]ruler of the kings of the earth. To Him who [d]loves us,
and released us from our sins [1]by His blood,
6 and He has made us *to be* a [a]kingdom, [a]priests to [1b]His God and
Father; [c]to Him *be* the glory and the dominion forever and ever.
Amen.
7 [a]BEHOLD, HE IS COMING WITH THE CLOUDS, and [b]every eye will see
Him, even those who pierced Him; and all the tribes of the earth will
[c]mourn over Him. Even so. Amen.
8 "I am [a]the Alpha and the Omega," says the [b]Lord God, "[c]who is
and who was and who is to come, the Almighty."
9 [a]I, John, your [b]brother and [c]fellow partaker in the tribulation and
[d]kingdom and [1e]perseverance *which are* in Jesus, was on the island
called Patmos, [f]because of the word of God and the testimony of
Jesus.
10 I was [1a]in the Spirit on [b]the Lord's day, and I heard behind me a
loud voice [c]like *the sound* of a trumpet,
11 saying, "[a]Write in a [1]book what you see, and send *it* to the [b]seven
churches: to [c]Ephesus and to [d]Smyrna and to [e]Pergamum and to
[f]Thyatira and to [g]Sardis and to [h]Philadelphia and to [i]Laodicea."
12 And I turned to see the voice that was speaking with me. And
having turned I saw [a]seven golden lampstands;
13 and [a]in the middle of the lampstands one [b]like [1]a son of man,
[c]clothed in a robe reaching to the feet, and [d]girded across His breast
with a golden girdle.
14 And His head and His [a]hair were white like white wool, like
snow; and [b]His eyes were like a flame of fire;
15 and His [a]feet *were* like burnished bronze, when it has been
caused to glow in a furnace, and His [b]voice *was* like the sound of
many waters.
16 And in His right hand He held [a]seven stars; and out of His

ignified [a]John Rev. 5:7 [b]Rev. an. 2:28f.; Rev. v. 17:1; 19:9f.; :16 [e]Rev. 1:4, 9; 22:8
:9; 6:9; 12:17; Cor. 1:6; Rev. 12:17
Or, *keep* [a]Luke v. 22:7 [b]Rom. Rev. 3:11; 22:7, 10, 12
ev. 1:1, 9; 22:8 1:11, 20 [c]Acts Rom. 1:7 [e]Rev. ; 4:8; 16:5 [f]Is. v. 3:1; 4:5; 5:6; 8:2
in [a]Rev. 3:14; [b]1 Cor. 15:20; 8 [c]Rev. 17:14; 16 [d]Rom. 8:37
r, *God and His* Rev. 5:10; 20:6 6 [c]Rom. 11:36
7:13; 1 Thess. Zech. 12:10-14; 37 [c]Luke 23:28
1:4; Rev. 21:6; Rev. 4:8; 11:17 [c]Rev. 1:4
steadfastness 1:1 [b]Acts 1:15 23; Acts 14:22; 1:7; Phil. 4:14 2:12; Rev. 1:6 Thess. 3:5; Rev. 3:10 [f]Rev. 1:2
in spirit [a]Matt. ; Rev. 4:2; 17:3; Acts 20:7 [c]Rev. 4:1
scroll [a]Rev. 1:2, v. 1:4, 20 [c]Rev. [d]Rev. 2:8 [e]Rev. Acts 16:14; Rev. 24 [g]Rev. 3:1, 4 [i]Col. 2:1; Rev. 3:14
x. 25:37; 37:23; 2; Rev. 1:20; 2:1
the Son of Man 2:1 [b]Ezek. 1:26; :13; 10:16; Rev. Dan. 10:5 [d]Rev. 15:6
7:9 [b]Dan. 7:9; Rev. 2:18; 19:12
[a]Ezek. 1:7; Dan. ev. 2:18 [b]Ezek. 43:2; Rev. 14:2; 19:6
ev. 1:20; 2:1; 3:1

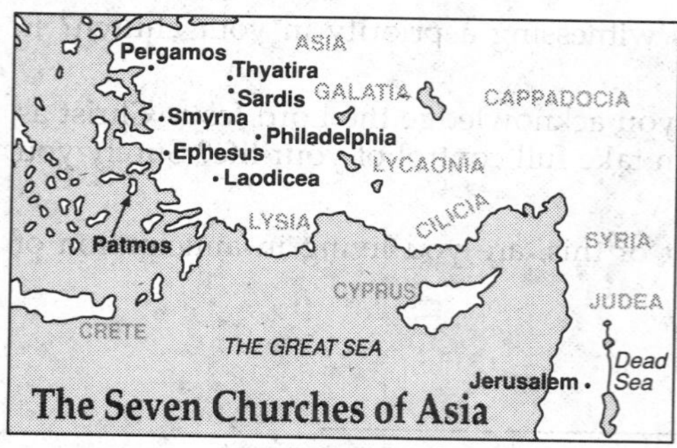

The Seven Churches of Asia

mouth came a [b]sharp two-edged sword;
and His [c]face was like [d]the sun [1]shining in
its strength.
17 And when I saw Him, I [a]fell at His feet
as a dead man. And He [b]laid His right hand
upon me, saying, "[c]Do not be afraid; [d]I am
the first and the last,
18 and the [a]living One; and I [1b]was dead,
and behold, I am alive forevermore, and I
have [c]the keys of death and of Hades.
19 "[a]Write therefore [b]the things which you
have seen, and the things which are, and
the things which shall take place [c]after these things.
20 "As for the [a]mystery of the [b]seven stars which you saw in My
right hand, and the [c]seven golden lampstands: the [b]seven stars are
the angels of [d]the seven churches, and the seven [e]lampstands are the
seven churches.

Chapter 2

2 "To the angel of the church in [a]Ephesus write:
The One who holds [b]the seven stars in His right hand, the One
who walks [1c]among the seven golden lampstands, says this:
2 '[a]I know your deeds and your toil and [1]perseverance, and that
you cannot endure evil men, and you [b]put to the test those who call
themselves [c]apostles, and they are not, and you found them *to be*
false;
3 and you have [1]perseverance and have endured [a]for My name's
sake, and have not grown weary.
4 'But I have *this* against you, that you have [a]left your first love.
5 'Remember therefore from where you have fallen, and [a]repent
and [b]do the [1]deeds you did at first; or else I am coming to you, and
will remove your [c]lampstand out of its place—unless you repent.
6 'Yet this you do have, that you hate the deeds of the [a]Nicolaitans,
which I also hate.
7 '[a]He who has an ear, let him hear what the Spirit says to the
churches. [b]To him who overcomes, I will grant to eat of [c]the tree of
life, which is in the [d]Paradise of God.'
8 "And to the angel of the church in [a]Smyrna write:
[b]The first and the last, who [1c]was dead, and has come to life, says
this:
9 'I know your [a]tribulation and your [b]poverty (but you are [b]rich),
and the blasphemy by those who [c]say they are Jews and are not, but
are a synagogue of [d]Satan.
10 'Do not fear what you are about to suffer. Behold, the devil is
about to cast some of you into prison, that you may be [a]tested, and
you will have tribulation [b]ten days. Be [c]faithful until death, and I will
give you [d]the crown of life.
11 '[a]He who has an ear, let him hear what the Spirit says to the
churches. [b]He who overcomes shall not be hurt by the [c]second
death.'
12 "And to the angel of the church in [a]Pergamum write:
The One who has [b]the sharp two-edged sword says this:
13 'I know where you dwell, where [a]Satan's throne is; and you hold
fast My name, and did not deny [b]My faith, even in the days of

16 [1]Lit., *shi*… 49:2; Heb. 4… 2:12, 16; 19… 17:2; Rev. 1… 5:31

17 [a]Dan. 8:… 15 [b]Dan. 8:… 12 [c]Matt. 14… [d]Is. 41:4; 44… Rev. 2:8; 22…

18 [1]Lit., *bec*… 24:5; Rev. 4:… 6:9; Rev. 2:8… [c]Job 38:17; … 16:19; Rev. …

19 [a]Rev. 1:1… 1:12-16 [c]Re…

20 [a]Rom. 11… 1:16; 2:1; 3:1… 25:37; 37:23… Rev. 1:12; 2:… 1:4, 11 [e]Mat…

2:1 [1]Lit., *in th*… *of* [a]Rev. 1:11… 1:16 [c]Rev. 1:…

2 [1]Or, *steadf*… [a]Rev. 2:19; 3… [b]John 6:6; 1 J… [c]2 Cor. 11:13

3 [1]V. 2, note… 15:21

4 [a]Jer. 2:2; M…

5 [1]Lit., *first de*… [a]Rev. 2:16, 22… [b]Heb. 10:32; … [c]Matt. 5:14ff.; … Rev. 1:20

6 [a]Rev. 2:15

7 [a]Matt. 11:15… 2:11, 17; 3:6, … 13:9 [b]Rev. 2:… 3:5, 12, 21; 21… 2:9; 3:22; Prov… 11:30; 13:12; … 22:2, 14 [d]Ezek… 31:8f.; Luke 23…

8 [1]Lit., *becam*… 1:11 [b]Is. 44:6; … Rev. 1:17; 22:… 1:18

9 [a]Rev. 1:9 [b]2… 6:10; 8:9; Jame… [c]Rev. 3:9 [d]Mat… Rev. 2:13, 24

10 [a]Rev. 3:10; … [b]Dan. 1:12, 14… 2:13; 12:11; 17:… [d]1 Cor. 9:25; Re…

11 [a]Matt. 11:15… 2:7, 17, 29; 3:6, … 13:9 [b]Rev. 2:7, … 3:5, 12, 21; 21:7… 20:6, 14; 21:8

12 [a]Rev. 1:11… 1:16; 2:16

13 [a]Matt. 4:10; … 2:24 [b]1 Tim. 5:… 14:12

Antipas, My [c]witness, My [d]faithful one, who was killed among you,
[e]where Satan dwells.
14 'But [a]I have a few things against you, because you have there
some who hold the [b]teaching of Balaam, who kept teaching Balak to
put a stumbling block before the sons of Israel, [c]to eat things
sacrificed to idols, and to commit *acts of* immorality.
15 'Thus you also have some who in the same way hold the teach-
ing of the [a]Nicolaitans.
16 '[a]Repent therefore; or else [b]I am coming to you quickly, and I will
make war against them with [c]the sword of My mouth.
17 '[a]He who has an ear, let him hear what the Spirit says to the
churches. [a]To him who overcomes, to him I will give *some* of the
hidden [b]manna, and I will give him a white stone, and a [c]new name
written on the stone [d]which no one knows but he who receives it.'
18 "And to the angel of the church in [a]Thyatira write:
[b]The Son of God, [c]who has [1]eyes like a flame of fire, and His feet
are like burnished bronze, says this:
19 '[a]I know your deeds, and your love and faith and service and
[1]perseverance, and that your [2]deeds of late are greater than [3]at first.
20 'But [a]I have *this* against you, that you tolerate the woman
[b]Jezebel, who calls herself a prophetess, and she teaches and leads
My bond-servants astray, so that they [c]commit *acts of* immorality and
eat things sacrificed to idols.
21 'And [a]I gave her time to repent; and she [b]does not want to repent
of her immorality.
22 'Behold, [1]I will cast her [2]upon a bed *of sickness*, and those who
[a]commit adultery with her into great tribulation, unless they repent
of [3]her deeds.
23 'And I will kill her children with [1]pestilence; and all the churches
will know that I am He who [a]searches the [2]minds and hearts; and [b]I
will give to each one of you according to your deeds.
24 'But I say to you, the rest who are in [a]Thyatira, who do not hold
this teaching, who have not known the [b]deep things of Satan, as they
call them—I [c]place no other burden on you.
25 'Nevertheless [a]what you have, hold fast [b]until I come.
26 'And [a]he who overcomes, and he who keeps My deeds [b]until the
end, [c]TO HIM I WILL GIVE AUTHORITY OVER THE [1]NATIONS;
27 AND HE SHALL [1a]RULE THEM WITH A ROD OF IRON, [b]AS THE VESSELS OF
THE POTTER ARE BROKEN TO PIECES, as I also have received *authority* from
My Father;
28 and I will give him [a]the morning star.
29 '[a]He who has an ear, let him hear what the Spirit says to the
churches.'

Chapter 3

3 "And to the angel of the church in [a]Sardis write:
He who has [b]the seven Spirits of God, and [c]the seven stars, says
this: '[d]I know your deeds, that you have a name that you are alive,
but you are [e]dead.
2 'Wake up, and strengthen the things that remain, which were
about to die; for I have not found your deeds completed in the sight
of My God.
3 '[a]Remember therefore [1]what you have received and heard; and
keep *it*, and [a]repent. If therefore you will not wake up, [a]I will come

2:20; Rev. 17:6 [d]Rev. 2:11; 17:14 [e]Rev. 2:9
:20 [b]Num. 2 Pet. 2:15 25:1f.; Acts Cor. 10:20; Rev. 2:20
5 [a]Rev. 2:6
. 2:5 [b]Rev. Thess. 2:8; Rev. 1:16
ev. 2:7 [b]Ex. 6:49f. [c]Is. 65:15 [d]Rev. 14:3; 19:12
eyes [a]Rev. 4 [b]Matt. 4:3 [c]Rev. 1:14f.
eadfastness deeds [3]Lit., *st* [a]Rev. 2:2
2:14 [b]1 Kin. 5; 2 Kin. 9:7, [c]Acts 15:29; 20; Rev. 2:14
n. 2:4; 2 Pet. om. 2:5; Rev. 20f.; 16:9, 11
., *I cast* [2]Lit., ne mss. read ev. 17:2; 18:9
., *death* [2]Lit., e., inner man ; 26:2; 139:1; ; 17:10; Matt. e 16:15; Acts om. 8:27 [b]Ps. 62:12
. 2:18 [b]1 Cor. 0 [c]Acts 15:28
ev. 3:11 [b]John 21:22
Gentiles [a]Rev. tt. 10:22; Heb. 2:8; Rev. 3:21; 20:4
shepherd [a]Ps. ev. 12:5; 19:15 0:14; Jer. 19:11
John 3:2; Rev. 22:16
29 [a]Rev. 2:7
Rev. 1:11 [b]Rev. Rev. 1:16 [d]Rev. 15 [e]1 Tim. 5:6
how [a]Rev. 2:5

[b]like a thief, and you will not know at [c]what hour I will come upon
you.
4 'But you have a few [1a]people in [b]Sardis who have not [c]soiled their
garments; and they will walk with Me [d]in white; for they are worthy.
5 '[a]He who overcomes shall thus be clothed in [b]white garments;
and I will not [c]erase his name from the book of life, and [d]I will
confess his name before My Father, and before His angels.
6 '[a]He who has an ear, let him hear what the Spirit says to the
churches.'
7 "And to the angel of the church in [a]Philadelphia write:
[b]**He** who is holy, [c]who is true, who has [d]the key of David, who
opens and no one will shut, and who shuts and no one opens, says
this:
8 '[a]I know your [1]deeds. Behold, I have put before you [b]an open
door which no one can shut, because you have a little power, and
have kept My word, and [c]have not denied My name.
9 'Behold, I [1]will cause *those* of [a]the synagogue of Satan, who say
that they are Jews, and are not, but lie—behold, I will make them to
[b]come and bow down [2]at your feet, and to know that [c]I have loved
you.
10 'Because you have [a]kept the word of [b]My [1]perseverance, [c]I also
will keep you from the hour of [2d]testing, that *hour* which is about to
come upon the whole [3e]world, to [4]test [f]those who dwell upon the
earth.
11 '[a]I am coming quickly; [b]hold fast what you have, in order that no
one take your [c]crown.
12 '[a]He who overcomes, I will make him a [b]pillar in the temple of
My God, and he will not go out from it anymore; and I will write
upon him the [c]name of My God, and [d]the name of the city of My
God, [e]the new Jerusalem, which comes down out of heaven from My
God, and My [f]new name.
13 '[a]He who has an ear, let him hear what the Spirit says to the
churches.'
14 "And to the angel of the church in [a]Laodicea write:
[b]The Amen, [c]the faithful and true Witness, [d]the [1]Beginning of the
creation of God, says this:
15 '[a]I know your deeds, that you are neither cold nor hot; [b]I would
that you were cold or hot.
16 'So because you are lukewarm, and neither hot nor cold, I will
[1]spit you out of My mouth.
17 'Because you say, "[a]I am rich, and have become wealthy, and
have need of nothing," and you do not know that you are wretched
and miserable and poor and blind and naked,
18 I advise you to [a]buy from Me [b]gold refined by fire, that you may
become rich, and [c]white garments, that you may clothe yourself, and
that [d]the shame of your nakedness may not be revealed; and eye
salve to anoint your eyes, that you may see.
19 '[a]Those whom I love, I reprove and discipline; be zealous there-
fore, and [b]repent.
20 'Behold, I stand [a]at the door and [b]knock; if anyone hears My
voice and opens the door, [c]I will come in to him, and will dine with
him, and he with Me.
21 '[a]He who overcomes, I will grant to him [b]to sit down with Me on

3 [b]1 Thess 3:10; Rev. 24:43; Luke

4 [1]Lit., *nam* 11:13 [b]Rev 23 [d]Eccl. 9 18; 4:4; 6:1 19:8, 14

5 [a]Rev. 2:7 [c]Ex. 32:32f. Luke 10:20; 17:8; 20:12, [d]Matt. 10:32

6 [a]Rev. 2:7

7 [a]Rev. 1:11 6:10 [c]1 Joh 3:14; 19:11 Is. 22:22; Ma Rev. 1:18

8 [1]Or, *deed* *. shut), that* 3:1 [b]Acts 14 2:13

9 [1]Lit., *give before* [a]Rev 45:14; 49:23 43:4; John 1

10 [1]Or, *stea* [2]Or, *temptati inhabited ea tempt* [a]John 3:8 [b]Rev. 1:9 2:12; 2 Pet. 2 2:10 [e]Matt. 2 16:14 [f]Rev. 6 11:10; 13:8,

11 [a]Rev. 1:3; 20 [b]Rev. 2:25 2:10

12 [a]Rev. 3:5 7:21; Jer. 1:18 [c]Rev. 14:1; 22 48:35; Rev. 2 4:26; Heb. 13 21:2, 10 [f]Is. 6 2:17

13 [a]Rev. 3:6

14 [1]I.e., origin source [a]Rev. [b]2 Cor. 1:20 3:7 [d]Gen. 49: 21:17; Prov. 8 1:3; Col. 1:18; 21:6; 22:13

15 [a]Rev. 3:1 12:11

16 [1]Lit., *vomit*

17 [a]Hos. 12:8; 11:5; Matt. 5:3;

18 [a]Is. 55:1; M 13:44 [b]1 Pet. 3:4 [d]Rev. 16:15

19 [a]Prov. 3:12; 11:32; Heb. 12 2:5

20 [a]Matt. 24:33 5:9 [b]Luke 12:3 10:3 [c]John 14:

21 [a]Rev. 2:7 [b] 19:28; 2 Tim. 2 2:26; 20:4

My throne, as [c]I also overcame and sat down with My Father on His
throne.
22 '[a]He who has an ear, let him hear what the Spirit says to the
churches.' "

Chapter 4

4 After [a]these things I looked, and behold, [b]a door *standing* open in
heaven, and the first voice which I had heard, [c]like *the sound* of a
trumpet speaking with me, [1]said, "[d]Come up here, and I will [e]show
you what must take place after these things."
2 Immediately I was [1a]in the Spirit; and behold, [b]a throne was
standing in heaven, and [c]One sitting on the throne.
3 And He who was sitting *was* like a [a]jasper stone and a [b]sardius in
appearance; and *there was* a [1c]rainbow around the throne, like an
[d]emerald in appearance.
4 And [a]around the throne *were* [b]twenty-four thrones; and upon the
thrones *I saw* [c]twenty-four elders [d]sitting, clothed in [e]white garments,
and [f]golden crowns on their heads.
5 And from the throne proceed [a]flashes of lightning and sounds
and peals of thunder. And *there were* [b]seven lamps of fire burning
before the throne, which are [c]the seven Spirits of God;
6 and before the throne *there was,* as it were, a [a]sea of glass like
crystal; and in the [1]center and [b]around the throne, [c]four living crea-
tures [d]full of eyes in front and behind.
7 [a]And the first creature *was* like a lion, and the second creature
like a calf, and the third creature had a face like that of a man, and
the fourth creature *was* like a flying eagle.
8 And the [a]four living creatures, each one of them having [b]six
wings, are [c]full of eyes around and within; and [d]day and night [1]they
do not cease to say,

> "[e]HOLY, HOLY, HOLY, *is* THE [f]LORD GOD, THE ALMIGHTY, [g]who was
> and who is and who is to come."

9 And when the living creatures give glory and honor and thanks
to Him who [a]sits on the throne, to [b]Him who lives forever and ever,
10 the [a]twenty-four elders will [b]fall down before Him who [c]sits on
the throne, and will worship [d]Him who lives forever and ever, and
will cast their [e]crowns before the throne, saying,
11 "[a]Worthy art Thou, our Lord and our God, to receive glory and
honor and power; for Thou [b]didst create all things, and be-
cause of Thy will they [1]existed, and were created."

Chapter 5

5 And I saw [1]in the right hand of Him who [a]sat on the throne a
[2b]book written inside and on the back, [c]sealed up with seven
seals.
2 And I saw a [a]strong angel proclaiming with a loud voice, "Who
is worthy to open the [1]book and to break its seals?"
3 And no one [a]in heaven, or on the earth, or under the earth, was
able to open the [1]book, or to look into it.
4 And I *began* to weep greatly, because no one was found worthy
to open the [1]book, or to look into it;
5 and one of the elders *said to me, "Stop weeping; behold, the
[a]Lion that is [b]from the tribe of Judah, the [c]Root of David, has over-
come so as to open the [1]book and its seven seals."

n 16:33; Rev.
:5; 6:2; 17:14
22 [a]Rev. 2:7
saying [a]Rev.
9 [b]Ezek. 1:1;
1 [c]Rev. 1:10
2 [e]Rev. 1:19;
22:6
n spirit [a]Rev.
Kin. 22:19; Is.
ek. 1:26; Dan.
:9f. [c]Rev. 4:9
Or, halo [a]Rev.
[b]Rev. 21:20
28; Rev. 10:1
[d]Rev. 21:19
4:6; 5:11; 7:11
6 [c]Rev. 4:10;
4; 19:4 [d]Matt.
ev. 20:4 [e]Rev.
18 [f]Rev. 4:10
:16; Rev. 8:5;
9; 16:18 [b]Ex.
ch. 4:2 [c]Rev.
1:4
middle of the
ne and around
22; Rev. 15:2;
21 [b]Rev. 4:4
:5; Rev. 4:8f.;
6; 7:11; 14:3;
[d]Ezek. 1:18;
10:12
k. 1:10; 10:14
, they have no
g, [a]Ezek. 1:5;
9; 5:6; 6:1, 6;
4:3; 15:7; 19:4
2 [c]Ezek. 1:18;
Rev. 14:11 [e]Is.
1:8 [g]Rev. 1:4
s. 47:8; Is. 6:1;
[b]Deut. 32:40;
:34; 12:7; Rev.
10:6; 15:7
4:4 [b]Rev. 5:8,
11; 11:16; 19:4
8; Is. 6:1; Rev.
ut. 32:40; Dan.
2:7 [e]Rev. 4:4;
10:6; 15:7
it., were [a]Rev.
2 [b]Acts 14:15;
Rev. 10:6; 14:7
Lit., *upon* [2]Or,
ev. 4:9; 5:7, 13
ek. 2:9, 10 [c]Is.
:11; Dan. 12:4
roll [a]Rev. 10:1;
18:21
roll [a]Phil. 2:10;
Rev. 5:13
4 [1]Or, *scroll*
Or, scroll [a]Gen.
[b]Heb. 7:14 [c]Is.
0; Rom. 15:12;
Rev. 22:16

6 And I saw [1]between the throne (with the four living creatures)
and [a]the elders a [b]Lamb standing, as if [c]slain, having seven [d]horns
and [e]seven eyes, which are [f]the seven Spirits of God, sent out into all
the earth.
7 And He came, and He took [a]*it* out of the right hand of Him who
[a]sat on the throne.
8 And when He had taken the [1]book, the [a]four living creatures and
the [b]twenty-four elders [c]fell down before the [d]Lamb, having each one
a [e]harp, and [f]golden bowls full of incense, which are the [g]prayers of
the [2]saints.
9 And they *sang a [a]new song, saying,
"[b]Worthy art Thou to take the [1]book, and to break its seals; for
Thou wast [c]slain, and didst [d]purchase for God with Thy blood
men from [e]every tribe and tongue and people and nation.
10 "And Thou hast made them *to be* a [a]kingdom and [a]priests to
our God; and they will [b]reign upon the earth."
11 And I looked, and I heard the voice of many angels [a]around the
throne and the [b]living creatures and the [c]elders; and the number of
them was [d]myriads of myriads, and thousands of thousands,
12 saying with a loud voice,
"[a]Worthy is the [b]Lamb that was [b]slain to receive power and
riches and wisdom and might and honor and glory and bless-
ing."
13 And [a]every created thing which is in heaven and on the earth
and under the earth and on the sea, and all things in them, I heard
saying,
"To Him who [b]sits on the throne, and to the [c]Lamb, [d]*be* blessing
and honor and glory and dominion forever and ever."
14 And the [a]four living creatures kept saying, "[b]Amen." And the
[c]elders [d]fell down and worshiped.

Chapter 6

6 And I saw when the [a]Lamb broke one of the [b]seven seals, and I
heard one of the [c]four living creatures saying as with a [d]voice of
thunder, "Come[1]."
2 And I looked, and behold, a [a]white horse, and he who sat on it
had a bow; and [b]a crown was given to him; and he went out [c]con-
quering, and to conquer.
3 And when He broke the second seal, I heard the [a]second living
creature saying, "Come[1]."
4 And another, [a]a red horse, went out; and to him who sat on it, it
was granted to [b]take peace from the earth, and that *men* should slay
one another; and a great sword was given to him.
5 And when He broke the third seal, I heard the [a]third living crea-
ture saying, "Come[1]." And I looked, and behold, a [b]black horse; and
he who sat on it had a [c]pair of scales in his hand.
6 And I heard as it were a voice in the center of the [a]four living
creatures saying, "A [1]quart of wheat for a [2]denarius, and three
[1]quarts of barley for a [2]denarius; and [b]do not harm the oil and the
wine."
7 And when He broke the fourth seal, I heard the voice of the
[a]fourth living creature saying, "Come[1]."
8 And I looked, and behold, an [1a]ashen horse; and he who sat on it
had the name [b]Death; and [b]Hades was following with him. And

6 [1]Lit., *in th* *the throne a* *four living c* *and in the m* *elders* [a]Re 14 [b]John 1 5:8, 12f.; 13 5:9, 12; 13: 8:3f. [e]Zech [f]Rev. 1:4

7 [a]Rev. 5:1

8 [1]Or, *scrol* *ones* [a]Rev. 14 [b]Rev. 4: [c]Rev. 4:10 Rev. 5:6, 12 [e]Rev. 14:2; 15:7 [g]Ps. 14 8:3f.

9 [1]Or, *scrol* 40:3; 98:1; 42:10; Rev. [b]Rev. 4:11 [c] 12; 13:8 [d]1 Rev. 14:3f. 5:19; Rev. 7 11:9; 13:7; 1

10 [a]Rev. 1:6 3:21; 20:4

11 [a]Rev. 4:4 5:6, 8, 14 [c]R 5:6, 14 [d]Dan Heb. 12:22; Rev. 9:16

12 [a]Rev. 1:6 [b]John 1:29; F 13; 13:8

13 [a]Phil. 2:1 [b]Rev. 5:1 [c]Jo Rev. 5:6, 12f. [d]Rom. 11:36;

14 [a]Rev. 4:6; [b]1 Cor. 14:16 19:4 [c]Rev. 4: [d]Rev. 4:10

6:1 [1]Some m *and see* [a]Joh Rev. 5:6, 12f.; [b]Rev. 5:1 [c]Re 8, 11, 14 [d]Re 19:6

2 [a]Zech. 1:8; 19:11 [b]Zech. 9:7; 14:14; 19 3:21

3 [1]Some mss *see* [a]Rev. 4:7

4 [a]Zech. 1:8; 10:34

5 [1]Some mss. *see* [a]Rev. 4:7 6:2, 6 [c]Ezek. 4

6 [1]Gr., *choeni* dry measure a equal to a qt. denarius was e to one day's wa [a]Rev. 4:6f. [b]Re

7 [1]Some mss. *see* [a]Rev. 4:7

8 [1]Or, *sickly p* [a]Zech. 6:3 [b]Pr Hos. 13:14; Ma Rev. 1:18; 20:1

authority was given to them over a fourth of the earth, [c]to kill with sword and with famine and with [2]pestilence and by the wild beasts of the earth.

9 And when He broke the fifth seal, I saw [a]underneath the [b]altar the [c]souls of those who had been slain [d]because of the word of God, and because of the [e]testimony which they had maintained;

10 and they cried out with a loud voice, saying, "[a]How long, O [1b]Lord, [c]holy and true, [2]wilt Thou refrain from [d]judging and avenging our blood on [e]those who dwell on the earth?"

11 And [a]there was given to each of them a white robe; and they were told that they should [b]rest for a little while longer, [c]until *the number of* their fellow servants and their brethren who were to be killed even as they had been, should be [d]completed also.

12 And I looked when He broke the sixth seal, and there was a great [a]earthquake; and the [b]sun became black as [c]sackcloth *made* of hair, and the whole moon became like blood;

13 and [a]the stars of the sky fell to the earth, [b]as a fig tree casts its unripe figs when shaken by a great wind.

14 And [a]the sky was split apart like a scroll when it is rolled up; and [b]every mountain and island were moved out of their places.

15 And [a]the kings of the earth and the great men and the [1]commanders and the rich and the strong and every slave and free man, hid themselves in the caves and among the rocks of the mountains;

16 and they *[a]said to the mountains and to the rocks, "Fall on us and hide us from the [1]presence of Him [b]who sits on the throne, and from the [c]wrath of the Lamb;

17 for [a]the great day of their wrath has come; and [b]who is able to stand?"

Chapter 7

7 After this I saw [a]four angels standing at the [b]four corners of the earth, holding back [c]the four winds of the earth, [d]so that no wind should blow on the earth or on the sea or on any tree.

2 And I saw another angel ascending [a]from the rising of the sun, having the [b]seal of [c]the living God; and he cried out with a loud voice to the [d]four angels to whom it was granted to harm the earth and the sea,

3 saying, "[a]Do not harm the earth or the sea or the trees, until we have [b]sealed the bond-servants of our God on their [c]foreheads."

4 And I heard the [a]number of those who were sealed, [b]one hundred and forty-four thousand sealed from every tribe of the sons of Israel:

5 from the tribe of Judah, twelve thousand *were* sealed, from the tribe of Reuben twelve thousand, from the tribe of Gad twelve thousand,

6 from the tribe of Asher twelve thousand, from the tribe of Naphtali twelve thousand, from the tribe of Manasseh twelve thousand,

7 from the tribe of Simeon twelve thousand, from the tribe of Levi twelve thousand, from the tribe of Issachar twelve thousand,

8 from the tribe of Zebulun twelve thousand, from the tribe of Joseph twelve thousand, from the tribe of Benjamin, twelve thousand *were* sealed.

9 After these things I looked, and behold, a great multitude, which no one could count, from [a]every nation and *all* tribes and peoples

r, *death* [c]Jer. 15:2f.; 24:10; zek. 5:12, 17; 14:21; 29:5

):12; Lev. 4:7; [b]Rev. 14:18; v. 20:4 [d]Rev. 9 [e]Rev. 12:17

Master [2]Lit., *not judge and e* [a]Zech. 1:12 :29; 2 Pet. 2:1 [d]Deut. 32:43; 10; Luke 18:7; 2 [e]Rev. 3:10

Rev. 3:4, 5; 7:9 ess. 1:7; Heb. . 14:13 [c]Heb.) [d]Acts 20:24; 2 Tim. 4:7

att. 24:7; Rev. :13; 16:18 [b]Is. Joel 2:10, 31; tt. 24:29; Mark [c]Is. 50:3; Matt. 11:21

tt. 24:29; Mark Rev. 8:10; 9:1 [b]Is. 34:4

Is. 34:4; 2 Pet. ev. 20:11; 21:1 4:10; Jer. 4:24; 8:20; Nah. 1:5; Rev. 16:20

., chiliarchs, in mmand of one and troops [a]Is. , 19, 21; 24:21; Rev. 19:18

Lit., *face* [a]Hos. ke 23:30; Rev. [b]Rev. 4:9; 5:1 [c]Mark 3:5

63:4; Jer. 30:7; 5; 2:1f., 11, 31; ph. 1:14f.; Rev. [b]Ps. 76:7; Nah. 3:2; Luke 21:36

[a]Rev. 9:14 [b]Is. Ezek. 7:2; Rev. Jer. 49:36; Dan. Zech. 6:5; Matt. ev. 7:3; 8:7; 9:4

41:2 [b]Rev. 7:3; att. 16:16 [d]Rev. 9:14

6:6 [b]John 3:33; 3-8 [c]Ezek. 9:4, . 13:16; 14:1, 9; 20:4; 22:4

Rev. 9:16 [b]Rev. 14:1, 3

9 [a]Rev. 5:9

and tongues, standing [b]before the throne and [c]before the Lamb,
clothed in [d]white robes, and [e]palm branches *were* in their hands;
10 and they cry out with a loud voice, saying,
"[a]Salvation to our God [b]who sits on the throne, and to the
Lamb."
11 And all the angels were standing [a]around the throne and *around*
[a]the elders and the [b]four living creatures; and they [c]fell on their faces
before the throne and worshiped God,
12 saying,
"[a]Amen, [b]blessing and glory and wisdom and thanksgiving and
honor and power and might, *be* to our God forever and ever.
[a]Amen."
13 And one of the elders [a]answered, saying to me, "These who are
clothed in the [b]white robes, who are they, and from where have they
come?"
14 And I [1]said to him, "My lord, you know." And he said to me,
"These are the ones who come out of the [a]great tribulation, and they
have [b]washed their robes and made them [c]white in the [d]blood of the
Lamb.
15 "For this reason, they are [a]before the throne of God; and they
[b]serve Him day and night in His [1c]temple; and [d]He who sits on the
throne shall spread His [e]tabernacle over them.
16 "[a]They shall hunger no more, neither thirst anymore; neither shall
the sun [1]beat down on them, nor any heat;
17 for the Lamb in the center of the throne shall be their [a]shepherd,
and shall guide them to springs of the [1b]water of life; and [c]God shall
wipe every tear from their eyes."

Chapter 8

8 And when He broke the [a]seventh seal, there was silence in heav-
en for about half an hour.
2 And I saw [a]the seven angels who stand before God; and seven
[b]trumpets were given to them.
3 And [a]another angel came and stood at the [b]altar, holding a [c]gold-
en censer; and much [d]incense was given to him, that he might [1]add it
to the [d]prayers of all the [2]saints upon the [e]golden altar which was
before the throne.
4 And [a]the smoke of the incense, [1]with the prayers of the [2]saints,
went up before God out of the angel's hand.
5 And the angel took the censer; and he [a]filled it with the fire of the
altar and [b]threw it to the earth; and there followed [c]peals of thunder
and sounds and flashes of lightning and an [d]earthquake.
6 [a]And the seven angels who had the seven trumpets prepared
themselves to sound them.
7 And the first sounded, and there came [a]hail and fire, mixed with
blood, and they were thrown to the earth; and [b]a third of the earth
was burned up, and [b]a third of the [c]trees were burned up, and all the
green [c]grass was burned up.
8 And the second angel sounded, and *something* like a great
[a]mountain burning with fire was thrown into the sea; and [b]a third of
the [c]sea became blood;
9 and [a]a third of the creatures, which were in the sea [1]and had life,
died; and a third of the [b]ships were destroyed.

9 [b]Rev. 7:1 22:3 [c]Rev. [e]Lev. 23:40
10 [a]Ps. 3:8 19:1 [b]Rev.
11 [a]Rev. 4: [c]Rev. 4:10
12 [a]Rev. 5: 5:12
13 [a]Acts 3:
14 [1]Lit., *hav* [a]Dan. 12:1; Mark 13:19 3:3-5; Rev. 6:11; 7:9 [d]H 1 John 1:7
15 [1]Or, *san* [a]Rev. 7:9 [b]R 22:3 [c]Rev. [d]Rev. 4:9 [e]L Ezek. 37:27; Rev. 21:3
16 [1]Lit., *fall* 121:5f.; Is. 4
17 [1]Lit., *wat* 23:1f.; Matt. 10:11 [b]John 21:6; 22:1 [c]Is Matt. 5:4; Re
8:1 [a]Rev. 5:1 7, 9, 12
2 [a]Rev. 1:4; 13; 11:15 [b]1 1 Thess. 4:16
3 [1]Lit., *give* *ones* [a]Rev. 7 9:1; Rev. 6:9 [d]Ex. 30:1; Rev 30:3; Num. 4: 8:5; 9:13
4 [1]Or, *for* [2]V. [a]Ps. 141:2
5 [a]Lev. 16:12 10:2 [c]Ex. 19: 4:5; 11:19; 16: 6:12
6 [a]Rev. 8:2
7 [a]Ex. 9:23ff.; Ezek. 38:22; J [b]Zech. 13:8, 9; 8:7-12; 9:15, 1 [c]Rev. 9:4
8 [a]Jer. 51:25 13:8, 9; Rev. 8: 9:15, 18; 12:4 7:17ff.; Rev. 11
9 [1]Lit., *those w* *had* [a]Zech. 13: Rev. 8:7-12; 9: 12:4 [b]Is. 2:16

10 And the third angel sounded, and a great star [a]fell from heaven, burning like a torch, and it fell on a [b]third of the rivers and on the [c]springs of waters;
11 and the name of the star is called Wormwood; and a [a]third of the waters became [b]wormwood; and many men died from the waters, because they were made bitter.
12 And the fourth angel sounded, and a [a]third of the [b]sun and a third of the [b]moon and a [a]third of the [b]stars were smitten, so that a [a]third of them might be darkened and the day might not shine for a [a]third of it, and the night in the same way.
13 And I looked, and I heard [1]an eagle flying in [a]midheaven, saying with a loud voice, "[b]Woe, woe, woe, to [c]those who dwell on the earth, because of the remaining blasts of the trumpet of the [d]three angels who are about to sound!"

Chapter 9

9 And the [a]fifth angel sounded, and I saw a [b]star from heaven which had fallen to the earth; and the [c]key of the [1d]bottomless pit was given to him.
2 And he opened the [1]bottomless pit; and [a]smoke went up out of the pit, like the smoke of a great furnace; and [b]the sun and the air were darkened by the smoke of the pit.
3 And out of the smoke came forth [a]locusts [1]upon the earth; and power was given them, as the [b]scorpions of the earth have power.
4 And they were told that they should not [a]hurt the [b]grass of the earth, nor any green thing, nor any tree, but only the men who do not have the [c]seal of God on their foreheads.
5 And [1]they were not permitted to kill [2]anyone, but to torment for [a]five months; and their torment was like the torment of a [b]scorpion when it [3]stings a man.
6 And in those days [a]men will seek death and will not find it; and they will long to die and death flees from them.
7 And the [1a]appearance of the locusts was like horses prepared for battle; and on their heads, as it were, crowns like gold, and their faces were like the faces of men.
8 And they had hair like the hair of women, and their [a]teeth were like *the teeth* of lions.
9 And they had breastplates like breastplates of iron; and the [a]sound of their wings was like the sound of chariots, of many horses rushing to battle.
10 And they have tails like [a]scorpions, and stings; and in their [b]tails is their power to hurt men for [c]five months.
11 They have as king over them, the angel of the [a]abyss; his name in [b]Hebrew is [1c]Abaddon, and in the Greek he has the name [2]Apollyon.
12 [a]The first woe is past; behold, two woes are still coming after these things.
13 And the sixth angel sounded, and I heard [1]a voice from the [2]four [a]horns of the [b]golden altar which is before God,
14 one saying to the sixth angel who had the trumpet, "Release the [a]four angels who are bound at the [b]great river Euphrates."
15 And the four angels, who had been prepared for the hour and day and month and year, were [a]released, so that they might kill a [b]third of [1]mankind.

4:12; Rev. Zech. 13:8, ; 9:15, 18; 14:7; 16:4
8:8, 9; Rev. 5, 18; 12:4 9:15; 23:15
8:8, 9; Rev. 5, 18; 12:4 ; Is. 13:10; ; Joel 2:10, Rev. 6:12f.
. *one eagle* 9:17 [b]Rev. 2:12 [c]Rev.) [d]Rev. 8:2
shaft of the v. 8:2 [b]Rev. 1:18 [d]Luke Rev. 9:2, 11
ote 1 [a]Gen. 19:18 [b]Joel 2:2, 10
it., *into* [a]Ex. 15; Rev. 9:7 1, 14; Ezek. Rev. 9:5, 10
:6 [b]Rev. 8:7 ; Rev. 7:2, 3
was given to ., *them* [3]Lit., s [a]Rev. 9:10 1, 14; Ezek. Rev. 9:3, 10
21; 7:15; Jer. :3; Rev. 6:16
appearances [a]Joel 2:4
8 [a]Joel 1:6
47:3; Joel 2:5
hr. 10:11, 14; 6; Rev. 9:3, 5 :19 [b]Rev. 9:5
e., destruction stroyer [a]Luke . 9:1, 2 [b]John v. 16:16 [c]Job 22; 31:12; Ps. g.; Prov. 15:11
ev. 8:13; 11:14
Lit., *one voice* ncient mss. do ntain *four* [a]Ex. , 10 [b]Rev. 8:3
Rev. 7:1 [b]Gen. eut. 1:7; Josh. :4; Rev. 16:12
Lit., *men* [a]Rev. [b]Rev. 8:7; 9:18

16 And the number of the armies of the horsemen was [a]two
hundred million; [b]I heard the number of them.
17 And [1]this is how I saw [a]in the vision the horses and those who
sat on them: *the riders* had breastplates *the color* of fire and of
hyacinth and of [2b]brimstone; and the heads of the horses are like the
heads of lions; and [c]out of their mouths proceed fire and smoke and
[2b]brimstone.
18 A [a]third of [1]mankind was killed by these three plagues, by the
[b]fire and the smoke and the [2]brimstone, which proceeded out of their
mouths.
19 For the power of the horses is in their mouths and in their tails;
for their tails are like serpents and have heads; and with them they
do harm.
20 And the rest of [1]mankind, who were not killed by these plagues,
[a]did not repent of [b]the works of their hands, so as not to [c]worship
demons, and [d]the idols of gold and of silver and of brass and of
stone and of wood, which can neither see nor hear nor walk;
21 and they [a]did not repent of their murders nor of their [b]sorceries
nor of their [c]immorality nor of their thefts.

Chapter 10

10 And I saw another [a]strong angel [b]coming down out of heav-
en, clothed with a cloud; and the [c]rainbow was upon his
head, and [d]his face was like the sun, and his [e]feet like pillars of fire;
2 and he had in his hand a [a]little book which was open. And he
placed [b]his right foot on the sea and his left on the land;
3 and he cried out with a loud voice, [a]as when a lion roars; and
when he had cried out, the [b]seven peals of thunder [1]uttered their
voices.
4 And when the seven peals of thunder had spoken, [a]I was about
to write; and I [b]heard a voice from heaven saying, "[c]Seal up the
things which the seven peals of thunder have spoken, and do not
write them."
5 And the angel whom I saw standing on the sea and on the land
[a]lifted up his right hand to heaven,
6 [a]and swore by [b]Him who lives forever and ever, [c]WHO CREATED
HEAVEN AND THE THINGS IN IT, AND THE EARTH AND THE THINGS IN IT, AND
THE SEA AND THE THINGS IN IT, that [d]there shall be delay no longer,
7 but in the days of the voice of the [a]seventh angel, when he is
about to sound, then [b]the mystery of God is finished, as He
[1]preached to His servants the prophets.
8 And [a]the voice which I heard from heaven, *I heard* again speak-
ing with me, and saying, "Go, take [b]the [1]book which is open in the
hand of the angel who [b]stands on the sea and on the land."
9 And I went to the angel, telling him to give me the little book.
And he *said to me, "[a]Take it, and eat it; and it will make your
stomach bitter, but in your mouth it will be sweet as honey."
10 And I took the little book out of the angel's hand and ate it, and
it was in my mouth sweet as honey; and when I had eaten it, my
stomach was made bitter.
11 And [a]they *said to me, "You must [b]prophesy again concerning
[c]many peoples and nations and tongues and [d]kings."

16 [a]Rev. 5:1

17 [1]Lit., *thus*
sulphur [a]Da
[b]Rev. 9:18; 1
19:20; 20:10
[c]Rev. 11:5

18 [1]Lit., *men*
sulphur [a]Re
[b]Rev. 9:17

20 [1]Lit., *men*
2:21 [b]Deut.
1:16; Mic. 5:1
7:41 [c]1 Cor.
115:4-7; 135:
Dan. 5:23

21 [a]Rev. 9:2
12; Rev. 18:2
17:2, 4, 5

10:1 [a]Rev. 5
18:1; 20:1 [c]R
[d]Matt. 17:2; R
[e]Rev. 1:15

2 [a]Rev. 5:1;
[b]Rev. 10:5, 8

3 [1]Or, *spoke*
Hos. 11:10 [b]R
Rev. 4:5

4 [a]Rev. 1:11,
10:8 [c]Dan. 8:2
9; Rev. 22:10

5 [a]Deut. 32:40
12:7

6 [a]Gen. 14:22
Num. 14:30; E
[b]Rev. 4:9 [c]Ex.
Rev. 4:11 [d]Rev
12:12; 16:17; 2

7 [1]Lit., *preach*
gospel [a]Rev.
[b]Amos 3:7; Ro

8 [1]Or, *scroll* [a]R
[b]Rev. 10:2

9 [a]Jer. 15:16;
3:1-3

11 [a]Rev. 11:1
37:4, 9 [c]Rev. 5
17:10, 12

Chapter 11

11 And there was given me a [1a]measuring rod like a staff; [2]and
[b]someone said, "Rise and measure the [3]temple of God, and
the altar, and those who worship in it.
2 "And [1]leave out the [a]court which is outside the [2]temple, and do
not measure it, for [b]it has been given to the nations; and they will
[b]tread under foot [c]the holy city for [d]forty-two months.
3 "And I will grant *authority* to my two [a]witnesses, and they will
prophesy for [b]twelve hundred and sixty days, clothed in [c]sackcloth."
4 These are the [a]two olive trees and the two lampstands that stand
before the Lord of the earth.
5 And if anyone desires to harm them, [a]fire proceeds out of their
mouth and devours their enemies; and if anyone would desire to
harm them, [b]in this manner he must be killed.
6 These have the power to [a]shut up the sky, in order that rain may
not fall during [b]the days of their prophesying; and they have power
over the waters to [c]turn them into blood, and [d]to smite the earth with
every plague, as often as they desire.
7 And when they have finished their testimony, [a]the beast that
comes up out of the [b]abyss will [c]make war with them, and overcome
them and kill them.
8 And their dead [1]bodies *will lie* in the street of the [a]great city
which [2]mystically is called [b]Sodom and [c]Egypt, where also their Lord
was crucified.
9 And those from [a]the peoples and tribes and tongues and nations
will look at their dead [1]bodies for three and a half days, and [2b]will
not permit their dead bodies to be laid in a tomb.
10 And [a]those who dwell on the earth *will* rejoice over them and
make merry; and they will [b]send gifts to one another, because these
two prophets tormented [a]those who dwell on the earth.
11 And after the three and a half days [a]the breath of life from God
came into them, and they stood on their feet; and great fear fell upon
those who were beholding them.
12 And they heard a loud voice from heaven saying to them,
"[a]Come up here." And they [b]went up into heaven in the cloud, and
their enemies beheld them.
13 And in that hour there was a great [a]earthquake, and a tenth of
the city fell; and [1]seven thousand people were killed in the
earthquake, and the rest were terrified and [b]gave glory to the [c]God of
heaven.
14 The second [a]woe is past; behold, the third woe is coming quickly.
15 And the [a]seventh angel sounded; and there arose [b]loud voices in
heaven, saying,
"[c]The kingdom of the world has become *the kingdom* of our Lord,
and of [d]His [1]Christ; and [e]He will reign forever and ever."
16 And the twenty-four elders, who [a]sit on their thrones before
God, [b]fell on their faces and worshiped God,
17 saying,
"We give Thee thanks, [a]O Lord God, the Almighty, who art and
who wast, because Thou hast taken Thy great power and [1]hast
begun to [b]reign.
18 "And [a]the nations were enraged, and [b]Thy wrath came, and [c]the
time *came* for the dead to be judged, and *the time* to give their reward
to Thy [d]bond-servants the prophets and to the [1]saints and to those

who fear Thy name, [e]the small and the great, and to destroy those
who destroy the earth."
19 And [a]the [1]temple of God which is in heaven was opened; and
[b]the ark of His covenant appeared in His [1]temple, and there were
flashes of [c]lightning and sounds and peals of thunder and an
earthquake and a [d]great [2]hailstorm.

Chapter 12

12 And a great [a]sign appeared [b]in heaven: [c]a woman [d]clothed
with the sun, and the moon under her feet, and on her head a
crown of twelve stars;
2 and she was with child; and she *[a]cried out, being in labor and in
pain to give birth.
3 And [a]another sign appeared in heaven: and behold, a great red
[b]dragon having [c]seven heads and [d]ten horns, and on his heads *were*
[e]seven diadems.
4 And his tail *swept away a [a]third of the stars of heaven, and
[b]threw them to the earth. And the [c]dragon stood before the woman
who was about to give birth, so that when she gave birth [d]he might
devour her child.
5 And [a]she gave birth to a son, a male *child*, who is to [1b]rule all the
[2]nations with a rod of iron; and her child was [c]caught up to God and
to His throne.
6 And the woman fled into the wilderness where she *had a place
prepared by God, so that there [1]she might be nourished for [a]one
thousand two hundred and sixty days.
7 And there was war in heaven, [a]Michael and his angels waging
war with the [b]dragon. And the dragon and [c]his angels waged war,
8 and they were not strong enough, and there was no longer a
place found for them in heaven.
9 And the great [a]dragon was thrown down, the [b]serpent of old
who is called the devil and [c]Satan, who [d]deceives the whole [1]world;
he was [e]thrown down to the earth, and his angels were thrown
down with him.
10 And I heard [a]a loud voice in heaven, saying,
"Now the [b]salvation, and the power, and the [a]kingdom of our God
and the authority of His Christ have come, for the [c]accuser of our
brethren has been thrown down, who accuses them before our God
day and night.
11 "And they [a]overcame him because of [b]the blood of the Lamb and
because of [c]the word of their testimony, and they [d]did not love their
life even to death.
12 "For this reason, [a]rejoice, O heavens and [b]you who [1]dwell in them.
[c]Woe to the earth and the sea, because [d]the devil has come down to
you, having great wrath, knowing that he has *only* [e]a short time."
13 And when the [a]dragon saw that he was thrown down to the
earth, he persecuted [b]the woman who gave birth to the male *child*.
14 And the [a]two wings of the great eagle were given to the woman,
in order that she might fly [b]into the wilderness to her place, where
she *was nourished for [c]a time and times and half a time, from the
[1]presence of the serpent.
15 And the [a]serpent [1]poured water like a river out of his mouth
after the woman, so that he might cause her to be swept away with
the flood.

18 [e]Ps. 11 13:16; 19:5

19 [1]Or, *sa* *hail* [a]Rev. [b]Heb. 9:4 8:5; 16:18

12:1 [a]Matt 12:3 [b]Rev. 4:26 [d]Ps. 1 6:10

2 [a]Is. 26:17 Mic. 4:9f.

3 [a]Rev. 12. 27:1; Rev. 1 16f.; 13:2, 4 20:2 [c]Rev. 7, 9ff. [d]Dan Rev. 13:1; 1 [e]Rev. 13:1;

4 [a]Rev. 8:7 8:10 [c]Is. 27 12:3, 7, 9, 1 4, 11; 16:13 2:16

5 [1]Or, *shep* *Gentiles* [a]Is 2:9; Rev. 2:2 12:2ff.

6 [1]Lit., *they nourish her* 11:3; 13:5

7 [a]Dan. 10:1 Jude 9 [b]Rev [c]Matt. 25:41

9 [1]Lit., *inhab* [a]Rev. 12:3 [b] 2 Cor. 11:3; F 20:2 [c]Matt. 4 [d]Rev. 13:14; [e]Luke 10:18;

10 [a]Rev. 11:1 7:10 [c]Job 1:1 Zech. 3:1; Lu 1 Pet. 5:8

11 [a]John 16:3 2:13; Rev. 15 7:14 [c]Rev. 6:9 14:26; Rev. 2.

12 [1]Or, *tabern* 96:11; Is. 44:2 18:20 [b]Rev. 1 8:13 [d]Rev. 12 10:6

13 [a]Rev. 12:3 12:5

14 [1]Lit., *face* Deut. 32:11; Is [b]Rev. 12:6 [c]Da 12:7

15 [1]Lit., *threw* 3:1; 2 Cor. 11:3 12:9; 20:2

16 And the earth helped the woman, and the earth opened its
mouth and drank up the river which the dragon [1]poured out of his
mouth.
17 And the dragon was enraged with the woman, and went off to
[a]make war with the rest of her [b]offspring, who [c]keep the command-
ments of God and [d]hold to the testimony of Jesus.

Chapter 13

13 And [1]he stood on the sand of the [2]seashore.
And I saw a [a]beast coming up out of the sea, having [b]ten
horns and [b]seven heads, and on his horns *were* [c]ten diadems, and on
his heads *were* [d]blasphemous names.
2 And the beast which I saw was [a]like a leopard, and his feet were
like *those* of [b]a bear, and his mouth like the mouth of [c]a lion. And the
[d]dragon gave him his power and his [e]throne and great authority.
3 And *I saw* one of his heads as if it had been [1]slain, and his [a]fatal
wound was healed. And the whole earth [b]was amazed *and followed*
after the beast;
4 and they worshiped the [a]dragon, because he [a]gave his authority
to the beast; and they worshiped the beast, saying, "[b]Who is like the
beast, and who is able to wage war with him?"
5 And there was given to him a mouth [a]speaking [1]arrogant words
and blasphemies; and authority to [2]act for [b]forty-two months was
given to him.
6 And he opened his mouth in blasphemies against God, to blas-
pheme His name and His tabernacle, *that is,* [a]those who [1]dwell in
heaven.
7 And it was given to him to [a]make war with the [1]saints and to
overcome them; and authority over [b]every tribe and people and
tongue and nation was given to him.
8 And all who [a]dwell on the earth will worship him, *everyone*
[b]whose name has not been [1]written [c]from the foundation of the
world in the [d]book of life of [e]the Lamb who has been slain.
9 [a]If anyone has an ear, let him hear.
10 [a]If anyone [1]*is destined* for captivity, to captivity he goes; [b]if
anyone kills with the sword, with the sword he must be killed. Here
is [c]the [2]perseverance and the faith of the [3]saints.
11 And [a]I saw another beast coming up out of the earth; and he
[1]had [b]two horns like a lamb, and he [2]spoke as a [c]dragon.
12 And he [a]exercises all the authority of the first beast [1b]in his pres-
ence. And he makes [c]the earth and those who dwell in it to [d]worship
the first beast, whose [e]fatal wound was healed.
13 And he [a]performs great signs, so that he even makes [b]fire come
down out of heaven to the earth in the presence of men.
14 And he [a]deceives [b]those who dwell on the earth because of
[c]the signs which it was given him to perform [1d]in the presence of the
beast, telling those who dwell on the earth to make an image to
the beast who *had the [e]wound of the sword and has come to life.
15 And there was given to him to give breath to the image of the
beast, that the image of the beast might even [1]speak and cause [a]as
many as do not [b]worship the image of the beast to be killed.
16 And he causes all, [a]the small and the great, and the rich and the
poor, and the free men and the slaves, [1]to be given a [b]mark on their
right hand, or on their forehead,

6 [1]Lit., *threw*
ev. 11:7; 13:7
[c]1 John 2:3;
12 [d]Rev. 1:2;
14:12; 19:10

e mss. read *I*
t., *sea* [a]Dan.
. 11:7; 13:14,
; 16:13; 17:8
3 [c]Rev. 12:3;
n. 7:8; 11:36;
Rev. 17:3

an. 7:6; Hos.
an. 7:5 [c]Dan.
v. 12:3; 13:4,
. 2:13; 16:10

itten to death
12, 14 [b]Rev.
17:8

12:3; 13:2, 12
Is. 46:5; Rev.
18:18

, *great things*
[a]Dan. 7:8, 11,
:36; 2 Thess.
3f. [b]Rev. 11:2

ernacle [a]Rev.
7:15; 12:12

y ones [a]Dan.
v. 11:7 [b]Rev.
5:9

written in the
slain from the
n of the world
:10; 13:12, 14
[c]Matt. 25:34;
:8 [d]Ps. 69:28
[e]Rev. 5:6

9 [a]Rev. 2:7

Or, *leads into*
captivity [2]Or,
ess [3]Or, *holy*
[a]Is. 33:1; Jer.
11 [b]Gen. 9:6;
52; Rev. 11:18
2; Rev. 14:12

t., *was having*
was speaking
; 16:13 [b]Dan.
:3 [c]Rev. 13:4

y his authority
[b]Rev. 13:14;
ev. 13:8 [d]Rev.
14:9, 11; 16:2;
:4 [e]Rev. 13:3

tt. 24:24; Rev.
19:20 [b]1 Kin.
uke 9:54; Rev.
11:5; 20:9

y the authority
ev. 12:9 [b]Rev.
2 Thess. 2:9f.
. 13:12; 19:20
[e]Rev. 13:3

e ancient mss.
ak, and he will
se [a]Dan. 3:3ff.
3:12; 14:9, 11;
2; 19:20; 20:4

that they give
a mark [a]Rev.
19:5, 18 [b]Gal.
7:3; 14:9; 20:4

17 and *he provides* that no one should be able to buy or to sell, except the one who has the [a]mark, *either* [b]the name of the beast or [c]the number of his name.

18 [a]Here is wisdom. Let him who has understanding calculate the number of the beast, for the number is that [b]of a man; and his number is [1]six hundred and sixty-six.

Chapter 14

14 And I looked, and behold, [a]the Lamb *was* standing on [b]Mount Zion, and with Him [c]one hundred and forty-four thousand, having [d]His name and the [d]name of His Father written [e]on their foreheads.

2 And I heard a voice from heaven, like [a]the sound of many waters and like the [b]sound of loud thunder, and the voice which I heard *was* like *the sound* of [c]harpists playing on their harps.

3 And they [1]*sang [a]a new song before the throne and before the [b]four living creatures and the [c]elders; and [d]no one could learn the song except the [e]one hundred and forty-four thousand who had been [a]purchased from the earth.

4 [a]These are the ones who have not been defiled with women, for they [1]have kept themselves chaste. These *are* the ones who [b]follow the Lamb wherever He goes. These have been [c]purchased from among men [d]as first fruits to God and to the Lamb.

5 And [a]no lie was found in their mouth; they are [b]blameless.

6 And I saw another angel flying in [a]midheaven, having [b]an eternal gospel to preach to [c]those who [1]live on the earth, and to [d]every nation and tribe and tongue and people;

7 and he said with a loud voice, "[a]Fear God, and [b]give Him glory, because the hour of His judgment has come; and worship Him who [c]made the heaven and the earth and sea and [d]springs of waters."

8 And another angel, a second one, followed, saying, "[a]Fallen, fallen is [b]Babylon the great, she who has [c]made all the nations drink of the [d]wine of the [1]passion of her immorality."

9 And another angel, a third one, followed them, saying with a loud voice, "If anyone [a]worships the beast and his [b]image, and receives a [c]mark on his forehead or upon his hand,

10 he also will drink of the [a]wine of the wrath of God, which is mixed [1]in full strength [b]in the cup of His anger; and he will be tormented with [c]fire and brimstone in the presence of the [d]holy angels and in the presence of the Lamb.

11 "And the [a]smoke of their torment goes up forever and ever; and [b]they have no rest day and night, those who [c]worship the beast and his [c]image, and whoever receives the [d]mark of his name."

12 Here is [a]the [1]perseverance of the [2]saints who [b]keep the commandments of God and [3c]their faith in Jesus.

13 And I heard a voice from heaven, saying, "Write, '[a]Blessed are the dead who [b]die in the Lord from now on!' " "Yes," [c]says the Spirit, "that they may [d]rest from their labors, for their [e]deeds follow with them."

14 And I looked, and behold, a [a]white cloud, and sitting on the cloud *was* one [b]like [1]a son of man, having a golden [c]crown on His head, and a sharp sickle in His hand.

17 [a]Gal. 6: 14:9; 20:4 [c]Rev. 15:2

18 [1]Some 616 [a]Rev. 21:17

14:1 [a]Rev. 2:6; Heb. 12 7:4; 14:3 [d] [e]Ezek. 9:4;

2 [a]Rev. 1:1 [c]Rev. 5:8

3 [1]Some an read *sing, a new song* [a] [b]Rev. 4:6 [c] [d]Rev. 2:17 14:1

4 [1]Lit., *are* [a]Matt. 19:12 11:2; Eph. 5: 3:4 [b]Rev. 3: 17:14 [c]Rev. 12:23; Jame

5 [a]Ps. 32:2; Mal. 2:6; Joh 1 Pet. 2:22 1 Pet. 1:19;

6 [1]Lit., *sit* [a] [b]1 Pet. 1:25; [c]Rev. 3:10

7 [a]Rev. 15:4 11:13 [c]Rev. 8:10

8 [1]Or, *wrath* Jer. 51:8; Rev [b]Dan. 4:30; R 17:5; 18:10 [d]Rev. 17:2, 4;

9 [a]Rev. 13:12 [b]Rev. 13:14f.; [c]Rev. 13:16

10 [1]Lit., *unmi* 51:17; Jer. 25 Rev. 16:19; 19 75:8; Rev. 18 19:24; Ezek. 3 2 Thess. 1:7; 19:20; 20:10, [d]Mark 8:38

11 [a]Is. 34:8-10 18:9, 18; 19:3 4:8 [c]Rev. 13:1 [d]Rev. 13:17

12 [1]Or, *steadf* [2]Or, *holy ones* *faith of* [a]Rev. [b]Rev. 12:17 [c]

13 [a]Rev. 20:6 15:18; 1 Thess [c]Rev. 2:7; 22:1 4:9ff.; Rev. 6:1 5:25

14 [1]Or, *the So* [a]Matt. 17:5 [b]D Rev. 1:13 [c]Ps. Rev. 6:2

tuary [2]Lit., [3]Lit., *has* dry [a]Rev. 4:17; 15:6; 3:13; Mark 4:18 [c]Jer. . 13:39-41

15 And another angel [a]came out of the [1]temple, crying out with a
loud voice to Him who sat on the cloud, "[2b]Put in your sickle and
reap, because the hour to reap has come, because the [c]harvest of the
earth [3]is ripe."

[1]Lit., *cast*

16 And He who sat on the cloud [1]swung His sickle over the earth;
and the earth was reaped.

tuary [2]Lit., *imself also* 4:15; 15:6; 16:17

17 And another angel [a]came out of the [1]temple which is in heaven,
[2]and he also had a sharp sickle.

Send forth [a]Rev. 16:8 ; 8:3 [c]Joel . 4:29; Rev. [d]Joel 3:13

18 And another angel, [a]the one who has power over fire, came out
from [b]the altar; and he called with a loud voice to him who had the
sharp sickle, saying, "[1c]Put in your sharp sickle, and gather the
clusters [2]from the vine of the earth, [d]because her grapes are ripe."

[a]Is. 63:2f.; Rev. 19:15

19 And the angel [1]swung his sickle to the earth, and gathered *the
clusters from* the vine of the earth, and threw them into [a]the great
wine press of the wrath of God.

t., *from two miles* [2]Lit., *dred stadia;* was approx. 63:3; Lam. 9:15 [b]Heb. 11:8 [c]Gen. Deut. 32:14

20 And [a]the wine press was trodden [b]outside the city, and [c]blood
came out from the wine press, up to the horses' bridles, [1]for a dis-
tance of [2]two hundred miles.

Chapter 15

Rev. 12:1, 3 ; 16:1; 17:1; 26:21 [d]Rev. 9:20

15 And I saw [a]another sign in heaven, great and marvelous,
[b]seven angels who had [c]seven plagues, *which are* [d]the last,
because in them the wrath of God is finished.

v. 4:6 [b]Rev. . 13:1 [d]Rev. [e]Rev. 13:17 [f]Rev. 5:8

2 And I saw, as it were, a [a]sea of glass mixed with fire, and those
who had [b]come off victorious from the [c]beast and from [d]his image
and from the [e]number of his name, standing on the [a]sea of glass,
holding [f]harps of God.

ancient mss. [a]Ex. 15:1ff. 2:5; Heb. 3:5 , 12f. [d]Deut. f.; Ps. 111:2; s. 14:9; Rev. [f]1 Tim. 1:17

3 And they *sang the [a]song of Moses [b]the bond-servant of God and
the [c]song of the Lamb, saying,

"[d]Great and marvelous are Thy works,
[e]O Lord God, the Almighty;
Righteous and true are Thy ways,
Thou [f]King of the [1]nations.

ments [a]Jer. ev. 14:7 [b]Ps. 66:23 [c]Rev. 19:8

4 "[a]Who will not fear, O Lord, and glorify Thy name?
For Thou alone art holy;
For [b]ALL THE NATIONS WILL COME AND WORSHIP BEFORE THEE,
For Thy [1c]righteous acts have been revealed."

ctuary [a]Rev. 38:21; Num. :5; Rev. 13:6

5 After these things I looked, and [a]the [1]temple of the [b]tabernacle of
testimony in heaven was opened,

Or, *sanctuary* s. read *stone* [b]Rev. 14:15 [c]Rev. 1:13

6 and the [a]seven angels who had the seven plagues [b]came out of
the [1]temple, clothed in [2]linen, clean *and* bright, and [c]girded around
their breasts with golden girdles.

6 [b]Rev. 15:1 [d]Rev. 14:10; 5:1 [e]Rev. 4:9

7 And one of the [a]four living creatures gave to the [b]seven angels
seven [c]golden bowls full of the [d]wrath of God, who [e]lives forever and
ever.

anctuary [a]Ex. ; 40:34f.; Lev. ; 1 Kin. 8:10f.; 5:13f.; Is. 6:4

8 And the [1]temple was filled with [a]smoke from the glory of God
and from His power; and no one was able to enter the [1]temple until
the seven plagues of the seven angels were finished.

Chapter 16

[1]Or, *sanctuary* 19 [b]Rev. 15:1 :6; Jer. 10:25; 31; Zeph. 3:8; Rev. 16:2ff.

16 And I heard a loud voice from [a]the [1]temple, saying to the
[b]seven angels, "Go and [c]pour out the seven bowls of the
wrath of God into the earth."

2 [a]Rev. 8:7

2 And the first *angel* went and poured out his bowl [a]into the earth;

and it became a loathsome and malignant [b]sore upon the men [c]who
had the mark of the beast and who worshiped his image.
3 And the second *angel* poured out his bowl [a]into the sea, and it
became blood like *that* of a dead man; and every living [1]thing in the
sea died.
4 And the third *angel* poured out his bowl into the [a]rivers and the
springs of waters; and [1]they [b]became blood.
5 And I heard the angel of the waters saying, "[a]Righteous art
Thou, [b]who art and who wast, O [c]Holy One, because Thou didst
[d]judge these things;
6 for they poured out [a]the blood of saints and prophets, and Thou
hast given them [b]blood to drink. They [1]deserve it."
7 And I heard [a]the altar saying, "Yes, O [b]Lord God, the Almighty,
[c]true and righteous are Thy judgments."
8 And the fourth *angel* poured out his bowl upon [a]the sun; [b]and it
was given to it to scorch men with fire.
9 And men were scorched with [1]fierce heat; and they [a]blasphemed
the name of God who has the power over these plagues; and they
[b]did not repent, so as to [c]give Him glory.
10 And the fifth *angel* poured out his bowl upon the [a]throne of the
beast; and his kingdom became [b]darkened; and they gnawed their
tongues because of pain,
11 and they [a]blasphemed the [b]God of heaven because of their pains
and their [c]sores; and they [d]did not repent of their deeds.
12 And the sixth *angel* poured out his bowl upon the [a]great river,
the Euphrates; and [b]its water was dried up, that [c]the way might be
prepared for the kings [d]from the [1]east.
13 And I saw *coming* out of the mouth of the [a]dragon and out of the
mouth of the [b]beast and out of the mouth of the [c]false prophet, three
[d]unclean spirits like [e]frogs;
14 for they are [a]spirits of demons, [b]performing signs, which go out
to the kings of the [c]whole [1]world, to [d]gather them together for the
war of the [e]great day of God, the Almighty.
15 ("Behold, [a]I am coming like a thief. [b]Blessed is the one who stays
awake and keeps his garments, [c]lest he walk about naked and [1]men
see his shame.")
16 And they [a]gathered them together to the place which [b]in Hebrew
is called [1]Har[c]Magedon.
17 And the seventh *angel* poured out his bowl upon [a]the air; and a
[b]loud voice came out of the [1c]temple from the throne, saying, "[d]It is
done."
18 And there were flashes of [a]lightning and sounds and peals of
thunder; and there was [b]a great earthquake, [c]such as there had not
been since man came to be upon the earth, so great an earthquake
was it, and so mighty.
19 And [a]the great city was split into three parts, and the cities of the
[1]nations fell. And [b]Babylon the great was [c]remembered before God,
to give her [d]the cup of the wine of His fierce wrath.
20 And [a]every island fled away, and the mountains were not found.
21 And [a]huge [1]hailstones, about [2]one hundred pounds each, *came
down from heaven upon men; and men [b]blasphemed God because
of the [c]plague of the hail, because its plague *was extremely [3]severe.

2 [b]Ex. 9:9 28:35; Rev 13:15-17; 1
3 [1]Lit., *sou* ancient ms *the things* [a]Ex. 7:17-2 11:6
4 [1]Some a read *it beca* 8:10 [b]Ex. 7 78:44; Rev.
5 [a]John 17 11:17 [c]Rev 6:10
6 [1]Lit., *are* [a]Rev. 17:6; 49:26; Luke
7 [a]Rev. 6:9 [b]Rev. 1:8 [c] 19:2
8 [a]Rev. 6:12 14:18
9 [1]Lit., *grea* 16:11, 21 [b]F [c]Rev. 11:13
10 [a]Rev. 13 10:21f.; Is. 8 8:12; 9:2
11 [a]Rev. 16. 11:13 [c]Rev. 2:21
12 [1]Lit., *risir sun* [a]Rev. 9: 11:15f.; 44:27 51:36 [c]Is. 41 46:11 [d]Rev.
13 [a]Rev. 12: 13:1 [c]Rev. 1: 19:20; 20:10 18:2 [e]Ex. 8:6
14 [1]Lit., *inha* [a]1 Tim. 4:1 [b] [c]Rev. 3:10 [d]1 22:21-23; Re 19:19; 20:8 [e]
15 [1]Lit., *they* 24:43f.; Luke Rev. 3:3, 11 [c] 12:37 [c]Rev. 3
16 [1]Some au read *Armaged* [a]Rev. 19:19 [b] [c]Judg. 5:19; 2 23:29f.; 2 Chr. Zech. 12:11
17 [1]Or, *sancti* [a]Eph. 2:2 [b]Re [c]Rev. 14:15 [d]F 21:6
18 [a]Rev. 4:5 6:12 [c]Dan. 12: 24:21
19 [1]Or, *Gentil* 11:8; 17:18; 18 21 [b]Rev. 14:8 18:5 [d]Rev. 14:
20 [a]Rev. 6:14;
21 [1]Lit., *hail* [2] *weight of a tale great* [a]Rev. 8:7 [b]Rev. 16:9, 11 9:18-25

Chapter 17

17 [a]And one of the [b]seven angels who had the [c]seven bowls came
and spoke with me, saying, "Come here, I shall show you [d]the
judgment of the [e]great harlot who [f]sits on many waters,
2 with whom [a]the kings of the earth committed *acts of* immorality,
and [b]those who dwell on the earth were [c]made drunk with the wine
of her immorality."
3 And [a]he carried me away [1b]in the Spirit [c]into a wilderness; and I
saw a woman sitting on a [d]scarlet beast, full of [e]blasphemous names,
having [f]seven heads and ten horns.
4 And the woman [a]was clothed in purple and scarlet, and
[1]adorned with gold and precious [2]stones and pearls, having in her
hand [b]a gold cup full of abominations and of the unclean things of
her immorality,
5 and upon her forehead a name *was* written, a [a]mystery,
"[b]BABYLON THE GREAT, THE MOTHER OF HARLOTS AND OF
[c]THE ABOMINATIONS OF THE EARTH."
6 And I saw the woman drunk with [a]the blood of the [1]saints, and
with the blood of the witnesses of Jesus. And when I saw her, I
wondered [2]greatly.
7 And the angel said to me, "Why [1]do you wonder? I shall tell you
the [a]mystery of the woman and of the beast that carries her, which
has the [b]seven heads and the ten horns.
8 "[a]The beast that you saw [b]was and is not, and is about to [c]come up
out of the [d]abyss and [1]to [e]go to destruction. And [f]those who dwell on
the earth will [g]wonder, [h]whose name has not been written in the
book of life [i]from the foundation of the world, when they see the
beast, that he was and is not and will come.
9 "[a]Here is the mind which has wisdom. The [b]seven heads are seven
mountains on which the woman sits,
10 and they are seven [a]kings; five have fallen, one is, the other has
not yet come; and when he comes, he must remain a little while.
11 "And the beast which [a]was and is not, is himself also an eighth,
and is *one* of the seven, and he [b]goes to destruction.
12 "And the [a]ten horns which you saw are ten kings, who have not
yet received a kingdom, but they receive authority as kings with the
beast [b]for one hour.
13 "These have [a]one [1]purpose and they give their power and
authority to the beast.
14 "These will wage [a]war against the Lamb, and the Lamb will [b]over-
come them, because He is [c]Lord of lords and [c]King of kings, and
[d]those who are with Him *are the* [e]called and chosen and faithful."
15 And he *said to me, "The [a]waters which you saw where the
harlot sits, are [b]peoples and multitudes and nations and tongues.
16 "And the [a]ten horns which you saw, and the beast, these will hate
the harlot and will make her [b]desolate and [c]naked, and will [d]eat her
flesh and will [e]burn her up with fire.
17 "For [a]God has put it in their hearts to execute His [1]purpose [2]by
[b]having a common purpose, and by giving their kingdom to the
beast, until the [c]words of God should be fulfilled.
18 "And the woman whom you saw is [a]the great city, which [1]reigns
over the kings of the earth."

v. 1:1; 21:9 [c]Rev. 15:7
9 [e]Is. 1:21;
h. 3:4; Rev.
; 19:2 [f]Jer.
Rev. 17:15

:22; 18:3, 9
17:8 [c]Rev.
14:8

spirit [a]Rev.
1:10 [c]Rev.
1:10 [d]Matt.
v. 18:12, 16
[f]Rev. 12:3;
:7, 9, 12, 16

gilded [2]Lit.,
Ezek. 28:13;
12, 16 [b]Jer.
7; Rev. 18:6

ss. 2:7; Rev.
[b]Rev. 14:8;
) [c]Rev. 17:2

y ones [2]Lit.,
onder [a]Rev.
16:6

it., *have you*
ed [a]2 Thess.
v. 1:20; 17:5
[b]Rev. 17:3

ancient mss.
es [a]Dan. 7:7
13:3, 12, 14;
ev. 11:7; 13:1
; 13:1 [e]Rev.
1 [f]Rev. 3:10
3 [h]Ps. 69:28;
[i]Matt. 25:34;
Rev. 13:8

13:18 [b]Rev.
17:3

) [a]Rev. 10:11

13:3, 12, 14;
v. 13:10; 17:8

an. 7:24; Rev.
; 17:16 [b]Rev.
18:10, 17, 19

r, mind [a]Rev.
17:17

/. 16:14 [b]Rev.
im. 6:15; Rev.
6 [d]Rev. 2:10f.
[e]Matt. 22:14

8:7; Jer. 47:2;
7:1 [b]Rev. 5:9

v. 17:12 [b]Rev.
[c]Ezek. 16:37,
v. 19:18 [e]Rev.
18:8

ind [2]Lit., *even*
ne mind and to
Cor. 8:16 [b]Rev.
:13 [c]Rev. 10:7

has a kingdom
Rev. 11:8; 16:19

Chapter 18

18 After these things I saw another [a]angel [b]coming down from
heaven, having great authority, and the earth was [c]illumined
with his glory.
2 And he cried out with a mighty voice, saying, "[a]Fallen, fallen is
Babylon the great! And she [b]has become a dwelling place of demons
and a [1]prison of every [c]unclean spirit, and a [1]prison of every unclean
and hateful bird.
3 "For all the nations [1]have drunk of the [a]wine of the [2]passion of her
immorality, and [b]the kings of the earth have committed *acts of* im-
morality with her, and the [c]merchants of the earth have become rich
by the [3]wealth of her [4d]sensuality."
4 And I heard another voice from heaven, saying, "[a]Come out of
her, my people, that you may not participate in her sins and that you
may not receive of her plagues;
5 for her sins have [1a]piled up as high as heaven, and God has
[b]remembered her iniquities.
6 "[a]Pay her back even as she has paid, and [1]give back *to her* double
according to her deeds; in the [b]cup which she has mixed, mix twice
as much for her.
7 "[a]To the degree that she glorified herself and [b]lived [1]sensuously, to
the same degree give her torment and mourning; for she says in her
heart, '[c]I SIT *as* A QUEEN AND I AM NOT A WIDOW, and will never see
mourning.'
8 "For this reason [a]in one day her plagues will come, [1]pestilence
and mourning and famine, and she will be [b]burned up with fire; for
the Lord God who judges her [c]is strong.
9 "And [a]the kings of the earth, who committed *acts of* immorality
and [b]lived [1]sensuously with her, will [c]weep and lament over her
when they [d]see the smoke of her burning,
10 [a]standing at a distance because of the fear of her torment, saying,
'[b]Woe, woe, [c]the great city, Babylon, the strong city! For in [d]one hour
your judgment has come.'
11 "And the [a]merchants of the earth [b]weep and mourn over her,
because no one buys their cargoes any more;
12 cargoes of [a]gold and silver and precious [1]stones and pearls and
fine linen and purple and silk and scarlet, and every *kind of* citron
wood and every article of ivory and every article *made* from very
costly wood and [2]bronze and iron and marble,
13 and cinnamon and [1]spice and incense and perfume and frankin-
cense and wine and olive oil and fine flour and wheat and cattle and
sheep, and *cargoes* of horses and chariots and [2]slaves and [3a]human
lives.
14 "And the fruit [1]you long for has gone from you, and all things
that were luxurious and splendid have passed away from you and
men will no longer find them.
15 "The [a]merchants of [b]these things, who became rich from her, will
[c]stand at a distance because of the fear of her torment, weeping and
mourning,
16 saying, '[a]Woe, woe, [b]the great city, she who [c]was clothed in fine
linen and purple and scarlet, and [1]adorned with gold and precious
[2]stones and pearls;
17 for in [a]one hour such great wealth has been laid [b]waste!' And

18:1 [a]Rev. [b]Rev. 10:1
2 [1]Or, *haun* Jer. 51:8; R 13:21f.; 34:1 Jer. 50:39; 5 2:14f. [c]Rev.
3 [1]Many an read *have fa* [2]Lit., *wrath* [4]Or, *luxury* Rev. 14:8 [b] 18:9 [c]Ezek. Rev. 18:11, [d]1 Tim. 5:11;
4 [a]Is. 52:11; 51:6, 9, 45; 2
5 [1]Lit., *joine* [a]Jer. 51:9 [b]R
6 [1]Lit., *doub* [a]Ps. 137:8; J 29 [b]Rev. 17:
7 [1]Or, *luxuri* [a]Ezek. 28:2-8 5:11; Rev. 18 47:7f.; Zeph.
8 [1]Or, *death* Jer. 50:31f.; F [b]Rev. 17:16 Rev. 11:17f.
9 [1]Or, *luxuri* 17:2; 18:3 [b]1 Rev. 18:3, 7 26:16f.; 27:35 14:11; 18:18;
10 [a]Rev. 18:1 [b]Rev. 18:16, 1 11:8; 16:19; 18 19, 21 [d]Rev. 1 18:8, 17, 19
11 [a]Ezek. 27: 18:3, 15, 19, 2 27:27-34
12 [1]Lit., *stone* *brass* [a]Ezek. 2 Rev. 17:4
13 [1]Gr., *amom* *bodies* [3]Lit., *so* *men* [a]1 Chr. 5: 27:13; 1 Tim. 1
14 [1]Lit., *of you* *desire*
15 [a]Rev. 18:3 18:12, 13 [c]Rev
16 [1]Lit., *gilded* *stone and pear* 18:10, 19 [b]Rev 18, 19, 21 [c]Re
17 [a]Rev. 18:10 17:16; 18:19

[c]every shipmaster and every [1]passenger and sailor, and as many as
make their living by the sea, [a]stood at a distance,
18 and were [a]crying out as they [b]saw the smoke of her burning,
saying, '[c]What *city* is like [d]the great city?'
19 "And they threw [a]dust on their heads and were crying out, weep-
ing and mourning, saying, '[b]Woe, woe, the great city, in which all
who had ships at sea [c]became rich by her [1]wealth, for in [b]one hour
she has been laid [d]waste!'
20 "[a]Rejoice over her, O heaven, and you [1]saints and [b]apostles and
prophets, because [c]God has [2]pronounced judgment for you against
her."
21 And [1]a [a]strong angel [b]took up a stone like a great millstone and
threw it into the sea, saying, "Thus will Babylon, [c]the great city, be
thrown down with violence, and [d]will not be found any longer.
22 "And [a]the sound of harpists and musicians and flute-players and
trumpeters will not be heard in you any longer; and no craftsman of
any craft will be found in you any longer; and the [b]sound of a mill
will not be heard in you any longer;
23 and the light of a lamp will not shine in you any longer; and the
[a]voice of the bridegroom and bride will not be heard in you any
longer; for your [b]merchants were the great men of the earth, because
all the nations were deceived [c]by your sorcery.
24 "And in her was found the [a]blood of prophets and of [1]saints and
of [b]all who have been slain on the earth."

Chapter 19

19 After these things I heard, as it were, a [a]loud voice of a great
multitude in heaven, saying,
"[b]**H**allelujah! [c]Salvation and [d]glory and power belong to our
God;
2 [a]BECAUSE HIS [b]JUDGMENTS ARE [c]TRUE AND RIGHTEOUS; for He has
judged the [d]great harlot who was corrupting the earth with her im-
morality, and HE HAS [e]AVENGED THE BLOOD OF HIS BOND-SERVANTS [1]ON
HER."
3 And a second time they said, "[a]Hallelujah! [b]HER SMOKE RISES UP
FOREVER AND EVER."
4 And the [a]twenty-four elders and the [b]four living creatures [c]fell
down and worshiped God who sits on the throne saying, "[d]Amen.
[e]Hallelujah!"
5 And a voice came from the throne, saying,
"[a]**G**ive praise to our God, all you His bond-servants, [b]you who
fear Him, the small and the great."
6 And I heard, as it were, [a]the voice of a great multitude and as
[b]the sound of many waters and as the [c]sound of mighty peals of
thunder, saying,
"[a]**H**allelujah! For the [d]Lord our God, the Almighty, reigns.
7 "Let us rejoice and be glad and [a]give the glory to Him, for [b]the
marriage of the Lamb has come and His [1c]bride has made herself
ready."
8 And it was given to her to clothe herself in [a]fine linen, bright *and*
clean; for the fine linen is the [b]righteous acts of the [1]saints.
9 And [a]he *said to me, "[b]Write, '[c]Blessed are those who are invited
to the marriage supper of the Lamb.'" And he *said to me, "[d]These
are true words of God."

10 And [a]I fell at his feet to worship him. [b]And he *said to me, "Do
not do that; I am a [c]fellow servant of yours and your brethren who
[d]hold the testimony of Jesus; worship God. For the testimony of
Jesus is the spirit of prophecy."
11 And I saw [a]heaven opened; and behold, a [b]white horse, and He
who sat upon it *is* called [c]Faithful and True; and in [d]righteousness He
judges and wages war.
12 And His [a]eyes *are* a flame of fire, and upon His head *are* many
[b]diadems; and He has a [c]name written *upon Him* which no one
knows except Himself.
13 And *He is* clothed with a [a]robe dipped in blood; and His name is
called [b]The Word of God.
14 And the armies which are in heaven, clothed in [a]fine linen,
[b]white *and* clean, were following Him on white horses.
15 And [a]from His mouth comes a sharp sword, so that [b]with it He
may smite the nations; and He will [1c]rule them with a rod of iron;
and [d]He treads the [2]wine press of the fierce wrath of God, the Al-
mighty.
16 And on His robe and on His thigh He has [a]a name written,
"[b]KING OF KINGS, AND LORD OF LORDS."
17 And I saw [1]an angel standing in the sun; and he cried out with a
loud voice, saying to [a]all the birds which fly in [b]midheaven, "[c]Come,
assemble for the great supper of God;
18 in order that you may [a]eat the flesh of kings and the flesh of
[1]commanders and the flesh of mighty men and the flesh of horses
and of those who sit on them and the flesh of all men, [b]both free men
and slaves, and [c]small and great."
19 And I saw [a]the beast and [b]the kings of the earth and their armies,
assembled to make war against Him who [c]sat upon the horse, and
against His army.
20 And the beast was seized, and with him the [a]false prophet who
[b]performed the signs [1c]in his presence, by which he [d]deceived those
who had received the [e]mark of the beast and those who [f]worshiped
his image; these two were thrown alive into the [g]lake of [h]fire which
burns with brimstone.
21 And the rest were killed with the sword which [a]came from the
mouth of Him who [b]sat upon the horse, and [c]all the birds were filled
with their flesh.

Chapter 20

20 And I saw [a]an angel coming down from heaven, having the
[b]key of the abyss and a great chain [1]in his hand.
2 And he laid hold of the [a]dragon, the serpent of old, who is the
devil and Satan, and [b]bound him for a thousand years,
3 and threw him into the [a]abyss, and shut *it* and [b]sealed *it* over
him, so that he should [c]not deceive the nations any longer, until the
thousand years were completed; after these things he must be
released for a short time.
4 And I saw [a]thrones, and [b]they sat upon them, and [c]judgment was
given to them. And I *saw* [d]the souls of those who had been beheaded
because of the [e]testimony of Jesus and because of the word of God,
and those who had not [f]worshiped the beast or his image, and had
not received the [g]mark upon their forehead and upon their hand;
and they [h]came to life and [i]reigned with Christ for a thousand years.

10 [a]Rev. 10:26; Re 1:1f. [d]Rev

11 [a]Ezek. 1:51; Rev. 6:2; 19:19 3:14 [d]Ps.

12 [a]Dan. 1:14 [b]Rev [c]Rev. 2:17

13 [a]Is. 63

14 [a]Rev. 1 3:4; 19:8

15 [1]Or, *sh wine press of His fierc* [a]Rev. 1:16 11:4; 2 The 2:9; Rev. 2 Joel 3:13;

16 [a]Rev. 2 [b]Rev. 17:14

17 [1]Lit., *or* 19:21 [b]Rev [c]1 Sam. 17 12:9; Ezek.

18 [1]I.e., ch command c thousand tr 39:18-20 [b] [c]Rev. 11:18

19 [a]Rev. 11 [b]Rev. 16:14 19:11, 21

20 [1]Or, *by* [a]Rev. 16:13 13:13 [c]Rev. [d]Rev. 13:14 13:16f. [f]Rev [g]Rev. 20:10, [h]Is. 30:33; D Rev. 14:10

21 [a]Rev. 19 19:11, 19 [c]F

20:1 [1]Lit., *u* 10:1 [b]Rev. 1

2 [a]Gen. 3:1; [b]Is. 24:22; 2 Jude 6

3 [a]Rev. 20:1 6:17; Matt. 2 12:9; 20:8, 1

4 [a]Dan. 7:9 19:28; Rev. 3 7:22; 1 Cor. 6:9 [e]Rev. 1: 13:12, 15 [g]R [h]John 14:19 5:10; 20:6; 2

5 The rest of the dead did not come to life until the thousand years
were completed. [a]This is the first resurrection.
6 [a]Blessed and holy is the one who has a part in the first resurrec-
tion; over these the [b]second death has no power, but they will be
[c]priests of God and of Christ and will [d]reign with Him for a
thousand years.
7 And when the thousand years are completed, Satan will be
[a]released from his prison,
8 and will come out to [a]deceive the nations which are in the [b]four
corners of the earth, [c]Gog and Magog, to [d]gather them together for
the war; the number of them is like the [e]sand of the [1]seashore.
9 And they [a]came up on the [1]broad plain of the earth and sur-
rounded the [b]camp of the [2]saints and the [c]beloved city, and [d]fire came
down from heaven and devoured them.
10 And [a]the devil who [a]deceived them was thrown into the [b]lake of
fire and brimstone, where the [c]beast and the [c]false prophet are also;
and they will be [d]tormented day and night forever and ever.
11 And I saw a great white [a]throne and Him who sat upon it, from
whose [1]presence [b]earth and heaven fled away, and [c]no place was
found for them.
12 And I saw the dead, the [a]great and the small, standing before the
throne, and [1b]books were opened; and another [2]book was opened,
which is [c]*the book* of life; and the dead [a]were judged from the things
which were written in the [1]books, [d]according to their deeds.
13 And the sea gave up the dead which were in it, and [a]death and
Hades [b]gave up the dead which were in them; and they were judged,
every one *of them* [c]according to their deeds.
14 And [a]death and Hades were thrown into [b]the lake of fire. This is
the [c]second death, the lake of fire.
15 And if [1]anyone's name was not found written in [a]the book of life,
he was thrown into the lake of fire.

Chapter 21

21 And I saw [a]a new heaven and a new earth; for [b]the first heav-
en and the first earth passed away, and there is no longer *any*
sea.
2 And I saw [a]the holy city, [b]new Jerusalem, [c]coming down out of
heaven from God, [d]made ready as a bride adorned for her husband.
3 And I heard a loud voice from the throne, saying, "Behold, [a]the
tabernacle of God is among men, and He shall [1b]dwell among them,
and they shall be His people, and God Himself shall be among
them,[2]
4 and He shall [a]wipe away every tear from their eyes; and [b]there
shall no longer be *any* death; [c]there shall no longer be *any* mourning,
or crying, or pain; [d]the first things have passed away."
5 And [a]He who sits on the throne said, "Behold, I am [b]making all
things new." And He *said, "Write, for [c]these words are faithful and
true."
6 And He said to me, "[1a]It is done. I am the [b]Alpha and the Omega,
the beginning and the end. [c]I will give to the one who thirsts from
the spring of the [d]water of life without cost.
7 "[a]He who overcomes shall inherit these things, and [b]I will be his
God and he will be My son.
8 "[a]But for the cowardly and [1]unbelieving and abominable and

murderers and immoral persons and sorcerers and idolaters and all
liars, their part *will be* in [b]the lake that burns with fire and brimstone,
which is the [c]second death."
9 [a]And one of the seven angels who had the [b]seven bowls [1]full of
the [c]seven last plagues, came and spoke with me, saying, "[a]Come
here, I shall show you the [d]bride, the wife of the Lamb."
10 And [a]he carried me away [1b]in the Spirit to a great and high
mountain, and showed me [c]the holy city, Jerusalem, coming down
out of heaven from God,
11 having [a]the glory of God. Her [1]brilliance was like a very costly
stone, as a [b]stone of [c]crystal-clear jasper.
12 [1]It had a great and high wall, [1a]with twelve [b]gates, and at the
gates twelve angels; and names *were* written on them, which are
those of the twelve tribes of the sons of Israel.
13 *There were* three gates on the east and three gates on the north
and three gates on the south and three gates on the west.
14 And the wall of the city had [a]twelve foundation stones, and on
them *were* the twelve names of the [b]twelve apostles of the Lamb.
15 And the one who spoke with me had a [1]gold measuring [a]rod to
measure the city, and its [b]gates and its wall.
16 And the city is laid out as a square, and its length is as great as
the width; and he measured the city with the [1]rod, [2]fifteen hundred
miles; its length and width and height are equal.
17 And he measured its wall, [1]seventy-two yards, *according to*
[a]human [2]measurements, which are *also* [b]angelic *measurements.*
18 And the material of the wall was [a]jasper; and the city was [b]pure
gold, like [1]clear [c]glass.
19 [a]The foundation stones of the city wall were adorned with every
kind of precious stone. The first foundation stone was [b]jasper; the
second, sapphire; the third, chalcedony; the fourth, [c]emerald;
20 the fifth, sardonyx; the sixth, [a]sardius; the seventh, chrysolite; the
eighth, beryl; the ninth, topaz; the tenth, chrysoprase; the eleventh,
jacinth; the twelfth, amethyst.
21 And the twelve [a]gates were twelve [b]pearls; each one of the gates
was a single pearl. And the street of the city was [c]pure gold, like
transparent [d]glass.
22 And I saw [a]no [1]temple in it, for the [b]Lord God, the Almighty, and
the [c]Lamb, are its [1]temple.
23 And the city [a]has no need of the sun or of the moon to shine
upon it, for [b]the glory of God has illumined it, and its lamp *is* the
[c]Lamb.
24 And [a]the nations shall walk by its light, and the [b]kings of the
earth [1]shall bring their glory into it.
25 And in the daytime (for [a]there shall be no night there) [b]its gates
[c]shall never be closed;
26 and [a]they shall bring the glory and the honor of the nations
into it;
27 and [a]nothing unclean and no one who practices abomination
and lying, shall ever come into it, but only those [1]whose names are
[b]written in the Lamb's book of life.

Chapter 22

22 And [a]he showed me a [b]river of the [c]water of life, [1]clear [d]as
crystal, coming from the throne of God and of [2]the Lamb,

8 [b]Rev. 1
2:11

9 [1]Lit., *w*
[a]Rev. 17:1
[c]Rev. 15:1
21:2

10 [1]Or, *in*
40:2; Rev.
1:10 [c]Rev

11 [1]Lit., *li*
60:1f.; Eze
15:8; 21:2
4:3; 21:18,

12 [1]Lit., *ha*
48:31-34
21, 25; 22:

14 [a]Heb. 1
1:26

15 [1]Lit., *m*
gold reed
Rev. 11:1
21, 25

16 [1]Lit., *re*
twelve thou
a stadion w
600 ft.

17 [1]Lit., *or*
forty-four c
measure [a]
Rev. 13:18

18 [1]Lit., *pu*
21:11 [b]Rev
[c]Rev. 4:6

19 [a]Ex. 28
54:11f.; Eze
[b]Rev. 21:11

20 [a]Rev. 4:

21 [a]Rev. 21
[b]Rev. 17:4
[d]Rev. 4:6

22 [1]Or, *san*
[a]Matt. 24:2;
[b]Rev. 1:8
7:17; 14:4

23 [a]Is. 24:2
Rev. 21:25;
21:11 [c]Rev.
14:4

24 [1]Lit., *brin*
5 [b]Ps. 72:10
49:23; 60:16;

25 [a]Zech. 14
21:23; 22:5
21:12, 15 [c]Is

26 [a]Ps. 72:1
49:23; 60:16

27 [1]Lit., *who*
52:1; Ezek. 4
14:21; Rev. 2
[b]Rev. 3:5

22:1 [1]Lit., *bri*
the Lamb. In
of its street, a
either side of
was [a]Rev. 1:
22:6 [b]Ps. 46:
47:1 [c]Zech.
7:17; 22:17

2 in the middle of [a]its street. And [b]on either side of the river was
[c]the tree of life, bearing twelve [1]*kinds of* fruit, yielding its fruit every
month; and the leaves of the tree were for the healing of the nations.
3 And [a]there shall no longer be any curse; and [b]the throne of God
and of the Lamb shall be in it, and His bond-servants shall [c]serve
Him;
4 and they shall [a]see His face, and His [b]name *shall be* on their
[c]foreheads.
5 And [a]there shall no longer be *any* night; and they [1]shall not have
need [b]of the light of a lamp nor the light of the sun, because the Lord
God shall illumine them; and they shall [c]reign forever and ever.
6 And [a]he said to me, "[b]These words are faithful and true"; and the
Lord, the [c]God of the spirits of the prophets, [d]sent His angel to show
to His bond-servants the things which must shortly take place.
7 "And behold, [a]I am coming quickly. [b]Blessed is he who [1]heeds [c]the
words of the prophecy of this book."
8 And [a]I, John, am the one who heard and saw these things. And
when I heard and saw, [b]I fell down to worship at the feet of the angel
who showed me these things.
9 And [a]he *said to me, "Do not do that; I am a [b]fellow servant of
yours and of your brethren the prophets and of those who [1]heed the
words of [c]this book; worship God."
10 And he *said to me, "[a]Do not seal up [b]the words of the prophecy
of this book, [c]for the time is near.
11 "[a]Let the one who does wrong, still do wrong; and let the one who
is filthy, still be filthy; and let the one who is righteous, still practice
righteousness; and let the one who is holy, still keep himself holy."
12 "Behold, [a]I am coming quickly, and My [b]reward *is* with Me, [c]to
render to every man [1]according to what he has done.
13 "I am the [a]Alpha and the Omega, [b]the first and the last, [c]the begin-
ning and the end."
14 Blessed are those who [a]wash their robes, that they may have the
right to [b]the tree of life, and may [c]enter by the [d]gates into the city.
15 [a]Outside are the [b]dogs and the sorcerers and the immoral per-
sons and the murderers and the idolaters, and everyone who loves
and practices lying.
16 "[a]I, Jesus, have sent [b]My angel to testify to you these things [1c]for
the churches. I am [d]the root and the [e]offspring of David, the bright
[f]morning star."
17 And the [a]Spirit and the [b]bride say, "Come." And let the one who
hears say, "Come." And [c]let the one who is thirsty come; let the one
who wishes take the [d]water of life without cost.
18 I testify to everyone who hears [a]the words of the prophecy of
this book: if anyone [b]adds to them, God shall add to him [c]the plagues
which are written in [d]this book;
19 and if anyone [a]takes away from the [b]words of the book of this
prophecy, God shall take away his part from [c]the tree of life and
[1]from the holy city, [d]which are written in this book.
20 He who [a]testifies to these things says, "Yes, [b]I am coming quick-
ly." Amen. [c]Come, Lord Jesus.
21 [a]The grace of the Lord Jesus be with [1]all. Amen.

rops of *fruit*
:21 [b]Ezek.
n. 2:9; Rev.
7; 22:14, 19
14:11 [b]Rev.
[c]Rev. 7:15
17:15; 42:2;
[b]Rev. 14:1
[c]Rev. 7:3
do not have
Rev. 21:25
, Rev. 21:23
8, 27; Matt.
. 5:17; Rev.
20:4
21:9 [b]Rev.
21:5 [c]1 Cor.
12:9 [d]Rev.
1:1; 22:16
s [a]Rev. 1:3;
6:15; 22:12,
. 1:3; 16:15
2:9, 10, 18f.
[b]Rev. 19:10
keep [a]Rev.
v. 1:1 [c]Rev.
, 22:10, 18f.
. 8:26; Rev.
. 1:11; 22:9,
f. [c]Rev. 1:3
. 3:27; Dan.
12:10
s his work is
[b]Is. 40:10;
s. 28:4; Jer.
16:27; Rev.
2:23
:8 [b]Is. 44:6;
ev. 1:17; 2:8
[c]Rev. 21:6
7:14 [b]Gen.
2; Rev. 22:2
[d]Rev. 21:12
8:12; 1 Cor.
5:19ff.; Rev.
23:18; Matt.
7:6; Phil. 3:2
, *concerning*
1 [b]Rev. 1:1;
1:4, 11; 3:22
5 [e]Matt. 1:1
2; Rev. 2:28
v. 2:7; 14:13
9 [c]Is. 55:1;
[d]Rev. 7:17;
22:1
22:7 [b]Deut.
2; Prov. 30:6
16:21 [d]Rev.
22:7
out of [a]Deut.
2; Prov. 30:6
7 [c]Rev. 22:2
. 21:10-22:5
ev. 1:2 [b]Rev.
[c]1Cor. 16:22
ancient mss.
saints [a]Rom.
16:20

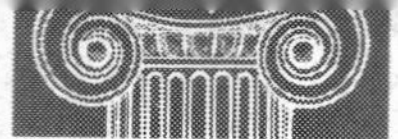

JESUS' MESSAGES TO THE CHURCHES

	Description of Jesus	Commendation to the Church	Reproof Given to the Church	Warnings and Instructions to the Church	Pro O
Ephesus					
Smyrna					
Pergamum					
Thyatira					
Sardis					
Philadelphia					
Laodicea					

What Revelation Teaches About

God	Jesus	The Holy Spirit

The Seven Seals, Trumpets, and Bowls

	Seals	Trumpets	Bowls
1st			
2nd			
3rd			
4th			
5th			
6th			
7th			

Revelation:

MENT DIVISIONS

			CHAPTER THEMES
			1
			2
			3
			4
			5
			6
			7
			8
			9
			10
			11
			12
			13
			14
			15
			16
			17
			18
			19
			20
			21
			22

Author:

Date:

Purpose:

Key Words:

God

Jesus (Christ)

Spirit

seven

churches

write

mystery

repent

overcome(s)

mark every reference to Satan (demons, devil) with a red pitchfork

angel

seals

trumpets

APPENDIX

THE GENEALOGY OF JESUS THE CHRIST

As proof of His right to the throne of David through Mary

FOR THE GENERATIONS FROM ADAM TO ABRAHAM, SEE LUKE 3:34-38

Abraham
Isaac
Jacob
Judah
Perez
Hezron
Ram
Admin
Amminadab
Nahshon
Salmon—Rahab
Boaz—Ruth
Obed
Jesse

David

Nathan
Mattatha
Menna
Melea
Eliakim
Jonam
Joseph
Judah
Simeon
Levi
Matthat
Jorim
Eliezer
Joshua
Er
Elmadam
Cosam
Addi
Melchi
Neri
Shealtiel
Zerubbabel
Rhesa
Joanan
Joda
Josech
Semein
Mattathias
Maath
Naggai
Hesli
Nahum
Amos
Mattathias
Joseph
Jannai
Melchi
Levi
Matthat
Eli
("Being supposedly the son of Joseph" [Luke 3:23])
Mary

Solomon
Rehoboam
Abijah
Asa
Jehoshaphat
Joram
Ahaziah
Joash
Amaziah
Uzziah (Azariah)
Jotham
Ahaz
Hezekiah
Manasseh
Amon
Josiah
Jehoiakim
Jeconiah
Shealtiel
Zerubbabel
Abuid
Eliakim
Azor
Zadok
Achim
Eliud
Eleazar
Matthan
Jacob
Joseph

The Hol
Luke

Jes

This information is taken from
1 Chronicles 3
Matthew 1
Luke 3

ERSE	LESSON FOR MY LIFE

WHAT THE BIBLE TEACHES ABOUT BABYLON

Its First Description in Scripture	Location of Babylon The City The Babylonian Empire *(see*
Worship Connected with Babylon	Warnings Given about Babylon

...ECIES REGARDING BABYLON	DESTRUCTION OF BABYLON
	HISTORY OF BABYLON'S DESTRUCTION THE CITY THE BABYLONIAN EMPIRE
	DETAILS CONCERNING BABYLON'S FINAL DESTRUCTION THE CITY THE BABYLONIAN SYSTEM

THE DAY OF THE LORD, THE

REFERENCE	HOW IS IT DESCRIBED

What Happens in Nature	Signs of Beginning or End

MATTHEW	MARK

LUKE	JOHN

THE ARREST, TRIAL, AND CRUCIFIXION OF JESUS CHRI[ST]

MATTHEW	MARK	LUKE	JOHN
		Luke gives chronological order of events in Jesus' life (Luke 1:3).	

The Account of Jesus' Resurrection

Matthew	Mark	Luke	John
		Luke gives chronological order of events in Jesus' life (Luke 1:3).	

Post-Resurrection Appearances

Matthew	Mark	Luke	John

OBSERVATIONS ON JOHN CHAPTER ONE

Chapter 1

1 [a]In the beginning was [b]the Word, and the Word was [c]w
and [d]the Word was God.
2 [1]He was in the beginning with God.
3 [a]All things came into being [1]by Him, and apart from H
ing came into being that has come into being.
4 [a]In Him was life, and the life was [b]the light of men.
5 And [a]the light shines in the darkness, and the darkness
[1]comprehend it.
6 There [1]came a man, sent from God, whose name was Joh
7 [1]He came [a]for a witness, that he might bear witness of t
[b]that all might believe through him.
8 [1][a]He was not the light, but *came* that he might bear witne
light.
9 There was [a]the true light [1]which, coming into the wo
lightens every man.
10 He was in the world, and [a]the world was made throug
and the world did not know Him.
11 He came to His [1]own, and those who were His own
receive Him.
12 But as many as received Him, to them He gave the
become [a]children of God, *even* [b]to those who believe in His na
13 [a]who were [1]born not of [2]blood, nor of the will of the flesh
the will of man, but of God.
14 And [a]the Word [b]became flesh, and [1][c]dwelt among us, a
beheld His glory, glory as of [2]the only begotten from the Fat
of [e]grace and [f]truth.
15 John [*][a]bore witness of Him, and cried out, saying, "This
of whom I said, '[b]He who comes after me [1]has a higher rank
[c]for He existed before me.'"
16 For of His [a]fulness [1]we have all received, and [2]grace upon
17 For [a]the Law was given through Moses; grace and [c]tru
realized through Jesus Christ.
18 [a]No man has seen God at any time; [b]the only begotten [1]G
is [c]in the bosom of the Father, [d]He has explained Him.
19 And this is [a]the witness of John, when [b]the Jews sent
priests and Levites [c]from Jerusalem to ask him, "Who are you
20 And he confessed, and did not deny, and he confessed,
not [1]the Christ."
21 And they asked him, "What then? Are you [a]Elijah?" A
[*]said, "I am not." "Are you [b]the Prophet?" And he answered,

ey said then to him, "Who are you, so that we may give an
to those who sent us? What do you say about yourself?"
said, "I am [a]A VOICE OF ONE CRYING IN THE WILDERNESS, 'MAKE
T THE WAY OF THE LORD,' as Isaiah the prophet said."
w they had been sent from the Pharisees.
d they asked him, and said to him, "Why then are you baptiz-
ou are not the [1]Christ, nor Elijah, nor [a]the Prophet?"
n answered them saying, "[a]I baptize [1]in water, *but* among you
One whom you do not know.
[a]He who comes after me, the [b]thong of whose sandal I am
rthy to untie."
se things took place in Bethany [a]beyond the Jordan, where
as baptizing.
next day he *saw Jesus coming to him, and *said, "Behold,
nb of God who [b]takes away the sin of the world!
s is He on behalf of whom I said, '[a]After me comes a Man
as a higher rank than I, [b]for He existed before me.'
d I did not recognize [1]Him, but in order that He might be
sted to Israel, I came baptizing [2]in water."
d John [a]bore witness saying, "[b]I have beheld the Spirit de-
g as a dove out of heaven, and He remained upon Him.
d I did not recognize [1]Him, but He who sent me to baptize [2]in
aid to me, 'He upon whom you see the Spirit descending and
ing upon Him, [a]this is the one who baptizes [2]in the Holy

d I have seen, and have borne witness that this is [a]the Son of

ain [a]the next day John was standing [1]with two of his disciples,
he looked upon Jesus as He walked, and *said, "Behold, [a]the
f God!"
d the two disciples heard him speak, and they followed Jesus.
d Jesus turned, and beheld them following, and *said to them,
do you seek?" And they said to Him, "[a]Rabbi (which trans-
eans Teacher), where are You staying?"
*said to them, "Come, and you will see." They came there-
d saw where He was staying; and they stayed with Him that
it was about the [1]tenth hour.
e of the two who heard John *speak*, and followed Him, was
v, Simon Peter's brother.
*found first his own brother Simon, and *said to him, "We
und the [a]Messiah" (which translated means [1]Christ).

JOHN AT A GLANCE

Theme of John: Eternal life through Jesus Christ, the Son of God

Author:
John

Date:
about A.D. 85

Purpose:
that his readers would believe that Jesus is the Christ, God's Son, and thus have eternal life

Key Words:
signs/miracles
believe
life
judge
judgment
witness
true, truth
king
kingdom
love
works
commandments
fruit
abide
ask

SEGMENT DIVISIONS

STRUCTURE OF BOOK	WRITTEN	SIGNS AND MIRACLES	MINISTRY	CHAPTER THEMES
Introduces Jesus as Christ, Son of God	That you may believe Jesus is the Christ, Son of God		To Israel	1:1-18 Prologue—The Word
				1:19 John the Baptist / calling disciples
Gives signs that prove Jesus is Christ, Son of God		Water to wine		2 wedding Cana / cleansing temple
				3 born again
		Heals nobleman's son.		4 woman at well / nobleman
		Heals lame man		5 father / son
		Feeds 5,000 walks on water		6 bread / feeding 5,000
				7 feast of tabernacles / thirst-drink
				8 adulterous woman / truth sets free
		Heals blind man		9 blind man
				10 sheep / shepherd
		Raises Lazarus from dead		11 raising Lazarus
Hour has come	Decision time		To disciples	12 King on donkey / dinner at Bethany
Life that belongs to those who believe	That you may have life			13 last supper / washing-disciples
				14 Father's house / hearts be troubled
				15 abide / vine and branches
				16 Holy Spirit / another comforter
			To all mankind	17 Lord's prayer / high-priestly prayer
Obtaining of that life—by death and resurrection				18 arrest and trial
				19 crucifixion
		Resurrection appearances		20 resurrection
Purpose of life: love and follow			To disciples	21 do you love Me?

Sidon
Mt. Lebanon
SYRIA
ABILENE
Mt. Harmon
Tyre
PHOENICIA
Caesarea Philippi
Kedesh
GALILEE
Ptolemais Acco
Chorazin
Bethsaida
Gennesaret
Capernaum
Magdala
Cana
Gergesa
Tiberias
Sepphoris
Mt. Tabor
The Great Sea
(Mediterranean Sea)
Nazareth
Sea of Galilee
Japhia
Gadara
Dora
Nain
Scythopolis
Caesarea
River Jordan
DECAPOLIS
Plain of Sharon
SAMARIA
Aenon
Samaria
Mt.Ebal
Shechem
Sychar
Apollonia
Mt. Gerizim
Jabbok River
Antipatris
Joppa
PEREA
Lydda,Lod
Ephraim
Emmaus
Ramah
Jericho
Mt. of Olives
Jerusalem
Bethany
Qumran
(Essene community)
Medeba
Bethlehem
JUDEA
Herodium
Tekoa
Hebron
Dibon
Gaza
En-gedi
Arnon River
Dead Sea (Salt Sea)
Masada
IDUMEA
Arad
NABATEANS
Beersheba
Zoar
Zered River

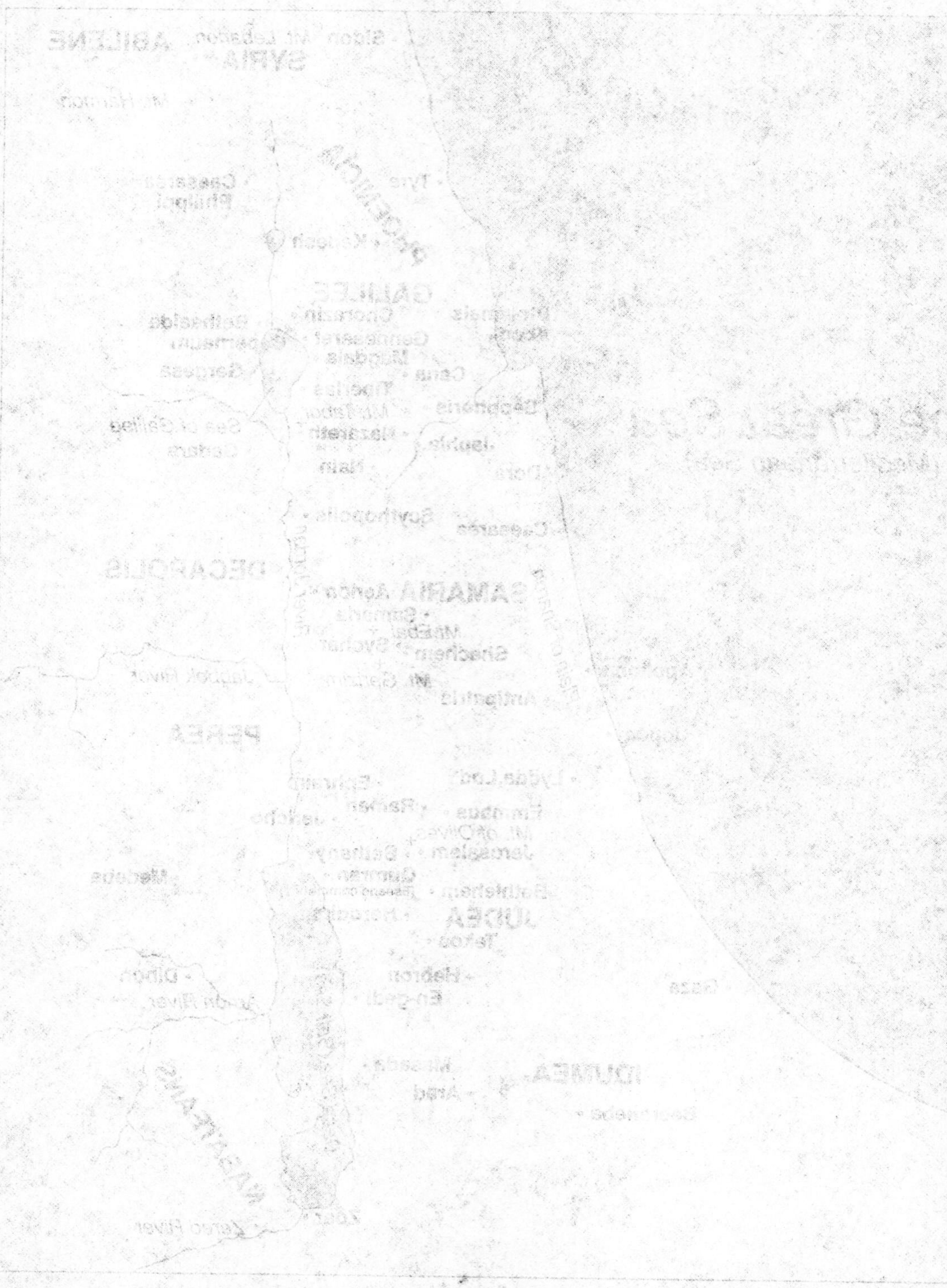

INDEX TO HISTORICAL CHARTS

OLD TESTAMENT

NEW TESTAMENT

INDEX TO TOPICAL STUDY CHARTS

OLD TESTAMENT

NEW TESTAMENT

Index to At a Glance Charts

Old Testament

New Testament

Index to Observations Charts

INDEX TO ILLUSTRATIONS

OLD TESTAMENT

NEW TESTAMENT

INDEX TO COLOR MAPS

Index to Maps

(All maps are approximate to scale.)

Old Testament

New Testament

BIBLE LANDS

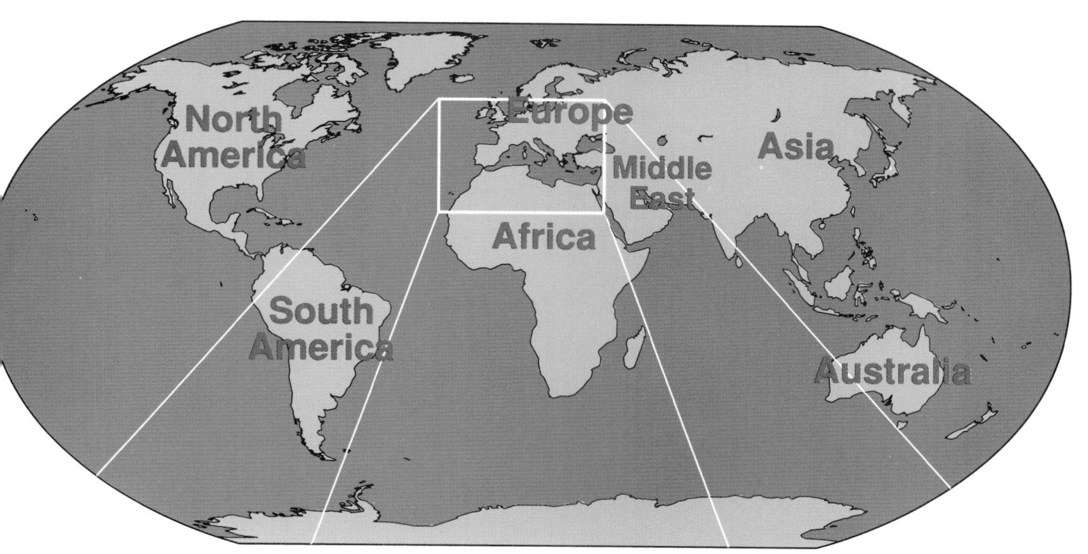

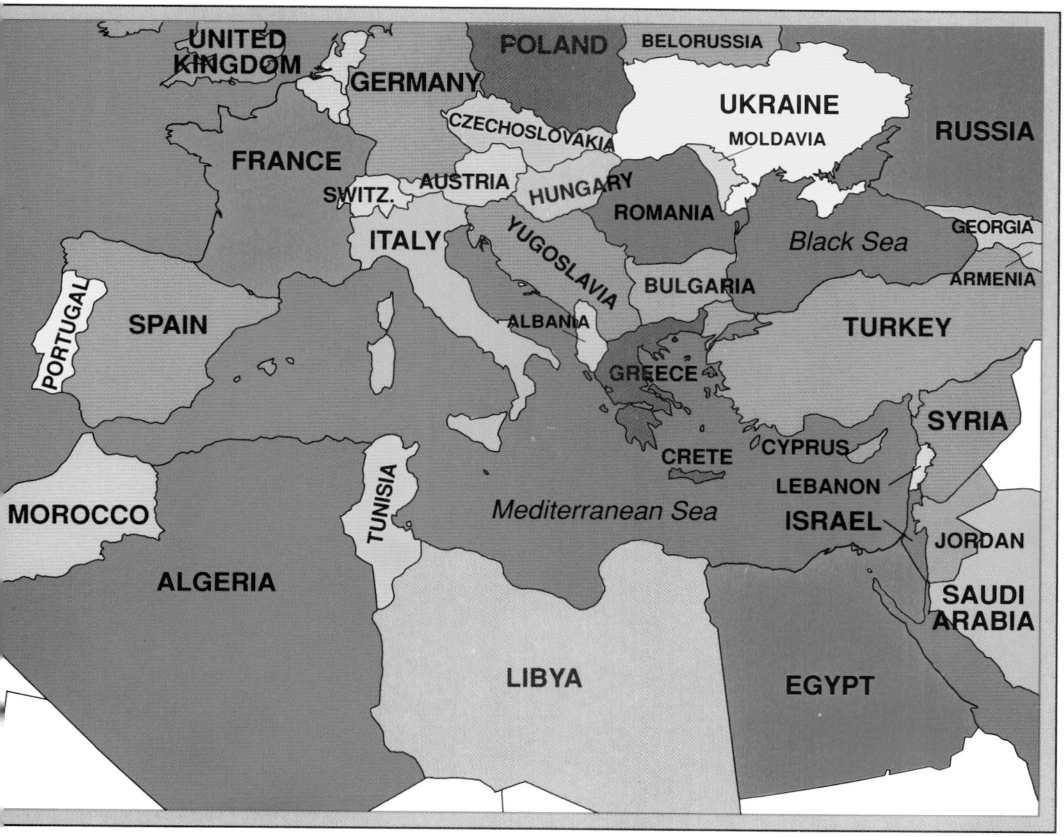

UNITED KINGDOM
POLAND
BELORUSSIA
GERMANY
UKRAINE
RUSSIA
CZECHOSLOVAKIA
MOLDAVIA
FRANCE
SWITZ.
AUSTRIA
HUNGARY
ROMANIA
ITALY
YUGOSLAVIA
Black Sea
GEORGIA
ARMENIA
BULGARIA
PORTUGAL
SPAIN
ALBANIA
TURKEY
GREECE
SYRIA
CRETE
CYPRUS
LEBANON
TUNISIA
MOROCCO
Mediterranean Sea
ISRAEL
JORDAN
ALGERIA
SAUDI ARABIA
LIBYA
EGYPT

THE TABLE OF NATIONS

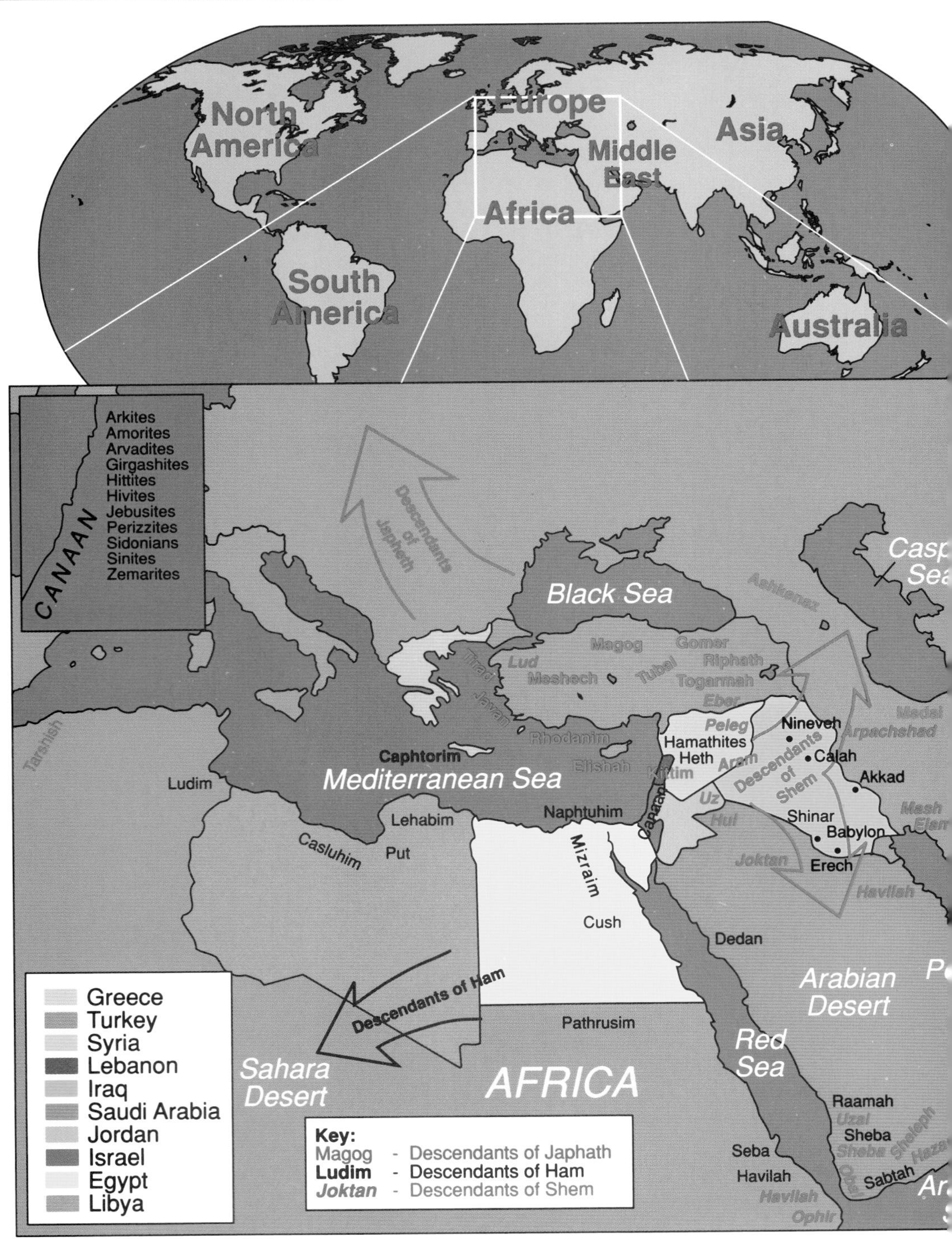

THE EXODUS

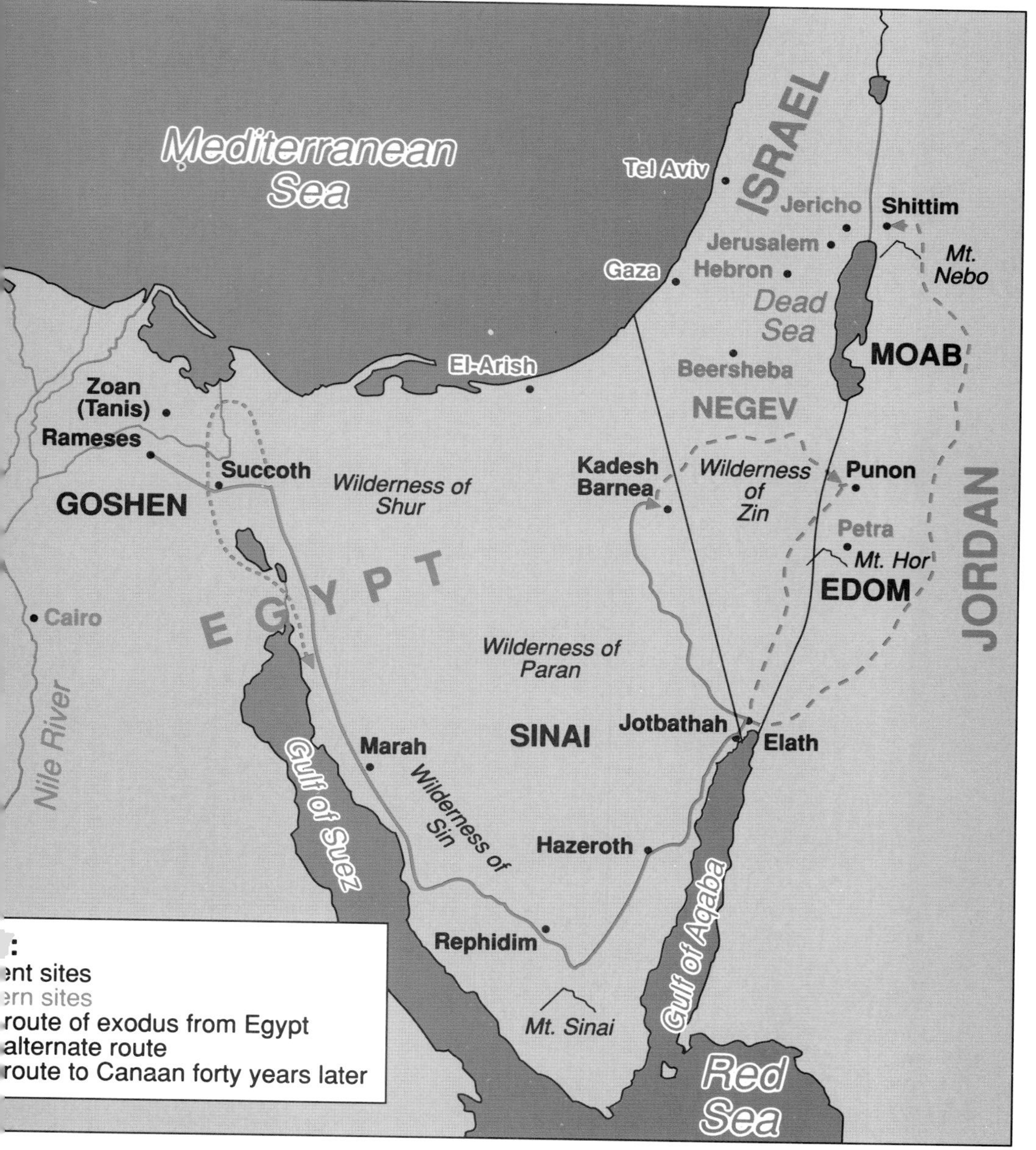
Mediterranean Sea
ISRAEL
Tel Aviv
Jericho
Shittim
Jerusalem
Mt. Nebo
Gaza
Hebron
Dead Sea
Beersheba
MOAB
El-Arish
Zoan (Tanis)
NEGEV
Rameses
Succoth
Wilderness of Shur
Kadesh Barnea
Wilderness of Zin
Punon
GOSHEN
Petra
Mt. Hor
EGYPT
EDOM
JORDAN
Cairo
Wilderness of Paran
Nile River
SINAI
Jotbathah
Elath
Marah
Gulf of Suez
Wilderness of Sin
Hazeroth
Gulf of Aqaba
Rephidim
Mt. Sinai
Red Sea
:
ent sites
ern sites
route of exodus from Egypt
alternate route
route to Canaan forty years later

BABYLONIAN EMPIRE

PERSIAN EMPIRE

GREEK EMPIRE

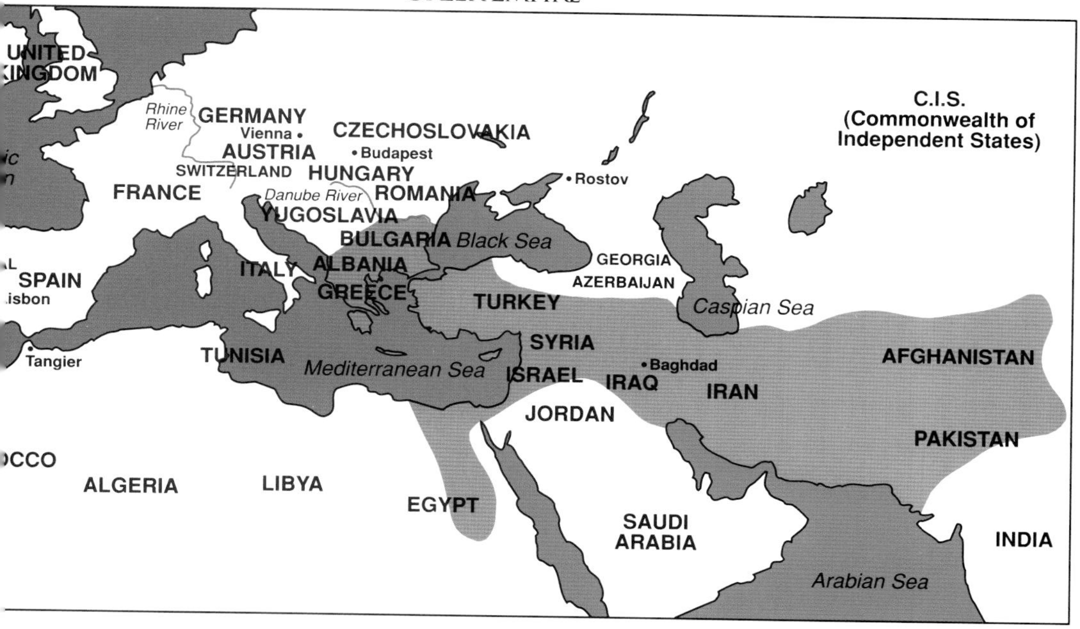

UNITED KINGDOM
C.I.S. (Commonwealth of Independent States)
Rhine River
GERMANY
Vienna
AUSTRIA
CZECHOSLOVAKIA
Budapest
SWITZERLAND
HUNGARY
FRANCE
Danube River
ROMANIA
Rostov
YUGOSLAVIA
BULGARIA
Black Sea
SPAIN
Lisbon
ITALY
ALBANIA
GREECE
GEORGIA
AZERBAIJAN
TURKEY
Caspian Sea
SYRIA
Tangier
TUNISIA
Mediterranean Sea
ISRAEL
Baghdad
IRAQ
IRAN
AFGHANISTAN
JORDAN
PAKISTAN
MOROCCO
ALGERIA
LIBYA
EGYPT
SAUDI ARABIA
INDIA
Arabian Sea

ROMAN EMPIRE

UNITED KINGDOM
C.I.S. (Commonwealth of Independent States)
Rhine River
GERMANY
Vienna
AUSTRIA
CZECHOSLOVAKIA
Budapest
SWITZERLAND
HUNGARY
FRANCE
Danube River
ROMANIA
Rostov
YUGOSLAVIA
BULGARIA
Black Sea
SPAIN
Lisbon
ITALY
ALBANIA
GREECE
GEORGIA
AZERBAIJAN
TURKEY
Caspian Sea
SYRIA
Tangier
TUNISIA
Mediterranean Sea
ISRAEL
Baghdad
IRAQ
IRAN
AFGHANISTAN
JORDAN
PAKISTAN
MOROCCO
ALGERIA
LIBYA
EGYPT
SAUDI ARABIA
INDIA
Arabian Sea

Israel's Territories: Ancient and Modern

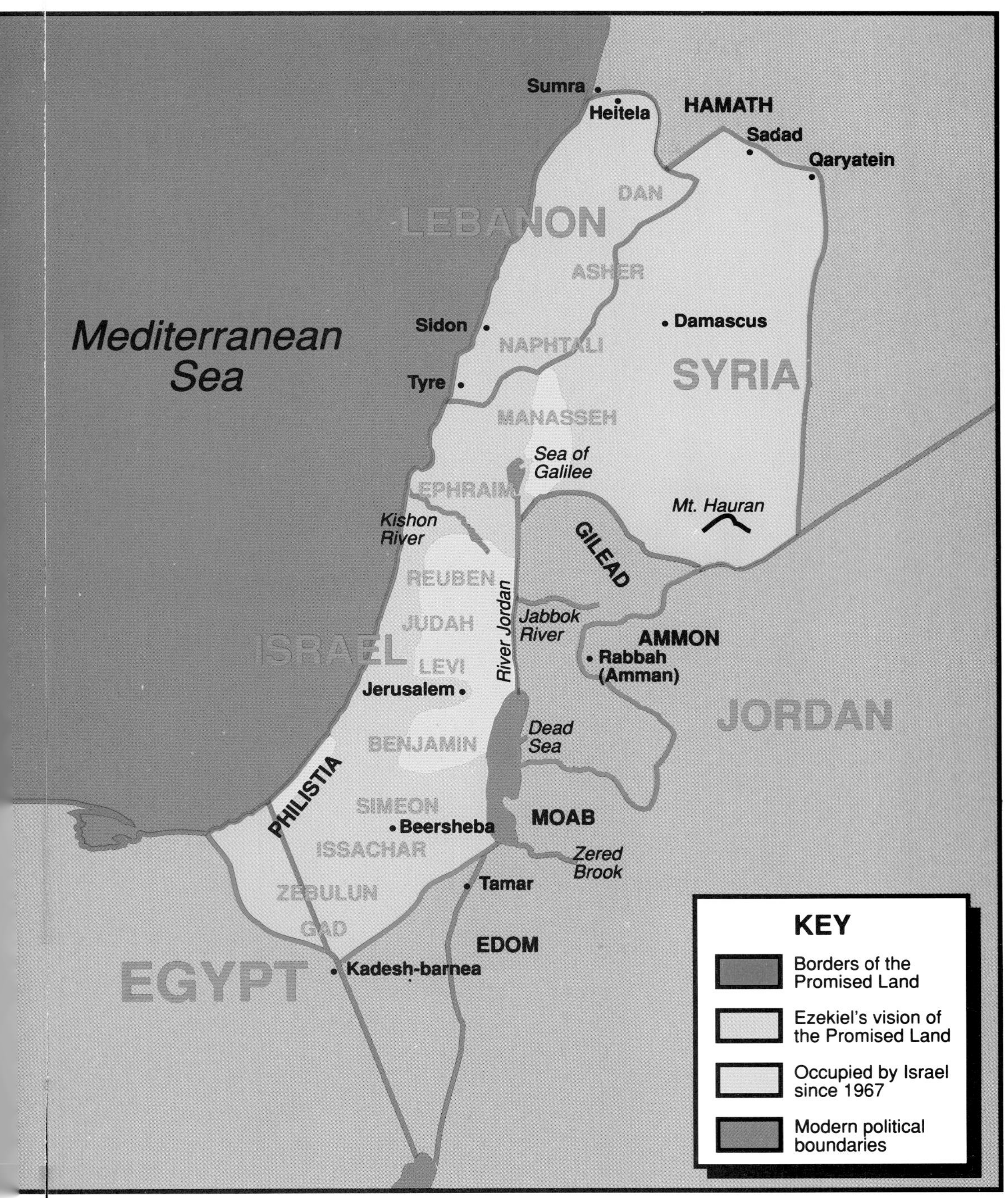
Sumra
Heitela
HAMATH
Sadad
Qaryatein
DAN
LEBANON
ASHER
Mediterranean Sea
Sidon
Damascus
NAPHTALI
SYRIA
Tyre
MANASSEH
Sea of Galilee
EPHRAIM
Mt. Hauran
Kishon River
GILEAD
REUBEN
River Jordan
Jabbok River
JUDAH
AMMON
ISRAEL
Rabbah (Amman)
LEVI
Jerusalem
JORDAN
Dead Sea
BENJAMIN
PHILISTIA
SIMEON
MOAB
Beersheba
ISSACHAR
Zered Brook
Tamar
ZEBULUN
GAD
EDOM
Kadesh-barnea
EGYPT
KEY
Borders of the Promised Land
Ezekiel's vision of the Promised Land
Occupied by Israel since 1967
Modern political boundaries

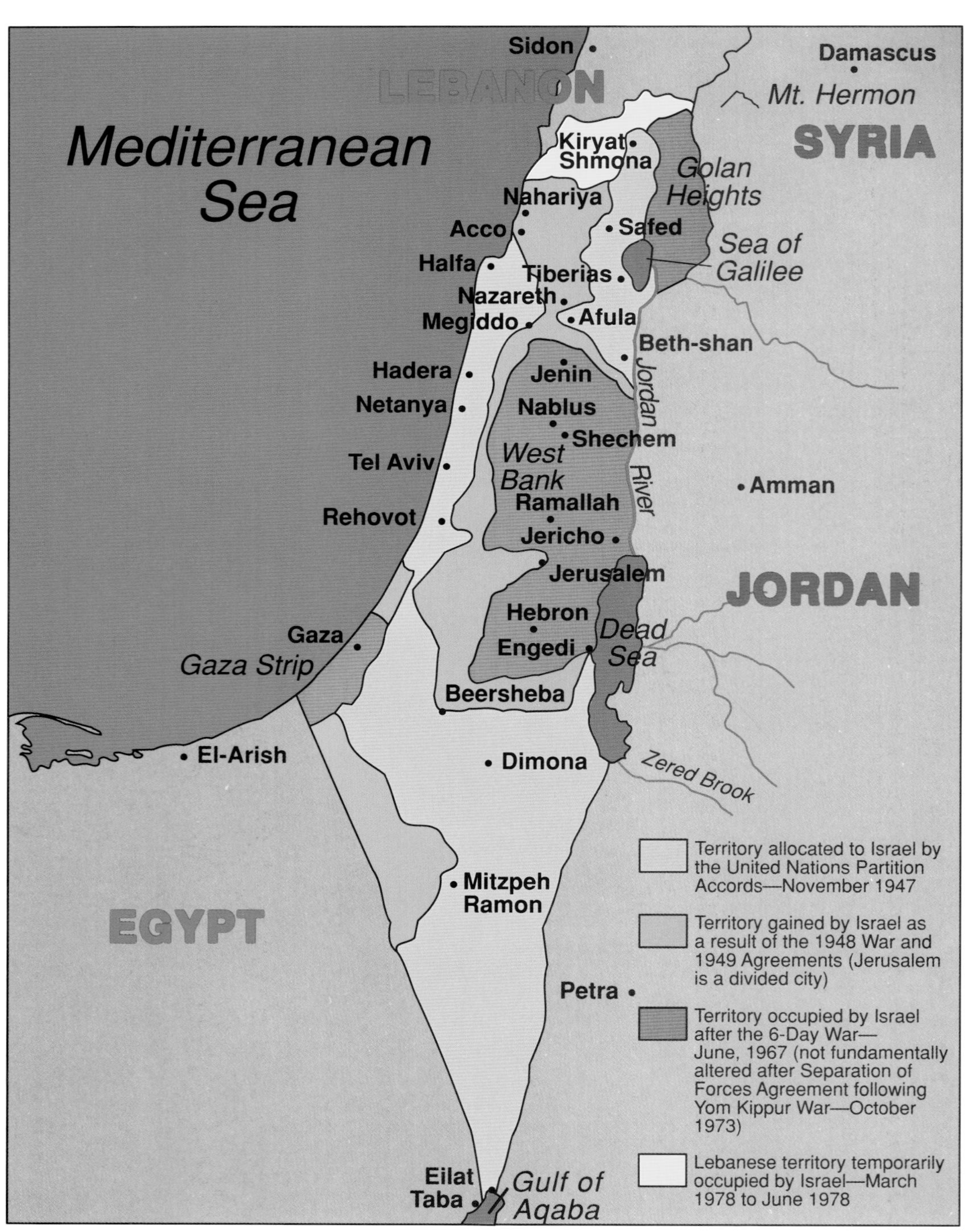

Sidon
LEBANON
Damascus
Mt. Hermon
SYRIA
Mediterranean Sea
Kiryat Shmona
Golan Heights
Nahariya
Acco
Safed
Sea of Galilee
Haifa
Tiberias
Nazareth
Megiddo
Afula
Beth-shan
Hadera
Jenin
Jordan River
Netanya
Nablus
Shechem
West Bank
Tel Aviv
Amman
Ramallah
Rehovot
Jericho
Jerusalem
JORDAN
Hebron
Gaza
Dead Sea
Engedi
Gaza Strip
Beersheba
El-Arish
Dimona
Zered Brook
Territory allocated to Israel by the United Nations Partition Accords—November 1947
Mitzpeh Ramon
EGYPT
Territory gained by Israel as a result of the 1948 War and 1949 Agreements (Jerusalem is a divided city)
Petra
Territory occupied by Israel after the 6-Day War—June, 1967 (not fundamentally altered after Separation of Forces Agreement following Yom Kippur War—October 1973)
Eilat
Taba
Gulf of Aqaba
Lebanese territory temporarily occupied by Israel—March 1978 to June 1978